PETERSON'S GRADUATE & PROFESSIONAL PROGRAMS

AN OVERVIEW

2008

BOOK 1

PETERSON'S

A nelnet COMPANY

PETERSON'S

A nelnet COMPANY

About Peterson's, a Nelnet company

Peterson's (www.petersons.com) is a leading provider of education information and advice, with books and online resources focusing on education search, test preparation, and financial aid. Its Web site offers searchable databases and interactive tools for contacting educational institutions, online practice tests and instruction, and planning tools for securing financial aid. Peterson's serves 110 million education consumers annually.

For more information, contact Peterson's, 2000 Lenox Drive, Lawrenceville, NJ 08648; 800-338-3282; or find us on the World Wide Web at www.petersons.com/about.

Editor: Fern A. Oram; Production Editor: Susan W. Dilts; Copy Editors: Bret Bollmann, Michael Haines, Brooke James, Sally Ross, Pam Sullivan, Valerie Bolus Vaughan; Research Project Manager: Ken Britschge; Research Associates: Cathleen Fee, James Ranish, Amy L. Weber; Programmer: Phyllis Johnson; Manufacturing Manager: Ray Golaszewski; Composition Manager: Linda M. Williams; Client Relations Representatives: Janet Garwo, Mimi Kaufman, Karen Mount, Danielle Vreeland

ISSN 1520-4359
ISBN-13: 978-0-7689-2404-6
ISBN-10: 0-7689-2404-9

Printed in the United States of America

10 9 8 7 6 5 4 3 2 1 10 09 08

Forty-second Edition

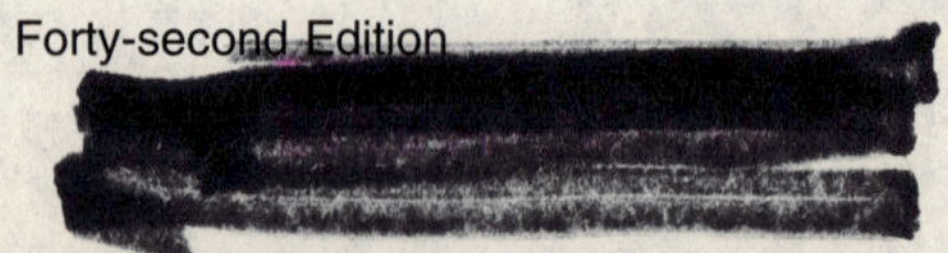

CONTENTS

A Note from the Peterson's Editors

The six volumes of *Peterson's Graduate and Professional Programs*, the only annually updated reference work of its kind, provide wide-ranging information on the graduate and professional programs offered by accredited colleges and universities in the United States, U.S. territories, and Canada and by those institutions outside the United States that are accredited by U.S. accrediting bodies. More than 44,000 individual academic and professional programs at more than 2,200 institutions are listed. *Peterson's Graduate and Professional Programs* have been used for more than forty years by prospective graduate and professional students, placement counselors, faculty advisers, and all others interested in postbaccalaureate education.

Book 1: *Graduate & Professional Programs: An Overview*, contains information on institutions as a whole, while Books 2 through 6 are devoted to specific academic and professional fields.

Book 2: *Graduate Programs in the Humanities, Arts & Social Sciences*

Book 3: *Graduate Programs in the Biological Sciences*

Book 4: *Graduate Programs in the Physical Sciences, Mathematics, Agricultural Sciences, the Environment & Natural Resources*

Book 5: *Graduate Programs in Engineering & Applied Sciences*

Book 6: *Graduate Programs in Business, Education, Health, Information Studies, Law & Social Work*

The books may be used individually or as a set. For example, if you have chosen a field of study but do not know what institution you want to attend or if you have a college or university in mind but have not chosen an academic field of study, it is best to begin with Book 1.

Book 1 presents several directories to help you identify programs of study that might interest you; you can then research those programs further in Books 2 through 6. The *Directory of Graduate and Professional Programs by Field* lists the 491 fields for which there are program directories in Books 2 through 6 and gives the names of those institutions that offer graduate degree programs in each.

For geographical or financial reasons, you may be interested in attending a particular institution and will want to know what it has to offer. You should turn to the *Directory of Institutions and Their Offerings*, which lists the degree programs available at each institution, again, in the 491 academic and professional fields for which Books 2 through 6 have program directories. As in the *Directory of Graduate and Professional Programs by Field*, the level of degrees offered is also indicated.

All books in the series include advice on graduate education, including topics such as admissions tests, financial aid, and accreditation. **The Graduate Adviser** includes two essays and information about accreditation. The first essay, "The Admissions Process," discusses general admission requirements, admission tests, factors to consider when selecting a graduate school or program, when and how to apply, and how admission decisions are made. Special information for international students and tips for minority students are also included. The second essay, "Financial Support," is an overview of the broad range of support available at the graduate level. Fellowships, scholarships, and grants; assistantships and internships; federal and private loan programs, as well as Federal Work-Study; and the GI bill are detailed. This essay concludes with advice on applying for need-based financial aid. "Accreditation and Accrediting Agencies" gives information on accreditation and its purpose and lists institutional accrediting agencies first and then specialized accrediting agencies relevant to each volume's specific fields of study.

With information on more than 44,000 graduate programs in 491 disciplines, *Peterson's Graduate and Professional Programs* give you all the information you need about the programs that are of interest to you in three formats: **Profiles** (capsule summaries of basic information), **Announcements** (information that an institution or program wants to emphasize, written by administrators), and **Close-Ups** (also written by administrators, with more expansive information than the **Profiles**, emphasizing different aspects of the programs). By using these various formats of program information, coupled with **Appendixes** and **Indexes** covering directories and subject areas for all six books, you will find that these guides provide the most comprehensive, accurate, and up-to-date graduate study information available.

Peterson's publishes a full line of resources with information you need to guide you through the graduate admissions process. Peterson's publications can be found at your local bookstore or library—or visit us on the Web at www.petersons.com.

Colleges and universities will be pleased to know that Peterson's helped you in your selection. Admissions staff members are more than happy to answer questions, address specific problems, and help in any way they can. The editors at Peterson's wish you great success in your graduate program search!

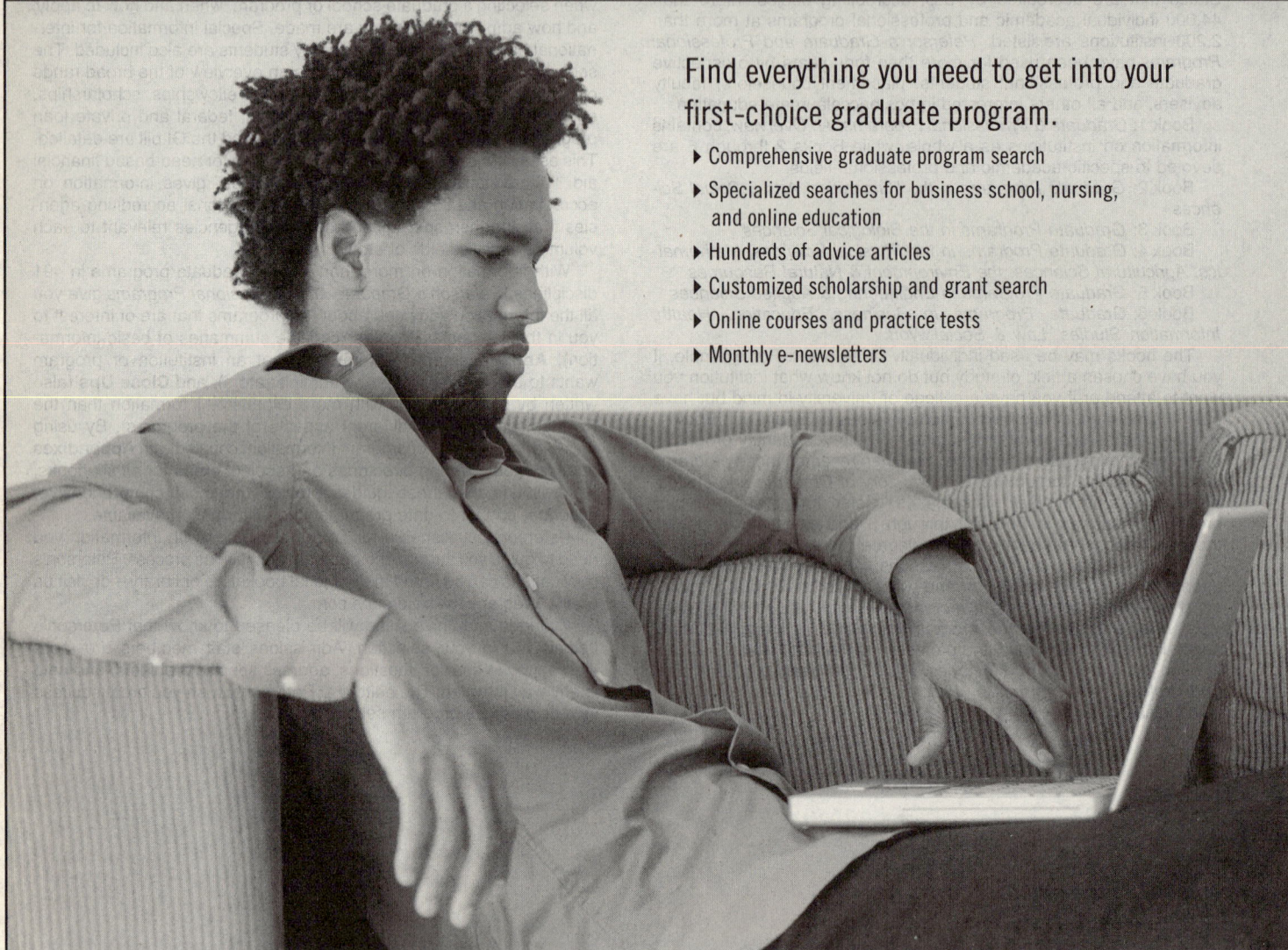

THE GRADUATE ADVISER

The Admissions Process

Generalizations about graduate admissions practices are not always helpful because each institution has its own set of guidelines and procedures. Nevertheless, some broad statements can be made about the admissions process that may help you plan your strategy.

Factors Involved in Selecting a Graduate School or Program

Selecting a graduate school and a specific program of study is a complex matter. Quality of the faculty; program and course offerings; the nature, size, and location of the institution; admission requirements; cost; and the availability of financial assistance are among the many factors that affect one's choice of institution. Other considerations are job placement and achievements of the program's graduates and the institution's resources, such as libraries, laboratories, and computer facilities. If you are to make the best possible choice, you need to learn as much as you can about the schools and programs you are considering before you apply. The following steps may help you narrow your choices.

- Talk to alumni of the programs or institutions you are considering to get their impressions of how well they were prepared for work in their fields of study.
- Remember that graduate school requirements change, so be sure to get the most up-to-date information possible.
- Talk to department faculty and the graduate adviser at your undergraduate institution. They often have information about programs of study at other institutions.
- Visit the Web sites of the graduate schools in which you are interested to request a graduate catalog. Contact the department chair in your chosen field of study for additional information about the department and the field.
- Visit as many campuses as possible. Call ahead for an appointment with the graduate adviser in your field of interest and be sure to check out the facilities and talk to students.

General Requirements

Graduate schools and departments have requirements that applicants for admission must meet. Typically, these requirements include undergraduate transcripts (which provide information about undergraduate grade point average and course work applied toward a major), admission test scores, and letters of recommendation. Most graduate programs also ask for an essay or personal statement that describes your personal reasons for seeking graduate study. In some fields, such as art and music, portfolios or auditions may be required in addition to other evidence of talent. Some institutions require that the applicant have an undergraduate degree in the same subject as the intended graduate major.

Most institutions evaluate each applicant on the basis of the applicant's total record, and the weight accorded any given factor varies widely from institution to institution and from program to program.

The Application Process

You should begin the application process at least one year before you expect to begin your graduate study. Find out the application deadline for each institution (many are provided in the **Profile** section of this guide). Go to the institution Web site and find out if you can apply online. If not, request a paper application form. Fill out this form thoroughly and neatly. Assume that the school needs all the information it is requesting and that the admissions officer will be sensitive to the neatness and overall quality of what you submit. Do not supply more information than the school requires.

The institution may ask at least one question that will require a three- or four-paragraph answer. Compose your response on the assumption that the admissions officer is interested in both what you think and how you express yourself. Keep your statement brief and to the point, but, at the same time, include all pertinent information about your past experiences and your educational goals. Individual statements vary greatly in style and content, which helps admissions officers differentiate among applicants. Many graduate departments give considerable weight to this statement in making their admissions decisions, so be sure to take the time to prepare a thoughtful and concise statement.

If recommendations are a part of the admissions requirements, carefully choose the individuals you ask to write them. It is generally best to ask current or former professors to write the recommendations, provided they are able to attest to your intellectual ability and motivation for doing the work required of a graduate student. It is advisable to provide stamped, preaddressed envelopes to people being asked to submit recommendations on your behalf.

Completed applications, including references, transcripts, and admission test scores, should be received at the institution by the specified date.

Be advised that institutions do not usually make admissions decisions until all materials have been received. Enclose a self-addressed postcard with your application, requesting confirmation of receipt. Allow at least 10 days for the return of the postcard before making further inquiries.

If you plan to apply for financial support, it is imperative that you file your application early.

ADMISSION TESTS

The major testing program used in graduate admissions is the Graduate Record Examinations (GRE) testing program, sponsored by the GRE Board and administered by Educational Testing Service, Princeton, New Jersey.

The Graduate Record Examinations testing program consists of a General Test and eight Subject Tests. The General Test measures critical thinking, verbal reasoning, quantitative reasoning, and analytical writing skills. It is offered as an Internet-based test (iBT) in the United States, Canada, and many other countries.

Plans for launching an entirely new GRE General Test were dropped by ETS in early 2007 in favor of introducing new question types and improvements gradually. Some revisions to the computerized General Test are planned for November 2007. (No changes are planned for the paper-based version or the split-test administration of the GRE General Test offered in China, Korea, and Taiwan.) The fall 2007 revisions are part of the first phase of improvements endorsed by graduate school educators. When completely incorporated, the improvements will test validity, provide faculty with better information regarding applicants' performance, address security concerns, increase worldwide access to the test, and make better use of advances in technology and psychometric design. Changes planned for the verbal reasoning section may eventually include greater emphasis on higher cognitive skills and less dependence on vocabulary; more text-based materials, such as reading passages; a broader selection of reading passages; emphasis on skills related to graduate work, such as complex reasoning; and expansion of computer-enabled tasks (e.g., clicking on a sentence in a passage to highlight it). The verbal reasoning section currently consists of one 30-minute section comprised of thirty questions; beginning in November 2007, test takers may encounter a new question type in the verbal reasoning section: a text completion question that requires test takers to fill in one blank within a passage from a single multiple-choice list. Verbal scores are reported on a 200–800 score scale in 10-point increments.

Changes to the quantitative reasoning section may eventually include quantitative reasoning skills that are closer to those generally used in graduate school, an increase in the proportion of questions involving real-life scenarios and data interpretation, a decrease in the proportion of geometry questions, and better use of technology (e.g., an on-screen calculator). Currently, the quantitative reasoning section consists of one 45-minute section comprised of twenty-eight questions; beginning in November 2007, however, test takers may encounter one new question type in the quantitative reasoning section: a numeric entry question that requires test takers to type their answer as a number in a box or as a fraction in two boxes. Quantitative scores are reported on a 200–800 score scale in 10-point increments.

Changes to the analytical writing section may eventually include new, more focused prompts that reduce the possibility of reliance on memorized materials. The length of time allotted for the issue and argument tasks remains at 45 minutes and 30 minutes, respectively. Analytical writing scores are reported on a 0–6 score scale, in half-point increments.

To prepare for the new question types, be sure to check the GRE Web site at www.ets.org/gre/newquestiontypes.html.

The Subject Tests measure achievement and assume undergraduate majors or extensive background in the following eight disciplines:

- Biochemistry, Cell and Molecular Biology
- Biology
- Chemistry
- Computer Science
- Literature in English
- Mathematics
- Physics
- Psychology

The Subject Tests are available three times per year as paper-based administrations around the world. Testing time is approximately 2 hours and 50 minutes. You can obtain more information about the GRE by visiting the ETS Web site at www.ets.org or consulting the *GRE Information and Registration Bulletin.* The *Bulletin* can be obtained at many undergraduate colleges. You can also download it from the ETS Web site or obtain it by contacting Graduate Record Examinations, Educational Testing Service, PO Box 6000, Princeton, NJ 08541-6000, telephone 1-609-771-7670 or 1-866-473-4373 (toll-free for the United States, U.S. Territories, and Canada).

If you expect to apply for admission to a program that requires any of the GRE tests, you should select a test date well in advance of the application deadline. Scores on the computer-based General Test are reported within ten to fifteen days; scores on the paper-based Subject Tests are reported within six weeks.

Another testing program, the Miller Analogies Test (MAT), is administered at more than 500 Controlled Testing Centers (CTC) in the United States, Canada, and other countries. The MAT computer-based test is now available. Testing time is 60 minutes. The test consists of 120 partial analogies. There are no nationally scheduled test administrations for the MAT. Each CTC determines its own test schedule. You can obtain the *Candidate Information Booklet,* which contains a list of test centers and instructions for taking the test, from http://harcourtassessment.com/haiweb/Cultures/en-US/Harcourt/Community/PostSecondary/Products/MAT/mathome.htm, by completing a request form on the Web site, or by calling Harcourt Assessment, Inc., at 1-800-211-8378.

Always check the specific requirements of the programs to which you are applying.

How Admission Decisions Are Made

The program you apply to is directly involved in the admissions process. Although the final decision is usually made by the graduate dean (or an associate) or the faculty admissions committee, recommendations from faculty members in your intended field are important. At some institutions, an interview is incorporated into the decision process.

A Special Note for International Students

In addition to the steps already described, there are some special considerations for international students who intend to apply for graduate study in the United States. All graduate schools require an indication of competence in English. The purpose of the Test of English as a Foreign Language (TOEFL) is to evaluate the English proficiency of people who are nonnative speakers of English and want to study at colleges and universities where English is the language of instruction. The TOEFL is administered by Educational Testing Service (ETS) under the general direction of a policy board established by the College Board and the Graduate Record Examinations Board.

The TOEFL is administered as a computer-based test throughout most of the world and is available year-round by appointment only. It is not necessary to have previous computer experience to take the test. The computer-based test consists of four sections—listening, reading, structure, and writing. Total testing time is approximately 4 hours.

The TOEFL is also offered in the paper-based format in areas of the world where computer- and Internet-based testing is not available. The paper-based TOEFL consists of three sections—listening comprehension, structure and written expression, and reading comprehension. Testing time is approximately 3 hours. The Test of Written English (TWE) is also given as part of the paper-based TOEFL. TWE is a 30-minute essay that measures the examinee's ability to compose in English. Examinees receive a TWE score separate from their TOEFL score. The *Information Bulletin* contains information on local fees and registration procedures.

A new TOEFL (TOEFL iBT) that assesses the four basic language skills: listening, reading, writing, and speaking, was administered for the first time in September 2005 in the United States, Canada, France, Germany, and Puerto Rico. The second phase began in March 2006 in Africa, Europe, Eurasia, and the Middle East. (ETS will continue to introduce the iBT in selected cities and will continue to deliver the paper-based test in other locations.) The Internet-based test is administered at secure, official test centers. Testing time is approximately 4 hours. Because the TOEFL iBT includes a speaking section, the TSE will no longer be needed.

Additional information and registration materials are available from TOEFL Services, Educational Testing Service, P.O. Box 6151, Princeton, New Jersey 08541-6151. Telephone: 1-609-771-7100. E-mail: toefl@ets.org. World Wide Web: http://www.toefl.org.

International students should apply especially early because of the number of steps required to complete the admissions process. Furthermore, many United States graduate schools have a limited number of spaces for international students, and many more students apply than the schools can accommodate.

International students may find financial assistance from institutions very limited. The U.S. government requires international applicants to submit a certification of support, which is a statement attesting to the applicant's financial resources. In addition, international students *must* have health insurance coverage.

Tips for Minority Students

Indicators of a university's values in terms of diversity are found both in its recruitment programs and its resources directed to student success. Important questions: Does the institution vigorously recruit minorities for its graduate programs? Is there funding available to help with the costs associated with visiting the school? Are minorities represented in the institution's brochures or Web site or on their faculty rolls? What campus-based resources or services (including assistance in locating housing or career counseling and placement) are available? Is funding available to members of underrepresented groups?

At the program level, it is particularly important for minority students to investigate the "climate" of a program under consideration. How many minority students are enrolled and how many have graduated? What opportunities are there to work with diverse faculty and mentors whose research interests match yours? How are conflicts resolved or concerns addressed? How interested are faculty in building strong and supportive relations with students? "Climate" concerns should be addressed by posing questions to various individuals, including faculty members, current students, and alumni.

Information is also available through various organizations, such as the Hispanic Association of Colleges and Universities (HACU), and publications, such as *Diverse Issues in Higher Education* and *Hispanic Outlook* magazine. There are also books devoted to this topic, such as *The Multicultural Student's Guide to Colleges* by Robert Mitchell.

Financial Support

The range of financial support at the graduate level is very broad. The following descriptions will give you a general idea of what you might expect and what will be expected of you as a financial support recipient.

Fellowships, Scholarships, and Grants

These are usually outright awards of a few hundred to many thousands of dollars with no service to the institution required in return. Fellowships and scholarships are usually awarded on the basis of merit and are highly competitive. Grants are made on the basis of financial need or special talent in a field of study. Many fellowships, scholarships, and grants not only cover tuition, fees, and supplies but also include stipends for living expenses with allowances for dependents. However, the terms of each should be examined because some do not permit recipients to supplement their income with outside work. Fellowships, scholarships, and grants may vary in the number of years for which they are awarded.

In addition to the availability of these funds at the university or program level, many excellent fellowship programs are available at the national level and may be applied for before and during enrollment in a graduate program. A listing of many of these programs can be found at the Council of Graduate Schools' Web site: http://www.cgsnet.org. There is a wealth of information in the "Programs and Awards" section.

Assistantships and Internships

Many graduate students receive financial support through assistantships, particularly involving teaching or research duties. It is important to recognize that such appointments should not be viewed simply as employment relationships but rather should constitute an integral and important part of a student's graduate education. As such, the appointments should be accompanied by strong faculty mentoring and increasingly responsible apprenticeship experiences. The specific nature of these appointments in a given program should be considered in selecting that graduate program.

TEACHING ASSISTANTSHIPS

These usually provide a salary and full or partial tuition remission and may also provide health benefits. Unlike fellowships, scholarships, and grants, which require no service to the institution, teaching assistantships require recipients to provide the institution with a specific amount of undergraduate teaching, ideally related to the student's field of study. Some teaching assistants are limited to grading papers, compiling bibliographies, taking notes, or monitoring laboratories. At some graduate schools, teaching assistants must carry lighter course loads than regular full-time students.

RESEARCH ASSISTANTSHIPS

These are very similar to teaching assistantships in the manner in which financial assistance is provided. The difference is that recipients are given basic research assignments in their disciplines rather than teaching responsibilities. The work required is normally related to the student's field of study; in most instances, the assistantship supports the student's thesis or dissertation research.

ADMINISTRATIVE INTERNSHIPS

These are similar to assistantships in application of financial assistance funds, but the student is given an assignment on a part-time basis, usually as a special assistant with one of the university's administrative offices. The assignment may not necessarily be directly related to the recipient's discipline.

RESIDENCE HALL AND COUNSELING ASSISTANTSHIPS

These assistantships are frequently assigned to graduate students in psychology, counseling, and social work, but may be offered to students in other disciplines, especially if they have worked in this capacity during their undergraduate years. Duties can vary from being available in a dean's office for a specific number of hours for consultation with undergraduates to living in campus residences and being responsible for both counseling and administrative tasks or advising student activity groups. Residence hall assistantships often include a room and board allowance and, in some cases, tuition assistance and stipends. Contact the Housing and Student Life Office for more information.

Health Insurance

The availability and affordability of health insurance is an important issue and one that should be considered in an applicant's choice of institution and program. While often included with assistantships and fellowships, this is not always the case and, even if provided, the benefits may be limited. It is important to note that the U.S. government requires international students to have health insurance.

The GI Bill

This provides financial assistance for students who are veterans of the United States armed forces. If you are a veteran, contact your local Veterans Administration office to determine your eligibility and to get full details about benefits. There are a number of programs that offer educational benefits to current military enlistees. Some states have tuition assistance programs for members of the National Guard. Contact the VA office at the college for more information.

Federal Work-Study Program (FWS)

Employment is another way some students finance their graduate studies. The federally funded Federal Work-Study Program provides eligible students with employment opportunities, usually in public and private nonprofit organizations. Federal funds pay up to 75 percent of the wages, with the remainder paid by the employing agency. FWS is available to graduate students who demonstrate financial need. Not all schools have these funds, and some only award them to undergraduates. Each school sets its application deadline and work-study earnings limits. Wages vary and are related to the type of work done. You must file the Free Application for Federal Student Aid (FAFSA) to be eligible for this program.

Loans

Many graduate students borrow to finance their graduate programs when other sources of assistance (which do not have to be repaid) prove insufficient. You should always read and understand the terms of any loan program before submitting your application.

FEDERAL LOANS

Federal Stafford Loans. The Federal Stafford Loan Program offers government-sponsored, low-interest loans to students through a private lender such as a bank, credit union, or savings and loan association.

There are two components of the Federal Stafford Loan program. Under the *subsidized* component of the program, the federal government pays the interest on the loan while you are enrolled in graduate school on at least a half-time basis. Under the *unsubsidized* component of the program, you pay the interest on the loan from the day proceeds are issued. Eligibility for the federal subsidy is based on demonstrated financial need as determined by the financial aid office from the information you provide on the FAFSA. A cosigner is not required, since the loan is not based on creditworthiness.

Although *unsubsidized* Federal Stafford Loans may not be as desirable as *subsidized* Federal Stafford Loans from the student's perspective, they are a useful source of support for those who may not qualify for the subsidized loans or who need additional financial assistance.

Graduate students may borrow up to $20,500 per year through the Stafford Loan Program, up to a cumulative maximum of $138,500, including undergraduate borrowing. This may include up to $8500 in *subsidized* Stafford Loans annually, depending on eligibility, up to a cumulative maximum of $65,500, including undergraduate borrowing. The amount of the loan borrowed through the *unsubsidized* Stafford Program equals the total amount of the loan (as much as $20,500) minus your eligibility for a *subsidized* Stafford Loan (as much as $8500). You may borrow up to the cost of attendance at the school in which you are enrolled or will attend, minus estimated financial assistance from other federal, state, and private sources, up to a maximum of $20,500.

Stafford Loans made on or after July 1, 2006, carry a fixed interest rate of 6.8% both for in-school and in-repayment borrowers.

Two fees may be deducted from the loan proceeds upon disbursement: a Federal Default Fee of 1 percent, which is deposited in an insurance pool to ensure repayment to the lender if the borrower defaults, and a federally mandated 1.5 percent origination fee, for loans made after July 1, 2007, which is used to offset the administrative cost of the Federal Stafford Loan Program. Many lenders do offer reduced-fee or "zero fee" loans. The origination fees are scheduled to be eliminated by July 1, 2010.

Under the *subsidized* Federal Stafford Loan Program, repayment begins six months after your last date of enrollment on at least a half-time basis. Under the *unsubsidized* program, repayment of interest begins within thirty days from disbursement of the loan proceeds, and repayment of the principal begins six months after your last enrollment on at least a half-time basis. Some borrowers may choose to defer interest payments while they are in school. The accrued interest is added to the loan balance when the borrower begins repayment. There are several repayment options.

Federal Direct Loans. Some schools participate in the Department of Education's William D. Ford Direct Lending Program instead of the Federal Stafford Loan Program. The two programs are essentially the same except that with the Direct Loans, schools themselves provide the loans with funds from the federal government. Terms and interest rates are virtually the same except that there are a few additional repayment options with Federal Direct Loans.

Federal Perkins Loans. The Federal Perkins Loan is available to students demonstrating financial need and is administered directly by the school. Not all schools have these funds, and some may award them to undergraduates only. Eligibility is determined from the information you provide on the FAFSA. The school will notify you of your eligibility.

Eligible graduate students may borrow up to $6000 per year, up to a maximum of $40,000, including undergraduate borrowing (even if your previous Perkins Loans have been repaid). The interest rate for Federal Perkins Loans is 5 percent, and no interest accrues while you remain in school at least half-time. There are no guarantee, loan, or disbursement fees. Repayment begins nine months after your last date of enrollment on at least a half-time basis and may extend over a maximum of ten years with no prepayment penalty.

Federal GRADUATE PLUS Loans. Identical to the Parent Loans for Undergraduate Students, this program allows students to borrow up to their cost of attendance, less any other aid received through this federal program. These loans have a fixed interest rate of 8.5% (7.9% for the Federal Direct PLUS), and interest begins to accrue at the time of disbursement. For more information, contact your FFELD lender or your college financial aid office.

Deferring Your Federal Loan Repayments. If you borrowed under the Federal Stafford Loan Program or the Federal Perkins Loan Program for previous undergraduate or graduate study, your repayments may be deferred when you return to graduate school, depending on when you borrowed and under which program.

There are other deferment options available if you are temporarily unable to repay your loan. Information about these deferments is provided at your entrance and exit interviews. If you believe you are eligible for a deferment of your loan repayments, you must contact your lender to complete a deferment form. The deferment must be filed prior to the time your repayment is due, and it must be refiled when it expires if you remain eligible for deferment at that time.

SUPPLEMENTAL (PRIVATE) LOANS

Many lending institutions offer supplemental loan programs and other financing plans, such as the ones described here, to students seeking additional assistance in meeting their educational expenses. Some loan programs target all types of graduate students; others are designed specifically for business, law, or medical students. In addition, you can use private loans not specifically designed for education to help finance your graduate degree.

If you are considering borrowing through a supplemental or private loan program, you should carefully consider the terms and be sure to "read the fine print." Check with the program sponsor for the most current terms that will be applicable to the amounts you intend to borrow for graduate study. Most supplemental loan programs for graduate study offer unsubsidized, credit-based loans. In general, a credit-ready borrower is one who has a satisfactory credit history or no credit history at all. A creditworthy borrower generally must pass a credit test to be eligible to borrow or act as a cosigner for the loan funds.

Many supplemental loan programs have minimum and maximum annual loan limits. Some offer amounts equal to the cost of attendance minus any other aid you will receive for graduate study. If you are planning to borrow for several years of graduate study, consider whether there is a cumulative or aggregate limit on the amount you may borrow. Often this cumulative or aggregate limit will include any amounts you borrowed and have not repaid for undergraduate or previous graduate study.

The combination of the annual interest rate, loan fees, and the repayment terms you choose will determine how much you will repay over time. Compare these features in combination before you decide which loan program to use. Some loans offer interest rates that are adjusted monthly, some quarterly, some annually. Some offer interest rates that are lower during the in-school, grace, and deferment periods, and then increase when you begin repayment. Some programs include a loan "origination" fee, which is usually deducted from the principal amount you receive when the loan is disbursed, and must be repaid along with the interest and other principal when you graduate, withdraw from school, or drop below half-time study. Sometimes the loan fees are reduced if you borrow with a qualified cosigner. Some programs allow you to defer interest and/or principal payments while you are enrolled in graduate school. Many programs allow you to capitalize your interest payments; the interest due on your loan is added to the outstanding balance of your loan, so you don't have to repay immediately, but this increases the amount you owe. Other programs allow you to pay the interest as you go, which reduces the amount you later have to repay.

Some examples of supplemental programs follow. The private loan market is very competitive and your financial aid office can help you evaluate these and other programs.

CitiAssist Loans. Offered by Citibank, these no-fee loans help graduate students fill the gap between the financial aid they receive and the money they need for school. Visit www.studentloan.com for more loan information from Citibank.

EXCEL Loan. This program, sponsored by Nellie Mae, is designed for students who are not ready to borrow on their own and wish to borrow with a creditworthy cosigner. Visit www.nelliemae.com for more information.

Key Alternative Loan. This loan can bridge the gap between education costs and traditional funding. Visit https://www.key.com/html/H-1.3.html for more information.

Graduate Access Loan. Sponsored by the Access Group, this is for graduate students enrolled at least half-time. The Web site is www.accessgroup.com.

Signature Student Loan. A loan program for students who are enrolled at least half-time, this is sponsored by Sallie Mae. Visit www.salliemae.com for more information.

Applying for Need-Based Financial Aid

Schools that award federal and institutional financial assistance based on need will require you to complete the FAFSA and, in some cases, an institutional financial aid application.

If you are applying for federal student assistance, you **must** complete the FAFSA. A service of the U.S. Department of Education, it is free to all applicants. Most applicants apply online at www.fafsa.ed.gov. Paper applications are available at the financial aid office of your local college.

After your FAFSA information has been processed, you will receive a Student Aid Report (SAR). If you provided an e-mail address on the FAFSA, this will be sent to you electronically; otherwise, it will be mailed to your home address.

Follow the instructions on the SAR if you need to correct information reported on your original application. If your situation changes after you file your FAFSA, contact your financial aid officer to discuss amending your information. You can also appeal your financial aid award if you have extenuating circumstances.

If you would like more information on federal student financial aid, visit the FAFSA Web site or download the most recent version of *The Student Guide* at http://studentaid.ed.gov/students/publications/student_guide/index.html. This guide is also available in Spanish.

The U.S. Department of Education also has a toll-free number for questions concerning federal student aid programs. The number is 1-800-4-FED AID (1-800-433-3243). If you are hearing impaired, call toll-free, 1-800-730-8913.

Summary

Remember that these are generalized statements about financial assistance at the graduate level. Because each institution allots its aid differently, you should communicate directly with the school and the specific department of interest to you. It is not unusual, for example, to find that an endowment vested within a specific department supports one or more fellowships. You may fit its requirements and specifications precisely.

Accreditation and Accrediting Agencies

Colleges and universities in the United States, and their individual academic and professional programs, are accredited by nongovernmental agencies concerned with monitoring the quality of education in this country. Agencies with both regional and national jurisdictions grant accreditation to institutions as a whole, while specialized bodies acting on a nationwide basis—often national professional associations—grant accreditation to departments and programs in specific fields.

Institutional and specialized accrediting agencies share the same basic concerns: the purpose an academic unit—whether university or program—has set for itself and how well it fulfills that purpose, the adequacy of its financial and other resources, the quality of its academic offerings, and the level of services it provides. Agencies that grant institutional accreditation take a broader view, of course, and examine university-wide or college-wide services with which a specialized agency may not concern itself.

Both types of agencies follow the same general procedures when considering an application for accreditation. The academic unit prepares a self-evaluation, focusing on the concerns mentioned above and usually including an assessment of both its strengths and weaknesses; a team of representatives of the accrediting body reviews this evaluation, visits the campus, and makes its own report; and finally, the accrediting body makes a decision on the application. Often, even when accreditation is granted, the agency makes a recommendation regarding how the institution or program can improve. All institutions and programs are also reviewed every few years to determine whether they continue to meet established standards; if they do not, they may lose their accreditation.

Accrediting agencies themselves are reviewed and evaluated periodically by the U.S. Department of Education and the Council for Higher Education Accreditation (CHEA). Recognized agencies adhere to certain standards and practices, and their authority in matters of accreditation is widely accepted in the educational community.

This does not mean, however, that accreditation is a simple matter, either for schools wishing to become accredited or for students deciding where to apply. Indeed, in certain fields the very meaning and methods of accreditation are the subject of a good deal of debate. For their part, those applying to graduate school should be aware of the safeguards provided by regional accreditation, especially in terms of degree acceptance and institutional longevity. Beyond this, applicants should understand the role that specialized accreditation plays in their field, as this varies considerably from one discipline to another. In certain professional fields, it is necessary to have graduated from a program that is accredited in order to be eligible for a license to practice, and in some fields the federal government also makes this a hiring requirement. In other disciplines, however, accreditation is not as essential, and there can be excellent programs that are not accredited. In fact, some programs choose not to seek accreditation, although most do.

Institutions and programs that present themselves for accreditation are sometimes granted the status of candidate for accreditation, or what is known as "preaccreditation." This may happen, for example, when an academic unit is too new to have met all the requirements for accreditation. Such status signifies initial recognition and indicates that the school or program in question is working to fulfill all requirements; it does not, however, guarantee that accreditation will be granted.

Institutional Accrediting Agencies—Regional

MIDDLE STATES ASSOCIATION OF COLLEGES AND SCHOOLS
Accredits institutions in Delaware, District of Columbia, Maryland, New Jersey, New York, Pennsylvania, Puerto Rico, and the Virgin Islands.
Jean Avnet Morse, President
Middle States Commission on Higher Education
3624 Market Street
Philadelphia, Pennsylvania 19104
Telephone: 267-284-5025
Fax: 215-662-5501
E-mail: info@msche.org
World Wide Web: www.msche.org

NEW ENGLAND ASSOCIATION OF SCHOOLS AND COLLEGES
Accredits institutions in Connecticut, Maine, Massachusetts, New Hampshire, Rhode Island, and Vermont.
Barbara E. Brittingham, Director
Commission on Institutions of Higher Education
209 Burlington Road
Bedford, Massachusetts 01730-1433
Telephone: 781-541-5447
Fax: 781-271-0950
E-mail: bbrittingham@neasc.org
World Wide Web: www.neasc.org

NORTH CENTRAL ASSOCIATION OF COLLEGES AND SCHOOLS
Accredits institutions in Arizona, Arkansas, Colorado, Illinois, Indiana, Iowa, Kansas, Michigan, Minnesota, Missouri, Nebraska, New Mexico, North Dakota, Ohio, Oklahoma, South Dakota, West Virginia, Wisconsin, and Wyoming.
Steven D. Crow, President
The Higher Learning Commission
30 North LaSalle Street, Suite 2400
Chicago, Illinois 60602
Telephone: 312-263-0456
Fax: 312-263-7462
E-mail: scrow@hlcommission.org
World Wide Web: www.ncahigherlearningcommission.org

NORTHWEST COMMISSION ON COLLEGES AND UNIVERSITIES
Accredits institutions in Alaska, Idaho, Montana, Nevada, Oregon, Utah, and Washington.
Sandra E. Elman, President
8060 165th Avenue, NE, Suite 100
Redmond, Washington 98052
Telephone: 425-558-4224
Fax: 425-376-0596
E-mail: selman@nwccu.org
World Wide Web: www.nwccu.org

SOUTHERN ASSOCIATION OF COLLEGES AND SCHOOLS
Accredits institutions in Alabama, Florida, Georgia, Kentucky, Louisiana, Mississippi, North Carolina, South Carolina, Tennessee, Texas, and Virginia.
Belle S. Wheelan, President
Commission on Colleges
1866 Southern Lane
Decatur, Georgia 30033
Telephone: 404-679-4512
Fax: 404-679-4558
E-mail: bwheelan@sacscoc.org
World Wide Web: www.sacscoc.org

WESTERN ASSOCIATION OF SCHOOLS AND COLLEGES
Accredits institutions in California, Guam, and Hawaii.
Ralph A. Wolff, President and Executive Director
The Senior College Commission
985 Atlantic Avenue, Suite 100
Alameda, California 94501
Telephone: 510-748-9001
Fax: 510-748-9797
E-mail: wascsr@wascsenior.org
World Wide Web: www.wascsenior.org/wasc/

Institutional Accrediting Agencies—Other

ACCREDITING COUNCIL FOR INDEPENDENT COLLEGES AND SCHOOLS
Sheryl L. Moody, Executive Director
750 First Street, NE, Suite 980
Washington, DC 20002-4242
Telephone: 202-336-6780
Fax: 202-842-2593
E-mail: smoody@acics.org
World Wide Web: www.acics.org

DISTANCE EDUCATION AND TRAINING COUNCIL
Accrediting Commission
Michael P. Lambert, Executive Director
1601 18th Street, NW
Washington, DC 20009
Telephone: 202-234-5100 Ext. 101
Fax: 202-332-1386
E-mail: detc@detc.org
World Wide Web: www.detc.org

Specialized Accrediting Agencies

[Only Book 1 of *Peterson's Graduate and Professional Programs* Series includes the complete list of specialized accrediting groups recognized by the U.S. Department of Education and the Council on Higher Education Accreditation (CHEA). The lists in Books 2, 3, 4, 5, and 6 are abridged.]

ACUPUNCTURE AND ORIENTAL MEDICINE
Dort S. Bigg, Executive Director
Accreditation Commission for Acupuncture and Oriental Medicine
Maryland Trade Center #3
7501 Greenway Center Drive, Suite 820
Greenbelt, Maryland 20770
Telephone: 301-313-0855
Fax: 301-313-0912
E-mail: acaom1@compuserve.com
World Wide Web: www.acaom.org

ART AND DESIGN
Samuel Hope, Executive Director
National Association of Schools of Art and Design
11250 Roger Bacon Drive, Suite 21
Reston, Virginia 20190
Telephone: 703-437-0700
Fax: 703-437-6312
E-mail: shope@arts-accredit.org
World Wide Web: nasad.arts-accredit.org

BUSINESS
Jerry E. Trapnell, Executive Vice President/Chief Accreditation Officer
AACSB International--The Association to Advance Collegiate Schools of Business
777 South Harbour Island Boulevard, Suite 750
Tampa, Florida 33602
Telephone: 813-769-6500
Fax: 813-769-6559
E-mail: jerryt@aacsb.edu
World Wide Web: www.aacsb.edu

CHIROPRACTIC
Martha S. O'Connor, Executive Director
Council on Chiropractic Education
8049 North 85th Way
Scottsdale, Arizona 85258-4321
Telephone: 480-443-8877
Fax: 480-483-7333
E-mail: cce@cce-usa.org
World Wide Web: www.cce-usa.org

CLINICAL LABORATORY SCIENCES
Dianne M. Cearlock, Chief Executive Officer
National Accrediting Agency for Clinical Laboratory Sciences
8410 West Bryn Mawr Avenue, Suite 670
Chicago, Illinois 60631
Telephone: 773-714-8880
Fax: 773-714-8886
E-mail: dcearlocknaacls.org
World Wide Web: www.naacls.org

CLINICAL PASTORAL EDUCATION
Teresa E. Snorton, Executive Director
Accreditation Commission
Association for Clinical Pastoral Education, Inc.
1549 Clairmont Road, Suite 103
Decatur, Georgia 30033-4611
Telephone: 404-320-1472
Fax: 404-320-0849
E-mail: acpe@acpe.edu
World Wide Web: www.acpe.edu

DANCE
Samuel Hope, Executive Director
National Association of Schools of Dance
11250 Roger Bacon Drive, Suite 21
Reston, Virginia 20190
Telephone: 703-437-0700
Fax: 703-437-6312
E-mail: shope@arts-accredit.org
World Wide Web: nasd.arts-accredit.org

DENTISTRY
Laura M. Neumann, Interim Director
Commission on Dental Accreditation
American Dental Association
211 East Chicago Avenue, 18th Floor
Chicago, Illinois 60611
Telephone: 312-440-2712
Fax: 312-440-2915
E-mail: neumannl@ada.org
World Wide Web: www.ada.org

DIETETICS
Beverly E. Mitchell, Director
American Dietetic Association
Commission on Accreditation for Dietetics Education (CADE-ADA)
120 South Riverside Plaza, Suite 2000
Chicago, Illinois 60606-6995
Phone: 312-899-4872
Fax: 312-899-4817
E-mail: bmitchell@eatright.org
Web: www.eatright.org/cade

ENGINEERING
George D. Peterson, Executive Director
Accreditation Board for Engineering and Technology, Inc.
111 Market Place, Suite 1050
Baltimore, Maryland 21202
Telephone: 410-347-7700
Fax: 410-625-2238
E-mail: info@abet.org
World Wide Web: www.abet.org

FORESTRY
Michael T. Goergen Jr.
Executive Vice President and CEO
Society of American Foresters
5400 Grosvenor Lane
Bethesda, Maryland 20814
Telephone: 301-897-8720
Fax: 301-897-3690
E-mail: goergenm@safnet.org
World Wide Web: www.safnet.org

HEALTH SERVICES ADMINISTRATION
Commission on Accreditation of Healthcare Management Education
Pamela S. Jenness
Director of Accreditation Operations
2000 14th Street North, Suite 780
Arlington, Virginia 22201
Telephone: 703-894-0960
Fax: 703-894-0941
E-mail: pjenness@cahme.org
World Wide Web: cahmeweb.org

INTERIOR DESIGN
Holly Mattson, Executive Director
Council for Interior Design Accreditation
146 Monroe Center, NW, Suite 1318
Grand Rapids, Michigan 49503
Telephone: 616-458-0400
Fax: 616-458-0460
E-mail: holly@accredit-id.org
World Wide Web: www.accredit-id.org

JOURNALISM AND MASS COMMUNICATIONS
Susanne Shaw, Executive Director
Accrediting Council on Education in Journalism and Mass Communications
School of Journalism
Stauffer-Flint Hall
University of Kansas
1435 Jayhawk Boulevard
Lawrence, Kansas 66045-7575
Telephone: 785-864-3973
Fax: 785-864-5225
E-mail: sshaw@ku.edu
World Wide Web: www.ku.edu/~acejmc

LANDSCAPE ARCHITECTURE
Ronald C. Leighton, Executive Director
Landscape Architectural Accreditation Board
American Society of Landscape Architects
636 Eye Street, NW
Washington, DC 20001
Telephone: 202-898-2444
Fax: 202-898-1185
E-mail: rleighton@asla.org
World Wide Web: www.asla.org

LAW
Hulett H. Askew, Consultant on Legal Education
American Bar Association
321 North Clark Street, 21st Floor
Chicago, Illinois 60610
Telephone: 312-988-6746
Fax: 312-988-5681
E-mail: askewh@staff.abanet.org
World Wide Web: www.abanet.org/legaled/

LIBRARY
Karen O'Brien, Executive Director
Office for Accreditation
American Library Association
50 East Huron Street
Chicago, Illinois 60611
Telephone: 312-280-2434
Fax: 312-280-2433
E-mail: kobrien@ala.org
World Wide Web: www.ala.org/ala/accreditation/accreditation.htm

MARRIAGE AND FAMILY THERAPY
Jeff S. Harmon, Director of Accreditation Services
Commission on Accreditation for Marriage and Family Therapy Education
American Association for Marriage and Family Therapy
112 South Alfred Street
Alexandria, Virginia 22314-3061
Telephone: 703-838-9808
Fax: 703-253-0508
E-mail: jharmon@aamft.org
World Wide Web: www.aamft.org

MEDICAL ILLUSTRATION
Commission on Accreditation of Allied Health Education Programs (CAAHEP)
Kathleen Megivern, Executive Director
1361 Park Street
Clearwater, Florida 33756
Telephone: 727-210-2350
Fax: 727-210-2354
E-mail: megivern@caahep.org
World Wide Web: www.caahep.org

MEDICINE
Liaison Committee on Medical Education (LCME)
In even-numbered years beginning each July 1, contact:
Robert H. Eaglen
Interim AAMC Secretary to the LCME
Association of American Medical Colleges
2450 N Street, NW
Washington, DC 20037
Telephone: 202-828-0596
Fax: 202-828-1125
E-mail: reaglen@aamc.org
World Wide Web: www.lcme.org

In odd-numbered years beginning each July 1, contact:
Barbara Barzansky
Interim AMA Secretary to the LCME
American Medical Association
Council on Medical Education
515 North State Street
Chicago, Illinois 60610
Telephone: 312-464-1690
Fax: 312-464-5830
E-mail: barbara_barzansky@ama-assn.org
World Wide Web: www.ama-assn.org

MUSIC
Samuel Hope, Executive Director
National Association of Schools of Music
11250 Roger Bacon Drive, Suite 21
Reston, Virginia 20190
Telephone: 703-437-0700
Fax: 703-437-6312
E-mail: shope@arts-accredit.org
World Wide Web: nasm.arts-accredit.org

NATUROPATHIC MEDICINE
Daniel Seitz, Executive Director
Council on Naturopathic Medical Education
P.O. Box 178
Great Barrington, Massachusetts 01230
Telephone: 413-528-8877
Fax: 413-528-8880
E-mail: council@cnme.org
World Wide Web: www.cnme.org

NURSE ANESTHESIA
Francis Gerbasi, Director of Accreditation and Education
Council on Accreditation of Nurse Anesthesia Educational Programs
222 South Prospect Avenue
Park Ridge, Illinois 60068
Telephone: 847-692-7050
Fax: 847-692-7137
E-mail: fgerbasi@aana.com
World Wide Web: www.aana.com

NURSE EDUCATION
Jennifer Butlin, Director
Commission on Collegiate Nursing Education (CCNE)
One Dupont Circle, NW, Suite 530

Washington, DC 20036-1120
Telephone: 202-887-6791
Fax: 202-887-8476
E-mail: jbutlin@aacn.nche.edu
World Wide Web: www.aacn.nche.edu/accreditation

NURSE MIDWIFERY
Diane Boyer, Chair
ACNM Division of Accreditation
American College of Nurse-Midwives
8403 Colesville Road, Suite 1550
Silver Spring, Maryland 20910
Telephone: 240-485-1800
Fax: 240-485-1818
E-mail: dboyer@luc.edu
World Wide Web: www.midwife.org

Mary Ann Baul, Executive Director
Midwifery Education Accreditation Council
20 East Cherry Avenue
Flagstaff, Arizona 86001-4607
Telephone: 928-214-0997
Fax: 928-773-9694
E-mail: info@meacschools.org
World Wide Web: www.meacschools.org

NURSE PRACTITIONER
Susan Wysocki, President
National Association of Nurse Practitioners in Women's Health
Council on Accreditation
505 C Street, NE
Washington, DC 20002
Telephone: 202-543-9693
Fax: 202-543-9858
E-mail: info@npwh.org
World Wide Web: www.npwh.org

NURSING
Sharon J. Tanner, Executive Director
National League for Nursing Accrediting Commission
61 Broadway, 33rd Floor
New York, New York 10006
Telephone: 800-669-1656 Ext. 451
Fax: 212-812-0364
E-mail: stanner@nlnac.org
World Wide Web: www.nlnac.org

OCCUPATIONAL THERAPY
Neil Harvison, Director of Accreditation
American Occupational Therapy Association
4720 Montgomery Lane
P.O. Box 31220
Bethesda, Maryland 20824-1220
Telephone: 301-652-2682 Ext. 2912
Fax: 301-652-7711
E-mail: nharvison@aota.org
World Wide Web: www.aota.org

OPTOMETRY
Joyce L. Urbeck, Administrative Director
Accreditation Council on Optometric Education
American Optometric Association
243 North Lindbergh Boulevard
St. Louis, Missouri 63141
Telephone: 314-991-4100 Ext. 246
Fax: 314-991-4101
E-mail: jlurbeck@aoa.org
World Wide Web: www.aoanet.org

OSTEOPATHIC MEDICINE
Konrad C. Miskowicz-Retz, Director
Commission on Osteopathic College Accreditation
American Osteopathic Association
142 East Ontario Street
Chicago, Illinois 60611
Telephone: 312-202-8048
Fax: 312-202-8202
E-mail: kretz@osteopathic.org
World Wide Web: www.osteopathic.org

PHARMACY
Peter H. Vlasses, Executive Director
Accreditation Council for Pharmacy Education
20 North Clark Street, Suite 2500
Chicago, Illinois 60602-5109
Telephone: 312-664-3575
Fax: 312-664-4652
E-mail: pvlasses@acpe-accredit.org
World Wide Web: www.acpe-accredit.org

PHYSICAL THERAPY
Mary Jane Harris, Director
Commission on Accreditation
American Physical Therapy Association
1111 North Fairfax Street
Alexandria, Virginia 22314
Telephone: 703-684-2782
Fax: 703-684-7343
E-mail: maryjaneharris@apta.org
World Wide Web: www.apta.org

PHYSICIAN ASSISTANT STUDIES
John McCarty, Executive Director
Accreditation Review Commission on Education for the Physician Assistant
12000 Findley Road, Suite 240
Duluth, Georgia 30097
Telephone: 770-476-1224
Fax: 770-476-1738
E-mail: johnmccarty@arc-pa.org
World Wide Web: www.arc-pa.org

PLANNING
Shonagh Merits, Executive Director
American Institute of Certified Planners/Association of Collegiate Schools of Planning/American Planning Association
Planning Accreditation Board (PAB)
122 South Michigan Avenue, Suite 1600
Chicago, Illinois 60603
Telephone: 312-334-1271
Fax: 312-334-1273
E-mail: pab@planning.org
World Wide Web: showcase.netins.net/web/pab_fi66/

PODIATRIC MEDICINE
Alan R. Tinkleman, Director
Council on Podiatric Medical Education
American Podiatric Medical Association
9312 Old Georgetown Road
Bethesda, Maryland 20814-1621
Telephone: 301-581-9200
Fax: 301-571-4903
E-mail: artinkleman@apma.org
World Wide Web: www.cpme.org

PSYCHOLOGY AND COUNSELING
Susan F. Zlotlow, Director
Office of Program Consultation and Accreditation
American Psychological Association
750 First Street, NE
Washington, DC 20002-4242
Telephone: 202-336-5979
Fax: 202-336-5978
E-mail: szlotlow@apa.org
World Wide Web: www.apa.org/ed/accreditation/
Carol L. Bobby, Executive Director
Council for Accreditation of Counseling and Related Educational Programs
1001 North Fairfax Street, Suite 510
Alexandria, Virginia 22314
Telephone: 703-535-5990

Fax: 703-739-6209
E-mail: cacrep@cacrep.org
World Wide Web: www.cacrep.org

PUBLIC AFFAIRS AND ADMINISTRATION
Crystal Calarusse, Academic Director
Commission on Peer Review and Accreditation
National Association of Schools of Public Affairs and Administration
1120 G Street, NW, Suite 730
Washington, DC 20005
Telephone: 202-628-8965 Ext. 103
Fax: 202-626-4978
E-mail: calarusse@naspaa.org
World Wide Web: www.naspaa.org

PUBLIC HEALTH
Laura Rasar King, Executive Director
Council on Education for Public Health
800 Eye Street, NW, Suite 202
Washington, DC 20001-3710
Telephone: 202-789-1050
Fax: 202-789-1895
E-mail: lking@ceph.org
World Wide Web: www.ceph.org

REHABILITATION EDUCATION
Marv Kuehn, Executive Director
Council on Rehabilitation Education
Commission on Standards and Accreditation
300 North Martingale Road, Suite 460
Schaumburg, Illinois 60173
Telephone: 847-944-1345
Fax: 847-944-1324
E-mail: mkuehn@emporia.edu
World Wide Web: www.core-rehab.org

SOCIAL WORK
Dean Pierce, Director
Office of Social Work Accreditation and Educational Excellence
Council on Social Work Education
1725 Duke Street, Suite 500
Alexandria, Virginia 22314
Telephone: 703-519-2044
Fax: 703-739-9048
E-mail: dpierce@cswe.org
World Wide Web: www.cswe.org

SPEECH-LANGUAGE PATHOLOGY AND AUDIOLOGY
Patrima Tice, Director of Credentialing
American Speech-Language-Hearing Association
10801 Rockville Pike
Rockville, Maryland 20852
Telephone: 301-897-5700
Fax: 301-571-0457
E-mail: ptice@asha.org
World Wide Web: www.asha.org

TEACHER EDUCATION
Arthur E. Wise, President
National Council for Accreditation of Teacher Education
2010 Massachusetts Avenue, NW, Suite 500
Washington, DC 20036
Telephone: 202-466-7496
Fax: 202-296-6620
E-mail: art@ncate.org
World Wide Web: www.ncate.org

Frank B. Murray, President
Teacher Education Accreditation Council (TEAC)
One Dupont Circle, Suite 320
Washington, DC 20036-0110
Telephone: 202-466-7236
Fax: 202-466-7238
E-mail: frank@teac.org
World Wide Web: www.teac.org

TECHNOLOGY
Elise Scanlon, Executive Director
Accrediting Commission of Career Schools and Colleges of Technology
2101 Wilson Boulevard, Suite 302
Arlington, Virginia 22201
Telephone: 703-247-4212
Fax: 703-247-4533
E-mail: escanlon@accsct.org
World Wide Web: www.accsct.org

THEATER
Samuel Hope, Executive Director
National Association of Schools of Theatre
11250 Roger Bacon Drive, Suite 21
Reston, Virginia 20190
Telephone: 703-437-0700
Fax: 703-437-6312
E-mail: shope@arts-accredit.org
World Wide Web: nast.arts-accredit.org

THEOLOGY
Bernard Fryshman, Executive Vice President
Association of Advanced Rabbinical and Talmudic Schools
11 Broadway, Suite 405
New York, New York 10004
Telephone: 212-363-1991
Fax: 212-533-5335

Daniel O. Aleshire, Executive Director
Association of Theological Schools in the United States and Canada
10 Summit Park Drive
Pittsburgh, Pennsylvania 15275
Telephone: 412-788-6505 Ext. 237
Fax: 412-788-6510
E-mail: ats@ats.edu
World Wide Web: www.ats.edu

Russell Guy Fitzgerald, Executive Director
Transnational Association of Christian Colleges and Schools
Accreditation Commission
15935 Forest Road
P.O. Box 328
Forest, Virginia 24551
Telephone: 434-525-9539
Fax: 434-525-9538
E-mail: rfitzgerald@tracs.org
World Wide Web: www.tracs.org

VETERINARY MEDICINE
Donald G. Simmons, Director of Education and Research Division
American Veterinary Medical Association
1931 North Meacham Road, Suite 100
Schaumburg, Illinois 60173
Telephone: 847-925-8070 Ext. 6674
Fax: 847-925-9329
E-mail: dsimmons@avma.org
World Wide Web: www.avma.org

How to Use This Guide

As you identify the particular programs and institutions that interest you, you can use both Book 1 and the specialized volumes (Books 2–6) to obtain detailed information—Book 1 for information on the institutions overall and Books 2 through 6 for details about the individual graduate units and their degree programs.

Directory of Graduate and Professional Programs by Field

This directory lists the 491 fields covered in *Peterson's Graduate and Professional Programs,* with an alphabetical listing of each of the institutions offering graduate or professional work in that field. Institutions in the United States and U.S. territories and those in Canada, Mexico, Europe, and Africa that are accredited by U.S. accrediting bodies are included. The directory enables readers who are interested in a particular academic area to quickly identify the colleges and universities that they might wish to attend. In each field, degree levels are given if an institution provided the information in response to *Peterson's Annual Survey of Graduate and Professional Institutions.* An *M* indicates that a master's degree program is offered; a *D* indicates that a doctoral program is offered; a *P* indicates that the first professional degree is offered; and an *O* signifies that other advanced degrees (e.g., certificates and specialist degrees) are offered. If no degree is listed, the school offers a degree in a subdiscipline of the field, not in the field itself.

All of the programs listed in this directory are profiled, and many are described in detail in **Close-Ups** or outlined briefly in **Announcements** in Books 2–6. These **Announcements** and **Close-Ups** are indicated in the directory listings by an asterisk, and their page numbers may be found by consulting the indexes of Books 2–6. The **Profiles, Announcements, and Close-Ups Index** at the back of this book indicates the institutions that chose to place a Close-Up or an Announcement in *this* volume.

Directory of Institutions and Their Offerings

This directory contains information identical to that in the **Directory of Graduate and Professional Programs by Field** but conversely presented. Accredited institutions in the United States and U.S. territories and those in Canada, Mexico, Europe, and Africa that are accredited by U.S. accrediting bodies are given here, with an alphabetical listing of which programs they offer out of the 491 selected fields that are covered in the guides. The directory will be of value to readers who are interested in the range of programs at particular institutions, as well as those who wish to compare programs and degree levels. The degree levels are shown if the institution provided information in response to *Peterson's Annual Survey of Graduate and Professional Institutions;* the degree levels included are master's, doctorate, first professional, and other advanced degrees (e.g., certificates and specialist degrees), included as *M, D, P,* and *O,* respectively.

All of the programs listed in this directory are profiled, and many are described in detail in **Close-Ups** or outlined briefly in **Announcements** in Books 2–6. A note at the end of each institution's listing refers the reader to the specific page number if an **Announcement** or **Close-Up** appears in **this** book. If there is such information in Books 2–6, an asterisk appears in the column that lists the degree level offered. The reader should then refer to the **Index of Close-Ups and Announcements** in the appropriate volume.

Profiles of Institutions Offering Graduate and Professional Work

This section presents profiles of accredited colleges and universities in the United States and U.S. territories and those in Canada, Mexico, Europe, and Africa that are accredited by U.S. accrediting bodies. Together with the other sections of Book 1, it is both a basic reference source and a foundation for the other five volumes of *Peterson's Graduate and Professional Programs.* (Books 2–6 provide descriptions of graduate programs in the humanities, arts, and social sciences; the biological sciences; the physical sciences, mathematics, agricultural sciences, the environment, and natural resources; engineering and applied sciences; and business, education, health, information studies, law, and social work, respectively.) The profiles in this section include the data on graduate and professional units that were submitted in 2007 by each institution in response to *Peterson's Annual Survey of Graduate and Professional Institutions.* If an institution provided all of the information requested, the profile includes all of the items listed below. A number of graduate school administrators have written brief **Announcements**, which follow their profiles. In these, readers will find information an institution wants to emphasize. In addition, bolded reference lines at the end of a profile indicate the page number on which the reader will find a **Close-Up**, if the institution has chosen to submit one. The absence of an **Announcement** or **Close-Up** does not reflect any type of editorial judgment on the part of Peterson's.

General Information

Type. An institution's control is indicated as independent (private nonprofit), independent with religious affiliation, proprietary (private profit-making), or state-supported or state-related (public). Whether an institution is coeducational or primarily for men or women is indicated. A few schools are designated as undergraduate: women (or men) only; graduate: coed. Institutional type is given as university, comprehensive, graduate only, or upper level.

CGS Membership. Membership in the Council of Graduate Schools in the United States and in Canada is indicated here.

Enrollment. Enrollment figures include total matriculated students (graduate, professional, and undergraduate), total full- and part-time matriculated graduate and professional students, and the number of women in each category.

Enrollment by Degree Level. Figures include the total number of students enrolled at each degree level—master's, doctoral, first-professional, and other advanced degrees.

Graduate Faculty. The numbers of full-time and part-time/adjunct faculty members actively involved with graduate students through teaching or research are given, followed by numbers of women.

Graduate Expenses. Tuition and fees for the overall institution for 2007–08 are indicated on a full-time (per academic year, semester, quarter, etc.) and/or a part-time (per credit, semester hour, quarter hour, course, etc.) basis. In-state and out-of-state figures are supplied where applicable. For exact costs at any given time, contact the schools and programs directly. Keep in mind that the tuition of Canadian institutions is usually given in Canadian dollars.

Graduate Housing. Institutions were asked to indicate whether housing for single and married students is guaranteed or available on a first-come, first-served basis and whether that includes board and to indicate the typical cost per year.

Student Services. Each institution was asked which of the following services are available to graduate and professional students: campus employment opportunities, campus safety program, career counseling, child day-care facilities, disabled student services, exercise/

wellness program, free psychological counseling, grant writing training, international student services, low-cost health insurance, multicultural affairs office, teacher training, and writing training.

Library Facilities. The main library name and the number of additional on-campus libraries, if any, are provided. Also provided are online resources, such as library catalog, Web page, and other libraries' catalogs, and numbers of titles, current serial subscriptions, and audiovisual materials.

Research Affiliations. Institutions were asked to name up to six independent research centers, laboratories, or institutes with which they maintain formal arrangements providing extra research or study opportunities for graduate students.

Computer Facilities

Institutions were asked to provide the total number of PCs and/or terminals available for student use, whether a campuswide network is available, and whether Internet access and/or online class registration is available. The institution's Web site also appears here if that information was supplied.

General Application Contact

The name, title, telephone number, fax number, and e-mail address of the person to contact for further information about applying to graduate and professional programs appear here.

Graduate Units

Each major graduate and professional unit within the institution (school, college, institute, center, etc.) is listed below the general information. These units are arranged to show the hierarchical structure of the institution. Those units offering advanced degree programs through the graduate school are listed immediately beneath it. Professional schools not connected with the graduate school are listed separately.

Enrollment. The number of full- and part-time matriculated students and the number of women, minority-group members, and international students are given. Average age is indicated, followed by the number of applicants, percentage accepted, and the number enrolled.

Faculty. Full-time and part-time/adjunct figures are given, and the number of women is indicated.

Expenses. For individual program expenses, readers are advised to contact the institution.

Financial Support. Information is given on the number of fellowships and assistantships awarded in 2006–07 and the availability of other types of aid. The financial aid application deadline is also indicated.

Degree Program Information. The number of degrees awarded in calendar year 2006 is given, broken down by degree level, followed by the availability of part-time and evening/weekend programs. Degree programs offered through the subunits and the specific degrees awarded are listed. Special degree information is also included, such as that a degree is offered jointly with another university.

Applying. The application deadline (for domestic and international students) and application fee are given, followed by a person to contact and a telephone number, fax number, and e-mail address (if provided).

Head. The head of the unit and his or her title are indicated, along with a telephone number, fax number, and e-mail address (if provided).

Close-Ups of Institutions Offering Graduate and Professional Work

The **Close-Ups** in this section present an overview of accredited graduate and professional schools in the United States and U.S. territories and institutions in Canada, Mexico, Europe, and Africa that are accredited by U.S. accrediting bodies. Critical information sought by all prospective graduate students—regardless of their intended field of study—has been supplied by the schools themselves.

In addition to listing the degree programs available, each entry gives valuable information on research facilities, financial aid opportunities, tuition rates, living and housing costs, students, the faculty, location, the university, and application criteria—in short, facts that all prospective graduate students need to know about an institution when selecting a graduate program.

After using the **Close-Ups** and the other sections of this volume to identify those universities that are appropriate to your needs, refer to the other five volumes for specific program information. Graduate and professional schools and colleges within the institutions represented in Book 1 are considered in detail in Books 2–6, which cover the humanities, arts, and social sciences; the biological sciences; the physical sciences, mathematics, agricultural sciences, the environment, and natural resources; engineering and applied sciences; and business, education, health, information studies, law, and social work, respectively.

Appendixes

This section contains two appendixes. The first, *Institutional Changes Since the 2007 Edition*, lists institutions that have closed, moved, merged, or changed their name or status since the last edition of the guides. The second, *Abbreviations Used in the Guides*, gives abbreviations of degree names, along with what those abbreviations stand for. These appendixes are identical in all six volumes of *Peterson's Graduate and Professional Programs.*

Indexes

There are two indexes in this section. The first, **Profiles, Announcements, and Close-Ups**, gives page references for all information on all graduate and professional schools in this volume. Location of the institution's **Profile** is indicated in normal type. An *italic* page number indicates that an **Announcement** follows the institution's **Profile**. A **boldface** page number indicates the location of an institution's **Close-Up**. The second, **Directories and Subject Areas in Books 2–6**, gives references to the directories in other volumes of this set and also includes cross-references for subject area names not used in the directory structure, for example, "Arabic (*see* Near and Middle Eastern Languages)."

Data Collection Procedures

The information published in the directories and **Profiles** of all the books is collected through *Peterson's Annual Survey of Graduate and Professional Institutions.* The survey is sent each spring to more than 2,200 institutions offering postbaccalaureate degree programs, including accredited institutions in the United States, U.S. territories, and Canada and those institutions outside the United States that are accredited by U.S. accrediting bodies. Deans and other administrators complete these surveys, providing information on programs in the 491 academic and professional fields covered in the guides as well as overall institutional information. While every effort has been made to ensure the accuracy and completeness of the data, information is sometimes unavailable or changes occur after publication deadlines. All usable information received in time for publication has been included. The omission of any particular item from a directory or **Profile** signifies either that the item is not applicable to the institution or program or that information was not available. **Profiles** of programs scheduled to begin during the 2007–08 academic year cannot, obviously, include statistics on enrollment or, in many cases, the number of faculty members. If no usable data were submitted by an institution, its name, address, and program name appear in order to indicate the availability of graduate work.

Criteria for Inclusion in This Guide

To be included in this guide, an institution must have full accreditation or be a candidate for accreditation (preaccreditation) status by an institutional or specialized accrediting body recognized by the U.S. Department of Education or the Council for Higher Education Accreditation (CHEA). Institutional accrediting bodies, which review each institution as a whole, include the six regional associations of schools and colleges (Middle States, New England, North Central, Northwest, Southern, and Western), each of which is responsible for a specified portion of the United States and its territories. Other institutional accrediting bodies are national in scope and accredit specific kinds of institutions (e.g., Bible colleges, independent colleges, and rabbinical and Talmudic schools). Program registration by the New York State Board of Regents is considered to be the equivalent of institutional accreditation, since the board requires that all programs offered by an institution meet its standards before recognition is granted. A Canadian institution must be chartered and authorized to grant degrees by the provincial government, affiliated with a chartered institution, or accredited by a recognized U.S. accrediting body. This guide also includes institutions outside the United States that are accredited by these U.S. accrediting bodies. There are recognized specialized or professional accrediting bodies in more than fifty different fields, each of which is authorized to accredit institutions or specific programs in its particular field. For specialized institutions that offer programs in one field only, we designate this to be the equivalent of institutional accreditation. A full explanation of the accrediting process and complete information on recognized institutional (regional and national) and specialized accrediting bodies can be found online at www.chea.org or at www.ed.gov/admins/finaid/accred/index.html.

DIRECTORY OF GRADUATE AND PROFESSIONAL PROGRAMS BY FIELD

ACCOUNTING

Institution	Degrees
Abilene Christian University	M
Adelphi University	M*
Alabama State University	M
American InterContinental University (FL)	M
American InterContinental University Buckhead Campus	M
American InterContinental University Online	M
American University	M*
Anderson University	M,D
Andrews University	M
Angelo State University	M
Appalachian State University	M
Argosy University, Atlanta Campus	M,D*
Argosy University, Chicago Campus	M,D*
Argosy University, Denver Campus	M,D*
Argosy University, Hawai'i Campus	M,D,O*
Argosy University, Inland Empire Campus	M,D*
Argosy University, Nashville Campus	D*
Argosy University, Orange County Campus	M,D,O*
Argosy University, Phoenix Campus	M,D*
Argosy University, San Diego Campus	M,D*
Argosy University, San Francisco Bay Area Campus	M,D*
Argosy University, Santa Monica Campus	M,D*
Argosy University, Sarasota Campus	M,D,O*
Argosy University, Schaumburg Campus	M,D,O*
Argosy University, Seattle Campus	M,D*
Argosy University, Tampa Campus	M,D,O*
Argosy University, Twin Cities Campus	M,D*
Argosy University, Washington DC Campus	M,D,O*
Arizona State University	M,D*
Arizona State University at the West campus	O
Arkansas State University	M
Auburn University	M*
Avila University	M*
Baker College Center for Graduate Studies	M
Baldwin-Wallace College	M
Ball State University	M*
Barry University	M*
Bayamón Central University	M
Baylor University	M*
Benedictine University	M
Bentley College	M,D*
Bernard M. Baruch College of the City University of New York	M,D*
Bob Jones University	P,M,D,O
Boise State University	M
Boston College	M*
Boston University	M,D,O*
Bowling Green State University	M*
Bradley University	M
Brenau University	M
Bridgewater State College	M
Brigham Young University	M*
Brock University	M
Brooklyn College of the City University of New York	M
Bryant University	M,O
Caldwell College	M
California State University, East Bay	M
California State University, Fresno	M
California State University, Fullerton	M
California State University, Los Angeles	M
California State University, Sacramento	M*
California Western School of Law	P,M
Canisius College	M
Capella University	M,D,O
Cardean University	M
Caribbean University	M,D
Carnegie Mellon University	D*
Case Western Reserve University	M,D*
Centenary College	M
Central Michigan University	M*
Central Washington University	M
Charleston Southern University	M
City University	M,O
Clark University	M*
Cleary University	M
Clemson University	M*
Cleveland State University	M
College of Charleston	M*
The College of Saint Rose	M*
The College of William and Mary	M
Colorado State University	M*
Colorado Technical University—Colorado Springs	M,D
Colorado Technical University—Denver	M
Columbia University	M,D*
Concordia University (Canada)	M,D,O
Cornell University	D*
Dallas Baptist University	M
Davenport University	M
Davenport University	M
Delta State University	M
DePaul University	M*
DeVry University	M*
Dominican University	M
Drexel University	M,D,O*
East Carolina University	M*
Eastern Illinois University	M,O
Eastern Michigan University	M
Eastern University	M*
East Tennessee State University	M
Elmhurst College	M
Fairfield University	M,O*
Fairleigh Dickinson University, College at Florham	M*
Fairleigh Dickinson University, Metropolitan Campus	M,O*
Fitchburg State College	M
Florida Agricultural and Mechanical University	M*
Florida Atlantic University	M
Florida Gulf Coast University	M
Florida International University	M*
Florida Metropolitan University–South Orlando Campus	M
Florida Metropolitan University–Tampa Campus	M
Florida Southern College	M
Florida State University	M,D*
Fontbonne University	M
Fordham University	M*
Fort Hays State University	M
Gannon University	O
The George Washington University	M,D*
Georgia College & State University	M
Georgia Institute of Technology	M,D,O*
Georgia Southern University	M
Georgia State University	M,D,O*
Golden Gate University	M,D,O
Gonzaga University	M
Governors State University	M
Graduate School and University Center of the City University of New York	D*
Grand Valley State University	M
Hawai'i Pacific University	M*
HEC Montreal	M,O
Hendrix College	M
Hofstra University	M*
Houston Baptist University	M
Howard University	M*
Hunter College of the City University of New York	M
Illinois State University	M*
Indiana Tech	M
Indiana University Northwest	M,O
Indiana University South Bend	M
Indiana University Southeast	M,O
Indiana Wesleyan University	M
Inter American University of Puerto Rico, Metropolitan Campus	M
Inter American University of Puerto Rico, Ponce Campus	M
Inter American University of Puerto Rico, San Germán Campus	M,D
Iowa State University of Science and Technology	M*
Ithaca College	M
Jackson State University	M
James Madison University	M
John Carroll University	M
Johnson & Wales University	M*
Jones International University	M*
Kansas State University	M*
Kean University	M
Kennesaw State University	M
Kent State University	M,D*
Lamar University	M*
Lehigh University	M*
Lehman College of the City University of New York	M
Lincoln University (MO)	M
Lindenwood University	M
Lipscomb University	M
Long Island University, Brooklyn Campus	M*
Long Island University, C.W. Post Campus	M,O*
Louisiana State University and Agricultural and Mechanical College	M,D*
Louisiana Tech University	M,D
Loyola University Chicago	M*
Marquette University	M
Maryville University of Saint Louis	M,O
McGill University	M,D,O*
Mercer University	M
Miami University	M*
Michigan State University	M,D*
Middle Tennessee State University	M*
Millsaps College	M
Minnesota State University Mankato	M
Mississippi College	M,O
Mississippi State University	M,D
Missouri State University	M*
Monmouth University	M,O
Montana State University	M
Montclair State University	M*
Murray State University	M
National University	M
New Jersey City University	M
New Mexico State University	M
New York Institute of Technology	M,O
New York University	M,D*
North Carolina State University	M*
Northeastern Illinois University	M
Northeastern State University	M
Northeastern University	M,O*
Northern Illinois University	M
Northern Kentucky University	M
Northwestern University	D*
Northwest Missouri State University	M
Notre Dame College (OH)	M,O
Nova Southeastern University	M*
Nyack College	M
Oakland University	M,O*
The Ohio State University	M,D*
Oklahoma City University	M
Oklahoma State University	M,D*
Old Dominion University	M*
Oral Roberts University	M
Pace University	M*
Pacific States University	M,D
Penn State University Park	M,D*
Pittsburg State University	M
Pontifical Catholic University of Puerto Rico	M,D
Prairie View A&M University	M
Purdue University	M,D*
Purdue University Calumet	M
Queens College of the City University of New York	M
Quinnipiac University	M*
Regis University	M,O
Rhode Island College	M
Rhodes College	M
Rider University	M*
Robert Morris University	M
Rochester Institute of Technology	M
Roosevelt University	M
Rutgers, The State University of New Jersey, Newark	M,D,O*
St. Ambrose University	M
St. Bonaventure University	M,O
St. Edward's University	M,O
St. John's University (NY)	M,O
St. Joseph's College, New York	M*
St. Joseph's College, Suffolk Campus	M
Saint Joseph's University	M*
Saint Leo University	M
Saint Louis University	M*
St. Mary's University of San Antonio	M
Saint Peter's College	M,O
St. Thomas University	M,O
Saint Vincent College	M
San Diego State University	M*
San Jose State University	M
Seattle University	M
Seton Hall University	M*
Southeastern University	M
Southeast Missouri State University	M
Southern Adventist University	M
Southern Illinois University Carbondale	M,D*
Southern Illinois University Edwardsville	M
Southern Methodist University	M*
Southern New Hampshire University	M,D,O*
Southern University and Agricultural and Mechanical College	M*
Southern Utah University	M
Southwestern Adventist University	M
State University of New York at Binghamton	M,D*
State University of New York at Fredonia	M
State University of New York at New Paltz	M
State University of New York College at Old Westbury	M*
State University of New York Institute of Technology	M
Stephen F. Austin State University	M
Stetson University	M
Stonehill College	M
Strayer University	M
Suffolk University	M,O*
Swedish Institute, College of Health Sciences	M
Syracuse University	M,D*
Tabor College	M
Tarleton State University	M
Temple University	M,D*
Texas A&M International University	M
Texas A&M University	M,D*
Texas A&M University–Corpus Christi	M
Texas A&M University–Texarkana	M
Texas Christian University	M
Texas State University-San Marcos	M*
Texas Tech University	M,D
Towson University	M
Trinity University	M*
Truman State University	M
Universidad Central del Este	M
Universidad del Este	M
Universidad del Turabo	M
Universidad Metropolitana	M,O
Universidad Nacional Pedro Henriquez Urena	P,M,D
Université de Sherbrooke	M
Université du Québec à Montréal	M,O
Université du Québec à Trois-Rivières	O
Université du Québec en Outaouais	M,O
Université Laval	M,O
University at Albany, State University of New York	M*
University at Buffalo, the State University of New York	M,D,O*
The University of Akron	M
The University of Alabama	M,D
The University of Alabama in Huntsville	M,O
University of Alberta	D*
The University of Arizona	M*
University of Arkansas	M*
University of Baltimore	M*
The University of British Columbia	D*
University of California, Berkeley	D*
University of Central Arkansas	M
University of Central Florida	M*
University of Central Missouri	M
University of Cincinnati	M,D
University of Colorado at Boulder	D*
University of Colorado at Colorado Springs	M
University of Colorado at Denver and Health Sciences Center	M*
University of Connecticut	M,D*
University of Dallas	M
University of Delaware	M*
University of Denver	M*
University of Florida	M,D*
University of Georgia	M*
University of Hartford	M,O*
University of Hawaii at Manoa	M,D*
University of Houston	M,D*
University of Houston–Clear Lake	M
University of Idaho	M*
University of Illinois at Chicago	M*
University of Illinois at Springfield	M
University of Illinois at Urbana–Champaign	M,D*
The University of Iowa	M,D*
University of Kansas	M*
University of Kentucky	M*
University of La Verne	M
University of Lethbridge	M,D
University of Louisville	M
University of Maine	M*
University of Mary Hardin-Baylor	M
University of Maryland University College	M,O
University of Massachusetts Amherst	M*
University of Massachusetts Dartmouth	M,O
University of Memphis	M,D*
University of Miami	M*
University of Michigan–Dearborn	M*
University of Minnesota, Twin Cities Campus	M,D*
University of Mississippi	M,D
University of Missouri–Columbia	M,D*
University of Missouri–Kansas City	M,D*
University of Missouri–St. Louis	M,O

The University of Montana M*
University of Nebraska at Omaha M
University of Nebraska–Lincoln M,D*
University of Nevada, Las Vegas M
University of Nevada, Reno M*
University of New Hampshire M*
University of New Haven M*
University of New Mexico M*
University of New Orleans M
The University of North Carolina at Chapel Hill M,D*
The University of North Carolina at Charlotte M*
The University of North Carolina at Greensboro M,O
The University of North Carolina Wilmington M*
University of Northern Iowa M
University of Northern Virginia M,D
University of North Florida M*
University of North Texas M,D*
University of Notre Dame M*
University of Oklahoma M*
University of Oregon M,D*
University of Pennsylvania M,D*
University of Phoenix–Augusta Campus M
University of Phoenix–Austin Campus M
University of Phoenix–Bay Area Campus M
University of Phoenix–Central Florida Campus M
University of Phoenix–Central Valley Campus M
University of Phoenix–Charlotte Campus M
University of Phoenix–Chattanooga Campus M
University of Phoenix–Cleveland Campus M
University of Phoenix–Columbus Georgia Campus M
University of Phoenix–Dallas Campus M
University of Phoenix–Denver Campus M
University of Phoenix–Des Moines Campus M
University of Phoenix–Detroit Campus M
University of Phoenix–Fort Lauderdale Campus M
University of Phoenix–Harrisburg Campus M
University of Phoenix–Hawaii Campus M
University of Phoenix–Idaho Campus M
University of Phoenix–Jersey City Campus M
University of Phoenix–Madison Campus M
University of Phoenix–Memphis Campus M
University of Phoenix–Minneapolis/St. Louis Park Campus M
University of Phoenix–Northern Nevada Campus M
University of Phoenix–Northern Virginia Campus M
University of Phoenix–North Florida Campus M
University of Phoenix–Northwest Arkansas Campus M
University of Phoenix–Omaha Campus M
University of Phoenix Online Campus M
University of Phoenix–Oregon Campus M
University of Phoenix–Pittsburgh Campus M
University of Phoenix–Puerto Rico Campus M
University of Phoenix–Raleigh Campus M
University of Phoenix–Renton Learning Center M
University of Phoenix–Richmond Campus M
University of Phoenix–Sacramento Valley Campus M
University of Phoenix–San Antonio Campus M
University of Phoenix–Savannah Campus M
University of Phoenix–Southern Arizona Campus M
University of Phoenix–Southern California Campus M
University of Phoenix–Springfield Campus M
University of Phoenix–West Michigan Campus M
University of Rhode Island M
University of St. Thomas (MN) M*
University of San Diego M,O*
University of Saskatchewan M
The University of Scranton M
University of South Alabama M*
University of South Carolina M*
The University of South Dakota M
University of Southern California M*
University of Southern Indiana M
University of Southern Maine M
University of Southern Mississippi M*
University of South Florida M*
The University of Tampa M
The University of Tennessee M,D*
The University of Tennessee at Chattanooga M
The University of Tennessee at Martin M
The University of Texas at Arlington M,D*
The University of Texas at Austin M,D*
The University of Texas at Dallas M,D*
The University of Texas at El Paso M
The University of Texas at San Antonio M,D*
The University of Texas of the Permian Basin M
The University of Toledo M*
University of Toronto M,D
University of Utah M,D*
University of Virginia M*
University of Washington M,D*
University of Waterloo M,D*
The University of Western Ontario M,D
University of West Florida M
University of West Georgia M
University of Wisconsin–Madison D*
University of Wisconsin–Whitewater M*
University of Wyoming M
Upper Iowa University M
Utah State University M
Utica College M
Villanova University M*
Virginia Commonwealth University M,D*
Virginia Polytechnic Institute and State University M,D*
Wagner College M
Wake Forest University M*
Walsh College of Accountancy and Business Administration M
Washington State University M,D*
Washington University in St. Louis M*
Wayne State College M
Wayne State University M,D*
Webber International University M*
Weber State University M*
Western Carolina University M*
Western Connecticut State University M*
Western Illinois University M*
Western Michigan University M*
Western New England College M*
West Texas A&M University M
West Virginia University M*
Wheeling Jesuit University M*
Wichita State University M*
Widener University M*
Wilkes University M
Worcester State College M
Wright State University M
Yale University D*
Youngstown State University M

ACOUSTICS

The Catholic University of America M,D*
Penn State University Park M,D*
University of Massachusetts Dartmouth M,D,O

ACTUARIAL SCIENCE

Ball State University M*
Boston University M*
Central Connecticut State University M,O
Columbia University M*
Georgia State University M*
Maryville University of Saint Louis M
Roosevelt University M
St. John's University (NY) M
Simon Fraser University M,D
Temple University M*
Université du Québec à Montréal O
University of Central Florida M,O*
University of Connecticut M,D*
The University of Iowa M,D*
University of Nebraska–Lincoln M*
University of Waterloo M,D*
University of Wisconsin–Madison M*

ACUPUNCTURE AND ORIENTAL MEDICINE

Academy of Chinese Culture and Health Sciences M
Academy of Oriental Medicine at Austin M
Acupuncture & Integrative Medicine College, Berkeley M
Acupuncture and Massage College M
American College of Acupuncture and Oriental Medicine M
American College of Traditional Chinese Medicine M,D,O
Atlantic Institute of Oriental Medicine M
Bastyr University M,D,O*
Colorado School of Traditional Chinese Medicine M
Dongguk Royal University M
East West College of Natural Medicine M
Emperor's College of Traditional Oriental Medicine M,D
Five Branches Institute: College of Traditional Chinese Medicine M
Florida College of Integrative Medicine M
Institute of Clinical Acupuncture and Oriental Medicine M
Midwest College of Oriental Medicine M,O
National College of Natural Medicine M
National University of Health Sciences P,M,D*
New England School of Acupuncture M*
New York Chiropractic College M*
New York College of Health Professions M
New York College of Traditional Chinese Medicine M
Northwestern Health Sciences University M
Oregon College of Oriental Medicine M,D*
Pacific College of Oriental Medicine M,D
Pacific College of Oriental Medicine-Chicago M
Pacific College of Oriental Medicine-New York M
Samra University of Oriental Medicine M,D
Seattle Institute of Oriental Medicine M
South Baylo University M
Southern California University of Health Sciences M
Southwest Acupuncture College M
Swedish Institute, College of Health Sciences M
Tai Sophia Institute for the Healing Arts M
Texas College of Traditional Chinese Medicine M
Traditional Chinese Medical College of Hawaii M
Tri State College of Acupuncture M,O
University of Bridgeport M
World Medicine Institute: College of Acupuncture and Herbal Medicine M
Yo San University of Traditional Chinese Medicine M

ACUTE CARE/CRITICAL CARE NURSING

Allen College M
Barry University M,O*
Case Western Reserve University M,D*
The College of New Rochelle M,O
Columbia University M,O*
Duke University M,D,O*
Duquesne University M,O*
Indiana University–Purdue University Indianapolis M*
The Johns Hopkins University M,O*
Loyola University Chicago M*
New York University M,O*
Northeastern University M,O*
Rush University M,D,O
Seton Hall University M*
Texas Tech University Health Sciences Center M,O
Universidad de Iberoamerica P,M
University at Buffalo, the State University of New York M,D,O*
University of Cincinnati M,D
University of Connecticut M,D,O*
University of Guelph M,D,O
University of Massachusetts Worcester M,D,O*
University of Miami M,D*
University of Michigan M*
University of Pennsylvania M*
University of Pittsburgh M,D*
University of South Carolina M,O*
Vanderbilt University M,D*
Wayne State University M*
Wright State University M*

ADDICTIONS/SUBSTANCE ABUSE COUNSELING

Adler School of Professional Psychology M,D,O*
Argosy University, Hawai'i Campus O*
Capella University M,D,O
The College of New Jersey M,O
College of St. Joseph M
The College of William and Mary M,D
Coppin State University M
East Carolina University M*
Eastern Kentucky University M*
Georgian Court University M,O
Governors State University M
Hofstra University M,O*
The Johns Hopkins University M,D,O*
Kean University M,O
Lewis & Clark College M
Loyola College in Maryland M,O
Marywood University M*
Mercy College M,O
Minnesota State University Mankato M
Monmouth University M,O
Montclair State University M,O*
National-Louis University M,O
Notre Dame de Namur University M,O
Pace University M*
Palm Beach Atlantic University M,O
St. Mary's University of San Antonio M,D,O
Southern New Hampshire University M,O*
Springfield College M,O*
Stony Brook University, State University of New York M*
Universidad Central del Caribe M
Université de Montréal M,D,O
University of Central Florida M,O*
University of Central Oklahoma M
University of Detroit Mercy M,O
University of Great Falls M,O
University of Illinois at Springfield M
University of Lethbridge M,D
University of Louisiana at Monroe M
University of New England M,O
Wayne State University O*

ADULT EDUCATION

Alverno College M
Armstrong Atlantic State University M
Athabasca University M,O
Auburn University M,D,O*
Ball State University M,D*
Buffalo State College, State University of New York M,O
Capella University M,D,O
Cheyney University of Pennsylvania M
Cleveland State University M,O
Concordia University (Canada) M,O
Coppin State University M,O
Cornell University M,D*
Curry College M,O
DePaul University M*
Drake University M*
East Carolina University M,O*
Eastern Washington University M
Florida Agricultural and Mechanical University M,D*
Florida Atlantic University M,D,O
Florida International University M,D*
Florida State University M,D,O*
Fordham University M,D,O*
Grand Valley State University M
Indiana University of Pennsylvania M
Jones International University M
Kansas State University M,D*
Kean University M
Marshall University M
Marygrove College M
Memorial University of Newfoundland M,D,O
Michigan State University M,D,O*
Morehead State University M,D,O
Mount Saint Vincent University M
National-Louis University M,D,O

*P—first professional degree; M—master's degree; D—doctorate; O—other advanced degree; *full description and/or announcement in Book 2, 3, 4, 5, or 6*

North Carolina Agricultural and Technical State University M
North Carolina State University M,D*
Northern Illinois University M,D
Northwestern Oklahoma State University M
Northwestern State University of Louisiana M
Nova Southeastern University D*
Oregon State University M*
Penn State Harrisburg M,D*
Penn State University Park M,D*
Portland State University M,D
Regis University M,O
Robert Morris University M
Rutgers, The State University of New Jersey, New Brunswick M*
St. Francis Xavier University M
San Francisco State University M,O
Seattle University M,O
Suffolk University M,O*
Teachers College Columbia University M,D*
Texas A&M University–Kingsville M
Texas A&M University–Texarkana M
Touro University International M
Troy University M
Tusculum College M
Université du Québec en Outaouais O
University of Alaska Anchorage M
University of Alberta M,D,O*
University of Arkansas M,D,O*
University of Arkansas at Little Rock M
The University of British Columbia M,D*
University of Central Oklahoma M
University of Cincinnati M,D,O
University of Connecticut M,D*
University of Denver M,D,O*
University of Georgia M,D,O*
University of Idaho M,D,O*
University of Manitoba M
University of Memphis M,D*
University of Minnesota, Twin Cities Campus M,D,O*
University of Missouri–Columbia M,D,O*
University of Missouri–St. Louis M,D,O
The University of North Carolina at Greensboro M,D,O
University of Oklahoma M,D*
University of Phoenix–Bay Area Campus M
University of Phoenix–Metro Detroit Campus M
University of Phoenix–Omaha Campus M
University of Phoenix Online Campus M
University of Phoenix–Sacramento Valley Campus M,O
University of Phoenix–Springfield Campus M
University of Regina M
University of Rhode Island M
University of St. Francis (IL) M
University of Southern Maine M,O
University of Southern Mississippi M,D,O*
University of South Florida M,D,O*
The University of Tennessee M,D*
The University of Texas at San Antonio M,D*
University of the Incarnate Word M,D,O
The University of West Alabama M
University of Wisconsin–Platteville M
University of Wyoming M,D,O
Valdosta State University M,D
Virginia Commonwealth University M*
Virginia Polytechnic Institute and State University M,D,O*
Walden University M,D
Wayne State University M,D,O*
Western Washington University M
Widener University M,D*
Wright State University O*

ADULT NURSING

Angelo State University M
Barnes-Jewish College of Nursing and Allied Health M
Bloomsburg University of Pennsylvania M
Boston College M,D*
Case Western Reserve University M,D*
The Catholic University of America M,D*
College of Mount Saint Vincent M,O
College of Staten Island of the City University of New York M,O
Columbia University M,O*
Daemen College M,O
DeSales University M
Duke University M,D,O*
Eastern Michigan University M,O
Emory University M*
Fairfield University M,O*
Felician College M,O*
The George Washington University M,D,O*
Georgia State University M,D,O*
Gwynedd-Mercy College M
Hunter College of the City University of New York M
The Johns Hopkins University M,O*
La Salle University M,O
Lehman College of the City University of New York M
Loma Linda University M
Long Island University, Brooklyn Campus M,O*
Louisiana State University Health Sciences Center M,D*
Loyola University Chicago M*
Madonna University M
Marian College of Fond du Lac M
Marquette University M,D,O
Medical College of Georgia M,D*
Medical University of South Carolina M*
Mercy College M,O
Molloy College M,O
Mount Carmel College of Nursing M*
Mount Saint Mary College M
New Mexico State University M
New York University M,O*
Oakland University M*
Oregon Health & Science University M,O*
Otterbein College M,O
Quinnipiac University M,O*
Rush University M,D,O
Rutgers, The State University of New Jersey, Newark M*
Sage Graduate School M,O
Saint Xavier University M,O
Seton Hall University M*
Southern Adventist University M
Spalding University M
State University of New York at New Paltz M,O
State University of New York Institute of Technology M,O
Stony Brook University, State University of New York M,O*
Texas Christian University M
Texas Woman's University M,D
University at Buffalo, the State University of New York M,D,O*
University of Central Florida D,O*
University of Cincinnati M,D
University of Colorado at Colorado Springs M,D
University of Connecticut M,D,O*
University of Delaware M,O*
University of Hawaii at Manoa M,D,O*
University of Massachusetts Lowell M*
University of Massachusetts Worcester M,D,O*
University of Medicine and Dentistry of New Jersey M,D,O*
University of Miami M,D*
University of Michigan M*
University of Minnesota, Twin Cities Campus M*
University of Missouri–Kansas City M,D*
The University of North Carolina at Charlotte M*
The University of North Carolina at Greensboro M,D,O
University of Pennsylvania M*
University of Pittsburgh M,D*
University of San Diego M,D,O*
University of San Francisco M
The University of Scranton M,O
University of South Alabama M,D*
University of South Carolina M*
University of Southern Maine M,O
University of Southern Mississippi M,D*
The University of Tampa M
The University of Tennessee at Chattanooga M
The University of Texas–Pan American M
University of Wisconsin–Oshkosh M
Vanderbilt University M,D*
Villanova University M,D,O*
Virginia Commonwealth University M,D,O*
Wayne State University M*
Western Connecticut State University M*
Wilmington College (DE) M
Winona State University M
Wright State University M*

ADVERTISING AND PUBLIC RELATIONS

Academy of Art University M*
Ball State University M*
Boston University M*
California State University, Fullerton M
Colorado State University M*
Emerson College M*
Golden Gate University M,D,O
Huron University USA in London M
Iona College M*
Marquette University M*
Michigan State University M,D*
Mississippi College M
Monmouth University M,O
Montana State University–Billings M
Montclair State University M*
New York Institute of Technology M,O
New York University M*
Northwestern University M*
Rowan University M*
Royal Roads University M*
San Diego State University M*
Savannah College of Art and Design M*
Syracuse University M*
Texas Christian University M
Towson University O
Université Laval O
The University of Alabama M
University of Colorado at Denver and Health Sciences Center M,O*
University of Denver M*
University of Florida M*
University of Houston M*
University of Illinois at Urbana–Champaign M*
University of Maryland, College Park M,D*
University of Miami M,D*
University of New Haven M*
University of Oklahoma M*
University of Southern California M*
University of Southern Mississippi M,D*
The University of Tennessee M,D*
The University of Texas at Austin M,D*
University of the Sacred Heart M
University of Wisconsin–Stevens Point M
Virginia Commonwealth University M*
Wayne State University M,D*
Webster University M

AEROSPACE/AERONAUTICAL ENGINEERING

Air Force Institute of Technology M,D
Arizona State University M,D*
Arizona State University at the Polytechnic Campus M
Auburn University M,D*
Boston University M,D*
Brown University M,D*
California Institute of Technology M,D,O*
California Polytechnic State University, San Luis Obispo M
California State University, Long Beach M
Carleton University M,D
Case Western Reserve University M,D*
Concordia University (Canada) M
Cornell University M,D*
École Polytechnique de Montréal M,D,O
Embry-Riddle Aeronautical University (FL) M*
Embry-Riddle Aeronautical University Worldwide M
Florida Institute of Technology M,D*
The George Washington University M,D,O*
Georgia Institute of Technology M,D*
Illinois Institute of Technology M,D*
Iowa State University of Science and Technology M,D*
Massachusetts Institute of Technology M,D,O*
McGill University M,D*
Middle Tennessee State University M*
Mississippi State University M
Naval Postgraduate School M
North Carolina State University M,D*
The Ohio State University M,D*
Oklahoma State University M*
Old Dominion University M*
Penn State University Park M,D*
Polytechnic University, Long Island Graduate Center M,D
Princeton University M,D*
Purdue University M,D*
Rensselaer Polytechnic Institute M,D*
Rutgers, The State University of New Jersey, New Brunswick M,D*
San Diego State University M,D*
San Jose State University M
Stanford University M,D,O*
Syracuse University M,D*
Texas A&M University M,D*
Université Laval M
University at Buffalo, the State University of New York M,D*
The University of Alabama M,D
The University of Alabama in Huntsville M,D
The University of Arizona M,D*
University of California, Davis M,D,O*
University of California, Irvine M,D*
University of California, Los Angeles M,D*
University of California, San Diego M,D*
University of Central Florida M*
University of Cincinnati M,D
University of Colorado at Boulder M,D*
University of Colorado at Colorado Springs M
University of Dayton M,D*
University of Florida M,D,O*
University of Houston M,D*
University of Illinois at Urbana–Champaign M,D*
University of Kansas M,D*
University of Maryland, College Park M,D,O*
University of Miami M,D*
University of Michigan M,D*
University of Minnesota, Twin Cities Campus M,D*
University of Missouri–Columbia M,D*
University of Missouri–Rolla M,D*
University of Notre Dame M,D*
University of Oklahoma M,D*
University of Ottawa M,D*
University of Southern California M,D,O*
The University of Tennessee M,D*
The University of Tennessee Space Institute M,D*
The University of Texas at Arlington M,D*
The University of Texas at Austin M,D*
University of Toronto M,D
University of Virginia M,D*
University of Washington M,D*
Utah State University M,D
Virginia Polytechnic Institute and State University M,D*
Webster University M,D
West Virginia University M,D*
Wichita State University M,D*

AFRICAN-AMERICAN STUDIES

Boston University M*
Clark Atlanta University M,D
Columbia University M*
Cornell University M,D*
Florida Agricultural and Mechanical University M*
Harvard University D*
Indiana University Bloomington M*
Michigan State University M,D*
Morgan State University M,D*
North Carolina Agricultural and Technical State University M
The Ohio State University M*
Syracuse University M*
Temple University M,D*
University at Albany, State University of New York M*
University of California, Berkeley D*
University of California, Los Angeles M*
The University of Iowa M*
University of Massachusetts Amherst M,D*
University of Wisconsin–Madison M*
West Virginia University M,D*
Yale University M,D*

AFRICAN STUDIES

Boston University M,O*
Claremont Graduate University M,D,O
Columbia University O*
Cornell University M,D*
Florida International University M*
Harvard University D*
Howard University M,D*
The Johns Hopkins University M,D,O*

Michigan State University M,D*
New York University M,D,O*
Northwestern University O*
The Ohio State University M*
Ohio University M*
Rutgers, The State University of New Jersey, New Brunswick D*
St. John's University (NY) M,O
Syracuse University M*
University at Albany, State University of New York M*
University of California, Los Angeles M*
University of Connecticut M*
University of Florida O*
University of Illinois at Urbana–Champaign M*
University of Louisville M
University of Pittsburgh O*
University of South Florida M*
University of Wisconsin–Madison M,D*
West Virginia University M,D*
Yale University M*

AGRICULTURAL ECONOMICS AND AGRIBUSINESS

Alabama Agricultural and Mechanical University M
Alcorn State University M
American University of Beirut M
Arizona State University at the Polytechnic Campus M
Auburn University M,D*
California Polytechnic State University, San Luis Obispo M
Colorado State University M,D*
Cornell University M,D*
Delaware Valley College
Florida Agricultural and Mechanical University M*
Illinois State University M*
Instituto Centroamericano de Administración de Empresas M
Iowa State University of Science and Technology M,D*
Kansas State University M,D*
Louisiana State University and Agricultural and Mechanical College M,D*
McGill University M*
Michigan State University M,D*
Mississippi State University M,D
Montana State University M
New Mexico State University M
North Carolina Agricultural and Technical State University M
North Carolina State University M*
North Dakota State University M,D
Northwest Missouri State University M
The Ohio State University M,D*
Oklahoma State University M,D*
Oregon State University M,D*
Penn State University Park M,D*
Prairie View A&M University M
Purdue University M,D*
Rutgers, The State University of New Jersey, New Brunswick M*
South Carolina State University M
Southern Illinois University Carbondale M*
Texas A&M University M,D*
Texas A&M University–Kingsville M
Texas Tech University M,D
Tuskegee University M
Université Laval M
University of Alberta M,D*
The University of Arizona M*
University of Arkansas M*
The University of British Columbia M*
University of California, Berkeley D*
University of California, Davis M,D*
University of California, Santa Barbara M,D*
University of Connecticut M,D*
University of Delaware M*
University of Florida M,D*
University of Georgia M,D*
University of Guelph M,D
University of Idaho M*
University of Illinois at Urbana–Champaign M,D*
University of Kentucky M,D*
University of Maine M*
University of Manitoba M,D
University of Maryland, College Park M,D*
University of Massachusetts Amherst M,D*
University of Missouri–Columbia M,D*
University of Nebraska–Lincoln M,D*
University of Nevada, Reno M,D*
University of Puerto Rico, Mayagüez Campus M*
University of Saskatchewan M,D
University of Vermont M*
University of Wisconsin–Madison M,D*
University of Wyoming M
Virginia Polytechnic Institute and State University M,D*
Washington State University M,D,O*
West Texas A&M University M
West Virginia University M*
William Woods University M,O

AGRICULTURAL EDUCATION

Alcorn State University M,O
Arkansas State University M,O
Clemson University M*
Cornell University M,D*
Eastern Kentucky University M*
Iowa State University of Science and Technology M,D*
Louisiana State University and Agricultural and Mechanical College M,D*
Mississippi State University M
Missouri State University M*
Murray State University M
New Mexico State University M
North Carolina Agricultural and Technical State University M
North Carolina State University M*
North Dakota State University M
Northwest Missouri State University M
The Ohio State University M,D*
Oklahoma State University M,D*
Oregon State University M*
Penn State University Park M,D*
Purdue University M,D,O*
State University of New York at Oswego M
Stephen F. Austin State University M
Tarleton State University M
Texas A&M University M,D*
Texas A&M University–Commerce M
Texas A&M University–Kingsville M
Texas State University-San Marcos M*
Texas Tech University M,D
The University of Arizona M*
University of Arkansas M*
University of Connecticut M,D*
University of Florida M,D*
University of Georgia M*
University of Idaho M,D*
University of Illinois at Urbana–Champaign M,D*
University of Minnesota, Twin Cities Campus M,D*
University of Missouri–Columbia M,D,O*
University of Nebraska–Lincoln M*
University of Puerto Rico, Mayagüez Campus M*
The University of Tennessee M*
University of Wisconsin–River Falls M
Utah State University M
West Virginia University M*

AGRICULTURAL ENGINEERING

Cornell University M,D*
Dalhousie University M,D
Illinois Institute of Technology M,D*
Instituto Tecnológico y de Estudios Superiores de Monterrey, Campus Monterrey M,D
Iowa State University of Science and Technology M,D*
Kansas State University M,D*
Louisiana State University and Agricultural and Mechanical College M,D*
McGill University M,D*
Michigan State University M,D*
New York University M,D*
North Carolina Agricultural and Technical State University M
North Carolina State University M,D*
North Dakota State University M,D
The Ohio State University M,D*
Oklahoma State University M,D*
Penn State Great Valley M
Penn State University Park M,D*
Purdue University M,D*
Rutgers, The State University of New Jersey, New Brunswick M*
South Dakota State University M,D
Texas A&M University M,D*
Université Laval M
The University of Arizona M,D*
University of Arkansas M,D*
University of Dayton M*
University of Florida M,D,O*
University of Georgia M,D*
University of Idaho M,D*
University of Illinois at Urbana–Champaign M,D*
University of Kentucky M,D*
University of Minnesota, Twin Cities Campus M,D*
University of Missouri–Columbia M,D*
University of Nebraska–Lincoln M,D*
University of Saskatchewan M,D
The University of Tennessee M*
University of Wisconsin–Madison M,D*
Utah State University M,D
Virginia Polytechnic Institute and State University M,D*
Washington State University M,D*

AGRICULTURAL SCIENCES—GENERAL

Alabama Agricultural and Mechanical University M,D
Alcorn State University M
Angelo State University M
Arkansas State University M,O
Auburn University M,D*
Brigham Young University M,D*
California Polytechnic State University, San Luis Obispo M
California State Polytechnic University, Pomona M
California State University, Fresno M
Clemson University M,D*
Colorado State University M,D*
Dalhousie University M
Florida Agricultural and Mechanical University M*
Illinois State University M*
Instituto Tecnológico y de Estudios Superiores de Monterrey, Campus Monterrey M,D
Iowa State University of Science and Technology M,D*
Kansas State University M,D*
Louisiana State University and Agricultural and Mechanical College M,D*
McGill University M,D,O*
McNeese State University M*
Michigan State University M,D*
Mississippi State University M,D
Missouri State University M*
Montana State University M,D
Murray State University M
New Mexico State University M
North Carolina Agricultural and Technical State University M
North Carolina State University M,D*
North Dakota State University M,D
Northwest Missouri State University M
Nova Scotia Agricultural College M
The Ohio State University M,D*
Oklahoma State University M,D*
Oregon State University M,D*
Penn State University Park M,D*
Prairie View A&M University M
Purdue University M,D*
Sam Houston State University M
South Dakota State University M,D
Southern Illinois University Carbondale M*
Southern University and Agricultural and Mechanical College M*
Tarleton State University M
Tennessee State University M*
Texas A&M University M,D*
Texas A&M University–Commerce M
Texas A&M University–Kingsville M,D
Texas Tech University M,D
Tropical Agriculture Research and Higher Education Center M,D
Tuskegee University M
Université Laval M,D,O
University of Alberta M,D*
The University of Arizona M,D*
University of Arkansas M,D*
The University of British Columbia M,D*
University of California, Davis M*
University of Connecticut M,D*
University of Delaware M,D*
University of Florida M,D*
University of Georgia M,D*
University of Guelph M,D,O
University of Hawaii at Manoa M,D*
University of Illinois at Urbana–Champaign M,D*
University of Kentucky M,D*
University of Lethbridge M,D
University of Maine M,D*
University of Manitoba M,D
University of Maryland, College Park P,M,D*
University of Maryland Eastern Shore M,D*
University of Minnesota, Twin Cities Campus M,D*
University of Missouri–Columbia M,D*
University of Nebraska–Lincoln M,D*
University of Nevada, Reno M,D*
University of Puerto Rico, Mayagüez Campus M*
University of Saskatchewan M,D
The University of Tennessee M,D*
The University of Tennessee at Martin M
University of Vermont M,D*
University of Wisconsin–Madison M,D*
University of Wisconsin–River Falls M
University of Wyoming M,D
Utah State University M,D
Virginia Polytechnic Institute and State University M,D*
Washington State University M*
Western Kentucky University M
West Texas A&M University M,D
West Virginia University M,D*

AGRONOMY AND SOIL SCIENCES

Alabama Agricultural and Mechanical University M,D
Alcorn State University M
American University of Beirut M
Auburn University M,D*
Brigham Young University M,D*
Colorado State University M,D*
Cornell University M,D*
Iowa State University of Science and Technology M,D*
Kansas State University M,D*
Louisiana State University and Agricultural and Mechanical College M,D*
McGill University M,D*
Michigan State University M,D*
Mississippi State University M,D
New Mexico State University M,D
North Carolina State University M,D*
North Dakota State University M,D
Nova Scotia Agricultural College M
The Ohio State University M,D*
Oklahoma State University M,D*
Oregon State University M,D*
Penn State University Park M,D*
Prairie View A&M University M
Purdue University M,D*
South Dakota State University M,D
Southern Illinois University Carbondale M*
Texas A&M University M,D*
Texas A&M University–Kingsville M,D
Texas Tech University M,D
Tuskegee University M
Université Laval M,D
University of Alberta M,D*
The University of Arizona M,D*
University of Arkansas M,D*
The University of British Columbia M,D*
University of California, Davis M,D*
University of California, Riverside M,D*
University of Connecticut M,D*
University of Delaware M,D*
University of Florida M,D*
University of Georgia M,D*
University of Guelph M,D
University of Idaho M,D*
University of Illinois at Urbana–Champaign M,D*
University of Kentucky M,D*
University of Maine M,D*
University of Manitoba M,D
University of Maryland, College Park M,D*
University of Massachusetts Amherst M,D*
University of Minnesota, Twin Cities Campus M,D*
University of Missouri–Columbia M,D*
University of Nebraska–Lincoln M,D*
University of New Hampshire M*
University of Puerto Rico, Mayagüez Campus M*
University of Saskatchewan M,D
University of Vermont M,D*
University of Wisconsin–Madison M,D*
University of Wyoming M,D
Utah State University M,D
Virginia Polytechnic Institute and State University M,D*
Washington State University M,D*

P—first professional degree; M—master's degree; D—doctorate; O—other advanced degree;
**full description and/or announcement in Book 2, 3, 4, 5, or 6*

West Virginia University M,D*

ALLIED HEALTH—GENERAL

Alabama State University D
Alderson-Broaddus College M
Andrews University M
Arkansas State University M,O
Athabasca University M,O
A.T. Still University of Health Sciences M,D
Barnes-Jewish College of Nursing and Allied Health M,O
Baylor University M,D*
Belmont University M,D
Bennington College O*
Boston University M,D*
Brock University M
Cleveland State University M
College Misericordia M,D
Creighton University P,M,D*
Dominican College M,D
Drexel University M,D,O*
Duquesne University M,D*
East Carolina University M,D*
Eastern Kentucky University M*
East Tennessee State University M,D,O
Emory University M,D*
Ferris State University M
Florida Agricultural and Mechanical University M*
Florida Gulf Coast University M
Georgia Southern University M,O
Georgia State University M,D,O*
Grand Valley State University M,D
Idaho State University M,D,O
Ithaca College M,D
Loma Linda University M,D
Long Island University, C.W. Post Campus M,O*
Louisiana State University Health Sciences Center M*
Marymount University M,D,O
Maryville University of Saint Louis M,D
Medical College of Georgia M,D*
Medical University of South Carolina M,D*
Mercy College M,O
MGH Institute of Health Professions M,D,O*
Midwestern University, Downers Grove Campus M,D*
Midwestern University, Glendale Campus P,M,O*
Minnesota State University Mankato M,O
Mountain State University M*
New Jersey City University M
Northeastern University P,M,D,O*
Northern Arizona University M,D,O
Nova Southeastern University M,D*
Oakland University M,D,O*
The Ohio State University M*
Old Dominion University M,D*
Quinnipiac University M,D,O*
Regis University M,D
Rosalind Franklin University of Medicine and Science M,D*
Saint Louis University M,D,O*
Seton Hall University M,D*
Shenandoah University M,D,O*
South Carolina State University M
Southwestern Oklahoma State University M
Temple University M,D*
Tennessee State University M,D*
Texas Christian University M
Texas State University-San Marcos M*
Texas Tech University Health Sciences Center M,D
Texas Woman's University M,D
Towson University M
University at Buffalo, the State University of New York M,D,O*
The University of Alabama at Birmingham M,D,O*
University of Connecticut M*
University of Detroit Mercy M,O
University of Florida M,D*
University of Illinois at Chicago M,D*
University of Kansas M,D,O*
University of Kentucky M,D*
University of Massachusetts Lowell M,D*
University of Medicine and Dentistry of New Jersey M,D,O*
University of Mississippi Medical Center M*
University of Nebraska Medical Center M,D,O*
The University of North Carolina at Chapel Hill M,D*
University of North Florida M,O
University of Oklahoma Health Sciences Center M,D,O
University of Phoenix–Charlotte Campus M
University of Phoenix–Las Vegas Campus M
University of Puerto Rico, Medical Sciences Campus M,O*
University of St. Francis (IL) M
University of Saint Francis (IN) M
University of South Alabama M,D*
The University of South Dakota M,D
The University of Tennessee Health Science Center M,D*
The University of Texas at El Paso M
The University of Texas Medical Branch M*
University of Vermont M,D*
University of Wisconsin–Milwaukee M,D
Virginia Commonwealth University D*
Washington University in St. Louis M,D,O*
Western University of Health Sciences M,D
Wichita State University M*

ALLOPATHIC MEDICINE

Albany Medical College P
Albert Einstein College of Medicine P*
American University of Beirut P,M
Baylor College of Medicine P*
Boston University P*
Brown University P*
Case Western Reserve University P*
Charles R. Drew University of Medicine and Science P
Columbia University P*
Cornell University, Joan and Sanford I. Weill Medical College and Graduate School of Medical Sciences P,M,D*
Creighton University P*
Dalhousie University P
Drexel University P*
Duke University P*
East Carolina University P*
Eastern Virginia Medical School P
East Tennessee State University P
Emory University P*
Florida State University P,D*
Georgetown University P*
The George Washington University P*
Harvard University P,D*
Howard University P,D*
Instituto Tecnologico de Santo Domingo P,M
The Johns Hopkins University P*
Loma Linda University P,M,D
Louisiana State University Health Sciences Center P,M*
Louisiana State University Health Sciences Center at Shreveport P*
Loyola University Chicago P*
Marshall University P
Mayo Medical School P
McGill University M,D*
Medical College of Georgia P*
Medical College of Wisconsin P*
Medical University of South Carolina P*
Meharry Medical College P
Memorial University of Newfoundland P
Mercer University P,M
Michigan State University P*
Morehouse School of Medicine P*
Mount Sinai School of Medicine of New York University P*
New York Medical College P*
New York University P*
Northeastern Ohio Universities College of Medicine P
Northwestern University *
The Ohio State University P*
Oregon Health & Science University P*
Penn State Hershey Medical Center P,M,D*
Ponce School of Medicine P
Pontificia Universidad Catolica Madre y Maestra P
Queen's University at Kingston P
Rosalind Franklin University of Medicine and Science P*
Rush University P*
Saint Louis University P*
San Juan Bautista School of Medicine P
Stanford University P*
State University of New York Downstate Medical Center P,M*
State University of New York Upstate Medical University P*
Stony Brook University, State University of New York P*
Temple University P*
Texas Tech University Health Sciences Center P
Thomas Jefferson University P*
Tufts University P*
Tulane University P*
Uniformed Services University of the Health Sciences P*
Universidad Autonoma de Guadalajara P
Universidad Central del Caribe P,M
Universidad Central del Este P
Universidad de Ciencias Medicas P,M
Universidad de Iberoamerica P,M
Universidad Iberoamericana P
Universidad Nacional Pedro Henriquez Urena P
Université de Montréal P,O
Université de Sherbrooke P
Université Laval P,O
University at Buffalo, the State University of New York P*
The University of Alabama at Birmingham P,M,D*
The University of Arizona P*
The University of British Columbia P,M*
University of Calgary P
University of California, Berkeley *
University of California, Davis P*
University of California, Irvine P*
University of California, Los Angeles P*
University of California, San Diego P*
University of California, San Francisco P
University of Chicago P*
University of Cincinnati P,M
University of Colorado at Denver and Health Sciences Center P*
University of Connecticut Health Center P*
University of Florida P*
University of Hawaii at Manoa P*
University of Illinois at Chicago P*
University of Illinois at Urbana–Champaign *
The University of Iowa P*
University of Kansas P*
University of Kentucky P*
University of Louisville P
University of Maryland, Baltimore P*
University of Massachusetts Worcester P*
University of Medicine and Dentistry of New Jersey P*
University of Miami P*
University of Michigan P*
University of Minnesota, Duluth P*
University of Minnesota, Twin Cities Campus P*
University of Mississippi Medical Center P*
University of Missouri–Columbia P*
University of Missouri–Kansas City P*
University of Nebraska Medical Center P*
University of New Mexico P*
The University of North Carolina at Chapel Hill P*
University of North Dakota P
University of Oklahoma Health Sciences Center P
University of Ottawa P,M,D*
University of Pennsylvania P*
University of Pittsburgh P*
University of Puerto Rico, Medical Sciences Campus P*
University of Rochester P*
University of Saskatchewan P
University of South Alabama P*
University of South Carolina P*
The University of South Dakota P
University of Southern California P*
The University of Tennessee Health Science Center P,M,D*
The University of Texas Health Science Center at Houston P*
The University of Texas Health Science Center at San Antonio P*
The University of Texas Medical Branch P*
The University of Texas Southwestern Medical Center at Dallas P*
The University of Toledo M*
University of Toronto P,M,D
University of Utah P*
University of Vermont P*
University of Virginia P,M,D*
University of Washington P*
The University of Western Ontario P,M
University of Wisconsin–Madison P*
Vanderbilt University M,D*
Virginia Commonwealth University P*
Wake Forest University P*
Washington University in St. Louis P*
Wayne State University P*
West Virginia University P*
Wright State University P*
Yale University P*

AMERICAN INDIAN/NATIVE AMERICAN STUDIES

Montana State University M
Trent University M,D
The University of Arizona M,D*
University of California, Davis M,D*
University of California, Los Angeles M*
University of Kansas M*
University of Lethbridge M,D
University of Manitoba M
University of Oklahoma M*
University of Regina M

AMERICAN STUDIES

American University M,D,O*
Appalachian State University M
Baylor University M*
Boston University D*
Bowling Green State University M,D*
Brandeis University M,D*
Brown University M,D*
California State University, Fullerton M
Claremont Graduate University M,D,O
The College of William and Mary M,D
Columbia University M*
Cornell University M,D*
Drake University M*
East Carolina University M*
Eastern Michigan University M
Emory & Henry College M
Fairfield University M*
Florida State University M,O*
The George Washington University M,D*
Harvard University D*
Lehigh University M*
Michigan State University M,D*
New Mexico Highlands University M
New York University M,D*
Northeastern State University M
Penn State Harrisburg M*
Pepperdine University M*
Purdue University M,D*
Saint Louis University M,D*
State University of New York College at Cortland O*
Stony Brook University, State University of New York M,O*
Trinity College M
Universidad de las Américas–Puebla M
University at Buffalo, the State University of New York M,D*
The University of Alabama M
University of Central Oklahoma M
University of Dallas M
University of Delaware M*
University of Hawaii at Manoa M,D,O*
The University of Iowa M,D*
University of Kansas M,D*
University of Louisiana at Lafayette D*
University of Maryland, College Park M,D*
University of Massachusetts Boston M
University of Michigan M,D
University of Michigan–Flint M*
University of Minnesota, Twin Cities Campus M,D*
University of Mississippi M
University of New Mexico M,D*
University of Pennsylvania M,D*
University of Southern California D*
University of Southern Maine M
University of South Florida M*
The University of Texas at Austin M,D*
University of Utah M,D*
University of Wyoming M
Utah State University M
Washington State University M,D*
Western Carolina University M*
West Virginia University M,D*
Wheaton College M
Yale University M,D*

ANALYTICAL CHEMISTRY

Auburn University M,D*

Brigham Young University M,D*
California State University, Fullerton M
California State University, Los Angeles M
Case Western Reserve University M,D*
Clarkson University M,D*
Cleveland State University M,D
Cornell University D*
Florida State University M,D*
Georgetown University M,D*
The George Washington University M,D*
Governors State University M
Howard University M,D*
Illinois Institute of Technology M,D*
Indiana University Bloomington M,D*
Kansas State University M,D*
Kent State University M,D*
Marquette University M,D
McMaster University M,D
Miami University M,D*
Northeastern University M,D*
Old Dominion University M,D*
Oregon State University M,D*
Purdue University M,D*
Rensselaer Polytechnic Institute M,D*
Rutgers, The State University of New Jersey, Newark M,D*
Rutgers, The State University of New Jersey, New Brunswick M,D*
Seton Hall University M,D*
Southern University and Agricultural and Mechanical College M*
State University of New York at Binghamton M,D*
Stevens Institute of Technology M,D,O*
Tufts University M,D*
University of Calgary M,D
University of Cincinnati M,D
University of Georgia M,D
University of Louisville M,D
University of Maryland, College Park M,D*
University of Michigan D*
University of Missouri–Columbia M,D*
University of Missouri–Kansas City M,D*
The University of Montana M,D*
University of Nebraska–Lincoln M,D*
University of Regina M,D
University of Southern Mississippi M,D*
University of South Florida M,D*
The University of Tennessee M,D*
The University of Texas at Austin M,D*
The University of Toledo M,D*
Vanderbilt University M,D*
Virginia Commonwealth University M,D*
Wake Forest University M,D*
West Virginia University M,D*

ANATOMY

Albert Einstein College of Medicine D*
Auburn University M,D*
Barry University M*
Boston University M,D*
Case Western Reserve University M,D*
Columbia University M,D*
Cornell University M,D*
Creighton University M*
Dalhousie University M,D*
Duke University D*
East Carolina University D*
East Tennessee State University M,D
Howard University M,D*
Indiana University–Purdue University Indianapolis M,D*
The Johns Hopkins University D*
Kansas State University M,D*
Loma Linda University M,D
Louisiana State University Health Sciences Center M,D*
Louisiana State University Health Sciences Center at Shreveport M,D*
Loyola University Chicago M,D*
McGill University M,D*
Medical College of Georgia M,D*
Medical University of South Carolina D*
New York Medical College M,D*
The Ohio State University M,D*
Palmer College of Chiropractic M*
Penn State Hershey Medical Center M,D*
Purdue University M,D*
Queen's University at Kingston M,D
Rosalind Franklin University of Medicine and Science M,D*
Rush University M,D*
Saint Louis University M,D*
State University of New York Upstate Medical University M,D*
Stony Brook University, State University of New York D*
Temple University M,D*
Texas A&M University M,D*
Universidad Central del Caribe M
Université Laval M,D,O
University at Buffalo, the State University of New York M,D*
The University of Arizona D*
University of Arkansas for Medical Sciences M,D*
The University of British Columbia M,D*
University of California, Irvine M,D*
University of California, Los Angeles D*
University of California, San Francisco D
University of Chicago D*
University of Georgia M*
University of Guelph M,D
University of Illinois at Chicago M,D*
The University of Iowa D*
University of Kansas M,D*
University of Kentucky D*
University of Louisville M,D
University of Manitoba M,D
University of Maryland, Baltimore *
University of Mississippi Medical Center M,D*
University of Nebraska Medical Center M,D*
University of North Dakota M,D
University of North Texas Health Science Center at Fort Worth M,D
University of Prince Edward Island M,D
University of Puerto Rico, Medical Sciences Campus M,D*
University of Rochester M,D*
University of Saskatchewan M,D
University of South Florida M,D*
The University of Tennessee M,D*
The University of Tennessee Health Science Center D*
University of Utah D*
University of Vermont D*
The University of Western Ontario M,D
University of Wisconsin–Madison M,D*
Virginia Commonwealth University M,D,O*
Wake Forest University D*
Wayne State University M,D*
Wright State University M*

ANESTHESIOLOGIST ASSISTANT STUDIES

Case Western Reserve University M*
Emory University M*
South University (GA) M*
Université Laval O
University of Guelph M,D,O

ANIMAL BEHAVIOR

Arizona State University M,D*
Bucknell University M
Cornell University D*
Emory University D*
Illinois State University M,D*
University of California, Davis D*
University of Colorado at Boulder M,D*
University of Minnesota, Twin Cities Campus M,D*
University of Missouri–St. Louis M,D,O
The University of Montana M,D,O*
The University of Tennessee M,D*
The University of Texas at Austin D*

ANIMAL SCIENCES

Alabama Agricultural and Mechanical University M,D
Alcorn State University M
American University of Beirut M
Angelo State University M
Auburn University M,D*
Boise State University M
Brigham Young University M,D*
California State Polytechnic University, Pomona M
California State University, Fresno M
Clemson University M,D*
Colorado State University M,D*
Cornell University M,D*
Florida Agricultural and Mechanical University M*
Fort Valley State University M
Iowa State University of Science and Technology M,D*
Kansas State University M,D*
Louisiana State University and Agricultural and Mechanical College M,D*
McGill University M,D*
Michigan State University M,D*
Mississippi State University M
Montana State University M,D
New Mexico State University M,D
North Carolina State University M,D*
North Dakota State University M,D
Nova Scotia Agricultural College M
The Ohio State University M,D*
Oklahoma State University M,D*
Oregon State University M,D*
Penn State University Park M,D*
Prairie View A&M University M
Purdue University M,D*
Rutgers, The State University of New Jersey, New Brunswick M,D*
South Dakota State University M,D
Southern Illinois University Carbondale M*
Sul Ross State University M*
Texas A&M University M,D*
Texas A&M University–Kingsville M
Texas Tech University M,D
Tuskegee University M
Universidad Nacional Pedro Henriquez Urena P,M,D
Université Laval M,D
The University of Arizona M,D*
University of Arkansas M,D*
The University of British Columbia M,D*
University of California, Davis M,D*
University of Connecticut M,D*
University of Delaware M,D*
University of Florida M,D*
University of Georgia M,D*
University of Guelph M,D
University of Hawaii at Manoa M*
University of Idaho M,D*
University of Illinois at Urbana–Champaign M,D*
University of Kentucky M,D*
University of Maine M*
University of Manitoba M,D
University of Maryland, College Park M,D*
University of Massachusetts Amherst M,D*
University of Minnesota, Twin Cities Campus M,D*
University of Missouri–Columbia M,D*
University of Nebraska–Lincoln M,D*
University of Nevada, Reno M*
University of New Hampshire M,D*
University of Puerto Rico, Mayagüez Campus M*
University of Rhode Island M,D
University of Saskatchewan M,D
The University of Tennessee M,D*
University of Vermont M,D*
University of Wisconsin–Madison M,D*
University of Wyoming M,D
Utah State University M,D
Virginia Polytechnic Institute and State University M,D*
Washington State University M,D*
West Texas A&M University M
West Virginia University M,D*

ANTHROPOLOGY

American University M,D,O*
The American University in Cairo M
American University of Beirut M
Arizona State University M,D*
Ball State University M*
Boston University M,D*
Brandeis University M,D*
Brigham Young University M*
Brown University M,D*
California Institute of Integral Studies M,D*
California State University, Bakersfield M
California State University, Chico M
California State University, East Bay M
California State University, Fullerton M
California State University, Long Beach M
California State University, Los Angeles M
California State University, Northridge M
California State University, Sacramento M*
Carleton University M
Case Western Reserve University M,D*
The Catholic University of America M,D*
Central European University M,D*
The College of William and Mary M,D
Colorado State University M*
Columbia University M,D*
Concordia University (Canada) M
Cornell University D*
Dalhousie University M,D
Duke University D*
East Carolina University M*
Eastern New Mexico University M
Emory University D*
Florida Atlantic University M
Florida State University M,D*
The George Washington University M,D*
Georgia State University M*
Graduate School and University Center of the City University of New York D*
Harvard University M,D*
Hunter College of the City University of New York M
Idaho State University M
Indiana University Bloomington M,D*
Iowa State University of Science and Technology M*
The Johns Hopkins University D*
Kent State University M*
Louisiana State University and Agricultural and Mechanical College M,D*
Marshall University M
McGill University M,D*
McMaster University M,D
Memorial University of Newfoundland M,D
Michigan State University M,D*
Minnesota State University Mankato M
Mississippi State University M,D
New Mexico Highlands University M
New Mexico State University M
The New School: A University M,D*
New York University M,D*
North Carolina State University M*
Northern Arizona University M
Northern Illinois University M
Northwestern University D*
The Ohio State University M,D*
Oregon State University M*
Penn State University Park M,D*
Portland State University M,D,O
Princeton University D*
Purdue University M,D*
Rice University M,D*
Roosevelt University M
Rutgers, The State University of New Jersey, New Brunswick M,D*
San Diego State University M*
San Francisco State University M
Simon Fraser University M,D
Southern Illinois University Carbondale M,D*
Southern Methodist University M,D*
Stanford University M,D*
State University of New York at Binghamton M,D*
Stony Brook University, State University of New York M,D*
Syracuse University M,D*
Teachers College Columbia University M,D*
Temple University D*
Texas A&M University M,D*
Texas State University-San Marcos M*
Texas Tech University M
Trent University M
Tulane University M,D*
Universidad de las Américas–Puebla M
Université de Montréal M,D
Université Laval M,D
University at Albany, State University of New York M,D*
University at Buffalo, the State University of New York M,D*
The University of Alabama M,D
The University of Alabama at Birmingham M*
University of Alaska Anchorage M
University of Alaska Fairbanks M,D
University of Alberta M,D*
The University of Arizona M,D*
University of Arkansas M*
The University of British Columbia M,D*
University of Calgary M,D

P—first professional degree; M—master's degree; D—doctorate; O—other advanced degree;
**full description and/or announcement in Book 2, 3, 4, 5, or 6*

University of California, Berkeley D*
University of California, Davis M,D*
University of California, Irvine M,D*
University of California, Los Angeles M,D*
University of California, Riverside M,D*
University of California, San Diego D*
University of California, San Francisco D
University of California, Santa Barbara M,D*
University of California, Santa Cruz D*
University of Central Florida M,D,O*
University of Chicago M,D*
University of Cincinnati M
University of Colorado at Boulder M,D*
University of Colorado at Denver and Health Sciences Center M*
University of Connecticut M,D*
University of Denver M*
University of Florida M,D*
University of Georgia M,D*
University of Guelph M
University of Hawaii at Manoa M,D*
University of Houston M*
University of Idaho M*
University of Illinois at Chicago M,D*
University of Illinois at Urbana–Champaign M,D*
The University of Iowa M,D*
University of Kansas M,D*
University of Kentucky M,D*
University of Lethbridge M,D
University of Manitoba M,D
University of Maryland, College Park M*
University of Massachusetts Amherst M,D*
University of Memphis M*
University of Michigan D*
University of Minnesota, Duluth M*
University of Minnesota, Twin Cities Campus M,D*
University of Mississippi M
University of Missouri–Columbia M,D*
The University of Montana M,D*
University of Nebraska–Lincoln M*
University of Nevada, Las Vegas M,D
University of Nevada, Reno M,D*
University of New Brunswick Fredericton M
University of New Mexico M,D*
The University of North Carolina at Chapel Hill M,D*
University of North Texas M*
University of Oklahoma M,D*
University of Oregon M,D*
University of Ottawa M*
University of Pennsylvania M,D*
University of Pittsburgh M,D*
University of Regina M
University of Saskatchewan M
University of South Carolina M,D*
University of Southern California M,D,O*
University of Southern Mississippi M*
University of South Florida M,D*
The University of Tennessee M,D*
The University of Texas at Arlington M*
The University of Texas at Austin M,D*
The University of Texas at San Antonio M,D*
University of Toronto M,D
University of Tulsa M*
University of Utah M,D*
University of Victoria M
University of Virginia M,D*
University of Washington M,D*
University of Waterloo M*
The University of Western Ontario M,D
University of West Florida M
University of Wisconsin–Madison M,D*
University of Wisconsin–Milwaukee M,D,O
University of Wyoming M,D
Vanderbilt University M,D*
Washington State University M,D*
Washington University in St. Louis M,D*
Wayne State University M,D*
West Chester University of Pennsylvania M,O
Western Kentucky University M
Western Michigan University M*
Western Washington University M
Wichita State University M*
Yale University M,D*
York University M,D*

APPLIED ARTS AND DESIGN—GENERAL

Academy of Art University M*
Alfred University M*
Arizona State University M*
Art Center College of Design M*
Bowling Green State University M*
Bradley University M
California College of the Arts M*
California Institute of the Arts M,O
California State University, Fresno M
California State University, Fullerton M,O
California State University, Los Angeles M
Cardinal Stritch University M*
Carnegie Mellon University D*
Concordia University (Canada) O
Cranbrook Academy of Art M*
Drexel University M*
Fashion Institute of Technology M*
Ferris State University M
Florida Atlantic University M
Florida State University M,D*
The George Washington University M,D*
Howard University M*
Illinois Institute of Technology M,D*
Indiana University–Purdue University Indianapolis M*
Iowa State University of Science and Technology M*
Lamar University M*
Louisiana State University and Agricultural and Mechanical College M*
Louisiana Tech University M
Massachusetts College of Art M
Memphis College of Art M*
Minneapolis College of Art and Design M
New Mexico State University M
The New School: A University M*
New York University M*
North Carolina State University M,D*
NSCAD University M
Oklahoma State University M,D*
Pratt Institute M*
Purdue University M*
Rhode Island School of Design M
Rutgers, The State University of New Jersey, New Brunswick M*
San Diego State University M*
San Francisco Art Institute M,O*
San Jose State University M
Savannah College of Art and Design M*
School of Visual Arts M
Southern Illinois University Carbondale M*
Stephen F. Austin State University M
Suffolk University M*
Sul Ross State University M*
Syracuse University M*
University of Alberta M*
University of California, Berkeley M*
University of California, Los Angeles M*
University of Central Oklahoma M
University of Cincinnati M
University of Delaware M*
University of Idaho M*
University of Illinois at Urbana–Champaign M,D*
University of Kansas M*
University of Kentucky M*
University of Massachusetts Dartmouth M
University of Michigan M*
University of Minnesota, Twin Cities Campus M,D,O*
University of Notre Dame M*
University of Oklahoma M*
The University of Texas at Austin M*
University of Wisconsin–Madison M,D*
Virginia Commonwealth University M*
Virginia Polytechnic Institute and State University M*
Wayne State University M*
Western Michigan University M*
Yale University M*
York University M*

APPLIED ECONOMICS

American University M,D,O*
Auburn University M,D*
Buffalo State College, State University of New York M
Clemson University M,D*
Cornell University D*
Eastern Michigan University M
HEC Montreal M
The Johns Hopkins University M*
Mississippi State University M,D
Montana State University M
New York University M,D,O*
North Carolina Agricultural and Technical State University M
Northeastern University M,D*
Ohio University M*
Portland State University M,D
Roosevelt University M
St. Cloud State University M
San Jose State University M
Southern Methodist University M,D*
Texas Tech University M,D
University of California, Santa Cruz M*
University of Georgia M,D*
University of Michigan M*
University of Minnesota, Twin Cities Campus M,D*
University of Nevada, Reno M,D*
The University of North Carolina at Greensboro M
University of North Dakota M
University of North Texas M*
The University of Texas at Dallas M,D*
University of Vermont M*
University of Wisconsin–Madison M,D*
University of Wyoming M
Utah State University M
Virginia Polytechnic Institute and State University M,D*
Washington State University M,D,O*
Western Michigan University M,D*
Wright State University M*

APPLIED MATHEMATICS

Acadia University M
Air Force Institute of Technology M,D
Arizona State University M,D*
Auburn University M,D*
Bowie State University M
Brown University M,D*
California Institute of Technology M,D*
California State Polytechnic University, Pomona M
California State University, Fullerton M
California State University, Long Beach M,D
California State University, Los Angeles M
California State University, Northridge M
Case Western Reserve University M,D*
Central European University M,D*
Claremont Graduate University M,D
Clark Atlanta University M
Clemson University M,D*
Columbia University M,D,O*
Cornell University M,D*
Dalhousie University M,D
DePaul University M,O*
East Carolina University M*
École Polytechnique de Montréal M,D
Florida Atlantic University M,D
Florida Institute of Technology M,D*
Florida State University M,D*
The George Washington University M,D*
Georgia Institute of Technology M,D*
Hampton University M,D*
Harvard University M,D*
Hofstra University M*
Howard University M,D*
Hunter College of the City University of New York M
Illinois Institute of Technology M,D*
Indiana University Bloomington M,D*
Indiana University of Pennsylvania M
Indiana University–Purdue University Fort Wayne M,O
Indiana University–Purdue University Indianapolis M,D*
Indiana University South Bend M
Inter American University of Puerto Rico, San Germán Campus M
Iowa State University of Science and Technology M,D*
The Johns Hopkins University M,D*
Kent State University M,D*
Lehigh University M,D*
Long Island University, C.W. Post Campus M*
McGill University M,D*
Michigan State University M,D*
Montclair State University M,O*
Naval Postgraduate School M,D
New Jersey Institute of Technology M
New Mexico Institute of Mining and Technology M,D
North Carolina State University M,D*
North Dakota State University M,D
Northeastern University M,D*
Northwestern University M,D*
Oakland University M,D*
Oklahoma State University M,D*
Penn State University Park M,D*
Princeton University M,D*
Rensselaer Polytechnic Institute M*
Rice University M,D*
Rochester Institute of Technology M
Rutgers, The State University of New Jersey, New Brunswick M,D*
St. John's University (NY) M
San Diego State University M*
Santa Clara University M
Simon Fraser University M,D
Southern Methodist University M,D*
Stevens Institute of Technology M,D*
Stony Brook University, State University of New York M,D*
Temple University M,D*
Texas A&M University–Corpus Christi M
Texas State University-San Marcos M*
Towson University M
Tulane University M,D*
The University of Akron M,D
The University of Alabama M,D
The University of Alabama at Birmingham M,D*
The University of Alabama in Huntsville M,D
University of Alberta M,D,O*
The University of Arizona M,D*
University of Arkansas at Little Rock M
The University of British Columbia M,D*
University of California, Berkeley D*
University of California, Davis M,D*
University of California, San Diego M,D*
University of California, Santa Barbara M,D*
University of Central Florida M,D,O*
University of Central Missouri M
University of Central Oklahoma M
University of Chicago M,D*
University of Cincinnati M,D
University of Colorado at Boulder M,D*
University of Colorado at Colorado Springs M
University of Colorado at Denver and Health Sciences Center M,D*
University of Connecticut M*
University of Dayton M*
University of Delaware M,D*
University of Denver M,D*
University of Georgia M,D*
University of Guelph M,D
University of Illinois at Chicago M,D*
University of Illinois at Urbana–Champaign M,D*
The University of Iowa D*
University of Kansas M,D*
University of Kentucky M,D*
University of Louisville M,D
University of Maryland, Baltimore County M,D*
University of Maryland, College Park M,D*
University of Massachusetts Amherst M*
University of Massachusetts Lowell M,D*
University of Memphis M,D*
University of Michigan–Dearborn M*
University of Minnesota, Duluth M*
University of Missouri–Columbia M*
University of Missouri–Rolla M*
University of Missouri–St. Louis M,D
University of Nevada, Las Vegas M,D
University of New Hampshire M,D*
The University of North Carolina at Charlotte M,D*
University of Notre Dame M,D*
University of Pittsburgh M,D*
University of Puerto Rico, Mayagüez Campus M*
University of Rhode Island M,D,O
University of Southern California M,D*
The University of Tennessee M,D*
The University of Tennessee Space Institute M*
The University of Texas at Austin M,D*
The University of Texas at Dallas M,D*
The University of Toledo M,D*
University of Washington M,D*
University of Waterloo M,D*
The University of Western Ontario M,D

Utah State University M,D
Virginia Commonwealth University M,O*
Virginia Polytechnic Institute and State University M,D*
Washington State University M,D*
Wayne State University M,D*
Western Illinois University M,O
Western Michigan University M*
West Virginia University M,D*
Wichita State University M,D*
Worcester Polytechnic Institute M,D,O*
Wright State University M*
Yale University M,D*
York University M,D*

APPLIED PHYSICS

Air Force Institute of Technology M,D
Alabama Agricultural and Mechanical University M,D
Appalachian State University M
Brooklyn College of the City University of New York M,D
California Institute of Technology M,D*
Christopher Newport University M
Colorado School of Mines M,D
Columbia University M,D,O*
Cornell University M,D*
DePaul University M*
George Mason University M*
Harvard University M,D*
Iowa State University of Science and Technology M,D*
The Johns Hopkins University M*
Laurentian University M
Naval Postgraduate School M,D
New Jersey Institute of Technology M,D
Northern Arizona University M
Pittsburg State University M
Princeton University M,D*
Rensselaer Polytechnic Institute M,D*
Rice University M,D*
Rutgers, The State University of New Jersey, Newark M,D*
Southern Illinois University Carbondale M,D*
Stanford University M,D*
State University of New York at Binghamton M*
Texas A&M University M,D*
Texas Tech University M,D*
The University of Arizona M*
University of Arkansas M*
University of California, San Diego M,D*
University of Maryland, Baltimore County M,D*
University of Massachusetts Boston M
University of Massachusetts Lowell M,D*
University of Michigan D*
University of Missouri–St. Louis M,D
The University of North Carolina at Charlotte M,D*
University of South Florida M,D*
University of Washington M,D*
Virginia Commonwealth University M,D*
Virginia Polytechnic Institute and State University M,D*
West Virginia University M,D*
Yale University M,D*

APPLIED SCIENCE AND TECHNOLOGY

American University M,O*
The College of William and Mary M,D
Colorado State University-Pueblo M
Harvard University M,O*
James Madison University M
Louisiana State University and Agricultural and Mechanical College M*
Naval Postgraduate School M*
Oklahoma State University M*
Rensselaer Polytechnic Institute M*
Southeastern Louisiana University M
Southern Methodist University M,D*
University of Arkansas at Little Rock M,D
University of California, Berkeley D*
University of California, Davis M,D*
University of Colorado at Denver and Health Sciences Center M*
University of Mississippi M,D
University of Northern Colorado M

APPLIED SOCIAL RESEARCH

American University M,O*
California State University, Dominguez Hills M,O
Hunter College of the City University of New York M
The New School: A University M,D*
Portland State University M,D
University of California, Los Angeles M,D*
Virginia Commonwealth University M,O*
West Virginia University M*

APPLIED STATISTICS

American University M,O*
Bowling Green State University M,D*
Brigham Young University M*
California State University, East Bay M
Cornell University M,D*
DePaul University M,O*
Florida State University M,D*
Indiana University–Purdue University Fort Wayne M,O
Indiana University–Purdue University Indianapolis M*
Instituto Tecnológico y de Estudios Superiores de Monterrey, Campus Monterrey M,D
Kennesaw State University M
Louisiana State University and Agricultural and Mechanical College M*
McMaster University M*
Michigan State University M,D*
Montclair State University M,O*
New Jersey Institute of Technology M
North Dakota State University M,D,O
Oakland University M*
Oregon State University M,D*
Penn State University Park M,D*
Rochester Institute of Technology M,O
St. Cloud State University M
Stevens Institute of Technology O*
Syracuse University M*
The University of Alabama M,D
University of California, Riverside M,D*
University of California, Santa Barbara M,D*
University of Guelph M,D
University of Memphis M,D
University of Michigan M,D*
University of Nevada, Las Vegas M,D
University of Northern Colorado M,D
University of Pittsburgh M,D*
University of South Carolina M,D,O*
The University of Texas at San Antonio M,D*
Villanova University M*
Worcester Polytechnic Institute M,D,O*
Wright State University M*

AQUACULTURE

American University of Beirut M
Auburn University M,D*
Clemson University M,D*
Kentucky State University M
Memorial University of Newfoundland M
Nova Scotia Agricultural College M
Purdue University M,D*
Texas A&M University–Corpus Christi M
University of Florida M,D*
University of Guelph M
University of Rhode Island M,D

ARCHAEOLOGY

American University of Beirut M
Boston University M,D*
Brown University M,D*
Bryn Mawr College M,D*
Columbia University M,D*
Cornell University M,D*
Florida State University M,D*
George Mason University M*
Graduate School and University Center of the City University of New York D*
Harvard University M,D*
Illinois State University M*
Memorial University of Newfoundland M,D
Michigan Technological University M,D*
New York University M,D*
Northern Arizona University M,D*
Northwestern State University of Louisiana M
Princeton University D*
Simon Fraser University M,D
Trinity International University P,M,D,O
Tufts University M*
Universidad de las Américas–Puebla M
Université Laval M,D
University of Alberta M,D*
The University of British Columbia M,D*
University of Calgary M,D
University of California, Berkeley M,D*
University of California, Los Angeles M,D*
University of California, Santa Barbara M,D*
University of Chicago M,D*
University of Lethbridge M,D
University of Massachusetts Boston M
University of Memphis M*
University of Michigan D*
University of Minnesota, Twin Cities Campus M,D*
University of Missouri–Columbia M,D*
The University of North Carolina at Chapel Hill M,D*
University of Pennsylvania M,D*
University of Saskatchewan M,D
The University of Tennessee M,D*
The University of Texas at Austin M,D*
University of Virginia M,D*
University of West Florida M
Washington State University M,D*
Washington University in St. Louis M,D*
Wheaton College M
Yale University M*

ARCHITECTURAL ENGINEERING

Illinois Institute of Technology M,D*
Kansas State University M*
North Carolina Agricultural and Technical State University M
Oklahoma State University M*
Penn State University Park M,D*
University of Colorado at Boulder M,D
University of Detroit Mercy M
University of Kansas M*
University of Louisiana at Lafayette M*
University of Miami M,D*
University of Nebraska–Lincoln M*
The University of Texas at Austin M*

ARCHITECTURAL HISTORY

Arizona State University D*
Cornell University M,D*
Graduate School and University Center of the City University of New York D*
Harvard University D*
Massachusetts Institute of Technology M,D*
Savannah College of Art and Design M*
University of California, Berkeley M,D*
University of Pittsburgh M,D*
University of Virginia M,D*
Virginia Commonwealth University M,D*

ARCHITECTURE

Academy of Art University M*
Andrews University M*
Arizona State University M,D*
Auburn University M*
Ball State University M*
Boston Architectural College M*
California College of the Arts M*
California Polytechnic State University, San Luis Obispo M
California State Polytechnic University, Pomona M
Carleton University M
Carnegie Mellon University M,D*
The Catholic University of America M*
City College of the City University of New York M*
Clemson University M*
Columbia College Chicago M
Columbia University M,D*
Cornell University M,D*
Cranbrook Academy of Art M*
Dalhousie University M
Drexel University M*
Florida Agricultural and Mechanical University M*
Florida International University M*
Frank Lloyd Wright School of Architecture M
Georgia Institute of Technology M,D*
Harvard University M,D*
Idaho State University M
Illinois Institute of Technology M,D*
Instituto Tecnológico y de Estudios Superiores de Monterrey, Campus Estado de México M,D
Instituto Tecnológico y de Estudios Superiores de Monterrey, Campus Irapuato M,D
Iowa State University of Science and Technology M*
Kansas State University M*
Kent State University M,O*
Lawrence Technological University M
Louisiana State University and Agricultural and Mechanical College M*
Massachusetts Institute of Technology M,D*
McGill University M,D,O*
Miami University M*
Mississippi State University M
Montana State University M*
Morgan State University M*
New Jersey Institute of Technology M
The New School: A University M*
Newschool of Architecture & Design M
New York Institute of Technology M
North Carolina State University M*
Northeastern University M*
The Ohio State University M*
Oklahoma State University M*
Penn State University Park M*
Pontificia Universidad Catolica Madre y Maestra M
Prairie View A&M University M
Pratt Institute M*
Princeton University M,D*
Rensselaer Polytechnic Institute M,D*
Rhode Island School of Design M
Rice University M,D*
Roger Williams University M*
Savannah College of Art and Design M*
Southern California Institute of Architecture M*
Syracuse University M*
Texas A&M University M,D*
Texas Tech University M
Tulane University M*
Universidad Autonoma de Guadalajara M,D
Universidad Central del Este M
Universidad Nacional Pedro Henriquez Urena P,M,D
Université Laval M
University at Buffalo, the State University of New York M*
The University of Arizona M*
The University of British Columbia M*
University of Calgary M,D
University of California, Berkeley M,D*
University of California, Los Angeles M,D*
University of Cincinnati M*
University of Colorado at Denver and Health Sciences Center M*
University of Florida M,D*
University of Hartford M*
University of Hawaii at Manoa D*
University of Houston M*
University of Idaho M*
University of Illinois at Chicago M*
University of Illinois at Urbana–Champaign M,D*
University of Kansas M*
University of Kentucky M*
University of Manitoba M
University of Maryland, College Park M*
University of Massachusetts Amherst M*
University of Miami M*
University of Michigan M,D*
University of Minnesota, Twin Cities Campus M*
University of Missouri–Columbia M*
University of Nebraska–Lincoln M*
University of Nevada, Las Vegas M
University of New Mexico M*
The University of North Carolina at Charlotte M*
The University of North Carolina at Greensboro M,O
University of Notre Dame M*
University of Oklahoma M*
University of Oregon M*
University of Pennsylvania M,D,O*

P—first professional degree; M—master's degree; D—doctorate; O—other advanced degree;
**full description and/or announcement in Book 2, 3, 4, 5, or 6*

University of Puerto Rico, Río Piedras M*
University of Southern California M,O*
University of South Florida M*
The University of Tennessee M*
The University of Texas at Arlington M*
The University of Texas at Austin M,D*
The University of Texas at San Antonio M*
University of Toronto M
University of Utah M*
University of Virginia M*
University of Washington M,O*
University of Waterloo M*
University of Wisconsin–Milwaukee M,D,O
Virginia Polytechnic Institute and State University M*
Washington State University M*
Washington State University Spokane M,D
Washington University in St. Louis M*
Woodbury University M
Yale University M*

ART/FINE ARTS

Academy of Art University M*
Adams State College M
Adelphi University M*
Alfred University M,D*
American Academy of Art M
American University M*
Anna Maria College M
Antioch University McGregor M*
Arizona State University M*
Arkansas State University M
Arkansas Tech University M
Art Center College of Design M*
The Art Institute of Boston at Lesley University M*
Azusa Pacific University M*
Ball State University M*
Bard College M*
Barry University M*
Bob Jones University P,M,D,O
Boise State University M
Boston University M*
Bowling Green State University M*
Bradley University M
Brandeis University O*
Brigham Young University M*
Brooklyn College of the City University of New York M,D
California College of the Arts M*
California Institute of the Arts M,O
California State University, Chico M
California State University, Fresno M
California State University, Fullerton M,O
California State University, Long Beach M
California State University, Los Angeles M
California State University, Northridge M
California State University, Sacramento M*
California State University, San Bernardino M
Carnegie Mellon University M*
Central Michigan University M*
Central Washington University M
City College of the City University of New York M*
Claremont Graduate University M
Clemson University M*
Cleveland State University M
The College of New Rochelle M*
Colorado State University M*
Columbia University M*
Concordia University (Canada) M*
Cornell University M*
Cranbrook Academy of Art M*
Drake University M*
East Carolina University M*
Eastern Illinois University M
Eastern Michigan University M
East Tennessee State University M
Edinboro University of Pennsylvania M
Fairleigh Dickinson University, Metropolitan Campus M*
Ferris State University M
Florida Atlantic University M*
Florida International University M*
Florida State University M*
Fontbonne University M
Fort Hays State University M
Framingham State College M*
The George Washington University M,D*
Georgia Southern University M*
Georgia State University M*
Governors State University M
Hofstra University M,O*
Hollins University M,O
Hood College M,O
Howard University M*
Hunter College of the City University of New York M
Idaho State University M
Illinois State University M*
Indiana State University M*
Indiana University Bloomington M,D*
Indiana University of Pennsylvania M
Indiana University–Purdue University Indianapolis M*
Inter American University of Puerto Rico, San Germán Campus M
James Madison University M
John F. Kennedy University M
Johnson State College M
Kansas State University M*
Kean University M
Kent State University M*
Lamar University M*
Lehman College of the City University of New York M
Lesley University M*
Lindenwood University M
Long Island University, C.W. Post Campus M*
Louisiana State University and Agricultural and Mechanical College M*
Louisiana Tech University M
Maine College of Art M*
Marshall University M
Maryland Institute College of Art M,O*
Marywood University M*
Massachusetts College of Art M
Massachusetts Institute of Technology M,D,O*
Memphis College of Art M*
Miami International University of Art & Design M*
Miami University M*
Michigan State University M*
Mills College M
Minneapolis College of Art and Design M,O
Minnesota State University Mankato M
Mississippi College M
Mississippi State University M
Missouri State University M*
Montana State University M
Montclair State University M*
Morehead State University M
National University M
New Jersey City University M
New Mexico State University M
The New School: A University M*
New York Academy of Art M
New York University M,D*
Norfolk State University M
Northern Illinois University M
Northwestern State University of Louisiana M
Northwestern University M*
NSCAD University M
The Ohio State University M*
Ohio University M*
Oklahoma City University M*
Old Dominion University M*
Otis College of Art and Design M
Penn State University Park M,D*
Pennsylvania Academy of the Fine Arts M,O*
Pittsburg State University M
Portland State University M
Pratt Institute M*
Purchase College, State University of New York M
Purdue University M*
Queens College of the City University of New York M
Radford University M
Regent University M,D
Regis University M,O
Rensselaer Polytechnic Institute M,D*
Rhode Island College M
Rhode Island School of Design M
Rochester Institute of Technology M
Rutgers, The State University of New Jersey, New Brunswick M*
Sam Houston State University M
San Diego State University M*
San Francisco Art Institute M,O*
San Francisco State University M
San Jose State University M
Savannah College of Art and Design M*
School of the Art Institute of Chicago M*
School of the Museum of Fine Arts, Boston M
School of Visual Arts M
Seattle Pacific University M
Seton Hall University M*
Southern Illinois University Carbondale M*
Southern Illinois University Edwardsville M
Southern Methodist University M*
Stanford University M,D*
State University of New York at New Paltz M
State University of New York at Oswego M
State University of New York College at Brockport M*
Stephen F. Austin State University M
Stony Brook University, State University of New York M*
Sul Ross State University M*
Syracuse University M*
Temple University M*
Texas A&M International University M
Texas A&M University–Commerce M
Texas A&M University–Corpus Christi M
Texas A&M University–Kingsville M
Texas Christian University M
Texas Tech University M
Texas Woman's University M
Towson University M
Troy University M
Tufts University M*
Tulane University M*
Union Institute & University M
United Theological Seminary of the Twin Cities M
Université du Québec à Chicoutimi M
Université du Québec à Montréal M
Université Laval M
University at Albany, State University of New York M*
University at Buffalo, the State University of New York M,O*
The University of Alabama M
University of Alaska Fairbanks M
University of Alberta M*
The University of Arizona M*
University of Arkansas M*
University of Arkansas at Little Rock M
The University of British Columbia M,D,O*
University of Calgary M
University of California, Berkeley M*
University of California, Davis M*
University of California, Irvine M*
University of California, Los Angeles M*
University of California, Riverside M*
University of California, San Diego M,D*
University of California, Santa Barbara M,D*
University of California, Santa Cruz M*
University of Central Florida M
University of Chicago M,D*
University of Cincinnati M
University of Colorado at Boulder M*
University of Connecticut M*
University of Dallas M*
University of Delaware M*
University of Denver M*
University of Florida M,D*
University of Georgia M,D*
University of Guam M
University of Guelph M*
University of Hartford M*
University of Hawaii at Manoa M*
University of Houston M*
University of Idaho M*
University of Illinois at Chicago M*
University of Illinois at Urbana–Champaign M*
University of Indianapolis M
The University of Iowa M*
University of Kansas M*
University of Kentucky M*
University of Lethbridge M,D
University of Louisville M
University of Maryland, Baltimore County M*
University of Maryland, College Park M*
University of Massachusetts Amherst M*
University of Massachusetts Dartmouth M,O
University of Memphis M*
University of Miami M*
University of Michigan M*
University of Minnesota, Duluth M*
University of Minnesota, Twin Cities Campus M*
University of Mississippi M
University of Missouri–Columbia M*
University of Missouri–Kansas City M,D*
The University of Montana M*
University of Nebraska–Lincoln M*
University of Nevada, Las Vegas M
University of Nevada, Reno M*
University of New Hampshire M*
University of New Mexico M*
University of New Orleans M
The University of North Carolina at Chapel Hill M*
The University of North Carolina at Greensboro M
University of North Dakota M
University of Northern Colorado M
University of Northern Iowa M
University of North Texas M,D*
University of Notre Dame M*
University of Oklahoma M*
University of Oregon M*
University of Pennsylvania M*
University of Regina M*
University of Rochester M,D*
University of Saint Francis (IN) M
University of Saskatchewan M
University of South Carolina M*
The University of South Dakota M
University of Southern California M*
University of South Florida M*
The University of Tennessee M*
The University of Texas at Austin M*
The University of Texas at El Paso M
The University of Texas at San Antonio M*
The University of Texas at Tyler M
The University of Texas–Pan American M
The University of the Arts M*
University of Tulsa M*
University of Utah M*
University of Victoria M*
University of Washington M*
University of Waterloo M*
University of Windsor M*
University of Wisconsin–Madison M*
University of Wisconsin–Milwaukee M
University of Wisconsin–Superior M
Utah State University M
Virginia Commonwealth University M,D*
Washington State University M*
Washington University in St. Louis M*
Wayne State University M*
Webster University M*
Western Carolina University M*
Western Connecticut State University M*
West Texas A&M University M*
West Virginia University M*
Wichita State University M*
William Paterson University of New Jersey M*
Winthrop University M*
Yale University M*
York University M,D*

ART EDUCATION

American University of Puerto Rico M
Arcadia University M,D,O
Art Academy of Cincinnati M
Austin College M
Averett University M
Ball State University M*
Bennington College M*
Boise State University M
Boston University M*
Bowling Green State University M*
Bridgewater State College M*
Brigham Young University M*
Brooklyn College of the City University of New York M,O
Buffalo State College, State University of New York M
California State University, Los Angeles M
California State University, Northridge M
Cape Breton University M
Carlow University O
Carthage College M,O
Case Western Reserve University M*
Central Connecticut State University M,O
Chatham University M
Christopher Newport University M
City University M,O

Cleveland State University M
College of Mount St. Joseph M
The College of New Rochelle M
The College of Saint Rose M,O*
The Colorado College M
Columbus State University M
Concordia University (Canada) M,D
Concordia University Wisconsin M
Converse College M,O
Corcoran College of Art and Design M
Eastern Illinois University M
Eastern Kentucky University M*
Eastern Michigan University M
East Tennessee State University M
Endicott College M
Fitchburg State College M,O
Florida Atlantic University M,D,O
Florida International University M,D*
Florida State University M,D,O*
Georgia Southern University M
Georgia State University M,D,O*
Harding University M,O
Harvard University M*
Hofstra University M*
Indiana University Bloomington M,D,O*
Indiana University–Purdue University Indianapolis M*
Iowa State University of Science and Technology M*
James Madison University M
Kean University M
Kent State University M*
Kutztown University of Pennsylvania M,O
LaGrange College M
Lesley University M,D,O*
Long Island University, C.W. Post Campus M*
Manhattanville College M*
Mansfield University of Pennsylvania M
Maryland Institute College of Art M*
Maryville University of Saint Louis M,D
Marywood University M*
Massachusetts College of Art M
Memphis College of Art M*
Miami University M*
Millersville University of Pennsylvania M
Minnesota State University Mankato M
Mississippi College M,O
Missouri State University M*
Montclair State University M,O*
Morehead State University M
Nazareth College of Rochester M
New Jersey City University M
New York University M,D*
North Carolina Agricultural and Technical State University M
North Georgia College & State University M,O
Nova Southeastern University M,O*
The Ohio State University M,D*
Ohio University M,D*
Penn State University Park M,D*
Pittsburg State University M
Pratt Institute M*
Purdue University M,D,O*
Queens College of the City University of New York M,O
Rhode Island College M
Rhode Island School of Design M
Rochester Institute of Technology M
Rockford College M
Sage Graduate School M
Saint Michael's College M,O
Salem State College M
Salisbury University M
School of the Art Institute of Chicago M,O*
School of Visual Arts M
Simon Fraser University M,D
Southern Connecticut State University M
Southern Illinois University Edwardsville M
Southwestern Oklahoma State University M
Stanford University M,D*
State University of New York at New Paltz M
State University of New York at Oswego M
Sul Ross State University M*
Syracuse University M,O*
Teachers College Columbia University M,D*
Temple University M*
Texas Tech University M
Towson University M
The University of Alabama at Birmingham M*
The University of Arizona M*
University of Arkansas at Little Rock M
The University of British Columbia M,D*
University of Central Florida M*
University of Cincinnati M*
University of Dayton M*
University of Florida M,D*
University of Georgia M,D,O*
University of Houston M,D*
University of Idaho M*
University of Illinois at Urbana–Champaign M,D*
University of Indianapolis M
The University of Iowa M,D*
University of Kansas M*
University of Kentucky M*
University of Louisville M*
University of Massachusetts Dartmouth M
University of Minnesota, Twin Cities Campus M,D,O*
University of Mississippi M
University of Missouri–Columbia M,D,O*
University of Nebraska at Kearney M*
University of New Mexico M*
The University of North Carolina at Charlotte M*
The University of North Carolina at Pembroke M
University of Northern Iowa M
University of North Texas M,D*
University of Rio Grande M
University of South Carolina M,D*
University of Southern Mississippi M*
The University of Tennessee M,D,O*
The University of Texas at Austin M,D*
The University of Texas at Tyler M
The University of the Arts M*
The University of Toledo M*
University of Utah M*
University of Victoria M,D
University of West Georgia M
University of Wisconsin–Madison M,D*
University of Wisconsin–Milwaukee M
University of Wisconsin–Superior M
Virginia Commonwealth University M*
Wayne State University M,D,O*
Western Carolina University M*
Western Kentucky University M*
West Virginia University M*
Wichita State University M*
William Carey University M,O
Winthrop University M

ART HISTORY

American University M*
American University of Puerto Rico M
Bard Graduate Center for Studies in the Decorative Arts, Design, and Culture M,D*
Boston University M,D,O*
Bowling Green State University M*
Brigham Young University M*
Brooklyn College of the City University of New York M,D
Brown University M,D*
Bryn Mawr College M,D*
California State University, Chico M
California State University, Fullerton M
California State University, Los Angeles M
California State University, Northridge M
Caribbean University M,D
Carleton University M
Case Western Reserve University M,D*
Christie's Education M
City College of the City University of New York M*
Cleveland State University M
Columbia University M,D*
Concordia University (Canada) M,D
Cornell University D*
Duke University D*
East Tennessee State University M
Emory University D*
Fashion Institute of Technology M*
Florida State University M,D,O*
The George Washington University M,D*
Georgia State University M*
Graduate School and University Center of the City University of New York D*
Graduate Theological Union M,D,O
Harvard University D*
Howard University M*
Hunter College of the City University of New York M
Illinois State University M*
Indiana University Bloomington M,D*
James Madison University M
The Johns Hopkins University M,D*
Kent State University M*
Lamar University M*
Louisiana State University and Agricultural and Mechanical College M*
Massachusetts Institute of Technology M,D*
McGill University M,D
Montclair State University M*
New Mexico State University M
New York University M,D*
Northwestern University D*
The Ohio State University M,D*
Ohio University M*
Penn State University Park M,D*
Pratt Institute M*
Purchase College, State University of New York M
Queens College of the City University of New York M
Richmond, The American International University in London M
Rutgers, The State University of New Jersey, New Brunswick M,D*
San Diego State University M*
San Francisco Art Institute M*
San Francisco State University M
San Jose State University M
Savannah College of Art and Design M*
School of the Art Institute of Chicago M,O*
Southern Methodist University M*
State University of New York at Binghamton M,D*
Stony Brook University, State University of New York M,D*
Sul Ross State University M*
Syracuse University M*
Temple University M,D*
Texas A&M University–Commerce M
Texas Christian University M
Tufts University M*
Tulane University M*
Université de Montréal M,D
Université du Québec à Montréal M,D
Université Laval M,D
University at Buffalo, the State University of New York M,O*
The University of Alabama M*
The University of Alabama at Birmingham M*
University of Alberta M*
The University of Arizona M,D*
University of Arkansas at Little Rock M
The University of British Columbia M,D,O*
University of California, Berkeley D*
University of California, Davis M*
University of California, Irvine M,D*
University of California, Los Angeles M,D*
University of California, Riverside M*
University of California, Santa Barbara D*
University of Chicago M,D*
University of Cincinnati M*
University of Colorado at Boulder M*
University of Connecticut M*
University of Delaware M,D*
University of Denver M*
University of Florida M,D*
University of Georgia M,D*
University of Hawaii at Manoa M*
University of Illinois at Chicago M,D*
University of Illinois at Urbana–Champaign M,D*
The University of Iowa M,D*
University of Kansas M,D*
University of Kentucky M*
University of Louisville M,D
University of Maryland, College Park M,D*
University of Massachusetts Amherst M*
University of Memphis M*
University of Miami M*
University of Michigan D*
University of Minnesota, Twin Cities Campus M,D*
University of Mississippi M
University of Missouri–Columbia M,D*
University of Missouri–Kansas City M,D*
University of Nebraska–Lincoln M*
University of New Mexico M,D*
The University of North Carolina at Chapel Hill M,D*
University of North Texas M,D*
University of Notre Dame M*
University of Oklahoma M*
University of Oregon M,D*
University of Pennsylvania M,D*
University of Pittsburgh M,D*
University of Rochester M,D*
University of St. Thomas (MN) M*
University of South Carolina M*
University of Southern California M,D,O*
University of South Florida M*
The University of Texas at Austin M,D*
The University of Texas at San Antonio M*
University of Toronto M,D
University of Utah M*
University of Victoria M,D
University of Virginia M,D*
University of Washington M,D*
University of Wisconsin–Madison M,D*
University of Wisconsin–Milwaukee M,O
University of Wisconsin–Superior M
Virginia Commonwealth University M,D*
Washington University in St. Louis M,D*
Wayne State University M*
West Virginia University M*
Williams College M
Yale University D*
York University M,D*

ARTIFICIAL INTELLIGENCE/ROBOTICS

Carnegie Mellon University M,D*
The Catholic University of America M,D*
Cornell University M,D*
Indiana University–Purdue University Indianapolis M,D*
Instituto Tecnológico y de Estudios Superiores de Monterrey, Campus Monterrey M,D
Portland State University M,D,O
University of California, Irvine M*
University of California, Riverside M,D*
University of California, San Diego M,D*
University of Georgia M*
University of Southern California M*
The University of Tennessee M,D*
Villanova University M,O*

ARTS ADMINISTRATION

American University M,O*
Boston University M,O*
Carnegie Mellon University M*
Claremont Graduate University M
Columbia College Chicago M
Drexel University M
Eastern Michigan University M
Fashion Institute of Technology M
Florida State University M,D*
Goucher College M
HEC Montreal O
Montclair State University M*
New York University M*
The Ohio State University M*
Pratt Institute M*
Regis University M,O
Rhode Island College M
Ryerson University M
Saint Mary's University of Minnesota M
Savannah College of Art and Design M*
School of the Art Institute of Chicago M*
Seton Hall University M*
Shenandoah University M,D,O*
Southern Methodist University *
Southern Utah University M
Teachers College Columbia University M*
Temple University M,D*
The University of Akron M
University of Cincinnati M
University of Florida M*
University of New Orleans M
University of Oregon M*
University of Southern California M*
University of Wisconsin–Madison M*
Virginia Polytechnic Institute and State University M*

P—first professional degree; M—master's degree; D—doctorate; O—other advanced degree;
**full description and/or announcement in Book 2, 3, 4, 5, or 6*

Webster University M
Winthrop University M

ART THERAPY

Adler School of Professional Psychology M,D,O*
Albertus Magnus College M
Avila University M*
Caldwell College M
California Institute of Integral Studies M,D*
California State University, Los Angeles M
The College of New Rochelle M
Concordia University (Canada) M
Drexel University M*
Eastern Virginia Medical School M
Emporia State University M
The George Washington University M,O*
Hofstra University M*
Lesley University M,D,O*
Long Island University, C.W. Post Campus M*
Marylhurst University M,O
Marywood University M,O*
Mount Mary College M
Naropa University M*
Nazareth College of Rochester M
New York University M*
Notre Dame de Namur University M
Ottawa University M
Pratt Institute M*
Saint Mary-of-the-Woods College M,O
Salve Regina University M,O
School of the Art Institute of Chicago M*
School of Visual Arts M
Seton Hill University M,O
Southern Illinois University Edwardsville M,O
Southwestern College (NM) M,O*
Springfield College M,O*
University of Louisville M
University of Wisconsin–Superior M
Ursuline College M

ASIAN-AMERICAN STUDIES

California State University, Long Beach M,O
San Francisco State University M
University of California, Los Angeles M*

ASIAN LANGUAGES

Columbia University M,D*
Cornell University M,D*
Harvard University M,D*
Indiana University Bloomington M,D*
Kent State University M*
Naropa University M*
The Ohio State University M,D*
St. John's College (NM) M
University of California, Berkeley M,D*
University of California, Irvine M,D*
University of California, Los Angeles M,D*
University of California, Santa Barbara D*
University of Chicago M,D*
University of Hawaii at Manoa M,D*
University of Illinois at Urbana–Champaign M,D*
University of Kansas M*
University of Michigan M,D*
University of Minnesota, Twin Cities Campus D*
University of Oregon M,D*
University of Southern California M,D*
The University of Texas at Austin M,D*
University of Washington M,D*
University of Wisconsin–Madison M,D*
Washington University in St. Louis M,D*
Yale University D*

ASIAN STUDIES

California Institute of Integral Studies M,D*
California State University, Long Beach M,O
Columbia University M,D,O*
Cornell University M,D*
Duke University M,D*
Florida State University M*
The George Washington University M*
Harvard University M,D*
Indiana University Bloomington M,D*
The Johns Hopkins University M,D,O*
Maharishi University of Management M,D
McGill University M,D*
Ohio University M*
Princeton University D*
St. John's College (NM) M
St. John's University (NY) M,O
San Diego State University M*
Seton Hall University M*
Stanford University M*
University of Alberta M*
The University of Arizona M,D*
The University of British Columbia M,D*
University of California, Berkeley M,D*
University of California, Los Angeles M,D*
University of California, Santa Barbara M,D*
University of Chicago M,D*
University of Colorado at Boulder M,D*
University of Hawaii at Manoa M,O*
University of Illinois at Urbana–Champaign M,D*
The University of Iowa M*
University of Kansas M*
University of Michigan M,D,O*
University of Minnesota, Twin Cities Campus D*
University of Oregon M,D*
University of Pennsylvania M,D*
University of Pittsburgh M,O*
University of San Francisco M
University of Southern California M,D*
The University of Texas at Austin M,D*
University of Toronto M,D
University of Victoria M
University of Virginia M*
University of Washington M*
University of Wisconsin–Madison M,D*
Valparaiso University M
Washington State University M,D*
Washington University in St. Louis M,D*
West Virginia University M,D*
Yale University M*

ASTRONOMY

Arizona State University M,D*
Boston University M,D*
Brigham Young University M,D*
California Institute of Technology D*
Case Western Reserve University M,D*
Clemson University M,D*
Columbia University M,D*
Cornell University D*
Dartmouth College M,D*
Georgia State University D*
Harvard University D*
Indiana University Bloomington M,D*
Iowa State University of Science and Technology M,D*
The Johns Hopkins University D*
Louisiana State University and Agricultural and Mechanical College M,D*
Michigan State University M,D*
Minnesota State University Mankato M
New Mexico State University M,D
Northwestern University M,D*
The Ohio State University M,D*
Ohio University M,D*
Penn State University Park M,D*
Rice University M,D*
Saint Mary's University M
San Diego State University M*
Stony Brook University, State University of New York M,D*
Texas Christian University M,D
Université de Moncton M
The University of Arizona M,D*
The University of British Columbia M,D*
University of Calgary M,D
University of California, Los Angeles M,D*
University of California, Santa Cruz D*
University of Chicago M,D*
University of Delaware M,D*
University of Florida M,D*
University of Georgia M,D*
University of Hawaii at Manoa M,D*
University of Illinois at Urbana–Champaign M,D*
The University of Iowa M*
University of Kansas M,D*
University of Kentucky M,D*
University of Maryland, College Park M,D*
University of Massachusetts Amherst M,D*
University of Michigan M,D*
University of Minnesota, Twin Cities Campus M,D*
University of Missouri–Columbia M,D*
University of Nebraska–Lincoln M,D*
The University of North Carolina at Chapel Hill M,D*
University of Rochester M,D*
University of South Carolina M,D*
The University of Texas at Austin M,D*
University of Toronto M,D
University of Victoria M,D
University of Virginia M,D*
University of Washington M,D*
The University of Western Ontario M,D
University of Wisconsin–Madison D*
Vanderbilt University M,D*
Wesleyan University M*
West Chester University of Pennsylvania M
Yale University M,D*
York University M,D*

ASTROPHYSICS

Air Force Institute of Technology M,D
Clemson University M,D*
Cornell University D*
Harvard University D*
ICR Graduate School M
Indiana University Bloomington M,D*
Iowa State University of Science and Technology M,D*
Louisiana State University and Agricultural and Mechanical College M,D*
McMaster University D
Michigan State University M,D*
New Mexico Institute of Mining and Technology M,D
Northwestern University M,D*
Penn State University Park M,D*
Princeton University D*
Rensselaer Polytechnic Institute M,D*
Texas Christian University M,D
University of Alaska Fairbanks M,D
University of Alberta M,D*
University of California, Berkeley D*
University of California, Los Angeles M,D*
University of California, Santa Cruz D*
University of Chicago M,D*
University of Colorado at Boulder M,D*
University of Maryland, Baltimore County M,D*
University of Minnesota, Twin Cities Campus M,D*
University of Missouri–St. Louis M,D
The University of North Carolina at Chapel Hill M,D*
University of Oklahoma M,D*
University of Pennsylvania M,D*
University of Victoria M,D

ATHLETIC TRAINING AND SPORTS MEDICINE

Armstrong Atlantic State University M
Barry University M*
Boston University D*
Brigham Young University M,D*
California University of Pennsylvania M
Eastern Michigan University M
Florida International University M*
Georgia State University M*
Humboldt State University M
Indiana State University M,D*
Indiana University Bloomington M,D,O*
Kent State University M*
Long Island University, Brooklyn Campus M*
Montana State University–Billings M
Ohio University M*
Old Dominion University M*
Plymouth State University M
Seton Hall University M*
Shenandoah University M*
Stephen F. Austin State University M
Texas Tech University Health Sciences Center M
United States Sports Academy M*
The University of Findlay M
University of Florida M,D*
University of Miami M*
The University of North Carolina at Chapel Hill M*
University of Pittsburgh M*
The University of Tennessee M,D*
The University of West Alabama M
University of Wisconsin–La Crosse M
Virginia Commonwealth University M,D*
West Chester University of Pennsylvania M
Western Michigan University M*
West Virginia University M,D*

ATMOSPHERIC SCIENCES

City College of the City University of New York M,D*
Clemson University M,D*
Colorado State University M,D*
Columbia University M,D*
Cornell University M,D*
Creighton University M*
George Mason University D*
Georgia Institute of Technology M,D*
Howard University M,D*
Massachusetts Institute of Technology M,D*
McGill University M,D*
New Mexico Institute of Mining and Technology M,D
North Carolina State University M,D*
The Ohio State University M,D*
Oregon State University M,D*
Princeton University D*
Purdue University M,D*
Rutgers, The State University of New Jersey, New Brunswick M,D*
South Dakota School of Mines and Technology M,D
Stony Brook University, State University of New York M,D*
Texas Tech University M,D
Université du Québec à Montréal M,D,O
University at Albany, State University of New York M,D*
The University of Alabama in Huntsville M,D
University of Alaska Fairbanks M,D
The University of Arizona M,D*
The University of British Columbia M,D*
University of California, Davis M,D*
University of California, Los Angeles M,D*
University of Chicago M,D*
University of Colorado at Boulder M,D*
University of Delaware D*
University of Guelph M,D
University of Illinois at Urbana–Champaign M,D*
University of Maryland, Baltimore County M,D*
University of Michigan M,D*
University of Missouri–Columbia M,D*
University of Nevada, Reno M,D*
University of New Hampshire *
The University of North Carolina at Chapel Hill M,D*
University of North Dakota M
University of Washington M,D*
University of Wisconsin–Madison M,D*
University of Wyoming M,D
Washington State University Tri-Cities M,D

AUTOMOTIVE ENGINEERING

Central Michigan University M,O*
Clemson University M,D*
Kettering University M
Lawrence Technological University M,D
Minnesota State University Mankato M
Old Dominion University M*
University of Detroit Mercy M,D
University of Michigan M*
University of Michigan–Dearborn M*

AVIATION

Everglades University M
Everglades University M
Middle Tennessee State University M*
Southeastern Oklahoma State University M
University of Central Missouri M
University of Illinois at Urbana–Champaign M*
University of North Dakota M
The University of Tennessee M*
The University of Tennessee Space Institute M*

AVIATION MANAGEMENT

Concordia University (Canada) M,D,O
Daniel Webster College M
Daniel Webster College–Portsmouth Campus M

Delta State University M
Dowling College M,O
Embry-Riddle Aeronautical University (FL) M*
Embry-Riddle Aeronautical University Worldwide M
Lynn University M,D
Southeastern Oklahoma State University M

BACTERIOLOGY

Illinois State University M,D*
The University of Iowa M,D*
University of Prince Edward Island M,D
The University of Texas Medical Branch D*
University of Virginia D*
University of Washington M,D*
University of Wisconsin–Madison M*

BIOCHEMICAL ENGINEERING

Cornell University M,D*
Dartmouth College M,D*
Drexel University M*
Hofstra University M,O*
Rutgers, The State University of New Jersey, New Brunswick M,D*
University of California, Irvine M,D*
The University of Iowa M,D*
University of Maryland, Baltimore County M,D,O*
University of Massachusetts Dartmouth D

BIOCHEMISTRY

Albert Einstein College of Medicine D*
American University of Beirut P,M
Arizona State University M,D*
Auburn University M,D*
Baylor College of Medicine D*
Boston College M,D*
Boston University M,D*
Brandeis University M,D*
Brigham Young University M,D*
Brown University M,D*
California Institute of Technology D*
California Polytechnic State University, San Luis Obispo M
California State University, East Bay M
California State University, Fullerton M
California State University, Long Beach M
California State University, Los Angeles M*
California State University, Northridge M
Carnegie Mellon University M,D*
Case Western Reserve University M,D*
City College of the City University of New York M,D*
Clemson University M,D*
Colorado State University M,D*
Colorado State University-Pueblo M
Columbia University M,D*
Cornell University D*
Cornell University, Joan and Sanford I. Weill Medical College and Graduate School of Medical Sciences D*
Dalhousie University M,D*
Dartmouth College D*
DePaul University M*
Drexel University M,D*
Duke University D,O*
Duquesne University M,D*
East Carolina University D*
East Tennessee State University M,D*
Emory University D*
Florida Atlantic University M,D*
Florida State University M,D*
Georgetown University M,D*
The George Washington University M,D*
Georgia Institute of Technology M,D*
Georgia State University M,D*
Graduate School and University Center of the City University of New York D*
Harvard University D*
Howard University M,D*
Hunter College of the City University of New York M
Illinois State University M,D*
Indiana University Bloomington M,D*
Indiana University–Purdue University Indianapolis D*
Iowa State University of Science and Technology M,D*
The Johns Hopkins University M,D*
Kansas State University M,D*
Kent State University M,D*
Laurentian University M
Lehigh University M,D*
Loma Linda University M,D
Louisiana State University and Agricultural and Mechanical College M,D*
Louisiana State University Health Sciences Center at Shreveport M,D*
Loyola University Chicago M,D*
Massachusetts Institute of Technology D*
Mayo Graduate School D*
McGill University M,D*
McMaster University M,D
Medical College of Georgia M,D*
Medical College of Wisconsin M,D*
Medical University of South Carolina M,D*
Meharry Medical College D
Memorial University of Newfoundland M,D
Miami University M,D*
Michigan State University M,D*
Mississippi State University M,D*
Montana State University M,D
Montclair State University M*
New Mexico Institute of Mining and Technology M,D
New Mexico State University M,D
New York Medical College M,D*
North Carolina State University M,D*
North Dakota State University M,D*
Northeastern University M,D*
Northern Arizona University M
Northern Michigan University M
Northwestern University D*
OGI School of Science & Engineering at Oregon Health & Science University M,D*
The Ohio State University M*
Ohio University M,D*
Oklahoma State University M,D*
Old Dominion University M,D
Oregon Health & Science University D*
Oregon State University M,D*
Penn State Hershey Medical Center M,D*
Penn State University Park M,D*
Purdue University M,D*
Queens College of the City University of New York M
Queen's University at Kingston M,D
Rensselaer Polytechnic Institute M,D*
Rice University M,D*
Rosalind Franklin University of Medicine and Science M,D*
Rush University D
Rutgers, The State University of New Jersey, Newark M,D*
Rutgers, The State University of New Jersey, New Brunswick M,D*
Saint Louis University D*
San Francisco State University M
The Scripps Research Institute D*
Seton Hall University M,D*
Simon Fraser University M,D
Southern Illinois University Carbondale M,D*
Southern University and Agricultural and Mechanical College M*
Stanford University D*
State University of New York College of Environmental Science and Forestry M,D
State University of New York Upstate Medical University M,D*
Stevens Institute of Technology M,D,O*
Stony Brook University, State University of New York D*
Syracuse University D*
Temple University M,D*
Texas A&M University M,D*
Texas State University-San Marcos M*
Texas Tech University Health Sciences Center M,D
Thomas Jefferson University D*
Tufts University D*
Tulane University M,D*
Universidad Central del Caribe M
Université de Moncton M
Université de Montréal M,D,O
Université de Sherbrooke M,D
Université Laval M,D,O
University at Albany, State University of New York M,D*
University at Buffalo, the State University of New York M,D*
The University of Alabama at Birmingham D*
University of Alaska Fairbanks M,D*
University of Alberta M,D*
The University of Arizona M,D*
University of Arkansas for Medical Sciences M,D*
The University of British Columbia M,D*
University of Calgary M,D
University of California, Berkeley D*
University of California, Davis M,D*
University of California, Irvine M,D*
University of California, Los Angeles M,D*
University of California, Riverside M,D*
University of California, San Diego M,D*
University of California, San Francisco D
University of California, Santa Barbara M,D*
University of California, Santa Cruz M,D*
University of Chicago D*
University of Cincinnati M,D
University of Colorado at Boulder M,D*
University of Colorado at Denver and Health Sciences Center D*
University of Connecticut M,D*
University of Connecticut Health Center D*
University of Delaware M,D*
University of Detroit Mercy M
University of Florida M,D*
University of Georgia M,D*
University of Guelph M,D*
University of Houston M,D*
University of Idaho M,D*
University of Illinois at Chicago M,D*
University of Illinois at Urbana–Champaign M,D*
The University of Iowa M,D*
University of Kansas M,D*
University of Kentucky M,D*
University of Lethbridge M,D
University of Louisville M,D
University of Maine M,D*
University of Manitoba M,D
University of Maryland, Baltimore D*
University of Maryland, Baltimore County M,D*
University of Maryland, College Park M,D*
University of Massachusetts Amherst M,D*
University of Massachusetts Lowell M,D*
University of Massachusetts Worcester D*
University of Medicine and Dentistry of New Jersey M,D*
University of Miami D*
University of Michigan D*
University of Minnesota, Duluth M,D*
University of Minnesota, Twin Cities Campus D*
University of Mississippi Medical Center M,D*
University of Missouri–Columbia M,D*
University of Missouri–Kansas City D*
University of Missouri–St. Louis M,D,O
The University of Montana M,D*
University of Nebraska–Lincoln M,D*
University of Nebraska Medical Center M,D*
University of Nevada, Las Vegas M,D
University of Nevada, Reno M,D*
University of New Hampshire M,D*
University of New Mexico M,D*
The University of North Carolina at Chapel Hill M,D*
The University of North Carolina at Greensboro M
University of North Dakota M,D
University of North Texas M,D
University of North Texas Health Science Center at Fort Worth M,D
University of Notre Dame M,D*
University of Oklahoma M,D*
University of Oklahoma Health Sciences Center M,D
University of Oregon M,D*
University of Ottawa M,D*
University of Pennsylvania D*
University of Pittsburgh M,D*
University of Puerto Rico, Medical Sciences Campus M,D
University of Regina M,D
University of Rhode Island M,D
University of Rochester M,D*
University of Saskatchewan M,D
The University of Scranton M
University of South Alabama D*
University of South Carolina M,D*
University of Southern California M,D*
University of Southern Mississippi M,D*
University of South Florida M,D*
The University of Tennessee M,D*
The University of Texas at Austin M,D*
The University of Texas Health Science Center at Houston M,D*
The University of Texas Health Science Center at San Antonio M,D*
The University of Texas Medical Branch D*
The University of Texas Southwestern Medical Center at Dallas D*
University of the Sciences in Philadelphia M,D*
The University of Toledo M,D*
University of Toronto M,D
University of Utah M,D*
University of Vermont M,D*
University of Victoria M,D
University of Virginia D*
University of Washington D*
The University of Western Ontario M,D*
University of West Florida M
University of Windsor M,D
University of Wisconsin–Madison M,D*
Utah State University M,D*
Vanderbilt University M,D*
Virginia Commonwealth University M,D,O*
Virginia Polytechnic Institute and State University M,D*
Wake Forest University D*
Washington State University M,D*
Washington University in St. Louis D*
Wayne State University M,D*
Wesleyan University M,D*
West Virginia University M,D*
Worcester Polytechnic Institute M,D*
Wright State University M*
Yale University M,D*

BIOENGINEERING

Alfred University M,D*
Arizona State University M,D*
Baylor College of Medicine D*
California Institute of Technology M,D*
Carnegie Mellon University M,D*
Clemson University M,D*
Cornell University M,D*
Dalhousie University M,D
Georgia Institute of Technology M,D,O*
Illinois Institute of Technology M,D*
Iowa State University of Science and Technology M,D*
The Johns Hopkins University M,D*
Kansas State University M,D*
Louisiana State University and Agricultural and Mechanical College M,D*
Massachusetts Institute of Technology M,D*
McGill University M,D*
Mississippi State University M,D
North Carolina State University M,D*
The Ohio State University M,D*
Oklahoma State University M,D*
Oregon State University M,D*
Penn State Hershey Medical Center M,D*
Penn State University Park M,D*
Rensselaer Polytechnic Institute M,D*
Rice University M,D*
Rutgers, The State University of New Jersey, New Brunswick M*
Stanford University M,D*
Syracuse University M,D*
Texas A&M University M,D*
Tufts University O*
University at Buffalo, the State University of New York M,D*
University of Arkansas M*
University of California, Berkeley D*
University of California, Davis M,D*
University of California, Riverside M,D*
University of California, San Diego M,D*
University of California, San Francisco D
University of California, Santa Barbara M,D*
University of Florida M,D,O*
University of Georgia M,D*
University of Guelph M,D
University of Hawaii at Manoa M,D*

*P—first professional degree; M—master's degree; D—doctorate; O—other advanced degree; *full description and/or announcement in Book 2, 3, 4, 5, or 6*

Institution	Degrees
University of Illinois at Chicago	M,D*
University of Illinois at Urbana–Champaign	M,D*
University of Maine	M*
University of Maryland, College Park	M,D*
University of Missouri–Columbia	M,D*
University of Nebraska–Lincoln	M,D*
University of Notre Dame	M,D*
University of Oklahoma	M,D*
University of Pennsylvania	M,D*
University of Pittsburgh	M,D*
The University of Toledo	M,D*
University of Utah	M,D*
University of Washington	M,D*
University of Wisconsin–Madison	M,D*
Virginia Commonwealth University	M,D*
Virginia Polytechnic Institute and State University	M,D*
Washington State University	M,D*

BIOETHICS

Institution	Degrees
Albany Medical College	M,O
Boston University	M*
Case Western Reserve University	M,D*
Cleveland State University	M,O
Drew University	M,D,O
Duquesne University	M,D,O*
Indiana University–Purdue University Indianapolis	M,D,O*
Kansas City University of Medicine and Biosciences	M
Loma Linda University	M,O
Loyola Marymount University	M
McGill University	M,D,O*
Medical College of Wisconsin	M*
Michigan State University	M*
Midwestern University, Glendale Campus	M,O*
Mount Sinai School of Medicine of New York University	M*
Rush University	M,O
Saint Louis University	D,O*
Trinity International University	M
Union Graduate College	M*
Université de Montréal	M,O
University of Pennsylvania	M*
University of Pittsburgh	M,D*
The University of Tennessee	M,D*
University of Virginia	M*

BIOINFORMATICS

Institution	Degrees
Boston University	M,D*
California State University Channel Islands	M*
California State University, Dominguez Hills	M
Duke University	D*
Eastern Michigan University	M
George Mason University	M,D,O*
The George Washington University	M*
Georgia Institute of Technology	M,D*
Grand Valley State University	M
Indiana University Bloomington	M,D*
Iowa State University of Science and Technology	D*
The Johns Hopkins University	M,D,O*
Marquette University	M,D*
McGill University	M,D*
Medical College of Wisconsin	M*
Medical University of South Carolina	M,D*
Mississippi Valley State University	M
Morgan State University	M*
North Carolina State University	M,D*
North Dakota State University	M,D
Northeastern University	M*
Northwestern University	M*
Oregon Health & Science University	M,D,O*
Polytechnic University, Brooklyn Campus	M*
Rochester Institute of Technology	M
Stevens Institute of Technology	M,D,O*
Texas Tech University	M,D
University of Arkansas at Little Rock	M,D
University of California, Riverside	D*
University of California, San Diego	D*
University of California, Santa Cruz	M,D*
University of Cincinnati	D
University of Colorado at Denver and Health Sciences Center	D*
University of Idaho	M,D*
University of Illinois at Urbana–Champaign	M,D,O*
University of Medicine and Dentistry of New Jersey	M,D*
University of Michigan	M,D*
University of Pittsburgh	M,D,O*
University of South Florida	M,D*
The University of Texas at El Paso	M
The University of Texas Medical Branch	D*
University of the Sciences in Philadelphia	M*
The University of Toledo	M,O*
University of Utah	M,D*
University of Washington	M,D*
Vanderbilt University	M,D*
Virginia Commonwealth University	M*
Virginia Polytechnic Institute and State University	D*
Yale University	D*

BIOLOGICAL AND BIOMEDICAL SCIENCES—GENERAL

Institution	Degrees
Acadia University	M
Adelphi University	M*
Alabama Agricultural and Mechanical University	M
Alabama State University	M
Albany Medical College	M,D
Albert Einstein College of Medicine	D*
Alcorn State University	M
American University	M*
The American University of Athens	M
American University of Beirut	M
Andrews University	M
Angelo State University	M
Appalachian State University	M
Arizona State University	M,D*
Arizona State University at the Polytechnic Campus	M
Arkansas State University	M,D,O
A.T. Still University of Health Sciences	P,M
Auburn University	M,D*
Austin Peay State University	M
Ball State University	M,D*
Barry University	M*
Baylor College of Medicine	M,D*
Baylor University	M,D*
Bemidji State University	M
Bloomsburg University of Pennsylvania	M
Boise State University	M
Boston College	M,D*
Boston University	M,D*
Bowling Green State University	M,D*
Bradley University	M
Brandeis University	M,D,O*
Brigham Young University	M,D*
Brock University	M,D
Brooklyn College of the City University of New York	M,D
Brown University	M,D*
Bucknell University	M
Buffalo State College, State University of New York	M
California Institute of Technology	M,D*
California Polytechnic State University, San Luis Obispo	M
California State Polytechnic University, Pomona	M
California State University, Bakersfield	M
California State University, Chico	M
California State University, Dominguez Hills	M
California State University, East Bay	M
California State University, Fresno	M
California State University, Fullerton	M
California State University, Long Beach	M
California State University, Los Angeles	M
California State University, Northridge	M
California State University, Sacramento	M*
California State University, San Bernardino	M
California State University, San Marcos	M
Carleton University	M,D
Carnegie Mellon University	M,D*
Case Western Reserve University	M,D*
The Catholic University of America	M,D*
Central Connecticut State University	M,O
Central Michigan University	M*
Central Washington University	M
Chatham University	M
Chicago State University	M
The Citadel, The Military College of South Carolina	M
City College of the City University of New York	M,D*
City of Hope National Medical Center/Beckman Research Institute	D*
Clarion University of Pennsylvania	M
Clark Atlanta University	M,D
Clark University	M,D*
Clemson University	M,D*
Cleveland State University	M,D
Cold Spring Harbor Laboratory, Watson School of Biological Sciences	D*
College of Staten Island of the City University of New York	M
The College of William and Mary	M
Colorado State University	M,D*
Colorado State University-Pueblo	M
Columbia University	M,D*
Concordia University (Canada)	M,D,O
Cornell University	P,M,D*
Cornell University, Joan and Sanford I. Weill Medical College and Graduate School of Medical Sciences	M,D*
Creighton University	M,D*
Dalhousie University	M,D*
Dartmouth College	D*
Delaware State University	M
Delta State University	M
DePaul University	M*
Drexel University	M,D,O*
Duke University	D,O*
Duquesne University	M,D*
East Carolina University	M,D*
Eastern Illinois University	M
Eastern Kentucky University	M*
Eastern Michigan University	M
Eastern New Mexico University	M
Eastern Virginia Medical School	M,D
Eastern Washington University	M
East Stroudsburg University of Pennsylvania	M
East Tennessee State University	M,D
Edinboro University of Pennsylvania	M
Emory University	D*
Emporia State University	M
Fairleigh Dickinson University, College at Florham	M*
Fairleigh Dickinson University, Metropolitan Campus	M*
Fayetteville State University	M
Fisk University	M
Fitchburg State College	M
Florida Agricultural and Mechanical University	M*
Florida Atlantic University	M,D
Florida Institute of Technology	M,D*
Florida International University	M,D*
Florida State University	P,M,D*
Fordham University	M,D*
Fort Hays State University	M
Framingham State College	M*
Frostburg State University	M
George Mason University	M,D,O*
Georgetown University	M,D*
The George Washington University	M,D*
Georgia Campus–Philadelphia College of Osteopathic Medicine	M,O
Georgia College & State University	M
Georgia Institute of Technology	M,D*
Georgian Court University	M,O
Georgia Southern University	M
Georgia State University	M,D*
Gerstner Sloan-Kettering Graduate School of Biomedical Sciences	D
Goucher College	O
Graduate School and University Center of the City University of New York	D*
Grand Valley State University	M
Hampton University	M
Harvard University	M,D,O*
Heritage University	M
Hofstra University	M*
Hood College	M
Howard University	M,D*
Humboldt State University	M
Hunter College of the City University of New York	M,D
ICR Graduate School	M
Idaho State University	M,D
Illinois Institute of Technology	M,D*
Illinois State University	M,D*
Indiana State University	M,D*
Indiana University Bloomington	M,D*
Indiana University of Pennsylvania	M
Indiana University–Purdue University Fort Wayne	M
Indiana University–Purdue University Indianapolis	M,D*
Iowa State University of Science and Technology	M,D*
Jackson State University	M,D
Jacksonville State University	M
James Madison University	M
John Carroll University	M
The Johns Hopkins University	M,D*
Kansas City University of Medicine and Biosciences	M
Kansas State University	M,D*
Keck Graduate Institute of Applied Life Sciences	M
Kent State University	M,D*
Lake Erie College of Osteopathic Medicine	P,M,O
Lakehead University	M
Lamar University	M*
Laurentian University	M
Lehigh University	M,D*
Lehman College of the City University of New York	M
Loma Linda University	M,D
Long Island University, Brooklyn Campus	M*
Long Island University, C.W. Post Campus	M*
Louisiana State University and Agricultural and Mechanical College	M,D*
Louisiana State University Health Sciences Center	M,D*
Louisiana State University Health Sciences Center at Shreveport	M,D*
Louisiana Tech University	M
Loyola University Chicago	M*
Marquette University	M,D
Marshall University	M,D
Massachusetts Institute of Technology	P,M,D*
Mayo Graduate School	D*
McGill University	M,D*
McMaster University	M,D
McNeese State University	M
Medical College of Georgia	M,D*
Medical College of Wisconsin	M,D*
Medical University of South Carolina	M,D*
Meharry Medical College	D
Memorial University of Newfoundland	M,D,O
Michigan State University	M,D*
Michigan Technological University	M,D*
Middle Tennessee State University	M*
Midwestern State University	M
Midwestern University, Downers Grove Campus	M*
Midwestern University, Glendale Campus	M*
Millersville University of Pennsylvania	M
Mills College	O
Minnesota State University Mankato	M
Mississippi College	M
Mississippi State University	M,D
Missouri State University	M*
Montana State University	M,D
Montclair State University	M,O*
Morehead State University	M
Morehouse School of Medicine	D*
Morgan State University	M,D*
Mount Allison University	M
Mount Sinai School of Medicine of New York University	M,D*
Murray State University	M,D
New Jersey Institute of Technology	M,D
New Mexico Highlands University	M
New Mexico Institute of Mining and Technology	M
New Mexico State University	M,D
New York Medical College	M,D*
New York University	M,D*
North Carolina Agricultural and Technical State University	M
North Carolina Central University	M
North Carolina State University	M,D*
North Dakota State University	M,D
Northeastern Illinois University	M
Northeastern University	M,D*
Northern Arizona University	M,D*
Northern Illinois University	M,D
Northern Michigan University	M
Northwestern University	D*
Northwest Missouri State University	M
Notre Dame de Namur University	O
Nova Southeastern University	M*
Oakland University	M*
Occidental College	M
The Ohio State University	M,D*
Ohio University	M,D*
Oklahoma State University Center for Health Sciences	M,D
Old Dominion University	M,D*
Oregon Health & Science University	M,D,O*

Penn State Hershey Medical Center M,D*
Penn State University Park M,D*
Philadelphia College of Osteopathic Medicine M,O*
Pittsburg State University M
Point Loma Nazarene University M
Polytechnic University, Long Island Graduate Center M,D,O
Ponce School of Medicine D
Pontifical Catholic University of Puerto Rico M
Portland State University M,D
Prairie View A&M University M
Princeton University M,D*
Purdue University M,D*
Purdue University Calumet M
Queens College of the City University of New York M
Queen's University at Kingston M,D
Quinnipiac University M*
Rensselaer Polytechnic Institute M,D*
Rhode Island College M
Rochester Institute of Technology M
The Rockefeller University D*
Rosalind Franklin University of Medicine and Science M,D*
Rutgers, The State University of New Jersey, Camden M
Rutgers, The State University of New Jersey, Newark M,D*
Rutgers, The State University of New Jersey, New Brunswick D*
St. Cloud State University M
Saint Francis University M
St. Francis Xavier University M
St. John's University (NY) M,D
Saint Joseph College M
Saint Joseph's University M*
Saint Louis University M,D*
Sam Houston State University M
San Diego State University M,D*
San Francisco State University M
San Jose State University M
The Scripps Research Institute D
Seton Hall University M,D*
Shippensburg University of Pennsylvania M
Simon Fraser University M,D
Smith College M*
Sonoma State University M
South Dakota State University M,D
Southeastern Louisiana University M
Southeast Missouri State University M
Southern Connecticut State University M
Southern Illinois University Carbondale M,D*
Southern Illinois University Edwardsville M
Southern Methodist University M,D*
Southern University and Agricultural and Mechanical College M*
Stanford University M,D*
State University of New York at Binghamton M,D*
State University of New York at Fredonia M
State University of New York at New Paltz M
State University of New York College at Brockport M*
State University of New York College at Oneonta M
State University of New York Downstate Medical Center M,D*
State University of New York Upstate Medical University M,D*
Stephen F. Austin State University M
Stony Brook University, State University of New York D*
Sul Ross State University M*
Syracuse University M,D*
Tarleton State University M*
Temple University M,D*
Tennessee State University M,D*
Tennessee Technological University M*
Texas A&M Health Science Center M,D*
Texas A&M International University M
Texas A&M University M,D*
Texas A&M University–Commerce M
Texas A&M University–Corpus Christi M
Texas A&M University–Kingsville M
Texas Christian University M
Texas Southern University M
Texas State University-San Marcos M*
Texas Tech University M,D
Texas Tech University Health Sciences Center M,D
Texas Woman's University M,D
Thomas Jefferson University M,D,O*
Touro College M
Towson University M
Trent University M,D
Truman State University M
Tufts University M,D*
Tulane University M,D*
Tuskegee University M,D
Uniformed Services University of the Health Sciences M,D*
Universidad Central del Caribe M
Université de Moncton M
Université de Montréal M,D
Université de Sherbrooke M,D,O
Université du Québec à Montréal M,D
Université du Québec, Institut National de la Recherche Scientifique M,D
Université Laval M,D,O
University at Albany, State University of New York M,D*
University at Buffalo, the State University of New York M,D*
The University of Akron M,D
The University of Alabama M,D
The University of Alabama at Birmingham M,D*
The University of Alabama in Huntsville M
University of Alaska Anchorage M
University of Alaska Fairbanks M,D
University of Alberta P,M,D*
The University of Arizona M,D*
University of Arkansas M,D*
University of Arkansas at Little Rock M
University of Arkansas for Medical Sciences M,D*
University of Calgary M,D
University of California, Berkeley D*
University of California, Irvine M,D*
University of California, Los Angeles M,D*
University of California, Riverside M,D*
University of California, San Diego M,D*
University of California, San Francisco D
University of Central Arkansas M
University of Central Florida M,D,O*
University of Central Missouri M
University of Central Oklahoma M
University of Chicago D*
University of Cincinnati M,D
University of Colorado at Denver and Health Sciences Center M,D*
University of Connecticut M,D*
University of Connecticut Health Center D*
University of Dayton M,D*
University of Delaware M,D*
University of Denver M,D*
University of Florida M,D*
University of Georgia D*
University of Guam M
University of Guelph M,D
University of Hartford M*
University of Hawaii at Manoa M,D*
University of Houston M,D*
University of Houston–Clear Lake M
University of Idaho M*
University of Illinois at Chicago M,D*
University of Illinois at Springfield M
University of Illinois at Urbana–Champaign M,D*
University of Indianapolis M
The University of Iowa M,D*
University of Kansas M,D*
University of Kentucky M,D*
University of Lethbridge M,D
University of Louisiana at Lafayette M,D*
University of Louisiana at Monroe M
University of Louisville M
University of Maine D*
University of Manitoba M,D
University of Maryland, Baltimore M,D*
University of Maryland, Baltimore County M,D*
University of Maryland, College Park M,D*
University of Massachusetts Amherst M,D*
University of Massachusetts Boston M
University of Massachusetts Dartmouth M
University of Massachusetts Lowell M,D*
University of Massachusetts Worcester D*
University of Medicine and Dentistry of New Jersey M,D,O*
University of Memphis M,D*
University of Miami M,D*
University of Michigan M,D*
University of Michigan–Flint M*
University of Minnesota, Duluth M*
University of Minnesota, Twin Cities Campus M,D*
University of Mississippi M,D
University of Mississippi Medical Center M,D*
University of Missouri–Columbia M,D*
University of Missouri–Kansas City M,D*
University of Missouri–Rolla M*
University of Missouri–St. Louis M,D,O
The University of Montana M,D*
University of Nebraska at Kearney M
University of Nebraska at Omaha M
University of Nebraska–Lincoln M,D*
University of Nebraska Medical Center M,D*
University of Nevada, Las Vegas M,D
University of Nevada, Reno M,D*
University of New Brunswick Fredericton M,D
University of New Brunswick Saint John M,D
University of New England M,D
University of New Mexico M,D*
University of New Orleans M,D*
The University of North Carolina at Chapel Hill M,D*
The University of North Carolina at Charlotte M,D*
The University of North Carolina at Greensboro M
The University of North Carolina Wilmington M,D*
University of North Dakota M,D
University of Northern Colorado M,D
University of Northern Iowa M
University of North Florida M
University of North Texas M,D*
University of North Texas Health Science Center at Fort Worth M,D
University of Notre Dame M,D*
University of Oklahoma Health Sciences Center M,D
University of Oregon M,D*
University of Ottawa M,D*
University of Pennsylvania M,D*
University of Pittsburgh D*
University of Prince Edward Island M
University of Puerto Rico, Mayagüez Campus M*
University of Puerto Rico, Medical Sciences Campus M,D*
University of Puerto Rico, Río Piedras M,D*
University of Regina M,D
University of Rhode Island M,D
University of Richmond M
University of Rochester M,D*
University of San Francisco M
University of Saskatchewan M,D,O
University of South Alabama M,D*
University of South Carolina M,D,O*
The University of South Dakota M,D
University of Southern California M,D*
University of Southern Maine M
University of Southern Mississippi M,D*
University of South Florida M,D*
The University of Tennessee M,D*
The University of Tennessee Health Science Center M,D*
The University of Tennessee–Oak Ridge National Laboratory Graduate School of Genome Science and Technology M,D*
The University of Texas at Arlington M,D*
The University of Texas at Austin M,D*
The University of Texas at Brownsville M
The University of Texas at Dallas M,D*
The University of Texas at El Paso M,D
The University of Texas at San Antonio M,D*
The University of Texas at Tyler M
The University of Texas Health Science Center at Houston M,D*
The University of Texas Health Science Center at San Antonio M,D*
The University of Texas Medical Branch M,D*
The University of Texas of the Permian Basin M
The University of Texas–Pan American M
The University of Texas Southwestern Medical Center at Dallas M,D*
University of the Incarnate Word M
University of the Pacific M
The University of Toledo M,D*
University of Toronto M,D,O
University of Tulsa M,D*
University of Utah M,D*
University of Vermont M,D*
University of Victoria M,D
University of Virginia M,D*
University of Washington M,D*
University of Waterloo M,D*
The University of Western Ontario M,D
University of West Florida M
University of West Georgia M
University of Windsor M,D
University of Wisconsin–Eau Claire M
University of Wisconsin–La Crosse M
University of Wisconsin–Madison M,D*
University of Wisconsin–Milwaukee M,D*
University of Wisconsin–Oshkosh M
Utah State University M,D
Vanderbilt University M,D
Villanova University M*
Virginia Commonwealth University M,D,O*
Virginia Polytechnic Institute and State University M,D*
Virginia State University M
Wagner College M
Wake Forest University M,D*
Walla Walla College M
Washington State University M*
Washington State University Tri-Cities M
Washington University in St. Louis D*
Wayne State University M,D*
Wesleyan University D*
West Chester University of Pennsylvania M
Western Carolina University M*
Western Connecticut State University M*
Western Illinois University M,O
Western Kentucky University M
Western Michigan University M,D*
Western Washington University M
West Texas A&M University M
West Virginia University M,D*
Wichita State University M*
Wilfrid Laurier University M
William Paterson University of New Jersey M*
Winthrop University M
Worcester Polytechnic Institute M,D*
Wright State University M,D*
Yale University D*
York University M,D*
Youngstown State University M

BIOLOGICAL ANTHROPOLOGY

Duke University D*
Kent State University D*
Mercyhurst College M

BIOMEDICAL ENGINEERING

Baylor College of Medicine D*
Baylor University M*
Boston University M,D*
Brown University M,D*
Carnegie Mellon University M,D*
Case Western Reserve University M,D*
The Catholic University of America M,D*
City College of the City University of New York M,D*
Cleveland State University D
Columbia University M,D*
Cornell University M,D*
Dalhousie University M,D
Dartmouth College M,D*
Drexel University M,D*
Duke University M,D*

P—first professional degree; M—master's degree; D—doctorate; O—other advanced degree;
**full description and/or announcement in Book 2, 3, 4, 5, or 6*

École Polytechnique de Montréal M,D,O
Florida Agricultural and Mechanical University M,D*
Florida International University M,D*
Florida State University M,D*
Georgia Institute of Technology M,D,O*
Graduate School and University Center of the City University of New York D*
Harvard University M,D*
Illinois Institute of Technology D*
Indiana University–Purdue University Indianapolis M,D,O*
The Johns Hopkins University M,D*
Louisiana Tech University M,D
Marquette University M,D
Massachusetts Institute of Technology M,D,O*
Mayo Graduate School D*
McGill University M,D*
Michigan Technological University D*
Mississippi State University M,D
New Jersey Institute of Technology M,D
North Carolina State University M,D*
Northwestern University M,D*
OGI School of Science & Engineering at Oregon Health & Science University M,D
The Ohio State University M,D*
Ohio University M,D*
Penn State University Park M,D*
Polytechnic University, Brooklyn Campus M,D*
Polytechnic University, Long Island Graduate Center M,D,O
Purdue University M,D*
Rensselaer Polytechnic Institute M,D*
Rice University M,D*
Rose-Hulman Institute of Technology M*
Rutgers, The State University of New Jersey, New Brunswick M,D*
Saint Louis University M,D*
Stanford University M*
State University of New York Downstate Medical Center M,D*
Stevens Institute of Technology M,O*
Stony Brook University, State University of New York M,D,O*
Syracuse University M,D*
Texas A&M University M,D*
Thomas Jefferson University D*
Tufts University M,D*
Tulane University M,D*
Université de Montréal M,D,O
The University of Akron M,D
The University of Alabama at Birmingham M,D*
University of Alberta M,D*
University of Arkansas M*
University of Calgary M,D
University of California, Davis M,D*
University of California, Irvine M,D*
University of California, Los Angeles M,D*
University of Cincinnati D
University of Connecticut M,D*
University of Florida M,D,O*
University of Houston M,D*
University of Illinois at Urbana–Champaign D*
The University of Iowa M,D*
University of Kentucky M,D*
University of Massachusetts Worcester D*
University of Medicine and Dentistry of New Jersey M,D*
University of Memphis M,D*
University of Miami M,D*
University of Michigan M,D*
University of Minnesota, Twin Cities Campus M,D*
University of Nevada, Reno M,D*
The University of North Carolina at Chapel Hill M,D*
University of Ottawa M*
University of Rochester M,D*
University of Saskatchewan M,D
University of Southern California M,D*
University of South Florida M,D*
The University of Tennessee M,D*
The University of Tennessee Health Science Center M,D*
The University of Texas at Arlington M,D*
The University of Texas at Austin M,D*
The University of Texas at San Antonio M,D*
The University of Texas Southwestern Medical Center at Dallas M,D
University of Toronto M,D
University of Vermont M*
University of Virginia M,D*
University of Wisconsin–Madison M,D*
Vanderbilt University M,D*
Virginia Commonwealth University M,D*
Virginia Polytechnic Institute and State University M,D*
Wake Forest University M,D*
Washington University in St. Louis M,D*
Wayne State University M,D*
Worcester Polytechnic Institute M,D,O*
Wright State University M*

BIOMETRICS

Cornell University M,D*
Louisiana State University Health Sciences Center M*
North Carolina State University M,D*
Oregon State University M,D*
San Diego State University D*
The University of Alabama at Birmingham M,D*
University of California, Los Angeles M,D*
University of Nebraska–Lincoln M*
University of Southern California M*
The University of Texas Health Science Center at Houston M,D*
University of Wisconsin–Madison M*

BIOPHYSICS

Albert Einstein College of Medicine D*
Baylor College of Medicine D*
Boston University M,D*
Brandeis University M,D*
California Institute of Technology D*
Carnegie Mellon University M,D*
Case Western Reserve University M,D*
Clemson University M,D*
Columbia University M,D*
Cornell University D*
Cornell University, Joan and Sanford I. Weill Medical College and Graduate School of Medical Sciences D*
Dalhousie University M,D
East Carolina University M,D*
East Tennessee State University M,D
Emory University D*
Georgetown University M,D*
Harvard University D*
Howard University D*
Illinois State University M,D*
Iowa State University of Science and Technology M,D*
The Johns Hopkins University M,D*
Medical College of Wisconsin D*
Mount Sinai School of Medicine of New York University M,D*
Northwestern University D*
The Ohio State University M,D*
Oregon State University M,D*
Princeton University D*
Purdue University M,D*
Rensselaer Polytechnic Institute M,D*
The Scripps Research Institute D
Simon Fraser University M,D
Stanford University D*
Stony Brook University, State University of New York D*
Syracuse University D*
Texas A&M University M,D*
Thomas Jefferson University D*
Université de Montréal M,D
Université de Sherbrooke M,D
Université du Québec à Trois-Rivières M,D
University at Buffalo, the State University of New York M,D*
The University of Alabama at Birmingham M,D*
University of Arkansas for Medical Sciences M,D*
University of California, Berkeley D*
University of California, Davis M,D*
University of California, Irvine D*
University of California, San Diego M,D*
University of California, San Francisco D
University of California, Santa Barbara M,D*
University of Chicago D*
University of Cincinnati D
University of Colorado at Denver and Health Sciences Center D*
University of Connecticut M,D*
University of Guelph M,D
University of Illinois at Chicago M,D*
University of Illinois at Urbana–Champaign D*
The University of Iowa M,D*
University of Kansas M,D*
University of Louisville M,D
University of Miami D*
University of Michigan D*
University of Minnesota, Duluth M,D*
University of Minnesota, Twin Cities Campus M,D*
University of Mississippi Medical Center M,D*
University of Missouri–Kansas City D*
University of New Mexico M,D*
The University of North Carolina at Chapel Hill M,D*
University of Rochester M,D*
University of Southern California M,D*
University of South Florida M,D*
The University of Texas Medical Branch D*
University of Toronto M,D
University of Vermont M,D*
University of Virginia M,D*
University of Washington D*
The University of Western Ontario M,D
University of Wisconsin–Madison D*
Vanderbilt University M,D*
Washington State University M,D*
Wright State University M*
Yale University M,D*

BIOPSYCHOLOGY

American University M*
Argosy University, Atlanta Campus M,D,O*
Argosy University, Twin Cities Campus M,D,O*
Boston University M*
Carnegie Mellon University D*
Columbia University M,D*
Cornell University D*
Drexel University M,D*
Duke University D*
Graduate School and University Center of the City University of New York D*
Harvard University D*
Howard University M,D*
Hunter College of the City University of New York M
Indiana University–Purdue University Indianapolis M,D*
Louisiana State University and Agricultural and Mechanical College M,D*
Memorial University of Newfoundland M,D
Northwestern University D*
Oregon Health & Science University M,D*
Pacific Graduate School of Psychology D*
Penn State University Park M,D*
Rutgers, The State University of New Jersey, Newark D*
Rutgers, The State University of New Jersey, New Brunswick D*
State University of New York at Binghamton M,D*
Stony Brook University, State University of New York D*
Texas A&M University M,D*
University at Albany, State University of New York M,D,O*
The University of British Columbia M,D*
University of Connecticut M,D*
University of Michigan D*
University of Minnesota, Twin Cities Campus D*
University of Nebraska at Omaha M,D,O
University of Oklahoma Health Sciences Center M,D
University of Oregon M,D*
The University of Texas at Austin M,D*
The University of Toledo M,D*
University of Windsor M,D
University of Wisconsin–Madison D*
Wayne State University M*

BIOSTATISTICS

Arizona State University M,D*
Boston University M,D*
Brown University M,D*
California State University, East Bay M
Case Western Reserve University M,D*
Columbia University M,D*
Drexel University M,D*
Emory University M,D*
Florida State University M,D*
Georgetown University M*
The George Washington University M,D*
Grand Valley State University M
Harvard University M,D*
Iowa State University of Science and Technology D*
The Johns Hopkins University M,D*
Loma Linda University M
McGill University M,D,O*
Medical College of Georgia M*
Medical College of Wisconsin D*
Medical University of South Carolina M,D*
New York Medical College M,D,O*
The Ohio State University D*
Oregon Health & Science University M*
Rice University M,D*
Rutgers, The State University of New Jersey, New Brunswick M,D*
San Diego State University M,D*
Tufts University M,D*
Tulane University M,D*
University at Albany, State University of New York M,D*
University at Buffalo, the State University of New York M,D*
The University of Alabama at Birmingham M,D*
University of Alberta M,D,O*
University of California, Berkeley M,D*
University of California, Davis M,D*
University of California, Los Angeles M,D*
University of Cincinnati M,D
University of Colorado at Denver and Health Sciences Center M,D*
University of Florida M*
University of Illinois at Chicago M,D*
The University of Iowa M,D*
University of Louisville M,D
University of Maryland, Baltimore M,D*
University of Medicine and Dentistry of New Jersey M,D,O*
University of Michigan M,D*
University of Minnesota, Twin Cities Campus M,D*
The University of North Carolina at Chapel Hill M,D*
University of North Texas Health Science Center at Fort Worth M,D
University of Oklahoma Health Sciences Center M,D
University of Pennsylvania M,D*
University of Pittsburgh M,D*
University of Puerto Rico, Medical Sciences Campus M*
University of Rochester M,D*
University of South Carolina M,D*
University of Southern California M,D*
University of Southern Mississippi M*
University of South Florida M,D*
The University of Texas Health Science Center at Houston M,D*
University of Utah M,D*
University of Vermont M*
University of Washington M,D*
University of Waterloo M,D*
The University of Western Ontario M,D
Virginia Commonwealth University M,D*
Western Michigan University M*
Yale University M,D*

BIOSYSTEMS ENGINEERING

Clemson University M,D*
Iowa State University of Science and Technology M,D*
Michigan State University M,D*
North Dakota State University M,D
South Dakota State University M,D
The University of Arizona M,D*
University of Manitoba M,D
The University of Tennessee M,D*

BIOTECHNOLOGY

Brigham Young University M,D*
Brock University M,D
Brown University M,D*
Cabrini College M,O
California State University Channel Islands M*
Claflin University M
Concordia University (Canada) M,D,O
Dartmouth College M,D*
East Carolina University M*
Florida Institute of Technology M,D*
The George Washington University M*
Harvard University M,D*
Howard University M,D*
Illinois State University M*

Instituto Tecnológico y de Estudios Superiores de Monterrey, Campus Monterrey M,D
The Johns Hopkins University M*
Kean University M
Marywood University M*
McGill University M,D,O*
North Carolina State University M*
Northeastern University M,D*
Northwestern University D*
Oklahoma State University M,D*
Penn State University Park M,D*
Polytechnic University, Brooklyn Campus M,D*
Polytechnic University, Long Island Graduate Center M,D,O
Purdue University Calumet M
Roosevelt University M
Simon Fraser University M,D
Southern Illinois University Edwardsville M
Stephen F. Austin State University M
Texas Tech University M
Texas Tech University Health Sciences Center M
Thomas Jefferson University D*
Tufts University O*
Universidad de las Américas–Puebla M
Université de Sherbrooke P,M,D,O
University at Buffalo, the State University of New York M*
The University of Alabama in Huntsville M,D
University of Alberta M,D*
University of Calgary M
University of California, Irvine M*
University of Connecticut M*
University of Delaware M,D*
University of Guelph M,D
University of Houston–Clear Lake M
University of Illinois at Chicago M,D*
University of Maryland University College M,O
University of Massachusetts Amherst M,D*
University of Massachusetts Boston M
University of Massachusetts Dartmouth D
University of Massachusetts Lowell M,D*
University of Minnesota, Twin Cities Campus M*
University of Missouri–St. Louis M,D,O
University of Nevada, Reno M*
University of North Texas Health Science Center at Fort Worth M,D
University of Pennsylvania M*
University of Saskatchewan M
The University of Texas at Dallas M,D*
The University of Texas at San Antonio M,D*
University of the Sciences in Philadelphia M*
University of Utah M*
University of Washington D*
The University of Western Ontario M,D
University of Wisconsin–Madison *
West Virginia State University M
William Paterson University of New Jersey M*
Worcester Polytechnic Institute M,D*
Worcester State College M

BOTANY

Auburn University M,D*
California State University, Chico M
California State University, Fullerton M
Claremont Graduate University M,D
Colorado State University M,D*
Connecticut College M
Emporia State University M
Illinois State University M,D*
Kent State University M*
Miami University M,D*
North Carolina State University M,D*
North Dakota State University M,D
Nova Scotia Agricultural College M
Oklahoma State University M,D*
Oregon State University M,D*
Purdue University M,D*
Texas A&M University M,D*
University of Alaska Fairbanks M,D
The University of British Columbia M,D*
University of California, Riverside M,D*
University of Connecticut M,D*
University of Florida M,D*
University of Guelph M,D
University of Hawaii at Manoa M,D*
University of Kansas M,D*
University of Maine M*
University of Manitoba M,D
University of Missouri–St. Louis M,D,O
The University of North Carolina at Chapel Hill M,D*
University of North Dakota M,D
University of Oklahoma M,D*
University of South Florida M,D*
University of Toronto M,D
University of Vermont M,D*
University of Washington M,D*
University of Wisconsin–Madison M,D*
University of Wisconsin–Oshkosh M
University of Wyoming M,D
Virginia Polytechnic Institute and State University M,D*
Washington State University M,D*

BUILDING SCIENCE

Arizona State University M*
Auburn University M*
Carnegie Mellon University M,D*
Cornell University M,D*
Georgia Institute of Technology M,D*
University of California, Berkeley M,D*
University of Florida M,D*
University of Southern California M,O*

BUSINESS ADMINISTRATION AND MANAGEMENT—GENERAL

Adelphi University M,O*
Adler Graduate School M,O
Alabama Agricultural and Mechanical University M
Alabama State University M
Alaska Pacific University M
Albany State University M
Albertus Magnus College M
Alcorn State University M
Alfred University M*
Alliant International University–Los Angeles D*
Alliant International University–México City M*
Alliant International University–San Francisco M*
Alvernia College M
Alverno College M
Amberton University M
American College of Computer & Information Sciences M
American College of Thessaloniki M,O
American Graduate University M,O
American InterContinental University (CA) M
American InterContinental University (FL) M
American InterContinental University Buckhead Campus M
American InterContinental University-London M
American InterContinental University Online M
American International College M
American Jewish University M
American Public University System M
American Sentinel University M
American University M,O*
The American University in Cairo M,O
The American University in Dubai M
The American University of Athens M
American University of Beirut M,D
Anderson University M
Andrew Jackson University M
Andrews University M
Angelo State University M
Anna Maria College M,O
Antioch University Los Angeles M
Antioch University McGregor M*
Antioch University New England M*
Antioch University Seattle M*
Appalachian State University M
Aquinas College M
Arcadia University M
Argosy University, Atlanta Campus M,D*
Argosy University, Chicago Campus M,D*
Argosy University, Dallas Campus M*
Argosy University, Denver Campus M,D*
Argosy University, Hawai'i Campus M,D,O*
Argosy University, Inland Empire Campus M,D*
Argosy University, Nashville Campus D*
Argosy University, Orange County Campus M,D,O*
Argosy University, Phoenix Campus M,D*
Argosy University, San Diego Campus M,D*
Argosy University, San Francisco Bay Area Campus M,D*
Argosy University, Santa Monica Campus M,D*
Argosy University, Sarasota Campus M,D,O*
Argosy University, Schaumburg Campus M,D,O*
Argosy University, Seattle Campus M,D*
Argosy University, Tampa Campus M,D,O*
Argosy University, Twin Cities Campus M,D*
Argosy University, Washington DC Campus M,D,O*
Arizona State University M,D*
Arizona State University at the West campus M
Arkansas State University M,O
Ashland University M
Aspen University M
Assumption College M,O*
Athabasca University M,O
Auburn University M,D*
Auburn University Montgomery M
Augsburg College M
Augusta State University M
Aurora University M
Austin Peay State University M
Averett University M
Avila University M*
Azusa Pacific University M
Babson College M
Baker College Center for Graduate Studies M
Baker University M
Baldwin-Wallace College M
Ball State University M*
Barry University M,O*
Bayamón Central University M
Baylor University M*
Belhaven College (MS) M
Bellarmine University M
Bellevue University M*
Belmont University M
Benedictine College M
Benedictine University M
Bentley College M,D,O*
Bernard M. Baruch College of the City University of New York M,D,O*
Berry College M
Bethel College (IN) M
Bethel University M
Biola University M
Birmingham-Southern College M
Black Hills State University M*
Bloomsburg University of Pennsylvania M
Bluffton University M
Bob Jones University P,M,D,O
Boise State University M
Boston College M*
Boston University M,D,O*
Bowie State University M
Bowling Green State University M*
Bradley University M
Brandeis University M*
Brenau University M
Brescia University M
Bridgewater State College M
Briercrest Seminary M
Brigham Young University M*
Brock University M,O
Bryant University M
Butler University M
Caldwell College M
California Baptist University M
California Lutheran University M,O
California National University for Advanced Studies M
California Polytechnic State University, San Luis Obispo M
California State Polytechnic University, Pomona M
California State University, Bakersfield M
California State University Channel Islands M*
California State University, Chico M
California State University, Dominguez Hills M
California State University, East Bay M
California State University, Fresno M
California State University, Fullerton M
California State University, Long Beach M
California State University, Los Angeles M
California State University, Northridge M
California State University, Sacramento M*
California State University, San Bernardino M
California State University, San Marcos M
California State University, Stanislaus M
California University of Pennsylvania M
Cambridge College M
Cameron University M
Campbellsville University M
Campbell University M
Canisius College M
Cape Breton University M
Capella University M,D,O
Capital University M
Capitol College M
Cardean University M
Cardinal Stritch University M*
Carleton University M,D
Carlos Albizu University, Miami Campus M,D
Carnegie Mellon University M,D*
Case Western Reserve University M,D*
The Catholic University of America M*
Centenary College M
Centenary College of Louisiana M
Central Connecticut State University M,O
Central European University M*
Central Michigan University M*
Chadron State College M
Chaminade University of Honolulu M
Chapman University M,O
Charleston Southern University M
Chatham University M
Christian Brothers University M,O
The Citadel, The Military College of South Carolina M
City University M,O
Claflin University M
Claremont Graduate University M,D,O
Clarion University of Pennsylvania M
Clark Atlanta University M
Clarke College M
Clarkson University M*
Clark University M*
Clayton State University M
Cleary University M
Clemson University M,D*
Cleveland State University M,D
Coastal Carolina University M
College of Charleston M*
College of Notre Dame of Maryland M
College of Saint Elizabeth M
College of St. Joseph M
The College of Saint Rose M*
The College of St. Scholastica M
College of Santa Fe M
College of Staten Island of the City University of New York M
The College of William and Mary M
Colorado Christian University M
Colorado State University M*
Colorado State University-Pueblo M
Colorado Technical University—Colorado Springs M,D
Colorado Technical University—Denver M
Colorado Technical University—Sioux Falls M
Columbia College (MO) M
Columbia Southern University M
Columbia University M,D*
Columbus State University M
Concordia University (CA) M
Concordia University (OR) M
Concordia University (Canada) M,D,O
Concordia University, St. Paul M
Concordia University Wisconsin M
Cornell University M,D*
Cornerstone University M,O
Creighton University M*
Cumberland University M
Curry College M
Daemen College M
Dalhousie University M
Dallas Baptist University M
Daniel Webster College M
Daniel Webster College–Portsmouth Campus M

P—first professional degree; M—master's degree; D—doctorate; O—other advanced degree;
**full description and/or announcement in Book 2, 3, 4, 5, or 6*

Institution	Degrees
Dartmouth College	M*
Davenport University	M
Davenport University	M
Davenport University	M
Defiance College	M
Delaware State University	M
Delta State University	M
DePaul University	M*
DeSales University	M
DeVry University	M
DeVry University	M
DeVry University	M
DeVry University	M
DeVry University	M
DeVry University	M
DeVry University	M
DeVry University	M
DeVry University	M
DeVry University	M
DeVry University	M
DeVry University	M
DeVry University	M
DeVry University	M
DeVry University	M
DeVry University	M
DeVry University	M
DeVry University	M
DeVry University	M
DeVry University	M
DeVry University	M
DeVry University	M
DeVry University	M
DeVry University	M
DeVry University	M
DeVry University (MD)	M,O
DeVry University	M
DeVry University	M
DeVry University	M
DeVry University (NV)	M
DeVry University	M
DeVry University	M
DeVry University (OR)	M
DeVry University	M
DeVry University	M
DeVry University	M
DeVry University	M
DeVry University	M
DeVry University	M
DeVry University	M
DeVry University	M
DeVry University	M
DeVry University	M
DeVry University	M
DeVry University	M
DeVry University	M
DeVry University	M
DeVry University	M
DeVry University	M*
DeVry University	M
Doane College	M
Dominican University	M
Dominican University of California	M
Dowling College	M,O
Drake University	M*
Drexel University	M,D,O*
Drury University	M
Duke University	M,D*
Duquesne University	M*
East Carolina University	M,D,O*
Eastern Illinois University	M,O
Eastern Kentucky University	M*
Eastern Mennonite University	M
Eastern Michigan University	M
Eastern New Mexico University	M
Eastern University	M*
Eastern Washington University	M
East Tennessee State University	M,O
Edgewood College	M
Elmhurst College	M
Elon University	M
Embry-Riddle Aeronautical University (FL)	M*
Emmanuel College	M
Emory University	M,D*
Emporia State University	M
Endicott College	M
Everglades University	M
Everglades University	M
Excelsior College	M
Fairfield University	M,O*
Fairleigh Dickinson University, College at Florham	M,O*
Fairleigh Dickinson University, Metropolitan Campus	M,O*
Fairmont State University	M
Fashion Institute of Technology	M*
Felician College	M*
Ferris State University	M
Fitchburg State College	M
Florida Agricultural and Mechanical University	M*
Florida Atlantic University	M
Florida Atlantic University, Jupiter Campus	M
Florida Gulf Coast University	M
Florida Institute of Technology	M*
Florida International University	M,D*
Florida Metropolitan University–Brandon Campus	M
Florida Metropolitan University–Jacksonville Campus	M
Florida Metropolitan University–Melbourne Campus	M
Florida Metropolitan University–North Orlando Campus	M
Florida Metropolitan University–Pinellas Campus	M
Florida Metropolitan University–Pompano Beach Campus	M
Florida Metropolitan University–South Orlando Campus	M
Florida Metropolitan University–Tampa Campus	M
Florida Southern College	M
Florida State University	M,D*
Fontbonne University	M
Fordham University	M*
Fort Hays State University	M
Framingham State College	M*
Franciscan University of Steubenville	M
Francis Marion University	M
Franklin Pierce University	M
Franklin University	M
Freed-Hardeman University	M
Fresno Pacific University	M
Friends University	M
Frostburg State University	M
Gannon University	M,O
Gardner-Webb University	P,M,D
Geneva College	M*
George Fox University	M,D*
George Mason University	M*
Georgetown University	M*
The George Washington University	M,D*
Georgia College & State University	M
Georgia Institute of Technology	M,D,O*
Georgian Court University	M
Georgia Southern University	M
Georgia Southwestern State University	M
Georgia State University	M,D*
Goddard College	M
Golden Gate University	M,D,O
Goldey-Beacom College	M
Gonzaga University	M
Governors State University	M
Graduate School and University Center of the City University of New York	D*
Grand Canyon University	M*
Grand Valley State University	M
Grantham University	M
Green Mountain College	M
Gwynedd-Mercy College	M
Hamline University	M
Hampton University	M*
Harding University	M
Hardin-Simmons University	M
Harvard University	M,D,O*
Hawai'i Pacific University	M*
HEC Montreal	M,D,O
Heidelberg College	M
Henderson State University	M
High Point University	M
Hodges University	M
Hofstra University	M,O*
Holy Family University	M
Holy Names University	M
Hood College	M
Houston Baptist University	M
Howard University	M*
Hult International Business School	M
Humboldt State University	M
Huron University USA in London	M
Husson College	M
Idaho State University	M,O
Illinois Institute of Technology	M,D*
Illinois State University	M*
IMCA–International Management Centres Association	M,D
Indiana State University	M*
Indiana Tech	M
Indiana University Bloomington	M,D*
Indiana University Kokomo	M
Indiana University Northwest	M,O
Indiana University of Pennsylvania	M
Indiana University–Purdue University Fort Wayne	M
Indiana University–Purdue University Indianapolis	M*
Indiana University South Bend	M
Indiana University Southeast	M,O
Indiana Wesleyan University	M
Instituto Centroamericano de Administración de Empresas	M
Instituto Tecnologico de Santo Domingo	M
Instituto Tecnológico y de Estudios Superiores de Monterrey, Campus Central de Veracruz	M
Instituto Tecnológico y de Estudios Superiores de Monterrey, Campus Ciudad de México	M,D
Instituto Tecnológico y de Estudios Superiores de Monterrey, Campus Ciudad Juárez	M
Instituto Tecnológico y de Estudios Superiores de Monterrey, Campus Ciudad Obregón	M
Instituto Tecnológico y de Estudios Superiores de Monterrey, Campus Cuernavaca	M
Instituto Tecnológico y de Estudios Superiores de Monterrey, Campus Estado de México	M,D
Instituto Tecnológico y de Estudios Superiores de Monterrey, Campus Guadalajara	M
Instituto Tecnológico y de Estudios Superiores de Monterrey, Campus Irapuato	M,D
Instituto Tecnológico y de Estudios Superiores de Monterrey, Campus Laguna	M
Instituto Tecnológico y de Estudios Superiores de Monterrey, Campus León	M
Instituto Tecnológico y de Estudios Superiores de Monterrey, Campus Monterrey	M,D
Instituto Tecnológico y de Estudios Superiores de Monterrey, Campus Querétaro	M
Instituto Tecnológico y de Estudios Superiores de Monterrey, Campus Sonora Norte	M
Instituto Tecnológico y de Estudios Superiores de Monterrey, Campus Toluca	M
Inter American University of Puerto Rico, Metropolitan Campus	M,D
Inter American University of Puerto Rico, San Germán Campus	M,D
International College of the Cayman Islands	M
International Technological University	M
International University in Geneva	M
The International University of Monaco	M
Iona College	M,O*
Iowa State University of Science and Technology	M*
Ithaca College	M
ITT Technical Institute (IN)	M
Jackson State University	M,D
Jacksonville State University	M
Jacksonville University	M
James Madison University	M
John Brown University	M
John Carroll University	M
John F. Kennedy University	M,O
The Johns Hopkins University	M,O*
Jones International University	M
Kansas State University	M*
Kansas Wesleyan University	M
Kean University	M
Keller Graduate School of Management	M
Keller Graduate School of Management	M
Kennesaw State University	M
Kent State University	M*
Kentucky State University	M
Kettering University	M
Keuka College	M
King College	M
King's College	M
Kutztown University of Pennsylvania	M
Lake Erie College	M
Lake Forest Graduate School of Management	M
Lakeland College	M
Lamar University	M*
La Salle University	M,O
Lasell College	M*
La Sierra University	M,O
Laurentian University	M
Lawrence Technological University	M,D
Lebanese American University	M
Lebanon Valley College	M
Lehigh University	M,D,O*
Le Moyne College	M
Lenoir-Rhyne College	M
LeTourneau University	M
Lewis University	M
Liberty University	M
Lincoln Memorial University	M
Lincoln University (CA)	M
Lincoln University (MO)	M
Lindenwood University	M
Lipscomb University	M
Long Island University, Brooklyn Campus	M*
Long Island University, C.W. Post Campus	M,O*
Long Island University, Rockland Graduate Campus	M,O
Long Island University, Westchester Graduate Campus	M
Longwood University	M*
Louisiana State University and Agricultural and Mechanical College	M,D*
Louisiana State University in Shreveport	M
Louisiana Tech University	M,D
Loyola College in Maryland	M
Loyola Marymount University	M
Loyola University Chicago	M*
Loyola University New Orleans	M
Lynchburg College	M
Lynn University	M,D
Madonna University	M
Maharishi University of Management	M,D
Malaspina University-College	M
Malone College	M
Marian College of Fond du Lac	M
Marist College	M,O*
Marlboro College	M
Marquette University	M
Marshall University	M
Marylhurst University	M
Marymount University	M,O
Maryville University of Saint Louis	M,O
Marywood University	M*
Massachusetts Institute of Technology	M,D*
McGill University	M,D,O*
McKendree College	M
McMaster University	M,D
McNeese State University	M
Medaille College	M
Memorial University of Newfoundland	M
Mercer University	M
Mercy College	M
Meredith College	M
Mesa State College	M
Methodist University	M
Metropolitan College of New York	M
Metropolitan State University	M
Miami University	M*
Michigan State University	M,D*
Michigan Technological University	M*
MidAmerica Nazarene University	M
Middle Tennessee State University	M*
Midwestern State University	M
Millersville University of Pennsylvania	M
Milligan College	M
Millikin University	M
Millsaps College	M
Mills College	M
Milwaukee School of Engineering	M*
Minnesota State University Mankato	M
Minot State University	M
Mississippi College	M,O
Mississippi State University	M,D
Missouri State University	M*
Monmouth University	M,O
Monroe College	M
Montclair State University	M*
Monterey Institute of International Studies	M*
Montreat College	M
Moravian College	M
Morehead State University	M
Morgan State University	D*
Morrison University	M
Mount Marty College	M
Mount Mary College	M
Mount Saint Mary College	M
Mount St. Mary's University	M
Mount Vernon Nazarene University	M
Murray State University	M
Myers University	M
National American University	M
The National Graduate School of Quality Management	M
National-Louis University	M
National University	M
Naval Postgraduate School	M
Nazareth College of Rochester	M
New England College	M
New Jersey City University	M
New Jersey Institute of Technology	M

Newman University M
New Mexico Highlands University M
New Mexico State University M,D
New York Institute of Technology M,O
New York University P,M,D,O*
Niagara University M
Nicholls State University M
Nichols College M
North Carolina Central University M
North Carolina State University M*
North Central College M
North Dakota State University M
Northeastern Illinois University M
Northeastern State University M
Northeastern University M,O*
Northern Arizona University M
Northern Illinois University M
Northern Kentucky University M
North Greenville University M
North Park University M
Northwest Christian College M
Northwestern Polytechnic University M
Northwestern University M*
Northwest Missouri State University M
Northwest Nazarene University M
Northwest University M
Northwood University M
Norwich University M
Notre Dame College (OH) M,O
Notre Dame de Namur University M
Nova Southeastern University M,D*
Nyack College M
Oakland City University M
Oakland University M,O*
OGI School of Science & Engineering at Oregon Health & Science University M,O
Oglala Lakota College M
Oglethorpe University M
Ohio Dominican University M
The Ohio State University M,D*
Ohio University M*
Oklahoma City University M
Oklahoma State University M,D*
Old Dominion University M,D*
Olivet Nazarene University M
Oral Roberts University M
Oregon State University M,O*
Ottawa University M
Otterbein College M
Our Lady of the Lake University of San Antonio M
Pace University M,D,O*
Pacific Lutheran University M
Pacific States University M,D
Palm Beach Atlantic University M
Park University M
Penn State Great Valley M
Penn State Harrisburg M*
Pepperdine University M*
Pepperdine University M*
Pfeiffer University M
Philadelphia University M*
Phillips Theological Seminary P,M,D
Piedmont College M
Pittsburg State University M
Plymouth State University M
Point Loma Nazarene University M
Point Park University M*
Polytechnic University, Brooklyn Campus M,D*
Polytechnic University, Long Island Graduate Center M,O
Polytechnic University of Puerto Rico M
Polytechnic University of the Americas–Miami Campus M
Polytechnic University of the Americas–Orlando Campus M
Polytechnic University, Westchester Graduate Center M
Pontifical Catholic University of Puerto Rico M,D
Pontificia Universidad Catolica Madre y Maestra M
Portland State University M,D,O
Prairie View A&M University M
Providence College M*
Purdue University M,D*
Purdue University Calumet M
Queen's University at Kingston M
Queens University of Charlotte M
Quincy University M
Quinnipiac University M*
Radford University M
Regent University M,D,O
Regis College (MA) M
Regis University M,O
Rensselaer at Hartford M
Rensselaer Polytechnic Institute M,D*
Rice University M*
The Richard Stockton College of New Jersey M
Rider University M*
Rivier College M
Robert Morris University M
Roberts Wesleyan College M,O
Rochester Institute of Technology M
Rockford College M
Rockhurst University M
Rollins College M
Roosevelt University M
Rosemont College M
Rowan University M
Royal Military College of Canada M
Royal Roads University M
Rutgers, The State University of New Jersey, Camden M
Rutgers, The State University of New Jersey, Newark M,D,O*
Sacred Heart University M
Sage Graduate School M
Saginaw Valley State University M
St. Ambrose University M,D
St. Bonaventure University M,O
St. Cloud State University M
St. Edward's University M,O
Saint Francis University M
St. John Fisher College M
St. John's University (NY) M,O
Saint Joseph College M
St. Joseph's College, New York M*
Saint Joseph's College of Maine M
St. Joseph's College, Suffolk Campus M,O
Saint Joseph's University M,O*
Saint Leo University M
Saint Louis University M*
Saint Martin's University M
Saint Mary's College of California M
Saint Mary's University M,D
Saint Mary's University of Minnesota M,O
St. Mary's University of San Antonio M
Saint Michael's College M,O
Saint Peter's College M
St. Thomas Aquinas College M*
St. Thomas University M,O
Saint Xavier University M,O
Salem International University M
Salem State College M
Salisbury University M
Salve Regina University M,O
Samford University M
Sam Houston State University M
San Diego State University M*
San Francisco State University M
San Jose State University M
Santa Clara University M
Schiller International University (United States) M
Schiller International University (Germany) M
Schiller International University M
Schiller International University (Spain) M
Schiller International University, American College of Switzerland M
School for International Training M
Seattle Pacific University M
Seattle University M,O
Seton Hall University M,O*
Seton Hill University M
Shenandoah University M,O*
Shippensburg University of Pennsylvania M
Shorter College M
Silver Lake College M
Simmons College M,O
Simon Fraser University M,D
Slippery Rock University of Pennsylvania M
Sonoma State University M
Southeastern Louisiana University M
Southeastern Oklahoma State University M
Southeastern University M
Southeast Missouri State University M
Southern Adventist University M
Southern Connecticut State University M
Southern Illinois University Carbondale M,D*
Southern Illinois University Edwardsville M
Southern Methodist University M*
Southern Nazarene University M
Southern New Hampshire University M,D,O*
Southern Oregon University M
Southern Polytechnic State University M
Southern University and Agricultural and Mechanical College M*
Southern Utah University M
Southern Wesleyan University M
Southwest Baptist University M
Southwestern Adventist University M
Southwestern Oklahoma State University M
Southwest Minnesota State University M
Spalding University M
Spring Arbor University M
Spring Hill College M
Stanford University M,D*
State University of New York at Binghamton M,D*
State University of New York at Fredonia M
State University of New York at New Paltz M
State University of New York at Oswego M
State University of New York Empire State College M
State University of New York Institute of Technology M
Stephen F. Austin State University M
Stephens College M
Stetson University M
Stevens Institute of Technology M*
Stony Brook University, State University of New York M,O*
Stratford University M
Strayer University M
Suffolk University M,O*
Sullivan University M
Sul Ross State University M*
Syracuse University M,D*
Tabor College M
Tarleton State University M
Taylor University Fort Wayne M
Temple University M,D*
Tennessee State University M*
Tennessee Technological University M*
Texas A&M International University M
Texas A&M University M,D*
Texas A&M University–Commerce M
Texas A&M University–Corpus Christi M
Texas A&M University–Kingsville M
Texas A&M University–Texarkana M
Texas Christian University M,D
Texas Southern University M
Texas State University-San Marcos M*
Texas Tech University M,D
Texas Wesleyan University M
Texas Woman's University M
Thomas College M
Thomas Edison State College M
Thomas More College M
Thomas University M
Thunderbird School of Global Management M
Tiffin University M
Touro University International M,D
Towson University M
Trevecca Nazarene University M
Trinity International University P,M,D,O
Trinity University M*
Trinity (Washington) University M
Troy University M
Tulane University M,D*
Union Graduate College M,O*
Union University M
United States International University M
Universidad Autonoma de Guadalajara M,D
Universidad Central del Este M
Universidad de las Americas, A.C. M
Universidad de las Américas–Puebla M
Universidad del Este M
Universidad del Turabo M,D
Universidad Metropolitana M,O
Universidad Nacional Pedro Henriquez Urena P,M,D
Université de Moncton M
Université de Sherbrooke P,M,D,O
Université du Québec à Chicoutimi M
Université du Québec à Montréal M,D,O
Université du Québec à Rimouski M,O
Université du Québec à Trois-Rivières M,D
Université du Québec en Abitibi-Témiscamingue M
Université Laval M,D,O
University at Albany, State University of New York M*
University at Buffalo, the State University of New York M,D,O*
The University of Akron M
The University of Alabama M,D
The University of Alabama at Birmingham M,D*
The University of Alabama in Huntsville M,O
University of Alaska Anchorage M
University of Alaska Fairbanks M
University of Alaska Southeast M
University of Alberta M,D*
The University of Arizona M,D*
University of Arkansas M,D*
University of Arkansas at Little Rock M
University of Baltimore M*
University of Bridgeport M
The University of British Columbia M,D*
University of Calgary M,D
University of California, Berkeley M,D*
University of California, Davis M*
University of California, Irvine M,D*
University of California, Los Angeles M,D*
University of California, Riverside M*
University of California, San Diego M*
University of Central Arkansas M
University of Central Florida M,D*
University of Central Missouri M
University of Central Oklahoma M
University of Charleston M
University of Chicago M,D*
University of Cincinnati M,D
University of Colorado at Boulder M,D*
University of Colorado at Colorado Springs M
University of Colorado at Denver and Health Sciences Center M*
University of Colorado at Denver and Health Sciences Center M*
University of Connecticut M,D*
University of Dallas M
University of Dayton M*
University of Delaware M*
University of Denver M,O*
University of Detroit Mercy M,O
University of Dubuque M
University of Evansville M
The University of Findlay M
University of Florida M,D,O*
University of Georgia M,D,O*
University of Guam M
University of Guelph M
University of Hartford M*
University of Hawaii at Manoa M*
University of Houston M,D*
University of Houston–Clear Lake M
University of Houston–Victoria M*
University of Idaho M*
University of Illinois at Chicago M,D*
University of Illinois at Springfield M
University of Illinois at Urbana–Champaign M,D*
University of Indianapolis M,O
The University of Iowa M,D*
University of Kansas M,D*
University of Kentucky M,D*
University of La Verne M,O
University of Lethbridge M,D
University of Louisiana at Lafayette M*
University of Louisiana at Monroe M
University of Louisville M
University of Maine M*
University of Management and Technology M,D,O
University of Manitoba M,D
University of Mary M
University of Mary Hardin-Baylor M
University of Maryland, College Park M,D*
University of Maryland University College M,D,O
University of Mary Washington M
University of Massachusetts Amherst M,D*
University of Massachusetts Boston M
University of Massachusetts Dartmouth M,O
University of Massachusetts Lowell M*
University of Memphis M,D*

P—first professional degree; M—master's degree; D—doctorate; O—other advanced degree;
**full description and/or announcement in Book 2, 3, 4, 5, or 6*

University of Miami M*
University of Michigan D*
University of Michigan–Dearborn M*
University of Michigan–Flint M*
University of Minnesota, Duluth M*
University of Minnesota, Twin Cities Campus M,D*
University of Mississippi M,D
University of Missouri–Columbia M,D*
University of Missouri–Kansas City M,D*
University of Missouri–St. Louis M,O
University of Mobile M
The University of Montana M*
University of Nebraska at Kearney M
University of Nebraska at Omaha M
University of Nebraska–Lincoln M,D*
University of Nevada, Las Vegas M
University of Nevada, Reno M*
University of New Brunswick Fredericton M
University of New Brunswick Saint John M
University of New Hampshire M*
University of New Hampshire at Manchester M,O
University of New Haven M*
University of New Mexico M*
University of New Orleans M
University of North Alabama M
The University of North Carolina at Chapel Hill M,D*
The University of North Carolina at Charlotte M,D*
The University of North Carolina at Greensboro M,O
The University of North Carolina at Pembroke M
The University of North Carolina Wilmington M*
University of North Dakota M
University of Northern Iowa M
University of Northern Virginia M,D
University of North Florida M
University of North Texas M,D*
University of Notre Dame M*
University of Oklahoma M,D*
University of Oregon M,D*
University of Ottawa M*
University of Pennsylvania M,D*
University of Phoenix–Atlanta Campus M
University of Phoenix–Augusta Campus M
University of Phoenix–Austin Campus M
University of Phoenix–Bay Area Campus M
University of Phoenix–Boston Campus M
University of Phoenix–Central Florida Campus M
University of Phoenix–Central Massachusetts Campus M
University of Phoenix–Central Valley Campus M
University of Phoenix–Charlotte Campus M
University of Phoenix–Chattanooga Campus M
University of Phoenix–Cheyenne Campus M
University of Phoenix–Chicago Campus M
University of Phoenix–Cincinnati Campus M
University of Phoenix–Cleveland Campus M
University of Phoenix–Columbia Campus M
University of Phoenix–Columbus Georgia Campus M
University of Phoenix–Columbus Ohio Campus M
University of Phoenix–Dallas Campus M
University of Phoenix–Denver Campus M
University of Phoenix–Des Moines Campus M
University of Phoenix–Detroit Campus M
University of Phoenix–Eastern Washington Campus M
University of Phoenix–Fairfield County M
University of Phoenix–Fort Lauderdale Campus M
University of Phoenix–Harrisburg Campus M
University of Phoenix–Hawaii Campus M
University of Phoenix–Houston Campus M
University of Phoenix–Idaho Campus M
University of Phoenix–Indianapolis Campus M
University of Phoenix–Jersey City Campus M
University of Phoenix–Kansas City Campus M
University of Phoenix–Las Vegas Campus M
University of Phoenix–Little Rock Campus M
University of Phoenix–Louisiana Campus M
University of Phoenix–Louisville Campus M
University of Phoenix–Madison Campus M
University of Phoenix–Maryland Campus M
University of Phoenix–Memphis Campus M
University of Phoenix–Metro Detroit Campus M
University of Phoenix–Minneapolis/St. Louis Park Campus M
University of Phoenix–Nashville Campus M
University of Phoenix–New Mexico Campus M
University of Phoenix—Northern Nevada Campus M
University of Phoenix–Northern Virginia Campus M
University of Phoenix–North Florida Campus M
University of Phoenix–Northwest Arkansas Campus M
University of Phoenix–Northwest Indiana M
University of Phoenix–Oklahoma City Campus M
University of Phoenix–Omaha Campus M
University of Phoenix Online Campus M,D
University of Phoenix–Oregon Campus M
University of Phoenix–Philadelphia Campus M
University of Phoenix–Phoenix Campus M
University of Phoenix–Pittsburgh Campus M
University of Phoenix–Puerto Rico Campus M
University of Phoenix–Raleigh Campus M
University of Phoenix–Renton Learning Center M
University of Phoenix–Richmond Campus M
University of Phoenix–Sacramento Valley Campus M
University of Phoenix–St. Louis Campus M
University of Phoenix–San Antonio Campus M
University of Phoenix–San Diego Campus M
University of Phoenix–Savannah Campus M
University of Phoenix–Southern Arizona Campus M
University of Phoenix–Southern California Campus M
University of Phoenix–Southern Colorado Campus M
University of Phoenix–Springfield Campus M
University of Phoenix–Tulsa Campus M
University of Phoenix–Utah Campus M
University of Phoenix–Vancouver Campus M
University of Phoenix–Washington Campus M
University of Phoenix–West Florida Campus M
University of Phoenix–West Michigan Campus M
University of Phoenix–Wichita Campus M
University of Phoenix–Wisconsin Campus M
University of Pittsburgh M,D*
University of Portland M
University of Puerto Rico, Mayagüez Campus M*
University of Puerto Rico, Río Piedras M,D*
University of Redlands M
University of Regina M,O
University of Rhode Island M,D
University of Richmond M
University of Rochester M,D*
University of St. Francis (IL) M
University of Saint Francis (IN) M
University of Saint Mary M
University of St. Thomas (MN) M*
University of St. Thomas (TX) M
University of San Diego M,O*
University of San Francisco M
University of Saskatchewan M
The University of Scranton M
University of Sioux Falls M
University of South Alabama M*
University of South Carolina M,D*
The University of South Dakota M
University of Southern California M,D*
University of Southern Indiana M
University of Southern Maine M
University of Southern Mississippi M*
University of South Florida M,D*
The University of Tampa M
The University of Tennessee M,D*
The University of Tennessee at Chattanooga M
The University of Tennessee at Martin M
The University of Texas at Arlington M,D*
The University of Texas at Austin M,D*
The University of Texas at Brownsville M
The University of Texas at Dallas M,D*
The University of Texas at El Paso M
The University of Texas at San Antonio M,D*
The University of Texas at Tyler M
The University of Texas of the Permian Basin M
The University of Texas–Pan American M,D
University of the District of Columbia M
University of the Incarnate Word M,O
University of the Pacific M
University of the Sacred Heart M
University of the Virgin Islands M
University of the West M
The University of Toledo M,D*
University of Toronto M,D
University of Tulsa M*
University of Utah M,D*
University of Vermont M*
University of Victoria M
University of Virginia M,D*
University of Washington M,D*
University of Washington, Bothell M
University of Waterloo M*
The University of Western Ontario M,D
University of West Florida M
University of West Georgia M
University of Windsor M
University of Wisconsin–Eau Claire M
University of Wisconsin–Green Bay M
University of Wisconsin–La Crosse M
University of Wisconsin–Madison M*
University of Wisconsin–Milwaukee M,D,O
University of Wisconsin–Oshkosh M
University of Wisconsin–Parkside M
University of Wisconsin–River Falls M
University of Wisconsin–Stevens Point M
University of Wisconsin–Whitewater M*
University of Wyoming M
Upper Iowa University M
Urbana University M
Ursuline College M
Utah State University M
Valdosta State University M
Valparaiso University M,O
Vanderbilt University M,D*
Vanguard University of Southern California M
Villanova University M*
Virginia College at Birmingham M
Virginia Commonwealth University M,D*
Virginia Polytechnic Institute and State University M,D*
Wagner College M
Wake Forest University M*
Walden University M,D,O
Walsh College of Accountancy and Business Administration M
Walsh University M
Warner Pacific College M
Warner Southern College M
Washburn University M
Washington State University M,D*
Washington State University Tri-Cities M
Washington State University Vancouver M
Washington University in St. Louis M,D*
Wayland Baptist University M
Waynesburg College M
Wayne State College M
Wayne State University M,D*
Webber International University M*
Weber State University M*
Webster University M,D
Wesleyan College M
Wesley College M
West Chester University of Pennsylvania M
Western Carolina University M*
Western Connecticut State University M*
Western Governors University M
Western Illinois University M
Western International University M
Western Kentucky University M
Western Michigan University M*
Western New England College M
Western New Mexico University M
Western Washington University M
Westminster College (UT) M,O
West Texas A&M University M
West Virginia University M*
West Virginia Wesleyan College M
Wheeling Jesuit University M
Whitworth University M
Wichita State University M*
Widener University M*
Wilfrid Laurier University M,D
Wilkes University M
Willamette University M
William Carey University M
William Paterson University of New Jersey M*
Wilmington College (DE) M
Wingate University M
Winston-Salem State University M
Winthrop University M
Woodbury University M
Worcester Polytechnic Institute M,O*
Worcester State College M
Wright State University M*
Xavier University M*
Yale University M,D*
York College of Pennsylvania M
York University M,D*
Youngstown State University M

BUSINESS EDUCATION

Albany State University M
Arkansas State University M,O
Armstrong Atlantic State University M
Auburn University M,D,O*
Ball State University M*
Bloomsburg University of Pennsylvania M
Bowling Green State University M*
Buffalo State College, State University of New York M
Canisius College M
Central Connecticut State University M,O
Central Michigan University M*
Chadron State College M,O
The College of Saint Rose M,O*
Drake University M*
Eastern Kentucky University M*
Emporia State University M
Florida Agricultural and Mechanical University M*
Georgia Southern University M*
Hofstra University M*
Inter American University of Puerto Rico, Metropolitan Campus M
Inter American University of Puerto Rico, San Germán Campus M
International College of the Cayman Islands M
Lehman College of the City University of New York M
Louisiana State University and Agricultural and Mechanical College M,D*
Louisiana Tech University M,D
Maryville University of Saint Louis M,O
Middle Tennessee State University M*
Mississippi College M,O
Nazareth College of Rochester M
New York University M,O*
Northwestern State University of Louisiana M
Old Dominion University M,D*
Penn State Harrisburg M,D*
Rider University M,O*
Salisbury University M

- South Carolina State University M
- Southern New Hampshire University M,O*
- State University of New York at Oswego M
- Thomas College M
- University of Delaware M,D*
- University of Minnesota, Twin Cities Campus M,D*
- University of Missouri–Columbia M,D,O*
- University of South Carolina M,D*
- The University of Toledo M*
- University of Washington M,D*
- University of West Georgia M,O
- University of Wisconsin–Whitewater M*
- Utah State University M,D
- Valdosta State University M,D
- Wayne State College M
- Wayne State University M,D,O*
- Western Kentucky University M,O
- Wright State University M*

CANADIAN STUDIES

- Carleton University M,D
- Collège universitaire de Saint-Boniface M
- The Johns Hopkins University M,D,O*
- Saint Mary's University M
- Trent University M
- Université de Sherbrooke M,D
- Université du Québec à Chicoutimi M
- Université du Québec à Trois-Rivières M,D
- University of Lethbridge M,D
- University of Manitoba M
- University of Ottawa D*
- University of Regina M,D
- University of Saskatchewan M,D

CANCER BIOLOGY/ONCOLOGY

- Baylor College of Medicine D*
- Brown University M,D*
- Dartmouth College D*
- Drexel University M,D*
- Duke University D*
- Georgetown University *
- Gerstner Sloan-Kettering Graduate School of Biomedical Sciences D
- Mayo Graduate School D*
- McMaster University M,D
- Medical University of South Carolina D*
- New York University M,D*
- Northwestern University D*
- Stanford University D*
- Université de Montréal O
- Université Laval O
- University at Buffalo, the State University of New York D*
- University of Alberta M,D*
- The University of Arizona D*
- University of Calgary M,D
- University of California, San Diego D*
- University of Chicago D*
- University of Cincinnati D
- University of Colorado at Denver and Health Sciences Center D*
- University of Delaware M,D*
- University of Maryland, Baltimore D*
- University of Massachusetts Worcester D*
- University of Medicine and Dentistry of New Jersey *
- University of Miami D*
- University of Nebraska Medical Center M,D*
- The University of North Carolina at Chapel Hill *
- University of Pennsylvania D*
- University of South Florida D*
- The University of Texas Health Science Center at Houston M,D*
- The University of Toledo M,D*
- University of Utah M,D*
- University of Wisconsin–Madison D*
- Vanderbilt University M,D*
- Wake Forest University D*
- Wayne State University M,D*
- West Virginia University M,D*
- Yale University D*

CARDIOVASCULAR SCIENCES

- Albany Medical College M,D
- Baylor College of Medicine D*
- Dartmouth College D*
- Long Island University, C.W. Post Campus M,O*
- McMaster University M,D
- Medical College of Georgia M,D*
- Midwestern University, Glendale Campus M*
- Milwaukee School of Engineering M*
- The Ohio State University M*
- Université Laval O
- University of Calgary M,D
- University of California, San Diego D*
- University of Maryland, Baltimore *
- University of Medicine and Dentistry of New Jersey M,D*
- The University of South Dakota M,D
- The University of Toledo M,D*
- University of Virginia *

CELL BIOLOGY

- Albany Medical College M,D
- Albert Einstein College of Medicine D*
- Arizona State University M,D*
- Auburn University M,D*
- Baylor College of Medicine D*
- Boston University M,D*
- Brandeis University M,D*
- Brown University M,D*
- California Institute of Technology D*
- Carnegie Mellon University M,D*
- Case Western Reserve University M,D*
- The Catholic University of America M,D*
- Colorado State University M,D*
- Columbia University M,D*
- Cornell University M,D*
- Cornell University, Joan and Sanford I. Weill Medical College and Graduate School of Medical Sciences D*
- Dartmouth College D*
- Drexel University M,D*
- Duke University D,O*
- East Carolina University D*
- Emory University D*
- Emporia State University M
- Florida Institute of Technology M,D*
- Florida State University M,D*
- George Mason University M,D,O*
- Georgetown University D*
- Georgia State University M,D*
- Grand Valley State University M
- Harvard University D*
- Illinois State University M,D*
- Indiana University Bloomington M,D*
- Indiana University–Purdue University Indianapolis M,D*
- Iowa State University of Science and Technology M,D*
- The Johns Hopkins University D*
- Kent State University M,D*
- Louisiana State University Health Sciences Center M,D*
- Louisiana State University Health Sciences Center at Shreveport M,D*
- Loyola University Chicago M,D*
- Marquette University M,D
- Massachusetts Institute of Technology D*
- Mayo Graduate School D*
- McGill University M,D*
- McMaster University M,D
- Medical College of Georgia M,D*
- Medical College of Wisconsin M,D*
- Medical University of South Carolina D*
- Michigan State University M,D*
- Missouri State University M*
- Mount Sinai School of Medicine of New York University M,D*
- New York Medical College M,D*
- New York University D*
- North Carolina State University M,D*
- North Dakota State University M,D
- Northwestern University D*
- Oakland University M*
- The Ohio State University M,D*
- Ohio University M,D*
- Oregon Health & Science University D*
- Oregon State University M,D*
- Penn State Hershey Medical Center M,D*
- Penn State University Park M,D*
- Purdue University M,D*
- Queen's University at Kingston M,D
- Quinnipiac University M*
- Rensselaer Polytechnic Institute M,D*
- Rice University M,D*
- Rosalind Franklin University of Medicine and Science M,D*
- Rush University M,D
- Rutgers, The State University of New Jersey, New Brunswick M,D*
- Saint Joseph College M
- San Diego State University M,D*
- San Francisco State University M
- State University of New York Downstate Medical Center D*
- State University of New York Upstate Medical University M,D*
- Stony Brook University, State University of New York M,D*
- Temple University M,D*
- Texas A&M Health Science Center D*
- Texas A&M University M,D*
- Texas Tech University Health Sciences Center M,D
- Thomas Jefferson University M,D*
- Tufts University D*
- Tulane University M,D*
- Uniformed Services University of the Health Sciences D*
- Universidad Central del Caribe M
- Université de Montréal M,D
- Université de Sherbrooke M,D
- Université Laval M,D
- University at Albany, State University of New York M,D*
- University at Buffalo, the State University of New York D*
- The University of Alabama at Birmingham M,D*
- University of Alberta M,D*
- The University of Arizona M,D*
- University of Arkansas M,D*
- The University of British Columbia M,D*
- University of California, Berkeley D*
- University of California, Davis M,D*
- University of California, Irvine M,D*
- University of California, Los Angeles M,D*
- University of California, Riverside M,D*
- University of California, San Diego D*
- University of California, San Francisco D
- University of California, Santa Barbara M,D*
- University of California, Santa Cruz M,D*
- University of Chicago D*
- University of Cincinnati D
- University of Colorado at Boulder M,D*
- University of Colorado at Denver and Health Sciences Center D*
- University of Connecticut M,D*
- University of Connecticut Health Center D*
- University of Delaware M,D*
- University of Florida M,D*
- University of Georgia M,D*
- University of Guelph M,D
- University of Illinois at Chicago M,D*
- University of Illinois at Urbana–Champaign D*
- The University of Iowa M,D*
- University of Kansas M,D*
- University of Maryland, Baltimore M,D*
- University of Maryland, Baltimore County D*
- University of Maryland, College Park M,D*
- University of Massachusetts Amherst D*
- University of Massachusetts Boston D
- University of Massachusetts Worcester D*
- University of Medicine and Dentistry of New Jersey M,D*
- University of Miami D*
- University of Michigan M,D*
- University of Minnesota, Twin Cities Campus M,D*
- University of Missouri–Columbia M,D*
- University of Missouri–Kansas City D*
- University of Missouri–St. Louis M,D,O
- University of Nebraska Medical Center M,D*
- University of Nevada, Reno M,D*
- University of New Haven M*
- University of New Mexico M,D*
- The University of North Carolina at Chapel Hill D*
- University of Notre Dame M,D*
- University of Oklahoma Health Sciences Center M,D
- University of Ottawa M,D*
- University of Pennsylvania D*
- University of Pittsburgh M,D
- University of Rhode Island M,D
- University of Saskatchewan M,D
- University of South Alabama D*
- University of South Carolina M,D*
- The University of South Dakota M,D
- University of Southern California M,D*
- The University of Texas at Austin D*
- The University of Texas at Dallas M,D*
- The University of Texas at San Antonio M,D
- The University of Texas Health Science Center at Houston M,D*
- The University of Texas Health Science Center at San Antonio M,D*
- The University of Texas Medical Branch D*
- The University of Texas Southwestern Medical Center at Dallas D*
- University of the Sciences in Philadelphia M*
- The University of Toledo M,D*
- University of Utah D*
- University of Vermont M,D*
- University of Virginia D*
- University of Washington D*
- The University of Western Ontario M,D
- University of Wisconsin–La Crosse M
- University of Wisconsin–Madison M,D*
- Vanderbilt University M,D*
- Washington State University M,D*
- Washington University in St. Louis D*
- Wesleyan University D*
- West Virginia University M,D*
- Yale University D*

CELTIC LANGUAGES

- Harvard University D*

CERAMIC SCIENCES AND ENGINEERING

- Alfred University M,D*
- Case Western Reserve University M,D*
- Penn State University Park M,D*
- Rensselaer Polytechnic Institute M,D*
- Rutgers, The State University of New Jersey, New Brunswick M,D*
- University of California, Los Angeles M,D*
- University of Cincinnati M,D
- University of Missouri–Rolla M,D*

CHEMICAL ENGINEERING

- Arizona State University M,D*
- Auburn University M,D*
- Brigham Young University M,D*
- Brown University M,D*
- Bucknell University M
- California Institute of Technology M,D*
- Carnegie Mellon University M,D*
- Case Western Reserve University M,D*
- City College of the City University of New York M,D*
- Clarkson University M,D*
- Clemson University M,D*
- Cleveland State University M,D
- Colorado School of Mines M,D*
- Colorado State University M,D*
- Columbia University M,D*
- Cooper Union for the Advancement of Science and Art M
- Cornell University M,D*
- Dalhousie University M,D
- Drexel University M,D*
- École Polytechnique de Montréal M,D,O
- Fairleigh Dickinson University, College at Florham M,O*
- Florida Agricultural and Mechanical University M,D*
- Florida Institute of Technology M,D*
- Florida State University M,D*
- Georgia Institute of Technology M,D*
- Graduate School and University Center of the City University of New York D*
- Howard University M*
- Illinois Institute of Technology M,D*
- Instituto Tecnológico y de Estudios Superiores de Monterrey, Campus Monterrey M,D
- Iowa State University of Science and Technology M,D*

*P—first professional degree; M—master's degree; D—doctorate; O—other advanced degree; *full description and/or announcement in Book 2, 3, 4, 5, or 6*

Institution	Degrees
The Johns Hopkins University	M,D*
Kansas State University	M,D*
Lamar University	M,D*
Lehigh University	M,D*
Louisiana State University and Agricultural and Mechanical College	M,D*
Louisiana Tech University	M,D
Manhattan College	M
Massachusetts Institute of Technology	M,D*
McGill University	M,D,O*
McMaster University	M,D
McNeese State University	M
Michigan State University	M,D*
Michigan Technological University	M,D*
Mississippi State University	M,D
Montana State University	M,D
New Jersey Institute of Technology	M,D
New Mexico State University	M,D
North Carolina Agricultural and Technical State University	M
North Carolina State University	M,D*
Northeastern University	M,D*
Northwestern University	M,D*
The Ohio State University	M,D*
Ohio University	M,D*
Oklahoma State University	M,D*
Oregon State University	M,D*
Penn State University Park	M,D*
Polytechnic University, Brooklyn Campus	M,D*
Polytechnic University, Long Island Graduate Center	M,D
Polytechnic University, Westchester Graduate Center	M
Princeton University	M,D*
Purdue University	M,D*
Queen's University at Kingston	M,D
Rensselaer Polytechnic Institute	M,D*
Rice University	M,D*
Rose-Hulman Institute of Technology	M*
Royal Military College of Canada	M,D
Rutgers, The State University of New Jersey, New Brunswick	M,D*
San Jose State University	M
South Dakota School of Mines and Technology	M,D
Stanford University	M,D,O*
Stevens Institute of Technology	M,D,O*
Syracuse University	M,D*
Tennessee Technological University	M,D*
Texas A&M University	M,D*
Texas A&M University–Kingsville	M
Texas Tech University	M,D
Tufts University	M,D*
Tulane University	M,D*
Universidad de las Américas–Puebla	M
Université de Sherbrooke	M,D
Université Laval	M,D
University at Buffalo, the State University of New York	M,D*
The University of Akron	M,D
The University of Alabama	M,D
The University of Alabama in Huntsville	M,D
University of Alberta	M,D*
The University of Arizona	M,D*
University of Arkansas	M,D*
The University of British Columbia	M,D*
University of Calgary	M,D
University of California, Berkeley	M,D*
University of California, Davis	M,D*
University of California, Irvine	M,D*
University of California, Los Angeles	M,D*
University of California, Riverside	M,D*
University of California, San Diego	M,D*
University of California, Santa Barbara	M,D*
University of Cincinnati	M,D
University of Colorado at Boulder	M,D*
University of Connecticut	M,D*
University of Dayton	M*
University of Delaware	M,D*
University of Detroit Mercy	M,D
University of Florida	M,D*
University of Houston	M,D*
University of Idaho	M,D*
University of Illinois at Chicago	M,D*
University of Illinois at Urbana–Champaign	M,D*
The University of Iowa	M,D*
University of Kansas	M,D*
University of Kentucky	M,D*
University of Louisiana at Lafayette	M*
University of Louisville	M,D
University of Maine	M,D*
University of Maryland, Baltimore County	M,D,O*
University of Maryland, College Park	M,D,O*
University of Massachusetts Amherst	M,D*
University of Massachusetts Lowell	M*
University of Michigan	M,D,O*
University of Minnesota, Twin Cities Campus	M,D*
University of Missouri–Columbia	M,D*
University of Missouri–Rolla	M,D*
University of Nebraska–Lincoln	M,D*
University of Nevada, Reno	M,D*
University of New Brunswick Fredericton	M,D
University of New Hampshire	M,D*
University of New Mexico	M,D*
University of North Dakota	M
University of Notre Dame	M,D*
University of Oklahoma	M,D*
University of Ottawa	M,D*
University of Pennsylvania	M,D*
University of Pittsburgh	M,D*
University of Puerto Rico, Mayagüez Campus	M,D*
University of Rhode Island	M,D
University of Rochester	M,D*
University of Saskatchewan	M,D
University of South Alabama	M*
University of South Carolina	M,D*
University of Southern California	M,D,O*
University of South Florida	M,D*
The University of Tennessee	M,D*
The University of Texas at Austin	M,D*
The University of Toledo	M,D*
University of Toronto	M,D
University of Tulsa	M,D*
University of Utah	M,D*
University of Virginia	M,D*
University of Washington	M,D*
University of Waterloo	M,D*
University of Wisconsin–Madison	M,D*
University of Wyoming	M,D
Vanderbilt University	M,D*
Villanova University	M*
Virginia Commonwealth University	M,D*
Virginia Polytechnic Institute and State University	M,D*
Washington State University	M,D*
Washington University in St. Louis	M,D*
Wayne State University	M,D*
Western Michigan University	M,D*
West Virginia University	M,D*
Widener University	M*
Worcester Polytechnic Institute	M,D*
Yale University	M,D*
Youngstown State University	M

CHEMICAL PHYSICS

Institution	Degrees
Columbia University	M,D*
Cornell University	D*
Florida State University	M,D*
Georgetown University	M,D*
Harvard University	D*
Kent State University	M,D*
Marquette University	M,D
McMaster University	M,D
Michigan State University	M,D*
The Ohio State University	M,D*
Princeton University	D*
Simon Fraser University	M,D
University of Colorado at Boulder	M,D*
University of Louisville	M,D
University of Maryland, College Park	M,D*
University of Nevada, Reno	D*
University of Southern California	D*
The University of Tennessee	M,D*
University of Utah	M,D*
Virginia Commonwealth University	M,D*
Wesleyan University	M,D*
West Virginia University	M,D*

CHEMISTRY

Institution	Degrees
Acadia University	M
American University	M*
American University of Beirut	M
Arizona State University	M,D*
Arkansas State University	M,O
Auburn University	M,D*
Ball State University	M*
Baylor University	M,D*
Boston College	M,D*
Boston University	M,D*
Bowling Green State University	M,D*
Bradley University	M
Brandeis University	M,D*
Brigham Young University	M,D*
Brock University	M,D
Brooklyn College of the City University of New York	M,D
Brown University	M,D*
Bryn Mawr College	M,D*
Bucknell University	M
Buffalo State College, State University of New York	M
California Institute of Technology	M,D*
California Polytechnic State University, San Luis Obispo	M
California State Polytechnic University, Pomona	M
California State University, East Bay	M
California State University, Fresno	M
California State University, Fullerton	M
California State University, Long Beach	M
California State University, Los Angeles	M
California State University, Northridge	M
California State University, Sacramento	M*
California State University, San Bernardino	M
Carleton University	M,D
Carnegie Mellon University	M,D*
Case Western Reserve University	M,D*
The Catholic University of America	M*
Central Connecticut State University	M
Central Michigan University	M*
Central Washington University	M
City College of the City University of New York	M,D*
Clark Atlanta University	M,D
Clarkson University	M,D*
Clark University	M,D*
Clemson University	M,D*
Cleveland State University	M,D
The College of William and Mary	M
Colorado School of Mines	M,D
Colorado State University	M,D*
Colorado State University-Pueblo	M
Columbia University	M,D*
Concordia University (Canada)	M,D
Cornell University	D*
Dalhousie University	M,D
Dartmouth College	D*
Delaware State University	M
DePaul University	M*
Drexel University	M,D*
Duke University	D*
Duquesne University	M,D*
East Carolina University	M*
Eastern Illinois University	M
Eastern Kentucky University	M*
Eastern Michigan University	M
Eastern New Mexico University	M
East Tennessee State University	M
Emory University	D*
Fairleigh Dickinson University, College at Florham	M*
Fairleigh Dickinson University, Metropolitan Campus	M*
Fisk University	M
Florida Agricultural and Mechanical University	M*
Florida Atlantic University	M,D
Florida Institute of Technology	M,D*
Florida International University	M,D*
Florida State University	M,D*
Furman University	M
Georgetown University	M,D*
The George Washington University	M,D*
Georgia Institute of Technology	M,D*
Georgia State University	M,D*
Graduate School and University Center of the City University of New York	D*
Hampton University	M*
Harvard University	D*
Howard University	M,D*
Idaho State University	M
Illinois Institute of Technology	M,D*
Illinois State University	M*
Indiana University Bloomington	M,D*
Indiana University of Pennsylvania	M
Indiana University–Purdue University Indianapolis	M,D*
Instituto Tecnológico y de Estudios Superiores de Monterrey, Campus Monterrey	M,D
Iowa State University of Science and Technology	M,D*
Jackson State University	M,D
The Johns Hopkins University	D*
Kansas State University	M,D*
Kent State University	M,D*
Lakehead University	M
Lamar University	M*
Laurentian University	M
Lehigh University	M,D*
Long Island University, Brooklyn Campus	M*
Louisiana State University and Agricultural and Mechanical College	M,D*
Louisiana Tech University	M
Loyola University Chicago	M,D*
Marquette University	M,D
Marshall University	M
Massachusetts College of Pharmacy and Health Sciences	M,D*
Massachusetts Institute of Technology	D*
McGill University	M,D*
McMaster University	M,D
McNeese State University	M
Memorial University of Newfoundland	M,D
Miami University	M,D*
Michigan State University	M,D*
Michigan Technological University	M,D*
Middle Tennessee State University	M,D*
Mississippi College	M
Mississippi State University	M,D
Missouri State University	M*
Montana State University	M,D
Montclair State University	M*
Morgan State University	M*
Mount Allison University	M
Murray State University	M
New Jersey Institute of Technology	M,D
New Mexico Highlands University	M
New Mexico Institute of Mining and Technology	M,D
New Mexico State University	M,D
New York University	M,D*
North Carolina Agricultural and Technical State University	M
North Carolina Central University	M
North Carolina State University	M,D*
North Dakota State University	M,D
Northeastern Illinois University	M
Northeastern University	M,D*
Northern Arizona University	M
Northern Illinois University	M,D
Northern Michigan University	M
Northwestern University	D*
Oakland University	M,D*
The Ohio State University	M,D*
Oklahoma State University	M,D*
Old Dominion University	M,D*
Oregon State University	M,D*
Penn State University Park	M,D*
Pittsburg State University	M
Polytechnic University, Brooklyn Campus	M,D*
Polytechnic University, Westchester Graduate Center	M
Pontifical Catholic University of Puerto Rico	M
Portland State University	M,D
Prairie View A&M University	M
Princeton University	M,D*
Purdue University	M,D*
Queens College of the City University of New York	M
Queen's University at Kingston	M,D
Rensselaer Polytechnic Institute	M,D*
Rice University	M,D*
Rochester Institute of Technology	M
Roosevelt University	M
Royal Military College of Canada	M,D
Rutgers, The State University of New Jersey, Camden	M
Rutgers, The State University of New Jersey, Newark	M,D*
Rutgers, The State University of New Jersey, New Brunswick	M,D*
Sacred Heart University	M
St. Francis Xavier University	M
St. John's University (NY)	M
Saint Joseph College	M
Saint Louis University	M*
Sam Houston State University	M
San Diego State University	M,D*
San Francisco State University	M
San Jose State University	M
The Scripps Research Institute	D
Seton Hall University	M,D*
Simon Fraser University	M,D
Smith College	M*
South Dakota School of Mines and Technology	M,D
South Dakota State University	M,D
Southeast Missouri State University	M

Southern Connecticut State University M
Southern Illinois University Carbondale M,D*
Southern Illinois University Edwardsville M
Southern Methodist University M,D*
Southern University and Agricultural and Mechanical College M*
Stanford University D*
State University of New York at Binghamton M,D*
State University of New York at Fredonia M
State University of New York at New Paltz M
State University of New York at Oswego M
State University of New York College of Environmental Science and Forestry M,D
Stephen F. Austin State University M
Stevens Institute of Technology M,D,O*
Stony Brook University, State University of New York M,D*
Sul Ross State University M*
Syracuse University M,D*
Temple University M,D*
Tennessee State University M*
Tennessee Technological University M*
Texas A&M University M,D*
Texas A&M University–Commerce M
Texas A&M University–Kingsville M
Texas Christian University M,D
Texas Southern University M
Texas State University-San Marcos M*
Texas Tech University M,D
Texas Woman's University M
Trent University M
Tufts University M,D*
Tulane University M,D*
Tuskegee University M
Université de Moncton M
Université de Montréal M,D
Université de Sherbrooke M,D,O
Université du Québec à Montréal M
Université du Québec à Trois-Rivières M
Université Laval M,D
University at Albany, State University of New York M,D*
University at Buffalo, the State University of New York M,D*
The University of Akron M,D
The University of Alabama M,D
The University of Alabama at Birmingham M,D*
The University of Alabama in Huntsville M
University of Alaska Fairbanks M,D
University of Alberta M,D*
The University of Arizona M,D*
University of Arkansas M,D*
University of Arkansas at Little Rock M
The University of British Columbia M,D*
University of Calgary M,D
University of California, Berkeley D*
University of California, Davis M,D*
University of California, Irvine M,D*
University of California, Los Angeles M,D*
University of California, Riverside M,D*
University of California, San Diego M,D*
University of California, San Francisco D
University of California, Santa Barbara M,D*
University of California, Santa Cruz M,D*
University of Central Florida M,D*
University of Central Oklahoma M
University of Chicago D*
University of Cincinnati M,D
University of Colorado at Boulder M,D*
University of Colorado at Denver and Health Sciences Center M*
University of Connecticut M,D*
University of Dayton M*
University of Delaware M,D*
University of Denver M,D*
University of Detroit Mercy M
University of Florida M,D*
University of Georgia M,D*
University of Guelph M,D
University of Hawaii at Manoa M,D*
University of Houston M,D*
University of Houston–Clear Lake M
University of Idaho M,D*
University of Illinois at Chicago M,D*
University of Illinois at Urbana–Champaign M,D*
The University of Iowa M,D*
University of Kansas M,D*
University of Kentucky M,D*
University of Lethbridge M,D
University of Louisville M,D
University of Maine M,D*
University of Manitoba M,D
University of Maryland, Baltimore County M,D*
University of Maryland, College Park M,D*
University of Massachusetts Amherst M,D*
University of Massachusetts Boston M
University of Massachusetts Dartmouth M
University of Massachusetts Lowell M,D*
University of Memphis M,D*
University of Miami M,D*
University of Michigan D*
University of Minnesota, Duluth M*
University of Minnesota, Twin Cities Campus M,D*
University of Mississippi M,D
University of Missouri–Columbia M,D*
University of Missouri–Kansas City M,D*
University of Missouri–Rolla M,D*
University of Missouri–St. Louis M,D
The University of Montana M,D*
University of Nebraska–Lincoln M,D*
University of Nevada, Las Vegas M,D
University of Nevada, Reno M,D*
University of New Brunswick Fredericton M,D
University of New Hampshire M,D*
University of New Mexico M,D*
University of New Orleans M,D
The University of North Carolina at Chapel Hill M,D*
The University of North Carolina at Charlotte M*
The University of North Carolina at Greensboro M
The University of North Carolina Wilmington M*
University of North Dakota M,D
University of Northern Colorado M,D
University of Northern Iowa M
University of North Texas M,D*
University of Notre Dame M,D*
University of Oklahoma M,D*
University of Oregon M,D*
University of Ottawa M,D*
University of Pennsylvania M,D*
University of Pittsburgh M,D*
University of Prince Edward Island M
University of Puerto Rico, Mayagüez Campus M,D*
University of Puerto Rico, Río Piedras M,D*
University of Regina M,D
University of Rhode Island M,D
University of Rochester M,D*
University of San Francisco M
University of Saskatchewan M,D
The University of Scranton M
University of South Carolina M,D*
The University of South Dakota M
University of Southern California M,D*
University of Southern Mississippi M,D*
University of South Florida M,D*
The University of Tennessee M,D*
The University of Texas at Arlington M,D*
The University of Texas at Austin M,D*
The University of Texas at Dallas M,D*
The University of Texas at El Paso M
The University of Texas at San Antonio M,D*
University of the Sciences in Philadelphia M,D*
The University of Toledo M,D*
University of Toronto M,D
University of Tulsa M*
University of Utah M,D*
University of Vermont M,D*
University of Victoria M,D
University of Virginia M,D*
University of Washington M,D*
University of Waterloo M,D*
The University of Western Ontario M,D
University of Windsor M,D
University of Wisconsin–Madison M,D*
University of Wisconsin–Milwaukee M,D
University of Wyoming M,D
Utah State University M,D
Vanderbilt University M,D*
Vassar College M
Villanova University M*
Virginia Commonwealth University M,D*
Virginia Polytechnic Institute and State University M,D*
Wake Forest University M,D*
Washington State University M,D*
Washington State University Tri-Cities M,D
Washington University in St. Louis M,D*
Wayne State University M,D*
Wesleyan University M,D*
West Chester University of Pennsylvania M
Western Carolina University M*
Western Illinois University M
Western Kentucky University M
Western Michigan University M,D*
Western Washington University M
West Texas A&M University M
West Virginia University M,D*
Wichita State University M,D*
Worcester Polytechnic Institute M,D*
Wright State University M*
Yale University D*
York University M,D*
Youngstown State University M

CHILD AND FAMILY STUDIES

Arizona State University M,D*
Auburn University M,D*
Bank Street College of Education M*
Bowling Green State University M*
Brandeis University M*
Brigham Young University M,D*
Brock University M
Capella University M,D,O
Central Michigan University M*
Central Washington University M
Clemson University D*
Colorado State University M*
Concordia University (Canada) M
Concordia University, St. Paul M,O
Concordia University Wisconsin M
Cornell University D*
East Carolina University M*
Florida State University M,D*
Indiana State University M*
Indiana University Bloomington M,D*
Iowa State University of Science and Technology M,D*
Kansas State University M,D*
Loma Linda University M,D,O
Miami University M*
Michigan State University M,D*
Middle Tennessee State University M*
Missouri State University M*
Mount Saint Vincent University M
North Dakota State University M,D
Northern Illinois University M
Nova Southeastern University M,D*
The Ohio State University M,D*
Ohio University M*
Oklahoma State University M,D*
Oregon State University M,D*
Oxford Graduate School M,D
Penn State University Park M,D*
Purdue University M,D*
Roberts Wesleyan College M
Sage Graduate School M
St. Cloud State University M
Saint Joseph College M,O
San Diego State University M*
San Jose State University M
South Carolina State University M
Spring Arbor University M
Springfield College M,O*
Stanford University D*
State University of New York at Oswego M
Syracuse University M,D*
Texas State University-San Marcos M*
Texas Tech University M,D
Texas Woman's University M,D
Towson University O
Tufts University M,D,O*
The University of Akron M
The University of Alabama M
The University of Arizona M,D*
The University of British Columbia M,D*
University of California, Santa Barbara M,D*
University of Central Florida M,O*
University of Connecticut M,D*
University of Delaware M,D*
University of Denver M,D,O*
University of Georgia M,D*
University of Guelph M,D
University of Illinois at Springfield M
University of Kentucky M,D*
University of La Verne M
University of Manitoba M
University of Maryland, College Park M,D*
University of Minnesota, Twin Cities Campus M,D*
University of Missouri–Columbia M,D*
University of Nebraska–Lincoln M,D*
University of Nevada, Reno M*
University of New Hampshire M*
University of New Mexico M,D*
The University of North Carolina at Greensboro M,D
University of North Texas M,D*
University of Rhode Island M
University of Southern Mississippi M*
The University of Tennessee M,D*
The University of Tennessee at Martin M
The University of Texas at Austin M,D*
The University of Texas at Dallas M,D*
University of Utah M*
University of Victoria M,D
University of Wisconsin–Madison M,D*
University of Wisconsin–Stout M*
Utah State University M,D
Vanderbilt University M*
Virginia Polytechnic Institute and State University M,D*
Wayne State University O*
West Virginia University M*
Wheelock College M

CHILD DEVELOPMENT

American International College M,D,O
Appalachian State University M
Arcadia University M,D,O
California State University, Los Angeles M
California State University, San Bernardino M
East Carolina University M*
Erikson Institute M*
Florida State University M,D*
Indiana State University M*
Michigan State University M,D*
Middle Tennessee State University M*
North Dakota State University M,D
Ohio University M*
Purdue University M,D*
Rutgers, The State University of New Jersey, Camden M,D
San Diego State University M*
Sarah Lawrence College M*
Southern New Hampshire University M,O*
Texas Woman's University M,D
Tufts University M,D,O*
The University of Akron M
University of California, Davis M*
University of La Verne M
University of Minnesota, Twin Cities Campus M,D*
The University of North Carolina at Charlotte M,D*
The University of Tennessee at Martin M
The University of Texas at Austin M,D*
Virginia Polytechnic Institute and State University M,D*
Whittier College M

CHINESE

Cornell University M,D*
Harvard University D*
Indiana University Bloomington M,D*
Middlebury College M
San Francisco State University M
Stanford University M,D*
University of Alberta M*
University of California, Berkeley D*
University of California, Irvine M,D*
University of Colorado at Boulder M,D*
University of Hawaii at Manoa M,D*
University of Kansas M*
University of Massachusetts Amherst M*
University of Oregon M,D*
University of Washington M,D*

P—first professional degree; M—master's degree; D—doctorate; O—other advanced degree;
**full description and/or announcement in Book 2, 3, 4, 5, or 6*

University of Wisconsin–Madison M,D*
Washington University in St. Louis M,D*

CHIROPRACTIC

Canadian Memorial Chiropractic College P,O
Cleveland Chiropractic College-Kansas City Campus P*
Cleveland Chiropractic College-Los Angeles Campus P*
D'Youville College P*
Institut Franco-Européen de Chiropratique P
Life Chiropractic College West P*
Life University P
Logan University-College of Chiropractic P,M
National University of Health Sciences P,M,D*
New York Chiropractic College P*
Northwestern Health Sciences University P
Palmer College of Chiropractic P*
Parker College of Chiropractic P
Sherman College of Straight Chiropractic P*
Southern California University of Health Sciences P
Texas Chiropractic College P
University of Bridgeport P
Western States Chiropractic College P

CIVIL ENGINEERING

American University of Beirut M
Arizona State University M,D*
Auburn University M,D*
Boise State University M
Bradley University M
Brigham Young University M,D*
Bucknell University M
California Institute of Technology M,D,O*
California Polytechnic State University, San Luis Obispo M
California State Polytechnic University, Pomona M
California State University, Fresno M
California State University, Fullerton M
California State University, Long Beach M
California State University, Los Angeles M
California State University, Northridge M
California State University, Sacramento M*
Carleton University M,D
Carnegie Mellon University M,D*
Case Western Reserve University M,D*
The Catholic University of America M,D*
City College of the City University of New York M,D*
Clarkson University M,D*
Clemson University M,D*
Cleveland State University M,D
Colorado State University M,D*
Columbia University M,D,O*
Concordia University (Canada) M,D,O
Cooper Union for the Advancement of Science and Art M
Cornell University M,D*
Dalhousie University M,D
Drexel University M,D*
Duke University M,D*
École Polytechnique de Montréal M,D,O
Florida Agricultural and Mechanical University M,D*
Florida Atlantic University M
Florida Institute of Technology M,D*
Florida International University M,D*
Florida State University M,D*
George Mason University M*
The George Washington University M,D,O*
Georgia Institute of Technology M,D*
Graduate School and University Center of the City University of New York D*
Howard University M*
Idaho State University M,D,O
Illinois Institute of Technology M,D*
Instituto Tecnológico y de Estudios Superiores de Monterrey, Campus Monterrey M,D
Iowa State University of Science and Technology M,D*
The Johns Hopkins University M,D*
Kansas State University M,D*
Lamar University M,D*
Lawrence Technological University M,D
Lehigh University M,D*
Louisiana State University and Agricultural and Mechanical College M,D*
Louisiana Tech University M,D
Loyola Marymount University M
Manhattan College M
Marquette University M,D
Massachusetts Institute of Technology M,D,O*
McGill University M,D*
McMaster University M,D
McNeese State University M
Memorial University of Newfoundland M,D
Michigan State University M,D*
Michigan Technological University M,D*
Mississippi State University M,D
Montana State University M,D
Morgan State University M,D*
New Jersey Institute of Technology M,D
New Mexico State University M,D
North Carolina Agricultural and Technical State University M
North Carolina State University M,D*
North Dakota State University M,D
Northeastern University M,D*
Northwestern University M,D*
Norwich University M
The Ohio State University M,D*
Ohio University M,D*
Oklahoma State University M,D*
Old Dominion University M,D*
Oregon State University M,D*
Penn State University Park M,D*
Polytechnic University, Brooklyn Campus M,D*
Polytechnic University, Long Island Graduate Center M,D
Polytechnic University of Puerto Rico M
Portland State University M,D,O
Princeton University M,D*
Purdue University M,D*
Queen's University at Kingston M,D
Rensselaer Polytechnic Institute M,D*
Rice University M,D*
Rose-Hulman Institute of Technology M*
Royal Military College of Canada M,D
Rutgers, The State University of New Jersey, New Brunswick M,D*
Saint Martin's University M
San Diego State University M*
San Jose State University M
Santa Clara University M
South Carolina State University M
South Dakota School of Mines and Technology M,D
South Dakota State University M
Southern Illinois University Carbondale M*
Southern Illinois University Edwardsville M
Southern Methodist University M,D*
Stanford University M,D,O*
Stevens Institute of Technology M,D,O*
Syracuse University M,D*
Temple University M*
Tennessee Technological University M,D*
Texas A&M University M,D*
Texas A&M University–Kingsville M
Texas Tech University M,D
Tufts University M,D*
Tulane University M,D*
Universidad Central del Este M
Université de Moncton M
Université de Sherbrooke M,D
Université Laval M,D,O
University at Buffalo, the State University of New York M,D*
The University of Akron M,D
The University of Alabama M,D
The University of Alabama at Birmingham M,D*
The University of Alabama in Huntsville M,D
University of Alaska Anchorage M,O
University of Alaska Fairbanks M,D
University of Alberta M,D*
The University of Arizona M,D*
University of Arkansas M,D*
The University of British Columbia M,D*
University of Calgary M,D
University of California, Berkeley M,D*
University of California, Davis M,D,O*
University of California, Irvine M,D*
University of California, Los Angeles M,D*
University of Central Florida M,D,O*
University of Cincinnati M,D
University of Colorado at Boulder M,D*
University of Colorado at Denver and Health Sciences Center M,D*
University of Connecticut M,D*
University of Dayton M*
University of Delaware M,D*
University of Detroit Mercy M
University of Florida M,D,O*
University of Hawaii at Manoa M,D*
University of Houston M,D*
University of Idaho M,D*
University of Illinois at Chicago M,D*
University of Illinois at Urbana–Champaign M,D*
The University of Iowa M,D*
University of Kansas M,D*
University of Kentucky M,D*
University of Louisiana at Lafayette M*
University of Louisville M,D
University of Maine M,D*
University of Manitoba M,D
University of Maryland, Baltimore County M,D*
University of Maryland, College Park M,D,O*
University of Massachusetts Amherst M,D*
University of Massachusetts Dartmouth M
University of Massachusetts Lowell M*
University of Memphis M,D*
University of Miami M,D*
University of Michigan M,D,O*
University of Minnesota, Twin Cities Campus M,D*
University of Missouri–Columbia M,D*
University of Missouri–Kansas City M,D*
University of Missouri–Rolla M,D*
University of Nebraska–Lincoln M,D*
University of Nevada, Las Vegas M,D
University of Nevada, Reno M,D*
University of New Brunswick Fredericton M,D
University of New Hampshire M,D*
University of New Mexico M,D*
The University of North Carolina at Charlotte M,D*
University of North Dakota M
University of Notre Dame M,D*
University of Oklahoma M,D*
University of Ottawa M,D*
University of Pittsburgh M,D*
University of Puerto Rico, Mayagüez Campus M,D*
University of Rhode Island M,D
University of Saskatchewan M,D
University of South Carolina M,D*
University of Southern California M,D,O*
University of South Florida M,D*
The University of Tennessee M,D*
The University of Texas at Arlington M,D*
The University of Texas at Austin M,D*
The University of Texas at El Paso M,D
The University of Texas at San Antonio M*
The University of Toledo M,D*
University of Toronto M,D
University of Utah M,D*
University of Vermont M,D*
University of Virginia M,D*
University of Washington M,D*
University of Waterloo M,D*
University of Windsor M,D
University of Wisconsin–Madison M,D*
University of Wyoming M,D
Utah State University M,D,O
Vanderbilt University M,D*
Villanova University M*
Virginia Polytechnic Institute and State University M,D*
Washington State University M,D*
Washington University in St. Louis M,D*
Wayne State University M,D*
West Virginia University M,D*
Widener University M*
Woods Hole Oceanographic Institution M,D,O
Worcester Polytechnic Institute M,D,O*
Youngstown State University M

CLASSICS

Boston College M*
Boston University M,D*
Brock University M
Brown University M,D*
Bryn Mawr College M,D*
The Catholic University of America M,D*
Columbia University M,D*
Connecticut College M
Cornell University D*
Dalhousie University M,D
Duke University D*
Florida State University M,D*
Fordham University M,D*
Graduate School and University Center of the City University of New York M,D*
Harvard University D*
Heritage Christian University M
Hunter College of the City University of New York M
Indiana University Bloomington M,D*
The Johns Hopkins University D*
Kent State University M*
McMaster University M,D
Memorial University of Newfoundland M
New York University M,D,O*
The Ohio State University M,D*
Princeton University D*
Queen's University at Kingston M
Rutgers, The State University of New Jersey, New Brunswick M,D*
San Francisco State University M
Stanford University M,D*
Texas Tech University M
Tufts University M*
Tulane University M*
University at Buffalo, the State University of New York M,D*
University of Alberta M,D*
The University of Arizona M*
The University of British Columbia M,D*
University of Calgary M,D
University of California, Berkeley M,D*
University of California, Irvine M,D*
University of California, Los Angeles M,D*
University of California, Riverside D*
University of California, Santa Barbara M,D*
University of Chicago M,D*
University of Cincinnati M,D
University of Colorado at Boulder M,D*
University of Florida M,D*
University of Georgia M*
University of Hawaii at Manoa M*
University of Illinois at Urbana–Champaign M,D*
The University of Iowa M,D*
University of Kansas M*
University of Kentucky M*
University of Manitoba M
University of Maryland, College Park M*
University of Massachusetts Amherst M*
University of Michigan M,D,O*
University of Minnesota, Twin Cities Campus M,D*
University of Mississippi M
University of Missouri–Columbia M,D*
University of Nebraska–Lincoln M*
University of New Brunswick Fredericton M
The University of North Carolina at Chapel Hill M,D*
The University of North Carolina at Greensboro M
University of Oregon M*
University of Ottawa M,D*
University of Pennsylvania M,D*
University of Pittsburgh M,D*
University of Southern California M,D*
The University of Texas at Austin M,D*
University of Toronto M,D
University of Vermont M*
University of Victoria M
University of Virginia M,D*
University of Washington M,D*
The University of Western Ontario M
University of Wisconsin–Madison M,D*
University of Wisconsin–Milwaukee M
Vanderbilt University M*
Villanova University M*
Washington University in St. Louis M*
Wayne State University M*
West Chester University of Pennsylvania M
Yale University D*

CLINICAL LABORATORY SCIENCES/MEDICAL TECHNOLOGY

Baylor College of Medicine M,D*

- The Catholic University of America M,D*
- Duke University M*
- Emory University M,D*
- Fairleigh Dickinson University, Metropolitan Campus M*
- Inter American University of Puerto Rico, Metropolitan Campus M
- Long Island University, C.W. Post Campus M*
- Medical College of Georgia M*
- Medical College of Wisconsin D*
- Michigan State University M*
- Milwaukee School of Engineering M*
- Pontifical Catholic University of Puerto Rico O
- Quinnipiac University M*
- Rochester Institute of Technology M
- Rosalind Franklin University of Medicine and Science M*
- Rush University M
- San Francisco State University M
- State University of New York Upstate Medical University M*
- Thomas Jefferson University M*
- Universidad de las Américas–Puebla M
- Université de Montréal O
- Université de Sherbrooke M,D
- University at Buffalo, the State University of New York M*
- The University of Alabama at Birmingham M*
- University of Alberta M,D*
- University of Colorado at Denver and Health Sciences Center M,D*
- University of Kentucky M,D*
- University of Maryland, Baltimore M*
- University of Massachusetts Lowell M*
- University of Medicine and Dentistry of New Jersey M,D*
- University of Mississippi Medical Center M,D*
- University of Nebraska Medical Center M,O*
- University of North Dakota M
- University of Puerto Rico, Medical Sciences Campus M,O*
- University of Rhode Island M
- University of Southern Mississippi M*
- The University of Texas Health Science Center at San Antonio M*
- University of the Sacred Heart O
- University of Utah M*
- University of Washington M*
- University of Wisconsin–Milwaukee M
- Virginia Commonwealth University M,D*
- Wayne State University M,O*

CLINICAL PSYCHOLOGY

- Abilene Christian University M
- Acadia University M
- Adelphi University D,O*
- Adler School of Professional Psychology M,D,O*
- Alabama Agricultural and Mechanical University M,O
- Alliant International University–Fresno D*
- Alliant International University–Los Angeles D*
- Alliant International University–Sacramento D*
- Alliant International University–San Diego M,D*
- Alliant International University–San Francisco D,O*
- American International College M
- American University D*
- Antioch University Los Angeles M
- Antioch University New England M,D*
- Antioch University Santa Barbara D
- Appalachian State University M
- Argosy University, Atlanta Campus M,D,O*
- Argosy University, Chicago Campus M*
- Argosy University, Dallas Campus M,D*
- Argosy University, Denver Campus M,D*
- Argosy University, Hawai'i Campus M,D,O*
- Argosy University, Inland Empire Campus M,D*
- Argosy University, Orange County Campus M,D,O*
- Argosy University, Phoenix Campus M,D,O*
- Argosy University, San Diego Campus M,D*
- Argosy University, San Francisco Bay Area Campus M,D*
- Argosy University, Santa Monica Campus M,D*
- Argosy University, Sarasota Campus M,D,O*
- Argosy University, Schaumburg Campus M,D,O*
- Argosy University, Seattle Campus M,D*
- Argosy University, Tampa Campus M,D*
- Argosy University, Twin Cities Campus M,D,O*
- Argosy University, Washington DC Campus M,D,O*
- Arizona State University D*
- Azusa Pacific University M,D
- Ball State University M*
- Barry University M,O*
- Baylor University M,D*
- Benedictine University M
- Bethany University M
- Bowling Green State University M,D*
- Brigham Young University M,D*
- Bryn Mawr College D*
- California Institute of Integral Studies M,D*
- California Lutheran University M
- California State University, Dominguez Hills M
- California State University, Fullerton M
- California State University, San Bernardino M
- Capella University M,D,O
- Cardinal Stritch University M*
- Carlos Albizu University M,D
- Carlos Albizu University, Miami Campus M,D
- Case Western Reserve University D*
- The Catholic University of America D*
- Central Michigan University D*
- Chestnut Hill College D
- The Chicago School of Professional Psychology M,D,O*
- City College of the City University of New York M,D*
- Clark University D*
- Cleveland State University M,O
- College of St. Joseph M
- The College of William and Mary D
- Concordia University (Canada) M,D,O
- Dalhousie University M,D
- DePaul University M,D*
- Drexel University M,D*
- Duke University D*
- Duquesne University D*
- East Carolina University M*
- Eastern Illinois University M,O
- Eastern Kentucky University M,O*
- Eastern Michigan University M,D
- Eastern Virginia Medical School D
- East Tennessee State University M
- Edinboro University of Pennsylvania M
- Emory University D*
- Emporia State University M
- Evangel University M
- Fairleigh Dickinson University, College at Florham M*
- Fairleigh Dickinson University, Metropolitan Campus M,D*
- Fielding Graduate University D,O*
- Fisk University M
- Florida Institute of Technology M,D*
- Florida State University D*
- Fordham University D*
- Forest Institute of Professional Psychology M,D,O
- Francis Marion University M
- Fuller Theological Seminary M,D
- Gallaudet University D
- George Fox University M,D*
- George Mason University M,D*
- The George Washington University D*
- Graduate School and University Center of the City University of New York D*
- Hofstra University M,D*
- Howard University M,D*
- Idaho State University D
- Illinois Institute of Technology M,D*
- Illinois State University M,D,O*
- Immaculata University M,D,O
- Indiana State University M,D*
- Indiana University of Pennsylvania D
- Indiana University–Purdue University Indianapolis M,D*
- Institute of Transpersonal Psychology M,D*
- Jackson State University D
- James Madison University D
- The Johns Hopkins University M,D*
- Kent State University M,D*
- Lakehead University M,D
- Lamar University M*
- La Salle University M,D
- Lesley University M,D,O*
- Long Island University, Brooklyn Campus D*
- Long Island University, C.W. Post Campus D*
- Louisiana State University and Agricultural and Mechanical College M,D*
- Loyola College in Maryland M,D,O
- Loyola University Chicago D*
- Madonna University M
- Marquette University M,D
- Marshall University M,D
- Marywood University M,D*
- Massachusetts School of Professional Psychology M,D*
- McGill University D*
- Miami University D*
- Michigan School of Professional Psychology M,D
- Midwestern University, Downers Grove Campus M,D*
- Millersville University of Pennsylvania M
- Minnesota State University Mankato M
- Mississippi State University M,D
- Montclair State University M,O*
- Morehead State University M
- Murray State University M
- Naropa University M*
- New College of California M*
- The New School: A University M,D*
- Norfolk State University M
- North Dakota State University M,D
- Northwestern State University of Louisiana M
- Northwestern University D*
- Nova Southeastern University D,O*
- The Ohio State University M,D*
- Ohio University D*
- Oklahoma State University M,D*
- Old Dominion University D*
- Pace University D*
- Pacifica Graduate Institute M,D
- Pacific Graduate School of Psychology D*
- Penn State Harrisburg M,D*
- Penn State University Park M,D*
- Pepperdine University M*
- Pepperdine University M*
- Philadelphia College of Osteopathic Medicine M,D*
- Ponce School of Medicine D
- Pontifical Catholic University of Puerto Rico M,D
- Prairie View A&M University M,D
- Queens College of the City University of New York M
- Queen's University at Kingston M,D
- Radford University M,D,O
- Regent University M,D,O
- Roosevelt University M,D
- Rosalind Franklin University of Medicine and Science M,D*
- Rutgers, The State University of New Jersey, New Brunswick M,D*
- St. John's University (NY) D
- Saint Louis University M,D*
- Saint Mary's University M
- St. Mary's University of San Antonio M
- Saint Michael's College M
- Sam Houston State University M,D
- San Diego State University M,D*
- San Jose State University M
- Seattle Pacific University D
- Southern Illinois University Carbondale M,D*
- Southern Illinois University Edwardsville M
- Southern Methodist University M,D*
- Southern New Hampshire University M,O*
- Spalding University M,D
- State University of New York at Binghamton M,D*
- Stony Brook University, State University of New York D*
- Suffolk University D*
- Syracuse University D*
- Teachers College Columbia University M,D*
- Temple University D*
- Texas A&M University M,D*
- Texas Tech University M,D
- Towson University M
- Troy University M
- Uniformed Services University of the Health Sciences D*
- Union Institute & University D
- Universidad de Iberoamerica P,M
- Université Laval D
- University at Albany, State University of New York M,D,O*
- University at Buffalo, the State University of New York M,D*
- The University of Alabama D
- The University of Alabama at Birmingham M,D*
- University of Alaska Anchorage M,D
- University of Alaska Fairbanks D
- The University of British Columbia M,D*
- University of Calgary M,D
- University of California, San Diego D*
- University of California, Santa Barbara M,D*
- University of Central Florida M,D*
- University of Cincinnati D
- University of Connecticut M,D*
- University of Dayton M*
- University of Delaware D*
- University of Denver M,D*
- University of Detroit Mercy M,D
- University of Florida D*
- University of Guelph M,D
- University of Hartford M,D*
- University of Hawaii at Manoa M,D,O*
- University of Houston M,D*
- University of Houston–Clear Lake M
- University of Indianapolis M,D
- University of Kansas M,D*
- University of Kentucky M,D*
- University of La Verne D
- University of Louisville D
- University of Maine M,D*
- University of Manitoba M,D
- University of Maryland, College Park M,D*
- University of Massachusetts Amherst M,D*
- University of Massachusetts Boston D
- University of Massachusetts Dartmouth M
- University of Memphis M,D*
- University of Miami M,D*
- University of Michigan D*
- University of Minnesota, Twin Cities Campus D*
- University of Mississippi M,D*
- University of Missouri–Kansas City M,D*
- University of Missouri–St. Louis M,D,O
- The University of Montana M,D,O*
- University of Nevada, Las Vegas M,D
- University of New Mexico M,D*
- The University of North Carolina at Chapel Hill D*
- The University of North Carolina at Charlotte M*
- The University of North Carolina at Greensboro M,D
- University of North Dakota M,D
- University of North Texas M,D*
- University of Oregon D*
- University of Pennsylvania D*
- University of Regina M,D
- University of Rhode Island D
- University of Rochester M,D*
- University of South Carolina M,D*
- University of South Carolina Aiken M
- The University of South Dakota M,D
- University of Southern California M,D*
- University of Southern Mississippi M,D*
- University of South Florida M,D*
- The University of Tennessee M,D*
- The University of Texas at El Paso M,D
- The University of Texas at Tyler M
- The University of Texas of the Permian Basin M
- The University of Texas–Pan American M
- The University of Texas Southwestern Medical Center at Dallas D*
- University of the District of Columbia M
- The University of Toledo M,D*
- University of Tulsa M,D*
- University of Vermont D*
- University of Victoria M,D
- University of Virginia M,D,O*
- University of Washington D*
- University of Windsor M,D
- University of Wisconsin–Madison D*
- University of Wisconsin–Milwaukee M,D

P—first professional degree; M—master's degree; D—doctorate; O—other advanced degree;
**full description and/or announcement in Book 2, 3, 4, 5, or 6*

Utah State University M,D
Valdosta State University M,O
Valparaiso University M,O
Vanguard University of Southern California M
Virginia Commonwealth University D*
Virginia Polytechnic Institute and State University M,D*
Washburn University M
Washington State University M,D*
Washington University in St. Louis M,D*
Wayne State University M,D,O*
West Chester University of Pennsylvania M
Western Carolina University M*
Western Illinois University M,O
Western Michigan University M,D,O*
West Virginia University M,D*
Wheaton College M,D
Wichita State University M,D*
Widener University D*
William Paterson University of New Jersey M*
Wisconsin School of Professional Psychology M,D
Wright Institute D
Wright State University D*
Xavier University M,D*
Yeshiva University D

CLINICAL RESEARCH

Case Western Reserve University M*
Duke University M*
Eastern Michigan University M
Emory University M*
The Johns Hopkins University M,D*
Medical University of South Carolina M*
MGH Institute of Health Professions M,O*
Morehouse School of Medicine M*
New York University P,M,D*
Northwestern University M,O*
Palmer College of Chiropractic M*
Texas Tech University Health Sciences Center M,O
Thomas Jefferson University O*
Touro University International M,D,O
Tufts University M,D*
University of California, Davis M*
University of California, Los Angeles M*
University of California, San Diego M*
University of Florida M*
The University of Iowa M,D*
University of Louisville M,D,O
University of Maryland, Baltimore M,D*
University of Massachusetts Worcester D*
University of Michigan M*
University of Minnesota, Twin Cities Campus M*
University of Pittsburgh M,O*
University of Virginia M*
Vanderbilt University M*
Washington University in St. Louis M*

CLOTHING AND TEXTILES

Academy of Art University M*
Auburn University M*
Cornell University M,D*
Eastern Michigan University M
Fashion Institute of Technology M*
Florida State University M,D*
Indiana State University M*
Iowa State University of Science and Technology M,D*
Kansas State University M,D*
North Carolina State University D*
The Ohio State University M,D*
Oklahoma State University M,D*
Oregon State University M,D*
Philadelphia University M*
Purdue University M,D*
South Dakota State University M
The University of Akron M
The University of Alabama M
University of Alberta M,D*
University of California, Davis M*
University of Georgia M,D*
University of Kentucky M*
University of Manitoba M
University of Minnesota, Twin Cities Campus M,D,O*
University of Missouri–Columbia M*
University of Nebraska–Lincoln M*
University of North Texas M*
University of Rhode Island M
The University of Tennessee M,D*
Virginia Polytechnic Institute and State University M,D*
Washington State University M,D*

COGNITIVE SCIENCES

Arizona State University D*
Ball State University M*
Boston University M,D*
Brandeis University M,D*
Brown University M,D*
Carleton University D
Carnegie Mellon University D*
Claremont Graduate University M,D,O
Cornell University D*
Dartmouth College D*
Duke University D*
Emory University D*
Florida State University D*
The George Washington University D*
Graduate School and University Center of the City University of New York D*
Harvard University M,D*
Hunter College of the City University of New York M
Indiana University Bloomington M,D*
Iowa State University of Science and Technology M,D*
The Johns Hopkins University D*
Louisiana State University and Agricultural and Mechanical College M,D*
Loyola University Chicago M*
Massachusetts Institute of Technology D*
Mississippi State University M,D
New Mexico Highlands University M
New York University M,D,O*
North Dakota State University M,D
Northwestern University D*
The Ohio State University M,D*
Penn State University Park M,D*
Queen's University at Kingston M,D
Rensselaer Polytechnic Institute D*
Rice University M,D*
Rutgers, The State University of New Jersey, Newark D*
Rutgers, The State University of New Jersey, New Brunswick D*
State University of New York at Binghamton M,D*
Stevens Institute of Technology O*
Temple University D*
Texas A&M University M,D*
University at Buffalo, the State University of New York M,D*
The University of Akron M,D
The University of British Columbia M,D*
University of California, San Diego D*
University of Colorado at Colorado Springs M,D
University of Connecticut M,D*
University of Delaware D*
University of Florida M,D*
University of Guelph M,D
University of Louisiana at Lafayette D*
University of Maryland, Baltimore County D*
University of Maryland, College Park D*
University of Minnesota, Twin Cities Campus D*
The University of North Carolina at Chapel Hill D*
The University of North Carolina at Greensboro M,D
University of Notre Dame D*
University of Oregon M,D*
University of Pittsburgh D*
University of Rochester M,D*
The University of Texas at Austin M,D*
The University of Texas at Dallas M,D*
The University of Toledo M,D*
University of Wisconsin–Madison D*
Wayne State University M,D*
Wilfrid Laurier University M,D

COMMUNICATION—GENERAL

Abilene Christian University M
American University M*
The American University in Cairo M,O
The American University of Paris M
Andrews University M
Angelo State University M
Arizona State University M,D*
Arizona State University at the West campus M,O
Arkansas State University M,O
Arkansas Tech University M
Auburn University M*
Austin Peay State University M
Ball State University M*
Barry University M,O*
Baylor University M*
Bellevue University M*
Bethel University M,O
Boise State University M
Boston University M*
Bowling Green State University M,D*
Brigham Young University M*
California State University, Chico M
California State University, East Bay M
California State University, Fresno M
California State University, Fullerton M
California State University, Long Beach M
California State University, Los Angeles M
California State University, Northridge M
California State University, Sacramento M*
California State University, San Bernardino M
Carleton University M,D
Carnegie Mellon University M,D*
Central Connecticut State University M
Central Michigan University M*
Clarion University of Pennsylvania M
Clark University M*
Clemson University M,D*
Cleveland State University M,O
The College of New Rochelle M,O
College of Notre Dame of Maryland M
Columbia University M,D*
Concordia University (Canada) M,D,O
Cornell University M,D*
DePaul University M*
DeVry University M*
Drake University M*
Drexel University M*
Drury University M
Duquesne University M,D*
Eastern Michigan University M
Eastern New Mexico University M
Eastern Washington University M
East Tennessee State University M
Edinboro University of Pennsylvania M
Emerson College M*
Fairleigh Dickinson University, Metropolitan Campus M*
Fitchburg State College M,O
Florida Atlantic University M
Florida Institute of Technology M*
Florida State University M,D*
Fordham University M*
Fort Hays State University M
George Mason University M*
Georgetown University M*
Georgia State University M,D*
Gonzaga University M
Governors State University M
Grand Valley State University M
Harvard University M,O*
Hawai'i Pacific University M*
Howard University M,D*
Illinois Institute of Technology M,D*
Illinois State University M*
Indiana State University M*
Indiana University Bloomington M,D*
Indiana University–Purdue University Fort Wayne M
Instituto Tecnológico y de Estudios Superiores de Monterrey, Campus Ciudad Obregón M
Instituto Tecnológico y de Estudios Superiores de Monterrey, Campus Monterrey M,D
International University in Geneva M
Ithaca College M
The Johns Hopkins University M*
Kean University M
Kent State University M,D*
Liberty University M
Lindenwood University M
Louisiana State University and Agricultural and Mechanical College M,D*
Loyola University New Orleans M
Marquette University M
Marshall University M
Marywood University M,O*
McGill University M,D*
Miami University M*
Michigan State University M,D*
Mississippi College M
Missouri State University M*
Monmouth University M,O
Montana State University–Billings M
Montclair State University M*
Morehead State University M
National University M
New Mexico State University M
The New School: A University M*
New York Institute of Technology M,O
New York University M,D*
Norfolk State University M
North Carolina State University M*
North Dakota State University M,D
Northeastern State University M
Northern Arizona University M
Northern Illinois University M
Northern Kentucky University M
Northwestern University M,D*
The Ohio State University M,D*
Ohio University M,D*
Penn State University Park M,D*
Pepperdine University M*
Pittsburg State University M
Point Park University M*
Polytechnic University, Brooklyn Campus O*
Purdue University M,D*
Purdue University Calumet M
Quinnipiac University M*
Regent University M,D
Regis University M,O
Rensselaer Polytechnic Institute M,D*
Rochester Institute of Technology M
Roosevelt University M
Rutgers, The State University of New Jersey, New Brunswick M,D*
Saginaw Valley State University M
St. John's University (NY) M,O
Saint Louis University M*
St. Mary's University of San Antonio M
St. Thomas University M,O
San Diego State University M*
San Jose State University M
Seton Hall University M*
Shippensburg University of Pennsylvania M
Simon Fraser University M,D
South Dakota State University M
Southeastern Louisiana University M
Southern Illinois University Carbondale M,D*
Southern Utah University M
Spalding University M
Spring Arbor University M
Stanford University M,D*
State University of New York College at Brockport M*
State University of New York College of Environmental Science and Forestry M,D
Stephen F. Austin State University M
Suffolk University M
Syracuse University M,D*
Teachers College Columbia University M,D*
Temple University M,D*
Texas A&M University M,D*
Texas Southern University M
Texas State University-San Marcos M*
Texas Tech University M
Towson University M,O
Trinity International University M
Trinity (Washington) University M
Troy University M
Université de Montréal M,D
Université du Québec à Montréal M,D
University at Albany, State University of New York M,D*
University at Buffalo, the State University of New York M,D*
The University of Akron M
The University of Alabama M,D
The University of Alabama at Birmingham M*
University of Alaska Fairbanks M
University of Alberta M*
The University of Arizona M,D*
University of Arkansas M*
University of Baltimore M,D*
University of Calgary M,D
University of California, Davis M*
University of California, San Diego M,D*
University of California, Santa Barbara D*
University of California, Santa Cruz O*
University of Central Florida M*
University of Central Missouri M
University of Cincinnati M
University of Colorado at Boulder M,D*
University of Colorado at Colorado Springs M

Institution	Degrees
University of Colorado at Denver and Health Sciences Center	M*
University of Connecticut	M,D*
University of Dayton	M*
University of Delaware	M*
University of Denver	M,D,O*
University of Dubuque	M
University of Florida	M,D*
University of Georgia	M,D*
University of Hartford	M*
University of Hawaii at Manoa	M,O*
University of Houston	M*
University of Illinois at Chicago	M*
University of Illinois at Springfield	M
University of Illinois at Urbana–Champaign	D*
The University of Iowa	M,D*
University of Kansas	M,D*
University of Kentucky	M,D*
University of Louisiana at Lafayette	M*
University of Louisiana at Monroe	M
University of Maine	M*
University of Maryland, Baltimore County	M*
University of Maryland, College Park	M,D*
University of Massachusetts Amherst	M,D*
University of Memphis	M,D*
University of Miami	M,D*
University of Michigan	D*
University of Minnesota, Twin Cities Campus	M,D,O*
University of Missouri–Columbia	M,D*
University of Missouri–St. Louis	M
The University of Montana	M*
University of Nebraska at Omaha	M
University of Nebraska–Lincoln	M,D*
University of Nevada, Las Vegas	M
University of New Mexico	M,D*
The University of North Carolina at Chapel Hill	M,D*
The University of North Carolina at Charlotte	M*
The University of North Carolina at Greensboro	M
University of North Dakota	M,D
University of Northern Colorado	M
University of Northern Iowa	M
University of North Texas	M*
University of Oklahoma	M,D*
University of Oregon	M,D*
University of Ottawa	M*
University of Pennsylvania	D*
University of Pittsburgh	M,D*
University of Portland	M
University of Rhode Island	M
University of South Alabama	M*
The University of South Dakota	M
University of Southern California	M,D*
University of South Florida	M,D*
The University of Tennessee	M,D*
The University of Texas at Arlington	M*
The University of Texas at Austin	M,D*
The University of Texas at Dallas	D*
The University of Texas at El Paso	M
The University of Texas at San Antonio	M*
The University of Texas at Tyler	M
The University of Texas–Pan American	M
University of the Incarnate Word	M,O
University of the Pacific	M
University of the Sacred Heart	M
The University of Toledo	O*
University of Utah	M,D*
University of Vermont	M*
University of Washington	M,D*
University of West Florida	M
University of Windsor	M
University of Wisconsin–Madison	M,D*
University of Wisconsin–Milwaukee	M,O
University of Wisconsin–Stevens Point	M
University of Wisconsin–Superior	M
University of Wisconsin–Whitewater	M*
University of Wyoming	M
Utah State University	M
Villanova University	M*
Virginia Commonwealth University	D*
Virginia Polytechnic Institute and State University	M*
Wake Forest University	M*
Washington State University	M,D*
Wayne State College	M
Wayne State University	M,D*
Webster University	M
West Chester University of Pennsylvania	M
Western Illinois University	M
Western Kentucky University	M
Western Michigan University	M*
Westminster College (UT)	M
West Texas A&M University	M
West Virginia University	M*
Wichita State University	M*
Wilfrid Laurier University	M
York University	M,D*

COMMUNICATION DISORDERS

Institution	Degrees
Abilene Christian University	M
Adelphi University	M,D*
Alabama Agricultural and Mechanical University	M
Appalachian State University	M
Arizona State University	M,D*
Arkansas State University	M
Armstrong Atlantic State University	M
A.T. Still University of Health Sciences	M,D
Auburn University	M,D*
Ball State University	M,D*
Barry University	M*
Baylor University	M*
Bloomsburg University of Pennsylvania	M,D
Boston University	M,D,O*
Bowling Green State University	M,D*
Brigham Young University	M*
Brooklyn College of the City University of New York	M,D
Buffalo State College, State University of New York	M
California State University, Chico	M
California State University, East Bay	M
California State University, Fresno	M
California State University, Fullerton	M
California State University, Long Beach	M
California State University, Los Angeles	M
California State University, Northridge	M
California State University, Sacramento	M*
California University of Pennsylvania	M
Canisius College	M
Carlos Albizu University	M,D
Case Western Reserve University	M,D,O*
Central Michigan University	M,D*
Clarion University of Pennsylvania	M
Cleveland State University	M
College Misericordia	M
The College of New Jersey	M
The College of New Rochelle	M
The College of Saint Rose	M*
Dalhousie University	M
Duquesne University	M,D*
East Carolina University	M,D*
Eastern Illinois University	M
Eastern Kentucky University	M*
Eastern Michigan University	M
Eastern New Mexico University	M
Eastern Washington University	M
East Stroudsburg University of Pennsylvania	M
East Tennessee State University	M,D
Edinboro University of Pennsylvania	M
Elms College	O
Emerson College	M*
Florida Atlantic University	M
Florida International University	M*
Florida State University	M,D*
Fontbonne University	M
Fort Hays State University	M
Gallaudet University	M,D
The George Washington University	M*
Georgia State University	M*
Governors State University	M
Graduate School and University Center of the City University of New York	D*
Hampton University	M*
Harvard University	D*
Hofstra University	M,D*
Howard University	M,D*
Hunter College of the City University of New York	M
Idaho State University	M,D
Illinois State University	M*
Indiana State University	M*
Indiana University Bloomington	M,D*
Indiana University of Pennsylvania	M
Ithaca College	M
Jackson State University	M
James Madison University	M,D
Kean University	M
Kent State University	M,D*
Lamar University	M,D*
La Salle University	M
Lehman College of the City University of New York	M
Lewis & Clark College	M
Loma Linda University	M
Long Island University, Brooklyn Campus	M*
Long Island University, C.W. Post Campus	M*
Longwood University	M*
Louisiana State University and Agricultural and Mechanical College	M,D*
Louisiana State University Health Sciences Center	M*
Louisiana Tech University	M*
Loyola College in Maryland	M,O
Marquette University	M
Marshall University	M
Marywood University	M*
Massachusetts Institute of Technology	D*
McGill University	M,D*
Medical University of South Carolina	M*
Mercy College	M
MGH Institute of Health Professions	M,O*
Miami University	M*
Michigan State University	M,D*
Minnesota State University Mankato	M
Minnesota State University Moorhead	M
Minot State University	M
Mississippi University for Women	M
Missouri State University	M,D*
Montclair State University	M,D*
Murray State University	M
National University	M
Nazareth College of Rochester	M
New Mexico State University	M,D
New York Medical College	M*
New York University	M,D*
North Carolina Central University	M
Northeastern State University	M
Northeastern University	M,D*
Northern Arizona University	M
Northern Illinois University	M,D
Northern Michigan University	M
Northwestern University	M,D*
Nova Southeastern University	M,D*
The Ohio State University	M,D*
Ohio University	M,D*
Oklahoma State University	M*
Old Dominion University	M*
Our Lady of the Lake University of San Antonio	M
Penn State University Park	M,D*
Pennsylvania College of Optometry	M,D,O
Portland State University	M
Purdue University	M,D*
Queens College of the City University of New York	M
Radford University	M
Rockhurst University	M
Rush University	M,D
St. Cloud State University	M
Saint Louis University	M*
Saint Xavier University	M
San Diego State University	M,D*
San Francisco State University	M
San Jose State University	M
Seton Hall University	M*
South Carolina State University	M
Southeastern Louisiana University	M
Southeast Missouri State University	M
Southern Connecticut State University	M
Southern Illinois University Carbondale	M*
Southern Illinois University Edwardsville	M
State University of New York at Fredonia	M
State University of New York at New Paltz	M
State University of New York at Plattsburgh	M
State University of New York College at Geneseo	M
Stephen F. Austin State University	M
Syracuse University	M,D*
Teachers College Columbia University	M,D*
Temple University	M*
Tennessee State University	M*
Texas A&M University–Kingsville	M
Texas Christian University	M
Texas State University-San Marcos	M*
Texas Tech University Health Sciences Center	M,D
Texas Woman's University	M,D
Towson University	M,D
Truman State University	M
Université de Montréal	M,O
Université Laval	M
University at Buffalo, the State University of New York	M,D*
The University of Akron	M,D
The University of Alabama	M
University of Alberta	M,D*
The University of Arizona	M,D*
University of Arkansas	M*
University of Arkansas for Medical Sciences	M,D*
The University of British Columbia	M,D*
University of California, San Diego	D*
University of Central Arkansas	M
University of Central Florida	M,D,O*
University of Central Missouri	M
University of Central Oklahoma	M
University of Cincinnati	M,D,O
University of Colorado at Boulder	M,D*
University of Connecticut	M,D*
University of Florida	M,D*
University of Georgia	M,D,O*
University of Hawaii at Manoa	M*
University of Houston	M*
University of Illinois at Urbana–Champaign	M,D*
The University of Iowa	M,D*
University of Kansas	M,D*
University of Kentucky	M*
University of Louisiana at Lafayette	M,D*
University of Louisiana at Monroe	M
University of Louisville	M,D
University of Maine	M*
University of Maryland, College Park	M,D*
University of Massachusetts Amherst	M,D*
University of Memphis	M,D*
University of Minnesota, Duluth	M*
University of Minnesota, Twin Cities Campus	M,D*
University of Mississippi	M
University of Missouri–Columbia	M*
University of Montevallo	M
University of Nebraska at Kearney	M
University of Nebraska at Omaha	M
University of Nebraska–Lincoln	M*
University of Nevada, Reno	M,D*
University of New Hampshire	M*
University of New Mexico	M*
The University of North Carolina at Chapel Hill	M,D*
The University of North Carolina at Greensboro	M,D
University of North Dakota	M,D
University of Northern Colorado	M,D
University of Northern Iowa	M
University of North Texas	M,D*
University of Oklahoma Health Sciences Center	M,D,O
University of Ottawa	M*
University of Pittsburgh	M,D*
University of Puerto Rico, Medical Sciences Campus	M*
University of Redlands	M
University of Rhode Island	M,D
University of South Alabama	M,D*
University of South Carolina	M,D*
The University of South Dakota	M,D
University of Southern Mississippi	M,D*
University of South Florida	D*
The University of Tennessee	M,D,O*
The University of Texas at Austin	M,D*
The University of Texas at Dallas	M,D*
The University of Texas at El Paso	M
The University of Texas–Pan American	M

*P—first professional degree; M—master's degree; D—doctorate; O—other advanced degree; *full description and/or announcement in Book 2, 3, 4, 5, or 6*

- University of the District of Columbia M
- University of the Pacific M
- The University of Toledo M,D,O*
- University of Toronto M,D
- University of Tulsa M*
- University of Utah M,D*
- University of Virginia M*
- University of Washington M,D*
- The University of Western Ontario M
- University of West Georgia M
- University of Wisconsin–Eau Claire M
- University of Wisconsin–Madison M,D*
- University of Wisconsin–Milwaukee M
- University of Wisconsin–River Falls M
- University of Wisconsin–Stevens Point M,D
- University of Wisconsin–Whitewater M*
- University of Wyoming M,D
- Utah State University M,D,O
- Valdosta State University M,O
- Vanderbilt University M,D*
- Washington State University Spokane M
- Washington University in St. Louis M,D*
- Wayne State University M,D*
- West Chester University of Pennsylvania M
- Western Carolina University M*
- Western Illinois University M*
- Western Kentucky University M
- Western Michigan University M*
- Western Washington University M
- West Texas A&M University M
- West Virginia University M,D*
- Wichita State University M,D*
- William Paterson University of New Jersey M*
- Worcester State College M

COMMUNITY COLLEGE EDUCATION

- Argosy University, Chicago Campus M,D,O*
- Argosy University, Inland Empire Campus M,D*
- Argosy University, Nashville Campus M,D*
- Argosy University, Orange County Campus M,D*
- Argosy University, Phoenix Campus M,D,O*
- Argosy University, San Diego Campus M,D*
- Argosy University, San Francisco Bay Area Campus M,D*
- Argosy University, Santa Monica Campus M,D*
- Argosy University, Schaumburg Campus M,D,O*
- Argosy University, Seattle Campus M,D*
- Argosy University, Tampa Campus M,D,O*
- Arkansas State University M,D,O
- Eastern Washington University M
- George Mason University D,O*
- Morgan State University D*
- North Carolina State University M,D*
- Northern Arizona University M,D
- Old Dominion University M,D*
- Pittsburg State University O
- Princeton University D*
- University of Central Florida M,D,O*
- University of South Florida M,D,O*
- Walden University M,D
- Western Carolina University M*

COMMUNITY HEALTH

- Adelphi University M,O*
- Arcadia University M
- Bloomsburg University of Pennsylvania M
- Brooklyn College of the City University of New York M
- Brown University M,D*
- California College for Health Sciences M
- Columbia University M,D*
- Dalhousie University M
- Eastern Kentucky University M*
- East Stroudsburg University of Pennsylvania M
- East Tennessee State University M,O
- The George Washington University M,O*
- Idaho State University O
- Indiana State University M*
- The Johns Hopkins University M,D*
- Long Island University, Brooklyn Campus M*
- McGill University M,D,O*
- Meharry Medical College M
- Memorial University of Newfoundland M,D,O
- Minnesota State University Mankato M
- Mount Sinai School of Medicine of New York University M,D*
- New Jersey City University M
- New York Medical College M*
- Old Dominion University M*
- Sage Graduate School M
- Saint Louis University M*
- Simon Fraser University M
- Southern Illinois University Carbondale M*
- Southern New Hampshire University M,O*
- State University of New York Downstate Medical Center M*
- Stony Brook University, State University of New York M,D,O*
- Temple University M*
- Université de Montréal M,D,O
- Université Laval M,D,O
- University at Buffalo, the State University of New York M,D*
- University of Alberta M,D*
- The University of British Columbia M,D*
- University of Calgary M,D,O
- University of California, Los Angeles M,D*
- University of Illinois at Chicago M,D*
- University of Illinois at Urbana–Champaign M,D*
- The University of Iowa M,D*
- University of Manitoba M,D
- University of Miami M,D*
- University of Minnesota, Twin Cities Campus M*
- The University of North Carolina at Greensboro M,D
- University of Northern British Columbia M,D,O
- University of Northern Colorado M
- University of Northern Iowa M,D
- University of North Florida M,O
- University of North Texas M*
- University of North Texas Health Science Center at Fort Worth M,D
- University of Ottawa M,D,O*
- University of Pittsburgh M,D,O*
- University of Saskatchewan M,D
- University of South Florida M,D*
- The University of Tennessee M,D*
- The University of Texas Medical Branch M,D*
- University of Wisconsin–La Crosse M
- University of Wisconsin–Madison M,D*
- Virginia Commonwealth University D*
- Wayne State University M,O*
- West Virginia University M*

COMMUNITY HEALTH NURSING

- Augsburg College M
- Augustana College M
- Boston College M,D*
- Case Western Reserve University M*
- Cleveland State University M,D
- D'Youville College M,O*
- Georgia Southern University M,O
- Hawai'i Pacific University M*
- Holy Names University M
- Hunter College of the City University of New York M
- Indiana University–Purdue University Indianapolis M,D*
- Indiana Wesleyan University M,O
- Inter American University of Puerto Rico, Arecibo Campus M
- The Johns Hopkins University M*
- Kean University M
- La Salle University M,O
- Louisiana State University Health Sciences Center M,D*
- Medical College of Georgia M,D*
- New Mexico State University M
- Northeastern University M,O*
- Oregon Health & Science University M,O*
- Rush University M,D,O
- Rutgers, The State University of New Jersey, Newark M*
- Sage Graduate School M
- Saint Xavier University M,O
- Seattle University M
- Southern Illinois University Edwardsville M,O
- University of Cincinnati M,D
- University of Colorado at Colorado Springs M
- University of Connecticut M,D,O*
- University of Hartford M*
- University of Hawaii at Manoa M,D,O*
- University of Illinois at Chicago M*
- University of Maryland, Baltimore M*
- University of Massachusetts Dartmouth M,D,O
- University of Massachusetts Lowell M*
- University of Massachusetts Worcester M,D,O*
- University of Michigan M*
- University of Minnesota, Twin Cities Campus M*
- The University of North Carolina at Chapel Hill M*
- The University of North Carolina at Charlotte M*
- University of South Alabama M,D*
- University of South Carolina M*
- University of Southern Mississippi M,D*
- The University of Texas at Brownsville M
- The University of Texas at El Paso M
- Wayne State University M*
- Worcester State College M
- Wright State University M*

COMPARATIVE AND INTERDISCIPLINARY ARTS

- Bradley University M
- Brigham Young University M*
- Columbia College Chicago M
- Florida Atlantic University D
- Goddard College M
- John F. Kennedy University M
- Ohio University D*
- Simon Fraser University M

COMPARATIVE LITERATURE

- American University M*
- The American University in Cairo M
- Antioch University McGregor M*
- Arizona State University M,D*
- Brigham Young University M*
- Brock University M
- Brown University M,D*
- California State University, Fullerton M
- California State University, Northridge M
- Carleton University D
- Carnegie Mellon University M,D*
- Case Western Reserve University M,D*
- The Catholic University of America M,D*
- Claremont Graduate University M,D
- College of the Humanities and Sciences, Harrison Middleton University M,D
- Columbia University M,D*
- Cornell University D*
- Dartmouth College M*
- Duke University D*
- Emory University D,O*
- Fairleigh Dickinson University, Metropolitan Campus M*
- Florida Atlantic University M
- Graduate School and University Center of the City University of New York M,D*
- Harvard University D*
- Hofstra University M*
- Indiana University Bloomington M,D*
- The Johns Hopkins University D*
- Kent State University M,D*
- Long Island University, Brooklyn Campus M*
- Louisiana State University and Agricultural and Mechanical College M,D*
- New York University M,D*
- Northwestern University M,D,O*
- Oklahoma City University M
- Penn State University Park M,D*
- Princeton University D*
- Purdue University M,D*
- Rutgers, The State University of New Jersey, New Brunswick M,D*
- San Francisco State University M
- San Jose State University M,O
- Stanford University D*
- State University of New York at Binghamton M,D*
- Stony Brook University, State University of New York M,D*
- Université de Montréal M,D
- Université de Sherbrooke M,D
- Université du Québec à Chicoutimi M
- Université du Québec à Montréal M,D
- Université du Québec à Rimouski M,D
- Université du Québec à Trois-Rivières M
- Université Laval M,D
- University at Buffalo, the State University of New York M,D*
- The University of Arizona M,D*
- University of Arkansas M,D*
- The University of British Columbia M,D*
- University of California, Berkeley D*
- University of California, Davis D*
- University of California, Irvine M,D*
- University of California, Los Angeles M,D*
- University of California, Riverside M,D*
- University of California, San Diego M,D*
- University of California, Santa Barbara D*
- University of California, Santa Cruz M,D*
- University of Chicago M,D*
- University of Colorado at Boulder M,D*
- University of Connecticut M,D*
- University of Dallas D
- University of Georgia M,D*
- University of Guelph D
- University of Illinois at Urbana–Champaign M,D*
- The University of Iowa M,D*
- University of Maryland, College Park M,D*
- University of Massachusetts Amherst M,D*
- University of Michigan D*
- University of Minnesota, Twin Cities Campus D*
- University of Missouri–Columbia M,D*
- University of New Hampshire M,D*
- University of New Mexico M,D*
- The University of North Carolina at Chapel Hill M,D*
- University of Notre Dame D*
- University of Oregon M,D*
- University of Pennsylvania M,D*
- University of Puerto Rico, Río Piedras M*
- University of South Carolina M,D*
- University of Southern California M,D*
- The University of Texas at Austin M,D*
- The University of Texas at Dallas M,D*
- University of Toronto M,D
- University of Utah M,D*
- University of Washington M,D*
- The University of Western Ontario M,D
- University of Wisconsin–Madison M,D*
- University of Wisconsin–Milwaukee M,D,O
- Washington University in St. Louis M,D*
- Wayne State University M*
- Western Kentucky University M
- West Virginia University M*
- Yale University D*

COMPUTATIONAL BIOLOGY

- Arizona State University M*
- Baylor College of Medicine D*
- Carnegie Mellon University M,D*
- Claremont Graduate University M,D
- Cornell University, Joan and Sanford I. Weill Medical College and Graduate School of Medical Sciences D*
- Florida State University D*
- George Mason University M,D,O*
- Iowa State University of Science and Technology D*
- Massachusetts Institute of Technology D*
- New Jersey Institute of Technology M
- New York University D*
- Northwestern University M*
- Princeton University D*
- Rutgers, The State University of New Jersey, Newark M*
- Rutgers, The State University of New Jersey, New Brunswick D*
- University of Idaho M,D*
- University of Illinois at Urbana–Champaign D*
- The University of Iowa M,D,O*
- University of Pennsylvania D*
- University of Pittsburgh D*
- University of Rochester M,D*
- University of Southern California D*
- The University of Texas Medical Branch D*
- Virginia Polytechnic Institute and State University D*
- Washington University in St. Louis D*

Yale University D*

COMPUTATIONAL SCIENCES

Arizona State University M,D*
California Institute of Technology M,D*
Carnegie Mellon University M,D*
Claremont Graduate University M,D
Clemson University M,D*
The College of William and Mary M
Cornell University M,D*
George Mason University M,D,O*
Kean University M
Lehigh University M,D*
Louisiana Tech University M,D
Massachusetts Institute of Technology M*
McGill University M,D*
Memorial University of Newfoundland M
Michigan Technological University D*
Northwestern University M*
Princeton University D*
Rice University M,D*
Sam Houston State University M
San Diego State University M,D*
Simon Fraser University M,D
South Dakota State University M,D
Southern Methodist University M,D*
Stanford University M,D*
State University of New York College at Brockport M*
Temple University M,D*
University of Alaska Fairbanks M,D
University of Central Florida M,D*
The University of Iowa D*
University of Lethbridge M,D
University of Manitoba M
University of Massachusetts Lowell M,D*
University of Michigan–Dearborn M*
University of Minnesota, Duluth M*
University of Minnesota, Twin Cities Campus M,D*
University of Mississippi M,D
University of Nevada, Las Vegas M,D
University of Puerto Rico, Mayagüez Campus M*
The University of South Dakota D
University of Southern Mississippi M,D*
University of South Florida M,D*
The University of Tennessee at Chattanooga D
The University of Texas at Austin M,D*
University of Utah M*
Western Michigan University M*

COMPUTER AND INFORMATION SYSTEMS SECURITY

American InterContinental University (FL) M
American InterContinental University Online M
Benedictine University M
Capella University M,D,O
Capitol College M
Carnegie Mellon University M*
Colorado Technical University—Colorado Springs M,D
Colorado Technical University—Denver M
Colorado Technical University—Sioux Falls M
Concordia University (Canada) M,O
DePaul University M,D*
Eastern Illinois University M,O
Eastern Michigan University M
The Johns Hopkins University M*
Jones International University M
Marymount University M,O
New Jersey City University M
Northern Kentucky University M,O
Nova Southeastern University M*
Polytechnic University, Brooklyn Campus O*
Purdue University M*
Rochester Institute of Technology M
Sacred Heart University M,O
Saint Leo University M
Salem International University M
Stevens Institute of Technology M,D,O*
Syracuse University O*
Towson University O
University of St. Thomas (MN) M,O*
University of Wisconsin–Madison M*
Worcester Polytechnic Institute M,O*

COMPUTER ART AND DESIGN

Academy of Art University M*
Alfred University M*
American Academy of Art M
Art Center College of Design M*
Bowling Green State University M*
Carnegie Mellon University M*
Chatham University M
Claremont Graduate University M
Clemson University M*
Columbia University M*
Concordia University (Canada) O
Cornell University M,D*
DePaul University M,D*
East Tennessee State University M
Indiana University Bloomington M,D*
Long Island University, Brooklyn Campus M*
Long Island University, C.W. Post Campus M*
Maryland Institute College of Art M*
Memphis College of Art M*
Miami International University of Art & Design M*
Minneapolis College of Art and Design O
Mississippi State University M
National University M
New Mexico Highlands University M
The New School: A University M*
New York University M*
Philadelphia University M*
Rensselaer Polytechnic Institute M,D*
Rhode Island School of Design M
Rochester Institute of Technology M
St. Edward's University M
San Jose State University M
Savannah College of Art and Design M*
School of Visual Arts M
Syracuse University M*
Universidad de las Américas–Puebla M
University of Baltimore M,D*
University of California, Santa Cruz M*
University of Central Florida M*
University of Denver M*
University of Florida M,D*
University of Missouri–Columbia M*
University of Pennsylvania M*
University of Victoria M
Washington State University M*

COMPUTER EDUCATION

Arcadia University M,D,O
California State University, Dominguez Hills M,O
California State University, Los Angeles M
Canadian Southern Baptist Seminary P,M
Cardinal Stritch University M*
Christopher Newport University M
Dalhousie University M
DeSales University M,O
Eastern Washington University M
Florida Institute of Technology M,D,O*
Fontbonne University M
Jacksonville University M
Kean University M
Lesley University M,D,O*
Long Island University, C.W. Post Campus M*
Maple Springs Baptist Bible College and Seminary P,M,D,O
Marlboro College M
Mississippi College M,O
Morningside College M
Nova Southeastern University M,D,O*
Ohio University M,D*
Providence College M*
Southern New Hampshire University M,O*
Stanford University M,D*
Stony Brook University, State University of New York M*
Teachers College Columbia University M*
Thomas College M
University of Bridgeport M,O
University of Central Oklahoma M
University of Maryland, Baltimore County M,O*
University of Michigan M,D*
University of North Texas M,D*
University of Phoenix–Fort Lauderdale Campus M
University of Phoenix–North Florida Campus M
University of Phoenix–Omaha Campus M
University of Phoenix–Springfield Campus M
The University of Texas at Tyler M
Wilkes University M
Wright State University M*

COMPUTER ENGINEERING

Air Force Institute of Technology M,D
American University of Beirut M
Arizona State University at the Polytechnic Campus M
Auburn University M,D*
Baylor University M*
Boise State University M,D
Boston University M,D*
California State University, Chico M
California State University, East Bay M
California State University, Long Beach M
Carnegie Mellon University M,D*
Case Western Reserve University M,D*
Clarkson University M,D*
Clemson University M,D*
Colorado Technical University—Colorado Springs M
Colorado Technical University—Denver M
Columbia University M,D,O*
Concordia University (Canada) M,D
Cornell University M,D*
Dalhousie University M,D
Dartmouth College M,D*
Drexel University M*
Duke University M,D*
École Polytechnique de Montréal M,D,O
Fairfield University M*
Fairleigh Dickinson University, Metropolitan Campus M*
Florida Atlantic University M,D
Florida Institute of Technology M,D*
Florida International University M*
George Mason University M,D*
The George Washington University M,D*
Georgia Institute of Technology M,D*
Grand Valley State University M
Illinois Institute of Technology M,D*
Indiana State University M*
Indiana University–Purdue University Indianapolis M,D*
Instituto Tecnológico y de Estudios Superiores de Monterrey, Campus Chihuahua M,O
International Technological University M
Iowa State University of Science and Technology M,D*
The Johns Hopkins University M,D*
Kansas State University M,D*
Kettering University M
Lawrence Technological University M,D
Lehigh University M,D*
Louisiana State University and Agricultural and Mechanical College M,D*
Manhattan College M
Marquette University M,D
Massachusetts Institute of Technology M,D,O*
McGill University M,D*
Memorial University of Newfoundland M,D
Mercer University M
Michigan Technological University D*
Mississippi State University M,D
Naval Postgraduate School M,D,O
New Jersey Institute of Technology M,D
New Mexico State University M,D
New York Institute of Technology M
Norfolk State University M
North Carolina State University M,D*
Northeastern University M,D*
Northwestern Polytechnic University M
Northwestern University M,D,O*
Oakland University M*
OGI School of Science & Engineering at Oregon Health & Science University M,D
Oklahoma State University M,D*
Old Dominion University M,D*
Penn State University Park M,D*
Polytechnic University, Brooklyn Campus M,O*
Polytechnic University, Long Island Graduate Center M
Polytechnic University of Puerto Rico M
Polytechnic University, Westchester Graduate Center M
Portland State University M,D
Purdue University M,D*
Queen's University at Kingston M,D
Rensselaer at Hartford M
Rensselaer Polytechnic Institute M,D*
Rice University M,D*
Rochester Institute of Technology M
Royal Military College of Canada M,D
Rutgers, The State University of New Jersey, New Brunswick M,D*
St. Cloud State University M
St. Mary's University of San Antonio M
San Jose State University M
Santa Clara University M,D,O
South Dakota School of Mines and Technology M
Southern Illinois University Carbondale M,D*
Southern Methodist University M,D*
Southern Polytechnic State University M
State University of New York at New Paltz M
Stevens Institute of Technology M,D,O*
Stony Brook University, State University of New York M,D*
Syracuse University M,D,O*
Temple University M*
Texas A&M University M,D*
The University of Akron M,D
The University of Alabama M,D
The University of Alabama at Birmingham D*
The University of Alabama in Huntsville M,D
University of Alaska Fairbanks M,D
University of Alberta M,D*
The University of Arizona M,D*
University of Arkansas M,D*
University of Bridgeport M,D
The University of British Columbia M,D*
University of Calgary M,D
University of California, Davis M,D*
University of California, Riverside M,D*
University of California, San Diego M,D*
University of California, Santa Barbara M,D*
University of California, Santa Cruz M,D*
University of Central Florida M,D*
University of Cincinnati M,D
University of Colorado at Boulder M,D*
University of Colorado at Denver and Health Sciences Center M,D*
University of Dayton M,D*
University of Delaware M,D*
University of Denver M,D*
University of Florida M,D,O*
University of Houston M,D*
University of Houston–Clear Lake M
University of Idaho M*
University of Illinois at Chicago M,D*
University of Illinois at Urbana–Champaign M,D*
The University of Iowa M,D*
University of Kansas M*
University of Louisiana at Lafayette M,D*
University of Louisville M,D
University of Maine M,D*
University of Manitoba M,D
University of Maryland, Baltimore County M,D*
University of Maryland, College Park M,D*
University of Massachusetts Amherst M,D*
University of Massachusetts Dartmouth M,D,O
University of Massachusetts Lowell M*
University of Memphis M,D*
University of Miami M,D*
University of Michigan M,D*
University of Michigan–Dearborn M*
University of Minnesota, Duluth M*
University of Minnesota, Twin Cities Campus M,D*
University of Missouri–Kansas City M,D*
University of Missouri–Rolla M,D*
University of Nebraska–Lincoln M,D*
University of Nevada, Las Vegas M,D
University of Nevada, Reno M,D*

*P—first professional degree; M—master's degree; D—doctorate; O—other advanced degree; *full description and/or announcement in Book 2, 3, 4, 5, or 6*

Institution	Degrees
University of New Brunswick Fredericton	M,D
University of New Mexico	M,D*
The University of North Carolina at Charlotte	M,D*
University of Notre Dame	M,D*
University of Oklahoma	M,D*
University of Ottawa	M,D*
University of Puerto Rico, Mayagüez Campus	M*
University of Regina	M,D
University of Rochester	M,D*
University of South Carolina	M,D*
University of Southern California	M,D*
University of South Florida	M,D*
The University of Tennessee	M,D*
The University of Texas at Arlington	M,D*
The University of Texas at Austin	M,D*
The University of Texas at Dallas	M,D*
The University of Texas at El Paso	M,D
University of Toronto	M,D
University of Virginia	M,D*
University of Waterloo	M,D*
Villanova University	M,O*
Virginia Polytechnic Institute and State University	M,D*
Walden University	M,O
Washington State University	M,D*
Washington State University Tri-Cities	M,D
Washington University in St. Louis	M,D*
Wayne State University	M,D*
Western Michigan University	M,D*
Western New England College	M
West Virginia University	D*
Widener University	M*
Worcester Polytechnic Institute	M,D,O*
Wright State University	M,D*

COMPUTER SCIENCE

Institution	Degrees
Acadia University	M
Air Force Institute of Technology	M,D
Alabama Agricultural and Mechanical University	M
Alcorn State University	M
American College of Computer & Information Sciences	M
American Sentinel University	M
American University	M,O*
The American University in Cairo	M
The American University of Athens	M
American University of Beirut	M
Appalachian State University	M
Arizona State University	M,D*
Arizona State University at the Polytechnic Campus	M
Arkansas State University	M
Armstrong Atlantic State University	M
Auburn University	M,D*
Ball State University	M*
Baylor University	M*
Boise State University	M
Boston University	M,D*
Bowie State University	M,D
Bowling Green State University	M*
Bradley University	M
Brandeis University	M,D,O*
Bridgewater State College	M
Brigham Young University	M,D*
Brock University	M
Brooklyn College of the City University of New York	M,D
Brown University	M,D*
California Institute of Technology	M,D*
California Polytechnic State University, San Luis Obispo	M
California State Polytechnic University, Pomona	M
California State University Channel Islands	M*
California State University, Chico	M
California State University, East Bay	M
California State University, Fresno	M
California State University, Fullerton	M
California State University, Long Beach	M
California State University, Los Angeles	M
California State University, Northridge	M
California State University, Sacramento	M*
California State University, San Bernardino	M
California State University, San Marcos	M
Capitol College	M
Carleton University	M,D
Carnegie Mellon University	M,D*
Case Western Reserve University	M,D*
The Catholic University of America	M,D*
Central Connecticut State University	M
Central Michigan University	M*
Chicago State University	M
Christopher Newport University	M
The Citadel, The Military College of South Carolina	M
City College of the City University of New York	M,D*
City University	M,O
Clark Atlanta University	M
Clarkson University	M,D*
Clemson University	M,D*
College of Charleston	M*
The College of Saint Rose	M*
College of Staten Island of the City University of New York	M
The College of William and Mary	M,D
Colorado School of Mines	M,D
Colorado State University	M,D*
Colorado Technical University—Colorado Springs	M,D
Colorado Technical University—Denver	M
Colorado Technical University—Sioux Falls	M
Columbia University	M,D,O*
Columbus State University	M
Concordia University (Canada)	M,D,O
Cornell University	M,D*
Dalhousie University	M,D
Dartmouth College	M,D*
DePaul University	M,D*
DigiPen Institute of Technology	M
Drexel University	M,D*
Duke University	M,D*
East Carolina University	M,D,O*
Eastern Illinois University	M,O
Eastern Michigan University	M
Eastern Washington University	M
East Stroudsburg University of Pennsylvania	M
East Tennessee State University	M
École Polytechnique de Montréal	M,D,O
Elmhurst College	M
Emory University	M,D*
Fairleigh Dickinson University, Metropolitan Campus	M*
Ferris State University	M
Fitchburg State College	M
Florida Atlantic University	M,D
Florida Gulf Coast University	M
Florida Institute of Technology	M,D*
Florida International University	M,D*
Florida State University	M,D*
Fordham University	M*
Franklin University	M
Frostburg State University	M
Gannon University	M
George Mason University	M,D*
The George Washington University	M,D,O*
Georgia Institute of Technology	M,D*
Georgia Southwestern State University	M
Georgia State University	M,D*
Governors State University	M
Graduate School and University Center of the City University of New York	D*
Grand Valley State University	M
Hampton University	M*
Harrisburg University of Science and Technology	O
Harvard University	M,D*
Hofstra University	M*
Hood College	M
Howard University	M*
Illinois Institute of Technology	M,D*
Indiana State University	M*
Indiana University Bloomington	M,D*
Indiana University–Purdue University Fort Wayne	M
Indiana University–Purdue University Indianapolis	M,D*
Indiana University South Bend	M
Instituto Tecnológico y de Estudios Superiores de Monterrey, Campus Central de Veracruz	M
Instituto Tecnológico y de Estudios Superiores de Monterrey, Campus Ciudad de México	M,D
Instituto Tecnológico y de Estudios Superiores de Monterrey, Campus Cuernavaca	M,D
Instituto Tecnológico y de Estudios Superiores de Monterrey, Campus Estado de México	M,D
Instituto Tecnológico y de Estudios Superiores de Monterrey, Campus Irapuato	M,D
Instituto Tecnológico y de Estudios Superiores de Monterrey, Campus Monterrey	M,D
Inter American University of Puerto Rico, Metropolitan Campus	M
Iona College	M*
Iowa State University of Science and Technology	M,D*
Jackson State University	M
Jacksonville State University	M
James Madison University	M
The Johns Hopkins University	M,D*
Kansas State University	M,D*
Kennesaw State University	M
Kent State University	M,D*
Kentucky State University	M
Knowledge Systems Institute	M
Kutztown University of Pennsylvania	M
Lakehead University	M
Lamar University	M*
La Salle University	M
Lawrence Technological University	M
Lebanese American University	M
Lehigh University	M,D*
Lehman College of the City University of New York	M
Long Island University, Brooklyn Campus	M*
Long Island University, C.W. Post Campus	M*
Louisiana State University and Agricultural and Mechanical College	M,D*
Louisiana Tech University	M
Loyola College in Maryland	M
Loyola Marymount University	M
Loyola University Chicago	M*
Maharishi University of Management	M
Marist College	M,O*
Marlboro College	M
Marquette University	M,D
Marymount University	M,O
Massachusetts Institute of Technology	M,D,O*
McGill University	M,D*
McMaster University	M,D
McNeese State University	M
Memorial University of Newfoundland	M,D
Michigan State University	M,D*
Michigan Technological University	M,D*
Middle Tennessee State University	M*
Midwestern State University	M
Mills College	M,O
Minnesota State University Mankato	M,O
Mississippi College	M
Mississippi State University	M,D
Missouri State University	M*
Monmouth University	M
Montana State University	M,D
Montclair State University	M,O*
National University	M
Naval Postgraduate School	M,D
New Jersey Institute of Technology	M,D
New Mexico Highlands University	M
New Mexico Institute of Mining and Technology	M,D
New Mexico State University	M,D
New York Institute of Technology	M
New York University	M,D*
Nicholls State University	M
Norfolk State University	M
North Carolina Agricultural and Technical State University	M
North Carolina State University	M,D*
North Central College	M
North Dakota State University	M,D,O
Northeastern Illinois University	M
Northeastern University	M,D*
Northern Illinois University	M
Northern Kentucky University	M
Northwestern Polytechnic University	M
Northwestern University	M,D,O*
Northwest Missouri State University	M
Nova Southeastern University	M,D*
Oakland University	M*
OGI School of Science & Engineering at Oregon Health & Science University	M,D
The Ohio State University	M,D*
Ohio University	M,D*
Oklahoma City University	M
Oklahoma State University	M,D*
Old Dominion University	M,D*
Oregon State University	M,D*
Pace University	M,D,O*
Pacific States University	M
Penn State Harrisburg	M*
Penn State University Park	M,D*
Polytechnic University, Brooklyn Campus	M,D*
Polytechnic University, Long Island Graduate Center	M,D
Polytechnic University, Westchester Graduate Center	M,D
Portland State University	M,D
Prairie View A&M University	M,D
Princeton University	M,D*
Purdue University	M,D*
Queens College of the City University of New York	M
Queen's University at Kingston	M,D
Regis University	M,O
Rensselaer at Hartford	M
Rensselaer Polytechnic Institute	M,D*
Rice University	M,D*
Rivier College	M
Rochester Institute of Technology	M,O
Roosevelt University	M
Royal Military College of Canada	M
Rutgers, The State University of New Jersey, Camden	M
Rutgers, The State University of New Jersey, New Brunswick	M,D*
Sacred Heart University	M,O
St. Cloud State University	M
St. Francis Xavier University	M
St. John's University (NY)	M
Saint Joseph's University	M,O*
St. Mary's University of San Antonio	M
Saint Xavier University	M
Sam Houston State University	M
San Diego State University	M*
San Francisco State University	M
San Jose State University	M,O
Santa Clara University	M,D,O
Shippensburg University of Pennsylvania	M
Simon Fraser University	M,D
South Dakota School of Mines and Technology	M
Southeastern University	M
Southern Arkansas University–Magnolia	M
Southern Connecticut State University	M
Southern Illinois University Carbondale	M,D*
Southern Illinois University Edwardsville	M
Southern Methodist University	M,D*
Southern Oregon University	M
Southern Polytechnic State University	M
Southern University and Agricultural and Mechanical College	M*
Stanford University	M,D*
State University of New York at Binghamton	M,D*
State University of New York at New Paltz	M
State University of New York Institute of Technology	M
Stephen F. Austin State University	M
Stevens Institute of Technology	M,D,O*
Stony Brook University, State University of New York	M,D,O*
Suffolk University	M*
Syracuse University	M,D,O*
Télé-université	M,D
Temple University	M,D*
Tennessee Technological University	M*
Texas A&M University	M,D*
Texas A&M University–Commerce	M
Texas A&M University–Corpus Christi	M
Texas A&M University–Kingsville	M
Texas Southern University	M
Texas State University-San Marcos	M*
Texas Tech University	M,D
Towson University	M
Trent University	M
Troy University	M
Tufts University	M,D,O*
Tulane University	M,D*
Union Graduate College	M*
Universidad Autonoma de Guadalajara	M,D
Universidad de las Américas–Puebla	M,D
Université de Moncton	M,O
Université de Montréal	M,D,O
Université du Québec à Trois-Rivières	M
Université du Québec en Outaouais	M,O

Université Laval M,D
University at Albany, State University of New York M,D*
University at Buffalo, the State University of New York M,D*
The University of Akron M
The University of Alabama M,D
The University of Alabama at Birmingham M,D*
The University of Alabama in Huntsville M,D,O
University of Alaska Fairbanks M
University of Alberta M,D*
The University of Arizona M,D*
University of Arkansas M,D*
University of Arkansas at Little Rock M
University of Bridgeport M,D
The University of British Columbia M,D*
University of Calgary M,D
University of California, Berkeley M,D*
University of California, Davis M,D*
University of California, Irvine M,D*
University of California, Los Angeles M,D*
University of California, Riverside M,D*
University of California, San Diego M,D*
University of California, Santa Cruz M,D*
University of Central Arkansas M
University of Central Florida M,D*
University of Central Oklahoma M
University of Chicago M*
University of Cincinnati M,D
University of Colorado at Boulder M,D*
University of Colorado at Colorado Springs M,D
University of Colorado at Denver and Health Sciences Center M,D*
University of Connecticut M,D*
University of Dayton M*
University of Delaware M,D*
University of Denver M,D,O*
University of Detroit Mercy M
University of Evansville M
University of Florida M,D*
University of Georgia M,D*
University of Guelph M,D
University of Hawaii at Manoa M,D*
University of Houston M,D*
University of Houston–Clear Lake M
University of Houston–Victoria M*
University of Idaho M,D*
University of Illinois at Chicago M,D*
University of Illinois at Springfield M
University of Illinois at Urbana–Champaign M,D*
The University of Iowa M,D*
University of Kansas M,D*
University of Kentucky M,D*
University of Lethbridge M,D
University of Louisiana at Lafayette M,D*
University of Louisville M,D
University of Maine M,D*
University of Management and Technology M,O
University of Manitoba M,D
University of Maryland, Baltimore County M,D*
University of Maryland, College Park M,D*
University of Maryland Eastern Shore M*
University of Massachusetts Amherst M,D*
University of Massachusetts Boston M,D
University of Massachusetts Dartmouth M,O
University of Massachusetts Lowell M,D*
University of Memphis M,D*
University of Miami M*
University of Michigan M,D*
University of Michigan–Dearborn M*
University of Michigan–Flint M*
University of Minnesota, Duluth M*
University of Minnesota, Twin Cities Campus M,D*
University of Missouri–Columbia M,D*
University of Missouri–Kansas City M,D*
University of Missouri–Rolla M,D*
University of Missouri–St. Louis M,D
The University of Montana M*
University of Nebraska at Omaha M
University of Nebraska–Lincoln M,D*
University of Nevada, Las Vegas M,D
University of Nevada, Reno M,D*
University of New Brunswick Fredericton M,D
University of New Hampshire M,D*
University of New Haven M*
University of New Mexico M,D*
University of New Orleans M
The University of North Carolina at Chapel Hill M,D*
The University of North Carolina at Charlotte M*
The University of North Carolina at Greensboro M
The University of North Carolina Wilmington M*
University of North Dakota M
University of Northern British Columbia M,D,O
University of Northern Iowa M
University of Northern Virginia M,D
University of North Florida M
University of North Texas M,D*
University of Notre Dame M,D*
University of Oklahoma M,D*
University of Oregon M,D*
University of Ottawa M,D*
University of Pennsylvania M,D*
University of Pittsburgh M,D*
University of Regina M,D
University of Rhode Island M,D,O
University of Rochester M,D*
University of San Francisco M
University of Saskatchewan M,D
University of South Alabama M*
University of South Carolina M,D*
The University of South Dakota M,D
University of Southern California M,D*
University of Southern Maine M
University of Southern Mississippi M,D*
University of South Florida M,D*
The University of Tennessee M,D*
The University of Tennessee at Chattanooga M,O
The University of Texas at Arlington M,D*
The University of Texas at Austin M,D*
The University of Texas at Dallas M,D*
The University of Texas at El Paso M
The University of Texas at San Antonio M,D*
The University of Texas at Tyler M
The University of Texas–Pan American M
The University of Toledo M,D*
University of Toronto M,D
University of Tulsa M,D*
University of Utah M,D*
University of Vermont M,D*
University of Victoria M,D
University of Virginia M,D*
University of Washington M,D*
University of Waterloo M,D*
The University of Western Ontario M,D
University of West Florida M
University of West Georgia M
University of Windsor M,D
University of Wisconsin–Madison M,D*
University of Wisconsin–Milwaukee M,D
University of Wisconsin–Parkside M
University of Wisconsin–Platteville M
University of Wyoming M,D
Utah State University M,D
Vanderbilt University M,D*
Villanova University M,O*
Virginia Commonwealth University M,D,O*
Virginia Polytechnic Institute and State University M,D*
Wake Forest University M*
Walden University M,O
Washington State University M,D*
Washington State University Tri-Cities M,D
Washington State University Vancouver M
Washington University in St. Louis M,D*
Wayne State University M,D,O*
Webster University M,O
West Chester University of Pennsylvania M,O
Western Carolina University M*
Western Illinois University M
Western Kentucky University M
Western Michigan University M,D*
Western Washington University M
West Virginia University M,D*
Wichita State University M*
Winston-Salem State University M
Worcester Polytechnic Institute M,D,O*
Wright State University M,D*
Yale University D*
York University M,D*

CONDENSED MATTER PHYSICS

Cleveland State University M
Emory University D*
Iowa State University of Science and Technology M,D*
Memorial University of Newfoundland M,D
Rutgers, The State University of New Jersey, New Brunswick M,D*
University of Alberta M,D*
University of Victoria M,D
West Virginia University M,D*

CONFLICT RESOLUTION AND MEDIATION/PEACE STUDIES

Abilene Christian University M,O
American Public University System M
American University M,D,O*
The American University of Paris M
Antioch University McGregor M*
Arcadia University M
Associated Mennonite Biblical Seminary P,M,O
Baker University M
Bethany Theological Seminary P,M,O
Brandeis University M*
California State University, Dominguez Hills M
Carleton University M,O
Chaminade University of Honolulu M
Columbia College (SC) M,O
Cornell University M,D*
Creighton University M*
Dallas Baptist University M
Duquesne University M,O*
Eastern Mennonite University M,O
Florida International University O*
Fresno Pacific University M
George Mason University M,D*
Georgetown University M,D*
Huron University USA in London M
The Johns Hopkins University M,D,O*
Jones International University M
Kennesaw State University M
Lipscomb University M,O
Montclair State University M,O*
Nova Southeastern University M,D*
Pepperdine University M*
Portland State University M
Regis University M,O
Royal Roads University M
St. Edward's University M,O
Saint Paul University M
School for International Training M
Sullivan University M
Touro University International M,D
Tufts University M,D*
Université de Sherbrooke P,M,D,O
University of Baltimore M*
University of Denver M*
University of Hawaii at Manoa O*
University of Massachusetts Boston M,O
University of Missouri–Columbia M*
University of Missouri–St. Louis M
University of New Brunswick Fredericton M
The University of North Carolina at Greensboro M,O
University of Notre Dame M*
University of Pittsburgh M*
University of San Diego M*
University of the Sacred Heart M
University of Victoria M
Wayne State University M,O*
Woodbury University M,O

CONSERVATION BIOLOGY

Arizona State University M,D*
Central Michigan University M*
Columbia University M,D,O*
Frostburg State University M
Illinois State University M,D*
North Dakota State University M,D
Oklahoma State University M,D*
San Francisco State University M
State University of New York College of Environmental Science and Forestry M,D
Texas State University-San Marcos M*
Tropical Agriculture Research and Higher Education Center M,D
University at Albany, State University of New York M*
University of Alberta M,D*
University of Central Florida M,D,O*
University of Hawaii at Manoa M,D*
University of Maryland, College Park M*
University of Michigan M,D*
University of Minnesota, Twin Cities Campus M,D*
University of Missouri–St. Louis M,D,O
University of Nevada, Reno D*
University of Wisconsin–Madison M*

CONSTRUCTION ENGINEERING

Arizona State University M*
Auburn University M,D*
Bradley University M
Carnegie Mellon University M,D*
Columbia University M,D,O*
Concordia University (Canada) M,D,O
Illinois Institute of Technology M,D*
Iowa State University of Science and Technology M,D*
Lawrence Technological University M,D
Marquette University M,D
Massachusetts Institute of Technology M,D,O*
Ohio University M,D*
Oregon State University M,D*
Pontificia Universidad Catolica Madre y Maestra M
Southern Polytechnic State University M
State University of New York College of Environmental Science and Forestry M,D
Stevens Institute of Technology M,O*
Texas A&M University M,D*
Universidad Nacional Pedro Henriquez Urena P,M,D
The University of Alabama M,D
University of Alberta M,D*
University of Central Florida M,D,O*
University of Colorado at Boulder M,D*
University of Denver M*
University of Florida M,D*
University of Michigan M,D,O*
University of Missouri–Rolla M,D*
University of Nevada, Las Vegas M,D
University of New Brunswick Fredericton M,D
University of Southern California M*
University of Southern Mississippi M*
University of Washington M,D*
Virginia Polytechnic Institute and State University M*
Western Michigan University M*
Worcester Polytechnic Institute M,D,O*

CONSTRUCTION MANAGEMENT

Auburn University M*
Bowling Green State University M*
Brigham Young University M*
The Catholic University of America M,D*
Central Connecticut State University M
Clemson University M*
Colorado State University M*
Columbia University M,D,O*
Eastern Michigan University M
Florida International University M*
Michigan State University M,D*
New York University M,O*
Polytechnic University, Brooklyn Campus M*
Stevens Institute of Technology M,O*
Texas A&M University M*
Universidad de las Américas–Puebla M
University of Cincinnati M,D
University of Denver M*
University of Kansas M*
University of Nevada, Las Vegas M,D
University of New Mexico M,D*
University of Southern California M*
Washington University in St. Louis M*
Western Carolina University M*

CONSUMER ECONOMICS

California State University, Long Beach M
Colorado State University M*
Cornell University M,D*
Eastern Illinois University M

*P—first professional degree; M—master's degree; D—doctorate; O—other advanced degree; *full description and/or announcement in Book 2, 3, 4, 5, or 6*

Florida State University M,D*
Indiana State University M*
Iowa State University of Science and Technology M,D*
North Dakota State University M,D
The Ohio State University M,D*
Purdue University M,D*
State University of New York at Oswego M
Texas Tech University D
Université Laval O
The University of Alabama M
The University of Arizona M,D*
University of Georgia M,D*
University of Guelph M
University of Idaho M*
University of Illinois at Urbana–Champaign M,D*
University of Missouri–Columbia M*
University of Nebraska–Lincoln M,D*
University of South Carolina M*
The University of Tennessee M,D*
University of Utah M*
University of Wisconsin–Madison M,D*
University of Wyoming M
Utah State University M
Virginia Polytechnic Institute and State University M,D*

CORPORATE AND ORGANIZATIONAL COMMUNICATION

The American University of Athens M
Antioch University Seattle M*
Barry University M,O*
Bernard M. Baruch College of the City University of New York M*
Bowie State University M,O
Canisius College M
Central Connecticut State University M
Central Michigan University M*
College of Charleston O*
Columbia University M*
Concordia University Wisconsin M
Dallas Baptist University M
DePaul University M*
Emerson College M*
Fairleigh Dickinson University, College at Florham M*
Florida State University M,D*
Fordham University M*
Franklin University M
Hawai'i Pacific University M*
HEC Montreal O
Howard University M,D*
Illinois Institute of Technology M*
Iowa State University of Science and Technology M,D*
John Carroll University M
Jones International University M
La Salle University M
Loyola University Chicago M*
Manhattanville College M*
Marietta College M
Marist College M*
Marywood University M,O*
Metropolitan College of New York M
Mississippi College M
Monmouth University M,O
Montclair State University M*
Murray State University M
New Mexico State University M,D
New York University M*
North Carolina State University M*
Northwestern University M*
Oklahoma City University M
Queens University of Charlotte M
Radford University M
Regis College (MA) M
Roosevelt University M
Royal Roads University M
Schiller International University (United Kingdom) M
Seton Hall University M*
Simmons College M
Southern Illinois University Edwardsville O
Spalding University M
Stevens Institute of Technology O*
Syracuse University M*
Temple University M,D*
Towson University M
University of Alaska Fairbanks M
University of Arkansas at Little Rock M
University of Connecticut M,D*
University of Portland M
University of St. Thomas (MN) M*
University of Southern California M,D*
University of Wisconsin–Stevens Point M
University of Wisconsin–Whitewater M*
Washington State University M,D*
Wayne State University M,D*
Webster University M
Western Michigan University M*
West Virginia University M*

COUNSELING PSYCHOLOGY

Abilene Christian University M
Adelphi University M*
Adler Graduate School M,O
Adler School of Professional Psychology M,D,O*
Alabama Agricultural and Mechanical University M,O
Alaska Pacific University M
Alliant International University–México City M*
Amberton University M
Andrews University D
Angelo State University M
Anna Maria College M
Antioch University McGregor M*
Antioch University New England M*
Antioch University Santa Barbara M
Argosy University, Chicago Campus M,D*
Argosy University, Dallas Campus M,D*
Argosy University, Denver Campus M,D*
Argosy University, Inland Empire Campus M,D*
Argosy University, Nashville Campus M,D*
Argosy University, Orange County Campus M,D*
Argosy University, Phoenix Campus M*
Argosy University, San Diego Campus M,D*
Argosy University, San Francisco Bay Area Campus M*
Argosy University, Santa Monica Campus M,D*
Argosy University, Sarasota Campus M,D,O*
Argosy University, Schaumburg Campus M,D,O*
Argosy University, Seattle Campus M,D*
Argosy University, Tampa Campus M,D*
Argosy University, Washington DC Campus M,D,O*
Arizona State University D*
Assumption College M,O*
Auburn University M,D,O*
Avila University M*
Ball State University M,D*
Beacon University P,M
Bemidji State University M
Bethel College (IN) M
Bethel University M,O
Boston College M,D*
Boston University M,D*
Bowie State University M
Bowling Green State University M*
Brigham Young University M,D,O*
Brooklyn College of the City University of New York M,D,O
Caldwell College M
California Baptist University M
California Institute of Integral Studies M,D*
California State University, Bakersfield M
California State University, Sacramento M*
California State University, San Bernardino M
Cambridge College M,O
Capella University M,D,O
Carlos Albizu University, Miami Campus M,D
Carlow University M
Centenary College M
Central Washington University M
Chaminade University of Honolulu M
Chatham University M
Chestnut Hill College M,O
City University M
Cleveland State University D
The College of New Rochelle M,O
College of Saint Elizabeth M,O
College of St. Joseph M
Colorado Christian University M
Columbus State University M,O
Concordia University (IL) M
Concordia University Wisconsin M
Dallas Baptist University M
Dominican University of California M
Eastern Nazarene College M
Eastern University M*
Eastern Washington University M
Emporia State University M
Evangel University M
Fitchburg State College M,O
Florida Atlantic University M,O
Florida International University M*
Florida State University M,D,O*
Fordham University M,D,O*
Fort Valley State University M
Franciscan University of Steubenville M
Frostburg State University M
Gallaudet University M
Gannon University D
Gardner-Webb University M
Geneva College M*
George Fox University M,O*
Georgian Court University M,O
Georgia State University M,D,O*
Goddard College M
Gonzaga University M
Governors State University M
Grace College M
Grace University M
Harding University M
Heidelberg College M
Hofstra University M,O*
Holy Family University M
Holy Names University M,O
Hope International University M
Houston Baptist University M
Howard University M,D,O*
Idaho State University M,D,O
Illinois State University M,D,O*
Immaculata University M,D,O
Indiana State University M,D*
Indiana University Bloomington M,D,O*
Indiana Wesleyan University M
Institute of Transpersonal Psychology M,D*
Inter American University of Puerto Rico, San Germán Campus M,D
Iona College M*
Iowa State University of Science and Technology M,D*
James Madison University M,O
John Carroll University M,O
John F. Kennedy University M
Kean University M
Kent State University M*
Kutztown University of Pennsylvania M
La Salle University M
Leadership Institute of Seattle M
Lee University M
Lehigh University M,D,O*
Lesley University M*
Lewis & Clark College M,O
Lewis University M
Liberty University M,D
Lindenwood University M,D,O
Lindsey Wilson College M
Lipscomb University M,O
Long Island University, Rockland Graduate Campus M
Long Island University, Westchester Graduate Campus M
Louisiana State University in Shreveport M,O
Louisiana Tech University M,D
Loyola College in Maryland M,O
Loyola University Chicago D*
Marist College M,O*
Marylhurst University M,O
Marymount University M,O
Marywood University M*
McGill University M,D*
McKendree College M
McNeese State University M
Medaille College M
Mercy College M,O
Michigan Theological Seminary P,M,D
MidAmerica Nazarene University M
Mississippi College M,O
Monmouth University M,O
Morehead State University M
Mount St. Mary's College M
Naropa University M*
National University M
New England College M
New Jersey City University M,O
New Mexico State University M,D,O
New York Institute of Technology M,O
New York University M,D,O*
Nicholls State University M,O
Northeastern State University M
Northeastern University M,D,O*
Northern Arizona University D
Northwestern Oklahoma State University M
Northwestern University M*
Northwest University M
Notre Dame de Namur University M,O
Nova Southeastern University M*
Oakland University M,D,O*
Ottawa University M
Our Lady of the Lake University of San Antonio M,D
Pacifica Graduate Institute M,D
Palm Beach Atlantic University M
Penn State University Park M,D*
Prescott College M
Providence College and Theological Seminary P,M,D,O
Radford University M,D,O
Regent University M,D,O
Regions University P,M,D
Regis University M,O
Rivier College M,O
Rosemont College M
Rowan University M,O
Rutgers, The State University of New Jersey, New Brunswick M*
St. Edward's University M
St. John Fisher College M
Saint Joseph College M,O
Saint Martin's University M
Saint Mary's University of Minnesota M
St. Mary's University of San Antonio M,D,O
St. Thomas University M
Saint Xavier University M,O
Salem State College M
Salve Regina University M,O
San Francisco State University M
Santa Clara University M,O
Seton Hall University M,D*
Sonoma State University M
Southern Adventist University M
Southern Arkansas University–Magnolia M
Southern California Seminary P,M,D
Southern Illinois University Carbondale M,D*
Southern Methodist University M*
Southern Nazarene University M*
South University (SC) M*
South University (GA) M*
South University (AL) M*
South University (FL) M*
Southwestern Assemblies of God University M
Southwestern College (NM) M,O*
Spring Arbor University M
Springfield College M,O*
Stanford University D*
State University of New York at New Paltz M
State University of New York at Oswego M,O
State University of New York College at Brockport M,O*
Tarleton State University M
Teachers College Columbia University M,D*
Temple University M,D*
Tennessee State University M,D*
Texas A&M International University M
Texas A&M University M,D*
Texas A&M University–Commerce M,D
Texas A&M University–Texarkana M
Texas Tech University M,D
Texas Wesleyan University M
Texas Woman's University M,D,O
Towson University M,O
Trevecca Nazarene University M
Trinity International University P,M,D,O
Trinity International University, South Florida Campus M
Trinity Western University M
United States International University M
University at Albany, State University of New York M,D,O*
University at Buffalo, the State University of New York M,D,O*
The University of Akron M,D
University of Alberta M,D*
University of Baltimore M*
The University of British Columbia M,D,O*
University of Calgary M,D
University of California, Santa Barbara M,D*
University of Central Arkansas M
University of Central Oklahoma M
University of Colorado at Denver and Health Sciences Center M,O*
University of Connecticut M,D*
University of Denver M,D,O*
University of Florida M,D*
University of Great Falls M
University of Houston M,D*
University of Indianapolis M,D
The University of Iowa M,D,O*
University of Kansas M,D*
University of Kentucky M,D,O*
University of La Verne M
University of Lethbridge M,D
University of Louisville M,D
University of Mary Hardin-Baylor M
University of Maryland, College Park M,D,O*
University of Massachusetts Boston M,O

- University of Medicine and Dentistry of New Jersey O*
- University of Memphis M,D*
- University of Miami D*
- University of Minnesota, Twin Cities Campus D*
- University of Missouri–Columbia M,D,O*
- University of Missouri–Kansas City M,D,O*
- The University of Montana M,D,O*
- The University of North Carolina at Greensboro M,D,O
- University of North Dakota M
- University of Northern Colorado D
- University of North Florida M
- University of North Texas M,D*
- University of Notre Dame D*
- University of Oklahoma D*
- University of Pennsylvania M*
- University of Phoenix–Las Vegas Campus M
- University of Phoenix–Puerto Rico Campus M
- University of Phoenix–Utah Campus M
- University of Rhode Island M
- University of Saint Francis (IN) M
- University of St. Thomas (MN) M,D,O*
- University of San Francisco M,D
- The University of Scranton M,O
- University of Southern Mississippi M,D*
- The University of Tennessee M,D*
- The University of Texas at Austin M,D*
- The University of Texas at Tyler M
- University of the District of Columbia M
- University of Utah M,D*
- University of Vermont M*
- University of Victoria M,D
- University of Wisconsin–Madison D*
- University of Wisconsin–Stout M*
- Utah State University M,D
- Valdosta State University M,O
- Valparaiso University M,O
- Virginia Commonwealth University M,D,O*
- Walden University M,D
- Walla Walla College M
- Walsh University M
- Washington State University M,D*
- Wayland Baptist University M
- Webster University M
- Western Michigan University M,D*
- Western Washington University M
- Westfield State College M
- Westminster College (UT) M
- West Virginia University D*
- William Carey University M
- Yeshiva University M

COUNSELOR EDUCATION

- Acadia University M
- Adams State College M
- Adler Graduate School M,O
- Alabama Agricultural and Mechanical University M,O
- Alabama State University M,O
- Albany State University M
- Alcorn State University M,O
- Alfred University M,O*
- Angelo State University M
- Appalachian State University M
- Argosy University, Atlanta Campus M,D,O*
- Argosy University, Chicago Campus D*
- Argosy University, Denver Campus M,D*
- Argosy University, Nashville Campus M,D*
- Argosy University, Sarasota Campus M,D,O*
- Argosy University, Schaumburg Campus M,D,O*
- Argosy University, Tampa Campus M,D*
- Argosy University, Washington DC Campus M,D,O*
- Arizona State University M*
- Arkansas State University M,O
- Auburn University M,D,O*
- Auburn University Montgomery M,O
- Augusta State University M
- Austin Peay State University M
- Azusa Pacific University M
- Baptist Bible College of Pennsylvania M
- Barry University M,D,O*
- Bayamón Central University M
- Bloomsburg University of Pennsylvania M
- Bob Jones University P,M,D,O
- Boise State University M
- Boston University M,O*
- Bowie State University M
- Bowling Green State University M*
- Bradley University M
- Brandon University M,O
- Bridgewater State College M,O
- Brooklyn College of the City University of New York M,O
- Bucknell University M
- Buena Vista University M
- Butler University M
- Caldwell College M
- California Lutheran University M
- California State University, Bakersfield M
- California State University, Dominguez Hills M
- California State University, East Bay M
- California State University, Fresno M
- California State University, Fullerton M
- California State University, Long Beach M
- California State University, Los Angeles M
- California State University, Northridge M
- California State University, Sacramento M*
- California State University, San Bernardino M
- California University of Pennsylvania M
- Campbell University M
- Canisius College M
- Cape Breton University O
- Carson-Newman College M
- Carthage College M,O
- The Catholic University of America M,D*
- Central Connecticut State University M,O
- Central Methodist University M
- Central Michigan University M*
- Central Washington University M
- Chadron State College M,O
- Chapman University M
- The Chicago School of Professional Psychology M,D,O*
- Chicago State University M
- The Citadel, The Military College of South Carolina M
- Clark Atlanta University M,D
- Clemson University M*
- Cleveland State University M,D,O
- The College of New Jersey M
- College of St. Joseph M
- The College of Saint Rose M*
- College of Santa Fe M
- College of the Southwest M
- The College of William and Mary M,D
- Columbia International University M,D,O
- Columbus State University M,O
- Concordia University (IL) M,O
- Concordia University Wisconsin M
- Creighton University M*
- Dallas Baptist University M
- Delta State University M
- DePaul University M,D*
- Doane College M
- Drake University M*
- Duquesne University M,D*
- East Carolina University M,O*
- East Central University M
- Eastern Illinois University M
- Eastern Kentucky University M*
- Eastern Michigan University M,O
- Eastern New Mexico University M
- Eastern University M*
- Eastern Washington University M
- East Tennessee State University M
- Edinboro University of Pennsylvania M,O
- Emporia State University M
- Evangel University M
- Fairfield University M,O*
- Fitchburg State College M,O
- Florida Agricultural and Mechanical University M,D*
- Florida Atlantic University M,O
- Florida Gulf Coast University M
- Florida International University M*
- Florida State University M,D,O*
- Fordham University M,D,O*
- Fort Hays State University M
- Fort Valley State University M,O
- Freed-Hardeman University M,O
- Fresno Pacific University M
- Frostburg State University M
- Gallaudet University M
- Gannon University M,O
- Geneva College M*
- George Fox University M,O*
- George Mason University M*
- The George Washington University M,D,O*
- Georgia Southern University M,O
- Georgia State University M,D,O*
- Gwynedd-Mercy College M
- Hampton University M*
- Harding University M,O
- Hardin-Simmons University M
- Henderson State University M
- Heritage University M
- Hofstra University M,O*
- Houston Baptist University M
- Howard University M,O*
- Hunter College of the City University of New York M
- Idaho State University M,D,O
- Illinois State University M,D*
- Immaculata University M,D,O
- Indiana State University M,D*
- Indiana University Bloomington M,D,O*
- Indiana University of Pennsylvania M
- Indiana University–Purdue University Fort Wayne M
- Indiana University South Bend M
- Indiana University Southeast M
- Indiana Wesleyan University M
- Inter American University of Puerto Rico, Arecibo Campus M
- Inter American University of Puerto Rico, Metropolitan Campus M
- Inter American University of Puerto Rico, San Germán Campus M
- Iowa State University of Science and Technology M,D*
- Jackson State University M,O
- Jacksonville State University M
- John Brown University M
- John Carroll University M,O
- The Johns Hopkins University M,O*
- Johnson State College M
- Kansas State University M,D*
- Kean University M,O
- Keene State College M,O
- Kent State University M,D,O*
- Kutztown University of Pennsylvania M
- Lamar University M,D,O*
- Lancaster Bible College M
- La Sierra University M,O
- Lee University M
- Lehigh University M,D,O*
- Lehman College of the City University of New York M
- Lenoir-Rhyne College M
- Lewis University M
- Liberty University M,D,O
- Lincoln Memorial University M,O
- Lincoln University (MO) M,O
- Loma Linda University M,D,O
- Long Island University, Brentwood Campus M
- Long Island University, Brooklyn Campus M,O*
- Long Island University, C.W. Post Campus M*
- Long Island University, Rockland Graduate Campus M
- Long Island University, Westchester Graduate Campus M
- Longwood University M*
- Louisiana State University and Agricultural and Mechanical College M,D,O*
- Louisiana Tech University M,D
- Loyola College in Maryland M,O
- Loyola Marymount University M
- Loyola University Chicago M,O*
- Loyola University New Orleans M
- Lynchburg College M
- Lyndon State College M
- Malone College M
- Manhattan College M,O
- Marshall University M,O
- Marymount University M
- Marywood University M,O*
- McDaniel College M
- McNeese State University M
- Mercy College M
- Michigan State University M,D,O*
- Middle Tennessee State University M,O*
- Midwestern State University M
- Minnesota State University Mankato M,O
- Minnesota State University Moorhead M
- Mississippi College M,O
- Mississippi State University M,D,O
- Missouri State University M*
- Montana State University–Billings M
- Montana State University–Northern M
- Montclair State University M,O*
- Morehead State University M,O
- Mount Mary College M
- Murray State University M,O
- National-Louis University M,O
- National University M
- New Mexico Highlands University M
- New Mexico State University M,D,O
- New York Institute of Technology M
- New York University M,D,O*
- Niagara University M,O
- Nicholls State University M
- North Carolina Agricultural and Technical State University M
- North Carolina Central University M
- North Carolina State University M,D*
- North Dakota State University M,D
- Northeastern Illinois University M
- Northeastern State University M
- Northeastern University M*
- Northern Arizona University M
- Northern Illinois University M,D
- Northern Kentucky University M
- Northern State University M
- Northwest Christian College M
- Northwestern Oklahoma State University M
- Northwestern State University of Louisiana M,O
- Northwest Missouri State University M
- Northwest Nazarene University M
- Ohio University M,D*
- Oklahoma State University M,D,O*
- Old Dominion University M,D,O*
- Oregon State University M,D*
- Ottawa University M
- Our Lady of Holy Cross College M
- Our Lady of the Lake University of San Antonio M
- Palm Beach Atlantic University M
- Penn State University Park M,D*
- Phillips Graduate Institute M
- Pittsburg State University M
- Plymouth State University M
- Portland State University M,D
- Prairie View A&M University M,D
- Providence College M*
- Purdue University M,D,O*
- Purdue University Calumet M
- Queens College of the City University of New York M
- Quincy University M
- Radford University M
- Regent University M,D,O
- Rhode Island College M,O
- Rider University M,O*
- Rivier College M,O
- Roberts Wesleyan College M
- Rollins College M
- Roosevelt University M
- Rosemont College M
- Rowan University M
- Sage Graduate School M,O
- St. Bonaventure University M,O
- St. Cloud State University M
- St. John's University (NY) M,O
- Saint Joseph College M,O
- St. Lawrence University M,O
- Saint Louis University M,D,O*
- Saint Martin's University M
- Saint Mary's College of California M
- St. Mary's University of San Antonio D
- St. Thomas University M,O
- Saint Xavier University M
- Salem State College M
- Sam Houston State University M,D
- San Diego State University M*
- San Jose State University M
- Santa Clara University M
- Seattle Pacific University M
- Seattle University M,O
- Seton Hall University M*
- Shippensburg University of Pennsylvania M,O
- Siena Heights University M,O
- Simmons College M,D,O
- Simon Fraser University M
- Slippery Rock University of Pennsylvania M
- Sonoma State University M
- South Carolina State University M
- South Dakota State University M
- Southeastern Louisiana University M
- Southeastern Oklahoma State University M
- Southeast Missouri State University M,O
- Southern Adventist University M
- Southern Arkansas University–Magnolia M
- Southern Connecticut State University M,O

P—first professional degree; M—master's degree; D—doctorate; O—other advanced degree;
**full description and/or announcement in Book 2, 3, 4, 5, or 6*

Southern Illinois University Carbondale M,D*
Southern Oregon University M
Southern University and Agricultural and Mechanical College M*
Southwestern Oklahoma State University M
Springfield College M,O*
State University of New York at Plattsburgh M,O
State University of New York College at Brockport M,O*
State University of New York College at Oneonta M,O
Stephen F. Austin State University M
Stephens College M
Stetson University M
Suffolk University M,O*
Sul Ross State University M*
Syracuse University D*
Tarleton State University M
Tennessee State University M,D*
Texas A&M International University M
Texas A&M University M,D*
Texas A&M University–Commerce M,D
Texas A&M University–Corpus Christi M,D
Texas A&M University–Kingsville M
Texas Christian University M,O
Texas Southern University M,D
Texas State University-San Marcos M*
Texas Tech University M,D,O
Texas Wesleyan University M
Texas Woman's University M,D
Trevecca Nazarene University M
Trinity (Washington) University M
Troy University M,O
Université de Moncton M
Université Laval M,D
University at Albany, State University of New York M,D,O*
University at Buffalo, the State University of New York M,D,O*
The University of Akron M,D
The University of Alabama M,D,O
The University of Alabama at Birmingham M*
University of Alaska Anchorage M
University of Alaska Fairbanks M
University of Alberta M,D*
University of Arkansas M,D,O*
University of Arkansas at Little Rock M
University of Central Arkansas M
University of Central Florida M,D*
University of Central Missouri M,O
University of Central Oklahoma M
University of Cincinnati M,D,O
University of Colorado at Colorado Springs M,D
University of Colorado at Denver and Health Sciences Center M,O*
University of Connecticut M,D*
University of Dayton M,O*
University of Delaware M,D*
University of Detroit Mercy M
University of Florida M,D,O*
University of Georgia M,D,O*
University of Guam M
University of Hartford M,O*
University of Hawaii at Manoa M*
University of Houston–Clear Lake M
University of Idaho M,D,O*
University of Illinois at Urbana–Champaign M,D,O*
The University of Iowa M,D*
University of La Verne M,O
University of Louisiana at Lafayette M*
University of Louisiana at Monroe M
University of Louisville M,D
University of Maine M,D,O*
University of Manitoba M
University of Mary Hardin-Baylor M
University of Maryland, College Park M,D,O*
University of Maryland Eastern Shore M*
University of Massachusetts Amherst M,D,O*
University of Massachusetts Boston M,O
University of Memphis M,D*
University of Miami M,O*
University of Minnesota, Twin Cities Campus M,D,O*
University of Mississippi M,D,O
University of Missouri–St. Louis M
The University of Montana M,D,O*
University of Montevallo M
University of Nebraska at Kearney M,O
University of Nebraska at Omaha M
University of Nevada, Las Vegas M,D,O
University of Nevada, Reno M,D,O*
University of New Hampshire M*
University of New Hampshire at Manchester M,O
University of New Mexico M,D*
University of New Orleans M,D,O
University of North Alabama M
The University of North Carolina at Chapel Hill M*
The University of North Carolina at Charlotte M,D*
The University of North Carolina at Greensboro M,D,O
The University of North Carolina at Pembroke M
University of Northern Colorado D
University of Northern Iowa M,D
University of Northern Virginia M,D
University of North Florida M
University of North Texas M,D*
University of Oklahoma M*
University of Phoenix–Southern Arizona Campus M,O
University of Puerto Rico, Río Piedras M,D*
University of Puget Sound M
University of Saint Francis (IN) M
University of San Diego M*
University of San Francisco M,D
The University of Scranton M
University of South Alabama M,D*
University of South Carolina D,O*
The University of South Dakota M,D,O
University of Southern Maine M,O
University of South Florida M,D*
The University of Tennessee M,D,O*
The University of Tennessee at Chattanooga M,D,O
The University of Tennessee at Martin M
The University of Texas at Austin M,D*
The University of Texas at Brownsville M
The University of Texas at San Antonio M,D*
The University of Texas of the Permian Basin M
The University of Texas–Pan American M
University of the District of Columbia M
The University of Toledo M,D,O*
University of Utah M,D*
University of Vermont M*
University of Victoria M,D
University of Virginia M,D,O*
University of Washington M,D*
The University of West Alabama M
The University of Western Ontario M
University of West Florida M
University of West Georgia M,O
University of Wisconsin–Madison M*
University of Wisconsin–Oshkosh M
University of Wisconsin–Platteville M
University of Wisconsin–River Falls M,O
University of Wisconsin–Stevens Point M
University of Wisconsin–Superior M
University of Wisconsin–Whitewater M*
University of Wyoming M,D
Utah State University M,D
Valdosta State University M,O
Vanderbilt University M*
Villanova University M*
Virginia Commonwealth University M*
Virginia Polytechnic Institute and State University M,D,O*
Virginia State University M
Wake Forest University M*
Walsh University M
Washington State University Tri-Cities M,D
Wayne State College M
Wayne State University M,D,O*
West Chester University of Pennsylvania M
Western Carolina University M*
Western Connecticut State University M*
Western Illinois University M
Western Kentucky University M,O
Western Michigan University M,D*
Western New Mexico University M
Western Washington University M
Westfield State College M
Westminster College (PA) M,O
West Texas A&M University M
West Virginia University M*
Whitworth University M
Wichita State University M,D,O*
Widener University M,D*
William Paterson University of New Jersey M*
Wilmington College (DE) M
Winona State University M
Winthrop University M
Wright State University M*
Xavier University M*
Xavier University of Louisiana M
Youngstown State University M

CRIMINAL JUSTICE AND CRIMINOLOGY

Albany State University M
American International College M
American Public University System M
American University M,D*
American University of Puerto Rico M
Andrew Jackson University M
Anna Maria College M
Appalachian State University M
Arizona State University at the West campus M
Arkansas State University M,O
Armstrong Atlantic State University M
Auburn University Montgomery M
Bayamón Central University M
Bellevue University M*
Boise State University M
Boston University M*
Bowling Green State University M*
Bridgewater State College M
Buffalo State College, State University of New York M
California State University, Fresno M
California State University, Long Beach M
California State University, Los Angeles M
California State University, Sacramento M*
California State University, San Bernardino M
California State University, Stanislaus M
California University of Pennsylvania M
Capella University M,D,O
Caribbean University M,D
Carnegie Mellon University M*
Central Connecticut State University M
Central Michigan University M*
Chaminade University of Honolulu M
Charleston Southern University M
Chicago State University M
Clark Atlanta University M
Colorado Technical University—Colorado Springs M
Colorado Technical University—Denver M
Colorado Technical University—Sioux Falls M
Columbia College (MO) M
Concordia University, St. Paul M
Coppin State University M
Curry College M
Dallas Baptist University M
Delta State University M
DeSales University M
Drury University M
East Carolina University M*
East Central University M
Eastern Kentucky University M*
Eastern Michigan University M
East Tennessee State University M
Fairmont State University M
Fayetteville State University M
Ferris State University M
Fitchburg State College M
Florida Agricultural and Mechanical University M*
Florida Atlantic University M*
Florida Gulf Coast University M
Florida International University M*
Florida Metropolitan University–Brandon Campus M
Florida Metropolitan University–Jacksonville Campus M
Florida Metropolitan University–Lakeland Campus M
Florida Metropolitan University–Pompano Beach Campus M
Florida State University M,D*
The George Washington University M*
Georgia College & State University M
Georgia State University M*
Graduate School and University Center of the City University of New York D*
Grambling State University M
Grand Valley State University M
Hodges University M
Illinois State University M*
Indiana State University M*
Indiana University Bloomington M,D*
Indiana University Northwest M,O
Indiana University of Pennsylvania M,D
Indiana University–Purdue University Indianapolis M*
Inter American University of Puerto Rico, Aguadilla Campus M
Inter American University of Puerto Rico, Metropolitan Campus M
Inter American University of Puerto Rico, Ponce Campus M
Iona College M*
Jackson State University M
Jacksonville State University M
John Jay College of Criminal Justice of the City University of New York M,D
The Johns Hopkins University M,O*
Kean University M
Kent State University M*
Keuka College M
Lamar University M*
Lewis University M
Lincoln University (MO) M
Lindenwood University M
Long Island University, Brentwood Campus M
Long Island University, C.W. Post Campus M*
Longwood University M*
Loyola University Chicago M*
Loyola University New Orleans M
Lynn University M,O
Madonna University M
Marshall University M
Marywood University M*
Mercyhurst College M,O
Methodist University M
Metropolitan State University M
Michigan State University M,D*
Middle Tennessee State University M*
Midwestern State University M
Minnesota State University Mankato M
Minot State University M
Mississippi College M,O
Mississippi Valley State University M
Missouri State University M*
Monmouth University M,O
Morehead State University M
Mountain State University M*
Mount Aloysius College M
New Jersey City University M
New Mexico State University M
Niagara University M
Norfolk State University M
North Carolina Central University M
North Dakota State University M,D
Northeastern State University M
Northeastern University M,D*
Northern Arizona University M,O
Northern Michigan University M
Norwich University M
Nova Southeastern University M*
Oklahoma City University M
Oklahoma State University M,D*
Old Dominion University D*
Penn State Harrisburg M,D*
Penn State University Park M,D*
Point Park University M*
Polytechnic University, Brooklyn Campus M,D,O*
Pontifical Catholic University of Puerto Rico M,D
Portland State University M,D
Radford University M
The Richard Stockton College of New Jersey M
Roger Williams University M*
Rosemont College M
Rutgers, The State University of New Jersey, Camden M
Rutgers, The State University of New Jersey, Newark M,D*
Sacred Heart University M
St. Ambrose University M
St. Cloud State University M
St. John's University (NY) M
Saint Joseph's University M,O*
Saint Leo University M
Saint Louis University M*
Saint Mary's University M
St. Thomas University M,O
Salem State College M
Salve Regina University M

Sam Houston State University M,D
San Diego State University M*
San Jose State University M
Seattle University M
Shippensburg University of Pennsylvania M
Simon Fraser University M,D
Southeast Missouri State University M
Southern Illinois University Carbondale M*
Southern University and Agricultural and Mechanical College M*
Suffolk University M*
Sul Ross State University M*
Tarleton State University M
Temple University M,D*
Tennessee State University M*
Texas A&M International University M
Texas State University-San Marcos M*
Tiffin University M
Touro University International M,D
Troy University M
Universidad del Este M
Universidad del Turabo M
Université de Montréal M,D
University at Albany, State University of New York M,D*
University College of the Fraser Valley M
The University of Alabama M
The University of Alabama at Birmingham M*
University of Alaska Fairbanks M
University of Alberta M,D*
University of Arkansas at Little Rock M
University of Baltimore M*
University of California, Irvine M,D*
University of Central Florida M,O*
University of Central Missouri M,O
University of Central Oklahoma M
University of Cincinnati M,D
University of Colorado at Colorado Springs M
University of Colorado at Denver and Health Sciences Center M*
University of Delaware M,D*
University of Denver M,O*
University of Detroit Mercy M
University of Florida M,D*
University of Great Falls M
University of Guelph M
University of Houston–Clear Lake M
University of Houston–Downtown M
University of Illinois at Chicago M*
University of Louisiana at Monroe M
University of Louisville M
University of Maryland, College Park M,D*
University of Maryland Eastern Shore M*
University of Massachusetts Lowell M*
University of Memphis M*
University of Minnesota, Duluth M*
University of Missouri–Kansas City M,D*
University of Missouri–St. Louis M,D
The University of Montana M*
University of Nebraska at Omaha M,D
University of Nevada, Las Vegas M
University of Nevada, Reno M*
University of New Haven M*
University of North Alabama M
The University of North Carolina at Charlotte M*
The University of North Carolina at Greensboro M
The University of North Carolina Wilmington M*
University of North Dakota D
University of Northern Iowa M
University of North Florida M
University of North Texas M*
University of Ottawa M,D*
University of Pennsylvania M,D*
University of Phoenix–Augusta Campus M
University of Phoenix–Austin Campus M
University of Phoenix–Bay Area Campus M
University of Phoenix–Chattanooga Campus M
University of Phoenix–Cheyenne Campus M
University of Phoenix–Cleveland Campus M
University of Phoenix–Des Moines Campus M
University of Phoenix–Detroit Campus M
University of Phoenix–Harrisburg Campus M
University of Phoenix–Hawaii Campus M
University of Phoenix–Indianapolis Campus M
University of Phoenix–Jersey City Campus M
University of Phoenix–Kansas City Campus M
University of Phoenix–Louisiana Campus M
University of Phoenix–Maryland Campus M
University of Phoenix–Memphis Campus M
University of Phoenix—Northern Nevada Campus M
University of Phoenix–Northern Virginia Campus M
University of Phoenix–Northwest Arkansas Campus M
University of Phoenix–Northwest Indiana M
University of Phoenix–Omaha Campus M
University of Phoenix Online Campus M
University of Phoenix–Oregon Campus M
University of Phoenix–Pittsburgh Campus M
University of Phoenix–Renton Learning Center M
University of Phoenix–Richmond Campus M
University of Phoenix–Sacramento Valley Campus M
University of Phoenix–San Antonio Campus M
University of Phoenix–San Diego Campus M
University of Phoenix–Savannah Campus M
University of Phoenix–Southern Arizona Campus M,O
University of Phoenix–Springfield Campus M
University of Pittsburgh D*
University of Regina M
University of South Carolina M*
University of Southern Mississippi M,D*
University of South Florida M,D*
The University of Tennessee M,D*
The University of Tennessee at Chattanooga M
The University of Texas at Arlington M*
The University of Texas at San Antonio M*
The University of Texas at Tyler M
The University of Texas of the Permian Basin M
The University of Texas–Pan American M
The University of Toledo M,O*
University of Toronto M,D
University of West Florida M
University of Wisconsin–Milwaukee M
University of Wisconsin–Platteville M
Upper Iowa University M
Utica College M
Valdosta State University M
Villanova University M*
Virginia College at Birmingham M
Virginia Commonwealth University M,O*
Washburn University M
Washington State University M,D*
Washington State University Spokane M,D
Wayland Baptist University M
Wayne State University M*
Webster University M,D
West Chester University of Pennsylvania M
Western Connecticut State University M*
Western Illinois University M,O
Western Oregon University M
Westfield State College M
West Texas A&M University M
Wichita State University M*
Widener University M*
Wilmington College (DE) M
Wright State University M*
Xavier University M*
Youngstown State University M

CULTURAL STUDIES

Asbury Theological Seminary M,D
Athabasca University M
Baptist Bible College P,M
Biola University M,D,O
Brock University M
Chapman University D
Claremont Graduate University M,D,O
Columbia International University P,M,D,O
Cornell University M,D*
Eastern Michigan University M
George Mason University D*
Graduate Theological Union M,D,O
Lewis & Clark College M,O
Maranatha Baptist Bible College M
McMaster University M,D
New York University M,D,O*
St. Francis Xavier University M
San Francisco State University M
Simmons College M
Simpson University P,M
Southern Illinois University Carbondale M*
Stony Brook University, State University of New York M,O*
Taylor University College and Seminary P,M,O
Union University M
University of Alaska Fairbanks M
University of California, Davis M,D*
University of Hawaii at Manoa M,O*
University of Houston–Clear Lake M
University of Minnesota, Twin Cities Campus D*
University of Pittsburgh M,D*
The University of Texas at San Antonio M,D*
University of the Sacred Heart M
Washington State University M,D*
Wheaton College M,O
Wilfrid Laurier University M

CURRICULUM AND INSTRUCTION

Acadia University M
American InterContinental University Online M
Andrews University M,D,O
Angelo State University M
Appalachian State University M
Arizona State University M,D*
Arizona State University at the Polytechnic Campus M,D
Arkansas State University M,D,O
Arkansas Tech University M,O
Armstrong Atlantic State University M
Ashland University M
Auburn University M,D,O*
Aurora University M,D
Austin Peay State University M,O
Averett University M
Azusa Pacific University M
Ball State University M,O*
Bank Street College of Education M*
Barry University D,O*
Baylor University M,D,O*
Benedictine University M
Berry College O
Black Hills State University M*
Bloomsburg University of Pennsylvania M
Bob Jones University P,M,D,O
Boise State University D
Boston College M,D,O*
Boston University M,D,O*
Bowling Green State University M*
Bradley University M
Brandon University M,O
Brescia University M
Bucknell University M
Caldwell College M
California Baptist University M
California State University, Bakersfield M
California State University, Chico M
California State University, Dominguez Hills M
California State University, East Bay M
California State University, Fresno M
California State University, Sacramento M*
California State University, San Bernardino M
California State University, Stanislaus M
Calvin College M
Campbellsville University M
Capella University M,D,O
Caribbean University M,D
Carson-Newman College M
Castleton State College M
The Catholic University of America M,D*
Centenary College of Louisiana M
Chapman University M,D
Christian Brothers University M
City University M,O
Clarion University of Pennsylvania M
Clark Atlanta University M,O
Clemson University D*
College Misericordia M
The College of St. Scholastica M
College of Santa Fe M
College of the Southwest M
The College of William and Mary M,D
Colorado Christian University M
Columbia International University M,D,O
Concordia University (CA) M
Concordia University (IL) M
Concordia University (OR) M
Concordia University (NE) M
Concordia University Wisconsin M
Converse College O
Coppin State University M
Cornell University M,D*
Dallas Baptist University M
Delaware State University M
DePaul University D*
Doane College M
Dominican University M
Dominican University of California M
Drexel University M*
Duquesne University M,D*
East Carolina University M*
Eastern Kentucky University M*
Eastern Michigan University M
Eastern Washington University M
East Tennessee State University M
Emporia State University M
Fairleigh Dickinson University, Metropolitan Campus M*
Ferris State University M
Florida Atlantic University M,D,O
Florida Gulf Coast University M
Florida International University M,D,O*
Fordham University M,D,O*
Framingham State College M*
Franciscan University of Steubenville M
Freed-Hardeman University M,O
Fresno Pacific University M
Frostburg State University M
Gannon University M
Gardner-Webb University D
The George Washington University M,D,O*
Georgia Southern University D
Grambling State University M,D
Harvard University M*
Henderson State University M,O
Holy Names University M,O
Hood College M,O
Houston Baptist University M
Idaho State University M,O
Illinois State University M,D*
Indiana State University M,D*
Indiana University Bloomington M,D,O*
Indiana University of Pennsylvania M,D
Indiana Wesleyan University M
Iowa State University of Science and Technology M,D*
The Johns Hopkins University M*
Johnson State College M
Jones International University M
Kansas State University M,D*
Kean University M
Keene State College M
Kent State University M,D,O*
Kutztown University of Pennsylvania M,O
LaGrange College M
Lake Erie College M
Lakehead University M,D
Lander University M
La Sierra University M,D,O
Lesley University M,D,O*
Lewis University M
Liberty University M,D,O
Lincoln Memorial University M,O
Lipscomb University M
Louisiana Tech University M,D
Loyola College in Maryland M,O
Loyola University Chicago M,D*
Lyndon State College M
Malone College M
Massachusetts College of Liberal Arts M
McDaniel College M
McGill University M,D,O*
McNeese State University M
Medaille College M
Memorial University of Newfoundland M,D,O
Miami University M*
Michigan State University M,D,O*

P—first professional degree; M—master's degree; D—doctorate; O—other advanced degree;
**full description and/or announcement in Book 2, 3, 4, 5, or 6*

Institution	Degrees
MidAmerica Nazarene University	M
Middle Tennessee State University	M,O*
Midwestern State University	M
Mills College	M,D
Minnesota State University Mankato	M,O
Minnesota State University Moorhead	M
Mississippi College	M,O
Mississippi State University	M,D,O
Missouri State University	M*
Montana State University–Billings	M
Montclair State University	M,D,O*
Moravian College	M
Morehead State University	O
Mount Saint Vincent University	M
National-Louis University	M,D,O
Newman University	M
New Mexico Highlands University	M
New Mexico State University	M,D,O
Nicholls State University	M
North Carolina State University	M,D*
Northern Arizona University	D
Northern Illinois University	M,D
Northwestern Oklahoma State University	M
Northwestern State University of Louisiana	M
Northwest Nazarene University	M
Nova Southeastern University	M,O*
Ohio University	M,D*
Oklahoma State University	M,D*
Old Dominion University	M,D*
Olivet Nazarene University	M
Oral Roberts University	M,D
Ottawa University	M
Our Lady of Holy Cross College	M
Our Lady of the Lake University of San Antonio	M,D
Pace University	M,O*
Pacific Lutheran University	M
Penn State Great Valley	M
Penn State Harrisburg	M,D*
Penn State University Park	M,D*
Philadelphia Biblical University	M
Piedmont College	M,O
Point Park University	M*
Pontifical Catholic University of Puerto Rico	M,D
Portland State University	M,D
Prairie View A&M University	M
Purdue University	M,D,O*
Purdue University Calumet	M
Regis University	M,O
Rider University	M,O*
Rivier College	M,O
Rosemont College	M
Rowan University	M
St. Cloud State University	M
St. Francis Xavier University	M
Saint Leo University	M
Saint Louis University	M,D*
Saint Mary's College of California	M
Saint Michael's College	M,O
Saint Peter's College	M,O
Saint Vincent College	M
Saint Xavier University	M,O
Salem International University	M
San Diego State University	M*
Seattle University	M,O
Shaw University	M
Shepherd University	M
Shippensburg University of Pennsylvania	M
Siena Heights University	M
Simon Fraser University	M,D
Sonoma State University	M
South Dakota State University	M
Southeastern Louisiana University	M
Southern Adventist University	M
Southern Illinois University Carbondale	M,D*
Southern Nazarene University	M
Southern New Hampshire University	M,O*
Southwestern Assemblies of God University	M
Stanford University	M,D*
State University of New York at Plattsburgh	M
State University of New York College at Brockport	M*
State University of New York College at Potsdam	M
Stephens College	M
Stetson University	O
Suffolk University	M,O*
Syracuse University	M,D,O*
Tarleton State University	M
Teachers College Columbia University	M,D*
Tennessee State University	M,D*
Tennessee Technological University	M,O*
Tennessee Temple University	M
Texas A&M International University	M,D
Texas A&M University	M,D*
Texas A&M University–Commerce	M,D
Texas A&M University–Corpus Christi	M,D
Texas A&M University–Texarkana	M
Texas Southern University	M,D
Texas Tech University	M,D
Trevecca Nazarene University	M
Universidad Metropolitana	M
Université de Montréal	M,D,O
Université Laval	M,D
University at Albany, State University of New York	M,D,O*
University of Alaska Fairbanks	M
University of Arkansas	D*
The University of British Columbia	M,D*
University of Calgary	M,D,O
University of California, Davis	M,D*
University of Central Florida	D*
University of Central Missouri	M,O
University of Cincinnati	M,D
University of Colorado at Boulder	M,D*
University of Colorado at Colorado Springs	M,D
University of Connecticut	M,D*
University of Delaware	M,D*
University of Denver	M,D,O*
University of Detroit Mercy	M
University of Florida	M,D,O*
University of Hawaii at Manoa	M,D*
University of Houston	M,D*
University of Houston–Clear Lake	M
University of Idaho	M,D*
University of Illinois at Chicago	M,D*
University of Illinois at Urbana–Champaign	M,D,O*
University of Indianapolis	M
The University of Iowa	M,D*
University of Kansas	M,D*
University of Kentucky	M,D*
University of Louisiana at Lafayette	M*
University of Louisiana at Monroe	M,D
University of Louisville	D
University of Maine	M*
University of Manitoba	M
University of Mary	M
University of Maryland, Baltimore County	M,O*
University of Maryland, College Park	M,D,O*
University of Massachusetts Amherst	M,D,O*
University of Massachusetts Boston	M
University of Massachusetts Lowell	M,D,O*
University of Memphis	M,D*
University of Michigan	M,D*
University of Minnesota, Twin Cities Campus	M,D,O*
University of Mississippi	M,D,O
University of Missouri–Columbia	M,D,O*
University of Missouri–Kansas City	M,D,O*
University of Missouri–St. Louis	M,D
The University of Montana	M,D*
University of Nebraska at Kearney	M
University of Nebraska–Lincoln	M,D,O*
University of Nevada, Las Vegas	M,D,O
University of Nevada, Reno	M,D,O*
University of New Orleans	M,D,O
The University of North Carolina at Chapel Hill	M,D*
The University of North Carolina at Charlotte	M,D,O*
The University of North Carolina at Greensboro	M,D,O
The University of North Carolina Wilmington	M*
University of Northern Iowa	M,D
University of North Texas	D*
University of Oklahoma	M,D,O*
University of Phoenix–Bay Area Campus	M
University of Phoenix–Central Florida Campus	M
University of Phoenix–Central Valley Campus	M
University of Phoenix–Denver Campus	M
University of Phoenix–Fort Lauderdale Campus	M
University of Phoenix–Hawaii Campus	M
University of Phoenix–Las Vegas Campus	M
University of Phoenix–Memphis Campus	M
University of Phoenix–Metro Detroit Campus	M
University of Phoenix–Nashville Campus	M
University of Phoenix–New Mexico Campus	M
University of Phoenix–North Florida Campus	M
University of Phoenix–Omaha Campus	M
University of Phoenix Online Campus	M
University of Phoenix–Phoenix Campus	M
University of Phoenix–Sacramento Valley Campus	M,O
University of Phoenix–San Diego Campus	M
University of Phoenix–Southern Arizona Campus	M,O
University of Phoenix–Southern California Campus	M
University of Phoenix–Southern Colorado Campus	M,O
University of Phoenix–Springfield Campus	M
University of Phoenix–Utah Campus	M
University of Phoenix–Vancouver Campus	M
University of Phoenix–West Florida Campus	M
University of Phoenix–West Michigan Campus	M
University of Puerto Rico, Río Piedras	M,D*
University of Regina	M
University of St. Francis (IL)	M
University of Saint Mary	M
University of St. Thomas (MN)	M,D,O*
University of San Diego	M,D*
University of San Francisco	M,D
University of Saskatchewan	M,D,O
The University of Scranton	M
University of South Carolina	M,D,O*
The University of South Dakota	M,D,O
University of Southern Mississippi	M,D,O*
The University of Tennessee	M,D,O*
The University of Texas at Arlington	M*
The University of Texas at Austin	M,D*
The University of Texas at Brownsville	M
The University of Texas at El Paso	M
The University of Texas at San Antonio	M*
The University of Texas at Tyler	M
University of the Pacific	M,D
The University of Toledo	M,D,O*
University of Vermont	M*
University of Victoria	M,D
University of Virginia	M,D,O*
University of Washington	M,D*
The University of Western Ontario	M
University of West Florida	M,D,O
University of Wisconsin–Madison	M,D*
University of Wisconsin–Milwaukee	M
University of Wisconsin–Oshkosh	M
University of Wisconsin–Superior	M
University of Wisconsin–Whitewater	M*
University of Wyoming	M,D
Utah State University	D
Valdosta State University	M,D,O
Vanderbilt University	M,D*
Virginia Commonwealth University	M,O*
Virginia Polytechnic Institute and State University	M,D,O*
Walden University	M,D
Walla Walla College	M
Washburn University	M
Washington State University	M,D*
Wayne State University	M,D,O*
Weber State University	M
Western Connecticut State University	M*
West Texas A&M University	M
West Virginia University	M,D*
Wichita State University	M*
William Woods University	M,O
Wright State University	M,O*
Xavier University of Louisiana	M

DANCE

Institution	Degrees
American University	M,O*
Arizona State University	M*
Bennington College	M*
California Institute of the Arts	M,O
California State University, Fullerton	M
California State University, Long Beach	M
California State University, Sacramento	M*
Case Western Reserve University	M*
Connecticut College	M
Florida State University	M*
George Mason University	M*
Hollins University	M
Mills College	M
New York University	M,D*
Northern Illinois University	M
The Ohio State University	M,D*
Purchase College, State University of New York	M
Sam Houston State University	M
Sarah Lawrence College	M*
Shenandoah University	M,D,O*
Smith College	M*
Southern Methodist University	M*
State University of New York College at Brockport	M*
Temple University	M,D*
Texas Tech University	M,D
Texas Woman's University	M,D
Tufts University	M,D*
Tulane University	M*
Université du Québec à Montréal	M
University of California, Irvine	M*
University of California, Los Angeles	M,D*
University of California, Riverside	M,D*
University of Colorado at Boulder	M,D*
University of Hawaii at Manoa	M,D*
University of Illinois at Urbana–Champaign	M*
The University of Iowa	M*
University of Maryland, College Park	M*
University of Michigan	M*
University of Minnesota, Twin Cities Campus	M,D*
University of New Mexico	M*
The University of North Carolina at Charlotte	M*
The University of North Carolina at Greensboro	M
University of Oklahoma	M*
University of Oregon	M*
The University of Texas at Austin	M,D*
University of Utah	M*
University of Washington	M*
University of Wisconsin–Milwaukee	M
York University	M*

DECORATIVE ARTS

Institution	Degrees
Bard Graduate Center for Studies in the Decorative Arts, Design, and Culture	M,D*
Corcoran College of Art and Design	M
The New School: A University	M*

DEMOGRAPHY AND POPULATION STUDIES

Institution	Degrees
American University of Beirut	M
Arizona State University	M,D*
Bowling Green State University	M,D*
Brown University	D*
Cornell University	M,D*
Duke University	D*
Florida State University	M,O*
Georgetown University	M*
Harvard University	M,D*
The Johns Hopkins University	M,D*
Princeton University	D,O*
Université de Montréal	M,D
Université du Québec, Institut National de la Recherche Scientifique	M,D
University at Albany, State University of New York	M,D,O*
University of Alberta	M,D*
University of California, Berkeley	M,D*
University of California, Irvine	M*
University of Hawaii at Manoa	O*
University of Illinois at Urbana–Champaign	M,D*
University of Pennsylvania	M,D*
University of Puerto Rico, Medical Sciences Campus	M*
The University of Texas at San Antonio	D*
Washington State University	M,D*

DENTAL HYGIENE

Institution	Degrees
Boston University	P,M,D,O*
Dalhousie University	O
Idaho State University	M,O
Medical College of Georgia	M*
Old Dominion University	M*
Texas A&M Health Science Center	M*

Université de Montréal M,O
University of Alberta O*
University of Maryland, Baltimore M*
University of Missouri–Kansas City P,M,D,O*
University of New Mexico M*
The University of Texas Health Science Center at San Antonio M*

DENTISTRY

Boston University P,M,D,O*
Case Western Reserve University P*
Columbia University P*
Creighton University P*
Dalhousie University P
Harvard University P,M,D,O*
Howard University P,O*
Idaho State University M,O
Indiana University–Purdue University Indianapolis P,M,D,O*
Loma Linda University P,M,O
Louisiana State University Health Sciences Center P*
Marquette University P
McGill University P,M,D,O*
Medical College of Georgia P*
Medical University of South Carolina P*
Meharry Medical College P
New York University P*
Nova Southeastern University P,M*
The Ohio State University P,M*
Oregon Health & Science University P*
Southern Illinois University Edwardsville P
Stony Brook University, State University of New York P,O*
Temple University P*
Texas A&M Health Science Center P*
Tufts University P*
Universidad Iberoamericana P,M
Universidad Nacional Pedro Henriquez Urena P
Université de Montréal M,O
Université Laval P
University at Buffalo, the State University of New York P,M,D,O*
The University of Alabama at Birmingham P*
University of Alberta P*
The University of British Columbia P*
University of California, Los Angeles P,O*
University of California, San Francisco P
University of Colorado at Denver and Health Sciences Center P*
University of Connecticut Health Center P,O*
University of Detroit Mercy P
University of Florida P,O*
University of Illinois at Chicago P*
The University of Iowa P,M,D,O*
University of Kentucky P,M*
University of Louisville P
University of Manitoba P
University of Maryland, Baltimore P,M,O*
University of Medicine and Dentistry of New Jersey P,M,D,O*
University of Michigan P*
University of Minnesota, Twin Cities Campus P*
University of Mississippi Medical Center P,M,D*
University of Missouri–Kansas City P,M,D,O*
University of Nebraska Medical Center P,O*
The University of North Carolina at Chapel Hill P*
University of Oklahoma Health Sciences Center P
University of Pennsylvania P*
University of Pittsburgh P,M,O*
University of Puerto Rico, Medical Sciences Campus P*
University of Saskatchewan P
University of Southern California P,O*
The University of Tennessee Health Science Center P,M,O*
The University of Texas Health Science Center at Houston P,M*
The University of Texas Health Science Center at San Antonio P,M,O*
University of the Pacific P,M,O
University of Toronto P
University of Washington P
The University of Western Ontario P
Virginia Commonwealth University P*
West Virginia University P*

DEVELOPMENTAL BIOLOGY

Albert Einstein College of Medicine D*
Arizona State University M,D*
Baylor College of Medicine D*
Brigham Young University M,D*
Brown University M,D*
California Institute of Technology D*
Carnegie Mellon University M,D*
Case Western Reserve University M,D*
Columbia University M,D*
Cornell University M,D*
Duke University D,O*
Emory University D*
Florida State University M,D*
Illinois State University M,D*
Iowa State University of Science and Technology M,D*
The Johns Hopkins University D*
Louisiana State University Health Sciences Center M,D*
Marquette University M,D
Massachusetts Institute of Technology D*
Medical College of Wisconsin M,D*
New York University M,D*
Northwestern University D*
The Ohio State University M,D*
Oregon Health & Science University D*
Penn State University Park M,D*
Purdue University M,D*
Rensselaer Polytechnic Institute M,D*
Rutgers, The State University of New Jersey, New Brunswick M,D*
Stanford University D*
Stony Brook University, State University of New York M,D*
Thomas Jefferson University M,D*
Tufts University D*
University at Albany, State University of New York M,D*
University of California, Davis M,D*
University of California, Irvine M,D*
University of California, Los Angeles M,D*
University of California, Riverside M,D*
University of California, San Diego D*
University of California, San Francisco D
University of California, Santa Barbara M,D*
University of Chicago D*
University of Cincinnati D
University of Colorado at Boulder M,D*
University of Colorado at Denver and Health Sciences Center D*
University of Connecticut M,D*
University of Connecticut Health Center D*
University of Delaware M,D*
University of Illinois at Chicago M,D*
University of Illinois at Urbana–Champaign D*
University of Kansas M,D*
University of Massachusetts Amherst D*
University of Miami D*
University of Michigan M,D*
University of Minnesota, Twin Cities Campus M,D*
University of Missouri–St. Louis M,D,O
The University of North Carolina at Chapel Hill M,D*
University of Pennsylvania D*
University of Pittsburgh D*
University of South Carolina M,D*
The University of Texas at Austin D*
The University of Texas Health Science Center at Houston M,D*
The University of Texas Southwestern Medical Center at Dallas D*
Virginia Polytechnic Institute and State University M,D*
Washington University in St. Louis D*
Wesleyan University D*
West Virginia University M,D*
Yale University D*

DEVELOPMENTAL EDUCATION

Edinboro University of Pennsylvania O
Ferris State University M
Grambling State University M,D
Instituto Tecnológico y de Estudios Superiores de Monterrey, Campus Ciudad Obregón M
National-Louis University M,O
North Carolina State University M*
Rutgers, The State University of New Jersey, New Brunswick M*
Texas State University-San Marcos M,D*
University of California, Berkeley *
The University of Iowa M,D*

DEVELOPMENTAL PSYCHOLOGY

Andrews University M,D
Arizona State University D*
Boston College M,D*
Bowling Green State University M,D*
Brandeis University M,D*
Bryn Mawr College D*
Carnegie Mellon University D*
Claremont Graduate University M,D,O
Clark University D*
Cornell University D*
Duke University D*
Emory University D*
Erikson Institute M,O*
Florida International University M,D*
Florida State University D*
Fordham University D*
Gallaudet University M,O
George Mason University M,D*
Graduate School and University Center of the City University of New York D*
Harvard University D*
Howard University M,D*
Illinois State University M,D,O*
Indiana University Bloomington M,D*
Louisiana State University and Agricultural and Mechanical College M,D*
Loyola University Chicago D*
McGill University M,D,O*
New York University M,D,O*
North Carolina State University D*
The Ohio State University M,D*
Penn State University Park M,D*
Queen's University at Kingston M,D
Rutgers, The State University of New Jersey, New Brunswick D*
Stanford University D*
Suffolk University D*
Teachers College Columbia University M,D*
Temple University D*
Texas A&M University M,D*
Tufts University M,D,O*
Université de Montréal M,D
The University of Alabama at Birmingham M,D*
The University of British Columbia M,D*
University of California, Santa Barbara M,D*
University of Connecticut M,D*
University of Florida M,D*
University of Kansas M,D*
University of Maine M,D*
University of Maryland, Baltimore County D*
University of Maryland, College Park M,D*
University of Miami M,D*
University of Michigan D*
The University of Montana M,D,O*
University of Nebraska at Omaha M,D,O
The University of North Carolina at Chapel Hill D*
The University of North Carolina at Greensboro M,D
University of Notre Dame D*
University of Oregon M,D*
University of Pittsburgh M,D*
University of Rochester M,D*
University of Wisconsin–Madison D*
Virginia Polytechnic Institute and State University M,D*
Wayne State University M,D*
West Virginia University M,D*
Wilfrid Laurier University M,D

DISABILITY STUDIES

Brock University M,O
Chapman University D
New York Medical College M*
Suffolk University M,O*
Syracuse University O*
University of Hawaii at Manoa O*
University of Illinois at Chicago M,D*
University of Manitoba M
University of Northern British Columbia M,D,O
University of Pittsburgh O*
Utah State University M,D,O
York University M,D*

DISTANCE EDUCATION DEVELOPMENT

Athabasca University M,O
Barry University O*
Endicott College M
Fairmont State University M
Florida State University M,D,O*
Jones International University M
New York Institute of Technology M,O
Nova Southeastern University M,D*
Télé-université M,D
University of Maryland, Baltimore County M,O*
University of Maryland University College M,O
University of Phoenix–Metro Detroit Campus M
University of Wyoming M,D,O
Western Illinois University M,O

EARLY CHILDHOOD EDUCATION

Adelphi University M,O*
Alabama Agricultural and Mechanical University M,O
Alabama State University M,O
Albany State University M
Albright College M
Anna Maria College M,O
Arcadia University M,D,O
Arkansas State University M,O
Armstrong Atlantic State University M
Ashland University M
Auburn University M,D,O*
Auburn University Montgomery M,O
Bank Street College of Education M*
Barry University M,D,O*
Bayamón Central University M
Bellarmine University M
Belmont University M
Bennington College M*
Berry College M
Bloomsburg University of Pennsylvania M
Boise State University M
Boston College M*
Boston University M,D,O*
Bowling Green State University M*
Brenau University M,O
Bridgewater State College M
Brooklyn College of the City University of New York M
Buffalo State College, State University of New York M
California State University, Bakersfield M
California State University, Fresno M
California State University, Northridge M
California State University, Sacramento M*
Canisius College M
Carlow University M
Central Connecticut State University M
Central Michigan University M*
Chatham University M
Chestnut Hill College M
Cheyney University of Pennsylvania O
Chicago State University M
City College of the City University of New York M*
Clarion University of Pennsylvania M
Clarke College M
Cleveland State University M
Coastal Carolina University M
College of Charleston M*
College of Mount St. Joseph M
The College of New Jersey M
The College of New Rochelle M
The College of Saint Rose M,O*
Columbia International University M,D,O
Columbus State University M,O
Concordia University (IL) M,D
Concordia University (NE) M
Concordia University, St. Paul M,O
Concordia University Wisconsin M
Converse College M,O
Daemen College M
Dallas Baptist University M
Dominican University M
Duquesne University M*
Eastern Connecticut State University M
Eastern Illinois University M
Eastern Michigan University M
Eastern Nazarene College M,O
Eastern Washington University M

P—first professional degree; M—master's degree; D—doctorate; O—other advanced degree;
**full description and/or announcement in Book 2, 3, 4, 5, or 6*

East Tennessee State University	M
Edinboro University of Pennsylvania	M
Elms College	M,O
Emporia State University	M
Erikson Institute	M,D*
Fitchburg State College	M
Five Towns College	M
Florida Agricultural and Mechanical University	M*
Florida International University	M,D*
Florida State University	M,D,O*
Fordham University	M,D,O*
Fort Valley State University	M
Framingham State College	M*
Francis Marion University	M
Furman University	M
Gallaudet University	M,D,O
Gannon University	M,O
George Mason University	M*
The George Washington University	M*
Georgia College & State University	M,O
Georgia Southern University	M
Georgia Southwestern State University	M,O
Georgia State University	M,D,O*
Golden Gate Baptist Theological Seminary	P,M,D,O
Governors State University	M
Grambling State University	M
Grand Valley State University	M
Harding University	M,O
Hebrew College	M,O
Henderson State University	M,O
Hofstra University	M,O*
Hood College	M,O
Howard University	M,O*
Hunter College of the City University of New York	M,O
Indiana State University	M*
Indiana University of Pennsylvania	M
Inter American University of Puerto Rico, Guayama Campus	M
Jackson State University	M,D,O
Jacksonville State University	M
Jacksonville University	M,O
James Madison University	M
John Carroll University	M
Kean University	M
Kennesaw State University	M
Kent State University	M*
Keuka College	M
Kutztown University of Pennsylvania	M,O
Lehman College of the City University of New York	M
Lenoir-Rhyne College	M
Lesley University	M,D,O*
Liberty University	M,D,O
Long Island University, C.W. Post Campus	M*
Long Island University, Southampton Graduate Campus	M
Long Island University, Westchester Graduate Campus	M
Loyola College in Maryland	M,O
Manhattan College	M
Manhattanville College	M*
Marshall University	M
Maryville University of Saint Louis	M,D
Marywood University	M*
McNeese State University	M
Mercer University	M,D,O
Mercy College	M
Miami University	M*
Middle Tennessee State University	M,O*
Millersville University of Pennsylvania	M
Mills College	M,D
Minnesota State University Mankato	M
Minot State University	M
Missouri State University	M*
Montana State University–Billings	M
Montclair State University	M,O*
Mount Saint Mary College	M
Murray State University	M
National-Louis University	M,O
Nazareth College of Rochester	M
New Jersey City University	M
New York University	M,D,O*
Norfolk State University	M
North Carolina Agricultural and Technical State University	M
Northeastern State University	M
Northern Arizona University	M
Northern Illinois University	M,D
North Georgia College & State University	M,O
Northwestern State University of Louisiana	M
Northwest Missouri State University	M
Nova Southeastern University	M,D,O*
Oakland University	M,D,O*
Oglethorpe University	M
The Ohio State University at Lima	M
The Ohio State University at Marion	M,D
The Ohio State University–Mansfield Campus	M
The Ohio State University–Newark Campus	M
Ohio University	M*
Oklahoma City University	M
Old Dominion University	M,D*
Ottawa University	M
Pacific University	M
Penn State University Park	M,D*
Piedmont College	M,O
Pittsburg State University	M
Portland State University	M,D
Queens College of the City University of New York	M,O
Regis University	M,O
Rhode Island College	M
Rivier College	M,O
Roberts Wesleyan College	M,O
Roosevelt University	M
Rutgers, The State University of New Jersey, New Brunswick	M,D*
Saginaw Valley State University	M
St. John's University (NY)	M
Saint Joseph College	M
St. Joseph's College, New York	M*
St. Joseph's College, Suffolk Campus	M
Saint Mary's College of California	M
Saint Xavier University	M,O
Salem College	M
Salem State College	M
Salisbury University	M
Samford University	M,D,O
Sam Houston State University	M
San Francisco State University	M
Siena Heights University	M
Slippery Rock University of Pennsylvania	M
South Carolina State University	M
Southern Oregon University	M
Southwestern Oklahoma State University	M
Spring Hill College	M
State University of New York at Binghamton	M*
State University of New York at New Paltz	M
State University of New York College at Cortland	M*
State University of New York College at Geneseo	M
Stephen F. Austin State University	M
Sunbridge College	M
Syracuse University	M*
Teachers College Columbia University	M,D*
Temple University	M,D*
Tennessee Technological University	M,O*
Texas A&M International University	M,D
Texas A&M University–Commerce	M,D
Texas A&M University–Corpus Christi	M,D
Texas A&M University–Kingsville	M
Texas Southern University	M,D
Texas State University-San Marcos	M*
Texas Woman's University	M,D
Touro University International	M
Towson University	M,O
Trinity (Washington) University	M
Troy University	M,O
Tufts University	M,D,O*
Universidad Metropolitana	M
University at Buffalo, the State University of New York	M,D,O*
The University of Alabama at Birmingham	M,D*
University of Alaska Anchorage	M,O
University of Alaska Southeast	M
University of Arkansas	M*
University of Arkansas at Little Rock	M
University of Bridgeport	M,O
The University of British Columbia	M,D*
University of Central Arkansas	M
University of Central Florida	M*
University of Central Oklahoma	M
University of Cincinnati	M
University of Colorado at Denver and Health Sciences Center	M*
University of Dayton	M*
University of Detroit Mercy	M
The University of Findlay	M
University of Florida	M,D,O*
University of Georgia	M,D,O*
University of Hartford	M*
University of Hawaii at Manoa	M*
University of Houston	M,D*
University of Houston–Clear Lake	M
The University of Iowa	M,D*
University of Kentucky	M,D*
University of Louisville	M
University of Mary	M
University of Maryland, Baltimore County	M*
University of Maryland, College Park	M,D*
University of Massachusetts Amherst	M,D,O*
University of Memphis	M,D*
University of Miami	M,O*
University of Michigan	M,D*
University of Michigan–Flint	M*
University of Minnesota, Twin Cities Campus	M,D,O*
University of Missouri–Columbia	M,D,O*
University of Montevallo	M
University of New Hampshire	M*
The University of North Carolina at Chapel Hill	M,D*
The University of North Carolina at Greensboro	M,D,O
University of North Dakota	M
University of Northern Colorado	M,D
University of Northern Iowa	M
University of Northern Virginia	M,D
University of North Texas	M,D*
University of Oklahoma	M,D,O*
University of Pennsylvania	M*
University of Phoenix–Louisiana Campus	M
University of Phoenix Online Campus	M
University of Phoenix–Oregon Campus	M
University of Phoenix–Puerto Rico Campus	M
University of Pittsburgh	M*
University of Portland	M
University of Puerto Rico, Río Piedras	M*
The University of Scranton	M
University of South Alabama	M,O*
University of South Carolina	M,D*
University of South Carolina Upstate	M
University of Southern Mississippi	M,D,O*
University of South Florida	M,D,O*
The University of Tennessee	M,D,O*
The University of Texas at Brownsville	M
The University of Texas at San Antonio	M*
The University of Texas at Tyler	M
The University of Texas of the Permian Basin	M
The University of Texas–Pan American	M
University of the Cumberlands	M
University of the District of Columbia	M
University of the Incarnate Word	M,D
University of the Sacred Heart	M
The University of Toledo	M,O*
University of Victoria	M,D
University of West Alabama	M
University of West Florida	M
University of West Georgia	M,O
University of Wisconsin–Milwaukee	M
University of Wisconsin–Oshkosh	M
Valdosta State University	M,O
Vanderbilt University	M,D*
Virginia Commonwealth University	M,O*
Wagner College	M
Walden University	M,D
Wayne State College	M
Wayne State University	M,D,O*
Webster University	M
Wesleyan College	M
Western Kentucky University	M
Western Michigan University	M*
Western Oregon University	M
Westfield State College	M
West Virginia University	M,D*
Wheelock College	M
Widener University	M,D*
Worcester State College	M
Wright State University	M*
Xavier University	M*
Youngstown State University	M

EAST EUROPEAN AND RUSSIAN STUDIES

Boston College	M*
Carleton University	M,O
Columbia University	M,O*
Cornell University	M,D*
Florida State University	M*
Georgetown University	M*
The George Washington University	M*
Harvard University	M*
Indiana University Bloomington	M,O*
The Johns Hopkins University	M,D,O*
La Salle University	M
The Ohio State University	M*
Stanford University	M*
University of Alberta	M,D*
The University of British Columbia	M,D*
University of Illinois at Chicago	M,D*
University of Illinois at Urbana–Champaign	M*
University of Kansas	M*
University of Michigan	M,O*
The University of North Carolina at Chapel Hill	M*
University of Pittsburgh	O*
University of Saskatchewan	M
The University of Texas at Austin	M*
University of Toronto	M
University of Washington	M*
Yale University	M*

ECOLOGY

Arizona State University	M,D*
Brown University	D*
Clemson University	M,D*
Colorado State University	M,D*
Columbia University	D,O*
Cornell University	M,D*
Dartmouth College	D*
Duke University	M,D,O*
Eastern Kentucky University	M*
Emory University	D*
Florida Institute of Technology	M*
Florida State University	M,D*
Frostburg State University	M
Illinois State University	M,D*
Indiana State University	M,D*
Indiana University Bloomington	M,D*
Iowa State University of Science and Technology	M,D*
Kent State University	M,D*
Lesley University	M,D,O*
Marquette University	M,D
Michigan State University	D*
Michigan Technological University	M*
Minnesota State University Mankato	M
Montana State University	M,D
North Carolina State University	M,D*
North Dakota State University	M,D
Northern Arizona University	M,O
Nova Scotia Agricultural College	M
The Ohio State University	M,D*
Ohio University	M,D*
Old Dominion University	D*
Penn State University Park	M,D*
Prescott College	M
Princeton University	D*
Purdue University	M,D*
Rice University	M,D*
Rutgers, The State University of New Jersey, New Brunswick	M,D*
San Diego State University	M,D*
San Francisco State University	M
San Jose State University	M
State University of New York College of Environmental Science and Forestry	M,D
Stony Brook University, State University of New York	D*
Texas Christian University	M
Tulane University	M,D*
University at Albany, State University of New York	M,D*
University at Buffalo, the State University of New York	M,D,O*
University of Alberta	M,D*
The University of Arizona	M,D*
University of California, Davis	M,D*
University of California, Irvine	M,D*
University of California, San Diego	D*
University of California, Santa Barbara	M,D*
University of California, Santa Cruz	M,D*
University of Chicago	D*
University of Colorado at Boulder	M,D*
University of Connecticut	M,D*

University of Delaware M,D*
University of Florida M,D*
University of Georgia M,D*
University of Guelph M,D
University of Hawaii at Manoa M,D*
University of Illinois at Chicago M,D*
University of Illinois at Urbana–Champaign M,D*
University of Kansas M,D*
University of Maine M,D*
University of Maryland, College Park M,D*
University of Michigan M,D*
University of Minnesota, Twin Cities Campus M,D*
University of Missouri–Columbia M,D*
University of Missouri–St. Louis M,D,O
The University of Montana M,D*
University of Nevada, Reno D*
The University of North Carolina at Chapel Hill M,D*
University of North Dakota M,D
University of Notre Dame M,D*
University of Oregon M,D*
University of Pittsburgh D*
University of St. Michael's College P,M,D,O
University of South Carolina M,D*
University of South Florida M,D*
The University of Tennessee M,D*
The University of Texas at Austin D*
The University of Toledo M,D*
University of Utah M,D*
University of Wisconsin–Madison M,D*
Utah State University M,D
Virginia Polytechnic Institute and State University M,D*
Washington University in St. Louis D*
William Paterson University of New Jersey M*
Yale University D*

ECONOMICS

Alabama Agricultural and Mechanical University M
Albany State University M
American University M,D,O*
The American University in Cairo M
American University of Beirut M
Andrews University M
Arizona State University M,D*
Auburn University M*
Baylor University M*
Bernard M. Baruch College of the City University of New York M*
Boston College D*
Boston University M,D*
Bowling Green State University M*
Brandeis University M,D*
Brock University M
Brooklyn College of the City University of New York M
Brown University M,D*
Buffalo State College, State University of New York M
California State Polytechnic University, Pomona M
California State University, East Bay M
California State University, Fullerton M
California State University, Long Beach M
California State University, Los Angeles M
Cardean University M
Carleton University M,D
Carnegie Mellon University M,D*
Case Western Reserve University M*
The Catholic University of America M*
Central European University M,D*
Central Michigan University M*
City College of the City University of New York M*
Claremont Graduate University M,D,O
Clark Atlanta University M
Clark University D*
Clemson University M,D*
Cleveland State University M,O
Colorado State University M,D*
Columbia University M,D*
Concordia University (Canada) M,D,O
Cornell University M,D*
Dalhousie University M,D
DePaul University M*
Drexel University M,D,O*
Duke University M,D*
East Carolina University M*
Eastern Illinois University M
Eastern Michigan University M
Eastern University M*
East Tennessee State University M
Emory University D*
Florida Agricultural and Mechanical University M*
Florida Atlantic University M
Florida International University M,D*
Florida State University M,D*
Fordham University M,D,O*
George Mason University M,D*
Georgetown University D*
The George Washington University M,D*
Georgia Institute of Technology M*
Georgia State University M,D*
Graduate School and University Center of the City University of New York D*
Harvard University D*
Hawai'i Pacific University M*
Howard University M,D*
Hunter College of the City University of New York M
Illinois State University M*
Indiana University Bloomington M,D*
Indiana University–Purdue University Indianapolis M*
Indiana University Southeast M,O
Instituto Centroamericano de Administración de Empresas M
Instituto Tecnológico y de Estudios Superiores de Monterrey, Campus Ciudad de México M,D
Iowa State University of Science and Technology M,D*
The Johns Hopkins University D*
Kansas State University M,D*
Kent State University M*
Lakehead University M
Lehigh University M,D*
Long Island University, Brooklyn Campus M*
Louisiana State University and Agricultural and Mechanical College M,D*
Louisiana Tech University M,D
Loyola College in Maryland M
Marquette University M
Massachusetts Institute of Technology M,D*
McGill University M,D*
McMaster University M,D
Memorial University of Newfoundland M
Miami University M*
Michigan State University M,D*
Middle Tennessee State University M,D*
Mississippi State University M,D
Montclair State University M*
Morgan State University M*
Murray State University M
National University M
New Mexico State University M
The New School: A University M,D*
New York Institute of Technology M,O
New York University M,D,O*
North Carolina State University M,D*
Northeastern University M,D*
Northern Illinois University M,D
Northwestern University M,D*
Oakland University O*
The Ohio State University M,D*
Ohio University M*
Oklahoma State University M,D*
Old Dominion University M*
Oregon State University M,D*
Pace University M*
Penn State University Park M,D*
Pepperdine University M*
Portland State University M,D,O
Princeton University D,O*
Purdue University D*
Quinnipiac University M*
Regent University M
Rensselaer Polytechnic Institute M*
Rice University M,D*
Roosevelt University M
Rutgers, The State University of New Jersey, Newark M*
Rutgers, The State University of New Jersey, New Brunswick M,D*
St. Cloud State University M
San Diego State University M*
San Francisco State University M
San Jose State University M
Seattle Pacific University M
Simon Fraser University M,D
South Dakota State University M
Southern Illinois University Carbondale M,D*
Southern Illinois University Edwardsville M
Southern Methodist University M,D*
Southern New Hampshire University M,D*
Stanford University D*
State University of New York at Binghamton M,D*
Stony Brook University, State University of New York M,D*
Suffolk University M,D*
Syracuse University M,D*
Tarleton State University M
Teachers College Columbia University M,D*
Temple University M,D*
Texas A&M University M,D*
Texas A&M University–Commerce M
Texas Tech University M,D
Trinity College M
Tufts University M*
Tulane University M,D*
Universidad de las Américas–Puebla M
Universidad Nacional Pedro Henriquez Urena P,M,D
Université de Moncton M
Université de Montréal M,D
Université de Sherbrooke M
Université du Québec à Montréal M,D
Université Laval M,D
University at Albany, State University of New York M,D,O*
University at Buffalo, the State University of New York M,D,O*
The University of Akron M
The University of Alabama M,D
University of Alaska Fairbanks M
University of Alberta M,D*
The University of Arizona M,D*
University of Arkansas M,D*
The University of British Columbia M,D*
University of Calgary M,D
University of California, Berkeley D*
University of California, Davis M,D*
University of California, Irvine M,D*
University of California, Los Angeles M,D*
University of California, Riverside M,D*
University of California, San Diego M,D*
University of California, Santa Barbara M,D*
University of California, Santa Cruz D*
University of Central Arkansas M
University of Central Florida M,D*
University of Chicago D*
University of Cincinnati M
University of Colorado at Boulder M,D*
University of Colorado at Denver and Health Sciences Center M*
University of Connecticut M,D*
University of Delaware M,D*
University of Denver M*
University of Florida M,D*
University of Georgia M,D*
University of Guelph M,D
University of Hawaii at Manoa M,D*
University of Houston M,D*
University of Illinois at Chicago M,D*
University of Illinois at Urbana–Champaign M,D*
The University of Iowa D*
University of Kansas M,D*
University of Kentucky M,D*
University of Lethbridge M,D
University of Maine M*
University of Manitoba M,D
University of Maryland, Baltimore County M*
University of Maryland, College Park M,D*
University of Massachusetts Amherst M,D*
University of Massachusetts Lowell M*
University of Memphis M,D*
University of Miami M,D*
University of Michigan M,D*
University of Minnesota, Twin Cities Campus D*
University of Mississippi M,D
University of Missouri–Columbia M,D*
University of Missouri–Kansas City M,D*
University of Missouri–St. Louis M,O
The University of Montana M*
University of Nebraska at Omaha M
University of Nebraska–Lincoln M,D*
University of Nevada, Las Vegas M
University of Nevada, Reno M*
University of New Brunswick Fredericton M
University of New Hampshire M,D*
University of New Mexico M,D*
University of New Orleans D
The University of North Carolina at Chapel Hill M,D*
The University of North Carolina at Charlotte M*
The University of North Carolina at Greensboro D
University of North Texas M*
University of Notre Dame M,D*
University of Oklahoma M,D*
University of Oregon M,D*
University of Ottawa M,D*
University of Pennsylvania M,D*
University of Pittsburgh M,D,O*
University of Puerto Rico, Río Piedras M*
University of Regina M,D,O
University of Rhode Island M,D
University of Rochester M,D*
University of San Francisco M
University of Saskatchewan M
University of South Carolina M,D*
University of Southern California M,D*
University of Southern Mississippi M,D*
University of South Florida M,D*
The University of Tampa M
The University of Tennessee M,D*
The University of Texas at Arlington M*
The University of Texas at Austin M,D*
The University of Texas at Dallas M,D*
The University of Texas at El Paso M
The University of Texas at San Antonio M*
The University of Toledo M*
University of Toronto M,D
University of Utah M,D*
University of Victoria M,D
University of Virginia M,D*
University of Washington M,D*
University of Waterloo M,D*
The University of Western Ontario M,D
University of Windsor M
University of Wisconsin–Madison D*
University of Wisconsin–Milwaukee M,D
University of Wyoming M,D
Utah State University M,D
Vanderbilt University P,M,D*
Virginia Commonwealth University M*
Virginia Polytechnic Institute and State University M,D*
Virginia State University M
Walsh College of Accountancy and Business Administration M
Washington State University M,D,O*
Washington University in St. Louis M,D*
Wayne State University M,D,O*
West Chester University of Pennsylvania M
Western Illinois University M
Western Michigan University M,D*
West Texas A&M University M
West Virginia University M,D*
Wichita State University M*
Wilfrid Laurier University M
Wright State University M*
Yale University M,D*
York University M,D*
Youngstown State University M

EDUCATION—GENERAL

Abilene Christian University M,O
Acadia University M
Adams State College M
Adelphi University M,D,O*
Alabama Agricultural and Mechanical University M,O
Alabama State University M,D,O
Alaska Pacific University M
Albany State University M,O
Albertson College of Idaho M
Albright College M
Alcorn State University M,O
Alfred University M,O*
Alliant International University–Fresno M*
Alliant International University–Irvine M,O*
Alliant International University–Los Angeles M*
Alliant International University–México City M*
Alliant International University–Sacramento M*

*P—first professional degree; M—master's degree; D—doctorate; O—other advanced degree; *full description and/or announcement in Book 2, 3, 4, 5, or 6*

Alliant International University–San Diego	M,O*
Alliant International University–San Francisco	M,O*
Alvernia College	M
Alverno College	M
American InterContinental University (CA)	M
American InterContinental University Online	M
American International College	M,D,O
American Jewish University	M
American University	M,D,O*
American University of Beirut	M
American University of Puerto Rico	M
Anderson University	M
Andrews University	M,D,O
Angelo State University	M
Anna Maria College	M,O
Antioch University Los Angeles	M
Antioch University McGregor	M*
Antioch University New England	M*
Antioch University Santa Barbara	M
Antioch University Seattle	M*
Appalachian State University	M,D,O
Aquinas College	M
Arcadia University	M,D,O
Argosy University, Atlanta Campus	M,D,O*
Argosy University, Chicago Campus	M,D,O*
Argosy University, Dallas Campus	M*
Argosy University, Denver Campus	M,D*
Argosy University, Hawai'i Campus	M,D*
Argosy University, Orange County Campus	M,D*
Argosy University, Phoenix Campus	M,D,O*
Argosy University, San Diego Campus	M,D*
Argosy University, San Francisco Bay Area Campus	M,D*
Argosy University, Santa Monica Campus	M,D*
Argosy University, Sarasota Campus	M,D,O*
Argosy University, Schaumburg Campus	M,D,O*
Argosy University, Seattle Campus	M,D*
Argosy University, Tampa Campus	M,D,O*
Argosy University, Twin Cities Campus	M,D,O*
Argosy University, Washington DC Campus	M,D,O*
Arizona State University	M,D*
Arizona State University at the Polytechnic Campus	M,D
Arizona State University at the West campus	M,D,O
Arkansas State University	M,D,O
Arkansas Tech University	M,O
Armstrong Atlantic State University	M
Ashland University	M,D
Athabasca University	M,O
Atlantic Union College	M
Auburn University	M,D,O*
Auburn University Montgomery	M,O
Augsburg College	M
Augustana College	M
Augusta State University	M,O
Aurora University	M,D
Austin College	M
Austin Peay State University	M,O
Averett University	M
Avila University	M,O*
Azusa Pacific University	M,D
Baker University	M,D
Baldwin-Wallace College	M
Ball State University	M,D,O*
Bank Street College of Education	M*
Bard College	M*
Barry University	M,D,O*
Bayamón Central University	M
Baylor University	M,D,O*
Belhaven College (MS)	M
Bellarmine University	M
Belmont University	M
Bemidji State University	M
Benedictine University	M
Bennington College	M*
Berry College	M,O
Bethany University	M
Bethel College (IN)	M
Bethel College (TN)	M
Bethel University	M,D,O
Biola University	M
Bishop's University	M,O
Black Hills State University	M*
Bloomsburg University of Pennsylvania	M
Bluffton University	M
Boise State University	M,D
Boston College	M,D,O*
Boston University	M,D,O*
Bowie State University	M
Bradley University	M,D
Brandon University	M,O
Brenau University	M,O
Briar Cliff University	M
Bridgewater State College	M,O
Brigham Young University	M,D,O*
Brock University	M,D
Brooklyn College of the City University of New York	M,O
Brown University	M*
Bucknell University	M
Buena Vista University	M
Butler University	M
Cabrini College	M,O
California Baptist University	M
California Lutheran University	M,O
California Polytechnic State University, San Luis Obispo	M
California State Polytechnic University, Pomona	M
California State University, Bakersfield	M,O
California State University, Chico	M
California State University, Dominguez Hills	M,O
California State University, East Bay	M
California State University, Fresno	M,D
California State University, Fullerton	M
California State University, Long Beach	M,D
California State University, Los Angeles	M
California State University, Monterey Bay	M
California State University, Northridge	M
California State University, Sacramento	M*
California State University, San Bernardino	M
California State University, San Marcos	M
California State University, Stanislaus	M
California University of Pennsylvania	M
Calvin College	M
Cambridge College	M,D,O
Cameron University	M
Campbellsville University	M
Campbell University	M
Canisius College	M
Cape Breton University	O
Capella University	M,D,O
Cardinal Stritch University	M,D*
Caribbean University	M,D
Carlow University	M
Carnegie Mellon University	M,D*
Carroll College	M
Carson-Newman College	M
Carthage College	M,O
Castleton State College	M,O
Catawba College	M
The Catholic University of America	M,D*
Cedar Crest College	M*
Cedarville University	M
Centenary College	M
Centenary College of Louisiana	M
Central Connecticut State University	M,D,O
Central Methodist University	M
Central Michigan University	M,D,O*
Central State University	M
Central Washington University	M
Chadron State College	M,O
Chaminade University of Honolulu	M
Chapman University	M,D,O
Charleston Southern University	M
Chatham University	M
Chestnut Hill College	M
Cheyney University of Pennsylvania	M,O
Chicago State University	M,D
Christian Brothers University	M
Christopher Newport University	M
The Citadel, The Military College of South Carolina	M,O
City College of the City University of New York	M,O*
City University	M,O
Claflin University	M
Claremont Graduate University	M,D,O
Clarion University of Pennsylvania	M,O
Clark Atlanta University	M,D,O
Clarke College	M
Clark University	M*
Clemson University	M,D,O*
Cleveland State University	M,D,O
Coastal Carolina University	M
Coe College	M
College Misericordia	M
College of Charleston	M,O*
College of Mount St. Joseph	M
College of Mount Saint Vincent	M,O
The College of New Jersey	M,O
The College of New Rochelle	M,O
College of Notre Dame of Maryland	M
College of St. Catherine	M*
College of Saint Elizabeth	M,O
College of St. Joseph	M
The College of Saint Rose	M,O*
The College of St. Scholastica	M,O
College of Santa Fe	M
College of Staten Island of the City University of New York	M,O
College of the Humanities and Sciences, Harrison Middleton University	M,D
College of the Southwest	M
The College of William and Mary	M,D,O
Collège universitaire de Saint-Boniface	M
Colorado Christian University	M
The Colorado College	M
Columbia College (MO)	M
Columbia College (SC)	M
Columbia College Chicago	M
Columbia International University	M,D,O
Columbus State University	M,O
Concordia University (CA)	M
Concordia University (IL)	M
Concordia University (OR)	M
Concordia University (NE)	M
Concordia University (Canada)	M,D,O
Concordia University at Austin	M
Concordia University, St. Paul	M,O
Concordia University Wisconsin	M
Connecticut College	M
Converse College	M,O
Coppin State University	M
Cornell University	M,D*
Cornerstone University	M,O
Covenant College	M
Creighton University	M*
Cumberland University	M
Curry College	M,O
Daemen College	M
Dakota State University	M*
Dallas Baptist University	M
Defiance College	M
Delaware State University	M
Delta State University	M,D,O
DePaul University	M*
DeSales University	M
Doane College	M
Dominican College	M
Dominican University	M
Dominican University of California	M,O
Dordt College	M
Dowling College	M,D,O
Drake University	M,D,O*
Drexel University	M,D,O*
Drury University	M*
Duke University	M*
Duquesne University	M,D,O*
D'Youville College	M,O*
Earlham College	M
East Carolina University	M,D,O*
East Central University	M
Eastern Connecticut State University	M
Eastern Illinois University	M,O
Eastern Kentucky University	M*
Eastern Mennonite University	M
Eastern Michigan University	M,D,O
Eastern Nazarene College	M,O
Eastern New Mexico University	M
Eastern Oregon University	M
Eastern University	M,O*
Eastern Washington University	M
East Stroudsburg University of Pennsylvania	M
East Tennessee State University	M,D,O
Edgewood College	M,D,O
Edinboro University of Pennsylvania	M,O
Elms College	M,O
Elon University	M
Emmanuel College	M,O
Emory University	M,D,O*
Emporia State University	M,O
Evangel University	M
The Evergreen State College	M
Fairfield University	M,O*
Fairleigh Dickinson University, College at Florham	M,O*
Fairleigh Dickinson University, Metropolitan Campus	M,O*
Fairmont State University	M
Felician College	M*
Ferris State University	M
Florida Agricultural and Mechanical University	M,D*
Florida Atlantic University	M,D,O
Florida Atlantic University, Jupiter Campus	M
Florida Gulf Coast University	M
Florida International University	M,D,O*
Florida Southern College	M
Florida State University	M,D,O*
Fontbonne University	M
Fordham University	M,D,O*
Fort Hays State University	M,O
Franciscan University of Steubenville	M
Francis Marion University	M
Freed-Hardeman University	M,O
Fresno Pacific University	M
Friends University	M
Frostburg State University	M
Furman University	M
Gallaudet University	M,D,O
Gannon University	M,O
Gardner-Webb University	M,D
Geneva College	M*
George Fox University	M,D,O*
George Mason University	M,D*
Georgetown College	M
The George Washington University	M,D,O*
Georgia College & State University	M,O
Georgian Court University	M,O
Georgia Southern University	M,D,O
Georgia Southwestern State University	M,O
Georgia State University	M,D,O*
Goddard College	M
Gonzaga University	M
Gordon College	M
Goucher College	M
Governors State University	M
Graceland University	M
Grambling State University	M,D
Grand Canyon University	M*
Grand Valley State University	M
Gratz College	M
Greensboro College	M
Greenville College	M
Gwynedd-Mercy College	M
Hamline University	M,D
Hampton University	M*
Harding University	M,O
Hardin-Simmons University	M
Harvard University	M,D*
Hastings College	M
Hebrew College	M,O
Hebrew Union College–Jewish Institute of Religion (CA)	M,D,O
Hebrew Union College–Jewish Institute of Religion (NY)	M
Heidelberg College	M
Henderson State University	M,O
Heritage University	M
Hodges University	M
Hofstra University	M,D,O*
Hollins University	M
Holy Family University	M
Holy Names University	M,O
Hood College	M,O
Hope International University	M
Houston Baptist University	M
Howard University	M,D,O*
Humboldt State University	M
Hunter College of the City University of New York	M,O
Idaho State University	M,D,O
Illinois State University	M,D*
Indiana State University	M,D,O*
Indiana University Bloomington	M,D,O*
Indiana University Kokomo	M
Indiana University Northwest	M
Indiana University of Pennsylvania	M,D,O
Indiana University–Purdue University Fort Wayne	M
Indiana University–Purdue University Indianapolis	M,O*
Indiana University South Bend	M
Indiana University Southeast	M
Indiana Wesleyan University	M
Institute for Christian Studies	M,D
Instituto Tecnologico de Santo Domingo	M
Instituto Tecnológico y de Estudios Superiores de Monterrey, Campus Central de Veracruz	M
Instituto Tecnológico y de Estudios Superiores de Monterrey, Campus Ciudad de México	M,D
Instituto Tecnológico y de Estudios Superiores de Monterrey, Campus Ciudad Juárez	M
Instituto Tecnológico y de Estudios Superiores de Monterrey, Campus Ciudad Obregón	M
Instituto Tecnológico y de Estudios Superiores de Monterrey, Campus Estado de México	M,D
Instituto Tecnológico y de Estudios Superiores de Monterrey, Campus Irapuato	M,D
Instituto Tecnológico y de Estudios Superiores de	

Monterrey, Campus Sonora Norte M
Inter American University of Puerto Rico, Arecibo Campus M
Inter American University of Puerto Rico, Barranquitas Campus M
Inter American University of Puerto Rico, Metropolitan Campus M,D
Jackson State University M,D,O
Jacksonville State University M,O
Jacksonville University M,O
John Carroll University M
John F. Kennedy University M
The Johns Hopkins University M,D,O*
Johnson & Wales University M*
Johnson Bible College M
Johnson State College M,O
Jones International University M
Kansas State University M,D*
Kean University M,O
Keene State College M,O
Kennesaw State University M
Kent State University M,D,O*
Kutztown University of Pennsylvania M,O
LaGrange College M
Lake Erie College M
Lakehead University M,D
Lakeland College M
Lamar University M,D,O*
Lander University M
Langston University M
La Salle University M
La Sierra University M,D,O
Lee University M
Lehigh University M,D,O*
Lehman College of the City University of New York M
Le Moyne College M
Lenoir-Rhyne College M
Lesley University M,D,O*
Lewis & Clark College M,D,O
Lewis University M,O
Liberty University M,D,O
Lincoln Memorial University M,O
Lincoln University (MO) M,O
Lindenwood University M,D,O
Lipscomb University M
Lock Haven University of Pennsylvania M
Long Island University, Brentwood Campus M
Long Island University, Brooklyn Campus M,O*
Long Island University, C.W. Post Campus M,O*
Long Island University, Southampton Graduate Campus M
Long Island University, Westchester Graduate Campus M
Longwood University M*
Louisiana State University and Agricultural and Mechanical College M,D,O*
Louisiana State University in Shreveport M
Louisiana Tech University M,D
Lourdes College M
Loyola College in Maryland M,O
Loyola Marymount University M,D
Loyola University Chicago M,D,O*
Loyola University New Orleans M
Lynchburg College M
Lyndon State College M
Madonna University M
Maharishi University of Management M
Malone College M
Manhattan College M,O
Manhattanville College M*
Mansfield University of Pennsylvania M
Marian College M
Marian College of Fond du Lac M,D
Marietta College M
Marist College M,O*
Marlboro College M
Marquette University M,D,O
Marshall University M,D,O
Mary Baldwin College M
Marygrove College M
Marymount University M,O
Maryville University of Saint Louis M,D
Marywood University M*
Massachusetts College of Liberal Arts M
McGill University M,D,O*
McKendree College M
McNeese State University M
Medaille College M
Memorial University of Newfoundland M,D,O
Mercer University M,D,O
Mercy College M
Meredith College M
Merrimack College M
Miami University M,D,O*
Michigan State University M,D,O*
MidAmerica Nazarene University M
Middle Tennessee State University M,D,O*
Midwestern State University M
Millersville University of Pennsylvania M
Milligan College M
Mills College M,D
Minnesota State University Mankato M,O
Minnesota State University Moorhead M,O
Mississippi College M,O
Mississippi State University M,D,O
Mississippi University for Women M
Mississippi Valley State University M
Missouri State University M*
Monmouth University M,O
Montana State University M,D,O
Montana State University–Billings M,O
Montana State University–Northern M
Montclair State University M,O*
Montreat College M
Moravian College M
Morehead State University M,O
Morgan State University M,D*
Morningside College M
Mount Mary College M
Mount Saint Mary College M
Mount St. Mary's College M
Mount St. Mary's University M
Mount Saint Vincent University M
Mount Vernon Nazarene University M
Murray State University M,D,O
Muskingum College M
Naropa University M*
National-Louis University M,D,O
National University M
Nazareth College of Rochester M
Neumann College M
New College of California M*
New England College M
Newman University M
New Mexico Highlands University M
New Mexico State University M,D,O
New York Institute of Technology M,O
New York University M,D,O*
Niagara University M,O
Nicholls State University M
Nipissing University M,O
Norfolk State University M
North Carolina Agricultural and Technical State University M
North Carolina Central University M
North Carolina State University M,D,O*
North Central College M
North Dakota State University M,D,O
Northeastern Illinois University M
Northeastern State University M
Northern Arizona University M,D,O
Northern Illinois University M,D,O
Northern Kentucky University M,O
Northern Michigan University M,O
Northern State University M
North Georgia College & State University M,O
North Park University M
Northwestern Oklahoma State University M
Northwestern State University of Louisiana M,O
Northwestern University M,D*
Northwest Missouri State University M,O
Northwest Nazarene University M
Northwest University M
Norwich University M
Notre Dame College (OH) M,O
Notre Dame de Namur University M
Nova Southeastern University M,D,O*
Nyack College M
Oakland City University M,D
Oakland University M,D,O*
Occidental College M
Oglethorpe University M
Ohio Dominican University M
The Ohio State University M,D*
The Ohio State University at Lima M
The Ohio State University at Marion M,D
The Ohio State University–Newark Campus M
Ohio University M,D*
Oklahoma City University M
Oklahoma State University M,D,O*
Old Dominion University M,D,O*
Olivet College M
Olivet Nazarene University M
Oral Roberts University M,D
Oregon State University M,D*
Oregon State University–Cascades M
Ottawa University M
Otterbein College M
Our Lady of Holy Cross College M
Our Lady of the Lake University of San Antonio M,D
Pace University M,O*
Pacific Lutheran University M
Pacific Union College M
Pacific University M
Palm Beach Atlantic University M
Park University M
Penn State Great Valley M
Penn State Harrisburg M,D*
Penn State University Park M,D*
Pepperdine University M,D*
Peru State College M
Pfeiffer University M
Philadelphia Biblical University M
Piedmont College M,O
Pittsburg State University M,O
Plymouth State University O
Point Loma Nazarene University M,O
Point Park University M*
Pontifical Catholic University of Puerto Rico M,D
Portland State University M,D
Prairie View A&M University M,D
Prescott College M,D
Providence College M*
Purdue University M,D,O*
Purdue University Calumet M
Purdue University North Central M
Queens College of the City University of New York M,O
Queen's University at Kingston M,D
Queens University of Charlotte M
Quincy University M
Quinnipiac University M*
Radford University M
Regent University M,D,O
Regis College (MA) M,O
Regis University M,O
Rhode Island College D
Rice University M*
The Richard Stockton College of New Jersey M
Rider University M,O*
Rivier College M,O
Roberts Wesleyan College M,O
Rockford College M
Rockhurst University M
Roger Williams University M*
Rollins College M
Roosevelt University M,D
Rowan University M,D,O
Rutgers, The State University of New Jersey, New Brunswick M,D*
Sacred Heart University M,O
Sage Graduate School M,O
Saginaw Valley State University M,O
St. Ambrose University M
St. Bonaventure University M,O
St. Cloud State University M,O
St. Edward's University M
Saint Francis University M
St. Francis Xavier University M
St. John Fisher College M,D,O
St. John's University (NY) M,D,O
Saint Joseph College M
St. Joseph's College, New York M*
Saint Joseph's College of Maine M
Saint Joseph's University M,D,O*
St. Lawrence University M,O
Saint Leo University M
Saint Louis University M,D*
Saint Martin's University M
Saint Mary's College of California M,D
Saint Mary's University of Minnesota M
St. Mary's University of San Antonio M,O
Saint Michael's College M,O
St. Norbert College M
Saint Peter's College M,O
St. Thomas Aquinas College M,O*
St. Thomas University M,D,O
Saint Vincent College M
Saint Xavier University M,O
Salem College M
Salem International University M
Salem State College M
Salisbury University M
Samford University M,D,O
San Diego State University M,D*
San Francisco State University M,D,O
San Jose State University M,O
Santa Clara University M,O
Sarah Lawrence College M*
School for International Training M
Schreiner University M
Seattle Pacific University M,D
Seattle University M,D,O
Seton Hall University M,D,O*
Seton Hill University M
Shenandoah University M,D,O*
Shippensburg University of Pennsylvania M,O
Siena Heights University M
Sierra Nevada College M
Silver Lake College M
Simmons College M,D,O
Simon Fraser University M,D
Simpson University M
Sinte Gleska University M
Slippery Rock University of Pennsylvania M
Smith College M*
Sonoma State University M
South Dakota State University M
Southeastern Louisiana University M,D
Southeastern Oklahoma State University M
Southern Adventist University M
Southern Arkansas University–Magnolia M
Southern Connecticut State University M,D,O
Southern Illinois University Carbondale M,D*
Southern Illinois University Edwardsville M,O
Southern Methodist University M*
Southern Nazarene University M
Southern New Hampshire University M,O*
Southern Oregon University M
Southern University and Agricultural and Mechanical College M,D*
Southern Utah University M
Southern Wesleyan University M
Southwest Baptist University M,O
Southwestern Adventist University M
Southwestern Assemblies of God University M
Southwestern College (KS) M
Southwestern Oklahoma State University M
Southwest Minnesota State University M
Spalding University M,D
Spring Arbor University M
Springfield College M*
Spring Hill College M
Stanford University M,D*
State University of New York at Binghamton M,D*
State University of New York at Fredonia M,O
State University of New York at New Paltz M,O
State University of New York at Oswego M,O
State University of New York College at Brockport M*
State University of New York College at Cortland M,O*
State University of New York College at Geneseo M
State University of New York College at Oneonta M,O
State University of New York Empire State College M
Stephen F. Austin State University M,D
Stetson University M,O
Suffolk University M,O*
Sul Ross State University M*
Sunbridge College M
Sweet Briar College M
Syracuse University M,D,O*
Tarleton State University M,D,O
Teachers College Columbia University M,D,O*
Temple University M,D*
Tennessee State University M,D,O*
Tennessee Technological University M,D,O*
Tennessee Temple University M
Texas A&M International University M,D
Texas A&M University M,D*
Texas A&M University–Commerce M,D
Texas A&M University–Corpus Christi M,D
Texas A&M University–Kingsville M,D
Texas A&M University–Texarkana M
Texas Christian University M,D,O
Texas Southern University M,D

P—first professional degree; M—master's degree; D—doctorate; O—other advanced degree;
**full description and/or announcement in Book 2, 3, 4, 5, or 6*

Texas State University-San Marcos M,D*
Texas Tech University M,D,O
Texas Wesleyan University M
Texas Woman's University M,D
Thomas University M
Touro University College of Osteopathic Medicine P,M
Touro University International M,D,O
Towson University M
Trevecca Nazarene University M,D
Trinity Baptist College M
Trinity International University M
Trinity University M*
Trinity (Washington) University M
Troy University M,O
Truman State University M
Tufts University M,D,O*
Tusculum College M
Union College (KY) M
Union Graduate College M*
Union Institute & University M,O
Union University M,D,O
Universidad Adventista de las Antillas M
Universidad Autonoma de Guadalajara M,D
Universidad de las Americas, A.C. M
Universidad de las Américas–Puebla M
Universidad del Este M
Universidad del Turabo M
Universidad Iberoamericana P,M
Universidad Metropolitana M
Universidad Nacional Pedro Henriquez Urena P,M,D
Université de Moncton M
Université de Montréal M,D,O
Université de Sherbrooke M,O
Université du Québec à Chicoutimi M,D
Université du Québec à Montréal M,D,O
Université du Québec à Rimouski M,D,O
Université du Québec à Trois-Rivières M,O
Université du Québec en Abitibi-Témiscamingue M,D
Université du Québec en Outaouais M,D,O
Université Laval M,D,O
University at Albany, State University of New York M,D,O*
University at Buffalo, the State University of New York M,D,O*
The University of Akron M,D
The University of Alabama at Birmingham M,D,O*
University of Alaska Anchorage M,O
University of Alaska Fairbanks M
University of Alaska Southeast M
The University of Arizona M,D,O*
University of Arkansas M,D,O*
University of Arkansas at Little Rock M,D,O
University of Arkansas at Monticello M
University of Arkansas at Pine Bluff M
University of Bridgeport M,D,O
The University of British Columbia M,D,O*
University of California, Berkeley M,D*
University of California, Davis M,D*
University of California, Irvine M,D*
University of California, Los Angeles M,D*
University of California, Riverside M,D*
University of California, San Diego M,D*
University of California, Santa Barbara M,D*
University of California, Santa Cruz M,D*
University of Central Arkansas M
University of Central Florida M,D,O*
University of Central Missouri M,D,O
University of Central Oklahoma M
University of Cincinnati M,D,O
University of Colorado at Boulder M,D*
University of Colorado at Colorado Springs M,D
University of Colorado at Denver and Health Sciences Center M,D,O*
University of Connecticut M,D*
University of Dayton M,D,O*
University of Delaware M,D*
University of Denver M,D,O*
University of Detroit Mercy M
University of Evansville M
The University of Findlay M
University of Florida M,D,O*
University of Georgia M,D,O*
University of Great Falls M
University of Guam M
University of Hartford M,D,O*
University of Hawaii at Manoa M,D,O*
University of Houston M,D*
University of Houston–Clear Lake M,D
University of Houston–Victoria M*
University of Idaho M,D,O*
University of Illinois at Chicago M,D*
University of Illinois at Urbana–Champaign M,D,O*
University of Indianapolis M
The University of Iowa M,D,O*
University of Kansas M,D,O*
University of Kentucky M,D,O*
University of La Verne M,O
University of Lethbridge M,D
University of Louisiana at Lafayette M,D*
University of Louisiana at Monroe M,D,O
University of Louisville M,D,O
University of Maine M,D,O*
University of Manitoba M,D
University of Mary M
University of Mary Hardin-Baylor M,D
University of Maryland, Baltimore County M,O*
University of Maryland, College Park M,D,O*
University of Maryland Eastern Shore M*
University of Maryland University College M
University of Mary Washington M
University of Massachusetts Amherst M,D,O*
University of Massachusetts Boston M,D,O
University of Massachusetts Dartmouth M,O
University of Massachusetts Lowell M,D,O*
University of Memphis M,D*
University of Miami M,D,O*
University of Michigan M,D*
University of Michigan–Dearborn M*
University of Michigan–Flint M*
University of Minnesota, Duluth D*
University of Minnesota, Twin Cities Campus M,D,O*
University of Mississippi M,D,O
University of Missouri–Columbia M,D,O*
University of Missouri–Kansas City M,D,O*
University of Missouri–St. Louis M,D,O
University of Mobile M
The University of Montana M,D,O*
University of Montevallo M,O
University of Nebraska at Kearney M,O
University of Nebraska at Omaha M,D,O
University of Nebraska–Lincoln M,D,O*
University of Nevada, Las Vegas M,D,O
University of Nevada, Reno M,D,O*
University of New Brunswick Fredericton M,D
University of New England M
University of New Hampshire M,D,O*
University of New Hampshire at Manchester M,O
University of New Haven M*
University of New Mexico M,O*
University of New Orleans M,D,O
University of North Alabama M,O
The University of North Carolina at Chapel Hill M,D*
The University of North Carolina at Charlotte M*
The University of North Carolina at Greensboro M,D,O
The University of North Carolina at Pembroke M
The University of North Carolina Wilmington M*
University of North Dakota M,D,O
University of Northern British Columbia M,D,O
University of Northern Colorado M,D,O
University of Northern Iowa M,D,O
University of North Florida M,D
University of North Texas M,D,O*
University of Notre Dame M*
University of Oklahoma M,D*
University of Oregon M,D*
University of Ottawa M,D,O*
University of Pennsylvania M,D*
University of Phoenix–Bay Area Campus M
University of Phoenix–Central Florida Campus M
University of Phoenix–Central Massachusetts Campus M
University of Phoenix–Central Valley Campus M
University of Phoenix–Denver Campus M
University of Phoenix–Fort Lauderdale Campus M
University of Phoenix–Hawaii Campus M
University of Phoenix–Idaho Campus M
University of Phoenix–Kansas City Campus M
University of Phoenix–Las Vegas Campus M
University of Phoenix–Louisiana Campus M
University of Phoenix–Memphis Campus M
University of Phoenix–Metro Detroit Campus M
University of Phoenix–Nashville Campus M
University of Phoenix–New Mexico Campus M
University of Phoenix—Northern Nevada Campus M
University of Phoenix–Northern Virginia Campus M
University of Phoenix–North Florida Campus M
University of Phoenix–Omaha Campus M
University of Phoenix Online Campus M,D
University of Phoenix–Oregon Campus M
University of Phoenix–Phoenix Campus M
University of Phoenix–Puerto Rico Campus M
University of Phoenix–Sacramento Valley Campus M,O
University of Phoenix–San Diego Campus M
University of Phoenix–Southern Arizona Campus M,O
University of Phoenix–Southern California Campus M
University of Phoenix–Southern Colorado Campus M,O
University of Phoenix–Springfield Campus M
University of Phoenix–Utah Campus M
University of Phoenix–Vancouver Campus M
University of Phoenix–West Florida Campus M
University of Phoenix–West Michigan Campus M
University of Pittsburgh M,D*
University of Portland M
University of Prince Edward Island M
University of Puerto Rico, Río Piedras M,D*
University of Puget Sound M
University of Redlands M,D,O
University of Regina M,D
University of Rhode Island M
University of Rio Grande M
University of Rochester M,D*
University of St. Francis (IL) M
University of Saint Francis (IN) M
University of Saint Mary M
University of St. Thomas (MN) M*
University of St. Thomas (TX) M
University of San Diego M,D,O*
University of San Francisco M,D
University of Saskatchewan M,D,O
The University of Scranton M
University of Sioux Falls M,O
University of South Alabama M,D,O*
University of South Carolina M,D,O*
University of South Carolina Aiken M
University of South Carolina Upstate M
The University of South Dakota M,D,O
University of Southern California M,D*
University of Southern Indiana M
University of Southern Maine M,D,O
University of Southern Mississippi M,D,O*
University of South Florida M,D,O*
The University of Tampa M
The University of Tennessee M,D,O*
The University of Tennessee at Chattanooga M,D,O
The University of Tennessee at Martin M
The University of Texas at Arlington M*
The University of Texas at Austin M,D*
The University of Texas at Brownsville M
The University of Texas at El Paso M,D
The University of Texas at San Antonio M,D*
The University of Texas at Tyler M
The University of Texas of the Permian Basin M
The University of Texas–Pan American M,D
University of the Cumberlands M,O
University of the District of Columbia M
University of the Incarnate Word M,D
University of the Pacific M,D,O
University of the Sacred Heart M
University of the Virgin Islands M
The University of Toledo M,D,O*
University of Toronto M,D
University of Tulsa M*
University of Utah M,D*
University of Vermont M,D*
University of Victoria M,D
University of Virginia M,D,O*
University of Washington M,D,O*
University of Washington, Bothell M
The University of West Alabama M
The University of Western Ontario M
University of West Georgia M,D,O
University of Windsor M,D
University of Wisconsin–Eau Claire M
University of Wisconsin–Green Bay M
University of Wisconsin–La Crosse M
University of Wisconsin–Madison M,D,O*
University of Wisconsin–Milwaukee M,D,O
University of Wisconsin–Oshkosh M
University of Wisconsin–Platteville M
University of Wisconsin–River Falls M
University of Wisconsin–Stevens Point M
University of Wisconsin–Stout M,O*
University of Wisconsin–Superior M
University of Wisconsin–Whitewater M*
Urbana University M
Ursuline College M
Utah State University M,D,O
Utica College M,O
Valdosta State University M,D,O
Valparaiso University M
Vanderbilt University M,D*
Vanguard University of Southern California M
Villanova University M*
Virginia Commonwealth University M,D,O*
Virginia State University M,O
Viterbo University M
Wagner College M,O
Wake Forest University M*
Walla Walla College M
Walsh University M
Warner Pacific College M
Washburn University M
Washington State University M,D*
Washington State University Spokane M,O
Washington State University Tri-Cities M,D
Washington State University Vancouver M,D
Washington University in St. Louis M,D*
Wayland Baptist University M
Wayne State College M,O
Wayne State University M,D,O*
Weber State University M
Webster University M,O
Wesleyan College M
Wesley College M
West Chester University of Pennsylvania M,O
Western Carolina University M,D,O*
Western Connecticut State University M*
Western Governors University M,O
Western Illinois University M,D,O
Western Michigan University M,D,O*
Western New Mexico University M
Western Oregon University M
Western Washington University M
Westfield State College M,O
Westminster College (PA) M,O
Westminster College (UT) M
West Texas A&M University M
West Virginia University M,D*
Wheaton College M
Wheelock College M
Whittier College M
Whitworth University M
Wichita State University M,D,O*
Widener University M,D*
Wilkes University M
Willamette University M

William Carey University M,O
William Howard Taft University M
William Paterson University of New Jersey M*
Wilmington College (DE) M
Wilmington College (OH) M
Wingate University M
Winona State University M
Winthrop University M
Wittenberg University M
Worcester State College M
Wright State University M,O*
Xavier University M*
Xavier University of Louisiana M
York College of Pennsylvania M
York University M,D*
Youngstown State University M,D

EDUCATIONAL ADMINISTRATION

Abilene Christian University M,O
Acadia University M
Adelphi University M,O*
Alabama Agricultural and Mechanical University M,O
Alabama State University M,D,O
Albany State University M,O
Alliant International University–Fresno D*
Alliant International University–Irvine M,D,O*
Alliant International University–Los Angeles M,D,O*
Alliant International University–San Diego M,D,O*
Alliant International University–San Francisco M,D,O*
Alverno College M
American InterContinental University Online M
American International College M,D,O
American University M,D*
Andrews University M,D,O
Angelo State University M
Antioch University McGregor M*
Antioch University New England M*
Appalachian State University M,D,O
Arcadia University M,D,O
Argosy University, Atlanta Campus M,D,O*
Argosy University, Chicago Campus M,D,O*
Argosy University, Dallas Campus M*
Argosy University, Denver Campus M,D*
Argosy University, Hawai'i Campus M,D*
Argosy University, Inland Empire Campus M,D*
Argosy University, Nashville Campus M,D*
Argosy University, Orange County Campus M,D*
Argosy University, Phoenix Campus M,D,O*
Argosy University, San Diego Campus M,D*
Argosy University, San Francisco Bay Area Campus M,D*
Argosy University, Santa Monica Campus M,D*
Argosy University, Sarasota Campus M,D,O*
Argosy University, Schaumburg Campus M,D,O*
Argosy University, Seattle Campus M,D*
Argosy University, Tampa Campus M,D,O*
Argosy University, Twin Cities Campus M,D,O*
Argosy University, Washington DC Campus M,D,O*
Arizona State University M,D*
Arizona State University at the Polytechnic Campus M,D
Arizona State University at the West campus M,D,O
Arkansas State University M,D,O
Arkansas Tech University M,O
Ashland University M,D
Auburn University M,D,O*
Auburn University Montgomery M,O
Augusta State University M,O
Aurora University M,D
Austin Peay State University M,O
Azusa Pacific University M,D
Baldwin-Wallace College M
Ball State University M,D,O*
Bank Street College of Education M*
Barry University M,D,O*
Bayamón Central University M
Baylor University M,O*
Bellarmine University M
Benedictine College M
Benedictine University M,D
Bernard M. Baruch College of the City University of New York M*
Bethany University M
Bethel College (TN) M
Bethel University M,D,O
Bob Jones University P,M,D,O
Boise State University M,D
Boston College M,D,O*
Boston University M,O*
Bowie State University M,D
Bowling Green State University M,D,O*
Bradley University M
Brandon University M,O
Bridgewater State College M,O
Brigham Young University M,D*
Brooklyn College of the City University of New York O
Bucknell University M
Buffalo State College, State University of New York O
Butler University M
Cabrini College M,O
Caldwell College M
California Baptist University M
California Lutheran University M
California State University, Bakersfield M
California State University Channel Islands M*
California State University, Chico M
California State University, Dominguez Hills M
California State University, East Bay M
California State University, Fresno M,D
California State University, Fullerton M
California State University, Northridge M
California State University, Sacramento M*
California State University, San Bernardino M
California University of Pennsylvania M
Calvin College M
Cambridge College M,D,O
Cameron University M
Campbell University M
Canisius College M
Capella University M,D,O
Cardinal Stritch University M,D*
Caribbean University M,D
Carlow University M
Carthage College M,O
Castleton State College M,O
The Catholic University of America M,D*
Centenary College M
Centenary College of Louisiana M
Central Connecticut State University M,D,O
Central Michigan University M,D,O*
Central State University M
Central Washington University M
Chadron State College M,O
Chapman University M
Charleston Southern University M
Chestnut Hill College M
Cheyney University of Pennsylvania M,O
Chicago State University M,D
Christian Brothers University M
The Citadel, The Military College of South Carolina M,O
City College of the City University of New York M,O*
City University M,O
Claremont Graduate University M,D,O
Clark Atlanta University M,D,O
Clarke College M
Clemson University M,D,O*
Cleveland State University M,D,O
College of Mount St. Joseph M
The College of New Jersey M,O
The College of New Rochelle M,O
College of Notre Dame of Maryland M,D
College of Saint Elizabeth M,O
The College of Saint Rose M,O*
College of Santa Fe M
College of Staten Island of the City University of New York O
College of the Southwest M
The College of William and Mary M,D
Columbia International University M,D,O
Columbus State University M,O
Concordia University (CA) M
Concordia University (IL) M,D,O
Concordia University (MI) M
Concordia University (OR) M
Concordia University (NE) M
Concordia University Wisconsin M
Converse College M,O
Creighton University M*
Curry College M,O
Dallas Baptist University M
Delaware Valley College M
Delta State University M,D,O
DePaul University D*
Doane College M
Dominican University M
Dowling College M,D,O
Drake University M,D,O*
Drexel University M,D*
Duquesne University M,D*
East Carolina University M,D,O*
Eastern Illinois University M,O
Eastern Kentucky University M*
Eastern Michigan University M,D,O
Eastern Nazarene College M,O
Eastern Washington University M
East Tennessee State University M,D,O
Edgewood College M,D,O
Edinboro University of Pennsylvania M,O
Elmhurst College M
Emmanuel College M,O
Emporia State University M
Evangel University M
Fairleigh Dickinson University, College at Florham M*
Fairleigh Dickinson University, Metropolitan Campus M*
Fairmont State University M
Fayetteville State University M,D
Felician College M*
Ferris State University M
Fielding Graduate University M,D*
Fitchburg State College M,O
Florida Agricultural and Mechanical University M,D*
Florida Atlantic University M,D,O
Florida Gulf Coast University M
Florida International University M,D,O*
Florida State University M,D,O*
Fordham University M,D,O*
Fort Hays State University M,O
Framingham State College M*
Franciscan University of Steubenville M
Freed-Hardeman University M,O
Fresno Pacific University M
Friends University M
Frostburg State University M
Furman University M
Gallaudet University M,D,O
Gannon University M,O
Gardner-Webb University M,D
Geneva College M*
George Fox University M,D,O*
George Mason University M*
The George Washington University M,D,O*
Georgia College & State University M,O
Georgian Court University M,O
Georgia Southern University M,D,O
Georgia State University M,D,O*
Golden Gate Baptist Theological Seminary P,M,D,O
Gonzaga University M,D
Governors State University M
Grambling State University M,D
Grand Valley State University M
Gwynedd-Mercy College M
Harding University M,O
Harvard University M,D*
Henderson State University M,O
Heritage University M
High Point University M
Hofstra University M,D,O*
Hood College M,O
Houston Baptist University M
Howard University M,D,O*
Hunter College of the City University of New York O
Idaho State University M,D,O
Illinois State University M,D*
Immaculata University M,D,O
Indiana State University M,D,O*
Indiana University Bloomington M,D,O*
Indiana University of Pennsylvania M,D,O
Indiana University–Purdue University Fort Wayne M
Instituto Tecnológico y de Estudios Superiores de Monterrey, Campus Central de Veracruz M
Instituto Tecnológico y de Estudios Superiores de Monterrey, Campus Estado de México M,D
Instituto Tecnológico y de Estudios Superiores de Monterrey, Campus Irapuato M,D
Inter American University of Puerto Rico, Aguadilla Campus M
Inter American University of Puerto Rico, Arecibo Campus M
Inter American University of Puerto Rico, Barranquitas Campus M
Inter American University of Puerto Rico, Metropolitan Campus M
Inter American University of Puerto Rico, San Germán Campus M
Iona College M*
Iowa State University of Science and Technology M,D*
Jackson State University M,D,O
Jacksonville State University M,O
James Madison University M
John Carroll University M
The Johns Hopkins University M,D,O*
Johnson & Wales University D*
Jones International University M
Kansas State University M,D*
Kean University M
Keene State College M,O
Kennesaw State University M,D,O
Kent State University M,D,O*
Kutztown University of Pennsylvania M
Lake Erie College M
Lakehead University M,D
Lamar University M,D,O*
La Sierra University M,D,O
Lee University M
Lehigh University M,D,O*
LeTourneau University M
Lewis & Clark College M,D
Lewis University M
Liberty University M,D,O
Lincoln Memorial University M,O
Lincoln University (MO) M,O
Lindenwood University M,D,O
Lipscomb University M
Long Island University, Brentwood Campus M
Long Island University, Brooklyn Campus M*
Long Island University, C.W. Post Campus M,O*
Long Island University, Rockland Graduate Campus M,O
Longwood University M*
Loras College M
Louisiana State University and Agricultural and Mechanical College M,D,O*
Louisiana Tech University M,D
Loyola College in Maryland M,O
Loyola Marymount University M,D
Loyola University Chicago M,D,O*
Lynchburg College M
Lynn University M,D
Madonna University M
Manhattan College M,O
Manhattanville College M*
Marian College of Fond du Lac M,D
Marshall University M,D,O
Marygrove College M
Marymount University M,O
Maryville University of Saint Louis M,D
Marywood University M,D*
Massachusetts College of Liberal Arts M
McDaniel College M
McGill University M,D,O*
McNeese State University M,O
Memorial University of Newfoundland M,D,O
Mercer University M,D,O
Mercy College M
Mercyhurst College M,O
Miami University M,D*
Michigan State University M,D,O*
Middle Tennessee State University M,O*
Midwestern State University M
Mills College M,D
Minnesota State University Mankato M,O
Minnesota State University Moorhead M,O
Mississippi College M,O
Mississippi State University M,D,O
Missouri State University M,O*
Monmouth University M,O
Montclair State University M,O*
Morehead State University M,O
Morgan State University M,D*
Mount St. Mary's College M
Murray State University M,O
National-Louis University M,D,O
National University M
New England College M
New Jersey City University M
Newman Theological College M,O

*P—first professional degree; M—master's degree; D—doctorate; O—other advanced degree; *full description and/or announcement in Book 2, 3, 4, 5, or 6*

Newman University	M
New Mexico Highlands University	M
New Mexico State University	M,D
New York Institute of Technology	O
New York University	M,D,O*
Niagara University	M,O
Nicholls State University	M
Norfolk State University	M
North Carolina Agricultural and Technical State University	M
North Carolina Central University	M
North Carolina State University	M,D*
North Central College	M
North Dakota State University	M,O
Northeastern Illinois University	M
Northeastern State University	M
Northern Arizona University	M,D
Northern Illinois University	M,D,O
Northern Kentucky University	M
Northern Michigan University	M,O
Northern State University	M
North Georgia College & State University	M,O
Northwestern Oklahoma State University	M
Northwestern State University of Louisiana	M,O
Northwest Missouri State University	M,O
Northwest Nazarene University	M
Notre Dame de Namur University	M,O
Nova Southeastern University	M,D,O*
Oakland City University	M,D
Oakland University	M,D,O*
Oglala Lakota College	M
The Ohio State University	M,D*
Ohio University	M,D*
Oklahoma State University	M,D*
Old Dominion University	M,D,O*
Oral Roberts University	M,D
Oregon State University	M*
Ottawa University	M
Our Lady of Holy Cross College	M
Our Lady of the Lake University of San Antonio	M,D
Pace University	M,O*
Pacific Lutheran University	M
Pacific Union College	M
Park University	M
Penn State University Park	M,D*
Pepperdine University	M,D*
Philadelphia Biblical University	M
Pittsburg State University	M
Plymouth State University	M
Point Park University	M*
Pontificia Universidad Catolica Madre y Maestra	M
Portland State University	M,D
Prairie View A&M University	M,D
Providence College	M*
Purdue University	M,D,O*
Purdue University Calumet	M
Queens College of the City University of New York	O
Radford University	M
Regent University	M,D,O
Regis University	M,O
Rhode Island College	M,O
Rider University	M,O*
Rivier College	M,O
Roosevelt University	M,D
Rowan University	M,D,O
Royal Roads University	M
Rutgers, The State University of New Jersey, Camden	M
Rutgers, The State University of New Jersey, New Brunswick	M,D*
Sacred Heart University	M,O
Saginaw Valley State University	M,O
St. Ambrose University	M
St. Bonaventure University	M,O
St. Cloud State University	M
Saint Francis University	M
St. Francis Xavier University	M
St. John Fisher College	M,D
St. John's University (NY)	M,D,O
Saint Joseph's University	M,D,O*
St. Lawrence University	M,O
Saint Leo University	M
Saint Louis University	M,D,O*
Saint Martin's University	M
Saint Mary's College of California	M,D
Saint Mary's University of Minnesota	M,D,O
St. Mary's University of San Antonio	M,O
Saint Michael's College	M,O
Saint Peter's College	M,O
St. Thomas University	M,D,O
Saint Vincent College	M
Saint Xavier University	M,O
Salem International University	M
Salem State College	M
Salisbury University	M
Samford University	M,D,O
Sam Houston State University	M,D
San Diego State University	M*
San Francisco State University	M,O
San Jose State University	M,O
Santa Clara University	M
Seattle Pacific University	M,D
Seattle University	M,D,O
Seton Hall University	M,D,O*
Shasta Bible College	M
Shenandoah University	M,D,O*
Shippensburg University of Pennsylvania	M
Silver Lake College	M
Simmons College	M,O
Simon Fraser University	M,D
Simpson University	M
Slippery Rock University of Pennsylvania	M
Sonoma State University	M
South Carolina State University	D,O
South Dakota State University	M
Southeastern Louisiana University	M,D
Southeastern Oklahoma State University	M
Southeast Missouri State University	M,O
Southern Adventist University	M
Southern Arkansas University–Magnolia	M
Southern Connecticut State University	D,O
Southern Illinois University Carbondale	M,D*
Southern Illinois University Edwardsville	M,O
Southern Nazarene University	M
Southern New Hampshire University	M,O*
Southern Oregon University	M
Southern University and Agricultural and Mechanical College	M*
Southwest Baptist University	M,O
Southwestern Assemblies of God University	M
Southwestern Oklahoma State University	M
Southwest Minnesota State University	M
Spalding University	M,D
Stanford University	M,D*
State University of New York at Fredonia	O
State University of New York at New Paltz	M,O
State University of New York at Oswego	O
State University of New York at Plattsburgh	O
State University of New York College at Brockport	M,O*
State University of New York College at Cortland	O*
Stephen F. Austin State University	M,D
Stetson University	M,O
Stony Brook University, State University of New York	M,O*
Suffolk University	M,O*
Sul Ross State University	M*
Syracuse University	M,D,O*
Tarleton State University	M,D,O
Teachers College Columbia University	M,D*
Temple University	M,D*
Tennessee State University	M,D,O*
Tennessee Technological University	M,O*
Tennessee Temple University	M
Texas A&M International University	M
Texas A&M University	M,D*
Texas A&M University–Commerce	M,D
Texas A&M University–Corpus Christi	M,D
Texas A&M University–Kingsville	M,D
Texas A&M University–Texarkana	M
Texas Christian University	M
Texas Southern University	M,D
Texas State University-San Marcos	M*
Texas Tech University	M,D,O
Texas Woman's University	M,D
Touro University International	M,D
Towson University	M,O
Trevecca Nazarene University	M,D
Trinity Baptist College	M
Trinity International University	M
Trinity University	M*
Trinity (Washington) University	M
Trinity Western University	M
Troy University	M,O
Union College (KY)	M,O
Union University	M,D,O
Universidad del Este	M
Universidad del Turabo	M
Universidad Metropolitana	M
Université de Moncton	M
Université de Montréal	M,D,O
Université de Sherbrooke	M
Université du Québec à Trois-Rivières	D
Université Laval	M,D,O
University at Albany, State University of New York	M,D,O*
University at Buffalo, the State University of New York	M,D,O*
The University of Akron	M,D
The University of Alabama	M,D,O
The University of Alabama at Birmingham	M,D,O*
University of Alaska Anchorage	M,O
University of Alberta	M,D,O*
The University of Arizona	M,D,O*
University of Arkansas	M,D,O*
University of Arkansas at Little Rock	M,D,O
University of Arkansas at Monticello	M
University of Bridgeport	D,O
The University of British Columbia	M,D*
University of Calgary	M,D,O
University of California, Berkeley	M,D*
University of California, Irvine	M,D*
University of California, Santa Barbara	M,D*
University of Central Arkansas	O
University of Central Florida	M,D,O*
University of Central Missouri	M,O
University of Central Oklahoma	M
University of Cincinnati	M,D,O
University of Colorado at Colorado Springs	M,D
University of Colorado at Denver and Health Sciences Center	M,D,O*
University of Connecticut	D*
University of Dayton	M,D,O*
University of Delaware	M,D*
University of Denver	M,D,O*
University of Detroit Mercy	M
The University of Findlay	M
University of Florida	M,D,O*
University of Georgia	M,D,O*
University of Guam	M
University of Hartford	D,O*
University of Hawaii at Manoa	M,D*
University of Houston	M,D*
University of Houston–Clear Lake	M,D
University of Idaho	M,D,O*
University of Illinois at Chicago	M,D*
University of Illinois at Springfield	M
University of Illinois at Urbana–Champaign	M,D,O*
University of Indianapolis	M
The University of Iowa	M,D,O*
University of Kansas	M,D,O*
University of Kentucky	M,D,O*
University of La Verne	M,D,O
University of Lethbridge	M,D
University of Louisiana at Lafayette	M,D*
University of Louisiana at Monroe	M,D
University of Louisville	M,D,O
University of Maine	M,D,O*
University of Manitoba	M
University of Mary	M
University of Mary Hardin-Baylor	M,D
University of Maryland, College Park	M,D,O*
University of Maryland Eastern Shore	D*
University of Massachusetts Amherst	M,D,O*
University of Massachusetts Boston	M,D,O
University of Massachusetts Lowell	M,D,O*
University of Memphis	M,D*
University of Miami	M,O*
University of Michigan	M,D*
University of Michigan–Dearborn	M,O*
University of Minnesota, Twin Cities Campus	M,D,O*
University of Mississippi	M,D,O
University of Missouri–Columbia	M,D,O*
University of Missouri–Kansas City	M,D,O*
University of Missouri–St. Louis	M,D,O
The University of Montana	M,D,O*
University of Montevallo	M,O
University of Nebraska at Kearney	M,O
University of Nebraska at Omaha	M,D,O
University of Nebraska–Lincoln	M,D,O*
University of Nevada, Las Vegas	M,D,O
University of Nevada, Reno	M,D,O*
University of New England	O
University of New Hampshire	M,O*
University of New Hampshire at Manchester	M,O
University of New Mexico	M,D,O*
University of New Orleans	M,D,O
University of North Alabama	M,O
The University of North Carolina at Chapel Hill	M,D*
The University of North Carolina at Charlotte	M,D,O*
The University of North Carolina at Greensboro	M,D,O
The University of North Carolina at Pembroke	M
The University of North Carolina Wilmington	M*
University of North Dakota	M,D,O
University of Northern Colorado	M,D,O
University of Northern Iowa	M,D
University of Northern Virginia	M,D
University of North Florida	M,D
University of North Texas	M,D*
University of Oklahoma	M,D*
University of Pennsylvania	M,D*
University of Phoenix–Central Florida Campus	M
University of Phoenix–Denver Campus	M
University of Phoenix–Fort Lauderdale Campus	M
University of Phoenix–Hawaii Campus	M
University of Phoenix–Las Vegas Campus	M
University of Phoenix–Metro Detroit Campus	M
University of Phoenix–Nashville Campus	M
University of Phoenix–New Mexico Campus	M
University of Phoenix—Northern Nevada Campus	M
University of Phoenix–Northern Virginia Campus	M
University of Phoenix–North Florida Campus	M
University of Phoenix–Omaha Campus	M
University of Phoenix Online Campus	M
University of Phoenix–Phoenix Campus	M
University of Phoenix–Puerto Rico Campus	M
University of Phoenix–Southern Colorado Campus	M,O
University of Phoenix–Springfield Campus	M
University of Phoenix–Utah Campus	M
University of Phoenix–Vancouver Campus	M
University of Phoenix–West Florida Campus	M
University of Phoenix–West Michigan Campus	M
University of Pittsburgh	M,D*
University of Prince Edward Island	M
University of Puerto Rico, Río Piedras	M,D*
University of Regina	M
University of St. Francis (IL)	M
University of St. Thomas (MN)	M,D,O*
University of San Diego	M,D,O*
University of San Francisco	M,D
University of Saskatchewan	M,D,O
The University of Scranton	M
University of Sioux Falls	M,O
University of South Alabama	M,O*
University of South Carolina	M,D,O*
The University of South Dakota	M,D,O
University of Southern Maine	M,O
University of Southern Mississippi	M,D,O*
University of South Florida	M,D,O*
The University of Tennessee	M,D,O*
The University of Tennessee at Chattanooga	M,D,O
The University of Tennessee at Martin	M
The University of Texas at Arlington	M*
The University of Texas at Austin	M,D*
The University of Texas at Brownsville	M
The University of Texas at El Paso	M,D
The University of Texas at San Antonio	M,D*
The University of Texas at Tyler	M
The University of Texas of the Permian Basin	M
The University of Texas–Pan American	M,D
University of the Cumberlands	M,O
University of the Pacific	M,D

The University of Toledo M,D,O*
University of Utah M,D*
University of Vermont M,D*
University of Victoria M,D
University of Virginia M,D,O*
University of Washington M,D,O*
The University of West Alabama M
University of West Florida M,O
University of West Georgia M,O
University of Wisconsin–Madison M,D,O*
University of Wisconsin–Milwaukee M,O
University of Wisconsin–Oshkosh M
University of Wisconsin–Stevens Point M
University of Wisconsin–Superior M,O
University of Wisconsin–Whitewater M*
University of Wyoming M,D,O
Ursuline College M
Valdosta State University M,D,O
Vanderbilt University M,D*
Villanova University M*
Virginia Commonwealth University D*
Virginia Polytechnic Institute and State University D,O*
Virginia State University M
Wagner College O
Walden University M,D
Walla Walla College M
Washburn University M
Washington State University M,D*
Washington State University Spokane M,O
Washington State University Tri-Cities M,D
Wayne State College M,O
Wayne State University M,D,O*
Webster University M,O
Western Carolina University M,D,O*
Western Connecticut State University D*
Western Governors University M,O
Western Illinois University M,D,O
Western Kentucky University M,O
Western Michigan University M,D,O*
Western New Mexico University M
Western Washington University M
Westfield State College M,O
Westminster College (PA) M,O
West Texas A&M University M
West Virginia University M,D*
Wheelock College M
Whittier College M
Whitworth University M
Wichita State University M,D,O*
Widener University M,D*
Wilkes University M
William Paterson University of New Jersey M*
William Woods University M,O
Wilmington College (DE) M,D
Wingate University M
Winona State University M,O
Winthrop University M
Worcester State College M
Wright State University M,O*
Xavier University M*
Xavier University of Louisiana M
Yeshiva University M,D,O
Youngstown State University M,D

EDUCATIONAL MEASUREMENT AND EVALUATION

Abilene Christian University M
American InterContinental University Online M
Angelo State University M
Arkansas State University M,O
Boston College M,D*
Bucknell University M
Claremont Graduate University M,D,O
College of the Southwest M
Florida State University M,D*
Gallaudet University O
George Mason University M*
Georgia State University M,D*
Harvard University D*
Hofstra University M*
Houston Baptist University M
Iowa State University of Science and Technology M,D*
Kent State University M,D*
Louisiana State University and Agricultural and Mechanical College M,D,O*
Loyola University Chicago M,D*
Michigan State University M,D,O*
New York University M,D,O*
North Carolina State University D*
Ohio University M,D*
Rutgers, The State University of New Jersey, New Brunswick M*
Southern Connecticut State University M
Southern Illinois University Carbondale M,D*
Southwestern Oklahoma State University M
Stanford University M,D*
Sul Ross State University M*
Syracuse University M,D,O*
Teachers College Columbia University M,D*
Texas A&M University M,D*
Texas Christian University M
Texas Southern University M,D
Université Laval M,D,O
University at Albany, State University of New York M,D,O*
The University of British Columbia M,D,O*
University of Calgary M,D,O
University of California, Berkeley M,D*
University of California, Santa Barbara M,D*
University of Colorado at Boulder D*
University of Connecticut M,D*
University of Denver M,D,O*
University of Florida M,D,O*
The University of Iowa M,D,O*
University of Kansas M,D*
University of Kentucky M,D*
University of Maryland, College Park M,D*
University of Massachusetts Amherst M,D,O*
University of Memphis M,D*
University of Miami M,D*
University of Michigan M,D*
University of Minnesota, Twin Cities Campus M,D*
University of Missouri–St. Louis M,D,O
University of New England M
The University of North Carolina at Chapel Hill M,D*
The University of North Carolina at Greensboro D
University of North Dakota D
University of Northern Colorado M,D
University of North Texas D*
University of Pennsylvania M,D*
University of Pittsburgh M,D*
University of Puerto Rico, Río Piedras M*
University of South Carolina M,D*
University of South Florida M,D,O*
The University of Tennessee M,D,O*
The University of Texas–Pan American M
The University of Toledo M,D*
University of Virginia M,D*
University of Washington M,D*
University of West Georgia D
Utah State University M,D
Vanderbilt University M,D*
Virginia Commonwealth University D*
Virginia Polytechnic Institute and State University D*
Washington University in St. Louis D*
Wayne State University M,D,O*
West Chester University of Pennsylvania M
Western Governors University M,O
Western Michigan University M,D*
West Texas A&M University M
Wilkes University M

EDUCATIONAL MEDIA/INSTRUCTIONAL TECHNOLOGY

Acadia University M
Adelphi University M,O*
Alabama State University M,O
Alliant International University–Irvine M,O*
Alverno College M
American InterContinental University (CA) M
American InterContinental University (FL) M
American InterContinental University Online M
American University M,D*
Appalachian State University M
Arcadia University M,D,O
Argosy University, Denver Campus M,D*
Argosy University, Nashville Campus M,D*
Argosy University, Orange County Campus M,D*
Argosy University, Sarasota Campus M,D,O*
Argosy University, Seattle Campus M,D*
Argosy University, Twin Cities Campus M,D,O*
Arizona State University M,D*
Ashland University M
Auburn University M,D,O*
Azusa Pacific University M
Baldwin-Wallace College M
Barry University M,D,O*
Belmont University M
Bloomsburg University of Pennsylvania M
Boise State University M
Boston University M,D,O*
Bowling Green State University M*
Bridgewater State College M
Brigham Young University M,D*
Buffalo State College, State University of New York M
Cabrini College M,O
California Baptist University M
California State University, Bakersfield M
California State University, Chico M
California State University, East Bay M
California State University, Fullerton M
California State University, Los Angeles M
California State University, San Bernardino M
Cape Breton University O
Capella University M,D,O
Cardinal Stritch University M*
Carlow University M
Central Connecticut State University M
Central Michigan University M*
Central State University M
Chestnut Hill College M,O
Chicago State University M
City University M,O
Clarke College M
College of Mount Saint Vincent M,O
The College of New Jersey M
College of Saint Elizabeth M,O
The College of Saint Rose M,O*
The College of St. Scholastica M
The College of William and Mary M,D
Columbia International University M,D,O
Concordia University (Canada) M,D,O
Dakota State University M*
DeSales University M,O
Dowling College M,D,O
Drexel University D*
Duquesne University M,D*
East Carolina University M,O*
Eastern Connecticut State University M
Eastern Michigan University M
Eastern Washington University M
East Stroudsburg University of Pennsylvania M
East Tennessee State University M
Emporia State University M
Fairfield University M,O*
Fairleigh Dickinson University, College at Florham M,O*
Fairleigh Dickinson University, Metropolitan Campus M,O*
Ferris State University M
Fitchburg State College M,O
Florida Atlantic University M
Florida Gulf Coast University M
Florida International University M,D,O*
Florida State University M,D,O*
Fort Hays State University M
Framingham State College M*
Fresno Pacific University M
Frostburg State University M
Gallaudet University O
Gannon University M,O
George Mason University M*
The George Washington University M*
Georgia College & State University M,O
Georgian Court University M,O
Georgia Southern University M
Georgia State University M,D,O*
Governors State University M
Grand Valley State University M
Harvard University M,O*
Hofstra University M*
Idaho State University M,D,O
Indiana State University M,D*
Indiana University Bloomington M,D,O*
Indiana University of Pennsylvania M
Instituto Tecnológico y de Estudios Superiores de Monterrey, Campus Central de Veracruz M
Instituto Tecnológico y de Estudios Superiores de Monterrey, Campus Ciudad de México M,D
Instituto Tecnológico y de Estudios Superiores de Monterrey, Campus Estado de México M,D
Instituto Tecnológico y de Estudios Superiores de Monterrey, Campus Irapuato M,D
Inter American University of Puerto Rico, Metropolitan Campus M
Iona College M,O*
Iowa State University of Science and Technology M,D*
Jackson State University M,D,O
Jacksonville State University M
Jacksonville University M
The Johns Hopkins University M,D,O*
Johnson Bible College M
Jones International University M
Kean University M
Kent State University M*
Kutztown University of Pennsylvania M,O
Lamar University M,D,O*
Lawrence Technological University M
Lehigh University M,D,O*
Lindenwood University M,D,O
Long Island University, Brooklyn Campus M*
Long Island University, C.W. Post Campus M*
Longwood University M*
Louisiana State University and Agricultural and Mechanical College M,D,O*
Lourdes College M
Loyola College in Maryland M
Loyola University Chicago M*
Malone College M
McDaniel College M
McNeese State University M
Memorial University of Newfoundland M,D,O
Mercy College M
Michigan State University M,D,O*
MidAmerica Nazarene University M
Midwestern State University M
Minnesota State University Mankato M,O
Mississippi State University M,D,O
Mississippi University for Women M
Missouri State University M*
Montana State University–Billings M
Montclair State University M,O*
National-Louis University M,O
National University M
Nazareth College of Rochester M
New Jersey City University M
New York Institute of Technology M,O
New York University M,D,O*
North Carolina Agricultural and Technical State University M
North Carolina Central University M
North Carolina State University M,D*
Northeastern State University M
Northern Arizona University M,O
Northern Illinois University M,D
Northern State University M
Northwestern State University of Louisiana M,O
Northwestern University M,D*
Northwest Missouri State University M
Notre Dame de Namur University M,O
Nova Southeastern University M,D,O*
Oakland University O*
Ohio University M,D*
Old Dominion University M,D*
Ottawa University M
Our Lady of the Lake University of San Antonio M
Penn State Great Valley M
Penn State University Park M,D*
Pepperdine University D*
Philadelphia University M*
Pittsburg State University M
Pontifical Catholic University of Puerto Rico M,D
Portland State University M,D
Purdue University M,D,O*
Purdue University Calumet M
Regis University M,O
The Richard Stockton College of New Jersey M
Rochester Institute of Technology M

P—first professional degree; M—master's degree; D—doctorate; O—other advanced degree;
**full description and/or announcement in Book 2, 3, 4, 5, or 6*

Rosemont College M
Rowan University M
Royal Roads University M
Sacred Heart University M,O
Saginaw Valley State University M
St. Cloud State University M
Saint Joseph's University M,D,O*
Saint Michael's College M,O
Saint Vincent College M
Salem International University M
Salem State College M
Salisbury University M
San Diego State University M,D*
San Francisco State University M,O
San Jose State University M,O
Seton Hall University M*
Seton Hill University M
Simmons College M,D,O
Simon Fraser University M,D
Southeastern Oklahoma State University M
Southern Connecticut State University M,O
Southern Illinois University Edwardsville M
Southern University and Agricultural and Mechanical College M*
State University of New York College at Potsdam M
Stony Brook University, State University of New York M,O*
Syracuse University M,O*
Teachers College Columbia University M,D*
Texas A&M University M,D*
Texas A&M University–Commerce M,D
Texas A&M University–Corpus Christi M,D
Texas A&M University–Texarkana M
Texas Tech University M,D,O
Thomas Edison State College M
Touro University International M,D
Towson University M,D
Université Laval M,D
University at Albany, State University of New York M,D,O*
The University of Akron M
University of Alaska Southeast M
University of Alberta M,D*
University of Arkansas M*
University of Arkansas at Little Rock M
University of Calgary M,D,O
University of Central Arkansas M
University of Central Florida M,D,O*
University of Central Missouri M
University of Central Oklahoma M
University of Colorado at Denver and Health Sciences Center M*
University of Connecticut M,D*
University of Dayton M*
The University of Findlay M*
University of Georgia M,D,O*
University of Hartford M*
University of Hawaii at Manoa M*
University of Houston–Clear Lake M
University of Kentucky M,D*
University of Louisville M
University of Maine M*
University of Maryland, Baltimore County M,O*
University of Maryland, College Park M,D,O*
University of Massachusetts Amherst M,D,O*
University of Memphis M,D*
University of Michigan M,D*
University of Michigan–Flint M*
University of Minnesota, Twin Cities Campus M,D,O*
University of Missouri–Columbia M,D,O*
University of Nebraska at Kearney M
University of Nebraska at Omaha M,O
University of Nevada, Las Vegas M,D,O
University of New Mexico M,D,O*
The University of North Carolina at Charlotte M,D,O*
The University of North Carolina at Greensboro M,D,O
The University of North Carolina Wilmington M*
University of North Dakota M
University of Northern Colorado M,D
University of Northern Iowa M
University of Northern Virginia M,D
University of Phoenix Online Campus M
University of Phoenix–West Florida Campus M
University of St. Thomas (MN) M,D,O*
University of San Francisco M,D
University of Sioux Falls M,O
University of South Alabama M,D*
University of South Carolina M*
University of South Carolina Aiken M
The University of South Dakota M,O
University of South Florida M,D,O*
The University of Tennessee M,D,O*
The University of Tennessee at Chattanooga O
The University of Texas at Brownsville M
The University of Texas at San Antonio M*
University of the Incarnate Word M,D,O
University of the Sacred Heart M
The University of Toledo M,D,O*
University of Washington M,D*
The University of West Alabama M
University of West Florida M
University of West Georgia M,O
University of Wyoming M,D,O
Utah State University M,D,O
Valdosta State University M,D,O
Virginia Polytechnic Institute and State University M*
Walden University M,D
Wayne State University M,D,O*
Webster University M,O
West Chester University of Pennsylvania M,O
Western Connecticut State University M*
Western Governors University M,O
Western Illinois University M,O
Western Kentucky University M
Western Oregon University M
Westfield State College M
West Texas A&M University M
Widener University M,D*
Wilkes University M
Wilmington College (DE) M

EDUCATIONAL POLICY

Alabama State University M,D,O
The College of William and Mary M,D
DeSales University M,O
The George Washington University M,D*
Georgia State University M,D,O*
Harvard University M,D*
Illinois State University M,D*
Indiana University Bloomington M,D,O*
Loyola University Chicago M,D*
Michigan State University D*
New York University M,D*
The Ohio State University M,D*
Portland State University M,D
Rutgers, The State University of New Jersey, Camden M
Rutgers, The State University of New Jersey, New Brunswick D*
University of Alberta M,D,O*
The University of British Columbia M,D*
University of Georgia M,D,O*
University of Hawaii at Manoa D*
University of Illinois at Chicago M,D*
University of Illinois at Urbana–Champaign M,D*
The University of Iowa M,D,O*
University of Kansas D*
University of Kentucky M,D*
University of Minnesota, Twin Cities Campus M,D,O*
University of Pennsylvania M,D*
University of St. Thomas (MN) M,D,O*
University of Virginia M,D*
University of Washington M,D*
The University of Western Ontario M
University of Wisconsin–Madison M,D,O*
University of Wisconsin–Milwaukee M
Vanderbilt University M,D*
Wayne State University M,D,O*

EDUCATIONAL PSYCHOLOGY

Alliant International University–Irvine M,D,O*
Alliant International University–Los Angeles M,D,O*
Alliant International University–San Diego M,D,O*
Alliant International University–San Francisco M,D,O*
American International College M,D,O
Andrews University M,D
Arcadia University M,D,O
Arizona State University M,D*
Auburn University M,D,O*
Ball State University M,D,O*
Baylor University M,D,O*
Boston College M,D*
Brigham Young University M,D*
California State University, Northridge M
California State University, San Bernardino M
Capella University M,D,O
The Catholic University of America M,D*
Chapman University M,O
Clark Atlanta University M,D
The College of Saint Rose M,O*
Eastern Michigan University M
Eastern University M*
Edinboro University of Pennsylvania M
Florida Atlantic University M,D,O
Florida State University M,D*
Fordham University M,D,O*
Georgian Court University M,O
Georgia State University M,D*
Graduate School and University Center of the City University of New York D*
Harvard University M*
Holy Names University M,O
Howard University M,D,O*
Illinois State University M,D,O*
Indiana State University M,D,O*
Indiana University Bloomington M,D,O*
Indiana University of Pennsylvania M,O
John Carroll University M
Johnson State College M
Kansas State University M,D*
Kean University M
Kent State University M,D*
La Sierra University M,O
Long Island University, Westchester Graduate Campus M
Loyola Marymount University M
Loyola University Chicago M*
Marist College M,O*
McGill University M,D*
Memorial University of Newfoundland M,D,O
Miami University M,O*
Michigan School of Professional Psychology M,D
Michigan State University M,D,O*
Mississippi State University M,D,O
Montclair State University M,O*
Mount Saint Vincent University M
National-Louis University M,D,O
New Jersey City University M,O
New York University M,D,O*
Northeastern University M*
Northern Arizona University D
Northern Illinois University M,D,O
Oklahoma City University M
Oklahoma State University M,D,O*
Penn State University Park M,D*
Purdue University M,D,O*
Rutgers, The State University of New Jersey, New Brunswick M,D*
Simon Fraser University M,D
Southern Illinois University Carbondale M,D*
Stanford University D*
State University of New York College at Oneonta M,O
Teachers College Columbia University M,D*
Temple University M,D*
Tennessee Technological University M,O*
Texas A&M University M,D*
Texas A&M University–Commerce M,D
Texas Christian University M,O
Texas Tech University M,D,O
Universidad de Iberoamerica P,M
Université de Moncton M
Université de Montréal M,D,O
Université du Québec à Trois-Rivières M
Université du Québec en Outaouais M
Université Laval M,D
University at Albany, State University of New York M,D,O*
University at Buffalo, the State University of New York M,D,O*
University of Alberta M,D*
The University of Arizona M,D*
University of Calgary M,D
University of California, Davis M,D*
University of Colorado at Boulder M,D*
University of Colorado at Denver and Health Sciences Center M*
University of Connecticut M,D*
University of Denver M,D,O*
University of Florida M,D,O*
University of Georgia M,D,O*
University of Hawaii at Manoa M,D*
University of Houston M,D*
University of Illinois at Chicago M,D*
University of Illinois at Urbana–Champaign M,D,O*
The University of Iowa M,D,O*
University of Kansas M,D*
University of Kentucky M,D,O*
University of Louisville M,D
University of Manitoba M
University of Mary Hardin-Baylor M,D
University of Maryland, College Park M,D*
University of Memphis M,D*
University of Minnesota, Twin Cities Campus M,D,O*
University of Missouri–Columbia M,D,O*
University of Missouri–St. Louis D,O
University of Nebraska at Omaha M,D,O
University of Nebraska–Lincoln M,O*
University of Nevada, Las Vegas M,D,O
University of Nevada, Reno M,D,O*
University of New Mexico M,D*
The University of North Carolina at Chapel Hill M,D*
University of Northern Colorado M,D
University of Northern Iowa M,O
University of Oklahoma M,D*
University of Pennsylvania M,D*
University of Phoenix–Southern Arizona Campus M,O
University of Regina M
University of Saskatchewan M,D,O
University of South Carolina M,D*
The University of South Dakota M,D,O
The University of Tennessee M,D,O*
The University of Texas at Austin M,D*
The University of Texas at San Antonio M*
The University of Texas–Pan American M
University of the Pacific M,D,O
The University of Toledo M,D*
University of Utah M,D*
University of Victoria M,D
University of Virginia M,D,O*
University of Washington M,D*
The University of Western Ontario M
University of Wisconsin–Madison M,D*
University of Wisconsin–Milwaukee M,O
Washington State University M,D*
Wayne State University M,D,O*
Western Kentucky University M,O
West Virginia University M*
Wichita State University M,D,O*
Widener University M,D*

EDUCATION OF THE GIFTED

Arkansas State University M,D,O
Arkansas Tech University M,O
Ashland University M
Barry University M,D,O*
Belmont University M
Bowling Green State University M*
Carlos Albizu University, Miami Campus M,D
Carthage College M,O
Clark Atlanta University M,O
The College of New Rochelle M,O
The College of William and Mary M
Converse College M
Drury University M
Elon University M
Emporia State University M
Grand Valley State University M
Hardin-Simmons University M
Hofstra University M,O*
The Johns Hopkins University M,D,O*
Johnson State College M
Kent State University M*
Liberty University M,D,O
Lynn University M,D
Maryville University of Saint Louis M,D
Minnesota State University Mankato M,O
Mississippi University for Women M
Northeastern Illinois University M
Nova Southeastern University M,O*
Purdue University M,D,O*
Saint Leo University M
Samford University M,D,O
Teachers College Columbia University M,D*
Tennessee Technological University D*
Texas A&M University M,D*
The University of Alabama M,D,O
University of Arkansas at Little Rock M
University of Calgary M,D,O
University of Connecticut M,D*
University of Houston M,D*

University of Louisiana at Lafayette	M*
University of Minnesota, Twin Cities Campus	M,D,O*
University of Missouri–Columbia	M,D*
University of Nevada, Las Vegas	M,D,O
The University of North Carolina at Charlotte	M,D*
University of St. Thomas (MN)	M,D,O*
University of Southern Mississippi	M,D,O*
University of South Florida	M*
The University of Texas–Pan American	M
The University of Toledo	O*
Western Washington University	M
West Virginia University	M,D*
Whitworth University	M
William Carey University	M,O
Wilmington College (DE)	M
Wright State University	M*
Youngstown State University	M

EDUCATION OF THE MULTIPLY HANDICAPPED

Cleveland State University	M
Fresno Pacific University	M
Gallaudet University	M,D,O
Georgia State University	M*
Hunter College of the City University of New York	M
Minot State University	M
Montclair State University	M,O*
Norfolk State University	M
University of Arkansas at Little Rock	M
University of Illinois at Urbana–Champaign	M,D,O*
Western Oregon University	M
West Virginia University	M,D*

ELECTRICAL ENGINEERING

Air Force Institute of Technology	M,D
Alfred University	M*
American University of Beirut	M
Arizona State University	M,D*
Arizona State University at the Polytechnic Campus	M
Auburn University	M,D*
Baylor University	M*
Boise State University	M,D
Boston University	M,D*
Bradley University	M
Brigham Young University	M,D*
Brown University	M,D*
Bucknell University	M
California Institute of Technology	M,D,O*
California Polytechnic State University, San Luis Obispo	M
California State Polytechnic University, Pomona	M
California State University, Chico	M
California State University, Fresno	M
California State University, Fullerton	M
California State University, Long Beach	M
California State University, Los Angeles	M
California State University, Northridge	M
California State University, Sacramento	M*
Capitol College	M
Carleton University	M,D
Carnegie Mellon University	M,D*
Case Western Reserve University	M,D*
The Catholic University of America	M,D*
City College of the City University of New York	M,D*
Clarkson University	M,D*
Clemson University	M,D*
Cleveland State University	M,D
Colorado State University	M,D*
Colorado Technical University—Colorado Springs	M
Colorado Technical University—Denver	M
Columbia University	M,D,O*
Concordia University (Canada)	M,D
Cooper Union for the Advancement of Science and Art	M
Cornell University	M,D*
Dalhousie University	M,D
Dartmouth College	M,D*
Drexel University	M,D*
Duke University	M,D*
École Polytechnique de Montréal	M,D,O
Fairfield University	M*
Fairleigh Dickinson University, Metropolitan Campus	M*
Florida Agricultural and Mechanical University	M,D*
Florida Atlantic University	M,D
Florida Institute of Technology	M,D*
Florida International University	M,D*
Florida State University	M,D*
Gannon University	M
George Mason University	M,D*
The George Washington University	M,D*
Georgia Institute of Technology	M,D*
Georgia Southern University	M
Graduate School and University Center of the City University of New York	D*
Grand Valley State University	M
Howard University	M,D*
Illinois Institute of Technology	M,D*
Indiana University–Purdue University Indianapolis	M,D*
Instituto Tecnológico y de Estudios Superiores de Monterrey, Campus Chihuahua	M,O
Instituto Tecnológico y de Estudios Superiores de Monterrey, Campus Monterrey	M,D
International Technological University	M
Iowa State University of Science and Technology	M,D*
The Johns Hopkins University	M,D*
Kansas State University	M,D*
Kettering University	M
Lamar University	M,D*
Lawrence Technological University	M,D
Lehigh University	M,D*
Louisiana State University and Agricultural and Mechanical College	M,D*
Louisiana Tech University	M,D
Loyola Marymount University	M
Manhattan College	M
Marquette University	M,D
Massachusetts Institute of Technology	M,D,O*
McGill University	M,D*
McMaster University	M,D
McNeese State University	M
Memorial University of Newfoundland	M,D
Mercer University	M
Michigan State University	M,D*
Michigan Technological University	M,D*
Minnesota State University Mankato	M
Mississippi State University	M,D
Montana State University	M,D
Montana Tech of The University of Montana	M
Morgan State University	M,D*
Naval Postgraduate School	M,D,O
New Jersey Institute of Technology	M,D
New Mexico Institute of Mining and Technology	M
New Mexico State University	M,D
New York Institute of Technology	M
Norfolk State University	M
North Carolina Agricultural and Technical State University	M,D
North Carolina State University	M,D*
North Dakota State University	M,D
Northeastern University	M,D*
Northern Illinois University	M
Northwestern Polytechnic University	M
Northwestern University	M,D,O*
Oakland University	M*
OGI School of Science & Engineering at Oregon Health & Science University	M,D
The Ohio State University	M,D*
Ohio University	M,D*
Oklahoma State University	M,D*
Old Dominion University	M,D*
Oregon State University	M,D*
Penn State Harrisburg	M*
Penn State University Park	M,D*
Polytechnic University, Brooklyn Campus	M,D*
Polytechnic University, Long Island Graduate Center	M,D
Polytechnic University of Puerto Rico	M
Polytechnic University, Westchester Graduate Center	M,D
Portland State University	M,D
Prairie View A&M University	M,D
Princeton University	M,D*
Purdue University	M,D*
Queen's University at Kingston	M,D
Rensselaer at Hartford	M
Rensselaer Polytechnic Institute	M,D*
Rice University	M,D*
Rochester Institute of Technology	M
Rose-Hulman Institute of Technology	M*
Royal Military College of Canada	M,D
Rutgers, The State University of New Jersey, New Brunswick	M,D*
St. Cloud State University	M
St. Mary's University of San Antonio	M
San Diego State University	M*
San Jose State University	M
Santa Clara University	M,D,O
South Dakota School of Mines and Technology	M,D
South Dakota State University	M,D
Southern Illinois University Carbondale	M,D*
Southern Illinois University Edwardsville	M
Southern Methodist University	M,D*
Southern Polytechnic State University	M
Stanford University	M,D,O*
State University of New York at Binghamton	M,D*
State University of New York at New Paltz	M
Stevens Institute of Technology	M,D,O*
Stony Brook University, State University of New York	M,D*
Syracuse University	M,D,O*
Temple University	M*
Tennessee Technological University	M,D*
Texas A&M University	M,D*
Texas A&M University–Kingsville	M
Texas Tech University	M,D
Tufts University	M,D,O*
Tulane University	M,D*
Tuskegee University	M
Union Graduate College	M*
Universidad de las Américas–Puebla	M
Université de Moncton	M
Université de Sherbrooke	M,D
Université du Québec à Trois-Rivières	M,D
Université Laval	M,D
University at Buffalo, the State University of New York	M,D*
The University of Akron	M,D
The University of Alabama	M,D
The University of Alabama at Birmingham	M*
The University of Alabama in Huntsville	M,D
University of Alaska Fairbanks	M,D
University of Alberta	M,D*
The University of Arizona	M,D*
University of Arkansas	M,D*
University of Bridgeport	M
The University of British Columbia	M,D*
University of Calgary	M,D
University of California, Berkeley	M,D*
University of California, Davis	M,D*
University of California, Irvine	M,D*
University of California, Los Angeles	M,D*
University of California, Riverside	M,D*
University of California, San Diego	M,D*
University of California, Santa Barbara	M,D*
University of California, Santa Cruz	M,D*
University of Central Florida	M,D,O*
University of Cincinnati	M,D
University of Colorado at Boulder	M,D*
University of Colorado at Colorado Springs	M,D
University of Colorado at Denver and Health Sciences Center	M*
University of Connecticut	M,D*
University of Dayton	M,D*
University of Delaware	M,D*
University of Denver	M,D*
University of Detroit Mercy	M,D
University of Evansville	M
University of Florida	M,D,O*
University of Hawaii at Manoa	M,D*
University of Houston	M,D*
University of Idaho	M,D*
University of Illinois at Chicago	M,D*
University of Illinois at Urbana–Champaign	M,D*
The University of Iowa	M,D*
University of Kansas	M,D*
University of Kentucky	M,D*
University of Louisville	M,D
University of Maine	M,D*
University of Manitoba	M,D
University of Maryland, Baltimore County	M,D*
University of Maryland, College Park	M,D,O*
University of Massachusetts Amherst	M,D*
University of Massachusetts Dartmouth	M,D,O
University of Massachusetts Lowell	M,D*
University of Memphis	M,D*
University of Miami	M,D*
University of Michigan	M,D*
University of Michigan–Dearborn	M*
University of Minnesota, Duluth	M*
University of Minnesota, Twin Cities Campus	M,D*
University of Missouri–Columbia	M,D*
University of Missouri–Kansas City	M,D*
University of Missouri–Rolla	M,D*
University of Nebraska–Lincoln	M,D*
University of Nevada, Las Vegas	M,D
University of Nevada, Reno	M,D*
University of New Brunswick Fredericton	M,D
University of New Hampshire	M,D*
University of New Haven	M*
University of New Mexico	M,D*
The University of North Carolina at Charlotte	M,D*
University of North Dakota	M
University of North Texas	M*
University of Notre Dame	M,D*
University of Oklahoma	M,D*
University of Ottawa	M,D*
University of Pennsylvania	M,D*
University of Pittsburgh	M,D*
University of Puerto Rico, Mayagüez Campus	M*
University of Rhode Island	M,D
University of Rochester	M,D*
University of Saskatchewan	M,D
University of South Alabama	M*
University of South Carolina	M,D*
University of Southern California	M,D,O*
University of South Florida	M,D*
The University of Tennessee	M,D*
The University of Tennessee Space Institute	M,D*
The University of Texas at Arlington	M,D*
The University of Texas at Austin	M,D*
The University of Texas at Dallas	M,D*
The University of Texas at El Paso	M,D
The University of Texas at San Antonio	M,D*
The University of Toledo	M,D*
University of Toronto	M,D
University of Tulsa	M*
University of Utah	M,D,O*
University of Vermont	M,D*
University of Victoria	M,D*
University of Virginia	M,D*
University of Washington	M,D*
University of Waterloo	M,D*
University of Windsor	M,D
University of Wisconsin–Madison	M,D*
University of Wyoming	M,D
Utah State University	M,D
Vanderbilt University	M,D*
Villanova University	M,O*
Virginia Commonwealth University	M,D*
Virginia Polytechnic Institute and State University	M,D*
Walden University	M,O
Washington State University	M,D*
Washington State University Tri-Cities	M,D
Washington University in St. Louis	M,D*
Wayne State University	M,D*
Western Michigan University	M,D*
Western New England College	M
West Virginia University	M,D*
Wichita State University	M,D*
Wilkes University	M
Woods Hole Oceanographic Institution	M,D,O
Worcester Polytechnic Institute	M,D,O*
Wright State University	M*
Yale University	M,D*
Youngstown State University	M

ELECTRONIC COMMERCE

Adelphi University	M*
American University	M*

*P—first professional degree; M—master's degree; D—doctorate; O—other advanced degree; *full description and/or announcement in Book 2, 3, 4, 5, or 6*

Arkansas State University	M,O
Boston University	M*
Bryant University	M,O
California State University, East Bay	M
Cambridge College	M
Cardean University	M
Carnegie Mellon University	M*
City University	M,O
Claremont Graduate University	M,D,O
Clemson University	M,D*
Cleveland State University	M,D,O
Columbia Southern University	M
Dalhousie University	M,D
Dallas Baptist University	M
Davenport University	M
Davenport University	M
DePaul University	M,D*
Eastern Michigan University	M
Fairleigh Dickinson University, Metropolitan Campus	M*
Ferris State University	M
Florida Atlantic University	M
Florida Institute of Technology	M*
Georgia Institute of Technology	M,O*
Hawai'i Pacific University	M*
HEC Montreal	M,O
Instituto Tecnológico y de Estudios Superiores de Monterrey, Campus Central de Veracruz	M
Instituto Tecnológico y de Estudios Superiores de Monterrey, Campus Estado de México	M,D
Instituto Tecnológico y de Estudios Superiores de Monterrey, Campus Irapuato	M,D
Inter American University of Puerto Rico, Bayamón Campus	M
International University in Geneva	M
Maryville University of Saint Louis	M,O
Marywood University	M,O*
Mercy College	M
The National Graduate School of Quality Management	M
National University	M
New York Institute of Technology	M,O
New York University	M,O*
Northwestern University	M*
Regis University	M,O
Rensselaer Polytechnic Institute	M,D*
Saint Joseph's University	M,O*
Saint Xavier University	M,O
Stevens Institute of Technology	M,O*
Temple University	M*
Université Laval	M,O
University at Buffalo, the State University of New York	M,D,O*
The University of Akron	M
University of Cincinnati	M
University of Denver	M*
University of Florida	M*
University of Massachusetts Dartmouth	M,O
University of New Brunswick Saint John	M
University of Ottawa	M,D,O*
University of Phoenix–Austin Campus	M
University of Phoenix–Bay Area Campus	M
University of Phoenix–Chicago Campus	M
University of Phoenix–Cincinnati Campus	M
University of Phoenix–Columbus Georgia Campus	M
University of Phoenix–Dallas Campus	M
University of Phoenix–Denver Campus	M
University of Phoenix–Detroit Campus	M
University of Phoenix–Houston Campus	M
University of Phoenix–Louisville Campus	M
University of Phoenix–Madison Campus	M
University of Phoenix–Maryland Campus	M
University of Phoenix–Memphis Campus	M
University of Phoenix–New Mexico Campus	M
University of Phoenix–Northern Virginia Campus	M
University of Phoenix–Oklahoma City Campus	M
University of Phoenix Online Campus	M
University of Phoenix–Pittsburgh Campus	M
University of Phoenix–Raleigh Campus	M
University of Phoenix–San Antonio Campus	M
University of Phoenix–West Michigan Campus	M
University of San Francisco	M
West Chester University of Pennsylvania	M
Xavier University	M*

ELECTRONIC MATERIALS

Colorado School of Mines	M,D
Massachusetts Institute of Technology	M,D,O*
Northwestern University	M,D,O*
Princeton University	D*
University of Arkansas	M,D*

ELEMENTARY EDUCATION

Adelphi University	M*
Alabama Agricultural and Mechanical University	M,O
Alabama State University	M,O
Alaska Pacific University	M
Albright College	M
Alcorn State University	M,O
American International College	M,D,O
American University	M,O*
American University of Puerto Rico	M
Andrews University	M,D,O
Anna Maria College	M,O
Appalachian State University	M
Arcadia University	M,D,O
Argosy University, Atlanta Campus	M,D,O*
Argosy University, Chicago Campus	M,D,O*
Argosy University, Denver Campus	M,D*
Argosy University, Hawai'i Campus	M,D*
Argosy University, Inland Empire Campus	M,D*
Argosy University, Nashville Campus	M,D*
Argosy University, Orange County Campus	M,D*
Argosy University, Phoenix Campus	M,D,O*
Argosy University, San Diego Campus	M,D*
Argosy University, San Francisco Bay Area Campus	M,D*
Argosy University, Santa Monica Campus	M,D*
Argosy University, Sarasota Campus	M,D,O*
Argosy University, Schaumburg Campus	M,D,O*
Argosy University, Seattle Campus	M,D*
Argosy University, Tampa Campus	M,D,O*
Argosy University, Twin Cities Campus	M,D,O*
Argosy University, Washington DC Campus	M,D,O*
Arizona State University at the West campus	M,D,O
Arkansas State University	M,O
Armstrong Atlantic State University	M
Auburn University	M,D,O*
Auburn University Montgomery	M,O
Augustana College	M
Augusta State University	M,O
Austin College	M
Averett University	M
Ball State University	M,D*
Bank Street College of Education	M*
Barry University	M,D,O*
Bayamón Central University	M
Belhaven College (MS)	M
Belmont University	M
Benedictine University	M
Bennington College	M*
Bethel College (TN)	M
Bloomsburg University of Pennsylvania	M
Bob Jones University	P,M,D,O
Boston College	M*
Boston University	M*
Bowie State University	M
Brandeis University	M*
Bridgewater State College	M
Brooklyn College of the City University of New York	M
Brown University	M*
Buffalo State College, State University of New York	M
Butler University	M
California State University, Fullerton	M
California State University, Los Angeles	M
California State University, Northridge	M
California State University, San Bernardino	M
California State University, Stanislaus	M
California University of Pennsylvania	M
Campbell University	M
Capella University	M,D,O
Carlow University	M
Carson-Newman College	M
Catawba College	M
Centenary College of Louisiana	M
Central Connecticut State University	M,O
Central Michigan University	M*
Chadron State College	M,O
Chapman University	M
Charleston Southern University	M
Chatham University	M
Chestnut Hill College	M
Cheyney University of Pennsylvania	M
Chicago State University	M
Christopher Newport University	M
Clarion University of Pennsylvania	M
Clemson University	M*
Coastal Carolina University	M
College of Charleston	M*
The College of New Jersey	M
The College of New Rochelle	M
College of St. Joseph	M
The College of Saint Rose	M,O*
College of Staten Island of the City University of New York	M
The College of William and Mary	M
The Colorado College	M
Columbia College (SC)	M
Columbia College Chicago	M
Columbia International University	M,D,O
Concordia University (OR)	M
Connecticut College	M
Converse College	M
Curry College	M,O
Dallas Baptist University	M
Delta State University	M,O
DePaul University	M,D*
Drake University	M*
Drury University	M
Duquesne University	M*
D'Youville College	M,O*
East Carolina University	M*
Eastern Connecticut State University	M
Eastern Illinois University	M
Eastern Kentucky University	M*
Eastern Michigan University	M
Eastern Nazarene College	M,O
Eastern Oregon University	M
Eastern Washington University	M
East Stroudsburg University of Pennsylvania	M
East Tennessee State University	M
Edinboro University of Pennsylvania	M
Elizabeth City State University	M
Elms College	M,O
Elon University	M
Emmanuel College	M,O
Emporia State University	M
Endicott College	M
Fairfield University	M,O*
Fayetteville State University	M
Felician College	M*
Ferris State University	M
Fitchburg State College	M
Florida Agricultural and Mechanical University	M*
Florida Atlantic University	M,D,O
Florida Gulf Coast University	M
Florida Institute of Technology	M,D,O*
Florida International University	M,D*
Florida State University	M,D,O*
Fordham University	M,D,O*
Fort Hays State University	M
Framingham State College	M*
Francis Marion University	M
Friends University	M
Frostburg State University	M
Furman University	M
Gallaudet University	M,D,O
Gardner-Webb University	M
The George Washington University	M*
Grambling State University	M
Grand Canyon University	M*
Grand Valley State University	M
Greensboro College	M
Greenville College	M
Hampton University	M*
Harding University	M,O
High Point University	M
Hofstra University	M,O*
Holy Family University	M
Hood College	M,O
Howard University	M*
Hunter College of the City University of New York	M
Idaho State University	M,O
Immaculata University	M,D,O
Indiana State University	M*
Indiana University Bloomington	M,D,O*
Indiana University Kokomo	M
Indiana University Northwest	M
Indiana University–Purdue University Fort Wayne	M
Indiana University South Bend	M
Indiana University Southeast	M
Inter American University of Puerto Rico, Aguadilla Campus	M
Inter American University of Puerto Rico, Barranquitas Campus	M
Inter American University of Puerto Rico, Metropolitan Campus	M
Inter American University of Puerto Rico, Ponce Campus	M
Inter American University of Puerto Rico, San Germán Campus	M
Iona College	M*
Iowa State University of Science and Technology	M,D*
Jackson State University	M,D,O
Jacksonville State University	M
Jacksonville University	M
The Johns Hopkins University	M*
Jones International University	M*
Kansas State University	M,D*
Kent State University	M,D,O*
Kutztown University of Pennsylvania	M,O
Lander University	M
Langston University	M
Lee University	M
Lehigh University	M,D*
Lehman College of the City University of New York	M
Lesley University	M,D,O*
Lewis & Clark College	M
Liberty University	M,D,O
Lincoln University (MO)	M,O
Lock Haven University of Pennsylvania	M
Long Island University, Brentwood Campus	M
Long Island University, Brooklyn Campus	M*
Long Island University, C.W. Post Campus	M*
Long Island University, Rockland Graduate Campus	M
Long Island University, Southampton Graduate Campus	M
Long Island University, Westchester Graduate Campus	M
Longwood University	M*
Louisiana State University and Agricultural and Mechanical College	M,D,O*
Loyola Marymount University	M
Loyola University Chicago	M*
Loyola University New Orleans	M
Lynchburg College	M
Maharishi University of Management	M
Manhattanville College	M*
Mansfield University of Pennsylvania	M
Marshall University	M
Mary Baldwin College	M
Marygrove College	M
Marymount University	M,O
Maryville University of Saint Louis	M,D
Marywood University	M*
McDaniel College	M
McNeese State University	M
Medaille College	M
Mercy College	M
Metropolitan College of New York	M
Miami University	M*
Middle Tennessee State University	M,O*
Millersville University of Pennsylvania	M
Mills College	M,D
Minnesota State University Mankato	M
Minot State University	M
Mississippi College	M,O
Mississippi State University	M,D,O
Mississippi Valley State University	M
Missouri State University	M,O*
Monmouth University	M,O
Montclair State University	M,O*
Montreat College	M
Morehead State University	M
Morgan State University	M*
Morningside College	M
Mount Saint Mary College	M
Mount St. Mary's College	M
Mount Saint Vincent University	M
Murray State University	M,O
National-Louis University	M
Nazareth College of Rochester	M

New Jersey City University M
New York Institute of Technology M,O
New York University M,D,O*
Niagara University M
North Carolina Agricultural and Technical State University M
North Carolina Central University M
Northern Arizona University M
Northern Illinois University M,D
Northern Michigan University M
Northern State University M
Northwestern Oklahoma State University M
Northwestern State University of Louisiana M,O
Northwestern University M*
Northwest Missouri State University M,O
Nova Southeastern University M,O*
Occidental College M
Oklahoma City University M
Old Dominion University M*
Olivet Nazarene University M
Oregon State University M*
Ottawa University M
Pacific University M
Palm Beach Atlantic University M
Penn State University Park M,D*
Pfeiffer University M
Pittsburg State University M
Plymouth State University M
Portland State University M,D
Purdue University M,D,O*
Purdue University Calumet M
Purdue University North Central M
Queens College of the City University of New York M,O
Queens University of Charlotte M
Quinnipiac University M*
Regent University M,D,O
Regis University M,O
Rhode Island College M
Rider University M,O*
Rivier College M,O
Rockford College M
Roger Williams University M*
Rollins College M
Roosevelt University M
Rosemont College M
Rutgers, The State University of New Jersey, New Brunswick M,D*
Sacred Heart University M,O
Sage Graduate School M
Saginaw Valley State University M
St. John Fisher College M
St. John's University (NY) M
Saint Joseph's University M,D,O*
Saint Mary's University of Minnesota M,O
Saint Peter's College M,O
St. Thomas Aquinas College M,O*
St. Thomas University M,D,O
Saint Xavier University M,O
Salem College M
Salem State College M
Salisbury University M
Samford University M,D,O
Sam Houston State University M
San Diego State University M*
San Francisco State University M
San Jose State University M,O
Seton Hill University M,O
Shenandoah University M,D,O*
Siena Heights University M
Sierra Nevada College M
Simmons College M,O
Sinte Gleska University M
Slippery Rock University of Pennsylvania M
Smith College M*
Sonoma State University M
South Carolina State University M
Southeastern Louisiana University M
Southeastern Oklahoma State University M
Southeast Missouri State University M
Southern Arkansas University–Magnolia M
Southern Connecticut State University M,O
Southern Illinois University Edwardsville M
Southern New Hampshire University M,O*
Southern Oregon University M
Southern University and Agricultural and Mechanical College M*
Southwestern Adventist University M
Southwestern Oklahoma State University M
Spalding University M
Spring Hill College M
State University of New York at Binghamton M*
State University of New York at Fredonia M
State University of New York at New Paltz M
State University of New York at Oswego M
State University of New York at Plattsburgh M
State University of New York College at Geneseo M
State University of New York College at Oneonta M
State University of New York College at Potsdam M
Stephen F. Austin State University M
Sul Ross State University M*
Sunbridge College M
Teachers College Columbia University M*
Temple University M,D*
Tennessee State University M,D*
Tennessee Technological University M,O*
Texas A&M University–Commerce M,D
Texas A&M University–Corpus Christi M
Texas A&M University–Kingsville M
Texas Christian University M,O
Texas Southern University M,D
Texas State University-San Marcos M*
Texas Tech University M,D
Texas Woman's University M,D
Towson University M
Trevecca Nazarene University M
Trinity (Washington) University M
Troy University M,O
Tufts University M,D*
Union College (KY) M
Universidad del Este M
Université de Sherbrooke M,O
University at Buffalo, the State University of New York M,D,O*
The University of Akron M,D
The University of Alabama at Birmingham M*
University of Alaska Southeast M
University of Alberta M,D*
The University of Arizona M,D*
University of Arkansas M,O*
University of Arkansas at Pine Bluff M
University of Bridgeport M,O
University of California, Irvine M,D*
University of Central Florida M,D*
University of Central Missouri M,O
University of Central Oklahoma M
University of Cincinnati M
University of Connecticut M,D*
The University of Findlay M
University of Florida M,D,O*
University of Georgia M,D,O*
University of Hartford M*
University of Houston M,D*
University of Illinois at Chicago M,D*
University of Indianapolis M
The University of Iowa M,D*
University of Louisiana at Monroe M
University of Louisville M
University of Maine M,O*
University of Maryland, Baltimore County M*
University of Massachusetts Amherst M,D,O*
University of Massachusetts Boston M,D,O
University of Memphis M,D*
University of Miami M*
University of Michigan M,D*
University of Michigan–Flint M*
University of Minnesota, Twin Cities Campus M,D,O*
University of Missouri–Columbia M,D,O*
University of Missouri–St. Louis M,D
University of Montevallo M
University of Nebraska at Omaha M
University of Nevada, Las Vegas M,D,O
University of Nevada, Reno M,D,O*
University of New Hampshire M*
University of New Mexico M,O*
University of North Alabama M,O
The University of North Carolina at Charlotte M*
The University of North Carolina at Greensboro D
The University of North Carolina at Pembroke M
The University of North Carolina Wilmington M*
University of North Dakota M,D
University of Northern Colorado M,D
University of Northern Iowa M
University of North Florida M
University of Oklahoma M,D,O*
University of Pennsylvania M*
University of Phoenix–Central Florida Campus M
University of Phoenix–Central Valley Campus M
University of Phoenix–Denver Campus M
University of Phoenix–Fort Lauderdale Campus M
University of Phoenix–Hawaii Campus M
University of Phoenix–Las Vegas Campus M
University of Phoenix–Metro Detroit Campus M
University of Phoenix–Nashville Campus M
University of Phoenix–New Mexico Campus M
University of Phoenix—Northern Nevada Campus M
University of Phoenix–North Florida Campus M
University of Phoenix–Omaha Campus M
University of Phoenix Online Campus M
University of Phoenix–Oregon Campus M
University of Phoenix–Phoenix Campus M
University of Phoenix–Sacramento Valley Campus M,O
University of Phoenix–San Diego Campus M
University of Phoenix–Southern Arizona Campus M,O
University of Phoenix–Southern California Campus M
University of Phoenix–Southern Colorado Campus M,O
University of Phoenix–Utah Campus M
University of Phoenix–West Florida Campus M
University of Pittsburgh M*
University of Puget Sound M
University of Rhode Island M
University of St. Francis (IL) M
The University of Scranton M
University of South Alabama M,O*
University of South Carolina M,D*
University of South Carolina Aiken M
University of South Carolina Upstate M
The University of South Dakota M
University of Southern Indiana M
University of Southern Mississippi M,D,O*
University of South Florida M,D,O*
The University of Tennessee M,D,O*
The University of Tennessee at Chattanooga M,D,O
The University of Tennessee at Martin M
The University of Texas at San Antonio M*
The University of Texas–Pan American M
University of the Cumberlands M,O
University of the Incarnate Word M
The University of Toledo D,O*
University of Utah M,D*
The University of West Alabama M
University of West Florida M
University of Wisconsin–Eau Claire M
University of Wisconsin–La Crosse M
University of Wisconsin–Milwaukee M
University of Wisconsin–Platteville M
University of Wisconsin–River Falls M
University of Wisconsin–Stevens Point M
Utah State University M
Vanderbilt University M,D*
Villanova University M*
Wagner College M
Walden University M,D
Washington State University M,D*
Washington University in St. Louis M*
Wayne State College M
Wayne State University M,D,O*
West Chester University of Pennsylvania M
Western Carolina University M*
Western Illinois University M
Western Kentucky University M,O
Western Michigan University M*
Western New England College M
Western New Mexico University M
Western Washington University M
Westfield State College M
West Virginia University M*
Wheaton College M
Wheelock College M
Whittier College M
Whitworth University M
Widener University M,D*
Wilkes University M
William Carey University M,O
William Paterson University of New Jersey M*
Wilmington College (DE) M
Wingate University M
Winston-Salem State University M
Worcester State College M
Wright State University M*
Xavier University M*
Youngstown State University M

EMERGENCY MANAGEMENT

Adelphi University O*
American Public University System M
Anna Maria College M,O
Arkansas Tech University M
Benedictine University M
California State University, Long Beach M
Drexel University M*
The George Washington University M,D,O*
Jacksonville State University M
Lynn University M,O
North Dakota State University M,D
Oklahoma State University M*
Park University M
San Diego State University M,D*
Touro University International M,D,O
University of Nevada, Las Vegas M,D,O
Virginia Commonwealth University M,O*
West Chester University of Pennsylvania M,O
York University M*

EMERGENCY MEDICAL SERVICES

Alderson-Broaddus College M
Drexel University M*
The George Washington University M,O*
Oklahoma State University M*
San Diego State University M,D*
Université Laval O

ENERGY AND POWER ENGINEERING

New York Institute of Technology M,O
Rensselaer Polytechnic Institute M,D*
Southern Illinois University Carbondale D*
University of Alberta M,D*
University of Massachusetts Lowell M,D*
University of Memphis M,D*
University of Wisconsin–Madison M,D*
Worcester Polytechnic Institute M,D*

ENERGY MANAGEMENT AND POLICY

Boston University M*
New York Institute of Technology M,O
Université du Québec à Trois-Rivières M,D
Université du Québec, Institut National de la Recherche Scientifique M,D
University of California, Berkeley M,D*

ENGINEERING AND APPLIED SCIENCES—GENERAL

Air Force Institute of Technology M,D
Alabama Agricultural and Mechanical University M
Alfred University M,D*
The American University in Cairo M,O
The American University of Athens M
Andrews University M
Arizona State University M,D*

*P—first professional degree; M—master's degree; D—doctorate; O—other advanced degree; *full description and/or announcement in Book 2, 3, 4, 5, or 6*

- Arizona State University at the Polytechnic Campus M
- Auburn University M,D*
- Baylor University M*
- Boise State University M,D
- Boston University M,D*
- Bradley University M
- Brigham Young University M,D*
- Brown University M,D*
- Bucknell University M
- California Institute of Technology M,D,O*
- California National University for Advanced Studies M
- California Polytechnic State University, San Luis Obispo M
- California State Polytechnic University, Pomona M
- California State University, Chico M
- California State University, Fresno M
- California State University, Fullerton M
- California State University, Los Angeles M
- California State University, Northridge M
- California State University, Sacramento M*
- Carleton University M,D
- Carnegie Mellon University M,D*
- Case Western Reserve University M,D*
- The Catholic University of America M,D*
- Central Connecticut State University M
- Central Washington University M
- Christian Brothers University M
- City College of the City University of New York M,D*
- Clarkson University M,D*
- Clemson University M,D*
- Cleveland State University M,D
- Colorado School of Mines M,D,O
- Colorado State University M,D*
- Colorado State University-Pueblo M
- Columbia University M,D,O*
- Concordia University (Canada) M,D,O
- Cooper Union for the Advancement of Science and Art M
- Cornell University M,D*
- Dalhousie University M,D
- Dartmouth College M,D*
- Drexel University M,D*
- Duke University M,D*
- Eastern Illinois University M,O
- Eastern Michigan University M
- École Polytechnique de Montréal M,D,O
- Fairfield University M*
- Fairleigh Dickinson University, Metropolitan Campus M*
- Florida Agricultural and Mechanical University M,D*
- Florida Atlantic University M,D
- Florida Institute of Technology M,D*
- Florida International University M,D*
- Florida State University M,D*
- George Mason University M,D,O*
- The George Washington University M,D,O*
- Georgia Institute of Technology M,D,O*
- Graduate School and University Center of the City University of New York D*
- Grand Valley State University M
- Harvard University M,D*
- Howard University M,D*
- Idaho State University M,D,O
- Illinois Institute of Technology M,D*
- Indiana State University M,D*
- Indiana University–Purdue University Fort Wayne M
- Instituto Tecnologico de Santo Domingo M
- Instituto Tecnológico y de Estudios Superiores de Monterrey, Campus Ciudad Obregón M
- Instituto Tecnológico y de Estudios Superiores de Monterrey, Campus Monterrey M,D
- Iowa State University of Science and Technology M,D*
- The Johns Hopkins University M,D,O*
- Kansas State University M,D*
- Kent State University M*
- Lakehead University M
- Lamar University M,D*
- Laurentian University M
- Lawrence Technological University M,D
- Lehigh University M,D*
- Louisiana State University and Agricultural and Mechanical College M,D*
- Louisiana Tech University M,D
- Loyola College in Maryland M
- Manhattan College M
- Marquette University M,D
- Marshall University M
- Massachusetts Institute of Technology M,D,O*
- McGill University M,D,O*
- McMaster University M,D
- McNeese State University M
- Memorial University of Newfoundland M,D
- Mercer University M
- Miami University M,O*
- Michigan State University M,D*
- Michigan Technological University M,D*
- Milwaukee School of Engineering M*
- Mississippi State University M,D
- Montana State University M,D
- Montana Tech of The University of Montana M
- Morgan State University M,D*
- National University M
- New Jersey Institute of Technology M,D,O
- New Mexico State University M,D
- New York Institute of Technology M,O
- North Carolina Agricultural and Technical State University M,D
- North Carolina State University M,D*
- North Dakota State University M,D
- Northeastern University M,D*
- Northern Arizona University M,D,O
- Northern Illinois University M
- Northwestern Polytechnic University M
- Northwestern University M,D,O*
- Oakland University M,D*
- The Ohio State University M,D*
- Ohio University M,D*
- Oklahoma State University M,D*
- Old Dominion University M,D*
- Oregon State University M,D*
- Penn State Harrisburg M*
- Penn State University Park M,D*
- Pittsburg State University M,O
- Pontificia Universidad Catolica Madre y Maestra M
- Portland State University M,D,O
- Prairie View A&M University M,D
- Purdue University M,D,O*
- Purdue University Calumet M
- Queen's University at Kingston M,D
- Rensselaer at Hartford M
- Rensselaer Polytechnic Institute M,D*
- Rice University M,D*
- Rochester Institute of Technology M,D,O
- Rose-Hulman Institute of Technology M*
- Rowan University M
- Royal Military College of Canada M,D
- Rutgers, The State University of New Jersey, New Brunswick M,D*
- Saginaw Valley State University M
- St. Cloud State University M
- St. Mary's University of San Antonio M
- San Diego State University M,D*
- San Francisco State University M
- San Jose State University M
- Santa Clara University M,D,O
- Seattle University M
- Simon Fraser University M,D
- Sonoma State University M
- South Dakota School of Mines and Technology M,D
- South Dakota State University M,D
- Southern Illinois University Carbondale M,D*
- Southern Illinois University Edwardsville M
- Southern Methodist University M,D*
- Southern Polytechnic State University M
- Southern University and Agricultural and Mechanical College M*
- Stanford University M,D,O*
- State University of New York at Binghamton M,D*
- State University of New York Institute of Technology M
- Stevens Institute of Technology M,D,O*
- Stony Brook University, State University of New York M,D,O*
- Syracuse University M,D,O*
- Temple University M,D*
- Tennessee State University M,D*
- Tennessee Technological University M,D*
- Texas A&M University M,D*
- Texas A&M University–Kingsville M,D
- Texas Tech University M,D
- Tri-State University M
- Tufts University M,D*
- Tuskegee University M,D
- Union Graduate College M*
- Universidad de las Américas–Puebla M,D
- Université de Moncton M
- Université de Sherbrooke M,D,O
- Université du Québec à Chicoutimi M,D
- Université du Québec à Rimouski M
- Université du Québec, École de technologie supérieure M,D,O
- Université Laval M,D,O
- University at Buffalo, the State University of New York M,D*
- The University of Akron M,D
- The University of Alabama M,D
- The University of Alabama at Birmingham M,D*
- The University of Alabama in Huntsville M,D
- University of Alaska Anchorage M,O
- University of Alaska Fairbanks M,D
- The University of Arizona M,D*
- University of Arkansas M,D*
- University of Bridgeport M,D
- The University of British Columbia M,D*
- University of Calgary M,D
- University of California, Berkeley M,D*
- University of California, Davis M,D,O*
- University of California, Irvine M,D*
- University of California, Los Angeles M,D*
- University of California, Santa Barbara M,D*
- University of California, Santa Cruz M,D*
- University of Central Florida M,D,O*
- University of Central Oklahoma M
- University of Cincinnati M,D
- University of Colorado at Boulder M,D*
- University of Colorado at Colorado Springs M,D
- University of Connecticut M,D*
- University of Dayton M,D*
- University of Delaware M,D*
- University of Denver M,D*
- University of Detroit Mercy M,D
- University of Evansville M
- University of Florida M,D,O*
- University of Guelph M,D
- University of Hartford M*
- University of Hawaii at Manoa M,D,O*
- University of Houston M,D*
- University of Idaho M,D*
- University of Illinois at Chicago M,D*
- University of Illinois at Urbana–Champaign M,D*
- The University of Iowa M,D*
- University of Kansas M,D*
- University of Kentucky M,D*
- University of Louisville M,D
- University of Maine M,D*
- University of Manitoba M,D
- University of Maryland, Baltimore County M,D,O*
- University of Maryland, College Park M*
- University of Massachusetts Amherst M,D*
- University of Massachusetts Dartmouth M,D,O
- University of Massachusetts Lowell M,D,O*
- University of Memphis M,D*
- University of Miami M,D*
- University of Michigan M,D,O*
- University of Michigan–Dearborn M*
- University of Minnesota, Twin Cities Campus M,D*
- University of Mississippi M,D
- University of Missouri–Columbia M,D*
- University of Missouri–Kansas City M,D*
- University of Missouri–Rolla M,D*
- University of Nebraska–Lincoln M,D*
- University of Nevada, Las Vegas M,D
- University of Nevada, Reno M,D,O*
- University of New Brunswick Fredericton M,D,O
- University of New Haven M,O*
- University of New Mexico M,D*
- University of New Orleans M,D,O
- The University of North Carolina at Charlotte M,D*
- University of North Dakota D
- University of North Texas M*
- University of Notre Dame M,D*
- University of Oklahoma M,D*
- University of Ottawa M,D,O*
- University of Pennsylvania M,D,O*
- University of Pittsburgh M,D*
- University of Portland M
- University of Puerto Rico, Mayagüez Campus M,D*
- University of Regina M,D
- University of Rhode Island M,D
- University of Rochester M,D*
- University of St. Thomas (MN) M,O*
- University of Saskatchewan M,D,O
- University of South Alabama M*
- University of South Carolina M,D*
- University of Southern California M,D,O*
- University of Southern Indiana M
- University of Southern Mississippi M,D*
- University of South Florida M,D*
- The University of Tennessee M,D*
- The University of Tennessee at Chattanooga M,D,O
- The University of Tennessee Space Institute M,D*
- The University of Texas at Arlington M,D*
- The University of Texas at Austin M,D*
- The University of Texas at Dallas M,D*
- The University of Texas at El Paso M,D
- The University of Texas at San Antonio M,D*
- The University of Texas at Tyler M
- The University of Toledo M*
- University of Toronto M,D
- University of Tulsa M,D*
- University of Utah M,D,O*
- University of Vermont M,D*
- University of Victoria M,D
- University of Virginia M,D*
- University of Washington M,D*
- University of Waterloo M,D*
- The University of Western Ontario M,D
- University of Windsor M,D
- University of Wisconsin–Madison M,D,O*
- University of Wisconsin–Milwaukee M,D,O
- University of Wisconsin–Platteville M
- University of Wyoming M,D
- Utah State University M,D,O
- Vanderbilt University M,D*
- Villanova University M,D,O*
- Virginia Commonwealth University M,D,O*
- Virginia Polytechnic Institute and State University M,D*
- Walden University M,O
- Washington State University M,D*
- Washington State University Tri-Cities M,D
- Washington State University Vancouver M
- Washington University in St. Louis M,D*
- Wayne State University M,D,O*
- Western Michigan University M,D*
- Western New England College M
- West Texas A&M University M
- West Virginia University M,D*
- West Virginia University Institute of Technology M
- Wichita State University M,D*
- Widener University M*
- Wilkes University M
- Wright State University M,D*
- Yale University M,D*
- Youngstown State University M

ENGINEERING DESIGN

- The Catholic University of America M,D*
- Kettering University M
- Polytechnic University, Long Island Graduate Center M
- Rochester Institute of Technology M
- San Diego State University M,D*
- Santa Clara University M,D,O
- Stanford University M*
- Stevens Institute of Technology M*
- University of Central Florida M,D,O*
- University of Illinois at Urbana–Champaign M*
- University of New Haven M,O*
- Worcester Polytechnic Institute M*

ENGINEERING MANAGEMENT

- Air Force Institute of Technology M
- American University of Beirut M
- California National University for Advanced Studies M
- California State Polytechnic University, Pomona M
- California State University, East Bay M
- California State University, Long Beach M,D
- California State University, Northridge M
- Carnegie Mellon University M,D*

Case Western Reserve University M*
The Catholic University of America M*
Clarkson University M*
Colorado School of Mines M,D
Columbia University M,D,O*
Cornell University M,D*
Dallas Baptist University M
Dartmouth College M*
Drexel University M,D*
Duke University M*
Eastern Michigan University M
Florida Institute of Technology M*
Gannon University M
The George Washington University M,D,O*
Hofstra University M*
Instituto Tecnológico y de Estudios Superiores de Monterrey, Campus Chihuahua M,O
Kansas State University M,D*
Kettering University M
Lamar University M,D*
Lawrence Technological University M,D
Long Island University, C.W. Post Campus M*
Loyola Marymount University M,O
Marquette University M,D
Massachusetts Institute of Technology M,D*
McNeese State University M
Mercer University M
Michigan State University M,D*
Milwaukee School of Engineering M*
National University M
New Jersey Institute of Technology M
New Mexico Institute of Mining and Technology M
Northeastern University M,D*
Northwestern University M*
Oakland University M*
Oklahoma State University M*
Old Dominion University M,D*
Point Park University M*
Polytechnic University of Puerto Rico M
Polytechnic University of the Americas–Miami Campus M
Polytechnic University of the Americas–Orlando Campus M
Portland State University M,D,O
Rensselaer Polytechnic Institute M,D*
Rochester Institute of Technology M
Rose-Hulman Institute of Technology M*
St. Cloud State University M
Saint Martin's University M
St. Mary's University of San Antonio M
Santa Clara University M
Southern Methodist University M,D*
Stanford University M,D*
Stevens Institute of Technology M,D,O*
Syracuse University M*
Texas Tech University M,D
Tufts University M*
Union Graduate College M*
Université de Sherbrooke M,O
The University of Akron M
University of Alaska Anchorage M
University of Alaska Fairbanks M
University of Alberta M,D*
University of California, Berkeley M,D*
University of Central Florida M,D,O*
University of Colorado at Boulder M*
University of Colorado at Colorado Springs M
University of Dayton M*
University of Detroit Mercy M*
University of Kansas M*
University of Louisiana at Lafayette M*
University of Louisville M
University of Maryland, Baltimore County M*
University of Massachusetts Amherst M*
University of Michigan–Dearborn M*
University of Minnesota, Duluth M*
University of Missouri–Rolla M,D*
University of New Haven M*
University of New Orleans M,O
The University of North Carolina at Charlotte M*
University of Ottawa M,O*
University of St. Thomas (MN) M,O*
University of Southern California M*
University of South Florida M,D*
The University of Tennessee M,D*
The University of Tennessee at Chattanooga M,O
The University of Tennessee Space Institute M,D*
University of Tulsa M*
University of Waterloo M,D*
University of Wisconsin–Madison M*
Valparaiso University M,O
Virginia Polytechnic Institute and State University M,D*
Walden University M,D,O
Washington State University Spokane M
Wayne State University M*
Webster University M
Western Michigan University M*
Widener University M*

ENGINEERING PHYSICS

Air Force Institute of Technology M,D
Cornell University M,D*
Dartmouth College M,D*
École Polytechnique de Montréal M,D,O
Embry-Riddle Aeronautical University (FL) M*
George Mason University M*
McMaster University M,D
Michigan Technological University D*
Mississippi State University M,D
Polytechnic University, Brooklyn Campus M*
Polytechnic University, Long Island Graduate Center M
Rensselaer Polytechnic Institute M,D*
Stevens Institute of Technology M,D,O*
The University of British Columbia M*
University of California, San Diego M,D*
University of Maine M*
University of Oklahoma M,D*
University of Saskatchewan M,D
University of Virginia M,D*
University of Wisconsin–Madison M,D*
Yale University M,D*

ENGLISH

Abilene Christian University M
Acadia University M
The American University in Cairo M
American University of Beirut M
Andrews University M
Angelo State University M
Appalachian State University M
Arcadia University M
Arizona State University M,D*
Arkansas State University M,O
Arkansas Tech University M
Asbury College M,O
Auburn University M,D*
Austin Peay State University M
Ball State University M,D*
Baylor University M,D*
Belmont University M
Bemidji State University M
Bennington College M*
Bob Jones University P,M,D,O
Boise State University M
Boston College M,D*
Boston University M,D*
Bowie State University M
Bowling Green State University M,D*
Bradley University M
Brandeis University M,D*
Bridgewater State College M
Brigham Young University M*
Brock University M
Brooklyn College of the City University of New York M,D
Brown University M,D*
Bucknell University M
Buffalo State College, State University of New York M
Butler University M
California Baptist University M
California Polytechnic State University, San Luis Obispo M
California State Polytechnic University, Pomona M
California State University, Bakersfield M
California State University, Chico M
California State University, Dominguez Hills M,O
California State University, East Bay M
California State University, Fresno M
California State University, Fullerton M
California State University, Long Beach M
California State University, Los Angeles M
California State University, Northridge M
California State University, Sacramento M*
California State University, San Bernardino M
California State University, San Marcos M
California State University, Stanislaus M
Carleton University M,D
Carnegie Mellon University M,D*
Case Western Reserve University M,D*
The Catholic University of America M,D*
Central Connecticut State University M,O
Central Michigan University M*
Central Washington University M
Chapman University M
Chicago State University M
The Citadel, The Military College of South Carolina M
City College of the City University of New York M*
Claremont Graduate University M,D
Clarion University of Pennsylvania M
Clark Atlanta University M
Clark University M*
Clemson University M*
Cleveland State University M
College of Charleston M*
The College of New Jersey M
The College of Saint Rose M*
College of Staten Island of the City University of New York M
Columbia University M,D*
Concordia University (Canada) M
Connecticut College M
Converse College M
Cornell University M,D*
Creighton University M*
Dalhousie University M,D
DePaul University M*
Drew University M,D
Duke University D*
Duquesne University M,D*
East Carolina University M*
Eastern Illinois University M
Eastern Kentucky University M*
Eastern Michigan University M
Eastern New Mexico University M
Eastern Washington University M
East Tennessee State University M
Elmhurst College M
Emory University D,O*
Emporia State University M
Fairleigh Dickinson University, Metropolitan Campus M*
Fayetteville State University M
Fitchburg State College M
Florida Atlantic University M
Florida Gulf Coast University M
Florida International University M*
Florida State University M,D*
Fordham University M,D*
Fort Hays State University M
Gannon University M
Gardner-Webb University P,M,D
George Mason University M*
Georgetown University M*
The George Washington University M,D*
Georgia College & State University M
Georgia Southern University M
Georgia State University M,D*
Governors State University M
Graduate School and University Center of the City University of New York D*
Grand Valley State University M
Hardin-Simmons University M
Harvard University M,D,O*
Heritage University M
Hofstra University M*
Hollins University M
Howard University M,D*
Humboldt State University M
Hunter College of the City University of New York M
Idaho State University M,D,O
Illinois State University M,D*
Indiana State University M*
Indiana University Bloomington M,D*
Indiana University of Pennsylvania M,D
Indiana University–Purdue University Fort Wayne M,O
Indiana University–Purdue University Indianapolis M*
Indiana University South Bend M
Iona College M*
Iowa State University of Science and Technology M,D*
Jackson State University M
Jacksonville State University M
James Madison University M
John Carroll University M
The Johns Hopkins University D*
Kansas State University M*
Kent State University M,D*
Kutztown University of Pennsylvania M
Lakehead University M
Lamar University M*
La Sierra University M
Lehigh University M,D*
Lehman College of the City University of New York M
Long Island University, Brooklyn Campus M*
Long Island University, C.W. Post Campus M*
Longwood University M*
Louisiana State University and Agricultural and Mechanical College M,D*
Louisiana Tech University M
Loyola Marymount University M
Loyola University Chicago M,D*
Marquette University M,D
Marshall University M
Mary Baldwin College M
Marymount University M
McGill University M,D*
McMaster University M,D
McNeese State University M
Memorial University of Newfoundland M,D
Mercy College M
Miami University M,D*
Michigan State University M,D*
Middlebury College M
Middle Tennessee State University M,D*
Midwestern State University M
Millersville University of Pennsylvania M
Mills College M
Minnesota State University Mankato M,O
Mississippi College M
Mississippi State University M
Missouri State University M*
Monmouth University M
Montana State University M
Montclair State University M*
Morehead State University M
Morgan State University M,D*
Mount Mary College M
Murray State University M
National University M
New Mexico Highlands University M
New Mexico State University M,D
New York University M,D*
North Carolina Agricultural and Technical State University M
North Carolina Central University M
North Carolina State University M*
North Dakota State University M
Northeastern Illinois University M
Northeastern State University M
Northeastern University M,D,O*
Northern Arizona University M
Northern Illinois University M,D
Northern Michigan University M
Northwestern State University of Louisiana M
Northwestern University M,D*
Northwest Missouri State University M
Notre Dame de Namur University M,O
Oakland University M*
The Ohio State University M,D*
Ohio University M,D*
Oklahoma State University M,D*
Old Dominion University M,D*
Oregon State University M*
Our Lady of the Lake University of San Antonio M
Penn State University Park M,D*
Pittsburg State University M
Portland State University M
Prairie View A&M University M
Princeton University D*
Purdue University M,D*
Purdue University Calumet M
Queens College of the City University of New York M
Queen's University at Kingston M,D
Radford University M
Rhode Island College M
Rice University M,D*
Rivier College M
Roosevelt University M
Rosemont College M
Rutgers, The State University of New Jersey, Camden M

*P—first professional degree; M—master's degree; D—doctorate; O—other advanced degree; *full description and/or announcement in Book 2, 3, 4, 5, or 6*

Institution	Degrees
Rutgers, The State University of New Jersey, Newark	M*
Rutgers, The State University of New Jersey, New Brunswick	D*
St. Bonaventure University	M
St. Cloud State University	M
St. John's University (NY)	M,D
Saint Louis University	M,D*
Saint Louis University, Madrid	M*
St. Mary's University of San Antonio	M
Saint Xavier University	M,O
Salem State College	M
Salisbury University	M
Sam Houston State University	M
San Diego State University	M*
San Francisco State University	M,O
San Jose State University	M,O
Seton Hall University	M*
Sewanee: The University of the South	M*
Simmons College	M
Simon Fraser University	M,D
Slippery Rock University of Pennsylvania	M
Sonoma State University	M
South Dakota State University	M
Southeastern Louisiana University	M
Southeast Missouri State University	M
Southern Connecticut State University	M
Southern Illinois University Carbondale	M,D*
Southern Illinois University Edwardsville	M,O
Southern Methodist University	M,D*
Stanford University	M,D*
State University of New York at Binghamton	M,D*
State University of New York at Fredonia	M
State University of New York at New Paltz	M
State University of New York at Oswego	M
State University of New York College at Brockport	M*
State University of New York College at Cortland	M*
State University of New York College at Potsdam	M
Stephen F. Austin State University	M
Stetson University	M
Stony Brook University, State University of New York	M,D,O*
Sul Ross State University	M*
Syracuse University	M,D*
Tarleton State University	M
Temple University	M,D*
Tennessee State University	M*
Tennessee Technological University	M*
Texas A&M International University	M,D
Texas A&M University	M,D*
Texas A&M University–Commerce	M,D
Texas A&M University–Corpus Christi	M
Texas A&M University–Kingsville	M
Texas A&M University–Texarkana	M
Texas Christian University	M,D
Texas Southern University	M
Texas State University-San Marcos	M*
Texas Tech University	M,D
Texas Woman's University	M,D
Trinity College	M
Truman State University	M
Tufts University	M,D*
Tulane University	M,D*
Universidad de las Américas–Puebla	M
Université de Montréal	M,D
Université Laval	M,D
University at Albany, State University of New York	M,D*
University at Buffalo, the State University of New York	M,D*
The University of Akron	M
The University of Alabama	M,D
The University of Alabama at Birmingham	M*
The University of Alabama in Huntsville	M,O
University of Alaska Anchorage	M
University of Alaska Fairbanks	M
University of Alberta	M,D*
The University of Arizona	M,D*
University of Arkansas	M,D*
The University of British Columbia	M,D*
University of Calgary	M,D
University of California, Berkeley	D*
University of California, Davis	M,D*
University of California, Irvine	M,D*
University of California, Los Angeles	M,D*
University of California, Riverside	M,D*
University of California, San Diego	M*
University of California, Santa Barbara	D*
University of Central Arkansas	M
University of Central Florida	M*
University of Central Missouri	M
University of Central Oklahoma	M
University of Chicago	M,D*
University of Cincinnati	M,D
University of Colorado at Boulder	M,D*
University of Colorado at Denver and Health Sciences Center	M,O*
University of Connecticut	M,D*
University of Dallas	M
University of Dayton	M*
University of Delaware	M,D*
University of Denver	M,D*
University of Florida	M,D*
University of Georgia	M,D*
University of Guelph	M
University of Hawaii at Manoa	M,D*
University of Houston	M,D*
University of Houston–Clear Lake	M
University of Idaho	M*
University of Illinois at Chicago	M,D*
University of Illinois at Springfield	M
University of Illinois at Urbana–Champaign	M,D*
University of Indianapolis	M
The University of Iowa	M,D*
University of Kansas	M,D*
University of Kentucky	M,D*
University of Lethbridge	M,D
University of Louisiana at Lafayette	M,D*
University of Louisiana at Monroe	M
University of Louisville	M,D
University of Maine	M*
University of Manitoba	M,D
University of Maryland, College Park	M,D*
University of Massachusetts Amherst	M,D*
University of Massachusetts Boston	M
University of Memphis	M,D*
University of Miami	M,D*
University of Michigan	M,D,O*
University of Michigan–Flint	M*
University of Minnesota, Duluth	M*
University of Minnesota, Twin Cities Campus	M,D*
University of Mississippi	M,D
University of Missouri–Columbia	M,D*
University of Missouri–Kansas City	M,D*
University of Missouri–St. Louis	M,O
The University of Montana	M*
University of Montevallo	M
University of Nebraska at Kearney	M
University of Nebraska at Omaha	M,O
University of Nebraska–Lincoln	M,D*
University of Nevada, Las Vegas	M,D
University of Nevada, Reno	M,D*
University of New Brunswick Fredericton	M,D
University of New Hampshire	M,D*
University of New Mexico	M,D*
University of New Orleans	M
University of North Alabama	M
The University of North Carolina at Chapel Hill	M,D*
The University of North Carolina at Charlotte	M*
The University of North Carolina at Greensboro	M,D
The University of North Carolina Wilmington	M*
University of North Dakota	M,D
University of Northern Colorado	M
University of Northern Iowa	M
University of North Florida	M
University of North Texas	M,D*
University of Notre Dame	M,D*
University of Oklahoma	M,D*
University of Oregon	M,D*
University of Ottawa	M,D*
University of Pennsylvania	M,D*
University of Pittsburgh	M,D*
University of Puerto Rico, Mayagüez Campus	M*
University of Puerto Rico, Río Piedras	M,D*
University of Regina	M,D
University of Rhode Island	M,D
University of Richmond	M
University of Rochester	M,D*
University of St. Thomas (MN)	M*
University of Saskatchewan	M,D
University of South Alabama	M*
University of South Carolina	M,D*
The University of South Dakota	M,D
University of Southern Mississippi	M,D*
University of South Florida	M,D*
The University of Tennessee	M,D*
The University of Tennessee at Chattanooga	M
The University of Texas at Arlington	M,D*
The University of Texas at Austin	M,D*
The University of Texas at Brownsville	M
The University of Texas at El Paso	M
The University of Texas at San Antonio	M,D*
The University of Texas at Tyler	M
The University of Texas of the Permian Basin	M
The University of Texas–Pan American	M
University of the District of Columbia	M
University of the Incarnate Word	M,O
The University of Toledo	M,O*
University of Toronto	M,D
University of Tulsa	M,D*
University of Utah	M,D*
University of Vermont	M*
University of Victoria	M,D
University of Virginia	M,D*
University of Washington	M,D*
University of Waterloo	M,D*
The University of Western Ontario	M,D
University of West Florida	M
University of West Georgia	M
University of Windsor	M
University of Wisconsin–Eau Claire	M
University of Wisconsin–Madison	M,D*
University of Wisconsin–Milwaukee	M,D,O
University of Wisconsin–Oshkosh	M
University of Wisconsin–Stevens Point	M
University of Wyoming	M
Utah State University	M
Valdosta State University	M
Valparaiso University	M,O
Vanderbilt University	M,D*
Villanova University	M*
Virginia Commonwealth University	M*
Virginia Polytechnic Institute and State University	M,D*
Virginia State University	M
Wake Forest University	M*
Washington College	M
Washington State University	M,D*
Washington University in St. Louis	M,D*
Wayne State University	M,D*
Weber State University	M
West Chester University of Pennsylvania	M
Western Carolina University	M*
Western Connecticut State University	M*
Western Illinois University	M
Western Kentucky University	M
Western Michigan University	M,D*
Western Washington University	M
Westfield State College	M
West Texas A&M University	M
West Virginia University	M,D*
Wichita State University	M*
Wilfrid Laurier University	M,D
William Paterson University of New Jersey	M*
Winona State University	M
Winthrop University	M
Wright State University	M*
Xavier University	M*
Yale University	M,D*
York University	M,D*
Youngstown State University	M

ENGLISH AS A SECOND LANGUAGE

Institution	Degrees
Adelphi University	M,O*
Albright College	M
Alliant International University–Fresno	M,D,O*
Alliant International University–Irvine	M,D*
Alliant International University–San Diego	M,D,O*
American University	M,O*
The American University in Cairo	M,O
Andrews University	M,D,O
Arizona State University	M,D*
Arkansas Tech University	M
Asbury College	M,O
Avila University	M,O*
Azusa Pacific University	M
Ball State University	M,D*
Barry University	M,D,O*
Biola University	M,D,O
Bishop's University	M,O
Boston University	M,O*
Brigham Young University	M,O*
Brock University	M
California State University, Dominguez Hills	M,O
California State University, Fresno	M
California State University, Fullerton	M
California State University, Los Angeles	M
California State University, Sacramento	M*
California State University, San Bernardino	M
Cardinal Stritch University	M*
Carlos Albizu University, Miami Campus	M,D
Carson-Newman College	M
The Catholic University of America	M,D*
Central Connecticut State University	O
Central Michigan University	M*
Central Washington University	M
City University	M,O
Cleveland State University	M
College of Charleston	O*
The College of New Jersey	M,O
The College of New Rochelle	M,O
College of Notre Dame of Maryland	M
Columbia International University	M,D,O
Concordia University (Canada)	M,O
Cornerstone University	M,O
Dallas Baptist University	M
DeSales University	M,O
Drexel University	M,D,O*
Duquesne University	M,D*
Eastern Michigan University	M
Eastern Nazarene College	M,O
Eastern University	O*
Elms College	M,O
Emporia State University	M
Erikson Institute	M,O*
Fairfield University	M,O*
Florida International University	M,D,O*
Fordham University	M,D,O*
Framingham State College	M*
Fresno Pacific University	M
Furman University	M
Gannon University	O
George Mason University	M*
Georgetown University	M,D,O*
Georgia State University	M,D,O*
Gonzaga University	M
Grand Canyon University	M*
Grand Valley State University	M
Greensboro College	M
Hawai'i Pacific University	M*
Henderson State University	M,O
Heritage University	M
Hofstra University	M,O*
Holy Names University	M,O
Houston Baptist University	M
Hunter College of the City University of New York	M
Indiana State University	M,O*
Indiana University of Pennsylvania	M,D
Indiana University–Purdue University Fort Wayne	M,O
Inter American University of Puerto Rico, Metropolitan Campus	M
Inter American University of Puerto Rico, Ponce Campus	M
Inter American University of Puerto Rico, San Germán Campus	M
The Johns Hopkins University	M*
Kean University	M
Kent State University	M,D*
Langston University	M
Lehman College of the City University of New York	M
Long Island University, Brooklyn Campus	M*
Long Island University, C.W. Post Campus	M*
Long Island University, Westchester Graduate Campus	M
Madonna University	M
Manhattanville College	M*
Marymount University	M,O
Mercy College	M
Michigan State University	M,D*

Middle Tennessee State University M,O*
Mississippi College M
Montclair State University M,O*
Monterey Institute of International Studies M*
Moody Bible Institute P,M,O
Mount Saint Vincent University M
Murray State University M
Nazareth College of Rochester M
New Jersey City University M
Newman University M
The New School: A University M*
New York University M,D,O*
Northern Arizona University M,D,O
Notre Dame de Namur University M,O
Nova Southeastern University M,O*
Oakland University M,O*
Ohio Dominican University M
Ohio University M*
Oklahoma City University M
Oral Roberts University M,D
Pontifical Catholic University of Puerto Rico M,D
Portland State University M
Prescott College M,D
Providence College and Theological Seminary P,M,D,O
Queens College of the City University of New York M
Regent University M,D,O
Regis University M,O
Rhode Island College M,O
Rider University M,O*
Rutgers, The State University of New Jersey, New Brunswick M,D*
St. Cloud State University M
St. John's University (NY) M
Saint Martin's University M
Saint Michael's College M,O
Salem College M
Salem International University M
Salem State College M
Salisbury University M
San Diego State University M,O*
San Francisco State University M
San Jose State University M,O
School for International Training M
Seattle Pacific University M
Seattle University M,O
Shenandoah University M,D,O*
Simmons College M
Simon Fraser University M
Southeast Missouri State University M
Southern Connecticut State University M
Southern Illinois University Carbondale M*
Southern Illinois University Edwardsville M,O
Southern New Hampshire University M,O*
State University of New York at Fredonia M
State University of New York at New Paltz M
State University of New York College at Cortland M*
Stony Brook University, State University of New York M,D*
Teachers College Columbia University M,D*
Temple University M,D*
Texas A&M University–Kingsville M
Trevecca Nazarene University M
Trinity (Washington) University M
Trinity Western University M
Universidad del Este M
Universidad del Turabo M
University at Buffalo, the State University of New York M,D,O*
The University of Alabama M,D
The University of Alabama in Huntsville M,O
University of Alberta M,D*
The University of Arizona M,D*
The University of British Columbia M,D*
University of Calgary M,D,O
University of California, Los Angeles M*
University of Central Florida M,O*
University of Central Missouri M
University of Central Oklahoma M
University of Cincinnati M,D,O
University of Colorado at Denver and Health Sciences Center M,O*
University of Delaware M,D*
The University of Findlay M
University of Florida M,D,O*
University of Guam M
University of Hawaii at Manoa M,D,O*
University of Houston M,D*
University of Idaho M*
University of Illinois at Chicago M*
University of Illinois at Urbana–Champaign M*
University of Manitoba M
University of Maryland, College Park M,D,O*
University of Massachusetts Boston M
University of Miami M,D*
University of Michigan M,D*
University of Minnesota, Twin Cities Campus M*
University of Nebraska at Omaha M,O
University of Nevada, Las Vegas M,D,O
University of Nevada, Reno M,D,O*
The University of North Carolina at Charlotte M*
The University of North Carolina at Greensboro M,D,O
University of Northern Iowa M
University of Northern Virginia M,D
University of Pennsylvania M,D*
University of Phoenix–Omaha Campus M
University of Phoenix Online Campus M
University of Phoenix–Springfield Campus M
University of Pittsburgh O*
University of Puerto Rico, Río Piedras M*
University of San Francisco M,D
The University of Scranton M
University of South Carolina M,D,O*
University of Southern Maine M,O
The University of Tennessee M,D,O*
The University of Texas at Arlington M*
The University of Texas at Brownsville M
The University of Texas at San Antonio M,D*
The University of Texas of the Permian Basin M
The University of Texas–Pan American M
The University of Toledo M,O*
University of Washington M,D*
Wayne State College M
Webster University M
West Chester University of Pennsylvania M
Western Kentucky University M
West Virginia University M*
Wheaton College M,O
Wright State University M*

ENGLISH EDUCATION

Agnes Scott College M*
Alabama State University M,O
Albany State University M
Andrews University M,D,O
Appalachian State University M
Arcadia University M,D,O
Arkansas State University M,O
Arkansas Tech University M,O
Armstrong Atlantic State University M
Auburn University M,D,O*
Averett University M
Belmont University M
Bennington College M*
Bethel College (TN) M
Bob Jones University P,M,D,O
Boston College M*
Boston University M,O*
Brooklyn College of the City University of New York M,O
Brown University M*
Buffalo State College, State University of New York M
California State University, San Bernardino M
Campbell University M
Carthage College M,O
Chadron State College M,O
Charleston Southern University M
Chatham University M
Christopher Newport University M
City College of the City University of New York M,O*
Clarion University of Pennsylvania M
Clemson University M*
College of St. Joseph M
The College of William and Mary M
The Colorado College M
Columbia College Chicago M
Columbus State University M,O
Connecticut College M
Converse College M
Delta State University M
DeSales University M,O
Drake University M*
East Carolina University M*
Eastern Kentucky University M*
Edinboro University of Pennsylvania M
Elms College M,O
Emory & Henry College M
Fitchburg State College M
Florida Agricultural and Mechanical University M*
Florida Gulf Coast University M
Florida International University M,D*
Florida State University M,D,O*
Framingham State College M*
Gardner-Webb University M
Georgia College & State University M,O
Georgia Southern University M
Georgia State University M,D,O*
Grand Valley State University M
Harding University M,O
Henderson State University M,O
Hofstra University M*
Hunter College of the City University of New York M
Indiana University of Pennsylvania M,D
Indiana University–Purdue University Fort Wayne M,O
Indiana University–Purdue University Indianapolis M*
Iona College M*
Ithaca College M
Jackson State University M
Kent State University M,D*
Kutztown University of Pennsylvania M,O
Lehman College of the City University of New York M
Long Island University, Brooklyn Campus M*
Long Island University, C.W. Post Campus M*
Longwood University M*
Louisiana Tech University M,D
Lynchburg College M
Manhattanville College M*
Marymount University M
Maryville University of Saint Louis M,D
Miami University M,D*
Millersville University of Pennsylvania M
Mills College M,D
Minnesota State University Mankato M,O
Mississippi College M,O
Montclair State University M,O*
National-Louis University M,O
New York University M,D,O*
North Carolina Agricultural and Technical State University M
Northeastern Illinois University M
Northern Arizona University M
Northern State University M
North Georgia College & State University M,O
Northwestern State University of Louisiana M
Northwest Missouri State University M
Nova Southeastern University M,O*
Occidental College M
Plymouth State University M
Purdue University M,D,O*
Queens College of the City University of New York M,O
Quinnipiac University M*
Rider University M,O*
Rockford College M
Rollins College M
Rutgers, The State University of New Jersey, New Brunswick M*
Sage Graduate School M
St. John Fisher College M
Salem State College M
Salisbury University M
San Francisco State University M,O
San Jose State University M,O
Smith College M*
South Carolina State University M
Southern Illinois University Edwardsville M,O
Southwestern Oklahoma State University M
Stanford University M,D*
State University of New York at Binghamton M*
State University of New York at Plattsburgh M
State University of New York College at Brockport M*
State University of New York College at Cortland M*
Stony Brook University, State University of New York M,O*
Syracuse University M,D*
Teachers College Columbia University M,D*
Temple University M,D*
Texas A&M University M,D*
Texas A&M University–Commerce M,D
Texas Tech University M,D
Trinity (Washington) University M
Union Graduate College M*
University at Buffalo, the State University of New York M,D,O*
University of Alaska Fairbanks M
The University of Arizona M,D*
University of Arkansas at Pine Bluff M
University of Central Florida M*
University of Colorado at Denver and Health Sciences Center M,O*
University of Connecticut M,D*
University of Florida M,D,O*
University of Illinois at Chicago M,D*
University of Indianapolis M
The University of Iowa M,D*
University of Manitoba M
University of Michigan M,D*
University of Minnesota, Twin Cities Campus M*
University of Missouri–Columbia M,D,O*
The University of Montana M*
University of Nevada, Las Vegas M,D,O
University of New Hampshire M,D*
University of New Orleans M
The University of North Carolina at Chapel Hill M*
The University of North Carolina at Charlotte M*
The University of North Carolina at Greensboro M,D
The University of North Carolina at Pembroke M
University of Oklahoma M,D,O*
University of Phoenix–Omaha Campus M
University of Phoenix Online Campus M
University of Phoenix–Springfield Campus M
University of Pittsburgh M,D*
University of Puerto Rico, Mayagüez Campus M*
University of Puerto Rico, Río Piedras M,D*
University of St. Francis (IL) M
University of South Carolina M,D*
University of South Florida M,D,O*
The University of Tennessee M,D,O*
The University of Texas at El Paso M
The University of Texas at Tyler M
The University of Toledo M*
University of Victoria M,D
University of Washington M,D*
The University of West Alabama M
University of West Georgia M,O
University of Wisconsin–Eau Claire M
Vanderbilt University M,D*
Washington State University M,D*
Wayne State College M
Wayne State University M,D,O*
Western Carolina University M*
Western Connecticut State University M*
Western Governors University M,O
Western Kentucky University M
Western Michigan University M,D*
Western New England College M
Widener University M,D*
Wilkes University M
William Carey University M,O
Worcester State College M

ENTOMOLOGY

Auburn University M,D*
Clemson University M,D*
Colorado State University M,D*
Cornell University M,D*
Florida Agricultural and Mechanical University M*
Illinois State University M,D*
Iowa State University of Science and Technology M,D*
Kansas State University M,D*
Louisiana State University and Agricultural and Mechanical College M,D*
McGill University M,D*
Michigan State University M,D*
Mississippi State University M,D
New Mexico State University M
North Carolina State University M,D*
North Dakota State University M,D
The Ohio State University M,D*
Oklahoma State University D*
Penn State University Park M,D*
Purdue University M,D*

*P—first professional degree; M—master's degree; D—doctorate; O—other advanced degree; *full description and/or announcement in Book 2, 3, 4, 5, or 6*

Rutgers, The State University of New Jersey, New Brunswick M,D*
Simon Fraser University M,D
State University of New York College of Environmental Science and Forestry M,D
Texas A&M University M,D*
Texas Tech University M,D
The University of Arizona M,D*
University of Arkansas M,D*
University of California, Davis M,D*
University of California, Riverside M,D*
University of Connecticut M,D*
University of Delaware M,D*
University of Florida M,D*
University of Georgia M,D*
University of Guelph M,D
University of Hawaii at Manoa M,D*
University of Idaho M,D*
University of Illinois at Urbana–Champaign M,D*
University of Kansas M,D*
University of Kentucky M,D*
University of Maine M*
University of Manitoba M,D
University of Maryland, College Park M,D*
University of Massachusetts Amherst M,D*
University of Minnesota, Twin Cities Campus M,D*
University of Missouri–Columbia M,D*
University of Nebraska–Lincoln M,D*
University of North Dakota M,D
University of Rhode Island M,D
The University of Tennessee M,D*
University of Wisconsin–Madison M,D*
University of Wyoming M,D
Virginia Polytechnic Institute and State University M,D*
Washington State University M,D*
West Virginia University M,D*

ENTREPRENEURSHIP

American College of Thessaloniki M,O
American University M*
Andrew Jackson University M
Baldwin-Wallace College M
Bay Path College M
Benedictine University M
Bernard M. Baruch College of the City University of New York M,D*
California Lutheran University M,O
California State University, East Bay M
Cameron University M
Carlos Albizu University, Miami Campus M,D
Columbia University M*
Concordia University (CA) M
Dallas Baptist University M
DePaul University M*
Eastern Michigan University M
Fairleigh Dickinson University, College at Florham M,O*
Fairleigh Dickinson University, Metropolitan Campus M,O*
Felician College M*
Florida Atlantic University M
Georgia Institute of Technology M,O*
Georgia State University M,D*
Huron University USA in London M
Illinois Institute of Technology M*
Inter American University of Puerto Rico, San Germán Campus D
The International University of Monaco M
Jones International University M
Lamar University M*
Lincoln University (MO) M
Lindenwood University M
McGill University M,D,O*
Northeastern University M*
Oakland University M,O*
Park University M
Penn State Great Valley M
Polytechnic University, Long Island Graduate Center M,D,O
Regent University M,D,O
Rensselaer Polytechnic Institute M,D*
St. Edward's University M,O
San Diego State University M*
Simmons College M,O
South Carolina State University M
Stevens Institute of Technology M,O*
Syracuse University M*
Texas Tech University M
Université du Québec à Trois-Rivières M
Université Laval M,O
The University of Akron M
University of Dallas M
University of Delaware M,D*
University of Florida M,D,O*
University of Hawaii at Manoa M*
University of Houston D*
The University of Iowa M*
University of Louisville D
University of Minnesota, Twin Cities Campus M*
University of San Francisco M
University of South Florida M,O*
The University of Tampa M
University of the Incarnate Word M,D
University of Waterloo M*
The University of Western Ontario M,D
University of Wisconsin–Madison M*
Western Carolina University M*
Wilkes University M

ENVIRONMENTAL AND OCCUPATIONAL HEALTH

American University of Beirut M
Anna Maria College M
Boston University M,D*
California State University, Fresno M
California State University, Northridge M
Colorado State University M,D*
Columbia Southern University M
Columbia University M,D*
Duke University M,D,O*
East Carolina University M*
Eastern Kentucky University M*
East Tennessee State University M
Emory University M*
Fort Valley State University M
Gannon University M,O
The George Washington University M,D*
Harvard University M,D*
Hunter College of the City University of New York M
Illinois Institute of Technology M*
Indiana State University M*
Indiana University of Pennsylvania M
The Johns Hopkins University M,D*
Loma Linda University M
Loyola University Chicago M*
McGill University M,D,O*
Medical College of Wisconsin M*
Meharry Medical College M
Mississippi Valley State University M
Montclair State University M,D,O*
Murray State University M
New Jersey Institute of Technology M
New York Medical College M*
New York University M,D*
Oakland University M*
OGI School of Science & Engineering at Oregon Health & Science University M,D
Old Dominion University M*
Oregon State University M*
Penn State University Park M,D*
Saint Joseph's University M,O*
Saint Mary's University of Minnesota M
San Diego State University M,D*
Stony Brook University, State University of New York M,O*
Temple University M*
Texas A&M Health Science Center M*
Touro University International M,D,O
Towson University D
Tufts University M,D*
Tulane University M,D*
Uniformed Services University of the Health Sciences M,D*
Université de Montréal M,O
Université du Québec à Montréal O
Université Laval O
University at Albany, State University of New York M,D*
The University of Alabama at Birmingham D*
University of Alberta M,D*
University of Arkansas for Medical Sciences M*
The University of British Columbia M,D*
University of California, Berkeley M,D*
University of California, Los Angeles M,D*
University of Central Missouri M,O
University of Cincinnati M,D
University of Connecticut M*
University of Florida M*
University of Georgia M,D*
University of Illinois at Chicago M,D*
The University of Iowa M,D,O*
University of Miami M*
University of Michigan M,D*
University of Minnesota, Twin Cities Campus M,D,O*
University of Nevada, Reno M,D*
University of New Haven M*
The University of North Carolina at Chapel Hill M,D*
University of North Texas Health Science Center at Fort Worth M,D
University of Oklahoma M,D*
University of Oklahoma Health Sciences Center M,D
University of Pittsburgh M*
University of Puerto Rico, Medical Sciences Campus M,D*
University of South Alabama M*
University of South Carolina M,D*
University of Southern Mississippi M*
University of South Florida M,D*
University of the Sacred Heart M
The University of Toledo M*
University of Washington M,D*
University of Wisconsin–Eau Claire M
University of Wisconsin–Whitewater M*
Virginia Commonwealth University M*
Washington State University Tri-Cities M,D
Wayne State University M,O*
West Chester University of Pennsylvania M,O
West Virginia University D*
Yale University M,D*

ENVIRONMENTAL BIOLOGY

Antioch University New England M*
Baylor University M,D*
Emporia State University M
Georgia State University M,D*
Governors State University M
Hood College M
Massachusetts Institute of Technology M,D,O*
Montana State University M,D
Morgan State University D*
Nicholls State University M
Nova Scotia Agricultural College M
Ohio University M,D*
Rutgers, The State University of New Jersey, New Brunswick M,D*
Sonoma State University M
State University of New York College of Environmental Science and Forestry M,D
Tennessee Technological University M*
University of Alberta M,D*
University of California, Santa Cruz M,D*
University of Guelph M,D
University of Louisiana at Lafayette M,D*
University of Louisville D
University of Massachusetts Amherst M,D*
University of Massachusetts Boston D
University of Missouri–Rolla M*
University of North Dakota M,D
University of Southern Mississippi M,D*
University of West Florida M
University of Wisconsin–Madison M,D*
Washington University in St. Louis D*
West Virginia University M,D*

ENVIRONMENTAL DESIGN

Arizona State University D*
Art Center College of Design M*
Clemson University D*
Columbia University M*
Cornell University M*
Kent State University M,O*
Michigan State University M,D*
Minnesota State University Mankato M,O
San Diego State University M*
Texas Tech University M,D
Université de Montréal M,D,O
University of Calgary M,D
University of California, Berkeley M*
University of Missouri–Columbia M*
Virginia Polytechnic Institute and State University D*
Yale University M*

ENVIRONMENTAL EDUCATION

Alaska Pacific University M
Antioch University New England M*
Arcadia University M,D,O
Brooklyn College of the City University of New York M
California State University, Fullerton M
California State University, San Bernardino M
Chatham University M
Concordia University Wisconsin M
Florida Institute of Technology M,D,O*
Gannon University M
Lesley University M,D,O*
Maryville University of Saint Louis M,D
New York University M*
Prescott College M
Saint Vincent College M
Slippery Rock University of Pennsylvania M
Southern Connecticut State University M,O
Southern Oregon University M
Universidad Metropolitana M
Université du Québec à Montréal M,D,O
University of Minnesota, Twin Cities Campus M,D,O*
University of New Hampshire M*
University of Victoria M,D
Western Washington University M
West Virginia University M*

ENVIRONMENTAL ENGINEERING

Air Force Institute of Technology M
Auburn University M,D*
California Institute of Technology M,D*
California Polytechnic State University, San Luis Obispo M
Carleton University M,D
Carnegie Mellon University M,D*
The Catholic University of America M,D*
Clarkson University M,D*
Clemson University M,D*
Cleveland State University M,D
Colorado School of Mines M,D
Columbia University M,D,O*
Concordia University (Canada) M,D,O
Cornell University M,D*
Drexel University M,D*
Duke University M,D*
École Polytechnique de Montréal M,D,O
Florida Agricultural and Mechanical University M,D*
Florida International University M*
Florida State University M,D*
Gannon University M
The George Washington University M,D,O*
Georgia Institute of Technology M,D*
Idaho State University M,D,O
Illinois Institute of Technology M,D*
Instituto Tecnologico de Santo Domingo M
Instituto Tecnológico y de Estudios Superiores de Monterrey, Campus Ciudad de México M,D
Instituto Tecnológico y de Estudios Superiores de Monterrey, Campus Monterrey M,D
Iowa State University of Science and Technology M,D*
The Johns Hopkins University M,D,O*
Lamar University M,D*
Lehigh University M,D*
Louisiana State University and Agricultural and Mechanical College M,D*
Manhattan College M
Marquette University M,D
Massachusetts Institute of Technology M,D,O*
McGill University M,D,O*
Memorial University of Newfoundland M
Michigan State University M,D*
Michigan Technological University M,D*
Milwaukee School of Engineering M*
Montana State University M,D
Montana Tech of The University of Montana M
National University M
New Jersey Institute of Technology M,D
New Mexico Institute of Mining and Technology M
New Mexico State University M,D
New York Institute of Technology M
North Carolina Agricultural and Technical State University M

North Dakota State University M,D
Northeastern University M,D*
Northwestern University M,D*
OGI School of Science & Engineering at Oregon Health & Science University M,D
Ohio University M,D*
Oklahoma State University M,D*
Old Dominion University M,D*
Oregon State University M,D*
Penn State Harrisburg M*
Penn State University Park M,D*
Polytechnic University, Brooklyn Campus M*
Polytechnic University, Long Island Graduate Center M
Pontificia Universidad Catolica Madre y Maestra M
Portland State University M,D
Princeton University M,D*
Rensselaer Polytechnic Institute M,D*
Rice University M,D*
Rose-Hulman Institute of Technology M*
Royal Military College of Canada M,D
Rutgers, The State University of New Jersey, New Brunswick M,D*
Southern Methodist University M,D*
Stanford University M,D,O*
State University of New York College of Environmental Science and Forestry M,D
Stevens Institute of Technology M,D,O*
Syracuse University M,D*
Texas A&M University M,D*
Texas A&M University–Kingsville M,D
Texas Tech University M,D
Tufts University M,D*
Tulane University M,D*
Universidad Nacional Pedro Henriquez Urena P,M,D
Université de Sherbrooke M
Université Laval M,D
University at Buffalo, the State University of New York M,D*
The University of Alabama M,D
The University of Alabama at Birmingham M*
The University of Alabama in Huntsville M,D
University of Alaska Anchorage M
University of Alaska Fairbanks M,D
University of Alberta M,D*
The University of Arizona M,D*
University of Arkansas M*
University of California, Berkeley M,D*
University of California, Davis M,D,O*
University of California, Irvine M,D*
University of California, Los Angeles M,D*
University of California, Riverside M,D*
University of Central Florida M,D,O*
University of Cincinnati M,D
University of Colorado at Boulder M,D*
University of Connecticut M,D*
University of Dayton M*
University of Delaware M,D*
University of Detroit Mercy M
University of Florida M,D,O*
University of Guelph M,D
University of Hawaii at Manoa M,D*
University of Houston M,D*
University of Idaho M*
University of Illinois at Urbana–Champaign M,D*
The University of Iowa M,D*
University of Kansas M,D*
University of Louisville M,D
University of Maine M,D*
University of Maryland, Baltimore County M,D*
University of Maryland, College Park M,D*
University of Massachusetts Amherst M*
University of Massachusetts Lowell M*
University of Memphis M,D*
University of Michigan M,D,O*
University of Missouri–Columbia M,D*
University of Missouri–Rolla M*
University of Nebraska–Lincoln M,D*
University of New Brunswick Fredericton M,D
University of New Haven M,O*
The University of North Carolina at Chapel Hill M,D*
The University of North Carolina at Charlotte D*
University of North Dakota M
University of Notre Dame M,D*
University of Oklahoma M,D*
University of Pittsburgh M,D*
University of Regina M,D
University of Rhode Island M
University of Saskatchewan M,D,O
University of Southern California M,D*
University of South Florida M,D*
The University of Tennessee M*
The University of Texas at Arlington M,D*
The University of Texas at Austin M*
The University of Texas at El Paso M,D
The University of Texas at San Antonio M,D*
University of Utah M,D*
University of Vermont M,D*
University of Washington M,D*
University of Waterloo M,D*
University of Windsor M,D
University of Wisconsin–Madison M,D*
University of Wyoming M
Utah State University M,D,O
Vanderbilt University M,D*
Villanova University M*
Virginia Polytechnic Institute and State University M,D*
Washington State University M*
Washington University in St. Louis M,D*
West Virginia University M,D*
Worcester Polytechnic Institute M,D,O*
Youngstown State University M

ENVIRONMENTAL MANAGEMENT AND POLICY

Adelphi University M*
Air Force Institute of Technology M
American Public University System M
American University M,D,O*
American University of Beirut M
Antioch University New England M,D*
Antioch University Seattle M*
Arizona State University at the Polytechnic Campus M
Bard College M*
Baylor University M*
Bemidji State University M
Boise State University M
Boston University M,D,O*
Brown University M*
California Polytechnic State University, San Luis Obispo M
California State University, Fullerton M
Central European University M,D*
Central Washington University M
Clark University M*
Clemson University M,D*
Cleveland State University M
College of the Atlantic M
Colorado State University M,D*
Columbia University M*
Concordia University (Canada) M,O
Cornell University M,D*
Dalhousie University M
Drexel University M*
Duke University M,D*
Duquesne University M,O*
East Carolina University D*
The Evergreen State College M
Florida Gulf Coast University M
Florida Institute of Technology M,D*
Florida International University M*
Friends University M
Gannon University M
The George Washington University M,D*
Georgia Institute of Technology M,D*
Goddard College M
Green Mountain College M
Hardin-Simmons University M
Harvard University M,O*
Illinois Institute of Technology M*
Indiana University–Purdue University Indianapolis M*
Instituto Tecnológico y de Estudios Superiores de Monterrey, Campus Estado de México M,D
Instituto Tecnológico y de Estudios Superiores de Monterrey, Campus Irapuato M,D
Iowa State University of Science and Technology M,D*
The Johns Hopkins University M*
Kansas State University M*
Kean University M
Lamar University M,D*
Long Island University, C.W. Post Campus M*
Louisiana State University and Agricultural and Mechanical College M*
McGill University M,D*
Michigan State University M,D*
Michigan Technological University M*
Missouri State University M*
Montana State University M,D
Montclair State University M,D*
Monterey Institute of International Studies M*
Morehead State University M
Naropa University M*
New Jersey Institute of Technology M,D
New Mexico Highlands University M
New York Institute of Technology M,O
North Dakota State University M,D
Northeastern Illinois University M
Northern Arizona University M,O
Nova Scotia Agricultural College M
The Ohio State University M,D*
Ohio University M*
Oregon State University M,D*
Penn State University Park M*
Plymouth State University M
Polytechnic University of Puerto Rico M
Portland State University M,D
Prescott College M
Princeton University M,D*
Purdue University M,D*
Rensselaer Polytechnic Institute M,D*
Rice University M*
Rochester Institute of Technology M
Royal Roads University M
St. Cloud State University M
Saint Joseph's University M,O*
Saint Mary-of-the-Woods College M
Samford University M
San Francisco State University M
San Jose State University M
Shippensburg University of Pennsylvania M
Simon Fraser University M,D
Slippery Rock University of Pennsylvania M
Southeast Missouri State University M
Southern Illinois University Edwardsville M
Stanford University M*
State University of New York College of Environmental Science and Forestry M,D
Stony Brook University, State University of New York M,O*
Texas State University-San Marcos M*
Texas Tech University M,D
Towson University M
Trent University M,D
Tropical Agriculture Research and Higher Education Center M,D
Troy University M
Tufts University M,D,O*
Universidad del Turabo M
Universidad Metropolitana M
Universidad Nacional Pedro Henriquez Urena P,M,D
Université de Montréal O
Université du Québec à Chicoutimi M
Université du Québec, Institut National de la Recherche Scientifique M,D
Université Laval M,D
University at Albany, State University of New York M*
University of Alaska Fairbanks M
University of Alberta M,D*
The University of British Columbia M,D*
University of Calgary M,D,O
University of California, Berkeley M,D*
University of California, Santa Barbara M,D*
University of California, Santa Cruz D*
University of Chicago M,D*
University of Colorado at Boulder M,D*
University of Connecticut M,D*
University of Delaware M,D*
University of Denver M,O*
The University of Findlay M
University of Guelph M,D
University of Hawaii at Manoa M,D,O*
University of Houston–Clear Lake M
University of Idaho M*
University of Illinois at Springfield M
University of Maine M,D*
University of Manitoba M,D
University of Maryland University College M,O
University of Massachusetts Lowell M,D,O*
University of Miami M,D*
University of Michigan M,D*
University of Minnesota, Twin Cities Campus M,D*
University of Missouri–St. Louis M,D,O
The University of Montana M,D*
University of Nevada, Reno M*
University of New Brunswick Saint John M
University of New Hampshire M*
The University of North Carolina at Chapel Hill M,D*
University of Northern British Columbia M,D,O
University of Oregon M,D*
University of Pennsylvania M*
University of Pittsburgh M*
University of Rhode Island M,D
University of San Francisco M
University of South Carolina M*
University of South Florida M*
The University of Tennessee M,D*
The University of Texas at Austin M*
University of Vermont M,D*
University of Washington M,D*
University of Waterloo M*
University of Wisconsin–Green Bay M
University of Wisconsin–Madison M,D*
Utah State University M,D
Vanderbilt University M,D*
Vermont Law School M
Virginia Commonwealth University M*
Webster University M,D
Wesley College M
West Virginia University M,D*
Yale University M,D*
York University M,D*
Youngstown State University M,O

ENVIRONMENTAL SCIENCES

Alabama Agricultural and Mechanical University M,D
Alaska Pacific University M
American University M*
American University of Beirut M
Antioch University New England M,D*
Arkansas State University M,D,O
California State Polytechnic University, Pomona M
California State University, Chico M
California State University, Fullerton M
California State University, Northridge M
California State University, San Bernardino M
Christopher Newport University M
City College of the City University of New York M,D*
Clarkson University M,D*
Clemson University M,D*
Cleveland State University M,D
College of Charleston M*
College of Staten Island of the City University of New York M
Columbia University M*
Columbus State University M
Cornell University M,D*
Drexel University M,D*
Duke University M,D*
Duquesne University M,O*
Florida Agricultural and Mechanical University M,D*
Florida Atlantic University M
Florida Gulf Coast University M
Florida Institute of Technology M,D*
Florida International University M*
Gannon University O
Georgia Institute of Technology M,D*
Graduate School and University Center of the City University of New York D*
Hawai'i Pacific University M*
Howard University M,D*
Humboldt State University M
Hunter College of the City University of New York M,O
Idaho State University M
Indiana University Bloomington M,D*
Indiana University Northwest M,O
Instituto Tecnologico de Santo Domingo M
Instituto Tecnológico y de Estudios Superiores de Monterrey, Campus Ciudad de México M,D

P—first professional degree; M—master's degree; D—doctorate; O—other advanced degree;
**full description and/or announcement in Book 2, 3, 4, 5, or 6*

Inter American University of Puerto Rico, San Germán Campus M
Iowa State University of Science and Technology M,D*
Jackson State University M,D
The Johns Hopkins University M*
Lehigh University M,D*
Long Island University, C.W. Post Campus M*
Louisiana State University and Agricultural and Mechanical College M,D*
Loyola Marymount University M
Marshall University M
Massachusetts Institute of Technology M,D,O*
McNeese State University M
Memorial University of Newfoundland M
Miami University M*
Michigan State University M,D*
Minnesota State University Mankato M
Montana State University M,D
Montclair State University M,D,O*
Murray State University M
New Jersey Institute of Technology M,D
New Mexico Institute of Mining and Technology M,D
North Carolina Agricultural and Technical State University M
North Dakota State University M,D
Northern Arizona University M,O
Nova Scotia Agricultural College M
Nova Southeastern University M*
Oakland University M,D*
OGI School of Science & Engineering at Oregon Health & Science University M,D
The Ohio State University M,D*
Oklahoma State University M,D*
Oregon State University M,D*
Pace University M*
Penn State Harrisburg M*
Penn State University Park M*
Polytechnic University, Brooklyn Campus M*
Pontifical Catholic University of Puerto Rico M
Portland State University M,D
Queens College of the City University of New York M
Rensselaer Polytechnic Institute M,D*
Rice University M,D*
Rochester Institute of Technology M
Royal Military College of Canada M,D
Rutgers, The State University of New Jersey, Newark M,D*
Rutgers, The State University of New Jersey, New Brunswick M,D*
South Dakota School of Mines and Technology D
Southern Illinois University Carbondale D*
Southern Illinois University Edwardsville M
Southern Methodist University M,D*
Southern University and Agricultural and Mechanical College M*
Stanford University M,D,O*
State University of New York College at Brockport M*
State University of New York College of Environmental Science and Forestry M,D
Stephen F. Austin State University M
Tarleton State University M
Taylor University M
Tennessee Technological University D*
Texas A&M University–Corpus Christi M
Texas Christian University M
Texas Tech University M,D
Towson University M,O
Tufts University M,D*
Tuskegee University M
Université de Sherbrooke M,O
Université du Québec à Montréal M,D
Université du Québec à Trois-Rivières M,D
Université Laval M,D
University at Albany, State University of New York M*
The University of Alabama in Huntsville M,D
University of Alaska Anchorage M
University of Alaska Fairbanks M,D
University of Alberta M,D*
The University of Arizona M,D*
University of California, Berkeley M,D*
University of California, Davis M,D*
University of California, Los Angeles D*
University of California, Riverside M,D*
University of California, Santa Barbara M,D*
University of Chicago M,D*
University of Cincinnati M,D
University of Colorado at Colorado Springs M
University of Colorado at Denver and Health Sciences Center M,O*
University of Guam M
University of Guelph M,D
University of Houston–Clear Lake M
University of Idaho M,D*
University of Illinois at Springfield M
University of Illinois at Urbana–Champaign M,D*
University of Kansas M,D*
University of Lethbridge M,D
University of Maine M,D*
University of Maryland, Baltimore M,D*
University of Maryland, Baltimore County M,D*
University of Maryland, College Park M,D*
University of Maryland Eastern Shore M,D*
University of Massachusetts Boston D
University of Massachusetts Lowell M,D,O*
University of Medicine and Dentistry of New Jersey D*
University of Michigan M,D*
University of Michigan–Dearborn M*
The University of Montana M*
University of Nevada, Las Vegas M,D
University of Nevada, Reno M,D*
University of New Haven M*
University of New Orleans M
The University of North Carolina at Chapel Hill M,D*
University of Northern Iowa M
University of North Texas M,D*
University of Oklahoma M,D*
University of Rhode Island M,D
University of South Carolina M,D*
University of South Florida M*
The University of Tennessee at Chattanooga M
The University of Texas at Arlington M,D*
The University of Texas at El Paso M,D
The University of Texas at San Antonio M,D*
University of Utah M*
University of Virginia M,D*
The University of Western Ontario M,D
University of West Florida M
University of Windsor M,D
University of Wisconsin–Green Bay M
University of Wisconsin–Madison M,D*
Vanderbilt University M*
Virginia Commonwealth University M*
Virginia Polytechnic Institute and State University M,D*
Washington State University M,D*
Washington State University Tri-Cities M,D
Washington State University Vancouver M
Western Connecticut State University M*
Western Washington University M
West Texas A&M University M
Wichita State University M*
Wright State University M,D*
Yale University M,D*

EPIDEMIOLOGY

American University of Beirut M
Boston University M,D*
Brown University M,D*
Case Western Reserve University M,D*
Columbia University M,D*
Cornell University M,D*
Cornell University, Joan and Sanford I. Weill Medical College and Graduate School of Medical Sciences M*
Dalhousie University M
East Tennessee State University M,O
Emory University M,D*
Georgetown University M*
The George Washington University M,D*
Harvard University M,D*
The Johns Hopkins University M,D*
Loma Linda University M
McGill University M,D,O*
Medical College of Wisconsin M*
Medical University of South Carolina M,D*
Memorial University of Newfoundland M,D,O
Michigan State University M,D*
New York Medical College M,D,O*
New York University M,D*
North Carolina State University M,D*
Oregon Health & Science University M*
Purdue University M,D*
Queen's University at Kingston M
San Diego State University M,D*
Stanford University M,D*
Temple University M*
Texas A&M Health Science Center M*
Texas A&M University M,D
Tufts University M,D,O*
Tulane University M,D*
Université Laval M,D
University at Albany, State University of New York M,D*
University at Buffalo, the State University of New York M,D*
The University of Alabama at Birmingham D*
University of Alberta M,D*
The University of British Columbia M,D*
University of Calgary M,D
University of California, Berkeley M,D*
University of California, Davis M,D*
University of California, Los Angeles M,D*
University of California, San Diego D*
University of Cincinnati M,D
University of Colorado at Denver and Health Sciences Center D*
University of Florida M*
University of Guelph M,D,O
University of Hawaii at Manoa D*
University of Illinois at Chicago M,D*
The University of Iowa M,D*
University of Maryland, Baltimore M,D*
University of Maryland, Baltimore County M*
University of Massachusetts Lowell M,D,O*
University of Massachusetts Worcester D*
University of Medicine and Dentistry of New Jersey M,D,O*
University of Miami D*
University of Michigan M,D*
University of Minnesota, Twin Cities Campus M,D*
The University of North Carolina at Chapel Hill M,D*
University of North Texas Health Science Center at Fort Worth M,D
University of Oklahoma Health Sciences Center M,D
University of Ottawa M*
University of Pennsylvania M,D*
University of Pittsburgh M,D*
University of Prince Edward Island M,D
University of Puerto Rico, Medical Sciences Campus M*
University of Rochester M,D*
University of Saskatchewan M,D
University of South Carolina M,D*
University of Southern California M,D*
University of Southern Mississippi M*
University of South Florida M,D*
University of Washington M,D*
The University of Western Ontario M,D
Virginia Commonwealth University D*
Yale University M,D*

ERGONOMICS AND HUMAN FACTORS

Bentley College M*
The Catholic University of America M*
Clemson University D*
Cornell University M*
Embry-Riddle Aeronautical University (FL) M*
Florida Institute of Technology M*
Indiana University Bloomington M,D,O*
New York University M,D*
North Carolina State University D*
Old Dominion University D*
San Jose State University M
Tufts University M,D*
Université de Montréal O
Université du Québec à Montréal O
University of Central Florida M,D,O*
University of Cincinnati M,D
The University of Iowa M,D*
University of Massachusetts Lowell M,D,O*
University of Miami M,D*
The University of Tennessee M,D*
University of Washington M,D*
Wright State University M,D*

ETHICS

American University M,D,O*
Azusa Pacific University M
Biola University P,M,D
Claremont Graduate University M,D
Drew University M,D
Duquesne University M*
Eastern Michigan University M
Fordham University O*
Graduate Theological Union M,D,O
Marquette University M,D
Northern Baptist Theological Seminary P,M,D
Phillips Theological Seminary P,M,D
St. Edward's University M
Southeastern Baptist Theological Seminary P,M,D
Université de Sherbrooke M,D,O
Université du Québec à Chicoutimi O
Université du Québec à Rimouski M,O
Université Laval O
University of Baltimore M*
University of Nevada, Las Vegas M
University of North Florida M,O
University of North Texas M,D*
Valparaiso University M,O
Warner Pacific College M
Wilfrid Laurier University P,M,D

ETHNIC STUDIES

Cornell University M,D*
Minnesota State University Mankato M
San Francisco State University M
Université Laval M,D
University of California, Berkeley D*
University of California, San Diego M,D*
Washington State University M,D*

EVOLUTIONARY BIOLOGY

Arizona State University M,D*
Brown University D*
Clemson University M,D*
Columbia University D,O*
Cornell University D*
Dartmouth College D*
Emory University D*
Florida State University M,D*
George Mason University M,D,O*
Harvard University D*
Illinois State University M,D*
Indiana University Bloomington M,D*
Iowa State University of Science and Technology M,D*
The Johns Hopkins University D*
Marquette University M,D
Michigan State University D*
Northwestern University D*
The Ohio State University M,D*
Ohio University M,D*
Penn State University Park M,D*
Princeton University D*
Purdue University M,D*
Rice University M,D*
Rutgers, The State University of New Jersey, New Brunswick M,D*
Stony Brook University, State University of New York D*
Tulane University M,D*
University at Albany, State University of New York M,D*
University at Buffalo, the State University of New York M,D,O*
University of Alberta M,D*
The University of Arizona M,D*
University of California, Davis D*
University of California, Irvine M,D*
University of California, Riverside M,D*
University of California, San Diego D*
University of California, Santa Barbara M,D*
University of California, Santa Cruz M,D*
University of Chicago D*
University of Colorado at Boulder M,D*
University of Delaware M,D*
University of Guelph M,D

University of Hawaii at Manoa	M,D*
University of Illinois at Chicago	M,D*
University of Illinois at Urbana–Champaign	M,D*
The University of Iowa	M,D*
University of Kansas	M,D*
University of Louisiana at Lafayette	M,D*
University of Maryland, College Park	M,D*
University of Massachusetts Amherst	M,D*
University of Miami	M,D*
University of Michigan	M,D*
University of Minnesota, Twin Cities Campus	M,D*
University of Missouri–Columbia	M,D*
University of Missouri–St. Louis	M,D,O
University of Nevada, Reno	D*
The University of North Carolina at Chapel Hill	M,D*
University of Notre Dame	M,D*
University of Oregon	M,D*
University of Pittsburgh	D*
University of South Carolina	M,D*
The University of Tennessee	M,D*
The University of Texas at Austin	D*
University of Utah	M,D*
Virginia Polytechnic Institute and State University	M,D*
Washington University in St. Louis	D*
Wesleyan University	D*
West Virginia University	M,D*
Yale University	D*

EXERCISE AND SPORTS SCIENCE

American University	M*
Appalachian State University	M
Arizona State University	D*
Arizona State University at the Polytechnic Campus	M,D
Arkansas State University	M,O
Armstrong Atlantic State University	M
Ashland University	M
A.T. Still University of Health Sciences	M,D
Auburn University	M,D,O*
Austin Peay State University	M
Ball State University	D*
Barry University	M*
Baylor University	M,D*
Bemidji State University	M
Benedictine University	M
Bloomsburg University of Pennsylvania	M
Boise State University	M
Brigham Young University	M,D*
Brooklyn College of the City University of New York	M
California State University, Fresno	M
California University of Pennsylvania	M
Central Connecticut State University	M,O
Central Michigan University	M*
Cleveland State University	M
The College of St. Scholastica	M
Colorado State University	M,D*
Concordia University (IL)	M
Concordia University (Canada)	M
East Carolina University	M,D*
Eastern Michigan University	M
East Stroudsburg University of Pennsylvania	M
East Tennessee State University	M
Florida Atlantic University	M
Florida International University	M*
Florida State University	M,D*
Gardner-Webb University	M
George Mason University	M*
The George Washington University	M*
Georgia State University	M,D*
High Point University	M
Howard University	M*
Humboldt State University	M
Indiana State University	M*
Indiana University Bloomington	M,D,O*
Indiana University of Pennsylvania	M
Iowa State University of Science and Technology	M,D*
Ithaca College	M
Kean University	M
Kent State University	M,D*
Lakehead University	M
Life University	M
Long Island University, Brooklyn Campus	M*
Louisiana Tech University	M
Manhattanville College	M*
Marshall University	M
Marywood University	M*
McNeese State University	M
Memorial University of Newfoundland	M
Miami University	M*
Middle Tennessee State University	M,D*
Mississippi State University	M
Montclair State University	M,O*
Morehead State University	M
Murray State University	M
New Mexico Highlands University	M
North Dakota State University	M
Northeastern University	M*
Northern Arizona University	M
Northern Michigan University	M
Oakland University	M,O*
Ohio University	M,D*
Old Dominion University	M*
Oregon State University	M,D*
Purdue University	M,D*
Queens College of the City University of New York	M
Queen's University at Kingston	M,D
St. Cloud State University	M
San Diego State University	M*
Smith College	M*
Southeast Missouri State University	M
Southern Connecticut State University	M
Springfield College	M,D,O*
State University of New York College at Cortland	M*
Syracuse University	M*
Tennessee State University	M*
Texas Tech University	M
Texas Woman's University	M
United States Sports Academy	M*
University at Buffalo, the State University of New York	M,D*
The University of Akron	M
The University of Alabama	M,D
University of Alberta	M,D*
University of Calgary	M,D
University of California, Davis	M*
University of Central Florida	M*
University of Central Missouri	M
University of Connecticut	M,D*
University of Dayton	M,D*
University of Delaware	M*
University of Florida	M,D*
University of Houston	M,D*
University of Houston–Clear Lake	M
The University of Iowa	M,D*
University of Kentucky	M,D*
University of Lethbridge	M,D
University of Louisiana at Monroe	M
University of Louisville	M
University of Mary Hardin-Baylor	M,D
University of Memphis	M*
University of Miami	M,D*
University of Minnesota, Twin Cities Campus	M,D,O*
University of Mississippi	M,D
University of Missouri–Columbia	M,D*
The University of Montana	M*
University of Nebraska at Kearney	M
University of Nevada, Las Vegas	M
University of New Brunswick Fredericton	M
The University of North Carolina at Chapel Hill	M*
The University of North Carolina at Charlotte	M*
The University of North Carolina at Greensboro	M,D
University of Northern Colorado	M,D
University of Oklahoma	M,D*
University of Pittsburgh	M,D*
University of Puerto Rico, Río Piedras	M*
University of Rhode Island	M,D
University of South Alabama	M*
University of South Carolina	M,D*
University of Southern Mississippi	M,D*
The University of Tennessee	M,D,O*
The University of Texas at Arlington	M*
The University of Texas at El Paso	M
The University of Texas at Tyler	M
University of the Pacific	M
The University of Toledo	M,D*
University of Utah	M,D*
University of West Florida	M
University of Wisconsin–La Crosse	M
Virginia Commonwealth University	M,D*
Wake Forest University	M*
Washington State University	M,D*
Washington State University Spokane	M,O
Wayne State College	M
West Chester University of Pennsylvania	M,O
Western Michigan University	M*
Western Washington University	M
West Texas A&M University	M
West Virginia University	M,D*
Wichita State University	M*

EXPERIMENTAL PSYCHOLOGY

American University	M*
Appalachian State University	M
Auburn University	M,D*
Bowling Green State University	M,D*
Brooklyn College of the City University of New York	M,D
California State University, San Bernardino	M
Case Western Reserve University	D*
The Catholic University of America	M,D*
Central Michigan University	M,D*
Central Washington University	M
City College of the City University of New York	M,D*
Cleveland State University	M,O
The College of William and Mary	M
Columbia University	M,D*
Cornell University	D*
Dallas Baptist University	M
DePaul University	M,D*
Duke University	D*
Eastern Michigan University	M,D
Fairleigh Dickinson University, Metropolitan Campus	M,O*
George Mason University	M,D*
Graduate School and University Center of the City University of New York	D*
Harvard University	D*
Howard University	M,D*
Illinois State University	M,D,O*
Iona College	M*
Kent State University	M,D*
Lakehead University	M,D
Long Island University, C.W. Post Campus	M,O*
McGill University	M,D*
Memorial University of Newfoundland	M,D
Miami University	D*
Mississippi State University	M,D
Morehead State University	M
North Carolina State University	D*
Northeastern University	M,D*
Ohio University	D*
Oklahoma State University	M,D*
Old Dominion University	D*
Radford University	M,D,O
St. John's University (NY)	M
Saint Louis University	M,D*
San Jose State University	M
Seton Hall University	M*
Southern Illinois University Carbondale	M,D*
Stony Brook University, State University of New York	D*
Syracuse University	D*
Texas Tech University	M,D
Towson University	M
University at Albany, State University of New York	M,D,O*
The University of Alabama	D
University of Central Florida	M,D*
University of Cincinnati	D
University of Connecticut	M,D*
University of Hartford	M*
University of Kentucky	M,D*
University of Louisville	D
University of Maine	M,D*
University of Maryland, College Park	M,D*
University of Memphis	M,D*
University of Michigan	D*
University of Mississippi	M,D
The University of Montana	M,D,O*
University of Nevada, Las Vegas	M,D
The University of North Carolina at Chapel Hill	D*
University of North Dakota	M,D
University of North Texas	M,D*
University of Regina	M,D
University of South Carolina	M,D*
University of Southern Mississippi	M,D*
University of South Florida	M,D*
The University of Tennessee	M,D*
The University of Tennessee at Chattanooga	M
The University of Texas at Arlington	M,D*
The University of Texas at El Paso	M,D
The University of Texas–Pan American	M
The University of Toledo	M,D*
University of Wisconsin–Oshkosh	M
Washington State University	M,D*
Washington University in St. Louis	M,D*
Western Michigan University	M,D,O*
Western Washington University	M

FACILITIES MANAGEMENT

Cornell University	M*
Indiana University of Pennsylvania	M
Massachusetts Maritime Academy	M
Pratt Institute	M*
Southern Methodist University	M,D*
Université Laval	M,O

FAMILY AND CONSUMER SCIENCES-GENERAL

Alabama Agricultural and Mechanical University	M,D
Appalachian State University	M
Ball State University	M*
Bowling Green State University	M*
California State University, Fresno	M
California State University, Long Beach	M
California State University, Northridge	M
Central Michigan University	M*
Central Washington University	M
Clemson University	D*
Cornell University	M,D*
Eastern Illinois University	M
Florida State University	M,D*
Fontbonne University	M
Illinois State University	M*
Indiana State University	M*
Iowa State University of Science and Technology	M*
Kansas State University	M,D*
Kent State University	M*
Lamar University	M,O*
Louisiana State University and Agricultural and Mechanical College	M,D*
Louisiana Tech University	M
Marshall University	M
Missouri State University	M*
New Mexico State University	M
North Carolina Central University	M
North Dakota State University	M
The Ohio State University	M*
Ohio University	M*
Oklahoma State University	M,D*
Oregon State University	M*
Prairie View A&M University	M
Purdue University	M,D*
Queens College of the City University of New York	M
Sam Houston State University	M
San Francisco State University	M
South Carolina State University	M
South Dakota State University	M
Southeast Missouri State University	M
State University of New York College at Oneonta	M
Stephen F. Austin State University	M
Tennessee State University	M*
Texas A&M University–Kingsville	M
Texas Southern University	M
Texas Tech University	M,D,O
Tufts University	M,D,O*
The University of Akron	M
The University of Alabama	M,D
University of Alberta	M,D*
The University of Arizona	M,D*
University of Arkansas	M*
University of Central Arkansas	M
University of Central Oklahoma	M
University of Florida	M*
University of Georgia	M,D*
University of Houston	M*
University of Louisiana at Lafayette	M*
University of Manitoba	M
University of Maryland, College Park	M,D*
University of Memphis	M*
University of Missouri–Columbia	M,D*
University of Nebraska–Lincoln	M,D*
The University of North Carolina at Greensboro	M,D,O
University of Puerto Rico, Río Piedras	M*
The University of Tennessee	D*

P—first professional degree; M—master's degree; D—doctorate; O—other advanced degree;
**full description and/or announcement in Book 2, 3, 4, 5, or 6*

The University of Tennessee at Martin M
The University of Texas at Austin M,D*
University of Wisconsin–Madison M,D*
University of Wisconsin–Stevens Point M
Utah State University M,D
Western Michigan University M*

FAMILY NURSE PRACTITIONER STUDIES

Allen College M
Barry University M,O*
Baylor University M*
Bloomsburg University of Pennsylvania M
Bowie State University M
Brenau University M
California State University, Fresno M
Carson-Newman College M
Case Western Reserve University M,D*
The Catholic University of America M,D*
Clarke College M,O
Clarkson College M
College of Mount Saint Vincent M,O
Columbia University M,O*
Concordia University Wisconsin M
Coppin State University M,O
DeSales University M
Duke University M,D,O*
Duquesne University M,O*
D'Youville College M,O*
Eastern Kentucky University M*
Edinboro University of Pennsylvania M
Emory University M*
Fairfield University M,O*
Felician College M,O*
Florida State University M,O*
George Mason University M,D,O*
The George Washington University M,D,O*
Georgia Southern University M,O
Georgia State University M,D,O*
Graceland University M,O
Grambling State University M,O
Gwynedd-Mercy College M
Hardin-Simmons University M
Hawai'i Pacific University M*
Holy Names University M
Howard University M,O*
Hunter College of the City University of New York M,O
Husson College M
The Johns Hopkins University M,O*
La Roche College M
La Salle University M,O
Long Island University, C.W. Post Campus M,O*
Loyola University Chicago M*
Loyola University New Orleans M*
Malone College M
Marymount University M,O
McGill University M,D,O*
Medical College of Georgia M,D*
Medical University of South Carolina M*
Midwestern State University M
Minnesota State University Mankato M
Molloy College M,O
Montana State University M,O
Mountain State University M,O*
Murray State University M
Northern Kentucky University M,O
North Georgia College & State University M
Oakland University M,O*
Otterbein College M,O
Pacific Lutheran University M
Prairie View A&M University M
Quinnipiac University M,O*
Regis College (MA) M,O
Research College of Nursing M
Rutgers, The State University of New Jersey, Newark M*
Sacred Heart University M
Sage Graduate School M,O
Saginaw Valley State University M
St. John Fisher College M,O
Saint Joseph College M,O
Saint Xavier University M,O
Samuel Merritt College M,O
San Francisco State University M
Seattle Pacific University O
Shenandoah University M,O*
Sonoma State University M
Southern Adventist University M
Southern Illinois University Edwardsville M,O
Southern University and Agricultural and Mechanical College M,D,O*
Spalding University M
State University of New York Downstate Medical Center M,O*
State University of New York Institute of Technology M,O
State University of New York Upstate Medical University M,O*
Stony Brook University, State University of New York M,O*
Texas A&M University–Corpus Christi M
Texas Tech University Health Sciences Center M,O
Uniformed Services University of the Health Sciences M*
University of Alaska Anchorage M,O
University of Central Arkansas M
University of Colorado at Colorado Springs M,D
University of Delaware M,O*
University of Detroit Mercy M,O
University of Hawaii at Manoa M,D,O*
University of Mary M
University of Medicine and Dentistry of New Jersey M,D,O*
University of Miami M,D*
University of Michigan M*
University of Minnesota, Twin Cities Campus M*
University of Missouri–Kansas City M,D*
University of Nevada, Las Vegas M,D,O
The University of North Carolina at Charlotte M*
University of Northern Colorado M,D
University of Pennsylvania M,O*
University of Phoenix–Bay Area Campus M
University of Phoenix–Detroit Campus M
University of Phoenix–Hawaii Campus M
University of Phoenix–Minneapolis/St. Louis Park Campus M
University of Phoenix–Phoenix Campus M,O
University of Phoenix–Sacramento Valley Campus M
University of Phoenix–Southern Arizona Campus M,O
University of Phoenix–Southern California Campus M,O
University of Pittsburgh M,D*
University of Puerto Rico, Medical Sciences Campus M*
University of Rhode Island M,D
University of San Diego M,D,O*
The University of Scranton M,O
University of South Carolina M*
University of Southern Maine M,O
University of Southern Mississippi M,D*
The University of Tampa M
The University of Tennessee at Chattanooga M
The University of Texas at Arlington M,D*
The University of Texas at El Paso M
The University of Texas at Tyler M
The University of Texas–Pan American M
The University of Toledo M,O*
University of Wisconsin–Oshkosh M
Vanderbilt University M,D*
Virginia Commonwealth University M,O*
Wagner College O
Western University of Health Sciences M
Westminster College (UT) M
Wichita State University M*
Wilmington College (DE) M
Winona State University M
Wright State University M*

FILM, TELEVISION, AND VIDEO PRODUCTION

Academy of Art University M*
American Film Institute Conservatory M
American University M*
Antioch University McGregor M*
Art Center College of Design M*
Bob Jones University P,M,D,O
Boston University M*
Bowling Green State University M,D*
Brigham Young University M*
Brooklyn College of the City University of New York M
California College of the Arts M*
California Institute of the Arts M,O
California State University, Fullerton M
California State University, Northridge M
Carleton University M
Carnegie Mellon University M*
Central Michigan University M*
Chapman University M
Chatham University M
Chestnut Hill College M,O
Columbia College Chicago M
Columbia University M*
Concordia University (Canada) M
Emerson College M*
Florida State University M*
George Mason University M*
Georgia State University M,D*
Hofstra University M*
Hollins University M
Howard University M*
Loyola Marymount University M
Marywood University M,O*
Massachusetts College of Art M
Miami International University of Art & Design M*
Minneapolis College of Art and Design M
Montana State University M
New Mexico Highlands University M
New York Film Academy M*
New York University M*
North Carolina School of the Arts M
Northwestern University M,D*
Ohio University M*
Polytechnic University, Brooklyn Campus O*
Regent University M,D
Rochester Institute of Technology M
San Diego State University M*
San Francisco Art Institute M,O*
San Francisco State University M
San Jose State University M
Savannah College of Art and Design M*
School of the Art Institute of Chicago M*
Southern Methodist University M*
Syracuse University M*
Temple University M*
The University of Alabama M
The University of British Columbia M*
University of California, Los Angeles M,D*
University of California, Santa Barbara *
University of Central Arkansas M
University of Denver M*
The University of Iowa M*
University of Memphis M,D*
University of Miami M,D*
University of Michigan O*
The University of Montana M*
University of Nevada, Las Vegas M
University of New Orleans M
University of North Texas M*
University of Oklahoma M*
University of Southern California M*
The University of Texas at Austin M,D*
University of Utah M*
University of Wisconsin–Milwaukee M
York University M,D*

FILM, TELEVISION, AND VIDEO THEORY AND CRITICISM

Boston University M*
California College of the Arts M*
Claremont Graduate University M,D
College of Staten Island of the City University of New York M
Concordia University (Canada) M
Emory University M,D,O*
Hollins University M
New York University M,D*
Ohio University M*
San Francisco State University M
Savannah College of Art and Design M*
Syracuse University M*
Université de Montréal M,D
Université Laval M,D
The University of British Columbia M*
University of Chicago M,D*
University of Georgia M,D*
The University of Iowa M,D*
University of Kansas M,D*
University of Miami M,D*
University of Michigan D,O*
University of Southern California M,D*
Wilfrid Laurier University M,D

FINANCE AND BANKING

Adelphi University M*
Alabama Agricultural and Mechanical University M
Alaska Pacific University M
Alliant International University–San Diego M,D*
The American College M
American College of Thessaloniki M,O
American InterContinental University (FL) M
American InterContinental University Buckhead Campus M
American InterContinental University Online M
American University M,D,O*
The American University of Paris M
Andrew Jackson University M
Andrews University M
Argosy University, Atlanta Campus M,D*
Argosy University, Chicago Campus M,D*
Argosy University, Denver Campus M,D*
Argosy University, Hawai'i Campus M,D,O*
Argosy University, Inland Empire Campus M,D*
Argosy University, Orange County Campus M,D,O*
Argosy University, Phoenix Campus M,D*
Argosy University, San Diego Campus M,D*
Argosy University, San Francisco Bay Area Campus M,D*
Argosy University, Santa Monica Campus M,D*
Argosy University, Sarasota Campus M,D,O*
Argosy University, Schaumburg Campus M,D,O*
Argosy University, Seattle Campus M,D*
Argosy University, Tampa Campus M,D,O*
Argosy University, Twin Cities Campus M,D*
Argosy University, Washington DC Campus M,D,O*
Arizona State University M,D*
Auburn University M*
Avila University M*
Baker College Center for Graduate Studies M
Barry University O*
Bayamón Central University M
Benedictine University M
Bentley College M*
Bernard M. Baruch College of the City University of New York M,D*
Boston College M,D*
Boston University P,M,D*
Brandeis University M,D*
Bridgewater State College M
Bryant University M,O
California Lutheran University M,O
California State University, East Bay M
California State University, Fullerton M
California State University, Los Angeles M
California State University, Stanislaus M
Capella University M,D,O
Cardean University M
Carnegie Mellon University D*
Case Western Reserve University M,D*
Central European University M*
Central Michigan University M*
Charleston Southern University M
Christian Brothers University M,O
City University M,O
Clark Atlanta University M
Clark University M*
Cleveland State University M,D,O
College for Financial Planning M
College of Santa Fe M
Columbia University M,D*
Concordia University Wisconsin M
Cornell University D*
Dallas Baptist University M
Davenport University M
Davenport University M
DePaul University M,O*
DeVry University M*
Dowling College M,O
Drexel University M,D,O*
Eastern Michigan University M
Eastern University M*
East Tennessee State University M
Fairfield University M,O*
Fairleigh Dickinson University, College at Florham M,O*
Fairleigh Dickinson University, Metropolitan Campus M,O*
Florida Agricultural and Mechanical University M*

Florida Atlantic University M
Florida International University M*
Florida State University M,D*
Fordham University M*
Gannon University O
The George Washington University M,D*
Georgia Institute of Technology M,D,O*
Georgia State University M,D,O*
Golden Gate University M,D,O
Goldey-Beacom College M
Graduate School and University Center of the City University of New York D*
Hawai'i Pacific University M*
HEC Montreal M,O
Hofstra University M*
Howard University M*
Huron University USA in London M
Illinois Institute of Technology P,M*
Indiana University Southeast M,O
Instituto Tecnologico de Santo Domingo M
Instituto Tecnológico y de Estudios Superiores de Monterrey, Campus Central de Veracruz M
Instituto Tecnológico y de Estudios Superiores de Monterrey, Campus Ciudad de México M,D
Instituto Tecnológico y de Estudios Superiores de Monterrey, Campus Ciudad Juárez M
Instituto Tecnológico y de Estudios Superiores de Monterrey, Campus Ciudad Obregón M
Instituto Tecnológico y de Estudios Superiores de Monterrey, Campus Cuernavaca M
Instituto Tecnológico y de Estudios Superiores de Monterrey, Campus Estado de México M,D
Instituto Tecnológico y de Estudios Superiores de Monterrey, Campus Guadalajara M
Instituto Tecnológico y de Estudios Superiores de Monterrey, Campus Irapuato M,D
Instituto Tecnológico y de Estudios Superiores de Monterrey, Campus Monterrey M
Inter American University of Puerto Rico, Metropolitan Campus M
Inter American University of Puerto Rico, Ponce Campus M
Inter American University of Puerto Rico, San Germán Campus M,D
The International University of Monaco M
Iona College M,O*
The Johns Hopkins University M,O*
Johnson & Wales University M,O*
Jones International University M
Kent State University D*
Lamar University M*
Lehigh University M*
Lindenwood University M
Lipscomb University M
Long Island University, C.W. Post Campus M,O*
Long Island University, Rockland Graduate Campus M,O
Louisiana State University and Agricultural and Mechanical College M,D*
Louisiana Tech University M,D
Loyola College in Maryland M
Marywood University M*
McGill University M,D,O*
Mercy College M
Metropolitan State University M
Miami University M*
Michigan State University M,D*
Middle Tennessee State University M,D*
Minnesota State University Mankato M
Mississippi State University M,D
Montclair State University M*
Mount Saint Mary College M
National University M
New Jersey City University M
New Mexico Highlands University M
The New School: A University M*
New York Institute of Technology M,O
New York University M,D,O*
Northeastern Illinois University M
Northeastern State University M
Northeastern University M*
Northwestern University D*
Notre Dame College (OH) M,O
Oakland University M,O*
The Ohio State University M,D*
Ohio University M*
Oklahoma City University M
Oklahoma State University M,D*
Old Dominion University D*
Oral Roberts University M
Ottawa University M
Our Lady of the Lake University of San Antonio M
Pace University M*
Pacific States University M,D
Penn State University Park M,D*
Philadelphia University M*
Polytechnic University, Brooklyn Campus M,O*
Polytechnic University, Westchester Graduate Center M,O
Pontifical Catholic University of Puerto Rico M,D
Pontificia Universidad Catolica Madre y Maestra M
Portland State University M
Princeton University M*
Purdue University M,D*
Quinnipiac University M*
Regis University M,O
Rensselaer Polytechnic Institute M,D*
Rhode Island College M
Robert Morris University M
Rochester Institute of Technology M
Rutgers, The State University of New Jersey, Newark M,D,O*
Rutgers, The State University of New Jersey, New Brunswick M,D*
Sage Graduate School M
St. Bonaventure University M,O
St. Cloud State University M
St. Edward's University M,O
St. John's University (NY) M,O
Saint Joseph's University M,O*
Saint Louis University M*
Saint Mary's University of Minnesota M,O
St. Mary's University of San Antonio M
Saint Peter's College M
St. Thomas Aquinas College M*
Saint Xavier University M,O
Sam Houston State University M
San Diego State University M*
Schiller International University (United States) M
Seattle University M,O
Seton Hall University M*
Simon Fraser University M,D
Southeastern University M
Southeast Missouri State University M
Southern Adventist University M
Southern Illinois University Edwardsville M
Southern New Hampshire University M,D,O*
State University of New York at Binghamton M,D*
Stevens Institute of Technology M*
Stony Brook University, State University of New York M,O*
Suffolk University M,O*
Syracuse University M,D*
Tarleton State University M
Télé-université M,D
Temple University M,D*
Texas A&M International University M
Texas A&M University M,D*
Texas Tech University M,D
Touro University International M,D
Union Graduate College M,O*
United States International University M
Universidad de las Americas, A.C. M
Universidad de las Américas–Puebla M
Universidad Metropolitana M
Université de Sherbrooke M
Université du Québec à Montréal O
Université du Québec à Trois-Rivières O
Université du Québec en Outaouais M,O
Université Laval M,O
University at Albany, State University of New York M*
University at Buffalo, the State University of New York M,D,O*
The University of Akron M
The University of Alabama M,D
University of Alaska Fairbanks M
University of Alberta M,D*
The University of Arizona M,D*
University of Baltimore M*
The University of British Columbia D*
University of California, Berkeley D*
University of Cincinnati M,D
University of Colorado at Boulder D*
University of Colorado at Colorado Springs M
University of Colorado at Denver and Health Sciences Center M*
University of Connecticut M,D,O*
University of Dallas M
University of Denver M*
The University of Findlay M
University of Florida M,D,O*
University of Hawaii at Manoa M,D*
University of Houston M*
University of Houston–Clear Lake M
University of Illinois at Urbana–Champaign M,D*
University of Indianapolis M,O
The University of Iowa M,D*
University of La Verne M
University of Lethbridge M,D
University of Maryland University College M,O
University of Massachusetts Dartmouth M,O
University of Memphis M,D*
University of Miami M*
University of Michigan–Dearborn M*
University of Minnesota, Twin Cities Campus M,D*
University of Missouri–St. Louis M,O
University of Nebraska–Lincoln M,D*
University of Nevada, Reno M*
University of New Haven M*
University of New Mexico M*
University of New Orleans M,D
The University of North Carolina at Chapel Hill D*
The University of North Carolina at Greensboro M,O
University of Northern Virginia M,D
University of North Texas M,D*
University of Oregon D*
University of Ottawa D,O*
University of Pennsylvania M,D*
University of Puerto Rico, Mayagüez Campus M*
University of Rhode Island D
University of San Diego M,O*
University of San Francisco M
University of Saskatchewan M
The University of Scranton M
University of Southern California M*
University of South Florida M*
The University of Tampa M
The University of Tennessee M,D*
The University of Texas at Arlington M,D*
The University of Texas at Austin D*
The University of Texas at San Antonio M,D*
University of the West M
The University of Toledo M*
University of Tulsa M*
University of Utah M,D*
University of Waterloo M,D*
The University of Western Ontario M,D
University of Wisconsin–Madison M,D*
University of Wisconsin–Whitewater M*
University of Wyoming M
Upper Iowa University M
Vanderbilt University M,D*
Villanova University M*
Virginia Commonwealth University M*
Virginia Polytechnic Institute and State University M,D*
Wagner College M
Walden University M,D
Walsh College of Accountancy and Business Administration M
Washington State University M,D*
Washington University in St. Louis M*
Webster University M
West Chester University of Pennsylvania M
Western International University M
West Texas A&M University M
Wilkes University M
Wilmington College (DE) M
Wright State University M*
Xavier University M*
Yale University D*
Youngstown State University M

FINANCIAL ENGINEERING

Claremont Graduate University M,D
Columbia University M,D,O*
HEC Montreal M
The International University of Monaco M
Kent State University M*
North Carolina State University M*
Polytechnic University, Brooklyn Campus M,O*
Polytechnic University, Long Island Graduate Center M,O
Polytechnic University, Westchester Graduate Center M,O
Princeton University M,D*
University of California, Berkeley M*
University of Michigan M*
University of Tulsa M*

FIRE PROTECTION ENGINEERING

Anna Maria College M
Indiana University School of Law-Indianapolis P,M
Oklahoma State University M*
University of Central Missouri M,O
University of Maryland, College Park M,O*
University of New Haven M*
Worcester Polytechnic Institute M,D,O*

FISH, GAME, AND WILDLIFE MANAGEMENT

Arkansas Tech University M
Auburn University M,D*
Brigham Young University M,D*
Clemson University M,D*
Colorado State University M,D*
Cornell University M,D*
Frostburg State University M
Iowa State University of Science and Technology M,D*
Louisiana State University and Agricultural and Mechanical College M,D*
McGill University M,D*
Memorial University of Newfoundland M,O
Michigan State University M,D*
Mississippi State University M
Montana State University M,D
New Mexico Highlands University M
New Mexico State University M
North Carolina State University M*
Oregon State University M,D*
Penn State University Park M,D*
Purdue University M,D*
South Dakota State University M,D
State University of New York College of Environmental Science and Forestry M,D
Sul Ross State University M*
Tennessee Technological University M*
Texas A&M University M,D*
Texas A&M University–Kingsville M,D
Texas State University-San Marcos M
Texas Tech University M,D
Université du Québec à Rimouski M,D,O
University of Alaska Fairbanks M,D
The University of Arizona M,D*
University of Delaware M,D*
University of Florida M,D*
University of Idaho M,D*
University of Maine M,D*
University of Massachusetts Amherst M,D*
University of Miami M,D
University of Minnesota, Twin Cities Campus M,D*
University of Missouri–Columbia M,D*
The University of Montana M,D*
University of New Hampshire M*
University of North Dakota M,D
University of Rhode Island M,D
The University of Tennessee M*
University of Washington M,D
Utah State University M,D
Virginia Polytechnic Institute and State University M,D*
West Virginia University M*

FOLKLORE

The George Washington University M*
Indiana University Bloomington M,D*
Memorial University of Newfoundland M,D
University of Alberta M,D*

*P—first professional degree; M—master's degree; D—doctorate; O—other advanced degree; *full description and/or announcement in Book 2, 3, 4, 5, or 6*

- University of California, Berkeley M*
- University of Louisiana at Lafayette M,D*
- The University of North Carolina at Chapel Hill M*
- University of Oregon M*
- University of Pennsylvania M,D*
- The University of Texas at Austin M,D*
- Utah State University M

FOOD SCIENCE AND TECHNOLOGY

- Alabama Agricultural and Mechanical University M,D
- American University of Beirut M
- Auburn University M,D*
- Brigham Young University M*
- California State Polytechnic University, Pomona M
- California State University, Fresno M
- Chapman University M
- Clemson University M,D*
- Colorado State University M,D*
- Cornell University M,D*
- Dalhousie University M,D
- Drexel University M,D*
- Florida Agricultural and Mechanical University M*
- Florida State University M,D*
- Framingham State College M*
- Illinois Institute of Technology M*
- Iowa State University of Science and Technology M,D*
- Kansas State University M,D*
- Louisiana State University and Agricultural and Mechanical College M,D*
- McGill University M,D*
- Memorial University of Newfoundland M,D
- Michigan State University M,D*
- Mississippi State University M,D
- Montclair State University M,O*
- New York University M,D*
- North Carolina State University M,D*
- North Dakota State University M,D
- Nova Scotia Agricultural College M
- The Ohio State University M,D*
- Oklahoma State University M,D*
- Oregon State University M,D*
- Penn State University Park M,D*
- Purdue University M,D*
- Rutgers, The State University of New Jersey, New Brunswick M,D*
- South Dakota State University M
- Texas A&M University M,D*
- Texas Tech University M,D
- Texas Woman's University M,D
- Tuskegee University M
- Universidad de las Américas–Puebla M
- Université de Moncton M
- Université Laval M,D
- University of Arkansas M,D*
- The University of British Columbia M,D*
- University of California, Davis M,D*
- University of Delaware M,D*
- University of Florida M,D*
- University of Georgia M,D*
- University of Guelph M,D
- University of Hawaii at Manoa M*
- University of Idaho M,D*
- University of Illinois at Urbana–Champaign M,D*
- University of Maine M,D*
- University of Manitoba M
- University of Maryland, College Park M,D*
- University of Maryland Eastern Shore M,D*
- University of Massachusetts Amherst M,D*
- University of Minnesota, Twin Cities Campus M,D*
- University of Missouri–Columbia M,D*
- University of Nebraska–Lincoln M,D*
- University of Puerto Rico, Mayagüez Campus M*
- University of Rhode Island M,D
- University of Saskatchewan M,D
- University of Southern Mississippi M,D*
- The University of Tennessee M,D*
- The University of Tennessee at Martin M
- University of Vermont D*
- University of Wisconsin–Madison M,D*
- University of Wisconsin–Stout M*
- University of Wyoming M
- Utah State University M,D
- Virginia Polytechnic Institute and State University M,D*
- Washington State University M,D*
- Wayne State University M,D*
- West Virginia University M,D*

FOREIGN LANGUAGES EDUCATION

- The American University in Cairo M
- Andrews University M,D,O
- Auburn University M,D,O*
- Bennington College M*
- Boston College M*
- Boston University M*
- Bowling Green State University M*
- Brigham Young University M*
- Brooklyn College of the City University of New York M,O
- California State University, Chico M
- California State University, Sacramento M*
- Central Connecticut State University M,O
- Christopher Newport University M
- Cleveland State University M
- College of Charleston M*
- The College of New Jersey M
- The College of William and Mary M
- The Colorado College M
- Colorado State University M*
- Connecticut College M
- Cornell University M,D*
- Eastern Washington University M
- Elms College M,O
- Fairfield University M,O*
- Florida Atlantic University M
- Florida International University M,D,O*
- Framingham State College M*
- George Mason University M*
- Georgia Southern University M
- Harding University M,O
- Hofstra University M*
- Hood College O
- Hunter College of the City University of New York M
- Indiana University Bloomington M,D*
- Iona College M*
- Ithaca College M*
- Long Island University, C.W. Post Campus M*
- Louisiana Tech University M,D
- Manhattanville College M*
- Marquette University M
- McGill University M,D,O*
- Michigan State University D*
- Middle Tennessee State University M*
- Mississippi State University M*
- Missouri State University M*
- Monterey Institute of International Studies M*
- New College of California M*
- New York University M,D,O*
- Northern Arizona University M
- Occidental College M
- Portland State University M
- Purdue University M,D,O*
- Queens College of the City University of New York M,O
- Quinnipiac University M*
- Rider University M,O*
- Rivier College M
- Rutgers, The State University of New Jersey, New Brunswick M,D*
- St. John Fisher College M
- Salisbury University M
- School for International Training M
- Smith College M*
- Southern Illinois University Edwardsville M
- Stanford University M*
- State University of New York at Binghamton M*
- State University of New York at Plattsburgh M
- State University of New York College at Cortland M*
- Stony Brook University, State University of New York M,O*
- Teachers College Columbia University M,D*
- Temple University M,D*
- Texas A&M International University M,D
- Texas A&M University–Kingsville M
- Union Graduate College M*
- Universidad del Este M
- University at Buffalo, the State University of New York M,D,O*
- The University of Arizona M,D*
- University of Calgary M,D,O
- University of California, Irvine M,D*
- University of Central Arkansas M
- University of Central Florida M,O*
- University of Connecticut M,D*
- University of Delaware M*
- University of Hawaii at Manoa M,D,O*
- University of Illinois at Urbana–Champaign M,D,O*
- University of Indianapolis M
- The University of Iowa M,D*
- University of Kentucky M*
- University of Louisville M,D
- University of Maine M*
- University of Maryland, College Park M,D*
- University of Massachusetts Amherst M,D*
- University of Massachusetts Boston M
- University of Michigan M,D*
- University of Minnesota, Twin Cities Campus M*
- University of Missouri–Columbia M,D,O*
- University of Nebraska at Kearney M
- University of Nebraska at Omaha M
- University of Nevada, Reno M*
- The University of North Carolina at Chapel Hill M*
- The University of North Carolina at Charlotte M*
- The University of North Carolina at Greensboro M,D,O
- University of Northern Colorado M
- University of Pittsburgh M,D*
- University of Puerto Rico, Río Piedras M,D*
- University of South Carolina M,D*
- University of Southern Mississippi M*
- University of South Florida M,D,O*
- The University of Tennessee M,D,O*
- The University of Texas at Austin M,D*
- The University of Toledo M*
- University of Utah M,D*
- University of Vermont M*
- University of Victoria M
- University of West Georgia M
- University of Wisconsin–Madison M,D*
- Vanderbilt University M,D*
- Wayne State University M,D,O*
- West Chester University of Pennsylvania M
- Worcester State College M

FORENSIC NURSING

- Cleveland State University M
- Duquesne University M,O*
- Fitchburg State College M,O
- Quinnipiac University M,O*
- University of Colorado at Colorado Springs M,D
- Vanderbilt University M,D*

FORENSIC PSYCHOLOGY

- Alliant International University–Fresno D*
- Alliant International University–Los Angeles D*
- American International College M
- Argosy University, Chicago Campus D*
- Argosy University, Denver Campus M,D*
- Argosy University, Orange County Campus M*
- Argosy University, Phoenix Campus M*
- Argosy University, San Francisco Bay Area Campus M*
- Argosy University, Sarasota Campus M,D,O*
- Argosy University, Schaumburg Campus M,D,O*
- Argosy University, Twin Cities Campus M,D,O*
- Argosy University, Washington DC Campus M,D,O*
- Castleton State College M
- The Chicago School of Professional Psychology M*
- Drexel University M,D*
- John Jay College of Criminal Justice of the City University of New York M,D
- Marymount University M
- Oklahoma State University Center for Health Sciences M
- Prairie View A&M University M,D
- Roger Williams University M*
- Sage Graduate School O
- Tiffin University M
- The University of British Columbia M,D*
- University of Massachusetts Boston M,O
- University of North Dakota M,D

FORENSIC SCIENCES

- Alliant International University–Irvine D*
- Arcadia University M
- Argosy University, Chicago Campus M,D,O*
- Boston University M*
- Cedar Crest College M*
- Chaminade University of Honolulu M
- Duquesne University M*
- Florida International University M,D*
- The George Washington University M*
- John Jay College of Criminal Justice of the City University of New York M,D
- Marshall University M
- McGill University M,D,O*
- Mercyhurst College M
- Michigan State University M,D*
- National University M
- Nebraska Wesleyan University M
- Oklahoma State University Center for Health Sciences M
- Pace University M*
- Philadelphia College of Osteopathic Medicine M*
- Sam Houston State University M,D
- Southern Utah University M
- University at Albany, State University of New York M,D*
- The University of Alabama at Birmingham M*
- University of California, Davis M*
- University of Central Florida M,O*
- University of Florida M,O*
- University of Illinois at Chicago M*
- University of New Haven M*
- University of North Texas Health Science Center at Fort Worth M,D
- University of Rhode Island M,D,O
- Villa Julie College M
- Virginia Commonwealth University M*

FORESTRY

- California Polytechnic State University, San Luis Obispo M
- Clemson University M,D*
- Colorado State University M,D*
- Cornell University M,D*
- Duke University M*
- Harvard University M*
- Iowa State University of Science and Technology M,D*
- Lakehead University M
- Louisiana State University and Agricultural and Mechanical College M,D*
- McGill University M,D*
- Michigan State University M,D*
- Michigan Technological University M,D*
- Mississippi State University M,D
- North Carolina State University M,D*
- Northern Arizona University M,D
- Oklahoma State University M*
- Oregon State University M,D*
- Penn State University Park M,D*
- Purdue University M,D*
- Southern Illinois University Carbondale M*
- Southern University and Agricultural and Mechanical College M*
- State University of New York College of Environmental Science and Forestry M,D
- Stephen F. Austin State University M,D
- Texas A&M University M,D*
- Tropical Agriculture Research and Higher Education Center M,D
- Université Laval M,D
- University of Alberta M,D*
- The University of Arizona M,D*
- University of Arkansas at Monticello M
- The University of British Columbia M,D*
- University of California, Berkeley M,D*
- University of Florida M,D*
- University of Georgia M,D*
- University of Idaho M*
- University of Kentucky M*
- University of Maine M,D*
- University of Massachusetts Amherst M,D*
- University of Michigan M,D,O*
- University of Minnesota, Twin Cities Campus M,D*
- University of Missouri–Columbia M,D*
- The University of Montana M,D*
- University of New Brunswick Fredericton M,D
- University of New Hampshire M*
- The University of Tennessee M*
- University of Toronto M,D
- University of Vermont M,D*
- University of Washington M,D*
- University of Wisconsin–Madison M,D*
- Utah State University M,D

Virginia Polytechnic Institute and State University M,D*
West Virginia University M,D*
Yale University M,D*

FOUNDATIONS AND PHILOSOPHY OF EDUCATION

Antioch University New England M*
Arizona State University M*
Arkansas State University M,D,O
Ashland University M
Ball State University D*
Bank Street College of Education M*
Brigham Young University M,D*
California State University, Los Angeles M
Central Connecticut State University M
Chicago State University M
Curry College M,O
Duquesne University M*
Eastern Michigan University M
Eastern Washington University M
Fairfield University M,O*
Fairleigh Dickinson University, Metropolitan Campus M*
Florida Atlantic University M,D,O
Florida State University M,D,O*
George Fox University M,D,O*
Georgia State University M,D*
Harvard University M,O*
Hofstra University M,O*
Indiana University Bloomington M,D,O*
Iowa State University of Science and Technology M,D*
Kent State University M,D*
McGill University M,D,O*
Millersville University of Pennsylvania M
Montclair State University M,D,O*
Mount Saint Vincent University M
New York University M,D*
Niagara University M
Northeastern State University M
Northern Illinois University M,D,O
Oakland University M*
Penn State University Park M,D*
Purdue University M,D,O*
Regis University M,O
Rutgers, The State University of New Jersey, New Brunswick M,D*
Saint Louis University M,D*
Simon Fraser University M,D
Southeast Missouri State University M
Southern Connecticut State University O
Southern Illinois University Edwardsville M
Stanford University M,D*
State University of New York at Binghamton D*
Suffolk University M,O*
Syracuse University M,D*
Teachers College Columbia University M,D*
Texas A&M University M,D*
University of Arkansas M,D*
The University of British Columbia M,D*
University of Calgary M,D,O
University of California, Berkeley M,D*
University of Cincinnati M,D
University of Colorado at Boulder M,D*
University of Connecticut D*
University of Florida M,D,O*
University of Georgia M,D,O*
University of Hawaii at Manoa M,D*
University of Houston M,D*
University of Houston–Clear Lake M
The University of Iowa M,D,O*
University of Kansas D*
University of Manitoba M
University of Maryland, College Park M,D,O*
University of Michigan M,D*
University of Minnesota, Twin Cities Campus M,D,O*
University of New Mexico M,D*
University of New Orleans M,D,O
University of Oklahoma M,D*
University of Pittsburgh M,D*
University of Saskatchewan M,D,O
University of South Carolina D*
The University of Tennessee M,D,O*
The University of Texas of the Permian Basin M
The University of Toledo M,D*
University of Utah M,D*
University of Victoria M,D*
University of Washington M,D*
The University of West Alabama M
University of Wisconsin–Milwaukee M
Wayne State University M,D,O*
Western Illinois University M
Widener University M,D*
Wilfrid Laurier University M
Youngstown State University M,D

FRENCH

American University O*
Appalachian State University M
Arizona State University M*
Asbury College M,O
Bennington College M*
Boston College M,D*
Boston University M,D*
Bowling Green State University M*
Brigham Young University M*
Brooklyn College of the City University of New York M,D
Brown University M,D*
Bryn Mawr College M,D*
California State University, Fullerton M
California State University, Long Beach M
California State University, Los Angeles M
California State University, Sacramento M*
Carleton University M*
Case Western Reserve University M,D*
The Catholic University of America M,D*
Central Connecticut State University M,O
Columbia University M,D*
Concordia University (Canada) M,O
Connecticut College M
Cornell University D*
Dalhousie University M,D
Duke University D*
Eastern Michigan University M
Emory University D,O*
Florida Atlantic University M
Florida State University M,D*
Georgia State University M*
Graduate School and University Center of the City University of New York D*
Harvard University M,D*
Hofstra University M*
Howard University M*
Hunter College of the City University of New York M
Illinois State University M*
Indiana State University M,O*
Indiana University Bloomington M,D*
The Johns Hopkins University D*
Kansas State University M*
Kent State University M*
Louisiana State University and Agricultural and Mechanical College M,D*
McGill University M,D*
McMaster University M
Memorial University of Newfoundland M
Miami University M*
Michigan State University M,D*
Middlebury College M,D
Millersville University of Pennsylvania M
Minnesota State University Mankato M
Mississippi State University M
Missouri State University M*
Montclair State University M,O*
New York University M,D,O*
North Carolina State University M*
Northern Illinois University M
Northwestern University D,O*
The Ohio State University M,D*
Ohio University M*
Penn State University Park M,D*
Portland State University M
Princeton University D*
Purdue University M,D*
Queens College of the City University of New York M
Queen's University at Kingston M,D
Rice University M,D*
Rutgers, The State University of New Jersey, New Brunswick M,D*
Saint Louis University M*
San Francisco State University M
San Jose State University M
Simon Fraser University M
Smith College M*
Southern Connecticut State University M
Stanford University M,D*
State University of New York at Binghamton M*
Stony Brook University, State University of New York M,D*
Syracuse University M*
Texas Tech University M
Tufts University M*
Tulane University M,D*
Université de Moncton M,D
Université de Montréal M,D
Université de Sherbrooke M,D
Université du Québec à Chicoutimi O
Université Laval M
University at Albany, State University of New York M,D*
University at Buffalo, the State University of New York M,D*
The University of Alabama M,D
University of Alberta M,D*
The University of Arizona M,D*
University of Arkansas M*
The University of British Columbia M,D*
University of California, Berkeley D*
University of California, Davis D*
University of California, Irvine M,D*
University of California, Los Angeles M,D*
University of California, San Diego M*
University of California, Santa Barbara M,D*
University of Chicago M,D*
University of Cincinnati M,D
University of Colorado at Boulder M,D*
University of Connecticut M,D*
University of Delaware M*
University of Florida M,D*
University of Georgia M*
University of Hawaii at Manoa M*
University of Houston M,D*
University of Illinois at Chicago M*
University of Illinois at Urbana–Champaign M,D*
The University of Iowa M,D*
University of Kansas M,D*
University of Kentucky M*
University of Lethbridge M,D
University of Louisiana at Lafayette M,D*
University of Louisville M
University of Maine M*
University of Manitoba M,D
University of Maryland, Baltimore County M*
University of Maryland, College Park M,D*
University of Massachusetts Amherst M,D*
University of Memphis M*
University of Miami D*
University of Michigan D*
University of Minnesota, Twin Cities Campus M,D*
University of Mississippi M
University of Missouri–Columbia M,D*
The University of Montana M*
University of Nebraska–Lincoln M,D*
University of Nevada, Reno M*
University of New Mexico M,D*
The University of North Carolina at Chapel Hill M,D*
The University of North Carolina at Greensboro M
University of Northern Iowa M
University of North Texas M*
University of Notre Dame M*
University of Oklahoma M,D*
University of Oregon M*
University of Ottawa M,D*
University of Pennsylvania M,D*
University of Pittsburgh M,D*
University of Regina M
University of Saskatchewan M
University of South Carolina M,D*
University of Southern California M,D*
University of South Florida M*
The University of Tennessee M,D*
The University of Texas at Arlington M*
The University of Texas at Austin M,D*
The University of Toledo M*
University of Toronto M,D
University of Utah M,D*
University of Vermont M*
University of Victoria M
University of Virginia M,D*
University of Washington M,D*
University of Waterloo M,D*
The University of Western Ontario M,D
University of Wisconsin–Madison M,D,O*
University of Wisconsin–Milwaukee M
University of Wyoming M
Vanderbilt University M,D*
Washington University in St. Louis M,D*
Wayne State University M*
West Chester University of Pennsylvania M
West Virginia University M*
Yale University M,D*
York University M*

GENDER STUDIES

Central European University M,D*
Cornell University M,D*
Eastern Michigan University M
Memorial University of Newfoundland M,D
Northwestern University *
Roosevelt University M,O
Rutgers, The State University of New Jersey, New Brunswick M,D*
Simmons College M
University of Central Florida M,D,O*
University of Florida M,O*
The University of North Carolina at Greensboro M,O
University of Northern British Columbia M,D,O
University of Northern Iowa M
University of Saskatchewan M,D
Virginia Commonwealth University M,O*

GENETIC COUNSELING

Arcadia University M
Brandeis University M*
California State University, Northridge M
Case Western Reserve University M*
The Johns Hopkins University M,D*
McGill University M,D*
Mount Sinai School of Medicine of New York University M,D*
Northwestern University M*
Sarah Lawrence College M*
University of Arkansas for Medical Sciences M*
University of California, Irvine M*
University of Cincinnati M
University of Colorado at Denver and Health Sciences Center M*
University of Minnesota, Twin Cities Campus M,D*
The University of North Carolina at Greensboro M
University of Oklahoma Health Sciences Center M
University of Pittsburgh M*
University of South Carolina M*
The University of Texas Health Science Center at Houston M*
University of Toronto M,D
Virginia Commonwealth University M,D*

GENETICS

Arizona State University M,D*
Baylor College of Medicine D*
Brandeis University M,D*
California Institute of Technology D*
Carnegie Mellon University M,D*
Case Western Reserve University D*
Clemson University M,D*
Columbia University M,D*
Cornell University D*
Dartmouth College D*
Drexel University M,D*
Duke University D*
Emory University D*
Florida State University M,D*
The George Washington University D*
Harvard University D*
Hunter College of the City University of New York
Illinois State University M,D*
Indiana University Bloomington M,D*
Iowa State University of Science and Technology M,D*
The Johns Hopkins University M,D*
Kansas State University M,D*
Marquette University M,D
Mayo Graduate School D*
McMaster University M,D
Michigan State University M,D*
Mount Sinai School of Medicine of New York University M,D*
New York University M,D*
North Carolina State University M,D*
Northwestern University D*
The Ohio State University M,D*
Oregon Health & Science University D*
Oregon State University M,D*

*P—first professional degree; M—master's degree; D—doctorate; O—other advanced degree; *full description and/or announcement in Book 2, 3, 4, 5, or 6*

Penn State Hershey Medical Center M,D*
Penn State University Park M,D*
Purdue University M,D*
Rutgers, The State University of New Jersey, New Brunswick M,D*
Stanford University D*
Stony Brook University, State University of New York D*
Temple University D*
Texas A&M University M,D*
Thomas Jefferson University D*
Tufts University D*
Université de Montréal O
Université du Québec à Chicoutimi M
University at Albany, State University of New York M,D*
The University of Alabama at Birmingham D*
University of Alberta M,D*
The University of Arizona M,D*
The University of British Columbia M,D*
University of California, Davis M,D*
University of California, Irvine D*
University of California, Riverside D*
University of California, San Diego D*
University of California, San Francisco D
University of Chicago D*
University of Colorado at Boulder M,D*
University of Colorado at Denver and Health Sciences Center D*
University of Connecticut M,D*
University of Connecticut Health Center D*
University of Delaware M,D*
University of Florida D*
University of Georgia M,D*
University of Hawaii at Manoa M,D*
University of Illinois at Chicago M,D*
The University of Iowa M,D*
University of Miami M,D*
University of Michigan *
University of Minnesota, Twin Cities Campus M,D*
University of Missouri–Columbia M,D*
University of Missouri–St. Louis M,D,O
University of New Hampshire M,D*
University of New Mexico M,D*
The University of North Carolina at Chapel Hill M,D*
University of North Dakota M,D
University of North Texas Health Science Center at Fort Worth M,D
University of Notre Dame M,D*
University of Oregon M,D*
University of Pennsylvania D*
University of Rochester M,D*
University of Southern California M,D*
The University of Tennessee M,D*
The University of Texas at Austin D*
The University of Texas Health Science Center at Houston M,D*
The University of Texas Medical Branch D*
The University of Texas Southwestern Medical Center at Dallas D*
The University of Toledo M*
University of Toronto M,D
University of Utah M,D*
University of Washington M,D*
University of Wisconsin–Madison M,D*
Virginia Commonwealth University M,D*
Virginia Polytechnic Institute and State University M,D*
Washington State University M,D*
Washington University in St. Louis M,D,O*
Wayne State University M,D*
Wesleyan University D*
West Virginia University M,D*
Yale University D*

GENOMIC SCIENCES

Case Western Reserve University D*
Concordia University (Canada) M,D,O
The George Washington University M*
Harvard University D*
Mount Sinai School of Medicine of New York University M,D*
North Carolina State University M,D*
North Dakota State University M,D
University of California, Riverside D*
University of California, San Francisco D
University of Cincinnati M,D
University of Connecticut M*
University of Florida D*
University of Pennsylvania D*
The University of Tennessee M,D*
The University of Tennessee–Oak Ridge National Laboratory Graduate School of Genome Science and Technology M,D*
The University of Toledo M,O*
University of Washington D*
Wake Forest University D*
Yale University D*

GEOCHEMISTRY

California Institute of Technology M,D*
California State University, Fullerton M
Colorado School of Mines M,D,O
Columbia University M,D*
Cornell University M,D*
Georgia Institute of Technology M,D*
Indiana University Bloomington M,D*
Massachusetts Institute of Technology M,D*
McMaster University M,D
Montana Tech of The University of Montana M
New Mexico Institute of Mining and Technology M,D
Ohio University M*
Rensselaer Polytechnic Institute M,D*
University of California, Los Angeles M,D*
University of Hawaii at Manoa M,D*
University of Illinois at Chicago M,D*
University of Illinois at Urbana–Champaign M,D*
University of Michigan M,D*
University of Missouri–Rolla M,D*
University of Nevada, Reno M,D,O*
University of New Hampshire M*
Washington University in St. Louis M,D*
Woods Hole Oceanographic Institution M,D,O
Yale University D*

GEODETIC SCIENCES

Columbia University M,D*
George Mason University M,D,O*
The Ohio State University M,D*
Université Laval M,D
University of New Brunswick Fredericton M,D,O

GEOGRAPHIC INFORMATION SYSTEMS

Boston University M*
Clark University M*
Cleveland State University M,O
Florida State University M,D*
George Mason University M,D,O*
Georgia Institute of Technology M,D*
Georgia State University O*
Hunter College of the City University of New York M,O
Idaho State University M,O
North Carolina State University M,D*
Northern Arizona University M,O
Northwest Missouri State University M
Saint Louis University M,D,O*
Saint Mary's University of Minnesota M,O
Texas State University-San Marcos M,D*
Université du Québec à Montréal O
University at Albany, State University of New York M,O*
University at Buffalo, the State University of New York M,D,O*
The University of Akron M
University of Central Arkansas O
University of Colorado at Denver and Health Sciences Center M,D,O*
University of Connecticut M,D,O*
University of Denver M,O*
University of Lethbridge M,D
University of Minnesota, Twin Cities Campus M*
The University of Montana M*
The University of North Carolina at Greensboro M,D,O
University of Pittsburgh M,D*
University of Redlands M
The University of Texas at Dallas M,D*
The University of Toledo D*
University of Wisconsin–Madison M,D,O*
Virginia Commonwealth University M,O*
West Virginia University M,D*

GEOGRAPHY

Appalachian State University M
Arizona State University M,D*
Boston University M,D*
Brock University M
California State University, Chico M
California State University, East Bay M
California State University, Fullerton M
California State University, Long Beach M
California State University, Los Angeles M
California State University, Northridge M
Carleton University M,D
Central Connecticut State University M
Chicago State University M
Clark University M,D*
Concordia University (Canada) M,D,O
East Carolina University M*
Eastern Michigan University M*
Florida Atlantic University M
Florida State University M,D*
George Mason University M*
The George Washington University M*
Georgia State University M*
Hunter College of the City University of New York M,O
Indiana State University M,D*
Indiana University Bloomington M,D*
Indiana University of Pennsylvania M
The Johns Hopkins University M,D*
Kansas State University M,D*
Kent State University M,D*
Louisiana State University and Agricultural and Mechanical College M,D*
Marshall University M
McGill University M,D*
McMaster University M,D
Memorial University of Newfoundland M,D
Miami University M*
Michigan State University M,D*
Minnesota State University Mankato M
Missouri State University M*
New Mexico State University M
Northeastern Illinois University M
Northern Arizona University M,O
Northern Illinois University M
Northwest Missouri State University M
The Ohio State University M,D*
Ohio University M*
Oklahoma State University M,D*
Oregon State University M,D*
Penn State University Park M,D*
Portland State University M,D
Queen's University at Kingston M,D
Rutgers, The State University of New Jersey, New Brunswick M,D*
St. Cloud State University M
Salem State College M
San Diego State University M,D*
San Francisco State University M
San Jose State University M,O
Simon Fraser University M,D
South Dakota State University M
Southern Illinois University Carbondale M,D*
Southern Illinois University Edwardsville M
State University of New York at Binghamton M*
Syracuse University M,D*
Temple University M*
Texas A&M University M,D*
Texas State University-San Marcos M,D*
Towson University M
Trent University M,D
Université de Montréal M,D,O
Université de Sherbrooke M,D
Université du Québec à Montréal M
Université Laval M,D
University at Albany, State University of New York M,O*
University at Buffalo, the State University of New York M,D,O*
The University of Akron M
The University of Alabama M
The University of Arizona M,D*
University of Arkansas M*
The University of British Columbia M,D*
University of Calgary M,D
University of California, Berkeley D*
University of California, Davis M,D*
University of California, Los Angeles M,D*
University of California, Santa Barbara M,D*
University of Central Arkansas O
University of Cincinnati M,D
University of Colorado at Boulder M,D*
University of Colorado at Colorado Springs M
University of Connecticut M,D*
University of Delaware M,D*
University of Denver M,D*
University of Florida M,D*
University of Georgia M,D*
University of Guelph M,D
University of Hawaii at Manoa M,D*
University of Idaho M,D*
University of Illinois at Chicago M*
University of Illinois at Urbana–Champaign M,D*
The University of Iowa M,D*
University of Kansas M,D*
University of Kentucky M,D*
University of Lethbridge M,D
University of Manitoba M,D
University of Maryland, College Park M,D*
University of Massachusetts Amherst M*
University of Miami M*
University of Minnesota, Twin Cities Campus M,D*
University of Missouri–Columbia M*
The University of Montana M*
University of Nebraska at Omaha M,O
University of Nebraska–Lincoln M,D*
University of Nevada, Reno M,D*
University of New Mexico M*
University of New Orleans M
The University of North Carolina at Chapel Hill M,D*
The University of North Carolina at Charlotte M,D*
The University of North Carolina at Greensboro M,D,O
University of North Dakota M
University of Northern Iowa M
University of North Texas M*
University of Oklahoma M,D*
University of Oregon M,D*
University of Ottawa M,D*
University of Prince Edward Island M
University of Regina M,D
University of Saskatchewan M,D
University of South Carolina M,D*
University of Southern California M,D*
University of Southern Mississippi M,D*
University of South Florida M*
The University of Tennessee M,D*
The University of Texas at Austin M,D*
The University of Toledo M,D,O*
University of Toronto M,D
University of Utah M,D*
University of Victoria M,D
University of Washington M,D*
University of Waterloo M,D*
The University of Western Ontario M,D
University of Wisconsin–Madison M,D,O*
University of Wisconsin–Milwaukee M,D
University of Wyoming M
Utah State University M,D
Virginia Polytechnic Institute and State University M,D*
Wayne State University M*
West Chester University of Pennsylvania M
Western Illinois University M,O
Western Kentucky University M
Western Michigan University M*
Western Washington University M
West Virginia University M,D*
Wilfrid Laurier University M,D
York University M,D*

GEOLOGICAL ENGINEERING

Arizona State University M,D*
Colorado School of Mines M,D,O
Drexel University M*
École Polytechnique de Montréal M,D,O
Michigan Technological University M,D*
Montana Tech of The University of Montana M
South Dakota School of Mines and Technology M,D
University of Alaska Anchorage M
University of Alaska Fairbanks M,O
The University of British Columbia M,D*

University of Connecticut M,D*
University of Hawaii at Manoa M,D*
University of Idaho M*
University of Minnesota, Twin Cities Campus M,D*
University of Missouri–Rolla M,D*
University of Nevada, Reno M,D,O*
University of North Dakota M
University of Oklahoma M,D*
University of Utah M,D*
University of Wisconsin–Madison M,D*

GEOLOGY

Acadia University M
American University of Beirut M
Auburn University M*
Ball State University M*
Baylor University M,D*
Boise State University M,D
Boston College M*
Bowling Green State University M*
Brigham Young University M*
Brooklyn College of the City University of New York M,D
California Institute of Technology M,D*
California State University, Bakersfield M
California State University, Chico M
California State University, East Bay M
California State University, Fresno M
California State University, Fullerton M
California State University, Long Beach M
California State University, Los Angeles M
California State University, Northridge M
Case Western Reserve University M,D*
Central Washington University M
Cornell University M,D*
Duke University M,D*
East Carolina University M*
Eastern Kentucky University M,D*
Eastern Michigan University M
Florida Atlantic University M
Florida State University M,D*
Fort Hays State University M
The George Washington University M,D*
Georgia State University M*
ICR Graduate School M
Idaho State University M,O
Indiana University Bloomington M,D*
Indiana University–Purdue University Indianapolis M*
Iowa State University of Science and Technology M,D*
Kansas State University M*
Kent State University M,D*
Lakehead University M
Laurentian University M
Lehigh University M,D*
Louisiana State University and Agricultural and Mechanical College M,D*
Massachusetts Institute of Technology M,D*
McMaster University M,D
Memorial University of Newfoundland M,D
Miami University M,D*
Michigan Technological University M,D*
Missouri State University M*
Montana Tech of The University of Montana M
New Mexico Institute of Mining and Technology M,D
New Mexico State University M
Northern Arizona University M
Northern Illinois University M,D
Northwestern University M,D*
The Ohio State University M,D*
Ohio University M*
Oklahoma State University M*
Oregon State University M,D*
Portland State University M,D
Princeton University D*
Queens College of the City University of New York M
Queen's University at Kingston M,D
Rensselaer Polytechnic Institute M,D*
Rutgers, The State University of New Jersey, Newark M*
Rutgers, The State University of New Jersey, New Brunswick M,D*
St. Francis Xavier University M
San Diego State University M*
San Jose State University M
South Dakota School of Mines and Technology M,D
Southern Illinois University Carbondale M,D*
Southern Methodist University M,D*
State University of New York at Binghamton M,D*
State University of New York at New Paltz M
Stephen F. Austin State University M
Sul Ross State University M*
Syracuse University M,D*
Temple University M*
Texas A&M University M,D*
Texas A&M University–Kingsville M
Texas Christian University M
Tulane University M,D*
Université du Québec à Montréal M,D,O
Université Laval M,D
University at Albany, State University of New York M,D*
University at Buffalo, the State University of New York M,D*
The University of Akron M
The University of Alabama M,D
University of Alaska Fairbanks M,D
University of Arkansas M*
The University of British Columbia M,D*
University of Calgary M,D
University of California, Berkeley M,D*
University of California, Davis M,D*
University of California, Los Angeles M,D*
University of California, Riverside M,D*
University of California, Santa Barbara M,D*
University of Cincinnati M,D
University of Colorado at Boulder M,D*
University of Connecticut M,D*
University of Delaware M,D*
University of Florida M,D*
University of Georgia M,D*
University of Hawaii at Manoa M,D*
University of Houston M,D*
University of Idaho M,D*
University of Illinois at Chicago M,D*
University of Illinois at Urbana–Champaign M,D*
University of Kansas M,D*
University of Kentucky M,D*
University of Louisiana at Lafayette M*
University of Maine M,D*
University of Manitoba M,D
University of Maryland, College Park M,D*
University of Memphis M,D*
University of Michigan M,D*
University of Minnesota, Duluth M,D*
University of Minnesota, Twin Cities Campus M,D*
University of Missouri–Columbia M,D*
University of Missouri–Kansas City M,D*
University of Missouri–Rolla M,D*
The University of Montana M,D*
University of Nevada, Reno M,D,O*
University of New Brunswick Fredericton M,D
University of New Hampshire M*
The University of North Carolina at Chapel Hill M,D*
The University of North Carolina Wilmington M*
University of North Dakota M,D
University of Oklahoma M,D*
University of Oregon M,D*
University of Pennsylvania M,D*
University of Pittsburgh M,D*
University of Puerto Rico, Mayagüez Campus M*
University of Regina M,D
University of Rochester M,D*
University of Saskatchewan M,D,O
University of South Carolina M,D*
University of Southern Mississippi M,D*
University of South Florida M,D*
The University of Tennessee M,D*
The University of Texas at Arlington M,D*
The University of Texas at Austin M,D*
The University of Texas at El Paso M,D
The University of Texas at San Antonio M,D*
The University of Texas of the Permian Basin M
The University of Toledo M,D*
University of Toronto M,D
University of Tulsa M*
University of Utah M,D*
University of Vermont M*
University of Washington M,D*
The University of Western Ontario M,D
University of Wisconsin–Madison M,D*
University of Wisconsin–Milwaukee M,D
University of Wyoming M,D
Utah State University M
Virginia Polytechnic Institute and State University M,D*
Washington State University M,D*
Washington University in St. Louis M,D*
Wayne State University M*
West Chester University of Pennsylvania M
Western Kentucky University M
Western Michigan University M,D*
Western Washington University M
West Virginia University M,D*
Wichita State University M*
Wright State University M*
Yale University D*

GEOPHYSICS

Boise State University M,D
Boston College M*
Bowling Green State University M*
California Institute of Technology M,D*
Columbia University M,D*
Cornell University M,D*
Florida State University D*
Georgia Institute of Technology M,D*
ICR Graduate School M
Idaho State University M,O
Indiana University Bloomington M,D*
Louisiana State University and Agricultural and Mechanical College M,D*
Massachusetts Institute of Technology M,D*
Memorial University of Newfoundland M,D
Michigan Technological University M*
New Mexico Institute of Mining and Technology M,D
Ohio University M*
Oregon State University M,D*
Princeton University D*
Rensselaer Polytechnic Institute M,D*
Rice University M*
Saint Louis University M,D*
Southern Methodist University M,D*
Stanford University M,D*
Texas A&M University M,D*
The University of Akron M
University of Alaska Fairbanks M,D
University of Alberta M,D*
The University of British Columbia M,D*
University of Calgary M,D
University of California, Berkeley M,D*
University of California, Los Angeles M,D*
University of California, Santa Barbara M,D*
University of Chicago M,D*
University of Colorado at Boulder M,D*
University of Hawaii at Manoa M,D*
University of Houston M,D*
University of Illinois at Chicago M,D*
University of Illinois at Urbana–Champaign M,D*
University of Manitoba M,D
University of Miami M,D*
University of Minnesota, Twin Cities Campus M,D*
University of Missouri–Rolla M,D*
University of Nevada, Reno M,D,O*
University of Oklahoma M*
The University of Texas at El Paso M
University of Utah M,D*
University of Victoria M,D
University of Washington M,D*
The University of Western Ontario M,D
University of Wisconsin–Madison M,D*
University of Wyoming M,D
Virginia Polytechnic Institute and State University M,D*
Washington University in St. Louis M,D*
West Virginia University M,D*
Woods Hole Oceanographic Institution M,D,O
Wright State University M*
Yale University D*

GEOSCIENCES

Arizona State University M,D*
Ball State University M*
Baylor University M,D*
Boise State University M
Boston University M,D*
Brock University M
Brown University M,D*
California State University, Chico M
California State University, Long Beach M
Carleton University M,D
Case Western Reserve University M,D*
Central Connecticut State University M
City College of the City University of New York M,D*
Colorado School of Mines M,D,O
Colorado State University M,D*
Columbia University M,D*
Cornell University M,D*
Dalhousie University M,D
Dartmouth College M,D*
Emporia State University M,O
Florida International University M,D*
The George Washington University M,D*
Georgia Institute of Technology M,D*
Georgia State University M,O*
Graduate School and University Center of the City University of New York D*
Harvard University M,D*
Hunter College of the City University of New York M,O
Idaho State University M,O
Indiana State University M,D*
Indiana University Bloomington M,D*
Iowa State University of Science and Technology M,D*
The Johns Hopkins University M,D*
Lehigh University M,D*
Loma Linda University M,D
Massachusetts Institute of Technology M,D*
McGill University M,D*
McMaster University M,D
Memorial University of Newfoundland M,D
Michigan State University M,D*
Middle Tennessee State University O*
Mississippi State University M
Missouri State University M*
Montana State University M,D
Montana Tech of The University of Montana M
Montclair State University M,D,O*
Murray State University M
New Mexico Institute of Mining and Technology M,D
North Carolina Central University M
North Carolina State University M,D*
Northeastern Illinois University M
Northern Arizona University M
Northwestern University M,D*
Oregon State University M,D*
Penn State University Park M,D*
Princeton University D*
Purdue University M,D*
Rensselaer Polytechnic Institute M,D*
Rice University M,D*
St. Francis Xavier University M
Saint Louis University M,D*
San Francisco State University M
Simon Fraser University M,D
South Dakota State University D
Stanford University M,D,O*
State University of New York College at Oneonta M
Stony Brook University, State University of New York M,D*
Texas A&M University–Commerce M
Texas Christian University M
Texas Tech University M,D
Université du Québec à Chicoutimi M
Université du Québec à Montréal M,D,O
Université du Québec, Institut National de la Recherche Scientifique M,D
Université Laval M,D
University at Albany, State University of New York M,D*
The University of Akron M
University of Alberta M,D*
The University of Arizona M,D*
University of California, Irvine M,D*
University of California, Los Angeles M,D*

*P—first professional degree; M—master's degree; D—doctorate; O—other advanced degree; *full description and/or announcement in Book 2, 3, 4, 5, or 6*

University of California, San Diego	M,D*
University of California, Santa Barbara	M,D*
University of California, Santa Cruz	M,D*
University of Chicago	M,D*
University of Florida	M,D*
University of Illinois at Chicago	M,D*
University of Illinois at Urbana–Champaign	M,D*
The University of Iowa	M,D*
University of Maine	M,D*
University of Massachusetts Amherst	M,D*
University of Missouri–Kansas City	M,D*
The University of Montana	M,D*
University of Nebraska–Lincoln	M,D*
University of Nevada, Las Vegas	M,D
University of New Hampshire	M*
University of New Mexico	M,D*
University of New Orleans	M
The University of North Carolina at Charlotte	M*
The University of North Carolina Wilmington	M*
University of North Dakota	M,D
University of Northern Colorado	M
University of Notre Dame	M,D*
University of Ottawa	M,D*
University of Rhode Island	M
University of Rochester	M,D*
University of South Carolina	M,D*
University of Southern California	M,D*
The University of Texas at Arlington	M,D*
The University of Texas at Austin	M,D*
The University of Texas at Dallas	M,D*
The University of Toledo	M,D*
University of Tulsa	M,D*
University of Victoria	M,D
University of Waterloo	M,D*
The University of Western Ontario	M,D
University of Windsor	M,D
Virginia Polytechnic Institute and State University	M,D*
Washington State University	M,D*
Washington State University Tri-Cities	M,D
Washington University in St. Louis	M,D*
Wesleyan University	M*
Western Connecticut State University	M*
Western Michigan University	M*
Yale University	D*
York University	M,D*

GEOTECHNICAL ENGINEERING

Auburn University	M,D*
The Catholic University of America	M,D*
Cornell University	M,D*
École Polytechnique de Montréal	M,D,O
Illinois Institute of Technology	M,D*
Iowa State University of Science and Technology	M,D*
Louisiana State University and Agricultural and Mechanical College	M,D*
Marquette University	M,D
Massachusetts Institute of Technology	M,D,O*
McGill University	M,D*
Northwestern University	M,D*
Ohio University	M,D*
Rensselaer Polytechnic Institute	M,D*
Texas A&M University	M,D*
Tufts University	M,D*
University of Alberta	M,D*
University of Calgary	M,D
University of California, Berkeley	M,D*
University of California, Los Angeles	M,D*
University of Colorado at Boulder	M,D*
University of Delaware	M,D*
University of Illinois at Chicago	D*
University of Maine	M,D*
University of Missouri–Columbia	M,D*
University of Missouri–Rolla	M,D*
University of New Brunswick Fredericton	M,D
University of Oklahoma	M,D*
University of Southern California	M*
The University of Texas at Austin	M,D*
University of Washington	M,D*
Worcester Polytechnic Institute	M,D,O*

GERMAN

Arizona State University	M*
Bowling Green State University	M*
Brigham Young University	M*
Brown University	M,D*
California State University, Fullerton	M
California State University, Long Beach	M
California State University, Sacramento	M*
Columbia University	M,D*
Cornell University	M,D*
Dalhousie University	M
Duke University	D*
Eastern Michigan University	M
Florida Atlantic University	M
Florida State University	M*
Georgetown University	M,D*
Georgia State University	M*
Graduate School and University Center of the City University of New York	M,D*
Harvard University	D*
Hofstra University	M*
Illinois State University	M*
Indiana University Bloomington	M,D*
The Johns Hopkins University	D*
Kansas State University	M*
Kent State University	M*
McGill University	M,D*
Memorial University of Newfoundland	M
Michigan State University	M,D*
Middlebury College	M,D
Millersville University of Pennsylvania	M
Mississippi State University	M
Missouri State University	M*
New York University	M,D*
Northwestern University	D*
The Ohio State University	M,D*
Penn State University Park	M,D*
Portland State University	M
Princeton University	D*
Purdue University	M,D*
Queen's University at Kingston	M,D
Rutgers, The State University of New Jersey, New Brunswick	M,D*
San Francisco State University	M
Stanford University	M,D*
Stony Brook University, State University of New York	M,D*
Texas Tech University	M
Tufts University	M*
Université de Montréal	M
The University of Alabama	M,D
University of Alberta	M,D*
The University of Arizona	M,D*
University of Arkansas	M*
The University of British Columbia	M,D*
University of Calgary	M
University of California, Berkeley	D*
University of California, Davis	M,D*
University of California, Irvine	M,D*
University of California, Los Angeles	M,D*
University of California, San Diego	M*
University of California, Santa Barbara	M,D*
University of Chicago	M,D*
University of Cincinnati	M,D
University of Colorado at Boulder	M*
University of Connecticut	M,D*
University of Delaware	M*
University of Florida	M,D*
University of Georgia	M*
University of Illinois at Chicago	M,D*
University of Illinois at Urbana–Champaign	M,D*
The University of Iowa	M,D*
University of Kansas	M,D*
University of Kentucky	M*
University of Lethbridge	M,D
University of Manitoba	M
University of Maryland, Baltimore County	M*
University of Maryland, College Park	M,D*
University of Massachusetts Amherst	M,D*
University of Michigan	M,D*
University of Minnesota, Twin Cities Campus	M,D*
University of Mississippi	M
University of Missouri–Columbia	M*
The University of Montana	M*
University of Nebraska–Lincoln	M,D*
University of Nevada, Reno	M*
University of New Mexico	M,D*
The University of North Carolina at Chapel Hill	M,D*
University of Northern Iowa	M
University of Oklahoma	M*
University of Oregon	M,D*
University of Pennsylvania	M,D*
University of Pittsburgh	M,D*
University of Saskatchewan	M
University of South Carolina	M,D*
The University of Tennessee	M,D*
The University of Texas at Austin	M,D*
The University of Toledo	M*
University of Toronto	M,D
University of Utah	M,D*
University of Vermont	M*
University of Victoria	M
University of Virginia	M,D*
University of Washington	M,D*
University of Waterloo	M,D*
University of Wisconsin–Madison	M,D*
University of Wisconsin–Milwaukee	M
University of Wyoming	M
Vanderbilt University	M,D*
Washington University in St. Louis	M,D*
Wayne State University	M,D*
West Chester University of Pennsylvania	M
West Virginia University	M*
Yale University	M,D*

GERONTOLOGICAL NURSING

Abilene Christian University	O
Arkansas State University	M,O
Barnes-Jewish College of Nursing and Allied Health	M
Boston College	M,D*
Caribbean University	M,D
Case Western Reserve University	M,D*
The Catholic University of America	M,D*
College of Mount Saint Vincent	M,O
College of Staten Island of the City University of New York	M,O
Columbia University	M,O*
Concordia University Wisconsin	M
Duke University	M,D,O*
Emory University	M*
Gwynedd-Mercy College	M
Hunter College of the City University of New York	M
Lehman College of the City University of New York	M
Loma Linda University	M
Marquette University	M,D,O
Medical University of South Carolina	M*
MGH Institute of Health Professions	M,O*
Nazareth College of Rochester	M
New York University	M,O*
Oakland University	M,O*
Oregon Health & Science University	M,D,O*
Rush University	M,D,O
Rutgers, The State University of New Jersey, Newark	M*
San Jose State University	M,O
Seton Hall University	M*
Southern University and Agricultural and Mechanical College	M,D,O*
State University of New York at New Paltz	M,O
State University of New York Institute of Technology	M,O
Stony Brook University, State University of New York	M*
Texas Tech University Health Sciences Center	M,O
Texas Wesleyan University	M
University at Buffalo, the State University of New York	M,D,O*
University of Colorado at Colorado Springs	M,D
University of Delaware	M,O*
University of Maryland, Baltimore	M*
University of Massachusetts Lowell	M*
University of Massachusetts Worcester	M,D,O*
University of Michigan	M*
University of Minnesota, Twin Cities Campus	M*
The University of North Carolina at Greensboro	M,D,O
University of Utah	M,O*
Vanderbilt University	M,D*
Villanova University	M,D,O*

GERONTOLOGY

Abilene Christian University	M,O
Adelphi University	M,O*
Adler School of Professional Psychology	M,D,O*
Appalachian State University	M
Arizona State University at the West campus	O
Arkansas State University	M,O
A.T. Still University of Health Sciences	M,D
Ball State University	M*
Bethel University	M
California State University, Dominguez Hills	M
California State University, Fullerton	M
California State University, Long Beach	M
Case Western Reserve University	M,D,O*
Chestnut Hill College	M,O
The College of New Rochelle	M,O
Concordia University (IL)	M
Dominican University of California	M
Eastern Illinois University	M
Eastern Michigan University	M,O
East Tennessee State University	M,O
Emory University	M*
Florida Gulf Coast University	M
Gannon University	O
George Mason University	M*
Georgia State University	M*
Hofstra University	M,O*
Kent State University	M*
Lakehead University	M
La Salle University	M,O
Lindenwood University	M
Long Island University, C.W. Post Campus	M,O*
Long Island University, Rockland Graduate Campus	M,O
Marywood University	M,O*
Miami University	M*
Middle Tennessee State University	O*
Minnesota State University Mankato	M,O
Morehead State University	M
Mount Saint Vincent University	M
National-Louis University	M,O
North Dakota State University	M,D
Northeastern Illinois University	M
Notre Dame de Namur University	M,O
Oklahoma State University	M*
Oregon State University	M*
Portland State University	O
Rochester Institute of Technology	O
Sacred Heart University	M
Sage Graduate School	M
St. Cloud State University	M
Saint Joseph College	O
Saint Joseph's University	M,O*
San Diego State University	M*
San Francisco State University	M
San Jose State University	M,O
Simon Fraser University	M,D
Texas A&M University–Kingsville	M
Texas Tech University	M,D
Towson University	M,O
Université de Sherbrooke	M
Université Laval	O
University of Arkansas at Little Rock	M,O
University of Central Florida	M,O*
University of Central Missouri	M
University of Central Oklahoma	M
University of Georgia	O*
University of Hawaii at Manoa	O*
University of Illinois at Springfield	M
University of Indianapolis	M,O
University of Kansas	M,D*
University of Kentucky	D*
University of La Verne	M,O
University of Louisiana at Monroe	M,O
University of Maryland, Baltimore	M,D*
University of Maryland, Baltimore County	M,D,O*
University of Massachusetts Boston	M,D,O
University of Missouri–St. Louis	M,O
University of Nebraska at Omaha	M,O
University of New England	M,O
The University of North Carolina at Charlotte	M*
The University of North Carolina at Greensboro	M,O
University of Northern Colorado	M
University of North Florida	M,O
University of North Texas	M,D,O*
University of Pittsburgh	M,D,O*
University of Puerto Rico, Medical Sciences Campus	M,O*
University of Regina	M
University of Rhode Island	M,D
University of South Alabama	O*
University of South Carolina	O*
University of Southern California	M,D,O*
University of South Florida	M,D*
The University of Tennessee	M*
The University of Toledo	O*

- University of Utah M,O*
- University of West Georgia M
- Valparaiso University M,O
- Virginia Commonwealth University M,D,O*
- Virginia Polytechnic Institute and State University M,D*
- Wayne State University O*
- Webster University M
- West Chester University of Pennsylvania M,O
- Wichita State University M*
- Wilmington College (DE) M

GRAPHIC DESIGN

- Academy of Art University M*
- Atlantic College M
- Bob Jones University P,M,D,O
- Boston University M*
- Bowling Green State University M*
- California Institute of the Arts M,O
- California State University, Los Angeles M
- Cardinal Stritch University M*
- City College of the City University of New York M*
- The College of New Rochelle M
- Cranbrook Academy of Art M*
- George Mason University M*
- Illinois State University M*
- Indiana State University M*
- Iowa State University of Science and Technology M*
- Kean University M
- Kent State University M*
- Louisiana State University and Agricultural and Mechanical College M*
- Louisiana Tech University M
- Maryland Institute College of Art M*
- Marywood University M*
- Miami International University of Art & Design M*
- Minneapolis College of Art and Design M
- New York University M*
- North Carolina State University M*
- Pittsburg State University M,O
- Pratt Institute M*
- Rhode Island School of Design M
- Rochester Institute of Technology M
- San Diego State University M*
- Savannah College of Art and Design M*
- School of the Art Institute of Chicago M*
- Suffolk University M*
- Syracuse University M*
- Temple University M*
- Université Laval M
- University of Baltimore M*
- University of Cincinnati M
- University of Florida M,D*
- University of Guam M
- University of Illinois at Chicago M*
- University of Illinois at Urbana–Champaign M*
- University of Memphis M*
- University of Miami M*
- University of Minnesota, Duluth M*
- University of North Texas M,D*
- University of Notre Dame M*
- The University of Tennessee M*
- University of Utah M*
- Western Illinois University M,O
- Western Michigan University M*
- West Virginia University M*
- Yale University M*

HAZARDOUS MATERIALS MANAGEMENT

- Idaho State University M
- New Mexico Institute of Mining and Technology M
- Rutgers, The State University of New Jersey, New Brunswick M,D*
- Southern Methodist University M,D*
- Stony Brook University, State University of New York M,O*
- Tufts University M,D*
- University of Oklahoma M,D*
- University of South Carolina M,D*
- Wayne State University M,O*

HEALTH COMMUNICATION

- Cleveland State University M,O
- East Carolina University M*
- Emerson College M*
- Marquette University M
- Marywood University M,O*
- Michigan State University M*
- Tufts University M*
- Tulane University M*
- University of Florida M,D,O*
- University of Southern California M*
- University of West Florida M
- Washington State University M,D*

HEALTH EDUCATION

- Adams State College M
- Adelphi University M,O*
- Alabama State University M
- Albany State University M
- Alcorn State University M,O
- Allen College M
- Arcadia University M
- Arkansas State University M,O
- A.T. Still University of Health Sciences M,D
- Auburn University M,D,O*
- Augusta State University M
- Austin Peay State University M
- Averett University M
- Ball State University M*
- Baylor University M,D*
- Benedictine University M
- Boston University M,O*
- Brigham Young University M*
- Brooklyn College of the City University of New York M,O
- California State University, Dominguez Hills M
- California State University, Long Beach M
- California State University, Los Angeles M
- California State University, Northridge M
- California State University, San Bernardino M
- Central Washington University M
- The Citadel, The Military College of South Carolina M
- Cleveland State University M
- The College of New Jersey M
- Dalhousie University M
- East Carolina University M*
- Eastern Kentucky University M*
- Eastern Michigan University M
- Eastern University M*
- East Stroudsburg University of Pennsylvania M
- Emory University M,D*
- Felician College M,O*
- Florida Agricultural and Mechanical University M*
- Florida State University M,D*
- Fort Hays State University M
- Framingham State College M*
- Georgia College & State University M,O
- Georgia Southern University M
- Georgia Southwestern State University M,O
- Georgia State University M*
- Harding University M,O
- Hofstra University M*
- Howard University M*
- Idaho State University M
- Illinois State University M*
- Indiana State University M*
- Indiana University Bloomington M,D*
- Indiana University of Pennsylvania M
- Indiana University–Purdue University Indianapolis M,D*
- Inter American University of Puerto Rico, Metropolitan Campus M
- Iowa State University of Science and Technology M,D*
- Ithaca College M
- Jackson State University M
- Jacksonville State University M
- James Madison University M
- John F. Kennedy University M
- The Johns Hopkins University M,D*
- Kent State University M,D*
- Lake Erie College of Osteopathic Medicine P,M,O
- Lehman College of the City University of New York M
- Loma Linda University M,D
- Long Island University, Brooklyn Campus M*
- Louisiana Tech University M,D
- Marshall University M
- Marywood University D*
- Middle Tennessee State University M,D*
- Midwestern University, Glendale Campus M*
- Mills College M,D
- Minnesota State University Mankato M
- Mississippi State University M
- Mississippi University for Women M
- Montana State University M
- Montclair State University M,O*
- Morehead State University M
- Mount Mary College M
- New Jersey City University M
- New Mexico Highlands University M
- New York University M,D*
- North Carolina Agricultural and Technical State University M
- Northeastern State University M
- Northern Arizona University M
- Northern State University M
- Northwestern State University of Louisiana M
- Northwest Missouri State University M
- Nova Southeastern University D*
- Oklahoma State University M,D,O*
- Penn State Harrisburg M,D*
- Plymouth State University M
- Portland State University M,O
- Prairie View A&M University M
- Rhode Island College M
- Rosalind Franklin University of Medicine and Science M*
- Sage Graduate School M
- Saint Francis University M
- Saint Joseph's University M*
- Salem International University M
- San Francisco State University M
- San Jose State University M,O
- Simmons College M,D,O
- South Dakota State University M
- Southeastern Louisiana University M
- Southern Connecticut State University M
- Southern Illinois University Carbondale M,D*
- Southern Illinois University Edwardsville M,O
- Springfield College M,D,O*
- State University of New York College at Brockport M*
- State University of New York College at Cortland M*
- Teachers College Columbia University M,D*
- Temple University M*
- Tennessee Technological University M*
- Texas A&M Health Science Center M*
- Texas A&M University M,D*
- Texas A&M University–Commerce M,D
- Texas A&M University–Kingsville M
- Texas Southern University M
- Texas State University-San Marcos M*
- Texas Woman's University M,D
- Touro University International M,D,O
- Tulane University M*
- Union College (KY) M
- The University of Alabama M,D
- The University of Alabama at Birmingham M,D*
- University of Arkansas M,D*
- University of Calgary M,D
- University of California, Berkeley M*
- University of Central Arkansas M
- University of Central Oklahoma M
- University of Cincinnati M,D
- University of Colorado at Denver and Health Sciences Center D*
- University of Florida M,D,O*
- University of Georgia M,D,O*
- University of Houston M,D*
- University of Illinois at Chicago M*
- University of Louisville M
- University of Maryland, Baltimore County M*
- University of Maryland, College Park M,D*
- University of Medicine and Dentistry of New Jersey M,D*
- University of Michigan–Flint M*
- University of Missouri–Columbia M,D,O*
- The University of Montana M*
- University of Nebraska at Omaha M
- University of Nebraska–Lincoln M*
- University of New Mexico M*
- The University of North Carolina at Chapel Hill M,D*
- University of Northern Iowa M,D
- University of Oklahoma Health Sciences Center D
- University of Pennsylvania M,D*
- University of Pittsburgh M,O*
- University of Puerto Rico, Medical Sciences Campus M,O*
- University of Rhode Island M,D
- University of South Alabama M*
- University of South Carolina M,D,O*
- The University of South Dakota M
- University of Southern Mississippi M*
- The University of Tennessee M*
- The University of Texas at Austin M,D*
- The University of Texas at El Paso M
- The University of Texas at Tyler M
- The University of Toledo M,D*
- University of Utah M,D*
- University of Virginia M,D*
- University of Waterloo M,D*
- University of West Florida M
- University of Wisconsin–La Crosse M
- University of Wyoming M
- Utah State University M
- Valdosta State University M
- Virginia Commonwealth University M,D*
- Virginia Polytechnic Institute and State University M,D,O*
- Wayne State University M,D,O*
- West Chester University of Pennsylvania M,O
- Western Illinois University M,O
- Western Oregon University M
- Western University of Health Sciences M
- West Virginia University M,D*
- Widener University M,D*
- Worcester State College M
- Wright State University M*

HEALTH INFORMATICS

- American Sentinel University M
- Barry University O*
- Benedictine University M
- The College of St. Scholastica M,O
- Emory University M,D*
- The George Washington University M*
- Indiana University Bloomington M,D*
- The Johns Hopkins University M*
- Loma Linda University M
- Medical College of Georgia M*
- Molloy College M,O
- New York Medical College M,D,O*
- Northeastern University M,D*
- Northern Kentucky University M
- Touro College M,O
- Touro University International M,D,O
- The University of Alabama at Birmingham M*
- University of Illinois at Urbana–Champaign M,D,O*
- The University of Iowa M,D,O*
- University of La Verne M
- University of Maryland University College M,O
- University of Minnesota, Twin Cities Campus M,D*
- University of Missouri–Columbia M*
- University of Pittsburgh M*
- University of Puerto Rico, Medical Sciences Campus M*
- The University of Texas Health Science Center at Houston M,D*
- University of Victoria M
- University of Virginia M*
- University of Washington M,D*
- University of Wisconsin–Milwaukee M

HEALTH PHYSICS/RADIOLOGICAL HEALTH

- Bloomsburg University of Pennsylvania M
- Drexel University M,D*
- Emory University D*
- Georgetown University M*
- Georgia Institute of Technology M,D*
- Illinois Institute of Technology M,D*
- McGill University M,D*
- McMaster University M,D
- Medical College of Georgia M*
- Midwestern State University M
- New York Chiropractic College M*
- Oregon State University M,D*
- San Diego State University M*
- Texas A&M University M,D*
- Université de Montréal O
- Université Laval O
- University of Alberta M,D*
- University of Cincinnati M
- University of Illinois at Urbana–Champaign M,D*
- University of Kentucky M*
- University of Massachusetts Lowell M,D*
- University of Medicine and Dentistry of New Jersey M*
- University of Michigan M,D,O*
- University of Missouri–Columbia M,D*
- University of Nevada, Las Vegas M
- University of Oklahoma Health Sciences Center M,D

P—first professional degree; M—master's degree; D—doctorate; O—other advanced degree;
**full description and/or announcement in Book 2, 3, 4, 5, or 6*

The University of Toledo M*
Virginia Commonwealth University D*
Wayne State University M,D*

HEALTH PROMOTION

Auburn University M,D,O*
Ball State University M*
Barnes-Jewish College of Nursing and Allied Health M,O
Benedictine University M
Boston University M,D*
Bridgewater State College M
Brigham Young University M,D*
California College for Health Sciences M
California State University, Fresno M
Canisius College M
Central Michigan University M*
Eastern Michigan University M
Emerson College M*
Emory University M*
Florida Atlantic University M
Georgetown University M,D*
The George Washington University M,O*
Georgia State University M,D,O*
Goddard College M
Harvard University M,D*
Indiana State University M*
Indiana University Bloomington M,D*
Lehman College of the City University of New York M
Loma Linda University M,D
Marymount University M
McNeese State University M
Missouri State University M*
Nebraska Methodist College M
New York Medical College M*
New York University M,D,O*
Northern Arizona University M
Oakland University O*
Old Dominion University M*
Oregon State University M*
Portland State University M,O
Purdue University M,D*
San Diego State University M,D*
Simmons College M,O
Université de Montréal M,D,O
The University of Alabama M,D
The University of Alabama at Birmingham D*
University of Alberta M,O*
University of Central Florida M,O*
University of Chicago M*
University of Delaware M*
University of Georgia M,D,O*
University of Kentucky M,D*
University of Massachusetts Lowell D*
University of Memphis M*
University of Michigan M,D*
The University of Montana M*
University of Nevada, Las Vegas M
The University of North Carolina at Chapel Hill M*
University of North Texas M*
University of Oklahoma Health Sciences Center M,D
University of Puerto Rico, Medical Sciences Campus O*
University of South Carolina M,D,O*
University of Southern California M*
The University of Tennessee M*
University of Utah M,D*
University of Wisconsin–Madison M,D*
University of Wisconsin–Stevens Point M
West Virginia University M,D*
Wright State University M*

HEALTH PSYCHOLOGY

Appalachian State University M
Argosy University, Atlanta Campus M,D,O*
Argosy University, Chicago Campus D*
Argosy University, Schaumburg Campus M,D,O*
Argosy University, Twin Cities Campus M,D,O*
Argosy University, Washington DC Campus M,D,O*
Bastyr University M*
California Institute of Integral Studies M,D*
Central Connecticut State University M
Drexel University M,D*
Duke University D*
East Carolina University D*
The George Washington University D*
Lesley University M*
National-Louis University M,O
Northern Arizona University M
Philadelphia College of Osteopathic Medicine M,D*
Rutgers, The State University of New Jersey, New Brunswick D*
San Diego State University M,D*
Saybrook Graduate School and Research Center M,D
Southwestern College (NM) O*
Stony Brook University, State University of New York D*
Texas State University-San Marcos M*
The University of British Columbia M,D*
University of Florida D*
University of Michigan–Dearborn M*
The University of North Carolina at Charlotte D*
University of North Texas M,D*
University of the Sciences in Philadelphia M*
West Chester University of Pennsylvania M,O
Yeshiva University D

HEALTH SERVICES MANAGEMENT AND HOSPITAL ADMINISTRATION

Alaska Pacific University M
Albany State University M
American InterContinental University Online M
American Sentinel University M
Andrew Jackson University M
Aquinas Institute of Theology P,M,D,O
Argosy University, Atlanta Campus M,D*
Argosy University, Chicago Campus M,D*
Argosy University, Denver Campus M,D*
Argosy University, Hawai'i Campus M,D,O*
Argosy University, Inland Empire Campus M,D*
Argosy University, Orange County Campus M,D,O*
Argosy University, Phoenix Campus M,D*
Argosy University, San Francisco Bay Area Campus M,D*
Argosy University, Santa Monica Campus M,D*
Argosy University, Sarasota Campus M,D,O*
Argosy University, Schaumburg Campus M,D,O*
Argosy University, Seattle Campus M,D*
Argosy University, Tampa Campus M,D,O*
Argosy University, Twin Cities Campus M,D*
Argosy University, Washington DC Campus M,D,O*
Arizona State University M*
Armstrong Atlantic State University M
A.T. Still University of Health Sciences M,D
Avila University M*
Baker College Center for Graduate Studies M
Baldwin-Wallace College M
Barnes-Jewish College of Nursing and Allied Health M,O
Barry University M,O*
Baylor University M*
Bellevue University M*
Benedictine University M*
Bernard M. Baruch College of the City University of New York M*
Boston University M,D,O*
Brandeis University M*
Brenau University M
Brooklyn College of the City University of New York M
California College for Health Sciences M
California State University, Bakersfield M
California State University, Chico M
California State University, East Bay M
California State University, Fresno M
California State University, Long Beach M,O
California State University, Los Angeles M
California State University, Northridge M
California State University, San Bernardino M
Capella University M,D,O
Cardean University M
Carnegie Mellon University M*
Case Western Reserve University M,D*
Central Michigan University M,D,O*
Charleston Southern University M
Clark University M*
Clayton State University M
Cleveland State University M
College of Saint Elizabeth M
Colorado Technical University—Sioux Falls M
Columbia Southern University M
Columbia University M*
Concordia University (Canada) M,D,O
Concordia University Wisconsin M
Cornell University M,D*
Dalhousie University M
Dallas Baptist University M
Davenport University M
Davenport University M
DePaul University M,O*
Des Moines University M
Duke University O*
Duquesne University M,D*
D'Youville College M,O*
Eastern Kentucky University M*
East Tennessee State University M,D,O
Emory University M,D*
Fairfield University M,O*
Fairleigh Dickinson University, Metropolitan Campus M*
Florida Atlantic University M
Florida International University M*
Framingham State College M*
Francis Marion University M
Friends University M
The George Washington University M,D,O*
Georgia Institute of Technology M*
Georgia Southern University M*
Georgia State University M*
Governors State University M
Grand Valley State University M
Harvard University M,D*
Hofstra University M,O*
Houston Baptist University M
Illinois Institute of Technology M*
Indiana University Northwest M,O
Indiana University–Purdue University Indianapolis M*
Indiana University South Bend M,O
Indiana Wesleyan University M
Institute of Public Administration M,O
Iona College M,O*
The Johns Hopkins University M,D,O*
Jones International University M
Kean University M
Kennesaw State University M
King's College M
Lake Erie College M
Lamar University M*
Lindenwood University M
Lipscomb University M
Loma Linda University M
Long Island University, Brooklyn Campus M*
Long Island University, C.W. Post Campus M,O*
Long Island University, Rockland Graduate Campus M,O
Louisiana State University in Shreveport M
Loyola University Chicago M*
Loyola University New Orleans M
Madonna University M
Marshall University M
Marymount University M
Marywood University M*
Massachusetts College of Pharmacy and Health Sciences M*
McGill University M,D,O*
Medical University of South Carolina M,D*
Meharry Medical College M
Mercy College M,O
Middle Tennessee State University O*
Midwestern State University M
Mississippi College M
Missouri State University M*
Monmouth University M,O
Montana State University–Billings M
Mount Aloysius College M
National University M
Nebraska Methodist College M
New England College M
New Jersey City University M
The New School: A University M,O*
New York Institute of Technology M,O
New York Medical College M,O*
New York University M,O*
Northeastern University M*
Northwest Missouri State University M
OGI School of Science & Engineering at Oregon Health & Science University M,O
The Ohio State University M*
Ohio University M*
Oklahoma City University M
Oklahoma State University M*
Old Dominion University M*
Oregon State University M*
Our Lady of the Lake University of San Antonio M
Pace University M*
Park University M
Penn State Great Valley M
Penn State Harrisburg M,D*
Penn State University Park M,D*
Pfeiffer University M
Philadelphia University M*
Portland State University M,O
Quinnipiac University M*
Regent University M
Regis University M,D
Roberts Wesleyan College M
Rochester Institute of Technology M,O
Rosalind Franklin University of Medicine and Science M*
Rush University M,D
Rutgers, The State University of New Jersey, Newark M,D*
Sage Graduate School M
St. Ambrose University M,D
Saint Joseph's College of Maine M
St. Joseph's College, Suffolk Campus M,O
Saint Joseph's University M*
Saint Louis University M,D*
Saint Mary's University of Minnesota M
St. Thomas University M,O
Saint Xavier University M,O
Salve Regina University M,O
San Diego State University M,D*
Seton Hall University M*
Shenandoah University M,O*
Simmons College M,O
Southeastern University M
Southeast Missouri State University M
Southern Adventist University M
Southwest Baptist University M
Springfield College M*
State University of New York at Binghamton M,D*
State University of New York Institute of Technology M
Stephens College O
Stony Brook University, State University of New York M,D,O*
Suffolk University M,O*
Syracuse University O*
Temple University M,D*
Texas A&M Health Science Center M*
Texas A&M University–Corpus Christi M
Texas State University-San Marcos M*
Texas Tech University M,D
Texas Tech University Health Sciences Center M
Texas Wesleyan University M
Texas Woman's University M,D
Touro College O
Touro University International M,D,O
Towson University O
Trinity University M*
Tulane University M,D*
Union Graduate College M,O*
Universidad de Ciencias Medicas P,M
Universidad de Iberoamerica P,M
Universidad Nacional Pedro Henriquez Urena P,M,D
Université de Montréal M,O
University at Albany, State University of New York M*
The University of Akron M
The University of Alabama at Birmingham M,D*
University of Alberta M,D*
University of Arkansas at Little Rock M
University of Baltimore M*
The University of British Columbia M,D*
University of California, Berkeley M,D*
University of California, Los Angeles M,D*
University of California, San Diego M*
University of Central Florida M,O*
University of Colorado at Colorado Springs M
University of Colorado at Denver and Health Sciences Center M*
University of Colorado at Denver and Health Sciences Center M*
University of Connecticut M,D*
University of Dallas M
University of Detroit Mercy M

University of Evansville	M
University of Florida	M,D*
University of Houston–Clear Lake	M
University of Illinois at Chicago	M,D*
The University of Iowa	M,D*
University of Kansas	M*
University of Kentucky	M*
University of La Verne	M,O
University of Louisiana at Lafayette	M*
University of Maryland, Baltimore County	M*
University of Maryland University College	M,O
University of Massachusetts Boston	M,D,O
University of Massachusetts Lowell	M*
University of Medicine and Dentistry of New Jersey	M*
University of Memphis	M*
University of Michigan	M,D*
University of Minnesota, Twin Cities Campus	M,D*
University of Missouri–Columbia	M*
University of Missouri–St. Louis	M,O
University of New Hampshire	M*
University of New Haven	M*
University of New Orleans	M
The University of North Carolina at Chapel Hill	M,D*
The University of North Carolina at Charlotte	M*
University of North Florida	M,O
University of North Texas Health Science Center at Fort Worth	M,D
University of Oklahoma	M*
University of Oklahoma Health Sciences Center	M,D
University of Ottawa	M*
University of Pennsylvania	M,D*
University of Phoenix–Atlanta Campus	M
University of Phoenix–Augusta Campus	M
University of Phoenix–Austin Campus	M
University of Phoenix–Bay Area Campus	M
University of Phoenix–Central Florida Campus	M
University of Phoenix–Central Valley Campus	M
University of Phoenix–Chattanooga Campus	M
University of Phoenix–Cheyenne Campus	M
University of Phoenix–Cincinnati Campus	M
University of Phoenix–Cleveland Campus	M
University of Phoenix–Columbus Georgia Campus	M
University of Phoenix–Columbus Ohio Campus	M
University of Phoenix–Dallas Campus	M
University of Phoenix–Denver Campus	M
University of Phoenix–Des Moines Campus	M
University of Phoenix–Detroit Campus	M
University of Phoenix–Eastern Washington Campus	M
University of Phoenix–Fort Lauderdale Campus	M
University of Phoenix–Harrisburg Campus	M
University of Phoenix–Hawaii Campus	M
University of Phoenix–Houston Campus	M
University of Phoenix–Idaho Campus	M
University of Phoenix–Indianapolis Campus	M
University of Phoenix–Jersey City Campus	M
University of Phoenix–Kansas City Campus	M
University of Phoenix–Louisiana Campus	M
University of Phoenix–Louisville Campus	M
University of Phoenix–Madison Campus	M
University of Phoenix–Memphis Campus	M
University of Phoenix–Metro Detroit Campus	M
University of Phoenix–Minneapolis/St. Louis Park Campus	M
University of Phoenix–Nashville Campus	M
University of Phoenix–New Mexico Campus	M
University of Phoenix–Northern Nevada Campus	M
University of Phoenix–Northern Virginia Campus	M
University of Phoenix–North Florida Campus	M
University of Phoenix–Northwest Arkansas Campus	M
University of Phoenix–Northwest Indiana	M
University of Phoenix–Omaha Campus	M
University of Phoenix Online Campus	M,D
University of Phoenix–Oregon Campus	M
University of Phoenix–Philadelphia Campus	M
University of Phoenix–Phoenix Campus	M,O
University of Phoenix–Pittsburgh Campus	M
University of Phoenix–Puerto Rico Campus	M
University of Phoenix–Raleigh Campus	M
University of Phoenix–Renton Learning Center	M
University of Phoenix–Richmond Campus	M
University of Phoenix–Sacramento Valley Campus	M
University of Phoenix–St. Louis Campus	M
University of Phoenix–San Antonio Campus	M
University of Phoenix–Savannah Campus	M
University of Phoenix–Southern Arizona Campus	M,O
University of Phoenix–Southern California Campus	M,O
University of Phoenix–Southern Colorado Campus	M
University of Phoenix–Springfield Campus	M
University of Phoenix–Vancouver Campus	M
University of Phoenix–Washington Campus	M
University of Phoenix–West Florida Campus	M
University of Phoenix–West Michigan Campus	M
University of Phoenix–Wisconsin Campus	M
University of Pittsburgh	M,D,O*
University of Puerto Rico, Medical Sciences Campus	M*
University of St. Francis (IL)	M*
University of St. Thomas (MN)	M*
University of San Francisco	M
University of Saskatchewan	M
The University of Scranton	M
University of South Carolina	M,D*
University of Southern California	M*
University of Southern Indiana	M
University of Southern Maine	M,O
University of Southern Mississippi	M*
University of South Florida	M,D*
The University of Tennessee	M*
The University of Texas at Arlington	M*
The University of Texas at Dallas	M*
The University of Texas at Tyler	M
University of the Sciences in Philadelphia	M,D*
The University of Toledo	M*
University of Virginia	M*
University of Washington	M*
University of Wisconsin–Oshkosh	M
Villanova University	M,D,O*
Virginia Commonwealth University	M,D*
Wagner College	M
Walden University	M,D
Washington State University	M*
Washington State University Spokane	M
Washington University in St. Louis	M*
Wayland Baptist University	M
Weber State University	M
Webster University	M,D
West Chester University of Pennsylvania	M,O
Western Carolina University	M*
Western Connecticut State University	M*
Western Illinois University	M,O
Western Kentucky University	M
Widener University	M*
William Woods University	M,O
Wilmington College (DE)	M
Worcester State College	M
Wright State University	M*
Xavier University	M*
Yale University	M,D*
Youngstown State University	M

HEALTH SERVICES RESEARCH

Arizona State University	M,D*
Brown University	M,D*
Clarkson University	M*
Cornell University, Joan and Sanford I. Weill Medical College and Graduate School of Medical Sciences	M*
Dartmouth College	M,D*
Emory University	M,D*
Florida State University	M*
The George Washington University	M,D,O*
The Johns Hopkins University	M,D*
McMaster University	M,D
Old Dominion University	D*
Penn State Hershey Medical Center	M*
Stanford University	M*
Texas State University-San Marcos	M*
Thomas Jefferson University	O*
University of Alberta	M,D*
The University of British Columbia	M,D*
University of Florida	M,D*
University of La Verne	M
University of Maryland, Baltimore	M,D*
University of Massachusetts Worcester	D*
University of Minnesota, Twin Cities Campus	M,D*
University of New Brunswick Fredericton	M
The University of North Carolina at Charlotte	D*
University of North Florida	M,O
University of Ottawa	D,O*
University of Puerto Rico, Medical Sciences Campus	M*
University of Rochester	D*
University of Southern California	D*
University of Virginia	M*
University of Washington	M,D*
Virginia Commonwealth University	D*
Wake Forest University	M*

HIGHER EDUCATION

Abilene Christian University	M
Alliant International University–Irvine	M,D,O*
Alliant International University–Los Angeles	M,D,O*
Alliant International University–San Diego	M,D,O*
Alliant International University–San Francisco	M,D,O*
Angelo State University	M
Appalachian State University	M,O
Argosy University, Atlanta Campus	M,D,O*
Argosy University, Chicago Campus	M,D,O*
Argosy University, Denver Campus	M,D*
Argosy University, Hawai'i Campus	M,D*
Argosy University, Inland Empire Campus	M,D*
Argosy University, Nashville Campus	M,D*
Argosy University, Orange County Campus	M,D*
Argosy University, Phoenix Campus	M,D,O*
Argosy University, San Diego Campus	M,D*
Argosy University, San Francisco Bay Area Campus	M,D*
Argosy University, Santa Monica Campus	M,D*
Argosy University, Sarasota Campus	M,D,O*
Argosy University, Schaumburg Campus	M,D,O*
Argosy University, Seattle Campus	M,D*
Argosy University, Tampa Campus	M,D,O*
Argosy University, Twin Cities Campus	M,D,O*
Argosy University, Washington DC Campus	M,D,O*
Arizona State University	M,D,O*
Auburn University	M,D,O*
Azusa Pacific University	M,D
Ball State University	M,D*
Barry University	M,D*
Benedictine University	D
Bernard M. Baruch College of the City University of New York	M*
Bethel University	M,O
Boston College	M,D*
Bowling Green State University	D*
Capella University	M,D,O
Chicago State University	M,D
Claremont Graduate University	M,D,O
College of Saint Elizabeth	M,O
Columbia International University	M,D,O
Dallas Baptist University	M
Drexel University	M*
Eastern Kentucky University	M*
Eastern Washington University	M
Fitchburg State College	M,O
Florida Atlantic University	M,D,O
Florida International University	D*
Florida State University	M,D,O*
Geneva College	M*
The George Washington University	M,D,O*
Georgia Southern University	M
Grand Valley State University	M
Harvard University	D*
Illinois State University	M,D*
Indiana University Bloomington	M,D,O*
Indiana University of Pennsylvania	M
Inter American University of Puerto Rico, Metropolitan Campus	M
Iowa State University of Science and Technology	M,D*
Jones International University	M
Kent State University	M*
Louisiana State University and Agricultural and Mechanical College	M,D,O*
Loyola University Chicago	M,D*
Marywood University	M,D*
Michigan State University	M,D,O*
Minnesota State University Mankato	M,O
Mississippi College	M,O
Morehead State University	M,O
Morgan State University	D*
New York University	M,D*
North Carolina State University	M,D*
Northeastern State University	M
Northern Illinois University	M,D
Northwestern University	M*
Nova Southeastern University	D*
Oakland University	M,D,O*
The Ohio State University	M*
Ohio University	M,D*
Oklahoma State University	M,D*
Old Dominion University	M,D,O*
Oral Roberts University	M,D
Penn State University Park	M,D*
Phillips Theological Seminary	P,M,D
Pittsburg State University	M,O
Portland State University	M,D
Purdue University	M,D,O*
Rowan University	M
St. Cloud State University	M
St. John's University (NY)	O
Saint Louis University	M,D,O*
Salem State College	M
San Diego State University	M*
San Jose State University	M,O
Seton Hall University	D*
Southeast Missouri State University	M,O
Southern Illinois University Carbondale	M*
Stanford University	M,D*
Syracuse University	M,D*
Teachers College Columbia University	M,D*
Texas A&M University–Commerce	M,D
Texas A&M University–Kingsville	D
Texas Southern University	M,D
Texas Tech University	M,D,O
Touro University International	M,D
Union University	M,D,O
Université de Sherbrooke	M,O
University at Buffalo, the State University of New York	M,D,O*
The University of Akron	M
The University of Alabama	M,D
The University of Arizona	M,D*
University of Arkansas	M,D,O*
University of Arkansas at Little Rock	D
The University of British Columbia	M,D*
University of Calgary	M,D,O
University of Central Oklahoma	M
University of Connecticut	M*
University of Delaware	M*
University of Denver	M,D,O*
University of Florida	M,D,O*
University of Georgia	D*
University of Houston	M,D*
University of Illinois at Urbana–Champaign	M,D,O*

*P—first professional degree; M—master's degree; D—doctorate; O—other advanced degree; *full description and/or announcement in Book 2, 3, 4, 5, or 6*

The University of Iowa M,D,O*
University of Kansas M,D*
University of Kentucky M,D*
University of Louisville M,O
University of Maine M,D,O*
University of Mary M
University of Massachusetts Amherst M,D,O*
University of Massachusetts Boston M,D,O
University of Memphis M,D*
University of Miami M,O*
University of Michigan M,D*
University of Minnesota, Twin Cities Campus M,D*
University of Mississippi M,D,O
University of Missouri–Columbia M,D,O*
University of Missouri–St. Louis M,D,O
University of New Hampshire M*
The University of North Carolina at Greensboro D
University of Northern Iowa M
University of North Texas M,D*
University of Oklahoma M,D*
University of Pittsburgh M,D*
University of South Carolina M*
University of Southern Mississippi M,D,O*
University of South Florida M,D,O*
The University of Texas at San Antonio M,D*
The University of Toledo M,D*
University of Virginia D,O*
University of Washington M,D*
University of Wisconsin–Whitewater M*
Vanderbilt University M,D*
Walden University M,D
Washington State University M,D*
Wayne State University M,D,O*
Western Governors University M,O
Western Washington University M
West Virginia University M,D*
Wright State University M,O*

HISPANIC STUDIES

Brown University M,D*
California State University, Los Angeles M
California State University, Northridge M
Connecticut College M
Eastern Michigan University M,O
La Salle University M
McGill University M,D*
Michigan State University M,D*
New Mexico Highlands University M
Pontifical Catholic University of Puerto Rico M
St. Thomas University M,O
San Jose State University M
Stony Brook University, State University of New York M,D*
Texas A&M International University M,D
Université de Montréal M,D
University of Alberta M,D*
The University of British Columbia M,D*
University of California, Berkeley M,D*
University of California, Los Angeles D*
University of California, Riverside M,D*
University of California, Santa Barbara M,D*
University of Illinois at Chicago M,D*
University of Kentucky M,D*
The University of North Carolina at Greensboro M,O
The University of North Carolina Wilmington O*
University of Pittsburgh M,D*
University of Puerto Rico, Mayagüez Campus M*
University of Puerto Rico, Río Piedras M,D*
The University of Texas at San Antonio M*
University of Victoria M
University of Washington M*
Villanova University M*

HISTORIC PRESERVATION

Ball State University M*
Boston University M*
Buffalo State College, State University of New York M,O
Clemson University M*
Columbia University M*
Cornell University M,D*
Eastern Michigan University M
The George Washington University M*
Georgia State University M*
Goucher College M
Michigan Technological University D*
Middle Tennessee State University M,D*
New York University *
Pratt Institute M*
Rensselaer Polytechnic Institute M*
Rutgers, The State University of New Jersey, New Brunswick M,D*
Savannah College of Art and Design M*
School of the Art Institute of Chicago M*
Texas Tech University M
Universidad Nacional Pedro Henriquez Urena P,M,D
University of California, Riverside M,D*
University of Delaware M,D*
University of Georgia M*
University of Hawaii at Manoa O*
University of Kentucky M*
University of Maryland, College Park M,O*
The University of North Carolina at Greensboro M,O
University of Oregon M*
University of Pennsylvania M,O*
University of South Carolina M,O*
University of Southern California O*
University of Vermont M*
University of Washington O*
Ursuline College M
Virginia Commonwealth University M,O*

HISTORY

American Public University System M
American University M,D*
American University of Beirut M
Andrews University M
Angelo State University M
Appalachian State University M
Arizona State University M,D*
Arkansas State University M,D,O
Arkansas Tech University M
Armstrong Atlantic State University M
Ashland Theological Seminary P,M,D,O
Ashland University M
Auburn University M,D*
Ball State University M*
Baylor University M*
Bob Jones University P,M,D,O
Boise State University M
Boston College M,D*
Boston University M,D*
Bowling Green State University M,D*
Brandeis University M,D*
Brigham Young University M*
Brock University M
Brooklyn College of the City University of New York M,D
Brown University M,D*
Buffalo State College, State University of New York M
Butler University M
California Polytechnic State University, San Luis Obispo M
California State Polytechnic University, Pomona M
California State University, Bakersfield M
California State University, Chico M
California State University, East Bay M
California State University, Fresno M
California State University, Fullerton M
California State University, Long Beach M
California State University, Los Angeles M
California State University, Northridge M
California State University, Stanislaus M
Cardinal Stritch University M*
Carleton University M,D
Carnegie Mellon University M,D*
Case Western Reserve University M,D*
The Catholic University of America M,D*
Central Connecticut State University M,O
Central European University M,D*
Central Michigan University M,D*
Central Washington University M
Centro de Estudios Avanzados de Puerto Rico y el Caribe M,D
Chicago State University M
Christopher Newport University M
The Citadel, The Military College of South Carolina M
City College of the City University of New York M*
Claremont Graduate University M,D,O
Clark Atlanta University M
Clark University M,D,O*
Clemson University M*
Cleveland State University M
College of Charleston M*
The College of Saint Rose M*
College of Staten Island of the City University of New York M
The College of William and Mary M,D
Colorado State University M*
Columbia University M,D*
Concordia University (Canada) M,D
Converse College M
Cornell University M,D*
Dalhousie University M,D
DePaul University M*
Drake University M*
Drew University M,D
Duke University M,D*
Duquesne University M*
East Carolina University M*
Eastern Illinois University M
Eastern Kentucky University M*
Eastern Michigan University M
Eastern Washington University M
East Stroudsburg University of Pennsylvania M
East Tennessee State University M
Emory & Henry College M
Emory University D*
Emporia State University M
Fairleigh Dickinson University, Metropolitan Campus M*
Fayetteville State University M
Fitchburg State College M
Florida Agricultural and Mechanical University M*
Florida Atlantic University M
Florida International University M,D*
Florida State University M,D*
Fordham University M,D*
Fort Hays State University M
George Mason University M,D*
Georgetown University M,D*
The George Washington University M,D*
Georgia College & State University M
Georgia Southern University M
Georgia State University M,D*
Graduate School and University Center of the City University of New York D*
Hardin-Simmons University M
Harvard University D*
High Point University M
Howard University M,D*
Hunter College of the City University of New York M
Idaho State University M
Illinois State University M*
Indiana State University M*
Indiana University Bloomington M,D*
Indiana University of Pennsylvania M
Indiana University–Purdue University Indianapolis M*
Iona College M*
Iowa State University of Science and Technology M,D*
Jackson State University M
Jacksonville State University M
James Madison University M
John Carroll University M
The Johns Hopkins University D*
Kansas State University M,D*
Kent State University M,D*
Lakehead University M
Lamar University M*
La Salle University M*
Laurentian University M
Lehigh University M,D*
Lehman College of the City University of New York M
Lincoln University (MO) M
Long Island University, Brooklyn Campus M,O*
Long Island University, C.W. Post Campus M*
Louisiana State University and Agricultural and Mechanical College M,D*
Louisiana Tech University M
Loyola University Chicago M,D*
Marquette University M,D
Marshall University M
McGill University M,D*
McMaster University M,D
Memorial University of Newfoundland M,D
Miami University M,D*
Michigan State University M,D*
Middle Tennessee State University M,D*
Midwestern State University M
Millersville University of Pennsylvania M
Minnesota State University Mankato M
Mississippi College M,O
Mississippi State University M,D
Missouri State University M*
Monmouth University M
Montana State University M,D
Montclair State University M*
Morgan State University M,D*
Murray State University M
Nebraska Wesleyan University M
New Jersey Institute of Technology M
New Mexico Highlands University M
New Mexico State University M
The New School: A University M,D*
New York University M,D,O*
North Carolina Central University M
North Carolina State University M*
North Dakota State University M,D
Northeastern Illinois University M
Northeastern University M,D*
Northern Arizona University M,D
Northern Illinois University M,D
Northwestern University D*
Northwest Missouri State University M
Oakland University M*
The Ohio State University M,D*
Ohio University M,D*
Oklahoma State University M,D*
Old Dominion University M*
Oregon State University M,D*
Penn State University Park M,D*
Pepperdine University M*
Pittsburg State University M
Pontifical Catholic University of Puerto Rico M
Portland State University M
Prescott College M
Princeton University D*
Providence College M*
Purdue University M,D*
Purdue University Calumet M
Queens College of the City University of New York M
Rhode Island College M
Rice University M,D*
Roosevelt University M
Rutgers, The State University of New Jersey, Camden M
Rutgers, The State University of New Jersey, Newark M*
Rutgers, The State University of New Jersey, New Brunswick D*
St. Cloud State University M
St. John's University (NY) M,D
Saint Louis University M,D*
Saint Mary's University M
Salem State College M
Salisbury University M
Sam Houston State University M
San Diego State University M*
San Francisco State University M
San Jose State University M
Sarah Lawrence College M*
Seton Hall University M*
Shippensburg University of Pennsylvania M,O
Simon Fraser University M,D
Slippery Rock University of Pennsylvania M
Smith College M*
Sonoma State University M
Southeastern Louisiana University M
Southeast Missouri State University M
Southern Connecticut State University M
Southern Illinois University Carbondale M,D*
Southern Illinois University Edwardsville M
Southern Methodist University M,D*
Southern University and Agricultural and Mechanical College M*
Stanford University M,D*
State University of New York at Binghamton M,D*
State University of New York at Oswego M
State University of New York College at Brockport M*
State University of New York College at Cortland M*
Stephen F. Austin State University M
Stony Brook University, State University of New York M,D*
Sul Ross State University M*
Syracuse University M,D*
Tarleton State University M
Teachers College Columbia University M,D*
Temple University M,D*
Texas A&M International University M

Texas A&M University M,D*
Texas A&M University–Commerce M
Texas A&M University–Corpus Christi M
Texas A&M University–Kingsville M
Texas A&M University–Texarkana M
Texas Christian University M,D
Texas Southern University M
Texas State University-San Marcos M*
Texas Tech University M,D
Texas Woman's University M
Trent University M
Trinity College M
Tufts University M,D*
Tulane University M,D*
Université de Moncton M
Université de Montréal M,D
Université de Sherbrooke M
Université du Québec à Montréal M,D
Université Laval M,D
University at Albany, State University of New York M,D,O*
University at Buffalo, the State University of New York M,D*
The University of Akron M,D
The University of Alabama M,D
The University of Alabama at Birmingham M*
The University of Alabama in Huntsville M
University of Alberta M,D*
The University of Arizona M,D*
University of Arkansas M,D*
The University of British Columbia M,D*
University of Calgary M,D
University of California, Berkeley M,D*
University of California, Davis M,D*
University of California, Irvine M,D*
University of California, Los Angeles M,D*
University of California, Riverside M,D*
University of California, San Diego M,D*
University of California, Santa Barbara D*
University of California, Santa Cruz M,D*
University of Central Arkansas M
University of Central Florida M*
University of Central Missouri M
University of Central Oklahoma M
University of Chicago D*
University of Cincinnati M,D
University of Colorado at Boulder M,D*
University of Colorado at Colorado Springs M
University of Colorado at Denver and Health Sciences Center M*
University of Connecticut M,D*
University of Delaware M,D*
University of Florida M,D*
University of Georgia M,D*
University of Guelph M,D
University of Hawaii at Manoa M,D*
University of Houston M,D*
University of Houston–Clear Lake M
University of Idaho M,D*
University of Illinois at Chicago M,D*
University of Illinois at Urbana–Champaign M,D*
University of Indianapolis M
The University of Iowa M,D*
University of Kansas M,D*
University of Kentucky M,D*
University of Lethbridge M,D
University of Louisiana at Lafayette M*
University of Louisiana at Monroe M
University of Louisville M
University of Maine M,D*
University of Manitoba M,D
University of Maryland, Baltimore County M*
University of Maryland, College Park M,D*
University of Massachusetts Amherst M,D*
University of Massachusetts Boston M
University of Memphis M,D*
University of Miami M,D*
University of Michigan D,O*
University of Minnesota, Twin Cities Campus M,D*
University of Mississippi M,D
University of Missouri–Columbia M,D*
University of Missouri–Kansas City M,D*
The University of Montana M,D*
University of Nebraska at Kearney M
University of Nebraska at Omaha M
University of Nebraska–Lincoln M,D*
University of Nevada, Las Vegas M,D
University of Nevada, Reno M,D*
University of New Brunswick Fredericton M,D
University of New Hampshire M,D*
University of New Mexico M,D*
University of New Orleans M
The University of North Carolina at Chapel Hill M,D*
The University of North Carolina at Charlotte M*
The University of North Carolina at Greensboro M,D,O
The University of North Carolina Wilmington M*
University of North Dakota M,D
University of Northern British Columbia M,D,O
University of Northern Colorado M
University of Northern Iowa M
University of North Florida M
University of North Texas M,D*
University of Notre Dame M,D*
University of Oklahoma M,D*
University of Oregon M,D*
University of Ottawa M,D*
University of Pennsylvania M,D*
University of Pittsburgh M,D*
University of Puerto Rico, Río Piedras M,D
University of Regina M,D
University of Rhode Island M
University of Richmond M
University of Rochester M,D*
University of San Diego M*
University of Saskatchewan M,D
The University of Scranton M
University of South Alabama M*
University of South Carolina M,D,O*
The University of South Dakota M
University of Southern California M,D*
University of Southern Mississippi M,D*
University of South Florida M*
The University of Tennessee M,D*
The University of Texas at Arlington M,D*
The University of Texas at Austin M,D*
The University of Texas at Brownsville M
The University of Texas at El Paso M,D
The University of Texas at San Antonio M*
The University of Texas at Tyler M
The University of Texas of the Permian Basin M
The University of Texas–Pan American M
The University of Toledo M,D*
University of Toronto M,D
University of Tulsa M*
University of Utah M,D*
University of Vermont M*
University of Victoria M,D
University of Virginia M,D*
University of Washington M,D*
University of Waterloo M,D*
The University of Western Ontario M,D
University of West Florida M
University of West Georgia M
University of Windsor M
The University of Winnipeg M
University of Wisconsin–Eau Claire M
University of Wisconsin–Madison M,D*
University of Wisconsin–Milwaukee M,D
University of Wisconsin–Stevens Point M
University of Wyoming M
Utah State University M
Valdosta State University M
Valparaiso University M,O
Vanderbilt University M,D*
Villanova University M*
Virginia Commonwealth University M,D*
Virginia Polytechnic Institute and State University M*
Virginia State University M
Washington College M
Washington State University M,D*
Washington State University Vancouver M,D
Washington University in St. Louis M,D*
Wayne State University M,D*
West Chester University of Pennsylvania M
Western Carolina University M*
Western Connecticut State University M*
Western Illinois University M
Western Kentucky University M
Western Michigan University M,D*
Western Washington University M
Westfield State College M
West Texas A&M University M
West Virginia University M,D*
Wichita State University M*
Wilfrid Laurier University M,D
William Paterson University of New Jersey M*
Winthrop University M*
Wright State University M*
Yale University M,D*
York University M,D*
Youngstown State University M

HISTORY OF MEDICINE

Duke University *
McGill University M,D*
Rutgers, The State University of New Jersey, New Brunswick D*
Uniformed Services University of the Health Sciences M*
University of Minnesota, Twin Cities Campus M,D*
Yale University M,D*

HISTORY OF SCIENCE AND TECHNOLOGY

Arizona State University M,D*
Brown University M,D*
Cornell University M,D*
Drexel University M*
Georgia Institute of Technology M,D*
Harvard University M,D*
Indiana University Bloomington M,D*
Iowa State University of Science and Technology M,D*
The Johns Hopkins University M,D*
Massachusetts Institute of Technology D*
Polytechnic University, Brooklyn Campus M*
Princeton University D*
Rensselaer Polytechnic Institute M,D*
Rutgers, The State University of New Jersey, New Brunswick D*
Uniformed Services University of the Health Sciences M,D*
University of California, Berkeley D*
University of California, San Diego M,D*
University of California, San Francisco M,D
University of Delaware M,D*
University of Massachusetts Amherst M,D*
University of Minnesota, Twin Cities Campus M,D*
University of Notre Dame M,D*
University of Oklahoma M,D*
University of Pennsylvania M,D*
University of Pittsburgh M,D*
University of Toronto M,D
University of Wisconsin–Madison M,D*
Virginia Polytechnic Institute and State University M,D*
West Virginia University M,D*
Yale University M,D*

HIV/AIDS NURSING

Duke University M,D,O*
University of Delaware M,O*

HOLOCAUST STUDIES

Clark University D*
Drew University M,D,O
Kean University M
Laura and Alvin Siegal College of Judaic Studies M
The Richard Stockton College of New Jersey M

HOME ECONOMICS EDUCATION

Appalachian State University M
Central Washington University M
Eastern Kentucky University M*
Harding University M,O
Indiana State University M*
Iowa State University of Science and Technology M,D*
Louisiana State University and Agricultural and Mechanical College M,D*
Montclair State University M,O*
Northwestern State University of Louisiana M
The Ohio State University M*
Purdue University M,D,O*
Queens College of the City University of New York M
South Carolina State University M
State University of New York College at Oneonta M
Texas Tech University M,D,O
The University of British Columbia M,D*
University of Central Oklahoma M
University of Indianapolis M,O
Utah State University M
Wayne State College M
Western Carolina University M*

HOMELAND SECURITY

American Public University System M
Arkansas Tech University M
The Johns Hopkins University M,O*
Long Island University, Southampton Graduate Campus M,O
National University M
Regent University M
Salve Regina University M,O
Tiffin University M
Towson University M,O
University of Connecticut M*
Upper Iowa University M
Virginia Commonwealth University M,O*

HORTICULTURE

Auburn University M,D*
Colorado State University M,D*
Cornell University M,D*
Iowa State University of Science and Technology M,D*
Kansas State University M,D*
Louisiana State University and Agricultural and Mechanical College M,D*
Michigan State University M,D*
New Mexico State University M,D
North Carolina State University M,D*
Nova Scotia Agricultural College M
The Ohio State University M,D*
Oklahoma State University M,D*
Oregon State University M,D*
Penn State University Park M,D*
Purdue University M,D*
Rutgers, The State University of New Jersey, New Brunswick M,D*
Southern Illinois University Carbondale M*
Texas A&M University M,D*
Texas Tech University M,D
Universidad Nacional Pedro Henriquez Urena P,M,D
University of Arkansas M*
University of California, Davis M*
University of Delaware M*
University of Florida M,D*
University of Georgia M,D*
University of Guelph M,D
University of Hawaii at Manoa M,D*
University of Maine M*
University of Manitoba M,D
University of Maryland, College Park D*
University of Missouri–Columbia M,D*
University of Nebraska–Lincoln M,D*
University of Puerto Rico, Mayagüez Campus M*
University of Vermont M,D*
University of Washington M,D*
University of Wisconsin–Madison M,D*
Virginia Polytechnic Institute and State University M,D*
Washington State University M,D*
West Virginia University M,D*

HOSPICE NURSING

Madonna University M

HOSPITALITY MANAGEMENT

Andrew Jackson University M
Central Michigan University M*
Cornell University M,D*
Eastern Michigan University M
East Stroudsburg University of Pennsylvania M
Endicott College M

*P—first professional degree; M—master's degree; D—doctorate; O—other advanced degree; *full description and/or announcement in Book 2, 3, 4, 5, or 6*

Institution	Degrees
Fairleigh Dickinson University, College at Florham	M*
Fairleigh Dickinson University, Metropolitan Campus	M*
Florida International University	M*
The George Washington University	M,O*
Iowa State University of Science and Technology	M,D*
Johnson & Wales University	M,O*
Kansas State University	M,D*
Lynn University	M,D
Michigan State University	M*
New York University	M,D,O*
The Ohio State University	M,D*
Oklahoma State University	M,D*
Penn State University Park	M,D*
Purdue University	M,D*
Rochester Institute of Technology	M
Roosevelt University	M
Schiller International University (United States)	M
Schiller International University (United Kingdom)	M
South Dakota State University	M
Southern New Hampshire University	M,D,O*
Temple University	M*
Texas Tech University	M,D
Texas Woman's University	M,D
The University of Alabama	M
University of Central Florida	M*
University of Delaware	M*
University of Guelph	M
University of Houston	M*
University of Kentucky	M*
University of Massachusetts Amherst	M*
University of Missouri–Columbia	M,D*
University of Nevada, Las Vegas	M,D
University of New Haven	M*
University of New Orleans	M
University of North Texas	M*
University of South Carolina	M*
The University of Tennessee	M*
Virginia Polytechnic Institute and State University	M,D*

HUMAN-COMPUTER INTERACTION

Institution	Degrees
Carnegie Mellon University	M,D*
Cornell University	D*
Dalhousie University	M
DePaul University	M,D*
Georgia Institute of Technology	M*
Indiana University Bloomington	M,D*
Iowa State University of Science and Technology	M,D*
Naval Postgraduate School	M,D
Rensselaer Polytechnic Institute	M*
State University of New York at Oswego	M
Tufts University	O*
University of Baltimore	M,D*
University of Illinois at Urbana–Champaign	M,D,O*
University of Michigan	M,D*

HUMAN DEVELOPMENT

Institution	Degrees
Argosy University, Chicago Campus	D*
Arizona State University	M,D*
Auburn University	M,D*
Boston University	M,D,O*
Bowling Green State University	M*
Bradley University	M
Brigham Young University	M,D*
Brock University	M,D
California State University, San Bernardino	M
The Catholic University of America	D*
Central Michigan University	M*
Claremont Graduate University	M,D,O
Clemson University	M*
Colorado State University	M*
Cornell University	D*
DePaul University	M,D*
Dowling College	M,D,O
Duke University	D*
East Tennessee State University	M
Erikson Institute	M,O*
Fielding Graduate University	M,D,O*
The George Washington University	M,D*
Harvard University	M,D*
Hood College	M,O
Howard University	M*
Indiana University Bloomington	M,D*
Iowa State University of Science and Technology	M,D*
Kansas State University	D*
Kent State University	M,D*
Laurentian University	M
Lehigh University	M,D*
Lindsey Wilson College	M
Marywood University	D*
Montana State University	M
National-Louis University	M,D,O
New York Institute of Technology	M
New York University	M,D,O*
North Dakota State University	D
Northwestern University	D*
The Ohio State University	M,D*
Oregon State University	M,D*
Our Lady of the Lake University of San Antonio	M
Pacific Oaks College	M
Penn State University Park	M,D*
Purdue University	M,D*
Saint Joseph College	O
St. Lawrence University	M,O
Saint Louis University	M,D,O*
Saint Mary's University of Minnesota	M
South Dakota State University	M
Southern Illinois University Carbondale	M,D*
Texas A&M University	M,D*
Texas Southern University	M
Texas Tech University	M,D
The University of Alabama	M
The University of Arizona	M,D*
University of Calgary	M,D
University of California, Berkeley	M,D*
University of California, Davis	D*
University of Central Arkansas	M
University of Central Oklahoma	M
University of Chicago	D*
University of Connecticut	M,D*
University of Dayton	M,O*
University of Delaware	M,D*
University of Guelph	M,D
University of Houston	M*
University of Illinois at Chicago	M,D*
University of Illinois at Springfield	M
University of Illinois at Urbana–Champaign	M,D*
University of Kansas	M,D*
University of Maine	M*
University of Maryland, College Park	M,D*
University of Missouri–Columbia	M,D*
University of Nevada, Reno	M*
The University of North Carolina at Greensboro	M,D
University of North Texas	M,D*
University of Pennsylvania	M,D*
University of Puerto Rico, Medical Sciences Campus	M,O*
University of St. Thomas (MN)	M,D,O*
The University of Texas at Austin	M,D*
University of Victoria	M,D
University of Washington	M,D*
University of Wisconsin–Madison	M,D*
University of Wisconsin–Stevens Point	M
University of Wisconsin–Stout	M*
Utah State University	M,D
Vanderbilt University	M*
Virginia Polytechnic Institute and State University	M,D*
Washington State University	M*
Wayne State University	M*
Wheelock College	M

HUMAN GENETICS

Institution	Degrees
Baylor College of Medicine	D*
Case Western Reserve University	D*
Drexel University	M,D*
The Johns Hopkins University	D*
Louisiana State University Health Sciences Center	M,D*
McGill University	M,D*
Memorial University of Newfoundland	M,D
Sarah Lawrence College	M*
Tulane University	M,D*
University of California, Los Angeles	M,D*
University of Chicago	D*
University of Manitoba	M,D
University of Maryland, Baltimore	M,D*
University of Michigan	M,D*
University of Pittsburgh	M,D,O*
The University of Texas Health Science Center at Houston	M,D*
University of Utah	M,D*
Virginia Commonwealth University	M,D,O*
Wake Forest University	D*
West Virginia University	M,D*

HUMANITIES

Institution	Degrees
American Public University System	M
Arcadia University	M
Arizona State University	M*
Brigham Young University	M*
California Institute of Integral Studies	M,D*
California State University, Dominguez Hills	M
Carlow University	M
Central European University	M,D*
Central Michigan University	M*
Claremont Graduate University	M,D,O
Clark Atlanta University	D
College of the Humanities and Sciences, Harrison Middleton University	M,D
Concordia University (Canada)	D
Dominican University of California	M
Drew University	M,D,O
Duke University	M*
Florida State University	M,D*
Hofstra University	M*
Hollins University	M,O
Hood College	M
Instituto Tecnológico y de Estudios Superiores de Monterrey, Campus Central de Veracruz	M
Instituto Tecnológico y de Estudios Superiores de Monterrey, Campus Ciudad de México	M,D
Instituto Tecnológico y de Estudios Superiores de Monterrey, Campus Estado de México	M,D
Instituto Tecnológico y de Estudios Superiores de Monterrey, Campus Irapuato	M,D
John Carroll University	M
Laura and Alvin Siegal College of Judaic Studies	M
Laurentian University	M
Marshall University	M
Marymount University	M
Massachusetts Institute of Technology	M*
Memorial University of Newfoundland	M
Michigan State University	M*
Mount St. Mary's College	M
National University	M
New College of California	M*
New York University	M,O*
Nova Southeastern University	M*
Old Dominion University	M*
Penn State Harrisburg	M*
Pepperdine University	M*
Polytechnic University, Brooklyn Campus	M,O*
Prescott College	M
Salve Regina University	M,D
Sam Houston State University	M,D
San Francisco State University	M
Stanford University	M*
Texas Tech University	M,D
Tiffin University	M
Towson University	M
Universidad Nacional Pedro Henriquez Urena	P,M,D
University of California, Santa Cruz	D*
University of Chicago	M*
University of Colorado at Denver and Health Sciences Center	M*
University of Dallas	M
University of Houston–Clear Lake	M
University of Louisville	M,D
The University of Texas at Arlington	M*
The University of Texas at Dallas	M,D*
The University of Texas Medical Branch	M,D*
University of West Florida	M
Wright State University	M*
York University	M,D*

HUMAN RESOURCES DEVELOPMENT

Institution	Degrees
Abilene Christian University	M
Amberton University	M
American International College	M
Antioch University Los Angeles	M
Azusa Pacific University	M
Barry University	M,D*
Bowie State University	M
California State University, Sacramento	M*
Clemson University	M*
The College of New Rochelle	M,O
Florida International University	M,D*
Florida State University	M,D,O*
Friends University	M
The George Washington University	M,D,O*
Illinois Institute of Technology	M,D*
Indiana State University	M*
Indiana Tech	M
Indiana University of Pennsylvania	M
Inter American University of Puerto Rico, Metropolitan Campus	M
Inter American University of Puerto Rico, San Germán Campus	M,D
Iowa State University of Science and Technology	M,D*
John F. Kennedy University	M,O
The Johns Hopkins University	M,O*
Johnson & Wales University	O*
Manhattanville College	M*
Marquette University	M
McDaniel College	M
Midwestern State University	M
Mississippi State University	M,D,O
National-Louis University	M
Naval Postgraduate School	M
New York University	M,O*
North Carolina Agricultural and Technical State University	M
Northeastern Illinois University	M
Oakland University	M*
Ottawa University	M
Palm Beach Atlantic University	M
Penn State University Park	M*
Pittsburg State University	M,O
Rochester Institute of Technology	M,O
Rollins College	M
Roosevelt University	M
St. John Fisher College	M
Salve Regina University	M,O
Siena Heights University	M
Southern New Hampshire University	M,O*
Suffolk University	M,O*
Syracuse University	D*
Texas A&M University	M,D*
Towson University	M,O
Universidad Central del Este	M
University of Bridgeport	M
University of Connecticut	M*
University of Illinois at Urbana–Champaign	M,D,O*
University of Louisville	M
University of Minnesota, Twin Cities Campus	M,D,O*
University of Missouri–St. Louis	M,O
University of Regina	M
The University of Scranton	M
The University of Tennessee	M*
The University of Texas at Austin	M*
The University of Texas at Tyler	M
University of Wisconsin–Milwaukee	M,O
University of Wisconsin–Stout	M*
Vanderbilt University	M,D*
Villanova University	M*
Virginia Commonwealth University	M*
Virginia Polytechnic Institute and State University	M,D*
Webster University	M,D
Western Carolina University	M*
Western Michigan University	M,D,O*
William Woods University	M,O
Xavier University	M*

HUMAN RESOURCES MANAGEMENT

Institution	Degrees
Adelphi University	M,O*
Alabama Agricultural and Mechanical University	M,O
Albany State University	M
Amberton University	M
American InterContinental University (FL)	M
American InterContinental University Online	M
Andrew Jackson University	M
Auburn University	M,D*
Baker College Center for Graduate Studies	M
Baldwin-Wallace College	M
Barry University	O*
Benedictine University	M
Bernard M. Baruch College of the City University of New York	M,D*
Boston University	M,O*
Briar Cliff University	M
Buffalo State College, State University of New York	M,O
California State University, East Bay	M
California State University, Sacramento	M*
Capella University	M,D,O
Cardean University	M
Caribbean University	M,D
Case Western Reserve University	M*
Central Michigan University	M,O*
Chapman University	M,O
City University	M,O
Claremont Graduate University	M
Clarkson University	M*
Cleveland State University	M

College of Santa Fe M
Colorado Technical University—Colorado Springs M,D
Colorado Technical University—Denver M
Colorado Technical University—Sioux Falls M
Columbia Southern University M
Columbia University M*
Concordia University, St. Paul M
Concordia University Wisconsin M
Cornell University M,D*
Cumberland University M
Dallas Baptist University M
Davenport University M
Davenport University M
DePaul University M*
DeVry University M*
East Central University M
Eastern Michigan University M
Emmanuel College M,O
Fairfield University M,O*
Fairleigh Dickinson University, College at Florham M*
Fairleigh Dickinson University, Metropolitan Campus M,O*
Fitchburg State College M
Florida Institute of Technology M*
Florida Metropolitan University–South Orlando Campus M
Florida Metropolitan University–Tampa Campus M
Fordham University M,D,O*
Framingham State College M*
Gannon University O
George Mason University M*
The George Washington University M,D,O*
Georgia State University M,D*
Golden Gate University M,D,O
Goldey-Beacom College M
Hawai'i Pacific University M*
HEC Montreal M
Hofstra University M,O*
Holy Family University M
Houston Baptist University M
Indiana Tech M
Instituto Tecnologico de Santo Domingo M
Instituto Tecnológico y de Estudios Superiores de Monterrey, Campus Cuernavaca M
Inter American University of Puerto Rico, Bayamón Campus M
Inter American University of Puerto Rico, Metropolitan Campus M
Inter American University of Puerto Rico, Ponce Campus M
Inter American University of Puerto Rico, San Germán Campus M,D
International College of the Cayman Islands M
International University in Geneva M
Iona College M,O*
La Roche College M,O
Lindenwood University M
Long Island University, Brooklyn Campus M*
Loyola University Chicago M*
Manhattanville College M*
Marquette University M*
Marshall University M
Marygrove College M
Marymount University M,O
McMaster University M,D
Mercy College M
Metropolitan State University M
Michigan State University M,D*
National-Louis University M
Nazareth College of Rochester M
New Mexico Highlands University M
The New School: A University M,O*
New York Institute of Technology M,O
New York University M,D,O*
North Carolina Agricultural and Technical State University M
Nova Southeastern University M*
Oakland University M,O*
The Ohio State University M,D*
Ottawa University M
Pontifical Catholic University of Puerto Rico M,D
Pontificia Universidad Catolica Madre y Maestra M
Purdue University M,D*
Regis University M,O
Rivier College M
Robert Morris University M
Rollins College M
Roosevelt University M
Royal Roads University M
Rutgers, The State University of New Jersey, Newark M,D*
Rutgers, The State University of New Jersey, New Brunswick M,D*
Sage Graduate School M
St. Ambrose University M,D
St. Edward's University M,O
Saint Francis University M
St. Joseph's College, Suffolk Campus M,O
Saint Joseph's University M*
Saint Leo University M
Saint Mary's University of Minnesota M
St. Thomas University M,O
Salve Regina University M,O
San Diego State University M*
Southern Adventist University M
Southern New Hampshire University M,D,O*
Stevens Institute of Technology M,O*
Stony Brook University, State University of New York M,O*
Suffolk University M,O*
Tarleton State University M
Temple University M,D*
Texas A&M University M,D*
Thomas College M
Thomas Edison State College M
Touro University International M,D
Trinity (Washington) University M
Troy University M
Universidad del Este M
Universidad Metropolitana M
University at Albany, State University of New York M*
University at Buffalo, the State University of New York M,D,O*
The University of Akron M
The University of Alabama in Huntsville M,O
University of Connecticut M*
University of Dallas M
University of Denver M,O*
The University of Findlay M
University of Florida M*
University of Hawaii at Manoa M*
University of Houston–Clear Lake M
University of Illinois at Urbana–Champaign M,D*
University of Lethbridge M,D
University of Minnesota, Twin Cities Campus M,D*
University of Missouri–St. Louis M,O
University of New Haven M*
University of New Mexico M*
University of Phoenix–Atlanta Campus M
University of Phoenix–Augusta Campus M
University of Phoenix–Austin Campus M
University of Phoenix–Bay Area Campus M
University of Phoenix–Central Valley Campus M
University of Phoenix–Chattanooga Campus M
University of Phoenix–Cheyenne Campus M
University of Phoenix–Cleveland Campus M
University of Phoenix–Columbus Georgia Campus M
University of Phoenix–Dallas Campus M
University of Phoenix–Denver Campus M
University of Phoenix–Des Moines Campus M
University of Phoenix–Detroit Campus M
University of Phoenix–Fort Lauderdale Campus M
University of Phoenix–Harrisburg Campus M
University of Phoenix–Hawaii Campus M
University of Phoenix–Houston Campus M
University of Phoenix–Jersey City Campus M
University of Phoenix–Louisiana Campus M
University of Phoenix–Madison Campus M
University of Phoenix–Maryland Campus M
University of Phoenix–Memphis Campus M
University of Phoenix–Minneapolis/St. Louis Park Campus M
University of Phoenix–Nashville Campus M
University of Phoenix–New Mexico Campus M
University of Phoenix—Northern Nevada Campus M
University of Phoenix–Northern Virginia Campus M
University of Phoenix–North Florida Campus M
University of Phoenix–Northwest Arkansas Campus M
University of Phoenix–Northwest Indiana M
University of Phoenix–Oklahoma City Campus M
University of Phoenix–Omaha Campus M
University of Phoenix Online Campus M
University of Phoenix–Oregon Campus M
University of Phoenix–Pittsburgh Campus M
University of Phoenix–Puerto Rico Campus M
University of Phoenix–Renton Learning Center M
University of Phoenix–Richmond Campus M
University of Phoenix–Sacramento Valley Campus M
University of Phoenix–San Antonio Campus M
University of Phoenix–Savannah Campus M
University of Phoenix–Southern California Campus M
University of Phoenix–Springfield Campus M
University of Phoenix–West Florida Campus M
University of Phoenix–West Michigan Campus M
University of Puerto Rico, Mayagüez Campus M*
University of Regina M,O
University of Rhode Island M
The University of Scranton M
University of South Carolina M*
The University of Texas at Arlington M*
University of the Sacred Heart M
The University of Toledo M*
University of Wisconsin–Madison M,D*
University of Wisconsin–Whitewater M*
Upper Iowa University M
Utah State University M
Walden University M,D
Wayland Baptist University M
Webster University M,D
Widener University M*
Wilkes University M
Wilmington College (DE) M
York University M,D*

HUMAN SERVICES

Abilene Christian University M,O
Andrews University M
Anna Maria College M
Bellevue University M*
Boricua College M
Brandeis University M*
California State University, Sacramento M*
Canisius College M
Capella University M,D,O
Chestnut Hill College M,O
Concordia University (IL) M
Concordia University Wisconsin M,D
Coppin State University M
DePaul University M,D*
Drury University M
Eastern New Mexico University M
Fairmont State University M
Ferris State University M
Georgia State University M*
Indiana University Northwest M,O
Kansas State University M*
Kent State University M,D,O*
Lehigh University M,D,O*
Lincoln University (PA) M
Louisiana State University in Shreveport M
McDaniel College M
Minnesota State University Mankato M
Minnesota State University Moorhead M,O
Montana State University–Billings M
Murray State University M
National-Louis University M,O
National University M
New England College M
Nova Southeastern University D*
Pontifical Catholic University of Puerto Rico M,D
Roberts Wesleyan College M
Rosemont College M
Sage Graduate School M
St. Edward's University M,O
St. John Fisher College M
Saint Joseph's University M,O*
St. Mary's University of San Antonio M,D,O
Sojourner-Douglass College M
South Carolina State University M
Southern Oregon University M
Springfield College M*
State University of New York at Oswego M
Texas Southern University M
Thomas University M
Universidad del Turabo M
Université de Montréal D
University of Baltimore M*
University of Bridgeport M
University of Central Missouri M,O
University of Colorado at Colorado Springs M,D
University of Great Falls M
University of Illinois at Springfield M
University of Maryland, Baltimore County M,D*
University of Massachusetts Boston M
University of Oklahoma M*
University of Phoenix–Maryland Campus M
University of Phoenix–Richmond Campus M
Upper Iowa University M
Walden University M,D
Wayne State University O*
West Virginia University M*
Wichita State University M*
Wilmington College (DE) M
Youngstown State University M

HYDRAULICS

Auburn University M,D*
École Polytechnique de Montréal M,D,O
Massachusetts Institute of Technology M,D,O*
McGill University M,D*
University of Missouri–Rolla M,D*

HYDROGEOLOGY

California State University, Chico M
Clemson University M*
Colorado School of Mines M,D,O
Georgia State University M,O*
Indiana University Bloomington M,D*
Montana Tech of The University of Montana M
Ohio University M*
University of Hawaii at Manoa M,D*
University of Illinois at Chicago M,D*
University of Nevada, Reno M,D*
West Virginia University M,D*

HYDROLOGY

Auburn University M,D*
California State University, Bakersfield M
California State University, Chico M
Colorado State University M,D*
Cornell University M,D*
Georgia Institute of Technology M,D*
Idaho State University M,O
Illinois State University M*
Massachusetts Institute of Technology M,D,O*
Murray State University M
New Mexico Institute of Mining and Technology M,D
State University of New York College of Environmental Science and Forestry M,D
Université du Québec, Institut National de la Recherche Scientifique M,D
The University of Arizona M,D*
University of California, Davis M,D*
University of California, Los Angeles M,D*
University of Idaho M*
University of Missouri–Rolla M,D*
University of Nevada, Reno M,D*
University of New Brunswick Fredericton M,D
University of New Hampshire M*
University of Southern Mississippi M,D*
University of Washington M,D*
West Virginia University M,D*

ILLUSTRATION

Academy of Art University M*
Bob Jones University P,M,D,O
Bradley University M

P—first professional degree; M—master's degree; D—doctorate; O—other advanced degree;
**full description and/or announcement in Book 2, 3, 4, 5, or 6*

Fashion Institute of Technology M*
Kent State University M*
Marywood University M*
Minneapolis College of Art and Design M
Savannah College of Art and Design M*
School of Visual Arts M
University of Utah M*
Western Connecticut State University M*

IMMUNOLOGY

Albany Medical College M,D
Albert Einstein College of Medicine D*
Baylor College of Medicine D*
Boston University D*
Brown University M,D*
California Institute of Technology D*
Case Western Reserve University M,D*
Colorado State University M,D*
Cornell University P,M,D*
Cornell University, Joan and Sanford I. Weill Medical College and Graduate School of Medical Sciences M,D*
Creighton University M,D*
Dalhousie University M,D
Dartmouth College D*
Drexel University M,D*
Duke University D*
East Carolina University D*
Emory University D*
Florida State University M,D*
Georgetown University M,D*
The George Washington University D*
Harvard University D*
Illinois State University M,D*
Indiana University–Purdue University Indianapolis M,D*
Iowa State University of Science and Technology M,D*
The Johns Hopkins University M,D*
Long Island University, C.W. Post Campus M*
Louisiana State University Health Sciences Center M,D*
Louisiana State University Health Sciences Center at Shreveport M,D*
Loyola University Chicago M,D*
Massachusetts Institute of Technology D*
Mayo Graduate School D*
McGill University M,D*
McMaster University M,D
Medical University of South Carolina M,D*
New York Medical College M,D*
New York University M,D*
North Carolina State University M,D*
Northwestern University D*
The Ohio State University M,D*
Oregon Health & Science University D*
Penn State Hershey Medical Center M,D*
Purdue University M,D*
Queen's University at Kingston M,D
Rosalind Franklin University of Medicine and Science M,D*
Rush University M,D
Rutgers, The State University of New Jersey, New Brunswick M,D*
Saint Louis University D*
Stanford University D*
State University of New York Upstate Medical University M,D*
Stony Brook University, State University of New York M,D*
Temple University M,D*
Texas A&M Health Science Center D*
Thomas Jefferson University D*
Tufts University D*
Tulane University M,D*
Uniformed Services University of the Health Sciences D*
Universidad Central del Caribe M
Université de Montréal M,D
Université de Sherbrooke M,D
Université du Québec, Institut National de la Recherche Scientifique M,D
Université Laval M,D
University at Albany, State University of New York M,D*
University at Buffalo, the State University of New York M,D*
University of Alberta M,D*
The University of Arizona M,D*
University of Arkansas for Medical Sciences M,D*
The University of British Columbia M,D*
University of Calgary M,D
University of California, Berkeley D*
University of California, Davis M,D*
University of California, Los Angeles M,D*
University of California, San Diego D*
University of California, San Francisco D
University of Chicago D*
University of Cincinnati M,D
University of Colorado at Denver and Health Sciences Center D*
University of Connecticut Health Center D*
University of Florida D*
University of Guelph M,D,O
University of Illinois at Chicago D*
The University of Iowa M,D*
University of Kansas D*
University of Louisville M,D
University of Manitoba M,D
University of Maryland, Baltimore D*
University of Massachusetts Worcester D*
University of Medicine and Dentistry of New Jersey M,D*
University of Miami D*
University of Michigan D*
University of Minnesota, Duluth M,D*
University of Missouri–Columbia M,D*
The University of North Carolina at Chapel Hill M,D*
University of North Dakota M,D
University of North Texas Health Science Center at Fort Worth M,D
University of Oklahoma Health Sciences Center M,D
University of Ottawa M,D*
University of Pennsylvania D*
University of Pittsburgh M,D*
University of Prince Edward Island M,D
University of Rochester M,D*
University of Saskatchewan M,D
University of South Alabama D*
The University of South Dakota M,D
University of Southern California M,D*
University of Southern Maine M
University of South Florida M,D*
The University of Texas at Austin D*
The University of Texas Health Science Center at Houston M,D*
The University of Texas Health Science Center at San Antonio D*
The University of Texas Medical Branch M,D*
The University of Texas Southwestern Medical Center at Dallas D*
The University of Toledo M,D*
University of Toronto M,D
University of Utah *
University of Virginia D*
University of Washington D*
The University of Western Ontario M,D
Vanderbilt University M,D*
Virginia Commonwealth University M,D*
Wake Forest University D*
Washington University in St. Louis D*
Wayne State University M,D*
West Virginia University M,D*
Wright State University M*
Yale University D*

INDUSTRIAL/MANAGEMENT ENGINEERING

Arizona State University M,D*
Auburn University M,D*
Bradley University M
Buffalo State College, State University of New York M
California Polytechnic State University, San Luis Obispo M
California State University, Fresno M
California State University, Northridge M
Central Washington University M
Clemson University M,D*
Cleveland State University M,D
Colorado State University-Pueblo M
Columbia University M,D,O*
Concordia University (Canada) M,D,O
Cornell University M,D*
Dalhousie University M,D
East Carolina University M,D,O*
Eastern Kentucky University M*
École Polytechnique de Montréal M,O
Florida Agricultural and Mechanical University M,D*
Florida International University M,D*
Florida State University M,D*
Georgia Institute of Technology M,D*
Illinois State University M*
Indiana State University M*
Instituto Tecnologico de Santo Domingo M
Instituto Tecnológico y de Estudios Superiores de Monterrey, Campus Chihuahua M,O
Instituto Tecnológico y de Estudios Superiores de Monterrey, Campus Ciudad de México M,D
Instituto Tecnológico y de Estudios Superiores de Monterrey, Campus Ciudad Juárez M
Instituto Tecnológico y de Estudios Superiores de Monterrey, Campus Laguna M
Instituto Tecnológico y de Estudios Superiores de Monterrey, Campus Monterrey M,D
Iowa State University of Science and Technology M,D*
Kansas State University M,D*
Lamar University M,D*
Lehigh University M,D*
Louisiana State University and Agricultural and Mechanical College M,D*
Louisiana Tech University M,D
Mississippi State University M,D
Montana State University M,D
Montana Tech of The University of Montana M
Morehead State University M
Morgan State University M,D*
New Jersey Institute of Technology M,D
New Mexico State University M,D
North Carolina Agricultural and Technical State University M,D
North Carolina State University M,D*
North Dakota State University M,D
Northeastern University M,D*
Northern Illinois University M
Northwestern University M,D*
The Ohio State University M,D*
Ohio University M,D*
Oklahoma State University M,D*
Oregon State University M,D*
Penn State University Park M,D*
Polytechnic University, Brooklyn Campus M*
Polytechnic University, Long Island Graduate Center M,D
Purdue University M,D*
Rensselaer Polytechnic Institute M,D*
Rochester Institute of Technology M
Rutgers, The State University of New Jersey, New Brunswick M,D*
St. Mary's University of San Antonio M
Sam Houston State University M
San Jose State University M
South Dakota State University M
Southern Polytechnic State University M
Stanford University M,D*
State University of New York at Binghamton M,D*
Texas A&M University M,D*
Texas A&M University–Commerce M
Texas A&M University–Kingsville M
Texas Southern University M
Texas State University-San Marcos M*
Texas Tech University M,D
Universidad Central del Este M
Universidad de las Américas–Puebla M
Université de Moncton M
Université du Québec à Trois-Rivières M,O
Université Laval O
University at Buffalo, the State University of New York M,D*
The University of Alabama M
The University of Alabama in Huntsville M,D
The University of Arizona M,D*
University of Arkansas M,D*
University of California, Berkeley M,D*
University of Central Florida M,D,O*
University of Central Missouri M
University of Cincinnati M,D
University of Dayton M*
University of Florida M,D,O*
University of Houston M,D*
University of Illinois at Chicago M,D*
University of Illinois at Urbana–Champaign M,D*
The University of Iowa M,D*
University of Louisville M,D
University of Manitoba M,D
University of Massachusetts Amherst M,D*
University of Massachusetts Lowell M,D,O*
University of Memphis M,D*
University of Miami M,D*
University of Michigan M,D*
University of Michigan–Dearborn M*
University of Minnesota, Twin Cities Campus M,D*
University of Missouri–Columbia M,D*
University of Nebraska–Lincoln M,D*
University of New Haven M,O*
University of Oklahoma M,D*
University of Pittsburgh M,D*
University of Puerto Rico, Mayagüez Campus M*
University of Regina M,D
University of Rhode Island D
University of Southern California M,D,O*
University of South Florida M,D*
The University of Tennessee M,D*
The University of Texas at Arlington M*
The University of Texas at Austin M,D*
The University of Texas at El Paso M
The University of Toledo M,D*
University of Toronto M,D
University of Washington M,D*
University of Windsor M,D
University of Wisconsin–Madison M,D*
University of Wisconsin–Stout M*
Virginia Polytechnic Institute and State University M,D*
Wayne State University M,D*
Western Carolina University M*
Western Michigan University M*
Western New England College M
West Virginia University M,D*
Wichita State University M,D*
Youngstown State University M

INDUSTRIAL AND LABOR RELATIONS

Bernard M. Baruch College of the City University of New York M*
Case Western Reserve University M*
Cleveland State University M
Cornell University M,D*
Georgia State University M,D*
Indiana University of Pennsylvania M
Inter American University of Puerto Rico, Metropolitan Campus M
Inter American University of Puerto Rico, San Germán Campus M,D
Loyola University Chicago M*
McMaster University M
Memorial University of Newfoundland M
Michigan State University M,D*
New York Institute of Technology M,O
The Ohio State University M,D*
Penn State University Park M*
Pontificia Universidad Catolica Madre y Maestra M
Queen's University at Kingston M
Rutgers, The State University of New Jersey, New Brunswick M,D*
State University of New York Empire State College M
Stony Brook University, State University of New York M,O*
Université de Montréal M,D
Université du Québec à Trois-Rivières O
Université du Québec en Outaouais M,D,O
Université Laval M,D
University of Alberta D*
University of California, Berkeley D*
University of Cincinnati M
University of Illinois at Urbana–Champaign M,D*
University of Louisville M
University of Massachusetts Amherst M*
University of Minnesota, Twin Cities Campus M,D*
University of New Haven M*
University of North Texas M,D*
University of Rhode Island M

University of Saskatchewan M
University of Toronto M,D
University of Wisconsin–Madison M,D*
University of Wisconsin–Milwaukee M,O
Wayne State University M*
West Virginia University M*

INDUSTRIAL AND MANUFACTURING MANAGEMENT

American InterContinental University Online M
Boston University D*
Bryant University M,O
California Polytechnic State University, San Luis Obispo M
California State University, East Bay M
Carnegie Mellon University M,D*
Case Western Reserve University M,D*
Central Michigan University M*
Clarkson University M*
Clemson University M,D*
Cleveland State University D
DePaul University M*
Eastern Michigan University M
Florida Institute of Technology M*
Friends University M
The George Washington University M*
HEC Montreal M
Illinois Institute of Technology M*
Indiana University Southeast M,O
Instituto Tecnológico y de Estudios Superiores de Monterrey, Campus Estado de México M,D
Instituto Tecnológico y de Estudios Superiores de Monterrey, Campus Irapuato M,D
Inter American University of Puerto Rico, Metropolitan Campus M
Kettering University M
Lawrence Technological University M,D
Marist College M,O*
McGill University M,D,O*
Northeastern State University M
Northern Illinois University M
Oakland University M,O*
Oklahoma State University M,D*
Penn State University Park M,D*
Polytechnic University of Puerto Rico M
Portland State University M,D
Purdue University M,D*
Regis University M,O
Rensselaer Polytechnic Institute M,D*
Rochester Institute of Technology M
San Diego State University M*
San Jose State University M
Southeastern Oklahoma State University M
Southeast Missouri State University M
Stevens Institute of Technology M*
Stony Brook University, State University of New York M,O*
Syracuse University D*
Texas A&M University M,D*
Texas Tech University M,D
Universidad de las Américas–Puebla M
University of Arkansas M*
University of Central Missouri M
University of Cincinnati M,D
The University of Iowa M*
University of Massachusetts Lowell M*
University of Minnesota, Twin Cities Campus M,D*
University of Missouri–St. Louis M,O
University of North Dakota M
University of North Texas M,D*
University of Puerto Rico, Mayagüez Campus M*
University of Rhode Island M,D
University of St. Thomas (MN) M,O*
University of Southern Indiana M
The University of Tennessee M,D*
The University of Texas at Tyler M
The University of Toledo M,D*
University of Wisconsin–Madison D*
Washington State University M,D*

INDUSTRIAL AND ORGANIZATIONAL PSYCHOLOGY

Adler Graduate School M,O
Adler School of Professional Psychology M,D,O*
Alliant International University–Los Angeles M,D*
Alliant International University–Sacramento D*
Alliant International University–San Diego M,D*
Alliant International University–San Francisco M,D*
American InterContinental University Online M
Angelo State University M
Antioch University Seattle M*
Appalachian State University M
Auburn University M,D*
Avila University M*
Bernard M. Baruch College of the City University of New York M,D,O*
Bowling Green State University M,D*
Brooklyn College of the City University of New York M,D
California State University, San Bernardino M
Capella University M,D,O
Carlos Albizu University M,D
Carlos Albizu University, Miami Campus M,D
Central Michigan University M,D*
The Chicago School of Professional Psychology M,D*
Claremont Graduate University M,D,O
Clemson University D*
Cleveland State University M,O
DePaul University M,D*
Eastern Kentucky University M,O*
Elmhurst College M
Emporia State University M
Fairleigh Dickinson University, College at Florham M*
Florida Institute of Technology M,D*
George Mason University M,D*
The George Washington University D*
Goddard College M
Graduate School and University Center of the City University of New York D*
Hofstra University M,D*
Illinois Institute of Technology M,D*
Illinois State University M,D,O*
Indiana University–Purdue University Indianapolis M,D*
Iona College M*
John F. Kennedy University M,O
Kean University M
Lamar University M*
Louisiana State University and Agricultural and Mechanical College M,D*
Louisiana Tech University M,D
Marshall University M,D
Middle Tennessee State University M,O*
Minnesota State University Mankato M
Montclair State University M,O*
National-Louis University M,O
National University M
New York University M,D,O*
North Carolina State University D*
Northern Kentucky University M
Ohio University D*
Old Dominion University D*
Penn State University Park M,D*
Philadelphia College of Osteopathic Medicine M,D*
Pontifical Catholic University of Puerto Rico M,D
Radford University M,D,O
Rice University M,D*
Roosevelt University M
Rutgers, The State University of New Jersey, New Brunswick M,D*
St. Cloud State University M
Saint Louis University M,D*
Saint Mary's University of San Antonio M
San Diego State University M,D*
San Jose State University M
Seattle Pacific University M,D
Southern Illinois University Edwardsville M
Springfield College M,O*
Teachers College Columbia University M,D*
Temple University M*
Texas A&M University M,D*
University at Albany, State University of New York M,D,O*
The University of Akron M,D
University of Baltimore M*
University of Central Florida M,D*
University of Connecticut M,D*
University of Detroit Mercy M
University of Guelph M,D
University of Houston M,D*
University of Maryland, College Park M,D*
University of Michigan D*
University of Minnesota, Twin Cities Campus D*
University of Missouri–St. Louis M,D,O
University of Nebraska at Omaha M,D,O
University of New Haven M,O*
The University of North Carolina at Charlotte M,D*
University of North Texas M,D*
University of South Florida M,D*
The University of Tennessee D*
The University of Tennessee at Chattanooga M
University of Tulsa M,D*
University of Wisconsin–Oshkosh M
Valdosta State University M,O
Virginia Polytechnic Institute and State University M,D*
Wayne State University M,D*
West Chester University of Pennsylvania M
Western Michigan University M,D,O*
Wright State University M,D*

INDUSTRIAL DESIGN

Academy of Art University M*
Art Center College of Design M*
Auburn University M*
Brigham Young University M*
North Carolina State University M*
The Ohio State University M*
Pratt Institute M*
Rhode Island School of Design M
Rochester Institute of Technology M
San Francisco State University M
Savannah College of Art and Design M*
University of Calgary M,D
University of Cincinnati M
University of Illinois at Chicago M*
University of Illinois at Urbana–Champaign M*
University of Notre Dame M*
The University of the Arts M*

INDUSTRIAL HYGIENE

California State University, Northridge M
Montana Tech of The University of Montana M
Murray State University M
New Jersey Institute of Technology M
The University of Alabama at Birmingham D*
University of Central Missouri M,O
University of Cincinnati M,D
University of Massachusetts Lowell M,D,O*
University of Michigan M,D*
University of Minnesota, Twin Cities Campus M,D*
University of New Haven M*
The University of North Carolina at Chapel Hill M,D*
University of Puerto Rico, Medical Sciences Campus M*
University of South Carolina M,D*
University of Washington M,D*
University of Wisconsin–Stout M*
West Virginia University M*

INFECTIOUS DISEASES

Cornell University M,D*
Georgetown University M,D*
The George Washington University M*
Harvard University D*
The Johns Hopkins University M,D*
Loyola University Chicago M*
Purdue University M,D*
Tulane University M,D,O*
Uniformed Services University of the Health Sciences D*
Université de Montréal O
Université Laval O
University of Calgary M,D
University of California, Berkeley M,D*
University of Georgia M,D*
University of Guelph M,D,O
University of Minnesota, Twin Cities Campus M,D*
The University of Montana D*
University of Pittsburgh M,D*
The University of Texas Medical Branch D*
Yale University D*

INFORMATION SCIENCE

Alcorn State University M
American College of Computer & Information Sciences M
American InterContinental University (FL) M
American InterContinental University Dunwoody Campus M
American InterContinental University Online M
Arizona State University at the Polytechnic Campus M
Arkansas Tech University M
Aspen University M
Athabasca University M
Ball State University M*
Barry University M*
Bellevue University M*
Bentley College M*
Bradley University M
Brigham Young University M*
Brooklyn College of the City University of New York M,D
Bryant University M
California State University, Fullerton M
Capitol College M
Carleton University M,D
Carnegie Mellon University M,D*
Case Western Reserve University M,D*
The Citadel, The Military College of South Carolina M
Claremont Graduate University M,D,O
Clark Atlanta University M
Clarkson University M*
Clark University M*
Coleman College M
The College of Saint Rose M*
Colorado Technical University—Colorado Springs M,D
Cornell University D*
Dakota State University M,D*
DePaul University M,D*
DeSales University M
Drexel University D*
East Carolina University M*
East Tennessee State University M
Everglades University M
Florida Gulf Coast University M
Florida International University M,D*
Gannon University M
George Mason University M,D,O*
Georgia Southwestern State University M
Georgia State University M*
Grand Valley State University M
Harrisburg University of Science and Technology O
Harvard University M,D,O*
Hood College M
Indiana University Bloomington M,D,O*
Indiana University–Purdue University Indianapolis M,D*
Instituto Tecnológico y de Estudios Superiores de Monterrey, Campus Cuernavaca M,D
Instituto Tecnológico y de Estudios Superiores de Monterrey, Campus Estado de México M,D
Instituto Tecnológico y de Estudios Superiores de Monterrey, Campus Irapuato M,D
Instituto Tecnológico y de Estudios Superiores de Monterrey, Campus Monterrey M,D
Instituto Tecnológico y de Estudios Superiores de Monterrey, Campus Sonora Norte M
Iowa State University of Science and Technology M*
Kansas State University M,D*
Kennesaw State University M
Kent State University M*
Kettering University M
Knowledge Systems Institute M
Lamar University M*
Lehigh University M*
Long Island University, C.W. Post Campus M*
Loyola University Chicago M*
Marlboro College M
Marshall University M
Marywood University M*
Massachusetts Institute of Technology M,D,O*
Montclair State University M,O*
National University M
Naval Postgraduate School M,O
New Jersey Institute of Technology M,D
Northeastern University M,D*
Northern Kentucky University M
Northwestern University M*
Nova Southeastern University M,D*
The Ohio State University M,D*
Pace University M,D,O*
Penn State Great Valley M

*P—first professional degree; M—master's degree; D—doctorate; O—other advanced degree; *full description and/or announcement in Book 2, 3, 4, 5, or 6*

Polytechnic University, Westchester Graduate Center M
Regis University M,O
Rensselaer at Hartford M
Rensselaer Polytechnic Institute M*
Robert Morris University M,D
Rochester Institute of Technology M
Sacred Heart University M,O
St. Mary's University of San Antonio M
Saint Xavier University M
Sam Houston State University M
Shippensburg University of Pennsylvania M
Simon Fraser University M,D
Southern Methodist University M,D*
Southern Polytechnic State University M
State University of New York Institute of Technology M
Stevens Institute of Technology M,O*
Strayer University M
Syracuse University D*
Temple University M,D*
Towson University O
Trevecca Nazarene University M
Université de Sherbrooke M,D
University at Albany, State University of New York M,D,O*
The University of Alabama at Birmingham M,D*
University of Baltimore M,D*
University of California, Irvine M,D*
University of Colorado at Colorado Springs M
University of Colorado at Denver and Health Sciences Center D*
University of Delaware M,D*
University of Detroit Mercy M
University of Florida M,D*
University of Great Falls M
University of Hawaii at Manoa M,D,O*
University of Houston M,D*
University of Houston–Clear Lake M
University of Illinois at Urbana–Champaign M,D,O*
The University of Iowa M,D,O*
University of Management and Technology M,O
University of Maryland, Baltimore County M,D*
University of Maryland University College M,O
University of Michigan M,D*
University of Michigan–Dearborn M*
University of Michigan–Flint M*
University of Minnesota, Twin Cities Campus M,D*
University of Missouri–Rolla M*
University of Nebraska at Omaha M,D
University of Nevada, Las Vegas M,D
University of New Haven M*
The University of North Carolina at Charlotte M,D*
University of North Florida M
University of Oregon M,D*
University of Ottawa M,O*
University of Pennsylvania M,D*
University of Phoenix–Cincinnati Campus M
University of Phoenix–Phoenix Campus M
University of Pittsburgh M,D,O*
University of Puerto Rico, Mayagüez Campus D*
University of South Alabama M*
The University of Tennessee M,D*
The University of Texas at El Paso M
The University of Texas at San Antonio M,D*
The University of Texas at Tyler M
University of Washington M,D*
University of Waterloo M,D*
University of Wisconsin–Parkside M
University of Wisconsin–Stout M*
Villa Julie College M
Virginia Polytechnic Institute and State University M*

INFORMATION STUDIES

The Catholic University of America M*
Central Connecticut State University M
Claremont Graduate University M,D,O
College of St. Catherine M*
Cornell University D*
Dalhousie University M
Dominican University M,O
Drexel University M,D,O*
Emporia State University M,D,O
Florida State University M,D,O*
Indiana University Bloomington M,D,O*
Long Island University, C.W. Post Campus M,D,O*
Long Island University, Westchester Graduate Campus M
Louisiana State University and Agricultural and Mechanical College M,O*
Mansfield University of Pennsylvania M
McGill University M,D,O*
Metropolitan State University M
North Carolina Central University M
Pratt Institute M,O*
Queens College of the City University of New York M,O
Rutgers, The State University of New Jersey, New Brunswick M,D*
St. John's University (NY) M,O
San Jose State University M
Simmons College M,D,O
Southern Connecticut State University M,O
Syracuse University M*
Université de Montréal M,D,O
University at Buffalo, the State University of New York M,O*
The University of Alabama M,D
University of Alberta M*
The University of Arizona M,D*
The University of British Columbia M*
University of California, Berkeley M,D*
University of California, Los Angeles M,D,O*
University of Central Missouri M,O
University of Denver M,O*
University of Hawaii at Manoa M,D,O*
University of Illinois at Urbana–Champaign M,D,O*
The University of Iowa M*
University of Maryland, College Park M,D*
University of Michigan M,D*
University of Missouri–Columbia M,D,O*
The University of North Carolina at Chapel Hill M,D,O*
The University of North Carolina at Greensboro M
University of North Texas M,D*
University of Oklahoma M,O*
University of Pittsburgh M,D,O*
University of Puerto Rico, Río Piedras M,O*
University of Rhode Island M
University of South Carolina M,O*
University of South Florida M*
The University of Texas at Austin M,D*
University of Toronto M,D,O
The University of Western Ontario M,D
University of Wisconsin–Madison M,D,O*
University of Wisconsin–Milwaukee M,O
Valdosta State University M
Wayne State University M,O*

INORGANIC CHEMISTRY

Auburn University M,D*
Boston College M,D*
Brandeis University M,D*
Brigham Young University M,D*
California State University, Fullerton M
California State University, Los Angeles M
Case Western Reserve University M,D*
Clark Atlanta University M,D
Clarkson University M,D*
Cleveland State University M,D
Columbia University M,D*
Cornell University D*
Florida State University M,D*
Georgetown University M,D*
The George Washington University M,D*
Harvard University D*
Howard University M,D*
Indiana University Bloomington M,D*
Kansas State University M,D*
Kent State University M,D*
Marquette University M,D
Massachusetts Institute of Technology D*
McMaster University M,D
Miami University M,D*
Northeastern University M,D*
Oregon State University M,D*
Purdue University M,D*
Rensselaer Polytechnic Institute M,D*
Rice University M,D*
Rutgers, The State University of New Jersey, Newark M,D*
Rutgers, The State University of New Jersey, New Brunswick M,D*
Seton Hall University M,D*
Southern University and Agricultural and Mechanical College M*
State University of New York at Binghamton M,D*
Tufts University M,D*
University of Calgary M,D
University of Cincinnati M,D
University of Georgia M,D*
University of Louisville M,D
University of Maryland, College Park M,D*
University of Miami M,D*
University of Michigan D*
University of Missouri–Columbia M,D*
University of Missouri–Kansas City M,D*
University of Missouri–St. Louis M,D
The University of Montana M,D*
University of Nebraska–Lincoln M,D*
University of Notre Dame M,D*
University of Regina M,D
University of Southern Mississippi M,D*
University of South Florida M,D*
The University of Tennessee M,D*
The University of Texas at Austin M,D*
The University of Toledo M,D*
Vanderbilt University M,D*
Virginia Commonwealth University M,D*
Wake Forest University M,D*
Wesleyan University M,D*
West Virginia University M,D*
Yale University D*

INSURANCE

Florida State University M,D*
Georgia State University M,D*
St. John's University (NY) M
Temple University M,D*
University of Florida M,D,O*
University of North Texas M,D*
University of Pennsylvania M,D*
University of Wisconsin–Madison M,D*
Virginia Commonwealth University M*
Washington State University D*

INTERDISCIPLINARY STUDIES

Alaska Pacific University M
Amberton University M
American University M*
Angelo State University M
Antioch University New England M*
Arizona State University at the West campus M
Athabasca University M
Baylor University M,D*
Boise State University M
Boston University M,D*
Bowling Green State University M,D*
Buffalo State College, State University of New York M
California State University, Bakersfield M
California State University, Chico M
California State University, East Bay M,O
California State University, Long Beach M
California State University, Northridge M
California State University, Sacramento M*
California State University, San Bernardino M
California State University, Stanislaus M
Campbell University M
Central Washington University M
Clemson University D,O*
Columbia University M*
Dalhousie University D
Dallas Baptist University M
DePaul University M*
Drew University M,D,O
Eastern Michigan University M
Eastern Washington University M
Emory University D*
Fitchburg State College O
Fresno Pacific University M
Frostburg State University M
George Mason University M*
Goddard College M
Graduate School and University Center of the City University of New York M,D*
Hodges University M
Hofstra University M*
Hollins University M,O
Idaho State University M
Iowa State University of Science and Technology M*
John F. Kennedy University M
Lesley University M*
Long Island University, C.W. Post Campus M*
Manchester College M
Marquette University D
Marylhurst University M
Marywood University M,O*
Minnesota State University Mankato M
Montana State University–Billings M
Mountain State University M*
New Mexico State University M,D
New York University M*
Nova Southeastern University M*
The Ohio State University M,D*
Ohio University D*
Oregon State University M*
Regis University M,O
Rensselaer Polytechnic Institute M,D*
Rochester Institute of Technology M
Rutgers, The State University of New Jersey, New Brunswick D*
San Diego State University M*
San Jose State University M
Sarah Lawrence College M*
Sonoma State University M
Southern Methodist University M*
Stanford University M,D*
State University of New York at Fredonia M
State University of New York at New Paltz M
Stephen F. Austin State University M
Teachers College Columbia University M,D*
Texas A&M University M,D*
Texas A&M University–Texarkana M
Texas State University-San Marcos M*
Texas Tech University M
Union Institute & University M,D
University of Alaska Anchorage M
University of Alaska Fairbanks M,D
The University of Arizona M,D*
University of Arkansas D*
University of Central Florida M*
University of Chicago D*
University of Cincinnati D
University of Houston–Victoria M*
University of Idaho M*
University of Illinois at Springfield M
University of Kansas M,D*
University of Louisville M
University of Maine D*
University of Manitoba M,D
University of Maryland, College Park D*
University of Medicine and Dentistry of New Jersey M,D*
University of Minnesota, Twin Cities Campus D*
University of Missouri–Kansas City D*
The University of Montana M,D*
University of New Brunswick Fredericton M,D
University of Northern British Columbia M,D,O
University of Northern Colorado M
University of North Texas M*
University of Oklahoma M,D*
University of Oregon M*
University of Ottawa D,O*
University of Pittsburgh D*
The University of South Dakota M
The University of Texas at Arlington M*
The University of Texas at Brownsville M
The University of Texas at Dallas M*
The University of Texas at El Paso M
The University of Texas at San Antonio M*
The University of Texas at Tyler M
The University of Texas–Pan American M
University of the Incarnate Word M
The University of Western Ontario M,D
University of Wisconsin–Milwaukee D
Villanova University D*

- Virginia Commonwealth University M*
- Virginia Polytechnic Institute and State University M,D*
- Virginia State University M
- Washington State University D*
- Wayland Baptist University M
- Wayne State University M,D*
- Western Kentucky University M
- Western New Mexico University M
- West Texas A&M University M
- Worcester Polytechnic Institute M,D*
- Wright State University M*
- York University M*

INTERIOR DESIGN

- Academy of Art University M*
- Boston Architectural College M*
- Chatham University M
- Columbia College Chicago M
- Corcoran College of Art and Design M
- Cornell University M*
- Drexel University M*
- Eastern Michigan University M
- Florida State University M*
- The George Washington University M,D*
- Iowa State University of Science and Technology M*
- Lawrence Technological University M
- Louisiana Tech University M
- Marymount University M
- Marywood University M*
- Miami International University of Art & Design M*
- Michigan State University M,D*
- The New School: A University M*
- New York School of Interior Design M*
- The Ohio State University M*
- Pontificia Universidad Catolica Madre y Maestra M
- Pratt Institute M*
- Rhode Island School of Design M
- San Diego State University M*
- Savannah College of Art and Design M*
- School of the Art Institute of Chicago M*
- South Dakota State University M
- Suffolk University M*
- The University of Alabama M
- University of Central Oklahoma M
- University of Cincinnati M
- University of Florida M,D*
- University of Georgia M,D*
- University of Houston M*
- University of Kentucky M*
- University of Manitoba M
- University of Massachusetts Amherst M*
- University of Memphis M*
- University of Minnesota, Twin Cities Campus M,D,O*
- The University of North Carolina at Greensboro M,O
- University of North Texas M,D*
- University of Oregon M*
- Utah State University M
- Virginia Commonwealth University M*
- Virginia Polytechnic Institute and State University M,D*
- Washington State University M,D*
- Washington State University Spokane M,D

INTERNATIONAL AFFAIRS

- Alliant International University–México City M*
- Alliant International University–San Diego M*
- American Graduate School of International Relations and Diplomacy M,D*
- American Public University System M
- American University M,D,O*
- The American University of Paris M
- Arcadia University M
- Baylor University M,D*
- Boston University M,O*
- Brandeis University M,D*
- Brock University M
- California State University, Fresno M
- California State University, Sacramento M*
- Carleton University M,D
- The Catholic University of America M,D*
- Central Connecticut State University M
- Central European University M,D*
- Central Michigan University M,O*
- City College of the City University of New York M*
- Claremont Graduate University M,D
- Clark Atlanta University M,D
- Colorado School of Mines M,O
- Columbia University M*
- Concordia University (CA) M
- Cornell University D*
- Creighton University M*
- East Carolina University M*
- Fairleigh Dickinson University, Metropolitan Campus M*
- Florida Agricultural and Mechanical University M*
- Florida International University M,D*
- Florida State University M*
- Fordham University M,O*
- George Mason University M*
- Georgetown University M,D*
- The George Washington University M*
- Georgia Institute of Technology M*
- Harvard University D*
- Huron University USA in London M
- Indiana State University M*
- Instituto Tecnológico y de Estudios Superiores de Monterrey, Campus Ciudad Obregón M
- The Johns Hopkins University M,D,O*
- Kansas State University M*
- Lebanese American University M
- Lesley University M,O*
- Long Island University, Brooklyn Campus M,O*
- Long Island University, C.W. Post Campus M*
- Loyola University Chicago M,D*
- Marquette University M
- McMaster University M,D
- Michigan State University M*
- Missouri State University M*
- Monterey Institute of International Studies M*
- Morgan State University M*
- Naval Postgraduate School M
- The New School: A University M*
- New York University M,D,O*
- North Carolina State University M*
- Northeastern University M,D*
- Northwestern University O*
- Norwich University M
- Ohio University M*
- Oklahoma State University M*
- Old Dominion University M,D*
- Pepperdine University M*
- Princeton University M,D*
- Rutgers, The State University of New Jersey, Camden M
- Rutgers, The State University of New Jersey, Newark M,D*
- Rutgers, The State University of New Jersey, New Brunswick D*
- St. John Fisher College M
- St. Mary's University of San Antonio M
- Salve Regina University M,O
- San Francisco State University M
- Schiller International University (United Kingdom) M
- Schiller International University M
- School for International Training M
- Seton Hall University M*
- Stanford University M*
- Syracuse University M*
- Texas A&M University M*
- Texas State University-San Marcos M*
- Troy University M
- Tufts University M,D*
- United States International University M
- Universidad de las Americas, A.C. M
- Universidad Nacional Pedro Henriquez Urena P,M,D
- Université Laval M
- The University of British Columbia M*
- University of California, Berkeley M*
- University of California, San Diego M,D*
- University of California, Santa Barbara M*
- University of California, Santa Cruz D*
- University of Central Oklahoma M
- University of Chicago M*
- University of Colorado at Boulder M,D*
- University of Connecticut M*
- University of Delaware M,D*
- University of Denver M,D*
- University of Florida M*
- University of Hawaii at Manoa O*
- University of Indianapolis M
- University of Kansas M*
- University of Kentucky M*
- University of Miami M,D*
- University of Northern British Columbia M,D,O
- University of Oklahoma M*
- University of Oregon M*
- University of Pennsylvania M*
- University of Pittsburgh M,D,O*
- University of Rhode Island M,O
- University of San Diego M*
- University of South Carolina M,D*
- University of Southern California M,D*
- University of Southern Mississippi M,D*
- University of South Florida M*
- University of the Pacific P,M,D
- University of Virginia M,D*
- University of Washington M*
- University of Waterloo M,D*
- University of Wyoming M
- Virginia Polytechnic Institute and State University M*
- Washington State University M,D*
- Webster University M
- West Virginia University M,D*
- Wilfrid Laurier University M,D
- Yale University M*
- York University M*

INTERNATIONAL AND COMPARATIVE EDUCATION

- American University M*
- Boston University M*
- California State University, Dominguez Hills M
- The College of New Jersey M,O
- Drexel University M*
- Endicott College M
- Florida International University M,D*
- Florida State University M,D,O*
- The George Washington University M*
- Harvard University M*
- Indiana University Bloomington M,D,O*
- Louisiana State University and Agricultural and Mechanical College M,D*
- Lynn University M,D
- Morehead State University M
- New York University M,D,O*
- School for International Training M
- Stanford University M,D*
- Teachers College Columbia University M,D*
- Tufts University M,D*
- University of Bridgeport M,O
- University of California, Santa Barbara M,D*
- University of Massachusetts Amherst M,D,O*
- University of Minnesota, Twin Cities Campus M,D*
- University of Pennsylvania M,D*
- University of Pittsburgh M,D*
- University of San Francisco M,D
- Vanderbilt University M,D*
- Wright State University M*

INTERNATIONAL BUSINESS

- Alliant International University–México City M*
- Alliant International University–San Diego M,D*
- American InterContinental University (FL) M
- American InterContinental University Dunwoody Campus M
- American InterContinental University-London M
- American InterContinental University Online M
- American University M*
- The American University in Dubai M
- Andrew Jackson University M
- Argosy University, Atlanta Campus M,D*
- Argosy University, Chicago Campus M,D*
- Argosy University, Denver Campus M,D*
- Argosy University, Hawai'i Campus M,D,O*
- Argosy University, Inland Empire Campus M,D*
- Argosy University, Nashville Campus D*
- Argosy University, Orange County Campus M,D,O*
- Argosy University, Phoenix Campus M,D*
- Argosy University, San Diego Campus M,D*
- Argosy University, San Francisco Bay Area Campus M,D*
- Argosy University, Santa Monica Campus M,D*
- Argosy University, Sarasota Campus M,D,O*
- Argosy University, Schaumburg Campus M,D,O*
- Argosy University, Seattle Campus M,D*
- Argosy University, Tampa Campus M,D,O*
- Argosy University, Twin Cities Campus M,D*
- Argosy University, Washington DC Campus M,D,O*
- Avila University M*
- Azusa Pacific University M
- Baldwin-Wallace College M
- Barry University O*
- Baylor University M*
- Benedictine University M
- Bernard M. Baruch College of the City University of New York M*
- Boston University M*
- Brandeis University M,D*
- California Lutheran University M,O
- California State University, East Bay M
- California State University, Fullerton M
- California State University, Los Angeles M
- Cardean University M
- Central Connecticut State University M
- Central European University M,D*
- Central Michigan University M*
- City University M,O
- Clark Atlanta University M,D
- Clark University M*
- Cleveland State University M,D,O
- Columbia Southern University M
- Columbia University M*
- Concordia University Wisconsin M
- Daemen College M
- Dallas Baptist University M
- Davenport University M
- DePaul University M*
- Dominican University of California M
- Drury University M
- D'Youville College M*
- Eastern Michigan University M
- Emerson College M*
- Fairfield University M,O*
- Fairleigh Dickinson University, College at Florham M,O*
- Fairleigh Dickinson University, Metropolitan Campus M*
- Florida Atlantic University M
- Florida International University M*
- Florida Metropolitan University–South Orlando Campus M
- Florida Metropolitan University–Tampa Campus M
- Florida Southern College M
- The George Washington University M,D*
- Georgia Institute of Technology M,O*
- Georgia State University M*
- Golden Gate University M,D,O
- Hawai'i Pacific University M*
- HEC Montreal M
- Hofstra University M,O*
- Hope International University M
- Howard University M*
- Huron University USA in London M
- Illinois Institute of Technology M*
- Instituto Tecnológico y de Estudios Superiores de Monterrey, Campus Central de Veracruz M
- Instituto Tecnológico y de Estudios Superiores de Monterrey, Campus Chihuahua M,O
- Instituto Tecnológico y de Estudios Superiores de Monterrey, Campus Ciudad de México M,D
- Instituto Tecnológico y de Estudios Superiores de Monterrey, Campus Cuernavaca M
- Instituto Tecnológico y de Estudios Superiores de Monterrey, Campus Irapuato M,D
- Instituto Tecnológico y de Estudios Superiores de Monterrey, Campus Monterrey M
- Inter American University of Puerto Rico, Ponce Campus M
- Inter American University of Puerto Rico, San Germán Campus M,D

*P—first professional degree; M—master's degree; D—doctorate; O—other advanced degree; *full description and/or announcement in Book 2, 3, 4, 5, or 6*

International University in Geneva M
The International University of Monaco M
Iona College M,O*
John Marshall Law School P,M
Johnson & Wales University M*
Kean University M
Lindenwood University M
Long Island University, C.W. Post Campus M,O*
Lynn University M,D
Madonna University M
Maine Maritime Academy M,O
Manhattanville College M*
McGill University M,D,O*
Metropolitan State University M
Minnesota State University Mankato M
Montclair State University M*
Monterey Institute of International Studies M*
Newman University M
New Mexico Highlands University M
The New School: A University M*
New York Institute of Technology M,O
New York University M,D*
Nova Southeastern University M,D*
Oakland University M,O*
Oklahoma City University M
Oral Roberts University M
Our Lady of the Lake University of San Antonio M
Pace University M*
Pacific States University M,D
Park University M
Pepperdine University M*
Philadelphia University M*
Polytechnic University of Puerto Rico M
Pontifical Catholic University of Puerto Rico M,D
Pontificia Universidad Catolica Madre y Maestra M
Portland State University M
Purdue University M*
Quinnipiac University M*
Regis University M,O
Rochester Institute of Technology M
Roosevelt University M
Rutgers, The State University of New Jersey, Newark M,D*
St. Edward's University M,O
St. John's University (NY) M,O
Saint Joseph's University M*
Saint Louis University M,D*
Saint Mary's University of Minnesota M
St. Mary's University of San Antonio M
Saint Peter's College M
St. Thomas University M,O
Salem International University M
San Diego State University M*
Schiller International University (United States) M
Schiller International University (Germany) M
Schiller International University (United Kingdom) M
Schiller International University M
Schiller International University (Spain) M
Schiller International University M
Schiller International University, American College of Switzerland M
School for International Training M
Seton Hall University M,O*
Simon Fraser University M,D
Southeastern University M
Southeast Missouri State University M
Southern New Hampshire University M,D,O*
Stevens Institute of Technology M*
Suffolk University M,D*
Sul Ross State University M*
Temple University M,D*
Texas A&M International University M
Texas A&M University–Corpus Christi M
Texas Christian University M
Texas Tech University M
Thunderbird School of Global Management M
Touro University International M,D
Tufts University M,D*
Universidad Autonoma de Guadalajara M,D
Universidad Iberoamericana P,M
Universidad Metropolitana M
Université de Sherbrooke M
Université du Québec, École nationale d'administration publique M,O
Université Laval M,O
The University of Akron M
University of Alberta M*
The University of British Columbia D*
University of Chicago M*
University of Colorado at Colorado Springs M
University of Colorado at Denver and Health Sciences Center M*
University of Dallas M
University of Denver M*
The University of Findlay M
University of Florida P,M,D*
University of Hawaii at Manoa M,D*
University of Kentucky M*
University of La Verne M
University of Lethbridge M,D
University of Maryland University College M,O
University of Memphis M*
University of Miami M*
University of Minnesota, Twin Cities Campus M*
University of New Brunswick Saint John M
University of New Haven M*
University of New Mexico M*
University of Oklahoma M*
University of Pennsylvania M*
University of Phoenix–Atlanta Campus M
University of Phoenix–Augusta Campus M
University of Phoenix–Austin Campus M
University of Phoenix–Bay Area Campus M
University of Phoenix–Boston Campus M
University of Phoenix–Central Florida Campus M
University of Phoenix–Central Valley Campus M
University of Phoenix–Charlotte Campus M
University of Phoenix–Chattanooga Campus M
University of Phoenix–Cheyenne Campus M
University of Phoenix–Chicago Campus M
University of Phoenix–Cleveland Campus M
University of Phoenix–Columbus Georgia Campus M
University of Phoenix–Denver Campus M
University of Phoenix–Des Moines Campus M
University of Phoenix–Detroit Campus M
University of Phoenix–Fort Lauderdale Campus M
University of Phoenix–Harrisburg Campus M
University of Phoenix–Hawaii Campus M
University of Phoenix–Houston Campus M
University of Phoenix–Jersey City Campus M
University of Phoenix–Madison Campus M
University of Phoenix–Maryland Campus M
University of Phoenix–Memphis Campus M
University of Phoenix–Metro Detroit Campus M
University of Phoenix–Minneapolis/St. Louis Park Campus M
University of Phoenix–New Mexico Campus M
University of Phoenix–Northern Nevada Campus M
University of Phoenix–Northern Virginia Campus M
University of Phoenix–North Florida Campus M
University of Phoenix–Northwest Arkansas Campus M
University of Phoenix–Omaha Campus M
University of Phoenix–Oregon Campus M
University of Phoenix–Philadelphia Campus M
University of Phoenix–Pittsburgh Campus M
University of Phoenix–Puerto Rico Campus M
University of Phoenix–Raleigh Campus M
University of Phoenix–Renton Learning Center M
University of Phoenix–Richmond Campus M
University of Phoenix–Sacramento Valley Campus M
University of Phoenix–San Antonio Campus M
University of Phoenix–San Diego Campus M
University of Phoenix–Savannah Campus M
University of Phoenix–Southern Arizona Campus M
University of Phoenix–Springfield Campus M
University of Phoenix–West Florida Campus M
University of Phoenix–West Michigan Campus M
University of Pittsburgh M*
University of Regina O
University of Rhode Island M,D
University of San Francisco M
University of Saskatchewan M
The University of Scranton M
University of South Carolina M*
University of Southern California M*
The University of Tampa M
The University of Texas at Dallas M,D*
The University of Texas at San Antonio M,D*
University of the Incarnate Word M,O
University of the West M
The University of Toledo M*
University of Washington M,D,O*
University of Wisconsin–Whitewater M*
Upper Iowa University M
Valparaiso University M
Wagner College M
Washington State University M,D,O*
Wayland Baptist University M
Webster University M
Western International University M
Whitworth University M
Wilkes University M
Wright State University M*
Xavier University M*

INTERNATIONAL DEVELOPMENT

American University M,D,O*
Andrews University M
Athabasca University M
Brandeis University M*
Clark Atlanta University M,D
Clark University M*
Cornell University M*
Dalhousie University M
Duke University M,O*
Fordham University M,O*
The George Washington University M*
Harvard University M*
Hope International University M
The Johns Hopkins University M,D,O*
McGill University M,D,O*
The New School: A University M*
Ohio University M*
Rutgers, The State University of New Jersey, Camden M
Saint Mary's University M
Tufts University M,D*
Tulane University M,D*
University of Florida M,D,O*
University of Guelph M
University of Ottawa M*
University of Pittsburgh M,O*
University of Southern Mississippi M,D*

INTERNATIONAL HEALTH

Boston University M,D,O*
Brandeis University M*
Emory University M,D*
The George Washington University M*
Harvard University M,D*
The Johns Hopkins University M,D*
Loma Linda University M
New York Medical College M*
New York University M,D*
Touro University International M,D,O
Tufts University M,D*
Tulane University M,D*
Uniformed Services University of the Health Sciences M,D*
University of Alberta M,D*
University of Michigan M,D*
University of South Florida M,D*
University of Washington M,D*
Yale University M*

INTERNET AND INTERACTIVE MULTIMEDIA

Alfred University M*
American Academy of Art M
Brooklyn College of the City University of New York M,O
California State University, East Bay M
Chestnut Hill College M,O
City University M,O
Concordia University (Canada) M,O
Duquesne University M,O*
Georgetown University M*
Georgia Institute of Technology M*
Indiana University–Purdue University Indianapolis M,D*
Long Island University, C.W. Post Campus M*
Marlboro College M
National University M
New Jersey Institute of Technology M
New Mexico Highlands University M
New York Institute of Technology M,O
New York University M*
Polytechnic University, Brooklyn Campus M,O*
Pratt Institute M*
Quinnipiac University M*
Robert Morris University M
Rochester Institute of Technology M,O
Sacred Heart University M,O
San Diego State University M*
Savannah College of Art and Design M*
Simon Fraser University M,D
Southern Polytechnic State University M
Syracuse University M*
Towson University M,D,O
University of Florida M,D*
University of Georgia M*
University of Miami M*
University of San Francisco M
University of Southern California M,D*
Virginia Commonwealth University M,D,O*
Western Illinois University M,O
Wilmington College (DE) M

INVESTMENT MANAGEMENT

Boston University M*
Concordia University (Canada) M,D,O
Gannon University O
The George Washington University M,D*
The Johns Hopkins University M,O*
Lindenwood University M
Lynn University M,D
Marywood University M*
Pace University M*
Quinnipiac University M*
The University of Iowa M*
University of Tulsa M*
University of Wisconsin–Madison D*

ITALIAN

Boston College M,D*
Brown University M,D*
The Catholic University of America M,D*
Central Connecticut State University M,O
Columbia University M,D*
Connecticut College M
Cornell University D*
Florida State University M*
Graduate School and University Center of the City University of New York M,D*
Harvard University M,D*
Hunter College of the City University of New York M
Indiana University Bloomington M,D*
The Johns Hopkins University D*
McGill University M,D*
Middlebury College M,D
New York University M,D*
Northwestern University D,O*
The Ohio State University M,D*
Princeton University D*
Queens College of the City University of New York M
Rutgers, The State University of New Jersey, New Brunswick M,D*
San Francisco State University M
Stanford University M,D*
State University of New York at Binghamton M*
Stony Brook University, State University of New York M,D*
University at Albany, State University of New York M*
University of Alberta M,D*
University of California, Berkeley D*
University of California, Los Angeles M,D*
University of Chicago M,D*
University of Connecticut M,D*
University of Manitoba M,D
University of Massachusetts Amherst M,D*

The University of North Carolina at Chapel Hill M,D*
University of Notre Dame M*
University of Oregon M*
University of Pennsylvania M,D*
University of Pittsburgh M*
The University of Tennessee D*
University of Toronto M,D
University of Victoria M
University of Virginia M*
University of Washington M,D*
University of Wisconsin–Madison M,D*
University of Wisconsin–Milwaukee M
Wayne State University M*
Yale University D*

JAPANESE

Cornell University M,D*
Harvard University D*
Indiana University Bloomington M,D*
The Ohio State University M,D*
Portland State University M
San Francisco State University M
Stanford University M,D*
University at Buffalo, the State University of New York M,D,O*
University of Alberta M*
University of California, Berkeley D*
University of California, Irvine M,D*
University of Colorado at Boulder M,D*
University of Hawaii at Manoa M,D*
University of Kansas M*
University of Maryland, College Park M,D*
University of Massachusetts Amherst M*
University of Oregon M,D*
University of Washington M,D*
University of Wisconsin–Madison M,D*
Washington University in St. Louis M,D*

JEWISH STUDIES

American Jewish University M
Baltimore Hebrew University M,D
Brandeis University M,D*
Brooklyn College of the City University of New York M
Brown University M,D*
Chicago Theological Seminary P,M,D
Columbia University M,D*
Concordia University (Canada) M
Cornell University M,D*
Emory University M,D*
Graduate Theological Union M,D,O
Gratz College M
Harvard University M,D*
Hebrew College M,O
Hebrew Union College–Jewish Institute of Religion (CA) M,D
Hebrew Union College–Jewish Institute of Religion (NY) M
Hebrew Union College–Jewish Institute of Religion (OH) P,M,D
The Jewish Theological Seminary M,D*
Jewish University of America P,D
Laura and Alvin Siegal College of Judaic Studies M
McGill University M,D*
New York University M,D,O*
Seton Hall University M*
Spertus Institute of Jewish Studies M,D
Touro College M
University of California, Berkeley D*
University of California, San Diego M,D*
University of Connecticut M*
University of Maryland, College Park M*
The University of Montana M*
University of St. Michael's College P,M,D,O
University of Wisconsin–Madison M,D*
University of Wisconsin–Milwaukee M
Washington University in St. Louis M*
Yeshiva University M,D

JOURNALISM

American University M*
The American University in Cairo M,O
Angelo State University M
Arizona State University M*
Arkansas State University M
Arkansas Tech University M
Ball State University M*
Baylor University M*
Bob Jones University P,M,D,O
Boston University M*
California State University, Fresno M
California State University, Fullerton M
California State University, Northridge M
Carleton University M,D
Columbia College Chicago M
Columbia University M,D*
Concordia University (Canada) O
CUNY Graduate School of Journalism M*
Drake University M*
Drexel University M*
Emerson College M*
Florida Agricultural and Mechanical University M*
Harvard University M,O*
Hofstra University M*
Indiana University Bloomington M,D*
Iona College M*
Iowa State University of Science and Technology M*
Kent State University M*
Marquette University M*
Marshall University M
Michigan State University M*
Middle Tennessee State University M*
New York University M,D,O*
Northeastern University M*
Northwestern University M*
Ohio University M,D*
Point Park University M*
Polytechnic University, Brooklyn Campus M*
Quinnipiac University M*
Regent University M,D
Roosevelt University M
South Dakota State University M
Southern Illinois University Carbondale D*
Stanford University M,D*
Syracuse University M*
Temple University M*
Texas A&M University M*
Texas Christian University M
Texas Southern University M
Université Laval O
The University of Alabama M
University of Arkansas M*
The University of British Columbia M*
University of California, Berkeley M*
University of Colorado at Boulder M,D*
University of Florida M*
University of Georgia M,D*
University of Illinois at Springfield M
University of Illinois at Urbana–Champaign M*
The University of Iowa M*
University of Kansas M*
University of Maryland, College Park M,D*
University of Memphis M*
University of Miami M,D*
University of Mississippi M
University of Missouri–Columbia M,D*
The University of Montana M*
University of Nebraska–Lincoln M*
University of Nevada, Las Vegas M
University of Nevada, Reno M*
University of North Texas M*
University of Oklahoma M*
University of Oregon M,D*
University of South Carolina M,D*
University of Southern California M*
The University of Tennessee M,D*
The University of Texas at Austin M,D*
The University of Texas at Tyler M
University of the Sacred Heart M
The University of Western Ontario M
University of Wisconsin–Madison M,D*
University of Wisconsin–Milwaukee M
Virginia Commonwealth University M*
West Virginia University M*

KINESIOLOGY AND MOVEMENT STUDIES

Acadia University M
Angelo State University M
Arizona State University M,D*
A.T. Still University of Health Sciences M,D
Barry University M*
Bowling Green State University M*
California Baptist University M
California Polytechnic State University, San Luis Obispo M
California State Polytechnic University, Pomona M
California State University, Chico M
California State University, Fresno M
California State University, Long Beach M
California State University, Los Angeles M
California State University, Northridge M
California State University, San Bernardino M
Columbia University M,D*
Dalhousie University M
Florida State University M,D*
Fresno Pacific University M
Georgia Southern University M
Humboldt State University M
Indiana University Bloomington M,D,O*
Inter American University of Puerto Rico, San Germán Campus M
James Madison University M
Kansas State University M*
Lamar University M*
Louisiana State University and Agricultural and Mechanical College M,D*
McGill University M,D,O*
McMaster University M,D
Memorial University of Newfoundland M
Michigan State University M,D*
Midwestern State University M
Mississippi State University M
New York University M,D*
Old Dominion University D*
Oregon State University M*
Penn State University Park M,D*
Saint Mary's College of California M
Sam Houston State University M
San Francisco State University M
San Jose State University M
Simon Fraser University M,D
Sonoma State University M
Southeastern Louisiana University M
Southern Arkansas University–Magnolia M
Southern Illinois University Edwardsville M,O
Southwestern Oklahoma State University M
Springfield College M,D*
Stephen F. Austin State University M
Teachers College Columbia University M,D*
Temple University M,D*
Tennessee Technological University M*
Texas A&M University M,D*
Texas A&M University–Commerce M,D
Texas A&M University–Corpus Christi M,D
Texas A&M University–Kingsville M
Texas Christian University M
Texas Woman's University M,D
Université de Montréal M,D,O
Université de Sherbrooke M,O
Université du Québec à Montréal M
Université Laval M,D
The University of Alabama M,D
University of Arkansas M,D*
The University of British Columbia M,D*
University of Calgary M,D
University of Central Arkansas M
University of Colorado at Boulder M,D*
University of Connecticut M,D*
University of Delaware M,D*
University of Florida M,D*
University of Georgia M,D,O*
University of Hawaii at Manoa M*
University of Houston M,D*
University of Illinois at Chicago M*
University of Illinois at Urbana–Champaign M,D*
University of Kentucky M,D*
University of Lethbridge M,D
University of Maine M*
University of Maryland, College Park M,D*
University of Massachusetts Amherst M,D*
University of Medicine and Dentistry of New Jersey M,D*
University of Michigan M,D*
University of Minnesota, Twin Cities Campus M,D*
University of Nevada, Las Vegas M
University of New Hampshire M*
The University of North Carolina at Chapel Hill M,D*
The University of North Carolina at Charlotte M*
University of North Dakota M
University of North Texas M*
University of Ottawa M*
University of Regina M,D
University of Saskatchewan M,D,O
University of Southern California M,D*
The University of Tennessee M,D*
The University of Texas at Austin M,D*
The University of Texas at El Paso M
The University of Texas at Tyler M
The University of Texas of the Permian Basin M
The University of Texas–Pan American M
University of the Incarnate Word M,D
University of Victoria M,D
University of Virginia M,D*
University of Waterloo M,D*
The University of Western Ontario M,D
University of Windsor M
University of Wisconsin–Madison M,D*
University of Wisconsin–Milwaukee M
Washington University in St. Louis D*
Wayne State University M*
West Chester University of Pennsylvania M,O
Western Illinois University M
Wilfrid Laurier University M
York University M,D*

LANDSCAPE ARCHITECTURE

Arizona State University M*
Auburn University M*
Ball State University M*
California State Polytechnic University, Pomona M
Chatham University M
City College of the City University of New York M,O*
Clemson University M*
Columbia University M*
Conway School of Landscape Design M
Cornell University M*
Florida Agricultural and Mechanical University M*
Florida International University M*
Harvard University M,D*
Iowa State University of Science and Technology M*
Kansas State University M*
Louisiana State University and Agricultural and Mechanical College M*
Mississippi State University M
Morgan State University M*
North Carolina State University M*
The Ohio State University M*
Oklahoma State University M,D*
Penn State University Park M*
Rhode Island School of Design M
State University of New York College of Environmental Science and Forestry M
Texas A&M University M,D*
Texas Tech University M
The University of Arizona M*
The University of British Columbia M*
University of California, Berkeley M*
University of Colorado at Denver and Health Sciences Center M*
University of Florida M,D*
University of Georgia M*
University of Guelph M
University of Idaho M*
University of Illinois at Urbana–Champaign M,D*
University of Manitoba M
University of Massachusetts Amherst M*
University of Michigan M,D*
University of Minnesota, Twin Cities Campus M*
University of New Mexico M*
University of Oklahoma M*
University of Oregon M*
University of Pennsylvania M,O*

*P—first professional degree; M—master's degree; D—doctorate; O—other advanced degree; *full description and/or announcement in Book 2, 3, 4, 5, or 6*

University of Southern California M,O*
The University of Tennessee M*
The University of Texas at Arlington M*
University of Virginia M*
University of Washington M*
University of Wisconsin–Madison M*
Utah State University M
Virginia Polytechnic Institute and State University M*
Washington State University M,D*
Washington State University Spokane M,D

LATIN AMERICAN STUDIES

American University M,O*
Arizona State University M,D*
Boricua College M
Brown University M,D*
California State University, Los Angeles M
Centro de Estudios Avanzados de Puerto Rico y el Caribe M,D
Columbia University O*
Cornell University M,D*
Duke University M,D,O*
Florida International University M*
Fordham University O*
Georgetown University M*
The George Washington University M*
Indiana University Bloomington M*
The Johns Hopkins University M,D,O*
La Salle University M
Michigan State University D*
New York University M,O*
Ohio University M*
San Diego State University M*
Simon Fraser University M
Tulane University M,D*
University at Albany, State University of New York M,O*
The University of Arizona M*
University of California, Berkeley M,D*
University of California, Los Angeles M*
University of California, San Diego M*
University of California, Santa Barbara M,D*
University of Central Florida M,D,O*
University of Chicago M*
University of Connecticut M*
University of Florida M,O*
University of Illinois at Urbana–Champaign M*
University of Kansas M,O*
University of Massachusetts Dartmouth M,D
University of New Mexico M,D*
The University of North Carolina at Chapel Hill M,D,O*
University of Notre Dame M*
University of Pittsburgh O*
University of South Florida M,O*
The University of Texas at Austin M,D*
University of Wisconsin–Madison M*
Vanderbilt University M*
West Virginia University M,D*

LAW

Albany Law School of Union University P,M
American University P,M,O*
Appalachian School of Law P
Arizona State University P*
Ave Maria School of Law P
Barry University P*
Baylor University P*
Boston College P*
Boston University P,M*
Brigham Young University P,M*
Brooklyn Law School P
California Western School of Law P,M
Campbell University P
Capital University P,M
Case Western Reserve University P,M*
The Catholic University of America P*
Central European University M,D*
Chapman University P,M
City University of New York School of Law at Queens College P
Cleveland State University P,M
The College of William and Mary P,M
Columbia University P,M,D*
Concord Law School P
Cornell University P,M,D*
Creighton University P,M*
Dalhousie University M,D
DePaul University P,M*
Drake University P*
Duke University P,M,D*
Duquesne University P,M*
Elon University P
Emory University P,M,O*
Facultad de derecho Eugenio María de Hostos P
Faulkner University P
Florida Agricultural and Mechanical University P*
Florida Coastal School of Law P
Florida International University P*
Florida State University P*
Fordham University P,M*
Franklin Pierce Law Center P,M,O
Friends University M
George Mason University P,M*
Georgetown University P,M,D*
The George Washington University P,M,D*
Georgia State University P*
Golden Gate University P,M,D
Gonzaga University P
Hamline University P,M
Harvard University P,M,D*
Hodges University M
Hofstra University P,M*
Howard University P,M*
Humphreys College P
Illinois Institute of Technology P,M*
Indiana University Bloomington P,M,D,O*
Indiana University–Purdue University Indianapolis P,M,D*
Indiana University School of Law-Bloomington P,M,D,O
Indiana University School of Law-Indianapolis P,M
Instituto Tecnológico y de Estudios Superiores de Monterrey, Campus Ciudad de México P
Inter American University of Puerto Rico School of Law P
John F. Kennedy University P
John Marshall Law School P,M
The Johns Hopkins University M,D,O*
The Judge Advocate General's School, U.S. Army M
Lewis & Clark College P,M
Liberty University P
Louisiana State University and Agricultural and Mechanical College P,M*
Loyola Marymount University P,M
Loyola University Chicago P,M,D*
Loyola University New Orleans P
Marquette University P
Massachusetts School of Law at Andover P*
McGill University M,D,O*
Mercer University P
Michigan State University College of Law P,M
Mississippi College P,O
New College of California P*
New England School of Law P*
New York Law School P,M
New York University P,M,D,O*
North Carolina Central University P
Northeastern University P*
Northern Illinois University P*
Northern Kentucky University P
Northwestern University P,M,O*
Nova Southeastern University P,M*
Ohio Northern University P
The Ohio State University P,M*
Oklahoma City University P
Pace University P,M,D*
Park University M
Penn State Dickinson School of Law P,M
Pepperdine University P*
Pontifical Catholic University of Puerto Rico P
Queen's University at Kingston P,M
Quinnipiac University P,M*
Regent University P,M
Roger Williams University P*
Rutgers, The State University of New Jersey, Camden P
Rutgers, The State University of New Jersey, Newark P*
St. John's University (NY) P
Saint Joseph's University M,O*
Saint Louis University P,M*
St. Mary's University of San Antonio P
St. Thomas University P,M
Samford University P,M
San Joaquin College of Law P
Santa Clara University P,M,O
Seattle University P
Seton Hall University P,M*
Southern Illinois University Carbondale P,M*
Southern Methodist University P,M,D*
Southern New England School of Law P
Southern University and Agricultural and Mechanical College P*
South Texas College of Law P
Southwestern Law School P,M
Stanford University P,M,D*
Stetson University P,M
Suffolk University P,M*
Syracuse University P*
Temple University P,M*
Texas Southern University P
Texas Tech University P
Texas Wesleyan University P
Thomas Jefferson School of Law P
Thomas M. Cooley Law School P,M
Touro College P,M
Trinity International University P
Tulane University P,M,D*
Universidad Central del Este P
Université de Moncton P,M,O
Université de Montréal P,M,D,O
Université de Sherbrooke P,M,D,O
Université du Québec à Montréal M
Université Laval M,D,O
University at Buffalo, the State University of New York P,M*
The University of Akron P
The University of Alabama P,M
University of Alberta P,M*
The University of Arizona P,M*
University of Arkansas P,M*
University of Arkansas at Little Rock P
University of Baltimore P,M*
The University of British Columbia M,D*
University of Calgary P,M,O
University of California, Berkeley P,M,D*
University of California, Davis P,M*
University of California, Hastings College of the Law P,M
University of California, Los Angeles P,M*
University of Chicago P,M,D*
University of Cincinnati P
University of Colorado at Boulder P*
University of Connecticut P*
University of Dayton P,M*
University of Denver P,M*
University of Detroit Mercy P
University of Florida P,M,D*
University of Georgia P,M*
University of Hawaii at Manoa P,O*
University of Houston P,M*
University of Idaho P*
University of Illinois at Urbana–Champaign P,M,D*
The University of Iowa P,M*
University of Kansas P*
University of Kentucky P*
University of La Verne P
University of Louisville P
University of Manitoba M
University of Maryland, Baltimore P*
University of Maryland, College Park *
University of Memphis P*
University of Miami P,M*
University of Michigan P,M,D*
University of Minnesota, Twin Cities Campus P,M*
University of Mississippi P
University of Missouri–Columbia P,M*
University of Missouri–Kansas City P,M*
The University of Montana P*
University of Nebraska–Lincoln P,M*
University of Nevada, Las Vegas P
University of New Brunswick Fredericton P
University of New Mexico P*
The University of North Carolina at Chapel Hill P*
University of North Dakota P
University of Notre Dame P,M,D*
University of Oklahoma P*
University of Oregon P,M*
University of Ottawa M,D*
University of Pennsylvania P,M,D*
University of Pittsburgh P,M,O*
University of Puerto Rico, Río Piedras P,M*
University of Richmond P
University of St. Thomas (MN) P*
University of San Diego P,M,O*
University of San Francisco P,M
University of Saskatchewan P,M
University of South Carolina P*
The University of South Dakota P
University of Southern California P,M*
University of Southern Maine P*
The University of Tennessee P*
The University of Texas at Austin P,M*
University of the District of Columbia P
University of the Pacific P,M,D
The University of Toledo P,M*
University of Toronto P,M,D
University of Tulsa P,M,O*
University of Utah P,M*
University of Victoria P,M,D
University of Virginia P,M,D*
University of Washington P,M,D*
The University of Western Ontario P,M,O
University of Wisconsin–Madison M,D*
University of Wyoming P
Valparaiso University P,M
Vanderbilt University P,M,D*
Vermont Law School P
Villanova University P*
Wake Forest University P,M*
Washburn University P
Washington and Lee University P,M
Washington University in St. Louis P,M,D*
Wayne State University P,M,D*
Western New England College P,M
Western State University College of Law P
West Virginia University P*
Whittier College P,M
Widener University P,M,D*
Willamette University P,M
William Howard Taft University P,M
William Mitchell College of Law P
Yale University P,M,D*
Yeshiva University P,M
York University P,M,D*

LEGAL AND JUSTICE STUDIES

American University M,D,O*
Arizona State University M,D*
Boston University M*
Brock University M
California University of Pennsylvania M
Capital University M
Carleton University M,O
Case Western Reserve University P,M*
The Catholic University of America D,O*
Central European University M,D*
College of Charleston M,O*
College of the Humanities and Sciences, Harrison Middleton University M,D
DePaul University M,O*
The George Washington University M,O*
Golden Gate University P,M,D
Governors State University M
Hofstra University P,M*
Indiana University School of Law-Bloomington P,M,D,O
John Jay College of Criminal Justice of the City University of New York M,D
John Marshall Law School P,M
Marygrove College M
Marymount University M,O
Michigan State University College of Law P,M
Mississippi College M,O
Montclair State University M,O*
New York University M,D*
Northeastern University M,D*
Nova Southeastern University M*
Pace University P,M,D*
Prairie View A&M University M,D
Quinnipiac University M*
Regis University M,O
The Richard Stockton College of New Jersey O
Rutgers, The State University of New Jersey, New Brunswick D*
St. John's University (NY) M
Salve Regina University M
San Francisco State University M,O
Southern Illinois University Carbondale P,M*
State University of New York at Binghamton M,D*
Texas State University-San Marcos M*
Touro University International M,D,O
Université Laval O
University of Baltimore M*
University of Calgary M,O
University of California, Berkeley D*
University of Denver M,O*
University of Illinois at Springfield M
University of Manitoba M
University of Nebraska–Lincoln M*
University of Nevada, Reno M*
University of New Hampshire M*
University of Pittsburgh M,O*
University of San Diego P,M,O*
University of the Pacific P,M,D
University of the Sacred Heart M
University of Washington P,M,D*

University of Windsor	M
University of Wisconsin–Madison	M*
Vermont Law School	M
Weber State University	M
Webster University	M
West Virginia University	M*
Whittier College	P,M
William Howard Taft University	P,M

LEISURE STUDIES

Aurora University	M
Bowling Green State University	M*
California State University, Long Beach	M
Central Michigan University	M*
Dalhousie University	M
East Carolina University	M*
Florida International University	M*
Gallaudet University	M
Howard University	M*
Indiana University Bloomington	M,D,O*
Murray State University	M
Oklahoma State University	M,D,O*
Penn State University Park	M,D*
Prescott College	M
San Francisco State University	M
Southeast Missouri State University	M
Southern Connecticut State University	M
State University of New York College at Brockport	M*
Temple University	M*
Texas State University-San Marcos	M*
Universidad Metropolitana	M
Université du Québec à Trois-Rivières	M,O
University of Connecticut	M,D*
University of Illinois at Urbana–Champaign	M,D*
The University of Iowa	M*
University of Memphis	M*
University of Minnesota, Twin Cities Campus	M,D*
University of Mississippi	M,D
University of Nevada, Las Vegas	M
The University of North Carolina at Chapel Hill	M*
University of Northern Iowa	M,D
University of North Texas	M,O*
University of South Alabama	M*
University of Southern Mississippi	M,D*
The University of Tennessee	M,D*
The University of Toledo	M*
University of Utah	M,D*
University of Victoria	M
University of Waterloo	M,D*
University of West Florida	M

LIBERAL STUDIES

Abilene Christian University	M
Alaska Pacific University	M
Albertus Magnus College	M
Alvernia College	M
Antioch University McGregor	M*
Armstrong Atlantic State University	M
Auburn University Montgomery	M
Baker University	M
Barry University	M*
Boston University	M*
Bradley University	M
Brooklyn College of the City University of New York	M
California State University, Sacramento	M*
Cardinal Stritch University	M*
Clark University	M*
Clayton State University	M
College of Notre Dame of Maryland	M
College of Staten Island of the City University of New York	M
Columbia University	M*
Concordia University (IL)	M*
Converse College	M
Creighton University	M*
Dallas Baptist University	M
Dartmouth College	M*
DePaul University	M*
Dowling College	M*
Duke University	M*
Duquesne University	M*
East Tennessee State University	M
Excelsior College	M
Fitchburg State College	M
Florida Atlantic University	M
Florida International University	M*
Fordham University	M*
Fort Hays State University	M
Friends University	M
George Mason University	M*
Georgetown University	M*
Graduate School and University Center of the City University of New York	M*
Hamline University	M,O
Harvard University	M,O*
Henderson State University	M
Hollins University	M,O
Houston Baptist University	M
Indiana University Kokomo	M
Indiana University–Purdue University Fort Wayne	M
Indiana University–Purdue University Indianapolis	M,D,O*
Indiana University South Bend	M
Indiana University Southeast	M
Jacksonville State University	M
The Johns Hopkins University	M,O*
Kean University	M
Kent State University	M*
Lake Forest College	M
Lock Haven University of Pennsylvania	M
Louisiana State University and Agricultural and Mechanical College	M*
Louisiana State University in Shreveport	M
Loyola College in Maryland	M
Madonna University	M
Manhattanville College	M*
McDaniel College	M
Minnesota State University Moorhead	M
Mississippi College	M
Monmouth University	M
Nazareth College of Rochester	M
The New School: A University	M*
North Carolina State University	M*
North Central College	M
Northern Arizona University	M
Northern Kentucky University	M
Northwestern University	M*
Oakland University	M*
Occidental College	M
Ohio Dominican University	M
Oklahoma City University	M
Queens College of the City University of New York	M
Ramapo College of New Jersey	M
Reed College	M
Rollins College	M
Rutgers, The State University of New Jersey, Camden	M
Rutgers, The State University of New Jersey, Newark	M*
St. Edward's University	M,O
St. John's College (MD)	M
St. John's College (NM)	M
St. John's University (NY)	M
Saint Mary's College of California	M
San Diego State University	M*
Simon Fraser University	M
Skidmore College	M
Spring Hill College	M
State University of New York at Plattsburgh	M
State University of New York College at Brockport	M*
State University of New York Empire State College	M
Stony Brook University, State University of New York	M,O*
Tarleton State University	M
Temple University	M*
Texas Christian University	M*
Thomas Edison State College	M
Towson University	M
Tulane University	M*
University at Albany, State University of New York	M*
University of Arkansas at Little Rock	M
University of Delaware	M*
University of Denver	M,O*
University of Detroit Mercy	M
The University of Findlay	M
University of Maine	M*
University of Memphis	M*
University of Miami	M*
University of Michigan–Dearborn	M*
University of Minnesota, Duluth	M*
University of New Hampshire	M*
The University of North Carolina at Asheville	M
The University of North Carolina at Charlotte	M*
The University of North Carolina at Greensboro	M
The University of North Carolina Wilmington	M*
University of Oklahoma	M*
University of Pennsylvania	M*
University of Richmond	M
University of St. Thomas (TX)	M
University of Southern Indiana	M
University of South Florida	M*
The University of Toledo	M*
University of Wisconsin–Milwaukee	M
Ursuline College	M
Utica College	M
Valparaiso University	M,O
Vanderbilt University	M*
Villanova University	M*
Wake Forest University	M*
Washburn University	M
Wesleyan University	M,O*
West Virginia University	M*
Wichita State University	M*
Widener University	M*
Winthrop University	M

LIBRARY SCIENCE

Appalachian State University	M
Azusa Pacific University	M
The Catholic University of America	M*
Chicago State University	M
Clarion University of Pennsylvania	M,O
College of St. Catherine	M*
Columbia University	M*
Dalhousie University	M
Dominican University	M,O
Drexel University	M,D,O*
East Carolina University	M,O*
Emporia State University	M,D,O
Florida State University	M,D,O*
Gratz College	O
Indiana University Bloomington	M,D,O*
Indiana University–Purdue University Indianapolis	M*
Instituto Tecnológico y de Estudios Superiores de Monterrey, Campus Irapuato	M,D
Inter American University of Puerto Rico, San Germán Campus	M
Kent State University	M*
Kutztown University of Pennsylvania	M,O
Long Island University, C.W. Post Campus	M,D,O*
Long Island University, Westchester Graduate Campus	M
Louisiana State University and Agricultural and Mechanical College	M,O*
Mansfield University of Pennsylvania	M
Marywood University	M,O*
McDaniel College	M
McGill University	M,D,O*
North Carolina Central University	M
Old Dominion University	M*
Pratt Institute	M,O*
Queens College of the City University of New York	M,O
Rowan University	M
Rutgers, The State University of New Jersey, New Brunswick	M*
St. John's University (NY)	M,O
Sam Houston State University	M
San Jose State University	M
Simmons College	M,D,O
Southern Arkansas University–Magnolia	M
Southern Connecticut State University	M,O
Syracuse University	M,O*
Tennessee Technological University	M,O*
Texas Woman's University	M,D
Trevecca Nazarene University	M
Université de Montréal	M,D,O
University at Albany, State University of New York	M,D,O*
University at Buffalo, the State University of New York	M,O*
The University of Alabama	M,D
University of Alberta	M*
The University of Arizona	M,D*
The University of British Columbia	M*
University of California, Los Angeles	M,D,O*
University of Central Arkansas	M
University of Central Missouri	M,O
University of Denver	M,D,O*
University of Hawaii at Manoa	M,D,O*
University of Houston–Clear Lake	M
University of Illinois at Urbana–Champaign	M,D,O*
The University of Iowa	M*
University of Kentucky	M*
University of Maryland, College Park	M*
University of Michigan	M,D*
University of Missouri–Columbia	M,D,O*
University of Nevada, Las Vegas	M,D,O
The University of North Carolina at Chapel Hill	M,D,O*
The University of North Carolina at Greensboro	M
University of North Texas	M,D*
University of Oklahoma	M,O*
University of Pittsburgh	M,D,O*
University of Puerto Rico, Río Piedras	M,O*
University of Rhode Island	M
University of South Carolina	M,O*
University of Southern Mississippi	M,O*
University of South Florida	M*
The University of Texas at Austin	M,D*
University of Toronto	M,D,O
University of Washington	M,D*
The University of Western Ontario	M,D
University of Wisconsin–Madison	M,D,O*
University of Wisconsin–Milwaukee	M,O
Valdosta State University	M
Wayne State University	M,O*
Wright State University	M*

LIMNOLOGY

Baylor University	M,D*
Cornell University	D*
University of Alaska Fairbanks	M,D
University of Florida	M,D*
University of Wisconsin–Madison	M,D*
William Paterson University of New Jersey	M*

LINGUISTICS

Arizona State University	M,D*
Ball State University	D*
Biola University	M,D,O
Boston College	M*
Boston University	M,D*
Brigham Young University	M,O*
Brown University	M,D*
California State University, Fresno	M
California State University, Fullerton	M
California State University, Long Beach	M
California State University, Northridge	M
Carleton University	M
Carnegie Mellon University	M,D*
Concordia University (Canada)	M,O
Cornell University	M,D*
Eastern Michigan University	M
Florida International University	M*
Gallaudet University	M
George Mason University	M*
Georgetown University	M,D,O*
Georgia State University	M,D*
Graduate Institute of Applied Linguistics	M,O
Graduate School and University Center of the City University of New York	M,D*
Harvard University	D*
Hofstra University	M*
Indiana State University	M,O*
Indiana University Bloomington	M,D*
Indiana University of Pennsylvania	M,D
Louisiana State University and Agricultural and Mechanical College	M,D*
Massachusetts Institute of Technology	D*
McGill University	M,D*
Memorial University of Newfoundland	M,D
Michigan State University	M,D*
Montclair State University	M*
New York University	M,D*
Northeastern Illinois University	M
Northern Arizona University	M,D,O
Northwestern University	M,D*
Oakland University	M,O*
The Ohio State University	M,D*
Ohio University	M*
Old Dominion University	M*
Purdue University	M,D*
Queens College of the City University of New York	M
Rice University	M,D*
Rutgers, The State University of New Jersey, New Brunswick	D*
San Diego State University	M,O*
San Francisco State University	M
San Jose State University	M,O
Simon Fraser University	M,D
Southern Illinois University Carbondale	M*
Stanford University	M,D*
Stony Brook University, State University of New York	M,D*

*P—first professional degree; M—master's degree; D—doctorate; O—other advanced degree; *full description and/or announcement in Book 2, 3, 4, 5, or 6*

Syracuse University M*
Teachers College Columbia University M,D*
Temple University M*
Texas Tech University M
Universidad de las Américas–Puebla M
Université de Montréal M,D,O
Université de Sherbrooke M,D
Université du Québec à Chicoutimi M
Université du Québec à Montréal M,D
Université Laval M,D
University at Buffalo, the State University of New York M,D*
University of Alaska Fairbanks M
University of Alberta M,D*
The University of Arizona M,D*
The University of British Columbia M,D*
University of Calgary M,D
University of California, Berkeley D*
University of California, Davis M,D*
University of California, Los Angeles M,D*
University of California, San Diego D*
University of California, Santa Barbara M,D*
University of California, Santa Cruz M,D*
University of Chicago M,D*
University of Colorado at Boulder M,D*
University of Colorado at Denver and Health Sciences Center M,O*
University of Connecticut D*
University of Delaware M,D*
University of Florida M,D,O*
University of Georgia M,D*
University of Hawaii at Manoa M,D*
University of Houston M,D*
University of Illinois at Chicago M*
University of Illinois at Urbana–Champaign M,D*
The University of Iowa M,D*
University of Kansas M,D*
University of Manitoba M,D
University of Maryland, Baltimore County M*
University of Maryland, College Park M,D*
University of Massachusetts Amherst M,D*
University of Massachusetts Boston M
University of Michigan D*
University of Minnesota, Twin Cities Campus M,D*
University of Missouri–St. Louis M,O
The University of Montana M,D*
University of New Hampshire M,D*
University of New Mexico M,D*
The University of North Carolina at Chapel Hill M,D*
University of North Dakota M
University of Oregon M,D*
University of Ottawa M,D*
University of Pennsylvania M,D*
University of Pittsburgh M,D*
University of Puerto Rico, Río Piedras M*
University of Regina M
University of South Carolina M,D,O*
University of Southern California M,D*
University of South Florida M*
The University of Tennessee D*
The University of Texas at Arlington M,D*
The University of Texas at Austin M,D*
The University of Texas at El Paso M
University of Toronto M,D
University of Utah M,D*
University of Victoria M,D
University of Virginia M*
University of Washington M,D*
University of Wisconsin–Madison M,D*
Wayne State University M*
West Virginia University M*
Yale University D*
York University M,D*

LOGISTICS

Air Force Institute of Technology M,D
American Public University System M
Benedictine University M
Case Western Reserve University M,D*
Colorado Technical University—Colorado Springs M,D
East Carolina University M,D,O*
Florida Institute of Technology M*
George Mason University M*
The George Washington University M*
Georgia College & State University M
HEC Montreal M
Maine Maritime Academy M,O
Massachusetts Institute of Technology M,D*
North Dakota State University M,D
The Ohio State University M*
Penn State University Park M,D*
Pontificia Universidad Catolica Madre y Maestra M
Stevens Institute of Technology M,D,O*
Touro University International M,D
Universidad del Turabo M
University at Buffalo, the State University of New York M,D,O*
University of Alaska Anchorage M,O
University of Arkansas M*
University of Dallas M
University of Houston M*
University of Minnesota, Twin Cities Campus M,D*
University of Missouri–St. Louis M,D,O
University of New Hampshire M,D*
University of New Haven M,O*
The University of Tennessee M,D*
The University of Texas at Arlington M*
University of Washington O*
Virginia Polytechnic Institute and State University M,D*
Wilmington College (DE) M
Wright State University M*

MANAGEMENT INFORMATION SYSTEMS

Adelphi University M*
Air Force Institute of Technology M
Alliant International University–San Diego M,D*
American InterContinental University (CA) M
American InterContinental University Dunwoody Campus M
American InterContinental University-London M
American Sentinel University M
American University M,O*
Argosy University, Atlanta Campus M,D*
Argosy University, Chicago Campus M,D*
Argosy University, Denver Campus M,D*
Argosy University, Hawai'i Campus M,D,O*
Argosy University, Inland Empire Campus M,D*
Argosy University, Nashville Campus D*
Argosy University, Orange County Campus M,D,O*
Argosy University, Phoenix Campus M,D*
Argosy University, San Diego Campus M,D*
Argosy University, San Francisco Bay Area Campus M,D*
Argosy University, Santa Monica Campus M,D*
Argosy University, Sarasota Campus M,D,O*
Argosy University, Schaumburg Campus M,D,O*
Argosy University, Seattle Campus M,D*
Argosy University, Tampa Campus M,D,O*
Argosy University, Twin Cities Campus M,D*
Argosy University, Washington DC Campus M,D,O*
Arizona State University M,D*
Arizona State University at the Polytechnic Campus M
Arkansas State University M,O
Aspen University M,O
Auburn University M,D*
Avila University M*
Baker College Center for Graduate Studies M
Barry University O*
Baylor University M*
Bay Path College M
Bellevue University M*
Benedictine University M
Bernard M. Baruch College of the City University of New York M,D*
Boise State University M
Boston University D*
Bowie State University M,O
Brigham Young University M*
Bryant University M,O
California Lutheran University M,O
California State University, East Bay M
California State University, Fullerton M
California State University, Los Angeles M
California State University, Monterey Bay M
California State University, Sacramento M*
Capella University M,D,O
Capitol College M
Cardean University M
Carnegie Mellon University M,D*
Case Western Reserve University M,D*
Central European University M*
Central Michigan University M,O*
Charleston Southern University M
City University M,O
Claremont Graduate University M,D,O
Clarkson University M*
Clark University M*
Cleveland State University M,D
The College of St. Scholastica M
Colorado State University M*
Colorado Technical University—Colorado Springs M,D
Colorado Technical University—Denver M
Colorado Technical University—Sioux Falls M
Concordia University Wisconsin M
Creighton University M*
Dalhousie University M
Dallas Baptist University M
DePaul University M,D*
DeVry University M*
Dominican University M
Duquesne University M*
East Carolina University M,D,O*
Eastern Michigan University M
Edinboro University of Pennsylvania M,O
Fairfield University M,O*
Fairleigh Dickinson University, Metropolitan Campus M,O*
Ferris State University M
Florida Agricultural and Mechanical University M*
Florida Institute of Technology M*
Florida International University D*
Florida State University M,D*
Fordham University M*
Franklin Pierce University M
Friends University M
The George Washington University M*
Georgia College & State University M
Georgia Institute of Technology M,D,O*
Georgia State University M,D*
Golden Gate University M,D,O
Goldey-Beacom College M
Governors State University M
Graduate School and University Center of the City University of New York D*
Grand Valley State University M*
Grantham University M
Harvard University D*
Hawai'i Pacific University M*
HEC Montreal M
Hodges University M
Hofstra University M*
Holy Family University M
Howard University M*
Idaho State University M,O
Illinois Institute of Technology M,D*
Illinois State University M*
Indiana University South Bend M
Indiana University Southeast M,O
Instituto Tecnológico y de Estudios Superiores de Monterrey, Campus Central de Veracruz M
Instituto Tecnológico y de Estudios Superiores de Monterrey, Campus Ciudad de México M,D
Instituto Tecnológico y de Estudios Superiores de Monterrey, Campus Ciudad Juárez M
Instituto Tecnológico y de Estudios Superiores de Monterrey, Campus Ciudad Obregón M
Instituto Tecnológico y de Estudios Superiores de Monterrey, Campus Estado de México M,D
Instituto Tecnológico y de Estudios Superiores de Monterrey, Campus Irapuato M,D
Instituto Tecnológico y de Estudios Superiores de Monterrey, Campus Laguna M
Inter American University of Puerto Rico, San Germán Campus M,D
Iowa State University of Science and Technology M*
John Marshall Law School P,M
The Johns Hopkins University M,O*
Kean University M
Kent State University D*
Lawrence Technological University M,D
Lindenwood University M
Long Island University, C.W. Post Campus M,O*
Louisiana State University and Agricultural and Mechanical College M,D*
Loyola University Chicago M*
Marist College M,O*
Marymount University M,O
Marywood University M*
McGill University M,D,O*
McMaster University D
Metropolitan State University M
Miami University M*
Michigan State University M,D*
Middle Tennessee State University M*
Minot State University M
Mississippi State University M
Missouri State University M*
Montclair State University M*
Morehead State University M
National University M
Naval Postgraduate School M,O
Newman University M
New York Institute of Technology M,O
New York University M,D,O*
North Central College M
Northeastern University M,D*
Northern Arizona University M
Northern Illinois University M
Northwestern University M*
Northwest Missouri State University M
Norwich University M
Notre Dame College (OH) M,O
Nova Southeastern University M,D*
Oakland University M,O*
The Ohio State University M,D*
Oklahoma City University M
Oklahoma State University M,D*
Pace University M*
Pacific States University M,D
Park University M
Penn State Harrisburg M*
Penn State University Park M,D*
Polytechnic University, Westchester Graduate Center M,O
Pontifical Catholic University of Puerto Rico M,D
Prairie View A&M University M,D
Purdue University M,D*
Quinnipiac University M*
Regis University M,O
Rensselaer Polytechnic Institute M,D*
Rivier College M
Robert Morris University M,D
Rochester Institute of Technology M,O
Roosevelt University M
Rutgers, The State University of New Jersey, Newark M,D*
Sacred Heart University M,O
St. Edward's University M,O
St. John's University (NY) M,O
Saint Joseph's University M*
Saint Peter's College M
San Diego State University M*
San Jose State University M
Santa Clara University M
Schiller International University (United States) M
Schiller International University (Germany) M
Schiller International University (United Kingdom) M
Seattle Pacific University M
Seton Hall University M*
Shenandoah University M,O*
Southeastern University M
Southern Illinois University Edwardsville M
Southern New Hampshire University M,D,O*
Stevens Institute of Technology M,D,O*
Stony Brook University, State University of New York M,D,O*
Stratford University M
Strayer University M
Syracuse University M,D,O*
Tarleton State University M
Temple University M,D*
Texas A&M International University M
Texas A&M University M,D*
Texas Tech University M,D
Touro University International M,D,O
Towson University M,D,O
United States International University M
Universidad del Turabo D

Université de Montréal M,D,O
Université de Sherbrooke M,O
Université du Québec à Montréal M
Université Laval M,O
University at Buffalo, the State University of New York M,D,O*
The University of Akron M
The University of Alabama in Huntsville M,O
The University of Arizona M,D*
University of Arkansas M*
University of Arkansas at Little Rock M
University of Baltimore M*
The University of British Columbia D*
University of Central Florida M*
University of Central Missouri M
University of Cincinnati M
University of Colorado at Colorado Springs M
University of Colorado at Denver and Health Sciences Center M,D*
University of Dallas M
University of Delaware M*
University of Denver M*
University of Detroit Mercy M*
University of Florida M,D*
University of Hawaii at Manoa M,D,O*
University of Houston–Clear Lake M
University of Illinois at Chicago M,D*
University of Illinois at Springfield M
The University of Iowa M*
University of Kansas M,D*
University of La Verne M
University of Lethbridge M,D
University of Maine M*
University of Management and Technology M,O
University of Mary Hardin-Baylor M
University of Maryland University College M,O
University of Mary Washington M
University of Memphis M,D*
University of Miami M*
University of Minnesota, Twin Cities Campus M,D*
University of Mississippi M,D
University of Missouri–St. Louis M,D
University of Nebraska at Omaha M,D
University of Nebraska–Lincoln M*
University of Nevada, Las Vegas M
University of New Haven M*
University of New Mexico M*
The University of North Carolina at Chapel Hill D*
The University of North Carolina at Greensboro M,D,O
University of Northern Virginia M,D
University of North Texas M,D*
University of Oklahoma M*
University of Oregon M*
University of Pennsylvania M,D*
University of Phoenix–Atlanta Campus M
University of Phoenix–Augusta Campus M
University of Phoenix–Austin Campus M
University of Phoenix–Bay Area Campus M
University of Phoenix–Boston Campus M
University of Phoenix–Central Florida Campus M
University of Phoenix–Charlotte Campus M
University of Phoenix–Cheyenne Campus M
University of Phoenix–Chicago Campus M
University of Phoenix–Cleveland Campus M
University of Phoenix–Denver Campus M
University of Phoenix–Des Moines Campus M
University of Phoenix–Detroit Campus M
University of Phoenix–Fort Lauderdale Campus M
University of Phoenix–Harrisburg Campus M
University of Phoenix–Hawaii Campus M
University of Phoenix–Idaho Campus M
University of Phoenix–Indianapolis Campus M
University of Phoenix–Jersey City Campus M
University of Phoenix–Las Vegas Campus M
University of Phoenix–Louisiana Campus M
University of Phoenix–Madison Campus M
University of Phoenix–Maryland Campus M
University of Phoenix–Memphis Campus M
University of Phoenix–Metro Detroit Campus M
University of Phoenix–Nashville Campus M
University of Phoenix–New Mexico Campus M
University of Phoenix—Northern Nevada Campus M
University of Phoenix–Northern Virginia Campus M
University of Phoenix–North Florida Campus M
University of Phoenix–Northwest Arkansas Campus M
University of Phoenix–Northwest Indiana M
University of Phoenix–Oklahoma City Campus M
University of Phoenix–Omaha Campus M
University of Phoenix Online Campus M
University of Phoenix–Oregon Campus M
University of Phoenix–Philadelphia Campus M
University of Phoenix–Pittsburgh Campus M
University of Phoenix–Raleigh Campus M
University of Phoenix–Renton Learning Center M
University of Phoenix–Richmond Campus M
University of Phoenix–Sacramento Valley Campus M
University of Phoenix–St. Louis Campus M
University of Phoenix–San Antonio Campus M
University of Phoenix–San Diego Campus M
University of Phoenix–Savannah Campus M
University of Phoenix–Southern Arizona Campus M
University of Phoenix–Southern California Campus M
University of Phoenix–Southern Colorado Campus M
University of Phoenix–Springfield Campus M
University of Phoenix–Utah Campus M
University of Phoenix–Vancouver Campus M
University of Phoenix–West Florida Campus M
University of Phoenix–West Michigan Campus M
University of Phoenix–Wisconsin Campus M
University of Pittsburgh M*
University of Redlands M
University of Rhode Island D
University of St. Thomas (MN) M,O*
University of San Francisco M
The University of Scranton M
University of South Alabama M*
University of Southern California M*
University of Southern Mississippi M*
University of South Florida M*
The University of Tampa M
The University of Texas at Arlington M,D*
The University of Texas at Austin D*
The University of Texas at Dallas M*
The University of Texas at San Antonio M,D*
The University of Texas–Pan American M,D
University of the Sacred Heart M
University of the West M
The University of Toledo M*
University of Virginia M*
University of Wisconsin–Madison M,D*
University of Wisconsin–Oshkosh M
Utah State University M,D
Virginia Commonwealth University M,D*
Virginia Polytechnic Institute and State University M,D*
Walden University M,D
Walsh College of Accountancy and Business Administration M
Washington State University M,D*
Wayland Baptist University M
Webster University M,D,O
Western Governors University M
Western International University M
Western New England College M
Wilmington College (DE) M
Winston-Salem State University M
Worcester Polytechnic Institute M,D*
Wright State University M*
Xavier University M*

MANAGEMENT OF TECHNOLOGY

Air Force Institute of Technology M,D
Alliant International University–San Diego M,D*
Athabasca University M,O
Boston University M*
Capella University M,D,O
Cardean University M
Carlow University M
Carnegie Mellon University M,D*
Central Connecticut State University M
Champlain College M
City University M,O
Coleman College M
Colorado School of Mines M,D
Colorado Technical University—Colorado Springs M,D
Colorado Technical University—Denver M
Colorado Technical University—Sioux Falls M
Columbia University M*
Dallas Baptist University M
East Carolina University M,D,O*
Eastern Michigan University D
École Polytechnique de Montréal M,O
Embry-Riddle Aeronautical University Worldwide M
Fairfield University M*
Fairleigh Dickinson University, College at Florham M,O*
George Mason University M,D*
The George Washington University M,D*
Georgia Institute of Technology M,O*
Golden Gate University M,D,O
Grantham University M
Harvard University D*
Hodges University M
Idaho State University M
Illinois Institute of Technology M*
Illinois State University M*
Indiana State University D*
Instituto Tecnológico y de Estudios Superiores de Monterrey, Campus Central de Veracruz M
Instituto Tecnológico y de Estudios Superiores de Monterrey, Campus Cuernavaca M,D
Instituto Tecnológico y de Estudios Superiores de Monterrey, Campus Irapuato M,D
Iona College M,O*
The Johns Hopkins University M,O*
Jones International University M
La Salle University M
Lawrence Technological University M,D
Marist College M,O*
Marquette University M,D
Marshall University M
Mercer University M
Murray State University M
National University M
New Jersey Institute of Technology M,D
New York Institute of Technology M,O
New York University M*
North Carolina Agricultural and Technical State University M
North Carolina State University D*
OGI School of Science & Engineering at Oregon Health & Science University M,O
Oklahoma State University M*
Pacific Lutheran University M
Pacific States University M,D
Pepperdine University M*
Polytechnic University, Brooklyn Campus M,D*
Polytechnic University of Puerto Rico M
Polytechnic University, Westchester Graduate Center M
Portland State University M,D
Regis University M,O
Rensselaer Polytechnic Institute M,D*
Saginaw Valley State University M
St. Ambrose University M
Simon Fraser University M,D
South Dakota School of Mines and Technology M
State University of New York Institute of Technology M
Stevens Institute of Technology M,D,O*
Stony Brook University, State University of New York M,O*
Sullivan University M
Texas A&M University–Commerce M
Texas State University-San Marcos M*
Université Laval O
University at Albany, State University of New York M*
University of Advancing Technology M
The University of Akron M
University of Bridgeport M
University of Cincinnati M,D
University of Colorado at Colorado Springs M
University of Dallas M
University of Delaware M*
University of Denver M,O*
University of Illinois at Urbana–Champaign M*
University of Indianapolis M,O
University of Maryland University College M,O
University of Miami M,D*
University of Minnesota, Twin Cities Campus M*
University of New Hampshire M*
University of New Haven M*
University of New Mexico M*
University of Pennsylvania M*
University of Phoenix–Atlanta Campus M
University of Phoenix–Augusta Campus M
University of Phoenix–Austin Campus M
University of Phoenix–Bay Area Campus M
University of Phoenix–Boston Campus M
University of Phoenix–Central Florida Campus M
University of Phoenix–Central Massachusetts Campus M
University of Phoenix–Central Valley Campus M
University of Phoenix–Charlotte Campus M
University of Phoenix–Chattanooga Campus M
University of Phoenix–Cheyenne Campus M
University of Phoenix–Chicago Campus M
University of Phoenix–Cincinnati Campus M
University of Phoenix–Cleveland Campus M
University of Phoenix–Columbus Georgia Campus M
University of Phoenix–Dallas Campus M
University of Phoenix–Denver Campus M
University of Phoenix–Des Moines Campus M
University of Phoenix–Detroit Campus M
University of Phoenix–Harrisburg Campus M
University of Phoenix–Hawaii Campus M
University of Phoenix–Houston Campus M
University of Phoenix–Idaho Campus M
University of Phoenix–Indianapolis Campus M
University of Phoenix–Jersey City Campus M
University of Phoenix–Kansas City Campus M
University of Phoenix–Las Vegas Campus M
University of Phoenix–Louisiana Campus M
University of Phoenix–Louisville Campus M
University of Phoenix–Madison Campus M
University of Phoenix–Maryland Campus M
University of Phoenix–Memphis Campus M
University of Phoenix–Metro Detroit Campus M

P—first professional degree; M—master's degree; D—doctorate; O—other advanced degree;
**full description and/or announcement in Book 2, 3, 4, 5, or 6*

University of Phoenix–Minneapolis/St. Louis Park Campus M

University of Phoenix–Nashville Campus M

University of Phoenix–New Mexico Campus M

University of Phoenix—Northern Nevada Campus M

University of Phoenix–Northern Virginia Campus M

University of Phoenix–Northwest Arkansas Campus M

University of Phoenix–Oklahoma City Campus M

University of Phoenix–Omaha Campus M

University of Phoenix Online Campus M

University of Phoenix–Oregon Campus M

University of Phoenix–Philadelphia Campus M

University of Phoenix–Pittsburgh Campus M

University of Phoenix–Puerto Rico Campus M

University of Phoenix–Raleigh Campus M

University of Phoenix–Renton Learning Center M

University of Phoenix–Richmond Campus M

University of Phoenix–Sacramento Valley Campus M

University of Phoenix–San Antonio Campus M

University of Phoenix–San Diego Campus M

University of Phoenix–Savannah Campus M

University of Phoenix–Southern Arizona Campus M

University of Phoenix–Southern California Campus M

University of Phoenix–Southern Colorado Campus M

University of Phoenix–Springfield Campus M

University of Phoenix–Vancouver Campus M

University of Phoenix–West Florida Campus M

University of Phoenix–West Michigan Campus M

University of Phoenix–Wisconsin Campus M

University of St. Thomas (MN) M,O*

The University of Scranton M

The University of Tampa M

University of Tulsa M*

University of Washington M,D*

University of Waterloo M,D*

University of Wisconsin–Madison M*

University of Wisconsin–Stout M*

University of Wisconsin–Whitewater M*

Villa Julie College M

Villanova University M*

Walden University M,D

Washington State University Tri-Cities M

Westminster College (UT) M,O

MANAGEMENT STRATEGY AND POLICY

Alliant International University–San Diego M,D*

Azusa Pacific University M

Bernard M. Baruch College of the City University of New York M,D*

Brenau University M

California State University, East Bay M

Cardean University M

Case Western Reserve University M*

Claremont Graduate University M,D,O

Clemson University M,D*

DePaul University M*

Dominican University of California M

Drexel University M,D,O*

Duquesne University M*

The George Washington University M,D*

Georgia Institute of Technology M,D,O*

HEC Montreal M

Illinois Institute of Technology M*

Lamar University M*

Manhattanville College M*

McGill University M,D,O*

Mountain State University M*

Neumann College M

New York Institute of Technology M,O

New York University M,D*

Northwestern University D*

Pace University M*

Purdue University M,D*

Regent University M,D,O

Roberts Wesleyan College M,O

Rutgers, The State University of New Jersey, Newark M*

Sage Graduate School M

Saint Mary-of-the-Woods College M

Stevens Institute of Technology M*

Syracuse University D*

Temple University M,D*

Tennessee Technological University M*

Towson University O

Tufts University O*

United States International University M

The University of Arizona M,D*

The University of British Columbia D*

University of Calgary M,D

University of Dallas M

University of Denver M,O*

University of Florida M*

The University of Iowa M*

University of Lethbridge M,D

University of Minnesota, Twin Cities Campus M,D*

University of New Haven M*

University of New Mexico M*

The University of North Carolina at Chapel Hill D*

University of North Texas M,D*

University of Oklahoma M*

University of Wisconsin–Madison M*

Western Governors University M

Western International University M

MANUFACTURING ENGINEERING

Arizona State University at the Polytechnic Campus M

Boston University M,D*

Bowling Green State University M*

Bradley University M

California State University, Northridge M

Clemson University M*

Cornell University M,D*

Dartmouth College M,D*

Drexel University M,D*

East Carolina University M,D,O*

Eastern Kentucky University M*

East Tennessee State University M

Florida State University M,D*

Grand Valley State University M

Illinois Institute of Technology M,D*

Instituto Tecnológico y de Estudios Superiores de Monterrey, Campus Monterrey M,D

Kansas State University M,D*

Kettering University M

Lawrence Technological University M,D

Lehigh University M*

Louisiana Tech University M,D

Marquette University M,D

Massachusetts Institute of Technology M,D,O*

Michigan State University M,D*

Minnesota State University Mankato M

New Jersey Institute of Technology M

North Carolina State University M*

North Dakota State University M,D

Northeastern University M,D*

Northwestern University M*

Ohio University M,D*

Oklahoma State University M*

Old Dominion University M,D*

Oregon State University M,D*

Penn State University Park M,D*

Polytechnic University, Brooklyn Campus M*

Polytechnic University, Long Island Graduate Center M,D

Polytechnic University of Puerto Rico M

Portland State University M

Rensselaer Polytechnic Institute M,D*

Rochester Institute of Technology M

Southern Illinois University Carbondale M*

Southern Methodist University M,D*

Stevens Institute of Technology M*

Texas A&M University M*

Texas Tech University M,D

Tufts University O*

Universidad Autonoma de Guadalajara M,D

Universidad de las Américas–Puebla M

University of Calgary M,D

University of California, Los Angeles M*

University of Central Florida M,D,O*

University of Colorado at Colorado Springs M

University of Detroit Mercy M,D

The University of Iowa M,D*

University of Kentucky M*

University of Maryland, College Park M,D*

University of Massachusetts Amherst M*

University of Massachusetts Lowell M,D,O*

University of Memphis M*

University of Michigan M,D*

University of Michigan–Dearborn M,D*

University of Missouri–Columbia M,D*

University of Missouri–Rolla M*

University of Nebraska–Lincoln M,D*

University of New Mexico M*

University of Regina M

University of Rhode Island M

University of St. Thomas (MN) M,O*

University of Southern California M*

University of Southern Maine M

The University of Tennessee M,D*

The University of Texas at Austin M,D*

University of Windsor M,D

University of Wisconsin–Madison M*

University of Wisconsin–Stout M*

Villanova University M,O*

Wayne State University M*

Western Illinois University M

Western Michigan University M*

Western New England College M

Wichita State University M,D*

Worcester Polytechnic Institute M,D,O*

MARINE AFFAIRS

Dalhousie University M

Duke University M*

East Carolina University D*

Florida Institute of Technology M,D*

Louisiana State University and Agricultural and Mechanical College M,D*

Memorial University of Newfoundland M,D,O

Nova Southeastern University M*

Oregon State University M*

Stevens Institute of Technology M*

Université du Québec à Rimouski M,O

University of Delaware M,D*

University of Maine M*

University of Miami M*

University of Rhode Island M,D

University of San Diego M*

University of Washington M*

University of West Florida M

MARINE BIOLOGY

California State University, Stanislaus M

College of Charleston M*

Florida Institute of Technology M*

Florida State University M,D*

Memorial University of Newfoundland M,D

Nicholls State University M

Northeastern University M,D*

Nova Southeastern University M,D*

Rutgers, The State University of New Jersey, New Brunswick M,D*

San Francisco State University M

Texas State University-San Marcos M*

University of Alaska Fairbanks M,D

University of California, San Diego M,D*

University of California, Santa Barbara M,D*

University of Colorado at Boulder M,D*

University of Guam M

University of Hawaii at Manoa M,D*

University of Maine M,D*

University of Massachusetts Dartmouth M

University of Miami M,D*

The University of North Carolina Wilmington M,D*

University of Oregon M,D*

University of Southern California D*

University of Southern Mississippi M,D*

Western Illinois University M,O

Woods Hole Oceanographic Institution M,D,O

MARINE GEOLOGY

Cornell University M,D*

Massachusetts Institute of Technology M,D*

University of Delaware M,D*

University of Hawaii at Manoa M,D*

University of Miami M,D*

University of Michigan M,D*

University of Washington M,D*

Woods Hole Oceanographic Institution M,D,O

MARINE SCIENCES

American University M*

California State University, East Bay M

California State University, Fresno M

California State University, Monterey Bay M

California State University, Sacramento M*

Coastal Carolina University M

The College of William and Mary M,D

Cornell University M,D*

Duke University M*

Florida Institute of Technology M,D*

Hawai'i Pacific University M*

Medical University of South Carolina D*

Memorial University of Newfoundland M,O

North Carolina State University M,D*

Nova Southeastern University M*

Oregon State University M*

San Francisco State University M

San Jose State University M

Savannah State University M

Stony Brook University, State University of New York M,D*

Texas A&M University at Galveston M

Texas A&M University–Corpus Christi D

University of Alaska Fairbanks M,D

The University of British Columbia M,D*

University of California, San Diego M*

University of California, Santa Barbara M,D*

University of California, Santa Cruz M,D*

University of Connecticut M,D*

University of Delaware M,D*

University of Florida M,D*

University of Georgia M,D*

University of Maine M,D*

University of Maryland, Baltimore M,D*

University of Maryland, Baltimore County M,D*

University of Maryland, College Park M,D*

University of Maryland Eastern Shore M,D*

University of Massachusetts Amherst M*

University of Massachusetts Boston D

University of Massachusetts Dartmouth M,D

University of Miami M,D*

University of Michigan M,D*

University of New England M

The University of North Carolina at Chapel Hill M,D*

The University of North Carolina Wilmington M,D*

University of Puerto Rico, Mayagüez Campus M,D*

University of Rhode Island M,D

University of San Diego M*

University of South Alabama M,D*

University of South Carolina M,D*

University of Southern California D*

University of Southern Mississippi M,D*

University of South Florida M,D*

The University of Texas at Austin M,D*

University of Wisconsin–La Crosse M

University of Wisconsin–Madison M,D*

Western Washington University M

MARKETING

Adelphi University M*

Alabama Agricultural and Mechanical University M

Alliant International University–San Diego M,D*

American College of Thessaloniki M,O

American InterContinental University (FL) M

American InterContinental University Buckhead Campus M

American InterContinental University Online M

American University M*

Andrew Jackson University M

Institution	Degrees
Andrews University	M
Argosy University, Atlanta Campus	M,D*
Argosy University, Chicago Campus	M,D*
Argosy University, Denver Campus	M,D*
Argosy University, Hawai'i Campus	M,D,O*
Argosy University, Inland Empire Campus	M,D*
Argosy University, Nashville Campus	D*
Argosy University, Orange County Campus	M,D,O*
Argosy University, Phoenix Campus	M,D*
Argosy University, San Diego Campus	M,D*
Argosy University, San Francisco Bay Area Campus	M,D*
Argosy University, Santa Monica Campus	M,D*
Argosy University, Sarasota Campus	M,D,O*
Argosy University, Schaumburg Campus	M,D,O*
Argosy University, Seattle Campus	M,D*
Argosy University, Tampa Campus	M,D,O*
Argosy University, Twin Cities Campus	M,D*
Argosy University, Washington DC Campus	M,D,O*
Arizona State University	M,D*
Avila University	M*
Baker College Center for Graduate Studies	M
Barry University	O*
Bayamón Central University	M
Benedictine University	M
Bentley College	M*
Bernard M. Baruch College of the City University of New York	M,D*
Boston University	D*
Bryant University	M,O
California Lutheran University	M,O
California State University, East Bay	M
California State University, Fullerton	M
California State University, Los Angeles	M
Canisius College	M
Capella University	M,D,O
Cardean University	M
Carnegie Mellon University	D*
Case Western Reserve University	M,D*
Central European University	M*
Central Michigan University	M*
City University	M,O
Clark Atlanta University	M
Clark University	M*
Clemson University	M*
Cleveland State University	M,D,O
Columbia Southern University	M
Columbia University	M,D*
Concordia University Wisconsin	M
Cornell University	D*
Dallas Baptist University	M
Davenport University	M
Delta State University	M
DePaul University	M*
Drexel University	M,D,O*
Eastern Michigan University	M
Eastern University	M*
Emerson College	M*
Fairfield University	M,O*
Fairleigh Dickinson University, College at Florham	M,O*
Fairleigh Dickinson University, Metropolitan Campus	M,O*
Fashion Institute of Technology	M*
Florida Agricultural and Mechanical University	M*
Florida Atlantic University	M
Florida State University	M,D*
Fordham University	M*
Franklin University	M
Gannon University	O
The George Washington University	M,D*
Georgia Institute of Technology	M,D,O*
Georgia State University	M,D*
Golden Gate University	M,D,O
Goldey-Beacom College	M
Hawai'i Pacific University	M*
HEC Montreal	M*
Hofstra University	M,O*
Howard University	M*
Huron University USA in London	M
Illinois Institute of Technology	M*
Indiana Tech	M
Indiana University Southeast	M,O
Instituto Tecnológico y de Estudios Superiores de Monterrey, Campus Central de Veracruz	M
Instituto Tecnológico y de Estudios Superiores de Monterrey, Campus Ciudad Obregón	M
Instituto Tecnológico y de Estudios Superiores de Monterrey, Campus Cuernavaca	M
Instituto Tecnológico y de Estudios Superiores de Monterrey, Campus Estado de México	M,D
Instituto Tecnológico y de Estudios Superiores de Monterrey, Campus Monterrey	M
Inter American University of Puerto Rico, Metropolitan Campus	M
Inter American University of Puerto Rico, San Germán Campus	M,D
International University in Geneva	M
The International University of Monaco	M
Iona College	M,O*
The Johns Hopkins University	M*
Johnson & Wales University	M*
Kent State University	D*
Lasell College	M*
Lindenwood University	M
Long Island University, C.W. Post Campus	M,O*
Louisiana State University and Agricultural and Mechanical College	D*
Louisiana Tech University	M,D
Loyola College in Maryland	M
Loyola University Chicago	M*
Lynn University	M,D
Manhattanville College	M*
Maryville University of Saint Louis	M,O
McGill University	M,D,O*
Mercy College	M
Metropolitan State University	M
Miami University	M*
Michigan State University	M,D*
Middle Tennessee State University	M*
Minnesota State University Mankato	M
Mississippi State University	M,D
Montclair State University	M*
New Mexico State University	D
New York Institute of Technology	M,O
New York University	M,D,O*
Northeastern Illinois University	M
Northwestern University	M,D*
Oakland University	M,O*
Oklahoma City University	M
Oklahoma State University	M,D*
Old Dominion University	D*
Oral Roberts University	M
Ottawa University	M
Pace University	M*
Penn State University Park	M,D*
Philadelphia University	M*
Pontifical Catholic University of Puerto Rico	M,D
Purdue University	M,D*
Quinnipiac University	M*
Regis University	M,O
Rensselaer Polytechnic Institute	M,D*
Roberts Wesleyan College	M,O
Rutgers, The State University of New Jersey, Newark	M,D*
Sage Graduate School	M
St. Bonaventure University	M,O
St. Cloud State University	M,O
St. Edward's University	M,O
St. John's University (NY)	M,O
Saint Joseph's University	M,O*
Saint Peter's College	M
St. Thomas Aquinas College	M*
Saint Xavier University	M,O
San Diego State University	M*
Seton Hall University	M*
Southeastern University	M
Southern Adventist University	M
Southern New Hampshire University	M,D,O*
Stephen F. Austin State University	M
Syracuse University	M,D*
Temple University	M,D*
Texas A&M University	M,D*
Texas Tech University	M,D
United States International University	M
Universidad del Turabo	M
Universidad Metropolitana	M
Université de Sherbrooke	M
Université Laval	M,O
University at Albany, State University of New York	M*
The University of Akron	M
The University of Alabama	M,D
University of Alberta	D*
The University of Arizona	D*
University of Baltimore	M*
The University of British Columbia	D*
University of California, Berkeley	D*
University of Cincinnati	M,D
University of Colorado at Boulder	D*
University of Colorado at Colorado Springs	M
University of Colorado at Denver and Health Sciences Center	M*
University of Connecticut	M,D*
University of Dallas	M*
University of Denver	M*
The University of Findlay	M*
University of Florida	M,D*
University of Georgia	M*
University of Hawaii at Manoa	M,D*
University of Houston	D*
University of Indianapolis	M,O
The University of Iowa	M,D*
University of La Verne	M
University of Massachusetts Dartmouth	M,O
University of Memphis	M,D*
University of Miami	M*
University of Minnesota, Twin Cities Campus	M,D*
University of Missouri–St. Louis	M,O
University of Nebraska–Lincoln	M,D*
University of New Brunswick Fredericton	M,D
University of New Haven	M*
University of New Mexico	M*
The University of North Carolina at Chapel Hill	D*
The University of North Carolina at Charlotte	M*
The University of North Carolina at Greensboro	M,D
University of Northern Virginia	M,D
University of North Texas	M,D*
University of Oregon	D*
University of Pennsylvania	M,D*
University of Phoenix–Augusta Campus	M
University of Phoenix–Austin Campus	M
University of Phoenix–Bay Area Campus	M
University of Phoenix–Central Florida Campus	M
University of Phoenix–Central Valley Campus	M
University of Phoenix–Chattanooga Campus	M
University of Phoenix–Cheyenne Campus	M
University of Phoenix–Cleveland Campus	M
University of Phoenix–Columbus Georgia Campus	M
University of Phoenix–Columbus Ohio Campus	M
University of Phoenix–Dallas Campus	M
University of Phoenix–Denver Campus	M
University of Phoenix–Des Moines Campus	M
University of Phoenix–Detroit Campus	M
University of Phoenix–Fort Lauderdale Campus	M
University of Phoenix–Harrisburg Campus	M
University of Phoenix–Hawaii Campus	M
University of Phoenix–Jersey City Campus	M
University of Phoenix–Madison Campus	M
University of Phoenix–Maryland Campus	M
University of Phoenix–Memphis Campus	M
University of Phoenix–Minneapolis/St. Louis Park Campus	M
University of Phoenix—Northern Nevada Campus	M
University of Phoenix–Northern Virginia Campus	M
University of Phoenix–North Florida Campus	M
University of Phoenix–Northwest Arkansas Campus	M
University of Phoenix–Omaha Campus	M
University of Phoenix Online Campus	M
University of Phoenix–Pittsburgh Campus	M
University of Phoenix–Puerto Rico Campus	M
University of Phoenix–Renton Learning Center	M
University of Phoenix–Richmond Campus	M
University of Phoenix–Sacramento Valley Campus	M
University of Phoenix–San Antonio Campus	M
University of Phoenix–Savannah Campus	M
University of Phoenix–Southern California Campus	M
University of Phoenix–Springfield Campus	M
University of Phoenix–West Florida Campus	M
University of Rhode Island	D
University of San Francisco	M
University of Saskatchewan	M
The University of Scranton	M
The University of Tampa	M
The University of Tennessee	M,D*
The University of Texas at Arlington	M,D*
The University of Texas at Austin	D*
The University of Texas at San Antonio	M*
University of the Sacred Heart	M
The University of Toledo	M*
University of Wisconsin–Whitewater	M*
Vanderbilt University	D*
Virginia Commonwealth University	O*
Virginia Polytechnic Institute and State University	M,D*
Wagner College	M
Walden University	M,D
Washington State University	M,D*
Webster University	M,D
Western International University	M
West Virginia University	M*
Wilkes University	M
Worcester Polytechnic Institute	M,O*
Wright State University	M*
Xavier University	M*
Yale University	D*
Youngstown State University	M

MARKETING RESEARCH

Institution	Degrees
Hofstra University	M,O*
Instituto Tecnológico y de Estudios Superiores de Monterrey, Campus Irapuato	M,D
Pace University	M*
Southern Illinois University Edwardsville	M
Universidad de las Americas, A.C.	M
University of Georgia	M*
The University of Texas at Arlington	M*
University of Wisconsin–Madison	M*

MARRIAGE AND FAMILY THERAPY

Institution	Degrees
Abilene Christian University	M,O
Adler Graduate School	M,O
Adler School of Professional Psychology	M,D,O*
Alliant International University–Irvine	M,D*
Alliant International University–Sacramento	M*
Alliant International University–San Diego	M,D*
Antioch University New England	M*
Appalachian State University	M
Argosy University, Atlanta Campus	M,D,O*
Argosy University, Chicago Campus	D*
Argosy University, Hawai'i Campus	M*
Argosy University, Inland Empire Campus	M,D*
Argosy University, Orange County Campus	M,D,O*
Argosy University, San Diego Campus	M,D*
Argosy University, Santa Monica Campus	M,D*
Argosy University, Sarasota Campus	M,D,O*
Argosy University, Schaumburg Campus	M,D,O*
Argosy University, Tampa Campus	M,D*
Argosy University, Twin Cities Campus	M,D,O*

*P—first professional degree; M—master's degree; D—doctorate; O—other advanced degree; *full description and/or announcement in Book 2, 3, 4, 5, or 6*

Argosy University, Washington DC Campus M,D,O*
Azusa Pacific University M,D
Barry University M,O*
Bethel College (IN) M
Bethel Seminary P,M,D,O
Briercrest Seminary M
Brigham Young University M,D*
California Baptist University M
California Lutheran University M
California State University, Chico M
California State University, Dominguez Hills M
California State University, Fresno M
California State University, Northridge M
Capella University M,D,O
Carlos Albizu University, Miami Campus M,D
Central Connecticut State University M,O
Chapman University M
Christian Theological Seminary P,M,D
The College of New Jersey O
The College of William and Mary M,D
Converse College O
Denver Seminary P,M,D,O
Drexel University M,D*
East Carolina University M*
Eastern Nazarene College M
Eastern University D*
East Tennessee State University M
Edgewood College M
Evangelical Theological Seminary P,M,O
Fairfield University M*
Fitchburg State College M,O
Florida Atlantic University M,O
Florida State University M,D*
Friends University M
Fuller Theological Seminary M
Geneva College M*
George Fox University M,O*
Harding University M
Hardin-Simmons University M
Hofstra University M,O*
Hope International University M
Idaho State University M,D,O
Indiana State University M,D*
Indiana Wesleyan University M
Iona College M,O*
Iowa State University of Science and Technology M,D*
John Brown University M
Johnson Bible College M
Kansas State University D*
Kean University O
Kutztown University of Pennsylvania M
La Salle University D
Lewis & Clark College M
Long Island University, Westchester Graduate Campus M
Loyola Marymount University M
Mennonite Brethren Biblical Seminary M,O
Mercy College M,O
Michigan State University M,D*
Minnesota State University Mankato M,O
Mississippi College M,O
Montclair State University M,O*
North Dakota State University M,D
Northwestern University M*
Northwest Nazarene University M
Notre Dame de Namur University M
Nova Southeastern University M,D,O*
Ottawa University M
Our Lady of Holy Cross College M
Our Lady of the Lake University of San Antonio M,D
Pacific Lutheran University M
Pacific Oaks College M
Palm Beach Atlantic University M
Phillips Graduate Institute M,D
Purdue University M,D*
Purdue University Calumet M
Reformed Theological Seminary–Jackson Campus P,M,D,O
Regions University P,M,D
Regis University M,O
St. Cloud State University M
Saint Joseph College M,O
Saint Louis University M,D,O*
Saint Mary's College of California M
Saint Mary's University of Minnesota M,O
St. Mary's University of San Antonio M,D
Saint Paul University M
St. Thomas University M,O
San Francisco State University M
Seattle Pacific University M
Seton Hall University M,O*
Seton Hill University M
Shippensburg University of Pennsylvania M,O
Sioux Falls Seminary M
Sonoma State University M
Southern Connecticut State University M
Southern Nazarene University M
Springfield College M,O*
Stetson University M
Syracuse University M,D*
Texas Tech University M,D,O
Texas Woman's University M,D
Thomas Jefferson University M*
Trevecca Nazarene University M
Universidad de las Americas, A.C. M
The University of Akron M
The University of Alabama at Birmingham M*
University of Central Florida M*
University of Florida M,D,O*
University of Great Falls M
University of Guelph M,D
University of Houston–Clear Lake M
University of La Verne M
University of Louisiana at Monroe M,D
University of Louisville M,D,O
University of Mary Hardin-Baylor M
University of Maryland, College Park M,D*
University of Massachusetts Boston M,O
University of Miami M,O*
University of Minnesota, Twin Cities Campus M,D*
University of Mobile M
University of Nevada, Las Vegas M,O
University of New Hampshire M*
The University of North Carolina at Greensboro M,D,O
University of Phoenix–Bay Area Campus M
University of Phoenix–Central Valley Campus M
University of Phoenix–Denver Campus M
University of Phoenix–Hawaii Campus M
University of Phoenix–Las Vegas Campus M
University of Phoenix–New Mexico Campus M
University of Phoenix—Northern Nevada Campus M
University of Phoenix–Puerto Rico Campus M
University of Phoenix–Sacramento Valley Campus M
University of Phoenix–San Diego Campus M
University of Phoenix–Southern Arizona Campus M,O
University of Phoenix–Southern California Campus M,O
University of Phoenix–Southern Colorado Campus M
University of Rochester M*
University of St. Thomas (MN) M,D,O*
University of San Diego M*
University of San Francisco M,D
University of Southern Mississippi M*
The University of Texas at Tyler M
The University of Winnipeg P,M,O
University of Wisconsin–Stout M*
Utah State University M,D
Valdosta State University M
Virginia Polytechnic Institute and State University M,D*
Wesley Biblical Seminary P,M
Western Michigan University M,D*
Western Seminary M

MASS COMMUNICATION

American University M*
The American University in Cairo M,O
Auburn University M*
Boston University M*
Brigham Young University M*
California State University, Fresno M
California State University, Northridge M
Central Michigan University M*
The College of Saint Rose M*
Florida International University M*
Florida State University M,D*
Fordham University M*
The George Washington University M*
Georgia State University M,D*
Grambling State University M
Howard University M,D*
Indiana University Bloomington M,D*
Iona College M*
Iowa State University of Science and Technology M*
Jackson State University M
Kansas State University M*
Kent State University M*
Louisiana State University and Agricultural and Mechanical College M,D*
Loyola University New Orleans M
Lynn University M,D
Marquette University M
Marshall University M
Miami University M*
Middle Tennessee State University M*
Murray State University M
The New School: A University M*
North Dakota State University M,D
Oklahoma City University M
Oklahoma State University M*
Penn State University Park M,D*
Point Park University M*
St. Cloud State University M
San Jose State University M
Seton Hall University M*
Southern Illinois University Carbondale M*
Southern Illinois University Edwardsville M
Southern University and Agricultural and Mechanical College M*
Stephen F. Austin State University M
Syracuse University M,D*
Temple University D*
Texas State University-San Marcos M*
Texas Tech University M,D
Université Laval M
University of Arkansas at Little Rock M
University of Central Missouri M
University of Colorado at Boulder M,D*
University of Denver M*
University of Florida M,D*
University of Georgia M,D*
University of Houston M*
University of Illinois at Chicago M*
The University of Iowa M,D*
University of Louisiana at Lafayette M*
University of Michigan D*
University of Minnesota, Twin Cities Campus M,D*
University of Nebraska–Lincoln M*
The University of North Carolina at Chapel Hill M,D*
University of Oklahoma M*
University of Puerto Rico, Río Piedras M*
University of Southern California M,D*
University of Southern Mississippi M,D*
University of South Florida M*
University of the Sacred Heart M
University of Wisconsin–Madison M,D*
University of Wisconsin–Milwaukee M
University of Wisconsin–Stevens Point M
University of Wisconsin–Superior M
University of Wisconsin–Whitewater M*
Virginia Commonwealth University M*

MATERIALS ENGINEERING

Arizona State University M,D*
Auburn University M,D*
Boise State University M
California State University, Northridge M
Carleton University M,D
Carnegie Mellon University M,D*
Case Western Reserve University M,D*
Clemson University M,D*
Colorado School of Mines M,D
Columbia University M,D,O*
Cornell University M,D*
Dartmouth College M,D*
Drexel University M,D*
École Polytechnique de Montréal M,D,O
Florida International University M,D*
Georgia Institute of Technology M,D*
Illinois Institute of Technology M,D*
Instituto Tecnológico y de Estudios Superiores de Monterrey, Campus Estado de México M,D
Iowa State University of Science and Technology M,D*
The Johns Hopkins University M,D*
Lehigh University M,D*
Massachusetts Institute of Technology M,D,O*
McGill University M,D*
McMaster University M,D
Michigan State University M,D*
Michigan Technological University M,D*
New Jersey Institute of Technology M,D
New Mexico Institute of Mining and Technology M,D
North Carolina State University M,D*
Northwestern University M,D,O*
The Ohio State University M,D*
Penn State University Park M,D*
Purdue University M,D*
Rensselaer Polytechnic Institute M,D*
Rochester Institute of Technology M
Rutgers, The State University of New Jersey, New Brunswick M,D*
San Jose State University M
Santa Clara University M,D,O
South Dakota School of Mines and Technology M,D
Stanford University M,D,O*
State University of New York at Binghamton M,D*
Stevens Institute of Technology M,D*
Stony Brook University, State University of New York M,D*
Texas A&M University M,D*
Tuskegee University D
The University of Alabama M,D
The University of Alabama at Birmingham M,D*
University of Alberta M,D*
The University of Arizona M,D*
The University of British Columbia M,D*
University of California, Berkeley M,D*
University of California, Davis M,D*
University of California, Irvine M,D*
University of California, Los Angeles M,D*
University of California, Santa Barbara M,D*
University of Central Florida M,D*
University of Cincinnati M,D
University of Connecticut M,D*
University of Dayton M,D*
University of Delaware M,D*
University of Florida M,D,O*
University of Houston M,D*
University of Idaho M,D*
University of Illinois at Chicago M,D*
University of Illinois at Urbana–Champaign M,D*
University of Maryland, College Park M,D,O*
University of Massachusetts Lowell M,D*
University of Michigan M,D*
University of Minnesota, Twin Cities Campus M,D*
University of Nebraska–Lincoln M,D*
University of Pennsylvania M,D*
University of Southern California M,D,O*
The University of Tennessee M,D*
The University of Tennessee Space Institute M*
The University of Texas at Arlington M,D*
The University of Texas at Austin M,D*
The University of Texas at Dallas M,D*
The University of Texas at El Paso D
University of Toronto M,D
University of Utah M,D*
University of Washington M,D*
University of Windsor M,D
University of Wisconsin–Madison M,D*
Virginia Polytechnic Institute and State University M,D*
Washington State University M*
Wayne State University M,D,O*
Worcester Polytechnic Institute M,D,O*
Wright State University M*

MATERIALS SCIENCES

Air Force Institute of Technology M,D
Alabama Agricultural and Mechanical University M,D
Alfred University M,D*
Arizona State University M,D*
Brown University M,D*
California Institute of Technology M,D*
Carnegie Mellon University M,D*
Case Western Reserve University M,D*
Clemson University M,D*
Colorado School of Mines M,D

Institution	Degrees
Columbia University	M,D,O*
Cornell University	M,D*
Dartmouth College	M,D*
Duke University	M,D*
École Polytechnique de Montréal	M,D,O
The George Washington University	M,D*
Illinois Institute of Technology	M,D*
Instituto Tecnológico y de Estudios Superiores de Monterrey, Campus Estado de México	M,D
Iowa State University of Science and Technology	M,D*
Jackson State University	M
The Johns Hopkins University	M,D*
Lehigh University	M,D*
Massachusetts Institute of Technology	M,D,O*
McMaster University	M,D
Michigan State University	M,D*
Missouri State University	M*
New Jersey Institute of Technology	M,D
Norfolk State University	M
North Carolina State University	M,D*
Northwestern University	M,D,O*
The Ohio State University	M,D*
Oregon State University	M,D*
Penn State University Park	M,D*
Polytechnic University, Brooklyn Campus	M*
Polytechnic University, Long Island Graduate Center	M,D
Polytechnic University, Westchester Graduate Center	D
Princeton University	*
Rensselaer Polytechnic Institute	M,D*
Rice University	M,D*
Rochester Institute of Technology	M
Royal Military College of Canada	M,D
Rutgers, The State University of New Jersey, New Brunswick	M,D*
South Dakota School of Mines and Technology	M,D
Stanford University	M,D,O*
State University of New York at Binghamton	M,D*
Stony Brook University, State University of New York	M,D*
Texas A&M Health Science Center	M*
Université du Québec, Institut National de la Recherche Scientifique	M,D
University at Buffalo, the State University of New York	M*
The University of Alabama	D
The University of Alabama at Birmingham	D*
The University of Alabama in Huntsville	M,D
The University of Arizona	M,D*
The University of British Columbia	M,D*
University of California, Berkeley	M,D*
University of California, Davis	M,D*
University of California, Irvine	M,D*
University of California, Los Angeles	M,D*
University of California, San Diego	M,D*
University of California, Santa Barbara	M,D*
University of Central Florida	M,D*
University of Cincinnati	M,D
University of Connecticut	M,D*
University of Delaware	M,D*
University of Denver	M,D*
University of Florida	M,D,O*
University of Idaho	M,D*
University of Illinois at Urbana–Champaign	M,D*
University of Kentucky	M,D*
University of Maryland, College Park	M,D,O*
University of Michigan	M,D*
University of Minnesota, Twin Cities Campus	M,D*
University of New Brunswick Fredericton	M,D
University of New Hampshire	M,D*
The University of North Carolina at Chapel Hill	M,D*
University of North Texas	M,D*
University of Pennsylvania	M,D*
University of Pittsburgh	M,D*
University of Rochester	M,D*
University of Southern California	M,D,O*
The University of Tennessee	M,D*
The University of Tennessee Space Institute	M*
The University of Texas at Arlington	M,D*
The University of Texas at Austin	M,D*
The University of Texas at El Paso	D
University of Toronto	M,D
University of Utah	M,D*
University of Vermont	M,D*
University of Virginia	M,D*
University of Washington	M,D*
University of Wisconsin–Madison	M,D*
Vanderbilt University	M,D*
Virginia Polytechnic Institute and State University	M,D*
Washington State University	M,D*
Wayne State University	M,D,O*
Worcester Polytechnic Institute	M,D,O*
Wright State University	M*

MATERNAL AND CHILD/NEONATAL NURSING

Institution	Degrees
Barnes-Jewish College of Nursing and Allied Health	M
Baylor University	M*
Boston College	M,D*
Columbia University	M,O*
Duke University	M,D,O*
Hardin-Simmons University	M
Hunter College of the City University of New York	M
Indiana University–Purdue University Indianapolis	M,D*
Lehman College of the City University of New York	M
Marquette University	M,D,O
Medical College of Georgia	M,D*
Medical University of South Carolina	M*
Northeastern University	M,O*
Rush University	M,D,O
Rutgers, The State University of New Jersey, Newark	M*
Saint Joseph College	M,O
Stony Brook University, State University of New York	M,O*
Université de Montréal	O
University at Buffalo, the State University of New York	M,D,O*
The University of Alabama in Huntsville	M,O
University of Alberta	P*
University of Cincinnati	M,D
University of Colorado at Colorado Springs	M,D
University of Connecticut	M,D,O*
University of Delaware	M,O*
University of Illinois at Chicago	M*
University of Maryland, Baltimore	M*
University of Missouri–Kansas City	M,D*
University of Pennsylvania	M,O*
University of South Alabama	M,D*
University of Southern Mississippi	M,D*
Vanderbilt University	M,D*
Wayne State University	M,O*

MATERNAL AND CHILD HEALTH

Institution	Degrees
Bank Street College of Education	M*
Boston University	M,O*
Columbia University	M*
The George Washington University	M,O*
New York Medical College	M*
Oakland University	M,D,O*
Tulane University	M,D*
The University of Alabama at Birmingham	M*
University of California, Berkeley	M*
University of California, Davis	M*
University of Minnesota, Twin Cities Campus	M*
University of Mississippi Medical Center	M*
The University of North Carolina at Chapel Hill	M,D*
University of Puerto Rico, Medical Sciences Campus	M*
University of Washington	M,D*

MATHEMATICAL AND COMPUTATIONAL FINANCE

Institution	Degrees
Bernard M. Baruch College of the City University of New York	M*
Boston University	M,D*
Carnegie Mellon University	M,D*
DePaul University	M,D*
Florida State University	M,D*
Georgia Institute of Technology	M,D*
Illinois Institute of Technology	M,D*
New York University	M*
North Carolina State University	M*
Polytechnic University, Brooklyn Campus	M,O*
Polytechnic University, Westchester Graduate Center	M,O
Rice University	M,D*
Stanford University	M,D*
University of Alberta	M,D,O*
University of California, Santa Barbara	M,D*
University of Chicago	M*
University of Connecticut	M*
University of Dayton	M*
The University of North Carolina at Charlotte	M*
University of Pittsburgh	M,D*

MATHEMATICAL PHYSICS

Institution	Degrees
New Mexico Institute of Mining and Technology	M,D
Princeton University	D*
University of Alberta	M,D,O*
University of Colorado at Boulder	M,D*
Virginia Polytechnic Institute and State University	M,D*

MATHEMATICS

Institution	Degrees
Alabama State University	M,O
American University	M*
American University of Beirut	M
Andrews University	M
Appalachian State University	M
Arizona State University	M,D*
Arkansas State University	M
Auburn University	M,D*
Aurora University	M
Ball State University	M*
Baylor University	M,D*
Boston College	M*
Boston University	M,D*
Bowling Green State University	M,D*
Brandeis University	M,D*
Brigham Young University	M,D*
Brock University	M
Brooklyn College of the City University of New York	M,D
Brown University	M,D*
Bryn Mawr College	M,D*
Bucknell University	M
California Institute of Technology	D*
California Polytechnic State University, San Luis Obispo	M
California State Polytechnic University, Pomona	M
California State University Channel Islands	M*
California State University, East Bay	M
California State University, Fresno	M
California State University, Fullerton	M
California State University, Long Beach	M
California State University, Los Angeles	M
California State University, Northridge	M
California State University, Sacramento	M*
California State University, San Bernardino	M
California State University, San Marcos	M
Carleton University	M,D
Carnegie Mellon University	M,D*
Case Western Reserve University	M,D*
Central Connecticut State University	M,O
Central Michigan University	M,D*
Central Washington University	M
Chicago State University	M
City College of the City University of New York	M*
Claremont Graduate University	M,D
Clarkson University	M,D*
Clemson University	M,D*
Cleveland State University	M
College of Charleston	M,O*
Colorado State University	M,D*
Columbia University	M,D*
Concordia University (Canada)	M,D
Cornell University	D*
Dalhousie University	M,D
Dartmouth College	D*
Delaware State University	M
DePaul University	M,O*
Dowling College	M
Drexel University	M,D*
Duke University	D*
Duquesne University	M*
East Carolina University	M*
Eastern Illinois University	M
Eastern Kentucky University	M*
Eastern Michigan University	M
Eastern New Mexico University	M
Eastern Washington University	M
East Tennessee State University	M
École Polytechnique de Montréal	M,D
Emory University	M,D*
Emporia State University	M
Fairfield University	M*
Fairleigh Dickinson University, Metropolitan Campus	M*
Fayetteville State University	M
Florida Atlantic University	M,D
Florida International University	M*
Florida State University	M,D*
The George Washington University	M,D*
Georgia Institute of Technology	M,D*
Georgian Court University	M,O
Georgia Southern University	M
Georgia State University	M*
Graduate School and University Center of the City University of New York	D*
Hardin-Simmons University	M,D
Harvard University	D*
Hofstra University	M*
Howard University	M,D*
Hunter College of the City University of New York	M
Idaho State University	M,D
Illinois State University	M*
Indiana State University	M*
Indiana University Bloomington	M,D*
Indiana University of Pennsylvania	M
Indiana University–Purdue University Fort Wayne	M,O
Iowa State University of Science and Technology	M,D*
Jackson State University	M
Jacksonville State University	M
James Madison University	M
John Carroll University	M
The Johns Hopkins University	D*
Kansas State University	M,D*
Kean University	M
Kent State University	M,D*
Lakehead University	M
Lamar University	M*
Lehigh University	M,D*
Lehman College of the City University of New York	M
Long Island University, C.W. Post Campus	M*
Louisiana State University and Agricultural and Mechanical College	M,D*
Louisiana Tech University	M
Loyola University Chicago	M*
Marquette University	M,D
Marshall University	M
Massachusetts Institute of Technology	D*
McGill University	M,D*
McMaster University	M,D*
McNeese State University	M
Memorial University of Newfoundland	M,D
Miami University	M*
Michigan State University	M,D*
Michigan Technological University	M,D*
Middle Tennessee State University	M*
Minnesota State University Mankato	M
Mississippi College	M
Mississippi State University	M,D
Missouri State University	M*
Montana State University	M,D
Montclair State University	M,O*
Morgan State University	M*
Murray State University	M
Naval Postgraduate School	M,D
New Jersey Institute of Technology	D
New Mexico Institute of Mining and Technology	M,D
New Mexico State University	M,D
New York University	M,D*
Nicholls State University	M
North Carolina Central University	M
North Carolina State University	M,D*
North Dakota State University	M,D
Northeastern Illinois University	M
Northeastern University	M,D*
Northern Arizona University	M
Northern Illinois University	M,D
Northwestern University	D*
Oakland University	M*
The Ohio State University	M,D*
Ohio University	M,D*
Oklahoma State University	M,D*
Old Dominion University	M,D*
Oregon State University	M,D*
Penn State University Park	M,D*
Pittsburg State University	M
Polytechnic University, Brooklyn Campus	M,D*

P—first professional degree; M—master's degree; D—doctorate; O—other advanced degree;
**full description and/or announcement in Book 2, 3, 4, 5, or 6*

Institution	Degrees
Portland State University	M,D,O
Prairie View A&M University	M
Princeton University	D*
Purdue University	M,D*
Purdue University Calumet	M
Queens College of the City University of New York	M
Queen's University at Kingston	M,D
Rensselaer Polytechnic Institute	M,D*
Rhode Island College	M
Rice University	M,D*
Rivier College	M
Roosevelt University	M
Rowan University	M
Royal Military College of Canada	M
Rutgers, The State University of New Jersey, Camden	M
Rutgers, The State University of New Jersey, Newark	D*
Rutgers, The State University of New Jersey, New Brunswick	M,D*
St. Cloud State University	M
St. John's University (NY)	M
Saint Joseph's University	M,O*
Saint Louis University	M,D*
Saint Xavier University	M
Salem State College	M
Sam Houston State University	M
San Diego State University	M,D*
San Francisco State University	M
San Jose State University	M
Simon Fraser University	M,D
South Dakota State University	M,D
Southeast Missouri State University	M
Southern Connecticut State University	M
Southern Illinois University Carbondale	M,D*
Southern Illinois University Edwardsville	M
Southern Methodist University	M,D*
Southern Oregon University	M
Southern University and Agricultural and Mechanical College	M*
Stanford University	M,D*
State University of New York at Binghamton	M,D*
State University of New York at Fredonia	M
State University of New York at New Paltz	M
State University of New York College at Brockport	M*
State University of New York College at Cortland	M*
State University of New York College at Potsdam	M
Stephen F. Austin State University	M
Stevens Institute of Technology	M,D*
Stony Brook University, State University of New York	M,D*
Syracuse University	M,D*
Tarleton State University	M
Temple University	M,D*
Tennessee State University	M*
Tennessee Technological University	M*
Texas A&M International University	M
Texas A&M University	M,D*
Texas A&M University–Commerce	M
Texas A&M University–Corpus Christi	M
Texas A&M University–Kingsville	M
Texas Christian University	M
Texas Southern University	M
Texas State University-San Marcos	M*
Texas Tech University	M,D
Texas Woman's University	M
Tufts University	M,D*
Tulane University	M,D*
Université de Moncton	M
Université de Montréal	M,D
Université de Sherbrooke	M,D
Université du Québec à Montréal	M,D
Université du Québec à Trois-Rivières	M
Université Laval	M,D
University at Albany, State University of New York	M,D*
University at Buffalo, the State University of New York	M,D*
The University of Akron	M
The University of Alabama	M,D
The University of Alabama at Birmingham	M,D*
The University of Alabama in Huntsville	M,D
University of Alaska Fairbanks	M,D
University of Alberta	M,D,O*
The University of Arizona	M,D*
University of Arkansas	M,D*
University of Arkansas at Little Rock	M
The University of British Columbia	M,D*
University of Calgary	M,D
University of California, Berkeley	M,D*
University of California, Davis	M,D*
University of California, Irvine	M,D*
University of California, Los Angeles	M,D*
University of California, Riverside	M,D*
University of California, San Diego	M,D*
University of California, Santa Barbara	M,D*
University of California, Santa Cruz	M,D*
University of Central Arkansas	M
University of Central Florida	M,D,O*
University of Central Missouri	M
University of Central Oklahoma	M
University of Chicago	M,D*
University of Cincinnati	M,D
University of Colorado at Boulder	M,D*
University of Colorado at Denver and Health Sciences Center	M*
University of Connecticut	M,D*
University of Delaware	M,D*
University of Denver	M,D*
University of Detroit Mercy	M
University of Florida	M,D*
University of Georgia	M,D*
University of Guelph	M,D
University of Hawaii at Manoa	M,D*
University of Houston	M,D*
University of Houston–Clear Lake	M
University of Idaho	M,D*
University of Illinois at Chicago	M,D*
University of Illinois at Urbana–Champaign	M,D*
The University of Iowa	M,D*
University of Kansas	M,D*
University of Kentucky	M,D*
University of Lethbridge	M,D
University of Louisiana at Lafayette	M,D*
University of Louisville	M,D
University of Maine	M*
University of Manitoba	M,D
University of Maryland, College Park	M,D*
University of Massachusetts Amherst	M,D*
University of Massachusetts Lowell	M,D*
University of Memphis	M,D*
University of Miami	M,D*
University of Michigan	M,D*
University of Minnesota, Twin Cities Campus	M,D*
University of Mississippi	M,D
University of Missouri–Columbia	M,D*
University of Missouri–Kansas City	M,D*
University of Missouri–Rolla	M,D*
University of Missouri–St. Louis	M,D
The University of Montana	M,D*
University of Nebraska at Omaha	M
University of Nebraska–Lincoln	M,D*
University of Nevada, Las Vegas	M,D
University of Nevada, Reno	M*
University of New Brunswick Fredericton	M,D
University of New Hampshire	M,D*
University of New Mexico	M,D*
University of New Orleans	M
The University of North Carolina at Chapel Hill	M,D*
The University of North Carolina at Charlotte	M,D*
The University of North Carolina at Greensboro	M
The University of North Carolina Wilmington	M*
University of North Dakota	M
University of Northern British Columbia	M,D,O
University of Northern Colorado	M,D
University of Northern Iowa	M
University of North Florida	M
University of North Texas	M,D*
University of Notre Dame	M,D*
University of Oklahoma	M,D*
University of Oregon	M,D*
University of Ottawa	M,D*
University of Pennsylvania	M,D*
University of Pittsburgh	M,D*
University of Puerto Rico, Mayagüez Campus	M*
University of Puerto Rico, Río Piedras	M,D*
University of Regina	M,D
University of Rhode Island	M,D
University of Rochester	M,D*
University of Saskatchewan	M,D
University of South Alabama	M*
University of South Carolina	M,D*
The University of South Dakota	M
University of Southern California	M,D*
University of Southern Mississippi	M,D*
University of South Florida	M,D,O*
The University of Tennessee	M,D*
The University of Texas at Arlington	M,D*
The University of Texas at Austin	M,D*
The University of Texas at Brownsville	M
The University of Texas at Dallas	M,D*
The University of Texas at El Paso	M
The University of Texas at Tyler	M
The University of Texas–Pan American	M
University of the Incarnate Word	M
The University of Toledo	M,D*
University of Toronto	M,D
University of Tulsa	M*
University of Utah	M,D*
University of Vermont	M,D*
University of Victoria	M,D
University of Virginia	M,D*
University of Washington	M,D*
University of Waterloo	M,D*
The University of Western Ontario	M,D
University of West Florida	M
University of Windsor	M,D
University of Wisconsin–Madison	M,D*
University of Wisconsin–Milwaukee	M,D
University of Wyoming	M,D
Utah State University	M,D
Vanderbilt University	M,D*
Villanova University	M*
Virginia Commonwealth University	M,O*
Virginia Polytechnic Institute and State University	M,D*
Virginia State University	M
Wake Forest University	M*
Washington State University	M,D*
Washington University in St. Louis	M,D*
Wayne State University	M,D*
Wesleyan University	M,D*
West Chester University of Pennsylvania	M
Western Carolina University	M*
Western Connecticut State University	M*
Western Illinois University	M,O
Western Kentucky University	M
Western Michigan University	M,D*
Western Washington University	M
West Texas A&M University	M
West Virginia University	M,D*
Wichita State University	M,D*
Wilfrid Laurier University	M
Wilkes University	M
Worcester Polytechnic Institute	M,D,O*
Wright State University	M*
Yale University	M,D*
York University	M,D*
Youngstown State University	M

MATHEMATICS EDUCATION

Institution	Degrees
Acadia University	M
Agnes Scott College	M*
Alabama State University	M,O
Albany State University	M
Appalachian State University	M
Arcadia University	M,D,O
Arkansas Tech University	M
Armstrong Atlantic State University	M
Asbury College	M,O
Auburn University	M,D,O*
Averett University	M
Ball State University	M*
Bank Street College of Education	M*
Belmont University	M
Bemidji State University	M
Bennington College	M*
Bob Jones University	P,M,D,O
Boston College	M*
Boston University	M,D,O*
Bowling Green State University	M,D*
Bridgewater State College	M
Brigham Young University	M*
Brooklyn College of the City University of New York	M,D,O
Buffalo State College, State University of New York	M
California State University, Bakersfield	M
California State University, Chico	M
California State University, Dominguez Hills	M
California State University, Fresno	M
California State University, Fullerton	M
California State University, Long Beach	M
California State University, Northridge	M
Campbell University	M
Chatham University	M
Cheyney University of Pennsylvania	O
Christopher Newport University	M
City College of the City University of New York	M,O*
Clemson University	M*
Cleveland State University	M
College of Charleston	M*
College of St. Joseph	M
The College of William and Mary	M
The Colorado College	M
Columbus State University	M,O
Concordia University (Canada)	M,D
Connecticut College	M
Converse College	M
Cornell University	M,D*
Delta State University	M
DePaul University	M,O*
DeSales University	M,O
Drake University	M*
East Carolina University	M*
Eastern Illinois University	M
Eastern Kentucky University	M*
Eastern Michigan University	M
Eastern Washington University	M
Edinboro University of Pennsylvania	M
Florida Agricultural and Mechanical University	M*
Florida Gulf Coast University	M
Florida Institute of Technology	M,D,O*
Florida International University	M,D*
Florida State University	M,D,O*
Framingham State College	M*
Fresno Pacific University	M
Georgia College & State University	M,O
Georgia Southern University	M
Georgia State University	M,D,O*
Harding University	M,O
Harvard University	M,O*
Henderson State University	M,O
Hofstra University	M*
Hood College	M,O
Hunter College of the City University of New York	M
Idaho State University	M,D
Illinois Institute of Technology	M,D*
Illinois State University	D*
Indiana University Bloomington	M,D,O*
Indiana University of Pennsylvania	M
Indiana University–Purdue University Indianapolis	M*
Instituto Tecnológico y de Estudios Superiores de Monterrey, Campus Ciudad Obregón	M
Inter American University of Puerto Rico, Ponce Campus	M
Iona College	M*
Iowa State University of Science and Technology	M,D*
Ithaca College	M
Jackson State University	M
Jacksonville University	M
Kean University	M
Kutztown University of Pennsylvania	M,O
Lehman College of the City University of New York	M
Long Island University, Brooklyn Campus	M*
Long Island University, C.W. Post Campus	M*
Louisiana Tech University	M,D
Loyola Marymount University	M
Manhattanville College	M*
Marquette University	M,D
Miami University	M*
Michigan State University	M,D*
Middle Tennessee State University	M*
Millersville University of Pennsylvania	M
Mills College	M,D
Minnesota State University Mankato	M
Minot State University	M
Mississippi College	M,O
Montclair State University	M,D,O*
Morgan State University	M,D*
National-Louis University	M,O
New Jersey City University	M
New York University	M*

Nicholls State University M
North Carolina Agricultural and Technical State University M
North Carolina State University M,D*
North Dakota State University M,D,O
Northeastern Illinois University M
Northeastern State University M
Northern Arizona University M
North Georgia College & State University M,O
Northwestern State University of Louisiana M
Northwest Missouri State University M
Nova Southeastern University M,O*
Oakland University M,D,O*
Occidental College M
Ohio University M,D*
Oklahoma State University M,D*
Oregon State University M,D*
Plymouth State University M
Portland State University M,D
Providence College M*
Purdue University M,D,O*
Purdue University Calumet M
Queens College of the City University of New York M,O
Quinnipiac University M*
Rider University M,O*
Rollins College M
Rutgers, The State University of New Jersey, New Brunswick M,D*
Sage Graduate School M
St. John Fisher College M
Salisbury University M
San Diego State University M,D*
San Francisco State University M
San Jose State University M
Simon Fraser University M,D
Slippery Rock University of Pennsylvania M
Smith College M*
South Carolina State University M
Southern Illinois University Edwardsville M
Southern University and Agricultural and Mechanical College D*
Southwestern Oklahoma State University M
Stanford University M,D*
State University of New York at Binghamton M*
State University of New York at Plattsburgh M
State University of New York College at Brockport M*
State University of New York College at Cortland M*
Stephen F. Austin State University M
Stony Brook University, State University of New York M,O*
Syracuse University M,D*
Teachers College Columbia University M,D*
Temple University M,D*
Texas A&M University M,D*
Texas A&M University–Corpus Christi M
Texas State University-San Marcos M*
Texas Woman's University M
Towson University M
Trinity (Washington) University M
Union Graduate College M*
University at Albany, State University of New York M,D*
University at Buffalo, the State University of New York M,D,O*
University of Arkansas M*
University of Arkansas at Pine Bluff M
The University of British Columbia M,D*
University of California, Berkeley M,D*
University of California, San Diego D*
University of Central Florida M,D,O*
University of Central Oklahoma M
University of Cincinnati M,D
University of Connecticut M,D*
University of Dayton M*
University of Detroit Mercy M
University of Florida M,D,O*
University of Georgia M,D,O*
University of Houston M,D*
University of Illinois at Chicago M*
University of Illinois at Urbana–Champaign M,D*
University of Indianapolis M
The University of Iowa M,D*
University of Massachusetts Lowell M,D,O*
University of Miami M,D,O*
University of Michigan M,D*
University of Minnesota, Twin Cities Campus M*
University of Missouri–Columbia M,D,O*
University of Missouri–Rolla M,D*
The University of Montana M,D*
University of Nevada, Las Vegas M,D,O
University of Nevada, Reno M*
University of New Hampshire M,D*
The University of North Carolina at Chapel Hill M*
The University of North Carolina at Charlotte M*
The University of North Carolina at Greensboro M,D,O
The University of North Carolina at Pembroke M
University of Northern Colorado M,D
University of Northern Iowa M
University of Oklahoma M,D,O*
University of Phoenix–Omaha Campus M
University of Phoenix Online Campus M
University of Phoenix–Springfield Campus M
University of Pittsburgh M,D*
University of Puerto Rico, Río Piedras M,D*
University of Rio Grande M
University of St. Francis (IL) M
University of South Carolina M,D*
University of Southern Mississippi M,D*
University of South Florida M,D,O*
The University of Tampa M
The University of Tennessee M,D,O*
The University of Texas at Austin M,D*
The University of Texas at Dallas M*
The University of Texas at San Antonio M*
The University of Texas at Tyler M
University of the District of Columbia M
University of the Incarnate Word M,D
University of the Virgin Islands M
The University of Toledo M*
University of Tulsa M*
University of Vermont M,D*
University of Victoria M,D
University of Washington M,D
The University of West Alabama M
University of West Georgia M,O
University of Wisconsin–Eau Claire M
University of Wisconsin–Madison M,D*
University of Wisconsin–Oshkosh M
University of Wisconsin–River Falls M
University of Wyoming M,D
Vanderbilt University M,D*
Virginia State University M
Walden University M,D
Washington State University M,D*
Washington University in St. Louis M,D*
Wayne State College M
Wayne State University M,D,O*
Webster University M,O
Wesleyan College M
Western Carolina University M*
Western Connecticut State University M*
Western Governors University M,O
Western Michigan University M,D*
Western New England College M
Western Oregon University M
West Virginia University M,D*
Widener University M,D*
Wilkes University M
Wright State University M*

MECHANICAL ENGINEERING

Alfred University M*
American University of Beirut M*
Arizona State University M,D*
Arizona State University at the Polytechnic Campus M
Auburn University M,D*
Baylor University M*
Boise State University M
Boston University M,D*
Bradley University M
Brigham Young University M,D*
Brown University M,D*
Bucknell University M
California Institute of Technology M,D,O*
California Polytechnic State University, San Luis Obispo M
California State Polytechnic University, Pomona M
California State University, Fresno M
California State University, Fullerton M
California State University, Long Beach M,D
California State University, Los Angeles M
California State University, Northridge M
California State University, Sacramento M*
Carleton University M,D
Carnegie Mellon University M,D*
Case Western Reserve University M,D*
The Catholic University of America M,D*
City College of the City University of New York M,D*
Clarkson University M,D*
Clemson University M,D*
Cleveland State University M,D
Colorado State University M,D*
Columbia University M,D,O*
Concordia University (Canada) M,D,O
Cooper Union for the Advancement of Science and Art M
Cornell University M,D*
Dalhousie University M,D
Dartmouth College M,D*
Drexel University M,D*
Duke University M,D*
École Polytechnique de Montréal M,D,O
Fairfield University M*
Florida Agricultural and Mechanical University M,D*
Florida Atlantic University M,D
Florida Institute of Technology M,D*
Florida International University M,D*
Florida State University M,D*
Gannon University M
The George Washington University M,D,O*
Georgia Institute of Technology M,D*
Georgia Southern University M
Graduate School and University Center of the City University of New York D*
Grand Valley State University M
Howard University M,D*
Idaho State University M,D,O
Illinois Institute of Technology M,D*
Indiana University–Purdue University Indianapolis M,D,O*
Instituto Tecnológico y de Estudios Superiores de Monterrey, Campus Chihuahua M,O
Instituto Tecnológico y de Estudios Superiores de Monterrey, Campus Monterrey M,D
Iowa State University of Science and Technology M,D*
The Johns Hopkins University M,D*
Kansas State University M,D*
Kettering University M
Lamar University M,D*
Lawrence Technological University M,D
Lehigh University M,D*
Louisiana State University and Agricultural and Mechanical College M,D*
Louisiana Tech University M,D
Loyola Marymount University M
Manhattan College M
Marquette University M,D
Massachusetts Institute of Technology M,D,O*
McGill University M,D*
McMaster University M,D
McNeese State University M
Memorial University of Newfoundland M,D
Mercer University M
Michigan State University M,D*
Michigan Technological University M,D*
Mississippi State University M,D
Montana State University M,D
Naval Postgraduate School M,D,O
New Jersey Institute of Technology M,D,O
New Mexico State University M,D
North Carolina Agricultural and Technical State University M,D
North Carolina State University M,D*
North Dakota State University M,D
Northeastern University M,D*
Northern Illinois University M
Northwestern University M,D*
Oakland University M,D*
The Ohio State University M,D*
Ohio University M,D*
Oklahoma State University M,D*
Old Dominion University M,D*
Oregon State University M,D*
Penn State University Park M,D*
Polytechnic University, Brooklyn Campus M,D*
Polytechnic University, Long Island Graduate Center M,D
Portland State University M,D,O
Princeton University M,D*
Purdue University M,D,O*
Queen's University at Kingston M,D
Rensselaer at Hartford M
Rensselaer Polytechnic Institute M,D*
Rice University M,D*
Rochester Institute of Technology M
Rose-Hulman Institute of Technology M*
Royal Military College of Canada M,D
Rutgers, The State University of New Jersey, New Brunswick M,D*
St. Cloud State University M
San Diego State University M,D*
San Jose State University M
Santa Clara University M,D,O
South Carolina State University M
South Dakota School of Mines and Technology M,D
South Dakota State University M
Southern Illinois University Carbondale M*
Southern Illinois University Edwardsville M
Southern Methodist University M,D*
Stanford University M,D,O*
State University of New York at Binghamton M,D*
Stevens Institute of Technology M,D,O*
Stony Brook University, State University of New York M,D,O*
Syracuse University M,D*
Temple University M*
Tennessee Technological University M,D*
Texas A&M University M,D*
Texas A&M University–Kingsville M
Texas Tech University M,D
Tufts University M,D*
Tulane University M,D*
Tuskegee University M
Union Graduate College M*
Universidad Central del Este M
Université de Moncton M
Université de Sherbrooke M,D
Université Laval M,D
University at Buffalo, the State University of New York M,D*
The University of Akron M,D
The University of Alabama M,D
The University of Alabama at Birmingham M,D*
The University of Alabama in Huntsville M,D
University of Alaska Fairbanks M,D
University of Alberta M,D*
The University of Arizona M,D*
University of Arkansas M,D*
University of Bridgeport M
The University of British Columbia M,D*
University of Calgary M,D
University of California, Berkeley M,D*
University of California, Davis M,D,O*
University of California, Irvine M,D*
University of California, Los Angeles M,D*
University of California, Riverside M,D*
University of California, San Diego M,D*
University of California, Santa Barbara M,D*
University of Central Florida M,D,O*
University of Cincinnati M,D
University of Colorado at Boulder M,D*
University of Colorado at Colorado Springs M
University of Colorado at Denver and Health Sciences Center M*
University of Connecticut M,D*
University of Dayton M,D*
University of Delaware M,D*
University of Denver M,D*
University of Detroit Mercy M,D
University of Florida M,D,O*
University of Hawaii at Manoa M,D*
University of Houston M,D*
University of Idaho M,D*
University of Illinois at Chicago M,D*
University of Illinois at Urbana–Champaign M,D*

P—first professional degree; M—master's degree; D—doctorate; O—other advanced degree;
**full description and/or announcement in Book 2, 3, 4, 5, or 6*

The University of Iowa M,D*
University of Kansas M,D*
University of Kentucky M,D*
University of Louisiana at Lafayette M*
University of Louisville M
University of Maine M,D*
University of Manitoba M,D
University of Maryland, Baltimore County M,D,O*
University of Maryland, College Park M,D,O*
University of Massachusetts Amherst M,D*
University of Massachusetts Dartmouth M
University of Massachusetts Lowell M,D,O*
University of Memphis M,D*
University of Miami M,D*
University of Michigan M,D*
University of Michigan–Dearborn M*
University of Minnesota, Twin Cities Campus M,D*
University of Missouri–Columbia M,D*
University of Missouri–Kansas City M,D*
University of Missouri–Rolla M,D*
University of Nebraska–Lincoln M,D*
University of Nevada, Las Vegas M,D
University of Nevada, Reno M,D*
University of New Brunswick Fredericton M,D
University of New Hampshire M,D*
University of New Haven M*
University of New Mexico M,D*
University of New Orleans M
The University of North Carolina at Charlotte M,D*
University of North Dakota M
University of Notre Dame M,D*
University of Oklahoma M,D*
University of Ottawa M,D*
University of Pennsylvania M,D*
University of Pittsburgh M,D*
University of Puerto Rico, Mayagüez Campus M*
University of Rhode Island M,D
University of Rochester M,D*
University of Saskatchewan M,D
University of South Alabama M*
University of South Carolina M,D*
University of Southern California M,D,O*
University of South Florida M,D*
The University of Tennessee M,D*
The University of Tennessee Space Institute M,D*
The University of Texas at Arlington M,D*
The University of Texas at Austin M,D*
The University of Texas at El Paso M
The University of Texas at San Antonio M*
The University of Toledo M,D*
University of Toronto M,D
University of Tulsa M,D*
University of Utah M,D*
University of Vermont M,D*
University of Victoria M,D
University of Virginia M,D*
University of Washington M,D*
University of Waterloo M,D*
University of Windsor M,D
University of Wisconsin–Madison M,D*
University of Wyoming M,D
Utah State University M,D
Vanderbilt University M,D*
Villanova University M,O*
Virginia Commonwealth University M,D*
Virginia Polytechnic Institute and State University M,D*
Washington State University M,D*
Washington State University Tri-Cities M,D
Washington State University Vancouver M
Washington University in St. Louis M,D*
Wayne State University M,D*
Western Michigan University M,D*
Western New England College M
West Virginia University M,D*
Wichita State University M,D*
Widener University M*
Woods Hole Oceanographic Institution M,D,O
Worcester Polytechnic Institute M,D,O*
Wright State University M*
Yale University M,D*
Youngstown State University M

MECHANICS

Brown University M,D*
California Institute of Technology M,D*
California State University, Fullerton M
Case Western Reserve University M,D*
The Catholic University of America M,D*
Columbia University M,D,O*
Cornell University M,D*
Drexel University M,D*
École Polytechnique de Montréal M,D,O
Georgia Institute of Technology M,D*
Idaho State University M,D,O
Iowa State University of Science and Technology M,D*
Lehigh University M,D*
Louisiana State University and Agricultural and Mechanical College M,D*
Massachusetts Institute of Technology M,D,O*
McGill University M,D*
Michigan State University M,D*
Michigan Technological University M*
Mississippi State University M
New Mexico Institute of Mining and Technology M
North Dakota State University M,D
Northwestern University M,D*
The Ohio State University M,D*
Penn State University Park M,D*
Rutgers, The State University of New Jersey, New Brunswick M,D*
San Diego State University M,D*
Southern Illinois University Carbondale M,D*
The University of Alabama M,D
The University of Arizona M,D*
University of California, Berkeley M,D*
University of California, San Diego M,D*
University of Cincinnati M,D
University of Dayton M*
University of Illinois at Urbana–Champaign M,D*
University of Maryland, College Park M,D*
University of Massachusetts Lowell M,D*
University of Minnesota, Twin Cities Campus M,D*
University of Missouri–Rolla M,D*
University of Nebraska–Lincoln M,D*
University of New Brunswick Fredericton M,D
University of Pennsylvania M,D*
University of Rhode Island M,D
University of Southern California M*
The University of Tennessee M,D*
The University of Tennessee Space Institute M,D*
The University of Texas at Austin M,D*
University of Virginia M*
University of Wisconsin–Madison M,D*
Virginia Polytechnic Institute and State University M,D*
Yale University M,D*

MEDIA STUDIES

American University M*
Arkansas State University M
Bob Jones University P,M,D,O
Boston University M*
California State University, Fullerton M
Carnegie Mellon University M*
Central Michigan University M*
City College of the City University of New York M*
College of Staten Island of the City University of New York M
Columbia College Chicago M
Concordia University (Canada) M,D,O
Dallas Theological Seminary M,D,O
Edinboro University of Pennsylvania M
Emerson College M*
Fairleigh Dickinson University, Metropolitan Campus M*
Florida State University M,D*
Fordham University M*
Governors State University M
Howard University M,D*
Hunter College of the City University of New York M
Indiana State University M*
International University in Geneva M
Kutztown University of Pennsylvania M
Louisiana State University and Agricultural and Mechanical College M,D*
Lynn University M,D
Marquette University M
Marywood University M,O*
Massachusetts Institute of Technology M,D*
Metropolitan College of New York M
Michigan State University M,D*
Monmouth University M,O
National University M
New College of California M*
The New School: A University M*
New York University M,D*
Norfolk State University M
Northwestern University M,D*
Ohio University M,D*
Rochester Institute of Technology M
Saginaw Valley State University M
San Diego State University M*
San Francisco State University M
Savannah College of Art and Design M*
Southern Illinois University Carbondale M*
Southern Illinois University Edwardsville O
Syracuse University M*
Temple University M,D*
Texas Southern University M
University at Buffalo, the State University of New York M,O*
The University of Alabama M
The University of Arizona M*
University of California, Santa Barbara M,D*
University of Chicago M,D*
University of Colorado at Boulder D*
University of Denver M*
University of Florida M,D*
The University of Iowa M,D*
University of Lethbridge M,D
University of Maryland, College Park M,D*
University of Michigan M*
University of Nevada, Las Vegas M
University of South Carolina M*
University of Southern California M*
The University of Tennessee M,D*
The University of Texas at Austin M,D*
The University of Western Ontario M,D
Virginia Commonwealth University D*
Washington State University M,D*
Wayne State University M,D*
Webster University M
William Paterson University of New Jersey M*

MEDICAL/SURGICAL NURSING

Angelo State University M
Case Western Reserve University M,D*
Columbia University M,O*
Daemen College M,O
Eastern Virginia Medical School O
Emory University M*
Gannon University M,O
George Mason University M,D,O*
Hunter College of the City University of New York M
Kent State University M,D*
La Salle University M,O
New Mexico State University M
Pontifical Catholic University of Puerto Rico M
Rush University M,D,O
Sage Graduate School M
Saint Francis Medical Center College of Nursing M,O
University of Illinois at Chicago M*
University of Maryland, Baltimore M*
University of Michigan M*
University of South Carolina M*
University of Southern Maine M,O
Vanderbilt University M,D*

MEDICAL ILLUSTRATION

The Johns Hopkins University M*
Medical College of Georgia M*
Rochester Institute of Technology M
University of Illinois at Chicago M*
The University of Texas Southwestern Medical Center at Dallas M*

MEDICAL IMAGING

MGH Institute of Health Professions O*
University of Cincinnati D
University of Florida M,D*
University of Medicine and Dentistry of New Jersey M*
University of Southern California M*

MEDICAL INFORMATICS

A.T. Still University of Health Sciences M,D
Columbia University M,D,O*
Excelsior College O
Grand Valley State University M
Harvard University M*
Marymount University M,O
Massachusetts Institute of Technology M*
Medical College of Wisconsin M*
Milwaukee School of Engineering M*
Oregon Health & Science University M,D,O*
Stanford University M,D*
University of California, Davis M*
University of California, San Francisco M,D
University of Illinois at Urbana–Champaign M,D,O*
University of Medicine and Dentistry of New Jersey M,D,O*
University of Washington M,D*
University of Wisconsin–Milwaukee D

MEDICAL MICROBIOLOGY

Creighton University M,D*
Idaho State University M,D
Rosalind Franklin University of Medicine and Science M,D*
Rutgers, The State University of New Jersey, New Brunswick M,D*
Texas Tech University Health Sciences Center M,D
Université du Québec, Institut National de la Recherche Scientifique M,D
University of Alberta M,D*
University of Hawaii at Manoa M,D*
University of Manitoba M,D
University of Minnesota, Duluth M,D*
University of South Florida M,D*
University of Wisconsin–La Crosse M
University of Wisconsin–Madison D*

MEDICAL PHYSICS

Cleveland State University M
Columbia University M,D,O*
Drexel University M,D*
East Carolina University M,D*
Georgia Institute of Technology M,D*
Harvard University D*
Massachusetts Institute of Technology D*
McGill University M,D*
McMaster University M,D
Oakland University M,D*
Rosalind Franklin University of Medicine and Science M,D*
Rush University M,D
Stony Brook University, State University of New York D*
University of Alberta M,D*
University of California, Los Angeles M,D*
University of Central Arkansas M
University of Cincinnati M
University of Colorado at Boulder M,D*
University of Kentucky M*
University of Massachusetts Worcester D*
University of Minnesota, Twin Cities Campus M,D*
University of Missouri–Columbia M,D*
University of Oklahoma Health Sciences Center M,D
University of Pennsylvania M,D*
The University of Texas Health Science Center at Houston M,D*
The University of Texas Health Science Center at San Antonio M,D*
The University of Toledo M*
University of Victoria M,D
University of Wisconsin–Madison M,D*
Vanderbilt University M*
Virginia Commonwealth University M,D*
Wayne State University M,D*
Wright State University M*

MEDICINAL AND PHARMACEUTICAL CHEMISTRY

Duquesne University M,D*
Florida Agricultural and Mechanical University M,D*

Idaho State University M,D
Lehigh University M,D*
Long Island University, C.W. Post Campus M*
The Ohio State University M,D*
Purdue University M,D*
Rutgers, The State University of New Jersey, New Brunswick M,D*
Temple University M,D*
University at Buffalo, the State University of New York M,D*
University of California, San Francisco D
University of Connecticut M,D*
University of Florida P,M,D*
University of Georgia M,D*
University of Kansas M,D*
University of Michigan D*
University of Minnesota, Twin Cities Campus M,D*
University of Mississippi M,D
University of Rhode Island M,D
University of the Sciences in Philadelphia M,D*
The University of Toledo M,D*
University of Utah M,D*
University of Washington D*
Wayne State University P,M,D*
West Virginia University M,D*

MEDIEVAL AND RENAISSANCE STUDIES

The Catholic University of America M,D,O*
Central European University M,D*
Columbia University M*
Cornell University M,D*
Duke University O*
Fordham University M,O*
Graduate School and University Center of the City University of New York M,D*
Harvard University D*
Indiana University Bloomington M,D*
Marquette University M,D
Rutgers, The State University of New Jersey, New Brunswick D*
Southern Methodist University M*
Tufts University M,D*
University of Colorado at Boulder M,D*
University of Connecticut M,D*
University of Guelph D
University of Minnesota, Twin Cities Campus M,D*
University of Notre Dame M,D*
University of Toronto M,D
Western Michigan University M*
Yale University M,D*

METALLURGICAL ENGINEERING AND METALLURGY

Colorado School of Mines M,D
Columbia University M,D,O*
Dalhousie University M,D
École Polytechnique de Montréal M,D,O
Laurentian University M
Massachusetts Institute of Technology M,D,O*
Michigan Technological University M,D*
Montana Tech of The University of Montana M
The Ohio State University M,D*
Penn State University Park M,D*
Rensselaer Polytechnic Institute M,D*
South Dakota School of Mines and Technology M,D
Université Laval M,D
The University of Alabama M,D
The University of British Columbia M,D*
University of California, Los Angeles M,D*
University of Cincinnati M,D
University of Connecticut M,D*
University of Idaho M*
University of Missouri–Rolla M,D*
University of Nevada, Reno M,D,O*
The University of Texas at El Paso M
University of Utah M,D*
Wayne State University M,D,O*

METEOROLOGY

Columbia University M*
Florida Institute of Technology M,D*
Florida State University M,D*
Iowa State University of Science and Technology M,D*
McGill University M,D*
Naval Postgraduate School M,D
North Carolina State University M,D*
Penn State University Park M,D*
Plymouth State University M
Saint Louis University M,D*
San Jose State University M
Texas A&M University M,D*
Université du Québec à Montréal M,D,O
University of Hawaii at Manoa M,D*
University of Maryland, College Park M,D*
University of Miami M,D*
University of Oklahoma M,D*
University of Utah M,D*
Utah State University M,D
Yale University D*

MICROBIOLOGY

Albany Medical College M,D
Albert Einstein College of Medicine D*
American University of Beirut P,M
Arizona State University M,D*
Auburn University M,D*
Baylor College of Medicine D*
Boston University M,D*
Brandeis University M,D*
Brigham Young University M,D*
Brown University M,D*
California State University, Fullerton M
California State University, Long Beach M
Case Western Reserve University D*
The Catholic University of America M,D*
Clemson University M,D*
Colorado State University M,D*
Columbia University M,D*
Cornell University D*
Dalhousie University M,D
Dartmouth College D*
Drexel University M,D*
Duke University D*
East Carolina University D*
East Tennessee State University M,D
Emory University D*
Emporia State University M
Florida State University M,D*
George Mason University M,D,O*
Georgetown University M,D*
The George Washington University M,D,O*
Georgia State University M,D*
Harvard University D*
Howard University D*
Idaho State University M,D
Illinois State University M,D*
Indiana State University M,D*
Indiana University Bloomington M,D*
Indiana University–Purdue University Indianapolis M,D*
Iowa State University of Science and Technology M,D*
The Johns Hopkins University M,D*
Kansas State University D*
Loma Linda University M,D
Long Island University, C.W. Post Campus M*
Louisiana State University Health Sciences Center M,D*
Louisiana State University Health Sciences Center at Shreveport M,D*
Loyola University Chicago M,D*
Marquette University M,D
McGill University M,D*
Medical College of Wisconsin M,D*
Medical University of South Carolina M,D*
Meharry Medical College D
Miami University M,D*
Michigan State University M,D*
Montana State University M,D
Mount Sinai School of Medicine of New York University M,D*
New York Medical College M,D*
New York University M,D*
North Carolina State University M,D*
North Dakota State University M,D
Northwestern University D*
The Ohio State University M,D*
Ohio University M,D*
Oklahoma State University M,D*
Oregon Health & Science University D*
Oregon State University M,D*
Penn State Hershey Medical Center M,D*
Penn State University Park M,D*
Purdue University M,D*
Queen's University at Kingston M,D
Quinnipiac University M*
Rensselaer Polytechnic Institute M,D*
Rosalind Franklin University of Medicine and Science M,D*
Rush University M,D
Rutgers, The State University of New Jersey, New Brunswick M,D*
Saint Louis University D*
San Diego State University M*
San Francisco State University M
San Jose State University M
Seton Hall University M,D*
South Dakota State University M,D
Southern Illinois University Carbondale M,D*
Southwestern Oklahoma State University M
Stanford University D*
State University of New York Upstate Medical University M,D*
Stony Brook University, State University of New York D*
Temple University M,D*
Texas A&M Health Science Center D*
Texas A&M University M,D*
Texas Tech University M,D
Thomas Jefferson University M,D*
Tufts University D*
Tulane University M,D*
Uniformed Services University of the Health Sciences D*
Universidad Central del Caribe M
Université de Montréal M,D,O
Université de Sherbrooke M,D
Université du Québec, Institut National de la Recherche Scientifique M,D
Université Laval M,D
University at Buffalo, the State University of New York M,D*
The University of Alabama at Birmingham D*
University of Alberta M,D*
The University of Arizona M,D*
University of Arkansas for Medical Sciences M,D*
The University of British Columbia M,D*
University of Calgary M,D
University of California, Berkeley D*
University of California, Davis M,D*
University of California, Irvine M,D*
University of California, Los Angeles M,D*
University of California, Riverside M,D*
University of California, San Diego D*
University of California, San Francisco D
University of Central Florida M*
University of Chicago D*
University of Cincinnati M,D
University of Colorado at Boulder M,D*
University of Colorado at Denver and Health Sciences Center D*
University of Connecticut M,D*
University of Delaware M,D*
University of Florida M,D*
University of Georgia M,D*
University of Guelph M,D
University of Hawaii at Manoa M,D*
University of Idaho M,D*
University of Illinois at Chicago D*
University of Illinois at Urbana–Champaign D*
The University of Iowa M,D*
University of Kansas M,D*
University of Kentucky D*
University of Louisville M,D
University of Maine M,D*
University of Manitoba M,D
University of Maryland, Baltimore D*
University of Massachusetts Amherst M,D*
University of Massachusetts Worcester D*
University of Medicine and Dentistry of New Jersey M,D*
University of Miami D*
University of Michigan D*
University of Minnesota, Twin Cities Campus D*
University of Mississippi Medical Center M,D*
University of Missouri–Columbia M,D*
The University of Montana M,D*
University of Nebraska Medical Center M,D*
University of New Hampshire M,D*
University of New Mexico M,D*
The University of North Carolina at Chapel Hill M,D*
University of North Dakota M,D
University of North Texas Health Science Center at Fort Worth M,D
University of Oklahoma M,D*
University of Oklahoma Health Sciences Center M,D
University of Ottawa M,D*
University of Pennsylvania D*
University of Pittsburgh M,D*
University of Puerto Rico, Medical Sciences Campus M,D*
University of Rhode Island M,D
University of Rochester M,D*
University of Saskatchewan M,D
University of South Alabama D*
The University of South Dakota M,D
University of Southern California M,D*
University of Southern Mississippi M,D*
University of South Florida M,D*
The University of Tennessee M,D*
The University of Texas at Austin M,D*
The University of Texas Health Science Center at Houston M,D*
The University of Texas Health Science Center at San Antonio D*
The University of Texas Medical Branch M,D*
The University of Texas Southwestern Medical Center at Dallas D*
The University of Toledo M*
University of Utah M,D*
University of Vermont M,D*
University of Victoria M,D
University of Virginia D*
University of Washington D*
The University of Western Ontario M,D
University of Wisconsin–La Crosse M
University of Wisconsin–Madison D*
University of Wisconsin–Oshkosh M
Utah State University M,D
Vanderbilt University M,D*
Virginia Commonwealth University M,D,O*
Virginia Polytechnic Institute and State University M,D*
Wagner College M
Wake Forest University D*
Washington State University M,D*
Washington University in St. Louis D*
Wayne State University M,D*
West Virginia University M,D*
Wright State University M*
Yale University D*

MIDDLE SCHOOL EDUCATION

Alaska Pacific University M
Albany State University M
Armstrong Atlantic State University M
Ashland University M
Augusta State University M,O
Austin College M
Bank Street College of Education M*
Bellarmine University M
Belmont University M
Berry College M
Brenau University M,O
Brooklyn College of the City University of New York M
California State University, Bakersfield M
California State University, Fullerton M
Campbell University M
Capella University M,D,O
Central Michigan University M*
Chicago State University M
City College of the City University of New York M,O*
Clemson University M*
Cleveland State University M
College of Mount St. Joseph M
College of Mount Saint Vincent M,O
Columbus State University M,O
Daemen College M
Drury University M
East Carolina University M*
Eastern Illinois University M
Eastern Michigan University M
Eastern Nazarene College M,O
Emory University M,D,O*
Fayetteville State University M
Fitchburg State College M
Fort Valley State University M
Furman University M
Gardner-Webb University M
George Mason University M*
Georgia College & State University M,O
Georgia Southern University M

*P—first professional degree; M—master's degree; D—doctorate; O—other advanced degree; *full description and/or announcement in Book 2, 3, 4, 5, or 6*

Georgia Southwestern State University M,O
Georgia State University M,O*
Grand Valley State University M
Hebrew College M,O
Henderson State University M,O
Hofstra University O*
James Madison University M
John Carroll University M
Kennesaw State University M
Kent State University M*
Lesley University M,D,O*
Long Island University, C.W. Post Campus M*
Manhattanville College M*
Mary Baldwin College M
Maryville University of Saint Louis M,D
Mercer University M,D,O
Mercy College M
Middle Tennessee State University M,O*
Montclair State University M,O*
Morehead State University M
Morgan State University M*
Mount Saint Mary College M
Mount Saint Vincent University M
Murray State University M,O
Nazareth College of Rochester M
North Carolina Agricultural and Technical State University M
North Carolina State University M*
North Georgia College & State University M,O
Northwestern State University of Louisiana M
Northwest Missouri State University M
The Ohio State University at Lima M
The Ohio State University at Marion M,D
The Ohio State University–Mansfield Campus M
The Ohio State University–Newark Campus M
Ohio University M,D*
Old Dominion University M,D*
Pacific University M
Park University M
Plymouth State University M
Quinnipiac University M*
Roberts Wesleyan College M,O
Rosemont College M
Saginaw Valley State University M
St. John Fisher College M
St. Thomas Aquinas College M,O*
Salem College M
Salem State College M
Shenandoah University M,D,O*
Siena Heights University M
Simmons College M,O
Smith College M*
Southeast Missouri State University M
Spalding University M
State University of New York College at Brockport M*
State University of New York College at Oneonta M
Tufts University M,D*
Union College (KY) M
University at Buffalo, the State University of New York M,D,O*
University of Arkansas M,D,O*
University of Arkansas at Little Rock M
University of Dayton M*
University of Georgia M,D,O*
University of Kentucky M,D*
University of Louisville M
University of Memphis M,D*
University of Missouri–St. Louis M,D
The University of North Carolina at Charlotte M*
The University of North Carolina at Greensboro M,D,O
The University of North Carolina at Pembroke M
The University of North Carolina Wilmington M*
University of Northern Iowa M
University of Puget Sound M
University of Southern Maine M,O
University of South Florida M,D,O*
University of the Cumberlands M
The University of Toledo M*
University of West Florida M
University of West Georgia M,O
University of Wisconsin–Milwaukee M
University of Wisconsin–Platteville M
Valdosta State University M,O
Virginia Commonwealth University M,O*
Wagner College M
Walden University M,D
Wesleyan College M
Western Carolina University M*
Western Kentucky University M,O
Western Michigan University M*
Widener University M,D*
Winthrop University M
Worcester State College M
Wright State University M*
Youngstown State University M

MILITARY AND DEFENSE STUDIES

American Public University System M
Austin Peay State University M
The George Washington University M*
Hawai'i Pacific University M*
The Institute of World Politics M,O*
Joint Military Intelligence College M,O
The Judge Advocate General's School, U.S. Army M
Missouri State University M*
National Defense University M
Naval Postgraduate School M,D
Norwich University M
Royal Military College of Canada M
School of Advanced Air and Space Studies M
United States Army Command and General Staff College M
University of Calgary M,D
University of Pittsburgh M*

MINERAL/MINING ENGINEERING

Colorado School of Mines M,D
Columbia University M,D,O*
Dalhousie University M,D
École Polytechnique de Montréal M,D,O
Laurentian University M
McGill University M,D,O*
Michigan Technological University M,D*
Montana Tech of The University of Montana M
New Mexico Institute of Mining and Technology M
Penn State University Park M,D*
Queen's University at Kingston M,D
Southern Illinois University Carbondale M*
Université Laval M,D
University of Alaska Fairbanks M
University of Alberta M,D*
The University of Arizona M,O*
The University of British Columbia M,D*
University of Kentucky M,D*
University of Missouri–Rolla M,D*
University of Nevada, Reno M,O*
University of North Dakota M
The University of Texas at Austin M*
University of Utah M,D*
Virginia Polytechnic Institute and State University M,D*
West Virginia University M,D*

MINERAL ECONOMICS

Colorado School of Mines M,D
Michigan Technological University M*
The University of Texas at Austin M*

MINERALOGY

Cornell University M,D*
Indiana University Bloomington M,D*
Université du Québec à Chicoutimi D
Université du Québec à Montréal M,D,O
University of Illinois at Chicago M,D*
University of Michigan M,D*
Yale University D*

MISSIONS AND MISSIOLOGY

Abilene Christian University M
Alliance Theological Seminary P,M
Alliance University College P,M,O
Anderson University P,M,D
Asbury Theological Seminary M,D
Associated Mennonite Biblical Seminary P,M,O
Bethel Seminary P,M,D,O
Biola University M,D,O
Briercrest Seminary M
Calvin Theological Seminary P,M,D
Catholic Theological Union at Chicago P,M,D,O
Central Baptist Theological Seminary P,M,O
Church of God Theological Seminary P,M
Columbia International University P,M,D,O
Dallas Baptist University M
Dallas Theological Seminary M,D,O
Eastern University D*
Fuller Theological Seminary M,D
Gardner-Webb University P,M,D
Global University of the Assemblies of God P,M
Gordon-Conwell Theological Seminary P,M,D
Grace Theological Seminary P,M,D,O
Grand Rapids Theological Seminary of Cornerstone University P,M
Knox Theological Seminary M
Luther Rice University P,M,D
Mennonite Brethren Biblical Seminary M
Midwest University P,M,D
Nazarene Theological Seminary P,M,D
Oral Roberts University P,M,D
Phillips Theological Seminary P,M,D
Providence College and Theological Seminary P,M,D,O
Reformed Theological Seminary–Jackson Campus P,M,D,O
Regent University P,M,D
Saint Paul University M
Simpson University P,M
Southeastern Baptist Theological Seminary P,M,D
Southern Adventist University M
Southern Baptist Theological Seminary P,M,D
Southern Evangelical Seminary P,M,O
Taylor University College and Seminary P,M,O
Trinity Episcopal School for Ministry P,M,D,O
Trinity International University P,M,D,O
Tyndale University College & Seminary P,M,O
Wesley Biblical Seminary P,M
Westminster Theological Seminary P,M,D,O
Wheaton College M,O

MOLECULAR BIOLOGY

Albany Medical College M,D
Albert Einstein College of Medicine D*
Arkansas State University M,D,O
Auburn University M,D*
Baylor College of Medicine D*
Boston University M,D*
Brandeis University M,D*
Brigham Young University M,D*
Brown University M,D*
California Institute of Technology D*
Carnegie Mellon University M,D*
Case Western Reserve University M,D*
Central Connecticut State University M
Clemson University M,D*
Colorado State University M,D*
Columbia University M,D*
Cornell University D*
Cornell University, Joan and Sanford I. Weill Medical College and Graduate School of Medical Sciences D*
Dartmouth College D*
Drexel University M,D*
Duke University D,O*
East Carolina University M,D*
Emory University D*
Florida Institute of Technology M,D*
Florida State University M,D*
George Mason University M,D,O*
Georgetown University D*
The George Washington University M,D*
Georgia State University M,D*
Grand Valley State University M
Harvard University D*
Howard University M,D*
Illinois Institute of Technology M,D*
Illinois State University M,D*
Indiana University Bloomington M,D*
Indiana University–Purdue University Indianapolis D*
Iowa State University of Science and Technology M,D*
The Johns Hopkins University M,D*
Kent State University M,D*
Lehigh University M,D*
Louisiana State University Health Sciences Center at Shreveport M,D*
Loyola University Chicago D*
Marquette University M,D
Mayo Graduate School D*
McMaster University M,D
Medical College of Georgia M,D*
Medical University of South Carolina M,D*
Michigan State University M,D*
Mississippi State University M,D
Missouri State University M*
Montana State University M,D
Montclair State University M,O*
Mount Sinai School of Medicine of New York University M,D*
New Mexico State University M,D
New York Medical College M,D*
New York University M,D*
North Dakota State University M,D
Northwestern University D*
OGI School of Science & Engineering at Oregon Health & Science University M,D
The Ohio State University M,D*
Ohio University M,D*
Oklahoma State University M,D*
Oklahoma State University Center for Health Sciences M
Oregon Health & Science University D*
Oregon State University M,D*
Penn State Hershey Medical Center M,D*
Penn State University Park M,D*
Princeton University D*
Purdue University M,D*
Quinnipiac University M*
Rensselaer Polytechnic Institute M,D*
Rutgers, The State University of New Jersey, New Brunswick M,D*
Saint Joseph College M
Saint Louis University D*
San Diego State University M,D*
San Francisco State University M
San Jose State University M
Seton Hall University M,D*
Simon Fraser University M,D
Southern Illinois University Carbondale M,D*
State University of New York Downstate Medical Center D*
State University of New York Upstate Medical University M,D*
Stony Brook University, State University of New York M,D*
Temple University D*
Texas A&M Health Science Center D*
Texas Woman's University M,D
Thomas Jefferson University D*
Tufts University D*
Tulane University M,D*
Uniformed Services University of the Health Sciences D*
Université de Montréal M,D
Université Laval M,D
University at Albany, State University of New York M,D*
University at Buffalo, the State University of New York D*
The University of Alabama at Birmingham M,D*
University of Alberta M,D*
The University of Arizona M,D*
University of Arkansas M,D*
University of Arkansas for Medical Sciences M,D*
The University of British Columbia M,D*
University of Calgary M,D
University of California, Berkeley D*
University of California, Davis M,D*
University of California, Irvine M,D*
University of California, Los Angeles M,D*
University of California, Riverside M,D*
University of California, San Diego D*
University of California, San Francisco D
University of California, Santa Barbara M,D*
University of California, Santa Cruz M,D*
University of Central Florida M*
University of Chicago D*
University of Cincinnati M,D
University of Colorado at Boulder M,D*
University of Colorado at Denver and Health Sciences Center D*
University of Connecticut M*
University of Connecticut Health Center D*
University of Delaware M,D*
University of Florida M,D*
University of Georgia M,D*
University of Guelph M,D
University of Hawaii at Manoa M,D*
University of Idaho M,D*
University of Illinois at Chicago M,D*
University of Illinois at Urbana–Champaign *
The University of Iowa D*
University of Kansas M,D*
University of Lethbridge M,D
University of Louisville M,D
University of Maine M,D*

University of Maryland, Baltimore D*
University of Maryland, Baltimore County M,D*
University of Maryland, College Park D*
University of Massachusetts Amherst D*
University of Massachusetts Boston D
University of Medicine and Dentistry of New Jersey M,D*
University of Miami D*
University of Michigan M,D*
University of Minnesota, Duluth M,D*
University of Minnesota, Twin Cities Campus M,D*
University of Missouri–Kansas City D*
University of Missouri–St. Louis M,D,O
University of Nebraska Medical Center M,D*
University of Nevada, Reno M,D*
University of New Haven M*
University of New Mexico M,D*
The University of North Carolina at Chapel Hill M,D*
University of North Texas M,D*
University of North Texas Health Science Center at Fort Worth M,D
University of Notre Dame M,D*
University of Oklahoma Health Sciences Center M,D
University of Oregon M,D*
University of Ottawa M,D*
University of Pennsylvania D*
University of Pittsburgh D*
University of Rhode Island M,D
University of South Alabama D*
University of South Carolina M,D*
The University of South Dakota M,D
University of Southern California M,D*
University of Southern Maine M
University of Southern Mississippi M,D*
University of South Florida M,D*
The University of Texas at Austin D*
The University of Texas at Dallas M,D*
The University of Texas at San Antonio M,D*
The University of Texas Health Science Center at Houston M,D*
The University of Toledo M,D*
University of Utah D*
University of Vermont M,D*
University of Washington D*
The University of Western Ontario M,D
University of Wisconsin–La Crosse M
University of Wisconsin–Madison M,D*
University of Wisconsin–Parkside M
University of Wyoming M,D
Utah State University M,D
Vanderbilt University M,D*
Virginia Commonwealth University M,D*
Wake Forest University D*
Washington State University M,D*
Washington University in St. Louis D*
Wayne State University M,D*
Wesleyan University D*
West Virginia University M,D*
William Paterson University of New Jersey M*
Wright State University M*
Yale University D*

MOLECULAR BIOPHYSICS

Baylor College of Medicine D*
California Institute of Technology M,D*
Duke University O*
Florida State University D*
Illinois Institute of Technology M,D*
Rutgers, The State University of New Jersey, New Brunswick D*
University of Michigan *
University of Pennsylvania D*
University of Pittsburgh D*
The University of Texas Medical Branch M,D*
The University of Texas Southwestern Medical Center at Dallas D*
Vanderbilt University *
Virginia Commonwealth University M,D*
Washington University in St. Louis D*
Yale University D*

MOLECULAR GENETICS

Albert Einstein College of Medicine D*
Duke University D*
Emory University D*
Georgia State University M,D*
Harvard University D*
Illinois State University M,D*
Indiana University–Purdue University Indianapolis M,D*
Medical College of Wisconsin M,D*
Michigan State University M,D*
New York University M,D*
The Ohio State University M,D*
Oklahoma State University M,D*
Rutgers, The State University of New Jersey, New Brunswick M,D*
Stony Brook University, State University of New York D*
Texas Tech University Health Sciences Center M,D
The University of Alabama at Birmingham D*
University of California, Irvine M,D*
University of California, Los Angeles M,D*
University of California, Riverside D*
University of Chicago D*
University of Cincinnati M,D
University of Florida M,D*
University of Guelph M,D
University of Illinois at Chicago D*
University of Kansas D*
University of Maryland, College Park M,D*
University of Massachusetts Worcester D*
University of Medicine and Dentistry of New Jersey M,D*
University of Pittsburgh M,D*
University of Rhode Island M,D
The University of Texas Health Science Center at Houston M,D*
University of Vermont M,D*
University of Virginia D*
Wake Forest University D*
Washington University in St. Louis D*

MOLECULAR MEDICINE

Baylor College of Medicine D*
Boston University D*
Cleveland State University M,D
Cornell University M,D*
Dartmouth College D*
The George Washington University D*
The Johns Hopkins University D*
Medical College of Georgia M,D*
North Shore–LIJ Graduate School of Molecular Medicine D
Penn State Hershey Medical Center M,D*
Penn State University Park M,D*
Texas A&M Health Science Center D*
University of Cincinnati D
University of Maryland, Baltimore D*
University of Medicine and Dentistry of New Jersey D*
University of Rochester *
The University of Texas Health Science Center at San Antonio M,D*
University of Washington M,D*
Wake Forest University M,D*
Yale University D*

MOLECULAR PATHOGENESIS

Dartmouth College D*
Emory University D*
Massachusetts Institute of Technology M,D*
North Dakota State University M,D
Texas A&M Health Science Center D*
University at Albany, State University of New York M,D*
Washington University in St. Louis D*

MOLECULAR PATHOLOGY

Texas Tech University Health Sciences Center M
University of California, San Diego D*
University of Medicine and Dentistry of New Jersey D*
University of Pittsburgh M,D*

The University of Texas Health Science Center at Houston M,D*
Yale University D*

MOLECULAR PHARMACOLOGY

Albert Einstein College of Medicine D*
Brown University M,D*
Dartmouth College D*
Harvard University D*
Massachusetts Institute of Technology M,D*
Mayo Graduate School D*
Medical University of South Carolina M,D*
New York University D*
Purdue University M,D*
Rosalind Franklin University of Medicine and Science M,D*
Rutgers, The State University of New Jersey, New Brunswick D*
Stanford University D*
Thomas Jefferson University D*
University at Buffalo, the State University of New York D*
University of Connecticut Health Center D*
University of Massachusetts Worcester D*
University of Medicine and Dentistry of New Jersey M,D*
University of Nevada, Reno M,D*
University of Pittsburgh D*
University of Southern California M,D*

MOLECULAR PHYSIOLOGY

Baylor College of Medicine D*
Loyola University Chicago M,D*
Stony Brook University, State University of New York D*
Thomas Jefferson University D*
Tufts University D*
The University of Alabama at Birmingham M,D*
University of Chicago D*
The University of North Carolina at Chapel Hill D*
University of Pittsburgh M,D*
University of Vermont M,D*
University of Virginia M,D*
Vanderbilt University M,D*
Yale University D*

MOLECULAR TOXICOLOGY

Massachusetts Institute of Technology M,D*
New York University M,D*
North Carolina State University M,D*
Oregon State University M,D*
Penn State Hershey Medical Center M,D*
University of California, Berkeley D*
University of California, Los Angeles D*
University of Cincinnati M,D
University of Pittsburgh M,D,O*

MULTILINGUAL AND MULTICULTURAL EDUCATION

Alliant International University–Irvine M,O*
Alliant International University–San Francisco M,O*
Azusa Pacific University M
Bank Street College of Education M*
Belhaven College (MS) M
Bennington College M*
Boston University M,O*
Brooklyn College of the City University of New York M
Brown University M,D*
Buffalo State College, State University of New York M
California Baptist University M
California State University, Bakersfield M
California State University, Chico M
California State University, Dominguez Hills M
California State University, Fullerton M
California State University, Sacramento M*
California State University, San Bernardino M
California State University, Stanislaus M
Capella University M,D,O
Chicago State University M
City College of the City University of New York M*
College of Mount St. Joseph M
College of Mount Saint Vincent M,O
The College of New Rochelle M,O
The College of Saint Rose M,O*
College of Santa Fe M
Columbia College Chicago M
Columbia International University M,D,O
DePaul University M,D*
DeSales University M,O
Eastern Michigan University M
Eastern University M*
Fairfield University M,O*
Fairleigh Dickinson University, Metropolitan Campus M*
Florida Atlantic University M,D,O
Florida State University M,D,O*
Fordham University M,D,O*
Fresno Pacific University M
George Mason University M*
Georgetown University M,D,O*
Graduate Institute of Applied Linguistics M,O
Harvard University D*
Heritage University M
Hofstra University M,O*
Howard University M,D*
Hunter College of the City University of New York M
Immaculata University M
Indiana State University M,O*
Iona College M*
Kean University M
Langston University M
Lehman College of the City University of New York M
Long Island University, Brooklyn Campus M*
Long Island University, C.W. Post Campus M*
Long Island University, Westchester Graduate Campus M
Loyola Marymount University M
McNeese State University M
Mercy College M,O
Mercyhurst College M,O
Minnesota State University Mankato M
National University M
New Jersey City University M
New York University M,D,O*
Northeastern Illinois University M
Northern Arizona University M,O
Nova Southeastern University M,O*
Park University M
Penn State University Park M,D*
Prescott College M,D
Queens College of the City University of New York M,O
Rhode Island College M,O
St. John's University (NY) M
Salem State College M
San Diego State University M,D*
Seton Hall University O*
Southern Connecticut State University M
Southern Methodist University M*
State University of New York at New Paltz M
State University of New York College at Brockport M*
Sul Ross State University M*
Teachers College Columbia University M*
Texas A&M International University M,D
Texas A&M University M,D*
Texas A&M University–Kingsville M,D
Texas Southern University M,D
Texas State University-San Marcos M*
Texas Tech University M,D
Universidad del Turabo M
University at Buffalo, the State University of New York M,D,O*
University of Alaska Fairbanks M
University of Alberta M*
The University of Arizona M,D,O*
University of California, Berkeley M,D*
University of Colorado at Boulder M,D*
University of Connecticut M,D*
University of Delaware M,D*
The University of Findlay M
University of Florida M,D,O*
University of Houston M,D*
University of Houston–Clear Lake M
University of La Verne O
University of Maryland, Baltimore County M,D,O*
University of Massachusetts Amherst M,D,O*
University of Massachusetts Boston M
University of Michigan M,D*
University of Michigan–Flint M*

P—first professional degree; M—master's degree; D—doctorate; O—other advanced degree;
**full description and/or announcement in Book 2, 3, 4, 5, or 6*

Institution	Degrees
University of Minnesota, Twin Cities Campus	M*
University of Nevada, Las Vegas	M,D,O
University of New Mexico	D,O*
The University of North Carolina at Greensboro	M,D,O
University of Oklahoma	M,D,O*
University of Pennsylvania	M,D*
University of San Francisco	M,D
The University of Tennessee	M,D,O*
The University of Texas at Brownsville	M
The University of Texas at San Antonio	M,D*
The University of Texas–Pan American	M
University of Washington	M,D*
Utah State University	M
Vanderbilt University	M,D*
Washington State University	M,D*
Wayne State University	M,D,O*
Western Oregon University	M
Xavier University	M*

MUSEUM EDUCATION

Institution	Degrees
Bank Street College of Education	M*
The College of New Rochelle	O
The George Washington University	M*
The University of the Arts	M*

MUSEUM STUDIES

Institution	Degrees
Bank Street College of Education	M*
Bard College	M*
Baylor University	M*
Boston University	M,D,O*
California College of the Arts	M*
California State University, Chico	M
California State University, Fullerton	M,O
Caribbean University	M,D
Case Western Reserve University	M,D*
Christie's Education	M
City College of the City University of New York	M*
Cleveland State University	M
Duquesne University	M*
Fashion Institute of Technology	M*
Florida State University	M,D,O*
The George Washington University	M,D,O*
Hampton University	M*
Harvard University	M,O*
John F. Kennedy University	M,O
New York University	M,D,O*
Rutgers, The State University of New Jersey, New Brunswick	M,D*
San Francisco Art Institute	M*
San Francisco State University	M
Seton Hall University	M*
Southern Illinois University Edwardsville	O
State University of New York College at Oneonta	M
Syracuse University	M*
Texas Tech University	M
Tufts University	O*
Université de Montréal	M
Université du Québec à Montréal	M
Université Laval	O
University at Buffalo, the State University of New York	M,O*
University of California, Riverside	M,D*
University of Central Oklahoma	M
University of Colorado at Boulder	M*
University of Delaware	O*
University of Denver	M,O*
University of Florida	M,D*
University of Hawaii at Manoa	O*
University of Kansas	M*
University of Missouri–St. Louis	M,O
University of Nebraska–Lincoln	M*
University of New Hampshire	M,D*
The University of North Carolina at Greensboro	M,D,O
University of Oklahoma	M*
University of South Carolina	M,O*
The University of the Arts	M*
University of Toronto	M
University of Washington	M*
University of Wisconsin–Milwaukee	M,O
Virginia Commonwealth University	M,D*

MUSIC

Institution	Degrees
Alabama Agricultural and Mechanical University	M
Alabama State University	M
Andrews University	M
Appalachian State University	M
Arizona State University	M,D*
Arkansas State University	M,O
Austin Peay State University	M
Azusa Pacific University	M
Baptist Theological Seminary at Richmond	P,D
Baylor University	M*
Belmont University	M
Bennington College	M*
Birmingham-Southern College	M
Bob Jones University	P,M,D,O
Boise State University	M
The Boston Conservatory	M,O
Boston University	M,D,O*
Bowling Green State University	M,D*
Brandeis University	M,D*
Brandon University	M
Brigham Young University	M*
Brooklyn College of the City University of New York	M,D,O
Brown University	M,D*
Butler University	M
California Baptist University	M
California Institute of the Arts	M,O
California State University, Chico	M
California State University, East Bay	M
California State University, Fresno	M
California State University, Fullerton	M
California State University, Long Beach	M
California State University, Los Angeles	M
California State University, Northridge	M
California State University, Sacramento	M*
Campbellsville University	M
Capital University	M
Cardinal Stritch University	M*
Carnegie Mellon University	M*
Case Western Reserve University	M,D*
The Catholic University of America	M,D*
Central Michigan University	M*
Central Washington University	M
City College of the City University of New York	M*
Claremont Graduate University	M,D
Cleveland Institute of Music	M,D,O
Cleveland State University	M
The College of Saint Rose	M*
Colorado State University	M*
Columbia University	M,D*
Concordia University (IL)	M
Concordia University (Canada)	O
Concordia University Wisconsin	M
Connecticut College	M
Conservatorio de Musica	O
Converse College	M
Cornell University	M,D*
The Curtis Institute of Music	M
Dartmouth College	M*
DePaul University	M,O*
Duke University	M,D*
Duquesne University	M,O*
East Carolina University	M*
Eastern Illinois University	M
Eastern Kentucky University	M*
Eastern Michigan University	M*
Eastern Washington University	M*
Emory University	M*
Emporia State University	M
Five Towns College	M,D
Florida Atlantic University	M
Florida International University	M*
Florida State University	M,D*
Garrett-Evangelical Theological Seminary	P,M,D
George Mason University	M*
Georgia Southern University	M*
Georgia State University	M*
Graduate School and University Center of the City University of New York	D*
Gratz College	M,O
Hardin-Simmons University	M
Harvard University	M,D*
Hebrew College	M,O
Hebrew Union College–Jewish Institute of Religion (NY)	M
Hofstra University	M*
Hollins University	M,O
Holy Names University	M,O
Hope International University	M
Houghton College	M
Howard University	M*
Hunter College of the City University of New York	M
Illinois State University	M*
Indiana State University	M*
Indiana University Bloomington	M,D*
Indiana University of Pennsylvania	M
Indiana University–Purdue University Indianapolis	M*
Indiana University South Bend	M
Ithaca College	M
Jacksonville State University	M
James Madison University	M
The Jewish Theological Seminary	M*
The Johns Hopkins University	M,D,O*
The Juilliard School	M,D,O
Kansas State University	M*
Kent State University	M,D*
Lamar University	M*
Lee University	M
Long Island University, C.W. Post Campus	M*
Longy School of Music	M,O
Louisiana State University and Agricultural and Mechanical College	M,D*
Loyola University New Orleans	M
Lynn University	M,O
Manhattan School of Music	M,D,O
Mansfield University of Pennsylvania	M
Marshall University	M
McGill University	M,D*
McMaster University	M
Memorial University of Newfoundland	M,D
Mercer University	M
Meredith College	M
Miami University	M*
Michigan State University	M,D*
Middle Tennessee State University	M*
Midwestern Baptist Theological Seminary	P,M,D
Midwest University	P,M,D
Mills College	M
Minnesota State University Mankato	M
Mississippi College	M
Missouri State University	M*
Montclair State University	M,O*
Morehead State University	M
Morgan State University	M*
Murray State University	M
New England Conservatory of Music	M,D,O
New Jersey City University	M
New Mexico State University	M
New Orleans Baptist Theological Seminary	M,D
The New School: A University	M,O*
New York University	M,D,O*
The Nigerian Baptist Theological Seminary	P,M,O
Norfolk State University	M
North Carolina School of the Arts	M
North Dakota State University	M,D
Northeastern Illinois University	M
Northern Arizona University	M
Northern Illinois University	M,O
Northwestern State University of Louisiana	M
Northwestern University	M,D,O*
Notre Dame de Namur University	M
Oakland University	M,D*
Oberlin College	M
The Ohio State University	M,D*
Ohio University	M,O*
Oklahoma City University	M
Oklahoma State University	M*
Penn State University Park	M,D*
Phillips Theological Seminary	P,M,D
Pittsburg State University	M
Point Park University	M*
Portland State University	M*
Princeton University	D*
Purchase College, State University of New York	M
Queens College of the City University of New York	M
Radford University	M
Regis University	M,O
Rice University	M,D*
Roosevelt University	M,O
Rowan University	M
Rutgers, The State University of New Jersey, Newark	M*
Rutgers, The State University of New Jersey, New Brunswick	M,D,O*
St. Cloud State University	M
Saint John's University (MN)	P,M
Saint Joseph's College	M,O
St. Vladimir's Orthodox Theological Seminary	P,M,D
Samford University	M
Sam Houston State University	M
San Diego State University	M*
San Francisco Conservatory of Music	M
San Francisco State University	M
San Jose State University	M
Santa Clara University	M
Savannah College of Art and Design	M*
Seton Hall University	M*
Shenandoah University	M,D,O*
Southeastern Baptist Theological Seminary	P,M,D
Southeastern Louisiana University	M
Southern Baptist Theological Seminary	P,M,D
Southern Illinois University Carbondale	M*
Southern Illinois University Edwardsville	M
Southern Methodist University	M,O*
Southern Oregon University	M
Southwestern Baptist Theological Seminary	M,D,O
Southwestern Oklahoma State University	M
Stanford University	M,D*
State University of New York at Binghamton	M*
State University of New York at Fredonia	M
State University of New York College at Potsdam	M
Stephen F. Austin State University	M
Stony Brook University, State University of New York	M,D*
Syracuse University	M*
Temple University	M,D*
Texas A&M International University	M
Texas A&M University–Commerce	M
Texas Christian University	M,O
Texas Southern University	M
Texas State University-San Marcos	M*
Texas Tech University	M,D
Texas Woman's University	M
Towson University	M
Trinity Lutheran Seminary	P,M
Truman State University	M
Tufts University	M*
Tulane University	M*
Université de Montréal	M,D,O
Université Laval	M,D
University at Buffalo, the State University of New York	M,D*
The University of Akron	M
The University of Alabama	M,D
University of Alaska Fairbanks	M
University of Alberta	M,D*
The University of Arizona	M,D*
University of Arkansas	M*
The University of British Columbia	M,D*
University of Calgary	M,D
University of California, Berkeley	D*
University of California, Davis	M,D*
University of California, Irvine	M*
University of California, Los Angeles	M,D*
University of California, Riverside	M*
University of California, San Diego	M,D*
University of California, Santa Barbara	M,D*
University of California, Santa Cruz	M,D*
University of Central Arkansas	M
University of Central Missouri	M
University of Central Oklahoma	M
University of Chicago	M,D*
University of Cincinnati	M,D,O
University of Colorado at Boulder	M,D*
University of Colorado at Denver and Health Sciences Center	M*
University of Connecticut	M,D,O*
University of Delaware	M*
University of Denver	M,O*
University of Florida	M,D*
University of Georgia	M,D*
University of Hartford	M,D,O*
University of Hawaii at Manoa	M,D*
University of Houston	M,D*
University of Idaho	M*
University of Illinois at Urbana–Champaign	M,D*
The University of Iowa	M,D*
University of Kansas	M,D*
University of Kentucky	M,D*
University of Lethbridge	M,D
University of Louisiana at Lafayette	M*
University of Louisiana at Monroe	M
University of Louisville	M,D
University of Maine	M*
University of Manitoba	M
University of Maryland, Baltimore County	O*
University of Maryland, College Park	M,D*
University of Massachusetts Amherst	M,D*
University of Massachusetts Lowell	M*
University of Memphis	M,D*

University of Miami M,D,O*
University of Michigan M,D,O*
University of Minnesota, Duluth M*
University of Minnesota, Twin Cities Campus M,D*
University of Mississippi M,D
University of Missouri–Columbia M*
University of Missouri–Kansas City M,D*
The University of Montana M*
University of Montevallo M
University of Nebraska at Omaha M
University of Nebraska–Lincoln M,D*
University of Nevada, Las Vegas M,D
University of Nevada, Reno M*
University of New Hampshire M*
University of New Mexico M*
University of New Orleans M
The University of North Carolina at Chapel Hill M,D*
The University of North Carolina at Greensboro M,D
University of North Dakota M,D
University of Northern Colorado M,D
University of Northern Iowa M
University of North Texas M,D*
University of Oklahoma M,D*
University of Oregon M,D*
University of Ottawa M,O*
University of Pennsylvania M,D*
University of Pittsburgh M,D*
University of Portland M
University of Redlands M
University of Regina M,D
University of Rhode Island M
University of Rochester M,D*
University of Saskatchewan M
University of South Carolina M,D,O*
The University of South Dakota M
University of Southern California M,D,O*
University of Southern Maine M
University of Southern Mississippi M,D*
University of South Florida M*
The University of Tennessee M*
The University of Tennessee at Chattanooga M
The University of Texas at Arlington M*
The University of Texas at Austin M,D*
The University of Texas at El Paso M
The University of Texas at San Antonio M*
The University of Texas at Tyler M
The University of Texas–Pan American M
The University of the Arts M*
University of the Pacific M
The University of Toledo M*
University of Toronto M,D
University of Trinity College P,M,D,O
University of Utah M,D*
University of Victoria M,D
University of Virginia M,D*
University of Washington M,D*
The University of Western Ontario M,D
University of West Georgia M
University of Wisconsin–Madison M,D*
University of Wisconsin–Milwaukee M,O
University of Wyoming M
Valdosta State University M
Virginia Commonwealth University M*
Washington State University M*
Washington University in St. Louis M,D*
Wayne State University M,O*
Webster University M
Wesleyan University M,D*
West Chester University of Pennsylvania M*
Western Carolina University M*
Western Illinois University M
Western Michigan University M*
Western Oregon University M
Western Washington University M
Westminster Choir College of Rider University M*
West Texas A&M University M
West Virginia University M,D*
Wichita State University M*
William Paterson University of New Jersey M*
Winthrop University M*
Wright State University M*
Yale University M,D,O*
York University M,D*
Youngstown State University M

MUSIC EDUCATION

Alabama Agricultural and Mechanical University M
Albany State University M
Appalachian State University M
Arcadia University M,D,O
Arkansas State University M,O
Auburn University M,D,O*
Austin College M
Austin Peay State University M
Azusa Pacific University M
Ball State University M,D*
Baylor University M*
Belmont University M
Bennington College M*
Bob Jones University P,M,D,O
Boise State University M
The Boston Conservatory M,O
Boston University M,D*
Bowling Green State University M,D*
Brandon University M
Brigham Young University M*
Brooklyn College of the City University of New York M,D,O
Butler University M
California State University, Fresno M
California State University, Fullerton M
California State University, Los Angeles M
California State University, Northridge M
Campbellsville University M
Capital University M
Carnegie Mellon University M*
Case Western Reserve University M,D*
The Catholic University of America M,D*
Central Connecticut State University M,O
Central Michigan University M*
Christopher Newport University M
Cleveland State University M
College of Mount St. Joseph M
The College of Saint Rose M,O*
The Colorado College M
Columbus State University M
Connecticut College M
Conservatorio de Musica M
Converse College M
DePaul University M,O*
Duquesne University M,O*
East Carolina University M*
Eastern Kentucky University M*
Eastern Michigan University M
Eastern Washington University M
Emporia State University M
Five Towns College M,D
Florida International University M*
Florida State University M,D*
George Mason University M*
Georgia State University M,D,O*
Gordon College M
Hardin-Simmons University M
Hebrew College M,O
Hofstra University M*
Holy Names University M,O
Howard University M*
Hunter College of the City University of New York M
Indiana University of Pennsylvania M
Inter American University of Puerto Rico, San Germán Campus M
Ithaca College M
Jackson State University M
Jacksonville University M
James Madison University M
Kansas State University M*
Kent State University M,D*
Kutztown University of Pennsylvania O
LaGrange College M
Lamar University M*
Lebanon Valley College M
Lee University M
Lehman College of the City University of New York M
Long Island University, C.W. Post Campus M*
Louisiana State University and Agricultural and Mechanical College M,D*
Manhattanville College M*
Marywood University M*
McGill University M,D*
McNeese State University M*
Miami University M*
Michigan State University M,D*
Minot State University M
Mississippi College M
Montclair State University M,O*
Morehead State University M
Murray State University M
Nazareth College of Rochester M
New Jersey City University M
New York University M,D,O*
Norfolk State University M
North Dakota State University M,D,O
Northern Arizona University M
Northwestern University M,D*
Northwest Missouri State University M
Notre Dame de Namur University M
Oakland University M,D*
Ohio University M,O*
Oklahoma State University M*
Old Dominion University M*
Oregon State University M*
Penn State University Park M,D*
Pittsburg State University M
Portland State University M
Queens College of the City University of New York M,O
Rhode Island College M
Rollins College M
Roosevelt University M,O
Rowan University M,O
Rutgers, The State University of New Jersey, New Brunswick M,D,O*
St. Cloud State University M
Salisbury University M
Samford University M
Sam Houston State University M
San Diego State University M*
San Francisco State University M
Shenandoah University M,D,O*
Silver Lake College M
Southeast Missouri State University M
Southern Illinois University Carbondale M*
Southern Illinois University Edwardsville M
Southern Methodist University M,O*
Southwestern Oklahoma State University M
State University of New York at Fredonia M
State University of New York College at Potsdam M
Syracuse University M*
Teachers College Columbia University M,D*
Temple University M,D*
Tennessee State University M*
Texas A&M University–Commerce M
Texas A&M University–Kingsville M
Texas Christian University M,O
Texas State University-San Marcos M*
Texas Tech University M,D
Towson University M,O
Union College (KY) M
Université Laval M,D
University at Buffalo, the State University of New York M,D,O*
The University of Akron M
The University of Alabama M,D,O
University of Alaska Fairbanks M
The University of Arizona M,D*
The University of British Columbia M,D*
University of Central Arkansas M
University of Central Florida M*
University of Central Oklahoma M
University of Cincinnati M
University of Colorado at Boulder M,D*
University of Connecticut M,D,O*
University of Dayton M*
University of Delaware M*
University of Denver M,O*
University of Florida M,D*
University of Georgia M,D,O*
University of Hartford M,D,O*
University of Houston M,D*
The University of Iowa M,D*
University of Kansas M,D*
University of Kentucky M,D*
University of Louisiana at Lafayette M*
University of Louisville M
University of Maryland, College Park M,D*
University of Massachusetts Lowell M*
University of Memphis M,D*
University of Miami M,D,O*
University of Michigan M,D,O*
University of Minnesota, Duluth M*
University of Missouri–Columbia M,D,O*
University of Missouri–Kansas City M,D*
University of Missouri–St. Louis M
The University of Montana M*
University of Nebraska at Kearney M
University of Nevada, Las Vegas M,D
University of New Hampshire M*
The University of North Carolina at Chapel Hill M*
The University of North Carolina at Charlotte M*
The University of North Carolina at Greensboro M,D
The University of North Carolina at Pembroke M
University of North Dakota M,D
University of Northern Colorado M,D
University of Northern Iowa M
University of North Texas M,D*
University of Oklahoma M,D*
University of Oregon M,D*
University of Ottawa M,O*
University of Rhode Island M
University of Rochester M,D*
University of St. Thomas (MN) M*
University of South Carolina M,D,O*
University of Southern California M,D*
University of Southern Mississippi M,D*
University of South Florida M*
The University of Tennessee M*
The University of Texas at El Paso M
The University of Texas at Tyler M
The University of Texas–Pan American M
The University of the Arts M*
University of the Pacific M
The University of Toledo M*
University of Toronto M,D
University of Victoria M,D
University of Washington M,D*
University of West Georgia M
University of Wisconsin–Madison M,D*
University of Wisconsin–Stevens Point M
University of Wyoming M
Valdosta State University M
VanderCook College of Music M
Virginia Commonwealth University M*
Washington State University M*
Wayne State College M
Wayne State University M,O*
Webster University M
West Chester University of Pennsylvania M
Western Carolina University M*
Western Connecticut State University M*
Western Kentucky University M
Westminster Choir College of Rider University M*
West Virginia University M,D*
Wichita State University M*
Winthrop University M*
Wright State University M*
Youngstown State University M

NANOTECHNOLOGY

George Mason University M,D,O*
Rice University M*
South Dakota School of Mines and Technology D
University at Albany, State University of New York M,D*
University of Alberta M,D*
University of Washington M,D*

NATIONAL SECURITY

American Public University System M
California State University, San Bernardino M
Georgetown University M*
Huron University USA in London M
The Institute of World Politics M,O*
National Defense University M
Naval Postgraduate School M
Naval War College M
New Jersey City University M
University of Pittsburgh M*

NATURAL RESOURCES

Auburn University M,D*
Ball State University M*
Cornell University M,D*
Duke University M,D*
Georgia Institute of Technology M,D*
Humboldt State University M
Iowa State University of Science and Technology M,D*
Louisiana State University and Agricultural and Mechanical College M,D*
McGill University M,D*
Memorial University of Newfoundland M
Montana State University M,D
North Carolina State University M*

*P—first professional degree; M—master's degree; D—doctorate; O—other advanced degree; *full description and/or announcement in Book 2, 3, 4, 5, or 6*

The Ohio State University M,D*
Oklahoma State University M,D*
Purdue University M,D*
State University of New York College of Environmental Science and Forestry M,D
Texas A&M University M,D*
Université du Québec à Montréal M,D,O
University of Alberta M,D*
The University of Arizona M,D*
University of Arkansas at Monticello M
University of Connecticut M,D*
University of Florida M,D*
University of Georgia M,D*
University of Guelph M,D
University of Hawaii at Manoa M,D*
University of Idaho M,D*
University of Illinois at Urbana–Champaign M,D*
University of Maine M,D*
University of Maryland, College Park M,D*
University of Michigan M,D,O*
The University of Montana M,D*
University of Nebraska–Lincoln M,D*
University of New Hampshire D*
University of Northern British Columbia M,D,O
University of Oklahoma M,D*
University of Rhode Island M,D
University of Vermont M,D*
University of Wisconsin–Stevens Point M
University of Wyoming M,D
Utah State University M
Virginia Polytechnic Institute and State University M*
Washington State University M,D*

NATUROPATHIC MEDICINE

Bastyr University D,O*
Canadian College of Naturopathic Medicine D*
National College of Natural Medicine D
National University of Health Sciences P,M,D*
Southwest College of Naturopathic Medicine and Health Sciences D*
University of Bridgeport D

NEAR AND MIDDLE EASTERN LANGUAGES

The American University in Cairo M,O
American University of Beirut M
Brandeis University M,D*
The Catholic University of America M,D*
Columbia University M,D*
Georgetown University M,D*
Harvard University M,D*
Hebrew Union College–Jewish Institute of Religion (NY) D
Indiana University Bloomington M,D*
The Ohio State University M,D*
University of California, Los Angeles M,D*
University of Chicago M,D*
University of Michigan M,D*
The University of Texas at Austin M,D*
University of Utah M,D*
University of Wisconsin–Madison M,D*
Yale University M,D*

NEAR AND MIDDLE EASTERN STUDIES

The American University in Cairo M,O
American University of Beirut M
The American University of Paris M
Brandeis University M,D*
Columbia University M,D,O*
Cornell University M,D*
Drew University M,D
Emory University D,O*
Georgetown University M,O*
Gratz College O
Harvard University M,D*
Hebrew Union College–Jewish Institute of Religion (OH) M,D
The Johns Hopkins University M,D,O*
McGill University M,D,O*
New York University M,D,O*
Princeton University M,D*
The University of Arizona M,D*
University of California, Berkeley M,D*
University of California, Los Angeles M,D*
University of Chicago M,D*
University of Kansas M*
University of Michigan M,D*
University of Pennsylvania M,D*
The University of Texas at Austin M,D*
University of Toronto M,D
University of Utah M,D*
University of Washington M,D*
Washington University in St. Louis M*
Wayne State University M*

NEUROBIOLOGY

Albert Einstein College of Medicine D*
Brandeis University M,D*
California Institute of Technology D*
Carnegie Mellon University M,D*
Case Western Reserve University D*
Columbia University M,D*
Cornell University D*
Dalhousie University M,D
Duke University D*
Georgia State University M,D*
Harvard University D*
Illinois State University M,D*
Louisiana State University Health Sciences Center M,D*
Loyola University Chicago M,D*
Marquette University M,D
Massachusetts Institute of Technology D*
New York University M,D*
Northwestern University M,D*
Purdue University M,D*
Rutgers, The State University of New Jersey, New Brunswick D*
Université Laval M,D
University at Albany, State University of New York M,D*
The University of Alabama at Birmingham D*
University of Arkansas for Medical Sciences M,D*
University of California, Irvine M,D*
University of California, Los Angeles D*
University of California, San Diego D*
University of Chicago D*
University of Colorado at Boulder M,D*
University of Connecticut M,D*
University of Illinois at Chicago M,D*
The University of Iowa M,D*
University of Kentucky D*
University of Louisville M,D
University of Maryland, Baltimore D*
University of Missouri–Columbia M,D*
The University of North Carolina at Chapel Hill D*
University of Pittsburgh M,D*
University of Puerto Rico, Medical Sciences Campus M,D*
University of Rochester M,D*
University of Southern California M,D*
The University of Tennessee Health Science Center D*
The University of Texas at Austin M,D*
The University of Texas at San Antonio M,D*
University of Utah D*
University of Vermont D*
University of Washington D*
University of Wisconsin–Madison D*
Virginia Commonwealth University D*
Wake Forest University D*
Wayne State University D*
Wesleyan University D*
Yale University D*

NEUROSCIENCE

Albany Medical College M,D
American University D*
American University of Beirut P,M
Argosy University, Tampa Campus M,D*
Arizona State University M,D*
Baylor College of Medicine D*
Baylor University M,D*
Boston University M,D*
Brandeis University M,D*
Brigham Young University M,D*
Brock University M,D
Brown University D*
California Institute of Technology M,D*
Carleton University M,D
Carnegie Mellon University D*
Case Western Reserve University D*
College of Staten Island of the City University of New York M
Colorado State University M,D*
Cornell University, Joan and Sanford I. Weill Medical College and Graduate School of Medical Sciences D*
Dalhousie University M,D
Dartmouth College D*
Drexel University D*
Duke University D,O*
Emory University D*
Florida Atlantic University D
Florida State University D*
George Mason University M,D,O*
Georgetown University D*
The George Washington University D*
Graduate School and University Center of the City University of New York D*
Harvard University D*
Illinois State University M,D*
Iowa State University of Science and Technology M,D*
The Johns Hopkins University D*
Kent State University M,D*
Louisiana State University Health Sciences Center M,D*
Loyola University Chicago M,D*
Massachusetts Institute of Technology D*
Mayo Graduate School D*
McGill University M,D*
McMaster University M,D
Medical College of Georgia M,D*
Medical University of South Carolina M,D*
Michigan State University M,D*
Montana State University M,D
Mount Sinai School of Medicine of New York University M,D*
New York Medical College M,D*
New York University D*
Northwestern University D*
The Ohio State University M,D*
Ohio University M,D*
Oregon Health & Science University M,D*
Penn State Hershey Medical Center M,D*
Penn State University Park M,D*
Princeton University D*
Rosalind Franklin University of Medicine and Science D*
Rush University M,D
Rutgers, The State University of New Jersey, Newark D*
Rutgers, The State University of New Jersey, New Brunswick D*
Seton Hall University M*
Stanford University D*
State University of New York Downstate Medical Center D*
State University of New York Upstate Medical University D*
Stony Brook University, State University of New York D*
Syracuse University M,D*
Teachers College Columbia University M,D*
Temple University M,D*
Texas A&M Health Science Center D*
Texas A&M University M,D*
Texas Tech University Health Sciences Center M,D
Thomas Jefferson University D*
Tufts University D*
Tulane University M,D*
Uniformed Services University of the Health Sciences D*
Université de Montréal M,D,O
University at Albany, State University of New York M,D*
University at Buffalo, the State University of New York M,D*
The University of Alabama at Birmingham M,D*
University of Alberta M,D*
The University of Arizona D*
The University of British Columbia M,D*
University of Calgary M,D
University of California, Berkeley D*
University of California, Davis D*
University of California, Los Angeles D*
University of California, Riverside D*
University of California, San Diego D*
University of California, San Francisco D
University of Chicago D*
University of Cincinnati D
University of Colorado at Denver and Health Sciences Center D*
University of Connecticut M,D*
University of Connecticut Health Center D*
University of Delaware D*
University of Florida M,D*
University of Georgia D*
University of Guelph M,D,O
University of Hartford M*
University of Idaho M,D*
University of Illinois at Chicago D*
University of Illinois at Urbana–Champaign D*
The University of Iowa D*
University of Kansas M,D*
University of Lethbridge M,D
University of Maryland, Baltimore D*
University of Maryland, Baltimore County D*
University of Maryland, College Park M,D*
University of Massachusetts Amherst M,D*
University of Massachusetts Worcester D*
University of Medicine and Dentistry of New Jersey M,D*
University of Miami M,D*
University of Michigan D*
University of Minnesota, Twin Cities Campus M,D*
University of Missouri–St. Louis M,D,O
University of Nebraska Medical Center M,D*
University of New Mexico M,D*
University of Oklahoma Health Sciences Center M,D
University of Oregon M,D*
University of Pennsylvania D*
University of Pittsburgh D*
University of Rochester M,D*
University of South Alabama D*
The University of South Dakota M,D
University of Southern California D*
The University of Texas at Austin M,D*
The University of Texas at Dallas M,D*
The University of Texas Health Science Center at Houston M,D*
The University of Texas Medical Branch D*
The University of Texas Southwestern Medical Center at Dallas D*
The University of Toledo M,D*
University of Utah D*
University of Vermont D*
University of Virginia D*
University of Washington D*
The University of Western Ontario M,D
University of Wisconsin–Madison M,D*
University of Wyoming D
Vanderbilt University D*
Virginia Commonwealth University M,D*
Wake Forest University D*
Washington State University M,D*
Washington University in St. Louis D*
Wayne State University M,D*
West Virginia University D*
Yale University D*

NONPROFIT MANAGEMENT

American Jewish University M
Azusa Pacific University M
Boston University M,O*
Capella University M,D,O
Carlos Albizu University, Miami Campus M,D
Carlow University M
Case Western Reserve University M,O*
Cleveland State University M,O
College of Notre Dame of Maryland M
The College of Saint Rose O*
Columbia University M*
DePaul University M,O*
Eastern Michigan University M
Eastern University M*
Fairleigh Dickinson University, Metropolitan Campus M,O*
Florida Atlantic University M
The George Washington University M*
Hamline University M
High Point University M
Hope International University M
Illinois Institute of Technology M*
Indiana University Bloomington M,D,O*
Indiana University Northwest M,O
Indiana University–Purdue University Indianapolis M*
Indiana University South Bend M,O
John Carroll University M
Kean University M
Lindenwood University M

Lipscomb University	M
Long Island University, C.W. Post Campus	M,O*
Long Island University, Rockland Graduate Campus	M,O
Metropolitan State University	M
New England College	M
New Mexico Highlands University	M
The New School: A University	M*
New York University	M,D,O*
North Central College	M
Northern Kentucky University	M,O
Oral Roberts University	M
Pace University	M*
Park University	M
Regis University	M,O
Robert Morris University	M
Roberts Wesleyan College	M,O
Rosemont College	M
St. Cloud State University	M
Saint Xavier University	M,O
San Francisco State University	M
Seattle University	M
Seton Hall University	M*
Southern New Hampshire University	M,D,O*
Spertus Institute of Jewish Studies	M
Suffolk University	M,O*
Trinity (Washington) University	M
Tufts University	O*
University of Central Florida	M,O*
University of Connecticut	M,O*
University of Dallas	M
University of Delaware	M,D*
University of Georgia	M,D,O*
The University of Iowa	M*
University of La Verne	M,O
University of Maryland, Baltimore County	M,O*
University of Memphis	M*
University of Michigan–Dearborn	M,O*
University of Missouri–St. Louis	M,O
The University of North Carolina at Greensboro	M,O
University of Northern Iowa	M
University of Notre Dame	M*
University of Pittsburgh	M*
University of San Diego	M,D,O*
University of San Francisco	M
University of Southern Maine	M,O
University of the Sacred Heart	M
University of the West	M
Virginia Commonwealth University	O*
Western Illinois University	M,O
Willamette University	M
Worcester State College	M

NORTHERN STUDIES

University of Alaska Fairbanks	M
University of Manitoba	M

NUCLEAR ENGINEERING

Air Force Institute of Technology	M,D
Cornell University	M,D*
École Polytechnique de Montréal	M,D,O
Georgia Institute of Technology	M,D*
Idaho State University	M,D,O
Kansas State University	M,D*
Massachusetts Institute of Technology	M,D,O*
McMaster University	M,D
North Carolina State University	M,D*
The Ohio State University	M,D*
Oregon State University	M,D*
Penn State University Park	M,D*
Purdue University	M,D*
Rensselaer Polytechnic Institute	M,D*
Royal Military College of Canada	M,D
Texas A&M University	M,D*
The University of Arizona	M,D*
University of California, Berkeley	M,D*
University of Cincinnati	M,D
University of Florida	M,D,O*
University of Idaho	M,D*
University of Illinois at Urbana–Champaign	M,D*
University of Maryland, College Park	M,D*
University of Massachusetts Lowell	M*
University of Michigan	M,D,O*
University of Missouri–Columbia	M,D*
University of Missouri–Rolla	M,D*
University of New Mexico	M,D*
The University of Tennessee	M,D*
University of Utah	M,D*
University of Wisconsin–Madison	M,D*

NURSE ANESTHESIA

Albany Medical College	M
Arkansas State University	M,O
Barry University	M*
Baylor College of Medicine	M*
Boston College	M,D*
Bradley University	M
Case Western Reserve University	M*
Central Connecticut State University	M,O
Columbia University	M,O*
DePaul University	M*
Drexel University	M*
Duke University	M,D,O*
Emory University	M,D*
Fairfield University	M,O*
Gannon University	M,O
Gonzaga University	M
Gooding Institute of Nurse Anesthesia	M
Inter American University of Puerto Rico, Arecibo Campus	M
La Roche College	M
Mayo School of Health Sciences	M
Medical College of Georgia	M,D*
Medical University of South Carolina	M*
Middle Tennessee School of Anesthesia	M
Midwestern University, Glendale Campus	M*
Missouri State University	M*
Mountain State University	M,O*
Mount Marty College	M
Murray State University	M
Newman University	M
Northeastern University	M*
Oakland University	M,O*
Rush University	M,D,O
Saint Joseph's University	M*
Saint Mary's University of Minnesota	M
Samuel Merritt College	M,O
Southern Illinois University Edwardsville	M,O
State University of New York Downstate Medical Center	M*
Texas Christian University	M
Texas Wesleyan University	M
Uniformed Services University of the Health Sciences	M*
Union University	M,O
Université de Montréal	O
University at Buffalo, the State University of New York	M,D,O*
The University of Alabama at Birmingham	M*
The University of British Columbia	M,D*
University of Cincinnati	M,D
University of Detroit Mercy	M
University of Kansas	M*
University of Medicine and Dentistry of New Jersey	M,D,O*
University of Miami	M,D*
University of Michigan–Flint	M*
University of Minnesota, Twin Cities Campus	M*
University of New England	M
The University of North Carolina at Charlotte	M*
The University of North Carolina at Greensboro	M,D,O
University of Pennsylvania	M*
University of Pittsburgh	M*
University of Puerto Rico, Medical Sciences Campus	M*
The University of Scranton	M,O
University of South Carolina	M*
The University of Tennessee at Chattanooga	M
University of Wisconsin–La Crosse	M
Villanova University	M,D,O*
Virginia Commonwealth University	M,D*
Wayne State University	M,O*
Webster University	M
Westminster College (UT)	M

NURSE MIDWIFERY

Bastyr University	D,O*
Boston University	M,O*
Case Western Reserve University	M,D*
Columbia University	M*
Emory University	M*
Frontier School of Midwifery and Family Nursing	M,O
Illinois State University	M,O*
Marquette University	M,D,O
Medical University of South Carolina	M*
National College of Midwifery	M,D
New York University	M,O*
Oregon Health & Science University	M,O*
Philadelphia University	M,O*
Shenandoah University	M,O*
Stony Brook University, State University of New York	M,O*
University of Cincinnati	M,D
University of Illinois at Chicago	M*
University of Indianapolis	M
University of Kansas	M,D,O*
University of Maryland, Baltimore	M*
University of Medicine and Dentistry of New Jersey	O*
University of Miami	M,D*
University of Michigan	M*
University of Minnesota, Twin Cities Campus	M*
University of Pennsylvania	M*
University of Puerto Rico, Medical Sciences Campus	M,O*
University of Rhode Island	M,D
The University of Texas at El Paso	M
Vanderbilt University	M,D*
Wichita State University	M*

NURSING—GENERAL

Abilene Christian University	M
Adelphi University	M,D,O*
Albany State University	M
Alcorn State University	M
Allen College	M
Alverno College	M
American International College	M
American Sentinel University	M
American University of Beirut	M
Andrews University	M
Arizona State University	M*
Arkansas State University	M,O
Armstrong Atlantic State University	M
Athabasca University	M,O
Augsburg College	M
Augustana College	M
Austin Peay State University	M
Azusa Pacific University	M,D
Ball State University	M*
Barnes-Jewish College of Nursing and Allied Health	M
Barry University	M,D,O*
Baylor University	M*
Bellarmine University	M,D
Belmont University	M
Bethel College (IN)	M
Bethel University	M,O
Bloomsburg University of Pennsylvania	M
Boston College	M,D*
Bowie State University	M
Bradley University	M
Briar Cliff University	M
Brigham Young University	M*
California State University, Bakersfield	M
California State University, Chico	M
California State University, Dominguez Hills	M
California State University, Fresno	M
California State University, Fullerton	M
California State University, Long Beach	M
California State University, Los Angeles	M
California State University, Sacramento	M*
California State University, San Bernardino	M
Capital University	M
Cardinal Stritch University	M*
Carlow University	M,O
Carson-Newman College	M
Case Western Reserve University	M,D*
The Catholic University of America	M,D*
Chatham University	M,D
Clarion University of Pennsylvania	M
Clarke College	M,O
Clarkson College	M,O
Clayton State University	M
Clemson University	M*
Cleveland State University	M
College Misericordia	M
College of Mount St. Joseph	M
College of Mount Saint Vincent	M,O
The College of New Jersey	M,O
The College of New Rochelle	M,O
College of St. Catherine	M*
The College of St. Scholastica	M,O
College of Staten Island of the City University of New York	M,O
Columbia University	M,D,O*
Concordia University Wisconsin	M
Coppin State University	M,O
Creighton University	M*
Daemen College	M,O
Dalhousie University	M
Delta State University	M
DePaul University	M*
DeSales University	M
Dominican College	M
Dominican University of California	M
Drexel University	M*
Duke University	D*
Duquesne University	M,D,O*
D'Youville College	M,O*
East Carolina University	M,D*
Eastern Kentucky University	M*
Eastern Washington University	M
East Tennessee State University	M,D,O
Edgewood College	M
Edinboro University of Pennsylvania	M
Elmhurst College	M
Emory University	M,D*
Excelsior College	M
Fairfield University	M,O*
Fairleigh Dickinson University, Metropolitan Campus	M,O*
Fairmont State University	M
Felician College	M,O*
Ferris State University	M
Florida Agricultural and Mechanical University	M*
Florida Atlantic University	M,D,O
Florida Gulf Coast University	M
Florida International University	M,D*
Florida Southern College	M
Florida State University	M,O*
Fort Hays State University	M
Franciscan University of Steubenville	M
Frontier School of Midwifery and Family Nursing	M,O
Gannon University	M,O
Gardner-Webb University	M,O
George Mason University	M,D,O*
Georgetown University	M*
Georgia College & State University	M
Georgia Southern University	M,O
Georgia State University	M,D,O*
Gonzaga University	M
Governors State University	M
Graceland University	M,O
Grambling State University	M,O
Grand Valley State University	M
Gwynedd-Mercy College	M
Hampton University	M*
Hardin-Simmons University	M
Hawai'i Pacific University	M*
Holy Family University	M
Holy Names University	M
Howard University	M,O*
Hunter College of the City University of New York	M,O
Husson College	M
Idaho State University	M,O
Illinois State University	M,O*
Immaculata University	M
Indiana State University	M*
Indiana University of Pennsylvania	M
Indiana University–Purdue University Fort Wayne	M,O
Indiana University–Purdue University Indianapolis	M,D*
Indiana Wesleyan University	M,O
Inter American University of Puerto Rico, Arecibo Campus	M
Jacksonville State University	M
Jacksonville University	M
James Madison University	M
Jefferson College of Health Sciences	M
The Johns Hopkins University	M,D,O*
Kean University	M
Kennesaw State University	M
Kent State University	M,D*
Lamar University	M*
La Roche College	M
La Salle University	M,O
Lehman College of the City University of New York	M
Le Moyne College	M
Lewis University	M
Liberty University	M,D
Lincoln Memorial University	M
Loma Linda University	M,O
Long Island University, Brooklyn Campus	M,O*
Long Island University, C.W. Post Campus	M,O*
Louisiana State University Health Sciences Center	M,D*
Loyola University Chicago	M*
Loyola University New Orleans	M
Madonna University	M
Malone College	M

P—first professional degree; M—master's degree; D—doctorate; O—other advanced degree;
**full description and/or announcement in Book 2, 3, 4, 5, or 6*

Institution	Degrees
Mansfield University of Pennsylvania	M
Marian College of Fond du Lac	M
Marquette University	M,D,O
Marshall University	M
Marymount University	M,O
Maryville University of Saint Louis	M
McGill University	M,D,O*
McKendree College	M
McMaster University	M,D
McNeese State University	M
Medical College of Georgia	M,D*
Medical University of South Carolina	D*
Memorial University of Newfoundland	M,O
Mercer University	M,O
Mercy College	M
Metropolitan State University	M
MGH Institute of Health Professions	M,O*
Michigan State University	M,D*
Middle Tennessee State University	M*
Midwestern State University	M
Millersville University of Pennsylvania	M
Minnesota State University Mankato	M
Minnesota State University Moorhead	M,O
Mississippi University for Women	M,O
Missouri State University	M*
Molloy College	M,O
Monmouth University	M,O
Montana State University	M,O
Mountain State University	M,O*
Mount Carmel College of Nursing	M*
Mount Saint Mary College	M
Mount St. Mary's College	M
Murray State University	M
Nazareth College of Rochester	M
Nebraska Methodist College	M
Nebraska Wesleyan University	M
Neumann College	M
New Jersey City University	M
New Mexico State University	M
New York University	M,O*
North Dakota State University	M,D
Northeastern University	M,O*
Northern Arizona University	M,O
Northern Illinois University	M
Northern Kentucky University	M,O
Northern Michigan University	M
North Park University	M
Northwestern State University of Louisiana	M
Nova Southeastern University	M*
Oakland University	M,D,O*
The Ohio State University	M,D*
The Ohio State University at Marion	M,D
Oklahoma City University	M
Old Dominion University	M*
Oregon Health & Science University	M,D,O*
Otterbein College	M,O
Pace University	M,O*
Pacific Lutheran University	M
Penn State University Park	M,D*
Pittsburg State University	M
Point Loma Nazarene University	M
Pontifical Catholic University of Puerto Rico	M
Prairie View A&M University	M
Purdue University Calumet	M
Queen's University at Kingston	M
Queens University of Charlotte	M
Radford University	M
Regis College (MA)	M,O
Regis University	M
Research College of Nursing	M
Rhode Island College	M
The Richard Stockton College of New Jersey	M
Rivier College	M
Robert Morris University	M
Roberts Wesleyan College	M
Rush University	M,D,O
Rutgers, The State University of New Jersey, Newark	M*
Sacred Heart University	M
Sage Graduate School	M,O
Saginaw Valley State University	M
St. Ambrose University	M
Saint Francis Medical Center College of Nursing	M,O
St. John Fisher College	M,O
Saint Joseph College	M,O
St. Joseph's College, New York	M*
Saint Joseph's College of Maine	M,O
St. Joseph's College, Suffolk Campus	M
Saint Louis University	M,D,O*
Saint Peter's College	M
Saint Xavier University	M,O
Salem State College	M
Salisbury University	M
Samford University	M
Samuel Merritt College	M,O
San Diego State University	M*
San Francisco State University	M
San Jose State University	M,O
Seattle Pacific University	M,O
Seattle University	M
Seton Hall University	M,D*
Shenandoah University	M,O*
Simmons College	M,D,O
Slippery Rock University of Pennsylvania	M
South Dakota State University	M,D
Southeastern Louisiana University	M
Southeast Missouri State University	M
Southern Adventist University	M
Southern Connecticut State University	M
Southern Illinois University Edwardsville	M,O
Southern Nazarene University	M
Southern University and Agricultural and Mechanical College	M,D,O*
Spalding University	M
Spring Hill College	M
State University of New York at Binghamton	M,D,O*
State University of New York at New Paltz	M,O
State University of New York Downstate Medical Center	M,O*
State University of New York Institute of Technology	M,O
State University of New York Upstate Medical University	M,O*
Stony Brook University, State University of New York	M,O*
Temple University	M*
Tennessee State University	M*
Tennessee Technological University	M*
Texas A&M International University	M
Texas A&M University–Corpus Christi	M
Texas Christian University	M
Texas Tech University Health Sciences Center	M,O
Texas Woman's University	M,D
Thomas Edison State College	M
Thomas Jefferson University	M*
Thomas University	M
Towson University	M,O
Troy University	M
Uniformed Services University of the Health Sciences	M*
Union University	M,O
Université de Montréal	M,D,O
Université du Québec à Rimouski	M,O
Université du Québec à Trois-Rivières	M,O
Université du Québec en Outaouais	M,O
Université Laval	M,O
University at Buffalo, the State University of New York	M,D,O*
The University of Akron	M,D
The University of Alabama	M
The University of Alabama at Birmingham	M,D*
The University of Alabama in Huntsville	M,O
University of Alaska Anchorage	M,O
University of Alberta	M,D*
The University of Arizona	M,D*
University of Arkansas	M*
University of Arkansas for Medical Sciences	M,D*
The University of British Columbia	M,D*
University of Calgary	M,D,O
University of California, Los Angeles	M,D*
University of California, San Francisco	M,D
University of Central Arkansas	M
University of Central Florida	D,O*
University of Central Missouri	M
University of Cincinnati	M,D
University of Colorado at Colorado Springs	M,D
University of Colorado at Denver and Health Sciences Center	M,D,O*
University of Connecticut	M,D,O*
University of Delaware	M,O*
University of Evansville	M
University of Florida	M,D*
University of Hartford	M*
University of Hawaii at Manoa	M,D,O*
University of Illinois at Chicago	M,D*
University of Indianapolis	M
The University of Iowa	M,D*
University of Kansas	M,D,O*
University of Kentucky	M,D*
University of Lethbridge	M,D
University of Louisiana at Lafayette	M*
University of Louisville	M,D
University of Maine	M,O*
University of Manitoba	M
University of Mary	M
University of Maryland, Baltimore	M,D*
University of Massachusetts Amherst	M,D*
University of Massachusetts Boston	M,D
University of Massachusetts Lowell	M,D*
University of Massachusetts Worcester	M,D,O*
University of Medicine and Dentistry of New Jersey	M,O*
University of Miami	M,D*
University of Michigan	M,D,O*
University of Michigan–Flint	M*
University of Minnesota, Twin Cities Campus	M,D*
University of Mississippi Medical Center	M,D*
University of Missouri–Columbia	M,D*
University of Missouri–Kansas City	M,D*
University of Missouri–St. Louis	M,D,O
University of Mobile	M
University of Nebraska Medical Center	M,D*
University of Nevada, Las Vegas	M,D,O
University of Nevada, Reno	M*
University of New Brunswick Fredericton	M
University of New Hampshire	M*
University of New Mexico	M,D*
University of North Alabama	M
The University of North Carolina at Chapel Hill	M,D*
The University of North Carolina at Charlotte	M*
The University of North Carolina at Greensboro	M,D,O
The University of North Carolina Wilmington	M*
University of North Dakota	M,D
University of Northern Colorado	M,D
University of North Florida	M,O
University of Oklahoma Health Sciences Center	M
University of Ottawa	M,D,O*
University of Pennsylvania	M,D,O*
University of Phoenix–Atlanta Campus	M
University of Phoenix–Augusta Campus	M
University of Phoenix–Central Florida Campus	M
University of Phoenix–Central Valley Campus	M
University of Phoenix–Charlotte Campus	M
University of Phoenix–Cheyenne Campus	M
University of Phoenix–Cleveland Campus	M
University of Phoenix–Denver Campus	M
University of Phoenix–Detroit Campus	M
University of Phoenix–Fort Lauderdale Campus	M
University of Phoenix–Harrisburg Campus	M
University of Phoenix–Hawaii Campus	M
University of Phoenix–Indianapolis Campus	M
University of Phoenix–Kansas City Campus	M
University of Phoenix–Louisiana Campus	M
University of Phoenix–Maryland Campus	M
University of Phoenix–Metro Detroit Campus	M
University of Phoenix–Minneapolis/St. Louis Park Campus	M
University of Phoenix–New Mexico Campus	M
University of Phoenix—Northern Nevada Campus	M
University of Phoenix–Northern Virginia Campus	M
University of Phoenix–North Florida Campus	M
University of Phoenix–Northwest Arkansas Campus	M
University of Phoenix–Northwest Indiana	M
University of Phoenix Online Campus	M
University of Phoenix–Phoenix Campus	M,O
University of Phoenix–Renton Learning Center	M
University of Phoenix–Richmond Campus	M
University of Phoenix–Sacramento Valley Campus	M
University of Phoenix–San Diego Campus	M
University of Phoenix–Savannah Campus	M
University of Phoenix–Southern California Campus	M,O
University of Phoenix–Southern Colorado Campus	M
University of Phoenix–Springfield Campus	M
University of Phoenix–Utah Campus	M
University of Phoenix–Vancouver Campus	M
University of Phoenix–West Florida Campus	M
University of Phoenix–West Michigan Campus	M
University of Pittsburgh	M*
University of Portland	M
University of Puerto Rico, Medical Sciences Campus	M*
University of Rhode Island	M,D
University of Rochester	M,D,O*
University of St. Francis (IL)	M
University of Saint Francis (IN)	M
University of San Diego	M,D,O*
University of San Francisco	M
University of Saskatchewan	M
The University of Scranton	M,O
University of South Alabama	M,D*
University of South Carolina	M,O*
University of Southern Indiana	M
University of Southern Maine	M,O
University of Southern Mississippi	M,D*
University of South Florida	M,D*
The University of Tampa	M
The University of Tennessee	M,D*
The University of Tennessee at Chattanooga	M
The University of Tennessee Health Science Center	M,D*
The University of Texas at Arlington	M,D*
The University of Texas at Austin	M,D*
The University of Texas at El Paso	M
The University of Texas at Tyler	M
The University of Texas Health Science Center at Houston	M,D*
The University of Texas Health Science Center at San Antonio	M,D*
The University of Texas Medical Branch	M,D*
The University of Texas–Pan American	M
University of the Incarnate Word	M
The University of Toledo	M,O*
University of Toronto	M,D,O
University of Utah	M,D*
University of Vermont	M*
University of Victoria	M
University of Virginia	M,D*
University of Washington	M,D*
University of Washington, Bothell	M
The University of Western Ontario	M,D
University of West Georgia	M
University of Windsor	M
University of Wisconsin–Eau Claire	M
University of Wisconsin–Madison	M,D*
University of Wisconsin–Milwaukee	M,D,O
University of Wisconsin–Oshkosh	M
University of Wyoming	M
Ursuline College	M
Valdosta State University	M
Valparaiso University	M,O
Vanderbilt University	M,D*
Villanova University	M,D,O*
Virginia Commonwealth University	M,D,O*
Viterbo University	M
Wagner College	M
Walden University	M,D
Washington State University Spokane	M
Washington State University Tri-Cities	M
Washington State University Vancouver	M
Wayne State University	D*
Webster University	M
Wesley College	M
West Chester University of Pennsylvania	M
Western Carolina University	M*

Western Connecticut State University M*
Western Kentucky University M
Western University of Health Sciences M
Westminster College (UT) M
West Texas A&M University M
West Virginia University M,D,O*
Wheeling Jesuit University M*
Wichita State University M*
Widener University M,D,O*
Wilkes University M
William Carey University M
William Paterson University of New Jersey M*
Wilmington College (DE) M
Winona State University M
Winston-Salem State University M
Wright State University M*
Xavier University M*
Yale University M,D,O*
York College of Pennsylvania M
York University M*
Youngstown State University M

NURSING AND HEALTHCARE ADMINISTRATION

Allen College M
Athabasca University M,O
Barry University M,D,O*
Baylor University M*
Bellarmine University M,D
Bloomsburg University of Pennsylvania M
Bowie State University M
Bradley University M
Capital University M
Carlow University M,O
The Catholic University of America M,D*
Clarke College M
Clarkson College M
College of Mount Saint Vincent M,O
The College of New Rochelle M,O
Daemen College M,O
Duke University M,D,O*
Duquesne University M,O*
D'Youville College M,O*
Eastern Michigan University M
Emory University M*
Excelsior College O
Fairmont State University M
Ferris State University M
Florida Agricultural and Mechanical University M*
Florida Atlantic University M*
Gannon University M,O
George Mason University M,D,O*
The George Washington University M,D,O*
Graceland University M,O
Grand Valley State University M
Indiana University–Purdue University Fort Wayne M,O
Indiana Wesleyan University M,O
Jefferson College of Health Sciences M
The Johns Hopkins University M*
Kean University M
Kent State University M,D*
Lamar University M*
La Roche College M
La Salle University M,O
Lewis University M
Loma Linda University M,O
Long Island University, Brooklyn Campus M*
Louisiana State University Health Sciences Center M,D*
Loyola University Chicago M*
Madonna University M
Marymount University M,O
Marywood University M*
Medical University of South Carolina M*
Mercy College M
Minnesota State University Mankato M
Molloy College M,O
Mountain State University M,O*
Mount Saint Mary College M*
Northeastern University M*
Norwich University M
Otterbein College M,O
Pacific Lutheran University M
Prairie View A&M University M
Queens University of Charlotte M
Rivier College M
Roberts Wesleyan College M
Sacred Heart University M
Saginaw Valley State University M
Saint Joseph's College of Maine M,O
Saint Xavier University M,O
Samuel Merritt College M,O
San Francisco State University M
San Jose State University M,O
Seattle Pacific University M
Seattle University M
Seton Hall University M*
Southern Adventist University M
Southern Connecticut State University M
Southern Illinois University Edwardsville M,O
Southern Nazarene University M
Southern University and Agricultural and Mechanical College M,D,O*
Spalding University M
State University of New York Institute of Technology M,O
Teachers College Columbia University M,D*
Texas A&M University–Corpus Christi M
Texas Tech University Health Sciences Center M,O
Touro University International M,D,O
University of Cincinnati M,D
University of Colorado at Colorado Springs M,D
University of Connecticut M,D,O*
University of Delaware M,O*
University of Hawaii at Manoa M,D,O*
University of Illinois at Chicago M*
University of Indianapolis M
University of Mary M
University of Maryland, Baltimore M*
University of Massachusetts Lowell D*
University of Michigan M*
University of Minnesota, Twin Cities Campus M*
University of Missouri–Kansas City M,D*
The University of North Carolina at Greensboro M,D,O
University of Pennsylvania M,D*
University of Phoenix–Springfield Campus M
University of Pittsburgh M*
University of Puerto Rico, Medical Sciences Campus M*
University of Rhode Island M,D
University of San Diego M,D,O*
University of San Francisco M
University of South Carolina M*
University of Southern Mississippi M,D*
The University of Tampa M
The University of Tennessee at Chattanooga M
The University of Texas at Arlington M,D*
The University of Texas at El Paso M
The University of Texas at Tyler M
Vanderbilt University M,D*
Villanova University M,D,O*
Virginia Commonwealth University M,D,O*
Wichita State University M*
Winona State University M*
Wright State University M*
Xavier University M*

NURSING EDUCATION

Angelo State University M
Azusa Pacific University M,D
Barnes-Jewish College of Nursing and Allied Health M
Barry University M,O*
Bellarmine University M,D
Bethel University M,O
Bowie State University M
Brenau University M
The Catholic University of America M,D*
Clarke College M,O
Clarkson College M
College of Mount Saint Vincent M,O
The College of New Rochelle M,O
Concordia University Wisconsin M
DeSales University M
Dominican University of California M
Duke University M,D,O*
Duquesne University M,O*
D'Youville College M,O*
Eastern Michigan University M,O
Eastern Washington University M
Fairmont State University M
Ferris State University M
Florida State University M,O*
George Mason University M,D,O*
Graceland University M,O
Grambling State University M,O
Grand Valley State University M
Indiana Wesleyan University M,O
Jefferson College of Health Sciences M
Kent State University M,D*
Lamar University M*
La Salle University M,O
Lewis University M
Marian College of Fond du Lac M
Marymount University M,O
Medical University of South Carolina M*
Mercy College M
MGH Institute of Health Professions M,O*
Midwestern State University M
Minnesota State University Mankato M
Minnesota State University Moorhead M
Molloy College M,O
Montana State University M,O
Mountain State University M,O*
Mount Carmel College of Nursing M*
Mount Saint Mary College M*
New York University M,O*
North Georgia College & State University M
Oakland University M,O*
Prairie View A&M University M
Regis College (MA) M,O
Research College of Nursing M
Rivier College M
Roberts Wesleyan College M
Saint Francis Medical Center College of Nursing M,O
St. John Fisher College M,O
Saint Joseph's College of Maine M,O
San Francisco State University M
San Jose State University M,O
Seton Hall University M*
Southern Connecticut State University M
Southern Illinois University Edwardsville M,O
Southern Nazarene University M
Southern University and Agricultural and Mechanical College M,D,O*
State University of New York Institute of Technology M,O
Teachers College Columbia University M,D*
Texas Tech University Health Sciences Center M,O
Texas Woman's University M,D
Union University M,O
University of Alaska Anchorage M,O
University of Central Florida D,O*
University of Hartford M*
University of Indianapolis M
University of Kansas M,D,O*
University of Mary M
University of Maryland, Baltimore M*
University of Massachusetts Worcester M,D,O*
University of Medicine and Dentistry of New Jersey M,O*
University of Missouri–Kansas City M,D*
University of Nevada, Las Vegas M,D,O
The University of North Carolina at Greensboro M,D,O
University of Northern Colorado M,D
University of Phoenix–Cheyenne Campus M
University of Phoenix–Fort Lauderdale Campus M
University of Phoenix–Harrisburg Campus M
University of Phoenix–Maryland Campus M
University of Phoenix—Northern Nevada Campus M
University of Phoenix–North Florida Campus M
University of Phoenix–Northwest Arkansas Campus M
University of Phoenix–Northwest Indiana M
University of Phoenix Online Campus M
University of Phoenix–Pittsburgh Campus M
University of Phoenix–Renton Learning Center M
University of Phoenix–Sacramento Valley Campus M
University of Phoenix–Savannah Campus M
University of Phoenix–Southern California Campus M,O
University of Phoenix–West Florida Campus M
University of Pittsburgh M*
University of Puerto Rico, Medical Sciences Campus M*
University of Rhode Island M,D
The University of Tampa M
The University of Tennessee at Chattanooga M
The University of Texas at Arlington M,D*
The University of Texas at Tyler M
Villanova University M,D,O*
Wayne State University M,O*
West Chester University of Pennsylvania M
Westminster College (UT) M
Winona State University M

NURSING INFORMATICS

Case Western Reserve University M*
Duke University M,D,O*
Ferris State University M
La Salle University M,O
Molloy College M,O
New York University M,O*
University of Medicine and Dentistry of New Jersey M*
Vanderbilt University M,D*

NUTRITION

American Health Sciences University M
American University of Beirut M
Andrews University M
Arizona State University at the Polytechnic Campus M
Auburn University M,D*
Barnes-Jewish College of Nursing and Allied Health M,O
Bastyr University M*
Baylor University M,D*
Benedictine University M
Boston University M,D*
Bowling Green State University M*
Brigham Young University M*
Brooklyn College of the City University of New York M
California State Polytechnic University, Pomona M
California State University, Chico M
California State University, Long Beach M
California State University, Los Angeles M
Case Western Reserve University M,D*
Central Michigan University M*
Central Washington University M*
Chapman University M
Clemson University M*
College of Saint Elizabeth M,O
Colorado State University M,D*
Columbia University M,D*
Cornell University M,D*
Drexel University M,D*
D'Youville College M*
East Carolina University M*
Eastern Illinois University M
Eastern Kentucky University M*
Eastern Michigan University M
East Tennessee State University M
Emory University M,D*
Florida International University M,D*
Florida State University M,D*
Framingham State College M*
Georgia State University M,O*
Harvard University D*
Howard University M,D*
Huntington College of Health Sciences M
Idaho State University M,O
Immaculata University M
Indiana State University M*
Indiana University Bloomington M,D*
Indiana University of Pennsylvania M
Indiana University–Purdue University Indianapolis M,D*
Iowa State University of Science and Technology M,D*
The Johns Hopkins University M,D*
Kansas State University M,D*
Kent State University M*
Lehman College of the City University of New York M
Loma Linda University M,D
Long Island University, C.W. Post Campus M,O*
Louisiana Tech University M
Marshall University M
Marywood University M*
McGill University M,D,O*
McMaster University M,D
Meredith College M
Michigan State University M,D*
Middle Tennessee State University M*
Mississippi State University M,D
Montclair State University M,O*
Mount Mary College M
Mount Saint Vincent University M

P—first professional degree; M—master's degree; D—doctorate; O—other advanced degree;
**full description and/or announcement in Book 2, 3, 4, 5, or 6*

New York Chiropractic College M*
New York Institute of Technology M
New York University M,D*
North Carolina Agricultural and Technical State University M
North Carolina State University M,D*
North Dakota State University M
Northern Illinois University M
The Ohio State University M,D*
Ohio University M*
Oklahoma State University M,D*
Oregon State University M,D*
Penn State University Park M,D*
Purdue University M,D*
Rosalind Franklin University of Medicine and Science M*
Rush University M
Rutgers, The State University of New Jersey, New Brunswick M,D*
Sage Graduate School M
Saint Louis University M*
San Diego State University M*
San Jose State University M
Simmons College M,O
South Carolina State University M
South Dakota State University M
Southeast Missouri State University M
Southern Illinois University Carbondale M*
Syracuse University M*
Teachers College Columbia University M,D*
Texas Southern University M
Texas Tech University M,D
Texas Woman's University M,D
Tufts University M,D*
Tulane University M*
Tuskegee University M
Université de Moncton M
Université de Montréal M,D
Université Laval M,D
University at Buffalo, the State University of New York M,D*
The University of Akron M
The University of Alabama M
The University of Alabama at Birmingham M,D,O*
University of Arkansas for Medical Sciences M*
University of Bridgeport M
The University of British Columbia M,D*
University of California, Berkeley M,D*
University of California, Davis M,D*
University of Central Oklahoma M
University of Chicago D*
University of Cincinnati M
University of Connecticut M,D*
University of Delaware M*
University of Florida M,D*
University of Georgia M,D*
University of Guelph M,D
University of Hawaii at Manoa M*
University of Illinois at Chicago M,D*
University of Illinois at Urbana–Champaign M,D*
University of Kansas M,O*
University of Kentucky M,D*
University of Maine M,D*
University of Manitoba M,D
University of Maryland, College Park M,D*
University of Massachusetts Amherst M,D*
University of Medicine and Dentistry of New Jersey M,D,O*
University of Memphis M*
University of Michigan M*
University of Minnesota, Twin Cities Campus M,D*
University of Missouri–Columbia M,D*
University of Nebraska–Lincoln M,D*
University of Nebraska Medical Center O*
University of Nevada, Reno M*
University of New Hampshire M,D*
University of New Haven M*
University of New Mexico M*
The University of North Carolina at Chapel Hill M,D*
The University of North Carolina at Greensboro M,D
University of North Florida M,O
University of Oklahoma Health Sciences Center M
University of Pittsburgh M*
University of Puerto Rico, Medical Sciences Campus M,D,O*
University of Puerto Rico, Río Piedras M*
University of Rhode Island M,D
University of Southern California M*
University of Southern Mississippi M,D*
The University of Tennessee M*
The University of Tennessee at Martin M
The University of Texas at Austin M,D*
University of the Incarnate Word M,O
University of Toronto M,D
University of Utah M*
University of Vermont M,D*
University of Washington M,D*
University of Wisconsin–Madison M,D*
University of Wisconsin–Stevens Point M
University of Wisconsin–Stout M*
University of Wyoming M
Utah State University M,D
Virginia Polytechnic Institute and State University M,D*
Washington State University M,D*
Wayne State University M,D*
West Virginia University M*
Winthrop University M

OCCUPATIONAL HEALTH NURSING

University of Cincinnati M,D
University of Massachusetts Lowell M*
University of Medicine and Dentistry of New Jersey M,D,O*
University of Michigan M*
University of Minnesota, Twin Cities Campus M,D*
The University of North Carolina at Chapel Hill M*
University of Pennsylvania M*

OCCUPATIONAL THERAPY

Alvernia College M
American International College M
A.T. Still University of Health Sciences M,D
Baker College Center for Graduate Studies M
Barry University M*
Bay Path College M
Belmont University M,D
Boston University M,D*
Brenau University M
California State University, Dominguez Hills M
Chatham University M,D
Cleveland State University M
College Misericordia M
College of St. Catherine M*
The College of St. Scholastica M*
Colorado State University M*
Columbia University M,D*
Concordia University Wisconsin M
Creighton University D*
Dalhousie University M
Dominican College M
Dominican University of California M
Duquesne University M,D*
D'Youville College M*
East Carolina University M*
Eastern Kentucky University M*
Eastern Michigan University M
Eastern Washington University M
Florida Gulf Coast University M
Florida International University M*
Gannon University M,O
Governors State University M
Grand Valley State University M
Idaho State University M
Indiana University–Purdue University Indianapolis M,D*
Ithaca College M
James Madison University M
Kean University M
Keuka College M
Maryville University of Saint Louis M
McMaster University M
Medical College of Georgia M*
Medical University of South Carolina M*
Mercy College M
Midwestern University, Downers Grove Campus M*
Midwestern University, Glendale Campus M*
Milligan College M
Mount Mary College M
New York Institute of Technology M
New York University M,D*
Nova Southeastern University M,D*
The Ohio State University M*
Pacific University M*
Philadelphia University M*
Quinnipiac University M*
The Richard Stockton College of New Jersey M
Rockhurst University M
Rush University M
Sacred Heart University M
Sage Graduate School M
Saginaw Valley State University M
St. Ambrose University M
Saint Francis University M
Saint Louis University M*
Salem State College M
Samuel Merritt College M
San Jose State University M
Seton Hall University M*
Shenandoah University M*
Spalding University M
Springfield College M,O*
Stony Brook University, State University of New York M,D,O*
Temple University M*
Texas Tech University Health Sciences Center M
Texas Woman's University M,D
Thomas Jefferson University M*
Touro College M*
Towson University M
Tufts University M,D,O*
University at Buffalo, the State University of New York M*
The University of Alabama at Birmingham M*
University of Alberta M,D*
University of Central Arkansas M
The University of Findlay M
University of Florida M*
University of Illinois at Chicago M*
University of Indianapolis M,D
University of Kansas M,D*
University of Mary M
University of Mississippi Medical Center M*
University of Missouri–Columbia M*
University of New England M
University of New Hampshire M*
University of New Mexico M*
The University of North Carolina at Chapel Hill M,D*
University of North Dakota M
University of Oklahoma Health Sciences Center M
University of Pittsburgh M*
University of Puget Sound M
University of St. Augustine for Health Sciences M,D
The University of Scranton M
University of South Alabama M*
The University of South Dakota M
University of Southern California M,D*
University of Southern Indiana M
University of Southern Maine M
The University of Texas Health Science Center at San Antonio M*
The University of Texas Medical Branch M*
The University of Texas–Pan American M
The University of Toledo M,D*
University of Utah M*
University of Washington M,D*
The University of Western Ontario M
University of Wisconsin–La Crosse M
University of Wisconsin–Madison M,D*
University of Wisconsin–Milwaukee M
Utica College M
Virginia Commonwealth University M,D*
Washington University in St. Louis M,D*
Wayne State University M*
Western Michigan University M*
West Virginia University M*
Winston-Salem State University M
Worcester State College M
Xavier University M*

OCEAN ENGINEERING

Florida Atlantic University M,D
Florida Institute of Technology M,D*
Georgia Institute of Technology M,D*
Massachusetts Institute of Technology M,D,O*
Memorial University of Newfoundland M,D
OGI School of Science & Engineering at Oregon Health & Science University M,D
Oregon State University M*
Stevens Institute of Technology M,D*
Texas A&M University M,D*
University of Alaska Anchorage M,O
University of California, San Diego M,D*
University of Delaware M,D*
University of Florida M,D,O*
University of Hawaii at Manoa M,D*
University of Michigan M,D,O*
University of New Hampshire M,D*
University of Rhode Island M,D
University of Southern California M*
Virginia Polytechnic Institute and State University M,D*
Woods Hole Oceanographic Institution M,D,O

OCEANOGRAPHY

Columbia University M,D*
Cornell University D*
Dalhousie University M,D
Florida Institute of Technology M,D*
Florida State University M,D*
Louisiana State University and Agricultural and Mechanical College M,D*
Massachusetts Institute of Technology M,D,O*
McGill University M,D*
Memorial University of Newfoundland M,D
Naval Postgraduate School M,D
North Carolina State University M,D*
Nova Southeastern University M,D*
Old Dominion University M,D*
Oregon State University M,D*
Princeton University D*
Rutgers, The State University of New Jersey, New Brunswick M,D*
Texas A&M University M,D*
Université du Québec à Rimouski M,D
Université Laval D
University of Alaska Fairbanks M,D
The University of British Columbia M,D*
University of California, San Diego M,D*
University of Colorado at Boulder M,D*
University of Connecticut M,D*
University of Delaware M,D*
University of Georgia M,D*
University of Hawaii at Manoa M,D*
University of Maine M,D*
University of Maryland, College Park M,D*
University of Miami M,D*
University of Michigan M,D*
University of New Hampshire M,D*
University of Rhode Island M,D
University of Southern California D*
University of South Florida M,D*
University of Victoria M,D
University of Washington M,D*
University of Wisconsin–Madison M,D*
Woods Hole Oceanographic Institution M,D,O
Yale University D*

ONCOLOGY NURSING

Barnes-Jewish College of Nursing and Allied Health M
Columbia University M,O*
Duke University M,D,O*
Emory University M*
Gwynedd-Mercy College M
Loyola University Chicago M*
University of Delaware M,O*
University of Pennsylvania M*

OPERATIONS RESEARCH

Air Force Institute of Technology M,D
Bowling Green State University M*
California State University, East Bay M
California State University, Fullerton M
Carnegie Mellon University D*
Case Western Reserve University M*
Claremont Graduate University M,D
Clemson University M,D*
The College of William and Mary M
Columbia University M,D,O*
Cornell University M,D*
École Polytechnique de Montréal M,D,O
Florida Institute of Technology M,D*
George Mason University M*
Georgia Institute of Technology M*
Georgia State University M,D*
Idaho State University M,D,O
Indiana University–Purdue University Fort Wayne M,O
Iowa State University of Science and Technology M,D*
The Johns Hopkins University M,D*
Kansas State University M,D*
Louisiana Tech University M,D
Massachusetts Institute of Technology M,D*
Miami University M*
Naval Postgraduate School M,D

New Mexico Institute of Mining and Technology M,D
North Carolina State University M,D*
North Dakota State University M,D,O
Northeastern University M,D*
Northwestern University M,D*
Oklahoma State University M,D*
Oregon State University M,D*
Princeton University M,D*
Rensselaer Polytechnic Institute M,D*
Rutgers, The State University of New Jersey, New Brunswick D*
St. Mary's University of San Antonio M
Southern Methodist University M,D*
Temple University D*
The University of Alabama in Huntsville M
University of Arkansas M*
The University of British Columbia M*
University of California, Berkeley M,D*
University of California, Los Angeles M,D*
University of Central Florida M,D,O*
University of Colorado at Boulder M*
University of Delaware M,D*
University of Illinois at Chicago D*
The University of Iowa M,D*
University of Massachusetts Amherst M,D*
University of Miami M*
University of Michigan M,D*
University of New Haven M*
The University of North Carolina at Chapel Hill M,D*
University of Southern California M*
The University of Texas at Austin M,D*
University of Waterloo M,D*
Virginia Commonwealth University M,O*
Virginia Polytechnic Institute and State University M,D*
Western Michigan University M*

OPTICAL SCIENCES

Air Force Institute of Technology M,D
Alabama Agricultural and Mechanical University M,D
Cleveland State University M
École Polytechnique de Montréal M,D,O
Norfolk State University M
The Ohio State University M,D*
Rochester Institute of Technology M,D
Rose-Hulman Institute of Technology M*
The University of Alabama in Huntsville D
The University of Arizona M,D*
University of Central Florida M,D*
University of Colorado at Boulder M,D*
University of Dayton M,D*
University of Maryland, Baltimore County M,D*
University of Massachusetts Lowell M,D*
University of New Mexico M,D*
The University of North Carolina at Charlotte M,D*
University of Rochester M,D*

OPTOMETRY

Ferris State University P
Illinois College of Optometry P
Indiana University Bloomington P,M,D*
Inter American University of Puerto Rico School of Optometry P
The New England College of Optometry P,M*
Northeastern State University P
Nova Southeastern University P,M*
The Ohio State University P*
Pennsylvania College of Optometry P
Southern California College of Optometry P
Southern College of Optometry P
State University of New York College of Optometry P
Université de Montréal P
The University of Alabama at Birmingham P*
University of California, Berkeley P,O*
University of Houston P*
University of Missouri–St. Louis P
University of Waterloo M,D*

ORAL AND DENTAL SCIENCES

A.T. Still University of Health Sciences P
Boston University P,M,D,O*
Case Western Reserve University M,O*
Columbia University M,D,O*
Dalhousie University P,M,O
The George Washington University M*
Harvard University M,D,O*
Howard University P,O*
Idaho State University M,O
Jacksonville University O
Loma Linda University M,O
Marquette University M
McGill University M,D*
Medical College of Georgia M,D*
New York University M,D,O*
The Ohio State University D*
Oregon Health & Science University M,O*
Saint Louis University M*
Stony Brook University, State University of New York P,D,O*
Temple University M,O*
Texas A&M Health Science Center P,M,D,O*
Tufts University M,O*
Université de Montréal M,O
Université Laval M,O
University at Buffalo, the State University of New York M,D,O*
The University of Alabama at Birmingham M*
University of Alberta P,M,D,O*
The University of British Columbia M,D,O*
University of California, Los Angeles M,D*
University of California, San Francisco M,D
University of Connecticut M*
University of Connecticut Health Center M,D*
University of Detroit Mercy M,O
University of Florida M,D,O*
University of Illinois at Chicago M*
The University of Iowa M,D,O*
University of Kentucky M*
University of Louisville M
University of Manitoba M,D
University of Maryland, Baltimore P,M,D,O*
University of Medicine and Dentistry of New Jersey P,M,D,O*
University of Michigan M,D,O*
University of Minnesota, Twin Cities Campus M,D,O*
University of Mississippi Medical Center M,D*
University of Missouri–Kansas City P,M,D,O*
The University of North Carolina at Chapel Hill M,D*
University of Oklahoma Health Sciences Center M
University of Pittsburgh M,O*
University of Puerto Rico, Medical Sciences Campus M,O*
University of Rochester M*
University of Southern California M,D*
The University of Tennessee Health Science Center P,M,O*
The University of Texas Health Science Center at San Antonio M,O*
University of the Pacific M,O
The University of Toledo M*
University of Toronto M,D
University of Washington M,D*
The University of Western Ontario M
West Virginia University M*

ORGANIC CHEMISTRY

Auburn University M,D*
Boston College M,D*
Brandeis University M,D*
Brigham Young University M,D*
California State University, Fullerton M
California State University, Los Angeles M
Case Western Reserve University M,D*
Clark Atlanta University M,D*
Clarkson University M,D*
Cleveland State University M,D
Columbia University M,D*
Cornell University D*
Florida State University M,D*
Georgetown University M,D*
The George Washington University M,D*
Harvard University D*
Howard University M,D*
Instituto Tecnológico y de Estudios Superiores de Monterrey, Campus Monterrey M,D
Kansas State University M,D*
Kent State University M,D*
Marquette University M,D
Massachusetts Institute of Technology M,D,O*
McMaster University M,D
Miami University M,D*
Northeastern University M,D*
Old Dominion University M,D*
Oregon State University M,D*
Purdue University M,D*
Rensselaer Polytechnic Institute M,D*
Rice University M,D*
Rutgers, The State University of New Jersey, Newark M,D*
Rutgers, The State University of New Jersey, New Brunswick M,D*
Seton Hall University M,D*
Southern University and Agricultural and Mechanical College M*
State University of New York at Binghamton M,D*
State University of New York College of Environmental Science and Forestry M,D
Stevens Institute of Technology M,D,O*
Tufts University M,D*
University of Calgary M,D
University of Cincinnati M,D
University of Georgia M,D*
University of Louisville M,D
University of Maryland, College Park M,D*
University of Miami M,D*
University of Michigan D*
University of Missouri–Columbia M,D*
University of Missouri–Kansas City M,D*
University of Missouri–St. Louis M,D
The University of Montana M,D*
University of Nebraska–Lincoln M,D*
University of Notre Dame M,D*
University of Regina M,D
University of Southern Mississippi M,D*
University of South Florida M,D*
The University of Tennessee M,D*
The University of Texas at Austin M,D*
The University of Toledo M,D*
Vanderbilt University M,D*
Virginia Commonwealth University M,D*
Wake Forest University M,D*
Wesleyan University M,D*
West Virginia University M,D*
Yale University D*

ORGANIZATIONAL BEHAVIOR

Benedictine University M
Bernard M. Baruch College of the City University of New York M,D*
Boston College D*
Boston University D*
California Lutheran University M,O
Carnegie Mellon University D*
Case Western Reserve University M*
Columbia College (SC) M,O
Cornell University M,D*
Drexel University M,D,O*
Fairleigh Dickinson University, College at Florham M,O*
The George Washington University M,D*
Georgia Institute of Technology M,D,O*
Graduate School and University Center of the City University of New York D*
Harvard University D*
John Jay College of Criminal Justice of the City University of New York M,D
Leadership Institute of Seattle M
Lindenwood University M
New York University M,D*
Northwestern University M,D*
Oral Roberts University M
Phillips Graduate Institute M
Polytechnic University, Brooklyn Campus M*
Purdue University M,D*
Regions University P,M,D
Saybrook Graduate School and Research Center M,D
Silver Lake College M
Syracuse University D*
Towson University O
Universidad de las Americas, A.C. M
Université de Sherbrooke M
The University of British Columbia D*
University of California, Berkeley D*
University of Hartford M*
University of Hawaii at Manoa M*
The University of North Carolina at Chapel Hill D*
University of Oklahoma M*
University of Pennsylvania M*
University of Saskatchewan M

ORGANIZATIONAL MANAGEMENT

Adler Graduate School M,O
American International College M
American University M*
Antioch University Los Angeles M
Antioch University New England O*
Antioch University Santa Barbara M
Antioch University Seattle M*
Argosy University, Chicago Campus D*
Argosy University, Denver Campus M,D*
Argosy University, Hawai'i Campus D*
Argosy University, Orange County Campus M,D,O*
Argosy University, San Francisco Bay Area Campus M,D*
Argosy University, Santa Monica Campus M,D*
Argosy University, Sarasota Campus M,D,O*
Argosy University, Schaumburg Campus M,D,O*
Argosy University, Tampa Campus M,D*
Argosy University, Washington DC Campus M,D,O*
Athabasca University M
Augsburg College M
Avila University M,O*
Azusa Pacific University M
Beacon University P,M
Benedictine University M,D
Bernard M. Baruch College of the City University of New York M,D*
Bethel University M
Biola University M
Bluffton University M
Boston College D*
Bowling Green State University M*
Brenau University M
Briercrest Seminary M
Cabrini College M,O
Capella University M,D,O
Cardean University M
Carlos Albizu University, Miami Campus M,D
Carlow University M
Carnegie Mellon University D*
Charleston Southern University M
Chatham University M
College Misericordia M
College of Mount St. Joseph M
College of St. Catherine M*
Colorado Technical University—Colorado Springs M,D
Colorado Technical University—Sioux Falls M
Concordia University (MI) M
Concordia University (Canada) M
Concordia University, St. Paul M
Cumberland University M
Defiance College M
Dominican University M
Duquesne University M*
Eastern Connecticut State University M
Eastern Michigan University M
Eastern University D*
Endicott College M
Evangel University M
Fairleigh Dickinson University, College at Florham M,O*
Fielding Graduate University M,D,O*
Gannon University O
Geneva College M*
George Fox University M*
George Mason University M*
The George Washington University M,O*
Georgia State University M,D*
Gonzaga University M
Hawai'i Pacific University M*
Immaculata University M
Indiana University–Purdue University Fort Wayne M
Indiana Wesleyan University D
International University in Geneva M
John F. Kennedy University M,O

P—first professional degree; M—master's degree; D—doctorate; O—other advanced degree;
**full description and/or announcement in Book 2, 3, 4, 5, or 6*

Johnson & Wales University M*
Jones International University M
Leadership Institute of Seattle M
Lehigh University M,D,O*
Lewis University M
Lindenwood University M
Lourdes College M
Manhattanville College M*
Marian College of Fond du Lac M
Medaille College M
Mercy College M
Mercyhurst College M,O
Metropolitan State University M
National University M
New England College M
Newman University M
The New School: A University M*
New York University M,D*
Northern Kentucky University M
Northwestern University M,D*
Norwich University M
Nova Southeastern University D*
Olivet Nazarene University M
Oxford Graduate School M,D
Palm Beach Atlantic University M
Pepperdine University M*
Pfeiffer University M
Philadelphia Biblical University M
Point Park University M*
Regent University M,D,O
Regions University P,M,D
Regis College (MA) M
Regis University M,O
Rider University M*
Rivier College M
Roosevelt University M,D
Royal Roads University M
Rutgers, The State University of New Jersey, Newark D*
Sage Graduate School M
St. Ambrose University M
St. Edward's University M
St. Joseph's College, Suffolk Campus M,O
Saint Joseph's University M,D,O*
Saint Louis University M,D,O*
Saint Mary's University of Minnesota M
Saybrook Graduate School and Research Center M,D
School for International Training M
Seattle University M,O
Shippensburg University of Pennsylvania M
Southern New Hampshire University M,D,O*
Spring Arbor University M
Thomas Edison State College M
Trevecca Nazarene University M
Trinity (Washington) University M
Trinity Western University M
Tusculum College M
Université Laval M,O
University of Alberta D*
University of Cincinnati M
University of Dallas M
University of Denver M,O*
University of Great Falls M
University of Hawaii at Manoa M,D*
University of La Verne M,D,O
University of Maryland Eastern Shore D*
University of Massachusetts Dartmouth M,O
University of New Mexico M*
University of North Texas M,D*
University of Pennsylvania M*
University of Phoenix Online Campus D
University of St. Thomas (MN) M,D,O*
University of San Francisco M
The University of Scranton M
University of the Incarnate Word M,D,O
Upper Iowa University M
Vanderbilt University M,D*
Walden University M,D
Warner Pacific College M
Wayland Baptist University M
Webster University M
Wilmington College (DE) M
Woodbury University M
Worcester Polytechnic Institute M*
Worcester State College M

OSTEOPATHIC MEDICINE

A.T. Still University of Health Sciences P,M
Des Moines University P
Edward Via Virginia College of Osteopathic Medicine P
Georgia Campus–Philadelphia College of Osteopathic Medicine P
Kansas City University of Medicine and Biosciences P
Lake Erie College of Osteopathic Medicine P,M,O
Michigan State University P*
Midwestern University, Downers Grove Campus P*
Midwestern University, Glendale Campus P*
New York Institute of Technology P
Nova Southeastern University P,M*
Ohio University P*
Oklahoma State University Center for Health Sciences P
Philadelphia College of Osteopathic Medicine P*
Pikeville College P
Touro University College of Osteopathic Medicine P,M
University of Medicine and Dentistry of New Jersey P*
University of New England P
University of North Texas Health Science Center at Fort Worth P,M
Western University of Health Sciences P
West Virginia School of Osteopathic Medicine P

PALEONTOLOGY

Cornell University M,D*
Duke University D*
South Dakota School of Mines and Technology M
Tulane University M,D*
University of Chicago M,D*
University of Illinois at Chicago M,D*
West Virginia University M,D*
Yale University D*

PAPER AND PULP ENGINEERING

Miami University M*
North Carolina State University M,D*
Oregon State University M,D*
State University of New York College of Environmental Science and Forestry M,D
Université du Québec à Trois-Rivières M,D
University of Washington M,D*
Western Michigan University M,D*

PARASITOLOGY

Illinois State University M,D*
Louisiana State University Health Sciences Center M,D*
McGill University M,D,O*
New York University D*
Purdue University M,D*
Texas A&M University M,D*
Tulane University M,D,O*
University of Notre Dame M,D*
University of Pennsylvania D*
University of Prince Edward Island M,D
University of Washington M,D*
Yale University D*

PASTORAL MINISTRY AND COUNSELING

Abilene Christian University M,D
Alliance Theological Seminary P,M
Alliance University College P,M,O
Andrews University P,M,D,O
Anna Maria College M
Aquinas Institute of Theology P,M,D,O
Argosy University, Sarasota Campus M,D,O*
Asbury Theological Seminary M,O
Ashland Theological Seminary P,M,D,O
Assemblies of God Theological Seminary P,M,D
The Athenaeum of Ohio P,M,O
Austin Presbyterian Theological Seminary P,M,D
Ave Maria University M,D
Azusa Pacific University P,M
Bakke Graduate University of Ministry M,D
Baptist Bible College P,M
Baptist Bible College of Pennsylvania P,M,D
Baptist Theological Seminary at Richmond P,D
Barry University M,D*
Bayamón Central University P,M
Beacon University P,M
Bethany Theological Seminary P,M,O
Bethel College (IN) M
Bethel Seminary P,M,D,O
Biblical Theological Seminary P,M,D
Bob Jones University P,M,D,O
Boston College M,D*
Briercrest Seminary P,M
Caldwell College M
California Baptist University M
Calvary Bible College and Theological Seminary P,M
Capital Bible Seminary P,M,O
Cardinal Stritch University M*
Catholic Theological Union at Chicago P,M,D,O
Chaminade University of Honolulu M
Chestnut Hill College M,O
Chicago Theological Seminary P,M,D
Christian Theological Seminary P,M,D
Christ the King Seminary P,M,O
Church of God Theological Seminary P,M
Cincinnati Christian University M
Claremont School of Theology D
Collège Dominicain de Philosophie et de Théologie M
College of Mount St. Joseph M
Columbia International University P,M,D,O
Concordia University (NE) M
Concordia University, St. Paul M,O
The Criswell College P,M
Dallas Baptist University M
Dallas Theological Seminary M,D,O
Denver Seminary P,M,D,O
Eastern Mennonite University P,M,O
Eastern University D*
Ecumenical Theological Seminary D
Episcopal Theological Seminary of the Southwest P,M,O
Evangelical Theological Seminary P,M,O
Faith Baptist Bible College and Theological Seminary P,M
Fordham University M,D,O*
Freed-Hardeman University M
Gannon University M,O
Gardner-Webb University P,M,D
Garrett-Evangelical Theological Seminary P,M,D
George Fox University P,M,D,O*
Golden Gate Baptist Theological Seminary P,M,D,O
Gonzaga University M
Gordon-Conwell Theological Seminary P,M,D
Graceland University M
Grace Theological Seminary P,M,D,O
Grace University M
Grand Rapids Theological Seminary of Cornerstone University P,M
Greenville College M
Hardin-Simmons University M
Hartford Seminary M,D,O
Heritage Christian University M
Hillsdale Free Will Baptist College M
Holmes Institute M
Holy Names University M,O
Hope International University M
Houston Baptist University M
Houston Graduate School of Theology P,M,D
Huntington University M
Iliff School of Theology P,M,D
International Baptist College M,D
Iona College M,O*
Jewish University of America M,D
John Brown University M
The Johns Hopkins University M,O*
Knox Theological Seminary D
Lancaster Bible College M
La Salle University M
Liberty University M,D
Lincoln Christian Seminary P,M
Loma Linda University M,O
Loras College M
Loyola College in Maryland M,D,O
Loyola Marymount University M
Loyola University Chicago M*
Lutheran School of Theology at Chicago P,M,D
Lutheran Theological Seminary P,M
Lutheran Theological Seminary at Gettysburg P,M,D
The Lutheran Theological Seminary at Philadelphia P,M,D,O
Luther Rice University P,M,D
Madonna University M
Malone College M
Maple Springs Baptist Bible College and Seminary P,M,D,O
Maranatha Baptist Bible College M
Martin University M
Marygrove College M
Marymount University M,O
The Master's College and Seminary P,M,D
McCormick Theological Seminary P,M,D,O
McMaster University P,M,D,O
Meadville Lombard Theological School P,M,D
Mennonite Brethren Biblical Seminary M
Midwestern Baptist Theological Seminary P,M,D
Midwest University P,M,D
Mount Marty College M
Multnomah Bible College and Biblical Seminary M
Neumann College M,O
New Brunswick Theological Seminary D
New Orleans Baptist Theological Seminary P,M,D
Northern Baptist Theological Seminary P,M,D
North Greenville University M
Northwest Nazarene University P,M
Notre Dame College (OH) M,O
Oblate School of Theology P,M,D,O
Oklahoma Christian University P,M
Olivet Nazarene University M
Oral Roberts University P,M,D
Ottawa University M
Philadelphia Biblical University M
Phillips Theological Seminary D
Providence College M*
Providence College and Theological Seminary P,M,D,O
Reformed Theological Seminary–Charlotte Campus P,M,D
Reformed Theological Seminary–Jackson Campus P,M,D,O
Reformed Theological Seminary–Orlando Campus P,M,D
Regent University P,M,D
Regions University P,M,D
Regis College (Canada) P,M,D,O
Roberts Wesleyan College M
Sacred Heart Major Seminary P,M
St. Ambrose University M
St. Augustine's Seminary of Toronto P,M,O
Saint Bernard's School of Theology and Ministry P,M,O
Saint Francis Seminary P,M
St. John's Seminary (CA) P,M
Saint John's University (MN) P,M
St. John's University (NY) P,M,O
Saint Joseph College M,O
Saint Leo University M
Saint Mary-of-the-Woods College M,O
Saint Mary's University of Minnesota M
St. Mary's University of San Antonio M
Saint Paul University M,D,O
Saints Cyril and Methodius Seminary P,M
St. Stephen's College P,M
St. Thomas University M,D,O
Santa Clara University M
Seattle University M
Seminary of the Immaculate Conception P,M,D,O
Seton Hall University P,M,O*
Shasta Bible College M
Simpson University P,M
Sioux Falls Seminary P,M
Southern Baptist Theological Seminary P,M,D
Southern Evangelical Seminary P,M,O
Southern Wesleyan University M
Southwestern Christian University M
Spring Arbor University M
Texas Christian University P,M,D,O
Trinity Baptist College M
Trinity Episcopal School for Ministry P,M,D,O
Trinity International University P,M,D,O
Trinity Western University P,M
Tyndale University College & Seminary P,M,O
United Theological Seminary of the Twin Cities M,D
University of Dallas M
University of Dayton M,D*
University of Portland M
University of Puget Sound M
University of Saint Francis (IN) M
University of St. Michael's College P,M,D,O
University of St. Thomas (MN) M*
University of San Diego M,O*
University of San Francisco M
University of Trinity College P,M,D,O
Wake Forest University M*
Warner Pacific College M
Wayland Baptist University M
Wesley Biblical Seminary P,M
Western Seminary P,M,D,O
Westminster Theological Seminary P,M,D,O
Wheaton College M,D
Wilfrid Laurier University P,M,D
Xavier University of Louisiana M

PATHOBIOLOGY

Auburn University M,D*
Brown University M,D*
Columbia University M,D*
Drexel University D*
The Johns Hopkins University D*
Kansas State University M,D*
Medical University of South Carolina D*
Michigan State University M,D*
New York University D*

The Ohio State University M,D*
Penn State University Park D*
Purdue University M,D*
Texas A&M University M,D*
Uniformed Services University of the Health Sciences D*
The University of Arizona M,D*
University of Cincinnati D
University of Connecticut M,D*
University of Illinois at Urbana–Champaign M,D*
University of Missouri–Columbia M,D*
University of Rochester *
University of Southern California M,D*
University of Toronto M,D
University of Washington M,D*
University of Wyoming M
Wake Forest University M,D*
Yale University D*

PATHOLOGY

Albert Einstein College of Medicine D*
Baylor College of Medicine D*
Boston University D*
Brown University M,D*
Case Western Reserve University M,D*
Colorado State University M,D*
Columbia University M,D*
Dalhousie University M
Duke University M,D*
East Carolina University D*
Georgetown University M,D*
Harvard University D*
Indiana University–Purdue University Indianapolis M,D*
Iowa State University of Science and Technology M,D*
The Johns Hopkins University D*
Loma Linda University M,D
Louisiana State University Health Sciences Center M,D*
McGill University M,D*
Medical College of Wisconsin M,D*
Medical University of South Carolina M,D*
Michigan State University M,D*
Mount Sinai School of Medicine of New York University M,D*
New York Medical College M,D*
North Carolina State University M,D*
North Dakota State University M,D
The Ohio State University M*
Oregon State University M*
Purdue University M,D*
Queen's University at Kingston M,D
Quinnipiac University M*
Rosalind Franklin University of Medicine and Science M,D*
Saint Louis University D*
Stony Brook University, State University of New York M,D*
Temple University D*
Texas A&M University M,D*
Uniformed Services University of the Health Sciences D*
Université de Montréal M,D
Université Laval O
University at Albany, State University of New York M,D*
University at Buffalo, the State University of New York M,D*
The University of Alabama at Birmingham D*
University of Alberta M,D*
University of Arkansas for Medical Sciences M*
The University of British Columbia M,D*
University of California, Davis M,D*
University of California, Los Angeles M,D*
University of California, San Francisco D
University of Chicago D*
University of Cincinnati D
University of Florida D*
University of Georgia M,D*
University of Guelph M,D,O
The University of Iowa M*
University of Kansas M,D*
University of Manitoba M
University of Maryland, Baltimore M,D*
University of Medicine and Dentistry of New Jersey D*
University of Michigan D*
University of Mississippi Medical Center M,D*
University of Nebraska Medical Center M,D*
University of New Mexico M,D*
The University of North Carolina at Chapel Hill D*
University of Oklahoma Health Sciences Center D
University of Pittsburgh M,D*
University of Prince Edward Island M,D
University of Rochester M,D*
University of Saskatchewan M,D
University of Southern California M,D*
University of South Florida M,D*
The University of Texas Medical Branch D*
The University of Toledo O*
University of Utah M,D*
University of Vermont M*
University of Washington M,D*
The University of Western Ontario M,D
University of Wisconsin–Madison D*
Vanderbilt University D*
Virginia Commonwealth University M,D*
Washington State University M,D*
Wayne State University M,D*
Yale University D*

PEDIATRIC NURSING

Baylor University M*
Caribbean University M,D
Case Western Reserve University M,D*
The Catholic University of America M,D*
Columbia University M,O*
Duke University M,D,O*
Emory University M*
Florida State University M,O*
Georgia State University M,D,O*
Gwynedd-Mercy College M
Hunter College of the City University of New York M,O
Indiana University–Purdue University Indianapolis M,D*
The Johns Hopkins University M,O*
Kent State University M,D*
Lehman College of the City University of New York M
Loma Linda University M
Louisiana State University Health Sciences Center M,D*
Marquette University M,D,O
MGH Institute of Health Professions M,O*
Molloy College M,O
New York University M,O*
Oregon Health & Science University M,O*
Rush University M,D,O
Seton Hall University M*
Spalding University M
Stony Brook University, State University of New York M,O*
Texas Tech University Health Sciences Center M,O
University at Buffalo, the State University of New York M,D,O*
University of Central Florida D,O*
University of Cincinnati M,D
University of Delaware M,O*
University of Illinois at Chicago M*
University of Maryland, Baltimore M*
University of Michigan M*
University of Minnesota, Twin Cities Campus M*
University of Missouri–Kansas City M,D*
University of Nevada, Las Vegas M,D,O
University of Pennsylvania M*
University of Pittsburgh M,D*
University of San Diego M,D,O*
University of South Carolina M*
The University of Texas–Pan American M
Vanderbilt University M,D*
Villanova University M,D,O*
Virginia Commonwealth University M,D,O*
Wayne State University M,O*
Wright State University M*

PETROLEUM ENGINEERING

Colorado School of Mines M,D
Louisiana State University and Agricultural and Mechanical College M,D*
Montana Tech of The University of Montana M
New Mexico Institute of Mining and Technology M,D
Penn State University Park M,D*
Stanford University M,D,O*
Texas A&M University M,D*
Texas A&M University–Kingsville M
Texas Tech University M,D
University of Alaska Fairbanks M
University of Alberta M,D*
University of Calgary M,D
University of Houston M,D*
University of Kansas M,D*
University of Louisiana at Lafayette M*
University of Missouri–Rolla M,D*
University of Oklahoma M,D*
University of Pittsburgh M,D*
University of Regina M,D
University of Southern California M,D,O*
The University of Texas at Austin M,D*
University of Tulsa M,D*
University of Wyoming M,D
West Virginia University M,D*

PHARMACEUTICAL ADMINISTRATION

Duquesne University M*
Fairleigh Dickinson University, Metropolitan Campus M,O*
Florida Agricultural and Mechanical University M,D*
Idaho State University P,M,D
Long Island University, Brooklyn Campus M*
Massachusetts College of Pharmacy and Health Sciences M*
The Ohio State University M,D*
Purdue University M,D,O*
St. John's University (NY) M
St. Louis College of Pharmacy M,O
San Diego State University M*
Seton Hall University M*
University of Arkansas for Medical Sciences M*
University of Colorado at Denver and Health Sciences Center M*
University of Florida M,D*
University of Georgia M,D*
University of Houston P,M,D*
University of Illinois at Chicago M,D*
University of Maryland, Baltimore M,D*
University of Michigan D*
University of Minnesota, Twin Cities Campus M,D*
University of Mississippi M,D
University of the Sciences in Philadelphia M*
The University of Toledo M*
University of Wisconsin–Madison M,D*
Wayne State University P,M,D,O*
West Virginia University M,D*

PHARMACEUTICAL ENGINEERING

New Jersey Institute of Technology M
University of Michigan M*

PHARMACEUTICAL SCIENCES

Auburn University M,D*
Boston University M,D*
Butler University P,M
Campbell University P,M
Creighton University M,D*
Dalhousie University M,D
Dartmouth College D*
Duquesne University M,D*
Florida Agricultural and Mechanical University M,D*
Idaho State University M,D
Long Island University, Brooklyn Campus M,D*
Long Island University, Rockland Graduate Campus M
Massachusetts College of Pharmacy and Health Sciences M,D*
Medical University of South Carolina P,D*
Memorial University of Newfoundland M,D
Mercer University P,M,D
North Dakota State University M,D
Northeastern University P,M,D*
The Ohio State University M,D*
Oregon State University P,M,D*
Purdue University M,D*
Rush University M,D
Rutgers, The State University of New Jersey, New Brunswick M,D*
St. John's University (NY) M,D
South Dakota State University M,D
Stevens Institute of Technology M,O*
Temple University M,D*
Texas Tech University Health Sciences Center M,D
Université de Montréal M,D,O
Université Laval M,D,O
University at Buffalo, the State University of New York M,D*
University of Alberta M,D*
The University of Arizona M,D*
University of Arkansas for Medical Sciences M*
The University of British Columbia P,M,D*
University of California, San Francisco D
University of Cincinnati M,D
University of Colorado at Denver and Health Sciences Center D*
University of Connecticut M,D*
University of Florida D*
University of Georgia M,D*
University of Houston P,M,D*
University of Illinois at Chicago M,D*
University of Kansas M*
University of Kentucky M,D*
University of Louisiana at Monroe M
University of Manitoba M,D
University of Maryland, Baltimore D*
University of Michigan D*
University of Minnesota, Twin Cities Campus M,D*
University of Mississippi M,D
University of Missouri–Kansas City P,M,D*
The University of Montana M,D*
University of Nebraska Medical Center M,D*
University of New Mexico M,D*
The University of North Carolina at Chapel Hill M,D*
University of Oklahoma Health Sciences Center M,D
University of Puerto Rico, Medical Sciences Campus P,M*
University of Rhode Island M,D
University of Saskatchewan M,D
University of South Carolina M,D*
University of Southern California M,D*
The University of Tennessee Health Science Center M,D*
The University of Texas at Austin M,D*
University of the Pacific M,D
University of the Sciences in Philadelphia M,D*
The University of Toledo M*
University of Toronto M,D
University of Washington M,D*
University of Wisconsin–Madison M,D*
Virginia Commonwealth University P,M,D*
Wayne State University P,M,D,O*
Western University of Health Sciences M
West Virginia University M,D*

PHARMACOLOGY

Albany Medical College M,D
Alliant International University–San Francisco M*
American University of Beirut P,M
Argosy University, Hawai'i Campus O*
Auburn University M,D*
Baylor College of Medicine D*
Boston University M,D*
Case Western Reserve University M,D*
Columbia University M,D*
Cornell University P,M,D*
Cornell University, Joan and Sanford I. Weill Medical College and Graduate School of Medical Sciences D*
Creighton University M,D*
Dalhousie University M,D
Dartmouth College D*
Drexel University M,D*
Duke University D*
Duquesne University M,D*
East Carolina University D*
East Tennessee State University M,D
Emory University D*
Fairleigh Dickinson University, College at Florham M,O*
Florida Agricultural and Mechanical University M,D*
Georgetown University D*
The George Washington University D*
Howard University M,D*
Idaho State University M,D
Indiana University–Purdue University Indianapolis M,D*
The Johns Hopkins University D*
Kent State University M,D*
Loma Linda University M,D
Long Island University, Brooklyn Campus M,D*
Louisiana State University Health Sciences Center M,D*

*P—first professional degree; M—master's degree; D—doctorate; O—other advanced degree; *full description and/or announcement in Book 2, 3, 4, 5, or 6*

Institution	Degrees
Louisiana State University Health Sciences Center at Shreveport	D*
Loyola University Chicago	M,D*
Massachusetts College of Pharmacy and Health Sciences	M,D*
McGill University	M,D*
McMaster University	M,D
Medical College of Georgia	M,D*
Medical College of Wisconsin	M,D*
Meharry Medical College	M,D
Michigan State University	M,D*
New York Medical College	M,D*
New York University	D*
North Carolina State University	M,D*
Northeastern University	M,D*
Northwestern University	D*
Nova Southeastern University	M*
The Ohio State University	M,D*
Oregon Health & Science University	D*
Penn State Hershey Medical Center	M,D*
Purdue University	M,D*
Queen's University at Kingston	M,D
Rush University	M,D
Saint Louis University	D*
Southern Illinois University Carbondale	M,D*
State University of New York Upstate Medical University	M,D*
Stony Brook University, State University of New York	M,D*
Temple University	M,D*
Texas Tech University Health Sciences Center	M,D
Thomas Jefferson University	M*
Tufts University	D*
Tulane University	M,D*
Universidad Central del Caribe	M
Université de Montréal	M,D
Université de Sherbrooke	M,D
University at Buffalo, the State University of New York	M,D*
The University of Alabama at Birmingham	D*
University of Alberta	M,D*
The University of Arizona	M,D*
University of Arkansas for Medical Sciences	M,D*
The University of British Columbia	M,D*
University of California, Davis	M,D*
University of California, Irvine	M,D*
University of California, Los Angeles	D*
University of California, San Diego	D*
University of California, San Francisco	D
University of Chicago	D*
University of Cincinnati	D
University of Colorado at Denver and Health Sciences Center	D*
University of Connecticut	M,D*
University of Florida	M,D*
University of Georgia	M,D*
University of Guelph	M,D
University of Houston	P,M,D*
University of Illinois at Chicago	D*
The University of Iowa	M,D*
University of Kansas	M,D*
University of Kentucky	D*
University of Louisville	M,D
University of Manitoba	M,D
University of Maryland, Baltimore	D*
University of Medicine and Dentistry of New Jersey	D,O*
University of Miami	D*
University of Michigan	D*
University of Minnesota, Duluth	M,D*
University of Minnesota, Twin Cities Campus	M,D*
University of Mississippi	M,D
University of Mississippi Medical Center	M,D*
University of Missouri–Columbia	M,D*
The University of Montana	M,D*
University of Nebraska Medical Center	M,D*
The University of North Carolina at Chapel Hill	D*
University of North Dakota	M,D
University of North Texas Health Science Center at Fort Worth	M,D
University of Pennsylvania	D*
University of Prince Edward Island	M,D
University of Puerto Rico, Medical Sciences Campus	M,D*
University of Rhode Island	M,D
University of Rochester	M,D*
University of Saskatchewan	M,D
University of South Alabama	D*
The University of South Dakota	M,D
University of South Florida	M,D*
The University of Texas Health Science Center at San Antonio	D*
The University of Texas Medical Branch	M,D*
University of the Sciences in Philadelphia	M,D*
The University of Toledo	M*
University of Toronto	M,D
University of Utah	M,D*
University of Vermont	M,D*
University of Virginia	D*
University of Washington	M,D*
University of Wisconsin–Madison	M,D*
Vanderbilt University	D*
Virginia Commonwealth University	M,D,O*
Wake Forest University	D*
Washington State University	M,D*
Wayne State University	P,M,D*
West Virginia University	M,D*
Wright State University	M*
Yale University	D*

PHARMACY

Institution	Degrees
Albany College of Pharmacy of Union University	P
Auburn University	P*
Butler University	P,M
Campbell University	P,M
Creighton University	P*
Drake University	P*
Duquesne University	P*
Ferris State University	P
Florida Agricultural and Mechanical University	P,D*
Harding University	P
Howard University	P*
Idaho State University	P,M,D
Lake Erie College of Osteopathic Medicine	P,M,O
Lebanese American University	P
Medical University of South Carolina	P,D*
Mercer University	P,M,D
Midwestern University, Downers Grove Campus	P*
Midwestern University, Glendale Campus	P*
Nova Southeastern University	P*
Ohio Northern University	P
The Ohio State University	P*
Oregon State University	P,M,D*
Pacific University	P
Palm Beach Atlantic University	P
Purdue University	P*
Rutgers, The State University of New Jersey, New Brunswick	P*
St. John Fisher College	P
St. John's University (NY)	P
St. Louis College of Pharmacy	P
Samford University	P
Shenandoah University	P
South Dakota State University	P*
Southern Illinois University Edwardsville	P
South University (GA)	P*
Southwestern Oklahoma State University	P
Temple University	P*
Texas Southern University	P,M
Thomas Jefferson University	P*
Touro University College of Osteopathic Medicine	P,M
Universidad de Ciencias Medicas	P,M
University at Buffalo, the State University of New York	P*
University of Alberta	M,D*
The University of Arizona	P,M,D*
University of Arkansas for Medical Sciences	P,M*
The University of British Columbia	P,M,D*
University of California, San Diego	P*
University of California, San Francisco	P
University of Charleston	P
University of Cincinnati	P
University of Colorado at Denver and Health Sciences Center	P,D*
University of Connecticut	P*
University of Florida	P*
University of Georgia	P*
University of Houston	P,M,D*
University of Illinois at Chicago	P,M,D*
The University of Iowa	M,D*
University of Kentucky	P*
University of Louisiana at Monroe	P,D
University of Maryland, Baltimore	P,M,D*
University of Michigan	P*
University of Minnesota, Twin Cities Campus	P*
University of Mississippi	P
University of Missouri–Kansas City	P,M,D*
University of Nebraska Medical Center	P*
University of New Mexico	P*
University of Oklahoma Health Sciences Center	P
University of Pittsburgh	P*
University of Puerto Rico, Medical Sciences Campus	P,M*
University of Rhode Island	M,D
University of South Alabama	P*
University of South Carolina	P*
University of Southern California	P*
University of Southern Nevada	P
The University of Tennessee Health Science Center	P,M,D*
The University of Texas at Austin	P*
University of the Incarnate Word	P
University of the Pacific	P
University of the Sciences in Philadelphia	P*
University of Utah	P,M*
University of Washington	P*
University of Wisconsin–Madison	P*
University of Wyoming	P
Virginia Commonwealth University	P*
Washington State University	P*
Washington State University Spokane	P
Wayne State University	P,M,D,O*
Western University of Health Sciences	P
West Virginia University	P,M,D*
Wilkes University	P
Wingate University	P
Xavier University of Louisiana	P

PHILANTHROPIC STUDIES

Institution	Degrees
Saint Mary's University of Minnesota	M

PHILOSOPHY

Institution	Degrees
American University	M*
American University of Beirut	M
Arizona State University	M,D*
Baylor University	M,D*
Boston College	M,D*
Boston University	M,D*
Bowling Green State University	M,D*
Brock University	M
Brown University	M,D*
California Institute of Integral Studies	M,D*
California State University, Long Beach	M
California State University, Los Angeles	M
Carleton University	M
Carnegie Mellon University	M,D*
The Catholic University of America	M,D,O*
Central European University	M,D*
Claremont Graduate University	M,D
Cleveland State University	M,O
Collège Dominicain de Philosophie et de Théologie	M,D
College of the Humanities and Sciences, Harrison Middleton University	M,D
Colorado State University	M*
Columbia University	M,D*
Concordia University (Canada)	M
Cornell University	D*
Dalhousie University	M,D
DePaul University	M,D*
Dominican School of Philosophy and Theology	M
Duke University	M,D*
Duquesne University	M,D*
Emory University	D,O*
Florida State University	M,D*
Fordham University	M,D*
Franciscan University of Steubenville	M
Georgetown University	M,D*
The George Washington University	M,D*
Georgia State University	M*
Gonzaga University	M
Graduate School and University Center of the City University of New York	M,D*
Harvard University	M,D*
Howard University	M*
Indiana University Bloomington	M,D*
Indiana University–Purdue University Indianapolis	M,D,O*
Institute for Christian Studies	M,D
The Johns Hopkins University	M,D*
Kent State University	M*
Lakehead University	M
Louisiana State University and Agricultural and Mechanical College	M*
Loyola Marymount University	M
Loyola University Chicago	M,D*
Marquette University	M,D
Massachusetts Institute of Technology	D*
McGill University	M,D*
McMaster University	M,D
Memorial University of Newfoundland	M
Miami University	M*
Michigan State University	M,D*
Montclair State University	M,D,O*
The New School: A University	M,D*
New York University	M,D*
Northern Illinois University	M
Northwestern University	D*
The Ohio State University	M,D*
Ohio University	M*
Oklahoma City University	M
Oklahoma State University	M*
Penn State University Park	M,D*
Princeton University	D*
Purdue University	M,D*
Purdue University Calumet	M
Queen's University at Kingston	M,D
Rice University	M,D*
Rutgers, The State University of New Jersey, New Brunswick	D*
St. John's University (NY)	M
Saint Louis University	M,D*
Saint Mary's University	M
San Diego State University	M*
San Francisco State University	M,O
San Jose State University	M,O
Simon Fraser University	M,D
Southeastern Baptist Theological Seminary	P,M,D
Southern Evangelical Seminary	M,D,O
Southern Illinois University Carbondale	M,D*
Stanford University	M,D*
State University of New York at Binghamton	M,D*
Stony Brook University, State University of New York	M,D*
Syracuse University	M,D*
Temple University	M,D*
Texas A&M University	M,D*
Texas Tech University	M
Tufts University	M*
Tulane University	M,D*
Université de Montréal	M,D
Université de Sherbrooke	M,D,O
Université du Québec à Montréal	M,D
Université du Québec à Trois-Rivières	M,D
Université Laval	M,D
University at Albany, State University of New York	M,D*
University at Buffalo, the State University of New York	M,D*
University of Alberta	M,D*
The University of Arizona	M,D*
University of Arkansas	M,D*
The University of British Columbia	M,D*
University of Calgary	M,D
University of California, Berkeley	D*
University of California, Davis	M,D*
University of California, Irvine	M,D*
University of California, Los Angeles	M,D*
University of California, Riverside	M,D*
University of California, San Diego	D*
University of California, Santa Barbara	D*
University of California, Santa Cruz	M,D*
University of Chicago	M,D*
University of Cincinnati	M,D
University of Colorado at Boulder	M,D*
University of Connecticut	M,D*
University of Dallas	M,D
University of Florida	M,D*
University of Georgia	M,D*
University of Guelph	M,D
University of Hawaii at Manoa	M,D*
University of Houston	M*
University of Illinois at Chicago	M,D*
University of Illinois at Urbana–Champaign	M,D*
The University of Iowa	M,D*
University of Kansas	M,D*
University of Kentucky	M,D*
University of Lethbridge	M,D
University of Louisville	M
University of Manitoba	M
University of Maryland, College Park	M,D*
University of Massachusetts Amherst	M,D*
University of Memphis	M,D*

- University of Miami M,D*
- University of Michigan M,D*
- University of Minnesota, Twin Cities Campus M,D*
- University of Mississippi M
- University of Missouri–Columbia M,D*
- University of Missouri–St. Louis M
- The University of Montana M*
- University of Nebraska–Lincoln M,D*
- University of Nevada, Reno M*
- University of New Brunswick Fredericton M
- University of New Mexico M,D*
- The University of North Carolina at Chapel Hill M,D*
- University of North Florida M,O
- University of North Texas M,D*
- University of Notre Dame D*
- University of Oklahoma M,D*
- University of Oregon M,D*
- University of Ottawa M,D*
- University of Pennsylvania M,D*
- University of Pittsburgh M,D*
- University of Puerto Rico, Río Piedras M*
- University of Regina M
- University of Rochester M,D*
- University of St. Thomas (TX) M,D
- University of Saskatchewan M
- University of South Carolina M,D*
- University of Southern California M,D*
- University of Southern Mississippi M*
- University of South Florida M,D*
- The University of Tennessee M,D*
- The University of Texas at Austin M,D*
- The University of Toledo M*
- University of Toronto M,D
- University of Utah M,D*
- University of Victoria M
- University of Virginia M,D*
- University of Washington M,D*
- University of Waterloo M,D*
- The University of Western Ontario M,D
- University of Windsor M
- University of Wisconsin–Madison M,D*
- University of Wisconsin–Milwaukee M
- University of Wyoming M
- Vanderbilt University M,D*
- Villanova University D*
- Virginia Polytechnic Institute and State University M*
- Washington State University M*
- Washington University in St. Louis M,D*
- Wayne State University M,D*
- West Chester University of Pennsylvania M
- Western Michigan University M*
- Wilfrid Laurier University M
- Yale University D*
- York University M,D*

PHOTOGRAPHY

- Academy of Art University M*
- Barry University M*
- Bradley University M
- Brooklyn College of the City University of New York M,D
- Brooks Institute of Photography M
- California College of the Arts M*
- California Institute of the Arts M,O
- California State University, Fullerton M,O
- California State University, Los Angeles M
- Claremont Graduate University M
- Columbia College Chicago M
- Columbia University M*
- Cornell University M*
- Cranbrook Academy of Art M*
- The George Washington University M,D*
- Georgia State University M,D*
- Howard University M*
- Illinois State University M*
- Indiana State University M*
- Inter American University of Puerto Rico, San Germán Campus M
- James Madison University M
- Lamar University M*
- Louisiana State University and Agricultural and Mechanical College M*
- Louisiana Tech University M
- Maryland Institute College of Art M*
- Marywood University M*
- Massachusetts College of Art M*
- Memphis College of Art M*
- Mills College M
- Minneapolis College of Art and Design M
- New Mexico State University M
- The New School: A University M*
- Ohio University M*
- Otis College of Art and Design M
- Penn State University Park M,D*
- Pratt Institute M*
- Rhode Island School of Design M
- Rochester Institute of Technology M
- San Francisco Art Institute M,O*
- San Jose State University M
- Savannah College of Art and Design M*
- School of the Art Institute of Chicago M*
- School of Visual Arts M*
- Southern Methodist University M*
- Syracuse University M*
- Temple University M*
- The University of Alabama M
- University of Colorado at Boulder M*
- University of Florida M,D*
- University of Houston M*
- University of Illinois at Chicago M*
- University of Illinois at Urbana–Champaign M*
- University of Memphis M*
- University of Miami M*
- The University of Montana M*
- University of North Texas M,D*
- University of Notre Dame M*
- University of Oklahoma M*
- The University of Tennessee M*
- University of Utah M*
- University of Victoria M
- Virginia Commonwealth University M*
- Washington State University M*
- Yale University M*

PHOTONICS

- Boston University M,D*
- Lehigh University M,D*
- Oklahoma State University M,D*
- Princeton University D*
- Stevens Institute of Technology O*
- University of Arkansas M,D*
- University of California, San Diego M,D*
- University of Central Florida M,D*

PHYSICAL CHEMISTRY

- Auburn University M,D*
- Boston College M,D*
- Brandeis University M,D*
- Brigham Young University M,D*
- California State University, Fullerton M
- California State University, Los Angeles M
- Case Western Reserve University M,D*
- Clark Atlanta University M,D
- Clarkson University M,D*
- Cleveland State University M,D
- Cornell University D*
- Florida State University M,D*
- Georgetown University M,D*
- The George Washington University M,D*
- Harvard University D*
- Howard University M,D*
- Indiana University Bloomington M,D*
- Kansas State University M,D*
- Kent State University M,D*
- Marquette University M,D
- Massachusetts Institute of Technology D*
- McMaster University M,D
- Miami University M,D*
- Northeastern University M,D*
- Old Dominion University M,D*
- Oregon State University M,D*
- Purdue University M,D*
- Rensselaer Polytechnic Institute M,D*
- Rice University M,D*
- Rutgers, The State University of New Jersey, Newark M,D*
- Rutgers, The State University of New Jersey, New Brunswick M,D*
- Seton Hall University M,D*
- Southern University and Agricultural and Mechanical College M*
- State University of New York at Binghamton M,D*
- Stevens Institute of Technology M,D,O*
- Tufts University M,D*
- University of Calgary M,D
- University of Cincinnati M,D
- University of Georgia M,D*
- University of Louisville M,D
- University of Maryland, College Park M,D*
- University of Miami M,D*
- University of Michigan D*
- University of Missouri–Columbia M,D*
- University of Missouri–Kansas City M,D*
- University of Missouri–St. Louis M,D
- The University of Montana M,D*
- University of Nebraska–Lincoln M,D*
- University of Notre Dame M,D*
- University of Regina M,D
- University of Southern Mississippi M,D*
- University of South Florida M,D*
- The University of Tennessee M,D*
- The University of Texas at Austin M,D*
- The University of Toledo M,D*
- Vanderbilt University M,D*
- Virginia Commonwealth University M,D*
- Wake Forest University M,D*
- West Virginia University M,D*
- Yale University D*

PHYSICAL EDUCATION

- Adams State College M
- Adelphi University M,O*
- Alabama Agricultural and Mechanical University M
- Alabama State University M
- Albany State University M
- Alcorn State University M,O
- American University of Puerto Rico M
- Arizona State University at the Polytechnic Campus M,D
- Arkansas State University M,O
- Ashland University M
- Auburn University M,D,O*
- Auburn University Montgomery M,O
- Augusta State University M
- Austin College M
- Austin Peay State University M
- Averett University M
- Azusa Pacific University M
- Ball State University M,D*
- Bayamón Central University M
- Baylor University M,D*
- Bethel College (TN) M
- Boston University M,D,O*
- Bridgewater State College M
- Brigham Young University M,D*
- Brooklyn College of the City University of New York M,O
- California State University, Dominguez Hills M
- California State University, East Bay M
- California State University, Fullerton M
- California State University, Long Beach M
- California State University, Los Angeles M
- California State University, Sacramento M*
- Campbell University M
- Canisius College M
- Caribbean University M,D
- Central Connecticut State University M,O
- Central Michigan University M*
- Central Washington University M
- Chicago State University M
- The Citadel, The Military College of South Carolina M
- Cleveland State University M
- The College of New Jersey M
- Columbus State University M,O
- Concordia University (CA) M
- Delta State University M
- DePaul University M,D*
- Drury University M
- Eastern Illinois University M
- Eastern Kentucky University M*
- Eastern Michigan University M
- Eastern New Mexico University M
- Eastern Washington University M
- East Stroudsburg University of Pennsylvania M
- East Tennessee State University M
- Emporia State University M
- Florida Agricultural and Mechanical University M*
- Florida International University M,D,O*
- Florida State University M,D,O*
- Fort Hays State University M
- Frostburg State University M
- Gardner-Webb University M
- Georgia College & State University M,O
- Georgia Southern University M
- Georgia Southwestern State University M,O
- Georgia State University M*
- Hardin-Simmons University M
- Henderson State University M
- Hofstra University M*
- Howard University M*
- Humboldt State University M
- Idaho State University M
- Illinois State University M*
- Indiana State University M*
- Indiana University Bloomington M,D,O*
- Indiana University of Pennsylvania M
- Indiana University–Purdue University Indianapolis M*
- Inter American University of Puerto Rico, Metropolitan Campus M
- Inter American University of Puerto Rico, San Germán Campus M
- Iowa State University of Science and Technology M,D*
- Ithaca College M
- Jackson State University M
- Jacksonville State University M
- Kent State University M,D*
- Lakehead University M
- Long Island University, Brooklyn Campus M*
- Louisiana Tech University M,D
- McDaniel College M
- McGill University M,D,O*
- Memorial University of Newfoundland M
- Middle Tennessee State University M,D*
- Minnesota State University Mankato M,O
- Mississippi State University M
- Missouri State University M*
- Montana State University–Billings M
- Montclair State University M,O*
- Morehead State University M
- Murray State University M,O
- North Carolina Agricultural and Technical State University M
- North Carolina Central University M
- North Dakota State University M
- Northern Arizona University M
- Northern Illinois University M
- Northern State University M
- North Georgia College & State University M,O
- Northwest Missouri State University M
- The Ohio State University M,D*
- Ohio University M*
- Oklahoma State University M,D,O*
- Old Dominion University M*
- Oregon State University M*
- Pittsburg State University M
- Prairie View A&M University M
- Purdue University M,D*
- Saginaw Valley State University M
- St. Cloud State University M
- Salem International University M
- Salem State College M
- San Diego State University M*
- Slippery Rock University of Pennsylvania M
- South Dakota State University M
- Southern Connecticut State University M
- Southern Illinois University Carbondale M*
- Springfield College M,D,O*
- State University of New York College at Brockport M*
- State University of New York College at Cortland M*
- Stony Brook University, State University of New York M,O*
- Sul Ross State University M*
- Tarleton State University M*
- Teachers College Columbia University M,D*
- Temple University M,D*
- Tennessee State University M*
- Tennessee Technological University M*
- Texas A&M University M,D*
- Texas A&M University–Commerce M,D
- Texas Southern University M
- Texas State University-San Marcos M*
- Union College (KY) M
- United States Sports Academy M*
- Universidad Metropolitana M
- Université de Montréal M,D,O
- Université de Sherbrooke M,O
- Université du Québec à Trois-Rivières M
- The University of Akron M
- The University of Alabama M,D
- The University of Alabama at Birmingham M*

P—first professional degree; M—master's degree; D—doctorate; O—other advanced degree;
**full description and/or announcement in Book 2, 3, 4, 5, or 6*

Institution	Degrees
University of Alberta	M,D*
University of Arkansas	M*
University of Arkansas at Pine Bluff	M
The University of British Columbia	M,D*
University of California, Berkeley	M,D*
University of Central Florida	M*
University of Central Missouri	M
University of Dayton	M,D*
University of Florida	M,D*
University of Houston	M,D*
University of Idaho	M,D*
University of Indianapolis	M
The University of Iowa	M,D*
University of Kansas	M,D*
University of Louisville	M
University of Maine	M*
University of Manitoba	M
University of Massachusetts Amherst	M,D,O*
University of Memphis	M*
University of Minnesota, Twin Cities Campus	M,D,O*
The University of Montana	M*
University of Nebraska at Kearney	M
University of Nebraska at Omaha	M
University of Nebraska–Lincoln	M*
University of Nevada, Las Vegas	M,D
University of New Brunswick Fredericton	M
University of New Mexico	M,D,O*
The University of North Carolina at Chapel Hill	M*
The University of North Carolina at Pembroke	M
University of Northern Colorado	M,D
University of Northern Iowa	M
University of Rhode Island	M,D
University of South Alabama	M*
University of South Carolina	M,D*
The University of South Dakota	M
University of Southern Mississippi	M,D*
University of South Florida	M*
The University of Tennessee at Chattanooga	M
The University of Texas at Arlington	M*
The University of Texas at El Paso	M
University of the Incarnate Word	M
The University of Toledo	M*
University of Toronto	M,D
University of Victoria	M
University of Virginia	M,D*
The University of West Alabama	M
University of West Florida	M
University of West Georgia	M,O
University of Wisconsin–La Crosse	M
University of Wyoming	M
Utah State University	M
Valdosta State University	M
Virginia Commonwealth University	M,D*
Virginia Polytechnic Institute and State University	M,D,O*
Wayne State College	M
Wayne State University	M*
West Chester University of Pennsylvania	M,O
Western Carolina University	M*
Western Kentucky University	M
Western Michigan University	M*
Western Washington University	M
Westfield State College	M
West Virginia University	M,D*
Wichita State University	M*
Wilfrid Laurier University	M
Wingate University	M
Winthrop University	M
Wright State University	M*

PHYSICAL THERAPY

Institution	Degrees
Alabama State University	D
American International College	M,D
Andrews University	D
Angelo State University	M
Arcadia University	D
Arkansas State University	M
Armstrong Atlantic State University	M
A.T. Still University of Health Sciences	M,D
Azusa Pacific University	D
Baylor University	M,D*
Bellarmine University	M,D
Belmont University	D
Boston University	D*
Bradley University	D
California State University, Fresno	M
California State University, Long Beach	M
California State University, Northridge	M
Carroll College	M,D
Central Michigan University	M,D*
Chapman University	D
Chatham University	D
Clarke College	M
Clarkson University	M,D*
Cleveland State University	D
College Misericordia	M,D
College of Mount St. Joseph	M,D
College of St. Catherine	M,D*
The College of St. Scholastica	D
Columbia University	D*
Concordia University Wisconsin	M,D
Creighton University	D*
Daemen College	D
Des Moines University	D
Dominican College	M,D
Drexel University	M,D,O*
Duke University	D*
Duquesne University	M,D*
D'Youville College	M,D,O*
East Carolina University	M,D*
Eastern Washington University	D
East Tennessee State University	D
Elon University	D
Emory University	D*
Florida Agricultural and Mechanical University	M*
Florida Gulf Coast University	M
Florida International University	M*
Franklin Pierce University	M
Gannon University	D
The George Washington University	D*
Georgia State University	D*
Governors State University	M,D
Grand Valley State University	M,D
Hampton University	D*
Hardin-Simmons University	D
Humboldt State University	M
Hunter College of the City University of New York	M
Husson College	M
Idaho State University	D
Indiana University–Purdue University Indianapolis	M,D*
Ithaca College	D
Langston University	D
Loma Linda University	M,D
Long Island University, Brooklyn Campus	D*
Louisiana State University Health Sciences Center	M*
Marquette University	D
Marymount University	D
Maryville University of Saint Louis	D
Mayo School of Health Sciences	D
McMaster University	M
Medical College of Georgia	M,D*
Medical University of South Carolina	D*
Mercy College	M
MGH Institute of Health Professions	M,D,O*
Midwestern University, Downers Grove Campus	D*
Missouri State University	M*
Mount St. Mary's College	D
Nazareth College of Rochester	M,D
Neumann College	M,D
New York Institute of Technology	M,D
New York Medical College	D*
New York University	M,D*
Northern Arizona University	D
Northern Illinois University	M
North Georgia College & State University	D
Northwestern University	D*
Nova Southeastern University	D*
Oakland University	M,D,O*
The Ohio State University	M*
Ohio University	D*
Old Dominion University	D*
Pacific University	D
Quinnipiac University	D*
Regis University	D
The Richard Stockton College of New Jersey	M,D
Rockhurst University	D
Rosalind Franklin University of Medicine and Science	M,D*
Rutgers, The State University of New Jersey, Camden	M
Sacred Heart University	D
Sage Graduate School	D
St. Ambrose University	D
Saint Francis University	D
Saint Louis University	M,D*
Samuel Merritt College	M
San Francisco State University	M,D
Seton Hall University	D*
Shenandoah University	D*
Simmons College	D
Slippery Rock University of Pennsylvania	D
Southwest Baptist University	D
Springfield College	M*
State University of New York Upstate Medical University	D*
Stony Brook University, State University of New York	M,D,O*
Temple University	D*
Tennessee State University	M,D*
Texas State University-San Marcos	M*
Texas Tech University Health Sciences Center	M,D
Texas Woman's University	M,D
Thomas Jefferson University	M,D*
Touro College	M
Université de Montréal	O
University at Buffalo, the State University of New York	D*
The University of Alabama at Birmingham	D*
University of Alberta	M,D*
University of California, San Francisco	M,D
University of Central Arkansas	D
University of Central Florida	M*
University of Colorado at Denver and Health Sciences Center	M,D*
University of Connecticut	M*
University of Delaware	D*
The University of Findlay	M
University of Florida	D*
University of Hartford	M,D*
University of Illinois at Chicago	M*
University of Indianapolis	M,D
The University of Iowa	D*
University of Kansas	M,D*
University of Kentucky	M*
University of Mary	D
University of Maryland, Baltimore	D*
University of Maryland Eastern Shore	D*
University of Massachusetts Lowell	M*
University of Medicine and Dentistry of New Jersey	M,D*
University of Miami	D*
University of Michigan–Flint	D*
University of Minnesota, Twin Cities Campus	D*
University of Mississippi Medical Center	M*
University of Missouri–Columbia	M*
The University of Montana	D*
University of Nebraska Medical Center	D*
University of Nevada, Las Vegas	M,D
University of New England	D
University of New Mexico	M*
The University of North Carolina at Chapel Hill	M,D*
University of North Dakota	M,D
University of North Florida	M
University of Oklahoma Health Sciences Center	M
University of Pittsburgh	M,D*
University of Puerto Rico, Medical Sciences Campus	M*
University of Puget Sound	D
University of Rhode Island	D
University of St. Augustine for Health Sciences	M,D,O
The University of Scranton	M,D
University of South Alabama	D*
The University of South Dakota	M,D
University of Southern California	M,D*
University of South Florida	M*
The University of Tennessee at Chattanooga	D
The University of Tennessee Health Science Center	M,D*
The University of Texas at El Paso	M
The University of Texas Health Science Center at San Antonio	M*
The University of Texas Medical Branch	M*
The University of Texas Southwestern Medical Center at Dallas	M*
University of the Pacific	M,D
University of the Sciences in Philadelphia	D*
The University of Toledo	M,D*
University of Utah	D,O*
University of Vermont	D*
University of Washington	M,D*
The University of Western Ontario	M
University of Wisconsin–La Crosse	M,D
Utica College	D
Virginia Commonwealth University	M,D*
Walsh University	M
Washington University in St. Louis	D,O*
Wayne State University	M*
Western Carolina University	M*
Western University of Health Sciences	D
West Virginia University	M*
Wheeling Jesuit University	D
Wichita State University	M*
Widener University	M,D*
Winston-Salem State University	M
Youngstown State University	M

PHYSICIAN ASSISTANT STUDIES

Institution	Degrees
Albany Medical College	M
A.T. Still University of Health Sciences	M,D
Augsburg College	M
Barry University	M*
Baylor College of Medicine	M*
Butler University	P,M
California State University, Dominguez Hills	M
Central Michigan University	M,D*
Chatham University	M
Daemen College	M
DeSales University	M
Des Moines University	M
Drexel University	M*
Duke University	M*
Duquesne University	M,D*
D'Youville College	M*
East Carolina University	M*
Eastern Virginia Medical School	M
Emory University	M*
Gannon University	M
The George Washington University	M*
Grand Valley State University	M*
Harding University	M
Idaho State University	M
James Madison University	M
King's College	M
Le Moyne College	M
Lock Haven University of Pennsylvania	M
Loma Linda University	M
Marietta College	M
Marquette University	M
Marywood University	M*
Medical College of Georgia	M*
Medical University of South Carolina	M*
Mercy College	M
Methodist University	M
Midwestern University, Downers Grove Campus	M*
Midwestern University, Glendale Campus	M*
Missouri State University	M*
Mountain State University	M*
New York Institute of Technology	M
Northeastern University	M*
Nova Southeastern University	M*
Pacific University	M
Philadelphia College of Osteopathic Medicine	M*
Philadelphia University	M*
Quinnipiac University	M*
Regis University	M,D
Rosalind Franklin University of Medicine and Science	M*
Saint Francis University	M
Saint Louis University	M*
Samuel Merritt College	M
Seton Hall University	M*
Seton Hill University	M
Shenandoah University	M*
South University (GA)	M*
Springfield College	M*
Texas Tech University Health Sciences Center	M
Touro University College of Osteopathic Medicine	P,M
Towson University	M
Trevecca Nazarene University	M
Union College (NE)	M
The University of Alabama at Birmingham	M*
University of Colorado at Denver and Health Sciences Center	M*
University of Detroit Mercy	M
University of Florida	M*
The University of Iowa	M*
University of Kentucky	M*
University of Medicine and Dentistry of New Jersey	M*
University of Nebraska Medical Center	M*
University of New England	M
University of North Dakota	M
University of North Texas Health Science Center at Fort Worth	M
University of St. Francis (IL)	M
University of Saint Francis (IN)	M

Institution	Degrees
University of South Alabama	M*
The University of South Dakota	M
University of Southern California	M*
The University of Texas Health Science Center at San Antonio	M*
The University of Texas Medical Branch	M*
The University of Texas Southwestern Medical Center at Dallas	M*
The University of Toledo	M*
University of Utah	M*
University of Wisconsin–La Crosse	M
Wagner College	M
Wayne State University	M*
Western Michigan University	M*
Western University of Health Sciences	M
Yale University	M*

PHYSICS

Institution	Degrees
Adelphi University	M*
Alabama Agricultural and Mechanical University	M,D
American University	M*
American University of Beirut	M
Arizona State University	M,D*
Auburn University	M,D*
Ball State University	M*
Baylor University	M,D*
Boston College	M,D*
Boston University	M,D*
Bowling Green State University	M*
Brandeis University	M,D*
Brigham Young University	M,D*
Brock University	M
Brooklyn College of the City University of New York	M,D
Brown University	M,D*
Bryn Mawr College	M,D*
California Institute of Technology	D*
California State University, Fresno	M
California State University, Fullerton	M
California State University, Long Beach	M
California State University, Los Angeles	M
California State University, Northridge	M
Carleton University	M,D
Carnegie Mellon University	D*
Case Western Reserve University	M,D*
The Catholic University of America	M,D*
Central Connecticut State University	M*
Central Michigan University	M*
Christopher Newport University	M
City College of the City University of New York	M,D*
Clark Atlanta University	M
Clarkson University	M,D*
Clark University	M,D*
Clemson University	M,D*
Cleveland State University	M
The College of William and Mary	M,D
Colorado State University	M,D*
Columbia University	M,D*
Concordia University (Canada)	M,D
Cornell University	M,D*
Creighton University	M*
Dalhousie University	M,D
Dartmouth College	M,D*
Delaware State University	M
DePaul University	M*
Drexel University	M,D*
Duke University	M,D*
East Carolina University	M,D*
Eastern Michigan University	M
Emory University	D*
Fisk University	M
Florida Agricultural and Mechanical University	M,D*
Florida Atlantic University	M,D
Florida Institute of Technology	M,D*
Florida International University	M,D*
Florida State University	M,D*
The George Washington University	M,D*
Georgia Institute of Technology	M,D*
Georgia State University	M,D*
Graduate School and University Center of the City University of New York	D*
Hampton University	M,D*
Harvard University	D*
Howard University	M,D*
Hunter College of the City University of New York	M,D
Idaho State University	M,D
Illinois Institute of Technology	M,D*
Indiana University Bloomington	M,D*
Indiana University of Pennsylvania	M
Indiana University–Purdue University Indianapolis	M,D*
Iowa State University of Science and Technology	M,D*
The Johns Hopkins University	D*
Kansas State University	M,D*
Kent State University	M,D*
Lakehead University	M
Lehigh University	M,D*
Louisiana State University and Agricultural and Mechanical College	M,D*
Louisiana Tech University	M,D
Marshall University	M
Massachusetts Institute of Technology	D*
McGill University	M,D*
McMaster University	D
Memorial University of Newfoundland	M,D
Miami University	M*
Michigan State University	M,D*
Michigan Technological University	M,D*
Minnesota State University Mankato	M
Mississippi State University	M,D
Montana State University	M,D
Morgan State University	M*
Naval Postgraduate School	M,D
New Mexico Institute of Mining and Technology	M,D
New Mexico State University	M,D
New York University	M,D*
North Carolina State University	M,D*
North Dakota State University	M,D
Northeastern University	M,D*
Northern Illinois University	M,D
Northwestern University	M,D*
Oakland University	M,D*
The Ohio State University	M,D*
Ohio University	M,D*
Oklahoma State University	M,D*
Old Dominion University	M,D*
Oregon State University	M,D*
Penn State University Park	M,D*
Pittsburg State University	M
Polytechnic University, Brooklyn Campus	M,D*
Portland State University	M,D
Princeton University	D*
Purdue University	M,D*
Queens College of the City University of New York	M,D
Queen's University at Kingston	M,D
Rensselaer Polytechnic Institute	M,D*
Rice University	M,D*
Royal Military College of Canada	M
Rutgers, The State University of New Jersey, New Brunswick	M,D*
St. Francis Xavier University	M
San Diego State University	M*
San Francisco State University	M
San Jose State University	M
Simon Fraser University	M,D
South Dakota School of Mines and Technology	M,D
South Dakota State University	M
Southern Illinois University Carbondale	M,D*
Southern Illinois University Edwardsville	M
Southern Methodist University	M,D*
Southern University and Agricultural and Mechanical College	M*
Stanford University	D*
State University of New York at Binghamton	M*
Stephen F. Austin State University	M
Stevens Institute of Technology	M,D,O*
Stony Brook University, State University of New York	M,D*
Syracuse University	M,D*
Temple University	M,D*
Texas A&M International University	M
Texas A&M University	M,D*
Texas A&M University–Commerce	M
Texas Christian University	M,D
Texas State University-San Marcos	M*
Texas Tech University	M,D
Trent University	M
Tufts University	M,D*
Tulane University	M,D*
Université de Moncton	M
Université de Montréal	M,D
Université de Sherbrooke	M,D
Université Laval	M,D
University at Albany, State University of New York	M,D*
University at Buffalo, the State University of New York	M,D*
The University of Akron	M
The University of Alabama	M,D
The University of Alabama at Birmingham	M,D*
The University of Alabama in Huntsville	M,D
University of Alaska Fairbanks	M,D
University of Alberta	M,D*
The University of Arizona	M,D*
University of Arkansas	M,D*
The University of British Columbia	M,D*
University of Calgary	M,D
University of California, Berkeley	D*
University of California, Davis	M,D*
University of California, Irvine	M,D*
University of California, Los Angeles	M,D*
University of California, Riverside	M,D*
University of California, San Diego	M,D*
University of California, Santa Barbara	D*
University of California, Santa Cruz	M,D*
University of Central Florida	M,D*
University of Central Oklahoma	M
University of Chicago	M,D*
University of Cincinnati	M,D
University of Colorado at Boulder	M,D*
University of Connecticut	M,D*
University of Delaware	M,D*
University of Denver	M,D*
University of Florida	M,D*
University of Georgia	M,D*
University of Guelph	M,D
University of Hawaii at Manoa	M,D*
University of Houston	M,D*
University of Houston–Clear Lake	M
University of Idaho	M,D*
University of Illinois at Chicago	M,D*
University of Illinois at Urbana–Champaign	M,D*
The University of Iowa	M,D*
University of Kansas	M,D*
University of Kentucky	M,D*
University of Lethbridge	M,D
University of Louisiana at Lafayette	M*
University of Louisville	M
University of Maine	M,D*
University of Manitoba	M,D
University of Maryland, Baltimore County	M,D*
University of Maryland, College Park	M,D*
University of Massachusetts Amherst	M,D*
University of Massachusetts Dartmouth	M
University of Massachusetts Lowell	M,D*
University of Memphis	M*
University of Miami	M,D*
University of Michigan	M,D*
University of Minnesota, Duluth	M*
University of Minnesota, Twin Cities Campus	M,D*
University of Mississippi	M,D
University of Missouri–Columbia	M,D*
University of Missouri–Kansas City	M,D*
University of Missouri–Rolla	M,D*
University of Missouri–St. Louis	M,D
University of Nebraska–Lincoln	M,D*
University of Nevada, Las Vegas	M,D
University of Nevada, Reno	M,D*
University of New Brunswick Fredericton	M,D
University of New Hampshire	M,D*
University of New Mexico	M,D*
University of New Orleans	M,D
The University of North Carolina at Chapel Hill	M,D*
University of North Dakota	M,D
University of Northern Iowa	M
University of North Texas	M,D*
University of Notre Dame	D*
University of Oklahoma	M,D*
University of Oregon	M,D*
University of Ottawa	M,D*
University of Pennsylvania	M,D*
University of Pittsburgh	M,D*
University of Puerto Rico, Mayagüez Campus	M*
University of Puerto Rico, Río Piedras	M,D*
University of Regina	M,D
University of Rhode Island	M,D
University of Rochester	M,D*
University of Saskatchewan	M,D
University of South Carolina	M,D*
University of Southern California	M,D*
University of Southern Mississippi	M,D*
University of South Florida	M,D*
The University of Tennessee	M,D*
The University of Tennessee Space Institute	M,D*
The University of Texas at Arlington	M,D*
The University of Texas at Austin	M,D*
The University of Texas at Brownsville	M
The University of Texas at Dallas	M,D*
The University of Texas at El Paso	M
The University of Texas at San Antonio	M,D*
The University of Toledo	M,D*
University of Toronto	M,D*
University of Utah	M,D*
University of Vermont	M*
University of Victoria	M,D
University of Virginia	M,D*
University of Washington	M,D*
University of Waterloo	M,D*
The University of Western Ontario	M,D
University of Windsor	M,D
University of Wisconsin–Madison	M,D*
University of Wisconsin–Milwaukee	M,D
Utah State University	M,D
Vanderbilt University	M,D*
Virginia Commonwealth University	M,D*
Virginia Polytechnic Institute and State University	M,D*
Virginia State University	M
Wake Forest University	M,D*
Washington State University	M,D*
Washington University in St. Louis	M,D*
Wayne State University	M,D*
Wesleyan University	M,D*
Western Illinois University	M
Western Michigan University	M,D*
West Virginia University	M,D*
Wichita State University	M*
Worcester Polytechnic Institute	M,D*
Wright State University	M*
Yale University	D*
York University	M,D*

PHYSIOLOGY

Institution	Degrees
Albert Einstein College of Medicine	D*
American University of Beirut	P,M
Arizona State University	M,D*
Ball State University	M*
Boston University	M,D*
Brigham Young University	M,D*
Brown University	M,D*
Case Western Reserve University	M,D*
Columbia University	M,D*
Cornell University	P,M,D*
Cornell University, Joan and Sanford I. Weill Medical College and Graduate School of Medical Sciences	D*
Dalhousie University	M,D
Dartmouth College	D*
East Carolina University	D*
East Tennessee State University	M,D
Florida State University	M,D*
Georgetown University	M,D*
Georgia Institute of Technology	M*
Georgia State University	M,D*
Harvard University	M,D*
Howard University	D*
Illinois State University	M,D*
Indiana State University	M,D*
The Johns Hopkins University	M,D*
Kansas State University	M,D*
Kent State University	M,D*
Loma Linda University	M,D
Louisiana State University Health Sciences Center	M,D*
Louisiana State University Health Sciences Center at Shreveport	M,D*
Maharishi University of Management	M,D
Marquette University	M,D
McGill University	M,D*
McMaster University	M,D*
Medical College of Georgia	M,D*
Medical College of Wisconsin	M,D*
Meharry Medical College	D
Michigan State University	M,D*
New York Medical College	M,D*

P—first professional degree; M—master's degree; D—doctorate; O—other advanced degree;
**full description and/or announcement in Book 2, 3, 4, 5, or 6*

New York University	D*
North Carolina State University	M,D*
Northwestern University	M*
Nova Scotia Agricultural College	M
The Ohio State University	M,D*
Ohio University	M,D*
Oregon Health & Science University	D*
Penn State Hershey Medical Center	M,D*
Penn State University Park	M,D*
Purdue University	M,D*
Queen's University at Kingston	M,D
Rosalind Franklin University of Medicine and Science	M,D*
Rush University	D
Rutgers, The State University of New Jersey, New Brunswick	D*
Saint Louis University	D*
Salisbury University	M
San Francisco State University	M
San Jose State University	M
Southern Illinois University Carbondale	M,D*
Stanford University	D*
State University of New York Upstate Medical University	M,D*
Stony Brook University, State University of New York	D*
Temple University	D*
Texas A&M University	M,D*
Texas Tech University Health Sciences Center	M,D
Tufts University	D*
Tulane University	M,D*
Universidad Central del Caribe	M
Université de Montréal	M,D
Université de Sherbrooke	M,D
Université Laval	M,D
University at Buffalo, the State University of New York	M,D*
The University of Alabama at Birmingham	M,D*
University of Alberta	M,D*
The University of Arizona	D*
University of Arkansas for Medical Sciences	M,D*
The University of British Columbia	M,D*
University of California, Berkeley	M,D*
University of California, Davis	M,D*
University of California, Irvine	D*
University of California, Los Angeles	M,D*
University of California, San Diego	D*
University of California, San Francisco	D
University of Chicago	D*
University of Cincinnati	D
University of Colorado at Boulder	M,D*
University of Colorado at Denver and Health Sciences Center	D*
University of Connecticut	M,D*
University of Delaware	M,D*
University of Florida	M,D*
University of Georgia	M,D*
University of Guelph	M,D
University of Hawaii at Manoa	M,D*
University of Illinois at Chicago	M,D*
University of Illinois at Urbana–Champaign	M,D*
The University of Iowa	M,D*
University of Kansas	M,D*
University of Kentucky	M,D*
University of Louisville	M,D
University of Manitoba	M,D
University of Maryland, Baltimore	D*
University of Massachusetts Worcester	D*
University of Medicine and Dentistry of New Jersey	M,D*
University of Miami	D*
University of Michigan	D*
University of Minnesota, Duluth	M,D*
University of Minnesota, Twin Cities Campus	M,D*
University of Mississippi Medical Center	M,D*
University of Missouri–Columbia	M,D*
University of Missouri–St. Louis	M,D,O
University of Nebraska Medical Center	M,D*
University of Nevada, Reno	M,D*
University of New Mexico	M,D*
University of North Dakota	M,D
University of North Texas Health Science Center at Fort Worth	M,D
University of Notre Dame	M,D*
University of Oklahoma Health Sciences Center	M,D
University of Oregon	M,D*
University of Pennsylvania	D*
University of Prince Edward Island	M,D
University of Puerto Rico, Medical Sciences Campus	M,D*
University of Rochester	M,D*
University of Saskatchewan	M,D
University of South Alabama	D*
The University of South Dakota	M,D
University of Southern California	M,D*
University of South Florida	M,D*
The University of Tennessee	M,D*
The University of Texas Health Science Center at San Antonio	M,D*
The University of Texas Medical Branch	M,D*
University of Toronto	M,D
University of Utah	D*
University of Virginia	D*
University of Washington	D*
The University of Western Ontario	M,D
University of Wisconsin–La Crosse	M
University of Wisconsin–Madison	M,D*
University of Wyoming	M,D
Virginia Commonwealth University	M,D,O*
Wake Forest University	D*
Washington State University Spokane	M,O
Wayne State University	M,D*
Wesleyan University	D*
West Virginia University	M,D*
William Paterson University of New Jersey	M*
Wright State University	M*
Yale University	D*

PLANETARY AND SPACE SCIENCES

Air Force Institute of Technology	M,D
California Institute of Technology	M,D*
Columbia University	M,D*
Cornell University	D*
Embry-Riddle Aeronautical University (FL)	M*
Florida Institute of Technology	M,D*
Harvard University	M,D*
Massachusetts Institute of Technology	M,D*
McGill University	M,D*
Stony Brook University, State University of New York	M,D*
The University of Arizona	M,D*
University of Arkansas	M,D*
University of California, Los Angeles	M,D*
University of Chicago	M,D*
University of Hawaii at Manoa	M,D*
University of Michigan	M,D*
University of New Mexico	M,D*
University of North Dakota	M
University of Pittsburgh	M,D*
Washington University in St. Louis	M,D*
Western Connecticut State University	M*
York University	M,D*

PLANT BIOLOGY

Clemson University	M,D*
Cornell University	M,D*
Florida State University	M,D*
Illinois State University	M,D*
Indiana University Bloomington	M,D*
Miami University	M,D*
Michigan State University	M,D*
New York University	M,D*
The Ohio State University	M,D*
Ohio University	M,D*
Rutgers, The State University of New Jersey, New Brunswick	M,D*
Southern Illinois University Carbondale	M,D*
Texas A&M University	M,D*
Université Laval	M,D
University of Alberta	M,D*
University of California, Berkeley	D*
University of California, Davis	M,D*
University of California, Riverside	M,D*
University of California, San Diego	D*
University of Connecticut	M,D*
University of Florida	M,D*
University of Georgia	M,D*
University of Illinois at Chicago	M,D*
University of Illinois at Urbana–Champaign	M,D*
The University of Iowa	M,D*
University of Maine	M,D*
University of Maryland, College Park	M,D*
University of Massachusetts Amherst	M,D*
University of Minnesota, Twin Cities Campus	M,D*
University of Missouri–Columbia	M,D*
University of New Hampshire	M,D*
The University of Texas at Austin	M,D*
University of Utah	M,D*
University of Vermont	M,D*
The University of Western Ontario	M,D
Washington University in St. Louis	D*
Yale University	D*

PLANT MOLECULAR BIOLOGY

Cornell University	M,D*
Illinois State University	M,D*
Michigan Technological University	M,D*
Rutgers, The State University of New Jersey, New Brunswick	M,D*
University of California, Los Angeles	M,D*
University of California, San Diego	D*
University of Connecticut	M,D*
University of Florida	M,D*
University of Massachusetts Amherst	M,D*
Washington State University	M,D*

PLANT PATHOLOGY

Auburn University	M,D*
Colorado State University	M,D*
Cornell University	M,D*
Iowa State University of Science and Technology	M,D*
Kansas State University	M,D*
Louisiana State University and Agricultural and Mechanical College	M,D*
Michigan State University	M,D*
Mississippi State University	M,D
Montana State University	M,D
New Mexico State University	M
North Carolina State University	M,D*
North Dakota State University	M,D
Nova Scotia Agricultural College	M
The Ohio State University	M,D*
Oklahoma State University	D*
Oregon State University	M,D*
Penn State University Park	M,D*
Purdue University	M,D*
Rutgers, The State University of New Jersey, New Brunswick	M,D*
State University of New York College of Environmental Science and Forestry	M,D
Texas A&M University	M,D*
The University of Arizona	M,D*
University of Arkansas	M*
University of California, Davis	M,D*
University of California, Riverside	M,D*
University of Florida	M,D*
University of Georgia	M,D*
University of Guelph	M,D
University of Hawaii at Manoa	M,D*
University of Kentucky	M,D*
University of Maine	M*
University of Minnesota, Twin Cities Campus	M,D*
University of Missouri–Columbia	M,D*
The University of Tennessee	M,D*
University of Wisconsin–Madison	M,D*
Virginia Polytechnic Institute and State University	M,D*
Washington State University	M,D*
West Virginia University	M,D*

PLANT PHYSIOLOGY

Cornell University	M,D*
Iowa State University of Science and Technology	M,D*
Nova Scotia Agricultural College	M
Oregon State University	M,D*
Penn State University Park	M,D*
Purdue University	M,D*
Rutgers, The State University of New Jersey, New Brunswick	M,D*
University of Kentucky	D*
University of Massachusetts Amherst	M,D*
The University of Tennessee	M,D*
Virginia Polytechnic Institute and State University	M,D*

PLANT SCIENCES

Alabama Agricultural and Mechanical University	M,D
American University of Beirut	M
Brigham Young University	M,D*
California State University, Fresno	M
Clemson University	M,D*
Colorado State University	M,D*
Cornell University	M,D*
Florida Agricultural and Mechanical University	M*
Illinois State University	M,D*
Lehman College of the City University of New York	D
McGill University	M,D,O*
Miami University	M,D*
Michigan State University	M,D*
Mississippi State University	M,D
Missouri State University	M*
Montana State University	M,D
New Mexico State University	M
North Carolina Agricultural and Technical State University	M
North Dakota State University	M,D
Oklahoma State University	M,D*
Rutgers, The State University of New Jersey, New Brunswick	M,D*
South Dakota State University	M,D
Southern Illinois University Carbondale	M*
State University of New York College of Environmental Science and Forestry	M,D
Texas A&M University	M,D*
Texas A&M University–Kingsville	M,D
Texas Tech University	M,D
Tuskegee University	M
The University of Arizona	M,D*
University of Arkansas	D*
The University of British Columbia	M,D*
University of California, Riverside	M,D*
University of Connecticut	M,D*
University of Delaware	M,D*
University of Florida	D*
University of Hawaii at Manoa	M,D*
University of Idaho	M,D*
University of Kentucky	M*
University of Maine	M,D*
University of Massachusetts Amherst	M,D*
University of Minnesota, Twin Cities Campus	M,D*
University of Missouri–Columbia	M,D*
University of Rhode Island	M,D
University of Saskatchewan	M,D
The University of Tennessee	M*
University of Vermont	M,D*
The University of Western Ontario	M,D
University of Wisconsin–Madison	M,D*
Utah State University	M,D
West Texas A&M University	M
West Virginia University	M,D*

PLASMA PHYSICS

Massachusetts Institute of Technology	M,D,O*
Princeton University	D*
University of Colorado at Boulder	M,D*
West Virginia University	M,D*

PODIATRIC MEDICINE

Barry University	P*
California School of Podiatric Medicine at Samuel Merritt College	P
Des Moines University	P
Midwestern University, Glendale Campus	P*
New York College of Podiatric Medicine	P
Ohio College of Podiatric Medicine	P
Rosalind Franklin University of Medicine and Science	P*
Temple University	P*

POLITICAL SCIENCE

Acadia University	M
American Public University System	M
American University	M,D,O*
The American University in Cairo	M
The American University of Athens	M
American University of Beirut	M
Appalachian State University	M
Arizona State University	M,D*
Arkansas State University	M,O
Ashland University	M
Auburn University	M,D*

- Auburn University Montgomery M,D
- Augusta State University M
- Ball State University M*
- Baylor University M,D*
- Boston College M,D*
- Boston University M,D*
- Bowling Green State University *
- Brandeis University M,D*
- Brock University M
- Brooklyn College of the City University of New York M,D
- Brown University M,D*
- California Polytechnic State University, San Luis Obispo M
- California State University, Chico M
- California State University, Fullerton M
- California State University, Long Beach M
- California State University, Los Angeles M
- California State University, Northridge M
- California State University, Sacramento M*
- California State University, Stanislaus M
- Carleton University M,D
- Case Western Reserve University M,D*
- The Catholic University of America M,D*
- Central European University M,D*
- Central Michigan University M*
- Claremont Graduate University M,D
- Clark Atlanta University M,D
- The College of Saint Rose M*
- Colorado State University M,D*
- Columbia University M,D*
- Concordia University (Canada) M,D
- Converse College M
- Cornell University D*
- Dalhousie University M,D
- Duke University M,D*
- East Carolina University M*
- Eastern Illinois University M
- Eastern Kentucky University M*
- East Stroudsburg University of Pennsylvania M
- Emory University D*
- Fairleigh Dickinson University, Metropolitan Campus M*
- Fayetteville State University M
- Florida Agricultural and Mechanical University M*
- Florida Atlantic University M
- Florida International University M,D*
- Florida State University M,D*
- Fordham University M*
- Georgetown University M,D*
- The George Washington University M,D*
- Georgia State University M,D*
- Governors State University M
- Graduate School and University Center of the City University of New York M,D*
- Harvard University M,D*
- Hawai'i Pacific University M*
- Howard University M,D*
- Huron University USA in London M
- Idaho State University M,D
- Illinois State University M*
- Indiana State University M*
- Indiana University Bloomington M,D*
- Indiana University of Pennsylvania M
- Indiana University–Purdue University Indianapolis M,O*
- Institute for Christian Studies M,D
- The Institute of World Politics M,O*
- Iowa State University of Science and Technology M*
- Jackson State University M
- Jacksonville State University M
- The Johns Hopkins University M,D,O*
- Kansas State University M*
- Kean University M
- Kent State University M,D*
- Lamar University M*
- Lehigh University M*
- Lincoln University (MO) M
- Long Island University, Brooklyn Campus M*
- Long Island University, C.W. Post Campus M*
- Louisiana State University and Agricultural and Mechanical College M,D*
- Loyola University Chicago M,D*
- Marquette University M
- Marshall University M
- Massachusetts Institute of Technology M,D*
- McGill University M,D*
- McMaster University M,D
- Memorial University of Newfoundland M
- Miami University M,D*
- Michigan State University M,D*
- Midwestern State University M
- Minnesota State University Mankato M
- Mississippi College M,O
- Mississippi State University M,D
- Missouri State University M*
- Naval Postgraduate School M
- New Mexico Highlands University M
- New Mexico State University M
- The New School: A University M,D*
- New York University M,D*
- North Dakota State University M,D
- Northeastern Illinois University M
- Northeastern University M,D*
- Northern Arizona University M,D,O
- Northern Illinois University M,D
- Northwestern University M,D*
- The Ohio State University M,D*
- Ohio University M*
- Oklahoma State University M*
- Penn State University Park M,D*
- Pepperdine University M*
- Portland State University M,D
- Princeton University D*
- Purdue University M,D*
- Purdue University Calumet M
- Queen's University at Kingston M,D
- Regent University M
- Rice University M,D*
- Roosevelt University M
- Rutgers, The State University of New Jersey, Newark M*
- Rutgers, The State University of New Jersey, New Brunswick M,D*
- St. John's University (NY) M,O
- St. Mary's University of San Antonio M
- Sam Houston State University M
- San Diego State University M*
- San Francisco State University M
- Simon Fraser University M,D
- Sonoma State University M
- Southern Connecticut State University M
- Southern Illinois University Carbondale M,D*
- Southern University and Agricultural and Mechanical College M*
- Stanford University M,D*
- State University of New York at Binghamton M,D*
- Stony Brook University, State University of New York M,D*
- Suffolk University M*
- Sul Ross State University M*
- Syracuse University M,D*
- Tarleton State University M
- Teachers College Columbia University M,D*
- Temple University M,D*
- Texas A&M International University M
- Texas A&M University M,D*
- Texas A&M University–Kingsville M
- Texas State University-San Marcos M*
- Texas Tech University M,D
- Texas Woman's University M
- Tulane University M,D*
- Université de Montréal M,D
- Université du Québec à Montréal M,D
- Université Laval M,D
- University at Albany, State University of New York M,D*
- University at Buffalo, the State University of New York M,D*
- The University of Akron M
- The University of Alabama M,D
- University of Alberta M,D*
- The University of Arizona M,D*
- University of Arkansas M*
- The University of British Columbia M,D*
- University of Calgary M,D
- University of California, Berkeley D*
- University of California, Davis M,D*
- University of California, Irvine D*
- University of California, Los Angeles M,D*
- University of California, Riverside M,D*
- University of California, San Diego M,D*
- University of California, Santa Barbara M,D*
- University of California, Santa Cruz D*
- University of Central Florida M*
- University of Central Oklahoma M
- University of Chicago D*
- University of Cincinnati M,D
- University of Colorado at Boulder M,D*
- University of Colorado at Denver and Health Sciences Center M*
- University of Connecticut M,D*
- University of Dallas M,D
- University of Delaware M,D*
- University of Florida M,D,O*
- University of Georgia M,D*
- University of Guelph M
- University of Hawaii at Manoa M,D*
- University of Houston M,D*
- University of Idaho M,D*
- University of Illinois at Chicago M,D*
- University of Illinois at Springfield M
- University of Illinois at Urbana–Champaign M,D*
- The University of Iowa M,D*
- University of Kansas M,D*
- University of Kentucky M,D*
- University of Lethbridge M,D
- University of Louisville M
- University of Manitoba M
- University of Maryland, College Park D*
- University of Massachusetts Amherst M,D*
- University of Massachusetts Boston M,D,O
- University of Memphis M*
- University of Miami M*
- University of Michigan M,D*
- University of Minnesota, Twin Cities Campus M,D*
- University of Mississippi M,D
- University of Missouri–Columbia M,D*
- University of Missouri–Kansas City M,D*
- University of Missouri–St. Louis M,D
- The University of Montana M*
- University of Nebraska at Omaha M
- University of Nebraska–Lincoln M,D*
- University of Nevada, Las Vegas M
- University of Nevada, Reno M,D*
- University of New Brunswick Fredericton M*
- University of New Hampshire M*
- University of New Mexico M,D*
- University of New Orleans M,D
- The University of North Carolina at Chapel Hill M,D*
- The University of North Carolina at Greensboro M,O
- University of Northern British Columbia M,D,O
- University of North Texas M,D*
- University of Notre Dame D*
- University of Oklahoma M,D*
- University of Oregon M,D*
- University of Ottawa M,D*
- University of Pennsylvania M,D*
- University of Pittsburgh M,D*
- University of Regina M,D
- University of Rhode Island M,O
- University of Rochester M,D*
- University of Saskatchewan M
- University of South Carolina M,D*
- The University of South Dakota M
- University of Southern California M,D*
- University of Southern Mississippi M,D*
- University of South Florida M*
- The University of Tennessee M,D*
- The University of Texas at Arlington M*
- The University of Texas at Austin M,D*
- The University of Texas at Brownsville M
- The University of Texas at Dallas M,D*
- The University of Texas at El Paso M
- The University of Texas at San Antonio M*
- The University of Texas at Tyler M
- The University of Toledo M*
- University of Toronto M,D
- University of Utah M,D*
- University of Victoria M,D
- University of Virginia M,D*
- University of Washington M,D*
- University of Waterloo M,D*
- The University of Western Ontario M,D
- University of West Florida M
- University of Windsor M
- University of Wisconsin–Madison M,D*
- University of Wisconsin–Milwaukee M,D
- University of Wisconsin–Oshkosh M
- University of Wyoming M
- Utah State University M
- Vanderbilt University M,D*
- Villanova University M*
- Virginia Polytechnic Institute and State University M,D*
- Washington State University M,D*
- Washington University in St. Louis M,D*
- Wayne State University M,D*
- Western Illinois University M,O
- Western Kentucky University M
- Western Michigan University M,D*
- Western Washington University M
- West Texas A&M University M
- West Virginia University M,D*
- Wichita State University M*
- Wilfrid Laurier University M
- Yale University D*
- York University M,D*

POLYMER SCIENCE AND ENGINEERING

- California Polytechnic State University, San Luis Obispo M
- Carnegie Mellon University M,D*
- Case Western Reserve University M,D*
- Clemson University M,D*
- Cornell University M,D*
- DePaul University M*
- Eastern Michigan University M
- Georgia Institute of Technology M,D*
- Illinois Institute of Technology *
- Lehigh University M,D*
- Massachusetts Institute of Technology M,D,O*
- North Carolina State University D*
- North Dakota State University M,D
- Penn State University Park M,D*
- Polytechnic University, Brooklyn Campus M*
- Princeton University M,D*
- Rensselaer Polytechnic Institute M,D*
- Stevens Institute of Technology M,D,O*
- The University of Akron M,D
- University of Cincinnati M,D
- University of Connecticut M,D*
- University of Detroit Mercy M,D
- University of Massachusetts Amherst M,D*
- University of Massachusetts Lowell M,D*
- University of Missouri–Kansas City M,D*
- University of Southern Mississippi M,D*
- The University of Tennessee M,D*
- University of Wisconsin–Madison M,D*
- Wayne State University M,D,O*

PORTUGUESE

- Brigham Young University M*
- Emory University D,O*
- Harvard University M,D*
- Indiana University Bloomington M,D*
- Michigan State University M,D*
- New York University M,D*
- The Ohio State University M,D*
- Princeton University D*
- Tulane University M,D*
- University of California, Los Angeles M*
- University of California, Santa Barbara M,D*
- University of Maryland, College Park M,D*
- University of Massachusetts Dartmouth M,D
- University of Minnesota, Twin Cities Campus M,D*
- University of New Mexico M,D*
- The University of North Carolina at Chapel Hill M,D*
- The University of Tennessee D*
- The University of Texas at Austin M,D*
- University of Toronto M,D
- University of Washington M*
- University of Wisconsin–Madison M,D*
- Vanderbilt University M,D*
- Yale University M,D*

PROJECT MANAGEMENT

- American Graduate University M,O
- American InterContinental University Online M
- Aspen University M,O
- Athabasca University M,O
- Avila University M,O*
- Boston University M*
- Cabrini College M,O
- Capella University M,D,O
- Cardean University M

P—first professional degree; M—master's degree; D—doctorate; O—other advanced degree;
**full description and/or announcement in Book 2, 3, 4, 5, or 6*

Christian Brothers University	M,O
City University	M,O
Colorado Technical University—Colorado Springs	M,D
Colorado Technical University—Denver	M
Colorado Technical University—Sioux Falls	M
Dallas Baptist University	M
DeVry University	M*
The George Washington University	M,D*
Grantham University	M
Harrisburg University of Science and Technology	M
Jones International University	M
Lehigh University	M,D,O*
Marymount University	M,O
Mississippi State University	M,D
Missouri State University	M*
Montana Tech of The University of Montana	M
New York Institute of Technology	M,O
Northwestern University	M*
Regis University	M,O
Rosemont College	M
St. Edward's University	M
Saint Mary's University of Minnesota	M
Southern New Hampshire University	M,D,O*
Stevens Institute of Technology	M,O*
Texas A&M University	M,D*
Universidad Nacional Pedro Henriquez Urena	P,M,D
Université du Québec à Chicoutimi	M
Université du Québec à Montréal	M,O
Université du Québec à Rimouski	M,O
Université du Québec à Trois-Rivières	M,O
Université du Québec en Abitibi-Témiscamingue	M
Université du Québec en Outaouais	M,O
University of Alaska Anchorage	M
University of Dallas	M
University of Denver	M,O*
University of Management and Technology	M,D,O
University of Northern Virginia	M,D
University of Ottawa	M,O*
University of San Francisco	M
University of the Incarnate Word	M,O
University of Wisconsin–Platteville	M
Western Carolina University	M*
Winthrop University	M,O
Worcester Polytechnic Institute	M*
Wright State University	M*

PSYCHIATRIC NURSING

Boston College	M,D*
Case Western Reserve University	M,D*
The Catholic University of America	M,D*
Columbia University	M,O*
Duquesne University	M,O*
Fairfield University	M,O*
Georgia State University	M,D,O*
Hunter College of the City University of New York	M
Husson College	M
Indiana University–Purdue University Indianapolis	M,D*
Kent State University	M,D*
Louisiana State University Health Sciences Center	M,D*
Medical College of Georgia	M,D*
Medical University of South Carolina	M*
MGH Institute of Health Professions	M,O*
Molloy College	M,O
New Mexico State University	M
New York University	M,O*
Northeastern University	M,O*
Oregon Health & Science University	M,O*
Pontifical Catholic University of Puerto Rico	M
Rush University	M,D,O
Rutgers, The State University of New Jersey, Newark	M*
Sage Graduate School	M
Saint Joseph College	M,O
Saint Xavier University	M,O
Seattle University	M
Shenandoah University	M,O*
Stony Brook University, State University of New York	M,O*
University at Buffalo, the State University of New York	M,D,O*
University of Alaska Anchorage	M,O
University of Cincinnati	M,D
University of Connecticut	M,D,O*
University of Delaware	M,O*
University of Illinois at Chicago	M*
University of Kansas	M,D,O*
University of Maryland, Baltimore	M*
University of Massachusetts Lowell	M*
University of Miami	M,D*
University of Michigan	M*
University of Minnesota, Twin Cities Campus	M*
University of Pennsylvania	M*
University of Pittsburgh	M,D*
University of Rhode Island	M,D
University of South Carolina	M,O*
University of Southern Maine	M,O
University of Southern Mississippi	M,D*
Vanderbilt University	M,D*
Virginia Commonwealth University	M,D,O*
Wayne State University	M,O*

PSYCHOANALYSIS AND PSYCHOTHERAPY

Adler Graduate School	M,O
Argosy University, Chicago Campus	D*
Boston Graduate School of Psychoanalysis	M,D,O*
Naropa University	M*
New York University	M,D,O*

PSYCHOLOGY—GENERAL

Abilene Christian University	M
Acadia University	M
Adelphi University	M,D,O*
Adler School of Professional Psychology	M,D,O*
Alabama Agricultural and Mechanical University	M,O
Alliant International University–Fresno	D*
Alliant International University–Los Angeles	D*
Alliant International University–Sacramento	M,D*
Alliant International University–San Diego	M,D*
Alliant International University–San Francisco	M,D,O*
American International College	M,D
American University	M,D*
American University of Beirut	M
Andrews University	M,D,O
Angelo State University	M
Anna Maria College	M
Antioch University Los Angeles	M
Antioch University McGregor	M*
Antioch University New England	M,O*
Antioch University Santa Barbara	M
Antioch University Seattle	M,D*
Appalachian State University	M,O
Arcadia University	M,D,O
Argosy University, Atlanta Campus	M,D,O*
Argosy University, Chicago Campus	M,D,O*
Argosy University, Dallas Campus	M,D*
Argosy University, Hawai'i Campus	M,D,O*
Argosy University, Orange County Campus	M,D,O*
Argosy University, Phoenix Campus	M,D,O*
Argosy University, San Diego Campus	M,D*
Argosy University, San Francisco Bay Area Campus	M,D*
Argosy University, Santa Monica Campus	M,D*
Argosy University, Sarasota Campus	M,D,O*
Argosy University, Schaumburg Campus	M,D,O*
Argosy University, Seattle Campus	M,D*
Argosy University, Tampa Campus	M,D*
Argosy University, Twin Cities Campus	M,D,O*
Argosy University, Washington DC Campus	M,D,O*
Arizona State University	D*
Arizona State University at the Polytechnic Campus	M
Auburn University	M,D*
Auburn University Montgomery	M
Augusta State University	M
Austin Peay State University	M
Avila University	M*
Azusa Pacific University	M,D
Ball State University	M*
Barry University	M,O*
Bastyr University	M*
Bayamón Central University	M
Baylor University	M,D*
Biola University	M,D
Boston College	M,D*
Boston University	M,D*
Bowling Green State University	M,D*
Brandeis University	M*
Brenau University	M
Bridgewater State College	M
Brigham Young University	M,D*
Brock University	M,D
Brooklyn College of the City University of New York	M,D
Brown University	M,D*
Bryn Mawr College	D*
Bucknell University	M
Caldwell College	M
California Institute of Integral Studies	M,D*
California Lutheran University	M
California Polytechnic State University, San Luis Obispo	M
California State Polytechnic University, Pomona	M
California State University, Bakersfield	M
California State University, Chico	M
California State University, Dominguez Hills	M
California State University, Fresno	M
California State University, Fullerton	M
California State University, Long Beach	M
California State University, Los Angeles	M
California State University, Northridge	M
California State University, Sacramento	M*
California State University, San Bernardino	M
California State University, San Marcos	M
California State University, Stanislaus	M
Cameron University	M
Capella University	M,D,O
Cardinal Stritch University	M*
Carleton University	M,D
Carlos Albizu University	M,D
Carlos Albizu University, Miami Campus	M,D
Carnegie Mellon University	D*
Case Western Reserve University	D*
Castleton State College	M
The Catholic University of America	M,D*
Central Connecticut State University	M
Central Michigan University	M,D,O*
Central Washington University	M
Chestnut Hill College	M,D,O
The Chicago School of Professional Psychology	M,D,O*
The Citadel, The Military College of South Carolina	M
City College of the City University of New York	M,D*
Claremont Graduate University	M,D,O
Clark University	D*
Clemson University	M,D*
Cleveland State University	M,O
College of Saint Elizabeth	M,O
College of St. Joseph	M
The College of William and Mary	M,D
Colorado State University	M,D*
Columbia University	M,D*
Concordia University (IL)	M
Concordia University (Canada)	M,D
Concordia University Wisconsin	M
Connecticut College	M
Cornell University	D*
Dalhousie University	M,D
Dartmouth College	D*
DePaul University	M,D*
Drexel University	M,D*
Duke University	D*
Duquesne University	D*
East Carolina University	M*
East Central University	M
Eastern Illinois University	M,O
Eastern Kentucky University	M,O*
Eastern Michigan University	M,D
Eastern Washington University	M
East Tennessee State University	M
Edinboro University of Pennsylvania	M
Emory University	D*
Emporia State University	M
Evangel University	M
Fairfield University	M,O*
Fairleigh Dickinson University, College at Florham	M,O*
Fairleigh Dickinson University, Metropolitan Campus	M,D,O*
Fayetteville State University	M
Fielding Graduate University	D,O*
Fisk University	M
Florida Agricultural and Mechanical University	M*
Florida Atlantic University	M,D
Florida Institute of Technology	M,D*
Florida International University	M,D*
Florida State University	M,D*
Fordham University	D*
Forest Institute of Professional Psychology	M,D,O
Fort Hays State University	M,O
Framingham State College	M*
Francis Marion University	M
Frostburg State University	M
Fuller Theological Seminary	M,D
Gallaudet University	M,D,O
Gardner-Webb University	M
Geneva College	M*
George Fox University	M,D*
George Mason University	M,D*
Georgetown University	D*
The George Washington University	D*
Georgia Institute of Technology	M,D*
Georgia Southern University	M
Georgia State University	M,D*
Golden Gate University	M,D,O
Governors State University	M
Graduate School and University Center of the City University of New York	D*
Hardin-Simmons University	M
Harvard University	D*
Hodges University	M
Hofstra University	M,D,O*
Hood College	M,O
Hope International University	M
Houston Baptist University	M
Howard University	M,D*
Humboldt State University	M
Hunter College of the City University of New York	M
Idaho State University	M,D
Illinois Institute of Technology	M,D*
Illinois State University	M,D,O*
Immaculata University	M,D,O
Indiana State University	M,D*
Indiana University Bloomington	M,D*
Indiana University of Pennsylvania	M,D
Indiana University–Purdue University Indianapolis	M,D*
Institute of Transpersonal Psychology	M,D,O*
Instituto Tecnologico de Santo Domingo	M
Inter American University of Puerto Rico, Metropolitan Campus	M
Inter American University of Puerto Rico, San Germán Campus	M,D
Iona College	M*
Iowa State University of Science and Technology	M,D*
Jackson State University	D
Jacksonville State University	M
James Madison University	M,D,O
John F. Kennedy University	M,D,O
The Johns Hopkins University	D*
Kansas State University	M,D*
Kent State University	M,D*
Lakehead University	M,D
Lamar University	M*
La Salle University	D
Leadership Institute of Seattle	M
Lehigh University	M,D*
Lesley University	M,D,O*
Lipscomb University	M,O
Loma Linda University	D
Long Island University, Brooklyn Campus	M,D*
Long Island University, C.W. Post Campus	M,D,O*
Loras College	M
Louisiana State University and Agricultural and Mechanical College	M,D*
Louisiana Tech University	M,D
Loyola College in Maryland	M,D,O
Loyola University Chicago	M,D*
Lynn University	M,O
Madonna University	M
Marietta College	M
Marist College	M,O*
Marquette University	M,D
Marshall University	M,D
Martin University	M
Marywood University	M*
Massachusetts School of Professional Psychology	M,D*
McGill University	M,D*
McMaster University	M,D
McNeese State University	M
Medaille College	M
Memorial University of Newfoundland	M,D
Mercy College	M
Miami University	D*
Michigan School of Professional Psychology	M,D
Michigan State University	M,D*

Middle Tennessee State University M*
Midwestern State University M
Millersville University of Pennsylvania M
Minnesota State University Mankato M
Mississippi State University M,D
Missouri State University M*
Monmouth University M,O
Montana State University M
Montana State University–Billings M
Montclair State University M,O*
Morehead State University M
Morgan State University M,D*
Mount Aloysius College M
Mount Holyoke College M
Murray State University M
National-Louis University M,O
National University M
New College of California M*
New Jersey City University M,O
New Mexico Highlands University M
New Mexico State University M,D
The New School: A University M,D*
New York University M,D,O*
Norfolk State University M,D
North Carolina Central University M
North Carolina State University D*
North Dakota State University M,D
Northeastern State University M
Northeastern University M,D,O*
Northern Arizona University M,D
Northern Illinois University M,D
Northern Michigan University M
Northwestern State University of Louisiana M
Northwestern University D*
Northwest Missouri State University M
Northwest University M
Notre Dame de Namur University M,O
Nova Southeastern University M,D,O*
The Ohio State University M,D*
Ohio University D*
Oklahoma State University M,D*
Old Dominion University M,D*
Our Lady of the Lake University of San Antonio M,D
Pace University M,D*
Pacifica Graduate Institute M,D
Pacific Graduate School of Psychology M,D*
Pacific University M,D
Penn State Harrisburg M,D*
Penn State University Park M,D*
Pepperdine University M,D*
Pepperdine University M*
Philadelphia College of Osteopathic Medicine M,D*
Pittsburg State University M
Polytechnic University, Brooklyn Campus M*
Pontifical Catholic University of Puerto Rico M,D
Portland State University M,D,O
Princeton University D*
Purdue University D*
Queens College of the City University of New York M
Queen's University at Kingston M,D
Radford University M,D,O
Regis University M,O
Rhode Island College M
Rice University M,D*
Rochester Institute of Technology M
Roosevelt University D
Rowan University M,O
Rutgers, The State University of New Jersey, Camden M
Rutgers, The State University of New Jersey, Newark D*
Rutgers, The State University of New Jersey, New Brunswick M,D*
Sage Graduate School M,O
St. Cloud State University M
St. John's University (NY) M,D
Saint Joseph's University M,O*
Saint Louis University M,D*
Saint Mary's University M
St. Mary's University of San Antonio M
Saint Xavier University M,O
Salem State College M
Sam Houston State University M,D
San Diego State University M,D*
San Francisco State University M
San Jose State University M
Saybrook Graduate School and Research Center M,D
Seattle University M
Seton Hall University M,D,O*
Shippensburg University of Pennsylvania M
Simon Fraser University M,D
Southeastern Baptist Theological Seminary P,M,D
Southeastern Louisiana University M
Southern Adventist University M
Southern California Seminary P,M,D
Southern Connecticut State University M
Southern Illinois University Carbondale M,D*
Southern Illinois University Edwardsville M,O
Southern Methodist University M,D*
Southern Nazarene University M
Southern New Hampshire University M,O*
Southern Oregon University M
Southern University and Agricultural and Mechanical College M*
Southwestern College (NM) O*
Spalding University M,D
Stanford University D*
State University of New York at Binghamton M,D*
State University of New York at New Paltz M
State University of New York at Plattsburgh M,O
State University of New York College at Brockport M*
Stephen F. Austin State University M
Stony Brook University, State University of New York M,D*
Suffolk University D*
Sul Ross State University M*
Syracuse University D*
Temple University D*
Tennessee State University M,D*
Texas A&M International University M
Texas A&M University M,D*
Texas A&M University–Commerce M,D
Texas A&M University–Corpus Christi M
Texas A&M University–Kingsville M
Texas A&M University–Texarkana M
Texas Christian University M,D
Texas Southern University M
Texas State University-San Marcos M*
Texas Tech University M,D*
Texas Woman's University M,D,O
Tufts University M,D*
Tulane University M,D*
Uniformed Services University of the Health Sciences D*
Union Institute & University M,D
Universidad de las Americas, A.C. M
Universidad de las Américas–Puebla M
Université de Moncton M
Université de Montréal M,D
Université de Sherbrooke M
Université du Québec à Montréal D
Université du Québec à Trois-Rivières M,D
Université Laval D
University at Albany, State University of New York M,D,O*
University at Buffalo, the State University of New York M,D*
The University of Akron M,D
The University of Alabama D
The University of Alabama at Birmingham M,D*
The University of Alabama in Huntsville M
University of Alaska Anchorage M,D
University of Alaska Fairbanks D
University of Alberta M,D*
The University of Arizona D*
University of Arkansas M,D*
University of Arkansas at Little Rock M
University of Baltimore M*
The University of British Columbia M,D*
University of Calgary M,D
University of California, Berkeley D*
University of California, Davis D*
University of California, Irvine D*
University of California, Los Angeles M,D*
University of California, Riverside M,D*
University of California, San Diego D*
University of California, Santa Barbara D*
University of California, Santa Cruz D*
University of Central Arkansas M,D
University of Central Florida M,D*
University of Central Missouri M
University of Central Oklahoma M
University of Chicago D*
University of Cincinnati D
University of Colorado at Boulder M,D*
University of Colorado at Colorado Springs M,D
University of Colorado at Denver and Health Sciences Center M*
University of Connecticut M,D*
University of Dallas M
University of Dayton M*
University of Delaware D*
University of Denver M,D*
University of Detroit Mercy M,D,O
University of Florida M,D*
University of Georgia M,D*
University of Guelph M,D
University of Hartford M,D*
University of Hawaii at Manoa M,D,O*
University of Houston M,D*
University of Houston–Clear Lake M
University of Houston–Victoria M*
University of Idaho M*
University of Illinois at Chicago D*
University of Illinois at Urbana–Champaign M,D*
University of Indianapolis M,D
The University of Iowa M,D,O*
University of Kansas M,D*
University of Kentucky M,D*
University of La Verne M,D
University of Lethbridge M,D
University of Louisiana at Lafayette M*
University of Louisiana at Monroe M,O
University of Louisville M,D
University of Maine M,D*
University of Manitoba M,D
University of Mary Hardin-Baylor M
University of Maryland, Baltimore County M,D*
University of Maryland, College Park M,D*
University of Massachusetts Amherst M,D*
University of Massachusetts Dartmouth M
University of Massachusetts Lowell M*
University of Memphis M,D*
University of Miami M,D*
University of Michigan D,O*
University of Minnesota, Twin Cities Campus D*
University of Mississippi M,D
University of Missouri–Columbia M,D*
University of Missouri–Kansas City M,D*
University of Missouri–St. Louis M,D,O
The University of Montana M,D,O*
University of Nebraska at Omaha M,D,O
University of Nebraska–Lincoln M,D*
University of Nevada, Las Vegas M,D
University of Nevada, Reno M,D*
University of New Brunswick Fredericton D
University of New Brunswick Saint John M
University of New Hampshire D*
University of New Mexico M,D*
University of New Orleans M,D
The University of North Carolina at Chapel Hill D*
The University of North Carolina at Charlotte M,D*
The University of North Carolina at Greensboro M,D
The University of North Carolina Wilmington M*
University of North Dakota M,D
University of Northern British Columbia M,D,O
University of Northern Colorado M,D
University of Northern Iowa M
University of North Florida M
University of North Texas M,D*
University of Notre Dame D*
University of Oklahoma M,D*
University of Oregon M,D*
University of Ottawa D*
University of Pennsylvania D*
University of Phoenix–Austin Campus M
University of Phoenix–Cheyenne Campus M
University of Phoenix–Cleveland Campus M
University of Phoenix–Harrisburg Campus M
University of Phoenix–Hawaii Campus M
University of Phoenix–Idaho Campus M
University of Phoenix–Indianapolis Campus M
University of Phoenix–Jersey City Campus M
University of Phoenix–Louisiana Campus M
University of Phoenix–Maryland Campus M
University of Phoenix–Northern Nevada Campus M
University of Phoenix–Northwest Indiana M
University of Phoenix Online Campus M
University of Phoenix–Oregon Campus M
University of Phoenix–Pittsburgh Campus M
University of Phoenix–Richmond Campus M
University of Phoenix–San Antonio Campus M
University of Pittsburgh M,D*
University of Puerto Rico, Río Piedras M,D*
University of Regina M,D
University of Rhode Island D
University of Richmond M
University of Rochester M,D*
University of Saint Francis (IN) M
University of Saint Mary M
University of St. Thomas (MN) M,D,O*
University of Saskatchewan M,D
University of South Alabama M*
University of South Carolina M,D*
The University of South Dakota M,D
University of Southern California M,D*
University of Southern Mississippi M,D*
University of South Florida M,D*
The University of Tennessee M,D*
The University of Tennessee at Chattanooga M
The University of Texas at Arlington M,D*
The University of Texas at Austin D*
The University of Texas at Brownsville M
The University of Texas at Dallas M,D*
The University of Texas at El Paso M,D
The University of Texas at San Antonio M*
The University of Texas at Tyler M
The University of Texas of the Permian Basin M
The University of Texas–Pan American M
University of the Pacific M,D*
The University of Toledo M,D*
University of Toronto M,D
University of Tulsa M,D*
University of Utah M,D*
University of Vermont D*
University of Victoria M,D
University of Virginia M,D*
University of Washington D*
University of Waterloo M,D*
The University of Western Ontario M,D
University of West Florida M
University of West Georgia M,D
University of Windsor M,D
University of Wisconsin–Eau Claire M,O
University of Wisconsin–La Crosse M,O
University of Wisconsin–Madison D*
University of Wisconsin–Milwaukee M,D
University of Wisconsin–Oshkosh M
University of Wisconsin–Stout M*
University of Wisconsin–Whitewater M,O*
University of Wyoming M,D*
Utah State University M,D
Valdosta State University M,O
Valparaiso University M,O
Vanderbilt University M,D*
Villanova University M*
Virginia Commonwealth University D*
Virginia Polytechnic Institute and State University M,D*
Virginia State University M
Wake Forest University M*
Washburn University M

P—first professional degree; M—master's degree; D—doctorate; O—other advanced degree;
**full description and/or announcement in Book 2, 3, 4, 5, or 6*

Washington College M
Washington State University M,D*
Washington University in St. Louis M,D*
Wayne State University M,D*
Wesleyan University M*
West Chester University of Pennsylvania M
Western Carolina University M*
Western Illinois University M,O
Western Kentucky University M,O
Western Michigan University M,D,O*
Western Washington University M
Westfield State College M
West Texas A&M University M
West Virginia University M,D*
Wheaton College M,D
Wichita State University M,D*
Widener University *
Wilfrid Laurier University M,D
William Carey University M
Winthrop University M,O
Wisconsin School of Professional Psychology M,D
Wright Institute D
Wright State University M,D*
Xavier University M,D*
Yale University D*
Yeshiva University M,D
York University M,D*

PUBLIC ADMINISTRATION

Adelphi University O*
Albany State University M
American International College M
American Public University System M
American University M,D*
American University of Beirut M
The American University of Paris M
Andrew Jackson University M
Angelo State University M
Appalachian State University M
Argosy University, Orange County Campus M,D,O*
Argosy University, San Diego Campus M,D*
Argosy University, Tampa Campus M,D,O*
Arkansas State University M,O
Auburn University M,D*
Auburn University Montgomery M,D
Ball State University M*
Barry University M*
Baylor University M,D*
Bernard M. Baruch College of the City University of New York M*
Birmingham-Southern College M
Boise State University M
Boston University M,O*
Bowie State University M
Bowling Green State University M*
Bridgewater State College M
Brigham Young University M*
Brock University M
California Baptist University M
California Lutheran University M
California State Polytechnic University, Pomona M
California State University, Bakersfield M
California State University, Chico M
California State University, Dominguez Hills M
California State University, East Bay M
California State University, Fresno M
California State University, Fullerton M
California State University, Long Beach M
California State University, Los Angeles M
California State University, Northridge M
California State University, Sacramento M*
California State University, San Bernardino M
California State University, Stanislaus M
Carleton University M,D
Carnegie Mellon University M*
Central Michigan University M,O*
Clark Atlanta University M
Clark University M,O*
Clemson University M*
Cleveland State University M,O
College of Charleston M*
Columbia University M*
Columbus State University M
Concordia University (Canada) M,D
Concordia University Wisconsin M
Cumberland University M
Dalhousie University M
DePaul University M,O*
DeVry University M*
Drake University M*
Duquesne University M,O*
East Carolina University M*
Eastern Kentucky University M*
Eastern Michigan University M
Eastern Washington University M
The Evergreen State College M
Fairleigh Dickinson University, College at Florham M*
Fairleigh Dickinson University, Metropolitan Campus M,O*
Florida Agricultural and Mechanical University M*
Florida Atlantic University M,D
Florida Atlantic University, Jupiter Campus M
Florida Gulf Coast University M
Florida Institute of Technology M*
Florida International University M,D*
Florida State University M,D,O*
Framingham State College M*
Gannon University M,O
The George Washington University M,D*
Georgia College & State University M
Georgia Southern University M
Georgia State University M*
Governors State University M
Grambling State University M
Grand Valley State University M
Hamline University M
Harvard University M*
Hodges University M
Howard University M*
Idaho State University M*
Illinois Institute of Technology M*
Indiana State University M*
Indiana University Bloomington M,D,O*
Indiana University Kokomo O
Indiana University Northwest M,O
Indiana University–Purdue University Indianapolis M*
Indiana University South Bend M,O
Institute of Public Administration M,O
Iowa State University of Science and Technology M*
Jackson State University M,D
James Madison University M
John Jay College of Criminal Justice of the City University of New York M
Kansas State University M*
Kean University M*
Kennesaw State University M
Kent State University M*
Kentucky State University M
Kutztown University of Pennsylvania M
Lamar University M*
Lewis University M
Lincoln University (MO) M
Lindenwood University M
Long Island University, Brooklyn Campus M*
Long Island University, C.W. Post Campus M,O*
Louisiana State University and Agricultural and Mechanical College M,D*
Marist College M*
Marquette University M
Marywood University M*
McMaster University M,D
Metropolitan College of New York M
Metropolitan State University M
Midwestern State University M
Minnesota State University Mankato M
Minnesota State University Moorhead M
Mississippi State University M,D
Missouri State University M*
Montana State University M
Montana State University–Billings M
Monterey Institute of International Studies M*
Morehead State University M
National University of Singapore M,D*
New York University M,D,O*
North Carolina Central University M
North Carolina State University M,D*
Northeastern University M*
Northern Arizona University M,D,O
Northern Illinois University M
Northern Kentucky University M
Northern Michigan University M
North Georgia College & State University M
Norwich University M
Notre Dame de Namur University M
Nova Southeastern University M,D*
Oakland University M*
Ohio University M*
Old Dominion University M,D*
Pace University M*
Park University M
Penn State Harrisburg M,D*
Pepperdine University M*
Pontifical Catholic University of Puerto Rico M,D
Portland State University M,D
Regent University M
Rhode Island College M
Roger Williams University M*
Roosevelt University M
Rutgers, The State University of New Jersey, Camden M
Rutgers, The State University of New Jersey, Newark M,D*
Sage Graduate School M
Saginaw Valley State University M
St. Edward's University M,O
Saint Louis University M,D,O*
Saint Mary's University of Minnesota M,O
St. Mary's University of San Antonio M
St. Thomas University M,O
Sam Houston State University M
San Diego State University M*
San Francisco State University M
San Jose State University M
Savannah State University M
Seattle University M
Seton Hall University M*
Shenandoah University M,D,O*
Shippensburg University of Pennsylvania M
Sojourner-Douglass College M
Sonoma State University M
Southeastern University M
Southeast Missouri State University M
Southern Illinois University Carbondale M*
Southern Illinois University Edwardsville M
Southern University and Agricultural and Mechanical College M,D*
State University of New York at Binghamton M*
State University of New York College at Brockport M*
Stephen F. Austin State University M
Suffolk University M,O*
Sul Ross State University M*
Syracuse University M,D,O*
Tennessee State University M,D*
Texas A&M International University M
Texas A&M University M*
Texas A&M University–Corpus Christi M
Texas Southern University M
Texas State University-San Marcos M*
Texas Tech University M,D
Thomas Edison State College M
Touro University International M,D
Troy University M
Tufts University O*
Universidad Nacional Pedro Henriquez Urena P,M,D
Université de Moncton M
Université du Québec à Montréal M
Université du Québec, École nationale d'administration publique D,O
University at Albany, State University of New York M,D,O*
The University of Akron M
The University of Alabama M,D
The University of Alabama at Birmingham M*
University of Alaska Anchorage M
University of Alaska Southeast M
The University of Arizona M,D*
University of Arkansas M*
University of Arkansas at Little Rock M
University of Baltimore D*
University of Central Florida M,O*
University of Colorado at Colorado Springs M
University of Colorado at Denver and Health Sciences Center M*
University of Connecticut M*
University of Dayton M*
University of Delaware M*
University of Evansville M
The University of Findlay M
University of Georgia M,D*
University of Guam M
University of Hawaii at Manoa M,O*
University of Idaho M*
University of Illinois at Chicago M,D*
University of Illinois at Springfield M,D
University of Kansas M,D*
University of Kentucky M,D*
University of La Verne M,D,O
University of Louisville M
University of Maine M,D*
University of Management and Technology M,O
University of Manitoba M
University of Maryland, College Park M*
University of Massachusetts Amherst M*
University of Memphis M*
University of Michigan–Dearborn M,O*
University of Michigan–Flint M*
University of Missouri–Kansas City M,D*
University of Missouri–St. Louis M,D,O
The University of Montana M*
University of Nebraska at Omaha M,D
University of Nevada, Las Vegas M,D,O
University of Nevada, Reno M*
University of New Brunswick Fredericton M
University of New Hampshire M*
University of New Hampshire at Manchester M,O
University of New Haven M*
University of New Mexico M*
University of New Orleans M
The University of North Carolina at Chapel Hill M*
The University of North Carolina at Charlotte M*
The University of North Carolina at Pembroke M
The University of North Carolina Wilmington M*
University of North Dakota M
University of Northern Virginia M,D
University of North Florida M
University of North Texas M*
University of Oklahoma M*
University of Ottawa D,O*
University of Pennsylvania M*
University of Phoenix–Augusta Campus M
University of Phoenix–Austin Campus M
University of Phoenix–Bay Area Campus M
University of Phoenix–Central Valley Campus M
University of Phoenix–Chattanooga Campus M
University of Phoenix–Cheyenne Campus M
University of Phoenix–Cleveland Campus M
University of Phoenix–Columbus Georgia Campus M
University of Phoenix–Dallas Campus M
University of Phoenix–Denver Campus M
University of Phoenix–Des Moines Campus M
University of Phoenix–Detroit Campus M
University of Phoenix–Fort Lauderdale Campus M
University of Phoenix–Harrisburg Campus M
University of Phoenix–Hawaii Campus M
University of Phoenix–Houston Campus M
University of Phoenix–Jersey City Campus M
University of Phoenix–Louisiana Campus M
University of Phoenix–Madison Campus M
University of Phoenix–Maryland Campus M
University of Phoenix–Memphis Campus M
University of Phoenix—Northern Nevada Campus M
University of Phoenix–Northern Virginia Campus M
University of Phoenix–North Florida Campus M
University of Phoenix–Northwest Arkansas Campus M
University of Phoenix–Northwest Indiana M
University of Phoenix–Omaha Campus M
University of Phoenix Online Campus M
University of Phoenix–Pittsburgh Campus M
University of Phoenix–Renton Learning Center M
University of Phoenix–Richmond Campus M
University of Phoenix–Sacramento Valley Campus M
University of Phoenix–San Antonio Campus M

- University of Phoenix–Savannah Campus M
- University of Phoenix–Springfield Campus M
- University of Phoenix–West Florida Campus M
- University of Pittsburgh M,D*
- University of Puerto Rico, Río Piedras M*
- University of Regina M,D,O
- University of Rhode Island M,O
- University of San Francisco M
- University of South Alabama M*
- University of South Carolina M*
- The University of South Dakota M
- University of Southern California M,D,O*
- University of Southern Indiana M
- University of South Florida M*
- The University of Tennessee M*
- The University of Tennessee at Chattanooga M
- The University of Texas at Arlington M*
- The University of Texas at Brownsville M
- The University of Texas at San Antonio M*
- The University of Texas at Tyler M
- The University of Texas–Pan American M
- University of the District of Columbia M
- University of the Virgin Islands M
- The University of Toledo M*
- University of Utah M,O*
- University of Vermont M*
- University of Victoria M,D
- University of West Georgia M
- The University of Winnipeg M
- University of Wisconsin–Milwaukee M
- University of Wyoming M
- Upper Iowa University M
- Valdosta State University M
- Villanova University M*
- Virginia Commonwealth University M,O*
- Virginia Polytechnic Institute and State University M,D,O*
- Walden University M,D
- Wayland Baptist University M
- Wayne State University M*
- Webster University M,D
- West Chester University of Pennsylvania M
- Western Illinois University M,O
- Western International University M
- Western Michigan University M,D*
- West Virginia University M*
- Wichita State University M*
- Widener University M*
- Willamette University M
- Wilmington College (DE) M
- Wright State University M*
- York University M*

PUBLIC AFFAIRS

- American University M*
- Arizona State University M,D*
- Concordia University (Canada) O
- Cornell University M*
- Dalhousie University M
- DePaul University M,O*
- George Mason University M*
- Georgia College & State University M
- Howard University M*
- Indiana University Bloomington M,D,O*
- Indiana University Northwest M,O
- Indiana University of Pennsylvania M
- Indiana University–Purdue University Fort Wayne M,O
- Indiana University–Purdue University Indianapolis M*
- Indiana University South Bend M,O
- The Institute of World Politics M,O*
- Jackson State University M
- McMaster University M,D
- Murray State University M
- National University of Singapore M,D*
- New Mexico Highlands University M
- Northeastern University M,D*
- The Ohio State University M,D*
- Park University M
- Princeton University M,D*
- Stony Brook University, State University of New York M,O*
- Texas A&M University M*
- The University of Alabama in Huntsville M
- University of Arkansas at Little Rock M
- University of Baltimore M,D*
- University of Central Florida D*
- University of Colorado at Colorado Springs M
- University of Colorado at Denver and Health Sciences Center D*
- University of Florida M,D,O*
- University of Idaho M,D*
- University of Louisville D
- University of Massachusetts Boston M
- University of Minnesota, Twin Cities Campus M*
- University of Missouri–Columbia M*
- University of Missouri–Kansas City M,D*
- University of Nevada, Las Vegas M,D,O
- The University of North Carolina at Greensboro M,O
- The University of Texas at Arlington D*
- The University of Texas at Austin M,D*
- The University of Texas at Dallas M,D*
- University of Washington M,D*
- University of Waterloo M*
- University of Wisconsin–Madison M*
- Washington State University Vancouver M
- Western Carolina University M*
- Western Michigan University M,D*
- York University M*

PUBLIC HEALTH—GENERAL

- Adelphi University O*
- American Public University System M
- American University of Beirut M
- Armstrong Atlantic State University M
- A.T. Still University of Health Sciences M,D
- Barry University M*
- Benedictine University M
- Boise State University M
- Boston University P,M,D,O*
- Bowling Green State University M*
- Brooklyn College of the City University of New York M
- Brown University M*
- California College for Health Sciences M
- California State University, Fresno M
- California State University, Fullerton M
- Case Western Reserve University M*
- College of St. Catherine M*
- Columbia University M,D*
- Dartmouth College M*
- Des Moines University M
- Dominican University of California M
- Drexel University M*
- East Carolina University M*
- Eastern Virginia Medical School M
- East Stroudsburg University of Pennsylvania M
- East Tennessee State University M,O
- Emerson College M*
- Emory University M,D*
- Florida Agricultural and Mechanical University M*
- Florida International University M*
- Fort Valley State University M
- Georgetown University M,D*
- The George Washington University M,D,O*
- Georgia Southern University M
- Georgia State University M,O*
- Harvard University M,D*
- Hunter College of the City University of New York M*
- Idaho State University M,O
- Indiana University Bloomington M,D*
- Indiana University–Purdue University Indianapolis M*
- The Johns Hopkins University M,D*
- Kansas State University M*
- Kent State University M*
- Loma Linda University M,D
- Louisiana State University Health Sciences Center M*
- Medical College of Wisconsin M*
- Missouri State University M*
- Morehouse School of Medicine M*
- Morgan State University M,D*
- New Jersey Institute of Technology M
- New Mexico State University M
- New York Medical College M,D,O*
- Northern Arizona University M
- Northern Illinois University M
- Northwestern University M*
- Nova Southeastern University M*
- The Ohio State University M,D*
- Old Dominion University M*
- Oregon State University M,D*
- Ponce School of Medicine M
- Portland State University M,O
- Purdue University M,D*
- Regis College (MA) M
- Rutgers, The State University of New Jersey, New Brunswick M,D*
- Saint Louis University M,D*
- Saint Xavier University M,O
- San Diego State University M,D*
- San Francisco State University M
- San Jose State University M,O
- Sarah Lawrence College M*
- Simon Fraser University M
- Southern Connecticut State University M
- State University of New York Downstate Medical Center M*
- Stony Brook University, State University of New York M*
- Temple University M,D*
- Texas A&M Health Science Center M*
- Texas A&M University M,D*
- Texas Wesleyan University M
- Thomas Jefferson University M*
- Touro University College of Osteopathic Medicine P,M
- Touro University International M,D,O
- Trinity (Washington) University M
- Tufts University M*
- Tulane University M,D,O*
- Uniformed Services University of the Health Sciences M,D*
- Universidad Central del Este M
- Université de Montréal M,D,O
- University at Albany, State University of New York M,D*
- University at Buffalo, the State University of New York M,D*
- The University of Akron M,D
- The University of Alabama at Birmingham M,D*
- University of Alaska Anchorage M
- University of Alberta M,D*
- The University of Arizona M*
- University of California, Berkeley M,D*
- University of California, Los Angeles M,D*
- University of California, San Diego D*
- University of Colorado at Denver and Health Sciences Center M*
- University of Connecticut M*
- University of Connecticut Health Center M*
- University of Florida M*
- University of Hawaii at Manoa M*
- University of Illinois at Chicago M,D*
- University of Illinois at Springfield M
- The University of Iowa M,D,O*
- University of Kansas M*
- University of Kentucky M*
- University of Louisville M,O
- University of Maryland, College Park M,D*
- University of Massachusetts Amherst M,D*
- University of Medicine and Dentistry of New Jersey M,D,O*
- University of Miami M*
- University of Michigan M,D*
- University of Minnesota, Twin Cities Campus M,D,O*
- University of Missouri–Columbia M*
- The University of Montana M,O*
- University of Nebraska at Omaha M
- University of Nebraska Medical Center M*
- University of Nevada, Las Vegas M
- University of Nevada, Reno M*
- University of New England M,O
- University of New Hampshire M*
- University of New Hampshire at Manchester M,O
- University of New Mexico M*
- The University of North Carolina at Chapel Hill M,D*
- The University of North Carolina at Charlotte M*
- University of Northern Colorado M
- University of North Florida M,O
- University of North Texas Health Science Center at Fort Worth M,D
- University of Oklahoma Health Sciences Center M,D
- University of Ottawa D*
- University of Pittsburgh M,D,O*
- University of Puerto Rico, Medical Sciences Campus M*
- University of Rochester M*
- University of South Carolina M*
- University of Southern California M*
- University of Southern Mississippi M*
- University of South Florida M,D*
- The University of Tennessee M*
- The University of Texas Health Science Center at Houston M,D,O*
- The University of Texas Medical Branch M*
- University of the Sciences in Philadelphia M*
- The University of Toledo M,D,O*
- University of Toronto M,D,O
- University of Utah M,D*
- University of Virginia M*
- University of Washington M,D*
- University of West Florida M
- University of Wisconsin–Eau Claire M
- University of Wisconsin–La Crosse M
- Vanderbilt University M*
- Virginia Commonwealth University M,D*
- Walden University M,D
- Wayne State University M,O*
- West Chester University of Pennsylvania M,O
- Western Kentucky University M*
- West Virginia University M*
- Wichita State University M*
- Wright State University M*
- Yale University M,D*

PUBLIC HISTORY

- Appalachian State University M
- Arizona State University M,D*
- California State University, Sacramento M*
- Eastern Illinois University M
- Florida State University M,D*
- Indiana University–Purdue University Indianapolis M*
- Loyola University Chicago M,D*
- New York University M,D,O*
- North Carolina State University M*
- Northeastern University M,D*
- Rutgers, The State University of New Jersey, Camden M
- Shippensburg University of Pennsylvania M,O
- Simmons College
- Sonoma State University M
- University at Albany, State University of New York M,D,O*
- University of Arkansas at Little Rock M
- The University of British Columbia M*
- University of California, Santa Barbara D*
- University of Houston M,D*
- University of Illinois at Springfield M
- University of Massachusetts Amherst M,D*
- University of Massachusetts Boston M
- University of South Carolina M,O*
- The University of Texas at Austin M,D*
- Washington State University M,D*

PUBLIC POLICY

- Albany State University M
- American University M*
- Baylor University M,D*
- Boise State University M
- Brandeis University M,D*
- Brooklyn College of the City University of New York M,D
- Brown University M*
- California Lutheran University M
- California State University, Long Beach M
- California State University, Monterey Bay M
- California State University, Sacramento M*
- Carleton University M,D
- Carnegie Mellon University M*
- Central European University M,D*
- Claremont Graduate University M,D,O
- Clemson University D,O*
- The College of William and Mary M
- Columbia University M*
- Concordia University (Canada) M,D
- Cornell University M,D*
- Duke University M,D,O*

*P—first professional degree; M—master's degree; D—doctorate; O—other advanced degree; *full description and/or announcement in Book 2, 3, 4, 5, or 6*

Institution	Degrees
Duquesne University	M,O*
Florida State University	M,D,O*
Frederick S. Pardee RAND Graduate School	D
George Mason University	M,D*
Georgetown University	M*
The George Washington University	M,D*
Georgia Institute of Technology	M,D*
Georgia State University	D*
Graduate School and University Center of the City University of New York	M,D*
Harvard University	M,D*
Indiana University Bloomington	D*
Indiana University–Purdue University Indianapolis	M*
The Institute of World Politics	M,O*
Jackson State University	M,D
John Jay College of Criminal Justice of the City University of New York	M,D
The Johns Hopkins University	M*
Kent State University	M,D*
Lincoln University (MO)	M
McMaster University	M,D
Mississippi State University	M,D
Monmouth University	M
National University of Singapore	M,D*
New England College	M
The New School: A University	D*
Northeastern University	M,D*
Northern Arizona University	M,D,O
Northwestern University	D*
Pepperdine University	M*
Queen's University at Kingston	M
Regent University	M
Rochester Institute of Technology	M
Rutgers, The State University of New Jersey, Camden	M
Rutgers, The State University of New Jersey, Newark	M,D*
Rutgers, The State University of New Jersey, New Brunswick	M*
Saint Louis University	M,D,O*
San Francisco State University	M
Seton Hall University	M*
Simon Fraser University	M
State University of New York at Binghamton	M,D*
State University of New York Empire State College	M
Stony Brook University, State University of New York	M,D*
Trinity College	M
Tufts University	M*
University at Albany, State University of New York	M,D,O*
The University of Arizona	M,D*
University of Arkansas	D*
University of California, Berkeley	M,D*
University of California, Los Angeles	M*
University of Chicago	M,D*
University of Colorado at Boulder	M,D*
University of Connecticut	M,O*
University of Delaware	M,D*
University of Denver	M*
University of Georgia	M,D*
University of Illinois at Chicago	M,D*
University of Louisville	M
University of Maryland, Baltimore County	M,D*
University of Maryland, College Park	M,D*
University of Massachusetts Amherst	M*
University of Massachusetts Boston	D
University of Massachusetts Dartmouth	M
University of Memphis	M*
University of Michigan	M,D*
University of Michigan–Dearborn	M*
University of Minnesota, Twin Cities Campus	M*
University of Missouri–St. Louis	M,D,O
University of Nevada, Las Vegas	M
University of New Brunswick Fredericton	M
The University of North Carolina at Chapel Hill	D*
The University of North Carolina at Charlotte	D*
University of Northern Iowa	M
University of Oregon	M*
University of Pennsylvania	M,D*
University of Pittsburgh	M,D*
University of Regina	M,D,O
University of Rhode Island	M,O
University of Southern California	M*
University of Southern Maine	M,D,O
The University of Texas at Austin	M,D*
The University of Texas at Brownsville	M
The University of Texas at Dallas	M*
University of the Pacific	P,M,D
University of Washington, Bothell	M
Vanderbilt University	M,D*
Virginia Commonwealth University	D*
Virginia Polytechnic Institute and State University	M,D,O*
Washington State University	M,D*
Washington University in St. Louis	M*
West Virginia University	M,D*
Wilfrid Laurier University	M
William Paterson University of New Jersey	M*
York University	M*

PUBLISHING

Institution	Degrees
Drexel University	M*
Emerson College	M*
The George Washington University	M*
New York University	M*
Northwestern University	M*
Pace University	M*
Rosemont College	M
Simon Fraser University	M
University of Baltimore	M*

QUALITY MANAGEMENT

Institution	Degrees
California State University, Dominguez Hills	M
Case Western Reserve University	M,D*
Dowling College	M,O
Eastern Michigan University	M
Ferris State University	M
Hofstra University	M,O*
Illinois Institute of Technology	M*
Instituto Tecnológico y de Estudios Superiores de Monterrey, Campus Ciudad de México	M,D
Instituto Tecnológico y de Estudios Superiores de Monterrey, Campus Ciudad Juárez	M
Instituto Tecnológico y de Estudios Superiores de Monterrey, Campus Estado de México	M,D
Instituto Tecnológico y de Estudios Superiores de Monterrey, Campus Irapuato	M,D
Madonna University	M
Marian College of Fond du Lac	M
The National Graduate School of Quality Management	M
Penn State University Park	M*
Rutgers, The State University of New Jersey, New Brunswick	M,D*
Saint Joseph's College of Maine	M
San Jose State University	M
Southern Polytechnic State University	M
Stevens Institute of Technology	M,O*
Touro University International	M,D,O
Universidad de las Americas, A.C.	M
University of Miami	M*
Upper Iowa University	M
Webster University	M,D

QUANTITATIVE ANALYSIS

Institution	Degrees
Bernard M. Baruch College of the City University of New York	M*
California State University, East Bay	M
Clark Atlanta University	M
Drexel University	M,D,O*
Hofstra University	M*
Lehigh University	M*
Loyola College in Maryland	M
New York University	M,D,O*
Purdue University	M,D*
St. John's University (NY)	M,O
Saint Joseph's University	M*
Syracuse University	D*
Texas Tech University	M,D
The University of British Columbia	M,D*
University of California, Santa Barbara	M,D*
University of Cincinnati	M,D
University of Florida	M*
University of Missouri–St. Louis	M,O
University of North Texas	M,D*
University of Oregon	M*
The University of Texas at Arlington	M,D*
Virginia Commonwealth University	M*
Walden University	M,D

RADIATION BIOLOGY

Institution	Degrees
Auburn University	M,D*
Colorado State University	M,D*
Georgetown University	M*
Université de Sherbrooke	M,D
The University of Iowa	M,D*
University of Oklahoma Health Sciences Center	M,D
The University of Texas Southwestern Medical Center at Dallas	M,D*

RANGE SCIENCE

Institution	Degrees
Colorado State University	M,D*
Kansas State University	M,D*
Montana State University	M,D
New Mexico State University	M,D
North Dakota State University	M,D
Oregon State University	M,D*
Sul Ross State University	M*
Texas A&M University	M,D*
Texas A&M University–Kingsville	M
Texas Tech University	M,D
The University of Arizona	M,D*
University of California, Berkeley	M*
University of Idaho	M*
University of Wyoming	M,D
Utah State University	M,D

READING EDUCATION

Institution	Degrees
Abilene Christian University	M
Adelphi University	M*
Albany State University	M
Alfred University	M,O*
Alverno College	M
American International College	M,D,O
Andrews University	M
Angelo State University	M
Anna Maria College	M,O
Appalachian State University	M
Arcadia University	M,D,O
Arkansas State University	M,O
Asbury College	M,O
Auburn University	M,D,O*
Auburn University Montgomery	M,O
Aurora University	M,D
Austin Peay State University	M,O
Averett University	M
Avila University	M,O*
Baldwin-Wallace College	M
Bank Street College of Education	M*
Barry University	M,D,O*
Bellarmine University	M
Benedictine University	M
Berry College	M
Bethel University	M,D,O
Bloomsburg University of Pennsylvania	M
Boise State University	M
Boston College	M,O*
Boston University	M,D,O*
Bowie State University	M
Bowling Green State University	M,O*
Bridgewater State College	M,O
Brigham Young University	M*
Bucknell University	M
Buffalo State College, State University of New York	M
Butler University	M
California Baptist University	M
California Lutheran University	M
California State University, Bakersfield	M,O
California State University, Chico	M
California State University, Fresno	M
California State University, Fullerton	M
California State University, Los Angeles	M
California State University, Sacramento	M*
California State University, San Bernardino	M
California State University, Stanislaus	M
California University of Pennsylvania	M
Calvin College	M
Canisius College	M
Capella University	M,D,O
Cardinal Stritch University	M*
Carthage College	M,O
Castleton State College	M,O
Central Connecticut State University	M,O
Central Michigan University	M*
Central State University	M
Central Washington University	M
Chapman University	M
Chicago State University	M
The Citadel, The Military College of South Carolina	M
City College of the City University of New York	M*
City University	M,O
Clarion University of Pennsylvania	M
Clarke College	M
Clemson University	M*
College of Mount St. Joseph	M
The College of New Jersey	M,O
The College of New Rochelle	M
College of St. Joseph	M
The College of Saint Rose	M,O*
The College of William and Mary	M
Concordia University (IL)	M
Concordia University (NE)	M
Concordia University Wisconsin	M
Coppin State University	M
Curry College	M,O
Dallas Baptist University	M
DePaul University	M,D*
Dominican University	M
Dowling College	M,D,O
Duquesne University	M*
East Carolina University	M*
Eastern Connecticut State University	M
Eastern Kentucky University	M*
Eastern Michigan University	M
Eastern Nazarene College	M,O
Eastern Washington University	M
East Stroudsburg University of Pennsylvania	M
East Tennessee State University	M
Edinboro University of Pennsylvania	M,O
Elms College	M,O
Emory & Henry College	M
Emporia State University	M
Endicott College	M
Evangel University	M
Fairleigh Dickinson University, College at Florham	M,O*
Fairleigh Dickinson University, Metropolitan Campus	M,O*
Fairmont State University	M
Fayetteville State University	M
Ferris State University	M
Florida Atlantic University	M,D,O
Florida Atlantic University, Jupiter Campus	M
Florida Gulf Coast University	M
Florida International University	M,D*
Florida State University	M,D,O*
Fordham University	M,D,O*
Framingham State College	M*
Fresno Pacific University	M
Frostburg State University	M
Furman University	M
Gannon University	M,O
George Mason University	M*
Georgia Southern University	M
Georgia Southwestern State University	M,O
Georgia State University	M,D,O*
Governors State University	M
Grand Canyon University	M*
Grand Valley State University	M
Gwynedd-Mercy College	M
Harding University	M,O
Hardin-Simmons University	M
Harvard University	M*
Henderson State University	M,O
Heritage University	M
Hofstra University	M,D,O*
Holy Family University	M
Hood College	M,O
Houston Baptist University	M
Howard University	M,O*
Hunter College of the City University of New York	M,O
Idaho State University	M,O
Illinois State University	M*
Indiana State University	M*
Indiana University Bloomington	M,D,O*
Indiana University of Pennsylvania	M
Jacksonville State University	M
Jacksonville University	M
James Madison University	M
The Johns Hopkins University	M,D,O*
Johnson State College	M
Kean University	M
Kent State University	M*
King's College	M
Kutztown University of Pennsylvania	M
Lake Erie College	M
Lehman College of the City University of New York	M
Lenoir-Rhyne College	M
Lesley University	M,D,O*
Liberty University	M,D,O
Long Island University, Brentwood Campus	M
Long Island University, Brooklyn Campus	M*

Long Island University, C.W. Post Campus M*
Long Island University, Rockland Graduate Campus M
Long Island University, Southampton Graduate Campus M
Long Island University, Westchester Graduate Campus M
Longwood University M*
Loyola College in Maryland M,O
Loyola Marymount University M
Loyola University Chicago M*
Loyola University New Orleans M
Lyndon State College M
Madonna University M
Malone College M
Manhattanville College M*
Marshall University M,O
Marygrove College M
Maryville University of Saint Louis M,D
Marywood University M*
Massachusetts College of Liberal Arts M
McDaniel College M
Medaille College M
Mercer University M,D,O
Mercy College M
MGH Institute of Health Professions M,O*
Miami University M*
Michigan State University M*
Middle Tennessee State University M*
Midwestern State University M
Millersville University of Pennsylvania M
Minnesota State University Moorhead M
Missouri State University M*
Monmouth University M,O
Montana State University–Billings M
Montclair State University M,O*
Morehead State University M
Morningside College M
Mount Saint Mary College M
Mount Saint Vincent University M
Murray State University M,O
National-Louis University M,D,O
Nazareth College of Rochester M
New Jersey City University M
New Mexico State University M,D,O
New York University M*
Niagara University M
North Carolina Agricultural and Technical State University M
Northeastern Illinois University M
Northeastern State University M
Northern Illinois University M,D
Northern State University M
Northwestern Oklahoma State University M
Northwestern State University of Louisiana M,O
Northwest Missouri State University M
Northwest Nazarene University M
Notre Dame College (OH) M,O
Notre Dame de Namur University M,O
Nova Southeastern University M,O*
Oakland University M,D,O*
Ohio University M,D*
Old Dominion University M,D*
Oregon State University M*
Penn State University Park M,D*
Pittsburg State University M
Plymouth State University M
Portland State University M,D
Providence College M*
Purdue University M,D,O*
Queens College of the City University of New York M
Radford University M
Regis University M,O
Rhode Island College M
Rider University M,O*
Rivier College M,O
Roberts Wesleyan College M,O
Rockford College M
Roger Williams University M*
Roosevelt University M
Rowan University M
Rutgers, The State University of New Jersey, New Brunswick M,D*
Sacred Heart University M,O
Sage Graduate School M
Saginaw Valley State University M
St. Bonaventure University M
Saint Francis University M
St. John Fisher College M
St. John's University (NY) M,O
St. Joseph's College, New York M*
St. Joseph's College, Suffolk Campus M
Saint Joseph's University M,D,O*
Saint Leo University M
Saint Martin's University M
Saint Mary's College of California M
Saint Mary's University of Minnesota M,O
St. Mary's University of San Antonio M
Saint Michael's College M,O
Saint Peter's College M
St. Thomas Aquinas College M,O*
St. Thomas University M,D,O
Saint Xavier University M,O
Salem College M
Salem State College M,O
Salisbury University M
Sam Houston State University M
San Diego State University M*
San Francisco State University M,O
Seattle Pacific University M
Seattle University M,O
Shippensburg University of Pennsylvania M
Siena Heights University M
Slippery Rock University of Pennsylvania M
Sojourner-Douglass College M
Southern Adventist University M
Southern Connecticut State University M,O
Southern Illinois University Edwardsville M
Southern Oregon University M
State University of New York at Binghamton M*
State University of New York at Fredonia M
State University of New York at New Paltz M
State University of New York at Oswego M
State University of New York at Plattsburgh M
State University of New York College at Brockport M*
State University of New York College at Cortland M*
State University of New York College at Geneseo M
State University of New York College at Oneonta M
State University of New York College at Potsdam M
Stetson University M
Sul Ross State University M*
Syracuse University M,D*
Teachers College Columbia University M*
Temple University M,D*
Tennessee Technological University M,O*
Texas A&M International University M,D
Texas A&M University M,D*
Texas A&M University–Commerce M,D
Texas A&M University–Corpus Christi M,D
Texas A&M University–Kingsville M
Texas Southern University M,D
Texas State University-San Marcos M*
Texas Tech University M,D
Texas Woman's University M,D
Touro University International M
Towson University M,O
Trevecca Nazarene University M
Trinity (Washington) University M
Union College (KY) M
University at Albany, State University of New York M,D,O*
University at Buffalo, the State University of New York M,D,O*
University of Alaska Fairbanks M
The University of Arizona M,D,O*
University of Arkansas at Little Rock M
University of Bridgeport M,O
The University of British Columbia M,D*
University of California, Berkeley M,D*
University of Central Arkansas M
University of Central Florida M,O*
University of Central Missouri M,O
University of Central Oklahoma M
University of Cincinnati M,D
University of Connecticut M,D*
University of Dayton M*
University of Florida M,D,O*
University of Georgia M,D,O*
University of Guam M
University of Houston M,D*
University of Houston–Clear Lake M
University of Illinois at Chicago M,D*
University of La Verne M,O
University of Louisiana at Monroe M
University of Louisville M
University of Maine M,D,O*
University of Mary M
University of Mary Hardin-Baylor M,D
University of Maryland, College Park M,D,O*
University of Massachusetts Amherst M,D,O*
University of Massachusetts Lowell M,D,O*
University of Memphis M,D*
University of Miami M,D,O*
University of Michigan M,D*
University of Michigan–Flint M*
University of Minnesota, Twin Cities Campus M,D,O*
University of Missouri–Columbia M,D,O*
University of Missouri–Kansas City M,D,O*
University of Missouri–St. Louis M,D
University of Nebraska at Kearney M
University of Nebraska at Omaha M
University of Nevada, Las Vegas M,D,O
University of Nevada, Reno M,D,O*
University of New England M
University of New Hampshire M*
The University of North Carolina at Chapel Hill M,D*
The University of North Carolina at Charlotte M*
The University of North Carolina at Greensboro M,D,O
The University of North Carolina at Pembroke M
The University of North Carolina Wilmington M*
University of North Dakota M
University of Northern Colorado M
University of Northern Iowa M
University of North Texas M,D*
University of Oklahoma M,D,O*
University of Pennsylvania M,D*
University of Pittsburgh M,D*
University of Rhode Island M
University of Rio Grande M
University of St. Francis (IL) M
University of St. Thomas (MN) M,D,O*
The University of Scranton M*
University of Sioux Falls M,O
University of South Alabama M,O*
University of South Carolina M,D*
University of Southern Maine M,O
University of Southern Mississippi M,D,O*
University of South Florida M*
The University of Tampa M
The University of Tennessee M,D,O*
The University of Texas at Brownsville M
The University of Texas at San Antonio M*
The University of Texas at Tyler M
The University of Texas of the Permian Basin M
The University of Texas–Pan American M
University of the Cumberlands M
University of the Incarnate Word M,D
University of Vermont M*
University of Victoria M,D
University of Washington M,D*
University of West Florida M
University of West Georgia M
University of Wisconsin–Eau Claire M
University of Wisconsin–La Crosse M
University of Wisconsin–Milwaukee M
University of Wisconsin–Oshkosh M
University of Wisconsin–River Falls M
University of Wisconsin–Stevens Point M
University of Wisconsin–Superior M
University of Wisconsin–Whitewater M*
Valdosta State University M,O
Vanderbilt University M,D*
Virginia Commonwealth University M*
Wagner College M
Walden University M,D
Walla Walla College M
Washburn University M
Washington State University M,D*
Washington State University Tri-Cities M,D
Wayne State University M,D,O*
West Chester University of Pennsylvania M
Western Carolina University M*
Western Connecticut State University M*
Western Illinois University M
Western Kentucky University M
Western Michigan University M*
Western New Mexico University M
Westfield State College M
Westminster College (PA) M,O
West Texas A&M University M
West Virginia University M*
Wheelock College M
Widener University M,D*
William Paterson University of New Jersey M*
Wilmington College (DE) M
Wilmington College (OH) M
Winthrop University M
Worcester State College M
Xavier University M*
Youngstown State University M

REAL ESTATE

American University M*
Bentley College M*
California State University, Sacramento M*
Central European University M*
Clemson University M*
Cleveland State University M,O
Columbia University M*
Cornell University M*
DePaul University M*
Florida Atlantic University M
The George Washington University M*
Georgia State University M,D,O*
John Marshall Law School P,M
The Johns Hopkins University M*
Massachusetts Institute of Technology M*
New York University M,O*
Nova Southeastern University M*
Pacific States University M,D
Penn State University Park M,D*
Roosevelt University M,O
Texas A&M University M*
University of California, Berkeley D*
University of Denver M*
University of Florida M,D,O*
University of Hawaii at Manoa M*
University of Memphis M,D*
University of Michigan M,O*
University of North Texas M,D*
University of Pennsylvania M,D*
University of St. Thomas (MN) M*
University of Southern California M*
The University of Texas at Arlington M,D*
University of Wisconsin–Madison M,D*
Virginia Commonwealth University M,O*
Washington State University D*
Woodbury University M

RECREATION AND PARK MANAGEMENT

Acadia University M
Arizona State University M*
Bowling Green State University M*
Brigham Young University M*
California State University, Chico M
California State University, Long Beach M
California State University, Northridge M
California State University, Sacramento M*
Central Michigan University M*
Clemson University M,D*
Colorado State University M,D*
Delta State University M
East Carolina University M*
Eastern Kentucky University M*
Florida Agricultural and Mechanical University M*
Florida Gulf Coast University M
Florida International University M*
Florida State University M,D,O*
Frostburg State University M
Georgia Southern University M
Hardin-Simmons University M
Indiana University Bloomington M,D,O*
Kent State University M*
Lehman College of the City University of New York M
Michigan State University M,D*
Middle Tennessee State University M,D*
Naropa University M*

*P—first professional degree; M—master's degree; D—doctorate; O—other advanced degree; *full description and/or announcement in Book 2, 3, 4, 5, or 6*

North Carolina Central University M
North Carolina State University M,D*
Northwest Missouri State University M
Ohio University M*
Old Dominion University M*
Penn State University Park M,D*
San Francisco State University M
San Jose State University M
South Dakota State University M
Southern Connecticut State University M
Southern Illinois University Carbondale M*
Southern University and Agricultural and Mechanical College M*
Southwestern Oklahoma State University M
Springfield College M*
State University of New York College at Brockport M*
State University of New York College at Cortland M*
State University of New York College of Environmental Science and Forestry M,D
Temple University M*
Texas A&M University M,D*
Texas State University-San Marcos M*
Universidad Metropolitana M
University of Alberta M,D*
University of Arkansas M,D*
University of Florida M,D*
University of Idaho M*
The University of Iowa M*
University of Manitoba M
University of Minnesota, Twin Cities Campus M,D*
University of Mississippi M,D
University of Missouri–Columbia M*
The University of Montana M,D*
University of Nebraska at Omaha M
University of Nebraska–Lincoln M*
University of New Brunswick Fredericton M
University of New Hampshire M*
The University of North Carolina at Chapel Hill M*
The University of North Carolina at Greensboro M
University of North Texas M,O*
University of Rhode Island M,D
University of South Alabama M*
University of Southern Mississippi M,D*
The University of Tennessee M,D*
University of Utah M,D*
University of Waterloo M,D*
University of Wisconsin–La Crosse M
University of Wisconsin–Madison M*
Utah State University M,D
Virginia Commonwealth University M*
Virginia Polytechnic Institute and State University M,D*
Wayne State University M*
Western Illinois University M
Western Kentucky University M
West Virginia University M*
Wright State University M*

REHABILITATION COUNSELING

Arkansas State University M,O
Assumption College M,O*
Auburn University M,D,O*
Barry University M,O*
Bowling Green State University M*
California State University, Fresno M
California State University, Los Angeles M
California State University, San Bernardino M
Central Connecticut State University M,O
Coppin State University M
Drake University M*
East Carolina University M*
East Central University M
Edinboro University of Pennsylvania M
Emporia State University M
Florida Atlantic University M,O
Florida International University M*
Florida State University M,D,O*
Fort Valley State University M
The George Washington University M*
Georgia State University M*
Hofstra University M,O*
Hunter College of the City University of New York M
Illinois Institute of Technology M,D*
Indiana University–Purdue University Indianapolis M,D*
Jackson State University M,O
Kent State University M,O*
Langston University M
La Salle University D
Louisiana State University Health Sciences Center M*
Maryville University of Saint Louis M
Michigan State University M,D,O*
Minnesota State University Mankato M
Montana State University–Billings M
Northeastern University M*
Ohio University M,D*
St. Cloud State University M
St. John's University (NY) M,O
Salve Regina University M,O
San Diego State University M*
San Francisco State University M
South Carolina State University M
Southern Illinois University Carbondale M,D*
Southern University and Agricultural and Mechanical College M*
Springfield College M,O*
Syracuse University M*
Texas Tech University Health Sciences Center M
Thomas University M
Troy University M,O
Université de Montréal O
University at Albany, State University of New York M*
University at Buffalo, the State University of New York M,D,O*
The University of Alabama at Birmingham M*
The University of Arizona M,D,O*
University of Arkansas M,D*
University of Florida M*
The University of Iowa M,D*
University of Kentucky M,D*
University of Louisiana at Lafayette M*
University of Maryland, College Park M,D,O*
University of Maryland Eastern Shore M*
University of Massachusetts Boston M,O
University of Medicine and Dentistry of New Jersey M,D*
University of Memphis M,D*
University of Nevada, Las Vegas M,O
The University of North Carolina at Chapel Hill M,D*
University of Northern Colorado M,D
University of North Florida M,O
University of North Texas M*
University of Pittsburgh M*
University of Puerto Rico, Río Piedras M*
The University of Scranton M
University of South Alabama M,D*
University of South Carolina M,O*
University of South Florida M*
The University of Tennessee M,D*
The University of Texas–Pan American M
The University of Texas Southwestern Medical Center at Dallas M*
University of Wisconsin–Madison M,D*
University of Wisconsin–Stout M*
Utah State University M
Virginia Commonwealth University M,O*
Wayne State University M,D,O*
Western Michigan University M*
Western Oregon University M
Western Washington University M
West Virginia University M*
Winston-Salem State University M
Wright State University M*

REHABILITATION SCIENCES

Boston University D*
California University of Pennsylvania M
Canisius College M
Central Michigan University M,D*
Clarion University of Pennsylvania M
Concordia University Wisconsin M
Drake University M*
East Carolina University M*
East Stroudsburg University of Pennsylvania M
Indiana University–Purdue University Indianapolis M,D*
McGill University M,D*
McMaster University M,D
Medical University of South Carolina M,D*
Northwestern Health Sciences University O
Pennsylvania College of Optometry M,D,O
Queen's University at Kingston M,D
University at Buffalo, the State University of New York M,D,O*
The University of Alabama at Birmingham O*
University of Alberta D*
The University of British Columbia M,D*
University of Cincinnati D
University of Florida D*
The University of Iowa D*
University of Kansas M,D*
University of Kentucky D*
University of Manitoba M
University of Maryland, Baltimore D*
University of Maryland Eastern Shore M*
University of Northern Iowa M,D
University of North Texas M*
University of Oklahoma Health Sciences Center M
University of Ottawa M*
University of Pittsburgh M,D,O*
University of South Carolina M,O*
University of Toronto M
University of Washington M,D*
University of Wisconsin–La Crosse M
University of Wisconsin–Madison M*
Virginia Commonwealth University M,D*
Wayne State University M,O*

RELIABILITY ENGINEERING

The University of Arizona M*
University of Maryland, College Park M,D,O*

RELIGION

Arizona State University M,D*
Azusa Pacific University M
Baylor University M,D*
Bellarmine University M
Bethany Theological Seminary P,M,O
Bethesda Christian University P,M
Biola University P,M,D
Bob Jones University P,M,D,O
Boston University M,D*
Briercrest Seminary P,M
Brown University M,D*
Bryn Athyn College of the New Church P,M
California Institute of Integral Studies M,D*
California State University, Long Beach M
Cardinal Stritch University M*
The Catholic University of America P,M,D,O*
Chestnut Hill College M,O
Chicago Theological Seminary P,M,D
Christian Brothers University M
Christian Theological Seminary P,M,D
Cincinnati Christian University P,M
Claremont Graduate University M,D
Claremont School of Theology M,D
College of the Humanities and Sciences, Harrison Middleton University M,D
Columbia University M,D*
Concordia University (IL) M
Concordia University (Canada) M,D
Cornell University D*
Denver Seminary P,M,D,O
Drew University M,D
Duke University M,D*
Earlham School of Religion P,M
Eastern Mennonite University P,M,O
Edgewood College M
Elms College M
Emmanuel School of Religion P,M,D
Emory University D,O*
Episcopal Theological Seminary of the Southwest P,M,O
Evangelical Theological Seminary P,M,O
Faith Baptist Bible College and Theological Seminary P,M
Florida International University M*
Florida State University M,D*
Fordham University M,D,O*
George Fox University P,M,D,O*
The George Washington University M*
Georgia State University M*
Gonzaga University M
Gordon-Conwell Theological Seminary P,M,D
Graceland University M
Graduate Theological Union M,D,O
Grand Rapids Theological Seminary of Cornerstone University P,M
Harding University Graduate School of Religion P,M,D
Hardin-Simmons University M
Hartford Seminary M,D,O
Harvard University D*
Hawai'i Theological Seminary P,M
Hebrew Union College–Jewish Institute of Religion (OH) M,D
Heritage Christian University M
Holy Names University M,O
Iliff School of Theology P,M,D
Indiana University Bloomington M,D*
The Jewish Theological Seminary M,D*
John Carroll University M
Kentucky Christian University M
Knox Theological Seminary M
La Salle University M
La Sierra University M
Lee University M
Liberty University P,M,D
Lipscomb University P,M
Loma Linda University M
Louisville Presbyterian Theological Seminary P,M,D
Loyola University Chicago P,M,O*
Loyola University New Orleans M
Lutheran Theological Seminary at Gettysburg P,M,D
The Lutheran Theological Seminary at Philadelphia P,M,D,O
McGill University M,D*
McMaster University M,D
Memorial University of Newfoundland M
Miami University M*
Missouri State University M*
Mount St. Mary's College M*
Naropa University M*
New Life Theological Seminary M*
New York University M,O*
Northern Baptist Theological Seminary P,M,D
Northwest Nazarene University P,M
Oblate School of Theology P,M,D,O
Oklahoma City University M
Olivet Nazarene University M
Oxford Graduate School M,D
Pacific School of Religion P,M,D,O
Pepperdine University P,M*
Point Loma Nazarene University M
Princeton Theological Seminary P,M,D
Princeton University D*
Providence College M*
Queen's University at Kingston M
Reformed Theological Seminary–Charlotte Campus P,M,D
Reformed Theological Seminary–Washington D.C. M
Regions University P,M,D
Rice University D*
Sacred Heart University M
St. Charles Borromeo Seminary, Overbrook M
Saint John's Seminary (MA) P,M
Santa Clara University M
Seton Hall University M*
Simpson University P,M
Sioux Falls Seminary M
Southern Adventist University M
Southern California Seminary P,M,D
Southern Evangelical Seminary P,M,D,O
Southern Methodist University M,D*
Southern Nazarene University M
Stanford University M,D*
Syracuse University M,D*
Temple University M,D*
Trevecca Nazarene University M
Trinity Episcopal School for Ministry P,M,D,O
Trinity International University P,M,D,O
Trinity International University, South Florida Campus M
Union University M
United Theological Seminary of the Twin Cities M,O
Université de Sherbrooke M,D,O
Université du Québec à Montréal M,D
Université Laval M,D
The University of British Columbia M,D*
University of Calgary M,D
University of California, Berkeley D*
University of California, Santa Barbara M,D*
University of Chicago P,M,D*
University of Colorado at Boulder M*
University of Denver M,D*
University of Detroit Mercy M
University of Florida M,D*
University of Georgia M*

University of Hawaii at Manoa M*
The University of Iowa M,D*
University of Kansas M*
University of Lethbridge M,D
University of Manitoba M,D
University of Minnesota, Twin Cities Campus M,D*
University of Missouri–Columbia M*
University of Mobile M
The University of North Carolina at Chapel Hill M,D*
The University of North Carolina at Charlotte M*
University of North Texas M,D*
University of Notre Dame M*
University of Ottawa M,D*
University of Pennsylvania D*
University of Pittsburgh M,D*
University of Regina M,D
University of St. Thomas (MN) M*
University of Saskatchewan M
University of South Carolina M*
University of Southern California M,D*
University of South Florida M*
The University of Tennessee M,D*
University of the Incarnate Word M
University of the West M,D
University of Toronto M,D
University of Virginia M,D*
University of Washington M*
The University of Winnipeg M
Vanderbilt University M,D*
Vanguard University of Southern California M
Virginia University of Lynchburg P
Wake Forest University M*
Warner Pacific College M
Washington University in St. Louis M*
Wayland Baptist University M
Western Michigan University M,D*
Western Seminary M,O
Westminster Seminary California P,M
Westminster Theological Seminary P,M,D,O
Wheaton College M
Wilfrid Laurier University M,D
Wycliffe College P,M,D,O
Yale University D*

RELIGIOUS EDUCATION

Alliance University College P,M,O
Andover Newton Theological School P,M,D
Andrews University M,D,O
Asbury Theological Seminary M,O
Azusa Pacific University M
Baptist Bible College of Pennsylvania M
Baptist Theological Seminary at Richmond P,D
Bethel Seminary P,M,D,O
Biola University P,M,D
Boston College M,D,O*
Brandeis University M*
Brigham Young University M*
Calvin Theological Seminary P,M,D
Campbell University P,M,D
Chicago Theological Seminary P,M,D
Claremont School of Theology M,D
Columbia International University P,M,D,O
Concordia University (IL) M
Concordia University (NE) M
Concordia University, St. Paul M,O
Dallas Baptist University M
Dallas Theological Seminary M,D,O
Felician College M,O*
Fordham University M,D,O*
Gardner-Webb University P,M,D
Garrett-Evangelical Theological Seminary P,M,D
Global University of the Assemblies of God P,M
Gordon-Conwell Theological Seminary P,M,D
Grand Rapids Theological Seminary of Cornerstone University P,M
Gratz College M,O
Harding University M,O
Hebrew College M,O
Hebrew Union College–Jewish Institute of Religion (CA) M,D,O
Hebrew Union College–Jewish Institute of Religion (NY) M
Indiana Wesleyan University M
The Jewish Theological Seminary M,D*
Jewish University of America M,D
La Sierra University M
Laura and Alvin Siegal College of Judaic Studies M
Loyola Marymount University M
Loyola University Chicago P,M,O*
Luther Rice University P,M,D
Michigan Theological Seminary P,M,D
Midwestern Baptist Theological Seminary P,M,D
Midwest University P,M,D
Nazarene Theological Seminary P,M,D
Newman Theological College M,O
New Orleans Baptist Theological Seminary P,M,D
North Park Theological Seminary M
Nova Southeastern University M,O*
Oral Roberts University P,M,D
Pfeiffer University M
Phillips Theological Seminary P,M,D
Pontifical Catholic University of Puerto Rico M,D
Providence College and Theological Seminary P,M,D,O
Reformed Theological Seminary–Charlotte Campus P,M,D
Reformed Theological Seminary–Jackson Campus P,M,D,O
Regent University M,D,O
St. Augustine's Seminary of Toronto P,M,O
Saints Cyril and Methodius Seminary P,M
St. Vladimir's Orthodox Theological Seminary P,M,D
Shasta Bible College M
Southeastern Baptist Theological Seminary P,M,D
Southern Adventist University M
Southern Baptist Theological Seminary P,M,D
Southern Evangelical Seminary P,M,O
Southwestern Assemblies of God University M
Southwestern Baptist Theological Seminary M,D,O
Spertus Institute of Jewish Studies M
Teachers College Columbia University M,D*
Trinity Baptist College M
Trinity International University P,M,D,O
Union Theological Seminary and Presbyterian School of Christian Education M
University of St. Michael's College P,M,D,O
University of St. Thomas (MN) M*
University of San Francisco M,D
Western Seminary M,D
Wheaton College M
Yeshiva University M,D,O

REPRODUCTIVE BIOLOGY

Cornell University M,D*
Eastern Virginia Medical School M
New York University D*
Northwestern University D*
The University of British Columbia M,D*
University of Saskatchewan M,D
University of Wyoming M,D
West Virginia University M,D*

RHETORIC

Abilene Christian University M
Ball State University M*
Bob Jones University P,M,D,O
Bowling Green State University M,D*
California State University, Dominguez Hills M,O
California State University, Northridge M
Carnegie Mellon University M*
The Catholic University of America M,D*
Clemson University D*
Duquesne University M,D*
Florida State University M,D*
Georgia State University M,D*
Indiana University of Pennsylvania M,D
Iowa State University of Science and Technology M,D*
Kansas State University M*
Kent State University M,D*
Miami University M,D*
Michigan State University M,D*
Michigan Technological University M,D*
New Mexico Highlands University M
New Mexico State University M,D
Northern Arizona University M
Rensselaer Polytechnic Institute M,D*
San Diego State University M*
Southern Illinois University Carbondale M,D*
Syracuse University M,D*
Texas State University-San Marcos M*
Texas Tech University M,D
Texas Woman's University M,D
The University of Alabama M,D
The University of Arizona M,D*
University of Arkansas at Little Rock M
University of California, Berkeley D*
University of Illinois at Chicago M,D*
The University of Iowa M,D*
University of Louisiana at Lafayette M,D*
University of Louisville D
The University of North Carolina at Greensboro M,D
The University of Texas at Arlington M,D*
The University of Texas at El Paso M
University of Utah M,D*
Virginia Commonwealth University M*
Wright State University M*

ROMANCE LANGUAGES

Appalachian State University M
Boston University M,D*
The Catholic University of America M,D*
Clark Atlanta University M
Columbia University M,D*
Cornell University M,D*
Hunter College of the City University of New York M
The Johns Hopkins University D*
Michigan State University M,D*
New York University M,D*
Northern Illinois University M
Queens College of the City University of New York M
San Diego State University M*
Southern Connecticut State University M
Stony Brook University, State University of New York M,D*
Texas Tech University M,D
University at Buffalo, the State University of New York M,D*
The University of Alabama M,D
University of California, Berkeley D*
University of California, Los Angeles M,D*
University of Chicago M,D*
University of Cincinnati M,D
University of Georgia M,D*
University of Michigan D*
University of Missouri–Columbia M,D*
University of Missouri–Kansas City M*
University of New Orleans M
The University of North Carolina at Chapel Hill M,D*
University of Notre Dame M*
University of Oregon M,D*
University of Pennsylvania M,D*
The University of Texas at Austin M,D*
University of Virginia M,D*
University of Washington M,D*
Washington University in St. Louis M,D*
Wayne State University M,D*

RURAL PLANNING AND STUDIES

Brandon University M,O
California State University, Chico M
Concordia University (Canada) M,D,O
Cornell University M*
Dalhousie University M
Iowa State University of Science and Technology M,D*
Université Laval O
University of Alaska Fairbanks M
University of Guelph M,D
The University of Montana M*
University of West Georgia M
University of Wyoming M

RURAL SOCIOLOGY

Auburn University M*
Cornell University M,D*
Iowa State University of Science and Technology M,D*
North Carolina State University M,D*
The Ohio State University M,D*
Penn State University Park M,D*
South Dakota State University M,D
University of Alberta M,D*
University of Missouri–Columbia M,D*
The University of Montana M*
University of Wisconsin–Madison M,D*

RUSSIAN

American University O*
Boston College M*
Brown University M,D*
Bryn Mawr College M,D*
Columbia University M,D*
Harvard University D*
Hofstra University M*
Kent State University M*
McGill University M,D*
Middlebury College M,D
New York University M*
Penn State University Park M,D*
Stanford University M,D*
University at Albany, State University of New York M,O*
The University of Arizona M*
University of California, Berkeley D*
University of Illinois at Urbana–Champaign M,D*
University of Maryland, Baltimore County M*
University of Michigan M,D*
The University of North Carolina at Chapel Hill M,D*
University of Oregon M*
The University of Tennessee D*
University of Washington M,D*
University of Waterloo M,D*
Wayne State University M,D*

SAFETY ENGINEERING

Embry-Riddle Aeronautical University (AZ) M*
Indiana University Bloomington M,D*
Murray State University M
National University M
New Jersey Institute of Technology M
University of Minnesota, Duluth M*
West Virginia University M*

SCANDINAVIAN LANGUAGES

Cornell University M,D*
Harvard University D*
University of California, Berkeley D*
University of California, Los Angeles M,D*
University of Minnesota, Twin Cities Campus M,D*
University of Washington M,D*
University of Wisconsin–Madison M,D*

SCHOOL NURSING

Kutztown University of Pennsylvania O
La Salle University M,O
Monmouth University M,O
Seton Hall University M*
Wright State University M*

SCHOOL PSYCHOLOGY

Abilene Christian University M
Adelphi University M*
Alabama Agricultural and Mechanical University M,O
Alfred University M,D,O*
Alliant International University–Irvine M,D,O*
Alliant International University–Los Angeles M,D,O*
Alliant International University–San Diego M,D,O*
Alliant International University–San Francisco M,D,O*
Andrews University M,O
Appalachian State University M,O
Arcadia University M
Argosy University, Hawai'i Campus M,D*
Argosy University, Phoenix Campus M,D*
Argosy University, Sarasota Campus M,D,O*
Arkansas State University M,O
Assumption College M,O*
Auburn University M,D,O*
Azusa Pacific University M
Ball State University M,D,O*
Barry University M,O*
Bowling Green State University M,O*
Brigham Young University M,D,O*
Brooklyn College of the City University of New York M,O
Bucknell University M
California State University, Los Angeles M
California State University, Northridge M
California State University, Sacramento M*
California University of Pennsylvania M
Canisius College M

*P—first professional degree; M—master's degree; D—doctorate; O—other advanced degree; *full description and/or announcement in Book 2, 3, 4, 5, or 6*

Capella University M,D,O
Carlos Albizu University, Miami Campus M,D
Central Connecticut State University M,O
Central Michigan University D,O*
Central Washington University M
Chapman University M,D,O
The Chicago School of Professional Psychology O*
The Citadel, The Military College of South Carolina M,O
City University M,O
Cleveland State University M,O
The College of New Rochelle M
College of St. Joseph M
The College of Saint Rose M,O*
The College of William and Mary M,O
Duquesne University M,D,O*
East Carolina University *
Eastern Illinois University M,O
Eastern Kentucky University M,O*
Eastern Washington University M
Emporia State University M,O
Evangel University M
Fairfield University M,O*
Fairleigh Dickinson University, Metropolitan Campus M,D*
Florida Agricultural and Mechanical University M*
Florida International University M,O*
Florida State University M,O*
Fordham University M,D,O*
Fort Hays State University O
Francis Marion University M
Fresno Pacific University M
Gallaudet University M,O
Gardner-Webb University M
George Fox University M,O*
George Mason University M*
Georgia Southern University M,O
Georgia State University M,D,O*
Grand Valley State University M
Hofstra University M,D,O*
Howard University M,D,O*
Idaho State University M,D,O
Illinois State University D,O*
Immaculata University M,D,O
Indiana State University M,D,O*
Indiana University Bloomington M,D,O*
Indiana University of Pennsylvania D,O
Inter American University of Puerto Rico, San Germán Campus M,D
Iona College M*
James Madison University M,D,O
Kean University O
Kent State University M,D,O*
La Sierra University M,O
Lehigh University D,O*
Lenoir-Rhyne College M
Lesley University M*
Lewis & Clark College M,O
Lindenwood University M,D,O
Long Island University, Brooklyn Campus M*
Long Island University, Westchester Graduate Campus M
Louisiana State University and Agricultural and Mechanical College M,D*
Louisiana State University in Shreveport M,O
Loyola Marymount University M
Loyola University Chicago M,D,O*
Marist College M,O*
Marshall University O
Marywood University M,O*
Massachusetts School of Professional Psychology M,D*
McGill University M,D,O*
McNeese State University M
Mercy College M
Miami University M,O*
Michigan State University M,D,O*
Middle Tennessee State University M,O*
Millersville University of Pennsylvania M
Minnesota State University Moorhead M,O
Minot State University O
Montclair State University M,O*
Mount Saint Vincent University M
National-Louis University M,D,O
National University M
New Jersey City University M,O
New Mexico State University M,D,O
New York University M,D,O*
Niagara University M
Nicholls State University M,O
North Carolina State University D*
Northeastern University M,D,O*
Northern Arizona University M,D
Northwest Nazarene University M
Nova Southeastern University M,D,O*
Oregon State University–Cascades M
Ottawa University M
Our Lady of the Lake University of San Antonio M,D
Pace University M*
Penn State University Park M,D*
Philadelphia College of Osteopathic Medicine M,D*
Pittsburg State University O
Pontifical Catholic University of Puerto Rico M,D
Queens College of the City University of New York M,O
Radford University O
Regent University M,D,O
Rider University M,O*
Roberts Wesleyan College M
Rochester Institute of Technology M,O
Rowan University M,O
Rutgers, The State University of New Jersey, New Brunswick M,D*
St. John's University (NY) M,D
St. Mary's University of San Antonio M
Sam Houston State University M,D
San Diego State University M*
Seattle University M,O
Seton Hall University O*
Southeast Missouri State University M,O
Southern Connecticut State University M,O
Southern Illinois University Edwardsville O
Southern New Hampshire University M,O*
Southwestern Oklahoma State University M
State University of New York at Oswego M,O
State University of New York at Plattsburgh M,O
Stephen F. Austin State University M
Syracuse University M,D*
Tarleton State University M
Teachers College Columbia University M,D*
Temple University M,D*
Tennessee State University M,D*
Texas A&M University M,D*
Texas State University-San Marcos M*
Texas Woman's University M,D,O
Towson University M,O
Trinity University M*
Troy University M
Tufts University M,O*
University at Albany, State University of New York M,D,O*
University at Buffalo, the State University of New York M,D,O*
The University of Akron M
The University of Alabama at Birmingham M*
University of Alberta M,D*
The University of British Columbia M,D,O*
University of Calgary M,D
University of California, Berkeley *
University of Central Arkansas M,D
University of Central Florida O*
University of Cincinnati D,O
University of Colorado at Denver and Health Sciences Center M,O*
University of Connecticut M,D*
University of Dayton M,O*
University of Delaware M,D*
University of Denver M,D,O*
University of Detroit Mercy O
University of Florida M,D,O*
University of Great Falls M
University of Hartford M*
University of Houston–Clear Lake M
University of Idaho O*
The University of Iowa M,D,O*
University of Kansas D,O*
University of Kentucky M,D,O*
University of Louisiana at Monroe O
University of Mary Hardin-Baylor M
University of Maryland, College Park M,D,O*
University of Massachusetts Amherst D*
University of Massachusetts Boston M,O
University of Memphis M,D*
University of Minnesota, Twin Cities Campus M,D,O*
University of Missouri–Columbia M,D,O*
University of Missouri–St. Louis D,O
The University of Montana M,D,O*
University of Nebraska at Kearney M,O
University of Nebraska at Omaha M,D,O
University of Nevada, Las Vegas M,D,O
The University of North Carolina at Chapel Hill M,D*
The University of North Carolina at Greensboro M,D,O
University of Northern Colorado D,O
University of Northern Iowa M,O
University of North Texas M,D*
University of Oklahoma M,D*
University of Pennsylvania D*
University of Phoenix–Denver Campus M
University of Phoenix–Las Vegas Campus M
University of Phoenix–Northern Nevada Campus M
University of Phoenix–Puerto Rico Campus M
University of Phoenix–Southern Colorado Campus M,O
University of Phoenix–Utah Campus M
University of Rhode Island M,D
University of South Alabama M,D*
University of South Carolina D*
University of Southern Maine M,D,O
University of Southern Mississippi M,D*
University of South Florida M,D,O*
The University of Tennessee M,D,O*
The University of Tennessee at Chattanooga O
The University of Texas at Austin M,D*
The University of Texas at Tyler M
The University of Texas–Pan American M
University of the Pacific M,D,O
The University of Toledo M,D,O*
University of Virginia M,D,O*
University of Washington M,D*
University of Wisconsin–Eau Claire M,O
University of Wisconsin–La Crosse M,O
University of Wisconsin–Milwaukee O
University of Wisconsin–River Falls M,O
University of Wisconsin–Stout M,O*
University of Wisconsin–Whitewater M,O*
Utah State University M,D
Valdosta State University M,O
Valparaiso University
Wayne State University M,D,O*
Western Carolina University M*
Western Illinois University M,O
Western Kentucky University M,O
Western Michigan University M,D,O*
Wichita State University M,D,O*
Yeshiva University D

SCIENCE EDUCATION

Acadia University M
Agnes Scott College M*
Alabama State University M,O
Albany State University M
Alverno College M
American University of Puerto Rico M
Andrews University M,D,O
Antioch University New England M*
Arcadia University M,D,O
Arizona State University M,D*
Arkansas State University M,D,O
Armstrong Atlantic State University M
Asbury College M,O
Auburn University M,D,O*
Averett University M
Ball State University M,D*
Belmont University M
Bemidji State University M
Benedictine University M
Bennington College M*
Bethel College (TN) M
Bloomsburg University of Pennsylvania M
Boise State University M,D
Boston College M,D*
Boston University M,D,O*
Bowling Green State University M*
Bridgewater State College M
Brigham Young University M,D*
Brooklyn College of the City University of New York M,O
Brown University M*
Buffalo State College, State University of New York M
California State University, Chico M
California State University, Fullerton M
California State University, Long Beach M
California State University, San Bernardino M
Carthage College M,O
Central Michigan University M*
Charleston Southern University M
Chatham University M
Christopher Newport University M
City College of the City University of New York M*
Clarion University of Pennsylvania M
Clark Atlanta University M,D
Clemson University M*
Cleveland State University M
College of Charleston M*
College of the Humanities and Sciences, Harrison Middleton University M,D
The College of William and Mary M
The Colorado College M
Columbia University M,D,O*
Columbus State University M,O
Connecticut College M
Converse College M
Cornell University M,D*
Delaware State University M
DeSales University M,O
Drake University M*
East Carolina University M*
Eastern Connecticut State University M
Eastern Kentucky University M*
Eastern Michigan University M
Eastern Washington University M
East Stroudsburg University of Pennsylvania M
Edinboro University of Pennsylvania M
Elms College M,O
Fairleigh Dickinson University, Metropolitan Campus M*
Fitchburg State College M
Florida Agricultural and Mechanical University M*
Florida Gulf Coast University M
Florida Institute of Technology M,D,O*
Florida International University M,D*
Florida State University M,D,O*
Framingham State College M*
Fresno Pacific University M
Gannon University M
Georgia College & State University M,O
Georgia Southern University M
Georgia State University M,D,O*
Grambling State University M,O
Harding University M,O
Hardin-Simmons University M,D
Harvard University M*
Heritage University M
Hofstra University M,O*
Hood College M,O
Hunter College of the City University of New York M,O
ICR Graduate School M
Illinois Institute of Technology M,D*
Indiana State University M,D*
Indiana Tech M
Indiana University Bloomington M,D,O*
Instituto Tecnológico y de Estudios Superiores de Monterrey, Campus Monterrey M,D
Inter American University of Puerto Rico, Metropolitan Campus M
Inter American University of Puerto Rico, Ponce Campus M
Inter American University of Puerto Rico, San Germán Campus M
Iona College M*
Ithaca College M
Jackson State University M,D
John Carroll University M
The Johns Hopkins University M,D,O*
Johnson State College M
Kean University M
Kutztown University of Pennsylvania M,O
Lawrence Technological University M
Lebanon Valley College M
Lehman College of the City University of New York M
Lesley University M,D,O*
Long Island University, C.W. Post Campus M*
Louisiana Tech University M,D
Loyola University Chicago M*
Lynchburg College M
Lyndon State College M
Manhattanville College M*
McNeese State University M
Michigan State University M*
Michigan Technological University M*
Middle Tennessee State University M*

Institution	Degrees
Mills College	M,D
Minnesota State University Mankato	M
Minot State University	M
Mississippi College	M,O
Missouri State University	M*
Montclair State University	M,D,O*
Morgan State University	M,D*
National-Louis University	M,O
New Mexico Institute of Mining and Technology	M
New York University	M*
North Carolina Agricultural and Technical State University	M
North Carolina State University	M,D*
North Dakota State University	M,D,O
Northeastern State University	M
Northern Arizona University	M,D
North Georgia College & State University	M,O
Northwestern State University of Louisiana	M
Northwest Missouri State University	M
Nova Southeastern University	M,O*
Occidental College	M
Ohio University	M*
Old Dominion University	M*
Oregon State University	M,D*
Penn State University Park	M,D*
Plymouth State University	M
Portland State University	M,D
Purdue University	M,D,O*
Purdue University Calumet	M
Queens College of the City University of New York	M,O
Quinnipiac University	M*
Regis University	M,O
Rider University	M,O*
Rutgers, The State University of New Jersey, New Brunswick	M,D*
Sage Graduate School	M
Saginaw Valley State University	M
St. John Fisher College	M
Salem State College	M
Salisbury University	M
San Diego State University	M,D*
Slippery Rock University of Pennsylvania	M
Smith College	M*
South Carolina State University	M
Southeast Missouri State University	M
Southern Connecticut State University	M,O
Southern Illinois University Edwardsville	M
Southern University and Agricultural and Mechanical College	D*
Southwestern Oklahoma State University	M
Stanford University	M,D*
State University of New York at Binghamton	M*
State University of New York at Fredonia	M
State University of New York at Plattsburgh	M
State University of New York College at Brockport	M*
State University of New York College at Cortland	M*
Stony Brook University, State University of New York	M,O*
Syracuse University	M,D*
Teachers College Columbia University	M,D*
Temple University	M,D*
Texas A&M University	M,D*
Texas Christian University	M,D
Texas State University-San Marcos	M*
Texas Woman's University	M,D
Towson University	M
Trinity (Washington) University	M
Union Graduate College	M*
University at Albany, State University of New York	M,D*
University at Buffalo, the State University of New York	M,D,O*
University of Arkansas at Pine Bluff	M
The University of British Columbia	M,D*
University of California, Berkeley	M,D*
University of California, Los Angeles	M,D*
University of California, San Diego	D*
University of Central Florida	M,O*
University of Chicago	D*
University of Cincinnati	M,D,O
University of Connecticut	M,D*
University of Florida	M,D,O*
University of Georgia	M,D,O*
University of Houston	M,D*
University of Idaho	M,D*
University of Indianapolis	M
The University of Iowa	M,D*
University of Maine	M,O*
University of Massachusetts Lowell	M,D,O*
University of Miami	M,D,O*
University of Michigan	M,D*
University of Minnesota, Twin Cities Campus	M*
University of Missouri–Columbia	M,D,O*
University of Nebraska at Kearney	M
University of New Hampshire	M,D*
University of New Orleans	M
The University of North Carolina at Chapel Hill	M*
The University of North Carolina at Greensboro	M,D,O
The University of North Carolina at Pembroke	M
University of Northern Colorado	M,D
University of Northern Iowa	M,O
University of North Texas Health Science Center at Fort Worth	M,D
University of Oklahoma	M,D,O*
University of Pittsburgh	M,D*
University of Puerto Rico, Río Piedras	M,D*
University of St. Francis (IL)	M
University of South Alabama	M,O*
University of South Carolina	M,D*
University of Southern Mississippi	M,D*
University of South Florida	M,D*
The University of Tampa	M
The University of Tennessee	M,D,O*
The University of Texas at Austin	M,D*
The University of Texas at Dallas	M*
The University of Texas at Tyler	M
University of the Incarnate Word	M
The University of Toledo	M*
University of Tulsa	M*
University of Utah	M,D*
University of Vermont	M,D*
University of Victoria	M,D*
University of Virginia	M,D*
University of Washington	M,D*
The University of West Alabama	M
University of West Florida	M
University of West Georgia	M,O
University of Wisconsin–Eau Claire	M
University of Wisconsin–Madison	M,D*
University of Wisconsin–River Falls	M
University of Wisconsin–Stevens Point	M
University of Wyoming	M
Vanderbilt University	M,D*
Walden University	M,D
Wayne State College	M
Wayne State University	M,D,O*
Wesleyan College	M
West Chester University of Pennsylvania	M
Western Carolina University	M*
Western Governors University	M,O
Western Kentucky University	M
Western Michigan University	D*
Western Oregon University	M
Western Washington University	M
Widener University	M,D*
Wilkes University	M
Wright State University	M*

SECONDARY EDUCATION

Institution	Degrees
Adelphi University	M*
Alabama Agricultural and Mechanical University	M,O
Alabama State University	M,O
Alcorn State University	M,O
American International College	M,D,O
American University	M,O*
Andrews University	M,D,O
Appalachian State University	M
Arcadia University	M,D,O
Argosy University, Atlanta Campus	M,D,O*
Argosy University, Chicago Campus	M,D,O*
Argosy University, Hawai'i Campus	M,D*
Argosy University, Inland Empire Campus	M,D*
Argosy University, Nashville Campus	M,D*
Argosy University, Orange County Campus	M,D*
Argosy University, Phoenix Campus	M,D,O*
Argosy University, San Diego Campus	M,D*
Argosy University, San Francisco Bay Area Campus	M,D*
Argosy University, Santa Monica Campus	M,D*
Argosy University, Sarasota Campus	M,D,O*
Argosy University, Schaumburg Campus	M,D,O*
Argosy University, Seattle Campus	M,D*
Argosy University, Tampa Campus	M,D,O*
Argosy University, Twin Cities Campus	M,D,O*
Argosy University, Washington DC Campus	M,D,O*
Arizona State University at the West campus	M,D,O
Arkansas Tech University	M,O
Armstrong Atlantic State University	M
Auburn University	M,D,O*
Auburn University Montgomery	M,O
Augustana College	M
Augusta State University	M,O
Austin College	M
Ball State University	M*
Belhaven College (MS)	M
Bellarmine University	M
Belmont University	M
Benedictine University	M
Bennington College	M*
Berry College	M
Bethel University	M,D,O
Bob Jones University	P,M,D,O
Boston College	M*
Bowie State University	M
Brandeis University	M*
Bridgewater State College	M
Brooklyn College of the City University of New York	M,O
Brown University	M*
Butler University	M
California State University, Bakersfield	M
California State University, Fullerton	M
California State University, Los Angeles	M
California State University, Northridge	M
California State University, San Bernardino	M
California State University, Stanislaus	M
California University of Pennsylvania	M
Campbell University	M
Canisius College	M
Carlow University	M
Carson-Newman College	M
Centenary College of Louisiana	M
Central Connecticut State University	M
Central Michigan University	M*
Chadron State College	M,O
Chapman University	M
Charleston Southern University	M
Chatham University	M
Chestnut Hill College	M
Chicago State University	M
The Citadel, The Military College of South Carolina	M
City College of the City University of New York	M,O*
Clemson University	M*
Coastal Carolina University	M
Colgate University	M
College of Mount St. Joseph	M
The College of New Jersey	M
College of St. Joseph	M
The College of Saint Rose	M,O*
College of Staten Island of the City University of New York	M
The College of William and Mary	M
The Colorado College	M
Columbus State University	M,O
Concordia University (OR)	M
Connecticut College	M
Converse College	M
Delta State University	M,O
DePaul University	M,D*
Dowling College	M,D,O
Drake University	M*
Drury University	M*
Duquesne University	M*
D'Youville College	M,O*
Eastern Connecticut State University	M
Eastern Kentucky University	M*
Eastern Michigan University	M
Eastern Nazarene College	M,O
Eastern Oregon University	M
East Stroudsburg University of Pennsylvania	M
East Tennessee State University	M
Edinboro University of Pennsylvania	M
Elms College	M,O
Emmanuel College	M,O
Emory University	M,D,O*
Emporia State University	M
Evangel University	M
Fairfield University	M,O*
Fayetteville State University	M
Fitchburg State College	M
Florida Agricultural and Mechanical University	M*
Florida Gulf Coast University	M
Fordham University	M,D,O*
Fort Hays State University	M
Francis Marion University	M
Friends University	M
Frostburg State University	M
Gallaudet University	M,D,O
George Mason University	M*
The George Washington University	M*
Georgia College & State University	M,O
Georgia Southwestern State University	M,O
Grand Canyon University	M*
Greenville College	M
Harding University	M,O
Hawai'i Pacific University	M*
Hofstra University	M,O*
Holy Family University	M
Hood College	M,O
Howard University	M,O*
Hunter College of the City University of New York	M
Idaho State University	M,O
Immaculata University	M,D,O
Indiana University Bloomington	M,D,O*
Indiana University Kokomo	M
Indiana University Northwest	M
Indiana University–Purdue University Fort Wayne	M
Indiana University South Bend	M
Indiana University Southeast	M
Iona College	M*
Ithaca College	M
Jackson State University	M,D,O
Jacksonville State University	M
James Madison University	M
John Carroll University	M
The Johns Hopkins University	M*
Johnson State College	M,O
Jones International University	M
Kansas State University	M,D*
Kent State University	M*
Kutztown University of Pennsylvania	M,O
LaGrange College	M
Lee University	M
Lehigh University	M,D*
Lewis & Clark College	M
Liberty University	M,D,O
Lincoln University (MO)	M,O
Long Island University, C.W. Post Campus	M*
Long Island University, Westchester Graduate Campus	M
Longwood University	M*
Louisiana State University and Agricultural and Mechanical College	M,D,O*
Louisiana Tech University	M,D
Loyola Marymount University	M
Loyola University Chicago	M*
Loyola University New Orleans	M
Maharishi University of Management	M
Manhattanville College	M*
Mansfield University of Pennsylvania	M
Marshall University	M
Marygrove College	M
Marymount University	M,O
Maryville University of Saint Louis	M,D
Marywood University	M*
McDaniel College	M
McNeese State University	M
Mercer University	M,D,O
Mercy College	M
Miami University	M*
Mills College	M,D
Mississippi College	M,O
Mississippi State University	M,D,O
Missouri State University	M,O*
Montana State University–Billings	M
Morehead State University	M
Morgan State University	M*
Mount Saint Mary College	M
Mount St. Mary's College	M
Murray State University	M,O
National-Louis University	M
New Jersey City University	M

*P—first professional degree; M—master's degree; D—doctorate; O—other advanced degree; *full description and/or announcement in Book 2, 3, 4, 5, or 6*

Niagara University M
Norfolk State University M
Northern Arizona University M
Northern Illinois University M,D
Northern Michigan University M
Northern State University M
North Georgia College & State University M,O
Northwestern Oklahoma State University M
Northwestern State University of Louisiana M,O
Northwestern University M*
Northwest Missouri State University M,O
Nova Southeastern University M,O*
Oakland University M*
Occidental College M
Ohio University M,D*
Old Dominion University M,D*
Olivet Nazarene University M
Pacific University M
Park University M
Piedmont College M,O
Pittsburg State University M
Plymouth State University M
Portland State University M,D
Purdue University Calumet M
Queens College of the City University of New York M,O
Quinnipiac University M*
Regis University M,O
Rhode Island College M,O
Roberts Wesleyan College M,O
Rochester Institute of Technology M
Rockford College M
Rollins College M
Roosevelt University M
Rowan University M
Sacred Heart University M,O
Saginaw Valley State University M
St. John's University (NY) M
Saint Joseph's University M,D,O*
Saint Mary's University of Minnesota M,O
St. Thomas Aquinas College M,O*
Saint Xavier University M,O
Salem College M
Salem State College M
Salisbury University M
Sam Houston State University M
San Diego State University M*
San Francisco State University M
San Jose State University M,O
Seattle Pacific University M
Shenandoah University M,D,O*
Siena Heights University M
Sierra Nevada College M
Simmons College M,O
Slippery Rock University of Pennsylvania M
Smith College M*
South Carolina State University M
Southeastern Louisiana University M
Southeastern Oklahoma State University M
Southeast Missouri State University M
Southern Arkansas University–Magnolia M
Southern Illinois University Edwardsville M
Southern New Hampshire University M,O*
Southern Oregon University M
Southern University and Agricultural and Mechanical College M*
Southwestern Oklahoma State University M
Spalding University M
Springfield College M*
Spring Hill College M
State University of New York at Binghamton M*
State University of New York at Fredonia M
State University of New York at New Paltz M
State University of New York at Oswego M
State University of New York at Plattsburgh M
State University of New York College at Cortland M*
State University of New York College at Geneseo M
State University of New York College at Oneonta M
State University of New York College at Potsdam M
Stephen F. Austin State University M,D
Suffolk University M*
Sul Ross State University M*
Tarleton State University M,D,O
Tennessee Technological University M,O*
Texas A&M University–Commerce M,D
Texas A&M University–Corpus Christi M
Texas A&M University–Kingsville M
Texas Southern University M,D
Texas State University-San Marcos M*
Texas Tech University M,D
Towson University M
Trevecca Nazarene University M
Trinity (Washington) University M
Troy University M,O
Tufts University M,D*
Union College (KY) M
The University of Akron M,D
The University of Alabama at Birmingham M*
University of Alaska Southeast M
University of Alberta M,D*
The University of Arizona M,D*
University of Arkansas M,O*
University of Arkansas at Little Rock M
University of Arkansas at Pine Bluff M
University of Bridgeport M,O
University of California, Irvine M,D*
University of Central Missouri M,O
University of Central Oklahoma M
University of Cincinnati M
University of Connecticut M,D*
University of Dayton M*
University of Guam M
University of Houston M,D*
University of Illinois at Chicago M,D*
University of Indianapolis M
The University of Iowa M,D*
University of Louisiana at Monroe M
University of Louisville M
University of Maine M,O*
University of Maryland, Baltimore County M*
University of Maryland, College Park M,D,O*
University of Massachusetts Amherst M,D,O*
University of Massachusetts Boston M,D,O
University of Memphis M,D*
University of Michigan M,D*
University of Mississippi M,D,O
University of Missouri–St. Louis M,D
University of Montevallo M
University of Nebraska at Omaha M
University of Nevada, Las Vegas M,D,O
University of Nevada, Reno M,D,O*
University of New Hampshire M*
University of New Mexico M,O*
University of North Alabama M
The University of North Carolina at Chapel Hill M*
The University of North Carolina at Charlotte M*
The University of North Carolina Wilmington M*
University of North Dakota D
University of North Florida M
University of North Texas M*
University of Oklahoma M,D,O*
University of Pennsylvania M*
University of Phoenix–Central Florida Campus M
University of Phoenix–Central Valley Campus M
University of Phoenix–Denver Campus M
University of Phoenix–Fort Lauderdale Campus M
University of Phoenix–Hawaii Campus M
University of Phoenix–Nashville Campus M
University of Phoenix–New Mexico Campus M
University of Phoenix–North Florida Campus M
University of Phoenix–Omaha Campus M
University of Phoenix Online Campus M
University of Phoenix–Oregon Campus M
University of Phoenix–Phoenix Campus M
University of Phoenix–Sacramento Valley Campus M,O
University of Phoenix–San Diego Campus M
University of Phoenix–Southern Arizona Campus M,O
University of Phoenix–Southern California Campus M
University of Phoenix–Southern Colorado Campus M,O
University of Phoenix–Utah Campus M
University of Phoenix–West Florida Campus M
University of Pittsburgh M,D*
University of Portland M
University of Puerto Rico, Río Piedras M,D*
University of Puget Sound M
University of Rhode Island M
University of St. Francis (IL) M
The University of Scranton M
University of South Alabama M,O*
University of South Carolina M,D*
The University of South Dakota M
University of Southern Indiana M
University of Southern Mississippi M,D,O*
University of South Florida M,D,O*
The University of Tennessee M,D,O*
The University of Tennessee at Chattanooga M,D,O
The University of Tennessee at Martin M
The University of Texas at Tyler M
The University of Texas–Pan American M
University of the Cumberlands M,O
University of the Incarnate Word M
The University of Toledo M,D,O*
University of Utah M,D*
The University of West Alabama M
University of West Florida M
University of West Georgia M,O
University of Wisconsin–Eau Claire M
University of Wisconsin–La Crosse M
University of Wisconsin–Milwaukee M
University of Wisconsin–Platteville M
University of Wisconsin–Whitewater M*
Utah State University M
Valdosta State University M,O
Vanderbilt University M,D*
Villanova University M*
Virginia Commonwealth University M,O*
Wagner College M
Wake Forest University M*
Washington State University M,D*
Washington State University Tri-Cities M,D
Washington University in St. Louis M*
Wayne State University M,D,O*
West Chester University of Pennsylvania M
Western Carolina University M*
Western Illinois University M
Western Kentucky University M,O
Western New Mexico University M
Western Oregon University M
Western Washington University M
Westfield State College M
West Virginia University M,D*
Wheaton College M
Whittier College M
Whitworth University M
Wilkes University M
William Carey University M,O
Wilmington College (DE) M
Winthrop University M
Worcester State College M
Wright State University M*
Xavier University M*
Youngstown State University M

SLAVIC LANGUAGES

Boston College M*
Brown University M,D*
Columbia University M,D*
Cornell University M,D*
Duke University M*
Florida State University M*
Harvard University D*
Indiana University Bloomington M,D*
New York University M*
Northwestern University D*
The Ohio State University M,D*
Princeton University D*
Stanford University M,D*
Stony Brook University, State University of New York M*
University of Alberta M,D*
University of California, Berkeley D*
University of California, Los Angeles M,D*
University of Chicago M,D*
University of Illinois at Chicago M,D*
University of Illinois at Urbana–Champaign M,D*
University of Kansas M,D*
University of Manitoba M
University of Michigan M,D*
The University of North Carolina at Chapel Hill M,D*
University of Pittsburgh M,D*
University of Southern California M,D*
The University of Texas at Austin M,D*
University of Toronto M,D
University of Virginia M,D*
University of Washington M,D*
University of Wisconsin–Madison M,D*
University of Wisconsin–Milwaukee M
Yale University D*

SOCIAL PSYCHOLOGY

Alvernia College M
American University M*
Andrews University M
Appalachian State University M
Arcadia University M
Argosy University, Atlanta Campus M,D,O*
Argosy University, Chicago Campus M,D,O*
Argosy University, Denver Campus M,D*
Argosy University, Sarasota Campus M,D,O*
Argosy University, Schaumburg Campus M,D,O*
Argosy University, Washington DC Campus M,D,O*
Arizona State University D*
Auburn University M,D,O*
Ball State University M*
Bowling Green State University M,D*
Brandeis University M,D*
Brigham Young University M,D*
Brock University M,D
Brooklyn College of the City University of New York M,D
California State University, Fullerton M
Canisius College M
Carnegie Mellon University D*
Central Connecticut State University M
Claremont Graduate University M,D,O
Clark University D*
The College of New Rochelle M
College of St. Joseph M
Columbia University M,D*
Cornell University M,D*
DePaul University M,D*
Eastern Illinois University M
Eastern Michigan University M,O
Florida Agricultural and Mechanical University M*
Florida State University D*
Francis Marion University M
The George Washington University D*
Graduate School and University Center of the City University of New York D*
Harvard University D*
Henderson State University M
Hofstra University M,D,O*
Howard University M,D*
Hunter College of the City University of New York M
Indiana University Bloomington M,D*
Indiana Wesleyan University M
Iowa State University of Science and Technology M,D*
Lamar University M*
Lesley University M,D,O*
Loyola University Chicago M,D*
Martin University M
Marymount University
Memorial University of Newfoundland M,D
Miami University D*
Minnesota State University Mankato M,O
Montclair State University M,O*
Naropa University M*
National-Louis University M,O
New College of California M*
New York University M,D,O*
Norfolk State University M
North Carolina State University M*
North Dakota State University M,D
Northern Kentucky University M
North Georgia College & State University M
Northwestern University D*
Northwest Nazarene University M
The Ohio State University M,D*
Oregon State University–Cascades M
Penn State Harrisburg M,D*
Penn State University Park M,D*
Prescott College M
Queen's University at Kingston M,D
Regent University M,D,O
Regis University M,O
Rutgers, The State University of New Jersey, Newark D*

Institution	Degrees
Rutgers, The State University of New Jersey, New Brunswick	D*
Sage Graduate School	M
St. Cloud State University	M
Saint Joseph College	M,O
Saint Martin's University	M
St. Mary's University of San Antonio	M
Southeast Missouri State University	M,O
Southwestern College (NM)	O*
Stony Brook University, State University of New York	D*
Syracuse University	M,D*
Teachers College Columbia University	M,D*
Temple University	D*
Texas A&M University	M,D*
Thomas University	M
Université du Québec à Rimouski	M
Université Laval	D
University at Albany, State University of New York	M,D,O*
University at Buffalo, the State University of New York	M,D*
University of Alaska Anchorage	M,D
University of Alaska Fairbanks	D
The University of British Columbia	M,D*
University of Central Arkansas	M
University of Connecticut	M,D*
University of Dayton	M,O*
University of Delaware	D*
University of Florida	M,D*
University of Guelph	M,D
University of Hawaii at Manoa	M,D,O*
University of Houston	M,D*
University of La Verne	D
University of Maine	M,D*
University of Mary Hardin-Baylor	M
University of Maryland, College Park	M,D*
University of Massachusetts Lowell	M*
University of Michigan	D*
University of Minnesota, Twin Cities Campus	D*
University of Missouri–Kansas City	M,D*
University of Missouri–St. Louis	M,D,O
University of Nevada, Reno	D*
University of New Haven	M,O*
The University of North Carolina at Chapel Hill	D*
The University of North Carolina at Charlotte	M*
The University of North Carolina at Greensboro	M,D
University of Oklahoma	M*
University of Oregon	M,D*
University of Pennsylvania	D*
University of Phoenix–Denver Campus	M
University of Phoenix–Hawaii Campus	M
University of Phoenix–Kansas City Campus	M
University of Phoenix–Phoenix Campus	M,O
University of Phoenix–Southern Colorado Campus	M
University of Puget Sound	M
University of Rochester	M,D*
The University of Scranton	M
University of South Carolina	M,D*
The University of Toledo	M,D,O*
University of Victoria	M,D
University of Windsor	M,D
University of Wisconsin–Madison	D*
University of Wisconsin–Superior	M
University of Wisconsin–Whitewater	M*
Washington State University	M,D*
Washington University in St. Louis	M,D*
Western Carolina University	M*
Western Connecticut State University	M*
Western Illinois University	M,O
Wichita State University	M,D*
Wilfrid Laurier University	M,D
Wilmington College (DE)	M

SOCIAL SCIENCES

Institution	Degrees
Arizona State University	M,D*
Arkansas Tech University	M
Ball State University	M*
California Institute of Technology	M,D*
California State University, Chico	M
California State University, San Bernardino	M
California University of Pennsylvania	M
Campbellsville University	M
Carnegie Mellon University	D*
Central European University	M,D*
The Citadel, The Military College of South Carolina	M
Cleveland State University	M
College of the Humanities and Sciences, Harrison Middleton University	M,D
Columbia University	M*
Eastern Michigan University	M
Edinboro University of Pennsylvania	M
Florida Agricultural and Mechanical University	M*
Florida State University	M*
George Mason University	M,D,O*
Graduate Theological Union	M,D,O
Hollins University	M,O
Humboldt State University	M
Indiana University Bloomington	P,M,D,O*
The Johns Hopkins University	M,D*
Lincoln University (MO)	M
Long Island University, Brooklyn Campus	M,O*
Long Island University, C.W. Post Campus	M*
Massachusetts Institute of Technology	D*
Michigan State University	M*
Mississippi College	M,O
Montclair State University	M,O*
The New School: A University	M,D*
North Dakota State University	M,D
Northwestern University	M,O*
Nova Southeastern University	M*
Ohio University	M*
Queens College of the City University of New York	M
Regis University	M,O
San Francisco State University	M
Southern Oregon University	M
Southern University and Agricultural and Mechanical College	M*
State University of New York at Binghamton	M*
Stony Brook University, State University of New York	M,O*
Syracuse University	M,D*
Texas A&M International University	M
Texas A&M University–Commerce	M
Towson University	M
Universidad Nacional Pedro Henriquez Urena	P,M,D
University of California, Irvine	M,D*
University of California, Santa Cruz	D*
University of Chicago	M,D*
University of Colorado at Denver and Health Sciences Center	M*
University of Florida	M*
University of Idaho	M*
University of Illinois at Springfield	M
University of Kansas	M,D*
University of Maryland, Baltimore County	D*
University of Michigan	D*
University of Michigan–Flint	M*
University of Regina	M,D
The University of Texas at Tyler	M
The University of Toledo	D*
University of Wisconsin–Madison	D*
Worcester Polytechnic Institute	M,D*
Yale University	M,D*
York University	M*

SOCIAL SCIENCES EDUCATION

Institution	Degrees
Acadia University	M
Alabama State University	M,O
Albany State University	M
Andrews University	M,D,O
Appalachian State University	M
Arcadia University	M,D,O
Arkansas State University	M,D,O
Arkansas Tech University	M
Armstrong Atlantic State University	M
Asbury College	M,O
Auburn University	M,D,O*
Averett University	M
Belmont University	M
Bennington College	M*
Bethel College (TN)	M
Bob Jones University	P,M,D,O
Boston College	M*
Boston University	M,D,O*
Bridgewater State College	M
Brooklyn College of the City University of New York	M,O
Brown University	M*
Buffalo State College, State University of New York	M
California State University, Chico	M
California State University, San Bernardino	M
Campbell University	M
Carthage College	M,O
Chadron State College	M,O
Chaminade University of Honolulu	M
Charleston Southern University	M
Chatham University	M
Christopher Newport University	M
City College of the City University of New York	M,O*
Clarion University of Pennsylvania	M
College of St. Joseph	M
The College of William and Mary	M
The Colorado College	M
Columbus State University	M,O
Converse College	M
Delta State University	M
Drake University	M*
East Carolina University	M*
Eastern Kentucky University	M*
Eastern Washington University	M
East Stroudsburg University of Pennsylvania	M
Emporia State University	M
Fayetteville State University	M
Fitchburg State College	M
Florida Agricultural and Mechanical University	M*
Florida Gulf Coast University	M
Florida International University	M,D*
Florida State University	M,D,O*
Framingham State College	M*
Georgia College & State University	M,O
Georgia Southern University	M,O
Georgia State University	M,D,O*
Grambling State University	M
Harding University	M,O
Henderson State University	M,O
Hofstra University	M*
Hunter College of the City University of New York	M
Indiana University Bloomington	M,D,O*
Instituto Tecnologico de Santo Domingo	M
Inter American University of Puerto Rico, Ponce Campus	M
Iona College	M*
Ithaca College	M
Kutztown University of Pennsylvania	M,O
Lehman College of the City University of New York	M
Louisiana Tech University	M,D
Manhattanville College	M*
McNeese State University	M*
Miami University	M*
Michigan State University	M,D*
Mills College	M,D
Minnesota State University Mankato	M
Mississippi College	M,O
Missouri State University	M*
Montclair State University	M*
New York University	M,D*
North Carolina Agricultural and Technical State University	M
North Dakota State University	M,D,O
North Georgia College & State University	M,O
Northwestern State University of Louisiana	M
Northwest Missouri State University	M
Nova Southeastern University	M,O*
Occidental College	M
Ohio University	M,D*
Penn State University Park	M,D*
Portland State University	M
Princeton University	D*
Purdue University	M,D,O*
Queens College of the City University of New York	M,O
Quinnipiac University	M*
Rider University	M,O*
Rivier College	M
Rockford College	M
Rutgers, The State University of New Jersey, New Brunswick	M,D*
Sage Graduate School	M
St. John Fisher College	M
Salisbury University	M
Smith College	M*
South Carolina State University	M
Southern Illinois University Edwardsville	M
Southwestern Oklahoma State University	M
Stanford University	M,D*
State University of New York at Binghamton	M*
State University of New York at Plattsburgh	M
State University of New York College at Brockport	M*
State University of New York College at Cortland	M*
Stony Brook University, State University of New York	M,O*
Syracuse University	M,O*
Teachers College Columbia University	M,D*
Texas A&M University–Commerce	M
Texas State University-San Marcos	D*
Trinity (Washington) University	M
Union Graduate College	M*
University at Buffalo, the State University of New York	M,D,O*
University of Arkansas at Pine Bluff	M
The University of British Columbia	M,D*
University of California, Santa Cruz	M*
University of Central Florida	M*
University of Cincinnati	M,D,O
University of Colorado at Denver and Health Sciences Center	M*
University of Connecticut	M,D*
University of Florida	M,D,O*
University of Georgia	M,D,O*
University of Houston	M,D*
University of Indianapolis	M
The University of Iowa	M,D*
University of Maine	M,O*
University of Michigan	M,D*
University of Minnesota, Twin Cities Campus	M*
University of Missouri–Columbia	M,D,O*
University of New Orleans	M
The University of North Carolina at Chapel Hill	M*
The University of North Carolina at Greensboro	M,D,O
The University of North Carolina at Pembroke	M
University of Oklahoma	M,D,O*
University of Pittsburgh	M,D*
University of Puerto Rico, Río Piedras	M,D*
University of St. Francis (IL)	M
University of South Carolina	M,D,O*
University of Southern Mississippi	M,D,O*
University of South Florida	M,D,O*
The University of Tennessee	M,D,O*
The University of Texas at Tyler	M
The University of Toledo	M,D*
University of Victoria	M,D
University of Washington	M,D*
The University of West Alabama	M
University of West Georgia	M,O
University of Wisconsin–Eau Claire	M
University of Wisconsin–River Falls	M
Virginia Commonwealth University	M,O*
Wayne State College	M
Wayne State University	M,D,O*
Webster University	M,O
Western Carolina University	M*
Western Oregon University	M
Widener University	M,D*
Wilkes University	M
William Carey University	M,O
Worcester State College	M

SOCIAL WORK

Institution	Degrees
Abilene Christian University	M
Adelphi University	M,D*
Alabama Agricultural and Mechanical University	M
American Jewish University	M
Andrews University	M
Appalachian State University	M
Arizona State University	M,D*
Arizona State University at the West campus	M
Arkansas State University	M
Augsburg College	M
Aurora University	M
Barry University	M,D*
Baylor University	M*
Boise State University	M
Boston College	M,D*
Boston University	M,D*
Bridgewater State College	M
Brigham Young University	M*
Bryn Mawr College	M,D*
California State University, Bakersfield	M

*P—first professional degree; M—master's degree; D—doctorate; O—other advanced degree; *full description and/or announcement in Book 2, 3, 4, 5, or 6*

- California State University, Chico M
- California State University, Dominguez Hills M
- California State University, East Bay M
- California State University, Fresno M
- California State University, Long Beach M
- California State University, Los Angeles M
- California State University, Northridge M
- California State University, Sacramento M*
- California State University, San Bernardino M
- California State University, Stanislaus M
- California University of Pennsylvania M
- Campbellsville University
- Carleton University M
- Case Western Reserve University M,D*
- The Catholic University of America M,D*
- Chicago State University M
- Clark Atlanta University M,D
- Cleveland State University M
- College of St. Catherine M*
- Colorado State University M*
- Columbia University M,D*
- Cornell University M,D*
- Dalhousie University M
- Delaware State University M
- Dominican University M
- East Carolina University M*
- Eastern Michigan University M,O
- Eastern Washington University M
- East Tennessee State University M
- Edinboro University of Pennsylvania M
- Fayetteville State University M
- Florida Agricultural and Mechanical University M*
- Florida Atlantic University M
- Florida Atlantic University, Jupiter Campus M
- Florida Gulf Coast University M
- Florida International University M,D*
- Florida State University M,D*
- Fordham University M,D*
- Gallaudet University M
- George Mason University M,D,O*
- Georgia State University M*
- Governors State University M
- Graduate School and University Center of the City University of New York D*
- Grambling State University M
- Grand Valley State University M
- Gratz College M,O
- Hawai'i Pacific University M*
- Hebrew Union College–Jewish Institute of Religion (CA) M,O
- Howard University M,D*
- Humboldt State University M
- Hunter College of the City University of New York M,D
- Illinois State University M*
- Indiana University Northwest M
- Indiana University–Purdue University Indianapolis M,D,O*
- Indiana University South Bend M
- Institute for Clinical Social Work D
- Inter American University of Puerto Rico, Metropolitan Campus M
- Jackson State University M,D
- Kean University M
- Kennesaw State University M
- Kutztown University of Pennsylvania M
- Lakehead University M
- Laurentian University M
- Loma Linda University M,D
- Louisiana State University and Agricultural and Mechanical College M,D*
- Loyola University Chicago M,D*
- Marywood University M,D*
- McGill University M,D,O*
- McMaster University M
- Memorial University of Newfoundland M
- Miami University M*
- Michigan State University M,D*
- Millersville University of Pennsylvania M
- Missouri State University M*
- Monmouth University M
- Morgan State University M,D*
- Nazareth College of Rochester M
- Newman University M
- New Mexico Highlands University M
- New Mexico State University M
- New York University M,D*
- Norfolk State University M,D
- North Carolina Agricultural and Technical State University M
- Northwest Nazarene University M
- The Ohio State University M,D*
- The Ohio State University at Lima M
- The Ohio State University at Marion M,D
- The Ohio State University–Mansfield Campus M
- The Ohio State University–Newark Campus M
- Ohio University M*
- Our Lady of the Lake University of San Antonio M
- Phillips Theological Seminary P,M,D
- Pontifical Catholic University of Puerto Rico M,D
- Portland State University M,D
- Radford University M
- Rhode Island College M
- Roberts Wesleyan College M
- Rutgers, The State University of New Jersey, New Brunswick M,D*
- St. Ambrose University M
- Saint Louis University M*
- Salem State College M
- Salisbury University M
- San Diego State University M*
- San Francisco State University M
- San Jose State University M,O
- Savannah State University M
- Shippensburg University of Pennsylvania M
- Simmons College M,D
- Smith College M,D*
- Southern Connecticut State University M
- Southern Illinois University Carbondale M*
- Southern Illinois University Edwardsville M
- Southern University at New Orleans M
- Spalding University M
- Springfield College M,O*
- State University of New York College at Brockport M*
- Stephen F. Austin State University M
- Stony Brook University, State University of New York M,D*
- Syracuse University M*
- Temple University M*
- Texas A&M University–Commerce M
- Texas State University-San Marcos M*
- Tulane University M*
- Universidad del Este M
- Université de Moncton M
- Université de Montréal O
- Université de Sherbrooke M
- Université du Québec à Montréal M
- Université du Québec en Outaouais M
- Université Laval M,D
- University at Albany, State University of New York M,D*
- University at Buffalo, the State University of New York M,D*
- The University of Akron M
- The University of Alabama M,D
- University of Alaska Anchorage M,O
- University of Arkansas M*
- University of Arkansas at Little Rock M
- The University of British Columbia M,D*
- University of Calgary M,D,O
- University of California, Berkeley M,D*
- University of California, Los Angeles M,D*
- University of Central Florida M,O*
- University of Chicago M,D*
- University of Cincinnati M
- University of Connecticut M,D*
- University of Denver M,D,O*
- University of Georgia M,D,O*
- University of Hawaii at Manoa M,D*
- University of Houston M,D*
- University of Illinois at Chicago M,D*
- University of Illinois at Urbana–Champaign M,D*
- The University of Iowa M,D*
- University of Kentucky M,D*
- University of Louisville M,D,O
- University of Maine M*
- University of Manitoba M
- University of Maryland, Baltimore M,D*
- University of Maryland, College Park *
- University of Michigan M,D*
- University of Minnesota, Duluth M*
- University of Minnesota, Twin Cities Campus M,D*
- University of Missouri–Columbia M*
- University of Missouri–Kansas City M*
- University of Missouri–St. Louis M
- University of Nebraska at Omaha M
- University of Nevada, Las Vegas M
- University of Nevada, Reno M*
- University of New England M,O
- University of New Hampshire M*
- University of New Hampshire at Manchester M,O
- The University of North Carolina at Chapel Hill M,D*
- The University of North Carolina at Charlotte M*
- The University of North Carolina at Greensboro M
- The University of North Carolina Wilmington M*
- University of North Dakota M
- University of Northern British Columbia M,D,O
- University of Northern Iowa M
- University of Oklahoma M*
- University of Ottawa M*
- University of Pennsylvania M,D*
- University of Pittsburgh M,D,O*
- University of Puerto Rico, Río Piedras M,D*
- University of Regina M,D
- University of St. Francis (IL) M
- University of St. Thomas (MN) M*
- University of South Carolina M,D*
- University of Southern California M,D*
- University of Southern Indiana M
- University of Southern Maine M
- University of Southern Mississippi M*
- University of South Florida M*
- The University of Tennessee M,D*
- The University of Texas at Arlington M,D*
- The University of Texas at Austin M,D*
- The University of Texas at San Antonio M*
- The University of Texas–Pan American M
- The University of Toledo M*
- University of Toronto M,D
- University of Utah M,D*
- University of Vermont M*
- University of Victoria M
- University of Washington M,D*
- University of Windsor M
- University of Wisconsin–Green Bay M
- University of Wisconsin–Madison M,D*
- University of Wisconsin–Milwaukee M,O
- University of Wisconsin–Oshkosh M
- University of Wyoming M
- Valdosta State University M
- Virginia Commonwealth University M,D*
- Walla Walla College M
- Washburn University M
- Washington University in St. Louis M,D*
- Wayne State University M,D,O*
- West Chester University of Pennsylvania M
- Western Kentucky University M
- Western Michigan University M*
- West Virginia University M*
- Wheelock College M
- Wichita State University M*
- Widener University M*
- Wilfrid Laurier University M,D
- Winthrop University M
- Yeshiva University M,D
- York University M,D*

SOCIOLOGY

- Acadia University M
- American University M,O*
- The American University in Cairo M
- American University of Beirut M
- Arizona State University M,D*
- Arkansas State University M,O
- Auburn University M*
- Ball State University M*
- Baylor University M,D*
- Boston College M,D*
- Boston University M,D*
- Bowling Green State University M,D*
- Brandeis University M,D*
- Brigham Young University M,D*
- Brooklyn College of the City University of New York M,D
- Brown University M,D*
- California State University, Bakersfield M
- California State University, Dominguez Hills M,O
- California State University, East Bay M
- California State University, Fullerton M
- California State University, Los Angeles M
- California State University, Northridge M
- California State University, Sacramento M*
- California State University, San Marcos M
- Carleton University M,D
- Case Western Reserve University D*
- The Catholic University of America M,D*
- Central European University M,D*
- Central Michigan University M*
- City College of the City University of New York M*
- Clark Atlanta University M
- Clemson University M*
- Cleveland State University M
- Colorado State University M,D*
- Columbia University M,D*
- Concordia University (Canada) M
- Cornell University M,D*
- Dalhousie University M,D
- DePaul University M*
- Drake University M*
- Duke University M,D*
- East Carolina University M*
- Eastern Michigan University M
- East Tennessee State University M
- Emory University M,D*
- Fayetteville State University M
- Fisk University M
- Florida Agricultural and Mechanical University M*
- Florida Atlantic University M
- Florida International University M,D*
- Florida State University M,D*
- Fordham University M,D*
- George Mason University M*
- The George Washington University M*
- Georgia Southern University M
- Georgia State University M,D*
- Graduate School and University Center of the City University of New York D*
- Harvard University D*
- Howard University M,D*
- Humboldt State University M
- Idaho State University M
- Illinois State University M*
- Indiana University Bloomington M,D*
- Indiana University of Pennsylvania M
- Indiana University–Purdue University Fort Wayne M
- Indiana University–Purdue University Indianapolis M*
- Iowa State University of Science and Technology M,D*
- Jackson State University M
- The Johns Hopkins University D*
- Kansas State University M,D*
- Kent State University M,D*
- Lakehead University M
- Laurentian University M
- Lehigh University M*
- Lincoln University (MO) M
- Louisiana State University and Agricultural and Mechanical College M,D*
- Loyola University Chicago M,D*
- Marshall University M
- McGill University M,D,O*
- McMaster University M,D
- Memorial University of Newfoundland M,D
- Michigan State University M,D*
- Middle Tennessee State University M,O*
- Minnesota State University Mankato M
- Mississippi College M
- Mississippi State University M,D
- Montclair State University M*
- Morehead State University M
- Morgan State University M*
- New Mexico Highlands University M
- New Mexico State University M
- The New School: A University M,D*
- New York University M,D*
- Norfolk State University M
- North Carolina Central University M*
- North Carolina State University M,D*
- North Dakota State University M,D
- Northeastern University M,D*
- Northern Arizona University M
- Northern Illinois University M
- Northwestern University D*
- The Ohio State University M,D*
- Ohio University M*

Oklahoma State University M,D*
Old Dominion University M*
Our Lady of the Lake University of San Antonio M
Penn State University Park M,D*
Portland State University M,D,O
Prairie View A&M University M
Princeton University D,O*
Purdue University M,D*
Queens College of the City University of New York M
Queen's University at Kingston M,D
Roosevelt University M
Rutgers, The State University of New Jersey, New Brunswick M,D*
St. John's University (NY) M
Sam Houston State University M
San Diego State University M*
San Jose State University M
Shippensburg University of Pennsylvania M
Simon Fraser University M,D
Southeastern Louisiana University M
Southern Connecticut State University M
Southern Illinois University Carbondale M,D*
Southern Illinois University Edwardsville M
Stanford University D*
State University of New York at Binghamton M,D*
State University of New York Institute of Technology M
Stony Brook University, State University of New York M,D*
Syracuse University M,D*
Teachers College Columbia University M,D*
Temple University M,D*
Texas A&M International University M
Texas A&M University M,D*
Texas A&M University–Commerce M
Texas A&M University–Kingsville M
Texas Southern University M
Texas State University-San Marcos M*
Texas Tech University M
Texas Woman's University M,D
Tulane University M,D*
Université de Montréal M,D
Université du Québec à Montréal M,D
Université Laval M,D
University at Albany, State University of New York M,D,O*
University at Buffalo, the State University of New York M,D*
The University of Akron M,D
The University of Alabama at Birmingham M,D*
University of Alberta M,D*
The University of Arizona M,D*
University of Arkansas M*
The University of British Columbia M,D*
University of Calgary M,D
University of California, Berkeley D*
University of California, Davis M,D*
University of California, Irvine M,D*
University of California, Los Angeles M,D*
University of California, Riverside M,D*
University of California, San Diego D*
University of California, San Francisco D
University of California, Santa Barbara D*
University of California, Santa Cruz D*
University of Central Florida M,D,O*
University of Central Missouri M
University of Chicago D*
University of Cincinnati M,D
University of Colorado at Boulder D*
University of Colorado at Colorado Springs M
University of Colorado at Denver and Health Sciences Center M*
University of Connecticut M,D*
University of Delaware M,D*
University of Florida M,D*
University of Georgia M,D*
University of Guelph M
University of Hawaii at Manoa M,D,O*
University of Houston M*
University of Houston–Clear Lake M
University of Illinois at Chicago M,D*
University of Illinois at Urbana–Champaign M,D*
University of Indianapolis M
The University of Iowa M,D*
University of Kansas M,D*
University of Kentucky M,D*
University of Lethbridge M,D
University of Louisville M
University of Manitoba M,D
University of Maryland, Baltimore County M,O*
University of Maryland, College Park M,D*
University of Massachusetts Amherst M,D*
University of Massachusetts Boston M
University of Massachusetts Lowell M*
University of Memphis M*
University of Miami M,D*
University of Michigan D*
University of Minnesota, Duluth M*
University of Minnesota, Twin Cities Campus M,D*
University of Mississippi M
University of Missouri–Columbia M,D*
University of Missouri–Kansas City M,D*
University of Missouri–St. Louis M
The University of Montana M*
University of Nebraska–Lincoln M,D*
University of Nevada, Las Vegas M,D
University of Nevada, Reno M*
University of New Brunswick Fredericton M,D
University of New Hampshire M,D*
University of New Mexico M,D*
University of New Orleans M
The University of North Carolina at Chapel Hill M,D*
The University of North Carolina at Charlotte M*
The University of North Carolina at Greensboro M
The University of North Carolina Wilmington M*
University of North Dakota M
University of Northern Colorado M
University of Northern Iowa M
University of North Florida M
University of North Texas M,D*
University of Notre Dame D*
University of Oklahoma M,D*
University of Oregon M,D*
University of Ottawa M*
University of Pennsylvania M,D*
University of Pittsburgh M,D*
University of Puerto Rico, Río Piedras M*
University of Regina M,D
University of Saskatchewan M,D
University of South Alabama M*
University of South Carolina M,D*
University of Southern California M,D*
University of South Florida M*
The University of Tennessee M,D*
The University of Texas at Arlington M*
The University of Texas at Austin M,D*
The University of Texas at Dallas M*
The University of Texas at El Paso M
The University of Texas at San Antonio M*
The University of Texas at Tyler M
The University of Texas–Pan American M
The University of Toledo M*
University of Toronto M,D
University of Utah M,D*
University of Victoria M,D
University of Virginia M,D*
University of Washington M,D*
University of Waterloo M,D*
The University of Western Ontario M,D
University of West Georgia M
University of Windsor M,D
University of Wisconsin–Madison M,D*
University of Wisconsin–Milwaukee M
University of Wyoming M
Utah State University M,D
Valdosta State University M
Vanderbilt University M,D*
Virginia Commonwealth University M,O*
Virginia Polytechnic Institute and State University M,D*
Washington State University M,D*
Wayne State University M,D*
West Chester University of Pennsylvania M,O
Western Illinois University M
Western Kentucky University M
Western Michigan University M,D*
West Virginia University M*
Wichita State University M*
Wilfrid Laurier University M
William Paterson University of New Jersey M*
Yale University D*
York University M,D*

SOFTWARE ENGINEERING

Andrews University M
Auburn University M,D*
Bowling Green State University M*
California State University, East Bay M
California State University, Fullerton M
California State University, Sacramento M*
Carnegie Mellon University M,D*
Carroll College M
Central Michigan University M,O*
Cleveland State University M,D
Colorado Technical University—Colorado Springs M,D
Colorado Technical University—Denver M
Colorado Technical University—Sioux Falls M
Concordia University (Canada) M,D,O
DePaul University M,D*
Drexel University M*
East Tennessee State University M
Embry-Riddle Aeronautical University (FL) M*
Fairfield University M*
Florida Agricultural and Mechanical University M*
Florida Institute of Technology M,D*
Florida State University M,D*
Gannon University M
George Mason University M*
Grand Valley State University M
Illinois Institute of Technology M,D*
International Technological University M
Jacksonville State University M
Kansas State University M,D*
Loyola College in Maryland M
Loyola University Chicago M*
Marist College M,O*
McMaster University M,D
Mercer University M
Miami University M,O*
Monmouth University M,O
National University M
Naval Postgraduate School M,D
North Dakota State University M,D,O
Northern Kentucky University M,O
Oakland University M*
Penn State Great Valley M
Polytechnic University, Brooklyn Campus O*
Polytechnic University, Long Island Graduate Center M
Portland State University M,D
Regis University M,O
Rochester Institute of Technology M
Royal Military College of Canada M,D
St. Mary's University of San Antonio M
San Jose State University M
Santa Clara University M,D,O
Seattle University M
Southern Methodist University M,D*
Southern Polytechnic State University M
Stevens Institute of Technology M,O*
Stony Brook University, State University of New York M,D,O*
Stratford University M
Texas State University-San Marcos M*
Texas Tech University M,D
Towson University M,D,O
Université du Québec en Outaouais O
Université Laval O
The University of Alabama in Huntsville M,D,O
University of Alaska Fairbanks M
The University of British Columbia M*
University of Calgary M,D
University of Colorado at Colorado Springs M
University of Connecticut M,D*
University of Houston–Clear Lake M
University of Management and Technology M,O
University of Michigan–Dearborn M*
University of Missouri–Kansas City M,D*
University of New Haven M*
University of St. Thomas (MN) M,O*
The University of Scranton M
University of South Carolina M,D*
University of Southern California M*
The University of Texas at Arlington M,D*
The University of Texas at Dallas M,D*
University of Waterloo M,D*
University of West Florida M
University of Wisconsin–La Crosse M
Walden University M,O
West Virginia University M*
Widener University M*
Winthrop University M,O

SPANISH

American University M,O*
Appalachian State University M
Arizona State University M,D*
Arkansas Tech University M
Asbury College M,O
Auburn University M*
Baylor University M*
Bennington College M*
Boston College M,D*
Boston University M,D*
Bowling Green State University M*
Brigham Young University M*
Brooklyn College of the City University of New York M,D
California State University, Bakersfield M
California State University, Fresno M
California State University, Fullerton M
California State University, Long Beach M
California State University, Los Angeles M
California State University, Northridge M
California State University, Sacramento M*
California State University, San Bernardino M
California State University, San Marcos M
The Catholic University of America M,D*
Central Connecticut State University M,O
Central Michigan University M*
City College of the City University of New York M*
Cleveland State University M
The College of New Jersey M
Columbia University M,D*
Cornell University D*
Duke University D*
Eastern Michigan University M
Emory University D,O*
Florida Atlantic University M
Florida International University M,D*
Florida State University M,D*
Framingham State College M*
Georgetown University M,D*
Georgia State University M*
Graduate School and University Center of the City University of New York D*
Harvard University M,D*
Hofstra University M*
Howard University M*
Hunter College of the City University of New York M
Illinois State University M*
Indiana State University M,O*
Indiana University Bloomington M,D*
Inter American University of Puerto Rico, Metropolitan Campus M
Inter American University of Puerto Rico, Ponce Campus M
Iona College M*
The Johns Hopkins University D*
Kansas State University M*
Kent State University M*
Lehman College of the City University of New York M
Long Island University, C.W. Post Campus M*
Louisiana State University and Agricultural and Mechanical College M*
Loyola University Chicago M*
Marquette University M
Miami University M*
Michigan State University M,D*
Middlebury College M,D

*P—first professional degree; M—master's degree; D—doctorate; O—other advanced degree; *full description and/or announcement in Book 2, 3, 4, 5, or 6*

Millersville University of Pennsylvania M
Minnesota State University Mankato M
Mississippi State University M
Missouri State University M*
Montclair State University M,O*
New Mexico Highlands University M
New Mexico State University M
New York University M,D*
North Carolina State University M*
Northern Illinois University M
Nova Southeastern University M,O*
The Ohio State University M,D*
Ohio University M*
Penn State University Park M,D*
Portland State University M
Princeton University D*
Purdue University M,D*
Queens College of the City University of New York M
Queen's University at Kingston M
Rice University M*
Roosevelt University M
Rutgers, The State University of New Jersey, New Brunswick M,D*
St. John's University (NY) M,O
Saint Louis University M*
Saint Louis University, Madrid M*
Salem State College M
San Diego State University M*
San Francisco State University M
San Jose State University M
Simmons College M
Southern Connecticut State University M
Stanford University M,D*
State University of New York at Binghamton M,O*
Syracuse University M*
Temple University M,D*
Texas A&M International University M,D
Texas A&M University M,D*
Texas A&M University–Commerce M,D
Texas A&M University–Kingsville M
Texas State University-San Marcos M*
Texas Tech University M,D*
Tulane University M,D*
Université de Montréal M
Université Laval M,D
University at Albany, State University of New York M,D*
University at Buffalo, the State University of New York M,D*
The University of Akron M
The University of Alabama M,D
The University of Arizona M,D*
University of Arkansas M*
University of California, Berkeley M,D*
University of California, Davis M,D*
University of California, Irvine M,D*
University of California, Los Angeles M*
University of California, Riverside M,D*
University of California, San Diego M*
University of California, Santa Barbara M,D*
University of Central Florida M*
University of Chicago M,D*
University of Cincinnati M,D
University of Colorado at Boulder M,D*
University of Colorado at Denver and Health Sciences Center M*
University of Connecticut M,D*
University of Delaware M*
University of Florida M,D*
University of Georgia M*
University of Hawaii at Manoa M*
University of Houston M,D*
The University of Iowa M,D*
University of Kansas M,D*
University of Lethbridge M,D
University of Louisville M
University of Manitoba M,D
University of Maryland, Baltimore County M*
University of Maryland, College Park M,D*
University of Massachusetts Amherst M,D*
University of Memphis M*
University of Miami M,D*
University of Michigan D*
University of Minnesota, Twin Cities Campus M,D*
University of Mississippi M
University of Missouri–Columbia M,D*
The University of Montana M*
University of Nebraska–Lincoln M,D*
University of Nevada, Las Vegas M
University of Nevada, Reno M*
University of New Hampshire M*
University of New Mexico M,D*
The University of North Carolina at Chapel Hill M,D*
The University of North Carolina at Charlotte M*
The University of North Carolina at Greensboro M,O
University of Northern Colorado M
University of Northern Iowa M
University of North Texas M*
University of Notre Dame M*
University of Oklahoma M,D*
University of Oregon M*
University of Ottawa M,D*
University of Pennsylvania M,D*
University of Pittsburgh M,D*
University of Rhode Island M
University of South Carolina M,D*
University of South Florida M*
The University of Tennessee M,D*
The University of Texas at Arlington M*
The University of Texas at Austin M,D*
The University of Texas at Brownsville M
The University of Texas at El Paso M
The University of Texas at San Antonio M*
The University of Texas–Pan American M
The University of Toledo M*
University of Toronto M,D
University of Utah M,D*
University of Virginia M,D*
University of Washington M*
The University of Western Ontario M,D
University of Wisconsin–Madison M,D*
University of Wisconsin–Milwaukee M
University of Wyoming M
Vanderbilt University M,D*
Washington State University M*
Washington University in St. Louis M,D*
Wayne State University M*
West Chester University of Pennsylvania M
Western Michigan University M*
West Virginia University M*
Wichita State University M*
Winthrop University M
Yale University M,D*

SPECIAL EDUCATION

Acadia University M
Adams State College M
Adelphi University M,O*
Alabama Agricultural and Mechanical University M,O
Alabama State University M,O
Albany State University M
Albright College M
Alcorn State University M,O
Alliant International University–Irvine M,O*
Alliant International University–San Francisco M,O*
American International College M,D,O
American University M*
American University of Puerto Rico M
Andrews University M,D,O
Appalachian State University M
Arcadia University M,D,O
Arizona State University M*
Arizona State University at the West campus M,D,O
Arkansas State University M,D,O
Armstrong Atlantic State University M
Asbury College M,O
Ashland University M
Assumption College M*
Auburn University M,D,O*
Auburn University Montgomery M,O
Augusta State University M,O
Averett University M
Azusa Pacific University M
Baldwin-Wallace College M
Ball State University M,D,O*
Bank Street College of Education M*
Barry University M,D,O*
Bayamón Central University M
Bellarmine University M
Bemidji State University M
Benedictine University M
Bethel College (TN) M
Bethel University M,D,O
Bloomsburg University of Pennsylvania M
Bob Jones University P,M,D,O
Boise State University M
Boston College M,O*
Boston University M,D,O*
Bowie State University M
Bowling Green State University M*
Brandon University M,O
Brenau University M,O
Bridgewater State College M
Brigham Young University M,D,O*
Brooklyn College of the City University of New York M
Buffalo State College, State University of New York M
Butler University M
Caldwell College M
California Baptist University M
California Lutheran University M
California State University, Bakersfield M
California State University, Chico M
California State University, Dominguez Hills M
California State University, East Bay M
California State University, Fresno M
California State University, Fullerton M
California State University, Long Beach M
California State University, Los Angeles M
California State University, Northridge M
California State University, Sacramento M*
California State University, San Bernardino M
California University of Pennsylvania M
Calvin College M
Campbellsville University M
Canisius College M
Cardinal Stritch University M*
Caribbean University M,D
Carlos Albizu University, Miami Campus M,D
Carlow University M
Castleton State College M,O
Centenary College M
Central Connecticut State University M
Central Michigan University M*
Central Washington University M
Chapman University M
Chatham University M
Cheyney University of Pennsylvania M
Chicago State University M
City College of the City University of New York M*
Clarion University of Pennsylvania M
Clarke College M
Clemson University M*
Cleveland State University M*
College of Charleston M*
The College of New Jersey M,O
The College of New Rochelle M
College of St. Joseph M
The College of Saint Rose M,O*
College of Santa Fe M
College of Staten Island of the City University of New York M
The College of William and Mary M
Columbia International University M,D,O
Columbus State University M,O
Concordia University, St. Paul M,O
Concordia University Wisconsin M
Converse College M
Coppin State University M
Creighton University M*
Curry College M,O
Daemen College M
Delaware State University M
Delta State University M
DePaul University M,D*
DeSales University M,O
Dominican College M
Dominican University M
Dominican University of California O
Dowling College M,D,O
Drake University M*
Duquesne University M*
D'Youville College M,O*
East Carolina University M*
Eastern Illinois University M
Eastern Kentucky University M*
Eastern Michigan University M,O
Eastern Nazarene College M,O
Eastern New Mexico University M
Eastern Washington University M
East Stroudsburg University of Pennsylvania M
East Tennessee State University M,D
Edgewood College M,D,O
Edinboro University of Pennsylvania M
Elmhurst College M
Elms College M,O
Elon University M
Emporia State University M
Endicott College M
Fairfield University M,O*
Fairleigh Dickinson University, Metropolitan Campus M*
Fairmont State University M
Felician College M*
Ferris State University M
Fitchburg State College M
Florida Atlantic University M,D
Florida Atlantic University, Jupiter Campus M
Florida Gulf Coast University M
Florida International University M,D,O*
Florida State University M,D,O*
Fontbonne University M
Fordham University M,D,O*
Fort Hays State University M
Framingham State College M*
Francis Marion University M
Fresno Pacific University M
Frostburg State University M
Furman University M
Gallaudet University M,D,O
Geneva College M*
George Mason University M*
The George Washington University M,D,O*
Georgia College & State University M
Georgian Court University M,O
Georgia Southern University M
Georgia Southwestern State University M,O
Georgia State University M,D*
Gonzaga University M
Governors State University M
Grambling State University M,D
Grand Valley State University M
Greensboro College M
Gwynedd-Mercy College M
Hampton University M*
Harding University M,O
Hebrew College M,O
Henderson State University M,O
Heritage University M
High Point University M
Hofstra University M,O*
Holy Names University M,O
Hood College M,O
Howard University M,O*
Hunter College of the City University of New York M
Idaho State University M,D,O
Illinois State University M,D*
Immaculata University M,D,O
Indiana University Bloomington M,D,O*
Indiana University of Pennsylvania M
Indiana University South Bend M
Inter American University of Puerto Rico, Metropolitan Campus M
Inter American University of Puerto Rico, San Germán Campus M
Iowa State University of Science and Technology M,D*
Jackson State University M,O
Jacksonville State University M
James Madison University M
The Johns Hopkins University M,D,O*
Johnson State College M
Kansas State University M,D*
Kean University M
Keene State College M,O
Kennesaw State University M
Kent State University M,D,O*
Kentucky State University M
Kutztown University of Pennsylvania M,O
Lamar University M,D*
Lancaster Bible College M
La Sierra University M,D,O
Lee University M
Lehigh University M,D,O*
Lehman College of the City University of New York M
Lesley University M,D,O*
Lewis & Clark College M
Lewis University M
Liberty University M,D,O
Lincoln University (MO) M,O
Lipscomb University M
Long Island University, Brentwood Campus M
Long Island University, Brooklyn Campus M*
Long Island University, C.W. Post Campus M*
Long Island University, Rockland Graduate Campus M
Long Island University, Southampton Graduate Campus M

Institution	Degrees
Long Island University, Westchester Graduate Campus	M
Longwood University	M*
Loras College	M
Louisiana Tech University	M,D
Loyola College in Maryland	M,O
Loyola Marymount University	M
Loyola University Chicago	M*
Lynchburg College	M
Lyndon State College	M
Lynn University	M,D
Madonna University	M
Malone College	M
Manhattan College	M
Manhattanville College	M*
Marshall University	M
Marymount University	M,O
Marywood University	M*
Massachusetts College of Liberal Arts	M
McDaniel College	M
Medaille College	M
Mercy College	M
Mercyhurst College	M,O
Miami University	M*
Michigan State University	M,D,O*
MidAmerica Nazarene University	M
Middle Tennessee State University	M,O*
Midwestern State University	M
Millersville University of Pennsylvania	M
Minnesota State University Mankato	M,O
Minnesota State University Moorhead	M
Minot State University	M
Mississippi College	M,O
Mississippi State University	M,D,O
Missouri State University	M,O*
Monmouth University	M,O
Montana State University–Billings	M
Montclair State University	M,O*
Morehead State University	M
Morningside College	M
Mount Saint Mary College	M
Mount St. Mary's College	M
Mount Saint Vincent University	M
Murray State University	M
National-Louis University	M,O
National University	M
New England College	M
New Jersey City University	M
New Mexico Highlands University	M
New Mexico State University	M,D
New York University	M*
Niagara University	M
Norfolk State University	M
North Carolina Central University	M
North Carolina State University	M*
Northeastern Illinois University	M
Northeastern University	M,D,O*
Northern Arizona University	M,O
Northern Illinois University	M,D
Northern Kentucky University	O
Northern Michigan University	M
Northern State University	M
North Georgia College & State University	M,O
Northwestern State University of Louisiana	M,O
Northwestern University	M,D*
Northwest Missouri State University	M
Northwest Nazarene University	M
Notre Dame College (OH)	M,O
Notre Dame de Namur University	M,O
Nova Southeastern University	M,D,O*
Oakland University	M,O*
Ohio University	M,D*
Old Dominion University	M,D*
Ottawa University	M
Our Lady of the Lake University of San Antonio	M
Pacific University	M
Park University	M
Penn State Great Valley	M
Penn State University Park	M,D*
Pennsylvania College of Optometry	M,D,O
Pittsburg State University	M
Plymouth State University	M,O
Portland State University	M,D
Prairie View A&M University	M
Pratt Institute	M*
Providence College	M*
Purdue University	M,D,O*
Queens College of the City University of New York	M
Radford University	M
Regent University	M,D,O
Regis University	M,O
Rhode Island College	M,O
Rider University	M,O*
Rivier College	M,O
Roberts Wesleyan College	M,O
Rochester Institute of Technology	M
Rockford College	M
Roosevelt University	M
Rowan University	M
Rutgers, The State University of New Jersey, New Brunswick	M,D*
Sage Graduate School	M
Saginaw Valley State University	M
St. Ambrose University	M
St. Cloud State University	M
St. John Fisher College	M,O
St. John's University (NY)	M
Saint Joseph College	M
St. Joseph's College, New York	M*
St. Joseph's College, Suffolk Campus	M
Saint Joseph's University	M,D,O*
Saint Louis University	M,D*
Saint Martin's University	M
Saint Mary's College of California	M
Saint Michael's College	M,O
St. Thomas Aquinas College	M,O*
St. Thomas University	M,D,O
Saint Vincent College	M
Saint Xavier University	M,O
Salem College	M
Salem State College	M
Sam Houston State University	M
San Diego State University	M*
San Francisco State University	M,D,O
San Jose State University	M,O
Santa Clara University	M,O
Seattle University	M,O
Seton Hill University	M,O
Shippensburg University of Pennsylvania	M
Silver Lake College	M
Simmons College	M,D,O
Slippery Rock University of Pennsylvania	M
Smith College	M*
Sonoma State University	M
South Carolina State University	M
Southeastern Louisiana University	M
Southeast Missouri State University	M
Southern Connecticut State University	M,O
Southern Illinois University Carbondale	M*
Southern Illinois University Edwardsville	M
Southern New Hampshire University	M,O*
Southern Oregon University	M
Southern University and Agricultural and Mechanical College	M,D*
Southwestern College (KS)	M
Southwestern Oklahoma State University	M
Southwest Minnesota State University	M
Spalding University	M
State University of New York at Binghamton	M*
State University of New York at New Paltz	M
State University of New York at Oswego	M
State University of New York at Plattsburgh	M
State University of New York College at Cortland	M*
State University of New York College at Potsdam	M
Stephen F. Austin State University	M
Stetson University	M
Syracuse University	M,D*
Tarleton State University	M,D,O
Teachers College Columbia University	M,D,O*
Temple University	M,D*
Tennessee State University	M,D*
Tennessee Technological University	M,O*
Texas A&M International University	M
Texas A&M University	M,D*
Texas A&M University–Commerce	M,D
Texas A&M University–Corpus Christi	M
Texas A&M University–Kingsville	M
Texas A&M University–Texarkana	M
Texas Christian University	M
Texas Southern University	M,D
Texas State University-San Marcos	M*
Texas Tech University	M,D,O
Texas Woman's University	M,D
Towson University	M
Trinity Baptist College	M
Trinity (Washington) University	M
Union College (KY)	M
Universidad del Turabo	M
Universidad Metropolitana	M
Université de Sherbrooke	M,O
University at Albany, State University of New York	M*
University at Buffalo, the State University of New York	M,D,O*
The University of Akron	M
The University of Alabama	M,D,O
The University of Alabama at Birmingham	M*
University of Alaska Anchorage	M,O
University of Alberta	M,D*
The University of Arizona	M,D,O*
University of Arkansas	M*
University of Arkansas at Little Rock	M
The University of British Columbia	M,D,O*
University of Calgary	M,D
University of California, Berkeley	D*
University of California, Los Angeles	D*
University of California, Santa Barbara	M,D*
University of Central Arkansas	M
University of Central Florida	M,D*
University of Central Missouri	M,O
University of Central Oklahoma	M
University of Cincinnati	M,D
University of Colorado at Colorado Springs	M,D
University of Connecticut	M,D*
University of Dayton	M*
University of Delaware	M,D*
University of Detroit Mercy	M
The University of Findlay	M
University of Florida	M,D,O*
University of Georgia	M,D,O*
University of Guam	M
University of Hawaii at Manoa	M,D*
University of Houston	M,D*
University of Idaho	M,O*
University of Illinois at Chicago	M,D*
University of Illinois at Urbana–Champaign	M,D,O*
The University of Iowa	M,D*
University of Kansas	M,D*
University of Kentucky	M,D*
University of La Verne	M
University of Louisiana at Monroe	M
University of Louisville	M,D
University of Maine	M,O*
University of Manitoba	M
University of Mary	M
University of Maryland, College Park	M,D,O*
University of Maryland Eastern Shore	M*
University of Massachusetts Amherst	M,D,O*
University of Massachusetts Boston	M
University of Memphis	M,D*
University of Miami	M,D,O*
University of Michigan	M,D*
University of Michigan–Dearborn	M*
University of Michigan–Flint	M*
University of Minnesota, Twin Cities Campus	M,D,O*
University of Missouri–Columbia	M,D*
University of Missouri–Kansas City	M,D,O*
University of Missouri–St. Louis	M,D
University of Nebraska at Kearney	M
University of Nebraska at Omaha	M
University of Nebraska–Lincoln	M*
University of Nevada, Las Vegas	M,D,O
University of Nevada, Reno	M,D,O*
University of New Hampshire	M*
University of New Mexico	M,D,O*
University of New Orleans	M,D,O
University of North Alabama	M
The University of North Carolina at Charlotte	M,D*
The University of North Carolina at Greensboro	M,D,O
The University of North Carolina Wilmington	M*
University of North Dakota	M,D
University of Northern Colorado	M,D
University of Northern Iowa	M,D
University of North Florida	M
University of North Texas	M,D*
University of Oklahoma	M,D*
University of Oklahoma Health Sciences Center	M,D,O
University of Phoenix–Metro Detroit Campus	M
University of Phoenix–Omaha Campus	M
University of Phoenix–Southern Arizona Campus	M,O
University of Pittsburgh	M,D*
University of Portland	M
University of Puerto Rico, Medical Sciences Campus	O*
University of Puerto Rico, Río Piedras	M*
University of Rio Grande	M
University of St. Francis (IL)	M
University of Saint Francis (IN)	M
University of Saint Mary	M
University of St. Thomas (MN)	M,O*
University of Saskatchewan	M,D,O
The University of Scranton	M
University of South Alabama	M,O*
University of South Carolina	M,D*
University of South Carolina Upstate	M
The University of South Dakota	M
University of Southern Maine	M
University of Southern Mississippi	M,D,O*
University of South Florida	M*
The University of Tennessee	M,D,O*
The University of Tennessee at Chattanooga	M,D,O
The University of Texas at Austin	M,D*
The University of Texas at Brownsville	M
The University of Texas at San Antonio	M*
The University of Texas at Tyler	M
The University of Texas of the Permian Basin	M
The University of Texas–Pan American	M
University of the Cumberlands	M
University of the District of Columbia	M
University of the Incarnate Word	M,D
University of the Pacific	M,D
The University of Toledo	M,D,O*
University of Utah	M,D*
University of Vermont	M*
University of Victoria	M,D
University of Virginia	M,D,O*
University of Washington	M,D*
The University of West Alabama	M
The University of Western Ontario	M
University of West Florida	M
University of West Georgia	M,O
University of Wisconsin–Eau Claire	M
University of Wisconsin–La Crosse	M
University of Wisconsin–Madison	M,D*
University of Wisconsin–Milwaukee	M
University of Wisconsin–Oshkosh	M
University of Wisconsin–Stevens Point	M
University of Wisconsin–Superior	M
University of Wisconsin–Whitewater	M*
University of Wyoming	M,O
Utah State University	M,D,O
Valdosta State University	M,O
Vanderbilt University	M,D*
Virginia Commonwealth University	M*
Virginia Polytechnic Institute and State University	D,O*
Walden University	M,D
Walla Walla College	M
Washburn University	M
Washington University in St. Louis	M,D*
Wayne State College	M
Wayne State University	M,D,O*
Webster University	M,O
West Chester University of Pennsylvania	M
Western Carolina University	M*
Western Connecticut State University	M*
Western Illinois University	M
Western Kentucky University	M
Western Michigan University	M,D*
Western New Mexico University	M
Western Oregon University	M
Westfield State College	M

P—first professional degree; M—master's degree; D—doctorate; O—other advanced degree;
**full description and/or announcement in Book 2, 3, 4, 5, or 6*

West Texas A&M University M
West Virginia University M,D*
Wheelock College M
Whitworth University M
Wichita State University M*
Widener University M,D*
Wilkes University M
William Carey University M,O
William Paterson University of New Jersey M*
Wilmington College (DE) M
Wilmington College (OH) M
Winona State University M
Winthrop University M
Worcester State College M
Wright State University M*
Xavier University M*
Youngstown State University M

SPEECH AND INTERPERSONAL COMMUNICATION

Abilene Christian University M
Arizona State University M,D*
Arkansas State University M,O
Ball State University M*
Bob Jones University P,M,D,O
Bowling Green State University M,D*
Brooklyn College of the City University of New York M,D
California State University, Fullerton M
California State University, Los Angeles M
California State University, Northridge M
Central Michigan University M*
Colorado State University M*
Drake University M*
Eastern Illinois University M
Eastern Michigan University M
Florida State University M,D*
Georgia State University M,D*
Hofstra University M*
Idaho State University M
Indiana University Bloomington M,D*
Kansas State University M*
Louisiana Tech University M
Marquette University M
Miami University M*
Minnesota State University Mankato M
Montclair State University M*
New York University M,D*
North Dakota State University M,D
Northeastern Illinois University M
Northeastern University D*
Northwestern University M,D*
Ohio University D*
Portland State University M,O
Rensselaer Polytechnic Institute M,D*
San Francisco State University M
San Jose State University M
Seton Hall University M*
Southern Illinois University Carbondale M,D*
Southern Illinois University Edwardsville M
Texas A&M University–Commerce M
Texas Christian University M
Texas Southern University M
The University of Alabama M
University of Arkansas at Little Rock M
University of Central Missouri M
University of Denver M,D*
University of Georgia M,D*
University of Hawaii at Manoa M*
University of Houston M*
University of Illinois at Urbana–Champaign M,D*
University of Maryland, College Park M,D*
University of Nevada, Reno M*
University of South Carolina M,D*
University of Southern California M,D*
University of Southern Mississippi M,D*
The University of Tennessee M,D*
The University of Texas at Tyler M
University of Wisconsin–Stevens Point M
University of Wisconsin–Superior M
Wake Forest University M*
Washington University in St. Louis M,D*
Wayne State University M,D*

SPORT PSYCHOLOGY

Argosy University, Phoenix Campus M,D,O*
Barry University M*
California State University, Fresno M
California University of Pennsylvania M
Capella University M,D,O
Cleveland State University M
Florida State University M,D*
John F. Kennedy University M
Memorial University of Newfoundland M
Purdue University M,D*
Queen's University at Kingston M,D
Southern Connecticut State University M
Springfield College M,D,O*
University of Florida M,D*
The University of Iowa M,D*
University of Rhode Island M,D
West Virginia University M,D*

SPORTS MANAGEMENT

American Public University System M
Ashland University M
Barry University M*
Belmont University M
Boise State University M
Bowling Green State University M*
Brooklyn College of the City University of New York M
California University of Pennsylvania M
Canisius College M
Central Michigan University M*
Cleveland State University M
Concordia University (CA) M
Concordia University (Canada) M,D,O
Duquesne University M*
Eastern Kentucky University M*
Eastern Michigan University M*
East Stroudsburg University of Pennsylvania M
East Tennessee State University M
Endicott College M
Florida Atlantic University M
Florida International University M*
Florida State University M,D,O*
The George Washington University M,O*
Georgia Southern University M
Georgia State University M*
Gonzaga University M
Grambling State University M
Hardin-Simmons University M
Henderson State University M
Howard University M*
Indiana State University M*
Indiana University Bloomington M,D,O*
Indiana University of Pennsylvania M
Ithaca College M
Kent State University M*
Lindenwood University M
Lynn University M,D
Manhattanville College M*
Marshall University M*
Millersville University of Pennsylvania M
Mississippi State University M
Missouri State University M*
Montana State University–Billings M
Montclair State University M,O*
Morehead State University M
Neumann College M
New Mexico Highlands University M
New York University M,O*
North Carolina State University M,D*
North Dakota State University M
Northern Illinois University M
Nova Southeastern University M,O*
Ohio University M*
Old Dominion University M*
Robert Morris University M
St. Cloud State University M
St. Edward's University M,O
Saint Leo University M
Seattle University M
Seton Hall University M*
Slippery Rock University of Pennsylvania M
Southern New Hampshire University M,D,O*
Springfield College M,D,O*
State University of New York College at Cortland M*
Temple University M*
Tiffin University M
Troy University M
United States Sports Academy M,D*
The University of Alabama M,D
University of Alberta M*
University of Central Florida M,O*
University of Dallas M
University of Florida M*
The University of Iowa M*
University of Louisville M
University of Mary Hardin-Baylor M
University of Massachusetts Amherst M,D*
University of Miami M*
University of Michigan M,D*
University of Minnesota, Twin Cities Campus M,D,O*
University of Nevada, Las Vegas M,D
University of New Brunswick Fredericton M
University of New Haven M*
The University of North Carolina at Chapel Hill M*
The University of North Carolina at Charlotte M*
University of Northern Colorado M,D
University of Northern Iowa M,D
University of Rhode Island M,D
University of San Francisco M
University of South Carolina M*
University of Southern Maine M,O
University of Southern Mississippi M,D*
The University of Tennessee M,D*
University of the Incarnate Word M,O
University of Wisconsin–La Crosse M
Valparaiso University M
Washington State University M,D*
Wayne State University M*
Webber International University M*
West Chester University of Pennsylvania M,O
Western Illinois University M
Western Michigan University M*
West Virginia University M,D*
Wichita State University M*
Wingate University M
Xavier University M*

STATISTICS

Acadia University M
American University M,O*
American University of Beirut M
Arizona State University M,D*
Auburn University M,D*
Ball State University M*
Baylor University M,D*
Bernard M. Baruch College of the City University of New York M*
Bowling Green State University M,D*
Brigham Young University M*
Brock University M
California State University, East Bay M
California State University, Fullerton M
California State University, Sacramento M*
Carnegie Mellon University M,D*
Case Western Reserve University M,D*
Central Connecticut State University M,O
Claremont Graduate University M,D
Clemson University M,D*
Colorado State University M,D*
Columbia University M,D*
Cornell University M,D*
Dalhousie University M,D
Duke University D*
Eastern Michigan University M
Florida Atlantic University M,D
Florida International University M*
Florida State University M,D*
George Mason University M,D,O*
The George Washington University M,D,O*
Georgia Institute of Technology M,D*
Harvard University M,D*
Indiana University Bloomington M,D*
Iowa State University of Science and Technology M,D*
James Madison University M
The Johns Hopkins University M,D*
Kansas State University M,D*
Kean University M
Lakehead University M
Lehigh University M,D*
Louisiana State University and Agricultural and Mechanical College M*
Louisiana Tech University M
Loyola University Chicago M*
Marquette University M,D
McGill University M,D,O*
McMaster University M
McNeese State University M
Memorial University of Newfoundland M,D
Miami University M*
Michigan State University M,D*
Minnesota State University Mankato M
Mississippi State University M,D
Montana State University M,D
Montclair State University M,O*
Murray State University M
New Mexico State University M
New York University M,D*
North Carolina State University M,D*
North Dakota State University M,D,O
Northern Arizona University M
Northern Illinois University M
Northwestern University M,D*
Oakland University O*
The Ohio State University M,D*
Oklahoma State University M,D*
Oregon State University M,D*
Penn State University Park M,D*
Portland State University M,D
Princeton University M,D*
Purdue University M,D,O*
Queen's University at Kingston M,D
Rensselaer Polytechnic Institute M,D*
Rice University M,D*
Rochester Institute of Technology M,O
Rutgers, The State University of New Jersey, New Brunswick M,D*
St. John's University (NY) M
Sam Houston State University M
San Diego State University M*
Simon Fraser University M,D
South Dakota State University M,D
Southern Illinois University Carbondale M,D*
Southern Methodist University M,D*
Stanford University M,D*
State University of New York at Binghamton M,D*
Stephen F. Austin State University M
Stevens Institute of Technology M,O*
Stony Brook University, State University of New York M,D*
Temple University M,D*
Texas A&M University M,D*
Texas Tech University M
Tulane University M,D*
Université de Montréal M,D
Université Laval M
University at Albany, State University of New York M,D,O*
The University of Akron M
The University of Alabama M,D
University of Alaska Fairbanks M,D
University of Alberta M,D,O*
The University of Arizona M,D*
University of Arkansas M*
University of Arkansas at Little Rock M
The University of British Columbia M,D*
University of Calgary M,D
University of California, Berkeley M,D*
University of California, Davis M,D*
University of California, Los Angeles M,D*
University of California, Riverside M,D*
University of California, San Diego M,D*
University of California, Santa Barbara M,D*
University of California, Santa Cruz M*
University of Central Florida M,O*
University of Central Oklahoma M
University of Chicago M,D*
University of Cincinnati M,D*
University of Connecticut M,D*
University of Delaware M*
University of Denver M*
University of Florida M,D*
University of Georgia M,D*
University of Guelph M,D
University of Houston–Clear Lake M
University of Idaho M*
University of Illinois at Chicago M,D*
University of Illinois at Urbana–Champaign M,D*
The University of Iowa M,D,O*
University of Kentucky M,D*
University of Manitoba M,D
University of Maryland, Baltimore County M,D*
University of Maryland, College Park M,D*
University of Massachusetts Amherst M,D*
University of Memphis M,D*
University of Miami M*
University of Michigan M,D*
University of Minnesota, Twin Cities Campus M,D*
University of Missouri–Columbia M,D*
University of Missouri–Kansas City M,D*
University of Missouri–Rolla M,D*
University of Nebraska–Lincoln M,D*
University of Nevada, Las Vegas M,D
University of New Brunswick Fredericton M,D
University of New Hampshire M,D*
University of New Hampshire at Manchester M,O

- University of New Mexico M,D*
- The University of North Carolina at Chapel Hill M,D*
- University of North Florida M
- University of Ottawa M,D*
- University of Pennsylvania M,D*
- University of Pittsburgh M,D*
- University of Puerto Rico, Mayagüez Campus M*
- University of Regina M,D
- University of Rhode Island M,D,O
- University of Rochester M,D*
- University of Saskatchewan M,D
- University of South Carolina M,D,O*
- The University of South Dakota D
- University of Southern California M*
- University of Southern Maine M
- The University of Tennessee M,D*
- The University of Texas at Austin M*
- The University of Texas at Dallas M,D*
- The University of Texas at El Paso M
- The University of Texas at San Antonio M,D*
- The University of Toledo M,D*
- University of Toronto M,D
- University of Utah M,D*
- University of Vermont M*
- University of Victoria M,D
- University of Virginia M,D*
- University of Washington M,D*
- University of Waterloo M,D*
- The University of Western Ontario M,D
- University of Windsor M,D
- University of Wisconsin–Madison M,D*
- University of Wyoming M,D
- Utah State University M,D
- Virginia Commonwealth University M,O*
- Virginia Polytechnic Institute and State University M,D*
- Washington State University M*
- Washington University in St. Louis M,D*
- Wayne State University M,D*
- Western Michigan University M,D*
- West Virginia University M,D*
- Wichita State University M,D*
- Yale University M,D*
- York University M,D*

STRUCTURAL BIOLOGY

- Baylor College of Medicine D*
- Brandeis University M,D*
- Cornell University M,D*
- Cornell University, Joan and Sanford I. Weill Medical College and Graduate School of Medical Sciences D*
- Duke University O*
- Florida State University D*
- Harvard University D*
- Illinois State University M,D*
- Iowa State University of Science and Technology D*
- Massachusetts Institute of Technology D*
- Mayo Graduate School D*
- Mount Sinai School of Medicine of New York University M,D*
- New York University D*
- Northwestern University D*
- Stanford University D*
- Stony Brook University, State University of New York D*
- Syracuse University D*
- Thomas Jefferson University D*
- Tulane University M,D*
- University at Albany, State University of New York M,D*
- University at Buffalo, the State University of New York M,D*
- University of California, San Diego D*
- University of Connecticut M,D*
- University of Pittsburgh D*
- The University of Texas Health Science Center at San Antonio M,D*
- The University of Texas Medical Branch D*
- University of Washington D*
- Yale University D*

STRUCTURAL ENGINEERING

- Auburn University M,D*
- California State University, Northridge M
- The Catholic University of America M,D*
- Cornell University M,D*
- École Polytechnique de Montréal M,D,O
- Illinois Institute of Technology M,D*
- Instituto Tecnologico de Santo Domingo M
- Iowa State University of Science and Technology M,D*
- Louisiana State University and Agricultural and Mechanical College M,D*
- Marquette University M,D
- Massachusetts Institute of Technology M,D,O*
- McGill University M,D*
- Milwaukee School of Engineering M*
- Northwestern University M,D*
- Ohio University M,D*
- Penn State University Park M,D*
- Princeton University M,D*
- Rensselaer Polytechnic Institute M,D*
- Stevens Institute of Technology M,D,O*
- Texas A&M University M,D*
- Tufts University M,D*
- University at Buffalo, the State University of New York M,D*
- University of Alberta M,D*
- University of California, Berkeley M,D*
- University of California, Los Angeles M,D*
- University of California, San Diego M,D*
- University of Central Florida M,D,O*
- University of Colorado at Boulder M,D*
- University of Dayton M*
- University of Delaware M,D*
- University of Maine M,D*
- University of Memphis M,D*
- University of Michigan M,D,O*
- University of Missouri–Columbia M,D*
- University of New Brunswick Fredericton M,D
- University of North Dakota M
- University of Oklahoma M,D*
- University of Rhode Island M,D
- University of Southern California M*
- University of Washington M,D*
- Washington University in St. Louis M,D*
- Western Michigan University M*
- Worcester Polytechnic Institute M,D,O*

STUDENT AFFAIRS

- Alliant International University–Los Angeles M,D,O*
- Alliant International University–San Diego M,D,O*
- Arkansas State University M,O
- Arkansas Tech University M,O
- Ashland University M
- Azusa Pacific University M
- Bloomsburg University of Pennsylvania M
- Bob Jones University P,M,D,O
- Bowling Green State University M*
- Buffalo State College, State University of New York M
- California State University, Bakersfield M
- Canisius College M
- Cleveland State University M,O
- College of Saint Elizabeth M,O
- The College of Saint Rose M,O*
- Colorado State University M,D*
- Concordia University Wisconsin M
- Eastern Illinois University M
- Fresno Pacific University M
- Hampton University M*
- Kansas State University M,D*
- Kent State University M*
- Lewis University M
- Miami University M*
- Minnesota State University Mankato M,O
- New York University M,D*
- Northeastern University M*
- Northwestern State University of Louisiana M,O
- Nova Southeastern University M*
- The Ohio State University M*
- Ohio University M,D*
- Oklahoma State University M,D,O*
- Oregon State University M*
- Penn State University Park M,D*
- Providence College and Theological Seminary P,M,D,O
- St. Cloud State University M
- Saint Louis University M,D,O*
- San Jose State University M
- Seton Hall University M*
- Slippery Rock University of Pennsylvania M
- Springfield College M,O*
- Teachers College Columbia University M,D*
- Tennessee Technological University M,O*
- University of Bridgeport M
- University of Central Arkansas M
- University of Central Missouri M
- University of Dayton M,O*
- University of Florida M,D,O*
- The University of Iowa M,D*
- University of Louisville M,D
- University of Maryland, College Park M,D,O*
- University of Memphis M,D*
- University of Miami M,O*
- University of Minnesota, Twin Cities Campus M,D,O*
- University of Mississippi M,D,O
- University of Northern Iowa M
- University of Rhode Island M
- University of St. Thomas (MN) M,D,O*
- University of South Carolina M*
- University of South Florida M,D,O*
- The University of Tennessee M*
- University of Wisconsin–La Crosse M
- Washington State University M,D*
- Western Illinois University M
- Western Kentucky University M,O

SUPPLY CHAIN MANAGEMENT

- Arizona State University M,D*
- California State University, East Bay M
- Case Western Reserve University M*
- Eastern Michigan University M
- Elmhurst College M
- HEC Montreal O
- Howard University M*
- Lehigh University M,D,O*
- Maine Maritime Academy M,O
- Michigan State University M,D*
- North Carolina State University M*
- Rutgers, The State University of New Jersey, Newark D*
- Syracuse University M,D*
- The University of Akron M
- University of Dallas M
- University of Florida M,D*
- University of Indianapolis M,O
- University of La Verne M
- University of Massachusetts Dartmouth M,O
- University of Memphis M,D*
- University of Minnesota, Twin Cities Campus M*
- University of Missouri–St. Louis M,D,O
- The University of North Carolina at Greensboro M,D,O
- University of San Diego M,O*
- University of Wisconsin–Madison M*
- University of Wisconsin–Whitewater M*
- Worcester Polytechnic Institute M*
- Wright State University M*

SURVEYING SCIENCE AND ENGINEERING

- The Ohio State University M,D*
- University of New Brunswick Fredericton M,D,O

SURVEY METHODOLOGY

- University of Maryland, College Park M,D*
- University of Michigan M,D,O*
- University of Nebraska–Lincoln M*

SUSTAINABLE DEVELOPMENT

- Brandeis University M*
- Carnegie Mellon University M*
- Clark University M*
- Columbia University M,D*
- Goddard College M
- Hawai'i Pacific University M*
- HEC Montreal O
- Illinois Institute of Technology M*
- Instituto Centroamericano de Administración de Empresas M
- Iowa State University of Science and Technology M,D*
- Michigan Technological University O*
- New College of California M*
- Prescott College M
- School for International Training M
- Slippery Rock University of Pennsylvania M
- University of Connecticut M*
- University of Georgia M,D*
- University of Maryland, College Park M*
- University of Michigan M,D*
- University of New Brunswick Fredericton M
- University of Washington P,M,D*
- University of Wisconsin–Madison M*
- Western Illinois University M,O
- West Virginia University D*

SYSTEMS BIOLOGY

- Cornell University, Joan and Sanford I. Weill Medical College and Graduate School of Medical Sciences D*
- Dartmouth College D*
- Harvard University D*
- Massachusetts Institute of Technology D*
- Rutgers, The State University of New Jersey, New Brunswick D*
- Texas A&M Health Science Center D*
- University of California, San Diego D*

SYSTEMS ENGINEERING

- Air Force Institute of Technology M,D
- The American University of Athens M
- Auburn University M,D*
- Boston University M,D*
- California Institute of Technology M,D*
- California State University, Fullerton M
- California State University, Northridge M
- Carleton University M,D
- Carnegie Mellon University M*
- Case Western Reserve University M,D*
- Colorado School of Mines M,D
- Colorado State University-Pueblo M
- Colorado Technical University—Colorado Springs M
- Colorado Technical University—Denver M
- Concordia University (Canada) M,O
- Cornell University M*
- Embry-Riddle Aeronautical University (FL) M*
- Florida Institute of Technology M*
- George Mason University M*
- The George Washington University M,D,O*
- Georgia Institute of Technology M,D*
- Instituto Tecnológico y de Estudios Superiores de Monterrey, Campus Chihuahua M,O
- Instituto Tecnológico y de Estudios Superiores de Monterrey, Campus Monterrey M,D
- Iowa State University of Science and Technology M*
- The Johns Hopkins University M,O*
- Lehigh University M,D*
- Louisiana State University in Shreveport M
- Loyola Marymount University M,O
- Massachusetts Institute of Technology M,D*
- Mississippi State University M,D
- National University M
- Naval Postgraduate School M,D,O
- North Carolina Agricultural and Technical State University M,D
- Northeastern University M*
- Oakland University M,D*
- The Ohio State University M,D*
- Ohio University M*
- Oklahoma State University M*
- Old Dominion University M*
- Penn State Great Valley M
- Polytechnic University, Brooklyn Campus M*
- Polytechnic University, Long Island Graduate Center M
- Portland State University M,O
- Regis University M,O
- Rensselaer Polytechnic Institute M,D*
- Rochester Institute of Technology M,D
- Rutgers, The State University of New Jersey, New Brunswick M,D*
- San Jose State University M
- Southern Methodist University M,D*
- Southern Polytechnic State University M
- Stevens Institute of Technology M,D,O*
- Stony Brook University, State University of New York M,D,O*
- Texas Tech University M,D
- University of Alberta M,D*

P—first professional degree; M—master's degree; D—doctorate; O—other advanced degree;
**full description and/or announcement in Book 2, 3, 4, 5, or 6*

The University of Arizona	M,D*
University of Central Florida	M,D,O*
University of Florida	M,D,O*
University of Houston	M,D*
University of Houston–Clear Lake	M
University of Idaho	M*
University of Illinois at Urbana–Champaign	M*
University of Maryland, Baltimore County	O*
University of Maryland, College Park	M,O*
University of Michigan	M,D*
University of Michigan–Dearborn	M*
University of Minnesota, Twin Cities Campus	M*
University of Missouri–Rolla	M,D*
The University of North Carolina at Charlotte	D*
University of Pennsylvania	M,D*
University of Regina	M,D
University of Rhode Island	M,D
University of St. Thomas (MN)	M,O*
University of Southern California	M,D,O*
The University of Texas at Arlington	M*
University of Virginia	M,D*
University of Waterloo	M,D*
University of Wisconsin–Madison	M,D*
Virginia Polytechnic Institute and State University	M*
Walden University	M,O
Western International University	M
West Virginia University Institute of Technology	M
Worcester Polytechnic Institute	M,D*

SYSTEMS SCIENCE

Arkansas Tech University	M
Carleton University	M,D
Claremont Graduate University	M,D,O
Eastern Illinois University	M,O
Fairleigh Dickinson University, Metropolitan Campus	M*
Florida Institute of Technology	M*
Hood College	M
Louisiana State University and Agricultural and Mechanical College	M,D*
Louisiana State University in Shreveport	M
Miami University	M*
Oakland University	M*
Portland State University	M,D,O
Rensselaer at Hartford	M
Southern Methodist University	M,D*
State University of New York at Binghamton	M,D*
Stevens Institute of Technology	M*
Universidad Autonoma de Guadalajara	M,D
University of Michigan–Dearborn	M*
The University of North Carolina at Charlotte	M,D*
The University of North Carolina Wilmington	M*
University of Ottawa	M,D,O*
Washington University in St. Louis	M,D*
Worcester Polytechnic Institute	M,O*

TAXATION

American University	M*
Bentley College	M*
Bernard M. Baruch College of the City University of New York	M*
Boise State University	M
Boston University	P,M*
Bryant University	M,O
California Polytechnic State University, San Luis Obispo	M
California State University, East Bay	M
California State University, Fullerton	M
California State University, Los Angeles	M
Capital University	M
Chapman University	P,M
Cleveland State University	M
DePaul University	M*
Drexel University	M*
Duquesne University	M*
Fairfield University	M,O*
Fairleigh Dickinson University, College at Florham	M,O*
Fairleigh Dickinson University, Metropolitan Campus	M*
Florida Atlantic University	M
Florida Gulf Coast University	M
Florida International University	M*
Florida State University	M,D*
Fontbonne University	M
Fordham University	M*
Georgetown University	P,M,D*
Georgia State University	M*
Golden Gate University	P,M,D,O
Grand Valley State University	M
HEC Montreal	M,O
Hofstra University	M*
Illinois Institute of Technology	P,M*
John Marshall Law School	P,M
Long Island University, Brooklyn Campus	M*
Long Island University, C.W. Post Campus	M,O*
Loyola Marymount University	P,M
Mississippi State University	M
National University	M
New York Law School	P,M
New York University	P,M,D,O*
Northeastern University	M,O*
Northern Illinois University	M
Nova Southeastern University	M*
Pace University	M*
Philadelphia University	M*
Robert Morris University	M
Rutgers, The State University of New Jersey, Newark	M*
St. John's University (NY)	M,O
St. Mary's University of San Antonio	M
St. Thomas University	P,M
San Jose State University	M
Seton Hall University	M*
Southeastern University	M
Southern Methodist University	P,M,D*
Southern New Hampshire University	M,D,O*
State University of New York College at Old Westbury	M*
Suffolk University	M,O*
Temple University	P,M*
Université de Sherbrooke	M,O
University at Albany, State University of New York	M*
The University of Akron	M
The University of Alabama	M,D
University of Baltimore	P,M*
University of Central Florida	M*
University of Cincinnati	M*
University of Denver	M*
University of Florida	P,M,D*
University of Hartford	M,O*
University of Hawaii at Manoa	M*
University of Memphis	M*
University of Miami	M*
University of Minnesota, Twin Cities Campus	M*
University of Mississippi	M,D
University of Missouri–Kansas City	P,M*
University of New Haven	M*
University of New Mexico	M*
University of New Orleans	M
The University of North Carolina at Greensboro	M,O
University of San Diego	P,M,O*
University of Southern California	M*
The University of Texas at Arlington	M*
The University of Texas at San Antonio	M,D*
University of the Sacred Heart	M
University of Tulsa	M*
University of Washington	P,M,D*
University of Waterloo	M,D*
Villanova University	M*
Virginia Commonwealth University	M,D*
Walsh College of Accountancy and Business Administration	M
Washington State University	M*
Wayne State University	M,D*
Widener University	M*
William Howard Taft University	P,M

TECHNICAL COMMUNICATION

Boise State University	M
Bowling Green State University	M,D*
Colorado State University	M*
Harvard University	M*
Lawrence Technological University	M
Michigan Technological University	M,D*
Minnesota State University Mankato	M,O
Montana Tech of The University of Montana	M
New Jersey Institute of Technology	M
North Carolina State University	M*
Polytechnic University, Brooklyn Campus	O*
Rensselaer Polytechnic Institute	M*
Rochester Institute of Technology	O
Southern Polytechnic State University	M
Texas State University-San Marcos	M*
University of Colorado at Denver and Health Sciences Center	M*
University of Houston–Downtown	M
University of Nebraska at Omaha	M,O
University of Washington	M,D*

TECHNICAL WRITING

Carnegie Mellon University	M*
Colorado State University	M*
Drexel University	M*
Fitchburg State College	M,O
Illinois Institute of Technology	M,D*
James Madison University	M
The Johns Hopkins University	M*
Massachusetts Institute of Technology	M*
Metropolitan State University	M
Miami University	M*
Oklahoma State University	M,D*
Polytechnic University, Brooklyn Campus	M*
Regis University	M,O
Texas Tech University	M,D
The University of Alabama in Huntsville	M,O
University of Arkansas at Little Rock	M
University of Central Florida	M,D,O*
The University of North Carolina at Greensboro	M,D,O
University of the Sciences in Philadelphia	M,O*
University of Waterloo	M,D*

TECHNOLOGY AND PUBLIC POLICY

Carnegie Mellon University	M,D*
Eastern Michigan University	M
The George Washington University	M*
Massachusetts Institute of Technology	M,D*
Rensselaer Polytechnic Institute	M,D*
Rochester Institute of Technology	M
St. Cloud State University	M
University of Minnesota, Twin Cities Campus	M*
The University of Texas at Austin	M*
Western Illinois University	M

TELECOMMUNICATIONS

The American University of Athens	M
Ball State University	M*
Boston University	M*
California State University, East Bay	M
Claremont Graduate University	M,D,O
DePaul University	M,D*
Drexel University	M*
Florida International University	M*
George Mason University	M,D,O*
The George Washington University	M,D*
Illinois Institute of Technology	M,D*
Indiana University Bloomington	M*
Instituto Tecnologico de Santo Domingo	M
Instituto Tecnológico y de Estudios Superiores de Monterrey, Campus Ciudad Juárez	M
International University in Geneva	M
Iona College	M,O*
The Johns Hopkins University	M*
Michigan State University	M*
National University	M
Ohio University	M*
Pace University	M,D,O*
Polytechnic University, Brooklyn Campus	M*
Polytechnic University, Long Island Graduate Center	M
Polytechnic University, Westchester Graduate Center	M
Rochester Institute of Technology	M
Roosevelt University	M
Saint Mary's University of Minnesota	M
Southern Illinois University Carbondale	M*
Southern Methodist University	M,D*
State University of New York Institute of Technology	M
Stevens Institute of Technology	M,D,O*
Syracuse University	M*
Université du Québec, Institut National de la Recherche Scientifique	M,D
University of Alberta	M,D*
University of Arkansas	M*
University of California, San Diego	M,D*
University of California, Santa Cruz	M,D*
University of Colorado at Boulder	M*
University of Denver	M,O*
University of Hawaii at Manoa	O*
University of Louisiana at Lafayette	M*
University of Maryland, College Park	M*
University of Massachusetts Dartmouth	M,D,O
University of Missouri–Kansas City	M,D*
University of Oklahoma	M,D*
University of Pennsylvania	M*
University of Pittsburgh	M,O*
The University of Texas at Dallas	M,D*
Widener University	M*

TELECOMMUNICATIONS MANAGEMENT

Alaska Pacific University	M
Capitol College	M
Carleton University	M
Carnegie Mellon University	M*
Concordia University (Canada)	M,O
DeVry University	M*
Instituto Tecnológico y de Estudios Superiores de Monterrey, Campus Ciudad de México	M
Instituto Tecnológico y de Estudios Superiores de Monterrey, Campus Ciudad Obregón	M
Instituto Tecnológico y de Estudios Superiores de Monterrey, Campus Estado de México	M,D
Instituto Tecnológico y de Estudios Superiores de Monterrey, Campus Irapuato	M,D
Morgan State University	M*
Murray State University	M
Northeastern University	M,D*
Oklahoma State University	M,D*
Polytechnic University, Brooklyn Campus	M*
San Diego State University	M*
Santa Clara University	M,D,O
Stevens Institute of Technology	M,D,O*
Syracuse University	M,O*
University of Colorado at Boulder	M*
University of Denver	M,O*
University of Management and Technology	M,O
University of Missouri–St. Louis	M,O
University of Pennsylvania	M*
University of San Francisco	M
University of Wisconsin–Stout	M*
Webster University	M,D

TEXTILE DESIGN

Academy of Art University	M*
California College of the Arts	M*
California State University, Los Angeles	M
Cornell University	M,D*
Cranbrook Academy of Art	M*
Drexel University	M*
Florida State University	M,D*
Illinois State University	M*
James Madison University	M
Kent State University	M*
Marywood University	M*
Massachusetts College of Art	M
Memphis College of Art	M*
Philadelphia University	M*
Rhode Island School of Design	M
Savannah College of Art and Design	M*
Sul Ross State University	M*
Temple University	M*
University of California, Davis	M*
University of Cincinnati	M
University of Minnesota, Twin Cities Campus	M,D,O*
The University of North Carolina at Greensboro	M,D
University of North Texas	M,D*
Western Michigan University	M*

TEXTILE SCIENCES AND ENGINEERING

Auburn University	M,D*
Clemson University	M,D*
Cornell University	M,D*
Georgia Institute of Technology	M,D*
North Carolina State University	M,D*
Philadelphia University	M,D*
University of Massachusetts Dartmouth	M

THANATOLOGY

Institution	Degrees
Brooklyn College of the City University of New York	M
Hood College	M,O
Southwestern College (NM)	M,O*

THEATER

Institution	Degrees
American Conservatory Theater	M,O
Antioch University McGregor	M*
Arcadia University	M,D,O
Arizona State University	M,D*
Arkansas State University	M,O
Baylor University	M*
Bennington College	M*
Bob Jones University	P,M,D,O
The Boston Conservatory	M
Boston University	M,O*
Bowling Green State University	M,D*
Brandeis University	M*
Brigham Young University	M*
Brooklyn College of the City University of New York	M,D
Brown University	M*
California Institute of the Arts	M,O
California State University, Fullerton	M
California State University, Long Beach	M
California State University, Los Angeles	M
California State University, Northridge	M
California State University, Sacramento	M*
California State University, San Bernardino	M
Carnegie Mellon University	M*
Case Western Reserve University	M*
The Catholic University of America	M*
Central Michigan University	M*
Central Washington University	M
Christopher Newport University	M
Columbia University	M,D*
Cornell University	D*
Dell'Arte School of Physical Theatre	M
DePaul University	M,O*
Drake University	M*
Eastern Kentucky University	M*
Eastern Michigan University	M*
Emerson College	M*
Florida Atlantic University	M
Florida State University	M,D*
Fontbonne University	M
The George Washington University	M*
Graduate School and University Center of the City University of New York	D*
Hollins University	M
Humboldt State University	M
Hunter College of the City University of New York	M
Idaho State University	M
Illinois State University	M*
Indiana State University	M*
Indiana University Bloomington	M,D*
Kansas State University	M*
Kent State University	M*
Lamar University	M*
Lindenwood University	M
Long Island University, C.W. Post Campus	M*
Louisiana State University and Agricultural and Mechanical College	M,D*
Mary Baldwin College	M
Massachusetts College of Art	M
Miami University	M*
Michigan State University	M*
Minnesota State University Mankato	M
Missouri State University	M*
Montclair State University	M*
Naropa University	M*
National Theatre Conservatory	M,O
The New School: A University	M*
New York University	M,D,O*
North Carolina School of the Arts	M
Northern Illinois University	M*
Northwestern University	M,D*
The Ohio State University	M,D*
Ohio University	M*
Oklahoma City University	M
Oklahoma State University	M*
Pace University	M*
Penn State University Park	M*
Pittsburg State University	M
Point Park University	M*
Portland State University	M
Purchase College, State University of New York	M
Purdue University	M*
Regent University	M,D
Rhode Island College	M
Roosevelt University	M
Rowan University	M
Rutgers, The State University of New Jersey, New Brunswick	M*
St. John's University (NY)	M,O
San Diego State University	M*
San Francisco State University	M
San Jose State University	M
Sarah Lawrence College	M*
Savannah College of Art and Design	M*
Smith College	M*
Southern Illinois University Carbondale	M,D*
Southern Methodist University	M*
Stanford University	D*
State University of New York at Binghamton	M*
Stony Brook University, State University of New York	M*
Temple University	M*
Texas A&M University–Commerce	M
Texas State University-San Marcos	M*
Texas Tech University	M,D
Texas Woman's University	M
Towson University	M
Tufts University	M,D*
Tulane University	M*
Université de Sherbrooke	M,D
Université du Québec à Montréal	M
Université Laval	M,D
University at Albany, State University of New York	M*
The University of Akron	M
The University of Alabama	M*
University of Alberta	M*
The University of Arizona	M*
University of Arkansas	M*
The University of British Columbia	M,D*
University of Calgary	M
University of California, Berkeley	D*
University of California, Davis	M,D*
University of California, Irvine	M,D*
University of California, Los Angeles	M,D*
University of California, San Diego	M,D*
University of California, Santa Barbara	M,D*
University of California, Santa Cruz	O*
University of Central Florida	M*
University of Central Missouri	M
University of Cincinnati	M
University of Colorado at Boulder	M,D*
University of Connecticut	M*
University of Delaware	M*
University of Florida	M*
University of Georgia	M,D*
University of Guelph	M
University of Hawaii at Manoa	M,D*
University of Houston	M*
University of Idaho	M*
University of Illinois at Urbana–Champaign	M,D*
The University of Iowa	M*
University of Kansas	M,D*
University of Kentucky	M*
University of Louisville	M
University of Maryland, College Park	M,D*
University of Massachusetts Amherst	M*
University of Memphis	M*
University of Michigan	M,D*
University of Minnesota, Twin Cities Campus	M,D*
University of Mississippi	M
University of Missouri–Columbia	M,D*
University of Missouri–Kansas City	M*
The University of Montana	M*
University of Nebraska at Omaha	M
University of Nebraska–Lincoln	M,D*
University of Nevada, Las Vegas	M
University of New Mexico	M*
University of New Orleans	M
The University of North Carolina at Chapel Hill	M*
The University of North Carolina at Charlotte	M*
The University of North Carolina at Greensboro	M
University of North Dakota	M
University of North Texas	M*
University of Oklahoma	M*
University of Oregon	M,D*
University of Ottawa	M*
University of Pittsburgh	M,D*
University of Portland	M
University of San Diego	M*
University of Saskatchewan	M
University of South Carolina	M,D*
The University of South Dakota	M
University of Southern California	M*
University of Southern Mississippi	M*
The University of Tennessee	M*
The University of Texas at Austin	M,D*
The University of Texas at El Paso	M
The University of Texas at Tyler	M
The University of Texas–Pan American	M
University of Toronto	M,D
University of Victoria	M,D
University of Virginia	M*
University of Washington	M,D*
University of Wisconsin–Madison	M,D*
University of Wisconsin–Milwaukee	M
University of Wisconsin–Superior	M
Utah State University	M
Villanova University	M*
Virginia Commonwealth University	M*
Virginia Polytechnic Institute and State University	M*
Washington University in St. Louis	M*
Wayne State University	M,D*
Western Illinois University	M
Western Washington University	M
West Virginia University	M*
Yale University	M,D,O*
York University	M,D*

THEOLOGY

Institution	Degrees
Abilene Christian University	P,M
Acadia University	P,M,D
Alliance Theological Seminary	P,M
Alliance University College	P,M,O
American Baptist Seminary of the West	P,M
American Jewish University	M
Anderson University	P,M,D
Andover Newton Theological School	P,M,D
Andrews University	P,M,D,O
Apex School of Theology	P,M
Aquinas Institute of Theology	P,M,D,O
Asbury Theological Seminary	M,D,O
Ashland Theological Seminary	P,M,D,O
Assemblies of God Theological Seminary	P,M,D
Associated Mennonite Biblical Seminary	P,M,O
The Athenaeum of Ohio	P,M,O
Atlantic School of Theology	P,M,O
Austin Graduate School of Theology	M
Austin Presbyterian Theological Seminary	P,M,D
Ave Maria University	M,D
Azusa Pacific University	M,D
Bangor Theological Seminary	P,M,D
Baptist Bible College	P,M
Baptist Bible College of Pennsylvania	P,M,D
Baptist Missionary Association Theological Seminary	P,M
Baptist Theological Seminary at Richmond	P,D
Barry University	M,D*
Bayamón Central University	P,M
Baylor University	P,M,D*
Beacon University	P,M
Bethany Theological Seminary	P,M,O
Beth Benjamin Academy of Connecticut	
Bethel College (IN)	M
Bethel Seminary	P,M,D,O
Bethesda Christian University	P,M
Beth HaMedrash Shaarei Yosher Institute	
Beth Hatalmud Rabbinical College	
Beth Medrash Govoha	
Bexley Hall Seminary	P,M
Biblical Theological Seminary	P,M,D
Biola University	P,M,D
Blessed John XXIII National Seminary	P
Bob Jones University	P,M,D,O
Boston College	M,D*
Boston University	P,M,D*
Briercrest Seminary	P,M
Bryn Athyn College of the New Church	P,M
California Institute of Integral Studies	M,D*
Calvary Bible College and Theological Seminary	P,M
Calvin Theological Seminary	P,M,D
Campbellsville University	M
Campbell University	P,M,D
Canadian Southern Baptist Seminary	P,M
Capital Bible Seminary	P,M,O
Carey Theological College	M,D
The Catholic Distance University	M
Catholic Theological Union at Chicago	P,M,D,O
The Catholic University of America	P,M,D,O*
Central Baptist Theological Seminary	P,M,O
Central Yeshiva Tomchei Tmimim-Lubavitch	
Chaminade University of Honolulu	M
Chicago Theological Seminary	P,M,D
Christendom College	M
Christian Theological Seminary	P,M,D
Christ the King Seminary	P,M,O
Church Divinity School of the Pacific	P,M,D,O
Church of God Theological Seminary	P,M
Cincinnati Christian University	P,M
Claremont Graduate University	M,D
Claremont School of Theology	P,M,D
Colgate Rochester Crozer Divinity School	P,M,D,O
Collège Dominicain de Philosophie et de Théologie	M,D,O
College of Emmanuel and St. Chad	P,M
College of Mount St. Joseph	M
College of St. Catherine	M*
College of Saint Elizabeth	M
Columbia International University	P,M,D,O
Columbia Theological Seminary	P,M,D
Concordia Lutheran Seminary	P,M
Concordia Seminary	P,M,D,O
Concordia Theological Seminary	P,M,D
Concordia University (CA)	M
Concordia University (Canada)	M
Concordia University, St. Paul	M,O
Covenant Theological Seminary	P,M,D,O
Creighton University	M*
The Criswell College	P,M
Crown College	M
Dallas Theological Seminary	M,D,O
Darkei Noam Rabbinical College	
Denver Seminary	P,M,D,O
Dominican House of Studies, Pontifical Faculty of the Immaculate Conception	P,M,O
Dominican School of Philosophy and Theology	P,O
Drew University	P,M,D,O
Duke University	P,M*
Duquesne University	M,D*
Earlham School of Religion	P,M
Eastern Mennonite University	P,M,O
Eastern University	P,M,D*
Ecumenical Theological Seminary	P
Eden Theological Seminary	P,M,D
Emmanuel School of Religion	P,M,D
Emory University	P,M,D*
Episcopal Divinity School	P,M,D,O
Episcopal Theological Seminary of the Southwest	P,M,O
Erskine Theological Seminary	P,M,D
Evangelical Seminary of Puerto Rico	P,M,D
Evangelical Theological Seminary	P,M,O
Faith Baptist Bible College and Theological Seminary	P,M
Faith Evangelical Lutheran Seminary	P,M,D
Fordham University	M,D*
Franciscan School of Theology	P,M
Franciscan University of Steubenville	M
Freed-Hardeman University	P,M
Friends University	M
Fuller Theological Seminary	P,M,D
Gardner-Webb University	P,M,D
Garrett-Evangelical Theological Seminary	P,M,D
General Theological Seminary	P,M,D
George Fox University	P,M,D,O*
Georgian Court University	M,O
Global University of the Assemblies of God	P,M
Golden Gate Baptist Theological Seminary	P,M,D,O
Gordon-Conwell Theological Seminary	P,M,D
Grace Theological Seminary	P,M,D,O
Grace University	M
Graduate Theological Union	M,D,O

*P—first professional degree; M—master's degree; D—doctorate; O—other advanced degree; *full description and/or announcement in Book 2, 3, 4, 5, or 6*

- Grand Rapids Theological Seminary of Cornerstone University P,M
- Harding University M
- Harding University Graduate School of Religion P,M,D
- Hardin-Simmons University P,M
- Hartford Seminary M,D,O
- Harvard University P,M,D*
- Hawai'i Theological Seminary P,M
- Hebrew College M
- Hebrew Theological College O
- Hebrew Union College–Jewish Institute of Religion (CA) P
- Hebrew Union College–Jewish Institute of Religion (NY) P,D
- Hebrew Union College–Jewish Institute of Religion (OH) P
- Heritage Baptist College and Heritage Theological Seminary M,O
- Holy Apostles College and Seminary P,M,O
- Holy Cross Greek Orthodox School of Theology P,M
- Hood Theological Seminary P,M,D
- Houston Baptist University M
- Houston Graduate School of Theology P,M,D
- Howard University P,M,D*
- Iliff School of Theology P,M,D
- Indiana Wesleyan University M
- Institute for Christian Studies M,D
- Inter American University of Puerto Rico, Metropolitan Campus D
- Interdenominational Theological Center P,M,D
- International Baptist College M
- Jesuit School of Theology at Berkeley P,M,D,O
- The Jewish Theological Seminary M,D,O*
- Johnson Bible College M
- Kehilath Yakov Rabbinical Seminary
- Kenrick-Glennon Seminary P,M,O
- Kentucky Christian University M
- Knox College P,M,D
- Knox Theological Seminary P,M,O
- Kol Yaakov Torah Center O
- Lakeland College M
- Lancaster Bible College M
- Lancaster Theological Seminary P,M,D,O
- La Salle University M
- Lee University M
- Lexington Theological Seminary P,M,D
- Liberty University P,M,D
- Lincoln Christian Seminary P,M
- Lipscomb University P,M
- Loras College M
- Louisville Presbyterian Theological Seminary P,M,D
- Loyola Marymount University M
- Loyola University Chicago P,M,D*
- Loyola University New Orleans M,O
- Lubbock Christian University M
- Lutheran School of Theology at Chicago P,M,D
- Lutheran Theological Seminary P,M
- Lutheran Theological Seminary at Gettysburg P,M,D
- The Lutheran Theological Seminary at Philadelphia P,M,D,O
- Lutheran Theological Southern Seminary P,M,D
- Luther Rice University P,M,D
- Luther Seminary P,M,D
- Machzikei Hadath Rabbinical College O
- Madonna University M
- Malone College M
- Maple Springs Baptist Bible College and Seminary P,M,D,O
- Maranatha Baptist Bible College M
- Marquette University M,D
- Marylhurst University P,M
- The Master's College and Seminary P,M,D
- McCormick Theological Seminary P,M,D,O
- McGill University M,D*
- McMaster University P,M,D,O
- Meadville Lombard Theological School P,M,D
- Memphis Theological Seminary P,M,D
- Mennonite Brethren Biblical Seminary P,M
- Mercer University P,D
- Mesivta of Eastern Parkway Rabbinical Seminary
- Mesivta Tifereth Jerusalem of America
- Mesivta Torah Vodaath Rabbinical Seminary
- Methodist Theological School in Ohio P,M
- Michigan Theological Seminary P,M,D
- Mid-America Baptist Theological Seminary P,M,D
- Mid-America Baptist Theological Seminary Northeast Branch P
- Midwestern Baptist Theological Seminary P,M,D
- Midwest University P,M,D
- Mirrer Yeshiva
- Moody Bible Institute P,M,O
- Moravian Theological Seminary P,M
- Mount Angel Seminary P,M
- Mount St. Mary's University P,M
- Mount Vernon Nazarene University M
- Multnomah Bible College and Biblical Seminary P,M,O
- Naropa University P*
- Nashotah House P,M,O
- Nazarene Theological Seminary P,M,D
- Ner Israel Rabbinical College M,D
- Ner Israel Yeshiva College of Toronto
- New Brunswick Theological Seminary P,M,D
- Newman Theological College P,M
- New Orleans Baptist Theological Seminary P,D
- New York Theological Seminary P,M,D
- The Nigerian Baptist Theological Seminary P,M,O
- Northeastern Seminary at Roberts Wesleyan College P,M,D
- Northern Baptist Theological Seminary P,M,D
- North Park Theological Seminary P,M,D,O
- Northwest Baptist Seminary P,M,D,O
- Notre Dame Seminary P,M
- Oakland City University P,D
- Oblate School of Theology P,M,D,O
- Ohio Dominican University M
- Ohr Hameir Theological Seminary
- Oklahoma Christian University P,M
- Olivet Nazarene University M
- Oral Roberts University P,M,D
- Pacific Lutheran Theological Seminary P,M,D,O
- Pacific School of Religion P,M,D,O
- Payne Theological Seminary P
- Philadelphia Biblical University P,M
- Phillips Theological Seminary P,M,D
- Piedmont Baptist College and Graduate School M,D
- Pittsburgh Theological Seminary P,M,D
- Pontifical Catholic University of Puerto Rico P
- Pontifical College Josephinum P,M
- Princeton Theological Seminary P,M,D
- The Protestant Episcopal Theological Seminary in Virginia P,M,D
- Providence College M*
- Providence College and Theological Seminary P,M,D,O
- Queen's University at Kingston P,M
- Quincy University M
- Rabbi Isaac Elchanan Theological Seminary O
- Rabbinical Academy Mesivta Rabbi Chaim Berlin O
- Rabbinical College Beth Shraga
- Rabbinical College Bobover Yeshiva B'nei Zion
- Rabbinical College Ch'san Sofer
- Rabbinical College of Long Island
- Rabbinical Seminary M'kor Chaim
- Rabbinical Seminary of America
- Reconstructionist Rabbinical College P,M,D,O
- Reformed Presbyterian Theological Seminary P,M,D
- Reformed Theological Seminary–Charlotte Campus P,M,D
- Reformed Theological Seminary–Jackson Campus P,M,D,O
- Reformed Theological Seminary–Orlando Campus P,M,D
- Regent College P,M,O
- Regent University P,M,D
- Regions University P,M,D
- Regis College (Canada) P,M,D,O
- Sacred Heart Major Seminary P,M
- Sacred Heart School of Theology P,M
- St. Andrew's College in Winnipeg P
- St. Augustine's Seminary of Toronto P,M,O
- Saint Bernard's School of Theology and Ministry P,M,O
- St. Bonaventure University M,O
- St. Charles Borromeo Seminary, Overbrook P,M
- Saint Francis Seminary P,M
- St. John's Seminary (CA) P,M
- Saint John's Seminary (MA) P,M
- Saint John's University (MN) P,M
- St. John's University (NY) P,M,O
- St. Joseph's Seminary P,M
- Saint Louis University M,D*
- Saint Mary-of-the-Woods College M,O
- Saint Mary Seminary and Graduate School of Theology P,M,D
- St. Mary's Seminary and University P,M,D,O*
- St. Mary's University of San Antonio M
- Saint Meinrad School of Theology P,M
- Saint Michael's College M,O
- St. Norbert College M
- St. Patrick's Seminary & University P,M
- Saint Paul School of Theology P,M,D
- Saint Paul University M,D,O
- St. Peter's Seminary P,M
- Saints Cyril and Methodius Seminary P,M
- St. Stephen's College M,D
- St. Thomas University M,D,O
- St. Tikhon's Orthodox Theological Seminary P
- Saint Vincent de Paul Regional Seminary P,M
- Saint Vincent Seminary P,M
- St. Vladimir's Orthodox Theological Seminary P,M,D
- Samford University P,M,D
- San Francisco Theological Seminary P,M,D
- Seabury-Western Theological Seminary P,M,D,O
- Seattle University P,M,O
- Seminary of the Immaculate Conception P,M,D,O
- Seton Hall University P,M,O*
- Sewanee: The University of the South P,M,D*
- Shaw University P,M
- Sh'or Yoshuv Rabbinical College
- Sioux Falls Seminary M,D,O
- Southeastern Baptist Theological Seminary P,M,D
- Southern Baptist Theological Seminary P,M,D
- Southern California Seminary P,M,D
- Southern Evangelical Seminary P,M,D,O
- Southern Methodist University P,M,D*
- Southern Nazarene University M
- Southwestern Assemblies of God University M
- Southwestern Baptist Theological Seminary P,M,D,O
- Spring Arbor University M
- Spring Hill College M
- Starr King School for the Ministry P
- Talmudic College of Florida M,D
- Taylor University College and Seminary P,M,O
- Temple Baptist Seminary P,M,D
- Texas Christian University P,M,D,O
- Toronto School of Theology P,M,D
- Trevecca Nazarene University M
- Trinity Episcopal School for Ministry P,M,D,O
- Trinity International University P,M,D,O
- Trinity Lutheran Seminary P,M
- Trinity Western University P,M
- Tyndale University College & Seminary P,M,O
- Unification Theological Seminary P,M,D
- Union Theological Seminary and Presbyterian School of Christian Education P,M,D
- Union Theological Seminary in the City of New York P,M,D
- United Talmudical Seminary
- United Theological Seminary P,M,D
- United Theological Seminary of the Twin Cities P,M,D
- Université de Montréal M,D,O
- Université de Sherbrooke M,D,O
- Université du Québec à Chicoutimi M,D
- Université Laval M,D
- University of Chicago P,M,D*
- University of Dallas M
- University of Dayton M,D*
- University of Denver D*
- University of Dubuque P,M,D
- University of Manitoba P
- University of Mobile M
- University of Notre Dame P,M,D*
- University of Saint Mary of the Lake–Mundelein Seminary P,D,O
- University of St. Michael's College P,M,D,O
- University of St. Thomas (MN) P,M*
- University of St. Thomas (TX) P,M
- University of San Francisco M
- The University of Scranton M
- University of Trinity College P,M,D,O
- The University of Winnipeg P,M,O
- Ursuline College M
- Valparaiso University M,O
- Vancouver School of Theology P,M,D,O
- Vanderbilt University P,M*
- Vanguard University of Southern California M
- Victoria University P,M,D,O
- Villanova University M*
- Virginia Union University P,D
- Walsh University M
- Warner Pacific College M
- Wartburg Theological Seminary P,M
- Washington Theological Union P,M
- Wesley Biblical Seminary P,M
- Wesley Theological Seminary P,M,D
- Western Seminary M,O
- Western Theological Seminary P,M,D
- Westminster Seminary California P,M
- Westminster Theological Seminary P,M,D,O
- Weston Jesuit School of Theology P,M,D,O*
- Wheaton College M,D
- Wilfrid Laurier University P,M,D
- Winebrenner Theological Seminary P,M,D
- Wycliffe College P,M,D,O
- Xavier University M*
- Xavier University of Louisiana M
- Yale University P,M*
- Yeshiva Beth Moshe O
- Yeshiva Karlin Stolin Rabbinical Institute O
- Yeshiva of Nitra Rabbinical College
- Yeshiva Shaar Hatorah Talmudic Research Institute
- Yeshivath Zichron Moshe O
- Yeshiva Toras Chaim Talmudical Seminary

THEORETICAL CHEMISTRY

- Cornell University D*
- Georgetown University M,D*
- University of Calgary M,D
- The University of Tennessee M,D*
- Vanderbilt University M,D*
- Wesleyan University M,D*
- West Virginia University M,D*

THEORETICAL PHYSICS

- Cornell University M,D*
- Harvard University D*
- Rutgers, The State University of New Jersey, New Brunswick M,D*
- University of Victoria M,D
- West Virginia University M,D*

THERAPIES—DANCE, DRAMA, AND MUSIC

- Antioch University New England M*
- Appalachian State University M
- California Institute of Integral Studies M,D*
- Columbia College Chicago M,O
- Drexel University M*
- East Carolina University M*
- Florida State University M,D*
- Georgia College & State University M,O
- Immaculata University M
- Lesley University M,D,O*
- Maryville University of Saint Louis M
- Marywood University M,O*
- Michigan State University M,D*
- Montclair State University M,O*
- Naropa University M*
- Nazareth College of Rochester M
- New York University M,D*
- Ohio University M,O*
- Pratt Institute M*
- Radford University M
- Saint Mary-of-the-Woods College M
- Shenandoah University M,D,O*
- Temple University M,D*
- University of Kansas M*
- University of Miami M,D,O*
- University of the Pacific M
- Wilfrid Laurier University M

TOXICOLOGY

- American University M,O*
- A.T. Still University of Health Sciences P,M
- Brown University M,D*
- Columbia University M,D*
- Cornell University M,D*

Dartmouth College D*
Duke University D,O*
Florida Agricultural and Mechanical University M,D*
The George Washington University M*
Indiana University–Purdue University Indianapolis M,D*
Iowa State University of Science and Technology M,D*
The Johns Hopkins University M,D*
Long Island University, Brooklyn Campus M,D*
Louisiana State University and Agricultural and Mechanical College M*
Massachusetts Institute of Technology M,D*
Medical College of Wisconsin M,D*
Michigan State University M,D*
New York University M,D*
North Carolina State University M,D*
Northeastern University M*
Northwestern University D*
The Ohio State University M,D*
Oklahoma State University Center for Health Sciences M
Oregon State University M,D*
Purdue University M,D*
Queen's University at Kingston M,D
Rutgers, The State University of New Jersey, New Brunswick M,D*
St. John's University (NY) M
San Diego State University M,D*
Simon Fraser University M,D
Texas A&M University M,D*
Texas Southern University M,D
Texas Tech University M,D
Université de Montréal O
University at Albany, State University of New York M,D*
University at Buffalo, the State University of New York M,D*
The University of Alabama at Birmingham M,D*
University of Arkansas for Medical Sciences M,D*
University of California, Davis M,D*
University of California, Irvine M,D*
University of California, Riverside M,D*
University of California, Santa Cruz M,D*
University of Cincinnati D
University of Colorado at Denver and Health Sciences Center P,D*
University of Connecticut M,D*
University of Florida M,D,O*
University of Georgia M,D*
University of Guelph M,D
The University of Iowa M,D*
University of Kansas M,D*
University of Kentucky M,D*
University of Louisville M,D
University of Maryland, Baltimore M,D*
University of Maryland Eastern Shore M,D*
University of Michigan M,D*
University of Minnesota, Duluth M,D*
University of Minnesota, Twin Cities Campus M,D*
University of Mississippi Medical Center M,D*
The University of Montana M,D*
University of Nebraska–Lincoln M,D*
University of Nebraska Medical Center M,D*
University of New Mexico M,D*
The University of North Carolina at Chapel Hill M,D*
University of Prince Edward Island M,D
University of Puerto Rico, Medical Sciences Campus M,D*
University of Rhode Island M,D
University of Rochester M,D*
University of Saskatchewan M,D,O
University of South Alabama M*
University of Southern California M,D*
The University of Texas Health Science Center at Houston M,D*
The University of Texas Medical Branch D*
University of the Sciences in Philadelphia M,D*
University of Utah M,D*
University of Washington M,D*
University of Wisconsin–Madison M,D*
Utah State University M,D
Vanderbilt University M*
Virginia Commonwealth University M,D*
Washington State University M,D*
Washington State University Tri-Cities M,D
Wayne State University M,D*
West Virginia University M,D*
Wright State University M*

TRANSCULTURAL NURSING

Augsburg College M
New Jersey City University M
University of Medicine and Dentistry of New Jersey D*

TRANSLATIONAL BIOLOGY

Baylor College of Medicine D*
The University of Iowa M,D*

TRANSLATION AND INTERPRETATION

American University M,O*
Babel University School of Translation M
Concordia University (Canada) M,O
Gallaudet University M
Georgia State University O*
Kent State University M*
Marygrove College M
Montclair State University M,O*
Monterey Institute of International Studies M*
Rutgers, The State University of New Jersey, New Brunswick M,D*
State University of New York at Binghamton M,O*
Université Laval M,O
University at Albany, State University of New York M,O*
University of Arkansas M*
University of Denver M,O*
The University of Iowa M*
University of Ottawa M,D*
University of Puerto Rico, Río Piedras M,O*
York University M*

TRANSPERSONAL AND HUMANISTIC PSYCHOLOGY

Atlantic University M
Institute of Transpersonal Psychology M,D,O*
Michigan School of Professional Psychology M,D
Naropa University M*
Saybrook Graduate School and Research Center M,D
Seattle University M

TRANSPORTATION AND HIGHWAY ENGINEERING

Auburn University M,D*
Cornell University M,D*
École Polytechnique de Montréal M,D,O
Illinois Institute of Technology M,D*
Iowa State University of Science and Technology M,D*
Louisiana State University and Agricultural and Mechanical College M,D*
Marquette University M,D
Massachusetts Institute of Technology M,D,O*
Morgan State University M,D*
New Jersey Institute of Technology M,D
Northwestern University M,D*
Ohio University M,D*
Penn State University Park M,D*
Polytechnic University, Brooklyn Campus M,D*
Polytechnic University, Long Island Graduate Center M
Princeton University M,D*
Rensselaer Polytechnic Institute M,D*
Texas A&M University M,D*
Texas Southern University M
University of Arkansas M*
University of California, Berkeley M,D*
University of California, Davis M,D*
University of California, Irvine M,D*
University of Central Florida M,D,O*
University of Dayton M*
University of Delaware M,D*
University of Memphis M,D*
University of Missouri–Columbia M,D*
University of Nevada, Las Vegas M,D
University of New Brunswick Fredericton M,D
University of Rhode Island M,D
University of Southern California M*
University of Washington M,D*
Villanova University M*
Western Michigan University M*
Worcester Polytechnic Institute M,D,O*

TRANSPORTATION MANAGEMENT

American Public University System M
Arizona State University O*
Arizona State University at the Polytechnic Campus M
Concordia University (Canada) M,D,O
Florida Institute of Technology M*
George Mason University M*
Iowa State University of Science and Technology M*
Maine Maritime Academy M,O
McGill University M,D*
Morgan State University M*
New Jersey Institute of Technology M,D
North Dakota State University M,D
Polytechnic University, Brooklyn Campus M*
San Jose State University M
State University of New York Maritime College M*
University at Buffalo, the State University of New York M,D,O*
University of Arkansas M*
The University of British Columbia D*
University of California, Davis M,D*
University of Central Missouri M,O
University of Denver M*
The University of Tennessee M,D*
University of Washington O*
Wilmington College (DE) M

TRAVEL AND TOURISM

Boston University M*
Clemson University M,D*
East Stroudsburg University of Pennsylvania M
The George Washington University M,O*
Indiana University–Purdue University Indianapolis M*
New York University M,O*
North Carolina State University M,D*
Old Dominion University M*
Purdue University M,D*
Rochester Institute of Technology M
Saint Xavier University M,O
Schiller International University (United States) M
Schiller International University (United Kingdom) M
Temple University M,D*
Université du Québec à Trois-Rivières M,O
University of Central Florida M*
University of Hawaii at Manoa M*
University of Massachusetts Amherst M*
University of New Haven M*
University of New Orleans M*
University of South Carolina M*
The University of Tennessee M*
University of Waterloo M*
Virginia Polytechnic Institute and State University M,D*
Western Illinois University M

URBAN AND REGIONAL PLANNING

Alabama Agricultural and Mechanical University M
American University of Beirut M
Arizona State University M*
Auburn University M*
Ball State University M*
Boston University M*
California Polytechnic State University, San Luis Obispo M
California State Polytechnic University, Pomona M
California State University, Chico M
The Catholic University of America M*
Clark University M*
Clemson University M*
Cleveland State University M,O
Columbia University M,D*
Concordia University (Canada) O
Cornell University M,D*
Dalhousie University M
Delta State University M
DePaul University M,O*
Eastern Kentucky University M*
Eastern Washington University M
East Tennessee State University M
Florida Atlantic University M
Florida State University M,D*
Georgia Institute of Technology M,D*
Harvard University M,D*
Hunter College of the City University of New York M
Iowa State University of Science and Technology M*
Jackson State University M
Kansas State University M*
Massachusetts Institute of Technology M,D*
McGill University M,D*
Michigan State University M,D*
Minnesota State University Mankato M,O
Missouri State University M*
Morgan State University M*
New York University M,O*
North Park University M
The Ohio State University M,D*
Old Dominion University M*
Pontificia Universidad Catolica Madre y Maestra M
Portland State University M
Pratt Institute M*
Queen's University at Kingston M
Rutgers, The State University of New Jersey, New Brunswick M,D*
San Diego State University M*
San Jose State University M,O
State University of New York College of Environmental Science and Forestry M,D
Temple University M*
Texas A&M University M,D*
Texas Southern University M
Texas Tech University M
Tufts University M*
Université du Québec à Rimouski M,D,O
Université du Québec en Outaouais M
Université Laval M,D
University at Albany, State University of New York M*
University at Buffalo, the State University of New York M*
The University of Akron M
The University of British Columbia M,D*
University of Calgary M,D
University of California, Berkeley M,D*
University of California, Davis M*
University of California, Irvine M,D*
University of California, Los Angeles M,D*
University of Central Florida M,O*
University of Cincinnati M
University of Colorado at Denver and Health Sciences Center M,D*
University of Florida M,D*
University of Hawaii at Manoa M,D,O*
University of Illinois at Chicago M,D*
University of Illinois at Urbana–Champaign M,D*
The University of Iowa M*
University of Kansas M*
University of Louisville M
University of Manitoba M
University of Maryland, College Park M,D*
University of Massachusetts Amherst M,D*
University of Memphis M*
University of Michigan M,D,O*
University of Minnesota, Twin Cities Campus M*
University of Nebraska–Lincoln M*
University of New Mexico M*
University of New Orleans M
The University of North Carolina at Chapel Hill M,D*
University of Oklahoma M*
University of Oregon M*
University of Pennsylvania M,D,O*
University of Pittsburgh M*
University of Puerto Rico, Río Piedras M*
University of Southern California M,D*
University of Southern Maine M,O
The University of Texas at Arlington M*
The University of Texas at Austin M,D*
The University of Toledo M,D,O*
University of Toronto M
University of Utah M*
University of Virginia M*
University of Washington M,D*
University of Waterloo M,D*
University of Wisconsin–Madison M,D*
University of Wisconsin–Milwaukee M,O
Utah State University M,D
Vanderbilt University M*
Virginia Commonwealth University M,O*
Virginia Polytechnic Institute and State University M*
Wayne State University M*
West Chester University of Pennsylvania M
West Virginia University M,D*

P—first professional degree; M—master's degree; D—doctorate; O—other advanced degree;
**full description and/or announcement in Book 2, 3, 4, 5, or 6*

URBAN DESIGN

American University of Beirut M
City College of the City University of New York M*
Cleveland State University M,O
Columbia University M*
Cornell University M,D*
Georgia Institute of Technology M,D*
Harvard University M*
New York Institute of Technology M
Prairie View A&M University M
Pratt Institute M*
Rice University M,D*
Savannah College of Art and Design M*
State University of New York College of Environmental Science and Forestry M
University at Buffalo, the State University of New York M*
University of Calgary M,D
University of California, Berkeley M,D*
University of California, Los Angeles M,D*
University of Colorado at Denver and Health Sciences Center M*
University of Miami M*
University of Michigan M*
University of Pennsylvania D*
University of Washington M,D,O*
Washington University in St. Louis M*

URBAN EDUCATION

Cardinal Stritch University M,D*
Claremont Graduate University M,D,O
Cleveland State University D
College of Mount Saint Vincent M,O
Columbia College Chicago M
Concordia University (IL) M
DePaul University M,D*
Florida International University M*
Graduate School and University Center of the City University of New York D*
Harvard University D*
Holy Names University M,O
The Johns Hopkins University M,D,O*
Langston University M
Marygrove College M
Mercy College M
New Jersey City University M
Norfolk State University M
Northeastern Illinois University M
Nova Southeastern University M,O*
Roberts Wesleyan College M,O
Saint Peter's College M
Simmons College M,O
Sojourner-Douglass College M
Temple University M,D*
Texas A&M University M,D*
Texas Southern University M,D
University of Houston–Downtown M
University of Illinois at Chicago M,D*
University of Massachusetts Boston M,D,O
University of Michigan–Flint M*
University of Nebraska at Omaha M,O
University of Wisconsin–Milwaukee M,D
Virginia Commonwealth University D*

URBAN STUDIES

Boston University M*
Brooklyn College of the City University of New York M,D
Cleveland State University M,D
Concordia University (Canada) M,O
East Tennessee State University M
Georgia State University M*
Graduate School and University Center of the City University of New York M,D*
Hunter College of the City University of New York M
Long Island University, Brooklyn Campus M*
Massachusetts Institute of Technology M,D*
Minnesota State University Mankato M,O
New Jersey City University M
New Jersey Institute of Technology D
The New School: A University M*
Norfolk State University M
Old Dominion University M,D*
Portland State University M,D
Queens College of the City University of New York M
Rutgers, The State University of New Jersey, Newark M,D*
Saint Louis University M,D,O*
San Francisco Art Institute M*
Savannah State University M
Simon Fraser University M,O
Southern Connecticut State University M
Temple University M*
Tufts University M*
Université du Québec à Montréal M,D
Université du Québec, École nationale d'administration publique M
Université du Québec, Institut National de la Recherche Scientifique M,D
University at Albany, State University of New York M,D,O*
The University of Akron M,D
University of California, Irvine M,D*
University of Central Oklahoma M
University of Delaware M,D*
University of Lethbridge M,D
University of Louisville D
University of New Orleans M,D
University of the Incarnate Word M,O
University of Wisconsin–Milwaukee M,D
Wright State University M*

VETERINARY MEDICINE

Auburn University P*
Colorado State University P*
Cornell University P,D*
Iowa State University of Science and Technology P,M*
Kansas State University P*
Louisiana State University and Agricultural and Mechanical College P*
Michigan State University P*
Mississippi State University P
North Carolina State University P,M*
The Ohio State University P*
Oklahoma State University P*
Oregon State University P*
Purdue University P*
Texas A&M University P,M*
Tufts University P*
Universidad Nacional Pedro Henriquez Urena P,M,D
Université de Montréal P
University of California, Davis P*
University of Florida P*
University of Georgia P*
University of Guelph M,D,O
University of Illinois at Urbana–Champaign P*
University of Maryland, College Park P*
University of Minnesota, Twin Cities Campus P*
University of Missouri–Columbia P*
University of Pennsylvania P*
University of Prince Edward Island P
University of Saskatchewan P,M,D
The University of Tennessee P*
University of Wisconsin–Madison P*
Virginia Polytechnic Institute and State University P*
Washington State University P*
Western University of Health Sciences P

VETERINARY SCIENCES

Auburn University M,D*
Clemson University M,D*
Colorado State University M,D*
Drexel University M*
Iowa State University of Science and Technology M,D*
Kansas State University M*
Louisiana State University and Agricultural and Mechanical College M,D*
Michigan State University M,D*
Mississippi State University M,D
Montana State University M,D
North Carolina State University M,D*
North Dakota State University M,D
The Ohio State University M,D*
Oklahoma State University M,D*
Oregon State University M,D*
Penn State Hershey Medical Center M*
Penn State University Park D*
Purdue University M,D*
South Dakota State University M,D
Texas A&M University M*
Tufts University M,D*
Tuskegee University P,M
Université de Montréal M,D,O
University of California, Davis M,D,O*
University of Florida M,D,O*
University of Georgia M,D*
University of Guelph M,D,O
University of Idaho M,D*
University of Illinois at Urbana–Champaign M,D*
University of Kentucky M,D*
University of Maryland, College Park M,D*
University of Minnesota, Twin Cities Campus M,D*
University of Missouri–Columbia M,D*
University of Nebraska–Lincoln M,D*
University of Prince Edward Island M,D
University of Saskatchewan M,D
University of Washington M*
University of Wisconsin–Madison M,D*
Utah State University M,D
Virginia Polytechnic Institute and State University M,D*
Washington State University M,D*

VIROLOGY

Baylor College of Medicine D*
Loyola University Chicago M,D*
Mayo Graduate School D*
McMaster University M,D
The Ohio State University M,D*
Penn State Hershey Medical Center M,D*
Purdue University M,D*
Rush University M,D
Rutgers, The State University of New Jersey, New Brunswick M,D*
Texas A&M Health Science Center D*
Université de Montréal D
Université du Québec, Institut National de la Recherche Scientifique M,D
University of California, San Diego D*
The University of Iowa M,D*
University of Massachusetts Worcester D*
University of Pennsylvania D*
University of Pittsburgh M,D*
University of Prince Edward Island M,D
The University of Texas Health Science Center at Houston M,D*
The University of Texas Medical Branch D*
University of Virginia D*
Yale University D*

VISION SCIENCES

Eastern Virginia Medical School O
Emory University M*
The New England College of Optometry P,M*
Nova Southeastern University P,M*
Pennsylvania College of Optometry M,D,O
State University of New York College of Optometry M,D
Université de Montréal M,O
The University of Alabama at Birmingham M,D*
The University of Alabama in Huntsville M,D
University of Alberta M,D*
University of California, Berkeley M,D*
University of Chicago D*
University of Guelph M,D,O
University of Houston M,D*
University of Louisville D
University of Missouri–St. Louis M,D
University of Waterloo M,D*

VOCATIONAL AND TECHNICAL EDUCATION

Alabama Agricultural and Mechanical University M
Alcorn State University M,O
Appalachian State University M
Ball State University M*
Bemidji State University M
Bowling Green State University M*
Buffalo State College, State University of New York M
California Baptist University M
California State University, Long Beach M
California State University, Sacramento M*
California State University, San Bernardino M
California University of Pennsylvania M
Central Connecticut State University M,O
Central Michigan University M*
Chicago State University M
Clarion University of Pennsylvania M
Colorado State University M,D*
East Carolina University M*
Eastern Kentucky University M*
Eastern Michigan University M
East Tennessee State University M
Fitchburg State College M
Florida Agricultural and Mechanical University M*
Georgia Southern University M
Idaho State University M
Indiana State University M*
Inter American University of Puerto Rico, Metropolitan Campus M
Iowa State University of Science and Technology M,D*
Jackson State University M
James Madison University M
Kent State University M,O*
Louisiana State University and Agricultural and Mechanical College M,D*
Marshall University M
Middle Tennessee State University M*
Millersville University of Pennsylvania M
Mississippi State University M,D,O
Morehead State University M
Murray State University M
North Carolina Agricultural and Technical State University M
Northern Arizona University M
Nova Southeastern University D*
The Ohio State University D*
Oklahoma State University M,D*
Old Dominion University M,D*
Penn State University Park M,D*
Pittsburg State University M,O
Purdue University M,D,O*
Saint Martin's University M
Sam Houston State University M
South Carolina State University M
Southern Illinois University Carbondale M,D*
Southern New Hampshire University M,O*
State University of New York at Oswego M
Sul Ross State University M*
Temple University M,D*
Texas A&M University–Corpus Christi M
Texas State University-San Marcos M*
Trevecca Nazarene University M
The University of Akron M
University of Arkansas M,D,O*
The University of British Columbia M,D*
University of Calgary M,D,O
University of Central Florida M*
University of Central Missouri M,O
University of Georgia M,D,O*
University of Idaho M,D,O*
University of Illinois at Urbana–Champaign M,D,O*
University of Kentucky M*
University of Louisville M
University of Maryland Eastern Shore M*
University of Minnesota, Twin Cities Campus M,D,O*
University of Missouri–Columbia M,D,O*
University of North Dakota M
University of Northern Iowa M,D
University of North Texas M,D*
University of South Carolina M,D,O*
University of Southern Maine M
University of Southern Mississippi M*
University of South Florida M,D,O*
The University of Texas at Tyler M
The University of Toledo M,O*
University of Victoria M,D
University of West Florida M
University of Wisconsin–Platteville M
University of Wisconsin–Stout M,O*
Utah State University M
Valdosta State University M,D
Virginia Polytechnic Institute and State University M,D,O*
Virginia State University M,O
Wayne State College M
Wayne State University M,D,O*
Western Michigan University M*
Westfield State College M,O
West Virginia University M*
Wilmington College (DE) M
Wright State University M*

WATER RESOURCES

Albany State University M
Colorado State University M,D*
Duke University M*
Iowa State University of Science and Technology M,D*

Montclair State University M,D,O*
Nova Scotia Agricultural College M
Rutgers, The State University of New Jersey, New Brunswick M,D*
South Dakota School of Mines and Technology D
State University of New York College of Environmental Science and Forestry M,D
Tropical Agriculture Research and Higher Education Center M,D
The University of Arizona M,D*
University of California, Riverside M,D*
University of Florida M,D*
University of Illinois at Chicago M,D*
University of Kansas M*
University of Minnesota, Twin Cities Campus M,D*
University of Missouri–Rolla M,D*
University of Nevada, Las Vegas M
University of New Brunswick Fredericton M,D
University of New Hampshire M*
University of New Mexico M*
University of Oklahoma M,D*
University of Wisconsin–Madison M*
University of Wyoming M,D
Utah State University M,D
Washington State University Tri-Cities M,D

WATER RESOURCES ENGINEERING

American University of Beirut M
Cornell University M,D*
Louisiana State University and Agricultural and Mechanical College M,D*
Marquette University M,D
McGill University M,D*
New Mexico Institute of Mining and Technology M
Ohio University M,D*
Oregon State University M,D*
Penn State University Park M,D*
Princeton University M,D*
Stevens Institute of Technology M,D,O*
Texas A&M University M,D*
Tufts University M,D*
University of Alberta M,D*
The University of Arizona M,D*
University of California, Berkeley M,D*
University of California, Los Angeles M,D*
University of Central Florida M,D,O*
University of Colorado at Boulder M,D*
University of Delaware M,D*
University of Guelph M,D
University of Memphis M,D*
University of Missouri–Columbia M,D*
University of Southern California M*
The University of Texas at Austin M*
University of Washington M,D*
Utah State University M,D
Villanova University M*

WESTERN EUROPEAN STUDIES

Boston College M,D*
Brown University M,D*
Carleton University M,O
The Catholic University of America M*
Claremont Graduate University M,D,O
Columbia University M,O*
Cornell University M,D*
East Carolina University M*
Georgetown University M*
The George Washington University M*
Indiana University Bloomington M*
The Johns Hopkins University M,D,O*
New York University M*
San Diego State University M*
University of California, Santa Barbara M*
University of Connecticut M*
University of Nevada, Reno D*
University of Pittsburgh O*
Washington State University M,D*

WOMEN'S HEALTH NURSING

Case Western Reserve University M,D*
Columbia University O*
Emory University M*
Frontier School of Midwifery and Family Nursing M,O
Georgia Southern University M,O
Georgia State University M,D,O*
Indiana University–Purdue University Indianapolis M,D*
Loyola University Chicago M*
MGH Institute of Health Professions M,O*
Oregon Health & Science University M,O*
Seton Hall University M*
Stony Brook University, State University of New York M,O*
University at Buffalo, the State University of New York M,D,O*
University of Cincinnati M,D
University of Colorado at Colorado Springs M,D
University of Delaware M,O*
University of Medicine and Dentistry of New Jersey M,D,O*
University of Michigan M,O*
University of Minnesota, Twin Cities Campus M*
University of Missouri–Kansas City M,D*
University of Pennsylvania M*
University of South Carolina M*
The University of Texas at El Paso M
Vanderbilt University M,D*
Virginia Commonwealth University M,D,O*
Wilmington College (DE) M

WOMEN'S STUDIES

Brandeis University M*
California Institute of Integral Studies M,D*
Claremont Graduate University M,D
Clark Atlanta University M,D
Cornell University M,D*
Dalhousie University M
Drew University M
Duke University O*
Eastern Michigan University M
Emory University D,O*
Florida Atlantic University M,O
The George Washington University M,D,O*
Georgia State University M*
Graduate School and University Center of the City University of New York M,D*
Lakehead University M
Lesley University M*
Minnesota State University Mankato M,O
Mount Saint Vincent University M
New College of California M*
The Ohio State University M,D*
Roosevelt University M,O
Rutgers, The State University of New Jersey, New Brunswick M,D*
Saint Mary's University M
San Diego State University M*
San Francisco State University M
Sarah Lawrence College M*
Shenandoah University M,D,O*
Simon Fraser University M,D
Southeastern Baptist Theological Seminary P,M,D
Southern Connecticut State University M
Stony Brook University, State University of New York M,O*
Texas Woman's University M
Towson University M
United Theological Seminary of the Twin Cities M
Université Laval O
University at Albany, State University of New York M,D*
The University of Alabama M
The University of Arizona M*
University of California, Los Angeles M,D*
University of California, Santa Barbara M,D*
University of Cincinnati M,O
University of Florida M,O*
University of Georgia O*
University of Hawaii at Manoa O*
The University of Iowa D*
University of Louisville M,O
University of Maryland, Baltimore County O*
University of Maryland, College Park M,D*
University of Massachusetts Boston M,D,O
University of Michigan D,O*
University of Minnesota, Twin Cities Campus D*
University of Nevada, Las Vegas O
The University of North Carolina at Greensboro M,D,O
University of Northern Iowa M
University of Ottawa M*
University of Pittsburgh O*
University of Saskatchewan M,D
University of South Carolina O*
University of South Florida M*
University of Washington M,D*
Washington State University M,D*
York University M,D*

WRITING

Abilene Christian University M
Adelphi University M*
American University M*
Antioch University Los Angeles M,O
Antioch University McGregor M*
Arizona State University M*
Asbury College M,O
Ball State University M,D*
Belmont University M
Bennington College M*
Boise State University M
Boston University M,D*
Bowling Green State University M,D*
Brooklyn College of the City University of New York M
Brown University M*
California College of the Arts M*
California Institute of the Arts M,O
California State University, Fresno M
California State University, Long Beach M
California State University, Northridge M
California State University, Sacramento M*
California State University, San Marcos M
Carlow University M
Carnegie Mellon University M*
Central Michigan University M*
Chapman University M
Chatham University M
Chicago State University M
City College of the City University of New York M*
Claremont Graduate University M,D
Clemson University M*
Cleveland State University M*
Colorado State University M*
Columbia College Chicago M
Columbia University M*
Concordia University (Canada) M
Cornell University M,D*
DePaul University M*
Eastern Kentucky University M*
Eastern Michigan University M
Eastern Washington University M
Emerson College M*
Fairleigh Dickinson University, College at Florham M*
Florida Atlantic University M
Florida International University M*
Florida State University M,D*
George Mason University M*
Georgia College & State University M
Georgia State University M,D*
Goddard College M
Goucher College M
Hofstra University M*
Hollins University M
Hunter College of the City University of New York M
Illinois State University M*
Indiana University Bloomington M,D*
Indiana University of Pennsylvania M,D
The Johns Hopkins University M*
Kennesaw State University M*
Kent State University M,D*
Lesley University M*
Lindenwood University M
Long Island University, Brooklyn Campus M*
Longwood University M*
Louisiana State University and Agricultural and Mechanical College M,D*
Loyola Marymount University M
Manhattanville College M*
Massachusetts Institute of Technology M*
McNeese State University M
Miami University M,D*
Michigan State University M,D*
Mills College M
Minnesota State University Mankato M,O
Minnesota State University Moorhead M
Murray State University M
Naropa University M*
National-Louis University M
National University M
New College of California M*
New England College M
New Mexico Highlands University M
New Mexico State University M,D
The New School: A University M*
New York University M*
North Carolina State University M*
Northeastern Illinois University M
Northern Arizona University M
Northern Michigan University M
Northwestern University M*
Oklahoma City University M
Oklahoma State University M,D*
Old Dominion University M*
Otis College of Art and Design M
Pacific Lutheran University M
Penn State University Park M,D*
Purdue University M,D*
Queens College of the City University of New York M
Queens University of Charlotte M
Rhode Island College M
Rivier College M
Roosevelt University M
Rowan University M
Rutgers, The State University of New Jersey, New Brunswick M*
Saint Joseph's University M*
Saint Mary's College of California M
Saint Xavier University M,O
Salisbury University M
San Diego State University M*
San Francisco State University M
San Jose State University M,O
Sarah Lawrence College M*
Savannah College of Art and Design M*
School of the Art Institute of Chicago M*
Seton Hill University M
Sewanee: The University of the South M*
Sonoma State University M
Southern Illinois University Carbondale M*
Southern Illinois University Edwardsville M
Southern New Hampshire University M,O*
Spalding University M
Syracuse University M,D*
Temple University M*
Texas State University-San Marcos M*
Towson University M
Union Institute & University M
The University of Akron M
The University of Alabama M,D
University of Alaska Anchorage M
University of Alaska Fairbanks M
The University of Arizona M*
University of Arkansas M*
University of Arkansas at Little Rock M
University of Baltimore M*
The University of British Columbia M*
University of California, Davis M,D*
University of California, Irvine M*
University of California, Riverside M*
University of California, Santa Cruz M*
University of Central Florida M*
University of Central Oklahoma M
University of Colorado at Boulder M,D*
University of Florida M,D*
University of Houston M,D*
University of Houston–Downtown M
University of Idaho M*
University of Illinois at Chicago M,D*
The University of Iowa M,D*
University of Kansas M,D*
University of Louisiana at Lafayette M,D*
University of Maryland, College Park M,D*
University of Massachusetts Amherst M,D*
University of Massachusetts Dartmouth M,O
University of Memphis M,D*
University of Miami M,D*
University of Michigan M*
University of Missouri–St. Louis M,O
The University of Montana M*
University of Nebraska at Kearney M
University of Nebraska at Omaha M,O
University of Nevada, Las Vegas M,D
University of New Hampshire M,D*
University of New Mexico M*
The University of North Carolina at Greensboro M
The University of North Carolina Wilmington M*
University of North Florida M
University of Notre Dame M*

P—first professional degree; M—master's degree; D—doctorate; O—other advanced degree;
**full description and/or announcement in Book 2, 3, 4, 5, or 6*

University of Oklahoma	M*
University of Oregon	M*
University of Pennsylvania	M,D*
University of Pittsburgh	M,D*
University of San Francisco	M
University of South Carolina	M,D*
University of Southern California	M*
University of Southern Maine	M
The University of Texas at Austin	M*
The University of Texas at El Paso	M
University of the Sacred Heart	M
The University of Toledo	M,O*
University of Utah	M*
University of Virginia	M*
University of West Florida	M
University of Windsor	M
University of Wyoming	M
Utah State University	M
Vanderbilt University	M*
Virginia Commonwealth University	M*
Warren Wilson College	M
Washington University in St. Louis	M*
Wayne State University	M,D*
Western Illinois University	M
Western Kentucky University	M
Western Michigan University	M,D*
Westminster College (UT)	M
West Virginia University	M*
Wichita State University	M*
Wilkes University	M
Wright State University	M*

ZOOLOGY

Auburn University	M,D*
Clemson University	M,D*
Colorado State University	M,D*
Connecticut College	M
Cornell University	P,M,D*
Emporia State University	M
Illinois State University	M,D*
Indiana University Bloomington	M,D*
Miami University	M,D*
Michigan State University	M,D*
Montana State University	M,D
North Carolina State University	M,D*
North Dakota State University	M,D
Oklahoma State University	M,D*
Oregon State University	M,D*
Southern Illinois University Carbondale	M,D*
Texas A&M University	M,D*
Texas Tech University	M,D
Uniformed Services University of the Health Sciences	M,D*
University of Alaska Fairbanks	M,D
The University of British Columbia	M,D*
University of California, Davis	M*
University of Chicago	D*
University of Connecticut	M,D*
University of Florida	M,D*
University of Guelph	M,D
University of Hawaii at Manoa	M,D*
University of Illinois at Urbana–Champaign	M,D*
University of Maine	M,D*
University of Manitoba	M,D
The University of Montana	M,D*
University of New Hampshire	M,D*
University of North Dakota	M,D
University of Oklahoma	M,D*
University of Puerto Rico, Medical Sciences Campus	M,D*
University of South Florida	M,D*
University of Toronto	M,D
University of Washington	D*
The University of Western Ontario	M,D
University of Wisconsin–Madison	M,D*
University of Wisconsin–Oshkosh	M
University of Wyoming	M,D
Virginia Polytechnic Institute and State University	M,D*
Washington State University	M,D*
Western Illinois University	M,O

DIRECTORY OF INSTITUTIONS AND THEIR OFFERINGS

ABILENE CHRISTIAN UNIVERSITY
Accounting M
Clinical Psychology M
Communication Disorders M
Communication—General M
Conflict Resolution and Mediation/Peace Studies M,O
Counseling Psychology M
Education—General M,O
Educational Administration M,O
Educational Measurement and Evaluation M
English M
Gerontological Nursing O
Gerontology M,O
Higher Education M
Human Resources Development M
Human Services M,O
Liberal Studies M
Marriage and Family Therapy M,O
Missions and Missiology M
Nursing—General M
Pastoral Ministry and Counseling M,D
Psychology—General M
Reading Education M
Rhetoric M
School Psychology M
Social Work M
Speech and Interpersonal Communication M
Theology P,M
Writing M

ACADEMY OF ART UNIVERSITY
Advertising and Public Relations M
Applied Arts and Design—General M*
Architecture M*
Art/Fine Arts M*
Clothing and Textiles M
Computer Art and Design M*
Film, Television, and Video Production M*
Graphic Design M*
Illustration M*
Industrial Design M*
Interior Design M*
Photography M*
Textile Design M*

ACADEMY OF CHINESE CULTURE AND HEALTH SCIENCES
Acupuncture and Oriental Medicine M

ACADEMY OF ORIENTAL MEDICINE AT AUSTIN
Acupuncture and Oriental Medicine M

ACADIA UNIVERSITY
Applied Mathematics M
Biological and Biomedical Sciences—General M
Chemistry M
Clinical Psychology M
Computer Science M
Counselor Education M
Curriculum and Instruction M
Education—General M
Educational Administration M
Educational Media/Instructional Technology M
English M
Geology M
Kinesiology and Movement Studies M
Mathematics Education M
Political Science M
Psychology—General M
Recreation and Park Management M
Science Education M
Social Sciences Education M
Sociology M
Special Education M
Statistics M
Theology P,M,D

ACUPUNCTURE & INTEGRATIVE MEDICINE COLLEGE, BERKELEY
Acupuncture and Oriental Medicine M

ACUPUNCTURE AND MASSAGE COLLEGE
Acupuncture and Oriental Medicine M

ADAMS STATE COLLEGE
Art/Fine Arts M
Counselor Education M
Education—General M
Health Education M
Physical Education M
Special Education M

ADELPHI UNIVERSITY
Accounting M
Art/Fine Arts M*
Biological and Biomedical Sciences—General M*
Business Administration and Management—General M,O
Clinical Psychology D,O
Communication Disorders M,D
Community Health M,O
Counseling Psychology M
Early Childhood Education M,O
Education—General M,D,O*
Educational Administration M,O
Educational Media/Instructional Technology M,O
Electronic Commerce M
Elementary Education M
Emergency Management O
English as a Second Language M,O
Environmental Management and Policy M*
Finance and Banking M
Gerontology M,O
Health Education M,O
Human Resources Management M,O
Management Information Systems M
Marketing M
Nursing—General M,D,O*
Physical Education M,O
Physics M
Psychology—General M,D,O*
Public Administration O
Public Health—General O
Reading Education M
School Psychology M
Secondary Education M
Social Work M,D*
Special Education M,O
Writing M*

ADLER GRADUATE SCHOOL
Business Administration and Management—General M,O
Counseling Psychology M,O
Counselor Education M,O
Industrial and Organizational Psychology M,O
Marriage and Family Therapy M,O
Organizational Management M,O
Psychoanalysis and Psychotherapy M,O

ADLER SCHOOL OF PROFESSIONAL PSYCHOLOGY
Addictions/Substance Abuse Counseling M,D,O
Art Therapy M,D,O
Clinical Psychology M,D,O
Counseling Psychology M,D,O
Gerontology M,D,O
Industrial and Organizational Psychology M,D,O
Marriage and Family Therapy M,D,O
Psychology—General M,D,O*

AGNES SCOTT COLLEGE
English Education M*
Mathematics Education M*
Science Education M

AIR FORCE INSTITUTE OF TECHNOLOGY
Aerospace/Aeronautical Engineering M,D
Applied Mathematics M,D
Applied Physics M,D
Astrophysics M,D
Computer Engineering M,D
Computer Science M,D
Electrical Engineering M,D
Engineering and Applied Sciences—General M,D
Engineering Management M
Engineering Physics M,D
Environmental Engineering M
Environmental Management and Policy M
Logistics M,D
Management Information Systems M
Management of Technology M,D
Materials Sciences M,D
Nuclear Engineering M,D
Operations Research M,D
Optical Sciences M,D
Planetary and Space Sciences M,D
Systems Engineering M,D

ALABAMA AGRICULTURAL AND MECHANICAL UNIVERSITY
Agricultural Economics and Agribusiness M
Agricultural Sciences—General M,D
Agronomy and Soil Sciences M,D
Animal Sciences M,D
Applied Physics M,D
Biological and Biomedical Sciences—General M
Business Administration and Management—General M
Clinical Psychology M,O
Communication Disorders M
Computer Science M
Counseling Psychology M,O
Counselor Education M,O
Early Childhood Education M,O
Economics M
Education—General M,O
Educational Administration M,O
Elementary Education M,O
Engineering and Applied Sciences—General M
Environmental Sciences M,D
Family and Consumer Sciences-General M,D
Finance and Banking M
Food Science and Technology M,D
Human Resources Management M,O
Marketing M
Materials Sciences M,D
Music Education M
Music M
Optical Sciences M,D
Physical Education M
Physics M,D
Plant Sciences M,D
Psychology—General M,O
School Psychology M,O
Secondary Education M,O
Social Work M
Special Education M,O
Urban and Regional Planning M
Vocational and Technical Education M

ALABAMA STATE UNIVERSITY
Accounting M
Allied Health—General D
Biological and Biomedical Sciences—General M
Business Administration and Management—General M
Counselor Education M,O
Early Childhood Education M,O
Education—General M,D,O
Educational Administration M,D,O
Educational Media/Instructional Technology M,O
Educational Policy M,D,O
Elementary Education M,O
English Education M,O
Health Education M
Mathematics Education M,O
Mathematics M,O
Music M
Physical Education M
Physical Therapy D
Science Education M,O
Secondary Education M,O
Social Sciences Education M,O
Special Education M

ALASKA PACIFIC UNIVERSITY
Business Administration and Management—General M
Counseling Psychology M
Education—General M
Elementary Education M
Environmental Education M
Environmental Sciences M
Finance and Banking M
Health Services Management and Hospital Administration M
Interdisciplinary Studies M
Liberal Studies M
Middle School Education M
Telecommunications Management M

ALBANY COLLEGE OF PHARMACY OF UNION UNIVERSITY
Pharmacy P

ALBANY LAW SCHOOL OF UNION UNIVERSITY
Law P,M

ALBANY MEDICAL COLLEGE
Allopathic Medicine P
Bioethics M,O
Biological and Biomedical Sciences—General M,D
Cardiovascular Sciences M,D
Cell Biology M,D
Immunology M,D
Microbiology M,D
Molecular Biology M,D
Neuroscience M,D
Nurse Anesthesia M
Pharmacology M,D
Physician Assistant Studies M

ALBANY STATE UNIVERSITY
Business Administration and Management—General M
Business Education M
Counselor Education M
Criminal Justice and Criminology M
Early Childhood Education M
Economics M
Education—General M,O
Educational Administration M,O
English Education M
Health Education M
Health Services Management and Hospital Administration M
Human Resources Management M
Mathematics Education M
Middle School Education M
Music Education M
Nursing—General M
Physical Education M
Public Administration M
Public Policy M
Reading Education M
Science Education M
Social Sciences Education M
Special Education M
Water Resources M

ALBERT EINSTEIN COLLEGE OF MEDICINE
Allopathic Medicine P
Anatomy D
Biochemistry D
Biological and Biomedical Sciences—General D*
Biophysics D
Cell Biology D
Developmental Biology D
Immunology D
Microbiology D
Molecular Biology D
Molecular Genetics D
Molecular Pharmacology D
Neurobiology D
Pathology D
Physiology D

ALBERTSON COLLEGE OF IDAHO
Education—General M

ALBERTUS MAGNUS COLLEGE
Art Therapy M
Business Administration and Management—General M
Liberal Studies M

ALBRIGHT COLLEGE
Early Childhood Education M
Education—General M
Elementary Education M
English as a Second Language M
Special Education M

ALCORN STATE UNIVERSITY
Agricultural Economics and Agribusiness M
Agricultural Education M,O
Agricultural Sciences—General M
Agronomy and Soil Sciences M
Animal Sciences M
Biological and Biomedical Sciences—General M
Business Administration and Management—General M
Computer Science M
Counselor Education M,O
Education—General M,O
Elementary Education M,O
Health Education M,O
Information Science M
Nursing—General M
Physical Education M,O
Secondary Education M,O
Special Education M,O
Vocational and Technical Education M,O

ALDERSON-BROADDUS COLLEGE
- Allied Health—General M
- Emergency Medical Services M

ALFRED UNIVERSITY
- Applied Arts and Design—General M
- Art/Fine Arts M,D
- Bioengineering M,D
- Business Administration and Management—General M
- Ceramic Sciences and Engineering M,D*
- Computer Art and Design M
- Counselor Education M,O
- Education—General M,O
- Electrical Engineering M
- Engineering and Applied Sciences—General M,D
- Internet and Interactive Multimedia M
- Materials Sciences M,D
- Mechanical Engineering M
- Reading Education M,O
- School Psychology M,D,O*

ALLEN COLLEGE
- Acute Care/Critical Care Nursing M
- Family Nurse Practitioner Studies M
- Health Education M
- Nursing and Healthcare Administration M
- Nursing—General M

ALLIANCE THEOLOGICAL SEMINARY
- Missions and Missiology P,M
- Pastoral Ministry and Counseling P,M
- Theology P,M

ALLIANCE UNIVERSITY COLLEGE
- Missions and Missiology P,M,O
- Pastoral Ministry and Counseling P,M,O
- Religious Education P,M,O
- Theology P,M,O

ALLIANT INTERNATIONAL UNIVERSITY–FRESNO
- Clinical Psychology D*
- Education—General M*
- Educational Administration D*
- English as a Second Language M,D,O*
- Forensic Psychology D*
- Psychology—General D

ALLIANT INTERNATIONAL UNIVERSITY–IRVINE
- Education—General M,O
- Educational Administration M,D,O*
- Educational Media/Instructional Technology M,O
- Educational Psychology M,D,O*
- English as a Second Language M,D*
- Forensic Sciences D
- Higher Education M,D,O
- Marriage and Family Therapy M,D*
- Multilingual and Multicultural Education M,O
- School Psychology M,D,O
- Special Education M,O

ALLIANT INTERNATIONAL UNIVERSITY–LOS ANGELES
- Business Administration and Management—General D*
- Clinical Psychology D*
- Education—General M*
- Educational Administration M,D,O*
- Educational Psychology M,D,O*
- Forensic Psychology D*
- Higher Education M,D,O
- Industrial and Organizational Psychology M,D*
- Psychology—General D
- School Psychology M,D,O
- Student Affairs M,D,O

ALLIANT INTERNATIONAL UNIVERSITY–MÉXICO CITY
- Business Administration and Management—General M*
- Counseling Psychology M
- Education—General M
- International Affairs M*
- International Business M

ALLIANT INTERNATIONAL UNIVERSITY–SACRAMENTO
- Clinical Psychology D*
- Education—General M*
- Industrial and Organizational Psychology D
- Marriage and Family Therapy M*
- Psychology—General M,D

ALLIANT INTERNATIONAL UNIVERSITY–SAN DIEGO
- Clinical Psychology M,D*
- Education—General M,O*
- Educational Administration M,D,O*
- Educational Psychology M,D,O*
- English as a Second Language M,D,O*
- Finance and Banking M,D
- Higher Education M,D,O
- Industrial and Organizational Psychology M,D*
- International Affairs M*
- International Business M,D
- Management Information Systems M,D
- Management of Technology M,D
- Management Strategy and Policy M,D
- Marketing M,D
- Marriage and Family Therapy M,D*
- Psychology—General M,D
- School Psychology M,D,O
- Student Affairs M,D,O

ALLIANT INTERNATIONAL UNIVERSITY–SAN FRANCISCO
- Business Administration and Management—General M
- Clinical Psychology D,O*
- Education—General M,O*
- Educational Administration M,D,O*
- Educational Psychology M,D,O*
- Higher Education M,D,O
- Industrial and Organizational Psychology M,D*
- Multilingual and Multicultural Education M,O
- Pharmacology M
- Psychology—General M,D,O
- School Psychology M,D,O
- Special Education M,O

ALVERNIA COLLEGE
- Business Administration and Management—General M
- Education—General M
- Liberal Studies M
- Occupational Therapy M
- Social Psychology M

ALVERNO COLLEGE
- Adult Education M
- Business Administration and Management—General M
- Education—General M
- Educational Administration M
- Educational Media/Instructional Technology M
- Nursing—General M
- Reading Education M
- Science Education M

AMBERTON UNIVERSITY
- Business Administration and Management—General M
- Counseling Psychology M
- Human Resources Development M
- Human Resources Management M
- Interdisciplinary Studies M

AMERICAN ACADEMY OF ART
- Art/Fine Arts M
- Computer Art and Design M
- Internet and Interactive Multimedia M

AMERICAN BAPTIST SEMINARY OF THE WEST
- Theology P,M

THE AMERICAN COLLEGE
- Finance and Banking M

AMERICAN COLLEGE OF ACUPUNCTURE AND ORIENTAL MEDICINE
- Acupuncture and Oriental Medicine M

AMERICAN COLLEGE OF COMPUTER & INFORMATION SCIENCES
- Business Administration and Management—General M
- Computer Science M
- Information Science M

AMERICAN COLLEGE OF THESSALONIKI
- Business Administration and Management—General M,O
- Entrepreneurship M,O
- Finance and Banking M,O
- Marketing M,O

AMERICAN COLLEGE OF TRADITIONAL CHINESE MEDICINE
- Acupuncture and Oriental Medicine M,D,O

AMERICAN CONSERVATORY THEATER
- Theater M,O

AMERICAN FILM INSTITUTE CONSERVATORY
- Film, Television, and Video Production M

AMERICAN GRADUATE SCHOOL OF INTERNATIONAL RELATIONS AND DIPLOMACY
- International Affairs M,D*

AMERICAN GRADUATE UNIVERSITY
- Business Administration and Management—General M,O
- Project Management M,O

AMERICAN HEALTH SCIENCES UNIVERSITY
- Nutrition M

AMERICAN INTERCONTINENTAL UNIVERSITY (CA)
- Business Administration and Management—General M
- Education—General M
- Educational Media/Instructional Technology M
- Management Information Systems M

AMERICAN INTERCONTINENTAL UNIVERSITY (FL)
- Accounting M
- Business Administration and Management—General M
- Computer and Information Systems Security M
- Educational Media/Instructional Technology M
- Finance and Banking M
- Human Resources Management M
- Information Science M
- International Business M
- Marketing M

AMERICAN INTERCONTINENTAL UNIVERSITY BUCKHEAD CAMPUS
- Accounting M
- Business Administration and Management—General M
- Finance and Banking M
- Marketing M

AMERICAN INTERCONTINENTAL UNIVERSITY DUNWOODY CAMPUS
- Information Science M
- International Business M
- Management Information Systems M

AMERICAN INTERCONTINENTAL UNIVERSITY-LONDON
- Business Administration and Management—General M
- International Business M
- Management Information Systems M

AMERICAN INTERCONTINENTAL UNIVERSITY ONLINE
- Accounting M
- Business Administration and Management—General M
- Computer and Information Systems Security M
- Curriculum and Instruction M
- Education—General M
- Educational Administration M
- Educational Measurement and Evaluation M
- Educational Media/Instructional Technology M
- Finance and Banking M
- Health Services Management and Hospital Administration M
- Human Resources Management M
- Industrial and Manufacturing Management M
- Industrial and Organizational Psychology M
- Information Science M
- International Business M
- Marketing M
- Project Management M

AMERICAN INTERNATIONAL COLLEGE
- Business Administration and Management—General M
- Child Development M,D,O
- Clinical Psychology M
- Criminal Justice and Criminology M
- Education—General M,D,O
- Educational Administration M,D,O
- Educational Psychology M,D,O
- Elementary Education M,D,O
- Forensic Psychology M
- Human Resources Development M
- Nursing—General M
- Occupational Therapy M
- Organizational Management M
- Physical Therapy M,D
- Psychology—General M,D
- Public Administration M
- Reading Education M,D,O
- Secondary Education M,D,O
- Special Education M,D,O

AMERICAN JEWISH UNIVERSITY
- Business Administration and Management—General M
- Education—General M
- Jewish Studies M
- Nonprofit Management M
- Social Work M
- Theology M

AMERICAN PUBLIC UNIVERSITY SYSTEM
- Business Administration and Management—General M
- Conflict Resolution and Mediation/Peace Studies M
- Criminal Justice and Criminology M
- Emergency Management M
- Environmental Management and Policy M
- History M
- Homeland Security M
- Humanities M
- International Affairs M
- Logistics M
- Military and Defense Studies M
- National Security M
- Political Science M
- Public Administration M
- Public Health—General M
- Sports Management M
- Transportation Management M

AMERICAN SENTINEL UNIVERSITY
- Business Administration and Management—General M
- Computer Science M
- Health Informatics M
- Health Services Management and Hospital Administration M
- Management Information Systems M
- Nursing—General M

AMERICAN UNIVERSITY
- Accounting M
- American Studies M,D,O
- Anthropology M,D,O
- Applied Economics M,D,O
- Applied Science and Technology M,O
- Applied Social Research M,O
- Applied Statistics M,O
- Art History M
- Art/Fine Arts M
- Arts Administration M,O
- Biological and Biomedical Sciences—General M
- Biopsychology M
- Business Administration and Management—General M,O
- Chemistry M
- Clinical Psychology D
- Communication—General M*
- Comparative Literature M
- Computer Science M,O
- Conflict Resolution and Mediation/Peace Studies M,D,O
- Criminal Justice and Criminology M,D
- Dance M,O
- Economics M,D,O
- Education—General M,D,O
- Educational Administration M,D
- Educational Media/Instructional Technology M,D

Electronic Commerce M
Elementary Education M,O
English as a Second Language M,O
Entrepreneurship M
Environmental Management and Policy M,D,O
Environmental Sciences M
Ethics M,D,O
Exercise and Sports Science M
Experimental Psychology M
Film, Television, and Video Production M
Finance and Banking M,D,O
French O
History M,D
Interdisciplinary Studies M
International Affairs M,D,O*
International and Comparative Education M
International Business M
International Development M,D,O
Journalism M
Latin American Studies M,O
Law P,M,O
Legal and Justice Studies M,D,O
Management Information Systems M,O
Marine Sciences M
Marketing M
Mass Communication M
Mathematics M
Media Studies M
Neuroscience D
Organizational Management M
Philosophy M
Physics M
Political Science M,D,O
Psychology—General M,D
Public Administration M,D
Public Affairs M
Public Policy M
Real Estate M
Russian O
Secondary Education M,O
Social Psychology M
Sociology M,O
Spanish M,O
Special Education M
Statistics M,O
Taxation M
Toxicology M,O
Translation and Interpretation M,O
Writing M

THE AMERICAN UNIVERSITY IN CAIRO

Anthropology M
Business Administration and Management—General M,O
Communication—General M,O
Comparative Literature M
Computer Science M
Economics M
Engineering and Applied Sciences—General M,O
English as a Second Language M,O
English M
Foreign Languages Education M
Journalism M,O
Mass Communication M,O
Near and Middle Eastern Languages M,O
Near and Middle Eastern Studies M,O
Political Science M
Sociology M

THE AMERICAN UNIVERSITY IN DUBAI

Business Administration and Management—General M
International Business M

THE AMERICAN UNIVERSITY OF ATHENS

Biological and Biomedical Sciences—General M
Business Administration and Management—General M
Computer Science M
Corporate and Organizational Communication M
Engineering and Applied Sciences—General M
Political Science M
Systems Engineering M
Telecommunications M

Close-Up on page 797.

AMERICAN UNIVERSITY OF BEIRUT

Agricultural Economics and Agribusiness M
Agronomy and Soil Sciences M
Allopathic Medicine P,M
Animal Sciences M
Anthropology M
Aquaculture M
Archaeology M
Biochemistry P,M
Biological and Biomedical Sciences—General M
Business Administration and Management—General M
Chemistry M
Civil Engineering M
Computer Engineering M
Computer Science M
Demography and Population Studies M
Economics M
Education—General M
Electrical Engineering M
Engineering Management M
English M
Environmental and Occupational Health M
Environmental Management and Policy M
Environmental Sciences M
Epidemiology M
Food Science and Technology M
Geology M
History M
Mathematics M
Mechanical Engineering M
Microbiology P,M
Near and Middle Eastern Languages M
Near and Middle Eastern Studies M
Neuroscience P,M
Nursing—General M
Nutrition M
Pharmacology P,M
Philosophy M
Physics M
Physiology P,M
Plant Sciences M
Political Science M
Psychology—General M
Public Administration M
Public Health—General M
Sociology M
Statistics M
Urban and Regional Planning M
Urban Design M
Water Resources Engineering M

THE AMERICAN UNIVERSITY OF PARIS

Communication—General M
Conflict Resolution and Mediation/Peace Studies M
Finance and Banking M
International Affairs M
Near and Middle Eastern Studies M
Public Administration M

AMERICAN UNIVERSITY OF PUERTO RICO

Art Education M
Art History M
Criminal Justice and Criminology M
Education—General M
Elementary Education M
Physical Education M
Science Education M
Special Education M

ANDERSON UNIVERSITY

Accounting M,D
Business Administration and Management—General M,D
Education—General M
Missions and Missiology P,M,D
Theology P,M,D

ANDOVER NEWTON THEOLOGICAL SCHOOL

Religious Education P,M,D
Theology P,M,D

ANDREW JACKSON UNIVERSITY

Business Administration and Management—General M
Criminal Justice and Criminology M
Entrepreneurship M
Finance and Banking M
Health Services Management and Hospital Administration M
Hospitality Management M
Human Resources Management M
International Business M
Marketing M
Public Administration M

ANDREWS UNIVERSITY

Accounting M
Allied Health—General M
Architecture M
Biological and Biomedical Sciences—General M
Business Administration and Management—General M
Communication—General M
Counseling Psychology D
Curriculum and Instruction M,D,O
Developmental Psychology M,D
Economics M
Education—General M,D,O
Educational Administration M,D,O
Educational Psychology M,D
Elementary Education M,D,O
Engineering and Applied Sciences—General M
English as a Second Language M,D,O
English Education M,D,O
English M
Finance and Banking M
Foreign Languages Education M,D,O
History M
Human Services M
International Development M
Marketing M
Mathematics M
Music M
Nursing—General M
Nutrition M
Pastoral Ministry and Counseling P,M,D,O
Physical Therapy D
Psychology—General M,D,O
Reading Education M
Religious Education M,D,O
School Psychology M,O
Science Education M,D,O
Secondary Education M,D,O
Social Psychology M
Social Sciences Education M,D,O
Social Work M
Software Engineering M
Special Education M,D,O
Theology P,M,D,O

ANGELO STATE UNIVERSITY

Accounting M
Adult Nursing M
Agricultural Sciences—General M
Animal Sciences M
Biological and Biomedical Sciences—General M
Business Administration and Management—General M
Communication—General M
Counseling Psychology M
Counselor Education M
Curriculum and Instruction M
Education—General M
Educational Administration M
Educational Measurement and Evaluation M
English M
Higher Education M
History M
Industrial and Organizational Psychology M
Interdisciplinary Studies M
Journalism M
Kinesiology and Movement Studies M
Medical/Surgical Nursing M
Nursing Education M
Physical Therapy M
Psychology—General M
Public Administration M
Reading Education M

Close-Up on page 799.

ANNA MARIA COLLEGE

Art/Fine Arts M
Business Administration and Management—General M,O
Counseling Psychology M
Criminal Justice and Criminology M
Early Childhood Education M,O
Education—General M,O
Elementary Education M,O
Emergency Management M,O
Environmental and Occupational Health M
Fire Protection Engineering M
Human Services M
Pastoral Ministry and Counseling M
Psychology—General M
Reading Education M,O

ANTIOCH UNIVERSITY LOS ANGELES

Business Administration and Management—General M
Clinical Psychology M
Education—General M
Human Resources Development M
Organizational Management M
Psychology—General M
Writing M,O

ANTIOCH UNIVERSITY MCGREGOR

Art/Fine Arts M
Business Administration and Management—General M
Comparative Literature M
Conflict Resolution and Mediation/Peace Studies M
Counseling Psychology M
Education—General M
Educational Administration M
Film, Television, and Video Production M
Liberal Studies M*
Psychology—General M
Theater M
Writing M

Announcement on page 293.

ANTIOCH UNIVERSITY NEW ENGLAND

Business Administration and Management—General M*
Clinical Psychology M,D*
Counseling Psychology M
Education—General M*
Educational Administration M
Environmental Biology M
Environmental Education M
Environmental Management and Policy M,D
Environmental Sciences M,D*
Foundations and Philosophy of Education M
Interdisciplinary Studies M
Marriage and Family Therapy M
Organizational Management O
Psychology—General M,O*
Science Education M
Therapies—Dance, Drama, and Music M

ANTIOCH UNIVERSITY SANTA BARBARA

Clinical Psychology D
Counseling Psychology M
Education—General M
Organizational Management M
Psychology—General M

ANTIOCH UNIVERSITY SEATTLE

Business Administration and Management—General M
Corporate and Organizational Communication M
Education—General M*
Environmental Management and Policy M
Industrial and Organizational Psychology M
Organizational Management M
Psychology—General M,D

APEX SCHOOL OF THEOLOGY

Theology P,M

APPALACHIAN SCHOOL OF LAW

Law P

APPALACHIAN STATE UNIVERSITY

Accounting M
American Studies M
Applied Physics M
Biological and Biomedical Sciences—General M
Business Administration and Management—General M
Child Development M
Clinical Psychology M
Communication Disorders M
Computer Science M
Counselor Education M
Criminal Justice and Criminology M
Curriculum and Instruction M
Education—General M,D,O
Educational Administration M,D,O
Educational Media/Instructional Technology M
Elementary Education M
English Education M
English M
Exercise and Sports Science M
Experimental Psychology M
Family and Consumer Sciences-General M
French M
Geography M
Gerontology M
Health Psychology M
Higher Education M,O
History M
Home Economics Education M
Industrial and Organizational Psychology M
Library Science M
Marriage and Family Therapy M
Mathematics Education M
Mathematics M
Music Education M
Music M

Political Science M
Psychology—General M,O
Public Administration M
Public History M
Reading Education M
Romance Languages M
School Psychology M,O
Secondary Education M
Social Psychology M
Social Sciences Education M
Social Work M
Spanish M
Special Education M
Therapies—Dance, Drama, and Music M
Vocational and Technical Education M

AQUINAS COLLEGE

Business Administration and Management—General M
Education—General M

AQUINAS INSTITUTE OF THEOLOGY

Health Services Management and Hospital Administration P,M,D,O
Pastoral Ministry and Counseling P,M,D,O
Theology P,M,D,O

ARCADIA UNIVERSITY

Art Education M,D,O
Business Administration and Management—General M
Child Development M,D,O
Community Health M
Computer Education M,D,O
Conflict Resolution and Mediation/Peace Studies M
Early Childhood Education M,D,O
Education—General M,D,O
Educational Administration M,D,O
Educational Media/Instructional Technology M,D,O
Educational Psychology M,D,O
Elementary Education M,D,O
English Education M,D,O
English M
Environmental Education M,D,O
Forensic Sciences M
Genetic Counseling M
Health Education M
Humanities M
International Affairs M
Mathematics Education M,D,O
Music Education M,D,O
Physical Therapy D
Psychology—General M,D,O
Reading Education M,D,O
School Psychology M
Science Education M,D,O
Secondary Education M,D,O
Social Psychology M
Social Sciences Education M,D,O
Special Education M,D,O
Theater M,D,O

Close-Up on page 801.

ARGOSY UNIVERSITY, ATLANTA CAMPUS

Accounting M,D
Biopsychology M,D,O
Business Administration and Management—General M,D*
Clinical Psychology M,D,O
Counselor Education M,D,O
Education—General M,D,O
Educational Administration M,D,O
Elementary Education M,D,O
Finance and Banking M,D
Health Psychology M,D,O
Health Services Management and Hospital Administration M,D
Higher Education M,D,O
International Business M,D
Management Information Systems M,D
Marketing M,D
Marriage and Family Therapy M,D,O
Psychology—General M,D,O*
Secondary Education M,D,O
Social Psychology M,D,O

ARGOSY UNIVERSITY, CHICAGO CAMPUS

Accounting M,D
Business Administration and Management—General M,D*
Clinical Psychology M*
Community College Education M,D,O
Counseling Psychology M,D
Counselor Education D
Education—General M,D,O*
Educational Administration M,D,O
Elementary Education M,D,O
Finance and Banking M,D
Forensic Psychology D
Forensic Sciences M,D,O
Health Psychology D
Health Services Management and Hospital Administration M,D
Higher Education M,D,O
Human Development D
International Business M,D
Management Information Systems M,D
Marketing M,D
Marriage and Family Therapy D
Organizational Management D
Psychoanalysis and Psychotherapy D
Psychology—General M,D,O
Secondary Education M,D,O
Social Psychology M,D,O

ARGOSY UNIVERSITY, DALLAS CAMPUS

Business Administration and Management—General M*
Clinical Psychology M,D*
Counseling Psychology M,D
Education—General M*
Educational Administration M
Psychology—General M,D

ARGOSY UNIVERSITY, DENVER CAMPUS

Accounting M,D
Business Administration and Management—General M,D*
Clinical Psychology M,D
Counseling Psychology M,D
Counselor Education M,D
Education—General M,D*
Educational Administration M,D
Educational Media/Instructional Technology M,D
Elementary Education M,D
Finance and Banking M,D
Forensic Psychology M,D
Health Services Management and Hospital Administration M,D
Higher Education M,D
International Business M,D
Management Information Systems M,D
Marketing M,D
Organizational Management M,D
Social Psychology M,D*

ARGOSY UNIVERSITY, HAWAI'I CAMPUS

Accounting M,D,O
Addictions/Substance Abuse Counseling O
Business Administration and Management—General M,D,O*
Clinical Psychology M,D,O
Education—General M,D*
Educational Administration M,D
Elementary Education M,D
Finance and Banking M,D,O
Health Services Management and Hospital Administration M,D,O
Higher Education M,D
International Business M,D,O
Management Information Systems M,D,O
Marketing M,D,O
Marriage and Family Therapy M
Organizational Management D
Pharmacology O
Psychology—General M,D,O*
School Psychology M,D
Secondary Education M,D

ARGOSY UNIVERSITY, INLAND EMPIRE CAMPUS

Accounting M,D
Business Administration and Management—General M,D*
Clinical Psychology M,D
Community College Education M,D
Counseling Psychology M,D*
Educational Administration M,D*
Elementary Education M,D
Finance and Banking M,D
Health Services Management and Hospital Administration M,D
Higher Education M,D
International Business M,D
Management Information Systems M,D
Marketing M,D
Marriage and Family Therapy M,D
Secondary Education M,D

ARGOSY UNIVERSITY, NASHVILLE CAMPUS

Accounting D
Business Administration and Management—General D*
Community College Education M,D
Counseling Psychology M,D*
Counselor Education M,D
Educational Administration M,D*
Educational Media/Instructional Technology M,D
Elementary Education M,D
Higher Education M,D
International Business D
Management Information Systems D
Marketing D
Secondary Education M,D

ARGOSY UNIVERSITY, ORANGE COUNTY CAMPUS

Accounting M,D,O
Business Administration and Management—General M,D,O*
Clinical Psychology M,D,O
Community College Education M,D
Counseling Psychology M,D
Education—General M,D*
Educational Administration M,D
Educational Media/Instructional Technology M,D
Elementary Education M,D
Finance and Banking M,D,O
Forensic Psychology M
Health Services Management and Hospital Administration M,D,O
Higher Education M,D
International Business M,D,O
Management Information Systems M,D,O
Marketing M,D,O
Marriage and Family Therapy M,D,O
Organizational Management M,D,O
Psychology—General M,D,O*
Public Administration M,D,O
Secondary Education M,D

ARGOSY UNIVERSITY, PHOENIX CAMPUS

Accounting M,D
Business Administration and Management—General M,D*
Clinical Psychology M,D,O
Community College Education M,D,O
Counseling Psychology M
Education—General M,D,O*
Educational Administration M,D,O
Elementary Education M,D,O
Finance and Banking M,D
Forensic Psychology M
Health Services Management and Hospital Administration M,D
Higher Education M,D,O
International Business M,D
Management Information Systems M,D
Marketing M,D
Psychology—General M,D,O*
School Psychology M,D
Secondary Education M,D,O
Sport Psychology M,D,O

ARGOSY UNIVERSITY, SAN DIEGO CAMPUS

Accounting M,D
Business Administration and Management—General M,D*
Clinical Psychology M,D
Community College Education M,D
Counseling Psychology M,D*
Education—General M,D*
Educational Administration M,D
Elementary Education M,D
Finance and Banking M,D
Higher Education M,D
International Business M,D
Management Information Systems M,D
Marketing M,D
Marriage and Family Therapy M,D
Psychology—General M,D
Public Administration M,D
Secondary Education M,D

ARGOSY UNIVERSITY, SAN FRANCISCO BAY AREA CAMPUS

Accounting M,D
Business Administration and Management—General M,D*
Clinical Psychology M,D
Community College Education M,D
Counseling Psychology M
Education—General M,D*
Educational Administration M,D
Elementary Education M,D
Finance and Banking M,D
Forensic Psychology M
Health Services Management and Hospital Administration M,D
Higher Education M,D
International Business M,D
Management Information Systems M,D
Marketing M,D
Organizational Management M,D
Psychology—General M,D*
Secondary Education M,D

ARGOSY UNIVERSITY, SANTA MONICA CAMPUS

Accounting M,D
Business Administration and Management—General M,D*
Clinical Psychology M,D*
Community College Education M,D
Counseling Psychology M,D
Education—General M,D*
Educational Administration M,D
Elementary Education M,D
Finance and Banking M,D
Health Services Management and Hospital Administration M,D
Higher Education M,D
International Business M,D
Management Information Systems M,D
Marketing M,D
Marriage and Family Therapy M,D
Organizational Management M,D
Psychology—General M,D
Secondary Education M,D

ARGOSY UNIVERSITY, SARASOTA CAMPUS

Accounting M,D,O
Business Administration and Management—General M,D,O*
Clinical Psychology M,D,O
Counseling Psychology M,D,O
Counselor Education M,D,O
Education—General M,D,O*
Educational Administration M,D,O
Educational Media/Instructional Technology M,D,O
Elementary Education M,D,O
Finance and Banking M,D,O
Forensic Psychology M,D,O
Health Services Management and Hospital Administration M,D,O
Higher Education M,D,O
International Business M,D,O
Management Information Systems M,D,O
Marketing M,D,O
Marriage and Family Therapy M,D,O
Organizational Management M,D,O
Pastoral Ministry and Counseling M,D,O
Psychology—General M,D,O*
School Psychology M,D,O
Secondary Education M,D,O
Social Psychology M,D,O

ARGOSY UNIVERSITY, SCHAUMBURG CAMPUS

Accounting M,D,O
Business Administration and Management—General M,D,O*
Clinical Psychology M,D,O*
Community College Education M,D,O
Counseling Psychology M,D,O
Counselor Education M,D,O
Education—General M,D,O*
Educational Administration M,D,O
Elementary Education M,D,O
Finance and Banking M,D,O
Forensic Psychology M,D,O
Health Psychology M,D,O
Health Services Management and Hospital Administration M,D,O
Higher Education M,D,O
International Business M,D,O
Management Information Systems M,D,O
Marketing M,D,O
Marriage and Family Therapy M,D,O
Organizational Management M,D,O
Psychology—General M,D,O
Secondary Education M,D,O
Social Psychology M,D,O

ARGOSY UNIVERSITY, SEATTLE CAMPUS

Accounting M,D
Business Administration and Management—General M,D*
Clinical Psychology M,D*
Community College Education M,D
Counseling Psychology M,D
Education—General M,D*
Educational Administration M,D
Educational Media/Instructional Technology M,D
Elementary Education M,D
Finance and Banking M,D
Health Services Management and Hospital Administration M,D
Higher Education M,D
International Business M,D
Management Information Systems M,D
Marketing M,D
Psychology—General M,D
Secondary Education M,D

ARGOSY UNIVERSITY, TAMPA CAMPUS

Accounting M,D,O
Business Administration and Management—General M,D,O*
Clinical Psychology M,D

Community College Education M,D,O
Counseling Psychology M,D
Counselor Education M,D
Education—General M,D,O*
Educational Administration M,D,O
Elementary Education M,D,O
Finance and Banking M,D,O
Health Services Management and Hospital Administration M,D,O
Higher Education M,D,O
International Business M,D,O
Management Information Systems M,D,O
Marketing M,D,O
Marriage and Family Therapy M,D
Neuroscience M,D
Organizational Management M,D
Psychology—General M,D*
Public Administration M,D,O
Secondary Education M,D,O

ARGOSY UNIVERSITY, TWIN CITIES CAMPUS

Accounting M,D
Biopsychology M,D,O
Business Administration and Management—General M,D*
Clinical Psychology M,D,O
Education—General M,D,O*
Educational Administration M,D,O
Educational Media/Instructional Technology M,D,O
Elementary Education M,D,O
Finance and Banking M,D
Forensic Psychology M,D,O
Health Psychology M,D,O
Health Services Management and Hospital Administration M,D
Higher Education M,D,O
International Business M,D
Management Information Systems M,D
Marketing M,D
Marriage and Family Therapy M,D,O
Psychology—General M,D,O*
Secondary Education M,D,O

ARGOSY UNIVERSITY, WASHINGTON DC CAMPUS

Accounting M,D,O
Business Administration and Management—General M,D,O*
Clinical Psychology M,D,O*
Counseling Psychology M,D,O
Counselor Education M,D,O
Education—General M,D,O*
Educational Administration M,D,O
Elementary Education M,D,O
Finance and Banking M,D,O
Forensic Psychology M,D,O
Health Psychology M,D,O
Health Services Management and Hospital Administration M,D,O
Higher Education M,D,O
International Business M,D,O
Management Information Systems M,D,O
Marketing M,D,O
Marriage and Family Therapy M,D,O
Organizational Management M,D,O
Psychology—General M,D,O
Secondary Education M,D,O
Social Psychology M,D,O

ARIZONA STATE UNIVERSITY

Accounting M,D
Aerospace/Aeronautical Engineering M,D
Animal Behavior M,D
Anthropology M,D
Applied Arts and Design—General M
Applied Mathematics M,D
Architectural History D
Architecture M
Art/Fine Arts M
Astronomy M,D
Biochemistry M,D
Bioengineering M,D
Biological and Biomedical Sciences—General M,D
Biostatistics M,D
Building Science M
Business Administration and Management—General M,D
Cell Biology M,D
Chemical Engineering M,D
Chemistry M,D
Child and Family Studies M,D
Civil Engineering M,D
Clinical Psychology D
Cognitive Sciences D
Communication Disorders M,D
Communication—General M,D
Comparative Literature M,D
Computational Biology M
Computational Sciences M,D
Computer Science M,D*
Conservation Biology M,D
Construction Engineering M
Counseling Psychology D
Counselor Education M
Curriculum and Instruction M,D
Dance M
Demography and Population Studies M,D
Developmental Biology M,D
Developmental Psychology D
Ecology M,D
Economics M,D
Education—General M,D
Educational Administration M,D
Educational Media/Instructional Technology M,D
Educational Psychology M,D
Electrical Engineering M,D
Engineering and Applied Sciences—General M,D
English as a Second Language M,D
English M,D
Environmental Design D
Evolutionary Biology M,D
Exercise and Sports Science D
Finance and Banking M,D
Foundations and Philosophy of Education M
French M
Genetics M,D
Geography M,D
Geological Engineering M,D
Geosciences M,D
German M
Health Services Management and Hospital Administration M
Health Services Research M,D
Higher Education M,D
History of Science and Technology M,D
History M,D
Human Development M,D
Humanities M
Industrial/Management Engineering M,D
Journalism M
Kinesiology and Movement Studies M,D*
Landscape Architecture M
Latin American Studies M,D
Law P
Legal and Justice Studies M,D
Linguistics M,D
Management Information Systems M,D
Marketing M,D
Materials Engineering M,D
Materials Sciences M,D*
Mathematics M,D
Mechanical Engineering M,D
Microbiology M,D
Music M,D
Neuroscience M,D
Nursing—General M
Philosophy M,D
Physics M,D
Physiology M,D
Political Science M,D
Psychology—General D
Public Affairs M,D
Public History M,D
Recreation and Park Management M
Religion M,D
Science Education M,D
Social Psychology D
Social Sciences M,D
Social Work M,D
Sociology M,D
Spanish M,D
Special Education M
Speech and Interpersonal Communication M,D
Statistics M,D
Supply Chain Management M,D
Theater M
Transportation Management O
Urban and Regional Planning M
Writing M

ARIZONA STATE UNIVERSITY AT THE POLYTECHNIC CAMPUS

Aerospace/Aeronautical Engineering M
Agricultural Economics and Agribusiness M
Biological and Biomedical Sciences—General M
Computer Engineering M
Computer Science M
Curriculum and Instruction M,D
Education—General M,D
Educational Administration M,D
Electrical Engineering M
Engineering and Applied Sciences—General M
Environmental Management and Policy M
Exercise and Sports Science M,D
Information Science M
Management Information Systems M
Manufacturing Engineering M
Mechanical Engineering M
Nutrition M,D
Physical Education M,D
Psychology—General M
Transportation Management M

ARIZONA STATE UNIVERSITY AT THE WEST CAMPUS

Accounting O
Business Administration and Management—General M
Communication—General M,O
Criminal Justice and Criminology M
Education—General M,D,O
Educational Administration M,D,O
Elementary Education M,D,O
Gerontology O
Interdisciplinary Studies M
Secondary Education M,D,O
Social Work M
Special Education M,D,O

ARKANSAS STATE UNIVERSITY

Accounting M
Agricultural Education M,O
Agricultural Sciences—General M,O
Allied Health—General M,O
Art/Fine Arts M
Biological and Biomedical Sciences—General M,D,O
Business Administration and Management—General M,O
Business Education M,O
Chemistry M,O
Communication Disorders M
Communication—General M,O
Community College Education M,D,O
Computer Science M
Counselor Education M,O
Criminal Justice and Criminology M,O
Curriculum and Instruction M,D,O
Early Childhood Education M,O
Education of the Gifted M,D,O
Education—General M,D,O
Educational Administration M,D,O
Educational Measurement and Evaluation M,O
Electronic Commerce M,O
Elementary Education M,O
English Education M,O
English M,O
Environmental Sciences M,D,O
Exercise and Sports Science M,O
Foundations and Philosophy of Education M,D,O
Gerontological Nursing M,O
Gerontology M,O
Health Education M,O
History M,D,O
Journalism M
Management Information Systems M,O
Mathematics M,O
Media Studies M
Molecular Biology M,D,O
Music Education M,O
Music M,O
Nurse Anesthesia M,O
Nursing—General M,O
Physical Education M,O
Physical Therapy M
Political Science M,O
Public Administration M,O
Reading Education M,O
Rehabilitation Counseling M,O
School Psychology M,O
Science Education M,D,O
Social Sciences Education M,D,O
Social Work M
Sociology M,O
Special Education M,D,O
Speech and Interpersonal Communication M,O
Student Affairs M,O
Theater M,O

ARKANSAS TECH UNIVERSITY

Art/Fine Arts M
Communication—General M
Curriculum and Instruction M,O
Education of the Gifted M,O
Education—General M,O
Educational Administration M,O
Emergency Management M
English as a Second Language M
English Education M,O
English M
Fish, Game, and Wildlife Management M
History M
Homeland Security M
Information Science M
Journalism M
Mathematics Education M
Secondary Education M,O
Social Sciences Education M
Social Sciences M
Spanish M
Student Affairs M,O
Systems Science M

ARMSTRONG ATLANTIC STATE UNIVERSITY

Adult Education M
Athletic Training and Sports Medicine M
Business Education M
Communication Disorders M
Computer Science M
Criminal Justice and Criminology M
Curriculum and Instruction M
Early Childhood Education M
Education—General M
Elementary Education M
English Education M
Exercise and Sports Science M
Health Services Management and Hospital Administration M
History M
Liberal Studies M
Mathematics Education M
Middle School Education M
Nursing—General M
Physical Therapy M
Public Health—General M
Science Education M
Secondary Education M
Social Sciences Education M
Special Education M

Close-Up on page 803.

ART ACADEMY OF CINCINNATI

Art Education M

ART CENTER COLLEGE OF DESIGN

Applied Arts and Design—General M*
Art/Fine Arts M
Computer Art and Design M
Environmental Design M
Film, Television, and Video Production M
Industrial Design M

THE ART INSTITUTE OF BOSTON AT LESLEY UNIVERSITY

Art/Fine Arts M*

ASBURY COLLEGE

English as a Second Language M,O
English M,O
French M,O
Mathematics Education M,O
Reading Education M,O
Science Education M,O
Social Sciences Education M,O
Spanish M,O
Special Education M,O
Writing M,O

ASBURY THEOLOGICAL SEMINARY

Cultural Studies M,D
Missions and Missiology M,D
Pastoral Ministry and Counseling M,O
Religious Education M,O
Theology M,D,O

ASHLAND THEOLOGICAL SEMINARY

History P,M,D,O
Pastoral Ministry and Counseling P,M,D,O
Theology P,M,D,O

ASHLAND UNIVERSITY

Business Administration and Management—General M
Curriculum and Instruction M
Early Childhood Education M
Education of the Gifted M
Education—General M,D
Educational Administration M,D
Educational Media/Instructional Technology M
Exercise and Sports Science M
Foundations and Philosophy of Education M
History M
Middle School Education M
Physical Education M
Political Science M
Special Education M
Sports Management M
Student Affairs M

ASPEN UNIVERSITY

Business Administration and Management—General M,O
Information Science M

- Management Information Systems M,O
- Project Management M,O

ASSEMBLIES OF GOD THEOLOGICAL SEMINARY
- Pastoral Ministry and Counseling P,M,D
- Theology P,M,D

ASSOCIATED MENNONITE BIBLICAL SEMINARY
- Conflict Resolution and Mediation/Peace Studies P,M,O
- Missions and Missiology P,M,O
- Theology P,M,O

ASSUMPTION COLLEGE
- Business Administration and Management—General M,O
- Counseling Psychology M,O
- Rehabilitation Counseling M,O*
- School Psychology M,O
- Special Education M

ATHABASCA UNIVERSITY
- Adult Education M
- Allied Health—General M,O
- Business Administration and Management—General M,O
- Cultural Studies M
- Distance Education Development M,O
- Education—General M,O
- Information Science M
- Interdisciplinary Studies M
- International Development M
- Management of Technology M,O
- Nursing and Healthcare Administration M,O
- Nursing—General M,O
- Organizational Management M
- Project Management M,O

THE ATHENAEUM OF OHIO
- Pastoral Ministry and Counseling P,M,O
- Theology P,M,O

ATLANTIC COLLEGE
- Graphic Design M

ATLANTIC INSTITUTE OF ORIENTAL MEDICINE
- Acupuncture and Oriental Medicine M

ATLANTIC SCHOOL OF THEOLOGY
- Theology P,M,O

ATLANTIC UNION COLLEGE
- Education—General M

ATLANTIC UNIVERSITY
- Transpersonal and Humanistic Psychology M

A.T. STILL UNIVERSITY OF HEALTH SCIENCES
- Allied Health—General M,D
- Biological and Biomedical Sciences—General P,M
- Communication Disorders M,D
- Exercise and Sports Science M,D
- Gerontology M,D
- Health Education M,D
- Health Services Management and Hospital Administration M,D
- Kinesiology and Movement Studies M,D
- Medical Informatics M,D
- Occupational Therapy M,D
- Oral and Dental Sciences P
- Osteopathic Medicine P,M
- Physical Therapy M,D
- Physician Assistant Studies M,D
- Public Health—General M,D
- Toxicology P,M

AUBURN UNIVERSITY
- Accounting M
- Adult Education M,D,O
- Aerospace/Aeronautical Engineering M,D
- Agricultural Economics and Agribusiness M,D
- Agricultural Sciences—General M,D
- Agronomy and Soil Sciences M,D
- Analytical Chemistry M,D
- Anatomy M,D
- Animal Sciences M,D
- Applied Economics M,D
- Applied Mathematics M,D
- Aquaculture M,D
- Architecture M
- Biochemistry M,D
- Biological and Biomedical Sciences—General M,D
- Botany M,D
- Building Science M
- Business Administration and Management—General M,D
- Business Education M,D,O
- Cell Biology M,D
- Chemical Engineering M,D
- Chemistry M,D
- Child and Family Studies M,D
- Civil Engineering M,D
- Clothing and Textiles M
- Communication Disorders M,D
- Communication—General M
- Computer Engineering M,D
- Computer Science M,D
- Construction Engineering M,D
- Construction Management M
- Counseling Psychology M,D,O
- Counselor Education M,D,O
- Curriculum and Instruction M,D,O
- Early Childhood Education M,D,O
- Economics M
- Education—General M,D,O*
- Educational Administration M,D,O
- Educational Media/Instructional Technology M,D,O
- Educational Psychology M,D,O
- Electrical Engineering M,D
- Elementary Education M,D,O
- Engineering and Applied Sciences—General M,D
- English Education M,D,O
- English M,D*
- Entomology M,D
- Environmental Engineering M,D
- Exercise and Sports Science M,D,O
- Experimental Psychology M,D
- Finance and Banking M
- Fish, Game, and Wildlife Management M,D
- Food Science and Technology M,D
- Foreign Languages Education M,D,O
- Geology M*
- Geotechnical Engineering M,D
- Health Education M,D,O
- Health Promotion M,D,O
- Higher Education M,D,O
- History M,D
- Horticulture M,D
- Human Development M,D
- Human Resources Management M,D
- Hydraulics M,D
- Hydrology M,D
- Industrial and Organizational Psychology M,D
- Industrial Design M
- Industrial/Management Engineering M,D
- Inorganic Chemistry M,D
- Landscape Architecture M
- Management Information Systems M,D
- Mass Communication M
- Materials Engineering M,D
- Mathematics Education M,D,O
- Mathematics M,D
- Mechanical Engineering M,D
- Microbiology M,D
- Molecular Biology M,D
- Music Education M,D,O
- Natural Resources M,D
- Nutrition M,D
- Organic Chemistry M,D
- Pathobiology M,D
- Pharmaceutical Sciences M,D
- Pharmacology M,D
- Pharmacy P
- Physical Chemistry M,D
- Physical Education M,D,O
- Physics M,D*
- Plant Pathology M,D
- Political Science M,D
- Psychology—General M,D
- Public Administration M,D*
- Radiation Biology M,D
- Reading Education M,D,O
- Rehabilitation Counseling M,D,O
- Rural Sociology M
- School Psychology M,D,O
- Science Education M,D,O
- Secondary Education M,D,O
- Social Psychology M,D,O
- Social Sciences Education M,D,O
- Sociology M
- Software Engineering M,D
- Spanish M
- Special Education M,D,O
- Statistics M,D
- Structural Engineering M,D
- Systems Engineering M,D
- Textile Sciences and Engineering M,D
- Transportation and Highway Engineering M,D
- Urban and Regional Planning M
- Veterinary Medicine P
- Veterinary Sciences M,D
- Zoology M,D

Close-Up on page 805.

AUBURN UNIVERSITY MONTGOMERY
- Business Administration and Management—General M
- Counselor Education M,O
- Criminal Justice and Criminology M
- Early Childhood Education M,O
- Education—General M,O
- Educational Administration M,O
- Elementary Education M,O
- Liberal Studies M
- Physical Education M,O
- Political Science M,D
- Psychology—General M
- Public Administration M,D
- Reading Education M,O
- Secondary Education M,O
- Special Education M,O

AUGSBURG COLLEGE
- Business Administration and Management—General M
- Community Health Nursing M
- Education—General M
- Nursing—General M
- Organizational Management M
- Physician Assistant Studies M
- Social Work M
- Transcultural Nursing M

AUGUSTANA COLLEGE
- Community Health Nursing M
- Education—General M
- Elementary Education M
- Nursing—General M
- Secondary Education M

AUGUSTA STATE UNIVERSITY
- Business Administration and Management—General M
- Counselor Education M
- Education—General M,O
- Educational Administration M,O
- Elementary Education M,O
- Health Education M
- Middle School Education M,O
- Physical Education M
- Political Science M
- Psychology—General M
- Secondary Education M,O
- Special Education M,O

AURORA UNIVERSITY
- Business Administration and Management—General M
- Curriculum and Instruction M,D
- Education—General M,D
- Educational Administration M,D
- Leisure Studies M
- Mathematics M
- Reading Education M,D
- Social Work M

AUSTIN COLLEGE
- Art Education M
- Education—General M
- Elementary Education M
- Middle School Education M
- Music Education M
- Physical Education M
- Secondary Education M

AUSTIN GRADUATE SCHOOL OF THEOLOGY
- Theology M

AUSTIN PEAY STATE UNIVERSITY
- Biological and Biomedical Sciences—General M
- Business Administration and Management—General M
- Communication—General M
- Counselor Education M
- Curriculum and Instruction M,O
- Education—General M,O
- Educational Administration M,O
- English M
- Exercise and Sports Science M
- Health Education M
- Military and Defense Studies M
- Music Education M
- Music M
- Nursing—General M
- Physical Education M
- Psychology—General M
- Reading Education M,O

AUSTIN PRESBYTERIAN THEOLOGICAL SEMINARY
- Pastoral Ministry and Counseling P,M,D
- Theology P,M,D

AVE MARIA SCHOOL OF LAW
- Law P

AVE MARIA UNIVERSITY
- Pastoral Ministry and Counseling M,D
- Theology M,D

AVERETT UNIVERSITY
- Art Education M
- Business Administration and Management—General M
- Curriculum and Instruction M
- Education—General M
- Elementary Education M
- English Education M
- Health Education M
- Mathematics Education M
- Physical Education M
- Reading Education M
- Science Education M
- Social Sciences Education M
- Special Education M

AVILA UNIVERSITY
- Accounting M
- Art Therapy M
- Business Administration and Management—General M
- Counseling Psychology M
- Education—General M,O
- English as a Second Language M,O
- Finance and Banking M
- Health Services Management and Hospital Administration M
- Industrial and Organizational Psychology M
- International Business M
- Management Information Systems M
- Marketing M
- Organizational Management M,O*
- Project Management M,O
- Psychology—General M
- Reading Education M,O

AZUSA PACIFIC UNIVERSITY
- Art/Fine Arts M
- Business Administration and Management—General M
- Clinical Psychology M,D
- Counselor Education M
- Curriculum and Instruction M
- Education—General M,D
- Educational Administration M,D
- Educational Media/Instructional Technology M
- English as a Second Language M
- Ethics M
- Higher Education M,D
- Human Resources Development M
- International Business M
- Library Science M
- Management Strategy and Policy M
- Marriage and Family Therapy M,D
- Multilingual and Multicultural Education M
- Music Education M
- Music M
- Nonprofit Management M
- Nursing Education M,D
- Nursing—General M,D
- Organizational Management M
- Pastoral Ministry and Counseling P,M
- Physical Education M
- Physical Therapy D
- Psychology—General M,D
- Religion M
- Religious Education M
- School Psychology M
- Special Education M
- Student Affairs M
- Theology M,D

BABEL UNIVERSITY SCHOOL OF TRANSLATION
- Translation and Interpretation M

BABSON COLLEGE
- Business Administration and Management—General M

BAKER COLLEGE CENTER FOR GRADUATE STUDIES
- Accounting M
- Business Administration and Management—General M
- Finance and Banking M
- Health Services Management and Hospital Administration M
- Human Resources Management M

- Management Information Systems M
- Marketing M
- Occupational Therapy M

BAKER UNIVERSITY

- Business Administration and Management—General M
- Conflict Resolution and Mediation/Peace Studies M
- Education—General M,D
- Liberal Studies M

BAKKE GRADUATE UNIVERSITY OF MINISTRY

- Pastoral Ministry and Counseling M,D

BALDWIN-WALLACE COLLEGE

- Accounting M
- Business Administration and Management—General M
- Education—General M
- Educational Administration M
- Educational Media/Instructional Technology M
- Entrepreneurship M
- Health Services Management and Hospital Administration M
- Human Resources Management M
- International Business M
- Reading Education M
- Special Education M

BALL STATE UNIVERSITY

- Accounting M
- Actuarial Science M
- Adult Education M,D
- Advertising and Public Relations M
- Anthropology M
- Architecture M
- Art Education M
- Art/Fine Arts M
- Biological and Biomedical Sciences—General M,D
- Business Administration and Management—General M
- Business Education M
- Chemistry M
- Clinical Psychology M
- Cognitive Sciences M
- Communication Disorders M,D
- Communication—General M
- Computer Science M
- Counseling Psychology M,D
- Curriculum and Instruction M,O
- Education—General M,D,O
- Educational Administration M,D,O
- Educational Psychology M,D,O
- Elementary Education M,D
- English as a Second Language M,D
- English M,D
- Exercise and Sports Science D
- Family and Consumer Sciences-General M
- Foundations and Philosophy of Education D
- Geology M
- Geosciences M
- Gerontology M
- Health Education M
- Health Promotion M
- Higher Education M,D
- Historic Preservation M
- History M
- Information Science M
- Journalism M
- Landscape Architecture M
- Linguistics D
- Mathematics Education M
- Mathematics M
- Music Education M,D
- Natural Resources M
- Nursing—General M
- Physical Education M,D
- Physics M
- Physiology M
- Political Science M
- Psychology—General M
- Public Administration M
- Rhetoric M
- School Psychology M,D,O
- Science Education M,D
- Secondary Education M
- Social Psychology M
- Social Sciences M
- Sociology M
- Special Education M,D,O
- Speech and Interpersonal Communication M
- Statistics M
- Telecommunications M
- Urban and Regional Planning M*
- Vocational and Technical Education M
- Writing M,D

BALTIMORE HEBREW UNIVERSITY

- Jewish Studies M,D

BANGOR THEOLOGICAL SEMINARY

- Theology P,M,D

BANK STREET COLLEGE OF EDUCATION

- Child and Family Studies M
- Curriculum and Instruction M
- Early Childhood Education M
- Education—General M*
- Educational Administration M
- Elementary Education M
- Foundations and Philosophy of Education M
- Maternal and Child Health M
- Mathematics Education M
- Middle School Education M
- Multilingual and Multicultural Education M
- Museum Education M
- Museum Studies M
- Reading Education M
- Special Education M

BAPTIST BIBLE COLLEGE

- Cultural Studies P,M
- Pastoral Ministry and Counseling P,M
- Theology P,M

BAPTIST BIBLE COLLEGE OF PENNSYLVANIA

- Counselor Education M
- Pastoral Ministry and Counseling P,M,D
- Religious Education M
- Theology P,M,D

BAPTIST MISSIONARY ASSOCIATION THEOLOGICAL SEMINARY

- Theology P,M

BAPTIST THEOLOGICAL SEMINARY AT RICHMOND

- Music P,D
- Pastoral Ministry and Counseling P,D
- Religious Education P,D
- Theology P,D

BARD COLLEGE

- Art/Fine Arts M
- Education—General M*
- Environmental Management and Policy M*
- Museum Studies M

BARD GRADUATE CENTER FOR STUDIES IN THE DECORATIVE ARTS, DESIGN, AND CULTURE

- Art History M,D*
- Decorative Arts M,D*

Announcement on page 310.

BARNES-JEWISH COLLEGE OF NURSING AND ALLIED HEALTH

- Adult Nursing M
- Allied Health—General M,O
- Gerontological Nursing M
- Health Promotion M,O
- Health Services Management and Hospital Administration M,O
- Maternal and Child/Neonatal Nursing M
- Nursing Education M
- Nursing—General M
- Nutrition M,O
- Oncology Nursing M

BARRY UNIVERSITY

- Accounting M
- Acute Care/Critical Care Nursing M,O
- Anatomy M
- Art/Fine Arts M
- Athletic Training and Sports Medicine M
- Biological and Biomedical Sciences—General M
- Business Administration and Management—General M,O
- Clinical Psychology M,O
- Communication Disorders M
- Communication—General M,O
- Corporate and Organizational Communication M,O
- Counselor Education M,D,O
- Curriculum and Instruction D,O
- Distance Education Development O
- Early Childhood Education M,D,O
- Education of the Gifted M,D,O
- Education—General M,D,O
- Educational Administration M,D,O
- Educational Media/Instructional Technology M,D,O
- Elementary Education M,D,O
- English as a Second Language M,D,O
- Exercise and Sports Science M
- Family Nurse Practitioner Studies M,O
- Finance and Banking O
- Health Informatics O
- Health Services Management and Hospital Administration M,O
- Higher Education M,D
- Human Resources Development M,D
- Human Resources Management O
- Information Science M
- International Business O
- Kinesiology and Movement Studies M
- Law P
- Liberal Studies M
- Management Information Systems O
- Marketing O
- Marriage and Family Therapy M,O
- Nurse Anesthesia M
- Nursing and Healthcare Administration M,D,O
- Nursing Education M,O
- Nursing—General M,D,O
- Occupational Therapy M
- Pastoral Ministry and Counseling M,D
- Photography M
- Physician Assistant Studies M
- Podiatric Medicine P
- Psychology—General M,O
- Public Administration M
- Public Health—General M
- Reading Education M,D,O
- Rehabilitation Counseling M,O
- School Psychology M,O
- Social Work M,D*
- Special Education M,D,O
- Sport Psychology M
- Sports Management M*
- Theology M,D

Close-Up on page 807.

BASTYR UNIVERSITY

- Acupuncture and Oriental Medicine M,D,O*
- Health Psychology M
- Naturopathic Medicine D,O*
- Nurse Midwifery D,O
- Nutrition M*
- Psychology—General M

BAYAMÓN CENTRAL UNIVERSITY

- Accounting M
- Business Administration and Management—General M
- Counselor Education M
- Criminal Justice and Criminology M
- Early Childhood Education M
- Education—General M
- Educational Administration M
- Elementary Education M
- Finance and Banking M
- Marketing M
- Pastoral Ministry and Counseling P,M
- Physical Education M
- Psychology—General M
- Special Education M
- Theology P,M

BAYLOR COLLEGE OF MEDICINE

- Allopathic Medicine P
- Biochemistry D*
- Bioengineering D
- Biological and Biomedical Sciences—General M,D*
- Biomedical Engineering D
- Biophysics D
- Cancer Biology/Oncology D
- Cardiovascular Sciences D*
- Cell Biology D*
- Clinical Laboratory Sciences/Medical Technology M,D
- Computational Biology D
- Developmental Biology D*
- Genetics D*
- Human Genetics D
- Immunology D*
- Microbiology D
- Molecular Biology D
- Molecular Biophysics D*
- Molecular Medicine D
- Molecular Physiology D*
- Neuroscience D*
- Nurse Anesthesia M
- Pathology D
- Pharmacology D
- Physician Assistant Studies M
- Structural Biology D
- Translational Biology D*
- Virology D*

BAYLOR UNIVERSITY

- Accounting M
- Allied Health—General M,D
- American Studies M
- Biological and Biomedical Sciences—General M,D
- Biomedical Engineering M
- Business Administration and Management—General M
- Chemistry M,D
- Clinical Psychology M,D
- Communication Disorders M
- Communication—General M
- Computer Engineering M
- Computer Science M
- Curriculum and Instruction M,D,O
- Economics M
- Education—General M,D,O
- Educational Administration M,O
- Educational Psychology M,D,O
- Electrical Engineering M
- Engineering and Applied Sciences—General M
- English M,D
- Environmental Biology M,D
- Environmental Management and Policy M
- Exercise and Sports Science M,D
- Family Nurse Practitioner Studies M
- Geology M,D
- Geosciences M,D
- Health Education M,D
- Health Services Management and Hospital Administration M
- History M
- Interdisciplinary Studies M,D
- International Affairs M,D
- International Business M
- Journalism M
- Law P
- Limnology M,D
- Management Information Systems M
- Maternal and Child/Neonatal Nursing M
- Mathematics M,D
- Mechanical Engineering M
- Museum Studies M
- Music Education M
- Music M
- Neuroscience M,D
- Nursing and Healthcare Administration M
- Nursing—General M
- Nutrition M,D
- Pediatric Nursing M
- Philosophy M,D
- Physical Education M,D
- Physical Therapy M,D
- Physics M,D
- Political Science M,D
- Psychology—General M,D
- Public Administration M,D
- Public Policy M,D
- Religion M,D*
- Social Work M
- Sociology M,D
- Spanish M
- Statistics M,D
- Theater M
- Theology P,M,D

BAY PATH COLLEGE

- Entrepreneurship M
- Management Information Systems M
- Occupational Therapy M

BEACON UNIVERSITY

- Counseling Psychology P,M
- Organizational Management P,M
- Pastoral Ministry and Counseling P,M
- Theology P,M

BELHAVEN COLLEGE (MS)

- Business Administration and Management—General M
- Education—General M
- Elementary Education M
- Multilingual and Multicultural Education M
- Secondary Education M

BELLARMINE UNIVERSITY

- Business Administration and Management—General M
- Early Childhood Education M
- Education—General M
- Educational Administration M
- Middle School Education M
- Nursing and Healthcare Administration M,D

Nursing Education M,D
Nursing—General M,D
Physical Therapy M,D
Reading Education M
Religion M
Secondary Education M
Special Education M

BELLEVUE UNIVERSITY

Business Administration and Management—General M
Communication—General M
Criminal Justice and Criminology M
Health Services Management and Hospital Administration M*
Human Services M
Information Science M*
Management Information Systems M

Close-Up on page 809.

BELMONT UNIVERSITY

Allied Health—General M,D
Business Administration and Management—General M
Early Childhood Education M
Education of the Gifted M
Education—General M
Educational Media/Instructional Technology M
Elementary Education M
English Education M
English M
Mathematics Education M
Middle School Education M
Music Education M
Music M
Nursing—General M
Occupational Therapy M,D
Physical Therapy D
Science Education M
Secondary Education M
Social Sciences Education M
Sports Management M
Writing M

BEMIDJI STATE UNIVERSITY

Biological and Biomedical Sciences—General M
Counseling Psychology M
Education—General M
English M
Environmental Management and Policy M
Exercise and Sports Science M
Mathematics Education M
Science Education M
Special Education M
Vocational and Technical Education M

BENEDICTINE COLLEGE

Business Administration and Management—General M
Educational Administration M

BENEDICTINE UNIVERSITY

Accounting M
Business Administration and Management—General M
Clinical Psychology M
Computer and Information Systems Security M
Curriculum and Instruction M
Education—General M
Educational Administration M,D
Elementary Education M
Emergency Management M
Entrepreneurship M
Exercise and Sports Science M
Finance and Banking M
Health Education M
Health Informatics M
Health Promotion M
Health Services Management and Hospital Administration M
Higher Education D
Human Resources Management M
International Business M
Logistics M
Management Information Systems M
Marketing M
Nutrition M
Organizational Behavior M
Organizational Management M,D
Public Health—General M
Reading Education M
Science Education M
Secondary Education M
Special Education M

BENNINGTON COLLEGE

Allied Health—General O
Art Education M
Dance M
Early Childhood Education M
Education—General M*
Elementary Education M
English Education M
English M
Foreign Languages Education M
French M
Mathematics Education M
Multilingual and Multicultural Education M
Music Education M
Music M
Science Education M
Secondary Education M
Social Sciences Education M
Spanish M
Theater M
Writing M

BENTLEY COLLEGE

Accounting M,D
Business Administration and Management—General M,D,O*
Ergonomics and Human Factors M
Finance and Banking M
Information Science M
Marketing M
Real Estate M
Taxation M

BERNARD M. BARUCH COLLEGE OF THE CITY UNIVERSITY OF NEW YORK

Accounting M,D
Business Administration and Management—General M,D,O*
Corporate and Organizational Communication M
Economics M
Educational Administration M
Entrepreneurship M,D
Finance and Banking M,D
Health Services Management and Hospital Administration M
Higher Education M
Human Resources Management M,D
Industrial and Labor Relations M
Industrial and Organizational Psychology M,D,O
International Business M
Management Information Systems M,D
Management Strategy and Policy M,D
Marketing M,D
Mathematical and Computational Finance M*
Organizational Behavior M,D
Organizational Management M,D
Public Administration M*
Quantitative Analysis M
Statistics M
Taxation M*

Close-Up on page 811.

BERRY COLLEGE

Business Administration and Management—General M
Curriculum and Instruction O
Early Childhood Education M
Education—General M,O
Middle School Education M
Reading Education M
Secondary Education M

BETHANY THEOLOGICAL SEMINARY

Conflict Resolution and Mediation/Peace Studies P,M,O
Pastoral Ministry and Counseling P,M,O
Religion P,M,O
Theology P,M,O

BETHANY UNIVERSITY

Clinical Psychology M
Education—General M
Educational Administration M

BETH BENJAMIN ACADEMY OF CONNECTICUT

Theology

BETHEL COLLEGE (IN)

Business Administration and Management—General M
Counseling Psychology M
Education—General M
Marriage and Family Therapy M
Nursing—General M
Pastoral Ministry and Counseling M
Theology M

BETHEL COLLEGE (TN)

Education—General M
Educational Administration M
Elementary Education M
English Education M
Physical Education M
Science Education M
Social Sciences Education M
Special Education M

BETHEL SEMINARY

Marriage and Family Therapy P,M,D,O
Missions and Missiology P,M,D,O
Pastoral Ministry and Counseling P,M,D,O
Religious Education P,M,D,O
Theology P,M,D,O

BETHEL UNIVERSITY

Business Administration and Management—General M
Communication—General M,O
Counseling Psychology M,O
Education—General M,D,O
Educational Administration M,D,O
Gerontology M
Higher Education M,O
Nursing Education M,O
Nursing—General M,O
Organizational Management M
Reading Education M,D,O
Secondary Education M,D,O
Special Education M,D,O

BETHESDA CHRISTIAN UNIVERSITY

Religion P,M
Theology P,M

BETH HAMEDRASH SHAAREI YOSHER INSTITUTE

Theology

BETH HATALMUD RABBINICAL COLLEGE

Theology

BETH MEDRASH GOVOHA

Theology

BEXLEY HALL SEMINARY

Theology P,M

BIBLICAL THEOLOGICAL SEMINARY

Pastoral Ministry and Counseling P,M,D
Theology P,M,D

BIOLA UNIVERSITY

Business Administration and Management—General M
Cultural Studies M,D,O
Education—General M
English as a Second Language M,D,O
Ethics P,M,D
Linguistics M,D,O
Missions and Missiology M,D,O
Organizational Management M
Psychology—General M,D
Religion P,M,D
Religious Education P,M,D
Theology P,M,D

BIRMINGHAM-SOUTHERN COLLEGE

Business Administration and Management—General M
Music M
Public Administration M

BISHOP'S UNIVERSITY

Education—General M,O
English as a Second Language M,O

BLACK HILLS STATE UNIVERSITY

Business Administration and Management—General M
Curriculum and Instruction M
Education—General M*

BLESSED JOHN XXIII NATIONAL SEMINARY

Theology P

BLOOMSBURG UNIVERSITY OF PENNSYLVANIA

Adult Nursing M
Biological and Biomedical Sciences—General M
Business Administration and Management—General M
Business Education M
Communication Disorders M,D
Community Health M
Counselor Education M
Curriculum and Instruction M
Early Childhood Education M
Education—General M
Educational Media/Instructional Technology M
Elementary Education M
Exercise and Sports Science M
Family Nurse Practitioner Studies M
Health Physics/Radiological Health M
Nursing and Healthcare Administration M
Nursing—General M
Reading Education M
Science Education M
Special Education M
Student Affairs M

BLUFFTON UNIVERSITY

Business Administration and Management—General M
Education—General M
Organizational Management M

BOB JONES UNIVERSITY

Accounting P,M,D,O
Art/Fine Arts P,M,D,O
Business Administration and Management—General P,M,D,O
Counselor Education P,M,D,O
Curriculum and Instruction P,M,D,O
Educational Administration P,M,D,O
Elementary Education P,M,D,O
English Education P,M,D,O
English P,M,D,O
Film, Television, and Video Production P,M,D,O
Graphic Design P,M,D,O
History P,M,D,O
Illustration P,M,D,O
Journalism P,M,D,O
Mathematics Education P,M,D,O
Media Studies P,M,D,O
Music Education P,M,D,O
Music P,M,D,O
Pastoral Ministry and Counseling P,M,D,O
Religion P,M,D,O
Rhetoric P,M,D,O
Secondary Education P,M,D,O
Social Sciences Education P,M,D,O
Special Education P,M,D,O
Speech and Interpersonal Communication P,M,D,O
Student Affairs P,M,D,O
Theater P,M,D,O
Theology P,M,D,O

BOISE STATE UNIVERSITY

Accounting M
Animal Sciences M
Art Education M
Art/Fine Arts M
Biological and Biomedical Sciences—General M
Business Administration and Management—General M
Civil Engineering M
Communication—General M
Computer Engineering M,D
Computer Science M
Counselor Education M
Criminal Justice and Criminology M
Curriculum and Instruction D
Early Childhood Education M
Education—General M,D
Educational Administration M,D
Educational Media/Instructional Technology M
Electrical Engineering M,D
Engineering and Applied Sciences—General M,D
English M
Environmental Management and Policy M
Exercise and Sports Science M
Geology M,D
Geophysics M,D
Geosciences M
History M
Interdisciplinary Studies M
Management Information Systems M
Materials Engineering M
Mechanical Engineering M
Music Education M
Music M
Public Administration M
Public Health—General M
Public Policy M
Reading Education M
Science Education M,D
Social Work M

Special Education M
Sports Management M
Taxation M
Technical Communication M
Writing M

BORICUA COLLEGE

Human Services M
Latin American Studies M

BOSTON ARCHITECTURAL COLLEGE

Architecture M*
Interior Design M

BOSTON COLLEGE

Accounting M
Adult Nursing M,D
Biochemistry M,D
Biological and Biomedical Sciences—General M,D*
Business Administration and Management—General M
Chemistry M,D
Classics M
Community Health Nursing M,D
Counseling Psychology M,D
Curriculum and Instruction M,D,O
Developmental Psychology M,D
Early Childhood Education M
East European and Russian Studies M
Economics D
Education—General M,D,O*
Educational Administration M,D,O
Educational Measurement and Evaluation M,D
Educational Psychology M,D
Elementary Education M
English Education M
English M,D
Finance and Banking M,D
Foreign Languages Education M
French M,D*
Geology M*
Geophysics M
Gerontological Nursing M,D
Higher Education M,D
History M,D
Inorganic Chemistry M,D
Italian M,D
Law P
Linguistics M
Maternal and Child/Neonatal Nursing M,D
Mathematics Education M
Mathematics M*
Nurse Anesthesia M,D
Nursing—General M,D
Organic Chemistry M,D
Organizational Behavior D
Organizational Management D
Pastoral Ministry and Counseling M,D
Philosophy M,D
Physical Chemistry M,D
Physics M,D*
Political Science M,D
Psychiatric Nursing M,D
Psychology—General M,D
Reading Education M,D
Religious Education M,D,O
Russian M
Science Education M,D
Secondary Education M
Slavic Languages M
Social Sciences Education M
Social Work M,D*
Sociology M,D
Spanish M,D
Special Education M,O
Theology M,D
Western European Studies M,D

THE BOSTON CONSERVATORY

Music Education M,O
Music M,O
Theater M

BOSTON GRADUATE SCHOOL OF PSYCHOANALYSIS

Psychoanalysis and Psychotherapy M,D,O

BOSTON UNIVERSITY

Accounting M,D,O
Actuarial Science M
Advertising and Public Relations M
Aerospace/Aeronautical Engineering M,D*
African Studies M,O
African-American Studies M
Allied Health—General M,D
Allopathic Medicine P
American Studies D
Anatomy M,D
Anthropology M,D
Archaeology M,D
Art Education M
Art History M,D,O
Art/Fine Arts M
Arts Administration M,O
Astronomy M,D
Athletic Training and Sports Medicine D
Biochemistry M,D*
Bioethics M
Bioinformatics M,D
Biological and Biomedical Sciences—General M,D
Biomedical Engineering M,D*
Biophysics M,D*
Biopsychology M
Biostatistics M,D
Business Administration and Management—General M,D,O
Cell Biology M,D*
Chemistry M,D
Classics M,D
Cognitive Sciences M,D
Communication Disorders M,D,O
Communication—General M*
Computer Engineering M,D
Computer Science M,D
Counseling Psychology M,D*
Counselor Education M,O
Criminal Justice and Criminology M
Curriculum and Instruction M,D,O
Dental Hygiene P,M,D,O
Dentistry P,M,D,O
Early Childhood Education M,D,O
Economics M,D
Education—General M,D,O*
Educational Administration M,O
Educational Media/Instructional Technology M,D,O
Electrical Engineering M,D*
Electronic Commerce M
Elementary Education M
Energy Management and Policy M
Engineering and Applied Sciences—General M,D*
English as a Second Language M,O
English Education M,O
English M,D
Environmental and Occupational Health M,D
Environmental Management and Policy M,D,O
Epidemiology M,D
Film, Television, and Video Production M
Film, Television, and Video Theory and Criticism M
Finance and Banking P,M,D
Foreign Languages Education M
Forensic Sciences M*
French M,D
Geographic Information Systems M
Geography M,D
Geosciences M,D
Graphic Design M
Health Education M,O
Health Promotion M,D
Health Services Management and Hospital Administration M,D,O
Historic Preservation M
History M,D
Human Development M,D,O
Human Resources Management M,O
Immunology D*
Industrial and Manufacturing Management D
Interdisciplinary Studies M,D
International Affairs M,O
International and Comparative Education M
International Business M
International Health M,D,O
Investment Management M
Journalism M
Law P,M
Legal and Justice Studies M
Liberal Studies M
Linguistics M,D
Management Information Systems D
Management of Technology M,D
Manufacturing Engineering M,D*
Marketing D
Mass Communication M
Maternal and Child Health M,O
Mathematical and Computational Finance M,D
Mathematics Education M,D,O
Mathematics M,D
Mechanical Engineering M,D
Media Studies M
Microbiology M,D*
Molecular Biology M,D
Molecular Medicine D*
Multilingual and Multicultural Education M,O
Museum Studies M,D,O
Music Education M,D
Music M,D,O*
Neuroscience M,D*
Nonprofit Management M,O
Nurse Midwifery M,O
Nutrition M,D*
Occupational Therapy M,D
Oral and Dental Sciences P,M,D,O*
Organizational Behavior D
Pathology D
Pharmaceutical Sciences M,D
Pharmacology M,D*
Philosophy M,D
Photonics M,D
Physical Education M,D,O
Physical Therapy D
Physics M,D*
Physiology M,D
Political Science M,D
Project Management M
Psychology—General M,D
Public Administration M,O
Public Health—General P,M,D,O
Reading Education M,D,O
Rehabilitation Sciences D
Religion M,D
Romance Languages M,D
Science Education M,D,O
Social Sciences Education M,D,O
Social Work M,D
Sociology M,D
Spanish M,D
Special Education M,D,O
Systems Engineering M,D
Taxation P,M
Telecommunications M
Theater M,O
Theology P,M,D
Travel and Tourism M
Urban and Regional Planning M
Urban Studies M
Writing M,D

Close-Up on page 813.

BOWIE STATE UNIVERSITY

Applied Mathematics M
Business Administration and Management—General M
Computer Science M,D
Corporate and Organizational Communication M,O
Counseling Psychology M
Counselor Education M
Education—General M
Educational Administration M,D
Elementary Education M
English M
Family Nurse Practitioner Studies M
Human Resources Development M
Management Information Systems M,O
Nursing and Healthcare Administration M
Nursing Education M
Nursing—General M
Public Administration M
Reading Education M
Secondary Education M
Special Education M

BOWLING GREEN STATE UNIVERSITY

Accounting M
American Studies M,D
Applied Arts and Design—General M
Applied Statistics M,D
Art Education M
Art History M
Art/Fine Arts M
Biological and Biomedical Sciences—General M,D*
Business Administration and Management—General M
Business Education M
Chemistry M,D
Child and Family Studies M
Clinical Psychology M,D
Communication Disorders M,D
Communication—General M,D
Computer Art and Design M
Computer Science M
Construction Management M
Counseling Psychology M
Counselor Education M
Criminal Justice and Criminology M
Curriculum and Instruction M
Demography and Population Studies M,D
Developmental Psychology M,D
Early Childhood Education M
Economics M
Education of the Gifted M
Educational Administration M,D,O
Educational Media/Instructional Technology M
English M,D
Experimental Psychology M,D
Family and Consumer Sciences-General M
Film, Television, and Video Production M,D
Foreign Languages Education M
French M
Geology M
Geophysics M
German M
Graphic Design M
Higher Education D
History M,D
Human Development M
Industrial and Organizational Psychology M,D
Interdisciplinary Studies M,D
Kinesiology and Movement Studies M
Leisure Studies M
Manufacturing Engineering M
Mathematics Education M,D
Mathematics M,D*
Music Education M,D
Music M,D
Nutrition M
Operations Research M
Organizational Management M
Philosophy M,D
Physics M
Political Science M
Psychology—General M,D
Public Administration M
Public Health—General M
Reading Education M,O
Recreation and Park Management M
Rehabilitation Counseling M
Rhetoric M,D
School Psychology M,O
Science Education M
Social Psychology M,D
Sociology M,D
Software Engineering M
Spanish M
Special Education M
Speech and Interpersonal Communication M,D
Sports Management M
Statistics M,D
Student Affairs M
Technical Communication M,D
Theater M,D
Vocational and Technical Education M
Writing M,D

Close-Up on page 815.

BRADLEY UNIVERSITY

Accounting M
Applied Arts and Design—General M
Art/Fine Arts M
Biological and Biomedical Sciences—General M
Business Administration and Management—General M
Chemistry M
Civil Engineering M
Comparative and Interdisciplinary Arts M
Computer Science M
Construction Engineering M
Counselor Education M
Curriculum and Instruction M
Education—General M,D
Educational Administration M
Electrical Engineering M
Engineering and Applied Sciences—General M
English M
Human Development M
Illustration M
Industrial/Management Engineering M
Information Science M
Liberal Studies M
Manufacturing Engineering M
Mechanical Engineering M
Nurse Anesthesia M
Nursing and Healthcare Administration M
Nursing—General M
Photography M
Physical Therapy D

BRANDEIS UNIVERSITY

American Studies M,D
Anthropology M,D
Art/Fine Arts O
Biochemistry M,D
Biological and Biomedical Sciences—General M,D,O
Biophysics M,D
Business Administration and Management—General M*
Cell Biology M,D
Chemistry M,D
Child and Family Studies M
Cognitive Sciences M,D
Computer Science M,D,O

- Conflict Resolution and Mediation/Peace Studies M
- Developmental Psychology M,D
- Economics M,D*
- Elementary Education M
- English M,D
- Finance and Banking M,D
- Genetic Counseling M
- Genetics M,D
- Health Services Management and Hospital Administration M
- History M,D
- Human Services M
- Inorganic Chemistry M,D
- International Affairs M,D
- International Business M,D
- International Development M*
- International Health M*
- Jewish Studies M,D
- Mathematics M,D*
- Microbiology M,D
- Molecular Biology M,D
- Music M,D
- Near and Middle Eastern Languages M,D
- Near and Middle Eastern Studies M,D
- Neurobiology M,D
- Neuroscience M,D
- Organic Chemistry M,D
- Physical Chemistry M,D
- Physics M,D
- Political Science M,D
- Psychology—General M
- Public Policy M,D*
- Religious Education M,D
- Secondary Education M,D
- Social Psychology M,D
- Sociology M,D
- Structural Biology M,D
- Sustainable Development M
- Theater M
- Women's Studies M

Close-Up on page 817.

BRANDON UNIVERSITY
- Counselor Education M,O
- Curriculum and Instruction M,O
- Education—General M,O
- Educational Administration M,O
- Music Education M
- Music M
- Rural Planning and Studies M,O
- Special Education M,O

BRENAU UNIVERSITY
- Accounting M
- Business Administration and Management—General M
- Early Childhood Education M,O
- Education—General M,O
- Family Nurse Practitioner Studies M
- Health Services Management and Hospital Administration M
- Management Strategy and Policy M
- Middle School Education M,O
- Nursing Education M
- Occupational Therapy M
- Organizational Management M
- Psychology—General M
- Special Education M,O

BRESCIA UNIVERSITY
- Business Administration and Management—General M
- Curriculum and Instruction M

BRIAR CLIFF UNIVERSITY
- Education—General M
- Human Resources Management M
- Nursing—General M

BRIDGEWATER STATE COLLEGE
- Accounting M
- Art Education M
- Business Administration and Management—General M
- Computer Science M
- Counselor Education M,O
- Criminal Justice and Criminology M
- Early Childhood Education M
- Education—General M,O
- Educational Administration M,O
- Educational Media/Instructional Technology M
- Elementary Education M
- English M
- Finance and Banking M
- Health Promotion M
- Mathematics Education M
- Physical Education M
- Psychology—General M
- Public Administration M
- Reading Education M,O
- Science Education M
- Secondary Education M
- Social Sciences Education M
- Social Work M
- Special Education M

BRIERCREST SEMINARY
- Business Administration and Management—General M
- Marriage and Family Therapy M
- Missions and Missiology M
- Organizational Management M
- Pastoral Ministry and Counseling P,M
- Religion P,M
- Theology P,M

BRIGHAM YOUNG UNIVERSITY
- Accounting M
- Agricultural Sciences—General M,D
- Agronomy and Soil Sciences M,D
- Analytical Chemistry M,D
- Animal Sciences M,D
- Anthropology M
- Applied Statistics M
- Art Education M
- Art History M
- Art/Fine Arts M
- Astronomy M,D
- Athletic Training and Sports Medicine M,D
- Biochemistry M,D
- Biological and Biomedical Sciences—General M,D
- Biotechnology M,D
- Business Administration and Management—General M
- Chemical Engineering M,D
- Chemistry M,D*
- Child and Family Studies M,D
- Civil Engineering M,D
- Clinical Psychology M,D
- Communication Disorders M
- Communication—General M
- Comparative and Interdisciplinary Arts M
- Comparative Literature M
- Computer Science M,D
- Construction Management M
- Counseling Psychology M,D,O
- Developmental Biology M,D
- Education—General M,D,O
- Educational Administration M,D
- Educational Media/Instructional Technology M,D
- Educational Psychology M,D
- Electrical Engineering M,D
- Engineering and Applied Sciences—General M,D
- English as a Second Language M,O
- English M
- Exercise and Sports Science M,D
- Film, Television, and Video Production M
- Fish, Game, and Wildlife Management M,D
- Food Science and Technology M
- Foreign Languages Education M
- Foundations and Philosophy of Education M,D
- French M
- Geology M
- German M
- Health Education M
- Health Promotion M,D
- History M
- Human Development M,D
- Humanities M
- Industrial Design M
- Information Science M
- Inorganic Chemistry M,D
- Law P,M
- Linguistics M,O
- Management Information Systems M
- Marriage and Family Therapy M,D
- Mass Communication M
- Mathematics Education M
- Mathematics M,D
- Mechanical Engineering M,D
- Microbiology M,D
- Molecular Biology M,D
- Music Education M
- Music M
- Neuroscience M,D
- Nursing—General M*
- Nutrition M
- Organic Chemistry M,D
- Physical Chemistry M,D
- Physical Education M,D
- Physics M,D
- Physiology M,D*
- Plant Sciences M,D
- Portuguese M
- Psychology—General M,D
- Public Administration M
- Reading Education M
- Recreation and Park Management M
- Religious Education M
- School Psychology M,D,O
- Science Education M,D
- Social Psychology M,D
- Social Work M
- Sociology M,D
- Spanish M
- Special Education M,D,O
- Statistics M
- Theater M

BROCK UNIVERSITY
- Accounting M
- Allied Health—General M
- Biological and Biomedical Sciences—General M,D
- Biotechnology M,D
- Business Administration and Management—General M
- Chemistry M,D
- Child and Family Studies M
- Classics M
- Comparative Literature M
- Computer Science M
- Cultural Studies M
- Disability Studies M,O
- Economics M
- Education—General M,D
- English as a Second Language M
- English M
- Geography M
- Geosciences M
- History M
- Human Development M,D
- International Affairs M
- Legal and Justice Studies M
- Mathematics M
- Neuroscience M,D
- Philosophy M
- Physics M
- Political Science M
- Psychology—General M,D
- Public Administration M
- Social Psychology M,D
- Statistics M

BROOKLYN COLLEGE OF THE CITY UNIVERSITY OF NEW YORK
- Accounting M
- Applied Physics M,D
- Art Education M,O
- Art History M,D
- Art/Fine Arts M,D
- Biological and Biomedical Sciences—General M,D
- Chemistry M,D
- Communication Disorders M,D
- Community Health M
- Computer Science M,D
- Counseling Psychology M,D,O
- Counselor Education M,O
- Early Childhood Education M
- Economics M
- Education—General M,O
- Educational Administration O
- Elementary Education M
- English Education M,O
- English M,D
- Environmental Education M
- Exercise and Sports Science M
- Experimental Psychology M,D
- Film, Television, and Video Production M
- Foreign Languages Education M,O
- French M,D
- Geology M,D
- Health Education M,O
- Health Services Management and Hospital Administration M
- History M,D
- Industrial and Organizational Psychology M,D
- Information Science M,D
- Internet and Interactive Multimedia M,O
- Jewish Studies M
- Liberal Studies M
- Mathematics Education M,D,O
- Mathematics M,D
- Middle School Education M
- Multilingual and Multicultural Education M
- Music Education M,D,O
- Music M,D,O
- Nutrition M
- Photography M,D
- Physical Education M,O
- Physics M,D
- Political Science M,D
- Psychology—General M,D
- Public Health—General M
- Public Policy M,D
- School Psychology M,O
- Science Education M,O
- Secondary Education M,O
- Social Psychology M,D
- Social Sciences Education M,O
- Sociology M,D
- Spanish M,D
- Special Education M
- Speech and Interpersonal Communication M,D
- Sports Management M
- Thanatology M
- Theater M,D
- Urban Studies M,D
- Writing M

Close-Up on page 819.

BROOKLYN LAW SCHOOL
- Law P

BROOKS INSTITUTE OF PHOTOGRAPHY
- Photography M

BROWN UNIVERSITY
- Aerospace/Aeronautical Engineering M,D
- Allopathic Medicine P
- American Studies M,D
- Anthropology M,D
- Applied Mathematics M,D*
- Archaeology M,D
- Art History M,D
- Biochemistry M,D
- Biological and Biomedical Sciences—General M,D
- Biomedical Engineering M,D
- Biostatistics M,D
- Biotechnology M,D
- Cancer Biology/Oncology M,D
- Cell Biology M,D
- Chemical Engineering M,D
- Chemistry M,D
- Classics M,D
- Cognitive Sciences M,D
- Community Health M,D
- Comparative Literature M,D
- Computer Science M,D
- Demography and Population Studies D
- Developmental Biology M,D
- Ecology D
- Economics M,D
- Education—General M
- Electrical Engineering M,D
- Elementary Education M
- Engineering and Applied Sciences—General M,D
- English Education M
- English M,D
- Environmental Management and Policy M
- Epidemiology M,D
- Evolutionary Biology D
- French M,D
- Geosciences M,D
- German M,D
- Health Services Research M,D
- Hispanic Studies M,D
- History of Science and Technology M,D
- History M,D
- Immunology M,D
- Italian M,D
- Jewish Studies M,D
- Latin American Studies M,D
- Linguistics M,D
- Materials Sciences M,D
- Mathematics M,D
- Mechanical Engineering M,D
- Mechanics M,D
- Microbiology M,D
- Molecular Biology M,D*
- Molecular Pharmacology M,D
- Multilingual and Multicultural Education M,D
- Music M,D
- Neuroscience D
- Pathobiology M,D
- Pathology M,D
- Philosophy M,D
- Physics M,D
- Physiology M,D
- Political Science M,D
- Psychology—General M,D
- Public Health—General M
- Public Policy M
- Religion M,D
- Russian M,D
- Science Education M
- Secondary Education M
- Slavic Languages M,D
- Social Sciences Education M
- Sociology M,D
- Theater M
- Toxicology M,D
- Western European Studies M,D
- Writing M

BRYANT UNIVERSITY
- Accounting M,O
- Business Administration and Management—General M,O
- Electronic Commerce M,O
- Finance and Banking M,O
- Industrial and Manufacturing Management M,O
- Information Science M

Management Information Systems M,O
Marketing M,O
Taxation M,O

BRYN ATHYN COLLEGE OF THE NEW CHURCH

Religion P,M
Theology P,M

BRYN MAWR COLLEGE

Archaeology M,D*
Art History M,D*
Chemistry M,D
Classics M,D*
Clinical Psychology D
Developmental Psychology D
French M,D
Mathematics M,D
Physics M,D
Psychology—General D
Russian M,D
Social Work M,D

Close-Up on page 821.

BUCKNELL UNIVERSITY

Animal Behavior M
Biological and Biomedical Sciences—General M
Chemical Engineering M
Chemistry M
Civil Engineering M
Counselor Education M
Curriculum and Instruction M
Education—General M
Educational Administration M
Educational Measurement and Evaluation M
Electrical Engineering M
Engineering and Applied Sciences—General M
English M
Mathematics M
Mechanical Engineering M
Psychology—General M
Reading Education M
School Psychology M

BUENA VISTA UNIVERSITY

Counselor Education M
Education—General M

BUFFALO STATE COLLEGE, STATE UNIVERSITY OF NEW YORK

Adult Education M,O
Applied Economics M
Art Education M
Biological and Biomedical Sciences—General M
Business Education M
Chemistry M
Communication Disorders M
Criminal Justice and Criminology M
Early Childhood Education M
Economics M
Educational Administration O
Educational Media/Instructional Technology M
Elementary Education M
English Education M
English M
Historic Preservation M,O
History M
Human Resources Management M,O
Industrial/Management Engineering M
Interdisciplinary Studies M
Mathematics Education M
Multilingual and Multicultural Education M
Reading Education M
Science Education M
Social Sciences Education M
Special Education M
Student Affairs M
Vocational and Technical Education M

BUTLER UNIVERSITY

Business Administration and Management—General M
Counselor Education M
Education—General M
Educational Administration M
Elementary Education M
English M
History M
Music Education M
Music M
Pharmaceutical Sciences P,M
Pharmacy P,M
Physician Assistant Studies P,M
Reading Education M
Secondary Education M
Special Education M

CABRINI COLLEGE

Biotechnology M,O
Education—General M,O
Educational Administration M,O
Educational Media/Instructional Technology M,O
Organizational Management M,O
Project Management M,O

CALDWELL COLLEGE

Accounting M
Art Therapy M
Business Administration and Management—General M
Counseling Psychology M
Counselor Education M
Curriculum and Instruction M
Educational Administration M
Pastoral Ministry and Counseling M
Psychology—General M
Special Education M

Close-Up on page 823.

CALIFORNIA BAPTIST UNIVERSITY

Business Administration and Management—General M
Counseling Psychology M
Curriculum and Instruction M
Education—General M
Educational Administration M
Educational Media/Instructional Technology M
English M
Kinesiology and Movement Studies M
Marriage and Family Therapy M
Multilingual and Multicultural Education M
Music M
Pastoral Ministry and Counseling M
Public Administration M
Reading Education M
Special Education M
Vocational and Technical Education M

CALIFORNIA COLLEGE FOR HEALTH SCIENCES

Community Health M
Health Promotion M
Health Services Management and Hospital Administration M
Public Health—General M

CALIFORNIA COLLEGE OF THE ARTS

Applied Arts and Design—General M
Architecture M
Art/Fine Arts M*
Film, Television, and Video Production M
Film, Television, and Video Theory and Criticism M
Museum Studies M
Photography M
Textile Design M
Writing M

CALIFORNIA INSTITUTE OF INTEGRAL STUDIES

Anthropology M,D
Art Therapy M,D
Asian Studies M,D
Clinical Psychology M,D
Counseling Psychology M,D
Health Psychology M,D
Humanities M,D*
Philosophy M,D
Psychology—General M,D*
Religion M,D
Theology M,D
Therapies—Dance, Drama, and Music M,D
Women's Studies M,D

CALIFORNIA INSTITUTE OF TECHNOLOGY

Aerospace/Aeronautical Engineering M,D,O
Applied Mathematics M,D
Applied Physics M,D
Astronomy D
Biochemistry M,D
Bioengineering M,D
Biological and Biomedical Sciences—General M,D*
Biophysics D
Cell Biology D
Chemical Engineering M,D
Chemistry M,D
Civil Engineering M,D,O
Computational Sciences M,D
Computer Science M,D
Developmental Biology D
Electrical Engineering M,D,O
Engineering and Applied Sciences—General M,D,O
Environmental Engineering M,D
Genetics D
Geochemistry M,D
Geology M,D
Geophysics M,D
Immunology D
Materials Sciences M,D
Mathematics D
Mechanical Engineering M,D,O
Mechanics M,D
Molecular Biology D
Molecular Biophysics M,D
Neurobiology D
Neuroscience M,D
Physics D
Planetary and Space Sciences M,D
Social Sciences M,D
Systems Engineering M,D

CALIFORNIA INSTITUTE OF THE ARTS

Applied Arts and Design—General M,O
Art/Fine Arts M,O
Dance M,O
Film, Television, and Video Production M,O
Graphic Design M,O
Music M,O
Photography M,O
Theater M,O
Writing M,O

CALIFORNIA LUTHERAN UNIVERSITY

Business Administration and Management—General M,O
Clinical Psychology M
Counselor Education M
Education—General M,O
Educational Administration M
Entrepreneurship M,O
Finance and Banking M,O
International Business M,O
Management Information Systems M,O
Marketing M,O
Marriage and Family Therapy M
Organizational Behavior M,O
Psychology—General M
Public Administration M
Public Policy M
Reading Education M
Special Education M

Close-Up on page 825.

CALIFORNIA NATIONAL UNIVERSITY FOR ADVANCED STUDIES

Business Administration and Management—General M
Engineering and Applied Sciences—General M
Engineering Management M

CALIFORNIA POLYTECHNIC STATE UNIVERSITY, SAN LUIS OBISPO

Aerospace/Aeronautical Engineering M
Agricultural Economics and Agribusiness M
Agricultural Sciences—General M
Architecture M
Biochemistry M
Biological and Biomedical Sciences—General M
Business Administration and Management—General M
Chemistry M
Civil Engineering M
Computer Science M
Education—General M
Electrical Engineering M
Engineering and Applied Sciences—General M
English M
Environmental Engineering M
Environmental Management and Policy M
Forestry M
History M
Industrial and Manufacturing Management M
Industrial/Management Engineering M
Kinesiology and Movement Studies M
Mathematics M
Mechanical Engineering M
Political Science M
Polymer Science and Engineering M
Psychology—General M
Taxation M
Urban and Regional Planning M

CALIFORNIA SCHOOL OF PODIATRIC MEDICINE AT SAMUEL MERRITT COLLEGE

Podiatric Medicine P

CALIFORNIA STATE POLYTECHNIC UNIVERSITY, POMONA

Agricultural Sciences—General M
Animal Sciences M
Applied Mathematics M
Architecture M
Biological and Biomedical Sciences—General M
Business Administration and Management—General M
Chemistry M
Civil Engineering M
Computer Science M
Economics M
Education—General M
Electrical Engineering M
Engineering and Applied Sciences—General M
Engineering Management M
English M
Environmental Sciences M
Food Science and Technology M
History M
Kinesiology and Movement Studies M
Landscape Architecture M
Mathematics M
Mechanical Engineering M
Nutrition M
Psychology—General M
Public Administration M
Urban and Regional Planning M

CALIFORNIA STATE UNIVERSITY, BAKERSFIELD

Anthropology M
Biological and Biomedical Sciences—General M
Business Administration and Management—General M
Counseling Psychology M
Counselor Education M
Curriculum and Instruction M
Early Childhood Education M
Education—General M,O
Educational Administration M
Educational Media/Instructional Technology M
English M
Geology M
Health Services Management and Hospital Administration M
History M
Hydrology M
Interdisciplinary Studies M
Mathematics Education M
Middle School Education M
Multilingual and Multicultural Education M
Nursing—General M
Psychology—General M
Public Administration M
Reading Education M,O
Secondary Education M
Social Work M
Sociology M
Spanish M
Special Education M
Student Affairs M

CALIFORNIA STATE UNIVERSITY CHANNEL ISLANDS

Bioinformatics M
Biotechnology M*
Business Administration and Management—General M
Computer Science M
Educational Administration M
Mathematics M

CALIFORNIA STATE UNIVERSITY, CHICO

Anthropology M
Art History M
Art/Fine Arts M
Biological and Biomedical Sciences—General M
Botany M
Business Administration and Management—General M
Communication Disorders M
Communication—General M
Computer Engineering M
Computer Science M
Curriculum and Instruction M
Education—General M
Educational Administration M
Educational Media/Instructional Technology M
Electrical Engineering M
Engineering and Applied Sciences—General M
English M
Environmental Sciences M
Foreign Languages Education M

Geography M
Geology M
Geosciences M
Health Services Management and Hospital Administration M
History M
Hydrogeology M
Hydrology M
Interdisciplinary Studies M
Kinesiology and Movement Studies M
Marriage and Family Therapy M
Mathematics Education M
Multilingual and Multicultural Education M
Museum Studies M
Music M
Nursing—General M
Nutrition M
Political Science M
Psychology—General M
Public Administration M
Reading Education M
Recreation and Park Management M
Rural Planning and Studies M
Science Education M
Social Sciences Education M
Social Sciences M
Social Work M
Special Education M
Urban and Regional Planning M

CALIFORNIA STATE UNIVERSITY, DOMINGUEZ HILLS

Applied Social Research M,O
Bioinformatics M
Biological and Biomedical Sciences—General M
Business Administration and Management—General M
Clinical Psychology M
Computer Education M,O
Conflict Resolution and Mediation/Peace Studies M
Counselor Education M
Curriculum and Instruction M
Education—General M,O
Educational Administration M
English as a Second Language M,O
English M,O
Gerontology M
Health Education M
Humanities M
International and Comparative Education M
Marriage and Family Therapy M
Mathematics Education M
Multilingual and Multicultural Education M
Nursing—General M
Occupational Therapy M
Physical Education M
Physician Assistant Studies M
Psychology—General M
Public Administration M
Quality Management M
Rhetoric M,O
Social Work M
Sociology M,O
Special Education M

Close-Up on page 827.

CALIFORNIA STATE UNIVERSITY, EAST BAY

Accounting M
Anthropology M
Applied Statistics M
Biochemistry M
Biological and Biomedical Sciences—General M
Biostatistics M
Business Administration and Management—General M
Chemistry M
Communication Disorders M
Communication—General M
Computer Engineering M
Computer Science M
Counselor Education M
Curriculum and Instruction M
Economics M
Education—General M
Educational Administration M
Educational Media/Instructional Technology M
Electronic Commerce M
Engineering Management M
English M
Entrepreneurship M
Finance and Banking M
Geography M
Geology M
Health Services Management and Hospital Administration M
History M
Human Resources Management M
Industrial and Manufacturing Management M
Interdisciplinary Studies M,O
International Business M
Internet and Interactive Multimedia M
Management Information Systems M
Management Strategy and Policy M
Marine Sciences M
Marketing M
Mathematics M
Music M
Operations Research M
Physical Education M
Public Administration M
Quantitative Analysis M
Social Work M
Sociology M
Software Engineering M
Special Education M
Statistics M
Supply Chain Management M
Taxation M
Telecommunications M

Announcement on page 332.

CALIFORNIA STATE UNIVERSITY, FRESNO

Accounting M
Agricultural Sciences—General M
Animal Sciences M
Applied Arts and Design—General M
Art/Fine Arts M
Biological and Biomedical Sciences—General M
Business Administration and Management—General M
Chemistry M
Civil Engineering M
Communication Disorders M
Communication—General M
Computer Science M
Counselor Education M
Criminal Justice and Criminology M
Curriculum and Instruction M
Early Childhood Education M
Education—General M,D
Educational Administration M,D
Electrical Engineering M
Engineering and Applied Sciences—General M
English as a Second Language M
English M
Environmental and Occupational Health M
Exercise and Sports Science M
Family and Consumer Sciences-General M
Family Nurse Practitioner Studies M
Food Science and Technology M
Geology M
Health Promotion M
Health Services Management and Hospital Administration M
History M
Industrial/Management Engineering M
International Affairs M
Journalism M
Kinesiology and Movement Studies M
Linguistics M
Marine Sciences M
Marriage and Family Therapy M
Mass Communication M
Mathematics Education M
Mathematics M
Mechanical Engineering M
Music Education M
Music M
Nursing—General M
Physical Therapy M
Physics M
Plant Sciences M
Psychology—General M
Public Administration M
Public Health—General M
Reading Education M
Rehabilitation Counseling M
Social Work M
Spanish M
Special Education M
Sport Psychology M
Writing M

CALIFORNIA STATE UNIVERSITY, FULLERTON

Accounting M
Advertising and Public Relations M
American Studies M
Analytical Chemistry M
Anthropology M
Applied Arts and Design—General M,O
Applied Mathematics M
Art History M,O
Art/Fine Arts M,O
Biochemistry M
Biological and Biomedical Sciences—General M
Botany M
Business Administration and Management—General M
Chemistry M
Civil Engineering M
Clinical Psychology M
Communication Disorders M
Communication—General M
Comparative Literature M
Computer Science M
Counselor Education M
Dance M
Economics M
Education—General M
Educational Administration M
Educational Media/Instructional Technology M
Electrical Engineering M
Elementary Education M
Engineering and Applied Sciences—General M
English as a Second Language M
English M
Environmental Education M
Environmental Management and Policy M
Environmental Sciences M
Film, Television, and Video Production M
Finance and Banking M
French M
Geochemistry M
Geography M
Geology M
German M
Gerontology M
History M
Information Science M
Inorganic Chemistry M
International Business M
Journalism M
Linguistics M
Management Information Systems M
Marketing M
Mathematics Education M
Mathematics M
Mechanical Engineering M
Mechanics M
Media Studies M
Microbiology M
Middle School Education M
Multilingual and Multicultural Education M
Museum Studies M,O
Music Education M
Music M
Nursing—General M
Operations Research M
Organic Chemistry M
Photography M,O
Physical Chemistry M
Physical Education M
Physics M
Political Science M
Psychology—General M
Public Administration M
Public Health—General M
Reading Education M
Science Education M
Secondary Education M
Social Psychology M
Sociology M
Software Engineering M
Spanish M
Special Education M
Speech and Interpersonal Communication M
Statistics M
Systems Engineering M
Taxation M
Theater M

CALIFORNIA STATE UNIVERSITY, LONG BEACH

Aerospace/Aeronautical Engineering M
Anthropology M
Applied Mathematics M,D
Art/Fine Arts M
Asian Studies M,O
Asian-American Studies M,O
Biochemistry M
Biological and Biomedical Sciences—General M
Business Administration and Management—General M
Chemistry M
Civil Engineering M
Communication Disorders M
Communication—General M
Computer Engineering M
Computer Science M
Consumer Economics M
Counselor Education M
Criminal Justice and Criminology M
Dance M
Economics M
Education—General M,D
Electrical Engineering M
Emergency Management M
Engineering Management M,D
English M
Family and Consumer Sciences-General M
French M
Geography M
Geology M
Geosciences M
German M
Gerontology M
Health Education M
Health Services Management and Hospital Administration M,O
History M
Interdisciplinary Studies M
Kinesiology and Movement Studies M
Leisure Studies M
Linguistics M
Mathematics Education M
Mathematics M
Mechanical Engineering M,D
Microbiology M
Music M
Nursing—General M
Nutrition M
Philosophy M
Physical Education M
Physical Therapy M
Physics M
Political Science M
Psychology—General M
Public Administration M
Public Policy M
Recreation and Park Management M
Religion M
Science Education M
Social Work M
Spanish M
Special Education M
Theater M
Vocational and Technical Education M
Writing M

CALIFORNIA STATE UNIVERSITY, LOS ANGELES

Accounting M
Analytical Chemistry M
Anthropology M
Applied Arts and Design—General M
Applied Mathematics M
Art Education M
Art History M
Art Therapy M
Art/Fine Arts M
Biochemistry M
Biological and Biomedical Sciences—General M
Business Administration and Management—General M
Chemistry M
Child Development M
Civil Engineering M
Communication Disorders M
Communication—General M
Computer Education M
Computer Science M
Counselor Education M
Criminal Justice and Criminology M
Economics M
Education—General M
Educational Media/Instructional Technology M
Electrical Engineering M
Elementary Education M
Engineering and Applied Sciences—General M
English as a Second Language M
English M
Finance and Banking M
Foundations and Philosophy of Education M
French M
Geography M
Geology M
Graphic Design M
Health Education M
Health Services Management and Hospital Administration M
Hispanic Studies M
History M
Inorganic Chemistry M
International Business M
Kinesiology and Movement Studies M
Latin American Studies M

Management Information Systems M
Marketing M
Mathematics M
Mechanical Engineering M
Music Education M
Music M
Nursing—General M
Nutrition M
Organic Chemistry M
Philosophy M
Photography M
Physical Chemistry M
Physical Education M
Physics M
Political Science M
Psychology—General M
Public Administration M
Reading Education M
Rehabilitation Counseling M
School Psychology M
Secondary Education M
Social Work M
Sociology M
Spanish M
Special Education M
Speech and Interpersonal Communication M
Taxation M
Textile Design M
Theater M

CALIFORNIA STATE UNIVERSITY, MONTEREY BAY

Education—General M
Management Information Systems M
Marine Sciences M
Public Policy M

CALIFORNIA STATE UNIVERSITY, NORTHRIDGE

Anthropology M
Applied Mathematics M
Art Education M
Art History M
Art/Fine Arts M
Biochemistry M
Biological and Biomedical Sciences—General M
Business Administration and Management—General M
Chemistry M
Civil Engineering M
Communication Disorders M
Communication—General M
Comparative Literature M
Computer Science M
Counselor Education M
Early Childhood Education M
Education—General M
Educational Administration M
Educational Psychology M
Electrical Engineering M
Elementary Education M
Engineering and Applied Sciences—General M
Engineering Management M
English M
Environmental and Occupational Health M
Environmental Sciences M
Family and Consumer Sciences-General M
Film, Television, and Video Production M
Genetic Counseling M
Geography M
Geology M
Health Education M
Health Services Management and Hospital Administration M
Hispanic Studies M
History M
Industrial Hygiene M
Industrial/Management Engineering M
Interdisciplinary Studies M
Journalism M
Kinesiology and Movement Studies M
Linguistics M
Manufacturing Engineering M
Marriage and Family Therapy M
Mass Communication M
Materials Engineering M
Mathematics Education M
Mathematics M
Mechanical Engineering M
Music Education M
Music M
Physical Therapy M
Physics M
Political Science M
Psychology—General M
Public Administration M
Recreation and Park Management M
Rhetoric M
School Psychology M
Secondary Education M
Social Work M
Sociology M
Spanish M
Special Education M
Speech and Interpersonal Communication M
Structural Engineering M
Systems Engineering M
Theater M
Writing M

CALIFORNIA STATE UNIVERSITY, SACRAMENTO

Accounting M
Anthropology M
Art/Fine Arts M
Biological and Biomedical Sciences—General M
Business Administration and Management—General M*
Chemistry M
Civil Engineering M
Communication Disorders M
Communication—General M
Computer Science M
Counseling Psychology M
Counselor Education M
Criminal Justice and Criminology M
Curriculum and Instruction M
Dance M
Early Childhood Education M
Education—General M
Educational Administration M
Electrical Engineering M
Engineering and Applied Sciences—General M
English as a Second Language M
English M
Foreign Languages Education M
French M
German M
Human Resources Development M
Human Resources Management M
Human Services M
Interdisciplinary Studies M
International Affairs M
Liberal Studies M
Management Information Systems M
Marine Sciences M
Mathematics M
Mechanical Engineering M
Multilingual and Multicultural Education M
Music M
Nursing—General M
Physical Education M
Political Science M
Psychology—General M
Public Administration M
Public History M
Public Policy M
Reading Education M
Real Estate M
Recreation and Park Management M
School Psychology M
Social Work M
Sociology M
Software Engineering M
Spanish M
Special Education M
Statistics M
Theater M
Vocational and Technical Education M
Writing M

CALIFORNIA STATE UNIVERSITY, SAN BERNARDINO

Art/Fine Arts M
Biological and Biomedical Sciences—General M
Business Administration and Management—General M
Chemistry M
Child Development M
Clinical Psychology M
Communication—General M
Computer Science M
Counseling Psychology M
Counselor Education M
Criminal Justice and Criminology M
Curriculum and Instruction M
Education—General M
Educational Administration M
Educational Media/Instructional Technology M
Educational Psychology M
Elementary Education M
English as a Second Language M
English Education M
English M
Environmental Education M
Environmental Sciences M
Experimental Psychology M
Health Education M
Health Services Management and Hospital Administration M
Human Development M
Industrial and Organizational Psychology M
Interdisciplinary Studies M
Kinesiology and Movement Studies M
Mathematics M
Multilingual and Multicultural Education M
National Security M
Nursing—General M
Psychology—General M
Public Administration M
Reading Education M
Rehabilitation Counseling M
Science Education M
Secondary Education M
Social Sciences Education M
Social Sciences M
Social Work M
Spanish M
Special Education M
Theater M
Vocational and Technical Education M

CALIFORNIA STATE UNIVERSITY, SAN MARCOS

Biological and Biomedical Sciences—General M
Business Administration and Management—General M
Computer Science M
Education—General M
English M
Mathematics M
Psychology—General M
Sociology M
Spanish M
Writing M

CALIFORNIA STATE UNIVERSITY, STANISLAUS

Business Administration and Management—General M
Criminal Justice and Criminology M
Curriculum and Instruction M
Education—General M
Elementary Education M
English M
Finance and Banking M
History M
Interdisciplinary Studies M
Marine Biology M
Multilingual and Multicultural Education M
Political Science M
Psychology—General M
Public Administration M
Reading Education M
Secondary Education M
Social Work M

CALIFORNIA UNIVERSITY OF PENNSYLVANIA

Athletic Training and Sports Medicine M
Business Administration and Management—General M
Communication Disorders M
Counselor Education M
Criminal Justice and Criminology M
Education—General M
Educational Administration M
Elementary Education M
Exercise and Sports Science M
Legal and Justice Studies M
Reading Education M
Rehabilitation Sciences M
School Psychology M
Secondary Education M
Social Sciences M
Social Work M
Special Education M
Sport Psychology M
Sports Management M
Vocational and Technical Education M

CALIFORNIA WESTERN SCHOOL OF LAW

Accounting P,M
Law P,M

CALVARY BIBLE COLLEGE AND THEOLOGICAL SEMINARY

Pastoral Ministry and Counseling P,M
Theology P,M

CALVIN COLLEGE

Curriculum and Instruction M
Education—General M
Educational Administration M
Reading Education M
Special Education M

CALVIN THEOLOGICAL SEMINARY

Missions and Missiology P,M,D
Religious Education P,M,D
Theology P,M,D

CAMBRIDGE COLLEGE

Business Administration and Management—General M
Counseling Psychology M,O
Education—General M,D,O
Educational Administration M,D,O
Electronic Commerce M

CAMERON UNIVERSITY

Business Administration and Management—General M
Education—General M
Educational Administration M
Entrepreneurship M
Psychology—General M

CAMPBELLSVILLE UNIVERSITY

Business Administration and Management—General M
Curriculum and Instruction M
Education—General M
Music Education M
Music M
Social Sciences M
Social Work
Special Education M
Theology M

CAMPBELL UNIVERSITY

Business Administration and Management—General M
Counselor Education M
Education—General M
Educational Administration M
Elementary Education M
English Education M
Interdisciplinary Studies M
Law P
Mathematics Education M
Middle School Education M
Pharmaceutical Sciences P,M
Pharmacy P,M
Physical Education M
Religious Education P,M,D
Secondary Education M
Social Sciences Education M
Theology P,M,D

CANADIAN COLLEGE OF NATUROPATHIC MEDICINE

Naturopathic Medicine D*

CANADIAN MEMORIAL CHIROPRACTIC COLLEGE

Chiropractic P,O

CANADIAN SOUTHERN BAPTIST SEMINARY

Computer Education P,M
Theology P,M

CANISIUS COLLEGE

Accounting M
Business Administration and Management—General M
Business Education M
Communication Disorders M
Corporate and Organizational Communication M
Counselor Education M
Early Childhood Education M
Education—General M
Educational Administration M
Health Promotion M
Human Services M
Marketing M
Physical Education M
Reading Education M
Rehabilitation Sciences M
School Psychology M
Secondary Education M
Social Psychology M
Special Education M
Sports Management M
Student Affairs M

CAPE BRETON UNIVERSITY

Art Education O
Business Administration and Management—General M
Counselor Education O
Education—General O
Educational Media/Instructional Technology O

CAPELLA UNIVERSITY

Accounting M,D,O
Addictions/Substance Abuse Counseling M,D,O
Adult Education M,D,O
Business Administration and Management—General M,D,O
Child and Family Studies M,D,O
Clinical Psychology M,D,O
Computer and Information Systems Security M,D,O
Counseling Psychology M,D,O
Criminal Justice and Criminology M,D,O
Curriculum and Instruction M,D,O
Education—General M,D,O
Educational Administration M,D,O
Educational Media/Instructional Technology M,D,O
Educational Psychology M,D,O
Elementary Education M,D,O
Finance and Banking M,D,O
Health Services Management and Hospital Administration M,D,O
Higher Education M,D,O
Human Resources Management M,D,O
Human Services M,D,O
Industrial and Organizational Psychology M,D,O
Management Information Systems M,D,O
Management of Technology M,D,O
Marketing M,D,O
Marriage and Family Therapy M,D,O
Middle School Education M,D,O
Multilingual and Multicultural Education M,D,O
Nonprofit Management M,D,O
Organizational Management M,D,O
Project Management M,D,O
Psychology—General M,D,O
Reading Education M,D,O
School Psychology M,D,O
Sport Psychology M,D,O

CAPITAL BIBLE SEMINARY

Pastoral Ministry and Counseling P,M,O
Theology P,M,O

CAPITAL UNIVERSITY

Business Administration and Management—General M
Law P,M
Legal and Justice Studies M
Music Education M
Music M
Nursing and Healthcare Administration M
Nursing—General M
Taxation M

CAPITOL COLLEGE

Business Administration and Management—General M
Computer and Information Systems Security M
Computer Science M
Electrical Engineering M
Information Science M
Management Information Systems M
Telecommunications Management M

CARDEAN UNIVERSITY

Accounting M
Business Administration and Management—General M
Economics M
Electronic Commerce M
Finance and Banking M
Health Services Management and Hospital Administration M
Human Resources Management M
International Business M
Management Information Systems M
Management of Technology M
Management Strategy and Policy M
Marketing M
Organizational Management M
Project Management M

CARDINAL STRITCH UNIVERSITY

Applied Arts and Design—General M*
Business Administration and Management—General M*
Clinical Psychology M
Computer Education M
Education—General M,D*
Educational Administration M,D
Educational Media/Instructional Technology M
English as a Second Language M
Graphic Design M
History M
Liberal Studies M
Music M
Nursing—General M*
Pastoral Ministry and Counseling M
Psychology—General M
Reading Education M
Religion M
Special Education M
Urban Education M,D

CAREY THEOLOGICAL COLLEGE

Theology M,D

CARIBBEAN UNIVERSITY

Accounting M,D
Art History M,D
Criminal Justice and Criminology M,D
Curriculum and Instruction M,D
Education—General M,D
Educational Administration M,D
Gerontological Nursing M,D
Human Resources Management M,D
Museum Studies M,D
Pediatric Nursing M,D
Physical Education M,D
Special Education M,D

CARLETON UNIVERSITY

Aerospace/Aeronautical Engineering M,D
Anthropology M
Architecture M
Art History M
Biological and Biomedical Sciences—General M,D
Business Administration and Management—General M,D
Canadian Studies M,D
Chemistry M,D
Civil Engineering M,D
Cognitive Sciences D
Communication—General M,D
Comparative Literature D
Computer Science M,D
Conflict Resolution and Mediation/Peace Studies M,O
East European and Russian Studies M,O
Economics M,D
Electrical Engineering M,D
Engineering and Applied Sciences—General M,D
English M,D
Environmental Engineering M,D
Film, Television, and Video Production M
French M
Geography M,D
Geosciences M,D
History M,D
Information Science M,D
International Affairs M,D
Journalism M,O
Legal and Justice Studies M,O
Linguistics M
Materials Engineering M,D
Mathematics M,D
Mechanical Engineering M,D
Neuroscience M,D
Philosophy M
Physics M,D
Political Science M,D
Psychology—General M,D
Public Administration M,D
Public Policy M,D
Social Work M
Sociology M,D
Systems Engineering M,D
Systems Science M,D
Telecommunications Management M
Western European Studies M,O

CARLOS ALBIZU UNIVERSITY

Clinical Psychology M,D
Communication Disorders M,D
Industrial and Organizational Psychology M,D
Psychology—General M,D

CARLOS ALBIZU UNIVERSITY, MIAMI CAMPUS

Business Administration and Management—General M,D
Clinical Psychology M,D
Counseling Psychology M,D
Education of the Gifted M,D
English as a Second Language M,D
Entrepreneurship M,D
Industrial and Organizational Psychology M,D
Marriage and Family Therapy M,D
Nonprofit Management M,D
Organizational Management M,D
Psychology—General M,D
School Psychology M,D
Special Education M,D

CARLOW UNIVERSITY

Art Education M
Counseling Psychology M
Early Childhood Education M
Education—General M
Educational Administration M
Educational Media/Instructional Technology M
Elementary Education M
Humanities M
Management of Technology M
Nonprofit Management M
Nursing and Healthcare Administration M,O
Nursing—General M,O
Organizational Management M
Secondary Education M
Special Education M
Writing M

CARNEGIE MELLON UNIVERSITY

Accounting D
Applied Arts and Design—General D
Architecture M,D
Art/Fine Arts M
Artificial Intelligence/Robotics M,D*
Arts Administration M*
Biochemistry M,D
Bioengineering M,D
Biological and Biomedical Sciences—General M,D*
Biomedical Engineering M,D
Biophysics M,D
Biopsychology D
Building Science M,D
Business Administration and Management—General M,D*
Cell Biology M,D
Chemical Engineering M,D
Chemistry M,D
Civil Engineering M,D*
Cognitive Sciences D
Communication—General M,D
Comparative Literature M,D
Computational Biology M,D*
Computational Sciences M,D
Computer and Information Systems Security M
Computer Art and Design M
Computer Engineering M,D*
Computer Science M,D*
Construction Engineering M,D
Criminal Justice and Criminology M
Developmental Biology M,D
Developmental Psychology D
Economics M,D
Education—General M,D
Electrical Engineering M,D
Electronic Commerce M
Engineering and Applied Sciences—General M,D
Engineering Management M,D
English M,D*
Environmental Engineering M,D
Film, Television, and Video Production M
Finance and Banking D
Genetics M,D
Health Services Management and Hospital Administration M*
History M,D
Human-Computer Interaction M,D*
Industrial and Manufacturing Management M,D
Information Science M,D*
Linguistics M,D
Management Information Systems M,D
Management of Technology M,D
Marketing D
Materials Engineering M,D
Materials Sciences M,D*
Mathematical and Computational Finance M,D
Mathematics M,D
Mechanical Engineering M,D
Media Studies M
Molecular Biology M,D
Music Education M
Music M
Neurobiology M,D
Neuroscience D*
Operations Research D
Organizational Behavior D
Organizational Management D
Philosophy M,D
Physics D
Polymer Science and Engineering M,D
Psychology—General D
Public Administration M*
Public Policy M*
Rhetoric M
Social Psychology D
Social Sciences D
Software Engineering M,D*
Statistics M,D*
Sustainable Development M
Systems Engineering M
Technical Writing M
Technology and Public Policy M,D*
Telecommunications Management M
Theater M
Writing M*

CARROLL COLLEGE

Education—General M
Physical Therapy M,D
Software Engineering M

CARSON-NEWMAN COLLEGE

Counselor Education M
Curriculum and Instruction M
Education—General M
Elementary Education M
English as a Second Language M
Family Nurse Practitioner Studies M
Nursing—General M
Secondary Education M

CARTHAGE COLLEGE

Art Education M,O
Counselor Education M,O
Education of the Gifted M,O
Education—General M,O
Educational Administration M,O
English Education M,O
Reading Education M,O
Science Education M,O
Social Sciences Education M,O

CASE WESTERN RESERVE UNIVERSITY

Accounting M,D
Acute Care/Critical Care Nursing M,D
Adult Nursing M,D
Aerospace/Aeronautical Engineering M,D
Allopathic Medicine P
Analytical Chemistry M,D
Anatomy M,D
Anesthesiologist Assistant Studies M
Anthropology M,D
Applied Mathematics M,D
Art Education M
Art History M,D
Astronomy M,D
Biochemistry M,D
Bioethics M,D
Biological and Biomedical Sciences—General M,D*
Biomedical Engineering M,D*
Biophysics M,D
Biostatistics M,D
Business Administration and Management—General M,D
Cell Biology M,D
Ceramic Sciences and Engineering M,D
Chemical Engineering M,D
Chemistry M,D
Civil Engineering M,D
Clinical Psychology D
Clinical Research M
Communication Disorders M,D,O
Community Health Nursing M
Comparative Literature M,D
Computer Engineering M,D
Computer Science M,D
Dance M
Dentistry P
Developmental Biology M,D
Economics M
Electrical Engineering M,D
Engineering and Applied Sciences—General M,D*
Engineering Management M
English M,D
Epidemiology M,D
Experimental Psychology D
Family Nurse Practitioner Studies M,D
Finance and Banking M,D
French M,D
Genetic Counseling M
Genetics D
Genomic Sciences D*
Geology M,D
Geosciences M,D
Gerontological Nursing M,D
Gerontology M,D,O
Health Services Management and Hospital Administration M,D
History M,D
Human Genetics D
Human Resources Management M

- Immunology M,D
- Industrial and Labor Relations M
- Industrial and Manufacturing Management M,D
- Information Science M,D
- Inorganic Chemistry M,D
- Law P,M
- Legal and Justice Studies P,M
- Logistics M,D
- Management Information Systems M,D
- Management Strategy and Policy M
- Marketing M,D
- Materials Engineering M,D
- Materials Sciences M,D
- Mathematics M,D
- Mechanical Engineering M,D
- Mechanics M,D
- Medical/Surgical Nursing M,D
- Microbiology D
- Molecular Biology M,D
- Museum Studies M,D
- Music Education M,D
- Music M,D
- Neurobiology D
- Neuroscience D*
- Nonprofit Management M,O*
- Nurse Anesthesia M
- Nurse Midwifery M,D
- Nursing Informatics M
- Nursing—General M,D
- Nutrition M,D*
- Operations Research M
- Oral and Dental Sciences M,O
- Organic Chemistry M,D
- Organizational Behavior M
- Pathology M,D
- Pediatric Nursing M,D
- Pharmacology M,D
- Physical Chemistry M,D
- Physics M,D
- Physiology M,D*
- Political Science M,D
- Polymer Science and Engineering M,D
- Psychiatric Nursing M,D
- Psychology—General D
- Public Health—General M
- Quality Management M,D
- Social Work M,D*
- Sociology D
- Statistics M,D
- Supply Chain Management M
- Systems Engineering M,D
- Theater M
- Women's Health Nursing M,D

CASTLETON STATE COLLEGE

- Curriculum and Instruction M
- Education—General M,O
- Educational Administration M,O
- Forensic Psychology M
- Psychology—General M
- Reading Education M,O
- Special Education M,O

CATAWBA COLLEGE

- Education—General M
- Elementary Education M

THE CATHOLIC DISTANCE UNIVERSITY

- Theology M

CATHOLIC THEOLOGICAL UNION AT CHICAGO

- Missions and Missiology P,M,D,O
- Pastoral Ministry and Counseling P,M,D,O
- Theology P,M,D,O

THE CATHOLIC UNIVERSITY OF AMERICA

- Acoustics M,D
- Adult Nursing M,D
- Anthropology M,D
- Architecture M
- Artificial Intelligence/Robotics M,D
- Biological and Biomedical Sciences—General M,D
- Biomedical Engineering M,D
- Business Administration and Management—General M
- Cell Biology M,D
- Chemistry M
- Civil Engineering M,D
- Classics M,D
- Clinical Laboratory Sciences/Medical Technology M,D
- Clinical Psychology D
- Comparative Literature M,D
- Computer Science M,D
- Construction Management M,D
- Counselor Education M,D
- Curriculum and Instruction M,D
- Economics M
- Education—General M,D
- Educational Administration M,D
- Educational Psychology M,D
- Electrical Engineering M,D
- Engineering and Applied Sciences—General M,D
- Engineering Design M,D
- Engineering Management M
- English as a Second Language M,D
- English M,D
- Environmental Engineering M,D
- Ergonomics and Human Factors M
- Experimental Psychology M,D
- Family Nurse Practitioner Studies M,D
- French M,D
- Geotechnical Engineering M,D
- Gerontological Nursing M,D
- History M,D
- Human Development D
- Information Studies M
- International Affairs M,D
- Italian M,D
- Law P
- Legal and Justice Studies D,O
- Library Science M
- Mechanical Engineering M,D
- Mechanics M,D
- Medieval and Renaissance Studies M,D,O
- Microbiology M,D
- Music Education M,D
- Music M,D
- Near and Middle Eastern Languages M,D
- Nursing and Healthcare Administration M,D
- Nursing Education M,D
- Nursing—General M,D
- Pediatric Nursing M,D
- Philosophy M,D,O
- Physics M,D
- Political Science M,D
- Psychiatric Nursing M,D
- Psychology—General M,D
- Religion P,M,D,O
- Rhetoric M,D
- Romance Languages M,D
- Social Work M,D*
- Sociology M,D
- Spanish M,D
- Structural Engineering M,D
- Theater M
- Theology P,M,D,O
- Urban and Regional Planning M
- Western European Studies M

CEDAR CREST COLLEGE

- Education—General M*
- Forensic Sciences M*

CEDARVILLE UNIVERSITY

- Education—General M

CENTENARY COLLEGE

- Accounting M
- Business Administration and Management—General M
- Counseling Psychology M
- Education—General M
- Educational Administration M
- Special Education M

CENTENARY COLLEGE OF LOUISIANA

- Business Administration and Management—General M
- Curriculum and Instruction M
- Education—General M
- Educational Administration M
- Elementary Education M
- Secondary Education M

CENTRAL BAPTIST THEOLOGICAL SEMINARY

- Missions and Missiology P,M,O
- Theology P,M,O

CENTRAL CONNECTICUT STATE UNIVERSITY

- Actuarial Science M,O
- Art Education M,O
- Biological and Biomedical Sciences—General M,O
- Business Administration and Management—General M,O
- Business Education M,O
- Chemistry M
- Communication—General M
- Computer Science M
- Construction Management M
- Corporate and Organizational Communication M
- Counselor Education M,O
- Criminal Justice and Criminology M
- Early Childhood Education M
- Education—General M,D,O
- Educational Administration M,D,O
- Educational Media/Instructional Technology M
- Elementary Education M,O
- Engineering and Applied Sciences—General M
- English as a Second Language O
- English M,O
- Exercise and Sports Science M,O
- Foreign Languages Education M,O
- Foundations and Philosophy of Education M
- French M,O
- Geography M
- Geosciences M
- Health Psychology M
- History M,O
- Information Studies M
- International Affairs M
- International Business M
- Italian M,O
- Management of Technology M
- Marriage and Family Therapy M,O
- Mathematics M,O
- Molecular Biology M
- Music Education M,O
- Nurse Anesthesia M,O
- Physical Education M,O
- Physics M
- Psychology—General M
- Reading Education M,O
- Rehabilitation Counseling M,O
- School Psychology M,O
- Secondary Education M
- Social Psychology M
- Spanish M,O
- Special Education M
- Statistics M,O
- Vocational and Technical Education M,O

CENTRAL EUROPEAN UNIVERSITY

- Anthropology M,D
- Applied Mathematics M,D
- Business Administration and Management—General M
- Economics M,D
- Environmental Management and Policy M,D
- Finance and Banking M
- Gender Studies M,D
- History M,D
- Humanities M,D*
- International Affairs M,D
- International Business M,D
- Law M,D
- Legal and Justice Studies M,D
- Management Information Systems M
- Marketing M
- Medieval and Renaissance Studies M,D
- Philosophy M,D
- Political Science M,D
- Public Policy M,D
- Real Estate M
- Social Sciences M,D
- Sociology M,D

CENTRAL METHODIST UNIVERSITY

- Counselor Education M
- Education—General M

CENTRAL MICHIGAN UNIVERSITY

- Accounting M
- Art/Fine Arts M
- Automotive Engineering M,O
- Biological and Biomedical Sciences—General M
- Business Administration and Management—General M*
- Business Education M
- Chemistry M
- Child and Family Studies M
- Clinical Psychology D
- Communication Disorders M,D
- Communication—General M
- Computer Science M
- Conservation Biology M
- Corporate and Organizational Communication M
- Counselor Education M
- Criminal Justice and Criminology M
- Early Childhood Education M
- Economics M
- Education—General M,D,O
- Educational Administration M,D,O
- Educational Media/Instructional Technology M
- Elementary Education M
- English as a Second Language M
- English M
- Exercise and Sports Science M
- Experimental Psychology M,D
- Family and Consumer Sciences-General M
- Film, Television, and Video Production M
- Finance and Banking M
- Health Promotion M
- Health Services Management and Hospital Administration M,D,O
- History M,D
- Hospitality Management M
- Human Development M
- Human Resources Management M,O
- Humanities M
- Industrial and Manufacturing Management M
- Industrial and Organizational Psychology M,D
- International Affairs M,O
- International Business M
- Leisure Studies M
- Management Information Systems M,O*
- Marketing M
- Mass Communication M
- Mathematics M,D
- Media Studies M
- Middle School Education M
- Music Education M
- Music M
- Nutrition M
- Physical Education M
- Physical Therapy M,D
- Physician Assistant Studies M,D
- Physics M
- Political Science M
- Psychology—General M,D,O
- Public Administration M,O
- Reading Education M
- Recreation and Park Management M
- Rehabilitation Sciences M,D
- School Psychology D,O
- Science Education M
- Secondary Education M
- Sociology M
- Software Engineering M,O
- Spanish M
- Special Education M
- Speech and Interpersonal Communication M
- Sports Management M
- Theater M
- Vocational and Technical Education M
- Writing M

CENTRAL STATE UNIVERSITY

- Education—General M
- Educational Administration M
- Educational Media/Instructional Technology M
- Reading Education M

CENTRAL WASHINGTON UNIVERSITY

- Accounting M
- Art/Fine Arts M
- Biological and Biomedical Sciences—General M
- Chemistry M
- Child and Family Studies M
- Counseling Psychology M
- Counselor Education M
- Education—General M
- Educational Administration M
- Engineering and Applied Sciences—General M
- English as a Second Language M
- English M
- Environmental Management and Policy M
- Experimental Psychology M
- Family and Consumer Sciences-General M
- Geology M
- Health Education M
- History M
- Home Economics Education M
- Industrial/Management Engineering M
- Interdisciplinary Studies M
- Mathematics M
- Music M
- Nutrition M
- Physical Education M
- Psychology—General M
- Reading Education M
- School Psychology M
- Special Education M
- Theater M

Close-Up on page 829 and Announcement on page 346.

CENTRAL YESHIVA TOMCHEI TMIMIM-LUBAVITCH

- Theology

CENTRO DE ESTUDIOS AVANZADOS DE PUERTO RICO Y EL CARIBE

- History M,D
- Latin American Studies M,D

CHADRON STATE COLLEGE
- Business Administration and Management—General M
- Business Education M,O
- Counselor Education M,O
- Education—General M,O
- Educational Administration M,O
- Elementary Education M,O
- English Education M,O
- Secondary Education M,O
- Social Sciences Education M,O

CHAMINADE UNIVERSITY OF HONOLULU
- Business Administration and Management—General M
- Conflict Resolution and Mediation/Peace Studies M
- Counseling Psychology M
- Criminal Justice and Criminology M
- Education—General M
- Forensic Sciences M
- Pastoral Ministry and Counseling M
- Social Sciences Education M
- Theology M

CHAMPLAIN COLLEGE
- Management of Technology M

CHAPMAN UNIVERSITY
- Business Administration and Management—General M,O
- Counselor Education M
- Cultural Studies D
- Curriculum and Instruction M,D
- Disability Studies D
- Education—General M,D,O
- Educational Administration M
- Educational Psychology M,O
- Elementary Education M
- English M
- Film, Television, and Video Production M
- Food Science and Technology M
- Human Resources Management M,O
- Law P,M
- Marriage and Family Therapy M
- Nutrition M
- Physical Therapy D
- Reading Education M
- School Psychology M,D,O
- Secondary Education M
- Special Education M
- Taxation P,M
- Writing M

Close-Up on page 831.

CHARLES R. DREW UNIVERSITY OF MEDICINE AND SCIENCE
- Allopathic Medicine P

CHARLESTON SOUTHERN UNIVERSITY
- Accounting M
- Business Administration and Management—General M
- Criminal Justice and Criminology M
- Education—General M
- Educational Administration M
- Elementary Education M
- English Education M
- Finance and Banking M
- Health Services Management and Hospital Administration M
- Management Information Systems M
- Organizational Management M
- Science Education M
- Secondary Education M
- Social Sciences Education M

CHATHAM UNIVERSITY
- Art Education M
- Biological and Biomedical Sciences—General M
- Business Administration and Management—General M
- Computer Art and Design M
- Counseling Psychology M
- Early Childhood Education M
- Education—General M
- Elementary Education M
- English Education M
- Environmental Education M
- Film, Television, and Video Production M
- Interior Design M
- Landscape Architecture M
- Mathematics Education M
- Nursing—General M,D
- Occupational Therapy M,D
- Organizational Management M
- Physical Therapy D
- Physician Assistant Studies M
- Science Education M
- Secondary Education M
- Social Sciences Education M
- Special Education M
- Writing M

CHESTNUT HILL COLLEGE
- Clinical Psychology D
- Counseling Psychology M,O
- Early Childhood Education M
- Education—General M
- Educational Administration M
- Educational Media/Instructional Technology M,O
- Elementary Education M
- Film, Television, and Video Production M,O
- Gerontology M,O
- Human Services M,O
- Internet and Interactive Multimedia M,O
- Pastoral Ministry and Counseling M,O
- Psychology—General M,D,O
- Religion M,O
- Secondary Education M

Close-Up on page 833.

CHEYNEY UNIVERSITY OF PENNSYLVANIA
- Adult Education M
- Early Childhood Education O
- Education—General M,O
- Educational Administration M,O
- Elementary Education M
- Mathematics Education O
- Special Education M

THE CHICAGO SCHOOL OF PROFESSIONAL PSYCHOLOGY
- Clinical Psychology M,D,O*
- Counselor Education M,D,O
- Forensic Psychology M*
- Industrial and Organizational Psychology M,D*
- Psychology—General M,D,O
- School Psychology O*

CHICAGO STATE UNIVERSITY
- Biological and Biomedical Sciences—General M
- Computer Science M
- Counselor Education M
- Criminal Justice and Criminology M
- Early Childhood Education M
- Education—General M,D
- Educational Administration M,D
- Educational Media/Instructional Technology M
- Elementary Education M
- English M
- Foundations and Philosophy of Education M
- Geography M
- Higher Education M,D
- History M
- Library Science M
- Mathematics M
- Middle School Education M
- Multilingual and Multicultural Education M
- Physical Education M
- Reading Education M
- Secondary Education M
- Social Work M
- Special Education M
- Vocational and Technical Education M
- Writing M

CHICAGO THEOLOGICAL SEMINARY
- Jewish Studies P,M,D
- Pastoral Ministry and Counseling P,M,D
- Religion P,M,D
- Religious Education P,M,D
- Theology P,M,D

CHRISTENDOM COLLEGE
- Theology M

CHRISTIAN BROTHERS UNIVERSITY
- Business Administration and Management—General M,O
- Curriculum and Instruction M
- Education—General M
- Educational Administration M
- Engineering and Applied Sciences—General M
- Finance and Banking M,O
- Project Management M,O
- Religion M

CHRISTIAN THEOLOGICAL SEMINARY
- Marriage and Family Therapy P,M,D
- Pastoral Ministry and Counseling P,M,D
- Religion P,M,D
- Theology P,M,D

CHRISTIE'S EDUCATION
- Art History M
- Museum Studies M

CHRISTOPHER NEWPORT UNIVERSITY
- Applied Physics M
- Art Education M
- Computer Education M
- Computer Science M
- Education—General M
- Elementary Education M
- English Education M
- Environmental Sciences M
- Foreign Languages Education M
- History M
- Mathematics Education M
- Music Education M
- Physics M
- Science Education M
- Social Sciences Education M
- Theater M

CHRIST THE KING SEMINARY
- Pastoral Ministry and Counseling P,M,O
- Theology P,M,O

CHURCH DIVINITY SCHOOL OF THE PACIFIC
- Theology P,M,D,O

CHURCH OF GOD THEOLOGICAL SEMINARY
- Missions and Missiology P,M
- Pastoral Ministry and Counseling P,M
- Theology P,M

CINCINNATI CHRISTIAN UNIVERSITY
- Pastoral Ministry and Counseling M
- Religion P,M
- Theology P,M

THE CITADEL, THE MILITARY COLLEGE OF SOUTH CAROLINA
- Biological and Biomedical Sciences—General M
- Business Administration and Management—General M
- Computer Science M
- Counselor Education M
- Education—General M,O
- Educational Administration M,O
- English M
- Health Education M
- History M
- Information Science M
- Physical Education M
- Psychology—General M
- Reading Education M
- School Psychology M,O
- Secondary Education M
- Social Sciences M

CITY COLLEGE OF THE CITY UNIVERSITY OF NEW YORK
- Architecture M
- Art History M
- Art/Fine Arts M
- Atmospheric Sciences M,D
- Biochemistry M,D
- Biological and Biomedical Sciences—General M,D
- Biomedical Engineering M,D
- Chemical Engineering M,D
- Chemistry M,D
- Civil Engineering M,D
- Clinical Psychology M,D
- Computer Science M,D
- Early Childhood Education M
- Economics M
- Education—General M,O
- Educational Administration M,O
- Electrical Engineering M,D
- Engineering and Applied Sciences—General M,D*
- English Education M,O
- English M
- Environmental Sciences M,D
- Experimental Psychology M,D
- Geosciences M,D
- Graphic Design M
- History M
- International Affairs M
- Landscape Architecture M,O
- Mathematics Education M,O
- Mathematics M
- Mechanical Engineering M,D
- Media Studies M
- Middle School Education M,O
- Multilingual and Multicultural Education M
- Museum Studies M
- Music M
- Physics M,D*
- Psychology—General M,D
- Reading Education M
- Science Education M
- Secondary Education M,O
- Social Sciences Education M,O
- Sociology M
- Spanish M
- Special Education M
- Urban Design M
- Writing M

Close-Up on page 835.

CITY OF HOPE NATIONAL MEDICAL CENTER/BECKMAN RESEARCH INSTITUTE
- Biological and Biomedical Sciences—General D*

CITY UNIVERSITY
- Accounting M,O
- Art Education M,O
- Business Administration and Management—General M,O
- Computer Science M,O
- Counseling Psychology M
- Curriculum and Instruction M,O
- Education—General M,O
- Educational Administration M,O
- Educational Media/Instructional Technology M,O
- Electronic Commerce M,O
- English as a Second Language M,O
- Finance and Banking M,O
- Human Resources Management M,O
- International Business M,O
- Internet and Interactive Multimedia M,O
- Management Information Systems M,O
- Management of Technology M,O
- Marketing M,O
- Project Management M,O
- Reading Education M,O
- School Psychology M,O

Close-Up on page 837.

CITY UNIVERSITY OF NEW YORK SCHOOL OF LAW AT QUEENS COLLEGE
- Law P

CLAFLIN UNIVERSITY
- Biotechnology M
- Business Administration and Management—General M
- Education—General M

CLAREMONT GRADUATE UNIVERSITY
- African Studies M,D,O
- American Studies M,D,O
- Applied Mathematics M,D
- Art/Fine Arts M
- Arts Administration M
- Botany M,D
- Business Administration and Management—General M,D,O
- Cognitive Sciences M,D,O
- Comparative Literature M,D
- Computational Biology M,D
- Computational Sciences M,D
- Computer Art and Design M
- Cultural Studies M,D,O
- Developmental Psychology M,D,O
- Economics M,D,O
- Education—General M,D,O
- Educational Administration M,D,O
- Educational Measurement and Evaluation M,D,O
- Electronic Commerce M,D,O
- English M,D
- Ethics M,D
- Film, Television, and Video Theory and Criticism M,D
- Financial Engineering M,D
- Higher Education M,D,O
- History M,D,O
- Human Development M,D,O
- Human Resources Management M
- Humanities M,D,O
- Industrial and Organizational Psychology M,D,O
- Information Science M,D,O
- Information Studies M,D,O
- International Affairs M,D
- Management Information Systems M,D,O
- Management Strategy and Policy M,D,O
- Mathematics M,D
- Music M,D
- Operations Research M,D

Program	Degrees
Philosophy	M,D
Photography	M
Political Science	M,D
Psychology—General	M,D,O
Public Policy	M,D,O
Religion	M,D
Social Psychology	M,D,O
Statistics	M,D
Systems Science	M,D,O
Telecommunications	M,D,O
Theology	M,D
Urban Education	M,D,O
Western European Studies	M,D,O
Women's Studies	M,D
Writing	M,D

CLAREMONT SCHOOL OF THEOLOGY

Program	Degrees
Pastoral Ministry and Counseling	D
Religion	M,D
Religious Education	M,D
Theology	P,M,D

CLARION UNIVERSITY OF PENNSYLVANIA

Program	Degrees
Biological and Biomedical Sciences—General	M
Business Administration and Management—General	M
Communication Disorders	M
Communication—General	M
Curriculum and Instruction	M
Early Childhood Education	M
Education—General	M,O
Elementary Education	M
English Education	M
English	M
Library Science	M,O
Nursing—General	M
Reading Education	M
Rehabilitation Sciences	M
Science Education	M
Social Sciences Education	M
Special Education	M
Vocational and Technical Education	M

Close-Up on page 839.

CLARK ATLANTA UNIVERSITY

Program	Degrees
African-American Studies	M,D
Applied Mathematics	M
Biological and Biomedical Sciences—General	M,D
Business Administration and Management—General	M
Chemistry	M,D
Computer Science	M
Counselor Education	M,D
Criminal Justice and Criminology	M
Curriculum and Instruction	M,O
Economics	M
Education of the Gifted	M,O
Education—General	M,D,O
Educational Administration	M,D,O
Educational Psychology	M,D
English	M
Finance and Banking	M
History	M
Humanities	D
Information Science	M
Inorganic Chemistry	M,D
International Affairs	M,D
International Business	M,D
International Development	M,D
Marketing	M
Organic Chemistry	M,D
Physical Chemistry	M,D
Physics	M
Political Science	M,D
Public Administration	M
Quantitative Analysis	M
Romance Languages	M
Science Education	M,D
Social Work	M,D
Sociology	M
Women's Studies	M,D

CLARKE COLLEGE

Program	Degrees
Business Administration and Management—General	M
Early Childhood Education	M
Education—General	M
Educational Administration	M
Educational Media/Instructional Technology	M
Family Nurse Practitioner Studies	M,O
Nursing and Healthcare Administration	M,O
Nursing Education	M,O
Nursing—General	M,O
Physical Therapy	M
Reading Education	M
Special Education	M

CLARKSON COLLEGE

Program	Degrees
Family Nurse Practitioner Studies	M
Nursing and Healthcare Administration	M
Nursing Education	M
Nursing—General	M

CLARKSON UNIVERSITY

Program	Degrees
Analytical Chemistry	M,D
Business Administration and Management—General	M
Chemical Engineering	M,D
Chemistry	M,D
Civil Engineering	M,D
Computer Engineering	M,D
Computer Science	M,D
Electrical Engineering	M,D
Engineering and Applied Sciences—General	M,D*
Engineering Management	M
Environmental Engineering	M,D
Environmental Sciences	M,D
Health Services Research	M
Human Resources Management	M
Industrial and Manufacturing Management	M
Information Science	M*
Inorganic Chemistry	M,D
Management Information Systems	M
Mathematics	M,D
Mechanical Engineering	M,D
Organic Chemistry	M,D
Physical Chemistry	M,D
Physical Therapy	M,D
Physics	M,D

CLARK UNIVERSITY

Program	Degrees
Accounting	M
Biological and Biomedical Sciences—General	M,D
Business Administration and Management—General	M*
Chemistry	M,D
Clinical Psychology	D
Communication—General	M
Developmental Psychology	D
Economics	D
Education—General	M
English	M
Environmental Management and Policy	M
Finance and Banking	M
Geographic Information Systems	M
Geography	M,D
Health Services Management and Hospital Administration	M
History	M,D,O
Holocaust Studies	D
Information Science	M
International Business	M
International Development	M
Liberal Studies	M
Management Information Systems	M
Marketing	M
Physics	M,D
Psychology—General	D
Public Administration	M,O
Social Psychology	D
Sustainable Development	M
Urban and Regional Planning	M

Close-Up on page 841.

CLAYTON STATE UNIVERSITY

Program	Degrees
Business Administration and Management—General	M
Health Services Management and Hospital Administration	M
Liberal Studies	M
Nursing—General	M

CLEARY UNIVERSITY

Program	Degrees
Accounting	M
Business Administration and Management—General	M

CLEMSON UNIVERSITY

Program	Degrees
Accounting	M*
Agricultural Education	M*
Agricultural Sciences—General	M,D
Animal Sciences	M,D*
Applied Economics	M,D*
Applied Mathematics	M,D
Aquaculture	M,D
Architecture	M*
Art/Fine Arts	M*
Astronomy	M,D
Astrophysics	M,D
Atmospheric Sciences	M,D
Automotive Engineering	M,D*
Biochemistry	M,D*
Bioengineering	M,D*
Biological and Biomedical Sciences—General	M,D*
Biophysics	M,D
Biosystems Engineering	M,D*
Business Administration and Management—General	M,D*
Chemical Engineering	M,D*
Chemistry	M,D*
Child and Family Studies	D*
Civil Engineering	M,D*
Communication—General	M,D*
Computational Sciences	M,D
Computer Art and Design	M*
Computer Engineering	M,D*
Computer Science	M,D*
Construction Management	M*
Counselor Education	M*
Curriculum and Instruction	D*
Ecology	M,D
Economics	M,D*
Education—General	M,D,O
Educational Administration	M,D,O*
Electrical Engineering	M,D
Electronic Commerce	M,D
Elementary Education	M*
Engineering and Applied Sciences—General	M,D
English Education	M
English	M*
Entomology	M,D*
Environmental Design	D*
Environmental Engineering	M,D*
Environmental Management and Policy	M,D
Environmental Sciences	M,D*
Ergonomics and Human Factors	D
Evolutionary Biology	M,D
Family and Consumer Sciences-General	D
Fish, Game, and Wildlife Management	M,D*
Food Science and Technology	M,D*
Forestry	M,D*
Genetics	M,D*
Historic Preservation	M*
History	M*
Human Development	M*
Human Resources Development	M*
Hydrogeology	M*
Industrial and Manufacturing Management	M,D
Industrial and Organizational Psychology	D*
Industrial/Management Engineering	M,D*
Interdisciplinary Studies	D,O
Landscape Architecture	M*
Management Strategy and Policy	M,D
Manufacturing Engineering	M*
Marketing	M*
Materials Engineering	M,D
Materials Sciences	M,D*
Mathematics Education	M
Mathematics	M,D*
Mechanical Engineering	M,D*
Microbiology	M,D*
Middle School Education	M*
Molecular Biology	M,D
Nursing—General	M*
Nutrition	M
Operations Research	M,D
Physics	M,D*
Plant Biology	M,D*
Plant Sciences	M,D
Polymer Science and Engineering	M,D
Psychology—General	M,D*
Public Administration	M*
Public Policy	D,O*
Reading Education	M*
Real Estate	M*
Recreation and Park Management	M,D*
Rhetoric	D*
Science Education	M
Secondary Education	M*
Sociology	M*
Special Education	M*
Statistics	M,D
Textile Sciences and Engineering	M,D*
Travel and Tourism	M,D
Urban and Regional Planning	M*
Veterinary Sciences	M,D
Writing	M
Zoology	M,D

Close-Up on page 843.

CLEVELAND CHIROPRACTIC COLLEGE-KANSAS CITY CAMPUS

Program	Degrees
Chiropractic	P*

CLEVELAND CHIROPRACTIC COLLEGE-LOS ANGELES CAMPUS

Program	Degrees
Chiropractic	P*

CLEVELAND INSTITUTE OF MUSIC

Program	Degrees
Music	M,D,O

CLEVELAND STATE UNIVERSITY

Program	Degrees
Accounting	M
Adult Education	M,O
Allied Health—General	M
Analytical Chemistry	M,D
Art Education	M
Art History	M
Art/Fine Arts	M
Bioethics	M,O
Biological and Biomedical Sciences—General	M,D
Biomedical Engineering	D
Business Administration and Management—General	M,D
Chemical Engineering	M,D
Chemistry	M,D
Civil Engineering	M,D
Clinical Psychology	M,O
Communication Disorders	M
Communication—General	M,O
Community Health Nursing	M
Condensed Matter Physics	M
Counseling Psychology	D
Counselor Education	M,D,O
Early Childhood Education	M
Economics	M,O
Education of the Multiply Handicapped	M
Education—General	M,D,O
Educational Administration	M,D,O
Electrical Engineering	M,D
Electronic Commerce	M,D,O
Engineering and Applied Sciences—General	M,D
English as a Second Language	M
English	M
Environmental Engineering	M,D
Environmental Management and Policy	M
Environmental Sciences	M,D
Exercise and Sports Science	M
Experimental Psychology	M,O
Finance and Banking	M,D,O
Foreign Languages Education	M
Forensic Nursing	M
Geographic Information Systems	M,O
Health Communication	M,O
Health Education	M
Health Services Management and Hospital Administration	M
History	M
Human Resources Management	M
Industrial and Labor Relations	M
Industrial and Manufacturing Management	D
Industrial and Organizational Psychology	M,O
Industrial/Management Engineering	M,D
Inorganic Chemistry	M,D
International Business	M,D,O
Law	P,M
Management Information Systems	M,D
Marketing	M,D,O
Mathematics Education	M
Mathematics	M
Mechanical Engineering	M,D
Medical Physics	M
Middle School Education	M
Molecular Medicine	M,D
Museum Studies	M
Music Education	M
Music	M
Nonprofit Management	M,O
Nursing—General	M
Occupational Therapy	M
Optical Sciences	M
Organic Chemistry	M,D
Philosophy	M,O
Physical Chemistry	M,D
Physical Education	M
Physical Therapy	D
Physics	M
Psychology—General	M,O
Public Administration	M,O
Real Estate	M,O
School Psychology	M,O
Science Education	M
Social Sciences	M
Social Work	M
Sociology	M
Software Engineering	M,D
Spanish	M
Special Education	M
Sport Psychology	M
Sports Management	M
Student Affairs	M,O
Taxation	M
Urban and Regional Planning	M,O
Urban Design	M,O
Urban Education	D
Urban Studies	M,D

- Writing M

COASTAL CAROLINA UNIVERSITY
- Business Administration and Management—General M
- Early Childhood Education M
- Education—General M
- Elementary Education M
- Marine Sciences M
- Secondary Education M

COE COLLEGE
- Education—General M

COLD SPRING HARBOR LABORATORY, WATSON SCHOOL OF BIOLOGICAL SCIENCES
- Biological and Biomedical Sciences—General D*

COLEMAN COLLEGE
- Information Science M
- Management of Technology M

COLGATE ROCHESTER CROZER DIVINITY SCHOOL
- Theology P,M,D,O

COLGATE UNIVERSITY
- Secondary Education M

COLLÈGE DOMINICAIN DE PHILOSOPHIE ET DE THÉOLOGIE
- Pastoral Ministry and Counseling M
- Philosophy M,D
- Theology M,D,O

COLLEGE FOR FINANCIAL PLANNING
- Finance and Banking M

COLLEGE MISERICORDIA
- Allied Health—General M,D
- Communication Disorders M
- Curriculum and Instruction M
- Education—General M
- Nursing—General M
- Occupational Therapy M
- Organizational Management M
- Physical Therapy M,D

COLLEGE OF CHARLESTON
- Accounting M
- Business Administration and Management—General M
- Computer Science M
- Corporate and Organizational Communication O
- Early Childhood Education M
- Education—General M,O
- Elementary Education M
- English as a Second Language O
- English M
- Environmental Sciences M*
- Foreign Languages Education M
- History M
- Legal and Justice Studies M,O
- Marine Biology M*
- Mathematics Education M
- Mathematics M,O
- Public Administration M
- Science Education M
- Special Education M

COLLEGE OF EMMANUEL AND ST. CHAD
- Theology P,M

COLLEGE OF MOUNT ST. JOSEPH
- Art Education M
- Early Childhood Education M
- Education—General M
- Educational Administration M
- Middle School Education M
- Multilingual and Multicultural Education M
- Music Education M
- Nursing—General M
- Organizational Management M
- Pastoral Ministry and Counseling M
- Physical Therapy M,D
- Reading Education M
- Secondary Education M
- Theology M

Close-Up on page 845.

COLLEGE OF MOUNT SAINT VINCENT
- Adult Nursing M,O
- Education—General M,O
- Educational Media/Instructional Technology M,O
- Family Nurse Practitioner Studies M,O
- Gerontological Nursing M,O
- Middle School Education M,O
- Multilingual and Multicultural Education M,O
- Nursing and Healthcare Administration M,O
- Nursing Education M,O
- Nursing—General M,O
- Urban Education M,O

THE COLLEGE OF NEW JERSEY
- Addictions/Substance Abuse Counseling M,O
- Communication Disorders M
- Counselor Education M
- Early Childhood Education M
- Education—General M,O
- Educational Administration M,O
- Educational Media/Instructional Technology M
- Elementary Education M
- English as a Second Language M,O
- English M
- Foreign Languages Education M
- Health Education M
- International and Comparative Education M,O
- Marriage and Family Therapy O
- Nursing—General M,O
- Physical Education M
- Reading Education M,O
- Secondary Education M
- Spanish M
- Special Education M,O

Close-Up on page 847.

THE COLLEGE OF NEW ROCHELLE
- Acute Care/Critical Care Nursing M,O
- Art Education M
- Art Therapy M
- Art/Fine Arts M
- Communication Disorders M
- Communication—General M,O
- Counseling Psychology M,O
- Early Childhood Education M
- Education of the Gifted M,O
- Education—General M,O
- Educational Administration M,O
- Elementary Education M
- English as a Second Language M,O
- Gerontology M,O
- Graphic Design M
- Human Resources Development M,O
- Multilingual and Multicultural Education M,O
- Museum Education O
- Nursing and Healthcare Administration M,O
- Nursing Education M,O
- Nursing—General M,O
- Reading Education M
- School Psychology M
- Social Psychology M
- Special Education M

Close-Up on page 849.

COLLEGE OF NOTRE DAME OF MARYLAND
- Business Administration and Management—General M
- Communication—General M
- Education—General M
- Educational Administration M,D
- English as a Second Language M
- Liberal Studies M
- Nonprofit Management M

COLLEGE OF ST. CATHERINE
- Education—General M
- Information Studies M
- Library Science M
- Nursing—General M
- Occupational Therapy M*
- Organizational Management M
- Physical Therapy M,D*
- Public Health—General M
- Social Work M
- Theology M

COLLEGE OF SAINT ELIZABETH
- Business Administration and Management—General M
- Counseling Psychology M,O
- Education—General M,O
- Educational Administration M,O
- Educational Media/Instructional Technology M,O
- Health Services Management and Hospital Administration M
- Higher Education M
- Nutrition M,O
- Psychology—General M,O
- Student Affairs M,O
- Theology M

COLLEGE OF ST. JOSEPH
- Addictions/Substance Abuse Counseling M
- Business Administration and Management—General M
- Clinical Psychology M
- Counseling Psychology M
- Counselor Education M
- Education—General M
- Elementary Education M
- English Education M
- Mathematics Education M
- Psychology—General M
- Reading Education M
- School Psychology M
- Secondary Education M
- Social Psychology M
- Social Sciences Education M
- Special Education M

THE COLLEGE OF SAINT ROSE
- Accounting M
- Art Education M,O
- Business Administration and Management—General M
- Business Education M,O
- Communication Disorders M
- Computer Science M
- Counselor Education M
- Early Childhood Education M,O
- Education—General M,O*
- Educational Administration M,O
- Educational Media/Instructional Technology M,O
- Educational Psychology M,O
- Elementary Education M,O
- English M
- History M
- Information Science M
- Mass Communication M
- Multilingual and Multicultural Education M,O
- Music Education M,O*
- Music M
- Nonprofit Management O
- Political Science M
- Reading Education M,O
- School Psychology M,O
- Secondary Education M,O
- Special Education M,O
- Student Affairs M,O

Close-Up on page 851.

THE COLLEGE OF ST. SCHOLASTICA
- Business Administration and Management—General M
- Curriculum and Instruction M
- Education—General M,O
- Educational Media/Instructional Technology M
- Exercise and Sports Science M
- Health Informatics M,O
- Management Information Systems M
- Nursing—General M,O
- Occupational Therapy M
- Physical Therapy D

COLLEGE OF SANTA FE
- Business Administration and Management—General M
- Counselor Education M
- Curriculum and Instruction M
- Education—General M
- Educational Administration M
- Finance and Banking M
- Human Resources Management M
- Multilingual and Multicultural Education M
- Special Education M

COLLEGE OF STATEN ISLAND OF THE CITY UNIVERSITY OF NEW YORK
- Adult Nursing M,O
- Biological and Biomedical Sciences—General M
- Business Administration and Management—General M
- Computer Science M
- Education—General M,O
- Educational Administration O
- Elementary Education M
- English M
- Environmental Sciences M
- Film, Television, and Video Theory and Criticism M
- Gerontological Nursing M,O
- History M
- Liberal Studies M
- Media Studies M
- Neuroscience M
- Nursing—General M,O
- Secondary Education M
- Special Education M

Close-Up on page 853.

COLLEGE OF THE ATLANTIC
- Environmental Management and Policy M

COLLEGE OF THE HUMANITIES AND SCIENCES, HARRISON MIDDLETON UNIVERSITY
- Comparative Literature M,D
- Education—General M,D
- Humanities M,D
- Legal and Justice Studies M,D
- Philosophy M,D
- Religion M,D
- Science Education M,D
- Social Sciences M,D

COLLEGE OF THE SOUTHWEST
- Counselor Education M
- Curriculum and Instruction M
- Education—General M
- Educational Administration M
- Educational Measurement and Evaluation M

THE COLLEGE OF WILLIAM AND MARY
- Accounting M
- Addictions/Substance Abuse Counseling M,D
- American Studies M,D
- Anthropology M,D
- Applied Science and Technology M,D
- Biological and Biomedical Sciences—General M
- Business Administration and Management—General M
- Chemistry M
- Clinical Psychology D
- Computational Sciences M
- Computer Science M,D
- Counselor Education M,D
- Curriculum and Instruction M,D
- Education of the Gifted M
- Education—General M,D,O
- Educational Administration M,D
- Educational Media/Instructional Technology M,D
- Educational Policy M,D
- Elementary Education M
- English Education M
- Experimental Psychology M
- Foreign Languages Education M
- History M,D
- Law P,M
- Marine Sciences M,D
- Marriage and Family Therapy M,D
- Mathematics Education M
- Operations Research M
- Physics M,D
- Psychology—General M,D
- Public Policy M
- Reading Education M
- School Psychology M,O
- Science Education M
- Secondary Education M
- Social Sciences Education M
- Special Education M

Close-Up on page 855.

COLLÈGE UNIVERSITAIRE DE SAINT-BONIFACE
- Canadian Studies M
- Education—General M

COLORADO CHRISTIAN UNIVERSITY
- Business Administration and Management—General M
- Counseling Psychology M
- Curriculum and Instruction M
- Education—General M

THE COLORADO COLLEGE
- Art Education M
- Education—General M
- Elementary Education M
- English Education M
- Foreign Languages Education M
- Mathematics Education M
- Music Education M
- Science Education M
- Secondary Education M
- Social Sciences Education M

COLORADO SCHOOL OF MINES
- Applied Physics M,D
- Chemical Engineering M,D
- Chemistry M,D
- Computer Science M,D
- Electronic Materials M,D
- Engineering and Applied Sciences—General M,D,O
- Engineering Management M,D
- Environmental Engineering M,D

Geochemistry M,D,O
Geological Engineering M,D,O
Geosciences M,D,O
Hydrogeology M,D,O
International Affairs M,O
Management of Technology M,D
Materials Engineering M,D
Materials Sciences M,D
Metallurgical Engineering and Metallurgy M,D
Mineral Economics M,D
Mineral/Mining Engineering M,D
Petroleum Engineering M,D
Systems Engineering M,D

Close-Up on page 857.

COLORADO SCHOOL OF TRADITIONAL CHINESE MEDICINE

Acupuncture and Oriental Medicine M

COLORADO STATE UNIVERSITY

Accounting M
Advertising and Public Relations M
Agricultural Economics and Agribusiness M,D
Agricultural Sciences—General M,D
Agronomy and Soil Sciences M,D
Animal Sciences M,D
Anthropology M
Art/Fine Arts M
Atmospheric Sciences M,D
Biochemistry M,D
Biological and Biomedical Sciences—General M,D
Botany M,D
Business Administration and Management—General M
Cell Biology M,D*
Chemical Engineering M,D
Chemistry M,D
Child and Family Studies M
Civil Engineering M,D
Computer Science M,D
Construction Management M
Consumer Economics M
Ecology M,D
Economics M,D
Electrical Engineering M,D
Engineering and Applied Sciences—General M,D
Entomology M,D
Environmental and Occupational Health M,D
Environmental Management and Policy M,D
Exercise and Sports Science M,D
Fish, Game, and Wildlife Management M,D
Food Science and Technology M,D
Foreign Languages Education M
Forestry M,D
Geosciences M,D
History M
Horticulture M,D
Human Development M
Hydrology M,D
Immunology M,D
Management Information Systems M
Mathematics M,D
Mechanical Engineering M,D
Microbiology M,D*
Molecular Biology M,D
Music M
Neuroscience M,D
Nutrition M,D
Occupational Therapy M
Pathology M,D
Philosophy M
Physics M,D
Plant Pathology M,D
Plant Sciences M,D
Political Science M,D
Psychology—General M,D
Radiation Biology M,D
Range Science M,D
Recreation and Park Management M,D
Social Work M
Sociology M,D
Speech and Interpersonal Communication M
Statistics M,D
Student Affairs M,D
Technical Communication M
Technical Writing M
Veterinary Medicine P
Veterinary Sciences M,D
Vocational and Technical Education M,D
Water Resources M,D
Writing M
Zoology M,D

COLORADO STATE UNIVERSITY-PUEBLO

Applied Science and Technology M
Biochemistry M
Biological and Biomedical Sciences—General M
Business Administration and Management—General M
Chemistry M
Engineering and Applied Sciences—General M
Industrial/Management Engineering M
Systems Engineering M

COLORADO TECHNICAL UNIVERSITY—COLORADO SPRINGS

Accounting M,D
Business Administration and Management—General M,D
Computer and Information Systems Security M,D
Computer Engineering M
Computer Science M,D
Criminal Justice and Criminology M
Electrical Engineering M
Human Resources Management M,D
Information Science M,D
Logistics M,D
Management Information Systems M,D
Management of Technology M,D
Organizational Management M,D
Project Management M,D
Software Engineering M,D
Systems Engineering M

COLORADO TECHNICAL UNIVERSITY—DENVER

Accounting M
Business Administration and Management—General M
Computer and Information Systems Security M
Computer Engineering M
Computer Science M
Criminal Justice and Criminology M
Electrical Engineering M
Human Resources Management M
Management Information Systems M
Management of Technology M
Project Management M
Software Engineering M
Systems Engineering M

COLORADO TECHNICAL UNIVERSITY—SIOUX FALLS

Business Administration and Management—General M
Computer and Information Systems Security M
Computer Science M
Criminal Justice and Criminology M
Health Services Management and Hospital Administration M
Human Resources Management M
Management Information Systems M
Management of Technology M
Organizational Management M
Project Management M
Software Engineering M

COLUMBIA COLLEGE (MO)

Business Administration and Management—General M
Criminal Justice and Criminology M
Education—General M

COLUMBIA COLLEGE (SC)

Conflict Resolution and Mediation/Peace Studies M,O
Education—General M
Elementary Education M
Organizational Behavior M,O

COLUMBIA COLLEGE CHICAGO

Architecture M
Arts Administration M
Comparative and Interdisciplinary Arts M
Education—General M
Elementary Education M
English Education M
Film, Television, and Video Production M
Interior Design M
Journalism M
Media Studies M
Multilingual and Multicultural Education M
Photography M
Therapies—Dance, Drama, and Music M,O
Urban Education M
Writing M

COLUMBIA INTERNATIONAL UNIVERSITY

Counselor Education M,D,O
Cultural Studies P,M,D,O
Curriculum and Instruction M,D,O
Early Childhood Education M,D,O
Education—General M,D,O
Educational Administration M,D,O
Educational Media/Instructional Technology M,D,O
Elementary Education M,D,O
English as a Second Language M,D,O
Higher Education M,D,O
Missions and Missiology P,M,D,O
Multilingual and Multicultural Education M,D,O
Pastoral Ministry and Counseling P,M,D,O
Religious Education P,M,D,O
Special Education M,D,O
Theology P,M,D,O

COLUMBIA SOUTHERN UNIVERSITY

Business Administration and Management—General M
Electronic Commerce M
Environmental and Occupational Health M
Health Services Management and Hospital Administration M
Human Resources Management M
International Business M
Marketing M

COLUMBIA THEOLOGICAL SEMINARY

Theology P,M,D

COLUMBIA UNIVERSITY

Accounting M,D
Actuarial Science M
Acute Care/Critical Care Nursing M,O
Adult Nursing M,O
African Studies O
African-American Studies M
Allopathic Medicine P
American Studies M
Anatomy M,D
Anthropology M,D
Applied Mathematics M,D,O
Applied Physics M,D,O*
Archaeology M,D
Architecture M,D
Art History M,D
Art/Fine Arts M
Asian Languages M,D
Asian Studies M,D,O
Astronomy M,D
Atmospheric Sciences M,D*
Biochemistry M,D
Biological and Biomedical Sciences—General M,D*
Biomedical Engineering M,D*
Biophysics M,D
Biopsychology M,D
Biostatistics M,D
Business Administration and Management—General M,D
Cell Biology M,D
Chemical Engineering M,D
Chemical Physics M,D
Chemistry M,D
Civil Engineering M,D,O
Classics M,D
Communication—General M,D
Community Health M,D
Comparative Literature M,D
Computer Art and Design M
Computer Engineering M,D,O
Computer Science M,D,O*
Conservation Biology M,D,O*
Construction Engineering M,D,O
Construction Management M,D,O
Corporate and Organizational Communication M
Dentistry P
Developmental Biology M,D
East European and Russian Studies M,O
Ecology D,O
Economics M,D
Electrical Engineering M,D,O*
Engineering and Applied Sciences—General M,D,O*
Engineering Management M,D,O
English M,D
Entrepreneurship M
Environmental and Occupational Health M,D
Environmental Design M
Environmental Engineering M,D,O*
Environmental Management and Policy M*
Environmental Sciences M
Epidemiology M,D
Evolutionary Biology D,O
Experimental Psychology M,D
Family Nurse Practitioner Studies M,O
Film, Television, and Video Production M
Finance and Banking M,D
Financial Engineering M,D,O
French M,D
Genetics M,D
Geochemistry M,D
Geodetic Sciences M,D
Geophysics M,D
Geosciences M,D
German M,D
Gerontological Nursing M,O
Health Services Management and Hospital Administration M
Historic Preservation M
History M,D
Human Resources Management M
Industrial/Management Engineering M,D,O*
Inorganic Chemistry M,D
Interdisciplinary Studies M
International Affairs M*
International Business M
Italian M,D
Jewish Studies M,D
Journalism M,D*
Kinesiology and Movement Studies M,D
Landscape Architecture M
Latin American Studies O
Law P,M,D
Liberal Studies M
Library Science M
Management of Technology M
Marketing M,D
Materials Engineering M,D,O
Materials Sciences M,D,O
Maternal and Child Health M
Maternal and Child/Neonatal Nursing M,O
Mathematics M,D*
Mechanical Engineering M,D,O
Mechanics M,D,O
Medical Informatics M,D,O*
Medical Physics M,D,O
Medical/Surgical Nursing M,O
Medieval and Renaissance Studies M
Metallurgical Engineering and Metallurgy M,D,O
Meteorology M*
Microbiology M,D
Mineral/Mining Engineering M,D,O
Molecular Biology M,D
Music M,D
Near and Middle Eastern Languages M,D
Near and Middle Eastern Studies M,D,O
Neurobiology M,D
Nonprofit Management M
Nurse Anesthesia M,O
Nurse Midwifery M
Nursing—General M,D,O*
Nutrition M,D*
Occupational Therapy M,D
Oceanography M,D
Oncology Nursing M,O
Operations Research M,D,O
Oral and Dental Sciences M,D,O
Organic Chemistry M,D
Pathobiology M,D
Pathology M,D
Pediatric Nursing M,O
Pharmacology M,D
Philosophy M,D
Photography M
Physical Therapy D
Physics M,D
Physiology M,D
Planetary and Space Sciences M,D
Political Science M,D
Psychiatric Nursing M,O
Psychology—General M,D
Public Administration M
Public Health—General M,D*
Public Policy M
Real Estate M
Religion M,D
Romance Languages M,D
Russian M,D
Science Education M,D,O
Slavic Languages M,D
Social Psychology M,D

Social Sciences M
Social Work M,D*
Sociology M,D
Spanish M,D
Statistics M,D
Sustainable Development M,D
Theater M,D*
Toxicology M,D
Urban and Regional Planning M,D
Urban Design M
Western European Studies M,O
Women's Health Nursing O
Writing M

COLUMBUS STATE UNIVERSITY

Art Education M
Business Administration and Management—General M
Computer Science M
Counseling Psychology M,O
Counselor Education M,O
Early Childhood Education M,O
Education—General M,O
Educational Administration M,O
English Education M,O
Environmental Sciences M
Mathematics Education M,O
Middle School Education M,O
Music Education M
Physical Education M,O
Public Administration M
Science Education M,O
Secondary Education M,O
Social Sciences Education M,O
Special Education M,O

CONCORDIA LUTHERAN SEMINARY

Theology P,M

CONCORDIA SEMINARY

Theology P,M,D,O

CONCORDIA THEOLOGICAL SEMINARY

Theology P,M,D

CONCORDIA UNIVERSITY (CA)

Business Administration and Management—General M
Curriculum and Instruction M
Education—General M
Educational Administration M
Entrepreneurship M
International Affairs M
Physical Education M
Sports Management M
Theology M

CONCORDIA UNIVERSITY (CANADA)

Accounting M,D,O
Adult Education M,O
Aerospace/Aeronautical Engineering M
Anthropology M
Applied Arts and Design—General O
Art Education M,D
Art History M,D
Art Therapy M
Art/Fine Arts M
Aviation Management M,D,O
Biological and Biomedical Sciences—General M,D,O
Biotechnology M,D,O
Business Administration and Management—General M,D,O
Chemistry M,D
Child and Family Studies M
Civil Engineering M,D,O
Clinical Psychology M,D,O
Communication—General M,D,O
Computer and Information Systems Security M,O
Computer Art and Design O
Computer Engineering M,D
Computer Science M,D,O
Construction Engineering M,D,O
Economics M,D,O
Education—General M,D,O
Educational Media/Instructional Technology M,D,O
Electrical Engineering M,D
Engineering and Applied Sciences—General M,D,O
English as a Second Language M,O
English M
Environmental Engineering M,D,O
Environmental Management and Policy M,O
Exercise and Sports Science M
Film, Television, and Video Production M
Film, Television, and Video Theory and Criticism M
French M,O
Genomic Sciences M,D,O
Geography M,D,O
Health Services Management and Hospital Administration M,D,O
History M,D
Humanities D
Industrial/Management Engineering M,D,O
Internet and Interactive Multimedia M,O
Investment Management M,D,O
Jewish Studies M
Journalism O
Linguistics M,O
Mathematics Education M,D
Mathematics M,D
Mechanical Engineering M,D,O
Media Studies M,D,O
Music O
Organizational Management M
Philosophy M
Physics M,D
Political Science M,D
Psychology—General M,D
Public Administration M,D
Public Affairs O
Public Policy M,D
Religion M,D
Rural Planning and Studies M,D,O
Sociology M
Software Engineering M,D,O
Sports Management M,D,O
Systems Engineering M,O
Telecommunications Management M,O
Theology M
Translation and Interpretation M,O
Transportation Management M,D,O
Urban and Regional Planning O
Urban Studies M,O
Writing M

Close-Up on page 859.

CONCORDIA UNIVERSITY (IL)

Counseling Psychology M
Counselor Education M,O
Curriculum and Instruction M
Early Childhood Education M,D
Education—General M
Educational Administration M,D,O
Exercise and Sports Science M
Gerontology M
Human Services M
Liberal Studies M
Music M
Psychology—General M
Reading Education M
Religion M
Religious Education M
Urban Education M

CONCORDIA UNIVERSITY (MI)

Educational Administration M
Organizational Management M

CONCORDIA UNIVERSITY (NE)

Curriculum and Instruction M
Early Childhood Education M
Education—General M
Educational Administration M
Pastoral Ministry and Counseling M
Reading Education M
Religious Education M

CONCORDIA UNIVERSITY (OR)

Business Administration and Management—General M
Curriculum and Instruction M
Education—General M
Educational Administration M
Elementary Education M
Secondary Education M

CONCORDIA UNIVERSITY AT AUSTIN

Education—General M

CONCORDIA UNIVERSITY, ST. PAUL

Business Administration and Management—General M
Child and Family Studies M,O
Criminal Justice and Criminology M
Early Childhood Education M,O
Education—General M,O
Human Resources Management M
Organizational Management M
Pastoral Ministry and Counseling M,O
Religious Education M,O
Special Education M,O
Theology M,O

CONCORDIA UNIVERSITY WISCONSIN

Art Education M
Business Administration and Management—General M
Child and Family Studies M
Corporate and Organizational Communication M
Counseling Psychology M
Counselor Education M
Curriculum and Instruction M
Early Childhood Education M
Education—General M
Educational Administration M
Environmental Education M
Family Nurse Practitioner Studies M
Finance and Banking M
Gerontological Nursing M
Health Services Management and Hospital Administration M
Human Resources Management M
Human Services M,D
International Business M
Management Information Systems M
Marketing M
Music M
Nursing Education M
Nursing—General M
Occupational Therapy M
Physical Therapy M,D
Psychology—General M
Public Administration M
Reading Education M
Rehabilitation Sciences M
Special Education M
Student Affairs M

CONCORD LAW SCHOOL

Law P

CONNECTICUT COLLEGE

Botany M
Classics M
Dance M
Education—General M
Elementary Education M
English Education M
English M
Foreign Languages Education M
French M
Hispanic Studies M
Italian M
Mathematics Education M
Music Education M
Music M
Psychology—General M
Science Education M
Secondary Education M
Zoology M

CONSERVATORIO DE MUSICA

Music Education M
Music O

CONVERSE COLLEGE

Art Education M,O
Curriculum and Instruction O
Early Childhood Education M,O
Education of the Gifted M
Education—General M,O
Educational Administration M,O
Elementary Education M
English Education M
English M
History M
Liberal Studies M
Marriage and Family Therapy O
Mathematics Education M
Music Education M
Music M
Political Science M
Science Education M
Secondary Education M
Social Sciences Education M
Special Education M

CONWAY SCHOOL OF LANDSCAPE DESIGN

Landscape Architecture M

COOPER UNION FOR THE ADVANCEMENT OF SCIENCE AND ART

Chemical Engineering M
Civil Engineering M
Electrical Engineering M
Engineering and Applied Sciences—General M
Mechanical Engineering M

COPPIN STATE UNIVERSITY

Addictions/Substance Abuse Counseling M
Adult Education M
Criminal Justice and Criminology M
Curriculum and Instruction M
Education—General M
Family Nurse Practitioner Studies M,O
Human Services M
Nursing—General M,O
Reading Education M
Rehabilitation Counseling M
Special Education M

CORCORAN COLLEGE OF ART AND DESIGN

Art Education M
Decorative Arts M
Interior Design M

CORNELL UNIVERSITY

Accounting D
Adult Education M,D
Aerospace/Aeronautical Engineering M,D
African Studies M,D
African-American Studies M,D
Agricultural Economics and Agribusiness M,D
Agricultural Education M,D
Agricultural Engineering M,D
Agronomy and Soil Sciences M,D
American Studies M,D
Analytical Chemistry D
Anatomy M,D
Animal Behavior D
Animal Sciences M,D
Anthropology D
Applied Economics D
Applied Mathematics M,D*
Applied Physics M,D
Applied Statistics M,D
Archaeology M,D
Architectural History M,D
Architecture M,D
Art History D
Art/Fine Arts M
Artificial Intelligence/Robotics M,D
Asian Languages M,D
Asian Studies M,D
Astronomy D
Astrophysics D
Atmospheric Sciences M,D
Biochemical Engineering M,D
Biochemistry D
Bioengineering M,D
Biological and Biomedical Sciences—General P,M,D
Biomedical Engineering M,D
Biometrics M,D
Biophysics D
Biopsychology D
Building Science M,D
Business Administration and Management—General M,D
Cell Biology M,D
Chemical Engineering M,D
Chemical Physics D
Chemistry D*
Child and Family Studies M,D
Chinese M,D
Civil Engineering M,D
Classics D
Clothing and Textiles M,D
Cognitive Sciences D
Communication—General M,D
Comparative Literature D
Computational Sciences M,D
Computer Art and Design M,D
Computer Engineering M,D
Computer Science M,D
Conflict Resolution and Mediation/Peace Studies M,D
Consumer Economics M,D
Cultural Studies M,D
Curriculum and Instruction M,D
Demography and Population Studies M,D
Developmental Biology M,D
Developmental Psychology D
East European and Russian Studies M,D
Ecology M,D
Economics M,D
Education—General M,D
Electrical Engineering M,D
Engineering and Applied Sciences—General M,D
Engineering Management M,D
Engineering Physics M,D
English M,D
Entomology M,D
Environmental Design M
Environmental Engineering M,D
Environmental Management and Policy M,D
Environmental Sciences M,D
Epidemiology M,D
Ergonomics and Human Factors M
Ethnic Studies M,D
Evolutionary Biology D
Experimental Psychology D
Facilities Management M
Family and Consumer Sciences-General M,D
Finance and Banking D
Fish, Game, and Wildlife Management M,D
Food Science and Technology M,D

- Foreign Languages Education M,D
- Forestry M,D
- French D
- Gender Studies M,D
- Genetics D
- Geochemistry M,D
- Geology M,D
- Geophysics M,D
- Geosciences M,D
- Geotechnical Engineering M,D
- German M,D
- Health Services Management and Hospital Administration M,D
- Historic Preservation M,D
- History of Science and Technology M,D
- History M,D
- Horticulture M,D
- Hospitality Management M,D
- Human Development D
- Human Resources Management M,D
- Human-Computer Interaction D
- Hydrology M,D
- Immunology P,M,D
- Industrial and Labor Relations M,D*
- Industrial/Management Engineering M,D
- Infectious Diseases M,D
- Information Science D
- Information Studies D
- Inorganic Chemistry D
- Interior Design M
- International Affairs D
- International Development M
- Italian D
- Japanese M,D
- Jewish Studies M,D
- Landscape Architecture M
- Latin American Studies M,D
- Law P,M,D
- Limnology D
- Linguistics M,D
- Manufacturing Engineering M,D
- Marine Geology M,D
- Marine Sciences M,D
- Marketing D
- Materials Engineering M,D
- Materials Sciences M,D
- Mathematics Education M,D
- Mathematics D
- Mechanical Engineering M,D
- Mechanics M,D
- Medieval and Renaissance Studies M,D
- Microbiology D
- Mineralogy M,D
- Molecular Biology D
- Molecular Medicine M,D
- Music M,D
- Natural Resources M,D
- Near and Middle Eastern Studies M,D
- Neurobiology D*
- Nuclear Engineering M,D
- Nutrition M,D
- Oceanography D
- Operations Research M,D*
- Organic Chemistry D
- Organizational Behavior M,D
- Paleontology M,D
- Pharmacology P,M,D*
- Philosophy D
- Photography M
- Physical Chemistry D
- Physics M,D
- Physiology P,M,D
- Planetary and Space Sciences D
- Plant Biology M,D
- Plant Molecular Biology M,D
- Plant Pathology M,D
- Plant Physiology M,D
- Plant Sciences M,D
- Political Science D
- Polymer Science and Engineering M,D
- Psychology—General D
- Public Affairs M*
- Public Policy M,D
- Real Estate M
- Religion D
- Reproductive Biology M,D
- Romance Languages M,D
- Rural Planning and Studies M
- Rural Sociology M,D
- Scandinavian Languages M,D
- Science Education M,D
- Slavic Languages M,D
- Social Psychology M,D
- Social Work M,D
- Sociology M,D
- Spanish D
- Statistics M,D
- Structural Biology M,D
- Structural Engineering M,D
- Systems Engineering M
- Textile Design M,D
- Textile Sciences and Engineering M,D
- Theater D
- Theoretical Chemistry D
- Theoretical Physics M,D
- Toxicology M,D
- Transportation and Highway Engineering M,D
- Urban and Regional Planning M,D
- Urban Design M,D
- Veterinary Medicine P,D
- Water Resources Engineering M,D
- Western European Studies M,D
- Women's Studies M,D
- Writing M,D
- Zoology P,M,D

CORNELL UNIVERSITY, JOAN AND SANFORD I. WEILL MEDICAL COLLEGE AND GRADUATE SCHOOL OF MEDICAL SCIENCES

- Allopathic Medicine P,M,D
- Biochemistry D*
- Biological and Biomedical Sciences—General M,D
- Biophysics D
- Cell Biology D
- Computational Biology D
- Epidemiology M
- Health Services Research M
- Immunology M,D*
- Molecular Biology D
- Neuroscience D*
- Pharmacology D*
- Physiology D*
- Structural Biology D
- Systems Biology D

CORNERSTONE UNIVERSITY

- Business Administration and Management—General M,O
- Education—General M,O
- English as a Second Language M,O

COVENANT COLLEGE

- Education—General M

COVENANT THEOLOGICAL SEMINARY

- Theology P,M,D,O

CRANBROOK ACADEMY OF ART

- Applied Arts and Design—General M
- Architecture M
- Art/Fine Arts M*
- Graphic Design M
- Photography M
- Textile Design M

CREIGHTON UNIVERSITY

- Allied Health—General P,M,D
- Allopathic Medicine P
- Anatomy M
- Atmospheric Sciences M
- Biological and Biomedical Sciences—General M,D*
- Business Administration and Management—General M
- Conflict Resolution and Mediation/Peace Studies M
- Counselor Education M
- Dentistry P
- Education—General M
- Educational Administration M
- English M
- Immunology M,D
- International Affairs M
- Law P,M
- Liberal Studies M
- Management Information Systems M
- Medical Microbiology M,D*
- Nursing—General M
- Occupational Therapy D
- Pharmaceutical Sciences M,D
- Pharmacology M,D
- Pharmacy P
- Physical Therapy D
- Physics M
- Special Education M
- Theology M

THE CRISWELL COLLEGE

- Pastoral Ministry and Counseling P,M
- Theology P,M

CROWN COLLEGE

- Theology M

CUMBERLAND UNIVERSITY

- Business Administration and Management—General M
- Education—General M
- Human Resources Management M
- Organizational Management M
- Public Administration M

CUNY GRADUATE SCHOOL OF JOURNALISM

- Journalism M*

CURRY COLLEGE

- Adult Education M,O
- Business Administration and Management—General M
- Criminal Justice and Criminology M
- Education—General M,O
- Educational Administration M,O
- Elementary Education M,O
- Foundations and Philosophy of Education M,O
- Reading Education M,O
- Special Education M,O

THE CURTIS INSTITUTE OF MUSIC

- Music M

DAEMEN COLLEGE

- Adult Nursing M,O
- Business Administration and Management—General M
- Early Childhood Education M
- Education—General M
- International Business M
- Medical/Surgical Nursing M,O
- Middle School Education M
- Nursing and Healthcare Administration M,O
- Nursing—General M,O
- Physical Therapy D
- Physician Assistant Studies M
- Special Education M

DAKOTA STATE UNIVERSITY

- Education—General M
- Educational Media/Instructional Technology M
- Information Science M,D*

DALHOUSIE UNIVERSITY

- Agricultural Engineering M,D
- Agricultural Sciences—General M
- Allopathic Medicine P
- Anatomy M,D
- Anthropology M,D
- Applied Mathematics M,D
- Architecture M
- Biochemistry M,D
- Bioengineering M,D
- Biological and Biomedical Sciences—General M,D
- Biomedical Engineering M
- Biophysics M,D
- Business Administration and Management—General M
- Chemical Engineering M,D
- Chemistry M,D
- Civil Engineering M,D
- Classics M,D
- Clinical Psychology M,D
- Communication Disorders M
- Community Health M
- Computer Education M
- Computer Engineering M,D
- Computer Science M,D
- Dental Hygiene O
- Dentistry P
- Economics M,D
- Electrical Engineering M,D
- Electronic Commerce M,D
- Engineering and Applied Sciences—General M,D
- English M,D
- Environmental Management and Policy M
- Epidemiology M
- Food Science and Technology M,D
- French M,D
- Geosciences M,D
- German M
- Health Education M
- Health Services Management and Hospital Administration M
- History M,D
- Human-Computer Interaction M
- Immunology M,D
- Industrial/Management Engineering M,D
- Information Studies M
- Interdisciplinary Studies D
- International Development M
- Kinesiology and Movement Studies M
- Law M,D
- Leisure Studies M
- Library Science M
- Management Information Systems M
- Marine Affairs M
- Mathematics M,D
- Mechanical Engineering M,D
- Metallurgical Engineering and Metallurgy M,D
- Microbiology M,D
- Mineral/Mining Engineering M,D
- Neurobiology M,D
- Neuroscience M,D
- Nursing—General M
- Occupational Therapy M
- Oceanography M,D
- Oral and Dental Sciences P,M,O
- Pathology M
- Pharmaceutical Sciences M,D
- Pharmacology M,D
- Philosophy M,D
- Physics M,D
- Physiology M,D
- Political Science M,D
- Psychology—General M,D
- Public Administration M
- Public Affairs M
- Rural Planning and Studies M
- Social Work M
- Sociology M,D
- Statistics M,D
- Urban and Regional Planning M
- Women's Studies M

DALLAS BAPTIST UNIVERSITY

- Accounting M
- Business Administration and Management—General M
- Conflict Resolution and Mediation/Peace Studies M
- Corporate and Organizational Communication M
- Counseling Psychology M
- Counselor Education M
- Criminal Justice and Criminology M
- Curriculum and Instruction M
- Early Childhood Education M
- Education—General M
- Educational Administration M
- Electronic Commerce M
- Elementary Education M
- Engineering Management M
- English as a Second Language M
- Entrepreneurship M
- Experimental Psychology M
- Finance and Banking M
- Health Services Management and Hospital Administration M
- Higher Education M
- Human Resources Management M
- Interdisciplinary Studies M
- International Business M
- Liberal Studies M
- Management Information Systems M
- Management of Technology M
- Marketing M
- Missions and Missiology M
- Pastoral Ministry and Counseling M
- Project Management M
- Reading Education M
- Religious Education M

DALLAS THEOLOGICAL SEMINARY

- Media Studies M,D,O
- Missions and Missiology M,D,O
- Pastoral Ministry and Counseling M,D,O
- Religious Education M,D,O
- Theology M,D,O

DANIEL WEBSTER COLLEGE

- Aviation Management M
- Business Administration and Management—General M

DANIEL WEBSTER COLLEGE–PORTSMOUTH CAMPUS

- Aviation Management M
- Business Administration and Management—General M

DARKEI NOAM RABBINICAL COLLEGE

- Theology

DARTMOUTH COLLEGE

- Astronomy M,D
- Biochemical Engineering M,D
- Biochemistry D*
- Biological and Biomedical Sciences—General D*
- Biomedical Engineering M,D
- Biotechnology M,D
- Business Administration and Management—General M
- Cancer Biology/Oncology D
- Cardiovascular Sciences D
- Cell Biology D
- Chemistry D
- Cognitive Sciences D
- Comparative Literature M
- Computer Engineering M,D

Computer Science M,D*
Ecology D
Electrical Engineering M,D
Engineering and Applied Sciences—General M,D*
Engineering Management M
Engineering Physics M,D
Evolutionary Biology D
Genetics D*
Geosciences M,D
Health Services Research M,D*
Immunology D*
Liberal Studies M*
Manufacturing Engineering M,D
Materials Engineering M,D
Materials Sciences M,D
Mathematics D*
Mechanical Engineering M,D
Microbiology D*
Molecular Biology D*
Molecular Medicine D*
Molecular Pathogenesis D
Molecular Pharmacology D
Music M
Neuroscience D*
Pharmaceutical Sciences D
Pharmacology D*
Physics M,D
Physiology D
Psychology—General D
Public Health—General M
Systems Biology D
Toxicology D

Close-Up on page 861.

DAVENPORT UNIVERSITY
Accounting M
Business Administration and Management—General M
Electronic Commerce M
Finance and Banking M
Health Services Management and Hospital Administration M
Human Resources Management M
International Business M
Marketing M

DAVENPORT UNIVERSITY
Business Administration and Management—General M

DAVENPORT UNIVERSITY
Accounting M
Business Administration and Management—General M
Electronic Commerce M
Finance and Banking M
Health Services Management and Hospital Administration M
Human Resources Management M

DEFIANCE COLLEGE
Business Administration and Management—General M
Education—General M
Organizational Management M

DELAWARE STATE UNIVERSITY
Biological and Biomedical Sciences—General M
Business Administration and Management—General M
Chemistry M
Curriculum and Instruction M
Education—General M
Mathematics M
Physics M
Science Education M
Social Work M
Special Education M

DELAWARE VALLEY COLLEGE
Agricultural Economics and Agribusiness
Educational Administration M

DELL'ARTE SCHOOL OF PHYSICAL THEATRE
Theater M

DELTA STATE UNIVERSITY
Accounting M
Aviation Management M
Biological and Biomedical Sciences—General M
Business Administration and Management—General M
Counselor Education M
Criminal Justice and Criminology M
Education—General M,D,O
Educational Administration M,D,O
Elementary Education M,O
English Education M
Marketing M
Mathematics Education M
Nursing—General M
Physical Education M
Recreation and Park Management M
Secondary Education M,O
Social Sciences Education M
Special Education M
Urban and Regional Planning M

DENVER SEMINARY
Marriage and Family Therapy P,M,D,O
Pastoral Ministry and Counseling P,M,D,O
Religion P,M,D,O
Theology P,M,D,O

DEPAUL UNIVERSITY
Accounting M
Adult Education M
Applied Mathematics M,O
Applied Physics M
Applied Statistics M,O
Biochemistry M
Biological and Biomedical Sciences—General M*
Business Administration and Management—General M
Chemistry M
Clinical Psychology M,D
Communication—General M
Computer and Information Systems Security M,D
Computer Art and Design M,D
Computer Science M,D
Corporate and Organizational Communication M
Counselor Education M,D
Curriculum and Instruction D
Economics M
Education—General M
Educational Administration D
Electronic Commerce M,D
Elementary Education M,D
English M
Entrepreneurship M
Experimental Psychology M,D
Finance and Banking M,O
Health Services Management and Hospital Administration M,O
History M
Human Development M,D
Human Resources Management M
Human Services M,D
Human-Computer Interaction M,D
Industrial and Manufacturing Management M
Industrial and Organizational Psychology M,D
Information Science M,D
Interdisciplinary Studies M,D
International Business M
Law P,M
Legal and Justice Studies M,O
Liberal Studies M
Management Information Systems M,D
Management Strategy and Policy M
Marketing M
Mathematical and Computational Finance M,D
Mathematics Education M,O
Mathematics M,O
Multilingual and Multicultural Education M,D
Music Education M,O
Music M,O
Nonprofit Management M,O
Nurse Anesthesia M
Nursing—General M
Philosophy M,D
Physical Education M,D
Physics M
Polymer Science and Engineering M
Psychology—General M,D
Public Administration M,O
Public Affairs M,O
Reading Education M,D
Real Estate M
Secondary Education M,D
Social Psychology M,D
Sociology M
Software Engineering M,D
Special Education M,D
Taxation M
Telecommunications M,D
Theater M,O*
Urban and Regional Planning M,O
Urban Education M,O
Writing M

DESALES UNIVERSITY
Adult Nursing M
Business Administration and Management—General M
Computer Education M,O
Criminal Justice and Criminology M
Education—General M,O
Educational Media/Instructional Technology M,O
Educational Policy M,O
English as a Second Language M,O
English Education M,O
Family Nurse Practitioner Studies M
Information Science M
Mathematics Education M,O
Multilingual and Multicultural Education M,O
Nursing Education M
Nursing—General M
Physician Assistant Studies M
Science Education M,O
Special Education M,O

DES MOINES UNIVERSITY
Health Services Management and Hospital Administration M
Osteopathic Medicine P
Physical Therapy D
Physician Assistant Studies M
Podiatric Medicine P
Public Health—General M

DEVRY UNIVERSITY
Business Administration and Management—General M

DEVRY UNIVERSITY
Business Administration and Management—General M

DEVRY UNIVERSITY
Business Administration and Management—General M

DEVRY UNIVERSITY
Business Administration and Management—General M

DEVRY UNIVERSITY
Business Administration and Management—General M

DEVRY UNIVERSITY
Business Administration and Management—General M

DEVRY UNIVERSITY
Business Administration and Management—General M

DEVRY UNIVERSITY
Business Administration and Management—General M

DEVRY UNIVERSITY
Business Administration and Management—General M

DEVRY UNIVERSITY
Business Administration and Management—General M

DEVRY UNIVERSITY
Business Administration and Management—General M

DEVRY UNIVERSITY
Business Administration and Management—General M

DEVRY UNIVERSITY
Business Administration and Management—General M

DEVRY UNIVERSITY
Business Administration and Management—General M

DEVRY UNIVERSITY
Business Administration and Management—General M

DEVRY UNIVERSITY
Business Administration and Management—General M

DEVRY UNIVERSITY
Business Administration and Management—General M

DEVRY UNIVERSITY
Business Administration and Management—General M

DEVRY UNIVERSITY
Business Administration and Management—General M

DEVRY UNIVERSITY
Business Administration and Management—General M

DEVRY UNIVERSITY
Business Administration and Management—General M

DEVRY UNIVERSITY
Business Administration and Management—General M

DEVRY UNIVERSITY
Business Administration and Management—General M

DEVRY UNIVERSITY
Business Administration and Management—General M

DEVRY UNIVERSITY
Business Administration and Management—General M

DEVRY UNIVERSITY
Business Administration and Management—General M

DEVRY UNIVERSITY
Business Administration and Management—General M

DEVRY UNIVERSITY
Accounting M
Business Administration and Management—General M*
Communication—General M
Finance and Banking M
Human Resources Management M
Management Information Systems M
Project Management M
Public Administration M
Telecommunications Management M

DEVRY UNIVERSITY
Business Administration and Management—General M

DEVRY UNIVERSITY
Business Administration and Management—General M

DEVRY UNIVERSITY
Business Administration and Management—General M

DEVRY UNIVERSITY
Business Administration and Management—General M

DEVRY UNIVERSITY (MD)
Business Administration and Management—General M,O

DEVRY UNIVERSITY
Business Administration and Management—General M

DEVRY UNIVERSITY (NV)
Business Administration and Management—General M

DEVRY UNIVERSITY
Business Administration and Management—General M

DEVRY UNIVERSITY
Business Administration and Management—General M

DEVRY UNIVERSITY
Business Administration and Management—General M

DEVRY UNIVERSITY
Business Administration and Management—General M

DEVRY UNIVERSITY (OR)

Program	Degree
Business Administration and Management—General	M

DEVRY UNIVERSITY

Program	Degree
Business Administration and Management—General	M

DEVRY UNIVERSITY

Program	Degree
Business Administration and Management—General	M

DEVRY UNIVERSITY

Program	Degree
Business Administration and Management—General	M

DEVRY UNIVERSITY

Program	Degree
Business Administration and Management—General	M

DEVRY UNIVERSITY

Program	Degree
Business Administration and Management—General	M

DEVRY UNIVERSITY

Program	Degree
Business Administration and Management—General	M

DEVRY UNIVERSITY

Program	Degree
Business Administration and Management—General	M

DEVRY UNIVERSITY

Program	Degree
Business Administration and Management—General	M

DEVRY UNIVERSITY

Program	Degree
Business Administration and Management—General	M

DEVRY UNIVERSITY

Program	Degree
Business Administration and Management—General	M

DIGIPEN INSTITUTE OF TECHNOLOGY

Program	Degree
Computer Science	M

DOANE COLLEGE

Program	Degree
Business Administration and Management—General	M
Counselor Education	M
Curriculum and Instruction	M
Education—General	M
Educational Administration	M

DOMINICAN COLLEGE

Program	Degree
Allied Health—General	M,D
Education—General	M
Nursing—General	M
Occupational Therapy	M
Physical Therapy	M,D
Special Education	M

Close-Up on page 863.

DOMINICAN HOUSE OF STUDIES, PONTIFICAL FACULTY OF THE IMMACULATE CONCEPTION

Program	Degree
Theology	P,M,O

DOMINICAN SCHOOL OF PHILOSOPHY AND THEOLOGY

Program	Degree
Philosophy	M
Theology	P,O

DOMINICAN UNIVERSITY

Program	Degree
Accounting	M
Business Administration and Management—General	M
Curriculum and Instruction	M
Early Childhood Education	M
Education—General	M
Educational Administration	M
Information Studies	M,O
Library Science	M,O
Management Information Systems	M
Organizational Management	M
Reading Education	M
Social Work	M
Special Education	M

DOMINICAN UNIVERSITY OF CALIFORNIA

Program	Degree
Business Administration and Management—General	M
Counseling Psychology	M
Curriculum and Instruction	M
Education—General	M,O
Gerontology	M
Humanities	M
International Business	M
Management Strategy and Policy	M
Nursing Education	M
Nursing—General	M
Occupational Therapy	M
Public Health—General	M
Special Education	O

DONGGUK ROYAL UNIVERSITY

Program	Degree
Acupuncture and Oriental Medicine	M

DORDT COLLEGE

Program	Degree
Education—General	M

DOWLING COLLEGE

Program	Degree
Aviation Management	M,O
Business Administration and Management—General	M,O
Education—General	M,D,O
Educational Administration	M,D,O
Educational Media/Instructional Technology	M,D,O
Finance and Banking	M,O
Human Development	M,D,O
Liberal Studies	M
Mathematics	M
Quality Management	M,O
Reading Education	M,D,O
Secondary Education	M,D,O
Special Education	M,D,O

DRAKE UNIVERSITY

Program	Degree
Adult Education	M
American Studies	M
Art/Fine Arts	M
Business Administration and Management—General	M
Business Education	M
Communication—General	M
Counselor Education	M
Education—General	M,D,O
Educational Administration	M,D,O
Elementary Education	M
English Education	M
History	M
Journalism	M
Law	P*
Mathematics Education	M
Pharmacy	P
Public Administration	M
Rehabilitation Counseling	M
Rehabilitation Sciences	M
Science Education	M
Secondary Education	M
Social Sciences Education	M
Sociology	M
Special Education	M
Speech and Interpersonal Communication	M
Theater	M

Close-Up on page 865.

DREW UNIVERSITY

Program	Degree
Bioethics	M,D,O
English	M,D
Ethics	M,D
History	M,D
Holocaust Studies	M,D,O
Humanities	M,D,O
Interdisciplinary Studies	M,D,O
Near and Middle Eastern Studies	M,D
Religion	M,D
Theology	P,M,D,O
Women's Studies	M

Close-Up on page 867.

DREXEL UNIVERSITY

Program	Degree
Accounting	M,D,O
Allied Health—General	M,D,O
Allopathic Medicine	P
Applied Arts and Design—General	M
Architecture	M
Art Therapy	M
Arts Administration	M
Biochemical Engineering	M
Biochemistry	M,D
Biological and Biomedical Sciences—General	M,D,O*
Biomedical Engineering	M,D
Biopsychology	M,D
Biostatistics	M,D
Business Administration and Management—General	M,D,O
Cancer Biology/Oncology	M,D
Cell Biology	M,D
Chemical Engineering	M,D
Chemistry	M,D
Civil Engineering	M,D
Clinical Psychology	M,D
Communication—General	M
Computer Engineering	M
Computer Science	M,D
Curriculum and Instruction	M
Economics	M,D,O
Education—General	M,D,O*
Educational Administration	M,D
Educational Media/Instructional Technology	D
Electrical Engineering	M,D*
Emergency Management	M
Emergency Medical Services	M
Engineering and Applied Sciences—General	M,D
Engineering Management	M,D
English as a Second Language	M,D,O
Environmental Engineering	M,D
Environmental Management and Policy	M
Environmental Sciences	M,D
Finance and Banking	M,D,O
Food Science and Technology	M,D
Forensic Psychology	M,D
Genetics	M,D
Geological Engineering	M
Health Physics/Radiological Health	M,D
Health Psychology	M,D
Higher Education	M
History of Science and Technology	M
Human Genetics	M,D
Immunology	M,D
Information Science	D
Information Studies	M,D,O*
Interior Design	M
International and Comparative Education	M
Journalism	M
Library Science	M,D,O
Management Strategy and Policy	M,D,O
Manufacturing Engineering	M,D
Marketing	M,D,O
Marriage and Family Therapy	M,D
Materials Engineering	M,D
Mathematics	M,D
Mechanical Engineering	M,D
Mechanics	M,D
Medical Physics	M,D
Microbiology	M,D
Molecular Biology	M,D
Neuroscience	D
Nurse Anesthesia	M
Nursing—General	M
Nutrition	M,D
Organizational Behavior	M,D,O
Pathobiology	D
Pharmacology	M,D
Physical Therapy	M,D,O
Physician Assistant Studies	M
Physics	M,D
Psychology—General	M,D
Public Health—General	M
Publishing	M
Quantitative Analysis	M,D,O
Software Engineering	M
Taxation	M
Technical Writing	M
Telecommunications	M
Textile Design	M
Therapies—Dance, Drama, and Music	M
Veterinary Sciences	M

Close-Up on page 869.

DRURY UNIVERSITY

Program	Degree
Business Administration and Management—General	M
Communication—General	M
Criminal Justice and Criminology	M
Education of the Gifted	M
Education—General	M
Elementary Education	M
Human Services	M
International Business	M
Middle School Education	M
Physical Education	M
Secondary Education	M

DUKE UNIVERSITY

Program	Degree
Acute Care/Critical Care Nursing	M,D,O
Adult Nursing	M,D,O
Allopathic Medicine	P
Anatomy	D
Anthropology	D
Art History	D
Asian Studies	M,O
Biochemistry	D,O
Bioinformatics	D
Biological and Biomedical Sciences—General	D,O
Biological Anthropology	D
Biomedical Engineering	M,D*
Biopsychology	D
Business Administration and Management—General	M,D
Cancer Biology/Oncology	D
Cell Biology	D,O*
Chemistry	D
Civil Engineering	M,D*
Classics	D
Clinical Laboratory Sciences/Medical Technology	M
Clinical Psychology	D
Clinical Research	M
Cognitive Sciences	D
Comparative Literature	D
Computer Engineering	M,D
Computer Science	M,D*
Demography and Population Studies	D
Developmental Biology	D,O*
Developmental Psychology	D
Ecology	M,D,O
Economics	M,D
Education—General	M
Electrical Engineering	M,D*
Engineering and Applied Sciences—General	M,D
Engineering Management	M*
English	D
Environmental and Occupational Health	M,D,O
Environmental Engineering	M,D
Environmental Management and Policy	M,D*
Environmental Sciences	M,D
Experimental Psychology	D
Family Nurse Practitioner Studies	M,D,O
Forestry	M
French	D
Genetics	D*
Geology	M,D
German	D
Gerontological Nursing	M,D,O
Health Psychology	D
Health Services Management and Hospital Administration	O
History of Medicine	
History	M,D
HIV/AIDS Nursing	M,D,O
Human Development	D
Humanities	M
Immunology	D*
International Development	M,O*
Latin American Studies	M,D,O
Law	P,M,D
Liberal Studies	M
Marine Affairs	M
Marine Sciences	M*
Materials Sciences	M,D
Maternal and Child/Neonatal Nursing	M,D,O
Mathematics	D
Mechanical Engineering	M,D*
Medieval and Renaissance Studies	O
Microbiology	D
Molecular Biology	D,O
Molecular Biophysics	O
Molecular Genetics	D*
Music	M,D
Natural Resources	M,D*
Neurobiology	D
Neuroscience	D,O
Nurse Anesthesia	M,D,O
Nursing and Healthcare Administration	M,D,O
Nursing Education	M,D,O
Nursing Informatics	M,D,O
Nursing—General	D
Oncology Nursing	M,D,O
Paleontology	D
Pathology	M,D*
Pediatric Nursing	M,D,O
Pharmacology	D
Philosophy	M,D
Physical Therapy	D
Physician Assistant Studies	M
Physics	M,D
Political Science	M,D
Psychology—General	D
Public Policy	M,D,O
Religion	M,D
Slavic Languages	M
Sociology	M,D
Spanish	D
Statistics	D
Structural Biology	O*
Theology	P,M
Toxicology	D,O
Water Resources	M
Women's Studies	O

DUQUESNE UNIVERSITY

Program	Degree
Acute Care/Critical Care Nursing	M,O
Allied Health—General	M,D
Biochemistry	M,D
Bioethics	M,D,O
Biological and Biomedical Sciences—General	M,D*
Business Administration and Management—General	M*
Chemistry	M,D*
Clinical Psychology	D
Communication Disorders	M,D
Communication—General	M,D
Conflict Resolution and Mediation/Peace Studies	M,O

Counselor Education M,D
Curriculum and Instruction M,D
Early Childhood Education M
Education—General M,D,O
Educational Administration M,D
Educational Media/Instructional Technology M,D
Elementary Education M
English as a Second Language M,D
English M,D
Environmental Management and Policy M,O
Environmental Sciences M,O
Ethics M
Family Nurse Practitioner Studies M,O
Forensic Nursing M,O
Forensic Sciences M
Foundations and Philosophy of Education M
Health Services Management and Hospital Administration M,D
History M
Internet and Interactive Multimedia M,O
Law P,M
Liberal Studies M
Management Information Systems M
Management Strategy and Policy M
Mathematics M
Medicinal and Pharmaceutical Chemistry M,D
Museum Studies M
Music Education M,O
Music M,O
Nursing and Healthcare Administration M,O
Nursing Education M,O
Nursing—General M,D,O
Occupational Therapy M,D
Organizational Management M
Pharmaceutical Administration M
Pharmaceutical Sciences M,D*
Pharmacology M,D
Pharmacy P
Philosophy M,D
Physical Therapy M,D
Physician Assistant Studies M,D
Psychiatric Nursing M,D
Psychology—General D
Public Administration M,O
Public Policy M,O
Reading Education M,O
Rhetoric M,D
School Psychology M,D,O
Secondary Education M
Special Education M
Sports Management M
Taxation M
Theology M,D

Close-Up on page 871.

D'YOUVILLE COLLEGE

Chiropractic P
Community Health Nursing M,O
Education—General M,O
Elementary Education M,O
Family Nurse Practitioner Studies M,O
Health Services Management and Hospital Administration M,O
International Business M
Nursing and Healthcare Administration M,O
Nursing Education M,O
Nursing—General M,O*
Nutrition M
Occupational Therapy M
Physical Therapy M,D,O
Physician Assistant Studies M
Secondary Education M,O
Special Education M,O

Close-Up on page 873.

EARLHAM COLLEGE

Education—General M

EARLHAM SCHOOL OF RELIGION

Religion P,M
Theology P,M

EAST CAROLINA UNIVERSITY

Accounting M
Addictions/Substance Abuse Counseling M
Adult Education M,O
Allied Health—General M,D
Allopathic Medicine P
American Studies M
Anatomy D
Anthropology M
Applied Mathematics M
Art/Fine Arts M
Biochemistry D
Biological and Biomedical Sciences—General M,D*
Biophysics M,D
Biotechnology M
Business Administration and Management—General M,D,O
Cell Biology D
Chemistry M
Child and Family Studies M
Child Development M
Clinical Psychology M
Communication Disorders M,D
Computer Science M,D,O
Counselor Education M,O
Criminal Justice and Criminology M
Curriculum and Instruction M
Economics M
Education—General M,D,O
Educational Administration M,D,O
Educational Media/Instructional Technology M,O
Elementary Education M
English Education M
English M
Environmental and Occupational Health M
Environmental Management and Policy D
Exercise and Sports Science M,D
Geography M
Geology M
Health Communication M
Health Education M
Health Psychology D
History M
Immunology D
Industrial/Management Engineering M,D,O
Information Science M
International Affairs M
Leisure Studies M
Library Science M,O
Logistics M,D,O
Management Information Systems M,D,O
Management of Technology M,D,O
Manufacturing Engineering M,D,O
Marine Affairs D
Marriage and Family Therapy M
Mathematics Education M
Mathematics M
Medical Physics M,D
Microbiology D
Middle School Education M
Molecular Biology M,D
Music Education M
Music M
Nursing—General M,D
Nutrition M
Occupational Therapy M
Pathology D
Pharmacology D
Physical Therapy M,D
Physician Assistant Studies M
Physics M,D*
Physiology D
Political Science M
Psychology—General M
Public Administration M
Public Health—General M
Reading Education M
Recreation and Park Management M
Rehabilitation Counseling M
Rehabilitation Sciences M
School Psychology M
Science Education M
Social Sciences Education M
Social Work M
Sociology M
Special Education M
Therapies—Dance, Drama, and Music M
Vocational and Technical Education M
Western European Studies M

Close-Up on page 875.

EAST CENTRAL UNIVERSITY

Counselor Education M
Criminal Justice and Criminology M
Education—General M
Human Resources Management M
Psychology—General M
Rehabilitation Counseling M

EASTERN CONNECTICUT STATE UNIVERSITY

Early Childhood Education M
Education—General M
Educational Media/Instructional Technology M
Elementary Education M
Organizational Management M
Reading Education M
Science Education M
Secondary Education M

Announcement on page 382.

EASTERN ILLINOIS UNIVERSITY

Accounting M,O
Art Education M
Art/Fine Arts M
Biological and Biomedical Sciences—General M
Business Administration and Management—General M,O
Chemistry M
Clinical Psychology M,O
Communication Disorders M
Computer and Information Systems Security M,O
Computer Science M,O
Consumer Economics M
Counselor Education M
Early Childhood Education M
Economics M
Education—General M,O
Educational Administration M,O
Elementary Education M
Engineering and Applied Sciences—General M,O
English M
Family and Consumer Sciences-General M
Gerontology M
History M
Mathematics Education M
Mathematics M
Middle School Education M
Music M
Nutrition M
Physical Education M
Political Science M
Psychology—General M,O
Public History M
School Psychology M,O
Social Psychology M
Special Education M
Speech and Interpersonal Communication M
Student Affairs M
Systems Science M,O

Close-Up on page 877.

EASTERN KENTUCKY UNIVERSITY

Addictions/Substance Abuse Counseling M
Agricultural Education M
Allied Health—General M
Art Education M
Biological and Biomedical Sciences—General M
Business Administration and Management—General M*
Business Education M
Chemistry M
Clinical Psychology M,O
Communication Disorders M
Community Health M
Counselor Education M
Criminal Justice and Criminology M
Curriculum and Instruction M
Ecology M
Education—General M
Educational Administration M
Elementary Education M
English Education M
English M
Environmental and Occupational Health M
Family Nurse Practitioner Studies M
Geology M,D
Health Education M
Health Services Management and Hospital Administration M
Higher Education M
History M
Home Economics Education M
Industrial and Organizational Psychology M,O
Industrial/Management Engineering M
Manufacturing Engineering M
Mathematics Education M
Mathematics M
Music Education M
Music M
Nursing—General M
Nutrition M
Occupational Therapy M
Physical Education M
Political Science M
Psychology—General M,O
Public Administration M
Reading Education M
Recreation and Park Management M
School Psychology M,O
Science Education M
Secondary Education M
Social Sciences Education M
Special Education M
Sports Management M
Theater M
Urban and Regional Planning M
Vocational and Technical Education M
Writing M

EASTERN MENNONITE UNIVERSITY

Business Administration and Management—General M
Conflict Resolution and Mediation/Peace Studies M,O
Education—General M
Pastoral Ministry and Counseling P,M,O
Religion P,M,O
Theology P,M,O

EASTERN MICHIGAN UNIVERSITY

Accounting M
Adult Nursing M,O
American Studies M
Applied Economics M
Art Education M
Art/Fine Arts M
Arts Administration M
Athletic Training and Sports Medicine M
Bioinformatics M
Biological and Biomedical Sciences—General M
Business Administration and Management—General M
Chemistry M
Clinical Psychology M,D
Clinical Research M
Clothing and Textiles M
Communication Disorders M
Communication—General M
Computer and Information Systems Security M
Computer Science M
Construction Management M
Counselor Education M,O
Criminal Justice and Criminology M
Cultural Studies M
Curriculum and Instruction M
Early Childhood Education M
Economics M
Education—General M,D,O
Educational Administration M,D,O
Educational Media/Instructional Technology M
Educational Psychology M
Electronic Commerce M
Elementary Education M
Engineering and Applied Sciences—General M
Engineering Management M
English as a Second Language M
English M
Entrepreneurship M
Ethics M
Exercise and Sports Science M
Experimental Psychology M,D
Finance and Banking M
Foundations and Philosophy of Education M
French M
Gender Studies M
Geography M
Geology M
German M
Gerontology M,O
Health Education M
Health Promotion M
Hispanic Studies M,O
Historic Preservation M
History M
Hospitality Management M
Human Resources Management M
Industrial and Manufacturing Management M
Interdisciplinary Studies M
Interior Design M
International Business M
Linguistics M
Management Information Systems M
Management of Technology D
Marketing M
Mathematics Education M
Mathematics M
Middle School Education M
Multilingual and Multicultural Education M
Music Education M
Music M
Nonprofit Management M
Nursing and Healthcare Administration M
Nursing Education M,O
Nutrition M
Occupational Therapy M
Organizational Management M
Physical Education M
Physics M
Polymer Science and Engineering M

- Psychology—General M,D
- Public Administration M
- Quality Management M
- Reading Education M
- Science Education M
- Secondary Education M
- Social Psychology M,O
- Social Sciences M
- Social Work M,O
- Sociology M
- Spanish M
- Special Education M,O
- Speech and Interpersonal Communication M
- Sports Management M
- Statistics M
- Supply Chain Management M
- Technology and Public Policy M
- Theater M
- Vocational and Technical Education M
- Women's Studies M
- Writing M

Close-Up on page 879.

EASTERN NAZARENE COLLEGE

- Counseling Psychology M
- Early Childhood Education M,O
- Education—General M,O
- Educational Administration M,O
- Elementary Education M,O
- English as a Second Language M,O
- Marriage and Family Therapy M
- Middle School Education M,O
- Reading Education M,O
- Secondary Education M,O
- Special Education M,O

EASTERN NEW MEXICO UNIVERSITY

- Anthropology M
- Biological and Biomedical Sciences—General M
- Business Administration and Management—General M
- Chemistry M
- Communication Disorders M
- Communication—General M
- Counselor Education M
- Education—General M
- English M
- Human Services M
- Mathematics M
- Physical Education M
- Special Education M

EASTERN OREGON UNIVERSITY

- Education—General M
- Elementary Education M
- Secondary Education M

EASTERN UNIVERSITY

- Accounting M
- Business Administration and Management—General M
- Counseling Psychology M*
- Counselor Education M
- Economics M
- Education—General M,O*
- Educational Psychology M
- English as a Second Language O
- Finance and Banking M
- Health Education M
- Marketing M
- Marriage and Family Therapy D
- Missions and Missiology D
- Multilingual and Multicultural Education M
- Nonprofit Management M
- Organizational Management D*
- Pastoral Ministry and Counseling D
- Theology P,M,D

EASTERN VIRGINIA MEDICAL SCHOOL

- Allopathic Medicine P
- Art Therapy M
- Biological and Biomedical Sciences—General M,D
- Clinical Psychology D
- Medical/Surgical Nursing O
- Physician Assistant Studies M
- Public Health—General M
- Reproductive Biology M
- Vision Sciences O

EASTERN WASHINGTON UNIVERSITY

- Adult Education M
- Biological and Biomedical Sciences—General M
- Business Administration and Management—General M
- Communication Disorders M
- Communication—General M
- Community College Education M
- Computer Education M
- Computer Science M
- Counseling Psychology M
- Counselor Education M
- Curriculum and Instruction M
- Early Childhood Education M
- Education—General M
- Educational Administration M
- Educational Media/Instructional Technology M
- Elementary Education M
- English M
- Foreign Languages Education M
- Foundations and Philosophy of Education M
- Higher Education M
- History M
- Interdisciplinary Studies M
- Mathematics Education M
- Mathematics M
- Music Education M
- Music M
- Nursing Education M
- Nursing—General M
- Occupational Therapy M
- Physical Education M
- Physical Therapy D
- Psychology—General M
- Public Administration M
- Reading Education M
- School Psychology M
- Science Education M
- Social Sciences Education M
- Social Work M
- Special Education M
- Urban and Regional Planning M
- Writing M

EAST STROUDSBURG UNIVERSITY OF PENNSYLVANIA

- Biological and Biomedical Sciences—General M
- Communication Disorders M
- Community Health M
- Computer Science M
- Education—General M
- Educational Media/Instructional Technology M
- Elementary Education M
- Exercise and Sports Science M
- Health Education M
- History M
- Hospitality Management M
- Physical Education M
- Political Science M
- Public Health—General M
- Reading Education M
- Rehabilitation Sciences M
- Science Education M
- Secondary Education M
- Social Sciences Education M
- Special Education M
- Sports Management M
- Travel and Tourism M

Close-Up on page 881.

EAST TENNESSEE STATE UNIVERSITY

- Accounting M
- Allied Health—General M,D,O
- Allopathic Medicine P
- Anatomy M,D
- Art Education M
- Art History M
- Art/Fine Arts M
- Biochemistry M,D
- Biological and Biomedical Sciences—General M,D
- Biophysics M,D
- Business Administration and Management—General M,O
- Chemistry M
- Clinical Psychology M
- Communication Disorders M,D
- Communication—General M
- Community Health M,O
- Computer Art and Design M
- Computer Science M
- Counselor Education M
- Criminal Justice and Criminology M
- Curriculum and Instruction M
- Early Childhood Education M
- Economics M
- Education—General M,D,O
- Educational Administration M,D,O
- Educational Media/Instructional Technology M
- Elementary Education M
- English M
- Environmental and Occupational Health M
- Epidemiology M,O
- Exercise and Sports Science M
- Finance and Banking M
- Gerontology M,O
- Health Services Management and Hospital Administration M,D,O
- History M
- Human Development M
- Information Science M
- Liberal Studies M
- Manufacturing Engineering M
- Marriage and Family Therapy M
- Mathematics M
- Microbiology M,D
- Nursing—General M,D,O
- Nutrition M
- Pharmacology M,D
- Physical Education M
- Physical Therapy D
- Physiology M,D
- Psychology—General M
- Public Health—General M,O
- Reading Education M
- Secondary Education M
- Social Work M
- Sociology M
- Software Engineering M
- Special Education M,D
- Sports Management M
- Urban and Regional Planning M
- Urban Studies M
- Vocational and Technical Education M

Close-Up on page 883.

EAST WEST COLLEGE OF NATURAL MEDICINE

- Acupuncture and Oriental Medicine M

ÉCOLE POLYTECHNIQUE DE MONTRÉAL

- Aerospace/Aeronautical Engineering M,D,O
- Applied Mathematics M,D,O
- Biomedical Engineering M,D,O
- Chemical Engineering M,D,O
- Civil Engineering M,D,O
- Computer Engineering M,D,O
- Computer Science M,D,O
- Electrical Engineering M,D,O
- Engineering and Applied Sciences—General M,D,O
- Engineering Physics M,D,O
- Environmental Engineering M,D,O
- Geological Engineering M,D,O
- Geotechnical Engineering M,D,O
- Hydraulics M,D,O
- Industrial/Management Engineering M,O
- Management of Technology M,O
- Materials Engineering M,D,O
- Materials Sciences M,D,O
- Mathematics M,D
- Mechanical Engineering M,D,O
- Mechanics M,D,O
- Metallurgical Engineering and Metallurgy M,D,O
- Mineral/Mining Engineering M,D,O
- Nuclear Engineering M,D,O
- Operations Research M,D,O
- Optical Sciences M,D,O
- Structural Engineering M,D,O
- Transportation and Highway Engineering M,D,O

ECUMENICAL THEOLOGICAL SEMINARY

- Pastoral Ministry and Counseling D
- Theology P

EDEN THEOLOGICAL SEMINARY

- Theology P,M,D

EDGEWOOD COLLEGE

- Business Administration and Management—General M
- Education—General M,D,O
- Educational Administration M,D,O
- Marriage and Family Therapy M
- Nursing—General M
- Religion M
- Special Education M,D,O

EDINBORO UNIVERSITY OF PENNSYLVANIA

- Art/Fine Arts M
- Biological and Biomedical Sciences—General M
- Clinical Psychology M
- Communication Disorders M
- Communication—General M
- Counselor Education M,O
- Developmental Education O
- Early Childhood Education M
- Education—General M,O
- Educational Administration M,O
- Educational Psychology M
- Elementary Education M
- English Education M
- Family Nurse Practitioner Studies M
- Management Information Systems M,O
- Mathematics Education M
- Media Studies M
- Nursing—General M
- Psychology—General M
- Reading Education M,O
- Rehabilitation Counseling M
- Science Education M
- Secondary Education M
- Social Sciences M
- Social Work M
- Special Education M

EDWARD VIA VIRGINIA COLLEGE OF OSTEOPATHIC MEDICINE

- Osteopathic Medicine P

ELIZABETH CITY STATE UNIVERSITY

- Elementary Education M

ELMHURST COLLEGE

- Accounting M
- Business Administration and Management—General M
- Computer Science M
- Educational Administration M
- English M
- Industrial and Organizational Psychology M
- Nursing—General M
- Special Education M
- Supply Chain Management M

ELMS COLLEGE

- Communication Disorders O
- Early Childhood Education M,O
- Education—General M,O
- Elementary Education M,O
- English as a Second Language M,O
- English Education M,O
- Foreign Languages Education M,O
- Reading Education M,O
- Religion M
- Science Education M,O
- Secondary Education M,O
- Special Education M,O

ELON UNIVERSITY

- Business Administration and Management—General M
- Education of the Gifted M
- Education—General M
- Elementary Education M
- Law P
- Physical Therapy D
- Special Education M

EMBRY-RIDDLE AERONAUTICAL UNIVERSITY (AZ)

- Safety Engineering M*

EMBRY-RIDDLE AERONAUTICAL UNIVERSITY (FL)

- Aerospace/Aeronautical Engineering M*
- Aviation Management M
- Business Administration and Management—General M
- Engineering Physics M
- Ergonomics and Human Factors M*
- Planetary and Space Sciences M
- Software Engineering M*
- Systems Engineering M

EMBRY-RIDDLE AERONAUTICAL UNIVERSITY WORLDWIDE

- Aerospace/Aeronautical Engineering M
- Aviation Management M
- Management of Technology M

EMERSON COLLEGE

- Advertising and Public Relations M
- Communication Disorders M*
- Communication—General M
- Corporate and Organizational Communication M*
- Film, Television, and Video Production M
- Health Communication M
- Health Promotion M
- International Business M*
- Journalism M*
- Marketing M*
- Media Studies M*
- Public Health—General M*
- Publishing M*
- Theater M*
- Writing M*

EMMANUEL COLLEGE

- Business Administration and Management—General M
- Education—General M,O
- Educational Administration M,O
- Elementary Education M,O

Human Resources Management M,O
Secondary Education M,O

EMMANUEL SCHOOL OF RELIGION

Religion P,M,D
Theology P,M,D

EMORY & HENRY COLLEGE

American Studies M
English Education M
History M
Reading Education M

EMORY UNIVERSITY

Adult Nursing M
Allied Health—General M,D
Allopathic Medicine P
Anesthesiologist Assistant Studies M
Animal Behavior D
Anthropology D
Art History D
Biochemistry D*
Biological and Biomedical Sciences—General D*
Biophysics D
Biostatistics M,D
Business Administration and Management—General M,D
Cell Biology D
Chemistry D
Clinical Laboratory Sciences/ Medical Technology M,D
Clinical Psychology D
Clinical Research M
Cognitive Sciences D
Comparative Literature D,O
Computer Science M,D*
Condensed Matter Physics D
Developmental Biology D
Developmental Psychology D
Ecology D*
Economics D
Education—General M,D,O
English D,O
Environmental and Occupational Health M
Epidemiology M,D
Evolutionary Biology D
Family Nurse Practitioner Studies M
Film, Television, and Video Theory and Criticism M,D,O
French D,O
Genetics D*
Gerontological Nursing M
Gerontology M
Health Education M,D
Health Informatics M,D
Health Physics/Radiological Health D
Health Promotion M
Health Services Management and Hospital Administration M,D
Health Services Research M,D
History D
Immunology D*
Interdisciplinary Studies D
International Health M,D
Jewish Studies M
Law P,M,O
Mathematics M,D*
Medical/Surgical Nursing M
Microbiology D*
Middle School Education M,D,O
Molecular Biology D
Molecular Genetics D
Molecular Pathogenesis D
Music M
Near and Middle Eastern Studies D,O
Neuroscience D*
Nurse Anesthesia M,D
Nurse Midwifery M
Nursing and Healthcare Administration M
Nursing—General M,D*
Nutrition M,D*
Oncology Nursing M
Pediatric Nursing M
Pharmacology D*
Philosophy D,O
Physical Therapy D
Physician Assistant Studies M
Physics D
Political Science D
Portuguese D,O
Psychology—General D
Public Health—General M,D*
Religion D,O
Secondary Education M,D,O
Sociology M,D*
Spanish D,O
Theology P,M,D
Vision Sciences M
Women's Health Nursing M
Women's Studies D,O

Close-Up on page 885.

EMPEROR'S COLLEGE OF TRADITIONAL ORIENTAL MEDICINE

Acupuncture and Oriental Medicine M,D

EMPORIA STATE UNIVERSITY

Art Therapy M
Biological and Biomedical Sciences—General M
Botany M
Business Administration and Management—General M
Business Education M
Cell Biology M
Clinical Psychology M
Counseling Psychology M
Counselor Education M
Curriculum and Instruction M
Early Childhood Education M
Education of the Gifted M
Education—General M,O
Educational Administration M
Educational Media/Instructional Technology M
Elementary Education M
English as a Second Language M
English M
Environmental Biology M
Geosciences M,O
History M
Industrial and Organizational Psychology M
Information Studies M,D,O
Library Science M,D,O
Mathematics M
Microbiology M
Music Education M
Music M
Physical Education M
Psychology—General M
Reading Education M
Rehabilitation Counseling M
School Psychology M,O
Secondary Education M
Social Sciences Education M
Special Education M
Zoology M

Close-Up on page 887.

ENDICOTT COLLEGE

Art Education M
Business Administration and Management—General M
Distance Education Development M
Elementary Education M
Hospitality Management M
International and Comparative Education M
Organizational Management M
Reading Education M
Special Education M
Sports Management M

EPISCOPAL DIVINITY SCHOOL

Theology P,M,D,O

EPISCOPAL THEOLOGICAL SEMINARY OF THE SOUTHWEST

Pastoral Ministry and Counseling P,M,O
Religion P,M,O
Theology P,M,O

ERIKSON INSTITUTE

Child Development M*
Developmental Psychology M,O
Early Childhood Education M,D*
English as a Second Language M,O
Human Development M,O

ERSKINE THEOLOGICAL SEMINARY

Theology P,M,D

EVANGELICAL SEMINARY OF PUERTO RICO

Theology P,M,D

EVANGELICAL THEOLOGICAL SEMINARY

Marriage and Family Therapy P,M,O
Pastoral Ministry and Counseling P,M,O
Religion P,M,O
Theology P,M,O

EVANGEL UNIVERSITY

Clinical Psychology M
Counseling Psychology M
Counselor Education M
Education—General M
Educational Administration M
Organizational Management M
Psychology—General M
Reading Education M
School Psychology M
Secondary Education M

EVERGLADES UNIVERSITY

Aviation M
Business Administration and Management—General M
Information Science M

EVERGLADES UNIVERSITY

Aviation M
Business Administration and Management—General M

THE EVERGREEN STATE COLLEGE

Education—General M
Environmental Management and Policy M
Public Administration M

EXCELSIOR COLLEGE

Business Administration and Management—General M
Liberal Studies M
Medical Informatics O
Nursing and Healthcare Administration O
Nursing—General M

FACULTAD DE DERECHO EUGENIO MARÍA DE HOSTOS

Law P

FAIRFIELD UNIVERSITY

Accounting M,O
Adult Nursing M,O
American Studies M
Business Administration and Management—General M,O*
Computer Engineering M
Counselor Education M,O
Education—General M,O*
Educational Media/Instructional Technology M,O
Electrical Engineering M
Elementary Education M,O
Engineering and Applied Sciences—General M
English as a Second Language M,O
Family Nurse Practitioner Studies M,O
Finance and Banking M,O
Foreign Languages Education M,O
Foundations and Philosophy of Education M,O
Health Services Management and Hospital Administration M,O
Human Resources Management M,O
International Business M,O
Management Information Systems M,O
Management of Technology M
Marketing M,O
Marriage and Family Therapy M
Mathematics M
Mechanical Engineering M
Multilingual and Multicultural Education M,O
Nurse Anesthesia M,O
Nursing—General M,O
Psychiatric Nursing M,O
Psychology—General M,O
School Psychology M,O
Secondary Education M,O
Software Engineering M
Special Education M,O
Taxation M,O

FAIRLEIGH DICKINSON UNIVERSITY, COLLEGE AT FLORHAM

Accounting M
Biological and Biomedical Sciences—General M
Business Administration and Management—General M,O*
Chemical Engineering M,O
Chemistry M
Clinical Psychology M*
Corporate and Organizational Communication M
Education—General M,O
Educational Administration M
Educational Media/Instructional Technology M,O
Entrepreneurship M,O
Finance and Banking M,O
Hospitality Management M*
Human Resources Management M,O
Industrial and Organizational Psychology M
International Business M,O
Management of Technology M,O
Marketing M,O
Organizational Behavior M,O
Organizational Management M,O
Pharmacology M,O
Psychology—General M,O
Public Administration M
Reading Education M,O
Taxation M,O
Writing M

Close-Up on page 889.

FAIRLEIGH DICKINSON UNIVERSITY, METROPOLITAN CAMPUS

Accounting M,O
Art/Fine Arts M
Biological and Biomedical Sciences—General M
Business Administration and Management—General M,O*
Chemistry M
Clinical Laboratory Sciences/ Medical Technology M
Clinical Psychology M,D*
Communication—General M
Comparative Literature M
Computer Engineering M
Computer Science M*
Curriculum and Instruction M
Education—General M,O*
Educational Administration M
Educational Media/Instructional Technology M,O
Electrical Engineering M*
Electronic Commerce M
Engineering and Applied Sciences—General M
English M
Entrepreneurship M,O
Experimental Psychology M,O
Finance and Banking M,O
Foundations and Philosophy of Education M
Health Services Management and Hospital Administration M
History M
Hospitality Management M*
Human Resources Management M,O
International Affairs M
International Business M
Management Information Systems M,O
Marketing M,O
Mathematics M
Media Studies M
Multilingual and Multicultural Education M,O
Nonprofit Management M,O
Nursing—General M,O
Pharmaceutical Administration M,O
Political Science M
Psychology—General M,D,O
Public Administration M,O
Reading Education M,O
School Psychology M,D
Science Education M
Special Education M
Systems Science M
Taxation M

Close-Up on page 889.

FAIRMONT STATE UNIVERSITY

Business Administration and Management—General M
Criminal Justice and Criminology M
Distance Education Development M
Education—General M
Educational Administration M
Human Services M
Nursing and Healthcare Administration M
Nursing Education M
Nursing—General M
Reading Education M
Special Education M

FAITH BAPTIST BIBLE COLLEGE AND THEOLOGICAL SEMINARY

Pastoral Ministry and Counseling P,M
Religion P,M
Theology P,M

FAITH EVANGELICAL LUTHERAN SEMINARY

Theology P,M,D

FASHION INSTITUTE OF TECHNOLOGY

Applied Arts and Design—General M*
Art History M
Arts Administration M
Business Administration and Management—General M
Clothing and Textiles M
Illustration M

Marketing M
Museum Studies M

FAULKNER UNIVERSITY

Law P

FAYETTEVILLE STATE UNIVERSITY

Biological and Biomedical Sciences—General M
Criminal Justice and Criminology M
Educational Administration M,D
Elementary Education M
English M
History M
Mathematics M
Middle School Education M
Political Science M
Psychology—General M
Reading Education M
Secondary Education M
Social Sciences Education M
Social Work M
Sociology M

FELICIAN COLLEGE

Adult Nursing M,O
Business Administration and Management—General M
Education—General M*
Educational Administration M
Elementary Education M
Entrepreneurship M
Family Nurse Practitioner Studies M,O*
Health Education M,O
Nursing—General M,O
Religious Education M,O
Special Education M

FERRIS STATE UNIVERSITY

Allied Health—General M
Applied Arts and Design—General M
Art/Fine Arts M
Business Administration and Management—General M
Computer Science M
Criminal Justice and Criminology M
Curriculum and Instruction M
Developmental Education M
Education—General M
Educational Administration M
Educational Media/Instructional Technology M
Electronic Commerce M
Elementary Education M
Human Services M
Management Information Systems M
Nursing and Healthcare Administration M
Nursing Education M
Nursing Informatics M
Nursing—General M
Optometry P
Pharmacy P
Quality Management M
Reading Education M
Special Education M

FIELDING GRADUATE UNIVERSITY

Clinical Psychology D,O
Educational Administration M,D*
Human Development M,D,O
Organizational Management M,D,O*
Psychology—General D,O*

FISK UNIVERSITY

Biological and Biomedical Sciences—General M
Chemistry M
Clinical Psychology M
Physics M
Psychology—General M
Sociology M

FITCHBURG STATE COLLEGE

Accounting M
Art Education M,O
Biological and Biomedical Sciences—General M
Business Administration and Management—General M
Communication—General M,O
Computer Science M
Counseling Psychology M,O
Counselor Education M,O
Criminal Justice and Criminology M
Early Childhood Education M
Educational Administration M,O
Educational Media/Instructional Technology M,O
Elementary Education M
English Education M
English M
Forensic Nursing M,O
Higher Education M,O
History M
Human Resources Management M
Interdisciplinary Studies O
Liberal Studies M
Marriage and Family Therapy M,O
Middle School Education M
Science Education M
Secondary Education M
Social Sciences Education M
Special Education M
Technical Writing M,O
Vocational and Technical Education M

FIVE BRANCHES INSTITUTE: COLLEGE OF TRADITIONAL CHINESE MEDICINE

Acupuncture and Oriental Medicine M

FIVE TOWNS COLLEGE

Early Childhood Education M
Music Education M,D
Music M,D

FLORIDA AGRICULTURAL AND MECHANICAL UNIVERSITY

Accounting M
Adult Education M,D
African-American Studies M
Agricultural Economics and Agribusiness M
Agricultural Sciences—General M
Allied Health—General M
Animal Sciences M
Architecture M
Biological and Biomedical Sciences—General M
Biomedical Engineering M,D
Business Administration and Management—General M
Business Education M
Chemical Engineering M,D
Chemistry M
Civil Engineering M,D
Counselor Education M,D
Criminal Justice and Criminology M
Early Childhood Education M
Economics M
Education—General M,D
Educational Administration M,D
Electrical Engineering M,D
Elementary Education M
Engineering and Applied Sciences—General M,D
English Education M
Entomology M
Environmental Engineering M,D
Environmental Sciences M,D
Finance and Banking M
Food Science and Technology M
Health Education M
History M
Industrial/Management Engineering M,D
International Affairs M
Journalism M
Landscape Architecture M
Law P
Management Information Systems M
Marketing M
Mathematics Education M
Mechanical Engineering M,D
Medicinal and Pharmaceutical Chemistry M,D
Nursing and Healthcare Administration M
Nursing—General M
Pharmaceutical Administration M,D
Pharmaceutical Sciences M,D*
Pharmacology M,D
Pharmacy P,D
Physical Education M
Physical Therapy M
Physics M,D
Plant Sciences M
Political Science M
Psychology—General M
Public Administration M
Public Health—General M
Recreation and Park Management M
School Psychology M
Science Education M
Secondary Education M
Social Psychology M
Social Sciences Education M
Social Sciences M
Social Work M
Sociology M
Software Engineering M
Toxicology M,D
Vocational and Technical Education M

FLORIDA ATLANTIC UNIVERSITY

Accounting M
Adult Education M,D,O
Anthropology M
Applied Arts and Design—General M
Applied Mathematics M,D
Art Education M,D,O
Art/Fine Arts M
Biochemistry M,D
Biological and Biomedical Sciences—General M,D
Business Administration and Management—General M
Chemistry M,D
Civil Engineering M
Communication Disorders M
Communication—General M
Comparative and Interdisciplinary Arts D
Comparative Literature M
Computer Engineering M,D
Computer Science M,D
Counseling Psychology M,O
Counselor Education M,O
Criminal Justice and Criminology M
Curriculum and Instruction M,D,O
Economics M
Education—General M,D,O
Educational Administration M,D,O
Educational Media/Instructional Technology M
Educational Psychology M,D,O
Electrical Engineering M,D
Electronic Commerce M
Elementary Education M,D,O
Engineering and Applied Sciences—General M,D
English M
Entrepreneurship M
Environmental Sciences M
Exercise and Sports Science M
Finance and Banking M
Foreign Languages Education M
Foundations and Philosophy of Education M,D,O
French M
Geography M
Geology M
German M
Health Promotion M
Health Services Management and Hospital Administration M
Higher Education M,D,O
History M
International Business M
Liberal Studies M
Marketing M
Marriage and Family Therapy M,O
Mathematics M,D
Mechanical Engineering M,D
Multilingual and Multicultural Education M,D,O
Music M
Neuroscience D
Nonprofit Management M
Nursing and Healthcare Administration M
Nursing—General M,D,O
Ocean Engineering M,D
Physics M,D
Political Science M
Psychology—General M,D
Public Administration M,D
Reading Education M,D,O
Real Estate M
Rehabilitation Counseling M,O
Social Work M
Sociology M
Spanish M
Special Education M,D
Sports Management M
Statistics M,D
Taxation M
Theater M
Urban and Regional Planning M
Women's Studies M,O
Writing M

FLORIDA ATLANTIC UNIVERSITY, JUPITER CAMPUS

Business Administration and Management—General M
Education—General M
Public Administration M
Reading Education M
Social Work M
Special Education M

FLORIDA COASTAL SCHOOL OF LAW

Law P

FLORIDA COLLEGE OF INTEGRATIVE MEDICINE

Acupuncture and Oriental Medicine M

FLORIDA GULF COAST UNIVERSITY

Accounting M
Allied Health—General M
Business Administration and Management—General M
Computer Science M
Counselor Education M
Criminal Justice and Criminology M
Curriculum and Instruction M
Education—General M
Educational Administration M
Educational Media/Instructional Technology M
Elementary Education M
English Education M
English M
Environmental Management and Policy M
Environmental Sciences M
Gerontology M
Information Science M
Mathematics Education M
Nursing—General M
Occupational Therapy M
Physical Therapy M
Public Administration M
Reading Education M
Recreation and Park Management M
Science Education M
Secondary Education M
Social Sciences Education M
Social Work M
Special Education M
Taxation M

FLORIDA INSTITUTE OF TECHNOLOGY

Aerospace/Aeronautical Engineering M,D*
Applied Mathematics M,D
Biological and Biomedical Sciences—General M,D
Biotechnology M,D
Business Administration and Management—General M
Cell Biology M,D*
Chemical Engineering M,D
Chemistry M,D
Civil Engineering M,D*
Clinical Psychology M,D
Communication—General M
Computer Education M,D,O
Computer Engineering M,D
Computer Science M,D*
Ecology M
Electrical Engineering M,D*
Electronic Commerce M
Elementary Education M,D,O
Engineering and Applied Sciences—General M,D
Engineering Management M*
Environmental Education M,D,O
Environmental Management and Policy M,D
Environmental Sciences M,D*
Ergonomics and Human Factors M
Human Resources Management M
Industrial and Manufacturing Management M
Industrial and Organizational Psychology M,D
Logistics M
Management Information Systems M
Marine Affairs M,D
Marine Biology M*
Marine Sciences M,D
Mathematics Education M,D,O
Mechanical Engineering M,D*
Meteorology M,D
Molecular Biology M,D
Ocean Engineering M,D*
Oceanography M,D*
Operations Research M,D
Physics M,D
Planetary and Space Sciences M,D
Psychology—General M,D*
Public Administration M
Science Education M,D,O
Software Engineering M,D
Systems Engineering M
Systems Science M
Transportation Management M

Close-Ups on pages 891 and 893.

FLORIDA INTERNATIONAL UNIVERSITY

Accounting M
Adult Education M,D
African Studies M
Architecture M
Art Education M,D
Art/Fine Arts M
Athletic Training and Sports Medicine M
Biological and Biomedical Sciences—General M,D
Biomedical Engineering M,D*

Business Administration and Management—General M,D
Chemistry M,D
Civil Engineering M,D*
Communication Disorders M
Computer Engineering M
Computer Science M,D*
Conflict Resolution and Mediation/Peace Studies O
Construction Management M*
Counseling Psychology M
Counselor Education M
Criminal Justice and Criminology M,D
Curriculum and Instruction M,D,O
Developmental Psychology M,D
Early Childhood Education M,D
Economics M,D
Education—General M,D,O*
Educational Administration M,D,O
Educational Media/Instructional Technology M,D,O
Electrical Engineering M,D*
Elementary Education M,D
Engineering and Applied Sciences—General M,D*
English as a Second Language M,D,O
English Education M,D
English M
Environmental Engineering M
Environmental Management and Policy M
Environmental Sciences M
Exercise and Sports Science M
Finance and Banking M
Foreign Languages Education M,D,O
Forensic Sciences M,D
Geosciences M,D
Health Services Management and Hospital Administration M
Higher Education D
History M,D
Hospitality Management M
Human Resources Development M,D
Industrial/Management Engineering M,D*
Information Science M,D
International Affairs M,D
International and Comparative Education M,D
International Business M
Landscape Architecture M
Latin American Studies M
Law P
Leisure Studies M
Liberal Studies M
Linguistics M
Management Information Systems D
Mass Communication M
Materials Engineering M,D
Mathematics Education M,D
Mathematics M
Mechanical Engineering M,D*
Music Education M
Music M
Nursing—General M,D*
Nutrition M,D*
Occupational Therapy M
Physical Education M,D,O
Physical Therapy M
Physics M,D
Political Science M,D
Psychology—General M,D
Public Administration M,D*
Public Health—General M*
Reading Education M,D
Recreation and Park Management M
Rehabilitation Counseling M
Religion M
School Psychology M,O
Science Education M,D
Social Sciences Education M,D
Social Work M,D*
Sociology M,D
Spanish M,D
Special Education M,D,O
Sports Management M
Statistics M
Taxation M
Telecommunications M*
Urban Education M
Writing M

Close-Up on page 895.

FLORIDA METROPOLITAN UNIVERSITY–BRANDON CAMPUS

Business Administration and Management—General M
Criminal Justice and Criminology M

FLORIDA METROPOLITAN UNIVERSITY–JACKSONVILLE CAMPUS

Business Administration and Management—General M
Criminal Justice and Criminology M

FLORIDA METROPOLITAN UNIVERSITY–LAKELAND CAMPUS

Criminal Justice and Criminology M

FLORIDA METROPOLITAN UNIVERSITY–MELBOURNE CAMPUS

Business Administration and Management—General M

FLORIDA METROPOLITAN UNIVERSITY–NORTH ORLANDO CAMPUS

Business Administration and Management—General M

FLORIDA METROPOLITAN UNIVERSITY–PINELLAS CAMPUS

Business Administration and Management—General M

FLORIDA METROPOLITAN UNIVERSITY–POMPANO BEACH CAMPUS

Business Administration and Management—General M
Criminal Justice and Criminology M

FLORIDA METROPOLITAN UNIVERSITY–SOUTH ORLANDO CAMPUS

Accounting M
Business Administration and Management—General M
Human Resources Management M
International Business M

FLORIDA METROPOLITAN UNIVERSITY–TAMPA CAMPUS

Accounting M
Business Administration and Management—General M
Human Resources Management M
International Business M

FLORIDA SOUTHERN COLLEGE

Accounting M
Business Administration and Management—General M
Education—General M
International Business M
Nursing—General M

FLORIDA STATE UNIVERSITY

Accounting M,D
Adult Education M,D,O
Allopathic Medicine P,D
American Studies M,O
Analytical Chemistry M,D
Anthropology M,D
Applied Arts and Design—General M,D
Applied Mathematics M,D
Applied Statistics M,D
Archaeology M,D
Art Education M,D,O
Art History M,D,O
Art/Fine Arts M
Arts Administration M,D
Asian Studies M
Biochemistry M,D
Biological and Biomedical Sciences—General P,M,D
Biomedical Engineering M,D
Biostatistics M,D
Business Administration and Management—General M,D
Cell Biology M,D
Chemical Engineering M,D
Chemical Physics M,D
Chemistry M,D*
Child and Family Studies M,D
Child Development M,D
Civil Engineering M,D
Classics M,D
Clinical Psychology D
Clothing and Textiles M,D
Cognitive Sciences D
Communication Disorders M,D
Communication—General M,D
Computational Biology D
Computer Science M,D
Consumer Economics M,D
Corporate and Organizational Communication M,D
Counseling Psychology M,D,O
Counselor Education M,D,O
Criminal Justice and Criminology M,D
Dance M
Demography and Population Studies M,O
Developmental Biology M,D
Developmental Psychology D
Distance Education Development M,D,O
Early Childhood Education M,D,O
East European and Russian Studies M
Ecology M,D
Economics M,D
Education—General M,D,O
Educational Administration M,D,O
Educational Measurement and Evaluation M,D
Educational Media/Instructional Technology M,D,O
Educational Psychology M,D
Electrical Engineering M,D
Elementary Education M,D,O
Engineering and Applied Sciences—General M,D
English Education M,D,O
English M,D
Environmental Engineering M,D
Evolutionary Biology M,D
Exercise and Sports Science M,D
Family and Consumer Sciences-General M,D*
Family Nurse Practitioner Studies M,O
Film, Television, and Video Production M
Finance and Banking M,D
Food Science and Technology M,D
Foundations and Philosophy of Education M,D,O
French M,D
Genetics M,D
Geographic Information Systems M,D
Geography M,D
Geology M,D
Geophysics D
German M,D
Health Education M,D
Health Services Research M
Higher Education M,D,O
History M,D
Human Resources Development M,D,O
Humanities M,D
Immunology M,D
Industrial/Management Engineering M,D
Information Studies M,D,O
Inorganic Chemistry M,D
Insurance M,D
Interior Design M
International Affairs M
International and Comparative Education M,D,O
Italian M
Kinesiology and Movement Studies M,D
Law P
Library Science M,D,O
Management Information Systems M,D
Manufacturing Engineering M,D
Marine Biology M,D
Marketing M,D
Marriage and Family Therapy M,D
Mass Communication M,D
Mathematical and Computational Finance M,D
Mathematics Education M,D,O
Mathematics M,D
Mechanical Engineering M,D
Media Studies M,D
Meteorology M,D
Microbiology M,D
Molecular Biology M,D
Molecular Biophysics D
Multilingual and Multicultural Education M,D,O
Museum Studies M,D,O
Music Education M,D
Music M,D
Neuroscience D
Nursing Education M,O
Nursing—General M,O
Nutrition M,D
Oceanography M,D*
Organic Chemistry M,D
Pediatric Nursing M,O
Philosophy M,D
Physical Chemistry M,D
Physical Education M,D,O
Physics M,D*
Physiology M,D
Plant Biology M,D
Political Science M,D
Psychology—General M,D
Public Administration M,D,O
Public History M,D
Public Policy M,D,O
Reading Education M,D,O
Recreation and Park Management M,D,O
Rehabilitation Counseling M,D,O
Religion M,D
Rhetoric M,D
School Psychology M,O
Science Education M,D,O
Slavic Languages M
Social Psychology D
Social Sciences Education M,D,O
Social Sciences M
Social Work M,D
Sociology M,D
Software Engineering M,D
Spanish M,D
Special Education M,D,O
Speech and Interpersonal Communication M,D
Sport Psychology M,D
Sports Management M,D,O
Statistics M,D
Structural Biology D
Taxation M,D
Textile Design M,D
Theater M,D
Therapies—Dance, Drama, and Music M,D
Urban and Regional Planning M,D
Writing M,D

Close-Up on page 897.

FONTBONNE UNIVERSITY

Accounting M
Art/Fine Arts M
Business Administration and Management—General M
Communication Disorders M
Computer Education M
Education—General M
Family and Consumer Sciences-General M
Special Education M
Taxation M
Theater M

FORDHAM UNIVERSITY

Accounting M
Adult Education M,D,O
Biological and Biomedical Sciences—General M,D*
Business Administration and Management—General M
Classics M,D
Clinical Psychology D
Communication—General M
Computer Science M
Corporate and Organizational Communication M
Counseling Psychology M,D,O
Counselor Education M,D,O
Curriculum and Instruction M,D,O
Developmental Psychology D
Early Childhood Education M,D,O
Economics M,D,O
Education—General M,D,O*
Educational Administration M,D,O
Educational Psychology M,D,O
Elementary Education M,D,O
English as a Second Language M,D,O
English M,D
Ethics O
Finance and Banking M
History M,D
Human Resources Management M,D,O
International Affairs M,O
International Development M,O*
Latin American Studies O
Law P,M
Liberal Studies M
Management Information Systems M
Marketing M
Mass Communication M
Media Studies M
Medieval and Renaissance Studies M,O
Multilingual and Multicultural Education M,D,O
Pastoral Ministry and Counseling M,D,O
Philosophy M,D
Political Science M
Psychology—General D
Reading Education M,D,O
Religion M,D,O
Religious Education M,D,O
School Psychology M,D,O
Secondary Education M,D,O
Social Work M,D*
Sociology M,D
Special Education M,D,O
Taxation M
Theology M,D

Close-Up on page 899.

FOREST INSTITUTE OF PROFESSIONAL PSYCHOLOGY

Clinical Psychology M,D,O
Psychology—General M,D,O

FORT HAYS STATE UNIVERSITY

Accounting M
Art/Fine Arts M

Biological and Biomedical Sciences—General	M
Business Administration and Management—General	M
Communication Disorders	M
Communication—General	M
Counselor Education	M
Education—General	M,O
Educational Administration	M,O
Educational Media/Instructional Technology	M
Elementary Education	M
English	M
Geology	M
Health Education	M
History	M
Liberal Studies	M
Nursing—General	M
Physical Education	M
Psychology—General	M,O
School Psychology	O
Secondary Education	M
Special Education	M

FORT VALLEY STATE UNIVERSITY

Animal Sciences	M
Counseling Psychology	M
Counselor Education	M,O
Early Childhood Education	M
Environmental and Occupational Health	M
Middle School Education	M
Public Health—General	M
Rehabilitation Counseling	M

FRAMINGHAM STATE COLLEGE

Art/Fine Arts	M
Biological and Biomedical Sciences—General	M
Business Administration and Management—General	M
Curriculum and Instruction	M
Early Childhood Education	M
Educational Administration	M
Educational Media/Instructional Technology	M
Elementary Education	M
English as a Second Language	M
English Education	M
Food Science and Technology	M*
Foreign Languages Education	M
Health Education	M
Health Services Management and Hospital Administration	M
Human Resources Management	M
Mathematics Education	M
Nutrition	M
Psychology—General	M
Public Administration	M
Reading Education	M
Science Education	M
Social Sciences Education	M
Spanish	M
Special Education	M

FRANCISCAN SCHOOL OF THEOLOGY

Theology	P,M

FRANCISCAN UNIVERSITY OF STEUBENVILLE

Business Administration and Management—General	M
Counseling Psychology	M
Curriculum and Instruction	M
Education—General	M
Educational Administration	M
Nursing—General	M
Philosophy	M
Theology	M

FRANCIS MARION UNIVERSITY

Business Administration and Management—General	M
Clinical Psychology	M
Early Childhood Education	M
Education—General	M
Elementary Education	M
Health Services Management and Hospital Administration	M
Psychology—General	M
School Psychology	M
Secondary Education	M
Social Psychology	M
Special Education	M

FRANKLIN PIERCE LAW CENTER

Law	P,M,O

FRANKLIN PIERCE UNIVERSITY

Business Administration and Management—General	M
Management Information Systems	M
Physical Therapy	M

FRANKLIN UNIVERSITY

Business Administration and Management—General	M
Computer Science	M
Corporate and Organizational Communication	M
Marketing	M

FRANK LLOYD WRIGHT SCHOOL OF ARCHITECTURE

Architecture	M

FREDERICK S. PARDEE RAND GRADUATE SCHOOL

Public Policy	D

FREED-HARDEMAN UNIVERSITY

Business Administration and Management—General	M
Counselor Education	M,O
Curriculum and Instruction	M,O
Education—General	M,O
Educational Administration	M,O
Pastoral Ministry and Counseling	M
Theology	P,M

FRESNO PACIFIC UNIVERSITY

Business Administration and Management—General	M
Conflict Resolution and Mediation/Peace Studies	M
Counselor Education	M
Curriculum and Instruction	M
Education of the Multiply Handicapped	M
Education—General	M
Educational Administration	M
Educational Media/Instructional Technology	M
English as a Second Language	M
Interdisciplinary Studies	M
Kinesiology and Movement Studies	M
Mathematics Education	M
Multilingual and Multicultural Education	M
Reading Education	M
School Psychology	M
Science Education	M
Special Education	M
Student Affairs	M

FRIENDS UNIVERSITY

Business Administration and Management—General	M
Education—General	M
Educational Administration	M
Elementary Education	M
Environmental Management and Policy	M
Health Services Management and Hospital Administration	M
Human Resources Development	M
Industrial and Manufacturing Management	M
Law	M
Liberal Studies	M
Management Information Systems	M
Marriage and Family Therapy	M
Secondary Education	M
Theology	M

FRONTIER SCHOOL OF MIDWIFERY AND FAMILY NURSING

Nurse Midwifery	M,O
Nursing—General	M,O
Women's Health Nursing	M,O

FROSTBURG STATE UNIVERSITY

Biological and Biomedical Sciences—General	M
Business Administration and Management—General	M
Computer Science	M
Conservation Biology	M
Counseling Psychology	M
Counselor Education	M
Curriculum and Instruction	M
Ecology	M
Education—General	M
Educational Administration	M
Educational Media/Instructional Technology	M
Elementary Education	M
Fish, Game, and Wildlife Management	M
Interdisciplinary Studies	M
Physical Education	M
Psychology—General	M
Reading Education	M
Recreation and Park Management	M
Secondary Education	M
Special Education	M

FULLER THEOLOGICAL SEMINARY

Clinical Psychology	M,D
Marriage and Family Therapy	M
Missions and Missiology	M,D
Psychology—General	M,D
Theology	P,M,D

FURMAN UNIVERSITY

Chemistry	M
Early Childhood Education	M
Education—General	M
Educational Administration	M
Elementary Education	M
English as a Second Language	M
Middle School Education	M
Reading Education	M
Special Education	M

GALLAUDET UNIVERSITY

Clinical Psychology	D
Communication Disorders	M,D
Counseling Psychology	M
Counselor Education	M
Developmental Psychology	M,O
Early Childhood Education	M,D,O
Education of the Multiply Handicapped	M,D,O
Education—General	M,D,O
Educational Administration	M,D,O
Educational Measurement and Evaluation	O
Educational Media/Instructional Technology	O
Elementary Education	M,D,O
Leisure Studies	M
Linguistics	M
Psychology—General	M,D,O
School Psychology	M,O
Secondary Education	M,D,O
Social Work	M
Special Education	M,D,O
Translation and Interpretation	M

GANNON UNIVERSITY

Accounting	O
Business Administration and Management—General	M,O
Computer Science	M
Counseling Psychology	D
Counselor Education	M,O
Curriculum and Instruction	M
Early Childhood Education	M,O
Education—General	M,O
Educational Administration	M,O
Educational Media/Instructional Technology	M,O
Electrical Engineering	M
Engineering Management	M
English as a Second Language	O
English	M
Environmental and Occupational Health	M,O
Environmental Education	M
Environmental Engineering	M
Environmental Management and Policy	M
Environmental Sciences	O
Finance and Banking	O
Gerontology	O
Human Resources Management	O
Information Science	M
Investment Management	O
Marketing	O
Mechanical Engineering	M
Medical/Surgical Nursing	M,O
Nurse Anesthesia	M,O
Nursing and Healthcare Administration	M,O
Nursing—General	M,O
Occupational Therapy	M,O
Organizational Management	O
Pastoral Ministry and Counseling	M,O
Physical Therapy	D
Physician Assistant Studies	M
Public Administration	M,O
Reading Education	M,O
Science Education	M
Software Engineering	M

GARDNER-WEBB UNIVERSITY

Business Administration and Management—General	P,M,D
Counseling Psychology	M
Curriculum and Instruction	D
Education—General	M,D
Educational Administration	M,D
Elementary Education	M
English Education	M
English	P,M,D
Exercise and Sports Science	M
Middle School Education	M
Missions and Missiology	P,M,D
Nursing—General	M,O
Pastoral Ministry and Counseling	P,M,D
Physical Education	M
Psychology—General	M
Religious Education	P,M,D
School Psychology	M
Theology	P,M,D

GARRETT-EVANGELICAL THEOLOGICAL SEMINARY

Music	P,M,D
Pastoral Ministry and Counseling	P,M,D
Religious Education	P,M,D
Theology	P,M,D

GENERAL THEOLOGICAL SEMINARY

Theology	P,M,D

GENEVA COLLEGE

Business Administration and Management—General	M
Counseling Psychology	M*
Counselor Education	M
Education—General	M
Educational Administration	M
Higher Education	M
Marriage and Family Therapy	M
Organizational Management	M
Psychology—General	M
Special Education	M

GEORGE FOX UNIVERSITY

Business Administration and Management—General	M,D
Clinical Psychology	M,D*
Counseling Psychology	M,O
Counselor Education	M,O
Education—General	M,D,O
Educational Administration	M,D,O
Foundations and Philosophy of Education	M,D,O
Marriage and Family Therapy	M,O
Organizational Management	M
Pastoral Ministry and Counseling	P,M,D,O
Psychology—General	M,D
Religion	P,M,D,O
School Psychology	M,O
Theology	P,M,D,O

Close-Up on page 901.

GEORGE MASON UNIVERSITY

Applied Physics	M
Archaeology	M
Atmospheric Sciences	D
Bioinformatics	M,D,O
Biological and Biomedical Sciences—General	M,D,O
Business Administration and Management—General	M
Cell Biology	M,D,O
Civil Engineering	M
Clinical Psychology	M,D
Communication—General	M
Community College Education	D,O
Computational Biology	M,D,O
Computational Sciences	M,D,O*
Computer Engineering	M,D
Computer Science	M,D
Conflict Resolution and Mediation/Peace Studies	M,D
Counselor Education	M
Cultural Studies	D*
Dance	M
Developmental Psychology	M,D
Early Childhood Education	M
Economics	M,D
Education—General	M,D
Educational Administration	M
Educational Measurement and Evaluation	M
Educational Media/Instructional Technology	M
Electrical Engineering	M,D
Engineering and Applied Sciences—General	M,D,O
Engineering Physics	M
English as a Second Language	M
English	M
Evolutionary Biology	M,D,O
Exercise and Sports Science	M
Experimental Psychology	M,D
Family Nurse Practitioner Studies	M,D,O
Film, Television, and Video Production	M
Foreign Languages Education	M
Geodetic Sciences	M,D,O
Geographic Information Systems	M,D,O
Geography	M
Gerontology	M
Graphic Design	M
History	M,D
Human Resources Management	M

Industrial and Organizational Psychology M,D
Information Science M,D,O
Interdisciplinary Studies M
International Affairs M
Law P,M
Liberal Studies M
Linguistics M
Logistics M
Management of Technology M,D
Medical/Surgical Nursing M,D,O
Microbiology M,D,O
Middle School Education M
Molecular Biology M,D,O
Multilingual and Multicultural Education M
Music Education M
Music M
Nanotechnology M,D,O
Neuroscience M,D,O
Nursing and Healthcare Administration M,D,O
Nursing Education M,D,O
Nursing—General M,D,O
Operations Research M
Organizational Management M
Psychology—General M,D
Public Affairs M
Public Policy M,D*
Reading Education M
School Psychology M
Secondary Education M
Social Sciences M,D,O
Social Work M,D,O
Sociology M
Software Engineering M
Special Education M
Statistics M,D,O
Systems Engineering M
Telecommunications M,D,O
Transportation Management M
Writing M

GEORGETOWN COLLEGE

Education—General M

GEORGETOWN UNIVERSITY

Allopathic Medicine P
Analytical Chemistry M,D
Biochemistry M,D
Biological and Biomedical Sciences—General M,D
Biophysics M,D
Biostatistics M
Business Administration and Management—General M
Cancer Biology/Oncology D
Cell Biology D
Chemical Physics M,D
Chemistry M,D
Communication—General M*
Conflict Resolution and Mediation/Peace Studies M,D
Demography and Population Studies M
East European and Russian Studies M
Economics D
English as a Second Language M,D,O
English M
Epidemiology M
German M,D
Health Physics/Radiological Health M
Health Promotion M,D
History M,D
Immunology M,D
Infectious Diseases M,D
Inorganic Chemistry M,D
International Affairs M,D
Internet and Interactive Multimedia M
Latin American Studies M
Law P,M,D
Liberal Studies M
Linguistics M,D,O
Microbiology M,D*
Molecular Biology D
Multilingual and Multicultural Education M,D,O
National Security M
Near and Middle Eastern Languages M,D
Near and Middle Eastern Studies M,O
Neuroscience D
Nursing—General M
Organic Chemistry M,D
Pathology M,D
Pharmacology D
Philosophy M,D
Physical Chemistry M,D
Physiology M,D
Political Science M,D
Psychology—General D
Public Health—General M,D
Public Policy M*
Radiation Biology M
Spanish M,D
Taxation P,M,D
Theoretical Chemistry M,D
Western European Studies M

THE GEORGE WASHINGTON UNIVERSITY

Accounting M,D
Adult Nursing M,D,O
Aerospace/Aeronautical Engineering M,D,O
Allopathic Medicine P
American Studies M,D
Analytical Chemistry M,D
Anthropology M,D
Applied Arts and Design—General M,D
Applied Mathematics M,D
Art History M,D
Art Therapy M,O
Art/Fine Arts M,D
Asian Studies M
Biochemistry M,D*
Bioinformatics M
Biological and Biomedical Sciences—General M,D*
Biostatistics M,D
Biotechnology M
Business Administration and Management—General M,D
Chemistry M,D
Civil Engineering M,D,O
Clinical Psychology D
Cognitive Sciences D
Communication Disorders M
Community Health M,O
Computer Engineering M,D
Computer Science M,D,O
Counselor Education M,D,O
Criminal Justice and Criminology M
Curriculum and Instruction M,D,O
Early Childhood Education M
East European and Russian Studies M
Economics M,D
Education—General M,D,O
Educational Administration M,D,O
Educational Media/Instructional Technology M
Educational Policy M,D
Electrical Engineering M,D
Elementary Education M
Emergency Management M,D,O
Emergency Medical Services M,O
Engineering and Applied Sciences—General M,D,O*
Engineering Management M,D,O
English M,D
Environmental and Occupational Health M,D
Environmental Engineering M,D,O
Environmental Management and Policy M,D
Epidemiology M,D
Exercise and Sports Science M
Family Nurse Practitioner Studies M,D,O
Finance and Banking M,D
Folklore M
Forensic Sciences M
Genetics M,D
Genomic Sciences M*
Geography M,D
Geology M,D
Geosciences M,D
Health Informatics M
Health Promotion M,O
Health Psychology D
Health Services Management and Hospital Administration M,D,O
Health Services Research M,D,O
Higher Education M,D,O
Historic Preservation M
History M,D
Hospitality Management M,O
Human Development M,D
Human Resources Development M,D,O
Human Resources Management M,D,O
Immunology D*
Industrial and Manufacturing Management M
Industrial and Organizational Psychology D
Infectious Diseases M,D
Inorganic Chemistry M,D
Interior Design M,D
International Affairs M
International and Comparative Education M
International Business M,D
International Development M
International Health M
Investment Management M,D
Latin American Studies M
Law P,M,D
Legal and Justice Studies M,O
Logistics M
Management Information Systems M
Management of Technology M,D
Management Strategy and Policy M,D
Marketing M,D
Mass Communication M
Materials Sciences M,D
Maternal and Child Health M,O
Mathematics M,D
Mechanical Engineering M,D,O
Microbiology M,D,O
Military and Defense Studies M
Molecular Biology M,D
Molecular Medicine D*
Museum Education M
Museum Studies M,D,O
Neuroscience D
Nonprofit Management M
Nursing and Healthcare Administration M,D,O
Oral and Dental Sciences M
Organic Chemistry M,D
Organizational Behavior M,D
Organizational Management M,O*
Pharmacology D
Philosophy M,D
Photography M,D
Physical Chemistry M,D
Physical Therapy D
Physician Assistant Studies M
Physics M,D
Political Science M,D
Project Management M,D
Psychology—General D
Public Administration M,D
Public Health—General M,D,O
Public Policy M,D
Publishing M
Real Estate M
Rehabilitation Counseling M
Religion M
Secondary Education M
Social Psychology D
Sociology M
Special Education M,D,O
Sports Management M,D,O
Statistics M,D,O
Systems Engineering M,D,O
Technology and Public Policy M
Telecommunications M,D
Theater M
Toxicology M
Travel and Tourism M,O
Western European Studies M
Women's Studies M,D,O

GEORGIA CAMPUS–PHILADELPHIA COLLEGE OF OSTEOPATHIC MEDICINE

Biological and Biomedical Sciences—General M,O
Osteopathic Medicine P

GEORGIA COLLEGE & STATE UNIVERSITY

Accounting M
Biological and Biomedical Sciences—General M
Business Administration and Management—General M
Criminal Justice and Criminology M
Early Childhood Education M,O
Education—General M,O
Educational Administration M,O
Educational Media/Instructional Technology M,O
English Education M,O
English M
Health Education M,O
History M
Logistics M
Management Information Systems M
Mathematics Education M,O
Middle School Education M,O
Nursing—General M
Physical Education M,O
Public Administration M
Public Affairs M
Science Education M,O
Secondary Education M,O
Social Sciences Education M,O
Special Education M,O
Therapies—Dance, Drama, and Music M,O
Writing M

GEORGIA INSTITUTE OF TECHNOLOGY

Accounting M,D,O
Aerospace/Aeronautical Engineering M,D
Applied Mathematics M,D
Architecture M,D
Atmospheric Sciences M,D
Biochemistry M,D
Bioengineering M,D,O
Bioinformatics M,D
Biological and Biomedical Sciences—General M,D*
Biomedical Engineering M,D,O
Building Science M,D*
Business Administration and Management—General M,D,O
Chemical Engineering M,D
Chemistry M,D
Civil Engineering M,D
Computer Engineering M,D
Computer Science M,D
Economics M
Electrical Engineering M,D
Electronic Commerce M,O
Engineering and Applied Sciences—General M,D,O
Entrepreneurship M,O
Environmental Engineering M,D
Environmental Management and Policy M,D
Environmental Sciences M,D
Finance and Banking M,D,O
Geochemistry M,D
Geographic Information Systems M,D
Geophysics M,D
Geosciences M,D*
Health Physics/Radiological Health M,D
Health Services Management and Hospital Administration M
History of Science and Technology M,D
Human-Computer Interaction M
Hydrology M,D
Industrial/Management Engineering M,D
International Affairs M*
International Business M,O
Internet and Interactive Multimedia M
Management Information Systems M,D,O
Management of Technology M,O
Management Strategy and Policy M,D,O
Marketing M,D,O
Materials Engineering M,D
Mathematical and Computational Finance M,D
Mathematics M,D
Mechanical Engineering M,D
Mechanics M,D
Medical Physics M,D
Natural Resources M,D
Nuclear Engineering M,D
Ocean Engineering M,D
Operations Research M
Organizational Behavior M,D,O
Physics M,D
Physiology M
Polymer Science and Engineering M,D
Psychology—General M,D
Public Policy M,D
Statistics M,D
Systems Engineering M,D
Textile Sciences and Engineering M,D
Urban and Regional Planning M,D
Urban Design M,D

GEORGIAN COURT UNIVERSITY

Addictions/Substance Abuse Counseling M,O
Biological and Biomedical Sciences—General M,O
Business Administration and Management—General M
Counseling Psychology M,O
Education—General M,O
Educational Administration M,O
Educational Media/Instructional Technology M,O
Educational Psychology M,O
Mathematics M,O
Special Education M,O
Theology M,O

GEORGIA SOUTHERN UNIVERSITY

Accounting M
Allied Health—General M,O
Art Education M
Art/Fine Arts M
Biological and Biomedical Sciences—General M
Business Administration and Management—General M
Business Education M
Community Health Nursing M,O
Counselor Education M,O
Curriculum and Instruction D
Early Childhood Education M
Education—General M,D,O
Educational Administration M,D,O
Educational Media/Instructional Technology M
Electrical Engineering M
English Education M
English M
Family Nurse Practitioner Studies M,O
Foreign Languages Education M
Health Education M

Health Services Management and Hospital Administration	M
Higher Education	M
History	M
Kinesiology and Movement Studies	M
Mathematics Education	M
Mathematics	M
Mechanical Engineering	M
Middle School Education	M
Music	M
Nursing—General	M,O
Physical Education	M
Psychology—General	M
Public Administration	M
Public Health—General	M
Reading Education	M
Recreation and Park Management	M
School Psychology	M,O
Science Education	M
Social Sciences Education	M
Sociology	M
Special Education	M
Sports Management	M
Vocational and Technical Education	M
Women's Health Nursing	M,O

GEORGIA SOUTHWESTERN STATE UNIVERSITY

Business Administration and Management—General	M
Computer Science	M
Early Childhood Education	M,O
Education—General	M,O
Health Education	M,O
Information Science	M
Middle School Education	M,O
Physical Education	M,O
Reading Education	M,O
Secondary Education	M,O
Special Education	M,O

GEORGIA STATE UNIVERSITY

Accounting	M,D,O
Actuarial Science	M
Adult Nursing	M,D,O
Allied Health—General	M,D,O
Anthropology	M
Art Education	M,D,O
Art History	M
Art/Fine Arts	M
Astronomy	D
Athletic Training and Sports Medicine	M
Biochemistry	M,D
Biological and Biomedical Sciences—General	M,D*
Business Administration and Management—General	M,D
Cell Biology	M,D
Chemistry	M,D
Communication Disorders	M
Communication—General	M,D
Computer Science	M,D
Counseling Psychology	M,D,O
Counselor Education	M,D,O
Criminal Justice and Criminology	M
Early Childhood Education	M,D,O
Economics	M,D
Education of the Multiply Handicapped	M
Education—General	M,D,O
Educational Administration	M,D,O
Educational Measurement and Evaluation	M,D
Educational Media/Instructional Technology	M,D,O
Educational Policy	M,D,O
Educational Psychology	M,D
English as a Second Language	M,D,O
English Education	M,D,O
English	M,D
Entrepreneurship	M,D
Environmental Biology	M,D
Exercise and Sports Science	M,D
Family Nurse Practitioner Studies	M,D,O
Film, Television, and Video Production	M,D
Finance and Banking	M,D,O
Foundations and Philosophy of Education	M,D
French	M
Geographic Information Systems	O
Geography	M
Geology	M
Geosciences	M,O
German	M
Gerontology	M
Health Education	M
Health Promotion	M,D,O
Health Services Management and Hospital Administration	M
Historic Preservation	M
History	M,D
Human Resources Management	M,D
Human Services	M
Hydrogeology	M,O
Industrial and Labor Relations	M,D
Information Science	M
Insurance	M,D
International Business	M
Law	P
Linguistics	M,D
Management Information Systems	M,D
Marketing	M,D
Mass Communication	M,D
Mathematics Education	M,D,O
Mathematics	M
Microbiology	M,D
Middle School Education	M,O
Molecular Biology	M,D
Molecular Genetics	M,D
Music Education	M,D,O
Music	M
Neurobiology	M,D*
Nursing—General	M,D,O
Nutrition	M,O
Operations Research	M,D
Organizational Management	M,D
Pediatric Nursing	M,D,O
Philosophy	M
Photography	M,D
Physical Education	M
Physical Therapy	D
Physics	M,D
Physiology	M,D
Political Science	M,D
Psychiatric Nursing	M,D,O
Psychology—General	M,D
Public Administration	M
Public Health—General	M,O
Public Policy	D
Reading Education	M,D,O
Real Estate	M,D,O
Rehabilitation Counseling	M
Religion	M
Rhetoric	M,D
School Psychology	M,D,O
Science Education	M,D,O
Social Sciences Education	M,D,O
Social Work	M
Sociology	M,D
Spanish	M
Special Education	M,D
Speech and Interpersonal Communication	M,D
Sports Management	M
Taxation	M
Translation and Interpretation	O
Urban Studies	M
Women's Health Nursing	M,D,O
Women's Studies	M
Writing	M,D

GERSTNER SLOAN-KETTERING GRADUATE SCHOOL OF BIOMEDICAL SCIENCES

Biological and Biomedical Sciences—General	D
Cancer Biology/Oncology	D

GLOBAL UNIVERSITY OF THE ASSEMBLIES OF GOD

Missions and Missiology	P,M
Religious Education	P,M
Theology	P,M

GODDARD COLLEGE

Business Administration and Management—General	M
Comparative and Interdisciplinary Arts	M
Counseling Psychology	M
Education—General	M
Environmental Management and Policy	M
Health Promotion	M
Industrial and Organizational Psychology	M
Interdisciplinary Studies	M
Sustainable Development	M
Writing	M

GOLDEN GATE BAPTIST THEOLOGICAL SEMINARY

Early Childhood Education	P,M,D,O
Educational Administration	P,M,D,O
Pastoral Ministry and Counseling	P,M,D,O
Theology	P,M,D,O

GOLDEN GATE UNIVERSITY

Accounting	M,D,O
Advertising and Public Relations	M,D,O
Business Administration and Management—General	M,D,O
Finance and Banking	M,D,O
Human Resources Management	M,D,O
International Business	M,D,O
Law	P,M,D
Legal and Justice Studies	P,M,D
Management Information Systems	M,D,O
Management of Technology	M,D,O
Marketing	M,D,O
Psychology—General	M,D,O
Taxation	P,M,D,O

GOLDEY-BEACOM COLLEGE

Business Administration and Management—General	M
Finance and Banking	M
Human Resources Management	M
Management Information Systems	M
Marketing	M

GONZAGA UNIVERSITY

Accounting	M
Business Administration and Management—General	M
Communication—General	M
Counseling Psychology	M
Education—General	M
Educational Administration	M,D
English as a Second Language	M
Law	P
Nurse Anesthesia	M
Nursing—General	M
Organizational Management	M
Pastoral Ministry and Counseling	M
Philosophy	M
Religion	M
Special Education	M
Sports Management	M

GOODING INSTITUTE OF NURSE ANESTHESIA

Nurse Anesthesia	M

GORDON COLLEGE

Education—General	M
Music Education	M

GORDON-CONWELL THEOLOGICAL SEMINARY

Missions and Missiology	P,M,D
Pastoral Ministry and Counseling	P,M,D
Religion	P,M,D
Religious Education	P,M,D
Theology	P,M,D

GOUCHER COLLEGE

Arts Administration	M
Biological and Biomedical Sciences—General	O
Education—General	M
Historic Preservation	M
Writing	M

GOVERNORS STATE UNIVERSITY

Accounting	M
Addictions/Substance Abuse Counseling	M
Analytical Chemistry	M
Art/Fine Arts	M
Business Administration and Management—General	M
Communication Disorders	M
Communication—General	M
Computer Science	M
Counseling Psychology	M
Early Childhood Education	M
Education—General	M
Educational Administration	M
Educational Media/Instructional Technology	M
English	M
Environmental Biology	M
Health Services Management and Hospital Administration	M
Legal and Justice Studies	M
Management Information Systems	M
Media Studies	M
Nursing—General	M
Occupational Therapy	M
Physical Therapy	M,D
Political Science	M
Psychology—General	M
Public Administration	M
Reading Education	M
Social Work	M
Special Education	M

GRACE COLLEGE

Counseling Psychology	M

GRACELAND UNIVERSITY

Education—General	M
Family Nurse Practitioner Studies	M,O
Nursing and Healthcare Administration	M,O
Nursing Education	M,O
Nursing—General	M,O
Pastoral Ministry and Counseling	M
Religion	M

GRACE THEOLOGICAL SEMINARY

Missions and Missiology	P,M,D,O
Pastoral Ministry and Counseling	P,M,D,O
Theology	P,M,D,O

GRACE UNIVERSITY

Counseling Psychology	M
Pastoral Ministry and Counseling	M
Theology	M

GRADUATE INSTITUTE OF APPLIED LINGUISTICS

Linguistics	M,O
Multilingual and Multicultural Education	M,O

GRADUATE SCHOOL AND UNIVERSITY CENTER OF THE CITY UNIVERSITY OF NEW YORK

Accounting	D
Anthropology	D
Archaeology	D
Architectural History	D
Art History	D
Biochemistry	D
Biological and Biomedical Sciences—General	D
Biomedical Engineering	D
Biopsychology	D
Business Administration and Management—General	D
Chemical Engineering	D
Chemistry	D
Civil Engineering	D
Classics	M,D
Clinical Psychology	D
Cognitive Sciences	D
Communication Disorders	D
Comparative Literature	M,D
Computer Science	D
Criminal Justice and Criminology	D
Developmental Psychology	D
Economics	D
Educational Psychology	D
Electrical Engineering	D
Engineering and Applied Sciences—General	D*
English	D
Environmental Sciences	D
Experimental Psychology	D
Finance and Banking	D
French	D
Geosciences	D
German	M,D
History	D
Industrial and Organizational Psychology	D
Interdisciplinary Studies	M,D
Italian	M,D
Liberal Studies	M
Linguistics	M,D
Management Information Systems	D
Mathematics	D
Mechanical Engineering	D
Medieval and Renaissance Studies	M,D
Music	D
Neuroscience	D
Organizational Behavior	D
Philosophy	M,D
Physics	D
Political Science	M,D
Psychology—General	D
Public Policy	M,D
Social Psychology	D
Social Work	D
Sociology	D
Spanish	D
Theater	D
Urban Education	D
Urban Studies	M,D
Women's Studies	M,D

GRADUATE THEOLOGICAL UNION

Art History	M,D,O
Cultural Studies	M,D,O
Ethics	M,D,O
Jewish Studies	M,D,O
Religion	M,D,O
Social Sciences	M,D,O
Theology	M,D,O

GRAMBLING STATE UNIVERSITY

- Criminal Justice and Criminology M
- Curriculum and Instruction M,D
- Developmental Education M,D
- Early Childhood Education M
- Education—General M,D
- Educational Administration M,D
- Elementary Education M
- Family Nurse Practitioner Studies M,O
- Mass Communication M
- Nursing Education M,O
- Nursing—General M,O
- Public Administration M
- Science Education M,O
- Social Sciences Education M
- Social Work M
- Special Education M,D
- Sports Management M

GRAND CANYON UNIVERSITY

- Business Administration and Management—General M
- Education—General M*
- Elementary Education M
- English as a Second Language M
- Reading Education M
- Secondary Education M

GRAND RAPIDS THEOLOGICAL SEMINARY OF CORNERSTONE UNIVERSITY

- Missions and Missiology P,M
- Pastoral Ministry and Counseling P,M
- Religion P,M
- Religious Education P,M
- Theology P,M

GRAND VALLEY STATE UNIVERSITY

- Accounting M
- Adult Education M
- Allied Health—General M,D
- Bioinformatics M
- Biological and Biomedical Sciences—General M
- Biostatistics M
- Business Administration and Management—General M
- Cell Biology M
- Communication—General M
- Computer Engineering M
- Computer Science M
- Criminal Justice and Criminology M
- Early Childhood Education M
- Education of the Gifted M
- Education—General M
- Educational Administration M
- Educational Media/Instructional Technology M
- Electrical Engineering M
- Elementary Education M
- Engineering and Applied Sciences—General M
- English as a Second Language M
- English Education M
- English M
- Health Services Management and Hospital Administration M
- Higher Education M
- Information Science M
- Management Information Systems M
- Manufacturing Engineering M
- Mechanical Engineering M
- Medical Informatics M
- Middle School Education M
- Molecular Biology M
- Nursing and Healthcare Administration M
- Nursing Education M
- Nursing—General M
- Occupational Therapy M
- Physical Therapy M,D
- Physician Assistant Studies M
- Public Administration M
- Reading Education M
- School Psychology M
- Social Work M
- Software Engineering M
- Special Education M
- Taxation M

Close-Up on page 903.

GRANTHAM UNIVERSITY

- Business Administration and Management—General M
- Management Information Systems M
- Management of Technology M
- Project Management M

GRATZ COLLEGE

- Education—General M
- Jewish Studies M
- Library Science O
- Music M,O
- Near and Middle Eastern Studies O
- Religious Education M,O
- Social Work M,O

GREEN MOUNTAIN COLLEGE

- Business Administration and Management—General M
- Environmental Management and Policy M

Close-Up on page 905.

GREENSBORO COLLEGE

- Education—General M
- Elementary Education M
- English as a Second Language M
- Special Education M

GREENVILLE COLLEGE

- Education—General M
- Elementary Education M
- Pastoral Ministry and Counseling M
- Secondary Education M

GWYNEDD-MERCY COLLEGE

- Adult Nursing M
- Business Administration and Management—General M
- Counselor Education M
- Education—General M
- Educational Administration M
- Family Nurse Practitioner Studies M
- Gerontological Nursing M
- Nursing—General M
- Oncology Nursing M
- Pediatric Nursing M
- Reading Education M
- Special Education M

HAMLINE UNIVERSITY

- Business Administration and Management—General M
- Education—General M,D
- Law P,M
- Liberal Studies M,O
- Nonprofit Management M
- Public Administration M

HAMPTON UNIVERSITY

- Applied Mathematics M
- Biological and Biomedical Sciences—General M
- Business Administration and Management—General M
- Chemistry M
- Communication Disorders M*
- Computer Science M
- Counselor Education M
- Education—General M
- Elementary Education M
- Museum Studies M
- Nursing—General M
- Physical Therapy D
- Physics M,D
- Special Education M
- Student Affairs M

Close-Up on page 907.

HARDING UNIVERSITY

- Art Education M,O
- Business Administration and Management—General M
- Counseling Psychology M
- Counselor Education M,O
- Early Childhood Education M,O
- Education—General M,O
- Educational Administration M,O
- Elementary Education M,O
- English Education M,O
- Foreign Languages Education M,O
- Health Education M,O
- Home Economics Education M,O
- Marriage and Family Therapy M
- Mathematics Education M,O
- Pharmacy P
- Physician Assistant Studies M
- Reading Education M,O
- Religious Education M,O
- Science Education M,O
- Secondary Education M,O
- Social Sciences Education M,O
- Special Education M,O
- Theology M

HARDING UNIVERSITY GRADUATE SCHOOL OF RELIGION

- Religion P,M,D
- Theology P,M,D

HARDIN-SIMMONS UNIVERSITY

- Business Administration and Management—General M
- Counselor Education M
- Education of the Gifted M
- Education—General M
- English M
- Environmental Management and Policy M
- Family Nurse Practitioner Studies M
- History M
- Marriage and Family Therapy M
- Maternal and Child/Neonatal Nursing M
- Mathematics M,D
- Music Education M
- Music M
- Nursing—General M
- Pastoral Ministry and Counseling M
- Physical Education M
- Physical Therapy D
- Psychology—General M
- Reading Education M
- Recreation and Park Management M
- Religion M
- Science Education M,D
- Sports Management M
- Theology P,M

HARRISBURG UNIVERSITY OF SCIENCE AND TECHNOLOGY

- Computer Science O
- Information Science O
- Project Management M

HARTFORD SEMINARY

- Pastoral Ministry and Counseling M,D,O
- Religion M,D,O
- Theology M,D,O

HARVARD UNIVERSITY

- African Studies D
- African-American Studies D
- Allopathic Medicine P,D
- American Studies D
- Anthropology M,D
- Applied Mathematics M,D
- Applied Physics M,D
- Applied Science and Technology M,O
- Archaeology M,D
- Architectural History D
- Architecture M,D
- Art Education M
- Art History D
- Asian Languages M,D
- Asian Studies M,D
- Astronomy D
- Astrophysics D
- Biochemistry D
- Biological and Biomedical Sciences—General M,D,O*
- Biomedical Engineering M,D*
- Biophysics D*
- Biopsychology D
- Biostatistics M,D
- Biotechnology M,O
- Business Administration and Management—General M,D,O
- Cell Biology D
- Celtic Languages D
- Chemical Physics D
- Chemistry D*
- Chinese D
- Classics D
- Cognitive Sciences M,D
- Communication Disorders D*
- Communication—General M,O
- Comparative Literature D
- Computer Science M,D
- Curriculum and Instruction M
- Demography and Population Studies M,D
- Dentistry P,M,D,O
- Developmental Psychology D
- East European and Russian Studies M
- Economics D
- Education—General M,D*
- Educational Administration M,D
- Educational Measurement and Evaluation D
- Educational Media/Instructional Technology M,O
- Educational Policy M,D
- Educational Psychology M
- Engineering and Applied Sciences—General M,D*
- English M,D,O
- Environmental and Occupational Health M,D
- Environmental Management and Policy M,O
- Epidemiology M,D
- Evolutionary Biology D*
- Experimental Psychology D
- Forestry M
- Foundations and Philosophy of Education M,O
- French M,D
- Genetics D
- Genomic Sciences D
- Geosciences M,D
- German D
- Health Promotion M,D
- Health Services Management and Hospital Administration M,D
- Higher Education D
- History of Science and Technology M,D
- History D
- Human Development M,D
- Immunology D
- Infectious Diseases D
- Information Science M,D,O
- Inorganic Chemistry D
- International Affairs D
- International and Comparative Education M
- International Development M
- International Health M,D
- Italian M,D
- Japanese D
- Jewish Studies M,D
- Journalism M,O
- Landscape Architecture M,D
- Law P,M,D
- Liberal Studies M,O
- Linguistics D
- Management Information Systems D
- Management of Technology D
- Mathematics Education M,O
- Mathematics D
- Medical Informatics M
- Medical Physics D
- Medieval and Renaissance Studies D
- Microbiology D
- Molecular Biology D
- Molecular Genetics D
- Molecular Pharmacology D
- Multilingual and Multicultural Education D
- Museum Studies M,O
- Music M,D
- Near and Middle Eastern Languages M,D
- Near and Middle Eastern Studies M,D
- Neurobiology D
- Neuroscience D*
- Nutrition D
- Oral and Dental Sciences M,D,O
- Organic Chemistry D
- Organizational Behavior D
- Pathology D
- Philosophy M,D
- Physical Chemistry D
- Physics D
- Physiology M,D
- Planetary and Space Sciences M,D
- Political Science M,D
- Portuguese M,D
- Psychology—General D
- Public Administration M
- Public Health—General M,D*
- Public Policy M,D
- Reading Education M
- Religion D
- Russian D
- Scandinavian Languages D
- Science Education M
- Slavic Languages D
- Social Psychology D
- Sociology D
- Spanish M,D
- Statistics M,D
- Structural Biology D
- Systems Biology D*
- Technical Communication M
- Theology P,M,D
- Theoretical Physics D
- Urban and Regional Planning M,D
- Urban Design M
- Urban Education D

Close-Up on page 909.

HASTINGS COLLEGE

- Education—General M

HAWAI'I PACIFIC UNIVERSITY

- Accounting M
- Business Administration and Management—General M*
- Communication—General M*
- Community Health Nursing M

Corporate and Organizational Communication M
Economics M
Electronic Commerce M
English as a Second Language M*
Environmental Sciences M
Family Nurse Practitioner Studies M
Finance and Banking M
Human Resources Management M
International Business M
Management Information Systems M
Marine Sciences M*
Marketing M
Military and Defense Studies M*
Nursing—General M*
Organizational Management M
Political Science M
Secondary Education M*
Social Work M
Sustainable Development M

Close-Up on page 911.

HAWAI'I THEOLOGICAL SEMINARY
Religion P,M
Theology P,M

HEBREW COLLEGE
Early Childhood Education M,O
Education—General M,O
Jewish Studies M,O
Middle School Education M,O
Music Education M,O
Music M,O
Religious Education M,O
Special Education M,O
Theology M

Close-Up on page 913.

HEBREW THEOLOGICAL COLLEGE
Theology O

HEBREW UNION COLLEGE–JEWISH INSTITUTE OF RELIGION (CA)
Education—General M,D,O
Jewish Studies M,D
Religious Education M,D,O
Social Work M,O
Theology P

HEBREW UNION COLLEGE–JEWISH INSTITUTE OF RELIGION (NY)
Education—General M
Jewish Studies M
Music M
Near and Middle Eastern Languages D
Religious Education M
Theology P,D

HEBREW UNION COLLEGE–JEWISH INSTITUTE OF RELIGION (OH)
Jewish Studies P,M,D
Near and Middle Eastern Studies M,D
Religion M,D
Theology P

HEC MONTREAL
Accounting M,O
Applied Economics M
Arts Administration O
Business Administration and Management—General M,D,O
Corporate and Organizational Communication O
Electronic Commerce M,O
Finance and Banking M,O
Financial Engineering M
Human Resources Management M
Industrial and Manufacturing Management M
International Business M
Logistics M
Management Information Systems M
Management Strategy and Policy M
Marketing M
Supply Chain Management O
Sustainable Development O
Taxation M,O

HEIDELBERG COLLEGE
Business Administration and Management—General M
Counseling Psychology M
Education—General M

HENDERSON STATE UNIVERSITY
Business Administration and Management—General M
Counselor Education M
Curriculum and Instruction M,O
Early Childhood Education M,O
Education—General M,O
Educational Administration M,O
English as a Second Language M,O
English Education M,O
Liberal Studies M
Mathematics Education M,O
Middle School Education M,O
Physical Education M
Reading Education M,O
Social Psychology M
Social Sciences Education M,O
Special Education M,O
Sports Management M

HENDRIX COLLEGE
Accounting M

HERITAGE BAPTIST COLLEGE AND HERITAGE THEOLOGICAL SEMINARY
Theology M,O

HERITAGE CHRISTIAN UNIVERSITY
Classics M
Pastoral Ministry and Counseling M
Religion M

HERITAGE UNIVERSITY
Biological and Biomedical Sciences—General M
Counselor Education M
Education—General M
Educational Administration M
English as a Second Language M
English M
Multilingual and Multicultural Education M
Reading Education M
Science Education M
Special Education M

HIGH POINT UNIVERSITY
Business Administration and Management—General M
Educational Administration M
Elementary Education M
Exercise and Sports Science M
History M
Nonprofit Management M
Special Education M

HILLSDALE FREE WILL BAPTIST COLLEGE
Pastoral Ministry and Counseling M

HODGES UNIVERSITY
Business Administration and Management—General M
Criminal Justice and Criminology M
Education—General M
Interdisciplinary Studies M
Law M
Management Information Systems M
Management of Technology M
Psychology—General M
Public Administration M

HOFSTRA UNIVERSITY
Accounting M
Addictions/Substance Abuse Counseling M,O
Applied Mathematics M
Art Education M
Art Therapy M
Art/Fine Arts M,O
Biochemical Engineering M,O
Biological and Biomedical Sciences—General M*
Business Administration and Management—General M,O*
Business Education M
Clinical Psychology M,D
Communication Disorders M,D
Comparative Literature M
Computer Science M
Counseling Psychology M,O
Counselor Education M,O
Early Childhood Education M,O
Education of the Gifted M,O
Education—General M,D,O*
Educational Administration M,D,O
Educational Measurement and Evaluation M
Educational Media/Instructional Technology M
Elementary Education M,O
Engineering Management M
English as a Second Language M,O
English Education M
English M
Film, Television, and Video Production M
Finance and Banking M
Foreign Languages Education M
Foundations and Philosophy of Education M,O
French M
German M
Gerontology M,O
Health Education M
Health Services Management and Hospital Administration M,O
Human Resources Management M,O
Humanities M
Industrial and Organizational Psychology M,D
Interdisciplinary Studies M
International Business M,O
Journalism M
Law P,M
Legal and Justice Studies P,M
Linguistics M
Management Information Systems M
Marketing Research M,O
Marketing M,O
Marriage and Family Therapy M,O
Mathematics Education M
Mathematics M
Middle School Education O
Multilingual and Multicultural Education M,O
Music Education M
Music M
Physical Education M
Psychology—General M,D,O
Quality Management M,O
Quantitative Analysis M
Reading Education M,D,O
Rehabilitation Counseling M,O
Russian M
School Psychology M,D,O
Science Education M,O
Secondary Education M,O
Social Psychology M,D,O
Social Sciences Education M
Spanish M
Special Education M,O
Speech and Interpersonal Communication M*
Taxation M
Writing M

Close-Up on page 915.

HOLLINS UNIVERSITY
Art/Fine Arts M,O
Dance M
Education—General M
English M
Film, Television, and Video Production M
Film, Television, and Video Theory and Criticism M
Humanities M,O
Interdisciplinary Studies M,O
Liberal Studies M,O
Music M,O
Social Sciences M,O
Theater M
Writing M

Close-Up on page 917.

HOLMES INSTITUTE
Pastoral Ministry and Counseling M

HOLY APOSTLES COLLEGE AND SEMINARY
Theology P,M,O

HOLY CROSS GREEK ORTHODOX SCHOOL OF THEOLOGY
Theology P,M

HOLY FAMILY UNIVERSITY
Business Administration and Management—General M
Counseling Psychology M
Education—General M
Elementary Education M
Human Resources Management M
Management Information Systems M
Nursing—General M
Reading Education M
Secondary Education M

HOLY NAMES UNIVERSITY
Business Administration and Management—General M
Community Health Nursing M
Counseling Psychology M,O
Curriculum and Instruction M,O
Education—General M,O
Educational Psychology M,O
English as a Second Language M,O
Family Nurse Practitioner Studies M
Music Education M,O
Music M,O
Nursing—General M
Pastoral Ministry and Counseling M,O
Religion M,O
Special Education M,O
Urban Education M,O

HOOD COLLEGE
Art/Fine Arts M,O
Biological and Biomedical Sciences—General M
Business Administration and Management—General M
Computer Science M
Curriculum and Instruction M,O
Early Childhood Education M,O
Education—General M,O
Educational Administration M,O
Elementary Education M,O
Environmental Biology M
Foreign Languages Education O
Human Development M,O
Humanities M
Information Science M
Mathematics Education M,O
Psychology—General M,O
Reading Education M,O
Science Education M,O
Secondary Education M,O
Special Education M,O
Systems Science M
Thanatology M,O

HOOD THEOLOGICAL SEMINARY
Theology P,M,D

HOPE INTERNATIONAL UNIVERSITY
Counseling Psychology M
Education—General M
International Business M
International Development M
Marriage and Family Therapy M
Music M
Nonprofit Management M
Pastoral Ministry and Counseling M
Psychology—General M

HOUGHTON COLLEGE
Music M

HOUSTON BAPTIST UNIVERSITY
Accounting M
Business Administration and Management—General M
Counseling Psychology M
Counselor Education M
Curriculum and Instruction M
Education—General M
Educational Administration M
Educational Measurement and Evaluation M
English as a Second Language M
Health Services Management and Hospital Administration M
Human Resources Management M
Liberal Studies M
Pastoral Ministry and Counseling M
Psychology—General M
Reading Education M
Theology M

HOUSTON GRADUATE SCHOOL OF THEOLOGY
Pastoral Ministry and Counseling P,M,D
Theology P,M,D

HOWARD UNIVERSITY
Accounting M
African Studies M,D
Allopathic Medicine P,D
Analytical Chemistry M,D
Anatomy M,D

- Applied Arts and Design—General M
- Applied Mathematics M,D
- Art History M
- Art/Fine Arts M
- Atmospheric Sciences M,D
- Biochemistry M,D*
- Biological and Biomedical Sciences—General M,D
- Biophysics D
- Biopsychology M,D
- Biotechnology M,D
- Business Administration and Management—General M
- Chemical Engineering M
- Chemistry M,D
- Civil Engineering M
- Clinical Psychology M,D
- Communication Disorders M,D
- Communication—General M,D
- Computer Science M
- Corporate and Organizational Communication M,D
- Counseling Psychology M,D,O
- Counselor Education M,O
- Dentistry P,O
- Developmental Psychology M,D
- Early Childhood Education M,O
- Economics M,D
- Education—General M,D,O
- Educational Administration M,D,O
- Educational Psychology M,D,O
- Electrical Engineering M,D
- Elementary Education M
- Engineering and Applied Sciences—General M,D
- English M,D
- Environmental Sciences M,D
- Exercise and Sports Science M
- Experimental Psychology M,D
- Family Nurse Practitioner Studies M,O
- Film, Television, and Video Production M
- Finance and Banking M
- French M
- Health Education M
- History M,D
- Human Development M
- Inorganic Chemistry M,D
- International Business M
- Law P,M
- Leisure Studies M
- Management Information Systems M
- Marketing M
- Mass Communication M,D
- Mathematics M,D
- Mechanical Engineering M,D
- Media Studies M,D
- Microbiology D
- Molecular Biology M,D
- Multilingual and Multicultural Education M,D
- Music Education M
- Music M
- Nursing—General M,O
- Nutrition M,D
- Oral and Dental Sciences P,O
- Organic Chemistry M,D
- Pharmacology M,D
- Pharmacy P
- Philosophy M
- Photography M
- Physical Chemistry M,D
- Physical Education M
- Physics M,D
- Physiology D
- Political Science M,D
- Psychology—General M,D
- Public Administration M
- Public Affairs M
- Reading Education M,O
- School Psychology M,D,O
- Secondary Education M,O
- Social Psychology M,D
- Social Work M,D
- Sociology M,D
- Spanish M
- Special Education M,O
- Sports Management M
- Supply Chain Management M
- Theology P,M,D

HULT INTERNATIONAL BUSINESS SCHOOL

- Business Administration and Management—General M

HUMBOLDT STATE UNIVERSITY

- Athletic Training and Sports Medicine M
- Biological and Biomedical Sciences—General M
- Business Administration and Management—General M
- Education—General M
- English M
- Environmental Sciences M
- Exercise and Sports Science M
- Kinesiology and Movement Studies M
- Natural Resources M
- Physical Education M
- Physical Therapy M
- Psychology—General M
- Social Sciences M
- Social Work M
- Sociology M
- Theater M

HUMPHREYS COLLEGE

- Law P

HUNTER COLLEGE OF THE CITY UNIVERSITY OF NEW YORK

- Accounting M
- Adult Nursing M
- Anthropology M
- Applied Mathematics M
- Applied Social Research M
- Art History M
- Art/Fine Arts M
- Biochemistry M
- Biological and Biomedical Sciences—General M,D
- Biopsychology M
- Classics M
- Cognitive Sciences M
- Communication Disorders M
- Community Health Nursing M
- Counselor Education M
- Early Childhood Education M,O
- Economics M
- Education of the Multiply Handicapped M
- Education—General M,O
- Educational Administration O
- Elementary Education M
- English as a Second Language M
- English Education M
- English M
- Environmental and Occupational Health M
- Environmental Sciences M,O
- Family Nurse Practitioner Studies M,O
- Foreign Languages Education M
- French M
- Genetics M
- Geographic Information Systems M,O
- Geography M,O
- Geosciences M,O
- Gerontological Nursing M
- History M
- Italian M
- Maternal and Child/Neonatal Nursing M
- Mathematics Education M
- Mathematics M
- Media Studies M
- Medical/Surgical Nursing M
- Multilingual and Multicultural Education M
- Music Education M
- Music M
- Nursing—General M,O
- Pediatric Nursing M,O
- Physical Therapy M
- Physics M,D
- Psychiatric Nursing M
- Psychology—General M
- Public Health—General M
- Reading Education M,O
- Rehabilitation Counseling M
- Romance Languages M
- Science Education M,O
- Secondary Education M
- Social Psychology M
- Social Sciences Education M
- Social Work M,D
- Spanish M
- Special Education M
- Theater M
- Urban and Regional Planning M
- Urban Studies M
- Writing M

HUNTINGTON COLLEGE OF HEALTH SCIENCES

- Nutrition M

HUNTINGTON UNIVERSITY

- Pastoral Ministry and Counseling M

HURON UNIVERSITY USA IN LONDON

- Advertising and Public Relations M
- Business Administration and Management—General M
- Conflict Resolution and Mediation/Peace Studies M
- Entrepreneurship M
- Finance and Banking M
- International Affairs M
- International Business M
- Marketing M
- National Security M
- Political Science M

HUSSON COLLEGE

- Business Administration and Management—General M
- Family Nurse Practitioner Studies M
- Nursing—General M
- Physical Therapy M
- Psychiatric Nursing M

ICR GRADUATE SCHOOL

- Astrophysics M
- Biological and Biomedical Sciences—General M
- Geology M
- Geophysics M
- Science Education M

IDAHO STATE UNIVERSITY

- Allied Health—General M,D,O
- Anthropology M
- Architecture M
- Art/Fine Arts M
- Biological and Biomedical Sciences—General M,D
- Business Administration and Management—General M,O
- Chemistry M
- Civil Engineering M,D,O
- Clinical Psychology D
- Communication Disorders M,D
- Community Health O
- Counseling Psychology M,D,O
- Counselor Education M,D,O
- Curriculum and Instruction M,O
- Dental Hygiene M,O
- Dentistry M,O
- Education—General M,D,O
- Educational Administration M,D,O
- Educational Media/Instructional Technology M,D,O
- Elementary Education M,O
- Engineering and Applied Sciences—General M,D,O
- English M,D,O
- Environmental Engineering M,D,O
- Environmental Sciences M
- Geographic Information Systems M,O
- Geology M,O
- Geophysics M,O
- Geosciences M,O
- Hazardous Materials Management M
- Health Education M
- History M
- Hydrology M,O
- Interdisciplinary Studies M
- Management Information Systems M,O
- Management of Technology M
- Marriage and Family Therapy M,D,O
- Mathematics Education M,D
- Mathematics M,D
- Mechanical Engineering M,D,O
- Mechanics M,D,O
- Medical Microbiology M,D
- Medicinal and Pharmaceutical Chemistry M,D
- Microbiology M,D
- Nuclear Engineering M,D,O
- Nursing—General M,O
- Nutrition M,O
- Occupational Therapy M
- Operations Research M,D,O
- Oral and Dental Sciences M,O
- Pharmaceutical Administration P,M,D
- Pharmaceutical Sciences M,D
- Pharmacology M,D
- Pharmacy P,M,D
- Physical Education M
- Physical Therapy D
- Physician Assistant Studies M
- Physics M,D
- Political Science M,D
- Psychology—General M,D
- Public Administration M
- Public Health—General M,O
- Reading Education M,O
- School Psychology M,D,O
- Secondary Education M,O
- Sociology M
- Special Education M,D,O
- Speech and Interpersonal Communication M
- Theater M
- Vocational and Technical Education M

ILIFF SCHOOL OF THEOLOGY

- Pastoral Ministry and Counseling P,M,D
- Religion P,M,D
- Theology P,M,D

ILLINOIS COLLEGE OF OPTOMETRY

- Optometry P

ILLINOIS INSTITUTE OF TECHNOLOGY

- Aerospace/Aeronautical Engineering M,D
- Agricultural Engineering M,D
- Analytical Chemistry M,D
- Applied Arts and Design—General M,D*
- Applied Mathematics M,D
- Architectural Engineering M,D
- Architecture M,D
- Bioengineering M,D
- Biological and Biomedical Sciences—General M,D
- Biomedical Engineering D
- Business Administration and Management—General M,D
- Chemical Engineering M,D
- Chemistry M,D
- Civil Engineering M,D
- Clinical Psychology M,D
- Communication—General M,D
- Computer Engineering M,D
- Computer Science M,D*
- Construction Engineering M,D
- Corporate and Organizational Communication M
- Electrical Engineering M,D*
- Engineering and Applied Sciences—General M,D
- Entrepreneurship M
- Environmental and Occupational Health M
- Environmental Engineering M,D
- Environmental Management and Policy M
- Finance and Banking P,M
- Food Science and Technology M
- Geotechnical Engineering M,D
- Health Physics/Radiological Health M,D
- Health Services Management and Hospital Administration M
- Human Resources Development M,D
- Industrial and Manufacturing Management M
- Industrial and Organizational Psychology M,D
- International Business M
- Law P,M
- Management Information Systems M,D
- Management of Technology M
- Management Strategy and Policy M
- Manufacturing Engineering M,D
- Marketing M
- Materials Engineering M,D
- Materials Sciences M,D
- Mathematical and Computational Finance M
- Mathematics Education M,D
- Mechanical Engineering M,D
- Molecular Biology M,D
- Molecular Biophysics M,D
- Nonprofit Management M
- Physics M,D
- Polymer Science and Engineering M,D
- Psychology—General M,D
- Public Administration M
- Quality Management M
- Rehabilitation Counseling M,D
- Science Education M,D
- Software Engineering M,D
- Structural Engineering M,D
- Sustainable Development M
- Taxation P,M
- Technical Writing M,D
- Telecommunications M,D
- Transportation and Highway Engineering M,D

ILLINOIS STATE UNIVERSITY

- Accounting M
- Agricultural Economics and Agribusiness M
- Agricultural Sciences—General M
- Animal Behavior M,D
- Archaeology M
- Art History M
- Art/Fine Arts M
- Bacteriology M,D
- Biochemistry M,D
- Biological and Biomedical Sciences—General M,D*
- Biophysics M,D
- Biotechnology M
- Botany M,D
- Business Administration and Management—General M
- Cell Biology M,D
- Chemistry M

Clinical Psychology M,D,O
Communication Disorders M
Communication—General M
Conservation Biology M,D
Counseling Psychology M,D,O
Counselor Education M,D
Criminal Justice and Criminology M
Curriculum and Instruction M,D
Developmental Biology M,D
Developmental Psychology M,D,O
Ecology M,D
Economics M
Education—General M,D
Educational Administration M,D
Educational Policy M,D
Educational Psychology M,D,O
English M,D
Entomology M,D
Evolutionary Biology M,D
Experimental Psychology M,D,O
Family and Consumer Sciences-General M
French M
Genetics M,D
German M
Graphic Design M
Health Education M
Higher Education M,D
History M
Hydrology M
Immunology M,D
Industrial and Organizational Psychology M,D,O
Industrial/Management Engineering M
Management Information Systems M
Management of Technology M
Mathematics Education D
Mathematics M
Microbiology M,D
Molecular Biology M,D
Molecular Genetics M,D
Music M
Neurobiology M,D
Neuroscience M,D
Nurse Midwifery M,O
Nursing—General M,O
Parasitology M,D
Photography M
Physical Education M
Physiology M,D
Plant Biology M,D
Plant Molecular Biology M,D
Plant Sciences M,D
Political Science M
Psychology—General M,D,O
Reading Education M
School Psychology D,O
Social Work M
Sociology M
Spanish M
Special Education M,D
Structural Biology M,D
Textile Design M
Theater M
Writing M
Zoology M,D

Close-Up on page 919.

IMCA–INTERNATIONAL MANAGEMENT CENTRES ASSOCIATION

Business Administration and Management—General M,D

IMMACULATA UNIVERSITY

Clinical Psychology M,D,O
Counseling Psychology M,D,O
Counselor Education M,D,O
Educational Administration M,D,O
Elementary Education M,D,O
Multilingual and Multicultural Education M
Nursing—General M
Nutrition M
Organizational Management M
Psychology—General M,D,O
School Psychology M,D,O
Secondary Education M,D,O
Special Education M,D,O
Therapies—Dance, Drama, and Music M

Close-Up on page 921.

INDIANA STATE UNIVERSITY

Art/Fine Arts M
Athletic Training and Sports Medicine M,D
Biological and Biomedical Sciences—General M,D*
Business Administration and Management—General M
Child and Family Studies M
Child Development M
Clinical Psychology M,D
Clothing and Textiles M
Communication Disorders M
Communication—General M
Community Health M
Computer Engineering M
Computer Science M
Consumer Economics M
Counseling Psychology M,D
Counselor Education M,D
Criminal Justice and Criminology M
Curriculum and Instruction M,D
Early Childhood Education M
Ecology M,D
Education—General M,D,O
Educational Administration M,D,O
Educational Media/Instructional Technology M,D
Educational Psychology M,D,O
Elementary Education M
Engineering and Applied Sciences—General M,D
English as a Second Language M,O
English M
Environmental and Occupational Health M
Exercise and Sports Science M
Family and Consumer Sciences-General M
French M,O
Geography M,D
Geosciences M,D
Graphic Design M
Health Education M
Health Promotion M
History M
Home Economics Education M
Human Resources Development M
Industrial/Management Engineering M
International Affairs M
Linguistics M,O
Management of Technology D
Marriage and Family Therapy M,D
Mathematics M
Media Studies M
Microbiology M,D
Multilingual and Multicultural Education M,O
Music M
Nursing—General M
Nutrition M
Photography M
Physical Education M
Physiology M,D
Political Science M
Psychology—General M,D
Public Administration M
Reading Education M
School Psychology M,D,O
Science Education M,D
Spanish M,O
Sports Management M
Theater M
Vocational and Technical Education M

Close-Up on page 923.

INDIANA TECH

Accounting M
Business Administration and Management—General M
Human Resources Development M
Human Resources Management M
Marketing M
Science Education M

INDIANA UNIVERSITY BLOOMINGTON

African-American Studies M
Analytical Chemistry M,D
Anthropology M,D
Applied Mathematics M,D
Art Education M,D,O
Art History M,D
Art/Fine Arts M,D
Asian Languages M,D
Asian Studies M,D
Astronomy M,D
Astrophysics M,D
Athletic Training and Sports Medicine M,D,O
Biochemistry M,D
Bioinformatics M,D
Biological and Biomedical Sciences—General M,D*
Business Administration and Management—General M,D
Cell Biology M,D
Chemistry M,D
Child and Family Studies M,D
Chinese M,D
Classics M,D
Cognitive Sciences M,D
Communication Disorders M,D
Communication—General M,D*
Comparative Literature M,D
Computer Art and Design M,D
Computer Science M,D
Counseling Psychology M,D,O
Counselor Education M,D,O
Criminal Justice and Criminology M,D*
Curriculum and Instruction M,D,O
Developmental Psychology M,D
East European and Russian Studies M,O
Ecology M,D
Economics M,D
Education—General M,D,O*
Educational Administration M,D,O
Educational Media/Instructional Technology M,D,O
Educational Policy M,D,O
Educational Psychology M,D,O
Elementary Education M,D,O
English M,D
Environmental Sciences M,D*
Ergonomics and Human Factors M,D,O
Evolutionary Biology M,D
Exercise and Sports Science M,D,O
Folklore M,D
Foreign Languages Education M,D
Foundations and Philosophy of Education M,D,O
French M,D
Genetics M,D
Geochemistry M,D
Geography M,D
Geology M,D
Geophysics M,D
Geosciences M,D
German M,D
Health Education M,D
Health Informatics M,D
Health Promotion M,D
Higher Education M,D,O
History of Science and Technology M,D
History M,D
Human Development M,D
Human-Computer Interaction M,D
Hydrogeology M,D
Information Science M,D,O*
Information Studies M,D,O
Inorganic Chemistry M,D
International and Comparative Education M,D,O
Italian M,D
Japanese M,D
Journalism M,D
Kinesiology and Movement Studies M,D,O
Latin American Studies M
Law P,M,D,O
Leisure Studies M,D,O
Library Science M,D,O*
Linguistics M,D
Mass Communication M,D
Mathematics Education M,D,O
Mathematics M,D
Medieval and Renaissance Studies M,D
Microbiology M,D
Mineralogy M,D
Molecular Biology M,D
Music M,D
Near and Middle Eastern Languages M,D
Nonprofit Management M,D,O
Nutrition M,D
Optometry P,M,D
Philosophy M,D
Physical Chemistry M,D
Physical Education M,D,O
Physics M,D
Plant Biology M,D
Political Science M,D
Portuguese M,D
Psychology—General M,D
Public Administration M,D,O
Public Affairs M,D,O*
Public Health—General M,D
Public Policy D
Reading Education M,D,O
Recreation and Park Management M,D,O
Religion M,D
Safety Engineering M,D
School Psychology M,D,O
Science Education M,D,O
Secondary Education M,D,O
Slavic Languages M,D
Social Psychology M,D
Social Sciences Education M,D,O
Social Sciences P,M,D,O
Sociology M,D
Spanish M,D
Special Education M,D,O
Speech and Interpersonal Communication M,D
Sports Management M,D,O
Statistics M,D
Telecommunications M
Theater M,D
Western European Studies M
Writing M,D
Zoology M,D

INDIANA UNIVERSITY KOKOMO

Business Administration and Management—General M
Education—General M
Elementary Education M
Liberal Studies M
Public Administration O
Secondary Education M

INDIANA UNIVERSITY NORTHWEST

Accounting M,O
Business Administration and Management—General M,O
Criminal Justice and Criminology M,O
Education—General M
Elementary Education M
Environmental Sciences M,O
Health Services Management and Hospital Administration M,O
Human Services M,O
Nonprofit Management M,O
Public Administration M,O
Public Affairs M,O
Secondary Education M
Social Work M

INDIANA UNIVERSITY OF PENNSYLVANIA

Adult Education M
Applied Mathematics M
Art/Fine Arts M
Biological and Biomedical Sciences—General M
Business Administration and Management—General M
Chemistry M
Clinical Psychology D
Communication Disorders M
Counselor Education M
Criminal Justice and Criminology M,D
Curriculum and Instruction M,D
Early Childhood Education M
Education—General M,D,O
Educational Administration M,D,O
Educational Media/Instructional Technology M
Educational Psychology M,O
English as a Second Language M,D
English Education M,D
English M,D
Environmental and Occupational Health M
Exercise and Sports Science M
Facilities Management M
Geography M
Health Education M
Higher Education M
History M
Human Resources Development M
Industrial and Labor Relations M
Linguistics M,D
Mathematics Education M
Mathematics M
Music Education M
Music M
Nursing—General M
Nutrition M
Physical Education M
Physics M
Political Science M
Psychology—General M,D
Public Affairs M
Reading Education M
Rhetoric M,D
School Psychology D,O
Sociology M
Special Education M
Sports Management M
Writing M,D

Close-Up on page 925.

INDIANA UNIVERSITY–PURDUE UNIVERSITY FORT WAYNE

Applied Mathematics M,O
Applied Statistics M,O
Biological and Biomedical Sciences—General M
Business Administration and Management—General M
Communication—General M
Computer Science M
Counselor Education M
Education—General M
Educational Administration M
Elementary Education M
Engineering and Applied Sciences—General M
English as a Second Language M,O
English Education M,O
English M,O
Liberal Studies M
Mathematics M,O

Nursing and Healthcare Administration M,O
Nursing—General M,O
Operations Research M,O
Organizational Management M
Public Affairs M,O
Secondary Education M
Sociology M

INDIANA UNIVERSITY–PURDUE UNIVERSITY INDIANAPOLIS

Acute Care/Critical Care Nursing M
Anatomy M,D
Applied Arts and Design—General M
Applied Mathematics M,D
Applied Statistics M
Art Education M
Art/Fine Arts M
Artificial Intelligence/Robotics M,D
Biochemistry D
Bioethics M,D,O
Biological and Biomedical Sciences—General M,D
Biomedical Engineering M,D,O
Biopsychology M,D
Business Administration and Management—General M
Cell Biology M,D
Chemistry M,D
Clinical Psychology M,D
Community Health Nursing M,D
Computer Engineering M,D
Computer Science M,D
Criminal Justice and Criminology M
Dentistry P,M,D,O
Economics M
Education—General M,O
Electrical Engineering M,D
English Education M
English M
Environmental Management and Policy M
Geology M
Health Education M,D
Health Services Management and Hospital Administration M
History M
Immunology M,D
Industrial and Organizational Psychology M,D
Information Science M,D
Internet and Interactive Multimedia M,D
Law P,M,D
Liberal Studies M,D,O
Library Science M
Maternal and Child/Neonatal Nursing M,D
Mathematics Education M
Mechanical Engineering M,D,O*
Microbiology M,D*
Molecular Biology D
Molecular Genetics M,D*
Music M
Nonprofit Management M
Nursing—General M,D
Nutrition M,D
Occupational Therapy M,D
Pathology M,D
Pediatric Nursing M,D
Pharmacology M,D
Philosophy M,D,O
Physical Education M
Physical Therapy M,D
Physics M,D
Political Science M,O
Psychiatric Nursing M,D
Psychology—General M,D
Public Administration M,D
Public Affairs M*
Public Health—General M
Public History M
Public Policy M
Rehabilitation Counseling M,D
Rehabilitation Sciences M,D
Social Work M,D,O
Sociology M
Toxicology M,D
Travel and Tourism M
Women's Health Nursing M,D

INDIANA UNIVERSITY SCHOOL OF LAW-BLOOMINGTON

Law P,M,D,O
Legal and Justice Studies P,M,D,O

INDIANA UNIVERSITY SCHOOL OF LAW-INDIANAPOLIS

Fire Protection Engineering P,M
Law P,M

INDIANA UNIVERSITY SOUTH BEND

Accounting M
Applied Mathematics M
Business Administration and Management—General M
Computer Science M
Counselor Education M
Education—General M
Elementary Education M
English M
Health Services Management and Hospital Administration M,O
Liberal Studies M
Management Information Systems M
Music M,O
Nonprofit Management M,O
Public Administration M,O
Public Affairs M,O
Secondary Education M
Social Work M
Special Education M

INDIANA UNIVERSITY SOUTHEAST

Accounting M,O
Business Administration and Management—General M,O
Counselor Education M
Economics M,O
Education—General M
Elementary Education M
Finance and Banking M,O
Industrial and Manufacturing Management M,O
Liberal Studies M
Management Information Systems M,O
Marketing M,O
Secondary Education M

INDIANA WESLEYAN UNIVERSITY

Accounting M
Business Administration and Management—General M
Community Health Nursing M,O
Counseling Psychology M
Counselor Education M
Curriculum and Instruction M
Education—General M
Health Services Management and Hospital Administration M
Marriage and Family Therapy M
Nursing and Healthcare Administration M,O
Nursing Education M,O
Nursing—General M,O
Organizational Management D
Religious Education M
Social Psychology M
Theology M

INSTITUTE FOR CHRISTIAN STUDIES

Education—General M,D
Philosophy M,D
Political Science M,D
Theology M,D

INSTITUTE FOR CLINICAL SOCIAL WORK

Social Work D

INSTITUTE OF CLINICAL ACUPUNCTURE AND ORIENTAL MEDICINE

Acupuncture and Oriental Medicine M

INSTITUTE OF PUBLIC ADMINISTRATION

Health Services Management and Hospital Administration M,O
Public Administration M,O

INSTITUTE OF TRANSPERSONAL PSYCHOLOGY

Clinical Psychology M,D
Counseling Psychology M,D
Psychology—General M,D,O
Transpersonal and Humanistic Psychology M,D,O*

THE INSTITUTE OF WORLD POLITICS

Military and Defense Studies M,O
National Security M,O
Political Science M,O*
Public Affairs M,O
Public Policy M,O

INSTITUT FRANCO-EUROPÉEN DE CHIROPRATIQUE

Chiropractic P

INSTITUTO CENTROAMERICANO DE ADMINISTRACIÓN DE EMPRESAS

Agricultural Economics and Agribusiness M
Business Administration and Management—General M
Economics M
Sustainable Development M

INSTITUTO TECNOLOGICO DE SANTO DOMINGO

Allopathic Medicine P,M
Business Administration and Management—General M
Education—General M
Engineering and Applied Sciences—General M
Environmental Engineering M
Environmental Sciences M
Finance and Banking M
Human Resources Management M
Industrial/Management Engineering M
Psychology—General M
Social Sciences Education M
Structural Engineering M
Telecommunications M

INSTITUTO TECNOLÓGICO Y DE ESTUDIOS SUPERIORES DE MONTERREY, CAMPUS CENTRAL DE VERACRUZ

Business Administration and Management—General M
Computer Science M
Education—General M
Educational Administration M
Educational Media/Instructional Technology M
Electronic Commerce M
Finance and Banking M
Humanities M
International Business M
Management Information Systems M
Management of Technology M
Marketing M

INSTITUTO TECNOLÓGICO Y DE ESTUDIOS SUPERIORES DE MONTERREY, CAMPUS CHIHUAHUA

Computer Engineering M,O
Electrical Engineering M,O
Engineering Management M,O
Industrial/Management Engineering M,O
International Business M,O
Mechanical Engineering M,O
Systems Engineering M,O

INSTITUTO TECNOLÓGICO Y DE ESTUDIOS SUPERIORES DE MONTERREY, CAMPUS CIUDAD DE MÉXICO

Business Administration and Management—General M,D
Computer Science M,D
Economics M,D
Education—General M,D
Educational Media/Instructional Technology M,D
Environmental Engineering M,D
Environmental Sciences M,D
Finance and Banking M,D
Humanities M,D
Industrial/Management Engineering M,D
International Business M,D
Law P
Management Information Systems M,D
Quality Management M,D
Telecommunications Management M

INSTITUTO TECNOLÓGICO Y DE ESTUDIOS SUPERIORES DE MONTERREY, CAMPUS CIUDAD JUÁREZ

Business Administration and Management—General M
Education—General M
Finance and Banking M
Industrial/Management Engineering M
Management Information Systems M
Quality Management M
Telecommunications M

INSTITUTO TECNOLÓGICO Y DE ESTUDIOS SUPERIORES DE MONTERREY, CAMPUS CIUDAD OBREGÓN

Business Administration and Management—General M
Communication—General M
Developmental Education M
Education—General M
Engineering and Applied Sciences—General M
Finance and Banking M
International Affairs M
Management Information Systems M
Marketing M
Mathematics Education M
Telecommunications Management M

INSTITUTO TECNOLÓGICO Y DE ESTUDIOS SUPERIORES DE MONTERREY, CAMPUS CUERNAVACA

Business Administration and Management—General M
Computer Science M,D
Finance and Banking M
Human Resources Management M
Information Science M,D
International Business M
Management of Technology M,D
Marketing M

INSTITUTO TECNOLÓGICO Y DE ESTUDIOS SUPERIORES DE MONTERREY, CAMPUS ESTADO DE MÉXICO

Architecture M,D
Business Administration and Management—General M,D
Computer Science M,D
Education—General M,D
Educational Administration M,D
Educational Media/Instructional Technology M,D
Electronic Commerce M,D
Environmental Management and Policy M,D
Finance and Banking M,D
Humanities M,D
Industrial and Manufacturing Management M,D
Information Science M,D
Management Information Systems M,D
Marketing M,D
Materials Engineering M,D
Materials Sciences M,D
Quality Management M,D
Telecommunications Management M,D

INSTITUTO TECNOLÓGICO Y DE ESTUDIOS SUPERIORES DE MONTERREY, CAMPUS GUADALAJARA

Business Administration and Management—General M
Finance and Banking M

INSTITUTO TECNOLÓGICO Y DE ESTUDIOS SUPERIORES DE MONTERREY, CAMPUS IRAPUATO

Architecture M,D
Business Administration and Management—General M,D
Computer Science M,D
Education—General M,D
Educational Administration M,D
Educational Media/Instructional Technology M,D
Electronic Commerce M,D
Environmental Management and Policy M,D
Finance and Banking M,D
Humanities M,D
Industrial and Manufacturing Management M,D
Information Science M,D
International Business M,D
Library Science M,D
Management Information Systems M,D
Management of Technology M,D
Marketing Research M,D
Quality Management M,D
Telecommunications Management M

INSTITUTO TECNOLÓGICO Y DE ESTUDIOS SUPERIORES DE MONTERREY, CAMPUS LAGUNA

Business Administration and Management—General M
Industrial/Management Engineering M
Management Information Systems M

INSTITUTO TECNOLÓGICO Y DE ESTUDIOS SUPERIORES DE MONTERREY, CAMPUS LEÓN

Business Administration and Management—General M

INSTITUTO TECNOLÓGICO Y DE ESTUDIOS SUPERIORES DE MONTERREY, CAMPUS MONTERREY

Agricultural Engineering M,D

- Agricultural Sciences—General M,D
- Applied Statistics M,D
- Artificial Intelligence/Robotics M,D
- Biotechnology M,D
- Business Administration and Management—General M,D
- Chemical Engineering M,D
- Chemistry M,D
- Civil Engineering M,D
- Communication—General M,D
- Computer Science M,D
- Electrical Engineering M,D
- Engineering and Applied Sciences—General M,D
- Environmental Engineering M,D
- Finance and Banking M
- Industrial/Management Engineering M,D
- Information Science M,D
- International Business M
- Manufacturing Engineering M,D
- Marketing M
- Mechanical Engineering M,D
- Organic Chemistry M,D
- Science Education M,D
- Systems Engineering M,D

INSTITUTO TECNOLÓGICO Y DE ESTUDIOS SUPERIORES DE MONTERREY, CAMPUS QUERÉTARO

- Business Administration and Management—General M

INSTITUTO TECNOLÓGICO Y DE ESTUDIOS SUPERIORES DE MONTERREY, CAMPUS SONORA NORTE

- Business Administration and Management—General M
- Education—General M
- Information Science M

INSTITUTO TECNOLÓGICO Y DE ESTUDIOS SUPERIORES DE MONTERREY, CAMPUS TOLUCA

- Business Administration and Management—General M

INTER AMERICAN UNIVERSITY OF PUERTO RICO, AGUADILLA CAMPUS

- Criminal Justice and Criminology M
- Educational Administration M
- Elementary Education M

INTER AMERICAN UNIVERSITY OF PUERTO RICO, ARECIBO CAMPUS

- Community Health Nursing M
- Counselor Education M
- Education—General M
- Educational Administration M
- Nurse Anesthesia M
- Nursing—General M

INTER AMERICAN UNIVERSITY OF PUERTO RICO, BARRANQUITAS CAMPUS

- Education—General M
- Educational Administration M
- Elementary Education M

INTER AMERICAN UNIVERSITY OF PUERTO RICO, BAYAMÓN CAMPUS

- Electronic Commerce M
- Human Resources Management M

INTER AMERICAN UNIVERSITY OF PUERTO RICO, GUAYAMA CAMPUS

- Early Childhood Education M

INTER AMERICAN UNIVERSITY OF PUERTO RICO, METROPOLITAN CAMPUS

- Accounting M
- Business Administration and Management—General M,D
- Business Education M
- Clinical Laboratory Sciences/ Medical Technology M
- Computer Science M
- Counselor Education M
- Criminal Justice and Criminology M
- Education—General M,D
- Educational Administration M
- Educational Media/Instructional Technology M
- Elementary Education M
- English as a Second Language M
- Finance and Banking M
- Health Education M
- Higher Education M
- Human Resources Development M
- Human Resources Management M
- Industrial and Labor Relations M
- Industrial and Manufacturing Management M
- Marketing M
- Physical Education M
- Psychology—General M
- Science Education M
- Social Work M
- Spanish M
- Special Education M
- Theology D
- Vocational and Technical Education M

INTER AMERICAN UNIVERSITY OF PUERTO RICO, PONCE CAMPUS

- Accounting M
- Criminal Justice and Criminology M
- Elementary Education M
- English as a Second Language M
- Finance and Banking M
- Human Resources Management M
- International Business M
- Mathematics Education M
- Science Education M
- Social Sciences Education M
- Spanish M

INTER AMERICAN UNIVERSITY OF PUERTO RICO, SAN GERMÁN CAMPUS

- Accounting M,D
- Applied Mathematics M
- Art/Fine Arts M
- Business Administration and Management—General M,D
- Business Education M
- Counseling Psychology M,D
- Counselor Education M
- Educational Administration M
- Elementary Education M
- English as a Second Language M
- Entrepreneurship D
- Environmental Sciences M
- Finance and Banking M,D
- Human Resources Development M,D
- Human Resources Management M,D
- Industrial and Labor Relations M,D
- International Business M,D
- Kinesiology and Movement Studies M
- Library Science M
- Management Information Systems M,D
- Marketing M,D
- Music Education M
- Photography M
- Physical Education M
- Psychology—General M,D
- School Psychology M,D
- Science Education M
- Special Education M

INTER AMERICAN UNIVERSITY OF PUERTO RICO SCHOOL OF LAW

- Law P

INTER AMERICAN UNIVERSITY OF PUERTO RICO SCHOOL OF OPTOMETRY

- Optometry P

INTERDENOMINATIONAL THEOLOGICAL CENTER

- Theology P,M,D

INTERNATIONAL BAPTIST COLLEGE

- Pastoral Ministry and Counseling M,D
- Theology M

INTERNATIONAL COLLEGE OF THE CAYMAN ISLANDS

- Business Administration and Management—General M
- Business Education M
- Human Resources Management M

INTERNATIONAL TECHNOLOGICAL UNIVERSITY

- Business Administration and Management—General M
- Computer Engineering M
- Electrical Engineering M
- Software Engineering M

INTERNATIONAL UNIVERSITY IN GENEVA

- Business Administration and Management—General M
- Communication—General M
- Electronic Commerce M
- Human Resources Management M
- International Business M
- Marketing M
- Media Studies M
- Organizational Management M
- Telecommunications M

THE INTERNATIONAL UNIVERSITY OF MONACO

- Business Administration and Management—General M
- Entrepreneurship M
- Finance and Banking M
- Financial Engineering M
- International Business M
- Marketing M

IONA COLLEGE

- Advertising and Public Relations M
- Business Administration and Management—General M,O*
- Computer Science M
- Counseling Psychology M
- Criminal Justice and Criminology M
- Educational Administration M
- Educational Media/Instructional Technology M,O
- Elementary Education M
- English Education M
- English M
- Experimental Psychology M
- Finance and Banking M,O
- Foreign Languages Education M
- Health Services Management and Hospital Administration M,O
- History M
- Human Resources Management M,O
- Industrial and Organizational Psychology M
- International Business M,O
- Journalism M
- Management of Technology M,O
- Marketing M,O
- Marriage and Family Therapy M,O
- Mass Communication M
- Mathematics Education M
- Multilingual and Multicultural Education M
- Pastoral Ministry and Counseling M,O
- Psychology—General M
- School Psychology M
- Science Education M
- Secondary Education M
- Social Sciences Education M
- Spanish M
- Telecommunications M,O

Close-Up on page 927.

IOWA STATE UNIVERSITY OF SCIENCE AND TECHNOLOGY

- Accounting M
- Aerospace/Aeronautical Engineering M,D
- Agricultural Economics and Agribusiness M,D
- Agricultural Education M,D
- Agricultural Engineering M,D
- Agricultural Sciences—General M,D
- Agronomy and Soil Sciences M,D
- Animal Sciences M,D
- Anthropology M
- Applied Arts and Design—General M
- Applied Mathematics M,D
- Applied Physics M,D
- Architecture M
- Art Education M
- Astronomy M,D
- Astrophysics M,D
- Biochemistry M,D*
- Bioengineering M,D
- Bioinformatics D*
- Biological and Biomedical Sciences—General M,D
- Biophysics M,D
- Biostatistics D
- Biosystems Engineering M,D
- Business Administration and Management—General M
- Cell Biology M,D
- Chemical Engineering M,D
- Chemistry M,D
- Child and Family Studies M,D
- Civil Engineering M,D
- Clothing and Textiles M,D
- Cognitive Sciences M,D
- Computational Biology D
- Computer Engineering M,D
- Computer Science M,D*
- Condensed Matter Physics M,D
- Construction Engineering M,D
- Consumer Economics M,D
- Corporate and Organizational Communication M,D
- Counseling Psychology M,D
- Counselor Education M,D
- Curriculum and Instruction M,D
- Developmental Biology M,D
- Ecology M,D
- Economics M,D
- Educational Administration M,D
- Educational Measurement and Evaluation M,D
- Educational Media/Instructional Technology M,D
- Electrical Engineering M,D
- Elementary Education M,D
- Engineering and Applied Sciences—General M,D
- English M,D
- Entomology M,D
- Environmental Engineering M,D
- Environmental Management and Policy M,D
- Environmental Sciences M,D
- Evolutionary Biology M,D
- Exercise and Sports Science M,D
- Family and Consumer Sciences-General M
- Fish, Game, and Wildlife Management M,D
- Food Science and Technology M,D
- Forestry M,D
- Foundations and Philosophy of Education M,D
- Genetics M,D*
- Geology M,D
- Geosciences M,D
- Geotechnical Engineering M,D
- Graphic Design M
- Health Education M,D
- Higher Education M,D
- History of Science and Technology M,D
- History M,D
- Home Economics Education M,D
- Horticulture M,D
- Hospitality Management M,D
- Human Development M,D
- Human Resources Development M,D
- Human-Computer Interaction M,D
- Immunology M,D
- Industrial/Management Engineering M,D
- Information Science M
- Interdisciplinary Studies M
- Interior Design M
- Journalism M
- Landscape Architecture M
- Management Information Systems M
- Marriage and Family Therapy M,D
- Mass Communication M
- Materials Engineering M,D
- Materials Sciences M,D
- Mathematics Education M,D
- Mathematics M,D
- Mechanical Engineering M,D
- Mechanics M,D
- Meteorology M,D
- Microbiology M,D
- Molecular Biology M,D
- Natural Resources M,D
- Neuroscience M,D
- Nutrition M,D
- Operations Research M,D
- Pathology M,D
- Physical Education M,D
- Physics M,D
- Plant Pathology M,D
- Plant Physiology M,D
- Political Science M
- Psychology—General M,D
- Public Administration M
- Rhetoric M,D
- Rural Planning and Studies M,D
- Rural Sociology M,D
- Social Psychology M,D
- Sociology M,D
- Special Education M,D
- Statistics M,D
- Structural Biology D
- Structural Engineering M,D
- Sustainable Development M,D
- Systems Engineering M
- Toxicology M,D
- Transportation and Highway Engineering M,D
- Transportation Management M
- Urban and Regional Planning M
- Veterinary Medicine P,M
- Veterinary Sciences M,D
- Vocational and Technical Education M,D

Water Resources M,D
Close-Up on page 929.

ITHACA COLLEGE
Accounting M
Allied Health—General M,D
Business Administration and Management—General M
Communication Disorders M
Communication—General M
English Education M
Exercise and Sports Science M
Foreign Languages Education M
Health Education M
Mathematics Education M
Music Education M
Music M
Occupational Therapy M
Physical Education M
Physical Therapy D
Science Education M
Secondary Education M
Social Sciences Education M
Sports Management M
Close-Up on page 931.

ITT TECHNICAL INSTITUTE (IN)
Business Administration and Management—General M

JACKSON STATE UNIVERSITY
Accounting M
Biological and Biomedical Sciences—General M,D
Business Administration and Management—General M,D
Chemistry M,D
Clinical Psychology D
Communication Disorders M
Computer Science M
Counselor Education M,O
Criminal Justice and Criminology M
Early Childhood Education M,D,O
Education—General M,D,O
Educational Administration M,D,O
Educational Media/Instructional Technology M,D,O
Elementary Education M,D,O
English Education M
English M
Environmental Sciences M,D
Health Education M
History M
Mass Communication M
Materials Sciences M
Mathematics Education M
Mathematics M
Music Education M
Physical Education M
Political Science M
Psychology—General D
Public Administration M,D
Public Affairs M
Public Policy M,D
Rehabilitation Counseling M,O
Science Education M,D
Secondary Education M,D,O
Social Work M,D
Sociology M
Special Education M,O
Urban and Regional Planning M
Vocational and Technical Education M

JACKSONVILLE STATE UNIVERSITY
Biological and Biomedical Sciences—General M
Business Administration and Management—General M
Computer Science M
Counselor Education M
Criminal Justice and Criminology M
Early Childhood Education M
Education—General M,O
Educational Administration M,O
Educational Media/Instructional Technology M
Elementary Education M
Emergency Management M
English M
Health Education M
History M
Liberal Studies M
Mathematics M
Music M
Nursing—General M
Physical Education M
Political Science M
Psychology—General M
Reading Education M
Secondary Education M
Software Engineering M
Special Education M

JACKSONVILLE UNIVERSITY
Business Administration and Management—General M
Computer Education M
Early Childhood Education M,O
Education—General M,O
Educational Media/Instructional Technology M
Elementary Education M
Mathematics Education M
Music Education M
Nursing—General M
Oral and Dental Sciences O
Reading Education M

JAMES MADISON UNIVERSITY
Accounting M
Applied Science and Technology M
Art Education M
Art History M
Art/Fine Arts M
Biological and Biomedical Sciences—General M
Business Administration and Management—General M
Clinical Psychology D
Communication Disorders M,D
Computer Science M
Counseling Psychology M,O
Early Childhood Education M
Educational Administration M
English M
Health Education M
History M
Kinesiology and Movement Studies M
Mathematics M
Middle School Education M
Music Education M
Music M
Nursing—General M
Occupational Therapy M
Photography M
Physician Assistant Studies M
Psychology—General M,D,O
Public Administration M
Reading Education M
School Psychology M,D,O
Secondary Education M
Special Education M
Statistics M
Technical Writing M
Textile Design M
Vocational and Technical Education M

JEFFERSON COLLEGE OF HEALTH SCIENCES
Nursing and Healthcare Administration M
Nursing Education M
Nursing—General M

JESUIT SCHOOL OF THEOLOGY AT BERKELEY
Theology P,M,D,O

THE JEWISH THEOLOGICAL SEMINARY
Jewish Studies M,D
Music M
Religion M,D*
Religious Education M,D*
Theology M,D,O

JEWISH UNIVERSITY OF AMERICA
Jewish Studies P,D
Pastoral Ministry and Counseling M,D
Religious Education M,D

JOHN BROWN UNIVERSITY
Business Administration and Management—General M
Counselor Education M
Marriage and Family Therapy M
Pastoral Ministry and Counseling M

JOHN CARROLL UNIVERSITY
Accounting M
Biological and Biomedical Sciences—General M
Business Administration and Management—General M
Corporate and Organizational Communication M
Counseling Psychology M,O
Counselor Education M,O
Early Childhood Education M
Education—General M
Educational Administration M
Educational Psychology M
English M
History M
Humanities M
Mathematics M
Middle School Education M
Nonprofit Management M
Religion M
Science Education M
Secondary Education M

JOHN F. KENNEDY UNIVERSITY
Art/Fine Arts M
Business Administration and Management—General M,O
Comparative and Interdisciplinary Arts M
Counseling Psychology M
Education—General M
Health Education M
Human Resources Development M,O
Industrial and Organizational Psychology M,O
Interdisciplinary Studies M
Law P
Museum Studies M,O
Organizational Management M,O
Psychology—General M,D,O
Sport Psychology M

JOHN JAY COLLEGE OF CRIMINAL JUSTICE OF THE CITY UNIVERSITY OF NEW YORK
Criminal Justice and Criminology M,D
Forensic Psychology M,D
Forensic Sciences M,D
Legal and Justice Studies M,D
Organizational Behavior M,D
Public Administration M
Public Policy M,D

JOHN MARSHALL LAW SCHOOL
International Business P,M
Law P,M
Legal and Justice Studies P,M
Management Information Systems P,M
Real Estate P,M
Taxation P,M

THE JOHNS HOPKINS UNIVERSITY
Acute Care/Critical Care Nursing M,O
Addictions/Substance Abuse Counseling M,D,O
Adult Nursing M,O
African Studies M,D,O
Allopathic Medicine P
Anatomy D
Anthropology D
Applied Economics M
Applied Mathematics M,D
Applied Physics M
Art History M,D
Asian Studies M,D,O
Astronomy D
Biochemistry M,D
Bioengineering M,D
Bioinformatics M,D,O
Biological and Biomedical Sciences—General M,D
Biomedical Engineering M,D
Biophysics M,D
Biostatistics M,D
Biotechnology M
Business Administration and Management—General M,O
Canadian Studies M,D,O
Cell Biology D
Chemical Engineering M,D
Chemistry D
Civil Engineering M,D
Classics D
Clinical Psychology M,D
Clinical Research M,D
Cognitive Sciences D
Communication—General M
Community Health Nursing M
Community Health M,D
Comparative Literature D
Computer and Information Systems Security M
Computer Engineering M,D
Computer Science M,D*
Conflict Resolution and Mediation/Peace Studies M,D,O
Counselor Education M,O
Criminal Justice and Criminology M,O
Curriculum and Instruction M
Demography and Population Studies M,D
Developmental Biology D
East European and Russian Studies M,D,O
Economics D
Education of the Gifted M,D,O
Education—General M,D,O
Educational Administration M,D,O
Educational Media/Instructional Technology M,D,O
Electrical Engineering M,D*
Elementary Education M
Engineering and Applied Sciences—General M,D,O*
English as a Second Language M
English D
Environmental and Occupational Health M,D
Environmental Engineering M,D,O
Environmental Management and Policy M
Environmental Sciences M
Epidemiology M,D
Evolutionary Biology D
Family Nurse Practitioner Studies M,O
Finance and Banking M,O
French D
Genetic Counseling M,D
Genetics M,D
Geography M,D
Geosciences M,D
German D
Health Education M,D
Health Informatics M
Health Services Management and Hospital Administration M,D,O
Health Services Research M,D
History of Science and Technology M,D
History D
Homeland Security M,O
Human Genetics D
Human Resources Development M,O
Immunology M,D*
Infectious Diseases M,D
International Affairs M,D,O
International Development M,D,O
International Health M,D
Investment Management M,O
Italian D
Latin American Studies M,D,O
Law M,D,O
Liberal Studies M,O
Management Information Systems M,O
Management of Technology M,O
Marketing M
Materials Engineering M,D
Materials Sciences M,D
Mathematics D*
Mechanical Engineering M,D
Medical Illustration M
Microbiology M,D
Molecular Biology M,D
Molecular Medicine D
Music M,D,O
Near and Middle Eastern Studies M,D,O
Neuroscience D
Nursing and Healthcare Administration M
Nursing—General M,D,O
Nutrition M,D
Operations Research M,D
Pastoral Ministry and Counseling M,O
Pathobiology D
Pathology D
Pediatric Nursing M,O
Pharmacology D*
Philosophy M,D
Physics D*
Physiology M,D
Political Science M,D,O
Psychology—General D
Public Health—General M,D*
Public Policy M*
Reading Education M,D,O
Real Estate M
Romance Languages D
Science Education M,D,O
Secondary Education M
Social Sciences M,D
Sociology D
Spanish D
Special Education M,D,O
Statistics M,D
Systems Engineering M,O
Technical Writing M
Telecommunications M
Toxicology M,D
Urban Education M,D,O
Western European Studies M,D,O
Writing M
Close-Up on page 933.

JOHNSON & WALES UNIVERSITY
Accounting M
Education—General M
Educational Administration D
Finance and Banking M,O
Hospitality Management M,O
Human Resources Development O

International Business M
Marketing M
Organizational Management M

Close-Up on page 935.

JOHNSON BIBLE COLLEGE
Education—General M
Educational Media/Instructional Technology M
Marriage and Family Therapy M
Theology M

JOHNSON STATE COLLEGE
Art/Fine Arts M
Counselor Education M
Curriculum and Instruction M
Education of the Gifted M
Education—General M,O
Educational Psychology M
Reading Education M
Science Education M
Secondary Education M,O
Special Education M

JOINT MILITARY INTELLIGENCE COLLEGE
Military and Defense Studies M,O

JONES INTERNATIONAL UNIVERSITY
Accounting M
Adult Education M
Business Administration and Management—General M
Computer and Information Systems Security M
Conflict Resolution and Mediation/Peace Studies M
Corporate and Organizational Communication M
Curriculum and Instruction M
Distance Education Development M
Education—General M
Educational Administration M
Educational Media/Instructional Technology M
Elementary Education M
Entrepreneurship M
Finance and Banking M
Health Services Management and Hospital Administration M
Higher Education M
Management of Technology M
Organizational Management M
Project Management M
Secondary Education M

THE JUDGE ADVOCATE GENERAL'S SCHOOL, U.S. ARMY
Law M
Military and Defense Studies M

THE JUILLIARD SCHOOL
Music M,D,O

KANSAS CITY UNIVERSITY OF MEDICINE AND BIOSCIENCES
Bioethics M
Biological and Biomedical Sciences—General M
Osteopathic Medicine P

KANSAS STATE UNIVERSITY
Accounting M
Adult Education M,D
Agricultural Economics and Agribusiness M,D
Agricultural Engineering M,D
Agricultural Sciences—General M,D
Agronomy and Soil Sciences M,D
Analytical Chemistry M,D
Anatomy M,D
Animal Sciences M,D
Architectural Engineering M
Architecture M
Art/Fine Arts M
Biochemistry M,D
Bioengineering M,D
Biological and Biomedical Sciences—General M,D
Business Administration and Management—General M
Chemical Engineering M,D
Chemistry M,D
Child and Family Studies M,D
Civil Engineering M,D
Clothing and Textiles M,D
Computer Engineering M,D
Computer Science M,D
Counselor Education M,D
Curriculum and Instruction M,D
Economics M,D
Education—General M,D
Educational Administration M,D
Educational Psychology M,D
Electrical Engineering M,D
Elementary Education M,D
Engineering and Applied Sciences—General M,D*
Engineering Management M,D
English M
Entomology M,D
Environmental Management and Policy M
Family and Consumer Sciences-General M,D
Food Science and Technology M,D
French M
Genetics M,D
Geography M,D
Geology M
German M
History M,D
Horticulture M,D
Hospitality Management M,D
Human Development D
Human Services M
Industrial/Management Engineering M,D
Information Science M,D
Inorganic Chemistry M,D
International Affairs M
Kinesiology and Movement Studies M
Landscape Architecture M
Manufacturing Engineering M,D
Marriage and Family Therapy D
Mass Communication M
Mathematics M,D
Mechanical Engineering M,D
Microbiology D
Music Education M
Music M
Nuclear Engineering M,D
Nutrition M,D
Operations Research M,D
Organic Chemistry M,D
Pathobiology M,D
Physical Chemistry M,D
Physics M,D
Physiology M,D
Plant Pathology M,D
Political Science M
Psychology—General M,D
Public Administration M
Public Health—General M
Range Science M,D
Rhetoric M
Secondary Education M,D
Sociology M,D
Software Engineering M,D
Spanish M
Special Education M,D
Speech and Interpersonal Communication M
Statistics M,D
Student Affairs M,D
Theater M
Urban and Regional Planning M
Veterinary Medicine P
Veterinary Sciences M

Close-Up on page 937.

KANSAS WESLEYAN UNIVERSITY
Business Administration and Management—General M

KEAN UNIVERSITY
Accounting M
Addictions/Substance Abuse Counseling M,O
Adult Education M
Art Education M
Art/Fine Arts M
Biotechnology M
Business Administration and Management—General M
Communication Disorders M
Communication—General M
Community Health Nursing M
Computational Sciences M
Computer Education M
Counseling Psychology M
Counselor Education M,O
Criminal Justice and Criminology M
Curriculum and Instruction M
Early Childhood Education M
Education—General M,O
Educational Administration M
Educational Media/Instructional Technology M
Educational Psychology M
English as a Second Language M
Environmental Management and Policy M
Exercise and Sports Science M
Graphic Design M
Health Services Management and Hospital Administration M
Holocaust Studies M
Industrial and Organizational Psychology M
International Business M
Liberal Studies M
Management Information Systems M
Marriage and Family Therapy O
Mathematics Education M
Mathematics M
Multilingual and Multicultural Education M
Nonprofit Management M
Nursing and Healthcare Administration M
Nursing—General M
Occupational Therapy M
Political Science M
Public Administration M
Reading Education M
School Psychology O
Science Education M
Social Work M
Special Education M
Statistics M

Close-Up on page 939.

KECK GRADUATE INSTITUTE OF APPLIED LIFE SCIENCES
Biological and Biomedical Sciences—General M

KEENE STATE COLLEGE
Counselor Education M,O
Curriculum and Instruction M
Education—General M,O
Educational Administration M,O
Special Education M,O

KEHILATH YAKOV RABBINICAL SEMINARY
Theology

KELLER GRADUATE SCHOOL OF MANAGEMENT
Business Administration and Management—General M

KELLER GRADUATE SCHOOL OF MANAGEMENT
Business Administration and Management—General M

KENNESAW STATE UNIVERSITY
Accounting M
Applied Statistics M
Business Administration and Management—General M
Computer Science M
Conflict Resolution and Mediation/Peace Studies M
Early Childhood Education M
Education—General M
Educational Administration M,D,O
Health Services Management and Hospital Administration M
Information Science M
Middle School Education M
Nursing—General M
Public Administration M
Social Work M
Special Education M
Writing M

KENRICK-GLENNON SEMINARY
Theology P,M,O

KENT STATE UNIVERSITY
Accounting M,D
Analytical Chemistry M,D
Anthropology M
Applied Mathematics M,D
Architecture M,O
Art Education M
Art History M
Art/Fine Arts M
Asian Languages M
Athletic Training and Sports Medicine M
Biochemistry M,D
Biological and Biomedical Sciences—General M,D*
Biological Anthropology D
Botany M,D
Business Administration and Management—General M*
Cell Biology M,D
Chemical Physics M,D
Chemistry M,D*
Classics M
Clinical Psychology M,D
Communication Disorders M,D
Communication—General M,D
Comparative Literature M,D
Computer Science M,D
Counseling Psychology M
Counselor Education M,D,O
Criminal Justice and Criminology M
Curriculum and Instruction M,D,O
Early Childhood Education M
Ecology M,D
Economics M
Education of the Gifted M
Education—General M,D,O
Educational Administration M,D,O
Educational Measurement and Evaluation M,D
Educational Media/Instructional Technology M
Educational Psychology M,D
Elementary Education M,D,O
Engineering and Applied Sciences—General M
English as a Second Language M,D
English Education M,D
English M,D*
Environmental Design M,O
Exercise and Sports Science M,D
Experimental Psychology M,D
Family and Consumer Sciences-General M
Finance and Banking D
Financial Engineering M
Foundations and Philosophy of Education M,D
French M
Geography M,D
Geology M,D
German M
Gerontology M
Graphic Design M
Health Education M,D
Higher Education M
History M,D
Human Development M,D
Human Services M,D,O
Illustration M
Information Science M
Inorganic Chemistry M,D
Journalism M
Liberal Studies M
Library Science M
Management Information Systems D
Marketing D
Mass Communication M
Mathematics M,D
Medical/Surgical Nursing M,D
Middle School Education M
Molecular Biology M,D
Music Education M,D
Music M,D
Neuroscience M,D
Nursing and Healthcare Administration M,D
Nursing Education M,D
Nursing—General M,D
Nutrition M
Organic Chemistry M,D
Pediatric Nursing M,D
Pharmacology M,D
Philosophy M
Physical Chemistry M,D
Physical Education M,D
Physics M,D*
Physiology M,D
Political Science M,D
Psychiatric Nursing M,D
Psychology—General M,D
Public Administration M
Public Health—General M
Public Policy M,D
Reading Education M
Recreation and Park Management M
Rehabilitation Counseling M,O
Rhetoric M,D
Russian M
School Psychology M,D,O
Secondary Education M,D
Sociology M,D
Spanish M
Special Education M,D,O
Sports Management M
Student Affairs M
Textile Design M
Theater M
Translation and Interpretation M
Vocational and Technical Education M,O
Writing M,D

KENTUCKY CHRISTIAN UNIVERSITY
Religion M
Theology M

KENTUCKY STATE UNIVERSITY
Aquaculture M
Business Administration and Management—General M
Computer Science M
Public Administration M
Special Education M

KETTERING UNIVERSITY
Automotive Engineering M
Business Administration and Management—General M
Computer Engineering M

- Electrical Engineering M
- Engineering Design M
- Engineering Management M
- Industrial and Manufacturing Management M
- Information Science M
- Manufacturing Engineering M
- Mechanical Engineering M

KEUKA COLLEGE
- Business Administration and Management—General M
- Criminal Justice and Criminology M
- Early Childhood Education M
- Occupational Therapy M

KING COLLEGE
- Business Administration and Management—General M

KING'S COLLEGE
- Business Administration and Management—General M
- Health Services Management and Hospital Administration M
- Physician Assistant Studies M
- Reading Education M

KNOWLEDGE SYSTEMS INSTITUTE
- Computer Science M
- Information Science M

KNOX COLLEGE
- Theology P,M,D

KNOX THEOLOGICAL SEMINARY
- Missions and Missiology M
- Pastoral Ministry and Counseling D
- Religion M
- Theology P,M,O

KOL YAAKOV TORAH CENTER
- Theology O

KUTZTOWN UNIVERSITY OF PENNSYLVANIA
- Art Education M,O
- Business Administration and Management—General M
- Computer Science M
- Counseling Psychology M
- Counselor Education M
- Curriculum and Instruction M,O
- Early Childhood Education M,O
- Education—General M,O
- Educational Administration M
- Educational Media/Instructional Technology M,O
- Elementary Education M,O
- English Education M,O
- English M
- Library Science M,O
- Marriage and Family Therapy M
- Mathematics Education M,O
- Media Studies M,O
- Music Education O
- Public Administration M
- Reading Education M
- School Nursing O
- Science Education M,O
- Secondary Education M,O
- Social Sciences Education M,O
- Social Work M
- Special Education M,O

Close-Up on page 941.

LAGRANGE COLLEGE
- Art Education M
- Curriculum and Instruction M
- Education—General M
- Music Education M
- Secondary Education M

LAKE ERIE COLLEGE
- Business Administration and Management—General M
- Curriculum and Instruction M
- Education—General M
- Educational Administration M
- Health Services Management and Hospital Administration M
- Reading Education M

LAKE ERIE COLLEGE OF OSTEOPATHIC MEDICINE
- Biological and Biomedical Sciences—General P,M,O
- Health Education P,M,O
- Osteopathic Medicine P,M,O
- Pharmacy P,M,O

LAKE FOREST COLLEGE
- Liberal Studies M

LAKE FOREST GRADUATE SCHOOL OF MANAGEMENT
- Business Administration and Management—General M

LAKEHEAD UNIVERSITY
- Biological and Biomedical Sciences—General M
- Chemistry M
- Clinical Psychology M,D
- Computer Science M
- Curriculum and Instruction M,D
- Economics M
- Education—General M,D
- Educational Administration M,D
- Engineering and Applied Sciences—General M
- English M
- Exercise and Sports Science M
- Experimental Psychology M,D
- Forestry M
- Geology M
- Gerontology M
- History M
- Mathematics M
- Philosophy M
- Physical Education M
- Physics M
- Psychology—General M,D
- Social Work M
- Sociology M
- Statistics M
- Women's Studies M

LAKELAND COLLEGE
- Business Administration and Management—General M
- Education—General M
- Theology M

LAMAR UNIVERSITY
- Accounting M
- Applied Arts and Design—General M
- Art History M
- Art/Fine Arts M
- Biological and Biomedical Sciences—General M
- Business Administration and Management—General M
- Chemical Engineering M,D
- Chemistry M
- Civil Engineering M,D
- Clinical Psychology M
- Communication Disorders M,D
- Computer Science M*
- Counselor Education M,D,O
- Criminal Justice and Criminology M
- Education—General M,D,O
- Educational Administration M,D,O
- Educational Media/Instructional Technology M,D,O
- Electrical Engineering M,D
- Engineering and Applied Sciences—General M,D
- Engineering Management M,D
- English M
- Entrepreneurship M
- Environmental Engineering M,D
- Environmental Management and Policy M,D
- Family and Consumer Sciences-General M,O
- Finance and Banking M
- Health Services Management and Hospital Administration M
- History M
- Industrial and Organizational Psychology M
- Industrial/Management Engineering M,D
- Information Science M
- Kinesiology and Movement Studies M
- Management Strategy and Policy M
- Mathematics M
- Mechanical Engineering M,D
- Music Education M
- Music M
- Nursing and Healthcare Administration M
- Nursing Education M
- Nursing—General M
- Photography M
- Political Science M
- Psychology—General M
- Public Administration M
- Social Psychology M
- Special Education M,D
- Theater M

Close-Up on page 943.

LANCASTER BIBLE COLLEGE
- Counselor Education M
- Pastoral Ministry and Counseling M
- Special Education M
- Theology M

LANCASTER THEOLOGICAL SEMINARY
- Theology P,M,D,O

LANDER UNIVERSITY
- Curriculum and Instruction M
- Education—General M
- Elementary Education M

LANGSTON UNIVERSITY
- Education—General M
- Elementary Education M
- English as a Second Language M
- Multilingual and Multicultural Education M
- Physical Therapy D
- Rehabilitation Counseling M
- Urban Education M

LA ROCHE COLLEGE
- Family Nurse Practitioner Studies M
- Human Resources Management M,O
- Nurse Anesthesia M
- Nursing and Healthcare Administration M
- Nursing—General M

LA SALLE UNIVERSITY
- Adult Nursing M,O
- Business Administration and Management—General M,O
- Clinical Psychology M,D
- Communication Disorders M
- Community Health Nursing M,O
- Computer Science M
- Corporate and Organizational Communication M
- Counseling Psychology M
- East European and Russian Studies M
- Education—General M
- Family Nurse Practitioner Studies M,O
- Gerontology M,O
- Hispanic Studies M
- History M
- Latin American Studies M
- Management of Technology M
- Marriage and Family Therapy D
- Medical/Surgical Nursing M,O
- Nursing and Healthcare Administration M,O
- Nursing Education M,O
- Nursing Informatics M,O
- Nursing—General M,O
- Pastoral Ministry and Counseling M
- Psychology—General D
- Rehabilitation Counseling D
- Religion M
- School Nursing M,O
- Theology M

LASELL COLLEGE
- Business Administration and Management—General M*
- Marketing M

LA SIERRA UNIVERSITY
- Business Administration and Management—General M,O
- Counselor Education M,O
- Curriculum and Instruction M,D,O
- Education—General M,D,O
- Educational Administration M,D,O
- Educational Psychology M,O
- English M
- Religion M
- Religious Education M
- School Psychology M,O
- Special Education M,D,O

LAURA AND ALVIN SIEGAL COLLEGE OF JUDAIC STUDIES
- Holocaust Studies M
- Humanities M
- Jewish Studies M
- Religious Education M

LAURENTIAN UNIVERSITY
- Applied Physics M
- Biochemistry M
- Biological and Biomedical Sciences—General M
- Business Administration and Management—General M
- Chemistry M
- Engineering and Applied Sciences—General M
- Geology M
- History M
- Human Development M
- Humanities M
- Metallurgical Engineering and Metallurgy M
- Mineral/Mining Engineering M
- Social Work M
- Sociology M

LAWRENCE TECHNOLOGICAL UNIVERSITY
- Architecture M
- Automotive Engineering M,D
- Business Administration and Management—General M,D
- Civil Engineering M,D
- Computer Engineering M,D
- Computer Science M
- Construction Engineering M,D
- Educational Media/Instructional Technology M
- Electrical Engineering M,D
- Engineering and Applied Sciences—General M,D
- Engineering Management M,D
- Industrial and Manufacturing Management M,D
- Interior Design M
- Management Information Systems M,D
- Management of Technology M,D
- Manufacturing Engineering M,D
- Mechanical Engineering M,D
- Science Education M
- Technical Communication M

LEADERSHIP INSTITUTE OF SEATTLE
- Counseling Psychology M
- Organizational Behavior M
- Organizational Management M
- Psychology—General M

LEBANESE AMERICAN UNIVERSITY
- Business Administration and Management—General M
- Computer Science M
- International Affairs M
- Pharmacy P

LEBANON VALLEY COLLEGE
- Business Administration and Management—General M
- Music Education M
- Science Education M

LEE UNIVERSITY
- Counseling Psychology M
- Counselor Education M
- Education—General M
- Educational Administration M
- Elementary Education M
- Music Education M
- Music M
- Religion M
- Secondary Education M
- Special Education M
- Theology M

LEHIGH UNIVERSITY
- Accounting M*
- American Studies M
- Applied Mathematics M,D
- Biochemistry M,D
- Biological and Biomedical Sciences—General M,D
- Business Administration and Management—General M,D,O*
- Chemical Engineering M,D
- Chemistry M,D
- Civil Engineering M,D
- Computational Sciences M,D
- Computer Engineering M,D
- Computer Science M,D*
- Counseling Psychology M,D,O
- Counselor Education M,D,O
- Economics M,D
- Education—General M,D,O
- Educational Administration M,D,O
- Educational Media/Instructional Technology M,D,O
- Electrical Engineering M,D
- Elementary Education M,D
- Engineering and Applied Sciences—General M,D*
- English M,D
- Environmental Engineering M,D
- Environmental Sciences M,D
- Finance and Banking M
- Geology M,D
- Geosciences M,D

History	M,D
Human Development	M,D
Human Services	M,D,O
Industrial/Management Engineering	M,D
Information Science	M
Manufacturing Engineering	M
Materials Engineering	M,D
Materials Sciences	M,D
Mathematics	M,D
Mechanical Engineering	M,D
Mechanics	M,D
Medicinal and Pharmaceutical Chemistry	M,D
Molecular Biology	M,D
Organizational Management	M,D,O
Photonics	M,D
Physics	M,D
Political Science	M
Polymer Science and Engineering	M,D*
Project Management	M,D,O
Psychology—General	M,D
Quantitative Analysis	M*
School Psychology	D,O
Secondary Education	M,D
Sociology	M
Special Education	M,D,O
Statistics	M,D
Supply Chain Management	M,D,O
Systems Engineering	M,D

LEHMAN COLLEGE OF THE CITY UNIVERSITY OF NEW YORK

Accounting	M
Adult Nursing	M
Art/Fine Arts	M
Biological and Biomedical Sciences—General	M
Business Education	M
Communication Disorders	M
Computer Science	M
Counselor Education	M
Early Childhood Education	M
Education—General	M
Elementary Education	M
English as a Second Language	M
English Education	M
English	M
Gerontological Nursing	M
Health Education	M
Health Promotion	M
History	M
Maternal and Child/Neonatal Nursing	M
Mathematics Education	M
Mathematics	M
Multilingual and Multicultural Education	M
Music Education	M
Nursing—General	M
Nutrition	M
Pediatric Nursing	M
Plant Sciences	D
Reading Education	M
Recreation and Park Management	M
Science Education	M
Social Sciences Education	M
Spanish	M
Special Education	M

LE MOYNE COLLEGE

Business Administration and Management—General	M
Education—General	M
Nursing—General	M
Physician Assistant Studies	M

LENOIR-RHYNE COLLEGE

Business Administration and Management—General	M
Counselor Education	M
Early Childhood Education	M
Education—General	M
Reading Education	M
School Psychology	M

LESLEY UNIVERSITY

Art Education	M,D,O
Art Therapy	M,D,O*
Art/Fine Arts	M*
Clinical Psychology	M,D,O
Computer Education	M,D,O
Counseling Psychology	M*
Curriculum and Instruction	M,D,O
Early Childhood Education	M,D,O
Ecology	M,D,O
Education—General	M,D,O*
Elementary Education	M,D,O
Environmental Education	M,D,O
Health Psychology	M
Interdisciplinary Studies	M
International Affairs	M,O
Middle School Education	M,D,O
Psychology—General	M,D,O
Reading Education	M,D,O
School Psychology	M
Science Education	M,D,O
Social Psychology	M,D,O
Special Education	M,D,O
Therapies—Dance, Drama, and Music	M,D,O
Women's Studies	M
Writing	M*

LETOURNEAU UNIVERSITY

Business Administration and Management—General	M
Educational Administration	M

LEWIS & CLARK COLLEGE

Addictions/Substance Abuse Counseling	M
Communication Disorders	M
Counseling Psychology	M,O
Cultural Studies	M,O
Education—General	M,D,O
Educational Administration	M,D
Elementary Education	M
Law	P,M
Marriage and Family Therapy	M
School Psychology	M,O
Secondary Education	M
Special Education	M

LEWIS UNIVERSITY

Business Administration and Management—General	M
Counseling Psychology	M
Counselor Education	M
Criminal Justice and Criminology	M
Curriculum and Instruction	M
Education—General	M,O
Educational Administration	M
Nursing and Healthcare Administration	M
Nursing Education	M
Nursing—General	M
Organizational Management	M
Public Administration	M
Special Education	M
Student Affairs	M

LEXINGTON THEOLOGICAL SEMINARY

Theology	P,M,D

LIBERTY UNIVERSITY

Business Administration and Management—General	M
Communication—General	M
Counseling Psychology	M,D
Counselor Education	M,D,O
Curriculum and Instruction	M,D,O
Early Childhood Education	M,D,O
Education of the Gifted	M,D,O
Education—General	M,D,O
Educational Administration	M,D,O
Elementary Education	M,D,O
Law	P
Nursing—General	M,D
Pastoral Ministry and Counseling	M,D
Reading Education	M,D,O
Religion	P,M,D
Secondary Education	M,D,O
Special Education	M,D,O
Theology	P,M,D

LIFE CHIROPRACTIC COLLEGE WEST

Chiropractic	P*

LIFE UNIVERSITY

Chiropractic	P
Exercise and Sports Science	M

LINCOLN CHRISTIAN SEMINARY

Pastoral Ministry and Counseling	P,M
Theology	P,M

LINCOLN MEMORIAL UNIVERSITY

Business Administration and Management—General	M
Counselor Education	M,O
Curriculum and Instruction	M,O
Education—General	M,O
Educational Administration	M,O
Nursing—General	M

LINCOLN UNIVERSITY (CA)

Business Administration and Management—General	M

LINCOLN UNIVERSITY (MO)

Accounting	M
Business Administration and Management—General	M
Counselor Education	M,O
Criminal Justice and Criminology	M
Education—General	M,O
Educational Administration	M,O
Elementary Education	M,O
Entrepreneurship	M
History	M
Political Science	M
Public Administration	M
Public Policy	M
Secondary Education	M,O
Social Sciences	M
Sociology	M
Special Education	M,O

LINCOLN UNIVERSITY (PA)

Human Services	M

LINDENWOOD UNIVERSITY

Accounting	M
Art/Fine Arts	M
Business Administration and Management—General	M
Communication—General	M
Counseling Psychology	M,D,O
Criminal Justice and Criminology	M
Education—General	M,D,O
Educational Administration	M,D,O
Educational Media/Instructional Technology	M,D,O
Entrepreneurship	M
Finance and Banking	M
Gerontology	M
Health Services Management and Hospital Administration	M
Human Resources Management	M
International Business	M
Investment Management	M
Management Information Systems	M
Marketing	M
Nonprofit Management	M
Organizational Behavior	M
Organizational Management	M
Public Administration	M
School Psychology	M,D,O
Sports Management	M
Theater	M
Writing	M

LINDSEY WILSON COLLEGE

Counseling Psychology	M
Human Development	M

LIPSCOMB UNIVERSITY

Accounting	M
Business Administration and Management—General	M
Conflict Resolution and Mediation/Peace Studies	M,O
Counseling Psychology	M,O
Curriculum and Instruction	M
Education—General	M
Educational Administration	M
Finance and Banking	M
Health Services Management and Hospital Administration	M
Nonprofit Management	M
Psychology—General	M,O
Religion	P,M
Special Education	M
Theology	P,M

LOCK HAVEN UNIVERSITY OF PENNSYLVANIA

Education—General	M
Elementary Education	M
Liberal Studies	M
Physician Assistant Studies	M

LOGAN UNIVERSITY-COLLEGE OF CHIROPRACTIC

Chiropractic	P,M

LOMA LINDA UNIVERSITY

Adult Nursing	M
Allied Health—General	M,D
Allopathic Medicine	P,M,D
Anatomy	M,D
Biochemistry	M,D
Bioethics	M,O
Biological and Biomedical Sciences—General	M,D
Biostatistics	M
Child and Family Studies	M,D,O
Communication Disorders	M
Counselor Education	M,D,O
Dentistry	P,M,O
Environmental and Occupational Health	M
Epidemiology	M
Geosciences	M,D
Gerontological Nursing	M
Health Education	M,D
Health Informatics	M
Health Promotion	M,D
Health Services Management and Hospital Administration	M
International Health	M
Microbiology	M,D
Nursing and Healthcare Administration	M,O
Nursing—General	M,O
Nutrition	M,D
Oral and Dental Sciences	M,O
Pastoral Ministry and Counseling	M,O
Pathology	M,D
Pediatric Nursing	M
Pharmacology	M,D
Physical Therapy	M,D
Physician Assistant Studies	M
Physiology	M,D
Psychology—General	D
Public Health—General	M,D
Religion	M
Social Work	M,D

LONG ISLAND UNIVERSITY, BRENTWOOD CAMPUS

Counselor Education	M
Criminal Justice and Criminology	M
Education—General	M
Educational Administration	M
Elementary Education	M
Reading Education	M
Special Education	M

LONG ISLAND UNIVERSITY, BROOKLYN CAMPUS

Accounting	M
Adult Nursing	M,O
Athletic Training and Sports Medicine	M
Biological and Biomedical Sciences—General	M
Business Administration and Management—General	M
Chemistry	M
Clinical Psychology	D
Communication Disorders	M
Community Health	M
Comparative Literature	M
Computer Art and Design	M*
Computer Science	M
Counselor Education	M,O
Economics	M
Education—General	M,O
Educational Administration	M
Educational Media/Instructional Technology	M
Elementary Education	M
English as a Second Language	M
English Education	M
English	M*
Exercise and Sports Science	M
Health Education	M
Health Services Management and Hospital Administration	M
History	M,O
Human Resources Management	M
International Affairs	M,O
Mathematics Education	M
Multilingual and Multicultural Education	M
Nursing and Healthcare Administration	M
Nursing—General	M,O
Pharmaceutical Administration	M
Pharmaceutical Sciences	M,D
Pharmacology	M,D
Physical Education	M
Physical Therapy	D
Political Science	M
Psychology—General	M,D
Public Administration	M
Reading Education	M
School Psychology	M
Social Sciences	M,O
Special Education	M
Taxation	M
Toxicology	M,D
Urban Studies	M
Writing	M

LONG ISLAND UNIVERSITY, C.W. POST CAMPUS

Accounting	M,O
Allied Health—General	M,O
Applied Mathematics	M
Art Education	M
Art Therapy	M
Art/Fine Arts	M
Biological and Biomedical Sciences—General	M
Business Administration and Management—General	M,O*
Cardiovascular Sciences	M,O
Clinical Laboratory Sciences/Medical Technology	M
Clinical Psychology	D
Communication Disorders	M
Computer Art and Design	M
Computer Education	M
Computer Science	M

- Counselor Education M
- Criminal Justice and Criminology M
- Early Childhood Education M
- Education—General M,O
- Educational Administration M,O
- Educational Media/Instructional Technology M
- Elementary Education M
- Engineering Management M
- English as a Second Language M
- English Education M
- English M
- Environmental Management and Policy M
- Environmental Sciences M
- Experimental Psychology M,O
- Family Nurse Practitioner Studies M,O
- Finance and Banking M,O
- Foreign Languages Education M
- Gerontology M,O
- Health Services Management and Hospital Administration M,O
- History M
- Immunology M
- Information Science M
- Information Studies M,D,O
- Interdisciplinary Studies M
- International Affairs M
- International Business M,O
- Internet and Interactive Multimedia M
- Library Science M,D,O*
- Management Information Systems M,O
- Marketing M,O
- Mathematics Education M
- Mathematics M
- Medicinal and Pharmaceutical Chemistry M
- Microbiology M
- Middle School Education M
- Multilingual and Multicultural Education M
- Music Education M
- Music M
- Nonprofit Management M,O
- Nursing—General M,O
- Nutrition M,O
- Political Science M
- Psychology—General M,D,O
- Public Administration M,O
- Reading Education M
- Science Education M
- Secondary Education M
- Social Sciences M
- Spanish M
- Special Education M
- Taxation M,O
- Theater M

Close-Up on page 945.

LONG ISLAND UNIVERSITY, ROCKLAND GRADUATE CAMPUS

- Business Administration and Management—General M,O
- Counseling Psychology M
- Counselor Education M
- Educational Administration M,O
- Elementary Education M
- Finance and Banking M,O
- Gerontology M,O
- Health Services Management and Hospital Administration M,O
- Nonprofit Management M,O
- Pharmaceutical Sciences M
- Reading Education M
- Special Education M

LONG ISLAND UNIVERSITY, SOUTHAMPTON GRADUATE CAMPUS

- Early Childhood Education M
- Education—General M
- Elementary Education M
- Homeland Security M,O
- Reading Education M
- Special Education M

LONG ISLAND UNIVERSITY, WESTCHESTER GRADUATE CAMPUS

- Business Administration and Management—General M
- Counseling Psychology M
- Counselor Education M
- Early Childhood Education M
- Education—General M
- Educational Psychology M
- Elementary Education M
- English as a Second Language M
- Information Studies M
- Library Science M
- Marriage and Family Therapy M
- Multilingual and Multicultural Education M
- Reading Education M
- School Psychology M
- Secondary Education M
- Special Education M

Close-Up on page 947.

LONGWOOD UNIVERSITY

- Business Administration and Management—General M
- Communication Disorders M*
- Counselor Education M
- Criminal Justice and Criminology M
- Education—General M
- Educational Administration M
- Educational Media/Instructional Technology M
- Elementary Education M
- English Education M
- English M*
- Reading Education M
- Secondary Education M
- Special Education M
- Writing M

LONGY SCHOOL OF MUSIC

- Music M,O

LORAS COLLEGE

- Educational Administration M
- Pastoral Ministry and Counseling M
- Psychology—General M
- Special Education M
- Theology M

LOUISIANA STATE UNIVERSITY AND AGRICULTURAL AND MECHANICAL COLLEGE

- Accounting M,D
- Agricultural Economics and Agribusiness M,D
- Agricultural Education M,D
- Agricultural Engineering M,D
- Agricultural Sciences—General M,D
- Agronomy and Soil Sciences M,D
- Animal Sciences M,D
- Anthropology M,D
- Applied Arts and Design—General M
- Applied Science and Technology M
- Applied Statistics M
- Architecture M
- Art History M
- Art/Fine Arts M
- Astronomy M,D
- Astrophysics M,D
- Biochemistry M,D
- Bioengineering M,D
- Biological and Biomedical Sciences—General M,D*
- Biopsychology M,D
- Business Administration and Management—General M,D
- Business Education M,D
- Chemical Engineering M,D*
- Chemistry M,D
- Civil Engineering M,D
- Clinical Psychology M,D
- Cognitive Sciences M,D
- Communication Disorders M,D
- Communication—General M,D
- Comparative Literature M,D
- Computer Engineering M,D
- Computer Science M,D
- Counselor Education M,D,O
- Developmental Psychology M,D
- Economics M,D
- Education—General M,D,O
- Educational Administration M,D,O
- Educational Measurement and Evaluation M,D,O
- Educational Media/Instructional Technology M,D,O
- Electrical Engineering M,D
- Elementary Education M,D,O
- Engineering and Applied Sciences—General M,D
- English M,D
- Entomology M,D
- Environmental Engineering M,D
- Environmental Management and Policy M
- Environmental Sciences M,D
- Family and Consumer Sciences-General M,D
- Finance and Banking M,D
- Fish, Game, and Wildlife Management M,D
- Food Science and Technology M,D
- Forestry M,D
- French M,D
- Geography M,D
- Geology M,D
- Geophysics M,D
- Geotechnical Engineering M,D
- Graphic Design M
- Higher Education M,D,O
- History M,D
- Home Economics Education M,D
- Horticulture M,D
- Industrial and Organizational Psychology M,D
- Industrial/Management Engineering M,D
- Information Studies M,O
- International and Comparative Education M,D
- Kinesiology and Movement Studies M,D
- Landscape Architecture M
- Law P,M
- Liberal Studies M
- Library Science M,O
- Linguistics M,D
- Management Information Systems M,D
- Marine Affairs M,D
- Marketing D
- Mass Communication M,D*
- Mathematics M,D
- Mechanical Engineering M,D
- Mechanics M,D
- Media Studies M,D
- Music Education M,D
- Music M,D
- Natural Resources M,D
- Oceanography M,D
- Petroleum Engineering M,D
- Philosophy M
- Photography M
- Physics M,D
- Plant Pathology M,D
- Political Science M,D
- Psychology—General M,D
- Public Administration M,D
- School Psychology M,D
- Secondary Education M,D,O
- Social Work M,D
- Sociology M,D
- Spanish M
- Statistics M
- Structural Engineering M,D
- Systems Science M,D
- Theater M,D
- Toxicology M
- Transportation and Highway Engineering M,D
- Veterinary Medicine P
- Veterinary Sciences M,D
- Vocational and Technical Education M,D
- Water Resources Engineering M,D
- Writing M,D

LOUISIANA STATE UNIVERSITY HEALTH SCIENCES CENTER

- Adult Nursing M,D
- Allied Health—General M
- Allopathic Medicine P,M
- Anatomy M,D
- Biological and Biomedical Sciences—General M,D
- Biometrics M
- Cell Biology M,D
- Communication Disorders M
- Community Health Nursing M,D
- Dentistry P
- Developmental Biology M,D
- Human Genetics M,D
- Immunology M,D
- Microbiology M,D
- Neurobiology M,D
- Neuroscience M,D*
- Nursing and Healthcare Administration M,D
- Nursing—General M,D
- Parasitology M,D
- Pathology M,D
- Pediatric Nursing M,D
- Pharmacology M,D
- Physical Therapy M
- Physiology M,D
- Psychiatric Nursing M,D
- Public Health—General M
- Rehabilitation Counseling M

LOUISIANA STATE UNIVERSITY HEALTH SCIENCES CENTER AT SHREVEPORT

- Allopathic Medicine P
- Anatomy M,D
- Biochemistry M,D
- Biological and Biomedical Sciences—General M,D*
- Cell Biology M,D
- Immunology M,D
- Microbiology M,D
- Molecular Biology M,D
- Pharmacology D
- Physiology M,D

LOUISIANA STATE UNIVERSITY IN SHREVEPORT

- Business Administration and Management—General M
- Counseling Psychology M,O
- Education—General M
- Health Services Management and Hospital Administration M
- Human Services M
- Liberal Studies M
- School Psychology M,O
- Systems Engineering M
- Systems Science M

LOUISIANA TECH UNIVERSITY

- Accounting M,D
- Applied Arts and Design—General M
- Art/Fine Arts M
- Biological and Biomedical Sciences—General M
- Biomedical Engineering M,D
- Business Administration and Management—General M,D
- Business Education M,D
- Chemical Engineering M,D
- Chemistry M
- Civil Engineering M,D
- Communication Disorders M
- Computational Sciences M,D
- Computer Science M
- Counseling Psychology M,D
- Counselor Education M,D
- Curriculum and Instruction M,D
- Economics M,D
- Education—General M,D
- Educational Administration M,D
- Electrical Engineering M,D
- Engineering and Applied Sciences—General M,D
- English Education M,D
- English M
- Exercise and Sports Science M
- Family and Consumer Sciences-General M
- Finance and Banking M,D
- Foreign Languages Education M,D
- Graphic Design M
- Health Education M,D
- History M
- Industrial and Organizational Psychology M,D
- Industrial/Management Engineering M,D
- Interior Design M
- Manufacturing Engineering M,D
- Marketing M,D
- Mathematics Education M,D
- Mathematics M
- Mechanical Engineering M,D
- Nutrition M
- Operations Research M,D
- Photography M
- Physical Education M,D
- Physics M,D
- Psychology—General M,D
- Science Education M,D
- Secondary Education M,D
- Social Sciences Education M,D
- Special Education M,D
- Speech and Interpersonal Communication M
- Statistics M

LOUISVILLE PRESBYTERIAN THEOLOGICAL SEMINARY

- Religion P,M,D
- Theology P,M,D

LOURDES COLLEGE

- Education—General M
- Educational Media/Instructional Technology M
- Organizational Management M

LOYOLA COLLEGE IN MARYLAND

- Addictions/Substance Abuse Counseling M,O
- Business Administration and Management—General M
- Clinical Psychology M,D,O
- Communication Disorders M,O
- Computer Science M
- Counseling Psychology M,O
- Counselor Education M,O
- Curriculum and Instruction M,O
- Early Childhood Education M,O
- Economics M
- Education—General M,O
- Educational Administration M,O
- Educational Media/Instructional Technology M
- Engineering and Applied Sciences—General M
- Finance and Banking M
- Liberal Studies M
- Marketing M
- Pastoral Ministry and Counseling M,D,O
- Psychology—General M,D,O
- Quantitative Analysis M
- Reading Education M,O
- Software Engineering M
- Special Education M,O

LOYOLA MARYMOUNT UNIVERSITY

- Bioethics M

Program	Degrees
Business Administration and Management—General	M
Civil Engineering	M
Computer Science	M
Counselor Education	M
Education—General	M,D
Educational Administration	M,D
Educational Psychology	M
Electrical Engineering	M
Elementary Education	M
Engineering Management	M,O
English	M
Environmental Sciences	M
Film, Television, and Video Production	M
Law	P,M
Marriage and Family Therapy	M
Mathematics Education	M
Mechanical Engineering	M
Multilingual and Multicultural Education	M
Pastoral Ministry and Counseling	M
Philosophy	M
Reading Education	M
Religious Education	M
School Psychology	M
Secondary Education	M
Special Education	M
Systems Engineering	M,O
Taxation	P,M
Theology	M
Writing	M

Close-Up on page 949.

LOYOLA UNIVERSITY CHICAGO

Program	Degrees
Accounting	M
Acute Care/Critical Care Nursing	M
Adult Nursing	M
Allopathic Medicine	P
Anatomy	M,D
Biochemistry	M,D*
Biological and Biomedical Sciences—General	M
Business Administration and Management—General	M
Cell Biology	M,D*
Chemistry	M,D
Clinical Psychology	D
Cognitive Sciences	M
Computer Science	M
Corporate and Organizational Communication	M
Counseling Psychology	D
Counselor Education	M,O
Criminal Justice and Criminology	M
Curriculum and Instruction	M,D
Developmental Psychology	D
Education—General	M,D,O
Educational Administration	M,D,O
Educational Measurement and Evaluation	M,D
Educational Media/Instructional Technology	M
Educational Policy	M,D
Educational Psychology	M
Elementary Education	M
English	M,D
Environmental and Occupational Health	M
Family Nurse Practitioner Studies	M
Health Services Management and Hospital Administration	M
Higher Education	M,D
History	M,D
Human Resources Management	M
Immunology	M,D
Industrial and Labor Relations	M
Infectious Diseases	M
Information Science	M
International Affairs	M,D
Law	P,M,D
Management Information Systems	M
Marketing	M
Mathematics	M
Microbiology	M,D*
Molecular Biology	D
Molecular Physiology	M,D*
Neurobiology	M,D
Neuroscience	M,D
Nursing and Healthcare Administration	M
Nursing—General	M
Oncology Nursing	M
Pastoral Ministry and Counseling	M
Pharmacology	M,D
Philosophy	M,D
Political Science	M,D
Psychology—General	M,D
Public History	M,D
Reading Education	M
Religion	P,M,O
Religious Education	P,M,O
School Psychology	M,D,O
Science Education	M
Secondary Education	M
Social Psychology	M,D
Social Work	M,D
Sociology	M,D
Software Engineering	M
Spanish	M
Special Education	M
Statistics	M
Theology	P,M,D
Virology	M,D
Women's Health Nursing	M

Close-Up on page 951.

LOYOLA UNIVERSITY NEW ORLEANS

Program	Degrees
Business Administration and Management—General	M
Communication—General	M
Counselor Education	M
Criminal Justice and Criminology	M
Education—General	M
Elementary Education	M
Family Nurse Practitioner Studies	M
Health Services Management and Hospital Administration	M
Law	P
Mass Communication	M
Music	M
Nursing—General	M
Reading Education	M
Religion	M
Secondary Education	M
Theology	M,O

LUBBOCK CHRISTIAN UNIVERSITY

Program	Degrees
Theology	M

LUTHERAN SCHOOL OF THEOLOGY AT CHICAGO

Program	Degrees
Pastoral Ministry and Counseling	P,M,D
Theology	P,M,D

LUTHERAN THEOLOGICAL SEMINARY

Program	Degrees
Pastoral Ministry and Counseling	P,M
Theology	P,M

LUTHERAN THEOLOGICAL SEMINARY AT GETTYSBURG

Program	Degrees
Pastoral Ministry and Counseling	P,M,D
Religion	P,M,D
Theology	P,M,D

THE LUTHERAN THEOLOGICAL SEMINARY AT PHILADELPHIA

Program	Degrees
Pastoral Ministry and Counseling	P,M,D,O
Religion	P,M,D,O
Theology	P,M,D,O

LUTHERAN THEOLOGICAL SOUTHERN SEMINARY

Program	Degrees
Theology	P,M,D

LUTHER RICE UNIVERSITY

Program	Degrees
Missions and Missiology	P,M,D
Pastoral Ministry and Counseling	P,M,D
Religious Education	P,M,D
Theology	P,M,D

LUTHER SEMINARY

Program	Degrees
Theology	P,M,D

LYNCHBURG COLLEGE

Program	Degrees
Business Administration and Management—General	M
Counselor Education	M
Education—General	M
Educational Administration	M
Elementary Education	M
English Education	M
Science Education	M
Special Education	M

LYNDON STATE COLLEGE

Program	Degrees
Counselor Education	M
Curriculum and Instruction	M
Education—General	M
Reading Education	M
Science Education	M
Special Education	M

LYNN UNIVERSITY

Program	Degrees
Aviation Management	M,D
Business Administration and Management—General	M,D
Criminal Justice and Criminology	M,O
Education of the Gifted	M,D
Educational Administration	M,D
Emergency Management	M,O
Hospitality Management	M,D
International and Comparative Education	M,D
International Business	M,D
Investment Management	M,D
Marketing	M,D
Mass Communication	M,D
Media Studies	M,D
Music	M,O
Psychology—General	M,O
Special Education	M,D
Sports Management	M,D

MACHZIKEI HADATH RABBINICAL COLLEGE

Program	Degrees
Theology	O

MADONNA UNIVERSITY

Program	Degrees
Adult Nursing	M
Business Administration and Management—General	M
Clinical Psychology	M
Criminal Justice and Criminology	M
Education—General	M
Educational Administration	M
English as a Second Language	M
Health Services Management and Hospital Administration	M
Hospice Nursing	M
International Business	M
Liberal Studies	M
Nursing and Healthcare Administration	M
Nursing—General	M
Pastoral Ministry and Counseling	M
Psychology—General	M
Quality Management	M
Reading Education	M
Special Education	M
Theology	M

MAHARISHI UNIVERSITY OF MANAGEMENT

Program	Degrees
Asian Studies	M,D
Business Administration and Management—General	M,D
Computer Science	M
Education—General	M
Elementary Education	M
Physiology	M,D
Secondary Education	M

MAINE COLLEGE OF ART

Program	Degrees
Art/Fine Arts	M*

MAINE MARITIME ACADEMY

Program	Degrees
International Business	M,O
Logistics	M,O
Supply Chain Management	M,O
Transportation Management	M,O

MALASPINA UNIVERSITY-COLLEGE

Program	Degrees
Business Administration and Management—General	M

MALONE COLLEGE

Program	Degrees
Business Administration and Management—General	M
Counselor Education	M
Curriculum and Instruction	M
Education—General	M
Educational Media/Instructional Technology	M
Family Nurse Practitioner Studies	M
Nursing—General	M
Pastoral Ministry and Counseling	M
Reading Education	M
Special Education	M
Theology	M

MANCHESTER COLLEGE

Program	Degrees
Interdisciplinary Studies	M

MANHATTAN COLLEGE

Program	Degrees
Chemical Engineering	M
Civil Engineering	M
Computer Engineering	M
Counselor Education	M,O
Early Childhood Education	M
Education—General	M,O
Educational Administration	M,O
Electrical Engineering	M
Engineering and Applied Sciences—General	M
Environmental Engineering	M
Mechanical Engineering	M
Special Education	M

MANHATTAN SCHOOL OF MUSIC

Program	Degrees
Music	M,D,O

MANHATTANVILLE COLLEGE

Program	Degrees
Art Education	M
Corporate and Organizational Communication	M
Early Childhood Education	M
Education—General	M*
Educational Administration	M
Elementary Education	M
English as a Second Language	M
English Education	M
Exercise and Sports Science	M
Foreign Languages Education	M
Human Resources Development	M
Human Resources Management	M
International Business	M
Liberal Studies	M
Management Strategy and Policy	M
Marketing	M
Mathematics Education	M
Middle School Education	M
Music Education	M
Organizational Management	M
Reading Education	M
Science Education	M
Secondary Education	M
Social Sciences Education	M
Special Education	M
Sports Management	M
Writing	M

Close-Up on page 953.

MANSFIELD UNIVERSITY OF PENNSYLVANIA

Program	Degrees
Art Education	M
Education—General	M
Elementary Education	M
Information Studies	M
Library Science	M
Music	M
Nursing—General	M
Secondary Education	M

MAPLE SPRINGS BAPTIST BIBLE COLLEGE AND SEMINARY

Program	Degrees
Computer Education	P,M,D,O
Pastoral Ministry and Counseling	P,M,D,O
Theology	P,M,D,O

MARANATHA BAPTIST BIBLE COLLEGE

Program	Degrees
Cultural Studies	M
Pastoral Ministry and Counseling	M
Theology	M

MARIAN COLLEGE

Program	Degrees
Education—General	M

MARIAN COLLEGE OF FOND DU LAC

Program	Degrees
Adult Nursing	M
Business Administration and Management—General	M
Education—General	M,D
Educational Administration	M,D
Nursing Education	M
Nursing—General	M
Organizational Management	M
Quality Management	M

MARIETTA COLLEGE

Program	Degrees
Corporate and Organizational Communication	M
Education—General	M
Physician Assistant Studies	M
Psychology—General	M

MARIST COLLEGE

Program	Degrees
Business Administration and Management—General	M,O*
Computer Science	M,O
Corporate and Organizational Communication	M
Counseling Psychology	M,O
Education—General	M,O
Educational Psychology	M,O
Industrial and Manufacturing Management	M,O
Management Information Systems	M,O
Management of Technology	M,O
Psychology—General	M,O
Public Administration	M
School Psychology	M,O
Software Engineering	M,O

MARLBORO COLLEGE

Business Administration and Management—General M
Computer Education M
Computer Science M
Education—General M
Information Science M
Internet and Interactive Multimedia M

MARQUETTE UNIVERSITY

Accounting M
Adult Nursing M,D,O
Advertising and Public Relations M
Analytical Chemistry M,D
Bioinformatics M
Biological and Biomedical Sciences—General M,D
Biomedical Engineering M,D
Business Administration and Management—General M
Cell Biology M,D
Chemical Physics M,D
Chemistry M,D
Civil Engineering M,D
Clinical Psychology M,D
Communication Disorders M
Communication—General M
Computer Engineering M,D
Computer Science M,D
Construction Engineering M,D
Dentistry P
Developmental Biology M,D
Ecology M,D
Economics M
Education—General M,D,O
Electrical Engineering M,D
Engineering and Applied Sciences—General M,D
Engineering Management M,D
English M,D
Environmental Engineering M,D
Ethics M,D
Evolutionary Biology M,D
Foreign Languages Education M
Genetics M,D
Geotechnical Engineering M,D
Gerontological Nursing M,D,O
Health Communication M
History M,D
Human Resources Development M
Human Resources Management M
Inorganic Chemistry M,D
Interdisciplinary Studies D
International Affairs M
Journalism M
Law P
Management of Technology M,D
Manufacturing Engineering M,D
Mass Communication M
Maternal and Child/Neonatal Nursing M,D,O
Mathematics Education M,D
Mathematics M,D
Mechanical Engineering M,D
Media Studies M
Medieval and Renaissance Studies M,D
Microbiology M,D
Molecular Biology M,D
Neurobiology M,D
Nurse Midwifery M,D,O
Nursing—General M,D,O
Oral and Dental Sciences M
Organic Chemistry M,D
Pediatric Nursing M,D,O
Philosophy M,D
Physical Chemistry M,D
Physical Therapy D
Physician Assistant Studies M
Physiology M,D
Political Science M
Psychology—General M,D
Public Administration M
Spanish M
Speech and Interpersonal Communication M
Statistics M,D
Structural Engineering M,D
Theology M,D
Transportation and Highway Engineering M,D
Water Resources Engineering M,D

MARSHALL UNIVERSITY

Adult Education M
Allopathic Medicine P
Anthropology M
Art/Fine Arts M
Biological and Biomedical Sciences—General M,D
Business Administration and Management—General M
Chemistry M
Clinical Psychology M,D
Communication Disorders M
Communication—General M
Counselor Education M,O
Criminal Justice and Criminology M
Early Childhood Education M
Education—General M,D,O
Educational Administration M,D,O
Elementary Education M
Engineering and Applied Sciences—General M
English M
Environmental Sciences M
Exercise and Sports Science M
Family and Consumer Sciences-General M
Forensic Sciences M
Geography M
Health Education M
Health Services Management and Hospital Administration M
History M
Human Resources Management M
Humanities M
Industrial and Organizational Psychology M,D
Information Science M
Journalism M
Management of Technology M
Mass Communication M
Mathematics M
Music M
Nursing—General M
Nutrition M
Physics M
Political Science M
Psychology—General M,D
Reading Education M,O
School Psychology O
Secondary Education M
Sociology M
Special Education M
Sports Management M
Vocational and Technical Education M

Close-Up on page 955.

MARTIN UNIVERSITY

Pastoral Ministry and Counseling M
Psychology—General M
Social Psychology M

MARY BALDWIN COLLEGE

Education—General M
Elementary Education M
English M
Middle School Education M
Theater M

MARYGROVE COLLEGE

Adult Education M
Education—General M
Educational Administration M
Elementary Education M
Human Resources Management M
Legal and Justice Studies M
Pastoral Ministry and Counseling M
Reading Education M
Secondary Education M
Translation and Interpretation M
Urban Education M

MARYLAND INSTITUTE COLLEGE OF ART

Art Education M
Art/Fine Arts M,O*
Computer Art and Design M
Graphic Design M
Photography M

MARYLHURST UNIVERSITY

Art Therapy M,O
Business Administration and Management—General M
Counseling Psychology M,O
Interdisciplinary Studies M
Theology P,M

MARYMOUNT UNIVERSITY

Allied Health—General M,D,O
Business Administration and Management—General M,O
Computer and Information Systems Security M,O
Computer Science M,O
Counseling Psychology M,O
Counselor Education M
Education—General M,O
Educational Administration M,O
Elementary Education M,O
English as a Second Language M,O
English Education M
English M
Family Nurse Practitioner Studies M,O
Forensic Psychology M
Health Promotion M
Health Services Management and Hospital Administration M
Human Resources Management M,O
Humanities M
Interior Design M
Legal and Justice Studies M,O
Management Information Systems M,O
Medical Informatics M,O
Nursing and Healthcare Administration M,O
Nursing Education M,O
Nursing—General M,O
Pastoral Ministry and Counseling M,O
Physical Therapy D
Project Management M,O
Secondary Education M,O
Social Psychology M
Special Education M,O

MARYVILLE UNIVERSITY OF SAINT LOUIS

Accounting M,O
Actuarial Science M
Allied Health—General M,D
Art Education M,D
Business Administration and Management—General M,O
Business Education M,O
Early Childhood Education M,D
Education of the Gifted M,D
Education—General M,D
Educational Administration M,D
Electronic Commerce M,O
Elementary Education M,D
English Education M,D
Environmental Education M,D
Marketing M,O
Middle School Education M,D
Nursing—General M
Occupational Therapy M
Physical Therapy D
Reading Education M,D
Rehabilitation Counseling M
Secondary Education M,D
Therapies—Dance, Drama, and Music M

MARYWOOD UNIVERSITY

Addictions/Substance Abuse Counseling M
Art Education M
Art Therapy M,O
Art/Fine Arts M
Biotechnology M*
Business Administration and Management—General M*
Clinical Psychology M,D
Communication Disorders M*
Communication—General M
Corporate and Organizational Communication M,O
Counseling Psychology M,O
Counselor Education M,O
Criminal Justice and Criminology M
Early Childhood Education M
Education—General M
Educational Administration M,D
Electronic Commerce M,O
Elementary Education M
Exercise and Sports Science M
Film, Television, and Video Production M,O
Finance and Banking M,O
Gerontology M,O
Graphic Design M
Health Communication M,O
Health Education D
Health Services Management and Hospital Administration M
Higher Education M,D
Human Development D
Illustration M
Information Science M
Interdisciplinary Studies M,O
Interior Design M
Investment Management M
Library Science M,O
Management Information Systems M
Media Studies M,O
Music Education M
Nursing and Healthcare Administration M
Nutrition M
Photography M
Physician Assistant Studies M
Psychology—General M*
Public Administration M
Reading Education M
School Psychology M,O
Secondary Education M
Social Work M,D*
Special Education M
Textile Design M
Therapies—Dance, Drama, and Music M,O

MASSACHUSETTS COLLEGE OF ART

Applied Arts and Design—General M
Art Education M
Art/Fine Arts M
Film, Television, and Video Production M
Photography M
Textile Design M
Theater M

MASSACHUSETTS COLLEGE OF LIBERAL ARTS

Curriculum and Instruction M
Education—General M
Educational Administration M
Reading Education M
Special Education M

MASSACHUSETTS COLLEGE OF PHARMACY AND HEALTH SCIENCES

Chemistry M,D
Health Services Management and Hospital Administration M
Pharmaceutical Administration M
Pharmaceutical Sciences M,D*
Pharmacology M,D

MASSACHUSETTS INSTITUTE OF TECHNOLOGY

Aerospace/Aeronautical Engineering M,D,O
Architectural History M,D
Architecture M,D*
Art History M,D
Art/Fine Arts M,D,O
Atmospheric Sciences M,D
Biochemistry D
Bioengineering M,D*
Biological and Biomedical Sciences—General P,M,D*
Biomedical Engineering M,D,O*
Business Administration and Management—General M,D
Cell Biology D
Chemical Engineering M,D
Chemistry D
Civil Engineering M,D,O
Cognitive Sciences D
Communication Disorders D*
Computational Biology D
Computational Sciences M*
Computer Engineering M,D,O
Computer Science M,D,O
Construction Engineering M,D,O
Developmental Biology D
Economics M,D
Electrical Engineering M,D,O
Electronic Materials M,D,O
Engineering and Applied Sciences—General M,D,O
Engineering Management M,D
Environmental Biology M,D,O
Environmental Engineering M,D,O
Environmental Sciences M,D,O
Geochemistry M,D
Geology M,D
Geophysics M,D
Geosciences M,D
Geotechnical Engineering M,D,O
History of Science and Technology D
Humanities M
Hydraulics M,D,O
Hydrology M,D,O
Immunology D
Information Science M,D,O
Inorganic Chemistry D
Linguistics D
Logistics M,D
Manufacturing Engineering M,D,O
Marine Geology M,D
Materials Engineering M,D,O
Materials Sciences M,D,O
Mathematics D
Mechanical Engineering M,D,O
Mechanics M,D,O
Media Studies M,D
Medical Informatics M
Medical Physics D
Metallurgical Engineering and Metallurgy M,D,O
Molecular Pathogenesis M,D
Molecular Pharmacology M,D
Molecular Toxicology M,D
Neurobiology D
Neuroscience D*
Nuclear Engineering M,D,O
Ocean Engineering M,D,O
Oceanography M,D,O
Operations Research M,D

Organic Chemistry M,D,O
Philosophy D
Physical Chemistry D
Physics D
Planetary and Space Sciences M,D
Plasma Physics M,D,O
Political Science M,D
Polymer Science and Engineering M,D,O
Real Estate M
Social Sciences D
Structural Biology D
Structural Engineering M,D,O
Systems Biology D
Systems Engineering M,D
Technical Writing M
Technology and Public Policy M,D
Toxicology M,D
Transportation and Highway Engineering M,D,O
Urban and Regional Planning M,D
Urban Studies M,D
Writing M

MASSACHUSETTS MARITIME ACADEMY
Facilities Management M

MASSACHUSETTS SCHOOL OF LAW AT ANDOVER
Law P*

MASSACHUSETTS SCHOOL OF PROFESSIONAL PSYCHOLOGY
Clinical Psychology M,D
Psychology—General M,D*
School Psychology M,D

THE MASTER'S COLLEGE AND SEMINARY
Pastoral Ministry and Counseling P,M,D
Theology P,M,D

MAYO GRADUATE SCHOOL
Biochemistry D*
Biological and Biomedical Sciences—General D*
Biomedical Engineering D*
Cancer Biology/Oncology D
Cell Biology D
Genetics D
Immunology D*
Molecular Biology D
Molecular Pharmacology D*
Neuroscience D
Structural Biology D
Virology D*

MAYO MEDICAL SCHOOL
Allopathic Medicine P

MAYO SCHOOL OF HEALTH SCIENCES
Nurse Anesthesia M
Physical Therapy D

MCCORMICK THEOLOGICAL SEMINARY
Pastoral Ministry and Counseling P,M,D,O
Theology P,M,D,O

MCDANIEL COLLEGE
Counselor Education M
Curriculum and Instruction M
Educational Administration M
Educational Media/Instructional Technology M
Elementary Education M
Human Resources Development M
Human Services M
Liberal Studies M
Library Science M
Physical Education M
Reading Education M
Secondary Education M
Special Education M

MCGILL UNIVERSITY
Accounting M,D,O
Aerospace/Aeronautical Engineering M,D
Agricultural Economics and Agribusiness M
Agricultural Engineering M,D
Agricultural Sciences—General M,D,O
Agronomy and Soil Sciences M,D
Allopathic Medicine M,D
Anatomy M,D
Animal Sciences M,D
Anthropology M,D
Applied Mathematics M,D
Architecture M,D,O
Art History M,D
Asian Studies M,D
Atmospheric Sciences M,D
Biochemistry M,D
Bioengineering M,D
Bioethics M,D,O
Bioinformatics M,D
Biological and Biomedical Sciences—General M,D*
Biomedical Engineering M,D
Biostatistics M,D,O
Biotechnology M,D,O
Business Administration and Management—General M,D,O
Cell Biology M,D
Chemical Engineering M,D,O
Chemistry M,D
Civil Engineering M,D
Clinical Psychology D
Communication Disorders M,D
Communication—General M,D
Community Health M,D,O
Computational Sciences M,D
Computer Engineering M,D
Computer Science M,D
Counseling Psychology M,D
Curriculum and Instruction M,D,O
Dentistry P,M,D,O
Developmental Psychology M,D,O
Economics M,D
Education—General M,D,O
Educational Administration M,D,O
Educational Psychology M,D
Electrical Engineering M,D
Engineering and Applied Sciences—General M,D,O
English M,D
Entomology M,D
Entrepreneurship M,D,O
Environmental and Occupational Health M,D,O
Environmental Engineering M,D,O
Environmental Management and Policy M,D
Epidemiology M,D,O
Experimental Psychology M,D
Family Nurse Practitioner Studies M,D,O
Finance and Banking M,D,O
Fish, Game, and Wildlife Management M,D
Food Science and Technology M,D
Foreign Languages Education M,D,O
Forensic Sciences M,D,O
Forestry M,D
Foundations and Philosophy of Education M,D,O
French M,D
Genetic Counseling M,D
Geography M,D
Geosciences M,D
Geotechnical Engineering M,D
German M,D
Health Physics/Radiological Health M,D
Health Services Management and Hospital Administration M,D,O
Hispanic Studies M,D
History of Medicine M,D
History M,D
Human Genetics M,D
Hydraulics M,D
Immunology M,D
Industrial and Manufacturing Management M,D,O*
Information Studies M,D,O
International Business M,D,O
International Development M,D,O
Italian M,D
Jewish Studies M,D
Kinesiology and Movement Studies M,D,O
Law M,D,O
Library Science M,D,O
Linguistics M,D
Management Information Systems M,D,O
Management Strategy and Policy M,D,O
Marketing M,D,O
Materials Engineering M,D
Mathematics M,D
Mechanical Engineering M,D
Mechanics M,D
Medical Physics M,D
Meteorology M,D
Microbiology M,D
Mineral/Mining Engineering M,D,O
Music Education M,D
Music M,D
Natural Resources M,D
Near and Middle Eastern Studies M,D,O
Neuroscience M,D
Nursing—General M,D,O
Nutrition M,D,O
Oceanography M,D
Oral and Dental Sciences M,D
Parasitology M,D,O
Pathology M,D
Pharmacology M,D
Philosophy M,D
Physical Education M,D,O
Physics M,D
Physiology M,D
Planetary and Space Sciences M,D
Plant Sciences M,D,O
Political Science M,D
Psychology—General M,D
Rehabilitation Sciences M,D
Religion M,D
Russian M,D
School Psychology M,D,O
Social Work M,D,O
Sociology M,D,O
Statistics M,D,O
Structural Engineering M,D
Theology M,D
Transportation Management M,D
Urban and Regional Planning M,D
Water Resources Engineering M,D

MCKENDREE COLLEGE
Business Administration and Management—General M
Counseling Psychology M
Education—General M
Nursing—General M

MCMASTER UNIVERSITY
Analytical Chemistry M,D
Anthropology M,D
Applied Statistics M
Astrophysics D
Biochemistry M,D
Biological and Biomedical Sciences—General M,D
Business Administration and Management—General M,D
Cancer Biology/Oncology M,D
Cardiovascular Sciences M,D
Cell Biology M,D
Chemical Engineering M,D
Chemical Physics M,D
Chemistry M,D
Civil Engineering M,D
Classics M,D
Computer Science M,D
Cultural Studies M,D
Economics M,D
Electrical Engineering M,D
Engineering and Applied Sciences—General M,D
Engineering Physics M,D
English M,D
French M
Genetics M,D
Geochemistry M,D
Geography M,D
Geology M,D
Geosciences M,D
Health Physics/Radiological Health M,D
Health Services Research M,D
History M,D
Human Resources Management M,D
Immunology M,D
Industrial and Labor Relations M
Inorganic Chemistry M,D
International Affairs M,D
Kinesiology and Movement Studies M,D
Management Information Systems D
Materials Engineering M,D
Materials Sciences M,D
Mathematics M,D
Mechanical Engineering M,D
Medical Physics M,D
Molecular Biology M,D
Music M
Neuroscience M,D
Nuclear Engineering M,D
Nursing—General M,D
Nutrition M,D
Occupational Therapy M
Organic Chemistry M,D
Pastoral Ministry and Counseling P,M,D,O
Pharmacology M,D
Philosophy M,D
Physical Chemistry M,D
Physical Therapy M
Physics D
Physiology M,D
Political Science M,D
Psychology—General M,D
Public Administration M,D
Public Affairs M,D
Public Policy M,D
Rehabilitation Sciences M,D
Religion M,D
Social Work M
Sociology M,D
Software Engineering M,D
Statistics M
Theology P,M,D,O
Virology M,D

MCNEESE STATE UNIVERSITY
Agricultural Sciences—General M
Biological and Biomedical Sciences—General M
Business Administration and Management—General M
Chemical Engineering M
Chemistry M
Civil Engineering M
Computer Science M
Counseling Psychology M
Counselor Education M
Curriculum and Instruction M
Early Childhood Education M
Education—General M
Educational Administration M,O
Educational Media/Instructional Technology M
Electrical Engineering M
Elementary Education M
Engineering and Applied Sciences—General M
Engineering Management M
English M
Environmental Sciences M
Exercise and Sports Science M
Health Promotion M
Mathematics M
Mechanical Engineering M
Multilingual and Multicultural Education M
Music Education M
Nursing—General M
Psychology—General M
School Psychology M
Science Education M
Secondary Education M
Social Sciences Education M
Statistics M
Writing M

MEADVILLE LOMBARD THEOLOGICAL SCHOOL
Pastoral Ministry and Counseling P,M,D
Theology P,M,D

MEDAILLE COLLEGE
Business Administration and Management—General M
Counseling Psychology M
Curriculum and Instruction M
Education—General M
Elementary Education M
Organizational Management M
Psychology—General M
Reading Education M
Special Education M

MEDICAL COLLEGE OF GEORGIA
Adult Nursing M,D
Allied Health—General M,D
Allopathic Medicine P
Anatomy M,D
Biochemistry M,D
Biological and Biomedical Sciences—General M,D*
Biostatistics M
Cardiovascular Sciences M,D
Cell Biology M,D
Clinical Laboratory Sciences/Medical Technology M
Community Health Nursing M,D
Dental Hygiene M
Dentistry P
Family Nurse Practitioner Studies M,D
Health Informatics M
Health Physics/Radiological Health M
Maternal and Child/Neonatal Nursing M,D
Medical Illustration M
Molecular Biology M,D
Molecular Medicine M,D
Neuroscience M,D
Nurse Anesthesia M,D
Nursing—General M,D
Occupational Therapy M
Oral and Dental Sciences M,D
Pharmacology M,D
Physical Therapy M,D
Physician Assistant Studies M
Physiology M,D
Psychiatric Nursing M,D

MEDICAL COLLEGE OF WISCONSIN
Allopathic Medicine P
Biochemistry M,D
Bioethics M
Bioinformatics M
Biological and Biomedical Sciences—General M,D*
Biophysics D*
Biostatistics D*
Cell Biology M,D
Clinical Laboratory Sciences/Medical Technology D
Developmental Biology M,D
Environmental and Occupational Health M
Epidemiology M
Medical Informatics M

- Microbiology M,D
- Molecular Genetics M,D
- Pathology M,D
- Pharmacology M,D
- Physiology M,D*
- Public Health—General M
- Toxicology M,D

MEDICAL UNIVERSITY OF SOUTH CAROLINA

- Adult Nursing M
- Allied Health—General M,D
- Allopathic Medicine P
- Anatomy D
- Biochemistry M,D
- Bioinformatics M,D
- Biological and Biomedical Sciences—General M,D
- Biostatistics M,D
- Cancer Biology/Oncology D
- Cell Biology D
- Clinical Research M
- Communication Disorders M
- Dentistry P
- Epidemiology M,D
- Family Nurse Practitioner Studies M
- Gerontological Nursing M
- Health Services Management and Hospital Administration M,D
- Immunology M,D
- Marine Sciences D
- Maternal and Child/Neonatal Nursing M
- Microbiology M,D*
- Molecular Biology M,D
- Molecular Pharmacology M,D
- Neuroscience M,D
- Nurse Anesthesia M
- Nurse Midwifery M
- Nursing and Healthcare Administration M
- Nursing Education M
- Nursing—General M,D
- Occupational Therapy M
- Pathobiology D
- Pathology M,D
- Pharmaceutical Sciences P,D
- Pharmacy P,D
- Physical Therapy D
- Physician Assistant Studies M
- Psychiatric Nursing M
- Rehabilitation Sciences D

MEHARRY MEDICAL COLLEGE

- Allopathic Medicine P
- Biochemistry D
- Biological and Biomedical Sciences—General D
- Community Health M
- Dentistry P
- Environmental and Occupational Health M
- Health Services Management and Hospital Administration M
- Microbiology D
- Pharmacology D
- Physiology D

MEMORIAL UNIVERSITY OF NEWFOUNDLAND

- Adult Education M,D,O
- Allopathic Medicine P
- Anthropology M,D
- Aquaculture M
- Archaeology M,D
- Biochemistry M,D
- Biological and Biomedical Sciences—General M,D,O
- Biopsychology M,D
- Business Administration and Management—General M
- Chemistry M,D
- Civil Engineering M,D
- Classics M
- Community Health M,D,O
- Computational Sciences M
- Computer Engineering M,D
- Computer Science M,D
- Condensed Matter Physics M,D
- Curriculum and Instruction M,D,O
- Economics M
- Education—General M,D,O
- Educational Administration M,D,O
- Educational Media/Instructional Technology M,D,O
- Educational Psychology M,D,O
- Electrical Engineering M,D
- Engineering and Applied Sciences—General M,D
- English M,D
- Environmental Engineering M
- Environmental Sciences M
- Epidemiology M,D,O
- Exercise and Sports Science M
- Experimental Psychology M,D
- Fish, Game, and Wildlife Management M,O
- Folklore M,D
- Food Science and Technology M,D
- French M
- Gender Studies M,D
- Geography M,D
- Geology M,D
- Geophysics M,D
- Geosciences M,D
- German M
- History M,D
- Human Genetics M,D
- Humanities M
- Industrial and Labor Relations M
- Kinesiology and Movement Studies M
- Linguistics M,D
- Marine Affairs M,D,O
- Marine Biology M,D
- Marine Sciences M,O
- Mathematics M,D
- Mechanical Engineering M,D
- Music M,D
- Natural Resources M,D
- Nursing—General M,O
- Ocean Engineering M,D
- Oceanography M,D
- Pharmaceutical Sciences M,D
- Philosophy M
- Physical Education M
- Physics M,D
- Political Science M
- Psychology—General M,D
- Religion M
- Social Psychology M,D
- Social Work M
- Sociology M,D
- Sport Psychology M
- Statistics M,D

MEMPHIS COLLEGE OF ART

- Applied Arts and Design—General M
- Art Education M
- Art/Fine Arts M*
- Computer Art and Design M
- Photography M
- Textile Design M

MEMPHIS THEOLOGICAL SEMINARY

- Theology P,M,D

MENNONITE BRETHREN BIBLICAL SEMINARY

- Marriage and Family Therapy M,O
- Missions and Missiology M
- Pastoral Ministry and Counseling M
- Theology P,M

MERCER UNIVERSITY

- Accounting M
- Allopathic Medicine P,M
- Business Administration and Management—General M
- Computer Engineering M
- Early Childhood Education M,D,O
- Education—General M,D,O
- Educational Administration M,D,O
- Electrical Engineering M
- Engineering and Applied Sciences—General M
- Engineering Management M
- Law P
- Management of Technology M
- Mechanical Engineering M
- Middle School Education M,D,O
- Music M
- Nursing—General M,O
- Pharmaceutical Sciences P,M,D
- Pharmacy P,M,D
- Reading Education M,D,O
- Secondary Education M,D,O
- Software Engineering M
- Theology P,D

MERCY COLLEGE

- Addictions/Substance Abuse Counseling M,O
- Adult Nursing M,O
- Allied Health—General M,O
- Business Administration and Management—General M
- Communication Disorders M
- Counseling Psychology M,O
- Counselor Education M
- Early Childhood Education M
- Education—General M
- Educational Administration M
- Educational Media/Instructional Technology M
- Electronic Commerce M
- Elementary Education M
- English as a Second Language M
- English M
- Finance and Banking M
- Health Services Management and Hospital Administration M,O
- Human Resources Management M
- Marketing M
- Marriage and Family Therapy M,O
- Middle School Education M
- Multilingual and Multicultural Education M,O
- Nursing and Healthcare Administration M
- Nursing Education M
- Nursing—General M
- Occupational Therapy M
- Organizational Management M
- Physical Therapy M
- Physician Assistant Studies M
- Psychology—General M
- Reading Education M
- School Psychology M
- Secondary Education M
- Special Education M
- Urban Education M

MERCYHURST COLLEGE

- Biological Anthropology M
- Criminal Justice and Criminology M,O
- Educational Administration M,O
- Forensic Sciences M
- Multilingual and Multicultural Education M,O
- Organizational Management M,O
- Special Education M,O

MEREDITH COLLEGE

- Business Administration and Management—General M
- Education—General M
- Music M
- Nutrition M

MERRIMACK COLLEGE

- Education—General M

MESA STATE COLLEGE

- Business Administration and Management—General M

MESIVTA OF EASTERN PARKWAY RABBINICAL SEMINARY

- Theology

MESIVTA TIFERETH JERUSALEM OF AMERICA

- Theology

MESIVTA TORAH VODAATH RABBINICAL SEMINARY

- Theology

METHODIST THEOLOGICAL SCHOOL IN OHIO

- Theology P,M

METHODIST UNIVERSITY

- Business Administration and Management—General M
- Criminal Justice and Criminology M
- Physician Assistant Studies M

METROPOLITAN COLLEGE OF NEW YORK

- Business Administration and Management—General M
- Corporate and Organizational Communication M
- Elementary Education M
- Media Studies M
- Public Administration M

METROPOLITAN STATE UNIVERSITY

- Business Administration and Management—General M
- Criminal Justice and Criminology M
- Finance and Banking M
- Human Resources Management M
- Information Studies M
- International Business M
- Management Information Systems M
- Marketing M
- Nonprofit Management M
- Nursing—General M
- Organizational Management M
- Public Administration M
- Technical Writing M

MGH INSTITUTE OF HEALTH PROFESSIONS

- Allied Health—General M,D,O
- Clinical Research M,O
- Communication Disorders M,O
- Gerontological Nursing M,O
- Medical Imaging O
- Nursing Education M,O
- Nursing—General M,O*
- Pediatric Nursing M,O
- Physical Therapy M,D,O
- Psychiatric Nursing M,O
- Reading Education M,O
- Women's Health Nursing M,O

MIAMI INTERNATIONAL UNIVERSITY OF ART & DESIGN

- Art/Fine Arts M
- Computer Art and Design M
- Film, Television, and Video Production M
- Graphic Design M*
- Interior Design M

MIAMI UNIVERSITY

- Accounting M
- Analytical Chemistry M,D
- Architecture M
- Art Education M
- Art/Fine Arts M*
- Biochemistry M,D
- Botany M,D*
- Business Administration and Management—General M
- Chemistry M,D
- Child and Family Studies M
- Clinical Psychology D
- Communication Disorders M
- Communication—General M
- Curriculum and Instruction M
- Early Childhood Education M
- Economics M
- Education—General M,D,O
- Educational Administration M,D
- Educational Psychology M,O
- Elementary Education M
- Engineering and Applied Sciences—General M,O
- English Education M,D
- English M,D
- Environmental Sciences M
- Exercise and Sports Science M
- Experimental Psychology D
- Finance and Banking M
- French M
- Geography M
- Geology M,D
- Gerontology M
- History M,D
- Inorganic Chemistry M,D
- Management Information Systems M
- Marketing M
- Mass Communication M
- Mathematics Education M
- Mathematics M*
- Microbiology M,D
- Music Education M
- Music M
- Operations Research M
- Organic Chemistry M,D
- Paper and Pulp Engineering M
- Philosophy M
- Physical Chemistry M,D
- Physics M
- Plant Biology M,D
- Plant Sciences M,D
- Political Science M,D
- Psychology—General D
- Reading Education M
- Religion M
- Rhetoric M,D
- School Psychology M,O
- Secondary Education M
- Social Psychology D
- Social Sciences Education M
- Social Work M
- Software Engineering M,O
- Spanish M
- Special Education M
- Speech and Interpersonal Communication M
- Statistics M
- Student Affairs M
- Systems Science M
- Technical Writing M
- Theater M
- Writing M,D
- Zoology M,D*

Close-Up on page 957.

MICHIGAN SCHOOL OF PROFESSIONAL PSYCHOLOGY

- Clinical Psychology M,D
- Educational Psychology M,D
- Psychology—General M,D
- Transpersonal and Humanistic Psychology M,D

MICHIGAN STATE UNIVERSITY

- Accounting M,D
- Adult Education M,D,O
- Advertising and Public Relations M,D
- African Studies M,D
- African-American Studies M,D

Agricultural Economics and Agribusiness M,D
Agricultural Engineering M,D
Agricultural Sciences—General M,D
Agronomy and Soil Sciences M,D
Allopathic Medicine P
American Studies M,D
Animal Sciences M,D
Anthropology M,D
Applied Mathematics M,D
Applied Statistics M,D
Art/Fine Arts M
Astronomy M,D
Astrophysics M,D
Biochemistry M,D*
Bioethics M
Biological and Biomedical Sciences—General M,D
Biosystems Engineering M,D
Business Administration and Management—General M,D
Cell Biology M,D
Chemical Engineering M,D
Chemical Physics M,D
Chemistry M,D
Child and Family Studies M,D
Child Development M,D
Civil Engineering M,D
Clinical Laboratory Sciences/Medical Technology M
Communication Disorders M,D
Communication—General M,D
Computer Science M,D
Construction Management M,D*
Counselor Education M,D,O
Criminal Justice and Criminology M,D*
Curriculum and Instruction M,D,O
Ecology D*
Economics M,D
Education—General M,D,O
Educational Administration M,D,O
Educational Measurement and Evaluation M,D,O
Educational Media/Instructional Technology M,D,O
Educational Policy D
Educational Psychology M,D,O
Electrical Engineering M,D
Engineering and Applied Sciences—General M,D
Engineering Management M,D
English as a Second Language M,D
English M,D
Entomology M,D
Environmental Design M,D
Environmental Engineering M,D
Environmental Management and Policy M,D
Environmental Sciences M,D
Epidemiology M,D
Evolutionary Biology D
Finance and Banking M,D
Fish, Game, and Wildlife Management M,D
Food Science and Technology M,D
Foreign Languages Education D
Forensic Sciences M,D
Forestry M,D
French M,D
Genetics M,D
Geography M,D
Geosciences M,D
German M,D
Health Communication M
Higher Education M,D,O
Hispanic Studies M,D
History M,D
Horticulture M,D
Hospitality Management M*
Human Resources Management M,D
Humanities M
Industrial and Labor Relations M,D
Interior Design M,D
International Affairs M
Journalism M
Kinesiology and Movement Studies M,D
Latin American Studies D
Linguistics M,D
Management Information Systems M,D
Manufacturing Engineering M,D
Marketing M,D
Marriage and Family Therapy M,D
Materials Engineering M,D
Materials Sciences M,D
Mathematics Education M,D
Mathematics M,D
Mechanical Engineering M,D
Mechanics M,D
Media Studies M,D
Microbiology M,D*
Molecular Biology M,D
Molecular Genetics M,D
Music Education M,D
Music M,D
Neuroscience M,D
Nursing—General M,D
Nutrition M,D
Osteopathic Medicine P
Pathobiology M,D
Pathology M,D
Pharmacology M,D
Philosophy M,D
Physics M,D
Physiology M,D
Plant Biology M,D
Plant Pathology M,D
Plant Sciences M,D
Political Science M,D
Portuguese M,D
Psychology—General M,D
Reading Education M
Recreation and Park Management M,D
Rehabilitation Counseling M,D,O
Rhetoric M,D
Romance Languages M,D
School Psychology M,D,O
Science Education M
Social Sciences Education M,D
Social Sciences M
Social Work M,D
Sociology M,D
Spanish M,D
Special Education M,D,O
Statistics M,D
Supply Chain Management M,D
Telecommunications M
Theater M
Therapies—Dance, Drama, and Music M,D
Toxicology M,D
Urban and Regional Planning M,D
Veterinary Medicine P
Veterinary Sciences M,D
Writing M,D
Zoology M,D

Close-Up on page 959.

MICHIGAN STATE UNIVERSITY COLLEGE OF LAW

Law P,M
Legal and Justice Studies P,M

MICHIGAN TECHNOLOGICAL UNIVERSITY

Archaeology M,D
Biological and Biomedical Sciences—General M,D
Biomedical Engineering D
Business Administration and Management—General M
Chemical Engineering M,D
Chemistry M,D
Civil Engineering M,D
Computational Sciences D
Computer Engineering D
Computer Science M,D
Ecology M
Electrical Engineering M,D
Engineering and Applied Sciences—General M,D
Engineering Physics D
Environmental Engineering M,D
Environmental Management and Policy M
Forestry M,D
Geological Engineering M,D
Geology M,D
Geophysics M
Historic Preservation D
Materials Engineering M,D
Mathematics M,D
Mechanical Engineering M,D*
Mechanics M
Metallurgical Engineering and Metallurgy M,D
Mineral Economics M
Mineral/Mining Engineering M,D
Physics M,D
Plant Molecular Biology M,D
Rhetoric M,D
Science Education M
Sustainable Development O
Technical Communication M,D

Close-Up on page 961.

MICHIGAN THEOLOGICAL SEMINARY

Counseling Psychology P,M,D
Religious Education P,M,D
Theology P,M,D

MID-AMERICA BAPTIST THEOLOGICAL SEMINARY

Theology P,M,D

MID-AMERICA BAPTIST THEOLOGICAL SEMINARY NORTHEAST BRANCH

Theology P

MIDAMERICA NAZARENE UNIVERSITY

Business Administration and Management—General M
Counseling Psychology M
Curriculum and Instruction M
Education—General M
Educational Media/Instructional Technology M
Special Education M

MIDDLEBURY COLLEGE

Chinese M
English M
French M,D
German M,D
Italian M,D
Russian M,D
Spanish M,D

MIDDLE TENNESSEE SCHOOL OF ANESTHESIA

Nurse Anesthesia M

MIDDLE TENNESSEE STATE UNIVERSITY

Accounting M
Aerospace/Aeronautical Engineering M
Aviation M
Biological and Biomedical Sciences—General M
Business Administration and Management—General M
Business Education M
Chemistry M,D
Child and Family Studies M
Child Development M
Computer Science M
Counselor Education M,O
Criminal Justice and Criminology M
Curriculum and Instruction M,O
Early Childhood Education M,O
Economics M,D*
Education—General M,D,O
Educational Administration M,O
Elementary Education M,O
English as a Second Language M,O
English M,D
Exercise and Sports Science M,D
Finance and Banking M,D
Foreign Languages Education M
Geosciences O
Gerontology O
Health Education M,D
Health Services Management and Hospital Administration O
Historic Preservation M,D
History M,D
Industrial and Organizational Psychology M,O
Journalism M
Management Information Systems M
Marketing M
Mass Communication M
Mathematics Education M
Mathematics M
Middle School Education M,O
Music M
Nursing—General M
Nutrition M
Physical Education M,D
Psychology—General M
Reading Education M
Recreation and Park Management M,D
School Psychology M,O
Science Education M
Sociology M,O
Special Education M,O
Vocational and Technical Education M

MIDWEST COLLEGE OF ORIENTAL MEDICINE

Acupuncture and Oriental Medicine M,O

MIDWESTERN BAPTIST THEOLOGICAL SEMINARY

Music P,M,D
Pastoral Ministry and Counseling P,M,D
Religious Education P,M,D
Theology P,M,D

MIDWESTERN STATE UNIVERSITY

Biological and Biomedical Sciences—General M
Business Administration and Management—General M
Computer Science M
Counselor Education M
Criminal Justice and Criminology M
Curriculum and Instruction M
Education—General M
Educational Administration M
Educational Media/Instructional Technology M
English M
Family Nurse Practitioner Studies M
Health Physics/Radiological Health M
Health Services Management and Hospital Administration M
History M
Human Resources Development M
Kinesiology and Movement Studies M
Nursing Education M
Nursing—General M
Political Science M
Psychology—General M
Public Administration M
Reading Education M
Special Education M

MIDWESTERN UNIVERSITY, DOWNERS GROVE CAMPUS

Allied Health—General M,D
Biological and Biomedical Sciences—General M*
Clinical Psychology M,D*
Occupational Therapy M*
Osteopathic Medicine P*
Pharmacy P*
Physical Therapy D*
Physician Assistant Studies M*

MIDWESTERN UNIVERSITY, GLENDALE CAMPUS

Allied Health—General P,M,O
Bioethics M,O
Biological and Biomedical Sciences—General M
Cardiovascular Sciences M
Health Education M
Nurse Anesthesia M
Occupational Therapy M
Osteopathic Medicine P*
Pharmacy P
Physician Assistant Studies M
Podiatric Medicine P

MIDWEST UNIVERSITY

Missions and Missiology P,M,D
Music P,M,D
Pastoral Ministry and Counseling P,M,D
Religious Education P,M,D
Theology P,M,D

MILLERSVILLE UNIVERSITY OF PENNSYLVANIA

Art Education M
Biological and Biomedical Sciences—General M
Business Administration and Management—General M
Clinical Psychology M
Early Childhood Education M
Education—General M
Elementary Education M
English Education M
English M
Foundations and Philosophy of Education M
French M
German M
History M
Mathematics Education M
Nursing—General M
Psychology—General M
Reading Education M
School Psychology M
Social Work M
Spanish M
Special Education M
Sports Management M
Vocational and Technical Education M

MILLIGAN COLLEGE

Business Administration and Management—General M
Education—General M
Occupational Therapy M

MILLIKIN UNIVERSITY

Business Administration and Management—General M

MILLSAPS COLLEGE

Accounting M
Business Administration and Management—General M

MILLS COLLEGE

Art/Fine Arts M
Biological and Biomedical Sciences—General O
Business Administration and Management—General M
Computer Science M,O
Curriculum and Instruction M,D

Dance M
Early Childhood Education M,D
Education—General M,D
Educational Administration M,D
Elementary Education M,D
English Education M,D
English M
Health Education M,D
Mathematics Education M,D
Music M
Photography M
Science Education M,D
Secondary Education M,D
Social Sciences Education M,D
Writing M

Close-Up on page 963.

MILWAUKEE SCHOOL OF ENGINEERING

Business Administration and Management—General M
Cardiovascular Sciences M
Clinical Laboratory Sciences/ Medical Technology M
Engineering and Applied Sciences—General M*
Engineering Management M
Environmental Engineering M
Medical Informatics M
Structural Engineering M

MINNEAPOLIS COLLEGE OF ART AND DESIGN

Applied Arts and Design—General M
Art/Fine Arts M
Computer Art and Design O
Film, Television, and Video Production M
Graphic Design M
Illustration M
Photography M

MINNESOTA STATE UNIVERSITY MANKATO

Accounting M
Addictions/Substance Abuse Counseling M
Allied Health—General M,O
Anthropology M
Art Education M
Art/Fine Arts M
Astronomy M
Automotive Engineering M
Biological and Biomedical Sciences—General M
Business Administration and Management—General M
Clinical Psychology M
Communication Disorders M
Community Health M
Computer Science M,O
Counselor Education M,O
Criminal Justice and Criminology M
Curriculum and Instruction M,O
Early Childhood Education M
Ecology M
Education of the Gifted M,O
Education—General M,O
Educational Administration M,O
Educational Media/Instructional Technology M,O
Electrical Engineering M
Elementary Education M
English Education M,O
English M,O
Environmental Design M,O
Environmental Sciences M
Ethnic Studies M
Family Nurse Practitioner Studies M
Finance and Banking M
French M
Geography M
Gerontology M,O
Health Education M
Higher Education M,O
History M
Human Services M
Industrial and Organizational Psychology M
Interdisciplinary Studies M
International Business M
Manufacturing Engineering M
Marketing M
Marriage and Family Therapy M,O
Mathematics Education M
Mathematics M
Multilingual and Multicultural Education M
Music M
Nursing and Healthcare Administration M
Nursing Education M
Nursing—General M
Physical Education M,O
Physics M
Political Science M
Psychology—General M
Public Administration M
Rehabilitation Counseling M
Science Education M
Social Psychology M,O
Social Sciences Education M
Sociology M
Spanish M
Special Education M,O
Speech and Interpersonal Communication M
Statistics M
Student Affairs M,O
Technical Communication M,O
Theater M
Urban and Regional Planning M,O
Urban Studies M,O
Women's Studies M,O
Writing M,O

MINNESOTA STATE UNIVERSITY MOORHEAD

Communication Disorders M
Counselor Education M
Curriculum and Instruction M
Education—General M,O
Educational Administration M,O
Human Services M
Liberal Studies M
Nursing Education M
Nursing—General M,O
Public Administration M
Reading Education M
School Psychology M,O
Special Education M
Writing M

MINOT STATE UNIVERSITY

Business Administration and Management—General M
Communication Disorders M
Criminal Justice and Criminology M
Early Childhood Education M
Education of the Multiply Handicapped M
Elementary Education M
Management Information Systems M
Mathematics Education M
Music Education M
School Psychology O
Science Education M
Special Education M

MIRRER YESHIVA

Theology

MISSISSIPPI COLLEGE

Accounting M,O
Advertising and Public Relations M
Art Education M,O
Art/Fine Arts M
Biological and Biomedical Sciences—General M
Business Administration and Management—General M,O
Business Education M,O
Chemistry M
Communication—General M
Computer Education M,O
Computer Science M
Corporate and Organizational Communication M
Counseling Psychology M,O
Counselor Education M,O
Criminal Justice and Criminology M,O
Curriculum and Instruction M,O
Education—General M,O
Educational Administration M,O
Elementary Education M,O
English as a Second Language M
English Education M,O
English M
Health Services Management and Hospital Administration M
Higher Education M,O
History M,O
Law P,O
Legal and Justice Studies M,O
Liberal Studies M
Marriage and Family Therapy M,O
Mathematics Education M,O
Mathematics M
Music Education M
Music M
Political Science M,O
Science Education M,O
Secondary Education M,O
Social Sciences Education M,O
Social Sciences M,O
Sociology M
Special Education M,O

MISSISSIPPI STATE UNIVERSITY

Accounting M,D
Aerospace/Aeronautical Engineering M
Agricultural Economics and Agribusiness M,D
Agricultural Education M
Agricultural Sciences—General M,D
Agronomy and Soil Sciences M,D
Animal Sciences M
Anthropology M,D
Applied Economics M,D
Architecture M
Art/Fine Arts M
Biochemistry M,D
Bioengineering M,D
Biological and Biomedical Sciences—General M,D
Biomedical Engineering M,D
Business Administration and Management—General M,D
Chemical Engineering M,D
Chemistry M,D
Civil Engineering M,D
Clinical Psychology M,D
Cognitive Sciences M,D
Computer Art and Design M
Computer Engineering M,D
Computer Science M,D
Counselor Education M,D,O
Curriculum and Instruction M,D,O
Economics M,D
Education—General M,D,O
Educational Administration M,D,O
Educational Media/Instructional Technology M,D,O
Educational Psychology M,D,O
Electrical Engineering M,D
Elementary Education M,D,O
Engineering and Applied Sciences—General M,D
Engineering Physics M,D
English M
Entomology M,D
Exercise and Sports Science M
Experimental Psychology M,D
Finance and Banking M,D
Fish, Game, and Wildlife Management M
Food Science and Technology M,D
Foreign Languages Education M
Forestry M,D
French M
Geosciences M
German M
Health Education M
History M,D
Human Resources Development M,D,O
Industrial/Management Engineering M,D
Kinesiology and Movement Studies M
Landscape Architecture M
Management Information Systems M
Marketing M,D
Mathematics M,D
Mechanical Engineering M,D
Mechanics M
Molecular Biology M,D
Nutrition M,D
Physical Education M
Physics M,D
Plant Pathology M,D
Plant Sciences M,D
Political Science M,D
Project Management M,D
Psychology—General M,D
Public Administration M,D
Public Policy M,D
Secondary Education M,D,O
Sociology M,D
Spanish M
Special Education M,D,O
Sports Management M
Statistics M,D
Systems Engineering M,D
Taxation M
Veterinary Medicine P
Veterinary Sciences M,D
Vocational and Technical Education M,D,O

MISSISSIPPI UNIVERSITY FOR WOMEN

Communication Disorders M
Education of the Gifted M
Education—General M
Educational Media/Instructional Technology M
Health Education M
Nursing—General M,O

MISSISSIPPI VALLEY STATE UNIVERSITY

Bioinformatics M
Criminal Justice and Criminology M
Education—General M
Elementary Education M
Environmental and Occupational Health M

MISSOURI STATE UNIVERSITY

Accounting M
Agricultural Education M
Agricultural Sciences—General M
Art Education M
Art/Fine Arts M
Biological and Biomedical Sciences—General M
Business Administration and Management—General M*
Cell Biology M
Chemistry M
Child and Family Studies M
Communication Disorders M,D
Communication—General M
Computer Science M
Counselor Education M
Criminal Justice and Criminology M
Curriculum and Instruction M
Early Childhood Education M
Education—General M
Educational Administration M,O
Educational Media/Instructional Technology M
Elementary Education M,O
English M
Environmental Management and Policy M
Family and Consumer Sciences-General M
Foreign Languages Education M
French M
Geography M
Geology M
Geosciences M
German M
Health Promotion M
Health Services Management and Hospital Administration M
History M
International Affairs M
Management Information Systems M
Materials Sciences M
Mathematics M
Military and Defense Studies M*
Molecular Biology M
Music M
Nurse Anesthesia M
Nursing—General M
Physical Education M
Physical Therapy M
Physician Assistant Studies M
Plant Sciences M
Political Science M
Project Management M
Psychology—General M
Public Administration M
Public Health—General M
Reading Education M
Religion M
Science Education M
Secondary Education M,O
Social Sciences Education M
Social Work M
Spanish M
Special Education M,O
Sports Management M
Theater M
Urban and Regional Planning M

Close-Up on page 965.

MOLLOY COLLEGE

Adult Nursing M,O
Family Nurse Practitioner Studies M,O
Health Informatics M,O
Nursing and Healthcare Administration M,O
Nursing Education M,O
Nursing Informatics M,O
Nursing—General M,O
Pediatric Nursing M,O
Psychiatric Nursing M,O

MONMOUTH UNIVERSITY

Accounting M,O
Addictions/Substance Abuse Counseling M,O
Advertising and Public Relations M,O
Business Administration and Management—General M,O
Communication—General M,O
Computer Science M
Corporate and Organizational Communication M,O
Counseling Psychology M,O
Criminal Justice and Criminology M,O
Education—General M,O
Educational Administration M,O
Elementary Education M,O
English M
Health Services Management and Hospital Administration M,O
History M
Liberal Studies M
Media Studies M,O

Nursing—General	M,O
Psychology—General	M,O
Public Policy	M
Reading Education	M,O
School Nursing	M,O
Social Work	M
Software Engineering	M,O
Special Education	M,O

Close-Up on page 967.

MONROE COLLEGE

Business Administration and Management—General	M

MONTANA STATE UNIVERSITY

Accounting	M
Agricultural Economics and Agribusiness	M
Agricultural Sciences—General	M,D
American Indian/Native American Studies	M
Animal Sciences	M,D
Applied Economics	M
Architecture	M
Art/Fine Arts	M
Biochemistry	M,D
Biological and Biomedical Sciences—General	M,D
Chemical Engineering	M,D
Chemistry	M,D
Civil Engineering	M,D
Computer Science	M,D
Ecology	M,D
Education—General	M,D,O
Electrical Engineering	M,D
Engineering and Applied Sciences—General	M,D
English	M
Environmental Biology	M,D
Environmental Engineering	M,D
Environmental Management and Policy	M,D
Environmental Sciences	M,D
Family Nurse Practitioner Studies	M,O
Film, Television, and Video Production	M
Fish, Game, and Wildlife Management	M,D
Geosciences	M,D
Health Education	M
History	M,D
Human Development	M
Industrial/Management Engineering	M,D
Mathematics	M,D
Mechanical Engineering	M,D
Microbiology	M,D
Molecular Biology	M,D
Natural Resources	M,D
Neuroscience	M,D
Nursing Education	M,O
Nursing—General	M,O
Physics	M,D
Plant Pathology	M,D
Plant Sciences	M,D
Psychology—General	M
Public Administration	M
Range Science	M,D
Statistics	M,D
Veterinary Sciences	M,D
Zoology	M,D

MONTANA STATE UNIVERSITY–BILLINGS

Advertising and Public Relations	M
Athletic Training and Sports Medicine	M
Communication—General	M
Counselor Education	M
Curriculum and Instruction	M
Early Childhood Education	M
Education—General	M,O
Educational Media/Instructional Technology	M
Health Services Management and Hospital Administration	M
Human Services	M
Interdisciplinary Studies	M
Physical Education	M
Psychology—General	M
Public Administration	M
Reading Education	M
Rehabilitation Counseling	M
Secondary Education	M
Special Education	M
Sports Management	M

MONTANA STATE UNIVERSITY–NORTHERN

Counselor Education	M
Education—General	M

MONTANA TECH OF THE UNIVERSITY OF MONTANA

Electrical Engineering	M
Engineering and Applied Sciences—General	M
Environmental Engineering	M
Geochemistry	M
Geological Engineering	M
Geology	M
Geosciences	M
Hydrogeology	M
Industrial Hygiene	M
Industrial/Management Engineering	M
Metallurgical Engineering and Metallurgy	M
Mineral/Mining Engineering	M
Petroleum Engineering	M
Project Management	M
Technical Communication	M

MONTCLAIR STATE UNIVERSITY

Accounting	M
Addictions/Substance Abuse Counseling	M,O
Advertising and Public Relations	M
Applied Mathematics	M,O
Applied Statistics	M,O
Art Education	M,O
Art History	M
Art/Fine Arts	M
Arts Administration	M
Biochemistry	M
Biological and Biomedical Sciences—General	M,O
Business Administration and Management—General	M*
Chemistry	M
Clinical Psychology	M,O
Communication Disorders	M,D
Communication—General	M
Computer Science	M,O
Conflict Resolution and Mediation/Peace Studies	M,O
Corporate and Organizational Communication	M
Counselor Education	M,O
Curriculum and Instruction	M,D,O*
Early Childhood Education	M,O
Economics	M
Education of the Multiply Handicapped	M,O
Education—General	M,O
Educational Administration	M,O
Educational Media/Instructional Technology	M,O
Educational Psychology	M,O
Elementary Education	M,O
English as a Second Language	M,O
English Education	M,O
English	M
Environmental and Occupational Health	M,D,O
Environmental Management and Policy	M,D*
Environmental Sciences	M,D,O
Exercise and Sports Science	M,O
Finance and Banking	M
Food Science and Technology	M,O
Foundations and Philosophy of Education	M,D,O
French	M,O
Geosciences	M,D,O
Health Education	M,O
History	M
Home Economics Education	M,O
Industrial and Organizational Psychology	M,O
Information Science	M,O
International Business	M
Legal and Justice Studies	M,O
Linguistics	M
Management Information Systems	M
Marketing	M
Marriage and Family Therapy	M,O
Mathematics Education	M,D,O
Mathematics	M,O
Middle School Education	M,O
Molecular Biology	M,O
Music Education	M,O
Music	M,O
Nutrition	M,O
Philosophy	M,D,O
Physical Education	M,O
Psychology—General	M,O
Reading Education	M,O
School Psychology	M,O
Science Education	M,D,O
Social Psychology	M,O
Social Sciences Education	M
Social Sciences	M,O
Sociology	M
Spanish	M,O
Special Education	M,O
Speech and Interpersonal Communication	M
Sports Management	M,O
Statistics	M,O
Theater	M
Therapies—Dance, Drama, and Music	M,O
Translation and Interpretation	M,O
Water Resources	M,D,O

Close-Up on page 969.

MONTEREY INSTITUTE OF INTERNATIONAL STUDIES

Business Administration and Management—General	M
English as a Second Language	M*
Environmental Management and Policy	M
Foreign Languages Education	M
International Affairs	M*
International Business	M
Public Administration	M
Translation and Interpretation	M*

MONTREAT COLLEGE

Business Administration and Management—General	M
Education—General	M
Elementary Education	M

MOODY BIBLE INSTITUTE

English as a Second Language	P,M,O
Theology	P,M,O

MORAVIAN COLLEGE

Business Administration and Management—General	M
Curriculum and Instruction	M
Education—General	M

MORAVIAN THEOLOGICAL SEMINARY

Theology	P,M

MOREHEAD STATE UNIVERSITY

Adult Education	M,O
Art Education	M
Art/Fine Arts	M
Biological and Biomedical Sciences—General	M
Business Administration and Management—General	M
Clinical Psychology	M
Communication—General	M
Counseling Psychology	M
Counselor Education	M,O
Criminal Justice and Criminology	M
Curriculum and Instruction	O
Education—General	M,O
Educational Administration	M,O
Elementary Education	M
English	M
Environmental Management and Policy	M
Exercise and Sports Science	M
Experimental Psychology	M
Gerontology	M
Health Education	M
Higher Education	M,O
Industrial/Management Engineering	M
International and Comparative Education	M
Management Information Systems	M
Middle School Education	M
Music Education	M
Music	M
Physical Education	M
Psychology—General	M
Public Administration	M
Reading Education	M
Secondary Education	M
Sociology	M
Special Education	M
Sports Management	M
Vocational and Technical Education	M

MOREHOUSE SCHOOL OF MEDICINE

Allopathic Medicine	P
Biological and Biomedical Sciences—General	D*
Clinical Research	M
Public Health—General	M

MORGAN STATE UNIVERSITY

African-American Studies	M,D
Architecture	M
Bioinformatics	M
Biological and Biomedical Sciences—General	M,D
Business Administration and Management—General	D
Chemistry	M
Civil Engineering	M,D
Community College Education	D
Economics	M
Education—General	M,D
Educational Administration	M,D
Electrical Engineering	M,D
Elementary Education	M
Engineering and Applied Sciences—General	M,D
English	M,D
Environmental Biology	D*
Higher Education	D
History	M,D
Industrial/Management Engineering	M,D
International Affairs	M
Landscape Architecture	M
Mathematics Education	M,D
Mathematics	M
Middle School Education	M
Music	M
Physics	M
Psychology—General	M,D
Public Health—General	M,D
Science Education	M,D
Secondary Education	M
Social Work	M,D
Sociology	M
Telecommunications Management	M
Transportation and Highway Engineering	M,D
Transportation Management	M
Urban and Regional Planning	M

MORNINGSIDE COLLEGE

Computer Education	M
Education—General	M
Elementary Education	M
Reading Education	M
Special Education	M

MORRISON UNIVERSITY

Business Administration and Management—General	M

MOUNTAIN STATE UNIVERSITY

Allied Health—General	M
Criminal Justice and Criminology	M
Family Nurse Practitioner Studies	M,O
Interdisciplinary Studies	M*
Management Strategy and Policy	M
Nurse Anesthesia	M,O
Nursing and Healthcare Administration	M,O
Nursing Education	M,O
Nursing—General	M,O*
Physician Assistant Studies	M*

MOUNT ALLISON UNIVERSITY

Biological and Biomedical Sciences—General	M
Chemistry	M

MOUNT ALOYSIUS COLLEGE

Criminal Justice and Criminology	M
Health Services Management and Hospital Administration	M
Psychology—General	M

MOUNT ANGEL SEMINARY

Theology	P,M

MOUNT CARMEL COLLEGE OF NURSING

Adult Nursing	M
Nursing Education	M
Nursing—General	M*

MOUNT HOLYOKE COLLEGE

Psychology—General	M

MOUNT MARTY COLLEGE

Business Administration and Management—General	M
Nurse Anesthesia	M
Pastoral Ministry and Counseling	M

MOUNT MARY COLLEGE

Art Therapy	M
Business Administration and Management—General	M
Counselor Education	M
Education—General	M
English	M
Health Education	M
Nutrition	M
Occupational Therapy	M

MOUNT SAINT MARY COLLEGE

Adult Nursing	M
Business Administration and Management—General	M
Early Childhood Education	M
Education—General	M
Elementary Education	M

- Finance and Banking M
- Middle School Education M
- Nursing and Healthcare Administration M
- Nursing Education M
- Nursing—General M
- Reading Education M
- Secondary Education M
- Special Education M

MOUNT ST. MARY'S COLLEGE
- Counseling Psychology M
- Education—General M
- Educational Administration M
- Elementary Education M
- Humanities M
- Nursing—General M
- Physical Therapy D
- Religion M
- Secondary Education M
- Special Education M

MOUNT ST. MARY'S UNIVERSITY
- Business Administration and Management—General M
- Education—General M
- Theology P,M

MOUNT SAINT VINCENT UNIVERSITY
- Adult Education M
- Child and Family Studies M
- Curriculum and Instruction M
- Education—General M
- Educational Psychology M
- Elementary Education M
- English as a Second Language M
- Foundations and Philosophy of Education M
- Gerontology M
- Middle School Education M
- Nutrition M
- Reading Education M
- School Psychology M
- Special Education M
- Women's Studies M

MOUNT SINAI SCHOOL OF MEDICINE OF NEW YORK UNIVERSITY
- Allopathic Medicine P
- Bioethics M*
- Biological and Biomedical Sciences—General M,D
- Biophysics M,D
- Cell Biology M,D
- Community Health M,D
- Genetic Counseling M,D
- Genetics M,D
- Genomic Sciences M,D
- Microbiology M,D
- Molecular Biology M,D
- Neuroscience M,D
- Pathology M,D
- Structural Biology M,D

MOUNT VERNON NAZARENE UNIVERSITY
- Business Administration and Management—General M
- Education—General M
- Theology M

MULTNOMAH BIBLE COLLEGE AND BIBLICAL SEMINARY
- Pastoral Ministry and Counseling M
- Theology P,M,O

MURRAY STATE UNIVERSITY
- Accounting M
- Agricultural Education M
- Agricultural Sciences—General M
- Biological and Biomedical Sciences—General M,D
- Business Administration and Management—General M
- Chemistry M
- Clinical Psychology M
- Communication Disorders M
- Corporate and Organizational Communication M
- Counselor Education M,O
- Early Childhood Education M
- Economics M
- Education—General M,D,O
- Educational Administration M,O
- Elementary Education M,O
- English as a Second Language M
- English M
- Environmental and Occupational Health M
- Environmental Sciences M
- Exercise and Sports Science M
- Family Nurse Practitioner Studies M
- Geosciences M
- History M
- Human Services M
- Hydrology M
- Industrial Hygiene M
- Leisure Studies M
- Management of Technology M
- Mass Communication M
- Mathematics M
- Middle School Education M,O
- Music Education M
- Music M
- Nurse Anesthesia M
- Nursing—General M
- Physical Education M,O
- Psychology—General M
- Public Affairs M
- Reading Education M,O
- Safety Engineering M
- Secondary Education M,O
- Special Education M
- Statistics M
- Telecommunications Management M
- Vocational and Technical Education M
- Writing M

MUSKINGUM COLLEGE
- Education—General M

MYERS UNIVERSITY
- Business Administration and Management—General M

NAROPA UNIVERSITY
- Art Therapy M
- Asian Languages M
- Clinical Psychology M
- Counseling Psychology M
- Education—General M
- Environmental Management and Policy M
- Psychoanalysis and Psychotherapy M
- Recreation and Park Management M
- Religion M
- Social Psychology M
- Theater M
- Theology P
- Therapies—Dance, Drama, and Music M
- Transpersonal and Humanistic Psychology M*
- Writing M

NASHOTAH HOUSE
- Theology P,M,O

NATIONAL AMERICAN UNIVERSITY
- Business Administration and Management—General M

NATIONAL COLLEGE OF MIDWIFERY
- Nurse Midwifery M,D

NATIONAL COLLEGE OF NATURAL MEDICINE
- Acupuncture and Oriental Medicine M
- Naturopathic Medicine D

NATIONAL DEFENSE UNIVERSITY
- Military and Defense Studies M
- National Security M

THE NATIONAL GRADUATE SCHOOL OF QUALITY MANAGEMENT
- Business Administration and Management—General M
- Electronic Commerce M
- Quality Management M

NATIONAL-LOUIS UNIVERSITY
- Addictions/Substance Abuse Counseling M,O
- Adult Education M,D,O
- Business Administration and Management—General M
- Counselor Education M,O
- Curriculum and Instruction M,D,O
- Developmental Education M,O
- Early Childhood Education M,O
- Education—General M,D,O
- Educational Administration M,D,O
- Educational Media/Instructional Technology M,O
- Educational Psychology M,D,O
- Elementary Education M
- English Education M,O
- Gerontology M,O
- Health Psychology M,O
- Human Development M,D,O
- Human Resources Development M
- Human Resources Management M
- Human Services M,O
- Industrial and Organizational Psychology M,O
- Mathematics Education M,O
- Psychology—General M,O
- Reading Education M,D,O
- School Psychology M,D,O
- Science Education M,O
- Secondary Education M
- Social Psychology M,O
- Special Education M,O
- Writing M

NATIONAL THEATRE CONSERVATORY
- Theater M,O

NATIONAL UNIVERSITY
- Accounting M
- Art/Fine Arts M
- Business Administration and Management—General M
- Communication Disorders M
- Communication—General M
- Computer Art and Design M
- Computer Science M
- Counseling Psychology M
- Counselor Education M
- Economics M
- Education—General M
- Educational Administration M
- Educational Media/Instructional Technology M
- Electronic Commerce M
- Engineering and Applied Sciences—General M
- Engineering Management M
- English M
- Environmental Engineering M
- Finance and Banking M
- Forensic Sciences M
- Health Services Management and Hospital Administration M
- Homeland Security M
- Human Services M
- Humanities M
- Industrial and Organizational Psychology M
- Information Science M
- Internet and Interactive Multimedia M
- Management Information Systems M
- Management of Technology M
- Media Studies M
- Multilingual and Multicultural Education M
- Organizational Management M
- Psychology—General M
- Safety Engineering M
- School Psychology M
- Software Engineering M
- Special Education M
- Systems Engineering M
- Taxation M
- Telecommunications M
- Writing M

NATIONAL UNIVERSITY OF HEALTH SCIENCES
- Acupuncture and Oriental Medicine P,M,D
- Chiropractic P,M,D*
- Naturopathic Medicine P,M,D

NATIONAL UNIVERSITY OF SINGAPORE
- Public Administration M,D
- Public Affairs M,D
- Public Policy M,D*

NAVAL POSTGRADUATE SCHOOL
- Aerospace/Aeronautical Engineering M
- Applied Mathematics M,D
- Applied Physics M,D
- Applied Science and Technology M
- Business Administration and Management—General M
- Computer Engineering M,D,O
- Computer Science M,D
- Electrical Engineering M,D,O
- Human Resources Development M
- Human-Computer Interaction M,D
- Information Science M,O
- International Affairs M
- Management Information Systems M,O
- Mathematics M,D
- Mechanical Engineering M,D,O
- Meteorology M,D
- Military and Defense Studies M,D
- National Security M
- Oceanography M,D
- Operations Research M,D
- Physics M,D
- Political Science M
- Software Engineering M,D
- Systems Engineering M,D,O

NAVAL WAR COLLEGE
- National Security M

NAZARENE THEOLOGICAL SEMINARY
- Missions and Missiology P,M,D
- Religious Education P,M,D
- Theology P,M,D

NAZARETH COLLEGE OF ROCHESTER
- Art Education M
- Art Therapy M
- Business Administration and Management—General M
- Business Education M
- Communication Disorders M
- Early Childhood Education M
- Education—General M
- Educational Media/Instructional Technology M
- Elementary Education M
- English as a Second Language M
- Gerontological Nursing M
- Human Resources Management M
- Liberal Studies M
- Middle School Education M
- Music Education M
- Nursing—General M
- Physical Therapy M,D
- Reading Education M
- Social Work M
- Therapies—Dance, Drama, and Music M

NEBRASKA METHODIST COLLEGE
- Health Promotion M
- Health Services Management and Hospital Administration M
- Nursing—General M

NEBRASKA WESLEYAN UNIVERSITY
- Forensic Sciences M
- History M
- Nursing—General M

NER ISRAEL RABBINICAL COLLEGE
- Theology M,D

NER ISRAEL YESHIVA COLLEGE OF TORONTO
- Theology

NEUMANN COLLEGE
- Education—General M
- Management Strategy and Policy M
- Nursing—General M
- Pastoral Ministry and Counseling M,O
- Physical Therapy M,D
- Sports Management M

NEW BRUNSWICK THEOLOGICAL SEMINARY
- Pastoral Ministry and Counseling D
- Theology P,M,D

NEW COLLEGE OF CALIFORNIA
- Clinical Psychology M
- Education—General M
- Foreign Languages Education M
- Humanities M
- Law P*
- Media Studies M
- Psychology—General M
- Social Psychology M
- Sustainable Development M
- Women's Studies M
- Writing M

Close-Up on page 971.

NEW ENGLAND COLLEGE
- Business Administration and Management—General M
- Counseling Psychology M
- Education—General M
- Educational Administration M
- Health Services Management and Hospital Administration M
- Human Services M
- Nonprofit Management M
- Organizational Management M
- Public Policy M
- Special Education M

Writing	M

THE NEW ENGLAND COLLEGE OF OPTOMETRY

Optometry	P,M*
Vision Sciences	P,M

NEW ENGLAND CONSERVATORY OF MUSIC

Music	M,D,O

NEW ENGLAND SCHOOL OF ACUPUNCTURE

Acupuncture and Oriental Medicine	M*

NEW ENGLAND SCHOOL OF LAW

Law	P

NEW JERSEY CITY UNIVERSITY

Accounting	M
Allied Health—General	M
Art Education	M
Art/Fine Arts	M
Business Administration and Management—General	M
Community Health	M
Computer and Information Systems Security	M
Counseling Psychology	M,O
Criminal Justice and Criminology	M
Early Childhood Education	M
Educational Administration	M
Educational Media/Instructional Technology	M
Educational Psychology	M,O
Elementary Education	M
English as a Second Language	M
Finance and Banking	M
Health Education	M
Health Services Management and Hospital Administration	M
Mathematics Education	M
Multilingual and Multicultural Education	M
Music Education	M
Music	M
National Security	M
Nursing—General	M
Psychology—General	M,O
Reading Education	M
School Psychology	M,O
Secondary Education	M
Special Education	M
Transcultural Nursing	M
Urban Education	M
Urban Studies	M

NEW JERSEY INSTITUTE OF TECHNOLOGY

Applied Mathematics	M
Applied Physics	M,D
Applied Statistics	M
Architecture	M
Biological and Biomedical Sciences—General	M,D
Biomedical Engineering	M,D
Business Administration and Management—General	M
Chemical Engineering	M,D
Chemistry	M,D
Civil Engineering	M,D
Computational Biology	M
Computer Engineering	M,D
Computer Science	M,D
Electrical Engineering	M,D
Engineering and Applied Sciences—General	M,D,O
Engineering Management	M
Environmental and Occupational Health	M
Environmental Engineering	M,D
Environmental Management and Policy	M,D
Environmental Sciences	M,D
History	M
Industrial Hygiene	M
Industrial/Management Engineering	M,D
Information Science	M,D
Internet and Interactive Multimedia	M
Management of Technology	M,D
Manufacturing Engineering	M
Materials Engineering	M,D
Materials Sciences	M,D
Mathematics	D
Mechanical Engineering	M,D,O
Pharmaceutical Engineering	M
Public Health—General	M
Safety Engineering	M
Technical Communication	M
Transportation and Highway Engineering	M,D
Transportation Management	M,D
Urban Studies	D

NEW LIFE THEOLOGICAL SEMINARY

Religion	M

NEWMAN THEOLOGICAL COLLEGE

Educational Administration	M,O
Religious Education	M,O
Theology	P,M

NEWMAN UNIVERSITY

Business Administration and Management—General	M
Curriculum and Instruction	M
Education—General	M
Educational Administration	M
English as a Second Language	M
International Business	M
Management Information Systems	M
Nurse Anesthesia	M
Organizational Management	M
Social Work	M

NEW MEXICO HIGHLANDS UNIVERSITY

American Studies	M
Anthropology	M
Biological and Biomedical Sciences—General	M
Business Administration and Management—General	M
Chemistry	M
Cognitive Sciences	M
Computer Art and Design	M
Computer Science	M
Counselor Education	M
Curriculum and Instruction	M
Education—General	M
Educational Administration	M
English	M
Environmental Management and Policy	M
Exercise and Sports Science	M
Film, Television, and Video Production	M
Finance and Banking	M
Fish, Game, and Wildlife Management	M
Health Education	M
Hispanic Studies	M
History	M
Human Resources Management	M
International Business	M
Internet and Interactive Multimedia	M
Nonprofit Management	M
Political Science	M
Psychology—General	M
Public Affairs	M
Rhetoric	M
Social Work	M
Sociology	M
Spanish	M
Special Education	M
Sports Management	M
Writing	M

NEW MEXICO INSTITUTE OF MINING AND TECHNOLOGY

Applied Mathematics	M,D
Astrophysics	M,D
Atmospheric Sciences	M,D
Biochemistry	M,D
Biological and Biomedical Sciences—General	M
Chemistry	M,D
Computer Science	M,D
Electrical Engineering	M
Engineering Management	M
Environmental Engineering	M
Environmental Sciences	M,D
Geochemistry	M,D
Geology	M,D
Geophysics	M,D
Geosciences	M,D
Hazardous Materials Management	M
Hydrology	M,D
Materials Engineering	M,D
Mathematical Physics	M,D
Mathematics	M,D
Mechanics	M
Mineral/Mining Engineering	M
Operations Research	M,D
Petroleum Engineering	M,D
Physics	M,D
Science Education	M
Water Resources Engineering	M

Close-Up on page 973.

NEW MEXICO STATE UNIVERSITY

Accounting	M
Adult Nursing	M
Agricultural Economics and Agribusiness	M
Agricultural Education	M
Agricultural Sciences—General	M
Agronomy and Soil Sciences	M,D
Animal Sciences	M,D
Anthropology	M
Applied Arts and Design—General	M
Art History	M
Art/Fine Arts	M
Astronomy	M,D
Biochemistry	M,D
Biological and Biomedical Sciences—General	M,D
Business Administration and Management—General	M,D
Chemical Engineering	M,D
Chemistry	M,D
Civil Engineering	M,D
Communication Disorders	M,D
Communication—General	M
Community Health Nursing	M
Computer Engineering	M,D
Computer Science	M,D
Corporate and Organizational Communication	M,D
Counseling Psychology	M,D,O
Counselor Education	M,D,O
Criminal Justice and Criminology	M
Curriculum and Instruction	M,D,O
Economics	M
Education—General	M,D,O
Educational Administration	M,D
Electrical Engineering	M,D
Engineering and Applied Sciences—General	M,D
English	M,D
Entomology	M
Environmental Engineering	M,D
Family and Consumer Sciences-General	M
Fish, Game, and Wildlife Management	M
Geography	M
Geology	M
History	M
Horticulture	M,D
Industrial/Management Engineering	M,D
Interdisciplinary Studies	M,D
Marketing	D
Mathematics	M,D
Mechanical Engineering	M,D
Medical/Surgical Nursing	M
Molecular Biology	M,D
Music	M
Nursing—General	M
Photography	M
Physics	M,D
Plant Pathology	M
Plant Sciences	M
Political Science	M
Psychiatric Nursing	M
Psychology—General	M,D
Public Health—General	M
Range Science	M,D
Reading Education	M,D,O
Rhetoric	M,D
School Psychology	M,D,O
Social Work	M
Sociology	M
Spanish	M
Special Education	M,D
Statistics	M
Writing	M,D

NEW ORLEANS BAPTIST THEOLOGICAL SEMINARY

Music	M,D
Pastoral Ministry and Counseling	P,M,D
Religious Education	P,M,D
Theology	P,D

THE NEW SCHOOL: A UNIVERSITY

Anthropology	M,D
Applied Arts and Design—General	M
Applied Social Research	M,D
Architecture	M*
Art/Fine Arts	M*
Clinical Psychology	M,D
Communication—General	M*
Computer Art and Design	M*
Decorative Arts	M*
Economics	M,D
English as a Second Language	M
Finance and Banking	M
Health Services Management and Hospital Administration	M,O*
History	M,D
Human Resources Management	M,O
Interior Design	M*
International Affairs	M*
International Business	M
International Development	M
Liberal Studies	M
Mass Communication	M
Media Studies	M
Music	M,O
Nonprofit Management	M*
Organizational Management	M*
Philosophy	M,D
Photography	M*
Political Science	M,D
Psychology—General	M,D
Public Policy	D*
Social Sciences	M,D*
Sociology	M,D
Theater	M*
Urban Studies	M*
Writing	M*

Close-Up on page 975.

NEWSCHOOL OF ARCHITECTURE & DESIGN

Architecture	M

NEW YORK ACADEMY OF ART

Art/Fine Arts	M

NEW YORK CHIROPRACTIC COLLEGE

Acupuncture and Oriental Medicine	M
Chiropractic	P*
Health Physics/Radiological Health	M
Nutrition	M

NEW YORK COLLEGE OF HEALTH PROFESSIONS

Acupuncture and Oriental Medicine	M

NEW YORK COLLEGE OF PODIATRIC MEDICINE

Podiatric Medicine	P

NEW YORK COLLEGE OF TRADITIONAL CHINESE MEDICINE

Acupuncture and Oriental Medicine	M

NEW YORK FILM ACADEMY

Film, Television, and Video Production	M*

NEW YORK INSTITUTE OF TECHNOLOGY

Accounting	M,O
Advertising and Public Relations	M,O
Architecture	M
Business Administration and Management—General	M,O
Communication—General	M,O
Computer Engineering	M
Computer Science	M
Counseling Psychology	M
Counselor Education	M
Distance Education Development	M,O
Economics	M,O
Education—General	M,O
Educational Administration	O
Educational Media/Instructional Technology	M,O
Electrical Engineering	M
Electronic Commerce	M,O
Elementary Education	M,O
Energy and Power Engineering	M,O
Energy Management and Policy	M,O
Engineering and Applied Sciences—General	M,O
Environmental Engineering	M
Environmental Management and Policy	M,O
Finance and Banking	M,O
Health Services Management and Hospital Administration	M,O
Human Development	M
Human Resources Management	M,O
Industrial and Labor Relations	M,O
International Business	M,O
Internet and Interactive Multimedia	M,O
Management Information Systems	M,O
Management of Technology	M,O
Management Strategy and Policy	M,O
Marketing	M,O
Nutrition	M
Occupational Therapy	M
Osteopathic Medicine	P
Physical Therapy	M,D
Physician Assistant Studies	M
Project Management	M,O
Urban Design	M

NEW YORK LAW SCHOOL

Law	P,M
Taxation	P,M

NEW YORK MEDICAL COLLEGE

Allopathic Medicine	P

Anatomy M,D
Biochemistry M,D
Biological and Biomedical Sciences—General M,D*
Biostatistics M,D,O
Cell Biology M,D*
Communication Disorders M*
Community Health M
Disability Studies M*
Environmental and Occupational Health M
Epidemiology M,D,O*
Health Informatics M,D,O
Health Promotion M
Health Services Management and Hospital Administration M*
Immunology M,D
International Health M
Maternal and Child Health M
Microbiology M,D
Molecular Biology M,D
Neuroscience M,D
Pathology M,D*
Pharmacology M,D
Physical Therapy D*
Physiology M,D*
Public Health—General M,D,O*

NEW YORK SCHOOL OF INTERIOR DESIGN

Interior Design M*

NEW YORK THEOLOGICAL SEMINARY

Theology P,M,D

NEW YORK UNIVERSITY

Accounting M,D
Acute Care/Critical Care Nursing M,O
Adult Nursing M,O
Advertising and Public Relations M
African Studies M,D,O
Agricultural Engineering M,D
Allopathic Medicine P
American Studies M,D
Anthropology M,D
Applied Arts and Design—General M
Applied Economics M,D,O
Archaeology M,D
Art Education M,D
Art History M,D
Art Therapy M
Art/Fine Arts M,D
Arts Administration M
Biological and Biomedical Sciences—General M,D*
Business Administration and Management—General P,M,D,O
Business Education M,O
Cancer Biology/Oncology M,D
Cell Biology D
Chemistry M,D*
Classics M,D,O
Clinical Research P,M,D
Cognitive Sciences M,D,O
Communication Disorders M,D
Communication—General M,D
Comparative Literature M,D
Computational Biology D
Computer Art and Design M*
Computer Science M,D*
Construction Management M,O
Corporate and Organizational Communication M*
Counseling Psychology M,D,O
Counselor Education M,D,O
Cultural Studies M,D,O
Dance M,D
Dentistry P
Developmental Biology M,D
Developmental Psychology M,D,O
Early Childhood Education M,D,O
Economics M,D,O
Education—General M,D,O*
Educational Administration M,D,O
Educational Measurement and Evaluation M,D,O
Educational Media/Instructional Technology M,D,O
Educational Policy M,D
Educational Psychology M,D,O
Electronic Commerce M,O
Elementary Education M,D,O
English as a Second Language M,D,O
English Education M,D,O
English M,D
Environmental and Occupational Health M,D
Environmental Education M
Epidemiology M,D
Ergonomics and Human Factors M,D
Film, Television, and Video Production M
Film, Television, and Video Theory and Criticism M,D
Finance and Banking M,D,O
Food Science and Technology M,D
Foreign Languages Education M,D,O
Foundations and Philosophy of Education M,D
French M,D,O
Genetics M,D
German M,D
Gerontological Nursing M,O
Graphic Design M*
Health Education M,D
Health Promotion M,D,O
Health Services Management and Hospital Administration M,O
Higher Education M,D
Historic Preservation
History M,D,O
Hospitality Management M,D,O*
Human Development M,D,O
Human Resources Development M,O
Human Resources Management M,D,O*
Humanities M,O
Immunology M,D*
Industrial and Organizational Psychology M,D,O
Interdisciplinary Studies M*
International Affairs M,D,O*
International and Comparative Education M,D,O
International Business M,D
International Health M,D
Internet and Interactive Multimedia M
Italian M,D
Jewish Studies M,D,O
Journalism M,D,O*
Kinesiology and Movement Studies M,D
Latin American Studies M,O
Law P,M,D,O
Legal and Justice Studies M,D
Linguistics M,D
Management Information Systems M,D,O*
Management of Technology M
Management Strategy and Policy M,D
Marketing M,D,O*
Mathematical and Computational Finance M,D
Mathematics Education M
Mathematics M,D*
Media Studies M,D
Microbiology M,D*
Molecular Biology M,D
Molecular Genetics M,D
Molecular Pharmacology D
Molecular Toxicology M,D
Multilingual and Multicultural Education M,D,O
Museum Studies M,D,O
Music Education M,D,O
Music M,D,O
Near and Middle Eastern Studies M,D,O
Neurobiology M,D
Neuroscience D*
Nonprofit Management M,D,O*
Nurse Midwifery M,O
Nursing Education M,O
Nursing Informatics M,O
Nursing—General M,D,O
Nutrition M,D
Occupational Therapy M,D
Oral and Dental Sciences M,D,O
Organizational Behavior M,D
Organizational Management M,D
Parasitology D
Pathobiology D
Pediatric Nursing M,O
Pharmacology D
Philosophy M,D
Physical Therapy M,D
Physics M,D
Physiology D
Plant Biology M,D
Political Science M,D
Portuguese M,D
Psychiatric Nursing M,O
Psychoanalysis and Psychotherapy M,D,O
Psychology—General M,D,O
Public Administration M,D,O*
Public History M,D,O
Publishing M*
Quantitative Analysis M,D,O
Reading Education M
Real Estate M,O*
Religion M,O
Reproductive Biology D
Romance Languages M,D
Russian M
School Psychology M,D,O
Science Education M
Slavic Languages M
Social Psychology M,D,O
Social Sciences Education M,D
Social Work M,D*
Sociology M,D
Spanish M,D
Special Education M
Speech and Interpersonal Communication M,D
Sports Management M,O
Statistics M,D
Structural Biology D
Student Affairs M,D
Taxation P,M,D,O
Theater M,D,O
Therapies—Dance, Drama, and Music M,D
Toxicology M,D
Travel and Tourism M,O
Urban and Regional Planning M,O
Western European Studies M
Writing M

Close-Up on page 977.

NIAGARA UNIVERSITY

Business Administration and Management—General M
Counselor Education M,O
Criminal Justice and Criminology M
Education—General M,O
Educational Administration M,O
Elementary Education M
Foundations and Philosophy of Education M
Reading Education M
School Psychology M
Secondary Education M
Special Education M

NICHOLLS STATE UNIVERSITY

Business Administration and Management—General M
Computer Science M
Counseling Psychology M,O
Counselor Education M
Curriculum and Instruction M
Education—General M
Educational Administration M
Environmental Biology M
Marine Biology M
Mathematics Education M
Mathematics M
School Psychology M,O

NICHOLS COLLEGE

Business Administration and Management—General M

THE NIGERIAN BAPTIST THEOLOGICAL SEMINARY

Music P,M,O
Theology P,M,O

NIPISSING UNIVERSITY

Education—General M,O

NORFOLK STATE UNIVERSITY

Art/Fine Arts M
Clinical Psychology M
Communication—General M
Computer Engineering M
Computer Science M
Criminal Justice and Criminology M
Early Childhood Education M
Education of the Multiply Handicapped M
Education—General M
Educational Administration M
Electrical Engineering M
Materials Sciences M
Media Studies M
Music Education M
Music M
Optical Sciences M
Psychology—General M,D
Secondary Education M
Social Psychology M
Social Work M,D
Sociology M
Special Education M
Urban Education M
Urban Studies M

NORTH CAROLINA AGRICULTURAL AND TECHNICAL STATE UNIVERSITY

Adult Education M
African-American Studies M
Agricultural Economics and Agribusiness M
Agricultural Education M
Agricultural Engineering M
Agricultural Sciences—General M
Applied Economics M
Architectural Engineering M
Art Education M
Biological and Biomedical Sciences—General M
Chemical Engineering M
Chemistry M
Civil Engineering M
Computer Science M
Counselor Education M
Early Childhood Education M
Education—General M
Educational Administration M
Educational Media/Instructional Technology M
Electrical Engineering M,D
Elementary Education M
Engineering and Applied Sciences—General M,D
English Education M
English M
Environmental Engineering M
Environmental Sciences M
Health Education M
Human Resources Development M
Human Resources Management M
Industrial/Management Engineering M,D
Management of Technology M
Mathematics Education M
Mechanical Engineering M,D
Middle School Education M
Nutrition M
Physical Education M
Plant Sciences M
Reading Education M
Science Education M
Social Sciences Education M
Social Work M
Systems Engineering M,D
Vocational and Technical Education M

Close-Up on page 979.

NORTH CAROLINA CENTRAL UNIVERSITY

Biological and Biomedical Sciences—General M
Business Administration and Management—General M
Chemistry M
Communication Disorders M
Counselor Education M
Criminal Justice and Criminology M
Education—General M
Educational Administration M
Educational Media/Instructional Technology M
Elementary Education M
English M
Family and Consumer Sciences-General M
Geosciences M
History M
Information Studies M
Law P
Library Science M
Mathematics M
Physical Education M
Psychology—General M
Public Administration M
Recreation and Park Management M
Sociology M
Special Education M

NORTH CAROLINA SCHOOL OF THE ARTS

Film, Television, and Video Production M
Music M
Theater M

NORTH CAROLINA STATE UNIVERSITY

Accounting M
Adult Education M,D
Aerospace/Aeronautical Engineering M,D
Agricultural Economics and Agribusiness M
Agricultural Education M
Agricultural Engineering M,D
Agricultural Sciences—General M,D
Agronomy and Soil Sciences M,D
Animal Sciences M,D
Anthropology M
Applied Arts and Design—General M,D
Applied Mathematics M,D
Architecture M
Atmospheric Sciences M,D
Biochemistry M,D*
Bioengineering M,D
Bioinformatics M,D*
Biological and Biomedical Sciences—General M,D
Biomedical Engineering M,D*
Biometrics M,D
Biotechnology M
Botany M,D
Business Administration and Management—General M
Cell Biology M,D
Chemical Engineering M,D
Chemistry M,D
Civil Engineering M,D

Clothing and Textiles D
Communication—General M
Community College Education M,D
Computer Engineering M,D
Computer Science M,D
Corporate and Organizational Communication M
Counselor Education M,D
Curriculum and Instruction M,D
Developmental Education M
Developmental Psychology D
Ecology M,D
Economics M,D
Education—General M,D,O
Educational Administration M,D
Educational Measurement and Evaluation D
Educational Media/Instructional Technology M,D
Electrical Engineering M,D
Engineering and Applied Sciences—General M,D*
English M
Entomology M,D
Epidemiology M,D
Ergonomics and Human Factors D
Experimental Psychology D
Financial Engineering M
Fish, Game, and Wildlife Management M
Food Science and Technology M,D
Forestry M,D
French M
Genetics M,D
Genomic Sciences M,D*
Geographic Information Systems M,D
Geosciences M,D*
Graphic Design M
Higher Education M,D
History M
Horticulture M,D
Immunology M,D
Industrial and Organizational Psychology D
Industrial Design M
Industrial/Management Engineering M,D
International Affairs M
Landscape Architecture M
Liberal Studies M
Management of Technology D
Manufacturing Engineering M
Marine Sciences M,D
Materials Engineering M,D
Materials Sciences M,D
Mathematical and Computational Finance M*
Mathematics Education M,D
Mathematics M,D
Mechanical Engineering M,D*
Meteorology M,D
Microbiology M,D
Middle School Education M
Molecular Toxicology M,D*
Natural Resources M
Nuclear Engineering M,D
Nutrition M,D
Oceanography M,D
Operations Research M,D
Paper and Pulp Engineering M,D
Pathology M,D
Pharmacology M,D
Physics M,D
Physiology M,D
Plant Pathology M,D
Polymer Science and Engineering D
Psychology—General D
Public Administration M,D
Public History M
Recreation and Park Management M,D
Rural Sociology M,D
School Psychology D
Science Education M,D
Social Psychology D
Sociology M,D
Spanish M
Special Education M
Sports Management M,D
Statistics M,D
Supply Chain Management M
Technical Communication M
Textile Sciences and Engineering M,D
Toxicology M,D
Travel and Tourism M,D
Veterinary Medicine P,M
Veterinary Sciences M,D
Writing M
Zoology M,D

NORTH CENTRAL COLLEGE

Business Administration and Management—General M
Computer Science M
Education—General M
Educational Administration M
Liberal Studies M
Management Information Systems M
Nonprofit Management M

NORTH DAKOTA STATE UNIVERSITY

Agricultural Economics and Agribusiness M,D
Agricultural Education M
Agricultural Engineering M,D
Agricultural Sciences—General M,D
Agronomy and Soil Sciences M,D
Animal Sciences M,D
Applied Mathematics M,D
Applied Statistics M,D,O
Biochemistry M,D
Bioinformatics M,D
Biological and Biomedical Sciences—General M,D
Biosystems Engineering M,D
Botany M,D
Business Administration and Management—General M
Cell Biology M,D
Chemistry M,D
Child and Family Studies M,D
Child Development M,D
Civil Engineering M,D
Clinical Psychology M,D
Cognitive Sciences M,D
Communication—General M,D
Computer Science M,D,O
Conservation Biology M,D
Consumer Economics M,D
Counselor Education M,D
Criminal Justice and Criminology M,D
Ecology M,D
Education—General M,D,O
Educational Administration M,O
Electrical Engineering M,D
Emergency Management M,D
Engineering and Applied Sciences—General M,D
English M
Entomology M,D
Environmental Engineering M,D
Environmental Management and Policy M,D
Environmental Sciences M,D
Exercise and Sports Science M
Family and Consumer Sciences-General M
Food Science and Technology M,D
Genomic Sciences M,D
Gerontology M,D
History M,D
Human Development D
Industrial/Management Engineering M,D
Logistics M,D
Manufacturing Engineering M,D
Marriage and Family Therapy M,D
Mass Communication M,D
Mathematics Education M,D,O
Mathematics M,D
Mechanical Engineering M,D
Mechanics M,D
Microbiology M,D
Molecular Biology M,D
Molecular Pathogenesis M,D
Music Education M,D,O
Music M,D
Nursing—General M,D
Nutrition M
Operations Research M,D,O
Pathology M,D
Pharmaceutical Sciences M,D
Physical Education M
Physics M,D
Plant Pathology M,D
Plant Sciences M,D
Political Science M,D
Polymer Science and Engineering M,D
Psychology—General M,D
Range Science M,D
Science Education M,D,O
Social Psychology M,D
Social Sciences Education M,D,O
Social Sciences M,D
Sociology M,D
Software Engineering M,D,O
Speech and Interpersonal Communication M,D
Sports Management M
Statistics M,D,O
Transportation Management M,D
Veterinary Sciences M,D
Zoology M,D

Close-Up on page 981.

NORTHEASTERN ILLINOIS UNIVERSITY

Accounting M
Biological and Biomedical Sciences—General M
Business Administration and Management—General M
Chemistry M
Computer Science M
Counselor Education M
Education of the Gifted M
Education—General M
Educational Administration M
English Education M
English M
Environmental Management and Policy M
Finance and Banking M
Geography M
Geosciences M
Gerontology M
History M
Human Resources Development M
Linguistics M
Marketing M
Mathematics Education M
Mathematics M
Multilingual and Multicultural Education M
Music M
Political Science M
Reading Education M
Special Education M
Speech and Interpersonal Communication M
Urban Education M
Writing M

NORTHEASTERN OHIO UNIVERSITIES COLLEGE OF MEDICINE

Allopathic Medicine P

NORTHEASTERN SEMINARY AT ROBERTS WESLEYAN COLLEGE

Theology P,M,D

NORTHEASTERN STATE UNIVERSITY

Accounting M
American Studies M
Business Administration and Management—General M
Communication Disorders M
Communication—General M
Counseling Psychology M
Counselor Education M
Criminal Justice and Criminology M
Early Childhood Education M
Education—General M
Educational Administration M
Educational Media/Instructional Technology M
English M
Finance and Banking M
Foundations and Philosophy of Education M
Health Education M
Higher Education M
Industrial and Manufacturing Management M
Mathematics Education M
Optometry P
Psychology—General M
Reading Education M
Science Education M

NORTHEASTERN UNIVERSITY

Accounting M,O
Acute Care/Critical Care Nursing M,O
Allied Health—General P,M,D,O
Analytical Chemistry M,D
Applied Economics M,D
Applied Mathematics M,D
Architecture M
Biochemistry M,D
Bioinformatics M
Biological and Biomedical Sciences—General M,D*
Biotechnology M,D
Business Administration and Management—General M,O
Chemical Engineering M,D
Chemistry M,D
Civil Engineering M,D
Communication Disorders M,D
Community Health Nursing M,O
Computer Engineering M,D
Computer Science M,D*
Counseling Psychology M,D,O
Counselor Education M
Criminal Justice and Criminology M,D
Economics M,D*
Educational Psychology M,D
Electrical Engineering M,D*
Engineering and Applied Sciences—General M,D*
Engineering Management M,D
English M,D,O
Entrepreneurship M
Environmental Engineering M,D
Exercise and Sports Science M
Experimental Psychology M,D
Finance and Banking M
Health Informatics M,D
Health Services Management and Hospital Administration M
History M,D*
Industrial/Management Engineering M,D
Information Science M,D
Inorganic Chemistry M,D
International Affairs M,D
Journalism M
Law P
Legal and Justice Studies M,D
Management Information Systems M,D
Manufacturing Engineering M,D
Marine Biology M,D
Maternal and Child/Neonatal Nursing M,O
Mathematics M,D
Mechanical Engineering M,D
Nurse Anesthesia M
Nursing and Healthcare Administration M
Nursing—General M,O
Operations Research M,D
Organic Chemistry M,D
Pharmaceutical Sciences P,M,D
Pharmacology M,D
Physical Chemistry M,D
Physician Assistant Studies M
Physics M,D*
Political Science M,D
Psychiatric Nursing M,O
Psychology—General M,D,O
Public Administration M
Public Affairs M,D
Public History M,D
Public Policy M,D
Rehabilitation Counseling M
School Psychology M,D,O
Sociology M,D
Special Education M,D,O
Speech and Interpersonal Communication D
Student Affairs M
Systems Engineering M
Taxation M,O
Telecommunications Management M,D
Toxicology M

Close-Up on page 983.

NORTHERN ARIZONA UNIVERSITY

Allied Health—General M,D,O
Anthropology M
Applied Physics M
Archaeology M
Biochemistry M
Biological and Biomedical Sciences—General M,D
Business Administration and Management—General M
Chemistry M
Communication Disorders M
Communication—General M
Community College Education M,D
Counseling Psychology D
Counselor Education M
Criminal Justice and Criminology M,O
Curriculum and Instruction D
Early Childhood Education M
Ecology M,O
Education—General M,D,O
Educational Administration M,D
Educational Media/Instructional Technology M,O
Educational Psychology D
Elementary Education M
Engineering and Applied Sciences—General M,D,O
English as a Second Language M,D,O
English Education M
English M
Environmental Management and Policy M,O
Environmental Sciences M,O
Exercise and Sports Science M
Foreign Languages Education M
Forestry M,D
Geographic Information Systems M,O
Geography M,O
Geology M
Geosciences M
Health Education M
Health Promotion M
Health Psychology M
History M,D
Liberal Studies M
Linguistics M,D,O
Management Information Systems M
Mathematics Education M
Mathematics M
Multilingual and Multicultural Education M,O
Music Education M
Music M
Nursing—General M,O
Physical Education M
Physical Therapy D
Political Science M,D,O

Psychology—General M
Public Administration M,D,O
Public Health—General M
Public Policy M,D,O
Rhetoric M
School Psychology M,D
Science Education M,D
Secondary Education M
Sociology M
Special Education M
Statistics M
Vocational and Technical Education M
Writing M

NORTHERN BAPTIST THEOLOGICAL SEMINARY

Ethics P,M,D
Pastoral Ministry and Counseling P,M,D
Religion P,M,D
Theology P,M,D

NORTHERN ILLINOIS UNIVERSITY

Accounting M
Adult Education M,D
Anthropology M
Art/Fine Arts M
Biological and Biomedical Sciences—General M,D
Business Administration and Management—General M
Chemistry M,D
Child and Family Studies M
Communication Disorders M,D
Communication—General M
Computer Science M
Counselor Education M,D
Curriculum and Instruction M,D
Dance M
Early Childhood Education M,D
Economics M,D
Education—General M,D,O
Educational Administration M,D,O
Educational Media/Instructional Technology M,D
Educational Psychology M,D,O
Electrical Engineering M
Elementary Education M,D
Engineering and Applied Sciences—General M
English M,D
Foundations and Philosophy of Education M,D,O
French M
Geography M
Geology M,D
Higher Education M,D
History M,D
Industrial and Manufacturing Management M
Industrial/Management Engineering M
Law P
Management Information Systems M
Mathematics M
Mechanical Engineering M
Music M,O
Nursing—General M
Nutrition M
Philosophy M
Physical Education M
Physical Therapy M
Physics M,D
Political Science M,D
Psychology—General M,D
Public Administration M
Public Health—General M
Reading Education M,D
Romance Languages M
Secondary Education M,D
Sociology M
Spanish M
Special Education M,D
Sports Management M
Statistics M
Taxation M
Theater M

NORTHERN KENTUCKY UNIVERSITY

Accounting M
Business Administration and Management—General M
Communication—General M
Computer and Information Systems Security M,O
Computer Science M
Counselor Education M
Education—General M,O
Educational Administration M
Family Nurse Practitioner Studies M,O
Health Informatics M
Industrial and Organizational Psychology M
Information Science M
Law P
Liberal Studies M

Nonprofit Management M,O
Nursing—General M,O
Organizational Management M
Public Administration M
Social Psychology M
Software Engineering M,O
Special Education O

NORTHERN MICHIGAN UNIVERSITY

Biochemistry M
Biological and Biomedical Sciences—General M
Chemistry M
Communication Disorders M
Criminal Justice and Criminology M
Education—General M,O
Educational Administration M,O
Elementary Education M
English M
Exercise and Sports Science M
Nursing—General M
Psychology—General M
Public Administration M
Secondary Education M
Special Education M
Writing M

NORTHERN STATE UNIVERSITY

Counselor Education M
Education—General M
Educational Administration M
Educational Media/Instructional Technology M
Elementary Education M
English Education M
Health Education M
Physical Education M
Reading Education M
Secondary Education M
Special Education M

NORTH GEORGIA COLLEGE & STATE UNIVERSITY

Art Education M,O
Early Childhood Education M,O
Education—General M,O
Educational Administration M,O
English Education M,O
Family Nurse Practitioner Studies M
Mathematics Education M,O
Middle School Education M,O
Nursing Education M
Physical Education M,O
Physical Therapy D
Public Administration M
Science Education M,O
Secondary Education M,O
Social Psychology M
Social Sciences Education M,O
Special Education M,O

NORTH GREENVILLE UNIVERSITY

Business Administration and Management—General M
Pastoral Ministry and Counseling M

NORTH PARK THEOLOGICAL SEMINARY

Religious Education M
Theology P,M,D,O

NORTH PARK UNIVERSITY

Business Administration and Management—General M
Education—General M
Nursing—General M
Urban and Regional Planning M

NORTH SHORE–LIJ GRADUATE SCHOOL OF MOLECULAR MEDICINE

Molecular Medicine D

NORTHWEST BAPTIST SEMINARY

Theology P,M,D,O

NORTHWEST CHRISTIAN COLLEGE

Business Administration and Management—General M
Counselor Education M

NORTHWESTERN HEALTH SCIENCES UNIVERSITY

Acupuncture and Oriental Medicine M
Chiropractic P
Rehabilitation Sciences O

NORTHWESTERN OKLAHOMA STATE UNIVERSITY

Adult Education M
Counseling Psychology M

Counselor Education M
Curriculum and Instruction M
Education—General M
Educational Administration M
Elementary Education M
Reading Education M
Secondary Education M

NORTHWESTERN POLYTECHNIC UNIVERSITY

Business Administration and Management—General M
Computer Engineering M
Computer Science M
Electrical Engineering M
Engineering and Applied Sciences—General M

NORTHWESTERN STATE UNIVERSITY OF LOUISIANA

Adult Education M
Archaeology M
Art/Fine Arts M
Business Education M
Clinical Psychology M
Counselor Education M,O
Curriculum and Instruction M
Early Childhood Education M
Education—General M,O
Educational Administration M,O
Educational Media/Instructional Technology M,O
Elementary Education M
English Education M
English M
Health Education M
Home Economics Education M
Mathematics Education M
Middle School Education M
Music M
Nursing—General M
Psychology—General M
Reading Education M,O
Science Education M
Secondary Education M,O
Social Sciences Education M
Special Education M,O
Student Affairs M,O

NORTHWESTERN UNIVERSITY

Accounting D
Advertising and Public Relations M
African Studies O
Allopathic Medicine
Anthropology D
Applied Mathematics M,D
Art History D
Art/Fine Arts M*
Astronomy M,D
Astrophysics M,D
Biochemistry D
Bioinformatics M
Biological and Biomedical Sciences—General D*
Biomedical Engineering M,D
Biophysics D
Biopsychology D
Biotechnology D
Business Administration and Management—General M
Cancer Biology/Oncology D
Cell Biology D
Chemical Engineering M,D
Chemistry D
Civil Engineering M,D
Clinical Psychology D
Clinical Research M,O
Cognitive Sciences D
Communication Disorders M,D*
Communication—General M,D
Comparative Literature M,D,O
Computational Biology M
Computational Sciences M
Computer Engineering M,D,O
Computer Science M,D,O
Corporate and Organizational Communication M
Counseling Psychology M*
Developmental Biology D
Economics M,D
Education—General M,D*
Educational Media/Instructional Technology M,D
Electrical Engineering M,D,O*
Electronic Commerce M
Electronic Materials M,D,O
Elementary Education M
Engineering and Applied Sciences—General M,D,O
Engineering Management M
English M,D*
Environmental Engineering M,D
Evolutionary Biology D
Film, Television, and Video Production M,D
Finance and Banking D
French D,O
Gender Studies

Genetic Counseling M
Genetics D
Geology M,D
Geosciences M,D
Geotechnical Engineering M,D
German D
Higher Education M
History D
Human Development D
Immunology D
Industrial/Management Engineering M,D
Information Science M
International Affairs O
Italian D,O
Journalism M*
Law P,M,O
Liberal Studies M
Linguistics M,D
Management Information Systems M
Management Strategy and Policy D
Manufacturing Engineering M
Marketing M,D*
Marriage and Family Therapy M
Materials Engineering M,D,O
Materials Sciences M,D,O
Mathematics D
Mechanical Engineering M,D
Mechanics M,D
Media Studies M,D
Microbiology D
Molecular Biology D
Music Education M,D
Music M,D,O
Neurobiology M,D
Neuroscience D*
Operations Research M,D
Organizational Behavior M,D
Organizational Management M,D
Pharmacology D
Philosophy D
Physical Therapy D
Physics M,D
Physiology M
Political Science M,D
Project Management M
Psychology—General D*
Public Health—General M
Public Policy D*
Publishing M
Reproductive Biology D
Secondary Education M
Slavic Languages D
Social Psychology D
Social Sciences M,O
Sociology D
Special Education M,D
Speech and Interpersonal Communication M,D
Statistics M,D
Structural Biology D
Structural Engineering M,D
Theater M,D
Toxicology D
Transportation and Highway Engineering M,D
Writing M

NORTHWEST MISSOURI STATE UNIVERSITY

Accounting M
Agricultural Economics and Agribusiness M
Agricultural Education M
Agricultural Sciences—General M
Biological and Biomedical Sciences—General M
Business Administration and Management—General M
Computer Science M
Counselor Education M
Early Childhood Education M
Education—General M,O
Educational Administration M,O
Educational Media/Instructional Technology M
Elementary Education M,O
English Education M
English M
Geographic Information Systems M
Geography M
Health Education M
Health Services Management and Hospital Administration M
History M
Management Information Systems M
Mathematics Education M
Middle School Education M
Music Education M
Physical Education M
Psychology—General M
Reading Education M
Recreation and Park Management M
Science Education M
Secondary Education M,O

Social Sciences Education M
Special Education M

NORTHWEST NAZARENE UNIVERSITY

Business Administration and Management—General M
Counselor Education M
Curriculum and Instruction M
Education—General M
Educational Administration M
Marriage and Family Therapy M
Pastoral Ministry and Counseling P,M
Reading Education M
Religion P,M
School Psychology M
Social Psychology M
Social Work M
Special Education M

NORTHWEST UNIVERSITY

Business Administration and Management—General M
Counseling Psychology M
Education—General M
Psychology—General M

NORTHWOOD UNIVERSITY

Business Administration and Management—General M

NORWICH UNIVERSITY

Business Administration and Management—General M
Civil Engineering M
Criminal Justice and Criminology M
Education—General M
International Affairs M
Management Information Systems M
Military and Defense Studies M
Nursing and Healthcare Administration M
Organizational Management M
Public Administration M

NOTRE DAME COLLEGE (OH)

Accounting M,O
Business Administration and Management—General M,O
Education—General M,O
Finance and Banking M,O
Management Information Systems M,O
Pastoral Ministry and Counseling M,O
Reading Education M,O
Special Education M,O

NOTRE DAME DE NAMUR UNIVERSITY

Addictions/Substance Abuse Counseling M,O
Art Therapy M
Biological and Biomedical Sciences—General O
Business Administration and Management—General M
Counseling Psychology M,O
Education—General M
Educational Administration M,O
Educational Media/Instructional Technology M,O
English as a Second Language M,O
English M,O
Gerontology M,O
Marriage and Family Therapy M
Music Education M
Music M
Psychology—General M,O
Public Administration M
Reading Education M,O
Special Education M,O

NOTRE DAME SEMINARY

Theology P,M

NOVA SCOTIA AGRICULTURAL COLLEGE

Agricultural Sciences—General M
Agronomy and Soil Sciences M
Animal Sciences M
Aquaculture M
Botany M
Ecology M
Environmental Biology M
Environmental Management and Policy M
Environmental Sciences M
Food Science and Technology M
Horticulture M
Physiology M
Plant Pathology M
Plant Physiology M
Water Resources M

NOVA SOUTHEASTERN UNIVERSITY

Accounting M
Adult Education D
Allied Health—General M,D
Art Education M,O
Biological and Biomedical Sciences—General M
Business Administration and Management—General M,D*
Child and Family Studies M,D
Clinical Psychology D,O*
Communication Disorders M,D
Computer and Information Systems Security M
Computer Education M,D,O
Computer Science M,D*
Conflict Resolution and Mediation/Peace Studies M,D*
Counseling Psychology M*
Criminal Justice and Criminology M*
Curriculum and Instruction M,O
Dentistry P,M
Distance Education Development M,D
Early Childhood Education M,D,O
Education of the Gifted M,O
Education—General M,D,O*
Educational Administration M,D,O
Educational Media/Instructional Technology M,D,O
Elementary Education M,O
English as a Second Language M,O
English Education M,O
Environmental Sciences M
Health Education D
Higher Education D
Human Resources Management M
Human Services D
Humanities M
Information Science M,D
Interdisciplinary Studies M
International Business M,D
Law P,M
Legal and Justice Studies M
Management Information Systems M,D
Marine Affairs M
Marine Biology M,D
Marine Sciences M
Marriage and Family Therapy M,D,O
Mathematics Education M,O
Multilingual and Multicultural Education M,O
Nursing—General M
Occupational Therapy M,D
Oceanography M,D*
Optometry P,M
Organizational Management D
Osteopathic Medicine P,M
Pharmacology M
Pharmacy P
Physical Therapy D
Physician Assistant Studies M
Psychology—General M,D,O
Public Administration M,D
Public Health—General M
Reading Education M,O
Real Estate M
Religious Education M,O
School Psychology M,D,O*
Science Education M,O
Secondary Education M,O
Social Sciences Education M,O
Social Sciences M
Spanish M,O
Special Education M,D,O
Sports Management M,O
Student Affairs M
Taxation M
Urban Education M,O
Vision Sciences P,M
Vocational and Technical Education D

NSCAD UNIVERSITY

Applied Arts and Design—General M
Art/Fine Arts M

NYACK COLLEGE

Accounting M
Business Administration and Management—General M
Education—General M

OAKLAND CITY UNIVERSITY

Business Administration and Management—General M
Education—General M,D
Educational Administration M,D
Theology P,D

OAKLAND UNIVERSITY

Accounting M,O
Adult Nursing M
Allied Health—General M,D,O
Applied Mathematics M,D
Applied Statistics M
Biological and Biomedical Sciences—General M
Business Administration and Management—General M,O*
Cell Biology M
Chemistry M,D
Computer Engineering M
Computer Science M
Counseling Psychology M,D,O*
Early Childhood Education M,D,O
Economics O
Education—General M,D,O
Educational Administration M,D,O*
Educational Media/Instructional Technology O
Electrical Engineering M
Engineering and Applied Sciences—General M,D
Engineering Management M
English as a Second Language M,O
English M
Entrepreneurship M,O
Environmental and Occupational Health M*
Environmental Sciences M,D
Exercise and Sports Science M,O
Family Nurse Practitioner Studies M,O
Finance and Banking M,O
Foundations and Philosophy of Education M
Gerontological Nursing M,O
Health Promotion O
Higher Education M,D,O
History M
Human Resources Development M
Human Resources Management M,O
Industrial and Manufacturing Management M,O
International Business M,O
Liberal Studies M*
Linguistics M,O
Management Information Systems M,O
Marketing M,O
Maternal and Child Health M,D,O
Mathematics Education M,D,O
Mathematics M
Mechanical Engineering M,D
Medical Physics M,D
Music Education M,D
Music M,D
Nurse Anesthesia M,O
Nursing Education M,O
Nursing—General M,D,O*
Physical Therapy M,D,O
Physics M,D
Public Administration M
Reading Education M,D,O
Secondary Education M
Software Engineering M
Special Education M,O
Statistics O
Systems Engineering M,D*
Systems Science M

Close-Up on page 985.

OBERLIN COLLEGE

Music M

OBLATE SCHOOL OF THEOLOGY

Pastoral Ministry and Counseling P,M,D,O
Religion P,M,D,O
Theology P,M,D,O

OCCIDENTAL COLLEGE

Biological and Biomedical Sciences—General M
Education—General M
Elementary Education M
English Education M
Foreign Languages Education M
Liberal Studies M
Mathematics Education M
Science Education M
Secondary Education M
Social Sciences Education M

OGI SCHOOL OF SCIENCE & ENGINEERING AT OREGON HEALTH & SCIENCE UNIVERSITY

Biochemistry M,D
Biomedical Engineering M,D
Business Administration and Management—General M,D
Computer Engineering M,D
Computer Science M,D
Electrical Engineering M,D
Environmental and Occupational Health M,D
Environmental Engineering M,D
Environmental Sciences M,D
Health Services Management and Hospital Administration M,O
Management of Technology M,O
Molecular Biology M,D
Ocean Engineering M,D

OGLALA LAKOTA COLLEGE

Business Administration and Management—General M
Educational Administration M

OGLETHORPE UNIVERSITY

Business Administration and Management—General M
Early Childhood Education M
Education—General M

OHIO COLLEGE OF PODIATRIC MEDICINE

Podiatric Medicine P

OHIO DOMINICAN UNIVERSITY

Business Administration and Management—General M
Education—General M
English as a Second Language M
Liberal Studies M
Theology M

OHIO NORTHERN UNIVERSITY

Law P
Pharmacy P

THE OHIO STATE UNIVERSITY

Accounting M,D
Aerospace/Aeronautical Engineering M,D
African Studies M
African-American Studies M
Agricultural Economics and Agribusiness M,D
Agricultural Education M,D
Agricultural Engineering M,D
Agricultural Sciences—General M,D
Agronomy and Soil Sciences M,D
Allied Health—General M
Allopathic Medicine P
Anatomy M,D
Animal Sciences M,D
Anthropology M,D
Architecture M*
Art Education M,D
Art History M,D
Art/Fine Arts M
Arts Administration M
Asian Languages M,D
Astronomy M,D
Atmospheric Sciences M,D
Biochemistry M
Bioengineering M,D
Biological and Biomedical Sciences—General M,D
Biomedical Engineering M,D
Biophysics M,D
Biostatistics D
Business Administration and Management—General M,D
Cardiovascular Sciences M
Cell Biology M,D
Chemical Engineering M,D
Chemical Physics M,D
Chemistry M,D
Child and Family Studies M,D
Civil Engineering M,D
Classics M,D
Clinical Psychology M,D
Clothing and Textiles M,D
Cognitive Sciences M,D
Communication Disorders M,D
Communication—General M,D*
Computer Science M,D
Consumer Economics M,D
Dance M,D
Dentistry P,M
Developmental Biology M,D
Developmental Psychology M,D
East European and Russian Studies M
Ecology M,D
Economics M,D
Education—General M,D*
Educational Administration M,D
Educational Policy M,D
Electrical Engineering M,D
Engineering and Applied Sciences—General M,D
English M,D
Entomology M,D
Environmental Management and Policy M,D
Environmental Sciences M,D
Evolutionary Biology M,D
Family and Consumer Sciences-General M
Finance and Banking M,D
Food Science and Technology M,D
French M,D

Program	Degrees
Genetics	M,D
Geodetic Sciences	M,D
Geography	M,D
Geology	M,D
German	M,D
Health Services Management and Hospital Administration	M
Higher Education	M
History	M,D
Home Economics Education	M
Horticulture	M,D
Hospitality Management	M,D
Human Development	M,D
Human Resources Management	M,D
Immunology	M,D
Industrial and Labor Relations	M,D
Industrial Design	M
Industrial/Management Engineering	M,D
Information Science	M,D
Interdisciplinary Studies	M,D
Interior Design	M
Italian	M,D
Japanese	M,D
Landscape Architecture	M
Law	P,M*
Linguistics	M,D
Logistics	M
Management Information Systems	M,D
Materials Engineering	M,D
Materials Sciences	M,D*
Mathematics	M,D
Mechanical Engineering	M,D
Mechanics	M,D
Medicinal and Pharmaceutical Chemistry	M,D
Metallurgical Engineering and Metallurgy	M,D
Microbiology	M,D
Molecular Biology	M,D
Molecular Genetics	M,D
Music	M,D
Natural Resources	M,D
Near and Middle Eastern Languages	M,D
Neuroscience	M,D
Nuclear Engineering	M,D
Nursing—General	M,D
Nutrition	M,D
Occupational Therapy	M
Optical Sciences	M,D
Optometry	P
Oral and Dental Sciences	D
Pathobiology	M,D
Pathology	M
Pharmaceutical Administration	M,D
Pharmaceutical Sciences	M,D*
Pharmacology	M,D
Pharmacy	P
Philosophy	M,D
Physical Education	M,D
Physical Therapy	M
Physics	M,D
Physiology	M,D
Plant Biology	M,D
Plant Pathology	M,D
Political Science	M,D
Portuguese	M,D
Psychology—General	M,D
Public Affairs	M,D*
Public Health—General	M,D
Rural Sociology	M,D
Slavic Languages	M,D
Social Psychology	M,D
Social Work	M,D
Sociology	M,D
Spanish	M,D
Statistics	M,D
Student Affairs	M
Surveying Science and Engineering	M,D
Systems Engineering	M,D
Theater	M,D
Toxicology	M,D
Urban and Regional Planning	M,D
Veterinary Medicine	P
Veterinary Sciences	M,D
Virology	M,D
Vocational and Technical Education	D
Women's Studies	M,D

THE OHIO STATE UNIVERSITY AT LIMA

Program	Degrees
Early Childhood Education	M
Education—General	M
Middle School Education	M
Social Work	M

THE OHIO STATE UNIVERSITY AT MARION

Program	Degrees
Early Childhood Education	M,D
Education—General	M,D
Middle School Education	M,D
Nursing—General	M,D
Social Work	M,D

THE OHIO STATE UNIVERSITY–MANSFIELD CAMPUS

Program	Degrees
Early Childhood Education	M
Middle School Education	M
Social Work	M

THE OHIO STATE UNIVERSITY–NEWARK CAMPUS

Program	Degrees
Early Childhood Education	M
Education—General	M
Middle School Education	M
Social Work	M

OHIO UNIVERSITY

Program	Degrees
African Studies	M
Applied Economics	M
Art Education	M
Art History	M
Art/Fine Arts	M
Asian Studies	M
Astronomy	M,D
Athletic Training and Sports Medicine	M
Biochemistry	M,D
Biological and Biomedical Sciences—General	M,D
Biomedical Engineering	M,D
Business Administration and Management—General	M
Cell Biology	M,D
Chemical Engineering	M,D
Child and Family Studies	M
Child Development	M
Civil Engineering	M,D
Clinical Psychology	D
Communication Disorders	M,D
Communication—General	M,D
Comparative and Interdisciplinary Arts	D
Computer Education	M,D
Computer Science	M,D
Construction Engineering	M,D
Counselor Education	M,D
Curriculum and Instruction	M,D
Early Childhood Education	M
Ecology	M,D
Economics	M
Education—General	M,D
Educational Administration	M,D
Educational Measurement and Evaluation	M,D
Educational Media/Instructional Technology	M,D
Electrical Engineering	M,D
Engineering and Applied Sciences—General	M,D
English as a Second Language	M
English	M,D
Environmental Biology	M,D
Environmental Engineering	M,D
Environmental Management and Policy	M
Evolutionary Biology	M,D
Exercise and Sports Science	M,D
Experimental Psychology	D
Family and Consumer Sciences-General	M
Film, Television, and Video Production	M
Film, Television, and Video Theory and Criticism	M
Finance and Banking	M
French	M
Geochemistry	M
Geography	M
Geology	M
Geophysics	M
Geotechnical Engineering	M,D
Health Services Management and Hospital Administration	M
Higher Education	M,D
History	M,D
Hydrogeology	M
Industrial and Organizational Psychology	D
Industrial/Management Engineering	M,D
Interdisciplinary Studies	D
International Affairs	M
International Development	M
Journalism	M,D
Latin American Studies	M
Linguistics	M
Manufacturing Engineering	M,D
Mathematics Education	M,D
Mathematics	M,D*
Mechanical Engineering	M,D
Media Studies	M,D
Microbiology	M,D
Middle School Education	M,D
Molecular Biology	M,D*
Music Education	M,O
Music	M,O
Neuroscience	M,D
Nutrition	M
Osteopathic Medicine	P
Philosophy	M
Photography	M
Physical Education	M
Physical Therapy	D
Physics	M,D*
Physiology	M,D
Plant Biology	M,D
Political Science	M
Psychology—General	D
Public Administration	M
Reading Education	M,D
Recreation and Park Management	M
Rehabilitation Counseling	M,D
Science Education	M
Secondary Education	M,D
Social Sciences Education	M,D
Social Sciences	M
Social Work	M
Sociology	M
Spanish	M
Special Education	M,D
Speech and Interpersonal Communication	D
Sports Management	M
Structural Engineering	M,D
Student Affairs	M,D
Systems Engineering	M
Telecommunications	M
Theater	M
Therapies—Dance, Drama, and Music	M,O
Transportation and Highway Engineering	M,D
Water Resources Engineering	M,D

OHR HAMEIR THEOLOGICAL SEMINARY

Program	Degrees
Theology	

OKLAHOMA CHRISTIAN UNIVERSITY

Program	Degrees
Pastoral Ministry and Counseling	P,M
Theology	P,M

OKLAHOMA CITY UNIVERSITY

Program	Degrees
Accounting	M
Art/Fine Arts	M
Business Administration and Management—General	M
Comparative Literature	M
Computer Science	M
Corporate and Organizational Communication	M
Criminal Justice and Criminology	M
Early Childhood Education	M
Education—General	M
Educational Psychology	M
Elementary Education	M
English as a Second Language	M
Finance and Banking	M
Health Services Management and Hospital Administration	M
International Business	M
Law	P
Liberal Studies	M
Management Information Systems	M
Marketing	M
Mass Communication	M
Music	M
Nursing—General	M
Philosophy	M
Religion	M
Theater	M
Writing	M

OKLAHOMA STATE UNIVERSITY

Program	Degrees
Accounting	M,D
Aerospace/Aeronautical Engineering	M
Agricultural Economics and Agribusiness	M,D
Agricultural Education	M,D
Agricultural Engineering	M,D
Agricultural Sciences—General	M,D
Agronomy and Soil Sciences	M,D
Animal Sciences	M,D
Applied Arts and Design—General	M,D
Applied Mathematics	M,D
Applied Science and Technology	M
Architectural Engineering	M
Architecture	M
Biochemistry	M,D*
Bioengineering	M,D
Biotechnology	M,D
Botany	M,D
Business Administration and Management—General	M,D*
Chemical Engineering	M,D
Chemistry	M,D
Child and Family Studies	M,D
Civil Engineering	M,D
Clinical Psychology	M,D
Clothing and Textiles	M,D
Communication Disorders	M
Computer Engineering	M,D
Computer Science	M,D*
Conservation Biology	M,D
Counselor Education	M,D,O
Criminal Justice and Criminology	M,D
Curriculum and Instruction	M,D
Economics	M,D
Education—General	M,D,O
Educational Administration	M,D
Educational Psychology	M,D,O
Electrical Engineering	M,D
Emergency Management	M
Emergency Medical Services	M
Engineering and Applied Sciences—General	M,D*
Engineering Management	M
English	M,D
Entomology	D
Environmental Engineering	M,D
Environmental Sciences	M,D
Experimental Psychology	M,D
Family and Consumer Sciences-General	M,D
Finance and Banking	M,D
Fire Protection Engineering	M
Food Science and Technology	M,D
Forestry	M
Geography	M,D
Geology	M
Gerontology	M
Health Education	M,D,O
Health Services Management and Hospital Administration	M
Higher Education	M,D
History	M,D
Horticulture	M,D
Hospitality Management	M,D
Industrial and Manufacturing Management	M,D
Industrial/Management Engineering	M,D
International Affairs	M
Landscape Architecture	M
Leisure Studies	M,D,O
Management Information Systems	M,D
Management of Technology	M
Manufacturing Engineering	M
Marketing	M,D
Mass Communication	M
Mathematics Education	M,D
Mathematics	M,D*
Mechanical Engineering	M,D
Microbiology	M,D
Molecular Biology	M,D
Molecular Genetics	M,D
Music Education	M
Music	M
Natural Resources	M,D
Nutrition	M,D
Operations Research	M,D
Philosophy	M
Photonics	M,D
Physical Education	M,D,O
Physics	M,D
Plant Pathology	D
Plant Sciences	M,D
Political Science	M
Psychology—General	M,D
Sociology	M,D
Statistics	M,D
Student Affairs	M,D,O
Systems Engineering	M
Technical Writing	M,D
Telecommunications Management	M,D
Theater	M
Veterinary Medicine	P
Veterinary Sciences	M,D
Vocational and Technical Education	M,D
Writing	M,D
Zoology	M,D

OKLAHOMA STATE UNIVERSITY CENTER FOR HEALTH SCIENCES

Program	Degrees
Biological and Biomedical Sciences—General	M,D
Forensic Psychology	M
Forensic Sciences	M
Molecular Biology	M,D
Osteopathic Medicine	P
Toxicology	M

OLD DOMINION UNIVERSITY

Program	Degrees
Accounting	M
Aerospace/Aeronautical Engineering	M
Allied Health—General	M,D
Analytical Chemistry	M,D
Art/Fine Arts	M
Athletic Training and Sports Medicine	M
Automotive Engineering	M
Biochemistry	M,D
Biological and Biomedical Sciences—General	M,D
Business Administration and Management—General	M,D*

Business Education M,D
Chemistry M,D
Civil Engineering M,D
Clinical Psychology D
Communication Disorders M
Community College Education M,D
Community Health M
Computer Engineering M,D
Computer Science M,D
Counselor Education M,D,O
Criminal Justice and Criminology D
Curriculum and Instruction M,D
Dental Hygiene M
Early Childhood Education M,D
Ecology D
Economics M
Education—General M,D,O
Educational Administration M,D,O
Educational Media/Instructional Technology M,D
Electrical Engineering M,D
Elementary Education M
Engineering and Applied Sciences—General M,D
Engineering Management M,D
English M,D
Environmental and Occupational Health M
Environmental Engineering M,D
Ergonomics and Human Factors D
Exercise and Sports Science M
Experimental Psychology D
Finance and Banking D
Health Promotion M
Health Services Management and Hospital Administration M
Health Services Research D
Higher Education M,D,O
History M
Humanities M
Industrial and Organizational Psychology D
International Affairs M,D
Kinesiology and Movement Studies D
Library Science M
Linguistics M
Manufacturing Engineering M,D
Marketing D
Mathematics M,D
Mechanical Engineering M,D
Middle School Education M,D
Music Education M
Nursing—General M
Oceanography M,D
Organic Chemistry M,D
Physical Chemistry M,D
Physical Education M
Physical Therapy D
Physics M,D
Psychology—General M,D
Public Administration M,D
Public Health—General M
Reading Education M,D
Recreation and Park Management M
Science Education M
Secondary Education M,D
Sociology M
Special Education M,D
Sports Management M
Systems Engineering M
Travel and Tourism M
Urban and Regional Planning M
Urban Studies M,D
Vocational and Technical Education M,D
Writing M

Close-Up on page 987.

OLIVET COLLEGE

Education—General M

OLIVET NAZARENE UNIVERSITY

Business Administration and Management—General M
Curriculum and Instruction M
Education—General M
Elementary Education M
Organizational Management M
Pastoral Ministry and Counseling M
Religion M
Secondary Education M
Theology M

ORAL ROBERTS UNIVERSITY

Accounting M
Business Administration and Management—General M
Curriculum and Instruction M,D
Education—General M,D
Educational Administration M,D
English as a Second Language M,D
Finance and Banking M
Higher Education M,D
International Business M
Marketing M
Missions and Missiology P,M,D
Nonprofit Management M
Organizational Behavior M
Pastoral Ministry and Counseling P,M,D
Religious Education P,M,D
Theology P,M,D

OREGON COLLEGE OF ORIENTAL MEDICINE

Acupuncture and Oriental Medicine M,D*

OREGON HEALTH & SCIENCE UNIVERSITY

Adult Nursing M,O
Allopathic Medicine P
Biochemistry D
Bioinformatics M,D,O
Biological and Biomedical Sciences—General M,D,O
Biopsychology M,D
Biostatistics M
Cell Biology D
Community Health Nursing M,O
Dentistry P
Developmental Biology D
Epidemiology M
Genetics D
Gerontological Nursing M,D,O
Immunology D
Medical Informatics M,D,O*
Microbiology D
Molecular Biology D
Neuroscience M,D*
Nurse Midwifery M,O
Nursing—General M,D,O
Oral and Dental Sciences M,O
Pediatric Nursing M,O
Pharmacology D
Physiology D
Psychiatric Nursing M,O
Women's Health Nursing M,O

OREGON STATE UNIVERSITY

Adult Education M
Agricultural Economics and Agribusiness M,D
Agricultural Education M
Agricultural Sciences—General M,D
Agronomy and Soil Sciences M,D
Analytical Chemistry M,D
Animal Sciences M,D
Anthropology M
Applied Statistics M,D
Atmospheric Sciences M,D
Biochemistry M,D
Bioengineering M,D
Biometrics M,D
Biophysics M,D
Botany M,D
Business Administration and Management—General M,O
Cell Biology M,D
Chemical Engineering M,D
Chemistry M,D
Child and Family Studies M,D
Civil Engineering M,D
Clothing and Textiles M,D
Computer Science M,D
Construction Engineering M,D
Counselor Education M,D
Economics M,D
Education—General M,D
Educational Administration M
Electrical Engineering M,D*
Elementary Education M
Engineering and Applied Sciences—General M,D*
English M
Environmental and Occupational Health M
Environmental Engineering M,D
Environmental Management and Policy M,D
Environmental Sciences M,D
Exercise and Sports Science M,D
Family and Consumer Sciences-General M
Fish, Game, and Wildlife Management M,D
Food Science and Technology M,D
Forestry M,D
Genetics M,D
Geography M,D
Geology M,D
Geophysics M,D
Geosciences M,D
Gerontology M
Health Physics/Radiological Health M,D
Health Promotion M
Health Services Management and Hospital Administration M
History M,D
Horticulture M,D
Human Development M,D
Industrial/Management Engineering M,D
Inorganic Chemistry M,D
Interdisciplinary Studies M
Kinesiology and Movement Studies M
Manufacturing Engineering M,D
Marine Affairs M
Marine Sciences M
Materials Sciences M,D
Mathematics Education M,D
Mathematics M,D
Mechanical Engineering M,D
Microbiology M,D
Molecular Biology M,D
Molecular Toxicology M,D
Music Education M
Nuclear Engineering M,D*
Nutrition M,D
Ocean Engineering M
Oceanography M,D
Operations Research M,D
Organic Chemistry M,D
Paper and Pulp Engineering M,D
Pathology M
Pharmaceutical Sciences P,M,D
Pharmacy P,M,D
Physical Chemistry M,D
Physical Education M
Physics M,D*
Plant Pathology M,D
Plant Physiology M,D
Public Health—General M,D
Range Science M,D
Reading Education M
Science Education M,D
Statistics M,D
Student Affairs M
Toxicology M,D
Veterinary Medicine P
Veterinary Sciences M,D
Water Resources Engineering M,D
Zoology M,D

OREGON STATE UNIVERSITY–CASCADES

Education—General M
School Psychology M
Social Psychology M

OTIS COLLEGE OF ART AND DESIGN

Art/Fine Arts M
Photography M
Writing M

OTTAWA UNIVERSITY

Art Therapy M
Business Administration and Management—General M
Counseling Psychology M
Counselor Education M
Curriculum and Instruction M
Early Childhood Education M
Education—General M
Educational Administration M
Educational Media/Instructional Technology M
Elementary Education M
Finance and Banking M
Human Resources Development M
Human Resources Management M
Marketing M
Marriage and Family Therapy M
Pastoral Ministry and Counseling M
School Psychology M
Special Education M

OTTERBEIN COLLEGE

Adult Nursing M,O
Business Administration and Management—General M
Education—General M
Family Nurse Practitioner Studies M,O
Nursing and Healthcare Administration M,O
Nursing—General M,O

OUR LADY OF HOLY CROSS COLLEGE

Counselor Education M
Curriculum and Instruction M
Education—General M
Educational Administration M
Marriage and Family Therapy M

OUR LADY OF THE LAKE UNIVERSITY OF SAN ANTONIO

Business Administration and Management—General M
Communication Disorders M
Counseling Psychology M,D
Counselor Education M
Curriculum and Instruction M,D
Education—General M,D
Educational Administration M,D
Educational Media/Instructional Technology M
English M
Finance and Banking M
Health Services Management and Hospital Administration M
Human Development M
International Business M
Marriage and Family Therapy M,D
Psychology—General M,D
School Psychology M,D
Social Work M
Sociology M
Special Education M

OXFORD GRADUATE SCHOOL

Child and Family Studies M,D
Organizational Management M,D
Religion M,D

PACE UNIVERSITY

Accounting M
Addictions/Substance Abuse Counseling M*
Business Administration and Management—General M,D,O*
Clinical Psychology D
Computer Science M,D,O*
Curriculum and Instruction M,O
Economics M
Education—General M,O*
Educational Administration M,O
Environmental Sciences M*
Finance and Banking M
Forensic Sciences M*
Health Services Management and Hospital Administration M
Information Science M,D,O
International Business M
Investment Management M
Law P,M,D*
Legal and Justice Studies P,M,D
Management Information Systems M
Management Strategy and Policy M
Marketing Research M
Marketing M
Nonprofit Management M
Nursing—General M,O*
Psychology—General M,D*
Public Administration M*
Publishing M*
School Psychology M
Taxation M
Telecommunications M,D,O
Theater M*

PACIFICA GRADUATE INSTITUTE

Clinical Psychology M,D
Counseling Psychology M,D
Psychology—General M,D

PACIFIC COLLEGE OF ORIENTAL MEDICINE

Acupuncture and Oriental Medicine M,D

PACIFIC COLLEGE OF ORIENTAL MEDICINE-CHICAGO

Acupuncture and Oriental Medicine M

PACIFIC COLLEGE OF ORIENTAL MEDICINE-NEW YORK

Acupuncture and Oriental Medicine M

PACIFIC GRADUATE SCHOOL OF PSYCHOLOGY

Biopsychology D
Clinical Psychology D*
Psychology—General M,D*

PACIFIC LUTHERAN THEOLOGICAL SEMINARY

Theology P,M,D,O

PACIFIC LUTHERAN UNIVERSITY

Business Administration and Management—General M
Curriculum and Instruction M
Education—General M
Educational Administration M
Family Nurse Practitioner Studies M
Management of Technology M
Marriage and Family Therapy M
Nursing and Healthcare Administration M
Nursing—General M
Writing M

Close-Up on page 989.

PACIFIC OAKS COLLEGE
- Human Development M
- Marriage and Family Therapy M

PACIFIC SCHOOL OF RELIGION
- Religion P,M,D,O
- Theology P,M,D,O

PACIFIC STATES UNIVERSITY
- Accounting M,D
- Business Administration and Management—General M,D
- Computer Science M
- Finance and Banking M,D
- International Business M,D
- Management Information Systems M,D
- Management of Technology M,D
- Real Estate M,D

PACIFIC UNION COLLEGE
- Education—General M
- Educational Administration M

PACIFIC UNIVERSITY
- Early Childhood Education M
- Education—General M
- Elementary Education M
- Middle School Education M
- Occupational Therapy M
- Pharmacy P
- Physical Therapy D
- Physician Assistant Studies M
- Psychology—General M,D
- Secondary Education M
- Special Education M

PALM BEACH ATLANTIC UNIVERSITY
- Addictions/Substance Abuse Counseling M
- Business Administration and Management—General M
- Counseling Psychology M
- Counselor Education M
- Education—General M
- Elementary Education M
- Human Resources Development M
- Marriage and Family Therapy M
- Organizational Management M
- Pharmacy P

PALMER COLLEGE OF CHIROPRACTIC
- Anatomy M
- Chiropractic P*
- Clinical Research M

PARKER COLLEGE OF CHIROPRACTIC
- Chiropractic P

PARK UNIVERSITY
- Business Administration and Management—General M
- Education—General M
- Educational Administration M
- Emergency Management M
- Entrepreneurship M
- Health Services Management and Hospital Administration M
- International Business M
- Law M
- Management Information Systems M
- Middle School Education M
- Multilingual and Multicultural Education M
- Nonprofit Management M
- Public Administration M
- Public Affairs M
- Secondary Education M
- Special Education M

PAYNE THEOLOGICAL SEMINARY
- Theology P

PENN STATE DICKINSON SCHOOL OF LAW
- Law P,M

PENN STATE GREAT VALLEY
- Agricultural Engineering M
- Business Administration and Management—General M
- Curriculum and Instruction M
- Education—General M
- Educational Media/Instructional Technology M
- Entrepreneurship M
- Health Services Management and Hospital Administration M
- Information Science M
- Software Engineering M
- Special Education M
- Systems Engineering M

PENN STATE HARRISBURG
- Adult Education M,D
- American Studies M
- Business Administration and Management—General M*
- Business Education M,D
- Clinical Psychology M,D
- Computer Science M
- Criminal Justice and Criminology M,D
- Curriculum and Instruction M,D
- Education—General M,D
- Electrical Engineering M
- Engineering and Applied Sciences—General M,D
- Environmental Engineering M
- Environmental Sciences M
- Health Education M,D
- Health Services Management and Hospital Administration M,D
- Humanities M
- Management Information Systems M,D
- Psychology—General M,D
- Public Administration M,D
- Social Psychology M,D

Close-Up on page 991.

PENN STATE HERSHEY MEDICAL CENTER
- Allopathic Medicine P,M,D
- Anatomy M,D
- Biochemistry M,D
- Bioengineering M,D
- Biological and Biomedical Sciences—General M,D*
- Cell Biology M,D
- Genetics M,D
- Health Services Research M
- Immunology M,D
- Microbiology M,D
- Molecular Biology M,D
- Molecular Medicine M,D
- Molecular Toxicology M,D
- Neuroscience M,D
- Pharmacology M,D
- Physiology M,D
- Veterinary Sciences M
- Virology M,D

PENN STATE UNIVERSITY PARK
- Accounting M,D
- Acoustics M,D
- Adult Education M,D
- Aerospace/Aeronautical Engineering M,D
- Agricultural Economics and Agribusiness M,D
- Agricultural Education M,D
- Agricultural Engineering M,D
- Agricultural Sciences—General M,D
- Agronomy and Soil Sciences M,D
- Animal Sciences M,D
- Anthropology M,D
- Applied Mathematics M,D
- Applied Statistics M,D
- Architectural Engineering M,D
- Architecture M
- Art Education M,D
- Art History M,D
- Art/Fine Arts M,D
- Astronomy M,D
- Astrophysics M,D
- Biochemistry M,D*
- Bioengineering M,D
- Biological and Biomedical Sciences—General M,D*
- Biomedical Engineering M,D
- Biopsychology M,D*
- Biotechnology M,D
- Cell Biology M,D*
- Ceramic Sciences and Engineering M,D
- Chemical Engineering M,D
- Chemistry M,D*
- Child and Family Studies M,D
- Civil Engineering M,D
- Clinical Psychology M,D
- Cognitive Sciences M,D
- Communication Disorders M,D
- Communication—General M,D
- Comparative Literature M,D
- Computer Engineering M,D
- Computer Science M,D*
- Counseling Psychology M,D
- Counselor Education M,D
- Criminal Justice and Criminology M,D
- Curriculum and Instruction M,D
- Developmental Biology M,D
- Developmental Psychology M,D
- Early Childhood Education M,D
- Ecology M,D
- Economics M,D
- Education—General M,D
- Educational Administration M,D
- Educational Media/Instructional Technology M,D
- Educational Psychology M,D
- Electrical Engineering M,D
- Elementary Education M,D
- Engineering and Applied Sciences—General M,D
- English M,D
- Entomology M,D
- Environmental and Occupational Health M,D
- Environmental Engineering M,D
- Environmental Management and Policy M
- Environmental Sciences M
- Evolutionary Biology M,D
- Finance and Banking M,D
- Fish, Game, and Wildlife Management M,D
- Food Science and Technology M,D
- Forestry M,D
- Foundations and Philosophy of Education M,D
- French M,D
- Genetics M,D
- Geography M,D
- Geosciences M,D
- German M,D
- Health Services Management and Hospital Administration M,D*
- Higher Education M,D
- History M,D
- Horticulture M,D
- Hospitality Management M,D
- Human Development M,D
- Human Resources Development M
- Industrial and Labor Relations M
- Industrial and Manufacturing Management M,D
- Industrial and Organizational Psychology M,D
- Industrial/Management Engineering M,D
- Kinesiology and Movement Studies M,D
- Landscape Architecture M
- Leisure Studies M,D
- Logistics M,D
- Management Information Systems M,D
- Manufacturing Engineering M,D
- Marketing M,D
- Mass Communication M,D
- Materials Engineering M,D
- Materials Sciences M,D
- Mathematics M,D
- Mechanical Engineering M,D
- Mechanics M,D
- Metallurgical Engineering and Metallurgy M,D
- Meteorology M,D
- Microbiology M,D
- Mineral/Mining Engineering M,D
- Molecular Biology M,D
- Molecular Medicine M,D
- Multilingual and Multicultural Education M,D
- Music Education M,D
- Music M,D
- Neuroscience M,D
- Nuclear Engineering M,D
- Nursing—General M,D
- Nutrition M,D
- Pathobiology D
- Petroleum Engineering M,D
- Philosophy M,D
- Photography M,D
- Physics M,D*
- Physiology M,D
- Plant Pathology M,D
- Plant Physiology M,D
- Political Science M,D
- Polymer Science and Engineering M,D
- Psychology—General M,D
- Quality Management M
- Reading Education M,D
- Real Estate M,D
- Recreation and Park Management M,D
- Rural Sociology M,D
- Russian M,D
- School Psychology M,D
- Science Education M,D
- Social Psychology M,D
- Social Sciences Education M,D
- Sociology M,D
- Spanish M,D
- Special Education M,D
- Statistics M,D
- Structural Engineering M,D
- Student Affairs M,D
- Theater M
- Transportation and Highway Engineering M,D
- Veterinary Sciences D
- Vocational and Technical Education M,D
- Water Resources Engineering M,D
- Writing M,D

Close-Up on page 993.

PENNSYLVANIA ACADEMY OF THE FINE ARTS
- Art/Fine Arts M,O*

PENNSYLVANIA COLLEGE OF OPTOMETRY
- Communication Disorders M,D,O
- Optometry P
- Rehabilitation Sciences M,D,O
- Special Education M,D,O
- Vision Sciences M,D,O

PEPPERDINE UNIVERSITY
- Business Administration and Management—General M
- Clinical Psychology M
- Education—General M,D*
- Educational Administration M,D
- Educational Media/Instructional Technology D
- Management of Technology M
- Organizational Management M
- Psychology—General M,D*

Close-Up on page 995.

PEPPERDINE UNIVERSITY
- American Studies M
- Business Administration and Management—General M*
- Clinical Psychology M
- Communication—General M
- Conflict Resolution and Mediation/Peace Studies M
- Economics M
- History M
- Humanities M
- International Affairs M
- International Business M
- Law P
- Political Science M
- Psychology—General M
- Public Administration M
- Public Policy M*
- Religion P,M

Close-Up on page 995.

PERU STATE COLLEGE
- Education—General M

PFEIFFER UNIVERSITY
- Business Administration and Management—General M
- Education—General M
- Elementary Education M
- Health Services Management and Hospital Administration M
- Organizational Management M
- Religious Education M

PHILADELPHIA BIBLICAL UNIVERSITY
- Curriculum and Instruction M
- Education—General M
- Educational Administration M
- Organizational Management M
- Pastoral Ministry and Counseling M
- Theology P,M

PHILADELPHIA COLLEGE OF OSTEOPATHIC MEDICINE
- Biological and Biomedical Sciences—General M,O
- Clinical Psychology M,D
- Forensic Sciences M
- Health Psychology M,D
- Industrial and Organizational Psychology M,D
- Osteopathic Medicine P
- Physician Assistant Studies M*
- Psychology—General M,D*
- School Psychology M,D

PHILADELPHIA UNIVERSITY
- Business Administration and Management—General M
- Clothing and Textiles M
- Computer Art and Design M
- Educational Media/Instructional Technology M*
- Finance and Banking M
- Health Services Management and Hospital Administration M
- International Business M
- Marketing M
- Nurse Midwifery M,O
- Occupational Therapy M
- Physician Assistant Studies M
- Taxation M
- Textile Design M

- Textile Sciences and Engineering M,D

PHILLIPS GRADUATE INSTITUTE
- Counselor Education M
- Marriage and Family Therapy M,D
- Organizational Behavior M

PHILLIPS THEOLOGICAL SEMINARY
- Business Administration and Management—General P,M,D
- Ethics P,M,D
- Higher Education P,M,D
- Missions and Missiology P,M,D
- Music P,M,D
- Pastoral Ministry and Counseling D
- Religious Education P,M,D
- Social Work P,M,D
- Theology P,M,D

PIEDMONT BAPTIST COLLEGE AND GRADUATE SCHOOL
- Theology M,D

PIEDMONT COLLEGE
- Business Administration and Management—General M
- Curriculum and Instruction M,O
- Early Childhood Education M,O
- Education—General M,O
- Secondary Education M,O

PIKEVILLE COLLEGE
- Osteopathic Medicine P

PITTSBURGH THEOLOGICAL SEMINARY
- Theology P,M,D

PITTSBURG STATE UNIVERSITY
- Accounting M
- Applied Physics M
- Art Education M
- Art/Fine Arts M
- Biological and Biomedical Sciences—General M
- Business Administration and Management—General M
- Chemistry M
- Communication—General M
- Community College Education O
- Counselor Education M
- Early Childhood Education M
- Education—General M,O
- Educational Administration M
- Educational Media/Instructional Technology M
- Elementary Education M
- Engineering and Applied Sciences—General M,O
- English M
- Graphic Design M,O
- Higher Education M,O
- History M
- Human Resources Development M,O
- Mathematics M
- Music Education M
- Music M
- Nursing—General M
- Physical Education M
- Physics M
- Psychology—General M
- Reading Education M
- School Psychology O
- Secondary Education M
- Special Education M
- Theater M
- Vocational and Technical Education M,O

PLYMOUTH STATE UNIVERSITY
- Athletic Training and Sports Medicine M
- Business Administration and Management—General M
- Counselor Education M
- Education—General O
- Educational Administration M
- Elementary Education M
- English Education M
- Environmental Management and Policy M
- Health Education M
- Mathematics Education M
- Meteorology M
- Middle School Education M
- Reading Education M
- Science Education M
- Secondary Education M
- Special Education M,O

POINT LOMA NAZARENE UNIVERSITY
- Biological and Biomedical Sciences—General M
- Business Administration and Management—General M
- Education—General M,O
- Nursing—General M
- Religion M

POINT PARK UNIVERSITY
- Business Administration and Management—General M
- Communication—General M*
- Criminal Justice and Criminology M
- Curriculum and Instruction M
- Education—General M
- Educational Administration M
- Engineering Management M
- Journalism M
- Mass Communication M
- Music M
- Organizational Management M
- Theater M

POLYTECHNIC UNIVERSITY, BROOKLYN CAMPUS
- Bioinformatics M*
- Biomedical Engineering M,D
- Biotechnology M,D
- Business Administration and Management—General M,D*
- Chemical Engineering M,D*
- Chemistry M,D
- Civil Engineering M,D*
- Communication—General O
- Computer and Information Systems Security O
- Computer Engineering M,O
- Computer Science M,D*
- Construction Management M
- Criminal Justice and Criminology M,D,O
- Electrical Engineering M,D*
- Engineering Physics M
- Environmental Engineering M
- Environmental Sciences M
- Film, Television, and Video Production O
- Finance and Banking M,O
- Financial Engineering M,O*
- History of Science and Technology M
- Humanities M,O
- Industrial/Management Engineering M
- Internet and Interactive Multimedia M,O*
- Journalism M
- Management of Technology M,D
- Manufacturing Engineering M,D
- Materials Sciences M
- Mathematical and Computational Finance M,O
- Mathematics M,D
- Mechanical Engineering M,D*
- Organizational Behavior M
- Physics M,D
- Polymer Science and Engineering M
- Psychology—General M
- Software Engineering O
- Systems Engineering M
- Technical Communication O
- Technical Writing M
- Telecommunications Management M
- Telecommunications M
- Transportation and Highway Engineering M,D
- Transportation Management M

POLYTECHNIC UNIVERSITY, LONG ISLAND GRADUATE CENTER
- Aerospace/Aeronautical Engineering M,D
- Biological and Biomedical Sciences—General M,D,O
- Biomedical Engineering M,D,O
- Biotechnology M,D,O
- Business Administration and Management—General M,O
- Chemical Engineering M,D
- Civil Engineering M,D
- Computer Engineering M
- Computer Science M,D
- Electrical Engineering M,D
- Engineering Design M
- Engineering Physics M
- Entrepreneurship M,D,O
- Environmental Engineering M
- Financial Engineering M,O
- Industrial/Management Engineering M,D
- Manufacturing Engineering M,D
- Materials Sciences M,D
- Mechanical Engineering M,D
- Software Engineering M
- Systems Engineering M
- Telecommunications M
- Transportation and Highway Engineering M

POLYTECHNIC UNIVERSITY OF PUERTO RICO
- Business Administration and Management—General M
- Civil Engineering M
- Computer Engineering M
- Electrical Engineering M
- Engineering Management M
- Environmental Management and Policy M
- Industrial and Manufacturing Management M
- International Business M
- Management of Technology M
- Manufacturing Engineering M

POLYTECHNIC UNIVERSITY OF THE AMERICAS–MIAMI CAMPUS
- Business Administration and Management—General M
- Engineering Management M

POLYTECHNIC UNIVERSITY OF THE AMERICAS–ORLANDO CAMPUS
- Business Administration and Management—General M
- Engineering Management M

POLYTECHNIC UNIVERSITY, WESTCHESTER GRADUATE CENTER
- Business Administration and Management—General M
- Chemical Engineering M
- Chemistry M
- Computer Engineering M
- Computer Science M,D
- Electrical Engineering M,D
- Finance and Banking M,O
- Financial Engineering M,O
- Information Science M
- Management Information Systems M,O
- Management of Technology M
- Materials Sciences D
- Mathematical and Computational Finance M,O
- Telecommunications M

PONCE SCHOOL OF MEDICINE
- Allopathic Medicine P
- Biological and Biomedical Sciences—General D
- Clinical Psychology D
- Public Health—General M

PONTIFICAL CATHOLIC UNIVERSITY OF PUERTO RICO
- Accounting M,D
- Biological and Biomedical Sciences—General M
- Business Administration and Management—General M,D
- Chemistry M
- Clinical Laboratory Sciences/Medical Technology O
- Clinical Psychology M,D
- Criminal Justice and Criminology M,D
- Curriculum and Instruction M,D
- Education—General M,D
- Educational Media/Instructional Technology M,D
- English as a Second Language M,D
- Environmental Sciences M
- Finance and Banking M,D
- Hispanic Studies M
- History M
- Human Resources Management M,D
- Human Services M,D
- Industrial and Organizational Psychology M,D
- International Business M,D
- Law P
- Management Information Systems M,D
- Marketing M,D
- Medical/Surgical Nursing M
- Nursing—General M
- Psychiatric Nursing M
- Psychology—General M,D
- Public Administration M,D
- Religious Education M,D
- School Psychology M,D
- Social Work M,D
- Theology P

PONTIFICAL COLLEGE JOSEPHINUM
- Theology P,M

PONTIFICIA UNIVERSIDAD CATOLICA MADRE Y MAESTRA
- Allopathic Medicine P
- Architecture M
- Business Administration and Management—General M
- Construction Engineering M
- Educational Administration M
- Engineering and Applied Sciences—General M
- Environmental Engineering M
- Finance and Banking M
- Human Resources Management M
- Industrial and Labor Relations M
- Interior Design M
- International Business M
- Logistics M
- Urban and Regional Planning M

PORTLAND STATE UNIVERSITY
- Adult Education M,D
- Anthropology M,D,O
- Applied Economics M,D
- Applied Social Research M,D
- Art/Fine Arts M
- Artificial Intelligence/Robotics M,D,O
- Biological and Biomedical Sciences—General M,D
- Business Administration and Management—General M,D,O
- Chemistry M,D
- Civil Engineering M,D,O
- Communication Disorders M
- Computer Engineering M,D
- Computer Science M,D
- Conflict Resolution and Mediation/Peace Studies M
- Counselor Education M,D
- Criminal Justice and Criminology M,D
- Curriculum and Instruction M,D
- Early Childhood Education M,D
- Economics M,D,O
- Education—General M,D
- Educational Administration M,D
- Educational Media/Instructional Technology M,D
- Educational Policy M,D
- Electrical Engineering M,D
- Elementary Education M,D
- Engineering and Applied Sciences—General M,D,O
- Engineering Management M,D,O
- English as a Second Language M
- English M
- Environmental Engineering M,D
- Environmental Management and Policy M,D
- Environmental Sciences M,D
- Finance and Banking M
- Foreign Languages Education M
- French M
- Geography M,D
- Geology M,D
- German M
- Gerontology O
- Health Education M,O
- Health Promotion M,O
- Health Services Management and Hospital Administration M,O
- Higher Education M,D
- History M
- Industrial and Manufacturing Management M,D
- International Business M
- Japanese M
- Management of Technology M,D
- Manufacturing Engineering M
- Mathematics Education M,D
- Mathematics M,D,O
- Mechanical Engineering M,D,O
- Music Education M
- Music M
- Physics M,D
- Political Science M,D
- Psychology—General M,D,O
- Public Administration M,D
- Public Health—General M,D
- Reading Education M,D
- Science Education M,D
- Secondary Education M,D
- Social Sciences Education M
- Social Work M,D
- Sociology M,D,O
- Software Engineering M,D
- Spanish M
- Special Education M,D
- Speech and Interpersonal Communication M,O
- Statistics M,D
- Systems Engineering M,O
- Systems Science M,D,O
- Theater M
- Urban and Regional Planning M
- Urban Studies M,D

PRAIRIE VIEW A&M UNIVERSITY
- Accounting M
- Agricultural Economics and Agribusiness M
- Agricultural Sciences—General M
- Agronomy and Soil Sciences M
- Animal Sciences M
- Architecture M

- Biological and Biomedical Sciences—General M
- Business Administration and Management—General M
- Chemistry M
- Clinical Psychology M,D
- Computer Science M,D
- Counselor Education M,D
- Curriculum and Instruction M
- Education—General M,D
- Educational Administration M,D
- Electrical Engineering M,D
- Engineering and Applied Sciences—General M,D
- English M
- Family and Consumer Sciences-General M
- Family Nurse Practitioner Studies M
- Forensic Psychology M,D
- Health Education M
- Legal and Justice Studies M,D
- Management Information Systems M,D
- Mathematics M
- Nursing and Healthcare Administration M
- Nursing Education M
- Nursing—General M
- Physical Education M
- Sociology M
- Special Education M
- Urban Design M

PRATT INSTITUTE

- Applied Arts and Design—General M
- Architecture M*
- Art Education M
- Art History M
- Art Therapy M
- Art/Fine Arts M*
- Arts Administration M
- Facilities Management M
- Graphic Design M
- Historic Preservation M
- Industrial Design M
- Information Studies M,O*
- Interior Design M
- Internet and Interactive Multimedia M
- Library Science M,O
- Photography M
- Special Education M
- Therapies—Dance, Drama, and Music M
- Urban and Regional Planning M
- Urban Design M

PRESCOTT COLLEGE

- Counseling Psychology M
- Ecology M
- Education—General M,D
- English as a Second Language M
- Environmental Education M
- Environmental Management and Policy M
- History M
- Humanities M
- Leisure Studies M
- Multilingual and Multicultural Education M,D
- Social Psychology M
- Sustainable Development M

PRINCETON THEOLOGICAL SEMINARY

- Religion P,M,D
- Theology P,M,D

PRINCETON UNIVERSITY

- Aerospace/Aeronautical Engineering M,D
- Anthropology D
- Applied Mathematics M,D
- Applied Physics M,D
- Archaeology D
- Architecture M,D
- Asian Studies D
- Astrophysics D
- Atmospheric Sciences D
- Biological and Biomedical Sciences—General D
- Biophysics D
- Chemical Engineering M,D
- Chemical Physics D
- Chemistry M,D*
- Civil Engineering M,D
- Classics D
- Community College Education D
- Comparative Literature D
- Computational Biology D*
- Computational Sciences D
- Computer Science M,D*
- Demography and Population Studies D,O
- Ecology D
- Economics D,O
- Electrical Engineering M,D*
- Electronic Materials D
- English D
- Environmental Engineering M,D
- Environmental Management and Policy M,D
- Evolutionary Biology D
- Finance and Banking M
- Financial Engineering M,D
- French D
- Geology D
- Geophysics D
- Geosciences D
- German D
- History of Science and Technology D
- History D
- International Affairs M,D
- Italian D
- Materials Sciences D
- Mathematical Physics D
- Mathematics D
- Mechanical Engineering M,D
- Molecular Biology D*
- Music D
- Near and Middle Eastern Studies M,D
- Neuroscience D
- Oceanography D
- Operations Research M,D
- Philosophy D
- Photonics D
- Physics D
- Plasma Physics D
- Political Science D
- Polymer Science and Engineering M,D
- Portuguese D
- Psychology—General D
- Public Affairs M,D
- Religion D
- Slavic Languages D
- Social Sciences Education D
- Sociology D,O
- Spanish D
- Statistics M,D
- Structural Engineering M,D
- Transportation and Highway Engineering M,D
- Water Resources Engineering M,D

THE PROTESTANT EPISCOPAL THEOLOGICAL SEMINARY IN VIRGINIA

- Theology P,M,D

PROVIDENCE COLLEGE

- Business Administration and Management—General M*
- Computer Education M
- Counselor Education M
- Education—General M
- Educational Administration M
- History M
- Mathematics Education M
- Pastoral Ministry and Counseling M
- Reading Education M
- Religion M
- Special Education M
- Theology M

PROVIDENCE COLLEGE AND THEOLOGICAL SEMINARY

- Counseling Psychology P,M,D,O
- English as a Second Language P,M,D,O
- Missions and Missiology P,M,D,O
- Pastoral Ministry and Counseling P,M,D,O
- Religious Education P,M,D,O
- Student Affairs P,M,D,O
- Theology P,M,D,O

PURCHASE COLLEGE, STATE UNIVERSITY OF NEW YORK

- Art History M
- Art/Fine Arts M
- Dance M
- Music M
- Theater M

PURDUE UNIVERSITY

- Accounting M,D
- Aerospace/Aeronautical Engineering M,D
- Agricultural Economics and Agribusiness M,D
- Agricultural Education M,D,O
- Agricultural Engineering M,D
- Agricultural Sciences—General M,D
- Agronomy and Soil Sciences M,D
- American Studies M,D
- Analytical Chemistry M,D
- Anatomy M,D
- Animal Sciences M,D
- Anthropology M,D
- Applied Arts and Design—General M
- Aquaculture M,D
- Art Education M,D,O
- Art/Fine Arts M
- Atmospheric Sciences M,D
- Biochemistry M,D
- Biological and Biomedical Sciences—General M,D
- Biomedical Engineering M,D*
- Biophysics M,D
- Botany M,D
- Business Administration and Management—General M,D
- Cell Biology M,D
- Chemical Engineering M,D
- Chemistry M,D
- Child and Family Studies M,D
- Child Development M,D
- Civil Engineering M,D
- Clothing and Textiles M,D
- Communication Disorders M,D
- Communication—General M,D
- Comparative Literature M,D
- Computer and Information Systems Security M,D
- Computer Engineering M,D
- Computer Science M,D
- Consumer Economics M,D
- Counselor Education M,D,O
- Curriculum and Instruction M,D,O
- Developmental Biology M,D
- Ecology M,D
- Economics D
- Education of the Gifted M,D,O
- Education—General M,D,O
- Educational Administration M,D,O
- Educational Media/Instructional Technology M,D,O
- Educational Psychology M,D,O
- Electrical Engineering M,D
- Elementary Education M,D,O
- Engineering and Applied Sciences—General M,D,O*
- English Education M,D,O
- English M,D
- Entomology M,D
- Environmental Management and Policy M,D
- Epidemiology M,D
- Evolutionary Biology M,D
- Exercise and Sports Science M,D
- Family and Consumer Sciences-General M,D
- Finance and Banking M,D
- Fish, Game, and Wildlife Management M,D
- Food Science and Technology M,D
- Foreign Languages Education M,D,O
- Forestry M,D
- Foundations and Philosophy of Education M,D,O
- French M,D
- Genetics M,D
- Geosciences M,D
- German M,D
- Health Promotion M,D
- Higher Education M,D,O
- History M,D
- Home Economics Education M,D,O
- Horticulture M,D
- Hospitality Management M,D
- Human Development M,D
- Human Resources Management M,D
- Immunology M,D
- Industrial and Manufacturing Management M,D
- Industrial/Management Engineering M,D
- Infectious Diseases M,D
- Inorganic Chemistry M,D
- International Business M
- Linguistics M,D
- Management Information Systems M,D
- Management Strategy and Policy M,D
- Marketing M,D
- Marriage and Family Therapy M,D
- Materials Engineering M,D
- Mathematics Education M,D,O
- Mathematics M,D
- Mechanical Engineering M,D,O*
- Medicinal and Pharmaceutical Chemistry M,D
- Microbiology M,D
- Molecular Biology M,D
- Molecular Pharmacology M,D
- Natural Resources M,D
- Neurobiology M,D
- Nuclear Engineering M,D
- Nutrition M,D
- Organic Chemistry M,D
- Organizational Behavior M,D
- Parasitology M,D
- Pathobiology M,D
- Pathology M,D
- Pharmaceutical Administration M,D,O
- Pharmaceutical Sciences M,D
- Pharmacology M,D
- Pharmacy P
- Philosophy M,D
- Physical Chemistry M,D
- Physical Education M,D
- Physics M,D
- Physiology M,D
- Plant Pathology M,D
- Plant Physiology M,D
- Political Science M,D
- Psychology—General D
- Public Health—General M,D
- Quantitative Analysis M,D
- Reading Education M,D,O
- Science Education M,D,O
- Social Sciences Education M,D,O
- Sociology M,D
- Spanish M,D
- Special Education M,D,O
- Sport Psychology M,D
- Statistics M,D,O
- Theater M
- Toxicology M,D
- Travel and Tourism M,D
- Veterinary Medicine P
- Veterinary Sciences M,D
- Virology M,D
- Vocational and Technical Education M,D,O
- Writing M,D

PURDUE UNIVERSITY CALUMET

- Accounting M
- Biological and Biomedical Sciences—General M
- Biotechnology M
- Business Administration and Management—General M
- Communication—General M
- Counselor Education M
- Curriculum and Instruction M
- Education—General M
- Educational Administration M
- Educational Media/Instructional Technology M
- Elementary Education M
- Engineering and Applied Sciences—General M
- English M
- History M
- Marriage and Family Therapy M
- Mathematics Education M
- Mathematics M
- Nursing—General M
- Philosophy M
- Political Science M
- Science Education M
- Secondary Education M

PURDUE UNIVERSITY NORTH CENTRAL

- Education—General M
- Elementary Education M

QUEENS COLLEGE OF THE CITY UNIVERSITY OF NEW YORK

- Accounting M
- Art Education M,O
- Art History M
- Art/Fine Arts M
- Biochemistry M
- Biological and Biomedical Sciences—General M
- Chemistry M
- Clinical Psychology M
- Communication Disorders M
- Computer Science M
- Counselor Education M
- Early Childhood Education M,O
- Education—General M,O
- Educational Administration O
- Elementary Education M,O
- English as a Second Language M
- English Education M,O
- English M
- Environmental Sciences M
- Exercise and Sports Science M
- Family and Consumer Sciences-General M
- Foreign Languages Education M,O
- French M
- Geology M
- History M
- Home Economics Education M
- Information Studies M,O
- Italian M
- Liberal Studies M
- Library Science M,O
- Linguistics M
- Mathematics Education M,O
- Mathematics M
- Multilingual and Multicultural Education M,O
- Music Education M,O
- Music M
- Physics M,D
- Psychology—General M
- Reading Education M
- Romance Languages M
- School Psychology M,O
- Science Education M,O
- Secondary Education M,O
- Social Sciences Education M,O
- Social Sciences M
- Sociology M
- Spanish M

Special Education M
Urban Studies M
Writing M

Close-Up on page 997.

QUEEN'S UNIVERSITY AT KINGSTON

Allopathic Medicine P
Anatomy M,D
Biochemistry M,D
Biological and Biomedical Sciences—General M,D
Business Administration and Management—General M
Cell Biology M,D
Chemical Engineering M,D
Chemistry M,D
Civil Engineering M,D
Classics M
Clinical Psychology M,D
Cognitive Sciences M,D
Computer Engineering M,D
Computer Science M,D
Developmental Psychology M,D
Education—General M,D
Electrical Engineering M,D
Engineering and Applied Sciences—General M,D
English M,D
Epidemiology M
Exercise and Sports Science M,D
French M,D
Geography M,D
Geology M,D
German M,D
Immunology M,D
Industrial and Labor Relations M
Law P,M
Mathematics M,D
Mechanical Engineering M,D
Microbiology M,D
Mineral/Mining Engineering M,D
Nursing—General M
Pathology M,D
Pharmacology M,D
Philosophy M,D
Physics M,D
Physiology M,D
Political Science M,D
Psychology—General M,D
Public Policy M
Rehabilitation Sciences M,D
Religion M
Social Psychology M,D
Sociology M,D
Spanish M
Sport Psychology M,D
Statistics M,D
Theology P,M
Toxicology M,D
Urban and Regional Planning M

QUEENS UNIVERSITY OF CHARLOTTE

Business Administration and Management—General M
Corporate and Organizational Communication M
Education—General M
Elementary Education M
Nursing and Healthcare Administration M
Nursing—General M
Writing M

QUINCY UNIVERSITY

Business Administration and Management—General M
Counselor Education M
Education—General M
Theology M

QUINNIPIAC UNIVERSITY

Accounting M
Adult Nursing M,O
Allied Health—General M,D,O*
Biological and Biomedical Sciences—General M
Business Administration and Management—General M*
Cell Biology M
Clinical Laboratory Sciences/Medical Technology M
Communication—General M*
Economics M
Education—General M*
Elementary Education M
English Education M
Family Nurse Practitioner Studies M,O
Finance and Banking M
Foreign Languages Education M
Forensic Nursing M,O
Health Services Management and Hospital Administration M
International Business M
Internet and Interactive Multimedia M
Investment Management M
Journalism M
Law P,M
Legal and Justice Studies M
Management Information Systems M
Marketing M
Mathematics Education M
Microbiology M
Middle School Education M
Molecular Biology M
Occupational Therapy M
Pathology M
Physical Therapy D
Physician Assistant Studies M
Science Education M
Secondary Education M
Social Sciences Education M

RABBI ISAAC ELCHANAN THEOLOGICAL SEMINARY

Theology O

RABBINICAL ACADEMY MESIVTA RABBI CHAIM BERLIN

Theology O

RABBINICAL COLLEGE BETH SHRAGA

Theology

RABBINICAL COLLEGE BOBOVER YESHIVA B'NEI ZION

Theology

RABBINICAL COLLEGE CH'SAN SOFER

Theology

RABBINICAL COLLEGE OF LONG ISLAND

Theology

RABBINICAL SEMINARY M'KOR CHAIM

Theology

RABBINICAL SEMINARY OF AMERICA

Theology

RADFORD UNIVERSITY

Art/Fine Arts M
Business Administration and Management—General M
Clinical Psychology M,D,O
Communication Disorders M
Corporate and Organizational Communication M
Counseling Psychology M,D,O
Counselor Education M
Criminal Justice and Criminology M
Education—General M
Educational Administration M
English M
Experimental Psychology M,D,O
Industrial and Organizational Psychology M,D,O
Music M
Nursing—General M
Psychology—General M,D,O
Reading Education M
School Psychology O
Social Work M
Special Education M
Therapies—Dance, Drama, and Music M

RAMAPO COLLEGE OF NEW JERSEY

Liberal Studies M

RECONSTRUCTIONIST RABBINICAL COLLEGE

Theology P,M,D,O

REED COLLEGE

Liberal Studies M

REFORMED PRESBYTERIAN THEOLOGICAL SEMINARY

Theology P,M,D

REFORMED THEOLOGICAL SEMINARY–CHARLOTTE CAMPUS

Pastoral Ministry and Counseling P,M,D
Religion P,M,D
Religious Education P,M,D
Theology P,M,D

REFORMED THEOLOGICAL SEMINARY–JACKSON CAMPUS

Marriage and Family Therapy P,M,D,O
Missions and Missiology P,M,D,O
Pastoral Ministry and Counseling P,M,D,O
Religious Education P,M,D,O
Theology P,M,D,O

REFORMED THEOLOGICAL SEMINARY–ORLANDO CAMPUS

Pastoral Ministry and Counseling P,M,D
Theology P,M,D

REFORMED THEOLOGICAL SEMINARY–WASHINGTON D.C.

Religion M

REGENT COLLEGE

Theology P,M,O

REGENT UNIVERSITY

Art/Fine Arts M,D
Business Administration and Management—General M,D,O
Clinical Psychology M,D,O
Communication—General M,D
Counseling Psychology M,D,O
Counselor Education M,D,O
Economics M
Education—General M,D,O
Educational Administration M,D,O
Elementary Education M,D,O
English as a Second Language M,D,O
Entrepreneurship M,D,O
Film, Television, and Video Production M,D
Health Services Management and Hospital Administration M
Homeland Security M
Journalism M,D
Law P,M
Management Strategy and Policy M,D,O
Missions and Missiology P,M,D
Organizational Management M,D,O
Pastoral Ministry and Counseling P,M,D
Political Science M
Public Administration M
Public Policy M
Religious Education M,D,O
School Psychology M,D,O
Social Psychology M,D,O
Special Education M,D,O
Theater M,D
Theology P,M,D

Close-Up on page 999 and Announcement on page 547.

REGIONS UNIVERSITY

Counseling Psychology P,M,D
Marriage and Family Therapy P,M,D
Organizational Behavior P,M,D
Organizational Management P,M,D
Pastoral Ministry and Counseling P,M,D
Religion P,M,D
Theology P,M,D

REGIS COLLEGE (CANADA)

Pastoral Ministry and Counseling P,M,D,O
Theology P,M,D,O

REGIS COLLEGE (MA)

Business Administration and Management—General M
Corporate and Organizational Communication M
Education—General M
Family Nurse Practitioner Studies M,O
Nursing Education M,O
Nursing—General M,O
Organizational Management M
Public Health—General M

REGIS UNIVERSITY

Accounting M,O
Adult Education M,O
Allied Health—General M,D
Art/Fine Arts M,D
Arts Administration M,O
Business Administration and Management—General M,O
Communication—General M,O
Computer Science M,O
Conflict Resolution and Mediation/Peace Studies M,O
Counseling Psychology M,O
Curriculum and Instruction M,O
Early Childhood Education M,O
Education—General M,O
Educational Administration M,O
Educational Media/Instructional Technology M,O
Electronic Commerce M,O
Elementary Education M,O
English as a Second Language M,O
Finance and Banking M,O
Foundations and Philosophy of Education M,O
Health Services Management and Hospital Administration M,D
Human Resources Management M,O
Industrial and Manufacturing Management M,O
Information Science M,O
Interdisciplinary Studies M,O
International Business M,O
Legal and Justice Studies M,O
Management Information Systems M,O
Management of Technology M,O
Marketing M,O
Marriage and Family Therapy M,O
Music M,O
Nonprofit Management M,O
Nursing—General M
Organizational Management M,O
Physical Therapy D
Physician Assistant Studies M,D
Project Management M,O
Psychology—General M,O
Reading Education M,O
Science Education M,O
Secondary Education M,O
Social Psychology M,O
Social Sciences M,O
Software Engineering M,O
Special Education M,O
Systems Engineering M,O
Technical Writing M,O

RENSSELAER AT HARTFORD

Business Administration and Management—General M
Computer Engineering M
Computer Science M
Electrical Engineering M
Engineering and Applied Sciences—General M
Information Science M
Mechanical Engineering M
Systems Science M

RENSSELAER POLYTECHNIC INSTITUTE

Aerospace/Aeronautical Engineering M,D
Analytical Chemistry M,D
Applied Mathematics M
Applied Physics M,D
Applied Science and Technology M
Architecture M,D*
Art/Fine Arts M,D
Astrophysics M,D
Biochemistry M,D
Bioengineering M,D
Biological and Biomedical Sciences—General M,D*
Biomedical Engineering M,D*
Biophysics M,D
Business Administration and Management—General M,D*
Cell Biology M,D
Ceramic Sciences and Engineering M,D
Chemical Engineering M,D*
Chemistry M,D*
Civil Engineering M,D*
Cognitive Sciences D*
Communication—General M,D*
Computer Art and Design M,D*
Computer Engineering M,D
Computer Science M,D*
Developmental Biology M,D
Economics M*
Electrical Engineering M,D*
Electronic Commerce M,D
Energy and Power Engineering M,D
Engineering and Applied Sciences—General M,D
Engineering Management M,D
Engineering Physics M,D
Entrepreneurship M,D
Environmental Engineering M,D
Environmental Management and Policy M,D
Environmental Sciences M,D*
Finance and Banking M,D
Geochemistry M,D
Geology M,D
Geophysics M,D
Geosciences M,D
Geotechnical Engineering M,D
Historic Preservation M
History of Science and Technology M,D
Human-Computer Interaction M
Industrial and Manufacturing Management M,D
Industrial/Management Engineering M,D
Information Science M*
Inorganic Chemistry M,D
Interdisciplinary Studies M,D
Management Information Systems M,D
Management of Technology M,D

Manufacturing Engineering	M,D
Marketing	M,D
Materials Engineering	M,D
Materials Sciences	M,D*
Mathematics	M,D*
Mechanical Engineering	M,D*
Metallurgical Engineering and Metallurgy	M,D
Microbiology	M,D
Molecular Biology	M,D
Nuclear Engineering	M,D
Operations Research	M,D
Organic Chemistry	M,D
Physical Chemistry	M,D
Physics	M,D*
Polymer Science and Engineering	M,D
Rhetoric	M,D
Speech and Interpersonal Communication	M,D
Statistics	M,D
Structural Engineering	M,D
Systems Engineering	M,D*
Technical Communication	M
Technology and Public Policy	M,D*
Transportation and Highway Engineering	M,D

Close-Up on page 1001.

RESEARCH COLLEGE OF NURSING

Family Nurse Practitioner Studies	M
Nursing Education	M
Nursing—General	M

RHODE ISLAND COLLEGE

Accounting	M
Art Education	M
Art/Fine Arts	M
Arts Administration	M
Biological and Biomedical Sciences—General	M
Counselor Education	M,O
Early Childhood Education	M
Education—General	D
Educational Administration	M,O
Elementary Education	M
English as a Second Language	M,O
English	M
Finance and Banking	M
Health Education	M
History	M
Mathematics	M
Multilingual and Multicultural Education	M,O
Music Education	M
Nursing—General	M
Psychology—General	M
Public Administration	M
Reading Education	M
Secondary Education	M,O
Social Work	M
Special Education	M,O
Theater	M
Writing	M

RHODE ISLAND SCHOOL OF DESIGN

Applied Arts and Design—General	M
Architecture	M
Art Education	M
Art/Fine Arts	M
Computer Art and Design	M
Graphic Design	M
Industrial Design	M
Interior Design	M
Landscape Architecture	M
Photography	M
Textile Design	M

RHODES COLLEGE

Accounting	M

RICE UNIVERSITY

Anthropology	M,D
Applied Mathematics	M,D
Applied Physics	M,D
Architecture	M,D
Astronomy	M,D
Biochemistry	M,D*
Bioengineering	M,D
Biomedical Engineering	M,D
Biostatistics	M,D
Business Administration and Management—General	M
Cell Biology	M,D
Chemical Engineering	M,D*
Chemistry	M,D
Civil Engineering	M,D
Cognitive Sciences	M,D
Computational Sciences	M,D
Computer Engineering	M,D
Computer Science	M,D
Ecology	M,D
Economics	M,D
Education—General	M
Electrical Engineering	M,D
Engineering and Applied Sciences—General	M,D
English	M,D
Environmental Engineering	M,D
Environmental Management and Policy	M*
Environmental Sciences	M,D
Evolutionary Biology	M,D
French	M,D
Geophysics	M
Geosciences	M,D
History	M,D
Industrial and Organizational Psychology	M,D
Inorganic Chemistry	M,D
Linguistics	M,D
Materials Sciences	M,D
Mathematical and Computational Finance	M,D
Mathematics	M,D
Mechanical Engineering	M,D
Music	M,D
Nanotechnology	M
Organic Chemistry	M,D
Philosophy	M,D
Physical Chemistry	M,D
Physics	M,D
Political Science	M,D
Psychology—General	M,D
Religion	D
Spanish	M,D
Statistics	M,D
Urban Design	M,D

THE RICHARD STOCKTON COLLEGE OF NEW JERSEY

Business Administration and Management—General	M
Criminal Justice and Criminology	M
Education—General	M
Educational Media/Instructional Technology	M
Holocaust Studies	M
Legal and Justice Studies	O
Nursing—General	M
Occupational Therapy	M
Physical Therapy	M,D

RICHMOND, THE AMERICAN INTERNATIONAL UNIVERSITY IN LONDON

Art History	M

RIDER UNIVERSITY

Accounting	M
Business Administration and Management—General	M*
Business Education	M,O
Counselor Education	M,O
Curriculum and Instruction	M,O
Education—General	M,O*
Educational Administration	M,O
Elementary Education	M,O
English as a Second Language	M,O
English Education	M,O
Foreign Languages Education	M,O
Mathematics Education	M,O
Organizational Management	M
Reading Education	M,O
School Psychology	M,O
Science Education	M,O
Social Sciences Education	M,O
Special Education	M,O

RIVIER COLLEGE

Business Administration and Management—General	M
Computer Science	M
Counseling Psychology	M,O
Counselor Education	M,O
Curriculum and Instruction	M,O
Early Childhood Education	M,O
Education—General	M,O
Educational Administration	M,O
Elementary Education	M,O
English	M
Foreign Languages Education	M
Human Resources Management	M
Management Information Systems	M
Mathematics	M
Nursing and Healthcare Administration	M
Nursing Education	M
Nursing—General	M
Organizational Management	M
Reading Education	M,O
Social Sciences Education	M
Special Education	M,O
Writing	M

ROBERT MORRIS UNIVERSITY

Accounting	M
Adult Education	M
Business Administration and Management—General	M
Finance and Banking	M
Human Resources Management	M
Information Science	M,D
Internet and Interactive Multimedia	M
Management Information Systems	M,D
Nonprofit Management	M
Nursing—General	M
Sports Management	M
Taxation	M

Close-Up on page 1003.

ROBERTS WESLEYAN COLLEGE

Business Administration and Management—General	M,O
Child and Family Studies	M
Counselor Education	M
Early Childhood Education	M,O
Education—General	M,O
Health Services Management and Hospital Administration	M
Human Services	M
Management Strategy and Policy	M,O
Marketing	M,O
Middle School Education	M,O
Nonprofit Management	M,O
Nursing and Healthcare Administration	M
Nursing Education	M
Nursing—General	M
Pastoral Ministry and Counseling	M
Reading Education	M,O
School Psychology	M,O
Secondary Education	M,O
Social Work	M
Special Education	M,O
Urban Education	M,O

ROCHESTER INSTITUTE OF TECHNOLOGY

Accounting	M
Applied Mathematics	M
Applied Statistics	M,O
Art Education	M
Art/Fine Arts	M
Bioinformatics	M
Biological and Biomedical Sciences—General	M
Business Administration and Management—General	M
Chemistry	M
Clinical Laboratory Sciences/Medical Technology	M
Communication—General	M
Computer and Information Systems Security	M
Computer Art and Design	M
Computer Engineering	M
Computer Science	M,O
Educational Media/Instructional Technology	M
Electrical Engineering	M
Engineering and Applied Sciences—General	M,D,O
Engineering Design	M
Engineering Management	M
Environmental Management and Policy	M
Environmental Sciences	M
Film, Television, and Video Production	M
Finance and Banking	M
Gerontology	O
Graphic Design	M
Health Services Management and Hospital Administration	M,O
Hospitality Management	M
Human Resources Development	M,O
Industrial and Manufacturing Management	M
Industrial Design	M
Industrial/Management Engineering	M
Information Science	M
Interdisciplinary Studies	M
International Business	M
Internet and Interactive Multimedia	M,O
Management Information Systems	M,O
Manufacturing Engineering	M
Materials Engineering	M
Materials Sciences	M
Mechanical Engineering	M
Media Studies	M
Medical Illustration	M
Optical Sciences	M,D
Photography	M
Psychology—General	M
Public Policy	M
School Psychology	M,O
Secondary Education	M
Software Engineering	M
Special Education	M
Statistics	M,O
Systems Engineering	M,D
Technical Communication	O
Technology and Public Policy	M
Telecommunications	M
Travel and Tourism	M

Close-Up on page 1005.

THE ROCKEFELLER UNIVERSITY

Biological and Biomedical Sciences—General	D*

ROCKFORD COLLEGE

Art Education	M
Business Administration and Management—General	M
Education—General	M
Elementary Education	M
English Education	M
Reading Education	M
Secondary Education	M
Social Sciences Education	M
Special Education	M

ROCKHURST UNIVERSITY

Business Administration and Management—General	M
Communication Disorders	M
Education—General	M
Occupational Therapy	M
Physical Therapy	D

ROGER WILLIAMS UNIVERSITY

Architecture	M
Criminal Justice and Criminology	M*
Education—General	M
Elementary Education	M
Forensic Psychology	M*
Law	P
Public Administration	M
Reading Education	M

ROLLINS COLLEGE

Business Administration and Management—General	M
Counselor Education	M
Education—General	M
Elementary Education	M
English Education	M
Human Resources Development	M
Human Resources Management	M
Liberal Studies	M
Mathematics Education	M
Music Education	M
Secondary Education	M

ROOSEVELT UNIVERSITY

Accounting	M
Actuarial Science	M
Anthropology	M
Applied Economics	M
Biotechnology	M
Business Administration and Management—General	M
Chemistry	M
Clinical Psychology	M,D
Communication—General	M
Computer Science	M
Corporate and Organizational Communication	M
Counselor Education	M
Early Childhood Education	M
Economics	M
Education—General	M,D
Educational Administration	M,D
Elementary Education	M
English	M
Gender Studies	M,O
History	M
Hospitality Management	M
Human Resources Development	M
Human Resources Management	M
Industrial and Organizational Psychology	M
International Business	M
Journalism	M
Management Information Systems	M
Mathematics	M
Music Education	M,O
Music	M,O
Organizational Management	M,D
Political Science	M
Psychology—General	D
Public Administration	M
Reading Education	M
Real Estate	M,O
Secondary Education	M
Sociology	M
Spanish	M
Special Education	M
Telecommunications	M
Theater	M

Women's Studies	M,O
Writing	M

Close-Up on page 1007.

ROSALIND FRANKLIN UNIVERSITY OF MEDICINE AND SCIENCE

Allied Health—General	M,D
Allopathic Medicine	P
Anatomy	M,D
Biochemistry	M,D
Biological and Biomedical Sciences—General	M,D*
Cell Biology	M,D
Clinical Laboratory Sciences/Medical Technology	M
Clinical Psychology	M,D
Health Education	M
Health Services Management and Hospital Administration	M
Immunology	M,D
Medical Microbiology	M,D
Medical Physics	M,D
Microbiology	M,D
Molecular Pharmacology	M,D
Neuroscience	D*
Nutrition	M
Pathology	M,D
Physical Therapy	M,D
Physician Assistant Studies	M
Physiology	M,D
Podiatric Medicine	P

ROSE-HULMAN INSTITUTE OF TECHNOLOGY

Biomedical Engineering	M
Chemical Engineering	M
Civil Engineering	M
Electrical Engineering	M
Engineering and Applied Sciences—General	M*
Engineering Management	M
Environmental Engineering	M
Mechanical Engineering	M
Optical Sciences	M

ROSEMONT COLLEGE

Business Administration and Management—General	M
Counseling Psychology	M
Counselor Education	M
Criminal Justice and Criminology	M
Curriculum and Instruction	M
Educational Media/Instructional Technology	M
Elementary Education	M
English	M
Human Services	M
Middle School Education	M
Nonprofit Management	M
Project Management	M
Publishing	M

Close-Up on page 1009.

ROWAN UNIVERSITY

Advertising and Public Relations	M
Business Administration and Management—General	M
Counseling Psychology	M,O
Counselor Education	M
Curriculum and Instruction	M
Education—General	M,D,O
Educational Administration	M,D,O
Educational Media/Instructional Technology	M
Engineering and Applied Sciences—General	M
Higher Education	M
Library Science	M
Mathematics	M
Music Education	M,O
Music	M
Psychology—General	M,O
Reading Education	M
School Psychology	M,O
Secondary Education	M
Special Education	M
Theater	M
Writing	M

ROYAL MILITARY COLLEGE OF CANADA

Business Administration and Management—General	M
Chemical Engineering	M,D
Chemistry	M,D
Civil Engineering	M,D
Computer Engineering	M,D
Computer Science	M
Electrical Engineering	M,D
Engineering and Applied Sciences—General	M,D
Environmental Engineering	M,D
Environmental Sciences	M,D
Materials Sciences	M,D
Mathematics	M
Mechanical Engineering	M,D
Military and Defense Studies	M
Nuclear Engineering	M,D
Physics	M
Software Engineering	M,D

ROYAL ROADS UNIVERSITY

Advertising and Public Relations	M
Business Administration and Management—General	M
Conflict Resolution and Mediation/Peace Studies	M
Corporate and Organizational Communication	M
Educational Administration	M
Educational Media/Instructional Technology	M
Environmental Management and Policy	M
Human Resources Management	M
Organizational Management	M

RUSH UNIVERSITY

Acute Care/Critical Care Nursing	M,D,O
Adult Nursing	M,D,O
Allopathic Medicine	P
Anatomy	M,D
Biochemistry	D
Bioethics	M,O
Cell Biology	M,D
Clinical Laboratory Sciences/Medical Technology	M
Communication Disorders	M,D
Community Health Nursing	M,D,O
Gerontological Nursing	M,D,O
Health Services Management and Hospital Administration	M,D
Immunology	M,D
Maternal and Child/Neonatal Nursing	M,D,O
Medical Physics	M,D
Medical/Surgical Nursing	M,D,O
Microbiology	M,D
Neuroscience	M,D
Nurse Anesthesia	M,D,O
Nursing—General	M,D,O
Nutrition	M
Occupational Therapy	M
Pediatric Nursing	M,D,O
Pharmaceutical Sciences	M,D
Pharmacology	M,D
Physiology	D
Psychiatric Nursing	M,D,O
Virology	M,D

RUTGERS, THE STATE UNIVERSITY OF NEW JERSEY, CAMDEN

Biological and Biomedical Sciences—General	M
Business Administration and Management—General	M
Chemistry	M
Child Development	M,D
Computer Science	M
Criminal Justice and Criminology	M
Educational Administration	M
Educational Policy	M
English	M
History	M
International Affairs	M
International Development	M
Law	P
Liberal Studies	M
Mathematics	M
Physical Therapy	M
Psychology—General	M
Public Administration	M
Public History	M
Public Policy	M

RUTGERS, THE STATE UNIVERSITY OF NEW JERSEY, NEWARK

Accounting	M,D,O
Adult Nursing	M
Analytical Chemistry	M,D
Applied Physics	M,D
Biochemistry	M,D
Biological and Biomedical Sciences—General	M,D
Biopsychology	D
Business Administration and Management—General	M,D,O
Chemistry	M,D
Cognitive Sciences	D*
Community Health Nursing	M
Computational Biology	M
Criminal Justice and Criminology	M,D
Economics	M
English	M
Environmental Sciences	M,D
Family Nurse Practitioner Studies	M
Finance and Banking	M,D,O
Geology	M
Gerontological Nursing	M
Health Services Management and Hospital Administration	M,D
History	M
Human Resources Management	M,D
Inorganic Chemistry	M,D
International Affairs	M,D*
International Business	M,D
Law	P
Liberal Studies	M
Management Information Systems	M,D
Management Strategy and Policy	M
Marketing	M,D
Maternal and Child/Neonatal Nursing	M
Mathematics	D
Music	M
Neuroscience	D
Nursing—General	M
Organic Chemistry	M,D
Organizational Management	D
Physical Chemistry	M,D
Political Science	M
Psychiatric Nursing	M
Psychology—General	D
Public Administration	M,D
Public Policy	M,D
Social Psychology	D
Supply Chain Management	D
Taxation	M
Urban Studies	M,D

Close-Up on page 1011.

RUTGERS, THE STATE UNIVERSITY OF NEW JERSEY, NEW BRUNSWICK

Adult Education	M
Aerospace/Aeronautical Engineering	M,D
African Studies	D
Agricultural Economics and Agribusiness	M
Agricultural Engineering	M
Analytical Chemistry	M,D
Animal Sciences	M,D
Anthropology	M,D
Applied Arts and Design—General	M
Applied Mathematics	M,D
Art History	M,D
Art/Fine Arts	M
Atmospheric Sciences	M,D
Biochemical Engineering	M,D
Biochemistry	M,D
Bioengineering	M
Biological and Biomedical Sciences—General	D
Biomedical Engineering	M,D
Biopsychology	D
Biostatistics	M,D
Cell Biology	M,D
Ceramic Sciences and Engineering	M,D
Chemical Engineering	M,D
Chemistry	M,D*
Civil Engineering	M,D
Classics	M,D
Clinical Psychology	M,D
Cognitive Sciences	D
Communication—General	M,D
Comparative Literature	M,D
Computational Biology	D
Computer Engineering	M,D
Computer Science	M,D*
Condensed Matter Physics	M,D
Counseling Psychology	M
Developmental Biology	M,D
Developmental Education	M
Developmental Psychology	D
Early Childhood Education	M,D
Ecology	M,D
Economics	M,D
Education—General	M,D
Educational Administration	M,D
Educational Measurement and Evaluation	M
Educational Policy	D
Educational Psychology	M,D
Electrical Engineering	M,D*
Elementary Education	M,D
Engineering and Applied Sciences—General	M,D
English as a Second Language	M,D
English Education	M
English	D
Entomology	M,D
Environmental Biology	M,D
Environmental Engineering	M,D
Environmental Sciences	M,D
Evolutionary Biology	M,D
Finance and Banking	M,D
Food Science and Technology	M,D
Foreign Languages Education	M,D
Foundations and Philosophy of Education	M,D
French	M,D
Gender Studies	M,D
Genetics	M,D
Geography	M,D
Geology	M,D
German	M,D
Hazardous Materials Management	M,D
Health Psychology	D
Historic Preservation	M,D
History of Medicine	D
History of Science and Technology	D
History	D
Horticulture	M,D
Human Resources Management	M,D*
Immunology	M,D
Industrial and Labor Relations	M,D*
Industrial and Organizational Psychology	M,D
Industrial/Management Engineering	M,D
Information Studies	M,D
Inorganic Chemistry	M,D
Interdisciplinary Studies	D
International Affairs	D
Italian	M,D
Legal and Justice Studies	D
Library Science	M
Linguistics	D
Marine Biology	M,D
Materials Engineering	M,D
Materials Sciences	M,D
Mathematics Education	M,D
Mathematics	M,D
Mechanical Engineering	M,D
Mechanics	M,D
Medical Microbiology	M,D
Medicinal and Pharmaceutical Chemistry	M,D
Medieval and Renaissance Studies	D
Microbiology	M,D
Molecular Biology	M,D*
Molecular Biophysics	D
Molecular Genetics	M,D
Molecular Pharmacology	D
Museum Studies	M,D
Music Education	M,D,O
Music	M,D,O
Neurobiology	D
Neuroscience	D
Nutrition	M,D
Oceanography	M,D*
Operations Research	D
Organic Chemistry	M,D
Pharmaceutical Sciences	M,D
Pharmacy	P
Philosophy	D
Physical Chemistry	M,D
Physics	M,D
Physiology	D
Plant Biology	M,D
Plant Molecular Biology	M,D
Plant Pathology	M,D
Plant Physiology	M,D
Plant Sciences	M,D
Political Science	M,D
Psychology—General	M,D
Public Health—General	M,D
Public Policy	M
Quality Management	M,D
Reading Education	M,D
School Psychology	M,D
Science Education	M,D
Social Psychology	D
Social Sciences Education	M,D
Social Work	M,D
Sociology	M,D
Spanish	M,D
Special Education	M,D
Statistics	M,D
Systems Biology	D
Systems Engineering	M,D
Theater	M
Theoretical Physics	M,D
Toxicology	M,D
Translation and Interpretation	M,D
Urban and Regional Planning	M,D
Virology	M,D
Water Resources	M,D
Women's Studies	M,D
Writing	M

RYERSON UNIVERSITY

Arts Administration	M

SACRED HEART MAJOR SEMINARY

Pastoral Ministry and Counseling	P,M
Theology	P,M

SACRED HEART SCHOOL OF THEOLOGY

Theology	P,M

SACRED HEART UNIVERSITY

Business Administration and Management—General	M
Chemistry	M
Computer and Information Systems Security	M,O

- Computer Science M,O
- Criminal Justice and Criminology M
- Education—General M,O
- Educational Administration M,O
- Educational Media/Instructional Technology M,O
- Elementary Education M,O
- Family Nurse Practitioner Studies M
- Gerontology M
- Information Science M,O
- Internet and Interactive Multimedia M,O
- Management Information Systems M,O
- Nursing and Healthcare Administration M
- Nursing—General M
- Occupational Therapy M
- Physical Therapy D
- Reading Education M,O
- Religion M
- Secondary Education M,O

Close-Up on page 1013.

SAGE GRADUATE SCHOOL

- Adult Nursing M,O
- Art Education M
- Business Administration and Management—General M
- Child and Family Studies M
- Community Health Nursing M
- Community Health M
- Counselor Education M,O
- Education—General M,O
- Elementary Education M
- English Education M
- Family Nurse Practitioner Studies M
- Finance and Banking M
- Forensic Psychology O
- Gerontology M
- Health Education M
- Health Services Management and Hospital Administration M
- Human Resources Management M
- Human Services M
- Management Strategy and Policy M
- Marketing M
- Mathematics Education M
- Medical/Surgical Nursing M
- Nursing—General M,O
- Nutrition M
- Occupational Therapy M
- Organizational Management M
- Physical Therapy D
- Psychiatric Nursing M
- Psychology—General M,O
- Public Administration M
- Reading Education M
- Science Education M
- Social Psychology M
- Social Sciences Education M
- Special Education M

SAGINAW VALLEY STATE UNIVERSITY

- Business Administration and Management—General M
- Communication—General M
- Early Childhood Education M
- Education—General M,O
- Educational Administration M,O
- Educational Media/Instructional Technology M
- Elementary Education M
- Engineering and Applied Sciences—General M
- Family Nurse Practitioner Studies M
- Management of Technology M
- Media Studies M
- Middle School Education M
- Nursing and Healthcare Administration M
- Nursing—General M
- Occupational Therapy M
- Physical Education M
- Public Administration M
- Reading Education M
- Science Education M
- Secondary Education M
- Special Education M

ST. AMBROSE UNIVERSITY

- Accounting M
- Business Administration and Management—General M,D
- Criminal Justice and Criminology M
- Education—General M
- Educational Administration M
- Health Services Management and Hospital Administration M,D
- Human Resources Management M,D
- Management of Technology M
- Nursing—General M
- Occupational Therapy M
- Organizational Management M
- Pastoral Ministry and Counseling M
- Physical Therapy D
- Social Work M
- Special Education M

ST. ANDREW'S COLLEGE IN WINNIPEG

- Theology P

ST. AUGUSTINE'S SEMINARY OF TORONTO

- Pastoral Ministry and Counseling P,M,O
- Religious Education P,M,O
- Theology P,M,O

SAINT BERNARD'S SCHOOL OF THEOLOGY AND MINISTRY

- Pastoral Ministry and Counseling P,M,O
- Theology P,M,O

ST. BONAVENTURE UNIVERSITY

- Accounting M,O
- Business Administration and Management—General M,O
- Counselor Education M,O
- Education—General M,O
- Educational Administration M,O
- English M
- Finance and Banking M,O
- Marketing M,O
- Reading Education M
- Theology M,O

ST. CHARLES BORROMEO SEMINARY, OVERBROOK

- Religion M
- Theology P,M

ST. CLOUD STATE UNIVERSITY

- Applied Economics M
- Applied Statistics M
- Biological and Biomedical Sciences—General M
- Business Administration and Management—General M
- Child and Family Studies M
- Communication Disorders M
- Computer Engineering M
- Computer Science M
- Counselor Education M
- Criminal Justice and Criminology M
- Curriculum and Instruction M
- Economics M
- Education—General M,O
- Educational Administration M
- Educational Media/Instructional Technology M
- Electrical Engineering M
- Engineering and Applied Sciences—General M
- Engineering Management M
- English as a Second Language M
- English M
- Environmental Management and Policy M
- Exercise and Sports Science M
- Finance and Banking M
- Geography M
- Gerontology M
- Higher Education M
- History M
- Industrial and Organizational Psychology M
- Marketing M
- Marriage and Family Therapy M
- Mass Communication M
- Mathematics M
- Mechanical Engineering M
- Music Education M
- Music M
- Nonprofit Management M
- Physical Education M
- Psychology—General M
- Rehabilitation Counseling M
- Social Psychology M
- Special Education M
- Sports Management M
- Student Affairs M
- Technology and Public Policy M

ST. EDWARD'S UNIVERSITY

- Accounting M,O
- Business Administration and Management—General M,O
- Computer Art and Design M
- Conflict Resolution and Mediation/Peace Studies M,O
- Counseling Psychology M
- Education—General M
- Entrepreneurship M,O
- Ethics M
- Finance and Banking M,O
- Human Resources Management M,O
- Human Services M,O
- International Business M,O
- Liberal Studies M,O
- Management Information Systems M,O
- Marketing M,O
- Organizational Management M
- Project Management M
- Public Administration M,O
- Sports Management M,O

SAINT FRANCIS MEDICAL CENTER COLLEGE OF NURSING

- Medical/Surgical Nursing M,O
- Nursing Education M,O
- Nursing—General M,O

SAINT FRANCIS SEMINARY

- Pastoral Ministry and Counseling P,M
- Theology P,M

SAINT FRANCIS UNIVERSITY

- Biological and Biomedical Sciences—General M
- Business Administration and Management—General M
- Education—General M
- Educational Administration M
- Health Education M
- Human Resources Management M
- Occupational Therapy M
- Physical Therapy D
- Physician Assistant Studies M
- Reading Education M

ST. FRANCIS XAVIER UNIVERSITY

- Adult Education M
- Biological and Biomedical Sciences—General M
- Chemistry M
- Computer Science M
- Cultural Studies M
- Curriculum and Instruction M
- Education—General M
- Educational Administration M
- Geology M
- Geosciences M
- Physics M

ST. JOHN FISHER COLLEGE

- Business Administration and Management—General M
- Counseling Psychology M
- Education—General M,D,O
- Educational Administration M,D
- Elementary Education M
- English Education M
- Family Nurse Practitioner Studies M,O
- Foreign Languages Education M
- Human Resources Development M
- Human Services M
- International Affairs M
- Mathematics Education M
- Middle School Education M
- Nursing Education M,O
- Nursing—General M,O
- Pharmacy P
- Reading Education M
- Science Education M
- Social Sciences Education M
- Special Education M,O

ST. JOHN'S COLLEGE (MD)

- Liberal Studies M

ST. JOHN'S COLLEGE (NM)

- Asian Languages M
- Asian Studies M
- Liberal Studies M

ST. JOHN'S SEMINARY (CA)

- Pastoral Ministry and Counseling P,M
- Theology P,M

SAINT JOHN'S SEMINARY (MA)

- Religion P,M
- Theology P,M

SAINT JOHN'S UNIVERSITY (MN)

- Music P,M
- Pastoral Ministry and Counseling P,M
- Theology P,M

ST. JOHN'S UNIVERSITY (NY)

- Accounting M,O
- Actuarial Science M
- African Studies M,O
- Applied Mathematics M
- Asian Studies M,O
- Biological and Biomedical Sciences—General M,D
- Business Administration and Management—General M,O
- Chemistry M
- Clinical Psychology D
- Communication—General M,O
- Computer Science M
- Counselor Education M,O
- Criminal Justice and Criminology M
- Early Childhood Education M
- Education—General M,D,O
- Educational Administration M,D,O
- Elementary Education M
- English as a Second Language M
- English M,D
- Experimental Psychology M
- Finance and Banking M
- Higher Education O
- History M,D
- Information Studies M,O
- Insurance M
- International Business M,O
- Law P
- Legal and Justice Studies M
- Liberal Studies M
- Library Science M,O
- Management Information Systems M,O
- Marketing M,O
- Mathematics M
- Multilingual and Multicultural Education M
- Pastoral Ministry and Counseling P,M,O
- Pharmaceutical Administration M
- Pharmaceutical Sciences M,D
- Pharmacy P
- Philosophy M
- Political Science M,O
- Psychology—General M,D
- Quantitative Analysis M,O
- Reading Education M,O
- Rehabilitation Counseling M,O
- School Psychology M,D
- Secondary Education M
- Sociology M
- Spanish M,O
- Special Education M
- Statistics M
- Taxation M,O
- Theater M
- Theology P,M,O
- Toxicology M

SAINT JOSEPH COLLEGE

- Biological and Biomedical Sciences—General M
- Business Administration and Management—General M
- Cell Biology M
- Chemistry M
- Child and Family Studies M,O
- Counseling Psychology M,O
- Counselor Education M,O
- Early Childhood Education M
- Education—General M
- Family Nurse Practitioner Studies M,O
- Gerontology O
- Human Development O
- Marriage and Family Therapy M,O
- Maternal and Child/Neonatal Nursing M,O
- Molecular Biology M
- Nursing—General M,O
- Pastoral Ministry and Counseling M,O
- Psychiatric Nursing M,O
- Social Psychology M,O
- Special Education M

SAINT JOSEPH'S COLLEGE

- Music M,O

ST. JOSEPH'S COLLEGE, NEW YORK

- Accounting M
- Business Administration and Management—General M*
- Early Childhood Education M
- Education—General M*
- Nursing—General M*
- Reading Education M
- Special Education M

SAINT JOSEPH'S COLLEGE OF MAINE

- Business Administration and Management—General M
- Education—General M
- Health Services Management and Hospital Administration M
- Nursing and Healthcare Administration M,O

Nursing Education M,O
Nursing—General M,O
Quality Management M

ST. JOSEPH'S COLLEGE, SUFFOLK CAMPUS

Accounting M
Business Administration and Management—General M,O
Early Childhood Education M
Health Services Management and Hospital Administration M,O
Human Resources Management M,O
Nursing—General M
Organizational Management M,O
Reading Education M
Special Education M

ST. JOSEPH'S SEMINARY

Theology P,M

SAINT JOSEPH'S UNIVERSITY

Accounting M
Biological and Biomedical Sciences—General M
Business Administration and Management—General M,O
Computer Science M,O
Criminal Justice and Criminology M,O
Education—General M,D,O
Educational Administration M,D,O
Educational Media/Instructional Technology M,D,O
Electronic Commerce M,O
Elementary Education M,D,O
Environmental and Occupational Health M,O
Environmental Management and Policy M,O
Finance and Banking M,O*
Gerontology M,O
Health Education M
Health Services Management and Hospital Administration M
Human Resources Management M*
Human Services M,O
International Business M
Law M,O
Management Information Systems M
Marketing M,O*
Mathematics M,O
Nurse Anesthesia M
Organizational Management M,D,O
Psychology—General M,O*
Quantitative Analysis M
Reading Education M,D,O
Secondary Education M,D,O
Special Education M,D,O
Writing M

ST. LAWRENCE UNIVERSITY

Counselor Education M,O
Education—General M,O
Educational Administration M,O
Human Development M,O

SAINT LEO UNIVERSITY

Accounting M
Business Administration and Management—General M
Computer and Information Systems Security M
Criminal Justice and Criminology M
Curriculum and Instruction M
Education of the Gifted M
Education—General M
Educational Administration M
Human Resources Management M
Pastoral Ministry and Counseling M
Reading Education M
Sports Management M

ST. LOUIS COLLEGE OF PHARMACY

Pharmaceutical Administration M,O
Pharmacy P

SAINT LOUIS UNIVERSITY

Accounting M
Allied Health—General M,D,O
Allopathic Medicine P
American Studies M,D
Anatomy M,D
Biochemistry D
Bioethics D,O
Biological and Biomedical Sciences—General M,D
Biomedical Engineering M,D
Business Administration and Management—General M*
Chemistry M
Clinical Psychology M,D
Communication Disorders M
Communication—General M
Community Health M
Counselor Education M,D,O
Criminal Justice and Criminology M
Curriculum and Instruction M,D
Education—General M,D
Educational Administration M,D,O
English M,D
Experimental Psychology M,D
Finance and Banking M
Foundations and Philosophy of Education M,D
French M
Geographic Information Systems M,D,O
Geophysics M,D
Geosciences M,D
Health Services Management and Hospital Administration M,D
Higher Education M,D,O
History M,D
Human Development M,D,O
Immunology D
Industrial and Organizational Psychology M,D
International Business M,D
Law P,M
Marriage and Family Therapy M,D,O
Mathematics M,D
Meteorology M,D
Microbiology D
Molecular Biology D
Nursing—General M,D,O
Nutrition M
Occupational Therapy M
Oral and Dental Sciences M
Organizational Management M,D,O
Pathology D
Pharmacology D
Philosophy M,D
Physical Therapy M,D
Physician Assistant Studies M
Physiology D
Psychology—General M,D
Public Administration M,D,O
Public Health—General M,D
Public Policy M,D,O
Social Work M
Spanish M
Special Education M,D
Student Affairs M,D,O
Theology M,D
Urban Studies M,D,O

Close-Up on page 1015.

SAINT LOUIS UNIVERSITY, MADRID

English M*
Spanish M*

SAINT MARTIN'S UNIVERSITY

Business Administration and Management—General M
Civil Engineering M
Counseling Psychology M
Counselor Education M
Education—General M
Educational Administration M
Engineering Management M
English as a Second Language M
Reading Education M
Social Psychology M
Special Education M
Vocational and Technical Education M

SAINT MARY-OF-THE-WOODS COLLEGE

Art Therapy M,O
Environmental Management and Policy M
Management Strategy and Policy M
Pastoral Ministry and Counseling M,O
Theology M,O
Therapies—Dance, Drama, and Music M

SAINT MARY'S COLLEGE OF CALIFORNIA

Business Administration and Management—General M
Counselor Education M
Curriculum and Instruction M
Early Childhood Education M
Education—General M,D
Educational Administration M,D
Kinesiology and Movement Studies M
Liberal Studies M
Marriage and Family Therapy M
Reading Education M
Special Education M
Writing M

SAINT MARY SEMINARY AND GRADUATE SCHOOL OF THEOLOGY

Theology P,M,D

ST. MARY'S SEMINARY AND UNIVERSITY

Theology P,M,D,O*

SAINT MARY'S UNIVERSITY

Astronomy M
Business Administration and Management—General M,D
Canadian Studies M
Clinical Psychology M
Criminal Justice and Criminology M
History M
Industrial and Organizational Psychology M
International Development M
Philosophy M
Psychology—General M
Women's Studies M

SAINT MARY'S UNIVERSITY OF MINNESOTA

Arts Administration M
Business Administration and Management—General M,O
Counseling Psychology M
Education—General M
Educational Administration M,D,O
Elementary Education M,O
Environmental and Occupational Health M
Finance and Banking M,O
Geographic Information Systems M,O
Health Services Management and Hospital Administration M
Human Development M
Human Resources Management M
International Business M
Marriage and Family Therapy M,O
Nurse Anesthesia M
Organizational Management M
Pastoral Ministry and Counseling M
Philanthropic Studies M
Project Management M
Public Administration M,O
Reading Education M,O
Secondary Education M,O
Telecommunications M

ST. MARY'S UNIVERSITY OF SAN ANTONIO

Accounting M
Addictions/Substance Abuse Counseling M,D,O
Business Administration and Management—General M
Clinical Psychology M
Communication—General M
Computer Engineering M
Computer Science M
Counseling Psychology M,D,O
Counselor Education D
Education—General M,O
Educational Administration M,O
Electrical Engineering M
Engineering and Applied Sciences—General M
Engineering Management M
English M
Finance and Banking M
Human Services M,D,O
Industrial and Organizational Psychology M
Industrial/Management Engineering M
Information Science M
International Affairs M
International Business M
Law P
Marriage and Family Therapy M,D
Operations Research M
Pastoral Ministry and Counseling M
Political Science M
Psychology—General M
Public Administration M
Reading Education M
School Psychology M
Social Psychology M
Software Engineering M
Taxation M
Theology M

SAINT MEINRAD SCHOOL OF THEOLOGY

Theology P,M

SAINT MICHAEL'S COLLEGE

Art Education M,O
Business Administration and Management—General M,O
Clinical Psychology M
Curriculum and Instruction M,O
Education—General M,O
Educational Administration M,O
Educational Media/Instructional Technology M,O
English as a Second Language M,O
Reading Education M,O
Special Education M,O
Theology M,O

ST. NORBERT COLLEGE

Education—General M
Theology M

ST. PATRICK'S SEMINARY & UNIVERSITY

Theology P,M

SAINT PAUL SCHOOL OF THEOLOGY

Theology P,M,D

SAINT PAUL UNIVERSITY

Conflict Resolution and Mediation/Peace Studies M
Marriage and Family Therapy M
Missions and Missiology M
Pastoral Ministry and Counseling M,D,O
Theology M,D,O

SAINT PETER'S COLLEGE

Accounting M,O
Business Administration and Management—General M
Curriculum and Instruction M,O
Education—General M,O
Educational Administration M,O
Elementary Education M,O
Finance and Banking M
International Business M
Management Information Systems M
Marketing M
Nursing—General M
Reading Education M
Urban Education M

Close-Up on page 1017.

ST. PETER'S SEMINARY

Theology P,M

SAINTS CYRIL AND METHODIUS SEMINARY

Pastoral Ministry and Counseling P,M
Religious Education P,M
Theology P,M

ST. STEPHEN'S COLLEGE

Pastoral Ministry and Counseling M,D
Theology M,D

ST. THOMAS AQUINAS COLLEGE

Business Administration and Management—General M*
Education—General M,O*
Elementary Education M,O
Finance and Banking M
Marketing M
Middle School Education M,O
Reading Education M,O
Secondary Education M,O
Special Education M,O

ST. THOMAS UNIVERSITY

Accounting M,O
Business Administration and Management—General M,O
Communication—General M,O
Counseling Psychology M
Counselor Education M,O
Criminal Justice and Criminology M,O
Education—General M,D,O
Educational Administration M,D,O
Elementary Education M,D,O
Health Services Management and Hospital Administration M,O
Hispanic Studies M,O
Human Resources Management M,O
International Business M,O
Law P,M
Marriage and Family Therapy M,O
Pastoral Ministry and Counseling M,D,O
Public Administration M,O
Reading Education M,D,O
Special Education M,D,O

- Taxation P,M
- Theology M,D,O

ST. TIKHON'S ORTHODOX THEOLOGICAL SEMINARY

- Theology P

SAINT VINCENT COLLEGE

- Accounting M
- Curriculum and Instruction M
- Education—General M
- Educational Administration M
- Educational Media/Instructional Technology M
- Environmental Education M
- Special Education M

SAINT VINCENT DE PAUL REGIONAL SEMINARY

- Theology P,M

SAINT VINCENT SEMINARY

- Theology P,M

ST. VLADIMIR'S ORTHODOX THEOLOGICAL SEMINARY

- Music P,M,D
- Religious Education P,M,D
- Theology P,M,D

SAINT XAVIER UNIVERSITY

- Adult Nursing M,O
- Business Administration and Management—General M,O
- Communication Disorders M
- Community Health Nursing M,O
- Computer Science M,O
- Counseling Psychology M,O
- Counselor Education M
- Curriculum and Instruction M,O
- Early Childhood Education M,O
- Education—General M,O
- Educational Administration M,O
- Electronic Commerce M,O
- Elementary Education M,O
- English M,O
- Family Nurse Practitioner Studies M,O
- Finance and Banking M,O
- Health Services Management and Hospital Administration M,O
- Information Science M
- Marketing M,O
- Mathematics M
- Nonprofit Management M,O
- Nursing and Healthcare Administration M,O
- Nursing—General M,O
- Psychiatric Nursing M,O
- Psychology—General M,O
- Public Health—General M,O
- Reading Education M,O
- Secondary Education M,O
- Special Education M,O
- Travel and Tourism M,O
- Writing M,O

SALEM COLLEGE

- Early Childhood Education M
- Education—General M
- Elementary Education M
- English as a Second Language M
- Middle School Education M
- Reading Education M
- Secondary Education M
- Special Education M

SALEM INTERNATIONAL UNIVERSITY

- Business Administration and Management—General M
- Computer and Information Systems Security M
- Curriculum and Instruction M
- Education—General M
- Educational Administration M
- Educational Media/Instructional Technology M
- English as a Second Language M
- Health Education M
- International Business M
- Physical Education M

SALEM STATE COLLEGE

- Art Education M
- Business Administration and Management—General M
- Counseling Psychology M
- Counselor Education M
- Criminal Justice and Criminology M
- Early Childhood Education M
- Education—General M
- Educational Administration M
- Educational Media/Instructional Technology M
- Elementary Education M
- English as a Second Language M
- English Education M
- English M
- Geography M
- Higher Education M
- History M
- Mathematics M
- Middle School Education M
- Multilingual and Multicultural Education M
- Nursing—General M
- Occupational Therapy M
- Physical Education M
- Psychology—General M
- Reading Education M,O
- Science Education M
- Secondary Education M
- Social Work M
- Spanish M
- Special Education M

SALISBURY UNIVERSITY

- Art Education M
- Business Administration and Management—General M
- Business Education M
- Early Childhood Education M
- Education—General M
- Educational Administration M
- Educational Media/Instructional Technology M
- Elementary Education M
- English as a Second Language M
- English Education M
- English M
- Foreign Languages Education M
- History M
- Mathematics Education M
- Music Education M
- Nursing—General M
- Physiology M
- Reading Education M
- Science Education M
- Secondary Education M
- Social Sciences Education M
- Social Work M
- Writing M

SALVE REGINA UNIVERSITY

- Art Therapy M,O
- Business Administration and Management—General M,O
- Counseling Psychology M,O
- Criminal Justice and Criminology M
- Health Services Management and Hospital Administration M,O
- Homeland Security M,O
- Human Resources Development M,O
- Human Resources Management M,O
- Humanities M,D
- International Affairs M,O
- Legal and Justice Studies M
- Rehabilitation Counseling M,O

Close-Up on page 1019.

SAMFORD UNIVERSITY

- Business Administration and Management—General M
- Early Childhood Education M,D,O
- Education of the Gifted M,D,O
- Education—General M,D,O
- Educational Administration M,D,O
- Elementary Education M,D,O
- Environmental Management and Policy M
- Law P,M
- Music Education M
- Music M
- Nursing—General M
- Pharmacy P
- Theology P,M,D

SAM HOUSTON STATE UNIVERSITY

- Agricultural Sciences—General M
- Art/Fine Arts M
- Biological and Biomedical Sciences—General M
- Business Administration and Management—General M
- Chemistry M
- Clinical Psychology M,D
- Computational Sciences M
- Computer Science M
- Counselor Education M,D
- Criminal Justice and Criminology M,D
- Dance M
- Early Childhood Education M
- Educational Administration M,D
- Elementary Education M
- English M
- Family and Consumer Sciences-General M
- Finance and Banking M
- Forensic Sciences M,D
- History M
- Humanities M,D
- Industrial/Management Engineering M
- Information Science M
- Kinesiology and Movement Studies M
- Library Science M
- Mathematics M
- Music Education M
- Music M
- Political Science M
- Psychology—General M,D
- Public Administration M
- Reading Education M
- School Psychology M,D
- Secondary Education M
- Sociology M
- Special Education M
- Statistics M
- Vocational and Technical Education M

SAMRA UNIVERSITY OF ORIENTAL MEDICINE

- Acupuncture and Oriental Medicine M,D

SAMUEL MERRITT COLLEGE

- Family Nurse Practitioner Studies M,O
- Nurse Anesthesia M,O
- Nursing and Healthcare Administration M,O
- Nursing—General M,O
- Occupational Therapy M
- Physical Therapy M
- Physician Assistant Studies M

SAN DIEGO STATE UNIVERSITY

- Accounting M
- Advertising and Public Relations M
- Aerospace/Aeronautical Engineering M,D
- Anthropology M
- Applied Arts and Design—General M
- Applied Mathematics M
- Art History M
- Art/Fine Arts M
- Asian Studies M
- Astronomy M
- Biological and Biomedical Sciences—General M,D*
- Biometrics D
- Biostatistics M,D
- Business Administration and Management—General M
- Cell Biology M,D
- Chemistry M,D
- Child and Family Studies M
- Child Development M
- Civil Engineering M
- Clinical Psychology M,D
- Communication Disorders M,D
- Communication—General M
- Computational Sciences M,D
- Computer Science M
- Counselor Education M
- Criminal Justice and Criminology M
- Curriculum and Instruction M
- Ecology M,D*
- Economics M
- Education—General M,D
- Educational Administration M
- Educational Media/Instructional Technology M,D
- Electrical Engineering M
- Elementary Education M
- Emergency Management M,D
- Emergency Medical Services M,D
- Engineering and Applied Sciences—General M,D
- Engineering Design M,D
- English as a Second Language M,O
- English M
- Entrepreneurship M
- Environmental and Occupational Health M,D
- Environmental Design M
- Epidemiology M,D
- Exercise and Sports Science M
- Film, Television, and Video Production M
- Finance and Banking M
- Geography M,D
- Geology M
- Gerontology M
- Graphic Design M
- Health Physics/Radiological Health M
- Health Promotion M,D
- Health Psychology M,D
- Health Services Management and Hospital Administration M,D
- Higher Education M
- History M
- Human Resources Management M
- Industrial and Manufacturing Management M
- Industrial and Organizational Psychology M,D
- Interdisciplinary Studies M
- Interior Design M
- International Business M
- Internet and Interactive Multimedia M
- Latin American Studies M
- Liberal Studies M
- Linguistics M,O
- Management Information Systems M
- Marketing M
- Mathematics Education M,D
- Mathematics M,D
- Mechanical Engineering M,D
- Mechanics M,D
- Media Studies M
- Microbiology M
- Molecular Biology M,D*
- Multilingual and Multicultural Education M,D
- Music Education M
- Music M
- Nursing—General M
- Nutrition M
- Pharmaceutical Administration M
- Philosophy M
- Physical Education M
- Physics M
- Political Science M
- Psychology—General M,D
- Public Administration M
- Public Health—General M,D
- Reading Education M
- Rehabilitation Counseling M
- Rhetoric M
- Romance Languages M
- School Psychology M
- Science Education M,D
- Secondary Education M
- Social Work M
- Sociology M
- Spanish M
- Special Education M
- Statistics M
- Telecommunications Management M
- Theater M
- Toxicology M,D
- Urban and Regional Planning M
- Western European Studies M
- Women's Studies M
- Writing M

SAN FRANCISCO ART INSTITUTE

- Applied Arts and Design—General M,O
- Art History M
- Art/Fine Arts M,O*
- Film, Television, and Video Production M,O
- Museum Studies M
- Photography M,O
- Urban Studies M

SAN FRANCISCO CONSERVATORY OF MUSIC

- Music M

SAN FRANCISCO STATE UNIVERSITY

- Adult Education M,O
- Anthropology M
- Art History M
- Art/Fine Arts M
- Asian-American Studies M
- Biochemistry M
- Biological and Biomedical Sciences—General M
- Business Administration and Management—General M
- Cell Biology M
- Chemistry M
- Chinese M
- Classics M
- Clinical Laboratory Sciences/Medical Technology M
- Communication Disorders M
- Comparative Literature M
- Computer Science M
- Conservation Biology M
- Counseling Psychology M
- Cultural Studies M
- Early Childhood Education M
- Ecology M
- Economics M
- Education—General M,D,O
- Educational Administration M,O
- Educational Media/Instructional Technology M,O
- Elementary Education M

- Engineering and Applied Sciences—General M
- English as a Second Language M
- English Education M,O
- English M,O
- Environmental Management and Policy M
- Ethnic Studies M
- Family and Consumer Sciences-General M
- Family Nurse Practitioner Studies M
- Film, Television, and Video Production M
- Film, Television, and Video Theory and Criticism M
- French M
- Geography M
- Geosciences M
- German M
- Gerontology M
- Health Education M
- History M
- Humanities M
- Industrial Design M
- International Affairs M
- Italian M
- Japanese M
- Kinesiology and Movement Studies M
- Legal and Justice Studies M,O
- Leisure Studies M
- Linguistics M
- Marine Biology M
- Marine Sciences M
- Marriage and Family Therapy M
- Mathematics Education M
- Mathematics M
- Media Studies M
- Microbiology M
- Molecular Biology M
- Museum Studies M
- Music Education M
- Music M
- Nonprofit Management M
- Nursing and Healthcare Administration M
- Nursing Education M
- Nursing—General M
- Philosophy M,O
- Physical Therapy M,D
- Physics M
- Physiology M
- Political Science M
- Psychology—General M
- Public Administration M
- Public Health—General M
- Public Policy M
- Reading Education M,O
- Recreation and Park Management M
- Rehabilitation Counseling M
- Secondary Education M
- Social Sciences M
- Social Work M
- Spanish M
- Special Education M,D,O
- Speech and Interpersonal Communication M
- Theater M
- Women's Studies M
- Writing M

SAN FRANCISCO THEOLOGICAL SEMINARY

- Theology P,M,D

SAN JOAQUIN COLLEGE OF LAW

- Law P

SAN JOSE STATE UNIVERSITY

- Accounting M
- Aerospace/Aeronautical Engineering M
- Applied Arts and Design—General M
- Applied Economics M
- Art History M
- Art/Fine Arts M
- Biological and Biomedical Sciences—General M
- Business Administration and Management—General M
- Chemical Engineering M
- Chemistry M
- Child and Family Studies M
- Civil Engineering M
- Clinical Psychology M
- Communication Disorders M
- Communication—General M
- Comparative Literature M,O
- Computer Art and Design M
- Computer Engineering M
- Computer Science M,O
- Counselor Education M
- Criminal Justice and Criminology M
- Ecology M
- Economics M
- Education—General M,O
- Educational Administration M,O
- Educational Media/Instructional Technology M,O
- Electrical Engineering M
- Elementary Education M,O
- Engineering and Applied Sciences—General M
- English as a Second Language M,O
- English Education M,O
- English M,O
- Environmental Management and Policy M
- Ergonomics and Human Factors M
- Experimental Psychology M
- Film, Television, and Video Production M
- French M
- Geography M,O
- Geology M
- Gerontological Nursing M,O
- Gerontology M,O
- Health Education M,O
- Higher Education M,O
- Hispanic Studies M
- History M
- Industrial and Manufacturing Management M
- Industrial and Organizational Psychology M
- Industrial/Management Engineering M
- Information Studies M
- Interdisciplinary Studies M
- Kinesiology and Movement Studies M
- Library Science M
- Linguistics M,O
- Management Information Systems M
- Marine Sciences M
- Mass Communication M
- Materials Engineering M
- Mathematics Education M
- Mathematics M
- Mechanical Engineering M
- Meteorology M
- Microbiology M
- Molecular Biology M
- Music M
- Nursing and Healthcare Administration M,O
- Nursing Education M,O
- Nursing—General M,O
- Nutrition M
- Occupational Therapy M
- Philosophy M,O
- Photography M
- Physics M
- Physiology M
- Psychology—General M
- Public Administration M
- Public Health—General M,O
- Quality Management M
- Recreation and Park Management M
- Secondary Education M,O
- Social Work M,O
- Sociology M
- Software Engineering M
- Spanish M
- Special Education M,O
- Speech and Interpersonal Communication M
- Student Affairs M
- Systems Engineering M
- Taxation M
- Theater M
- Transportation Management M
- Urban and Regional Planning M,O
- Writing M,O

SAN JUAN BAUTISTA SCHOOL OF MEDICINE

- Allopathic Medicine P

SANTA CLARA UNIVERSITY

- Applied Mathematics M
- Business Administration and Management—General M
- Civil Engineering M
- Computer Engineering M,D,O
- Computer Science M,D,O
- Counseling Psychology M,O
- Counselor Education M
- Education—General M,O
- Educational Administration M,O
- Electrical Engineering M,D,O
- Engineering and Applied Sciences—General M,D,O
- Engineering Design M,D,O
- Engineering Management M
- Law P,M,O
- Management Information Systems M
- Materials Engineering M,D,O
- Mechanical Engineering M,D,O
- Music M
- Pastoral Ministry and Counseling M
- Religion M
- Software Engineering M,D,O
- Special Education M,O
- Telecommunications Management M,D,O

SARAH LAWRENCE COLLEGE

- Child Development M
- Dance M*
- Education—General M
- Genetic Counseling M
- History M
- Human Genetics M
- Interdisciplinary Studies M
- Public Health—General M*
- Theater M
- Women's Studies M*
- Writing M

Close-Up on page 1021.

SAVANNAH COLLEGE OF ART AND DESIGN

- Advertising and Public Relations M
- Applied Arts and Design—General M
- Architectural History M
- Architecture M
- Art History M
- Art/Fine Arts M*
- Arts Administration M
- Computer Art and Design M
- Film, Television, and Video Production M
- Film, Television, and Video Theory and Criticism M
- Graphic Design M
- Historic Preservation M
- Illustration M
- Industrial Design M
- Interior Design M
- Internet and Interactive Multimedia M
- Media Studies M
- Music M
- Photography M
- Textile Design M
- Theater M
- Urban Design M
- Writing M

SAVANNAH STATE UNIVERSITY

- Marine Sciences M
- Public Administration M
- Social Work M
- Urban Studies M

SAYBROOK GRADUATE SCHOOL AND RESEARCH CENTER

- Health Psychology M,D
- Organizational Behavior M,D
- Organizational Management M,D
- Psychology—General M,D
- Transpersonal and Humanistic Psychology M,D

SCHILLER INTERNATIONAL UNIVERSITY (GERMANY)

- Business Administration and Management—General M
- International Business M
- Management Information Systems M

SCHILLER INTERNATIONAL UNIVERSITY

- Business Administration and Management—General M
- International Affairs M
- International Business M

SCHILLER INTERNATIONAL UNIVERSITY (SPAIN)

- Business Administration and Management—General M
- International Business M

SCHILLER INTERNATIONAL UNIVERSITY

- Business Administration and Management—General M
- International Business M

SCHILLER INTERNATIONAL UNIVERSITY (UNITED KINGDOM)

- Corporate and Organizational Communication M
- Hospitality Management M
- International Affairs M
- International Business M
- Management Information Systems M
- Travel and Tourism M

SCHILLER INTERNATIONAL UNIVERSITY (UNITED STATES)

- Business Administration and Management—General M
- Finance and Banking M
- Hospitality Management M
- International Business M
- Management Information Systems M
- Travel and Tourism M

SCHILLER INTERNATIONAL UNIVERSITY, AMERICAN COLLEGE OF SWITZERLAND

- Business Administration and Management—General M
- International Business M

SCHOOL FOR INTERNATIONAL TRAINING

- Business Administration and Management—General M
- Conflict Resolution and Mediation/Peace Studies M
- Education—General M
- English as a Second Language M
- Foreign Languages Education M
- International Affairs M
- International and Comparative Education M
- International Business M
- Organizational Management M
- Sustainable Development M

Close-Up on page 1023.

SCHOOL OF ADVANCED AIR AND SPACE STUDIES

- Military and Defense Studies M

SCHOOL OF THE ART INSTITUTE OF CHICAGO

- Art Education M,O
- Art History M,O
- Art Therapy M
- Art/Fine Arts M*
- Arts Administration M
- Film, Television, and Video Production M
- Graphic Design M
- Historic Preservation M
- Interior Design M
- Photography M
- Writing M

SCHOOL OF THE MUSEUM OF FINE ARTS, BOSTON

- Art/Fine Arts M

SCHOOL OF VISUAL ARTS

- Applied Arts and Design—General M
- Art Education M
- Art Therapy M
- Art/Fine Arts M
- Computer Art and Design M
- Illustration M
- Photography M

Close-Up on page 1025.

SCHREINER UNIVERSITY

- Education—General M

THE SCRIPPS RESEARCH INSTITUTE

- Biochemistry D
- Biological and Biomedical Sciences—General D
- Biophysics D
- Chemistry D

SEABURY-WESTERN THEOLOGICAL SEMINARY

- Theology P,M,D,O

SEATTLE INSTITUTE OF ORIENTAL MEDICINE

- Acupuncture and Oriental Medicine M

SEATTLE PACIFIC UNIVERSITY

- Art/Fine Arts M
- Business Administration and Management—General M
- Clinical Psychology D
- Counselor Education M
- Economics M
- Education—General M,D
- Educational Administration M,D
- English as a Second Language M
- Family Nurse Practitioner Studies O

- Industrial and Organizational Psychology M,D
- Management Information Systems M
- Marriage and Family Therapy M
- Nursing and Healthcare Administration M
- Nursing—General M,O
- Reading Education M
- Secondary Education M

SEATTLE UNIVERSITY

- Accounting M
- Adult Education M,O
- Business Administration and Management—General M,O
- Community Health Nursing M
- Counselor Education M,O
- Criminal Justice and Criminology M
- Curriculum and Instruction M,O
- Education—General M,D,O
- Educational Administration M,D,O
- Engineering and Applied Sciences—General M
- English as a Second Language M,O
- Finance and Banking M,O
- Law P
- Nonprofit Management M
- Nursing and Healthcare Administration M
- Nursing—General M
- Organizational Management M,O
- Pastoral Ministry and Counseling M
- Psychiatric Nursing M
- Psychology—General M
- Public Administration M
- Reading Education M,O
- School Psychology M,O
- Software Engineering M
- Special Education M,O
- Sports Management M
- Theology P,M,O
- Transpersonal and Humanistic Psychology M

SEMINARY OF THE IMMACULATE CONCEPTION

- Pastoral Ministry and Counseling P,M,D,O
- Theology P,M,D,O

SETON HALL UNIVERSITY

- Accounting M
- Acute Care/Critical Care Nursing M
- Adult Nursing M
- Allied Health—General M,D*
- Analytical Chemistry M,D
- Art/Fine Arts M
- Arts Administration M
- Asian Studies M*
- Athletic Training and Sports Medicine M*
- Biochemistry M,D
- Biological and Biomedical Sciences—General M,D
- Business Administration and Management—General M,O
- Chemistry M,D*
- Communication Disorders M*
- Communication—General M
- Corporate and Organizational Communication M*
- Counseling Psychology M,D
- Counselor Education M
- Education—General M,D,O
- Educational Administration M,D,O
- Educational Media/Instructional Technology M
- English M*
- Experimental Psychology M*
- Finance and Banking M
- Gerontological Nursing M
- Health Services Management and Hospital Administration M,D*
- Higher Education D
- History M*
- Inorganic Chemistry M,D
- International Affairs M*
- International Business M,O
- Jewish Studies M
- Law P,M
- Management Information Systems M
- Marketing M
- Marriage and Family Therapy M,O
- Mass Communication M
- Microbiology M,D
- Molecular Biology M,D*
- Multilingual and Multicultural Education O
- Museum Studies M*
- Music M
- Neuroscience M
- Nonprofit Management M
- Nursing and Healthcare Administration M
- Nursing Education M
- Nursing—General M,D
- Occupational Therapy M*
- Organic Chemistry M,D
- Pastoral Ministry and Counseling P,M,O
- Pediatric Nursing M
- Pharmaceutical Administration M
- Physical Chemistry M,D
- Physical Therapy D*
- Physician Assistant Studies M*
- Psychology—General M,D,O
- Public Administration M
- Public Policy M*
- Religion M*
- School Nursing M
- School Psychology O
- Speech and Interpersonal Communication M
- Sports Management M
- Student Affairs M
- Taxation M
- Theology P,M,O
- Women's Health Nursing M

SETON HILL UNIVERSITY

- Art Therapy M,O
- Business Administration and Management—General M
- Education—General M
- Educational Media/Instructional Technology M
- Elementary Education M,O
- Marriage and Family Therapy M
- Physician Assistant Studies M
- Special Education M,O
- Writing M

Close-Up on page 1027.

SEWANEE: THE UNIVERSITY OF THE SOUTH

- English M*
- Theology P,M,D
- Writing M

SHASTA BIBLE COLLEGE

- Educational Administration M
- Pastoral Ministry and Counseling M
- Religious Education M

SHAW UNIVERSITY

- Curriculum and Instruction M
- Theology P,M

SHENANDOAH UNIVERSITY

- Allied Health—General M,D,O*
- Arts Administration M,D,O
- Athletic Training and Sports Medicine M
- Business Administration and Management—General M,O*
- Dance M,D,O
- Education—General M,D,O*
- Educational Administration M,D,O
- Elementary Education M,D,O
- English as a Second Language M,D,O
- Family Nurse Practitioner Studies M,O
- Health Services Management and Hospital Administration M,O
- Management Information Systems M,O
- Middle School Education M,D,O
- Music Education M,D,O
- Music M,D,O*
- Nurse Midwifery M,O
- Nursing—General M,O
- Occupational Therapy M
- Pharmacy P
- Physical Therapy D
- Physician Assistant Studies M
- Psychiatric Nursing M,O
- Public Administration M,D,O
- Secondary Education M,D,O
- Therapies—Dance, Drama, and Music M,D,O
- Women's Studies M,D,O

SHEPHERD UNIVERSITY

- Curriculum and Instruction M

SHERMAN COLLEGE OF STRAIGHT CHIROPRACTIC

- Chiropractic P*

SHIPPENSBURG UNIVERSITY OF PENNSYLVANIA

- Biological and Biomedical Sciences—General M
- Business Administration and Management—General M
- Communication—General M
- Computer Science M
- Counselor Education M,O
- Criminal Justice and Criminology M
- Curriculum and Instruction M
- Education—General M,O
- Educational Administration M
- Environmental Management and Policy M
- History M,O
- Information Science M
- Marriage and Family Therapy M,O
- Organizational Management M
- Psychology—General M
- Public Administration M
- Public History M,O
- Reading Education M
- Social Work M
- Sociology M
- Special Education M

Close-Up on page 1029.

SHORTER COLLEGE

- Business Administration and Management—General M

SH'OR YOSHUV RABBINICAL COLLEGE

- Theology

SIENA HEIGHTS UNIVERSITY

- Counselor Education M,O
- Curriculum and Instruction M
- Early Childhood Education M
- Education—General M
- Elementary Education M
- Human Resources Development M
- Middle School Education M
- Reading Education M
- Secondary Education M

SIERRA NEVADA COLLEGE

- Education—General M
- Elementary Education M
- Secondary Education M

SILVER LAKE COLLEGE

- Business Administration and Management—General M
- Education—General M
- Educational Administration M
- Music Education M
- Organizational Behavior M
- Special Education M

SIMMONS COLLEGE

- Business Administration and Management—General M,O
- Corporate and Organizational Communication M
- Counselor Education M,D,O
- Cultural Studies M
- Education—General M,D,O
- Educational Administration M,O
- Educational Media/Instructional Technology M,D,O
- Elementary Education M,O
- English as a Second Language M
- English M
- Entrepreneurship M
- Gender Studies M
- Health Education M,D,O
- Health Promotion M,O
- Health Services Management and Hospital Administration M,O
- Information Studies M,D,O
- Library Science M,D,O
- Middle School Education M,D,O
- Nursing—General M,D,O
- Nutrition M,O
- Physical Therapy D
- Public History M
- Secondary Education M,O
- Social Work M,D
- Spanish M
- Special Education M,D,O
- Urban Education M,O

SIMON FRASER UNIVERSITY

- Actuarial Science M,D
- Anthropology M,D
- Applied Mathematics M,D
- Archaeology M,D
- Art Education M,D
- Biochemistry M,D
- Biological and Biomedical Sciences—General M,D
- Biophysics M,D
- Biotechnology M,D
- Business Administration and Management—General M,D
- Chemical Physics M,D
- Chemistry M,D
- Communication—General M,D
- Community Health M
- Comparative and Interdisciplinary Arts M
- Computational Sciences M,D
- Computer Science M,D
- Counselor Education M
- Criminal Justice and Criminology M,D
- Curriculum and Instruction M,D
- Economics M,D
- Education—General M,D
- Educational Administration M,D
- Educational Media/Instructional Technology M,D
- Educational Psychology M,D
- Engineering and Applied Sciences—General M,D
- English as a Second Language M
- English M,D
- Entomology M,D
- Environmental Management and Policy M,D
- Finance and Banking M,D
- Foundations and Philosophy of Education M,D
- French M
- Geography M,D
- Geosciences M,D
- Gerontology M,D
- History M,D
- Information Science M,D
- International Business M,D
- Internet and Interactive Multimedia M,D
- Kinesiology and Movement Studies M,D
- Latin American Studies M
- Liberal Studies M
- Linguistics M,D
- Management of Technology M,D
- Mathematics Education M,D
- Mathematics M,D
- Molecular Biology M,D
- Philosophy M,D
- Physics M,D
- Political Science M,D
- Psychology—General M,D
- Public Health—General M
- Public Policy M
- Publishing M
- Sociology M,D
- Statistics M,D
- Toxicology M,D
- Urban Studies M,O
- Women's Studies M,D

SIMPSON UNIVERSITY

- Cultural Studies P,M
- Education—General M
- Educational Administration M
- Missions and Missiology P,M
- Pastoral Ministry and Counseling P,M
- Religion P,M

SINTE GLESKA UNIVERSITY

- Education—General M
- Elementary Education M

SIOUX FALLS SEMINARY

- Marriage and Family Therapy P,M
- Pastoral Ministry and Counseling P,M
- Religion P,M
- Theology M,D,O

SKIDMORE COLLEGE

- Liberal Studies M

SLIPPERY ROCK UNIVERSITY OF PENNSYLVANIA

- Business Administration and Management—General M
- Counselor Education M
- Early Childhood Education M
- Education—General M
- Educational Administration M
- Elementary Education M
- English M
- Environmental Education M
- Environmental Management and Policy M
- History M
- Mathematics Education M
- Nursing—General M
- Physical Education M
- Physical Therapy D
- Reading Education M
- Science Education M
- Secondary Education M
- Special Education M
- Sports Management M
- Student Affairs M
- Sustainable Development M

Close-Up on page 1031.

SMITH COLLEGE

- Biological and Biomedical Sciences—General M
- Chemistry M

Dance M
Education—General M
Elementary Education M
English Education M
Exercise and Sports Science M
Foreign Languages Education M
French M
History M
Mathematics Education M
Middle School Education M
Science Education M
Secondary Education M
Social Sciences Education M
Social Work M,D*
Special Education M
Theater M

SOJOURNER-DOUGLASS COLLEGE

Human Services M
Public Administration M
Reading Education M
Urban Education M

SONOMA STATE UNIVERSITY

Biological and Biomedical Sciences—General M
Business Administration and Management—General M
Counseling Psychology M
Counselor Education M
Curriculum and Instruction M
Education—General M
Educational Administration M
Elementary Education M
Engineering and Applied Sciences—General M
English M
Environmental Biology M
Family Nurse Practitioner Studies M
History M
Interdisciplinary Studies M
Kinesiology and Movement Studies M
Marriage and Family Therapy M
Political Science M
Public Administration M
Public History M
Special Education M
Writing M

SOUTH BAYLO UNIVERSITY

Acupuncture and Oriental Medicine M

SOUTH CAROLINA STATE UNIVERSITY

Agricultural Economics and Agribusiness M
Allied Health—General M
Business Education M
Child and Family Studies M
Civil Engineering M
Communication Disorders M
Counselor Education M
Early Childhood Education M
Educational Administration D,O
Elementary Education M
English Education M
Entrepreneurship M
Family and Consumer Sciences-General M
Home Economics Education M
Human Services M
Mathematics Education M
Mechanical Engineering M
Nutrition M
Rehabilitation Counseling M
Science Education M
Secondary Education M
Social Sciences Education M
Special Education M
Vocational and Technical Education M

SOUTH DAKOTA SCHOOL OF MINES AND TECHNOLOGY

Atmospheric Sciences M,D
Chemical Engineering M,D
Chemistry M,D
Civil Engineering M,D
Computer Engineering M
Computer Science M
Electrical Engineering M,D
Engineering and Applied Sciences—General M,D
Environmental Sciences D
Geological Engineering M,D
Geology M,D
Management of Technology M
Materials Engineering M,D
Materials Sciences M,D
Mechanical Engineering M,D
Metallurgical Engineering and Metallurgy M,D
Nanotechnology D
Paleontology M
Physics M,D
Water Resources D

Close-Up on page 1033.

SOUTH DAKOTA STATE UNIVERSITY

Agricultural Engineering M,D
Agricultural Sciences—General M,D
Agronomy and Soil Sciences M,D
Animal Sciences M,D
Biological and Biomedical Sciences—General M,D
Biosystems Engineering M,D
Chemistry M,D
Civil Engineering M
Clothing and Textiles M
Communication—General M
Computational Sciences M,D
Counselor Education M
Curriculum and Instruction M
Economics M
Education—General M
Educational Administration M
Electrical Engineering M,D
Engineering and Applied Sciences—General M,D
English M
Family and Consumer Sciences-General M
Fish, Game, and Wildlife Management M,D
Food Science and Technology M
Geography M
Geosciences D
Health Education M
Hospitality Management M
Human Development M
Industrial/Management Engineering M
Interior Design M
Journalism M
Mathematics M,D
Mechanical Engineering M
Microbiology M,D
Nursing—General M,D
Nutrition M
Pharmaceutical Sciences M,D
Pharmacy P
Physical Education M
Physics M
Plant Sciences M,D
Recreation and Park Management M
Rural Sociology M,D
Statistics M,D
Veterinary Sciences M,D

SOUTHEASTERN BAPTIST THEOLOGICAL SEMINARY

Ethics P,M,D
Missions and Missiology P,M,D
Music P,M,D
Philosophy P,M,D
Psychology—General P,M,D
Religious Education P,M,D
Theology P,M,D
Women's Studies P,M,D

SOUTHEASTERN LOUISIANA UNIVERSITY

Applied Science and Technology M
Biological and Biomedical Sciences—General M
Business Administration and Management—General M
Communication Disorders M
Communication—General M
Counselor Education M
Curriculum and Instruction M
Education—General M,D
Educational Administration M,D
Elementary Education M
English M
Health Education M
History M
Kinesiology and Movement Studies M
Music M
Nursing—General M
Psychology—General M
Secondary Education M
Sociology M
Special Education M

SOUTHEASTERN OKLAHOMA STATE UNIVERSITY

Aviation Management M
Aviation M
Business Administration and Management—General M
Counselor Education M
Education—General M
Educational Administration M
Educational Media/Instructional Technology M
Elementary Education M
Industrial and Manufacturing Management M
Secondary Education M

SOUTHEASTERN UNIVERSITY

Accounting M
Business Administration and Management—General M
Computer Science M
Finance and Banking M
Health Services Management and Hospital Administration M
International Business M
Management Information Systems M
Marketing M
Public Administration M
Taxation M

SOUTHEAST MISSOURI STATE UNIVERSITY

Accounting M
Biological and Biomedical Sciences—General M
Business Administration and Management—General M
Chemistry M
Communication Disorders M
Counselor Education M,O
Criminal Justice and Criminology M
Educational Administration M,O
Elementary Education M
English as a Second Language M
English M
Environmental Management and Policy M
Exercise and Sports Science M
Family and Consumer Sciences-General M
Finance and Banking M
Foundations and Philosophy of Education M
Health Services Management and Hospital Administration M
Higher Education M,O
History M
Industrial and Manufacturing Management M
International Business M
Leisure Studies M
Mathematics M
Middle School Education M
Music Education M
Nursing—General M
Nutrition M
Public Administration M
School Psychology M,O
Science Education M
Secondary Education M
Social Psychology M,O
Special Education M

SOUTHERN ADVENTIST UNIVERSITY

Accounting M
Adult Nursing M
Business Administration and Management—General M
Counseling Psychology M
Counselor Education M
Curriculum and Instruction M
Education—General M
Educational Administration M
Family Nurse Practitioner Studies M
Finance and Banking M
Health Services Management and Hospital Administration M
Human Resources Management M
Marketing M
Missions and Missiology M
Nursing and Healthcare Administration M
Nursing—General M
Psychology—General M
Reading Education M
Religion M
Religious Education M

SOUTHERN ARKANSAS UNIVERSITY–MAGNOLIA

Computer Science M
Counseling Psychology M
Counselor Education M
Education—General M
Educational Administration M
Elementary Education M
Kinesiology and Movement Studies M
Library Science M
Secondary Education M

SOUTHERN BAPTIST THEOLOGICAL SEMINARY

Missions and Missiology P,M,D
Music P,M,D
Pastoral Ministry and Counseling P,M,D
Religious Education P,M,D
Theology P,M,D

SOUTHERN CALIFORNIA COLLEGE OF OPTOMETRY

Optometry P

SOUTHERN CALIFORNIA INSTITUTE OF ARCHITECTURE

Architecture M*

SOUTHERN CALIFORNIA SEMINARY

Counseling Psychology P,M,D
Psychology—General P,M,D
Religion P,M,D
Theology P,M,D

SOUTHERN CALIFORNIA UNIVERSITY OF HEALTH SCIENCES

Acupuncture and Oriental Medicine M
Chiropractic P

SOUTHERN COLLEGE OF OPTOMETRY

Optometry P

SOUTHERN CONNECTICUT STATE UNIVERSITY

Art Education M
Biological and Biomedical Sciences—General M
Business Administration and Management—General M
Chemistry M
Communication Disorders M
Computer Science M
Counselor Education M,O
Education—General M,D,O
Educational Administration D,O
Educational Measurement and Evaluation M
Educational Media/Instructional Technology M,O
Elementary Education M,O
English as a Second Language M
English M
Environmental Education M,O
Exercise and Sports Science M
Foundations and Philosophy of Education O
French M
Health Education M
History M
Information Studies M,O
Leisure Studies M
Library Science M,O
Marriage and Family Therapy M
Mathematics M
Multilingual and Multicultural Education M
Nursing and Healthcare Administration M
Nursing Education M
Nursing—General M
Physical Education M
Political Science M
Psychology—General M
Public Health—General M
Reading Education M,O
Recreation and Park Management M
Romance Languages M
School Psychology M,O
Science Education M,O
Social Work M
Sociology M
Spanish M
Special Education M,O
Sport Psychology M
Urban Studies M
Women's Studies M

Close-Up on page 1035 and Announcement on page 585.

SOUTHERN EVANGELICAL SEMINARY

Missions and Missiology P,M,O
Pastoral Ministry and Counseling P,M,O
Philosophy M,D,O
Religion P,M,D,O
Religious Education P,M,O
Theology P,M,D,O

SOUTHERN ILLINOIS UNIVERSITY CARBONDALE

Accounting M,D
Agricultural Economics and Agribusiness M
Agricultural Sciences—General M
Agronomy and Soil Sciences M
Animal Sciences M
Anthropology M,D*
Applied Arts and Design—General M*
Applied Physics M,D*
Art/Fine Arts M
Biochemistry M,D

- Biological and Biomedical Sciences—General M,D
- Business Administration and Management—General M,D*
- Chemistry M,D*
- Civil Engineering M*
- Clinical Psychology M,D
- Communication Disorders M
- Communication—General M,D*
- Community Health M
- Computer Engineering M,D
- Computer Science M,D*
- Counseling Psychology M,D*
- Counselor Education M,D
- Criminal Justice and Criminology M
- Cultural Studies M
- Curriculum and Instruction M,D*
- Economics M,D*
- Education—General M,D
- Educational Administration M,D*
- Educational Measurement and Evaluation M,D
- Educational Psychology M,D*
- Electrical Engineering M,D*
- Energy and Power Engineering D*
- Engineering and Applied Sciences—General M,D*
- English as a Second Language M
- English M,D*
- Environmental Sciences D*
- Experimental Psychology M,D
- Forestry M
- Geography M,D
- Geology M,D
- Health Education M,D*
- Higher Education M
- History M,D*
- Horticulture M
- Human Development M,D
- Journalism D
- Law P,M
- Legal and Justice Studies P,M
- Linguistics M
- Manufacturing Engineering M*
- Mass Communication M
- Mathematics M,D*
- Mechanical Engineering M*
- Mechanics M,D
- Media Studies M
- Microbiology M,D
- Mineral/Mining Engineering M*
- Molecular Biology M,D*
- Music Education M
- Music M
- Nutrition M
- Pharmacology M,D*
- Philosophy M,D*
- Physical Education M,D
- Physics M,D
- Physiology M,D*
- Plant Biology M,D
- Plant Sciences M
- Political Science M,D*
- Psychology—General M,D*
- Public Administration M
- Recreation and Park Management M
- Rehabilitation Counseling M,D*
- Rhetoric M,D
- Social Work M
- Sociology M,D*
- Special Education M
- Speech and Interpersonal Communication M,D*
- Statistics M,D
- Telecommunications M
- Theater M,D*
- Vocational and Technical Education M,D*
- Writing M*
- Zoology M,D*

SOUTHERN ILLINOIS UNIVERSITY EDWARDSVILLE

- Accounting M
- Art Education M
- Art Therapy M,O
- Art/Fine Arts M
- Biological and Biomedical Sciences—General M
- Biotechnology M
- Business Administration and Management—General M
- Chemistry M
- Civil Engineering M
- Clinical Psychology M
- Communication Disorders M
- Community Health Nursing M,O
- Computer Science M
- Corporate and Organizational Communication O
- Dentistry P
- Economics M
- Education—General M,O
- Educational Administration M,O
- Educational Media/Instructional Technology M
- Electrical Engineering M
- Elementary Education M
- Engineering and Applied Sciences—General M
- English as a Second Language M,O
- English Education M,O
- English M,O
- Environmental Management and Policy M
- Environmental Sciences M
- Family Nurse Practitioner Studies M,O
- Finance and Banking M
- Foreign Languages Education M
- Foundations and Philosophy of Education M
- Geography M
- Health Education M,O
- History M
- Industrial and Organizational Psychology M
- Kinesiology and Movement Studies M,O
- Management Information Systems M
- Marketing Research M
- Mass Communication M
- Mathematics Education M
- Mathematics M
- Mechanical Engineering M
- Media Studies O
- Museum Studies O
- Music Education M
- Music M
- Nurse Anesthesia M,O
- Nursing and Healthcare Administration M,O
- Nursing Education M,O
- Nursing—General M,O
- Pharmacy P
- Physics M
- Psychology—General M,O
- Public Administration M
- Reading Education M
- School Psychology O
- Science Education M
- Secondary Education M
- Social Sciences Education M
- Social Work M
- Sociology M
- Special Education M
- Speech and Interpersonal Communication M
- Writing M

Close-Up on page 1037.

SOUTHERN METHODIST UNIVERSITY

- Accounting M
- Anthropology M,D
- Applied Economics M,D
- Applied Mathematics M,D
- Applied Science and Technology M,D
- Art History M
- Art/Fine Arts M
- Arts Administration M
- Biological and Biomedical Sciences—General M,D*
- Business Administration and Management—General M
- Chemistry M,D
- Civil Engineering M,D
- Clinical Psychology M,D
- Computational Sciences M,D
- Computer Engineering M,D
- Computer Science M,D
- Counseling Psychology M
- Dance M
- Economics M,D
- Education—General M
- Electrical Engineering M,D
- Engineering and Applied Sciences—General M,D*
- Engineering Management M,D
- English M,D
- Environmental Engineering M,D
- Environmental Sciences M,D
- Facilities Management M,D
- Film, Television, and Video Production M
- Geology M,D
- Geophysics M,D
- Hazardous Materials Management M,D
- History M,D
- Information Science M,D
- Interdisciplinary Studies M
- Law P,M,D
- Manufacturing Engineering M,D
- Mathematics M,D
- Mechanical Engineering M,D
- Medieval and Renaissance Studies M
- Multilingual and Multicultural Education M
- Music Education M,O
- Music M,O
- Operations Research M,D
- Photography M
- Physics M,D
- Psychology—General M,D
- Religion M,D
- Software Engineering M,D
- Statistics M,D
- Systems Engineering M,D
- Systems Science M,D
- Taxation P,M,D
- Telecommunications M,D
- Theater M
- Theology P,M,D

SOUTHERN NAZARENE UNIVERSITY

- Business Administration and Management—General M
- Counseling Psychology M
- Curriculum and Instruction M
- Education—General M
- Educational Administration M
- Marriage and Family Therapy M
- Nursing and Healthcare Administration M
- Nursing Education M
- Nursing—General M
- Psychology—General M
- Religion M
- Theology M

SOUTHERN NEW ENGLAND SCHOOL OF LAW

- Law P

SOUTHERN NEW HAMPSHIRE UNIVERSITY

- Accounting M,D,O
- Addictions/Substance Abuse Counseling M,O
- Business Administration and Management—General M,D,O*
- Business Education M,O
- Child Development M,O
- Clinical Psychology M,O
- Community Health M,O
- Computer Education M,O
- Curriculum and Instruction M,O
- Economics M,D
- Education—General M,O
- Educational Administration M,O
- Elementary Education M,O
- English as a Second Language M,O
- Finance and Banking M,D,O
- Hospitality Management M,D,O
- Human Resources Development M,O
- Human Resources Management M,D,O
- International Business M,D,O
- Management Information Systems M,D,O
- Marketing M,D,O
- Nonprofit Management M,D,O
- Organizational Management M,D,O
- Project Management M,D,O
- Psychology—General M,O
- School Psychology M,O
- Secondary Education M,O
- Special Education M,O
- Sports Management M,D,O
- Taxation M,D,O
- Vocational and Technical Education M,O
- Writing M,O

SOUTHERN OREGON UNIVERSITY

- Business Administration and Management—General M
- Computer Science M
- Counselor Education M
- Early Childhood Education M
- Education—General M
- Educational Administration M
- Elementary Education M
- Environmental Education M
- Human Services M
- Mathematics M
- Music M
- Psychology—General M
- Reading Education M
- Secondary Education M
- Social Sciences M
- Special Education M

SOUTHERN POLYTECHNIC STATE UNIVERSITY

- Business Administration and Management—General M
- Computer Engineering M
- Computer Science M
- Construction Engineering M
- Electrical Engineering M
- Engineering and Applied Sciences—General M
- Industrial/Management Engineering M
- Information Science M
- Internet and Interactive Multimedia M
- Quality Management M
- Software Engineering M
- Systems Engineering M
- Technical Communication M

SOUTHERN UNIVERSITY AND AGRICULTURAL AND MECHANICAL COLLEGE

- Accounting M
- Agricultural Sciences—General M
- Analytical Chemistry M
- Biochemistry M
- Biological and Biomedical Sciences—General M
- Business Administration and Management—General M
- Chemistry M
- Computer Science M
- Counselor Education M
- Criminal Justice and Criminology M
- Education—General M,D
- Educational Administration M
- Educational Media/Instructional Technology M
- Elementary Education M
- Engineering and Applied Sciences—General M
- Environmental Sciences M
- Family Nurse Practitioner Studies M,D,O
- Forestry M
- Gerontological Nursing M,D,O
- History M
- Inorganic Chemistry M
- Law P*
- Mass Communication M
- Mathematics Education D
- Mathematics M
- Nursing and Healthcare Administration M,D,O
- Nursing Education M,D,O
- Nursing—General M,D,O
- Organic Chemistry M
- Physical Chemistry M
- Physics M
- Political Science M
- Psychology—General M
- Public Administration M,D
- Recreation and Park Management M
- Rehabilitation Counseling M*
- Science Education D
- Secondary Education M
- Social Sciences M
- Special Education M,D

SOUTHERN UNIVERSITY AT NEW ORLEANS

- Social Work M

SOUTHERN UTAH UNIVERSITY

- Accounting M
- Arts Administration M
- Business Administration and Management—General M
- Communication—General M
- Education—General M
- Forensic Sciences M

SOUTHERN WESLEYAN UNIVERSITY

- Business Administration and Management—General M
- Education—General M
- Pastoral Ministry and Counseling M

SOUTH TEXAS COLLEGE OF LAW

- Law P

SOUTH UNIVERSITY (AL)

- Counseling Psychology M*

SOUTH UNIVERSITY (FL)

- Counseling Psychology M*

SOUTH UNIVERSITY (GA)

- Anesthesiologist Assistant Studies M
- Counseling Psychology M*
- Pharmacy P*
- Physician Assistant Studies M*

SOUTH UNIVERSITY (SC)

- Counseling Psychology M*

SOUTHWEST ACUPUNCTURE COLLEGE

- Acupuncture and Oriental Medicine M

SOUTHWEST BAPTIST UNIVERSITY

- Business Administration and Management—General M
- Education—General M,O
- Educational Administration M,O
- Health Services Management and Hospital Administration M
- Physical Therapy D

SOUTHWEST COLLEGE OF NATUROPATHIC MEDICINE AND HEALTH SCIENCES
Naturopathic Medicine D*

SOUTHWESTERN ADVENTIST UNIVERSITY
Accounting M
Business Administration and Management—General M
Education—General M
Elementary Education M

SOUTHWESTERN ASSEMBLIES OF GOD UNIVERSITY
Counseling Psychology M
Curriculum and Instruction M
Education—General M
Educational Administration M
Religious Education M
Theology M

SOUTHWESTERN BAPTIST THEOLOGICAL SEMINARY
Music M,D,O
Religious Education M,D,O
Theology P,M,D,O

SOUTHWESTERN CHRISTIAN UNIVERSITY
Pastoral Ministry and Counseling M

SOUTHWESTERN COLLEGE (KS)
Education—General M
Special Education M

SOUTHWESTERN COLLEGE (NM)
Art Therapy M,O
Counseling Psychology M,O*
Health Psychology O
Psychology—General O
Social Psychology O
Thanatology M,O

SOUTHWESTERN LAW SCHOOL
Law P,M

SOUTHWESTERN OKLAHOMA STATE UNIVERSITY
Allied Health—General M
Art Education M
Business Administration and Management—General M
Counselor Education M
Early Childhood Education M
Education—General M
Educational Administration M
Educational Measurement and Evaluation M
Elementary Education M
English Education M
Kinesiology and Movement Studies M
Mathematics Education M
Microbiology M
Music Education M
Music M
Pharmacy P
Recreation and Park Management M
School Psychology M
Science Education M
Secondary Education M
Social Sciences Education M
Special Education M

SOUTHWEST MINNESOTA STATE UNIVERSITY
Business Administration and Management—General M
Education—General M
Educational Administration M
Special Education M

SPALDING UNIVERSITY
Adult Nursing M
Business Administration and Management—General M
Clinical Psychology M,D
Communication—General M
Corporate and Organizational Communication M
Education—General M,D
Educational Administration M,D
Elementary Education M
Family Nurse Practitioner Studies M
Middle School Education M
Nursing and Healthcare Administration M
Nursing—General M
Occupational Therapy M
Pediatric Nursing M
Psychology—General M,D
Secondary Education M
Social Work M
Special Education M
Writing M

Close-Up on page 1039.

SPERTUS INSTITUTE OF JEWISH STUDIES
Jewish Studies M,D
Nonprofit Management M
Religious Education M

SPRING ARBOR UNIVERSITY
Business Administration and Management—General M
Child and Family Studies M
Communication—General M
Counseling Psychology M
Education—General M
Organizational Management M
Pastoral Ministry and Counseling M
Theology M

SPRINGFIELD COLLEGE
Addictions/Substance Abuse Counseling M,O
Art Therapy M,O
Child and Family Studies M,O
Counseling Psychology M,O
Counselor Education M,O
Education—General M
Exercise and Sports Science M,D,O
Health Education M,D,O
Health Services Management and Hospital Administration M
Human Services M
Industrial and Organizational Psychology M,O
Kinesiology and Movement Studies M,D
Marriage and Family Therapy M,O
Occupational Therapy M,O
Physical Education M,D,O
Physical Therapy M
Physician Assistant Studies M
Recreation and Park Management M
Rehabilitation Counseling M,O
Secondary Education M
Social Work M,O*
Sport Psychology M,D,O
Sports Management M,D,O
Student Affairs M,O

Close-Up on page 1041.

SPRING HILL COLLEGE
Business Administration and Management—General M
Early Childhood Education M
Education—General M
Elementary Education M
Liberal Studies M
Nursing—General M
Secondary Education M
Theology M

STANFORD UNIVERSITY
Aerospace/Aeronautical Engineering M,D,O
Allopathic Medicine P
Anthropology M,D
Applied Physics M,D
Art Education M,D
Art/Fine Arts M,D
Asian Studies M
Biochemistry D
Bioengineering M,D
Biological and Biomedical Sciences—General M,D
Biomedical Engineering M
Biophysics D
Business Administration and Management—General M,D
Cancer Biology/Oncology D
Chemical Engineering M,D,O
Chemistry D*
Child and Family Studies D
Chinese M,D
Civil Engineering M,D,O
Classics M,D
Communication—General M,D
Comparative Literature D
Computational Sciences M,D
Computer Education M,D
Computer Science M,D
Counseling Psychology D
Curriculum and Instruction M,D
Developmental Biology D
Developmental Psychology D
East European and Russian Studies M
Economics D
Education—General M,D
Educational Administration M,D
Educational Measurement and Evaluation M,D
Educational Psychology D
Electrical Engineering M,D,O
Engineering and Applied Sciences—General M,D,O
Engineering Design M
Engineering Management M,D*
English Education M,D
English M,D
Environmental Engineering M,D,O
Environmental Management and Policy M
Environmental Sciences M,D,O
Epidemiology M,D
Foreign Languages Education M
Foundations and Philosophy of Education M,D
French M,D
Genetics D
Geophysics M,D
Geosciences M,D,O
German M,D
Health Services Research M
Higher Education M,D
History M,D
Humanities M
Immunology D
Industrial/Management Engineering M,D
Interdisciplinary Studies M,D
International Affairs M
International and Comparative Education M,D
Italian M,D
Japanese M,D
Journalism M,D
Law P,M,D
Linguistics M,D
Materials Engineering M,D,O
Materials Sciences M,D,O
Mathematical and Computational Finance M,D
Mathematics Education M,D
Mathematics M,D
Mechanical Engineering M,D,O*
Medical Informatics M,D*
Microbiology D
Molecular Pharmacology D
Music M,D
Neuroscience D
Petroleum Engineering M,D,O
Philosophy M,D
Physics D
Physiology D
Political Science M,D
Psychology—General D
Religion M,D
Russian M,D
Science Education M,D
Slavic Languages M,D
Social Sciences Education M,D
Sociology D
Spanish M,D
Statistics M,D
Structural Biology D
Theater D

STARR KING SCHOOL FOR THE MINISTRY
Theology P

STATE UNIVERSITY OF NEW YORK AT BINGHAMTON
Accounting M,D
Analytical Chemistry M,D
Anthropology M,D
Applied Physics M
Art History M,D*
Biological and Biomedical Sciences—General M,D
Biopsychology M,D
Business Administration and Management—General M,D
Chemistry M,D
Clinical Psychology M,D
Cognitive Sciences M,D
Comparative Literature M,D
Computer Science M,D
Early Childhood Education M
Economics M,D
Education—General M,D
Electrical Engineering M,D
Elementary Education M
Engineering and Applied Sciences—General M,D*
English Education M
English M,D
Finance and Banking M,D
Foreign Languages Education M
Foundations and Philosophy of Education D
French M
Geography M
Geology M,D
Health Services Management and Hospital Administration M,D
History M,D
Industrial/Management Engineering M,D
Inorganic Chemistry M,D
Italian M
Legal and Justice Studies M,D
Materials Engineering M,D
Materials Sciences M,D
Mathematics Education M
Mathematics M,D
Mechanical Engineering M,D
Music M
Nursing—General M,D,O
Organic Chemistry M,D
Philosophy M,D
Physical Chemistry M,D
Physics M
Political Science M,D
Psychology—General M,D
Public Administration M
Public Policy M,D
Reading Education M
Science Education M
Secondary Education M
Social Sciences Education M
Social Sciences M
Sociology M,D
Spanish M,O
Special Education M
Statistics M,D
Systems Science M,D
Theater M
Translation and Interpretation M,O

STATE UNIVERSITY OF NEW YORK AT FREDONIA
Accounting M
Biological and Biomedical Sciences—General M
Business Administration and Management—General M
Chemistry M
Communication Disorders M
Education—General M,O
Educational Administration O
Elementary Education M
English as a Second Language M
English M
Interdisciplinary Studies M
Mathematics M
Music Education M
Music M
Reading Education M
Science Education M
Secondary Education M

STATE UNIVERSITY OF NEW YORK AT NEW PALTZ
Accounting M
Adult Nursing M,O
Art Education M
Art/Fine Arts M
Biological and Biomedical Sciences—General M
Business Administration and Management—General M
Chemistry M
Communication Disorders M
Computer Engineering M
Computer Science M
Counseling Psychology M
Early Childhood Education M
Education—General M,O
Educational Administration M,O
Electrical Engineering M
Elementary Education M
English as a Second Language M
English M
Geology M
Gerontological Nursing M,O
Interdisciplinary Studies M
Mathematics M
Multilingual and Multicultural Education M
Nursing—General M,O
Psychology—General M
Reading Education M
Secondary Education M
Special Education M

STATE UNIVERSITY OF NEW YORK AT OSWEGO
Agricultural Education M
Art Education M
Art/Fine Arts M
Business Administration and Management—General M
Business Education M
Chemistry M
Child and Family Studies M
Consumer Economics M
Counseling Psychology M,O
Education—General M,O
Educational Administration O
Elementary Education M
English M
History M
Human Services M
Human-Computer Interaction M
Reading Education M
School Psychology M,O
Secondary Education M
Special Education M
Vocational and Technical Education M

STATE UNIVERSITY OF NEW YORK AT PLATTSBURGH

Communication Disorders M
Counselor Education M,O
Curriculum and Instruction M
Educational Administration O
Elementary Education M
English Education M
Foreign Languages Education M
Liberal Studies M
Mathematics Education M
Psychology—General M,O
Reading Education M
School Psychology M,O
Science Education M
Secondary Education M
Social Sciences Education M
Special Education M

STATE UNIVERSITY OF NEW YORK COLLEGE AT BROCKPORT

Art/Fine Arts M
Biological and Biomedical Sciences—General M
Communication—General M
Computational Sciences M
Counseling Psychology M,O
Counselor Education M,O
Curriculum and Instruction M
Dance M
Education—General M
Educational Administration M,O
English Education M
English M
Environmental Sciences M
Health Education M
History M
Leisure Studies M
Liberal Studies M
Mathematics Education M
Mathematics M*
Middle School Education M
Multilingual and Multicultural Education M
Physical Education M
Psychology—General M
Public Administration M
Reading Education M
Recreation and Park Management M
Science Education M
Social Sciences Education M
Social Work M

Close-Up on page 1043.

STATE UNIVERSITY OF NEW YORK COLLEGE AT CORTLAND

American Studies O
Early Childhood Education M
Education—General M,O
Educational Administration O
English as a Second Language M
English Education M
English M
Exercise and Sports Science M*
Foreign Languages Education M
Health Education M
History M
Mathematics Education M
Mathematics M
Physical Education M
Reading Education M
Recreation and Park Management M
Science Education M
Secondary Education M
Social Sciences Education M
Special Education M
Sports Management M*

STATE UNIVERSITY OF NEW YORK COLLEGE AT GENESEO

Communication Disorders M
Early Childhood Education M
Education—General M
Elementary Education M
Reading Education M
Secondary Education M

STATE UNIVERSITY OF NEW YORK COLLEGE AT OLD WESTBURY

Accounting M*
Taxation M

STATE UNIVERSITY OF NEW YORK COLLEGE AT ONEONTA

Biological and Biomedical Sciences—General M
Counselor Education M,O
Education—General M,O
Educational Psychology M,O
Elementary Education M
Family and Consumer Sciences-General M
Geosciences M
Home Economics Education M
Middle School Education M
Museum Studies M
Reading Education M
Secondary Education M

STATE UNIVERSITY OF NEW YORK COLLEGE AT POTSDAM

Curriculum and Instruction M
Educational Media/Instructional Technology M
Elementary Education M
English M
Mathematics M
Music Education M
Music M
Reading Education M
Secondary Education M
Special Education M

STATE UNIVERSITY OF NEW YORK COLLEGE OF ENVIRONMENTAL SCIENCE AND FORESTRY

Biochemistry M,D
Chemistry M,D
Communication—General M,D
Conservation Biology M,D
Construction Engineering M,D
Ecology M,D
Entomology M,D
Environmental Biology M,D
Environmental Engineering M,D
Environmental Management and Policy M,D
Environmental Sciences M,D
Fish, Game, and Wildlife Management M,D
Forestry M,D
Hydrology M,D
Landscape Architecture M
Natural Resources M,D
Organic Chemistry M,D
Paper and Pulp Engineering M,D
Plant Pathology M,D
Plant Sciences M,D
Recreation and Park Management M,D
Urban and Regional Planning M,D
Urban Design M
Water Resources M,D

STATE UNIVERSITY OF NEW YORK COLLEGE OF OPTOMETRY

Optometry P
Vision Sciences M,D

STATE UNIVERSITY OF NEW YORK DOWNSTATE MEDICAL CENTER

Allopathic Medicine P,M
Biological and Biomedical Sciences—General M,D*
Biomedical Engineering M,D
Cell Biology D
Community Health M
Family Nurse Practitioner Studies M,O
Molecular Biology D
Neuroscience D
Nurse Anesthesia M
Nursing—General M,O
Public Health—General M*

STATE UNIVERSITY OF NEW YORK EMPIRE STATE COLLEGE

Business Administration and Management—General M
Education—General M
Industrial and Labor Relations M
Liberal Studies M
Public Policy M

STATE UNIVERSITY OF NEW YORK INSTITUTE OF TECHNOLOGY

Accounting M
Adult Nursing M,O
Business Administration and Management—General M
Computer Science M
Engineering and Applied Sciences—General M
Family Nurse Practitioner Studies M,O
Gerontological Nursing M,O
Health Services Management and Hospital Administration M
Information Science M
Management of Technology M
Nursing and Healthcare Administration M,O
Nursing Education M,O
Nursing—General M,O
Sociology M
Telecommunications M

Close-Up on page 1045.

STATE UNIVERSITY OF NEW YORK MARITIME COLLEGE

Transportation Management M*

STATE UNIVERSITY OF NEW YORK UPSTATE MEDICAL UNIVERSITY

Allopathic Medicine P
Anatomy M,D
Biochemistry M,D
Biological and Biomedical Sciences—General M,D*
Cell Biology M,D
Clinical Laboratory Sciences/Medical Technology M
Family Nurse Practitioner Studies M,O
Immunology M,D
Microbiology M,D
Molecular Biology M,D
Neuroscience D
Nursing—General M,O
Pharmacology M,D
Physical Therapy D
Physiology M,D

STEPHEN F. AUSTIN STATE UNIVERSITY

Accounting M
Agricultural Education M
Applied Arts and Design—General M
Art/Fine Arts M
Athletic Training and Sports Medicine M
Biological and Biomedical Sciences—General M
Biotechnology M
Business Administration and Management—General M
Chemistry M
Communication Disorders M
Communication—General M
Computer Science M
Counselor Education M
Early Childhood Education M
Education—General M,D
Educational Administration M,D
Elementary Education M
English M
Environmental Sciences M
Family and Consumer Sciences-General M
Forestry M,D
Geology M
History M
Interdisciplinary Studies M
Kinesiology and Movement Studies M
Marketing M
Mass Communication M
Mathematics Education M
Mathematics M
Music M
Physics M
Psychology—General M
Public Administration M
School Psychology M
Secondary Education M,D
Social Work M
Special Education M
Statistics M

STEPHENS COLLEGE

Business Administration and Management—General M
Counselor Education M
Curriculum and Instruction M
Health Services Management and Hospital Administration O

STETSON UNIVERSITY

Accounting M
Business Administration and Management—General M
Counselor Education M
Curriculum and Instruction O
Education—General M,O
Educational Administration M,O
English M
Law P,M
Marriage and Family Therapy M
Reading Education M
Special Education M

STEVENS INSTITUTE OF TECHNOLOGY

Analytical Chemistry M,D,O
Applied Mathematics M,D
Applied Statistics O
Biochemistry M,D,O
Bioinformatics M,D,O
Biomedical Engineering M,O
Business Administration and Management—General M
Chemical Engineering M,D,O
Chemistry M,D,O
Civil Engineering M,D,O
Cognitive Sciences O
Computer and Information Systems Security M,D,O
Computer Engineering M,D,O
Computer Science M,D,O
Construction Engineering M,O
Construction Management M,O
Corporate and Organizational Communication O
Electrical Engineering M,D,O
Electronic Commerce M,O
Engineering and Applied Sciences—General M,D,O*
Engineering Design M
Engineering Management M,D,O
Engineering Physics M,D,O
Entrepreneurship M,O
Environmental Engineering M,D,O
Finance and Banking M
Human Resources Management M,O
Industrial and Manufacturing Management M
Information Science M,O
International Business M
Logistics M,D,O
Management Information Systems M,D,O
Management of Technology M,D,O
Management Strategy and Policy M
Manufacturing Engineering M
Marine Affairs M
Materials Engineering M,D
Mathematics M,D
Mechanical Engineering M,D,O
Ocean Engineering M,D
Organic Chemistry M,D,O
Pharmaceutical Sciences M,O
Photonics O
Physical Chemistry M,D,O
Physics M,D,O
Polymer Science and Engineering M,D,O
Project Management M,O
Quality Management M,O
Software Engineering M,O
Statistics M,O
Structural Engineering M,D,O
Systems Engineering M,D,O
Systems Science M
Telecommunications Management M,D,O
Telecommunications M,D,O
Water Resources Engineering M,D,O

STONEHILL COLLEGE

Accounting M

STONY BROOK UNIVERSITY, STATE UNIVERSITY OF NEW YORK

Addictions/Substance Abuse Counseling M
Adult Nursing M,O
Allopathic Medicine P
American Studies M,O
Anatomy D*
Anthropology M,D*
Applied Mathematics M,D*
Art History M,D*
Art/Fine Arts M*
Astronomy M,D
Atmospheric Sciences M,D*
Biochemistry D*
Biological and Biomedical Sciences—General D*
Biomedical Engineering M,D,O*
Biophysics D*
Biopsychology D*
Business Administration and Management—General M,O*
Cell Biology M,D
Chemistry M,D*
Clinical Psychology D*
Community Health M,D,O
Comparative Literature M,D*
Computer Education M*
Computer Engineering M,D
Computer Science M,D,O*
Cultural Studies M,O
Dentistry P,O
Developmental Biology M,D*
Ecology D*
Economics M,D*
Educational Administration M,O
Educational Media/Instructional Technology M,O
Electrical Engineering M,D*
Engineering and Applied Sciences—General M,D,O
English as a Second Language M,D
English Education M,O
English M,D,O*
Environmental and Occupational Health M,O
Environmental Management and Policy M,O*
Evolutionary Biology D
Experimental Psychology D*
Family Nurse Practitioner Studies M,O
Finance and Banking M,O
Foreign Languages Education M,O
French M,D
Genetics D*
Geosciences M,D*
German M,D

- Gerontological Nursing M
- Hazardous Materials Management M,O
- Health Psychology D
- Health Services Management and Hospital Administration M,D,O
- Hispanic Studies M,D*
- History M,D*
- Human Resources Management M,O
- Immunology M,D
- Industrial and Labor Relations M,O
- Industrial and Manufacturing Management M,O
- Italian M,D
- Liberal Studies M,O
- Linguistics M,D*
- Management Information Systems M,D,O
- Management of Technology M,O*
- Marine Sciences M,D*
- Materials Engineering M,D
- Materials Sciences M,D*
- Maternal and Child/Neonatal Nursing M,O
- Mathematics Education M,O
- Mathematics M,D*
- Mechanical Engineering M,D,O*
- Medical Physics D*
- Microbiology D*
- Molecular Biology M,D*
- Molecular Genetics D*
- Molecular Physiology D*
- Music M,D*
- Neuroscience D*
- Nurse Midwifery M,O
- Nursing—General M,O
- Occupational Therapy M,D,O
- Oral and Dental Sciences P,D,O*
- Pathology M,D
- Pediatric Nursing M,O
- Pharmacology D*
- Philosophy M,D*
- Physical Education M,O
- Physical Therapy M,D,O
- Physics M,D*
- Physiology D*
- Planetary and Space Sciences M,D
- Political Science M,D*
- Psychiatric Nursing M,O
- Psychology—General M,D
- Public Affairs M,O
- Public Health—General M*
- Public Policy M,D
- Romance Languages M,D
- Science Education M,D
- Slavic Languages M
- Social Psychology D*
- Social Sciences Education M,D
- Social Sciences M,O
- Social Work M,D*
- Sociology M,D*
- Software Engineering M,D,O
- Statistics M,D
- Structural Biology D
- Systems Engineering M,D,O
- Theater M*
- Women's Health Nursing M,O
- Women's Studies M,O

Close-Up on page 1047.

STRATFORD UNIVERSITY

- Business Administration and Management—General M
- Management Information Systems M
- Software Engineering M

STRAYER UNIVERSITY

- Accounting M
- Business Administration and Management—General M
- Information Science M
- Management Information Systems M

SUFFOLK UNIVERSITY

- Accounting M,O
- Adult Education M,O
- Applied Arts and Design—General M
- Business Administration and Management—General M,O
- Clinical Psychology D
- Communication—General M
- Computer Science M
- Counselor Education M,O
- Criminal Justice and Criminology M
- Curriculum and Instruction M,O
- Developmental Psychology D
- Disability Studies M,O
- Economics M,D*
- Education—General M,O
- Educational Administration M,O
- Finance and Banking M,O
- Foundations and Philosophy of Education M,O
- Graphic Design M
- Health Services Management and Hospital Administration M,O
- Human Resources Development M,O
- Human Resources Management M,O
- Interior Design M
- International Business M,D
- Law P,M
- Nonprofit Management M,O
- Political Science M
- Psychology—General D
- Public Administration M,O
- Secondary Education M
- Taxation M,O

SULLIVAN UNIVERSITY

- Business Administration and Management—General M
- Conflict Resolution and Mediation/Peace Studies M
- Management of Technology M

SUL ROSS STATE UNIVERSITY

- Animal Sciences M
- Applied Arts and Design—General M
- Art Education M
- Art History M
- Art/Fine Arts M
- Biological and Biomedical Sciences—General M
- Business Administration and Management—General M
- Chemistry M
- Counselor Education M
- Criminal Justice and Criminology M
- Education—General M
- Educational Administration M
- Educational Measurement and Evaluation M
- Elementary Education M
- English M
- Fish, Game, and Wildlife Management M
- Geology M*
- History M
- International Business M
- Multilingual and Multicultural Education M
- Physical Education M
- Political Science M
- Psychology—General M
- Public Administration M
- Range Science M
- Reading Education M
- Secondary Education M
- Textile Design M
- Vocational and Technical Education M

SUNBRIDGE COLLEGE

- Early Childhood Education M
- Education—General M
- Elementary Education M

SWEDISH INSTITUTE, COLLEGE OF HEALTH SCIENCES

- Accounting M
- Acupuncture and Oriental Medicine M

SWEET BRIAR COLLEGE

- Education—General M

SYRACUSE UNIVERSITY

- Accounting M,D
- Advertising and Public Relations M
- Aerospace/Aeronautical Engineering M,D
- African Studies M
- African-American Studies M
- Anthropology M,D
- Applied Arts and Design—General M
- Applied Statistics M
- Architecture M
- Art Education M,O
- Art History M*
- Art/Fine Arts M
- Biochemistry D
- Bioengineering M,D
- Biological and Biomedical Sciences—General M,D*
- Biomedical Engineering M,D*
- Biophysics D
- Business Administration and Management—General M,D*
- Chemical Engineering M,D*
- Chemistry M,D
- Child and Family Studies M,D
- Civil Engineering M,D
- Clinical Psychology D
- Communication Disorders M,D
- Communication—General M,D*
- Computer and Information Systems Security O
- Computer Art and Design M
- Computer Engineering M,D,O*
- Computer Science M,D,O
- Corporate and Organizational Communication M
- Counselor Education D
- Curriculum and Instruction M,D,O
- Disability Studies O
- Early Childhood Education M
- Economics M,D
- Education—General M,D,O*
- Educational Administration M,D,O
- Educational Measurement and Evaluation M,D,O
- Educational Media/Instructional Technology M,O
- Electrical Engineering M,D,O
- Engineering and Applied Sciences—General M,D,O*
- Engineering Management M
- English Education M,D
- English M,D
- Entrepreneurship M
- Environmental Engineering M,D
- Exercise and Sports Science M
- Experimental Psychology D
- Film, Television, and Video Production M
- Film, Television, and Video Theory and Criticism M
- Finance and Banking M,D
- Foundations and Philosophy of Education M,D
- French M
- Geography M,D
- Geology M,D
- Graphic Design M
- Health Services Management and Hospital Administration O
- Higher Education M,D
- History M,D
- Human Resources Development D
- Industrial and Manufacturing Management D
- Information Science D
- Information Studies M*
- International Affairs M
- Internet and Interactive Multimedia M
- Journalism M
- Law P
- Library Science M,O
- Linguistics M
- Management Information Systems M,D,O
- Management Strategy and Policy D
- Marketing M,D
- Marriage and Family Therapy M,D
- Mass Communication M,D
- Mathematics Education M,D
- Mathematics M,D
- Mechanical Engineering M,D
- Media Studies M
- Museum Studies M
- Music Education M
- Music M
- Neuroscience M,D
- Nutrition M
- Organizational Behavior D
- Philosophy M,D
- Photography M
- Physics M,D
- Political Science M,D
- Psychology—General D
- Public Administration M,D,O*
- Quantitative Analysis D
- Reading Education M,D
- Rehabilitation Counseling M
- Religion M,D
- Rhetoric M,D
- School Psychology M,D
- Science Education M,D
- Social Psychology M,D
- Social Sciences Education M,O
- Social Sciences M,D
- Social Work M
- Sociology M,D
- Spanish M
- Special Education M,D
- Structural Biology D
- Supply Chain Management M,D
- Telecommunications Management M,O
- Telecommunications M
- Writing M,D

TABOR COLLEGE

- Accounting M
- Business Administration and Management—General M

TAI SOPHIA INSTITUTE FOR THE HEALING ARTS

- Acupuncture and Oriental Medicine M

TALMUDIC COLLEGE OF FLORIDA

- Theology M,D

TARLETON STATE UNIVERSITY

- Accounting M
- Agricultural Education M
- Agricultural Sciences—General M
- Biological and Biomedical Sciences—General M
- Business Administration and Management—General M
- Counseling Psychology M
- Counselor Education M
- Criminal Justice and Criminology M
- Curriculum and Instruction M
- Economics M
- Education—General M,D,O
- Educational Administration M,D,O
- English M
- Environmental Sciences M
- Finance and Banking M
- History M
- Human Resources Management M
- Liberal Studies M
- Management Information Systems M
- Mathematics M
- Physical Education M
- Political Science M
- School Psychology M
- Secondary Education M,D,O
- Special Education M,D,O

TAYLOR UNIVERSITY

- Environmental Sciences M

TAYLOR UNIVERSITY COLLEGE AND SEMINARY

- Cultural Studies P,M,O
- Missions and Missiology P,M,O
- Theology P,M,O

TAYLOR UNIVERSITY FORT WAYNE

- Business Administration and Management—General M

TEACHERS COLLEGE COLUMBIA UNIVERSITY

- Adult Education M,D
- Anthropology M,D*
- Art Education M,D
- Arts Administration M*
- Clinical Psychology M,D
- Communication Disorders M,D*
- Communication—General M,D
- Computer Education M
- Counseling Psychology M,D*
- Curriculum and Instruction M,D*
- Developmental Psychology M,D*
- Early Childhood Education M,D
- Economics M,D
- Education of the Gifted M,D
- Education—General M,D,O
- Educational Administration M,D*
- Educational Measurement and Evaluation M,D
- Educational Media/Instructional Technology M,D
- Educational Psychology M,D*
- Elementary Education M
- English as a Second Language M,D
- English Education M,D
- Foreign Languages Education M,D
- Foundations and Philosophy of Education M,D
- Health Education M,D
- Higher Education M,D
- History M,D
- Industrial and Organizational Psychology M,D
- Interdisciplinary Studies M,D
- International and Comparative Education M,D
- Kinesiology and Movement Studies M,D
- Linguistics M,D
- Mathematics Education M,D*
- Multilingual and Multicultural Education M
- Music Education M,D
- Neuroscience M,D
- Nursing and Healthcare Administration M,D
- Nursing Education M,D
- Nutrition M,D
- Physical Education M,D
- Political Science M,D
- Reading Education M
- Religious Education M,D
- School Psychology M,D
- Science Education M,D
- Social Psychology M,D
- Social Sciences Education M,D
- Sociology M,D
- Special Education M,D,O

- Student Affairs M,D

Close-Up on page 1049.

TÉLÉ-UNIVERSITÉ

- Computer Science M,D
- Distance Education Development M,D
- Finance and Banking M,D

TEMPLE BAPTIST SEMINARY

- Theology P,M,D

TEMPLE UNIVERSITY

- Accounting M,D
- Actuarial Science M
- African-American Studies M,D
- Allied Health—General M,D*
- Allopathic Medicine P
- Anatomy M,D
- Anthropology D
- Applied Mathematics M,D
- Art Education M
- Art History M,D*
- Art/Fine Arts M
- Arts Administration M,D
- Biochemistry M,D*
- Biological and Biomedical Sciences—General M,D*
- Business Administration and Management—General M,D
- Cell Biology M,D
- Chemistry M,D
- Civil Engineering M
- Clinical Psychology D
- Cognitive Sciences D
- Communication Disorders M,D
- Communication—General M,D
- Community Health M
- Computational Sciences M,D
- Computer Engineering M
- Computer Science M,D
- Corporate and Organizational Communication M,D
- Counseling Psychology M,D
- Criminal Justice and Criminology M,D
- Dance M,D
- Dentistry P
- Developmental Psychology D
- Early Childhood Education M,D
- Economics M,D
- Education—General M,D
- Educational Administration M,D
- Educational Psychology M,D
- Electrical Engineering M
- Electronic Commerce M
- Elementary Education M,D
- Engineering and Applied Sciences—General M,D*
- English as a Second Language M,D
- English Education M,D
- English M,D
- Environmental and Occupational Health M
- Epidemiology M
- Film, Television, and Video Production M
- Finance and Banking M,D
- Foreign Languages Education M,D
- Genetics D
- Geography M
- Geology M
- Graphic Design M
- Health Education M
- Health Services Management and Hospital Administration M,D
- History M,D
- Hospitality Management M
- Human Resources Management M,D
- Immunology M,D
- Industrial and Organizational Psychology M
- Information Science M,D
- Insurance M,D
- International Business M,D
- Journalism M
- Kinesiology and Movement Studies M,D
- Law P,M
- Leisure Studies M
- Liberal Studies M
- Linguistics M
- Management Information Systems M,D
- Management Strategy and Policy M,D
- Marketing M,D
- Mass Communication D
- Mathematics Education M,D
- Mathematics M,D
- Mechanical Engineering M
- Media Studies M,D
- Medicinal and Pharmaceutical Chemistry M,D
- Microbiology M,D*
- Molecular Biology D
- Music Education M,D
- Music M,D
- Neuroscience M,D
- Nursing—General M
- Occupational Therapy M
- Operations Research D
- Oral and Dental Sciences M,O
- Pathology D
- Pharmaceutical Sciences M,D*
- Pharmacology M,D
- Pharmacy P
- Philosophy M,D
- Photography M
- Physical Education M,D
- Physical Therapy D
- Physics M,D*
- Physiology D
- Podiatric Medicine P
- Political Science M,D
- Psychology—General D
- Public Health—General M,D
- Reading Education M,D
- Recreation and Park Management M
- Religion M,D
- School Psychology M,D
- Science Education M,D
- Social Psychology D
- Social Work M
- Sociology M,D
- Spanish M,D
- Special Education M,D
- Sports Management M
- Statistics M,D
- Taxation P,M
- Textile Design M
- Theater M
- Therapies—Dance, Drama, and Music M,D
- Travel and Tourism M,D*
- Urban and Regional Planning M
- Urban Education M,D
- Urban Studies M
- Vocational and Technical Education M,D
- Writing M

Close-Up on page 1051 and Announcement on page 604.

TENNESSEE STATE UNIVERSITY

- Agricultural Sciences—General M
- Allied Health—General M,D
- Biological and Biomedical Sciences—General M,D
- Business Administration and Management—General M
- Chemistry M*
- Communication Disorders M
- Counseling Psychology M,D
- Counselor Education M,D
- Criminal Justice and Criminology M
- Curriculum and Instruction M
- Education—General M,D,O
- Educational Administration M,D,O
- Elementary Education M,D
- Engineering and Applied Sciences—General M,D
- English M
- Exercise and Sports Science M
- Family and Consumer Sciences-General M
- Mathematics M
- Music Education M
- Nursing—General M
- Physical Education M
- Physical Therapy M,D
- Psychology—General M,D
- Public Administration M,D
- School Psychology M,D
- Special Education M,D

TENNESSEE TECHNOLOGICAL UNIVERSITY

- Biological and Biomedical Sciences—General M
- Business Administration and Management—General M*
- Chemical Engineering M,D
- Chemistry M
- Civil Engineering M,D
- Computer Science M
- Curriculum and Instruction M,O
- Early Childhood Education M,O
- Education of the Gifted D
- Education—General M,D,O
- Educational Administration M,O
- Educational Psychology M,O
- Electrical Engineering M,D
- Elementary Education M,O
- Engineering and Applied Sciences—General M,D
- English M
- Environmental Biology M
- Environmental Sciences D
- Fish, Game, and Wildlife Management M
- Health Education M
- Kinesiology and Movement Studies M
- Library Science M,O
- Management Strategy and Policy M
- Mathematics M
- Mechanical Engineering M,D
- Nursing—General M
- Physical Education M
- Reading Education M,O
- Secondary Education M,O
- Special Education M,O
- Student Affairs M,O

TENNESSEE TEMPLE UNIVERSITY

- Curriculum and Instruction M
- Education—General M
- Educational Administration M

TEXAS A&M HEALTH SCIENCE CENTER

- Biological and Biomedical Sciences—General M,D*
- Cell Biology D
- Dental Hygiene M
- Dentistry P
- Environmental and Occupational Health M
- Epidemiology M
- Health Education M
- Health Services Management and Hospital Administration M
- Immunology D
- Materials Sciences D
- Microbiology D
- Molecular Biology D
- Molecular Medicine D
- Molecular Pathogenesis D
- Neuroscience D*
- Oral and Dental Sciences P,M,D,O
- Public Health—General M
- Systems Biology D
- Virology D

TEXAS A&M INTERNATIONAL UNIVERSITY

- Accounting M
- Art/Fine Arts
- Biological and Biomedical Sciences—General M
- Business Administration and Management—General M
- Counseling Psychology M
- Counselor Education M
- Criminal Justice and Criminology M
- Curriculum and Instruction M,D
- Early Childhood Education M,D
- Education—General M,D
- Educational Administration M
- English M,D
- Finance and Banking M
- Foreign Languages Education M,D
- Hispanic Studies M,D
- History M
- International Business M
- Management Information Systems M
- Mathematics M
- Multilingual and Multicultural Education M,D
- Music M
- Nursing—General M
- Physics M
- Political Science M
- Psychology—General M
- Public Administration M
- Reading Education M,D
- Social Sciences M
- Sociology M
- Spanish M,D
- Special Education M

TEXAS A&M UNIVERSITY

- Accounting M,D
- Aerospace/Aeronautical Engineering M,D
- Agricultural Economics and Agribusiness M,D
- Agricultural Education M,D
- Agricultural Engineering M,D
- Agricultural Sciences—General M,D
- Agronomy and Soil Sciences M,D
- Anatomy M,D
- Animal Sciences M,D
- Anthropology M,D
- Applied Physics M,D
- Architecture M,D
- Biochemistry M,D
- Bioengineering M,D
- Biological and Biomedical Sciences—General M,D
- Biomedical Engineering M,D
- Biophysics M,D
- Biopsychology M,D
- Botany M,D
- Business Administration and Management—General M,D
- Cell Biology M,D
- Chemical Engineering M,D
- Chemistry M,D*
- Civil Engineering M,D
- Clinical Psychology M,D
- Cognitive Sciences M,D
- Communication—General M,D
- Computer Engineering M,D
- Computer Science M,D*
- Construction Engineering M,D
- Construction Management M
- Counseling Psychology M,D
- Counselor Education M,D
- Curriculum and Instruction M,D
- Developmental Psychology M,D
- Economics M,D
- Education of the Gifted M,D
- Education—General M,D
- Educational Administration M,D
- Educational Measurement and Evaluation M,D
- Educational Media/Instructional Technology M,D
- Educational Psychology M,D
- Electrical Engineering M,D
- Engineering and Applied Sciences—General M,D
- English Education M,D
- English M,D
- Entomology M,D
- Environmental Engineering M,D
- Epidemiology M,D
- Finance and Banking M,D
- Fish, Game, and Wildlife Management M,D
- Food Science and Technology M,D
- Forestry M,D
- Foundations and Philosophy of Education M,D
- Genetics M,D
- Geography M,D
- Geology M,D
- Geophysics M,D
- Geotechnical Engineering M,D
- Health Education M,D
- Health Physics/Radiological Health M,D
- History M,D
- Horticulture M,D
- Human Development M,D
- Human Resources Development M,D
- Human Resources Management M,D
- Industrial and Manufacturing Management M,D
- Industrial and Organizational Psychology M,D
- Industrial/Management Engineering M,D
- Interdisciplinary Studies M,D
- International Affairs M
- Journalism M
- Kinesiology and Movement Studies M,D
- Landscape Architecture M,D
- Management Information Systems M,D
- Manufacturing Engineering M
- Marketing M,D
- Materials Engineering M,D
- Mathematics Education M,D
- Mathematics M,D
- Mechanical Engineering M,D
- Meteorology M,D
- Microbiology M,D
- Multilingual and Multicultural Education M,D
- Natural Resources M,D
- Neuroscience M,D*
- Nuclear Engineering M,D
- Ocean Engineering M,D
- Oceanography M,D
- Parasitology M,D
- Pathobiology M,D
- Pathology M,D
- Petroleum Engineering M,D
- Philosophy M,D
- Physical Education M,D
- Physics M,D
- Physiology M,D
- Plant Biology M,D
- Plant Pathology M,D
- Plant Sciences M,D
- Political Science M,D
- Project Management M,D
- Psychology—General M,D
- Public Administration M
- Public Affairs M*
- Public Health—General M,D
- Range Science M,D
- Reading Education M,D
- Real Estate M
- Recreation and Park Management M,D
- School Psychology M,D
- Science Education M,D
- Social Psychology M,D
- Sociology M,D*
- Spanish M,D
- Special Education M,D
- Statistics M,D
- Structural Engineering M,D
- Toxicology M,D
- Transportation and Highway Engineering M,D
- Urban and Regional Planning M,D

Program	Degrees
Urban Education	M,D
Veterinary Medicine	P,M
Veterinary Sciences	M
Water Resources Engineering	M,D
Zoology	M,D

TEXAS A&M UNIVERSITY AT GALVESTON

Program	Degrees
Marine Sciences	M

TEXAS A&M UNIVERSITY–COMMERCE

Program	Degrees
Agricultural Education	M
Agricultural Sciences—General	M
Art History	M
Art/Fine Arts	M
Biological and Biomedical Sciences—General	M
Business Administration and Management—General	M
Chemistry	M
Computer Science	M
Counseling Psychology	M,D
Counselor Education	M,D
Curriculum and Instruction	M,D
Early Childhood Education	M,D
Economics	M
Education—General	M,D
Educational Administration	M,D
Educational Media/Instructional Technology	M,D
Educational Psychology	M,D
Elementary Education	M,D
English Education	M,D
English	M,D
Geosciences	M
Health Education	M,D
Higher Education	M,D
History	M
Industrial/Management Engineering	M
Kinesiology and Movement Studies	M,D
Management of Technology	M
Mathematics	M
Music Education	M
Music	M
Physical Education	M,D
Physics	M
Psychology—General	M,D
Reading Education	M,D
Secondary Education	M,D
Social Sciences Education	M
Social Sciences	M
Social Work	M
Sociology	M
Spanish	M,D
Special Education	M,D
Speech and Interpersonal Communication	M
Theater	M

TEXAS A&M UNIVERSITY–CORPUS CHRISTI

Program	Degrees
Accounting	M
Applied Mathematics	M
Aquaculture	M
Art/Fine Arts	M
Biological and Biomedical Sciences—General	M
Business Administration and Management—General	M
Computer Science	M
Counselor Education	M,D
Curriculum and Instruction	M,D
Early Childhood Education	M,D
Education—General	M,D
Educational Administration	M,D
Educational Media/Instructional Technology	M,D
Elementary Education	M
English	M
Environmental Sciences	M
Family Nurse Practitioner Studies	M
Health Services Management and Hospital Administration	M
History	M
International Business	M
Kinesiology and Movement Studies	M,D
Marine Sciences	D
Mathematics Education	M
Mathematics	M
Nursing and Healthcare Administration	M
Nursing—General	M
Psychology—General	M
Public Administration	M
Reading Education	M,D
Secondary Education	M
Special Education	M
Vocational and Technical Education	M

TEXAS A&M UNIVERSITY–KINGSVILLE

Program	Degrees
Adult Education	M
Agricultural Economics and Agribusiness	M
Agricultural Education	M
Agricultural Sciences—General	M,D
Agronomy and Soil Sciences	M,D
Animal Sciences	M
Art/Fine Arts	M
Biological and Biomedical Sciences—General	M
Business Administration and Management—General	M
Chemical Engineering	M
Chemistry	M
Civil Engineering	M
Communication Disorders	M
Computer Science	M
Counselor Education	M
Early Childhood Education	M
Education—General	M,D
Educational Administration	M,D
Electrical Engineering	M
Elementary Education	M
Engineering and Applied Sciences—General	M,D
English as a Second Language	M
English	M
Environmental Engineering	M,D
Family and Consumer Sciences-General	M
Fish, Game, and Wildlife Management	M,D
Foreign Languages Education	M
Geology	M
Gerontology	M
Health Education	M
Higher Education	D
History	M
Industrial/Management Engineering	M
Kinesiology and Movement Studies	M
Mathematics	M
Mechanical Engineering	M
Multilingual and Multicultural Education	M,D
Music Education	M
Petroleum Engineering	M
Plant Sciences	M,D
Political Science	M
Psychology—General	M
Range Science	M
Reading Education	M
Secondary Education	M
Sociology	M
Spanish	M
Special Education	M

Close-Up on page 1053.

TEXAS A&M UNIVERSITY–TEXARKANA

Program	Degrees
Accounting	M
Adult Education	M
Business Administration and Management—General	M
Counseling Psychology	M
Curriculum and Instruction	M
Education—General	M
Educational Administration	M
Educational Media/Instructional Technology	M
English	M
History	M
Interdisciplinary Studies	M
Psychology—General	M
Special Education	M

TEXAS CHIROPRACTIC COLLEGE

Program	Degrees
Chiropractic	P

TEXAS CHRISTIAN UNIVERSITY

Program	Degrees
Accounting	M
Adult Nursing	M
Advertising and Public Relations	M
Allied Health—General	M
Art History	M
Art/Fine Arts	M
Astronomy	M,D
Astrophysics	M,D
Biological and Biomedical Sciences—General	M
Business Administration and Management—General	M,D
Chemistry	M,D
Communication Disorders	M
Counselor Education	M,O
Ecology	M
Education—General	M,D,O
Educational Administration	M
Educational Measurement and Evaluation	M
Educational Psychology	M,O
Elementary Education	M,O
English	M,D
Environmental Sciences	M
Geology	M
Geosciences	M
History	M,D
International Business	M
Journalism	M
Kinesiology and Movement Studies	M
Liberal Studies	M
Mathematics	M
Music Education	M,O
Music	M,O
Nurse Anesthesia	M
Nursing—General	M
Pastoral Ministry and Counseling	P,M,D,O
Physics	M,D
Psychology—General	M,D
Science Education	M,D
Special Education	M
Speech and Interpersonal Communication	M
Theology	P,M,D,O

TEXAS COLLEGE OF TRADITIONAL CHINESE MEDICINE

Program	Degrees
Acupuncture and Oriental Medicine	M

TEXAS SOUTHERN UNIVERSITY

Program	Degrees
Biological and Biomedical Sciences—General	M
Business Administration and Management—General	M
Chemistry	M
Communication—General	M
Computer Science	M
Counselor Education	M,D
Curriculum and Instruction	M,D
Early Childhood Education	M,D
Education—General	M,D
Educational Administration	M,D
Educational Measurement and Evaluation	M,D
Elementary Education	M,D
English	M
Family and Consumer Sciences-General	M
Health Education	M
Higher Education	M,D
History	M
Human Development	M
Human Services	M
Industrial/Management Engineering	M
Journalism	M
Law	P
Mathematics	M
Media Studies	M
Multilingual and Multicultural Education	M,D
Music	M
Nutrition	M
Pharmacy	P,M
Physical Education	M
Psychology—General	M
Public Administration	M
Reading Education	M,D
Secondary Education	M,D
Sociology	M
Special Education	M,D
Speech and Interpersonal Communication	M
Toxicology	M,D
Transportation and Highway Engineering	M
Urban and Regional Planning	M
Urban Education	M,D

TEXAS STATE UNIVERSITY-SAN MARCOS

Program	Degrees
Accounting	M
Agricultural Education	M
Allied Health—General	M
Anthropology	M
Applied Mathematics	M
Biochemistry	M
Biological and Biomedical Sciences—General	M
Business Administration and Management—General	M
Chemistry	M
Child and Family Studies	M
Communication Disorders	M
Communication—General	M
Computer Science	M*
Conservation Biology	M
Counselor Education	M
Criminal Justice and Criminology	M
Developmental Education	M,D
Early Childhood Education	M
Education—General	M,D
Educational Administration	M
Elementary Education	M
English	M
Environmental Management and Policy	M
Fish, Game, and Wildlife Management	M
Geographic Information Systems	M,D
Geography	M,D
Health Education	M
Health Psychology	M
Health Services Management and Hospital Administration	M
Health Services Research	M
History	M
Industrial/Management Engineering	M
Interdisciplinary Studies	M
International Affairs	M
Legal and Justice Studies	M
Leisure Studies	M
Management of Technology	M
Marine Biology	M
Mass Communication	M
Mathematics Education	M
Mathematics	M
Multilingual and Multicultural Education	M
Music Education	M
Music	M
Physical Education	M
Physical Therapy	M
Physics	M
Political Science	M
Psychology—General	M
Public Administration	M
Reading Education	M
Recreation and Park Management	M
Rhetoric	M
School Psychology	M
Science Education	M
Secondary Education	M
Social Sciences Education	D
Social Work	M
Sociology	M
Software Engineering	M
Spanish	M
Special Education	M
Technical Communication	M
Theater	M
Vocational and Technical Education	M
Writing	M

TEXAS TECH UNIVERSITY

Program	Degrees
Accounting	M,D
Agricultural Economics and Agribusiness	M,D
Agricultural Education	M,D
Agricultural Sciences—General	M,D
Agronomy and Soil Sciences	M,D
Animal Sciences	M,D
Anthropology	M
Applied Economics	M,D
Applied Physics	M,D
Architecture	M
Art Education	M
Art/Fine Arts	M
Atmospheric Sciences	M,D
Bioinformatics	M,D
Biological and Biomedical Sciences—General	M,D
Biotechnology	M
Business Administration and Management—General	M,D
Chemical Engineering	M,D
Chemistry	M,D
Child and Family Studies	M,D
Civil Engineering	M,D
Classics	M
Clinical Psychology	M,D
Communication—General	M
Computer Science	M,D
Consumer Economics	D
Counseling Psychology	M,D
Counselor Education	M,D,O
Curriculum and Instruction	M,D
Dance	M,D
Economics	M,D
Education—General	M,D,O
Educational Administration	M,D,O
Educational Media/Instructional Technology	M,D,O
Educational Psychology	M,D,O
Electrical Engineering	M,D
Elementary Education	M,D
Engineering and Applied Sciences—General	M,D
Engineering Management	M,D
English Education	M,D
English	M,D
Entomology	M,D
Entrepreneurship	M
Environmental Design	M,D
Environmental Engineering	M,D
Environmental Management and Policy	M,D
Environmental Sciences	M,D
Exercise and Sports Science	M
Experimental Psychology	M,D
Family and Consumer Sciences-General	M,D,O
Finance and Banking	M,D
Fish, Game, and Wildlife Management	M,D
Food Science and Technology	M,D
French	M
Geosciences	M,D
German	M
Gerontology	M,D
Health Services Management and Hospital Administration	M,D
Higher Education	M,D,O
Historic Preservation	M

History M,D
Home Economics Education M,D,O
Horticulture M,D
Hospitality Management M,D
Human Development M,D
Humanities M,D
Industrial and Manufacturing Management M,D
Industrial/Management Engineering M,D
Interdisciplinary Studies M
International Business M
Landscape Architecture M
Law P
Linguistics M
Management Information Systems M,D
Manufacturing Engineering M,D
Marketing M,D
Marriage and Family Therapy M,D,O
Mass Communication M,D
Mathematics M,D
Mechanical Engineering M,D
Microbiology M,D
Multilingual and Multicultural Education M,D
Museum Studies M
Music Education M,D
Music M,D
Nutrition M,D
Petroleum Engineering M,D
Philosophy M
Physics M,D
Plant Sciences M,D
Political Science M,D
Psychology—General M,D
Public Administration M,D
Quantitative Analysis M,D
Range Science M,D
Reading Education M,D
Rhetoric M,D
Romance Languages M,D
Secondary Education M,D
Sociology M
Software Engineering M,D
Spanish M,D
Special Education M,D,O
Statistics M
Systems Engineering M,D
Technical Writing M,D
Theater M,D
Toxicology M,D
Urban and Regional Planning M
Zoology M,D
Close-Up on page 1055.

TEXAS TECH UNIVERSITY HEALTH SCIENCES CENTER
Acute Care/Critical Care Nursing M,O
Allied Health—General M,D
Allopathic Medicine P
Athletic Training and Sports Medicine M
Biochemistry M,D
Biological and Biomedical Sciences—General M,D
Biotechnology M
Cell Biology M,D
Clinical Research M,O
Communication Disorders M,D
Family Nurse Practitioner Studies M,O
Gerontological Nursing M,O
Health Services Management and Hospital Administration M
Medical Microbiology M,D
Molecular Genetics M,D
Molecular Pathology M
Neuroscience M,D
Nursing and Healthcare Administration M,O
Nursing Education M,O
Nursing—General M,O
Occupational Therapy M
Pediatric Nursing M,O
Pharmaceutical Sciences M,D
Pharmacology M,D
Physical Therapy M,D
Physician Assistant Studies M
Physiology M,D
Rehabilitation Counseling M

TEXAS WESLEYAN UNIVERSITY
Business Administration and Management—General M
Counseling Psychology M
Counselor Education M
Education—General M
Gerontological Nursing M
Health Services Management and Hospital Administration M
Law P
Nurse Anesthesia M
Public Health—General M

TEXAS WOMAN'S UNIVERSITY
Adult Nursing M,D
Allied Health—General M,D
Art/Fine Arts M
Biological and Biomedical Sciences—General M,D
Business Administration and Management—General M
Chemistry M
Child and Family Studies M,D
Child Development M,D
Communication Disorders M
Counseling Psychology M,D,O
Counselor Education M,D
Dance M,D
Early Childhood Education M,D
Education—General M,D
Educational Administration M,D
Elementary Education M,D
English M,D
Exercise and Sports Science M,D
Food Science and Technology M,D
Health Education M,D
Health Services Management and Hospital Administration M,D
History M
Hospitality Management M,D
Kinesiology and Movement Studies M,D
Library Science M,D
Marriage and Family Therapy M,D
Mathematics Education M,D
Mathematics M
Molecular Biology M,D
Music M
Nursing Education M,D
Nursing—General M,D
Nutrition M,D
Occupational Therapy M,D
Physical Therapy M,D
Political Science M
Psychology—General M,D,O
Reading Education M,D
Rhetoric M,D
School Psychology M,D,O
Science Education M,D
Sociology M,D
Special Education M,D
Theater M
Women's Studies M

THOMAS COLLEGE
Business Administration and Management—General M
Business Education M
Computer Education M
Human Resources Management M

THOMAS EDISON STATE COLLEGE
Business Administration and Management—General M
Educational Media/Instructional Technology M
Human Resources Management M
Liberal Studies M
Nursing—General M
Organizational Management M
Public Administration M
Close-Up on page 1057.

THOMAS JEFFERSON SCHOOL OF LAW
Law P

THOMAS JEFFERSON UNIVERSITY
Allopathic Medicine P
Biochemistry D*
Biological and Biomedical Sciences—General M,D,O*
Biomedical Engineering D
Biophysics D
Biotechnology D
Cell Biology M,D
Clinical Laboratory Sciences/Medical Technology M
Clinical Research O
Developmental Biology M,D
Genetics D*
Health Services Research O
Immunology D*
Marriage and Family Therapy M*
Microbiology M,D
Molecular Biology D
Molecular Pharmacology D
Molecular Physiology D
Neuroscience D
Nursing—General M*
Occupational Therapy M
Pharmacology M*
Pharmacy P*
Physical Therapy M,D
Public Health—General M
Structural Biology D
Close-Up on page 1059.

THOMAS M. COOLEY LAW SCHOOL
Law P,M

THOMAS MORE COLLEGE
Business Administration and Management—General M

THOMAS UNIVERSITY
Business Administration and Management—General M
Education—General M
Human Services M
Nursing—General M
Rehabilitation Counseling M
Social Psychology M

THUNDERBIRD SCHOOL OF GLOBAL MANAGEMENT
Business Administration and Management—General M
International Business M

TIFFIN UNIVERSITY
Business Administration and Management—General M
Criminal Justice and Criminology M
Forensic Psychology M
Homeland Security M
Humanities M
Sports Management M

TORONTO SCHOOL OF THEOLOGY
Theology P,M,D

TOURO COLLEGE
Biological and Biomedical Sciences—General M
Health Informatics M,O
Health Services Management and Hospital Administration O
Jewish Studies M
Law P,M
Occupational Therapy M
Physical Therapy M

TOURO UNIVERSITY COLLEGE OF OSTEOPATHIC MEDICINE
Education—General P,M
Osteopathic Medicine P,M
Pharmacy P,M
Physician Assistant Studies P,M
Public Health—General P,M

TOURO UNIVERSITY INTERNATIONAL
Adult Education M
Business Administration and Management—General M,D
Clinical Research M,D,O
Conflict Resolution and Mediation/Peace Studies M,D
Criminal Justice and Criminology M,D
Early Childhood Education M
Education—General M,D,O
Educational Administration M,D
Educational Media/Instructional Technology M,D
Emergency Management M,D,O
Environmental and Occupational Health M,D,O
Finance and Banking M,D
Health Education M,D,O
Health Informatics M,D,O
Health Services Management and Hospital Administration M,D,O
Higher Education M,D
Human Resources Management M,D
International Business M,D
International Health M,D,O
Legal and Justice Studies M,D,O
Logistics M,D
Management Information Systems M,D,O
Nursing and Healthcare Administration M,D,O
Public Administration M,D,O
Public Health—General M,D,O
Quality Management M,D,O
Reading Education M

TOWSON UNIVERSITY
Accounting M
Advertising and Public Relations O
Allied Health—General M
Applied Mathematics M
Art Education M
Art/Fine Arts M
Biological and Biomedical Sciences—General M
Business Administration and Management—General M
Child and Family Studies O
Clinical Psychology M
Communication Disorders M,D
Communication—General M,O
Computer and Information Systems Security O
Computer Science M
Corporate and Organizational Communication M
Counseling Psychology M,O
Early Childhood Education M,O
Education—General M
Educational Administration M,O
Educational Media/Instructional Technology M,D
Elementary Education M
Environmental and Occupational Health D
Environmental Management and Policy M
Environmental Sciences M,O
Experimental Psychology M
Geography M
Gerontology M,O
Health Services Management and Hospital Administration O
Homeland Security M,O
Human Resources Development M,O
Humanities M
Information Science O
Internet and Interactive Multimedia M,D,O
Liberal Studies M
Management Information Systems M,D,O
Management Strategy and Policy O
Mathematics Education M
Music Education M,O
Music M
Nursing—General M,O
Occupational Therapy M
Organizational Behavior O
Physician Assistant Studies M
Reading Education M,O
School Psychology M,O
Science Education M
Secondary Education M
Social Sciences M
Software Engineering M,D,O
Special Education M
Theater M
Women's Studies M
Writing M

TRADITIONAL CHINESE MEDICAL COLLEGE OF HAWAII
Acupuncture and Oriental Medicine M

TRENT UNIVERSITY
American Indian/Native American Studies M,D
Anthropology M
Biological and Biomedical Sciences—General M,D
Canadian Studies M
Chemistry M
Computer Science M
Environmental Management and Policy M,D
Geography M,D
History M
Physics M

TREVECCA NAZARENE UNIVERSITY
Business Administration and Management—General M
Counseling Psychology M
Counselor Education M
Curriculum and Instruction M
Education—General M,D
Educational Administration M,D
Elementary Education M
English as a Second Language M
Information Science M
Library Science M
Marriage and Family Therapy M
Organizational Management M
Physician Assistant Studies M
Reading Education M
Religion M
Secondary Education M
Theology M
Vocational and Technical Education M

TRINITY BAPTIST COLLEGE
Education—General M
Educational Administration M
Pastoral Ministry and Counseling M
Religious Education M
Special Education M

TRINITY COLLEGE
American Studies M
Economics M
English M

History M
Public Policy M

TRINITY EPISCOPAL SCHOOL FOR MINISTRY

Missions and Missiology P,M,D,O
Pastoral Ministry and Counseling P,M,D,O
Religion P,M,D,O
Theology P,M,D,O

TRINITY INTERNATIONAL UNIVERSITY

Archaeology P,M,D,O
Bioethics M
Business Administration and Management—General P,M,D,O
Communication—General M
Counseling Psychology P,M,D,O
Education—General M
Educational Administration M
Law P
Missions and Missiology P,M,D,O
Pastoral Ministry and Counseling P,M,D,O
Religion P,M,D,O
Religious Education P,M,D,O
Theology P,M,D,O

TRINITY INTERNATIONAL UNIVERSITY, SOUTH FLORIDA CAMPUS

Counseling Psychology M
Religion M

TRINITY LUTHERAN SEMINARY

Music P,M
Theology P,M

TRINITY UNIVERSITY

Accounting M
Business Administration and Management—General M
Education—General M
Educational Administration M
Health Services Management and Hospital Administration M*
School Psychology M

TRINITY (WASHINGTON) UNIVERSITY

Business Administration and Management—General M
Communication—General M
Counselor Education M
Early Childhood Education M
Education—General M
Educational Administration M
Elementary Education M
English as a Second Language M
English Education M
Human Resources Management M
Mathematics Education M
Nonprofit Management M
Organizational Management M
Public Health—General M
Reading Education M
Science Education M
Secondary Education M
Social Sciences Education M
Special Education M

TRINITY WESTERN UNIVERSITY

Counseling Psychology M
Educational Administration M
English as a Second Language M
Organizational Management M
Pastoral Ministry and Counseling P,M
Theology P,M

TRI STATE COLLEGE OF ACUPUNCTURE

Acupuncture and Oriental Medicine M,O

TRI-STATE UNIVERSITY

Engineering and Applied Sciences—General M

TROPICAL AGRICULTURE RESEARCH AND HIGHER EDUCATION CENTER

Agricultural Sciences—General M,D
Conservation Biology M,D
Environmental Management and Policy M,D
Forestry M,D
Water Resources M,D

TROY UNIVERSITY

Adult Education M
Art/Fine Arts M
Business Administration and Management—General M
Clinical Psychology M
Communication—General M
Computer Science M
Counselor Education M,O
Criminal Justice and Criminology M
Early Childhood Education M,O
Education—General M,O
Educational Administration M,O
Elementary Education M,O
Environmental Management and Policy M
Human Resources Management M
International Affairs M
Nursing—General M
Public Administration M
Rehabilitation Counseling M,O
School Psychology M
Secondary Education M,O
Sports Management M

TRUMAN STATE UNIVERSITY

Accounting M
Biological and Biomedical Sciences—General M
Communication Disorders M
Education—General M
English M
Music M

Close-Up on page 1061.

TUFTS UNIVERSITY

Allopathic Medicine P
Analytical Chemistry M,D
Archaeology M
Art History M
Art/Fine Arts M
Biochemistry D
Bioengineering O
Biological and Biomedical Sciences—General M,D*
Biomedical Engineering M,D
Biostatistics M,D
Biotechnology O
Cell Biology D
Chemical Engineering M,D
Chemistry M,D*
Child and Family Studies M,D,O
Child Development M,D,O*
Civil Engineering M,D
Classics M
Clinical Research M,D
Computer Science M,D,O
Conflict Resolution and Mediation/Peace Studies M,D
Dance M,D
Dentistry P
Developmental Biology D
Developmental Psychology M,D,O
Early Childhood Education M,D,O
Economics M
Education—General M,D,O
Electrical Engineering M,D,O
Elementary Education M,D
Engineering and Applied Sciences—General M,D*
Engineering Management M
English M,D
Environmental and Occupational Health M,D
Environmental Engineering M,D
Environmental Management and Policy M,D,O
Environmental Sciences M,D
Epidemiology M,D,O
Ergonomics and Human Factors M,D
Family and Consumer Sciences-General M,D,O
French M
Genetics D
Geotechnical Engineering M,D
German M
Hazardous Materials Management M,D
Health Communication M
History M,D
Human-Computer Interaction O
Immunology D
Inorganic Chemistry M,D
International Affairs M,D*
International and Comparative Education M,D
International Business M,D
International Development M,D
International Health M,D
Management Strategy and Policy O
Manufacturing Engineering O
Mathematics M,D
Mechanical Engineering M,D
Medieval and Renaissance Studies M,D
Microbiology D
Middle School Education M,D
Molecular Biology D
Molecular Physiology D
Museum Studies O
Music M
Neuroscience D
Nonprofit Management O
Nutrition M,D
Occupational Therapy M,D,O
Oral and Dental Sciences M,O
Organic Chemistry M,D
Pharmacology D
Philosophy M
Physical Chemistry M,D
Physics M,D
Physiology D
Psychology—General M,D
Public Administration O
Public Health—General M
Public Policy M*
School Psychology M,O
Secondary Education M,D
Structural Engineering M,D
Theater M,D*
Urban and Regional Planning M
Urban Studies M
Veterinary Medicine P
Veterinary Sciences M,D
Water Resources Engineering M,D

Close-Up on page 1063.

TULANE UNIVERSITY

Allopathic Medicine P
Anthropology M,D
Applied Mathematics M,D
Architecture M
Art History M
Art/Fine Arts M
Biochemistry M,D
Biological and Biomedical Sciences—General M,D
Biomedical Engineering M,D
Biostatistics M,D
Business Administration and Management—General M,D
Cell Biology M,D
Chemical Engineering M,D
Chemistry M,D
Civil Engineering M,D
Classics M
Computer Science M,D
Dance M
Ecology M,D
Economics M,D
Electrical Engineering M,D
English M,D
Environmental and Occupational Health M,D
Environmental Engineering M,D
Epidemiology M,D
Evolutionary Biology M,D
French M,D
Geology M,D
Health Communication M
Health Education M
Health Services Management and Hospital Administration M,D
History M,D
Human Genetics M,D
Immunology M,D
Infectious Diseases M,D,O
International Development M,D
International Health M,D
Latin American Studies M,D*
Law P,M,D
Liberal Studies M
Maternal and Child Health M,D
Mathematics M,D
Mechanical Engineering M,D
Microbiology M,D
Molecular Biology M,D
Music M
Neuroscience M,D
Nutrition M
Paleontology M,D
Parasitology M,D,O
Pharmacology M,D
Philosophy M,D
Physics M,D
Physiology M,D
Political Science M,D
Portuguese M,D
Psychology—General M,D
Public Health—General M,D,O
Social Work M
Sociology M,D
Spanish M,D
Statistics M,D
Structural Biology M,D
Theater M

TUSCULUM COLLEGE

Adult Education M
Education—General M
Organizational Management M

TUSKEGEE UNIVERSITY

Agricultural Economics and Agribusiness M
Agricultural Sciences—General M
Agronomy and Soil Sciences M
Animal Sciences M
Biological and Biomedical Sciences—General M,D
Chemistry M
Electrical Engineering M
Engineering and Applied Sciences—General M,D
Environmental Sciences M
Food Science and Technology M
Materials Engineering D
Mechanical Engineering M
Nutrition M
Plant Sciences M
Veterinary Sciences P,M

TYNDALE UNIVERSITY COLLEGE & SEMINARY

Missions and Missiology P,M,O
Pastoral Ministry and Counseling P,M,O
Theology P,M,O

UNIFICATION THEOLOGICAL SEMINARY

Theology P,M,D

UNIFORMED SERVICES UNIVERSITY OF THE HEALTH SCIENCES

Allopathic Medicine P
Biological and Biomedical Sciences—General M,D*
Cell Biology D
Clinical Psychology D
Environmental and Occupational Health M,D
Family Nurse Practitioner Studies M
History of Medicine M
History of Science and Technology M,D
Immunology D
Infectious Diseases D*
International Health M,D
Microbiology D*
Molecular Biology D*
Neuroscience D*
Nurse Anesthesia M
Nursing—General M
Pathobiology D
Pathology D
Psychology—General D
Public Health—General M,D
Zoology M,D

UNION COLLEGE (KY)

Education—General M
Educational Administration M,O
Elementary Education M
Health Education M
Middle School Education M
Music Education M
Physical Education M
Reading Education M
Secondary Education M
Special Education M

UNION COLLEGE (NE)

Physician Assistant Studies M

UNION GRADUATE COLLEGE

Bioethics M*
Business Administration and Management—General M,O*
Computer Science M
Education—General M*
Electrical Engineering M
Engineering and Applied Sciences—General M
Engineering Management M
English Education M
Finance and Banking M,O
Foreign Languages Education M
Health Services Management and Hospital Administration M,O
Mathematics Education M
Mechanical Engineering M
Science Education M
Social Sciences Education M

UNION INSTITUTE & UNIVERSITY

Art/Fine Arts M
Clinical Psychology D
Education—General M,O
Interdisciplinary Studies M,D
Psychology—General M,D
Writing M

UNION THEOLOGICAL SEMINARY AND PRESBYTERIAN SCHOOL OF CHRISTIAN EDUCATION

Religious Education M
Theology P,M,D

UNION THEOLOGICAL SEMINARY IN THE CITY OF NEW YORK

Theology P,M,D

UNION UNIVERSITY

Business Administration and Management—General M

Cultural Studies M
Education—General M,D,O
Educational Administration M,D,O
Higher Education M,D,O
Nurse Anesthesia M,O
Nursing Education M,O
Nursing—General M,O
Religion M

UNITED STATES ARMY COMMAND AND GENERAL STAFF COLLEGE

Military and Defense Studies M

UNITED STATES INTERNATIONAL UNIVERSITY

Business Administration and Management—General M
Counseling Psychology M
Finance and Banking M
International Affairs M
Management Information Systems M
Management Strategy and Policy M
Marketing M

UNITED STATES SPORTS ACADEMY

Athletic Training and Sports Medicine M
Exercise and Sports Science M
Physical Education M
Sports Management M,D*

UNITED TALMUDICAL SEMINARY

Theology

UNITED THEOLOGICAL SEMINARY

Theology P,M,D

UNITED THEOLOGICAL SEMINARY OF THE TWIN CITIES

Art/Fine Arts M
Pastoral Ministry and Counseling M,D
Religion M,O
Theology P,M,O
Women's Studies M

UNIVERSIDAD ADVENTISTA DE LAS ANTILLAS

Education—General M

UNIVERSIDAD AUTONOMA DE GUADALAJARA

Allopathic Medicine P
Architecture M,D
Business Administration and Management—General M,D
Computer Science M,D
Education—General M,D
International Business M,D
Manufacturing Engineering M,D
Systems Science M,D

UNIVERSIDAD CENTRAL DEL CARIBE

Addictions/Substance Abuse Counseling M
Allopathic Medicine P,M
Anatomy M
Biochemistry M
Biological and Biomedical Sciences—General M
Cell Biology M
Immunology M
Microbiology M
Pharmacology M
Physiology M

UNIVERSIDAD CENTRAL DEL ESTE

Accounting M
Allopathic Medicine P
Architecture M
Business Administration and Management—General M
Civil Engineering M
Human Resources Development M
Industrial/Management Engineering M
Law P
Mechanical Engineering M
Public Health—General M

UNIVERSIDAD DE CIENCIAS MEDICAS

Allopathic Medicine P,M
Health Services Management and Hospital Administration P,M
Pharmacy P,M

UNIVERSIDAD DE IBEROAMERICA

Acute Care/Critical Care Nursing P,M
Allopathic Medicine P,M
Clinical Psychology P,M
Educational Psychology P,M
Health Services Management and Hospital Administration P,M

UNIVERSIDAD DE LAS AMERICAS, A.C.

Business Administration and Management—General M
Education—General M
Finance and Banking M
International Affairs M
Marketing Research M
Marriage and Family Therapy M
Organizational Behavior M
Psychology—General M
Quality Management M

UNIVERSIDAD DE LAS AMÉRICAS–PUEBLA

American Studies M
Anthropology M
Archaeology M
Biotechnology M
Business Administration and Management—General M
Chemical Engineering M
Clinical Laboratory Sciences/Medical Technology M
Computer Art and Design M
Computer Science M,D
Construction Management M
Economics M
Education—General M
Electrical Engineering M
Engineering and Applied Sciences—General M,D
English M
Finance and Banking M
Food Science and Technology M
Industrial and Manufacturing Management M
Industrial/Management Engineering M
Linguistics M
Manufacturing Engineering M
Psychology—General M

UNIVERSIDAD DEL ESTE

Accounting M
Business Administration and Management—General M
Criminal Justice and Criminology M
Education—General M
Educational Administration M
Elementary Education M
English as a Second Language M
Foreign Languages Education M
Human Resources Management M
Social Work M

UNIVERSIDAD DEL TURABO

Accounting M
Business Administration and Management—General M,D
Criminal Justice and Criminology M
Education—General M
Educational Administration M
English as a Second Language M
Environmental Management and Policy M
Human Services M
Logistics M
Management Information Systems D
Marketing M
Multilingual and Multicultural Education M
Special Education M

UNIVERSIDAD IBEROAMERICANA

Allopathic Medicine P
Dentistry P,M
Education—General P,M
International Business P,M

UNIVERSIDAD METROPOLITANA

Accounting M,O
Business Administration and Management—General M,O
Curriculum and Instruction M
Early Childhood Education M
Education—General M
Educational Administration M
Environmental Education M
Environmental Management and Policy M
Finance and Banking M
Human Resources Management M
International Business M
Leisure Studies M
Marketing M
Physical Education M
Recreation and Park Management M
Special Education M

UNIVERSIDAD NACIONAL PEDRO HENRIQUEZ URENA

Accounting P,M,D
Allopathic Medicine P
Animal Sciences P,M,D
Architecture P,M,D
Business Administration and Management—General P,M,D
Construction Engineering P,M,D
Dentistry P
Economics P,M,D
Education—General P,M,D
Environmental Engineering P,M,D
Environmental Management and Policy P,M,D
Health Services Management and Hospital Administration P,M,D
Historic Preservation P,M,D
Horticulture P,M,D
Humanities P,M,D
International Affairs P,M,D
Project Management P,M,D
Public Administration P,M,D
Social Sciences P,M,D
Veterinary Medicine P,M,D

UNIVERSITÉ DE MONCTON

Astronomy M
Biochemistry M
Biological and Biomedical Sciences—General M
Business Administration and Management—General M
Chemistry M
Civil Engineering M
Computer Science M,O
Counselor Education M
Economics M
Education—General M
Educational Administration M
Educational Psychology M
Electrical Engineering M
Engineering and Applied Sciences—General M
Food Science and Technology M
French M,D
History M
Industrial/Management Engineering M
Law P,M,O
Mathematics M
Mechanical Engineering M
Nutrition M
Physics M
Psychology—General M
Public Administration M
Social Work M

UNIVERSITÉ DE MONTRÉAL

Addictions/Substance Abuse Counseling M,D,O
Allopathic Medicine P,O
Anthropology M,D
Art History M,D
Biochemistry M,D,O
Bioethics M,O
Biological and Biomedical Sciences—General M,D
Biomedical Engineering M,D,O
Biophysics M,D
Cancer Biology/Oncology O
Cell Biology M,D
Chemistry M,D
Clinical Laboratory Sciences/Medical Technology O
Communication Disorders M,O
Communication—General M,D
Community Health M,D,O
Comparative Literature M,D
Computer Science M,D,O
Criminal Justice and Criminology M,D
Curriculum and Instruction M,D,O
Demography and Population Studies M,D
Dental Hygiene M,O
Dentistry M,O
Developmental Psychology M,D
Economics M,D
Education—General M,D,O
Educational Administration M,D,O
Educational Psychology M,D,O
English M,D
Environmental and Occupational Health M,O
Environmental Design M,D,O
Environmental Management and Policy O
Ergonomics and Human Factors O
Film, Television, and Video Theory and Criticism M,D
French M,D
Genetics O
Geography M,D,O
German M
Health Physics/Radiological Health O
Health Promotion M,D,O
Health Services Management and Hospital Administration M,O
Hispanic Studies M,D
History M,D
Human Services D
Immunology M,D
Industrial and Labor Relations M,D
Infectious Diseases O
Information Studies M,D,O
Kinesiology and Movement Studies M,D,O
Law P,M,D,O
Library Science M,D,O
Linguistics M,D,O
Management Information Systems M,D,O
Maternal and Child/Neonatal Nursing O
Mathematics M,D
Microbiology M,D,O
Molecular Biology M,D
Museum Studies M
Music M,D,O
Neuroscience M,D,O
Nurse Anesthesia O
Nursing—General M,D,O
Nutrition M,D
Optometry M,O
Oral and Dental Sciences M,O
Pathology M,D,O
Pharmaceutical Sciences M,D,O
Pharmacology M,D
Philosophy M,D
Physical Education M,D,O
Physical Therapy O
Physics M,D
Physiology M,D
Political Science M,D
Psychology—General M,D
Public Health—General M,D,O
Rehabilitation Counseling O
Social Work O
Sociology M,D
Spanish M
Statistics M,D
Theology M,D,O
Toxicology O
Veterinary Medicine P
Veterinary Sciences M,D,O
Virology D
Vision Sciences M,O

UNIVERSITÉ DE SHERBROOKE

Accounting M
Allopathic Medicine P
Biochemistry M,D
Biological and Biomedical Sciences—General M,D,O
Biophysics M,D
Biotechnology P,M,D,O
Business Administration and Management—General P,M,D,O
Canadian Studies M,D
Cell Biology M,D
Chemical Engineering M,D
Chemistry M,D,O
Civil Engineering M,D
Clinical Laboratory Sciences/Medical Technology M,D
Comparative Literature M,D
Conflict Resolution and Mediation/Peace Studies P,M,D,O
Economics M
Education—General M,O
Educational Administration M
Electrical Engineering M,D
Elementary Education M,O
Engineering and Applied Sciences—General M,D,O
Engineering Management M,O
Environmental Engineering M
Environmental Sciences M,O
Ethics M,D,O
Finance and Banking M
French M,D
Geography M,D
Gerontology M
Higher Education M,O
History M
Immunology M,D
Information Science M,D
International Business M
Kinesiology and Movement Studies M,O
Law P,M,D,O
Linguistics M,D
Management Information Systems M,O
Marketing M
Mathematics M,D
Mechanical Engineering M,D
Microbiology M,D
Organizational Behavior M
Pharmacology M,D
Philosophy M,D,O
Physical Education M,O
Physics M,D
Physiology M,D

Psychology—General M
Radiation Biology M,D
Religion M,D,O
Social Work M
Special Education M,O
Taxation M,O
Theater M,D
Theology M,D,O

UNIVERSITÉ DU QUÉBEC À CHICOUTIMI

Art/Fine Arts M
Business Administration and Management—General M
Canadian Studies M
Comparative Literature M
Education—General M,D
Engineering and Applied Sciences—General M,D
Environmental Management and Policy M
Ethics O
French O
Genetics M
Geosciences M
Linguistics M
Mineralogy D
Project Management M
Theology M,D

UNIVERSITÉ DU QUÉBEC À MONTRÉAL

Accounting M,O
Actuarial Science O
Art History M,D
Art/Fine Arts M
Atmospheric Sciences M,D,O
Biological and Biomedical Sciences—General M,D
Business Administration and Management—General M,D,O
Chemistry M
Communication—General M,D
Comparative Literature M,D
Dance M
Economics M,D
Education—General M,D,O
Environmental and Occupational Health O
Environmental Education M,D,O
Environmental Sciences M,D
Ergonomics and Human Factors O
Finance and Banking O
Geographic Information Systems O
Geography M
Geology M,D,O
Geosciences M,D,O
History M,D
Kinesiology and Movement Studies M
Law M
Linguistics M,D
Management Information Systems M
Mathematics M,D
Meteorology M,D,O
Mineralogy M,D,O
Museum Studies M
Natural Resources M,D,O
Philosophy M,D
Political Science M,D
Project Management M,O
Psychology—General D
Public Administration M
Religion M,D
Social Work M
Sociology M,D
Theater M
Urban Studies M,D

UNIVERSITÉ DU QUÉBEC À RIMOUSKI

Business Administration and Management—General M,O
Comparative Literature M,D
Education—General M,D,O
Engineering and Applied Sciences—General M
Ethics M,O
Fish, Game, and Wildlife Management M,D,O
Marine Affairs M,O
Nursing—General M,O
Oceanography M,D
Project Management M,O
Social Psychology M
Urban and Regional Planning M,D,O

UNIVERSITÉ DU QUÉBEC À TROIS-RIVIÈRES

Accounting O
Biophysics M,D
Business Administration and Management—General M,D
Canadian Studies M,D
Chemistry M
Comparative Literature M
Computer Science M
Education—General M,O
Educational Administration D
Educational Psychology M
Electrical Engineering M,D
Energy Management and Policy M,D
Entrepreneurship M
Environmental Sciences M,D
Finance and Banking O
Industrial and Labor Relations O
Industrial/Management Engineering M,O
Leisure Studies M,O
Mathematics M
Nursing—General M,O
Paper and Pulp Engineering M,D
Philosophy M,D
Physical Education M
Project Management M,O
Psychology—General M,D
Travel and Tourism M,O

UNIVERSITÉ DU QUÉBEC, ÉCOLE DE TECHNOLOGIE SUPÉRIEURE

Engineering and Applied Sciences—General M,D,O

UNIVERSITÉ DU QUÉBEC, ÉCOLE NATIONALE D'ADMINISTRATION PUBLIQUE

International Business M,O
Public Administration D,O
Urban Studies M

UNIVERSITÉ DU QUÉBEC EN ABITIBI-TÉMISCAMINGUE

Business Administration and Management—General M
Education—General M,D
Project Management M

UNIVERSITÉ DU QUÉBEC EN OUTAOUAIS

Accounting M,O
Adult Education O
Computer Science M,O
Education—General M,D,O
Educational Psychology M
Finance and Banking M,O
Industrial and Labor Relations M,D,O
Nursing—General M,O
Project Management M,O
Social Work M
Software Engineering O
Urban and Regional Planning M

UNIVERSITÉ DU QUÉBEC, INSTITUT NATIONAL DE LA RECHERCHE SCIENTIFIQUE

Biological and Biomedical Sciences—General M,D
Demography and Population Studies M,D
Energy Management and Policy M,D
Environmental Management and Policy M,D
Geosciences M,D
Hydrology M,D
Immunology M,D
Materials Sciences M,D
Medical Microbiology M,D
Microbiology M,D
Telecommunications M,D
Urban Studies M,D
Virology M,D

UNIVERSITÉ LAVAL

Accounting M,O
Advertising and Public Relations O
Aerospace/Aeronautical Engineering M
Agricultural Economics and Agribusiness M
Agricultural Engineering M
Agricultural Sciences—General M,D,O
Agronomy and Soil Sciences M,D
Allopathic Medicine P,O
Anatomy M,D,O
Anesthesiologist Assistant Studies O
Animal Sciences M,D
Anthropology M,D
Archaeology M,D
Architecture M
Art History M,D
Art/Fine Arts M
Biochemistry M,D,O
Biological and Biomedical Sciences—General M,D,O
Business Administration and Management—General M,D,O
Cancer Biology/Oncology O
Cardiovascular Sciences O
Cell Biology M,D
Chemical Engineering M,D
Chemistry M,D
Civil Engineering M,D,O
Clinical Psychology D
Communication Disorders M
Community Health M,D,O
Comparative Literature M,D
Computer Science M,D
Consumer Economics O
Counselor Education M,D
Curriculum and Instruction M,D
Dentistry P
Economics M,D
Education—General M,D,O
Educational Administration M,D,O
Educational Measurement and Evaluation M,D,O
Educational Media/Instructional Technology M,D
Educational Psychology M,D
Electrical Engineering M,D
Electronic Commerce M,O
Emergency Medical Services O
Engineering and Applied Sciences—General M,D,O
English M,D
Entrepreneurship M,O
Environmental and Occupational Health O
Environmental Engineering M,D
Environmental Management and Policy M,D
Environmental Sciences M,D
Epidemiology M,D
Ethics O
Ethnic Studies M,D
Facilities Management M,O
Film, Television, and Video Theory and Criticism M,D
Finance and Banking M,O
Food Science and Technology M,D
Forestry M,D
French M
Geodetic Sciences M,D
Geography M,D
Geology M,D
Geosciences M,D
Gerontology O
Graphic Design M
Health Physics/Radiological Health O
History M,D
Immunology M,D
Industrial and Labor Relations M,D
Industrial/Management Engineering O
Infectious Diseases O
International Affairs M
International Business M,O
Journalism O
Kinesiology and Movement Studies M,D
Law M,D,O
Legal and Justice Studies O
Linguistics M,D
Management Information Systems M,O
Management of Technology O
Marketing M,O
Mass Communication M
Mathematics M,D
Mechanical Engineering M,D
Metallurgical Engineering and Metallurgy M,D
Microbiology M,D
Mineral/Mining Engineering M,D
Molecular Biology M,D
Museum Studies O
Music Education M,D
Music M,D
Neurobiology M,D
Nursing—General M,O
Nutrition M,D
Oceanography D
Oral and Dental Sciences M,O
Organizational Management M,O
Pathology O
Pharmaceutical Sciences M,D,O
Philosophy M,D
Physics M,D
Physiology M,D
Plant Biology M,D
Political Science M,D
Psychology—General D
Religion M,D
Rural Planning and Studies O
Social Psychology D
Social Work M,D
Sociology M,D
Software Engineering O
Spanish M,D
Statistics M
Theater M,D
Theology M,D
Translation and Interpretation M,O
Urban and Regional Planning M,O
Women's Studies O

UNIVERSITY AT ALBANY, STATE UNIVERSITY OF NEW YORK

Accounting M
African Studies M
African-American Studies M
Anthropology M,D
Art/Fine Arts M
Atmospheric Sciences M,D
Biochemistry M,D
Biological and Biomedical Sciences—General M,D*
Biopsychology M,D,O
Biostatistics M,D
Business Administration and Management—General M
Cell Biology M,D
Chemistry M,D
Clinical Psychology M,D,O
Communication—General M,D
Computer Science M,D
Conservation Biology M
Counseling Psychology M,D,O
Counselor Education M,D,O
Criminal Justice and Criminology M,D
Curriculum and Instruction M,D,O
Demography and Population Studies M,D,O
Developmental Biology M,D
Ecology M,D
Economics M,D,O
Education—General M,D,O
Educational Administration M,D,O
Educational Measurement and Evaluation M,D,O
Educational Media/Instructional Technology M,D,O
Educational Psychology M,D,O
English M,D
Environmental and Occupational Health M,D
Environmental Management and Policy M
Environmental Sciences M
Epidemiology M,D
Evolutionary Biology M,D
Experimental Psychology M,D,O
Finance and Banking M
Forensic Sciences M,D
French M,D
Genetics M,D
Geographic Information Systems M,O
Geography M,O
Geology M,D
Geosciences M,D
Health Services Management and Hospital Administration M
History M,D,O
Human Resources Management M
Immunology M,D
Industrial and Organizational Psychology M,D,O
Information Science M,D,O
Italian M
Latin American Studies M,O
Liberal Studies M
Library Science M,D,O
Management of Technology M
Marketing M
Mathematics Education M,D
Mathematics M,D
Molecular Biology M,D
Molecular Pathogenesis M,D
Nanotechnology M,D
Neurobiology M,D
Neuroscience M,D
Pathology M,D
Philosophy M,D
Physics M,D
Political Science M,D
Psychology—General M,D,O
Public Administration M,D,O
Public Health—General M,D
Public History M,D,O
Public Policy M,D,O
Reading Education M,D,O
Rehabilitation Counseling M
Russian M,O
School Psychology M,D,O
Science Education M,D
Social Psychology M,D,O
Social Work M,D
Sociology M,D,O
Spanish M,D
Special Education M
Statistics M,D,O
Structural Biology M,D
Taxation M
Theater M
Toxicology M,D*
Translation and Interpretation M,O
Urban and Regional Planning M
Urban Studies M,D,O
Women's Studies M,D

UNIVERSITY AT BUFFALO, THE STATE UNIVERSITY OF NEW YORK

Accounting M,D,O
Acute Care/Critical Care Nursing M,D,O
Adult Nursing M,D,O
Aerospace/Aeronautical Engineering M,D
Allied Health—General M,D,O
Allopathic Medicine P
American Studies M,D

Anatomy M,D
Anthropology M,D
Architecture M
Art History M,O
Art/Fine Arts M,O
Biochemistry M,D
Bioengineering M,D
Biological and Biomedical Sciences—General M,D*
Biophysics M,D
Biostatistics M,D
Biotechnology M
Business Administration and Management—General M,D,O
Cancer Biology/Oncology D
Cell Biology D
Chemical Engineering M,D
Chemistry M,D
Civil Engineering M,D
Classics M,D
Clinical Laboratory Sciences/Medical Technology M
Clinical Psychology M,D
Cognitive Sciences M,D
Communication Disorders M,D
Communication—General M,D
Community Health M,D
Comparative Literature M,D
Computer Science M,D
Counseling Psychology M,D,O
Counselor Education M,D,O
Dentistry P,M,D,O
Early Childhood Education M,D,O
Ecology M,D,O
Economics M,D,O
Education—General M,D,O
Educational Administration M,D,O
Educational Psychology M,D,O
Electrical Engineering M,D
Electronic Commerce M,D,O
Elementary Education M,D,O
Engineering and Applied Sciences—General M,D*
English as a Second Language M,D,O
English Education M,D,O
English M,D
Environmental Engineering M,D
Epidemiology M,D
Evolutionary Biology M,D,O
Exercise and Sports Science M,D
Finance and Banking M,D,O
Foreign Languages Education M,D,O
French M,D
Geographic Information Systems M,D,O
Geography M,D,O
Geology M,D
Gerontological Nursing M,D,O
Higher Education M,D,O
History M,D
Human Resources Management M,D,O
Immunology M,D
Industrial/Management Engineering M,D
Information Studies M,O
Japanese M,D,O
Law P,M
Library Science M,O
Linguistics M,D
Logistics M,D,O
Management Information Systems M,D,O
Materials Sciences M
Maternal and Child/Neonatal Nursing M,D,O
Mathematics Education M,D,O
Mathematics M,D
Mechanical Engineering M,D
Media Studies M,O
Medicinal and Pharmaceutical Chemistry M,D
Microbiology M,D
Middle School Education M,D,O
Molecular Biology D
Molecular Pharmacology D*
Multilingual and Multicultural Education M,D,O
Museum Studies M,O
Music Education M,D,O
Music M,D
Neuroscience M,D
Nurse Anesthesia M,D,O
Nursing—General M,D,O
Nutrition M,D
Occupational Therapy M
Oral and Dental Sciences M,D,O
Pathology M,D
Pediatric Nursing M,D,O
Pharmaceutical Sciences M,D*
Pharmacology M,D
Pharmacy P
Philosophy M,D
Physical Therapy D
Physics M,D
Physiology M,D
Political Science M,D
Psychiatric Nursing M,D,O
Psychology—General M,D
Public Health—General M,D
Reading Education M,D,O
Rehabilitation Counseling M,D,O
Rehabilitation Sciences M,D,O
Romance Languages M,D
School Psychology M,D,O
Science Education M,D,O
Social Psychology M,D
Social Sciences Education M,D,O
Social Work M,D
Sociology M,D
Spanish M,D
Special Education M,D,O
Structural Biology M,D
Structural Engineering M,D
Toxicology M,D
Transportation Management M,D,O
Urban and Regional Planning M
Urban Design M
Women's Health Nursing M,D,O

Close-Up on page 1065.

UNIVERSITY COLLEGE OF THE FRASER VALLEY

Criminal Justice and Criminology M

UNIVERSITY OF ADVANCING TECHNOLOGY

Management of Technology M

THE UNIVERSITY OF AKRON

Accounting M
Applied Mathematics M,D
Arts Administration M
Biological and Biomedical Sciences—General M,D
Biomedical Engineering M,D
Business Administration and Management—General M
Chemical Engineering M,D
Chemistry M,D
Child and Family Studies M
Child Development M
Civil Engineering M,D
Clothing and Textiles M
Cognitive Sciences M,D
Communication Disorders M,D
Communication—General M
Computer Engineering M,D
Computer Science M
Counseling Psychology M,D
Counselor Education M,D
Economics M
Education—General M,D
Educational Administration M,D
Educational Media/Instructional Technology M
Electrical Engineering M,D
Electronic Commerce M
Elementary Education M,D
Engineering and Applied Sciences—General M,D
Engineering Management M
English M
Entrepreneurship M
Exercise and Sports Science M
Family and Consumer Sciences-General M
Finance and Banking M
Geographic Information Systems M
Geography M
Geology M
Geophysics M
Geosciences M
Health Services Management and Hospital Administration M
Higher Education M
History M,D
Human Resources Management M
Industrial and Organizational Psychology M,D
International Business M
Law P
Management Information Systems M
Management of Technology M
Marketing M
Marriage and Family Therapy M
Mathematics M
Mechanical Engineering M,D
Music Education M
Music M
Nursing—General M,D
Nutrition M
Physical Education M
Physics M
Political Science M
Polymer Science and Engineering M,D
Psychology—General M,D
Public Administration M
Public Health—General M,D
School Psychology M
Secondary Education M,D
Social Work M
Sociology M,D
Spanish M
Special Education M
Statistics M
Supply Chain Management M
Taxation M
Theater M
Urban and Regional Planning M
Urban Studies M,D
Vocational and Technical Education M
Writing M

THE UNIVERSITY OF ALABAMA

Accounting M,D
Advertising and Public Relations M
Aerospace/Aeronautical Engineering M,D
American Studies M
Anthropology M,D
Applied Mathematics M,D
Applied Statistics M,D
Art History M
Art/Fine Arts M
Biological and Biomedical Sciences—General M,D
Business Administration and Management—General M,D
Chemical Engineering M,D
Chemistry M,D
Child and Family Studies M
Civil Engineering M,D
Clinical Psychology D
Clothing and Textiles M
Communication Disorders M
Communication—General M,D
Computer Engineering M,D
Computer Science M,D
Construction Engineering M,D
Consumer Economics M
Counselor Education M,D,O
Criminal Justice and Criminology M
Economics M,D
Education of the Gifted M,D,O
Educational Administration M,D,O
Electrical Engineering M,D
Engineering and Applied Sciences—General M,D
English as a Second Language M,D
English M,D
Environmental Engineering M,D
Exercise and Sports Science M,D
Experimental Psychology D
Family and Consumer Sciences-General M,D
Film, Television, and Video Production M
Finance and Banking M,D
French M,D
Geography M
Geology M,D
German M,D
Health Education M,D
Health Promotion M,D
Higher Education M,D
History M,D
Hospitality Management M
Human Development M
Industrial/Management Engineering M
Information Studies M,D
Interior Design M
Journalism M
Kinesiology and Movement Studies M,D
Law P,M
Library Science M,D
Marketing M,D
Materials Engineering M,D
Materials Sciences D
Mathematics M,D
Mechanical Engineering M,D
Mechanics M,D
Media Studies M
Metallurgical Engineering and Metallurgy M,D
Music Education M,D,O
Music M,D
Nursing—General M
Nutrition M
Photography M
Physical Education M,D
Physics M,D
Political Science M,D
Psychology—General D
Public Administration M,D
Rhetoric M,D
Romance Languages M,D
Social Work M,D
Spanish M,D
Special Education M,D,O
Speech and Interpersonal Communication M
Sports Management M,D
Statistics M,D
Taxation M,D
Theater M
Women's Studies M
Writing M,D

THE UNIVERSITY OF ALABAMA AT BIRMINGHAM

Allied Health—General M,D,O
Allopathic Medicine P,M,D
Anthropology M
Applied Mathematics M,D
Art Education M
Art History M
Biochemistry D*
Biological and Biomedical Sciences—General M,D*
Biomedical Engineering M,D
Biometrics M,D
Biophysics M,D
Biostatistics M,D
Business Administration and Management—General M,D
Cell Biology M,D*
Chemistry M,D
Civil Engineering M,D
Clinical Laboratory Sciences/Medical Technology M
Clinical Psychology M,D
Communication—General M
Computer Engineering D
Computer Science M,D
Counselor Education M
Criminal Justice and Criminology M
Dentistry P
Developmental Psychology M,D
Early Childhood Education M,D
Education—General M,D,O
Educational Administration M,D,O
Electrical Engineering M
Elementary Education M
Engineering and Applied Sciences—General M,D
English M
Environmental and Occupational Health D
Environmental Engineering M
Epidemiology D
Forensic Sciences M
Genetics D
Health Education M,D
Health Informatics M
Health Promotion D
Health Services Management and Hospital Administration M,D
History M
Industrial Hygiene D
Information Science M,D
Marriage and Family Therapy M
Materials Engineering M,D
Materials Sciences D
Maternal and Child Health M
Mathematics M,D
Mechanical Engineering M,D
Microbiology D*
Molecular Biology M,D
Molecular Genetics D
Molecular Physiology M,D
Neurobiology D*
Neuroscience M,D*
Nurse Anesthesia M
Nursing—General M,D
Nutrition M,D,O
Occupational Therapy M
Optometry P
Oral and Dental Sciences M
Pathology D
Pharmacology D
Physical Education M
Physical Therapy D
Physician Assistant Studies M
Physics M,D
Physiology M,D
Psychology—General M,D
Public Administration M
Public Health—General M,D
Rehabilitation Counseling M
Rehabilitation Sciences O
School Psychology M
Secondary Education M
Sociology M,D
Special Education M
Toxicology M,D
Vision Sciences M,D

Close-Up on page 1067.

THE UNIVERSITY OF ALABAMA IN HUNTSVILLE

Accounting M,O
Aerospace/Aeronautical Engineering M,D
Applied Mathematics M,D
Atmospheric Sciences M,D
Biological and Biomedical Sciences—General M
Biotechnology M,D
Business Administration and Management—General M,O
Chemical Engineering M,D
Chemistry M
Civil Engineering M,D

- Computer Engineering M,D
- Computer Science M,D,O
- Electrical Engineering M,D
- Engineering and Applied Sciences—General M,D
- English as a Second Language M,O
- English M,O
- Environmental Engineering M,D
- Environmental Sciences M,D
- History M
- Human Resources Management M,O
- Industrial/Management Engineering M,D
- Management Information Systems M,O
- Materials Sciences M,D
- Maternal and Child/Neonatal Nursing M,O
- Mathematics M,D
- Mechanical Engineering M,D
- Nursing—General M,O
- Operations Research M
- Optical Sciences D
- Physics M,D
- Psychology—General M
- Public Affairs M
- Software Engineering M,D,O
- Technical Writing M,O
- Vision Sciences M,D

UNIVERSITY OF ALASKA ANCHORAGE

- Adult Education M
- Anthropology M
- Biological and Biomedical Sciences—General M
- Business Administration and Management—General M
- Civil Engineering M,O
- Clinical Psychology M,D
- Counselor Education M
- Early Childhood Education M,O
- Education—General M,O
- Educational Administration M,O
- Engineering and Applied Sciences—General M,O
- Engineering Management M
- English M
- Environmental Engineering M
- Environmental Sciences M
- Family Nurse Practitioner Studies M,O
- Geological Engineering M
- Interdisciplinary Studies M
- Logistics M,O
- Nursing Education M,O
- Nursing—General M,O
- Ocean Engineering M,O
- Project Management M
- Psychiatric Nursing M,O
- Psychology—General M,D
- Public Administration M
- Public Health—General M
- Social Psychology M,D
- Social Work M,O
- Special Education M,O
- Writing M

UNIVERSITY OF ALASKA FAIRBANKS

- Anthropology M,D
- Art/Fine Arts M
- Astrophysics M,D
- Atmospheric Sciences M,D
- Biochemistry M,D
- Biological and Biomedical Sciences—General M,D
- Botany M,D
- Business Administration and Management—General M
- Chemistry M,D
- Civil Engineering M,D
- Clinical Psychology D
- Communication—General M
- Computational Sciences M,D
- Computer Engineering M,D
- Computer Science M
- Corporate and Organizational Communication M
- Counselor Education M
- Criminal Justice and Criminology M
- Cultural Studies M
- Curriculum and Instruction M
- Economics M
- Education—General M
- Electrical Engineering M,D
- Engineering and Applied Sciences—General M,D
- Engineering Management M
- English Education M
- English M
- Environmental Engineering M,D
- Environmental Management and Policy M
- Environmental Sciences M,D
- Finance and Banking M
- Fish, Game, and Wildlife Management M,D
- Geological Engineering M,O
- Geology M,D
- Geophysics M,D
- Interdisciplinary Studies M,D
- Limnology M,D
- Linguistics M
- Marine Biology M,D
- Marine Sciences M,D
- Mathematics M,D
- Mechanical Engineering M,D
- Mineral/Mining Engineering M
- Multilingual and Multicultural Education M
- Music Education M
- Music M
- Northern Studies M
- Oceanography M,D
- Petroleum Engineering M
- Physics M,D
- Psychology—General D
- Reading Education M
- Rural Planning and Studies M
- Social Psychology D
- Software Engineering M
- Statistics M,D
- Writing M
- Zoology M,D

UNIVERSITY OF ALASKA SOUTHEAST

- Business Administration and Management—General M
- Early Childhood Education M
- Education—General M
- Educational Media/Instructional Technology M
- Elementary Education M
- Public Administration M
- Secondary Education M

UNIVERSITY OF ALBERTA

- Accounting D
- Adult Education M,D,O
- Agricultural Economics and Agribusiness M,D
- Agricultural Sciences—General M,D
- Agronomy and Soil Sciences M,D
- Anthropology M,D
- Applied Arts and Design—General M
- Applied Mathematics M,D,O
- Archaeology M,D
- Art History M
- Art/Fine Arts M
- Asian Studies M
- Astrophysics M,D
- Biochemistry M,D
- Biological and Biomedical Sciences—General P,M,D
- Biomedical Engineering M,D
- Biostatistics M,D,O
- Biotechnology M,D
- Business Administration and Management—General M,D*
- Cancer Biology/Oncology M,D
- Cell Biology M,D
- Chemical Engineering M,D
- Chemistry M,D
- Chinese M
- Civil Engineering M,D
- Classics M,D
- Clinical Laboratory Sciences/Medical Technology M,D
- Clothing and Textiles M,D
- Communication Disorders M,D
- Communication—General M
- Community Health M,D
- Computer Engineering M,D
- Computer Science M,D
- Condensed Matter Physics M,D
- Conservation Biology M,D
- Construction Engineering M,D
- Counseling Psychology M,D
- Counselor Education M,D
- Criminal Justice and Criminology M,D
- Demography and Population Studies M,D
- Dental Hygiene O
- Dentistry P
- East European and Russian Studies M,D
- Ecology M,D
- Economics M,D
- Educational Administration M,D,O
- Educational Media/Instructional Technology M,D
- Educational Policy M,D,O
- Educational Psychology M,D
- Electrical Engineering M,D
- Elementary Education M,D
- Energy and Power Engineering M,D
- Engineering Management M,D
- English as a Second Language M,D
- English M,D
- Environmental and Occupational Health M,D
- Environmental Biology M,D
- Environmental Engineering M,D
- Environmental Management and Policy M,D
- Environmental Sciences M,D
- Epidemiology M,D
- Evolutionary Biology M,D
- Exercise and Sports Science M,D
- Family and Consumer Sciences-General M,D
- Finance and Banking M,D
- Folklore M,D
- Forestry M,D
- French M,D
- Genetics M,D
- Geophysics M,D
- Geosciences M,D
- Geotechnical Engineering M,D
- German M,D
- Health Physics/Radiological Health M,D
- Health Promotion M,O
- Health Services Management and Hospital Administration M,D
- Health Services Research M,D
- Hispanic Studies M,D
- History M,D
- Immunology M,D
- Industrial and Labor Relations D
- Information Studies M
- International Business M
- International Health M,D
- Italian M,D
- Japanese M
- Law P,M
- Library Science M
- Linguistics M,D
- Marketing D
- Materials Engineering M,D
- Maternal and Child/Neonatal Nursing P
- Mathematical and Computational Finance M,D,O
- Mathematical Physics M,D,O
- Mathematics M,D,O
- Mechanical Engineering M,D
- Medical Microbiology M,D
- Medical Physics M,D
- Microbiology M,D
- Mineral/Mining Engineering M,D
- Molecular Biology M,D
- Multilingual and Multicultural Education M
- Music M,D
- Nanotechnology M,D
- Natural Resources M,D
- Neuroscience M,D
- Nursing—General M,D
- Occupational Therapy M,D
- Oral and Dental Sciences P,M,D,O
- Organizational Management D
- Pathology M,D
- Petroleum Engineering M,D
- Pharmaceutical Sciences M,D
- Pharmacology M,D
- Pharmacy M,D
- Philosophy M,D
- Physical Education M,D
- Physical Therapy M,D
- Physics M,D
- Physiology M,D
- Plant Biology M,D
- Political Science M,D
- Psychology—General M,D
- Public Health—General M,D
- Recreation and Park Management M,D
- Rehabilitation Sciences D
- Rural Sociology M,D
- School Psychology M,D
- Secondary Education M,D
- Slavic Languages M,D
- Sociology M,D
- Special Education M,D
- Sports Management M
- Statistics M,D,O
- Structural Engineering M,D
- Systems Engineering M,D
- Telecommunications M,D
- Theater M
- Vision Sciences M,D
- Water Resources Engineering M,D

THE UNIVERSITY OF ARIZONA

- Accounting M
- Aerospace/Aeronautical Engineering M,D
- Agricultural Economics and Agribusiness M
- Agricultural Education M
- Agricultural Engineering M,D
- Agricultural Sciences—General M,D
- Agronomy and Soil Sciences M,D
- Allopathic Medicine P
- American Indian/Native American Studies M,D
- Anatomy D
- Animal Sciences M,D
- Anthropology M,D
- Applied Mathematics M,D*
- Applied Physics M
- Architecture M
- Art Education M
- Art History M,D
- Art/Fine Arts M
- Asian Studies M,D
- Astronomy M,D
- Atmospheric Sciences M,D
- Biochemistry M,D
- Biological and Biomedical Sciences—General M,D
- Biosystems Engineering M,D
- Business Administration and Management—General M,D
- Cancer Biology/Oncology D
- Cell Biology M,D
- Chemical Engineering M,D
- Chemistry M,D
- Child and Family Studies M,D
- Civil Engineering M,D
- Classics M
- Communication Disorders M,D
- Communication—General M,D
- Comparative Literature M,D
- Computer Engineering M,D
- Computer Science M,D
- Consumer Economics M,D
- Ecology M,D
- Economics M,D
- Education—General M,D,O
- Educational Administration M,D,O
- Educational Psychology M,D
- Electrical Engineering M,D*
- Elementary Education M,D
- Engineering and Applied Sciences—General M,D
- English as a Second Language M,D
- English Education M,D
- English M,D
- Entomology M,D
- Environmental Engineering M,D
- Environmental Sciences M,D
- Evolutionary Biology M,D
- Family and Consumer Sciences-General M,D
- Finance and Banking M,D
- Fish, Game, and Wildlife Management M,D
- Foreign Languages Education M,D
- Forestry M,D
- French M,D
- Genetics M,D
- Geography M,D
- Geosciences M,D
- German M,D
- Higher Education M,D
- History M,D
- Human Development M,D
- Hydrology M,D
- Immunology M,D*
- Industrial/Management Engineering M,D
- Information Studies M,D
- Interdisciplinary Studies M,D
- Landscape Architecture M
- Latin American Studies M
- Law P,M
- Library Science M,D
- Linguistics M,D
- Management Information Systems M,D
- Management Strategy and Policy M,D
- Marketing D
- Materials Engineering M,D
- Materials Sciences M,D
- Mathematics M,D
- Mechanical Engineering M,D
- Mechanics M,D
- Media Studies M
- Microbiology M,D
- Mineral/Mining Engineering M,O
- Molecular Biology M,D
- Multilingual and Multicultural Education M,D,O
- Music Education M,D
- Music M,D
- Natural Resources M,D
- Near and Middle Eastern Studies M,D
- Neuroscience D
- Nuclear Engineering M,D
- Nursing—General M,D
- Optical Sciences M,D
- Pathobiology M,D
- Pharmaceutical Sciences M,D
- Pharmacology M,D
- Pharmacy P,M,D
- Philosophy M,D
- Physics M,D
- Physiology D
- Planetary and Space Sciences M,D*
- Plant Pathology M,D
- Plant Sciences M,D
- Political Science M,D
- Psychology—General D
- Public Administration M,D
- Public Health—General M
- Public Policy M,D
- Range Science M,D
- Reading Education M,D,O
- Rehabilitation Counseling M,D,O
- Reliability Engineering M
- Rhetoric M,D
- Russian M
- Secondary Education M,D
- Sociology M,D
- Spanish M,D

Special Education	M,D,O
Statistics	M,D
Systems Engineering	M,D
Theater	M
Water Resources Engineering	M,D
Water Resources	M,D
Women's Studies	M
Writing	M

UNIVERSITY OF ARKANSAS

Accounting	M
Adult Education	M,D,O
Agricultural Economics and Agribusiness	M
Agricultural Education	M
Agricultural Engineering	M,D
Agricultural Sciences—General	M,D
Agronomy and Soil Sciences	M,D
Animal Sciences	M,D
Anthropology	M
Applied Physics	M
Art/Fine Arts	M
Bioengineering	M
Biological and Biomedical Sciences—General	M,D
Biomedical Engineering	M
Business Administration and Management—General	M,D
Cell Biology	M,D
Chemical Engineering	M,D
Chemistry	M,D
Civil Engineering	M,D
Communication Disorders	M
Communication—General	M
Comparative Literature	M,D
Computer Engineering	M,D
Computer Science	M,D
Counselor Education	M,D,O
Curriculum and Instruction	D
Early Childhood Education	M
Economics	M,D
Education—General	M,D,O
Educational Administration	M,D,O
Educational Media/Instructional Technology	M
Electrical Engineering	M,D*
Electronic Materials	M,D
Elementary Education	M,O
Engineering and Applied Sciences—General	M,D
English	M,D
Entomology	M,D
Environmental Engineering	M
Family and Consumer Sciences-General	M
Food Science and Technology	M,D
Foundations and Philosophy of Education	M,D
French	M
Geography	M
Geology	M
German	M
Health Education	M,D
Higher Education	M,D,O
History	M,D
Horticulture	M
Industrial and Manufacturing Management	M
Industrial/Management Engineering	M,D
Interdisciplinary Studies	D
Journalism	M
Kinesiology and Movement Studies	M,D
Law	P,M
Logistics	M
Management Information Systems	M
Mathematics Education	M
Mathematics	M,D
Mechanical Engineering	M,D
Middle School Education	M,D,O
Molecular Biology	M,D
Music	M
Nursing—General	M
Operations Research	M
Philosophy	M,D
Photonics	M,D
Physical Education	M
Physics	M,D
Planetary and Space Sciences	M,D
Plant Pathology	M
Plant Sciences	D
Political Science	M
Psychology—General	M,D
Public Administration	M
Public Policy	D
Recreation and Park Management	M,D
Rehabilitation Counseling	M,D
Secondary Education	M,O
Social Work	M
Sociology	M
Spanish	M
Special Education	M
Statistics	M
Telecommunications	M
Theater	M
Translation and Interpretation	M
Transportation and Highway Engineering	M
Transportation Management	M
Vocational and Technical Education	M,D,O
Writing	M

Close-Up on page 1069.

UNIVERSITY OF ARKANSAS AT LITTLE ROCK

Adult Education	M
Applied Mathematics	M
Applied Science and Technology	M,D
Art Education	M
Art History	M
Art/Fine Arts	M
Bioinformatics	M,D
Biological and Biomedical Sciences—General	M
Business Administration and Management—General	M
Chemistry	M
Computer Science	M
Corporate and Organizational Communication	M
Counselor Education	M
Criminal Justice and Criminology	M
Early Childhood Education	M
Education of the Gifted	M
Education of the Multiply Handicapped	M
Education—General	M,D,O
Educational Administration	M,D,O
Educational Media/Instructional Technology	M
Gerontology	M,O
Health Services Management and Hospital Administration	M
Higher Education	D
Law	P
Liberal Studies	M
Management Information Systems	M
Mass Communication	M
Mathematics	M
Middle School Education	M
Psychology—General	M
Public Administration	M
Public Affairs	M
Public History	M
Reading Education	M
Rhetoric	M
Secondary Education	M
Social Work	M
Special Education	M
Speech and Interpersonal Communication	M
Statistics	M
Technical Writing	M
Writing	M

UNIVERSITY OF ARKANSAS AT MONTICELLO

Education—General	M
Educational Administration	M
Forestry	M
Natural Resources	M

UNIVERSITY OF ARKANSAS AT PINE BLUFF

Education—General	M
Elementary Education	M
English Education	M
Mathematics Education	M
Physical Education	M
Science Education	M
Secondary Education	M
Social Sciences Education	M

UNIVERSITY OF ARKANSAS FOR MEDICAL SCIENCES

Anatomy	M,D
Biochemistry	M,D
Biological and Biomedical Sciences—General	M,D
Biophysics	M,D
Communication Disorders	M,D
Environmental and Occupational Health	M
Genetic Counseling	M
Immunology	M,D
Microbiology	M,D
Molecular Biology	M,D
Neurobiology	M,D*
Nursing—General	M,D
Nutrition	M
Pathology	M
Pharmaceutical Administration	M
Pharmaceutical Sciences	M
Pharmacology	M,D
Pharmacy	P,M
Physiology	M,D
Toxicology	M,D

UNIVERSITY OF BALTIMORE

Accounting	M
Business Administration and Management—General	M
Communication—General	M,D
Computer Art and Design	M,D
Conflict Resolution and Mediation/Peace Studies	M
Counseling Psychology	M
Criminal Justice and Criminology	M
Ethics	M
Finance and Banking	M
Graphic Design	M
Health Services Management and Hospital Administration	M
Human Services	M
Human-Computer Interaction	M,D*
Industrial and Organizational Psychology	M
Information Science	M,D
Law	P,M
Legal and Justice Studies	M
Management Information Systems	M
Marketing	M
Psychology—General	M
Public Administration	D
Public Affairs	M,D
Publishing	M
Taxation	P,M
Writing	M

UNIVERSITY OF BRIDGEPORT

Acupuncture and Oriental Medicine	M
Business Administration and Management—General	M
Chiropractic	P
Computer Education	M,O
Computer Engineering	M,D
Computer Science	M,D
Early Childhood Education	M,O
Education—General	M,D,O
Educational Administration	D,O
Electrical Engineering	M
Elementary Education	M,O
Engineering and Applied Sciences—General	M,D
Human Resources Development	M
Human Services	M
International and Comparative Education	M,O
Management of Technology	M
Mechanical Engineering	M
Naturopathic Medicine	D
Nutrition	M
Reading Education	M,O
Secondary Education	M,O
Student Affairs	M

THE UNIVERSITY OF BRITISH COLUMBIA

Accounting	D
Adult Education	M,D
Agricultural Economics and Agribusiness	M
Agricultural Sciences—General	M,D
Agronomy and Soil Sciences	M,D
Allopathic Medicine	P,M
Anatomy	M,D
Animal Sciences	M,D
Anthropology	M,D
Applied Mathematics	M,D
Archaeology	M,D
Architecture	M
Art Education	M,D
Art History	M,D,O
Art/Fine Arts	M,D,O
Asian Studies	M,D
Astronomy	M,D
Atmospheric Sciences	M,D
Biochemistry	M,D
Biopsychology	M,D
Botany	M,D
Business Administration and Management—General	M,D
Cell Biology	M,D
Chemical Engineering	M,D
Chemistry	M,D
Child and Family Studies	M,D
Civil Engineering	M,D
Classics	M,D
Clinical Psychology	M,D
Cognitive Sciences	M,D
Communication Disorders	M,D
Community Health	M,D
Comparative Literature	M,D
Computer Engineering	M,D
Computer Science	M,D
Counseling Psychology	M,D,O
Curriculum and Instruction	M,D
Dentistry	P
Developmental Psychology	M,D
Early Childhood Education	M,D
East European and Russian Studies	M,D
Economics	M,D
Education—General	M,D,O
Educational Administration	M,D
Educational Measurement and Evaluation	M,D,O
Educational Policy	M,D
Electrical Engineering	M,D
Engineering and Applied Sciences—General	M,D
Engineering Physics	M
English as a Second Language	M,D
English	M,D
Environmental and Occupational Health	M,D
Environmental Management and Policy	M,D
Epidemiology	M,D
Film, Television, and Video Production	M
Film, Television, and Video Theory and Criticism	M
Finance and Banking	D
Food Science and Technology	M,D
Forensic Psychology	M,D
Forestry	M,D
Foundations and Philosophy of Education	M,D
French	M,D
Genetics	M,D
Geography	M,D
Geological Engineering	M,D
Geology	M,D
Geophysics	M,D
German	M,D
Health Psychology	M,D
Health Services Management and Hospital Administration	M,D
Health Services Research	M,D
Higher Education	M,D
Hispanic Studies	M,D
History	M,D
Home Economics Education	M,D
Immunology	M,D
Information Studies	M
International Affairs	M
International Business	D
Journalism	M
Kinesiology and Movement Studies	M,D
Landscape Architecture	M
Law	M,D
Library Science	M
Linguistics	M,D
Management Information Systems	D
Management Strategy and Policy	D
Marine Sciences	M,D
Marketing	D
Materials Engineering	M,D
Materials Sciences	M,D
Mathematics Education	M,D
Mathematics	M,D
Mechanical Engineering	M,D
Metallurgical Engineering and Metallurgy	M,D
Microbiology	M,D
Mineral/Mining Engineering	M,D
Molecular Biology	M,D
Music Education	M,D
Music	M,D
Neuroscience	M,D
Nurse Anesthesia	M,D
Nursing—General	M,D
Nutrition	M,D
Oceanography	M,D
Operations Research	M*
Oral and Dental Sciences	M,D,O
Organizational Behavior	D
Pathology	M,D
Pharmaceutical Sciences	P,M,D
Pharmacology	M,D
Pharmacy	P,M,D
Philosophy	M,D
Physical Education	M,D
Physics	M,D
Physiology	M,D
Plant Sciences	M,D
Political Science	M,D
Psychology—General	M,D
Public History	M
Quantitative Analysis	M,D
Reading Education	M,D
Rehabilitation Sciences	M,D
Religion	M,D
Reproductive Biology	M,D
School Psychology	M,D,O
Science Education	M,D
Social Psychology	M,D
Social Sciences Education	M,D
Social Work	M,D
Sociology	M,D
Software Engineering	M
Special Education	M,D,O
Statistics	M,D
Theater	M,D
Transportation Management	D
Urban and Regional Planning	M,D
Vocational and Technical Education	M,D
Writing	M
Zoology	M,D

UNIVERSITY OF CALGARY

Allopathic Medicine	P
Analytical Chemistry	M,D
Anthropology	M,D

Archaeology M,D
Architecture M,D
Art/Fine Arts M
Astronomy M,D
Biochemistry M,D
Biological and Biomedical Sciences—General M,D
Biomedical Engineering M,D
Biotechnology M
Business Administration and Management—General M,D
Cancer Biology/Oncology M,D
Cardiovascular Sciences M,D
Chemical Engineering M,D
Chemistry M,D
Civil Engineering M,D
Classics M,D
Clinical Psychology M,D
Communication—General M,D
Community Health M,D,O
Computer Engineering M,D
Computer Science M,D
Counseling Psychology M,D
Curriculum and Instruction M,D,O
Economics M,D
Education of the Gifted M,D,O
Educational Administration M,D,O
Educational Measurement and Evaluation M,D,O
Educational Media/Instructional Technology M,D,O
Educational Psychology M,D
Electrical Engineering M,D
Engineering and Applied Sciences—General M,D
English as a Second Language M,D,O
English M,D
Environmental Design M,D
Environmental Management and Policy M,D,O
Epidemiology M,D
Exercise and Sports Science M,D
Foreign Languages Education M,D,O
Foundations and Philosophy of Education M,D,O
Geography M,D
Geology M,D
Geophysics M,D
Geotechnical Engineering M,D
German M
Health Education M,D
Higher Education M,D,O
History M,D
Human Development M,D
Immunology M,D
Industrial Design M,D
Infectious Diseases M,D
Inorganic Chemistry M,D
Kinesiology and Movement Studies M,D
Law P,M,O
Legal and Justice Studies M,O
Linguistics M,D
Management Strategy and Policy M,D
Manufacturing Engineering M,D
Mathematics M,D
Mechanical Engineering M,D
Microbiology M,D
Military and Defense Studies M,D
Molecular Biology M,D
Music M,D
Neuroscience M,D
Nursing—General M,D,O
Organic Chemistry M,D
Petroleum Engineering M,D
Philosophy M,D
Physical Chemistry M,D
Physics M,D
Political Science M,D
Psychology—General M,D
Religion M,D
School Psychology M,D
Social Work M,D,O
Sociology M,D
Software Engineering M,D
Special Education M,D
Statistics M,D
Theater M
Theoretical Chemistry M,D
Urban and Regional Planning M,D
Urban Design M,D
Vocational and Technical Education M,D,O

UNIVERSITY OF CALIFORNIA, BERKELEY

Accounting D
African-American Studies D
Agricultural Economics and Agribusiness D
Allopathic Medicine
Anthropology D
Applied Arts and Design—General M
Applied Mathematics D
Applied Science and Technology D
Archaeology M,D
Architectural History M,D
Architecture M,D
Art History D
Art/Fine Arts M
Asian Languages M,D
Asian Studies M,D
Astrophysics D
Biochemistry D
Bioengineering D
Biological and Biomedical Sciences—General D
Biophysics D
Biostatistics M,D
Building Science M,D
Business Administration and Management—General M,D
Cell Biology D
Chemical Engineering M,D
Chemistry D
Chinese D
Civil Engineering M,D
Classics M,D
Comparative Literature D
Computer Science M,D
Demography and Population Studies M,D
Developmental Education
Economics D
Education—General M,D
Educational Administration M,D
Educational Measurement and Evaluation M,D
Electrical Engineering M,D
Energy Management and Policy M,D
Engineering and Applied Sciences—General M,D
Engineering Management M,D
English D
Environmental and Occupational Health M,D
Environmental Design M
Environmental Engineering M,D
Environmental Management and Policy M,D
Environmental Sciences M,D
Epidemiology M,D
Ethnic Studies D
Finance and Banking D
Financial Engineering M
Folklore M
Forestry M,D
Foundations and Philosophy of Education M,D
French D
Geography D
Geology M,D
Geophysics M,D
Geotechnical Engineering M,D
German D
Health Education M
Health Services Management and Hospital Administration M,D
Hispanic Studies M,D
History of Science and Technology D
History M,D
Human Development M,D
Immunology D
Industrial and Labor Relations D
Industrial/Management Engineering M,D
Infectious Diseases M,D
Information Studies M,D
International Affairs M
Italian D
Japanese D
Jewish Studies D
Journalism M
Landscape Architecture M
Latin American Studies M,D
Law P,M,D
Legal and Justice Studies D
Linguistics D
Marketing D
Materials Engineering M,D
Materials Sciences M,D
Maternal and Child Health M
Mathematics Education M,D
Mathematics M,D
Mechanical Engineering M,D
Mechanics M,D
Microbiology D
Molecular Biology D
Molecular Toxicology D
Multilingual and Multicultural Education M,D
Music D
Near and Middle Eastern Studies M,D
Neuroscience D*
Nuclear Engineering M,D
Nutrition M,D*
Operations Research M,D
Optometry P,O
Organizational Behavior D
Philosophy D
Physical Education M,D
Physics D
Physiology M,D
Plant Biology D
Political Science D
Psychology—General D
Public Health—General M,D
Public Policy M,D
Range Science M
Reading Education M,D
Real Estate D
Religion D
Rhetoric D
Romance Languages D
Russian D
Scandinavian Languages D
School Psychology D
Science Education M,D
Slavic Languages D
Social Work M,D
Sociology D
Spanish M,D
Special Education D
Statistics M,D
Structural Engineering M,D
Theater D
Transportation and Highway Engineering M,D
Urban and Regional Planning M,D
Urban Design M,D
Vision Sciences M,D
Water Resources Engineering M,D

UNIVERSITY OF CALIFORNIA, DAVIS

Aerospace/Aeronautical Engineering M,D,O
Agricultural Economics and Agribusiness M,D
Agricultural Sciences—General M
Agronomy and Soil Sciences M,D
Allopathic Medicine P
American Indian/Native American Studies M,D
Animal Behavior D
Animal Sciences M,D
Anthropology M,D
Applied Mathematics M,D
Applied Science and Technology M,D
Art History M*
Art/Fine Arts M
Atmospheric Sciences M,D
Biochemistry M,D
Bioengineering M,D
Biomedical Engineering M,D
Biophysics M,D
Biostatistics M,D
Business Administration and Management—General M
Cell Biology M,D
Chemical Engineering M,D
Chemistry M,D
Child Development M
Civil Engineering M,D,O
Clinical Research M
Clothing and Textiles M
Communication—General M
Comparative Literature D
Computer Engineering M,D
Computer Science M,D
Cultural Studies M,D
Curriculum and Instruction M,D
Developmental Biology M,D
Ecology M,D
Economics M,D
Education—General M,D
Educational Psychology M,D
Electrical Engineering M,D
Engineering and Applied Sciences—General M,D,O
English M,D
Entomology M,D
Environmental Engineering M,D,O
Environmental Sciences M,D
Epidemiology M,D
Evolutionary Biology D
Exercise and Sports Science M
Food Science and Technology M,D
Forensic Sciences M
French D
Genetics M,D
Geography M,D
Geology M,D
German M,D
History M,D
Horticulture M
Human Development D
Hydrology M,D
Immunology M,D
Law P,M
Linguistics M,D
Materials Engineering M,D
Materials Sciences M,D
Maternal and Child Health M
Mathematics M,D
Mechanical Engineering M,D,O
Medical Informatics M
Microbiology M,D*
Molecular Biology M,D
Music M,D
Neuroscience D*
Nutrition M,D
Pathology M,D
Pharmacology M,D
Philosophy M,D
Physics M,D
Physiology M,D
Plant Biology M,D
Plant Pathology M,D
Political Science M,D
Psychology—General D
Sociology M,D
Spanish M,D
Statistics M,D
Textile Design M
Theater M,D
Toxicology M,D
Transportation and Highway Engineering M,D
Transportation Management M,D
Urban and Regional Planning M
Veterinary Medicine P
Veterinary Sciences M,O
Writing M,D
Zoology M

UNIVERSITY OF CALIFORNIA, HASTINGS COLLEGE OF THE LAW

Law P,M

UNIVERSITY OF CALIFORNIA, IRVINE

Aerospace/Aeronautical Engineering M,D
Allopathic Medicine P
Anatomy M,D
Anthropology M,D
Art History M,D
Art/Fine Arts M
Artificial Intelligence/Robotics M
Asian Languages M,D
Biochemical Engineering M,D
Biochemistry M,D
Biological and Biomedical Sciences—General M,D
Biomedical Engineering M,D
Biophysics D
Biotechnology M
Business Administration and Management—General M,D
Cell Biology M,D
Chemical Engineering M,D
Chemistry M,D
Chinese M,D
Civil Engineering M,D
Classics M,D
Comparative Literature M,D
Computer Science M,D*
Criminal Justice and Criminology M,D
Dance M
Demography and Population Studies M
Developmental Biology M,D
Ecology M,D
Economics M,D
Education—General M,D
Educational Administration M,D
Electrical Engineering M,D
Elementary Education M,D
Engineering and Applied Sciences—General M,D
English M,D
Environmental Engineering M,D
Evolutionary Biology M,D
Foreign Languages Education M,D
French M,D
Genetic Counseling M
Genetics D
Geosciences M,D
German M,D
History M,D
Information Science M,D
Japanese M,D
Materials Engineering M,D
Materials Sciences M,D
Mathematics M,D
Mechanical Engineering M,D
Microbiology M,D
Molecular Biology M,D
Molecular Genetics M,D
Music M
Neurobiology M,D
Pharmacology M,D*
Philosophy M,D
Physics M,D
Physiology D
Political Science D
Psychology—General D
Secondary Education M,D
Social Sciences M,D
Sociology M,D
Spanish M,D
Theater M,D
Toxicology M,D
Transportation and Highway Engineering M,D
Urban and Regional Planning M,D*
Urban Studies M,D
Writing M

UNIVERSITY OF CALIFORNIA, LOS ANGELES

Aerospace/Aeronautical Engineering M,D
African Studies M
African-American Studies M
Allopathic Medicine P

American Indian/Native American Studies M
Anatomy D
Anthropology M,D
Applied Arts and Design—General M
Applied Social Research M,D
Archaeology M,D
Architecture M,D
Art History M,D
Art/Fine Arts M
Asian Languages M,D
Asian Studies M,D
Asian-American Studies M
Astronomy M,D
Astrophysics M,D
Atmospheric Sciences M,D
Biochemistry M,D
Biological and Biomedical Sciences—General M,D
Biomedical Engineering M,D
Biometrics M,D*
Biostatistics M,D
Business Administration and Management—General M,D*
Cell Biology M,D*
Ceramic Sciences and Engineering M,D
Chemical Engineering M,D
Chemistry M,D
Civil Engineering M,D
Classics M,D
Clinical Research M
Community Health M,D
Comparative Literature M,D
Computer Science M,D
Dance M,D
Dentistry P,O
Developmental Biology M,D
Economics M,D
Education—General M,D
Electrical Engineering M,D
Engineering and Applied Sciences—General M,D
English as a Second Language M
English M,D
Environmental and Occupational Health M,D
Environmental Engineering M,D
Environmental Sciences D*
Epidemiology M,D
Film, Television, and Video Production M,D
French M,D
Geochemistry M,D
Geography M,D
Geology M,D
Geophysics M,D
Geosciences M,D
Geotechnical Engineering M,D
German M,D
Health Services Management and Hospital Administration M,D
Hispanic Studies D
History M,D
Human Genetics M,D
Hydrology M,D
Immunology M,D
Information Studies M,D,O
Italian M,D
Latin American Studies M
Law P,M
Library Science M,D,O
Linguistics M,D
Manufacturing Engineering M
Materials Engineering M,D
Materials Sciences M,D
Mathematics M,D
Mechanical Engineering M,D
Medical Physics M,D
Metallurgical Engineering and Metallurgy M,D
Microbiology M,D
Molecular Biology M,D
Molecular Genetics M,D
Molecular Toxicology D*
Music M,D
Near and Middle Eastern Languages M,D
Near and Middle Eastern Studies M,D
Neurobiology D
Neuroscience D
Nursing—General M,D
Operations Research M,D
Oral and Dental Sciences M,D
Pathology M,D
Pharmacology D*
Philosophy M,D
Physics M,D*
Physiology M,D
Planetary and Space Sciences M,D
Plant Molecular Biology M,D
Political Science M,D
Portuguese M
Psychology—General M,D
Public Health—General M,D
Public Policy M
Romance Languages M,D
Scandinavian Languages M,D
Science Education M,D
Slavic Languages M,D
Social Work M,D
Sociology M,D
Spanish M
Special Education D
Statistics M,D
Structural Engineering M,D
Theater M,D*
Urban and Regional Planning M,D
Urban Design M,D
Water Resources Engineering M,D
Women's Studies M,D

UNIVERSITY OF CALIFORNIA, RIVERSIDE

Agronomy and Soil Sciences M,D
Anthropology M,D
Applied Statistics M,D
Art History M
Art/Fine Arts M
Artificial Intelligence/Robotics M,D
Biochemistry M,D
Bioengineering M,D*
Bioinformatics D
Biological and Biomedical Sciences—General M,D
Botany M,D
Business Administration and Management—General M
Cell Biology M,D
Chemical Engineering M,D*
Chemistry M,D
Classics D
Comparative Literature M,D
Computer Engineering M,D
Computer Science M,D*
Dance M,D
Developmental Biology M,D
Economics M,D*
Education—General M,D
Electrical Engineering M,D*
English M,D
Entomology M,D
Environmental Engineering M,D
Environmental Sciences M,D
Evolutionary Biology M,D
Genetics D
Genomic Sciences D
Geology M,D*
Hispanic Studies M,D
Historic Preservation M,D
History M,D
Mathematics M,D
Mechanical Engineering M,D*
Microbiology M,D
Molecular Biology M,D
Molecular Genetics D
Museum Studies M,D
Music M
Neuroscience D
Philosophy M,D
Physics M,D
Plant Biology M,D
Plant Pathology M,D
Plant Sciences M,D
Political Science M,D
Psychology—General M,D
Sociology M,D
Spanish M,D
Statistics M,D
Toxicology M,D
Water Resources M,D
Writing M

UNIVERSITY OF CALIFORNIA, SAN DIEGO

Aerospace/Aeronautical Engineering M,D
Allopathic Medicine P
Anthropology D
Applied Mathematics M,D
Applied Physics M,D
Art/Fine Arts M,D
Artificial Intelligence/Robotics M,D
Biochemistry M,D
Bioengineering M,D*
Bioinformatics D*
Biological and Biomedical Sciences—General M,D*
Biophysics M,D
Business Administration and Management—General M
Cancer Biology/Oncology D
Cardiovascular Sciences D
Cell Biology D*
Chemical Engineering M,D*
Chemistry M,D*
Clinical Psychology D
Clinical Research M
Cognitive Sciences D
Communication Disorders D
Communication—General M,D
Comparative Literature M,D
Computer Engineering M,D
Computer Science M,D*
Developmental Biology D
Ecology D
Economics M,D
Education—General M,D
Electrical Engineering M,D*
Engineering Physics M,D
English M
Epidemiology D
Ethnic Studies M,D
Evolutionary Biology D
French M
Genetics D
Geosciences M,D
German M
Health Services Management and Hospital Administration M
History of Science and Technology M,D
History M,D
Immunology D
International Affairs M,D*
Jewish Studies M,D
Latin American Studies M
Linguistics D
Marine Biology M,D
Marine Sciences M
Materials Sciences M,D
Mathematics Education D
Mathematics M,D
Mechanical Engineering M,D*
Mechanics M,D
Microbiology D
Molecular Biology D
Molecular Pathology D
Music M,D*
Neurobiology D
Neuroscience D*
Ocean Engineering M,D
Oceanography M,D
Pharmacology D*
Pharmacy P
Philosophy D
Photonics M,D
Physics M,D
Physiology D
Plant Biology D
Plant Molecular Biology D
Political Science M,D
Psychology—General D
Public Health—General D
Science Education D
Sociology D
Spanish M
Statistics M,D
Structural Biology D
Structural Engineering M,D
Systems Biology D
Telecommunications M,D
Theater M,D
Virology D

UNIVERSITY OF CALIFORNIA, SAN FRANCISCO

Allopathic Medicine P
Anatomy D
Anthropology D
Biochemistry D
Bioengineering D
Biological and Biomedical Sciences—General D
Biophysics D
Cell Biology D
Chemistry D
Dentistry P
Developmental Biology D
Genetics D
Genomic Sciences D
History of Science and Technology M,D
Immunology D
Medical Informatics M,D
Medicinal and Pharmaceutical Chemistry D
Microbiology D
Molecular Biology D
Neuroscience D
Nursing—General M,D
Oral and Dental Sciences M,D
Pathology D
Pharmaceutical Sciences D
Pharmacology D
Pharmacy P
Physical Therapy M,D
Physiology D
Sociology D

UNIVERSITY OF CALIFORNIA, SANTA BARBARA

Agricultural Economics and Agribusiness M,D
Anthropology M,D
Applied Mathematics M,D
Applied Statistics M,D
Archaeology M,D
Art History D
Art/Fine Arts M,D
Asian Languages D
Asian Studies M,D
Biochemistry M,D
Bioengineering M,D
Biophysics M,D
Cell Biology M,D
Chemical Engineering M,D
Chemistry M,D
Child and Family Studies M,D
Classics M,D
Clinical Psychology M,D
Communication—General D
Comparative Literature D
Computer Engineering M,D
Counseling Psychology M,D
Developmental Biology M,D
Developmental Psychology M,D
Ecology M,D
Economics M,D
Education—General M,D
Educational Administration M,D
Educational Measurement and Evaluation M,D
Electrical Engineering M,D
Engineering and Applied Sciences—General M,D
English D
Environmental Management and Policy M,D
Environmental Sciences M,D*
Evolutionary Biology M,D
Film, Television, and Video Production
French M,D
Geography M,D
Geology M,D
Geophysics M,D
Geosciences M,D
German M,D
Hispanic Studies M,D
History D
International Affairs M
International and Comparative Education M,D
Latin American Studies M,D
Linguistics M,D
Marine Biology M,D
Marine Sciences M,D
Materials Engineering M,D
Materials Sciences M,D
Mathematical and Computational Finance M,D
Mathematics M,D
Mechanical Engineering M,D
Media Studies M,D
Molecular Biology M,D
Music M,D
Philosophy D
Physics D
Political Science M,D
Portuguese M,D
Psychology—General D
Public History D
Quantitative Analysis M,D
Religion M,D
Sociology D
Spanish M,D
Special Education M,D
Statistics M,D
Theater M,D
Western European Studies M
Women's Studies M,D

UNIVERSITY OF CALIFORNIA, SANTA CRUZ

Anthropology D
Applied Economics M
Art/Fine Arts M
Astronomy D
Astrophysics D
Biochemistry M,D
Bioinformatics M,D*
Cell Biology M,D
Chemistry M,D
Communication—General O
Comparative Literature M,D
Computer Art and Design M
Computer Engineering M,D*
Computer Science M,D*
Ecology M,D
Economics D
Education—General M,D
Electrical Engineering M,D*
Engineering and Applied Sciences—General M,D
Environmental Biology M,D
Environmental Management and Policy D
Evolutionary Biology M,D
Geosciences M,D
History D
Humanities D
International Affairs D
Linguistics M,D
Marine Sciences M,D
Mathematics M,D
Molecular Biology M,D
Music M,D
Philosophy M,D
Physics M,D
Political Science D
Psychology—General D
Social Sciences Education M
Social Sciences D
Sociology D
Statistics M*
Telecommunications M,D
Theater O

Toxicology M,D
Writing M

UNIVERSITY OF CENTRAL ARKANSAS

Accounting M
Biological and Biomedical Sciences—General M
Business Administration and Management—General M
Communication Disorders M
Computer Science M
Counseling Psychology M
Counselor Education M
Early Childhood Education M
Economics M
Education—General M
Educational Administration O
Educational Media/Instructional Technology M
English M
Family and Consumer Sciences-General M
Family Nurse Practitioner Studies M
Film, Television, and Video Production M
Foreign Languages Education M
Geographic Information Systems O
Geography O
Health Education M
History M
Human Development M
Kinesiology and Movement Studies M
Library Science M
Mathematics M
Medical Physics M
Music Education M
Music M
Nursing—General M
Occupational Therapy M
Physical Therapy D
Psychology—General M,D
Reading Education M
School Psychology M,D
Social Psychology M
Special Education M
Student Affairs M

UNIVERSITY OF CENTRAL FLORIDA

Accounting M
Actuarial Science M,O
Addictions/Substance Abuse Counseling M,O
Adult Nursing D,O
Aerospace/Aeronautical Engineering M
Anthropology M,D,O
Applied Mathematics M,D,O
Art Education M
Art/Fine Arts M
Biological and Biomedical Sciences—General M,D,O
Business Administration and Management—General M,D*
Chemistry M,D
Child and Family Studies M,O
Civil Engineering M,D,O
Clinical Psychology M,D
Communication Disorders M,D,O
Communication—General M
Community College Education M,D,O
Computational Sciences M,D
Computer Art and Design M
Computer Engineering M,D
Computer Science M,D
Conservation Biology M,D,O
Construction Engineering M,D,O
Counselor Education M,D
Criminal Justice and Criminology M,O
Curriculum and Instruction D
Early Childhood Education M
Economics M,D
Education—General M,D,O
Educational Administration M,D,O
Educational Media/Instructional Technology M,D,O
Electrical Engineering M,D,O
Elementary Education M,D
Engineering and Applied Sciences—General M,D,O
Engineering Design M,D,O
Engineering Management M,D,O
English as a Second Language M,O
English Education M
English M
Environmental Engineering M,D,O
Ergonomics and Human Factors M,D,O
Exercise and Sports Science M
Experimental Psychology M,D
Foreign Languages Education M,O
Forensic Sciences M,O
Gender Studies M,D,O
Gerontology M,O
Health Promotion M,O
Health Services Management and Hospital Administration M,O
History M
Hospitality Management M
Industrial and Organizational Psychology M,D
Industrial/Management Engineering M,D,O
Interdisciplinary Studies M
Latin American Studies M,D,O
Management Information Systems M
Manufacturing Engineering M,D,O
Marriage and Family Therapy M
Materials Engineering M,D
Materials Sciences M,D
Mathematics Education M,D,O
Mathematics M,D,O
Mechanical Engineering M,D,O
Microbiology M
Molecular Biology M
Music Education M
Nonprofit Management M,O
Nursing Education D,O
Nursing—General D,O
Operations Research M,D,O
Optical Sciences M,D
Pediatric Nursing D,O
Photonics M,D
Physical Education M
Physical Therapy M
Physics M,D
Political Science M
Psychology—General M,D
Public Administration M,O
Public Affairs D
Reading Education M,O
School Psychology O
Science Education M,O
Social Sciences Education M
Social Work M,O
Sociology M,D,O
Spanish M
Special Education M,D
Sports Management M,O
Statistics M,O
Structural Engineering M,D,O
Systems Engineering M,D,O
Taxation M
Technical Writing M,D,O
Theater M
Transportation and Highway Engineering M,D,O
Travel and Tourism M
Urban and Regional Planning M,O
Vocational and Technical Education M
Water Resources Engineering M,D,O
Writing M

UNIVERSITY OF CENTRAL MISSOURI

Accounting M
Applied Mathematics M
Aviation M
Biological and Biomedical Sciences—General M
Business Administration and Management—General M
Communication Disorders M
Communication—General M
Counselor Education M,O
Criminal Justice and Criminology M,O
Curriculum and Instruction M,O
Education—General M,D,O
Educational Administration M,O
Educational Media/Instructional Technology M
Elementary Education M,O
English as a Second Language M
English M
Environmental and Occupational Health M,O
Exercise and Sports Science M
Fire Protection Engineering M,O
Gerontology M
History M
Human Services M,O
Industrial and Manufacturing Management M
Industrial Hygiene M,O
Industrial/Management Engineering M
Information Studies M,O
Library Science M,O
Management Information Systems M
Mass Communication M
Mathematics M
Music M
Nursing—General M
Physical Education M
Psychology—General M
Reading Education M,O
Secondary Education M,O
Sociology M
Special Education M,O
Speech and Interpersonal Communication M
Student Affairs M
Theater M
Transportation Management M,O
Vocational and Technical Education M,O

Close-Up on page 1071.

UNIVERSITY OF CENTRAL OKLAHOMA

Addictions/Substance Abuse Counseling M
Adult Education M
American Studies M
Applied Arts and Design—General M
Applied Mathematics M
Biological and Biomedical Sciences—General M
Business Administration and Management—General M
Chemistry M
Communication Disorders M
Computer Education M
Computer Science M
Counseling Psychology M
Counselor Education M
Criminal Justice and Criminology M
Early Childhood Education M
Education—General M
Educational Administration M
Educational Media/Instructional Technology M
Elementary Education M
Engineering and Applied Sciences—General M
English as a Second Language M
English M
Family and Consumer Sciences-General M
Gerontology M
Health Education M
Higher Education M
History M
Home Economics Education M
Human Development M
Interior Design M
International Affairs M
Mathematics Education M
Mathematics M
Museum Studies M
Music Education M
Music M
Nutrition M
Physics M
Political Science M
Psychology—General M
Reading Education M
Secondary Education M
Special Education M
Statistics M
Urban Studies M
Writing M

UNIVERSITY OF CHARLESTON

Business Administration and Management—General M
Pharmacy P

UNIVERSITY OF CHICAGO

Allopathic Medicine P
Anatomy D
Anthropology M,D
Applied Mathematics M,D
Archaeology M,D
Art History M,D
Art/Fine Arts M,D
Asian Languages M,D
Asian Studies M,D
Astronomy M,D
Astrophysics M,D
Atmospheric Sciences M,D
Biochemistry D
Biological and Biomedical Sciences—General D
Biophysics D
Business Administration and Management—General M,D
Cancer Biology/Oncology D
Cell Biology D
Chemistry D
Classics M,D
Comparative Literature M,D
Computer Science M
Developmental Biology D
Ecology D
Economics D
English M,D
Environmental Management and Policy M,D
Environmental Sciences M,D
Evolutionary Biology D
Film, Television, and Video Theory and Criticism M,D
French M,D
Genetics D
Geophysics M,D
Geosciences M,D
German M,D
Health Promotion M
History D
Human Development D
Human Genetics D
Humanities M
Immunology D
Interdisciplinary Studies D
International Affairs M
International Business M
Italian M,D
Latin American Studies M
Law P,M,D
Linguistics M,D
Mathematical and Computational Finance M
Mathematics M,D
Media Studies M,D
Microbiology D
Molecular Biology D
Molecular Genetics D
Molecular Physiology D
Music M,D
Near and Middle Eastern Languages M,D
Near and Middle Eastern Studies M,D
Neurobiology D
Neuroscience D
Nutrition D
Paleontology M,D
Pathology D
Pharmacology D
Philosophy M,D
Physics M,D
Physiology D
Planetary and Space Sciences M,D
Political Science D
Psychology—General D
Public Policy M,D*
Religion P,M,D
Romance Languages M,D
Science Education D
Slavic Languages M,D
Social Sciences M,D*
Social Work M,D*
Sociology D
Spanish M,D
Statistics M,D
Theology P,M,D
Vision Sciences D
Zoology D

UNIVERSITY OF CINCINNATI

Accounting M,D
Acute Care/Critical Care Nursing M,D
Adult Education M,D,O
Adult Nursing M,D
Aerospace/Aeronautical Engineering M,D
Allopathic Medicine P,M
Analytical Chemistry M,D
Anthropology M
Applied Arts and Design—General M
Applied Mathematics M,D
Architecture M
Art Education M
Art History M
Art/Fine Arts M
Arts Administration M
Biochemistry M,D
Bioinformatics D
Biological and Biomedical Sciences—General M,D
Biomedical Engineering D
Biophysics D
Biostatistics M,D
Business Administration and Management—General M,D
Cancer Biology/Oncology D
Cell Biology D
Ceramic Sciences and Engineering M,D
Chemical Engineering M,D
Chemistry M,D
Civil Engineering M,D
Classics M,D
Clinical Psychology D
Communication Disorders M,D,O
Communication—General M
Community Health Nursing M,D
Computer Engineering M,D
Computer Science M,D
Construction Management M,D
Counselor Education M,D,O
Criminal Justice and Criminology M,D
Curriculum and Instruction M,D
Developmental Biology D
Early Childhood Education M
Economics M
Education—General M,D,O
Educational Administration M,D,O
Electrical Engineering M,D
Electronic Commerce M
Elementary Education M
Engineering and Applied Sciences—General M,D
English as a Second Language M,D,O
English M,D
Environmental and Occupational Health M,D

Environmental Engineering M,D
Environmental Sciences M,D
Epidemiology M,D
Ergonomics and Human Factors M,D
Experimental Psychology D
Finance and Banking M,D
Foundations and Philosophy of Education M,D
French M,D
Genetic Counseling M
Genomic Sciences M,D
Geography M,D
Geology M,D
German M,D
Graphic Design M
Health Education M,D
Health Physics/Radiological Health M
History M,D
Immunology M,D
Industrial and Labor Relations M
Industrial and Manufacturing Management M,D
Industrial Design M
Industrial Hygiene M,D
Industrial/Management Engineering M,D
Inorganic Chemistry M,D
Interdisciplinary Studies D
Interior Design M
Law P
Management Information Systems M
Management of Technology M,D
Marketing M,D
Materials Engineering M,D
Materials Sciences M,D
Maternal and Child/Neonatal Nursing M,D
Mathematics Education M,D
Mathematics M,D
Mechanical Engineering M,D
Mechanics M,D
Medical Imaging D
Medical Physics M
Metallurgical Engineering and Metallurgy M,D
Microbiology M,D
Molecular Biology M,D
Molecular Genetics M,D
Molecular Medicine D
Molecular Toxicology M,D
Music Education M
Music M,D,O
Neuroscience D
Nuclear Engineering M,D
Nurse Anesthesia M,D
Nurse Midwifery M,D
Nursing and Healthcare Administration M,D
Nursing—General M,D
Nutrition M
Occupational Health Nursing M,D
Organic Chemistry M,D
Organizational Management M
Pathobiology D
Pathology D
Pediatric Nursing M,D
Pharmaceutical Sciences M,D
Pharmacology D
Pharmacy P
Philosophy M,D
Physical Chemistry M,D
Physics M,D
Physiology D
Political Science M,D
Polymer Science and Engineering M,D
Psychiatric Nursing M,D
Psychology—General D
Quantitative Analysis M,D
Reading Education M,D
Rehabilitation Sciences D
Romance Languages M,D
School Psychology D,O
Science Education M,D,O
Secondary Education M
Social Sciences Education M,D,O
Social Work M
Sociology M,D
Spanish M,D
Special Education M,D
Statistics M,D
Taxation M
Textile Design M
Theater M
Toxicology D
Urban and Regional Planning M
Women's Health Nursing M,D
Women's Studies M,O

UNIVERSITY OF COLORADO AT BOULDER

Accounting D
Aerospace/Aeronautical Engineering M,D
Animal Behavior M,D
Anthropology M,D
Applied Mathematics M,D
Architectural Engineering M,D
Art History M
Art/Fine Arts M
Asian Studies M,D
Astrophysics M,D
Atmospheric Sciences M,D
Biochemistry M,D
Business Administration and Management—General M,D*
Cell Biology M,D
Chemical Engineering M,D
Chemical Physics M,D
Chemistry M,D
Chinese M,D
Civil Engineering M,D
Classics M,D
Communication Disorders M,D
Communication—General M,D
Comparative Literature M,D
Computer Engineering M,D
Computer Science M,D
Construction Engineering M,D
Curriculum and Instruction M,D
Dance M,D
Developmental Biology M,D
Ecology M,D
Economics M,D
Education—General M,D
Educational Measurement and Evaluation D
Educational Psychology M,D
Electrical Engineering M,D
Engineering and Applied Sciences—General M,D*
Engineering Management M
English M,D
Environmental Engineering M,D
Environmental Management and Policy M,D
Evolutionary Biology M,D
Finance and Banking D
Foundations and Philosophy of Education M,D
French M,D
Genetics M,D
Geography M,D
Geology M,D
Geophysics M,D
Geotechnical Engineering M,D
German M
History M,D
International Affairs M,D
Japanese M,D
Journalism M,D
Kinesiology and Movement Studies M,D
Law P
Linguistics M,D
Marine Biology M,D
Marketing D
Mass Communication M,D
Mathematical Physics M,D
Mathematics M,D
Mechanical Engineering M,D
Media Studies D
Medical Physics M,D
Medieval and Renaissance Studies M,D
Microbiology M,D
Molecular Biology M,D
Multilingual and Multicultural Education M,D
Museum Studies M
Music Education M,D
Music M,D
Neurobiology M,D
Oceanography M,D
Operations Research M
Optical Sciences M,D
Philosophy M,D
Photography M
Physics M,D
Physiology M,D
Plasma Physics M,D
Political Science M,D
Psychology—General M,D
Public Policy M,D
Religion M
Sociology D
Spanish M,D
Structural Engineering M,D
Telecommunications Management M
Telecommunications M
Theater M,D
Water Resources Engineering M,D
Writing M,D

UNIVERSITY OF COLORADO AT COLORADO SPRINGS

Accounting M
Adult Nursing M,D
Aerospace/Aeronautical Engineering M
Applied Mathematics M
Business Administration and Management—General M
Cognitive Sciences M
Communication—General M
Community Health Nursing M,D
Computer Science M,D
Counselor Education M,D
Criminal Justice and Criminology M
Curriculum and Instruction M,D
Education—General M,D
Educational Administration M,D
Electrical Engineering M,D
Engineering and Applied Sciences—General M,D
Engineering Management M
Environmental Sciences M
Family Nurse Practitioner Studies M,D
Finance and Banking M
Forensic Nursing M,D
Geography M
Gerontological Nursing M,D
Health Services Management and Hospital Administration M
History M
Human Services M,D
Information Science M
International Business M
Management Information Systems M
Management of Technology M
Manufacturing Engineering M
Marketing M
Maternal and Child/Neonatal Nursing M,D
Mechanical Engineering M
Nursing and Healthcare Administration M,D
Nursing—General M,D
Psychology—General M,D
Public Administration M
Public Affairs M
Sociology M
Software Engineering M
Special Education M,D
Women's Health Nursing M,D

UNIVERSITY OF COLORADO AT DENVER AND HEALTH SCIENCES CENTER

Accounting M
Advertising and Public Relations M,O
Allopathic Medicine P
Anthropology M
Applied Mathematics M,D
Applied Science and Technology M
Architecture M
Biochemistry D
Bioinformatics D
Biological and Biomedical Sciences—General M,D
Biophysics D
Biostatistics M,D
Business Administration and Management—General M
Cancer Biology/Oncology D
Cell Biology D
Chemistry M
Civil Engineering M,D
Clinical Laboratory Sciences/Medical Technology M,D
Communication—General M
Computer Engineering M,D
Computer Science M,D
Counseling Psychology M,O
Counselor Education M,O
Criminal Justice and Criminology M*
Dentistry P
Developmental Biology D
Early Childhood Education M
Economics M
Education—General M,D,O
Educational Administration M,D,O
Educational Media/Instructional Technology M
Educational Psychology M
Electrical Engineering M
English as a Second Language M,O
English Education M,O
English M,O
Environmental Sciences M,O
Epidemiology D
Finance and Banking M
Genetic Counseling M
Genetics D
Geographic Information Systems M,D,O
Health Education D
Health Services Management and Hospital Administration M
History M
Humanities M
Immunology D*
Information Science D
International Business M
Landscape Architecture M
Linguistics M,O
Management Information Systems M,D
Marketing M
Mathematics M
Mechanical Engineering M
Microbiology D*
Molecular Biology D
Music M
Neuroscience D*
Nursing—General M,D,O
Pharmaceutical Administration M
Pharmaceutical Sciences D*
Pharmacology D
Pharmacy P,D
Physical Therapy M,D
Physician Assistant Studies M
Physiology D
Political Science M
Psychology—General M
Public Administration M*
Public Affairs D
Public Health—General M*
School Psychology M,O
Social Sciences Education M
Social Sciences M
Sociology M
Spanish M
Technical Communication M
Toxicology P,D
Urban and Regional Planning M,D
Urban Design M

UNIVERSITY OF CONNECTICUT

Accounting M,D
Actuarial Science M,D
Acute Care/Critical Care Nursing M,D,O
Adult Education M,D
Adult Nursing M,D,O
African Studies M
Agricultural Economics and Agribusiness M,D
Agricultural Education M,D
Agricultural Sciences—General M,D
Agronomy and Soil Sciences M,D
Allied Health—General M
Animal Sciences M,D
Anthropology M,D
Applied Mathematics M
Art History M
Art/Fine Arts M
Biochemistry M,D
Biological and Biomedical Sciences—General M,D
Biomedical Engineering M,D
Biophysics M,D
Biopsychology M,D
Biotechnology M
Botany M,D
Business Administration and Management—General M,D*
Cell Biology M,D*
Chemical Engineering M,D
Chemistry M,D
Child and Family Studies M,D
Civil Engineering M,D
Clinical Psychology M,D
Cognitive Sciences M,D
Communication Disorders M,D
Communication—General M,D
Community Health Nursing M,D,O
Comparative Literature M,D
Computer Science M,D
Corporate and Organizational Communication M,D
Counseling Psychology M,D
Counselor Education M,D
Curriculum and Instruction M,D
Developmental Biology M,D
Developmental Psychology M,D
Ecology M,D
Economics M,D
Education of the Gifted M,D
Education—General M,D
Educational Administration D
Educational Measurement and Evaluation M,D
Educational Media/Instructional Technology M,D
Educational Psychology M,D
Electrical Engineering M,D
Elementary Education M,D
Engineering and Applied Sciences—General M,D
English Education M,D
English M,D*
Entomology M,D
Environmental and Occupational Health M
Environmental Engineering M,D
Environmental Management and Policy M,D
Exercise and Sports Science M,D
Experimental Psychology M,D
Finance and Banking M,D,O
Foreign Languages Education M,D
Foundations and Philosophy of Education D
French M,D
Genetics M,D
Genomic Sciences M
Geographic Information Systems M,D,O
Geography M,D
Geological Engineering M,D
Geology M,D
German M,D

Health Services Management and Hospital Administration M,D
Higher Education M
History M,D
Homeland Security M*
Human Development M,D
Human Resources Development M
Human Resources Management M*
Industrial and Organizational Psychology M,D
International Affairs M
Italian M,D
Jewish Studies M
Kinesiology and Movement Studies M,D
Latin American Studies M
Law P
Leisure Studies M,D
Linguistics D
Marine Sciences M,D
Marketing M,D
Materials Engineering M,D
Materials Sciences M,D
Maternal and Child/Neonatal Nursing M,D,O
Mathematical and Computational Finance M
Mathematics Education M,D
Mathematics M,D
Mechanical Engineering M,D
Medicinal and Pharmaceutical Chemistry M,D
Medieval and Renaissance Studies M,D
Metallurgical Engineering and Metallurgy M,D
Microbiology M,D
Molecular Biology M
Multilingual and Multicultural Education M,D
Music Education M,D,O
Music M,D,O
Natural Resources M,D
Neurobiology M,D
Neuroscience M,D
Nonprofit Management M,O
Nursing and Healthcare Administration M,D,O
Nursing—General M,D,O
Nutrition M,D
Oceanography M,D
Oral and Dental Sciences M
Pathobiology M,D
Pharmaceutical Sciences M,D
Pharmacology M,D
Pharmacy P
Philosophy M,D
Physical Therapy M
Physics M,D
Physiology M,D*
Plant Biology M,D
Plant Molecular Biology M,D
Plant Sciences M,D
Political Science M,D
Polymer Science and Engineering M,D*
Psychiatric Nursing M,D,O
Psychology—General M,D
Public Administration M
Public Health—General M
Public Policy M,O
Reading Education M,D
School Psychology M,D
Science Education M,D
Secondary Education M,D
Social Psychology M,D
Social Sciences Education M,D
Social Work M,D
Sociology M,D
Software Engineering M,D
Spanish M,D
Special Education M,D
Statistics M,D
Structural Biology M,D
Sustainable Development M*
Theater M
Toxicology M,D
Western European Studies M
Zoology M,D

Close-Up on page 1073.

UNIVERSITY OF CONNECTICUT HEALTH CENTER

Allopathic Medicine P
Biochemistry D
Biological and Biomedical Sciences—General D*
Cell Biology D*
Dentistry P,O
Developmental Biology D
Genetics D*
Immunology D*
Molecular Biology D*
Molecular Pharmacology D
Neuroscience D*
Oral and Dental Sciences M,D*
Public Health—General M

UNIVERSITY OF DALLAS

Accounting M
American Studies M
Art/Fine Arts M
Business Administration and Management—General M
Comparative Literature D
English M
Entrepreneurship M
Finance and Banking M
Health Services Management and Hospital Administration M
Human Resources Management M
Humanities M
International Business M
Logistics M
Management Information Systems M
Management of Technology M
Management Strategy and Policy M
Marketing M
Nonprofit Management M
Organizational Management M
Pastoral Ministry and Counseling M
Philosophy M,D
Political Science M,D
Project Management M
Psychology—General M
Sports Management M
Supply Chain Management M
Theology M

UNIVERSITY OF DAYTON

Aerospace/Aeronautical Engineering M,D
Agricultural Engineering M
Applied Mathematics M
Art Education M
Biological and Biomedical Sciences—General M,D*
Business Administration and Management—General M
Chemical Engineering M
Chemistry M
Civil Engineering M
Clinical Psychology M
Communication—General M
Computer Engineering M,D
Computer Science M
Counselor Education M,O
Early Childhood Education M
Education—General M,D,O
Educational Administration M,D,O
Educational Media/Instructional Technology M
Electrical Engineering M,D
Engineering and Applied Sciences—General M,D*
Engineering Management M
English M
Environmental Engineering M
Exercise and Sports Science M,D
Human Development M,O
Industrial/Management Engineering M
Law P,M
Materials Engineering M,D
Mathematical and Computational Finance M
Mathematics Education M
Mechanical Engineering M,D
Mechanics M
Middle School Education M
Music Education M
Optical Sciences M,D
Pastoral Ministry and Counseling M,D
Physical Education M,D
Psychology—General M
Public Administration M
Reading Education M
School Psychology M,O
Secondary Education M
Social Psychology M,O
Special Education M
Structural Engineering M
Student Affairs M,O
Theology M,D
Transportation and Highway Engineering M

UNIVERSITY OF DELAWARE

Accounting M
Adult Nursing M,O
Agricultural Economics and Agribusiness M
Agricultural Sciences—General M,D
Agronomy and Soil Sciences M,D
American Studies M
Animal Sciences M,D
Applied Arts and Design—General M
Applied Mathematics M,D
Art History M,D
Art/Fine Arts M*
Astronomy M,D
Atmospheric Sciences D
Biochemistry M,D
Biological and Biomedical Sciences—General M,D
Biotechnology M,D
Business Administration and Management—General M,D*
Business Education M,D
Cancer Biology/Oncology M,D
Cell Biology M,D
Chemical Engineering M,D
Chemistry M,D
Child and Family Studies M,D
Civil Engineering M,D
Clinical Psychology D
Cognitive Sciences D
Communication—General M
Computer Engineering M,D
Computer Science M,D*
Counselor Education M,D
Criminal Justice and Criminology M,D
Curriculum and Instruction M,D
Developmental Biology M,D
Ecology M,D
Economics M,D
Education—General M,D
Educational Administration M,D
Electrical Engineering M,D
Engineering and Applied Sciences—General M,D
English as a Second Language M,D
English M,D*
Entomology M,D
Entrepreneurship M,D
Environmental Engineering M,D
Environmental Management and Policy M,D*
Evolutionary Biology M,D
Exercise and Sports Science M
Family Nurse Practitioner Studies M,O
Fish, Game, and Wildlife Management M,D
Food Science and Technology M,D
Foreign Languages Education M
French M
Genetics M,D
Geography M,D
Geology M,D
Geotechnical Engineering M,D
German M
Gerontological Nursing M,O
Health Promotion M
Higher Education M
Historic Preservation M,D
History of Science and Technology M,D*
History M,D
HIV/AIDS Nursing M,O
Horticulture M
Hospitality Management M
Human Development M,D
Information Science M,D
International Affairs M,D
Kinesiology and Movement Studies M,D
Liberal Studies M
Linguistics M,D
Management Information Systems M*
Management of Technology M
Marine Affairs M,D
Marine Geology M,D
Marine Sciences M,D
Materials Engineering M,D
Materials Sciences M,D
Maternal and Child/Neonatal Nursing M,O
Mathematics M,D*
Mechanical Engineering M,D
Microbiology M,D
Molecular Biology M,D
Multilingual and Multicultural Education M,D
Museum Studies O
Music Education M
Music M
Neuroscience D
Nonprofit Management M,D
Nursing and Healthcare Administration M,O
Nursing—General M,O
Nutrition M
Ocean Engineering M,D
Oceanography M,D
Oncology Nursing M,O
Operations Research M,D*
Pediatric Nursing M,O
Physical Therapy D
Physics M,D
Physiology M,D
Plant Sciences M,D
Political Science M,D
Psychiatric Nursing M,O
Psychology—General D
Public Administration M*
Public Policy M,D
School Psychology M,D
Social Psychology D
Sociology M,D
Spanish M
Special Education M,D
Statistics M
Structural Engineering M,D
Theater M*
Transportation and Highway Engineering M,D
Urban Studies M,D
Water Resources Engineering M,D
Women's Health Nursing M,O

UNIVERSITY OF DENVER

Accounting M
Adult Education M,D,O
Advertising and Public Relations M
Anthropology M
Applied Mathematics M,D
Art History M
Art/Fine Arts M
Biological and Biomedical Sciences—General M,D
Business Administration and Management—General M,O*
Chemistry M,D
Child and Family Studies M,D,O
Clinical Psychology M,D
Communication—General M,D,O*
Computer Art and Design M
Computer Engineering M,D
Computer Science M,D,O
Conflict Resolution and Mediation/Peace Studies M
Construction Engineering M
Construction Management M
Counseling Psychology M,D,O
Criminal Justice and Criminology M,O
Curriculum and Instruction M,D,O
Economics M
Education—General M,D,O
Educational Administration M,D,O
Educational Measurement and Evaluation M,D,O
Educational Psychology M,D,O
Electrical Engineering M,D
Electronic Commerce M
Engineering and Applied Sciences—General M,D
English M,D
Environmental Management and Policy M,O
Film, Television, and Video Production M
Finance and Banking M
Geographic Information Systems M,O
Geography M,D
Higher Education M,D,O
Human Resources Management M,O
Information Studies M,O
International Affairs M,D
International Business M
Law P,M
Legal and Justice Studies M,O
Liberal Studies M,O
Library Science M,D,O
Management Information Systems M
Management of Technology M,O
Management Strategy and Policy M,O
Marketing M
Mass Communication M
Materials Sciences M,D
Mathematics M,D
Mechanical Engineering M,D
Media Studies M
Museum Studies M
Music Education M,O
Music M,O
Organizational Management M,O
Physics M,D
Project Management M,O
Psychology—General M,D
Public Policy M
Real Estate M
Religion M,D
School Psychology M,D,O
Social Work M,D,O*
Speech and Interpersonal Communication M,D
Statistics M
Taxation M
Telecommunications Management M,O
Telecommunications M,O
Theology D
Translation and Interpretation M,O
Transportation Management M

Close-Up on page 1075.

UNIVERSITY OF DETROIT MERCY

Addictions/Substance Abuse Counseling M,O
Allied Health—General M,O
Architectural Engineering M
Automotive Engineering M,D
Biochemistry M

Business Administration and Management—General M,O
Chemical Engineering M,D
Chemistry M
Civil Engineering M
Clinical Psychology M,D
Computer Science M
Counselor Education M
Criminal Justice and Criminology M
Curriculum and Instruction M
Dentistry P
Early Childhood Education M
Education—General M
Educational Administration M
Electrical Engineering M,D
Engineering and Applied Sciences—General M,D
Engineering Management M
Environmental Engineering M
Family Nurse Practitioner Studies M,O
Health Services Management and Hospital Administration M
Industrial and Organizational Psychology M
Information Science M
Law P
Liberal Studies M
Management Information Systems M
Manufacturing Engineering M,D
Mathematics Education M
Mathematics M
Mechanical Engineering M,D
Nurse Anesthesia M
Oral and Dental Sciences M,O
Physician Assistant Studies M
Polymer Science and Engineering M,D
Psychology—General M,D,O
Religion M
School Psychology O
Special Education M

UNIVERSITY OF DUBUQUE

Business Administration and Management—General M
Communication—General M
Theology P,M,D

UNIVERSITY OF EVANSVILLE

Business Administration and Management—General M
Computer Science M
Education—General M
Electrical Engineering M
Engineering and Applied Sciences—General M
Health Services Management and Hospital Administration M
Nursing—General M
Public Administration M

THE UNIVERSITY OF FINDLAY

Athletic Training and Sports Medicine M
Business Administration and Management—General M
Early Childhood Education M
Education—General M
Educational Administration M
Educational Media/Instructional Technology M
Elementary Education M
English as a Second Language M
Environmental Management and Policy M
Finance and Banking M
Human Resources Management M
International Business M
Liberal Studies M
Marketing M
Multilingual and Multicultural Education M
Occupational Therapy M
Physical Therapy M
Public Administration M
Special Education M

UNIVERSITY OF FLORIDA

Accounting M,D
Advertising and Public Relations M
Aerospace/Aeronautical Engineering M,D,O
African Studies O
Agricultural Economics and Agribusiness M,D
Agricultural Education M,D
Agricultural Engineering M,D,O
Agricultural Sciences—General M,D
Agronomy and Soil Sciences M,D
Allied Health—General M,D
Allopathic Medicine P
Animal Sciences M,D
Anthropology M,D
Aquaculture M,D
Architecture M,D
Art Education M,D
Art History M,D
Art/Fine Arts M,D
Arts Administration M
Astronomy M,D
Athletic Training and Sports Medicine M,D
Biochemistry M,D*
Bioengineering M,D,O
Biological and Biomedical Sciences—General D
Biomedical Engineering M,D,O
Biostatistics M
Botany M,D
Building Science M,D
Business Administration and Management—General M,D,O
Cell Biology M,D*
Chemical Engineering M,D*
Chemistry M,D
Civil Engineering M,D,O
Classics M,D
Clinical Psychology D
Clinical Research M
Cognitive Sciences M,D
Communication Disorders M,D
Communication—General M,D
Computer Art and Design M,D
Computer Engineering M,D,O
Computer Science M,D
Construction Engineering M,D
Counseling Psychology M,D
Counselor Education M,D,O
Criminal Justice and Criminology M,D
Curriculum and Instruction M,D,O
Dentistry P,O
Developmental Psychology M,D
Early Childhood Education M,D,O
Ecology M,D
Economics M,D
Education—General M,D,O
Educational Administration M,D,O
Educational Measurement and Evaluation M,D,O
Educational Psychology M,D,O
Electrical Engineering M,D,O
Electronic Commerce M
Elementary Education M,D,O
Engineering and Applied Sciences—General M,D,O*
English as a Second Language M,D,O
English Education M,D,O
English M,D
Entomology M,D
Entrepreneurship M,D,O
Environmental and Occupational Health M
Environmental Engineering M,D,O
Epidemiology M
Exercise and Sports Science M,D
Family and Consumer Sciences-General M
Finance and Banking M,D,O
Fish, Game, and Wildlife Management M,D
Food Science and Technology M,D
Forensic Sciences M,O
Forestry M,D
Foundations and Philosophy of Education M,D,O
French M,D
Gender Studies M,O
Genetics D*
Genomic Sciences D
Geography M,D
Geology M,D
Geosciences M,D
German M,D
Graphic Design M,D
Health Communication M,D,O
Health Education M,D,O
Health Psychology D
Health Services Management and Hospital Administration M,D*
Health Services Research M,D
Higher Education M,D,O
History M,D
Horticulture M,D
Human Resources Management M
Immunology D*
Industrial/Management Engineering M,D,O
Information Science M,D
Insurance M,D,O
Interior Design M,D
International Affairs M
International Business P,M,D
International Development M,D,O
Internet and Interactive Multimedia M,D
Journalism M
Kinesiology and Movement Studies M,D
Landscape Architecture M,D
Latin American Studies M,D
Law P,M,D
Limnology M,D
Linguistics M,D,O
Management Information Systems M,D
Management Strategy and Policy M
Marine Sciences M,D
Marketing M,D
Marriage and Family Therapy M,D,O
Mass Communication M,D
Materials Engineering M,D,O
Materials Sciences M,D,O
Mathematics Education M,D,O
Mathematics M,D
Mechanical Engineering M,D,O
Media Studies M
Medical Imaging M,D
Medicinal and Pharmaceutical Chemistry P,M,D
Microbiology M,D
Molecular Biology M,D
Molecular Genetics M,D
Multilingual and Multicultural Education M,D,O
Museum Studies M,D
Music Education M,D
Music M,D
Natural Resources M,D
Neuroscience M,D*
Nuclear Engineering M,D,O
Nursing—General M,D
Nutrition M,D
Occupational Therapy M
Ocean Engineering M,D,O
Oral and Dental Sciences M,D,O
Pathology D
Pharmaceutical Administration M,D
Pharmaceutical Sciences D
Pharmacology M,D
Pharmacy P
Philosophy M,D
Photography M,D
Physical Education M,D
Physical Therapy D
Physician Assistant Studies M
Physics M,D
Physiology M,D*
Plant Biology M,D
Plant Molecular Biology M,D
Plant Pathology M,D
Plant Sciences D
Political Science M,D,O
Psychology—General M,D
Public Affairs M,D,O
Public Health—General M
Quantitative Analysis M
Reading Education M,D,O
Real Estate M,D,O
Recreation and Park Management M,D
Rehabilitation Counseling M
Rehabilitation Sciences D
Religion M,D
School Psychology M,D,O
Science Education M,D,O
Social Psychology M,D
Social Sciences Education M,D,O
Social Sciences M
Sociology M,D
Spanish M,D
Special Education M,D,O
Sport Psychology M,D
Sports Management M
Statistics M,D
Student Affairs M,D,O
Supply Chain Management M,D
Systems Engineering M,D,O
Taxation P,M,D
Theater M
Toxicology M,D,O
Urban and Regional Planning M,D
Veterinary Medicine P
Veterinary Sciences M,D,O
Water Resources M,D
Women's Studies M,O
Writing M,D
Zoology M,D

Close-Up on page 1077.

UNIVERSITY OF GEORGIA

Accounting M
Adult Education M,D,O
Agricultural Economics and Agribusiness M,D
Agricultural Education M
Agricultural Engineering M,D
Agricultural Sciences—General M,D
Agronomy and Soil Sciences M,D
Analytical Chemistry M,D
Anatomy M
Animal Sciences M,D
Anthropology M,D
Applied Economics M,D
Applied Mathematics M,D
Art Education M,D,O
Art History M
Art/Fine Arts M,D
Artificial Intelligence/Robotics M*
Astronomy M,D
Biochemistry M,D
Bioengineering M,D
Biological and Biomedical Sciences—General D
Business Administration and Management—General M,D,O
Cell Biology M,D
Chemistry M,D
Child and Family Studies M,D
Classics M
Clothing and Textiles M,D
Communication Disorders M,D,O
Communication—General M,D
Comparative Literature M,D
Computer Science M,D
Consumer Economics M,D
Counselor Education M,D,O
Early Childhood Education M,D,O
Ecology M,D
Economics M,D
Education—General M,D,O
Educational Administration M,D,O
Educational Media/Instructional Technology M,D,O
Educational Policy M,D,O
Educational Psychology M,D,O
Elementary Education M,D,O
English M,D
Entomology M,D
Environmental and Occupational Health M,D
Family and Consumer Sciences-General M,D
Film, Television, and Video Theory and Criticism M,D
Food Science and Technology M,D
Forestry M,D
Foundations and Philosophy of Education M,D,O
French M
Genetics M,D
Geography M,D
Geology M,D
German M
Gerontology O
Health Education M,D,O
Health Promotion M,D,O
Higher Education D
Historic Preservation M
History M,D
Horticulture M,D
Infectious Diseases M,D
Inorganic Chemistry M,D
Interior Design M,D
Internet and Interactive Multimedia M
Journalism M,D
Kinesiology and Movement Studies M,D,O
Landscape Architecture M
Law P,M
Linguistics M,D
Marine Sciences M,D
Marketing Research M
Marketing M
Mass Communication M,D
Mathematics Education M,D,O
Mathematics M,D
Medicinal and Pharmaceutical Chemistry M,D
Microbiology M,D*
Middle School Education M,D,O
Molecular Biology M,D
Music Education M,D,O
Music M,D
Natural Resources M,D
Neuroscience D
Nonprofit Management M,D,O
Nutrition M,D
Oceanography M,D
Organic Chemistry M,D
Pathology M,D
Pharmaceutical Administration M,D
Pharmaceutical Sciences M,D
Pharmacology M,D
Pharmacy P
Philosophy M,D
Physical Chemistry M,D
Physics M,D
Physiology M,D
Plant Biology M,D
Plant Pathology M,D
Political Science M,D
Psychology—General M,D
Public Administration M,D
Public Policy M,D
Reading Education M,D,O
Religion M
Romance Languages M,D
Science Education M,D,O
Social Sciences Education M,D,O
Social Work M,D,O
Sociology M,D
Spanish M
Special Education M,D,O
Speech and Interpersonal Communication M,D
Statistics M,D
Sustainable Development M,D
Theater M,D
Toxicology M,D
Veterinary Medicine P
Veterinary Sciences M,D

Vocational and Technical Education M,D,O
Women's Studies O

UNIVERSITY OF GREAT FALLS

Addictions/Substance Abuse Counseling M,O
Counseling Psychology M
Criminal Justice and Criminology M
Education—General M
Human Services M
Information Science M
Marriage and Family Therapy M
Organizational Management M
School Psychology M

UNIVERSITY OF GUAM

Art/Fine Arts M
Biological and Biomedical Sciences—General M
Business Administration and Management—General M
Counselor Education M
Education—General M
Educational Administration M
English as a Second Language M
Environmental Sciences M
Graphic Design M
Marine Biology M
Public Administration M
Reading Education M
Secondary Education M
Special Education M

UNIVERSITY OF GUELPH

Acute Care/Critical Care Nursing M,D,O
Agricultural Economics and Agribusiness M,D
Agricultural Sciences—General M,D,O
Agronomy and Soil Sciences M,D
Anatomy M,D
Anesthesiologist Assistant Studies M,D,O
Animal Sciences M,D
Anthropology M
Applied Mathematics M,D
Applied Statistics M,D
Aquaculture M
Art/Fine Arts M
Atmospheric Sciences M,D
Biochemistry M,D
Bioengineering M,D
Biological and Biomedical Sciences—General M,D
Biophysics M,D
Biotechnology M,D
Botany M,D
Business Administration and Management—General M
Cell Biology M,D
Chemistry M,D
Child and Family Studies M,D
Clinical Psychology M,D
Cognitive Sciences M,D
Comparative Literature D
Computer Science M,D
Consumer Economics M
Criminal Justice and Criminology M
Ecology M,D
Economics M,D
Engineering and Applied Sciences—General M,D
English M
Entomology M,D
Environmental Biology M,D
Environmental Engineering M,D
Environmental Management and Policy M,D
Environmental Sciences M,D
Epidemiology M,D,O
Evolutionary Biology M,D
Food Science and Technology M,D
Geography M,D
History M,D
Horticulture M,D
Hospitality Management M
Human Development M,D
Immunology M,D,O
Industrial and Organizational Psychology M,D
Infectious Diseases M,D,O
International Development M
Landscape Architecture M
Marriage and Family Therapy M,D
Mathematics M,D
Medieval and Renaissance Studies D
Microbiology M,D
Molecular Biology M,D
Molecular Genetics M,D
Natural Resources M,D
Neuroscience M,D,O
Nutrition M,D
Pathology M,D,O
Pharmacology M,D
Philosophy M,D
Physics M,D
Physiology M,D
Plant Pathology M,D
Political Science M
Psychology—General M,D
Rural Planning and Studies M,D
Social Psychology M,D
Sociology M
Statistics M,D
Theater M
Toxicology M,D
Veterinary Medicine M,D,O
Veterinary Sciences M,D,O
Vision Sciences M,D,O
Water Resources Engineering M,D
Zoology M,D

UNIVERSITY OF HARTFORD

Accounting M,O
Architecture M
Art/Fine Arts M
Biological and Biomedical Sciences—General M
Business Administration and Management—General M
Clinical Psychology M,D
Communication—General M
Community Health Nursing M
Counselor Education M,O
Early Childhood Education M
Education—General M,D,O
Educational Administration D,O
Educational Media/Instructional Technology M
Elementary Education M
Engineering and Applied Sciences—General M
Experimental Psychology M
Music Education M,D,O
Music M,D,O
Neuroscience M*
Nursing Education M
Nursing—General M
Organizational Behavior M
Physical Therapy M,D
Psychology—General M,D
School Psychology M
Taxation M,O

UNIVERSITY OF HAWAII AT MANOA

Accounting M,D
Adult Nursing M,D,O
Agricultural Sciences—General M,D
Allopathic Medicine P
American Studies M,D,O
Animal Sciences M
Anthropology M,D
Architecture D
Art History M
Art/Fine Arts M
Asian Languages M,D
Asian Studies M,O
Astronomy M,D
Bioengineering M,D
Biological and Biomedical Sciences—General M,D
Botany M,D
Business Administration and Management—General M
Chemistry M,D
Chinese M,D
Civil Engineering M,D
Classics M
Clinical Psychology M,D,O
Communication Disorders M
Communication—General M,O
Community Health Nursing M,D,O
Computer Science M,D
Conflict Resolution and Mediation/Peace Studies O
Conservation Biology M,D
Counselor Education M
Cultural Studies M,O
Curriculum and Instruction M,D
Dance M,D
Demography and Population Studies O
Disability Studies O
Early Childhood Education M
Ecology M,D
Economics M,D
Education—General M,D,O
Educational Administration M,D
Educational Media/Instructional Technology M
Educational Policy D
Educational Psychology M,D
Electrical Engineering M,D
Engineering and Applied Sciences—General M,D,O
English as a Second Language M,D,O
English M,D
Entomology M,D
Entrepreneurship M
Environmental Engineering M,D
Environmental Management and Policy M,D,O
Epidemiology D
Evolutionary Biology M,D
Family Nurse Practitioner Studies M,D,O
Finance and Banking M,D
Food Science and Technology M
Foreign Languages Education M,D,O
Foundations and Philosophy of Education M,D
French M
Genetics M,D
Geochemistry M,D
Geography M,D
Geological Engineering M,D
Geology M,D
Geophysics M,D
Gerontology O
Historic Preservation O
History M,D
Horticulture M,D
Human Resources Management M
Hydrogeology M,D
Information Science M,D,O
Information Studies M,D,O
International Affairs O
International Business M,D
Japanese M,D
Kinesiology and Movement Studies M
Law P,O
Library Science M,D,O*
Linguistics M,D
Management Information Systems M,D,O
Marine Biology M,D
Marine Geology M,D
Marketing M,D
Mathematics M,D
Mechanical Engineering M,D
Medical Microbiology M,D
Meteorology M,D
Microbiology M,D
Molecular Biology M,D
Museum Studies O
Music M,D
Natural Resources M,D
Nursing and Healthcare Administration M,D,O
Nursing—General M,D,O
Nutrition M
Ocean Engineering M,D
Oceanography M,D
Organizational Behavior M
Organizational Management M,D
Philosophy M,D
Physics M,D
Physiology M,D
Planetary and Space Sciences M,D
Plant Pathology M,D
Plant Sciences M,D
Political Science M,D
Psychology—General M,D,O
Public Administration M,O
Public Health—General M
Real Estate M
Religion M
Social Psychology M,D,O
Social Work M,D
Sociology M,D,O
Spanish M
Special Education M,D
Speech and Interpersonal Communication M
Taxation M
Telecommunications O
Theater M,D*
Travel and Tourism M
Urban and Regional Planning M,D,O
Women's Studies O
Zoology M,D

UNIVERSITY OF HOUSTON

Accounting M,D
Advertising and Public Relations M
Aerospace/Aeronautical Engineering M,D
Anthropology M
Architecture M
Art Education M,D
Art/Fine Arts M
Biochemistry M,D
Biological and Biomedical Sciences—General M,D
Biomedical Engineering M,D
Business Administration and Management—General M,D
Chemical Engineering M,D
Chemistry M,D
Civil Engineering M,D
Clinical Psychology M,D
Communication Disorders M
Communication—General M
Computer Engineering M,D
Computer Science M,D*
Counseling Psychology M,D
Curriculum and Instruction M,D
Early Childhood Education M,D
Economics M,D
Education of the Gifted M,D
Education—General M,D
Educational Administration M,D
Educational Psychology M,D
Electrical Engineering M,D
Elementary Education M,D
Engineering and Applied Sciences—General M,D
English as a Second Language M,D
English M,D
Entrepreneurship D
Environmental Engineering M,D
Exercise and Sports Science M,D
Family and Consumer Sciences-General M
Finance and Banking M
Foundations and Philosophy of Education M,D
French M,D
Geology M,D
Geophysics M,D
Health Education M,D
Higher Education M,D
History M,D
Hospitality Management M
Human Development M
Industrial and Organizational Psychology M,D
Industrial/Management Engineering M,D
Information Science M,D
Interior Design M
Kinesiology and Movement Studies M,D
Law P,M
Linguistics M,D
Logistics M
Marketing D
Mass Communication M
Materials Engineering M,D
Mathematics Education M,D
Mathematics M,D
Mechanical Engineering M,D
Multilingual and Multicultural Education M,D
Music Education M,D
Music M,D
Optometry P
Petroleum Engineering M,D
Pharmaceutical Administration P,M,D
Pharmaceutical Sciences P,M,D
Pharmacology P,M,D
Pharmacy P,M,D
Philosophy M
Photography M
Physical Education M,D
Physics M,D
Political Science M,D
Psychology—General M,D
Public History M,D
Reading Education M,D
Science Education M,D
Secondary Education M,D
Social Psychology M,D
Social Sciences Education M,D
Social Work M,D
Sociology M
Spanish M,D
Special Education M,D
Speech and Interpersonal Communication M
Systems Engineering M,D
Theater M
Vision Sciences M,D
Writing M,D

UNIVERSITY OF HOUSTON–CLEAR LAKE

Accounting M
Biological and Biomedical Sciences—General M
Biotechnology M
Business Administration and Management—General M
Chemistry M
Clinical Psychology M
Computer Engineering M
Computer Science M
Counselor Education M
Criminal Justice and Criminology M
Cultural Studies M
Curriculum and Instruction M
Early Childhood Education M
Education—General M,D
Educational Administration M,D
Educational Media/Instructional Technology M
English M
Environmental Management and Policy M
Environmental Sciences M
Exercise and Sports Science M
Finance and Banking M
Foundations and Philosophy of Education M
Health Services Management and Hospital Administration M
History M
Human Resources Management M
Humanities M
Information Science M

Library Science M
Management Information Systems M
Marriage and Family Therapy M
Mathematics M
Multilingual and Multicultural Education M
Physics M
Psychology—General M
Reading Education M
School Psychology M
Sociology M
Software Engineering M
Statistics M
Systems Engineering M

UNIVERSITY OF HOUSTON–DOWNTOWN

Criminal Justice and Criminology M
Technical Communication M
Urban Education M
Writing M

UNIVERSITY OF HOUSTON–VICTORIA

Business Administration and Management—General M*
Computer Science M
Education—General M
Interdisciplinary Studies M
Psychology—General M

UNIVERSITY OF IDAHO

Accounting M
Adult Education M,D,O
Agricultural Economics and Agribusiness M
Agricultural Education M,D
Agricultural Engineering M,D*
Agronomy and Soil Sciences M,D
Animal Sciences M,D
Anthropology M
Applied Arts and Design—General M
Architecture M
Art Education M
Art/Fine Arts M
Biochemistry M,D
Bioinformatics M,D
Biological and Biomedical Sciences—General M
Business Administration and Management—General M
Chemical Engineering M,D*
Chemistry M,D
Civil Engineering M,D*
Computational Biology M,D
Computer Engineering M
Computer Science M,D*
Consumer Economics M
Counselor Education M,D,O
Curriculum and Instruction M,D
Education—General M,D,O
Educational Administration M,D,O
Electrical Engineering M,D*
Engineering and Applied Sciences—General M,D
English as a Second Language M
English M
Entomology M,D
Environmental Engineering M
Environmental Management and Policy M
Environmental Sciences M,D
Fish, Game, and Wildlife Management M,D
Food Science and Technology M,D
Forestry M
Geography M,D
Geological Engineering M
Geology M,D
History M,D
Hydrology M
Interdisciplinary Studies M
Landscape Architecture M
Law P
Materials Engineering M,D
Materials Sciences M,D*
Mathematics M,D
Mechanical Engineering M,D*
Metallurgical Engineering and Metallurgy M
Microbiology M,D
Molecular Biology M,D
Music M
Natural Resources M,D
Neuroscience M,D
Nuclear Engineering M,D
Physical Education M,D
Physics M,D
Plant Sciences M,D
Political Science M,D
Psychology—General M
Public Administration M
Public Affairs M,D
Range Science M
Recreation and Park Management M
School Psychology O
Science Education M,D

Social Sciences M
Special Education M,O
Statistics M
Systems Engineering M
Theater M
Veterinary Sciences M,D
Vocational and Technical Education M,D,O
Writing M

UNIVERSITY OF ILLINOIS AT CHICAGO

Accounting M
Allied Health—General M,D
Allopathic Medicine P
Anatomy M,D
Anthropology M,D
Applied Mathematics M,D
Architecture M
Art History M,D
Art/Fine Arts M
Biochemistry M,D
Bioengineering M,D
Biological and Biomedical Sciences—General M,D
Biophysics M,D
Biostatistics M,D
Biotechnology M,D
Business Administration and Management—General M,D
Cell Biology M,D
Chemical Engineering M,D
Chemistry M,D
Civil Engineering M,D
Communication—General M
Community Health Nursing M
Community Health M,D
Computer Engineering M,D
Computer Science M,D
Criminal Justice and Criminology M
Curriculum and Instruction M,D
Dentistry P
Developmental Biology M,D
Disability Studies M,D
East European and Russian Studies M,D
Ecology M,D
Economics M,D
Education—General M,D
Educational Administration M,D
Educational Policy M,D
Educational Psychology M,D
Electrical Engineering M,D*
Elementary Education M,D
Engineering and Applied Sciences—General M,D
English as a Second Language M
English Education M,D
English M,D
Environmental and Occupational Health M,D
Epidemiology M,D
Evolutionary Biology M,D
Forensic Sciences M
French M
Genetics M,D
Geochemistry M,D
Geography M
Geology M,D
Geophysics M,D
Geosciences M,D
Geotechnical Engineering D
German M,D
Graphic Design M
Health Education M
Health Services Management and Hospital Administration M,D
Hispanic Studies M,D
History M,D
Human Development M,D
Hydrogeology M,D
Immunology D
Industrial Design M
Industrial/Management Engineering M,D
Kinesiology and Movement Studies M
Linguistics M
Management Information Systems M
Mass Communication M
Materials Engineering M,D
Maternal and Child/Neonatal Nursing M
Mathematics Education M
Mathematics M,D*
Mechanical Engineering M,D*
Medical Illustration M
Medical/Surgical Nursing D
Microbiology D
Mineralogy M,D
Molecular Biology M,D
Molecular Genetics D
Neurobiology M,D*
Neuroscience D
Nurse Midwifery M
Nursing and Healthcare Administration M
Nursing—General M,D
Nutrition M,D

Occupational Therapy M
Operations Research D
Oral and Dental Sciences M
Paleontology M,D
Pediatric Nursing M
Pharmaceutical Administration M,D
Pharmaceutical Sciences M,D
Pharmacology D*
Pharmacy P,M,D
Philosophy M,D
Photography M
Physical Therapy M
Physics M,D
Physiology M,D
Plant Biology M,D
Political Science M,D
Psychiatric Nursing M
Psychology—General D
Public Administration M,D
Public Health—General M,D
Public Policy M,D
Reading Education M,D
Rhetoric M,D
Secondary Education M,D
Slavic Languages M,D
Social Work M,D
Sociology M,D
Special Education M,D
Statistics M,D
Urban and Regional Planning M,D
Urban Education M,D
Water Resources M,D
Writing M,D

UNIVERSITY OF ILLINOIS AT SPRINGFIELD

Accounting M
Addictions/Substance Abuse Counseling M
Biological and Biomedical Sciences—General M
Business Administration and Management—General M
Child and Family Studies M
Communication—General M
Computer Science M
Educational Administration M
English M
Environmental Management and Policy M
Environmental Sciences M
Gerontology M
Human Development M
Human Services M
Interdisciplinary Studies M
Journalism M
Legal and Justice Studies M
Management Information Systems M
Political Science M
Public Administration M,D
Public Health—General M
Public History M
Social Sciences M

UNIVERSITY OF ILLINOIS AT URBANA–CHAMPAIGN

Accounting M,D
Advertising and Public Relations M
Aerospace/Aeronautical Engineering M,D
African Studies M
Agricultural Economics and Agribusiness M,D
Agricultural Education M,D
Agricultural Engineering M,D
Agricultural Sciences—General M,D
Agronomy and Soil Sciences M,D
Allopathic Medicine
Animal Sciences M,D
Anthropology M,D
Applied Arts and Design—General M,D
Applied Mathematics M,D
Architecture M,D
Art Education M,D
Art History M,D
Art/Fine Arts M
Asian Languages M,D
Asian Studies M,D
Astronomy M,D
Atmospheric Sciences M,D
Aviation M
Biochemistry M,D*
Bioengineering M,D
Bioinformatics M,D,O
Biological and Biomedical Sciences—General M,D
Biomedical Engineering D
Biophysics D*
Business Administration and Management—General M,D
Cell Biology D
Chemical Engineering M,D
Chemistry M,D
Civil Engineering M,D*
Classics M,D
Communication Disorders M,D
Communication—General D
Community Health M,D

Comparative Literature M,D
Computational Biology D
Computer Engineering M,D
Computer Science M,D
Consumer Economics M,D
Counselor Education M,D,O
Curriculum and Instruction M,D,O
Dance M
Demography and Population Studies M,D
Developmental Biology D
East European and Russian Studies M
Ecology M,D
Economics M,D*
Education of the Multiply Handicapped M,D,O
Education—General M,D,O
Educational Administration M,D,O
Educational Policy M,D
Educational Psychology M,D,O
Electrical Engineering M,D
Engineering and Applied Sciences—General M,D
Engineering Design M
English as a Second Language M
English M,D
Entomology M,D*
Environmental Engineering M,D
Environmental Sciences M,D
Evolutionary Biology M,D
Finance and Banking M,D
Food Science and Technology M,D
Foreign Languages Education M,D,O
French M,D
Geochemistry M,D
Geography M,D
Geology M,D
Geophysics M,D
Geosciences M,D
German M,D
Graphic Design M
Health Informatics M,D,O
Health Physics/Radiological Health M,D
Higher Education M,D,O
History M,D
Human Development M,D
Human Resources Development M,D,O
Human Resources Management M,D*
Human-Computer Interaction M,D,O
Industrial and Labor Relations M,D
Industrial Design M
Industrial/Management Engineering M,D*
Information Science M,D,O
Information Studies M,D,O
Journalism M
Kinesiology and Movement Studies M,D
Landscape Architecture M,D
Latin American Studies M
Law P,M,D
Leisure Studies M,D
Library Science M,D,O*
Linguistics M,D
Management of Technology M
Materials Engineering M,D
Materials Sciences M,D
Mathematics Education M,D
Mathematics M,D
Mechanical Engineering M,D*
Mechanics M,D
Medical Informatics M,D,O
Microbiology D*
Molecular Biology D
Music M,D
Natural Resources M,D
Neuroscience D
Nuclear Engineering M,D*
Nutrition M,D
Pathobiology M,D
Philosophy M,D
Photography M
Physics M,D
Physiology M,D
Plant Biology M,D
Political Science M,D
Psychology—General M,D
Russian M,D
Slavic Languages M,D
Social Work M,D
Sociology M,D
Special Education M,D,O
Speech and Interpersonal Communication M,D
Statistics M,D
Systems Engineering M
Theater M,D
Urban and Regional Planning M,D
Veterinary Medicine P
Veterinary Sciences M,D
Vocational and Technical Education M,D,O
Zoology M,D

UNIVERSITY OF INDIANAPOLIS

Art Education M

Art/Fine Arts M
Biological and Biomedical Sciences—General M
Business Administration and Management—General M,O
Clinical Psychology M,D
Counseling Psychology M,D
Curriculum and Instruction M
Education—General M
Educational Administration M
Elementary Education M
English Education M
English M
Finance and Banking M,O
Foreign Languages Education M
Gerontology M,O
History M
Home Economics Education M,O
International Affairs M
Management of Technology M,O
Marketing M,O
Mathematics Education M
Nurse Midwifery M
Nursing and Healthcare Administration M
Nursing Education M
Nursing—General M
Occupational Therapy M,D
Physical Education M
Physical Therapy M,D
Psychology—General M,D
Science Education M
Secondary Education M
Social Sciences Education M
Sociology M
Supply Chain Management M,O

THE UNIVERSITY OF IOWA

Accounting M,D
Actuarial Science M,D
African-American Studies M
Allopathic Medicine P
American Studies M,D
Anatomy D
Anthropology M,D
Applied Mathematics D
Art Education M,D
Art History M,D
Art/Fine Arts M
Asian Studies M
Astronomy M
Bacteriology M,D
Biochemical Engineering M,D
Biochemistry M,D
Biological and Biomedical Sciences—General M,D*
Biomedical Engineering M,D
Biophysics M,D
Biostatistics M,D
Business Administration and Management—General M,D
Cell Biology M,D
Chemical Engineering M,D
Chemistry M,D
Civil Engineering M,D
Classics M,D
Clinical Research M,D
Communication Disorders M,D
Communication—General M,D
Community Health M,D
Comparative Literature M,D
Computational Biology M,D,O
Computational Sciences D
Computer Engineering M,D
Computer Science M,D*
Counseling Psychology M,D,O
Counselor Education M,D
Curriculum and Instruction M,D
Dance M
Dentistry P,M,D,O
Developmental Education M,D
Early Childhood Education M,D
Economics D
Education—General M,D,O
Educational Administration M,D,O
Educational Measurement and Evaluation M,D,O
Educational Policy M,D,O
Educational Psychology M,D,O
Electrical Engineering M,D
Elementary Education M,D
Engineering and Applied Sciences—General M,D*
English Education M,D
English M,D
Entrepreneurship M
Environmental and Occupational Health M,D,O
Environmental Engineering M,D
Epidemiology M,D
Ergonomics and Human Factors M,D
Evolutionary Biology M,D
Exercise and Sports Science M,D
Film, Television, and Video Production M
Film, Television, and Video Theory and Criticism M,D
Finance and Banking M,D
Foreign Languages Education M,D
Foundations and Philosophy of Education M,D,O
French M,D
Genetics M,D*
Geography M,D
Geosciences M,D
German M,D
Health Informatics M,D,O
Health Services Management and Hospital Administration M,D
Higher Education M,D,O
History M,D
Immunology M,D
Industrial and Manufacturing Management M
Industrial/Management Engineering M,D
Information Science M,D,O
Information Studies M
Investment Management M
Journalism M
Law P,M
Leisure Studies M
Library Science M
Linguistics M,D
Management Information Systems M
Management Strategy and Policy M
Manufacturing Engineering M,D
Marketing M,D
Mass Communication M,D
Mathematics Education M,D
Mathematics M,D
Mechanical Engineering M,D
Media Studies M,D
Microbiology M,D
Molecular Biology D*
Music Education M,D
Music M,D
Neurobiology M,D
Neuroscience D*
Nonprofit Management M
Nursing—General M,D
Operations Research M,D
Oral and Dental Sciences M,D,O
Pathology M
Pharmacology M,D
Pharmacy M,D
Philosophy M,D
Physical Education M,D
Physical Therapy D
Physician Assistant Studies M
Physics M,D
Physiology M,D*
Plant Biology M,D
Political Science M,D
Psychology—General M,D,O
Public Health—General M,D,O
Radiation Biology M,D*
Recreation and Park Management M
Rehabilitation Counseling M,D
Rehabilitation Sciences D
Religion M,D
Rhetoric M,D
School Psychology M,D,O
Science Education M,D
Secondary Education M,D
Social Sciences Education M,D
Social Work M,D
Sociology M,D
Spanish M,D
Special Education M,D
Sport Psychology M,D
Sports Management M
Statistics M,D,O
Student Affairs M,D
Theater M
Toxicology M,D
Translation and Interpretation M
Translational Biology M
Urban and Regional Planning M
Virology M,D
Women's Studies D
Writing M,D

UNIVERSITY OF KANSAS

Accounting M
Aerospace/Aeronautical Engineering M,D
Allied Health—General M,D,O
Allopathic Medicine P
American Indian/Native American Studies M
American Studies M,D
Anatomy M,D
Anthropology M,D
Applied Arts and Design—General M
Applied Mathematics M,D
Architectural Engineering M
Architecture M
Art Education M
Art History M,D
Art/Fine Arts M
Asian Languages M
Asian Studies M
Astronomy M,D
Biochemistry M,D
Biological and Biomedical Sciences—General M,D*
Biophysics M,D
Botany M,D
Business Administration and Management—General M,D
Cell Biology M,D
Chemical Engineering M,D
Chemistry M,D
Chinese M
Civil Engineering M,D
Classics M
Clinical Psychology M,D
Communication Disorders M,D
Communication—General M,D
Computer Engineering M
Computer Science M,D
Construction Management M
Counseling Psychology M,D
Curriculum and Instruction M,D
Developmental Biology M,D
Developmental Psychology M,D
East European and Russian Studies M
Ecology M,D
Economics M,D
Education—General M,D,O
Educational Administration M,D,O
Educational Measurement and Evaluation M,D
Educational Policy D
Educational Psychology M,D
Electrical Engineering M,D
Engineering and Applied Sciences—General M,D
Engineering Management M
English M,D
Entomology M,D
Environmental Engineering M,D
Environmental Sciences M,D
Evolutionary Biology M,D
Film, Television, and Video Theory and Criticism M,D
Foundations and Philosophy of Education D
French M,D
Geography M,D
Geology M,D
German M,D
Gerontology M,D
Health Services Management and Hospital Administration M
Higher Education M,D
History M,D
Human Development M,D
Immunology D
Interdisciplinary Studies M,D
International Affairs M
Japanese M
Journalism M
Latin American Studies M,O
Law P
Linguistics M,D
Management Information Systems M,D
Mathematics M,D
Mechanical Engineering M,D
Medicinal and Pharmaceutical Chemistry M,D
Microbiology M,D
Molecular Biology M,D
Molecular Genetics D
Museum Studies M
Music Education M,D
Music M,D
Near and Middle Eastern Studies M
Neuroscience M,D
Nurse Anesthesia M
Nurse Midwifery M,D,O
Nursing Education M,D,O
Nursing—General M,D,O
Nutrition M,O
Occupational Therapy M,D
Pathology M,D
Petroleum Engineering M,D
Pharmaceutical Sciences M
Pharmacology M,D
Philosophy M,D
Physical Education M,D
Physical Therapy M,D
Physics M,D*
Physiology M,D
Political Science M,D
Psychiatric Nursing M,D,O
Psychology—General M,D
Public Administration M,D
Public Health—General M
Rehabilitation Sciences M,D
Religion M
School Psychology D,O
Slavic Languages M,D
Social Sciences M,D
Sociology M,D
Spanish M,D
Special Education M,D
Theater M,D
Therapies—Dance, Drama, and Music M
Toxicology M,D
Urban and Regional Planning M
Water Resources M
Writing M,D

UNIVERSITY OF KENTUCKY

Accounting M
Agricultural Economics and Agribusiness M,D
Agricultural Engineering M,D
Agricultural Sciences—General M,D
Agronomy and Soil Sciences M,D
Allied Health—General M,D
Allopathic Medicine P
Anatomy D
Animal Sciences M,D
Anthropology M,D
Applied Arts and Design—General M
Applied Mathematics M,D
Architecture M
Art Education M
Art History M
Art/Fine Arts M
Astronomy M,D
Biochemistry D
Biological and Biomedical Sciences—General M,D
Biomedical Engineering M,D
Business Administration and Management—General M,D
Chemical Engineering M,D
Chemistry M,D
Child and Family Studies M,D
Civil Engineering M,D
Classics M
Clinical Laboratory Sciences/Medical Technology M,D
Clinical Psychology M,D
Clothing and Textiles M
Communication Disorders M
Communication—General M,D
Computer Science M,D
Counseling Psychology M,D,O
Curriculum and Instruction M,D
Dentistry P,M
Early Childhood Education M,D
Economics M,D
Education—General M,D,O
Educational Administration M,D,O
Educational Measurement and Evaluation M,D
Educational Media/Instructional Technology M,D
Educational Policy M,D
Educational Psychology M,D,O
Electrical Engineering M,D
Engineering and Applied Sciences—General M,D
English M,D
Entomology M,D
Exercise and Sports Science M,D
Experimental Psychology M,D
Foreign Languages Education M
Forestry M
French M
Geography M,D
Geology M,D
German M
Gerontology D
Health Physics/Radiological Health M
Health Promotion M,D
Health Services Management and Hospital Administration M
Higher Education M,D
Hispanic Studies M,D
Historic Preservation M
History M,D
Hospitality Management M
Interior Design M
International Affairs M
International Business M
Kinesiology and Movement Studies M,D
Law P
Library Science M
Manufacturing Engineering M
Materials Sciences M,D
Mathematics M,D
Mechanical Engineering M,D
Medical Physics M
Microbiology D*
Middle School Education M,D
Mineral/Mining Engineering M,D
Music Education M,D
Music M,D
Neurobiology D
Nursing—General M,D
Nutrition M,D*
Oral and Dental Sciences M
Pharmaceutical Sciences M,D
Pharmacology D
Pharmacy P
Philosophy M,D
Physical Therapy M
Physician Assistant Studies M
Physics M,D*
Physiology M,D
Plant Pathology M,D
Plant Physiology D
Plant Sciences M
Political Science M,D
Psychology—General M,D

Public Administration M,D
Public Health—General M
Rehabilitation Counseling M,D
Rehabilitation Sciences D
School Psychology M,D,O
Social Work M,D
Sociology M,D
Special Education M,D
Statistics M,D
Theater M
Toxicology M,D*
Veterinary Sciences M,D
Vocational and Technical Education M

UNIVERSITY OF LA VERNE

Accounting M
Business Administration and Management—General M,O
Child and Family Studies M
Child Development M
Clinical Psychology D
Counseling Psychology M
Counselor Education M,O
Education—General M,O
Educational Administration M,D,O
Finance and Banking M
Gerontology M,O
Health Informatics M
Health Services Management and Hospital Administration M,O
Health Services Research M
International Business M
Law P
Management Information Systems M
Marketing M
Marriage and Family Therapy M
Multilingual and Multicultural Education O
Nonprofit Management M,O
Organizational Management M,D,O
Psychology—General M,O
Public Administration M,D,O
Reading Education M,O
Social Psychology D
Special Education M
Supply Chain Management M

UNIVERSITY OF LETHBRIDGE

Accounting M,D
Addictions/Substance Abuse Counseling M,D
Agricultural Sciences—General M,D
American Indian/Native American Studies M,D
Anthropology M,D
Archaeology M,D
Art/Fine Arts M,D
Biochemistry M,D
Biological and Biomedical Sciences—General M,D
Business Administration and Management—General M,D
Canadian Studies M,D
Chemistry M,D
Computational Sciences M,D
Computer Science M,D
Counseling Psychology M,D
Economics M,D
Education—General M,D
Educational Administration M,D
English M,D
Environmental Sciences M,D
Exercise and Sports Science M,D
Finance and Banking M,D
French M,D
Geographic Information Systems M,D
Geography M,D
German M,D
History M,D
Human Resources Management M,D
International Business M,D
Kinesiology and Movement Studies M,D
Management Information Systems M,D
Management Strategy and Policy M,D
Mathematics M,D
Media Studies M,D
Molecular Biology M,D
Music M,D
Neuroscience M,D
Nursing—General M,D
Philosophy M,D
Physics M,D
Political Science M,D
Psychology—General M,D
Religion M,D
Sociology M,D
Spanish M,D
Urban Studies M,D

UNIVERSITY OF LOUISIANA AT LAFAYETTE

American Studies D
Architectural Engineering M
Biological and Biomedical Sciences—General M,D
Business Administration and Management—General M
Chemical Engineering M
Civil Engineering M
Cognitive Sciences D
Communication Disorders M,D
Communication—General M
Computer Engineering M,D
Computer Science M,D*
Counselor Education M
Curriculum and Instruction M
Education of the Gifted M
Education—General M,D
Educational Administration M,D
Engineering Management M
English M,D
Environmental Biology M,D
Evolutionary Biology M,D
Family and Consumer Sciences-General M
Folklore M,D
French M,D
Geology M
Health Services Management and Hospital Administration M
History M
Mass Communication M
Mathematics M,D
Mechanical Engineering M
Music Education M
Music M
Nursing—General M
Petroleum Engineering M
Physics M
Psychology—General M
Rehabilitation Counseling M
Rhetoric M,D
Telecommunications M
Writing M,D

UNIVERSITY OF LOUISIANA AT MONROE

Addictions/Substance Abuse Counseling M
Biological and Biomedical Sciences—General M
Business Administration and Management—General M
Communication Disorders M
Communication—General M
Counselor Education M
Criminal Justice and Criminology M
Curriculum and Instruction M,D
Education—General M,D,O
Educational Administration M,D
Elementary Education M
English M
Exercise and Sports Science M
Gerontology M,O
History M
Marriage and Family Therapy M,D
Music M
Pharmaceutical Sciences M
Pharmacy P,D
Psychology—General M,O
Reading Education M
School Psychology O
Secondary Education M
Special Education M

UNIVERSITY OF LOUISVILLE

Accounting M
African Studies M
Allopathic Medicine P
Analytical Chemistry M,D
Anatomy M,D
Applied Mathematics M,D
Art Education M
Art History M,D
Art Therapy M
Art/Fine Arts M
Biochemistry M,D
Biological and Biomedical Sciences—General M
Biophysics M,D
Biostatistics M,D
Business Administration and Management—General M
Chemical Engineering M,D
Chemical Physics M,D
Chemistry M,D
Civil Engineering M,D
Clinical Psychology D
Clinical Research M,D,O
Communication Disorders M,D
Computer Engineering M,D
Computer Science M,D
Counseling Psychology M,D
Counselor Education M,D
Criminal Justice and Criminology M
Curriculum and Instruction D
Dentistry P
Early Childhood Education M
Education—General M,D,O
Educational Administration M,D,O
Educational Media/Instructional Technology M
Educational Psychology M,D
Electrical Engineering M,D
Elementary Education M
Engineering and Applied Sciences—General M,D
Engineering Management M
English M,D
Entrepreneurship M
Environmental Biology D
Environmental Engineering M,D
Exercise and Sports Science M
Experimental Psychology D
Foreign Languages Education M,D
French M
Health Education M
Higher Education M,O
History M
Human Resources Development M
Humanities M,D
Immunology M,D
Industrial and Labor Relations M
Industrial/Management Engineering M,D
Inorganic Chemistry M,D
Interdisciplinary Studies M
Law P
Marriage and Family Therapy M,D,O
Mathematics M,D
Mechanical Engineering M
Microbiology M,D
Middle School Education M
Molecular Biology M,D
Music Education M
Music M,D
Neurobiology M,D
Nursing—General M,D
Oral and Dental Sciences M
Organic Chemistry M,D
Pharmacology M,D
Philosophy M
Physical Chemistry M,D
Physical Education M
Physics M
Physiology M,D
Political Science M
Psychology—General M,D
Public Administration M
Public Affairs D
Public Health—General M,O
Public Policy M
Reading Education M
Rhetoric D
Secondary Education M
Social Work M,D,O
Sociology M
Spanish M
Special Education M,D
Sports Management M
Student Affairs M,D
Theater M
Toxicology M,D
Urban and Regional Planning M
Urban Studies D
Vision Sciences D
Vocational and Technical Education M
Women's Studies M,O

Close-Up on page 1079.

UNIVERSITY OF MAINE

Accounting M
Agricultural Economics and Agribusiness M
Agricultural Sciences—General M,D
Agronomy and Soil Sciences M,D
Animal Sciences M
Biochemistry M,D
Bioengineering M
Biological and Biomedical Sciences—General D
Botany M
Business Administration and Management—General M
Chemical Engineering M,D
Chemistry M,D
Civil Engineering M,D
Clinical Psychology M,D
Communication Disorders M
Communication—General M
Computer Engineering M,D
Computer Science M,D
Counselor Education M,D,O
Curriculum and Instruction M
Developmental Psychology M,D
Ecology M,D
Economics M
Education—General M,D,O*
Educational Administration M,D,O
Educational Media/Instructional Technology M
Electrical Engineering M,D
Elementary Education M,O
Engineering and Applied Sciences—General M,D
Engineering Physics M
English M
Entomology M
Environmental Engineering M,D
Environmental Management and Policy M,D
Environmental Sciences M,D
Experimental Psychology M,D
Fish, Game, and Wildlife Management M,D
Food Science and Technology M,D
Foreign Languages Education M
Forestry M,D
French M
Geology M,D
Geosciences M,D
Geotechnical Engineering M,D
Higher Education M,D,O
History M,D
Horticulture M
Human Development M
Interdisciplinary Studies D
Kinesiology and Movement Studies M
Liberal Studies M
Management Information Systems M
Marine Affairs M
Marine Biology M,D
Marine Sciences M,D
Mathematics M
Mechanical Engineering M,D
Microbiology M,D
Molecular Biology M,D
Music M
Natural Resources M,D
Nursing—General M,O
Nutrition M,D
Oceanography M,D
Physical Education M
Physics M,D
Plant Biology M,D
Plant Pathology M
Plant Sciences M,D
Psychology—General M,D
Public Administration M,D*
Reading Education M,D,O
Science Education M,O
Secondary Education M,O
Social Psychology M,D
Social Sciences Education M,O
Social Work M
Special Education M,O
Structural Engineering M,D
Zoology M,D

UNIVERSITY OF MANAGEMENT AND TECHNOLOGY

Business Administration and Management—General M,D,O
Computer Science M,O
Information Science M,O
Management Information Systems M,O
Project Management M,D,O
Public Administration M,O
Software Engineering M,O
Telecommunications Management M,O

UNIVERSITY OF MANITOBA

Adult Education M
Agricultural Economics and Agribusiness M,D
Agricultural Sciences—General M,D
Agronomy and Soil Sciences M,D
American Indian/Native American Studies M
Anatomy M,D
Animal Sciences M,D
Anthropology M,D
Architecture M
Biochemistry M,D
Biological and Biomedical Sciences—General M,D
Biosystems Engineering M,D
Botany M,D
Business Administration and Management—General M,D
Canadian Studies M
Chemistry M,D
Child and Family Studies M
Civil Engineering M,D
Classics M
Clinical Psychology M,D
Clothing and Textiles M
Community Health M,D
Computational Sciences M
Computer Engineering M,D
Computer Science M,D
Counselor Education M
Curriculum and Instruction M
Dentistry P
Disability Studies M
Economics M,D
Education—General M,D
Educational Administration M
Educational Psychology M
Electrical Engineering M,D
Engineering and Applied Sciences—General M,D
English as a Second Language M
English Education M
English M,D
Entomology M,D

Environmental Management and Policy M,D
Family and Consumer Sciences-General M
Food Science and Technology M
Foundations and Philosophy of Education M
French M,D
Geography M,D
Geology M,D
Geophysics M,D
German M
History M,D
Horticulture M,D
Human Genetics M,D
Immunology M,D
Industrial/Management Engineering M,D
Interdisciplinary Studies M,D
Interior Design M
Italian M,D
Landscape Architecture M
Law M
Legal and Justice Studies M
Linguistics M,D
Mathematics M,D
Mechanical Engineering M,D
Medical Microbiology M,D
Microbiology M,D
Music M
Northern Studies M
Nursing—General M
Nutrition M,D
Oral and Dental Sciences M,D
Pathology M
Pharmaceutical Sciences M,D
Pharmacology M,D
Philosophy M
Physical Education M
Physics M,D
Physiology M,D
Political Science M
Psychology—General M,D
Public Administration M
Recreation and Park Management M
Rehabilitation Sciences M
Religion M,D
Slavic Languages M
Social Work M
Sociology M,D
Spanish M,D
Special Education M
Statistics M,D
Theology P
Urban and Regional Planning M
Zoology M,D

UNIVERSITY OF MARY

Business Administration and Management—General M
Curriculum and Instruction M
Early Childhood Education M
Education—General M
Educational Administration M
Family Nurse Practitioner Studies M
Higher Education M
Nursing and Healthcare Administration M
Nursing Education M
Nursing—General M
Occupational Therapy M
Physical Therapy D
Reading Education M
Special Education M

UNIVERSITY OF MARY HARDIN-BAYLOR

Accounting M
Business Administration and Management—General M
Counseling Psychology M
Counselor Education M
Education—General M,D
Educational Administration M,D
Educational Psychology M,D
Exercise and Sports Science M,D
Management Information Systems M
Marriage and Family Therapy M
Psychology—General M
Reading Education M,D
School Psychology M
Social Psychology M
Sports Management M

UNIVERSITY OF MARYLAND, BALTIMORE

Allopathic Medicine P
Anatomy
Biochemistry D*
Biological and Biomedical Sciences—General M,D
Biostatistics M,D
Cancer Biology/Oncology D
Cardiovascular Sciences
Cell Biology M,D
Clinical Laboratory Sciences/Medical Technology M
Clinical Research M,D
Community Health Nursing M
Dental Hygiene M
Dentistry P,M,O
Environmental Sciences M,D
Epidemiology M,D
Gerontological Nursing M
Gerontology M,D
Health Services Research M,D
Human Genetics M,D
Immunology D*
Law P
Marine Sciences M,D*
Maternal and Child/Neonatal Nursing M
Medical/Surgical Nursing M
Microbiology D
Molecular Biology D
Molecular Medicine D*
Neurobiology D
Neuroscience D*
Nurse Midwifery M
Nursing and Healthcare Administration M
Nursing Education M
Nursing—General M,D
Oral and Dental Sciences P,M,D,O
Pathology M,D
Pediatric Nursing M
Pharmaceutical Administration M,D
Pharmaceutical Sciences D
Pharmacology D
Pharmacy P,M,D
Physical Therapy D
Physiology D
Psychiatric Nursing M
Rehabilitation Sciences D
Social Work M,D
Toxicology M,D

UNIVERSITY OF MARYLAND, BALTIMORE COUNTY

Applied Mathematics M,D
Applied Physics M,D
Art/Fine Arts M
Astrophysics M,D
Atmospheric Sciences M,D
Biochemical Engineering M,D,O
Biochemistry M,D
Biological and Biomedical Sciences—General M,D
Cell Biology D
Chemical Engineering M,D,O
Chemistry M,D
Civil Engineering M,D
Cognitive Sciences D
Communication—General M
Computer Education M,O
Computer Engineering M,D
Computer Science M,D
Curriculum and Instruction M,O
Developmental Psychology D
Distance Education Development M,O
Early Childhood Education M
Economics M
Education—General M,O
Educational Media/Instructional Technology M,O
Electrical Engineering M,D
Elementary Education M
Engineering and Applied Sciences—General M,D,O*
Engineering Management M
Environmental Engineering M,D
Environmental Sciences M,D
Epidemiology M
French M
German M
Gerontology M,D,O
Health Education M
Health Services Management and Hospital Administration M
History M
Human Services M,D
Information Science M,D
Linguistics M
Marine Sciences M,D*
Mechanical Engineering M,D,O
Molecular Biology M,D
Multilingual and Multicultural Education M,D,O
Music O
Neuroscience D
Nonprofit Management M,O
Optical Sciences M,D
Physics M,D
Psychology—General M,D
Public Policy M,D*
Russian M
Secondary Education M
Social Sciences D
Sociology M,O
Spanish M
Statistics M,D
Systems Engineering O
Women's Studies O

Close-Up on page 1081.

UNIVERSITY OF MARYLAND, COLLEGE PARK

Advertising and Public Relations M,D
Aerospace/Aeronautical Engineering M,D,O
Agricultural Economics and Agribusiness M,D
Agricultural Sciences—General P,M,D
Agronomy and Soil Sciences M,D
American Studies M,D
Analytical Chemistry M,D
Animal Sciences M,D
Anthropology M
Applied Mathematics M,D
Architecture M
Art History M,D
Art/Fine Arts M
Astronomy M,D
Biochemistry M,D
Bioengineering M,D*
Biological and Biomedical Sciences—General M,D
Business Administration and Management—General M,D
Cell Biology M,D
Chemical Engineering M,D,O
Chemical Physics M,D
Chemistry M,D
Child and Family Studies M,D*
Civil Engineering M,D,O
Classics M
Clinical Psychology M,D
Cognitive Sciences D
Communication Disorders M,D
Communication—General M,D
Comparative Literature M,D
Computer Engineering M,D
Computer Science M,D
Conservation Biology M
Counseling Psychology M,D,O
Counselor Education M,D,O
Criminal Justice and Criminology M,D
Curriculum and Instruction M,D,O
Dance M
Developmental Psychology M,D
Early Childhood Education M,D
Ecology M,D
Economics M,D
Education—General M,D,O*
Educational Administration M,D,O
Educational Measurement and Evaluation M,D
Educational Media/Instructional Technology M,D,O
Educational Psychology M,D
Electrical Engineering M,D,O
Engineering and Applied Sciences—General M*
English as a Second Language M,D,O
English M,D
Entomology M,D
Environmental Engineering M,D
Environmental Sciences M,D
Evolutionary Biology M,D
Experimental Psychology M,D
Family and Consumer Sciences-General M,D
Fire Protection Engineering M,O
Food Science and Technology M,D
Foreign Languages Education M,D
Foundations and Philosophy of Education M,D,O
French M,D
Geography M,D
Geology M,D
German M,D
Health Education M,D
Historic Preservation M,O
History M,D
Horticulture D
Human Development M,D
Industrial and Organizational Psychology M,D
Information Studies M,D
Inorganic Chemistry M,D
Interdisciplinary Studies D
Japanese M,D
Jewish Studies M
Journalism M,D*
Kinesiology and Movement Studies M,D
Law
Library Science *
Linguistics M,D
Manufacturing Engineering M,D
Marine Sciences M,D*
Marriage and Family Therapy M,D
Materials Engineering M,D,O
Materials Sciences M,D,O
Mathematics M,D
Mechanical Engineering M,D,O
Mechanics M,D
Media Studies M,D
Meteorology M,D
Molecular Biology D
Molecular Genetics M,D
Music Education M,D
Music M,D
Natural Resources M,D
Neuroscience M,D
Nuclear Engineering M,D
Nutrition M,D
Oceanography M,D
Organic Chemistry M,D
Philosophy M,D
Physical Chemistry M,D
Physics M,D*
Plant Biology M,D
Political Science D
Portuguese M,D
Psychology—General M,D
Public Administration M*
Public Health—General M,D
Public Policy M,D
Reading Education M,D,O
Rehabilitation Counseling M,D,O
Reliability Engineering M,D,O
School Psychology M,D,O
Secondary Education M,D,O
Social Psychology M,D
Social Work
Sociology M,D
Spanish M,D
Special Education M,D,O
Speech and Interpersonal Communication M,D
Statistics M,D
Student Affairs M,D,O
Survey Methodology M,D
Sustainable Development M
Systems Engineering M,O
Telecommunications M*
Theater M,D
Urban and Regional Planning M,D
Veterinary Medicine P
Veterinary Sciences M,D
Women's Studies M,D
Writing M,D

UNIVERSITY OF MARYLAND EASTERN SHORE

Agricultural Sciences—General M,D
Computer Science M
Counselor Education M
Criminal Justice and Criminology M
Education—General M
Educational Administration D
Environmental Sciences M,D
Food Science and Technology M,D
Marine Sciences M,D*
Organizational Management D
Physical Therapy D
Rehabilitation Counseling M
Rehabilitation Sciences M
Special Education M
Toxicology M,D
Vocational and Technical Education M

Close-Up on page 1083.

UNIVERSITY OF MARYLAND UNIVERSITY COLLEGE

Accounting M,O
Biotechnology M,O
Business Administration and Management—General M,D,O
Distance Education Development M,O
Education—General M
Environmental Management and Policy M,O
Finance and Banking M,O
Health Informatics M,O
Health Services Management and Hospital Administration M,O
Information Science M,O
International Business M,O
Management Information Systems M,O
Management of Technology M,O

UNIVERSITY OF MARY WASHINGTON

Business Administration and Management—General M
Education—General M
Management Information Systems M

UNIVERSITY OF MASSACHUSETTS AMHERST

Accounting M
African-American Studies M,D
Agricultural Economics and Agribusiness M,D
Agronomy and Soil Sciences M,D
Animal Sciences M,D
Anthropology M,D
Applied Mathematics M
Architecture M

Program	Degrees
Art History	M
Art/Fine Arts	M
Astronomy	M,D
Biochemistry	M,D
Biological and Biomedical Sciences—General	M,D
Biotechnology	M,D
Business Administration and Management—General	M,D
Cell Biology	D
Chemical Engineering	M,D
Chemistry	M,D
Chinese	M*
Civil Engineering	M,D
Classics	M
Clinical Psychology	M,D
Communication Disorders	M,D
Communication—General	M,D
Comparative Literature	M,D
Computer Engineering	M,D
Computer Science	M,D*
Counselor Education	M,D,O
Curriculum and Instruction	M,D,O
Developmental Biology	D
Early Childhood Education	M,D,O
Economics	M,D
Education—General	M,D,O
Educational Administration	M,D,O
Educational Measurement and Evaluation	M,D,O
Educational Media/Instructional Technology	M,D,O
Electrical Engineering	M,D
Elementary Education	M,D,O
Engineering and Applied Sciences—General	M,D
Engineering Management	M
English	M,D
Entomology	M,D
Environmental Biology	M,D
Environmental Engineering	M
Evolutionary Biology	M,D
Fish, Game, and Wildlife Management	M,D
Food Science and Technology	M,D
Foreign Languages Education	M,D
Forestry	M,D
French	M,D
Geography	M
Geosciences	M,D
German	M,D
Higher Education	M,D,O
History of Science and Technology	M,D
History	M,D
Hospitality Management	M
Industrial and Labor Relations	M
Industrial/Management Engineering	M,D
Interior Design	M
International and Comparative Education	M,D,O
Italian	M,D
Japanese	M
Kinesiology and Movement Studies	M,D
Landscape Architecture	M
Linguistics	M,D
Manufacturing Engineering	M
Marine Sciences	M
Mathematics	M,D
Mechanical Engineering	M,D
Microbiology	M,D*
Molecular Biology	D*
Multilingual and Multicultural Education	M,D,O
Music	M,D
Neuroscience	M,D
Nursing—General	M,D
Nutrition	M,D
Operations Research	M,D
Philosophy	M,D
Physical Education	M,D,O
Physics	M,D
Plant Biology	M,D
Plant Molecular Biology	M,D
Plant Physiology	M,D
Plant Sciences	M,D
Political Science	M,D
Polymer Science and Engineering	M,D
Psychology—General	M,D
Public Administration	M
Public Health—General	M,D
Public History	M,D
Public Policy	M
Reading Education	M,D,O
School Psychology	D
Secondary Education	M,D,O
Sociology	M,D
Spanish	M,D
Special Education	M,D,O
Sports Management	M,D
Statistics	M,D
Theater	M
Travel and Tourism	M
Urban and Regional Planning	M,D
Writing	M,D

UNIVERSITY OF MASSACHUSETTS BOSTON

Program	Degrees
American Studies	M
Applied Physics	M
Archaeology	M
Biological and Biomedical Sciences—General	M
Biotechnology	M
Business Administration and Management—General	M
Cell Biology	D
Chemistry	M
Clinical Psychology	D
Computer Science	M,D
Conflict Resolution and Mediation/Peace Studies	M,O
Counseling Psychology	M,O
Counselor Education	M,O
Curriculum and Instruction	M
Education—General	M,D,O
Educational Administration	M,D,O
Elementary Education	M,D,O
English as a Second Language	M
English	M
Environmental Biology	D
Environmental Sciences	D
Foreign Languages Education	M
Forensic Psychology	M,O
Gerontology	M,D,O
Health Services Management and Hospital Administration	M,D,O
Higher Education	M,D,O
History	M
Human Services	M
Linguistics	M
Marine Sciences	D
Marriage and Family Therapy	M,O
Molecular Biology	D
Multilingual and Multicultural Education	M
Nursing—General	M,D
Political Science	M,D,O
Public Affairs	M
Public History	M
Public Policy	D
Rehabilitation Counseling	M,O
School Psychology	M,O
Secondary Education	M,D,O
Sociology	M
Special Education	M
Urban Education	M,D,O
Women's Studies	M,D,O

Close-Up on page 1085.

UNIVERSITY OF MASSACHUSETTS DARTMOUTH

Program	Degrees
Accounting	M,O
Acoustics	M,D,O
Applied Arts and Design—General	M
Art Education	M
Art/Fine Arts	M,O
Biochemical Engineering	D
Biological and Biomedical Sciences—General	M
Biotechnology	D
Business Administration and Management—General	M,O
Chemistry	M
Civil Engineering	M
Clinical Psychology	M
Community Health Nursing	M,D,O
Computer Engineering	M,D,O
Computer Science	M,O
Education—General	M,O
Electrical Engineering	M,D,O
Electronic Commerce	M,O
Engineering and Applied Sciences—General	M,D,O
Finance and Banking	M,O
Latin American Studies	M,D
Marine Biology	M
Marine Sciences	M,D
Marketing	M,O
Mechanical Engineering	M
Organizational Management	M,O
Physics	M
Portuguese	M,D
Psychology—General	M
Public Policy	M
Supply Chain Management	M,O
Telecommunications	M,D,O
Textile Sciences and Engineering	M
Writing	M,O

UNIVERSITY OF MASSACHUSETTS LOWELL

Program	Degrees
Adult Nursing	M
Allied Health—General	M,D
Applied Mathematics	M,D
Applied Physics	M,D
Biochemistry	M,D
Biological and Biomedical Sciences—General	M,D
Biotechnology	M,D
Business Administration and Management—General	M
Chemical Engineering	M
Chemistry	M,D
Civil Engineering	M
Clinical Laboratory Sciences/Medical Technology	M
Community Health Nursing	M
Computational Sciences	M,D
Computer Engineering	M
Computer Science	M,D
Criminal Justice and Criminology	M
Curriculum and Instruction	M,D,O
Economics	M
Education—General	M,D,O
Educational Administration	M,D,O
Electrical Engineering	M,D
Energy and Power Engineering	M,D
Engineering and Applied Sciences—General	M,D,O
Environmental Engineering	M
Environmental Management and Policy	M,D,O
Environmental Sciences	M,D,O
Epidemiology	M,D,O
Ergonomics and Human Factors	M,D,O
Gerontological Nursing	M
Health Physics/Radiological Health	M,D
Health Promotion	D
Health Services Management and Hospital Administration	M
Industrial and Manufacturing Management	M
Industrial Hygiene	M,D,O
Industrial/Management Engineering	M,D,O
Manufacturing Engineering	M,D,O
Materials Engineering	M,D
Mathematics Education	M,D,O
Mathematics	M,D
Mechanical Engineering	M,D,O
Mechanics	M,D
Music Education	M
Music	M
Nuclear Engineering	M
Nursing and Healthcare Administration	D
Nursing—General	M,D
Occupational Health Nursing	M
Optical Sciences	M,D
Physical Therapy	M
Physics	M,D*
Polymer Science and Engineering	M,D
Psychiatric Nursing	M
Psychology—General	M
Reading Education	M,D,O
Science Education	M,D,O
Social Psychology	M
Sociology	M

Close-Up on page 1087.

UNIVERSITY OF MASSACHUSETTS WORCESTER

Program	Degrees
Acute Care/Critical Care Nursing	M,D,O
Adult Nursing	M,D,O
Allopathic Medicine	P
Biochemistry	D
Biological and Biomedical Sciences—General	D*
Biomedical Engineering	D
Cancer Biology/Oncology	D
Cell Biology	D
Clinical Research	D
Community Health Nursing	M,D,O
Epidemiology	D
Gerontological Nursing	M,D,O
Health Services Research	D*
Immunology	D
Medical Physics	D
Microbiology	D
Molecular Genetics	D
Molecular Pharmacology	D
Neuroscience	D
Nursing Education	M,D,O
Nursing—General	M,D,O
Physiology	D
Virology	D

UNIVERSITY OF MEDICINE AND DENTISTRY OF NEW JERSEY

Program	Degrees
Adult Nursing	M,D,O
Allied Health—General	M,D,O
Allopathic Medicine	P
Biochemistry	M,D
Bioinformatics	M,D
Biological and Biomedical Sciences—General	M,D,O*
Biomedical Engineering	M,D
Biostatistics	M,D,O
Cancer Biology/Oncology	
Cardiovascular Sciences	M,D
Cell Biology	M,D
Clinical Laboratory Sciences/Medical Technology	M,D
Counseling Psychology	O
Dentistry	P,M,D,O
Environmental Sciences	D
Epidemiology	M,D,O
Family Nurse Practitioner Studies	M,D,O
Health Education	M,D
Health Physics/Radiological Health	M
Health Services Management and Hospital Administration	M
Immunology	M,D
Interdisciplinary Studies	M,D
Kinesiology and Movement Studies	M,D
Medical Imaging	M
Medical Informatics	M,D,O
Microbiology	M,D*
Molecular Biology	M,D*
Molecular Genetics	M,D
Molecular Medicine	D
Molecular Pathology	D
Molecular Pharmacology	M,D
Neuroscience	M,D
Nurse Anesthesia	M,D,O
Nurse Midwifery	O
Nursing Education	M,O
Nursing Informatics	M
Nursing—General	M,O
Nutrition	M,D,O
Occupational Health Nursing	M,D,O
Oral and Dental Sciences	P,M,D,O
Osteopathic Medicine	P
Pathology	D
Pharmacology	D,O
Physical Therapy	M,D
Physician Assistant Studies	M
Physiology	M,D
Public Health—General	M,D,O*
Rehabilitation Counseling	M,D
Transcultural Nursing	D
Women's Health Nursing	M,D,O

UNIVERSITY OF MEMPHIS

Program	Degrees
Accounting	M,D
Adult Education	M,D
Anthropology	M
Applied Mathematics	M,D
Applied Statistics	M,D
Archaeology	M
Art History	M
Art/Fine Arts	M
Biological and Biomedical Sciences—General	M,D
Biomedical Engineering	M,D*
Business Administration and Management—General	M,D
Chemistry	M,D
Civil Engineering	M,D
Clinical Psychology	M,D
Communication Disorders	M,D
Communication—General	M,D
Computer Engineering	M,D
Computer Science	M,D
Counseling Psychology	M,D
Counselor Education	M,D
Criminal Justice and Criminology	M
Curriculum and Instruction	M,D
Early Childhood Education	M,D
Economics	M,D
Education—General	M,D
Educational Administration	M,D
Educational Measurement and Evaluation	M,D
Educational Media/Instructional Technology	M,D
Educational Psychology	M,D
Electrical Engineering	M,D
Elementary Education	M,D
Energy and Power Engineering	M,D
Engineering and Applied Sciences—General	M,D
English	M,D
Environmental Engineering	M,D
Exercise and Sports Science	M
Experimental Psychology	M,D
Family and Consumer Sciences-General	M
Film, Television, and Video Production	M,D
Finance and Banking	M,D
French	M
Geology	M,D
Graphic Design	M
Health Promotion	M
Health Services Management and Hospital Administration	M
Higher Education	M,D
History	M,D
Industrial/Management Engineering	M,D
Interior Design	M
International Business	M
Journalism	M
Law	P
Leisure Studies	M
Liberal Studies	M
Management Information Systems	M,D

Manufacturing Engineering M
Marketing M,D
Mathematics M,D
Mechanical Engineering M,D
Middle School Education M,D
Music Education M,D
Music M,D
Nonprofit Management M
Nutrition M
Philosophy M,D
Photography M
Physical Education M
Physics M
Political Science M
Psychology—General M,D
Public Administration M
Public Policy M
Reading Education M,D
Real Estate M,D
Rehabilitation Counseling M,D
School Psychology M,D
Secondary Education M,D
Sociology M
Spanish M
Special Education M,D
Statistics M,D
Structural Engineering M,D
Student Affairs M,D
Supply Chain Management M,D
Taxation M
Theater M
Transportation and Highway Engineering M,D
Urban and Regional Planning M
Water Resources Engineering M,D
Writing M,D

Close-Up on page 1089.

UNIVERSITY OF MIAMI

Accounting M
Acute Care/Critical Care Nursing M,D
Adult Nursing M,D
Advertising and Public Relations M,D
Aerospace/Aeronautical Engineering M,D
Allopathic Medicine P
Architectural Engineering M,D
Architecture M*
Art History M
Art/Fine Arts M
Athletic Training and Sports Medicine M
Biochemistry D
Biological and Biomedical Sciences—General M,D*
Biomedical Engineering M,D
Biophysics D
Business Administration and Management—General M*
Cancer Biology/Oncology D*
Cell Biology D
Chemistry M,D
Civil Engineering M,D
Clinical Psychology M,D
Communication—General M,D*
Community Health M,D
Computer Engineering M,D
Computer Science M
Counseling Psychology D
Counselor Education M,O
Developmental Biology D
Developmental Psychology M,D
Early Childhood Education M,O
Economics M,D
Education—General M,D,O*
Educational Administration M,O
Educational Measurement and Evaluation M,D
Electrical Engineering M,D
Elementary Education M
Engineering and Applied Sciences—General M,D
English as a Second Language M,D
English M,D
Environmental and Occupational Health M
Environmental Management and Policy M,D
Epidemiology D
Ergonomics and Human Factors M,D
Evolutionary Biology M,D
Exercise and Sports Science M,D
Family Nurse Practitioner Studies M,D
Film, Television, and Video Production M,D
Film, Television, and Video Theory and Criticism M,D
Finance and Banking M
Fish, Game, and Wildlife Management M,D
French D
Genetics M,D
Geography M
Geophysics M,D
Graphic Design M
Higher Education M,O
History M,D
Immunology D
Industrial/Management Engineering M,D
Inorganic Chemistry M,D
International Affairs M,D
International Business M
Internet and Interactive Multimedia M
Journalism M,D
Law P,M
Liberal Studies M
Management Information Systems M
Management of Technology M,D
Marine Affairs M
Marine Biology M,D
Marine Geology M,D
Marine Sciences M,D
Marketing M
Marriage and Family Therapy M,O
Mathematics Education M,D,O
Mathematics M,D
Mechanical Engineering M,D
Meteorology M,D*
Microbiology D*
Molecular Biology D
Music Education M,D,O
Music M,D,O
Neuroscience M,D*
Nurse Anesthesia M,D
Nurse Midwifery M,D
Nursing—General M,D
Oceanography M,D
Operations Research M
Organic Chemistry M,D
Pharmacology D*
Philosophy M,D
Photography M
Physical Chemistry M,D
Physical Therapy D
Physics M,D*
Physiology D
Political Science M
Psychiatric Nursing M,D
Psychology—General M,D
Public Health—General M*
Quality Management M
Reading Education M,D,O
Science Education M,D,O
Sociology M,D
Spanish M,D
Special Education M,D,O
Sports Management M
Statistics M
Student Affairs M,O
Taxation M
Therapies—Dance, Drama, and Music M,D,O
Urban Design M
Writing M,D

Close-Up on page 1091.

UNIVERSITY OF MICHIGAN

Acute Care/Critical Care Nursing M
Adult Nursing M
Aerospace/Aeronautical Engineering M,D
Allopathic Medicine P
American Studies M,D
Analytical Chemistry D
Anthropology D
Applied Arts and Design—General M*
Applied Economics M
Applied Physics D
Applied Statistics M,D
Archaeology D
Architecture M,D
Art History D
Art/Fine Arts M
Asian Languages M,D
Asian Studies M,D,O
Astronomy M,D
Atmospheric Sciences M,D
Automotive Engineering M
Biochemistry D
Bioinformatics M,D
Biological and Biomedical Sciences—General M,D
Biomedical Engineering M,D
Biophysics D
Biopsychology D
Biostatistics M,D
Business Administration and Management—General D
Cell Biology M,D*
Chemical Engineering M,D,O*
Chemistry D
Civil Engineering M,D,O
Classics M,D,O
Clinical Psychology D
Clinical Research M
Communication—General D
Community Health Nursing M
Comparative Literature D
Computer Education M,D
Computer Engineering M,D
Computer Science M,D
Conservation Biology M,D
Construction Engineering M,D,O
Curriculum and Instruction M,D
Dance M
Dentistry P
Developmental Biology M,D
Developmental Psychology D
Early Childhood Education M,D
East European and Russian Studies M,O
Ecology M,D
Economics M,D
Education—General M,D*
Educational Administration M,D
Educational Measurement and Evaluation M,D
Educational Media/Instructional Technology M,D
Electrical Engineering M,D
Elementary Education M,D
Engineering and Applied Sciences—General M,D,O
English as a Second Language M,D
English Education M,D
English M,D,O
Environmental and Occupational Health M,D
Environmental Engineering M,D,O
Environmental Management and Policy M,D
Environmental Sciences M,D
Epidemiology M,D
Evolutionary Biology M,D
Experimental Psychology D
Family Nurse Practitioner Studies M
Film, Television, and Video Production O
Film, Television, and Video Theory and Criticism D,O
Financial Engineering M
Foreign Languages Education M,D
Forestry M,D,O
Foundations and Philosophy of Education M,D
French D
Genetics
Geochemistry M,D
Geology M,D
German M,D
Gerontological Nursing M
Health Physics/Radiological Health M,D,O
Health Promotion M,D
Health Services Management and Hospital Administration M,D
Higher Education M,D
History D,O
Human Genetics M,D
Human-Computer Interaction M,D
Immunology D
Industrial and Organizational Psychology D
Industrial Hygiene M,D
Industrial/Management Engineering M,D
Information Science M,D
Information Studies M,D*
Inorganic Chemistry D
International Health M,D
Kinesiology and Movement Studies M,D
Landscape Architecture M,D
Law P,M,D
Library Science M,D
Linguistics D
Manufacturing Engineering M,D
Marine Geology M,D
Marine Sciences M,D
Mass Communication D
Materials Engineering M,D
Materials Sciences M,D*
Mathematics Education M,D
Mathematics M,D
Mechanical Engineering M,D
Media Studies M
Medical/Surgical Nursing M
Medicinal and Pharmaceutical Chemistry D
Microbiology D
Mineralogy M,D
Molecular Biology M,D
Molecular Biophysics
Multilingual and Multicultural Education M,D
Music Education M,D,O
Music M,D,O
Natural Resources M,D,O
Near and Middle Eastern Languages M,D
Near and Middle Eastern Studies M,D
Neuroscience D
Nuclear Engineering M,D,O
Nurse Midwifery M
Nursing and Healthcare Administration M
Nursing—General M,D,O
Nutrition M
Occupational Health Nursing M
Ocean Engineering M,D,O
Oceanography M,D
Operations Research M,D
Oral and Dental Sciences M,D,O
Organic Chemistry D
Pathology D
Pediatric Nursing M
Pharmaceutical Administration D
Pharmaceutical Engineering M
Pharmaceutical Sciences D
Pharmacology D
Pharmacy P
Philosophy M,D
Physical Chemistry D
Physics M,D*
Physiology D
Planetary and Space Sciences M,D
Political Science M,D
Psychiatric Nursing M
Psychology—General D,O
Public Health—General M,D
Public Policy M,D
Reading Education M,D
Real Estate M,O
Romance Languages D
Russian M,D
Science Education M,D
Secondary Education M,D
Slavic Languages M,D
Social Psychology D
Social Sciences Education M,D
Social Sciences D
Social Work M,D*
Sociology D
Spanish D
Special Education M,D
Sports Management M,D
Statistics M,D
Structural Engineering M,D,O
Survey Methodology M,D,O
Sustainable Development M,D
Systems Engineering M,D
Theater M,D
Toxicology M,D
Urban and Regional Planning M,D,O
Urban Design M
Women's Health Nursing M,O
Women's Studies D,O
Writing M

UNIVERSITY OF MICHIGAN–DEARBORN

Accounting M
Applied Mathematics M
Automotive Engineering M
Business Administration and Management—General M
Computational Sciences M
Computer Engineering M
Computer Science M
Education—General M
Educational Administration M,O
Electrical Engineering M
Engineering and Applied Sciences—General M*
Engineering Management M
Environmental Sciences M
Finance and Banking M
Health Psychology M
Industrial/Management Engineering M
Information Science M
Liberal Studies M
Manufacturing Engineering M,D
Mechanical Engineering M
Nonprofit Management M,O
Public Administration M,O
Public Policy M
Software Engineering M
Special Education M
Systems Engineering M
Systems Science M

Close-Up on page 1093.

UNIVERSITY OF MICHIGAN–FLINT

American Studies M
Biological and Biomedical Sciences—General M
Business Administration and Management—General M
Computer Science M
Early Childhood Education M
Education—General M
Educational Media/Instructional Technology M*
Elementary Education M
English M
Health Education M
Information Science M
Multilingual and Multicultural Education M
Nurse Anesthesia M
Nursing—General M
Physical Therapy D
Public Administration M
Reading Education M
Social Sciences M*
Special Education M
Urban Education M

UNIVERSITY OF MINNESOTA, DULUTH

Allopathic Medicine P

Program	Degrees
Anthropology	M
Applied Mathematics	M*
Art/Fine Arts	M
Biochemistry	M,D
Biological and Biomedical Sciences—General	M
Biophysics	M,D
Business Administration and Management—General	M
Chemistry	M
Communication Disorders	M
Computational Sciences	M
Computer Engineering	M
Computer Science	M
Criminal Justice and Criminology	M
Education—General	D
Electrical Engineering	M
Engineering Management	M
English	M
Geology	M,D
Graphic Design	M
Immunology	M,D
Liberal Studies	M
Medical Microbiology	M,D
Molecular Biology	M,D
Music Education	M
Music	M
Pharmacology	M,D
Physics	M*
Physiology	M,D
Safety Engineering	M
Social Work	M
Sociology	M
Toxicology	M,D

UNIVERSITY OF MINNESOTA, TWIN CITIES CAMPUS

Program	Degrees
Accounting	M,D
Adult Education	M,D,O
Adult Nursing	M
Aerospace/Aeronautical Engineering	M,D
Agricultural Education	M,D
Agricultural Engineering	M,D
Agricultural Sciences—General	M,D
Agronomy and Soil Sciences	M,D
Allopathic Medicine	P
American Studies	M,D
Animal Behavior	M,D
Animal Sciences	M,D
Anthropology	M,D
Applied Arts and Design—General	M,D,O
Applied Economics	M,D
Archaeology	M,D
Architecture	M
Art Education	M,D,O
Art History	M,D
Art/Fine Arts	M
Asian Languages	D
Asian Studies	D
Astronomy	M,D
Astrophysics	M,D
Biochemistry	D
Biological and Biomedical Sciences—General	M,D
Biomedical Engineering	M,D
Biophysics	M,D
Biopsychology	D
Biostatistics	M,D
Biotechnology	M*
Business Administration and Management—General	M,D*
Business Education	M,D
Cell Biology	M,D
Chemical Engineering	M,D
Chemistry	M,D
Child and Family Studies	M,D
Child Development	M,D
Civil Engineering	M,D
Classics	M,D
Clinical Psychology	D
Clinical Research	M
Clothing and Textiles	M,D,O
Cognitive Sciences	D
Communication Disorders	M,D
Communication—General	M,D,O
Community Health Nursing	M
Community Health	M
Comparative Literature	D
Computational Sciences	M,D
Computer Engineering	M,D
Computer Science	M,D
Conservation Biology	M,D
Counseling Psychology	D
Counselor Education	M,D,O
Cultural Studies	D
Curriculum and Instruction	M,D,O
Dance	M,D
Dentistry	P
Developmental Biology	M,D
Early Childhood Education	M,D,O
Ecology	M,D
Economics	D
Education of the Gifted	M,D,O
Education—General	M,D,O
Educational Administration	M,D,O
Educational Measurement and Evaluation	M,D
Educational Media/Instructional Technology	M,D,O
Educational Policy	M,D,O
Educational Psychology	M,D,O
Electrical Engineering	M,D
Elementary Education	M,D,O
Engineering and Applied Sciences—General	M,D
English as a Second Language	M
English Education	M
English	M,D
Entomology	M,D
Entrepreneurship	M
Environmental and Occupational Health	M,D,O
Environmental Education	M,D,O
Environmental Management and Policy	M,D
Epidemiology	M,D
Evolutionary Biology	M,D
Exercise and Sports Science	M,D,O
Family Nurse Practitioner Studies	M
Finance and Banking	M,D
Fish, Game, and Wildlife Management	M,D
Food Science and Technology	M,D
Foreign Languages Education	M
Forestry	M,D
Foundations and Philosophy of Education	M,D,O
French	M,D
Genetic Counseling	M,D
Genetics	M,D
Geographic Information Systems	M
Geography	M,D
Geological Engineering	M,D
Geology	M,D
Geophysics	M,D
German	M,D
Gerontological Nursing	M
Health Informatics	M,D*
Health Services Management and Hospital Administration	M,D*
Health Services Research	M,D
Higher Education	M,D
History of Medicine	M,D
History of Science and Technology	M,D
History	M,D
Human Resources Development	M,D,O
Human Resources Management	M,D*
Industrial and Labor Relations	M,D
Industrial and Manufacturing Management	M,D
Industrial and Organizational Psychology	D
Industrial Hygiene	M,D
Industrial/Management Engineering	M,D
Infectious Diseases	M,D
Information Science	M,D
Interdisciplinary Studies	D
Interior Design	M,D,O
International and Comparative Education	M,D
International Business	M
Kinesiology and Movement Studies	M,D
Landscape Architecture	M
Law	P,M
Leisure Studies	M,D
Linguistics	M,D
Logistics	M,D
Management Information Systems	M,D
Management of Technology	M
Management Strategy and Policy	M,D
Marketing	M,D
Marriage and Family Therapy	M,D
Mass Communication	M,D
Materials Engineering	M,D
Materials Sciences	M,D
Maternal and Child Health	M
Mathematics Education	M,D
Mathematics	M,D
Mechanical Engineering	M,D
Mechanics	M,D
Medical Physics	M,D*
Medicinal and Pharmaceutical Chemistry	M,D
Medieval and Renaissance Studies	M,D
Microbiology	D*
Molecular Biology	M,D
Multilingual and Multicultural Education	M
Music	M,D
Neuroscience	M,D
Nurse Anesthesia	M
Nurse Midwifery	M
Nursing and Healthcare Administration	M
Nursing—General	M,D
Nutrition	M,D
Occupational Health Nursing	M,D
Oral and Dental Sciences	M,D,O
Pediatric Nursing	M
Pharmaceutical Administration	M,D
Pharmaceutical Sciences	M,D
Pharmacology	M,D
Pharmacy	P
Philosophy	M,D
Physical Education	M,D,O
Physical Therapy	D
Physics	M,D
Physiology	M,D
Plant Biology	M,D
Plant Pathology	M,D
Plant Sciences	M,D
Political Science	M,D
Portuguese	M,D
Psychiatric Nursing	M
Psychology—General	D
Public Affairs	M*
Public Health—General	M,D,O
Public Policy	M
Reading Education	M,D,O
Recreation and Park Management	M,D
Religion	M,D
Scandinavian Languages	M,D
School Psychology	M,D,O
Science Education	M
Social Psychology	D
Social Sciences Education	M
Social Work	M,D
Sociology	M,D
Spanish	M,D
Special Education	M,D,O
Sports Management	M,D,O
Statistics	M,D
Student Affairs	M,D,O
Supply Chain Management	M
Systems Engineering	M
Taxation	M
Technology and Public Policy	M
Textile Design	M,D,O
Theater	M,D
Toxicology	M,D
Urban and Regional Planning	M
Veterinary Medicine	P
Veterinary Sciences	M,D
Vocational and Technical Education	M,D,O
Water Resources	M,D
Women's Health Nursing	M
Women's Studies	D

UNIVERSITY OF MISSISSIPPI

Program	Degrees
Accounting	M,D
American Studies	M
Anthropology	M
Applied Science and Technology	M,D
Art Education	M
Art History	M
Art/Fine Arts	M
Biological and Biomedical Sciences—General	M,D
Business Administration and Management—General	M,D
Chemistry	M,D
Classics	M
Clinical Psychology	M,D
Communication Disorders	M
Computational Sciences	M,D
Counselor Education	M,D,O
Curriculum and Instruction	M,D,O
Economics	M,D
Education—General	M,D,O
Educational Administration	M,D,O
Engineering and Applied Sciences—General	M,D
English	M,D
Exercise and Sports Science	M,D
Experimental Psychology	M,D
French	M
German	M
Higher Education	M,D,O
History	M,D
Journalism	M
Law	P
Leisure Studies	M,D
Management Information Systems	M,D
Mathematics	M,D
Medicinal and Pharmaceutical Chemistry	M,D
Music	M,D
Pharmaceutical Administration	M,D
Pharmaceutical Sciences	M,D
Pharmacology	M,D
Pharmacy	P
Philosophy	M
Physics	M,D
Political Science	M,D
Psychology—General	M,D
Recreation and Park Management	M,D
Secondary Education	M,D,O
Sociology	M
Spanish	M
Student Affairs	M,D,O
Taxation	M,D
Theater	M

UNIVERSITY OF MISSISSIPPI MEDICAL CENTER

Program	Degrees
Allied Health—General	M
Allopathic Medicine	P
Anatomy	M,D
Biochemistry	M,D*
Biological and Biomedical Sciences—General	M,D*
Biophysics	M,D
Clinical Laboratory Sciences/Medical Technology	M,D
Dentistry	P,M,D
Maternal and Child Health	M
Microbiology	M,D
Nursing—General	M,D
Occupational Therapy	M
Oral and Dental Sciences	M,D
Pathology	M,D
Pharmacology	M,D*
Physical Therapy	M
Physiology	M,D
Toxicology	M,D

UNIVERSITY OF MISSOURI–COLUMBIA

Program	Degrees
Accounting	M,D
Adult Education	M,D,O
Aerospace/Aeronautical Engineering	M,D
Agricultural Economics and Agribusiness	M,D
Agricultural Education	M,D,O
Agricultural Engineering	M,D
Agricultural Sciences—General	M,D
Agronomy and Soil Sciences	M,D
Allopathic Medicine	P
Analytical Chemistry	M,D
Animal Sciences	M,D
Anthropology	M,D
Applied Mathematics	M
Archaeology	M,D
Architecture	M
Art Education	M,D,O
Art History	M,D
Art/Fine Arts	M
Astronomy	M,D
Atmospheric Sciences	M,D
Biochemistry	M,D
Bioengineering	M,D
Biological and Biomedical Sciences—General	M,D*
Business Administration and Management—General	M,D*
Business Education	M,D,O
Cell Biology	M,D
Chemical Engineering	M,D
Chemistry	M,D
Child and Family Studies	M,D
Civil Engineering	M,D
Classics	M,D
Clothing and Textiles	M
Communication Disorders	M
Communication—General	M,D
Comparative Literature	M,D
Computer Art and Design	M
Computer Science	M,D*
Conflict Resolution and Mediation/Peace Studies	M
Consumer Economics	M
Counseling Psychology	M,D,O
Curriculum and Instruction	M,D,O
Early Childhood Education	M,D,O
Ecology	M,D
Economics	M,D
Education of the Gifted	M,D
Education—General	M,D,O
Educational Administration	M,D,O
Educational Media/Instructional Technology	M,D,O
Educational Psychology	M,D,O
Electrical Engineering	M,D
Elementary Education	M,D,O
Engineering and Applied Sciences—General	M,D
English Education	M,D,O
English	M,D
Entomology	M,D
Environmental Design	M
Environmental Engineering	M,D
Evolutionary Biology	M,D
Exercise and Sports Science	M,D
Family and Consumer Sciences-General	M,D
Fish, Game, and Wildlife Management	M,D
Food Science and Technology	M,D
Foreign Languages Education	M,D,O
Forestry	M,D
French	M,D
Genetics	M,D
Geography	M
Geology	M,D
Geotechnical Engineering	M,D
German	M
Health Education	M,D,O
Health Informatics	M
Health Physics/Radiological Health	M,D
Health Services Management and Hospital Administration	M
Higher Education	M,D,O

History M,D
Horticulture M,D
Hospitality Management M,D
Human Development M,D
Immunology M,D
Industrial/Management Engineering M,D
Information Studies M,D,O
Inorganic Chemistry M,D
Journalism M,D
Law P,M
Library Science M,D,O
Manufacturing Engineering M,D
Mathematics Education M,D,O
Mathematics M,D
Mechanical Engineering M,D
Medical Physics M,D
Microbiology M,D
Music Education M,D,O
Music M
Neurobiology M,D
Nuclear Engineering M,D
Nursing—General M,D
Nutrition M,D
Occupational Therapy M
Organic Chemistry M,D
Pathobiology M,D
Pharmacology M,D
Philosophy M,D
Physical Chemistry M,D
Physical Therapy M
Physics M,D
Physiology M,D
Plant Biology M,D
Plant Pathology M,D
Plant Sciences M,D
Political Science M,D
Psychology—General M,D
Public Affairs M*
Public Health—General M
Reading Education M,D,O
Recreation and Park Management M
Religion M
Romance Languages M,D
Rural Sociology M,D
School Psychology M,D,O
Science Education M,D,O
Social Sciences Education M,D,O
Social Work M
Sociology M,D
Spanish M,D
Special Education M,D
Statistics M,D
Structural Engineering M,D
Theater M,D
Transportation and Highway Engineering M,D
Veterinary Medicine P
Veterinary Sciences M,D
Vocational and Technical Education M,D,O
Water Resources Engineering M,D

UNIVERSITY OF MISSOURI–KANSAS CITY

Accounting M,D
Adult Nursing M,D
Allopathic Medicine P
Analytical Chemistry M,D
Art History M,D
Art/Fine Arts M,D
Biochemistry D
Biological and Biomedical Sciences—General M,D
Biophysics D
Business Administration and Management—General M,D
Cell Biology D*
Chemistry M,D
Civil Engineering M,D
Clinical Psychology M,D
Computer Engineering M,D
Computer Science M,D
Counseling Psychology M,D,O
Criminal Justice and Criminology M,D
Curriculum and Instruction M,D,O
Dental Hygiene P,M,D,O
Dentistry P,M,D,O
Economics M,D
Education—General M,D,O
Educational Administration M,D,O
Electrical Engineering M,D
Engineering and Applied Sciences—General M,D
English M,D
Family Nurse Practitioner Studies M,D
Geology M,D
Geosciences M,D
History M,D
Inorganic Chemistry M,D
Interdisciplinary Studies D
Law P,M
Maternal and Child/Neonatal Nursing M,D
Mathematics M,D
Mechanical Engineering M,D
Molecular Biology D*
Music Education M,D
Music M,D
Nursing and Healthcare Administration M,D
Nursing Education M,D
Nursing—General M,D
Oral and Dental Sciences P,M,D,O
Organic Chemistry M,D
Pediatric Nursing M,D
Pharmaceutical Sciences P,M,D
Pharmacy P,M,D
Physical Chemistry M,D
Physics M,D
Political Science M,D
Polymer Science and Engineering M,D
Psychology—General M,D
Public Administration M,D
Public Affairs M,D
Reading Education M,D,O
Romance Languages M
Social Psychology M,D
Social Work M
Sociology M,D
Software Engineering M,D
Special Education M,D,O
Statistics M,D
Taxation P,M
Telecommunications M,D
Theater M
Women's Health Nursing M,D

UNIVERSITY OF MISSOURI–ROLLA

Aerospace/Aeronautical Engineering M,D
Applied Mathematics M
Biological and Biomedical Sciences—General M
Ceramic Sciences and Engineering M,D
Chemical Engineering M,D
Chemistry M,D
Civil Engineering M,D
Computer Engineering M,D
Computer Science M,D
Construction Engineering M,D
Electrical Engineering M,D
Engineering and Applied Sciences—General M,D*
Engineering Management M,D
Environmental Biology M
Environmental Engineering M,D
Geochemistry M,D
Geological Engineering M,D
Geology M,D
Geophysics M,D
Geotechnical Engineering M,D
Hydraulics M,D
Hydrology M,D
Information Science M
Manufacturing Engineering M
Mathematics Education M,D
Mathematics M,D
Mechanical Engineering M,D
Mechanics M,D
Metallurgical Engineering and Metallurgy M,D
Mineral/Mining Engineering M,D
Nuclear Engineering M,D
Petroleum Engineering M,D
Physics M,D
Statistics M,D
Systems Engineering M,D
Water Resources M,D

UNIVERSITY OF MISSOURI–ST. LOUIS

Accounting M,O
Adult Education M,D,O
Animal Behavior M,D,O
Applied Mathematics M,D
Applied Physics M,D
Astrophysics M,D
Biochemistry M,D,O
Biological and Biomedical Sciences—General M,D,O
Biotechnology M,D,O
Botany M,D,O
Business Administration and Management—General M,O
Cell Biology M,D,O
Chemistry M,D
Clinical Psychology M,D,O
Communication—General M
Computer Science M,D
Conflict Resolution and Mediation/Peace Studies M
Conservation Biology M,D,O
Counselor Education M
Criminal Justice and Criminology M,D
Curriculum and Instruction M,D
Developmental Biology M,D,O
Ecology M,D,O
Economics M,O
Education—General M,D,O
Educational Administration M,D,O
Educational Measurement and Evaluation M,D,O
Educational Psychology D,O
Elementary Education M,D
English M,O
Environmental Management and Policy M,D,O
Evolutionary Biology M,D,O
Finance and Banking M,O
Genetics M,D,O
Gerontology M,O
Health Services Management and Hospital Administration M,O
Higher Education M,D,O
Human Resources Development M,O
Human Resources Management M,O
Industrial and Manufacturing Management M,O
Industrial and Organizational Psychology M,D,O
Inorganic Chemistry M,D
Linguistics M,O
Logistics M,D,O
Management Information Systems M,D
Marketing M,O
Mathematics M,D
Middle School Education M,D
Molecular Biology M,D,O
Museum Studies M,O
Music Education M
Neuroscience M,D,O
Nonprofit Management M,O
Nursing—General M,D,O
Optometry P
Organic Chemistry M,D
Philosophy M
Physical Chemistry M,D
Physics M,D
Physiology M,D,O
Political Science M,D
Psychology—General M,D,O
Public Administration M,D,O
Public Policy M,D,O
Quantitative Analysis M,O
Reading Education M,D
School Psychology D,O
Secondary Education M,D
Social Psychology M,D,O
Social Work M
Sociology M
Special Education M,D
Supply Chain Management M,D,O
Telecommunications Management M,O
Vision Sciences M,D
Writing M,O

Close-Up on page 1095.

UNIVERSITY OF MOBILE

Business Administration and Management—General M
Education—General M
Marriage and Family Therapy M
Nursing—General M
Religion M
Theology M

THE UNIVERSITY OF MONTANA

Accounting M
Analytical Chemistry M,D
Animal Behavior M,D,O
Anthropology M,D
Art/Fine Arts M
Biochemistry M,D
Biological and Biomedical Sciences—General M,D
Business Administration and Management—General M
Chemistry M,D
Clinical Psychology M,D,O
Communication—General M
Computer Science M
Counseling Psychology M,D,O
Counselor Education M,D,O
Criminal Justice and Criminology M
Curriculum and Instruction M,D
Developmental Psychology M,D,O
Ecology M,D
Economics M
Education—General M,D,O
Educational Administration M,D,O
English Education M
English M
Environmental Management and Policy M,D
Environmental Sciences M*
Exercise and Sports Science M
Experimental Psychology M,D,O
Film, Television, and Video Production M
Fish, Game, and Wildlife Management M,D
Forestry M,D
French M
Geographic Information Systems M
Geography M
Geology M,D
Geosciences M,D
German M
Health Education M
Health Promotion M
History M,D
Infectious Diseases D
Inorganic Chemistry M,D
Interdisciplinary Studies M,D
Jewish Studies M
Journalism M
Law P
Linguistics M,D
Mathematics Education M,D
Mathematics M,D
Microbiology M,D
Music Education M
Music M
Natural Resources M,D
Organic Chemistry M,D
Pharmaceutical Sciences M,D
Pharmacology M,D
Philosophy M
Photography M
Physical Chemistry M,D
Physical Education M
Physical Therapy D
Political Science M
Psychology—General M,D,O
Public Administration M
Public Health—General M,O
Recreation and Park Management M,D
Rural Planning and Studies M
Rural Sociology M
School Psychology M,D,O
Sociology M
Spanish M
Theater M
Toxicology M,D
Writing M
Zoology M,D

UNIVERSITY OF MONTEVALLO

Communication Disorders M
Counselor Education M
Early Childhood Education M
Education—General M,O
Educational Administration M,O
Elementary Education M
English M
Music M
Secondary Education M

UNIVERSITY OF NEBRASKA AT KEARNEY

Art Education M
Biological and Biomedical Sciences—General M
Business Administration and Management—General M
Communication Disorders M
Counselor Education M,O
Curriculum and Instruction M
Education—General M,O
Educational Administration M,O
Educational Media/Instructional Technology M
English M
Exercise and Sports Science M
Foreign Languages Education M
History M
Music Education M
Physical Education M
Reading Education M
School Psychology M,O
Science Education M
Special Education M
Writing M

UNIVERSITY OF NEBRASKA AT OMAHA

Accounting M
Biological and Biomedical Sciences—General M
Biopsychology M,D,O
Business Administration and Management—General M
Communication Disorders M
Communication—General M
Computer Science M
Counselor Education M
Criminal Justice and Criminology M,D
Developmental Psychology M,D,O
Economics M
Education—General M,D,O
Educational Administration M,D,O
Educational Media/Instructional Technology M,O
Educational Psychology M,D,O
Elementary Education M
English as a Second Language M,O
English M,O
Foreign Languages Education M
Geography M,O
Gerontology M,O
Health Education M
History M
Industrial and Organizational Psychology M,D,O
Information Science M,D
Management Information Systems M,D

Mathematics M
Music M
Physical Education M
Political Science M
Psychology—General M,D,O
Public Administration M,D
Public Health—General M
Reading Education M
Recreation and Park Management M
School Psychology M,D,O
Secondary Education M
Social Work M
Special Education M
Technical Communication M,O
Theater M
Urban Education M,O
Writing M,O

UNIVERSITY OF NEBRASKA–LINCOLN

Accounting M,D
Actuarial Science M
Agricultural Economics and Agribusiness M,D
Agricultural Education M
Agricultural Engineering M,D
Agricultural Sciences—General M,D
Agronomy and Soil Sciences M,D
Analytical Chemistry M,D
Animal Sciences M,D
Anthropology M
Architectural Engineering M
Architecture M
Art History M
Art/Fine Arts M
Astronomy M,D
Biochemistry M,D
Bioengineering M,D
Biological and Biomedical Sciences—General M,D
Biometrics M
Business Administration and Management—General M,D
Chemical Engineering M,D
Chemistry M,D
Child and Family Studies M,D
Civil Engineering M,D
Classics M
Clothing and Textiles M
Communication Disorders M
Communication—General M,D
Computer Engineering M,D
Computer Science M,D*
Consumer Economics M,D
Curriculum and Instruction M,D,O
Economics M,D
Education—General M,D,O
Educational Administration M,D,O
Educational Psychology M,O
Electrical Engineering M,D
Engineering and Applied Sciences—General M,D
English M,D
Entomology M,D
Environmental Engineering M,D
Family and Consumer Sciences-General M,D
Finance and Banking M,D
Food Science and Technology M,D
French M,D
Geography M,D
Geosciences M,D
German M,D
Health Education M
History M,D
Horticulture M,D
Industrial/Management Engineering M,D
Inorganic Chemistry M,D
Journalism M
Law P,M
Legal and Justice Studies M
Management Information Systems M
Manufacturing Engineering M,D
Marketing M,D
Mass Communication M
Materials Engineering M,D
Mathematics M,D
Mechanical Engineering M,D*
Mechanics M,D*
Museum Studies M
Music M,D
Natural Resources M,D
Nutrition M,D
Organic Chemistry M,D
Philosophy M,D
Physical Chemistry M,D
Physical Education M,D
Physics M,D
Political Science M,D
Psychology—General M,D
Recreation and Park Management M
Sociology M,D
Spanish M,D
Special Education M
Statistics M,D
Survey Methodology M
Theater M
Toxicology M,D
Urban and Regional Planning M
Veterinary Sciences M,D

UNIVERSITY OF NEBRASKA MEDICAL CENTER

Allied Health—General M,D,O
Allopathic Medicine P,O
Anatomy M,D
Biochemistry M,D
Biological and Biomedical Sciences—General M,D*
Cancer Biology/Oncology M,D
Cell Biology M,D
Clinical Laboratory Sciences/Medical Technology M,O
Dentistry P,O
Microbiology M,D
Molecular Biology M,D
Neuroscience M,D
Nursing—General M,D
Nutrition O
Pathology M,D
Pharmaceutical Sciences M,D
Pharmacology M,D
Pharmacy P
Physical Therapy D
Physician Assistant Studies M
Physiology M,D
Public Health—General M
Toxicology M,D

UNIVERSITY OF NEVADA, LAS VEGAS

Accounting M
Anthropology M,D
Applied Mathematics M,D
Applied Statistics M,D
Architecture M
Art/Fine Arts M
Biochemistry M,D
Biological and Biomedical Sciences—General M,D
Business Administration and Management—General M
Chemistry M,D
Civil Engineering M,D
Clinical Psychology M,D
Communication—General M
Computational Sciences M,D
Computer Engineering M,D
Computer Science M,D
Construction Engineering M,D
Construction Management M,D
Counselor Education M,D,O
Criminal Justice and Criminology M
Curriculum and Instruction M,D,O
Economics M
Education of the Gifted M,D,O
Education—General M,D,O
Educational Administration M,D,O
Educational Media/Instructional Technology M,D,O
Educational Psychology M,D,O
Electrical Engineering M,D
Elementary Education M,D,O
Emergency Management M,D,O
Engineering and Applied Sciences—General M,D
English as a Second Language M,D,O
English Education M,D,O
English M,D
Environmental Sciences M,D
Ethics M
Exercise and Sports Science M
Experimental Psychology M,D
Family Nurse Practitioner Studies M,D,O
Film, Television, and Video Production M
Geosciences M,D
Health Physics/Radiological Health M
Health Promotion M
History M,D
Hospitality Management M,D
Information Science M,D
Journalism M
Kinesiology and Movement Studies M
Law P
Leisure Studies M
Library Science M,D,O
Management Information Systems M
Marriage and Family Therapy M,O
Mathematics Education M,D,O
Mathematics M,D
Mechanical Engineering M,D
Media Studies M
Multilingual and Multicultural Education M,D,O
Music Education M,D
Music M,D
Nursing Education M,D,O
Nursing—General M,D,O
Pediatric Nursing M,D,O
Physical Education M,D
Physical Therapy M,D
Physics M,D
Political Science M
Psychology—General M,D
Public Administration M,D,O
Public Affairs M,D,O
Public Health—General M
Public Policy M,D
Reading Education M,D,O
Rehabilitation Counseling M,O
School Psychology M,D,O
Secondary Education M,D,O
Social Work M
Sociology M,D
Spanish M
Special Education M,D,O
Sports Management M,D
Statistics M,D
Theater M
Transportation and Highway Engineering M,D
Water Resources M
Women's Studies O
Writing M,D

Close-Up on page 1097.

UNIVERSITY OF NEVADA, RENO

Accounting M
Agricultural Economics and Agribusiness M,D
Agricultural Sciences—General M,D
Animal Sciences M
Anthropology M,D
Applied Economics M,D
Art/Fine Arts M
Atmospheric Sciences M,D
Biochemistry M,D*
Biological and Biomedical Sciences—General M,D
Biomedical Engineering M,D
Biotechnology M
Business Administration and Management—General M
Cell Biology M,D
Chemical Engineering M,D
Chemical Physics D
Chemistry M,D
Child and Family Studies M
Civil Engineering M,D
Communication Disorders M,D
Computer Engineering M,D
Computer Science M,D
Conservation Biology D
Counselor Education M,D,O
Criminal Justice and Criminology M
Curriculum and Instruction M,D,O
Ecology D
Economics M
Education—General M,D,O
Educational Administration M,D,O
Educational Psychology M,D,O
Electrical Engineering M,D
Elementary Education M,D,O
Engineering and Applied Sciences—General M,D,O*
English as a Second Language M,D,O
English M,D
Environmental and Occupational Health M,D
Environmental Management and Policy M
Environmental Sciences M,D
Evolutionary Biology D
Finance and Banking M
Foreign Languages Education M
French M
Geochemistry M,D,O
Geography M,D
Geological Engineering M,D,O
Geology M,D,O
Geophysics M,D,O
German M
History M,D
Human Development M
Hydrogeology M,D
Hydrology M,D
Journalism M
Legal and Justice Studies M
Mathematics Education M
Mathematics M
Mechanical Engineering M,D
Metallurgical Engineering and Metallurgy M,D,O
Mineral/Mining Engineering M,O
Molecular Biology M,D
Molecular Pharmacology M,D
Music M
Nursing—General M
Nutrition M
Philosophy M
Physics M,D
Physiology M,D
Political Science M,D
Psychology—General M,D
Public Administration M
Public Health—General M
Reading Education M,D,O
Secondary Education M,D,O
Social Psychology D
Social Work M
Sociology M
Spanish M
Special Education M,D,O
Speech and Interpersonal Communication M
Western European Studies D

UNIVERSITY OF NEW BRUNSWICK FREDERICTON

Anthropology M
Biological and Biomedical Sciences—General M,D
Business Administration and Management—General M
Chemical Engineering M,D
Chemistry M,D
Civil Engineering M,D
Classics M
Computer Engineering M,D
Computer Science M,D
Conflict Resolution and Mediation/Peace Studies M
Construction Engineering M,D
Economics M
Education—General M,D
Electrical Engineering M,D
Engineering and Applied Sciences—General M,D,O
English M,D
Environmental Engineering M,D
Exercise and Sports Science M
Forestry M,D
Geodetic Sciences M,D,O
Geology M,D
Geotechnical Engineering M,D
Health Services Research M
History M,D
Hydrology M,D
Interdisciplinary Studies M,D
Law P
Marketing M,D
Materials Sciences M,D
Mathematics M,D
Mechanical Engineering M,D
Mechanics M,D
Nursing—General M
Philosophy M
Physical Education M
Physics M,D
Political Science M
Psychology—General D
Public Administration M
Public Policy M
Recreation and Park Management M
Sociology M,D
Sports Management M
Statistics M,D
Structural Engineering M,D
Surveying Science and Engineering M,D,O
Sustainable Development M
Transportation and Highway Engineering M,D
Water Resources M,D

UNIVERSITY OF NEW BRUNSWICK SAINT JOHN

Biological and Biomedical Sciences—General M,D
Business Administration and Management—General M
Electronic Commerce M
Environmental Management and Policy M
International Business M
Psychology—General M

UNIVERSITY OF NEW ENGLAND

Addictions/Substance Abuse Counseling M,O
Biological and Biomedical Sciences—General M
Education—General M
Educational Administration O
Educational Measurement and Evaluation M
Gerontology M,O
Marine Sciences M
Nurse Anesthesia M
Occupational Therapy M
Osteopathic Medicine P
Physical Therapy D
Physician Assistant Studies M
Public Health—General M,O
Reading Education M
Social Work M,O

UNIVERSITY OF NEW HAMPSHIRE

Accounting M*
Agronomy and Soil Sciences M
Animal Sciences M,D
Applied Mathematics M,D
Art/Fine Arts M
Atmospheric Sciences M
Biochemistry M,D
Business Administration and Management—General M
Chemical Engineering M,D
Chemistry M,D
Child and Family Studies M

Civil Engineering M,D
Communication Disorders M
Comparative Literature M,D
Computer Science M,D
Counselor Education M
Early Childhood Education M
Economics M,D*
Education—General M,D,O
Educational Administration M,O
Electrical Engineering M,D
Elementary Education M
English Education M,D
English M,D
Environmental Education M
Environmental Management and Policy M
Fish, Game, and Wildlife Management M
Forestry M
Genetics M,D
Geochemistry M
Geology M
Geosciences M
Health Services Management and Hospital Administration M
Higher Education M
History M,D
Hydrology M
Kinesiology and Movement Studies M
Legal and Justice Studies M
Liberal Studies M
Linguistics M,D
Logistics M,D
Management of Technology M
Marriage and Family Therapy M
Materials Sciences M,D
Mathematics Education M,D
Mathematics M,D
Mechanical Engineering M,D
Microbiology M,D
Museum Studies M,D
Music Education M
Music M
Natural Resources D
Nursing—General M
Nutrition M,D
Occupational Therapy M
Ocean Engineering M,D
Oceanography M,D
Physics M,D
Plant Biology M,D
Political Science M
Psychology—General D
Public Administration M
Public Health—General M
Reading Education M
Recreation and Park Management M
Science Education M,D
Secondary Education M
Social Work M
Sociology M,D
Spanish M
Special Education M
Statistics M,D
Water Resources M
Writing M,D
Zoology M,D

Close-Up on page 1099.

UNIVERSITY OF NEW HAMPSHIRE AT MANCHESTER

Business Administration and Management—General M,O
Counselor Education M,O
Education—General M,O
Educational Administration M,O
Public Administration M,O
Public Health—General M,O
Social Work M,O
Statistics M,O

UNIVERSITY OF NEW HAVEN

Accounting M
Advertising and Public Relations M
Business Administration and Management—General M
Cell Biology M*
Computer Science M
Criminal Justice and Criminology M*
Education—General M
Electrical Engineering M
Engineering and Applied Sciences—General M,O*
Engineering Design M,O
Engineering Management M
Environmental and Occupational Health M
Environmental Engineering M,O
Environmental Sciences M*
Finance and Banking M
Fire Protection Engineering M
Forensic Sciences M
Health Services Management and Hospital Administration M
Hospitality Management M
Human Resources Management M
Industrial and Labor Relations M
Industrial and Organizational Psychology M,O*
Industrial Hygiene M
Industrial/Management Engineering M,O
Information Science M
International Business M
Logistics M,O
Management Information Systems M
Management of Technology M
Management Strategy and Policy M
Marketing M
Mechanical Engineering M
Molecular Biology M
Nutrition M
Operations Research M
Public Administration M
Social Psychology M,O
Software Engineering M
Sports Management M
Taxation M
Travel and Tourism M

Close-Up on page 1101.

UNIVERSITY OF NEW MEXICO

Accounting M
Allopathic Medicine P
American Studies M,D
Anthropology M,D
Architecture M
Art Education M
Art History M,D
Art/Fine Arts M
Biochemistry M,D
Biological and Biomedical Sciences—General M,D
Biophysics M,D
Business Administration and Management—General M
Cell Biology M,D
Chemical Engineering M,D
Chemistry M,D
Child and Family Studies M,D
Civil Engineering M,D
Clinical Psychology M,D
Communication Disorders M
Communication—General M,D
Comparative Literature M,D
Computer Engineering M,D
Computer Science M,D
Construction Management M,D
Counselor Education M,D
Dance M
Dental Hygiene M
Economics M,D
Education—General M,O
Educational Administration M,D,O
Educational Media/Instructional Technology M,D,O
Educational Psychology M,D
Electrical Engineering M,D*
Elementary Education M,O
Engineering and Applied Sciences—General M,D
English M,D
Finance and Banking M
Foundations and Philosophy of Education M,D
French M,D
Genetics M,D
Geography M
Geosciences M,D
German M,D
Health Education M
History M,D
Human Resources Management M
International Business M
Landscape Architecture M
Latin American Studies M,D
Law P
Linguistics M,D
Management Information Systems M
Management of Technology M
Management Strategy and Policy M
Manufacturing Engineering M*
Marketing M
Mathematics M,D
Mechanical Engineering M,D*
Microbiology M,D
Molecular Biology M,D
Multilingual and Multicultural Education D,O
Music M
Neuroscience M,D
Nuclear Engineering M,D
Nursing—General M,D
Nutrition M
Occupational Therapy M
Optical Sciences M,D
Organizational Management M
Pathology M,D
Pharmaceutical Sciences M,D
Pharmacy P
Philosophy M,D
Physical Education M,D,O
Physical Therapy M
Physics M,D
Physiology M,D
Planetary and Space Sciences M,D
Political Science M,D
Portuguese M,D
Psychology—General M,D
Public Administration M
Public Health—General M
Secondary Education M,O
Sociology M,D
Spanish M,D
Special Education M,D,O
Statistics M,D
Taxation M
Theater M
Toxicology M,D
Urban and Regional Planning M
Water Resources M
Writing M

Close-Up on page 1103.

UNIVERSITY OF NEW ORLEANS

Accounting M
Art/Fine Arts M
Arts Administration M
Biological and Biomedical Sciences—General M,D
Business Administration and Management—General M,D
Chemistry M,D
Computer Science M
Counselor Education M,D,O
Curriculum and Instruction M,D,O
Economics D
Education—General M,D,O
Educational Administration M,D,O
Engineering and Applied Sciences—General M,D,O
Engineering Management M
English Education M
English M
Environmental Sciences M
Film, Television, and Video Production M
Finance and Banking M,D
Foundations and Philosophy of Education M,D,O
Geography M
Geosciences M
Health Services Management and Hospital Administration M
History M
Hospitality Management M
Mathematics M
Mechanical Engineering M
Music M
Physics M,D
Political Science M,D
Psychology—General M,D
Public Administration M
Romance Languages M
Science Education M
Social Sciences Education M
Sociology M
Special Education M,D,O
Taxation M
Theater M
Travel and Tourism M
Urban and Regional Planning M
Urban Studies M,D

UNIVERSITY OF NORTH ALABAMA

Business Administration and Management—General M
Counselor Education M
Criminal Justice and Criminology M
Education—General M,O
Educational Administration M,O
Elementary Education M,O
English M
Nursing—General M
Secondary Education M
Special Education M

THE UNIVERSITY OF NORTH CAROLINA AT ASHEVILLE

Liberal Studies M*

THE UNIVERSITY OF NORTH CAROLINA AT CHAPEL HILL

Accounting M,D
Allied Health—General M,D
Allopathic Medicine P
Anthropology M,D
Archaeology M,D
Art History M,D
Art/Fine Arts M
Astronomy M,D
Astrophysics M,D
Athletic Training and Sports Medicine M
Atmospheric Sciences M,D
Biochemistry M,D
Biological and Biomedical Sciences—General M,D*
Biomedical Engineering M,D*
Biophysics M,D
Biostatistics M,D
Botany M,D
Business Administration and Management—General M,D
Cancer Biology/Oncology D
Cell Biology D
Chemistry M,D
Classics M,D
Clinical Psychology D
Cognitive Sciences D
Communication Disorders M,D
Communication—General M,D
Community Health Nursing M
Comparative Literature M,D
Computer Science M,D*
Counselor Education M
Curriculum and Instruction M,D
Dentistry P
Developmental Biology M,D
Developmental Psychology D
Early Childhood Education M,D
East European and Russian Studies M
Ecology M,D
Economics M,D
Education—General M,D
Educational Administration M,D
Educational Measurement and Evaluation M,D
Educational Psychology M,D
English Education M
English M,D
Environmental and Occupational Health M,D
Environmental Engineering M,D
Environmental Management and Policy M,D
Environmental Sciences M,D
Epidemiology M,D
Evolutionary Biology M,D
Exercise and Sports Science M
Experimental Psychology D
Finance and Banking D
Folklore M
Foreign Languages Education M
French M,D
Genetics M,D
Geography M,D
Geology M,D
German M,D
Health Education M,D
Health Promotion M
Health Services Management and Hospital Administration M,D
History M,D
Immunology M,D
Industrial Hygiene M,D
Information Studies M,D,O
Italian M,D
Kinesiology and Movement Studies M,D
Latin American Studies M,D,O
Law P
Leisure Studies M
Library Science M,D,O
Linguistics M,D
Management Information Systems D
Management Strategy and Policy D
Marine Sciences M,D
Marketing D
Mass Communication M,D
Materials Sciences M,D
Maternal and Child Health M,D
Mathematics Education M
Mathematics M,D*
Microbiology M,D
Molecular Biology M,D
Molecular Physiology D
Music Education M
Music M,D
Neurobiology D
Nursing—General M,D
Nutrition M,D
Occupational Health Nursing M
Occupational Therapy M,D
Operations Research M,D
Oral and Dental Sciences M,D
Organizational Behavior D
Pathology D
Pharmaceutical Sciences M,D
Pharmacology D
Philosophy M,D
Physical Education M
Physical Therapy M,D
Physics M,D
Political Science M,D
Portuguese M,D
Psychology—General D
Public Administration M
Public Health—General M,D
Public Policy D
Reading Education M,D
Recreation and Park Management M
Rehabilitation Counseling M,D
Religion M,D
Romance Languages M,D
Russian M,D

School Psychology M,D
Science Education M
Secondary Education M
Slavic Languages M,D
Social Psychology D
Social Sciences Education M
Social Work M,D
Sociology M,D
Spanish M,D
Sports Management M
Statistics M,D
Theater M
Toxicology M,D*
Urban and Regional Planning M,D

THE UNIVERSITY OF NORTH CAROLINA AT CHARLOTTE

Accounting M
Adult Nursing M
Applied Mathematics M,D
Applied Physics M,D
Architecture M
Art Education M
Biological and Biomedical Sciences—General M,D
Business Administration and Management—General M,D*
Chemistry M
Child Development M,D
Civil Engineering M,D
Clinical Psychology M,D
Communication—General M
Community Health Nursing M
Computer Engineering M,D
Computer Science M
Counselor Education M,D
Criminal Justice and Criminology M
Curriculum and Instruction M,D,O
Dance M
Economics M
Education of the Gifted M,D
Education—General M
Educational Administration M,D,O
Educational Media/Instructional Technology M,D,O
Electrical Engineering M,D
Elementary Education M
Engineering and Applied Sciences—General M,D*
Engineering Management M
English as a Second Language M
English Education M
English M
Environmental Engineering D
Exercise and Sports Science M
Family Nurse Practitioner Studies M
Foreign Languages Education M
Geography M,D
Geosciences M
Gerontology M
Health Psychology D
Health Services Management and Hospital Administration M
Health Services Research D
History M
Industrial and Organizational Psychology M,D
Information Science M,D
Kinesiology and Movement Studies M
Liberal Studies M
Marketing M
Mathematical and Computational Finance M
Mathematics Education M
Mathematics M,D*
Mechanical Engineering M,D
Middle School Education M
Music Education M
Nurse Anesthesia M
Nursing—General M
Optical Sciences M,D
Psychology—General M,D
Public Administration M
Public Health—General M
Public Policy D
Reading Education M
Religion M
Secondary Education M
Social Psychology M
Social Work M
Sociology M
Spanish M
Special Education M,D
Sports Management M
Systems Engineering D
Systems Science M,D
Theater M

THE UNIVERSITY OF NORTH CAROLINA AT GREENSBORO

Accounting M,O
Adult Education M,D,O
Adult Nursing M,D,O
Applied Economics M
Architecture M,O
Art/Fine Arts M
Biochemistry M
Biological and Biomedical Sciences—General M
Business Administration and Management—General M,O
Chemistry M
Child and Family Studies M,D
Classics M
Clinical Psychology M,D
Cognitive Sciences M,D
Communication Disorders M,D
Communication—General M
Community Health M,D
Computer Science M
Conflict Resolution and Mediation/Peace Studies M,O
Counseling Psychology M,D,O
Counselor Education M,D,O
Criminal Justice and Criminology M
Curriculum and Instruction M,D,O
Dance M
Developmental Psychology M,D
Early Childhood Education M,D,O
Economics D
Education—General M,D,O
Educational Administration M,D,O
Educational Measurement and Evaluation D
Educational Media/Instructional Technology M,D,O
Elementary Education D
English as a Second Language M,D,O
English Education M,D
English M,D
Exercise and Sports Science M,D
Family and Consumer Sciences-General M,D,O
Finance and Banking M,O
Foreign Languages Education M,D,O
French M
Gender Studies M,O
Genetic Counseling M
Geographic Information Systems M,D,O
Geography M,D,O
Gerontological Nursing M,D,O
Gerontology M,O
Higher Education D
Hispanic Studies M,O
Historic Preservation M,O
History M,D,O
Human Development M,D
Information Studies M
Interior Design M,O
Liberal Studies M
Library Science M
Management Information Systems M,D,O
Marketing M,D
Marriage and Family Therapy M,D,O
Mathematics Education M,D,O
Mathematics M
Middle School Education M,D,O
Multilingual and Multicultural Education M,D,O
Museum Studies M,D,O
Music Education M,D
Music M,D
Nonprofit Management M,O
Nurse Anesthesia M,D,O
Nursing and Healthcare Administration M,D,O
Nursing Education M,D,O
Nursing—General M,D,O
Nutrition M,D
Political Science M,O
Psychology—General M,D
Public Affairs M,O
Reading Education M,D,O
Recreation and Park Management M
Rhetoric M,D
School Psychology M,D,O
Science Education M,D,O
Social Psychology M,D
Social Sciences Education M,D,O
Social Work M
Sociology M
Spanish M,O
Special Education M,D,O
Supply Chain Management M,D,O
Taxation M,O
Technical Writing M,D,O
Textile Design M,D
Theater M
Women's Studies M,D,O
Writing M

Close-Up on page 1105.

THE UNIVERSITY OF NORTH CAROLINA AT PEMBROKE

Art Education M
Business Administration and Management—General M
Counselor Education M
Education—General M
Educational Administration M
Elementary Education M
English Education M
Mathematics Education M
Middle School Education M
Music Education M
Physical Education M
Public Administration M
Reading Education M
Science Education M
Social Sciences Education M

THE UNIVERSITY OF NORTH CAROLINA WILMINGTON

Accounting M
Biological and Biomedical Sciences—General M,D
Business Administration and Management—General M
Chemistry M
Computer Science M*
Criminal Justice and Criminology M
Curriculum and Instruction M
Education—General M
Educational Administration M
Educational Media/Instructional Technology M
Elementary Education M
English M
Geology M
Geosciences M
Hispanic Studies O
History M
Liberal Studies M
Marine Biology M,D*
Marine Sciences M,D
Mathematics M
Middle School Education M
Nursing—General M
Psychology—General M
Public Administration M
Reading Education M
Secondary Education M
Social Work M
Sociology M*
Special Education M
Systems Science M
Writing M*

UNIVERSITY OF NORTH DAKOTA

Allopathic Medicine P
Anatomy M,D
Applied Economics M
Art/Fine Arts M
Atmospheric Sciences M
Aviation M
Biochemistry M,D
Biological and Biomedical Sciences—General M,D
Botany M,D
Business Administration and Management—General M
Chemical Engineering M
Chemistry M,D
Civil Engineering M
Clinical Laboratory Sciences/Medical Technology M
Clinical Psychology M,D
Communication Disorders M,D
Communication—General M,D
Computer Science M
Counseling Psychology M
Criminal Justice and Criminology D
Early Childhood Education M
Ecology M,D
Education—General M,D,O
Educational Administration M,D,O
Educational Measurement and Evaluation D
Educational Media/Instructional Technology M
Electrical Engineering M
Elementary Education M,D
Engineering and Applied Sciences—General D
English M,D
Entomology M,D
Environmental Biology M,D
Environmental Engineering M
Experimental Psychology M,D
Fish, Game, and Wildlife Management M,D
Forensic Psychology M,D
Genetics M,D
Geography M
Geological Engineering M
Geology M,D
Geosciences M,D
History M,D
Immunology M,D
Industrial and Manufacturing Management M
Kinesiology and Movement Studies M
Law P
Linguistics M
Mathematics M
Mechanical Engineering M
Microbiology M,D
Mineral/Mining Engineering M
Music Education M,D
Music M,D
Nursing—General M,D
Occupational Therapy M
Pharmacology M,D
Physical Therapy M,D
Physician Assistant Studies M
Physics M,D
Physiology M,D
Planetary and Space Sciences M
Psychology—General M,D
Public Administration M
Reading Education M
Secondary Education D
Social Work M
Sociology M
Special Education M,D
Structural Engineering M
Theater M
Vocational and Technical Education M
Zoology M,D

UNIVERSITY OF NORTHERN BRITISH COLUMBIA

Community Health M,D,O
Computer Science M,D,O
Disability Studies M,D,O
Education—General M,D,O
Environmental Management and Policy M,D,O
Gender Studies M,D,O
History M,D,O
Interdisciplinary Studies M,D,O
International Affairs M,D,O
Mathematics M,D,O
Natural Resources M,D,O
Political Science M,D,O
Psychology—General M,D,O
Social Work M,D,O

UNIVERSITY OF NORTHERN COLORADO

Applied Science and Technology M
Applied Statistics M,D
Art/Fine Arts M
Biological and Biomedical Sciences—General M,D
Chemistry M,D
Communication Disorders M,D
Communication—General M
Community Health M
Counseling Psychology D
Counselor Education D
Early Childhood Education M,D
Education—General M,D,O
Educational Administration M,D,O
Educational Measurement and Evaluation M,D
Educational Media/Instructional Technology M,D
Educational Psychology M,D
Elementary Education M,D
English M
Exercise and Sports Science M,D
Family Nurse Practitioner Studies M,D
Foreign Languages Education M
Geosciences M
Gerontology M
History M
Interdisciplinary Studies M
Mathematics Education M,D
Mathematics M,D
Music Education M,D
Music M,D
Nursing Education M,D
Nursing—General M,D
Physical Education M,D
Psychology—General M,D
Public Health—General M
Reading Education M
Rehabilitation Counseling M,D
School Psychology D,O
Science Education M,D
Sociology M
Spanish M
Special Education M,D
Sports Management M,D

Close-Up on page 1107.

UNIVERSITY OF NORTHERN IOWA

Accounting M
Art Education M
Art/Fine Arts M
Biological and Biomedical Sciences—General M
Business Administration and Management—General M
Chemistry M
Communication Disorders M
Communication—General M
Community Health M,D
Computer Science M
Counselor Education M,D
Criminal Justice and Criminology M
Curriculum and Instruction M,D
Early Childhood Education M

Program	Degrees
Education—General	M,D,O
Educational Administration	M,D
Educational Media/Instructional Technology	M
Educational Psychology	M,O
Elementary Education	M
English as a Second Language	M
English	M
Environmental Sciences	M
French	M
Gender Studies	M
Geography	M
German	M
Health Education	M,D
Higher Education	M
History	M
Leisure Studies	M,D
Mathematics Education	M
Mathematics	M
Middle School Education	M
Music Education	M
Music	M
Nonprofit Management	M
Physical Education	M
Physics	M
Psychology—General	M
Public Policy	M
Reading Education	M
Rehabilitation Sciences	M,D
School Psychology	M,O
Science Education	M,O
Social Work	M
Sociology	M
Spanish	M
Special Education	M,D
Sports Management	M,D
Student Affairs	M
Vocational and Technical Education	M,D
Women's Studies	M

UNIVERSITY OF NORTHERN VIRGINIA

Program	Degrees
Accounting	M,D
Business Administration and Management—General	M,D
Computer Science	M,D
Counselor Education	M,D
Early Childhood Education	M,D
Educational Administration	M,D
Educational Media/Instructional Technology	M,D
English as a Second Language	M,D
Finance and Banking	M,D
Management Information Systems	M,D
Marketing	M,D
Project Management	M,D
Public Administration	M,D

UNIVERSITY OF NORTH FLORIDA

Program	Degrees
Accounting	M
Allied Health—General	M,O
Biological and Biomedical Sciences—General	M
Business Administration and Management—General	M
Community Health	M,O
Computer Science	M
Counseling Psychology	M
Counselor Education	M
Criminal Justice and Criminology	M
Education—General	M,D
Educational Administration	M,D
Elementary Education	M
English	M
Ethics	M,O
Gerontology	M,O
Health Services Management and Hospital Administration	M,O
Health Services Research	M,O
History	M
Information Science	M
Mathematics	M
Nursing—General	M,O
Nutrition	M,O
Philosophy	M,O
Physical Therapy	M
Psychology—General	M
Public Administration	M
Public Health—General	M,O
Rehabilitation Counseling	M,O
Secondary Education	M
Sociology	M
Special Education	M
Statistics	M
Writing	M

UNIVERSITY OF NORTH TEXAS

Program	Degrees
Accounting	M,D
Anthropology	M
Applied Economics	M
Art Education	M,D
Art History	M,D
Art/Fine Arts	M,D
Biochemistry	M,D
Biological and Biomedical Sciences—General	M,D
Business Administration and Management—General	M,D
Chemistry	M,D
Child and Family Studies	M,D
Clinical Psychology	M,D
Clothing and Textiles	M
Communication Disorders	M,D
Communication—General	M
Community Health	M
Computer Education	M,D
Computer Science	M,D*
Counseling Psychology	M,D
Counselor Education	M,D
Criminal Justice and Criminology	M
Curriculum and Instruction	D
Early Childhood Education	M,D
Economics	M
Education—General	M,D,O
Educational Administration	M,D
Educational Measurement and Evaluation	D
Electrical Engineering	M
Engineering and Applied Sciences—General	M
English	M,D
Environmental Sciences	M,D
Ethics	M,D
Experimental Psychology	M,D
Film, Television, and Video Production	M
Finance and Banking	M,D
French	M
Geography	M
Gerontology	M,D,O
Graphic Design	M,D
Health Promotion	M
Health Psychology	M,D
Higher Education	M,D
History	M,D
Hospitality Management	M
Human Development	M,D
Industrial and Labor Relations	M,D
Industrial and Manufacturing Management	M,D
Industrial and Organizational Psychology	M,D
Information Studies	M,D
Insurance	M,D
Interdisciplinary Studies	M
Interior Design	M,D
Journalism	M
Kinesiology and Movement Studies	M
Leisure Studies	M,O
Library Science	M,D
Management Information Systems	M,D
Management Strategy and Policy	M,D
Marketing	M,D
Materials Sciences	M,D
Mathematics	M,D
Molecular Biology	M,D
Music Education	M,D
Music	M,D
Organizational Management	M,D
Philosophy	M,D
Photography	M,D
Physics	M,D
Political Science	M,D
Psychology—General	M,D
Public Administration	M
Quantitative Analysis	M,D
Reading Education	M,D
Real Estate	M,D
Recreation and Park Management	M,O
Rehabilitation Counseling	M
Rehabilitation Sciences	M
Religion	M,D
School Psychology	M,D
Secondary Education	M
Sociology	M,D
Spanish	M
Special Education	M,D
Textile Design	M,D
Theater	M
Vocational and Technical Education	M,D

Close-Up on page 1109.

UNIVERSITY OF NORTH TEXAS HEALTH SCIENCE CENTER AT FORT WORTH

Program	Degrees
Anatomy	M,D
Biochemistry	M,D
Biological and Biomedical Sciences—General	M,D
Biostatistics	M,D
Biotechnology	M,D
Community Health	M,D
Environmental and Occupational Health	M,D
Epidemiology	M,D
Forensic Sciences	M,D
Genetics	M,D
Health Services Management and Hospital Administration	M,D
Immunology	M,D
Microbiology	M,D
Molecular Biology	M,D
Osteopathic Medicine	P,M
Pharmacology	M,D
Physician Assistant Studies	M
Physiology	M,D
Public Health—General	M,D
Science Education	M,D

UNIVERSITY OF NOTRE DAME

Program	Degrees
Accounting	M
Aerospace/Aeronautical Engineering	M,D
Applied Arts and Design—General	M
Applied Mathematics	M,D
Architecture	M*
Art History	M
Art/Fine Arts	M
Biochemistry	M,D
Bioengineering	M,D
Biological and Biomedical Sciences—General	M,D*
Business Administration and Management—General	M*
Cell Biology	M,D
Chemical Engineering	M,D
Chemistry	M,D
Civil Engineering	M,D
Cognitive Sciences	D
Comparative Literature	D
Computer Engineering	M,D
Computer Science	M,D
Conflict Resolution and Mediation/Peace Studies	M
Counseling Psychology	D
Developmental Psychology	D
Ecology	M,D
Economics	M,D
Education—General	M
Electrical Engineering	M,D*
Engineering and Applied Sciences—General	M,D
English	M,D
Environmental Engineering	M,D
Evolutionary Biology	M,D
French	M
Genetics	M,D
Geosciences	M,D
Graphic Design	M
History of Science and Technology	M,D
History	M,D
Industrial Design	M
Inorganic Chemistry	M,D
Italian	M
Latin American Studies	M
Law	P,M,D
Mathematics	M,D
Mechanical Engineering	M,D
Medieval and Renaissance Studies	M,D
Molecular Biology	M,D
Nonprofit Management	M
Organic Chemistry	M,D
Parasitology	M,D
Philosophy	D
Photography	M
Physical Chemistry	M,D
Physics	D*
Physiology	M,D
Political Science	D
Psychology—General	D
Religion	M
Romance Languages	M
Sociology	D
Spanish	M
Theology	P,M,D
Writing	M

UNIVERSITY OF OKLAHOMA

Program	Degrees
Accounting	M
Adult Education	M,D
Advertising and Public Relations	M
Aerospace/Aeronautical Engineering	M,D
American Indian/Native American Studies	M
Anthropology	M,D
Applied Arts and Design—General	M
Architecture	M
Art History	M
Art/Fine Arts	M
Astrophysics	M,D
Biochemistry	M,D
Bioengineering	M,D
Botany	M,D
Business Administration and Management—General	M,D*
Chemical Engineering	M,D
Chemistry	M,D
Civil Engineering	M,D
Communication—General	M,D
Computer Engineering	M,D
Computer Science	M,D
Counseling Psychology	D
Counselor Education	M
Curriculum and Instruction	M,D,O
Dance	M
Early Childhood Education	M,D,O
Economics	M,D
Education—General	M,D
Educational Administration	M,D
Educational Psychology	M,D
Electrical Engineering	M,D
Elementary Education	M,D,O
Engineering and Applied Sciences—General	M,D
Engineering Physics	M,D
English Education	M,D,O
English	M,D
Environmental and Occupational Health	M,D
Environmental Engineering	M,D
Environmental Sciences	M,D
Exercise and Sports Science	M,D
Film, Television, and Video Production	M
Foundations and Philosophy of Education	M,D
French	M,D
Geography	M,D
Geological Engineering	M,D
Geology	M,D
Geophysics	M
Geotechnical Engineering	M,D
German	M
Hazardous Materials Management	M,D
Health Services Management and Hospital Administration	M
Higher Education	M,D
History of Science and Technology	M,D
History	M,D
Human Services	M
Industrial/Management Engineering	M,D
Information Studies	M,O
Interdisciplinary Studies	M,D
International Affairs	M
International Business	M
Journalism	M
Landscape Architecture	M
Law	P
Liberal Studies	M
Library Science	M,O
Management Information Systems	M
Management Strategy and Policy	M
Mass Communication	M
Mathematics Education	M,D,O
Mathematics	M,D*
Mechanical Engineering	M,D
Meteorology	M,D
Microbiology	M,D
Multilingual and Multicultural Education	M,D,O
Museum Studies	M
Music Education	M,D
Music	M,D
Natural Resources	M,D
Organizational Behavior	M
Petroleum Engineering	M,D
Philosophy	M,D
Photography	M
Physics	M,D
Political Science	M,D
Psychology—General	M,D
Public Administration	M
Reading Education	M,D,O
School Psychology	M,D
Science Education	M,D,O
Secondary Education	M,D,O
Social Psychology	M
Social Sciences Education	M,D,O
Social Work	M
Sociology	M,D
Spanish	M,D
Special Education	M,D
Structural Engineering	M,D
Telecommunications	M,D
Theater	M
Urban and Regional Planning	M
Water Resources	M,D
Writing	M
Zoology	M,D*

Close-Up on page 1111.

UNIVERSITY OF OKLAHOMA HEALTH SCIENCES CENTER

Program	Degrees
Allied Health—General	M,D,O
Allopathic Medicine	P
Biochemistry	M,D
Biological and Biomedical Sciences—General	M,D
Biopsychology	M,D
Biostatistics	M,D
Cell Biology	M,D
Communication Disorders	M,D,O
Dentistry	P
Environmental and Occupational Health	M,D
Epidemiology	M,D
Genetic Counseling	M
Health Education	D
Health Physics/Radiological Health	M,D
Health Promotion	M,D
Health Services Management and Hospital Administration	M,D

Immunology M,D
Medical Physics M,D
Microbiology M,D
Molecular Biology M,D
Neuroscience M,D
Nursing—General M
Nutrition M
Occupational Therapy M
Oral and Dental Sciences M
Pathology D
Pharmaceutical Sciences M,D
Pharmacy P
Physical Therapy M
Physiology M,D
Public Health—General M,D
Radiation Biology M,D
Rehabilitation Sciences M
Special Education M,D,O

UNIVERSITY OF OREGON

Accounting M,D
Anthropology M,D
Architecture M
Art History M,D
Art/Fine Arts M
Arts Administration M*
Asian Languages M,D
Asian Studies M
Biochemistry M,D
Biological and Biomedical Sciences—General M,D
Biopsychology M,D
Business Administration and Management—General M,D
Chemistry M,D
Chinese M,D
Classics M
Clinical Psychology D
Cognitive Sciences M,D
Communication—General M,D
Comparative Literature M,D
Computer Science M,D*
Dance M
Developmental Psychology M,D
Ecology M,D
Economics M,D
Education—General M,D
English M,D
Environmental Management and Policy M,D*
Evolutionary Biology M,D
Finance and Banking D
Folklore M
French M
Genetics M,D
Geography M,D
Geology M,D
German M,D
Historic Preservation M
History M,D
Information Science M,D
Interdisciplinary Studies M
Interior Design M
International Affairs M
Italian M
Japanese M,D
Journalism M,D
Landscape Architecture M
Law P,M
Linguistics M,D
Management Information Systems M
Marine Biology M,D
Marketing D
Mathematics M,D
Molecular Biology M,D
Music Education M,D
Music M,D
Neuroscience M,D
Philosophy M,D
Physics M,D
Physiology M,D
Political Science M,D
Psychology—General M,D
Public Policy M
Quantitative Analysis M
Romance Languages M,D
Russian M
Social Psychology M,D
Sociology M,D
Spanish M
Theater M,D
Urban and Regional Planning M
Writing M

UNIVERSITY OF OTTAWA

Aerospace/Aeronautical Engineering M,D
Allopathic Medicine P,M,D
Anthropology M
Biochemistry M,D
Biological and Biomedical Sciences—General M,D
Biomedical Engineering M
Business Administration and Management—General M*
Canadian Studies D
Cell Biology M,D
Chemical Engineering M,D
Chemistry M,D
Civil Engineering M,D
Classics M,D
Communication Disorders M
Communication—General M
Community Health M,D,O
Computer Engineering M,D
Computer Science M,D
Criminal Justice and Criminology M,D
Economics M,D
Education—General M,D,O
Electrical Engineering M,D
Electronic Commerce M,D,O
Engineering and Applied Sciences—General M,D,O
Engineering Management M,O
English M,D
Epidemiology M
Finance and Banking D,O
French M,D
Geography M,D
Geosciences M,D
Health Services Management and Hospital Administration M
Health Services Research D,O
History M,D
Immunology M,D
Information Science M,O
Interdisciplinary Studies D,O
International Development M
Kinesiology and Movement Studies M
Law M,D
Linguistics M,D
Mathematics M,D
Mechanical Engineering M,D
Microbiology M,D
Molecular Biology M,D
Music Education M,O
Music M,O
Nursing—General M,D,O
Philosophy M,D
Physics M,D
Political Science M,D
Project Management M,O
Psychology—General D
Public Administration D,O
Public Health—General M
Rehabilitation Sciences M
Religion M,D
Social Work M
Sociology M
Spanish M,D
Statistics M,D
Systems Science M,D,O
Theater M
Translation and Interpretation M,D
Women's Studies M

UNIVERSITY OF PENNSYLVANIA

Accounting M,D
Acute Care/Critical Care Nursing M
Adult Nursing M
Allopathic Medicine P
American Studies M,D
Anthropology M,D
Archaeology M,D
Architecture M,D,O*
Art History M,D
Art/Fine Arts M
Asian Studies M,D
Astrophysics M,D
Biochemistry D
Bioengineering M,D
Bioethics M
Biological and Biomedical Sciences—General M,D
Biostatistics M,D
Biotechnology M*
Business Administration and Management—General M,D
Cancer Biology/Oncology D
Cell Biology D
Chemical Engineering M,D
Chemistry M,D
Classics M,D
Clinical Psychology D
Communication—General D
Comparative Literature M,D
Computational Biology D
Computer Art and Design M
Computer Science M,D*
Counseling Psychology M
Criminal Justice and Criminology M,D
Demography and Population Studies M,D
Dentistry P
Developmental Biology D
Early Childhood Education M
Economics M,D
Education—General M,D*
Educational Administration M,D
Educational Measurement and Evaluation M,D
Educational Policy M,D
Educational Psychology M,D
Electrical Engineering M,D
Elementary Education M
Engineering and Applied Sciences—General M,D,O*
English as a Second Language M,D
English M,D
Environmental Management and Policy M
Epidemiology M,D
Family Nurse Practitioner Studies M,O
Finance and Banking M,D
Folklore M,D
French M,D
Genetics D
Genomic Sciences D
Geology M,D
German M,D
Health Education M,D
Health Services Management and Hospital Administration M,D
Historic Preservation M,O
History of Science and Technology M,D
History M,D
Human Development M,D
Immunology D
Information Science M,D
Insurance M,D
International Affairs M
International and Comparative Education M,D
International Business M
Italian M,D
Landscape Architecture M,O
Law P,M,D
Liberal Studies M
Linguistics M,D
Management Information Systems M,D
Management of Technology M,D
Marketing M,D
Materials Engineering M,D
Materials Sciences M,D
Maternal and Child/Neonatal Nursing M,O
Mathematics M,D
Mechanical Engineering M,D
Mechanics M,D
Medical Physics M,D
Microbiology D
Molecular Biology D
Molecular Biophysics D
Multilingual and Multicultural Education M,D
Music M,D
Near and Middle Eastern Studies M,D
Neuroscience D
Nurse Anesthesia M
Nurse Midwifery M
Nursing and Healthcare Administration M,D
Nursing—General M,D,O
Occupational Health Nursing M
Oncology Nursing M
Organizational Behavior M
Organizational Management M
Parasitology D
Pediatric Nursing M
Pharmacology D
Philosophy M,D
Physics M,D
Physiology D
Political Science M,D
Psychiatric Nursing M
Psychology—General D
Public Administration M*
Public Policy M,D*
Reading Education M,D
Real Estate M,D
Religion D
Romance Languages M,D
School Psychology D
Secondary Education M
Social Psychology D
Social Work M,D*
Sociology M,D
Spanish M,D
Statistics M,D
Systems Engineering M,D
Telecommunications Management M
Telecommunications M
Urban and Regional Planning M,D,O
Urban Design D
Veterinary Medicine P
Virology D
Women's Health Nursing M
Writing M,D

Close-Up on page 1113.

UNIVERSITY OF PHOENIX–ATLANTA CAMPUS

Business Administration and Management—General M
Health Services Management and Hospital Administration M
Human Resources Management M
International Business M
Management Information Systems M
Management of Technology M
Nursing—General M

UNIVERSITY OF PHOENIX–AUGUSTA CAMPUS

Accounting M
Business Administration and Management—General M
Criminal Justice and Criminology M
Health Services Management and Hospital Administration M
Human Resources Management M
International Business M
Management Information Systems M
Management of Technology M
Marketing M
Nursing—General M
Public Administration M

UNIVERSITY OF PHOENIX–AUSTIN CAMPUS

Accounting M
Business Administration and Management—General M
Criminal Justice and Criminology M
Electronic Commerce M
Health Services Management and Hospital Administration M
Human Resources Management M
International Business M
Management Information Systems M
Management of Technology M
Marketing M
Psychology—General M
Public Administration M

UNIVERSITY OF PHOENIX–BAY AREA CAMPUS

Accounting M
Adult Education M
Business Administration and Management—General M
Criminal Justice and Criminology M
Curriculum and Instruction M
Education—General M
Electronic Commerce M
Family Nurse Practitioner Studies M
Health Services Management and Hospital Administration M
Human Resources Management M
International Business M
Management Information Systems M
Management of Technology M
Marketing M
Marriage and Family Therapy M
Public Administration M

UNIVERSITY OF PHOENIX–BOSTON CAMPUS

Business Administration and Management—General M
International Business M
Management Information Systems M
Management of Technology M

UNIVERSITY OF PHOENIX–CENTRAL FLORIDA CAMPUS

Accounting M
Business Administration and Management—General M
Curriculum and Instruction M
Education—General M
Educational Administration M
Elementary Education M
Health Services Management and Hospital Administration M
International Business M
Management Information Systems M
Management of Technology M
Marketing M
Nursing—General M
Secondary Education M

UNIVERSITY OF PHOENIX–CENTRAL MASSACHUSETTS CAMPUS

Business Administration and Management—General M
Education—General M
Management of Technology M

UNIVERSITY OF PHOENIX–CENTRAL VALLEY CAMPUS

Accounting M
Business Administration and Management—General M
Curriculum and Instruction M

Education—General M
Elementary Education M
Health Services Management and Hospital Administration M
Human Resources Management M
International Business M
Management of Technology M
Marketing M
Marriage and Family Therapy M
Nursing—General M
Public Administration M
Secondary Education M

UNIVERSITY OF PHOENIX–CHARLOTTE CAMPUS

Accounting M
Allied Health—General M
Business Administration and Management—General M
International Business M
Management Information Systems M
Management of Technology M
Nursing—General M

UNIVERSITY OF PHOENIX–CHATTANOOGA CAMPUS

Accounting M
Business Administration and Management—General M
Criminal Justice and Criminology M
Health Services Management and Hospital Administration M
Human Resources Management M
International Business M
Management of Technology M
Marketing M
Public Administration M

UNIVERSITY OF PHOENIX–CHEYENNE CAMPUS

Business Administration and Management—General M
Criminal Justice and Criminology M
Health Services Management and Hospital Administration M
Human Resources Management M
International Business M
Management Information Systems M
Management of Technology M
Marketing M
Nursing Education M
Nursing—General M
Psychology—General M
Public Administration M

UNIVERSITY OF PHOENIX–CHICAGO CAMPUS

Business Administration and Management—General M
Electronic Commerce M
International Business M
Management Information Systems M
Management of Technology M

UNIVERSITY OF PHOENIX–CINCINNATI CAMPUS

Business Administration and Management—General M
Electronic Commerce M
Health Services Management and Hospital Administration M
Information Science M
Management of Technology M

UNIVERSITY OF PHOENIX–CLEVELAND CAMPUS

Accounting M
Business Administration and Management—General M
Criminal Justice and Criminology M
Health Services Management and Hospital Administration M
Human Resources Management M
International Business M
Management Information Systems M
Management of Technology M
Marketing M
Nursing—General M
Psychology—General M
Public Administration M

UNIVERSITY OF PHOENIX–COLUMBIA CAMPUS

Business Administration and Management—General M

UNIVERSITY OF PHOENIX–COLUMBUS GEORGIA CAMPUS

Accounting M
Business Administration and Management—General M
Electronic Commerce M
Health Services Management and Hospital Administration M
Human Resources Management M
International Business M
Management of Technology M
Marketing M
Public Administration M

UNIVERSITY OF PHOENIX–COLUMBUS OHIO CAMPUS

Business Administration and Management—General M
Health Services Management and Hospital Administration M
Marketing M

UNIVERSITY OF PHOENIX–DALLAS CAMPUS

Accounting M
Business Administration and Management—General M
Electronic Commerce M
Health Services Management and Hospital Administration M
Human Resources Management M
Management of Technology M
Marketing M
Public Administration M

UNIVERSITY OF PHOENIX–DENVER CAMPUS

Accounting M
Business Administration and Management—General M
Curriculum and Instruction M
Education—General M
Educational Administration M
Electronic Commerce M
Elementary Education M
Health Services Management and Hospital Administration M
Human Resources Management M
International Business M
Management Information Systems M
Management of Technology M
Marketing M
Marriage and Family Therapy M
Nursing—General M
Public Administration M
School Psychology M
Secondary Education M
Social Psychology M

UNIVERSITY OF PHOENIX–DES MOINES CAMPUS

Accounting M
Business Administration and Management—General M
Criminal Justice and Criminology M
Health Services Management and Hospital Administration M
Human Resources Management M
International Business M
Management Information Systems M
Management of Technology M
Marketing M
Public Administration M

UNIVERSITY OF PHOENIX–DETROIT CAMPUS

Accounting M
Business Administration and Management—General M
Criminal Justice and Criminology M
Electronic Commerce M
Family Nurse Practitioner Studies M
Health Services Management and Hospital Administration M
Human Resources Management M
International Business M
Management Information Systems M
Management of Technology M
Marketing M
Nursing—General M
Public Administration M

UNIVERSITY OF PHOENIX–EASTERN WASHINGTON CAMPUS

Business Administration and Management—General M
Health Services Management and Hospital Administration M

UNIVERSITY OF PHOENIX–FAIRFIELD COUNTY

Business Administration and Management—General M

UNIVERSITY OF PHOENIX–FORT LAUDERDALE CAMPUS

Accounting M
Business Administration and Management—General M
Computer Education M
Curriculum and Instruction M
Education—General M
Educational Administration M
Elementary Education M
Health Services Management and Hospital Administration M
Human Resources Management M
International Business M
Management Information Systems M
Marketing M
Nursing Education M
Nursing—General M
Public Administration M
Secondary Education M

UNIVERSITY OF PHOENIX–HARRISBURG CAMPUS

Accounting M
Business Administration and Management—General M
Criminal Justice and Criminology M
Health Services Management and Hospital Administration M
Human Resources Management M
International Business M
Management Information Systems M
Management of Technology M
Marketing M
Nursing Education M
Nursing—General M
Psychology—General M
Public Administration M

UNIVERSITY OF PHOENIX–HAWAII CAMPUS

Accounting M
Business Administration and Management—General M
Criminal Justice and Criminology M
Curriculum and Instruction M
Education—General M
Educational Administration M
Elementary Education M
Family Nurse Practitioner Studies M
Health Services Management and Hospital Administration M
Human Resources Management M
International Business M
Management Information Systems M
Management of Technology M
Marketing M
Marriage and Family Therapy M
Nursing—General M
Psychology—General M
Public Administration M
Secondary Education M
Social Psychology M

UNIVERSITY OF PHOENIX–HOUSTON CAMPUS

Business Administration and Management—General M
Electronic Commerce M
Health Services Management and Hospital Administration M
Human Resources Management M
International Business M
Management of Technology M
Public Administration M

UNIVERSITY OF PHOENIX–IDAHO CAMPUS

Accounting M
Business Administration and Management—General M
Education—General M
Health Services Management and Hospital Administration M

Management Information Systems M
Management of Technology M
Psychology—General M

UNIVERSITY OF PHOENIX–INDIANAPOLIS CAMPUS

Business Administration and Management—General M
Criminal Justice and Criminology M
Health Services Management and Hospital Administration M
Management Information Systems M
Management of Technology M
Nursing—General M
Psychology—General M

UNIVERSITY OF PHOENIX–JERSEY CITY CAMPUS

Accounting M
Business Administration and Management—General M
Criminal Justice and Criminology M
Health Services Management and Hospital Administration M
Human Resources Management M
International Business M
Management Information Systems M
Management of Technology M
Marketing M
Psychology—General M
Public Administration M

UNIVERSITY OF PHOENIX–KANSAS CITY CAMPUS

Business Administration and Management—General M
Criminal Justice and Criminology M
Education—General M
Health Services Management and Hospital Administration M
Management of Technology M
Nursing—General M
Social Psychology M

UNIVERSITY OF PHOENIX–LAS VEGAS CAMPUS

Allied Health—General M
Business Administration and Management—General M
Counseling Psychology M
Curriculum and Instruction M
Education—General M
Educational Administration M
Elementary Education M
Management Information Systems M
Management of Technology M
Marriage and Family Therapy M
School Psychology M

UNIVERSITY OF PHOENIX–LITTLE ROCK CAMPUS

Business Administration and Management—General M

UNIVERSITY OF PHOENIX–LOUISIANA CAMPUS

Business Administration and Management—General M
Criminal Justice and Criminology M
Early Childhood Education M
Education—General M
Health Services Management and Hospital Administration M
Human Resources Management M
Management Information Systems M
Management of Technology M
Nursing—General M
Psychology—General M
Public Administration M

UNIVERSITY OF PHOENIX–LOUISVILLE CAMPUS

Business Administration and Management—General M
Electronic Commerce M
Health Services Management and Hospital Administration M
Management of Technology M

UNIVERSITY OF PHOENIX–MADISON CAMPUS

Accounting M
Business Administration and Management—General M

Electronic Commerce M
Health Services Management and Hospital Administration M
Human Resources Management M
International Business M
Management Information Systems M
Management of Technology M
Marketing M
Public Administration M

UNIVERSITY OF PHOENIX–MARYLAND CAMPUS

Business Administration and Management—General M
Criminal Justice and Criminology M
Electronic Commerce M
Human Resources Management M
Human Services M
International Business M
Management Information Systems M
Management of Technology M
Marketing M
Nursing Education M
Nursing—General M
Psychology—General M
Public Administration M

UNIVERSITY OF PHOENIX–MEMPHIS CAMPUS

Accounting M
Business Administration and Management—General M
Criminal Justice and Criminology M
Curriculum and Instruction M
Education—General M
Electronic Commerce M
Health Services Management and Hospital Administration M
Human Resources Management M
International Business M
Management Information Systems M
Management of Technology M
Marketing M
Public Administration M

UNIVERSITY OF PHOENIX–METRO DETROIT CAMPUS

Adult Education M
Business Administration and Management—General M
Curriculum and Instruction M
Distance Education Development M
Education—General M
Educational Administration M
Elementary Education M
Health Services Management and Hospital Administration M
International Business M
Management Information Systems M
Management of Technology M
Nursing—General M
Special Education M

UNIVERSITY OF PHOENIX–MINNEAPOLIS/ST. LOUIS PARK CAMPUS

Accounting M
Business Administration and Management—General M
Family Nurse Practitioner Studies M
Health Services Management and Hospital Administration M
Human Resources Management M
International Business M
Management of Technology M
Marketing M
Nursing—General M

UNIVERSITY OF PHOENIX–NASHVILLE CAMPUS

Business Administration and Management—General M
Curriculum and Instruction M
Education—General M
Educational Administration M
Elementary Education M
Health Services Management and Hospital Administration M
Human Resources Management M
Management Information Systems M
Management of Technology M
Secondary Education M

UNIVERSITY OF PHOENIX–NEW MEXICO CAMPUS

Business Administration and Management—General M
Curriculum and Instruction M
Education—General M
Educational Administration M
Electronic Commerce M
Elementary Education M
Health Services Management and Hospital Administration M
Human Resources Management M
International Business M
Management Information Systems M
Management of Technology M
Marriage and Family Therapy M
Nursing—General M
Secondary Education M

UNIVERSITY OF PHOENIX—NORTHERN NEVADA CAMPUS

Accounting M
Business Administration and Management—General M
Criminal Justice and Criminology M
Education—General M
Educational Administration M
Elementary Education M
Health Services Management and Hospital Administration M
Human Resources Management M
International Business M
Management Information Systems M
Management of Technology M
Marketing M
Marriage and Family Therapy M
Nursing Education M
Nursing—General M
Psychology—General M
Public Administration M
School Psychology M

UNIVERSITY OF PHOENIX–NORTHERN VIRGINIA CAMPUS

Accounting M
Business Administration and Management—General M
Criminal Justice and Criminology M
Education—General M
Educational Administration M
Electronic Commerce M
Health Services Management and Hospital Administration M
Human Resources Management M
International Business M
Management Information Systems M
Management of Technology M
Marketing M
Nursing—General M
Public Administration M

UNIVERSITY OF PHOENIX–NORTH FLORIDA CAMPUS

Accounting M
Business Administration and Management—General M
Computer Education M
Curriculum and Instruction M
Education—General M
Educational Administration M
Elementary Education M
Health Services Management and Hospital Administration M
Human Resources Management M
International Business M
Management Information Systems M
Marketing M
Nursing Education M
Nursing—General M
Public Administration M
Secondary Education M

UNIVERSITY OF PHOENIX–NORTHWEST ARKANSAS CAMPUS

Accounting M
Business Administration and Management—General M
Criminal Justice and Criminology M
Health Services Management and Hospital Administration M
Human Resources Management M
International Business M
Management Information Systems M
Management of Technology M
Marketing M
Nursing Education M
Nursing—General M
Public Administration M

UNIVERSITY OF PHOENIX–NORTHWEST INDIANA

Business Administration and Management—General M
Criminal Justice and Criminology M
Health Services Management and Hospital Administration M
Human Resources Management M
Management Information Systems M
Nursing Education M
Nursing—General M
Psychology—General M
Public Administration M

UNIVERSITY OF PHOENIX–OKLAHOMA CITY CAMPUS

Business Administration and Management—General M
Electronic Commerce M
Human Resources Management M
Management Information Systems M
Management of Technology M

UNIVERSITY OF PHOENIX–OMAHA CAMPUS

Accounting M
Adult Education M
Business Administration and Management—General M
Computer Education M
Criminal Justice and Criminology M
Curriculum and Instruction M
Education—General M
Educational Administration M
Elementary Education M
English as a Second Language M
English Education M
Health Services Management and Hospital Administration M
Human Resources Management M
International Business M
Management Information Systems M
Management of Technology M
Marketing M
Mathematics Education M
Public Administration M
Secondary Education M
Special Education M

UNIVERSITY OF PHOENIX ONLINE CAMPUS

Accounting M
Adult Education M
Business Administration and Management—General M,D
Criminal Justice and Criminology M
Curriculum and Instruction M
Early Childhood Education M
Education—General M,D
Educational Administration M
Educational Media/Instructional Technology M
Electronic Commerce M
Elementary Education M
English as a Second Language M
English Education M
Health Services Management and Hospital Administration M,D
Human Resources Management M
Management Information Systems M
Management of Technology M
Marketing M
Mathematics Education M
Nursing Education M
Nursing—General M
Organizational Management D
Psychology—General M
Public Administration M
Secondary Education M

UNIVERSITY OF PHOENIX–OREGON CAMPUS

Accounting M
Business Administration and Management—General M
Criminal Justice and Criminology M
Early Childhood Education M
Education—General M
Elementary Education M
Health Services Management and Hospital Administration M
Human Resources Management M
International Business M
Management Information Systems M
Management of Technology M
Psychology—General M
Secondary Education M

UNIVERSITY OF PHOENIX–PHILADELPHIA CAMPUS

Business Administration and Management—General M
Health Services Management and Hospital Administration M
International Business M
Management Information Systems M
Management of Technology M

UNIVERSITY OF PHOENIX–PHOENIX CAMPUS

Business Administration and Management—General M
Curriculum and Instruction M
Education—General M
Educational Administration M
Elementary Education M
Family Nurse Practitioner Studies M,O
Health Services Management and Hospital Administration M,O
Information Science M
Nursing—General M,O
Secondary Education M
Social Psychology M,O

UNIVERSITY OF PHOENIX–PITTSBURGH CAMPUS

Accounting M
Business Administration and Management—General M
Criminal Justice and Criminology M
Electronic Commerce M
Health Services Management and Hospital Administration M
Human Resources Management M
International Business M
Management Information Systems M
Management of Technology M
Marketing M
Nursing Education M
Psychology—General M
Public Administration M

UNIVERSITY OF PHOENIX–PUERTO RICO CAMPUS

Accounting M
Business Administration and Management—General M
Counseling Psychology M
Early Childhood Education M
Education—General M
Educational Administration M
Health Services Management and Hospital Administration M
Human Resources Management M
International Business M
Management of Technology M
Marketing M
Marriage and Family Therapy M
School Psychology M

UNIVERSITY OF PHOENIX–RALEIGH CAMPUS

Accounting M
Business Administration and Management—General M
Electronic Commerce M
Health Services Management and Hospital Administration M
International Business M
Management Information Systems M
Management of Technology M

UNIVERSITY OF PHOENIX–RENTON LEARNING CENTER

Accounting M
Business Administration and Management—General M
Criminal Justice and Criminology M
Health Services Management and Hospital Administration M
Human Resources Management M
International Business M

Management Information Systems M
Management of Technology M
Marketing M
Nursing Education M
Nursing—General M
Public Administration M

UNIVERSITY OF PHOENIX–RICHMOND CAMPUS

Accounting M
Business Administration and Management—General M
Criminal Justice and Criminology M
Health Services Management and Hospital Administration M
Human Resources Management M
Human Services M
International Business M
Management Information Systems M
Management of Technology M
Marketing M
Nursing—General M
Psychology—General M
Public Administration M

UNIVERSITY OF PHOENIX–SACRAMENTO VALLEY CAMPUS

Accounting M
Adult Education M,O
Business Administration and Management—General M
Criminal Justice and Criminology M
Curriculum and Instruction M,O
Education—General M,O
Elementary Education M,O
Family Nurse Practitioner Studies M
Health Services Management and Hospital Administration M
Human Resources Management M
International Business M
Management Information Systems M
Management of Technology M
Marketing M
Marriage and Family Therapy M
Nursing Education M
Nursing—General M
Public Administration M
Secondary Education M,O

UNIVERSITY OF PHOENIX–ST. LOUIS CAMPUS

Business Administration and Management—General M
Health Services Management and Hospital Administration M
Management Information Systems M

UNIVERSITY OF PHOENIX–SAN ANTONIO CAMPUS

Accounting M
Business Administration and Management—General M
Criminal Justice and Criminology M
Electronic Commerce M
Health Services Management and Hospital Administration M
Human Resources Management M
International Business M
Management Information Systems M
Management of Technology M
Marketing M
Psychology—General M
Public Administration M

UNIVERSITY OF PHOENIX–SAN DIEGO CAMPUS

Business Administration and Management—General M
Criminal Justice and Criminology M
Curriculum and Instruction M
Education—General M
Elementary Education M
International Business M
Management Information Systems M
Management of Technology M
Marriage and Family Therapy M
Nursing—General M
Secondary Education M

UNIVERSITY OF PHOENIX–SAVANNAH CAMPUS

Accounting M
Business Administration and Management—General M
Criminal Justice and Criminology M
Health Services Management and Hospital Administration M
Human Resources Management M
International Business M
Management Information Systems M
Management of Technology M
Marketing M
Nursing Education M
Nursing—General M
Public Administration M

UNIVERSITY OF PHOENIX–SOUTHERN ARIZONA CAMPUS

Accounting M
Business Administration and Management—General M
Counselor Education M,O
Criminal Justice and Criminology M,O
Curriculum and Instruction M,O
Education—General M,O
Educational Psychology M,O
Elementary Education M,O
Family Nurse Practitioner Studies M,O
Health Services Management and Hospital Administration M,O
International Business M
Management Information Systems M
Management of Technology M
Marriage and Family Therapy M,O
Secondary Education M,O
Special Education M,O

UNIVERSITY OF PHOENIX–SOUTHERN CALIFORNIA CAMPUS

Accounting M
Business Administration and Management—General M
Curriculum and Instruction M
Education—General M
Elementary Education M
Family Nurse Practitioner Studies M,O
Health Services Management and Hospital Administration M,O
Human Resources Management M
Management Information Systems M
Management of Technology M
Marketing M
Marriage and Family Therapy M,O
Nursing Education M,O
Nursing—General M,O
Secondary Education M

UNIVERSITY OF PHOENIX–SOUTHERN COLORADO CAMPUS

Business Administration and Management—General M
Curriculum and Instruction M,O
Education—General M,O
Educational Administration M,O
Elementary Education M,O
Health Services Management and Hospital Administration M
Management Information Systems M
Management of Technology M
Marriage and Family Therapy M
Nursing—General M
School Psychology M,O
Secondary Education M,O
Social Psychology M

UNIVERSITY OF PHOENIX–SPRINGFIELD CAMPUS

Accounting M
Adult Education M
Business Administration and Management—General M
Computer Education M
Criminal Justice and Criminology M
Curriculum and Instruction M
Education—General M
Educational Administration M
English as a Second Language M
English Education M
Health Services Management and Hospital Administration M
Human Resources Management M
International Business M
Management Information Systems M
Management of Technology M
Marketing M
Mathematics Education M
Nursing and Healthcare Administration M
Nursing—General M
Public Administration M

UNIVERSITY OF PHOENIX–TULSA CAMPUS

Business Administration and Management—General M

UNIVERSITY OF PHOENIX–UTAH CAMPUS

Business Administration and Management—General M
Counseling Psychology M
Curriculum and Instruction M
Education—General M
Educational Administration M
Elementary Education M
Management Information Systems M
Nursing—General M
School Psychology M
Secondary Education M

UNIVERSITY OF PHOENIX–VANCOUVER CAMPUS

Business Administration and Management—General M
Curriculum and Instruction M
Education—General M
Educational Administration M
Health Services Management and Hospital Administration M
Management Information Systems M
Management of Technology M
Nursing—General M

UNIVERSITY OF PHOENIX–WASHINGTON CAMPUS

Business Administration and Management—General M
Health Services Management and Hospital Administration M

UNIVERSITY OF PHOENIX–WEST FLORIDA CAMPUS

Business Administration and Management—General M
Curriculum and Instruction M
Education—General M
Educational Administration M
Educational Media/Instructional Technology M
Elementary Education M
Health Services Management and Hospital Administration M
Human Resources Management M
International Business M
Management Information Systems M
Management of Technology M
Marketing M
Nursing Education M
Nursing—General M
Public Administration M
Secondary Education M

UNIVERSITY OF PHOENIX–WEST MICHIGAN CAMPUS

Accounting M
Business Administration and Management—General M
Curriculum and Instruction M
Education—General M
Educational Administration M
Electronic Commerce M
Health Services Management and Hospital Administration M
Human Resources Management M
International Business M
Management Information Systems M
Management of Technology M
Nursing—General M

UNIVERSITY OF PHOENIX–WICHITA CAMPUS

Business Administration and Management—General M

UNIVERSITY OF PHOENIX–WISCONSIN CAMPUS

Business Administration and Management—General M
Health Services Management and Hospital Administration
Management Information Systems M
Management of Technology M

UNIVERSITY OF PITTSBURGH

Acute Care/Critical Care Nursing M,D
Adult Nursing M,D
African Studies O
Allopathic Medicine P
Anthropology M,D
Applied Mathematics M,D
Applied Statistics M,D
Architectural History M,D
Art History M,D
Asian Studies M,O
Athletic Training and Sports Medicine M
Biochemistry M,D
Bioengineering M,D
Bioethics M
Bioinformatics M,D,O
Biological and Biomedical Sciences—General D*
Biostatistics M,D
Business Administration and Management—General M,D
Cell Biology M,D
Chemical Engineering M,D
Chemistry M,D*
Civil Engineering M,D
Classics M,D
Clinical Research M,O
Cognitive Sciences D
Communication Disorders M,D
Communication—General M,D
Community Health M,D,O
Computational Biology D*
Computer Science M,D
Conflict Resolution and Mediation/Peace Studies M
Criminal Justice and Criminology D
Cultural Studies M,D
Dentistry P,M,O
Developmental Biology D*
Developmental Psychology M,D
Disability Studies O
Early Childhood Education M
East European and Russian Studies O
Ecology D*
Economics M,D,O
Education—General M,D
Educational Administration M,D
Educational Measurement and Evaluation M,D
Electrical Engineering M,D
Elementary Education M
Engineering and Applied Sciences—General M,D
English as a Second Language O
English Education M,D
English M,D*
Environmental and Occupational Health M
Environmental Engineering M,D
Environmental Management and Policy M
Epidemiology M,D
Evolutionary Biology D
Exercise and Sports Science M,D
Family Nurse Practitioner Studies M,D
Foreign Languages Education M,D
Foundations and Philosophy of Education M,D
French M,D
Genetic Counseling M
Geographic Information Systems M,D
Geology M,D
German M,D
Gerontology M,D,O
Health Education M,O
Health Informatics M
Health Services Management and Hospital Administration M,D,O
Higher Education M,D
Hispanic Studies M,D
History of Science and Technology M,D
History M,D
Human Genetics M,D,O
Immunology M,D
Industrial/Management Engineering M,D
Infectious Diseases M,D
Information Science M,D,O
Information Studies M,D,O
Interdisciplinary Studies D
International Affairs M,D,O
International and Comparative Education M,D
International Business M
International Development M,O
Italian M
Latin American Studies O
Law P,M,O
Legal and Justice Studies M,O
Library Science M,D,O
Linguistics M,D
Management Information Systems M
Materials Sciences M,D
Mathematical and Computational Finance M,D
Mathematics Education M,D
Mathematics M,D
Mechanical Engineering M,D

Microbiology M,D*
Military and Defense Studies M
Molecular Biology D*
Molecular Biophysics D*
Molecular Genetics M,D
Molecular Pathology M,D
Molecular Pharmacology D
Molecular Physiology M,D
Molecular Toxicology M,D,O
Music M,D
National Security M
Neurobiology M,D
Neuroscience D*
Nonprofit Management M
Nurse Anesthesia M
Nursing and Healthcare Administration M
Nursing Education M
Nursing—General M
Nutrition M
Occupational Therapy M
Oral and Dental Sciences M,O
Pathology M,D
Pediatric Nursing M,D
Petroleum Engineering M,D
Pharmacy P
Philosophy M,D
Physical Therapy M,D
Physics M,D*
Planetary and Space Sciences M,D
Political Science M,D
Psychiatric Nursing M,D
Psychology—General M,D
Public Administration M,D*
Public Health—General M,D,O*
Public Policy M,D
Reading Education M,D
Rehabilitation Counseling M
Rehabilitation Sciences M,D,O
Religion M,D
Science Education M,D
Secondary Education M,D
Slavic Languages M,D
Social Sciences Education M,D
Social Work M,D,O
Sociology M,D
Spanish M,D
Special Education M,D
Statistics M,D
Structural Biology D
Telecommunications M,O
Theater M,D
Urban and Regional Planning M
Virology M,D
Western European Studies O
Women's Studies O
Writing M,D

UNIVERSITY OF PORTLAND

Business Administration and Management—General M
Communication—General M
Corporate and Organizational Communication M
Early Childhood Education M
Education—General M
Engineering and Applied Sciences—General M
Music M
Nursing—General M
Pastoral Ministry and Counseling M
Secondary Education M
Special Education M
Theater M

UNIVERSITY OF PRINCE EDWARD ISLAND

Anatomy M,D
Bacteriology M,D
Biological and Biomedical Sciences—General M
Chemistry M
Education—General M
Educational Administration M
Epidemiology M,D
Geography M
Immunology M,D
Parasitology M,D
Pathology M,D
Pharmacology M,D
Physiology M,D
Toxicology M,D
Veterinary Medicine P
Veterinary Sciences M,D
Virology M,D

UNIVERSITY OF PUERTO RICO, MAYAGÜEZ CAMPUS

Agricultural Economics and Agribusiness M
Agricultural Education M
Agricultural Sciences—General M
Agronomy and Soil Sciences M
Animal Sciences M
Applied Mathematics M
Biological and Biomedical Sciences—General M
Business Administration and Management—General M
Chemical Engineering M,D
Chemistry M,D
Civil Engineering M,D
Computational Sciences M
Computer Engineering M
Electrical Engineering M
Engineering and Applied Sciences—General M,D
English Education M
English M
Finance and Banking M
Food Science and Technology M
Geology M
Hispanic Studies M
Horticulture M
Human Resources Management M
Industrial and Manufacturing Management M
Industrial/Management Engineering M
Information Science D
Marine Sciences M,D*
Mathematics M
Mechanical Engineering M
Physics M
Statistics M

UNIVERSITY OF PUERTO RICO, MEDICAL SCIENCES CAMPUS

Allied Health—General M,O
Allopathic Medicine P
Anatomy M,D
Biochemistry M,D
Biological and Biomedical Sciences—General M,D*
Biostatistics M
Clinical Laboratory Sciences/Medical Technology M,O
Communication Disorders M
Demography and Population Studies M
Dentistry P
Environmental and Occupational Health M,D
Epidemiology M
Family Nurse Practitioner Studies M
Gerontology M,O
Health Education M,O
Health Informatics M
Health Promotion O
Health Services Management and Hospital Administration M
Health Services Research M
Human Development M,O
Industrial Hygiene M
Maternal and Child Health M
Microbiology M,D
Neurobiology M,D
Nurse Anesthesia M
Nurse Midwifery M,O
Nursing and Healthcare Administration M
Nursing Education M
Nursing—General M
Nutrition M,D,O
Oral and Dental Sciences M,O
Pharmaceutical Sciences P,M
Pharmacology M,D
Pharmacy P,M
Physical Therapy M
Physiology M,D
Public Health—General M
Special Education O
Toxicology M,D
Zoology M,D

UNIVERSITY OF PUERTO RICO, RÍO PIEDRAS

Architecture M
Biological and Biomedical Sciences—General M,D
Business Administration and Management—General M,D
Chemistry M,D*
Comparative Literature M
Counselor Education M,D
Curriculum and Instruction M,D
Early Childhood Education M
Economics M
Education—General M,D
Educational Administration M,D
Educational Measurement and Evaluation M
English as a Second Language M
English Education M,D
English M,D
Exercise and Sports Science M
Family and Consumer Sciences-General M
Foreign Languages Education M,D
Hispanic Studies M,D
History M,D
Information Studies M,O
Law P,M
Library Science M,O
Linguistics M
Mass Communication M
Mathematics Education M,D
Mathematics M,D
Nutrition M
Philosophy M
Physics M,D
Psychology—General M,D
Public Administration M
Rehabilitation Counseling M
Science Education M,D
Secondary Education M,D
Social Sciences Education M,D
Social Work M,D
Sociology M
Special Education M
Translation and Interpretation M,O
Urban and Regional Planning M

UNIVERSITY OF PUGET SOUND

Counselor Education M
Education—General M
Elementary Education M
Middle School Education M
Occupational Therapy M
Pastoral Ministry and Counseling M
Physical Therapy D
Secondary Education M
Social Psychology M

UNIVERSITY OF REDLANDS

Business Administration and Management—General M
Communication Disorders M
Education—General M,D,O
Geographic Information Systems M
Management Information Systems M
Music M

UNIVERSITY OF REGINA

Adult Education M
American Indian/Native American Studies M
Analytical Chemistry M,D
Anthropology M
Art/Fine Arts M
Biochemistry M,D
Biological and Biomedical Sciences—General M,D
Business Administration and Management—General M,O
Canadian Studies M,D
Chemistry M,D
Clinical Psychology M,D
Computer Engineering M,D
Computer Science M,D
Criminal Justice and Criminology M
Curriculum and Instruction M
Economics M,D,O
Education—General M,D
Educational Administration M
Educational Psychology M
Engineering and Applied Sciences—General M,D
English M,D
Environmental Engineering M,D
Experimental Psychology M,D
French M
Geography M,D
Geology M,D
Gerontology M
History M,D
Human Resources Development M
Human Resources Management M,O
Industrial/Management Engineering M,D
Inorganic Chemistry M,D
International Business O
Kinesiology and Movement Studies M,D
Linguistics M
Manufacturing Engineering M
Mathematics M,D
Music M,D
Organic Chemistry M,D
Petroleum Engineering M,D
Philosophy M
Physical Chemistry M,D
Physics M,D
Political Science M,D
Psychology—General M,D
Public Administration M,D,O
Public Policy M,D,O
Religion M,D
Social Sciences M,D
Social Work M,D
Sociology M,D
Statistics M,D
Systems Engineering M,D

UNIVERSITY OF RHODE ISLAND

Accounting M
Adult Education M
Animal Sciences M,D
Applied Mathematics M,D,O
Aquaculture M,D
Biochemistry M,D
Biological and Biomedical Sciences—General M,D
Business Administration and Management—General M,D
Cell Biology M,D
Chemical Engineering M,D
Chemistry M,D
Child and Family Studies M
Civil Engineering M,D
Clinical Laboratory Sciences/Medical Technology M
Clinical Psychology D
Clothing and Textiles M
Communication Disorders M,D
Communication—General M
Computer Science M,D,O
Counseling Psychology M
Economics M,D
Education—General M
Electrical Engineering M,D
Elementary Education M
Engineering and Applied Sciences—General M,D
English M,D
Entomology M,D
Environmental Engineering M
Environmental Management and Policy M,D
Environmental Sciences M,D
Exercise and Sports Science M,D
Family Nurse Practitioner Studies M,D
Finance and Banking D
Fish, Game, and Wildlife Management M,D
Food Science and Technology M,D
Forensic Sciences M,D,O
Geosciences M
Gerontology M,D
Health Education M,D
History M
Human Resources Management M
Industrial and Labor Relations M
Industrial and Manufacturing Management M,D
Industrial/Management Engineering D
Information Studies M
International Affairs M,O
International Business M,D
Library Science M
Management Information Systems D
Manufacturing Engineering M
Marine Affairs M,D
Marine Sciences M,D
Marketing D
Mathematics M,D
Mechanical Engineering M,D
Mechanics M,D
Medicinal and Pharmaceutical Chemistry M,D
Microbiology M,D
Molecular Biology M,D
Molecular Genetics M,D
Music Education M
Music M
Natural Resources M,D
Nurse Midwifery M,D
Nursing and Healthcare Administration M,D
Nursing Education M,D
Nursing—General M,D
Nutrition M,D
Ocean Engineering M,D
Oceanography M,D
Pharmaceutical Sciences M,D
Pharmacology M,D
Pharmacy M,D
Physical Education M,D
Physical Therapy D
Physics M,D
Plant Sciences M,D
Political Science M,O
Psychiatric Nursing M,D
Psychology—General D
Public Administration M,O
Public Policy M,O
Reading Education M
Recreation and Park Management M,D
School Psychology M,D
Secondary Education M
Spanish M
Sport Psychology M,D
Sports Management M,D
Statistics M,D,O
Structural Engineering M,D
Student Affairs M
Systems Engineering M,D
Toxicology M,D
Transportation and Highway Engineering M,D

UNIVERSITY OF RICHMOND

Biological and Biomedical Sciences—General M
Business Administration and Management—General M

English M
History M
Law P
Liberal Studies M
Psychology—General M

Close-Up on page 1115.

UNIVERSITY OF RIO GRANDE

Art Education M
Education—General M
Mathematics Education M
Reading Education M
Special Education M

UNIVERSITY OF ROCHESTER

Allopathic Medicine P
Anatomy M,D
Art History M,D
Art/Fine Arts M,D*
Astronomy M,D
Biochemistry M,D
Biological and Biomedical Sciences—General M,D*
Biomedical Engineering M,D
Biophysics M,D
Biostatistics M,D
Business Administration and Management—General M,D
Chemical Engineering M,D*
Chemistry M,D
Clinical Psychology M,D
Cognitive Sciences M,D
Computational Biology M,D
Computer Engineering M,D
Computer Science M,D*
Developmental Psychology M,D
Economics M,D
Education—General M,D
Electrical Engineering M,D
Engineering and Applied Sciences—General M,D*
English M,D
Epidemiology M,D
Genetics M,D
Geology M,D
Geosciences M,D*
Health Services Research D
History M,D
Immunology M,D
Marriage and Family Therapy M
Materials Sciences M,D
Mathematics M,D
Mechanical Engineering M,D
Microbiology M,D
Molecular Medicine
Music Education M,D
Music M,D
Neurobiology M,D
Neuroscience M,D
Nursing—General M,D,O
Optical Sciences M,D
Oral and Dental Sciences M
Pathobiology
Pathology M,D*
Pharmacology M,D
Philosophy M,D
Physics M,D*
Physiology M,D
Political Science M,D
Psychology—General M,D
Public Health—General M
Social Psychology M,D
Statistics M,D
Toxicology M,D

UNIVERSITY OF ST. AUGUSTINE FOR HEALTH SCIENCES

Occupational Therapy M,D
Physical Therapy M,D,O

UNIVERSITY OF ST. FRANCIS (IL)

Adult Education M
Allied Health—General M
Business Administration and Management—General M
Curriculum and Instruction M
Education—General M
Educational Administration M
Elementary Education M
English Education M
Health Services Management and Hospital Administration M
Mathematics Education M
Nursing—General M
Physician Assistant Studies M
Reading Education M
Science Education M
Secondary Education M
Social Sciences Education M
Social Work M
Special Education M

UNIVERSITY OF SAINT FRANCIS (IN)

Allied Health—General M
Art/Fine Arts M
Business Administration and Management—General M
Counseling Psychology M
Counselor Education M
Education—General M
Nursing—General M
Pastoral Ministry and Counseling M
Physician Assistant Studies M
Psychology—General M
Special Education M

UNIVERSITY OF SAINT MARY

Business Administration and Management—General M
Curriculum and Instruction M
Education—General M
Psychology—General M
Special Education M

UNIVERSITY OF SAINT MARY OF THE LAKE–MUNDELEIN SEMINARY

Theology P,D,O

UNIVERSITY OF ST. MICHAEL'S COLLEGE

Ecology P,M,D,O
Jewish Studies P,M,D,O
Pastoral Ministry and Counseling P,M,D,O
Religious Education P,M,D,O
Theology P,M,D,O

UNIVERSITY OF ST. THOMAS (MN)

Accounting M
Art History M
Business Administration and Management—General M*
Computer and Information Systems Security M,O
Corporate and Organizational Communication M
Counseling Psychology M,D,O
Curriculum and Instruction M,D,O
Education of the Gifted M,D,O
Education—General M
Educational Administration M,D,O
Educational Media/Instructional Technology M,D,O
Educational Policy M,D,O
Engineering and Applied Sciences—General M,O
Engineering Management M,O
English M*
Health Services Management and Hospital Administration M
Human Development M,D,O
Industrial and Manufacturing Management M,O
Law P
Management Information Systems M,O
Management of Technology M,O
Manufacturing Engineering M,O
Marriage and Family Therapy M,D,O
Music Education M
Organizational Management M,D,O
Pastoral Ministry and Counseling M
Psychology—General M,D,O
Reading Education M,D,O
Real Estate M
Religion M
Religious Education M
Social Work M
Software Engineering M,O*
Special Education M,O
Student Affairs M,D,O
Systems Engineering M,O
Theology P,M

UNIVERSITY OF ST. THOMAS (TX)

Business Administration and Management—General M
Education—General M
Liberal Studies M
Philosophy M,D
Theology P,M

UNIVERSITY OF SAN DIEGO

Accounting M,O
Adult Nursing M,D,O
Business Administration and Management—General M,O
Conflict Resolution and Mediation/Peace Studies M
Counselor Education M
Curriculum and Instruction M,D
Education—General M,D,O
Educational Administration M,D,O
Family Nurse Practitioner Studies M,D,O
Finance and Banking M,O
History M
International Affairs M
Law P,M,O
Legal and Justice Studies P,M,O
Marine Affairs M
Marine Sciences M
Marriage and Family Therapy M
Nonprofit Management M,D,O
Nursing and Healthcare Administration M,D,O
Nursing—General M,D,O*
Pastoral Ministry and Counseling M,O
Pediatric Nursing M,D,O
Supply Chain Management M,O
Taxation P,M,O
Theater M

Close-Up on page 1117.

UNIVERSITY OF SAN FRANCISCO

Adult Nursing M
Asian Studies M
Biological and Biomedical Sciences—General M
Business Administration and Management—General M
Chemistry M
Computer Science M
Counseling Psychology M,D
Counselor Education M,D
Curriculum and Instruction M,D
Economics M
Education—General M,D
Educational Administration M,D
Educational Media/Instructional Technology M,D
Electronic Commerce M
English as a Second Language M,D
Entrepreneurship M
Environmental Management and Policy M
Finance and Banking M
Health Services Management and Hospital Administration M
International and Comparative Education M,D
International Business M
Internet and Interactive Multimedia M
Law P,M
Management Information Systems M
Marketing M
Marriage and Family Therapy M,D
Multilingual and Multicultural Education M,D
Nonprofit Management M
Nursing and Healthcare Administration M
Nursing—General M
Organizational Management M
Pastoral Ministry and Counseling M
Project Management M
Public Administration M
Religious Education M,D
Sports Management M
Telecommunications Management M
Theology M
Writing M

UNIVERSITY OF SASKATCHEWAN

Accounting M
Agricultural Economics and Agribusiness M,D
Agricultural Engineering M,D
Agricultural Sciences—General M,D
Agronomy and Soil Sciences M,D
Allopathic Medicine P
Anatomy M,D
Animal Sciences M,D
Anthropology M
Archaeology M,D
Art/Fine Arts M
Biochemistry M,D
Biological and Biomedical Sciences—General M,D,O
Biomedical Engineering M,D
Biotechnology M
Business Administration and Management—General M
Canadian Studies M,D
Cell Biology M,D
Chemical Engineering M,D
Chemistry M,D
Civil Engineering M,D
Community Health M,D
Computer Science M,D
Curriculum and Instruction M,D,O
Dentistry P
East European and Russian Studies M
Economics M
Education—General M,D,O
Educational Administration M,D,O
Educational Psychology M,D,O
Electrical Engineering M,D
Engineering and Applied Sciences—General M,D,O
Engineering Physics M,D
English M,D
Environmental Engineering M,D,O
Epidemiology M,D
Finance and Banking M
Food Science and Technology M,D
Foundations and Philosophy of Education M,D,O
French M
Gender Studies M,D
Geography M,D
Geology M,D,O
German M
Health Services Management and Hospital Administration M
History M,D
Immunology M,D
Industrial and Labor Relations M
International Business M
Kinesiology and Movement Studies M,D,O
Law P,M
Marketing M
Mathematics M,D
Mechanical Engineering M,D
Microbiology M,D
Music M
Nursing—General M
Organizational Behavior M
Pathology M,D
Pharmaceutical Sciences M,D
Pharmacology M,D
Philosophy M
Physics M,D
Physiology M,D
Plant Sciences M,D
Political Science M
Psychology—General M,D
Religion M
Reproductive Biology M,D
Sociology M,D
Special Education M,D,O
Statistics M,D
Theater M
Toxicology M,D,O
Veterinary Medicine P,M,D
Veterinary Sciences M,D
Women's Studies M,D

Announcement on page 731.

THE UNIVERSITY OF SCRANTON

Accounting M
Adult Nursing M,O
Biochemistry M
Business Administration and Management—General M
Chemistry M
Counseling Psychology M,O
Counselor Education M
Curriculum and Instruction M
Early Childhood Education M
Education—General M
Educational Administration M
Elementary Education M
English as a Second Language M
Family Nurse Practitioner Studies M,O
Finance and Banking M
Health Services Management and Hospital Administration M
History M
Human Resources Development M
Human Resources Management M
International Business M
Management Information Systems M
Management of Technology M
Marketing M
Nurse Anesthesia M,O
Nursing—General M,O
Occupational Therapy M
Organizational Management M
Physical Therapy M,D
Reading Education M
Rehabilitation Counseling M
Secondary Education M
Social Psychology M
Software Engineering M
Special Education M
Theology M

UNIVERSITY OF SIOUX FALLS

Business Administration and Management—General M
Education—General M,O
Educational Administration M,O
Educational Media/Instructional Technology M,O
Reading Education M,O

UNIVERSITY OF SOUTH ALABAMA

Accounting M
Adult Nursing M,D
Allied Health—General M,D
Allopathic Medicine P
Biochemistry D
Biological and Biomedical Sciences—General M,D*
Business Administration and Management—General M
Cell Biology D
Chemical Engineering M

Communication Disorders M,D
Communication—General M
Community Health Nursing M,D
Computer Science M
Counselor Education M,D
Early Childhood Education M,O
Education—General M,D,O
Educational Administration M,O
Educational Media/Instructional Technology M,D
Electrical Engineering M
Elementary Education M,O
Engineering and Applied Sciences—General M
English M
Environmental and Occupational Health M
Exercise and Sports Science M
Gerontology O
Health Education M
History M
Immunology D
Information Science M
Leisure Studies M
Management Information Systems M
Marine Sciences M,D
Maternal and Child/Neonatal Nursing M,D
Mathematics M
Mechanical Engineering M
Microbiology D
Molecular Biology D
Neuroscience D
Nursing—General M,D
Occupational Therapy M
Pharmacology D
Pharmacy P
Physical Education M
Physical Therapy D
Physician Assistant Studies M
Physiology D
Psychology—General M
Public Administration M
Reading Education M,O
Recreation and Park Management M
Rehabilitation Counseling M,D
School Psychology M,D
Science Education M,O
Secondary Education M,O
Sociology M
Special Education M,O
Toxicology M

Close-Up on page 1119.

UNIVERSITY OF SOUTH CAROLINA

Accounting M
Acute Care/Critical Care Nursing M,O
Adult Nursing M
Allopathic Medicine P
Anthropology M,D
Applied Statistics M,D,O
Art Education M,D
Art History M
Art/Fine Arts M
Astronomy M,D
Biochemistry M,D
Biological and Biomedical Sciences—General M,D,O*
Biostatistics M,D
Business Administration and Management—General M,D
Business Education M,D
Cell Biology M,D
Chemical Engineering M,D
Chemistry M,D
Civil Engineering M,D
Clinical Psychology M,D
Communication Disorders M,D
Community Health Nursing M
Comparative Literature M,D
Computer Engineering M,D
Computer Science M,D
Consumer Economics M
Counselor Education D,O
Criminal Justice and Criminology M
Curriculum and Instruction M,D,O
Developmental Biology M,D
Early Childhood Education M,D
Ecology M,D*
Economics M,D
Education—General M,D,O
Educational Administration M,D,O
Educational Measurement and Evaluation M,D
Educational Media/Instructional Technology M
Educational Psychology M,D
Electrical Engineering M,D
Elementary Education M,D
Engineering and Applied Sciences—General M,D
English as a Second Language M,D,O
English Education M,D
English M,D
Environmental and Occupational Health M,D*
Environmental Management and Policy M
Environmental Sciences M,D
Epidemiology M,D
Evolutionary Biology M,D
Exercise and Sports Science M,D
Experimental Psychology M,D
Family Nurse Practitioner Studies M
Foreign Languages Education M,D
Foundations and Philosophy of Education D
French M,D
Genetic Counseling M
Geography M,D
Geology M,D
Geosciences M,D
German M,D
Gerontology O
Hazardous Materials Management M,D
Health Education M,D,O
Health Promotion M,D,O
Health Services Management and Hospital Administration M,D
Higher Education M
Historic Preservation M,O
History M,D,O
Hospitality Management M
Human Resources Management M
Industrial Hygiene M,D
Information Studies M,O
International Affairs M,D
International Business M
Journalism M,D
Law P
Library Science M,O
Linguistics M,D,O
Marine Sciences M,D
Mathematics Education M,D
Mathematics M,D
Mechanical Engineering M,D
Media Studies M
Medical/Surgical Nursing M
Molecular Biology M,D*
Museum Studies M,O
Music Education M,D,O
Music M,D,O
Nurse Anesthesia M
Nursing and Healthcare Administration M
Nursing—General M,O
Pediatric Nursing M
Pharmaceutical Sciences M,D
Pharmacy P
Philosophy M,D
Physical Education M,D
Physics M,D
Political Science M,D
Psychiatric Nursing M,O
Psychology—General M,D
Public Administration M
Public Health—General M,D
Public History M,O
Reading Education M,D
Rehabilitation Counseling M,O
Rehabilitation Sciences M,O
Religion M
School Psychology D
Science Education M,D
Secondary Education M,D
Social Psychology M,D
Social Sciences Education M,D,O
Social Work M,D
Sociology M,D
Software Engineering M,D
Spanish M,D
Special Education M,D
Speech and Interpersonal Communication M,D
Sports Management M
Statistics M,D,O
Student Affairs M
Theater M,D
Travel and Tourism M
Vocational and Technical Education M,D,O
Women's Health Nursing M
Women's Studies O
Writing M,D

Close-Up on page 1121.

UNIVERSITY OF SOUTH CAROLINA AIKEN

Clinical Psychology M
Education—General M
Educational Media/Instructional Technology M
Elementary Education M

UNIVERSITY OF SOUTH CAROLINA UPSTATE

Early Childhood Education M
Education—General M
Elementary Education M
Special Education M

THE UNIVERSITY OF SOUTH DAKOTA

Accounting M
Allied Health—General M,D
Allopathic Medicine P
Art/Fine Arts M
Biological and Biomedical Sciences—General M,D
Business Administration and Management—General M
Cardiovascular Sciences M,D
Cell Biology M,D
Chemistry M
Clinical Psychology M,D
Communication Disorders M,D
Communication—General M
Computational Sciences D
Computer Science M,D
Counselor Education M,D,O
Curriculum and Instruction M,D,O
Education—General M,D,O
Educational Administration M,D,O
Educational Media/Instructional Technology M,O
Educational Psychology M,D,O
Elementary Education M
English M,D
Health Education M
History M
Immunology M,D
Interdisciplinary Studies M
Law P
Mathematics M
Microbiology M,D
Molecular Biology M,D
Music M
Neuroscience M,D
Occupational Therapy M
Pharmacology M,D
Physical Education M
Physical Therapy M,D
Physician Assistant Studies M
Physiology M,D
Political Science M
Psychology—General M,D
Public Administration M
Secondary Education M
Special Education M
Statistics D
Theater M

Close-Up on page 1123.

UNIVERSITY OF SOUTHERN CALIFORNIA

Accounting M
Advertising and Public Relations M
Aerospace/Aeronautical Engineering M,D,O
Allopathic Medicine P
American Studies D
Anthropology M,D,O
Applied Mathematics M,D
Architecture M,O*
Art History M,D,O
Art/Fine Arts M
Artificial Intelligence/Robotics M
Arts Administration M
Asian Languages M,D
Asian Studies M,D
Biochemistry M,D
Biological and Biomedical Sciences—General M,D*
Biomedical Engineering M,D
Biometrics M
Biophysics M,D
Biostatistics M,D*
Building Science M,O
Business Administration and Management—General M,D
Cell Biology M,D
Chemical Engineering M,D,O
Chemical Physics D
Chemistry M,D
Civil Engineering M,D,O*
Classics M,D
Clinical Psychology M,D
Communication—General M,D*
Comparative Literature M,D
Computational Biology D
Computer Engineering M,D
Computer Science M,D*
Construction Engineering M
Construction Management M
Corporate and Organizational Communication M,D
Dentistry P,O
Economics M,D
Education—General M,D
Electrical Engineering M,D,O*
Engineering and Applied Sciences—General M,D,O*
Engineering Management M
Environmental Engineering M,D
Epidemiology M,D
Film, Television, and Video Production M
Film, Television, and Video Theory and Criticism M,D
Finance and Banking M
French M,D
Genetics M,D
Geography M,D
Geosciences M,D
Geotechnical Engineering M
Gerontology M,D,O
Health Communication M
Health Promotion M
Health Services Management and Hospital Administration M
Health Services Research D
Historic Preservation O
History M,D
Immunology M,D
Industrial/Management Engineering M,D,O
International Affairs M,D
International Business M
Internet and Interactive Multimedia M,D
Journalism M*
Kinesiology and Movement Studies M,D
Landscape Architecture M,O
Law P,M
Linguistics M,D
Management Information Systems M
Manufacturing Engineering M
Marine Biology D
Marine Sciences D
Mass Communication M,D
Materials Engineering M,D,O
Materials Sciences M,D,O
Mathematics M,D
Mechanical Engineering M,D,O
Mechanics M
Media Studies M
Medical Imaging M
Microbiology M,D
Molecular Biology M,D*
Molecular Pharmacology M,D
Music Education M,D
Music M,D,O
Neurobiology M,D
Neuroscience D
Nutrition M
Occupational Therapy M,D
Ocean Engineering M
Oceanography D
Operations Research M
Oral and Dental Sciences M,D
Pathobiology M,D*
Pathology M,D
Petroleum Engineering M,D,O
Pharmaceutical Sciences M,D*
Pharmacy P
Philosophy M,D
Physical Therapy M,D
Physician Assistant Studies M
Physics M,D
Physiology M,D
Political Science M,D
Psychology—General M,D
Public Administration M,D,O
Public Health—General M*
Public Policy M
Real Estate M
Religion M,D
Slavic Languages M,D
Social Work M,D
Sociology M,D
Software Engineering M
Speech and Interpersonal Communication M,D
Statistics M
Structural Engineering M
Systems Engineering M,D,O
Taxation M
Theater M*
Toxicology M,D
Transportation and Highway Engineering M
Urban and Regional Planning M,D
Water Resources Engineering M
Writing M

UNIVERSITY OF SOUTHERN INDIANA

Accounting M
Business Administration and Management—General M
Education—General M
Elementary Education M
Engineering and Applied Sciences—General M
Health Services Management and Hospital Administration M
Industrial and Manufacturing Management M
Liberal Studies M
Nursing—General M
Occupational Therapy M
Public Administration M
Secondary Education M
Social Work M

UNIVERSITY OF SOUTHERN MAINE

Accounting M
Adult Education M,O
Adult Nursing M,O
American Studies M

Biological and Biomedical Sciences—General M
Business Administration and Management—General M
Computer Science M
Counselor Education M,O
Education—General M,D,O
Educational Administration M,O
English as a Second Language M,O
Family Nurse Practitioner Studies M,O
Health Services Management and Hospital Administration M,O
Immunology M
Law P
Manufacturing Engineering M
Medical/Surgical Nursing M,O
Middle School Education M,O
Molecular Biology M
Music M
Nonprofit Management M,O
Nursing—General M,O
Occupational Therapy M
Psychiatric Nursing M,O
Public Policy M,D,O
Reading Education M,O
School Psychology M,D,O
Social Work M
Special Education M
Sports Management M,O
Statistics M
Urban and Regional Planning M,O
Vocational and Technical Education M
Writing M

UNIVERSITY OF SOUTHERN MISSISSIPPI

Accounting M
Adult Education M,D,O
Adult Nursing M,D
Advertising and Public Relations M,D
Analytical Chemistry M,D
Anthropology M
Art Education M
Biochemistry M,D
Biological and Biomedical Sciences—General M,D*
Biostatistics M
Business Administration and Management—General M
Chemistry M,D
Child and Family Studies M
Clinical Laboratory Sciences/Medical Technology M
Clinical Psychology M,D
Communication Disorders M,D
Community Health Nursing M,D
Computational Sciences M,D
Computer Science M,D
Construction Engineering M
Counseling Psychology M,D
Criminal Justice and Criminology M,D
Curriculum and Instruction M,D,O
Early Childhood Education M,D,O
Economics M,D
Education of the Gifted M,D,O
Education—General M,D,O
Educational Administration M,D,O
Elementary Education M,D,O
Engineering and Applied Sciences—General M,D
English M,D
Environmental and Occupational Health M
Environmental Biology M,D
Epidemiology M
Exercise and Sports Science M,D
Experimental Psychology M,D
Family Nurse Practitioner Studies M,D
Food Science and Technology M,D
Foreign Languages Education M
Geography M,D
Geology M,D
Health Education M
Health Services Management and Hospital Administration M
Higher Education M,D,O
History M,D
Hydrology M,D
Inorganic Chemistry M,D
International Affairs M,D
International Development M,D
Leisure Studies M,D
Library Science M,O
Management Information Systems M
Marine Biology M,D
Marine Sciences M,D
Marriage and Family Therapy M
Mass Communication M,D
Maternal and Child/Neonatal Nursing M,D
Mathematics Education M,D
Mathematics M,D
Microbiology M,D
Molecular Biology M,D
Music Education M,D
Music M,D
Nursing and Healthcare Administration M,D
Nursing—General M,D
Nutrition M,D
Organic Chemistry M,D
Philosophy M
Physical Chemistry M,D
Physical Education M,D
Physics M,D
Political Science M,D
Polymer Science and Engineering M,D
Psychiatric Nursing M,D
Psychology—General M,D
Public Health—General M
Reading Education M,D,O
Recreation and Park Management M,D
School Psychology M,D
Science Education M,D
Secondary Education M,D,O
Social Sciences Education M,D,O
Social Work M
Special Education M,D,O
Speech and Interpersonal Communication M,D
Sports Management M,D
Theater M
Vocational and Technical Education M

UNIVERSITY OF SOUTHERN NEVADA

Pharmacy P

UNIVERSITY OF SOUTH FLORIDA

Accounting M
Adult Education M,D,O
African Studies M
American Studies M
Analytical Chemistry M,D
Anatomy M,D
Anthropology M,D
Applied Physics M,D
Architecture M
Art History M
Art/Fine Arts M
Biochemistry M,D
Bioinformatics M,D
Biological and Biomedical Sciences—General M,D
Biomedical Engineering M,D
Biophysics M,D
Biostatistics M,D
Botany M,D
Business Administration and Management—General M,D
Cancer Biology/Oncology D*
Chemical Engineering M,D
Chemistry M,D
Civil Engineering M,D
Clinical Psychology M,D
Communication Disorders D
Communication—General M,D
Community College Education M,D,O
Community Health M,D
Computational Sciences M,D
Computer Engineering M,D
Computer Science M,D
Counselor Education M,D
Criminal Justice and Criminology M,D
Early Childhood Education M,D,O
Ecology M,D
Economics M,D
Education of the Gifted M
Education—General M,D,O*
Educational Administration M,D,O
Educational Measurement and Evaluation M,D,O
Educational Media/Instructional Technology M,D,O
Electrical Engineering M,D
Elementary Education M,D,O
Engineering and Applied Sciences—General M,D*
Engineering Management M,D
English Education M,D,O
English M,D
Entrepreneurship M,O
Environmental and Occupational Health M,D
Environmental Engineering M,D
Environmental Management and Policy M
Environmental Sciences M
Epidemiology M,D
Experimental Psychology M,D
Finance and Banking M
Foreign Languages Education M,D,O
French M
Geography M
Geology M,D
Gerontology M,D
Health Services Management and Hospital Administration M,D
Higher Education M,D,O
History M
Immunology M,D
Industrial and Organizational Psychology M,D
Industrial/Management Engineering M,D
Information Studies M
Inorganic Chemistry M,D
International Affairs M
International Health M,D
Latin American Studies M,O
Liberal Studies M
Library Science M
Linguistics M
Management Information Systems M
Marine Sciences M,D
Mass Communication M
Mathematics Education M,D,O
Mathematics M,D,O
Mechanical Engineering M,D
Medical Microbiology M,D
Microbiology M,D
Middle School Education M,D,O
Molecular Biology M,D
Music Education M
Music M
Nursing—General M,D*
Oceanography M,D
Organic Chemistry M,D
Pathology M,D
Pharmacology M,D
Philosophy M,D
Physical Chemistry M,D
Physical Education M
Physical Therapy M
Physics M,D
Physiology M,D
Political Science M
Psychology—General M,D
Public Administration M
Public Health—General M,D
Reading Education M
Rehabilitation Counseling M
Religion M
School Psychology M,D,O
Science Education M,D
Secondary Education M,D,O
Social Sciences Education M,D,O
Social Work M
Sociology M
Spanish M
Special Education M
Student Affairs M,D,O
Vocational and Technical Education M,D,O
Women's Studies M
Zoology M,D

Close-Up on page 1125.

THE UNIVERSITY OF TAMPA

Accounting M
Adult Nursing M
Business Administration and Management—General M
Economics M
Education—General M
Entrepreneurship M
Family Nurse Practitioner Studies M
Finance and Banking M
International Business M
Management Information Systems M
Management of Technology M
Marketing M
Mathematics Education M
Nursing and Healthcare Administration M
Nursing Education M
Nursing—General M
Reading Education M
Science Education M

THE UNIVERSITY OF TENNESSEE

Accounting M,D
Adult Education M,D
Advertising and Public Relations M,D
Aerospace/Aeronautical Engineering M,D
Agricultural Education M
Agricultural Engineering M
Agricultural Sciences—General M,D
Analytical Chemistry M,D
Anatomy M,D
Animal Behavior M,D
Animal Sciences M,D
Anthropology M,D
Applied Mathematics M,D
Archaeology M,D
Architecture M*
Art Education M,D,O
Art/Fine Arts M
Artificial Intelligence/Robotics M,D
Athletic Training and Sports Medicine M,D
Aviation M
Biochemistry M,D
Bioethics M,D
Biological and Biomedical Sciences—General M,D
Biomedical Engineering M,D
Biosystems Engineering M,D
Business Administration and Management—General M,D
Chemical Engineering M,D
Chemical Physics M,D
Chemistry M,D
Child and Family Studies M,D
Civil Engineering M,D
Clinical Psychology M,D
Clothing and Textiles M,D
Communication Disorders M,D,O
Communication—General M,D*
Community Health M,D
Computer Engineering M,D
Computer Science M,D*
Consumer Economics M,D
Counseling Psychology M,D
Counselor Education M,D,O
Criminal Justice and Criminology M,D
Curriculum and Instruction M,D,O
Early Childhood Education M,D,O
Ecology M,D
Economics M,D
Education—General M,D,O
Educational Administration M,D,O
Educational Measurement and Evaluation M,D,O
Educational Media/Instructional Technology M,D,O
Educational Psychology M,D,O
Electrical Engineering M,D
Elementary Education M,D,O
Engineering and Applied Sciences—General M,D
Engineering Management M,D
English as a Second Language M,D,O
English Education M,D,O
English M,D
Entomology M,D
Environmental Engineering M
Environmental Management and Policy M,D
Ergonomics and Human Factors M,D
Evolutionary Biology M,D
Exercise and Sports Science M,D,O
Experimental Psychology M,D
Family and Consumer Sciences-General D
Finance and Banking M,D
Fish, Game, and Wildlife Management M
Food Science and Technology M,D
Foreign Languages Education M,D,O
Forestry M
Foundations and Philosophy of Education M,D,O
French M,D
Genetics M,D
Genomic Sciences M,D
Geography M,D
Geology M,D
German M,D
Gerontology M
Graphic Design M
Health Education M
Health Promotion M
Health Services Management and Hospital Administration M
History M,D
Hospitality Management M
Human Resources Development M
Industrial and Manufacturing Management M,D
Industrial and Organizational Psychology D
Industrial/Management Engineering M,D
Information Science M,D
Inorganic Chemistry M,D
Italian D
Journalism M,D
Kinesiology and Movement Studies M,D
Landscape Architecture M
Law P
Leisure Studies M,D
Linguistics D
Logistics M,D
Manufacturing Engineering M,D
Marketing M,D
Materials Engineering M,D
Materials Sciences M,D
Mathematics Education M,D,O
Mathematics M,D
Mechanical Engineering M,D
Mechanics M,D
Media Studies M,D
Microbiology M,D
Multilingual and Multicultural Education M,D,O
Music Education M
Music M
Nuclear Engineering M,D
Nursing—General M,D
Nutrition M
Organic Chemistry M,D
Philosophy M,D
Photography M
Physical Chemistry M,D

Physics M,D
Physiology M,D
Plant Pathology M,D
Plant Physiology M,D
Plant Sciences M
Political Science M,D
Polymer Science and Engineering M,D
Portuguese D
Psychology—General M,D
Public Administration M
Public Health—General M
Reading Education M,D,O
Recreation and Park Management M,D
Rehabilitation Counseling M,D
Religion M,D
Russian D
School Psychology M,D,O
Science Education M,D,O
Secondary Education M,D,O
Social Sciences Education M,D,O
Social Work M,D
Sociology M,D
Spanish M,D
Special Education M,D,O
Speech and Interpersonal Communication M,D
Sports Management M,D
Statistics M,D
Student Affairs M
Theater M
Theoretical Chemistry M,D
Transportation Management M,D
Travel and Tourism M
Veterinary Medicine P

THE UNIVERSITY OF TENNESSEE AT CHATTANOOGA

Accounting M
Adult Nursing M
Business Administration and Management—General M
Computational Sciences D
Computer Science M,O
Counselor Education M,D,O
Criminal Justice and Criminology M
Education—General M,D,O
Educational Administration M,D,O
Educational Media/Instructional Technology O
Elementary Education M,D,O
Engineering and Applied Sciences—General M,D,O
Engineering Management M,O
English M
Environmental Sciences M
Experimental Psychology M
Family Nurse Practitioner Studies M
Industrial and Organizational Psychology M
Music M
Nurse Anesthesia M
Nursing and Healthcare Administration M
Nursing Education M
Nursing—General M
Physical Education M
Physical Therapy D
Psychology—General M
Public Administration M
School Psychology O
Secondary Education M,D,O
Special Education M,D,O

Announcement on page 740.

THE UNIVERSITY OF TENNESSEE AT MARTIN

Accounting M
Agricultural Sciences—General M
Business Administration and Management—General M
Child and Family Studies M
Child Development M
Counselor Education M
Education—General M
Educational Administration M
Elementary Education M
Family and Consumer Sciences-General M
Food Science and Technology M
Nutrition M
Secondary Education M

THE UNIVERSITY OF TENNESSEE HEALTH SCIENCE CENTER

Allied Health—General M,D
Allopathic Medicine P,M,D
Anatomy D
Biological and Biomedical Sciences—General M,D*
Biomedical Engineering M,D*
Dentistry P,M,O
Neurobiology D*
Nursing—General M,D
Oral and Dental Sciences P,M,O
Pharmaceutical Sciences M,D
Pharmacy P,M,D
Physical Therapy M,D

THE UNIVERSITY OF TENNESSEE–OAK RIDGE NATIONAL LABORATORY GRADUATE SCHOOL OF GENOME SCIENCE AND TECHNOLOGY

Biological and Biomedical Sciences—General M,D
Genomic Sciences M,D*

THE UNIVERSITY OF TENNESSEE SPACE INSTITUTE

Aerospace/Aeronautical Engineering M,D
Applied Mathematics M
Aviation M
Electrical Engineering M,D
Engineering and Applied Sciences—General M,D*
Engineering Management M
Materials Engineering M
Materials Sciences M
Mechanical Engineering M,D
Mechanics M,D
Physics M,D

THE UNIVERSITY OF TEXAS AT ARLINGTON

Accounting M,D
Aerospace/Aeronautical Engineering M,D
Anthropology M
Architecture M*
Biological and Biomedical Sciences—General M,D
Biomedical Engineering M,D
Business Administration and Management—General M,D*
Chemistry M,D*
Civil Engineering M,D
Communication—General M
Computer Engineering M,D
Computer Science M,D
Criminal Justice and Criminology M
Curriculum and Instruction M
Economics M
Education—General M
Educational Administration M
Electrical Engineering M,D
Engineering and Applied Sciences—General M,D
English as a Second Language M
English M,D
Environmental Engineering M,D
Environmental Sciences M,D
Exercise and Sports Science M
Experimental Psychology M,D
Family Nurse Practitioner Studies M,D
Finance and Banking M,D
French M
Geology M,D
Geosciences M,D
Health Services Management and Hospital Administration M
History M,D
Human Resources Management M
Humanities M
Industrial/Management Engineering M
Interdisciplinary Studies M
Landscape Architecture M
Linguistics M,D
Logistics M
Management Information Systems M,D
Marketing Research M
Marketing M,D
Materials Engineering M,D
Materials Sciences M,D
Mathematics M,D
Mechanical Engineering M,D
Music M
Nursing and Healthcare Administration M,D
Nursing Education M,D
Nursing—General M,D
Physical Education M
Physics M,D
Political Science M
Psychology—General M,D
Public Administration M
Public Affairs D
Quantitative Analysis M,D
Real Estate M,D
Rhetoric M,D
Social Work M,D
Sociology M
Software Engineering M,D
Spanish M
Systems Engineering M
Taxation M
Urban and Regional Planning M

THE UNIVERSITY OF TEXAS AT AUSTIN

Accounting M,D
Advertising and Public Relations M,D
Aerospace/Aeronautical Engineering M,D*
American Studies M,D
Analytical Chemistry M,D
Animal Behavior D
Anthropology M,D
Applied Arts and Design—General M
Applied Mathematics M,D
Archaeology M,D
Architectural Engineering M
Architecture M,D
Art Education M
Art History M,D
Art/Fine Arts M
Asian Languages M,D
Asian Studies M,D
Astronomy M,D
Biochemistry M,D
Biological and Biomedical Sciences—General M,D
Biomedical Engineering M,D*
Biopsychology M,D
Business Administration and Management—General M,D
Cell Biology D
Chemical Engineering M,D
Chemistry M,D
Child and Family Studies M,D
Child Development M,D
Civil Engineering M,D
Classics M,D
Cognitive Sciences M,D
Communication Disorders M,D
Communication—General M,D
Comparative Literature M,D
Computational Sciences M,D
Computer Engineering M,D
Computer Science M,D
Counseling Psychology M,D
Counselor Education M,D
Curriculum and Instruction M,D
Dance M
Developmental Biology D
East European and Russian Studies M
Ecology D
Economics M,D
Education—General M,D
Educational Administration M,D
Educational Psychology M,D
Electrical Engineering M,D*
Engineering and Applied Sciences—General M,D*
English M,D
Environmental Engineering M
Environmental Management and Policy M
Evolutionary Biology D
Family and Consumer Sciences-General M,D
Film, Television, and Video Production M,D
Finance and Banking D
Folklore M,D
Foreign Languages Education M,D
French M,D
Genetics D
Geography M,D
Geology M,D
Geosciences M,D
Geotechnical Engineering M,D
German M,D
Health Education M,D
History M,D
Human Development M,D
Human Resources Development M
Immunology D
Industrial/Management Engineering M,D
Information Studies M,D
Inorganic Chemistry M,D
Journalism M,D
Kinesiology and Movement Studies M,D
Latin American Studies M,D
Law P,M
Library Science M,D
Linguistics M,D
Management Information Systems D
Manufacturing Engineering M,D
Marine Sciences M,D*
Marketing D
Materials Engineering M,D
Materials Sciences M,D
Mathematics Education M,D
Mathematics M,D
Mechanical Engineering M,D
Mechanics M,D
Media Studies M,D
Microbiology M,D*
Mineral Economics M
Mineral/Mining Engineering M
Molecular Biology D*
Music M,D
Near and Middle Eastern Languages M,D
Near and Middle Eastern Studies M,D
Neurobiology M,D
Neuroscience M,D*
Nursing—General M,D
Nutrition M,D
Operations Research M,D
Organic Chemistry M,D
Petroleum Engineering M,D*
Pharmaceutical Sciences M,D
Pharmacy P
Philosophy M,D
Physical Chemistry M,D
Physics M,D
Plant Biology M,D
Political Science M,D
Portuguese M,D
Psychology—General D
Public Affairs M,D
Public History M,D
Public Policy M,D
Romance Languages M,D
School Psychology M,D
Science Education M,D
Slavic Languages M,D
Social Work M,D
Sociology M,D
Spanish M,D
Special Education M,D
Statistics M
Technology and Public Policy M
Theater M,D
Urban and Regional Planning M,D
Water Resources Engineering M
Writing M

THE UNIVERSITY OF TEXAS AT BROWNSVILLE

Biological and Biomedical Sciences—General M
Business Administration and Management—General M
Community Health Nursing M
Counselor Education M
Curriculum and Instruction M
Early Childhood Education M
Education—General M
Educational Administration M
Educational Media/Instructional Technology M
English as a Second Language M
English M
History M
Interdisciplinary Studies M
Mathematics M
Multilingual and Multicultural Education M
Physics M
Political Science M
Psychology—General M
Public Administration M
Public Policy M
Reading Education M
Spanish M
Special Education M

THE UNIVERSITY OF TEXAS AT DALLAS

Accounting M
Applied Economics M,D
Applied Mathematics M,D
Biological and Biomedical Sciences—General M,D
Biotechnology M,D
Business Administration and Management—General M,D*
Cell Biology M,D
Chemistry M,D
Child and Family Studies M,D
Cognitive Sciences M,D
Communication Disorders M,D
Communication—General D
Comparative Literature M,D
Computer Engineering M,D
Computer Science M,D*
Economics M,D*
Electrical Engineering M,D
Engineering and Applied Sciences—General M,D
Geographic Information Systems M,D
Geosciences M,D
Health Services Management and Hospital Administration M
Humanities M,D
Interdisciplinary Studies M
International Business M,D
Management Information Systems M
Materials Engineering M,D
Mathematics Education M
Mathematics M,D*
Molecular Biology M,D*
Neuroscience M,D
Physics M,D
Political Science M,D

Psychology—General M,D
Public Affairs M,D
Public Policy M
Science Education M
Sociology M
Software Engineering M,D
Statistics M,D
Telecommunications M,D

THE UNIVERSITY OF TEXAS AT EL PASO

Accounting M
Allied Health—General M
Art/Fine Arts M
Bioinformatics M
Biological and Biomedical Sciences—General M,D
Business Administration and Management—General M
Chemistry M
Civil Engineering M,D
Clinical Psychology M,D
Communication Disorders M
Communication—General M
Community Health Nursing M
Computer Engineering M,D
Computer Science M
Curriculum and Instruction M
Economics M
Education—General M,D
Educational Administration M,D
Electrical Engineering M,D
Engineering and Applied Sciences—General M,D
English Education M
English M
Environmental Engineering M,D
Environmental Sciences M,D
Exercise and Sports Science M
Experimental Psychology M,D
Family Nurse Practitioner Studies M
Geology M,D
Geophysics M
Health Education M
History M,D
Industrial/Management Engineering M
Information Science M
Interdisciplinary Studies M
Kinesiology and Movement Studies M
Linguistics M
Materials Engineering D
Materials Sciences D
Mathematics M
Mechanical Engineering M
Metallurgical Engineering and Metallurgy M
Music Education M
Music M
Nurse Midwifery M
Nursing and Healthcare Administration M
Nursing—General M
Physical Education M
Physical Therapy M
Physics M
Political Science M
Psychology—General M,D
Rhetoric M
Sociology M
Spanish M
Statistics M
Theater M
Women's Health Nursing M
Writing M

THE UNIVERSITY OF TEXAS AT SAN ANTONIO

Accounting M,D
Adult Education M,D
Anthropology M,D
Applied Statistics M,D
Architecture M
Art History M
Art/Fine Arts M
Biological and Biomedical Sciences—General M,D*
Biomedical Engineering M,D
Biotechnology M,D
Business Administration and Management—General M,D
Cell Biology M,D
Chemistry M,D*
Civil Engineering M
Communication—General M
Computer Science M,D
Counselor Education M,D
Criminal Justice and Criminology M
Cultural Studies M,D
Curriculum and Instruction M
Demography and Population Studies D
Early Childhood Education M
Economics M
Education—General M,D
Educational Administration M,D
Educational Media/Instructional Technology M
Educational Psychology M
Electrical Engineering M,D
Elementary Education M
Engineering and Applied Sciences—General M,D
English as a Second Language M,D
English M,D
Environmental Engineering M,D
Environmental Sciences M,D
Finance and Banking M,D
Geology M,D
Higher Education M,D
Hispanic Studies M
History M
Information Science M,D
Interdisciplinary Studies M
International Business M,D
Management Information Systems M,D
Marketing M
Mathematics Education M
Mechanical Engineering M
Molecular Biology M,D
Multilingual and Multicultural Education M,D
Music M
Neurobiology M,D
Physics M,D
Political Science M
Psychology—General M
Public Administration M
Reading Education M
Social Work M
Sociology M
Spanish M
Special Education M
Statistics M,D
Taxation M,D

THE UNIVERSITY OF TEXAS AT TYLER

Art Education M
Art/Fine Arts M
Biological and Biomedical Sciences—General M
Business Administration and Management—General M
Clinical Psychology M
Communication—General M
Computer Education M
Computer Science M
Counseling Psychology M
Criminal Justice and Criminology M
Curriculum and Instruction M
Early Childhood Education M
Education—General M
Educational Administration M
Engineering and Applied Sciences—General M
English Education M
English M
Exercise and Sports Science M
Family Nurse Practitioner Studies M
Health Education M
Health Services Management and Hospital Administration M
History M
Human Resources Development M
Industrial and Manufacturing Management M
Information Science M
Interdisciplinary Studies M
Journalism M
Kinesiology and Movement Studies M
Marriage and Family Therapy M
Mathematics Education M
Mathematics M
Music Education M
Music M
Nursing and Healthcare Administration M
Nursing Education M
Nursing—General M
Political Science M
Psychology—General M
Public Administration M
Reading Education M
School Psychology M
Science Education M
Secondary Education M
Social Sciences Education M
Social Sciences M
Sociology M
Special Education M
Speech and Interpersonal Communication M
Theater M
Vocational and Technical Education M

THE UNIVERSITY OF TEXAS HEALTH SCIENCE CENTER AT HOUSTON

Allopathic Medicine P
Biochemistry M,D
Biological and Biomedical Sciences—General M,D*
Biometrics M,D
Biostatistics M,D
Cancer Biology/Oncology M,D
Cell Biology M,D
Dentistry P,M
Developmental Biology M,D
Genetic Counseling M
Genetics M,D
Health Informatics M,D
Human Genetics M,D
Immunology M,D
Medical Physics M,D
Microbiology M,D
Molecular Biology M,D
Molecular Genetics M,D
Molecular Pathology M,D
Neuroscience M,D
Nursing—General M,D
Public Health—General M,D,O
Toxicology M,D
Virology M,D

THE UNIVERSITY OF TEXAS HEALTH SCIENCE CENTER AT SAN ANTONIO

Allopathic Medicine P
Biochemistry M,D
Biological and Biomedical Sciences—General M,D
Cell Biology M,D
Clinical Laboratory Sciences/Medical Technology M
Dental Hygiene M
Dentistry P,M,O
Immunology D
Medical Physics M,D
Microbiology D*
Molecular Medicine M,D*
Nursing—General M,D
Occupational Therapy M
Oral and Dental Sciences M,O
Pharmacology D
Physical Therapy M
Physician Assistant Studies M
Physiology M,D
Structural Biology M,D

THE UNIVERSITY OF TEXAS MEDICAL BRANCH

Allied Health—General M
Allopathic Medicine P
Bacteriology D
Biochemistry D
Bioinformatics D
Biological and Biomedical Sciences—General M,D*
Biophysics D
Cell Biology D*
Community Health M,D
Computational Biology D
Genetics D
Humanities M,D
Immunology M,D
Infectious Diseases D*
Microbiology M,D
Molecular Biophysics M,D*
Neuroscience D*
Nursing—General M,D
Occupational Therapy M
Pathology D*
Pharmacology M,D*
Physical Therapy M
Physician Assistant Studies M
Physiology M,D
Public Health—General M
Structural Biology D
Toxicology D
Virology D

THE UNIVERSITY OF TEXAS OF THE PERMIAN BASIN

Accounting M
Biological and Biomedical Sciences—General M
Business Administration and Management—General M
Clinical Psychology M
Counselor Education M
Criminal Justice and Criminology M
Early Childhood Education M
Education—General M
Educational Administration M
English as a Second Language M
English M
Foundations and Philosophy of Education M
Geology M
History M
Kinesiology and Movement Studies M
Psychology—General M
Reading Education M
Special Education M

THE UNIVERSITY OF TEXAS–PAN AMERICAN

Adult Nursing M
Art/Fine Arts M
Biological and Biomedical Sciences—General M
Business Administration and Management—General M,D
Clinical Psychology M
Communication Disorders M
Communication—General M
Computer Science M
Counselor Education M
Criminal Justice and Criminology M
Early Childhood Education M
Education of the Gifted M
Education—General M,D
Educational Administration M,D
Educational Measurement and Evaluation M
Educational Psychology M
Elementary Education M
English as a Second Language M
English M
Experimental Psychology M
Family Nurse Practitioner Studies M
History M
Interdisciplinary Studies M
Kinesiology and Movement Studies M
Management Information Systems M,D
Mathematics M
Multilingual and Multicultural Education M
Music Education M
Music M
Nursing—General M
Occupational Therapy M
Pediatric Nursing M
Psychology—General M
Public Administration M
Reading Education M
Rehabilitation Counseling M
School Psychology M
Secondary Education M
Social Work M
Sociology M
Spanish M
Special Education M
Theater M

THE UNIVERSITY OF TEXAS SOUTHWESTERN MEDICAL CENTER AT DALLAS

Allopathic Medicine P
Biochemistry D
Biological and Biomedical Sciences—General M,D*
Biomedical Engineering M,D
Cell Biology D
Clinical Psychology D
Developmental Biology D
Genetics D
Immunology D
Medical Illustration M
Microbiology D
Molecular Biophysics D
Neuroscience D
Pharmacology
Physical Therapy M
Physician Assistant Studies M
Radiation Biology M,D
Rehabilitation Counseling M

THE UNIVERSITY OF THE ARTS

Art Education M
Art/Fine Arts M*
Industrial Design M
Museum Education M
Museum Studies M
Music Education M
Music M

UNIVERSITY OF THE CUMBERLANDS

Early Childhood Education M
Education—General M,O
Educational Administration M,O
Elementary Education M,O
Middle School Education M
Reading Education M
Secondary Education M,O
Special Education M

UNIVERSITY OF THE DISTRICT OF COLUMBIA

Business Administration and Management—General M
Clinical Psychology M
Communication Disorders M
Counseling Psychology M
Counselor Education M
Early Childhood Education M
Education—General M
English M
Law P
Mathematics Education M
Public Administration M
Special Education M

UNIVERSITY OF THE INCARNATE WORD

- Adult Education M,D,O
- Biological and Biomedical Sciences—General M
- Business Administration and Management—General M,O
- Communication—General M,O
- Early Childhood Education M,D
- Education—General M,D
- Educational Media/Instructional Technology M,D,O
- Elementary Education M
- English M,O
- Entrepreneurship M,D
- Interdisciplinary Studies M
- International Business M,O
- Kinesiology and Movement Studies M,D
- Mathematics Education M,D
- Mathematics M
- Nursing—General M
- Nutrition M,O
- Organizational Management M,D,O
- Pharmacy P
- Physical Education M
- Project Management M,O
- Reading Education M,D
- Religion M
- Science Education M
- Secondary Education M
- Special Education M,D
- Sports Management M,O
- Urban Studies M,O

UNIVERSITY OF THE PACIFIC

- Biological and Biomedical Sciences—General M
- Business Administration and Management—General M
- Communication Disorders M
- Communication—General M
- Curriculum and Instruction M,D
- Dentistry P,M,O
- Education—General M,D,O
- Educational Administration M,D
- Educational Psychology M,D,O
- Exercise and Sports Science M
- International Affairs P,M,D
- Law P,M,D
- Legal and Justice Studies P,M,D
- Music Education M
- Music M
- Oral and Dental Sciences M,O
- Pharmaceutical Sciences M,D
- Pharmacy P
- Physical Therapy M,D
- Psychology—General M
- Public Policy P,M,D
- School Psychology M,D,O
- Special Education M,D
- Therapies—Dance, Drama, and Music M

UNIVERSITY OF THE SACRED HEART

- Advertising and Public Relations M
- Business Administration and Management—General M
- Clinical Laboratory Sciences/Medical Technology O
- Communication—General M
- Conflict Resolution and Mediation/Peace Studies M
- Cultural Studies M
- Early Childhood Education M
- Education—General M
- Educational Media/Instructional Technology M
- Environmental and Occupational Health M
- Human Resources Management M
- Journalism M
- Legal and Justice Studies M
- Management Information Systems M
- Marketing M
- Mass Communication M
- Nonprofit Management M
- Taxation M
- Writing M

UNIVERSITY OF THE SCIENCES IN PHILADELPHIA

- Biochemistry M,D
- Bioinformatics M
- Biotechnology M
- Cell Biology M
- Chemistry M,D
- Health Psychology M
- Health Services Management and Hospital Administration M,D
- Medicinal and Pharmaceutical Chemistry M,D
- Pharmaceutical Administration M
- Pharmaceutical Sciences M,D*
- Pharmacology M,D
- Pharmacy P
- Physical Therapy D
- Public Health—General M
- Technical Writing M,O
- Toxicology M,D

UNIVERSITY OF THE VIRGIN ISLANDS

- Business Administration and Management—General M
- Education—General M
- Mathematics Education M
- Public Administration M

UNIVERSITY OF THE WEST

- Business Administration and Management—General M
- Finance and Banking M
- International Business M
- Management Information Systems M
- Nonprofit Management M
- Religion M,D

THE UNIVERSITY OF TOLEDO

- Accounting M
- Allopathic Medicine M
- Analytical Chemistry M,D
- Applied Mathematics M,D
- Art Education M
- Biochemistry M,D*
- Bioengineering M,D
- Bioinformatics M,O
- Biological and Biomedical Sciences—General M,D*
- Biopsychology M,D
- Business Administration and Management—General M,D*
- Business Education M
- Cancer Biology/Oncology M,D
- Cardiovascular Sciences M,D
- Cell Biology M,D
- Chemical Engineering M,D
- Chemistry M,D*
- Civil Engineering M,D
- Clinical Psychology M,D
- Cognitive Sciences M,D
- Communication Disorders M,D,O
- Communication—General O
- Computer Science M,D
- Counselor Education M,D,O
- Criminal Justice and Criminology M,O
- Curriculum and Instruction M,D,O
- Early Childhood Education M,O
- Ecology M,D*
- Economics M
- Education of the Gifted O
- Education—General M,D,O
- Educational Administration M,D,O
- Educational Measurement and Evaluation M,D
- Educational Media/Instructional Technology M,D,O
- Educational Psychology M,D
- Electrical Engineering M,D
- Elementary Education D,O
- Engineering and Applied Sciences—General M*
- English as a Second Language M,O
- English Education M
- English M,O
- Environmental and Occupational Health M
- Exercise and Sports Science M,D
- Experimental Psychology M,D
- Family Nurse Practitioner Studies M,O
- Finance and Banking M
- Foreign Languages Education M
- Foundations and Philosophy of Education M,D
- French M
- Genetics M
- Genomic Sciences M,O
- Geographic Information Systems D
- Geography M,D,O*
- Geology M,D
- Geosciences M,D
- German M
- Gerontology O
- Health Education M,D
- Health Physics/Radiological Health M
- Health Services Management and Hospital Administration M
- Higher Education M,D
- History M,D*
- Human Resources Management M
- Immunology M,D
- Industrial and Manufacturing Management M,D
- Industrial/Management Engineering M,D
- Inorganic Chemistry M,D
- International Business M
- Law P,M
- Leisure Studies M
- Liberal Studies M
- Management Information Systems M
- Marketing M
- Mathematics Education M
- Mathematics M,D*
- Mechanical Engineering M,D
- Medical Physics M
- Medicinal and Pharmaceutical Chemistry M,D
- Microbiology M
- Middle School Education M
- Molecular Biology M,D
- Music Education M
- Music M
- Neuroscience M,D
- Nursing—General M,O
- Occupational Therapy M,D
- Oral and Dental Sciences M
- Organic Chemistry M,D
- Pathology O
- Pharmaceutical Administration M
- Pharmaceutical Sciences M
- Pharmacology M
- Philosophy M
- Physical Chemistry M,D
- Physical Education M
- Physical Therapy M,D
- Physician Assistant Studies M
- Physics M,D*
- Political Science M
- Psychology—General M,D*
- Public Administration M
- Public Health—General M,D,O
- School Psychology M,D,O
- Science Education M
- Secondary Education M,D,O
- Social Psychology M,D,O
- Social Sciences Education M,D
- Social Sciences D
- Social Work M
- Sociology M
- Spanish M
- Special Education M,D,O
- Statistics M,D
- Urban and Regional Planning M,D,O
- Vocational and Technical Education M,O
- Writing M,O

Close-Up on page 1127.

UNIVERSITY OF TORONTO

- Accounting M,D
- Aerospace/Aeronautical Engineering M,D
- Allopathic Medicine P,M,D
- Anthropology M,D
- Architecture M
- Art History M,D
- Asian Studies M,D
- Astronomy M,D
- Biochemistry M,D
- Biological and Biomedical Sciences—General M,D,O
- Biomedical Engineering M,D
- Biophysics M,D
- Botany M,D
- Business Administration and Management—General M,D
- Chemical Engineering M,D
- Chemistry M,D
- Civil Engineering M,D
- Classics M,D
- Communication Disorders M,D
- Comparative Literature M,D
- Computer Engineering M,D
- Computer Science M,D
- Criminal Justice and Criminology M,D
- Dentistry P
- East European and Russian Studies M
- Economics M,D
- Education—General M,D
- Electrical Engineering M,D
- Engineering and Applied Sciences—General M,D
- English M,D
- Forestry M,D
- French M,D
- Genetic Counseling M,D
- Genetics M,D
- Geography M,D
- Geology M,D
- German M,D
- History of Science and Technology M,D
- History M,D
- Immunology M,D
- Industrial and Labor Relations M,D
- Industrial/Management Engineering M,D
- Information Studies M,D,O
- Italian M,D
- Law P,M,D
- Library Science M,D,O
- Linguistics M,D
- Materials Engineering M,D
- Materials Sciences M,D
- Mathematics M,D
- Mechanical Engineering M,D
- Medieval and Renaissance Studies M,D
- Museum Studies M
- Music Education M,D
- Music M,D
- Near and Middle Eastern Studies M,D
- Nursing—General M,D,O
- Nutrition M,D
- Oral and Dental Sciences M,D
- Pathobiology M,D
- Pharmaceutical Sciences M,D
- Pharmacology M,D
- Philosophy M,D
- Physical Education M,D
- Physics M,D
- Physiology M,D
- Political Science M,D
- Portuguese M,D
- Psychology—General M,D
- Public Health—General M,D,O
- Rehabilitation Sciences M
- Religion M,D
- Slavic Languages M,D
- Social Work M,D
- Sociology M,D
- Spanish M,D
- Statistics M,D
- Theater M,D
- Urban and Regional Planning M
- Zoology M,D

UNIVERSITY OF TRINITY COLLEGE

- Music P,M,D,O
- Pastoral Ministry and Counseling P,M,D,O
- Theology P,M,D,O

UNIVERSITY OF TULSA

- Anthropology M
- Art/Fine Arts M
- Biological and Biomedical Sciences—General M,D
- Business Administration and Management—General M
- Chemical Engineering M,D
- Chemistry M
- Clinical Psychology M,D
- Communication Disorders M
- Computer Science M,D
- Education—General M
- Electrical Engineering M
- Engineering and Applied Sciences—General M,D
- Engineering Management M
- English M,D
- Finance and Banking M*
- Financial Engineering M
- Geology M
- Geosciences M,D
- History M
- Industrial and Organizational Psychology M,D
- Investment Management M
- Law P,M,O
- Management of Technology M
- Mathematics Education M
- Mathematics M
- Mechanical Engineering M,D
- Petroleum Engineering M,D
- Psychology—General M,D
- Science Education M
- Taxation M

Close-Up on page 1129.

UNIVERSITY OF UTAH

- Accounting M,D
- Allopathic Medicine P
- American Studies M,D
- Anatomy D
- Anthropology M,D
- Architecture M
- Art Education M
- Art History M
- Art/Fine Arts M
- Biochemistry M,D*
- Bioengineering M,D*
- Bioinformatics M,D
- Biological and Biomedical Sciences—General M,D*
- Biostatistics M,D
- Biotechnology M
- Business Administration and Management—General M,D
- Cancer Biology/Oncology M,D
- Cell Biology
- Chemical Engineering M,D
- Chemical Physics M,D
- Chemistry M,D
- Child and Family Studies M
- Civil Engineering M,D
- Clinical Laboratory Sciences/Medical Technology M
- Communication Disorders M,D
- Communication—General M,D
- Comparative Literature M,D*
- Computational Sciences M
- Computer Science M,D
- Consumer Economics M
- Counseling Psychology M,D
- Counselor Education M,D
- Dance M

Ecology M,D
Economics M,D
Education—General M,D
Educational Administration M,D
Educational Psychology M,D
Electrical Engineering M,D,O
Elementary Education M,D
Engineering and Applied Sciences—General M,D,O
English M,D
Environmental Engineering M,D
Environmental Sciences M
Evolutionary Biology M,D
Exercise and Sports Science M,D
Film, Television, and Video Production M
Finance and Banking M,D
Foreign Languages Education M,D
Foundations and Philosophy of Education M,D
French M,D
Genetics M,D
Geography M,D
Geological Engineering M,D
Geology M,D
Geophysics M,D
German M,D
Gerontological Nursing M,O
Gerontology M,O
Graphic Design M
Health Education M,D
Health Promotion M,D
History M,D
Human Genetics M,D
Illustration M
Immunology
Law P,M
Leisure Studies M,D
Linguistics M,D
Materials Engineering M,D
Materials Sciences M,D
Mathematics M,D*
Mechanical Engineering M,D
Medicinal and Pharmaceutical Chemistry M,D
Metallurgical Engineering and Metallurgy M,D
Meteorology M,D
Microbiology M,D
Mineral/Mining Engineering M,D
Molecular Biology D*
Music M,D
Near and Middle Eastern Languages M,D
Near and Middle Eastern Studies M,D
Neurobiology D
Neuroscience D*
Nuclear Engineering M,D
Nursing—General M,D
Nutrition M
Occupational Therapy M
Pathology M,D
Pharmacology M,D
Pharmacy P,M
Philosophy M,D
Photography M
Physical Therapy D,O
Physician Assistant Studies M
Physics M,D
Physiology D
Plant Biology M,D
Political Science M,D
Psychology—General M,D
Public Administration M,O
Public Health—General M,D
Recreation and Park Management M,D
Rhetoric M,D
Science Education M,D
Secondary Education M,D
Social Work M,D
Sociology M,D
Spanish M,D
Special Education M,D
Statistics M,D
Toxicology M,D
Urban and Regional Planning M
Writing M

UNIVERSITY OF VERMONT

Agricultural Economics and Agribusiness M
Agricultural Sciences—General M,D
Agronomy and Soil Sciences M,D
Allied Health—General M,D
Allopathic Medicine P
Anatomy D
Animal Sciences M,D
Applied Economics M
Biochemistry M,D*
Biological and Biomedical Sciences—General M,D
Biomedical Engineering M
Biophysics M,D
Biostatistics M
Botany M,D
Business Administration and Management—General M
Cell Biology M,D*
Chemistry M,D
Civil Engineering M,D
Classics M
Clinical Psychology D
Communication—General M
Computer Science M,D
Counseling Psychology M
Counselor Education M
Curriculum and Instruction M
Education—General M,D
Educational Administration M,D
Electrical Engineering M,D
Engineering and Applied Sciences—General M,D
English M
Environmental Engineering M,D
Environmental Management and Policy M,D
Food Science and Technology D
Foreign Languages Education M
Forestry M,D
French M
Geology M
German M
Historic Preservation M
History M
Horticulture M,D
Materials Sciences M,D
Mathematics Education M,D
Mathematics M,D
Mechanical Engineering M,D
Microbiology M,D
Molecular Biology M,D
Molecular Genetics M,D*
Molecular Physiology M,D
Natural Resources M,D
Neurobiology D
Neuroscience D
Nursing—General M
Nutrition M,D
Pathology M
Pharmacology M,D
Physical Therapy D
Physics M
Plant Biology M,D
Plant Sciences M,D
Psychology—General D
Public Administration M
Reading Education M
Science Education M
Social Work M
Special Education M
Statistics M

UNIVERSITY OF VICTORIA

Anthropology M
Art Education M
Art History M,D
Art/Fine Arts M
Asian Studies M
Astronomy M,D
Astrophysics M,D
Biochemistry M,D
Biological and Biomedical Sciences—General M,D
Business Administration and Management—General M
Chemistry M,D
Child and Family Studies M,D
Classics M
Clinical Psychology M,D
Computer Art and Design M
Computer Science M,D
Condensed Matter Physics M,D
Conflict Resolution and Mediation/Peace Studies M
Counseling Psychology M,D
Counselor Education M,D
Curriculum and Instruction M,D
Early Childhood Education M,D
Economics M,D
Education—General M,D
Educational Administration M,D
Educational Psychology M,D
Electrical Engineering M,D
Engineering and Applied Sciences—General M,D
English Education M,D
English M,D
Environmental Education M,D
Foreign Languages Education M
Foundations and Philosophy of Education M,D
French M
Geography M,D
Geophysics M,D
Geosciences M,D
German M
Health Informatics M
Hispanic Studies M
History M,D
Human Development M,D
Italian M
Kinesiology and Movement Studies M
Law P,M,D
Leisure Studies M
Linguistics M,D
Mathematics Education M,D
Mathematics M,D
Mechanical Engineering M,D
Medical Physics M,D
Microbiology M,D
Music Education M,D
Music M,D
Nursing—General M
Oceanography M,D
Philosophy M
Photography M
Physical Education M
Physics M,D
Political Science M,D
Psychology—General M,D
Public Administration M,D
Reading Education M,D
Science Education M,D
Social Psychology M,D
Social Sciences Education M,D
Social Work M
Sociology M,D
Special Education M,D
Statistics M,D
Theater M,D
Theoretical Physics M,D
Vocational and Technical Education M,D

UNIVERSITY OF VIRGINIA

Accounting M
Aerospace/Aeronautical Engineering M,D
Allopathic Medicine P,M,D
Anthropology M,D
Archaeology M,D
Architectural History M,D
Architecture M
Art History M,D
Asian Studies M
Astronomy M,D
Bacteriology D
Biochemistry D
Bioethics M
Biological and Biomedical Sciences—General M,D
Biomedical Engineering M,D
Biophysics M,D
Business Administration and Management—General M,D
Cardiovascular Sciences
Cell Biology D
Chemical Engineering M,D
Chemistry M,D
Civil Engineering M,D
Classics M,D
Clinical Psychology M,D,O
Clinical Research M
Communication Disorders M
Computer Engineering M,D
Computer Science M,D
Counselor Education M,D,O
Curriculum and Instruction M,D,O
Economics M,D
Education—General M,D,O
Educational Administration M,D,O
Educational Measurement and Evaluation M,D
Educational Policy M,D
Educational Psychology M,D,O
Electrical Engineering M,D
Engineering and Applied Sciences—General M,D
Engineering Physics M,D
English M,D
Environmental Sciences M,D
French M,D
German M,D
Health Education M,D
Health Informatics M
Health Services Management and Hospital Administration M
Health Services Research M
Higher Education D,O
History M,D
Immunology D*
International Affairs M,D
Italian M
Kinesiology and Movement Studies M,D
Landscape Architecture M
Law P,M,D
Linguistics M
Management Information Systems M
Materials Sciences M,D
Mathematics M,D
Mechanical Engineering M,D
Mechanics M
Microbiology D
Molecular Genetics D
Molecular Physiology M,D
Music M,D
Neuroscience D
Nursing—General M,D
Pharmacology D
Philosophy M,D
Physical Education M,D
Physics M,D
Physiology D
Political Science M,D
Psychology—General M,D
Public Health—General M
Religion M,D
Romance Languages M,D
School Psychology M,D,O
Science Education M,D
Slavic Languages M,D
Sociology M,D
Spanish M,D
Special Education M,D,O
Statistics M,D
Systems Engineering M,D
Theater M
Urban and Regional Planning M
Virology D
Writing M

UNIVERSITY OF WASHINGTON

Accounting M,D
Aerospace/Aeronautical Engineering M,D
Allopathic Medicine P
Anthropology M,D
Applied Mathematics M,D
Applied Physics M,D
Architecture M,O
Art History M,D
Art/Fine Arts M
Asian Languages M,D
Asian Studies M
Astronomy M,D
Atmospheric Sciences M,D
Bacteriology M,D
Biochemistry D
Bioengineering M,D
Bioinformatics M,D
Biological and Biomedical Sciences—General M,D
Biophysics D
Biostatistics M,D
Biotechnology D
Botany M,D
Business Administration and Management—General M,D
Business Education M,D
Cell Biology D*
Chemical Engineering M,D*
Chemistry M,D
Chinese M,D
Civil Engineering M,D
Classics M,D
Clinical Laboratory Sciences/Medical Technology M
Clinical Psychology D
Communication Disorders M,D
Communication—General M,D
Comparative Literature M,D
Computer Science M,D
Construction Engineering M,D
Counselor Education M,D
Curriculum and Instruction M,D
Dance M
Dentistry P
East European and Russian Studies M
Economics M,D
Education—General M,D,O
Educational Administration M,D,O
Educational Measurement and Evaluation M,D
Educational Media/Instructional Technology M,D
Educational Policy M,D
Educational Psychology M,D
Electrical Engineering M,D*
Engineering and Applied Sciences—General M,D
English as a Second Language M,D
English Education M,D
English M,D
Environmental and Occupational Health M,D*
Environmental Engineering M,D
Environmental Management and Policy M,D
Epidemiology M,D
Ergonomics and Human Factors M,D
Fish, Game, and Wildlife Management M,D
Forestry M,D
Foundations and Philosophy of Education M,D
French M,D
Genetics M,D
Genomic Sciences D
Geography M,D
Geology M,D
Geophysics M,D
Geotechnical Engineering M,D
German M,D
Health Informatics M,D
Health Services Management and Hospital Administration M
Health Services Research M,D
Higher Education M,D
Hispanic Studies M,D
Historic Preservation O
History M,D
Horticulture M,D
Human Development M,D
Hydrology M,D
Immunology D
Industrial Hygiene M,D

- Industrial/Management Engineering M,D
- Information Science M,D
- International Affairs M
- International Business M,D,O
- International Health M,D
- Italian M,D
- Japanese M,D
- Landscape Architecture M
- Law P,M,D
- Legal and Justice Studies P,M,D
- Library Science M,D
- Linguistics M,D
- Logistics O
- Management of Technology M,D
- Marine Affairs M
- Marine Geology M,D
- Materials Engineering M,D
- Materials Sciences M,D
- Maternal and Child Health M,D
- Mathematics Education M,D
- Mathematics M,D
- Mechanical Engineering M,D
- Medical Informatics M,D
- Medicinal and Pharmaceutical Chemistry D
- Microbiology D
- Molecular Biology D
- Molecular Medicine M,D
- Multilingual and Multicultural Education M,D
- Museum Studies M
- Music Education M,D
- Music M,D
- Nanotechnology M,D
- Near and Middle Eastern Studies M,D
- Neurobiology D
- Neuroscience D
- Nursing—General M,D
- Nutrition M,D
- Occupational Therapy M,D
- Oceanography M,D
- Oral and Dental Sciences M,D
- Paper and Pulp Engineering M,D
- Parasitology M,D
- Pathobiology M,D*
- Pathology M,D
- Pharmaceutical Sciences M,D
- Pharmacology M,D*
- Pharmacy P
- Philosophy M,D
- Physical Therapy M,D
- Physics M,D
- Physiology D
- Political Science M,D
- Portuguese M
- Psychology—General D
- Public Affairs M,D*
- Public Health—General M,D
- Reading Education M,D
- Rehabilitation Sciences M,D
- Religion M
- Romance Languages M,D
- Russian M,D
- Scandinavian Languages M,D
- School Psychology M,D
- Science Education M,D
- Slavic Languages M,D
- Social Sciences Education M,D
- Social Work M,D
- Sociology M,D
- Spanish M
- Special Education M,D
- Statistics M,D
- Structural Biology D
- Structural Engineering M,D
- Sustainable Development P,M,D
- Taxation P,M,D
- Technical Communication M,D
- Theater M,D
- Toxicology M,D
- Transportation and Highway Engineering M,D
- Transportation Management O
- Urban and Regional Planning M,D
- Urban Design M,D,O
- Veterinary Sciences M
- Water Resources Engineering M,D
- Women's Studies M,D
- Zoology D

UNIVERSITY OF WASHINGTON, BOTHELL

- Business Administration and Management—General M
- Education—General M
- Nursing—General M
- Public Policy M

UNIVERSITY OF WATERLOO

- Accounting M,D
- Actuarial Science M,D
- Anthropology M
- Applied Mathematics M,D
- Architecture M
- Art/Fine Arts M
- Biological and Biomedical Sciences—General M,D
- Biostatistics M,D
- Business Administration and Management—General M
- Chemical Engineering M,D*
- Chemistry M,D
- Civil Engineering M,D
- Computer Engineering M,D
- Computer Science M,D
- Economics M,D
- Electrical Engineering M,D
- Engineering and Applied Sciences—General M,D
- Engineering Management M,D
- English M,D
- Entrepreneurship M
- Environmental Engineering M,D
- Environmental Management and Policy M
- Finance and Banking M,D
- French M,D
- Geography M,D
- Geosciences M,D
- German M,D
- Health Education M,D
- History M,D
- Information Science M,D
- International Affairs M,D
- Kinesiology and Movement Studies M,D
- Leisure Studies M,D
- Management of Technology M,D
- Mathematics M,D
- Mechanical Engineering M,D
- Operations Research M,D
- Optometry M,D
- Philosophy M,D
- Physics M,D
- Political Science M,D
- Psychology—General M,D
- Public Affairs M
- Recreation and Park Management M,D
- Russian M,D
- Sociology M,D
- Software Engineering M,D
- Statistics M,D
- Systems Engineering M,D
- Taxation M,D
- Technical Writing M,D
- Travel and Tourism M
- Urban and Regional Planning M,D
- Vision Sciences M,D

THE UNIVERSITY OF WEST ALABAMA

- Adult Education M
- Athletic Training and Sports Medicine M
- Counselor Education M
- Early Childhood Education M
- Education—General M
- Educational Administration M
- Educational Media/Instructional Technology M
- Elementary Education M
- English Education M
- Foundations and Philosophy of Education M
- Mathematics Education M
- Physical Education M
- Science Education M
- Secondary Education M
- Social Sciences Education M
- Special Education M

THE UNIVERSITY OF WESTERN ONTARIO

- Accounting M,D
- Allopathic Medicine P,M
- Anatomy M,D
- Anthropology M,D
- Applied Mathematics M,D
- Astronomy M,D
- Biochemistry M,D
- Biological and Biomedical Sciences—General M,D
- Biophysics M,D
- Biostatistics M,D
- Biotechnology M,D
- Business Administration and Management—General M,D
- Cell Biology M,D
- Chemistry M,D
- Classics M
- Communication Disorders M
- Comparative Literature M,D
- Computer Science M,D
- Counselor Education M
- Curriculum and Instruction M
- Dentistry P
- Economics M,D
- Education—General M
- Educational Policy M
- Educational Psychology M
- Engineering and Applied Sciences—General M,D
- English M,D
- Entrepreneurship M,D
- Environmental Sciences M,D
- Epidemiology M,D
- Finance and Banking M,D
- French M,D
- Geography M,D
- Geology M,D
- Geophysics M,D
- Geosciences M,D
- History M,D
- Immunology M,D
- Information Studies M,D
- Interdisciplinary Studies M,D
- Journalism M
- Kinesiology and Movement Studies M,D
- Law P,M,O
- Library Science M,D
- Mathematics M,D
- Media Studies M,D
- Microbiology M,D
- Molecular Biology M,D
- Music M,D
- Neuroscience M,D
- Nursing—General M,D
- Occupational Therapy M
- Oral and Dental Sciences M
- Pathology M,D
- Philosophy M,D
- Physical Therapy M
- Physics M,D
- Physiology M,D
- Plant Biology M,D
- Plant Sciences M,D
- Political Science M,D
- Psychology—General M,D
- Sociology M,D
- Spanish M,D
- Special Education M
- Statistics M,D
- Zoology M,D

UNIVERSITY OF WEST FLORIDA

- Accounting M
- Anthropology M
- Archaeology M
- Biochemistry M
- Biological and Biomedical Sciences—General M
- Business Administration and Management—General M
- Communication—General M
- Computer Science M
- Counselor Education M
- Criminal Justice and Criminology M
- Curriculum and Instruction M,D,O
- Early Childhood Education M
- Educational Administration M,O
- Educational Media/Instructional Technology M
- Elementary Education M
- English M
- Environmental Biology M
- Environmental Sciences M
- Exercise and Sports Science M
- Health Communication M
- Health Education M
- History M
- Humanities M
- Leisure Studies M
- Marine Affairs M
- Mathematics M
- Middle School Education M
- Physical Education M
- Political Science M
- Psychology—General M
- Public Health—General M
- Reading Education M
- Science Education M
- Secondary Education M
- Software Engineering M
- Special Education M
- Vocational and Technical Education M
- Writing M

UNIVERSITY OF WEST GEORGIA

- Accounting M
- Art Education M
- Biological and Biomedical Sciences—General M
- Business Administration and Management—General M
- Business Education M,O
- Communication Disorders M
- Computer Science M
- Counselor Education M,O
- Early Childhood Education M,O
- Education—General M,D,O
- Educational Administration M,O
- Educational Measurement and Evaluation D
- Educational Media/Instructional Technology M,O
- English Education M,O
- English M
- Foreign Languages Education M
- Gerontology M
- History M
- Mathematics Education M,O
- Middle School Education M,O
- Music Education M
- Music M
- Nursing—General M
- Physical Education M,O
- Psychology—General M,D
- Public Administration M
- Reading Education M
- Rural Planning and Studies M
- Science Education M,O
- Secondary Education M,O
- Social Sciences Education M,O
- Sociology M
- Special Education M,O

UNIVERSITY OF WINDSOR

- Art/Fine Arts M
- Biochemistry M,D
- Biological and Biomedical Sciences—General M,D
- Biopsychology M,D
- Business Administration and Management—General M
- Chemistry M,D
- Civil Engineering M,D
- Clinical Psychology M,D
- Communication—General M
- Computer Science M,D
- Economics M
- Education—General M,D
- Electrical Engineering M,D
- Engineering and Applied Sciences—General M,D
- English M
- Environmental Engineering M,D
- Environmental Sciences M,D
- Geosciences M,D
- History M
- Industrial/Management Engineering M,D
- Kinesiology and Movement Studies M
- Legal and Justice Studies M
- Manufacturing Engineering M,D
- Materials Engineering M,D
- Mathematics M,D
- Mechanical Engineering M,D
- Nursing—General M
- Philosophy M
- Physics M,D
- Political Science M
- Psychology—General M,D
- Social Psychology M,D
- Social Work M
- Sociology M,D
- Statistics M,D
- Writing M

THE UNIVERSITY OF WINNIPEG

- History M
- Marriage and Family Therapy P,M,O
- Public Administration M
- Religion M
- Theology P,M,O

UNIVERSITY OF WISCONSIN–EAU CLAIRE

- Biological and Biomedical Sciences—General M
- Business Administration and Management—General M
- Communication Disorders M
- Education—General M
- Elementary Education M
- English Education M
- English M
- Environmental and Occupational Health M
- History M
- Mathematics Education M
- Nursing—General M
- Psychology—General M,O
- Public Health—General M
- Reading Education M
- School Psychology M,O
- Science Education M
- Secondary Education M
- Social Sciences Education M
- Special Education M

Announcement on page 757.

UNIVERSITY OF WISCONSIN–GREEN BAY

- Business Administration and Management—General M
- Education—General M
- Environmental Management and Policy M
- Environmental Sciences M
- Social Work M

UNIVERSITY OF WISCONSIN–LA CROSSE

- Athletic Training and Sports Medicine M
- Biological and Biomedical Sciences—General M
- Business Administration and Management—General M
- Cell Biology M
- Community Health M
- Education—General M
- Elementary Education M
- Exercise and Sports Science M

Health Education	M
Marine Sciences	M
Medical Microbiology	M
Microbiology	M
Molecular Biology	M
Nurse Anesthesia	M
Occupational Therapy	M
Physical Education	M
Physical Therapy	M,D
Physician Assistant Studies	M
Physiology	M
Psychology—General	M,O
Public Health—General	M
Reading Education	M
Recreation and Park Management	M
Rehabilitation Sciences	M
School Psychology	M,O
Secondary Education	M
Software Engineering	M
Special Education	M
Sports Management	M
Student Affairs	M

Close-Up on page 1131.

UNIVERSITY OF WISCONSIN–MADISON

Accounting	D
Actuarial Science	M
African Studies	M,D
African-American Studies	M
Agricultural Economics and Agribusiness	M,D
Agricultural Engineering	M,D
Agricultural Sciences—General	M,D
Agronomy and Soil Sciences	M,D
Allopathic Medicine	P
Anatomy	M,D
Animal Sciences	M,D
Anthropology	M,D
Applied Arts and Design—General	M,D
Applied Economics	M,D
Art Education	M,D
Art History	M,D
Art/Fine Arts	M
Arts Administration	M
Asian Languages	M,D
Asian Studies	M,D
Astronomy	D
Atmospheric Sciences	M,D
Bacteriology	M
Biochemistry	M,D
Bioengineering	M,D
Biological and Biomedical Sciences—General	M,D
Biomedical Engineering	M,D
Biometrics	M
Biophysics	D
Biopsychology	D
Biotechnology	
Botany	M,D
Business Administration and Management—General	M
Cancer Biology/Oncology	D
Cell Biology	M,D*
Chemical Engineering	M,D
Chemistry	M,D
Child and Family Studies	M,D
Chinese	M,D
Civil Engineering	M,D
Classics	M,D
Clinical Psychology	D
Cognitive Sciences	D
Communication Disorders	M,D
Communication—General	M,D
Community Health	M,D
Comparative Literature	M,D
Computer and Information Systems Security	M
Computer Science	M,D
Conservation Biology	M
Consumer Economics	M,D
Counseling Psychology	D
Counselor Education	M
Curriculum and Instruction	M,D
Developmental Psychology	D
Ecology	M,D
Economics	D
Education—General	M,D,O
Educational Administration	M,D,O
Educational Policy	M,D,O
Educational Psychology	M,D
Electrical Engineering	M,D
Energy and Power Engineering	M,D
Engineering and Applied Sciences—General	M,D,O
Engineering Management	M
Engineering Physics	M,D
English	M,D
Entomology	M,D
Entrepreneurship	M
Environmental Biology	M,D
Environmental Engineering	M,D
Environmental Management and Policy	M,D
Environmental Sciences	M,D
Family and Consumer Sciences-General	M,D
Finance and Banking	M,D
Food Science and Technology	M,D
Foreign Languages Education	M,D
Forestry	M,D
French	M,D,O
Genetics	M,D*
Geographic Information Systems	M,D,O
Geography	M,D,O
Geological Engineering	M,D
Geology	M,D
Geophysics	M,D
German	M,D
Health Promotion	M,D
History of Science and Technology	M,D
History	M,D
Horticulture	M,D
Human Development	M,D
Human Resources Management	M,D
Industrial and Labor Relations	M,D
Industrial and Manufacturing Management	D
Industrial/Management Engineering	M,D
Information Studies	M,D,O
Insurance	M,D
Investment Management	D
Italian	M,D
Japanese	M,D
Jewish Studies	M,D
Journalism	M,D
Kinesiology and Movement Studies	M,D
Landscape Architecture	M
Latin American Studies	M
Law	M,D
Legal and Justice Studies	M
Library Science	M,D,O
Limnology	M,D
Linguistics	M,D
Management Information Systems	M,D
Management of Technology	M
Management Strategy and Policy	M
Manufacturing Engineering	M
Marine Sciences	M,D
Marketing Research	M
Mass Communication	M,D
Materials Engineering	M,D
Materials Sciences	M,D
Mathematics Education	M,D
Mathematics	M,D
Mechanical Engineering	M,D
Mechanics	M,D
Medical Microbiology	D
Medical Physics	M,D
Microbiology	D*
Molecular Biology	M,D
Music Education	M,D
Music	M,D
Near and Middle Eastern Languages	M,D
Neurobiology	D
Neuroscience	M,D
Nuclear Engineering	M,D
Nursing—General	M,D
Nutrition	M,D
Occupational Therapy	M,D
Oceanography	M,D
Pathology	D*
Pharmaceutical Administration	M,D
Pharmaceutical Sciences	M,D
Pharmacology	M,D*
Pharmacy	P
Philosophy	M,D
Physics	M,D
Physiology	M,D
Plant Pathology	M,D
Plant Sciences	M,D
Political Science	M,D
Polymer Science and Engineering	M,D
Portuguese	M,D
Psychology—General	D
Public Affairs	M
Real Estate	M,D
Recreation and Park Management	M
Rehabilitation Counseling	M,D
Rehabilitation Sciences	M
Rural Sociology	M,D
Scandinavian Languages	M,D
Science Education	M,D
Slavic Languages	M,D
Social Psychology	D
Social Sciences	D
Social Work	M,D
Sociology	M,D
Spanish	M,D
Special Education	M,D
Statistics	M,D
Supply Chain Management	M
Sustainable Development	M
Systems Engineering	M,D
Theater	M,D
Toxicology	M,D
Urban and Regional Planning	M,D
Veterinary Medicine	P
Veterinary Sciences	M,D
Water Resources	M
Zoology	M,D

UNIVERSITY OF WISCONSIN–MILWAUKEE

Allied Health—General	M,D
Anthropology	M,D,O
Architecture	M,D,O
Art Education	M
Art History	M,O
Art/Fine Arts	M
Biological and Biomedical Sciences—General	M,D
Business Administration and Management—General	M,D,O
Chemistry	M,D
Classics	M
Clinical Laboratory Sciences/Medical Technology	M
Clinical Psychology	M,D
Communication Disorders	M
Communication—General	M,O
Comparative Literature	M,D,O
Computer Science	M,D
Criminal Justice and Criminology	M
Curriculum and Instruction	M
Dance	M
Early Childhood Education	M
Economics	M,D
Education—General	M,D,O
Educational Administration	M,O
Educational Policy	M
Educational Psychology	M,O
Elementary Education	M
Engineering and Applied Sciences—General	M,D,O
English	M,D,O
Film, Television, and Video Production	M
Foundations and Philosophy of Education	M
French	M
Geography	M,D
Geology	M,D
German	M
Health Informatics	M
History	M,D
Human Resources Development	M,O
Industrial and Labor Relations	M,O
Information Studies	M,O
Interdisciplinary Studies	D
Italian	M
Jewish Studies	M
Journalism	M
Kinesiology and Movement Studies	M
Liberal Studies	M
Library Science	M,O
Mass Communication	M
Mathematics	M,D
Medical Informatics	D
Middle School Education	M
Museum Studies	M,O
Music	M,O
Nursing—General	M,D,O
Occupational Therapy	M
Philosophy	M
Physics	M,D
Political Science	M,D
Psychology—General	M,D
Public Administration	M
Reading Education	M
School Psychology	O
Secondary Education	M
Slavic Languages	M
Social Work	M,O
Sociology	M
Spanish	M
Special Education	M
Theater	M
Urban and Regional Planning	M,O
Urban Education	M,D
Urban Studies	M,D

UNIVERSITY OF WISCONSIN–OSHKOSH

Adult Nursing	M
Biological and Biomedical Sciences—General	M
Botany	M
Business Administration and Management—General	M
Counselor Education	M
Curriculum and Instruction	M
Early Childhood Education	M
Education—General	M
Educational Administration	M
English	M
Experimental Psychology	M
Family Nurse Practitioner Studies	M
Health Services Management and Hospital Administration	M
Industrial and Organizational Psychology	M
Management Information Systems	M
Mathematics Education	M
Microbiology	M
Nursing—General	M
Political Science	M
Psychology—General	M
Reading Education	M
Social Work	M
Special Education	M
Zoology	M

UNIVERSITY OF WISCONSIN–PARKSIDE

Business Administration and Management—General	M
Computer Science	M
Information Science	M
Molecular Biology	M

UNIVERSITY OF WISCONSIN–PLATTEVILLE

Adult Education	M
Computer Science	M
Counselor Education	M
Criminal Justice and Criminology	M
Education—General	M
Elementary Education	M
Engineering and Applied Sciences—General	M
Middle School Education	M
Project Management	M
Secondary Education	M
Vocational and Technical Education	M

UNIVERSITY OF WISCONSIN–RIVER FALLS

Agricultural Education	M
Agricultural Sciences—General	M
Business Administration and Management—General	M
Communication Disorders	M
Counselor Education	M,O
Education—General	M
Elementary Education	M
Mathematics Education	M
Reading Education	M
School Psychology	M,O
Science Education	M
Social Sciences Education	M

UNIVERSITY OF WISCONSIN–STEVENS POINT

Advertising and Public Relations	M
Business Administration and Management—General	M
Communication Disorders	M,D
Communication—General	M
Corporate and Organizational Communication	M
Counselor Education	M
Education—General	M
Educational Administration	M
Elementary Education	M
English	M
Family and Consumer Sciences-General	M
Health Promotion	M
History	M
Human Development	M
Mass Communication	M
Music Education	M
Natural Resources	M
Nutrition	M
Reading Education	M
Science Education	M
Special Education	M
Speech and Interpersonal Communication	M

UNIVERSITY OF WISCONSIN–STOUT

Child and Family Studies	M
Counseling Psychology	M
Education—General	M,O
Food Science and Technology	M
Human Development	M
Human Resources Development	M
Industrial Hygiene	M
Industrial/Management Engineering	M*
Information Science	M*
Management of Technology	M
Manufacturing Engineering	M
Marriage and Family Therapy	M
Nutrition	M
Psychology—General	M
Rehabilitation Counseling	M
School Psychology	M,O
Telecommunications Management	M
Vocational and Technical Education	M,O

UNIVERSITY OF WISCONSIN–SUPERIOR

Art Education	M
Art History	M
Art Therapy	M
Art/Fine Arts	M
Communication—General	M
Counselor Education	M
Curriculum and Instruction	M
Education—General	M
Educational Administration	M,O

Mass Communication M
Reading Education M
Social Psychology M
Special Education M
Speech and Interpersonal Communication M
Theater M

UNIVERSITY OF WISCONSIN–WHITEWATER

Accounting M
Business Administration and Management—General M*
Business Education M
Communication Disorders M
Communication—General M
Corporate and Organizational Communication M
Counselor Education M
Curriculum and Instruction M
Education—General M
Educational Administration M
Environmental and Occupational Health M
Finance and Banking M
Higher Education M
Human Resources Management M
International Business M
Management of Technology M
Marketing M
Mass Communication M
Psychology—General M,O
Reading Education M
School Psychology M,O
Secondary Education M
Social Psychology M
Special Education M
Supply Chain Management M

UNIVERSITY OF WYOMING

Accounting M
Adult Education M,D,O
Agricultural Economics and Agribusiness M
Agricultural Sciences—General M,D
Agronomy and Soil Sciences M,D
American Studies M
Animal Sciences M,D
Anthropology M,D
Applied Economics M
Atmospheric Sciences M,D
Botany M,D
Business Administration and Management—General M
Chemical Engineering M,D
Chemistry M,D
Civil Engineering M,D
Communication Disorders M,D
Communication—General M
Computer Science M,D
Consumer Economics M
Counselor Education M,D
Curriculum and Instruction M,D
Distance Education Development M,D,O
Economics M,D
Educational Administration M,D,O
Educational Media/Instructional Technology M,D,O
Electrical Engineering M,D
Engineering and Applied Sciences—General M,D
English M
Entomology M,D
Environmental Engineering M
Finance and Banking M
Food Science and Technology M
French M
Geography M
Geology M,D
Geophysics M,D
German M
Health Education M
History M
International Affairs M
Law P
Mathematics Education M,D
Mathematics M,D
Mechanical Engineering M,D
Molecular Biology M,D
Music Education M
Music M
Natural Resources M,D
Neuroscience D
Nursing—General M
Nutrition M
Pathobiology M
Petroleum Engineering M,D
Pharmacy P
Philosophy M
Physical Education M
Physiology M,D
Political Science M
Psychology—General M,D
Public Administration M
Range Science M,D
Reproductive Biology M,D
Rural Planning and Studies M
Science Education M
Social Work M
Sociology M
Spanish M
Special Education M,O
Statistics M,D
Water Resources M,D
Writing M
Zoology M,D

UPPER IOWA UNIVERSITY

Accounting M
Business Administration and Management—General M
Criminal Justice and Criminology M
Finance and Banking M
Homeland Security M
Human Resources Management M
Human Services M
International Business M
Organizational Management M
Public Administration M
Quality Management M

URBANA UNIVERSITY

Business Administration and Management—General M
Education—General M

URSULINE COLLEGE

Art Therapy M
Business Administration and Management—General M
Education—General M
Educational Administration M
Historic Preservation M
Liberal Studies M
Nursing—General M
Theology M

UTAH STATE UNIVERSITY

Accounting M
Aerospace/Aeronautical Engineering M,D
Agricultural Education M
Agricultural Engineering M,D
Agricultural Sciences—General M,D
Agronomy and Soil Sciences M,D
American Studies M
Animal Sciences M,D
Applied Economics M
Applied Mathematics M,D
Art/Fine Arts M
Biochemistry M,D
Biological and Biomedical Sciences—General M,D
Business Administration and Management—General M
Business Education M,D
Chemistry M,D
Child and Family Studies M,D
Civil Engineering M,D,O
Clinical Psychology M,D
Communication Disorders M,D,O
Communication—General M
Computer Science M,D
Consumer Economics M,D
Counseling Psychology M,D
Counselor Education M,D
Curriculum and Instruction D
Disability Studies M,D,O
Ecology M,D
Economics M,D
Education—General M,D,O
Educational Measurement and Evaluation M,D
Educational Media/Instructional Technology M,D,O
Electrical Engineering M,D
Elementary Education M
Engineering and Applied Sciences—General M,D,O
English M
Environmental Engineering M,D,O
Environmental Management and Policy M,D
Family and Consumer Sciences-General M,D
Fish, Game, and Wildlife Management M,D
Folklore M
Food Science and Technology M,D
Forestry M,D
Geography M,D
Geology M
Health Education M
History M
Home Economics Education M
Human Development M,D
Human Resources Management M
Interior Design M
Landscape Architecture M
Management Information Systems M,D
Marriage and Family Therapy M,D
Mathematics M,D
Mechanical Engineering M,D
Meteorology M,D
Microbiology M,D
Molecular Biology M,D
Multilingual and Multicultural Education M
Natural Resources M
Nutrition M,D
Physical Education M
Physics M,D
Plant Sciences M,D
Political Science M
Psychology—General M,D
Range Science M,D
Recreation and Park Management M,D
Rehabilitation Counseling M
School Psychology M,D
Secondary Education M
Sociology M,D
Special Education M,D,O
Statistics M,D
Theater M
Toxicology M,D
Urban and Regional Planning M,D
Veterinary Sciences M,D
Vocational and Technical Education M
Water Resources Engineering M,D
Water Resources M,D
Writing M

UTICA COLLEGE

Accounting M
Criminal Justice and Criminology M
Education—General M,O
Liberal Studies M
Occupational Therapy M
Physical Therapy D

VALDOSTA STATE UNIVERSITY

Adult Education M,D
Business Administration and Management—General M
Business Education M,D
Clinical Psychology M,O
Communication Disorders M,O
Counseling Psychology M,O
Counselor Education M,O
Criminal Justice and Criminology M
Curriculum and Instruction M,D,O
Early Childhood Education M,O
Education—General M,D,O
Educational Administration M,D,O
Educational Media/Instructional Technology M,D,O
English M
Health Education M
History M
Industrial and Organizational Psychology M,O
Information Studies M
Library Science M
Marriage and Family Therapy M
Middle School Education M,O
Music Education M
Music M
Nursing—General M
Physical Education M
Psychology—General M,O
Public Administration M,D
Reading Education M,O
School Psychology M,O
Secondary Education M,O
Social Work M
Sociology M
Special Education M,O
Vocational and Technical Education M,D

VALPARAISO UNIVERSITY

Asian Studies M
Business Administration and Management—General M,O
Clinical Psychology M,O
Counseling Psychology M,O
Education—General M
Engineering Management M,O
English M,O
Ethics M,O
Gerontology M,O
History M,O
International Business M
Law P,M
Liberal Studies M,O
Nursing—General M,O
Psychology—General M,O
School Psychology
Sports Management M
Theology M,O

VANCOUVER SCHOOL OF THEOLOGY

Theology P,M,D,O

VANDERBILT UNIVERSITY

Acute Care/Critical Care Nursing M,D
Adult Nursing M,D
Allopathic Medicine M,D
Analytical Chemistry M,D
Anthropology M,D
Astronomy M,D
Biochemistry M,D
Bioinformatics M,D
Biological and Biomedical Sciences—General M,D*
Biomedical Engineering M,D*
Biophysics M,D
Business Administration and Management—General M,D
Cancer Biology/Oncology M,D
Cell Biology M,D
Chemical Engineering M,D
Chemistry M,D
Child and Family Studies M
Civil Engineering M,D
Classics M
Clinical Research M
Communication Disorders M,D
Computer Science M,D
Counselor Education M
Curriculum and Instruction M,D
Early Childhood Education M,D
Economics P,M,D
Education—General M,D*
Educational Administration M,D
Educational Measurement and Evaluation M,D
Educational Policy M,D
Electrical Engineering M,D
Elementary Education M,D
Engineering and Applied Sciences—General M,D*
English Education M,D
English M,D
Environmental Engineering M,D
Environmental Management and Policy M,D
Environmental Sciences M
Family Nurse Practitioner Studies M,D
Finance and Banking M,D
Foreign Languages Education M,D
Forensic Nursing M,D
French M,D
German M,D
Gerontological Nursing M,D
Higher Education M,D
History M,D
Human Development M
Human Resources Development M,D
Immunology M,D
Inorganic Chemistry M,D
International and Comparative Education M,D
Latin American Studies M
Law P,M,D
Liberal Studies M
Marketing D
Materials Sciences M,D
Maternal and Child/Neonatal Nursing M,D
Mathematics Education M,D
Mathematics M,D
Mechanical Engineering M,D
Medical Physics M
Medical/Surgical Nursing M,D
Microbiology M,D
Molecular Biology M,D
Molecular Biophysics
Molecular Physiology M,D
Multilingual and Multicultural Education M,D
Neuroscience D
Nurse Midwifery M,D
Nursing and Healthcare Administration M,D
Nursing Informatics M,D
Nursing—General M,D
Organic Chemistry M,D
Organizational Management M,D
Pathology D
Pediatric Nursing M,D
Pharmacology D
Philosophy M,D
Physical Chemistry M,D
Physics M,D
Political Science M,D
Portuguese M,D
Psychiatric Nursing M,D
Psychology—General M,D
Public Health—General M
Public Policy M,D
Reading Education M,D
Religion M,D
Science Education M,D
Secondary Education M,D
Sociology M,D
Spanish M,D
Special Education M,D
Theology P,M
Theoretical Chemistry M,D
Toxicology M
Urban and Regional Planning M
Women's Health Nursing M,D
Writing M

VANDERCOOK COLLEGE OF MUSIC

Music Education M

VANGUARD UNIVERSITY OF SOUTHERN CALIFORNIA

Program	Degrees
Business Administration and Management—General	M
Clinical Psychology	M
Education—General	M
Religion	M
Theology	M

VASSAR COLLEGE

Program	Degrees
Chemistry	M

VERMONT LAW SCHOOL

Program	Degrees
Environmental Management and Policy	M
Law	P
Legal and Justice Studies	M

VICTORIA UNIVERSITY

Program	Degrees
Theology	P,M,D,O

VILLA JULIE COLLEGE

Program	Degrees
Forensic Sciences	M
Information Science	M
Management of Technology	M

VILLANOVA UNIVERSITY

Program	Degrees
Accounting	M
Adult Nursing	M,D,O
Applied Statistics	M
Artificial Intelligence/Robotics	M,O
Biological and Biomedical Sciences—General	M*
Business Administration and Management—General	M
Chemical Engineering	M
Chemistry	M*
Civil Engineering	M
Classics	M
Communication—General	M
Computer Engineering	M,O
Computer Science	M,O*
Counselor Education	M*
Criminal Justice and Criminology	M
Education—General	M*
Educational Administration	M
Electrical Engineering	M,O
Elementary Education	M
Engineering and Applied Sciences—General	M,D,O
English	M*
Environmental Engineering	M
Finance and Banking	M
Gerontological Nursing	M,D,O
Health Services Management and Hospital Administration	M,D,O
Hispanic Studies	M
History	M*
Human Resources Development	M
Interdisciplinary Studies	D
Law	P
Liberal Studies	M
Management of Technology	M
Manufacturing Engineering	M,O
Mathematics	M
Mechanical Engineering	M,O
Nurse Anesthesia	M,D,O
Nursing and Healthcare Administration	M,D,O
Nursing Education	M,D,O
Nursing—General	M,D,O*
Pediatric Nursing	M,D,O
Philosophy	D
Political Science	M*
Psychology—General	M*
Public Administration	M
Secondary Education	M
Taxation	M
Theater	M*
Theology	M
Transportation and Highway Engineering	M
Water Resources Engineering	M

Close-Up on page 1133.

VIRGINIA COLLEGE AT BIRMINGHAM

Program	Degrees
Business Administration and Management—General	M
Criminal Justice and Criminology	M

VIRGINIA COMMONWEALTH UNIVERSITY

Program	Degrees
Accounting	M,D*
Adult Education	M*
Adult Nursing	M,D,O
Advertising and Public Relations	M
Allied Health—General	D*
Allopathic Medicine	P
Analytical Chemistry	M,D
Anatomy	M,D,O*
Applied Arts and Design—General	M*
Applied Mathematics	M,O
Applied Physics	M,D
Applied Social Research	M,O
Architectural History	M,D
Art Education	M*
Art History	M,D*
Art/Fine Arts	M,D*
Athletic Training and Sports Medicine	M,D*
Biochemistry	M,D,O*
Bioengineering	M,D
Bioinformatics	M*
Biological and Biomedical Sciences—General	M,D,O*
Biomedical Engineering	M,D
Biostatistics	M,D*
Business Administration and Management—General	M,D*
Chemical Engineering	M,D
Chemical Physics	M,D
Chemistry	M,D*
Clinical Laboratory Sciences/Medical Technology	M,D*
Clinical Psychology	D*
Communication—General	D
Community Health	D
Computer Science	M,D,O
Counseling Psychology	M,D,O*
Counselor Education	M*
Criminal Justice and Criminology	M,O*
Curriculum and Instruction	M,O*
Dentistry	P*
Early Childhood Education	M,O
Economics	M*
Education—General	M,D,O*
Educational Administration	D*
Educational Measurement and Evaluation	D
Electrical Engineering	M,D
Emergency Management	M,O
Engineering and Applied Sciences—General	M,D,O*
English	M*
Environmental and Occupational Health	M
Environmental Management and Policy	M
Environmental Sciences	M*
Epidemiology	D*
Exercise and Sports Science	M,D*
Family Nurse Practitioner Studies	M,O
Finance and Banking	M
Forensic Sciences	M*
Gender Studies	M,O*
Genetic Counseling	M,D*
Genetics	M,D
Geographic Information Systems	M,O*
Gerontology	M,D,O*
Health Education	M,D
Health Physics/Radiological Health	D
Health Services Management and Hospital Administration	M,D*
Health Services Research	D*
Historic Preservation	M,O*
History	M,D*
Homeland Security	M,O*
Human Genetics	M,D,O*
Human Resources Development	M
Immunology	M,D
Inorganic Chemistry	M,D
Insurance	M
Interdisciplinary Studies	M*
Interior Design	M
Internet and Interactive Multimedia	M,D,O
Journalism	M
Management Information Systems	M,D*
Marketing	O
Mass Communication	M*
Mathematics	M,O*
Mechanical Engineering	M,D
Media Studies	D*
Medical Physics	M,D*
Microbiology	M,D,O*
Middle School Education	M,O
Molecular Biology	M,D*
Molecular Biophysics	M,D
Museum Studies	M,D
Music Education	M*
Music	M
Neurobiology	D
Neuroscience	M,D*
Nonprofit Management	O*
Nurse Anesthesia	M,D*
Nursing and Healthcare Administration	M,D,O
Nursing—General	M,D,O*
Occupational Therapy	M,D*
Operations Research	M,O
Organic Chemistry	M,D
Pathology	M,D*
Pediatric Nursing	M,D,O
Pharmaceutical Sciences	P,M,D*
Pharmacology	M,D,O*
Pharmacy	P
Photography	M
Physical Chemistry	M,D
Physical Education	M,D
Physical Therapy	M,D*
Physics	M,D*
Physiology	M,D,O*
Psychiatric Nursing	M,D,O
Psychology—General	D*
Public Administration	M,O*
Public Health—General	M,D*
Public Policy	D*
Quantitative Analysis	M
Reading Education	M*
Real Estate	M,O*
Recreation and Park Management	M*
Rehabilitation Counseling	M,O*
Rehabilitation Sciences	M,D*
Rhetoric	M
Secondary Education	M,O
Social Sciences Education	M,O
Social Work	M,D*
Sociology	M,O*
Special Education	M*
Statistics	M,O
Taxation	M,D*
Theater	M*
Toxicology	M,D
Urban and Regional Planning	M,O*
Urban Education	D
Women's Health Nursing	M,D,O
Writing	M*

Close-Up on page 1135.

VIRGINIA POLYTECHNIC INSTITUTE AND STATE UNIVERSITY

Program	Degrees
Accounting	M,D*
Adult Education	M,D,O
Aerospace/Aeronautical Engineering	M,D
Agricultural Economics and Agribusiness	M,D
Agricultural Engineering	M,D
Agricultural Sciences—General	M,D
Agronomy and Soil Sciences	M,D
Animal Sciences	M,D
Applied Arts and Design—General	M
Applied Economics	M,D
Applied Mathematics	M,D
Applied Physics	M,D
Architecture	M*
Arts Administration	M
Biochemistry	M,D*
Bioengineering	M,D
Bioinformatics	D
Biological and Biomedical Sciences—General	M,D
Biomedical Engineering	M,D
Botany	M,D
Business Administration and Management—General	M,D
Chemical Engineering	M,D
Chemistry	M,D
Child and Family Studies	M,D
Child Development	M,D
Civil Engineering	M,D*
Clinical Psychology	M,D
Clothing and Textiles	M,D
Communication—General	M
Computational Biology	D
Computer Engineering	M,D
Computer Science	M,D*
Construction Engineering	M
Consumer Economics	M,D
Counselor Education	M,D,O
Curriculum and Instruction	M,D,O
Developmental Biology	M,D
Developmental Psychology	M,D
Ecology	M,D
Economics	M,D
Educational Administration	D,O
Educational Measurement and Evaluation	D
Educational Media/Instructional Technology	M
Electrical Engineering	M,D
Engineering and Applied Sciences—General	M,D
Engineering Management	M,D
English	M,D
Entomology	M,D
Environmental Design	D
Environmental Engineering	M,D
Environmental Sciences	M,D
Evolutionary Biology	M,D
Finance and Banking	M,D
Fish, Game, and Wildlife Management	M,D
Food Science and Technology	M,D
Forestry	M,D
Genetics	M,D
Geography	M,D
Geology	M,D
Geophysics	M,D
Geosciences	M,D
Gerontology	M,D
Health Education	M,D,O
History of Science and Technology	M,D
History	M
Horticulture	M,D
Hospitality Management	M,D
Human Development	M,D
Human Resources Development	M,D
Industrial and Organizational Psychology	M,D
Industrial/Management Engineering	M,D
Information Science	M
Interdisciplinary Studies	M,D
Interior Design	M,D
International Affairs	M
Landscape Architecture	M
Logistics	M,D
Management Information Systems	M,D
Marketing	M,D
Marriage and Family Therapy	M,D
Materials Engineering	M,D
Materials Sciences	M,D
Mathematical Physics	M,D
Mathematics	M,D
Mechanical Engineering	M,D
Mechanics	M,D
Microbiology	M,D
Mineral/Mining Engineering	M,D
Natural Resources	M
Nutrition	M,D
Ocean Engineering	M,D
Operations Research	M,D
Philosophy	M
Physical Education	M,D,O
Physics	M,D
Plant Pathology	M,D
Plant Physiology	M,D
Political Science	M
Psychology—General	M,D
Public Administration	M,D,O
Public Policy	M,D,O
Recreation and Park Management	M,D
Sociology	M,D
Special Education	D,O
Statistics	M,D
Systems Engineering	M
Theater	M
Travel and Tourism	M,D
Urban and Regional Planning	M
Veterinary Medicine	P
Veterinary Sciences	M,D
Vocational and Technical Education	M,D,O
Zoology	M,D

VIRGINIA STATE UNIVERSITY

Program	Degrees
Biological and Biomedical Sciences—General	M
Counselor Education	M
Economics	M
Education—General	M,O
Educational Administration	M
English	M
History	M
Interdisciplinary Studies	M
Mathematics Education	M
Mathematics	M
Physics	M
Psychology—General	M
Vocational and Technical Education	M,O

VIRGINIA UNION UNIVERSITY

Program	Degrees
Theology	P,D

VIRGINIA UNIVERSITY OF LYNCHBURG

Program	Degrees
Religion	P

VITERBO UNIVERSITY

Program	Degrees
Education—General	M
Nursing—General	M

WAGNER COLLEGE

Program	Degrees
Accounting	M
Biological and Biomedical Sciences—General	M
Business Administration and Management—General	M
Early Childhood Education	M
Education—General	M,O
Educational Administration	O
Elementary Education	M
Family Nurse Practitioner Studies	O
Finance and Banking	M
Health Services Management and Hospital Administration	M
International Business	M
Marketing	M
Microbiology	M
Middle School Education	M
Nursing—General	M
Physician Assistant Studies	M
Reading Education	M
Secondary Education	M

WAKE FOREST UNIVERSITY

Program	Degrees
Accounting	M
Allopathic Medicine	P

- Analytical Chemistry M,D
- Anatomy D
- Biochemistry D
- Biological and Biomedical Sciences—General M,D
- Biomedical Engineering M,D
- Business Administration and Management—General M
- Cancer Biology/Oncology D*
- Chemistry M,D
- Communication—General M
- Computer Science M
- Counselor Education M
- Education—General M
- English M
- Exercise and Sports Science M
- Genomic Sciences D
- Health Services Research M
- Human Genetics D
- Immunology D
- Inorganic Chemistry M,D
- Law P,M
- Liberal Studies M
- Mathematics M
- Microbiology D*
- Molecular Biology D
- Molecular Genetics D*
- Molecular Medicine M,D
- Neurobiology D
- Neuroscience D
- Organic Chemistry M,D
- Pastoral Ministry and Counseling M
- Pathobiology M,D*
- Pharmacology D
- Physical Chemistry M,D
- Physics M,D*
- Physiology D
- Psychology—General M
- Religion M
- Secondary Education M
- Speech and Interpersonal Communication M

Close-Up on page 1137.

WALDEN UNIVERSITY

- Adult Education M,D
- Business Administration and Management—General M,D,O
- Community College Education M,D
- Computer Engineering M,O
- Computer Science M,O
- Counseling Psychology M,D
- Curriculum and Instruction M,D
- Early Childhood Education M,D
- Educational Administration M,D
- Educational Media/Instructional Technology M,D
- Electrical Engineering M,O
- Elementary Education M,D
- Engineering and Applied Sciences—General M,O
- Engineering Management M,D,O
- Finance and Banking M,D
- Health Services Management and Hospital Administration M,D
- Higher Education M,D
- Human Resources Management M,D
- Human Services M,D
- Management Information Systems M,D
- Management of Technology M,D
- Marketing M,D
- Mathematics Education M,D
- Middle School Education M,D
- Nursing—General M,D
- Organizational Management M,D
- Public Administration M,D
- Public Health—General M,D
- Quantitative Analysis M,D
- Reading Education M,D
- Science Education M,D
- Software Engineering M,O
- Special Education M,D
- Systems Engineering M,O

Close-Up on page 1139.

WALLA WALLA COLLEGE

- Biological and Biomedical Sciences—General M
- Counseling Psychology M
- Curriculum and Instruction M
- Education—General M
- Educational Administration M
- Reading Education M
- Social Work M
- Special Education M

WALSH COLLEGE OF ACCOUNTANCY AND BUSINESS ADMINISTRATION

- Accounting M
- Business Administration and Management—General M
- Economics M
- Finance and Banking M
- Management Information Systems M
- Taxation M

WALSH UNIVERSITY

- Business Administration and Management—General M
- Counseling Psychology M
- Counselor Education M
- Education—General M
- Physical Therapy M
- Theology M

WARNER PACIFIC COLLEGE

- Business Administration and Management—General M
- Education—General M
- Ethics M
- Organizational Management M
- Pastoral Ministry and Counseling M
- Religion M
- Theology M

WARNER SOUTHERN COLLEGE

- Business Administration and Management—General M

WARREN WILSON COLLEGE

- Writing M

WARTBURG THEOLOGICAL SEMINARY

- Theology P,M

WASHBURN UNIVERSITY

- Business Administration and Management—General M
- Clinical Psychology M
- Criminal Justice and Criminology M
- Curriculum and Instruction M
- Education—General M
- Educational Administration M
- Law P
- Liberal Studies M
- Psychology—General M
- Reading Education M
- Social Work M
- Special Education M

WASHINGTON AND LEE UNIVERSITY

- Law P,M

WASHINGTON COLLEGE

- English M
- History M
- Psychology—General M

WASHINGTON STATE UNIVERSITY

- Accounting M,D
- Agricultural Economics and Agribusiness M,D,O
- Agricultural Engineering M,D
- Agricultural Sciences—General M
- Agronomy and Soil Sciences M,D
- American Studies M,D
- Animal Sciences M,D
- Anthropology M,D
- Applied Economics M,D,O
- Applied Mathematics M,D
- Archaeology M,D
- Architecture M
- Art/Fine Arts M
- Asian Studies M,D
- Biochemistry M,D
- Bioengineering M,D
- Biological and Biomedical Sciences—General M
- Biophysics M,D
- Botany M,D
- Business Administration and Management—General M,D*
- Cell Biology M,D
- Chemical Engineering M,D
- Chemistry M,D
- Civil Engineering M,D
- Clinical Psychology M,D
- Clothing and Textiles M,D
- Communication—General M,D
- Computer Art and Design M
- Computer Engineering M,D
- Computer Science M,D
- Corporate and Organizational Communication M,D
- Counseling Psychology M,D
- Criminal Justice and Criminology M,D
- Cultural Studies M,D
- Curriculum and Instruction M,D
- Demography and Population Studies M,D
- Economics M,D,O
- Education—General M,D
- Educational Administration M,D
- Educational Psychology M,D
- Electrical Engineering M,D
- Elementary Education M,D
- Engineering and Applied Sciences—General M,D
- English Education M,D
- English M,D
- Entomology M,D
- Environmental Engineering M
- Environmental Sciences M,D*
- Ethnic Studies M,D
- Exercise and Sports Science M,D
- Experimental Psychology M,D
- Finance and Banking M,D
- Food Science and Technology M,D
- Genetics M,D
- Geology M,D
- Geosciences M,D
- Health Communication M,D
- Health Services Management and Hospital Administration M
- Higher Education M,D
- History M,D
- Horticulture M,D
- Human Development M
- Industrial and Manufacturing Management M,D
- Insurance D
- Interdisciplinary Studies D
- Interior Design M,D
- International Affairs M,D
- International Business M,D,O
- Landscape Architecture M,D
- Management Information Systems M,D
- Marketing M,D
- Materials Engineering M
- Materials Sciences M,D
- Mathematics Education M,D
- Mathematics M,D*
- Mechanical Engineering M,D
- Media Studies M,D
- Microbiology M,D
- Molecular Biology M,D
- Multilingual and Multicultural Education M,D
- Music Education M
- Music M
- Natural Resources M,D
- Neuroscience M,D
- Nutrition M,D
- Pathology M,D
- Pharmacology M,D
- Pharmacy P
- Philosophy M
- Photography M
- Physics M,D
- Plant Molecular Biology M,D
- Plant Pathology M,D
- Political Science M,D
- Psychology—General M,D
- Public History M,D
- Public Policy M,D
- Reading Education M,D
- Real Estate D
- Secondary Education M,D
- Social Psychology M,D
- Sociology M,D
- Spanish M
- Sports Management M,D
- Statistics M
- Student Affairs M,D
- Taxation M
- Toxicology M,D
- Veterinary Medicine P
- Veterinary Sciences M,D
- Western European Studies M,D
- Women's Studies M,D
- Zoology M,D

WASHINGTON STATE UNIVERSITY SPOKANE

- Architecture M,D
- Communication Disorders M
- Criminal Justice and Criminology M,D
- Education—General M,O
- Educational Administration M,O
- Engineering Management M
- Exercise and Sports Science M,O
- Health Services Management and Hospital Administration M
- Interior Design M,D
- Landscape Architecture M,D
- Nursing—General M
- Pharmacy P
- Physiology M,O

WASHINGTON STATE UNIVERSITY TRI-CITIES

- Atmospheric Sciences M,D
- Biological and Biomedical Sciences—General M
- Business Administration and Management—General M
- Chemistry M,D
- Computer Engineering M,D
- Computer Science M,D
- Counselor Education M,D
- Education—General M,D
- Educational Administration M,D
- Electrical Engineering M,D
- Engineering and Applied Sciences—General M,D
- Environmental and Occupational Health M,D
- Environmental Sciences M,D
- Geosciences M,D
- Management of Technology M
- Mechanical Engineering M,D
- Nursing—General M
- Reading Education M,D
- Secondary Education M,D
- Toxicology M,D
- Water Resources M,D

WASHINGTON STATE UNIVERSITY VANCOUVER

- Business Administration and Management—General M
- Computer Science M
- Education—General M,D
- Engineering and Applied Sciences—General M
- Environmental Sciences M
- History M,D
- Mechanical Engineering M
- Nursing—General M
- Public Affairs M

WASHINGTON THEOLOGICAL UNION

- Theology P,M

WASHINGTON UNIVERSITY IN ST. LOUIS

- Accounting M
- Allied Health—General M,D,O
- Allopathic Medicine P
- Anthropology M,D
- Archaeology M,D
- Architecture M*
- Art History M,D
- Art/Fine Arts M
- Asian Languages M,D
- Asian Studies M,D*
- Biochemistry D
- Biological and Biomedical Sciences—General D
- Biomedical Engineering M,D
- Business Administration and Management—General M,D*
- Cell Biology D
- Chemical Engineering M,D
- Chemistry M,D
- Chinese M,D
- Civil Engineering M,D
- Classics M
- Clinical Psychology M,D
- Clinical Research M
- Communication Disorders M,D
- Comparative Literature M,D
- Computational Biology D
- Computer Engineering M,D
- Computer Science M,D*
- Construction Management M
- Developmental Biology D
- Ecology D
- Economics M,D*
- Education—General M,D*
- Educational Measurement and Evaluation D
- Electrical Engineering M,D*
- Elementary Education M
- Engineering and Applied Sciences—General M,D
- English M,D
- Environmental Biology D
- Environmental Engineering M,D
- Evolutionary Biology D
- Experimental Psychology M,D
- Finance and Banking M
- French M,D
- Genetics M,D,O
- Geochemistry M,D
- Geology M,D
- Geophysics M,D
- Geosciences M,D
- German M,D
- Health Services Management and Hospital Administration M
- History M,D
- Immunology D
- Japanese M,D
- Jewish Studies M
- Kinesiology and Movement Studies D
- Law P,M,D
- Mathematics Education M,D
- Mathematics M,D
- Mechanical Engineering M,D*
- Microbiology D
- Molecular Biology D
- Molecular Biophysics D
- Molecular Genetics D
- Molecular Pathogenesis D
- Music M,D
- Near and Middle Eastern Studies M
- Neuroscience D
- Occupational Therapy M,D
- Philosophy M,D
- Physical Therapy D,O
- Physics M,D
- Planetary and Space Sciences M,D
- Plant Biology D
- Political Science M,D
- Psychology—General M,D
- Public Policy M

Religion M
Romance Languages M,D
Secondary Education M
Social Psychology M,D
Social Work M,D*
Spanish M,D
Special Education M,D
Speech and Interpersonal Communication M,D
Statistics M,D
Structural Engineering M,D
Systems Science M,D
Theater M
Urban Design M
Writing M

Close-Up on page 1141.

WAYLAND BAPTIST UNIVERSITY

Business Administration and Management—General M
Counseling Psychology M
Criminal Justice and Criminology M
Education—General M
Health Services Management and Hospital Administration M
Human Resources Management M
Interdisciplinary Studies M
International Business M
Management Information Systems M
Organizational Management M
Pastoral Ministry and Counseling M
Public Administration M
Religion M

WAYNESBURG COLLEGE

Business Administration and Management—General M

WAYNE STATE COLLEGE

Accounting M
Business Administration and Management—General M
Business Education M
Communication—General M
Counselor Education M
Early Childhood Education M
Education—General M,O
Educational Administration M,O
Elementary Education M
English as a Second Language M
English Education M
Exercise and Sports Science M
Home Economics Education M
Mathematics Education M
Music Education M
Physical Education M
Science Education M
Social Sciences Education M
Special Education M
Vocational and Technical Education M

WAYNE STATE UNIVERSITY

Accounting M,D
Acute Care/Critical Care Nursing M
Addictions/Substance Abuse Counseling O
Adult Education M,D,O
Adult Nursing M
Advertising and Public Relations M,D
Allopathic Medicine P
Anatomy M,D
Anthropology M,D
Applied Arts and Design—General M
Applied Mathematics M,D
Art Education M,D,O
Art History M
Art/Fine Arts M
Biochemistry M,D
Biological and Biomedical Sciences—General M,D
Biomedical Engineering M,D
Biopsychology M,D
Business Administration and Management—General M,D*
Business Education M,D,O
Cancer Biology/Oncology M,D*
Chemical Engineering M,D
Chemistry M,D
Child and Family Studies O
Civil Engineering M,D
Classics M
Clinical Laboratory Sciences/Medical Technology M,O
Clinical Psychology M,D,O
Cognitive Sciences M,D
Communication Disorders M,D
Communication—General M,D
Community Health Nursing M
Community Health M,O
Comparative Literature M
Computer Engineering M,D
Computer Science M,D,O
Conflict Resolution and Mediation/Peace Studies M,O
Corporate and Organizational Communication M,D
Counselor Education M,D,O
Criminal Justice and Criminology M
Curriculum and Instruction M,D,O
Developmental Psychology M,D
Early Childhood Education M,D,O
Economics M,D,O
Education—General M,D,O*
Educational Administration M,D,O
Educational Measurement and Evaluation M,D,O
Educational Media/Instructional Technology M,D,O
Educational Policy M,D,O
Educational Psychology M,D,O
Electrical Engineering M,D
Elementary Education M,D,O
Engineering and Applied Sciences—General M,D,O*
Engineering Management M
English Education M,D,O
English M,D
Environmental and Occupational Health M,O
Food Science and Technology M,D
Foreign Languages Education M,D,O
Foundations and Philosophy of Education M,D,O
French M
Genetics M,D*
Geography M
Geology M
German M,D
Gerontology O
Hazardous Materials Management M,O
Health Education M,D,O
Health Physics/Radiological Health M,D
Higher Education M,D,O
History M,D
Human Development M
Human Services O
Immunology M,D
Industrial and Labor Relations M
Industrial and Organizational Psychology M,D
Industrial/Management Engineering M,D
Information Studies M,O
Interdisciplinary Studies M,D
Italian M
Kinesiology and Movement Studies M
Law P,M,D
Library Science M,O
Linguistics M
Manufacturing Engineering M
Materials Engineering M,D,O
Materials Sciences M,D,O
Maternal and Child/Neonatal Nursing M,O
Mathematics Education M,D,O
Mathematics M,D
Mechanical Engineering M,D
Media Studies M,D
Medical Physics M,D
Medicinal and Pharmaceutical Chemistry P,M,D
Metallurgical Engineering and Metallurgy M,D,O
Microbiology M,D
Molecular Biology M,D*
Multilingual and Multicultural Education M,D,O
Music Education M,O
Music M,O
Near and Middle Eastern Studies M
Neurobiology D
Neuroscience M,D
Nurse Anesthesia M,O
Nursing Education M,O
Nursing—General D
Nutrition M,D
Occupational Therapy M
Pathology M,D
Pediatric Nursing M,O
Pharmaceutical Administration P,M,D,O
Pharmaceutical Sciences P,M,D,O
Pharmacology P,M,D
Pharmacy P,M,D,O
Philosophy M,D
Physical Education M
Physical Therapy M
Physician Assistant Studies M
Physics M,D
Physiology M,D
Political Science M,D
Polymer Science and Engineering M,D,O
Psychiatric Nursing M,O
Psychology—General M,D*
Public Administration M
Public Health—General M,O
Reading Education M,D,O
Recreation and Park Management M
Rehabilitation Counseling M,D,O
Rehabilitation Sciences M,O
Romance Languages M,D
Russian M,D
School Psychology M,D,O
Science Education M,D,O
Secondary Education M,D,O
Social Sciences Education M,D,O
Social Work M,D,O
Sociology M,D
Spanish M
Special Education M,D,O
Speech and Interpersonal Communication M,D
Sports Management M
Statistics M,D
Taxation M,D
Theater M,D
Toxicology M,D*
Urban and Regional Planning M
Vocational and Technical Education M,D,O
Writing M,D

WEBBER INTERNATIONAL UNIVERSITY

Accounting M
Business Administration and Management—General M*
Sports Management M

WEBER STATE UNIVERSITY

Accounting M
Business Administration and Management—General M
Curriculum and Instruction M
Education—General M
English M
Health Services Management and Hospital Administration M
Legal and Justice Studies M

WEBSTER UNIVERSITY

Advertising and Public Relations M
Aerospace/Aeronautical Engineering M,D
Art/Fine Arts M
Arts Administration M
Business Administration and Management—General M,D
Communication—General M
Computer Science M,O
Corporate and Organizational Communication M
Counseling Psychology M
Criminal Justice and Criminology M,D
Early Childhood Education M
Education—General M,O
Educational Administration M,O
Educational Media/Instructional Technology M,O
Engineering Management M
English as a Second Language M
Environmental Management and Policy M,D
Finance and Banking M
Gerontology M
Health Services Management and Hospital Administration M,D
Human Resources Development M,D
Human Resources Management M,D
International Affairs M
International Business M
Legal and Justice Studies M
Management Information Systems M,D,O
Marketing M,D
Mathematics Education M,O
Media Studies M
Music Education M
Music M
Nurse Anesthesia M
Nursing—General M
Organizational Management M
Public Administration M,D
Quality Management M,D
Social Sciences Education M,O
Special Education M,O
Telecommunications Management M,D

WESLEYAN COLLEGE

Business Administration and Management—General M
Early Childhood Education M
Education—General M
Mathematics Education M
Middle School Education M
Science Education M

WESLEYAN UNIVERSITY

Astronomy M
Biochemistry M,D
Biological and Biomedical Sciences—General D
Cell Biology D
Chemical Physics M,D
Chemistry M,D*
Developmental Biology D
Evolutionary Biology D
Genetics D
Geosciences M
Inorganic Chemistry M,D
Liberal Studies M,O
Mathematics M,D*
Molecular Biology D
Music M,D
Neurobiology D
Organic Chemistry M,D
Physics M,D
Physiology D
Psychology—General M
Theoretical Chemistry M,D

WESLEY BIBLICAL SEMINARY

Marriage and Family Therapy P,M
Missions and Missiology P,M
Pastoral Ministry and Counseling P,M
Theology P,M

WESLEY COLLEGE

Business Administration and Management—General M
Education—General M
Environmental Management and Policy M
Nursing—General M

WESLEY THEOLOGICAL SEMINARY

Theology P,M,D

WEST CHESTER UNIVERSITY OF PENNSYLVANIA

Anthropology M,O
Astronomy M
Athletic Training and Sports Medicine M
Biological and Biomedical Sciences—General M
Business Administration and Management—General M
Chemistry M
Classics M
Clinical Psychology M
Communication Disorders M
Communication—General M
Computer Science M,O
Counselor Education M
Criminal Justice and Criminology M
Economics M
Education—General M,O
Educational Measurement and Evaluation M
Educational Media/Instructional Technology M,O
Electronic Commerce M
Elementary Education M
Emergency Management M,O
English as a Second Language M
English M
Environmental and Occupational Health M,O
Exercise and Sports Science M,O
Finance and Banking M
Foreign Languages Education M
French M
Geography M
Geology M
German M
Gerontology M,O
Health Education M,O
Health Psychology M,O
Health Services Management and Hospital Administration M,O
History M
Industrial and Organizational Psychology M
Kinesiology and Movement Studies M,O
Mathematics M
Music Education M
Music M
Nursing Education M
Nursing—General M
Philosophy M
Physical Education M,O
Psychology—General M
Public Administration M
Public Health—General M,O
Reading Education M
Science Education M
Secondary Education M
Social Work M
Sociology M,O
Spanish M
Special Education M
Sports Management M,O
Urban and Regional Planning M

Close-Up on page 1143.

WESTERN CAROLINA UNIVERSITY

Accounting M
American Studies M
Art Education M
Art/Fine Arts M
Biological and Biomedical Sciences—General M
Business Administration and Management—General M
Chemistry M
Clinical Psychology M
Communication Disorders M
Community College Education M
Computer Science M
Construction Management M
Counselor Education M
Education—General M,D,O
Educational Administration M,D,O
Elementary Education M
English Education M
English M
Entrepreneurship M*
Health Services Management and Hospital Administration M
History M
Home Economics Education M
Human Resources Development M
Industrial/Management Engineering M
Mathematics Education M
Mathematics M
Middle School Education M
Music Education M
Music M
Nursing—General M
Physical Education M
Physical Therapy M
Project Management M
Psychology—General M
Public Affairs M
Reading Education M
School Psychology M
Science Education M
Secondary Education M
Social Psychology M
Social Sciences Education M
Special Education M

WESTERN CONNECTICUT STATE UNIVERSITY

Accounting M
Adult Nursing M
Art/Fine Arts M
Biological and Biomedical Sciences—General M
Business Administration and Management—General M
Counselor Education M
Criminal Justice and Criminology M
Curriculum and Instruction M
Education—General M
Educational Administration D
Educational Media/Instructional Technology M
English Education M
English M
Environmental Sciences M
Geosciences M
Health Services Management and Hospital Administration M
History M
Illustration M
Mathematics Education M
Mathematics M
Music Education M
Nursing—General M*
Planetary and Space Sciences M
Reading Education M
Social Psychology M
Special Education M

WESTERN GOVERNORS UNIVERSITY

Business Administration and Management—General M
Education—General M,O
Educational Administration M,O
Educational Measurement and Evaluation M,O
Educational Media/Instructional Technology M,O
English Education M,O
Higher Education M,O
Management Information Systems M
Management Strategy and Policy M
Mathematics Education M,O
Science Education M,O

WESTERN ILLINOIS UNIVERSITY

Accounting M
Applied Mathematics M,O
Biological and Biomedical Sciences—General M,O
Business Administration and Management—General M
Chemistry M
Clinical Psychology M,O
Communication Disorders M
Communication—General M
Computer Science M
Counselor Education M
Criminal Justice and Criminology M,O
Distance Education Development M,O
Economics M
Education—General M,D,O
Educational Administration M,D,O
Educational Media/Instructional Technology M,O
Elementary Education M
English M
Foundations and Philosophy of Education M
Geography M,O
Graphic Design M,O
Health Education M,O
Health Services Management and Hospital Administration M,O
History M
Internet and Interactive Multimedia M,O
Kinesiology and Movement Studies M
Manufacturing Engineering M
Marine Biology M,O
Mathematics M,O
Music M
Nonprofit Management M,O
Physics M
Political Science M,O
Psychology—General M,O
Public Administration M,O
Reading Education M
Recreation and Park Management M
School Psychology M,O
Secondary Education M
Social Psychology M,O
Sociology M
Special Education M
Sports Management M
Student Affairs M
Sustainable Development M,O
Technology and Public Policy M
Theater M
Travel and Tourism M
Writing M
Zoology M,O

WESTERN INTERNATIONAL UNIVERSITY

Business Administration and Management—General M
Finance and Banking M
International Business M
Management Information Systems M
Management Strategy and Policy M
Marketing M
Public Administration M
Systems Engineering M

WESTERN KENTUCKY UNIVERSITY

Agricultural Sciences—General M
Anthropology M
Art Education M
Biological and Biomedical Sciences—General M
Business Administration and Management—General M
Business Education M,O
Chemistry M
Communication Disorders M
Communication—General M
Comparative Literature M
Computer Science M
Counselor Education M,O
Early Childhood Education M,O
Educational Administration M,O
Educational Media/Instructional Technology M
Educational Psychology M,O
Elementary Education M,O
English as a Second Language M
English Education M
English M
Geography M
Geology M
Health Services Management and Hospital Administration M
History M
Interdisciplinary Studies M
Mathematics M
Middle School Education M,O
Music Education M
Nursing—General M
Physical Education M
Political Science M
Psychology—General M,O
Public Health—General M
Reading Education M
Recreation and Park Management M
School Psychology M,O
Science Education M
Secondary Education M,O
Social Work M
Sociology M
Special Education M,O
Student Affairs M
Writing M

WESTERN MICHIGAN UNIVERSITY

Accounting M
Anthropology M
Applied Arts and Design—General M
Applied Economics M,D
Applied Mathematics M
Athletic Training and Sports Medicine M
Biological and Biomedical Sciences—General M,D
Biostatistics M
Business Administration and Management—General M
Chemical Engineering M,D
Chemistry M,D
Clinical Psychology M,D,O
Communication Disorders M
Communication—General M
Computational Sciences M
Computer Engineering M,D
Computer Science M,D
Construction Engineering M
Corporate and Organizational Communication M
Counseling Psychology M,D
Counselor Education M,D
Early Childhood Education M
Economics M,D
Education—General M,D,O
Educational Administration M,D,O
Educational Measurement and Evaluation M,D
Electrical Engineering M,D
Elementary Education M
Engineering and Applied Sciences—General M,D*
Engineering Management M
English Education M,D
English M,D
Exercise and Sports Science M
Experimental Psychology M,D,O
Family and Consumer Sciences-General M
Geography M
Geology M,D
Geosciences M
Graphic Design M
History M,D
Human Resources Development M,D,O
Industrial and Organizational Psychology M,D,O
Industrial/Management Engineering M
Manufacturing Engineering M
Marriage and Family Therapy M,D
Mathematics Education M,D
Mathematics M,D
Mechanical Engineering M,D
Medieval and Renaissance Studies M
Middle School Education M
Music M
Occupational Therapy M
Operations Research M
Paper and Pulp Engineering M,D
Philosophy M
Physical Education M
Physician Assistant Studies M
Physics M,D
Political Science M,D
Psychology—General M,D,O
Public Administration M,D
Public Affairs M,D
Reading Education M
Rehabilitation Counseling M
Religion M,D
School Psychology M,D,O
Science Education D*
Social Work M
Sociology M,D
Spanish M
Special Education M,D
Sports Management M
Statistics M,D
Structural Engineering M
Textile Design M
Transportation and Highway Engineering M
Vocational and Technical Education M
Writing M,D

WESTERN NEW ENGLAND COLLEGE

Accounting M
Business Administration and Management—General M
Computer Engineering M
Electrical Engineering M
Elementary Education M
Engineering and Applied Sciences—General M
English Education M
Industrial/Management Engineering M
Law P,M
Management Information Systems M
Manufacturing Engineering M
Mathematics Education M
Mechanical Engineering M

WESTERN NEW MEXICO UNIVERSITY

Business Administration and Management—General M
Counselor Education M
Education—General M
Educational Administration M
Elementary Education M
Interdisciplinary Studies M
Reading Education M
Secondary Education M
Special Education M

WESTERN OREGON UNIVERSITY

Criminal Justice and Criminology M
Early Childhood Education M
Education of the Multiply Handicapped M
Education—General M
Educational Media/Instructional Technology M
Health Education M
Mathematics Education M
Multilingual and Multicultural Education M
Music M
Rehabilitation Counseling M
Science Education M
Secondary Education M
Social Sciences Education M
Special Education M

WESTERN SEMINARY

Marriage and Family Therapy M
Pastoral Ministry and Counseling P,M,D,O
Religion M,O
Religious Education M,D
Theology M,O

WESTERN STATES CHIROPRACTIC COLLEGE

Chiropractic P

WESTERN STATE UNIVERSITY COLLEGE OF LAW

Law P

WESTERN THEOLOGICAL SEMINARY

Theology P,M,D

WESTERN UNIVERSITY OF HEALTH SCIENCES

Allied Health—General M,D
Family Nurse Practitioner Studies M
Health Education M
Nursing—General M
Osteopathic Medicine P
Pharmaceutical Sciences M
Pharmacy P
Physical Therapy D
Physician Assistant Studies M
Veterinary Medicine P

WESTERN WASHINGTON UNIVERSITY

Adult Education M
Anthropology M
Biological and Biomedical Sciences—General M
Business Administration and Management—General M
Chemistry M
Communication Disorders M
Computer Science M
Counseling Psychology M
Counselor Education M
Education of the Gifted M
Education—General M
Educational Administration M
Elementary Education M
English M
Environmental Education M
Environmental Sciences M
Exercise and Sports Science M
Experimental Psychology M
Geography M
Geology M
Higher Education M
History M
Marine Sciences M
Mathematics M
Music M
Physical Education M
Political Science M
Psychology—General M
Rehabilitation Counseling M
Science Education M

Secondary Education M
Theater M

WESTFIELD STATE COLLEGE
Counseling Psychology M
Counselor Education M
Criminal Justice and Criminology M
Early Childhood Education M
Education—General M,O
Educational Administration M,O
Educational Media/Instructional Technology M
Elementary Education M
English M
History M
Physical Education M
Psychology—General M
Reading Education M
Secondary Education M
Special Education M
Vocational and Technical Education M,O

WESTMINSTER CHOIR COLLEGE OF RIDER UNIVERSITY
Music Education M*
Music M

WESTMINSTER COLLEGE (PA)
Counselor Education M,O
Education—General M,O
Educational Administration M,O
Reading Education M,O

WESTMINSTER COLLEGE (UT)
Business Administration and Management—General M,O
Communication—General M
Counseling Psychology M
Education—General M
Family Nurse Practitioner Studies M
Management of Technology M,O
Nurse Anesthesia M
Nursing Education M
Nursing—General M
Writing M

WESTMINSTER SEMINARY CALIFORNIA
Religion P,M
Theology P,M

WESTMINSTER THEOLOGICAL SEMINARY
Missions and Missiology P,M,D,O
Pastoral Ministry and Counseling P,M,D,O
Religion P,M,D,O
Theology P,M,D,O

WESTON JESUIT SCHOOL OF THEOLOGY
Theology P,M,D,O*

WEST TEXAS A&M UNIVERSITY
Accounting M
Agricultural Economics and Agribusiness M
Agricultural Sciences—General M,D
Animal Sciences M
Art/Fine Arts M
Biological and Biomedical Sciences—General M
Business Administration and Management—General M
Chemistry M
Communication Disorders M
Communication—General M
Counselor Education M
Criminal Justice and Criminology M
Curriculum and Instruction M
Economics M
Education—General M
Educational Administration M
Educational Measurement and Evaluation M
Educational Media/Instructional Technology M
Engineering and Applied Sciences—General M
English M
Environmental Sciences M
Exercise and Sports Science M
Finance and Banking M
History M
Interdisciplinary Studies M
Mathematics M
Music M
Nursing—General M
Plant Sciences M
Political Science M
Psychology—General M
Reading Education M
Special Education M

WEST VIRGINIA SCHOOL OF OSTEOPATHIC MEDICINE
Osteopathic Medicine P

WEST VIRGINIA STATE UNIVERSITY
Biotechnology M

WEST VIRGINIA UNIVERSITY
Accounting M
Aerospace/Aeronautical Engineering M,D
African Studies M,D
African-American Studies M,D
Agricultural Economics and Agribusiness M
Agricultural Education M
Agricultural Sciences—General M,D
Agronomy and Soil Sciences M,D
Allopathic Medicine P
American Studies M,D
Analytical Chemistry M,D
Animal Sciences M,D
Applied Mathematics M,D
Applied Physics M,D
Applied Social Research M
Art Education M
Art History M
Art/Fine Arts M
Asian Studies M,D
Athletic Training and Sports Medicine M,D
Biochemistry M,D*
Biological and Biomedical Sciences—General M,D*
Business Administration and Management—General M
Cancer Biology/Oncology M,D*
Cell Biology M,D
Chemical Engineering M,D
Chemical Physics M,D
Chemistry M,D
Child and Family Studies M
Civil Engineering M,D
Clinical Psychology M,D
Communication Disorders M,D
Communication—General M*
Community Health M
Comparative Literature M
Computer Engineering D
Computer Science M,D
Condensed Matter Physics M,D
Corporate and Organizational Communication M
Counseling Psychology D
Counselor Education M
Curriculum and Instruction M,D
Dentistry P
Developmental Biology M,D
Developmental Psychology M,D
Early Childhood Education M,D
Economics M,D
Education of the Gifted M,D
Education of the Multiply Handicapped M,D
Education—General M,D
Educational Administration M,D
Educational Psychology M
Electrical Engineering M,D
Elementary Education M
Engineering and Applied Sciences—General M,D*
English as a Second Language M
English M,D
Entomology M,D
Environmental and Occupational Health D
Environmental Biology M,D
Environmental Education M
Environmental Engineering M,D
Environmental Management and Policy M,D
Evolutionary Biology M,D
Exercise and Sports Science M,D*
Fish, Game, and Wildlife Management M
Food Science and Technology M,D
Forestry M,D
French M
Genetics M,D*
Geographic Information Systems M,D
Geography M,D
Geology M,D
Geophysics M,D
German M
Graphic Design M
Health Education M,D
Health Promotion M,D
Higher Education M,D
History of Science and Technology M,D
History M,D
Horticulture M,D
Human Genetics M,D
Human Services M
Hydrogeology M,D
Hydrology M,D
Immunology M,D
Industrial and Labor Relations M
Industrial Hygiene M
Industrial/Management Engineering M,D
Inorganic Chemistry M,D
International Affairs M,D
Journalism M
Latin American Studies M,D
Law P
Legal and Justice Studies M
Liberal Studies M
Linguistics M
Marketing M
Mathematics Education M,D
Mathematics M,D
Mechanical Engineering M,D
Medicinal and Pharmaceutical Chemistry M,D
Microbiology M,D*
Mineral/Mining Engineering M,D
Molecular Biology M,D
Music Education M,D
Music M,D
Neuroscience D
Nursing—General M,D,O
Nutrition M
Occupational Therapy M
Oral and Dental Sciences M
Organic Chemistry M,D
Paleontology M,D
Petroleum Engineering M,D
Pharmaceutical Administration M,D
Pharmaceutical Sciences M,D*
Pharmacology M,D
Pharmacy P,M,D
Physical Chemistry M,D
Physical Education M,D
Physical Therapy M
Physics M,D
Physiology M,D*
Plant Pathology M,D
Plant Sciences M,D
Plasma Physics M,D
Political Science M,D
Psychology—General M,D
Public Administration M
Public Health—General M
Public Policy M,D
Reading Education M
Recreation and Park Management M
Rehabilitation Counseling M
Reproductive Biology M,D
Safety Engineering M
Secondary Education M,D
Social Work M
Sociology M
Software Engineering M
Spanish M
Special Education M,D
Sport Psychology M,D
Sports Management M,D
Statistics M,D
Sustainable Development D
Theater M
Theoretical Chemistry M,D
Theoretical Physics M,D
Toxicology M,D
Urban and Regional Planning M,D
Vocational and Technical Education M
Writing M

WEST VIRGINIA UNIVERSITY INSTITUTE OF TECHNOLOGY
Engineering and Applied Sciences—General M
Systems Engineering M

WEST VIRGINIA WESLEYAN COLLEGE
Business Administration and Management—General M

WHEATON COLLEGE
American Studies M
Archaeology M
Clinical Psychology M,D
Cultural Studies M,O
Education—General M
Elementary Education M
English as a Second Language M,O
Missions and Missiology M,O
Pastoral Ministry and Counseling M,D
Psychology—General M,D
Religion M
Religious Education M
Secondary Education M
Theology M,D

Close-Up on page 1145.

WHEELING JESUIT UNIVERSITY
Accounting M
Business Administration and Management—General M
Nursing—General M
Physical Therapy D

WHEELOCK COLLEGE
Child and Family Studies M
Early Childhood Education M
Education—General M
Educational Administration M
Elementary Education M
Human Development M
Reading Education M
Social Work M
Special Education M

WHITTIER COLLEGE
Child Development M
Education—General M
Educational Administration M
Elementary Education M
Law P,M
Legal and Justice Studies P,M
Secondary Education M

WHITWORTH UNIVERSITY
Business Administration and Management—General M
Counselor Education M
Education of the Gifted M
Education—General M
Educational Administration M
Elementary Education M
International Business M
Secondary Education M
Special Education M

WICHITA STATE UNIVERSITY
Accounting M
Aerospace/Aeronautical Engineering M,D
Allied Health—General M
Anthropology M
Applied Mathematics M,D
Art Education M
Art/Fine Arts M
Biological and Biomedical Sciences—General M*
Business Administration and Management—General M
Chemistry M,D
Clinical Psychology M,D
Communication Disorders M,D
Communication—General M
Computer Science M
Counselor Education M,D,O
Criminal Justice and Criminology M
Curriculum and Instruction M
Economics M
Education—General M,D,O
Educational Administration M,D,O
Educational Psychology M,D,O
Electrical Engineering M,D
Engineering and Applied Sciences—General M,D
English M
Environmental Sciences M
Exercise and Sports Science M
Family Nurse Practitioner Studies M
Geology M
Gerontology M
History M
Human Services M
Industrial/Management Engineering M,D
Liberal Studies M
Manufacturing Engineering M,D
Mathematics M,D
Mechanical Engineering M,D
Music Education M
Music M
Nurse Midwifery M
Nursing and Healthcare Administration M
Nursing—General M
Physical Education M
Physical Therapy M
Physics M
Political Science M
Psychology—General M,D
Public Administration M
Public Health—General M
School Psychology M,D,O
Social Psychology M,D
Social Work M
Sociology M
Spanish M
Special Education M
Sports Management M
Statistics M,D
Writing M

WIDENER UNIVERSITY
Accounting M
Adult Education M,D
Business Administration and Management—General M

Chemical Engineering M
Civil Engineering M
Clinical Psychology D*
Computer Engineering M
Counselor Education M,D
Criminal Justice and Criminology M
Early Childhood Education M,D
Education—General M,D
Educational Administration M,D
Educational Media/Instructional Technology M,D
Educational Psychology M,D
Elementary Education M,D
Engineering and Applied Sciences—General M*
Engineering Management M
English Education M,D
Foundations and Philosophy of Education M,D
Health Education M,D
Health Services Management and Hospital Administration M
Human Resources Management M
Law P,M,D*
Liberal Studies M
Mathematics Education M,D
Mechanical Engineering M
Middle School Education M,D
Nursing—General M,D,O
Physical Therapy M,D
Psychology—General
Public Administration M
Reading Education M,D
Science Education M,D
Social Sciences Education M,D
Social Work M*
Software Engineering M
Special Education M,D
Taxation M
Telecommunications M

Close-Up on page 1147 and Announcement on page 786.

WILFRID LAURIER UNIVERSITY

Biological and Biomedical Sciences—General M
Business Administration and Management—General M,D
Cognitive Sciences M,D
Communication—General M
Cultural Studies M
Developmental Psychology M,D
Economics M
English M,D
Ethics P,M,D
Film, Television, and Video Theory and Criticism M,D
Foundations and Philosophy of Education M
Geography M,D
History M,D
International Affairs M,D
Kinesiology and Movement Studies M
Mathematics M
Pastoral Ministry and Counseling P,M,D
Philosophy M
Physical Education M
Political Science M
Psychology—General M,D
Public Policy M
Religion M,D
Social Psychology M,D
Social Work M,D
Sociology M
Theology P,M,D
Therapies—Dance, Drama, and Music M

WILKES UNIVERSITY

Accounting M
Business Administration and Management—General M
Computer Education M
Education—General M
Educational Administration M
Educational Measurement and Evaluation M
Educational Media/Instructional Technology M
Electrical Engineering M
Elementary Education M
Engineering and Applied Sciences—General M
English Education M
Entrepreneurship M
Finance and Banking M
Human Resources Management M
International Business M
Marketing M
Mathematics Education M
Mathematics M
Nursing—General M
Pharmacy P
Science Education M
Secondary Education M
Social Sciences Education M
Special Education M
Writing M

WILLAMETTE UNIVERSITY

Business Administration and Management—General M
Education—General M
Law P,M
Nonprofit Management M
Public Administration M

WILLIAM CAREY UNIVERSITY

Art Education M,O
Business Administration and Management—General M
Counseling Psychology M
Education of the Gifted M,O
Education—General M,O
Elementary Education M,O
English Education M,O
Nursing—General M
Psychology—General M
Secondary Education M,O
Social Sciences Education M,O
Special Education M,O

WILLIAM HOWARD TAFT UNIVERSITY

Education—General M
Law P,M
Legal and Justice Studies P,M
Taxation P,M

WILLIAM MITCHELL COLLEGE OF LAW

Law P

WILLIAM PATERSON UNIVERSITY OF NEW JERSEY

Art/Fine Arts M
Biological and Biomedical Sciences—General M*
Biotechnology M
Business Administration and Management—General M
Clinical Psychology M
Communication Disorders M
Counselor Education M
Ecology M
Education—General M
Educational Administration M
Elementary Education M
English M
History M
Limnology M
Media Studies M
Molecular Biology M
Music M
Nursing—General M
Physiology M
Public Policy M
Reading Education M
Sociology M
Special Education M

Close-Up on page 1149.

WILLIAMS COLLEGE

Art History M

WILLIAM WOODS UNIVERSITY

Agricultural Economics and Agribusiness M,O
Curriculum and Instruction M,O
Educational Administration M,O
Health Services Management and Hospital Administration M,O
Human Resources Development M,O

WILMINGTON COLLEGE (DE)

Adult Nursing M
Business Administration and Management—General M
Counselor Education M
Criminal Justice and Criminology M
Education of the Gifted M
Education—General M
Educational Administration M,D
Educational Media/Instructional Technology M
Elementary Education M
Family Nurse Practitioner Studies M
Finance and Banking M
Gerontology M
Health Services Management and Hospital Administration M
Human Resources Management M
Human Services M
Internet and Interactive Multimedia M
Logistics M
Management Information Systems M
Nursing—General M
Organizational Management M
Public Administration M
Reading Education M
Secondary Education M
Social Psychology M
Special Education M
Transportation Management M
Vocational and Technical Education M
Women's Health Nursing M

WILMINGTON COLLEGE (OH)

Education—General M
Reading Education M
Special Education M

WINEBRENNER THEOLOGICAL SEMINARY

Theology P,M,D

WINGATE UNIVERSITY

Business Administration and Management—General M
Education—General M
Educational Administration M
Elementary Education M
Pharmacy P
Physical Education M
Sports Management M

WINONA STATE UNIVERSITY

Adult Nursing M
Counselor Education M
Education—General M
Educational Administration M,O
English M
Family Nurse Practitioner Studies M
Nursing and Healthcare Administration M
Nursing Education M
Nursing—General M
Special Education M

WINSTON-SALEM STATE UNIVERSITY

Business Administration and Management—General M
Computer Science M
Elementary Education M
Management Information Systems M
Nursing—General M
Occupational Therapy M
Physical Therapy M
Rehabilitation Counseling M

WINTHROP UNIVERSITY

Art Education M
Art/Fine Arts M
Arts Administration M
Biological and Biomedical Sciences—General M
Business Administration and Management—General M
Counselor Education M
Education—General M
Educational Administration M
English M
History M
Liberal Studies M
Middle School Education M
Music Education M
Music M
Nutrition M
Physical Education M
Project Management M,O
Psychology—General M,O
Reading Education M
Secondary Education M
Social Work M
Software Engineering M,O
Spanish M
Special Education M

WISCONSIN SCHOOL OF PROFESSIONAL PSYCHOLOGY

Clinical Psychology M,D
Psychology—General M,D

WITTENBERG UNIVERSITY

Education—General M

WOODBURY UNIVERSITY

Architecture M
Business Administration and Management—General M
Conflict Resolution and Mediation/Peace Studies M,O
Organizational Management M
Real Estate M

WOODS HOLE OCEANOGRAPHIC INSTITUTION

Civil Engineering M,D,O
Electrical Engineering M,D,O
Geochemistry M,D,O
Geophysics M,D,O
Marine Biology M,D,O
Marine Geology M,D,O
Mechanical Engineering M,D,O
Ocean Engineering M,D,O
Oceanography M,D,O

WORCESTER POLYTECHNIC INSTITUTE

Applied Mathematics M,D,O
Applied Statistics M,D,O
Biochemistry M,D
Biological and Biomedical Sciences—General M,D*
Biomedical Engineering M,D,O*
Biotechnology M,D
Business Administration and Management—General M,O*
Chemical Engineering M,D*
Chemistry M,D*
Civil Engineering M,D,O*
Computer and Information Systems Security M,O
Computer Engineering M,D,O
Computer Science M,D,O*
Construction Engineering M,D,O
Electrical Engineering M,D,O*
Energy and Power Engineering M,D
Engineering Design M
Environmental Engineering M,D,O
Fire Protection Engineering M,D,O*
Geotechnical Engineering M,D,O
Interdisciplinary Studies M,D
Management Information Systems M,D
Manufacturing Engineering M,D,O*
Marketing M,O
Materials Engineering M,D,O
Materials Sciences M,D,O*
Mathematics M,D,O*
Mechanical Engineering M,D,O*
Organizational Management M
Physics M,D*
Project Management M
Social Sciences M,D
Structural Engineering M,D,O
Supply Chain Management M
Systems Engineering M,D
Systems Science M,O
Transportation and Highway Engineering M,D,O

Close-Up on page 1151.

WORCESTER STATE COLLEGE

Accounting M
Biotechnology M
Business Administration and Management—General M
Communication Disorders M
Community Health Nursing M
Early Childhood Education M
Education—General M
Educational Administration M
Elementary Education M
English Education M
Foreign Languages Education M
Health Education M
Health Services Management and Hospital Administration M
Middle School Education M
Nonprofit Management M
Occupational Therapy M
Organizational Management M
Reading Education M
Secondary Education M
Social Sciences Education M
Special Education M

WORLD MEDICINE INSTITUTE: COLLEGE OF ACUPUNCTURE AND HERBAL MEDICINE

Acupuncture and Oriental Medicine M

WRIGHT INSTITUTE

Clinical Psychology D
Psychology—General D

WRIGHT STATE UNIVERSITY

Accounting M
Acute Care/Critical Care Nursing M
Adult Education O
Adult Nursing M
Allopathic Medicine P
Anatomy M
Applied Economics M
Applied Mathematics M
Applied Statistics M
Biochemistry M
Biological and Biomedical Sciences—General M,D*
Biomedical Engineering M
Biophysics M
Business Administration and Management—General M
Business Education M
Chemistry M

Clinical Psychology D
Community Health Nursing M
Computer Education M
Computer Engineering M,D
Computer Science M,D
Counselor Education M
Criminal Justice and Criminology M
Curriculum and Instruction M,O
Early Childhood Education M
Economics M
Education of the Gifted M
Education—General M,O
Educational Administration M,O
Electrical Engineering M
Elementary Education M
Engineering and Applied Sciences—General M,D
English as a Second Language M
English M
Environmental Sciences M,D
Ergonomics and Human Factors M,D
Family Nurse Practitioner Studies M
Finance and Banking M
Geology M
Geophysics M
Health Education M
Health Promotion M
Health Services Management and Hospital Administration M
Higher Education M,O
History M
Humanities M
Immunology M
Industrial and Organizational Psychology M,D
Interdisciplinary Studies M
International and Comparative Education M
International Business M
Library Science M
Logistics M
Management Information Systems M
Marketing M
Materials Engineering M
Materials Sciences M
Mathematics Education M
Mathematics M
Mechanical Engineering M
Medical Physics M
Microbiology M
Middle School Education M
Molecular Biology M
Music Education M
Music M
Nursing and Healthcare Administration M
Nursing—General M
Pediatric Nursing M
Pharmacology M
Physical Education M
Physics M
Physiology M
Project Management M
Psychology—General M,D
Public Administration M
Public Health—General M
Recreation and Park Management M
Rehabilitation Counseling M
Rhetoric M
School Nursing M
Science Education M
Secondary Education M
Special Education M
Supply Chain Management M
Toxicology M
Urban Studies M
Vocational and Technical Education M
Writing M

WYCLIFFE COLLEGE

Religion P,M,D,O
Theology P,M,D,O

XAVIER UNIVERSITY

Business Administration and Management—General M
Clinical Psychology M,D
Counselor Education M
Criminal Justice and Criminology M
Early Childhood Education M
Education—General M
Educational Administration M
Electronic Commerce M
Elementary Education M
English M
Finance and Banking M
Health Services Management and Hospital Administration M*
Human Resources Development M
International Business M
Management Information Systems M
Marketing M
Multilingual and Multicultural Education M
Nursing and Healthcare Administration M
Nursing—General M
Occupational Therapy M
Psychology—General M,D
Reading Education M
Secondary Education M
Special Education M
Sports Management M
Theology M

XAVIER UNIVERSITY OF LOUISIANA

Counselor Education M
Curriculum and Instruction M
Education—General M
Educational Administration M
Pastoral Ministry and Counseling M
Pharmacy P
Theology M

YALE UNIVERSITY

Accounting D
African Studies M
African-American Studies M,D
Allopathic Medicine P
American Studies M,D
Anthropology M,D
Applied Arts and Design—General M
Applied Mathematics M,D
Applied Physics M,D
Archaeology M
Architecture M
Art History D
Art/Fine Arts M
Asian Languages D
Asian Studies M
Astronomy M,D
Biochemistry M,D
Bioinformatics D
Biological and Biomedical Sciences—General D*
Biophysics M,D
Biostatistics M,D
Business Administration and Management—General M,D
Cancer Biology/Oncology D
Cell Biology D
Chemical Engineering M,D*
Chemistry D*
Classics D
Comparative Literature D
Computational Biology D
Computer Science D*
Developmental Biology D
East European and Russian Studies M
Ecology D
Economics M,D
Electrical Engineering M,D*
Engineering and Applied Sciences—General M,D*
Engineering Physics M,D
English M,D
Environmental and Occupational Health M,D
Environmental Design M
Environmental Management and Policy M,D
Environmental Sciences M,D
Epidemiology M,D
Evolutionary Biology D
Finance and Banking D
Forestry M,D*
French M,D
Genetics D
Genomic Sciences D
Geochemistry D
Geology D
Geophysics D
Geosciences D
German M,D
Graphic Design M
Health Services Management and Hospital Administration M,D
History of Medicine M,D
History of Science and Technology M,D
History M,D
Immunology D
Infectious Diseases D
Inorganic Chemistry D
International Affairs M
International Health M
Italian D
Law P,M,D
Linguistics D
Marketing D
Mathematics M,D
Mechanical Engineering M,D
Mechanics M,D
Medieval and Renaissance Studies M,D
Meteorology D
Microbiology D
Mineralogy D
Molecular Biology D
Molecular Biophysics D
Molecular Medicine D
Molecular Pathology D
Molecular Physiology D
Music M,D,O
Near and Middle Eastern Languages M,D
Neurobiology D
Neuroscience D
Nursing—General M,D,O
Oceanography D
Organic Chemistry D
Paleontology D
Parasitology D*
Pathobiology D
Pathology D
Pharmacology D
Philosophy D
Photography M
Physical Chemistry D
Physician Assistant Studies M
Physics D*
Physiology D
Plant Biology D*
Political Science D
Portuguese M,D
Psychology—General D
Public Health—General M,D*
Religion D
Slavic Languages D
Social Sciences M,D
Sociology D
Spanish M,D
Statistics M,D
Structural Biology D
Theater M,D,O
Theology P,M
Virology D

YESHIVA BETH MOSHE

Theology O

YESHIVA KARLIN STOLIN RABBINICAL INSTITUTE

Theology O

YESHIVA OF NITRA RABBINICAL COLLEGE

Theology

YESHIVA SHAAR HATORAH TALMUDIC RESEARCH INSTITUTE

Theology

YESHIVATH ZICHRON MOSHE

Theology O

YESHIVA TORAS CHAIM TALMUDICAL SEMINARY

Theology

YESHIVA UNIVERSITY

Clinical Psychology D
Counseling Psychology M
Educational Administration M,D,O
Health Psychology D
Jewish Studies M,D
Law P,M
Psychology—General M,D
Religious Education M,D,O
School Psychology D
Social Work M,D

YORK COLLEGE OF PENNSYLVANIA

Business Administration and Management—General M
Education—General M
Nursing—General M

YORK UNIVERSITY

Anthropology M,D
Applied Arts and Design—General M
Applied Mathematics M,D
Art History M,D
Art/Fine Arts M,D
Astronomy M,D
Biological and Biomedical Sciences—General M,D
Business Administration and Management—General M,D*
Chemistry M,D
Communication—General M,D
Computer Science M,D
Dance M
Disability Studies M,D
Economics M,D
Education—General M,D
Emergency Management M
English M,D
Environmental Management and Policy M,D
Film, Television, and Video Production M,D
French M
Geography M,D
Geosciences M,D
History M,D
Human Resources Management M,D
Humanities M,D
Interdisciplinary Studies M
International Affairs M
Kinesiology and Movement Studies M,D
Law P,M,D
Linguistics M,D
Mathematics M,D
Music M,D
Nursing—General M
Philosophy M,D
Physics M,D
Planetary and Space Sciences M,D
Political Science M,D
Psychology—General M,D
Public Administration M
Public Affairs M
Public Policy M
Social Sciences M
Social Work M,D
Sociology M,D
Statistics M,D
Theater M,D
Translation and Interpretation M
Women's Studies M,D

YO SAN UNIVERSITY OF TRADITIONAL CHINESE MEDICINE

Acupuncture and Oriental Medicine M

YOUNGSTOWN STATE UNIVERSITY

Accounting M
Biological and Biomedical Sciences—General M
Business Administration and Management—General M
Chemical Engineering M
Chemistry M
Civil Engineering M
Counselor Education M
Criminal Justice and Criminology M
Early Childhood Education M
Economics M
Education of the Gifted M
Education—General M,D
Educational Administration M,D
Electrical Engineering M
Elementary Education M
Engineering and Applied Sciences—General M
English M
Environmental Engineering M
Environmental Management and Policy M,O
Finance and Banking M
Foundations and Philosophy of Education M,D
Health Services Management and Hospital Administration M
History M
Human Services M
Industrial/Management Engineering M
Marketing M
Mathematics M
Mechanical Engineering M
Middle School Education M
Music Education M
Music M
Nursing—General M
Physical Therapy M
Reading Education M
Secondary Education M
Special Education M

PROFILES OF INSTITUTIONS OFFERING GRADUATE AND PROFESSIONAL WORK

ABILENE CHRISTIAN UNIVERSITY, Abilene, TX 79699-9100

General Information Independent-religious, coed, comprehensive institution. CGS member. *Enrollment:* 4,777 graduate, professional, and undergraduate students; 299 full-time matriculated graduate/professional students (147 women), 317 part-time matriculated graduate/professional students (139 women). *Enrollment by degree level:* 82 first professional, 409 master's, 24 doctoral, 101 other advanced degrees. *Graduate faculty:* 14 full-time (2 women), 72 part-time/adjunct (27 women). *Tuition:* Full-time $12,504; part-time $521 per hour. *Required fees:* $700; $34 per hour. *Graduate housing:* Rooms and/or apartments available to single students and available on a first-come, first-served basis to married students. Typical cost: $2,850 per year ($6,120 including board) for single students; $5,250 per year ($8,520 including board) for married students. Room and board charges vary according to board plan and housing facility selected. Housing application deadline: 5/11. *Student services:* Campus employment opportunities, campus safety program, career counseling, disabled student services, exercise/wellness program, grant writing training, international student services, low-cost health insurance, multicultural affairs office, teacher training, writing training. *Library facilities:* Brown Library. *Online resources:* library catalog, web page, access to other libraries' catalogs. *Collection:* 503,707 titles, 2,771 serial subscriptions, 65,246 audiovisual materials. *Research affiliation:* Los Alamos National Laboratory (particle physics), Fermilab (peanut toxins).

Computer facilities: 700 computers available on campus for general student use. A campuswide network can be accessed from student residence rooms and from off campus. Internet access and online class registration are available. *Web address:* http://www.acu.edu/.

General Application Contact: William Horn, Graduate Admissions Counselor, 325-674-2656, Fax: 325-674-6717, E-mail: gradinfo@acu.edu.

GRADUATE UNITS

Graduate School Students: 299 full-time (147 women), 317 part-time (139 women); includes 58 minority (25 African Americans, 1 American Indian/Alaska Native, 9 Asian Americans or Pacific Islanders, 23 Hispanic Americans), 22 international. Average age 31. 482 applicants, 71% accepted, 286 enrolled. *Faculty:* 14 full-time (2 women), 72 part-time/adjunct (27 women). Expenses: Contact institution. *Financial support:* In 2006–07, 345 students received support, including 35 research assistantships with partial tuition reimbursements available (averaging $5,800 per year), 10 teaching assistantships with partial tuition reimbursements available (averaging $5,800 per year); career-related internships or fieldwork, Federal Work-Study, institutionally sponsored loans, scholarships/grants, and tuition waivers (partial) also available. Support available to part-time students. Financial award application deadline: 4/1; financial award applicants required to submit FAFSA. In 2006, 25 M Divs, 154 master's, 4 doctorates, 24 other advanced degrees awarded. *Degree program information:* Part-time and evening/weekend programs available. Offers communication sciences and disorders (MS); education and human services (M Ed, MS, MSSW, Certificate); educational diagnostician (M Ed); higher education (M Ed); leadership of learning (M Ed, Certificate); liberal arts (MLA); reading specialist (M Ed); social work (MSSW). *Application deadline:* For fall admission, 4/1 priority date for domestic students; for spring admission, 11/1 priority date for domestic students. Applications are processed on a rolling basis. *Application fee:* $40 ($45 for international students). *Application Contact:* William Horn, Graduate Admissions Counselor, 325-674-2656, Fax: 325-674-3717, E-mail: gradinfo@acu.edu. *Graduate Dean,* Dr. Carol G. Williams, 325-674-2223, Fax: 325-674-6717, E-mail: gradinfo@acu.edu.

College of Arts and Sciences Students: 94 full-time (54 women), 53 part-time (29 women); includes 24 minority (12 African Americans, 3 Asian Americans or Pacific Islanders, 9 Hispanic Americans), 5 international. 104 applicants, 65% accepted, 37 enrolled. *Faculty:* 36 part-time/adjunct (9 women). Expenses: Contact institution. *Financial support:* Research assistantships, teaching assistantships, career-related internships or fieldwork, Federal Work-Study, and tuition waivers (partial) available. Support available to part-time students. Financial award application deadline: 4/1; financial award applicants required to submit FAFSA. In 2006, 57 master's, 1 other advanced degree awarded. *Degree program information:* Part-time programs available. Offers arts and sciences (MA, MS, Certificate); clinical psychology (MS); composition/rhetoric (MA); conflict resolution and reconciliation (MA, Certificate); counseling psychology (MS); family studies (MS, Certificate); general psychology (MS); gerontology (MS, Certificate); human communication (MA); literature (MA); organizational and human resource development (MS); school psychology (MS); writing (MA). *Application deadline:* For fall admission, 4/1 priority date for domestic students; for spring admission, 11/1 for domestic students. Applications are processed on a rolling basis. *Application fee:* $40 ($45 for international students). Electronic applications accepted. *Application Contact:* William Horn, Graduate Admissions Counselor, 325-674-2656, Fax: 325-674-6717, E-mail: gradinfo@acu.edu. *Dean,* 325-674-2209.

College of Biblical Studies Students: 131 full-time (44 women), 109 part-time (10 women); includes 16 minority (6 African Americans, 1 American Indian/Alaska Native, 4 Asian Americans or Pacific Islanders, 5 Hispanic Americans), 12 international. 115 applicants, 77% accepted, 80 enrolled. *Faculty:* 13 full-time (2 women), 17 part-time/adjunct (4 women). Expenses: Contact institution. *Financial support:* Teaching assistantships, career-related internships or fieldwork and Federal Work-Study available. Support available to part-time students. Financial award application deadline: 4/1. In 2006, 25 M Divs, 31 master's, 4 doctorates awarded. *Degree program information:* Part-time and evening/weekend programs available. Offers biblical studies (M Div, MA, MACM, MMFT, D Min); Christian ministry (MACM); divinity (M Div); history and theology (MA); marriage and family therapy (MMFT); ministry (D Min); missions (MA); New Testament (MA); Old Testament (MA). *Application deadline:* For fall admission, 4/1 priority date for domestic students; for spring admission, 11/1 for domestic students. Applications are processed on a rolling basis. *Application fee:* $40 ($45 for international students). *Application Contact:* William Horn, Graduate Admissions Counselor, 325-674-2656, Fax: 325-674-6717, E-mail: gradinfo@acu.edu. *Dean,* Dr. Jack Reese, 325-674-3700.

College of Business Administration Students: 22 full-time (7 women), 4 part-time (1 woman); includes 1 minority (African American), 3 international. 23 applicants, 83% accepted, 16 enrolled. *Faculty:* 6 part-time/adjunct (0 women). Expenses: Contact institution. *Financial support:* Teaching assistantships, Federal Work-Study available. Support available to part-time students. Financial award application deadline: 4/1. In 2006, 26 degrees awarded. *Degree program information:* Part-time programs available. Offers business administration (M Acc). *Application deadline:* For fall admission, 4/1 priority date for domestic students; for spring admission, 11/1 for domestic students. Applications are processed on a rolling basis. *Application fee:* $40 ($45 for international students). Electronic applications accepted. *Application Contact:* William Horn, Graduate Admissions Counselor, 325-674-2656, Fax: 325-674-6717, E-mail: gradinfo@acu.edu. *Department Chair,* Bill Fowler, 325-674-2080, Fax: 325-674-2564, E-mail: bill.fowler@coba.acu.edu.

School of Nursing Students: 4 full-time (3 women), 7 part-time (6 women); includes 1 minority (Hispanic American) 11 applicants, 64% accepted, 7 enrolled. *Faculty:* 5 part-time/adjunct (all women). Expenses: Contact institution. *Financial support:* Application deadline: 4/1. In 2006, 7 degrees awarded. Offers nursing (MSN). *Application deadline:* For fall admission, 4/1 priority date for domestic students; for spring admission, 11/1 for domestic students. Applications are processed on a rolling basis. *Application fee:* $40 ($45 for international students). Electronic applications accepted. *Application Contact:* William Horn, Graduate Admissions Counselor, 325-674-2656, Fax: 325-674-6717, E-mail: gradinfo@acu.edu. *Dean,* Dr. Jan Noles, 325-671-2399.

ACADEMY FOR FIVE ELEMENT ACUPUNCTURE, Hallandale, FL 33009

General Information Independent, coed, graduate-only institution.

GRADUATE UNITS

Graduate Program

ACADEMY OF ART UNIVERSITY, San Francisco, CA 94105-3410

General Information Proprietary, coed, comprehensive institution. *Enrollment:* 9,483 graduate, professional, and undergraduate students; 1,343 full-time matriculated graduate/professional students (698 women), 702 part-time matriculated graduate/professional students (401 women). *Enrollment by degree level:* 2,045 master's. *Graduate faculty:* 80 full-time (30 women), 252 part-time/adjunct (83 women). *Tuition:* Full-time $15,600; part-time $650 per unit. *Required fees:* $280. *Graduate housing:* Room and/or apartments guaranteed to single students; on-campus housing not available to married students. Typical cost: $12,600 (including board). Room and board charges vary according to campus/location and housing facility selected. Housing application deadline: 9/7. *Student services:* Campus employment opportunities, campus safety program, career counseling, disabled student services, international student services, low-cost health insurance, teacher training, writing training. *Library facilities:* Academy of Art University Library. *Online resources:* library catalog, web page, access to other libraries' catalogs. *Collection:* 36,000 titles, 476 serial subscriptions, 3,500 audiovisual materials.

Computer facilities: Computer purchase and lease plans are available. 600 computers available on campus for general student use. Internet access and online class registration are available. *Web address:* http://www.academyart.edu/.

General Application Contact: Cindy Cai, Director of Graduate Domestic Admissions, 800-544-ARTS, Fax: 415-263-4130, E-mail: info@academyart.edu.

GRADUATE UNITS

Graduate Program Students: 1,139 full-time (577 women), 518 part-time (287 women); includes 236 minority (58 African Americans, 3 American Indian/Alaska Native, 120 Asian Americans or Pacific Islanders, 55 Hispanic Americans), 632 international. Average age 31. 580 applicants, 84% accepted, 397 enrolled. *Faculty:* 58 full-time (28 women), 145 part-time/adjunct (60 women). Expenses: Contact institution. *Financial support:* In 2006–07, 765 students received support. Career-related internships or fieldwork and Federal Work-Study available. Support available to part-time students. Financial award application deadline: 8/10; financial award applicants required to submit FAFSA. In 2006, 250 degrees awarded. *Degree program information:* Part-time and evening/weekend programs available. Postbaccalaureate distance learning degree programs offered (no on-campus study). *Application deadline:* For fall admission, 9/7 for domestic and international students; for spring admission, 2/2 for domestic and international students. Applications are processed on a rolling basis. *Application fee:* $100 ($500 for international students). Electronic applications accepted. *Application Contact:* 800-544-ARTS, Fax: 415-263-4130, E-mail: info@academyart.edu. *Executive Vice President,* Melissa Marshall, 800-544-ARTS, E-mail: info@academyart.edu.

School of Advertising Students: 95 full-time (47 women), 45 part-time (26 women); includes 8 African Americans, 10 Asian Americans or Pacific Islanders, 4 Hispanic Americans, 49 international. Average age 28. 44 applicants. *Faculty:* 4 full-time (2 women), 30 part-time/adjunct (11 women). Expenses: Contact institution. *Financial support:* In 2006–07, 78 students received support; fellowships, career-related internships or fieldwork and Federal Work-Study available. Support available to part-time students. Financial award application deadline: 8/10; financial award applicants required to submit FAFSA. In 2006, 26 degrees awarded. *Degree program information:* Part-time programs available. Postbaccalaureate distance learning degree programs offered (no on-campus study). Offers advertising (MFA). *Application deadline:* For fall admission, 9/7 for domestic and international students; for spring admission, 2/2 for domestic and international students. Applications are processed on a rolling basis. *Application fee:* $100 ($500 for international students). Electronic applications accepted. *Application Contact:* 800-544-ARTS, Fax: 415-263-4130, E-mail: info@academyart.edu. *Director,* Melinda Mettler, 800-544-ARTS, E-mail: mmettler@academyart.edu.

School of Animation and Visual Effects Students: 311 full-time (97 women), 120 part-time (35 women); includes 63 minority (15 African Americans, 2 American Indian/Alaska Native, 31 Asian Americans or Pacific Islanders, 15 Hispanic Americans), 204 international. Average age 30. 105 applicants. *Faculty:* 12 full-time (2 women), 43 part-time/adjunct (6 women). Expenses: Contact institution. *Financial support:* In 2006–07, 156 students received support. Career-related internships or fieldwork and Federal Work-Study available. Support available to part-time students. Financial award application deadline: 8/10; financial award applicants required to submit FAFSA. In 2006, 54 degrees awarded. *Degree program information:* Part-time programs available. Postbaccalaureate distance learning degree programs offered (no on-campus study). Offers 2D animation (MFA); 3D animation (MFA); 3D modeling (MFA); games (MFA); visual effects (MFA). *Application deadline:* For fall admission, 9/7 for domestic and international students; for spring admission, 2/2 for domestic and international students. Applications are processed on a rolling basis. *Application fee:* $100 ($500 for international students). Electronic applications accepted. *Application Contact:* Information Contact, 800-544-ARTS, Fax: 415-263-4130, E-mail: info@academyart.edu. *Director of Animation 3D,* Tom Bertino, 800-544-ARTS, Fax: 415-263-4130, E-mail: info@academyart.edu.

School of Architecture Students: 19 full-time (8 women), 11 part-time (6 women); includes 2 African Americans, 1 Asian American or Pacific Islander, 1 Hispanic American, 14 international. Average age 28. 9 applicants. *Faculty:* 1 (woman) full-time, 11 part-time/adjunct (4 women). Expenses: Contact institution. *Financial support:* In 2006–07, 4 students received support. Career-related internships or fieldwork and Federal Work-Study available. Support available to part-time students. Financial award application deadline: 8/10; financial award applicants required to submit FAFSA. In 2006, 7 degrees awarded. *Degree program information:* Part-time programs available. Postbaccalaureate distance learning degree programs offered (no on-campus study). Offers architecture (M Arch, MFA). *Application deadline:* For fall admission, 9/7 for domestic and international students; for spring admission, 2/2 for domestic and international students. Applications are processed on a rolling basis. *Application fee:* $100 ($500 for international students). Electronic applications accepted. *Application Contact:* Prospective Students Services, 800-544-ARTS, Fax: 415-263-4131, E-mail: info@academyart.edu. *Director,* Mimi Sullivan, 800-544-ARTS, E-mail: info@academyart.edu.

School of Computer Arts/New Media Students: 106 full-time (51 women), 71 part-time (41 women); includes 32 minority (9 African Americans, 17 Asian Americans or Pacific Islanders, 6 Hispanic Americans), 73 international. Average age 30. 64 applicants. *Faculty:* 1 (woman) full-time, 13 part-time/adjunct (5 women). Expenses: Contact institution. *Financial support:* In 2006–07, 53 students received support. Career-related internships or fieldwork and Federal Work-Study available. Support available to part-time students. Financial award application deadline: 8/10; financial award applicants required to submit FAFSA. In 2006, 28 degrees awarded. *Degree program information:* Part-time and evening/weekend programs available. Offers computer arts/new media (MFA). *Application deadline:* For fall admission, 9/7 for domestic and international students; for spring admission, 2/2 for domestic students, 9/2 for international students. Applications are processed on a rolling basis. *Application fee:* $100 ($500 for international students). Electronic applications accepted. *Application Contact:* 800-544-ARTS, Fax: 415-263-4130, E-mail: info@academyart.edu. *Director,* Lourdes Livingston, 800-544-ARTS, E-mail: info@academyart.edu.

School of Fashion Students: 181 full-time (164 women), 75 part-time (71 women); includes 46 minority (18 African Americans, 1 American Indian/Alaska Native, 20 Asian Americans or Pacific Islanders, 7 Hispanic Americans), 112 international. Average age 28. 64 applicants. *Faculty:* 12 full-time (7 women), 20 part-time/adjunct (18 women). Expenses: Contact institution. *Financial support:* In 2006–07, 86 students received support. Career-related internships or fieldwork and Federal Work-Study available. Support available to part-time students. Financial award application deadline: 8/10; financial award applicants required to submit FAFSA. In 2006, 35 degrees awarded. *Degree program information:* Part-time programs available. Postbaccalaureate distance learning degree programs offered (no on-campus study). Offers fashion design (MFA); fashion merchandising (MFA); fashion textiles (MFA); knitwear (MFA). *Application deadline:* For fall admission, 9/7 for domestic and international students; for spring admission, 2/2 for domestic and international students. Applications are processed on a rolling basis. *Application fee:* $100 ($500 for international students). Electronic applications accepted. *Application Contact:* Prospective Student Services, 800-544-ARTS, Fax: 415-263-4130, E-mail: info@academyart.edu. *Director,* Simon Ungless, 800-544-ARTS, Fax: 415-296-2089, E-mail: info@academyart.edu.

School of Fine Art Students: 95 full-time (51 women), 90 part-time (63 women); includes 26 minority (4 African Americans, 1 American Indian/Alaska Native, 14 Asian Americans or Pacific Islanders, 7 Hispanic Americans), 30 international. Average age 37. 48 applicants.

Faculty: 11 full-time (5 women), 20 part-time/adjunct (8 women). Expenses: Contact institution. *Financial support:* In 2006–07, 72 students received support. Career-related internships or fieldwork and Federal Work-Study available. Support available to part-time students. Financial award application deadline: 8/10; financial award applicants required to submit FAFSA. In 2006, 19 degrees awarded. *Degree program information:* Part-time programs available. Postbaccalaureate distance learning degree programs offered (no on-campus study). Offers figurative painting (MFA); non-figurative painting (MFA); printmaking (MFA); sculpture (MFA). *Application deadline:* For fall admission, 9/7 for domestic and international students; for spring admission, 2/2 for domestic and international students. Applications are processed on a rolling basis. *Application fee:* $100 ($500 for international students). Electronic applications accepted. *Application Contact:* Prospective Student Services, 800-544-ARTS, Fax: 415-263-4130, E-mail: info@academyart.edu. *Director*, William Maughan, 800-544-ARTS, Fax: 415-263-4124, E-mail: info@academyart.edu.

School of Graphic Design Students: 128 full-time (92 women), 67 part-time (44 women); includes 34 minority (8 African Americans, 1 American Indian/Alaska Native, 17 Asian Americans or Pacific Islanders, 8 Hispanic Americans), 69 international. Average age 28. 58 applicants. *Faculty:* 12 full-time (7 women), 13 part-time/adjunct (2 women). Expenses: Contact institution. *Financial support:* In 2006–07, 57 students received support. Career-related internships or fieldwork and Federal Work-Study available. Support available to part-time students. Financial award application deadline: 8/10; financial award applicants required to submit FAFSA. In 2006, 17 degrees awarded. *Degree program information:* Part-time programs available. Postbaccalaureate distance learning degree programs offered (no on-campus study). Offers graphic design (MFA). *Application deadline:* For fall admission, 9/7 for domestic and international students; for spring admission, 2/2 for domestic and international students. Applications are processed on a rolling basis. *Application fee:* $100 ($500 for international students). Electronic applications accepted. *Application Contact:* Prospective Student Services, 800-544-ARTS, Fax: 415-263-4130, E-mail: info@academyart.edu. *Director*, Phil Hamlett, 800-544-ARTS, Fax: 415-263-4124.

School of Illustration Students: 68 full-time (32 women), 31 part-time (12 women); includes 14 minority (6 African Americans, 2 American Indian/Alaska Native, 2 Asian Americans or Pacific Islanders, 4 Hispanic Americans), 22 international. Average age 30. 42 applicants. *Faculty:* 5 full-time (2 women), 12 part-time/adjunct (2 women). Expenses: Contact institution. *Financial support:* In 2006–07, 48 students received support. Career-related internships or fieldwork and Federal Work-Study available. Support available to part-time students. Financial award application deadline: 8/10; financial award applicants required to submit FAFSA. In 2006, 10 degrees awarded. *Degree program information:* Part-time programs available. Postbaccalaureate distance learning degree programs offered (no on-campus study). Offers illustration (MFA). *Application deadline:* For fall admission, 9/7 for domestic and international students; for spring admission, 2/2 for domestic and international students. Applications are processed on a rolling basis. *Application fee:* $100 ($500 for international students). Electronic applications accepted. *Application Contact:* Prospective Student Services, 800-544-ARTS, Fax: 415-263-4130, E-mail: info@academyart.edu. *Director*, William Maughan, 800-544-ARTS, Fax: 415-263-4124, E-mail: info@academyart.edu.

School of Industrial Design Students: 47 full-time (15 women), 3 part-time (1 woman); includes 1 African American, 3 Asian Americans or Pacific Islanders, 36 international. Average age 28. 17 applicants. *Faculty:* 3 full-time (1 woman), 11 part-time/adjunct (1 woman). Expenses: Contact institution. *Financial support:* In 2006–07, 9 students received support. Career-related internships or fieldwork and Federal Work-Study available. Support available to part-time students. Financial award application deadline: 8/10; financial award applicants required to submit FAFSA. In 2006, 7 degrees awarded. *Degree program information:* Part-time programs available. Postbaccalaureate distance learning degree programs offered (no on-campus study). Offers industrial design (MFA). *Application deadline:* For fall admission, 9/7 for domestic and international students; for spring admission, 2/2 for domestic and international students. Applications are processed on a rolling basis. *Application fee:* $100 ($500 for international students). Electronic applications accepted. *Application Contact:* 800-544-ARTS, Fax: 415-263-4130, E-mail: info@academyart.edu. *Director*, Carol Keffel, 800-544-ARTS, Fax: 415-263-4130, E-mail: info@academyart.edu.

School of Interior Architecture and Design Students: 39 full-time (31 women), 37 part-time (30 women); includes 10 minority (5 African Americans, 4 Asian Americans or Pacific Islanders, 1 Hispanic American), 33 international. Average age 33. 32 applicants. *Faculty:* 3 full-time (all women), 15 part-time/adjunct (4 women). Expenses: Contact institution. *Financial support:* In 2006–07, 24 students received support. Career-related internships or fieldwork and Federal Work-Study available. Support available to part-time students. Financial award application deadline: 8/10; financial award applicants required to submit FAFSA. In 2006, 11 degrees awarded. *Degree program information:* Part-time programs available. Postbaccalaureate distance learning degree programs offered (no on-campus study). Offers interior architecture and design (MFA). *Application deadline:* For fall admission, 9/7 for domestic and international students; for spring admission, 2/2 for domestic and international students. Applications are processed on a rolling basis. *Application fee:* $100 ($500 for international students). Electronic applications accepted. *Application Contact:* 800-544-ARTS, Fax: 415-263-4130, E-mail: info@academyart.edu. *Director*, Marlene Farrell, 800-544-ARTS, Fax: 415-263-4130, E-mail: info@academyart.edu.

School of Motion Pictures and Television Students: 133 full-time (48 women), 65 part-time (23 women); includes 34 minority (14 African Americans, 1 American Indian/Alaska Native, 11 Asian Americans or Pacific Islanders, 8 Hispanic Americans), 49 international. Average age 30. 45 applicants. *Faculty:* 5 full-time (1 woman), 31 part-time/adjunct (12 women). Expenses: Contact institution. *Financial support:* In 2006–07, 95 students received support. Career-related internships or fieldwork and Federal Work-Study available. Support available to part-time students. Financial award application deadline: 8/10; financial award applicants required to submit FAFSA. In 2006, 22 degrees awarded. *Degree program information:* Part-time programs available. Postbaccalaureate distance learning degree programs offered (no on-campus study). Offers motion pictures and television (MFA). *Application deadline:* For fall admission, 9/7 for domestic and international students; for spring admission, 2/2 for domestic and international students. Applications are processed on a rolling basis. *Application fee:* $100 ($500 for international students). Electronic applications accepted. *Application Contact:* 800-544-ARTS, Fax: 415-263-4130, E-mail: info@academyart.edu. *Director*, Jack Isgro, 800-544-ARTS, E-mail: info@academyart.edu.

School of Photography Students: 111 full-time (59 women), 85 part-time (49 women); includes 27 minority (6 African Americans, 2 American Indian/Alaska Native, 11 Asian Americans or Pacific Islanders, 8 Hispanic Americans), 27 international. Average age 34. 52 applicants. *Faculty:* 5 full-time (1 woman), 16 part-time/adjunct (5 women). Expenses: Contact institution. *Financial support:* In 2006–07, 83 students received support. Career-related internships or fieldwork and Federal Work-Study available. Support available to part-time students. Financial award application deadline: 8/10; financial award applicants required to submit FAFSA. In 2006, 14 degrees awarded. *Degree program information:* Part-time programs available. Postbaccalaureate distance learning degree programs offered (no on-campus study). Offers photography (MFA). *Application deadline:* For fall admission, 9/7 for domestic and international students; for spring admission, 2/2 for domestic and international students. Applications are processed on a rolling basis. *Application fee:* $100 ($500 for international students). Electronic applications accepted. *Application Contact:* 800-544-ARTS, Fax: 415-263-4130, E-mail: info@academyart.edu. *Director*, William Musgrove, 800-544-ARTS, E-mail: info@academyart.edu.

ACADEMY OF CHINESE CULTURE AND HEALTH SCIENCES, Oakland, CA 94612

General Information Private, coed, graduate-only institution. *Graduate housing:* On-campus housing not available.

GRADUATE UNITS

Program in Traditional Chinese Medicine *Degree program information:* Part-time and evening/weekend programs available. Offers traditional Chinese medicine (MS).

ACADEMY OF ORIENTAL MEDICINE AT AUSTIN, Austin, TX 78757

General Information Proprietary, coed, graduate-only institution.

GRADUATE UNITS

Program in Acupuncture and Oriental Medicine Offers acupuncture and oriental medicine (MAOM).

ACADIA UNIVERSITY, Wolfville, NS B4P 2R6, Canada

General Information Province-supported, coed, comprehensive institution. *Enrollment:* 3,699 graduate, professional, and undergraduate students; 152 full-time matriculated graduate/professional students (69 women), 214 part-time matriculated graduate/professional students (141 women). *Enrollment by degree level:* 366 master's. *Graduate faculty:* 113 full-time (38 women), 29 part-time/adjunct (7 women). *Graduate housing:* Room and/or apartments available on a first-come, first-served basis to single students; on-campus housing not available to married students. Typical cost: $7,799 (including board). Room and board charges vary according to board plan, campus/location and housing facility selected. Housing application deadline: 5/31. *Student services:* Campus employment opportunities, campus safety program, career counseling, disabled student services, exercise/wellness program, free psychological counseling, international student services, low-cost health insurance, writing training. *Library facilities:* Vaughan Memorial Library. *Online resources:* library catalog, web page, access to other libraries' catalogs. *Collection:* 686,223 titles, 8,581 serial subscriptions, 10,062 audiovisual materials. *Research affiliation:* Atlantic Research Laboratory.

Computer facilities: 3,700 computers available on campus for general student use. A campuswide network can be accessed from student residence rooms and from off campus. Internet access and online class registration, online course and grade information are available. *Web address:* http://www.acadiau.ca/.

General Application Contact: Anne Scott, Manager, Admissions, 902-585-1016, Fax: 902-585-1092, E-mail: admissions@acadiau.ca.

GRADUATE UNITS

Divinity College Students: 65 full-time (18 women), 22 part-time (4 women); includes 7 minority (5 African Americans, 1 American Indian/Alaska Native, 1 Asian American or Pacific Islander). 33 applicants, 91% accepted, 28 enrolled. *Faculty:* 8 full-time (0 women), 12 part-time/adjunct (3 women). Expenses: Contact institution. *Financial support:* In 2006–07, 8 teaching assistantships (averaging $1,000 per year) were awarded; research assistantships, career-related internships or fieldwork, scholarships/grants, and tuition waivers (partial) also available. Financial award application deadline: 8/12. In 2006, 18 master's, 3 doctorates awarded. *Degree program information:* Part-time programs available. Offers divinity (M Div); theology (MA, D Min). *Application deadline:* For fall admission, 5/31 priority date for domestic students, 4/1 priority date for international students; for spring admission, 4/15 priority date for domestic students. Applications are processed on a rolling basis. *Application fee:* $25. *Application Contact:* Gail Noel, Office of Student Services, 902-585-2215, Fax: 902-585-2233, E-mail: gail.noel@acadiau.ca. *President*, Dr. Lee M. McDonald, 902-585-2212, Fax: 902-585-2233, E-mail: lee.mcdonald@acadiau.ca.

Faculty of Arts Students: 11 full-time (9 women), 9 part-time (5 women); includes 1 African American. Average age 25. *Faculty:* 29 full-time (12 women), 2 part-time/adjunct (1 woman). Expenses: Contact institution. *Financial support:* Research assistantships, teaching assistantships, career-related internships or fieldwork, scholarships/grants, and unspecified assistantships available. Financial award application deadline: 2/1. In 2006, 7 degrees awarded. Offers arts (MA); English (MA); political science (MA); sociology (MA). *Application deadline:* For fall admission, 2/1 for domestic and international students. *Application fee:* $50. Electronic applications accepted. *Dean*, Dr. Robert J. Perrins, 902-585-1485, Fax: 902-585-1070, E-mail: robert.perrins@acadiau.ca.

Faculty of Professional Studies Students: 24 full-time (18 women), 154 part-time (122 women). *Faculty:* 20 full-time (10 women). Expenses: Contact institution. *Financial support:* Research assistantships, teaching assistantships available. Financial award application deadline: 2/1. *Degree program information:* Part-time and evening/weekend programs available. *Application fee:* $50. *Application Contact:* Rosie Hare, Administrative Assistant, 902-585-1597, Fax: 902-585-1086, E-mail: rosie.hare@acadiau.ca. *Dean*, Dr. William McLeod, 902-585-1597, Fax: 902-585-1086, E-mail: bill.mcleod@acadiau.ca.

School of Education Students: 24 full-time (18 women), 152 part-time (121 women). *Faculty:* 20 full-time (10 women). Expenses: Contact institution. *Financial support:* In 2006–07, 7 teaching assistantships (averaging $4,000 per year) were awarded; research assistantships. Financial award application deadline: 2/1. In 2006, 101 master's awarded. *Degree program information:* Part-time and evening/weekend programs available. Offers counseling (M Ed); cultural and media studies (M Ed); curriculum studies (M Ed); inclusive education (M Ed); learning and technology (M Ed); organizational leadership (M Ed); science, math and technology (M Ed); special education (M Ed). *Application fee:* $50. Electronic applications accepted. *Application Contact:* Sheila Langille, Secretary, 902-585-1229, Fax: 902-585-1071, E-mail: sheila.langille@acadiau.ca.

School of Recreation Management and Kinesiology Expenses: Contact institution. In 2006, 2 degrees awarded. Offers recreation management and kinesiology (MR). *Application fee:* $50. *Application Contact:* Krista Robertson, Secretary, 902-585-1457, Fax: 902-585-1702, E-mail: krista.robertson@acadiau.ca. *Director*, Dr. Gary Ness, 902-585-1566, Fax: 902-585-1702, E-mail: gary.ness@acadiau.ca.

Faculty of Pure and Applied Science Students: 52 full-time (24 women), 29 part-time (10 women). *Faculty:* 56 full-time (16 women), 15 part-time/adjunct (3 women). Expenses: Contact institution. *Financial support:* Fellowships, research assistantships, teaching assistantships, career-related internships or fieldwork and scholarships/grants available. Financial award application deadline: 2/1. In 2006, 32 degrees awarded. Offers applied mathematics and statistics (M Sc); biology (M Sc); chemistry (M Sc); clinical psychology (M Sc); geology (M Sc); pure and applied science (M Sc). *Application deadline:* For fall admission, 2/1 for domestic students. *Application fee:* $50. *Dean*, Dr. George K. Iwama, 902-585-1472, Fax: 902-585-1637, E-mail: george.iwama@acadiau.ca.

Jodrey School of Computer Science Students: 9 full-time (1 woman), 13 part-time (2 women), 13 international. Average age 28. *Faculty:* 10 full-time (0 women), 1 part-time/adjunct (0 women). Expenses: Contact institution. *Financial support:* Teaching assistantships, career-related internships or fieldwork available. Financial award application deadline: 1/15. In 2006, 5 degrees awarded. Offers computer science (M Sc). *Application deadline:* For fall admission, 1/15 for domestic students. *Application fee:* $50. *Acting Director*, Dr. Colin W. Wightman, 902-585-1331, Fax: 902-585-1067, E-mail: cs@acadiau.ca.

ACUPUNCTURE & INTEGRATIVE MEDICINE COLLEGE, BERKELEY, Berkeley, CA 94704

General Information Independent, coed, graduate-only institution. *Enrollment by degree level:* 114 master's. *Graduate faculty:* 1 full-time (0 women), 20 part-time/adjunct (10 women). *Tuition:* Full-time $13,500; part-time $224 per term. *Graduate housing:* On-campus housing not available. *Library facilities:* Main library plus 1 other. *Online resources:* library catalog. *Collection:* 1,850 titles, 20 serial subscriptions, 100 audiovisual materials.

Computer facilities: 2 computers available on campus for general student use. A campuswide network can be accessed. Internet access, Medline are available. *Web address:* http://www.aimc.edu/.

General Application Contact: Nellie E. Wilson, Admissions and Programs Director, 510-666-8248 Ext. 106, Fax: 510-666-0111, E-mail: nwilson@aimc.edu.

GRADUATE UNITS

Program in Oriental Medicine Students: 90 full-time (74 women), 32 part-time (26 women); includes 36 minority (8 African Americans, 17 Asian Americans or Pacific Islanders, 11 Hispanic Americans). Average age 41. 36 applicants, 86% accepted, 26 enrolled. *Faculty:* 1 full-time (0 women), 20 part-time/adjunct (10 women). Expenses: Contact institution. *Financial support:* In 2006–07, 98 students received support. Application deadline: 7/31. *Degree program information:* Part-time programs available. Offers Oriental medicine (MS). *Application deadline:* For fall admission, 8/1 priority date for domestic students; for winter admission, 12/1 priority date for domestic students; for spring admission, 3/1 priority date for domestic students. Applications are processed on a rolling basis. *Application fee:* $100 ($200 for inter-

Acupuncture & Integrative Medicine College, Berkeley (continued)
national students). *Application Contact:* Nellie E. Wilson, Admissions and Programs Director, 510-666-8248 Ext. 106, Fax: 510-666-0111, E-mail: nwilson@aimc.edu. *President,* Skye Sturgeon, 510-666-8248 Ext. 132, Fax: 510-666-0111, E-mail: ssturgeon@aimc.edu.

ACUPUNCTURE AND MASSAGE COLLEGE, Miami, FL 33176

General Information Proprietary, coed, graduate-only institution.

GRADUATE UNITS

Program in Oriental Medicine Offers Oriental medicine (MOM).

ADAMS STATE COLLEGE, Alamosa, CO 81102

General Information State-supported, coed, comprehensive institution. *Graduate housing:* Rooms and/or apartments available to single and married students. Housing application deadline: 5/15. *Research affiliation:* Sandia National Laboratories (science education).

GRADUATE UNITS

The Graduate School *Degree program information:* Part-time programs available. Postbaccalaureate distance learning degree programs offered. Offers art (MA); counseling (MA); education (MA); health and physical education (MA); special education (MA).

ADELPHI UNIVERSITY, Garden City, NY 11530-0701

General Information Independent, coed, university. *Enrollment:* 8,053 graduate, professional, and undergraduate students; 900 full-time matriculated graduate/professional students (762 women), 2,195 part-time matriculated graduate/professional students (1,738 women). *Enrollment by degree level:* 2,856 master's, 198 doctoral, 41 other advanced degrees. *Graduate faculty:* 280 full-time (136 women), 623 part-time/adjunct (407 women). *Graduate housing:* Room and/or apartments available on a first-come, first-served basis to single students; on-campus housing not available to married students. Typical cost: $6,350 per year ($9,500 including board). *Student services:* Campus employment opportunities, campus safety program, career counseling, child daycare facilities, disabled student services, exercise/wellness program, free psychological counseling, international student services, low-cost health insurance, multicultural affairs office, teacher training. *Library facilities:* Swirbul Library plus 1 other. *Online resources:* library catalog, web page. *Collection:* 667,293 titles, 28,856 serial subscriptions, 30,372 audiovisual materials. *Research affiliation:* Albert Einstein College of Medicine, The Horace Hagedorn Foundation, The Research Corporation, The National Science Foundation, World Anti-doping Agency.

Computer facilities: Computer purchase and lease plans are available. 540 computers available on campus for general student use. A campuswide network can be accessed from student residence rooms and from off campus. Internet access and online class registration, payment, grades, drop/add classes, check application status are available. *Web address:* http://www.adelphi.edu/.

General Application Contact: Christine Murphy, Director of Admissions, 516-877-3050, Fax: 516-877-3039, E-mail: graduateadmissions@adelphi.edu.

GRADUATE UNITS

Derner Institute of Advanced Psychological Studies Students: 174 full-time (144 women), 201 part-time (161 women); includes 37 minority (20 African Americans, 9 Asian Americans or Pacific Islanders, 8 Hispanic Americans), 21 international. Average age 31. 541 applicants, 42% accepted, 118 enrolled. *Faculty:* 23 full-time (10 women). Expenses: Contact institution. *Financial support:* In 2006–07, 74 research assistantships with full and partial tuition reimbursements (averaging $6,343 per year) were awarded; teaching assistantships, career-related internships or fieldwork, Federal Work-Study, institutionally sponsored loans, unspecified assistantships, and clinical placements also available. Financial award application deadline: 2/15; financial award applicants required to submit FAFSA. In 2006, 98 master's, 27 doctorates, 12 other advanced degrees awarded. Offers clinical psychology (PhD, Post-Doctoral Certificate); general psychology (MA); mental health counseling (MA); school psychology (MA). *Application deadline:* For fall admission, 1/15 priority date for domestic students, 5/1 priority date for international students; for spring admission, 12/1 priority date for international students. *Application fee:* $50. Electronic applications accepted. *Application Contact:* Christine Murphy, Director of Admissions, 516-877-3050, Fax: 516-877-3039, E-mail: graduateadmissions@adelphi.edu. *Dean,* Dr. Jeau Lau Chir, 516-877-4800, E-mail: Chir@adelphi.edu.

Graduate School of Arts and Sciences Students: 8 full-time (5 women), 83 part-time (49 women); includes 19 minority (5 African Americans, 4 Asian Americans or Pacific Islanders, 10 Hispanic Americans), 2 international. Average age 33. 92 applicants, 67% accepted, 38 enrolled. *Faculty:* 109 full-time (37 women). Expenses: Contact institution. *Financial support:* In 2006–07, 24 research assistantships with full and partial tuition reimbursements (averaging $10,570 per year) were awarded; fellowships, teaching assistantships, career-related internships or fieldwork, Federal Work-Study, institutionally sponsored loans, tuition waivers (full and partial), and unspecified assistantships also available. Support available to part-time students. Financial award application deadline: 2/15; financial award applicants required to submit FAFSA. In 2006, 25 master's, 4 other advanced degrees awarded. *Degree program information:* Part-time and evening/weekend programs available. Offers art and art history (MA); arts and sciences (MA, MFA, MS, Certificate); biology (MS); creative writing (MFA); emergency management (Certificate); environmental studies (MS); physics (MS). *Application deadline:* For fall admission, 5/1 for international students; for spring admission, 12/1 for international students. Applications are processed on a rolling basis. *Application fee:* $50. Electronic applications accepted. *Application Contact:* Christine Murphy, Director of Admissions, 516-877-3050, Fax: 516-877-3039, E-mail: graduateadmissions@adelphi.edu. *Dean,* Dr. Gayle Insler, 516-877-4124, Fax: 516-877-4191, E-mail: insler@adelphi.edu.

School of Business Students: 68 full-time (35 women), 181 part-time (89 women); includes 47 minority (25 African Americans, 1 American Indian/Alaska Native, 13 Asian Americans or Pacific Islanders, 8 Hispanic Americans), 53 international. Average age 31. 222 applicants, 51% accepted, 76 enrolled. *Faculty:* 37 full-time (8 women). Expenses: Contact institution. *Financial support:* In 2006–07, 33 teaching assistantships (averaging $4,617 per year) were awarded; research assistantships with partial tuition reimbursements, career-related internships or fieldwork, Federal Work-Study, institutionally sponsored loans, scholarships/grants, and unspecified assistantships also available. Financial award application deadline: 3/1; financial award applicants required to submit FAFSA. In 2006, 132 degrees awarded. *Degree program information:* Part-time and evening/weekend programs available. Offers accounting (MBA); business (MBA, MS, Certificate); finance (MBA, MS); human resource management (Certificate); management information systems (MBA); management/human resource management (MBA); marketing/e-commerce (MBA). *Application deadline:* For fall admission, 5/1 for international students; for spring admission, 12/1 for international students. Applications are processed on a rolling basis. *Application fee:* $50. Electronic applications accepted. *Application Contact:* Christine Murphy, Director of Admissions, 516-877-3050, Fax: 516-877-3039, E-mail: graduateadmissions@adelphi.edu. *Dean,* Dr. Anthony F. Libertella, 516-877-4690, Fax: 516-877-4607, E-mail: libertel@adelphi.edu.

School of Education Students: 432 full-time (379 women), 869 part-time (679 women); includes 186 minority (73 African Americans, 27 Asian Americans or Pacific Islanders, 86 Hispanic Americans), 6 international. Average age 30. 1,111 applicants, 53% accepted, 424 enrolled. *Faculty:* 62 full-time (43 women). Expenses: Contact institution. *Financial support:* In 2006–07, 104 teaching assistantships (averaging $5,816 per year) were awarded; fellowships, research assistantships with full and partial tuition reimbursements, career-related internships or fieldwork, Federal Work-Study, institutionally sponsored loans, tuition waivers (full), and unspecified assistantships also available. Support available to part-time students. Financial award application deadline: 2/15; financial award applicants required to submit FAFSA. In 2006, 599 master's, 9 other advanced degrees awarded. *Degree program information:* Part-time and evening/weekend programs available. Offers adolescent education (MA); aging (Certificate); audiology (MS, DA); birth through grade 2 (Certificate); birth-grade 12 (MS); birth-grade 6 (MS); childhood special education (Certificate); childhood special education studies (MS); community health education (MA, Certificate); early childhood education (Certificate); education (MA, MS, DA, Certificate); educational leadership and technology (MA, Certificate); elementary teachers pre K-6 (MA); grades 1-6 (MA, MS); grades 5-12 (MS); in-service (MA, MS); inclusive setting, grades 1-6 preservice or in-service track (MS); physical/educational human performance science (MA); pre-certification (MA); preservice (MS); school health education (MA); speech-language pathology (MS, DA); teaching English to speakers of other languages (MA, Certificate). *Application deadline:* Applications are processed on a rolling basis. *Application fee:* $50. Electronic applications accepted. *Application Contact:* Christine Murphy, Director of Admissions, 516-877-3050, Fax: 516-877-3039, E-mail: graduateadmissions@adelphi.edu. *Dean,* Dr. Ronald Feingold, 516-877-4100, E-mail: feingold@adelphi.edu.

School of Nursing Students: 5 full-time (all women), 171 part-time (161 women); includes 56 minority (33 African Americans, 1 American Indian/Alaska Native, 17 Asian Americans or Pacific Islanders, 5 Hispanic Americans). Average age 44. 94 applicants, 48% accepted, 45 enrolled. *Faculty:* 27 full-time (24 women). Expenses: Contact institution. *Financial support:* In 2006–07, 1 research assistantship with full and partial tuition reimbursement (averaging $1,180 per year), 3 teaching assistantships (averaging $7,800 per year) were awarded; career-related internships or fieldwork, unspecified assistantships, and graduate achievement awards also available. Support available to part-time students. Financial award application deadline: 2/15; financial award applicants required to submit FAFSA. In 2006, 31 master's, 5 other advanced degrees awarded. *Degree program information:* Part-time and evening/weekend programs available. Offers nursing (MS, PhD, Certificate). *Application deadline:* For fall admission, 3/15 for domestic students. *Application fee:* $50. Electronic applications accepted. *Application Contact:* Christine Murphy, Director of Admissions, 516-877-3050, Fax: 516-877-3039, E-mail: graduateadmissions@adelphi.edu. *Dean,* Dr. Patrick Coonan, 516-877-4511, E-mail: coonan@adelphi.edu.

School of Social Work Students: 212 full-time (193 women), 688 part-time (597 women); includes 270 minority (187 African Americans, 1 American Indian/Alaska Native, 15 Asian Americans or Pacific Islanders, 67 Hispanic Americans), 7 international. Average age 36. 624 applicants, 71% accepted, 297 enrolled. *Faculty:* 22 full-time (14 women). Expenses: Contact institution. *Financial support:* In 2006–07, 72 research assistantships with full and partial tuition reimbursements (averaging $2,317 per year) were awarded; career-related internships or fieldwork, Federal Work-Study, institutionally sponsored loans, scholarships/grants, traineeships, tuition waivers (full and partial), and unspecified assistantships also available. Financial award application deadline: 2/15; financial award applicants required to submit FAFSA. In 2006, 280 master's, 4 doctorates awarded. *Degree program information:* Part-time and evening/weekend programs available. Offers social welfare (DSW); social work (MSW). *Application deadline:* For fall admission, 5/1 for international students; for spring admission, 12/1 for domestic and international students. *Application fee:* $50. Electronic applications accepted. *Application Contact:* Christine Murphy, Director of Admissions, 516-877-3050, Fax: 516-877-3039, E-mail: graduateadmissions@adelphi.edu. *Dean,* Dr. Andrew Safyer, 516-877-4300, E-mail: asafyer@adelphi.edu.

ADLER GRADUATE SCHOOL, Richfield, MN 55423

General Information Independent, coed, graduate-only institution. *Enrollment by degree level:* 187 master's. *Graduate faculty:* 4 full-time (1 woman), 36 part-time/adjunct (21 women). *Graduate housing:* On-campus housing not available. *Student services:* Career counseling, disabled student services, multicultural affairs office. *Library facilities:* Adler Graduate School Library. *Online resources:* web page. *Collection:* 4,700 titles, 16 serial subscriptions, 260 audiovisual materials.

Computer facilities: 8 computers available on campus for general student use. A campuswide network can be accessed. Internet access and online class registration are available. *Web address:* http://www.alfredadler.edu/.

General Application Contact: Evelyn B. Haas, Director of Student Services and Admissions, 612-861-7554 Ext. 103, Fax: 612-861-7559, E-mail: ev@alfredadler.edu.

GRADUATE UNITS

Program in Adlerian Studies Average age 37. 48 applicants, 98% accepted, 46 enrolled. *Faculty:* 4 full-time (1 woman), 36 part-time/adjunct (21 women). Expenses: Contact institution. *Financial support:* In 2006–07, 121 students received support. Career-related internships or fieldwork and tuition waivers available. Support available to part-time students. Financial award applicants required to submit FAFSA. In 2006, 37 degrees awarded. *Degree program information:* Part-time and evening/weekend programs available. Offers art therapy specialization (MA); clinical counseling track (MA); coaching and consulting in organizations (Certificate); management consulting and organizational leadership (MA); marriage and family track (MA); non-clinical Adlerian studies track (MA); personal and professional life coaching (Certificate); school counseling (MA). *Application deadline:* For fall admission, 10/1 priority date for domestic students; for winter admission, 1/1 priority date for domestic students; for spring admission, 4/1 priority date for domestic students. Applications are processed on a rolling basis. *Application fee:* $50. *Application Contact:* Evelyn B. Haas, Director of Student Services and Admissions, 612-861-7554 Ext. 103, Fax: 612-861-7559, E-mail: ev@alfredadler.edu. *President,* Dr. Dennis Rislove, 612-861-7554 Ext. 106, Fax: 612-861-7559, E-mail: rislove@alfredadler.edu.

ADLER SCHOOL OF PROFESSIONAL PSYCHOLOGY, Chicago, IL 60601-7203

General Information Independent, coed, graduate-only institution. *Enrollment by degree level:* 250 master's, 252 doctoral, 16 other advanced degrees. *Graduate faculty:* 17 full-time (9 women), 47 part-time/adjunct (20 women). *Tuition:* Part-time $690 per credit. *Required fees:* $160 per term. *Graduate housing:* On-campus housing not available. *Student services:* Campus employment opportunities, career counseling, disabled student services, international student services. *Library facilities:* Sol and Elaine Mosak Library. *Online resources:* library catalog, web page, access to other libraries' catalogs. *Collection:* 15,000 titles, 170 serial subscriptions, 1,800 audiovisual materials.

Computer facilities: 12 computers available on campus for general student use. A campuswide network can be accessed. Internet access is available. *Web address:* http://www.adler.edu/.

General Application Contact: Craig A. Hines, Director of Admissions, 312-201-5900 Ext. 226, Fax: 312-201-5917, E-mail: admissions@adler.edu.

GRADUATE UNITS

Programs in Psychology Students: 415 full-time (309 women), 103 part-time (77 women); includes 98 minority (45 African Americans, 2 American Indian/Alaska Native, 19 Asian Americans or Pacific Islanders, 32 Hispanic Americans), 7 international. Average age 27. 293 applicants, 100% accepted. *Faculty:* 23 full-time (6 women), 47 part-time/adjunct (18 women). Expenses: Contact institution. *Financial support:* In 2006–07, 180 students received support. Career-related internships or fieldwork, Federal Work-Study, scholarships/grants, and tuition waivers (full and partial) available. Support available to part-time students. Financial award application deadline: 5/15; financial award applicants required to submit FAFSA. In 2006, 62 master's, 54 doctorates awarded. *Degree program information:* Part-time and evening/weekend programs available. Offers art therapy (Certificate); clinical hypnosis (Certificate); clinical psychology (Psy D); counseling psychology (MACP); counseling psychology/art therapy (MACAT); gerontology (MAGP); marriage and family counseling (MAMFC); marriage and family therapy (Certificate); organizational psychology (MAO); substance abuse counseling (MASAC, Certificate). *Application deadline:* For fall admission, 1/1 priority date for domestic students. Applications are processed on a rolling basis. *Application fee:* $50. *Application Contact:* Susan E. Greenwald, Director of Admissions, 312-201-5900 Ext. 226, Fax: 312-201-5917, E-mail: seg@adler.edu. *Vice President of Academic Affairs,* Dr. Frank Gruba-McAllister, 312-201-5900, Fax: 312-207-5917.

AGNES SCOTT COLLEGE, Decatur, GA 30030-3797

General Information Independent-religious, Undergraduate: women only; graduate: coed, comprehensive institution. *Enrollment:* 902 graduate, professional, and undergraduate students; 15 full-time matriculated graduate/professional students (14 women), 1 (woman) part-time matriculated graduate/professional student. *Enrollment by degree level:* 16 master's. *Gradu-*

ate faculty: 6 full-time (2 women), 3 part-time/adjunct (all women). *Tuition:* Full-time $21,840; part-time $445 per hour. *Required fees:* $375. *Graduate housing:* On-campus housing not available. *Student services:* Campus safety program, career counseling, disabled student services, low-cost health insurance, multicultural affairs office, teacher training, writing training. *Library facilities:* McCain Library. *Online resources:* library catalog, web page, access to other libraries' catalogs. *Collection:* 218,046 titles, 1,842 serial subscriptions, 19,989 audiovisual materials.

Computer facilities: 558 computers available on campus for general student use. A campuswide network can be accessed from student residence rooms and from off campus. Internet access is available. *Web address:* http://www.agnesscott.edu/.

General Application Contact: Lisa M. Flowers, Education Faculty Coordinator, 404-471-5168, Fax: 404-471-5152, E-mail: lflowers@agnesscott.edu.

GRADUATE UNITS

Secondary English Program Students: 12 full-time (11 women), 1 (woman) part-time; includes 3 minority (2 African Americans, 1 Asian American or Pacific Islander). Average age 32. 17 applicants, 88% accepted, 13 enrolled. *Faculty:* 5 full-time (3 women), 3 part-time/adjunct (2 women). Expenses: Contact institution. *Financial support:* Applicants required to submit FAFSA. In 2006, 25 degrees awarded. *Degree program information:* Evening/weekend programs available. Offers secondary English (MAT). *Application deadline:* For spring admission, 4/1 priority date for domestic and international students. Applications are processed on a rolling basis. *Application fee:* $35. *Application Contact:* Lisa M. Flowers, Education Faculty Coordinator, 404-471-5168, Fax: 404-471-5152, E-mail: lflowers@agnesscott.edu. *Director,* Dr. Willie Tolliver, 404-471-5181, Fax: 404-471-5152, E-mail: wtolliver@agnesscott.edu.

Secondary Mathematics and Science Program Students: 3 full-time (all women). Average age 38. 3 applicants, 100% accepted, 3 enrolled. *Faculty:* 5 full-time (3 women), 3 part-time/adjunct (2 women). Expenses: Contact institution. Offers secondary biology (MAT); secondary chemistry (MAT); secondary math (MAT); secondary physics (MAT). *Application deadline:* For spring admission, 4/1 priority date for domestic and international students. *Application fee:* $35. *Application Contact:* Lisa M. Flowers, Education Faculty Coordinator, 404-471-5168, Fax: 404-471-5152, E-mail: lflowers@agnesscott.edu. *Professor and Chair,* Dr. Myrtle H. Lewin, 404-471-6201, Fax: 404-471-5152, E-mail: mlewin@agnesscott.edu.

AIR FORCE INSTITUTE OF TECHNOLOGY, Dayton, OH 45433-7765

General Information Federally supported, coed, primarily men, graduate-only institution. CGS member. *Graduate housing:* On-campus housing not available. *Research affiliation:* U.S. Air Force Office of Scientific Research, U.S. Air Force Research Laboratory, Dayton Area Graduate Studies Institute (aerospace), Department of Energy, National Security Agency.

GRADUATE UNITS

Graduate School of Engineering and Management *Degree program information:* Part-time programs available. Offers aeronautical engineering (MS, PhD); applied mathematics (MS, PhD); applied physics (MS, PhD); astronautical engineering (MS, PhD); computer engineering (MS, PhD); computer systems/science (MS); cost analysis (MS); electrical engineering (MS, PhD); electro-optics (MS, PhD); engineering and management (MS, PhD); environmental and engineering management (MS); environmental engineering science (MS); information resource/systems management (MS); logistics management (MS); materials science (MS, PhD); nuclear engineering (MS, PhD); operations research (MS, PhD); space operations (MS); space physics (MS); systems engineering (MS, PhD).

ALABAMA AGRICULTURAL AND MECHANICAL UNIVERSITY, Huntsville, AL 35811

General Information State-supported, coed, university. CGS member. *Enrollment:* 6,076 graduate, professional, and undergraduate students; 390 full-time matriculated graduate/professional students (295 women), 708 part-time matriculated graduate/professional students (496 women). *Enrollment by degree level:* 945 master's, 97 doctoral. *Graduate faculty:* 183. *Graduate housing:* Rooms and/or apartments available on a first-come, first-served basis to single students and available to married students. Housing application deadline: 5/1. *Student services:* Campus employment opportunities, campus safety program, career counseling, child daycare facilities, disabled student services, international student services, low-cost health insurance. *Library facilities:* J. F. Drake Learning Resources Center. *Online resources:* library catalog, access to other libraries' catalogs. *Collection:* 507,500 titles, 2,500 serial subscriptions. *Research affiliation:* Hughes Aircraft Corporation (physics), Nichols Research Corporation (computer science), Alabama Supercomputer Network, Lawrence Livermore National Laboratory (chemistry, physics), Boeing Defense and Space Group (plant science), NASA (utilization of space resources).

Computer facilities: 1,000 computers available on campus for general student use. A campuswide network can be accessed from student residence rooms and from off campus. Internet access is available. *Web address:* http://www.aamu.edu/.

General Application Contact: Dr. Caula Beyl, Dean, School of Graduate Studies, 256-372-5266, Fax: 256-372-5269, E-mail: caula.beyl@aamu.edu.

GRADUATE UNITS

School of Graduate Studies Students: 390 full-time (295 women), 708 part-time (496 women); includes 754 minority (714 African Americans, 2 American Indian/Alaska Native, 14 Asian Americans or Pacific Islanders, 24 Hispanic Americans), 111 international. Average age 33. 151 applicants, 56% accepted. *Faculty:* 183. Expenses: Contact institution. *Financial support:* In 2006–07, fellowships with tuition reimbursements (averaging $18,000 per year), research assistantships with tuition reimbursements (averaging $13,500 per year), teaching assistantships with tuition reimbursements (averaging $9,000 per year) were awarded; career-related internships or fieldwork, Federal Work-Study, and institutionally sponsored loans also available. Support available to part-time students. Financial award application deadline: 4/1. In 2006, 336 master's, 16 doctorates, 5 other advanced degrees awarded. *Application deadline:* For fall admission, 5/1 priority date for domestic students. Applications are processed on a rolling basis. *Application fee:* $25. Electronic applications accepted. *Dean, School of Graduate Studies,* Dr. Caula Beyl, 256-372-5266, Fax: 256-372-5269, E-mail: caula.beyl@aamu.edu.

School of Agricultural and Environmental Sciences Students: 50 full-time (33 women), 146 part-time (85 women); includes 136 minority (129 African Americans, 5 Asian Americans or Pacific Islanders, 2 Hispanic Americans), 44 international. *Faculty:* 30 full-time (6 women). Expenses: Contact institution. *Financial support:* Fellowships, research assistantships, teaching assistantships, career-related internships or fieldwork and Federal Work-Study available. Support available to part-time students. Financial award application deadline:4/1. *Degree program information:* Part-time and evening/weekend programs available. Offers agribusiness (MS); agricultural and environmental sciences (MS, MURP, PhD); animal sciences (MS); environmental science (MS); family and consumer sciences (MS); food science (MS, PhD); plant and soil science (PhD); urban and regional planning (MURP). *Application deadline:* For fall admission, 5/1 for domestic students. Applications are processed on a rolling basis. *Application fee:* $25. Electronic applications accepted. *Dean,* Dr. James W. Shuford, 256-372-5783, Fax: 256-372-5906.

School of Arts and Sciences Students: 104 full-time (84 women), 43 part-time (30 women); includes 115 minority (111 African Americans, 3 Asian Americans or Pacific Islanders, 1 Hispanic American), 10 international. *Faculty:* 38. Expenses: Contact institution. *Financial support:* In 2006–07, 2 fellowships with tuition reimbursements (averaging $15,000 per year), 15 research assistantships with tuition reimbursements (averaging $9,000 per year), 6 teaching assistantships with tuition reimbursements (averaging $9,000 per year) were awarded; career-related internships or fieldwork and Federal Work-Study also available. Financial award application deadline: 4/1. In 2006, 3 degrees awarded. *Degree program information:* Part-time and evening/weekend programs available. Offers arts and sciences (MS, MSW, PhD); biology (MS); physics (MS, PhD); social work (MSW). *Application deadline:* For fall admission, 5/1 priority date for domestic students. Applications are processed on a rolling basis. *Application fee:* $25. Electronic applications accepted. *Dean,* Dr. Jerry Shipman, 256-372-5300.

School of Business Students: 4 full-time (3 women), 7 part-time (4 women); all minorities (all African Americans) Average age 26. *Faculty:* 24 full-time (2 women). Expenses: Contact institution. *Financial support:* Research assistantships, teaching assistantships, career-related internships or fieldwork, Federal Work-Study, and institutionally sponsored loans available. Financial award application deadline: 4/1. In 2006, 21 degrees awarded. *Degree program information:* Part-time and evening/weekend programs available. Offers business (MBA, MS); economics and finance (MS); management and marketing (MBA). *Application deadline:* For fall admission, 5/1 for domestic students. Applications are processed on a rolling basis. *Application fee:* $25. Electronic applications accepted. *Dean,* Dr. Barbara A. P. Jones, 256-372-5485, Fax: 256-372-5081.

School of Education Students: 177 full-time (143 women), 376 part-time (284 women); includes 372 minority (355 African Americans, 2 American Indian/Alaska Native, 4 Asian Americans or Pacific Islanders, 11 Hispanic Americans), 22 international. *Faculty:* 36 full-time (18 women), 4 part-time/adjunct (1 woman). Expenses: Contact institution. *Financial support:* Fellowships, research assistantships, career-related internships or fieldwork, Federal Work-Study, institutionally sponsored loans, and traineeships available. Support available to part-time students. Financial award application deadline: 4/1. In 2006, 94 degrees awarded. *Degree program information:* Part-time and evening/weekend programs available. Offers communicative disorders (M Ed, MS); early childhood education (MS Ed, Ed S); education (M Ed, Ed S); elementary and early childhood education (MS Ed, Ed S); elementary education (MS Ed, Ed S); health and physical education (M Ed, MS); higher administration (MS); music (MS); music education (M Ed, MS); physical education (M Ed, MS); psychology and counseling (MS, Ed S); secondary education (M Ed, MS, Ed S); special education (M Ed, MS). *Application deadline:* For fall admission, 5/1 for domestic students. Applications are processed on a rolling basis. *Application fee:* $25. Electronic applications accepted. *Interim Dean,* Dr. John Vickers, 256-372-5500.

School of Engineering and Technology Students: 31 full-time (14 women), 35 part-time (20 women); includes 39 minority (38 African Americans, 1 Asian American or Pacific Islander), 23 international. *Faculty:* 4 full-time (1 woman). Expenses: Contact institution. *Financial support:* Research assistantships with tuition reimbursements, career-related internships or fieldwork available. Financial award application deadline: 4/1. *Degree program information:* Part-time and evening/weekend programs available. Offers computer science (MS); engineering and technology (M Ed, MS); industrial technology (M Ed, MS). *Application deadline:* For fall admission, 5/1 for domestic students. Applications are processed on a rolling basis. *Application fee:* $25. Electronic applications accepted. *Dean,* Dr. Arthur Bond, 256-372-5560.

ALABAMA STATE UNIVERSITY, Montgomery, AL 36101-0271

General Information State-supported, coed, comprehensive institution. *Enrollment:* 5,565 graduate, professional, and undergraduate students; 291 full-time matriculated graduate/professional students (184 women), 682 part-time matriculated graduate/professional students (512 women). *Enrollment by degree level:* 742 master's, 111 doctoral, 120 other advanced degrees. *Graduate faculty:* 73 full-time (36 women), 56 part-time/adjunct (34 women). Tuition, state resident: full-time $1,728; part-time $192 per hour. Tuition, nonresident: full-time $3,456; part-time $334 per hour. *Graduate housing:* Rooms and/or apartments available on a first-come, first-served basis to single and married students. Typical cost: $2,230 per year ($3,800 including board) for single students; $4,800 per year for married students. Housing application deadline: 7/15. *Student services:* Campus employment opportunities, career counseling, child daycare facilities, disabled student services, free psychological counseling, international student services, low-cost health insurance. *Library facilities:* Levi Watkins Learning Center. *Online resources:* library catalog, web page, access to other libraries' catalogs. *Collection:* 417,404 titles, 2,082 serial subscriptions, 43,318 audiovisual materials.

Computer facilities: Computer purchase and lease plans are available. 380 computers available on campus for general student use. A campuswide network can be accessed from off campus. Internet access and online class registration, e-mail are available. *Web address:* http://www.alasu.edu/.

General Application Contact: Dr. Nathaniel Alan Sheppard, Dean of Graduate Studies, 334-229-4274, Fax: 334-229-4928, E-mail: nsheppard@alasu.edu.

GRADUATE UNITS

School of Graduate Studies Students: 217 full-time (158 women), 787 part-time (612 women); includes 711 minority (703 African Americans, 1 American Indian/Alaska Native, 3 Asian Americans or Pacific Islanders, 4 Hispanic Americans), 6 international. Average age 33. 278 applicants, 95% accepted, 220 enrolled. *Faculty:* 72 full-time (31 women), 29 part-time/adjunct (18 women). Expenses: Contact institution. *Financial support:* In 2006–07, 20 research assistantships (averaging $9,450 per year) were awarded; Federal Work-Study, scholarships/grants, and unspecified assistantships also available. Support available to part-time students. In 2006, 227 master's, 7 other advanced degrees awarded. *Degree program information:* Part-time and evening/weekend programs available. Offers instrumental music (M Ed); vocal/choral music (M Ed). *Application deadline:* For fall admission, 7/15 for domestic students; for spring admission, 12/15 for domestic students. Applications are processed on a rolling basis. *Application fee:* $10. *Dean of Graduate Studies,* Dr. Nathaniel Alan Sheppard, 334-229-4274, Fax: 334-229-4928, E-mail: nsheppard@alasu.edu.

College of Arts and Sciences Students: 8 full-time (4 women), 9 part-time (6 women); includes 14 minority (all African Americans), 1 international. 10 applicants, 70% accepted. *Faculty:* 16 full-time (4 women). Expenses: Contact institution. *Financial support:* In 2006–07, 2 research assistantships (averaging $9,450 per year) were awarded. In 2006, 5 degrees awarded. *Degree program information:* Part-time programs available. Offers arts and sciences (M Ed, MS, Ed S); biological sciences (MS); mathematics (M Ed, MS, Ed S). *Application deadline:* For fall admission, 7/15 for domestic students; for spring admission, 12/15 for domestic students. Applications are processed on a rolling basis. *Application fee:* $10. *Dean,* Dr. Thelma Ivery, 334-229-4316, Fax: 334-229-4916, E-mail: tivery@asunet.alasu.edu.

College of Business Administration Students: 1 full-time (0 women), 9 part-time (5 women); includes 8 minority (all African Americans) 12 applicants, 83% accepted. *Faculty:* 9 full-time (2 women). Expenses: Contact institution. *Financial support:* In 2006–07, 2 research assistantships (averaging $9,450 per year) were awarded. In 2006, 6 degrees awarded. *Degree program information:* Part-time programs available. Offers accountancy (M Acc); business administration (M Acc). *Application deadline:* For fall admission, 7/15 for domestic students; for spring admission, 12/15 for domestic students. Applications are processed on a rolling basis. *Application fee:* $10. *Dean,* Dr. Percy Vaughn, 334-229-4124, Fax: 334-229-4870, E-mail: pvaughn@asunet.alasu.edu.

College of Education Students: 160 full-time (125 women), 739 part-time (581 women); includes 640 minority (635 African Americans, 1 American Indian/Alaska Native, 2 Asian Americans or Pacific Islanders, 2 Hispanic Americans), 4 international. *Faculty:* 26 full-time (17 women), 22 part-time/adjunct (13 women). Expenses: Contact institution. *Financial support:* In 2006–07, 2 research assistantships (averaging $9,450 per year) were awarded. In 2006, 201 master's, 7 other advanced degrees awarded. *Degree program information:* Part-time programs available. Offers biology education (M Ed, Ed S); early childhood education (M Ed, Ed S); education (M Ed, MS, Ed D, Ed S); educational administration (M Ed, Ed D, Ed S); educational leadership, policy and law (Ed D); elementary education (M Ed, Ed S); English/language arts (M Ed); general counseling (MS, Ed S); guidance and counseling (M Ed, MS, Ed S); health education (M Ed); history education (M Ed, Ed S); library education media (M Ed, Ed S); mathematics education (M Ed); physical education (M Ed); school counseling (M Ed, Ed S); secondary education (M Ed, Ed S); social studies (Ed S); special education (M Ed). *Application deadline:* For fall admission, 7/15 for domestic students; for spring admission, 12/15 for domestic students. Applications are processed on a rolling basis. *Application fee:* $10. *Acting Dean,* Dr. Katie Bell, 334-229-4250, Fax: 334-229-4904.

College of Health Sciences Students: 16 full-time (9 women); includes 10 minority (9 African Americans, 1 Hispanic American). *Faculty:* 7 full-time (5 women). Expenses: Contact institution. *Financial support:* In 2006–07, 4 research assistantships (averaging $9,450 per

Alabama State University (continued)

year) were awarded. Offers health sciences (DPT); physical therapy (DPT). *Application deadline:* For fall admission, 7/15 for domestic students; for spring admission, 12/15 for domestic students. Applications are processed on a rolling basis. *Application fee:* $10. *Dean*, Dr. Denise Chapman, 334-229-4707, Fax: 334-229-4964, E-mail: dchapman@alasu.edu.

ALASKA PACIFIC UNIVERSITY, Anchorage, AK 99508-4672

General Information Independent, coed, comprehensive institution. *Enrollment:* 733 graduate, professional, and undergraduate students; 74 full-time matriculated graduate/professional students (55 women), 99 part-time matriculated graduate/professional students (56 women). *Enrollment by degree level:* 173 master's. *Graduate faculty:* 21 full-time (11 women), 9 part-time/adjunct (3 women). *Tuition:* Part-time $550 per credit hour. *Required fees:* $100 per semester. Tuition and fees vary according to program. *Graduate housing:* Room and/or apartments available on a first-come, first-served basis to single students; on-campus housing not available to married students. Housing application deadline: 8/15. *Student services:* Campus employment opportunities, campus safety program, career counseling, exercise/wellness program, free psychological counseling, international student services, low-cost health insurance, multicultural affairs office, teacher training. *Library facilities:* Consortium Library. *Online resources:* library catalog, web page, access to other libraries' catalogs. *Collection:* 788,708 titles, 3,434 serial subscriptions.

Computer facilities: 40 computers available on campus for general student use. A campuswide network can be accessed from student residence rooms. Internet access is available. *Web address:* http://www.alaskapacific.edu/.

General Application Contact: Michael Warner, Director of Admissions, 907-564-8248, Fax: 907-564-8317, E-mail: mikew@alaskapacific.edu.

GRADUATE UNITS

Graduate Programs Students: 74 full-time (55 women), 99 part-time (56 women); includes 32 minority (7 African Americans, 14 American Indian/Alaska Native, 7 Asian Americans or Pacific Islanders, 4 Hispanic Americans), 3 international. Average age 35. 153 applicants, 56% accepted, 82 enrolled. *Faculty:* 21 full-time (11 women), 9 part-time/adjunct (3 women). Expenses: Contact institution. *Financial support:* Research assistantships, teaching assistantships, career-related internships or fieldwork, Federal Work-Study, scholarships/grants, and unspecified assistantships available. Support available to part-time students. Financial award application deadline: 4/15; financial award applicants required to submit FAFSA. In 2006, 75 degrees awarded. *Degree program information:* Part-time and evening/weekend programs available. Offers business administration (MBA); counseling psychology (MSCP); environmental science (MSES); global finance (MBA); health services administration (MBA); information and communication technology (MBAICT, MBATM); outdoor and environmental education (MSOEE); self-designed study (MA); teaching (MAT); teaching (K-8) (MAT). *Application deadline:* For fall admission, 6/1 priority date for international students; for spring admission, 9/1 priority date for international students. Applications are processed on a rolling basis. *Application fee:* $25. Electronic applications accepted. *Application Contact:* Michael Warner, Director of Admissions, 907-564-8248, Fax: 907-564-8317, E-mail: mikew@alaskapacific.edu. *Academic Dean*, Dr. Marilyn Barry, 907-564-8242, Fax: 907-562-4276.

ALBANY COLLEGE OF PHARMACY OF UNION UNIVERSITY, Albany, NY 12208-3425

General Information Independent, coed, comprehensive institution. *Enrollment:* 1,230 graduate, professional, and undergraduate students; 336 full-time matriculated graduate/professional students (195 women), 2 part-time matriculated graduate/professional students. *Enrollment by degree level:* 338 first professional. *Graduate faculty:* 72 full-time, 12 part-time/adjunct. *Tuition:* Full-time $19,350. *Required fees:* $635. One-time fee: $145 full-time. *Graduate housing:* Room and/or apartments available on a first-come, first-served basis to single students; on-campus housing not available to married students. Typical cost: $5,100 per year ($6,900 including board). Room and board charges vary according to board plan and housing facility selected. Housing application deadline: 8/1. *Student services:* Campus employment opportunities, career counseling, free psychological counseling, international student services, low-cost health insurance, writing training. *Library facilities:* George and Leona Lewis Library. *Online resources:* library catalog, web page, access to other libraries' catalogs. *Collection:* 16,124 titles, 3,576 serial subscriptions.

Computer facilities: Computer purchase and lease plans are available. 47 computers available on campus for general student use. A campuswide network can be accessed from student residence rooms and from off campus. Internet access is available. *Web address:* http://www.acp.edu/.

General Application Contact: Carly Connors, Director of Admissions, 518-694-7221, Fax: 518-694-7322, E-mail: admissions@acp.edu.

GRADUATE UNITS

Program in Pharmacy Students: 336 full-time (195 women), 2 part-time; includes 43 minority (7 African Americans, 2 American Indian/Alaska Native, 30 Asian Americans or Pacific Islanders, 4 Hispanic Americans), 20 international. Average age 26. 1,808 applicants, 7% accepted, 73 enrolled. *Faculty:* 72 full-time, 12 part-time/adjunct. Expenses: Contact institution. *Financial support:* In 2006–07, 145 students received support, including 1 fellowship with tuition reimbursement available (averaging $40,000 per year); Federal Work-Study also available. Support available to part-time students. Financial award application deadline: 3/1; financial award applicants required to submit FAFSA. In 2006, 132 Pharm Ds awarded. *Degree program information:* Part-time programs available. Offers pharmacy (Pharm D). *Application deadline:* For fall admission, 3/1 for domestic and international students. Applications are processed on a rolling basis. *Application fee:* $100. Electronic applications accepted. *Application Contact:* Carly Connors, Director of Admissions, 518-694-7221, Fax: 518-694-7322, E-mail: admissions@acp.edu. *Dean*, Dr. Mehdi Boroujerdi, 518-694-7212, Fax: 518-694-7063.

ALBANY LAW SCHOOL OF UNION UNIVERSITY, Albany, NY 12208-3494

General Information Independent, coed, graduate-only institution. *Graduate housing:* On-campus housing not available.

GRADUATE UNITS

Professional Program *Degree program information:* Part-time programs available. Offers law (JD, LL M, MSLS).

ALBANY MEDICAL COLLEGE, Albany, NY 12208-3479

General Information Independent, coed, graduate-only institution. *Enrollment by degree level:* 542 first professional, 119 master's, 69 doctoral. *Graduate faculty:* 80 full-time (24 women), 15 part-time/adjunct (6 women). *Graduate housing:* On-campus housing not available. *Student services:* Campus employment opportunities, campus safety program, child daycare facilities, exercise/wellness program, free psychological counseling, international student services, low-cost health insurance. *Library facilities:* Schaffer Library of the Health Sciences. *Online resources:* library catalog, web page, access to other libraries' catalogs. *Collection:* 150,462 titles, 13,197 serial subscriptions, 447 audiovisual materials. *Research affiliation:* Wadsworth Center for Laboratories and Research (biomedical research), ORDWAY Research Institute (Biomedical research), General Electric Corporation (imaging), X-Ray Optical Systems (diagnostic equipment), Albany Molecular Research, Inc. (biomedical research), Living MicroSystems, Inc. (biomedical research).

Computer facilities: 95 computers available on campus for general student use. A campuswide network can be accessed from student residence rooms and from off campus. Internet access and online class registration are available. *Web address:* http://www.amc.edu/.

General Application Contact: Jean M. Cornwell, Admissions Coordinator, 518-262-5253, Fax: 518-262-5183, E-mail: graduate-studies@mail.amc.edu.

GRADUATE UNITS

Alden March Bioethics Institute 1 applicant, 100% accepted, 1 enrolled. Expenses: Contact institution. *Degree program information:* Part-time programs available. Postbaccalaureate distance learning degree programs offered (no on-campus study). Offers bioethics (MS); clinical ethics (Certificate). *Application deadline:* For fall admission, 7/1 priority date for domestic students. Applications are processed on a rolling basis. *Application fee:* $50. Electronic applications accepted. *Application Contact:* Dr. Summer Johnson, Interim Director of Graduate Studies, 518-262-6082, Fax: 518-262-6856, E-mail: summer.johnson@bioethics.net. *Director, Alden March Bioethics Institute*, Dr. Glenn E. McGee, 518-262-6082, Fax: 518-262-6856, E-mail: mcgeeoffice@bioethics.net.

Center for Nurse Anesthesiology Students: 45 full-time (26 women), 3 part-time (all women); includes 4 minority (1 African American, 2 Asian Americans or Pacific Islanders, 1 Hispanic American). Average age 33. 52 applicants, 38% accepted, 17 enrolled. *Faculty:* 4 full-time (all women). Expenses: Contact institution. *Financial support:* Scholarships/grants and traineeships available. Financial award applicants required to submit FAFSA. In 2006, 16 master's awarded. Postbaccalaureate distance learning degree programs offered (minimal on-campus study). Offers nurse anesthesiology (MS). *Application deadline:* For fall admission, 3/15 priority date for domestic students. Applications are processed on a rolling basis. *Application fee:* $60. *Application Contact:* Helene M. Gregory, Coordinator, 518-262-4303, Fax: 518-262-5170, E-mail: amcnap@mail.amc.edu. *Graduate Director*, Dr. Denise Martin-Sheridan, 518-262-4303, Fax: 518-262-5170, E-mail: amcnap@mail.amc.edu.

Center for Physician Assistant Studies Students: 63 full-time (48 women); includes 1 minority (Asian American or Pacific Islander) Average age 32. 363 applicants, 12% accepted, 30 enrolled. *Faculty:* 9 full-time (5 women), 3 part-time/adjunct (1 woman). Expenses: Contact institution. *Financial support:* In 2006–07, 4 students received support. Scholarships/grants available. Financial award application deadline: 10/1; financial award applicants required to submit FAFSA. In 2006, 25 degrees awarded. Offers physician assistant studies (MS). *Application deadline:* For winter admission, 11/1 for domestic and international students. Applications are processed on a rolling basis. *Application fee:* $50. *Application Contact:* Rosalyn Green, Secretary, 518-262-5251, E-mail: greenr@mail.amc.edu. *Director*, Dr. David F. Irvine, 518-262-5251, Fax: 518-262-6698, E-mail: irvined@mail.amc.edu.

Graduate Programs in the Biological Sciences Students: 185 full-time (130 women), 13 part-time (7 women); includes 28 minority (5 African Americans, 2 American Indian/Alaska Native, 19 Asian Americans or Pacific Islanders, 2 Hispanic Americans), 24 international. Average age 30. 115 applicants, 81% accepted, 35 enrolled. *Faculty:* 80 full-time (24 women), 15 part-time/adjunct (6 women). Expenses: Contact institution. *Financial support:* In 2006–07, 70 research assistantships with full tuition reimbursements (averaging $18,000 per year) were awarded; Federal Work-Study, scholarships/grants, and tuition waivers (full) also available. Financial award applicants required to submit FAFSA. In 2006, 41 master's, 9 doctorates awarded. *Degree program information:* Part-time programs available. Offers biological sciences (MS, PhD). *Application deadline:* For fall admission, 3/15 priority date for domestic students. Applications are processed on a rolling basis. *Application fee:* $0 ($60 for international students). *Application Contact:* Jean M. Cornwell, Admissions Coordinator, 518-262-5253, Fax: 518-262-5183, E-mail: graduate-studies@mail.amc.edu. *Associate Dean for Graduate Studies and Medical Student Research*, Dr. Thomas A. Andersen, 518-262-5253, Fax: 518-262-5183.

Center for Cardiovascular Sciences Students: 15 full-time (12 women); includes 6 minority (2 African Americans, 4 Asian Americans or Pacific Islanders). Average age 25. 6 applicants, 33% accepted, 2 enrolled. *Faculty:* 19 full-time (3 women), 1 part-time/adjunct (0 women). Expenses: Contact institution. *Financial support:* In 2006–07, 11 research assistantships (averaging $23,000 per year) were awarded; Federal Work-Study, scholarships/grants, and tuition waivers (full) also available. Financial award applicants required to submit FAFSA. In 2006, 2 master's, 5 doctorates awarded. *Degree program information:* Part-time programs available. Offers cardiovascular sciences (MS, PhD). *Application deadline:* For fall admission, 3/15 priority date for domestic students. Applications are processed on a rolling basis. *Application fee:* $0 ($60 for international students). *Application Contact:* Wendy M. Hobb, Administrative Coordinator, 518-262-8102, Fax: 518-262-8101, E-mail: hobbw@mail.amc.edu. *Graduate Director*, Dr. Peter A. Vincent, 518-262-6296, Fax: 518-262-8101, E-mail: vincenp@mail.amc.edu.

Center for Cell Biology and Cancer Research Students: 23 full-time (16 women); includes 4 minority (1 African American, 2 Asian Americans or Pacific Islanders, 1 Hispanic American), 6 international. Average age 24. 16 applicants, 88% accepted, 5 enrolled. *Faculty:* 15 full-time (4 women). Expenses: Contact institution. *Financial support:* In 2006–07, 10 research assistantships (averaging $23,000 per year) were awarded; Federal Work-Study, scholarships/grants, and tuition waivers (full) also available. Financial award applicants required to submit FAFSA. In 2006, 5 master's, 1 doctorate awarded. *Degree program information:* Part-time programs available. Offers cell biology and cancer research (MS, PhD). *Application deadline:* For fall admission, 3/15 priority date for domestic students. Applications are processed on a rolling basis. *Graduate Director*, Dr. C. Michael DiPersio, 518-262-5916, Fax: 518-262-5669, E-mail: dipersm@mail.amc.edu.

Center for Immunology and Microbial Disease Students: 15 full-time (9 women); includes 1 minority (African American) Average age 25. 23 applicants, 87% accepted, 5 enrolled. *Faculty:* 18 full-time (2 women), 11 part-time/adjunct (6 women). Expenses: Contact institution. *Financial support:* In 2006–07, 10 research assistantships (averaging $23,000 per year) were awarded; Federal Work-Study, scholarships/grants, and tuition waivers (full) also available. Financial award applicants required to submit FAFSA. In 2006, 4 master's, 3 doctorates awarded. *Degree program information:* Part-time programs available. Offers immunology and microbial disease (MS, PhD). *Application deadline:* For fall admission, 3/15 priority date for domestic students. Applications are processed on a rolling basis. *Application fee:* $0 ($60 for international students). *Graduate Director*, Dr. Thomas D. Friedrich, 518-262-6750, Fax: 518-262-6161, E-mail: dgs_cimd@mail.amc.edu.

Center for Neuropharmacology and Neuroscience Students: 16 full-time (8 women); includes 2 minority (1 African American, 1 Asian American or Pacific Islander), 3 international. Average age 26. 28 applicants, 89% accepted, 5 enrolled. *Faculty:* 21 full-time (6 women). Expenses: Contact institution. *Financial support:* In 2006–07, 16 students received support, including 6 fellowships (averaging $23,000 per year), 10 research assistantships (averaging $23,000 per year); Federal Work-Study, scholarships/grants, and tuition waivers (full) also available. Financial award applicants required to submit FAFSA. In 2006, 4 degrees awarded. *Degree program information:* Part-time programs available. Offers neuropharmacology and neuroscience (MS, PhD). *Application deadline:* For fall admission, 3/15 priority date for domestic students. Applications are processed on a rolling basis. *Application fee:* $0 ($60 for international students). *Application Contact:* Dr. Richard Keller, Graduate Director, 518-262-5303, Fax: 518-262-5799, E-mail: cnninfo@mail.amc.edu. *Director*, Dr. Stanley D. Glick, 518-262-5303, Fax: 518-262-5799, E-mail: cnninfo@mail.amc.edu.

Professional Program Students: 542 full-time (292 women); includes 193 minority (24 African Americans, 4 American Indian/Alaska Native, 156 Asian Americans or Pacific Islanders, 9 Hispanic Americans), 11 international. Average age 26. 7,189 applicants, 4% accepted. *Faculty:* 97 full-time (31 women), 33 part-time/adjunct (13 women). Expenses: Contact institution. *Financial support:* Federal Work-Study, institutionally sponsored loans, and tuition waivers (partial) available. Financial award application deadline: 3/15; financial award applicants required to submit FAFSA. In 2006, 131 degrees awarded. Offers medicine (MD). *Application deadline:* For fall admission, 11/15 for domestic students. Applications are processed on a rolling basis. *Application fee:* $100. Electronic applications accepted. *Application Contact:* Joanne H. Nanos, Director of Admissions and Student Records, 518-262-5521, Fax: 518-262-5887. *Dean*, Dr. Vincent Verdile, 518-262-6008.

ALBANY STATE UNIVERSITY, Albany, GA 31705-2717

General Information State-supported, coed, comprehensive institution. CGS member. *Graduate housing:* On-campus housing not available.

GRADUATE UNITS

College of Arts and Sciences *Degree program information:* Part-time programs available. Offers arts and sciences (MPA, MS); community and economic development (MPA); criminal justice (MPA, MS); fiscal management (MPA); general management (MPA); health administration and policy (MPA); human resources management (MPA); public policy (MPA); water resource management and policy (MPA). Electronic applications accepted.

College of Education *Degree program information:* Part-time programs available. Offers biology (M Ed); business education (M Ed); chemistry (M Ed); early childhood education (M Ed); education (M Ed, Certificate, Ed S); educational administration and supervision (M Ed, Certificate, Ed S); English education (M Ed); health and physical education (M Ed); mathematics education (M Ed); middle grades education (M Ed); music education (M Ed); reading education (M Ed); school counseling (M Ed); social science education (M Ed); special education (M Ed). Electronic applications accepted.

College of Health Professions *Degree program information:* Part-time programs available. Offers nursing (MS). Electronic applications accepted.

School of Business *Degree program information:* Part-time and evening/weekend programs available. Postbaccalaureate distance learning degree programs offered (no on-campus study). Offers water policy (MBA). Electronic applications accepted.

ALBERT EINSTEIN COLLEGE OF MEDICINE, Bronx, NY 10461

General Information Independent, coed, graduate-only institution.

GRADUATE UNITS

Medical Scientist Training Program

Professional Program in Medicine Offers medicine (MD).

Sue Golding Graduate Division of Medical Sciences Offers anatomy (PhD); biochemistry (PhD); cell and developmental biology (PhD); medical sciences (PhD); microbiology and immunology (PhD); neuroscience (PhD); pathology (PhD); physiology and biophysics (PhD).

Division of Biological Sciences Offers cell biology (PhD); developmental and molecular biology (PhD); molecular genetics (PhD); molecular pharmacology (PhD).

ALBERTSON COLLEGE OF IDAHO, Caldwell, ID 83605-4494

General Information Independent, coed, comprehensive institution. *Enrollment:* 822 graduate, professional, and undergraduate students; 29 full-time matriculated graduate/professional students (23 women). *Enrollment by degree level:* 29 master's. *Graduate faculty:* 3 full-time (2 women), 1 part-time/adjunct (0 women). *Tuition:* Full-time $12,450; part-time $670 per credit. *Graduate housing:* Rooms and/or apartments available on a first-come, first-served basis to single and married students. Typical cost: $2,700 per year ($6,025 including board) for single students; $4,250 per year ($7,575 including board) for married students. *Student services:* Campus employment opportunities, career counseling, free psychological counseling, low-cost health insurance. *Library facilities:* Terteling Library. *Online resources:* library catalog, web page. *Collection:* 183,308 titles, 703 serial subscriptions.

Computer facilities: 240 computers available on campus for general student use. A campuswide network can be accessed from student residence rooms and from off campus. Internet access, online course syllabi, course assignments, course discussion are available. *Web address:* http://www.albertson.edu/.

General Application Contact: Dr. Dennis Cartwright, Director of Education Programs, 208-459-5814, E-mail: dcartwright@albertson.edu.

GRADUATE UNITS

Program in Teacher Education Students: 29 full-time (23 women); includes 1 minority (Hispanic American) Average age 27. *Faculty:* 3 full-time (2 women), 1 part-time/adjunct (0 women). Expenses: Contact institution. In 2006, 9 degrees awarded. Offers teacher education (MAT). *Application deadline:* For fall admission, 3/15 priority date for domestic students. *Chair,* Dr. Donald W. Burwell, 208-459-5222, E-mail: dburwell@albertson.edu.

ALBERTUS MAGNUS COLLEGE, New Haven, CT 06511-1189

General Information Independent-religious, coed, comprehensive institution. *Enrollment:* 2,186 graduate, professional, and undergraduate students; 322 full-time matriculated graduate/professional students (162 women), 95 part-time matriculated graduate/professional students (77 women). *Enrollment by degree level:* 417 master's. *Graduate faculty:* 27 full-time (12 women), 47 part-time/adjunct (21 women). *Tuition:* Full-time $10,800; part-time $1,080 per course. Tuition and fees vary according to program. *Graduate housing:* Room and/or apartments available to single students; on-campus housing not available to married students. Typical cost: $8,402 (including board). Housing application deadline: 8/31. *Student services:* Campus employment opportunities, career counseling, free psychological counseling, international student services, teacher training. *Library facilities:* Rosary Hall. *Online resources:* library catalog, web page, access to other libraries' catalogs. *Collection:* 538 serial subscriptions.

Computer facilities: 150 computers available on campus for general student use. A campuswide network can be accessed from student residence rooms and from off campus. Internet access is available. *Web address:* http://www.albertus.edu/.

General Application Contact: Amy Kwiatkowski, Director of Program Development, 203-777-0800 Ext. 123, Fax: 203-777-2112, E-mail: akwiatkowski@cc.albertus.edu.

GRADUATE UNITS

Liberal Studies Program Average age 39. 5 applicants, 60% accepted, 3 enrolled. *Faculty:* 5 full-time (3 women), 3 part-time/adjunct (1 woman). Expenses: Contact institution. *Financial support:* Available to part-time students. Application deadline: 8/17. In 2006, 3 degrees awarded. *Degree program information:* Part-time and evening/weekend programs available. Offers liberal studies (MALS). *Application deadline:* For fall admission, 8/31 priority date for domestic students; for spring admission, 1/10 for domestic students. Applications are processed on a rolling basis. *Application fee:* $25. *Director,* Dr. Paul Robichaud, 203-773-8556, Fax: 203-773-3117, E-mail: probichaud@albertus.edu.

Program in Art Therapy Students: 13 full-time (11 women), 29 part-time (26 women); includes 14 minority (5 African Americans, 9 Hispanic Americans). Average age 35. 12 applicants, 67% accepted, 8 enrolled. *Faculty:* 7 full-time (5 women), 6 part-time/adjunct (4 women). Expenses: Contact institution. *Financial support:* Available to part-time students. Application deadline: 8/17. In 2006, 5 degrees awarded. *Degree program information:* Part-time and evening/weekend programs available. Offers art therapy (MAAT). *Application deadline:* For fall admission, 8/30 for domestic students; for spring admission, 12/30 for domestic students. *Application fee:* $35. *Director,* Donna Kaiser, 203-773-8903, Fax: 203-773-3117.

Program in Leadership *Faculty:* 3 full-time (1 woman). Expenses: Contact institution. Offers leadership (MA). *Application Contact:* Joseph Chadwick, Director of Program Development, 203-777-0800 Ext. 114, Fax: 203-777-2112, E-mail: joe.chadwick@apollo.grp.edu. *Director of Masters in Leadership,* Dr. Howard Fero, 203-977-7100, Fax: 203-777-2112, E-mail: hfero@albertus.edu.

Program in Management Students: 351 full-time, 11 part-time. Average age 35. 90 applicants, 78% accepted, 66 enrolled. *Faculty:* 14 full-time (6 women), 36 part-time/adjunct (14 women). Expenses: Contact institution. *Financial support:* Available to part-time students. In 2006, 233 degrees awarded. *Degree program information:* Evening/weekend programs available. Offers business administration (MBA); management (MSM). Program also offered in East Hartford, CT. *Application deadline:* Applications are processed on a rolling basis. *Application fee:* $75. *Application Contact:* Joseph Chadwick, Director of Program Development, 203-777-0800 Ext. 114, Fax: 203-777-2112, E-mail: joe.chadwick@apollo.grp.edu. *Vice President, Academic Affairs,* Dr. John Donohue, 203-773-8068, Fax: 203-773-8525, E-mail: jdonohue@albertus.edu.

ALBRIGHT COLLEGE, Reading, PA 19612-5234

General Information Independent-religious, coed, comprehensive institution. *Graduate housing:* On-campus housing not available.

GRADUATE UNITS

Department of Education—Graduate Division *Degree program information:* Part-time and evening/weekend programs available. Offers early childhood education (MS); elementary education (MS); English as a second language (MA); general education (MA); special education (MS). Electronic applications accepted.

ALCORN STATE UNIVERSITY, Alcorn State, MS 39096-7500

General Information State-supported, coed, comprehensive institution. CGS member. *Enrollment:* 3,584 graduate, professional, and undergraduate students; 165 full-time matriculated graduate/professional students (100 women), 404 part-time matriculated graduate/professional students (323 women). *Enrollment by degree level:* 569 master's. *Graduate faculty:* 55 full-time (16 women), 23 part-time/adjunct (15 women). *Graduate housing:* Room and/or apartments available on a first-come, first-served basis to single students; on-campus housing not available to married students. *Student services:* Campus employment opportunities, career counseling, child daycare facilities. *Library facilities:* John Dewey Boyd Library. *Online resources:* library catalog, access to other libraries' catalogs. *Collection:* 229,238 titles, 1,046 serial subscriptions, 8,878 audiovisual materials.

Computer facilities: 500 computers available on campus for general student use. A campuswide network can be accessed from student residence rooms and from off campus. Internet access and online class registration are available. *Web address:* http://www.alcorn.edu/.

General Application Contact: Lula Russell, Administrative Assistant to the Dean, School of Graduate Studies, 601-877-6122, Fax: 601-877-6995, E-mail: lulagr@alcorn.edu.

GRADUATE UNITS

School of Graduate Studies Students: 165 full-time (100 women), 404 part-time (323 women); includes 492 minority (491 African Americans, 1 Asian American or Pacific Islander), 26 international. *Faculty:* 55 full-time (16 women), 23 part-time/adjunct (15 women). Expenses: Contact institution. *Financial support:* Career-related internships or fieldwork available. Support available to part-time students. In 2006, 169 degrees awarded. *Degree program information:* Part-time programs available. Offers workforce education leadership (MS). *Application deadline:* For fall admission, 7/15 priority date for domestic students; for spring admission, 11/25 for domestic students. Applications are processed on a rolling basis. *Application fee:* $0 ($10 for international students). Electronic applications accepted. *Application Contact:* Lula Russell, Administrative Assistant to the Dean, School of Graduate Studies, 601-877-6122, Fax: 601-877-6995, E-mail: lulagr@alcorn.edu. *Dean,* Dr. Donzell Lee, 601-877-6122, Fax: 601-877-6995, E-mail: dlee@alcorn.edu.

School of Agriculture and Applied Science Students: 3 full-time (1 woman), 11 part-time (5 women); includes 12 minority (all African Americans), 2 international. *Faculty:* 11 full-time (2 women). Expenses: Contact institution. *Financial support:* Career-related internships or fieldwork available. Support available to part-time students. In 2006, 3 degrees awarded. Offers agricultural economics (MS Ag); agronomy (MS Ag); animal science (MS Ag). *Application deadline:* For fall admission, 7/15 priority date for domestic students; for spring admission, 11/25 for domestic students. Applications are processed on a rolling basis. *Application fee:* $0 ($10 for international students). *Interim Dean,* Dalton McAfee, 601-877-6137, Fax: 601-877-6219.

School of Arts and Sciences Expenses: Contact institution. *Financial support:* Career-related internships or fieldwork available. Support available to part-time students. Offers arts and sciences (MS); biology (MS); computer and information sciences (MS). *Application deadline:* Applications are processed on a rolling basis. *Dean,* Reginald Lindsey, 601-877-6120.

School of Business Students: 28 full-time (14 women), 36 part-time (28 women); includes 35 minority (34 African Americans, 1 Asian American or Pacific Islander), 15 international. *Faculty:* 7 full-time (1 woman). Expenses: Contact institution. In 2006, 21 degrees awarded. Offers business (MBA). *Application deadline:* For fall admission, 7/15 for domestic students; for spring admission, 11/25 for domestic students. *Dean,* Dr. Steve Wells, 601-304-4300 Ext. 4309.

School of Nursing Students: 25 full-time (22 women), 17 part-time (15 women); includes 22 minority (all African Americans) *Faculty:* 3 full-time (all women), 2 part-time/adjunct (both women). Expenses: Contact institution. In 2006, 18 degrees awarded. Offers rural nursing (MSN). *Application deadline:* For fall admission, 7/15 priority date for domestic students; for spring admission, 11/25 for domestic students. Applications are processed on a rolling basis. *Application fee:* $0 ($10 for international students). *Dean,* Dr. Mary Hill, 601-304-4304.

School of Psychology and Education Students: 76 full-time (44 women), 271 part-time (226 women); includes 333 minority (all African Americans) *Faculty:* 14 full-time (9 women), 21 part-time/adjunct (13 women). Expenses: Contact institution. *Financial support:* Career-related internships or fieldwork available. Support available to part-time students. In 2006, 119 degrees awarded. Offers agricultural education (MS Ed); elementary education (MS Ed, Ed S); guidance and counseling (MS Ed); industrial education (MS Ed); secondary education (MS Ed); special education (MS Ed). *Application deadline:* For fall admission, 7/15 priority date for domestic students; for spring admission, 11/25 for domestic students. Applications are processed on a rolling basis. *Application fee:* $0 ($10 for international students). *Dean,* Dr. Josephine M. Posey, 601-877-6141, Fax: 601-877-3867.

ALDERSON-BROADDUS COLLEGE, Philippi, WV 26416

General Information Independent-religious, coed, comprehensive institution. *Graduate housing:* Rooms and/or apartments available on a first-come, first-served basis to single and married students. Housing application deadline: 8/21.

GRADUATE UNITS

Medical Science Department Postbaccalaureate distance learning degree programs offered (minimal on-campus study). Offers emergency medical care (MS); rural primary care (MS); surgery (MS).

ALFRED UNIVERSITY, Alfred, NY 14802-1205

General Information Independent, coed, university. CGS member. *Enrollment:* 2,310 graduate, professional, and undergraduate students; 182 full-time matriculated graduate/professional students (111 women), 105 part-time matriculated graduate/professional students (63 women). *Graduate faculty:* 87 full-time (24 women), 7 part-time/adjunct (2 women). *Tuition:* Full-time $29,600; part-time $630 per credit hour. *Required fees:* $850; $70 per semester. Tuition and fees vary according to program. *Graduate housing:* Room and/or apartments available on a first-come, first-served basis to single students; on-campus housing not available to married students. Typical cost: $9,900 (including board). Housing application deadline: 7/1. *Student services:* Campus employment opportunities, campus safety program, career counseling, exercise/wellness program, free psychological counseling, international student services, low-cost health insurance, multicultural affairs office, writing training. *Library facilities:* Herrick Memorial Library plus 1 other. *Online resources:* library catalog, web page, access to other libraries' catalogs. *Collection:* 288,667 titles, 1,478 serial subscriptions, 4,191 audiovisual materials. *Research affiliation:* Laboratory for Electronic Ceramics, Polymer-Assisted Ceramics Manufacturing Center, New York State Center for Advanced Ceramic Technology, National Science Foundation Industry-University Center for Glass Research, Whitewares Research Center Industry University Center (whitewares processing, traditional ceramics), National Science Foundation Industry-University Center for Biosurfaces (bioceramics).

Computer facilities: Computer purchase and lease plans are available. 450 computers available on campus for general student use. A campuswide network can be accessed from student residence rooms and from off campus. Internet access is available. *Web address:* http://www.alfred.edu/.

General Application Contact: Valerie Stephens, Coordinator of Graduate Admissions, 607-871-2141, Fax: 607-871-2198, E-mail: gradinquiry@alfred.edu.

GRADUATE UNITS

Graduate School Students: 182 full-time (111 women), 105 part-time (63 women). Average age 25. 683 applicants, 30% accepted, 139 enrolled. *Faculty:* 87 full-time (24 women), 7 part-time/adjunct (2 women). Expenses: Contact institution. *Financial support:* In 2006–07, 173 students received support; fellowships with tuition reimbursements available, research assistantships with tuition reimbursements available, teaching assistantships with tuition

Alfred University (continued)

reimbursements available, career-related internships or fieldwork, tuition waivers (full and partial), and unspecified assistantships available. Financial award applicants required to submit FAFSA. In 2006, 124 master's, 15 doctorates awarded. *Degree program information:* Part-time programs available. Offers school psychology (MA, Psy D, CAS). *Application deadline:* For fall admission, 5/1 priority date for international students; for spring admission, 10/1 priority date for international students. Applications are processed on a rolling basis. *Application fee:* $50. Electronic applications accepted. *Application Contact:* Cathleen R. Johnson, Coordinator of Graduate Admissions, 607-871-2141, Fax: 607-871-2198, E-mail: gradinquiry@alfred.edu. *Associate Provost for Graduate and Professional Programs,* Dr. William Hall, 607-871-2141, Fax: 607-871-2198, E-mail: fhall@alfred.edu.

College of Business Students: 6 full-time (0 women), 12 part-time (5 women). Average age 28. 33 applicants, 14 enrolled. Expenses: Contact institution. *Financial support:* In 2006–07, 6 students received support, including research assistantships (averaging $14,225 per year); tuition waivers (partial) and unspecified assistantships also available. Financial award applicants required to submit FAFSA. In 2006, 11 degrees awarded. *Degree program information:* Part-time programs available. Offers business administration (MBA). *Application deadline:* For fall admission, 6/1 priority date for international students; for spring admission, 11/1 priority date for international students. Applications are processed on a rolling basis. *Application fee:* $50. Electronic applications accepted. *Application Contact:* Valerie Stephens, Coordinator of Graduate Admissions, 607-871-2141, Fax: 607-871-2198, E-mail: gradinquiry@alfred.edu. *Director of MBA Program,* Lori Hollenbeck, 607-871-2630, Fax: 607-871-2114, E-mail: hollenl@alfred.edu.

Division of Education Students: 12 full-time (all women), 26 part-time (18 women). Average age 24. 62 applicants, 61% accepted, 30 enrolled. Expenses: Contact institution. *Financial support:* In 2006–07, 12 students received support, including research assistantships (averaging $14,225 per year); tuition waivers (partial) and unspecified assistantships also available. Financial award applicants required to submit FAFSA. In 2006, 48 master's, 19 other advanced degrees awarded. *Degree program information:* Part-time programs available. Offers counseling (MS Ed, CAS); literacy teacher (MS Ed). *Application deadline:* Applications are processed on a rolling basis. *Application fee:* $50. Electronic applications accepted. *Application Contact:* Valerie Stephens, Coordinator of Graduate Admissions, 607-871-2141, Fax: 607-871-2198, E-mail: gradinquiry@alfred.edu. *Chair,* Dr. James Curl, 607-871-2219, E-mail: fcurl@alfred.edu.

New York State College of Ceramics Students: 73 full-time (32 women), 8 part-time (3 women). Average age 25. 297 applicants, 16% accepted, 37 enrolled. Expenses: Contact institution. *Financial support:* In 2006–07, 73 students received support; fellowships with tuition reimbursements available, research assistantships with tuition reimbursements available, teaching assistantships with full tuition reimbursements available, tuition waivers (full and partial) available. Financial award applicants required to submit FAFSA. In 2006, 13 master's, 5 doctorates awarded. Offers biomedical materials engineering science (MS); ceramic art (MFA); ceramic engineering (MS); ceramics (PhD); electrical engineering (MS); electronic integrated arts (MFA); glass art (MFA); glass science (MS, PhD); materials science and engineering (MS, PhD); mechanical engineering (MS); sculpture (MFA). *Application deadline:* For fall admission, 6/1 priority date for international students; for spring admission, 11/1 priority date for international students. Applications are processed on a rolling basis. *Application fee:* $50. Electronic applications accepted. *Application Contact:* Valerie Stephens, Coordinator of Graduate Admissions, 607-871-2141, Fax: 607-871-2198, E-mail: gradinquiry@alfred.edu. *Dean of School of Engineering,* Dr. Alastair Cormack, 607-871-2141, Fax: 607-871-2339, E-mail: cormack@alfred.edu.

ALLEN COLLEGE, Waterloo, IA 50703

General Information Independent, coed, primarily women, comprehensive institution. *Enrollment:* 426 graduate, professional, and undergraduate students; 19 full-time matriculated graduate/professional students (17 women), 42 part-time matriculated graduate/professional students (39 women). *Enrollment by degree level:* 61 master's. *Graduate faculty:* 2 full-time (both women), 4 part-time/adjunct (all women). *Tuition:* Full-time $9,824; part-time $562 per credit hour. *Required fees:* $481. One-time fee: $220 part-time. Tuition and fees vary according to course load. *Graduate housing:* Room and/or apartments available on a first-come, first-served basis to single students; on-campus housing not available to married students. Typical cost: $5,712 (including board). *Student services:* Career counseling, child daycare facilities, exercise/wellness program, free psychological counseling, low-cost health insurance. *Library facilities:* Barrett Library. *Online resources:* library catalog, web page, access to other libraries' catalogs. *Collection:* 2,797 titles, 199 serial subscriptions.

Computer facilities: 26 computers available on campus for general student use. Internet access is available. *Web address:* http://www.allencollege.edu/.

General Application Contact: Dina Dowden, Education Secretary, 319-226-2000, Fax: 319-226-2051, E-mail: allcucollegeadmissions@ihs.org.

GRADUATE UNITS

Program in Nursing Students: 19 full-time (17 women), 42 part-time (39 women). Average age 37. 62 applicants, 94% accepted, 46 enrolled. *Faculty:* 2 full-time (both women), 4 part-time/adjunct (all women). Expenses: Contact institution. *Financial support:* In 2006–07, 58 students received support, including 1 teaching assistantship (averaging $10,116 per year); institutionally sponsored loans, scholarships/grants, and traineeships also available. Support available to part-time students. Financial award application deadline: 8/15; financial award applicants required to submit FAFSA. In 2006, 3 degrees awarded. *Degree program information:* Part-time and evening/weekend programs available. Offers acute care nurse practitioner (MSN); family nurse practitioner (MSN); health education (MSN); leadership in health care delivery (MSN). *Application deadline:* For fall admission, 7/15 priority date for domestic students; for spring admission, 12/1 priority date for domestic students. Applications are processed on a rolling basis. *Application fee:* $50. Electronic applications accepted. *Chair,* Nancy Kramer, 319-226-2040, Fax: 319-226-2070, E-mail: kramerna@ihs.org.

ALLIANCE THEOLOGICAL SEMINARY, Nyack, NY 10960

General Information Independent-religious, coed, graduate-only institution. *Graduate housing:* Rooms and/or apartments available on a first-come, first-served basis to single and married students. Housing application deadline: 9/1.

GRADUATE UNITS

Graduate and Professional Programs *Degree program information:* Part-time programs available. Offers Christian ministry (MPS); counseling (MA); intercultural studies (MA); missions (MPS); New Testament (MA); Old Testament (MA); theology (M Div); urban ministry (MPS).

ALLIANCE UNIVERSITY COLLEGE, Calgary, AB T2P 3T5, Canada

General Information Independent-religious, coed, comprehensive institution. *Graduate housing:* Room and/or apartments available to single students; on-campus housing not available to married students. Housing application deadline: 8/20.

GRADUATE UNITS

Canadian Theological Seminary *Degree program information:* Part-time programs available. Postbaccalaureate distance learning degree programs offered (minimal on-campus study). Offers biblical/theological studies (MA); Chinese ministries (Certificate); Christian studies (Diploma); church education (M Div); intercultural ministries (M Div, MA, Diploma); leadership and ministry (MA); pastoral ministries (M Div). Electronic applications accepted.

ALLIANT INTERNATIONAL UNIVERSITY–FRESNO, Fresno, CA 93727

General Information Independent, coed, graduate-only institution. *Enrollment by degree level:* 22 master's, 257 doctoral. *Graduate housing:* On-campus housing not available. *Student services:* Campus employment opportunities, career counseling, low-cost health insurance. *Library facilities:* Kauffman Library. *Online resources:* library catalog, web page, access to other libraries' catalogs. *Collection:* 18,000 titles, 250 serial subscriptions.

Computer facilities: 20 computers available on campus for general student use. A campuswide network can be accessed from off campus. Internet access and online class registration are available. *Web address:* http://www.alliant.edu/.

General Application Contact: Alliant International University Central Contact Center, 866-U-ALLIANT, Fax: 858-635-4555, E-mail: admissions@alliant.edu.

GRADUATE UNITS

California School of Professional Psychology Students: 88 full-time (63 women), 5 part-time (all women); includes 21 minority (7 African Americans, 9 Asian Americans or Pacific Islanders, 5 Hispanic Americans), 6 international. Average age 31. 42 applicants, 69% accepted, 20 enrolled. *Faculty:* 4 full-time (3 women), 18 part-time/adjunct (8 women). Expenses: Contact institution. *Financial support:* Research assistantships, teaching assistantships available. Financial award application deadline: 2/15; financial award applicants required to submit FAFSA. In 2006, 23 degrees awarded. Offers clinical psychology (PhD, Psy D); professional psychology (PhD, Psy D). *Application deadline:* For fall admission, 1/15 priority date for domestic and international students. *Application fee:* $70. *Application Contact:* Alliant International University Central Contact Center, 866-U-ALLIANT, Fax: 858-635-4555, E-mail: admissions@alliant.edu. *Interim Dean,* Dr. Steven Bucky, 866-825-5426, E-mail: admissions@alliant.edu.

Center for Forensic Studies Students: 84 full-time (65 women), 8 part-time (7 women); includes 19 minority (3 African Americans, 3 American Indian/Alaska Native, 6 Asian Americans or Pacific Islanders, 7 Hispanic Americans). Average age 28. 77 applicants, 40% accepted, 19 enrolled. *Faculty:* 3 full-time (2 women), 15 part-time/adjunct (2 women). Expenses: Contact institution. *Financial support:* Research assistantships, teaching assistantships, career-related internships or fieldwork, Federal Work-Study, institutionally sponsored loans, and scholarships/grants available. Financial award application deadline: 2/15; financial award applicants required to submit FAFSA. In 2006, 14 degrees awarded. Offers forensic psychology (PhD, Psy D). *Application deadline:* For fall admission, 1/15 priority date for domestic and international students. Applications are processed on a rolling basis. *Application fee:* $70. Electronic applications accepted. *Application Contact:* Alliant International University Central Contact Center, 866-U-ALLIANT, Fax: 858-635-4555, E-mail: admissions@alliant.edu. *Interim Director,* Dr. Jana Price–Sharps, 866-825-5426, Fax: 559-253-2267, E-mail: admissions@alliant.edu.

Graduate School of Education Students: 4 full-time (3 women), 37 part-time (31 women); includes 20 minority (6 African Americans, 1 American Indian/Alaska Native, 3 Asian Americans or Pacific Islanders, 10 Hispanic Americans), 2 international. Average age 43. 10 applicants, 90% accepted, 8 enrolled. *Faculty:* 1 (woman) full-time, 5 part-time/adjunct (2 women). Expenses: Contact institution. *Financial support:* Research assistantships, teaching assistantships, career-related internships or fieldwork, Federal Work-Study, institutionally sponsored loans, and scholarships/grants available. Financial award application deadline: 2/15; financial award applicants required to submit FAFSA. In 2006, 5 master's, 2 doctorates awarded. *Degree program information:* Part-time and evening/weekend programs available. Postbaccalaureate distance learning degree programs offered (no on-campus study). Offers education (MA, Ed D, Certificate, Credential); educational leadership and management (Ed D); teaching (MA); teaching English to speakers of other languages (MA, Ed D, Certificate). *Application deadline:* For fall admission, 7/1 priority date for domestic and international students; for spring admission, 12/1 priority date for domestic and international students. Applications are processed on a rolling basis. *Application fee:* $55. Electronic applications accepted. *Application Contact:* Alliant International University Central Contact Center, 866-U-ALLIANT, Fax: 858-635-4555, E-mail: admissions@alliant.edu. *Systemwide Dean,* Dr. Karen Schuster Webb, 866-825-5426, Fax: 559-253-2267, E-mail: admissions@alliant.edu.

Marshall Goldsmith School of Management Students: 40 full-time (19 women), 13 part-time (7 women); includes 21 minority (8 African Americans, 6 Asian Americans or Pacific Islanders, 7 Hispanic Americans), 2 international. Average age 36. 13 applicants, 77% accepted, 0 enrolled. *Faculty:* 2 full-time (both women), 10 part-time/adjunct (4 women). Expenses: Contact institution. *Financial support:* In 2006–07, 20 students received support. Career-related internships or fieldwork and Federal Work-Study available. Financial award application deadline: 2/15. In 2006, 1 master's, 3 doctorates awarded. *Degree program information:* Part-time and evening/weekend programs available. Offers management (MA, Psy D). *Application deadline:* Applications are processed on a rolling basis. *Application fee:* $70. *Application Contact:* Alliant International University Central Contact Center, 866-U-ALLIANT, Fax: 858-635-4555, E-mail: admissions@alliant.edu. *Systemwide Dean,* Dr. Jim Goodrich, 858-623-2777, Fax: 559-253-2267, E-mail: admissions@alliant.edu.

Organizational Psychology Division Students: 40 full-time (19 women), 13 part-time (7 women); includes 21 minority (8 African Americans, 6 Asian Americans or Pacific Islanders, 7 Hispanic Americans), 2 international. Average age 36. 13 applicants, 77% accepted, 10 enrolled. *Faculty:* 2 full-time (both women), 10 part-time/adjunct (4 women). Expenses: Contact institution. *Financial support:* Career-related internships or fieldwork, Federal Work-Study, institutionally sponsored loans, and scholarships/grants available. Financial award application deadline: 2/15; financial award applicants required to submit FAFSA. In 2006, 1 master's, 3 doctorates awarded. *Degree program information:* Part-time and evening/weekend programs available. Offers organizational behavior (MA); organizational development (Psy D). *Application deadline:* For fall admission, 4/1 priority date for domestic and international students; for spring admission, 11/1 priority date for domestic and international students. Applications are processed on a rolling basis. *Application fee:* $70. Electronic applications accepted. *Application Contact:* Alliant International University Central Contact Center, 866-U-ALLIANT, Fax: 858-635-4555, E-mail: admissions@alliant.edu. *Program Director,* Dr. Toni Knott, 866-825-5426, Fax: 559-253-2267, E-mail: admissions@alliant.edu.

ALLIANT INTERNATIONAL UNIVERSITY–IRVINE, Irvine, CA 92612

General Information Independent, coed, graduate-only institution. *Enrollment by degree level:* 92 master's, 121 doctoral, 3 other advanced degrees. *Student services:* Campus employment opportunities, campus safety program, career counseling, disabled student services, low-cost health insurance, teacher training, writing training. *Library facilities:* Alliant Library plus 1 other. *Online resources:* library catalog, web page, access to other libraries' catalogs. *Collection:* 221,000 titles, 1,149 serial subscriptions, 3,097 audiovisual materials.

Computer facilities: 41 computers available on campus for general student use. A campuswide network can be accessed from off campus. Online class registration is available. *Web address:* http://www.alliant.edu/.

General Application Contact: Alliant International University Central Contact Center, 866-U-ALLIANT, Fax: 858-635-4555, E-mail: admissions@alliant.edu.

GRADUATE UNITS

California School of Professional Psychology Students: 93 full-time (81 women), 44 part-time (33 women); includes 39 minority (8 African Americans, 2 American Indian/Alaska Native, 15 Asian Americans or Pacific Islanders, 14 Hispanic Americans), 1 international. Average age 29. 70 applicants, 86% accepted, 39 enrolled. *Faculty:* 4 full-time (1 woman), 11 part-time/adjunct (9 women). Expenses: Contact institution. *Financial support:* In 2006–07, 80 students received support. Career-related internships or fieldwork, Federal Work-Study, institutionally sponsored loans, and scholarships/grants available. Financial award application deadline: 2/15; financial award applicants required to submit FAFSA. In 2006, 6 master's, 22 doctorates awarded. *Degree program information:* Part-time programs available. Offers marital and family therapy (MA, Psy D); professional psychology (MA, Psy D). *Application deadline:* For fall admission, 2/1 priority date for domestic and international students. Applications are processed on a rolling basis. *Application fee:* $70. Electronic applications accepted. *Application Contact:* Alliant International University Central Contact Center, 866-U-ALLIANT, Fax: 858-635-4555, E-mail: admissions@alliant.edu. *Interim Dean,* Dr. Steven Bucky, 866-825-5426, Fax: 949-833-3507, E-mail: admissions@alliant.edu.

Center for Forensic Studies Offers forensic studies (Psy D).

Graduate School of Education Students: 32 full-time (25 women), 47 part-time (37 women); includes 28 minority (6 African Americans, 1 American Indian/Alaska Native, 8 Asian Americans or Pacific Islanders, 13 Hispanic Americans). Average age 32. 151 applicants, 61% accepted, 65 enrolled. *Faculty:* 15 full-time (7 women), 106 part-time/adjunct (55 women). Expenses: Contact institution. *Financial support:* Research assistantships, teaching assistantships, career-related internships or fieldwork, Federal Work-Study, institutionally sponsored loans, and scholarships/grants available. Financial award application deadline: 2/15; financial award applicants required to submit FAFSA. In 2006, 29 master's, 5 doctorates awarded. *Degree program information:* Part-time and evening/weekend programs available. Postbaccalaureate distance learning degree programs offered. Offers auditory oral education (Certificate); CLAD (Certificate); education (MA, Ed D, Psy D, Certificate, Credential); educational administration (MA, Credential); educational leadership and management (K-12) (Ed D); educational psychology (Psy D); higher education (Ed D); preliminary administrative services (Credential); preliminary multiple subject (Credential); preliminary multiple subject with BCLAD (Credential); preliminary single subject (Credential); professional clear multiple subject (Credential); professional clear single subject (Credential); pupil personnel services (Credential); school psychology (MA); teaching (MA, Credential); teaching English to speakers of other languages (MA, Ed D); technology and learning (MA). *Application deadline:* For fall admission, 7/1 priority date for domestic and international students; for spring admission, 12/1 priority date for domestic and international students. Applications are processed on a rolling basis. *Application fee:* $55. Electronic applications accepted. *Application Contact:* Alliant International University Central Contact Center, 866-U-ALLIANT, Fax: 858-635-4555, E-mail: admissions@alliant.edu. *Systemwide Dean,* Dr. Karen Schuster Webb, 866-825-5426, Fax: 949-833-3507, E-mail: admissions@alliant.edu.

ALLIANT INTERNATIONAL UNIVERSITY–LOS ANGELES, Alhambra, CA 91803-1360

General Information Independent, coed, graduate-only institution. *Enrollment by degree level:* 54 master's, 573 doctoral, 5 other advanced degrees. *Graduate faculty:* 40 full-time (19 women), 40 part-time/adjunct (17 women). *Graduate housing:* Room and/or apartments available to single students; on-campus housing not available to married students. *Student services:* Campus employment opportunities, campus safety program, career counseling, disabled student services, low-cost health insurance, multicultural affairs office, teacher training, writing training. *Library facilities:* Los Angeles Library. *Online resources:* library catalog, web page, access to other libraries' catalogs. *Collection:* 221,000 titles, 1,149 serial subscriptions, 3,097 audiovisual materials.

Computer facilities: 41 computers available on campus for general student use. A campuswide network can be accessed from student residence rooms and from off campus. Internet access and online class registration are available. *Web address:* http://www.alliant.edu/.

General Application Contact: Alliant International University Central Contact Center, 866-U-ALLIANT, Fax: 858-635-4555, E-mail: admissions@alliant.edu.

GRADUATE UNITS

California School of Professional Psychology Students: 435 full-time (350 women), 8 part-time (5 women); includes 165 minority (39 African Americans, 1 American Indian/Alaska Native, 61 Asian Americans or Pacific Islanders, 64 Hispanic Americans), 11 international. Average age 28. 333 applicants, 44% accepted, 102 enrolled. Expenses: Contact institution. *Financial support:* Research assistantships, teaching assistantships, career-related internships or fieldwork, Federal Work-Study, institutionally sponsored loans, and scholarships/grants available. Financial award application deadline: 2/15; financial award applicants required to submit FAFSA. In 2006, 80 degrees awarded. Offers clinical psychology (PhD, Psy D); professional psychology (PhD, Psy D). *Application deadline:* For fall admission, 1/15 priority date for domestic and international students; for spring admission, 11/1 priority date for domestic and international students. Applications are processed on a rolling basis. *Application fee:* $70. Electronic applications accepted. *Application Contact:* Alliant International University Central Contact Center, 866-U-ALLIANT, Fax: 858-635-4555, E-mail: admissions@alliant.edu. *Interim Dean,* Dr. Steven Bucky, 866-825-5426, Fax: 626-284-0550, E-mail: admissions@alliant.edu.

Center for Forensic Studies Students: 48 full-time (39 women), 3 part-time (2 women); includes 15 minority (2 African Americans, 3 Asian Americans or Pacific Islanders, 10 Hispanic Americans), 1 international. Average age 28. 50 applicants, 34% accepted, 13 enrolled. *Faculty:* 1 full-time (0 women), 11 part-time/adjunct (2 women). Expenses: Contact institution. *Financial support:* Research assistantships, teaching assistantships, career-related internships or fieldwork, Federal Work-Study, institutionally sponsored loans, and scholarships/grants available. Financial award application deadline: 2/15; financial award applicants required to submit FAFSA. In 2006, 1 degree awarded. Offers forensic psychology (Psy D). *Application deadline:* For fall admission, 1/2 priority date for domestic and international students. *Application fee:* $70. *Application Contact:* Alliant International University Central Contact Center, 866-U-ALLIANT, Fax: 858-635-4555, E-mail: admissions@alliant.edu. *Interim Director,* Dr. Jana Price Sharpe, 626-284-2777 Ext. 3064, Fax: 626-284-1552, E-mail: admissions@alliant.edu.

Graduate School of Education Students: 30 full-time (18 women), 38 part-time (24 women); includes 45 minority (16 African Americans, 6 Asian Americans or Pacific Islanders, 23 Hispanic Americans), 1 international. Average age 28. 50 applicants, 34% accepted, 13 enrolled. Expenses: Contact institution. *Financial support:* Research assistantships, teaching assistantships, career-related internships or fieldwork, Federal Work-Study, institutionally sponsored loans, and scholarships/grants available. Financial award application deadline: 2/15; financial award applicants required to submit FAFSA. In 2006, 2 degrees awarded. *Degree program information:* Part-time and evening/weekend programs available. Postbaccalaureate distance learning degree programs offered (no on-campus study). Offers education (MA, Ed D, Psy D, Credential); educational administration (MA); educational leadership and management (K-12) (Ed D); educational psychology (Psy D); higher education (Ed D); preliminary administrative services (Credential); pupil personnel services (Credential); school psychology (MA); teaching (MA). *Application deadline:* For fall admission, 7/1 priority date for domestic and international students; for spring admission, 12/1 priority date for domestic and international students. Applications are processed on a rolling basis. *Application fee:* $55. Electronic applications accepted. *Application Contact:* Alliant International University Central Contact Center, 866-U-ALLIANT, Fax: 858-635-4555, E-mail: admissions@alliant.edu. *Systemwide Dean,* Dr. Karen Schuster Webb, 866-825-5426, Fax: 626-284-0550, E-mail: admissions@alliant.edu.

Marshall Goldsmith School of Management Students: 64 full-time (44 women), 6 part-time (1 woman); includes 19 minority (9 African Americans, 6 Asian Americans or Pacific Islanders, 4 Hispanic Americans), 1 international. Average age 24. 55 applicants, 44% accepted, 15 enrolled. *Faculty:* 6 full-time (2 women), 7 part-time/adjunct (3 women). Expenses: Contact institution. *Financial support:* In 2006–07, 70 students received support; research assistantships, teaching assistantships, career-related internships or fieldwork and Federal Work-Study available. Financial award application deadline: 2/15; financial award applicants required to submit FAFSA. In 2006, 5 master's, 2 doctorates awarded. Offers management (MA, DBA, PhD). *Application deadline:* For fall admission, 1/2 priority date for domestic students. *Application fee:* $70. *Application Contact:* Alliant International University Central Contact Center, 866-U-ALLIANT, Fax: 858-635-4555, E-mail: admissions@alliant.edu. *Systemwide Dean,* Dr. Jim Goodrich, 866-825-5426, Fax: 858-552-1974, E-mail: admissions@alliant.edu.

Business Division Offers business (DBA).

Organizational Psychology Division Students: 64 full-time (44 women), 6 part-time (1 woman); includes 19 minority (9 African Americans, 6 Asian Americans or Pacific Islanders, 4 Hispanic Americans), 1 international. Average age 24. 55 applicants, 44% accepted, 15 enrolled. *Faculty:* 4 full-time (0 women), 5 part-time/adjunct (all women). Expenses: Contact institution. *Financial support:* In 2006–07, 60 students received support; research assistantships, teaching assistantships, career-related internships or fieldwork, Federal Work-Study, institutionally sponsored loans, and scholarships/grants available. Financial award application deadline: 2/15; financial award applicants required to submit FAFSA. In 2006, 5 master's, 2 doctorates awarded. *Degree program information:* Part-time programs available. Offers industrial/organizational psychology (MA, PhD). *Application deadline:* For fall admission, 4/1 priority date for domestic and international students; for spring admission, 11/1 priority date for domestic and international students. Applications are processed on a rolling basis. *Application fee:* $70. Electronic applications accepted. *Application Contact:* Alliant International University Central Contact Center, 866-U-ALLIANT, Fax: 858-635-4555, E-mail: admissions@alliant.edu. *Program Director,* Dr. Jay Finkelman, 866-825-5426, Fax: 626-284-0550, E-mail: admissions@alliant.edu.

ALLIANT INTERNATIONAL UNIVERSITY–MÉXICO CITY, CP06700 Mexico City, Mexico

General Information Independent, coed, comprehensive institution. *Enrollment:* 122 graduate, professional, and undergraduate students; 29 full-time matriculated graduate/professional students (18 women), 25 part-time matriculated graduate/professional students (16 women). *Enrollment by degree level:* 54 master's. *Graduate faculty:* 5 full-time (3 women), 21 part-time/adjunct (7 women). *Tuition:* Full-time $5,640; part-time $235 per unit. *Required fees:* $300; $150 per semester. *Graduate housing:* On-campus housing not available. *Student services:* Campus employment opportunities. *Library facilities:* Campus Library. *Collection:* 12,000 titles.

Computer facilities: 15 computers available on campus for general student use. Internet access is available. *Web address:* http://www.alliantmexico.edu/.

General Application Contact: Alliant International University Central Contact Center, 866-U-ALLIANT, Fax: 858-635-4555, E-mail: admissions@alliant.edu.

GRADUATE UNITS

Graduate School of Education Expenses: Contact institution. *Financial support:* Career-related internships or fieldwork, Federal Work-Study, institutionally sponsored loans, and scholarships/grants available. Financial award application deadline: 2/15; financial award applicants required to submit FAFSA. *Degree program information:* Part-time and evening/weekend programs available. Postbaccalaureate distance learning degree programs offered (no on-campus study). Offers teaching (MA). *Application deadline:* For fall admission, 8/1 priority date for domestic and international students; for spring admission, 12/1 priority date for domestic and international students. *Application fee:* $50. *Application Contact:* Alliant International University Central Contact Center, 866-U-ALLIANT, Fax: 858-635-4555, E-mail: admissions@alliant.edu. *Systemwide Dean,* Dr. Karen Schuster Webb, 888-824-4421, E-mail: kwebb@alliant.edu.

International Studies Division Offers international relations (MA).

Marshall Goldsmith School of Management Students: 15 full-time (7 women), 11 part-time (6 women); includes 4 minority (all Hispanic Americans), 10 international. Average age 25. 17 applicants, 41% accepted. *Faculty:* 1 full-time (0 women), 11 part-time/adjunct (3 women). Expenses: Contact institution. *Financial support:* Research assistantships, teaching assistantships, career-related internships or fieldwork, Federal Work-Study, institutionally sponsored loans, and scholarships/grants available. Support available to part-time students. Financial award application deadline: 2/15; financial award applicants required to submit FAFSA. *Degree program information:* Part-time and evening/weekend programs available. Offers international business administration (MIBA); international relations (MA). *Application deadline:* For fall admission, 8/1 priority date for domestic and international students; for spring admission, 12/1 priority date for domestic and international students. Applications are processed on a rolling basis. *Application fee:* $55. Electronic applications accepted. *Application Contact:* Alliant International University Central Contact Center, 866-U-ALLIANT, Fax: 858-635-4555, E-mail: admissions@alliant.edu. *Dean,* Dr. Jim Goodrich, 525-5264-2187, Fax: 525-5264-2188, E-mail: admissions@alliant.edu.

Programs in Arts and Science *Degree program information:* Part-time programs available. Offers counseling psychology (MA); international relations (MA). Electronic applications accepted.

ALLIANT INTERNATIONAL UNIVERSITY–SACRAMENTO, Sacramento, CA 95825

General Information Independent, coed, graduate-only institution. *Enrollment by degree level:* 14 master's, 72 doctoral. *Graduate faculty:* 4 full-time (2 women), 9 part-time/adjunct (4 women). *Tuition:* Part-time $825 per unit. Tuition and fees vary according to degree level. *Student services:* Campus employment opportunities, campus safety program, disabled student services, international student services, low-cost health insurance, teacher training, writing training. *Library facilities:* Alliant Library. *Online resources:* library catalog, web page, access to other libraries' catalogs.

Computer facilities: 10 computers available on campus for general student use. A campuswide network can be accessed. Internet access and online class registration are available. *Web address:* http://www.alliant.edu/.

General Application Contact: Alliant International University Central Contact Center, 866-U-ALLIANT, Fax: 858-635-4555, E-mail: admissions@alliant.edu.

GRADUATE UNITS

California School of Professional Psychology Average age 30. 57 applicants, 88% accepted, 27 enrolled. Expenses: Contact institution. In 2006, 6 degrees awarded. Offers clinical psychology (Psy D); marital and family therapy (MA); professional psychology (MA, Psy D). *Application deadline:* For fall admission, 1/15 priority date for domestic and international students. Applications are processed on a rolling basis. *Application fee:* $70. Electronic applications accepted. *Application Contact:* Alliant International University Central Contact Center, 866-U-ALLIANT, Fax: 858-635-4555, E-mail: admissions@alliant.edu. *Interim Dean,* Dr. Steven Bucky, 866-825-5426, Fax: 916-565-2959, E-mail: admissions@alliant.edu.

Graduate School of Education Offers education (MA); teaching (MA).

Marshall Goldsmith School of Management Students: 5 full-time (3 women), 3 part-time; includes 1 African American, 1 Asian American or Pacific Islander, 1 Hispanic American. Expenses: Contact institution. Offers management (Psy D); organizational development (Psy D). *Application fee:* $70. *Application Contact:* Alliant International University Central Contact Center, 866-U-ALLIANT, Fax: 858-635-4555, E-mail: admissions@alliant.edu. *Systemwide Dean,* Dr. Jim Goodrich, 866-824-5426, Fax: 916-565-2959, E-mail: admissions@alliant.edu.

ALLIANT INTERNATIONAL UNIVERSITY–SAN DIEGO, San Diego, CA 92131-1799

General Information Independent, coed, graduate-only institution. *Graduate faculty:* 49 full-time (23 women), 102 part-time/adjunct (50 women). *Tuition:* Part-time $825 per unit. Tuition and fees vary according to course load, degree level and program. *Graduate housing:* Rooms and/or apartments available on a first-come, first-served basis to single and married students. *Student services:* Campus employment opportunities, campus safety program, career counseling, disabled student services, exercise/wellness program, free psychological counseling, low-cost health insurance, multicultural affairs office, teacher training, writing training. *Library facilities:* Walter Library. *Online resources:* library catalog, web page, access to other libraries' catalogs. *Collection:* 221,000 titles, 1,149 serial subscriptions, 3,097 audiovisual materials.

Computer facilities: 55 computers available on campus for general student use. A campuswide network can be accessed from student residence rooms and from off campus. Internet access and online class registration are available. *Web address:* http://www.alliant.edu/.

General Application Contact: Alliant International University Central Contact Center, 866-U-ALLIANT, Fax: 858-635-4555, E-mail: admissions@alliant.edu.

GRADUATE UNITS

California School of Professional Psychology Students: 495 full-time (401 women), 154 part-time (122 women); includes 129 minority (25 African Americans, 9 American Indian/Alaska Native, 42 Asian Americans or Pacific Islanders, 53 Hispanic Americans), 26 international. Average age 29. 491 applicants, 43% accepted, 144 enrolled. *Faculty:* 19

Alliant International University–San Diego (continued)

full-time (6 women), 66 part-time/adjunct (29 women). Expenses: Contact institution. *Financial support:* In 2006–07, 475 students received support; research assistantships, teaching assistantships, career-related internships or fieldwork, Federal Work-Study, institutionally sponsored loans, and scholarships/grants available. Financial award application deadline: 2/15. In 2006, 24 master's, 76 doctorates awarded. *Degree program information:* Part-time programs available. Offers clinical psychology (PhD, Psy D); marital and family therapy (MA, Psy D); professional psychology (MA, PhD, Psy D). *Application deadline:* For fall admission, 1/15 priority date for domestic and international students. *Application fee:* $70. *Application Contact:* Alliant International University Central Contact Center, 866-U-ALLIANT, Fax: 858-635-4555, E-mail: admissions@alliant.edu. *Interim Systemwide Dean,* Dr. Steven Bucky, 866-825-5426, Fax: 858-635-4739, E-mail: admissions@alliant.edu.

Graduate School of Education Students: 97 full-time (75 women), 106 part-time (78 women); includes 59 minority (18 African Americans, 3 American Indian/Alaska Native, 15 Asian Americans or Pacific Islanders, 23 Hispanic Americans), 37 international. Average age 35. 158 applicants, 58% accepted, 66 enrolled. *Faculty:* 7 full-time (4 women), 15 part-time/adjunct (9 women). Expenses: Contact institution. *Financial support:* Research assistantships, teaching assistantships, career-related internships or fieldwork, Federal Work-Study, institutionally sponsored loans, and scholarships/grants available. Financial award application deadline: 2/15; financial award applicants required to submit FAFSA. In 2006, 58 master's, 14 doctorates awarded. *Degree program information:* Part-time and evening/weekend programs available. Postbaccalaureate distance learning degree programs offered (no on-campus study). Offers education (MA, Ed D, Psy D, Certificate, Credential); educational administration (MA); educational leadership and management (K-12) (Ed D); educational psychology (Psy D); higher education (Ed D, Certificate); preliminary administrative services (Credential); preliminary single subject (Credential); professional clear multiple subject (Credential); professional clear single subject (Credential); pupil personnel services (Credential); school psychology (MA); student personnel services (Certificate); teacher education (MA); teaching English to speakers of other languages (MA, Ed D, Certificate). *Application deadline:* For fall admission, 7/1 priority date for domestic and international students; for spring admission, 12/1 priority date for domestic and international students. Applications are processed on a rolling basis. *Application fee:* $55. Electronic applications accepted. *Application Contact:* Alliant International University Central Contact Center, 866-U-ALLIANT, Fax: 858-635-4555, E-mail: admissions@alliant.edu. *Systemwide Dean,* Dr. Karen Schuster Webb, 866-825-5426, Fax: 858-635-4739, E-mail: admissions@alliant.edu.

Marshall Goldsmith School of Management Students: 194 full-time (90 women), 82 part-time (36 women); includes 60 minority (18 African Americans, 2 American Indian/Alaska Native, 19 Asian Americans or Pacific Islanders, 21 Hispanic Americans), 82 international. Average age 30. 213 applicants, 60% accepted, 67 enrolled. *Faculty:* 13 full-time (5 women), 26 part-time/adjunct (10 women). Expenses: Contact institution. *Financial support:* In 2006–07, 58 students received support; research assistantships, teaching assistantships, career-related internships or fieldwork and Federal Work-Study available. Financial award application deadline: 2/15; financial award applicants required to submit FAFSA. In 2006, 29 master's, 30 doctorates awarded. *Degree program information:* Part-time and evening/weekend programs available. Offers management (MA, MBA, MIBA, MS, DBA, PhD). *Application deadline:* For fall admission, 2/1 priority date for domestic students. *Application fee:* $55. *Application Contact:* Alliant International University Central Contact Center, 866-U-ALLIANT, Fax: 858-635-4555, E-mail: admissions@alliant.edu. *Systemwide Dean,* Dr. Jim Goodrich, 866-825-5426, Fax: 858-635-4739.

Business and Management Division Students: 87 full-time (22 women), 51 part-time (17 women); includes 27 minority (8 African Americans, 2 American Indian/Alaska Native, 8 Asian Americans or Pacific Islanders, 9 Hispanic Americans), 68 international. Average age 32. 104 applicants, 66% accepted, 40 enrolled. Expenses: Contact institution. *Financial support:* Research assistantships, teaching assistantships, career-related internships or fieldwork, Federal Work-Study, institutionally sponsored loans, scholarships/grants, and tuition waivers (partial) available. Support available to part-time students. Financial award application deadline: 2/15; financial award applicants required to submit FAFSA. *Degree program information:* Part-time and evening/weekend programs available. Offers business administration (MBA); information and technology management (DBA); international business (MIBA, DBA); strategic business (DBA); sustainable management (MBA). *Application deadline:* For fall admission, 8/1 priority date for domestic and international students; for spring admission, 12/1 priority date for domestic and international students. Applications are processed on a rolling basis. *Application fee:* $55. Electronic applications accepted. *Application Contact:* Alliant International University Central Contact Center, 866-U-ALLIANT, Fax: 858-635-4555, E-mail: admissions@alliant.edu. *Associate Dean,* Dr. Fred Phillips, 866-825-5426, Fax: 855-635-4739, E-mail: admissions@alliant.edu.

International Studies Division Students: 7 full-time (5 women), 1 part-time. Average age 30. 42 applicants, 48% accepted, 6 enrolled. *Faculty:* 2 full-time (0 women), 2 part-time/adjunct (1 woman). Expenses: Contact institution. *Financial support:* In 2006–07, 6 students received support; research assistantships, teaching assistantships, Federal Work-Study and scholarships/grants available. Support available to part-time students. Financial award applicants required to submit FAFSA. In 2006, 6 degrees awarded. *Degree program information:* Part-time programs available. Offers international relations (MA). *Application deadline:* For fall admission, 8/1 priority date for domestic and international students; for spring admission, 12/1 priority date for domestic and international students. *Application fee:* $55. *Application Contact:* Alliant International University Central Contact Center, 866-U-ALLIANT, Fax: 858-635-4555, E-mail: admissions@alliant.edu. *Acting Director,* Dr. Ilya Adler, 866-825-5426, Fax: 858-635-4737, E-mail: admissions@alliant.edu.

Organizational Psychology Division Students: 100 full-time (63 women), 30 part-time (19 women); includes 30 minority (10 African Americans, 10 Asian Americans or Pacific Islanders, 10 Hispanic Americans), 5 international. Average age 27. 67 applicants, 58% accepted, 21 enrolled. *Faculty:* 7 full-time (1 woman), 15 part-time/adjunct (6 women). Expenses: Contact institution. *Financial support:* In 2006–07, 10 students received support; research assistantships, teaching assistantships, career-related internships or fieldwork, Federal Work-Study, institutionally sponsored loans, and scholarships/grants available. Financial award application deadline: 2/15; financial award applicants required to submit FAFSA. In 2006, 6 master's, 13 doctorates awarded. *Degree program information:* Part-time and evening/weekend programs available. Offers clinical/industrial organizational psychology (PhD); consulting psychology (PhD); industrial/organizational psychology (MA, MS, PhD); organizational behavior (MA). *Application deadline:* For fall admission, 4/1 priority date for domestic and international students; for spring admission, 11/1 priority date for domestic and international students. Applications are processed on a rolling basis. *Application fee:* $70. Electronic applications accepted. *Application Contact:* Alliant International University Central Contact Center, 866-U-ALLIANT, Fax: 858-635-4555, E-mail: admissions@alliant.edu. *Director,* Dr. Herbert Baker, 866-825-5426, Fax: 858-635-4739, E-mail: admissions@alliant.edu.

ALLIANT INTERNATIONAL UNIVERSITY–SAN FRANCISCO, San Francisco, CA 94133-1221

General Information Independent, coed, graduate-only institution. *Enrollment by degree level:* 305 master's, 594 doctoral, 73 other advanced degrees. *Graduate faculty:* 26 full-time (14 women). *Tuition:* Part-time $825 per unit. Tuition and fees vary according to course load, degree level and program. *Graduate housing:* On-campus housing not available. *Student services:* Campus employment opportunities, campus safety program, disabled student services, international student services, low-cost health insurance, teacher training, writing training. *Library facilities:* Hurwich Library. *Online resources:* library catalog, web page, access to other libraries' catalogs. *Collection:* 221,000 titles, 1,149 serial subscriptions, 3,097 audiovisual materials.

Computer facilities: 55 computers available on campus for general student use. A campuswide network can be accessed from off campus. Internet access and online class registration are available. *Web address:* http://www.alliant.edu/.

General Application Contact: Alliant International University Central Contact Center, 866-U-ALLIANT, Fax: 858-635-4555, E-mail: admissions@alliant.edu.

GRADUATE UNITS

California School of Professional Psychology Students: 424 full-time (339 women), 239 part-time (158 women); includes 155 minority (28 African Americans, 2 American Indian/Alaska Native, 71 Asian Americans or Pacific Islanders, 54 Hispanic Americans), 23 international. Average age 35. 320 applicants, 70% accepted, 139 enrolled. *Faculty:* 16 full-time (7 women), 66 part-time/adjunct (30 women). Expenses: Contact institution. *Financial support:* Research assistantships, teaching assistantships, career-related internships or fieldwork, Federal Work-Study, institutionally sponsored loans, and scholarships/grants available. Financial award application deadline: 2/15; financial award applicants required to submit FAFSA. In 2006, 19 master's, 75 doctorates awarded. Offers clinical psychology (PhD, Psy D, Certificate); professional psychology (Post-Doctoral MS, PhD, Psy D, Certificate); psychopharmacology (Post-Doctoral MS). *Application deadline:* For fall admission, 1/15 priority date for domestic and international students; for spring admission, 11/1 priority date for domestic and international students. Applications are processed on a rolling basis. *Application fee:* $70. Electronic applications accepted. *Application Contact:* Alliant International University Central Contact Center, 866-U-ALLIANT, Fax: 858-635-4555, E-mail: admissions@alliant.edu. *Interim Systemwide Dean,* Dr. Steven Bucky, 866-825-5426, E-mail: admissions@alliant.edu.

Graduate School of Education Students: 30 full-time (24 women), 99 part-time (60 women); includes 37 minority (15 African Americans, 1 American Indian/Alaska Native, 12 Asian Americans or Pacific Islanders, 9 Hispanic Americans), 3 international. Average age 29. 137 applicants, 72% accepted, 85 enrolled. *Faculty:* 4 full-time (2 women), 17 part-time/adjunct (9 women). Expenses: Contact institution. *Financial support:* Research assistantships, teaching assistantships, career-related internships or fieldwork, Federal Work-Study, institutionally sponsored loans, and scholarships/grants available. Financial award application deadline: 2/15; financial award applicants required to submit FAFSA. In 2006, 17 master's, 2 doctorates awarded. *Degree program information:* Part-time and evening/weekend programs available. Postbaccalaureate distance learning degree programs offered (no on-campus study). Offers auditory oral education (Certificate); CLAD (Certificate); community college administration (Ed D); education (MA, Ed D, Psy D, Certificate, Credential); educational administration (MA); educational leadership and management (K-12) (Ed D); educational psychology (Psy D); higher education (Ed D); preliminary administrative services (Credential); preliminary multiple subject (Credential); preliminary multiple subject with BCLAD (Credential); preliminary single subject (Credential); professional clear multiple subject (Credential); professional clear single subject (Credential); pupil personnel services (Credential); school psychology (MA); teaching (MA); university administration (Ed D). *Application deadline:* For fall admission, 7/1 priority date for domestic and international students; for spring admission, 12/1 priority date for domestic and international students. Applications are processed on a rolling basis. *Application fee:* $55. Electronic applications accepted. *Application Contact:* Alliant International University Central Contact Center, 866-U-ALLIANT, Fax: 858-635-4555, E-mail: admissions@alliant.edu. *System-wide Dean,* Dr. Karen Schuster Webb, 866-825-5426, Fax: 415-955-2179, E-mail: admissions@alliant.edu.

Marshall Goldsmith School of Management Students: 103 full-time (53 women), 77 part-time (46 women); includes 35 minority (10 African Americans, 3 American Indian/Alaska Native, 15 Asian Americans or Pacific Islanders, 7 Hispanic Americans), 2 international. Average age 38. 89 applicants, 72% accepted, 58 enrolled. *Faculty:* 5 full-time (all women), 13 part-time/adjunct (4 women). Expenses: Contact institution. *Financial support:* Research assistantships, teaching assistantships, career-related internships or fieldwork, Federal Work-Study, institutionally sponsored loans, and scholarships/grants available. Financial award application deadline: 2/15; financial award applicants required to submit FAFSA. In 2006, 23 master's, 6 doctorates awarded. *Degree program information:* Part-time and evening/weekend programs available. Offers management (MA, MBA, PhD); sustainable management (MBA). *Application deadline:* For fall admission, 4/1 priority date for domestic and international students; for spring admission, 11/1 priority date for domestic and international students. Applications are processed on a rolling basis. *Application fee:* $70. Electronic applications accepted. *Application Contact:* Alliant International University Central Contact Center, 866-U-ALLIANT, Fax: 858-635-4555, E-mail: admissions@alliant.edu. *Systemwide Dean,* Dr. Jim Goodrich, E-mail: admissions@alliant.edu.

Organizational Psychology Division Students: 28 full-time (16 women), 43 part-time (26 women); includes 21 minority (8 African Americans, 1 American Indian/Alaska Native, 10 Asian Americans or Pacific Islanders, 2 Hispanic Americans), 2 international. Average age 39. 24 applicants, 58% accepted, 10 enrolled. *Faculty:* 3 full-time (all women), 7 part-time/adjunct (2 women). Expenses: Contact institution. *Financial support:* In 2006–07, 32 students received support; research assistantships, teaching assistantships, career-related internships or fieldwork, Federal Work-Study, institutionally sponsored loans, and scholarships/grants available. Financial award application deadline: 2/15; financial award applicants required to submit FAFSA. In 2006, 3 master's, 6 doctorates awarded. *Degree program information:* Part-time and evening/weekend programs available. Offers organization development (MA); organizational psychology (MA, PhD). *Application deadline:* For fall admission, 4/1 priority date for domestic and international students; for spring admission, 11/1 priority date for domestic and international students. Applications are processed on a rolling basis. *Application fee:* $70. Electronic applications accepted. *Application Contact:* Alliant International University Central Contact Center, 866-U-ALLIANT, Fax: 858-635-4555, E-mail: admissions@alliant.edu. *Director,* Dr. Ira Levin, 866-825-5426, Fax: 415-955-2179, E-mail: admissions@alliant.edu.

ALVERNIA COLLEGE, Reading, PA 19607-1799

General Information Independent-religious, coed, comprehensive institution. *Graduate housing:* On-campus housing not available.

GRADUATE UNITS

Graduate and Continuing Studies *Degree program information:* Part-time and evening/weekend programs available. Offers business (MBA); community counseling (MA); education (M Ed); liberal studies (MALS); occupational therapy (MSOT). Electronic applications accepted.

ALVERNO COLLEGE, Milwaukee, WI 53234-3922

General Information Independent-religious, Undergraduate: women only; graduate: coed, comprehensive institution. *Enrollment:* 2,480 graduate, professional, and undergraduate students; 127 full-time matriculated graduate/professional students (109 women), 87 part-time matriculated graduate/professional students (73 women). *Enrollment by degree level:* 214 master's. *Graduate faculty:* 18 full-time (13 women), 19 part-time/adjunct (16 women). *Tuition:* Full-time $9,288; part-time $516 per credit. *Required fees:* $250; $125 per semester. Tuition and fees vary according to program. *Graduate housing:* On-campus housing not available. *Student services:* Campus employment opportunities, campus safety program, career counseling, child daycare facilities, disabled student services, exercise/wellness program, multicultural affairs office. *Library facilities:* Alverno College Library. *Online resources:* library catalog, web page, access to other libraries' catalogs. *Collection:* 95,622 titles, 3,932 serial subscriptions, 4,191 audiovisual materials.

Computer facilities: 400 computers available on campus for general student use. A campuswide network can be accessed from student residence rooms and from off campus. Internet access, e-mail are available. *Web address:* http://www.alverno.edu/.

General Application Contact: Dianna K. Gaebler, Director, Graduate and Adult Admissions, 414-382-6133, Fax: 414-382-6354, E-mail: dianna.gaebler@alverno.edu.

GRADUATE UNITS

School of Business Students: 26 full-time (25 women); includes 3 minority (all African Americans) Average age 37. 36 applicants, 72% accepted, 26 enrolled. *Faculty:* 5 full-time (1 woman), 1 part-time/adjunct (0 women). Expenses: Contact institution. *Financial support:* Federal Work-Study available. Support available to part-time students. Financial award application deadline: 4/15; financial award applicants required to submit FAFSA. *Degree program information:* Evening/weekend programs available. Offers business (MBA). *Application deadline:* For fall admission, 8/1 priority date for domestic students; for spring admission, 12/15 priority date for domestic students. Applications are processed on a rolling basis. *Application fee:* $20. Electronic applications accepted. *Application Contact:* Carolyn Wise, Graduate Recruiter,

800-933-3401, Fax: 414-382-6354, E-mail: carolyn.wise@alverno.edu. *MBA Program Director*, William McEachern, 414-382-6238, E-mail: william.mceachern@alverno.edu.

School of Education Students: 83 full-time (68 women), 74 part-time (60 women); includes 37 minority (32 African Americans, 2 American Indian/Alaska Native, 3 Hispanic Americans). Average age 35. 61 applicants, 82% accepted, 41 enrolled. *Faculty:* 12 full-time (11 women), 12 part-time/adjunct (10 women). Expenses: Contact institution. *Financial support:* In 2006–07, 92 students received support. Federal Work-Study available. Support available to part-time students. Financial award application deadline: 4/15; financial award applicants required to submit FAFSA. In 2006, 46 degrees awarded. *Degree program information:* Part-time and evening/weekend programs available. Offers adaptive education (MA); administrative leadership (MA); adult education and organizational development (MA); adult educational and instructional design (MA); adult educational and instructional technology (MA); instructional leadership (MA); instructional technology for K-12 settings (MA); professional development (MA); reading education (MA); reading education with adaptive education (MA); science education (MA); teaching in alternative schools (MA). *Application deadline:* For fall admission, 8/1 priority date for domestic and international students; for spring admission, 12/15 priority date for domestic and international students. Applications are processed on a rolling basis. *Application fee:* $20. Electronic applications accepted. *Application Contact:* Sarajane Kennedy, Associate Director, Admissions Graduate Programs, 414-382-6104, Fax: 414-382-6332, E-mail: sarajane.kennedy@alverno.edu. *Graduate Dean*, Dr. Mary Diez, 414-382-6214, Fax: 414-382-6332, E-mail: mary.diez@alverno.edu.

School of Nursing Students: 18 full-time (16 women), 13 part-time (all women); includes 4 minority (1 African American, 1 American Indian/Alaska Native, 1 Asian American or Pacific Islander, 1 Hispanic American). Average age 35. 23 applicants, 65% accepted, 9 enrolled. *Faculty:* 1 (woman) full-time, 6 part-time/adjunct (all women). Expenses: Contact institution. *Financial support:* In 2006–07, 21 students received support. Federal Work-Study available. Support available to part-time students. Financial award application deadline: 4/15. *Degree program information:* Part-time and evening/weekend programs available. Offers nursing (MSN). *Application deadline:* For fall admission, 8/1 priority date for domestic students; for spring admission, 12/25 priority date for domestic students. Applications are processed on a rolling basis. *Application fee:* $20. Electronic applications accepted. *Application Contact:* Carolyn Wise, Graduate Recruiter, 800-933-3401, Fax: 414-382-6354, E-mail: carolyn.wise@alverno.edu. *Program Director*, Julie Millenbruch, Fax: 414-382-6354, E-mail: julie.millenbruch@alverno.edu.

AMBERTON UNIVERSITY, Garland, TX 75041-5595

General Information Independent-religious, coed, upper-level institution. *Enrollment:* 1,648 graduate, professional, and undergraduate students; 289 full-time matriculated graduate/professional students (139 women), 700 part-time matriculated graduate/professional students (450 women). *Enrollment by degree level:* 989 master's. *Graduate faculty:* 16 full-time (7 women), 45 part-time/adjunct (20 women). *Tuition:* Full-time $4,800; part-time $600 per course. *Graduate housing:* On-campus housing not available. *Library facilities:* Library Resource Center plus 1 other. *Online resources:* library catalog, web page. *Collection:* 21,000 titles, 120 serial subscriptions.

Computer facilities: 30 computers available on campus for general student use. Internet access is available. *Web address:* http://www.amberton.edu/.

General Application Contact: Adviser, 972-279-6511 Ext. 180, Fax: 972-279-9773, E-mail: advisor@amberton.edu.

GRADUATE UNITS

Graduate School Students: 289 full-time (139 women), 700 part-time (450 women); includes 123 minority (77 African Americans, 5 American Indian/Alaska Native, 3 Asian Americans or Pacific Islanders, 38 Hispanic Americans), 15 international. Average age 35. *Faculty:* 16 full-time (7 women), 45 part-time/adjunct (20 women). Expenses: Contact institution. In 2006, 200 degrees awarded. *Degree program information:* Part-time and evening/weekend programs available. Offers counseling (MA); general business (MBA); human relations and business (MA, MS); management (MBA); professional development (MA). *Application deadline:* Applications are processed on a rolling basis. *Application Contact:* Adviser, 972-279-6511 Ext. 180, Fax: 972-279-9773, E-mail: advisor@amberton.edu. *Academic Dean*, Dr. Algia Allen, 972-279-6511 Ext. 135, Fax: 972-279-9773, E-mail: allen@ambernet.amberu.edu.

AMERICAN ACADEMY OF ART, Chicago, IL 60604-4302

General Information Proprietary, coed, comprehensive institution.

GRADUATE UNITS

Graduate Programs *Degree program information:* Part-time and evening/weekend programs available. Offers digital media and design (MFA); painting and drawing (MFA).

AMERICAN BAPTIST SEMINARY OF THE WEST, Berkeley, CA 94704-3029

General Information Independent-religious, coed, graduate-only institution. *Enrollment by degree level:* 51 first professional, 4 master's, 1 other advanced degree. *Graduate faculty:* 4 full-time (all women), 6 part-time/adjunct (1 woman). *Tuition:* Full-time $12,870; part-time $495 per unit. *Graduate housing:* Rooms and/or apartments available on a first-come, first-served basis to single and married students. Typical cost: $8,400 per year for single students; $8,400 per year for married students. Room charges vary according to housing facility selected. Housing application deadline: 6/1. *Student services:* Campus employment opportunities, international student services, writing training. *Library facilities:* Graduate Theological Union Library.

Computer facilities: 3 computers available on campus for general student use. Internet access and online class registration are available. *Web address:* http://www.absw.edu/.

General Application Contact: Rev. Michelle M. Holmes, Vice President, 510-841-1905 Ext. 225, Fax: 510-841-2446, E-mail: mmholmes@absw.edu.

GRADUATE UNITS

Graduate and Professional Programs Students: 56 (31 women); includes 42 minority (38 African Americans, 2 Asian Americans or Pacific Islanders, 2 Hispanic Americans) 3 international. 26 applicants, 92% accepted, 18 enrolled. *Faculty:* 4 full-time (all women), 6 part-time/adjunct (1 woman). Expenses: Contact institution. *Financial support:* In 2006–07, 38 students received support. Career-related internships or fieldwork, institutionally sponsored loans, scholarships/grants, tuition waivers (partial), and tuition discount available. Support available to part-time students. Financial award application deadline: 3/15; financial award applicants required to submit FAFSA. In 2006, 26 degrees awarded. *Degree program information:* Part-time and evening/weekend programs available. Offers theology (M Div, MA). *Application deadline:* For fall admission, 3/15 priority date for domestic students, 3/15 for international students; for spring admission, 11/1 for international students. Applications are processed on a rolling basis. *Application fee:* $25. Electronic applications accepted. *Application Contact:* Rev. Michelle M. Holmes, Vice President, 510-841-1905 Ext. 225, Fax: 510-841-2446, E-mail: mmholmes@absw.edu. *President*, Dr. Keith Russell, 510-841-1905 Ext. 224, Fax: 510-841-2446, E-mail: krussell@absw.edu.

THE AMERICAN COLLEGE, Bryn Mawr, PA 19010-2105

General Information Independent, coed, graduate-only institution. *Enrollment by degree level:* 582 master's. *Graduate faculty:* 19 full-time (1 woman), 9 part-time/adjunct (1 woman). *Graduate housing:* On-campus housing not available. *Student services:* Career counseling, international student services. *Library facilities:* Lucas Memorial Library plus 1 other. *Online resources:* library catalog. *Collection:* 12,500 titles, 620 serial subscriptions.

Computer facilities: 3 computers available on campus for general student use. Online class registration is available. *Web address:* http://www.theamericancollege.edu/.

General Application Contact: Joanne F. Patterson, Associate Director of Graduate Administration, 610-526-1366, Fax: 610-526-1359, E-mail: joanne.patterson@theamericancollege.edu.

GRADUATE UNITS

Richard D. Irwin Graduate School 130 applicants, 92% accepted. *Faculty:* 19 full-time (1 woman), 9 part-time/adjunct (1 woman). Expenses: Contact institution. In 2006, 79 degrees awarded. *Degree program information:* Part-time and evening/weekend programs available. Postbaccalaureate distance learning degree programs offered (minimal on-campus study). Offers financial sciences (MSFS). *Application deadline:* Applications are processed on a rolling basis. *Application fee:* $300. Electronic applications accepted. *Application Contact:* Joanne F. Patterson, Associate Director of Graduate Administration, 610-526-1366, Fax: 610-526-1359, E-mail: joanne.patterson@theamericancollege.edu. *Executive Vice President and Dean*, Dr. Walter Woerheide, 610-526-1398, Fax: 610-526-1359, E-mail: walt.woerheide@theamericancollege.edu.

AMERICAN COLLEGE OF ACUPUNCTURE AND ORIENTAL MEDICINE, Houston, TX 77063

General Information Proprietary, coed, graduate-only institution. *Research affiliation:* Baylor College of Medicine (acupuncture for osteoarthritis of the knee), Memorial Herman Healthcare System, Tianjing Hospital, China (traditional Chinese medicine), Montrose Clinic (HIV/AIDS research and treatment), Rice University Wellness Center (student and staff care).

GRADUATE UNITS

Graduate Studies *Degree program information:* Part-time programs available.

AMERICAN COLLEGE OF THESSALONIKI, GR-555-10 Pylea, Thessaloniki, Greece

General Information Independent, coed, comprehensive institution. *Enrollment:* 418 graduate, professional, and undergraduate students; 9 full-time matriculated graduate/professional students (6 women), 39 part-time matriculated graduate/professional students (24 women). *Enrollment by degree level:* 48 master's. *Graduate faculty:* 6 full-time (1 woman), 10 part-time/adjunct (4 women). *Tuition:* Full-time $10,560; part-time $660 per course. Part-time tuition and fees vary according to course load. *Student services:* Career counseling, free psychological counseling, international student services, writing training. *Library facilities:* Bissell Library plus 1 other. *Online resources:* library catalog, web page, access to other libraries' catalogs. *Collection:* 22,000 titles, 16,500 serial subscriptions, 700 audiovisual materials.

Computer facilities: 170 computers available on campus for general student use. A campuswide network can be accessed from off campus. Internet access is available. *Web address:* http://www.act.edu/.

General Application Contact: Vasilis Blatsas, Coordinator of Business Programs and MBA Advisor, 30-310-398206 Ext. 206.

GRADUATE UNITS

Department of Business Administration Students: 9 full-time (6 women), 39 part-time (24 women), 22 international. 36 applicants, 97% accepted, 26 enrolled. *Faculty:* 6 full-time (1 woman), 10 part-time/adjunct (4 women). Expenses: Contact institution. In 2006, 25 degrees awarded. *Degree program information:* Part-time and evening/weekend programs available. Offers banking and finance (MBA); entrepreneurship (MBA, Certificate); finance (Certificate); management (MBA, Certificate); marketing (MBA, Certificate). *Application deadline:* For fall admission, 9/30 priority date for domestic students; for spring admission, 1/31 priority date for domestic students. Applications are processed on a rolling basis. *Application fee:* $70. Electronic applications accepted. *Application Contact:* Vasilis Blatsas, Coordinator of Business Programs and MBA Advisor, 30-310-398206 Ext. 206. *Chair, Business Division*, Dr. Nikolaos Kourkoumelis, E-mail: nikolaos@act.edu.

AMERICAN COLLEGE OF TRADITIONAL CHINESE MEDICINE, San Francisco, CA 94107

General Information Independent, coed, graduate-only institution. *Enrollment by degree level:* 255 master's, 15 doctoral, 2 other advanced degrees. *Graduate faculty:* 36 full-time (17 women), 27 part-time/adjunct (17 women). *Tuition:* Part-time $185 per credit. *Graduate housing:* On-campus housing not available. *Student services:* Campus employment opportunities, campus safety program, career counseling, disabled student services, free psychological counseling, international student services. *Library facilities:* American College of Traditional Chinese Medicine Library. *Online resources:* library catalog. *Collection:* 4,850 titles, 65 serial subscriptions, 615 audiovisual materials.

Computer facilities: 10 computers available on campus for general student use. A campuswide network can be accessed. Internet access is available. *Web address:* http://www.actcm.edu/.

General Application Contact: Matt Munday, Admissions Officer, 415-282-7600 Ext. 14, Fax: 415-282-0856, E-mail: admissions@actcm.edu.

GRADUATE UNITS

Graduate Program Students: 176 full-time (131 women), 96 part-time (70 women); includes 99 minority (6 African Americans, 77 Asian Americans or Pacific Islanders, 16 Hispanic Americans), 9 international. Average age 33. 62 applicants, 82% accepted, 35 enrolled. *Faculty:* 36 full-time (17 women), 27 part-time/adjunct (17 women). Expenses: Contact institution. *Financial support:* In 2006–07, 190 students received support, including 14 teaching assistantships (averaging $3,200 per year); career-related internships or fieldwork, Federal Work-Study, institutionally sponsored loans, and scholarships/grants also available. Support available to part-time students. Financial award application deadline: 3/2; financial award applicants required to submit FAFSA. In 2006, 90 master's awarded. *Degree program information:* Part-time programs available. Offers acupuncture and Oriental medicine (DAOM); shiatsu massage (Certificate); traditional Chinese medicine (MSTCM); tui na massage (Certificate). *Application deadline:* For fall admission, 9/1 for domestic and international students; for winter admission, 12/1 for domestic and international students; for spring admission, 3/1 for domestic and international students. Applications are processed on a rolling basis. *Application fee:* $100 ($150 for international students). *Application Contact:* Matt Munday, Admissions Officer, 415-282-7600 Ext. 14, Fax: 415-282-0856, E-mail: admissions@actcm.edu. *President*, Lixin Huang, 415-282-7600 Ext. 12, Fax: 415-282-0856, E-mail: lixinhuang@actcm.edu.

AMERICAN CONSERVATORY THEATER, San Francisco, CA 94108-5800

General Information Independent, coed, graduate-only institution. *Enrollment by degree level:* 46 master's, 4 other advanced degrees. *Graduate faculty:* 9 full-time (3 women), 13 part-time/adjunct (8 women). *Tuition:* Full-time $15,366. *Graduate housing:* On-campus housing not available. *Student services:* Campus employment opportunities, campus safety program, career counseling, multicultural affairs office. *Library facilities:* Allen Fletcher Theater Collection. *Collection:* 15,500 titles, 43 serial subscriptions, 708 audiovisual materials.

Computer facilities: 3 computers available on campus for general student use. A campuswide network can be accessed. Internet access is available. *Web address:* http://www.act-sfbay.org/.

General Application Contact: Dr. Jack F. Sharrar, Director of Academic Affairs, 415-439-2350, Fax: 415-834-3300, E-mail: jsharrar@act-sf.org.

GRADUATE UNITS

Program in Acting Students: 46 full-time (22 women); includes 10 minority (9 African Americans, 1 Asian American or Pacific Islander), 1 international. Average age 24. 326 applicants, 4% accepted, 14 enrolled. *Faculty:* 9 full-time (3 women), 13 part-time/adjunct (8 women). Expenses: Contact institution. *Financial support:* In 2006–07, 40 students received support. Federal Work-Study, scholarships/grants, and tuition waivers (full and partial) available. Financial award application deadline: 2/16; financial award applicants required to submit FAFSA. In 2006, 17 degrees awarded. Offers acting (MFA, Certificate). Certificate open only to applicants with undergraduate degree from a non-accredited institution. *Application deadline:* For fall admission, 1/16 for domestic students. *Application fee:* $65. *Application Contact:* Dr.

American Conservatory Theater (continued)

Jack F. Sharrar, Director of Academic Affairs, 415-439-2350, Fax: 415-834-3300, E-mail: jsharrar@act-sf.org. *Conservatory Director*, Melissa Smith, 415-439-2350, E-mail: mysmith@act-sf.org.

AMERICAN FILM INSTITUTE CONSERVATORY, Los Angeles, CA 90027-1657

General Information Independent, coed, graduate-only institution. *Enrollment by degree level:* 326 master's. *Graduate faculty:* 10 full-time (1 woman), 57 part-time/adjunct (13 women). *Tuition:* Full-time $30,975. *Required fees:* $2,100. *Graduate housing:* On-campus housing not available. *Student services:* Campus employment opportunities, campus safety program, career counseling, disabled student services, free psychological counseling, international student services, writing training. *Library facilities:* Louis B. Mayer Library. *Online resources:* library catalog, web page, access to other libraries' catalogs. *Collection:* 9,450 titles, 112 serial subscriptions, 3,550 audiovisual materials.

Computer facilities: 30 computers available on campus for general student use. A campuswide network can be accessed from off campus. Internet access, online class schedule are available. *Web address:* http://www.afi.com/.

General Application Contact: Scott Hardman, Admissions Manager, 323-856-7609, Fax: 323-856-7720, E-mail: shardman@afi.com.

GRADUATE UNITS

Graduate Program Students: 326 full-time (106 women); includes 56 minority (21 African Americans, 2 American Indian/Alaska Native, 21 Asian Americans or Pacific Islanders, 12 Hispanic Americans), 71 international. Average age 27. 591 applicants, 32% accepted, 133 enrolled. *Faculty:* 10 full-time (1 woman), 57 part-time/adjunct (13 women). Expenses: Contact institution. *Financial support:* In 2006–07, 51 students received support, including 14 teaching assistantships with partial tuition reimbursements available (averaging $3,000 per year); career-related internships or fieldwork, scholarships/grants, and unspecified assistantships also available. Financial award application deadline: 4/15; financial award applicants required to submit FAFSA. In 2006, 115 degrees awarded. Offers cinematography (MFA); directing (MFA); editing (MFA); producing (MFA); production design (MFA); screenwriting (MFA). *Application deadline:* For fall admission, 12/1 for domestic and international students. *Application fee:* $75. *Application Contact:* Scott Hardman, Admissions Counselor, 323-856-7714, Fax: 323-856-7720, E-mail: shardman@afi.com. *Dean*, Robert Mandel, 323-856-7600, Fax: 323-467-4578.

AMERICAN GRADUATE SCHOOL OF INTERNATIONAL RELATIONS AND DIPLOMACY, F-75006 Paris, France

General Information Independent, coed, graduate-only institution.

GRADUATE UNITS

Program in International Relations and Diplomacy Offers international relations and diplomacy (MA, PhD).

AMERICAN GRADUATE UNIVERSITY, Covina, CA 91724

General Information Proprietary, coed, graduate-only institution. *Enrollment by degree level:* 951 master's. *Graduate faculty:* 20. *Library facilities:* American Graduate University Library. *Collection:* 11,000 titles, 33 serial subscriptions.

Computer facilities: Internet access and online class registration are available. *Web address:* http://www.agu.edu/.

General Application Contact: Linda Olsen, Registrar, 626-966-4576, Fax: 626-915-1709, E-mail: lindaolsen@agu.edu.

GRADUATE UNITS

Program in Acquisition Management *Faculty:* 2 full-time (1 woman), 12 part-time/adjunct (2 women). Expenses: Contact institution. In 2006, 30 master's, 3 other advanced degrees awarded. *Degree program information:* Part-time programs available. Postbaccalaureate distance learning degree programs offered (no on-campus study). Offers acquisition management (MAM, Certificate). *Application deadline:* Applications are processed on a rolling basis. *Application fee:* $50. Electronic applications accepted. *Application Contact:* Marie J. Sirney, Executive Vice President, 626-966-4576, Fax: 626-915-1709, E-mail: mariesirney@agu.edu. *President*, Paul McDonald, 626-966-4576 Ext. 1006, E-mail: paulmcdonald@agu.edu.

Program in Business Administration *Faculty:* 2 full-time (1 woman), 12 part-time/adjunct (2 women). Expenses: Contact institution. *Degree program information:* Part-time programs available. Postbaccalaureate distance learning degree programs offered (no on-campus study). Offers business administration (MBA). *Application deadline:* Applications are processed on a rolling basis. *Application fee:* $50. Electronic applications accepted. *Application Contact:* Marie J. Sirney, Executive Vice President, 626-966-4576, Fax: 626-915-1709, E-mail: mariesirney@agu.edu. *President*, Paul McDonald, 626-966-4576 Ext. 1006, E-mail: paulmcdonald@agu.edu.

Program in Contract Management *Faculty:* 2 full-time (1 woman), 12 part-time/adjunct (2 women). Expenses: Contact institution. In 2006, 9 degrees awarded. *Degree program information:* Part-time programs available. Postbaccalaureate distance learning degree programs offered (no on-campus study). Offers contract management (MCM, Certificate). *Application deadline:* Applications are processed on a rolling basis. *Application fee:* $50. Electronic applications accepted. *Application Contact:* Marie J. Sirney, Executive Vice President, 626-966-4576, Fax: 626-915-1709, E-mail: mariesirney@agu.edu. *President*, Paul McDonald, 626-966-4576 Ext. 1006, E-mail: paulmcdonald@agu.edu.

Program in Project Management *Faculty:* 2 full-time (1 woman), 12 part-time/adjunct (2 women). Expenses: Contact institution. In 2006, 13 degrees awarded. *Degree program information:* Part-time programs available. Postbaccalaureate distance learning degree programs offered (no on-campus study). Offers project management (MPM, Certificate). *Application deadline:* Applications are processed on a rolling basis. *Application fee:* $50. Electronic applications accepted. *Application Contact:* Marie J. Sirney, Executive Vice President, 626-966-4576, Fax: 626-915-1709, E-mail: mariesirney@agu.edu. *President*, Paul McDonald, 626-966-4576 Ext. 1006, E-mail: paulmcdonald@agu.edu.

AMERICAN HEALTH SCIENCES UNIVERSITY, Aurora, CO 80012

General Information Proprietary, coed, primarily women, graduate-only institution. *Enrollment by degree level:* 24 master's. *Graduate faculty:* 1 (woman) full-time, 4 part-time/adjunct (3 women).

Computer facilities: Online class registration is available. *Web address:* http://www.ahsu.edu/.

General Application Contact: Ann L Peterson, Academic Dean, 800-530-8079, Fax: 303-367-2577, E-mail: dean@ahsu.edu.

GRADUATE UNITS

Program in Nutrition Science Average age 35. *Faculty:* 4 part-time/adjunct (3 women). Expenses: Contact institution. *Degree program information:* Part-time and evening/weekend programs available. Postbaccalaureate distance learning degree programs offered (no on-campus study). Offers nutrition science (MS). *Application fee:* $100. Electronic applications accepted. *Application Contact:* Dr. Chaitali Adhikari, Director of Graduate Program, 303-340-2054, Fax: 303-367-2577, E-mail: masters@ahsu.edu. *Academic Dean*, Ann L Peterson, 800-530-8079, Fax: 303-367-2577, E-mail: dean@ahsu.edu.

AMERICAN INTERCONTINENTAL UNIVERSITY, Los Angeles, CA 90066

General Information Proprietary, coed, comprehensive institution. *Enrollment:* 56 full-time matriculated graduate/professional students (25 women), 6 part-time matriculated graduate/professional students (4 women). *Enrollment by degree level:* 62 master's. *Graduate faculty:* 11 full-time (2 women). *Tuition:* Full-time $26,400. *Graduate housing:* Room and/or apartments available on a first-come, first-served basis to single students; on-campus housing not available to married students. *Student services:* Campus employment opportunities, campus safety program, career counseling, disabled student services, international student services, low-cost health insurance. *Library facilities:* Library plus 1 other. *Collection:* 20,000 titles, 228 serial subscriptions.

Computer facilities: Computer purchase and lease plans are available. 40 computers available on campus for general student use. A campuswide network can be accessed from off campus. Internet access is available. *Web address:* http://www.aiuniv.edu/.

General Application Contact: Admissions Advisor, 888-594-9888, Fax: 310-302-2001.

GRADUATE UNITS

Program in Business Administration Students: 44 full-time (19 women), 4 part-time (3 women); includes 6 minority (3 African Americans, 1 Asian American or Pacific Islander, 2 Hispanic Americans), 10 international. Average age 34. *Faculty:* 5 full-time (0 women). Expenses: Contact institution. *Financial support:* Institutionally sponsored loans, scholarships/grants, and health care benefits available. Support available to part-time students. Financial award applicants required to submit FAFSA. In 2006, 32 degrees awarded. *Degree program information:* Part-time and evening/weekend programs available. Postbaccalaureate distance learning degree programs offered. Offers business administration (MBA); global technology management (MBA). *Application deadline:* Applications are processed on a rolling basis. *Application fee:* $50. Electronic applications accepted. *Application Contact:* Admissions Advisor, 310-302-2000, Fax: 310-302-2410. *Dean of School of Business*, Dr. James Carroll, 310-302-2639, E-mail: james.carroll@la.aiuniv.edu.

Program in Education Students: 4 full-time (3 women); includes 1 minority (African American) Average age 33. *Faculty:* 2 full-time (1 woman). Expenses: Contact institution. *Financial support:* Institutionally sponsored loans, scholarships/grants, and health care benefits available. Support available to part-time students. Financial award applicants required to submit FAFSA. In 2006, 4 degrees awarded. *Degree program information:* Part-time and evening/weekend programs available. Offers instructional technology (M Ed). *Application deadline:* Applications are processed on a rolling basis. *Application fee:* $50. Electronic applications accepted. *Application Contact:* Admissions Advisor, Fax: 310-302-2001. *Associate Dean of Education*, Dr. Eleanore Miller, 310-302-2634, E-mail: emiller@la.aiuniv.edu.

Program in Information Technology Students: 8 full-time (3 women), 2 part-time (1 woman); includes 2 minority (both African Americans), 1 international. Average age 38. *Faculty:* 4 full-time (1 woman). Expenses: Contact institution. *Financial support:* Institutionally sponsored loans, scholarships/grants, and health care benefits available. Support available to part-time students. Financial award applicants required to submit FAFSA. In 2006, 15 degrees awarded. *Degree program information:* Part-time programs available. Offers information technology (MIT). *Application deadline:* Applications are processed on a rolling basis. *Application fee:* $50. Electronic applications accepted. *Application Contact:* Admissions Advisor, Fax: 310-302-2001. *Dean of Information Technology*, Dr. Shantaram Vasikarla, 310-302-2646, E-mail: svasikarla@la.aiuniv.edu.

AMERICAN INTERCONTINENTAL UNIVERSITY, Weston, FL 33326

General Information Proprietary, coed, comprehensive institution. *Enrollment:* 1,844 graduate, professional, and undergraduate students; 99 full-time matriculated graduate/professional students (58 women), 8 part-time matriculated graduate/professional students (5 women). *Enrollment by degree level:* 107 master's. *Graduate faculty:* 8 full-time (1 woman), 4 part-time/adjunct (0 women). *Student services:* Campus employment opportunities, career counseling. *Library facilities:* AIU Fort Lauderdale Library. *Online resources:* library catalog, access to other libraries' catalogs. *Collection:* 3,256 titles, 100 serial subscriptions.

Computer facilities: Computer purchase and lease plans are available. 35 computers available on campus for general student use. A campuswide network can be accessed from off campus. Internet access is available. *Web address:* http://www.aiufl.edu/.

General Application Contact: Dr. Tom Takach, Vice President, Academic Affairs, 954-446-6119, Fax: 954-446-6303, E-mail: ttakach@aiufl.edu.

GRADUATE UNITS

Program in Information Technology Students: 2 full-time (0 women), 1 (woman) part-time; includes 2 minority (1 African American, 1 Hispanic American). Average age 37. *Faculty:* 2 full-time (0 women), 1 part-time/adjunct (0 women). Expenses: Contact institution. *Financial support:* Federal Work-Study and scholarships/grants available. Financial award application deadline: 1/15; financial award applicants required to submit FAFSA. In 2006, 3 degrees awarded. *Degree program information:* Part-time and evening/weekend programs available. Offers Internet security (MIT); wireless computer forensics (MIT). *Application deadline:* Applications are processed on a rolling basis. *Application fee:* $50. Electronic applications accepted. *Associate Dean*, Andy Blitz, 954-446-6100, Fax: 954-446-6393, E-mail: ablitz@aiufl.edu.

Program in Instructional Technology Students: 11 full-time; includes 7 minority (3 African Americans, 1 Asian American or Pacific Islander, 3 Hispanic Americans). *Faculty:* 3 full-time (1 woman), 1 part-time/adjunct (0 women). Expenses: Contact institution. *Financial support:* Federal Work-Study and scholarships/grants available. Financial award application deadline: 1/15; financial award applicants required to submit FAFSA. In 2006, 12 degrees awarded. *Degree program information:* Part-time and evening/weekend programs available. Offers instructional technology (M Ed). *Application deadline:* Applications are processed on a rolling basis. *Application fee:* $50. Electronic applications accepted. *Director of Institutional Effectiveness*, Dr. Fabian Cone, 954-446-6118, Fax: 954-446-6392, E-mail: fcone@aiufl.edu.

Program in International Business Students: 87 full-time (51 women), 7 part-time (4 women); includes 62 minority (42 African Americans, 1 American Indian/Alaska Native, 1 Asian American or Pacific Islander, 18 Hispanic Americans), 5 international. Average age 34. *Faculty:* 3 full-time (0 women), 2 part-time/adjunct (0 women). Expenses: Contact institution. *Financial support:* Federal Work-Study and scholarships/grants available. Financial award application deadline: 1/15; financial award applicants required to submit FAFSA. In 2006, 51 degrees awarded. *Degree program information:* Part-time and evening/weekend programs available. Postbaccalaureate distance learning degree programs offered. Offers accounting and finance (MBA); human resource management (MBA); management (MBA); marketing (MBA). *Application deadline:* Applications are processed on a rolling basis. *Application fee:* $50. Electronic applications accepted. *Acting Dean, School of Business*, Dr. David Kalichavan, 954-446-6100, Fax: 954-446-6393, E-mail: dkalichavan@aiufl.edu.

AMERICAN INTERCONTINENTAL UNIVERSITY BUCKHEAD CAMPUS, Atlanta, GA 30326-1016

General Information Proprietary, coed, comprehensive institution. *Enrollment:* 1,152 graduate, professional, and undergraduate students; 19 full-time matriculated graduate/professional students (16 women). *Enrollment by degree level:* 19 master's. *Graduate faculty:* 2 full-time (1 woman), 1 part-time/adjunct (0 women). *Graduate housing:* Room and/or apartments available on a first-come, first-served basis to single students; on-campus housing not available to married students. *Student services:* Campus employment opportunities, career counseling, free psychological counseling, international student services. *Library facilities:* American Intercontinental University Library-Buckhead Campus. *Online resources:* library catalog. *Collection:* 30,699 titles, 245 serial subscriptions, 2,716 audiovisual materials.

Computer facilities: 86 computers available on campus for general student use. A campuswide network can be accessed from off campus. Internet access is available. *Web address:* http://buckhead.aiuniv.edu/.

General Application Contact: Mike Betz, Vice President Admissions and Marketing, 404-965-5719, Fax: 404-965-5997, E-mail: mbetz@aiuniv.edu.

GRADUATE UNITS

Program in Business Administration Students: 19 full-time (16 women); includes 1 minority (African American) Average age 28. 10 applicants, 60% accepted, 5 enrolled. *Faculty:* 2 full-time (1 woman), 1 part-time/adjunct (0 women). Expenses: Contact institution. *Financial support:* In 2006–07, 14 students received support. Career-related internships or fieldwork, Federal Work-Study, institutionally sponsored loans, and scholarships/grants available. Financial award applicants required to submit FAFSA. In 2006, 25 degrees awarded. *Degree program information:* Evening/weekend programs available. Postbaccalaureate distance learning degree programs offered. Offers accounting and finance (MBA); management (MBA); marketing (MBA). *Application deadline:* Applications are processed on a rolling basis. *Application fee:* $50. Electronic applications accepted. *Application Contact:* Mike Betz, Vice President Admissions and Marketing, 404-965-5719, Fax: 404-965-5997, E-mail: mbetz@aiuniv.edu. *Dean of Business,* Dr. Sonia Heywood, 404-965-5764, Fax: 404-965-5957, E-mail: sonia.heywood@buckhead.aiuniv.edu.

AMERICAN INTERCONTINENTAL UNIVERSITY DUNWOODY CAMPUS, Atlanta, GA 30328

General Information Proprietary, coed, comprehensive institution. *Graduate housing:* On-campus housing not available.

GRADUATE UNITS

Program in Global Technology Management *Degree program information:* Part-time and evening/weekend programs available. Postbaccalaureate distance learning degree programs offered. Offers global technology management (MBA). Electronic applications accepted.

Program in Information Technology *Degree program information:* Part-time and evening/weekend programs available. Offers information technology (MIT). Electronic applications accepted.

AMERICAN INTERCONTINENTAL UNIVERSITY-LONDON, London W1U 4RY, United Kingdom

General Information Proprietary, coed, comprehensive institution. *Graduate housing:* Room and/or apartments available on a first-come, first-served basis to single students. Housing application deadline: 9/18.

GRADUATE UNITS

Program in Business Administration Offers international business (MBA). Electronic applications accepted.

Program in Information Technology Offers information technology (MIT). Electronic applications accepted.

AMERICAN INTERCONTINENTAL UNIVERSITY ONLINE, Hoffman Estates, IL 60192

General Information Proprietary, coed, comprehensive institution. *Student services:* Career counseling. *Web address:* http://www.aiuonline.edu/.

General Application Contact: Information Contact, 877-701-3800, E-mail: info@aiuonline.edu.

GRADUATE UNITS

Program in Business Administration Expenses: Contact institution. *Financial support:* Institutionally sponsored loans and scholarships/grants available. Financial award applicants required to submit FAFSA. *Degree program information:* Evening/weekend programs available. Postbaccalaureate distance learning degree programs offered (no on-campus study). Offers accounting and finance (MBA); healthcare management (MBA); human resource management (MBA); international business (MBA); management (MBA); marketing (MBA); operations management (MBA); organizational psychology and development (MBA); project management (MBA). *Application deadline:* Applications are processed on a rolling basis. *Application fee:* $50. Electronic applications accepted. *Application Contact:* 877-701-3800, E-mail: info@aiuonline.edu. *Vice President of Academic Affairs,* Kerri J Holloway, 847-851-5000 Ext. 15399, Fax: 847-586-6309, E-mail: kholloway@aivonline.edu.

Program in Education Expenses: Contact institution. *Financial support:* Institutionally sponsored loans and scholarships/grants available. Financial award applicants required to submit FAFSA. *Degree program information:* Evening/weekend programs available. Postbaccalaureate distance learning degree programs offered (no on-campus study). Offers curriculum and instruction (M Ed); educational assessment and evaluation (M Ed); instructional technology (M Ed); leadership of educational organizations (M Ed). *Application deadline:* Applications are processed on a rolling basis. *Application fee:* $50. Electronic applications accepted. *Application Contact:* 877-701-3800, E-mail: info@aiuonline.edu. *Vice President of Academic Affairs,* Kerri J Holloway, 847-851-5000 Ext. 15399, Fax: 847-586-6309, E-mail: kholloway@aivonline.edu.

Program in Information Technology Expenses: Contact institution. *Financial support:* Institutionally sponsored loans and scholarships/grants available. Financial award applicants required to submit FAFSA. *Degree program information:* Evening/weekend programs available. Postbaccalaureate distance learning degree programs offered (no on-campus study). Offers Internet security (MIT). *Application deadline:* Applications are processed on a rolling basis. *Application fee:* $50. Electronic applications accepted. *Application Contact:* 877-701-3800, E-mail: info@aiuonline.edu. *Vice President of Academic Affairs,* Kerri J Holloway, 847-851-5000 Ext. 15399, Fax: 847-586-6309, E-mail: kholloway@aivonline.edu.

AMERICAN INTERNATIONAL COLLEGE, Springfield, MA 01109-3189

General Information Independent, coed, comprehensive institution. *Enrollment:* 173 full-time matriculated graduate/professional students (116 women), 398 part-time matriculated graduate/professional students (310 women). *Enrollment by degree level:* 469 master's, 32 doctoral, 70 other advanced degrees. *Graduate faculty:* 55 full-time (28 women), 60 part-time/adjunct (27 women). *Tuition:* Part-time $585 per semester hour. *Required fees:* $100 per year. Full-time tuition and fees vary according to program. *Graduate housing:* Room and/or apartments available on a first-come, first-served basis to single students; on-campus housing not available to married students. Typical cost: $8,510 (including board). Room and board charges vary according to board plan. Housing application deadline: 6/1. *Student services:* Campus employment opportunities, campus safety program, career counseling, disabled student services, exercise/wellness program, free psychological counseling, grant writing training, international student services, low-cost health insurance, multicultural affairs office, writing training. *Library facilities:* James J. Shea Jr. Library. *Online resources:* library catalog, web page, access to other libraries' catalogs. *Collection:* 118,000 titles, 390 serial subscriptions.

Computer facilities: 125 computers available on campus for general student use. A campuswide network can be accessed. Internet access is available. *Web address:* http://www.aic.edu/.

General Application Contact: Keshawn Dodds, Associate Director of Graduate Admissions, 413-205-3549, Fax: 413-205-3911, E-mail: keshawn.dodds@aic.edu.

GRADUATE UNITS

School of Business Administration Students: 28 full-time (13 women), 55 part-time (34 women); includes 24 minority (14 African Americans, 6 Asian Americans or Pacific Islanders, 4 Hispanic Americans), 3 international. Average age 32. *Faculty:* 14 full-time (4 women), 10 part-time/adjunct (6 women). Expenses: Contact institution. *Financial support:* Career-related internships or fieldwork, Federal Work-Study, and unspecified assistantships available. Support available to part-time students. Financial award application deadline: 4/1; financial award applicants required to submit FAFSA. In 2006, 34 degrees awarded. *Degree program information:* Part-time and evening/weekend programs available. Offers business administration (MBA, MSAT). *Application deadline:* For fall admission, 7/1 priority date for domestic and international students; for spring admission, 12/1 priority date for domestic and international students. Applications are processed on a rolling basis. *Application fee:* $50. *Application Contact:* Keshawn Dodds, Associate Director of Graduate Admissions, 413-205-3549, Fax: 413-205-3911, E-mail: keshawn.dodds@aic.edu. *Dean,* Dr. John Rogers, 413-205-3230, E-mail: john.rogers@aic.edu.

School of Continuing Education and Graduate Studies Students: 11 full-time (3 women), 16 part-time (7 women); includes 5 minority (all African Americans), 1 international. Average age 36. *Faculty:* 8 full-time (5 women), 10 part-time/adjunct (5 women). Expenses: Contact institution. *Financial support:* Career-related internships or fieldwork available. Support available to part-time students. Financial award application deadline: 7/1; financial award applicants required to submit FAFSA. In 2006, 12 degrees awarded. *Degree program information:* Part-time and evening/weekend programs available. Offers organization development (MSOD); public administration (MPA). *Application deadline:* For fall admission, 7/1 priority date for domestic and international students; for spring admission, 12/1 priority date for domestic and international students. Applications are processed on a rolling basis. *Application fee:* $50. *Application Contact:* Keshawn Dodds, Associate Director of Graduate Admissions, 413-205-3549, Fax: 413-205-3911, E-mail: keshawn.dodds@aic.edu. *Dean,* Dr. Roland E. Holstead, 413-205-3440, Fax: 413-205-3911, E-mail: roland.holstead@aic.edu.

School of Health Sciences Students: 47 full-time (32 women), 12 part-time (all women); includes 7 minority (5 African Americans, 1 Asian American or Pacific Islander, 1 Hispanic American), 2 international. Average age 34. *Faculty:* 12 full-time (10 women). Expenses: Contact institution. In 2006, 13 degrees awarded. Offers health sciences (MPT, MSN, MSOT, DPT); nursing (MSN); occupational therapy (MSOT); physical therapy (MPT, DPT). *Application deadline:* For fall admission, 7/1 priority date for domestic and international students; for spring admission, 12/1 priority date for domestic and international students. Applications are processed on a rolling basis. *Application fee:* $50. *Application Contact:* Keshawn Dodds, Associate Director of Graduate Admissions, 413-205-3549, Fax: 413-205-3911, E-mail: keshawn.dodds@aic.edu. *Dean,* Dr. Carol Jobe, 413-205-3056, Fax: 413-205-3911, E-mail: carol.jobe@aic.edu.

School of Psychology and Education Students: 87 full-time (68 women), 315 part-time (258 women); includes 54 minority (29 African Americans, 1 American Indian/Alaska Native, 8 Asian Americans or Pacific Islanders, 16 Hispanic Americans), 3 international. Average age 37. *Faculty:* 19 full-time (9 women), 35 part-time/adjunct (16 women). Expenses: Contact institution. *Financial support:* In 2006–07, 6 fellowships were awarded; career-related internships or fieldwork and Federal Work-Study also available. Support available to part-time students. Financial award application deadline: 4/1; financial award applicants required to submit FAFSA. In 2006, 83 master's, 2 doctorates, 5 other advanced degrees awarded. *Degree program information:* Part-time and evening/weekend programs available. Offers administration (M Ed, CAGS); child development (MA, Ed D); clinical psychology (MA); criminal justice studies (MS); elementary education (M Ed, CAGS); forensic psychology (MS); psychology and education (M Ed, MA, MAT, MS, Ed D, CAGS); reading (M Ed, CAGS); secondary education (M Ed, CAGS); special education (M Ed, CAGS); teaching (MAT). *Application deadline:* For fall admission, 7/1 priority date for domestic and international students; for spring admission, 12/1 priority date for domestic and international students. Applications are processed on a rolling basis. *Application fee:* $50. *Application Contact:* Keshawn Dodds, Associate Director of Graduate Admissions, 413-205-3549, Fax: 413-205-3911, E-mail: keshawn.dodds@aic.edu. *Dean,* Dr. Gregory Schmutte, 413-205-3449, Fax: 413-205-3943, E-mail: gregory.schmutte@aic.edu.

Center for Human Resource Development Students: 6 full-time (4 women), 4 part-time (3 women); includes 4 minority (2 African Americans, 2 Hispanic Americans). Average age 36. *Faculty:* 2 full-time (both women), 2 part-time/adjunct (1 woman). Expenses: Contact institution. *Financial support:* Institutionally sponsored loans available. Financial award applicants required to submit FAFSA. In 2006, 9 degrees awarded. *Degree program information:* Evening/weekend programs available. Offers human resource development (MA). *Application deadline:* For fall admission, 7/1 priority date for domestic and international students; for spring admission, 12/1 priority date for domestic and international students. Applications are processed on a rolling basis. *Application fee:* $50. *Application Contact:* Keshawn Dodds, Associate Director of Graduate Admissions, 413-205-3549, Fax: 413-205-3911, E-mail: keshawn.dodds@aic.edu. *Director,* Dr. Debra D. Anderson, 413-205-3374, Fax: 413-205-3943, E-mail: debra.anderson@aic.edu.

AMERICAN JEWISH UNIVERSITY, Bel Air, CA 90077-1599

General Information Independent-religious, coed, comprehensive institution. *Graduate housing:* Rooms and/or apartments available on a first-come, first-served basis to single and married students. Housing application deadline: 6/1.

GRADUATE UNITS

Graduate School *Degree program information:* Part-time and evening/weekend programs available.

David Lieber School of Graduate Studies *Degree program information:* Part-time and evening/weekend programs available. Offers general nonprofit administration (MBA); Jewish communal studies (MAJCS); Jewish nonprofit administration (MBA).

Fingerhut School of Education Offers education (MA Ed); education for working professionals (MA Ed).

Ziegler School of Rabbinic Studies Offers rabbinic studies (MARS).

AMERICAN PUBLIC UNIVERSITY SYSTEM, Charles Town, WV 25414

General Information Proprietary, coed, comprehensive institution. *Enrollment:* 16,718 graduate, professional, and undergraduate students; 498 full-time matriculated graduate/professional students (104 women), 5,272 part-time matriculated graduate/professional students (1,209 women). *Enrollment by degree level:* 5,770 master's. *Graduate faculty:* 10 full-time (3 women), 188 part-time/adjunct (57 women). *Tuition:* Part-time $275 per credit. *Graduate housing:* On-campus housing not available. *Student services:* International student services. *Web address:* http://www.apus.edu/.

General Application Contact: Terry Grant, Director of Enrollment Management, 877-468-6268, Fax: 304-724-3780, E-mail: info@apus.edu.

GRADUATE UNITS

AMU/APU Graduate Programs Students: 498 full-time (104 women), 5,272 part-time (1,209 women). Average age 34. 6,574 applicants, 100% accepted, 3508 enrolled. *Faculty:* 10 full-time (3 women), 188 part-time/adjunct (57 women). Expenses: Contact institution. *Financial support:* Applicants required to submit FAFSA. In 2006, 358 degrees awarded. *Degree program information:* Part-time and evening/weekend programs available. Postbaccalaureate distance learning degree programs offered (no on-campus study). Offers business administration (MBA); criminal justice (MA); emergency and disaster management (MA); environmental policy and management (MS); history (MA); homeland security (MA); humanities (MA); intelligence (MA Strategic Intelligence); international relations and conflict resolution (MA); management (MA); military history (MA); national security studies (MA); political science (MA); public administration (MA); public health (MA); security management (MA); space studies (MS); sports management (MA); transportation and logistics management (MA). Programs offered via distance learning only. *Application deadline:* For fall admission, 9/1 priority date for domestic students; for winter admission, 1/1 priority date for domestic students; for spring admission, 5/1 priority date for domestic students. Applications are processed on a rolling basis. *Application fee:* $0. Electronic applications accepted. *Application Contact:* Terry Grant, Director of Enrollment Management, 877-468-6268, Fax: 304-724-3780, E-mail: info@apus.edu. *Provost,* Dr. Frank McCluskey, 877-468-6268, Fax: 304-724-3780.

AMERICAN SENTINEL UNIVERSITY, Englewood, CO 80112

General Information Private, coed, upper-level institution. *Graduate faculty:* 40. *Web address:* http://www.americansentinel.edu/.

General Application Contact: Janette D. Marshall, Registrar, 800-729-2427 Ext. 2211, Fax: 205-326-3822, E-mail: jan.marshall@americansentinel.edu.

GRADUATE UNITS

Graduate Programs Students: 400. Average age 36. *Faculty:* 40. Expenses: Contact institution. In 2006, 47 degrees awarded. *Degree program information:* Part-time and evening/weekend programs available. Postbaccalaureate distance learning degree programs offered (no on-campus study). *Application deadline:* Applications are processed on a rolling basis. *Applica-*

American Sentinel University (continued)

tion fee: $50. Electronic applications accepted. *Application Contact:* Natalie A. Nixon, Director of Admissions, 800-729-2427, Fax: 205-328-2229, E-mail: natalie.nixon@americansentinel.edu. *Registrar,* Janette D. Marshall, 800-729-2427 Ext. 2211, Fax: 205-326-3822, E-mail: jan.marshall@americansentinel.edu.

AMERICAN UNIVERSITY, Washington, DC 20016-8001

General Information Independent-religious, coed, university. CGS member. *Enrollment:* 11,279 graduate, professional, and undergraduate students; 2,732 full-time matriculated graduate/professional students (1,652 women), 2,468 part-time matriculated graduate/professional students (1,499 women). *Enrollment by degree level:* 1,483 first professional, 2,944 master's, 494 doctoral, 279 other advanced degrees. *Graduate faculty:* 554 full-time (250 women), 429 part-time/adjunct (190 women). *Tuition:* Full-time $18,864; part-time $1,048 per credit. *Required fees:* $380. Tuition and fees vary according to program. *Graduate housing:* Rooms and/or apartments available on a first-come, first-served basis to single and married students. Housing application deadline: 5/1. *Student services:* Campus employment opportunities, campus safety program, career counseling, child daycare facilities, disabled student services, free psychological counseling, international student services, low-cost health insurance, multicultural affairs office, teacher training. *Library facilities:* American University Bender Library plus 1 other. *Online resources:* library catalog, web page, access to other libraries' catalogs. *Collection:* 1 million titles, 23,955 serial subscriptions, 48,300 audiovisual materials.

Computer facilities: Computer purchase and lease plans are available. 760 computers available on campus for general student use. A campuswide network can be accessed from student residence rooms and from off campus. Internet access and online class registration, printers, scanners, online course support, wireless campus, USENET feed are available. *Web address:* http://www.american.edu/.

General Application Contact: Information Contact, 202-885-6000.

GRADUATE UNITS

College of Arts and Sciences Students: 461 full-time (330 women), 888 part-time (602 women); includes 255 minority (151 African Americans, 3 American Indian/Alaska Native, 43 Asian Americans or Pacific Islanders, 58 Hispanic Americans), 125 international. Average age 29. 1,652 applicants, 51% accepted, 391 enrolled. *Faculty:* 248 full-time (120 women), 159 part-time/adjunct (97 women). Expenses: Contact institution. *Financial support:* Fellowships, research assistantships, teaching assistantships, career-related internships or fieldwork, Federal Work-Study, institutionally sponsored loans, scholarships/grants, traineeships, tuition waivers (full and partial), and unspecified assistantships available. Support available to part-time students. Financial award applicants required to submit FAFSA. In 2006, 386 master's, 44 doctorates, 76 other advanced degrees awarded. *Degree program information:* Part-time and evening/weekend programs available. Offers anthropology (PhD); applied economics (Certificate); applied science (MS); applied statistics (Certificate); art history (MA); arts and sciences (MA, MAT, MFA, MS, PhD, Certificate); arts management (MA, Certificate); behavior, cognition, and neuroscience (PhD); biology (MA, MS); chemistry (MS); clinical psychology (PhD); computer science (MS, Certificate); creative writing (MFA); dance (MA, Certificate); economics (MA, PhD, Certificate); environmental science (MS); ethics, peace, and global affairs (MA); experimental/biological psychology (MA); French studies (Certificate); general psychology (MA); history (MA, PhD); interdisciplinary studies (MA); international economic relations (Certificate); literature (MA); marine science (MS); mathematics (MA); painting, sculpture and printmaking (MFA); personality/social psychology (MA); philosophy (MA); psychology (MA); public anthropology (MA, Certificate); Russian studies (Certificate); social research (Certificate); sociology (MA, Certificate); Spanish: Latin American studies (MA, Certificate); statistics (MS, Certificate); statistics for policy analysis (MS); teaching English to speakers of other languages (MA, Certificate); toxicology (Certificate); translation (Certificate). *Application deadline:* For fall admission, 2/1 for domestic students; for spring admission, 10/1 for domestic students. *Application fee:* $50. Electronic applications accepted. *Application Contact:* Kathleen Clowery, Director, Graduate Admissions, 202-885-3621, Fax: 202-885-1505. *Dean,* Dr. Kay Mussell, 202-885-2446, Fax: 202-885-2429.

School of Education, Teaching, and Health Students: 67 full-time (60 women), 402 part-time (295 women); includes 116 minority (81 African Americans, 13 Asian Americans or Pacific Islanders, 22 Hispanic Americans), 11 international. Average age 27. 265 applicants, 82% accepted, 149 enrolled. *Faculty:* 15 full-time (8 women), 41 part-time/adjunct (31 women). Expenses: Contact institution. *Financial support:* Fellowships with full tuition reimbursements, research assistantships with partial tuition reimbursements, teaching assistantships, career-related internships or fieldwork, Federal Work-Study, and institutionally sponsored loans available. Support available to part-time students. Financial award application deadline: 2/1; financial award applicants required to submit FAFSA. In 2006, 156 master's, 6 doctorates, 10 other advanced degrees awarded. *Degree program information:* Part-time and evening/weekend programs available. Offers education (PhD); educational leadership (MA); educational technology (MA); elementary education (MAT, Certificate); English for speakers of other languages (MAT, Certificate); health promotion management (MS); international education (MA); learning disabilities (MA); secondary teaching (MAT, Certificate). *Application deadline:* For fall admission, 2/1 priority date for domestic students; for spring admission, 10/1 priority date for domestic students. Applications are processed on a rolling basis. *Application fee:* $50. *Dean,* Dr. Sarah Irvine-Belson, 202-885-3714, Fax: 202-885-1187, E-mail: educate@american.edu.

Kogod School of Business Students: 152 full-time (67 women), 261 part-time (107 women); includes 90 minority (47 African Americans, 1 American Indian/Alaska Native, 27 Asian Americans or Pacific Islanders, 15 Hispanic Americans), 69 international. Average age 31. 518 applicants, 60% accepted, 125 enrolled. *Faculty:* 58 full-time (16 women), 21 part-time/adjunct (4 women). Expenses: Contact institution. *Financial support:* In 2006–07, 28 students received support; fellowships, research assistantships with partial tuition reimbursements available, career-related internships or fieldwork, Federal Work-Study, institutionally sponsored loans, and tuition waivers (partial) available. Support available to part-time students. Financial award application deadline: 2/1; financial award applicants required to submit FAFSA. In 2006, 187 degrees awarded. *Degree program information:* Part-time and evening/weekend programs available. Postbaccalaureate distance learning degree programs offered. Offers accounting (MBA); business (MBA, MS, Certificate); business administration (MBA); entrepreneurship and management (MBA); finance (MBA); information systems (MS, Certificate); interdisciplinary (MBA); international finance (MBA); international management (MBA); international marketing (MBA); law and business); management of global information technology (MBA); marketing (MBA); marketing information and technology (MBA); marketing management (MBA); real estate (MBA); taxation (MS). *Application deadline:* For fall admission, 2/1 priority date for domestic students. Applications are processed on a rolling basis. *Application fee:* $50. *Application Contact:* Sondra Smith, Acting Director of Graduate Programs, 202-885-1907, Fax: 202-885-1078, E-mail: sondra@american.edu. *Dean,* Dr. Richard Durand, 202-885-1900, Fax: 202-885-1955.

School of Communication Students: 123 full-time (84 women), 196 part-time (125 women); includes 84 minority (57 African Americans, 2 American Indian/Alaska Native, 13 Asian Americans or Pacific Islanders, 12 Hispanic Americans), 25 international. 601 applicants, 64% accepted, 179 enrolled. *Faculty:* 45 full-time (22 women), 50 part-time/adjunct. Expenses: Contact institution. *Financial support:* In 2006–07, 30 students received support, including 4 fellowships, 12 research assistantships with partial tuition reimbursements available, 12 teaching assistantships with partial tuition reimbursements available; career-related internships or fieldwork, Federal Work-Study, institutionally sponsored loans, scholarships/grants, tuition waivers (partial), and unspecified assistantships also available. Financial award application deadline: 2/1. In 2006, 159 degrees awarded. *Degree program information:* Part-time and evening/weekend programs available. Offers broadcast journalism (MA); communication (MA, MFA); film and electronic media (MFA); film and video (MA); interactive journalism (MA); news media studies (MA); print journalism (MA); producing film and video (MA); producing for film and video (MA); public communication (MA). *Application deadline:* For fall admission, 2/1 priority date for domestic and international students. Applications are processed on a rolling basis. *Application fee:* $50. Electronic applications accepted. *Application Contact:* Irene Moyer, Graduate Admissions Office, 202-885-6000, Fax: 202-885-2019, E-mail: imoyer@american.edu. *Dean,* Prof. Larry Kirkman, 202-885-2058, Fax: 202-885-2099, E-mail: larry@american.edu.

School of International Service Students: 506 full-time (326 women), 398 part-time (252 women); includes 123 minority (33 African Americans, 3 American Indian/Alaska Native, 44 Asian Americans or Pacific Islanders, 43 Hispanic Americans), 147 international. Average age 27. 1,806 applicants, 63% accepted, 307 enrolled. *Faculty:* 72 full-time (28 women), 34 part-time/adjunct (11 women). Expenses: Contact institution. *Financial support:* Career-related internships or fieldwork, Federal Work-Study, and institutionally sponsored loans available. Financial award application deadline: 1/15. In 2006, 400 master's, 8 doctorates, 4 other advanced degrees awarded. *Degree program information:* Part-time and evening/weekend programs available. Offers comparative and regional studies (MA); cross-cultural communication (Certificate); development management (MS); environmental policy (MA); ethics, peace, and global affairs (MA); global environmental policy (MA); international communication (MA); international development (MA); international development management (Certificate); international economic policy (MA); international economic relations (Certificate); international peace and conflict resolution (MA); international politics (MA); international relations (PhD); international service (MIS); the Americas (Certificate); U.S. foreign policy (MA). *Application deadline:* For fall admission, 1/15 priority date for domestic students; for spring admission, 10/1 priority date for domestic students. Applications are processed on a rolling basis. *Application fee:* $50. *Application Contact:* Amanda Taylor, Director of Graduate Admissions and Financial Aid, 202-885-1599, Fax: 202-885-2494. *Dean,* Dr. Louis W. Goodman, 202-885-1600, Fax: 202-885-2494.

School of Public Affairs Students: 226 full-time (145 women), 295 part-time (183 women); includes 96 minority (57 African Americans, 2 American Indian/Alaska Native, 19 Asian Americans or Pacific Islanders, 18 Hispanic Americans), 43 international. Average age 30. 916 applicants, 94% accepted, 178 enrolled. *Faculty:* 65 full-time (31 women), 45 part-time/adjunct (13 women). Expenses: Contact institution. *Financial support:* Fellowships, research assistantships, teaching assistantships, career-related internships or fieldwork, Federal Work-Study, institutionally sponsored loans, and tuition waivers (full and partial) available. Financial award application deadline: 2/1. In 2006, 238 master's, 9 doctorates, 12 other advanced degrees awarded. *Degree program information:* Part-time and evening/weekend programs available. Offers advanced leadership studies (Certificate); justice, law and society (MS, PhD); organization development (MSOD); organizational change (Certificate); political science (MA, PhD); public administration (MPA, PhD); public affairs (MA, MPA, MPP, MS, MSOD, PhD, Certificate); public financial management (Certificate); public management (Certificate); public policy (MPP). *Application deadline:* For fall admission, 2/1 for domestic students; for spring admission, 10/1 for domestic students. *Application fee:* $50. *Application Contact:* Brenda Manley, Admissions and Financial Aid Manager, 202-885-6202, Fax: 202-885-2355, E-mail: bmanley@american.edu. *Dean,* Dr. William Leo Grande, 202-885-6234.

Washington College of Law Students: 1,257 full-time (699 women), 419 part-time (218 women); includes 458 minority (118 African Americans, 15 American Indian/Alaska Native, 145 Asian Americans or Pacific Islanders, 180 Hispanic Americans), 155 international. Average age 26. 9,012 applicants, 26% accepted, 562 enrolled. *Faculty:* 72 full-time (36 women), 126 part-time/adjunct (47 women). Expenses: Contact institution. *Financial support:* In 2006–07, 379 students received support; fellowships with full tuition reimbursements available, career-related internships or fieldwork, Federal Work-Study, institutionally sponsored loans, and tuition waivers (full and partial) available. Support available to part-time students. Financial award application deadline: 2/15; financial award applicants required to submit FAFSA. In 2006, 407 first professional degrees, 143 master's, 2 doctorates awarded. *Degree program information:* Part-time and evening/weekend programs available. Offers human rights and the law (Certificate); international legal studies (LL M, Certificate); judicial sciences (SJD); law (JD); law and government (LL M). *Application deadline:* Applications are processed on a rolling basis. *Application fee:* $55. *Application Contact:* Brooke Sandoval, Associate Director, Graduate Admissions (WCL), 202-274-4103, Fax: 202-274-4107, E-mail: wcladmit@american.edu. *Dean,* Dr. Claudio Grossman, 202-274-4000, Fax: 202-274-4107, E-mail: wcladmit@american.edu.

AMERICAN UNIVERSITY IN BULGARIA, Blagoevgrad 2700, Bulgaria

General Information Independent, coed, comprehensive institution.

GRADUATE UNITS

Executive MBA Program

THE AMERICAN UNIVERSITY IN CAIRO, 11511 Cairo, Egypt

General Information Independent, coed, comprehensive institution. CGS member. *Graduate housing:* Room and/or apartments available to single students; on-campus housing not available to married students.

GRADUATE UNITS

Graduate Studies and Research *Degree program information:* Part-time programs available. Electronic applications accepted.

School of Business, Economics and Communication *Degree program information:* Part-time programs available. Offers business, economics and communication (MA, MBA, MPA, Diploma); economics (MA); journalism/mass communication (MA); management (MBA, MPA, Diploma); television journalism (MA, Diploma). Electronic applications accepted.

School of Humanities and Social Sciences *Degree program information:* Part-time programs available. Offers Arab language and literature (MA); English and comparative literature (MA); humanities and social sciences (MA, Diploma); Islamic art and architecture (MA); Islamic studies (Diploma); Middle East studies (MA, Diploma); Middle Eastern history (MA); political science (MA); sociology and anthropology (MA); teaching Arabic as a foreign language (MA); teaching English as a foreign language (MA, Diploma). Electronic applications accepted.

School of Sciences and Engineering Offers computer science (MS); engineering (MS, Diploma); sciences and engineering (MS, Diploma). Electronic applications accepted.

THE AMERICAN UNIVERSITY IN DUBAI, Dubai, United Arab Emirates

General Information Proprietary, coed, comprehensive institution. *Graduate housing:* Room and/or apartments available on a first-come, first-served basis to single students. Housing application deadline: 7/31.

GRADUATE UNITS

Program in International Business *Degree program information:* Part-time programs available. Offers international business (MBA). Electronic applications accepted.

AMERICAN UNIVERSITY OF ARMENIA, Yerevan 3750198, Armenia

General Information Independent, coed, graduate-only institution.

GRADUATE UNITS

Graduate Programs

THE AMERICAN UNIVERSITY OF ATHENS, GR-115 25 Athens, Greece

General Information Independent, coed, comprehensive institution. *Graduate housing:* Room and/or apartments guaranteed to single students; on-campus housing not available to married students. *Research affiliation:* Dimokritos (engineering and physics), Pasteur Institute (biomedical sciences).

GRADUATE UNITS

The School of Graduate Studies Offers biomedical sciences (MS); business (MBA); business communication (MA); computer sciences (MS); engineering and applied sciences (MS); politics and policy making (MA); systems engineering (MS); telecommunications (MS).

See Close-Up on page 797.

AMERICAN UNIVERSITY OF BEIRUT, Beirut 1107 2020, Lebanon

General Information Independent, coed, university. *Enrollment:* 7,048 graduate, professional, and undergraduate students; 488 full-time matriculated graduate/professional students (218 women), 816 part-time matriculated graduate/professional students (528 women). *Enrollment by degree level:* 313 first professional, 991 master's. *Graduate faculty:* 374 full-time (91 women), 83 part-time/adjunct (13 women). *Graduate housing:* Room and/or apartments available on a first-come, first-served basis to single students; on-campus housing not available to married students. Typical cost: $3,540 per year. Room charges vary according to housing facility selected. Housing application deadline: 8/7. *Student services:* Campus employment opportunities, campus safety program, career counseling, disabled student services, exercise/wellness program, free psychological counseling, grant writing training, international student services, low-cost health insurance, teacher training, writing training. *Library facilities:* Jafet Memorial Library plus 2 others. *Online resources:* library catalog, web page. *Collection:* 628,636 titles, 23,792 serial subscriptions, 2,456 audiovisual materials. *Research affiliation:* University of Paris—7 Denis Diderot (medicine), University of Poitiers (medicine), University of Cornell (agriculture), K.L.K. SARL (IBSAR), University of California Davis (UC DAVIS) (engineering), Lebanese American University (LAU) (student exchange).

Computer facilities: Computer purchase and lease plans are available. 739 computers available on campus for general student use. A campuswide network can be accessed from student residence rooms and from off campus. Internet access and online class registration, e-Learning (WEB CT) are available. *Web address:* http://www.aub.edu.lb/.

General Application Contact: Dr. Salim Kanaan, Director of Admissions Office, 961-1-374374 Ext. 2592, Fax: 961-1-750775, E-mail: admissions@aub.edu.lb.

GRADUATE UNITS

Graduate Programs Average age 25. 1,181 applicants, 70% accepted, 328 enrolled. *Faculty:* 374 full-time (91 women), 83 part-time/adjunct (13 women). Expenses: Contact institution. *Financial support:* In 2006–07, 52 students received support. Career-related internships or fieldwork, institutionally sponsored loans, scholarships/grants, health care benefits, and unspecified assistantships available. Financial award application deadline: 2/2; financial award applicants required to submit FAFSA. In 2006, 76 first professional degrees, 350 master's awarded. *Degree program information:* Part-time and evening/weekend programs available. Offers business administration (MBA); executive business administration (EMBA). *Application deadline:* For fall admission, 4/30 for domestic and international students; for spring admission, 11/1 for domestic and international students. *Application fee:* $50. *Application Contact:* Dr. Salim Kanaan, Director of Admissions Office, 961-1-374374 Ext. 2592, Fax: 961-1-750775, E-mail: admissions@aub.edu.lb.

Faculty of Agricultural and Food Sciences Students: 13 full-time (8 women), 76 part-time (61 women). Average age 24. 85 applicants, 78% accepted, 22 enrolled. *Faculty:* 22 full-time (6 women), 3 part-time/adjunct (0 women). Expenses: Contact institution. *Financial support:* In 2006–07, 3 students received support. Career-related internships or fieldwork, institutionally sponsored loans, scholarships/grants, health care benefits, and unspecified assistantships available. Financial award application deadline: 2/2. In 2006, 29 degrees awarded. *Degree program information:* Part-time programs available. Offers agricultural economics (MS); animal sciences (MS); ecosystem management (MSES); food technology (MS); irrigation (MS); mechanization (MS); nutrition (MS); plant protection (MS); plant science (MS); poultry science (MS); soils (MS). *Application deadline:* For fall admission, 4/30 for domestic and international students; for spring admission, 11/1 for domestic and international students. *Application fee:* $50. *Application Contact:* Dr. Salim Kanaan, Director of Admissions Office, 961-1-374374 Ext. 2592, Fax: 961-1-750775, E-mail: admissions@aub.edu.lb. *Dean,* Nahla Houalla, 961-1374444 Ext. 4400, Fax: 961-1744460, E-mail: nahla@aub.edu.lb.

Faculty of Arts and Sciences Students: 46 full-time (24 women), 368 part-time (269 women). Average age 25. 389 applicants, 71% accepted, 102 enrolled. *Faculty:* 101 full-time (28 women), 4 part-time/adjunct (1 woman). Expenses: Contact institution. *Financial support:* In 2006–07, 23 students received support. Career-related internships or fieldwork, institutionally sponsored loans, scholarships/grants, health care benefits, and unspecified assistantships available. Financial award application deadline: 2/2; financial award applicants required to submit FAFSA. In 2006, 131 degrees awarded. *Degree program information:* Part-time programs available. Offers anthropology (MA); Arabic language and literature (MA); archaeology (MA); biology (MS); chemistry (MS); computer science (MS); economics (MA); education (MA); English language (MA); English literature (MA); environmental policy planning (MSES); financial economics (MAFE); geology (MS); history (MA); mathematics (MA, MS); Middle Eastern studies (MA); philosophy (MA); physics (MS); political studies (MA); psychology (MA); public administration (MA); sociology (MA); statistics (MA, MS). *Application deadline:* For fall admission, 4/30 for domestic and international students; for spring admission, 11/1 for domestic and international students. *Application fee:* $50. *Application Contact:* Dr. Salim Kanaan, Director of Admissions Office, 961-1-374374 Ext. 2592, Fax: 961-1-750775, E-mail: admissions@aub.edu.lb. *Dean,* Khalil Bitar, 961-1374374 Ext. 3800, Fax: 961-1744461, E-mail: kmb@aub.edu.lb.

Faculty of Engineering and Architecture Students: 39 full-time (17 women), 159 part-time (51 women). Average age 25. 192 applicants, 84% accepted, 28 enrolled. *Faculty:* 40 full-time (4 women), 6 part-time/adjunct (0 women). Expenses: Contact institution. *Financial support:* In 2006–07, 6 students received support. Career-related internships or fieldwork, institutionally sponsored loans, scholarships/grants, health care benefits, and unspecified assistantships available. Financial award application deadline: 2/2. In 2006, 76 degrees awarded. *Degree program information:* Part-time and evening/weekend programs available. Offers civil engineering (ME); computer and communications engineering (ME); electrical engineering (ME); engineering management (MEM); environmental and water resources (ME); environmental technology (MSES); mechanical engineering (ME); urban design (MUD); urban planning (MUP). *Application deadline:* For fall admission, 4/30 for domestic and international students; for spring admission, 11/1 for domestic and international students. *Application fee:* $50. *Application Contact:* Dr. Salim Kanaan, Director of Admissions Office, 961-1-374374 Ext. 2592, Fax: 961-1-750775, E-mail: admissions@aub.edu.lb. *Dean,* Ibrahim Hajj, 961-1350000 Ext. 3400, Fax: 961-1744462, E-mail: ibajj@aub.edu.lb.

Faculty of Health Sciences Students: 42 full-time (34 women), 63 part-time (54 women). Average age 27. 158 applicants, 74% accepted, 47 enrolled. *Faculty:* 21 full-time (16 women), 4 part-time/adjunct (0 women). Expenses: Contact institution. *Financial support:* In 2006–07, 6 students received support. Career-related internships or fieldwork, institutionally sponsored loans, scholarships/grants, health care benefits, and unspecified assistantships available. Financial award application deadline: 2/2. In 2006, 47 degrees awarded. *Degree program information:* Part-time programs available. Offers environmental health (MSES); epidemiology (MS); population health (MS); population science (MS); public health (MPH). *Application deadline:* For fall admission, 4/30 for domestic and international students; for spring admission, 11/1 for domestic and international students. *Application fee:* $50. *Application Contact:* Dr. Salim Kanaan, Director of Admissions Office, 961-1-374374 Ext. 2592, Fax: 961-1-750775, E-mail: admissions@aub.edu.lb. *Dean,* Huda Zurayls, 961-1340119 Ext. 4600, Fax: 961-1744470, E-mail: hzurayk@aub.edu.lb.

Faculty of Medicine Students: 322 full-time (123 women), 34 part-time (22 women). Average age 23. *Faculty:* 166 full-time (30 women), 64 part-time/adjunct (12 women). Expenses: Contact institution. *Financial support:* In 2006–07, 4 students received support. Career-related internships or fieldwork, institutionally sponsored loans, scholarships/grants, health care benefits, and unspecified assistantships available. Financial award application deadline: 2/2. In 2006, 76 first professional degrees, 25 master's awarded. *Degree program information:* Part-time programs available. Offers biochemistry (MS); human morphology (MS); medicine (MD); microbiology and immunology (MS); neuroscience (MS); pharmacology and therapeutics (MS); physiology (MS). *Application deadline:* For fall admission, 4/30 for domestic and international students; for spring admission, 11/1 for domestic and international students. *Application fee:* $50. *Application Contact:* Dr. Salim Kanaan, Director of Admissions Office, 961-1-374374 Ext. 2592, Fax: 961-1-750775, E-mail: admissions@aub.edu.lb. *Dean,* Nadim Cortas, 961-1350000 Ext. 4700, Fax: 961-1744464, E-mail: cortasn@aub.edu.lb.

School of Nursing Students: 4 full-time (3 women), 32 part-time (28 women). Average age 27. 20 applicants, 65% accepted, 9 enrolled. *Faculty:* 5 full-time (4 women). Expenses: Contact institution. *Financial support:* In 2006–07, 1 student received support. Career-related internships or fieldwork, institutionally sponsored loans, scholarships/grants, health care benefits, and unspecified assistantships available. Financial award application deadline: 2/2. In 2006, 3 degrees awarded. *Degree program information:* Part-time programs available. Offers nursing (MSN). *Application deadline:* For fall admission, 4/30 for domestic and international students; for spring admission, 11/1 for domestic and international students. *Application fee:* $50. *Application Contact:* Dr. Salim Kanaan, Director of Admissions Office, 961-1-374374 Ext. 2592, Fax: 961-1-750775, E-mail: admissions@aub.edu.lb. *Director of School of Nursing,* Dr. Huda Huijer Abu-Saad, 961-1374374 Ext. 5952, Fax: 961-1744476, E-mail: hh35@aub.edu.lb.

THE AMERICAN UNIVERSITY OF PARIS, F-75007 Paris, France

General Information Independent, coed, comprehensive institution. *Enrollment:* 1,062 graduate, professional, and undergraduate students; 72 full-time matriculated graduate/professional students (47 women). *Enrollment by degree level:* 72 master's. *Graduate faculty:* 14 full-time (5 women). *Graduate tuition:* Tuition charges are reported in euros. *Tuition:* Full-time 22,200 euros. *Student services:* Campus employment opportunities, career counseling, writing training. *Library facilities:* The American University of Paris Library. *Online resources:* library catalog, web page. *Collection:* 70,000 titles, 2,000 serial subscriptions.

Computer facilities: 98 computers available on campus for general student use. A campuswide network can be accessed from off campus. Internet access is available. *Web address:* http://www.aup.edu/.

General Application Contact: Lynn Richardson, International Admissions Counselor, 33-140620720, Fax: 33-147053432, E-mail: lynn.richardson@aup.edu.

GRADUATE UNITS

Graduate Programs Students: 72 full-time (47 women). 71 applicants, 92% accepted, 34 enrolled. *Faculty:* 2 full-time (1 woman), 8 part-time/adjunct (2 women). Expenses: Contact institution. *Financial support:* In 2006–07, 25 students received support. Scholarships/grants available. Financial award applicants required to submit FAFSA. *Application deadline:* For fall admission, 4/15 priority date for international students; for spring admission, 11/15 priority date for international students. Applications are processed on a rolling basis. *Application fee:* $75. *Application Contact:* Lynn Richardson, International Admissions Counselor, 33-140620720, Fax: 33-147053432, E-mail: lynn.richardson@aup.edu. *President,* Gerardo Della Paolera, 331-40620739, E-mail: gerry@aup.edu.

AMERICAN UNIVERSITY OF PUERTO RICO, Bayamón, PR 00960-2037

General Information Independent, coed, comprehensive institution.

GRADUATE UNITS

Program in Criminal Justice Offers criminal justice (MA).

Program in Education Offers art history (M Ed); elementary education (4-6) (M Ed); elementary education (k-3) (M Ed); general science education (M Ed); physical education (k-12) (M Ed); special education at secondary level (transition) (M Ed).

AMERICAN UNIVERSITY OF SHARJAH, Sharjah, United Arab Emirates

General Information Independent, coed, comprehensive institution.

GRADUATE UNITS

Graduate Programs

ANDERSON UNIVERSITY, Anderson, IN 46012-3495

General Information Independent-religious, coed, comprehensive institution. *Graduate housing:* Room and/or apartments available to single students; on-campus housing not available to married students. Housing application deadline: 6/1.

GRADUATE UNITS

Falls School of Business Offers accountancy (MA); business administration (MBA, DBA).

School of Education Offers education (M Ed).

School of Theology *Degree program information:* Part-time programs available. Offers missions (MA); theology (M Div, MTS, D Min).

ANDOVER NEWTON THEOLOGICAL SCHOOL, Newton Centre, MA 02459-2243

General Information Independent-religious, coed, graduate-only institution. *Graduate housing:* Rooms and/or apartments available on a first-come, first-served basis to single and married students. Housing application deadline: 7/1.

GRADUATE UNITS

Graduate and Professional Programs *Degree program information:* Part-time programs available. Offers divinity (M Div); general (MA); psychology and religion (MA); religious education (MA); research (MA); sacred theology (STM); theology (D Min); theology and the arts (MA). Electronic applications accepted.

ANDREW JACKSON UNIVERSITY, Birmingham, AL 35244

General Information Private, coed, comprehensive institution. *Enrollment:* 425 graduate, professional, and undergraduate students; 250 part-time matriculated graduate/professional students (75 women). *Enrollment by degree level:* 250 master's. *Graduate faculty:* 48 part-time/adjunct (17 women). *Tuition:* Part-time $705 per course. *Graduate housing:* On-campus housing not available.

Computer facilities: A campuswide network can be accessed. *Web address:* http://www.aju.edu/.

General Application Contact: Betty Howell, Director of Student Affairs, 205-871-9288 Ext. 108, Fax: 205-871-9294, E-mail: bhowell@aju.edu.

GRADUATE UNITS

Brian Tracy College of Business and Entrepreneurship Average age 40. *Faculty:* 13 part-time/adjunct (1 woman). Expenses: Contact institution. In 2006, 6 degrees awarded. *Degree program information:* Part-time and evening/weekend programs available. Postbaccalaureate distance learning degree programs offered (no on-campus study). Offers entrepreneurship (MBA); finance (MBA); health services management (MBA); hospitality and tourism management (MBA); human resource management (MBA); international business (MBA); management (MBA); marketing (MBA). *Application deadline:* Applications are processed on a rolling basis. *Application fee:* $75. *Application Contact:* Betty Howell, Director of Student Affairs, 205-871-9288 Ext. 108, Fax: 205-871-9294, E-mail: bhowell@aju.edu.

Jeffrey D. Rubenstein College of Criminal Justice Average age 40. *Faculty:* 10 part-time/adjunct (0 women). Expenses: Contact institution. In 2006, 5 degrees awarded. *Degree program information:* Part-time and evening/weekend programs available. Postbaccalaureate distance learning degree programs offered (no on-campus study). Offers criminal justice (MPA, MS); public administration (MPA). *Application deadline:* Applications are processed on a rolling basis. *Application fee:* $75. Electronic applications accepted. *Application Contact:* Betty Howell, Director of Student Affairs, 205-871-9288 Ext. 108, Fax: 205-871-9294, E-mail: bhowell@aju.edu.

ANDREWS UNIVERSITY, Berrien Springs, MI 49104

General Information Independent-religious, coed, university. CGS member. *Graduate housing:* Rooms and/or apartments available to single and married students. *Research affiliation:* Deutches Electronen Synchroton (physics), Argonne National Laboratory (physics), RAND Corporation (drug abuse).

GRADUATE UNITS

School of Graduate Studies *Degree program information:* Part-time and evening/weekend programs available.

College of Arts and Sciences *Degree program information:* Part-time and evening/weekend programs available. Offers allied health (MSMT); arts and sciences (M Mus, MA, MAT, MS, MSA, MSMT, MSW, Dr Sc PT, TDPT); biology (MAT, MS); communication (MA); community services management (MSA); English (MA, MAT); history (MA, MAT); international development (MSA); international language studies (MAT); mathematics and physical science (MS); music (M Mus, MA); nursing (MS); nutrition (MS); physical therapy (DPT, Dr Sc PT, TDPT); social work (MSW).

College of Technology Offers software engineering (MS); technology (MS).

Division of Architecture Offers architecture (M Arch).

School of Business *Degree program information:* Part-time programs available. Offers accounting, economics and finance (MBA, MSA); business (MBA, MSA); management and marketing (MBA, MSA).

School of Education *Degree program information:* Part-time programs available. Offers community counseling (MA); counseling psychology (PhD); curriculum and instruction (MA, Ed D, PhD, Ed S); education (MA, MAT, MS, Ed D, PhD, Ed S); educational administration and leadership (MA, Ed D, PhD, Ed S); educational and developmental psychology (MA, Ed D, PhD); educational psychology (Ed D, PhD); elementary education (MAT); leadership (MA, Ed D, PhD); reading (MA); school counseling (MA); school psychology (Ed S); secondary education (MAT); special education (MS); special education/learning disabilities (MS); teacher education (MAT).

Seventh-day Adventist Theological Seminary Offers ministry (M Div, D Min); pastoral ministry (MA); religious education (MA, Ed D, PhD, Ed S); theology (M Th, Th D).

ANGELO STATE UNIVERSITY, San Angelo, TX 76909

General Information State-supported, coed, comprehensive institution. CGS member. *Enrollment:* 6,265 graduate, professional, and undergraduate students; 179 full-time matriculated graduate/professional students (114 women), 275 part-time matriculated graduate/professional students (168 women). *Enrollment by degree level:* 454 master's. *Graduate faculty:* 124 full-time (51 women). Tuition, state resident: full-time $2,340; part-time $130 per hour. Tuition, nonresident: full-time $7,290; part-time $405 per hour. *Required fees:* $906; $56 per hour. *Graduate housing:* Room and/or apartments available on a first-come, first-served basis to single students; on-campus housing not available to married students. Typical cost: $3,556 per year ($5,364 including board). Housing application deadline: 7/15. *Student services:* Campus employment opportunities, campus safety program, career counseling, free psychological counseling, international student services, low-cost health insurance, multicultural affairs office. *Library facilities:* Porter Henderson Library plus 1 other. *Online resources:* library catalog, web page, access to other libraries' catalogs. *Collection:* 50,963 titles, 22,004 serial subscriptions, 27,149 audiovisual materials.

Computer facilities: 600 computers available on campus for general student use. A campuswide network can be accessed from student residence rooms and from off campus. Internet access and online class registration are available. *Web address:* http://www.angelo.edu/.

General Application Contact: Brenda Stewart, Assistant to the Dean, College of Graduate Studies, 325-942-2169, Fax: 325-942-2194, E-mail: brenda.stewart@angelo.edu.

GRADUATE UNITS

College of Graduate Studies Students: 179 full-time (114 women), 275 part-time (168 women); includes 81 minority (14 African Americans, 2 American Indian/Alaska Native, 6 Asian Americans or Pacific Islanders, 59 Hispanic Americans), 7 international. Average age 33. 211 applicants, 78% accepted, 128 enrolled. *Faculty:* 124 full-time (51 women). Expenses: Contact institution. *Financial support:* In 2006–07, 274 students received support, including 9 research assistantships (averaging $9,887 per year), 16 teaching assistantships (averaging $10,251 per year); career-related internships or fieldwork, Federal Work-Study, scholarships/grants, and unspecified assistantships also available. Support available to part-time students. Financial award application deadline: 3/1. In 2006, 162 degrees awarded. *Degree program information:* Part-time and evening/weekend programs available. Postbaccalaureate distance learning degree programs offered (minimal on-campus study). Offers interdisciplinary studies (MA, MS). *Application deadline:* For fall admission, 7/15 priority date for domestic students, 6/15 for international students; for spring admission, 12/1 priority date for domestic students, 11/1 for international students. Applications are processed on a rolling basis. *Application fee:* $40 ($50 for international students). Electronic applications accepted. *Application Contact:* Brenda Stewart, Assistant to the Dean, College of Graduate Studies, 325-942-2169, Fax: 325-942-2194, E-mail: brenda.stewart@angelo.edu. *Dean of the College of Graduate Studies,* Dr. Carol B. Diminnie, 325-942-2169, Fax: 325-942-2194, E-mail: carol.diminnie@angelo.edu.

College of Business and Professional Studies Students: 21 full-time (12 women), 38 part-time (20 women); includes 9 minority (1 African American, 1 Asian American or Pacific Islander, 7 Hispanic Americans), 3 international. Average age 29. 24 applicants, 88% accepted, 16 enrolled. *Faculty:* 18 full-time (3 women). Expenses: Contact institution. *Financial support:* In 2006–07, 36 students received support. Career-related internships or fieldwork, Federal Work-Study, and scholarships/grants available. Support available to part-time students. Financial award application deadline: 3/1; financial award applicants required to submit FAFSA. In 2006, 16 degrees awarded. *Degree program information:* Part-time and evening/weekend programs available. Offers accounting (MBA); business (MBA, MPAC); business administration (MBA); professional accountancy (MPAC). *Application deadline:* For fall admission, 7/15 priority date for domestic students, 6/15 for international students; for spring admission, 12/8 for domestic students, 11/1 for international students. Applications are processed on a rolling basis. *Application fee:* $40 ($50 for international students). Electronic applications accepted. *Application Contact:* Brenda Stewart, Assistant to the Dean, College of Graduate Studies, 325-942-2169, Fax: 325-942-2194, E-mail: brenda.stewart@angelo.edu. *Dean,* Dr. Corbett Gaulden, 325-942-2337, E-mail: corbett.gaulden@angelo.edu.

College of Education Students: 26 full-time (15 women), 139 part-time (90 women); includes 26 minority (3 African Americans, 1 American Indian/Alaska Native, 1 Asian American or Pacific Islander, 21 Hispanic Americans). Average age 37. 65 applicants, 88% accepted, 47 enrolled. *Faculty:* 23 full-time (15 women). Expenses: Contact institution. *Financial support:* In 2006–07, 73 students received support. Career-related internships or fieldwork, Federal Work-Study, scholarships/grants, and unspecified assistantships available. Support available to part-time students. Financial award application deadline: 3/1; financial award applicants required to submit FAFSA. In 2006, 57 degrees awarded. *Degree program information:* Part-time and evening/weekend programs available. Offers curriculum and instruction (M Ed, MA); education (M Ed, MA, MS); educational diagnostics (M Ed); guidance and counseling (M Ed); kinesiology (MS); reading specialist (M Ed); school administration (M Ed); student development and leadership in higher education (M Ed); teacher education (M Ed, MA). *Application deadline:* For fall admission, 7/15 priority date for domestic students, 6/15 for international students; for spring admission, 12/8 for domestic students, 11/1 for international students. Applications are processed on a rolling basis. *Application fee:* $40 ($50 for international students). Electronic applications accepted. *Application Contact:* Brenda Stewart, Assistant to the Dean, College of Graduate Studies, 325-942-2169, Fax: 325-942-2194, E-mail: brenda.stewart@angelo.edu. *Dean of the College of Education,* Dr. John J. Miazga, 325-942-2212, E-mail: john.miazga@angelo.edu.

College of Liberal and Fine Arts Students: 55 full-time (38 women), 41 part-time (18 women); includes 19 minority (7 African Americans, 1 Asian American or Pacific Islander, 11 Hispanic Americans), 3 international. Average age 31. 58 applicants, 69% accepted, 30 enrolled. *Faculty:* 37 full-time (12 women). Expenses: Contact institution. *Financial support:* In 2006–07, 68 students received support, including 10 teaching assistantships (averaging $10,251 per year); career-related internships or fieldwork, Federal Work-Study, scholarships/grants, and unspecified assistantships also available. Support available to part-time students. Financial award application deadline: 3/1; financial award applicants required to submit FAFSA. In 2006, 49 degrees awarded. *Degree program information:* Part-time and evening/weekend programs available. Offers communication systems management (MA); English (MA); history (MA); liberal and fine arts (MA, MPA, MS); psychology (MS); public administration (MPA). *Application deadline:* For fall admission, 7/15 priority date for domestic students, 6/10 for international students; for spring admission, 12/8 for domestic students, 11/1 for international students. Applications are processed on a rolling basis. *Application fee:* $40 ($50 for international students). Electronic applications accepted. *Application Contact:* Brenda Stewart, Assistant to the Dean, College of Graduate Studies, 325-942-2169, Fax: 325-942-2194, E-mail: brenda.stewart@angelo.edu. *Dean,* Dr. Kevin Lambert, 325-942-2115, E-mail: kevin.lambert@angelo.edu.

College of Sciences Students: 76 full-time (49 women), 56 part-time (39 women); includes 27 minority (3 African Americans, 1 American Indian/Alaska Native, 3 Asian Americans or Pacific Islanders, 20 Hispanic Americans), 1 international. Average age 30. 91 applicants, 62% accepted, 47 enrolled. *Faculty:* 35 full-time (17 women). Expenses: Contact institution. *Financial support:* In 2006–07, 96 students received support, including 9 research assistantships (averaging $9,887 per year), 2 teaching assistantships (averaging $10,251 per year); career-related internships or fieldwork, Federal Work-Study, scholarships/grants, and unspecified assistantships also available. Support available to part-time students. Financial award application deadline: 8/1; financial award applicants required to submit FAFSA. In 2006, 38 degrees awarded. *Degree program information:* Part-time and evening/weekend programs available. Offers adult nurse practitioner (MSN); animal science (MS); biology (MS); nurse educator (MSN); physical therapy (MPT); sciences (MPT, MS, MSN). *Application deadline:* For fall admission, 7/5 priority date for domestic students, 6/15 for international students; for spring admission, 12/8 priority date for domestic students, 11/1 for international students. Applications are processed on a rolling basis. *Application fee:* $40 ($50 for international students). Electronic applications accepted. *Application Contact:* Brenda Stewart, Assistant to the Dean, College of Graduate Studies, 325-942-2169, Fax: 325-942-2194, E-mail: brenda.stewart@angelo.edu. *Dean,* Dr. Grady Blount, 325-942-2024 Ext. 242, E-mail: grady.blount@angelo.edu.

See Close-Up on page 799.

ANNA MARIA COLLEGE, Paxton, MA 01612

General Information Independent-religious, coed, comprehensive institution. *Enrollment:* 1,200 graduate, professional, and undergraduate students; 52 full-time matriculated graduate/professional students (32 women), 313 part-time matriculated graduate/professional students (210 women). *Enrollment by degree level:* 352 master's, 13 other advanced degrees. *Graduate faculty:* 16 full-time (8 women), 60 part-time/adjunct (31 women). *Graduate housing:* On-campus housing not available. *Student services:* Career counseling, disabled student services, free psychological counseling, teacher training. *Library facilities:* Mondor-Eagen Library. *Online resources:* library catalog, access to other libraries' catalogs. *Collection:* 79,039 titles, 318 serial subscriptions.

Computer facilities: 59 computers available on campus for general student use. A campuswide network can be accessed from student residence rooms and from off campus. Internet access, online class schedules, student account information are available. *Web address:* http://www.annamaria.edu/.

General Application Contact: Janet LaPointe, Admissions Coordinator, Graduate and Continuing Education, 508-849-3234, Fax: 508-819-3362, E-mail: jlapointe@annamaria.edu.

GRADUATE UNITS

Graduate Division Students: 52 full-time (32 women), 313 part-time (210 women); includes 11 minority (6 African Americans, 2 Asian Americans or Pacific Islanders, 3 Hispanic Americans), 6 international. Average age 36. *Faculty:* 16 full-time (8 women), 60 part-time/adjunct (31 women). Expenses: Contact institution. *Financial support:* Applicants required to submit FAFSA. In 2006, 98 master's, 6 other advanced degrees awarded. *Degree program information:* Part-time and evening/weekend programs available. Offers business administration (MBA, AC); counseling psychology (MA); criminal justice (MS); early childhood development (M Ed); education (CAGS); elementary education (M Ed); emergency management (MS, Graduate Certificate); fire science (MA); human services administration (MS); justice administration (MS); occupational and environmental health and safety (MS); pastoral ministry (MA); psychology (MA); reading (M Ed); visual art (MA). *Application deadline:* For fall admission, 3/1 priority date for domestic and international students; for spring admission, 11/1 priority date for domestic and international students. Applications are processed on a rolling basis. *Application fee:* $40. Electronic applications accepted. *Application Contact:* Janet LaPointe, Admissions Coordinator, Graduate and Continuing Education, 508-849-3234, Fax: 508-819-3362, E-mail: jlapointe@annamaria.edu. *Academic Dean,* Dr. Paul Erickson, 508-349-3359, Fax: 508-849-3343, E-mail: perickson@annamaria.edu.

ANTIOCH UNIVERSITY LOS ANGELES, Culver City, CA 90230

General Information Independent, coed, upper-level institution. *Graduate housing:* On-campus housing not available.

GRADUATE UNITS

Graduate Programs *Degree program information:* Part-time and evening/weekend programs available. Postbaccalaureate distance learning degree programs offered. Offers clinical psychology (MA); creative writing (MFA); education (MA); human resource development (MA); leadership (MA); organizational development (MA); pedagogy of creative writing (Certificate); psychology (MA).

ANTIOCH UNIVERSITY MCGREGOR, Yellow Springs, OH 45387-1609

General Information Independent, coed, upper-level institution. *Enrollment:* 679 graduate, professional, and undergraduate students; 304 full-time matriculated graduate/professional students (222 women), 215 part-time matriculated graduate/professional students (160 women). *Enrollment by degree level:* 519 master's. *Graduate faculty:* 19 full-time (11 women), 40 part-time/adjunct (20 women). *Graduate housing:* On-campus housing not available. *Student services:* International student services, teacher training. *Library facilities:* Olive Kettering Library. *Online resources:* library catalog, web page, access to other libraries' catalogs. *Collection:* 325,000 titles, 1,000 serial subscriptions.

Computer facilities: 49 computers available on campus for general student use. A campuswide network can be accessed from off campus. Internet access is available. *Web address:* http://www.mcgregor.edu/.

General Application Contact: Seth Gordon, Enrollment Services Officer, 937-769-1800 Ext. 1825, Fax: 937-769-1804, E-mail: sgordon@mcgregor.edu.

GRADUATE UNITS

Graduate Programs Students: 304 full-time (222 women), 215 part-time (160 women); includes 163 minority (149 African Americans, 5 Asian Americans or Pacific Islanders, 9 Hispanic Americans). Average age 40. 281 applicants, 82% accepted, 223 enrolled. *Faculty:* 19 full-time (11 women), 40 part-time/adjunct (20 women). Expenses: Contact institution. *Financial support:* Federal Work-Study available. Financial award applicants required to submit FAFSA. In 2006, 240 degrees awarded. *Degree program information:* Part-time and evening/weekend programs available. Postbaccalaureate distance learning degree programs offered (minimal on-campus study). Offers community college management (MA); conflict resolution (MA); liberal and professional studies (MA); management (MA); teacher education (M Ed). *Application deadline:* For fall admission, 8/1 for domestic students; for winter admission, 12/1 for domestic students; for spring admission, 3/10 for domestic students. Applications are processed on a rolling basis. *Application fee:* $50. Electronic applications accepted. *Application Contact:* Seth Gordon, Enrollment Services Officer, 937-769-1800 Ext. 1825, Fax:

937-769-1804, E-mail: sgordon@mcgregor.edu. *Director of Operations*, Darlene Robertson, 937-769-180, Fax: 937-769-1804, E-mail: drobertson@mcgregor.edu.

Announcement: Antioch University McGregor's graduate offerings serve busy adult learners through both local and distance programs that focus on community change and civic leadership, conflict resolution, education, and management. In addition, Antioch offers an individualized Master of Arts program for the motivated learner who wants a tailored degree to meet unique educational and lifestyle needs. McGregor seeks to pass on to its students a passion for lifelong learning and a commitment to the betterment of the workplace, the community, and the wider society.

ANTIOCH UNIVERSITY NEW ENGLAND, Keene, NH 03431-3552

General Information Independent, coed, graduate-only institution. *Enrollment by degree level:* 648 master's, 220 doctoral. *Graduate faculty:* 54 full-time (33 women), 34 part-time/adjunct (18 women). *Tuition:* Full-time $22,000. Tuition and fees vary according to program and student level. *Graduate housing:* On-campus housing not available. *Student services:* Campus employment opportunities, career counseling, disabled student services, international student services, multicultural affairs office, teacher training, writing training. *Library facilities:* Antioch New England Graduate School Library. *Online resources:* library catalog, web page, access to other libraries' catalogs. *Collection:* 38,320 titles, 1,625 serial subscriptions, 1,122 audiovisual materials. *Research affiliation:* Harris Center for Conservation Education (environmental studies), Cheshire Medical Center Cardiac Rehabilitation Program (clinical psychology), Northeast Foundation for Children (education), Pine Hill Waldorf School (education).

Computer facilities: 12 computers available on campus for general student use. A campuswide network can be accessed from off campus. Internet access, e-mail, intranet services are available. *Web address:* http://www.antiochne.edu/.

General Application Contact: Leatrice A. Oram, Co-Director of Admissions, 800-490-3310, Fax: 603-357-0718, E-mail: admissions@antiochne.edu.

GRADUATE UNITS

Graduate School Students: 676 full-time (519 women), 192 part-time (146 women); includes 24 minority (5 African Americans, 2 American Indian/Alaska Native, 5 Asian Americans or Pacific Islanders, 12 Hispanic Americans), 21 international. Average age 36. 705 applicants, 76% accepted, 377 enrolled. *Faculty:* 54 full-time (33 women), 34 part-time/adjunct (18 women). Expenses: Contact institution. *Financial support:* In 2006–07, 665 students received support, including 47 fellowships (averaging $1,138 per year), 21 research assistantships (averaging $1,381 per year), 21 teaching assistantships (averaging $923 per year); career-related internships or fieldwork, Federal Work-Study, and scholarships/grants also available. Financial award application deadline: 8/1; financial award applicants required to submit FAFSA. In 2006, 291 master's, 29 doctorates awarded. *Degree program information:* Evening/weekend programs available. Offers autism spectrum disorders (Certificate); clinical mental health counseling (MA); clinical psychology (Psy D); conservation biology (MS); dance/movement therapy and counseling (M Ed, MA); educational administration and supervision (M Ed); environmental advocacy (MS); environmental education (MS); environmental studies (MS, PhD); experienced educators (M Ed); integrated learning (M Ed); leadership and management (MS); marriage and family therapy (MA); organization development (Certificate); organizational and environmental sustainability (MBA); resource management and conservation (MS); teacher certification in biology (7th-12th grade) (MS); teacher certification in general science (5th-9th grade) (MS); Waldorf teacher training (M Ed). *Application deadline:* For fall admission, 8/1 for domestic and international students; for spring admission, 12/1 for domestic and international students. Applications are processed on a rolling basis. *Application fee:* $50. Electronic applications accepted. *Application Contact:* Leatrice A. Oram, Co-Director of Admissions, 800-490-3310, Fax: 603-357-0718, E-mail: admissions@antiochne.edu. *President*, Dr. David A. Caruso, 603-283-2435, Fax: 603-357-0718, E-mail: dcaruso@antiochne.edu.

Interdisciplinary Studies *Faculty:* 3 full-time (1 woman), 5 part-time/adjunct (3 women). Expenses: Contact institution. *Financial support:* Fellowships, career-related internships or fieldwork and Federal Work-Study available. Financial award applicants required to submit FAFSA. Offers interdisciplinary studies (MA). *Application deadline:* For fall admission, 8/1 for domestic and international students; for spring admission, 12/1 for domestic and international students. Applications are processed on a rolling basis. *Application fee:* $50. Electronic applications accepted. *Application Contact:* Leatrice A. Oram, Co-Director of Admissions, 800-490-3310, Fax: 603-357-0718, E-mail: admissions@antiochne.edu.

ANTIOCH UNIVERSITY SANTA BARBARA, Santa Barbara, CA 93101-1581

General Information Independent, coed, upper-level institution. *Enrollment:* 284 graduate, professional, and undergraduate students; 155 full-time matriculated graduate/professional students (130 women), 63 part-time matriculated graduate/professional students (53 women). *Enrollment by degree level:* 190 master's, 28 doctoral. *Graduate faculty:* 16 full-time (11 women), 55 part-time/adjunct (21 women). *Tuition:* Part-time $515 per unit. Part-time tuition and fees vary according to course load and program. *Graduate housing:* On-campus housing not available. *Student services:* Campus employment opportunities, international student services, low-cost health insurance.

Computer facilities: 14 computers available on campus for general student use. A campuswide network can be accessed from off campus. *Web address:* http://www.antiochsb.edu/.

General Application Contact: Director of Admissions, 805-962-8179, Fax: 805-962-4786, E-mail: admissions@antiochsb.edu.

GRADUATE UNITS

Master's Program in Psychology Students: 98 full-time (88 women), 29 part-time (24 women); includes 39 minority (4 African Americans, 6 Asian Americans or Pacific Islanders, 29 Hispanic Americans), 3 international. *Faculty:* 16 full-time (11 women), 55 part-time/adjunct (21 women). Expenses: Contact institution. *Financial support:* Federal Work-Study and traineeships available. Support available to part-time students. Financial award application deadline: 8/8; financial award applicants required to submit FAFSA. In 2006, 49 degrees awarded. *Degree program information:* Part-time and evening/weekend programs available. Offers psychology (MA). *Application deadline:* For fall admission, 7/16 priority date for domestic students; for winter admission, 11/5 priority date for domestic students. Applications are processed on a rolling basis. *Application fee:* $60 ($100 for international students). Electronic applications accepted. *Application Contact:* Director of Admissions, 805-962-8179, Fax: 805-962-4786, E-mail: admissions@antiochsb.edu. *Chair*, Dr. Catherine Radecki-Bush, 805-962-8179 Ext. 229, Fax: 805-962-4786, E-mail: cradecki-bush@antiochsb.edu.

Program in Education/Teacher Credentialing Students: 14 full-time (13 women), 17 part-time (14 women); includes 8 minority (3 African Americans, 5 Hispanic Americans). *Faculty:* 16 full-time (11 women), 55 part-time/adjunct (21 women). Expenses: Contact institution. *Financial support:* Federal Work-Study available. Support available to part-time students. Financial award application deadline: 8/8; financial award applicants required to submit FAFSA. In 2006, 9 degrees awarded. *Degree program information:* Part-time programs available. Offers education/teacher credentialing (MA). *Application fee:* $60 ($100 for international students). *Application Contact:* Director of Admissions, 805-962-8179 Ext. 330, Fax: 805-962-4786, E-mail: admissions@antiochsb.edu. *Chair*, Dr. Michele Britton Bass, 805-962-8179 Ext. 114, Fax: 805-962-4786, E-mail: britbass@antiochsb.edu.

Program in Organizational Management Students: 14 full-time (10 women), 14 part-time (12 women); includes 8 minority (1 Asian American or Pacific Islander, 7 Hispanic Americans). *Faculty:* 16 full-time (11 women), 55 part-time/adjunct (21 women). Expenses: Contact institution. *Financial support:* Federal Work-Study available. Support available to part-time students. Financial award application deadline: 8/8; financial award applicants required to submit FAFSA. In 2006, 12 degrees awarded. *Degree program information:* Part-time and evening/weekend programs available. Postbaccalaureate distance learning degree programs offered (minimal on-campus study). Offers organizational management (MA). *Application deadline:* For fall admission, 8/6 priority date for domestic students; for winter admission, 11/5 priority date for domestic students. Applications are processed on a rolling basis. *Application fee:* $60 ($100 for international students). Electronic applications accepted. *Application Contact:* Director of Admissions, 805-962-8179, Fax: 805-962-4786, E-mail: admissions@antiochsb.edu. *Chair*, Dr. Esther Lopez-Mulnix, 805-962-8179 Ext. 328, Fax: 805-962-4786, E-mail: emulnix@antiochsb.edu.

Psychology Program Students: 1 (woman) full-time, 3 part-time (all women); includes 2 minority (1 African American, 1 Hispanic American). *Faculty:* 16 full-time (11 women), 55 part-time/adjunct (21 women). Expenses: Contact institution. *Financial support:* Federal Work-Study and traineeships available. Support available to part-time students. Financial award application deadline: 8/8; financial award applicants required to submit FAFSA. In 2006, 7 degrees awarded. *Degree program information:* Part-time and evening/weekend programs available. Offers professional development and career counseling (MA). *Application deadline:* Applications are processed on a rolling basis. *Application fee:* $60 ($100 for international students). Electronic applications accepted. *Application Contact:* Director of Admissions, 805-962-8179, Fax: 805-962-4786, E-mail: admissions@antiochsb.edu. *Chair*, Dr. Catherine Radecki-Bush, 805-962-8179 Ext. 229, Fax: 805-962-4786, E-mail: cradecki-bush@antiochsb.edu.

ANTIOCH UNIVERSITY SEATTLE, Seattle, WA 98121-1814

General Information Independent, coed, upper-level institution. *Graduate housing:* On-campus housing not available.

GRADUATE UNITS

Graduate Programs *Degree program information:* Part-time and evening/weekend programs available. Offers education (MA); psychology (MA, Psy D). Electronic applications accepted.

Center for Creative Change *Degree program information:* Evening/weekend programs available. Offers environment and community (MA); management (MS); organizational psychology (MA); strategic communications (MA); whole system design (MA). Electronic applications accepted.

APEX SCHOOL OF THEOLOGY, Durham, NC 27713

General Information Independent-religious, coed, comprehensive institution. *Graduate housing:* On-campus housing not available.

GRADUATE UNITS

Graduate Programs

APPALACHIAN SCHOOL OF LAW, Grundy, VA 24614

General Information Independent, coed, graduate-only institution. *Enrollment by degree level:* 369 first professional. *Graduate faculty:* 25 full-time (10 women), 2 part-time/adjunct (1 woman). *Tuition:* Full-time $22,500. *Required fees:* $275. *Graduate housing:* On-campus housing not available. *Student services:* Campus employment opportunities, career counseling, disabled student services, writing training. *Library facilities:* ASL Library. *Online resources:* library catalog, web page, access to other libraries' catalogs. *Collection:* 100,657 titles, 2,730 serial subscriptions, 729 audiovisual materials.

Computer facilities: 27 computers available on campus for general student use. A campuswide network can be accessed. Internet access, printing access are available. *Web address:* http://www.asl.edu/.

General Application Contact: Nancy M. Pruitt, Director of Student Services and Registrar, 276-935-4349 Ext. 1229, Fax: 276-935-8261, E-mail: npruitt@asl.edu.

GRADUATE UNITS

Professional Program in Law Students: 369 full-time (114 women); includes 21 minority (5 African Americans, 1 American Indian/Alaska Native, 4 Asian Americans or Pacific Islanders, 11 Hispanic Americans). Average age 27. 1,714 applicants, 42% accepted, 163 enrolled. *Faculty:* 20 full-time, 4 part-time/adjunct. Expenses: Contact institution. *Financial support:* In 2006–07, 205 students received support, including 12 research assistantships (averaging $1,000 per year); career-related internships or fieldwork, Federal Work-Study, institutionally sponsored loans, scholarships/grants, and tuition waivers (full and partial) also available. Financial award application deadline: 7/1; financial award applicants required to submit FAFSA. In 2006, 108 degrees awarded. *Degree program information:* Part-time programs available. Offers law (JD). *Application deadline:* For spring admission, 4/15 priority date for domestic students. Applications are processed on a rolling basis. *Application fee:* $60. Electronic applications accepted. *Application Contact:* Nancy M. Pruitt, Director of Student Services and Registrar, 276-935-4349 Ext. 1229, Fax: 276-935-8261, E-mail: npruitt@asl.edu. *Dean*, Clinton W. Shinn, 276-935-4349, Fax: 276-935-8261, E-mail: wshinn@asl.edu.

APPALACHIAN STATE UNIVERSITY, Boone, NC 28608

General Information State-supported, coed, comprehensive institution. CGS member. *Enrollment:* 15,117 graduate, professional, and undergraduate students; 685 full-time matriculated graduate/professional students (440 women), 1,058 part-time matriculated graduate/professional students (740 women). *Enrollment by degree level:* 1,661 master's, 56 doctoral, 26 other advanced degrees. *Graduate faculty:* 530 full-time (213 women), 30 part-time/adjunct (15 women). Tuition, state resident: full-time $2,600; part-time $127 per hour. Tuition, nonresident: full-time $13,200; part-time $597 per hour. *Required fees:* $2,000; $546 per term. *Graduate housing:* Rooms and/or apartments available on a first-come, first-served basis to single and married students. Typical cost: $5,100 per year for single students; $5,100 per year for married students. Room charges vary according to campus/location. Housing application deadline: 2/28. *Student services:* Campus employment opportunities, campus safety program, career counseling, child daycare facilities, disabled student services, exercise/wellness program, free psychological counseling, grant writing training, international student services, low-cost health insurance, multicultural affairs office, teacher training, writing training. *Library facilities:* Carol Grotnes Belk Library plus 1 other. *Online resources:* library catalog, web page, access to other libraries' catalogs. *Collection:* 906,756 titles, 5,543 serial subscriptions, 11,974 audiovisual materials.

Computer facilities: Computer purchase and lease plans are available. 500 computers available on campus for general student use. A campuswide network can be accessed from student residence rooms and from off campus. Internet access is available. *Web address:* http://www.appstate.edu/.

General Application Contact: Dr. Holly Hirst, Associate Dean for Graduate Studies, 828-262-2130, Fax: 828-262-2709, E-mail: hirsthp@appstate.edu.

GRADUATE UNITS

Cratis D. Williams Graduate School Students: 685 full-time (440 women), 1,058 part-time (740 women); includes 94 minority (80 African Americans, 1 American Indian/Alaska Native, 9 Asian Americans or Pacific Islanders, 4 Hispanic Americans), 36 international. Average age 29. 1,097 applicants, 79% accepted, 725 enrolled. *Faculty:* 530 full-time (213 women), 30 part-time/adjunct (15 women). Expenses: Contact institution. *Financial support:* In 2006–07, 10 fellowships (averaging $10,000 per year), 135 research assistantships (averaging $8,000 per year), 150 teaching assistantships (averaging $8,000 per year) were awarded; career-related internships or fieldwork, Federal Work-Study, institutionally sponsored loans, scholarships/grants, tuition waivers (partial), and unspecified assistantships also available. Support available to part-time students. Financial award application deadline: 7/1; financial award applicants required to submit FAFSA. In 2006, 663 master's, 3 doctorates, 7 other advanced degrees awarded. *Degree program information:* Part-time and evening/weekend programs available. Postbaccalaureate distance learning degree programs offered (minimal on-campus study). *Application deadline:* For fall admission, 7/1 for domestic students, 1/1 for international students; for spring admission, 11/1 for domestic students, 6/1 for international students. Applications are processed on a rolling basis. *Application fee:* $50. Electronic applications accepted. *Application Contact:* Dr. Holly Hirst, Associate Dean for Graduate Studies, 828-262-2130, Fax: 828-262-2709, E-mail: hirsthp@appstate.edu. *Dean of Graduate Studies and Research*, Dr. E. D. Huntley, 828-262-2130, E-mail: huntleyed@appstate.edu.

Appalachian State University (continued)

College of Arts and Sciences Students: 250 full-time (139 women), 183 part-time (87 women); includes 20 minority (13 African Americans, 5 Asian Americans or Pacific Islanders, 2 Hispanic Americans), 13 international. 329 applicants, 71% accepted, 185 enrolled. *Faculty:* 254 full-time (88 women), 1 (woman) part-time/adjunct. Expenses: Contact institution. *Financial support:* In 2006–07, research assistantships (averaging $7,000 per year); fellowships, teaching assistantships, career-related internships or fieldwork, Federal Work-Study, scholarships/grants, and unspecified assistantships also available. Support available to part-time students. Financial award application deadline: 7/1; financial award applicants required to submit FAFSA. In 2006, 137 degrees awarded. *Degree program information:* Part-time programs available. Offers Appalachian studies (MA); applied physics (MS); arts and sciences (MA, MPA, MS, MSW, SSP); biology (MS); clinical health psychology (MA); computer science (MS); criminal justice (MS); English (MA); English education (MA); general experimental psychology (MA); geography (MA); gerontology (MA); history (MA); history education (MA); industrial and organizational psychology (MA); mathematics (MA); mathematics education (MA); political science (MA); political science and criminal justice (MA, MS); public administration (MPA); public history (MA); romance languages-French (MA); romance languages-Spanish (MA); school psychology (MA, SSP); social work (MSW). *Application deadline:* For fall admission, 7/1 for domestic students, 1/1 for international students; for spring admission, 11/1 for domestic students, 6/1 for international students. Applications are processed on a rolling basis. *Application fee:* $50. *Dean,* Dr. Robert Lyman, 828-262-3078.

College of Education Students: 310 full-time (243 women), 827 part-time (634 women); includes 68 minority (65 African Americans, 1 American Indian/Alaska Native, 2 Hispanic Americans), 18 international. 622 applicants, 82% accepted, 436 enrolled. *Faculty:* 137 full-time (78 women), 14 part-time/adjunct (9 women). Expenses: Contact institution. *Financial support:* In 2006–07, research assistantships (averaging $7,000 per year), teaching assistantships (averaging $7,000 per year) were awarded; fellowships, career-related internships or fieldwork, Federal Work-Study, scholarships/grants, and unspecified assistantships also available. Support available to part-time students. Financial award application deadline: 7/1; financial award applicants required to submit FAFSA. In 2006, 438 master's, 3 doctorates awarded. *Degree program information:* Part-time and evening/weekend programs available. Postbaccalaureate distance learning degree programs offered (minimal on-campus study). Offers communication disorders (MA); community counseling (MA); curriculum specialist (MA); education (MA, MLS, MSA, Ed D, Ed S); educational administration (Ed S); educational leadership (Ed D); educational media (MA); elementary education (MA); higher education (MA, Ed S); library science (MLS); marriage and family therapy (MA); reading education (MA); school administration (MSA, Ed S); school counseling (MA); secondary education (MA); special education (MA); student development (MA). *Application deadline:* For fall admission, 7/1 for domestic students, 1/1 for international students; for spring admission, 11/1 for domestic students, 6/1 for international students. *Application fee:* $50. *Application Contact:* Dr. Holly Hirst, Associate Dean for Graduate Studies, 828-262-2130, Fax: 828-262-2709, E-mail: hirsthp@appstate.edu. *Dean,* Dr. Charles Duke, 828-262-2232.

College of Fine and Applied Arts Students: 55 full-time (26 women), 18 part-time (9 women); includes 2 minority (both Asian Americans or Pacific Islanders) 52 applicants, 87% accepted, 37 enrolled. *Faculty:* 63 full-time (29 women). Expenses: Contact institution. *Financial support:* Fellowships, research assistantships, teaching assistantships, career-related internships or fieldwork, Federal Work-Study, institutionally sponsored loans, scholarships/grants, and unspecified assistantships available. Support available to part-time students. Financial award application deadline: 7/1; financial award applicants required to submit FAFSA. In 2006, 50 degrees awarded. *Degree program information:* Part-time programs available. Offers child development (MA); exercise science (MS); family and consumer science (MA); family and consumer science education (MA); fine and applied arts (MA, MS); industrial technology (MA); technology education (MA). *Application deadline:* For fall admission, 7/1 for domestic students, 1/1 for international students; for spring admission, 6/1 for international students. *Application fee:* $50. *Dean,* Dr. Mark Estepp, 828-262-3036.

John A. Walker College of Business Students: 51 full-time (21 women), 25 part-time (8 women); includes 1 minority (Asian American or Pacific Islander), 2 international. 80 applicants, 80% accepted, 54 enrolled. *Faculty:* 60 full-time (14 women). Expenses: Contact institution. *Financial support:* Fellowships, research assistantships, teaching assistantships, career-related internships or fieldwork, Federal Work-Study, scholarships/grants, and unspecified assistantships available. Support available to part-time students. Financial award application deadline: 7/1; financial award applicants required to submit FAFSA. In 2006, 48 degrees awarded. *Degree program information:* Part-time programs available. Postbaccalaureate distance learning degree programs offered (minimal on-campus study). Offers accounting (MS); business (MBA, MS); business administration (MBA). *Application deadline:* For fall admission, 3/1 for domestic students, 1/1 for international students; for spring admission, 6/1 for international students. *Application fee:* $50. *Dean,* Dr. Randy Edwards, 828-262-2058, E-mail: edwardsrk@appstate.edu.

School of Music Students: 19 full-time (11 women), 5 part-time (2 women); includes 3 minority (2 African Americans, 1 Asian American or Pacific Islander), 3 international. 14 applicants, 100% accepted, 13 enrolled. *Faculty:* 26 full-time (7 women). Expenses: Contact institution. *Financial support:* In 2006–07, fellowships (averaging $1,000 per year), 11 research assistantships (averaging $7,000 per year) were awarded; teaching assistantships, career-related internships or fieldwork, Federal Work-Study, scholarships/grants, tuition waivers (partial), and unspecified assistantships available. Support available to part-time students. Financial award application deadline: 7/1. In 2006, 15 degrees awarded. Offers music performance (MM); music therapy (MMT). *Application deadline:* For fall admission, 7/1 for domestic students, 1/1 for international students; for spring admission, 11/1 for domestic students, 6/1 for international students. *Application fee:* $50. *Application Contact:* Dr. Nancy Schneeloch-Bingham, Graduate Program Director, 828-262-6463, E-mail: schneelochna@appstate.edu. *Dean,* Dr. William Harbinson, 828-262-3020, Fax: 828-262-6446, E-mail: harbinsonwg@appstate.edu.

AQUINAS COLLEGE, Grand Rapids, MI 49506-1799

General Information Independent-religious, coed, comprehensive institution. *Enrollment:* 2,098 graduate, professional, and undergraduate students; 76 full-time matriculated graduate/professional students (53 women), 242 part-time matriculated graduate/professional students (182 women). *Enrollment by degree level:* 318 master's. *Graduate faculty:* 36 full-time (21 women), 39 part-time/adjunct (29 women). *Tuition:* Part-time $450 per credit. *Graduate housing:* On-campus housing not available. *Student services:* Campus employment opportunities, campus safety program, career counseling, child daycare facilities, disabled student services, exercise/wellness program, free psychological counseling, multicultural affairs office, teacher training. *Library facilities:* Grace Hauenstein Library. *Online resources:* library catalog, web page, access to other libraries' catalogs. *Collection:* 112,458 titles, 14,725 serial subscriptions.

Computer facilities: 176 computers available on campus for general student use. A campuswide network can be accessed from student residence rooms and from off campus. Internet access is available. *Web address:* http://www.aquinas.edu/.

General Application Contact: Lynn Atkins-Rykert, Executive Assistant, School of Management, 616-632-2924, Fax: 616-732-4489, E-mail: atkinlyn@aquinas.edu.

GRADUATE UNITS

School of Education Students: 65 full-time (46 women), 186 part-time (148 women); includes 25 minority (4 African Americans, 2 American Indian/Alaska Native, 2 Asian Americans or Pacific Islanders, 17 Hispanic Americans). Average age 35. 41 applicants, 80% accepted, 30 enrolled. *Faculty:* 24 full-time (16 women), 34 part-time/adjunct (28 women). Expenses: Contact institution. *Financial support:* In 2006–07, 141 students received support. Scholarships/grants available. Support available to part-time students. Financial award application deadline: 3/15; financial award applicants required to submit FAFSA. In 2006, 117 degrees awarded. *Degree program information:* Part-time and evening/weekend programs available. Offers education (MAT, ME, MS). *Application deadline:* Applications are processed on a rolling basis. *Application fee:* $0. *Application Contact:* Sandy Rademaker, Coordinator of Graduate Education Programs, 616-632-2443 Ext. 5400, E-mail: rademsan@aquinas.edu. *Dean,* Nanette Clatterbuck, 616-632-2973, Fax: 616-732-4465, E-mail: clattnan@aquinas.edu.

School of Management Students: 11 full-time (7 women), 56 part-time (34 women); includes 2 minority (1 African American, 1 American Indian/Alaska Native), 3 international. Average age 35. 28 applicants, 79% accepted, 17 enrolled. *Faculty:* 12 full-time (5 women), 5 part-time/adjunct (1 woman). Expenses: Contact institution. *Financial support:* In 2006–07, 38 students received support. Scholarships/grants available. Support available to part-time students. Financial award application deadline: 3/15; financial award applicants required to submit FAFSA. In 2006, 26 degrees awarded. *Degree program information:* Part-time and evening/weekend programs available. Offers management (M Mgt). *Application deadline:* Applications are processed on a rolling basis. *Application Contact:* Lynn Atkins-Rykert, Executive Assistant, School of Management, 616-632-2924, Fax: 616-732-4489, E-mail: atkinlyn@aquinas.edu. *Dean,* Cynthia VanGelderen, 616-632-2922, Fax: 616-732-4489, E-mail: vangecyn@aquinas.edu.

AQUINAS INSTITUTE OF THEOLOGY, St. Louis, MO 63108

General Information Independent-religious, coed, graduate-only institution. *Graduate housing:* On-campus housing not available.

GRADUATE UNITS

Graduate and Professional Programs *Degree program information:* Part-time and evening/weekend programs available. Postbaccalaureate distance learning degree programs offered (minimal on-campus study). Offers health care mission (MAHCM); ministry (M Div); pastoral care (Certificate); pastoral ministry (MAPM); pastoral studies (MAPS); preaching (D Min); spiritual direction (Certificate); theology (M Div, MA).

ARCADIA UNIVERSITY, Glenside, PA 19038-3295

General Information Independent-religious, coed, comprehensive institution. CGS member. *Enrollment:* 3,595 graduate, professional, and undergraduate students; 464 full-time matriculated graduate/professional students (369 women), 1,017 part-time matriculated graduate/professional students (760 women). *Enrollment by degree level:* 1,273 master's, 208 doctoral. *Graduate faculty:* 71 full-time, 135 part-time/adjunct. *Graduate housing:* On-campus housing not available. *Student services:* Campus safety program, career counseling, international student services, low-cost health insurance, multicultural affairs office, writing training. *Library facilities:* Landman Library. *Online resources:* library catalog, web page. *Collection:* 137,347 titles, 932 serial subscriptions, 2,580 audiovisual materials.

Computer facilities: Computer purchase and lease plans are available. 110 computers available on campus for general student use. A campuswide network can be accessed from student residence rooms and from off campus. Internet access is available. *Web address:* http://www.arcadia.edu/.

General Application Contact: Information Contact, 215-572-2910, Fax: 215-572-4049, E-mail: admiss@arcadia.edu.

GRADUATE UNITS

Graduate Studies Students: 464 full-time (369 women), 1,017 part-time (760 women); includes 215 minority (160 African Americans, 1 American Indian/Alaska Native, 26 Asian Americans or Pacific Islanders, 28 Hispanic Americans), 14 international. Average age 31. *Faculty:* 71 full-time, 135 part-time/adjunct. Expenses: Contact institution. *Financial support:* Research assistantships, teaching assistantships, career-related internships or fieldwork, scholarships/grants, tuition waivers (partial), and unspecified assistantships available. Support available to part-time students. In 2006, 443 master's, 45 doctorates awarded. *Degree program information:* Part-time and evening/weekend programs available. Postbaccalaureate distance learning degree programs offered (minimal on-campus study). Offers allied health (MSHE, MSPH); art education (M Ed, MA Ed); biology education (MA Ed); business administration (MBA); chemistry education (MA Ed); child development (CAS); community counseling (MACP); computer education (M Ed, CAS); computer education 7–12 (MA Ed); early childhood education (M Ed, CAS); educational leadership (M Ed, CAS); educational psychology (CAS); elementary education (M Ed, CAS); English (MAE); English education (MA Ed); environmental education (MA Ed, CAS); fine arts, theater, and music (MAH); forensic science (MSFS); genetic counseling (MSGC); history education (MA Ed); history, philosophy, and religion (MAH); international peace and conflict management (MAIPCR); international relations and diplomacy (MA); language arts (M Ed, CAS); literature and language (MAH); mathematics education (M Ed, MA Ed, CAS); medical science and community health (MM Sc, MSHE, MSPH); music education (MA Ed); physical therapy (DPT); psychology (MA Ed); pupil personnel services (CAS); reading (M Ed, CAS); school counseling (MACP); school library science (M Ed); science education (M Ed, CAS); secondary education (M Ed, CAS); special education (M Ed, Ed D, CAS); theater arts (MA Ed); written communication (MA Ed). Electronic applications accepted. *Application Contact:* 215-572-2910, Fax: 215-572-4049, E-mail: admiss@arcadia.edu. *Dean of Graduate and Professional Studies,* Mark Curchack, 215-572-2928, Fax: 215-572-2126, E-mail: curchack@arcadia.edu.

See Close-Up on page 801.

ARGOSY UNIVERSITY, ATLANTA CAMPUS, Atlanta, GA 30328

General Information Proprietary, coed, upper-level institution. CGS member. *Enrollment:* 979 full-time matriculated graduate/professional students (817 women), 582 part-time matriculated graduate/professional students (481 women). *Enrollment by degree level:* 704 master's, 846 doctoral, 11 other advanced degrees. *Graduate faculty:* 27 full-time (16 women), 66 part-time/adjunct (31 women). *Graduate housing:* On-campus housing not available. *Student services:* Campus employment opportunities, campus safety program. *Web address:* http://www.argosyu.edu/.

General Application Contact: Christa Holton, Director of Admissions, 770-671-1200 Ext. 1014, Fax: 770-671-9050, E-mail: cholton@argosy.edu.

GRADUATE UNITS

College of Business Students: 53 full-time (38 women), 35 part-time (28 women); includes 73 minority (66 African Americans, 3 Asian Americans or Pacific Islanders, 4 Hispanic Americans). Expenses: Contact institution. *Financial support:* Applicants required to submit FAFSA. *Degree program information:* Part-time programs available. Offers accounting (DBA); customized professional concentration (MBA, DBA); finance (MBA); healthcare administration (MBA); information systems (DBA); information systems management (MBA); international business (MBA, DBA); management (MBA, DBA); marketing (MBA, DBA). *Application deadline:* For fall admission, 7/1 priority date for domestic students, 6/1 for international students; for spring admission, 11/1 priority date for domestic students, 10/1 for international students. Applications are processed on a rolling basis. *Application fee:* $50. Electronic applications accepted. *Application Contact:* Christa Holton, Director of Admissions, 770-671-1200 Ext. 1014, Fax: 770-671-9050, E-mail: cholton@argosy.edu. *Department Chair,* Dr. Robert A. Berg, 770-407-1042, E-mail: rberg@argosy.edu.

College of Education Students: 459 full-time (377 women), 324 part-time (255 women); includes 388 minority (335 African Americans, 10 American Indian/Alaska Native, 14 Asian Americans or Pacific Islanders, 29 Hispanic Americans). Expenses: Contact institution. *Financial support:* Teaching assistantships, Federal Work-Study available. *Degree program information:* Evening/weekend programs available. Offers educational leadership (MAEd, Ed D, Ed S); instructional leadership (MAEd, Ed D, Ed S). *Application deadline:* For fall admission, 8/1 for domestic students; for spring admission, 10/1 for domestic students. *Application fee:* $50. *Application Contact:* Christa Holton, Director of Admissions, 770-671-1200, Fax: 770-671-9050, E-mail: inquiry@argosy.edu. *Department Chair,* Jacqueline Jenkins, 770-407-1067, Fax: 770-671-0476, E-mail: jbeard@argosy.edu.

College of Psychology and Behavioral Sciences Students: 467 full-time (402 women), 223 part-time (198 women); includes 362 minority (315 African Americans, 5 American Indian/Alaska Native, 10 Asian Americans or Pacific Islanders, 32 Hispanic Americans). Average age 26. 272 applicants, 46% accepted. *Faculty:* 11 full-time (6 women), 16 part-time/adjunct (6 women). Expenses: Contact institution. *Financial support:* In 2006–07, 280 students received support, including 40 teaching assistantships (averaging $700 per year); career-related internships or fieldwork and Federal Work-Study also available. Support available to part-time students. Financial award application deadline: 6/30; financial award applicants required to submit FAFSA. In 2006, 40 degrees awarded. *Degree program information:* Part-time and evening/weekend programs available. Offers clinical psychology (MA, Psy D, Postdoctoral Respecialization Certificate); community counseling (MA); counselor education and supervision (Ed D); marriage and family therapy (Certificate). *Application deadline:* For fall admission, 7/1 priority date for domestic students; for spring admission, 10/15 priority date for domestic students. Applications are processed on a rolling basis. *Application fee:* $50. Electronic applications accepted. *Application Contact:* Christa Holton, Director of Admissions, 770-671-1200 Ext. 1014, Fax: 770-671-9050, E-mail: cholton@argosy.edu. *Vice President for the Academic Affairs,* Dr. Edward Bouie, 770-671-1200 Ext. 1052, Fax: 770-671-0476, E-mail: ebouie@argosy.edu.

ARGOSY UNIVERSITY, CHICAGO CAMPUS, Chicago, IL 60603

General Information Proprietary, coed, upper-level institution. CGS member. *Enrollment:* 665 full-time matriculated graduate/professional students (513 women), 298 part-time matriculated graduate/professional students (222 women). *Enrollment by degree level:* 280 master's, 683 doctoral. *Graduate faculty:* 27 full-time (17 women), 94 part-time/adjunct (50 women). *Graduate housing:* On-campus housing not available. *Student services:* Campus employment opportunities, career counseling, disabled student services, international student services, low-cost health insurance, writing training. *Library facilities:* Argosy University Chicago Library. *Online resources:* library catalog, access to other libraries' catalogs. *Collection:* 20,000 titles, 150 serial subscriptions, 550 audiovisual materials.

Computer facilities: 15 computers available on campus for general student use. A campuswide network can be accessed from off campus. Internet access and online class registration, campus Web site are available. *Web address:* http://www.argosyu.edu/.

General Application Contact: Ashley Delaney, Director of Admissions, 800-626-4123, Fax: 312-777-7750, E-mail: argosyadmissions@argosy.edu.

GRADUATE UNITS

College of Business Students: 52 full-time (30 women), 18 part-time (7 women); includes 37 minority (24 African Americans, 7 Asian Americans or Pacific Islanders, 6 Hispanic Americans). Average age 37. 32 applicants, 81% accepted, 25 enrolled. *Faculty:* 2 full-time (both women), 4 part-time/adjunct (3 women). Expenses: Contact institution. *Financial support:* In 2006–07, 3 students received support. Scholarships/grants available. Financial award application deadline: 4/1. In 2006, 9 master's, 2 doctorates awarded. *Degree program information:* Part-time and evening/weekend programs available. Offers accounting (DBA); customized professional concentration (MBA, DBA); finance (MBA); healthcare administration (MBA); information systems (DBA); information systems management (MBA); international business (MBA, DBA); management (MBA, DBA); marketing (MBA, DBA). *Application deadline:* For fall admission, 2/28 for domestic and international students; for spring admission, 10/30 for domestic and international students. Applications are processed on a rolling basis. *Application fee:* $50. Electronic applications accepted. *Application Contact:* Ashley Delaney, Director of Admissions, 800-626-4123, Fax: 312-777-7750, E-mail: argosyadmissions@argosy.edu. *Associate Head,* Dr. Cynthia Scarlett, 800-626-4123, Fax: 212-727-7750, E-mail: cscarlett@argosy.edu.

College of Education Students: 116 full-time (96 women), 42 part-time (32 women); includes 112 minority (108 African Americans, 1 Asian American or Pacific Islander, 3 Hispanic Americans). Average age 45. 56 applicants, 84% accepted, 45 enrolled. *Faculty:* 3 full-time (1 woman), 7 part-time/adjunct (0 women). Expenses: Contact institution. *Financial support:* In 2006–07, 35 students received support. Scholarships/grants available. Financial award application deadline: 4/1. In 2006, 4 master's, 10 doctorates awarded. *Degree program information:* Part-time and evening/weekend programs available. Offers community college executive leadership (Ed D); educational leadership (MA Ed, Ed D, Ed S); instructional leadership (MA Ed, Ed D, Ed S). *Application deadline:* For fall admission, 2/28 for domestic and international students; for spring admission, 10/30 for domestic and international students. Applications are processed on a rolling basis. *Application fee:* $50. Electronic applications accepted. *Application Contact:* Ashley Delaney, Director of Admissions, 800-626-4123, Fax: 312-777-7750, E-mail: argosyadmissions@argosy.edu. *Head,* Dr. Paul Busceni, 800-626-4123, Fax: 312-777-7750, E-mail: pbusceni@argosy.edu.

College of Psychology and Behavioral Sciences Students: 496 full-time (387 women), 217 part-time (162 women); includes 194 minority (121 African Americans, 1 American Indian/Alaska Native, 35 Asian Americans or Pacific Islanders, 37 Hispanic Americans). Average age 32. 541 applicants, 58% accepted, 163 enrolled. *Faculty:* 25 full-time (16 women), 84 part-time/adjunct (44 women). Expenses: Contact institution. *Financial support:* In 2006–07, 200 students received support, including 8 fellowships with partial tuition reimbursements available (averaging $4,200 per year), 10 research assistantships with partial tuition reimbursements available (averaging $500 per year), 150 teaching assistantships with partial tuition reimbursements available (averaging $600 per year); career-related internships or fieldwork, Federal Work-Study, scholarships/grants, tuition waivers (partial), and unspecified assistantships also available. Support available to part-time students. Financial award application deadline: 4/1; financial award applicants required to submit FAFSA. In 2006, 104 master's, 78 doctorates awarded. *Degree program information:* Part-time programs available. Offers child and adolescent psychology (Psy D); client-centered and experiential psychotherapies (Psy D); client-centered and experiential psychotherapy (Certificate); clinical psychology (MA, Psy D); community counseling (MA); counseling psychology (Ed D); counselor education and supervision (Ed D); diversity and multicultural psychology (Psy D); family psychology (Psy D); forensic psychology (MA, Psy D); health psychology (Psy D); organizational leadership (Ed D); psychoanalytic psychology (Psy D); psychology and spirituality (Psy D). *Application deadline:* For fall admission, 5/15 for domestic and international students; for spring admission, 10/15 for domestic and international students. Applications are processed on a rolling basis. *Application fee:* $50. Electronic applications accepted. *Application Contact:* Ashley Delaney, Director of Admissions, 800-626-4123, Fax: 312-777-7750, E-mail: argosyadmissions@argosy.edu. *Dean,* 800-626-4123, Fax: 312-777-7250, E-mail: argosyadmissions@argosy.edu.

ARGOSY UNIVERSITY, DALLAS CAMPUS, Dallas, TX 75231

General Information Proprietary, coed, upper-level institution. CGS member. *Enrollment:* 141 full-time matriculated graduate/professional students (120 women), 251 part-time matriculated graduate/professional students (201 women). *Enrollment by degree level:* 170 master's, 222 doctoral. *Graduate faculty:* 14 full-time (7 women), 12 part-time/adjunct (7 women). *Graduate housing:* On-campus housing not available. *Student services:* Campus employment opportunities, career counseling, disabled student services.

Computer facilities: Internet access and online class registration are available. *Web address:* http://www.argosyu.edu/.

General Application Contact: Kara Smith, Director of Admissions, 866-954-9900, Fax: 214-378-8555, E-mail: dallasadmissions@argosy.edu.

GRADUATE UNITS

College of Business Expenses: Contact institution. *Financial support:* Federal Work-Study and scholarships/grants available. *Degree program information:* Part-time and evening/weekend programs available. Offers management (MBA). *Application deadline:* For fall admission, 5/15 priority date for domestic students, 1/15 priority date for international students; for spring admission, 10/15 priority date for domestic and international students. Applications are processed on a rolling basis. *Application fee:* $50. Electronic applications accepted. *Application Contact:* Kara Smith, Director of Admissions, 866-954-9900, Fax: 214-378-8555, E-mail: dallasadmissions@argosy.edu.

College of Education Expenses: Contact institution. *Financial support:* Federal Work-Study and scholarships/grants available. *Degree program information:* Part-time and evening/weekend programs available. Offers educational leadership (MA Ed); instructional leadership (MA Ed). *Application deadline:* For fall admission, 5/15 priority date for international students; for spring admission, 10/15 priority date for international students. Applications are processed on a rolling basis. *Application fee:* $50. Electronic applications accepted. *Application Contact:* Kara Smith, Director of Admissions, 214-459-2208, Fax: 214-378-8555, E-mail: dallas.admissions@argosyu.edu. *Education Program Chair,* Dr. Susan Bryza, E-mail: sbryza@argosy.edu.

College of Psychology and Behavioral Sciences Expenses: Contact institution. Offers clinical psychology (MA, Psy D); professional counseling (MA); psychology and behavioral sciences (MA, Psy D). *Application deadline:* For fall admission, 1/15 priority date for domestic and international students; for spring admission, 10/15 priority date for domestic and international students. Applications are processed on a rolling basis. *Application fee:* $50. Electronic applications accepted. *Application Contact:* Kara Smith, Director of Admissions, 866-954-9900, Fax: 214-378-8555, E-mail: dallasadmissions@argosy.edu. *Program Chair,* Dr. Marilyn Kissinger, 215-459-2214, E-mail: mkissinger@argosy.edu.

ARGOSY UNIVERSITY, DENVER CAMPUS, Denver, CO 80203

General Information Proprietary, coed, university. *Web address:* http://www.argosyu.edu/.

GRADUATE UNITS

College of Business Expenses: Contact institution. Offers accounting (DBA); customized professional concentraion (DBA); customized professional concentration (MBA); finance (MBA); healthcare administration (MBA); information systems (DBA); information systems management (MBA); international business (MBA, DBA); management (MBA, MSM, DBA); marketing (MBA, DBA).

College of Education Expenses: Contact institution. Offers educational leadership (MA Ed, Ed D); instructional leadership (MA Ed, Ed D).

College of Psychology and Behavioral Sciences Expenses: Contact institution. Offers clinical psychology (Psy D); community counseling (MA); counseling psychology (Ed D); counselor education and supervision (Ed D); forensic psychology (MA); organizational leadership (Ed D).

ARGOSY UNIVERSITY, HAWAI'I CAMPUS, Honolulu, HI 96813

General Information Proprietary, coed, upper-level institution. CGS member. *Enrollment by degree level:* 125 master's, 230 doctoral, 10 other advanced degrees. *Graduate faculty:* 13 full-time, 40 part-time/adjunct. *Graduate housing:* On-campus housing not available. *Student services:* Campus employment opportunities, career counseling, international student services, low-cost health insurance, writing training. *Web address:* http://www.argosyu.edu/honolulu/.

General Application Contact: Cherie Andrade, Director of Admissions, 888-323-2777, Fax: 808-536-5505, E-mail: candrade@argosy.edu.

GRADUATE UNITS

College of Business Students: 3 full-time (2 women), 1 part-time; includes 2 minority (1 Asian American or Pacific Islander, 1 Hispanic American). 6 applicants, 67% accepted, 3 enrolled. *Faculty:* 12 part-time/adjunct (2 women). Expenses: Contact institution. *Financial support:* Teaching assistantships, Federal Work-Study and scholarships/grants available. Support available to part-time students. *Degree program information:* Evening/weekend programs available. Offers accounting (DBA); customized professional concentration (MBA, DBA); finance (MBA, Certificate); healthcare administration (MBA, Certificate); information systems (DBA); information systems management (MBA, Certificate); international business (MBA, DBA, Certificate); management (MBA, DBA); marketing (MBA, DBA, Certificate). *Application deadline:* For fall admission, 1/15 priority date for domestic students; for spring admission, 10/15 for domestic students. Applications are processed on a rolling basis. *Application fee:* $50. *Application Contact:* Cherie Andrade, Director of Admissions, 888-323-2777, Fax: 808-536-5505, E-mail: candrade@argosy.edu. *Interim Chair, College of Business and Information Technology,* Lisa Parker, 888-323-2777, Fax: 808-536-5505, E-mail: lparker@argosy.edu.

College of Education Students: 26 full-time (18 women), 4 part-time (all women); includes 16 minority (13 Asian Americans or Pacific Islanders, 3 Hispanic Americans). 17 applicants, 94% accepted, 14 enrolled. *Faculty:* 9 part-time/adjunct (4 women). Expenses: Contact institution. Offers educational leadership (MAEd, Ed D); instructional leadership (MAEd, Ed D). *Application deadline:* For fall admission, 1/15 priority date for domestic students; for spring admission, 10/15 for domestic students. Applications are processed on a rolling basis. *Application fee:* $50. Electronic applications accepted. *Application Contact:* Cherie Andrade, Director of Admissions, 888-323-2777, Fax: 808-536-5505, E-mail: candrade@argosy.edu. *Chair,* Dr. Kristine Lesperance, 888-323-2777, Fax: 808-536-5505, E-mail: klesperance@argosy.edu.

College of Psychology and Behavioral Sciences Expenses: Contact institution. Offers clinical psychology (MA, Psy D, Postdoctoral Respecialization Certificate); marriage and family therapy (MA); organizational leadership (Ed D); psychology and behavioral sciences (MA, Ed D, Psy D, Certificate, Postdoctoral Respecialization Certificate); psychopharmacology (Certificate); school psychology (MA, Psy D); substance abuse counseling (Certificate).

ARGOSY UNIVERSITY, INLAND EMPIRE CAMPUS, San Bernardino, CA 92408

General Information Proprietary, coed, university. *Web address:* http://www.argosyu.edu/inlandempire/.

GRADUATE UNITS

College of Business Expenses: Contact institution. Offers accounting (DBA); customized professional concentration (MBA, DBA); finance (MBA); healthcare administration (MBA); information systems (DBA); information systems management (MBA); international business (MBA, DBA); management (DBA); mangement (MBA); marketing (MBA, DBA).

College of Education Expenses: Contact institution. Offers community college executive leadership (Ed D); educational leadership (MA Ed, Ed D); instructional leadership (MA Ed, Ed D).

College of Psychology and Behavioral Sciences Expenses: Contact institution. Offers clinical psychology (MA); clinical psychology/marriage and family therapy (MA); counseling psychology (MA, Ed D); counseling psychology/marriage and family therapy (MA).

ARGOSY UNIVERSITY, NASHVILLE CAMPUS, Franklin, TN 37067-7226

General Information Proprietary, coed, upper-level institution. CGS member. *Enrollment by degree level:* 125 master's. *Graduate faculty:* 4 full-time, 29 part-time/adjunct. *Student services:* Career counseling, disabled student services, low-cost health insurance. *Web address:* http://www.argosyu.edu/.

General Application Contact: Mary Quinn Neal, Director of Admissions, 615-369-0616, Fax: 615-503-9952, E-mail: mquinn@argosy.edu.

GRADUATE UNITS

College of Business Offers accounting (DBA); customized professional concentration (DBA); information systems (DBA); international business (DBA); management (DBA); marketing (DBA).

Doctoral Program in Counselor Education and Supervision Expenses: Contact institution. Offers counselor education and supervision (Ed D).

Program in Professional Counseling Students: 125 full-time. *Faculty:* 4 full-time, 29 part-time/adjunct. Expenses: Contact institution. *Financial support:* Scholarships/grants available. In 2006, 17 degrees awarded. *Degree program information:* Evening/weekend programs available. Offers mental health counseling (MA). *Application deadline:* Applications are processed on a rolling basis. *Application fee:* $50. *Application Contact:* Marie Quinn Neal, Director of Admissions, 615-369-0616, Fax: 615-369-9952, E-mail: mquinn@argosy.edu. *Director,* Dr. Cecelia Burrill, 770-407-1028, Fax: 770-671-0146, E-mail: cburrill@argosy.edu.

ARGOSY UNIVERSITY, ORANGE COUNTY CAMPUS, Santa Ana, CA 92704

General Information Proprietary, coed, university. CGS member. *Enrollment:* 646 graduate, professional, and undergraduate students; 507 full-time matriculated graduate/professional students (293 women), 132 part-time matriculated graduate/professional students (75 women). *Enrollment by degree level:* 219 master's, 420 doctoral. *Graduate faculty:* 15 full-time (8 women), 72 part-time/adjunct (28 women). *Student services:* Campus employment opportunities, disabled student services, international student services, low-cost health insurance, teacher training, writing training. *Library facilities:* Carrie Lixey. *Online resources:* library catalog, access to other libraries' catalogs. *Collection:* 1,200 titles, 50 serial subscriptions.

Computer facilities: 12 computers available on campus for general student use. Internet access and online class registration are available. *Web address:* http://www.argosyu.edu/.

General Application Contact: Mark Betz, Director of Admissions, 800-716-9598, Fax: 714-437-1697, E-mail: mbetz@argosy.edu.

GRADUATE UNITS

College of Business Students: 163 full-time (64 women), 41 part-time (16 women). Average age 42. 72 applicants, 51 enrolled. *Faculty:* 4 full-time (1 woman), 20 part-time/adjunct (7 women). Expenses: Contact institution. *Financial support:* Federal Work-Study, institutionally sponsored loans, and scholarships/grants available. Support available to part-time students. Financial award applicants required to submit FAFSA. In 2006, 6 master's, 23 doctorates awarded. *Degree program information:* Part-time and evening/weekend programs available. Offers accounting (DBA, Adv C); customized professional concentration (MBA, DBA); finance (MBA, Certificate); healthcare administration (MBA, Certificate); information systems (DBA, Adv C); information systems management (MBA); international business (MBA, DBA, Adv C, Certificate); management (MBA, MSM, DBA, EDBA); mangement (Adv C); marketing (MBA, DBA, Adv C, Certificate); organizational leadership (Ed D); public administration (MBA, Certificate). *Application deadline:* Applications are processed on a rolling basis. *Application fee:* $50. Electronic applications accepted. *Application Contact:* Mark Betz, Director of Admissions, 800-716-9598, Fax: 714-437-1697, E-mail: mbetz@argosy.edu. *Dean,* Dr. Ray London, 800-716-9598, Fax: 714-437-1284, E-mail: auocadmissions@argosy.edu.

College of Education Students: 185 full-time (112 women), 49 part-time (28 women). Average age 37. 91 applicants, 76 enrolled. *Faculty:* 3 full-time (2 women), 33 part-time/adjunct (15 women). Expenses: Contact institution. *Financial support:* Federal Work-Study and scholarships/grants available. Support available to part-time students. Financial award applicants required to submit FAFSA. In 2006, 58 master's, 17 doctorates awarded. *Degree program information:* Part-time and evening/weekend programs available. Offers community college executive leadership (Ed D); educational leadership (MA Ed, Ed D); instructional leadership (MA Ed, Ed D). *Application deadline:* Applications are processed on a rolling basis. *Application fee:* $50. Electronic applications accepted. *Application Contact:* Mark Betz, Director of Admissions, 800-716-9598, Fax: 714-437-1697, E-mail: mbetz@argosy.edu. *Dean,* Dr. Christine Zeppos, 800-7196-9598, Fax: 714-437-1287, E-mail: czeppos@argosy.edu.

College of Psychology and Behavioral Sciences Students: 160 full-time (118 women), 41 part-time (30 women). Average age 30. 217 applicants, 69 enrolled. *Faculty:* 8 full-time (5 women), 19 part-time/adjunct (6 women). Expenses: Contact institution. *Financial support:* In 2006–07, 15 students received support. Career-related internships or fieldwork, Federal Work-Study, institutionally sponsored loans, and scholarships/grants available. Support available to part-time students. Financial award applicants required to submit FAFSA. In 2006, 6 master's, 2 doctorates awarded. *Degree program information:* Part-time and evening/weekend programs available. Offers child and adolescent psychology (Psy D); clinical psychology (Postdoctoral Respecialization Certificate); counseling psychology (Ed D); forensic psychology (Psy D); marriage and family therapy (MA); psychology and behavioral sciences (MA, Ed D, Psy D, Postdoctoral Respecialization Certificate). *Application deadline:* Applications are processed on a rolling basis. *Application fee:* $50. Electronic applications accepted. *Application Contact:* Mark Betz, Director of Admissions, 800-716-9598, Fax: 714-437-1697, E-mail: mbetz@argosy.edu. *Dean,* Dr. Gary Bruss, 800-716-9598, Fax: 714-437-1284, E-mail: gbruss@argosy.edu.

ARGOSY UNIVERSITY, PHOENIX CAMPUS, Phoenix, AZ 85021

General Information Proprietary, coed, upper-level institution. CGS member. *Enrollment:* 319 matriculated graduate/professional students. *Graduate faculty:* 64. *Graduate housing:* On-campus housing not available. *Student services:* Campus employment opportunities, career counseling, disabled student services, international student services, writing training. *Web address:* http://www.argosyu.edu/.

General Application Contact: Andy Hughes, Director of Admissions, 866-216-2777, Fax: 602-216-2601, E-mail: ahughes@argosy.edu.

GRADUATE UNITS

College of Business Students: 7 full-time (4 women); includes 2 minority (1 African American, 1 Hispanic American). *Faculty:* 1 full-time (0 women). Expenses: Contact institution. *Financial support:* In 2006–07, 2 students received support. Federal Work-Study, institutionally sponsored loans, and scholarships/grants available. Support available to part-time students. Financial award applicants required to submit FAFSA. *Degree program information:* Part-time and evening/weekend programs available. Offers accounting (DBA); customized professional concentration (MBA, DBA); finance (MBA); healthcare administration (MBA); information systems (DBA); information systems management (MBA); international business (MBA, DBA); management (MBA, DBA); marketing (MBA, DBA). *Application fee:* $50. *Application Contact:* Andy Hughes, Director of Admissions, 866-216-2777 Ext. 3110, Fax: 602-216-2601, E-mail: ahughes@argosyu.edu. *Program Chair,* Dr. Gary Berg, 866-216-2777, Fax: 602-216-2601.

College of Education Students: 26 full-time (17 women), 2 part-time (1 woman); includes 3 minority (2 African Americans, 1 Hispanic American). Average age 44. 10 applicants, 100% accepted, 9 enrolled. *Faculty:* 13 part-time/adjunct (4 women). Expenses: Contact institution. *Financial support:* Federal Work-Study available. Financial award applicants required to submit FAFSA. *Degree program information:* Part-time and evening/weekend programs available. Offers community college executive leadership (Ed D); educational leadership (MA Ed, Ed D, Ed S); instructional leadership (MA Ed, Ed D, Ed S). *Application deadline:* Applications are processed on a rolling basis. *Application fee:* $50. Electronic applications accepted. *Application Contact:* Andy Hughes, Director of Admissions, 866-216-2777, Fax: 602-216-2601, E-mail: ahughes@argosy.edu. *Director,* Dr. Gayle Schou, 866-216-2777, E-mail: argosyadmissions@argosy.edu.

College of Psychology and Behavioral Sciences Expenses: Contact institution. Offers clinical psychology (MA, Postdoctoral Respecialization Certificate); forensic psychology (MA); mental health counseling (MA); psychology and behavioral sciences (MA, Psy D, Postdoctoral Respecialization Certificate); school psychology (MA, Psy D); sport–exercise psychology (MA, Postdoctoral Respecialization Certificate); sports-exercise psychology (Psy D).

ARGOSY UNIVERSITY, SAN DIEGO CAMPUS, San Diego, CA 92108

General Information Proprietary, coed, upper-level institution. *Web address:* http://www.argosyu.edu/sandiego/.

GRADUATE UNITS

College of Business Expenses: Contact institution. Offers accounting (DBA); customized professional concentration (MBA, DBA); finance (MBA); information systems (DBA); information systems management (MBA); international business (MBA, DBA); management (MBA, MSM, DBA); marketing (MBA, DBA); public administration (MBA).

College of Education Expenses: Contact institution. Offers community college executive leadership (Ed D); educational leadership (MA Ed, Ed D); instructional leadership (MA Ed, Ed D).

College of Psychology and Behavioral Sciences Expenses: Contact institution. Offers clinical psychology (Psy D); clnical psychology/marriage and family therapy (MA); counseling psychology (MA, Ed D); counseling psychology/marriage and family therapy (MA).

ARGOSY UNIVERSITY, SAN FRANCISCO BAY AREA CAMPUS, Point Richmond, CA 94804-3547

General Information Proprietary, coed, upper-level institution. CGS member. *Enrollment:* 670 graduate, professional, and undergraduate students; 421 full-time matriculated graduate/professional students (323 women), 118 part-time matriculated graduate/professional students (75 women). *Enrollment by degree level:* 191 master's, 348 doctoral. *Graduate faculty:* 24 full-time (15 women), 57 part-time/adjunct (31 women). *Graduate housing:* On-campus housing not available. *Student services:* Campus employment opportunities, career counseling, disabled student services, international student services, low-cost health insurance, writing training. *Library facilities:* Argosy University. *Online resources:* library catalog, web page. *Collection:* 6,500 titles, 95 serial subscriptions, 950 audiovisual materials. *Web address:* http://www.argosyu.edu/.

General Application Contact: John Vincent Stofan, Director, Admissions, 510-215-0277, Fax: 510-215-0299, E-mail: jstofan@argosy.edu.

GRADUATE UNITS

College of Business Students: 29 full-time (8 women), 9 part-time (2 women); includes 30 minority (5 African Americans, 24 Asian Americans or Pacific Islanders, 1 Hispanic American). 21 applicants, 76% accepted, 13 enrolled. *Faculty:* 2 full-time (0 women), 9 part-time/adjunct (0 women). Expenses: Contact institution. *Financial support:* Federal Work-Study and scholarships/grants available. Support available to part-time students. Financial award applicants required to submit FAFSA. In 2006, 3 master's, 2 doctorates awarded. *Degree program information:* Part-time and evening/weekend programs available. Offers accounting (DBA); corporate compliance (MBA); customized professional concentration (MBA, DBA); finance (MBA); healthcare administration (MBA); information systems (DBA); information systems management (MBA); international business (MBA, DBA); management (MBA, MSM, DBA); marketing (MBA, DBA). *Application deadline:* For fall admission, 7/1 priority date for domestic and international students; for winter admission, 11/1 priority date for domestic and international students; for spring admission, 4/1 priority date for domestic and international students. Applications are processed on a rolling basis. *Application fee:* $50. Electronic applications accepted. *Application Contact:* John Vincent Stofan, Director of Admissions, 866-215-2727 Ext. 205, Fax: 510-215-0299, E-mail: jstofan@argosyu.edu. *Department Chair, Business and Information Technology,* Dr. Anthony Martinez, 866-215-0277, Fax: 510-215-0299, E-mail: amartinez@argosy.edu.

College of Education Students: 59 full-time (41 women), 30 part-time (14 women); includes 26 minority (11 African Americans, 11 Asian Americans or Pacific Islanders, 4 Hispanic Americans), 1 international. 34 applicants, 82% accepted, 20 enrolled. *Faculty:* 1 (woman) full-time, 14 part-time/adjunct. Expenses: Contact institution. *Financial support:* Career-related internships or fieldwork, Federal Work-Study, and scholarships/grants available. Support available to part-time students. Financial award application deadline: 4/20; financial award applicants required to submit FAFSA. In 2006, 7 degrees awarded. *Degree program information:* Part-time and evening/weekend programs available. Postbaccalaureate distance learning degree programs offered (minimal on-campus study). Offers community college executive leadership (Ed D); educational leadership (MA Ed, Ed D); instructional leadership (MA Ed, Ed D). *Application deadline:* For fall admission, 7/1 priority date for domestic students, 7/1 for international students; for winter admission, 11/1 priority date for domestic and international students; for spring admission, 4/1 priority date for domestic and international students. Applications are processed on a rolling basis. *Application fee:* $50. Electronic applications accepted. *Application Contact:* John Vincent Stofan, Director, Admissions, 510-215-0277, Fax: 510-215-0299, E-mail: jstofan@argosy.edu. Dr. Keyes Kelly, 510-837-3740, E-mail: kkelly@argosy.edu.

College of Psychology and Behavioral Sciences Students: 98 full-time (76 women), 57 part-time (41 women); includes 44 minority (8 African Americans, 3 American Indian/Alaska Native, 22 Asian Americans or Pacific Islanders, 11 Hispanic Americans). Average age 30. 230 applicants, 61% accepted, 59 enrolled. *Faculty:* 8 full-time (5 women), 5 part-time/adjunct (3 women). Expenses: Contact institution. *Financial support:* In 2006–07, teaching assistantships (averaging $1,200 per year); Federal Work-Study and scholarships/grants also available. Support available to part-time students. Financial award application deadline: 3/1; financial award applicants required to submit FAFSA. In 2006, 21 master's, 16 doctorates awarded. *Degree program information:* Part-time programs available. Offers clinical psychology (MA, Psy D); counseling psychology (MA); forensic psychology (MA); organizational leadership (Ed D). *Application deadline:* For fall admission, 1/15 priority date for domestic students, 3/1 priority date for international students; for spring admission, 10/15 priority date for domestic students, 11/1 priority date for international students. Applications are processed on a rolling basis. *Application fee:* $50. Electronic applications accepted. *Application Contact:* John Vincent Stofan, Director, Admissions, 510-215-0277, Fax: 510-215-0299, E-mail: jstofan@argosy.edu. *Clinical Psychology Department Head,* Dr. Andrea Morrison, 866-215-2777, Fax: 510-215-0299, E-mail: argosyadmissions@argosy.edu.

ARGOSY UNIVERSITY, SANTA MONICA CAMPUS, Santa Monica, CA 90405

General Information Proprietary, coed, university. *Web address:* http://www.argosyu.edu/santamonica/.

GRADUATE UNITS

College of Business Expenses: Contact institution. Offers accounting (DBA); customized professional concentration (MBA, DBA); finance (MBA); healthcare administration (MBA); information systems (DBA); information systems management (MBA); international business (MBA, DBA); management (MBA, MS, MSM, DBA); marketing (MBA, DBA).

College of Education Expenses: Contact institution. Offers community college executive leadership (Ed D); educational leadership (MA Ed, Ed D); instructional leadership (MA Ed, Ed D).

College of Psychology and Behavioral Sciences Expenses: Contact institution. Offers clinical psychology (MA); clinical psychology/marriage and family therapy (MA); counseling psychology (Ed D); counseling psychology/marriage and family therapy (MA); organizational leadership (Ed D).

ARGOSY UNIVERSITY, SARASOTA CAMPUS, Sarasota, FL 34235-8246

General Information Proprietary, coed, upper-level institution. CGS member. *Enrollment:* 1,400 full-time matriculated graduate/professional students (1,000 women), 600 part-time matriculated graduate/professional students (400 women). *Graduate faculty:* 37 full-time (19 women), 100 part-time/adjunct (44 women). *Graduate housing:* On-campus housing not available. *Student services:* Campus employment opportunities, campus safety program, career counseling, disabled student services, international student services. *Library facilities:* Doris Pickett Library. *Online resources:* library catalog, web page, access to other libraries' catalogs. *Collection:* 10,000 titles, 18,000 serial subscriptions, 300 audiovisual materials.

Computer facilities: 80 computers available on campus for general student use. A campuswide network can be accessed. Internet access and online class registration are available. *Web address:* http://www.sarasota.edu/.

General Application Contact: Dr. Linda Volz, Director of Admissions, 800-331-5995 Ext. 222, Fax: 941-379-5964, E-mail: lvolz@argosy.edu.

GRADUATE UNITS

College of Business 71 applicants, 92% accepted, 64 enrolled. *Faculty:* 6 full-time (3 women), 13 part-time/adjunct (5 women). Expenses: Contact institution. *Financial support:* Federal Work-Study and scholarships/grants available. Support available to part-time students. Financial award application deadline: 4/1; financial award applicants required to submit FAFSA. In 2006, 7 master's, 30 doctorates awarded. *Degree program information:* Part-time and evening/weekend programs available. Postbaccalaureate distance learning degree programs offered (minimal on-campus study). Offers accounting (DBA, Adv C); customized professional concentration (MBA, DBA); finance (MBA, Certificate); healtcare administration (Certificate);

healthcare administration (MBA); information systems (DBA, Adv C); information systems management (MBA, Certificate); international business (MBA, DBA, Adv C, Certificate); management (MBA, MSM, DBA); mangement (Adv C); marketing (MBA, DBA, Adv C, Certificate). *Application deadline:* Applications are processed on a rolling basis. *Application fee:* $50. Electronic applications accepted. *Application Contact:* Admissions Representative, 800-331-5995 Ext. 221, Fax: 941-379-5964. *Dean,* Dr. Kathleen Cornett, 800-331-5995, Fax: 941-379-9464, E-mail: kcornett@argosy.edu.

College of Education 149 applicants, 96% accepted, 121 enrolled. *Faculty:* 15 full-time (8 women), 49 part-time/adjunct (21 women). Expenses: Contact institution. *Financial support:* Federal Work-Study available. Support available to part-time students. Financial award application deadline: 4/1; financial award applicants required to submit FAFSA. In 2006, 9 master's, 141 doctorates awarded. *Degree program information:* Part-time and evening/weekend programs available. Postbaccalaureate distance learning degree programs offered (minimal on-campus study). Offers community college educational leadership (Ed D); educational leadership (MA Ed, Ed D, Ed S); instructional leadership (MA Ed, Ed D, Ed S). *Application deadline:* Applications are processed on a rolling basis. *Application fee:* $50. Electronic applications accepted. *Application Contact:* Admissions Representative, 800-331-5995 Ext. 221, Fax: 941-371-8910. *Dean,* Dr. Chuck Mlynarczyk, 800-331-5995, Fax: 941-371-9464, E-mail: cmlynarczyk@argosy.edu.

College of Psychology and Behavioral Sciences 183 applicants, 75% accepted, 108 enrolled. *Faculty:* 16 full-time (7 women), 38 part-time/adjunct (17 women). Expenses: Contact institution. *Financial support:* Federal Work-Study available. Support available to part-time students. Financial award application deadline: 4/1; financial award applicants required to submit FAFSA. In 2006, 14 master's, 24 doctorates awarded. *Degree program information:* Part-time and evening/weekend programs available. Postbaccalaureate distance learning degree programs offered (minimal on-campus study). Offers clinical psychology (Psy D); community counseling (MA); counseling psychology (Ed D); counselor education and supervision (Ed D); forensic psychology (MA); marriage and family therapy (MA); mental health counseling (MA); organizational leadership (Ed D); pastoral community counseling (Ed D); school counseling (MA, Ed S); school psychology (MA). *Application deadline:* Applications are processed on a rolling basis. *Application fee:* $50. Electronic applications accepted. *Application Contact:* Admissions Representative, 800-331-5995 Ext. 221, Fax: 941-371-8910. *Dean,* Dr. Douglas Riedmiller, 800-331-5995, Fax: 941-379-9464, E-mail: driedmiller@argosy.edu.

ARGOSY UNIVERSITY, SCHAUMBURG CAMPUS, Schaumburg, IL 60173-5403

General Information Proprietary, coed, upper-level institution. CGS member. *Enrollment by degree level:* 150 master's, 306 doctoral, 3 other advanced degrees. *Graduate faculty:* 47. *Graduate housing:* On-campus housing not available. *Student services:* Campus employment opportunities, campus safety program, career counseling, disabled student services, international student services. *Web address:* http://www.argosyu.edu/.

General Application Contact: Jamal Scott, Director of Admissions, 847-598-6159, Fax: 630-598-6191, E-mail: jscott@argosy.edu.

GRADUATE UNITS

College of Business Students: 36 full-time, 23 part-time. 13 applicants, 69% accepted, 9 enrolled. *Faculty:* 1 (woman) full-time, 7 part-time/adjunct (0 women). Expenses: Contact institution. *Financial support:* Federal Work-Study and scholarships/grants available. In 2006, 5 master's, 4 doctorates awarded. *Degree program information:* Part-time and evening/weekend programs available. Offers accounting (DBA, Adv C); corporate compliance (MBA); customized professional concentration (MBA, DBA); finance (MBA, Certificate); healthcare administration (MBA, Certificate); information systems (DBA, Adv C); information systems management (MBA, Certificate); international business (MBA, DBA, Adv C, Certificate); management (MBA, DBA, Adv C, Certificate); marketing (MBA, DBA, Adv C, Certificate). *Application deadline:* For fall admission, 3/15 priority date for domestic and international students; for spring admission, 10/15 priority date for domestic and international students. Applications are processed on a rolling basis. *Application fee:* $50. Electronic applications accepted. *Application Contact:* Jamal Scott, Director of Admissions, 847-598-6159, Fax: 630-598-6191, E-mail: jscott@argosy.edu. *Dean,* Dr. Harriet Kandelman, 866-290-2777, Fax: 847-548-6159, E-mail: agrosyadmissions@argosy.edu.

College of Education Students: 19 full-time, 19 part-time. 15 applicants, 80% accepted, 10 enrolled. *Faculty:* 1 (woman) full-time, 7 part-time/adjunct (3 women). Expenses: Contact institution. *Financial support:* Federal Work-Study and scholarships/grants available. In 2006, 1 master's, 3 doctorates, 2 other advanced degrees awarded. *Degree program information:* Part-time and evening/weekend programs available. Offers community college executive leadership (Ed D); educational leadership (MA Ed, Ed D, Ed S); instructional leadership (MA Ed, Ed D, Ed S). *Application deadline:* For fall admission, 3/15 priority date for domestic and international students; for spring admission, 10/15 priority date for domestic and international students. Applications are processed on a rolling basis. *Application fee:* $50. Electronic applications accepted. *Application Contact:* Jamal Scott, Application Contact, 866-290-7400, Fax: 630-598-6191, E-mail: jscott@argosy.edu. *Program Chair,* Dr. Narjis Hyder, 866-290-7400, Fax: 847-598-6158, E-mail: nhyder@argosy.edu.

College of Psychology and Behavioral Sciences Students: 273 full-time, 89 part-time. 220 applicants, 57% accepted, 83 enrolled. Expenses: Contact institution. *Financial support:* In 2006–07, 40 students received support, including 2 fellowships, 30 teaching assistantships; career-related internships or fieldwork, Federal Work-Study, and scholarships/grants also available. Support available to part-time students. In 2006, 52 master's, 18 doctorates awarded. *Degree program information:* Evening/weekend programs available. Offers clinical health psychology (Post-Graduate Certificate); clinical psychology (MA, Psy D); community counseling (MA); counseling psychology (Ed D); counselor education and supervision (Ed D); forensic psychology (MA, Post-Graduate Certificate); organizational leadership (Ed D); professional counseling (MA). *Application deadline:* For fall admission, 1/15 priority date for domestic and international students; for spring admission, 10/15 priority date for domestic and international students. Applications are processed on a rolling basis. *Application fee:* $50. Electronic applications accepted. *Application Contact:* Jamal Scott, Director of Admissions, 866-290-2777, Fax: 847-598-6191, E-mail: jscott@argosy.edu. *Dean,* Dr. Jim Wasner, 866-290-2777, Fax: 847-598-6158, E-mail: argosyadmissions@argosy.edu.

ARGOSY UNIVERSITY, SEATTLE CAMPUS, Seattle, WA 98121

General Information Proprietary, coed, upper-level institution. CGS member. *Enrollment:* 235 full-time matriculated graduate/professional students (180 women), 149 part-time matriculated graduate/professional students (101 women). *Enrollment by degree level:* 195 master's, 189 doctoral. *Graduate faculty:* 17 full-time (11 women), 19 part-time/adjunct (11 women). *Graduate housing:* On-campus housing not available. *Student services:* Campus employment opportunities, career counseling, disabled student services, international student services, low-cost health insurance, writing training. *Web address:* http://www.argosyu.edu/.

General Application Contact: Josh Pond, Director of Admissions, 206-283-4500, Fax: 206-283-5777, E-mail: jpond@argosy.edu.

GRADUATE UNITS

College of Business 1 applicant, 100% accepted, 1 enrolled. Expenses: Contact institution. *Financial support:* Federal Work-Study and unspecified assistantships available. Support available to part-time students. Financial award applicants required to submit FAFSA. In 2006, 1 degree awarded. *Degree program information:* Part-time and evening/weekend programs available. Offers accounting (DBA); customized professional concentration (MBA, DBA); finance (MBA); healthcare administration (MBA); information systems (DBA); information systems management (MBA); international business (MBA, DBA); management (MSM, DBA); mangement (MBA); marketing (MBA, DBA). *Application deadline:* For fall admission, 4/15 priority date for domestic students, 4/15 for international students; for winter admission, 10/15 priority date for domestic students. Applications are processed on a rolling basis. *Application fee:* $50. Electronic applications accepted. *Application Contact:* Heather Simpson, Director of Admissions, 866-283-4500, Fax: 206-283-5777, E-mail: hsimpson@argosy.edu. *Chair,* Dr. Kylene Quinn, 206-393-3543, Fax: 206-283-5777, E-mail: kquinn@argosy.edu.

College of Education Students: 29 full-time, 15 part-time. Expenses: Contact institution. *Financial support:* Teaching assistantships with partial tuition reimbursements, Federal Work-Study, scholarships/grants, and unspecified assistantships available. Support available to part-time students. Financial award application deadline: 4/19; financial award applicants required to submit FAFSA. *Degree program information:* Part-time and evening/weekend programs available. Offers community college executive leadership (Ed D); education (MA Ed); educational leadership (MA Ed, Ed D); instructional leadership (MA Ed, Ed D). *Application deadline:* For fall admission, 4/15 priority date for domestic students, 4/15 for international students. *Application fee:* $50. *Application Contact:* Josh Pond, Director of Admissions, 206-283-4500, Fax: 206-283-5777, E-mail: jpond@argosyu.edu. *Chair of Education,* Dr. Leslie Aune Oja, 206-393-3570, Fax: 206-283-5777, E-mail: ioja@argosy.edu.

College of Psychology and Behavioral Sciences Expenses: Contact institution. Offers clinical psychology (MA, Psy D); counseling psychology (MA, Ed D); psychology and behavioral sciences (MA, Ed D, Psy D). *Chair,* Dr. Francine Parks, 206-283-4500.

ARGOSY UNIVERSITY, TAMPA CAMPUS, Tampa, FL 33614

General Information Proprietary, coed, upper-level institution. CGS member. *Enrollment:* 385 full-time matriculated graduate/professional students (304 women), 184 part-time matriculated graduate/professional students (146 women). *Enrollment by degree level:* 272 master's, 285 doctoral, 12 other advanced degrees. *Graduate faculty:* 6. *Student services:* Campus employment opportunities, disabled student services, international student services. *Library facilities:* Main library plus 1 other. *Online resources:* library catalog, web page. *Collection:* 10,000 serial subscriptions. *Web address:* http://www.argosyu.edu/.

General Application Contact: Susan Beecroft, Campus Administration Coordinator, 800-850-6488, Fax: 813-246-4045, E-mail: argosyadmissions@argosy.edu.

GRADUATE UNITS

College of Business Expenses: Contact institution. Offers accounting (DBA); customized professional concentration (MBA, DBA); finance (MBA, Certificate); healthcare administration (MBA, Certificate); information systems (DBA); information systems management (MBA); international business (MBA, DBA, Certificate); management (MBA, MSM, DBA); marketing (MBA, DBA, Certificate); public administration (MBA). *Dean,* Dr. Andrew Ghillyer, 813-393-5270, E-mail: aghillyer@argosy.edu.

College of Education *Faculty:* 1 (woman) full-time, 8 part-time/adjunct (3 women). Expenses: Contact institution. Offers community college executive leadership (Ed D); educational leadership (MA Ed, Ed D, Ed S); instructional leadership (MA Ed, Ed D, Ed S). *Application deadline:* Applications are processed on a rolling basis. *Application fee:* $50. Electronic applications accepted. *Head,* Dr. Patty O'Grady, 813-246-4419, Fax: 813-246-4045, E-mail: pogrady@argosy.edu.

College of Psychology and Behavioral Sciences Expenses: Contact institution. Offers clinical psychology (MA, Psy D); counselor education and supervision (Ed D); marriage and family therapy (MA); mental health counseling (MA); organizational leadership (Ed D); school counseling (MA).

Program in Clinical Psychology Students: 110 full-time (80 women), 20 part-time (16 women). Average age 32. 135 applicants, 26% accepted, 22 enrolled. *Faculty:* 6 full-time (3 women), 4 part-time/adjunct (2 women). Expenses: Contact institution. *Financial support:* In 2006–07, 3 research assistantships with partial tuition reimbursements were awarded; teaching assistantships with partial tuition reimbursements, Federal Work-Study, scholarships/grants, and unspecified assistantships also available. Support available to part-time students. Financial award applicants required to submit FAFSA. In 2006, 12 master's, 2 doctorates awarded. Offers child and adolescent psychology (MA); clinical psychology (Psy D); geropsychology (MA); marriage/couples and family therapy (MA); neuropsychology (MA). *Application deadline:* For fall admission, 1/15 priority date for domestic students; for spring admission, 10/15 priority date for domestic students. Applications are processed on a rolling basis. *Application fee:* $50. *Department Head,* Dr. Melanie Storms, 813-246-4419, Fax: 813-246-4045, E-mail: mstorms@argosy.edu.

ARGOSY UNIVERSITY, TWIN CITIES CAMPUS, Eagan, MN 55121

General Information Proprietary, coed, university. *Enrollment:* 1,700 graduate, professional, and undergraduate students; 406 full-time matriculated graduate/professional students (309 women), 219 part-time matriculated graduate/professional students (178 women). *Enrollment by degree level:* 266 master's, 316 doctoral. *Graduate faculty:* 19 full-time (10 women), 73 part-time/adjunct (33 women). *Student services:* Campus safety program, career counseling, disabled student services, free psychological counseling, international student services, low-cost health insurance, writing training. *Library facilities:* Argosy University/Twin Cities Library. *Online resources:* library catalog, web page, access to other libraries' catalogs. *Collection:* 9,000 titles, 160 serial subscriptions.

Computer facilities: 50 computers available on campus for general student use. Internet access and online class registration are available. *Web address:* http://www.argosyu.edu/.

General Application Contact: Jennifer Radke, 2nd Director of Graduate Admissions, 651-846-3300, Fax: 651-994-7954, E-mail: tcadmissions@argosy.edu.

GRADUATE UNITS

College of Business Students: 47 full-time (23 women), 20 part-time (11 women); includes 21 minority (10 African Americans, 1 American Indian/Alaska Native, 9 Asian Americans or Pacific Islanders, 1 Hispanic American). Average age 39. 72 applicants, 76% accepted, 45 enrolled. *Faculty:* 1 (woman) full-time, 20 part-time/adjunct (6 women). Expenses: Contact institution. *Financial support:* In 2006–07, 3 fellowships with partial tuition reimbursements, 3 teaching assistantships with partial tuition reimbursements were awarded; Federal Work-Study and scholarships/grants also available. Financial award applicants required to submit FAFSA. In 2006, 6 degrees awarded. *Degree program information:* Part-time and evening/weekend programs available. Offers accounting (DBA); corporate compliance (MBA); customized professional certification (DBA); customized professional concentration (MBA); finance (MBA); healthcare administration (MBA); information systems (DBA); information systems management (MBA); international business (MBA, DBA); management (MBA, MSM, DBA, EDBA); marketing (MBA, DBA). *Application deadline:* For fall admission, 5/15 priority date for domestic students, 5/15 for international students; for spring admission, 10/15 priority date for domestic students, 10/15 for international students. Applications are processed on a rolling basis. *Application fee:* $50. Electronic applications accepted. *Application Contact:* Jennifer Radke, 2nd Director of Graduate Admissions, 651-846-3300, Fax: 651-994-7954, E-mail: tcadmissions@argosy.edu. *Department Head,* Dr. Paula King, 651-846-3377, E-mail: pking@argosy.edu.

College of Education Students: 30 full-time (22 women), 12 part-time (9 women); includes 3 minority (1 African American, 1 American Indian/Alaska Native, 1 Asian American or Pacific Islander). Average age 45. 35 applicants, 86% accepted, 12 enrolled. *Faculty:* 1 full-time (0 women), 10 part-time/adjunct (4 women). Expenses: Contact institution. *Financial support:* In 2006–07, 12 fellowships with partial tuition reimbursements, 3 teaching assistantships with partial tuition reimbursements were awarded; Federal Work-Study and scholarships/grants also available. Financial award applicants required to submit FAFSA. In 2006, 1 master's, 6 doctorates awarded. *Degree program information:* Part-time and evening/weekend programs available. Offers educational leadership (MA Ed, Ed D, Ed S); instructional leadership (MA Ed, Ed D, Ed S). *Application deadline:* For fall admission, 5/15 priority date for domestic students, 5/15 for international students; for spring admission, 10/15 priority date for domestic students, 10/15 for international students. Applications are processed on a rolling basis. *Application fee:* $50. Electronic applications accepted. *Application Contact:* Jennifer Radke, 2nd Director of Graduate Admissions, 651-846-3300, Fax: 651-994-7954, E-mail: tcadmissions@argosy.edu. *Program Chair,* Dr. David Lange, 888-844-2004.

College of Psychology and Behavioral Sciences Students: 331 full-time (266 women), 149 part-time (121 women); includes 46 minority (7 African Americans, 5 American Indian/

Argosy University, Twin Cities Campus (continued)

Alaska Native, 19 Asian Americans or Pacific Islanders, 15 Hispanic Americans). Average age 32. 349 applicants, 63% accepted, 161 enrolled. *Faculty:* 17 full-time (9 women), 33 part-time/adjunct (13 women). Expenses: Contact institution. *Financial support:* In 2006–07, 454 students received support, including 8 fellowships with partial tuition reimbursements available (averaging $3,000 per year), 40 teaching assistantships with partial tuition reimbursements available (averaging $1,950 per year); career-related internships or fieldwork, Federal Work-Study, and scholarships/grants also available. Support available to part-time students. Financial award application deadline: 3/15; financial award applicants required to submit FAFSA. In 2006, 46 master's, 47 doctorates awarded. *Degree program information:* Part-time programs available. Offers clinical psychology (MA, Psy D, Postdoctoral Respecialization Certificate); forensic counseling (Post-Graduate Certificate); marriage and family therapy (MA, Post-Graduate Certificate). *Application deadline:* For fall admission, 5/15 priority date for domestic students, 5/15 for international students; for spring admission, 10/15 priority date for domestic students, 10/15 for international students. Applications are processed on a rolling basis. *Application fee:* $50. Electronic applications accepted. *Application Contact:* Jennifer Radke, 2nd Director of Admissions, 651-846-3300, Fax: 651-994-7954, E-mail: tcadmissions@argusyu.edu. *Dean,* Dr. Kenneth Solberg, 888-844-2004, E-mail: tcadmissions@argosy.edu.

ARGOSY UNIVERSITY, WASHINGTON DC CAMPUS, Arlington, VA 22209

General Information Proprietary, coed, upper-level institution. CGS member. *Enrollment:* 687 full-time matriculated graduate/professional students (572 women), 239 part-time matriculated graduate/professional students (190 women). *Enrollment by degree level:* 392 master's, 532 doctoral, 2 other advanced degrees. *Graduate faculty:* 26 full-time (17 women), 50 part-time/adjunct (34 women). *Graduate housing:* On-campus housing not available. *Student services:* Campus employment opportunities, career counseling, disabled student services, free psychological counseling, international student services, low-cost health insurance, writing training. *Web address:* http://www.argosyu.edu/.

General Application Contact: Emily Peck, Director of Admissions, 866-703-2777 Ext. 5851, Fax: 703-526-5850, E-mail: dcadmissions@argosy.edu.

GRADUATE UNITS

College of Business Students: 5 full-time (4 women), 4 part-time (1 woman); includes 4 minority (3 African Americans, 1 Asian American or Pacific Islander). 21 applicants, 86% accepted. *Faculty:* 1 full-time (0 women), 5 part-time/adjunct (2 women). Expenses: Contact institution. *Financial support:* Federal Work-Study and scholarships/grants available. Financial award applicants required to submit FAFSA. Offers accounting (DBA); customized professional concentration (MBA, DBA); finance (MBA); healthcare administration (MBA); information systems (DBA); information systems management (MBA); international business (MBA, DBA); international business marketing (Graduate Certificate); management (MBA, DBA); marketing (MBA, DBA). *Application deadline:* For fall admission, 6/15 priority date for domestic students; for spring admission, 10/15 priority date for domestic students. *Application fee:* $50. *Application Contact:* Emily Peck, Director of Admissions, 866-703-2777 Ext. 5851, Fax: 703-526-5850, E-mail: dcadmissions@argosy.edu. *Academic Affairs Officer,* Dr. Colleen Logan, 866-703-2777, Fax: 703-521-5850, E-mail: dcadmissions@argosy.edu.

College of Education Students: 22 full-time (16 women), 11 part-time (6 women); includes 24 minority (all African Americans) Average age 45. 16 applicants, 69% accepted, 9 enrolled. *Faculty:* 2 full-time (1 woman), 2 part-time/adjunct (0 women). Expenses: Contact institution. *Financial support:* Federal Work-Study and scholarships/grants available. Financial award applicants required to submit FAFSA. In 2006, 1 degree awarded. *Degree program information:* Part-time and evening/weekend programs available. Offers educational leadership (MA Ed, Ed D, Ed S); instructional leadership (MA Ed, Ed D, Ed S). *Application deadline:* For fall admission, 6/15 priority date for domestic and international students; for spring admission, 10/15 priority date for domestic and international students. Applications are processed on a rolling basis. *Application fee:* $50. Electronic applications accepted. *Application Contact:* Emily Peck, Director of Admissions, 866-703-2777 Ext. 5851, Fax: 703-526-5850, E-mail: dcadmissions@argosy.edu. *Academic Affairs Officer,* Dr. Colleen Logan, 866-703-2777, Fax: 703-521-5850, E-mail: dcadmissions@argosy.edu.

College of Psychology and Behavioral Sciences 585 applicants, 56% accepted, 218 enrolled. Expenses: Contact institution. Postbaccalaureate distance learning degree programs offered (minimal on-campus study). Offers psychology and behavioral sciences (MA, Ed D, Psy D, Postdoctoral Respecialization Certificate). *Application deadline:* For fall admission, 8/1 priority date for domestic students; for winter admission, 11/1 priority date for domestic students; for spring admission, 4/1 priority date for domestic students. Applications are processed on a rolling basis. *Application fee:* $50. Electronic applications accepted. *Application Contact:* Emily Peck, Director of Admissions, 866-703-2777 Ext. 5851, Fax: 703-526-5850, E-mail: dcadmissions@argosy.edu. *President,* Dr. Steve Sorkin, 866-703-2777.

Professional Programs in Psychology Students: 620 full-time (521 women), 209 part-time (173 women); includes 316 minority (239 African Americans, 5 American Indian/Alaska Native, 35 Asian Americans or Pacific Islanders, 37 Hispanic Americans). Average age 34. 518 applicants, 59% accepted, 193 enrolled. *Faculty:* 23 full-time (15 women), 51 part-time/adjunct (34 women). Expenses: Contact institution. *Financial support:* In 2006–07, 462 students received support, including 2 fellowships with tuition reimbursements available (averaging $3,600 per year), 50 teaching assistantships with full and partial tuition reimbursements available (averaging $2,040 per year); research assistantships, career-related internships or fieldwork, Federal Work-Study, and scholarships/grants also available. Support available to part-time students. Financial award applicants required to submit FAFSA. In 2006, 46 master's, 67 doctorates awarded. Postbaccalaureate distance learning degree programs offered (minimal on-campus study). Offers clinical psychology (MA, Psy D, Postdoctoral Respecialization Certificate); community counseling (MA); counseling psychology (Ed D); forensic psychology (MA); organizational leadership (Ed D). *Application deadline:* For fall admission, 1/15 priority date for domestic students. Applications are processed on a rolling basis. *Application fee:* $50. Electronic applications accepted. *Application Contact:* Emily Peck, Director of Admissions, 866-703-2777 Ext. 5851, Fax: 703-526-5850, E-mail: dcadmissions@argosy.edu.

ARIZONA SCHOOL OF ACUPUNCTURE AND ORIENTAL MEDICINE, Tucson, AZ 85712

General Information Proprietary, coed, graduate-only institution.

GRADUATE UNITS

Graduate Programs

ARIZONA STATE UNIVERSITY, Tempe, AZ 85287

General Information State-supported, coed, university. CGS member. *Graduate housing:* Room and/or apartments available to single students; on-campus housing not available to married students. *Research affiliation:* Semiconductor Industries, Aerospace Industries, Arizona State University Research Park Facilities and Partnerships with Industry, Architecture Research Centers Consortium, Southwest Center for Environmental Research and Policy, Industrial University Cooperative Center for Health Management Research.

GRADUATE UNITS

College of Law Offers law (JD).

Division of Graduate Studies *Degree program information:* Part-time programs available. Offers science and engineering of materials (MS, PhD); statistics (MS); transportation systems (Certificate).

College of Architecture and Environmental Design Offers architecture (M Arch); architecture and environmental design (M Arch, MEP, MS, MSD, PhD); building design (MS); design (MSD, PhD); history, theory, and criticism (PhD); planning (MEP, PhD).

College of Education *Degree program information:* Part-time programs available. Offers counseling (M Ed, MC); counseling psychology (PhD); curriculum and instruction (M Ed, MA, Ed D, PhD); education (M Ed, MA, MC, Ed D, PhD); educational administration and supervision (M Ed, Ed D); educational leadership and policy studies (M Ed, MA, Ed D, PhD); educational psychology (M Ed, MA, PhD); higher and post-secondary education (M Ed, Ed D); learning and instructional technology (M Ed, MA, PhD); psychology in education (M Ed, MA, MC, PhD); social and philosophical foundations of education (MA); special education (M Ed, MA).

College of Fine Arts Offers art (MA, MFA); dance (MFA); fine arts (MA, MFA, MM, DMA, PhD); music (MA, MM, DMA); theater (MA, MFA, PhD).

College of Liberal Arts and Sciences Offers anthropology (MA, PhD); applied mathematics (MA, PhD); Asian history (MA, PhD); audiology (Au D); behavior (MS, PhD); behavioral neuroscience (PhD); biology (MNS); biology education (MS, PhD); British history (MA, PhD); cell and developmental biology (MS, PhD); chemistry and biochemistry (MNS, MS, PhD); clinical psychology (PhD); cognitive/behavioral systems (PhD); communication (PhD); communication disorders (MS); computational biosciences (MS, PSM); computational, statistical, and mathematical biology (MS, PhD); conservation (MS, PhD); creative writing (MFA); demography and population studies (MA, PhD); developmental psychology (PhD); ecology (MS, PhD); English (MA, PhD); environmental psychology (PhD); European history (MA, PhD); evolution (MS, PhD); exercise science (PhD); family and human development (MS); family science (PhD); French (MA); genetics (MS, PhD); geography (MA, MAS, PhD); geological engineering (MS, PhD); German (MA); history and philosophy of biology (MS, PhD); humanities (MA, MFA, MTESL, PhD); justice and social inquiry (MS, PhD); kinesiology (MS, PhD); Latin American studies (MA, PhD); liberal arts and sciences (MA, MAS, MFA, MNS, MPE, MS, MTESL, PSM, Au D, PhD); mathematics (MA, MNS, PhD); microbiology (MNS, MS, PhD); molecular and cellular biology (MS, PhD); natural science (MNS); natural sciences and mathematics (MA, MNS, MS, PSM, Au D, PhD); neuroscience (MS, PhD); philosophy (MA, PhD); physics and astronomy (MNS, MS, PhD); physiology (MS, PhD); political science (MA, PhD); public history (MA); quantitative research methods (PhD); religious studies (MA, PhD); social psychology (PhD); social sciences (MA, MAS, MS, PhD); sociology (MA, PhD); Spanish (MA, PhD); speech and hearing science (MS, Au D, PhD); speech and interpersonal communication (MA); statistics (MA, PhD); teaching English as a second language (MTESL); U.S. history (PhD); U.S. western history (MA).

College of Nursing Offers nursing (MS).

College of Public Programs Offers journalism and mass communication (MMC); public affairs (MPA, PhD); public programs (MA, MMC, MPA, MS, MSW, PhD); recreation (MS); social work (MSW, PhD).

The Ira A. Fulton School of Engineering *Degree program information:* Part-time programs available. Offers aerospace engineering (MS, MSE, PhD); bioengineering (MS, PhD); chemical engineering (MS, MSE, PhD); civil engineering (MS, MSE, PhD); computer science (MCS, MS, PhD); construction (MS); electrical engineering (MS, MSE, PhD); engineering (M Eng, MCS, MS, MSE, PhD); engineering science (MS, MSE, PhD); industrial engineering (MS, MSE, PhD); materials science and engineering (MS, MSE, PhD); mechanical engineering (MS, MSE, PhD).

W.P. Carey School of Business *Degree program information:* Part-time programs available. Offers accountancy (PhD); accountancy and information management (M Tax, MAIS); business (M Tax, MAIS, MBA, MHSM, MPH, MS, PhD); business administration (MBA); economics (MS, PhD); finance (PhD); health management and policy (MHSM, MPH); health services research (PhD); information management (PhD); information systems (MS); management (PhD); marketing (PhD); supply chain management (PhD).

ARIZONA STATE UNIVERSITY AT THE DOWNTOWN PHOENIX CAMPUS, Phoenix, AZ 85004

General Information State-supported, coed, comprehensive institution.

ARIZONA STATE UNIVERSITY AT THE POLYTECHNIC CAMPUS, Mesa, AZ 85212

General Information State-supported, coed, comprehensive institution. *Enrollment:* 6,545 graduate, professional, and undergraduate students; 268 full-time matriculated graduate/professional students (178 women), 446 part-time matriculated graduate/professional students (234 women). *Enrollment by degree level:* 701 master's, 13 doctoral. *Graduate faculty:* 97 full-time (23 women). Tuition, state resident: part-time $310 per credit hour. Tuition, nonresident: part-time $688 per credit hour. *Graduate housing:* Rooms and/or apartments available on a first-come, first-served basis to single and married students. Typical cost: $5,150 per year ($7,050 including board) for single students; $4,450 per year ($6,350 including board) for married students. Room and board charges vary according to board plan, campus/location and housing facility selected. Housing application deadline: 3/31. *Student services:* Campus employment opportunities, career counseling, child daycare facilities, disabled student services, exercise/wellness program, free psychological counseling, grant writing training, international student services, low-cost health insurance, teacher training, writing training. *Library facilities:* ASU East Library Services at the Polytechnic campus plus 1 other. *Online resources:* library catalog, web page, access to other libraries' catalogs. *Collection:* 4.1 million titles, 33,122 serial subscriptions, 100,838 audiovisual materials.

Computer facilities: Computer purchase and lease plans are available. 456 computers available on campus for general student use. A campuswide network can be accessed from off campus. Internet access and online class registration, specialized software applications are available. *Web address:* http://www.poly.asu.edu/.

General Application Contact: Dr. Glenn Irvin, Vice Provost Academic Programs, 480-727-1435, Fax: 480-727-1876, E-mail: glenn.irvin@asu.edu.

GRADUATE UNITS

College of Science and Technology Students: 104 full-time (48 women), 278 part-time (112 women); includes 52 minority (9 African Americans, 7 American Indian/Alaska Native, 16 Asian Americans or Pacific Islanders, 20 Hispanic Americans), 105 international. Average age 33. 295 applicants, 91% accepted, 110 enrolled. *Faculty:* 38 full-time (4 women). Expenses: Contact institution. *Financial support:* In 2006–07, 32 research assistantships with full and partial tuition reimbursements (averaging $8,965 per year), 3 teaching assistantships with full and partial tuition reimbursements (averaging $6,166 per year) were awarded; career-related internships or fieldwork, Federal Work-Study, scholarships/grants, health care benefits, tuition waivers (full and partial), and unspecified assistantships also available. Support available to part-time students. Financial award application deadline: 3/1; financial award applicants required to submit FAFSA. In 2006, 74 degrees awarded. *Degree program information:* Part-time and evening/weekend programs available. Offers aeronautical management technology (MS); electronic systems (MS); mechanical and manufacturing engineering technology (MS); science and technology (MCST, MS); technology management (MS). *Application deadline:* Applications are processed on a rolling basis. *Application fee:* $50. Electronic applications accepted. *Interim Dean,* Dr. Timothy Lindquist, 480-727-2783, Fax: 480-727-1089, E-mail: timothy.lindquist@asu.edu.

Division of Computing Studies Students: 37 full-time (22 women), 36 part-time (21 women); includes 8 minority (1 African American, 6 Asian Americans or Pacific Islanders, 1 Hispanic American), 47 international. Average age 27. 58 applicants, 71% accepted, 15 enrolled. *Faculty:* 6 full-time (0 women). Expenses: Contact institution. *Financial support:* In 2006–07, 6 research assistantships with full and partial tuition reimbursements (averaging $9,500 per year), 2 teaching assistantships with full and partial tuition reimbursements (averaging $6,875 per year) were awarded; career-related internships or fieldwork, Federal Work-Study, scholarships/grants, health care benefits, tuition waivers (full and partial), and unspecified assistantships also available. Support available to part-time students. Financial award application deadline: 3/1; financial award applicants required to submit FAFSA. In 2006, 24 degrees awarded. *Degree program information:* Part-time programs available. Offers computing studies (MCST); technology (MS). *Application fee:* $50. *Application Contact:* Betsy Allen, Coordinator of Academic Programs, 480-727-1029, Fax: 480-727-1248, E-mail: emallen@asu.edu. *Division Chair,* Dr. Ben Huey, 480-727-1590, Fax: 480-727-1248, E-mail: ben.huey@asu.edu.

East College Students: 150 full-time (124 women), 155 part-time (114 women); includes 24 minority (3 African Americans, 2 American Indian/Alaska Native, 6 Asian Americans or Pacific Islanders, 13 Hispanic Americans), 4 international. Average age 33. 189 applicants, 73% accepted, 104 enrolled. *Faculty:* 44 full-time (17 women). Expenses: Contact institution. *Financial support:* In 2006–07, 1 fellowship (averaging $15,000 per year), 8 research assistantships with partial tuition reimbursements (averaging $13,622 per year), 20 teaching assistantships (averaging $11,758 per year) were awarded; career-related internships or fieldwork and unspecified assistantships also available. Financial award application deadline: 3/1. In 2006, 41 degrees awarded. Offers applied biological sciences (MS); applied psychology (MS); exercise and wellness (MS); human nutrition (MS); physical activity, nutrition and wellness (PhD). *Application deadline:* Applications are processed on a rolling basis. *Application fee:* $50. Electronic applications accepted. *Dean,* Dr. David Schwalm, 480-727-1418, E-mail: david.schwalm@asu.edu.

Morrison School of Management and Agribusiness Students: 14 full-time (6 women), 13 part-time (8 women); includes 4 minority (1 African American, 1 American Indian/Alaska Native, 1 Asian American or Pacific Islander, 1 Hispanic American), 6 international. Average age 33. 19 applicants, 74% accepted, 11 enrolled. *Faculty:* 15 full-time (2 women). Expenses: Contact institution. *Financial support:* In 2006–07, 12 research assistantships with full and partial tuition reimbursements (averaging $7,457 per year) were awarded; fellowships, teaching assistantships with partial tuition reimbursements, career-related internships or fieldwork, Federal Work-Study, institutionally sponsored loans, scholarships/grants, health care benefits, and tuition waivers (full and partial) also available. Support available to part-time students. Financial award application deadline: 3/1; financial award applicants required to submit CSS PROFILE or FAFSA. In 2006, 13 degrees awarded. *Degree program information:* Part-time and evening/weekend programs available. Offers agribusiness (MS). *Application deadline:* Applications are processed on a rolling basis. *Application fee:* $50. Electronic applications accepted. *Application Contact:* Dr. Troy Schmitz, Associate Professor of Agribusiness, 480-727-1566, Fax: 480-727-1946, E-mail: troy.schmitz@asu.edu. *Dean,* Dr. Paul Patterson, 480-727-1124, Fax: 480-727-1961, E-mail: paul.patterson@asu.edu.

ARIZONA STATE UNIVERSITY AT THE WEST CAMPUS, Phoenix, AZ 85069-7100

General Information State-supported, coed, comprehensive institution. *Enrollment:* 8,211 graduate, professional, and undergraduate students; 372 full-time matriculated graduate/professional students (285 women), 623 part-time matriculated graduate/professional students (385 women). *Enrollment by degree level:* 768 master's, 20 doctoral, 207 other advanced degrees. *Graduate faculty:* 81 full-time (40 women), 41 part-time/adjunct (30 women). Tuition, state resident: full-time $5,930. Tuition, nonresident: full-time $16,516. Tuition and fees vary according to course load. *Graduate housing:* Room and/or apartments available on a first-come, first-served basis to single students; on-campus housing not available to married students. Typical cost: $4,700 per year. *Student services:* Campus employment opportunities, campus safety program, career counseling, child daycare facilities, disabled student services, exercise/wellness program, free psychological counseling, international student services, low-cost health insurance, multicultural affairs office, writing training. *Library facilities:* Fletcher Library at the West campus. *Online resources:* library catalog, web page, access to other libraries' catalogs. *Collection:* 348,697 titles, 2,422 serial subscriptions.

Computer facilities: 400 computers available on campus for general student use. A campuswide network can be accessed from off campus. Internet access and online class registration are available. *Web address:* http://www.west.asu.edu/.

General Application Contact: Marge A. Williams, Student Support Coordinator, 602-543-4567, Fax: 602-543-4561, E-mail: marge.williams@asu.edu.

GRADUATE UNITS

College of Human Services Students: 144 full-time (122 women), 59 part-time (44 women); includes 47 minority (13 African Americans, 6 American Indian/Alaska Native, 6 Asian Americans or Pacific Islanders, 22 Hispanic Americans), 2 international. Average age 34. 136 applicants, 71% accepted, 70 enrolled. *Faculty:* 21 full-time (10 women), 12 part-time/adjunct (9 women). Expenses: Contact institution. *Financial support:* In 2006–07, 3 research assistantships with partial tuition reimbursements (averaging $7,025 per year) were awarded; career-related internships or fieldwork, Federal Work-Study, scholarships/grants, traineeships, tuition waivers (full and partial), and unspecified assistantships also available. Support available to part-time students. Financial award applicants required to submit FAFSA. In 2006, 83 degrees awarded. *Degree program information:* Part-time and evening/weekend programs available. Offers communication (MA); communication/human relations (Certificate); criminal justice (MA); gerontology (Certificate); human services (MA, MSW, Certificate); social work (MSW). *Application deadline:* Applications are processed on a rolling basis. *Application fee:* $50. Electronic applications accepted. *Application Contact:* Information Contact, 602-543-6600, Fax: 602-543-6651, E-mail: cohs@asu.edu. *Dean,* Dr. John Hepburn, 602-543-6600.

College of Teacher Education and Leadership Students: 169 full-time (133 women), 245 part-time (200 women); includes 76 minority (16 African Americans, 8 American Indian/Alaska Native, 7 Asian Americans or Pacific Islanders, 45 Hispanic Americans), 3 international. Average age 35. 308 applicants, 63% accepted, 171 enrolled. *Faculty:* 25 full-time (18 women), 27 part-time/adjunct (21 women). Expenses: Contact institution. *Financial support:* In 2006–07, 2 research assistantships with partial tuition reimbursements (averaging $16,413 per year) were awarded; fellowships with tuition reimbursements, career-related internships or fieldwork, institutionally sponsored loans, scholarships/grants, tuition waivers (full and partial), and unspecified assistantships also available. Support available to part-time students. Financial award application deadline: 4/1; financial award applicants required to submit FAFSA. In 2006, 84 degrees awarded. *Degree program information:* Part-time and evening/weekend programs available. Offers educational administration and supervision (M Ed); elementary education (M Ed, Certificate); leadership/innovation (administration) (Ed D); leadership/innovation (teaching) (Ed D); secondary education (M Ed, Certificate); special education (M Ed). *Application deadline:* Applications are processed on a rolling basis. *Application fee:* $50. Electronic applications accepted. *Application Contact:* Marie Wright, Administrative Assistant, 602-543-3634, Fax: 602-543-6350, E-mail: marie.wright@asu.edu or ctelgrad@asu.edu. *Dean,* Dr. Mari Koerner, 602-543-6352, Fax: 602-543-6350, E-mail: mari.koerner@asu.edu.

New College of Interdisciplinary Arts and Sciences Students: 4 full-time (3 women), 24 part-time (13 women); includes 6 minority (2 African Americans, 1 American Indian/Alaska Native, 1 Asian American or Pacific Islander, 2 Hispanic Americans), 2 international. Average age 38. 13 applicants, 46% accepted, 5 enrolled. *Faculty:* 16 full-time (6 women). Expenses: Contact institution. *Financial support:* Federal Work-Study, scholarships/grants, and tuition waivers (full and partial) available. Support available to part-time students. Financial award applicants required to submit FAFSA. In 2006, 6 degrees awarded. *Degree program information:* Part-time and evening/weekend programs available. Offers interdisciplinary studies (MA). *Application deadline:* For fall admission, 5/1 priority date for domestic students; for spring admission, 11/1 priority date for domestic students. Applications are processed on a rolling basis. *Application fee:* $50. Electronic applications accepted. *Application Contact:* Sheryl Gordon, Coordinator, Student Support Services, 602-543-6241, Fax: 602-543-6032, E-mail: sheryl.gordon@asu.edu. *Interim Dean,* Dr. Barry G. Ritchie, 602-543-6033, Fax: 602-543-6032, E-mail: barry.ritchie@asu.edu.

School of Global Management and Leadership Students: 55 full-time (27 women), 295 part-time (128 women); includes 60 minority (8 African Americans, 2 American Indian/Alaska Native, 19 Asian Americans or Pacific Islanders, 31 Hispanic Americans), 9 international. Average age 33. 177 applicants, 87% accepted, 127 enrolled. *Faculty:* 19 full-time (6 women), 2 part-time/adjunct (0 women). Expenses: Contact institution. *Financial support:* In 2006–07, 7 research assistantships with partial tuition reimbursements (averaging $6,400 per year) were awarded; fellowships, career-related internships or fieldwork, scholarships/grants, tuition waivers (full and partial), and unspecified assistantships also available. Financial award applicants required to submit FAFSA. In 2006, 54 degrees awarded. *Degree program information:* Part-time and evening/weekend programs available. Offers business administration (MBA); global management and leadership (MBA, Certificate); professional accountancy (Certificate). *Application deadline:* For fall admission, 6/1 priority date for domestic students, 5/1 priority date for international students; for spring admission, 11/1 priority date for domestic students, 10/1 priority date for international students. Applications are processed on a rolling basis. *Application fee:* $50. Electronic applications accepted. *Application Contact:* Information Contact, 602-543-4622, Fax: 602-543-6220, E-mail: gradprograms@asu.edu. *Dean,* Dr. Gary Waissi, 602-543-6661, Fax: 602-543-6220, E-mail: gary.waissi@asu.edu.

ARKANSAS STATE UNIVERSITY, Jonesboro, State University, AR 72467

General Information State-supported, coed, comprehensive institution. CGS member. *Enrollment:* 10,727 graduate, professional, and undergraduate students; 425 full-time matriculated graduate/professional students (254 women), 962 part-time matriculated graduate/professional students (640 women). *Enrollment by degree level:* 1,074 master's, 118 doctoral, 195 other advanced degrees. *Graduate faculty:* 212 full-time (76 women), 32 part-time/adjunct (13 women). Tuition, state resident: full-time $3,393; part-time $189 per hour. Tuition, nonresident: full-time $8,577; part-time $477 per hour. *Required fees:* $752; $39 per hour. $25 per semester. *Graduate housing:* Rooms and/or apartments available on a first-come, first-served basis to single and married students. Typical cost: $4,500 per year for single students; $4,500 per year for married students. Housing application deadline: 8/20. *Student services:* Campus employment opportunities, campus safety program, career counseling, child daycare facilities, disabled student services, exercise/wellness program, free psychological counseling, international student services. *Library facilities:* Dean B. Ellis Library. *Online resources:* library catalog, web page. *Collection:* 604,568 titles, 1,712 serial subscriptions, 18,949 audiovisual materials. *Research affiliation:* Radiance Technologies, Alaka'i Consulting and Engineering.

Computer facilities: 510 computers available on campus for general student use. A campuswide network can be accessed from student residence rooms and from off campus. Internet access and online class registration are available. *Web address:* http://www.astate.edu/.

General Application Contact: Dr. Andrew Sustich, Dean of the Graduate School, 870-972-3029, Fax: 870-972-3857, E-mail: sustich@astate.edu.

GRADUATE UNITS

Graduate School Students: 425 full-time (254 women), 962 part-time (640 women); includes 212 minority (186 African Americans, 7 American Indian/Alaska Native, 7 Asian Americans or Pacific Islanders, 12 Hispanic Americans), 50 international. Average age 32. 974 applicants, 68% accepted, 450 enrolled. *Faculty:* 212 full-time (76 women), 32 part-time/adjunct (13 women). Expenses: Contact institution. *Financial support:* Fellowships, research assistantships, teaching assistantships, career-related internships or fieldwork, scholarships/grants, and unspecified assistantships available. Financial award application deadline: 7/1; financial award applicants required to submit FAFSA. In 2006, 386 master's, 19 doctorates, 30 other advanced degrees awarded. *Degree program information:* Part-time programs available. *Application deadline:* Applications are processed on a rolling basis. *Application fee:* $30 ($40 for international students). Electronic applications accepted. *Dean of the Graduate School,* Dr. Andrew Sustich, 870-972-3029, Fax: 870-972-3857, E-mail: sustich@astate.edu.

College of Agriculture Students: 7 full-time (0 women), 19 part-time (11 women); includes 1 minority (African American) Average age 30. 13 applicants, 77% accepted, 7 enrolled. *Faculty:* 10 full-time (1 woman), 3 part-time/adjunct (1 woman). Expenses: Contact institution. *Financial support:* Teaching assistantships, scholarships/grants and unspecified assistantships available. Financial award application deadline: 7/1; financial award applicants required to submit FAFSA. In 2006, 17 degrees awarded. *Degree program information:* Part-time programs available. Offers agricultural education (MSA, SCCT); agriculture (MSA); vocational-technical administration (MS, SCCT). *Application deadline:* Applications are processed on a rolling basis. *Application fee:* $30 ($40 for international students). Electronic applications accepted. *Dean,* Dr. Gregory Phillips, 870-972-2085, Fax: 870-972-3885, E-mail: gphillips@astate.edu.

College of Business Students: 69 full-time (36 women), 126 part-time (64 women); includes 34 minority (30 African Americans, 1 American Indian/Alaska Native, 2 Asian Americans or Pacific Islanders, 1 Hispanic American), 21 international. Average age 29. 151 applicants, 75% accepted, 86 enrolled. *Faculty:* 24 full-time (5 women), 4 part-time/adjunct (1 woman). Expenses: Contact institution. *Financial support:* Teaching assistantships, career-related internships or fieldwork, scholarships/grants, and unspecified assistantships available. Financial award application deadline: 7/1; financial award applicants required to submit FAFSA. In 2006, 77 master's, 1 other advanced degree awarded. *Degree program information:* Part-time programs available. Offers accountancy (M Acc); business (EMBA, M Acc, MBA, MS, MSE, SCCT); business administration (EMBA, MBA, SCCT); business education (SCCT); business technology education (MSE); information systems and e-commerce (MS). *Application deadline:* Applications are processed on a rolling basis. *Application fee:* $30 ($40 for international students). Electronic applications accepted. *Dean,* Dr. Len Frey, 870-972-3035, Fax: 870-972-3744, E-mail: lfrey@astate.edu.

College of Communications Students: 13 full-time (9 women), 7 part-time (all women); includes 11 minority (all African Americans), 1 international. Average age 26. 16 applicants, 63% accepted, 8 enrolled. *Faculty:* 9 full-time (4 women). Expenses: Contact institution. *Financial support:* Career-related internships or fieldwork, scholarships/grants, and unspecified assistantships available. Financial award application deadline: 7/1; financial award applicants required to submit FAFSA. In 2006, 9 master's, 2 other advanced degrees awarded. *Degree program information:* Part-time programs available. Offers communications (MA, MSMC, SCCT); journalism (MSMC); radio-television (MSMC); speech communications and theater (MA, SCCT). *Application deadline:* Applications are processed on a rolling basis. *Application fee:* $30 ($40 for international students). Electronic applications accepted. *Dean,* Dr. Russell Shain, 870-972-2468, Fax: 870-972-3856, E-mail: rshain@astate.edu.

College of Education Students: 96 full-time (67 women), 423 part-time (307 women); includes 94 minority (85 African Americans, 3 American Indian/Alaska Native, 2 Asian Americans or Pacific Islanders, 4 Hispanic Americans), 3 international. Average age 34. 289 applicants, 75% accepted, 128 enrolled. *Faculty:* 37 full-time (17 women), 9 part-time/adjunct (3 women). Expenses: Contact institution. *Financial support:* Teaching assistantships, career-related internships or fieldwork, scholarships/grants, and unspecified assistantships available. Financial award application deadline: 7/1; financial award applicants required to submit FAFSA. In 2006, 141 master's, 13 doctorates, 25 other advanced degrees awarded. *Degree program information:* Part-time programs available. Offers college student personnel services (MS); community college administration education (SCCT); counselor education (Ed S); early childhood education (MSE); early childhood services (MS); education (MRC, MS, MSE, Ed D, Certificate, Ed S, SCCT); education theory and practice (MSE); educational leadership (MSE, Ed D, Ed S); elementary education (MSE); exercise science (MS); physical education (MS, MSE, SCCT); reading (MSE, SCCT); rehabilitation counseling (MRC); school counseling (MSE); special education (MSE); special education program administration (Ed S); student affairs (Certificate). *Application deadline:* Applications are processed on a rolling basis. *Application fee:* $30 ($40 for international students). Electronic applications accepted. *Dean,* Dr. John Beineke, 870-972-3057, Fax: 870-972-3828, E-mail: jbeineke@astate.edu.

College of Fine Arts Students: 12 full-time (9 women), 22 part-time (9 women), 1 international. Average age 29. 26 applicants, 77% accepted, 15 enrolled. *Faculty:* 23 full-time (6 women), 3 part-time/adjunct (0 women). Expenses: Contact institution. *Financial support:* Teaching assistantships, career-related internships or fieldwork, scholarships/grants, and unspecified assistantships available. Financial award application deadline: 7/1; financial award applicants required to submit FAFSA. In 2006, 6 master's, 2 other advanced degrees awarded. *Degree program information:* Part-time programs available. Offers art (MA); fine arts (MA, MM, MME, SCCT); music education (MME, SCCT); performance (MM); speech communication and theater (MA, SCCT). *Application deadline:* Applications are processed on a rolling basis. *Application fee:* $30 ($40 for international students). Electronic applications accepted. *Dean,* Dr. Daniel Reeves, 870-972-3053, Fax: 870-972-3932, E-mail: dreeves@astate.edu.

College of Humanities and Social Sciences Students: 49 full-time (26 women), 97 part-time (68 women); includes 22 minority (all African Americans), 7 international. Average age

Arkansas State University (continued)

34. 75 applicants, 84% accepted, 49 enrolled. *Faculty:* 48 full-time (19 women), 4 part-time/adjunct (1 woman). Expenses: Contact institution. *Financial support:* Fellowships, teaching assistantships, career-related internships or fieldwork, scholarships/grants, and unspecified assistantships available. Financial award application deadline: 7/1; financial award applicants required to submit FAFSA. In 2006, 42 master's, 2 doctorates awarded. *Degree program information:* Part-time programs available. Offers criminal justice (Certificate); English (MA); English education (MSE, SCCT); heritage studies (PhD); history (MA, SCCT); humanities and social sciences (MA, MPA, MSE, PhD, Certificate, SCCT); political science (MA, SCCT); public administration (MPA); social science (MSE); sociology (MA, SCCT). *Application deadline:* Applications are processed on a rolling basis. *Application fee:* $30 ($40 for international students). Electronic applications accepted. *Dean,* Dr. Gloria Gibson, 870-972-3973, Fax: 870-972-3976, E-mail: ggibson@astate.edu.

College of Nursing and Health Professions Students: 118 full-time (78 women), 154 part-time (103 women); includes 37 minority (30 African Americans, 2 Asian Americans or Pacific Islanders, 5 Hispanic Americans), 2 international. Average age 31. 140 applicants, 74% accepted, 103 enrolled. *Faculty:* 19 full-time (12 women), 4 part-time/adjunct (all women). Expenses: Contact institution. *Financial support:* Career-related internships or fieldwork, scholarships/grants, and unspecified assistantships available. Financial award application deadline: 7/1; financial award applicants required to submit FAFSA. In 2006, 70 degrees awarded. *Degree program information:* Part-time programs available. Offers aging studies (Certificate); communication disorders (MCD); health sciences (MS, Certificate); health sciences education (Certificate); nurse anesthesia (MSN); nursing (MSN, Certificate); physical therapy (MPT); social work (MSW). *Application deadline:* Applications are processed on a rolling basis. *Application fee:* $30 ($40 for international students). Electronic applications accepted. *Dean,* Dr. Susan Hanrahan, 870-972-3112, Fax: 870-972-2040, E-mail: hanrahan@astate.edu.

College of Sciences and Mathematics Students: 54 full-time (25 women), 42 part-time (18 women); includes 8 minority (4 African Americans, 2 American Indian/Alaska Native, 2 Hispanic Americans), 13 international. Average age 28. 68 applicants, 50% accepted, 27 enrolled. *Faculty:* 40 full-time (10 women), 4 part-time/adjunct (2 women). Expenses: Contact institution. *Financial support:* Fellowships, teaching assistantships, career-related internships or fieldwork, scholarships/grants, and unspecified assistantships available. Financial award application deadline: 7/1; financial award applicants required to submit FAFSA. In 2006, 24 master's, 4 doctorates awarded. *Degree program information:* Part-time programs available. Offers biological sciences (MA); biology (MS); biology education (MSE, SCCT); chemistry (MS); chemistry education (MSE, SCCT); computer science (MS); environmental sciences (MS, PhD); mathematics (MS, MSE); molecular biosciences (PhD); sciences and mathematics (MA, MS, MSE, PhD, SCCT). *Application deadline:* Applications are processed on a rolling basis. *Application fee:* $30 ($40 for international students). Electronic applications accepted. *Dean,* Dr. Gregory Phillips, 870-972-3079, Fax: 870-972-3827, E-mail: gphillips@astate.edu.

ARKANSAS TECH UNIVERSITY, Russellville, AR 72801

General Information State-supported, coed, comprehensive institution. *Enrollment:* 7,038 graduate, professional, and undergraduate students; 147 full-time matriculated graduate/professional students (83 women), 456 part-time matriculated graduate/professional students (326 women). *Enrollment by degree level:* 578 master's, 25 other advanced degrees. *Graduate faculty:* 62 full-time (26 women), 5 part-time/adjunct (4 women). Tuition, state resident: full-time $3,060; part-time $170 per hour. Tuition, nonresident: full-time $6,120; part-time $340 per hour. *Required fees:* $312; $4 per hour. $84 per term. Part-time tuition and fees vary according to course load. *Graduate housing:* Room and/or apartments available on a first-come, first-served basis to single students; on-campus housing not available to married students. Typical cost: $2,412 per year ($4,422 including board). Room and board charges vary according to board plan and housing facility selected. Housing application deadline: 8/1. *Student services:* Campus employment opportunities, campus safety program, career counseling, disabled student services, exercise/wellness program, free psychological counseling, international student services, low-cost health insurance, multicultural affairs office, teacher training. *Library facilities:* Ross Pendergraft Library and Technology Center. *Online resources:* library catalog, web page. *Collection:* 278,540 titles, 1,069 serial subscriptions, 6,975 audiovisual materials.

Computer facilities: 700 computers available on campus for general student use. A campuswide network can be accessed from student residence rooms and from off campus. Internet access and online class registration are available. *Web address:* http://www.atu.edu/.

General Application Contact: Dr. Eldon G. Clary, Dean of Graduate School, 479-968-0398, Fax: 479-964-0542, E-mail: graduate.school@atu.edu.

GRADUATE UNITS

Graduate School Students: 147 full-time (83 women), 456 part-time (326 women); includes 35 minority (16 African Americans, 5 American Indian/Alaska Native, 5 Asian Americans or Pacific Islanders, 9 Hispanic Americans), 80 international. Average age 33. *Faculty:* 62 full-time (26 women), 5 part-time/adjunct (4 women). Expenses: Contact institution. *Financial support:* In 2006–07, teaching assistantships with full tuition reimbursements (averaging $4,000 per year); research assistantships, career-related internships or fieldwork, Federal Work-Study, scholarships/grants, health care benefits, and unspecified assistantships also available. Support available to part-time students. Financial award application deadline: 4/15; financial award applicants required to submit FAFSA. In 2006, 126 master's, 4 other advanced degrees awarded. *Degree program information:* Part-time and evening/weekend programs available. Postbaccalaureate distance learning degree programs offered (no on-campus study). *Application deadline:* For fall admission, 3/1 priority date for domestic students, 5/1 priority date for international students; for winter admission, 10/1 priority date for international students; for spring admission, 10/1 priority date for domestic and international students. Applications are processed on a rolling basis. *Application fee:* $0 ($30 for international students). Electronic applications accepted. *Dean of Graduate School,* Dr. Eldon G. Clary, 479-968-0398, Fax: 479-964-0542, E-mail: graduate.school@atu.edu.

School of Community Education Students: 10 full-time (6 women), 19 part-time (9 women); includes 1 American Indian/Alaska Native, 1 international. Average age 33. Expenses: Contact institution. *Financial support:* In 2006–07, teaching assistantships with full tuition reimbursements (averaging $4,000 per year); career-related internships or fieldwork, Federal Work-Study, scholarships/grants, health care benefits, and unspecified assistantships also available. Support available to part-time students. Financial award application deadline: 4/15; financial award applicants required to submit FAFSA. *Degree program information:* Part-time programs available. Offers emergency management and homeland security (MS). *Application deadline:* For fall admission, 3/1 priority date for domestic students, 5/1 priority date for international students; for winter admission, 10/1 priority date for international students; for spring admission, 10/1 priority date for domestic and international students. Applications are processed on a rolling basis. *Application fee:* $0 ($30 for international students). Electronic applications accepted. *Application Contact:* Dr. Eldon G. Clary, Dean of Graduate School, 479-968-0398, Fax: 479-964-0542, E-mail: graduate.school@atu.edu. *Dean,* Dr. Mary Ann Rollans, 479-968-0234 Ext. 479, E-mail: maryann.rollans@atu.edu.

School of Education Students: 44 full-time (33 women), 244 part-time (181 women); includes 20 minority (14 African Americans, 1 American Indian/Alaska Native, 3 Asian Americans or Pacific Islanders, 2 Hispanic Americans), 18 international. Average age 34. Expenses: Contact institution. *Financial support:* In 2006–07, teaching assistantships with full tuition reimbursements (averaging $4,000 per year); career-related internships or fieldwork, Federal Work-Study, scholarships/grants, health care benefits, and unspecified assistantships also available. Support available to part-time students. Financial award application deadline: 4/15; financial award applicants required to submit FAFSA. In 2006, 72 master's, 4 other advanced degrees awarded. *Degree program information:* Part-time programs available. Offers college student personnel (MSE); educational leadership (M Ed, Ed S); English education (M Ed); gifted education (MSE); instructional improvement (M Ed); secondary education (M Ed); teaching, learning and leadership (M Ed). *Application deadline:* For fall admission, 3/1 priority date for domestic students, 5/1 priority date for international students; for winter admission, 10/1 priority date for international students; for spring admission, 10/1 priority date for domestic and international students. Applications are processed on a rolling basis. *Application fee:* $0 ($30 for international students). Electronic applications accepted. *Application Contact:* Dr. Eldon G. Clary, Dean of Graduate School, 479-968-0398, Fax: 479-964-0542, E-mail: graduate.school@atu.edu. *Dean,* Dr. C. Glenn Sheets, 479-968-0350, Fax: 479-968-0350, E-mail: glenn.sheets@atu.edu.

School of Liberal and Fine Arts Students: 47 full-time (36 women), 102 part-time (82 women); includes 9 minority (2 African Americans, 1 American Indian/Alaska Native, 1 Asian American or Pacific Islander, 5 Hispanic Americans), 20 international. Average age 33. Expenses: Contact institution. *Financial support:* In 2006–07, teaching assistantships with full tuition reimbursements (averaging $4,000 per year); career-related internships or fieldwork, Federal Work-Study, scholarships/grants, health care benefits, and unspecified assistantships also available. Support available to part-time students. Financial award application deadline: 4/15; financial award applicants required to submit FAFSA. In 2006, 20 degrees awarded. *Degree program information:* Part-time programs available. Offers communication (MLA); English (M Ed, MA); fine arts (MLA); history (MA); multi-media journalism (MA); social science (MLA); social studies (M Ed); Spanish (MA, MLA); teaching English as a second language (MA, MLA). *Application deadline:* For fall admission, 3/1 priority date for domestic students, 5/1 priority date for international students; for winter admission, 10/1 priority date for international students; for spring admission, 10/1 priority date for domestic and international students. Applications are processed on a rolling basis. *Application fee:* $0 ($30 for international students). Electronic applications accepted. *Application Contact:* Dr. Eldon G. Clary, Dean of Graduate School, 479-968-0398, Fax: 479-964-0542, E-mail: graduate.school@atu.edu. *Dean,* Dr. Georgena Duncan, 479-968-0266, Fax: 479-968-0275, E-mail: georgena.duncan@atu.edu.

School of Physical and Life Sciences Students: 1 full-time (0 women), 6 part-time (2 women). Average age 26. Expenses: Contact institution. *Financial support:* In 2006–07, teaching assistantships with full tuition reimbursements (averaging $4,000 per year); career-related internships or fieldwork, Federal Work-Study, scholarships/grants, health care benefits, and unspecified assistantships also available. Support available to part-time students. Financial award application deadline: 4/15; financial award applicants required to submit FAFSA. In 2006, 5 degrees awarded. Offers fisheries and wildlife biology (MS). *Application deadline:* For fall admission, 3/1 priority date for domestic students, 5/1 priority date for international students; for winter admission, 10/1 priority date for international students; for spring admission, 10/1 priority date for domestic and international students. Applications are processed on a rolling basis. *Application fee:* $0 ($30 for international students). Electronic applications accepted. *Application Contact:* Dr. Eldon G. Clary, Dean of Graduate School, 479-968-0398, Fax: 479-964-0542, E-mail: graduate.school@atu.edu. *Dean,* Dr. Richard Cohoon, 479-964-0816, E-mail: richard.cohoon@atu.edu.

School of System Science Students: 45 full-time (8 women), 30 part-time (8 women); includes 2 minority (1 American Indian/Alaska Native, 1 Asian American or Pacific Islander), 40 international. Average age 29. Expenses: Contact institution. *Financial support:* In 2006–07, teaching assistantships with full tuition reimbursements (averaging $4,000 per year); career-related internships or fieldwork, Federal Work-Study, scholarships/grants, health care benefits, and unspecified assistantships also available. Support available to part-time students. Financial award application deadline: 4/15; financial award applicants required to submit FAFSA. In 2006, 29 degrees awarded. *Degree program information:* Part-time programs available. Offers information technology (MS); mathematics (M Ed). *Application deadline:* For fall admission, 3/1 priority date for domestic students, 5/1 priority date for international students; for winter admission, 10/1 priority date for international students; for spring admission, 10/1 priority date for domestic and international students. Applications are processed on a rolling basis. *Application fee:* $0 ($30 for international students). Electronic applications accepted. *Application Contact:* Dr. Eldon G. Clary, Dean of Graduate School, 479-968-0398, Fax: 479-964-0542, E-mail: graduate.school@atu.edu. *Dean,* Dr. John Watson, 479-968-0353 Ext. 501, E-mail: john.watson@atu.edu.

ARMSTRONG ATLANTIC STATE UNIVERSITY, Savannah, GA 31419-1997

General Information State-supported, coed, comprehensive institution. CGS member. *Enrollment:* 6,728 graduate, professional, and undergraduate students; 195 full-time matriculated graduate/professional students (153 women), 447 part-time matriculated graduate/professional students (338 women). *Enrollment by degree level:* 642 master's. *Graduate faculty:* 62 full-time (29 women). Tuition, state resident: full-time $2,286; part-time $127 per credit. Tuition, nonresident: full-time $9,144; part-time $508 per credit. One-time fee: $257. *Graduate housing:* Room and/or apartments available on a first-come, first-served basis to single students; on-campus housing not available to married students. Typical cost: $4,500 per year. Room charges vary according to board plan and housing facility selected. *Student services:* Campus employment opportunities, campus safety program, career counseling, disabled student services, exercise/wellness program, free psychological counseling, international student services, low-cost health insurance, multicultural affairs office, teacher training, writing training. *Library facilities:* Lane Library. *Online resources:* library catalog, web page, access to other libraries' catalogs. *Collection:* 227,439 titles, 990 serial subscriptions.

Computer facilities: 160 computers available on campus for general student use. A campuswide network can be accessed from student residence rooms and from off campus. Internet access and online class registration are available. *Web address:* http://www.armstrong.edu/.

General Application Contact: Dr. Michael Price, Assistant Vice President of Graduate Studies, 912-921-5711, Fax: 912-921-5729, E-mail: pricemic@mail.armstrong.edu.

GRADUATE UNITS

School of Graduate Studies Students: 195 full-time (153 women), 447 part-time (338 women); includes 163 minority (149 African Americans, 1 American Indian/Alaska Native, 9 Asian Americans or Pacific Islanders, 4 Hispanic Americans), 30 international. Average age 35. *Faculty:* 62 full-time (29 women). Expenses: Contact institution. *Financial support:* In 2006–07, 34 research assistantships with partial tuition reimbursements (averaging $2,500 per year) were awarded; Federal Work-Study, scholarships/grants, and unspecified assistantships also available. Financial award applicants required to submit FAFSA. In 2006, 231 degrees awarded. *Degree program information:* Part-time and evening/weekend programs available. Postbaccalaureate distance learning degree programs offered (minimal on-campus study). Offers adult education (M Ed); computer science (MS); criminal justice (MS); early childhood education (M Ed); education (M Ed); elementary education (M Ed); health services administration (MHSA); history (MA); liberal and professional studies (MALPS); middle grades education (M Ed); nursing (MSN); physical therapy (MSPT); public health (MPH); secondary education (M Ed); special education (M Ed); sports health sciences (MSSM). *Application deadline:* For fall admission, 7/1 priority date for domestic and international students; for spring admission, 11/15 priority date for domestic and international students. Applications are processed on a rolling basis. *Application fee:* $25. Electronic applications accepted. *Application Contact:* Dr. Michael Price, Assistant Vice President of Graduate Studies, 912-921-5711, Fax: 912-921-5729, E-mail: pricemic@mail.armstrong.edu. *Assistant Vice President of Graduate Studies,* Dr. Michael Price, 912-921-5711, Fax: 912-921-5729, E-mail: pricemic@mail.armstrong.edu.

See Close-Up on page 803.

ART ACADEMY OF CINCINNATI, Cincinnati, OH 45202

General Information Independent, coed, comprehensive institution. *Enrollment:* 164 graduate, professional, and undergraduate students; 12 full-time matriculated graduate/professional students (6 women), 1 (woman) part-time matriculated graduate/professional student. *Enrollment by degree level:* 13 master's. *Graduate faculty:* 3 full-time (1 woman), 6 part-time/adjunct (5 women). *Tuition:* Full-time $9,240; part-time $840 per hour. *Graduate housing:* Room and/or apartments available on a first-come, first-served basis to single students; on-campus housing not available to married students. Housing application deadline: 5/1.

Student services: Career counseling, free psychological counseling, international student services, low-cost health insurance. *Library facilities:* Mary Schiff Library. *Collection:* 66,404 titles, 150 serial subscriptions, 588 audiovisual materials.

Computer facilities: 40 computers available on campus for general student use. Internet access is available. *Web address:* http://www.artacademy.edu/.

General Application Contact: John J. Wadell, Director of Admissions, 513-562-8744, Fax: 513-562-8778, E-mail: jwadell@artacademy.edu.

GRADUATE UNITS

Program in Art Education Students: 12 full-time (6 women), 1 (woman) part-time. Average age 36. 5 applicants, 80% accepted, 4 enrolled. *Faculty:* 3 full-time (1 woman), 6 part-time/adjunct (5 women). Expenses: Contact institution. *Financial support:* In 2006–07, 9 students received support. Institutionally sponsored loans and scholarships/grants available. Support available to part-time students. Financial award applicants required to submit FAFSA. In 2006, 2 degrees awarded. *Degree program information:* Part-time programs available. Offers art education (MA). Offered during summer only. *Application deadline:* For fall admission, 5/1 priority date for domestic students. Applications are processed on a rolling basis. *Application fee:* $25. Electronic applications accepted. *Application Contact:* John J. Wadell, Director of Admissions, 513-562-8744, Fax: 513-562-8778, E-mail: jwadell@artacademy.edu. *Chair,* Keith Benjamin, 513-562-6262, E-mail: kbenjamin@artacademy.edu.

ART CENTER COLLEGE OF DESIGN, Pasadena, CA 91103-1999

General Information Independent, coed, comprehensive institution. *Enrollment:* 1,631 graduate, professional, and undergraduate students; 100 full-time matriculated graduate/professional students (42 women), 29 part-time matriculated graduate/professional students (14 women). *Enrollment by degree level:* 129 master's. *Graduate faculty:* 8 full-time (3 women), 32 part-time/adjunct (11 women). *Tuition:* Full-time $29,288. *Graduate housing:* On-campus housing not available. *Student services:* Campus employment opportunities, career counseling, free psychological counseling, international student services, low-cost health insurance. *Library facilities:* James LeMont Fogg Library. *Collection:* 93,038 titles, 450 serial subscriptions.

Computer facilities: 225 computers available on campus for general student use. A campuswide network can be accessed from off campus. Internet access is available. *Web address:* http://www.artcenter.edu/.

General Application Contact: Kit Baron, Vice President, Admissions, 626-396-2373, Fax: 626-795-0578, E-mail: cbaron@artcenter.edu.

GRADUATE UNITS

Graduate Division Students: 100 full-time (42 women), 29 part-time (14 women); includes 32 minority (2 African Americans, 3 American Indian/Alaska Native, 24 Asian Americans or Pacific Islanders, 3 Hispanic Americans), 37 international. Average age 28. 202 applicants, 43% accepted, 46 enrolled. *Faculty:* 8 full-time (3 women), 32 part-time/adjunct (11 women). Expenses: Contact institution. *Financial support:* In 2006–07, 63 students received support, including 26 teaching assistantships; career-related internships or fieldwork, Federal Work-Study, and scholarships/grants also available. Financial award application deadline: 3/1. In 2006, 32 degrees awarded. Offers art and design theory and criticism (MA); broadcast cinema (MFA); environmental design (MS); fine arts (MFA); media design (MFA); product design (MS). *Application deadline:* For fall admission, 2/1 priority date for domestic and international students; for spring admission, 10/1 priority date for domestic and international students. Applications are processed on a rolling basis. *Application fee:* $50 ($70 for international students). *Application Contact:* Kit Baron, Vice President, Admissions, 626-396-2373, Fax: 626-795-0578, E-mail: cbaron@artcenter.edu.

THE ART INSTITUTE OF BOSTON AT LESLEY UNIVERSITY, Boston, MA 02215-2598

General Information Independent, coed, comprehensive institution.

GRADUATE UNITS

Program in Visual Arts Offers visual arts (MFA).

ASBURY COLLEGE, Wilmore, KY 40390-1198

General Information Independent-religious, coed, comprehensive institution. *Enrollment:* 1,220 graduate, professional, and undergraduate students; 67 part-time matriculated graduate/professional students (48 women). *Enrollment by degree level:* 67 master's. *Graduate faculty:* 8 full-time (7 women), 9 part-time/adjunct (4 women). *Tuition:* Part-time $335 per credit hour. *Graduate housing:* On-campus housing not available. *Student services:* Disabled student services, teacher training. *Library facilities:* Kinlaw Library. *Online resources:* library catalog, web page. *Collection:* 146,708 titles, 511 serial subscriptions, 9,280 audiovisual materials.

Computer facilities: Computer purchase and lease plans are available. 189 computers available on campus for general student use. A campuswide network can be accessed from student residence rooms and from off campus. Internet access is available. *Web address:* http://www.asbury.edu/.

General Application Contact: Melanie S. Kinnell, Graduate Program Assistant and Certification Specialist, 859-858-3511 Ext. 2304, Fax: 859-858-3921, E-mail: graded@asbury.edu.

GRADUATE UNITS

Graduate Programs Average age 36. 14 applicants, 100% accepted, 10 enrolled. *Faculty:* 8 full-time (7 women), 9 part-time/adjunct (4 women). Expenses: Contact institution. *Financial support:* Scholarships/grants and traineeships available. Financial award applicants required to submit FAFSA. In 2006, 17 degrees awarded. *Degree program information:* Part-time programs available. *Application deadline:* Applications are processed on a rolling basis. *Application fee:* $25. *Application Contact:* Melanie S. Kinnell, Graduate Program Assistant and Certification Specialist, 859-858-3511 Ext. 2304, Fax: 859-858-3921, E-mail: graded@asbury.edu. *Director,* Dr. Bonnie J. Banker, 859-858-3511 Ext. 2221, Fax: 859-858-3921, E-mail: bonnie.banker@asbury.edu.

ASBURY THEOLOGICAL SEMINARY, Wilmore, KY 40390-1199

General Information Independent-religious, coed, primarily men, graduate-only institution. *Enrollment by degree level:* 909 first professional, 423 master's, 303 doctoral, 52 other advanced degrees. *Graduate faculty:* 57 full-time (14 women), 116 part-time/adjunct (21 women). *Graduate housing:* Rooms and/or apartments available on a first-come, first-served basis to single and married students. Housing application deadline: 3/1. *Student services:* Campus employment opportunities, campus safety program, disabled student services, exercise/wellness program, free psychological counseling, international student services, low-cost health insurance, multicultural affairs office, writing training. *Library facilities:* B. L. Fisher Library. *Online resources:* library catalog, web page, access to other libraries' catalogs. *Collection:* 416,119 titles, 1,054 serial subscriptions, 21,680 audiovisual materials.

Computer facilities: 106 computers available on campus for general student use. A campuswide network can be accessed from student residence rooms. Internet access and online class registration, e-mail are available. *Web address:* http://www.asburyseminary.edu/.

General Application Contact: Janelle Vernon, Admissions Director, 859-858-2211, Fax: 859-858-2287, E-mail: admissions_office@asburyseminary.edu.

GRADUATE UNITS

Graduate and Professional Programs Students: 829 full-time (260 women), 858 part-time (289 women); includes 108 minority (62 African Americans, 12 American Indian/Alaska Native, 9 Asian Americans or Pacific Islanders, 25 Hispanic Americans), 183 international. Average age 25. 908 applicants, 69% accepted, 330 enrolled. *Faculty:* 57 full-time (14 women), 116 part-time/adjunct (21 women). Expenses: Contact institution. *Financial support:* In 2006–07, 1,198 students received support. Career-related internships or fieldwork, Federal Work-Study, institutionally sponsored loans, scholarships/grants, and tuition waivers (full and partial) available. Support available to part-time students. Financial award application deadline: 4/15; financial award applicants required to submit FAFSA. In 2006, 87 master's, 41 doctorates awarded. *Degree program information:* Part-time programs available. Postbaccalaureate distance learning degree programs offered (minimal on-campus study). *Application deadline:* For fall admission, 7/1 priority date for domestic students; for spring admission, 12/1 priority date for domestic students. Applications are processed on a rolling basis. *Application fee:* $25. Electronic applications accepted. *Application Contact:* Janelle Vernon, Admissions Director, 859-858-2211, Fax: 859-858-2287, E-mail: admissions_office@asburyseminary.edu. *VP of Academic Affairs/Provost,* Dr. Bill T. Arnold, 859-858-2206, Fax: 859-858-2025, E-mail: bill_arnold@asburyseminary.edu.

E. Stanley Jones School of World Mission and Evangelism Expenses: Contact institution. Offers intercultural studies (MA, PhD); missiology (D Miss); mission and evangelism (Th M); world mission and evangelism (MA). *Application Contact:* Janelle Vernon, Admissions Director, 859-858-2211, Fax: 859-858-2287, E-mail: admissions_office@asburyseminary.edu. *Dean,* Dr. Ronald K. Crandall, 859-858-2252, Fax: 859-858-2375, E-mail: ron_crandall@asburyseminary.edu.

School of Practical Theology Expenses: Contact institution. Offers Christian education (MACE); Christian leadership (MA); Christian studies (Certificate); counseling (MAC); pastoral counseling (MAPC); youth ministry (MA). *Application Contact:* Janelle Vernon, Admissions Director, 859-858-2211, Fax: 859-858-2287, E-mail: admissions_office@asburyseminary.edu. *Dean,* Dr. Catherine Stonehouse.

ASHLAND THEOLOGICAL SEMINARY, Ashland, OH 44805

General Information Independent-religious, coed, graduate-only institution. *Enrollment by degree level:* 284 first professional, 357 master's, 98 doctoral, 25 other advanced degrees. *Graduate faculty:* 22 full-time (5 women), 35 part-time/adjunct (13 women). *Tuition:* Full-time $9,288; part-time $1,244 per course. *Graduate housing:* Rooms and/or apartments available on a first-come, first-served basis to single and married students. Typical cost: $3,600 per year for single students; $6,000 per year for married students. Housing application deadline: 6/30. *Student services:* Campus employment opportunities, free psychological counseling, international student services, low-cost health insurance, writing training. *Library facilities:* Darling Memorial Library. *Online resources:* library catalog, web page, access to other libraries' catalogs. *Collection:* 88,354 titles, 331 serial subscriptions, 1,256 audiovisual materials.

Computer facilities: 20 computers available on campus for general student use. A campuswide network can be accessed from student residence rooms. Internet access and online class registration are available. *Web address:* http://www.ashland.edu/seminary/.

General Application Contact: Dr. S Robert Rosa, Dean, Student Development, 419-289-5164, Fax: 419-289-5969, E-mail: brosa@ashland.edu.

GRADUATE UNITS

Graduate Programs Students: 602 full-time (328 women), 164 part-time (87 women); includes 277 minority (266 African Americans, 2 American Indian/Alaska Native, 9 Asian Americans or Pacific Islanders), 18 international. Average age 41. 231 applicants, 87% accepted, 168 enrolled. *Faculty:* 22 full-time (5 women), 35 part-time/adjunct (13 women). Expenses: Contact institution. *Financial support:* In 2006–07, 554 students received support, including 17 teaching assistantships; research assistantships, career-related internships or fieldwork, institutionally sponsored loans, scholarships/grants, and unspecified assistantships also available. Support available to part-time students. Financial award application deadline: 5/15. In 2006, 42 M Divs, 102 master's, 20 doctorates awarded. *Degree program information:* Part-time programs available. Offers biblical and theological studies (MA, MAR); Christian ministry (MAPT); Christian studies (Diploma); clinical pastoral counseling (MACPC); historical studies (MA); ministry (D Min); pastoral counseling (MAPC); pastoral ministry (M Div); theological studies (MA). *Application deadline:* For fall admission, 8/30 for domestic students. Applications are processed on a rolling basis. *Application fee:* $30. Electronic applications accepted. *Application Contact:* Dr. S Robert Rosa, Dean, Student Development, 419-289-5164, Fax: 419-289-5969, E-mail: brosa@ashland.edu. *President,* Dr. John C. Shultz, 419-289-5160, Fax: 419-289-5969, E-mail: ffinks@ashland.edu.

ASHLAND UNIVERSITY, Ashland, OH 44805-3702

General Information Independent-religious, coed, comprehensive institution. CGS member. *Enrollment:* 6,648 graduate, professional, and undergraduate students; 738 full-time matriculated graduate/professional students (466 women), 1,191 part-time matriculated graduate/professional students (786 women). *Enrollment by degree level:* 1,890 master's, 39 doctoral. *Graduate faculty:* 67 full-time (29 women), 196 part-time/adjunct (111 women). *Tuition:* Part-time $403 per credit. Tuition and fees vary according to degree level and program. *Graduate housing:* On-campus housing not available. *Student services:* Campus employment opportunities, campus safety program, career counseling, disabled student services, exercise/wellness program, free psychological counseling, international student services, low-cost health insurance, multicultural affairs office, teacher training, writing training. *Library facilities:* Ashland Library plus 2 others. *Online resources:* library catalog, web page. *Collection:* 205,200 titles, 1,625 serial subscriptions, 3,550 audiovisual materials. *Research affiliation:* Teacher Quality Project (TQP) (Education).

Computer facilities: Computer purchase and lease plans are available. 600 computers available on campus for general student use. A campuswide network can be accessed from student residence rooms and from off campus. *Web address:* http://www.exploreashland.com.

General Application Contact: Dr. John P. Sikula, Associate Provost, 419-289-5751, Fax: 419-289-5738, E-mail: jsikula@ashland.edu.

GRADUATE UNITS

College of Arts and Sciences Students: 31 full-time (17 women), 13 part-time (5 women); includes 2 minority (both Hispanic Americans) *Faculty:* 4 full-time (0 women), 17 part-time/adjunct (1 woman). Expenses: Contact institution. *Financial support:* In 2006–07, 16 students received support. Application deadline: 4/15. *Degree program information:* Part-time programs available. Offers American history and government (MAHG); arts and sciences (MAHG). *Application deadline:* Applications are processed on a rolling basis. *Application fee:* $30. Electronic applications accepted. *Head,* Dr. John Bee, 419-289-5107.

College of Education Students: 460 full-time (337 women), 856 part-time (646 women); includes 80 minority (63 African Americans, 2 American Indian/Alaska Native, 6 Asian Americans or Pacific Islanders, 9 Hispanic Americans), 11 international. Average age 33. *Faculty:* 51 full-time (25 women), 176 part-time/adjunct (105 women). Expenses: Contact institution. *Financial support:* In 2006–07, 447 students received support; teaching assistantships with partial tuition reimbursements available, scholarships/grants available. Financial award application deadline: 4/15. In 2006, 624 master's, 5 doctorates awarded. *Degree program information:* Part-time and evening/weekend programs available. Offers education (M Ed, Ed D); educational leadership studies (Ed D). *Application deadline:* For fall admission, 8/27 for domestic students; for spring admission, 1/14 for domestic students. Applications are processed on a rolling basis. *Application fee:* $30. *Application Contact:* Dr. Ann C. Shelly, Director and Chair, Graduate Studies in Education and Associate Dean, 419-289-5388, Fax: 419-289-5331, E-mail: ashelly@ashland.edu. *Dean,* Dr. Frank E. Pettigrew, 419-289-5365, E-mail: fpettig@ashland.edu.

Graduate Studies in Education Students: 442 full-time (327 women), 835 part-time (634 women); includes 74 minority (59 African Americans, 1 American Indian/Alaska Native, 6 Asian Americans or Pacific Islanders, 8 Hispanic Americans), 11 international. Average age 33. *Faculty:* 43 full-time (21 women), 175 part-time/adjunct (104 women). Expenses: Contact institution. *Financial support:* In 2006–07, 435 students received support, including 5 teaching assistantships with partial tuition reimbursements available (averaging $3,500 per year); institutionally sponsored loans and scholarships/grants also available. Financial award application deadline: 4/15. In 2006, 619 degrees awarded. *Degree program information:* Part-time and evening/weekend programs available. Offers adapted physical education (M Ed); administration (M Ed); applied exercise science (M Ed); business manager (M Ed); classroom instruction (M Ed); curriculum specialist (M Ed); early childhood education (M Ed); early childhood intervention (M Ed); educational administration (M Ed); educational foundations (M Ed); educational technology (M Ed); intervention specialist-mild/moderate (M Ed); intervention specialist-moderate/intensive (M Ed); middle school education (M Ed); principalship (M Ed); pupil services (M Ed); school treasurer (M Ed); sport education (M Ed); sport management (M Ed); sport sciences (M Ed);

Ashland University (continued)

superintendency (M Ed); talent development (M Ed). *Application deadline:* For fall admission, 8/27 for domestic students; for spring admission, 1/14 for domestic students. Applications are processed on a rolling basis. *Application fee:* $30. *Associate Dean,* Dr. Ann C. Shelly, 419-289-5388, Fax: 419-289-5331, E-mail: ashelly@ashland.edu.

Dauch College of Business and Economics Students: 278 full-time (129 women), 335 part-time (140 women); includes 77 minority (65 African Americans, 2 American Indian/Alaska Native, 4 Asian Americans or Pacific Islanders, 6 Hispanic Americans), 28 international. Average age 34. *Faculty:* 16 full-time (4 women), 20 part-time/adjunct (6 women). Expenses: Contact institution. *Financial support:* In 2006–07, 189 students received support. Tuition waivers (partial) and unspecified assistantships available. Financial award application deadline: 4/15; financial award applicants required to submit FAFSA. In 2006, 218 degrees awarded. *Degree program information:* Part-time and evening/weekend programs available. Offers business and economics (MBA). *Application deadline:* For fall admission, 8/1 priority date for domestic students; for spring admission, 12/1 priority date for domestic students. Applications are processed on a rolling basis. *Application fee:* $30. Electronic applications accepted. *Application Contact:* Stephen W. Krispinsky, Executive Director of MBA Program, 419-289-5236, Fax: 419-289-5910, E-mail: skrispin@ashland.edu. *Chair,* Dr. Beverly Heimann, 419-289-5216, E-mail: bheimann@ashland.edu.

ASPEN UNIVERSITY, Denver, CO 80246

General Information Independent, coed, upper-level institution. *Graduate housing:* On-campus housing not available.

GRADUATE UNITS

Program in Business Administration Postbaccalaureate distance learning degree programs offered (no on-campus study). Offers business administration (MBA); information management (MBA); project management (MBA, Certificate). Electronic applications accepted.

Program in Information Technology *Degree program information:* Part-time and evening/weekend programs available. Postbaccalaureate distance learning degree programs offered (no on-campus study). Offers information technology (MS). Electronic applications accepted.

Programs in Information Management *Degree program information:* Part-time and evening/weekend programs available. Postbaccalaureate distance learning degree programs offered (no on-campus study). Offers information management (MS); information systems (Certificate). Electronic applications accepted.

ASSEMBLIES OF GOD THEOLOGICAL SEMINARY, Springfield, MO 65802

General Information Independent-religious, coed, graduate-only institution. *Enrollment by degree level:* 144 first professional, 210 master's, 84 doctoral. *Graduate faculty:* 15 full-time (3 women), 29 part-time/adjunct (6 women). *Tuition:* Full-time $9,144; part-time $381 per credit. One-time fee: $195 full-time. *Graduate housing:* On-campus housing not available. *Student services:* Career counseling, free psychological counseling, international student services. *Library facilities:* Cordas C. Burnett Library. *Online resources:* library catalog, web page, access to other libraries' catalogs. *Collection:* 89,853 titles, 452 serial subscriptions, 5,027 audiovisual materials.

Computer facilities: 23 computers available on campus for general student use. A campuswide network can be accessed. Internet access is available. *Web address:* http://www.agts.edu/.

General Application Contact: Information Contact, 417-268-1000, Fax: 417-268-1001.

GRADUATE UNITS

Graduate and Professional Programs Students: 208 full-time (78 women), 230 part-time (58 women); includes 63 minority (23 African Americans, 3 American Indian/Alaska Native, 17 Asian Americans or Pacific Islanders, 20 Hispanic Americans), 6 international. Average age 35. 190 applicants, 68% accepted, 103 enrolled. *Faculty:* 15 full-time (3 women), 29 part-time/adjunct (6 women). Expenses: Contact institution. *Financial support:* Career-related internships or fieldwork, Federal Work-Study, and scholarships/grants available. Support available to part-time students. Financial award application deadline: 7/15; financial award applicants required to submit FAFSA. In 2006, 24 M Divs, 76 master's, 13 doctorates awarded. *Degree program information:* Part-time and evening/weekend programs available. Postbaccalaureate distance learning degree programs offered (minimal on-campus study). Offers Christian ministries (MA); counseling (MA); divinity (M Div); intercultural ministries (MA); theological studies (MA); vocational ministry (D Min). *Application deadline:* For fall admission, 7/1 priority date for domestic students, 6/1 priority date for international students; for spring admission, 12/1 priority date for domestic students, 11/1 priority date for international students. Applications are processed on a rolling basis. *Application fee:* $35. Electronic applications accepted. *Academic Dean,* Joseph Castleberry, 417-268-1000, Fax: 417-268-1001, E-mail: jcastleberry@agts.edu.

ASSOCIATED MENNONITE BIBLICAL SEMINARY, Elkhart, IN 46517-1999

General Information Independent-religious, coed, graduate-only institution. *Graduate housing:* Rooms and/or apartments available on a first-come, first-served basis to single and married students. Housing application deadline: 5/1.

GRADUATE UNITS

Graduate and Professional Programs *Degree program information:* Part-time programs available. Offers Christian formation (MA); divinity (M Div); mission and evangelism (MA); peace studies (MA); theological studies (MA, Certificate). Electronic applications accepted.

ASSUMPTION COLLEGE, Worcester, MA 01609-1296

General Information Independent-religious, coed, comprehensive institution. *Enrollment:* 2,498 graduate, professional, and undergraduate students; 133 full-time matriculated graduate/professional students (103 women), 264 part-time matriculated graduate/professional students (174 women). *Enrollment by degree level:* 390 master's, 7 other advanced degrees. *Graduate faculty:* 16 full-time (4 women), 34 part-time/adjunct (12 women). *Graduate housing:* On-campus housing not available. *Student services:* Campus safety program, disabled student services, exercise/wellness program, international student services, low-cost health insurance, multicultural affairs office. *Library facilities:* Emmanuel d'Alzon Library. *Online resources:* library catalog, web page, access to other libraries' catalogs. *Collection:* 133,030 titles, 1,892 serial subscriptions, 2,820 audiovisual materials.

Computer facilities: Computer purchase and lease plans are available. 190 computers available on campus for general student use. A campuswide network can be accessed from student residence rooms and from off campus. Internet access is available. *Web address:* http://www.assumption.edu/.

General Application Contact: Adrian O. Dumas, Director of Graduate Enrollment Management and Services, 508-767-7365, Fax: 508-767-7030, E-mail: adumas@assumption.edu.

GRADUATE UNITS

Graduate School Students: 133 full-time (103 women), 264 part-time (174 women); includes 30 minority (13 African Americans, 8 Asian Americans or Pacific Islanders, 9 Hispanic Americans), 7 international. Average age 27. 310 applicants, 89% accepted. *Faculty:* 16 full-time (4 women), 34 part-time/adjunct (12 women). Expenses: Contact institution. *Financial support:* In 2006–07, 232 students received support, including 62 fellowships with partial tuition reimbursements available (averaging $7,364 per year), 2 teaching assistantships with partial tuition reimbursements available (averaging $9,900 per year); scholarships/grants, traineeships, and unspecified assistantships also available. Financial award application deadline: 7/1; financial award applicants required to submit FAFSA. In 2006, 92 master's, 4 other advanced degrees awarded. *Degree program information:* Part-time and evening/weekend programs available. Offers business administration (MBA, CAGS); counseling psychology (MA, CAGS); rehabilitation counseling (MA, CAGS); school counseling (MA, CAGS); special education (MA). *Application deadline:* For fall admission, 6/1 priority date for domestic students, 5/1 priority date for international students; for spring admission, 11/1 priority date for domestic students, 10/1 priority date for international students. Applications are processed on a rolling basis. *Application fee:* $30. Electronic applications accepted. *Application Contact:* Adrian O. Dumas, Director of Graduate Enrollment Management and Services, 508-767-7365, Fax: 508-767-7030, E-mail: adumas@assumption.edu. *Dean,* Dr. MaryLou Anderson, 508-767-7276, Fax: 508-767-7053, E-mail: mlanders@assumption.edu.

ATHABASCA UNIVERSITY, Athabasca, AB T9S 3A3, Canada

General Information Province-supported, coed, comprehensive institution. *Enrollment:* 34,171 graduate, professional, and undergraduate students; 2,914 part-time matriculated graduate/professional students (1,752 women). *Enrollment by degree level:* 2,914 master's. *Graduate faculty:* 43 full-time, 175 part-time/adjunct. *Student services:* Disabled student services. *Library facilities:* Athabasca University Library. *Online resources:* library catalog, web page, access to other libraries' catalogs. *Collection:* 178,808 titles, 32,619 serial subscriptions, 17,628 audiovisual materials. *Research affiliation:* IBM (software), SAP (software).

Computer facilities: 28 computers available on campus for general student use. A campuswide network can be accessed from off campus. Internet access and online class registration, computing services help desk are available. *Web address:* http://www.athabascau.ca/.

General Application Contact: Information Contact, 800-788-9041, Fax: 780-675-6437, E-mail: inquire@athabascau.ca.

GRADUATE UNITS

Centre for Distance Education Average age 41. 88 applicants, 93% accepted. *Faculty:* 10 full-time (3 women), 22 part-time/adjunct (8 women). Expenses: Contact institution. In 2006, 42 degrees awarded. *Degree program information:* Part-time programs available. Postbaccalaureate distance learning degree programs offered (no on-campus study). Offers distance education (MDE); distance education technology (Advanced Diploma). *Application deadline:* For fall admission, 3/1 for domestic and international students. *Application fee:* $65. Electronic applications accepted. *Application Contact:* Glenda Hawryluk, Administrative Assistant, 780-675-6179, Fax: 780-675-6170, E-mail: glendah@athabascau.ca. *Head,* Dr. Bob Spencer, 780-675-6238, Fax: 780-675-6170, E-mail: bobs@athabascau.ca.

Centre for Innovative Management Average age 39. 264 applicants, 82% accepted, 184 enrolled. *Faculty:* 11 full-time (7 women), 63 part-time/adjunct (18 women). Expenses: Contact institution. *Financial support:* In 2006–07, 34 students received support. Scholarships/grants available. In 2006, 228 degrees awarded. *Degree program information:* Part-time and evening/weekend programs available. Postbaccalaureate distance learning degree programs offered (no on-campus study). Offers business administration (MBA); information technology management (MBA); management (GDM); project management (MBA, GDM). *Application deadline:* For fall admission, 8/1 for domestic and international students; for winter admission, 10/15 for domestic and international students; for spring admission, 2/15 for domestic and international students. Applications are processed on a rolling basis. *Application fee:* $165. Electronic applications accepted. *Application Contact:* Shannon LaRose, Customer Service Representative, 800-561-4650, Fax: 800-561-4660, E-mail: cimoffice@athabascau.ca. *Executive Director,* Dr. Lindsay Redpath, 780-459-1144, Fax: 780-459-2093, E-mail: lindsayr@athabascau.ca.

Centre for Integrated Studies Average age 39. 150 applicants, 87% accepted, 112 enrolled. *Faculty:* 4 full-time (0 women), 50 part-time/adjunct (27 women). Expenses: Contact institution. In 2006, 40 degrees awarded. *Degree program information:* Part-time and evening/weekend programs available. Postbaccalaureate distance learning degree programs offered (no on-campus study). Offers adult education (MA); community studies (MA); cultural studies (MA); educational studies (MA); global change (MA); work, organization, and leadership (MA). *Application deadline:* For fall admission, 3/1 for domestic and international students; for winter admission, 10/1 for domestic and international students. *Application fee:* $65. Electronic applications accepted. *Application Contact:* Derek Stovin, Program Administrator, 780-675-6236, Fax: 780-675-6921, E-mail: mais@athabascau.ca. *Program Director,* Dr. Derek Briton, 780-675-6218, Fax: 780-675-6921, E-mail: derekb@athabascau.ca.

Centre for Nursing and Health Studies Average age 40. 460 applicants, 81% accepted, 335 enrolled. *Faculty:* 6 full-time (all women), 40 part-time/adjunct (37 women). Expenses: Contact institution. In 2006, 124 degrees awarded. *Degree program information:* Part-time programs available. Postbaccalaureate distance learning degree programs offered. Offers advanced nursing practice (MN, Advanced Diploma); generalist (MN); health studies-leadership (MHS). *Application deadline:* For fall admission, 3/1 for domestic and international students. *Application fee:* $60. Electronic applications accepted. *Application Contact:* Lisa Bodnarchuk, Administrative Assistant, 780-675-6381, Fax: 780-675-6468, E-mail: mhs@athabascau.ca. *Director,* Dr. Donna Romyn, 780-675-6794, Fax: 780-675-6468, E-mail: dromyn@athabascau.ca.

School of Computing and Information Systems Average age 36. 93 applicants, 96% accepted. *Faculty:* 13 full-time (0 women), 1 part-time/adjunct (0 women). Expenses: Contact institution. In 2006, 14 degrees awarded. *Degree program information:* Part-time programs available. Postbaccalaureate distance learning degree programs offered (no on-campus study). Offers information systems (M Sc). *Application deadline:* For fall admission, 3/1 for domestic students; for winter admission, 10/1 for domestic students. *Application fee:* $250. Electronic applications accepted. *Application Contact:* Claire Gemmell, Administration and Production Coordinator, 780-675-6777, Fax: 780-675-6148, E-mail: claire@athabascau.ca. *Director,* Dr. Kinshuk Kinshuk, 780-675-6812, E-mail: kinshuk@athabascau.ca.

THE ATHENAEUM OF OHIO, Cincinnati, OH 45230-5900

General Information Independent-religious, coed, graduate-only institution. *Graduate housing:* Room and/or apartments guaranteed to single students; on-campus housing not available to married students.

GRADUATE UNITS

Graduate Programs *Degree program information:* Part-time and evening/weekend programs available. Offers biblical studies (MABS); divinity (M Div); pastoral counseling (MAPC); religion (MAR); theology (MA Th).

ATLANTIC COLLEGE, Guaynabo, PR 00970

General Information Independent, comprehensive institution.

GRADUATE UNITS

Program in Graphic Arts *Degree program information:* Part-time programs available. Offers digital graphic design (UA Undergraduate Associate).

ATLANTIC INSTITUTE OF ORIENTAL MEDICINE, Fort Lauderdale, FL 33301

General Information Independent, coed, graduate-only institution. *Enrollment by degree level:* 94 master's. *Graduate faculty:* 7 full-time (2 women), 14 part-time/adjunct (2 women). *Tuition:* Full-time $12,000. *Required fees:* $1,200. *Student services:* Campus employment opportunities, campus safety program, career counseling, exercise/wellness program, international student services. *Collection:* 2,030 titles.

Computer facilities: 3 computers available on campus for general student use. Internet access is available. *Web address:* http://www.atom.edu/.

General Application Contact: Milafros Ferreira, Registrar, 954-763-9840 Ext. 207, Fax: 954-763-9844, E-mail: registrar@atom.edu.

GRADUATE UNITS

Graduate Program Students: 94 full-time (69 women); includes 33 minority (3 African Americans, 18 Asian Americans or Pacific Islanders, 12 Hispanic Americans), 3 international. 62 applicants, 52% accepted, 32 enrolled. *Faculty:* 7 full-time (2 women), 14 part-time/adjunct (2 women). Expenses: Contact institution. In 2006, 28 degrees awarded. *Degree* *program information:* Evening/weekend programs available. Offers Oriental medicine (MS). *Application deadline:* For fall admission, 7/1 for domestic students, 5/1 for international students; for spring admission, 11/30 for domestic students, 2/28 for international students. Applications are processed on a rolling basis. *Application fee:* $20 ($100 for international students). *Application Contact:* Milafros Ferreira, Registrar, 954-763-9840 Ext. 207, Fax: 954-763-9844, E-mail: registrar@atom.edu. *President,* Dr. Johanna C. Yen, 954-763-9840 Ext. 202, Fax: 954-763-9844, E-mail: president@atom.edu.

ATLANTIC SCHOOL OF THEOLOGY, Halifax, NS B3H 3B5, Canada

General Information Independent, coed, graduate-only institution. *Graduate faculty:* 5 full-time, 9 part-time/adjunct. *Graduate housing:* Rooms and/or apartments available on a first-come, first-served basis to single and married students. Housing application deadline:6/1. *Student services:* Campus employment opportunities, international student services, low-cost health insurance. *Library facilities:* Atlantic School of Theology Library. *Online resources:* library catalog, access to other libraries' catalogs. *Collection:* 71,910 titles, 365 serial subscriptions.

Computer facilities: 3 computers available on campus for general student use. A campuswide network can be accessed. Internet access is available. *Web address:* http://www.astheology.ns.ca/.

General Application Contact: Rev. Dr. David MacLachlan, Academic Dean/Registrar, 902-496-7941, Fax: 902-492-4048, E-mail: dmaclachlan@astheology.ns.ca.

GRADUATE UNITS

Graduate and Professional Programs Students: 60 full-time (33 women), 97 part-time (58 women). Average age 38. *Faculty:* 7 full-time (4 women), 3 part-time/adjunct (0 women). Expenses: Contact institution. *Financial support:* In 2006–07, 27 students received support. Career-related internships or fieldwork available. Support available to part-time students. Financial award application deadline: 9/30. In 2006, 14 first professional degrees, 4 master's awarded. *Degree program information:* Part-time programs available. Postbaccalaureate distance learning degree programs offered (minimal on-campus study). Offers theology (M Div, MTS, Graduate Certificate). *Application deadline:* For fall admission, 2/28 priority date for domestic students. Applications are processed on a rolling basis. *Application fee:* $40. *Application Contact:* Cynthia Thomson, Academic Secretary, 902-423-5592, Fax: 902-492-4048, E-mail: cthomson@astheology.ns.ca. *Academic Dean/Registrar,* Rev. Dr. David MacLachlan, 902-496-7941, Fax: 902-492-4048, E-mail: dmaclachlan@astheology.ns.ca.

ATLANTIC UNION COLLEGE, South Lancaster, MA 01561-1000

General Information Independent-religious, coed, comprehensive institution. *Graduate housing:* Room and/or apartments available to single students; on-campus housing not available to married students.

GRADUATE UNITS

Graduate Education Program *Degree program information:* Part-time programs available. Postbaccalaureate distance learning degree programs offered (minimal on-campus study). Offers education (M Ed). Offered during summer only.

ATLANTIC UNIVERSITY, Virginia Beach, VA 23451-2061

General Information Independent, coed, primarily women, graduate-only institution. *Enrollment by degree level:* 164 master's. *Graduate faculty:* 14 part-time/adjunct (5 women). *Tuition:* Full-time $4,170; part-time $695 per course. *Graduate housing:* On-campus housing not available. *Web address:* http://www.atlanticuniv.edu/.

General Application Contact: R. Gregory Deming, Director of Admissions, 757-631-8101 Ext. 7173, Fax: 757-631-8096, E-mail: gdeming@atlanticuniv.edu.

GRADUATE UNITS

Program in Transpersonal Studies Average age 45. 66 applicants, 65% accepted. *Faculty:* 14 part-time/adjunct (5 women). Expenses: Contact institution. In 2006, 11 degrees awarded. *Degree program information:* Part-time and evening/weekend programs available. Postbaccalaureate distance learning degree programs offered (no on-campus study). Offers transpersonal studies (MA). *Application deadline:* Applications are processed on a rolling basis. *Application fee:* $50. Electronic applications accepted. *Application Contact:* R. Gregory Deming, Director of Admissions, 757-631-8101 Ext. 210, Fax: 757-631-8096, E-mail: admissions@atlanticuniv.edu. *Chief Executive Officer,* Kevin Todeschi, 757-631-8101, Fax: 757-631-8096, E-mail: info@atlanticuniv.edu.

A.T. STILL UNIVERSITY OF HEALTH SCIENCES, Kirksville, MO 63501

General Information Independent, coed, graduate-only institution. *Enrollment by degree level:* 899 first professional, 555 master's, 863 doctoral. *Graduate faculty:* 145 full-time (59 women), 389 part-time/adjunct (149 women). *Graduate housing:* Rooms and/or apartments available on a first-come, first-served basis to single and married students. Typical cost: $4,560 per year for single students; $5,100 per year for married students. Housing application deadline: 4/1. *Student services:* Campus employment opportunities, career counseling, disabled student services, exercise/wellness program, free psychological counseling. *Library facilities:* A. T. Still Memorial Library plus 1 other. *Online resources:* library catalog, web page, access to other libraries' catalogs. *Collection:* 84,224 titles, 4,628 serial subscriptions, 8,183 audiovisual materials. *Research affiliation:* Ridgway Integrative Medicine (osteopathic clinical research), McGovern Capital, LLC (osteopathic/biomedical clinical research), European School of Osteopathy (osteopathic manual medicine), Unitec New Zealand (osteopathic manual medicine), Doctors Hospital (osteopathic clinical research), Mount Clemens Regional Medical Center (osteopathic clinical research).

Computer facilities: 38 computers available on campus for general student use. A campuswide network can be accessed from student residence rooms and from off campus. Internet access is available. *Web address:* http://www.atsu.edu/.

General Application Contact: Donna Sparks, Associate Director for Admissions, 660-626-2237, Fax: 660-626-2969, E-mail: admissions@atsu.edu.

GRADUATE UNITS

Arizona School of Dentistry and Oral Health Students: 216 full-time (100 women); includes 56 minority (2 African Americans, 12 American Indian/Alaska Native, 28 Asian Americans or Pacific Islanders, 14 Hispanic Americans). Average age 25. 2,915 applicants, 54 enrolled. *Faculty:* 26 full-time (12 women), 226 part-time/adjunct (71 women). Expenses: Contact institution. *Financial support:* In 2006–07, 214 students received support. Federal Work-Study and scholarships/grants available. Financial award application deadline: 5/1; financial award applicants required to submit FAFSA. Offers dental medicine (DMD). *Application deadline:* For fall admission, 12/1 for domestic students. Applications are processed on a rolling basis. *Application fee:* $60. Electronic applications accepted. *Application Contact:* Donna Sparks, Associate Director for Admissions, 660-626-2237, Fax: 660-626-2969, E-mail: admissions@atsu.edu. *Dean,* Dr. Jack Dillenberg, 480-219-6000, Fax: 480-219-6110, E-mail: jdillenberg@atsu.edu.

Arizona School of Health Sciences Students: 442 full-time (277 women), 732 part-time (579 women); includes 143 minority (38 African Americans, 11 American Indian/Alaska Native, 55 Asian Americans or Pacific Islanders, 39 Hispanic Americans), 4 international. Average age 33. 1,471 applicants, 547 enrolled. *Faculty:* 47 full-time (27 women), 101 part-time/adjunct (60 women). Expenses: Contact institution. *Financial support:* In 2006–07, 382 students received support. Federal Work-Study and scholarships/grants available. Financial award application deadline: 5/1. In 2006, 104 master's, 432 doctorates awarded. Postbaccalaureate distance learning degree programs offered (no on-campus study). Offers advanced occupational therapy (MS); advanced physician assistant (MS); audiology (Au D); human movement (MS); medical informatics (MS); occupational therapy (MS); physical therapy (MS, DPT); physician assistant (MS); sports health care (MS); transitional physical therapy (DPT). *Application deadline:* For fall admission, 2/1 priority date for domestic and international students. Applications are processed on a rolling basis. *Application fee:* $60. *Application Contact:* Donna Sparks, Associate Director for Admissions, 660-626-2237, Fax: 660-626-2969, E-mail: admissions@atsu.edu. *Dean,* Dr. Randy Danielsen, 480-219-6000, Fax: 480-219-6110, E-mail: rdanielsen@atsu.edu.

Kirksville College of Osteopathic Medicine Students: 695 full-time (285 women), 20 part-time (11 women); includes 117 minority (7 African Americans, 5 American Indian/Alaska Native, 93 Asian Americans or Pacific Islanders, 12 Hispanic Americans), 12 international. Average age 27. 2,911 applicants, 184 enrolled. *Faculty:* 71 full-time (20 women), 17 part-time/adjunct (1 woman). Expenses: Contact institution. *Financial support:* In 2006–07, 624 students received support, including 8 fellowships with full tuition reimbursements available (averaging $12,000 per year); career-related internships or fieldwork, Federal Work-Study, institutionally sponsored loans, and scholarships/grants also available. Financial award application deadline: 5/1; financial award applicants required to submit FAFSA. In 2006, 156 DOs, 4 master's awarded. Offers biomedical sciences (MS); osteopathic medicine (DO). *Application deadline:* For fall admission, 2/1 for domestic and international students. Applications are processed on a rolling basis. *Application fee:* $60. Electronic applications accepted. *Application Contact:* Donna Sparks, Associate Director for Admissions, 660-626-2237, Fax: 660-626-2969, E-mail: admissions@atsu.edu. *Vice President for Medical Affairs and Dean,* Dr. Philip C. Slocum, 660-626-2354, Fax: 660-626-2080, E-mail: pslocum@atsu.edu.

School of Health Management Students: 18 full-time (14 women), 194 part-time (130 women); includes 39 minority (20 African Americans, 8 American Indian/Alaska Native, 9 Asian Americans or Pacific Islanders, 2 Hispanic Americans). Average age 34. *Faculty:* 1 full-time (0 women), 45 part-time/adjunct (17 women). Expenses: Contact institution. *Financial support:* Application deadline: 5/1; In 2006, 75 degrees awarded. *Degree program information:* Part-time and evening/weekend programs available. Postbaccalaureate distance learning degree programs offered (no on-campus study). Offers geriatric healthcare (MGH); health administration (MHA); health education (MH Ed, DH Ed); public health (MPH). *Application deadline:* For fall admission, 8/27 for domestic students, 8/4 for international students; for winter admission, 10/25 for domestic students, 11/26 for international students; for spring admission, 2/10 for domestic students, 3/17 for international students. Applications are processed on a rolling basis. Electronic applications accepted. *Application Contact:* Donna Sparks, Associate Director for Admissions, 660-626-2237, Fax: 660-626-2969, E-mail: admissions@atsu.edu. *Dean,* Dr. Jon Persavich, 660-626-2820, Fax: 660-626-2826, E-mail: jpersavich@atsu.edu.

AUBURN UNIVERSITY, Auburn University, AL 36849

General Information State-supported, coed, university. CGS member. *Enrollment:* 23,547 graduate, professional, and undergraduate students; 2,303 full-time matriculated graduate/professional students (1,219 women), 1,823 part-time matriculated graduate/professional students (911 women). *Enrollment by degree level:* 918 first professional, 1,938 master's, 1,248 doctoral, 22 other advanced degrees. *Graduate faculty:* 1,054 full-time (270 women), 3 part-time/adjunct (0 women). Tuition, state resident: full-time $5,000. Tuition, nonresident: full-time $15,000. *Required fees:* $416. Tuition and fees vary according to program. *Graduate housing:* Rooms and/or apartments available on a first-come, first-served basis to single students and available to married students. Typical cost: $3,250 per year ($7,564 including board) for single students. Room and board charges vary according to board plan and housing facility selected. Housing application deadline: 7/1. *Student services:* Campus employment opportunities, campus safety program, career counseling, disabled student services, international student services, low-cost health insurance, teacher training. *Library facilities:* R. B. Draughon Library plus 2 others. *Online resources:* library catalog, web page, access to other libraries' catalogs. *Collection:* 3.7 million titles, 29,355 serial subscriptions, 14,760 audiovisual materials. *Research affiliation:* National Asphalt Pavement Association (asphalt technology), National Textile Center, Air Transportation Center of Excellence (airliner cabin environment research).

Computer facilities: 1,722 computers available on campus for general student use. A campuswide network can be accessed from student residence rooms and from off campus. Internet access and online class registration, online grades, pay Bursar online, course materials are available. *Web address:* http://www.auburn.edu/.

General Application Contact: Dr. Joe Pittman, Interim Dean of the Graduate School, 334-844-4700.

GRADUATE UNITS

College of Veterinary Medicine Students: 390 full-time (266 women), 34 part-time (24 women); includes 16 minority (7 African Americans, 4 Asian Americans or Pacific Islanders, 5 Hispanic Americans), 18 international. Average age 27. 917 applicants, 12% accepted, 102 enrolled. *Faculty:* 84 full-time (29 women), 1 part-time/adjunct (0 women). Expenses: Contact institution. *Financial support:* Fellowships, research assistantships, teaching assistantships, Federal Work-Study available. Support available to part-time students. Financial award application deadline: 3/15. In 2006, 91 DVMs, 8 master's, 4 doctorates awarded. *Degree program information:* Part-time programs available. Offers veterinary medicine (DVM, MS, PhD). *Application deadline:* For fall admission, 7/7 for domestic students. Applications are processed on a rolling basis. *Application fee:* $25 ($50 for international students). *Application Contact:* Dr. Joe Pittman, Interim Dean of the Graduate School, 334-844-4700. *Dean,* Dr. Timothy R. Boosinger, 334-844-4546.

Graduate Programs in Veterinary Medicine Students: 19 full-time (10 women), 34 part-time (24 women); includes 2 minority (both Hispanic Americans), 18 international. Average age 32. 49 applicants, 39% accepted, 9 enrolled. *Faculty:* 84 full-time (29 women), 1 part-time/adjunct (0 women). Expenses: Contact institution. *Financial support:* Research assistantships, teaching assistantships, Federal Work-Study available. Support available to part-time students. Financial award application deadline: 3/15. In 2006, 8 master's, 4 doctorates awarded. *Degree program information:* Part-time programs available. Offers biomedical sciences (MS, PhD). *Application deadline:* For fall admission, 7/7 for domestic students; for spring admission, 11/24 for domestic students. Applications are processed on a rolling basis. *Application fee:* $25 ($50 for international students). Electronic applications accepted. *Application Contact:* Dr. Joe Pittman, Interim Dean of the Graduate School, 334-844-4700.

Graduate School Students: 2,303 full-time (1,219 women), 1,823 part-time (911 women); includes 468 minority (308 African Americans, 13 American Indian/Alaska Native, 86 Asian Americans or Pacific Islanders, 61 Hispanic Americans), 715 international. Average age 30. 3,857 applicants, 56% accepted, 1160 enrolled. *Faculty:* 1,054 full-time (270 women), 3 part-time/adjunct (0 women). Expenses: Contact institution. *Financial support:* Fellowships, research assistantships, teaching assistantships, career-related internships or fieldwork and Federal Work-Study available. Support available to part-time students. In 2006, 867 master's, 164 doctorates, 25 other advanced degrees awarded. *Degree program information:* Part-time and evening/weekend programs available. Offers cell and molecular biology (PhD); integrated textile and apparel sciences (MS, PhD); rural sociology (MS); sociology (MA, MS); sociology, anthropology, criminology, and social work (MA, MS); textile science (MS). *Application deadline:* For fall admission, 7/7 for domestic students; for spring admission, 11/24 for domestic students. *Application fee:* $25 ($50 for international students). *Interim Dean of the Graduate School,* Dr. Joe Pittman, 334-844-4700.

College of Agriculture Students: 129 full-time (54 women), 105 part-time (47 women); includes 15 minority (8 African Americans, 1 American Indian/Alaska Native, 3 Asian Americans or Pacific Islanders, 3 Hispanic Americans), 84 international. Average age 31. 133 applicants, 72% accepted, 56 enrolled. *Faculty:* 150 full-time (24 women). Expenses: Contact institution. *Financial support:* Fellowships, research assistantships, teaching assistantships, Federal Work-Study available. Support available to part-time students. Financial award application deadline: 3/15. In 2006, 45 master's, 14 doctorates awarded. *Degree program information:* Part-time programs available. Offers agricultural economics (M Ag, MS); agriculture (M Ag, M Aq, MS, PhD); agronomy and soils (M Ag, MS, PhD); animal sciences (M Ag, MS, PhD); applied economics (PhD); entomology (M Ag, MS, PhD); fisheries and allied aquacultures (M Aq, MS, PhD); horticulture (M Ag, MS, PhD); plant pathology (M Ag, MS, PhD); poultry science (M Ag, MS, PhD). *Application deadline:* For fall admission, 7/7 for domestic students; for spring admission, 11/24 for domestic students. Applications are processed on a rolling basis. *Application fee:* $25 ($50 for

Auburn University (continued)

international students). Electronic applications accepted. *Application Contact:* Dr. Joe Pittman, Interim Dean of the Graduate School, 334-844-4700. *Dean,* Dr. Richard Guthrie, 334-844-2345.

College of Architecture, Design, and Construction Students: 79 full-time (27 women), 23 part-time (12 women); includes 17 minority (11 African Americans, 4 Asian Americans or Pacific Islanders, 2 Hispanic Americans), 18 international. Average age 28. 111 applicants, 71% accepted, 45 enrolled. *Faculty:* 50 full-time (9 women). Expenses: Contact institution. *Financial support:* Fellowships, Federal Work-Study available. Support available to part-time students. Financial award application deadline: 3/15. In 2006, 58 degrees awarded. *Degree program information:* Part-time programs available. Offers architecture, design, and construction (MBS, MCP, MID, MLA); building science (MBS); community planning (MCP); construction management (MBS); industrial design (MID); landscape architecture (MLA). *Application deadline:* For fall admission, 7/7 for domestic students; for spring admission, 11/24 for domestic students. Applications are processed on a rolling basis. *Application fee:* $25 ($50 for international students). Electronic applications accepted. *Application Contact:* Dr. Joe Pittman, Interim Dean of the Graduate School, 334-844-4700. *Dean,* Dan D. Bennett, 334-844-4524.

College of Business Students: 158 full-time (62 women), 342 part-time (99 women); includes 50 minority (23 African Americans, 1 American Indian/Alaska Native, 17 Asian Americans or Pacific Islanders, 9 Hispanic Americans), 23 international. Average age 31. 636 applicants, 55% accepted, 231 enrolled. *Faculty:* 78 full-time (12 women). Expenses: Contact institution. *Financial support:* Fellowships, research assistantships, teaching assistantships, career-related internships or fieldwork and Federal Work-Study available. Support available to part-time students. Financial award application deadline: 3/15. In 2006, 229 master's, 10 doctorates awarded. *Degree program information:* Part-time programs available. Offers accountancy (M Acc); business (M Acc, MBA, MMIS, MS, PhD); business administration (MBA); economics (MS); finance (MS); human resource management (PhD); management (MS, PhD); management information systems (MMIS, PhD). *Application deadline:* For fall admission, 7/7 for domestic students; for spring admission, 11/24 for domestic students. Applications are processed on a rolling basis. *Application fee:* $25 ($50 for international students). Electronic applications accepted. *Application Contact:* Dr. Joe Pittman, Interim Dean of the Graduate School, 334-844-4700. *Dean,* Dr. Paul M Bobrowski, 334-844-4832.

College of Education Students: 292 full-time (202 women), 419 part-time (293 women); includes 162 minority (144 African Americans, 6 American Indian/Alaska Native, 4 Asian Americans or Pacific Islanders, 8 Hispanic Americans), 18 international. Average age 33. 558 applicants, 58% accepted, 200 enrolled. *Faculty:* 85 full-time (48 women). Expenses: Contact institution. *Financial support:* Fellowships, research assistantships, teaching assistantships, career-related internships or fieldwork and Federal Work-Study available. Support available to part-time students. Financial award application deadline: 3/15. In 2006, 196 master's, 34 doctorates, 25 other advanced degrees awarded. *Degree program information:* Part-time programs available. Offers adult education (M Ed, MS, Ed D); business education (M Ed, MS, PhD); collaborative teacher special education (M Ed, MS); community agency counseling (M Ed, MS, Ed D, PhD, Ed S); counseling psychology (PhD); counselor education (Ed D, PhD); curriculum and instruction (M Ed, MS, Ed D, Ed S); curriculum supervision (M Ed, MS, Ed D, Ed S); early childhood education (M Ed, MS, PhD, Ed S); early childhood special education (M Ed, MS); education (M Ed, MS, Ed D, PhD, Ed S); educational psychology (PhD); elementary education (M Ed, MS, PhD, Ed S); exercise science (M Ed, MS, PhD); foreign languages (M Ed, MS); health promotion (M Ed, MS); higher education administration (M Ed, MS, Ed D, Ed S); media instructional design (MS); media specialist (M Ed); music education (M Ed, MS, PhD, Ed S); physical education/teacher education (M Ed, MS, Ed D, Ed S); postsecondary education (PhD); reading education (PhD, Ed S); rehabilitation counseling (M Ed, MS, PhD); school administration (M Ed, MS, Ed D, Ed S); school counseling (M Ed, MS, Ed D, PhD, Ed S); school psychometry (M Ed, MS, Ed D, PhD, Ed S); secondary education (M Ed, MS, PhD, Ed S). *Application fee:* $25 ($50 for international students). Electronic applications accepted. *Application Contact:* Dr. Joe Pittman, Interim Dean of the Graduate School, 334-844-4700. *Dean,* Dr. Frances Kochan, 334-844-4446.

College of Engineering Students: 351 full-time (72 women), 301 part-time (68 women); includes 43 minority (27 African Americans, 7 Asian Americans or Pacific Islanders, 9 Hispanic Americans), 339 international. Average age 28. 966 applicants, 59% accepted, 163 enrolled. *Faculty:* 147 full-time (13 women). Expenses: Contact institution. *Financial support:* Fellowships, research assistantships, teaching assistantships, Federal Work-Study available. Support available to part-time students. Financial award application deadline: 3/15. In 2006, 120 master's, 46 doctorates awarded. *Degree program information:* Part-time programs available. Offers aerospace engineering (MAE, MS, PhD); chemical engineering (M Ch E, MS, PhD); computer science and software engineering (MS, MSWE, PhD); construction engineering and management (MCE, MS, PhD); electrical and computer engineering (MEE, MS, PhD); engineering (M Ch E, M Mtl E, MAE, MCE, MEE, MISE, MME, MS, MSWE, PhD); environmental engineering (MCE, MS, PhD); geotechnical/materials engineering (MCE, MS, PhD); hydraulics/hydrology (MCE, MS, PhD); industrial and systems engineering (MISE, MS, PhD); materials engineering (M Mtl E, MS, PhD); mechanical engineering (MME, MS, PhD); structural engineering (MCE, MS, PhD); transportation engineering (MCE, MS, PhD). *Application deadline:* For fall admission, 7/7 for domestic students; for spring admission, 11/24 for domestic students. Applications are processed on a rolling basis. *Application fee:* $25 ($50 for international students). Electronic applications accepted. *Application Contact:* Dr. Joe Pittman, Interim Dean of the Graduate School, 334-844-4700. *Dean,* Dr. Larry Benefield, 334-844-2308.

College of Human Sciences Students: 58 full-time (49 women), 43 part-time (33 women); includes 13 minority (9 African Americans, 4 Asian Americans or Pacific Islanders), 23 international. Average age 28. 106 applicants, 60% accepted, 32 enrolled. *Faculty:* 37 full-time (24 women), 1 part-time/adjunct (0 women). Expenses: Contact institution. *Financial support:* Fellowships, research assistantships, teaching assistantships, career-related internships or fieldwork and Federal Work-Study available. Support available to part-time students. Financial award application deadline: 3/15. In 2006, 29 master's, 9 doctorates awarded. *Degree program information:* Part-time programs available. Offers apparel and textiles (MS); human development and family studies (MS, PhD); human sciences (MS, PhD); nutrition and food science (MS, PhD). *Application deadline:* For fall admission, 7/7 for domestic students; for spring admission, 11/24 for domestic students. Applications are processed on a rolling basis. *Application fee:* $25 ($50 for international students). Electronic applications accepted. *Application Contact:* Dr. Joe Pittman, Interim Dean of the Graduate School, 334-844-4700. *Dean,* Dr. June Henton, 334-844-3790, E-mail: jhenton@humsci.auburn.edu.

College of Liberal Arts Students: 209 full-time (136 women), 232 part-time (144 women); includes 52 minority (32 African Americans, 1 American Indian/Alaska Native, 4 Asian Americans or Pacific Islanders, 15 Hispanic Americans), 16 international. Average age 30. 676 applicants, 37% accepted, 139 enrolled. *Faculty:* 216 full-time (75 women), 1 part-time/adjunct (0 women). Expenses: Contact institution. *Financial support:* Fellowships, research assistantships, teaching assistantships, career-related internships or fieldwork and Federal Work-Study available. Support available to part-time students. Financial award application deadline: 3/15. In 2006, 115 master's, 15 doctorates awarded. *Degree program information:* Part-time programs available. Offers applied behavior analysis in developmental disabilities (MS); audiology (MCD, MS, Au D); clinical psychology (PhD); communication (MA); English (MA, MTPC, PhD); experimental psychology (PhD); history (MA, PhD); industrial/organizational psychology (PhD); liberal arts (MA, MCD, MFA, MHS, MPA, MS, MTPC, Au D, PhD); mass communications (MA); public administration (MPA, PhD); Spanish (MA, MHS); speech pathology (MCD, MS). *Application deadline:* For fall admission, 7/7 for domestic students; for spring admission, 11/24 for domestic students. Applications are processed on a rolling basis. *Application fee:* $25 ($50 for international students). Electronic applications accepted. *Application Contact:* Dr. Joe Pittman, Interim Dean of the Graduate School, 334-844-4700. *Dean,* Dr. Anne-Katrin Gramberg, 334-844-2185.

College of Sciences and Mathematics Students: 159 full-time (60 women), 142 part-time (70 women); includes 23 minority (11 African Americans, 2 American Indian/Alaska Native, 6 Asian Americans or Pacific Islanders, 4 Hispanic Americans), 127 international. Average age 28. 271 applicants, 54% accepted, 72 enrolled. *Faculty:* 144 full-time (19 women). Expenses: Contact institution. *Financial support:* Fellowships, research assistantships, teaching assistantships, career-related internships or fieldwork and Federal Work-Study available. Support available to part-time students. In 2006, 47 master's, 17 doctorates awarded. *Degree program information:* Part-time programs available. Offers analytical chemistry (MS, PhD); applied mathematics (MAM, MS); biochemistry (MS, PhD); botany (MS, PhD); geology (MS); inorganic chemistry (MS, PhD); mathematics (MS, PhD); microbiology (MS, PhD); organic chemistry (MS, PhD); physical chemistry (MS, PhD); physics (MS, PhD); probability and statistics (M Prob S); sciences and mathematics (M Prob S, MAM, MS, PhD); statistics (MS); zoology (MS, PhD). *Application deadline:* For fall admission, 7/7 for domestic students; for spring admission, 11/24 for domestic students. Applications are processed on a rolling basis. *Application fee:* $25 ($50 for international students). *Application Contact:* Dr. Joe Pittman, Interim Dean of the Graduate School, 334-844-4700. *Dean,* Dr. Stewart W. Schneller, 334-844-5737.

School of Forestry and Wildlife Sciences Students: 16 full-time (6 women), 27 part-time (13 women); includes 2 minority (both Hispanic Americans), 9 international. Average age 30. 18 applicants, 67% accepted, 8 enrolled. *Faculty:* 28 full-time (3 women). Expenses: Contact institution. *Financial support:* Fellowships, research assistantships, teaching assistantships, Federal Work-Study available. Support available to part-time students. Financial award application deadline: 3/15. In 2006, 10 master's, 5 doctorates awarded. *Degree program information:* Part-time programs available. Offers forest economics (PhD); forestry (MS, PhD); natural resource conservation (MNR); wildlife sciences (MS, PhD). *Application deadline:* For fall admission, 7/7 for domestic students; for spring admission, 11/24 for domestic students. Applications are processed on a rolling basis. *Application fee:* $25 ($50 for international students). Electronic applications accepted. *Application Contact:* Dr. Joe Pittman, Interim Dean of the Graduate School, 334-844-4700. *Dean,* Richard W. Brinker, 334-844-1007, Fax: 334-844-1084, E-mail: brinker@forestry.auburn.edu.

School of Pharmacy Students: 415 full-time (254 women), 121 part-time (80 women); includes 66 minority (31 African Americans, 2 American Indian/Alaska Native, 30 Asian Americans or Pacific Islanders, 3 Hispanic Americans), 17 international. Average age 25. 927 applicants, 16% accepted, 128 enrolled. *Faculty:* 19 full-time (5 women). Expenses: Contact institution. *Financial support:* Fellowships, research assistantships, teaching assistantships, Federal Work-Study available. Support available to part-time students. In 2006, 106 Pharm Ds, 4 doctorates awarded. *Degree program information:* Part-time programs available. Offers pharmacal sciences (MS, PhD); pharmaceutical sciences (PhD); pharmacy (Pharm D, MS, PhD); pharmacy care systems (MS, PhD). *Application deadline:* For fall admission, 7/7 for domestic students; for spring admission, 11/24 for domestic students. Applications are processed on a rolling basis. *Application fee:* $25. Electronic applications accepted. *Application Contact:* Dr. Joe Pittman, Interim Dean of the Graduate School, 334-844-4700. *Dean,* Dr. R. Lee Evans, 334-844-8348.

See Close-Up on page 805.

AUBURN UNIVERSITY MONTGOMERY, Montgomery, AL 36124-4023

General Information State-supported, coed, comprehensive institution. *Enrollment:* 5,079 graduate, professional, and undergraduate students; 213 full-time matriculated graduate/professional students (156 women), 562 part-time matriculated graduate/professional students (404 women). *Graduate faculty:* 97 full-time (35 women), 7 part-time/adjunct (1 woman). *Graduate housing:* Rooms and/or apartments available to single students and available on a first-come, first-served basis to married students. *Student services:* Campus employment opportunities, campus safety program, career counseling, disabled student services, free psychological counseling, international student services, low-cost health insurance. *Library facilities:* Auburn University Montgomery Library. *Online resources:* library catalog, web page, access to other libraries' catalogs. *Collection:* 347,044 titles, 2,303 serial subscriptions.

Computer facilities: 285 computers available on campus for general student use. A campuswide network can be accessed from student residence rooms and from off campus. Internet access and online class registration are available. *Web address:* http://www.aum.edu/.

General Application Contact: Valerie Crawford, Associate Director of Enrollment Services, 334-244-3614, Fax: 334-244-3762.

GRADUATE UNITS

School of Business Students: 51 full-time (28 women), 123 part-time (63 women); includes 55 minority (39 African Americans, 9 Asian Americans or Pacific Islanders, 7 Hispanic Americans). Average age 29. *Faculty:* 22 full-time (3 women). Expenses: Contact institution. *Financial support:* Research assistantships, career-related internships or fieldwork and scholarships/grants available. Support available to part-time students. Financial award application deadline: 3/1; financial award applicants required to submit FAFSA. In 2006, 94 degrees awarded. *Degree program information:* Part-time and evening/weekend programs available. Offers business (MBA). *Application deadline:* Applications are processed on a rolling basis. *Application fee:* $25. Electronic applications accepted. *Dean,* Dr. Jane Goodson, 334-244-3478, Fax: 334-244-3792, E-mail: jgoodson@mail.aum.edu.

School of Education Students: 94 full-time (73 women), 238 part-time (199 women); includes 151 minority (142 African Americans, 2 American Indian/Alaska Native, 3 Asian Americans or Pacific Islanders, 4 Hispanic Americans), 1 international. Average age 34. *Faculty:* 23 full-time (15 women), 2 part-time/adjunct (1 woman). Expenses: Contact institution. *Financial support:* In 2006–07, 2 teaching assistantships were awarded; career-related internships or fieldwork and scholarships/grants also available. Support available to part-time students. Financial award application deadline: 3/1; financial award applicants required to submit FAFSA. In 2006, 78 master's, 18 other advanced degrees awarded. *Degree program information:* Part-time and evening/weekend programs available. Offers counseling (M Ed, Ed S); early childhood education (M Ed, Ed S); education (M Ed, Ed S); education administration (M Ed, Ed S); elementary education (M Ed, Ed S); physical education (M Ed); reading education (M Ed, Ed S); secondary education (M Ed, Ed S); special education (M Ed, Ed S). *Application deadline:* Applications are processed on a rolling basis. *Application fee:* $25. Electronic applications accepted. *Application Contact:* Dr. Sam Flynt, Associate Graduate Coordinator, 334-244-3270, Fax: 334-244-3835, E-mail: sflynt@mail.aum.edu. *Dean,* Dr. Jennifer A. Brown, 334-244-3413, Fax: 334-244-3835, E-mail: jbrown@mail.aum.edu.

School of Liberal Arts Students: 5 full-time (all women), 24 part-time (17 women); includes 6 minority (3 African Americans, 1 American Indian/Alaska Native, 2 Asian Americans or Pacific Islanders). Average age 32. *Faculty:* 23 full-time (8 women). Expenses: Contact institution. *Financial support:* In 2006–07, 2 teaching assistantships were awarded; career-related internships or fieldwork and scholarships/grants also available. Support available to part-time students. Financial award application deadline: 3/1; financial award applicants required to submit FAFSA. In 2006, 7 degrees awarded. *Degree program information:* Part-time and evening/weekend programs available. Offers liberal arts (MLA). *Application deadline:* Applications are processed on a rolling basis. *Application fee:* $25. Electronic applications accepted. *Application Contact:* Dr. Susan L. Willis, Graduate Coordinator, 334-244-3406, Fax: 334-244-3740, E-mail: swillis1@mail.aum.edu. *Dean,* Dr. Larry C. Mullins, 334-244-3382, Fax: 334-244-3740, E-mail: lmullins@mail.aum.edu.

School of Sciences Students: 62 full-time (49 women), 138 part-time (97 women); includes 94 minority (81 African Americans, 6 Asian Americans or Pacific Islanders, 7 Hispanic Americans). Average age 38. *Faculty:* 29 full-time (9 women), 5 part-time/adjunct (0 women). Expenses: Contact institution. *Financial support:* In 2006–07, 8 teaching assistantships were awarded; career-related internships or fieldwork and scholarships/grants also available. Support available to part-time students. Financial award application deadline: 3/1; financial award applicants required to submit FAFSA. In 2006, 50 degrees awarded. *Degree program information:* Part-time and evening/weekend programs available. Offers justice and public safety (MSJPS); psychology (MSPG); public administration and political science (MPA, MPS, PhD); sciences (MPA, MPS, MSJPS, MSPG, PhD). *Application deadline:* Applications are processed on a rolling basis. *Application fee:* $25. Electronic applications accepted. *Application Contact:* Dr.

Glen Ray, Acting Graduate Coordinator, 334-244-3590, Fax: 334-244-3826, E-mail: gray@mail.aum.edu. *Dean*, Dr. Bayo Lawal, 334-224-3678, Fax: 334-244-3826, E-mail: blawal@mail.aum.edu.

AUGSBURG COLLEGE, Minneapolis, MN 55454-1351

General Information Independent-religious, coed, comprehensive institution. *Enrollment:* 3,732 graduate, professional, and undergraduate students; 573 full-time matriculated graduate/professional students (342 women), 238 part-time matriculated graduate/professional students (175 women). *Enrollment by degree level:* 811 master's. *Graduate faculty:* 30 full-time (19 women), 18 part-time/adjunct (8 women). *Tuition:* Full-time $10,584; part-time $1,764 per course. *Required fees:* $300; $35 per course. Tuition and fees vary according to program. *Graduate housing:* On-campus housing not available. *Student services:* Career counseling, free psychological counseling. *Library facilities:* James G. Lindell Library. *Online resources:* library catalog, web page, access to other libraries' catalogs. *Collection:* 146,166 titles, 754 serial subscriptions.

Computer facilities: 260 computers available on campus for general student use. A campuswide network can be accessed from student residence rooms and from off campus. Internet access and online class registration are available. *Web address:* http://www.augsburg.edu/.

General Application Contact: Mike Bilden, Director, Weekend College and Graduate Admissions, 612-330-1101 Ext. 1792, E-mail: bilden@augsburg.edu.

GRADUATE UNITS

Program in Business Administration Students: 289 full-time (133 women), 9 part-time (2 women); includes 23 minority (11 African Americans, 1 American Indian/Alaska Native, 9 Asian Americans or Pacific Islanders, 2 Hispanic Americans), 5 international. Average age 34. 715 applicants, 13% accepted, 85 enrolled. *Faculty:* 2 full-time (1 woman), 5 part-time/adjunct (2 women). Expenses: Contact institution. *Degree program information:* Evening/weekend programs available. Offers business administration (MBA). *Application deadline:* For fall admission, 8/15 priority date for domestic students; for winter admission, 12/15 priority date for domestic students; for spring admission, 3/25 priority date for domestic students. Applications are processed on a rolling basis. *Application fee:* $35. Electronic applications accepted. *Application Contact:* Mike Bilden, Graduate Recruiter, 612-330-1434, E-mail: bilden@augsburg.edu. *Director*, Dr. Robert Kramarczuk, 612-330-1606, E-mail: kramarc@augsburg.edu.

Program in Education Students: 97 full-time (59 women), 91 part-time (66 women); includes 17 minority (7 African Americans, 3 American Indian/Alaska Native, 6 Asian Americans or Pacific Islanders, 1 Hispanic American), 2 international. Average age 33. 405 applicants, 17% accepted, 43 enrolled. *Faculty:* 4 full-time (3 women), 3 part-time/adjunct (all women). Expenses: Contact institution. In 2006, 1 degree awarded. *Degree program information:* Part-time and evening/weekend programs available. Offers education (MAE). *Application deadline:* For fall admission, 8/15 for domestic and international students; for winter admission, 12/15 for domestic and international students; for spring admission, 3/26 for domestic and international students. Applications are processed on a rolling basis. *Application fee:* $35. Electronic applications accepted. *Application Contact:* Karen Howell, Program Coordinator, 612-330-1354, E-mail: howell@augsburg.edu. *Professor*, Vicki Olson, 612-330-1131, E-mail: olsonv@augsburg.edu.

Program in Leadership Students: 22 full-time (14 women), 79 part-time (52 women); includes 13 minority (10 African Americans, 2 American Indian/Alaska Native, 1 Hispanic American). Average age 38. 213 applicants, 17% accepted, 31 enrolled. *Faculty:* 7 full-time (2 women), 2 part-time/adjunct (1 woman). Expenses: Contact institution. *Financial support:* In 2006–07, 9 students received support. Available to part-time students. Application deadline: 8/1; In 2006, 10 degrees awarded. *Degree program information:* Part-time and evening/weekend programs available. Offers leadership (MA). *Application deadline:* For fall admission, 8/9 priority date for domestic students; for winter admission, 12/15 for domestic students; for spring admission, 3/7 for domestic students. Applications are processed on a rolling basis. *Application fee:* $35. *Application Contact:* Patricia Park, Program Coordinator, 612-330-1150, E-mail: parkp@augsburg.edu. *Director*, Dr. Norma Noonan, 612-330-1198, Fax: 612-330-1355, E-mail: noonan@augsburg.edu.

Program in Physicians Assistant Studies Students: 85 full-time (69 women); includes 8 minority (1 African American, 7 Asian Americans or Pacific Islanders). Average age 29. 130 applicants, 22% accepted, 28 enrolled. *Faculty:* 7 full-time (6 women), 1 part-time/adjunct (0 women). Expenses: Contact institution. *Financial support:* In 2006–07, 26 students received support. Application deadline: 8/1; In 2006, 25 degrees awarded. Offers physicians assistant studies (MS). *Application deadline:* For spring admission, 10/1 for domestic students. *Application fee:* $20. *Application Contact:* Carrie Benton, Information Contact, 612-330-1039, Fax: 612-330-1757, E-mail: paprog@augsburg.edu. *Director*, Dawn B. Ludwig, 612-330-1331, Fax: 612-330-1757, E-mail: ludwig@augsburg.edu.

Program in Social Work Students: 74 full-time (61 women), 16 part-time (13 women); includes 15 minority (8 African Americans, 1 American Indian/Alaska Native, 2 Asian Americans or Pacific Islanders, 4 Hispanic Americans). Average age 31. 359 applicants, 20% accepted, 36 enrolled. *Faculty:* 8 full-time (5 women), 5 part-time/adjunct (2 women). Expenses: Contact institution. *Financial support:* In 2006–07, 38 students received support. Career-related internships or fieldwork, institutionally sponsored loans, and tuition waivers (partial) available. Support available to part-time students. Financial award application deadline: 4/15. In 2006, 32 degrees awarded. *Degree program information:* Part-time and evening/weekend programs available. Offers social work (MSW). *Application deadline:* For fall admission, 1/15 for domestic students; for spring admission, 10/1 for domestic students. *Application fee:* $35. *Application Contact:* Holley Locher, Program Coordinator, 612-330-1763, Fax: 612-330-1493, E-mail: locherh@augsburg.edu. *Director*, Dr. Tony Bibus, 612-330-1746, Fax: 612-330-1493, E-mail: bibus@augsburg.edu.

Program in Transcultural Community Health Nursing Students: 6 full-time (all women), 43 part-time (42 women); includes 2 minority (both African Americans), 1 international. Average age 45. 120 applicants, 18% accepted, 20 enrolled. *Faculty:* 2 full-time (both women). Expenses: Contact institution. *Financial support:* In 2006–07, 5 students received support. Application deadline: 8/1; In 2006, 8 degrees awarded. Offers transcultural community health nursing (MA). *Application deadline:* For fall admission, 8/1 for domestic students; for winter admission, 12/4 for domestic students; for spring admission, 3/9 for domestic students. *Application fee:* $35. *Application Contact:* Sharon Wade, Coordinator, 612-330-1209, E-mail: wades@augsburg.edu. *Director*, Dr. Cheryl J. Leuning, 612-330-1214, E-mail: leuning@augsburg.edu.

AUGUSTANA COLLEGE, Sioux Falls, SD 57197

General Information Independent-religious, coed, comprehensive institution. *Graduate housing:* Room and/or apartments available on a first-come, first-served basis to single students.

GRADUATE UNITS

Department of Education *Degree program information:* Part-time and evening/weekend programs available. Offers education (MA); elementary (MA); secondary (MA).

Program in Advanced Nursing Practice in Emerging Health Systems *Degree program information:* Part-time programs available. Postbaccalaureate distance learning degree programs offered (minimal on-campus study). Offers community health nursing (MA).

AUGUSTA STATE UNIVERSITY, Augusta, GA 30904-2200

General Information State-supported, coed, comprehensive institution. *Enrollment:* 6,552 graduate, professional, and undergraduate students; 189 full-time matriculated graduate/professional students (133 women), 370 part-time matriculated graduate/professional students (276 women). *Enrollment by degree level:* 397 master's, 162 other advanced degrees. *Graduate faculty:* 39 full-time (23 women), 13 part-time/adjunct (11 women). Tuition, state resident: full-time $3,044; part-time $127 per credit hour. Tuition, nonresident: full-time $12,172; part-time $508 per credit hour. *Graduate housing:* Room and/or apartments available on a first-come, first-served basis to single students; on-campus housing not available to married students. Typical cost: $4,900 per year. *Student services:* Campus employment opportunities, career counseling, child daycare facilities, disabled student services, low-cost health insurance, teacher training. *Library facilities:* Reese Library plus 1 other. *Online resources:* library catalog, web page, access to other libraries' catalogs. *Collection:* 478,420 titles, 29,468 serial subscriptions, 4,738 audiovisual materials. *Research affiliation:* Veterans Administration Hospital (psychology).

Computer facilities: 325 computers available on campus for general student use. A campuswide network can be accessed from off campus. Internet access and online class registration are available. *Web address:* http://www.aug.edu/.

General Application Contact: Katherine Sweeney, Director of Admissions/Registrar, 706-737-1405, Fax: 706-667-4355, E-mail: ksweeney@aug.edu.

GRADUATE UNITS

Graduate Studies Students: 189 full-time (133 women), 370 part-time (276 women); includes 136 minority (111 African Americans, 2 American Indian/Alaska Native, 12 Asian Americans or Pacific Islanders, 11 Hispanic Americans). Average age 34. 176 applicants, 89% accepted, 113 enrolled. *Faculty:* 39 full-time (23 women), 13 part-time/adjunct (11 women). Expenses: Contact institution. *Financial support:* Research assistantships with partial tuition reimbursements, career-related internships or fieldwork, Federal Work-Study, institutionally sponsored loans, and unspecified assistantships available. Support available to part-time students. Financial award application deadline: 4/15; financial award applicants required to submit FAFSA. In 2006, 107 master's, 49 other advanced degrees awarded. *Degree program information:* Part-time and evening/weekend programs available. *Application deadline:* Applications are processed on a rolling basis. *Application fee:* $20. *Vice President for Academic Affairs*, Dr. Samuel Sullivan, 706-737-1422, Fax: 706-737-1585, E-mail: ssullivan@aug.edu.

College of Arts and Sciences Students: 30 full-time (19 women), 37 part-time (27 women); includes 21 minority (15 African Americans, 2 Asian Americans or Pacific Islanders, 4 Hispanic Americans). Average age 30. 41 applicants, 68% accepted, 24 enrolled. *Faculty:* 9 full-time (5 women), 3 part-time/adjunct (2 women). Expenses: Contact institution. *Financial support:* Research assistantships with partial tuition reimbursements, career-related internships or fieldwork, Federal Work-Study, and institutionally sponsored loans available. Financial award application deadline: 4/15; financial award applicants required to submit FAFSA. In 2006, 20 degrees awarded. *Degree program information:* Part-time and evening/weekend programs available. Offers arts and sciences (MPA, MS); political science (MPA); psychology (MS). *Application deadline:* Applications are processed on a rolling basis. *Application fee:* $20. *Dean*, Dr. Robert R. Parham, 706-737-1738, Fax: 706-737-1773, E-mail: rparham@aug.edu.

College of Business Administration Students: 31 full-time (16 women), 64 part-time (22 women); includes 20 minority (12 African Americans, 6 Asian Americans or Pacific Islanders, 2 Hispanic Americans). Average age 30. 44 applicants, 86% accepted, 28 enrolled. *Faculty:* 9 full-time (6 women). Expenses: Contact institution. *Financial support:* Research assistantships with partial tuition reimbursements, Federal Work-Study and institutionally sponsored loans available. Support available to part-time students. Financial award application deadline: 4/15; financial award applicants required to submit FAFSA. In 2006, 31 degrees awarded. *Degree program information:* Part-time and evening/weekend programs available. Offers business administration (MBA). *Application deadline:* For fall admission, 7/15 priority date for domestic students, 7/1 for international students; for spring admission, 12/1 priority date for domestic students, 11/15 for international students. Applications are processed on a rolling basis. *Application fee:* $20. *Application Contact:* Dr. Todd A Schultz, Acting Associate Dean, 706-737-1562, Fax: 706-667-4064, E-mail: tschultz@aug.edu. *Dean*, Dr. Marc D Miller, 706-737-1418, Fax: 706-667-4064, E-mail: mmiller@aug.edu.

College of Education Students: 128 full-time (98 women), 269 part-time (227 women); includes 95 minority (84 African Americans, 2 American Indian/Alaska Native, 4 Asian Americans or Pacific Islanders, 5 Hispanic Americans). Average age 36. 91 applicants, 100% accepted, 61 enrolled. *Faculty:* 21 full-time (12 women), 10 part-time/adjunct (9 women). Expenses: Contact institution. *Financial support:* Career-related internships or fieldwork, Federal Work-Study, institutionally sponsored loans, and unspecified assistantships available. Support available to part-time students. Financial award application deadline: 4/15; financial award applicants required to submit FAFSA. In 2006, 56 master's, 49 other advanced degrees awarded. *Degree program information:* Part-time and evening/weekend programs available. Offers counseling/guidance (M Ed); education (M Ed, Ed S); educational leadership (M Ed, Ed S); elementary education (M Ed, Ed S); health and physical education (M Ed); middle grades education (M Ed, Ed S); secondary education (M Ed, Ed S); special education (M Ed, Ed S). *Application deadline:* For fall admission, 7/16 priority date for domestic students. Applications are processed on a rolling basis. *Application fee:* $20. *Application Contact:* Andrea M. Scott, Secretary to the Dean, 706-737-1499, Fax: 706-667-4706, E-mail: ascott1@aug.edu. *Dean*, Dr. Thomas E. Deering, 706-737-1499, Fax: 706-667-4706, E-mail: tdeering@aug.edu.

AURORA UNIVERSITY, Aurora, IL 60506-4892

General Information Independent, coed, comprehensive institution. *Enrollment:* 3,791 graduate, professional, and undergraduate students; 378 full-time matriculated graduate/professional students (297 women), 1,384 part-time matriculated graduate/professional students (987 women). *Enrollment by degree level:* 1,614 master's, 109 doctoral, 39 other advanced degrees. *Graduate faculty:* 38 full-time (19 women), 126 part-time/adjunct (72 women). *Tuition:* Part-time $330 per credit hour. Tuition and fees vary according to campus/location and program. *Graduate housing:* On-campus housing not available. *Student services:* Campus employment opportunities, campus safety program, career counseling, disabled student services, exercise/wellness program, free psychological counseling, international student services, low-cost health insurance, multicultural affairs office. *Library facilities:* Charles B. Phillips Library plus 1 other. *Online resources:* library catalog, web page, access to other libraries' catalogs. *Collection:* 92,025 titles, 210 serial subscriptions, 7,621 audiovisual materials.

Computer facilities: 90 computers available on campus for general student use. A campuswide network can be accessed from student residence rooms and from off campus. Internet access is available. *Web address:* http://www.aurora.edu/.

General Application Contact: Donna DeSpain, Dean of Adult and Graduate Studies, 800-742-5281, Fax: 630-844-5535, E-mail: auadmission@aurora.edu.

GRADUATE UNITS

College of Education Students: 144 full-time (102 women), 1,156 part-time (832 women); includes 169 minority (32 African Americans, 2 American Indian/Alaska Native, 10 Asian Americans or Pacific Islanders, 125 Hispanic Americans). Average age 36. 451 applicants, 99% accepted, 421 enrolled. *Faculty:* 20 full-time (10 women), 99 part-time/adjunct (55 women). Expenses: Contact institution. *Financial support:* In 2006–07, 355 students received support; fellowships, research assistantships, teaching assistantships, Federal Work-Study and scholarships/grants available. Support available to part-time students. Financial award application deadline: 4/15; financial award applicants required to submit FAFSA. In 2006, 439 master's, 9 doctorates awarded. *Degree program information:* Part-time and evening/weekend programs available. Offers curriculum and instruction (Ed D); education (MAT); education and administration (Ed D); educational leadership (MEL); reading instruction (MA). *Application deadline:* For fall admission, 8/23 priority date for domestic students. Applications are processed on a rolling basis. *Application fee:* $25. Electronic applications accepted. *Application Contact:* Donna DeSpain, Dean of Adult and Graduate Studies, 800-742-5281, Fax: 630-844-5535, E-mail: auadmission@aurora.edu. *Dean*, Dr. Donald C. Wold, 630-844-1542, Fax: 630-844-5530, E-mail: dwold@aurora.edu.

College of Professional Studies Students: 213 full-time (182 women), 199 part-time (137 women); includes 73 minority (37 African Americans, 7 Asian Americans or Pacific Islanders, 29 Hispanic Americans), 1 international. Average age 34. 274 applicants, 98% accepted, 166 enrolled. *Faculty:* 16 full-time (8 women), 24 part-time/adjunct (15 women). Expenses: Contact institution. *Financial support:* In 2006–07, 267 students received support; fellowships, research assistantships, teaching assistantships available. Financial award application deadline: 4/15; financial award applicants required to submit FAFSA. In 2006, 170 degrees awarded. *Degree program information:* Part-time and evening/weekend programs available. *Application deadline:* For fall admission, 8/25 priority date for domestic students.

Aurora University (continued)
Applications are processed on a rolling basis. *Application fee:* $25. Electronic applications accepted. *Dean,* Dr. Michael Carroll.

Dunham School of Business Students: 27 full-time (15 women), 92 part-time (48 women); includes 23 minority (13 African Americans, 2 Asian Americans or Pacific Islanders, 8 Hispanic Americans), 1 international. Average age 36. 46 applicants, 100% accepted, 33 enrolled. *Faculty:* 6 full-time (0 women), 12 part-time/adjunct (4 women). Expenses: Contact institution. *Financial support:* In 2006–07, 43 students received support; fellowships, research assistantships, teaching assistantships, Federal Work-Study and scholarships/grants available. Support available to part-time students. Financial award application deadline: 4/15; financial award applicants required to submit FAFSA. In 2006, 48 degrees awarded. *Degree program information:* Part-time and evening/weekend programs available. Offers business (MBA). *Application deadline:* For fall admission, 8/25 priority date for domestic students. Applications are processed on a rolling basis. *Application fee:* $25. Electronic applications accepted. *Application Contact:* Donna DeSpain, Dean of Adult and Graduate Studies, 800-742-5281, Fax: 630-844-5535, E-mail: auadmission@aurora.edu. *Director,* Dr. Shawn Green, 630-844-5527, Fax: 630-844-7830, E-mail: sgreen@aurora.edu.

School of Social Work Students: 186 full-time (167 women), 107 part-time (89 women); includes 50 minority (24 African Americans, 5 Asian Americans or Pacific Islanders, 21 Hispanic Americans). Average age 33. 228 applicants, 97% accepted, 133 enrolled. *Faculty:* 10 full-time (8 women), 12 part-time/adjunct (11 women). Expenses: Contact institution. *Financial support:* In 2006–07, 224 students received support; fellowships, research assistantships, teaching assistantships, Federal Work-Study and scholarships/grants available. Support available to part-time students. Financial award application deadline: 4/15; financial award applicants required to submit FAFSA. In 2006, 122 degrees awarded. *Degree program information:* Part-time and evening/weekend programs available. Offers social work (MSW). *Application deadline:* For fall admission, 8/25 priority date for domestic students. Applications are processed on a rolling basis. *Application fee:* $25. Electronic applications accepted. *Application Contact:* Melissa Yovich-Whattam, Graduate Recruiter for MSW Program, 630-844-5292, E-mail: auadmission@aurora.edu. *Dean,* Dr. Fred Mckenzie, 630-844-5420, E-mail: mckenzie@aurora.edu.

School of Experiential Leadership Students: 21 full-time (13 women), 15 part-time (10 women); includes 3 minority (2 African Americans, 1 Asian American or Pacific Islander). Average age 31. 30 applicants, 100% accepted, 22 enrolled. *Faculty:* 2 full-time (1 woman), 2 part-time/adjunct (1 woman). Expenses: Contact institution. *Financial support:* In 2006–07, 27 students received support, including 6 fellowships (averaging $5,609 per year); research assistantships, teaching assistantships, Federal Work-Study, scholarships/grants, and unspecified assistantships also available. Support available to part-time students. Financial award application deadline: 4/15. In 2006, 30 degrees awarded. *Degree program information:* Part-time and evening/weekend programs available. Offers administration of leisure services (MS); outdoor pursuits recreation administration (MS). *Application deadline:* For fall admission, 8/25 priority date for domestic students. Applications are processed on a rolling basis. *Application fee:* $25. Electronic applications accepted. *Application Contact:* Dr. Rita Yerkes, Dean, 262-245-8572, E-mail: ryerkes@aurora.edu.

AUSTIN COLLEGE, Sherman, TX 75090-4400

General Information Independent-religious, coed, comprehensive institution. *Enrollment:* 1,354 graduate, professional, and undergraduate students; 33 full-time matriculated graduate/professional students (26 women). *Enrollment by degree level:* 33 master's. *Graduate faculty:* 5 full-time (3 women), 1 (woman) part-time/adjunct. *Tuition:* Full-time $27,385. *Required fees:* $160. *Graduate housing:* Room and/or apartments available on a first-come, first-served basis to single students; on-campus housing not available to married students. Typical cost: $3,554 per year ($7,741 including board). Housing application deadline: 5/1. *Student services:* Campus employment opportunities, career counseling, free psychological counseling, teacher training. *Library facilities:* Abell Library. *Online resources:* library catalog, web page, access to other libraries' catalogs. *Collection:* 240,944 titles, 2,181 serial subscriptions.

Computer facilities: 165 computers available on campus for general student use. A campuswide network can be accessed from student residence rooms and from off campus. Internet access is available. *Web address:* http://www.austincollege.edu/.

General Application Contact: Dr. Barbara Sylvester, Director of Teaching Program, 903-813-2498, Fax: 903-813-2326, E-mail: bsylvester@austincollege.edu.

GRADUATE UNITS

Program in Education Students: 33 full-time (26 women); includes 3 minority (2 Asian Americans or Pacific Islanders, 1 Hispanic American). Average age 25. *Faculty:* 5 full-time (3 women), 1 (woman) part-time/adjunct. Expenses: Contact institution. *Financial support:* In 2006–07, 27 students received support. Career-related internships or fieldwork, Federal Work-Study, scholarships/grants, and unspecified assistantships available. Support available to part-time students. Financial award application deadline: 4/1; financial award applicants required to submit FAFSA. In 2006, 24 degrees awarded. *Degree program information:* Part-time programs available. Offers art education (MA); elementary education (MA); middle school education (MA); music education (MA); physical education and coaching (MA); secondary education (MA). Applicants must meet Austin College's undergraduate curriculum requirements. *Application deadline:* For fall admission, 5/1 priority date for domestic students; for spring admission, 1/15 priority date for domestic students. Applications are processed on a rolling basis. *Application fee:* $35. Electronic applications accepted. *Director of Teaching Program,* Dr. Barbara Sylvester, 903-813-2498, Fax: 903-813-2326, E-mail: bsylvester@austincollege.edu.

AUSTIN GRADUATE SCHOOL OF THEOLOGY, Austin, TX 78705-5610

General Information Independent-religious, coed, upper-level institution. *Graduate housing:* On-campus housing not available.

GRADUATE UNITS

Program in Theological Studies *Degree program information:* Part-time programs available. Offers theological studies (MATS).

AUSTIN PEAY STATE UNIVERSITY, Clarksville, TN 37044

General Information State-supported, coed, comprehensive institution. CGS member. *Enrollment:* 9,207 graduate, professional, and undergraduate students; 228 full-time matriculated graduate/professional students (164 women), 488 part-time matriculated graduate/professional students (356 women). *Enrollment by degree level:* 673 master's, 43 other advanced degrees. *Graduate faculty:* 109 full-time (46 women), 21 part-time/adjunct (10 women). Tuition, state resident: full-time $5,138; part-time $272 per credit hour. Tuition, nonresident: full-time $14,832; part-time $693 per credit hour. *Required fees:* $1,009. *Graduate housing:* Rooms and/or apartments available on a first-come, first-served basis to single and married students. Typical cost: $3,200 per year ($5,190 including board) for single students; $5,100 per year ($7,090 including board) for married students. Room and board charges vary according to board plan and housing facility selected. Housing application deadline: 4/1. *Student services:* Campus employment opportunities, campus safety program, career counseling, child daycare facilities, disabled student services, exercise/wellness program, free psychological counseling, international student services, low-cost health insurance, multicultural affairs office, teacher training, writing training. *Library facilities:* Felix G. Woodward Library. *Online resources:* library catalog, web page, access to other libraries' catalogs. *Collection:* 400,000 titles, 1,754 serial subscriptions.

Computer facilities: Computer purchase and lease plans are available. 650 computers available on campus for general student use. A campuswide network can be accessed from student residence rooms and from off campus. Internet access and online class registration are available. *Web address:* http://www.apsu.edu/.

General Application Contact: Dr. Charles Pinder, Dean, College of Graduate Studies, 931-221-7414, Fax: 931-221-7641, E-mail: pinderc@apsu.edu.

GRADUATE UNITS

College of Graduate Studies Students: 228 full-time (164 women), 488 part-time (356 women); includes 154 minority (125 African Americans, 3 American Indian/Alaska Native, 5 Asian Americans or Pacific Islanders, 21 Hispanic Americans), 9 international. Average age 34. *Faculty:* 109 full-time (46 women), 21 part-time/adjunct (10 women). Expenses: Contact institution. *Financial support:* In 2006–07, 102 students received support, including fellowships (averaging $9,000 per year), research assistantships (averaging $9,250 per year), teaching assistantships (averaging $6,000 per year); career-related internships or fieldwork, Federal Work-Study, institutionally sponsored loans, scholarships/grants, and unspecified assistantships also available. Support available to part-time students. Financial award application deadline: 3/1; financial award applicants required to submit FAFSA. In 2006, 219 master's, 16 other advanced degrees awarded. *Degree program information:* Part-time and evening/weekend programs available. Postbaccalaureate distance learning degree programs offered. *Application deadline:* For fall admission, 7/31 priority date for domestic students; for spring admission, 12/17 priority date for domestic students. Applications are processed on a rolling basis. *Application fee:* $25. Electronic applications accepted. *Dean, College of Graduate Studies,* Dr. Charles Pinder, 931-221-7414, Fax: 931-221-7641, E-mail: pinderc@apsu.edu.

College of Arts and Letters Students: 42 full-time (25 women), 94 part-time (66 women); includes 34 minority (28 African Americans, 2 Asian Americans or Pacific Islanders, 4 Hispanic Americans), 2 international. Average age 32. *Faculty:* 47 full-time (18 women), 9 part-time/adjunct (3 women). Expenses: Contact institution. *Financial support:* In 2006–07, research assistantships (averaging $10,270 per year); career-related internships or fieldwork, Federal Work-Study, institutionally sponsored loans, scholarships/grants, and unspecified assistantships also available. Support available to part-time students. Financial award application deadline: 3/1; financial award applicants required to submit FAFSA. In 2006, 32 degrees awarded. *Degree program information:* Part-time programs available. Postbaccalaureate distance learning degree programs offered. Offers arts and letters (M Mu, MA); communication arts (MA); English (MA); military history (MA); music education (M Mu); performance (M Mu). *Application deadline:* For fall admission, 7/31 priority date for domestic students; for spring admission, 12/17 priority date for domestic students. Applications are processed on a rolling basis. *Application fee:* $25. Electronic applications accepted. *Dean,* James Diehr, 931-221-6445, Fax: 931-221-1024.

College of Professional Programs and Social Sciences Students: 176 full-time (131 women), 370 part-time (275 women); includes 115 minority (95 African Americans, 2 American Indian/Alaska Native, 3 Asian Americans or Pacific Islanders, 15 Hispanic Americans), 4 international. Average age 34. *Faculty:* 49 full-time (25 women), 11 part-time/adjunct (7 women). Expenses: Contact institution. *Financial support:* In 2006–07, fellowships (averaging $9,000 per year), research assistantships (averaging $10,270 per year) were awarded; career-related internships or fieldwork, Federal Work-Study, institutionally sponsored loans, scholarships/grants, and unspecified assistantships also available. Support available to part-time students. Financial award application deadline: 3/1; financial award applicants required to submit FAFSA. In 2006, 179 master's, 16 other advanced degrees awarded. *Degree program information:* Part-time and evening/weekend programs available. Postbaccalaureate distance learning degree programs offered. Offers curriculum and instruction (MA Ed); education (M Ed, Ed S); educational leadership studies (MA Ed); guidance and counseling (MS); health and physical education (MS); management (MS); nursing (MS); psychology (MA); reading (MA Ed); social sciences (M Ed, MA, MA Ed, MS, Ed S). *Application deadline:* For fall admission, 7/31 priority date for domestic students; for spring admission, 12/17 priority date for domestic students. Applications are processed on a rolling basis. *Application fee:* $25. Electronic applications accepted. *Dean,* Dr. David Denton, 931-221-6380, E-mail: dentond@apsu.edu.

College of Science and Mathematics Students: 9 full-time (7 women), 17 part-time (11 women); includes 4 minority (1 African American, 1 American Indian/Alaska Native, 2 Hispanic Americans), 3 international. Average age 29. *Faculty:* 13 full-time (3 women), 1 part-time/adjunct (0 women). Expenses: Contact institution. *Financial support:* In 2006–07, research assistantships with partial tuition reimbursements (averaging $10,270 per year), teaching assistantships (averaging $6,000 per year) were awarded; career-related internships or fieldwork, Federal Work-Study, institutionally sponsored loans, scholarships/grants, and unspecified assistantships also available. Support available to part-time students. Financial award application deadline: 3/1; financial award applicants required to submit FAFSA. In 2006, 8 degrees awarded. *Degree program information:* Part-time programs available. Offers biology (MS); science and mathematics (MS). *Application deadline:* For fall admission, 7/31 priority date for domestic students; for spring admission, 12/17 priority date for domestic students. Applications are processed on a rolling basis. *Application fee:* $25. Electronic applications accepted. *Interim Dean,* Dr. Susan Calovini, 931-221-7971, E-mail: calovinis@apsu.edu.

AUSTIN PRESBYTERIAN THEOLOGICAL SEMINARY, Austin, TX 78705-5797

General Information Independent-religious, coed, graduate-only institution. *Enrollment by degree level:* 145 first professional, 9 master's, 72 doctoral, 3 other advanced degrees. *Graduate faculty:* 21 full-time (7 women), 3 part-time/adjunct (0 women). *Tuition:* Full-time $9,600; part-time $160 per credit. Tuition and fees vary according to course load and degree level. *Graduate housing:* Rooms and/or apartments available on a first-come, first-served basis to single and married students. Typical cost: $2,000 per year for single students; $5,000 per year for married students. Housing application deadline: 5/31. *Student services:* Campus employment opportunities, career counseling, free psychological counseling, international student services. *Library facilities:* David and Jane Stitt Library. *Online resources:* library catalog, web page, access to other libraries' catalogs. *Collection:* 161,982 titles, 534 serial subscriptions, 6,956 audiovisual materials.

Computer facilities: 8 computers available on campus for general student use. A campuswide network can be accessed. Internet access and online class registration, Biblical Theological Research are available. *Web address:* http://www.austinseminary.edu/.

General Application Contact: Jack Barden, Director of Admissions, 512-404-4827, Fax: 512-479-0738, E-mail: jbarden@austinseminary.edu.

GRADUATE UNITS

Graduate and Professional Programs Students: 108 full-time (55 women), 121 part-time (43 women); includes 26 minority (17 African Americans, 4 Asian Americans or Pacific Islanders, 5 Hispanic Americans), 6 international. Average age 42. 102 applicants, 66% accepted, 42 enrolled. *Faculty:* 21 full-time (7 women), 3 part-time/adjunct (0 women). Expenses: Contact institution. *Financial support:* In 2006–07, 125 students received support, including 6 research assistantships (averaging $1,040 per year), 6 teaching assistantships (averaging $1,040 per year); career-related internships or fieldwork, institutionally sponsored loans, scholarships/grants, and tutorships also available. Support available to part-time students. Financial award application deadline: 6/1; financial award applicants required to submit FAFSA. In 2006, 52 M Divs, 10 master's, 5 doctorates awarded. *Degree program information:* Part-time programs available. Offers divinity (M Div); ministry (D Min); religious studies (MATS). *Application deadline:* For fall admission, 5/15 priority date for domestic students; for spring admission, 11/15 for domestic students. Applications are processed on a rolling basis. *Application fee:* $65. *Application Contact:* Jack Barden, Director of Admissions, 512-404-4827, Fax: 512-479-0738, E-mail: jbarden@austinseminary.edu. *Academic Dean,* Rev. Dr. Michael Jinkins, 512-404-4821, Fax: 512-479-0738, E-mail: mjinkins@austinseminary.edu.

AVE MARIA SCHOOL OF LAW, Ann Arbor, MI 48105-2550

General Information Independent-religious, coed, graduate-only institution. *Enrollment by degree level:* 381 first professional. *Graduate faculty:* 29 full-time (13 women), 8 part-time/adjunct (2 women). *Tuition:* Full-time $30,345. Tuition and fees vary according to student level. *Graduate housing:* On-campus housing not available. *Student services:* Campus employment opportunities, campus safety program, career counseling, disabled student services, exercise/wellness program, international student services, writing training. *Library facilities:*

Ave Maria School of Law Library. *Online resources:* library catalog, web page. *Collection:* 79,909 titles, 46,616 serial subscriptions, 1,219 audiovisual materials.

Computer facilities: 40 computers available on campus for general student use. A campuswide network can be accessed. Internet access and online class registration are available. *Web address:* http://www.avemarialaw.edu/.

General Application Contact: Rachele Conner, Assistant Director of Admissions, 734-827-8063, Fax: 734-622-0123, E-mail: rconner@avemarialaw.edu.

GRADUATE UNITS

School of Law Students: 380 full-time (126 women), 1 (woman) part-time; includes 62 minority (6 African Americans, 4 American Indian/Alaska Native, 28 Asian Americans or Pacific Islanders, 24 Hispanic Americans), 8 international. Average age 26. 941 applicants, 53% accepted, 131 enrolled. *Faculty:* 29 full-time (13 women), 8 part-time/adjunct (2 women). Expenses: Contact institution. *Financial support:* In 2006–07, 220 students received support. Career-related internships or fieldwork, Federal Work-Study, and scholarships/grants available. Financial award application deadline: 6/1; financial award applicants required to submit FAFSA. In 2006, 88 degrees awarded. Offers law (JD). *Application deadline:* For fall admission, 6/10 priority date for domestic and international students. Applications are processed on a rolling basis. *Application fee:* $50. Electronic applications accepted. *Application Contact:* Rachele Conner, Assistant Director of Admissions, 734-827-8063, Fax: 734-622-0123, E-mail: rconner@avemarialaw.edu.

AVE MARIA UNIVERSITY, Naples, FL 34119

General Information Independent-religious, coed, comprehensive institution. *Graduate housing:* Room and/or apartments available on a first-come, first-served basis to single students; on-campus housing not available to married students. Housing application deadline: 7/15.

GRADUATE UNITS

Graduate Programs

Institute for Pastoral Theology *Degree program information:* Part-time and evening/weekend programs available. Offers pastoral theology (MTS).

AVERETT UNIVERSITY, Danville, VA 24541-3692

General Information Independent-religious, coed, comprehensive institution. *Enrollment:* 883 graduate, professional, and undergraduate students; 216 full-time matriculated graduate/professional students (146 women), 457 part-time matriculated graduate/professional students (292 women). *Enrollment by degree level:* 673 master's. *Graduate faculty:* 20 full-time (5 women), 44 part-time/adjunct (17 women). *Graduate housing:* On-campus housing not available. *Student services:* Campus employment opportunities, campus safety program, career counseling, disabled student services, exercise/wellness program, free psychological counseling, international student services, teacher training, writing training. *Library facilities:* Mary B. Blount Library. *Online resources:* library catalog, web page, access to other libraries' catalogs. *Collection:* 109,414 titles, 19,495 serial subscriptions, 312 audiovisual materials.

Computer facilities: 100 computers available on campus for general student use. A campuswide network can be accessed. Internet access, online courses through Blackboard are available. *Web address:* http://www.averett.edu/.

General Application Contact: Katherine Pappas-Smith, Marketing and Enrollment Manager, 434-791-5844, Fax: 434-791-5850, E-mail: kapappas@averett.edu.

GRADUATE UNITS

Graduate Studies in Education Students: 14 full-time (10 women), 85 part-time (67 women); includes 20 minority (18 African Americans, 2 Asian Americans or Pacific Islanders). Average age 33. 52 applicants, 100% accepted, 40 enrolled. *Faculty:* 10 full-time (4 women), 7 part-time/adjunct (6 women). Expenses: Contact institution. *Financial support:* In 2006–07, 23 students received support. Federal Work-Study and scholarships/grants available. Financial award application deadline: 4/1; financial award applicants required to submit FAFSA. In 2006, 48 degrees awarded. *Degree program information:* Part-time and evening/weekend programs available. Offers art education (M Ed); biology (M Ed); chemistry (M Ed); curriculum and instruction (M Ed); elementary education (M Ed); English (M Ed); health and physical education (M Ed); history and social studies (M Ed); mathematics education (M Ed); physical science (M Ed); reading (M Ed); special education (learning disabilities specialization PK-12) (M Ed). Program also offered at Richmond, VA regional campus location. *Application deadline:* Applications are processed on a rolling basis. *Application fee:* $20. *Chair,* Dr. Lynn H. Wolf, 434-793-3995, Fax: 434-791-4392, E-mail: lynn.wolf@averett.edu.

Program in Business Administration Students: 202 full-time (136 women), 372 part-time (225 women); includes 238 minority (207 African Americans, 4 American Indian/Alaska Native, 13 Asian Americans or Pacific Islanders, 14 Hispanic Americans). Average age 38. 41 applicants, 100% accepted, 40 enrolled. *Faculty:* 12 full-time (3 women), 37 part-time/adjunct (11 women). Expenses: Contact institution. *Financial support:* In 2006–07, 187 students received support. Federal Work-Study and scholarships/grants available. Financial award application deadline: 4/1; financial award applicants required to submit FAFSA. In 2006, 210 degrees awarded. *Degree program information:* Part-time and evening/weekend programs available. Offers business administration (MBA). Program also offered at Richmond, VA regional campus location. *Application deadline:* Applications are processed on a rolling basis. *Application fee:* $50. *Application Contact:* Katherine Pappas-Smith, Marketing and Enrollment Manager, 434-791-5844, Fax: 434-791-5850, E-mail: kapappas@averett.edu. *Acting Dean,* Dr. Fred Bolton, 804-673-9675, Fax: 434-799-0658, E-mail: fbolton@averett.edu.

AVILA UNIVERSITY, Kansas City, MO 64145-1698

General Information Independent-religious, coed, comprehensive institution. *Enrollment:* 1,683 graduate, professional, and undergraduate students; 370 full-time matriculated graduate/professional students (273 women), 183 part-time matriculated graduate/professional students (112 women). *Enrollment by degree level:* 553 master's. *Graduate faculty:* 22 full-time (15 women), 42 part-time/adjunct (22 women). *Tuition:* Full-time $7,470; part-time $415 per credit. *Graduate housing:* Room and/or apartments available on a first-come, first-served basis to single students; on-campus housing not available to married students. Typical cost: $5,500 (including board). Housing application deadline: 7/31. *Student services:* Campus employment opportunities, campus safety program, career counseling, child daycare facilities, disabled student services, exercise/wellness program, free psychological counseling, international student services, low-cost health insurance, multicultural affairs office, teacher training, writing training. *Library facilities:* Hooley Bundshu Library. *Online resources:* library catalog, web page, access to other libraries' catalogs. *Collection:* 80,865 titles, 7,179 serial subscriptions.

Computer facilities: 68 computers available on campus for general student use. A campuswide network can be accessed from student residence rooms. Internet access is available. *Web address:* http://www.avila.edu/.

General Application Contact: Office of Admissions, 816-501-2400.

GRADUATE UNITS

Department of Psychology Students: 74 full-time (60 women), 35 part-time (28 women). Average age 35. 42 applicants, 64% accepted, 21 enrolled. *Faculty:* 7 full-time (6 women), 8 part-time/adjunct (5 women). Expenses: Contact institution. *Financial support:* Career-related internships or fieldwork and scholarships/grants available. Support available to part-time students. Financial award applicants required to submit FAFSA. In 2006, 25 degrees awarded. *Degree program information:* Part-time and evening/weekend programs available. Offers counseling and art therapy (MS); counseling psychology (MS); general psychology (MS); organizational development (MS). *Application deadline:* Applications are processed on a rolling basis. *Application fee:* $0. *Application Contact:* Regina Staves, PhD, Director of Graduate Psychology, 816-501-3665, Fax: 816-501-2455, E-mail: gradpsych@mail.avila.edu. *Director of Graduate Psychology,* Regina Staves, PhD, 816-501-3665, Fax: 816-501-2455, E-mail: gradpsych@mail.avila.edu.

Program in Organizational Development Students: 75. Average age 33. *Faculty:* 3 full-time (2 women), 20 part-time/adjunct. Expenses: Contact institution. *Financial support:* Unspecified assistantships available. Support available to part-time students. Financial award applicants required to submit FAFSA. In 2006, 5 degrees awarded. *Degree program information:* Part-time and evening/weekend programs available. Offers organizational development (MS); project management (Graduate Certificate). *Application deadline:* Applications are processed on a rolling basis. *Application fee:* $0. Electronic applications accepted. *Assistant Dean,* Lacey Smith, 816-501-3737, Fax: 816-941-4650, E-mail: advantage@avila.edu.

School of Business Students: 31 full-time (19 women), 165 part-time (96 women); includes 18 minority (14 African Americans, 1 American Indian/Alaska Native, 3 Hispanic Americans), 16 international. Average age 32. 77 applicants, 81% accepted, 62 enrolled. *Faculty:* 8 full-time (4 women), 17 part-time/adjunct (4 women). Expenses: Contact institution. *Financial support:* In 2006–07, 78 students received support. Career-related internships or fieldwork available. Support available to part-time students. Financial award applicants required to submit FAFSA. In 2006, 54 degrees awarded. *Degree program information:* Part-time and evening/weekend programs available. Offers accounting (MBA); finance (MBA); general management (MBA); health care administration (MBA); international business (MBA); management information systems (MBA); marketing (MBA). *Application deadline:* For fall admission, 7/30 priority date for domestic students; for winter admission, 11/30 priority date for domestic students; for spring admission, 2/28 priority date for domestic students. Applications are processed on a rolling basis. *Application fee:* $20. Electronic applications accepted. *Application Contact:* JoAnna Giffin, MBA Admissions Director, 816-501-3601, Fax: 816-501-2463, E-mail: joanna.giffin@avila.edu. *Dean,* Dr. Richard Woodall, 816-501-3798, Fax: 816-501-2463.

School of Education Students: 144 full-time (112 women), 42 part-time (24 women); includes 17 minority (15 African Americans, 2 Hispanic Americans). Average age 37. 72 applicants, 42% accepted, 14 enrolled. *Faculty:* 7 full-time (5 women), 17 part-time/adjunct (13 women). Expenses: Contact institution. *Financial support:* In 2006–07, 1 research assistantship was awarded; career-related internships or fieldwork also available. Support available to part-time students. Financial award applicants required to submit FAFSA. In 2006, 34 degrees awarded. *Degree program information:* Part-time and evening/weekend programs available. Offers education (MA); English for speakers of other languages (Advanced Certificate); special reading (Advanced Certificate). *Application deadline:* Applications are processed on a rolling basis. *Application fee:* $0. Electronic applications accepted. *Application Contact:* Deana Angotti, Director of Graduate Education, 816-501-2446, Fax: 816-501-2915, E-mail: deana.augotti@avila.edu. *Dean,* Dr. Laura Sloan, 816-501-3663, Fax: 816-501-2455, E-mail: laura.sloan@avila.edu.

AZUSA PACIFIC UNIVERSITY, Azusa, CA 91702-7000

General Information Independent-religious, coed, comprehensive institution. CGS member. *Enrollment:* 8,128 graduate, professional, and undergraduate students; 504 full-time matriculated graduate/professional students (320 women), 2,902 part-time matriculated graduate/professional students (1,907 women). *Enrollment by degree level:* 186 first professional, 2,910 master's, 310 doctoral. *Graduate faculty:* 129 full-time (74 women). *Tuition:* Part-time $475 per credit. *Graduate housing:* On-campus housing not available. *Student services:* Campus employment opportunities, campus safety program, career counseling, disabled student services, exercise/wellness program, free psychological counseling, international student services, low-cost health insurance, multicultural affairs office, teacher training. *Library facilities:* Marshburn Memorial Library plus 2 others. *Online resources:* library catalog, web page. *Collection:* 185,708 titles, 14,031 serial subscriptions.

Computer facilities: Computer purchase and lease plans are available. 300 computers available on campus for general student use. A campuswide network can be accessed from off campus. Internet access and online class registration are available. *Web address:* http://www.apu.edu/.

General Application Contact: Linda Witte, Graduate Admissions Office, 626-969-3434.

GRADUATE UNITS

College of Liberal Arts and Sciences Students: 12 full-time (all women), 91 part-time (68 women); includes 12 minority (1 American Indian/Alaska Native, 10 Asian Americans or Pacific Islanders, 1 Hispanic American), 21 international. Average age 32. *Faculty:* 13 full-time (6 women). Expenses: Contact institution. *Financial support:* Teaching assistantships, career-related internships or fieldwork available. Support available to part-time students. In 2006, 28 degrees awarded. *Degree program information:* Part-time and evening/weekend programs available. Postbaccalaureate distance learning degree programs offered. Offers fine arts in visual art (MFA); liberal arts and sciences (MA, MFA); teaching English to speakers of other languages (MA). *Application deadline:* Applications are processed on a rolling basis. *Application fee:* $45 ($65 for international students). *Application Contact:* Director of Graduate Admissions, 626-812-3037, Fax: 626-969-7180. *Dean,* Dr. David Weeks, 626-969-3434 Ext. 3500, E-mail: dweeks@apu.edu.

Haggard School of Theology Students: 115 full-time (28 women), 226 part-time (73 women); includes 147 minority (28 African Americans, 3 American Indian/Alaska Native, 48 Asian Americans or Pacific Islanders, 68 Hispanic Americans), 56 international. Average age 38. *Faculty:* 13 full-time (4 women). Expenses: Contact institution. *Financial support:* Teaching assistantships, career-related internships or fieldwork available. Support available to part-time students. Financial award application deadline: 6/4; financial award applicants required to submit FAFSA. In 2006, 42 first professional degrees, 41 master's, 1 doctorate awarded. *Degree program information:* Part-time and evening/weekend programs available. Offers Christian education (MA); Christian non-profit leadership (MA); divinity (M Div); ministry (D Min); ministry management (MAMM); pastoral studies (MAPS); religion: Biblical studies (MAR); religion: theology and ethics (MAR); theology (M Div, MA, MAMM, MAPS, MAR, MAWL, D Min); worship leadership (MAWL). *Application deadline:* For fall admission, 6/1 for international students; for spring admission, 10/7 for international students. *Application fee:* $45 ($65 for international students). *Associate Dean,* Dr. Enrique Zone, 626-815-6060 Ext. 5653, E-mail: ezone@apu.edu.

School of Business and Management Students: 24 full-time (11 women), 126 part-time (51 women); includes 50 minority (8 African Americans, 1 American Indian/Alaska Native, 12 Asian Americans or Pacific Islanders, 29 Hispanic Americans), 24 international. Average age 31. *Faculty:* 3 full-time (0 women). Expenses: Contact institution. *Financial support:* Scholarships/grants available. In 2006, 54 degrees awarded. *Degree program information:* Part-time and evening/weekend programs available. Offers business administration (MBA); human and organizational development (MA); international business (MBA); strategic management (MBA). *Application deadline:* For fall admission, 8/15 priority date for domestic students. Applications are processed on a rolling basis. *Application fee:* $45 ($65 for international students). *Dean,* Dr. Ilene Bezjian, 626-815-3090, Fax: 626-815-3802, E-mail: ibezjian@apu.edu.

School of Education Students: 59 full-time (55 women), 1,878 part-time (1,352 women); includes 676 minority (101 African Americans, 11 American Indian/Alaska Native, 93 Asian Americans or Pacific Islanders, 471 Hispanic Americans), 28 international. Average age 35. Expenses: Contact institution. *Financial support:* Career-related internships or fieldwork available. Support available to part-time students. Financial award applicants required to submit FAFSA. In 2006, 859 master's, 12 doctorates awarded. *Degree program information:* Part-time and evening/weekend programs available. Offers curriculum and instruction in a multicultural setting (MA); education (M Ed, MA, Ed D); educational counseling (MA); educational leadership (Ed D); educational psychology (MA); educational technology (M Ed); language development (MA); physical education (M Ed); pupil personnel services (MA); school administration (MA); school librarianship (MA); special education (MA); teaching (MA). *Application fee:* $45 ($65 for international students). *Dean,* Dr. Paul Gray, 626-815-5439, E-mail: pgray@apu.edu.

School of Music Students: 16 full-time (12 women), 29 part-time (15 women); includes 12 minority (1 African American, 5 Asian Americans or Pacific Islanders, 6 Hispanic Americans), 11 international. 35 applicants, 94% accepted, 33 enrolled. Expenses: Contact institution. *Financial support:* In 2006–07, 7 students received support, including 1 teaching assistantship with partial tuition reimbursement available (averaging $4,000 per year); career-related internships or fieldwork also available. Support available to part-time students. Financial award applicants required to submit FAFSA. In 2006, 11 degrees awarded. *Degree program information:* Part-time and evening/weekend programs available. Offers education (M Mus);

Azusa Pacific University (continued)

performance (M Mus). *Application fee:* $45 ($65 for international students). *Application Contact:* Graduate Admissions, 626-815-5470, Fax: 626-815-3867, E-mail: dfunderburk@apu.edu. *Dean,* Dr. Duane Funderburk, 626-812-3020, E-mail: dfunderburk@apu.edu.

School of Nursing Students: 56 full-time (49 women), 100 part-time (96 women); includes 73 minority (12 African Americans, 1 American Indian/Alaska Native, 33 Asian Americans or Pacific Islanders, 27 Hispanic Americans), 5 international. *Faculty:* 12 full-time (11 women). Expenses: Contact institution. *Financial support:* Teaching assistantships, scholarships/grants, traineeships, and unspecified assistantships available. Support available to part-time students. Financial award application deadline: 10/15. In 2006, 16 degrees awarded. *Degree program information:* Part-time and evening/weekend programs available. Offers nursing (MSN); nursing education (PhD). *Application deadline:* Applications are processed on a rolling basis. *Application fee:* $45 ($65 for international students). *Application Contact:* Barb Barthelmess, Graduate Program Secretary, 626-815-5391, Fax: 626-815-5414. *Interim Dean/Professor,* Dr. Aja Lesh, 626-815-5386, E-mail: alesh@apu.edu.

BABEL UNIVERSITY SCHOOL OF TRANSLATION, Honolulu, HI 96815-1302

General Information Proprietary, coed, primarily women, graduate-only institution. *Graduate housing:* On-campus housing not available.

GRADUATE UNITS

Program in Translation *Degree program information:* Part-time and evening/weekend programs available. Postbaccalaureate distance learning degree programs offered (no on-campus study). Offers translation (MS).

BABSON COLLEGE, Wellesley, Babson Park, MA 02457-0310

General Information Independent, coed, comprehensive institution. *Enrollment:* 3,359 graduate, professional, and undergraduate students; 414 full-time matriculated graduate/professional students (107 women), 1,169 part-time matriculated graduate/professional students (331 women). *Enrollment by degree level:* 1,583 master's. *Graduate faculty:* 137 full-time (37 women), 28 part-time/adjunct (3 women). *Tuition:* Full-time $35,110. *Required fees:* $1,140. Full-time tuition and fees vary according to program. *Graduate housing:* Rooms and/or apartments available on a first-come, first-served basis to single and married students. Typical cost: $10,125 per year ($14,265 including board) for single students. Housing application deadline: 6/20. *Student services:* Campus employment opportunities, campus safety program, career counseling, disabled student services, free psychological counseling, international student services, low-cost health insurance, writing training. *Library facilities:* Horn Library plus 1 other. *Online resources:* library catalog, web page, access to other libraries' catalogs. *Collection:* 131,436 titles, 626 serial subscriptions.

Computer facilities: 290 computers available on campus for general student use. A campuswide network can be accessed from student residence rooms and from off campus. Internet access and online class registration, network drives and folders are available. *Web address:* http://www.babson.edu/.

General Application Contact: Martha Snelling, Admissions Services Team, 781-239-4317, Fax: 781-239-4194, E-mail: mbaadmissions@babson.edu.

GRADUATE UNITS

F. W. Olin Graduate School of Business Students: 414 full-time (107 women), 1,169 part-time (331 women); includes 189 minority (21 African Americans, 3 American Indian/Alaska Native, 138 Asian Americans or Pacific Islanders, 27 Hispanic Americans), 288 international. Average age 29. 580 applicants, 58% accepted, 166 enrolled. *Faculty:* 137 full-time (37 women), 28 part-time/adjunct (3 women). Expenses: Contact institution. *Financial support:* In 2006–07, 54 fellowships (averaging $32,810 per year), 18 research assistantships (averaging $6,000 per year) were awarded; career-related internships or fieldwork, Federal Work-Study, scholarships/grants, tuition waivers (partial), and unspecified assistantships also available. Financial award application deadline: 4/15; financial award applicants required to submit FAFSA. In 2006, 604 degrees awarded. *Degree program information:* Part-time and evening/weekend programs available. Postbaccalaureate distance learning degree programs offered (minimal on-campus study). Offers business administration (MBA). *Application deadline:* For fall admission, 4/15 priority date for domestic students. Applications are processed on a rolling basis. *Application fee:* $100. Electronic applications accepted. *Application Contact:* Martha Snelling, Admission Services Team, 781-239-4317, Fax: 781-239-4194, E-mail: mbaadmission@babson.edu. *Dean,* Mark P. Rice, 781-239-4542, Fax: 781-239-4194.

BAKER COLLEGE CENTER FOR GRADUATE STUDIES, Flint, MI 48507-9843

General Information Independent, coed, graduate-only institution. *Enrollment by degree level:* 1,430 master's. *Graduate faculty:* 15 full-time (6 women), 425 part-time/adjunct (200 women). *Tuition:* Full-time $7,200; part-time $300 per credit hour. *Graduate housing:* On-campus housing not available. *Student services:* Campus employment opportunities, campus safety program, career counseling, child daycare facilities, disabled student services, exercise/wellness program, international student services. *Library facilities:* Baker Online Library plus 1 other. *Online resources:* library catalog, web page, access to other libraries' catalogs.

Computer facilities: A campuswide network can be accessed. Internet access and online class registration are available. *Web address:* http://online.baker.edu.

General Application Contact: Chuck J. Gurden, Vice President for Graduate and Online Admissions, 800-469-3165, Fax: 810-766-2051, E-mail: chuck@baker.edu.

GRADUATE UNITS

Graduate Programs Students: 370 full-time (190 women), 1,060 part-time (560 women); includes 372 minority (205 African Americans, 27 American Indian/Alaska Native, 66 Asian Americans or Pacific Islanders, 74 Hispanic Americans), 30 international. Average age 38. 780 applicants, 85% accepted, 567 enrolled. *Faculty:* 15 full-time (6 women), 425 part-time/adjunct (200 women). Expenses: Contact institution. *Financial support:* In 2006–07, 410 students received support. Scholarships/grants available. Support available to part-time students. Financial award applicants required to submit FAFSA. In 2006, 202 degrees awarded. *Degree program information:* Part-time and evening/weekend programs available. Postbaccalaureate distance learning degree programs offered. Offers accounting (MBA); finance (MBA); general business (MBA); health care management (MBA); human resources management (MBA); information management (MBA); leadership studies (MBA); management information systems (MSIS); marketing (MBA); occupational therapy (MOT). *Application deadline:* For fall admission, 8/6 priority date for domestic students; for winter admission, 12/15 priority date for domestic students; for spring admission, 2/15 priority date for domestic students. Applications are processed on a rolling basis. *Application fee:* $25. Electronic applications accepted. *Application Contact:* Chuck J. Gurden, Vice President for Graduate and Online Admissions, 800-469-3165, Fax: 810-766-2051, E-mail: chuck@baker.edu. *President,* Dr. Michael Heberling, 800-469-3165, Fax: 810-766-4399, E-mail: heberling@baker.edu.

BAKER UNIVERSITY, Baldwin City, KS 66006-0065

General Information Independent-religious, coed, comprehensive institution. *Enrollment:* 1,210 full-time matriculated graduate/professional students (718 women), 339 part-time matriculated graduate/professional students (232 women). *Enrollment by degree level:* 1,499 master's, 50 doctoral. *Graduate faculty:* 9 full-time (3 women), 358 part-time/adjunct (174 women). *Graduate housing:* On-campus housing not available. *Student services:* Campus safety program, disabled student services, international student services. *Library facilities:* Collins Library. *Online resources:* library catalog, web page, access to other libraries' catalogs. *Collection:* 132,325 titles, 678 serial subscriptions, 4,992 audiovisual materials.

Computer facilities: 222 computers available on campus for general student use. A campuswide network can be accessed from student residence rooms. Internet access and online class registration are available. *Web address:* http://www.bakeru.edu/.

General Application Contact: Kelly Belk, Director of Marketing, 913-491-4432, Fax: 913-491-0470, E-mail: kbelk@bakeru.edu.

GRADUATE UNITS

School of Education Students: 455 full-time (344 women), 284 part-time (194 women); includes 48 minority (30 African Americans, 3 American Indian/Alaska Native, 3 Asian Americans or Pacific Islanders, 12 Hispanic Americans). Average age 36. *Faculty:* 7 full-time (2 women), 89 part-time/adjunct (58 women). Expenses: Contact institution. *Financial support:* Applicants required to submit FAFSA. In 2006, 362 degrees awarded. *Degree program information:* Part-time and evening/weekend programs available. Offers education (MA Ed, MASL, Ed D). MA Ed and MASL programs also offered in Wichita, KS. *Application deadline:* Applications are processed on a rolling basis. *Application fee:* $20. *Interim Dean, School of Education,* Dr. Peggy Harris, 785-594-8492, Fax: 785-594-8363, E-mail: peggy.harris@bakeru.edu.

School of Professional and Graduate Studies Students: 755 full-time (374 women), 55 part-time (38 women); includes 128 minority (62 African Americans, 19 American Indian/Alaska Native, 17 Asian Americans or Pacific Islanders, 30 Hispanic Americans). Average age 34. *Faculty:* 2 full-time (1 woman), 269 part-time/adjunct (116 women). Expenses: Contact institution. *Financial support:* Applicants required to submit FAFSA. In 2006, 417 degrees awarded. *Degree program information:* Part-time and evening/weekend programs available. Postbaccalaureate distance learning degree programs offered (minimal on-campus study). Offers business (MBA, MSM); conflict management and dispute resolution (MA); liberal arts (MLA). *Application deadline:* Applications are processed on a rolling basis. *Application fee:* $45. *Application Contact:* Kelly Belk, Director of Marketing, 913-491-4432, Fax: 913-491-0470, E-mail: kbelk@bakeru.edu. *Acting Vice President and Dean,* Dr. Steve M. Cohen, 913-491-4432, Fax: 913-491-0470, E-mail: steve.cohen@bakeru.edu.

BAKKE GRADUATE UNIVERSITY OF MINISTRY, Seattle, WA 98104

General Information Independent-religious, coed, primarily men, graduate-only institution. *Graduate faculty:* 3 full-time (1 woman), 29 part-time/adjunct (2 women). *Graduate housing:* On-campus housing not available. *Student services:* Career counseling, writing training. *Library facilities:* Bakke Research Center. *Online resources:* library catalog, web page, access to other libraries' catalogs. *Collection:* 5,000 titles, 69 serial subscriptions, 125 audiovisual materials.

Computer facilities: 2 computers available on campus for general student use. A campuswide network can be accessed. Online class registration is available. *Web address:* http://www.bgu.edu/.

General Application Contact: Judith A. Melton, Registrar, 206-246-9100, Fax: 206-246-8828, E-mail: judim@bgu.edu.

GRADUATE UNITS

Program in Pastoral Ministry Students: 48 full-time (8 women), 134 part-time (26 women); includes 79 minority (45 African Americans, 34 American Indian/Alaska Native). Average age 36. *Faculty:* 3 full-time (1 woman), 29 part-time/adjunct (2 women). Expenses: Contact institution. *Financial support:* In 2006–07, 46 students received support. Scholarships/grants and tuition waivers (partial) available. Financial award applicants required to submit CSS PROFILE. In 2006, 8 master's, 19 doctorates awarded. *Degree program information:* Part-time programs available. Postbaccalaureate distance learning degree programs offered (minimal on-campus study). Offers pastoral ministry (MTS, D Min). *Application deadline:* For fall admission, 7/1 priority date for domestic students; for winter admission, 12/1 for domestic students; for spring admission, 3/15 for domestic students. Applications are processed on a rolling basis. *Application fee:* $75. Electronic applications accepted. *Application Contact:* Judith A. Melton, Registrar, 206-246-9100, Fax: 206-246-8828, E-mail: judim@bgu.edu. *Director of Academic Programs,* Dr. Grace Barnes, 206-264-9100 Ext. 19, Fax: 206-624-8828, E-mail: graceb@bgu.edu.

BALDWIN-WALLACE COLLEGE, Berea, OH 44017-2088

General Information Independent-religious, coed, comprehensive institution. *Enrollment:* 4,365 graduate, professional, and undergraduate students; 373 full-time matriculated graduate/professional students (208 women), 367 part-time matriculated graduate/professional students (259 women). *Enrollment by degree level:* 740 master's. *Graduate faculty:* 30 full-time (8 women), 24 part-time/adjunct (6 women). *Tuition:* Part-time $760 per credit hour. Tuition and fees vary according to program. *Graduate housing:* Room and/or apartments available to single students; on-campus housing not available to married students. *Student services:* Campus employment opportunities, career counseling, child daycare facilities, disabled student services, exercise/wellness program, free psychological counseling, international student services, low-cost health insurance, multicultural affairs office, teacher training, writing training. *Library facilities:* Ritter Library plus 2 others. *Online resources:* library catalog, web page, access to other libraries' catalogs. *Collection:* 200,000 titles, 22,000 serial subscriptions. *Research affiliation:* Ohio Department of Education (to create and offer courses for Intervention Specialists to gain Highly Qualified Teacher Status), Ohio Department of Education (to refine our assessment systems to improve programs and meet the standards set by state and national organizations), Ohio board of Regents (to provide training in educational technology to arts and sciences and educational faculty).

Computer facilities: Computer purchase and lease plans are available. 460 computers available on campus for general student use. A campuswide network can be accessed from student residence rooms. Internet access and online class registration are available. *Web address:* http://www.bw.edu/.

General Application Contact: Winifred W. Gerhardt, Director of Admission for the Evening and Weekend College, 440-826-2222, Fax: 440-826-3830, E-mail: admission@bw.edu.

GRADUATE UNITS

Graduate Programs Students: 373 full-time (208 women), 367 part-time (259 women); includes 79 minority (45 African Americans, 2 American Indian/Alaska Native, 20 Asian Americans or Pacific Islanders, 12 Hispanic Americans), 23 international. Average age 33. 306 applicants, 85% accepted, 194 enrolled. *Faculty:* 30 full-time (8 women), 24 part-time/adjunct (6 women). Expenses: Contact institution. *Financial support:* In 2006–07, 362 students received support. Career-related internships or fieldwork available. Support available to part-time students. Financial award applicants required to submit FAFSA. In 2006, 311 degrees awarded. *Degree program information:* Part-time and evening/weekend programs available. *Application deadline:* Applications are processed on a rolling basis. *Application fee:* $25. Electronic applications accepted. *Application Contact:* Winifred W. Gerhardt, Director of Admission for the Evening and Weekend College, 440-826-2222, Fax: 440-826-3830, E-mail: admission@bw.edu. *Dean of the College,* Mary Lou Higgerson, 440-826-2251, Fax: 440-826-2329, E-mail: mhiggers@bw.edu.

Division of Business Administration Students: 281 full-time (141 women), 165 part-time (98 women); includes 47 minority (27 African Americans, 2 American Indian/Alaska Native, 12 Asian Americans or Pacific Islanders, 6 Hispanic Americans), 22 international. Average age 33. 168 applicants, 89% accepted, 122 enrolled. *Faculty:* 19 full-time (4 women), 19 part-time/adjunct (3 women). Expenses: Contact institution. *Financial support:* Career-related internships or fieldwork available. Support available to part-time students. Financial award applicants required to submit FAFSA. In 2006, 174 degrees awarded. *Degree program information:* Part-time and evening/weekend programs available. Offers accounting (MBA); business administration-systems management (MBA); entrepreneurship (MBA); executive management (MBA); health care executive management (MBA); human resources (MBA); international management (MBA). *Application deadline:* For fall admission, 7/25 priority date for domestic students; for spring admission, 12/15 priority date for domestic students. Applications are processed on a rolling basis. *Application fee:* $25. Electronic applications accepted. *Application Contact:* Winifred W. Gerhardt, Director of Admission for the Evening and Weekend College, 440-826-2222, Fax: 440-826-3830, E-mail: admission@bw.edu. *Chairperson, Business Administration,* 440-826-2391, Fax: 440-826-3868, E-mail: pkelly@bw.edu.

Division of Education Students: 92 full-time (67 women), 202 part-time (161 women); includes 32 minority (18 African Americans, 8 Asian Americans or Pacific Islanders, 6

Hispanic Americans), 1 international. Average age 33. 138 applicants, 81% accepted, 72 enrolled. *Faculty:* 11 full-time (4 women), 5 part-time/adjunct (3 women). Expenses: Contact institution. *Financial support:* Career-related internships or fieldwork available. Financial award applicants required to submit FAFSA. In 2006, 137 degrees awarded. *Degree program information:* Part-time and evening/weekend programs available. Offers educational technology (MA Ed); mild/moderate educational needs (MA Ed); pre-administration (MA Ed); reading (MA Ed). *Application deadline:* For fall admission, 8/15 priority date for domestic students; for spring admission, 12/15 priority date for domestic students. Applications are processed on a rolling basis. *Application fee:* $25. Electronic applications accepted. *Application Contact:* Winifred W. Gerhardt, Director of Admission for the Evening and Weekend College, 440-826-2222, Fax: 440-826-3830, E-mail: admission@bw.edu. *Chair,* Karen Kaye, 440-826-2168, Fax: 440-826-3779, E-mail: kkaye@bw.edu.

BALL STATE UNIVERSITY, Muncie, IN 47306-1099

General Information State-supported, coed, university. CGS member. *Enrollment:* 17,082 graduate, professional, and undergraduate students; 1,044 full-time matriculated graduate/professional students (613 women), 1,729 part-time matriculated graduate/professional students (1,095 women). *Enrollment by degree level:* 2,398 master's, 297 doctoral, 78 other advanced degrees. *Graduate faculty:* 712. *Graduate housing:* Rooms and/or apartments available on a first-come, first-served basis to single and married students. Typical cost: $6,898 (including board) for single students; $6,300 per year for married students. Housing application deadline: 3/1. *Student services:* Campus employment opportunities, campus safety program, career counseling, child daycare facilities, disabled student services, exercise/wellness program, free psychological counseling, international student services, low-cost health insurance, multicultural affairs office, teacher training. *Library facilities:* Bracken Library plus 3 others. *Online resources:* library catalog, web page, access to other libraries' catalogs. *Collection:* 1.1 million titles, 2,937 serial subscriptions, 516,000 audiovisual materials.

Computer facilities: 1,500 computers available on campus for general student use. A campuswide network can be accessed from student residence rooms and from off campus. *Web address:* http://www.bsu.edu/.

General Application Contact: Dr. Mary E. Kite, Acting Dean, 765-285-1300, Fax: 765-285-1994, E-mail: mkite@bsu.edu.

GRADUATE UNITS

Graduate School Students: 1,044 full-time (613 women), 1,729 part-time (1,095 women); includes 171 minority (94 African Americans, 14 American Indian/Alaska Native, 27 Asian Americans or Pacific Islanders, 36 Hispanic Americans), 251 international. 2,002 applicants, 63% accepted, 771 enrolled. *Faculty:* 705. Expenses: Contact institution. *Financial support:* In 2006–07, 9 fellowships with full tuition reimbursements (averaging $11,428 per year), 78 research assistantships with full and partial tuition reimbursements (averaging $8,967 per year), 728 teaching assistantships with full and partial tuition reimbursements (averaging $8,411 per year) were awarded; career-related internships or fieldwork, Federal Work-Study, tuition waivers (partial), and unspecified assistantships also available. Support available to part-time students. Financial award application deadline: 3/1. In 2006, 922 master's, 59 doctorates, 17 other advanced degrees awarded. *Degree program information:* Part-time and evening/weekend programs available. Postbaccalaureate distance learning degree programs offered. *Application deadline:* For fall admission, 3/1 priority date for domestic students, 1/1 priority date for international students; for spring admission, 12/1 priority date for domestic students, 7/1 priority date for international students. Applications are processed on a rolling basis. *Application fee:* $35 ($40 for international students). Electronic applications accepted. *Application Contact:* Dr. Mary E. Kite, Acting Dean, 765-285-1300, Fax: 765-285-1994, E-mail: mkite@bsu.edu. *Acting Dean,* Dr. Mary E. Kite, 765-285-1300, Fax: 765-285-1994, E-mail: mkite@bsu.edu.

College of Applied Science and Technology Students: 97 full-time (65 women), 454 part-time (316 women); includes 26 minority (13 African Americans, 2 American Indian/Alaska Native, 5 Asian Americans or Pacific Islanders, 6 Hispanic Americans), 17 international. Average age 29. 280 applicants, 63% accepted, 122 enrolled. *Faculty:* 80. Expenses: Contact institution. *Financial support:* In 2006–07, research assistantships with full tuition reimbursements (averaging $10,585 per year), 97 teaching assistantships with full tuition reimbursements (averaging $9,149 per year) were awarded; fellowships with full tuition reimbursements, career-related internships or fieldwork and tuition waivers (full) also available. Financial award application deadline: 3/1. In 2006, 174 master's, 2 doctorates awarded. *Degree program information:* Part-time programs available. Offers applied gerontology (MA); applied science and technology (MA, MAE, MS, PhD); family and consumer sciences (MA, MS); human bioenergetics (PhD); industry and technology (MA, MAE); nursing (MS); physical education (MA, MAE, MS, PhD); wellness management (MA, MS). *Application fee:* $25 ($35 for international students). *Dean,* Dr. Nancy Kingsbury, 765-285-5818, Fax: 765-285-1071.

College of Architecture and Planning Students: 99 full-time (49 women), 12 part-time (6 women); includes 5 minority (4 African Americans, 1 Hispanic American), 12 international. Average age 27. 141 applicants, 79% accepted, 59 enrolled. *Faculty:* 47. Expenses: Contact institution. *Financial support:* In 2006–07, 10 research assistantships with full tuition reimbursements (averaging $7,919 per year), 44 teaching assistantships with full tuition reimbursements (averaging $6,532 per year) were awarded; fellowships with full tuition reimbursements, career-related internships or fieldwork also available. Support available to part-time students. Financial award application deadline: 3/1. In 2006, 26 degrees awarded. *Degree program information:* Part-time programs available. Offers architecture (M Arch); architecture and planning (M Arch, MLA, MS, MURP); historic preservation (M Arch, MS); landscape architecture (MLA); urban planning (MURP). *Application fee:* $25 ($35 for international students). *Dean,* Dr. Joseph Bilello, 765-285-5861, Fax: 765-285-3726.

College of Communication, Information, and Media Students: 136 full-time (69 women), 66 part-time (43 women); includes 20 minority (14 African Americans, 1 American Indian/Alaska Native, 2 Asian Americans or Pacific Islanders, 3 Hispanic Americans), 55 international. Average age 25. 163 applicants, 76% accepted, 88 enrolled. *Faculty:* 31. Expenses: Contact institution. *Financial support:* In 2006–07, 10 research assistantships with full tuition reimbursements (averaging $7,560 per year), 62 teaching assistantships with full tuition reimbursements (averaging $7,101 per year) were awarded; career-related internships or fieldwork also available. Financial award application deadline: 3/1. In 2006, 86 degrees awarded. Offers communication, information, and media (MA, MS); digital storytelling (MA); information and communication sciences (MS); journalism (MA); public relations (MA); speech, public address, forensics, and rhetoric (MA). *Application fee:* $25 ($35 for international students). *Dean,* Roger Lavery, 765-285-6000, Fax: 765-285-6002.

College of Fine Arts Students: 43 full-time (23 women), 45 part-time (22 women); includes 6 minority (3 African Americans, 1 American Indian/Alaska Native, 1 Asian American or Pacific Islander, 1 Hispanic American), 21 international. Average age 26. 68 applicants, 74% accepted, 32 enrolled. *Faculty:* 69. Expenses: Contact institution. *Financial support:* In 2006–07, 3 research assistantships (averaging $7,000 per year), 45 teaching assistantships with full tuition reimbursements (averaging $6,641 per year) were awarded; fellowships with full tuition reimbursements also available. Support available to part-time students. Financial award application deadline: 3/1. In 2006, 27 master's, 5 doctorates awarded. *Degree program information:* Part-time programs available. Offers art (MA); art education (MA, MAE); fine arts (MA, MAE, MM, DA); music education (MA, MM, DA). *Application fee:* $25 ($35 for international students). *Dean,* Dr. Robert Kvam, 765-285-5495, Fax: 765-285-3790, E-mail: rkvam@bsu.edu.

College of Sciences and Humanities Students: 351 full-time (216 women), 187 part-time (100 women); includes 35 minority (11 African Americans, 3 American Indian/Alaska Native, 10 Asian Americans or Pacific Islanders, 11 Hispanic Americans), 90 international. Average age 26. 596 applicants, 68% accepted, 197 enrolled. *Faculty:* 301. Expenses: Contact institution. *Financial support:* In 2006–07, 17 research assistantships with full tuition reimbursements (averaging $10,536 per year), 195 teaching assistantships with full tuition reimbursements (averaging $8,898 per year) were awarded; career-related internships or fieldwork and Federal Work-Study also available. Support available to part-time students. Financial award application deadline: 3/1. In 2006, 211 master's, 16 doctorates awarded. *Degree program information:* Part-time programs available. Offers actuarial science (MA); anthropology (MA); applied linguistics (PhD); biology (MA, MAE, MS); biology education (Ed D); chemistry (MA, MS); clinical psychology (MA); cognitive and social processes (MA); computer science (MA, MS); earth sciences (MA); English (MA, PhD); geology (MA, MS); health education (MA, MAE); history (MA); linguistics (MA, PhD); linguistics and teaching English to speakers of other languages (MA); mathematical statistics (MA); mathematics (MA, MAE, MS); mathematics education (MAE); natural resources (MA, MS); physics (MA, MS); physiology (MA, MS); political science (MA); public administration (MPA); sciences and humanities (MA, MAE, MPA, MS, Au D, Ed D, PhD); social sciences (MA); sociology (MA); speech pathology and audiology (MA, Au D); teaching English to speakers of other languages (MA). *Application fee:* $25 ($35 for international students). *Dean,* Dr. Michael Maggioto, 765-285-1042, Fax: 765-285-8980.

Miller College of Business Students: 78 full-time (26 women), 162 part-time (52 women); includes 9 minority (5 African Americans, 1 American Indian/Alaska Native, 3 Hispanic Americans), 15 international. Average age 26. 152 applicants, 68% accepted, 81 enrolled. *Faculty:* 60. Expenses: Contact institution. *Financial support:* In 2006–07, 1 fellowship with full tuition reimbursement (averaging $8,356 per year), 1 research assistantship (averaging $8,356 per year), 34 teaching assistantships with full tuition reimbursements (averaging $8,356 per year) were awarded; unspecified assistantships also available. Support available to part-time students. Financial award application deadline: 3/1. In 2006, 102 degrees awarded. *Degree program information:* Part-time and evening/weekend programs available. Offers accounting (MS); business (MAE, MBA, MS); business administration (MBA); information systems and operations management (MAE). *Application fee:* $25 ($35 for international students). *Application Contact:* Tamara Estep, Graduate Coordinator, 765-285-1931, Fax: 765-285-8818, E-mail: testep@bsu.edu. *Dean,* Dr. Lynne D. Richardson, 765-285-8192, Fax: 765-285-5117.

Teachers College Students: 241 full-time (165 women), 800 part-time (557 women); includes 69 minority (44 African Americans, 6 American Indian/Alaska Native, 8 Asian Americans or Pacific Islanders, 11 Hispanic Americans), 41 international. Average age 28. 752 applicants, 51% accepted, 256 enrolled. *Faculty:* 98. Expenses: Contact institution. *Financial support:* In 2006–07, 4 fellowships with full tuition reimbursements (averaging $12,000 per year), 5 research assistantships with full tuition reimbursements (averaging $7,887 per year), 130 teaching assistantships with full tuition reimbursements (averaging $7,376 per year) were awarded; career-related internships or fieldwork and Federal Work-Study also available. Support available to part-time students. Financial award application deadline: 3/1. In 2006, 296 master's, 36 doctorates, 17 other advanced degrees awarded. *Degree program information:* Part-time and evening/weekend programs available. Offers adult and community education (MA); adult education (MA, Ed D); adult, community, and higher education (Ed D); counseling psychology (MA, PhD); curriculum (MAE, Ed S); curriculum and instruction (MAE, Ed S); education (MA, MAE, Ed D, PhD, Ed S); educational administration (MAE, Ed D); educational psychology (MA, PhD, Ed S); educational studies (MAE, PhD); elementary education (MAE, Ed D, PhD); executive development (MA); school psychology (MA, PhD, Ed S); school superintendency (Ed S); secondary education (MA); social psychology (MA); special education (MA, MAE, Ed D, Ed S); student affairs administration in higher education (MA). *Application fee:* $25 ($35 for international students). *Dean,* Dr. Roy Weaver, 765-285-5251, Fax: 765-285-5455, E-mail: rweaver@bsu.edu.

BALTIMORE HEBREW UNIVERSITY, Baltimore, MD 21215-3996

General Information Independent, coed, comprehensive institution. *Graduate housing:* On-campus housing not available. *Research affiliation:* American Schools of Oriental Research (archaeology).

GRADUATE UNITS

Peggy Meyerhoff Pearlstone School of Graduate Studies *Degree program information:* Part-time programs available. Offers Jewish communal service (MAJCS); Jewish education (MAJE); Jewish studies (MAJS, PhD).

BANGOR THEOLOGICAL SEMINARY, Bangor, ME 04401-4699

General Information Independent-religious, coed, graduate-only institution. *Graduate housing:* Rooms and/or apartments available on a first-come, first-served basis to single and married students. Housing application deadline: 5/1.

GRADUATE UNITS

Professional Program *Degree program information:* Part-time programs available. Offers theology (M Div, MA, MTS, D Min). M Div not offered at Portland, ME campus.

BANK STREET COLLEGE OF EDUCATION, New York, NY 10025

General Information Independent, coed, graduate-only institution. *Enrollment by degree level:* 930 master's. *Graduate faculty:* 78 full-time (67 women), 56 part-time/adjunct (43 women). *Tuition:* Part-time $940 per credit. *Required fees:* $100 per term. *Student services:* Campus employment opportunities, campus safety program, career counseling, child daycare facilities, international student services, teacher training, writing training. *Library facilities:* Bank Street College Library. *Online resources:* library catalog, web page, access to other libraries' catalogs. *Collection:* 127,457 titles, 17,465 serial subscriptions, 1,543 audiovisual materials. *Research affiliation:* Educational Development Corporation (education).

Computer facilities: 52 computers available on campus for general student use. A campuswide network can be accessed from off campus. Internet access and online class registration are available. *Web address:* http://www.bankstreet.edu/.

General Application Contact: Ann Morgan, Director of Graduate Admissions, 212-875-4403, Fax: 212-873-4678, E-mail: gradcourses@bankstreet.edu.

GRADUATE UNITS

Graduate School Students: 337 full-time (291 women), 593 part-time (526 women); includes 231 minority (85 African Americans, 1 American Indian/Alaska Native, 46 Asian Americans or Pacific Islanders, 99 Hispanic Americans), 9 international. Average age 30. 610 applicants, 80% accepted, 386 enrolled. *Faculty:* 78 full-time (67 women), 56 part-time/adjunct (43 women). Expenses: Contact institution. *Financial support:* In 2006–07, 579 students received support. Career-related internships or fieldwork, Federal Work-Study, scholarships/grants, and unspecified assistantships available. Support available to part-time students. Financial award application deadline: 4/15; financial award applicants required to submit FAFSA. In 2006, 357 degrees awarded. Offers advanced literacy specialization (Ed M); bilingual childhood special education (Ed M, MS Ed); bilingual early childhood education (MS Ed); bilingual early childhood special and general education (MS Ed); bilingual early childhood special education (Ed M, MS Ed); bilingual education (Ed M, MS Ed); bilingual elementary/childhood general education (MS Ed); bilingual elementary/childhood special and general education (MS Ed); bilingual middle school general education (MS Ed); bilingual middle school special and general education (Ed M, MS Ed); bilingual middle school special education (MS Ed); child life (MS); early childhood and elementary/childhood education (MS Ed); early childhood education (MS Ed); early childhood leadership (MS Ed); early childhood special and general education (MS Ed); early childhood special education (Ed M, MS Ed); education (Ed M, MS, MS Ed); educational leadership (MS Ed); elementary/childhood education (MS Ed); elementary/childhood special and general education (MS Ed); elementary/childhood special education (MS Ed); elementary/childhood special education certification (Ed M); infant and parent development and early intervention (Ed M, MS Ed); infant and parent development and early intervention/early childhood special and general education (MS Ed); infant and parent development and early intervention/early childhood special education (Ed M); leadership for educational change (Ed M, MS Ed); leadership in mathematics education (MS Ed); leadership in museum education (MS Ed); leadership in the arts (MS Ed); middle school education (MS Ed); middle school special and general education (MS Ed); middle school special education (Ed M); museum education (MS Ed); museum education: elementary education certification (MS Ed); museum education: middle school certification (MS Ed); museum studies (MS Ed); reading and literacy (Ed M, MS Ed); special education (Ed M, MS Ed); teaching literacy (MS Ed); teaching literacy and elementary education (MS Ed). *Application deadline:* For fall admission,

Bank Street College of Education (continued)

3/1 priority date for domestic and international students; for spring admission, 11/1 priority date for domestic and international students. Applications are processed on a rolling basis. *Application fee:* $50. *Application Contact:* Ann Morgan, Director of Graduate Admissions, 212-875-4403, Fax: 212-875-4678, E-mail: amorgan@bankstreet.edu. *Dean*, Dr. Jon Snyder, 212-875-4466, Fax: 212-875-4753, E-mail: jsnyder@bankstreet.edu.

BAPTIST BIBLE COLLEGE, Springfield, MO 65803-3498

General Information Independent-religious, coed, comprehensive institution. *Graduate housing:* Rooms and/or apartments available on a first-come, first-served basis to single students and available to married students.

GRADUATE UNITS

Graduate School of Theology *Degree program information:* Part-time programs available. Offers biblical counseling (MA); biblical studies (MA); church ministries (MA); intercultural studies (MA); theology (M Div). Electronic applications accepted.

BAPTIST BIBLE COLLEGE OF PENNSYLVANIA, Clarks Summit, PA 18411-1297

General Information Independent-religious, coed, comprehensive institution. *Graduate housing:* Rooms and/or apartments guaranteed to single and married students.

GRADUATE UNITS

Baptist Bible Seminary *Degree program information:* Part-time programs available. Postbaccalaureate distance learning degree programs offered (minimal on-campus study). Offers ministry (M Min, D Min); theology (M Div, Th M, PhD). Electronic applications accepted.

Graduate School *Degree program information:* Part-time and evening/weekend programs available. Offers Christian school education (MS); counseling (MS).

BAPTIST MISSIONARY ASSOCIATION THEOLOGICAL SEMINARY, Jacksonville, TX 75766-5407

General Information Independent-religious, coed, primarily men, comprehensive institution. *Graduate housing:* Rooms and/or apartments available on a first-come, first-served basis to single and married students. Housing application deadline: 6/1.

GRADUATE UNITS

Graduate and Professional Programs *Degree program information:* Part-time programs available. Offers theology (M Div, MAR). Electronic applications accepted.

BAPTIST THEOLOGICAL SEMINARY AT RICHMOND, Richmond, VA 23227

General Information Independent-religious, coed, graduate-only institution. *Enrollment by degree level:* 141 first professional, 32 doctoral. *Graduate faculty:* 14 full-time (6 women), 8 part-time/adjunct (1 woman). *Tuition:* Full-time $6,500; part-time $650 per credit. *Required fees:* $45 per term. Full-time tuition and fees vary according to degree level. *Graduate housing:* Rooms and/or apartments available on a first-come, first-served basis to single and married students. Housing application deadline: 6/1. *Student services:* Campus employment opportunities, campus safety program, disabled student services, free psychological counseling, international student services, writing training. *Library facilities:* Morton at Union Theological Seminary-PSCE. *Online resources:* library catalog, web page, access to other libraries' catalogs. *Collection:* 427,679 titles, 982 serial subscriptions, 50,893 audiovisual materials.

Computer facilities: 20 computers available on campus for general student use. Internet access is available. *Web address:* http://www.btsr.edu/.

General Application Contact: Director of Admissions, 888-345-2877, Fax: 804-355-8182.

GRADUATE UNITS

Graduate and Professional Program Students: 146 full-time (70 women), 27 part-time (18 women); includes 15 minority (13 African Americans, 1 American Indian/Alaska Native, 1 Hispanic American), 4 international. Average age 39. 66 applicants, 88% accepted, 45 enrolled. *Faculty:* 14 full-time (6 women), 8 part-time/adjunct (1 woman). Expenses: Contact institution. *Financial support:* In 2006–07, 135 students received support, including 16 teaching assistantships (averaging $1,300 per year); scholarships/grants and tuition waivers (partial) also available. Financial award application deadline: 2/1. In 2006, 26 M Divs, 7 doctorates awarded. *Degree program information:* Part-time programs available. Postbaccalaureate distance learning degree programs offered (minimal on-campus study). Offers children and family ministry (M Div); Christian education (M Div); church music (M Div); theology (D Min); youth and student ministry (M Div). *Application deadline:* For fall admission, 8/1 priority date for domestic students, 5/1 priority date for international students; for winter admission, 12/1 priority date for domestic students, 9/1 priority date for international students; for spring admission, 1/1 priority date for domestic students, 10/1 priority date for international students. Applications are processed on a rolling basis. *Application fee:* $35. *Application Contact:* Director of Admissions, 804-355-8135, Fax: 804-355-8182. *President*, Dr. Ronald W. Crawford, 804-355-8135, Fax: 804-355-8182.

BARD COLLEGE, Annandale-on-Hudson, NY 12504

General Information Independent, coed, comprehensive institution. *Graduate housing:* Room and/or apartments available on a first-come, first-served basis to single students; on-campus housing not available to married students.

GRADUATE UNITS

Bard Center for Environmental Policy Students: 38 full-time (28 women); includes 2 minority (both African Americans), 9 international. Average age 28. *Faculty:* 3 full-time (2 women), 7 part-time/adjunct (5 women). Expenses: Contact institution. *Financial support:* In 2006–07, 37 students received support, including 30 fellowships (averaging $5,000 per year); career-related internships or fieldwork and scholarships/grants also available. Financial award applicants required to submit FAFSA. In 2006, 13 degrees awarded. Offers environmental policy (MS). *Application deadline:* For fall admission, 2/1 for domestic and international students. Applications are processed on a rolling basis. *Application fee:* $50. *Application Contact:* Jennifer Murray, Assistant Director for Graduate Admissions and Student Affairs, 845-758-7073, Fax: 845-758-7636, E-mail: cep@bard.edu. *Interim Director*, Mara Ranville, 845-758-7321, Fax: 845-758-7636, E-mail: ranville@bard.edu.

Center for Curatorial Studies Offers curatorial studies (MA).

Milton Avery Graduate School of the Arts Offers arts (MFA).

Program in Teaching Offers teaching (MAT).

BARD GRADUATE CENTER FOR STUDIES IN THE DECORATIVE ARTS, DESIGN, AND CULTURE, New York, NY 10024-3602

General Information Independent, coed, primarily women, graduate-only institution. *Enrollment by degree level:* 77 master's, 36 doctoral. *Graduate faculty:* 11 full-time (6 women), 17 part-time/adjunct (8 women). *Tuition:* Full-time $24,570; part-time $910 per credit. *Graduate housing:* Rooms and/or apartments available on a first-come, first-served basis to single and married students. Typical cost: $11,520 per year for single students. Housing application deadline: 5/1. *Student services:* Campus employment opportunities, career counseling, free psychological counseling, grant writing training, low-cost health insurance, writing training. *Library facilities:* BGC Decorative Arts Library. *Online resources:* library catalog, web page. *Collection:* 40,000 titles, 195 serial subscriptions. *Research affiliation:* Brooklyn Museum of Art, Metropolitan Museum of Art, New York Historical Society.

Computer facilities: 12 computers available on campus for general student use. A campuswide network can be accessed from student residence rooms and from off campus. Internet access is available. *Web address:* http://www.bgc.bard.edu/.

General Application Contact: Elena Pinto Simon, Dean, Academic Administration and Student Affairs, 212-501-3057, Fax: 212-501-3065, E-mail: simon@bgc.bard.edu.

GRADUATE UNITS

Program in History of the Decorative Arts, Design and Culture Students: 84 full-time (75 women), 29 part-time (21 women). Average age 25. 99 applicants, 38% accepted, 30 enrolled. *Faculty:* 11 full-time (6 women), 17 part-time/adjunct (8 women). Expenses: Contact institution. *Financial support:* In 2006–07, 25 students received support, including 20 fellowships with tuition reimbursements available, 3 research assistantships, 2 teaching assistantships; career-related internships or fieldwork, Federal Work-Study, scholarships/grants, health care benefits, and unspecified assistantships also available. Financial award application deadline: 2/1; financial award applicants required to submit FAFSA. In 2006, 30 master's, 2 doctorates awarded. *Degree program information:* Part-time programs available. Offers history of the decorative arts, design and culture (MA, PhD). Bard Graduate Center for Studies in the Decorative Arts is a unit of Bard College. *Application deadline:* For fall admission, 1/16 for domestic and international students. *Application fee:* $50. *Application Contact:* Elena Pinto Simon, Dean, Academic Administration and Student Affairs, 212-501-3057, Fax: 212-501-3065, E-mail: simon@bgc.bard.edu. *Director*, Susan Weber Soros, 212-501-3000, Fax: 212-501-3079.

Announcement: The Bard Graduate Center's (BGC) MA and PhD programs offer advanced training in the history of the decorative arts, design, and culture; American art and culture; museum history and practice; garden history and landscape studies; and renaissance and early modern studies. Interdisciplinary curriculum focuses on the roles objects and places play in people's lives. Hands-on study is integral to the program. Internship and thesis required for MA; qualifying examinations and dissertation required for PhD.

BARNES-JEWISH COLLEGE OF NURSING AND ALLIED HEALTH, St. Louis, MO 63110-1091

General Information Independent, coed, primarily women, comprehensive institution. *Graduate housing:* Room and/or apartments available on a first-come, first-served basis to single students; on-campus housing not available to married students.

GRADUATE UNITS

Division of Allied Health *Degree program information:* Part-time and evening/weekend programs available. Offers dietetic internship (Certificate); education (MSAH); management (MSAH); nutrition (MSAH).

Division of Nursing *Degree program information:* Part-time and evening/weekend programs available. Offers adult nurse practitioner (MSN); education (MSN); gerontology nurse practitioner (MSN); holistics (MSN); management/administration (MSN); neonatal nurse practitioner (MSN); oncology (MSN).

BARRY UNIVERSITY, Miami Shores, FL 33161-6695

General Information Independent-religious, coed, university. *Enrollment:* 8,885 graduate, professional, and undergraduate students; 1,935 full-time matriculated graduate/professional students (1,249 women), 1,497 part-time matriculated graduate/professional students (1,111 women). *Enrollment by degree level:* 772 first professional, 2,106 master's, 444 doctoral, 110 other advanced degrees. *Graduate faculty:* 142 full-time (80 women). *Graduate housing:* On-campus housing not available. *Student services:* Campus employment opportunities, campus safety program, career counseling, disabled student services, exercise/wellness program, free psychological counseling, international student services, low-cost health insurance, multicultural affairs office. *Library facilities:* Monsignor William Barry Memorial Library plus 1 other. *Online resources:* library catalog, web page. *Collection:* 233,938 titles, 2,880 serial subscriptions. *Research affiliation:* Baxter Corporation (immunology, diagnostics), Coulter Corporation (immunology, cytology), Cordis Corporation (cardiac product development), Diamedix (immunological diagnostics), Noven Pharmaceutical, Sano Pharmaceuticals.

Computer facilities: Computer purchase and lease plans are available. 368 computers available on campus for general student use. A campuswide network can be accessed from student residence rooms and from off campus. Internet access is available. *Web address:* http://www.barry.edu/.

General Application Contact: Dave Fletcher, Director of Graduate Admissions, 305-899-3113, Fax: 305-899-2971, E-mail: dfletcher@mail.barry.edu.

GRADUATE UNITS

Andreas School of Business Students: 35 full-time (18 women), 43 part-time (17 women); includes 35 minority (9 African Americans, 6 Asian Americans or Pacific Islanders, 20 Hispanic Americans), 20 international. Average age 29. 154 applicants, 35% accepted, 33 enrolled. *Faculty:* 24. Expenses: Contact institution. *Financial support:* Career-related internships or fieldwork and scholarships/grants available. Support available to part-time students. Financial award applicants required to submit FAFSA. In 2006, 43 degrees awarded. *Degree program information:* Part-time and evening/weekend programs available. Offers accounting (MSA); business (MBA, MSA, MSM, Certificate); business administration (MBA); finance (Certificate); health services administration (Certificate); international business (Certificate); management (Certificate); management information systems (Certificate); marketing (Certificate). *Application deadline:* Applications are processed on a rolling basis. *Application fee:* $30. Electronic applications accepted. *Application Contact:* Dave Fletcher, Director of Graduate Admissions, 305-899-3113, Fax: 305-899-2971, E-mail: dfletcher@mail.barry.edu. *Dean*, Dr. Jack Scarborough, 305-899-3500, Fax: 305-892-6412, E-mail: jscarborough@mail.barry.edu.

School of Adult and Continuing Education Students: 23 full-time (5 women), 35 part-time (14 women); includes 38 minority (21 African Americans, 2 American Indian/Alaska Native, 15 Hispanic Americans). Average age 39. 72 applicants, 56% accepted, 37 enrolled. Expenses: Contact institution. *Financial support:* Applicants required to submit FAFSA. In 2006, 20 degrees awarded. *Degree program information:* Part-time and evening/weekend programs available. Offers administrative studies (MA); adult and continuing education (MA, MPA, MS); information technology (MS); public administration (MPA). *Application deadline:* Applications are processed on a rolling basis. *Application fee:* $30. Electronic applications accepted. *Application Contact:* Dave Fletcher, Director of Graduate Admissions, 305-899-3113, Fax: 305-899-2971, E-mail: dfletcher@mail.barry.edu. *Dean*, Dr. Carol Rae Sodano, 305-899-3310.

School of Arts and Sciences Students: 44 full-time (34 women), 109 part-time (75 women); includes 60 minority (25 African Americans, 2 Asian Americans or Pacific Islanders, 33 Hispanic Americans), 12 international. Average age 38. *Faculty:* 36. Expenses: Contact institution. *Financial support:* Research assistantships, career-related internships or fieldwork, scholarships/grants, and tuition waivers (partial) available. Support available to part-time students. Financial award applicants required to submit FAFSA. In 2006, 24 master's, 9 other advanced degrees awarded. *Degree program information:* Part-time and evening/weekend programs available. Offers arts and sciences (MA, MFA, MS, D Min, Certificate, SSP); broadcasting (Certificate); clinical psychology (MS); communication (MA); liberal studies (MA); ministry (D Min); organizational communication (MS); pastoral ministry for Hispanics (MA); pastoral theology (MA); photography (MA, MFA); practical theology (MA); school psychology (MS, SSP). *Application deadline:* Applications are processed on a rolling basis. *Application fee:* $30. Electronic applications accepted. *Application Contact:* Dave Fletcher, Director of Graduate Admissions, 305-899-3113, Fax: 305-899-2971, E-mail: dfletcher@mail.barry.edu. *Interim Dean*, Dr. Christopher Starratt, 305-899-3402, Fax: 305-899-3466.

School of Education Students: 292 full-time (250 women), 717 part-time (546 women); includes 512 minority (269 African Americans, 1 American Indian/Alaska Native, 12 Asian Americans or Pacific Islanders, 230 Hispanic Americans), 35 international. Average age 39. *Faculty:* 70. Expenses: Contact institution. *Financial support:* Career-related internships or fieldwork and scholarships/grants available. Support available to part-time students. Financial award applicants required to submit FAFSA. In 2006, 284 master's, 29 doctorates, 30 other advanced degrees awarded. *Degree program information:* Part-time and evening/weekend programs available. Postbaccalaureate distance learning degree programs offered. Offers accomplished teacher (Ed S); advanced teaching and learning with technology (Certificate);

counseling (MS, PhD, Ed S); culture, language and literacy (TESOL) (PhD); curriculum evaluation and research (PhD); distance education (Certificate); early childhood (Ed S); early childhood education (PhD); education (MS, Ed D, PhD, Certificate, Ed S); education for teachers of students with hearing impairments (MS); educational computing and technology (MS, Ed S); educational leadership (MS, Ed D, Certificate, Ed S); educational technology (PhD); elementary (Ed S); elementary education (MS, PhD); elementary education/ESOL (MS); ESOL (Ed S); exceptional student education (MS, PhD, Ed S); gifted (Ed S); higher education administration (MS, PhD); higher education technology integration (Certificate); human resource development (PhD); human resource development and administration (MS); human resources: not for profit and religious organizations (Certificate); K-12 technology integration (Certificate); leadership (PhD); marital, couple and family counseling/therapy (MS, Ed S); mental health counseling (MS, Ed S); Montessori (Ed S); Montessori education (MS, Ed S); PKP/elementary (Ed S); pre-k/primary (MS); pre-k/primary/ESOL (MS); reading (Ed S); reading, language and cognition (PhD); rehabilitation counseling (MS, Ed S); school counseling (MS, Ed S); technology and TESOL (MS, Ed S); TESOL (MS); TESOL international (MS). *Application deadline:* For fall admission, 5/1 priority date for domestic students. Applications are processed on a rolling basis. *Application fee:* $30. Electronic applications accepted. *Application Contact:* Dave Fletcher, Director of Graduate Admissions, 305-899-3113, Fax: 305-899-2971, E-mail: dfletcher@mail.barry.edu. *Dean,* Dr. Terry Piper, 305-899-3649, Fax: 305-899-3630, E-mail: tpiper@mail.barry.edu.

School of Graduate Medical Sciences Students: 379 full-time (238 women), 27 part-time (19 women); includes 167 minority (65 African Americans, 2 American Indian/Alaska Native, 23 Asian Americans or Pacific Islanders, 77 Hispanic Americans), 4 international. Average age 28. 7 applicants, 86% accepted, 5 enrolled. *Faculty:* 26. Expenses: Contact institution. *Financial support:* Career-related internships or fieldwork and scholarships/grants available. Support available to part-time students. Financial award applicants required to submit FAFSA. In 2006, 49 DPMs, 61 master's awarded. Offers anatomy (MS); medical sciences (DPM, MCMS, MPH, MS); physician assistant (MCMS); podiatric medicine and surgery (DPM); public health (MPH). *Application deadline:* For fall admission, 6/1 for domestic students. Applications are processed on a rolling basis. *Application fee:* $30. Electronic applications accepted. *Application Contact:* Marc A. Weiner, Director of Graduate and Medical Sciences Admissions and Marketing, 305-899-3130, Fax: 305-899-3253, E-mail: mweiner@mail.barry.edu. *Dean,* Dr. Chet Evans, 305-899-3251, Fax: 305-899-3253, E-mail: cevans@mail.barry.edu.

School of Human Performance and Leisure Sciences Students: 55 full-time (30 women), 46 part-time (26 women); includes 19 minority (11 African Americans, 8 Hispanic Americans), 20 international. Average age 27. *Faculty:* 17. Expenses: Contact institution. *Financial support:* Career-related internships or fieldwork available. In 2006, 36 degrees awarded. *Degree program information:* Part-time and evening/weekend programs available. Offers athletic training (MS); biomechanics (MS); exercise science (MS); human performance and leisure sciences (MS); movement science (MS); sport and exercise psychology (MS); sport management (MS). *Application deadline:* Applications are processed on a rolling basis. *Application fee:* $30. Electronic applications accepted. *Application Contact:* Dave Fletcher, Director of Graduate Admissions, 305-899-3113, Fax: 305-899-2971, E-mail: dfletcher@mail.barry.edu. *Dean,* Dr. G. Jean Cerra, 305-899-3554, Fax: 305-899-3556, E-mail: jcerra@mail.barry.edu.

School of Law Students: 556 full-time (267 women), 19 part-time (9 women); includes 108 minority (26 African Americans, 4 American Indian/Alaska Native, 25 Asian Americans or Pacific Islanders, 53 Hispanic Americans), 3 international. Average age 29. 2,122 applicants, 46% accepted, 207 enrolled. Expenses: Contact institution. In 2006, 102 degrees awarded. Offers law (JD). *Application deadline:* For fall admission, 4/1 priority date for domestic students. *Application Contact:* Sheri Lagomarsino, Director of Admissions, 321-206-5654, Fax: 321-206-5620, E-mail: slagomarsino@mail.barry.edu. *Dean,* Leticia Diaz, 321-206-5602, E-mail: ldiaz@mail.barry.edu.

School of Natural and Health Sciences Students: 372 full-time (252 women), 136 part-time (94 women); includes 261 minority (79 African Americans, 52 Asian Americans or Pacific Islanders, 130 Hispanic Americans), 12 international. Average age 31. 698 applicants, 45% accepted, 235 enrolled. *Faculty:* 37. Expenses: Contact institution. *Financial support:* Teaching assistantships, tuition waivers (partial) available. Financial award application deadline: 5/1; financial award applicants required to submit FAFSA. In 2006, 190 degrees awarded. *Degree program information:* Part-time and evening/weekend programs available. Offers anesthesiology (MS); biology (MS); biomedical sciences (MS); health care leadership (Certificate); health care planning and informatics (Certificate); health services administration (MS); histotechnology (Certificate); long term care management (Certificate); medical group practice management (Certificate); natural and health sciences (MS, Certificate); occupational therapy (MS); quality improvement and outcomes management (Certificate). *Application deadline:* Applications are processed on a rolling basis. *Application fee:* $30. Electronic applications accepted. *Application Contact:* Jocelyn Goulet, Director, Health Services Admissions Operation, 305-899-3541, Fax: 305-899-3232, E-mail: jgoulet@mail.barry.edu. *Dean,* Sr. John Karen Frei, 305-899-3200, Fax: 305-899-3225, E-mail: jfrei@mail.barry.edu.

School of Nursing Students: 36 full-time (33 women), 204 part-time (174 women); includes 128 minority (44 African Americans, 7 Asian Americans or Pacific Islanders, 77 Hispanic Americans), 2 international. Average age 41. *Faculty:* 28. Expenses: Contact institution. *Financial support:* In 2006–07, 3 research assistantships (averaging $5,000 per year), 3 teaching assistantships (averaging $5,000 per year) were awarded; scholarships/grants and tuition waivers (full) also available. Financial award application deadline: 5/1; financial award applicants required to submit FAFSA. In 2006, 63 master's, 6 doctorates awarded. *Degree program information:* Part-time and evening/weekend programs available. Offers acute care nurse practitioner (MSN); family nurse practitioner (MSN); nurse practitioner (Certificate); nursing (MSN, PhD, Certificate); nursing administration (MSN, PhD, Certificate); nursing education (MSN, Certificate). *Application deadline:* For fall admission, 5/1 priority date for domestic students. Applications are processed on a rolling basis. *Application fee:* $30. Electronic applications accepted. *Application Contact:* Dave Fletcher, Director of Graduate Admissions, 305-899-3113, Fax: 305-899-2971, E-mail: dfletcher@mail.barry.edu. *Dean,* Dr. Pegge L. Bell, 305-899-3840, Fax: 305-899-3831, E-mail: pbell@mail.barry.edu.

School of Social Work Students: 143 full-time (122 women), 161 part-time (137 women); includes 187 minority (129 African Americans, 1 American Indian/Alaska Native, 5 Asian Americans or Pacific Islanders, 52 Hispanic Americans), 12 international. Average age 34. 250 applicants, 64% accepted, 117 enrolled. *Faculty:* 26. Expenses: Contact institution. *Financial support:* Available to part-time students. Applicants required to submit FAFSA. In 2006, 152 master's, 8 doctorates awarded. *Degree program information:* Part-time and evening/weekend programs available. Offers social work (MSW, PhD). *Application deadline:* For fall admission, 7/1 for domestic and international students; for spring admission, 12/1 for domestic and international students. Applications are processed on a rolling basis. *Application fee:* $30. Electronic applications accepted. *Application Contact:* Phillip Mack, Director of Admissions, 305-899-3919, Fax: 305-899-3934, E-mail: pmack@mail.barry.edu. *Dean,* Dr. Debra McPhee, 305-899-3196, Fax: 305-899-3934, E-mail: dmcphee@mail.barry.edu.

See Close-Up on page 807.

BASTYR UNIVERSITY, Kenmore, WA 98028-4966

General Information Independent, coed, upper-level institution. *Enrollment:* 1,126 graduate, professional, and undergraduate students; 795 full-time matriculated graduate/professional students (645 women), 68 part-time matriculated graduate/professional students (55 women). *Enrollment by degree level:* 490 first professional, 363 master's, 10 doctoral. *Tuition:* Full-time $18,845; part-time $325 per credit hour. *Required fees:* $1,365. Tuition and fees vary according to course load and degree level. *Graduate housing:* Room and/or apartments available on a first-come, first-served basis to single students; on-campus housing not available to married students. Typical cost: $2,460 per year. *Student services:* Campus employment opportunities, career counseling, child daycare facilities, free psychological counseling, international student services, low-cost health insurance. *Library facilities:* Bastyr University Library. *Online resources:* library catalog, web page. *Collection:* 14,000 titles, 265 serial subscriptions. *Research affiliation:* University of Washington (health), University of Minnesota (health), Child Health Institute (health).

Computer facilities: 28 computers available on campus for general student use. A campuswide network can be accessed from student residence rooms and from off campus. Internet access is available. *Web address:* http://www.bastyr.edu/.

General Application Contact: Information Contact, 425-602-3330, Fax: 425-602-2090, E-mail: admiss@bastyr.edu.

GRADUATE UNITS

Graduate and Professional Programs Students: 795 full-time (645 women), 68 part-time (55 women); includes 98 minority (20 African Americans, 3 American Indian/Alaska Native, 51 Asian Americans or Pacific Islanders, 24 Hispanic Americans), 36 international. Average age 32. 444 applicants, 76% accepted, 203 enrolled. Expenses: Contact institution. *Financial support:* In 2006–07, 826 students received support; teaching assistantships, career-related internships or fieldwork, Federal Work-Study, and scholarships/grants available. Support available to part-time students. Financial award application deadline: 4/15; financial award applicants required to submit FAFSA. In 2006, 137 master's, 5 doctorates, 4 other advanced degrees awarded. *Degree program information:* Part-time programs available. *Application deadline:* For winter admission, 3/15 priority date for domestic students. Applications are processed on a rolling basis. *Application fee:* $75. *Application Contact:* Ted Olsen, Director, Admissions, 425-602-3080, Fax: 425-602-3090. *Interim Vice President of Academics,* Daniel D. Leahy, 425-939-8100, Fax: 425-939-8110.

School of Acupuncture and Oriental Medicine Students: 94 full-time (63 women), 33 part-time (25 women); includes 20 minority (2 American Indian/Alaska Native, 14 Asian Americans or Pacific Islanders, 4 Hispanic Americans), 13 international. Average age 36. 75 applicants, 73% accepted, 32 enrolled. Expenses: Contact institution. *Financial support:* Career-related internships or fieldwork, Federal Work-Study, and scholarships/grants available. Support available to part-time students. Financial award application deadline: 4/15; financial award applicants required to submit FAFSA. In 2006, 41 master's, 5 doctorates, 3 other advanced degrees awarded. Offers acupuncture (MS); acupuncture and Oriental medicine (MS, DAOM); Chinese herbal medicine (Certificate). *Application deadline:* For fall admission, 3/15 priority date for domestic and international students. Applications are processed on a rolling basis. *Application fee:* $75. *Application Contact:* Admissions Office, 425-602-3330, Fax: 425-602-3090, E-mail: admiss@bastyr.edu. *Chair,* Terry Courtney, 425-823-1300, Fax: 425-823-6222.

School of Applied Behavioral Science Students: 129 full-time (102 women), 8 part-time (7 women); includes 9 minority (4 African Americans, 1 American Indian/Alaska Native, 4 Asian Americans or Pacific Islanders). Average age 37. 94 applicants, 97% accepted, 76 enrolled. Expenses: Contact institution. In 2006, 64 degrees awarded. Offers applied behavioral science (MA). Program offered jointly with Leadership Institute of Seattle. *Application deadline:* Applications are processed on a rolling basis. *Application fee:* $75. *Application Contact:* Scott Harris, Academic and Professional Admissions Director, E-mail: sharris@lios.org.

School of Naturopathic Medicine Students: 488 full-time (400 women), 2 part-time (1 woman); includes 64 minority (15 African Americans, 32 Asian Americans or Pacific Islanders, 17 Hispanic Americans), 13 international. Average age 29. 271 applicants, 73% accepted, 120 enrolled. Expenses: Contact institution. *Financial support:* Career-related internships or fieldwork, Federal Work-Study, and scholarships/grants available. Support available to part-time students. Financial award application deadline: 4/15; financial award applicants required to submit FAFSA. In 2006, 83 doctorates, 1 other advanced degree awarded. Offers midwifery (Certificate); naturopathic medicine (ND). *Application deadline:* For fall admission, 2/1 priority date for domestic and international students. Applications are processed on a rolling basis. *Application fee:* $75. *Application Contact:* Admissions Office, 425-602-3330, Fax: 425-602-3090, E-mail: admiss@bastyr.edu. *Dean,* Dr. Gannady Raskin, 425-823-1300, Fax: 425-823-6222.

School of Nutrition and Exercise Science Students: 84 full-time (80 women), 26 part-time (23 women); includes 5 minority (1 African American, 1 Asian American or Pacific Islander, 3 Hispanic Americans), 10 international. Average age 30. 98 applicants, 89% accepted, 51 enrolled. Expenses: Contact institution. *Financial support:* Career-related internships or fieldwork, Federal Work-Study, and scholarships/grants available. Support available to part-time students. Financial award application deadline: 4/15; financial award applicants required to submit FAFSA. In 2006, 32 degrees awarded. *Degree program information:* Part-time programs available. Offers nutrition (MS); nutrition and clinical health psychology (MS). *Application deadline:* For fall admission, 3/15 priority date for domestic and international students. Applications are processed on a rolling basis. *Application fee:* $75. *Application Contact:* Admissions Office, 425-602-3330, Fax: 425-602-3090, E-mail: admiss@bastyr.edu. *Chair,* Dr. Jennifer Lovejoy, 425-823-1300, Fax: 425-823-6222.

BAYAMÓN CENTRAL UNIVERSITY, Bayamón, PR 00960-1725

General Information Independent-religious, coed, comprehensive institution. *Graduate housing:* On-campus housing not available.

GRADUATE UNITS

Graduate Programs *Degree program information:* Part-time and evening/weekend programs available. Offers accounting (MBA); administration and supervision (MA Ed); biblical studies (MA); commercial education (MA Ed); divinity (M Div); education of the autistic (MA Ed); elementary education (K–3) (MA Ed); elementary education (K–6) (MA Ed); elementary physical education (MA Ed); finance (MBA); general business (MBA); guidance and counseling (MA Ed); management (MBA); management of security and protection (MBA); marketing (MBA); pastoral theology (MA); pre-elementary teacher (MA Ed); psychology (MA); special education (MA Ed); theological studies (MA); theology (MA).

BAYLOR COLLEGE OF MEDICINE, Houston, TX 77030-3498

General Information Independent, coed, graduate-only institution. CGS member. *Enrollment by degree level:* 678 first professional, 129 master's, 533 doctoral. *Graduate faculty:* 1,785 full-time, 343 part-time/adjunct. *Graduate housing:* On-campus housing not available. *Student services:* Campus employment opportunities, campus safety program, career counseling, disabled student services, exercise/wellness program, free psychological counseling, international student services, low-cost health insurance. *Library facilities:* Houston Academy of Medicine–Texas Medical Center Library. *Online resources:* library catalog, web page, access to other libraries' catalogs. *Collection:* 333,115 titles, 5,019 serial subscriptions, 713 audiovisual materials. *Research affiliation:* Children's Nutrition Research Center (pediatric nutrition), Harris County Hospital District (biomedical research), National Space Biomedical Research Institute, The Methodist Hospital (biomedical research), Texas Children's Hospital (pediatric biomedical research), Veterans Affairs Medical Center (biomedical research).

Computer facilities: 60 computers available on campus for general student use. A campuswide network can be accessed from off campus. Internet access is available. *Web address:* http://www.bcm.edu/.

General Application Contact: Dr. Lloyd H. Michael, Senior Associate Dean of the Medical School, 713-798-4842, Fax: 713-798-5563, E-mail: lmichael@bcm.edu.

GRADUATE UNITS

Graduate School of Biomedical Sciences Students: 556 full-time (276 women); includes 122 minority (22 African Americans, 2 American Indian/Alaska Native, 58 Asian Americans or Pacific Islanders, 40 Hispanic Americans), 208 international. Average age 29. 900 applicants, 18% accepted, 97 enrolled. *Faculty:* 380 full-time (89 women). Expenses: Contact institution. *Financial support:* In 2006–07, 556 students received support, including 208 fellowships (averaging $23,000 per year), 328 research assistantships (averaging $23,000 per year), 1 teaching assistantship; career-related internships or fieldwork, Federal Work-Study, institutionally sponsored loans, health care benefits, tuition waivers (full and partial), and stipends also available. Financial award applicants required to submit FAFSA. In 2006, 7 master's, 49 doctorates awarded. Offers biochemistry (PhD); biochemistry and molecular biology (PhD); biomedical sciences (MS, PhD); cardiovascular sciences (PhD); cell and molecular biology (PhD); clinical scientist training (MS, PhD); developmental biology (PhD); genetics (PhD); human genetics (PhD); immunology (PhD); microbiology (PhD); molecular and cellular biology (PhD); molecular and human genetics (PhD); molecular physiology and biophysics

Baylor College of Medicine (continued)

(PhD); molecular virology and microbiology (PhD); neuroscience (PhD); pharmacology (PhD); structural and computational biology and molecular biophysics (PhD); translational biology and molecular medicine (PhD); virology (PhD). *Application deadline:* For fall admission, 2/1 priority date for domestic students. Applications are processed on a rolling basis. *Application fee:* $30. Electronic applications accepted. *Application Contact:* Donna Otwell, Director of Administrative Operations, 713-798-4029, Fax: 713-798-6325, E-mail: dotwell@bcm.edu. *Dean of Graduate Sciences,* Dr. William R. Brinkley, 713-798-5263, Fax: 713-798-6325, E-mail: brinkley@bcm.tmc.edu.

Medical School Students: 678 full-time (326 women); includes 367 minority (59 African Americans, 11 American Indian/Alaska Native, 230 Asian Americans or Pacific Islanders, 67 Hispanic Americans), 3 international. Average age 24. 4,326 applicants, 6% accepted, 168 enrolled. Expenses: Contact institution. *Financial support:* In 2006–07, 503 students received support. Career-related internships or fieldwork, Federal Work-Study, institutionally sponsored loans, scholarships/grants, traineeships, and tuition waivers (full and partial) available. Financial award application deadline: 5/11; financial award applicants required to submit FAFSA. In 2006, 156 degrees awarded. Offers medicine (MD). *Application deadline:* For fall admission, 11/1 for domestic students. Applications are processed on a rolling basis. *Application fee:* $70. Electronic applications accepted. *Application Contact:* Dr. Lloyd H. Michael, Senior Associate Dean of the Medical School, 713-798-4842, Fax: 713-798-5563, E-mail: lmichael@bcm.edu. *President and CEO,* Dr. Peter G. Traber, 713-798-6363, Fax: 713-798-6353, E-mail: pgtraber@bcm.edu.

School of Allied Health Sciences Students: 130 full-time (103 women); includes 27 minority (7 African Americans, 1 American Indian/Alaska Native, 13 Asian Americans or Pacific Islanders, 6 Hispanic Americans). 682 applicants, 8% accepted, 45 enrolled. *Faculty:* 14 full-time (10 women), 4 part-time/adjunct (2 women). Expenses: Contact institution. *Financial support:* In 2006–07, 104 students received support. Institutionally sponsored loans and scholarships/grants available. Financial award application deadline: 5/11. In 2006, 39 degrees awarded. Offers allied health sciences (MS); nurse anesthesia (MS); physician assistant (MS). *Application deadline:* For fall admission, 11/1 for domestic students. Applications are processed on a rolling basis. Electronic applications accepted. *Head/Professor,* Dr. J. David Holcomb, 713-798-4613, Fax: 713-798-7694, E-mail: jholcomb@bcm.edu.

BAYLOR UNIVERSITY, Waco, TX 76798

General Information Independent-religious, coed, university. CGS member. *Enrollment:* 14,040 graduate, professional, and undergraduate students; 1,867 full-time matriculated graduate/professional students (826 women), 330 part-time matriculated graduate/professional students (176 women). *Enrollment by degree level:* 730 first professional, 860 master's, 589 doctoral, 18 other advanced degrees. *Graduate faculty:* 350. *Graduate housing:* Rooms and/or apartments available to single and married students. *Student services:* Campus employment opportunities, campus safety program, career counseling, disabled student services, exercise/wellness program, free psychological counseling, international student services, low-cost health insurance, multicultural affairs office. *Library facilities:* Moody Memorial Library plus 8 others. *Online resources:* library catalog, web page, access to other libraries' catalogs. *Collection:* 2.3 million titles, 8,429 serial subscriptions. *Research affiliation:* Fermi National Accelerator Laboratory (physics), Brookhaven National Laboratory (physics), OXiGENE, Inc. (pharmaceuticals), Zyvex Corporation (physics), National Center for Supercomputing Applications (physics), Sandia National Laboratory (physics).

Computer facilities: Computer purchase and lease plans are available. 1,500 computers available on campus for general student use. A campuswide network can be accessed from student residence rooms and from off campus. Internet access and online class registration are available. *Web address:* http://www.baylor.edu/.

General Application Contact: Suzanne Keener, Administrative Assistant, 254-710-3588, Fax: 254-710-3870.

GRADUATE UNITS

George W. Truett Seminary Students: 307 full-time (96 women), 69 part-time (15 women); includes 60 minority (31 African Americans, 1 American Indian/Alaska Native, 4 Asian Americans or Pacific Islanders, 24 Hispanic Americans), 20 international. 144 applicants, 94% accepted, 102 enrolled. *Faculty:* 14 full-time (3 women), 7 part-time/adjunct (1 woman). Expenses: Contact institution. *Financial support:* In 2006–07, 207 students received support, including 1 research assistantship, 12 teaching assistantships; career-related internships or fieldwork, Federal Work-Study, institutionally sponsored loans, scholarships/grants, tuition waivers (partial), and unspecified assistantships also available. Support available to part-time students. Financial award application deadline: 8/1; financial award applicants required to submit FAFSA. In 2006, 54 M Divs, 3 master's, 6 doctorates awarded. Offers theology (M Div, MTS, D Min). *Application deadline:* For fall admission, 7/1 priority date for domestic students, 7/1 for international students; for spring admission, 11/1 priority date for domestic students, 11/1 for international students. Applications are processed on a rolling basis. *Application fee:* $25. *Application Contact:* Dr. Grear Howard, Director of Student Services, 254-710-3755, Fax: 254-710-7233, E-mail: grear_howard@baylor.edu. *Dean,* Dr. Paul W. Powell, 254-710-3755, Fax: 254-710-3753.

Graduate School Students: 1,169 full-time (562 women), 254 part-time (157 women); includes 178 minority (65 African Americans, 10 American Indian/Alaska Native, 41 Asian Americans or Pacific Islanders, 62 Hispanic Americans), 169 international. 1,435 applicants, 46% accepted, 465 enrolled. *Faculty:* 350. Expenses: Contact institution. *Financial support:* Fellowships, research assistantships with full and partial tuition reimbursements, teaching assistantships with full and partial tuition reimbursements, career-related internships or fieldwork, Federal Work-Study, institutionally sponsored loans, scholarships/grants, tuition waivers (full and partial), and unspecified assistantships available. Support available to part-time students. In 2006, 488 master's, 99 doctorates, 1 other advanced degree awarded. *Degree program information:* Part-time and evening/weekend programs available. Postbaccalaureate distance learning degree programs offered (minimal on-campus study). *Application deadline:* Applications are processed on a rolling basis. *Application fee:* $25. *Application Contact:* Suzanne Keener, Administrative Assistant, 254-710-3588, Fax: 254-710-3870. *Dean,* Dr. Larry Lyon, 254-710-3588, Fax: 254-710-3870, E-mail: larry_lyon@baylor.edu.

Academy of Health Sciences Students: 150 full-time (49 women); includes 17 minority (7 African Americans, 5 Asian Americans or Pacific Islanders, 5 Hispanic Americans). Expenses: Contact institution. In 2006, 42 master's, 16 doctorates awarded. Offers health care administration (MHA); health sciences (MHA, MPT, DPT, Dr Sc PT); physical therapy (MPT, DPT, Dr Sc PT). *Application deadline:* Applications are processed on a rolling basis. *Application fee:* $25. *Dean,* Col. Darwin L. Fretwell, 210-221-8715, Fax: 210-221-7306.

College of Arts and Sciences Students: 533 full-time (259 women), 88 part-time (52 women); includes 56 minority (6 African Americans, 4 American Indian/Alaska Native, 15 Asian Americans or Pacific Islanders, 31 Hispanic Americans), 78 international. Expenses: Contact institution. *Financial support:* Fellowships, research assistantships with partial tuition reimbursements, teaching assistantships, career-related internships or fieldwork, Federal Work-Study, institutionally sponsored loans, scholarships/grants, tuition waivers (full and partial), unspecified assistantships, and laboratory assistantships, practicum stipends available. Support available to part-time students. In 2006, 126 master's, 57 doctorates awarded. *Degree program information:* Part-time and evening/weekend programs available. Offers American studies (MA); applied sociology (PhD); arts and sciences (MA, MES, MFA, MIJ, MPPA, MS, MSCP, MSCSD, MSL, MSW, PhD, Psy D); biology (MA, MS, PhD); chemistry (MS, PhD); church-state studies (MA, PhD); clinical psychology (MSCP, Psy D); communication sciences and disorders (MA, MSCSD); communication studies (MA); directing (MFA); earth science (MA); English (MA, PhD); environmental biology (MS); environmental studies (MES, MS); geology (MS, PhD); history (MA); international journalism (MIJ); international studies (MA); journalism (MA); limnology (MSL); mathematics (MS, PhD); museum studies (MA); neuroscience (MA, PhD); philosophy (MA, PhD); physics (MA, MS, PhD); political science (MA, PhD); public policy and administration (MPPA); religion (MA, PhD); social work (MSW); sociology (MA); Spanish (MA); statistics (MA, PhD). *Application deadline:* Applications are processed on a rolling basis. *Application fee:* $25. Electronic applications accepted.

Hankamer School of Business Students: 182 full-time (57 women), 11 part-time (5 women); includes 31 minority (15 African Americans, 10 Asian Americans or Pacific Islanders, 6 Hispanic Americans), 47 international. Expenses: Contact institution. *Financial support:* Research assistantships, teaching assistantships, career-related internships or fieldwork, Federal Work-Study, and institutionally sponsored loans available. In 2006, 145 degrees awarded. *Degree program information:* Part-time programs available. Offers accounting and business law (M Acc, MT); business (M Acc, MA, MBA, MBAIM, MIM, MS, MS Eco, MSIS, MT); business administration (MBA); economics (MS Eco); information systems (MSIS); information systems management (MBA); international economics (MA, MS); international management (MBA, MBAIM, MIM). *Application deadline:* For fall admission, 8/1 for domestic students; for spring admission, 12/1 for domestic students. Applications are processed on a rolling basis. *Application fee:* $25. *Application Contact:* Vicky Todd, Administrative Assistant, 254-710-3718, Fax: 254-710-1066, E-mail: mba@hsb.baylor.edu. *Director of Graduate Programs,* Dr. Gary Carini, 254-710-3718, Fax: 254-710-1092.

Institute of Biomedical Studies Students: 23 full-time (9 women), 1 part-time; includes 4 minority (all Asian Americans or Pacific Islanders), 12 international. Expenses: Contact institution. *Financial support:* Research assistantships, teaching assistantships available. In 2006, 4 degrees awarded. Offers biomedical studies (MS, PhD). *Application deadline:* Applications are processed on a rolling basis. *Application fee:* $25. *Application Contact:* Suzanne Keener, Administrative Assistant, 254-710-3588, Fax: 254-710-3870. *Interim Director,* Dr. Robert Kane, 254-710-2514, Fax: 254-710-3878, E-mail: robert_kane@baylor.edu.

Louise Herrington School of Nursing Students: 10 full-time (all women), 27 part-time (26 women); includes 6 minority (1 African American, 1 Asian American or Pacific Islander, 4 Hispanic Americans), 1 international. Expenses: Contact institution. In 2006, 13 degrees awarded. Offers family nurse practitioner (MSN); neonatal nurse practitioner (MSN); nursing administration and management (MSN). *Application deadline:* For fall admission, 8/1 for domestic students; for spring admission, 12/1 for domestic students. Applications are processed on a rolling basis. *Application fee:* $25. *Application Contact:* Suzanne Keener, Administrative Assistant, 254-710-3588, Fax: 254-710-3870. *Graduate Program Director,* Dr. Pauline Johnson, 214-820-3361, Fax: 214-818-8692, E-mail: pauline_johnson@baylor.edu.

School of Education Students: 170 full-time (115 women), 77 part-time (50 women); includes 43 minority (27 African Americans, 5 American Indian/Alaska Native, 4 Asian Americans or Pacific Islanders, 7 Hispanic Americans), 13 international. Expenses: Contact institution. *Financial support:* Research assistantships, teaching assistantships, career-related internships or fieldwork, Federal Work-Study, institutionally sponsored loans, scholarships/grants, and tuition waivers (partial) available. In 2006, 81 master's, 18 doctorates, 1 other advanced degree awarded. *Degree program information:* Part-time programs available. Postbaccalaureate distance learning degree programs offered (minimal on-campus study). Offers curriculum and instruction (MA, MS Ed, Ed D, Ed S); education (MA, MS Ed, Ed D, PhD, Ed S); educational administration (MS Ed, Ed S); educational psychology (MA, MS Ed, PhD, Ed S); exercise, nutrition and preventive health (PhD); health, human performance and recreation (MS Ed). *Application deadline:* Applications are processed on a rolling basis. *Application fee:* $25. Electronic applications accepted. *Application Contact:* Suzanne Keener, Administrative Assistant, 254-710-3588, Fax: 254-710-3870. *Interim Dean,* 254-710-3111, Fax: 254-710-3987.

School of Engineering and Computer Science Students: 33 full-time (8 women), 3 part-time; includes 5 minority (2 African Americans, 1 Asian American or Pacific Islander, 2 Hispanic Americans), 7 international. Expenses: Contact institution. *Financial support:* Teaching assistantships available. Financial award application deadline: 3/15. In 2006, 10 degrees awarded. *Degree program information:* Part-time programs available. Offers biomedical engineering (MSBE); computer science (MS); electrical and computer engineering (MSECE); engineering (ME, MSBE, MSECE, MSME); mechanical engineering (MSME). *Application deadline:* For fall admission, 8/1 for domestic students; for spring admission, 12/1 for domestic students. Applications are processed on a rolling basis. *Application fee:* $25. *Application Contact:* Suzanne Keener, Administrative Assistant, 254-710-3588, Fax: 254-710-3870. *Graduate Program Director,* Dr. Greg Speegle, 254-710-3876, Fax: 254-710-3839, E-mail: greg_speegle@baylor.edu.

School of Music Students: 14 full-time (9 women), 40 part-time (19 women); includes 6 minority (1 African American, 1 American Indian/Alaska Native, 4 Hispanic Americans), 11 international. Expenses: Contact institution. *Financial support:* Federal Work-Study and institutionally sponsored loans available. In 2006, 32 degrees awarded. Offers church music (MM); composition (MM); conducting (MM); music education (MM); music history and literature (MM); music theory (MM); performance (MM); piano accompanying (MM); piano pedagogy and performance (MM). *Application deadline:* For fall admission, 8/1 for domestic students; for spring admission, 12/1 for domestic students. Applications are processed on a rolling basis. *Application fee:* $25. *Application Contact:* Suzanne Keener, Administrative Assistant, 254-710-3588, Fax: 254-710-3870. *Graduate Program Director,* Dr. Harry Elzinga, 254-710-1161, Fax: 254-710-1191, E-mail: harry_elzinga@baylor.edu.

School of Law Students: 391 full-time (168 women), 7 part-time (4 women); includes 42 minority (5 African Americans, 1 American Indian/Alaska Native, 22 Asian Americans or Pacific Islanders, 14 Hispanic Americans), 3 international. Average age 24. 2,082 applicants, 21% accepted, 94 enrolled. *Faculty:* 24 full-time (4 women), 36 part-time/adjunct (2 women). Expenses: Contact institution. *Financial support:* In 2006–07, 394 students received support. Career-related internships or fieldwork, Federal Work-Study, institutionally sponsored loans, and scholarships/grants available. Financial award applicants required to submit FAFSA. In 2006, 151 degrees awarded. Offers law (JD). *Application deadline:* For fall admission, 3/1 for domestic students; for spring admission, 11/1 for domestic students. Applications are processed on a rolling basis. *Application fee:* $40. Electronic applications accepted. *Application Contact:* Heather Creed, Director of Student Relations, 254-710-1911, Fax: 254-710-2316, E-mail: heather_creed@baylor.edu. *Dean,* Dr. Bradley J. B. Toben, 254-710-1911, Fax: 254-710-2316.

BAY PATH COLLEGE, Longmeadow, MA 01106-2292

General Information Independent, Undergraduate: women only; graduate: coed, comprehensive institution. *Graduate housing:* Room and/or apartments available on a first-come, first-served basis to single students; on-campus housing not available to married students. Housing application deadline: 7/2.

GRADUATE UNITS

Program in Communications and Information Management *Degree program information:* Part-time and evening/weekend programs available. Offers information management (MS); information systems (MS). Electronic applications accepted.

Program in Entrepreneurial Thinking and Innovative Practices *Degree program information:* Part-time and evening/weekend programs available. Offers entrepreneurial thinking and innovative practices (MBA). Electronic applications accepted.

Program in Occupational Therapy *Degree program information:* Part-time and evening/weekend programs available. Offers occupational therapy (MOT, MS). Electronic applications accepted.

BEACON UNIVERSITY, Columbus, GA 31909

General Information Independent-religious, coed, comprehensive institution.

GRADUATE UNITS

Graduate Programs Offers cell church development (MAPM); counseling (MAC); counseling ministry (MAPM); military chaplaincy (MAPM); organizational leadership (MAPM); organizational leadership and management (MAOL); pastoral ministry (MAPM); theology (M Div, MABS).

BELHAVEN COLLEGE, Jackson, MS 39202-1789

General Information Independent-religious, coed, comprehensive institution. *Graduate housing:* On-campus housing not available.

GRADUATE UNITS

School of Business *Degree program information:* Evening/weekend programs available. Offers business administration (MBA); business management (MSM). MBA program also offered in Houston, TX; Memphis, TN; and Orlando, FL.

School of Education Offers elementary education (M Ed, MAT); secondary education (M Ed, MAT). M Ed program also offered in Memphis, TN and Orlando, FL; MAT program in Orlando, FL.

BELLARMINE UNIVERSITY, Louisville, KY 40205-0671

General Information Independent-religious, coed, comprehensive institution. *Enrollment:* 2,627 graduate, professional, and undergraduate students; 290 full-time matriculated graduate/professional students (198 women), 341 part-time matriculated graduate/professional students (226 women). *Enrollment by degree level:* 520 master's, 111 doctoral. *Graduate faculty:* 44 full-time (24 women), 32 part-time/adjunct (17 women). *Tuition:* Part-time $490 per credit hour. Tuition and fees vary according to program. *Graduate housing:* Room and/or apartments available on a first-come, first-served basis to single students; on-campus housing not available to married students. Typical cost: $3,860 per year ($3,020 including board). Room and board charges vary according to board plan and housing facility selected. Housing application deadline: 7/15. *Student services:* Campus employment opportunities, campus safety program, career counseling, disabled student services, exercise/wellness program, free psychological counseling, grant writing training, international student services, low-cost health insurance, multicultural affairs office, teacher training, writing training. *Library facilities:* W.L. Lyons Brown Library. *Online resources:* library catalog, web page. *Collection:* 118,707 titles, 19,687 serial subscriptions, 3,172 audiovisual materials.

Computer facilities: 160 computers available on campus for general student use. A campuswide network can be accessed from student residence rooms. Internet access is available. *Web address:* http://www.bellarmine.edu/.

General Application Contact: Dr. Julie F. Toner, Graduate School Dean, 502-452-8494, Fax: 502-452-8162, E-mail: jtoner@bellarmine.edu.

GRADUATE UNITS

Annsley Frazier Thornton School of Education Students: 92 full-time (68 women), 140 part-time (104 women); includes 16 minority (11 African Americans, 1 Asian American or Pacific Islander, 4 Hispanic Americans). Average age 32. *Faculty:* 10 full-time (8 women), 5 part-time/adjunct (all women). Expenses: Contact institution. In 2006, 98 degrees awarded. *Degree program information:* Part-time and evening/weekend programs available. Offers early elementary education (MA, MAT); education (MA, MAT); instructional leadership and school administration/school principal (MA); learning and behavior disorders (MA); middle school education (MA, MAT); reading and writing endorsement (MA); secondary school education (MAT); Waldorf inspired curriculum (MA). *Application deadline:* Applications are processed on a rolling basis. *Application fee:* $25. Electronic applications accepted. *Application Contact:* Theresa Klapheke, Director of Graduate Programs, 502-452-8033, Fax: 502-452-8189, E-mail: tklapheke@bellarmine.edu. *Dean (Interim),* Dr. Milton Brown, 502-452-8486, Fax: 502-452-8189, E-mail: mbrown@bellarmine.edu.

Bellarmine Center for Interdisciplinary Technology and Entrepreneurship Students: 12 full-time (5 women), 2 part-time (both women). Average age 33. *Faculty:* 1 full-time (0 women), 11 part-time/adjunct (3 women). Expenses: Contact institution. In 2006, 9 degrees awarded. *Degree program information:* Part-time and evening/weekend programs available. Offers technology and entrepreneurship (MAIT). *Application fee:* $25. *Executive Director,* Dr. Michael D. Mattei, 502-452-8441, E-mail: mmattei@bellarmine.edu.

Bellarmine College of Arts and Sciences Average age 50. *Faculty:* 4 full-time (1 woman), 2 part-time/adjunct (0 women). Expenses: Contact institution. In 2006, 9 degrees awarded. *Application fee:* $25. *Application Contact:* Pat Allen, Office Receptionist, 502-452-8188, E-mail: pallen@bellarmine.edu. *Dean,* Dr. Robert Kingsolver, 502-452-8359, E-mail: kingsolver@bellarmine.edu.

Donna and Allan Lansing School of Nursing and Health Sciences Students: 112 full-time (87 women), 70 part-time (66 women); includes 12 minority (7 African Americans, 4 Asian Americans or Pacific Islanders, 1 Hispanic American), 1 international. Average age 31. *Faculty:* 15 full-time (11 women), 8 part-time/adjunct (7 women). Expenses: Contact institution. *Financial support:* Career-related internships or fieldwork and scholarships/grants available. In 2006, 44 degrees awarded. Offers nursing administration (MSN); nursing education (MSN); physical therapy (DPT). *Application deadline:* For fall admission, 10/15 priority date for domestic students. Applications are processed on a rolling basis. *Application fee:* $25. Electronic applications accepted. *Application Contact:* Julie Armstrong-Binnix, Health Science Recruiter, 800-274-4723 Ext. 8364, E-mail: julieab@bellarmine.edu. *Dean,* Dr. Susan H. Davis, 800-274-4723 Ext. 8217, E-mail: sdavis@bellarmine.edu.

W. Fielding Rubel School of Business Students: 74 full-time (36 women), 110 part-time (44 women); includes 16 minority (8 African Americans, 5 Asian Americans or Pacific Islanders, 3 Hispanic Americans), 4 international. Average age 30. *Faculty:* 14 full-time (4 women), 6 part-time/adjunct (2 women). Expenses: Contact institution. *Financial support:* Career-related internships or fieldwork, scholarships/grants, and unspecified assistantships available. Support available to part-time students. Financial award application deadline: 7/1. In 2006, 50 degrees awarded. *Degree program information:* Part-time and evening/weekend programs available. Offers business (EMBA, MBA). *Application deadline:* Applications are processed on a rolling basis. *Application fee:* $25. Electronic applications accepted. *Application Contact:* Laura Richardson, Director, 800-274-4723 Ext. 8258, Fax: 502-452-8012, E-mail: lrichardson@bellarmine.edu. *Dean,* Daniel L. Bauer, 800-274-4723 Ext. 8026, Fax: 502-452-8013, E-mail: dbauer@bellarmine.edu.

BELLEVUE UNIVERSITY, Bellevue, NE 68005-3098

General Information Independent, coed, comprehensive institution. *Graduate housing:* Room and/or apartments available on a first-come, first-served basis to single students; on-campus housing not available to married students.

GRADUATE UNITS

Graduate School *Degree program information:* Part-time and evening/weekend programs available. Postbaccalaureate distance learning degree programs offered (no on-campus study). Offers business (MBA); communications studies (MA, MS); computer information systems (MS); health care administration (MS); human services (MS); leadership (MA); management (MA); security management (MS). MA is delivered in an accelerated executive format.

See Close-Up on page 809.

BELMONT UNIVERSITY, Nashville, TN 37212-3757

General Information Independent-religious, coed, comprehensive institution. *Enrollment:* 4,481 graduate, professional, and undergraduate students; 302 full-time matriculated graduate/professional students (236 women), 405 part-time matriculated graduate/professional students (221 women). *Enrollment by degree level:* 561 master's, 146 doctoral. *Graduate faculty:* 89 full-time (47 women), 52 part-time/adjunct (33 women). *Graduate housing:* On-campus housing not available. *Student services:* Campus employment opportunities, career counseling, exercise/wellness program, free psychological counseling, international student services, low-cost health insurance, multicultural affairs office. *Library facilities:* Lila D. Bunch Library. *Online resources:* library catalog, web page, access to other libraries' catalogs. *Collection:* 200,630 titles, 1,415 serial subscriptions, 29,312 audiovisual materials.

Computer facilities: 350 computers available on campus for general student use. A campuswide network can be accessed from student residence rooms and from off campus. Internet access and online class registration, individual student information via BANNER Web are available. *Web address:* http://www.belmont.edu/.

General Application Contact: Dr. Kathryn Baugher, Dean of Enrollment Services, 615-460-6785, Fax: 615-460-5434, E-mail: baugherk@mail.belmont.edu.

GRADUATE UNITS

College of Arts and Sciences Students: 52 full-time (37 women), 166 part-time (110 women); includes 31 minority (27 African Americans, 1 Asian American or Pacific Islander, 3 Hispanic Americans), 1 international. Average age 31. 70 applicants, 66% accepted, 40 enrolled. *Faculty:* 25 full-time (19 women), 12 part-time/adjunct (8 women). Expenses: Contact institution. *Financial support:* Fellowships with tuition reimbursements, tuition waivers (partial) available. In 2006, 97 degrees awarded. Offers arts and sciences (M Ed, MA, MAT, MSA); literature (MA); writing (MA). *Application deadline:* For fall admission, 8/1 for domestic students; for spring admission, 12/1 for domestic students. Applications are processed on a rolling basis. *Application fee:* $50. Electronic applications accepted. *Dean,* Dr. Larry M. Hall, 615-460-6437, Fax: 615-385-5084, E-mail: hall@mail.belmont.edu.

School of Education Students: 50 full-time (36 women), 116 part-time (76 women); includes 23 minority (20 African Americans, 1 Asian American or Pacific Islander, 2 Hispanic Americans), 1 international. Average age 30. 55 applicants, 60% accepted, 30 enrolled. *Faculty:* 9 full-time (7 women), 20 part-time/adjunct (15 women). Expenses: Contact institution. *Financial support:* In 2006–07, 25 students received support; fellowships with partial tuition reimbursements available, institutionally sponsored loans and tuition waivers (partial) available. Financial award application deadline: 4/15; financial award applicants required to submit FAFSA. In 2006, 82 degrees awarded. *Degree program information:* Part-time and evening/weekend programs available. Offers education (MAT); elementary education (M Ed); English (M Ed); history (M Ed); mathematics (M Ed); middle grade education (M Ed); science (M Ed); secondary education (M Ed); sports administration (MSA); technology (M Ed). *Application deadline:* For fall admission, 8/1 priority date for domestic students, 5/1 for international students; for spring admission, 12/1 priority date for domestic students, 9/1 for international students. Applications are processed on a rolling basis. *Application fee:* $50. *Application Contact:* Julie Hullett, Admission/Licensure Officer, 615-460-6879, Fax: 615-460-5556, E-mail: hullettj@email.belmont.edu. *Associate Dean,* Dr. Trevor F. Hutchins, 615-460-6232, Fax: 615-460-6414, E-mail: hutchinst@mail.belmont.edu.

College of Health Sciences Students: 215 full-time (180 women), 10 part-time (9 women); includes 10 minority (9 African Americans, 1 Asian American or Pacific Islander), 2 international. Average age 27. 342 applicants, 42% accepted, 92 enrolled. *Faculty:* 18 full-time (13 women), 29 part-time/adjunct (22 women). Expenses: Contact institution. *Financial support:* In 2006–07, 123 students received support, including teaching assistantships with full tuition reimbursements available (averaging $7,020 per year); career-related internships or fieldwork, scholarships/grants, and traineeships also available. Financial award application deadline: 3/1; financial award applicants required to submit FAFSA. In 2006, 27 master's, 37 doctorates awarded. *Degree program information:* Part-time programs available. Postbaccalaureate distance learning degree programs offered (minimal on-campus study). Offers health sciences (MSN, MSOT, DPT, OTD). *Application deadline:* Applications are processed on a rolling basis. *Application fee:* $50. Electronic applications accepted. *Application Contact:* Dr. Kathryn Baugher, Dean of Enrollment Services, 615-460-6785, Fax: 615-460-5434, E-mail: baugherk@mail.belmont.edu. *Dean,* Dr. Debra B. Wollaber, 615-460-6106, Fax: 615-460-6125, E-mail: wollaberd@mail.belmont.edu.

School of Nursing Students: 4 full-time (all women), 8 part-time (all women). Average age 30. 16 applicants, 94% accepted, 5 enrolled. *Faculty:* 1 (woman) full-time, 3 part-time/adjunct (all women). Expenses: Contact institution. *Financial support:* In 2006–07, 6 students received support. Scholarships/grants and traineeships available. Financial award application deadline: 3/1; financial award applicants required to submit FAFSA. In 2006, 3 degrees awarded. *Degree program information:* Part-time programs available. Offers nursing (MSN). *Application deadline:* For fall admission, 8/1 for domestic students; for spring admission, 10/15 priority date for domestic students. Applications are processed on a rolling basis. *Application fee:* $50. Electronic applications accepted. *Application Contact:* Cathy Hendon, Admissions Coordinator, 615-460-6107, Fax: 615-460-6125, E-mail: hendonc@mail.belmont.edu. *Director, Graduate Program,* Dr. Leslie J. Higgins, 615-460-6027, Fax: 615-460-5644, E-mail: higginsl@mail.belmont.edu.

School of Occupational Therapy Students: 112 full-time (98 women), 1 part-time; includes 9 minority (8 African Americans, 1 Asian American or Pacific Islander). Average age 29. 158 applicants, 46% accepted, 52 enrolled. *Faculty:* 8 full-time (7 women), 11 part-time/adjunct (9 women). Expenses: Contact institution. *Financial support:* Application deadline: 3/1; In 2006, 24 master's, 9 doctorates awarded. *Degree program information:* Evening/weekend programs available. Offers occupational therapy (MSOT, OTD). *Application deadline:* For fall admission, 3/31 priority date for domestic students. Applications are processed on a rolling basis. *Application fee:* $50. Electronic applications accepted. *Application Contact:* Vicki Bourne, Program Assistant, 615-460-6705, Fax: 615-460-6475, E-mail: bournev@mail.belmont.edu. *Associate Dean,* Dr. Ruth Ford, 615-460-6700, Fax: 615-460-6475, E-mail: fordr@mail.belmont.edu.

School of Physical Therapy Students: 99 full-time (78 women); includes 3 minority (2 African Americans, 1 Asian American or Pacific Islander), 1 international. Average age 25. 168 applicants, 35% accepted, 35 enrolled. *Faculty:* 9 full-time (5 women), 15 part-time/adjunct (10 women). Expenses: Contact institution. *Financial support:* In 2006–07, 74 students received support. Scholarships/grants available. Financial award applicants required to submit FAFSA. In 2006, 28 degrees awarded. Offers physical therapy (DPT). *Application deadline:* For fall admission, 8/31 priority date for domestic and international students. Applications are processed on a rolling basis. *Application fee:* $50. Electronic applications accepted. *Application Contact:* Lucy Baltimore, Program Assistant, 615-460-6726, Fax: 615-460-6729, E-mail: baltimorel@mail.belmont.edu. *Associate Dean,* Dr. John S. Halle, 615-460-6727, Fax: 615-460-6729, E-mail: hallej@mail.belmont.edu.

College of Visual and Performing Arts Students: 12 full-time (7 women), 34 part-time (17 women); includes 3 minority (1 Asian American or Pacific Islander, 2 Hispanic Americans), 2 international. Average age 27. 19 applicants, 89% accepted, 13 enrolled. *Faculty:* 24 full-time (7 women), 7 part-time/adjunct (3 women). Expenses: Contact institution. *Financial support:* In 2006–07, 33 fellowships (averaging $1,000 per year), 5 teaching assistantships (averaging $2,000 per year) were awarded; career-related internships or fieldwork, scholarships/grants, and unspecified assistantships also available. Financial award application deadline: 3/1; financial award applicants required to submit FAFSA. In 2006, 11 degrees awarded. *Degree program information:* Part-time programs available. Offers visual and performing arts (MM). *Application deadline:* For fall admission, 5/1 priority date for domestic students, 5/11 for international students; for spring admission, 11/1 priority date for domestic students, 11/1 for international students. Applications are processed on a rolling basis. *Application fee:* $50. Electronic applications accepted. *Application Contact:* Tish Mosley, Graduate Secretary, 615-460-8117, Fax: 615-386-0239, E-mail: mosleyt@mail.belmont.edu. *Dean,* Dr. Cynthia R. Curtis.

School of Music Students: 12 full-time (7 women), 34 part-time (17 women); includes 3 minority (1 Asian American or Pacific Islander, 2 Hispanic Americans), 2 international. Average age 27. 19 applicants, 89% accepted, 13 enrolled. *Faculty:* 24 full-time (7 women), 16 part-time/adjunct (8 women). Expenses: Contact institution. *Financial support:* In 2006–07, 33 fellowships (averaging $1,000 per year), 5 teaching assistantships (averaging $2,000 per year) were awarded; career-related internships or fieldwork, scholarships/grants, and unspecified assistantships also available. Financial award application deadline: 3/1; financial award applicants required to submit FAFSA. In 2006, 11 degrees awarded. *Degree program information:* Part-time programs available. Offers church music (MM); composition (MM); music education (MM); pedagogy (MM); performance (MM). *Application deadline:* For fall admission, 5/1 priority date for domestic students, 5/1 for international students; for spring admission, 11/1 priority date for domestic students, 11/1 for international students. Applications are processed on a rolling basis. *Application fee:* $50. Electronic applications accepted. *Application Contact:* Tish Mosley, Graduate Secretary, 615-460-8117, Fax: 615-386-0239, E-mail: mosleyt@mail.belmont.edu. *Director,* Dr. Robert Gregg, 615-460-8106, Fax: 615-386-0239, E-mail: greggr@mail.belmont.edu.

Jack C. Massey Graduate School of Business Students: 21 full-time (10 women), 189 part-time (82 women); includes 32 minority (20 African Americans, 11 Asian Americans or Pacific Islanders, 1 Hispanic American), 4 international. Average age 29. 55 applicants, 80% accepted, 34 enrolled. *Faculty:* 22 full-time (8 women), 4 part-time/adjunct (0 women).

Belmont University (continued)

Expenses: Contact institution. *Financial support:* In 2006–07, 22 students received support. Scholarships/grants, tuition waivers (full), and unspecified assistantships available. Financial award application deadline: 7/1; financial award applicants required to submit FAFSA. In 2006, 81 degrees awarded. *Degree program information:* Part-time and evening/weekend programs available. Offers business (M Acc, MBA). *Application deadline:* For fall admission, 7/1 for domestic and international students; for spring admission, 11/1 for domestic and international students. Applications are processed on a rolling basis. *Application fee:* $50. Electronic applications accepted. *Application Contact:* Tonya Hollin, Admissions Assistant, 615-460-6480, Fax: 615-460-6353, E-mail: masseyadmissions@mail.belmont.edu. *Dean,* Dr. Patrick Raines, 615-460-6480, Fax: 615-460-6455, E-mail: rainesp@mail.belmont.edu.

BEMIDJI STATE UNIVERSITY, Bemidji, MN 56601-2699

General Information State-supported, coed, comprehensive institution. *Enrollment:* 4,918 graduate, professional, and undergraduate students; 43 full-time matriculated graduate/professional students (27 women), 196 part-time matriculated graduate/professional students (125 women). *Enrollment by degree level:* 239 master's. *Graduate faculty:* 156 part-time/adjunct (59 women). Tuition, nonresident: part-time $284 per credit. *Required fees:* $86 per credit. *Graduate housing:* Room and/or apartments available on a first-come, first-served basis to single students; on-campus housing not available to married students. Typical cost: $4,400 per year ($6,400 including board). Housing application deadline: 4/25. *Student services:* Campus employment opportunities, campus safety program, career counseling, child daycare facilities, disabled student services, exercise/wellness program, free psychological counseling, grant writing training, international student services, low-cost health insurance, multicultural affairs office, teacher training, writing training. *Library facilities:* A. C. Clark Library. *Online resources:* library catalog, web page, access to other libraries' catalogs. *Collection:* 554,087 titles, 991 serial subscriptions.

Computer facilities: 1,200 computers available on campus for general student use. A campuswide network can be accessed from student residence rooms and from off campus. Internet access and online class registration are available. *Web address:* http://www.bemidjistate.edu/.

General Application Contact: Carol Nielsen, Interim Dean, School of Graduate/Professional Studies, 218-755-3732, Fax: 218-755-3788, E-mail: cnielsen@bemidjistate.edu.

GRADUATE UNITS

School of Graduate Studies Students: 43 full-time (27 women), 196 part-time (125 women); includes 15 minority (3 African Americans, 5 American Indian/Alaska Native, 7 Asian Americans or Pacific Islanders). Average age 34. 105 applicants, 95% accepted, 71 enrolled. *Faculty:* 94 full-time (36 women), 1 part-time/adjunct (0 women). Expenses: Contact institution. *Financial support:* In 2006–07, 32 research assistantships with partial tuition reimbursements (averaging $8,250 per year), 37 teaching assistantships with partial tuition reimbursements (averaging $8,250 per year) were awarded; career-related internships or fieldwork, Federal Work-Study, scholarships/grants, health care benefits, and unspecified assistantships also available. Support available to part-time students. Financial award application deadline: 5/1. In 2006, 55 degrees awarded. *Degree program information:* Part-time programs available. Postbaccalaureate distance learning degree programs offered (no on-campus study). *Application deadline:* For fall admission, 5/1 for domestic students. Applications are processed on a rolling basis. *Application fee:* $20. Electronic applications accepted. *Application Contact:* Joan Miller, Administrative Assistant, 218-755-2027, Fax: 218-755-3788, E-mail: jmiller@bemidjistate.edu. *Interim Dean, School of Graduate/Professional Studies,* Carol Nielsen, 218-755-3732, Fax: 218-755-3788, E-mail: cnielsen@bemidjistate.edu.

College of Arts and Letters Students: 7 full-time (5 women), 18 part-time (14 women). Average age 32. 8 applicants, 100% accepted. *Faculty:* 13 full-time (9 women). Expenses: Contact institution. *Financial support:* In 2006–07, 3 research assistantships with partial tuition reimbursements (averaging $8,250 per year), 9 teaching assistantships with partial tuition reimbursements (averaging $8,250 per year) were awarded; career-related internships or fieldwork, Federal Work-Study, scholarships/grants, health care benefits, and unspecified assistantships also available. Support available to part-time students. Financial award application deadline: 5/1. In 2006, 8 degrees awarded. *Degree program information:* Part-time programs available. Offers arts and letters (MA, MS); English (MA, MS). *Application deadline:* For fall admission, 5/1 priority date for domestic students. Applications are processed on a rolling basis. *Application fee:* $20. Electronic applications accepted. *Dean,* Dr. Nancy Erickson, 218-755-2988, E-mail: nerickson@bemidjistate.edu.

College of Professional Studies Students: 22 full-time (16 women), 122 part-time (75 women); includes 9 minority (3 African Americans, 5 American Indian/Alaska Native, 1 Asian American or Pacific Islander). Average age 35. 54 applicants, 98% accepted. *Faculty:* 42 full-time (17 women). Expenses: Contact institution. *Financial support:* In 2006–07, 18 research assistantships with partial tuition reimbursements (averaging $8,250 per year), 15 teaching assistantships with partial tuition reimbursements (averaging $8,250 per year) were awarded; career-related internships or fieldwork, Federal Work-Study, scholarships/grants, health care benefits, and unspecified assistantships also available. Support available to part-time students. Financial award application deadline: 5/1. In 2006, 34 degrees awarded. *Degree program information:* Part-time programs available. Postbaccalaureate distance learning degree programs offered (minimal on-campus study). Offers education (M Ed, MS); professional studies (M Ed, M Sp Ed, MS); special education (M Sp Ed, MS); sport studies (MS); technical education (MS); technology/career technical education (MS). *Application deadline:* For fall admission, 5/1 for domestic students. Applications are processed on a rolling basis. *Application fee:* $20. Electronic applications accepted. *Application Contact:* Joan Miller, Administrative Assistant, 218-755-2027, Fax: 218-755-3788, E-mail: jmiller@bemidjistate.edu.

College of Social and Natural Sciences Students: 20 full-time (12 women), 50 part-time (30 women); includes 6 minority (all Asian Americans or Pacific Islanders) Average age 31. 43 applicants, 91% accepted. *Faculty:* 39 full-time (10 women), 1 part-time/adjunct (0 women). Expenses: Contact institution. *Financial support:* In 2006–07, 2 research assistantships with partial tuition reimbursements (averaging $8,250 per year), 11 teaching assistantships with partial tuition reimbursements (averaging $8,250 per year) were awarded; career-related internships or fieldwork, Federal Work-Study, scholarships/grants, health care benefits, and unspecified assistantships also available. Support available to part-time students. Financial award application deadline: 5/1. In 2006, 13 degrees awarded. *Degree program information:* Part-time programs available. Offers biology (MS); environmental studies (MS); mathematics (MS); psychology (MS); science (MS); social and natural sciences (MS). *Application deadline:* For fall admission, 5/1 for domestic students. Applications are processed on a rolling basis. *Application fee:* $20. Electronic applications accepted. *Dean,* Dr. Ranae Womack, 218-755-2965, Fax: 218-755-2822, E-mail: rwomack@bemidjistate.edu.

BENEDICTINE COLLEGE, Atchison, KS 66002-1499

General Information Independent-religious, coed, comprehensive institution. *Graduate housing:* On-campus housing not available.

GRADUATE UNITS

Executive Master of Business Administration Program *Degree program information:* Part-time and evening/weekend programs available. Offers business administration (EMBA). Electronic applications accepted.

Program in Business Administration *Degree program information:* Evening/weekend programs available. Offers business administration (MBA).

Program in Educational Administration *Degree program information:* Part-time and evening/weekend programs available. Offers educational administration (MA).

BENEDICTINE UNIVERSITY, Lisle, IL 60532-0900

General Information Independent-religious, coed, comprehensive institution. *Enrollment:* 3,900 graduate, professional, and undergraduate students; 275 full-time matriculated graduate/professional students (165 women), 968 part-time matriculated graduate/professional students (596 women). *Enrollment by degree level:* 1,189 master's, 54 doctoral. *Graduate faculty:* 20 full-time (7 women), 92 part-time/adjunct (50 women). *Tuition:* Full-time $12,150; part-time $450 per credit hour. *Graduate housing:* Rooms and/or apartments available to single students and available on a first-come, first-served basis to married students. Typical cost: $4,450 (including board) for single students; $4,450 (including board) for married students. *Student services:* Campus employment opportunities, campus safety program, career counseling, disabled student services, free psychological counseling, international student services. *Library facilities:* Benedictine Library. *Online resources:* library catalog, web page, access to other libraries' catalogs. *Collection:* 201,190 titles, 14,177 serial subscriptions, 2,500 audiovisual materials.

Computer facilities: A campuswide network can be accessed from student residence rooms and from off campus. Internet access is available. *Web address:* http://www.ben.edu/.

General Application Contact: Kari Gibbons, Director, Admissions, 630-829-6200, Fax: 630-829-6584, E-mail: kgibbons@ben.edu.

GRADUATE UNITS

Graduate Programs Students: 275 full-time (165 women), 968 part-time (596 women); includes 206 minority (90 African Americans, 2 American Indian/Alaska Native, 62 Asian Americans or Pacific Islanders, 52 Hispanic Americans), 25 international. Average age 33. 674 applicants, 88% accepted, 470 enrolled. *Faculty:* 20 full-time (7 women), 92 part-time/adjunct (50 women). Expenses: Contact institution. *Financial support:* Career-related internships or fieldwork and health care benefits available. Support available to part-time students. In 2006, 365 master's, 22 doctorates awarded. *Degree program information:* Part-time and evening/weekend programs available. Postbaccalaureate distance learning degree programs offered (no on-campus study). Offers accounting (MBA); administration of health care institutions (MPH); clinical exercise physiology (MS); clinical psychology (MS); curriculum and instruction and collaborative teaching (M Ed); dietetics (MPH); disaster management (MPH); elementary education (MA Ed); entrepreneurship and managing innovation (MBA); financial management (MBA); health administration (MBA); health education (MPH); health information systems (MPH); higher education and organizational change (Ed D); human resource management (MBA); information systems security (MBA); international business (MBA); leadership and administration (M Ed); management and organizational behavior (MS); management consulting (MBA); management information systems (MBA); marketing management (MBA); nutrition and wellness (MS); operations management and logistics (MBA); organizational development (PhD); organizational leadership (MBA); reading and literacy (M Ed); science content and process (MS); secondary education (MA Ed); special education (MA Ed). *Application deadline:* For fall admission, 9/1 for domestic students; for winter admission, 12/1 for domestic students; for spring admission, 2/15 for domestic students. Applications are processed on a rolling basis. *Application fee:* $40. Electronic applications accepted. *Application Contact:* Kari Gibbons, Director, Admissions, 630-829-6200, Fax: 630-829-6584, E-mail: kgibbons@ben.edu. *Provost and Vice President for Academic Affairs,* Dr. Daniel Julius, 630-829-6240, Fax: 630-829-6369, E-mail: djulius@ben.edu.

BENNINGTON COLLEGE, Bennington, VT 05201

General Information Independent, coed, comprehensive institution. *Enrollment:* 657 graduate, professional, and undergraduate students; 120 full-time matriculated graduate/professional students (78 women), 14 part-time matriculated graduate/professional students (10 women). *Enrollment by degree level:* 123 master's, 11 other advanced degrees. *Graduate faculty:* 39 full-time (18 women), 16 part-time/adjunct (8 women). *Tuition:* Full-time $20,000; part-time $2,800 per course. One-time fee: $75 full-time. Tuition and fees vary according to program. *Graduate housing:* Room and/or apartments available on a first-come, first-served basis to single students; on-campus housing not available to married students. Typical cost: $2,700 per year ($6,750 including board). *Student services:* Campus employment opportunities, campus safety program, career counseling, child daycare facilities, exercise/wellness program, free psychological counseling, international student services, low-cost health insurance, teacher training, writing training. *Library facilities:* Crossett Library plus 1 other. *Online resources:* library catalog, web page, access to other libraries' catalogs. *Collection:* 121,500 titles, 13,500 serial subscriptions.

Computer facilities: 61 computers available on campus for general student use. A campuswide network can be accessed from student residence rooms and from off campus. Internet access is available. *Web address:* http://www.bennington.edu/.

General Application Contact: Ken Himmelman, Dean of Admissions, 802-440-4312, Fax: 802-440-4320, E-mail: admissions@bennington.edu.

GRADUATE UNITS

Graduate Programs Students: 120 full-time (78 women), 14 part-time (10 women); includes 17 minority (4 African Americans, 7 Asian Americans or Pacific Islanders, 6 Hispanic Americans), 2 international. Average age 37. 156 applicants, 51% accepted, 48 enrolled. *Faculty:* 39 full-time (18 women), 16 part-time/adjunct (8 women). Expenses: Contact institution. *Financial support:* In 2006–07, 23 students received support, including 4 fellowships (averaging $6,875 per year), 5 teaching assistantships; scholarships/grants and unspecified assistantships also available. Financial award application deadline: 4/1; financial award applicants required to submit FAFSA. In 2006, 71 master's, 10 other advanced degrees awarded. *Degree program information:* Part-time programs available. Postbaccalaureate distance learning degree programs offered (minimal on-campus study). Offers allied and health sciences (Certificate); art education (MAT); creative writing (MFA); dance (MFA); drama (MFA); early childhood (MAT); education (MATSL); elementary education (MAT); English education (MAT); foreign language education (MAT, MATSL); French (MATSL); mathematics education (MAT); music (MFA); music education (MAT); science education (MAT); secondary education (MAT); social science education (MAT); Spanish (MATSL). *Application deadline:* Applications are processed on a rolling basis. *Application fee:* $60. *Application Contact:* Ken Himmelman, Dean of Admissions, 802-440-4312, Fax: 802-440-4320, E-mail: admissions@bennington.edu. *Associate Dean,* Dr. Wendy Hirsch, 802-440-4400, Fax: 802-440-4876, E-mail: whirsch@bennington.edu.

BENTLEY COLLEGE, Waltham, MA 02452-4705

General Information Independent, coed, comprehensive institution. *Enrollment:* 5,497 graduate, professional, and undergraduate students; 236 full-time matriculated graduate/professional students (114 women), 1,020 part-time matriculated graduate/professional students (474 women). *Enrollment by degree level:* 1,221 master's, 11 doctoral, 24 other advanced degrees. *Graduate faculty:* 271 full-time (105 women), 202 part-time/adjunct (72 women). *Tuition:* Full-time $28,440; part-time $2,844 per course. *Required fees:* $404; $105 per year. *Graduate housing:* Room and/or apartments available on a first-come, first-served basis to single students; on-campus housing not available to married students. Typical cost: $8,740 per year ($12,390 including board). Housing application deadline: 5/1. *Student services:* Campus employment opportunities, campus safety program, career counseling, disabled student services, free psychological counseling, international student services, low-cost health insurance, multicultural affairs office. *Library facilities:* Baker Library. *Online resources:* library catalog, web page, access to other libraries' catalogs. *Collection:* 146,104 titles, 30,800 serial subscriptions, 7,002 audiovisual materials.

Computer facilities: Computer purchase and lease plans are available. 4,441 computers available on campus for general student use. A campuswide network can be accessed from student residence rooms and from off campus. Internet access and online class registration, grade checking, online admission, Blackboard, resume review, student employment, interlibrary loan are available. *Web address:* http://www.bentley.edu.

General Application Contact: Sharon Hill, Director of Graduate Admissions, 781-891-2108, Fax: 781-891-2464, E-mail: shill@bentley.edu.

GRADUATE UNITS

The Elkin B. McCallum Graduate School of Business Students: 236 full-time (114 women), 1,020 part-time (474 women); includes 143 minority (24 African Americans, 1 American Indian/Alaska Native, 92 Asian Americans or Pacific Islanders, 26 Hispanic Americans), 120 international. Average age 30. 1,013 applicants, 70% accepted, 456 enrolled. *Faculty:* 271 full-time (105 women), 202 part-time/adjunct (72 women). Expenses: Contact institution. *Financial support:* In 2006–07, 24 research assistantships (averaging $18,131 per year) were awarded; scholarships/grants, tuition waivers, and unspecified assistantships also available.

Financial award application deadline: 4/12; financial award applicants required to submit CSS PROFILE or FAFSA. In 2006, 227 degrees awarded. *Degree program information:* Part-time and evening/weekend programs available. Offers accountancy (PhD); accounting (GBC); accounting information systems (GBC); business (GSS); business administration (MBA); business ethics (GBC); data analysis (GBC); finance (MSF); financial planning (GBC); human factors in information design (MSHFID); information technology (MSIT); marketing analytics (GBC); real estate management (MSREM); taxation (GBC). *Application deadline:* For fall admission, 6/1 priority date for domestic students, 3/1 priority date for international students; for spring admission, 11/1 priority date for domestic and international students. Applications are processed on a rolling basis. *Application fee:* $50. Electronic applications accepted. *Application Contact:* Sharon Hill, Director of Graduate Admissions, 781-891-2108, Fax: 781-891-2464, E-mail: shill@bentley.edu. *Dean,* Dr. Margrethe H. Olson, 781-891-2921, Fax: 781-891-2464, E-mail: molson@bentley.edu.

BERNARD M. BARUCH COLLEGE OF THE CITY UNIVERSITY OF NEW YORK, New York, NY 10010-5585

General Information State and locally supported, coed, comprehensive institution. *Enrollment:* 15,730 graduate, professional, and undergraduate students; 829 full-time matriculated graduate/professional students (417 women), 2,083 part-time matriculated graduate/professional students (1,039 women). *Enrollment by degree level:* 1,861 master's, 63 doctoral. *Graduate faculty:* 271 full-time (66 women), 259 part-time/adjunct (59 women). *Graduate housing:* On-campus housing not available. *Student services:* Campus employment opportunities, campus safety program, career counseling, child daycare facilities, disabled student services, exercise/wellness program, free psychological counseling, international student services, low-cost health insurance, multicultural affairs office, teacher training, writing training. *Library facilities:* The William and Anita Newman Library plus 1 other. *Online resources:* library catalog, web page, access to other libraries' catalogs. *Collection:* 456,132 titles, 35,000 serial subscriptions.

Computer facilities: 1,294 computers available on campus for general student use. A campuswide network can be accessed. Internet access and online class registration are available. *Web address:* http://www.baruch.cuny.edu/.

General Application Contact: Frances Murphy, Office of Graduate Admissions, 646-312-1300, Fax: 646-312-1301, E-mail: zicklingradadmissions@baruch.cuny.edu.

GRADUATE UNITS

School of Public Affairs Students: 152 full-time (104 women), 539 part-time (374 women); includes 334 minority (172 African Americans, 57 Asian Americans or Pacific Islanders, 105 Hispanic Americans). Average age 34. 558 applicants, 61% accepted, 265 enrolled. *Faculty:* 43 full-time (15 women), 27 part-time/adjunct (12 women). Expenses: Contact institution. *Financial support:* In 2006–07, 58 students received support, including 14 fellowships (averaging $2,200 per year), 22 research assistantships (averaging $9,000 per year); teaching assistantships, career-related internships or fieldwork, Federal Work-Study, scholarships/grants, tuition waivers (partial), and unspecified assistantships also available. Support available to part-time students. Financial award application deadline: 5/30; financial award applicants required to submit FAFSA. In 2006, 311 master's awarded. *Degree program information:* Part-time and evening/weekend programs available. Offers educational administration and supervision (MS Ed); higher education administration (MS Ed); public administration (MPA); public affairs (MPA, MS Ed). *Application deadline:* For fall admission, 4/1 priority date for domestic and international students; for spring admission, 11/1 priority date for domestic and international students. Applications are processed on a rolling basis. *Application fee:* $125. Electronic applications accepted. *Application Contact:* Michael J. Lovaglio, Director of Graduate Admissions and Student Services, 646-660-6750, Fax: 646-660-6751, E-mail: michael_lovaglio@baruch.cuny.edu. *Dean,* David Birdsell, 646-660-6700, Fax: 646-660-6721, E-mail: david_birdsell@baruch.cuny.edu.

Weissman School of Arts and Sciences Students: 64. Expenses: Contact institution. Offers arts and sciences (MA, MS); corporate communication (MA); financial engineering (MS); industrial organizational psychology (MS). *Application Contact:* 646-312-4490, Fax: 646-312-4491, E-mail: wsas_graduate_studies@baruch.cuny.edu. *Director,* Gary Hentzi, 646-312-1000.

Zicklin School of Business Students: 754 full-time (353 women), 1,499 part-time (656 women); includes 476 minority (96 African Americans, 293 Asian Americans or Pacific Islanders, 87 Hispanic Americans), 664 international. Average age 29. 1,497 applicants, 46% accepted, 482 enrolled. *Faculty:* 198 full-time (46 women), 196 part-time/adjunct (35 women). Expenses: Contact institution. *Financial support:* In 2006–07, 163 students received support, including 59 fellowships (averaging $4,000 per year), 20 research assistantships (averaging $16,000 per year), 84 teaching assistantships (averaging $5,000 per year); career-related internships or fieldwork, Federal Work-Study, institutionally sponsored loans, scholarships/grants, and unspecified assistantships also available. Financial award application deadline: 4/30; financial award applicants required to submit FAFSA. In 2006, 1,351 master's, 6 doctorates awarded. *Degree program information:* Part-time and evening/weekend programs available. Offers accounting (MBA, MS, PhD); business (MBA, MS, PhD, Certificate); business administration (MBA); computer information systems (MBA, MS, PhD); decision sciences (MBA, MS); economics (MBA); entrepreneurship (MBA); finance (MBA, MS, PhD); general business (MBA); general management and policy (MBA); health care administration (MBA); human resources management (MBA); industrial and labor relations (MS); industrial and organizational psychology (MBA, MS, PhD, Certificate); international executive education (MBA); management planning systems (PhD); management science (MBA); marketing (MBA, MS, PhD); organization and policy studies (PhD); organizational behavior (MBA); statistics (MBA, MS); taxation (MBA, MS). *Application deadline:* For fall admission, 5/31 for domestic students, 4/30 for international students; for spring admission, 10/31 for domestic and international students. Applications are processed on a rolling basis. *Application fee:* $125. Electronic applications accepted. *Application Contact:* Frances Murphy, Office of Graduate Admissions, 646-312-1300, Fax: 646-312-1301, E-mail: zicklingradadmissions@baruch.cuny.edu. *Vice President and Dean,* John Elliott, 646-312-3030, Fax: 646-312-3031, E-mail: john_elliott@baruch.cuny.edu.

See Close-Up on page 811.

BERRY COLLEGE, Mount Berry, GA 30149-0159

General Information Independent-religious, coed, comprehensive institution. *Enrollment:* 1,842 graduate, professional, and undergraduate students; 11 full-time matriculated graduate/professional students (7 women), 113 part-time matriculated graduate/professional students (82 women). *Enrollment by degree level:* 105 master's, 19 other advanced degrees. *Graduate faculty:* 16 part-time/adjunct (8 women). *Tuition:* Full-time $6,174; part-time $343 per credit hour. *Graduate housing:* On-campus housing not available. *Student services:* Campus employment opportunities, campus safety program, career counseling, child daycare facilities, exercise/wellness program, free psychological counseling, grant writing training, international student services, low-cost health insurance. *Library facilities:* Memorial Library plus 1 other. *Online resources:* library catalog, web page, access to other libraries' catalogs. *Collection:* 203,522 titles, 2,082 serial subscriptions, 3,596 audiovisual materials. *Research affiliation:* Gulf Coast Research Laboratory (marine science), University of Georgia (animal science), Auburn University (marketing), Georgia State University (psychology), National Geographic Society (conservation), Georgia Forestry Commission (biology).

Computer facilities: 134 computers available on campus for general student use. A campuswide network can be accessed from student residence rooms and from off campus. Internet access is available. *Web address:* http://www.berry.edu/.

General Application Contact: Richard D. Paul, Dean of Admissions and Financial Aid, 706-236-2215, Fax: 706-290-2178, E-mail: dpaul@berry.edu.

GRADUATE UNITS

Graduate Programs Students: 11 full-time (7 women), 113 part-time (82 women); includes 4 minority (1 African American, 1 Asian American or Pacific Islander, 2 Hispanic Americans), 4 international. Average age 33. *Faculty:* 16 part-time/adjunct (8 women). Expenses: Contact institution. *Financial support:* In 2006–07, 72 students received support, including 8 research assistantships with full tuition reimbursements available (averaging $3,500 per year); scholarships/grants and unspecified assistantships also available. Support available to part-time students. Financial award application deadline: 4/1; financial award applicants required to submit FAFSA. In 2006, 55 degrees awarded. *Degree program information:* Part-time and evening/weekend programs available. Offers curriculum and instruction (Ed S); early childhood education (M Ed); middle-grades education and reading (M Ed); secondary education (M Ed). *Application deadline:* For fall admission, 7/27 for domestic students; for spring admission, 12/16 for domestic students. Applications are processed on a rolling basis. *Application fee:* $25 ($30 for international students). *Application Contact:* Richard D. Paul, Dean of Admissions and Financial Aid, 706-236-2215, Fax: 706-290-2178, E-mail: dpaul@berry.edu. *Provost,* Dr. Thomas E. Dasher, 706-236-2216, Fax: 706-290-2179, E-mail: tdasher@berry.edu.

Campbell School of Business Students: 5 full-time (2 women), 21 part-time (7 women); includes 1 minority (Asian American or Pacific Islander), 3 international. Average age 29. *Faculty:* 5 part-time/adjunct (3 women). Expenses: Contact institution. *Financial support:* In 2006–07, 13 students received support, including 5 research assistantships with full tuition reimbursements available (averaging $3,500 per year); scholarships/grants and unspecified assistantships also available. Support available to part-time students. Financial award application deadline: 4/1; financial award applicants required to submit FAFSA. In 2006, 11 degrees awarded. *Degree program information:* Part-time and evening/weekend programs available. Offers business (MBA). *Application deadline:* For fall admission, 7/27 for domestic students; for spring admission, 12/16 for domestic students. Applications are processed on a rolling basis. *Application fee:* $25 ($30 for international students). *Application Contact:* Richard D. Paul, Dean of Admissions and Financial Aid, 706-236-2215, Fax: 706-290-2178, E-mail: dpaul@berry.edu. *Dean,* Dr. Krishna Dhir, 706-236-2233, Fax: 706-802-6728, E-mail: kdhir@campbell.berry.edu.

BETHANY THEOLOGICAL SEMINARY, Richmond, IN 47374-4019

General Information Independent-religious, coed, graduate-only institution. *Graduate housing:* On-campus housing not available.

GRADUATE UNITS

Graduate and Professional Programs *Degree program information:* Part-time programs available. Postbaccalaureate distance learning degree programs offered (minimal on-campus study). Offers biblical studies (MA Th); ministry studies (M Div); peace studies (M Div, MA Th); theological studies (MA Th, CATS); youth ministry (M Div).

BETHANY UNIVERSITY, Scotts Valley, CA 95066-2820

General Information Independent-religious, coed, comprehensive institution. *Graduate housing:* Rooms and/or apartments available to single students and available on a first-come, first-served basis to married students. Housing application deadline: 7/31.

GRADUATE UNITS

Program in Clinical Psychology *Degree program information:* Part-time and evening/weekend programs available. Offers clinical psychology (MS).

Program in Teacher Education *Degree program information:* Part-time and evening/weekend programs available. Offers education (MA); educational leadership (MA).

BETH BENJAMIN ACADEMY OF CONNECTICUT, Stamford, CT 06901-1202

General Information Independent-religious, men only, comprehensive institution. *Graduate housing:* Rooms and/or apartments available to single and married students.

GRADUATE UNITS

Graduate and Professional Programs

BETHEL COLLEGE, Mishawaka, IN 46545-5591

General Information Independent-religious, coed, comprehensive institution. *Enrollment:* 43 full-time matriculated graduate/professional students (17 women), 150 part-time matriculated graduate/professional students (80 women). *Enrollment by degree level:* 193 master's. *Graduate faculty:* 36 part-time/adjunct (18 women). *Tuition:* Full-time $5,940; part-time $330 per credit hour. *Graduate housing:* On-campus housing not available. *Student services:* Campus employment opportunities, career counseling. *Library facilities:* Otis and Elizabeth Bowen Library. *Online resources:* library catalog, web page, access to other libraries' catalogs. *Collection:* 106,584 titles, 450 serial subscriptions, 3,926 audiovisual materials.

Computer facilities: 110 computers available on campus for general student use. A campuswide network can be accessed from student residence rooms and from off campus. Internet access is available. *Web address:* http://www.bethelcollege.edu.

General Application Contact: Dr. Bradley D. Smith, Dean, 574-257-3363, Fax: 574-257-7616, E-mail: smithb@bethelcollege.edu.

GRADUATE UNITS

Division of Graduate Studies Students: 43 full-time (17 women), 150 part-time (80 women); includes 18 minority (15 African Americans, 1 Asian American or Pacific Islander, 2 Hispanic Americans), 5 international. Average age 37. 168 applicants, 72% accepted, 93 enrolled. *Faculty:* 36 part-time/adjunct (18 women). Expenses: Contact institution. *Financial support:* Career-related internships or fieldwork and unspecified assistantships available. Financial award applicants required to submit FAFSA. In 2006, 37 degrees awarded. *Degree program information:* Part-time programs available. Offers business administration (MBA); Christian ministries (M Min); education (M Ed, MAT); marriage and family counseling/therapy (MA); mental health counseling (MA); nursing (MSN); theological studies (MATS). *Application deadline:* Applications are processed on a rolling basis. *Application fee:* $25. Electronic applications accepted. *Dean,* Dr. Bradley D. Smith, 574-257-3363, Fax: 574-257-3357, E-mail: smithb@bethelcollege.edu.

BETHEL COLLEGE, McKenzie, TN 38201

General Information Independent-religious, coed, comprehensive institution. *Graduate housing:* Room and/or apartments available on a first-come, first-served basis to single students; on-campus housing not available to married students. Housing application deadline: 7/31.

GRADUATE UNITS

Program in Education *Degree program information:* Part-time and evening/weekend programs available. Offers administration and supervision (MA Ed); biology education K8-12 (MAT); elementary education (MAT); English education K8-12 (MAT); history education K8-12 (MAT); physical education K8-12 (MAT); special education K8-12 (MAT).

BETHEL SEMINARY, St. Paul, MN 55112-6998

General Information Independent-religious, coed, graduate-only institution. *Enrollment by degree level:* 460 first professional, 514 master's, 88 doctoral, 14 other advanced degrees. *Graduate faculty:* 26 full-time (3 women), 72 part-time/adjunct. *Tuition:* Full-time $10,080; part-time $280 per credit. *Graduate housing:* Rooms and/or apartments available on a first-come, first-served basis to single and married students. Typical cost: $3,375 per year for single students; $5,490 per year for married students. Housing application deadline: 6/1. *Student services:* Campus employment opportunities, campus safety program, career counseling, child daycare facilities, free psychological counseling, multicultural affairs office. *Library facilities:* Carl H. Lundquist Library plus 1 other. *Online resources:* library catalog, web page, access to other libraries' catalogs. *Collection:* 230,800 titles, 593 serial subscriptions, 8,165 audiovisual materials.

Computer facilities: 19 computers available on campus for general student use. A campuswide network can be accessed from student residence rooms and from off campus. Internet access and online class registration are available. *Web address:* http://www.bethel.edu/seminary/btshome.htm.

General Application Contact: Joseph V. Dworak, Director of Admissions, 651-638-6288, Fax: 651-638-6002, E-mail: j-dworak@bethel.edu.

Bethel Seminary (continued)

GRADUATE UNITS

Graduate and Professional Programs Students: 494 full-time (148 women), 582 part-time (242 women); includes 164 minority (77 African Americans, 1 American Indian/Alaska Native, 60 Asian Americans or Pacific Islanders, 26 Hispanic Americans), 6 international. Average age 36. 314 applicants, 86% accepted. *Faculty:* 26 full-time (3 women), 72 part-time/adjunct. Expenses: Contact institution. *Financial support:* In 2006–07, 375 students received support, including 20 teaching assistantships; career-related internships or fieldwork, Federal Work-Study, institutionally sponsored loans, and scholarships/grants also available. Financial award application deadline: 7/15; financial award applicants required to submit FAFSA. In 2006, 62 M Divs, 102 master's, 14 doctorates awarded. *Degree program information:* Part-time and evening/weekend programs available. Postbaccalaureate distance learning degree programs offered (minimal on-campus study). Offers biblical studies (MATS, Certificate); children's and family ministry (MACFM); Christian education (MACE); Christian thought (M Div, MACT); church leadership (D Min); congregation and family care (D Min); global and contextual studies (MA); global missions (Certificate); lay ministry (Certificate); marriage and family studies (M Div); marriage and family therapy (MAMFT); missions (MATS); pastoral ministries (M Div); theological studies (MATS, Certificate); transformational leadership (MATL); youth ministries (MACE). *Application deadline:* For fall admission, 8/1 priority date for domestic students; for winter admission, 12/1 priority date for domestic students; for spring admission, 1/1 priority date for domestic students. Applications are processed on a rolling basis. *Application fee:* $20. Electronic applications accepted. *Application Contact:* Joseph V. Dworak, Director of Admissions, 651-638-6288, Fax: 651-638-6002, E-mail: j-dworak@bethel.edu. *Executive Vice President and Provost,* Dr. Leland Eliason, 651-638-6182.

BETHEL UNIVERSITY, St. Paul, MN 55112-6999

General Information Independent-religious, coed, comprehensive institution. *Enrollment:* 5,185 graduate, professional, and undergraduate students; 634 full-time matriculated graduate/professional students (428 women), 155 part-time matriculated graduate/professional students (103 women). *Enrollment by degree level:* 722 master's, 49 doctoral, 18 other advanced degrees. *Graduate faculty:* 59 full-time (26 women), 79 part-time/adjunct (30 women). *Tuition:* Part-time $395 per credit. Tuition and fees vary according to program. *Graduate housing:* On-campus housing not available. *Student services:* Campus employment opportunities, campus safety program, career counseling, disabled student services, free psychological counseling, low-cost health insurance, multicultural affairs office, writing training. *Library facilities:* Bethel College Library plus 1 other. *Online resources:* library catalog, web page, access to other libraries' catalogs. *Collection:* 184,000 titles, 21,343 serial subscriptions, 14,171 audiovisual materials.

Computer facilities: Computer purchase and lease plans are available. 124 computers available on campus for general student use. A campuswide network can be accessed from student residence rooms and from off campus. Internet access and online class registration are available. *Web address:* http://www.bethel.edu/.

General Application Contact: Michael Price, Director of Admissions, 651-635-8000 Ext. 8017, Fax: 651-635-8004, E-mail: m_price@bethel.edu.

GRADUATE UNITS

Graduate School Students: 634 full-time (428 women), 155 part-time (103 women); includes 55 minority (25 African Americans, 3 American Indian/Alaska Native, 13 Asian Americans or Pacific Islanders, 14 Hispanic Americans), 1 international. Average age 36. *Faculty:* 59 full-time (26 women), 79 part-time/adjunct (30 women). Expenses: Contact institution. *Financial support:* Institutionally sponsored loans available. Financial award applicants required to submit FAFSA. In 2006, 136 master's, 31 other advanced degrees awarded. *Degree program information:* Part-time and evening/weekend programs available. Postbaccalaureate distance learning degree programs offered (minimal on-campus study). Offers business administration (MBA); child and adolescent mental health (Certificate); Christian health ministry (MA); communication (MA); counseling psychology (MA); education K-12 (MA); educational administration (Ed D); gerontology (MA); healthcare leadership (MA); literacy (Certificate); literacy education (MA); nursing education (MA, Certificate); organizational leadership (MA); postsecondary teaching (Certificate); secondary education (MA); special education (M Ed). *Application deadline:* Applications are processed on a rolling basis. *Application fee:* $25. Electronic applications accepted. *Application Contact:* Michael Price, Director of Admissions, 651-635-8000 Ext. 8017, Fax: 651-635-8004, E-mail: m_price@bethel.edu. *Dean,* Dr. Carl Polding, 651-635-8000, Fax: 651-635-1464, E-mail: c-polding@bethel.edu.

BETHESDA CHRISTIAN UNIVERSITY, Anaheim, CA 92801

General Information Independent-religious, coed, comprehensive institution.

GRADUATE UNITS

Graduate and Professional Programs Offers biblical studies (MA); theology (M Div).

BETH HAMEDRASH SHAAREI YOSHER INSTITUTE, Brooklyn, NY 11204

General Information Independent-religious, men only, comprehensive institution.

GRADUATE UNITS

Graduate Programs

BETH HATALMUD RABBINICAL COLLEGE, Brooklyn, NY 11214

General Information Independent-religious, men only, comprehensive institution.

GRADUATE UNITS

Graduate Programs

BETH MEDRASH GOVOHA, Lakewood, NJ 08701-2797

General Information Independent-religious, men only, upper-level institution.

GRADUATE UNITS

Graduate Programs

BEXLEY HALL SEMINARY, Rochester, NY 14620-2589

General Information Independent-religious, coed, graduate-only institution.

GRADUATE UNITS

Graduate Programs Offers ministry (M Div, MA).

BIBLICAL THEOLOGICAL SEMINARY, Hatfield, PA 19440-2499

General Information Independent-religious, coed, graduate-only institution. *Graduate housing:* Rooms and/or apartments available to single students and available on a first-come, first-served basis to married students. *Research affiliation:* Christian Counseling and Education Foundation (psychology).

GRADUATE UNITS

Graduate and Professional Programs *Degree program information:* Part-time programs available. Offers counseling (MA); ministry (MA); theology (M Div, D Min).

BIOLA UNIVERSITY, La Mirada, CA 90639-0001

General Information Independent-religious, coed, university. *Graduate housing:* Rooms and/or apartments available on a first-come, first-served basis to single and married students.

GRADUATE UNITS

Crowell School of Business *Degree program information:* Part-time and evening/weekend programs available. Offers business (MBA).

Rosemead School of Psychology Offers psychology (MA, PhD, Psy D).

School of Arts and Sciences *Degree program information:* Part-time and evening/weekend programs available. Offers arts and sciences (MA Ed).

School of Intercultural Studies *Degree program information:* Part-time and evening/weekend programs available. Offers applied linguistics (MA); intercultural education (PhD); intercultural studies (MAICS); missiology (D Miss); missions (MA); teaching English to speakers of other languages (MA, Certificate). Electronic applications accepted.

School of Professional Studies *Degree program information:* Part-time and evening/weekend programs available. Offers Christian apologetics (MA); organizational leadership (MA).

Talbot School of Theology *Degree program information:* Part-time and evening/weekend programs available. Offers Bible exposition (MA); biblical and theological studies (MA); Christian education (MACE); Christian ministry and leadership (MA); divinity (M Div); education (PhD); ministry (MA Min); New Testament (MA); Old Testament (MA); philosophy of religion and ethics (MA); spiritual formation (MA); spiritual formation and soul care (MA); theology (MA, Th M, D Min).

BIRMINGHAM-SOUTHERN COLLEGE, Birmingham, AL 35254

General Information Independent-religious, coed, comprehensive institution. *Graduate housing:* On-campus housing not available.

GRADUATE UNITS

Program in Music Offers music (MM).

Program in Public and Private Management *Degree program information:* Part-time and evening/weekend programs available. Offers public and private management (MPPM).

BISHOP'S UNIVERSITY, Sherbrooke, QC J1M 0C8, Canada

General Information Province-supported, coed, comprehensive institution. *Graduate housing:* Room and/or apartments available on a first-come, first-served basis to single students; on-campus housing not available to married students. Housing application deadline: 7/1.

GRADUATE UNITS

School of Education *Degree program information:* Part-time programs available. Postbaccalaureate distance learning degree programs offered (minimal on-campus study). Offers advanced studies in education (Diploma); education (M Ed, MA); teaching English as a second language (Certificate).

BLACK HILLS STATE UNIVERSITY, Spearfish, SD 57799

General Information State-supported, coed, comprehensive institution. *Graduate housing:* Rooms and/or apartments available on a first-come, first-served basis to single and married students. Housing application deadline: 3/1.

GRADUATE UNITS

College of Business and Technology *Degree program information:* Part-time programs available. Offers business services management (MS).

College of Education *Degree program information:* Part-time programs available. Offers curriculum and instruction (MS).

BLESSED JOHN XXIII NATIONAL SEMINARY, Weston, MA 02493-2618

General Information Independent-religious, men only, graduate-only institution. *Enrollment by degree level:* 66 first professional. *Graduate faculty:* 11 full-time (0 women), 12 part-time/adjunct (3 women). *Graduate housing:* Room and/or apartments available to single students; on-campus housing not available to married students. *Student services:* Campus safety program, career counseling. *Library facilities:* Main library plus 1 other. *Collection:* 64,000 titles, 330 serial subscriptions.

Computer facilities: 6 computers available on campus for general student use. A campuswide network can be accessed from student residence rooms and from off campus. Internet access is available. *Web address:* http://www.blessedjohnxxiii.edu/.

General Application Contact: Rev. Peter J. Uglietto, President and Rector, 781-899-5500, Fax: 781-891-9057, E-mail: rev.uglietto@blessedjohnxxiii.edu.

GRADUATE UNITS

School of Theology Students: 65 full-time (0 women); includes 10 minority (3 African Americans, 1 American Indian/Alaska Native, 4 Asian Americans or Pacific Islanders, 2 Hispanic Americans). Average age 45. *Faculty:* 11 full-time (0 women), 11 part-time/adjunct (4 women). Expenses: Contact institution. *Financial support:* Career-related internships or fieldwork available. Offers theology (M Div). *Application deadline:* For fall admission, 7/15 priority date for domestic students. Applications are processed on a rolling basis. *Application fee:* $0. *President and Rector,* Rev. Peter J. Uglietto, 781-899-5500, Fax: 781-891-9057, E-mail: rev.uglietto@blessedjohnxxiii.edu.

BLOOMSBURG UNIVERSITY OF PENNSYLVANIA, Bloomsburg, PA 17815-1301

General Information State-supported, coed, comprehensive institution. CGS member. *Enrollment:* 8,723 graduate, professional, and undergraduate students; 344 full-time matriculated graduate/professional students (244 women), 394 part-time matriculated graduate/professional students (270 women). *Enrollment by degree level:* 685 master's, 53 doctoral. *Graduate faculty:* 186 full-time (65 women). Tuition, state resident: full-time $6,048; part-time $336 per credit. Tuition, nonresident: full-time $9,678; part-time $538 per credit. *Required fees:* $1,415. *Graduate housing:* Room and/or apartments available to single students; on-campus housing not available to married students. Typical cost: $3,282 per year ($5,616 including board). *Student services:* Campus employment opportunities, campus safety program, career counseling, child daycare facilities, disabled student services, free psychological counseling, international student services, low-cost health insurance, multicultural affairs office. *Library facilities:* Andruss Library. *Online resources:* library catalog, web page, access to other libraries' catalogs. *Collection:* 472,982 titles, 1,747 serial subscriptions, 13,125 audiovisual materials. *Research affiliation:* Marine Science Consortium.

Computer facilities: 1,250 computers available on campus for general student use. A campuswide network can be accessed from student residence rooms and from off campus. Internet access and online class registration are available. *Web address:* http://www.bloomu.edu/.

General Application Contact: Carol Arnold, Administrative Assistant, 570-389-4015, Fax: 570-389-3054, E-mail: carnold@bloomu.edu.

GRADUATE UNITS

School of Graduate Studies Students: 344 full-time (244 women), 394 part-time (270 women); includes 23 minority (14 African Americans, 5 Asian Americans or Pacific Islanders, 4 Hispanic Americans), 38 international. Average age 30. 329 applicants, 100% accepted, 228 enrolled. *Faculty:* 178 full-time (60 women). Expenses: Contact institution. *Financial support:* In 2006–07, 218 research assistantships were awarded; teaching assistantships with partial tuition reimbursements, career-related internships or fieldwork, Federal Work-Study, institutionally sponsored loans, and minority assistantships also available. In 2006, 325 master's, 7 doctorates awarded. *Degree program information:* Part-time and evening/weekend programs available. *Application fee:* $30. Electronic applications accepted. *Application Contact:* Carol Arnold, Administrative Assistant, 570-389-4015, Fax: 570-389-3054, E-mail: carnold@bloomu.edu. *Dean of Graduate Studies,* Dr. James F. Matta, 570-389-4015, Fax: 570-389-3054.

College of Business Students: 32 full-time (15 women), 51 part-time (15 women); includes 4 minority (2 African Americans, 1 Asian American or Pacific Islander, 1 Hispanic American), 11 international. Average age 31. 32 applicants, 100% accepted, 21 enrolled. *Faculty:* 24 full-time (2 women). Expenses: Contact institution. *Financial support:* Unspecified assistantships available. In 2006, 48 degrees awarded. Offers business (M Ed, MBA); business administration (MBA); business education (M Ed). *Application deadline:* Applications are processed on a rolling basis. *Application fee:* $30. Electronic applications accepted. *Dean,* Dr. David Martin, 570-389-4745, Fax: 570-389-3892, E-mail: dmarti2@bloomu.edu.

College of Liberal Arts Students: 16 full-time (10 women), 6 part-time (4 women). Average age 25. 17 applicants, 100% accepted, 11 enrolled. *Faculty:* 68 full-time (25 women). Expenses: Contact institution. *Financial support:* Unspecified assistantships available. In 2006, 12 degrees awarded. *Degree program information:* Part-time programs available. Offers exercise science (MS); liberal arts (MS). *Application deadline:* Applications are processed on a rolling basis. *Application fee:* $30. Electronic applications accepted. *Dean,* Dr. George Agbango, 570-389-4410, Fax: 570-389-3026, E-mail: gagbango@bloomu.edu.

College of Professional Studies Students: 241 full-time (192 women), 260 part-time (204 women); includes 8 minority (4 African Americans, 3 Asian Americans or Pacific Islanders, 1 Hispanic American), 13 international. Average age 30. 214 applicants, 100% accepted, 142 enrolled. *Faculty:* 50 full-time (28 women). Expenses: Contact institution. *Financial support:* Unspecified assistantships available. In 2006, 211 master's, 7 doctorates awarded. Offers adult and family nurse practitioner (MSN); adult health and illness (MSN); audiology (Au D); community health (MSN); curriculum and instruction (M Ed); early childhood education (MS); education (M Ed, MS); education of the deaf/hard of hearing (MS); elementary education (M Ed); exceptionality programs (MS); guidance counseling and student affairs (M Ed); health sciences (MS, MSN, Au D); nursing (MSN); nursing administration (MSN); reading (M Ed); special education (MS); speech pathology (MS). *Application fee:* $30. Electronic applications accepted. *Dean,* Dr. Dianne Mark, 570-389-4005, Fax: 570-389-5049, E-mail: dmark@bloomu.edu.

College of Science and Technology Students: 55 full-time (27 women), 77 part-time (47 women); includes 11 minority (8 African Americans, 1 Asian American or Pacific Islander, 2 Hispanic Americans), 14 international. Average age 30. 66 applicants, 100% accepted, 54 enrolled. *Faculty:* 43 full-time (9 women). Expenses: Contact institution. *Financial support:* Unspecified assistantships available. In 2006, 54 degrees awarded. Offers biology (MS); biology education (M Ed); instructional technology (MS); radiologist assistant (MS); science and technology (M Ed, MS). *Application fee:* $30. *Dean,* Dr. Robert Marande, 570-389-5333, Fax: 570-389-5063, E-mail: rmarande@bloomu.edu.

BLUFFTON UNIVERSITY, Bluffton, OH 45817

General Information Independent-religious, coed, comprehensive institution. *Enrollment:* 1,155 graduate, professional, and undergraduate students; 104 full-time matriculated graduate/professional students (58 women), 31 part-time matriculated graduate/professional students (24 women). *Enrollment by degree level:* 135 master's. *Graduate faculty:* 14 full-time (5 women), 6 part-time/adjunct (1 woman). *Student services:* Campus employment opportunities, career counseling, disabled student services, international student services, low-cost health insurance, multicultural affairs office, writing training. *Library facilities:* Musselman Library. *Online resources:* library catalog, web page, access to other libraries' catalogs. *Collection:* 168,888 titles, 263 serial subscriptions.

Computer facilities: Computer purchase and lease plans are available. 150 computers available on campus for general student use. A campuswide network can be accessed from student residence rooms and from off campus. Internet access and online class registration are available. *Web address:* http://www.bluffton.edu/.

General Application Contact: Betty Dills, Office of Adult and Graduate Education, 800-488-3257 Ext. 4, Fax: 419-358-3399, E-mail: adulted@bluffton.edu.

GRADUATE UNITS

Program in Education Students: 33 full-time (28 women), 21 part-time (19 women); includes 3 minority (2 African Americans, 1 Hispanic American). 32 applicants, 69% accepted, 20 enrolled. *Faculty:* 6 full-time (3 women), 2 part-time/adjunct (1 woman). Expenses: Contact institution. *Financial support:* In 2006–07, 2 students received support. Health care benefits available. Support available to part-time students. Financial award application deadline: 9/15; financial award applicants required to submit FAFSA. In 2006, 10 degrees awarded. *Degree program information:* Part-time programs available. Offers education (MA Ed). *Application deadline:* For fall admission, 8/15 priority date for domestic students, 6/15 priority date for international students; for spring admission, 12/15 priority date for domestic students, 9/15 priority date for international students. Applications are processed on a rolling basis. *Application fee:* $20. Electronic applications accepted. *Application Contact:* Susan White, Program Representative, 419-358-3560, Fax: 419-358-3399, E-mail: whites@bluffton.edu. *Director of Teacher Education,* Dr. Gayle M. Trollinger, 419-358-3331, Fax: 419-358-3074, E-mail: trollingerg@bluffton.edu.

Programs in Business Students: 71 full-time (30 women), 10 part-time (5 women); includes 11 minority (8 African Americans, 2 Asian Americans or Pacific Islanders, 1 Hispanic American). Average age 37. 42 applicants, 100% accepted, 41 enrolled. *Faculty:* 8 full-time (2 women), 4 part-time/adjunct (0 women). Expenses: Contact institution. In 2006, 43 degrees awarded. *Degree program information:* Evening/weekend programs available. Offers business administration (MBA); organizational management (MA). *Application deadline:* For fall admission, 7/31 priority date for domestic and international students. Applications are processed on a rolling basis. *Application fee:* $20. Electronic applications accepted. *Application Contact:* Betty Dills, Information Contact, 800-488-3257, Fax: 419-358-3399, E-mail: adulted@bluffton.edu. *Director of Graduate Programs in Business,* Dr. George Lehman, 419-358-3302, E-mail: lehmang@bluffton.edu.

BOB JONES UNIVERSITY, Greenville, SC 29614

General Information Independent-religious, coed, university.

GRADUATE UNITS

Graduate Programs

BOISE STATE UNIVERSITY, Boise, ID 83725-0399

General Information State-supported, coed, comprehensive institution. CGS member. *Enrollment:* 18,826 graduate, professional, and undergraduate students; 372 full-time matriculated graduate/professional students (206 women), 1,184 part-time matriculated graduate/professional students (676 women). *Enrollment by degree level:* 1,507 master's, 49 doctoral. *Graduate faculty:* 658. *Graduate housing:* Rooms and/or apartments available on a first-come, first-served basis to single and married students. *Student services:* Campus employment opportunities, campus safety program, career counseling, child daycare facilities, disabled student services, exercise/wellness program, free psychological counseling, grant writing training, international student services, low-cost health insurance, multicultural affairs office, writing training. *Library facilities:* Albertsons Library. *Online resources:* library catalog, web page. *Collection:* 838,932 titles, 5,575 serial subscriptions, 58,047 audiovisual materials. *Research affiliation:* American Chemical Society (petroleum research), Arsonne National Laboratory (energy policy analysis), Bechtel BWXT Idaho, LLC (energy policy analysis), Prewitt & Associates, Inc. (C-130 drop zones), Lee Pesky Learning Center (elementary mathematics education), Federal Aviation Administration (airliner cabin environment research).

Computer facilities: 900 computers available on campus for general student use. A campuswide network can be accessed from student residence rooms and from off campus. Internet access and online class registration are available. *Web address:* http://www.boisestate.edu/.

General Application Contact: Dr. John R. Pelton, Dean, 208-426-3647, Fax: 208-426-2789, E-mail: jpelton@boisestate.edu.

GRADUATE UNITS

Graduate College Students: 372 full-time (206 women), 1,184 part-time (676 women); includes 112 minority (21 African Americans, 10 American Indian/Alaska Native, 30 Asian Americans or Pacific Islanders, 51 Hispanic Americans), 54 international. Average age 37. 675 applicants, 84% accepted, 226 enrolled. *Faculty:* 415 full-time (132 women), 242 part-time/adjunct (94 women). Expenses: Contact institution. *Financial support:* In 2006–07, 11 fellowships (averaging $11,333 per year), 81 research assistantships with full and partial tuition reimbursements (averaging $10,498 per year), 84 teaching assistantships with full and partial tuition reimbursements (averaging $8,522 per year) were awarded; career-related internships or fieldwork, Federal Work-Study, institutionally sponsored loans, scholarships/grants, tuition waivers (full and partial), and unspecified assistantships also available. Support available to part-time students. Financial award application deadline: 3/1; financial award applicants required to submit FAFSA. In 2006, 386 master's, 3 doctorates awarded. *Degree program information:* Part-time programs available. Postbaccalaureate distance learning degree programs offered (no on-campus study). *Application deadline:* For fall admission, 3/1 priority date for domestic students; for spring admission, 10/1 priority date for domestic students. Applications are processed on a rolling basis. *Application fee:* $55. Electronic applications accepted. *Application Contact:* Linda Platt, Office Services Supervisor, Graduate Admission and Degree Services, 208-426-1074, Fax: 208-426-2789, E-mail: lplatt@boisestate.edu. *Dean,* Dr. John R. Pelton, 208-426-3647, Fax: 208-426-2789, E-mail: jpelton@boisestate.edu.

College of Arts and Sciences Students: 105 full-time (59 women), 156 part-time (89 women); includes 10 minority (3 African Americans, 3 Asian Americans or Pacific Islanders, 4 Hispanic Americans), 9 international. Average age 36. 176 applicants, 69% accepted, 56 enrolled. *Faculty:* 170 full-time (50 women), 101 part-time/adjunct (22 women). Expenses: Contact institution. *Financial support:* In 2006–07, 11 fellowships (averaging $11,333 per year), 21 research assistantships with full and partial tuition reimbursements (averaging $11,900 per year), 67 teaching assistantships with full and partial tuition reimbursements (averaging $11,090 per year) were awarded; career-related internships or fieldwork, Federal Work-Study, institutionally sponsored loans, scholarships/grants, tuition waivers (partial), and unspecified assistantships also available. Support available to part-time students. Financial award application deadline: 3/1. In 2006, 46 degrees awarded. *Degree program information:* Part-time programs available. Offers art education (MA); arts and sciences (MA, MFA, MM, MS, PhD); biology (MA, MS); creative writing (MFA); earth science (MS); English (MA); geology (MS, PhD); geophysics (MS, PhD); interdisciplinary studies (MA, MS); music (MM); music education (MM); pedagogy (MM); performance (MM); raptor biology (MS); technical communication (MA); visual arts (MFA). *Application deadline:* For fall admission, 3/1 priority date for domestic students; for spring admission, 10/1 priority date for domestic students. Applications are processed on a rolling basis. *Application fee:* $0. Electronic applications accepted. *Dean,* Martin E. Schimpf, 208-426-1414, Fax: 208-426-3006.

College of Business and Economics Students: 44 full-time (16 women), 149 part-time (64 women); includes 8 minority (4 Asian Americans or Pacific Islanders, 4 Hispanic Americans), 11 international. Average age 33. 82 applicants, 88% accepted, 32 enrolled. *Faculty:* 41 full-time (5 women), 8 part-time/adjunct (3 women). Expenses: Contact institution. *Financial support:* In 2006–07, 16 students received support, including 12 research assistantships (averaging $9,324 per year), 4 teaching assistantships (averaging $8,100 per year); career-related internships or fieldwork, Federal Work-Study, institutionally sponsored loans, and unspecified assistantships also available. Support available to part-time students. Financial award application deadline: 3/1. In 2006, 67 degrees awarded. *Degree program information:* Part-time programs available. Offers accountancy (MSA); business administration (MBA); business and economics (MBA, MSA); information technology management (MBA); taxation (MSA). *Application deadline:* For fall admission, 3/1 priority date for domestic students; for spring admission, 10/1 priority date for domestic students. Applications are processed on a rolling basis. *Application fee:* $0. Electronic applications accepted. *Application Contact:* J. Renee Anchustegui, Coordinator, 208-426-3116, Fax: 208-426-1135, E-mail: ranchust@boisestate.edu. *Dean,* Howard Smith, 208-426-2321, Fax: 208-426-1135, E-mail: howardsmith@boisestate.edu.

College of Education Students: 97 full-time (62 women), 426 part-time (289 women); includes 37 minority (2 African Americans, 5 American Indian/Alaska Native, 4 Asian Americans or Pacific Islanders, 26 Hispanic Americans), 4 international. Average age 38. 178 applicants, 92% accepted, 57 enrolled. *Faculty:* 84 full-time (39 women), 47 part-time/adjunct (29 women). Expenses: Contact institution. *Financial support:* In 2006–07, 40 students received support, including 13 research assistantships with full tuition reimbursements available (averaging $12,268 per year); fellowships with full tuition reimbursements available, career-related internships or fieldwork, Federal Work-Study, institutionally sponsored loans, and unspecified assistantships also available. Support available to part-time students. Financial award application deadline: 3/1; financial award applicants required to submit FAFSA. In 2006, 123 master's, 3 doctorates awarded. *Degree program information:* Part-time programs available. Offers athletic administration (MPE); counseling (MA); counselor education (MA); curriculum and instruction (Ed D); curriculum instruction (MA); early childhood education (M Ed, MA); education (M Ed, MA, MET, MPE, MS, MS Ed, Ed D); educational leadership (M Ed); educational technology (MET, MS, MS Ed); exercise and sports studies (MS); physical education (MPE); reading (MA); special education (M Ed, MA). *Application deadline:* For fall admission, 7/1 priority date for domestic students; for spring admission, 11/15 priority date for domestic students. Applications are processed on a rolling basis. *Application fee:* $0. Electronic applications accepted. *Application Contact:* Dr. Philip P. Kelly, Chair, 208-426-4977, Fax: 208-426-4365. *Dean,* Diane Boothe, 208-426-1134, Fax: 208-426-4365.

College of Engineering Students: 40 full-time (16 women), 265 part-time (120 women); includes 32 minority (12 African Americans, 1 American Indian/Alaska Native, 13 Asian Americans or Pacific Islanders, 6 Hispanic Americans), 28 international. Average age 40. 98 applicants, 84% accepted, 61 enrolled. *Faculty:* 33 full-time (6 women), 24 part-time/adjunct (12 women). Expenses: Contact institution. *Financial support:* In 2006–07, 32 research assistantships with full and partial tuition reimbursements (averaging $10,900 per year), 8 teaching assistantships with partial tuition reimbursements (averaging $6,800 per year) were awarded; career-related internships or fieldwork, Federal Work-Study, institutionally sponsored loans, tuition waivers (full), and unspecified assistantships also available. Support available to part-time students. Financial award application deadline: 3/1. In 2006, 71 degrees awarded. *Degree program information:* Part-time programs available. Postbaccalaureate distance learning degree programs offered (no on-campus study). Offers civil engineering (M Engr, MS); computer engineering (M Engr, MS); computer science (MS); electrical and computer engineering (PhD); electrical engineering (M Engr, MS); engineering (M Engr, MS, PhD); instructional and performance technology (MS); materials science and engineering (M Engr, MS); mechanical engineering (M Engr, MS). *Application deadline:* For fall admission, 3/1 priority date for domestic students; for spring admission, 10/1 priority date for domestic students. Applications are processed on a rolling basis. *Application fee:* $0. Electronic applications accepted. *Dean,* Dr. Cheryl B. Schrader, 208-426-1153, Fax: 208-426-3637.

College of Health Science Students: 6 full-time (5 women), 60 part-time (38 women); includes 5 minority (1 African American, 1 American Indian/Alaska Native, 2 Asian Americans or Pacific Islanders, 1 Hispanic American), 1 international. Average age 38. 30 applicants, 100% accepted, 16 enrolled. *Faculty:* 11 full-time (5 women), 41 part-time/adjunct (24 women). Expenses: Contact institution. *Financial support:* In 2006–07, 2 research assistantships with partial tuition reimbursements (averaging $4,080 per year) were awarded; career-related internships or fieldwork, Federal Work-Study, institutionally sponsored loans, and unspecified assistantships also available. Support available to part-time students. Financial award application deadline: 3/1. In 2006, 11 degrees awarded. *Degree program information:* Part-time programs available. Offers health science (MHS). *Application deadline:* For fall admission, 3/1 priority date for domestic students; for spring admission, 10/1 priority date for domestic students. Applications are processed on a rolling basis. *Application fee:* $0. Electronic applications accepted. *Application Contact:* Dr. Tedd McDonald, Program Director, 208-426-2425, E-mail: tmcdonal@boisestate.edu. *Dean,* Dr. James T. Girvan, 208-426-4116, Fax: 208-426-3469.

College of Social Sciences and Public Affairs Students: 80 full-time (48 women), 128 part-time (76 women); includes 20 minority (3 African Americans, 3 American Indian/Alaska Native, 4 Asian Americans or Pacific Islanders, 10 Hispanic Americans), 1 international. Average age 36. 111 applicants, 79% accepted, 44 enrolled. *Faculty:* 60 full-time (22 women), 19 part-time/adjunct (5 women). Expenses: Contact institution. *Financial support:* In 2006–07, 25 students received support, including 1 research assistantship with full tuition reimbursement available (averaging $8,096 per year), 5 teaching assistantships with full tuition reimbursements available (averaging $8,096 per year); career-related internships or fieldwork, Federal Work-Study, institutionally sponsored loans, and unspecified assistantships also available. Support available to part-time students. Financial award

Boise State University (continued)

application deadline: 3/1. In 2006, 68 degrees awarded. *Degree program information:* Part-time programs available. Offers communication (MA); criminal justice administration (MA); environmental and natural resources policy and administration (MPA); general public administration (MPA); history (MA); social sciences and public affairs (MA, MPA, MSW); social work (MSW); state and local government policy and administration (MPA). *Application deadline:* For fall admission, 3/1 priority date for domestic students; for spring admission, 10/1 priority date for domestic students. Applications are processed on a rolling basis. *Application fee:* $0. Electronic applications accepted. *Interim Associate Dean,* Joanne Klein, 208-426-1368, Fax: 208-426-4318, E-mail: jklein@boisestate.edu.

BORICUA COLLEGE, New York, NY 10032-1560

General Information Independent, coed, comprehensive institution. *Enrollment:* 37 full-time matriculated graduate/professional students (32 women). *Enrollment by degree level:* 37 master's. *Graduate faculty:* 3 full-time (2 women). *Tuition:* Full-time $9,000. *Required fees:* $50. One-time fee: $100 full-time. Full-time tuition and fees vary according to degree level and program. *Student services:* Career counseling. *Library facilities:* Boricua College Library plus 1 other. *Collection:* 112,600 titles, 780 serial subscriptions.

Computer facilities: 63 computers available on campus for general student use. Internet access is available. *Web address:* http://www.boricuacollege.edu/.

General Application Contact: Miriam Pfeiffer, Director of Student Services, 718-782-2200 Ext. 211, E-mail: mpfeiffer@boricuacollege.edu.

GRADUATE UNITS

Program in Human Services Students: 37 full-time (32 women); includes 32 minority (all Hispanic Americans), 5 international. 31 applicants, 65% accepted, 20 enrolled. *Faculty:* 3 full-time (2 women). Expenses: Contact institution. *Financial support:* Career-related internships or fieldwork and Federal Work-Study available. Financial award applicants required to submit FAFSA. In 2006, 41 degrees awarded. *Degree program information:* Evening/weekend programs available. Offers human services (MS). *Application deadline:* Applications are processed on a rolling basis. *Application fee:* $100. *Application Contact:* Miriam Pfeiffer, Director of Student Services, 718-782-2200 Ext. 211, E-mail: mpfeiffer@boricuacollege.edu. *Chair,* Dr. Basilisa Colón, 212-694-7000 Ext. 655, E-mail: bcolon@boricuacollege.edu.

Program in Latin American and Caribbean Studies Students: 1 (woman) full-time; minority (Hispanic American) *Faculty:* 1 (woman) full-time. Expenses: Contact institution. *Financial support:* Career-related internships or fieldwork and Federal Work-Study available. Financial award applicants required to submit FAFSA. In 2006, 1 degree awarded. *Degree program information:* Evening/weekend programs available. Offers Latin American and Caribbean studies (MA). *Application deadline:* Applications are processed on a rolling basis. *Application fee:* $100. *Application Contact:* Miriam Pfeiffer, Director of Student Services, 718-782-2200 Ext. 211, E-mail: mpfeiffer@boricuacollege.edu. *Unit Head,* Dr. Shivaji Sengupta, 212-694-1000 Ext. 617.

BOSTON ARCHITECTURAL COLLEGE, Boston, MA 02115-2795

General Information Independent, coed, comprehensive institution.

GRADUATE UNITS

Graduate Programs Offers architecture (M Arch); interior design (MID). Electronic applications accepted.

BOSTON COLLEGE, Chestnut Hill, MA 02467-3800

General Information Independent-religious, coed, university. CGS member. *Enrollment:* 13,652 graduate, professional, and undergraduate students; 2,383 full-time matriculated graduate/professional students (1,462 women), 2,249 part-time matriculated graduate/professional students (1,241 women). *Graduate faculty:* 679. *Graduate housing:* On-campus housing not available. *Student services:* Campus employment opportunities, campus safety program, career counseling, child daycare facilities, disabled student services, exercise/wellness program, free psychological counseling, grant writing training, international student services, low-cost health insurance, multicultural affairs office, teacher training, writing training. *Library facilities:* Thomas P. O'Neill Library plus 6 others. *Online resources:* library catalog, web page, access to other libraries' catalogs. *Collection:* 2.1 million titles, 52,338 serial subscriptions, 171,099 audiovisual materials.

Computer facilities: Computer purchase and lease plans are available. 1,000 computers available on campus for general student use. A campuswide network can be accessed from student residence rooms and from off campus. Internet access and online class registration are available. *Web address:* http://www.bc.edu/.

General Application Contact: Robert V. Howe, Associate Dean, 617-552-3265, Fax: 617-552-3700, E-mail: hower@bc.edu.

GRADUATE UNITS

The Carroll School of Management Students: 369 full-time (141 women), 597 part-time (193 women); includes 107 minority (23 African Americans, 2 American Indian/Alaska Native, 63 Asian Americans or Pacific Islanders, 19 Hispanic Americans), 149 international. Average age 28. 1,002 applicants, 48% accepted, 282 enrolled. *Faculty:* 65. Expenses: Contact institution. *Financial support:* Fellowships with full tuition reimbursements, research assistantships with full and partial tuition reimbursements, teaching assistantships, career-related internships or fieldwork, Federal Work-Study, institutionally sponsored loans, scholarships/grants, tuition waivers (full and partial), and unspecified assistantships available. Support available to part-time students. Financial award application deadline: 3/1; financial award applicants required to submit FAFSA. In 2006, 414 master's, 9 doctorates awarded. *Degree program information:* Part-time and evening/weekend programs available. Offers accounting (MSA); business administration (MBA); finance (MSF, PhD); management (MBA, MSA, MSF, PhD); organization studies (PhD). *Application fee:* $100. Electronic applications accepted. *Application Contact:* Shelley A. Burt, Director of Graduate Enrollment, 617-552-3920, Fax: 617-552-8078, E-mail: bcmba@bc.edu. *Associate Dean for Graduate Programs,* Dr. Jeffrey L. Ringuest, 617-552-9100, Fax: 617-552-0514, E-mail: jeffrey.ringuest@bc.edu.

Graduate School of Arts and Sciences Students: 343 full-time (161 women), 727 part-time (338 women); includes 93 minority (18 African Americans, 2 American Indian/Alaska Native, 41 Asian Americans or Pacific Islanders, 32 Hispanic Americans), 229 international. 2,567 applicants, 35% accepted, 320 enrolled. *Faculty:* 422 full-time (128 women). Expenses: Contact institution. *Financial support:* Fellowships with full and partial tuition reimbursements, research assistantships with full and partial tuition reimbursements, teaching assistantships with full and partial tuition reimbursements, career-related internships or fieldwork, Federal Work-Study, scholarships/grants, and tuition waivers (full and partial) available. Support available to part-time students. Financial award application deadline: 3/1; financial award applicants required to submit FAFSA. In 2006, 195 master's, 70 doctorates awarded. *Degree program information:* Part-time programs available. Offers arts and sciences (MA, MS, MST, PhD); biochemistry (MS, PhD); biology (PhD); classics (MA); economics (PhD); English (MA, PhD); European national studies (MA); French (MA, PhD); geology and geophysics (MS); Greek (MA); history (MA, PhD); inorganic chemistry (PhD); Italian (MA); Latin (MA); linguistics (MA); mathematics (MA); medieval language (PhD); medieval studies (MA); organic chemistry (PhD); philosophy (MA, PhD); physical chemistry (PhD); physics (MS, PhD); political science (MA, PhD); psychology (MA, PhD); Russian and Slavic languages and literature (MA); science education (MST); Slavic studies (MA); sociology (MA, PhD); Spanish (MA, PhD); theology (MA, PhD). *Application deadline:* For fall admission, 1/15 priority date for domestic and international students. *Application fee:* $70. Electronic applications accepted. *Application Contact:* Robert V. Howe, Associate Dean, 617-552-3265, Fax: 617-552-3700, E-mail: hower@bc.edu. *Dean,* Dr. Michael A. Smyer, 617-552-3265, Fax: 617-552-3700.

Institute of Religious Education and Pastoral Ministry 103 applicants, 54% accepted, 46 enrolled. Expenses: Contact institution. *Financial support:* Fellowships with tuition reimbursements, career-related internships or fieldwork, Federal Work-Study, and tuition waivers (full and partial) available. Support available to part-time students. Financial award application deadline: 3/1; financial award applicants required to submit FAFSA. In 2006, 37 master's, 4 doctorates awarded. *Degree program information:* Part-time programs available. Offers church leadership (MA); pastoral ministry (MA); religious education (MA, PhD); social justice/social ministry (MA); youth ministry (MA). *Application deadline:* For fall admission, 3/1 priority date for domestic students. *Application fee:* $70. Electronic applications accepted. *Application Contact:* Dr. Jennifer Bader, Assistant Director, Academic Affairs, 617-552-4478, Fax: 617-552-0811, E-mail: jennifer.bader@bc.edu. *Chairperson,* Dr. Thomas Groome, 617-552-8449, Fax: 617-552-0811.

Graduate School of Social Work Students: 391 full-time (351 women), 125 part-time (112 women); includes 86 minority (32 African Americans, 2 American Indian/Alaska Native, 27 Asian Americans or Pacific Islanders, 25 Hispanic Americans), 11 international. 733 applicants, 67% accepted, 208 enrolled. *Faculty:* 21 full-time (12 women), 35 part-time/adjunct (21 women). Expenses: Contact institution. *Financial support:* In 2006–07, 354 students received support, including 15 fellowships with full tuition reimbursements available (averaging $18,000 per year), 2 research assistantships with full tuition reimbursements available (averaging $6,000 per year); teaching assistantships, career-related internships or fieldwork, Federal Work-Study, institutionally sponsored loans, scholarships/grants, traineeships, tuition waivers (partial), and unspecified assistantships also available. Support available to part-time students. Financial award applicants required to submit FAFSA. In 2006, 179 master's, 4 doctorates awarded. *Degree program information:* Part-time programs available. Offers social work (MSW, PhD). *Application deadline:* For fall admission, 3/1 for domestic students. Applications are processed on a rolling basis. *Application fee:* $40. *Application Contact:* Dr. William Howard, Director of Admission, 617-552-4024, Fax: 617-552-1690, E-mail: william.howard@bc.edu. *Dean,* Dr. Alberto Godenzi, 617-552-0866, Fax: 617-552-2374, E-mail: godenzi@bc.edu.

Law School Students: 781 full-time (353 women); includes 187 minority (40 African Americans, 1 American Indian/Alaska Native, 94 Asian Americans or Pacific Islanders, 52 Hispanic Americans), 22 international. Average age 25. 6,321 applicants, 19% accepted, 254 enrolled. *Faculty:* 52 full-time (22 women), 35 part-time/adjunct (10 women). Expenses: Contact institution. *Financial support:* In 2006–07, 448 students received support. Career-related internships or fieldwork, Federal Work-Study, institutionally sponsored loans, scholarships/grants, and tuition waivers (partial) available. Financial award application deadline: 3/15; financial award applicants required to submit FAFSA. In 2006, 288 degrees awarded. Offers law (JD). *Application deadline:* For fall admission, 3/1 for domestic and international students. Applications are processed on a rolling basis. *Application fee:* $75. Electronic applications accepted. *Application Contact:* Rita C. Jones, Assistant Dean for Admissions and Financial Aid, 617-522-4351, Fax: 617-522-2917, E-mail: rita.jones@bc.edu. *Dean,* John H. Garvey, 617-552-4340.

Lynch Graduate School of Education Students: 629 full-time (499 women), 248 part-time (168 women); includes 130 minority (50 African Americans, 2 American Indian/Alaska Native, 49 Asian Americans or Pacific Islanders, 29 Hispanic Americans), 89 international. 1,622 applicants, 54% accepted, 860 enrolled. *Faculty:* 62 full-time (31 women), 33 part-time/adjunct (20 women). Expenses: Contact institution. *Financial support:* In 2006–07, 940 fellowships with full and partial tuition reimbursements, 324 research assistantships with full and partial tuition reimbursements, 126 teaching assistantships with full and partial tuition reimbursements were awarded; career-related internships or fieldwork, Federal Work-Study, institutionally sponsored loans, scholarships/grants, traineeships, tuition waivers (full and partial), and unspecified assistantships also available. Support available to part-time students. Financial award applicants required to submit FAFSA. In 2006, 385 master's, 35 doctorates, 4 other advanced degrees awarded. Offers biology (MST); chemistry (MST); counseling psychology (MA, PhD); curriculum and instruction (M Ed, PhD, CAES); developmental and educational psychology (MA, PhD); early childhood education/teacher option (M Ed); early childhood/specialist option (MA); education (M Ed, MA, MAT, MST, Ed D, PhD, CAES); educational administration (M Ed, Ed D, PhD, CAES); educational research, measurement, and evaluation (M Ed, PhD); elementary education (M Ed); English (MAT); French (MAT); geology (MST); higher education (MA, PhD); history (MAT); Latin and classical humanities (MAT); mathematics (MST); physics (MST); professional school administrator (Ed D); reading specialist (M Ed, CAES); religious education (M Ed, CAES); secondary education (M Ed, MAT, MST); secondary teaching (M Ed); Spanish (MAT); special needs: moderate disabilities (M Ed, CAES); special needs: severe disabilities (M Ed). *Application fee:* $60. *Application Contact:* Timothy P. Blackman, Director, Graduate Admission and Financial Aid, 617-552-4214, Fax: 617-552-0398, E-mail: timothy.blackman.1@bc.edu. *Dean,* Rev. Joseph O'Keefe, SJ, 617-552-8426, Fax: 617-552-0812, E-mail: okeefejo@bc.edu.

William F. Connell School of Nursing Students: 155 full-time (137 women), 56 part-time (54 women); includes 10 minority (4 African Americans, 5 Asian Americans or Pacific Islanders, 1 Hispanic American), 6 international. Average age 34. 276 applicants, 47% accepted, 67 enrolled. *Faculty:* 46 full-time (44 women), 34 part-time/adjunct (all women). Expenses: Contact institution. *Financial support:* In 2006–07, 104 students received support, including 15 fellowships with partial tuition reimbursements available (averaging $10,045 per year), 3 research assistantships (averaging $10,000 per year), 4 teaching assistantships (averaging $12,548 per year); Federal Work-Study, institutionally sponsored loans, scholarships/grants, traineeships, and tuition waivers (partial) also available. Support available to part-time students. Financial award application deadline: 3/1; financial award applicants required to submit FAFSA. In 2006, 61 master's, 4 doctorates awarded. *Degree program information:* Part-time programs available. Offers adult health nursing (MS); community health nursing (MS); family health (MS); gerontology (MS); maternal/child health nursing (MS); nurse anesthesia (MS); nursing (PhD); psychiatric-mental health nursing (MS). *Application deadline:* For fall admission, 10/15 for domestic and international students; for spring admission, 3/15 for domestic and international students. *Application fee:* $40. Electronic applications accepted. *Application Contact:* Zanifer John-Bayard, Graduate Programs Assistant, 617-552-4059, Fax: 617-552-0745, E-mail: johnza@bc.edu. *Dean,* Dr. Barbara Hazard, 617-552-4251, Fax: 617-552-0931, E-mail: barbara.munro@bc.edu.

THE BOSTON CONSERVATORY, Boston, MA 02215

General Information Independent, coed, comprehensive institution. *Graduate housing:* Room and/or apartments available on a first-come, first-served basis to single students; on-campus housing not available to married students. Housing application deadline: 12/1.

GRADUATE UNITS

Graduate Division *Degree program information:* Part-time programs available. Offers choral conducting (MM); composition (MM); music (MM, ADP, Certificate); music education (MM); music performance (MM, ADP, Certificate); opera (MM, ADP, Certificate); theater (MM). Electronic applications accepted.

BOSTON GRADUATE SCHOOL OF PSYCHOANALYSIS, Brookline, MA 02446-4602

General Information Independent, coed, graduate-only institution.

GRADUATE UNITS

Master's, Certificate, and Doctoral Programs *Degree program information:* Part-time programs available. Offers psychoanalysis (MA, Psya D, Certificate). Electronic applications accepted.

Master's Program—New York *Degree program information:* Part-time programs available. Offers psychoanalysis (MA).

Program in the Study of Violence *Degree program information:* Evening/weekend programs available. Offers the study of violence (Psya D). Electronic applications accepted.

Vermont Graduate School of Psychoanalysis *Degree program information:* Evening/weekend programs available. Offers psychoanalysis (Psya D).

BOSTON UNIVERSITY, Boston, MA 02215

General Information Independent, coed, university. CGS member. *Enrollment:* 31,574 graduate, professional, and undergraduate students; 8,508 full-time matriculated graduate/professional students (4,624 women), 4,330 part-time matriculated graduate/professional students (2,271 women). *Enrollment by degree level:* 2,195 first professional, 8,046 master's, 2,433 doctoral, 164 other advanced degrees. *Graduate faculty:* 3,856. *Tuition:* Full-time $33,330; part-time $1,042 per credit. *Required fees:* $462; $40. *Graduate housing:* Rooms and/or apartments available on a first-come, first-served basis to single and married students. Typical cost: $6,760 per year ($10,480 including board) for single students; $6,760 per year ($10,480 including board) for married students. *Student services:* Campus employment opportunities, campus safety program, career counseling, child daycare facilities, disabled student services, free psychological counseling, international student services, low-cost health insurance, writing training. *Library facilities:* Mugar Memorial Library plus 18 others. *Online resources:* library catalog, web page, access to other libraries' catalogs. *Collection:* 2.4 million titles, 33,983 serial subscriptions. *Research affiliation:* Woods Hole Oceanographic Institution–Marine Biological Laboratory, Massachusetts Historical Society, Society for the Preservation of New England Antiquities, NASA–Ames Research Center.

Computer facilities: Computer purchase and lease plans are available. 750 computers available on campus for general student use. A campuswide network can be accessed from student residence rooms and from off campus. Internet access and online class registration, research and educational networks are available. *Web address:* http://www.bu.edu/.

General Application Contact: Information Contact, 617-353-2000.

GRADUATE UNITS

College of Communication Students: 346 full-time (254 women), 40 part-time (32 women); includes 45 minority (17 African Americans, 17 Asian Americans or Pacific Islanders, 11 Hispanic Americans), 61 international. Average age 24. 800 applicants, 50% accepted. *Faculty:* 57 full-time, 81 part-time/adjunct. Expenses: Contact institution. *Financial support:* In 2006–07, 290 students received support, including 18 teaching assistantships with partial tuition reimbursements available; career-related internships or fieldwork, Federal Work-Study, institutionally sponsored loans, scholarships/grants, and unspecified assistantships also available. Support available to part-time students. Financial award application deadline: 2/1; financial award applicants required to submit FAFSA. In 2006, 166 degrees awarded. *Degree program information:* Part-time programs available. Offers advertising (MS); broadcast journalism (MS); business and economics journalism (MS); communication (MFA, MS); communication research (MS); communication studies (MS); film production (MFA); film studies (MFA); photo journalism (MS); print journalism (MS); public relations (MS); science journalism (MS); screenwriting (MFA); television (MS); television management (MS). *Application deadline:* For fall admission, 2/1 for domestic students. Electronic applications accepted. *Application Contact:* William A. Taylor, Assistant Director, Graduate Services and Financial Aid, 617-353-3481, Fax: 617-358-0399, E-mail: comgrad@bu.edu. *Dean,* Dr. John J. Schulz, 617-353-3450, Fax: 617-358-0399, E-mail: com@bu.edu.

College of Engineering Students: 468 full-time (111 women), 52 part-time (12 women); includes 53 minority (8 African Americans, 33 Asian Americans or Pacific Islanders, 12 Hispanic Americans), 218 international. Average age 25. 1,435 applicants, 28% accepted, 180 enrolled. *Faculty:* 117 full-time (13 women). Expenses: Contact institution. *Financial support:* In 2006–07, 434 students received support, including 27 fellowships with full tuition reimbursements available (averaging $24,000 per year), 261 research assistantships with full tuition reimbursements available (averaging $16,000 per year), 76 teaching assistantships with full tuition reimbursements available (averaging $16,000 per year); career-related internships or fieldwork, Federal Work-Study, institutionally sponsored loans, scholarships/grants, traineeships, health care benefits, and tuition waivers (full and partial) also available. Financial award application deadline: 1/15; financial award applicants required to submit FAFSA. In 2006, 93 master's, 42 doctorates awarded. *Degree program information:* Part-time programs available. Postbaccalaureate distance learning degree programs offered (no on-campus study). Offers aerospace engineering (MS, PhD); biomedical engineering (MS, PhD); computer engineering (PhD); computer systems engineering (MS); electrical engineering (MS, PhD); engineering (MS, PhD); general engineering (MS); global manufacturing (MS); manufacturing (MS); manufacturing engineering (PhD); mechanical engineering (MS, PhD); photonics (MS); systems engineering (PhD). *Application deadline:* For fall admission, 4/1 for domestic and international students; for spring admission, 10/1 for domestic and international students. Applications are processed on a rolling basis. *Application fee:* $70. Electronic applications accepted. *Application Contact:* Cheryl Kelley, Director of Graduate Programs, 617-353-9760, Fax: 617-353-0259, E-mail: enggrad@bu.edu. *Dean,* Dr. Kenneth R. Lutchen, 617-353-2800, Fax: 617-358-3468, E-mail: klutch@bu.edu.

College of Fine Arts Students: 729 full-time (418 women), 167 part-time (85 women); includes 97 minority (49 African Americans, 8 American Indian/Alaska Native, 15 Asian Americans or Pacific Islanders, 25 Hispanic Americans), 148 international. Average age 32. 1,229 applicants, 42% accepted. *Faculty:* 68 full-time, 38 part-time/adjunct. Expenses: Contact institution. *Financial support:* Fellowships, teaching assistantships, Federal Work-Study and scholarships/grants available. Support available to part-time students. Financial award application deadline: 2/1. In 2006, 117 master's, 14 doctorates, 14 other advanced degrees awarded. *Degree program information:* Part-time programs available. Offers art education (MFA); collaborative piano (MM, DMA); composition (MM, DMA); conducting (MM, Artist Diploma, Performance Diploma); costume design (MFA); costume production (MFA); directing (MFA); fine arts (MFA, MM, DMA, Artist Diploma, Certificate, Performance Diploma); graphic design (MFA); historical performance (MM, DMA, Artist Diploma, Performance Diploma); lighting design (MFA); music education (MM, DMA); music theory (MM); musicology (MM); opera performance (Certificate); painting (MFA); performance (MM, DMA, Artist Diploma, Performance Diploma); scene design (MFA); sculpture (MFA); studio teaching (MFA); technical production (MFA, Certificate); theatre crafts (Certificate); theatre education (MFA). *Application deadline:* For fall admission, 2/1 priority date for domestic and international students. *Application fee:* $65. Electronic applications accepted. *Application Contact:* Mark Krone, Manager, Graduate Admissions, 617-353-3350, E-mail: arts@bu.edu. *Interim Dean,* Walt Meissner, 617-353-3350.

College of Health and Rehabilitation Sciences—Sargent College Students: 380 full-time (337 women), 274 part-time (210 women); includes 70 minority (8 African Americans, 1 American Indian/Alaska Native, 46 Asian Americans or Pacific Islanders, 15 Hispanic Americans), 31 international. Average age 29. 690 applicants, 58% accepted, 120 enrolled. *Faculty:* 54 full-time (42 women), 44 part-time/adjunct (28 women). Expenses: Contact institution. *Financial support:* In 2006–07, 250 students received support, including 10 fellowships with full tuition reimbursements available (averaging $12,000 per year), 15 research assistantships with full tuition reimbursements available (averaging $14,000 per year), 40 teaching assistantships with partial tuition reimbursements available (averaging $8,000 per year); career-related internships or fieldwork, Federal Work-Study, institutionally sponsored loans, scholarships/grants, and health care benefits also available. Support available to part-time students. Financial award application deadline: 4/15; financial award applicants required to submit FAFSA. In 2006, 104 master's, 216 doctorates awarded. Postbaccalaureate distance learning degree programs offered (minimal on-campus study). Offers applied anatomy and physiology (MS, PhD); audiology (PhD); health and rehabilitation sciences (MS, MSOT, D Sc, DPT, PhD, CAGS); nutrition (MS); occupational therapy (MS, MSOT); physical therapy (DPT); rehabilitation sciences (D Sc); speech-language pathology (MS, PhD, CAGS). *Application deadline:* For fall admission, 2/1 priority date for domestic students. Applications are processed on a rolling basis. *Application fee:* $65. Electronic applications accepted. *Application Contact:* Sharon Sankey, Director, Student Services, 617-353-2713, Fax: 617-353-7500, E-mail: ssankey@bu.edu. *Dean,* Dr. Gloria S. Waters, 617-353-2704, Fax: 617-353-7500, E-mail: gwaters@bu.edu.

Goldman School of Dental Medicine Students: 788 full-time (362 women); includes 189 minority (11 African Americans, 2 American Indian/Alaska Native, 155 Asian Americans or Pacific Islanders, 21 Hispanic Americans), 269 international. Average age 26. Expenses: Contact institution. *Financial support:* In 2006–07, 480 students received support. Career-related internships or fieldwork and institutionally sponsored loans available. Financial award application deadline: 4/15; financial award applicants required to submit CSS PROFILE or FAFSA. In 2006, 149 DMDs, 3 master's, 2 doctorates, 63 other advanced degrees awarded. Offers advanced general dentistry (CAGS); dental medicine (DMD, MS, MSD, D Sc, D Sc D, PhD, CAGS); dental public health (MS, MSD, D Sc D, CAGS); dentistry (DMD); endodontics (MSD, D Sc D, CAGS); implantology (CAGS); operative dentistry (MSD, D Sc D, CAGS); oral and maxillofacial surgery (MSD, D Sc D, CAGS); oral biology (MSD, D Sc, D Sc D, PhD); orthodontics (MSD, D Sc D, CAGS); pediatric dentistry (MSD, D Sc D, CAGS); periodontology (MSD, D Sc D, CAGS); prosthodontics (MSD, D Sc D, CAGS). *Application deadline:* For fall admission, 3/1 for domestic students. Applications are processed on a rolling basis. *Application fee:* $60. *Application Contact:* 617-638-4787, Fax: 617-638-4798. *Dean,* Dr. Spencer Frankl, 617-638-4780.

Graduate School of Arts and Sciences Students: 1,743 full-time (862 women), 236 part-time (134 women); includes 137 minority (34 African Americans, 2 American Indian/Alaska Native, 67 Asian Americans or Pacific Islanders, 34 Hispanic Americans), 653 international. Average age 28. 6,616 applicants, 29% accepted, 634 enrolled. Expenses: Contact institution. *Financial support:* In 2006–07, 1,200 students received support, including 102 fellowships with full tuition reimbursements available, 499 research assistantships with full tuition reimbursements available, 408 teaching assistantships with full tuition reimbursements available; career-related internships or fieldwork, Federal Work-Study, scholarships/grants, traineeships, and unspecified assistantships also available. Support available to part-time students. Financial award application deadline: 1/15; financial award applicants required to submit FAFSA. In 2006, 337 master's, 140 doctorates awarded. Offers African American studies (MA); African studies (Certificate); American and New England studies (PhD); anthropology (PhD); applied anthropology (MA); applied linguistics (MA, PhD); archaeological heritage management (MA); archaeology (MA, PhD); art history (MA, PhD); arts and sciences (MA, MAEP, MAPE, MS, PhD, Certificate); astronomy (MA, PhD); bioinformatics (MS, PhD); biology (MA, PhD); biostatistics (MA, PhD); cellular biophysics (PhD); chemistry (MA, PhD); classical studies (MA, PhD); cognitive and neural systems (MA, PhD); composition (MA); computer science (MA, PhD); creative writing (MA); earth sciences (MA, PhD); economic policy (MAEP); economics (MA, PhD); energy and environmental analysis (MA); English (MA, PhD); environmental remote sensing and geographic information systems (MA); French language and literature (MA, PhD); geoarchaeology (MA); geography and environment (MA, PhD); Hispanic language and literatures (MA, PhD); history (MA, PhD); international relations (MA); international relations and environmental policy (MA); international relations and environmental policy management (MA); international relations and international communication (MA); mathematical finance (MA); mathematics (MA, PhD); molecular biology, cell biology, and biochemistry (MA, PhD); museum studies (Certificate); music education (MA); music history/theory (PhD); musicology (MA, PhD); neuroscience (MA, PhD); philosophy (MA, PhD); physics (MA, PhD); political economy (MAPE); political science (MA, PhD); preservation studies (MA); psychology (MA, PhD); religious and theological studies (MA, PhD); sociology (MA, PhD); sociology and social work (PhD). *Application deadline:* For fall admission, 1/15 priority date for domestic and international students; for spring admission, 10/15 priority date for domestic and international students. *Application fee:* $70. Electronic applications accepted. *Application Contact:* Patricia A. Schiavoni, Admissions Officer, 617-353-2696, Fax: 617-358-0540, E-mail: grs@bu.edu. *Associate Dean,* J. Scott Whittaker, 617-353-2690, Fax: 617-358-0540.

Editorial Institute Students: 12 full-time (8 women), 1 part-time; includes 1 minority (Hispanic American), 1 international. Average age 30. 11 applicants, 64% accepted, 7 enrolled. Expenses: Contact institution. *Financial support:* In 2006–07, 12 students received support, including 3 teaching assistantships with partial tuition reimbursements available (averaging $15,500 per year); Federal Work-Study, scholarships/grants, and unspecified assistantships also available. Support available to part-time students. Financial award application deadline: 1/15; financial award applicants required to submit FAFSA. Offers editorial studies (MA, PhD). *Application deadline:* For fall admission, 3/30 for domestic and international students. *Application fee:* $70. *Application Contact:* Alex Effgen, Administrative Assistant, 617-353-6631, Fax: 617-353-6917, E-mail: editinst@bu.edu. *Co-Director,* Archie Burnett, 617-353-6631, E-mail: burnetta@bu.edu.

Metropolitan College (Continuing Education) Students: 197 full-time (95 women), 1,941 part-time (780 women); includes 207 minority (53 African Americans, 2 American Indian/Alaska Native, 106 Asian Americans or Pacific Islanders, 46 Hispanic Americans), 255 international. Average age 32. *Faculty:* 22 full-time (3 women), 221 part-time/adjunct. Expenses: Contact institution. *Financial support:* Fellowships, research assistantships, teaching assistantships, career-related internships or fieldwork, Federal Work-Study, institutionally sponsored loans, and tuition waivers (full and partial) available. Support available to part-time students. In 2006, 833 degrees awarded. *Degree program information:* Part-time and evening/weekend programs available. Offers actuarial science (MS); advertising (MS); arts administration (MS, Graduate Certificate); banking and financial management (MSM); business continuity in emergency management (MSM); city planning (MCP); computer information systems (MS); computer science (MS); continuing education (MCJ, MCP, MLA, MS, MSAS, MSM, MUA, Graduate Certificate); criminal justice (MCJ); economics development and tourism management (MSAS); electronic commerce, systems, and technology (MSAS); financial economics (MSAS); fundraising management (Graduate Certificate); human resource management (MSM); innovation and technology (MSAS); insurance management (MSM); international market management (MSM); liberal studies (MLA); multinational commerce (MSAS); project management (MSM); telecommunications (MS); urban affairs (MUA). *Application deadline:* Applications are processed on a rolling basis. *Application fee:* $65. *Application Contact:* Dr. Jay Halfond, Dean, 617-353-6776, Fax: 617-353-6066, E-mail: jhalfond@bu.edu. *Dean,* Dr. Jay Halfond, 617-353-6776, Fax: 617-353-6066, E-mail: jhalfond@bu.edu.

School of Education Students: 265 full-time (209 women), 256 part-time (196 women). Average age 31. *Faculty:* 31 full-time, 57 part-time/adjunct. Expenses: Contact institution. *Financial support:* In 2006–07, 325 students received support, including 7 fellowships, 9 research assistantships, 32 teaching assistantships with partial tuition reimbursements available; career-related internships or fieldwork, Federal Work-Study, and scholarships/grants also available. Support available to part-time students. Financial award application deadline: 2/15; financial award applicants required to submit FAFSA. In 2006, 298 master's, 23 doctorates, 5 other advanced degrees awarded. *Degree program information:* Part-time programs available. Offers administration, training, and policy studies (Ed D); bilingual education (Ed M, CAGS); counseling (Ed M, CAGS); counseling psychology (Ed D); curriculum and teaching (Ed M, MAT, Ed D, CAGS); developmental studies (Ed M, Ed D, CAGS); early childhood education (Ed M, Ed D, CAGS); education (Ed M, MAT, Ed D, CAGS); education of the deaf (Ed M, CAGS); educational administration (Ed M); educational media and technology (Ed M, Ed D, CAGS); elementary education (Ed M); English and language arts education (Ed M, CAGS); health education (Ed M, CAGS); human resource education (Ed M, CAGS); international educational development (Ed M); Latin and classical studies (MAT); literacy and language (Ed D); mathematics education (Ed M, MAT, Ed D, CAGS); modern foreign language education (Ed M, MAT); physical education and coaching (Ed M, Ed D, CAGS); policy, planning, and administration (Ed M, CAGS); reading education (Ed M, Ed D, CAGS); science education (Ed M, MAT, Ed D, CAGS); social studies education (Ed M, MAT, Ed D, CAGS); special education (Ed M, Ed D, CAGS); teaching of English to speakers of other languages (Ed M, CAGS). *Application deadline:* For fall admission, 2/15 priority date for domestic and international students; for winter admission, 10/1 priority date for domestic and international students. Applications are processed on a rolling basis. *Application fee:* $65. Electronic applications accepted. *Application Contact:* Margaret Sullivan, Graduate Admissions Office, 617-353-4237, Fax: 617-353-8937, E-mail: sedgrad@bu.edu. *Dean ad interim,* Dr. Charles L. Glenn, 617-353-3212, E-mail: glennsed@bu.edu.

School of Law Students: 987 full-time (495 women), 103 part-time (52 women); includes 195 minority (38 African Americans, 2 American Indian/Alaska Native, 125 Asian Americans or Pacific Islanders, 30 Hispanic Americans), 132 international. Average age 27. 7,265 applicants, 19% accepted, 285 enrolled. *Faculty:* 69 full-time (21 women), 72 part-time/adjunct (20 women). Expenses: Contact institution. *Financial support:* In 2006–07, 681 students received support. Career-related internships or fieldwork, Federal Work-Study, institutionally sponsored loans, and scholarships/grants available. Financial award application deadline: 3/1; financial award applicants required to submit CSS PROFILE or FAFSA. In 2006, 262 JDs, 162 master's awarded. *Degree program information:* Part-time and evening/weekend programs available. Offers American law (LL M); banking law (LL M); intellectual property law (LL M); law (JD); taxation (LL M). *Application deadline:* For fall admission, 3/1 for domestic and international students. Applications are processed on a rolling basis. *Application fee:* $60. Electronic applications accepted. *Application Contact:* Joan Horgan, Director of Admissions and Financial Aid, 617-353-3100, Fax: 617-353-0578, E-mail: bulawadm@bu.edu. *Interim Dean,* Maureen O'Rourke, 617-353-3112, Fax: 617-353-7400.

Boston University (continued)

School of Management Students: 419 full-time (161 women), 544 part-time (198 women); includes 138 minority (15 African Americans, 2 American Indian/Alaska Native, 102 Asian Americans or Pacific Islanders, 19 Hispanic Americans), 171 international. Average age 33. 1,737 applicants, 42% accepted, 378 enrolled. *Faculty:* 104 full-time (21 women). Expenses: Contact institution. *Financial support:* Career-related internships or fieldwork, Federal Work-Study, institutionally sponsored loans, and tuition waivers (partial) available. Support available to part-time students. Financial award applicants required to submit FAFSA. In 2006, 395 master's, 8 doctorates awarded. *Degree program information:* Part-time and evening/weekend programs available. Offers accounting (DBA); advanced accounting (Certificate); business administration (Exec MBA, MBA, DBA, Certificate); general management (MBA); healthcare management (MBA); information systems (DBA); investment management (MSIM); management policy (DBA); marketing (DBA); operations management (DBA); organizational behavior (DBA); public and nonprofit management (MBA). *Application deadline:* For fall admission, 5/1 for domestic students. Applications are processed on a rolling basis. *Application fee:* $125. Electronic applications accepted. *Application Contact:* Hayden Estrada, Assistant Dean, Admissions, 617-353-2670, Fax: 617-353-7368, E-mail: mba@bu.edu. *Dean,* Louis Lataif, 617-353-2668, Fax: 617-353-5581, E-mail: lelataif@bu.edu.

School of Medicine Students: 1,365 full-time (769 women), 98 part-time (59 women); includes 366 minority (79 African Americans, 1 American Indian/Alaska Native, 230 Asian Americans or Pacific Islanders, 56 Hispanic Americans), 153 international. Average age 27. Expenses: Contact institution. *Financial support:* Fellowships, research assistantships, teaching assistantships, career-related internships or fieldwork, Federal Work-Study, and institutionally sponsored loans available. Support available to part-time students. In 2006, 153 MDs, 193 master's, 36 doctorates awarded. *Degree program information:* Part-time and evening/weekend programs available. Offers biomedical forensics (MS); medicine (MD, MA, MS, PhD). *Application Contact:* Dr. Robert Witzburg, Associate Dean for Admissions, 617-638-4630. *Dean,* Dr. Karen H. Antman, 617-638-5300.

Division of Graduate Medical Sciences Students: 520 full-time (268 women), 39 part-time (21 women); includes 131 minority (21 African Americans, 86 Asian Americans or Pacific Islanders, 24 Hispanic Americans), 71 international. Average age 25. *Faculty:* 80 full-time (20 women), 134 part-time/adjunct (19 women). Expenses: Contact institution. *Financial support:* In 2006–07, 38 fellowships with tuition reimbursements, 121 research assistantships with tuition reimbursements, 6 teaching assistantships with tuition reimbursements were awarded; Federal Work-Study, scholarships/grants, and traineeships also available. *Degree program information:* Part-time programs available. Offers biochemistry (MA, PhD); cell and molecular biology (PhD); experimental pathology (PhD); immunology (PhD); medical nutrition sciences (MA, PhD); medical sciences (MA, MS, PhD); mental health and behavioral medicine (MA); microbiology (MA, PhD); molecular medicine (PhD); pharmacology and experimental therapeutics (MA, PhD); physiology and biophysics (MA, PhD). *Application deadline:* For spring admission, 10/15 priority date for domestic students. Electronic applications accepted. *Application Contact:* Michelle Hall, Assistant Director of Admissions, 617-638-5121, Fax: 617-638-5740, E-mail: natashah@bu.edu. *Associate Dean,* Dr. Carl Franzblau, 617-638-5120, Fax: 617-638-4842, E-mail: medsci@bu.edu.

School of Public Health Students: 304 full-time (238 women), 404 part-time (323 women); includes 136 minority (40 African Americans, 77 Asian Americans or Pacific Islanders, 19 Hispanic Americans), 75 international. Average age 28. *Faculty:* 90 full-time (45 women), 223 part-time/adjunct (98 women). Expenses: Contact institution. *Financial support:* Career-related internships or fieldwork, Federal Work-Study, institutionally sponsored loans, and scholarships/grants available. Support available to part-time students. In 2006, 246 master's, 9 doctorates awarded. *Degree program information:* Part-time and evening/weekend programs available. Offers biostatistics (MA, MPH, PhD); environmental health (MPH, D Sc); epidemiology (M Sc, MPH, D Sc); health behavior, health promotion, and disease prevention (MPH); health law, bioethics and human rights (MPH); health policy and management (M Sc, MPH, D Sc); international health (MPH, Dr PH, Certificate); maternal and child health (MPH); nurse midwifery education (Certificate); public health (M Sc, MA, MPH, D Sc, Dr PH, PhD, Certificate); social behavioral sciences (Dr PH). *Application deadline:* For fall admission, 2/1 for domestic students; for spring admission, 10/15 for domestic students. Applications are processed on a rolling basis. *Application fee:* $95. Electronic applications accepted. *Application Contact:* LePhan Quan, Assistant Director of Admissions, 617-638-4640, Fax: 617-638-5299, E-mail: asksph@bu.edu. *Dean,* Dr. Robert F. Meenan, 617-638-4640, Fax: 617-638-5299.

School of Social Work Students: 165 full-time (144 women), 194 part-time (169 women); includes 41 minority (16 African Americans, 1 American Indian/Alaska Native, 5 Asian Americans or Pacific Islanders, 19 Hispanic Americans), 4 international. Average age 30. 507 applicants, 87% accepted, 192 enrolled. *Faculty:* 22 full-time (16 women), 29 part-time/adjunct (23 women). Expenses: Contact institution. *Financial support:* In 2006–07, 95 students received support, including 1 research assistantship with full tuition reimbursement available (averaging $8,000 per year); career-related internships or fieldwork, Federal Work-Study, institutionally sponsored loans, and scholarships/grants also available. Support available to part-time students. Financial award application deadline: 3/1; financial award applicants required to submit FAFSA. In 2006, 161 degrees awarded. *Degree program information:* Part-time programs available. Offers clinical practice with groups (MSW); clinical practice with individuals and families (MSW); macro social work practice (MSW); social work and sociology (PhD). *Application deadline:* For fall admission, 3/1 for domestic and international students. Applications are processed on a rolling basis. *Application fee:* $70. Electronic applications accepted. *Application Contact:* Edward M. Greene, Director of Admissions, 617-353-3765, Fax: 617-353-5612, E-mail: busswad@bu.edu. *Dean,* Wilma Peebles-Wilkins, 617-353-3760, Fax: 617-353-5612.

School of Theology Students: 254 full-time (117 women), 42 part-time (16 women); includes 33 minority (16 African Americans, 10 Asian Americans or Pacific Islanders, 7 Hispanic Americans), 72 international. Average age 34. 229 applicants, 70% accepted. *Faculty:* 24 full-time (10 women), 18 part-time/adjunct (5 women). Expenses: Contact institution. *Financial support:* In 2006–07, 7 fellowships (averaging $4,000 per year), 9 research assistantships (averaging $3,000 per year), 27 teaching assistantships (averaging $5,500 per year) were awarded; Federal Work-Study, institutionally sponsored loans, and scholarships/grants also available. Support available to part-time students. Financial award application deadline: 7/15; financial award applicants required to submit FAFSA. In 2006, 26 M Divs, 24 master's, 5 doctorates awarded. *Degree program information:* Part-time programs available. Offers theology (M Div, MSM, MTS, STM, D Min, Th D). *Application deadline:* For fall admission, 2/15 priority date for domestic students; for spring admission, 10/15 priority date for domestic students. Applications are processed on a rolling basis. *Application fee:* $60. Electronic applications accepted. *Application Contact:* Rev. Earl R. Beane, Director of Admissions, 617-353-3036, Fax: 617-358-0140, E-mail: sthadmis@bu.edu. *Interim Dean,* Dr. Ray Hart, 617-353-3050, Fax: 617-353-3061.

University Professors Program Students: 36 full-time (18 women), 3 part-time (all women); includes 2 minority (both Asian Americans or Pacific Islanders), 5 international. Average age 32. 29 applicants, 45% accepted. *Faculty:* 30 full-time (4 women), 1 part-time/adjunct (0 women). Expenses: Contact institution. *Financial support:* In 2006–07, 27 students received support, including 5 fellowships with tuition reimbursements available (averaging $13,000 per year), 6 teaching assistantships with tuition reimbursements available (averaging $14,500 per year); research assistantships, Federal Work-Study, institutionally sponsored loans, scholarships/grants, and tuition waivers (partial) also available. Support available to part-time students. Financial award application deadline: 4/1. In 2006, 6 master's, 6 doctorates awarded. *Degree program information:* Part-time programs available. Offers interdisciplinary studies (MA, PhD). *Application deadline:* For fall admission, 1/15 for domestic and international students; for spring admission, 10/15 for domestic and international students. Applications are processed on a rolling basis. *Application fee:* $65. *Application Contact:* Edna Newmark, Coordinator, 617-353-4020, Fax: 617-353-5084, E-mail: enewmark@bu.edu. *Director,* Bruce Redford, 617-353-4020, Fax: 617-353-5084.

See Close-Up on page 813.

BOWIE STATE UNIVERSITY, Bowie, MD 20715-9465

General Information State-supported, coed, comprehensive institution. CGS member. *Enrollment:* 5,291 graduate, professional, and undergraduate students; 304 full-time matriculated graduate/professional students (236 women), 835 part-time matriculated graduate/professional students (628 women). *Enrollment by degree level:* 1,039 master's, 91 doctoral, 9 other advanced degrees. *Graduate faculty:* 61 full-time (32 women), 57 part-time/adjunct (20 women). Tuition, state resident: full-time $7,344; part-time $306 per credit. Tuition, nonresident: full-time $14,304; part-time $396 per credit. *Required fees:* $1,078; $77 per credit. $539 per term. One-time fee: $40. *Graduate housing:* Room and/or apartments available on a first-come, first-served basis to single students; on-campus housing not available to married students. Typical cost: $4,736 per year ($7,096 including board). Room and board charges vary according to board plan and housing facility selected. Housing application deadline: 8/1. *Student services:* Campus employment opportunities, campus safety program, career counseling, free psychological counseling, international student services, low-cost health insurance, writing training. *Library facilities:* Thurgood Marshall Library. *Online resources:* library catalog, web page, access to other libraries' catalogs. *Collection:* 331,640 titles, 3,152 serial subscriptions.

Computer facilities: 3,144 computers available on campus for general student use. A campuswide network can be accessed from student residence rooms and from off campus. Internet access and online class registration are available. *Web address:* http://www.bowiestate.edu/.

General Application Contact: Dr. Beverly O'Bryant, Dean, 301-860-3406, Fax: 301-860-3414, E-mail: graduatestudiesandresearch@bowiestate.edu.

GRADUATE UNITS

Graduate Programs Students: 303 full-time (236 women), 827 part-time (620 women); includes 941 minority (917 African Americans, 1 American Indian/Alaska Native, 11 Asian Americans or Pacific Islanders, 12 Hispanic Americans), 12 international. Average age 34. 381 applicants, 93% accepted, 284 enrolled. *Faculty:* 61 full-time (32 women), 57 part-time/adjunct (26 women). Expenses: Contact institution. *Financial support:* In 2006–07, 21 research assistantships (averaging $2,880 per year) were awarded; fellowships, career-related internships or fieldwork, Federal Work-Study, institutionally sponsored loans, and unspecified assistantships also available. Support available to part-time students. Financial award application deadline: 4/1. In 2006, 309 master's, 9 doctorates awarded. *Degree program information:* Part-time and evening/weekend programs available. Offers administration of nursing services (MS); applied and computational mathematics (MS); business administration (MBA); computer science (MS, App Sc D); counseling psychology (MA); educational leadership (Ed D); elementary and secondary school administration (M Ed); elementary education (M Ed); English (MA); family nurse practitioner (MS); guidance and counseling (M Ed); human resource development (MA); information systems analyst (Certificate); management information systems (MS); mental halth counseling (MA); nursing education (MS); organizational communication (MA, Certificate); public administration (MPA); reading education (M Ed); school administration and supervision (M Ed); secondary education (M Ed); special education (M Ed); teaching (MAT). *Application deadline:* For fall admission, 4/1 priority date for domestic and international students; for spring admission, 11/1 priority date for domestic and international students. Applications are processed on a rolling basis. *Application fee:* $40. Electronic applications accepted. *Application Contact:* Angela Issac, Information Contact. *Dean,* Dr. Beverly O'Bryant, 301-860-3406, Fax: 301-860-3414, E-mail: graduatestudiesandresearch@bowiestate.edu.

BOWLING GREEN STATE UNIVERSITY, Bowling Green, OH 43403

General Information State-supported, coed, university. CGS member. *Enrollment:* 19,108 graduate, professional, and undergraduate students; 1,527 full-time matriculated graduate/professional students (881 women), 1,047 part-time matriculated graduate/professional students (734 women). *Enrollment by degree level:* 1,885 master's, 606 doctoral, 83 other advanced degrees. Tuition, state resident: part-time $535 per hour. Tuition, nonresident: part-time $884 per hour. *Graduate housing:* On-campus housing not available. *Student services:* Campus employment opportunities, campus safety program, career counseling, child daycare facilities, disabled student services, exercise/wellness program, free psychological counseling, grant writing training, international student services, low-cost health insurance, multicultural affairs office, teacher training, writing training. *Library facilities:* Jerome Library plus 2 others. *Online resources:* library catalog, web page, access to other libraries' catalogs. *Research affiliation:* Spectra Group, Inc. (photoscience).

Computer facilities: 6,240 computers available on campus for general student use. A campuswide network can be accessed from student residence rooms and from off campus. Internet access and online class registration are available. *Web address:* http://www.bgsu.edu/.

General Application Contact: Dr. Terry L. Lawrence, Assistant Dean for Graduate Admissions and Studies, 419-372-7713, Fax: 419-372-8569, E-mail: tlawren@bgnet.bgsu.edu.

GRADUATE UNITS

Graduate College Students: 1,527 full-time (881 women), 1,047 part-time (734 women); includes 223 minority (130 African Americans, 6 American Indian/Alaska Native, 33 Asian Americans or Pacific Islanders, 54 Hispanic Americans), 394 international. Average age 30. 2,541 applicants, 54% accepted, 711 enrolled. *Faculty:* 598 full-time (231 women), 396 part-time/adjunct (166 women). Expenses: Contact institution. *Financial support:* In 2006–07, 503 research assistantships with full and partial tuition reimbursements (averaging $7,688 per year), 658 teaching assistantships with full and partial tuition reimbursements (averaging $9,274 per year) were awarded; fellowships with full tuition reimbursements, career-related internships or fieldwork, Federal Work-Study, institutionally sponsored loans, tuition waivers (full and partial), and unspecified assistantships also available. Support available to part-time students. Financial award applicants required to submit FAFSA. In 2006, 1,015 master's, 98 doctorates awarded. *Degree program information:* Part-time and evening/weekend programs available. *Application fee:* $30. Electronic applications accepted. *Application Contact:* Dr. Terry L. Lawrence, Assistant Dean for Graduate Admissions and Studies, 419-372-7713, Fax: 419-372-8569, E-mail: tlawren@bgnet.bgsu.edu. *Vice Provost for Research and Dean,* Dr. Heinz Bulmahn, 419-372-7714, Fax: 419-372-8569, E-mail: bulmahn@bgnet.bgsu.edu.

College of Arts and Sciences Students: 821 full-time (430 women), 180 part-time (107 women); includes 82 minority (41 African Americans, 5 American Indian/Alaska Native, 18 Asian Americans or Pacific Islanders, 18 Hispanic Americans), 245 international. Average age 29. 1,306 applicants, 48% accepted, 264 enrolled. *Faculty:* 317 full-time (112 women), 165 part-time/adjunct (54 women). Expenses: Contact institution. *Financial support:* In 2006–07, 209 research assistantships with full and partial tuition reimbursements (averaging $9,131 per year), 475 teaching assistantships with full and partial tuition reimbursements (averaging $10,282 per year) were awarded; career-related internships or fieldwork, Federal Work-Study, institutionally sponsored loans, tuition waivers (full and partial), and unspecified assistantships also available. Support available to part-time students. Financial award applicants required to submit FAFSA. In 2006, 256 master's, 83 doctorates awarded. *Degree program information:* Part-time programs available. Offers 2-D studio art (MA, MFA); 3-D studio art (MA, MFA); American culture studies (MA, MAT, PhD); applied philosophy (PhD); applied statistics (MS); art education (MA); art history (MA); arts and sciences (MA, MAT, MFA, MPA, MS, PhD); biological sciences (MAT, MS, PhD); chemistry (MAT, MS); clinical psychology (MA, PhD); communication studies (MA, PhD); computer art (MA, MFA); computer science (MS); creative writing (MFA); demography and population studies (MA); design (MFA); developmental psychology (MA, PhD); English (MA, PhD); experimental psychology (MA, PhD); fiction (MFA); French (MA, MAT); French education (MAT); geology (MS); geophysics (MS); German (MA, MAT); graphics (MFA); history (MA, MAT, PhD); industrial/organizational psychology (MA, PhD); institutional theory and history (PhD); literature (MA); mathematics (MA, MAT, PhD); philosophy (MA); photochemical sciences (PhD); physics (MAT, MS); poetry (MFA); popular culture (MA); probability and statistics (PhD); public administration (MPA); public history (MA); quantitative psychology (MA, PhD); rhetoric and writing (PhD); scientific and technical communication (MA); social psychology (MA); sociology (PhD); Spanish (MA, MAT); Spanish education (MAT); theatre and film (MA, MAT, PhD). *Application fee:* $30. Electronic applications accepted. *Dean,* Dr. Donald Nieman, 419-372-2340.

College of Business Administration Students: 165 full-time (82 women), 71 part-time (27 women); includes 21 minority (8 African Americans, 4 Asian Americans or Pacific Islanders, 9 Hispanic Americans), 74 international. Average age 28. 247 applicants, 56% accepted, 87 enrolled. *Faculty:* 65 full-time (19 women), 4 part-time/adjunct (2 women). Expenses: Contact institution. *Financial support:* In 2006–07, 86 research assistantships with full tuition reimbursements (averaging $5,382 per year), 19 teaching assistantships with full tuition reimbursements (averaging $5,212 per year) were awarded; career-related internships or fieldwork, Federal Work-Study, institutionally sponsored loans, and unspecified assistantships also available. Financial award applicants required to submit FAFSA. In 2006, 174 degrees awarded. *Degree program information:* Part-time and evening/weekend programs available. Offers accountancy (M Acc); applied statistics (MS); business (MBA); business administration (M Acc, MA, MBA, MOD, MS); economics (MA); organization development (MOD). *Application deadline:* Applications are processed on a rolling basis. *Application fee:* $30. Electronic applications accepted. *Dean,* Dr. Rodney Rogers, 419-372-2747.

College of Education and Human Development Students: 336 full-time (247 women), 691 part-time (537 women); includes 82 minority (55 African Americans, 1 American Indian/Alaska Native, 7 Asian Americans or Pacific Islanders, 19 Hispanic Americans), 23 international. Average age 32. 602 applicants, 65% accepted, 236 enrolled. *Faculty:* 112 full-time (67 women), 194 part-time/adjunct (97 women). Expenses: Contact institution. *Financial support:* In 2006–07, 169 research assistantships with full tuition reimbursements (averaging $7,188 per year), 46 teaching assistantships with full tuition reimbursements (averaging $8,246 per year) were awarded; career-related internships or fieldwork, Federal Work-Study, institutionally sponsored loans, tuition waivers (full and partial), and unspecified assistantships also available. Support available to part-time students. Financial award applicants required to submit FAFSA. In 2006, 484 master's, 14 doctorates awarded. *Degree program information:* Part-time and evening/weekend programs available. Offers assistive technology (M Ed); business education (M Ed); classroom technology (M Ed); college student personnel (MA); counseling (M Ed, MA); curriculum (M Ed); curriculum and teaching (M Ed); developmental kinesiology (M Ed); early childhood intervention (M Ed); education and human development (M Ed, MA, MFCS, MRC, Ed D, PhD, Ed S, Sp Ed); education and intervention services (M Ed, MA, MRC, Ed S, Sp Ed); educational administration and supervision (M Ed, Ed S); food and nutrition (MFCS); gifted education (M Ed); hearing impaired intervention (M Ed); higher education administration (PhD); human development and family studies (MFCS); leadership and policy studies (M Ed, MA, Ed D, PhD, Ed S); leadership studies (Ed D); master teaching (M Ed); mental health counseling (MA); mild/moderate intervention (M Ed); moderate/intensive intervention (M Ed); reading (M Ed, Ed S); recreation and leisure (M Ed); rehabilitation counseling (MRC); school counseling (M Ed); school psychology (M Ed, Sp Ed); special education (M Ed); sport administration (M Ed). *Application deadline:* Applications are processed on a rolling basis. *Application fee:* $30. Electronic applications accepted. *Dean,* Dr. Josué Cruz, 419-372-7403.

College of Health and Human Services Students: 66 full-time (58 women), 63 part-time (44 women); includes 22 minority (15 African Americans, 3 Asian Americans or Pacific Islanders, 4 Hispanic Americans), 15 international. Average age 29. 171 applicants, 47% accepted, 64 enrolled. *Faculty:* 26 full-time (9 women), 6 part-time/adjunct (3 women). Expenses: Contact institution. *Financial support:* In 2006–07, 15 research assistantships with full tuition reimbursements (averaging $9,105 per year), 27 teaching assistantships with full tuition reimbursements (averaging $6,129 per year) were awarded; career-related internships or fieldwork, Federal Work-Study, institutionally sponsored loans, and unspecified assistantships also available. Financial award applicants required to submit FAFSA. In 2006, 31 degrees awarded. *Degree program information:* Part-time and evening/weekend programs available. Offers communication disorders (PhD); criminal justice (MSCJ); health and human services (MPH, MS, MSCJ, PhD); public health (MPH); speech-language pathology (MS). *Application fee:* $30. Electronic applications accepted. *Dean,* Dr. Linda Petrosino, 419-372-8243.

College of Musical Arts Students: 109 full-time (56 women), 19 part-time (11 women); includes 7 minority (5 African Americans, 2 Hispanic Americans), 31 international. Average age 26. 176 applicants, 55% accepted, 49 enrolled. *Faculty:* 55 full-time (20 women), 14 part-time/adjunct (6 women). Expenses: Contact institution. *Financial support:* In 2006–07, 14 research assistantships with full tuition reimbursements (averaging $4,923 per year), 74 teaching assistantships with full tuition reimbursements (averaging $5,479 per year) were awarded; career-related internships or fieldwork, Federal Work-Study, and unspecified assistantships also available. Financial award applicants required to submit FAFSA. In 2006, 45 degrees awarded. *Degree program information:* Part-time programs available. Offers composition (MM); contemporary music (DMA); ethnomusicology (MM); music education (MM); music history (MM); music theory (MM); performance (MM). *Application deadline:* For fall admission, 3/1 priority date for domestic students. *Application fee:* $30. Electronic applications accepted. *Application Contact:* Dr. Robert Satterlee, Graduate Coordinator, 419-372-2360. *Dean,* Dr. Richard Kennell, 419-372-2188.

College of Technology Students: 30 full-time (8 women), 22 part-time (7 women); includes 9 minority (6 African Americans, 1 Asian American or Pacific Islander, 2 Hispanic Americans), 6 international. Average age 32. 39 applicants, 74% accepted, 11 enrolled. *Faculty:* 23 full-time (4 women), 13 part-time/adjunct (4 women). Expenses: Contact institution. *Financial support:* In 2006–07, 10 research assistantships with full tuition reimbursements (averaging $7,568 per year), 17 teaching assistantships with full tuition reimbursements (averaging $8,827 per year) were awarded; career-related internships or fieldwork, Federal Work-Study, institutionally sponsored loans, tuition waivers (full and partial), and unspecified assistantships also available. Financial award applicants required to submit FAFSA. In 2006, 24 degrees awarded. *Degree program information:* Part-time programs available. Offers career and technology education (M Ed); construction management (MIT); manufacturing technology (MIT); technology (M Ed, MIT). *Application fee:* $30. Electronic applications accepted. *Dean,* Dr. C. Wayne Unsell, 419-372-2438.

Interdisciplinary Studies Average age 28. Expenses: Contact institution. *Financial support:* Fellowships with full tuition reimbursements, research assistantships with full tuition reimbursements, teaching assistantships with full tuition reimbursements, Federal Work-Study and unspecified assistantships available. Financial award applicants required to submit FAFSA. In 2006, 1 master's, 1 doctorate awarded. *Degree program information:* Part-time programs available. Offers interdisciplinary studies (M Ed, MA, MS, PhD). *Application fee:* $30. Electronic applications accepted. *Application Contact:* Dr. Terry L. Lawrence, Assistant Dean for Graduate Admissions and Studies, 419-372-7713, Fax: 419-372-8569, E-mail: tlawren@bgnet.bgsu.edu.

See Close-Up on page 815.

BRADLEY UNIVERSITY, Peoria, IL 61625-0002

General Information Independent, coed, comprehensive institution. CGS member. *Enrollment:* 6,126 graduate, professional, and undergraduate students; 226 full-time matriculated graduate/professional students (105 women), 481 part-time matriculated graduate/professional students (213 women). *Enrollment by degree level:* 667 master's, 40 doctoral. *Graduate faculty:* 245. *Graduate housing:* Room and/or apartments available to single students; on-campus housing not available to married students. *Student services:* Campus employment opportunities, campus safety program, career counseling, disabled student services, exercise/wellness program, free psychological counseling, international student services, low-cost health insurance, multicultural affairs office, teacher training. *Library facilities:* Cullom-Davis Library. *Online resources:* library catalog, web page, access to other libraries' catalogs. *Collection:* 518,000 titles, 3,529 serial subscriptions. *Research affiliation:* Northern Research Laboratory, Peoria School of Medicine, Caterpillar, Inc., Ford Motor Credit/Visteon, Illinois Manufacturing Extension Center.

Computer facilities: 2,000 computers available on campus for general student use. A campuswide network can be accessed from student residence rooms and from off campus. Internet access and online class registration are available. *Web address:* http://www.bradley.edu/.

General Application Contact: Leslie M. Betz, Director, Graduate Admissions, 309-677-2375, Fax: 309-677-3343, E-mail: lbetz@bradley.edu.

GRADUATE UNITS

Graduate School Students: 226 full-time (105 women), 481 part-time (213 women); includes 28 minority (7 African Americans, 3 American Indian/Alaska Native, 16 Asian Americans or Pacific Islanders, 2 Hispanic Americans), 206 international. 628 applicants, 60% accepted, 196 enrolled. *Faculty:* 240. Expenses: Contact institution. *Financial support:* In 2006–07, 300 students received support, including 5 research assistantships with full tuition reimbursements available (averaging $11,000 per year); fellowships, teaching assistantships, career-related internships or fieldwork, institutionally sponsored loans, scholarships/grants, tuition waivers (partial), and unspecified assistantships also available. Support available to part-time students. Financial award application deadline: 4/1. In 2006, 280 degrees awarded. *Degree program information:* Part-time and evening/weekend programs available. *Application deadline:* For fall admission, 5/15 priority date for domestic and international students; for spring admission, 10/15 priority date for domestic and international students. Applications are processed on a rolling basis. *Application fee:* $40 ($50 for international students). *Application Contact:* Leslie M. Betz, Director, Graduate Admissions, 309-677-2375, Fax: 309-677-3343, E-mail: lbetz@bradley.edu. *Dean of the Graduate School,* Dr. Robert I. Bolla, 309-677-2375, Fax: 309-677-3343.

College of Education and Health Sciences Students: 69 full-time (57 women), 173 part-time (122 women); includes 13 minority (1 African American, 1 American Indian/Alaska Native, 10 Asian Americans or Pacific Islanders, 1 Hispanic American), 1 international. 61 applicants, 61% accepted, 27 enrolled. *Faculty:* 78. Expenses: Contact institution. *Financial support:* In 2006–07, 13 research assistantships with full and partial tuition reimbursements (averaging $5,060 per year) were awarded; teaching assistantships, career-related internships or fieldwork, institutionally sponsored loans, scholarships/grants, tuition waivers (partial), and unspecified assistantships also available. Support available to part-time students. Financial award application deadline: 4/1. In 2006, 84 degrees awarded. *Degree program information:* Part-time and evening/weekend programs available. Offers curriculum and instruction (MA); education and health sciences (MA, MSN, DPT); human development counseling (MA); leadership in educational administration (MA); leadership in human service administration (MA); nurse administered anesthesia (MSN); nursing administration (MSN); physical therapy (DPT). *Application deadline:* For fall admission, 5/15 priority date for domestic students, 5/15 for international students; for spring admission, 10/15 priority date for domestic students, 10/15 for international students. Applications are processed on a rolling basis. *Application fee:* $40 ($50 for international students). *Dean,* Dr. Joan Sattler, 309-677-3180.

College of Engineering and Technology Students: 68 full-time (9 women), 100 part-time (23 women), 118 international. 292 applicants, 57% accepted, 73 enrolled. *Faculty:* 43. Expenses: Contact institution. *Financial support:* In 2006–07, 17 research assistantships with full and partial tuition reimbursements (averaging $5,680 per year) were awarded; teaching assistantships, institutionally sponsored loans, scholarships/grants, tuition waivers (partial), and unspecified assistantships also available. Support available to part-time students. Financial award application deadline: 4/1. In 2006, 88 degrees awarded. *Degree program information:* Part-time and evening/weekend programs available. Offers civil engineering and construction (MSCE); electrical engineering (MSEE); engineering and technology (MSCE, MSEE, MSIE, MSME, MSMFE); industrial engineering (MSIE); manufacturing engineering (MSIE); mechanical engineering (MSME). *Application deadline:* For fall admission, 5/15 priority date for domestic and international students; for spring admission, 10/15 priority date for domestic and international students. Applications are processed on a rolling basis. *Application fee:* $40 ($50 for international students). *Dean,* Dr. Richard Johnson, 309-677-2721.

College of Liberal Arts and Sciences Students: 30 full-time (15 women), 78 part-time (33 women); includes 4 minority (1 African American, 3 Asian Americans or Pacific Islanders), 60 international. 178 applicants, 61% accepted, 43 enrolled. *Faculty:* 65. Expenses: Contact institution. *Financial support:* In 2006–07, 18 research assistantships with full and partial tuition reimbursements (averaging $5,060 per year) were awarded; teaching assistantships, career-related internships or fieldwork, institutionally sponsored loans, scholarships/grants, tuition waivers (partial), and unspecified assistantships also available. Support available to part-time students. Financial award application deadline: 4/1. In 2006, 52 degrees awarded. *Degree program information:* Part-time and evening/weekend programs available. Offers biology (MS); chemistry (MS); computer information systems (MS); computer science (MS); English (MA); liberal arts and sciences (MA, MLS, MS); liberal studies (MLS). *Application deadline:* For fall admission, 5/15 priority date for domestic and international students; for spring admission, 10/15 priority date for domestic and international students. Applications are processed on a rolling basis. *Application fee:* $40 ($50 for international students). *Dean,* Dr. Claire Etaugh, 309-677-2380.

Foster College of Business Administration Students: 48 full-time (18 women), 130 part-time (35 women); includes 11 minority (5 African Americans, 2 American Indian/Alaska Native, 3 Asian Americans or Pacific Islanders, 1 Hispanic American), 26 international. 76 applicants, 74% accepted, 49 enrolled. *Faculty:* 44. Expenses: Contact institution. *Financial support:* In 2006–07, 21 research assistantships with full and partial tuition reimbursements (averaging $5,460 per year), 15 teaching assistantships with full and partial tuition reimbursements (averaging $5,460 per year) were awarded; fellowships, career-related internships or fieldwork, scholarships/grants, tuition waivers (partial), and unspecified assistantships also available. Support available to part-time students. Financial award application deadline: 4/1. In 2006, 55 degrees awarded. *Degree program information:* Part-time and evening/weekend programs available. Offers accounting (MSA); business administration (MBA, MSA). *Application deadline:* For fall admission, 5/15 priority date for domestic and international students; for spring admission, 10/15 priority date for domestic and international students. Applications are processed on a rolling basis. *Application fee:* $40 ($50 for international students). *Application Contact:* Janet Davidson, Assistant Director of Graduate Programs, 309-677-2256, Fax: 309-677-3374, E-mail: jldavids@bradley.edu. *Dean,* Dr. Rob Baer, 309-677-2255, Fax: 309-677-3374.

Slane College of Communications and Fine Arts Students: 11 full-time (6 women), 1 international. 21 applicants, 29% accepted, 4 enrolled. *Faculty:* 10. Expenses: Contact institution. *Financial support:* In 2006–07, 3 research assistantships with full and partial tuition reimbursements (averaging $5,060 per year) were awarded; scholarships/grants, tuition waivers (partial), and unspecified assistantships also available. Support available to part-time students. Financial award application deadline: 4/1. In 2006, 1 degree awarded. *Degree program information:* Part-time and evening/weekend programs available. Offers ceramics (MA, MFA); communications and fine arts (MA, MFA); drawing/illustration (MA, MFA); interdisciplinary art (MA, MFA); painting (MA, MFA); photography (MA, MFA); printmaking (MA, MFA); sculpture (MA, MFA); visual communication and design (MA, MFA). *Application deadline:* For fall admission, 4/1 priority date for domestic students, 4/11 priority date for international students; for spring admission, 11/1 priority date for domestic and international students. Applications are processed on a rolling basis. *Application fee:* $40 ($50 for international students). *Dean,* Dr. Jeffrey Huberman, 309-677-2360.

BRANDEIS UNIVERSITY, Waltham, MA 02454-9110

General Information Independent, coed, university. CGS member. *Enrollment:* 5,313 graduate, professional, and undergraduate students; 1,323 full-time matriculated graduate/professional students (731 women), 255 part-time matriculated graduate/professional students (94 women). *Graduate faculty:* 348 full-time (130 women), 153 part-time/adjunct (75 women). *Graduate housing:* Room and/or apartments available on a first-come, first-served basis to single students; on-campus housing not available to married students. Housing application deadline: 6/1. *Student services:* Campus employment opportunities, campus safety program, career counseling, child daycare facilities, disabled student services, exercise/wellness program, free psychological counseling, grant writing training, international student services, low-cost health insurance, multicultural affairs office, teacher training, writing training. *Library facilities:* Goldfarb Library plus 2 others. *Online resources:* library catalog, web page, access to other libraries' catalogs. *Collection:* 1.2 million titles, 38,717 audiovisual materials.

Brandeis University (continued)

Computer facilities: Computer purchase and lease plans are available. 104 computers available on campus for general student use. A campuswide network can be accessed from student residence rooms and from off campus. Internet access and online class registration, educational software are available. *Web address:* http://www.brandeis.edu/.

General Application Contact: Margaret Haley, Assistant Dean, Graduate Admissions, 781-736-3406, Fax: 781-736-3412, E-mail: haley@brandeis.edu.

GRADUATE UNITS

Graduate School of Arts and Sciences Students: 1,323 full-time (731 women), 255 part-time (94 women); includes 114 minority (31 African Americans, 9 American Indian/Alaska Native, 45 Asian Americans or Pacific Islanders, 29 Hispanic Americans), 429 international. Average age 30. 1,400 applicants, 17% accepted. *Faculty:* 348 full-time (130 women), 153 part-time/adjunct (75 women). Expenses: Contact institution. *Financial support:* Fellowships, research assistantships, teaching assistantships, career-related internships or fieldwork, institutionally sponsored loans, scholarships/grants, and tuition waivers (full and partial) available. Support available to part-time students. Financial award application deadline: 4/15; financial award applicants required to submit CSS PROFILE or FAFSA. In 2006, 261 master's, 102 doctorates awarded. *Degree program information:* Part-time programs available. Offers acting (MFA); American history (MA, PhD); anthropology (MA, PhD); anthropology and women's and gender studies (MA); arts and sciences (MA, MAT, MFA, MS, PhD, Certificate); biochemistry (MS, PhD); biophysics and structural biology (MS, PhD); coexistence and conflict (MA); cognitive neuroscience (PhD); comparative history (MA, PhD); composition and theory (MA, MFA, PhD); design (MFA); English and American literature (MA, PhD); English and women's and gender studies (MA); English and women's studies (MA); general psychology (MA); genetic counseling (MS); genetics (PhD); inorganic chemistry (MS, PhD); Jewish day school (MAT); Jewish professional leadership); mathematics (MA, PhD); microbiology (PhD); molecular and cell biology (MS, PhD); molecular biology (PhD); music and women's and gender studies (MA); music and women's studies (MA); musicology (MA, MFA, PhD); Near Eastern and Judaic studies (MA, PhD); Near Eastern and Judaic studies and sociology (PhD); Near Eastern and Judaic studies and women's and gender studies (MA); Near Eastern and Judaic studies and women's studies (MA); neurobiology (PhD); neuroscience (MS, PhD); organic chemistry (MS, PhD); physical chemistry (MS, PhD); physics (MS, PhD); politics (MA, PhD); premedical studies (Certificate); public education elementary (MAT); secondary education (English, history, biology, Bible) (MAT); social policy and sociology (PhD); social/developmental psychology (PhD); sociology (MA, PhD); sociology and women's and gender studies (MA); studio art (Certificate); teaching of Hebrew (MAT). *Application deadline:* For fall admission, 1/15 priority date for domestic and international students; for spring admission, 12/1 for domestic and international students. Applications are processed on a rolling basis. *Application fee:* $55. Electronic applications accepted. *Application Contact:* Margaret Haley, Assistant Dean, Graduate Admissions, 781-736-3406, Fax: 781-736-3412, E-mail: haley@brandeis.edu. *Dean*, Dr. Gregory L. Freeze, 781-736-2766, Fax: 781-736-3412.

Michtom School of Computer Science Students: 44 full-time (14 women), 3 part-time; includes 11 minority (1 African American, 10 Asian Americans or Pacific Islanders), 13 international. Average age 26. 120 applicants, 27% accepted. *Faculty:* 10 full-time (1 woman). Expenses: Contact institution. *Financial support:* In 2006–07, 40 students received support, including research assistantships with tuition reimbursements available (averaging $20,400 per year), teaching assistantships with tuition reimbursements available (averaging $20,400 per year); institutionally sponsored loans and tuition waivers (full and partial) also available. Financial award application deadline: 4/15; financial award applicants required to submit CSS PROFILE or FAFSA. In 2006, 14 master's, 4 doctorates awarded. *Degree program information:* Part-time programs available. Offers computer science (MA, PhD, Certificate). *Application deadline:* For fall admission, 2/15 for domestic students. *Application fee:* $55. Electronic applications accepted. *Application Contact:* Myrna Fox, Information Contact, 781-736-2701, E-mail: maf@cs.brandeis.edu. *Director of Graduate Studies*, Dr. James Pustejovsky, 781-736-2709, Fax: 781-736-2741.

The Heller School for Social Policy and Management *Degree program information:* Part-time programs available. Offers child, youth, and family policy and management (MBA); health care policy and management (MBA); international development (MA); international health policy and management (MS); social policy (MPP, PhD); social policy and management (MBA); sustainable development (MA, MBA). Electronic applications accepted.

International Business School *Degree program information:* Part-time and evening/weekend programs available. Offers finance (MSF); international business (MBAi); international economics and finance (MA, PhD); international finance/international economics (MBAi). Electronic applications accepted.

See Close-Up on page 817.

BRANDON UNIVERSITY, Brandon, MB R7A 6A9, Canada

General Information Province-supported, coed, comprehensive institution. *Graduate housing:* Room and/or apartments available on a first-come, first-served basis to single students; on-campus housing not available to married students.

GRADUATE UNITS

Department of Rural Development Offers rural development (MRD, Diploma). Electronic applications accepted.

Faculty of Education Offers curriculum (Diploma); curriculum studies (M Ed); education administration (M Ed, Diploma); guidance and counseling (M Ed, Diploma); special education (M Ed, Diploma).

School of Music *Degree program information:* Part-time programs available. Offers music education (M Mus); performance and literature (M Mus). Electronic applications accepted.

BRENAU UNIVERSITY, Gainesville, GA 30501

General Information Independent, Undergraduate: women only; graduate: coed, comprehensive institution. *Enrollment:* 846 graduate, professional, and undergraduate students; 209 full-time matriculated graduate/professional students (173 women), 344 part-time matriculated graduate/professional students (264 women). *Enrollment by degree level:* 526 master's, 27 other advanced degrees. *Graduate faculty:* 45 full-time (33 women), 38 part-time/adjunct (16 women). *Student services:* Campus employment opportunities, career counseling, child daycare facilities, exercise/wellness program, teacher training. *Library facilities:* Trustee Library. *Online resources:* library catalog, web page.

Computer facilities: 200 computers available on campus for general student use. A campuswide network can be accessed from student residence rooms and from off campus. Internet access and online class registration are available. *Web address:* http://www.brenau.edu/.

General Application Contact: Nathan Goss, Admissions Coordinator, 770-534-6162, Fax: 770-538-4701, E-mail: ngoss@brenau.edu.

GRADUATE UNITS

Graduate Programs Students: 209 full-time (173 women), 344 part-time (264 women); includes 108 minority (91 African Americans, 1 American Indian/Alaska Native, 7 Asian Americans or Pacific Islanders, 9 Hispanic Americans), 5 international. Average age 39. 485 applicants, 49% accepted, 216 enrolled. *Faculty:* 45 full-time (33 women), 38 part-time/adjunct (16 women). Expenses: Contact institution. *Financial support:* In 2006–07, 14 students received support. Scholarships/grants available. Support available to part-time students. Financial award application deadline: 7/15; financial award applicants required to submit FAFSA. In 2006, 196 master's, 24 other advanced degrees awarded. *Degree program information:* Part-time and evening/weekend programs available. Postbaccalaureate distance learning degree programs offered (no on-campus study). *Application deadline:* Applications are processed on a rolling basis. *Application fee:* $30. *Application Contact:* Nathan Goss, Admissions Coordinator, 770-534-6162, Fax: 770-538-4701, E-mail: ngoss@brenau.edu. *Dean*, Dr. Helen Ray, 770-534-6119.

School of Business and Mass Communication Students: 49 full-time (32 women), 148 part-time (89 women); includes 52 minority (45 African Americans, 2 Asian Americans or Pacific Islanders, 5 Hispanic Americans), 2 international. Average age 35. 222 applicants, 55% accepted, 111 enrolled. *Faculty:* 12 full-time (6 women), 16 part-time/adjunct (5 women). Expenses: Contact institution. *Financial support:* Career-related internships or fieldwork available. Financial award application deadline: 7/15; financial award applicants required to submit FAFSA. In 2006, 64 degrees awarded. *Degree program information:* Part-time and evening/weekend programs available. Postbaccalaureate distance learning degree programs offered (no on-campus study). Offers accounting (MBA); healthcare management (MBA); leadership development (MBA); management (MBA); organizational development (MS). *Application deadline:* Applications are processed on a rolling basis. *Application fee:* $30. Electronic applications accepted. *Application Contact:* Nathan Goss, Admissions Coordinator, 770-534-6162, Fax: 770-538-4701, E-mail: ngoss@brenau.edu. *Dean*, Dr. Bill Haney, 770-538-4707, Fax: 770-537-4701, E-mail: whaney@brenau.edu.

School of Education Students: 104 full-time (89 women), 160 part-time (140 women); includes 34 minority (28 African Americans, 3 Asian Americans or Pacific Islanders, 3 Hispanic Americans), 2 international. Average age 37. 187 applicants. *Faculty:* 12 full-time (9 women), 17 part-time/adjunct (9 women). Expenses: Contact institution. *Financial support:* Career-related internships or fieldwork available. Financial award application deadline: 7/15; financial award applicants required to submit FAFSA. In 2006, 92 master's, 24 other advanced degrees awarded. *Degree program information:* Part-time and evening/weekend programs available. Offers early childhood education (M Ed, Ed S); learning disabilities (M Ed); middle grades education (M Ed, Ed S). *Application deadline:* Applications are processed on a rolling basis. *Application fee:* $30. *Application Contact:* Nathan Goss, Admissions Coordinator, 770-534-6162, Fax: 770-538-4701, E-mail: ngoss@brenau.edu. *Dean*, Dr. William B. Ware, 770-534-6220, Fax: 770-534-6221, E-mail: bware@brenau.edu.

School of Health and Science Students: 56 full-time (52 women), 36 part-time (35 women); includes 22 minority (18 African Americans, 1 American Indian/Alaska Native, 2 Asian Americans or Pacific Islanders, 1 Hispanic American), 1 international. Average age 31. 76 applicants, 51% accepted, 28 enrolled. *Faculty:* 21 full-time (18 women), 5 part-time/adjunct (2 women). Expenses: Contact institution. *Financial support:* In 2006–07, 14 students received support. Scholarships/grants available. Support available to part-time students. Financial award application deadline: 7/15; financial award applicants required to submit FAFSA. In 2006, 40 degrees awarded. *Degree program information:* Part-time and evening/weekend programs available. Offers family nurse practitioner (MS); nurse educator (MS); occupational therapy (MS); psychology (MS). *Application deadline:* Applications are processed on a rolling basis. *Application fee:* $30. *Application Contact:* Nathan Goss, Admissions Coordinator, 770-534-6162, Fax: 770-538-4701, E-mail: ngoss@brenau.edu. *Dean*, Dr. Gale Starich, 777-718-5305, Fax: 770-297-5929, E-mail: gstarich@brenau.edu.

BRESCIA UNIVERSITY, Owensboro, KY 42301-3023

General Information Independent-religious, coed, comprehensive institution.

GRADUATE UNITS

Program in Curriculum and Instruction *Degree program information:* Part-time and evening/weekend programs available. Offers curriculum and instruction (MSCI). Electronic applications accepted.

Program in Management *Degree program information:* Part-time and evening/weekend programs available. Offers management (MSM).

BRIAR CLIFF UNIVERSITY, Sioux City, IA 51104-0100

General Information Independent-religious, coed, comprehensive institution. *Graduate housing:* Room and/or apartments available on a first-come, first-served basis to single students; on-campus housing not available to married students. Housing application deadline: 6/1.

GRADUATE UNITS

Program in Education Postbaccalaureate distance learning degree programs offered (minimal on-campus study). Offers education (MA). Program offered during the summer only. Electronic applications accepted.

Program in Human Resource Management *Degree program information:* Part-time and evening/weekend programs available. Offers human resource management (MA).

Program in Nursing *Degree program information:* Part-time and evening/weekend programs available. Offers nursing (MSN).

BRIDGEWATER STATE COLLEGE, Bridgewater, MA 02325-0001

General Information State-supported, coed, comprehensive institution. *Enrollment:* 9,655 graduate, professional, and undergraduate students; 2,150 matriculated graduate/professional students. *Enrollment by degree level:* 1,900 master's, 250 other advanced degrees. *Graduate faculty:* 140 full-time. *Graduate housing:* On-campus housing not available. *Student services:* Campus employment opportunities, career counseling, child daycare facilities, disabled student services, exercise/wellness program, free psychological counseling, international student services, low-cost health insurance, multicultural affairs office, teacher training, writing training. *Library facilities:* Clement Maxwell Library. *Online resources:* library catalog, web page, access to other libraries' catalogs. *Collection:* 577,881 titles, 31,617 serial subscriptions.

Computer facilities: Computer purchase and lease plans are available. 780 computers available on campus for general student use. A campuswide network can be accessed from student residence rooms and from off campus. Internet access and online class registration, student account information, application software are available. *Web address:* http://www.bridgew.edu/.

General Application Contact: Dr. Raymond Charles Guillette, Assistant Dean School of Graduate Studies, 508-531-2919, Fax: 508-531-6162, E-mail: rguillette@bridgew.edu.

GRADUATE UNITS

School of Graduate Studies Students: 1,900. *Faculty:* 140 full-time. Expenses: Contact institution. *Financial support:* Career-related internships or fieldwork, health care benefits, and unspecified assistantships available. Support available to part-time students. *Degree program information:* Part-time and evening/weekend programs available. *Application deadline:* For fall admission, 2/15 priority date for domestic students; for spring admission, 10/1 priority date for domestic students. *Application fee:* $50. *Application Contact:* Dr. Raymond Charles Guillette, Assistant Dean School of Graduate Studies, 508-531-2919, Fax: 508-531-6162, E-mail: rguillette@bridgew.edu. *Dean*, Dr. William Smith, 508-531-1300, Fax: 508-531-6162, E-mail: wismith@bridgew.edu.

School of Arts and Sciences Students: 275. Expenses: Contact institution. *Financial support:* Career-related internships or fieldwork, health care benefits, and unspecified assistantships available. Support available to part-time students. *Degree program information:* Part-time and evening/weekend programs available. Offers art (MAT); arts and sciences (MA, MAT, MPA, MS, MSW); biological sciences (MAT); computer science (MS); criminal justice (MS); English (MA, MAT); history (MAT); mathematics (MAT); physical sciences (MAT); physics (MAT); psychology (MA); public administration (MPA); social work (MSW). *Application deadline:* For fall admission, 3/1 priority date for domestic students; for spring admission, 10/1 priority date for domestic students. *Application fee:* $50. *Application Contact:* Dr. Raymond Charles Guillette, Assistant Dean School of Graduate Studies, 508-531-2919, Fax: 508-531-6162, E-mail: rguillette@bridgew.edu. *Dean*, Dr. Howard London, 508-531-1218.

School of Business Students: 50. Expenses: Contact institution. *Financial support:* Health care benefits and unspecified assistantships available. Support available to part-time students. *Degree program information:* Part-time and evening/weekend programs available. Offers accounting and finance (MSM); business (MSM); management (MSM). *Application deadline:* For fall admission, 3/1 priority date for domestic students; for spring admission, 10/1 priority date for domestic students. *Application fee:* $50. *Application Contact:* Dr. Raymond Charles Guillette, Assistant Dean School of Graduate Studies, 508-531-

2919, Fax: 508-531-6162, E-mail: rguillette@bridgew.edu. *Dean,* Dr. Catherine Morgan, 508-531-6151, E-mail: cmorgan@bridgew.edu.

School of Education and Allied Science Students: 1,575. Expenses: Contact institution. *Financial support:* Career-related internships or fieldwork, health care benefits, and unspecified assistantships available. Support available to part-time students. *Degree program information:* Part-time and evening/weekend programs available. Offers counseling (M Ed, CAGS); early childhood education (M Ed); education and allied science (M Ed, MAT, MS, CAGS); educational leadership (M Ed, CAGS); elementary education (M Ed); health promotion (M Ed); instructional technology (M Ed); physical education (MS); reading (M Ed, CAGS); secondary education (MAT); special education (M Ed). *Application deadline:* For fall admission, 3/1 priority date for domestic students; for spring admission, 10/1 priority date for domestic students. *Application fee:* $50. *Application Contact:* Dr. Raymond Charles Guillette, Assistant Dean School of Graduate Studies, 508-531-2919, Fax: 508-531-6162, E-mail: rguillette@bridgew.edu. *Dean,* Dr. Anna Bradfield, 508-697-1347.

BRIERCREST SEMINARY, Caronport, SK S0H 0S0, Canada

General Information Independent-religious, coed, graduate-only institution. *Enrollment by degree level:* 151 master's. *Graduate faculty:* 6 full-time (0 women), 25 part-time/adjunct (2 women). *Graduate housing:* Rooms and/or apartments guaranteed to single students and available on a first-come, first-served basis to married students. Typical cost: $4,800 (including board) for single students. *Student services:* Campus employment opportunities, career counseling, exercise/wellness program, free psychological counseling. *Library facilities:* Archibald Library. *Online resources:* library catalog, web page. *Collection:* 79,000 titles, 326 serial subscriptions, 5,600 audiovisual materials.

Computer facilities: 29 computers available on campus for general student use. A campuswide network can be accessed from off campus. Internet access and online class registration are available. *Web address:* http://www.briercrest.ca/.

General Application Contact: Kevin Weeks, Enrollment Management Officer, 306-756-3221, Fax: 306-756-5500, E-mail: kweeks@briercrest.ca.

GRADUATE UNITS

Graduate Programs Students: 35 full-time (13 women), 123 part-time (41 women). Average age 40. 104 applicants, 72% accepted, 46 enrolled. *Faculty:* 5 full-time (0 women), 23 part-time/adjunct (2 women). Expenses: Contact institution. *Financial support:* Teaching assistantships, career-related internships or fieldwork available. In 2006, 44 degrees awarded. *Degree program information:* Part-time programs available. Offers Biblical studies (M Div); leadership (MA); leadership and management (M Div); marriage and family counseling (MA); missions (MA); New Testament (MATS); Old Testament (MATS); organizational leadership (MA); pastoral counseling (M Div, MA); pastoral ministry (M Div); theological studies (M Div); theology (MATS); worship (M Div, MA); youth and family ministry (M Div, MA). *Application deadline:* Applications are processed on a rolling basis. *Application fee:* $25. *Application Contact:* Kevin Weeks, Enrollment Management Officer, 306-756-3221, Fax: 306-756-5500, E-mail: kweeks@briercrest.ca. *Dean of the Seminary,* Dr. David Guretzki, 306-756-3231, Fax: 306-756-5500, E-mail: dguretzki@briercrest.ca.

BRIGHAM YOUNG UNIVERSITY, Provo, UT 84602-1001

General Information Independent-religious, coed, university. CGS member. *Enrollment:* 34,185 graduate, professional, and undergraduate students; 2,674 full-time matriculated graduate/professional students (995 women), 727 part-time matriculated graduate/professional students (248 women). *Graduate faculty:* 1,100 full-time (181 women), 149 part-time/adjunct (50 women). *Graduate housing:* Rooms and/or apartments available on a first-come, first-served basis to single and married students. *Student services:* Campus employment opportunities, campus safety program, career counseling, disabled student services, exercise/wellness program, free psychological counseling, international student services, low-cost health insurance, multicultural affairs office, teacher training, writing training. *Library facilities:* Main library plus 2 others. *Online resources:* library catalog, web page, access to other libraries' catalogs. *Collection:* 3.5 million titles, 27,161 serial subscriptions.

Computer facilities: Computer purchase and lease plans are available. 2,000 computers available on campus for general student use. A campuswide network can be accessed from student residence rooms and from off campus. Internet access and online class registration, intranet are available. *Web address:* http://www.byu.edu/.

General Application Contact: Adviser, 801-422-4541, Fax: 801-422-0270, E-mail: gradstudies@byu.edu.

GRADUATE UNITS

Graduate Studies Students: 2,674 full-time (995 women), 727 part-time (248 women); includes 348 minority (25 African Americans, 24 American Indian/Alaska Native, 186 Asian Americans or Pacific Islanders, 113 Hispanic Americans), 240 international. 3,554 applicants, 47% accepted, 1298 enrolled. *Faculty:* 1,077 full-time (172 women), 165 part-time/adjunct (41 women). Expenses: Contact institution. *Financial support:* In 2006–07, 1,881 students received support, including 291 fellowships, 739 research assistantships, 766 teaching assistantships; career-related internships or fieldwork, institutionally sponsored loans, and tuition waivers (full and partial) also available. Support available to part-time students. Financial award applicants required to submit FAFSA. In 2006, 164 first professional degrees, 963 master's, 79 doctorates, 23 other advanced degrees awarded. *Degree program information:* Part-time and evening/weekend programs available. *Application deadline:* For fall admission, 1/10 priority date for domestic students; for winter admission, 2/1 priority date for domestic students; for spring admission, 2/1 priority date for domestic students. Applications are processed on a rolling basis. *Application fee:* $50. Electronic applications accepted. *Application Contact:* Adviser, 801-422-4541, Fax: 801-378-5238, E-mail: gradstudies@byu.edu. *Dean,* Bonnie Brinton, 801-422-4465, Fax: 801-422-0270, E-mail: gradstudies@byu.edu.

College of Family, Home, and Social Sciences Students: 330 full-time (164 women), 26 part-time (11 women); includes 43 minority (5 African Americans, 5 American Indian/Alaska Native, 22 Asian Americans or Pacific Islanders, 11 Hispanic Americans), 15 international. Average age 28. 425 applicants, 29% accepted, 111 enrolled. *Faculty:* 135 full-time (30 women), 17 part-time/adjunct (7 women). Expenses: Contact institution. *Financial support:* In 2006–07, 153 students received support, including 4 fellowships with tuition reimbursements available (averaging $5,000 per year), 73 research assistantships with partial tuition reimbursements available, 72 teaching assistantships with partial tuition reimbursements available (averaging $5,367 per year); career-related internships or fieldwork, institutionally sponsored loans, tuition waivers (full and partial), and administrative aides, paid field practica also available. Support available to part-time students. Financial award applicants required to submit FAFSA. In 2006, 74 master's, 19 doctorates awarded. Offers anthropology (MA); clinical psychology (PhD); family, home, and social sciences (MA, MS, MSW, PhD); general psychology (MS); history (MA); marriage and family therapy (MS, PhD); marriage, family and human development (MS, PhD); psychology (PhD); social work (MSW); sociology (MS, PhD). *Application fee:* $50. Electronic applications accepted. *Dean,* Dr. David B. Magleby, 801-422-2083, Fax: 801-422-2084, E-mail: david_magleby@byu.edu.

College of Fine Arts and Communications Students: 121 full-time (68 women), 38 part-time (21 women); includes 13 minority (9 Asian Americans or Pacific Islanders, 4 Hispanic Americans), 1 international. Average age 28. 121 applicants, 51% accepted, 55 enrolled. *Faculty:* 101 full-time (23 women), 5 part-time/adjunct (2 women). Expenses: Contact institution. *Financial support:* In 2006–07, 24 research assistantships (averaging $3,390 per year), 87 teaching assistantships (averaging $4,587 per year) were awarded; career-related internships or fieldwork, institutionally sponsored loans, tuition waivers (partial), and administrative aides, supplementary awards also available. Support available to part-time students. Financial award applicants required to submit FAFSA. In 2006, 47 degrees awarded. Offers art education (MA); art history (MA); composition (MM); conducting (MM); fine arts and communications (MA, MFA, MM); mass communication (MA); music education (MA, MM); musicology (MA); performance (MM); production design (MFA); studio art (MFA); theatre and media arts (MA). *Application fee:* $50. Electronic applications accepted. *Dean,* Dr. Stephen M. Jones, 801-422-2819, Fax: 801-422-0253.

College of Health and Human Performance Students: 55 full-time (33 women), 60 part-time (28 women); includes 12 minority (1 African American, 3 American Indian/Alaska Native, 5 Asian Americans or Pacific Islanders, 3 Hispanic Americans). Average age 28. 87 applicants, 47% accepted, 31 enrolled. *Faculty:* 40 full-time (7 women), 1 (woman) part-time/adjunct. Expenses: Contact institution. *Financial support:* In 2006–07, 45 research assistantships with full and partial tuition reimbursements (averaging $7,943 per year), 45 teaching assistantships with full and partial tuition reimbursements (averaging $11,080 per year) were awarded; fellowships, career-related internships or fieldwork, institutionally sponsored loans, scholarships/grants, tuition waivers (full and partial), and administrative aides also available. Support available to part-time students. Financial award application deadline: 3/1. In 2006, 27 master's, 3 doctorates awarded. Offers athletic training (MS); exercise physiology (MS, PhD); health and human performance (MPH, MS, PhD); health promotion (MS, PhD); health science (MPH); physical medicine and rehabilitation (PhD); sports pedagogy (MS); youth and family recreation (MS). *Application deadline:* For fall admission, 2/1 for domestic students. *Application fee:* $50. Electronic applications accepted. *Application Contact:* Sandra L. Alger, Graduate Secretary, 801-422-4271, Fax: 801-422-0557, E-mail: sandy_alger@byu.edu. *Dean,* Sara Lee Gibb, 801-422-2645, Fax: 801-422-0557, E-mail: sara_lee_gibb@byu.edu.

College of Humanities Students: 211 full-time (132 women), 53 part-time (35 women); includes 22 minority (8 Asian Americans or Pacific Islanders, 14 Hispanic Americans), 22 international. Average age 27. 198 applicants, 61% accepted, 99 enrolled. *Faculty:* 152 full-time (33 women). Expenses: Contact institution. *Financial support:* In 2006–07, 15 fellowships with partial tuition reimbursements (averaging $1,710 per year), 32 research assistantships with partial tuition reimbursements (averaging $2,890 per year), 164 teaching assistantships with partial tuition reimbursements (averaging $12,970 per year) were awarded; career-related internships or fieldwork, institutionally sponsored loans, tuition waivers (full and partial), and student instructorships also available. Support available to part-time students. In 2006, 72 master's, 23 other advanced degrees awarded. *Degree program information:* Part-time programs available. Offers comparative literature (MA); comparative studies (MA); English (MA); French studies (MA); general linguistics (MA); German studies (MA); humanities (MA); language acquisition and teaching (MA); Portuguese linguistics (MA); Portuguese literature (MA); Spanish linguistics (MA); Spanish teaching (MA); Spanish/Latin American Literature (MA); Spanish/Peninsular literature (MA); teaching English as a second language (MA, Certificate). *Application fee:* $50. Electronic applications accepted. *Dean,* Dr. John R. Rosenberg, 801-422-2779, Fax: 801-422-0308, E-mail: john_rosenberg@byu.edu.

College of Life Sciences Students: 117 full-time (59 women), 21 part-time (5 women); includes 10 minority (1 African American, 1 American Indian/Alaska Native, 4 Asian Americans or Pacific Islanders, 4 Hispanic Americans), 4 international. Average age 25. 104 applicants, 56% accepted, 55 enrolled. *Faculty:* 93 full-time (10 women), 4 part-time/adjunct (2 women). Expenses: Contact institution. *Financial support:* In 2006–07, 126 students received support, including fellowships with full and partial tuition reimbursements available (averaging $5,500 per year), research assistantships with full and partial tuition reimbursements available (averaging $12,943 per year), teaching assistantships with full and partial tuition reimbursements available (averaging $12,823 per year); career-related internships or fieldwork, institutionally sponsored loans, scholarships/grants, and tuition awards also available. Support available to part-time students. Financial award application deadline: 4/15. In 2006, 35 master's, 3 doctorates awarded. *Degree program information:* Part-time programs available. Offers agronomy (MS); biological science education (MS); food science (MS); genetics and biotechnology (MS); integrative biology (MS, PhD); life sciences (MS, PhD); microbiology (MS, PhD); molecular biology (MS, PhD); neuroscience (MS, PhD); nutrition (MS); physiology and developmental biology (MS, PhD); wildlife and wildlands conservation (MS, PhD). *Application deadline:* For fall admission, 1/31 for domestic and international students. *Application fee:* $50. Electronic applications accepted. *Application Contact:* Sue Pratley, Application Contact, 801-422-3963, Fax: 801-422-0050, E-mail: sue_pratley@byu.edu. *Dean,* Dr. Rodney J. Brown, 801-422-3963, Fax: 801-422-0050.

College of Nursing Students: 12 full-time (10 women), 15 part-time (12 women); includes 3 minority (2 Asian Americans or Pacific Islanders, 1 Hispanic American). Average age 25. 28 applicants, 54% accepted, 15 enrolled. *Faculty:* 26 full-time (24 women). Expenses: Contact institution. *Financial support:* In 2006–07, 21 students received support, including 2 research assistantships with full and partial tuition reimbursements available (averaging $10,000 per year), 3 teaching assistantships with full and partial tuition reimbursements available (averaging $10,000 per year); institutionally sponsored loans, scholarships/grants, tuition waivers (full), and unspecified assistantships also available. Support available to part-time students. Financial award application deadline: 2/1; financial award applicants required to submit FAFSA. In 2006, 9 degrees awarded. Offers family nurse practitioner (MS). *Application deadline:* For spring admission, 12/1 for domestic students. Applications are processed on a rolling basis. *Application fee:* $50. Electronic applications accepted. *Interim Dean,* Dr. Mary Williams, 801-422-5626, Fax: 801-422-0536, E-mail: mary_williams@byu.edu.

College of Physical and Mathematical Sciences Students: 338 full-time (76 women), 19 part-time (10 women); includes 3 African Americans, 17 Asian Americans or Pacific Islanders, 3 Hispanic Americans, 83 international. Average age 25. 203 applicants, 48% accepted, 72 enrolled. *Faculty:* 157 full-time (6 women). Expenses: Contact institution. *Financial support:* In 2006–07, 293 students received support, including 17 fellowships with full tuition reimbursements available (averaging $20,333 per year), 136 research assistantships with full and partial tuition reimbursements available (averaging $14,917 per year), 139 teaching assistantships with full and partial tuition reimbursements available (averaging $14,493 per year); career-related internships or fieldwork, institutionally sponsored loans, scholarships/grants, health care benefits, tuition waivers (full and partial), and unspecified assistantships also available. Support available to part-time students. In 2006, 77 master's, 19 doctorates awarded. *Degree program information:* Part-time programs available. Offers analytical chemistry (MS, PhD); applied statistics (MS); biochemistry (MS, PhD); computer science (MS, PhD); geology (MS); inorganic chemistry (MS, PhD); mathematics (MS, PhD); mathematics education (MA); organic chemistry (MS, PhD); physical and mathematical sciences (MA, MS, PhD); physical chemistry (MS, PhD); physics (MS, PhD); physics and astronomy (PhD). *Application fee:* $50. *Application Contact:* Lynn Patten, Executive Secretary, 801-422-4022, Fax: 801-422-0550, E-mail: lynn_patten@byu.edu. *Dean,* Earl M. Woolley, 801-422-2674, Fax: 801-422-0550, E-mail: emwoolle@chemdept.byu.edu.

College of Religious Education Students: 8 full-time (1 woman), 6 part-time. *Faculty:* 63 full-time (5 women). Expenses: Contact institution. *Financial support:* In 2006–07, 14 students received support. Scholarships/grants available. In 2006, 3 degrees awarded. Offers religious education (MRE). *Application deadline:* For fall admission, 12/1 for international students; for winter admission, 12/1 for domestic students. *Application fee:* $50. *Application Contact:* Dr. Clyde J. Williams, Professor of Ancient Scripture, 801-422-2124, Fax: 801-422-0616. *Dean,* Dr. Terry B. Ball, 801-422-2736, Fax: 801-422-0616, E-mail: terry_ball@byu.edu.

David O. McKay School of Education Students: 187 full-time (119 women), 112 part-time (64 women); includes 34 minority (2 African Americans, 5 American Indian/Alaska Native, 22 Asian Americans or Pacific Islanders, 5 Hispanic Americans), 25 international. Average age 34. 250 applicants, 57% accepted, 105 enrolled. *Faculty:* 63 full-time (25 women), 28 part-time/adjunct (9 women). Expenses: Contact institution. *Financial support:* In 2006–07, 108 students received support, including 58 research assistantships (averaging $25,120 per year), 34 teaching assistantships (averaging $18,000 per year); fellowships, career-related internships or fieldwork, institutionally sponsored loans, scholarships/grants, tuition waivers (partial), and unspecified assistantships also available. Support available to part-time students. Financial award applicants required to submit FAFSA. In 2006, 73 master's, 19 doctorates awarded. *Degree program information:* Part-time programs available. Offers counseling psychology (PhD); education (M Ed, MA, MS, PhD, Ed S); educational leadership and foundations (M Ed, PhD); instructional psychology and technology (MS, PhD); literacy education (M Ed, MA); school psychology (Ed S); special education (MS); speech-language pathology (MS); teacher education (M Ed, MA). *Application deadline:* For fall admission, 2/1 for domestic and international students; for winter admission, 2/1 for domestic and international students; for spring admission, 2/15 for domestic and international students.

Brigham Young University (continued)

Application fee: $50. Electronic applications accepted. *Application Contact:* Linda Parker, Director, Education Advisement Center, 801-422-3428, Fax: 801-422-0195, E-mail: linda_parker@byu.edu. *Dean,* Dr. K. Richard Young, 801-422-3695, Fax: 801-422-0200, E-mail: richard_young@byu.edu.

Ira A. Fulton College of Engineering and Technology Students: 267 full-time (22 women), 136 part-time (11 women); includes 52 minority (3 African Americans, 2 American Indian/Alaska Native, 34 Asian Americans or Pacific Islanders, 13 Hispanic Americans), 26 international. Average age 25. 223 applicants, 63% accepted, 109 enrolled. *Faculty:* 105 full-time (0 women), 13 part-time/adjunct (0 women). Expenses: Contact institution. *Financial support:* In 2006–07, 4 fellowships with partial tuition reimbursements (averaging $18,750 per year), 196 research assistantships with partial tuition reimbursements (averaging $13,342 per year), 93 teaching assistantships with partial tuition reimbursements (averaging $9,025 per year) were awarded; career-related internships or fieldwork, institutionally sponsored loans, and scholarships/grants also available. Support available to part-time students. Financial award application deadline: 3/15; financial award applicants required to submit FAFSA. In 2006, 115 master's, 15 doctorates awarded. Offers chemical engineering (MS, PhD); civil engineering (MS, PhD); construction management (MS); electrical and computer engineering (MS, PhD); engineering and technology (MS, PhD); information technology (MS); manufacturing systems (MS); mechanical engineering (MS, PhD); technology teacher education (MS). *Application deadline:* For fall admission, 1/15 for domestic and international students; for winter admission, 9/15 for domestic students, 2/15 for international students. Applications are processed on a rolling basis. *Application fee:* $50. Electronic applications accepted. *Dean,* Dr. Alan R. Parkinson, 801-422-4327, Fax: 801-422-0218, E-mail: college@et.byu.edu.

J. Reuben Clark Law School Students: 472 full-time (179 women); includes 82 minority (6 African Americans, 5 American Indian/Alaska Native, 38 Asian Americans or Pacific Islanders, 33 Hispanic Americans), 6 international. Average age 26. 940 applicants, 27% accepted, 153 enrolled. *Faculty:* 37 full-time (7 women), 33 part-time/adjunct (14 women). Expenses: Contact institution. *Financial support:* In 2006–07, 252 students received support, including 243 fellowships (averaging $1,500 per year); research assistantships, teaching assistantships, career-related internships or fieldwork, institutionally sponsored loans, scholarships/grants, and health care benefits also available. Financial award application deadline: 6/1; financial award applicants required to submit FAFSA. In 2006, 164 degrees awarded. Offers law (JD, LL M). *Application deadline:* For fall admission, 3/1 for domestic students. Applications are processed on a rolling basis. *Application fee:* $50. *Application Contact:* GaeLynn Kuchar, Admissions Director, 801-422-4277, Fax: 801-422-0389, E-mail: kucharg@lawgate.byu.edu. *Dean,* Kevin J Worthen, 801-422-6383, Fax: 801-422-0389, E-mail: worthenk@lawgate.byu.edu.

Marriott School of Management Students: 556 full-time (132 women), 241 part-time (51 women); includes 56 minority (4 African Americans, 5 American Indian/Alaska Native, 25 Asian Americans or Pacific Islanders, 22 Hispanic Americans), 58 international. Average age 29. 975 applicants, 63% accepted, 493 enrolled. *Faculty:* 128 full-time (11 women), 48 part-time/adjunct (15 women). Expenses: Contact institution. *Financial support:* In 2006–07, 491 students received support, including 114 research assistantships with full and partial tuition reimbursements available (averaging $3,855 per year), 18 teaching assistantships with full and partial tuition reimbursements available (averaging $1,277 per year); career-related internships or fieldwork, institutionally sponsored loans, scholarships/grants, and tuition waivers (full and partial) also available. Financial award application deadline: 4/15; financial award applicants required to submit FAFSA. In 2006, 438 degrees awarded. Offers accountancy (M Acc); business administration (MBA); information systems (MISM); management (EMPA, M Acc, MBA, MISM, MPA); public management (EMPA, MPA). *Application fee:* $50. Electronic applications accepted. *Dean,* Dr. Ned C. Hill, 801-422-4122, Fax: 801-422-0499.

BROCK UNIVERSITY, St. Catharines, ON L2S 3A1, Canada

General Information Province-supported, coed, university. *Enrollment:* 17,453 graduate, professional, and undergraduate students; 644 full-time matriculated graduate/professional students (377 women), 525 part-time matriculated graduate/professional students (386 women). *Enrollment by degree level:* 1,100 master's, 69 doctoral. *Graduate faculty:* 523 full-time (205 women), 64 part-time/adjunct (29 women). *Graduate housing:* Room and/or apartments available on a first-come, first-served basis to single students; on-campus housing not available to married students. Typical cost: $5,860 per year ($9,000 including board). Room and board charges vary according to board plan and housing facility selected. Housing application deadline: 5/28. *Student services:* Campus employment opportunities, campus safety program, career counseling, child daycare facilities, disabled student services, exercise/wellness program, free psychological counseling, grant writing training, international student services, low-cost health insurance, multicultural affairs office, teacher training, writing training. *Library facilities:* James A. Gibson Library plus 1 other. *Online resources:* library catalog, web page, access to other libraries' catalogs. *Collection:* 769,873 titles, 27,251 audiovisual materials. *Research affiliation:* Registered Nurses Association of Ontario (nursing best practices), Canadian Honey Council (agriculture/therapeutic product development), Fly Fishing Canada/Trout Unlimited Canada (fisheries management), Henry Ford Health Centre (cance epidemiology).

Computer facilities: Computer purchase and lease plans are available. 379 computers available on campus for general student use. A campuswide network can be accessed from student residence rooms and from off campus. Internet access and online class registration are available. *Web address:* http://www.brocku.ca/.

General Application Contact: Charlotte F. Sheridan, Associate Director, Faculty of Graduate Studies, 905-688-5550 Ext. 4390, Fax: 905-688-0748, E-mail: csherida@brocku.ca.

GRADUATE UNITS

Faculty of Graduate Studies Students: 644 full-time (377 women), 525 part-time (386 women). 1,278 applicants, 59% accepted, 534 enrolled. *Faculty:* 523 full-time (205 women), 64 part-time/adjunct (29 women). Expenses: Contact institution. *Financial support:* Fellowships, research assistantships, teaching assistantships, career-related internships or fieldwork, scholarships/grants, unspecified assistantships, and bursaries available. In 2006, 352 master's, 7 doctorates awarded. *Degree program information:* Part-time and evening/weekend programs available. *Application deadline:* Applications are processed on a rolling basis. *Application fee:* $75. Electronic applications accepted. *Application Contact:* Charlotte F. Sheridan, Associate Director, Faculty of Graduate Studies, 905-688-5550 Ext. 4390, Fax: 905-688-0748, E-mail: csherida@brocku.ca. *Dean, Faculty of Graduate Studies,* Dr. Marilyn Rose, 905-688-5550 Ext. 3884, Fax: 905-378-5705, E-mail: mrose@brocku.ca.

Faculty of Applied Health Sciences Students: 75 full-time (50 women), 4 part-time (1 woman). 93 applicants, 55% accepted, 42 enrolled. *Faculty:* 67 full-time (40 women), 4 part-time/adjunct (0 women). Expenses: Contact institution. *Financial support:* Fellowships, research assistantships, teaching assistantships, career-related internships or fieldwork, scholarships/grants, unspecified assistantships, and bursaries available. Support available to part-time students. In 2006, 22 degrees awarded. Offers applied health sciences (M Sc, MA). *Application deadline:* For fall admission, 2/15 for domestic students. *Application fee:* $75. Electronic applications accepted. *Application Contact:* Michael I. Plyley, Associate Dean, Research and Graduate Studies, 905-688-5550 Ext. 3383, Fax: 905-984-4851, E-mail: mplyley@brocku.ca. *Dean,* Dr. John Corlett, 905-688-5550 Ext. 3385, Fax: 905-984-4851, E-mail: john.corlett@brocku.ca.

Faculty of Business Students: 226 full-time (113 women), 32 part-time (15 women). 315 applicants, 87% accepted, 156 enrolled. *Faculty:* 69 full-time (16 women). Expenses: Contact institution. In 2006, 97 degrees awarded. *Degree program information:* Part-time programs available. Offers accountancy (M Acc); business administration (MBA); management (M Sc). *Application deadline:* Applications are processed on a rolling basis. Electronic applications accepted. *Application Contact:* Shari Sekel, Director, 905-688-5550 Ext. 3916, Fax: 905-688-4286, E-mail: shari.sekel@brocku.ca. *Dean,* Dr. Martin Kusy, 905-688-5550 Ext. 4006, Fax: 905-688-2593, E-mail: mkusy@brocku.ca.

Faculty of Education Students: 73 full-time (62 women), 356 part-time (275 women). 277 applicants, 72% accepted, 141 enrolled. *Faculty:* 40 full-time (24 women), 37 part-time/adjunct (18 women). Expenses: Contact institution. *Financial support:* Fellowships, research assistantships, teaching assistantships, scholarships/grants available. In 2006, 156 master's, 4 doctorates awarded. *Degree program information:* Part-time and evening/weekend programs available. Offers education (M Ed, PhD). *Application deadline:* For fall admission, 4/15 for domestic students. *Application fee:* $100. Electronic applications accepted. *Application Contact:* Lynn Duhaime, Administrative Coordinator, 905-688-5550 Ext. 3340, Fax: 905-688-5091, E-mail: lynn.duhaime@brocku.ca. *Dean,* Dr. James Heap, 905-688-5550 Ext. 3712, Fax: 905-685-4131, E-mail: jheap@brocku.ca.

Faculty of Humanities Students: 46 full-time (20 women), 19 part-time (7 women). 92 applicants, 68% accepted, 43 enrolled. *Faculty:* 109 full-time (45 women). Expenses: Contact institution. *Financial support:* Fellowships, research assistantships, teaching assistantships, scholarships/grants, unspecified assistantships, and bursaries available. In 2006, 20 master's awarded. *Degree program information:* Part-time programs available. Offers applied linguistics (MA); classics (MA); English (MA); history (MA); philosophy (MA); studies in comparative literatures and arts (MA). *Application fee:* $75. Electronic applications accepted. *Application Contact:* Charlotte F. Sheridan, Associate Director, Faculty of Graduate Studies, 905-688-5550 Ext. 4390, Fax: 905-688-0748, E-mail: csherida@brocku.ca. *Dean,* Dr. Rosemary Hale, 905-688-5550 Ext. 4562, Fax: 905-984-4848, E-mail: rhale@brocku.ca.

Faculty of Mathematics and Science Students: 88 full-time (41 women), 6 part-time (1 woman). 189 applicants, 35% accepted, 48 enrolled. *Faculty:* 115 full-time (21 women), 10 part-time/adjunct (3 women). Expenses: Contact institution. *Financial support:* Fellowships, research assistantships, teaching assistantships, scholarships/grants, unspecified assistantships, and bursaries available. In 2006, 12 master's, 2 doctorates awarded. *Degree program information:* Part-time programs available. Offers biological sciences (M Sc, PhD); biology (M Sc, PhD); biotechnology (M Sc, PhD); chemistry (M Sc, PhD); computer science (M Sc); earth sciences (M Sc); mathematics and statistics (M Sc); physics (M Sc). *Application deadline:* Applications are processed on a rolling basis. *Application fee:* $75. Electronic applications accepted. *Application Contact:* Charlotte F. Sheridan, Associate Director, Faculty of Graduate Studies, 905-688-5550 Ext. 4390, Fax: 905-688-0748, E-mail: csherida@brocku.ca. *Dean,* Dr. Ian Brindle, 905-688-5550 Ext. 3421, Fax: 905-641-0406, E-mail: ibrindle@brocku.ca.

Faculty of Social Sciences Students: 126 full-time (84 women), 91 part-time (73 women). 349 applicants, 50% accepted, 125 enrolled. *Faculty:* 123 full-time (59 women), 13 part-time/adjunct (8 women). Expenses: Contact institution. *Financial support:* Fellowships, research assistantships, teaching assistantships, career-related internships or fieldwork, scholarships/grants, unspecified assistantships, and bursaries available. In 2006, 45 master's, 1 doctorate awarded. *Degree program information:* Part-time programs available. Offers applied disability studies (MA, MADS, Diploma); behavioral neuroscience (MA, PhD); business economics (MBE); Canadian politics (MA); child and youth studies (MA); geography (MA); international and comparative politics (MA); life span development (MA, PhD); political philosophy (MA); political science (MA); popular culture (MA); psychology (MA, PhD); public administration (MA); social justice and equity studies (MA); social personality (MA, PhD). *Application fee:* $75. Electronic applications accepted. *Application Contact:* Charlotte F. Sheridan, Associate Director, Faculty of Graduate Studies, 905-688-5550 Ext. 4390, Fax: 905-688-0748, E-mail: csherida@brocku.ca. *Dean,* Dr. David Siegel, 905-688-5550 Ext. 3425, Fax: 905-641-5076, E-mail: dsiegel@brocku.ca.

BROOKLYN COLLEGE OF THE CITY UNIVERSITY OF NEW YORK, Brooklyn, NY 11210-2889

General Information State and locally supported, coed, comprehensive institution. CGS member. *Enrollment:* 15,947 graduate, professional, and undergraduate students; 356 full-time matriculated graduate/professional students (268 women), 2,883 part-time matriculated graduate/professional students (1,959 women). *Enrollment by degree level:* 3,066 master's, 173 other advanced degrees. Tuition, state resident: full-time $6,400; part-time $270 per credit. Tuition, nonresident: full-time $12,000; part-time $500 per credit. *Required fees:* $118 per semester. *Graduate housing:* On-campus housing not available. *Student services:* Campus employment opportunities, career counseling, child daycare facilities, disabled student services, exercise/wellness program, free psychological counseling, international student services, low-cost health insurance, multicultural affairs office, writing training. *Library facilities:* Brooklyn College Library plus 1 other. *Online resources:* library catalog, web page, access to other libraries' catalogs. *Collection:* 1.3 million titles, 13,500 serial subscriptions, 21,731 audiovisual materials. *Research affiliation:* The After School Corporation (Psychology), Solazyme (Biology), Childrens Progress Inc. (Education), Knowles Science Teaching Foundation (Science and Mathematics Education), Petroleum Research Fund (fundamental research is currently supported in chemistry, the earth sciences, chemical and petroleum engineering).

Computer facilities: 800 computers available on campus for general student use. A campuswide network can be accessed from off campus. Internet access and online class registration are available. *Web address:* http://www.brooklyn.cuny.edu/.

General Application Contact: Karen Alleyne-Pierre, Director of Admissions Services and Enrollment Communications, 718-951-5902, Fax: 718-951-4506, E-mail: grads@brooklyn.cuny.edu.

GRADUATE UNITS

Division of Graduate Studies Students: 356 full-time (268 women), 2,883 part-time (1,959 women); includes 1,319 minority (866 African Americans, 3 American Indian/Alaska Native, 159 Asian Americans or Pacific Islanders, 291 Hispanic Americans), 278 international. 2,725 applicants, 60% accepted, 901 enrolled. Expenses: Contact institution. *Financial support:* Career-related internships or fieldwork, Federal Work-Study, institutionally sponsored loans, and scholarships/grants available. Support available to part-time students. Financial award application deadline: 5/1; financial award applicants required to submit FAFSA. In 2006, 1,167 master's, 171 other advanced degrees awarded. *Degree program information:* Part-time and evening/weekend programs available. Offers accounting (MA, MS); acting (MFA); applied biology (MA); applied chemistry (MA); applied geology (MA); applied physics (MA); art history (MA, PhD); audiology (Au D); biology (MA, PhD); chemistry (MA, PhD); community health (MA, MPH, MS); community health education (MA); computer and information science (MA, PhD); computer science and health science (MS); creative writing (MFA); criticism and history (MA); design and technical production (MFA); digital art (MFA); directing (MFA); dramaturgy (MFA); drawing and painting (MFA); economics (MA); economics and computer and information science (MPS); economics/accounting (MA); English (MA, PhD); exercise science and rehabilitation (MS); experimental psychology (MA); fiction (MFA); French (MA); geology (MA, PhD); grief counseling (CAS); health care management (MPH); health care policy and administration (MPH); history (MA, PhD); industrial and organizational psychology (MA); information systems (MS); Judaic studies (MA); liberal studies (MA); mathematics (MA, PhD); mental health counseling (MA); modern languages and literature (PhD); nutrition (MS); nutrition sciences (MS); performance and interactive media arts (MFA, CAS); performing arts management (MFA); photography (MFA); physical education (MS, MS Ed); physics (MA, PhD); playwriting (MFA); poetry (MFA); political science (MA, PhD); political science, urban policy and administration (MA); printmaking (MFA); psychology (PhD); public health (MPH); sculpture (MFA); secondary mathematics education (MA); sociology (MA, PhD); Spanish (MA); speech (MA, MS Ed); speech and hearing sciences (PhD); speech pathology (MS); television and radio (MS); television production (MFA); thanatology (MA); theater (PhD). The division offers courses at Brooklyn College that are creditable toward the CUNY doctoral program. *Application deadline:* For fall admission, 3/1 for domestic students, 2/1 for international students; for spring admission, 11/1 for domestic students, 10/1 for international students. *Application fee:* $125. Electronic applications accepted. *Application Contact:* Karen Alleyne-Pierre, Director of Admissions Services and Enrollment Communications, 718-951-5902, Fax: 718-951-4506, E-mail: grads@brooklyn.cuny.edu. *Dean,* Dr. Louise Hainline, 718-951-5252, Fax: 718-951-4727, E-mail: louiseh@brooklyn.cuny.edu.

Conservatory of Music Students: 2 full-time (1 woman), 52 part-time (32 women); includes 10 minority (3 African Americans, 1 Asian American or Pacific Islander, 6 Hispanic Americans), 25 international. 46 applicants, 74% accepted, 20 enrolled. Expenses: Contact institution.

Financial support: Career-related internships or fieldwork, Federal Work-Study, institutionally sponsored loans, and scholarships/grants available. Support available to part-time students. Financial award application deadline: 5/1; financial award applicants required to submit FAFSA. In 2006, 24 degrees awarded. *Degree program information:* Part-time programs available. Offers composition (MM); music (DMA, PhD); music education (MA); musicology (MA); performance practice (MM). The department offers courses at Brooklyn College that are creditable toward the CUNY doctoral degree (with permission of the executive officer of the doctoral program). *Application deadline:* For fall admission, 3/1 priority date for domestic students, 2/1 priority date for international students; for spring admission, 11/1 priority date for domestic students, 10/1 priority date for international students. Applications are processed on a rolling basis. *Application fee:* $125. Electronic applications accepted. *Application Contact:* Karen Alleyne-Pierre, Director of Admissions Services and Enrollment Communications, 718-951-5902, Fax: 718-951-4506, E-mail: grads@brooklyn.cuny.edu. *Chairperson,* Dr. Bruce MacIntyre, 718-951-5286, E-mail: brucem@brooklyn.cuny.edu.

School of Education Students: 148 full-time (114 women), 1,688 part-time (1,233 women); includes 823 minority (546 African Americans, 2 American Indian/Alaska Native, 73 Asian Americans or Pacific Islanders, 202 Hispanic Americans), 66 international. 1,178 applicants, 73% accepted, 516 enrolled. Expenses: Contact institution. *Financial support:* Fellowships, career-related internships or fieldwork, Federal Work-Study, institutionally sponsored loans, scholarships/grants, and tuition waivers (full and partial) available. Support available to part-time students. Financial award application deadline: 5/1; financial award applicants required to submit FAFSA. In 2006, 731 master's, 170 other advanced degrees awarded. *Degree program information:* Part-time and evening/weekend programs available. Offers art teacher (MA); bilingual education (MS Ed); bilingual special education (MS Ed); biology teacher (MA); birth-grade 2 (MS Ed); chemistry teacher (MA); children with emotional handicaps (MS Ed); children with neuropsychological learning disabilities (MS Ed); children with retarded mental development (MS Ed); education (MA, MS Ed, CAS); educational leadership (CAS); English teacher (MA); French teacher (MA); guidance and counseling (CAS); health and nutrition sciences: health teacher (MS Ed); liberal arts (MS Ed); mathematics (MS Ed); mathematics teacher (MA); middle childhood education (math) (MS Ed); middle childhood education (science) (MS Ed); music education (CAS); music teacher (MA); physical education teacher (MS Ed); physics teacher (MA); school psychologist (MS Ed, CAS); school psychologist-bilingual (CAS); science/environmental education (MS Ed); social studies teacher (MA); Spanish teacher (MA); teacher of students with disabilities (MS Ed). *Application deadline:* For fall admission, 3/1 priority date for domestic students, 2/1 priority date for international students; for spring admission, 11/1 priority date for domestic students, 10/1 priority date for international students. Applications are processed on a rolling basis. *Application fee:* $125. Electronic applications accepted. *Application Contact:* Karen Alleyne-Pierre, Director of Admissions Services and Enrollment Communications, 718-951-5902, Fax: 718-951-4506, E-mail: grads@brooklyn.cuny.edu. *Dean,* Dr. Deborah Shanley, 718-951-5214, Fax: 718-951-4816, E-mail: dshanley@brooklyn.cuny.edu.

See Close-Up on page 819.

BROOKLYN LAW SCHOOL, Brooklyn, NY 11201-3798

General Information Independent, coed, graduate-only institution. *Enrollment by degree level:* 1,500 first professional, 1 other advanced degree. *Graduate faculty:* 66 full-time (30 women), 70 part-time/adjunct (19 women). *Graduate housing:* Rooms and/or apartments available to single and married students. Housing application deadline: 5/1. *Student services:* Campus employment opportunities, campus safety program, career counseling, disabled student services, free psychological counseling, international student services, low-cost health insurance, writing training. *Library facilities:* Brooklyn Law School Library plus 2 others. *Online resources:* library catalog, web page, access to other libraries' catalogs. *Collection:* 260,341 titles, 2,404 serial subscriptions, 1,535 audiovisual materials.

Computer facilities: 138 computers available on campus for general student use. A campuswide network can be accessed from student residence rooms and from off campus. Internet access and online class registration are available. *Web address:* http://www.brooklaw.edu/.

General Application Contact: Henry W. Haverstick, Dean of Admissions and Financial Aid, 718-780-7906, Fax: 718-780-0395, E-mail: admitq@brooklaw.edu.

GRADUATE UNITS

Professional Program Students: 1,156 full-time (571 women), 345 part-time (164 women); includes 394 minority (88 African Americans, 2 American Indian/Alaska Native, 221 Asian Americans or Pacific Islanders, 83 Hispanic Americans), 8 international. Average age 26. 5,003 applicants, 29% accepted, 493 enrolled. *Faculty:* 66 full-time (30 women), 70 part-time/adjunct (19 women). Expenses: Contact institution. *Financial support:* In 2006–07, 1,280 students received support, including 48 fellowships with partial tuition reimbursements available (averaging $5,000 per year), 91 research assistantships with partial tuition reimbursements available (averaging $2,680 per year); career-related internships or fieldwork, Federal Work-Study, scholarships/grants, and tuition waivers (partial) also available. Support available to part-time students. Financial award application deadline: 4/28; financial award applicants required to submit FAFSA. In 2006, 494 degrees awarded. *Degree program information:* Part-time and evening/weekend programs available. Offers law (JD). *Application deadline:* For fall admission, 2/1 priority date for domestic and international students. Applications are processed on a rolling basis. *Application fee:* $65. Electronic applications accepted. *Application Contact:* Henry W. Haverstick, Dean of Admissions and Financial Aid, 718-780-7906, Fax: 718-780-0395, E-mail: admitq@brooklaw.edu. *Dean,* Joan G. Wexler, 718-780-7900, Fax: 718-780-0393.

BROOKS INSTITUTE OF PHOTOGRAPHY, Santa Barbara, CA 93108-2399

General Information Proprietary, coed, comprehensive institution. *Graduate housing:* On-campus housing not available.

GRADUATE UNITS

Graduate Program in Professional Photography *Degree program information:* Evening/weekend programs available. Offers professional photography (MFA).

BROWN UNIVERSITY, Providence, RI 02912

General Information Independent, coed, university. CGS member. *Graduate housing:* Room and/or apartments available to single students; on-campus housing not available to married students. *Research affiliation:* Woods Hole Oceanographic Institution–Marine Biological Laboratory, Rhode Island Reactor, International Center for Numismatic Studies, Meeting Street School.

GRADUATE UNITS

Graduate School *Degree program information:* Part-time programs available. Offers American civilization (AM, PhD); anthropology (AM, PhD); art history (AM, PhD); biochemistry (PhD); chemistry (Sc M, PhD); classics (AM, PhD); cognitive science (Sc M, PhD); comparative literature (AM, PhD); comparative study of development (AM); computer science (Sc M, PhD); economics (AM, PhD); Egyptology (AM, PhD); elementary education 1-6 (MAT); English literature and language (AM, PhD); French studies (AM, PhD); geological sciences (MA, Sc M, PhD); German (AM, PhD); Hispanic studies (AM, PhD); history (AM, PhD); history of mathematics (AM, PhD); Italian studies (AM, PhD); Judaic studies (AM, PhD); linguistics (AM, PhD); mathematics (M Sc, MA, PhD); music (AM, PhD); neuroscience (PhD); old world archaeology and art (AM, PhD); philosophy (AM, PhD); physics (Sc M, PhD); political science (AM, PhD); population studies (PhD); psychology (AM, Sc M, PhD); religious studies (AM, PhD); Russian (AM, PhD); secondary biology (MAT); secondary English (MAT); secondary social studies/history (MAT); Slavic languages (AM, PhD); sociology (AM, PhD); theatre arts (AM); writing (MFA).

A. Alfred Taubman Center for Public Policy and American Institutions Offers public policy and American institutions (MPA, MPP).

Center for Environmental Studies Students: 16 full-time (12 women); includes 1 minority (Hispanic American), 3 international. Average age 25. 29 applicants, 66% accepted, 8 enrolled. *Faculty:* 4 full-time (2 women), 11 part-time/adjunct (3 women). Expenses: Contact institution. *Financial support:* In 2006–07, 16 students received support, including 2 teaching assistantships with full tuition reimbursements available (averaging $14,000 per year); career-related internships or fieldwork, Federal Work-Study, institutionally sponsored loans, scholarships/grants, health care benefits, and tuition waivers (partial) also available. Financial award application deadline: 1/2; financial award applicants required to submit FAFSA. In 2006, 8 degrees awarded. *Degree program information:* Part-time programs available. Offers environmental studies (AM). *Application deadline:* For fall admission, 1/2 priority date for domestic and international students. Applications are processed on a rolling basis. *Application fee:* $70. Electronic applications accepted. *Application Contact:* Patricia-Ann Caton, Administrative Manager, 401-863-3449, Fax: 401-863-3503, E-mail: patti_caton@brown.edu. *Director,* Osvaldo Sala, 401-863-3449, Fax: 401-863-3503, E-mail: osvaldo_sala@brown.edu.

Center for Old World Archaeology and Art Offers old world archaeology and art (AM, PhD).

Center for Portuguese and Brazilian Studies Offers Brazilian studies (AM); Luso-Brazilian studies (PhD); Portuguese studies and bilingual education (AM).

Division of Applied Mathematics Offers applied mathematics (Sc M, PhD).

Division of Biology and Medicine *Degree program information:* Part-time programs available. Offers artificial organs, biomaterials, and cell technology (MA, Sc M, PhD); biochemistry (M Med Sc, Sc M, PhD); biology (MA, PhD); biology and medicine (M Med Sc, MA, MPH, MS, Sc M, PhD); biomedical engineering (MS, PhD); biostatistics (MS, PhD); cancer biology (PhD); cell biology (M Med Sc, Sc M, PhD); developmental biology (M Med Sc, Sc M, PhD); ecology and evolutionary biology (PhD); epidemiology (MS, PhD); health services research (MS, PhD); immunology (M Med Sc, Sc M, PhD); immunology and infection (PhD); medical science (PhD); molecular microbiology (M Med Sc, Sc M, PhD); molecular pharmacology and physiology (MA, Sc M, PhD); neuroscience (PhD); pathobiology (Sc M); public health (MPH); statistical science (MS, PhD); toxicology and environmental pathology (PhD). Electronic applications accepted.

Division of Engineering Offers aerospace engineering (Sc M, PhD); biomedical engineering (Sc M); electrical sciences (Sc M, PhD); fluid mechanics, thermodynamics, and chemical processes (Sc M, PhD); materials science (Sc M, PhD); mechanics of solids and structures (Sc M, PhD).

National Institutes of Health Sponsored Programs Offers neuroscience (PhD).

Program in Medicine Offers medicine (MD).

BRYANT UNIVERSITY, Smithfield, RI 02917-1284

General Information Independent, coed, comprehensive institution. *Enrollment:* 3,651 graduate, professional, and undergraduate students; 420 part-time matriculated graduate/professional students (151 women). *Enrollment by degree level:* 411 master's, 9 other advanced degrees. *Graduate faculty:* 49 full-time (13 women), 8 part-time/adjunct (1 woman). *Tuition:* Part-time $1,998 per course. *Graduate housing:* On-campus housing not available. *Student services:* Campus employment opportunities, campus safety program, career counseling, disabled student services, exercise/wellness program, free psychological counseling, international student services, low-cost health insurance, multicultural affairs office, writing training. *Library facilities:* Douglas and Judith Krupp Library. *Online resources:* library catalog, web page, access to other libraries' catalogs. *Collection:* 143,393 titles, 26,451 serial subscriptions, 1,208 audiovisual materials.

Computer facilities: Computer purchase and lease plans are available. 467 computers available on campus for general student use. A campuswide network can be accessed from student residence rooms and from off campus. Internet access and online class registration, e-mail, online library, wireless network, student Web hosts are available. *Web address:* http://www.bryant.edu/.

General Application Contact: Kristopher T. Sullivan, Assistant Dean of the Graduate School, 401-232-6230, Fax: 401-232-6494, E-mail: gradprog@bryant.edu.

GRADUATE UNITS

Graduate School Average age 31. 180 applicants, 49% accepted, 67 enrolled. *Faculty:* 49 full-time (13 women), 8 part-time/adjunct (1 woman). Expenses: Contact institution. *Financial support:* In 2006–07, 11 research assistantships with full tuition reimbursements were awarded; unspecified assistantships also available. Support available to part-time students. Financial award applicants required to submit FAFSA. In 2006, 134 master's, 10 other advanced degrees awarded. *Degree program information:* Part-time and evening/weekend programs available. *Application deadline:* For fall admission, 7/15 for domestic students, 4/1 for international students; for spring admission, 11/15 for domestic and international students. Applications are processed on a rolling basis. *Application fee:* $80. Electronic applications accepted. *Assistant Dean of the Graduate School,* Kristopher T. Sullivan, 401-232-6230, Fax: 401-232-6494, E-mail: gradprog@bryant.edu.

Graduate School of Business Average age 31. 180 applicants, 49% accepted, 67 enrolled. *Faculty:* 49 full-time (13 women), 8 part-time/adjunct (1 woman). Expenses: Contact institution. *Financial support:* In 2006–07, 11 research assistantships with full tuition reimbursements were awarded; unspecified assistantships also available. Support available to part-time students. Financial award applicants required to submit FAFSA. In 2006, 134 master's, 10 other advanced degrees awarded. *Degree program information:* Part-time and evening/weekend programs available. Offers accounting (MBA, CAGS); business administration (MBA, CAGS); computer information systems (MBA, CAGS); e-strategy (MBA, CAGS); finance (MBA, CAGS); general business (MBA); information systems (MSIS); management (MBA, CAGS); marketing (MBA, CAGS); operations management (MBA); professional accounting (MPAC); taxation (MST, CAGS). *Application deadline:* For fall admission, 7/15 for domestic students, 4/1 for international students; for spring admission, 11/15 for domestic and international students. Applications are processed on a rolling basis. *Application fee:* $60 ($80 for international students). Electronic applications accepted. *Dean of the College of Business,* Dr. Jack W. Trifts, 401-232-6308, Fax: 401-232-6573, E-mail: jtrifts@bryant.edu.

BRYN ATHYN COLLEGE OF THE NEW CHURCH, Bryn Athyn, PA 19009-0717

General Information Independent-religious, coed, comprehensive institution. *Graduate housing:* Room and/or apartments available on a first-come, first-served basis to single students; on-campus housing not available to married students. Housing application deadline: 1/31.

GRADUATE UNITS

Academy of the New Church Theological School *Degree program information:* Part-time programs available. Postbaccalaureate distance learning degree programs offered (minimal on-campus study). Offers divinity (M Div); religious studies (MA).

BRYN MAWR COLLEGE, Bryn Mawr, PA 19010-2899

General Information Independent, Undergraduate: women only; graduate: coed, university. CGS member. *Enrollment:* 1,799 graduate, professional, and undergraduate students; 65 full-time matriculated graduate/professional students (50 women), 99 part-time matriculated graduate/professional students (80 women). *Enrollment by degree level:* 86 master's, 78 doctoral. *Graduate housing:* Room and/or apartments available on a first-come, first-served basis to single students. *Student services:* Campus employment opportunities, career counseling, disabled student services, exercise/wellness program, international student services, low-cost health insurance, multicultural affairs office. *Library facilities:* Miriam Coffin Canaday Library plus 2 others. *Online resources:* library catalog, web page, access to other libraries' catalogs. *Collection:* 1.1 million titles, 4,400 serial subscriptions.

Computer facilities: Computer purchase and lease plans are available. 200 computers available on campus for general student use. A campuswide network can be accessed from student residence rooms and from off campus. Internet access and online class registration are available. *Web address:* http://www.brynmawr.edu/.

Bryn Mawr College (continued)

General Application Contact: Graduate School, 610-526-5072.

GRADUATE UNITS

Graduate School of Arts and Sciences Students: 65 full-time (50 women), 99 part-time (80 women); includes 12 minority (3 African Americans, 7 Asian Americans or Pacific Islanders, 2 Hispanic Americans), 22 international. *Faculty:* 52. Expenses: Contact institution. *Financial support:* Fellowships, research assistantships, teaching assistantships, career-related internships or fieldwork, Federal Work-Study, institutionally sponsored loans, unspecified assistantships, and tuition awards available. Support available to part-time students. In 2006, 20 master's, 23 doctorates awarded. *Degree program information:* Part-time programs available. Offers arts and sciences (MA, PhD); chemistry (MA, PhD); classical and Near Eastern archaeology (MA, PhD); clinical developmental psychology (PhD); French (MA, PhD); Greek, Latin, and Classical studies (MA, PhD); history of art (MA, PhD); mathematics (MA, PhD); physics (MA, PhD); Russian (MA, PhD). *Application deadline:* Applications are processed on a rolling basis. *Application fee:* $25. *Application Contact:* Lea R. Miller, Secretary, 610-526-5072, Fax: 610-526-5076, E-mail: lrmiller@brynmawr.edu. *Dean,* Dr. Dale Kinney, 610-526-5073, Fax: 610-526-5076, E-mail: graddean@brynmawr.edu.

Graduate School of Social Work and Social Research Students: 163 full-time (142 women), 89 part-time (79 women); includes 63 minority (52 African Americans, 7 Asian Americans or Pacific Islanders, 4 Hispanic Americans), 7 international. Average age 34. 208 applicants, 74% accepted, 90 enrolled. *Faculty:* 14 full-time (8 women), 39 part-time/adjunct (33 women). Expenses: Contact institution. *Financial support:* In 2006–07, 190 students received support, including 17 fellowships with full and partial tuition reimbursements available (averaging $3,271 per year), 12 teaching assistantships with full and partial tuition reimbursements available (averaging $9,722 per year); research assistantships with full and partial tuition reimbursements available, career-related internships or fieldwork, Federal Work-Study, institutionally sponsored loans, scholarships/grants, tuition waivers (full and partial), and PhD dissertation award also available. Support available to part-time students. Financial award application deadline: 3/1; financial award applicants required to submit FAFSA. In 2006, 108 master's, 4 doctorates awarded. *Degree program information:* Part-time programs available. Offers social work and social research (MLSP, MSS, PhD). *Application deadline:* For fall admission, 3/31 priority date for domestic and international students. Applications are processed on a rolling basis. *Application fee:* $50. *Application Contact:* Nancy J. Kirby, Assistant Dean and Director of Admissions, 610-520-2601, Fax: 610-520-2655, E-mail: swadmiss@brynmawr.edu. *Co-Dean,* Dr. Marcia L. Martin, 610-520-2603, Fax: 610-520-2613, E-mail: mmartin@brynmawr.edu.

See Close-Up on page 821.

BUCKNELL UNIVERSITY, Lewisburg, PA 17837

General Information Independent, coed, comprehensive institution. *Graduate housing:* On-campus housing not available.

GRADUATE UNITS

Graduate Studies *Degree program information:* Part-time programs available.

College of Arts and Sciences *Degree program information:* Part-time programs available. Offers animal behavior (MA, MS); arts and sciences (MA, MS, MS Ed); biology (MA, MS); chemistry (MA, MS); classroom teaching (MS Ed); educational research (MS Ed); elementary and secondary counseling (MA, MS Ed); elementary and secondary principalship (MA, MS Ed); English (MA); mathematics (MA, MS); psychology (MA, MS); reading (MA, MS Ed); school psychology (MS Ed); supervision of curriculum and instruction (MA, MS Ed).

College of Engineering *Degree program information:* Part-time programs available. Offers chemical engineering (MS, MS Ch E); civil and environmental engineering (MS, MSCE, MSEV); electrical engineering (MS, MSEE); engineering (MS, MS Ch E, MSCE, MSEE, MSEV, MSME); mechanical engineering (MS, MSME).

BUENA VISTA UNIVERSITY, Storm Lake, IA 50588

General Information Independent-religious, coed, comprehensive institution. *Enrollment:* 1,229 graduate, professional, and undergraduate students; 105 full-time matriculated graduate/professional students (95 women). *Enrollment by degree level:* 105 master's. *Graduate faculty:* 3 full-time (2 women), 13 part-time/adjunct (10 women). *Graduate housing:* Room and/or apartments available on a first-come, first-served basis to single students; on-campus housing not available to married students. Housing application deadline: 5/1. *Student services:* Campus employment opportunities, campus safety program, career counseling, disabled student services, exercise/wellness program, free psychological counseling, multicultural affairs office, writing training. *Library facilities:* BVU Library. *Online resources:* library catalog, web page. *Collection:* 144,000 titles, 632 serial subscriptions, 5,648 audiovisual materials.

Computer facilities: Computer purchase and lease plans are available. 400 computers available on campus for general student use. A campuswide network can be accessed from student residence rooms and from off campus. Internet access and online class registration are available. *Web address:* http://www.bvu.edu/.

General Application Contact: Rita Mckenzie, Director of Graduate Studies, 712-749-2156, Fax: 712-749-1408, E-mail: mckenzie@bvu.edu.

GRADUATE UNITS

School of Education Students: 105 full-time (95 women). Average age 36. 38 applicants, 58% accepted, 20 enrolled. *Faculty:* 3 full-time (2 women), 13 part-time/adjunct (10 women). Expenses: Contact institution. *Financial support:* In 2006–07, teaching assistantships with full tuition reimbursements (averaging $6,000 per year); career-related internships or fieldwork also available. Financial award application deadline: 5/15; financial award applicants required to submit FAFSA. In 2006, 24 degrees awarded. *Degree program information:* Part-time and evening/weekend programs available. Postbaccalaureate distance learning degree programs offered (minimal on-campus study). Offers school guidance and counseling (MS Ed). Offered in summer only. *Application deadline:* For spring admission, 4/15 for domestic students. *Application fee:* $0. Electronic applications accepted. *Application Contact:* Rita Mckenzie, Director of Graduate Studies, 712-749-2156, Fax: 712-749-1408, E-mail: mckenzie@bvu.edu. *Dean,* Dr. Kline Capps, 712-749-2275, Fax: 712-749-1408, E-mail: capps@bvu.edu.

BUFFALO STATE COLLEGE, STATE UNIVERSITY OF NEW YORK, Buffalo, NY 14222-1095

General Information State-supported, coed, comprehensive institution. CGS member. *Graduate housing:* Room and/or apartments available on a first-come, first-served basis to single students; on-campus housing not available to married students. Housing application deadline: 8/15. *Research affiliation:* Roswell Park Memorial Institute, Research Institute on Addictions at the University of Buffalo, Phillip Morris Foundation, Ecology and Environment Corporation, Malcolm Pirnie, Friends of Buffalo River.

GRADUATE UNITS

Graduate Studies and Research *Degree program information:* Part-time and evening/weekend programs available. Postbaccalaureate distance learning degree programs offered (no on-campus study). Offers multidisciplinary studies (MA, MS).

Faculty of Applied Science and Education *Degree program information:* Part-time and evening/weekend programs available. Postbaccalaureate distance learning degree programs offered (no on-campus study). Offers adult education (MS, Certificate); applied science and education (MPS, MS, MS Ed, CAS, Certificate); business and marketing education (MS Ed); career and technical education (MS Ed); childhood education (grades 1-6) (MS Ed); creative studies (MS); criminal justice (MS); early childhood and childhood curriculum and instruction (MS Ed); early childhood education (birth-grade 2) (MS Ed); educational computing (MS Ed); educational leadership and facilitation (CAS); elementary education (MS Ed); human resources development (Certificate); industrial technology (MS); literacy specialist (MPS, MS Ed); literacy specialist (birth-grade 6) (MS Ed); literacy specialist (grades 5-12) (MPS); special education (MS Ed); special education: adolescents (MS Ed); special education: childhood (MS Ed); special education: early childhood (MS Ed); speech language pathology (MS Ed); student personnel administration (MS); teaching bilingual exceptional individuals (MS Ed); technology education (MS Ed).

Faculty of Arts and Humanities *Degree program information:* Part-time and evening/weekend programs available. Offers art conservation (CAS); art education (MS Ed); arts and humanities (MA, MS Ed, CAS); conservation of historic works and art works (MA); English (MA); secondary education (MS Ed).

Faculty of Natural and Social Sciences *Degree program information:* Part-time and evening/weekend programs available. Offers applied economics (MA); biology (MA); chemistry (MA); history (MA); mathematics education (MS Ed); natural and social sciences (MA, MS Ed); secondary education (MS Ed); secondary education physics (MS Ed).

BUTLER UNIVERSITY, Indianapolis, IN 46208-3485

General Information Independent, coed, comprehensive institution. *Enrollment:* 4,437 graduate, professional, and undergraduate students; 429 full-time matriculated graduate/professional students (304 women), 355 part-time matriculated graduate/professional students (211 women). *Enrollment by degree level:* 287 first professional, 497 master's. *Graduate faculty:* 84 full-time (33 women), 33 part-time/adjunct (18 women). *Tuition:* Full-time $6,030; part-time $335 per credit. Tuition and fees vary according to program. *Graduate housing:* Room and/or apartments available on a first-come, first-served basis to single students; on-campus housing not available to married students. Typical cost: $4,180 per year ($8,530 including board). Housing application deadline: 8/1. *Student services:* Campus employment opportunities, campus safety program, career counseling, child daycare facilities, free psychological counseling, international student services, low-cost health insurance, multicultural affairs office. *Library facilities:* Irwin Library System plus 1 other. *Online resources:* library catalog, web page, access to other libraries' catalogs. *Collection:* 346,805 titles, 13,441 serial subscriptions, 15,268 audiovisual materials.

Computer facilities: 430 computers available on campus for general student use. A campuswide network can be accessed from student residence rooms and from off campus. Internet access, e-mail are available. *Web address:* http://www.butler.edu/.

General Application Contact: Pamela Bender, Student Services Specialist, 317-940-8100, Fax: 317-940-8250, E-mail: pbender@butler.edu.

GRADUATE UNITS

College of Business Administration Students: 21 full-time (10 women), 150 part-time (54 women); includes 11 minority (6 African Americans, 1 American Indian/Alaska Native, 1 Asian American or Pacific Islander, 3 Hispanic Americans), 20 international. Average age 30. 79 applicants, 57% accepted, 26 enrolled. *Faculty:* 11 full-time (3 women), 2 part-time/adjunct (0 women). Expenses: Contact institution. *Financial support:* Career-related internships or fieldwork and institutionally sponsored loans available. Support available to part-time students. Financial award application deadline: 7/15; financial award applicants required to submit FAFSA. In 2006, 62 degrees awarded. *Degree program information:* Part-time and evening/weekend programs available. Offers business administration (MBA, MP Acc). *Application deadline:* For fall admission, 8/15 priority date for domestic students. Applications are processed on a rolling basis. *Application fee:* $35. Electronic applications accepted. *Application Contact:* Dr. Stephanie Judge, Director—Marketing, CBA, 317-940-9886, Fax: 317-940-9455, E-mail: sjudge@butler.edu. *Dean,* Dr. Richard Fetter, 317-940-9221, Fax: 317-940-9455, E-mail: rfetter@butler.edu.

College of Education Students: 18 full-time (10 women), 156 part-time (125 women); includes 21 minority (16 African Americans, 2 Asian Americans or Pacific Islanders, 3 Hispanic Americans), 7 international. Average age 31. 56 applicants, 57% accepted, 29 enrolled. *Faculty:* 12 full-time (6 women), 11 part-time/adjunct (8 women). Expenses: Contact institution. *Financial support:* Institutionally sponsored loans available. Support available to part-time students. Financial award application deadline: 7/15; financial award applicants required to submit FAFSA. In 2006, 72 degrees awarded. *Degree program information:* Part-time and evening/weekend programs available. Offers administration (MS); elementary education (MS); reading (MS); school counseling (MS); secondary education (MS); special education (MS). *Application deadline:* For fall admission, 8/15 priority date for domestic students. Applications are processed on a rolling basis. *Application fee:* $35. Electronic applications accepted. *Application Contact:* Karen Farrell, Department Secretary, 317-940-9220, E-mail: kfarrell@butler.edu. *Dean,* Dr. Ena Shelley, 317-940-9752, Fax: 317-940-6481.

College of Liberal Arts and Sciences Students: 5 full-time (3 women), 14 part-time (8 women); includes 2 minority (both African Americans), 5 international. Average age 34. 14 applicants, 50% accepted, 3 enrolled. *Faculty:* 8 full-time (3 women). Expenses: Contact institution. *Financial support:* Career-related internships or fieldwork, institutionally sponsored loans, and tuition waivers (full and partial) available. Support available to part-time students. Financial award applicants required to submit FAFSA. In 2006, 3 degrees awarded. *Degree program information:* Part-time and evening/weekend programs available. Offers English (MA); history (MA); liberal arts and sciences (MA). *Application deadline:* For fall admission, 8/15 priority date for domestic students. Applications are processed on a rolling basis. *Application fee:* $35. Electronic applications accepted. *Dean,* Dr. Michael Zimmerman, 317-940-9874, E-mail: mzimmerm@butler.edu.

College of Pharmacy Students: 369 full-time (275 women), 9 part-time (7 women); includes 26 minority (7 African Americans, 1 American Indian/Alaska Native, 17 Asian Americans or Pacific Islanders, 1 Hispanic American), 9 international. Average age 24. 135 applicants, 82% accepted, 87 enrolled. *Faculty:* 34 full-time (17 women), 9 part-time/adjunct (7 women). Expenses: Contact institution. *Financial support:* Applicants required to submit FAFSA. In 2006, 84 degrees awarded. *Degree program information:* Part-time and evening/weekend programs available. Offers pharmaceutical science (Pharm D, MS); physician assistance studies (MS). *Application deadline:* For fall admission, 8/1 priority date for domestic students; for spring admission, 12/15 for domestic students. Applications are processed on a rolling basis. *Application fee:* $35. Electronic applications accepted. *Application Contact:* Dr. Kent VanTyle, Professor, 317-940-9580, E-mail: kvantyle@butler.edu. *Dean,* Dr. Mary Andritz, 317-940-9451, Fax: 317-940-6172, E-mail: mandritz@butler.edu.

Jordan College of Fine Arts Students: 16 full-time (6 women), 26 part-time (17 women); includes 3 minority (2 Asian Americans or Pacific Islanders, 1 Hispanic American), 3 international. Average age 28. 37 applicants, 62% accepted, 15 enrolled. *Faculty:* 19 full-time (4 women), 11 part-time/adjunct (3 women). Expenses: Contact institution. *Financial support:* In 2006–07, 15 teaching assistantships with full tuition reimbursements (averaging $2,500 per year) were awarded; fellowships, career-related internships or fieldwork, institutionally sponsored loans, and scholarships/grants also available. Support available to part-time students. Financial award application deadline: 7/15; financial award applicants required to submit FAFSA. In 2006, 17 degrees awarded. *Degree program information:* Part-time and evening/weekend programs available. Offers composition (MM); conducting (MM); fine arts (MM); music (MM); music education (MM); music history (MM); organ (MM); performance (MM). *Application deadline:* For fall admission, 8/15 priority date for domestic students. Applications are processed on a rolling basis. *Application fee:* $35. Electronic applications accepted. *Application Contact:* Kathy Lang, Admission Representative, 317-940-9646, Fax: 317-940-9658, E-mail: klang@butler.edu. *Dean,* Dr. Peter Alexander, 317-940-9231, Fax: 317-940-9658, E-mail: palexand@butler.edu.

CABRINI COLLEGE, Radnor, PA 19087-3698

General Information Independent-religious, coed, comprehensive institution. *Enrollment:* 2,389 graduate, professional, and undergraduate students; 91 full-time matriculated graduate/professional students (63 women), 484 part-time matriculated graduate/professional students (364 women). *Enrollment by degree level:* 575 master's. *Graduate faculty:* 11 full-time (7 women), 25 part-time/adjunct (11 women). *Tuition:* Part-time $310 per credit. *Required fees:* $45 per term. Tuition and fees vary according to course load. *Graduate housing:* On-campus housing not available. *Student services:* Campus safety program, career counseling, disabled student services, exercise/wellness program, free psychological counseling, international student services, low-cost health insurance, multicultural affairs office, teacher training. *Library* *facilities:* Holy Spirit Library. *Online resources:* library catalog, web page, access to other libraries' catalogs. *Collection:* 229,204 titles, 21,695 serial subscriptions, 1,067 audiovisual materials.

Computer facilities: 195 computers available on campus for general student use. A campuswide network can be accessed from student residence rooms. Internet access and online class registration, student access to account balances, grades and other services are available. *Web address:* http://www.cabrini.edu/.

General Application Contact: Bruce D. Bryde, Director of Enrollment and Recruiting, 610-902-8291, Fax: 610-902-8522, E-mail: bruce.d.bryde@cabrini.edu.

GRADUATE UNITS

Graduate and Professional Studies Students: 91 full-time (63 women), 484 part-time (364 women); includes 43 minority (28 African Americans, 6 Asian Americans or Pacific Islanders, 9 Hispanic Americans), 6 international. Average age 32. *Faculty:* 11 full-time (7 women), 25 part-time/adjunct (11 women). Expenses: Contact institution. *Financial support:* Career-related internships or fieldwork and unspecified assistantships available. Support available to part-time students. Financial award applicants required to submit FAFSA. In 2006, 143 degrees awarded. *Degree program information:* Part-time and evening/weekend programs available. Offers biotechnology (Certificate); education (M Ed); educational leadership (Certificate); instructional systems technology (MS); organization leadership (MS); project management (Certificate). *Application deadline:* For fall admission, 7/29 priority date for domestic students; for spring admission, 12/9 for domestic students. Applications are processed on a rolling basis. *Application fee:* $50. Electronic applications accepted. *Application Contact:* Bruce D. Bryde, Director of Enrollment and Recruiting, 610-902-8291, Fax: 610-902-8522, E-mail: bruce.d.bryde@cabrini.edu. *Dean for Graduate and Professional Studies,* Dr. Michael W. Markowitz, 610-902-8501, Fax: 610-902-8522, E-mail: michael.w.markowitz@cabrini.edu.

CALDWELL COLLEGE, Caldwell, NJ 07006-6195

General Information Independent-religious, coed, comprehensive institution. CGS member. *Graduate housing:* On-campus housing not available.

GRADUATE UNITS

Graduate Studies *Degree program information:* Part-time and evening/weekend programs available. Postbaccalaureate distance learning degree programs offered (minimal on-campus study). Offers accounting (MBA); applied behavior analysis (MA); art therapy (MA); business administration (MBA); counseling psychology (MA); curriculum and instruction (MA); educational administration (MA); pastoral ministry (MA); school counseling (MA); special education (MA). Electronic applications accepted.

See Close-Up on page 823.

CALIFORNIA BAPTIST UNIVERSITY, Riverside, CA 92504-3206

General Information Independent-religious, coed, comprehensive institution. *Enrollment:* 3,409 graduate, professional, and undergraduate students; 268 full-time matriculated graduate/professional students (186 women), 518 part-time matriculated graduate/professional students (414 women). *Enrollment by degree level:* 786 master's. *Graduate faculty:* 44 full-time (22 women), 29 part-time/adjunct (19 women). *Tuition:* Full-time $7,812; part-time $434 per unit. *Required fees:* $120 per semester. Tuition and fees vary according to program. *Graduate housing:* On-campus housing not available. *Student services:* Campus employment opportunities, campus safety program, career counseling, exercise/wellness program, free psychological counseling, international student services, low-cost health insurance, teacher training. *Library facilities:* Annie Gabriel Library. *Online resources:* library catalog, web page, access to other libraries' catalogs. *Collection:* 180,946 titles, 11,166 serial subscriptions, 3,633 audiovisual materials.

Computer facilities: 154 computers available on campus for general student use. A campuswide network can be accessed from student residence rooms and from off campus. Internet access and online class registration, intranet are available. *Web address:* http://www.calbaptist.edu/.

General Application Contact: Gail Ronveaux, Dean of Graduate Enrollment, 951-343-5045, Fax: 951-343-5095, E-mail: graduateadmissions@calbaptist.edu.

GRADUATE UNITS

Program in Business Administration Students: 39 full-time (15 women), 25 part-time (10 women); includes 18 minority (7 African Americans, 1 American Indian/Alaska Native, 5 Asian Americans or Pacific Islanders, 5 Hispanic Americans), 6 international. 53 applicants, 38% accepted, 16 enrolled. *Faculty:* 7 full-time (1 woman), 3 part-time/adjunct (1 woman). Expenses: Contact institution. *Financial support:* In 2006–07, 30 students received support. Federal Work-Study available. Support available to part-time students. Financial award applicants required to submit FAFSA. In 2006, 4 degrees awarded. *Degree program information:* Part-time and evening/weekend programs available. Offers business administration (MBA). *Application deadline:* For fall admission, 9/1 for domestic students, 7/15 priority date for international students; for spring admission, 1/3 for domestic students, 11/1 priority date for international students. Applications are processed on a rolling basis. *Application fee:* $45. Electronic applications accepted. *Application Contact:* Gail Ronveaux, Dean of Graduate Enrollment, 951-343-5045, Fax: 951-343-5095, E-mail: graduateadmissions@calbaptist.edu. *Dean, School of Business,* Dr. Andrew Herrity, 951-343-4427, Fax: 951-343-4361, E-mail: aherrity@calbaptist.edu.

Program in Education Students: 77 full-time (64 women), 408 part-time (342 women); includes 157 minority (41 African Americans, 12 American Indian/Alaska Native, 18 Asian Americans or Pacific Islanders, 86 Hispanic Americans), 2 international. 282 applicants, 70% accepted, 171 enrolled. *Faculty:* 16 full-time (10 women), 16 part-time/adjunct (13 women). Expenses: Contact institution. *Financial support:* In 2006–07, 19 students received support. Career-related internships or fieldwork, Federal Work-Study, and scholarships/grants available. Support available to part-time students. Financial award applicants required to submit FAFSA. In 2006, 63 degrees awarded. *Degree program information:* Part-time programs available. Offers cross-cultural language and academic development (MA Ed); educational leadership (MS Ed); educational technology (MS Ed); instructional computer applications (MS Ed); reading (MS Ed); special education (MS Ed); teaching (MS Ed). *Application deadline:* For fall admission, 9/1 for domestic students, 7/15 priority date for international students; for spring admission, 1/3 for domestic students, 11/1 priority date for international students. Applications are processed on a rolling basis. *Application fee:* $45. Electronic applications accepted. *Application Contact:* Gail Ronveaux, Dean of Graduate Enrollment, 951-343-5045, Fax: 951-343-5095, E-mail: graduateadmissions@calbaptist.edu. *Dean, School of Education,* Dr. Mary Crist, 951-343-4313, Fax: 951-343-4516, E-mail: mcrist@calbaptist.edu.

Program in English Students: 6 full-time (4 women), 26 part-time (21 women); includes 6 minority (1 African American, 1 Asian American or Pacific Islander, 4 Hispanic Americans), 5 international. 20 applicants, 85% accepted, 8 enrolled. *Faculty:* 5 full-time (3 women), 1 (woman) part-time/adjunct. Expenses: Contact institution. *Financial support:* Federal Work-Study available. Support available to part-time students. Financial award applicants required to submit FAFSA. In 2006, 9 degrees awarded. *Degree program information:* Part-time programs available. Offers English (MA). *Application deadline:* For fall admission, 9/1 for domestic students, 7/15 priority date for international students; for spring admission, 1/3 for domestic students, 11/1 priority date for international students. Applications are processed on a rolling basis. *Application fee:* $45. Electronic applications accepted. *Application Contact:* Gail Ronveaux, Dean of Graduate Enrollment, 951-343-5045, Fax: 951-343-5095, E-mail: graduateadmissions@calbaptist.edu. *Director,* Dr. Jennifer Newton, 951-343-4276, Fax: 951-343-4661, E-mail: jnewton@calbaptist.edu.

Program in Kinesiology Students: 23 full-time (7 women), 14 part-time (5 women); includes 14 minority (3 African Americans, 1 American Indian/Alaska Native, 3 Asian Americans or Pacific Islanders, 7 Hispanic Americans), 1 international. 30 applicants, 70% accepted, 14 enrolled. *Faculty:* 2 full-time (1 woman), 1 (woman) part-time/adjunct. Expenses: Contact institution. *Financial support:* Federal Work-Study available. Support available to part-time students. Financial award applicants required to submit FAFSA. In 2006, 22 degrees awarded. *Degree program information:* Part-time programs available. Offers kinesiology (MS). *Application deadline:* For fall admission, 9/1 for domestic students, 7/15 priority date for international students; for spring admission, 1/3 for domestic students, 11/1 priority date for international students. Applications are processed on a rolling basis. *Application fee:* $45. Electronic applications accepted. *Application Contact:* Gail Ronveaux, Dean of Graduate Enrollment, 951-343-5045, Fax: 951-343-5095, E-mail: graduateadmissions@calbaptist.edu. *Chair, Department of Kinesiology,* Dr. Sean Sullivan, 951-343-4528, E-mail: ssullivan@calbaptist.edu.

Program in Marriage and Family Therapy: Counseling Psychology Students: 104 full-time (85 women), 38 part-time (34 women); includes 67 minority (29 African Americans, 6 American Indian/Alaska Native, 2 Asian Americans or Pacific Islanders, 30 Hispanic Americans). 93 applicants, 56% accepted, 36 enrolled. *Faculty:* 9 full-time (4 women), 8 part-time/adjunct (3 women). Expenses: Contact institution. *Financial support:* Career-related internships or fieldwork and Federal Work-Study available. Support available to part-time students. Financial award applicants required to submit FAFSA. In 2006, 39 degrees awarded. *Degree program information:* Part-time programs available. Offers counseling psychology (MS). *Application deadline:* For fall admission, 9/1 for domestic students, 7/15 priority date for international students; for spring admission, 1/3 for domestic students, 11/1 priority date for international students. Applications are processed on a rolling basis. *Application fee:* $45. Electronic applications accepted. *Application Contact:* Gail Ronveaux, Dean of Graduate Enrollment, 951-343-5045, Fax: 951-343-5095, E-mail: graduateadmissions@calbaptist.edu. *Director and Associate Dean, School of Business,* Dr. Gary Collins, 951-343-4304, Fax: 951-343-4569, E-mail: gcollins@calbaptist.edu.

Program in Music Students: 6 full-time (3 women), 1 part-time; includes 2 minority (1 Asian American or Pacific Islander, 1 Hispanic American), 2 international. 8 applicants, 63% accepted, 5 enrolled. *Faculty:* 3 full-time (2 women). Expenses: Contact institution. *Financial support:* Federal Work-Study available. Support available to part-time students. In 2006, 3 degrees awarded. *Degree program information:* Part-time programs available. Offers music (MM). *Application deadline:* For fall admission, 9/1 for domestic students, 7/15 for international students; for spring admission, 1/3 for domestic students, 11/1 for international students. Applications are processed on a rolling basis. *Application fee:* $45. Electronic applications accepted. *Application Contact:* Gail Ronveaux, Dean of Graduate Enrollment, 951-343-5045, Fax: 951-343-5095, E-mail: graduateadmissions@calbaptist.edu. *Dean, School of Music,* Dr. Gary Bonner, 951-343-4251, Fax: 951-343-4570, E-mail: gbonner@calbaptist.edu.

CALIFORNIA COAST UNIVERSITY, Santa Ana, CA 92701

General Information Proprietary, coed, comprehensive institution.

GRADUATE UNITS

Program in Business Administration Offers business administration (MBA).

CALIFORNIA COLLEGE FOR HEALTH SCIENCES, Salt Lake City, UT 84107

General Information Proprietary, coed, comprehensive institution. *Graduate housing:* On-campus housing not available.

GRADUATE UNITS

Program in Business Administration in Healthcare *Degree program information:* Part-time and evening/weekend programs available. Postbaccalaureate distance learning degree programs offered (no on-campus study). Offers healthcare administration (MBA).

Program in Healthcare Administration *Degree program information:* Part-time and evening/weekend programs available. Postbaccalaureate distance learning degree programs offered (no on-campus study). Offers healthcare administration (MSHCA).

Program in Health Services *Degree program information:* Part-time and evening/weekend programs available. Postbaccalaureate distance learning degree programs offered (no on-campus study). Offers community health (MSHS); wellness promotion (MSHS).

Program in Public Health *Degree program information:* Part-time and evening/weekend programs available. Postbaccalaureate distance learning degree programs offered (no on-campus study). Offers public health (MPH).

CALIFORNIA COLLEGE OF THE ARTS, San Francisco, CA 94107

General Information Independent, coed, comprehensive institution. *Enrollment:* 1,622 graduate, professional, and undergraduate students; 280 full-time matriculated graduate/professional students (173 women), 32 part-time matriculated graduate/professional students (23 women). *Enrollment by degree level:* 312 master's. *Graduate faculty:* 10 full-time (4 women), 69 part-time/adjunct (34 women). *Tuition:* Full-time $30,510; part-time $959 per unit. *Required fees:* $290. *Graduate housing:* Room and/or apartments available on a first-come, first-served basis to single students; on-campus housing not available to married students. Typical cost: $6,400 per year. Room charges vary according to housing facility selected. Housing application deadline: 4/1. *Student services:* Campus employment opportunities, career counseling, disabled student services, free psychological counseling, international student services, low-cost health insurance. *Library facilities:* Meyer Library plus 1 other. *Online resources:* library catalog, web page, access to other libraries' catalogs. *Collection:* 39,000 titles, 340 serial subscriptions.

Computer facilities: 180 computers available on campus for general student use. A campuswide network can be accessed from student residence rooms and from off campus. Internet access is available. *Web address:* http://www.cca.edu/.

General Application Contact: Kathryn Ward, Assistant Director of Graduate Admissions, 415-703-9523 Ext. 9593, Fax: 415-703-9539, E-mail: graduateprograms@cca.edu.

GRADUATE UNITS

Graduate Programs Students: 280 full-time (173 women), 32 part-time (23 women); includes 62 minority (15 African Americans, 1 American Indian/Alaska Native, 28 Asian Americans or Pacific Islanders, 18 Hispanic Americans), 28 international. 714 applicants, 45% accepted, 144 enrolled. *Faculty:* 10 full-time (4 women), 69 part-time/adjunct (34 women). Expenses: Contact institution. *Financial support:* In 2006–07, teaching assistantships (averaging $2,000 per year). In 2006, 87 master's awarded. Offers architecture (M Arch); ceramics (MFA); curatorial practice (MA); design (MFA); film/video/performance (MFA); glass (MFA); jewelry/metal arts (MFA); painting/drawing (MFA); photography (MFA); printmaking (MFA); sculpture (MFA); textiles (MFA); visual criticism (MA); wood/furniture (MFA); writing (MFA). *Application deadline:* For fall admission, 1/15 for domestic and international students. *Application fee:* $50. *Unit Head,* Larry Rinder, 800-477-1ART.

CALIFORNIA INSTITUTE OF INTEGRAL STUDIES, San Francisco, CA 94103

General Information Independent, coed, upper-level institution. CGS member. *Enrollment:* 1,034 matriculated graduate/professional students. *Enrollment by degree level:* 551 master's, 483 doctoral. *Graduate faculty:* 55 full-time (28 women), 154 part-time/adjunct. *Tuition:* Part-time $750 per unit. Tuition and fees vary according to course load, degree level and program. *Graduate housing:* On-campus housing not available. *Student services:* Campus employment opportunities, career counseling, disabled student services, grant writing training, international student services, low-cost health insurance. *Library facilities:* The Laurance S. Rockefeller. *Collection:* 4,000 titles. *Research affiliation:* Bay Area Reference Service.

Computer facilities: A campuswide network can be accessed from off campus. Internet access is available. *Web address:* http://www.ciis.edu/.

General Application Contact: Gwyneth Merner, Admissions Inquiries Coordinator, 415-575-6151, Fax: 415-575-1268, E-mail: gmerner@ciis.edu.

GRADUATE UNITS

Graduate Programs Students: 1,013. Average age 37. 603 applicants, 65% accepted, 263 enrolled. *Faculty:* 55 full-time (28 women), 154 part-time/adjunct. Expenses: Contact institution. *Financial support:* In 2006–07, 656 students received support; research assistant-

California Institute of Integral Studies (continued)

ships, teaching assistantships, career-related internships or fieldwork, Federal Work-Study, institutionally sponsored loans, scholarships/grants, tuition waivers (partial), and unspecified assistantships available. Support available to part-time students. Financial award application deadline: 3/15; financial award applicants required to submit FAFSA. In 2006, 159 master's, 56 doctorates awarded. *Degree program information:* Part-time and evening/weekend programs available. Postbaccalaureate distance learning degree programs offered (minimal on-campus study). *Application deadline:* For fall admission, 2/1 priority date for domestic and international students; for spring admission, 10/15 priority date for domestic and international students. Applications are processed on a rolling basis. *Application fee:* $65. Electronic applications accepted. *Application Contact:* Gwyneth Merner, Admissions Inquiries Coordinator, 415-575-6151, Fax: 415-575-1268, E-mail: gmerner@ciis.edu. *Academic Vice President,* Dr. Judie Wexler, 415-575-6124, Fax: 415-575-1264, E-mail: jwexler@ciis.edu.

School of Consciousness and Transformation Students: 440. Average age 42. 184 applicants, 85% accepted, 123 enrolled. *Faculty:* 30 full-time, 47 part-time/adjunct. Expenses: Contact institution. *Financial support:* In 2006–07, 255 students received support; research assistantships, teaching assistantships, career-related internships or fieldwork, Federal Work-Study, institutionally sponsored loans, scholarships/grants, and tuition waivers (partial) available. Support available to part-time students. Financial award application deadline: 3/15; financial award applicants required to submit FAFSA. In 2006, 37 master's, 24 doctorates awarded. *Degree program information:* Part-time and evening/weekend programs available. Postbaccalaureate distance learning degree programs offered (minimal on-campus study). Offers cultural anthropology and social transformation (MA); East-West psychology (MA, PhD); integrative health studies (MA); philosophy and religion (MA, PhD); social and cultural anthropology (PhD); transformative leadership (MA); transformative studies (PhD). *Application deadline:* For fall admission, 2/15 priority date for domestic and international students; for spring admission, 10/15 priority date for domestic and international students. Applications are processed on a rolling basis. *Application fee:* $65. Electronic applications accepted. *Application Contact:* Allyson Werner, Senior Admissions Counselor, 415-575-6155, Fax: 415-575-1268. *Academic Vice President,* Dr. Judie Wexler, 415-575-6124, Fax: 415-575-1264, E-mail: jwexler@ciis.edu.

School of Professional Psychology Students: 573; includes 94 minority (16 African Americans, 2 American Indian/Alaska Native, 39 Asian Americans or Pacific Islanders, 37 Hispanic Americans), 44 international. Average age 34. 419 applicants, 57% accepted, 137 enrolled. *Faculty:* 28 full-time, 101 part-time/adjunct. Expenses: Contact institution. *Financial support:* In 2006–07, 401 students received support; research assistantships with tuition reimbursements available, teaching assistantships with tuition reimbursements available, career-related internships or fieldwork, Federal Work-Study, institutionally sponsored loans, scholarships/grants, and tuition waivers (partial) available. Support available to part-time students. Financial award application deadline: 3/15; financial award applicants required to submit FAFSA. In 2006, 122 master's, 32 doctorates awarded. *Degree program information:* Part-time programs available. Offers drama therapy (MA); expressive arts therapy (MA); integral counseling psychology (MA); psychology (Psy D); somatic psychology (MA). *Application deadline:* For fall admission, 2/1 priority date for domestic and international students; for spring admission, 10/15 priority date for domestic and international students. Applications are processed on a rolling basis. *Application fee:* $65. Electronic applications accepted. *Application Contact:* David Townes, Senior Admissions Counselor, 415-575-6152, Fax: 415-575-1268, E-mail: dtownes@ciis.edu. *Academic Vice President,* Dr. Judie Wexler, 415-575-6124, Fax: 415-575-1264, E-mail: jwexler@ciis.edu.

CALIFORNIA INSTITUTE OF TECHNOLOGY, Pasadena, CA 91125-0001

General Information Independent, coed, university. CGS member. *Graduate housing:* Rooms and/or apartments available on a first-come, first-served basis to single students and available to married students. Housing application deadline: 5/1. *Research affiliation:* Scripps Institute of Oceanography, Stanford Linear Accelerator Center (high-energy physics), European Center for Nuclear Research (high-energy physics), National Science Foundation Center for Research in Parallel Computing, Cosmic Gravitational Waves Observatory (laser interferometer gravitational waves).

GRADUATE UNITS

Division of Biology Students: 79 full-time (42 women); includes 2 American Indian/Alaska Native, 7 Hispanic Americans. 197 applicants, 18% accepted, 18 enrolled. *Faculty:* 39 full-time (8 women). Expenses: Contact institution. *Financial support:* In 2006–07, fellowships with full tuition reimbursements (averaging $21,680 per year), teaching assistantships with full tuition reimbursements (averaging $4,320 per year) were awarded; research assistantships with full tuition reimbursements, institutionally sponsored loans also available. Financial award application deadline: 1/1. In 2006, 1 master's, 21 doctorates awarded. Offers biochemistry and molecular biophysics (MS, PhD); cell biology and biophysics (PhD); developmental biology (PhD); genetics (PhD); immunology (PhD); molecular biology (PhD); neurobiology (PhD). *Application deadline:* For fall admission, 1/1 for domestic and international students. *Application fee:* $80. Electronic applications accepted. *Application Contact:* Elizabeth Ayala, Graduate Program Coordinator, 626-395-4497, Fax: 626-683-3343, E-mail: biograd@cco.caltech.edu. *Chairman,* Elliot Meyerowitz, 626-395-4951, Fax: 626-683-3343, E-mail: biograd@cco.caltech.edu.

Division of Chemistry and Chemical Engineering Students: 336 full-time (116 women). Average age 24. 647 applicants, 26% accepted, 46 enrolled. *Faculty:* 40 full-time (8 women), 1 part-time/adjunct (0 women). Expenses: Contact institution. *Financial support:* Fellowships, research assistantships, teaching assistantships, Federal Work-Study, institutionally sponsored loans, scholarships/grants, traineeships, health care benefits, and unspecified assistantships available. Financial award application deadline: 1/1. In 2006, 18 master's, 50 doctorates awarded. Offers biochemistry and molecular biophysics (MS, PhD); chemical engineering (MS, PhD); chemistry (MS, PhD). *Application deadline:* For fall admission, 1/1 for domestic and international students. *Application fee:* $50. Electronic applications accepted. *Chairman,* Dr. David A. Tirrell, 626-395-3646, Fax: 626-568-8824, E-mail: tirrell@caltech.edu.

Division of Engineering and Applied Science Students: 563 full-time (122 women), 3 part-time; includes 72 minority (13 African Americans, 2 American Indian/Alaska Native, 42 Asian Americans or Pacific Islanders, 15 Hispanic Americans), 284 international. *Faculty:* 84 full-time (9 women). Expenses: Contact institution. *Financial support:* In 2006–07, 166 fellowships, 372 research assistantships, 173 teaching assistantships were awarded; Federal Work-Study and institutionally sponsored loans also available. Support available to part-time students. In 2006, 75 master's, 67 doctorates awarded. Offers aeronautics (MS, PhD, Engr); applied and computational mathematics (MS, PhD); applied mechanics (MS, PhD); applied physics (MS, PhD); bioengineering (MS, PhD); civil engineering (MS, PhD, Engr); computation and neural systems (MS, PhD); computer science (MS, PhD); control and dynamical systems (MS, PhD); electrical engineering (MS, PhD, Engr); environmental science and engineering (MS, PhD); materials science (MS, PhD); mechanical engineering (MS, PhD, Engr). *Application deadline:* For fall admission, 1/1 for domestic students. *Application fee:* $50. Electronic applications accepted. *Chair to Division of Engineering and Applied Science,* Dr. David Rutledge, 626-395-4100, E-mail: rutledge@caltech.edu.

Division of Geological and Planetary Sciences Students: 69 full-time (28 women); includes 23 minority (20 Asian Americans or Pacific Islanders, 3 Hispanic Americans). Average age 26. 92 applicants, 26% accepted, 14 enrolled. *Faculty:* 35 full-time (4 women). Expenses: Contact institution. *Financial support:* In 2006–07, 21 fellowships with full tuition reimbursements (averaging $25,000 per year), 49 research assistantships with full tuition reimbursements (averaging $25,000 per year) were awarded; teaching assistantships with full tuition reimbursements, institutionally sponsored loans, scholarships/grants, health care benefits, and unspecified assistantships also available. Financial award applicants required to submit FAFSA. In 2006, 10 master's, 11 doctorates awarded. Offers geobiology (PhD); geochemistry (MS, PhD); geology (MS, PhD); geophysics (MS, PhD); planetary science (MS, PhD). *Application deadline:* For fall admission, 1/15 for domestic and international students. *Application fee:* $80. Electronic applications accepted. *Application Contact:* Dr. George R. Rossman, Academic Officer, 626-395-6125, Fax: 626-568-0935, E-mail: divgps@gps.caltech.edu. *Chairman,* Dr. Kenneth A. Farley, 626-395-6108, Fax: 626-795-6028, E-mail: divgps@gps.caltech.edu.

Division of Physics, Mathematics and Astronomy Offers astronomy (PhD); mathematics (PhD); physics (PhD).

Division of the Humanities and Social Sciences Students: 35 full-time (13 women); includes 5 minority (4 Asian Americans or Pacific Islanders, 1 Hispanic American), 15 international. Average age 26. 170 applicants, 12% accepted, 8 enrolled. *Faculty:* 31 full-time (3 women). Expenses: Contact institution. *Financial support:* In 2006–07, 35 students received support, including 11 fellowships (averaging $25,000 per year), 14 research assistantships (averaging $25,000 per year), 10 teaching assistantships (averaging $25,000 per year); Federal Work-Study, institutionally sponsored loans, and scholarships/grants also available. In 2006, 10 master's, 2 doctorates awarded. Offers economics (PhD); humanities and social sciences (MS, PhD); political science (PhD); social science (MS). *Application deadline:* For fall admission, 12/15 for domestic and international students. *Application fee:* $50. Electronic applications accepted. *Application Contact:* Laurel Auchampaugh, Graduate Secretary, 626-395-4206, Fax: 626-405-9841, E-mail: gradsec@hss.caltech.edu. *Chair,* Peter L. Bossaerts, Fax: 626-405-9841.

CALIFORNIA INSTITUTE OF THE ARTS, Valencia, CA 91355-2340

General Information Independent, coed, comprehensive institution. *Enrollment:* 1,349 graduate, professional, and undergraduate students; 500 full-time matriculated graduate/professional students (266 women), 5 part-time matriculated graduate/professional students (3 women). *Enrollment by degree level:* 505 master's. *Graduate faculty:* 147 full-time (68 women), 140 part-time/adjunct (41 women). *Graduate housing:* Room and/or apartments available on a first-come, first-served basis to single students; on-campus housing not available to married students. Typical cost: $3,470 per year ($6,710 including board). Room and board charges vary according to board plan, campus/location and housing facility selected. Housing application deadline: 7/1. *Student services:* Campus employment opportunities, career counseling, free psychological counseling, international student services, low-cost health insurance. *Library facilities:* California Institute of the Arts Library plus 1 other. *Online resources:* library catalog, web page, access to other libraries' catalogs. *Collection:* 98,415 titles, 324 serial subscriptions.

Computer facilities: 40 computers available on campus for general student use. A campuswide network can be accessed from student residence rooms and from off campus. Internet access is available. *Web address:* http://www.calarts.edu/.

General Application Contact: Carol Kim, Dean of Enrollment Management, 661-255-1050, Fax: 661-253-7710, E-mail: admiss@calarts.edu.

GRADUATE UNITS

School of Art Students: 86 full-time (49 women); includes 32 minority (6 African Americans, 10 Asian Americans or Pacific Islanders, 16 Hispanic Americans), 9 international. Average age 27. 383 applicants, 17% accepted, 38 enrolled. *Faculty:* 30 full-time (15 women), 15 part-time/adjunct (8 women). Expenses: Contact institution. *Financial support:* Teaching assistantships, career-related internships or fieldwork, Federal Work-Study, institutionally sponsored loans, scholarships/grants, and tuition waivers (partial) available. Support available to part-time students. Financial award application deadline: 3/2; financial award applicants required to submit FAFSA. In 2006, 40 degrees awarded. Offers art (MFA, Adv C); graphic design (MFA, Adv C); photography (MFA, Adv C). *Application deadline:* For fall admission, 1/5 priority date for domestic and international students; for spring admission, 11/15 priority date for domestic and international students. Applications are processed on a rolling basis. *Application fee:* $70 ($85 for international students). Electronic applications accepted. *Application Contact:* Taryn Wolf, Assistant Director of Admissions, 661-255-1050 Ext. 7857, Fax: 661-253-7710, E-mail: twolf@calarts.edu. *Dean,* Thomas Lawson, 661-253-7801, Fax: 661-259-5871, E-mail: tlawson@calarts.edu.

School of Critical Studies Students: 35 full-time (23 women); includes 11 minority (4 African Americans, 3 Asian Americans or Pacific Islanders, 4 Hispanic Americans), 1 international. Average age 27. 119 applicants, 43% accepted, 18 enrolled. *Faculty:* 15 full-time (7 women), 19 part-time/adjunct (6 women). Expenses: Contact institution. *Financial support:* Research assistantships, teaching assistantships, career-related internships or fieldwork, Federal Work-Study, scholarships/grants, and tuition waivers (partial) available. Support available to part-time students. Financial award application deadline: 3/2; financial award applicants required to submit FAFSA. In 2006, 22 degrees awarded. Offers writing (MFA, Adv C). *Application deadline:* For fall admission, 2/1 priority date for domestic and international students; for spring admission, 11/15 for domestic students, 11/15 priority date for international students. Applications are processed on a rolling basis. *Application fee:* $70 ($85 for international students). *Application Contact:* Matt Timmons, Admissions Counselor, 661-253-7716, Fax: 661-253-7710, E-mail: mtimmons@calarts.edu. *Dean,* Nancy Wood, 661-253-7802.

School of Dance Students: 9 full-time (all women); includes 2 minority (1 African American, 1 Hispanic American), 5 international. Average age 27. 19 applicants, 32% accepted, 3 enrolled. *Faculty:* 6 full-time (3 women), 11 part-time/adjunct (5 women). Expenses: Contact institution. *Financial support:* Fellowships, teaching assistantships, career-related internships or fieldwork and Federal Work-Study available. Financial award application deadline: 3/2; financial award applicants required to submit FAFSA. In 2006, 5 degrees awarded. Offers dance (MFA, Adv C). *Application deadline:* For fall admission, 1/5 priority date for domestic and international students; for spring admission, 11/15 priority date for domestic and international students. Applications are processed on a rolling basis. *Application fee:* $70 ($85 for international students). *Application Contact:* Clyde Howell, Admissions Counselor, 661-255-1050 Ext. 3046, Fax: 660-253-7710, E-mail: chowell@calarts.edu. *Dean,* Stephan Koplowitz, 661-253-7899.

School of Film/Video Students: 131 full-time (71 women), 1 (woman) part-time; includes 27 minority (7 African Americans, 1 American Indian/Alaska Native, 13 Asian Americans or Pacific Islanders, 6 Hispanic Americans), 41 international. Average age 27. 246 applicants, 30% accepted, 35 enrolled. *Faculty:* 29 full-time (12 women), 51 part-time/adjunct (9 women). Expenses: Contact institution. *Financial support:* Career-related internships or fieldwork, Federal Work-Study, and scholarships/grants available. Financial award application deadline: 3/2; financial award applicants required to submit FAFSA. In 2006, 42 degrees awarded. Offers experimental animation (MFA); film directing (MFA, Adv C); film/video (Adv C). *Application deadline:* For fall admission, 1/5 priority date for domestic and international students; for spring admission, 11/15 priority date for domestic and international students. Applications are processed on a rolling basis. *Application fee:* $70 ($85 for international students). Electronic applications accepted. *Application Contact:* Libby Hux, Admissions Counselor, 661-253-7884, Fax: 661-253-7710, E-mail: lhux@calarts.edu. *Dean,* Steve Anker, 661-253-7822.

School of Music Students: 106 full-time (29 women); includes 17 minority (5 African Americans, 9 Asian Americans or Pacific Islanders, 3 Hispanic Americans), 10 international. Average age 27. 113 applicants, 75% accepted, 53 enrolled. *Faculty:* 30 full-time (8 women), 32 part-time/adjunct (11 women). Expenses: Contact institution. *Financial support:* In 2006–07, 60 students received support, including 20 teaching assistantships; career-related internships or fieldwork, Federal Work-Study, institutionally sponsored loans, and scholarships/grants also available. Support available to part-time students. Financial award application deadline: 3/2; financial award applicants required to submit FAFSA. In 2006, 36 degrees awarded. *Degree program information:* Part-time programs available. Offers African music (MFA, Adv C); composition (MFA, Adv C); composition/new media (MFA, Adv C); Indonesian music (MFA, Adv C); jazz (MFA, Adv C); North Indian music (MFA, Adv C); performance (MFA, Adv C); performer/composer (MFA, Adv C); voice (MFA, Adv C); world music performance (MFA). *Application deadline:* For fall admission, 1/5 priority date for domestic and international students; for spring admission, 11/15 priority date for domestic and international students. Applications are processed on a rolling basis. *Application fee:* $70 ($85 for international students). Electronic applications accepted. *Application Contact:* Natalie Brejcha, Admissions Counselor, 661-255-1050 Ext. 7841, Fax: 661-253-7710, E-mail: nbrejcha@calarts.edu. *Dean,* David Rosenboom, 661-253-7816, Fax: 661-255-0938.

School of Theatre Students: 130 full-time (83 women); includes 33 minority (14 African Americans, 1 American Indian/Alaska Native, 10 Asian Americans or Pacific Islanders, 8 Hispanic Americans), 12 international. Average age 27. 255 applicants, 25% accepted, 39 enrolled. *Faculty:* 31 full-time (18 women), 13 part-time/adjunct (3 women). Expenses: Contact institution. *Financial support:* Teaching assistantships, career-related internships or fieldwork, Federal Work-Study, institutionally sponsored loans, and scholarships/grants available. Support available to part-time students. Financial award application deadline: 3/2; financial award applicants required to submit FAFSA. In 2006, 30 degrees awarded. Offers acting (MFA, Adv C); design and technology (Adv C); directing (MFA); performing arts design and technology (MFA); theater management (Adv C); theatre management (MFA); writing for performance (MFA). *Application deadline:* For fall admission, 1/5 priority date for domestic and international students. Applications are processed on a rolling basis. *Application fee:* $70 ($85 for international students). Electronic applications accepted. *Application Contact:* Damion Parran, Admissions Counselor, 661-222-2761, Fax: 661-253-7710, E-mail: dparran@calarts.edu. *Dean,* Erik Ehn, 661-255-1050.

CALIFORNIA LUTHERAN UNIVERSITY, Thousand Oaks, CA 91360-2787

General Information Independent-religious, coed, comprehensive institution. *Graduate housing:* On-campus housing not available.

GRADUATE UNITS

Graduate Studies *Degree program information:* Part-time and evening/weekend programs available. Offers clinical psychology (MS); marital and family therapy (MS); public policy and administration (MPPA).

School of Business *Degree program information:* Evening/weekend programs available. Postbaccalaureate distance learning degree programs offered. Offers business (IMBA); finance (MBA); financial planning (MBA, MS, Certificate); general business (MBA); information technology management (MBA); international business (MBA); management and organization behavior (MBA); marketing (MBA); small business/entrepreneurship (MBA).

School of Education *Degree program information:* Part-time and evening/weekend programs available. Offers counseling and guidance (MS); curriculum and instruction (MA); education (M Ed); educational administration (MA); reading education (MA); special education (MS); teacher preparation (Certificate).

See Close-Up on page 825.

CALIFORNIA NATIONAL UNIVERSITY FOR ADVANCED STUDIES, Northridge, CA 91325-3576

General Information Proprietary, coed, comprehensive institution.

GRADUATE UNITS

College of Business Administration *Degree program information:* Part-time programs available. Postbaccalaureate distance learning degree programs offered (no on-campus study). Offers business administration (MBA, MHRM). Electronic applications accepted.

College of Engineering *Degree program information:* Part-time programs available. Postbaccalaureate distance learning degree programs offered (no on-campus study). Offers engineering (MS Eng). Electronic applications accepted.

College of Quality and Engineering Management *Degree program information:* Part-time programs available. Offers quality and engineering management (MEM).

CALIFORNIA POLYTECHNIC STATE UNIVERSITY, SAN LUIS OBISPO, San Luis Obispo, CA 93407

General Information State-supported, coed, comprehensive institution. *Enrollment:* 18,722 graduate, professional, and undergraduate students; 508 full-time matriculated graduate/professional students (229 women), 292 part-time matriculated graduate/professional students (130 women). *Enrollment by degree level:* 800 master's. *Graduate faculty:* 131 full-time (34 women), 54 part-time/adjunct (15 women). *Student services:* Campus employment opportunities, campus safety program, career counseling, child daycare facilities, disabled student services, exercise/wellness program, free psychological counseling, grant writing training, international student services, low-cost health insurance, multicultural affairs office, teacher training, writing training. *Library facilities:* Kennedy Library plus 1 other. *Online resources:* library catalog, web page, access to other libraries' catalogs. *Collection:* 763,651 titles, 5,529 serial subscriptions.

Computer facilities: 1,880 computers available on campus for general student use. A campuswide network can be accessed from student residence rooms and from off campus. *Web address:* http://www.calpoly.edu/.

General Application Contact: Dr. Jim Maraviglia, Assistant Vice President of Admissions, Recruitment and Financial Aid, 805-756-2311, Fax: 805-756-5400, E-mail: admissions@calpoly.edu.

GRADUATE UNITS

College of Agriculture, Food and Environmental Sciences Students: 73 full-time (52 women), 47 part-time (26 women); includes 22 minority (1 African American, 1 American Indian/Alaska Native, 9 Asian Americans or Pacific Islanders, 11 Hispanic Americans), 4 international. 73 applicants, 60% accepted, 41 enrolled. *Faculty:* 30 full-time (7 women), 12 part-time/adjunct (1 woman). Expenses: Contact institution. *Financial support:* In 2006–07, 40 students received support; fellowships, research assistantships, teaching assistantships, career-related internships or fieldwork, Federal Work-Study, institutionally sponsored loans, and scholarships/grants available. Support available to part-time students. Financial award application deadline: 3/2; financial award applicants required to submit FAFSA. In 2006, 42 degrees awarded. *Degree program information:* Part-time programs available. Offers agribusiness (MS); agriculture (MS); agriculture, food and environmental sciences (MS); forestry science (MS). *Application deadline:* For fall admission, 7/1 for domestic students, 11/30 for international students; for winter admission, 11/1 for domestic students, 6/30 for international students; for spring admission, 2/1 for domestic students. Applications are processed on a rolling basis. *Application fee:* $55. Electronic applications accepted. *Application Contact:* Dr. Mark Shelton, Associate Dean/Graduate Coordinator, 805-756-2161, Fax: 805-756-6577, E-mail: mshelton@calpoly.edu. *Dean,* Dr. David J. Wehner, 805-756-2161, Fax: 805-756-6577, E-mail: dwehner@calpoly.edu.

College of Architecture and Environmental Design Students: 43 full-time (15 women), 12 part-time (6 women); includes 12 minority (1 African American, 6 Asian Americans or Pacific Islanders, 5 Hispanic Americans), 3 international. 71 applicants, 69% accepted, 25 enrolled. *Faculty:* 9 full-time (2 women), 5 part-time/adjunct (2 women). Expenses: Contact institution. *Financial support:* Research assistantships, teaching assistantships, career-related internships or fieldwork, Federal Work-Study, and institutionally sponsored loans available. Support available to part-time students. Financial award application deadline: 3/2; financial award applicants required to submit FAFSA. In 2006, 14 degrees awarded. *Degree program information:* Part-time programs available. Offers architecture (MS); architecture and environmental design (MCRP, MS); city and regional planning (MCRP). *Application deadline:* For fall admission, 7/1 for domestic students, 11/30 for international students; for winter admission, 11/1 for domestic students, 6/30 for international students. Applications are processed on a rolling basis. *Application fee:* $55. Electronic applications accepted. *Dean,* R. Thomas Jones, 805-756-1414, Fax: 805-756-2765, E-mail: rtjones@calpoly.edu.

College of Education Students: 76 full-time (58 women), 25 part-time (22 women); includes 26 minority (1 African American, 6 Asian Americans or Pacific Islanders, 19 Hispanic Americans). 108 applicants, 62% accepted, 61 enrolled. *Faculty:* 5 full-time (2 women), 8 part-time/adjunct (6 women). Expenses: Contact institution. *Financial support:* Research assistantships, career-related internships or fieldwork, Federal Work-Study, and institutionally sponsored loans available. Support available to part-time students. Financial award application deadline: 3/2; financial award applicants required to submit FAFSA. In 2006, 66 degrees awarded. *Degree program information:* Part-time and evening/weekend programs available. Offers education (MA). *Application deadline:* For fall admission, 4/1 priority date for domestic students, 11/30 for international students. *Application fee:* $55. *Dean,* Dr. Bonnie Konopak, 805-756-2126, Fax: 805-756-5682, E-mail: bkonopak@calpoly.edu.

College of Engineering Students: 172 full-time (39 women), 99 part-time (20 women); includes 75 minority (3 African Americans, 1 American Indian/Alaska Native, 59 Asian Americans or Pacific Islanders, 12 Hispanic Americans), 7 international. 170 applicants, 69% accepted, 81 enrolled. *Faculty:* 52 full-time (11 women), 13 part-time/adjunct (2 women). Expenses: Contact institution. *Financial support:* Fellowships, research assistantships, teaching assistantships, career-related internships or fieldwork, Federal Work-Study, and institutionally sponsored loans available. Support available to part-time students. Financial award application deadline: 3/2; financial award applicants required to submit FAFSA. In 2006, 91 degrees awarded. *Degree program information:* Part-time programs available. Offers aerospace engineering (MS); civil and environmental engineering (MS); computer science (MS); electrical engineering (MS); engineering (MS); general engineering (MS); industrial engineering (MS); mechanical engineering (MS). *Application deadline:* For fall admission, 7/1 for domestic students, 11/30 for international students; for winter admission, 11/1 for domestic students, 6/30 for international students; for spring admission, 2/1 for domestic students. Applications are processed on a rolling basis. *Application fee:* $55. Electronic applications accepted. *Dean,* Dr. Mohammad Noori, 805-756-2131, Fax: 805-756-6503, E-mail: mnoori@calpoly.edu.

College of Liberal Arts Students: 54 full-time (35 women), 60 part-time (31 women); includes 21 minority (2 African Americans, 1 American Indian/Alaska Native, 8 Asian Americans or Pacific Islanders, 10 Hispanic Americans). 115 applicants, 58% accepted, 37 enrolled. *Faculty:* 8 full-time (5 women), 4 part-time/adjunct (2 women). Expenses: Contact institution. *Financial support:* Teaching assistantships, career-related internships or fieldwork, Federal Work-Study, institutionally sponsored loans, scholarships/grants, and tutorships, writing laboratory assistantships available. Support available to part-time students. Financial award application deadline: 3/2; financial award applicants required to submit FAFSA. In 2006, 45 degrees awarded. *Degree program information:* Part-time programs available. Offers English (MA); history (MA); liberal arts (MA, MPP, MS); political science (MPP); psychology (MS). *Application deadline:* For fall admission, 5/1 for domestic students, 11/30 for international students; for winter admission, 11/1 for domestic students, 6/30 for international students; for spring admission, 2/1 for domestic students. *Application fee:* $55. *Dean,* Dr. Linda Halisky, 805-756-2706, Fax: 805-756-5748, E-mail: lhalisky@calpoly.edu.

College of Science and Mathematics Students: 39 full-time (16 women), 30 part-time (16 women); includes 8 minority (1 African American, 4 Asian Americans or Pacific Islanders, 3 Hispanic Americans). 76 applicants, 50% accepted, 23 enrolled. *Faculty:* 23 full-time (6 women), 6 part-time/adjunct (2 women). Expenses: Contact institution. *Financial support:* Research assistantships, teaching assistantships, career-related internships or fieldwork and Federal Work-Study available. Support available to part-time students. Financial award application deadline: 3/2; financial award applicants required to submit FAFSA. In 2006, 32 degrees awarded. *Degree program information:* Part-time programs available. Offers biological sciences (MS); kinesiology (MS); mathematics (MS); polymers and coating science (MS); science and mathematics (MS). *Application deadline:* For fall admission, 7/1 for domestic students, 11/30 for international students; for winter admission, 11/1 for domestic students, 6/30 for international students; for spring admission, 2/1 for domestic students. *Application fee:* $55. Electronic applications accepted. *Dean,* Dr. Philip S. Bailey, 805-756-2226, Fax: 805-756-1670, E-mail: pbailey@calpoly.edu.

Orfalea College of Business Students: 51 full-time (14 women), 19 part-time (9 women); includes 4 minority (3 Asian Americans or Pacific Islanders, 1 Hispanic American), 4 international. 104 applicants, 49% accepted, 46 enrolled. *Faculty:* 4 full-time (1 woman), 6 part-time/adjunct (0 women). Expenses: Contact institution. *Financial support:* Career-related internships or fieldwork, Federal Work-Study, institutionally sponsored loans, scholarships/grants, and unspecified assistantships available. Support available to part-time students. Financial award application deadline: 3/2; financial award applicants required to submit FAFSA. In 2006, 42 degrees awarded. Offers business (MBA); industrial and technical studies (MS); taxation (MS Acct). *Application deadline:* For fall admission, 7/1 for domestic students, 11/30 for international students. Applications are processed on a rolling basis. *Application fee:* $55. Electronic applications accepted. *Application Contact:* Dr. Chris Carr, Associate Dean, 805-756-2637, Fax: 805-756-0110, E-mail: ccarr@calpoly.edu. *Dean,* Dr. David P. Christy, 805-756-2705, Fax: 805-756-5452, E-mail: dchristy@calpoly.edu.

CALIFORNIA SCHOOL OF PODIATRIC MEDICINE AT SAMUEL MERRITT COLLEGE, Oakland, CA 94609

General Information Independent, coed, graduate-only institution. *Enrollment by degree level:* 132 first professional. *Graduate faculty:* 12 full-time (2 women), 10 part-time/adjunct (2 women). *Tuition:* Full-time $25,599. *Required fees:* $370. One-time fee: $2,100 full-time. *Graduate housing:* Room and/or apartments available on a first-come, first-served basis to single students; on-campus housing not available to married students. Typical cost: $8,849 per year. Room charges vary according to campus/location. *Student services:* Campus employment opportunities, career counseling, disabled student services, exercise/wellness program, free psychological counseling, low-cost health insurance, writing training. *Library facilities:* John A. Graziano Memorial Library. *Online resources:* web page. *Collection:* 36,995 titles, 2,970 serial subscriptions, 1,947 audiovisual materials. *Research affiliation:* University of Southern California–Los Angeles County Medical Center, University of California, San Francisco Health Sciences Center, University of Texas Health Science Center–San Antonio.

Computer facilities: 50 computers available on campus for general student use. A campuswide network can be accessed from student residence rooms and from off campus. Internet access is available. *Web address:* http://www.ccpm.edu/.

General Application Contact: Dr. David Tran, Director of Recruitment, 800-334-2276 Ext. 407, Fax: 415-292-0439, E-mail: ldavis@ccpm.edu.

GRADUATE UNITS

Graduate and Professional Programs Students: 132 full-time (51 women); includes 42 minority (5 African Americans, 32 Asian Americans or Pacific Islanders, 5 Hispanic Americans), 4 international. Average age 27. 243 applicants, 42% accepted, 40 enrolled. *Faculty:* 12 full-time (2 women), 10 part-time/adjunct (2 women). Expenses: Contact institution. *Financial support:* In 2006–07, 112 fellowships were awarded; Federal Work-Study and institutionally sponsored loans also available. Financial award application deadline: 3/2; financial award applicants required to submit FAFSA. In 2006, 100 degrees awarded. Offers podiatric medicine (DPM). *Application deadline:* For fall admission, 4/1 priority date for domestic students. Applications are processed on a rolling basis. *Application fee:* $50. *Application Contact:* Dr. David Tran, Associate Director of Admissions, 800-334-2276 Ext. 483, Fax: 415-292-0439, E-mail: pwhite@ccpm.edu. *Vice President and Dean of Student Services,* Irma Walker-Adame, 415-292-0481 Ext. 413, E-mail: iadame@ccpm.edu.

CALIFORNIA STATE POLYTECHNIC UNIVERSITY, POMONA, Pomona, CA 91768-2557

General Information State-supported, coed, comprehensive institution. CGS member. *Enrollment:* 20,510 graduate, professional, and undergraduate students; 654 full-time matriculated graduate/professional students (335 women), 475 part-time matriculated graduate/professional students (210 women). *Enrollment by degree level:* 1,129 master's. *Graduate faculty:* 533 full-time (192 women), 602 part-time/adjunct (238 women). Tuition, state resident: part-time $226 per unit. Tuition, nonresident: part-time $226 per unit. *Required fees:* $2,486 per year. *Graduate housing:* Room and/or apartments available on a first-come, first-served basis to single students; on-campus housing not available to married students. Typical cost: $8,493 (including board). Room and board charges vary according to board plan and housing facility selected. Housing application deadline: 5/1. *Student services:* Campus employment opportunities, campus safety program, career counseling, child daycare facilities, disabled student services, free psychological counseling, international student services, low-cost health insurance. *Library facilities:* University Library. *Online resources:* library catalog, web page, access to other libraries' catalogs. *Collection:* 748,154 titles, 4,603 serial subscriptions, 6,062 audiovisual materials.

California State Polytechnic University, Pomona (continued)

Computer facilities: 1,864 computers available on campus for general student use. A campuswide network can be accessed from student residence rooms and from off campus. Internet access is available. *Web address:* http://www.csupomona.edu/.

General Application Contact: Scott Duncan, Associate Director, Admissions and Outreach, 909-869-3258, Fax: 909-869-4529, E-mail: sjduncan@csupomona.edu.

GRADUATE UNITS

Academic Affairs Students: 654 full-time (335 women), 475 part-time (210 women); includes 532 minority (42 African Americans, 1 American Indian/Alaska Native, 267 Asian Americans or Pacific Islanders, 222 Hispanic Americans), 99 international. Average age 32. 930 applicants, 47% accepted, 284 enrolled. *Faculty:* 533 full-time (192 women), 602 part-time/adjunct (238 women). Expenses: Contact institution. *Financial support:* In 2006–07, 4 fellowships, 5 research assistantships, 3 teaching assistantships were awarded; career-related internships or fieldwork, Federal Work-Study, institutionally sponsored loans, and unspecified assistantships also available. Support available to part-time students. Financial award application deadline: 3/2; financial award applicants required to submit FAFSA. In 2006, 396 degrees awarded. *Degree program information:* Part-time and evening/weekend programs available. *Application deadline:* Applications are processed on a rolling basis. *Application fee:* $55. Electronic applications accepted. *Provost/Vice President for Academic Affairs,* Dr. Tomas D. Morales, 909-869-3405, E-mail: tdmorales@csupomona.edu.

College of Agriculture Students: 25 full-time (18 women), 39 part-time (35 women); includes 23 minority (1 African American, 11 Asian Americans or Pacific Islanders, 11 Hispanic Americans), 5 international. Average age 30. 58 applicants, 76% accepted, 20 enrolled. *Faculty:* 34 full-time (9 women), 23 part-time/adjunct (13 women). Expenses: Contact institution. *Financial support:* Career-related internships or fieldwork, Federal Work-Study, and institutionally sponsored loans available. Support available to part-time students. Financial award application deadline: 3/2; financial award applicants required to submit FAFSA. In 2006, 13 degrees awarded. *Degree program information:* Part-time programs available. Offers agricultural science (MS); animal science (MS); foods and nutrition (MS). *Application deadline:* For fall admission, 5/1 priority date for domestic students; for winter admission, 10/15 priority date for domestic students; for spring admission, 1/2 priority date for domestic students. Applications are processed on a rolling basis. *Application fee:* $55. Electronic applications accepted. *Dean,* Dr. Wayne R. Bidlack, 909-869-2204, E-mail: wrbidlack@csupomona.edu.

College of Business Administration Students: 92 full-time (32 women), 68 part-time (27 women); includes 63 minority (3 African Americans, 43 Asian Americans or Pacific Islanders, 17 Hispanic Americans), 30 international. Average age 30. 132 applicants, 33% accepted, 27 enrolled. *Faculty:* 76 full-time (26 women), 57 part-time/adjunct (14 women). Expenses: Contact institution. *Financial support:* In 2006–07, 5 research assistantships, 3 teaching assistantships were awarded; career-related internships or fieldwork, Federal Work-Study, and institutionally sponsored loans also available. Support available to part-time students. Financial award application deadline: 3/2; financial award applicants required to submit FAFSA. In 2006, 58 degrees awarded. *Degree program information:* Part-time programs available. Offers business administration (MBA, MSBA). *Application deadline:* For fall admission, 5/1 priority date for domestic students; for winter admission, 10/15 priority date for domestic students; for spring admission, 1/2 priority date for domestic students. Applications are processed on a rolling basis. *Application fee:* $55. Electronic applications accepted. *Application Contact:* Dr. Eric J. McLaughlin, Director, Graduate Program, 909-869-2362, E-mail: ejmclaughlin@csupomona.edu. *Dean,* Dr. David Klock, 909-869-2400.

College of Education and Integrative Studies Students: 55 full-time (36 women), 48 part-time (36 women); includes 50 minority (3 African Americans, 14 Asian Americans or Pacific Islanders, 33 Hispanic Americans), 2 international. Average age 35. 56 applicants, 80% accepted, 25 enrolled. *Faculty:* 40 full-time (25 women), 44 part-time/adjunct (28 women). Expenses: Contact institution. *Financial support:* Career-related internships or fieldwork, Federal Work-Study, and institutionally sponsored loans available. Support available to part-time students. Financial award application deadline: 3/2; financial award applicants required to submit FAFSA. In 2006, 123 degrees awarded. *Degree program information:* Part-time programs available. Offers education and integrative studies (MA). *Application deadline:* For fall admission, 5/1 priority date for domestic students; for winter admission, 10/15 priority date for domestic students; for spring admission, 1/20 priority date for domestic students. Applications are processed on a rolling basis. *Application fee:* $55. Electronic applications accepted. *Application Contact:* Dr. Gary Kinsey, Associate Dean, 909-869-2316, Fax: 909-869-4963, E-mail: gwkinsey@csupomona.edu. *Interim Dean,* Dr. Barbara J. Way, 909-869-2307, E-mail: bjway@csupomona.edu.

College of Engineering Students: 61 full-time (14 women), 93 part-time (10 women); includes 96 minority (7 African Americans, 53 Asian Americans or Pacific Islanders, 36 Hispanic Americans), 12 international. Average age 30. 113 applicants, 69% accepted, 37 enrolled. *Faculty:* 83 full-time (14 women), 72 part-time/adjunct (3 women). Expenses: Contact institution. *Financial support:* In 2006–07, 1 fellowship, 6 research assistantships, 5 teaching assistantships were awarded; career-related internships or fieldwork, Federal Work-Study, institutionally sponsored loans, and unspecified assistantships also available. Support available to part-time students. Financial award application deadline: 3/2; financial award applicants required to submit FAFSA. In 2006, 45 degrees awarded. *Degree program information:* Part-time programs available. Offers civil engineering (MS); electrical engineering (MSEE); engineering (MSE); engineering management (MS); mechanical engineering (MS). *Application deadline:* For fall admission, 5/1 priority date for domestic students; for winter admission, 10/15 priority date for domestic students; for spring admission, 1/2 priority date for domestic students. Applications are processed on a rolling basis. *Application fee:* $55. Electronic applications accepted. *Application Contact:* Dr. Rajan Chandra, Director, 909-869-2476, Fax: 909-869-4687, E-mail: rmchandra@csupomona.edu. *Dean,* Dr. Edward Hohmann, 909-869-2472, Fax: 909-869-4370, E-mail: echohmann@csupomona.edu.

College of Environmental Design Students: 157 full-time (81 women), 36 part-time (18 women); includes 68 minority (6 African Americans, 37 Asian Americans or Pacific Islanders, 25 Hispanic Americans), 11 international. Average age 31. 265 applicants, 29% accepted, 49 enrolled. *Faculty:* 46 full-time (19 women), 41 part-time/adjunct (17 women). Expenses: Contact institution. *Financial support:* Career-related internships or fieldwork, Federal Work-Study, and institutionally sponsored loans available. Support available to part-time students. Financial award application deadline: 3/2; financial award applicants required to submit FAFSA. In 2006, 39 degrees awarded. *Degree program information:* Part-time programs available. Offers architecture (M Arch); environmental design (M Arch, M Land Arch, MS, MURP); landscape architecture (M Land Arch); regenerative studies (MS); urban and regional planning (MURP). *Application deadline:* For fall admission, 5/1 priority date for domestic students; for winter admission, 10/15 priority date for domestic students; for spring admission, 1/20 priority date for domestic students. Applications are processed on a rolling basis. *Application fee:* $55. Electronic applications accepted. *Dean,* Karen C. Hanna, 909-869-2667, E-mail: kchanna@csupomona.edu.

College of Letters, Arts, and Social Sciences Students: 149 full-time (97 women), 78 part-time (41 women); includes 110 minority (15 African Americans, 36 Asian Americans or Pacific Islanders, 59 Hispanic Americans), 13 international. Average age 32. 191 applicants, 53% accepted, 73 enrolled. *Faculty:* 120 full-time (61 women), 196 part-time/adjunct (95 women). Expenses: Contact institution. *Financial support:* In 2006–07, 2 fellowships were awarded; Federal Work-Study and institutionally sponsored loans also available. Support available to part-time students. Financial award application deadline: 3/2; financial award applicants required to submit FAFSA. In 2006, 58 degrees awarded. *Degree program information:* Part-time and evening/weekend programs available. Offers economics (MS); English (MA); history (MA); kinesiology (MS); letters, arts, and social sciences (MA, MPA, MS); psychology (MS); public administration (MPA). *Application deadline:* Applications are processed on a rolling basis. *Application fee:* $55. Electronic applications accepted. *Dean,* Dr. Barbara J. Way, 909-869-3943, E-mail: bjway@csupomona.edu.

College of Science Students: 115 full-time (57 women), 113 part-time (43 women); includes 122 minority (7 African Americans, 1 American Indian/Alaska Native, 73 Asian Americans or Pacific Islanders, 41 Hispanic Americans), 26 international. Average age 28. 123 applicants, 52% accepted, 50 enrolled. *Faculty:* 114 full-time (31 women), 165 part-time/adjunct (66 women). Expenses: Contact institution. *Financial support:* Career-related internships or fieldwork, Federal Work-Study, and institutionally sponsored loans available. Support available to part-time students. Financial award application deadline: 3/2; financial award applicants required to submit FAFSA. In 2006, 49 degrees awarded. *Degree program information:* Part-time and evening/weekend programs available. Offers applied mathematics (MS); biological sciences (MS); chemistry (MS); computer science (MS); pure mathematics (MS); science (MS). *Application deadline:* For fall admission, 5/1 priority date for domestic students; for winter admission, 10/15 priority date for domestic students; for spring admission, 1/20 priority date for domestic students. Applications are processed on a rolling basis. *Application fee:* $55. Electronic applications accepted. *Dean,* Dr. Donald O. Straney, 909-869-3600, E-mail: dostraney@csupomona.edu.

CALIFORNIA STATE UNIVERSITY, BAKERSFIELD, Bakersfield, CA 93311-1022

General Information State-supported, coed, comprehensive institution. CGS member. *Enrollment:* 948 full-time matriculated graduate/professional students (673 women), 658 part-time matriculated graduate/professional students (466 women). *Enrollment by degree level:* 1,606 master's. *Graduate faculty:* 165 full-time (96 women), 103 part-time/adjunct (63 women). *Graduate housing:* Room and/or apartments available on a first-come, first-served basis to single students; on-campus housing not available to married students. Housing application deadline: 8/1. *Student services:* Campus employment opportunities, campus safety program, career counseling, child daycare facilities, disabled student services, free psychological counseling, grant writing training, international student services, teacher training. *Library facilities:* Walter W. Stiern Library. *Online resources:* web page. *Collection:* 354,016 titles, 2,260 serial subscriptions.

Computer facilities: 600 computers available on campus for general student use. A campuswide network can be accessed from student residence rooms and from off campus. Internet access and online class registration are available. *Web address:* http://www.csubak.edu/.

General Application Contact: Dr. Kendyl Magnoson, Associate Dean, 661-664-2161, E-mail: kmagnuson@csub.edu.

GRADUATE UNITS

Division of Graduate Studies *Degree program information:* Part-time and evening/weekend programs available. Postbaccalaureate distance learning degree programs offered (no on-campus study). Offers administration (MS); interdisciplinary studies (MA).

School of Business and Public Administration Students: 86 full-time (39 women), 54 part-time (28 women); includes 57 minority (14 African Americans, 4 American Indian/Alaska Native, 14 Asian Americans or Pacific Islanders, 25 Hispanic Americans), 9 international. Average age 30. Expenses: Contact institution. *Financial support:* Career-related internships or fieldwork available. In 2006, 59 degrees awarded. Offers business administration (MBA); business and public administration (MBA, MPA, MSA); health care management (MSA); public administration (MPA). *Application deadline:* Applications are processed on a rolling basis. *Application fee:* $55. *Application Contact:* Thomas Mishoe, Student Adviser, 661-664-3099, E-mail: tmishoe@csub.edu. *Interim Dean,* Dr. Mark O. Evans, 661-654-2326, E-mail: mevans@csub.edu.

School of Education Offers bilingual/multicultural education (MA Ed); curriculum and instruction (MA Ed); early childhood education (MA); education (MA, MA Ed, MS, Certificate); educational administration (MA); educational technology (MA Ed); reading/literacy (MA Ed, Certificate); school counseling (MS); special education (MA); student affairs (MS).

School of Humanities and Social Sciences *Degree program information:* Part-time and evening/weekend programs available. Offers anthropology (MA); counseling psychology (MS); English (MA); history (MA); humanities and social sciences (MA, MS, MSW); psychology (MA); social work (MSW); sociology (MA); Spanish (MA).

School of Natural Sciences and Mathematics Students: 42 full-time (27 women), 42 part-time (31 women); includes 34 minority (5 African Americans, 1 American Indian/Alaska Native, 14 Asian Americans or Pacific Islanders, 14 Hispanic Americans), 2 international. Expenses: Contact institution. In 2006, 21 degrees awarded. Offers biology (MS); geology (MS); hydrogeology (MS); natural sciences and mathematics (MA, MS); nursing (MS); petroleum geology (MS); teaching mathematics (MA). *Application fee:* $55. *Dean,* Dr. Julio R. Blanco, 661-654-3450, E-mail: jblanco@csub.edu.

CALIFORNIA STATE UNIVERSITY CHANNEL ISLANDS, Camarillo, CA 93012

General Information State-supported, coed, comprehensive institution. *Enrollment:* 3,123 graduate, professional, and undergraduate students; 74 matriculated graduate/professional students. *Enrollment by degree level:* 74 master's. *Graduate housing:* On-campus housing not available. *Student services:* Career counseling. *Library facilities:* John Spoor Broome Library at Channel Islands. *Online resources:* library catalog, web page. *Web address:* http://www.csuci.edu/.

General Application Contact: Maribel Aguilera, Application Contact, 805-437-2748, Fax: 805-437-8859, E-mail: exed@csuci.edu.

GRADUATE UNITS

Extended Education Students: 74. Expenses: Contact institution. Offers biotechnology and bioinformatics (MS); business administration (MBA); computer science (MS); educational leadership (MAEd); mathematics (MS). *Application Contact:* Maribel Aguilera, Application Contact, 805-437-2748, Fax: 805-437-8859, E-mail: exed@csuci.edu. *Dean of Extended Education,* Dr. Gary A. Berg, 805-437-8580, Fax: 805-437-8859, E-mail: gary.berg@csuci.edu.

CALIFORNIA STATE UNIVERSITY, CHICO, Chico, CA 95929-0722

General Information State-supported, coed, comprehensive institution. CGS member. *Enrollment:* 16,250 graduate, professional, and undergraduate students; 470 full-time matriculated graduate/professional students (289 women), 365 part-time matriculated graduate/professional students (219 women). *Enrollment by degree level:* 835 master's. *Graduate faculty:* 533 full-time (203 women), 432 part-time/adjunct (212 women). *Graduate housing:* Room and/or apartments available to single students; on-campus housing not available to married students. Housing application deadline: 3/22. *Student services:* Campus employment opportunities, campus safety program, career counseling, child daycare facilities, disabled student services, free psychological counseling, grant writing training, international student services, low-cost health insurance, teacher training. *Library facilities:* Meriam Library. *Online resources:* library catalog, web page, access to other libraries' catalogs. *Collection:* 957,181 titles, 24,244 serial subscriptions, 28,500 audiovisual materials. *Research affiliation:* Hewlett-Packard Company (computer science).

Computer facilities: 840 computers available on campus for general student use. A campuswide network can be accessed from student residence rooms and from off campus. Internet access and online class registration, student account information, e-mail, calendar, transcripts are available. *Web address:* http://www.csuchico.edu/.

General Application Contact: Dr. Susan E. Place, School of Graduate, International, and Interdisciplinary Studies, 530-898-6880, Fax: 530-898-6889, E-mail: splace@csuchico.edu.

GRADUATE UNITS

Graduate School Students: 470 full-time (289 women), 365 part-time (219 women); includes 127 minority (15 African Americans, 16 American Indian/Alaska Native, 32 Asian Americans or Pacific Islanders, 64 Hispanic Americans), 80 international. Average age 32. 637 applicants, 99% accepted, 337 enrolled. Expenses: Contact institution. *Financial support:* Fellowships, research assistantships, teaching assistantships, career-related internships or fieldwork, Federal Work-Study, and stipends available. Support available to part-time students. In 2006, 352 degrees awarded. *Degree program information:* Part-time programs available. Offers interdisciplinary studies (MA, MS); science teaching (MS); simulation science (MS); teaching international languages (MA). *Application deadline:* For fall admission, 3/1 for domestic and international students; for spring admission, 9/15 for domestic and international students. Applications are processed on a rolling basis. *Application fee:* $55. Electronic applications accepted. *School of Graduate, International, and Interdisciplinary Studies,* Dr. Susan E. Place, 530-898-6880, Fax: 530-898-6889, E-mail: splace@csuchico.edu.

College of Behavioral and Social Sciences Students: 189 full-time (132 women), 113 part-time (64 women); includes 65 minority (9 African Americans, 8 American Indian/Alaska Native, 14 Asian Americans or Pacific Islanders, 34 Hispanic Americans), 4 international. Average age 32. 220 applicants, 99% accepted, 137 enrolled. Expenses: Contact institution. *Financial support:* Fellowships, teaching assistantships, career-related internships or fieldwork and Federal Work-Study available. Support available to part-time students. In 2006, 87 degrees awarded. *Degree program information:* Part-time programs available. Offers applied psychology (MA); behavioral and social sciences (MA, MPA, MS, MSW); geography (MA); health administration (MPA); local government management (MPA); marriage and family therapy (MS); museum studies (MA); political science (MA); psychological science (MA); psychology (MA); public administration (MPA); rural and town planning (MA); social science (MA); social science education (MA); social work (MSW). *Application deadline:* For fall admission, 3/1 for domestic and international students. Applications are processed on a rolling basis. *Application fee:* $55. Electronic applications accepted. *Dean,* Gayle Hutchinson, 530-898-6171.

College of Business Students: 27 full-time (16 women), 13 part-time (3 women); includes 5 minority (3 Asian Americans or Pacific Islanders, 2 Hispanic Americans), 12 international. Average age 29. 31 applicants, 100% accepted, 16 enrolled. Expenses: Contact institution. In 2006, 17 degrees awarded. Offers business (MBA); business administration (MBA). *Application deadline:* For fall admission, 3/1 for domestic and international students; for spring admission, 9/15 for domestic and international students. Applications are processed on a rolling basis. *Application fee:* $55. Electronic applications accepted. *Application Contact:* Dr. Ray Boykin, 530-898-5895. *Dean,* Dr. Willie Hopkins, 530-898-6271.

College of Communication and Education Students: 106 full-time (75 women), 99 part-time (73 women); includes 23 minority (3 African Americans, 4 American Indian/Alaska Native, 4 Asian Americans or Pacific Islanders, 12 Hispanic Americans), 3 international. Average age 32. 103 applicants, 99% accepted, 80 enrolled. Expenses: Contact institution. *Financial support:* Fellowships, teaching assistantships, career-related internships or fieldwork, Federal Work-Study, and stipends available. Support available to part-time students. In 2006, 89 degrees awarded. *Degree program information:* Part-time programs available. Offers communication and education (MA, MS); communication science and disorders (MA); communication studies (MA); curriculum and instruction (MA); education (MA); educational administration (MA); instructional technology (MS); kinesiology (MA); linguistically and culturally diverse learners (MA); reading/language arts (MA); recreation administration (MA); special education (MA). *Application deadline:* For fall admission, 3/1 for domestic and international students; for spring admission, 9/15 for domestic and international students. Applications are processed on a rolling basis. *Application fee:* $55. Electronic applications accepted. *Dean,* Dr. Phyllis Fernlund, 530-898-4015.

College of Engineering, Computer Science, and Technology Students: 46 full-time (8 women), 29 part-time (7 women); includes 7 minority (1 African American, 6 Asian Americans or Pacific Islanders), 52 international. Average age 26. 168 applicants, 99% accepted, 28 enrolled. Expenses: Contact institution. *Financial support:* Fellowships, research assistantships, teaching assistantships, career-related internships or fieldwork and Federal Work-Study available. Support available to part-time students. In 2006, 71 degrees awarded. *Degree program information:* Part-time programs available. Offers computer engineering (MS); computer science (MS); electronics engineering (MS); engineering, computer science, and technology (MS). *Application deadline:* For fall admission, 3/1 for domestic and international students; for spring admission, 9/15 for domestic and international students. Applications are processed on a rolling basis. *Application fee:* $55. Electronic applications accepted. *Dean,* Dr. Kenneth Derucher, 530-898-5963.

College of Humanities and Fine Arts Students: 44 full-time (21 women), 31 part-time (17 women); includes 6 minority (2 American Indian/Alaska Native, 4 Hispanic Americans), 1 international. Average age 33. 37 applicants, 100% accepted, 24 enrolled. Expenses: Contact institution. *Financial support:* Teaching assistantships, career-related internships or fieldwork and Federal Work-Study available. Support available to part-time students. In 2006, 33 degrees awarded. *Degree program information:* Part-time programs available. Offers art history (MA); English (MA); fine arts (MFA); history (MA); humanities and fine arts (MA, MFA); music (MA). *Application deadline:* For fall admission, 3/1 for domestic and international students. Applications are processed on a rolling basis. *Application fee:* $55. Electronic applications accepted. *Dean,* Dr. Sarah Blackstone, 530-898-5351.

College of Natural Sciences Students: 31 full-time (18 women), 50 part-time (40 women); includes 10 minority (2 African Americans, 4 Asian Americans or Pacific Islanders, 4 Hispanic Americans), 4 international. Average age 35. 50 applicants, 100% accepted, 38 enrolled. Expenses: Contact institution. *Financial support:* Fellowships, research assistantships, teaching assistantships, career-related internships or fieldwork and Federal Work-Study available. Support available to part-time students. In 2006, 21 degrees awarded. *Degree program information:* Part-time programs available. Offers biological sciences (MS); botany (MS); environmental science (MS); geosciences (MS); hydrology/hydrogeology (MS); math education (MS); natural sciences (MS); nursing (MS); nutrition education (MS); nutritional and food science (MS). *Application deadline:* For fall admission, 3/1 for domestic and international students; for spring admission, 9/15 for domestic and international students. Applications are processed on a rolling basis. *Application fee:* $55. Electronic applications accepted. *Dean,* Dr. James Houpis, 530-898-6121.

CALIFORNIA STATE UNIVERSITY, DOMINGUEZ HILLS, Carson, CA 90747-0001

General Information State-supported, coed, comprehensive institution. CGS member. *Enrollment:* 12,068 graduate, professional, and undergraduate students; 1,372 full-time matriculated graduate/professional students (990 women), 1,634 part-time matriculated graduate/professional students (1,216 women). *Enrollment by degree level:* 2,184 master's, 822 other advanced degrees. *Graduate faculty:* 101 full-time (57 women), 132 part-time/adjunct (100 women). Tuition, nonresident: part-time $339 per unit. *Required fees:* $1,148 per term. Tuition and fees vary according to program. *Graduate housing:* Rooms and/or apartments available on a first-come, first-served basis to single and married students. Typical cost: $4,200 per year for single students; $11,700 per year for married students. Housing application deadline: 4/15. *Student services:* Campus employment opportunities, career counseling, child daycare facilities, disabled student services, free psychological counseling, low-cost health insurance. *Library facilities:* Leo F. Cain Educational Resource Center. *Online resources:* library catalog, web page, access to other libraries' catalogs. *Collection:* 428,840 titles, 49,130 serial subscriptions, 4,999 audiovisual materials. *Research affiliation:* Drew Medical School.

Computer facilities: 200 computers available on campus for general student use. *Web address:* http://www.csudh.edu/.

General Application Contact: Linda Wise, Associate Director, 310-243-3613, E-mail: lwise@csudh.edu.

GRADUATE UNITS

College of Business Administration and Public Policy Students: 64 full-time (42 women), 143 part-time (96 women); includes 147 minority (85 African Americans, 17 Asian Americans or Pacific Islanders, 45 Hispanic Americans), 16 international. Average age 35. 248 applicants, 74% accepted, 41 enrolled. *Faculty:* 27 full-time (5 women), 5 part-time/adjunct (3 women). Expenses: Contact institution. In 2006, 95 degrees awarded. *Degree program information:* Part-time and evening/weekend programs available. Postbaccalaureate distance learning degree programs offered (no on-campus study). Offers business administration (MBA); business administration and public policy (MBA, MPA); public administration (MPA). *Application deadline:* For fall admission, 4/1 for domestic and international students; for spring admission, 11/1 for domestic students, 10/1 for international students. *Application fee:* $55. *Application Contact:* Eileen Hall, Graduate Advisor, 310-243-3465, E-mail: ehall@csudh.edu. *Dean,* Dr. James Strong, 310-243-3548, E-mail: jstrong@csudh.edu.

College of Education Students: 968 full-time (689 women), 850 part-time (593 women); includes 1,076 minority (384 African Americans, 11 American Indian/Alaska Native, 147 Asian Americans or Pacific Islanders, 534 Hispanic Americans), 7 international. Average age 35. 831 applicants, 84% accepted, 434 enrolled. *Faculty:* 20 full-time (13 women), 39 part-time/adjunct (24 women). Expenses: Contact institution. In 2006, 365 degrees awarded. *Degree program information:* Part-time and evening/weekend programs available. Offers education (MA, Certificate). *Application deadline:* For fall admission, 8/1 priority date for domestic students; for spring admission, 10/1 priority date for domestic students. Applications are processed on a rolling basis. *Application fee:* $55. *Application Contact:* Jeanette Perez, Admissions Office, 310-243-3530, Fax: 310-243-2800, E-mail: jperez@csudh.edu. *Dean,* Dr. Lynne Cook, 310-243-3510, Fax: 310-243-3518, E-mail: lcook@csudh.edu.

Division of Graduate Education Students: 313 full-time (216 women), 338 part-time (245 women); includes 414 minority (161 African Americans, 6 American Indian/Alaska Native, 50 Asian Americans or Pacific Islanders, 197 Hispanic Americans), 4 international. Average age 36. 305 applicants, 81% accepted, 116 enrolled. *Faculty:* 16 full-time (10 women), 19 part-time/adjunct (14 women). Expenses: Contact institution. In 2006, 288 degrees awarded. *Degree program information:* Part-time and evening/weekend programs available. Offers counseling (MA); curriculum and instruction (MA); early childhood (MA); educational administration (MA); individualized education (MA); mild/moderate (MA); moderate/severe (MA); multicultural education (MA); special education (MA); technology-based education (MA, Certificate). *Application deadline:* For fall admission, 6/1 for domestic students. *Application fee:* $55. *Application Contact:* Admissions Office, 310-243-3530. *Chairperson,* Dr. Farah Fisher, 310-243-3926, E-mail: ffisher@csudh.edu.

College of Health and Human Services Students: 221 full-time (178 women), 380 part-time (340 women); includes 283 minority (121 African Americans, 4 American Indian/Alaska Native, 86 Asian Americans or Pacific Islanders, 72 Hispanic Americans), 6 international. Average age 40. 250 applicants, 86% accepted, 140 enrolled. *Faculty:* 26 full-time (21 women), 32 part-time/adjunct (25 women). Expenses: Contact institution. In 2006, 80 degrees awarded. Offers health and human services (MA, MS, MSN, MSW); marital and family therapy (MS); nursing (MSN); occupational therapy (MS); physical education administration (MA); social work (MSW). *Application deadline:* For fall admission, 6/1 for domestic students. *Application fee:* $55. *Dean,* Dr. Mitchell T. Maki, 301-243-2046, E-mail: mmaki@csudh.edu.

Division of Health Sciences Students: 7 full-time (5 women), 19 part-time (16 women); includes 16 minority (9 African Americans, 7 Hispanic Americans), 1 international. Average age 39. 14 applicants, 71% accepted, 5 enrolled. *Faculty:* 1 (woman) full-time, 3 part-time/adjunct (all women). Expenses: Contact institution. In 2006, 4 degrees awarded. *Degree program information:* Part-time programs available. Offers gerontology (MA); health sciences (MS). *Application deadline:* For fall admission, 8/15 priority date for domestic students. Applications are processed on a rolling basis. Electronic applications accepted. *Dean, College of Health and Human Services,* Dr. Mitchell T. Maki, 301-243-2046, E-mail: mmaki@csudh.edu.

College of Liberal Arts Students: 34 full-time (23 women), 109 part-time (81 women); includes 72 minority (39 African Americans, 1 American Indian/Alaska Native, 10 Asian Americans or Pacific Islanders, 22 Hispanic Americans), 12 international. Average age 37. 145 applicants, 90% accepted, 43 enrolled. *Faculty:* 25 full-time, 8 part-time/adjunct. Expenses: Contact institution. *Financial support:* Institutionally sponsored loans available. Support available to part-time students. In 2006, 67 degrees awarded. *Degree program information:* Part-time and evening/weekend programs available. Offers English (MA); humanities (MA); liberal arts (MA, MS, Certificate); negotiation, conflict resolution and peacebuilding (MA); rhetoric and composition (Certificate); teaching English as a second language (Certificate). *Application deadline:* For fall admission, 6/1 for domestic students. *Application fee:* $55. *Acting Dean,* Dr. Garry Hart, 310-243-3389, E-mail: ghart@csudh.edu.

College of Natural and Behavioral Science Students: 51 full-time (37 women), 91 part-time (61 women); includes 97 minority (56 African Americans, 9 Asian Americans or Pacific Islanders, 32 Hispanic Americans), 1 international. Average age 36. 142 applicants, 73% accepted, 31 enrolled. *Faculty:* 28 full-time, 16 part-time/adjunct. Expenses: Contact institution. In 2006, 68 degrees awarded. Offers biology (MS); clinical psychology (MA); general psychology (MA); natural and behavioral science (MA, MS, Certificate); quality assurance (MS); social research (Certificate); sociology (MA); teaching of mathematics (MA). *Dean,* Dr. Charles Hohm, 310-243-2547, E-mail: chohm@csudh.edu.

See Close-Up on page 827.

CALIFORNIA STATE UNIVERSITY, EAST BAY, Hayward, CA 94542-3000

General Information State-supported, coed, comprehensive institution. CGS member. *Enrollment:* 983 full-time matriculated graduate/professional students (679 women), 1,410 part-time matriculated graduate/professional students (870 women). *Enrollment by degree level:* 2,393 master's. *Graduate faculty:* 368. *Graduate housing:* Room and/or apartments available on a first-come, first-served basis to single students; on-campus housing not available to married students. Typical cost: $6,702 per year ($8,402 including board). Housing application deadline: 4/30. *Student services:* Campus employment opportunities, campus safety program, career counseling, child daycare facilities, disabled student services, free psychological counseling, international student services, low-cost health insurance. *Library facilities:* California State University, East Bay Library plus 1 other. *Online resources:* library catalog, web page, access to other libraries' catalogs. *Collection:* 916,564 titles, 2,035 serial subscriptions, 29,857 audiovisual materials. *Research affiliation:* Pacific Telesis (urban education), Academy of Economy, Moscow (business management training), NASA–Ames Research Center, Lawrence Livermore National Laboratory (technology transfer), Stanford University (complex learning), Sandia National Laboratories (technology marketing assessment).

Computer facilities: 700 computers available on campus for general student use. A campuswide network can be accessed from student residence rooms and from off campus. Internet access and online class registration are available. *Web address:* http://www.csueastbay.edu/.

General Application Contact: My Huynh, Graduate Prospect Specialist, 510-885-2989, Fax: 510-885-4059, E-mail: my.huynh@csueastbay.edu.

GRADUATE UNITS

Academic Programs and Graduate Studies Students: 983 full-time (679 women), 1,410 part-time (870 women); includes 941 minority (230 African Americans, 9 American Indian/Alaska Native, 493 Asian Americans or Pacific Islanders, 209 Hispanic Americans), 354 international. Average age 34. 2,040 applicants, 86% accepted. Expenses: Contact institution. *Financial support:* Fellowships, teaching assistantships, career-related internships or fieldwork, Federal Work-Study, institutionally sponsored loans, and scholarships/grants available. Support available to part-time students. Financial award application deadline: 3/2; financial award applicants required to submit FAFSA. In 2006, 950 degrees awarded. *Degree program information:* Part-time and evening/weekend programs available. Offers interdisciplinary studies (MA, MS, Certificate); multimedia (MA). *Application deadline:* For fall admission, 5/31 for domestic students, 2/29 for international students; for winter admission, 9/30 for domestic students, 8/31 for international students; for spring admission, 11/30 for domestic and international students. Applications are processed on a rolling basis. *Application fee:* $55. Electronic applications accepted. *Application Contact:* My Huynh, Graduate Prospect Specialist, 510-885-2989, Fax: 510-885-4059, E-mail: my.huynh@csueastbay.edu. *Associate Vice President,* Dr. Carl Bellone, 510-885-3716, Fax: 510-885-4777, E-mail: cbellone@csuhayward.edu.

College of Business and Economics Students: 229 full-time, 424 part-time; includes 259 minority (22 African Americans, 209 Asian Americans or Pacific Islanders, 28 Hispanic Americans), 179 international. Average age 32. 420 applicants, 45% accepted, 117 enrolled. *Faculty:* 37 full-time (7 women), 8 part-time/adjunct (3 women). Expenses: Contact institution. *Financial support:* Career-related internships or fieldwork, Federal Work-Study, and institution-

California State University, East Bay (continued)

ally sponsored loans available. Support available to part-time students. Financial award application deadline: 3/2. In 2006, 299 degrees awarded. *Degree program information:* Part-time and evening/weekend programs available. Offers accounting (MBA); business administration (MBA); business and economics (MA, MBA, MS); business economics (MBA); computer information systems (MBA, MS); e-business (MBA); economics (MA, MBA); economics for teachers (MBA); entrepreneurship (MBA); finance (MBA); human resources management (MBA); international business (MBA); management sciences (MBA); marketing management (MBA); new ventures/small business management (MBA); operations and material management (MBA); operations research (MBA); quantitative business methods (MS); strategic management (MBA); supply chain management (MBA); taxation (MBA, MS); telecommunications (MS). *Application deadline:* For fall admission, 5/31 for domestic students, 4/30 for international students; for winter admission, 9/30 for domestic and international students; for spring admission, 12/31 for domestic students, 11/30 for international students. Applications are processed on a rolling basis. *Application fee:* $55. Electronic applications accepted. *Application Contact:* Doris Duncan, Director of Graduate Programs, 510-885-3364, Fax: 510-885-2176, E-mail: doris.duncan@csueastbay.edu. *Dean,* John Kohl, 510-885-3291, Fax: 510-885-4884, E-mail: john.kohl@csueastbay.edu.

College of Education and Allied Studies Students: 306 full-time, 293 part-time; includes 203 minority (60 African Americans, 7 American Indian/Alaska Native, 55 Asian Americans or Pacific Islanders, 81 Hispanic Americans), 11 international. Average age 35. 385 applicants, 65% accepted, 216 enrolled. Expenses: Contact institution. *Financial support:* Career-related internships or fieldwork, Federal Work-Study, and institutionally sponsored loans available. Support available to part-time students. Financial award application deadline:3/2. In 2006, 159 degrees awarded. *Degree program information:* Part-time and evening/weekend programs available. Offers counseling (MS); education (MS); education and allied studies (MS); educational leadership (MS); physical education (MS); special education (MS); specializing in urban teaching leadership (MS). *Application deadline:* For fall admission, 5/31 for domestic students, 4/30 for international students; for winter admission, 9/30 for domestic and international students; for spring admission, 12/31 for domestic students, 11/30 for international students. *Application fee:* $55. Electronic applications accepted. *Application Contact:* My Huynh, Graduate Prospect Specialist, 510-885-2989, Fax: 510-885-4059, E-mail: my.huynh@csueastbay.edu. *Interim Dean,* Dr. Emily Brizendine, 510-885-3942, E-mail: emily.brizendine@csueastbay.edu.

College of Letters, Arts, and Social Sciences Students: 318 full-time (260 women), 414 part-time (312 women); includes 320 minority (133 African Americans, 2 American Indian/Alaska Native, 106 Asian Americans or Pacific Islanders, 79 Hispanic Americans), 49 international. Average age 34. 600 applicants, 59% accepted, 249 enrolled. Expenses: Contact institution. *Financial support:* Fellowships, research assistantships, teaching assistantships, career-related internships or fieldwork, Federal Work-Study, institutionally sponsored loans, and scholarships/grants available. Support available to part-time students. Financial award application deadline: 3/2. In 2006, 289 degrees awarded. *Degree program information:* Part-time and evening/weekend programs available. Offers anthropology (MA); communication (MA); English (MA); geography (MA); health care administration (MS); history (MA); letters, arts, and social sciences (MA, MPA, MS, MSW); music (MA); public administration (MPA); social work (MSW); sociology (MA); speech pathology and audiology (MS). *Application deadline:* For fall admission, 5/31 for domestic students, 4/30 for international students; for winter admission, 9/30 for domestic and international students; for spring admission, 11/30 for international students. Applications are processed on a rolling basis. *Application fee:* $55. Electronic applications accepted. *Application Contact:* My Huynh, Graduate Prospect Specialist, 510-885-2989, Fax: 510-885-4059, E-mail: my.huynh@csueastbay.edu. *Interim Dean,* Dr. Benjamin Bowser, 510-885-3161, Fax: 510-885-3164, E-mail: benjamin.bowser@csueastbay.edu.

College of Science Students: 112 full-time (62 women), 253 part-time (140 women); includes 145 minority (13 African Americans, 117 Asian Americans or Pacific Islanders, 15 Hispanic Americans), 108 international. Average age 32. 255 applicants, 62% accepted, 98 enrolled. Expenses: Contact institution. *Financial support:* Career-related internships or fieldwork, Federal Work-Study, and institutionally sponsored loans available. Support available to part-time students. Financial award application deadline: 3/2. In 2006, 174 degrees awarded. *Degree program information:* Part-time and evening/weekend programs available. Offers actuarial statistics (MS); biochemistry (MS); biological sciences (MS); biostatistics (MS); chemistry (MS); computational statistics (MS); computer science (MS); engineering management (MS); geology (MS); marine sciences (MS); mathematical statistics (MS); mathematics (MS); multimedia (MA); science (MA, MS); statistics (MS); telecommunication (MS); theoretical and applied statistics (MS). *Application deadline:* For fall admission, 5/31 for domestic students, 4/30 for international students; for winter admission, 9/30 for domestic and international students; for spring admission, 12/31 for domestic students, 11/30 for international students. *Application fee:* $55. Electronic applications accepted. *Application Contact:* My Huynh, Graduate Prospect Specialist, 510-885-2989, Fax: 510-885-4059, E-mail: my.huynh@csueastbay.edu. *Dean,* Dr. Michael Leung, 510-885-3441, Fax: 510-885-2035, E-mail: michael.leung@csueastbay.edu.

Announcement: California State University, East Bay, has 30 professional and research-oriented master's degree programs that have strong contacts with industry, government, and education. These programs have a proven track record for placing graduates in new and better careers. Most programs are designed for working students and offer evening courses. Cal State East Bay is located in the center of the culturally rich San Francisco Bay Area. The campus has modern research facilities, including electronic library services and well-equipped science and computer labs. www.csueastbay.edu/gradprograms.

CALIFORNIA STATE UNIVERSITY, FRESNO, Fresno, CA 93740-8027

General Information State-supported, coed, comprehensive institution. CGS member. *Graduate housing:* Room and/or apartments available on a first-come, first-served basis to single students; on-campus housing not available to married students. Housing application deadline: 4/1. *Research affiliation:* Coleman Foundation (administration), Starburst Foundation (engineering), Garabedian Foundation (agribusiness), California Endowment (arts and humanities).

GRADUATE UNITS

Division of Graduate Studies *Degree program information:* Part-time and evening/weekend programs available. Electronic applications accepted.

College of Agricultural Sciences and Technology *Degree program information:* Part-time and evening/weekend programs available. Offers agricultural sciences and technology (MA, MS); animal science (MA); family and consumer sciences (MS); food science and nutritional sciences (MS); industrial technology (MS); plant science (MS); viticulture and enology (MS). Electronic applications accepted.

College of Arts and Humanities *Degree program information:* Part-time and evening/weekend programs available. Offers art (MA); arts and humanities (MA, MFA); communication (MA); composition theory (MA); creative writing (MFA); linguistics (MA); literature (MA); mass communication and journalism (MA); music (MA); music education (MA); performance (MA); Spanish (MA). Electronic applications accepted.

College of Engineering and Computer Science *Degree program information:* Part-time and evening/weekend programs available. Offers civil engineering (MS); computer science (MS); electrical engineering (MS); engineering and computer science (MS); mechanical engineering (MS). Electronic applications accepted.

College of Health and Human Services *Degree program information:* Part-time and evening/weekend programs available. Offers communicative disorders (MA); environmental/occupational health (MPH); exercise science (MA); health administration (MPH); health and human services (MA, MPH, MPT, MS, MSW); health promotion (MPH); nursing (MS); physical therapy (MPT); social work education (MSW); sport psychology (MA). Electronic applications accepted.

College of Science and Mathematics *Degree program information:* Part-time and evening/weekend programs available. Offers biology (MA); chemistry (MS); geology (MS); marine sciences (MS); mathematics (MA); physics (MS); psychology (MA, MS); science and mathematics (MA, MS); teaching (MA). Electronic applications accepted.

College of Social Sciences *Degree program information:* Part-time and evening/weekend programs available. Offers criminology (MS); history (MA); international relations (MA); public administration (MPA); social sciences (MA, MPA, MS). Electronic applications accepted.

Craig School of Business *Degree program information:* Part-time programs available. Offers accountancy (MS); business (MBA, MS); business administration (MBA). Electronic applications accepted.

School of Education and Human Development *Degree program information:* Part-time and evening/weekend programs available. Offers counseling and student services (MS); education (MA); education and human development (MA, MS, Ed D); educational leadership (Ed D); marriage and family therapy (MS); rehabilitation counseling (MS); special education (MA). Electronic applications accepted.

CALIFORNIA STATE UNIVERSITY, FULLERTON, Fullerton, CA 92834-9480

General Information State-supported, coed, comprehensive institution. CGS member. *Enrollment:* 35,921 graduate, professional, and undergraduate students; 1,309 full-time matriculated graduate/professional students (856 women), 2,802 part-time matriculated graduate/professional students (1,727 women). *Enrollment by degree level:* 4,111 master's. Tuition, nonresident: part-time $339 per unit. *Required fees:* $1,155 per semester. *Graduate housing:* Room and/or apartments available on a first-come, first-served basis to single students; on-campus housing not available to married students. *Student services:* Campus employment opportunities, campus safety program, career counseling, child daycare facilities, disabled student services, exercise/wellness program, free psychological counseling, international student services, low-cost health insurance, multicultural affairs office, teacher training, writing training. *Library facilities:* California State University, Fullerton Pollak Library. *Online resources:* library catalog, web page, access to other libraries' catalogs. *Collection:* 1.2 million titles, 29,888 serial subscriptions.

Computer facilities: 1,993 computers available on campus for general student use. A campuswide network can be accessed from student residence rooms and from off campus. Internet access is available. *Web address:* http://www.fullerton.edu/.

General Application Contact: Admissions/Applications, 714-278-2300.

GRADUATE UNITS

Graduate Studies Students: 1,309 full-time (856 women), 2,802 part-time (1,727 women); includes 1,555 minority (89 African Americans, 17 American Indian/Alaska Native, 773 Asian Americans or Pacific Islanders, 676 Hispanic Americans), 388 international. Average age 32. 4,009 applicants, 58% accepted, 1507 enrolled. Expenses: Contact institution. *Financial support:* Research assistantships, teaching assistantships, career-related internships or fieldwork, Federal Work-Study, institutionally sponsored loans, and scholarships/grants available. Support available to part-time students. Financial award application deadline: 3/1. In 2006, 1323 degrees awarded. *Degree program information:* Part-time and evening/weekend programs available. *Application deadline:* Applications are processed on a rolling basis. *Application fee:* $55. *Application Contact:* Admissions/Applications, 714-278-2300. *Associate Vice President, Academic Programs,* Dr. Ray Young, 714-278-3602.

College of Business and Economics Students: 215 full-time (115 women), 369 part-time (156 women); includes 225 minority (7 African Americans, 177 Asian Americans or Pacific Islanders, 41 Hispanic Americans), 137 international. Average age 30. 731 applicants, 48% accepted, 198 enrolled. Expenses: Contact institution. *Financial support:* Teaching assistantships, career-related internships or fieldwork, Federal Work-Study, institutionally sponsored loans, and scholarships/grants available. Support available to part-time students. Financial award application deadline: 3/1. In 2006, 155 degrees awarded. *Degree program information:* Part-time and evening/weekend programs available. Offers accounting (MBA, MS); business administration (MBA); business and economics (MA, MBA, MS); business economics (MBA); economics (MA); finance (MBA); international business (MBA); management (MBA); management information systems (MS); management science (MBA, MS); marketing (MBA); operations research (MS); statistics (MS); taxation (MS). *Application fee:* $55. *Application Contact:* Robert Miyake, Assistant Dean, 714-278-2211. *Dean,* Dr. Anil Puri, 714-773-2592.

College of Communications Students: 96 full-time (86 women), 71 part-time (52 women); includes 46 minority (4 African Americans, 14 Asian Americans or Pacific Islanders, 28 Hispanic Americans), 15 international. Average age 30. 308 applicants, 31% accepted, 48 enrolled. Expenses: Contact institution. *Financial support:* Teaching assistantships, career-related internships or fieldwork, Federal Work-Study, institutionally sponsored loans, and scholarships/grants available. Support available to part-time students. Financial award application deadline: 3/1. In 2006, 93 degrees awarded. *Degree program information:* Part-time programs available. Offers advertising (MA); communications (MA); communicative disorders (MA); journalism education (MA); news editorial (MA); photo communication (MA); public relations (MA); radio, television and film (MA); speech communication (MA); technical communication (MA); theory and process (MA). *Application fee:* $55. *Dean,* Dr. Rick Pullen, 714-278-3355.

College of Education Students: 123 full-time (112 women), 824 part-time (681 women); includes 313 minority (10 African Americans, 4 American Indian/Alaska Native, 101 Asian Americans or Pacific Islanders, 198 Hispanic Americans), 4 international. Average age 35. 687 applicants, 74% accepted, 390 enrolled. Expenses: Contact institution. In 2006, 344 degrees awarded. Offers bilingual/bicultural education (MS); education (MS); educational leadership (MS); elementary curriculum and instruction (MS); instructional design and technology (MS); middle school mathematics (MS); reading (MS); secondary education (MS); special education (MS); teacher induction (MS). *Dean,* Dr. Claire Cavallaro, 714-278-4021.

College of Engineering and Computer Science Students: 129 full-time (34 women), 358 part-time (75 women); includes 238 minority (10 African Americans, 194 Asian Americans or Pacific Islanders, 34 Hispanic Americans), 119 international. Average age 32. 430 applicants, 70% accepted, 164 enrolled. Expenses: Contact institution. *Financial support:* Career-related internships or fieldwork, Federal Work-Study, institutionally sponsored loans, and scholarships/grants available. Support available to part-time students. Financial award application deadline: 3/1. In 2006, 178 degrees awarded. *Degree program information:* Part-time programs available. Offers applications administrative information systems (MS); applications mathematical methods (MS); civil engineering and engineering mechanics (MS); computer science (MS); electrical engineering (MS); engineering and computer science (MS); engineering science (MS); information processing systems (MS); mechanical engineering (MS); software engineering (MS); systems engineering (MS). *Application fee:* $55. *Application Contact:* Dr. Dorota Huizinga, Associate Dean, 714-278-3362. *Dean,* Dr. Raman Unnikrishnan, 714-278-3362.

College of Health and Human Development Students: 293 full-time (209 women), 323 part-time (268 women); includes 255 minority (25 African Americans, 4 American Indian/Alaska Native, 111 Asian Americans or Pacific Islanders, 115 Hispanic Americans), 15 international. Average age 32. 689 applicants, 54% accepted, 269 enrolled. Expenses: Contact institution. *Financial support:* Teaching assistantships, career-related internships or fieldwork, Federal Work-Study, institutionally sponsored loans, and scholarships/grants available. Support available to part-time students. Financial award application deadline:3/1. In 2006, 176 degrees awarded. *Degree program information:* Part-time programs available. Offers counseling (MS); health and human development (MPH, MS); nursing (MS); physical education (MS); public health (MPH). *Application fee:* $55. *Dean,* Dr. Roberta Rikli, 714-278-3311.

College of Humanities and Social Sciences Students: 346 full-time (239 women), 607 part-time (353 women); includes 338 minority (22 African Americans, 6 American Indian/Alaska Native, 108 Asian Americans or Pacific Islanders, 202 Hispanic Americans), 65 international. Average age 32. 809 applicants, 66% accepted, 340 enrolled. Expenses:

Contact institution. *Financial support:* Teaching assistantships, career-related internships or fieldwork, Federal Work-Study, institutionally sponsored loans, and scholarships/grants available. Support available to part-time students. Financial award application deadline:3/1. In 2006, 259 degrees awarded. *Degree program information:* Part-time programs available. Offers American studies (MA); analysis of specific language structures (MA); anthropological linguistics (MA); anthropology (MA); applied linguistics (MA); clinical/community psychology (MS); communication and semantics (MA); comparative literature (MA); disorders of communication (MA); English (MA); environmental education and communication (MS); environmental policy and planning (MS); environmental sciences (MS); experimental phonetics (MA); French (MA); geography (MA); German (MA); gerontology (MS); history (MA); humanities and social sciences (MA, MPA, MS); political science (MA); psychology (MA); public administration (MPA); sociology (MA); Spanish (MA); teaching English to speakers of other languages (MS); technological studies (MS). *Application fee:* $55. *Dean,* Dr. Thomas Klammer, 714-278-3256.

College of Natural Science and Mathematics Students: 31 full-time (18 women), 167 part-time (94 women); includes 101 minority (5 African Americans, 2 American Indian/Alaska Native, 50 Asian Americans or Pacific Islanders, 44 Hispanic Americans), 12 international. Average age 30. 197 applicants, 52% accepted, 50 enrolled. Expenses: Contact institution. *Financial support:* Research assistantships, teaching assistantships, career-related internships or fieldwork, Federal Work-Study, institutionally sponsored loans, and scholarships/grants available. Support available to part-time students. Financial award application deadline: 3/1. In 2006, 61 degrees awarded. *Degree program information:* Part-time programs available. Offers analytical chemistry (MS); applied mathematics (MA); biochemistry (MS); biological science (MS); botany (MS); geochemistry (MS); geological sciences (MS); inorganic chemistry (MS); mathematics (MA); mathematics for secondary school teachers (MA); microbiology (MS); natural science and mathematics (MA, MAT, MS); organic chemistry (MS); physical chemistry (MS); physics (MA); teaching science (MAT). *Application fee:* $55. *Dean,* Dr. Steven Murray, 714-278-2638.

College of the Arts Students: 76 full-time (43 women), 83 part-time (48 women); includes 16 minority (2 African Americans, 1 American Indian/Alaska Native, 6 Asian Americans or Pacific Islanders, 7 Hispanic Americans), 8 international. Average age 32. 158 applicants, 47% accepted, 48 enrolled. Expenses: Contact institution. *Financial support:* Teaching assistantships, career-related internships or fieldwork, Federal Work-Study, institutionally sponsored loans, and scholarships/grants available. Support available to part-time students. Financial award application deadline: 3/1. In 2006, 57 degrees awarded. *Degree program information:* Part-time programs available. Offers acting (MFA); acting and directing (MA); art (MA, MFA); art history (MA); arts (MA, MFA, MM, Certificate); dance (MA); design (MA); directing (MFA); dramatic literature/criticism (MA); museum studies (Certificate); music education (MA); music history and literature (MA); oral interpretation (MA); performance (MM); playwriting (MA); technical theater (MA); theater and design (MFA); television (MA); theatre for children (MA); theatre history (MA); theory-composition (MM). *Application fee:* $55. *Dean,* Jerry Samuelson, 714-278-3256.

CALIFORNIA STATE UNIVERSITY, LONG BEACH, Long Beach, CA 90840

General Information State-supported, coed, comprehensive institution. CGS member. *Enrollment:* 35,574 graduate, professional, and undergraduate students; 1,975 full-time matriculated graduate/professional students (1,297 women), 2,884 part-time matriculated graduate/professional students (1,634 women). *Enrollment by degree level:* 4,859 master's. *Graduate faculty:* 852 full-time (345 women), 1,179 part-time/adjunct (614 women). *Graduate housing:* Room and/or apartments available on a first-come, first-served basis to single students; on-campus housing not available to married students. Typical cost: $6,648 (including board). Housing application deadline: 4/1. *Student services:* Campus employment opportunities, campus safety program, career counseling, child daycare facilities, disabled student services, exercise/wellness program, free psychological counseling, grant writing training, international student services, low-cost health insurance, multicultural affairs office, teacher training, writing training. *Library facilities:* University Library. *Online resources:* library catalog, web page, access to other libraries' catalogs. *Collection:* 1.5 million titles, 18,749 serial subscriptions. *Research affiliation:* Boeing Company (aerospace engineering and manufacturing).

Computer facilities: 2,000 computers available on campus for general student use. A campuswide network can be accessed from off campus. Internet access is available. *Web address:* http://www.csulb.edu/.

General Application Contact: Rachel Brophy, Students Programs Coordinator, 562-985-4546, Fax: 562-985-7786, E-mail: rpbrophy@csulb.edu.

GRADUATE UNITS

Graduate Studies Students: 1,975 full-time (1,297 women), 2,884 part-time (1,634 women); includes 2,051 minority (294 African Americans, 27 American Indian/Alaska Native, 762 Asian Americans or Pacific Islanders, 968 Hispanic Americans), 466 international. Average age 33. 4,741 applicants, 50% accepted, 1554 enrolled. *Faculty:* 903 full-time, 625 part-time/adjunct. Expenses: Contact institution. *Financial support:* Fellowships, research assistantships, teaching assistantships, career-related internships or fieldwork, Federal Work-Study, institutionally sponsored loans, scholarships/grants, traineeships, tuition waivers (partial), and unspecified assistantships available. Financial award application deadline: 3/2; financial award applicants required to submit FAFSA. In 2006, 1128 degrees awarded. *Degree program information:* Part-time and evening/weekend programs available. Postbaccalaureate distance learning degree programs offered (no on-campus study). Offers interdisciplinary studies (MA, MS). *Application deadline:* For fall admission, 7/1 for domestic and international students; for spring admission, 12/1 for domestic and international students. Applications are processed on a rolling basis. *Application fee:* $55. Electronic applications accepted. *Application Contact:* Rachel Brophy, Students Programs Coordinator, 562-985-4546, Fax: 562-985-7786, E-mail: rpbrophy@csulb.edu. *Director,* Dr. Cecile Lindsay, 562-985-8225, Fax: 562-985-1680, E-mail: clindsay@csulb.edu.

College of Business Administration Students: 100 full-time (48 women), 171 part-time (73 women); includes 73 minority (3 African Americans, 48 Asian Americans or Pacific Islanders, 22 Hispanic Americans), 42 international. Average age 32. 468 applicants, 30% accepted, 91 enrolled. *Faculty:* 8 full-time (3 women), 6 part-time/adjunct (2 women). Expenses: Contact institution. *Financial support:* Career-related internships or fieldwork and scholarships/grants available. Financial award application deadline: 3/2; financial award applicants required to submit FAFSA. In 2006, 123 degrees awarded. *Degree program information:* Part-time and evening/weekend programs available. Offers business administration (MBA). *Application deadline:* For fall admission, 7/1 for domestic students; for spring admission, 12/1 for domestic students. Applications are processed on a rolling basis. *Application fee:* $55. Electronic applications accepted. *Application Contact:* Dr. Philip Chong, Interim Associate Dean, 562-985-7696, Fax: 562-985-5742. *Interim Dean,* Dr. Mohammed B. Khan, 562-985-5306, Fax: 562-985-5742, E-mail: mkhan@csulb.edu.

College of Education Students: 202 full-time (144 women), 483 part-time (401 women); includes 360 minority (49 African Americans, 4 American Indian/Alaska Native, 101 Asian Americans or Pacific Islanders, 206 Hispanic Americans), 11 international. Average age 33. 718 applicants, 42% accepted, 216 enrolled. *Faculty:* 70 full-time (54 women), 82 part-time/adjunct (59 women). Expenses: Contact institution. *Financial support:* Federal Work-Study, institutionally sponsored loans, and scholarships/grants available. Financial award application deadline: 3/2. In 2006, 236 degrees awarded. *Degree program information:* Part-time and evening/weekend programs available. Offers counseling (MS); counseling-guidance (MS); education (MA); special education (MS). *Application deadline:* For fall admission, 7/1 for domestic students; for spring admission, 12/1 for domestic students. Applications are processed on a rolling basis. *Application fee:* $55. Electronic applications accepted. *Application Contact:* Nancy L. McGlothin, Coordinator for Graduate Studies, 562-985-4547, Fax: 562-985-4951, E-mail: nmcgloth@csulb.edu. *Dean,* Dr. Jean Houck, 562-985-4513, Fax: 562-985-4951, E-mail: houck@csulb.edu.

College of Engineering Students: 180 full-time (29 women), 350 part-time (55 women); includes 210 minority (19 African Americans, 140 Asian Americans or Pacific Islanders, 51 Hispanic Americans), 160 international. Average age 32. 539 applicants, 62% accepted, 155 enrolled. *Faculty:* 83 full-time (7 women), 44 part-time/adjunct (3 women). Expenses: Contact institution. *Financial support:* Research assistantships, teaching assistantships, career-related internships or fieldwork, Federal Work-Study, institutionally sponsored loans, scholarships/grants, and unspecified assistantships available. Financial award application deadline: 3/2. In 2006, 109 degrees awarded. *Degree program information:* Part-time and evening/weekend programs available. Offers aerospace engineering (MSAE); civil engineering (MSCE); computer engineering and computer science (MS); electrical engineering (MSEE); engineering (MS, MSAE, MSCE, MSE, MSEE, MSME, PhD); engineering and industrial applied mathematics (PhD); interdisciplinary engineering (MSE); management engineering (MSE); mechanical engineering (MSME). *Application deadline:* For fall admission, 7/1 for domestic students; for spring admission, 12/1 for domestic students. *Application fee:* $55. Electronic applications accepted. *Application Contact:* Dr. Sandra Cynar, Associate Dean for Instruction, 562-985-1512, Fax: 562-985-7561, E-mail: cynar@csulb.edu. *Dean,* 562-985-5123, Fax: 562-985-7561.

College of Health and Human Services Students: 834 full-time (681 women), 760 part-time (563 women); includes 831 minority (159 African Americans, 10 American Indian/Alaska Native, 253 Asian Americans or Pacific Islanders, 409 Hispanic Americans), 33 international. Average age 33. 1,717 applicants, 58% accepted, 694 enrolled. *Faculty:* 154 full-time, 115 part-time/adjunct. Expenses: Contact institution. *Financial support:* Fellowships, research assistantships, teaching assistantships, career-related internships or fieldwork, Federal Work-Study, institutionally sponsored loans, and scholarships/grants available. Financial award application deadline: 3/2; financial award applicants required to submit FAFSA. In 2006, 450 degrees awarded. *Degree program information:* Part-time and evening/weekend programs available. Postbaccalaureate distance learning degree programs offered (no on-campus study). Offers communicative disorders (MA); criminal justice (MS); emergency services administration (MS); family and consumer sciences (MA); gerontology (MS); health and human services (MA, MPA, MPH, MPT, MS, MSW, Certificate); health care administration (MS, Certificate); health science (MPH); kinesiology (MA, MS); nursing (MS); nursing-health care administration (MS); nutritional sciences (MS); nutritional sciences/dietetics and food administration (MS); occupational studies (MA); physical therapy (MPT); public policy and administration (MPA); recreation administration (MS); social work (MSW). *Application deadline:* For fall admission, 7/1 for domestic students; for spring admission, 12/1 for domestic students. Applications are processed on a rolling basis. *Application fee:* $55. Electronic applications accepted. *Application Contact:* Dr. Michael Lacourse, Chair, 562-985-4066, Fax: 562-985-7581, E-mail: mlacourse@csulb.edu. *Dean,* Dr. Ronald Vogel, 562-985-4691, Fax: 562-985-7581, E-mail: rvogel@csulb.edu.

College of Liberal Arts Students: 315 full-time (202 women), 429 part-time (239 women); includes 247 minority (25 African Americans, 8 American Indian/Alaska Native, 87 Asian Americans or Pacific Islanders, 127 Hispanic Americans), 81 international. Average age 33. 835 applicants, 46% accepted, 233 enrolled. *Faculty:* 167 full-time, 122 part-time/adjunct. Expenses: Contact institution. *Financial support:* Research assistantships, teaching assistantships, career-related internships or fieldwork, Federal Work-Study, institutionally sponsored loans, and scholarships/grants available. Financial award application deadline: 3/2. In 2006, 127 degrees awarded. *Degree program information:* Part-time and evening/weekend programs available. Offers anthropology (MA); Asian American studies (Certificate); Asian studies (MA); communication studies (MA); creative writing (MFA); economics (MA); English (MA); French (MA); geography (MA); German (MA); history (MA); liberal arts (MA, MFA, MS, Certificate); linguistics (MA); philosophy (MA); political science (MA); psychology (MA, MS); religious studies (MA); Spanish (MA). *Application deadline:* For fall admission, 7/1 for domestic and international students; for spring admission, 12/1 for domestic and international students. Applications are processed on a rolling basis. *Application fee:* $55. Electronic applications accepted. *Application Contact:* Dr. Frank Fata, Associate Dean, 562-985-5381, Fax: 562-985-2463, E-mail: ffata@csulb.edu. *Dean,* Dr. Gerry Riposa, 562-985-5381, Fax: 562-985-2463, E-mail: griposa@csulb.edu.

College of Natural Sciences and Mathematics Students: 150 full-time (104 women), 150 part-time (92 women); includes 114 minority (6 African Americans, 1 American Indian/Alaska Native, 66 Asian Americans or Pacific Islanders, 41 Hispanic Americans), 38 international. Average age 31. 239 applicants, 56% accepted, 93 enrolled. *Faculty:* 118 full-time, 94 part-time/adjunct. Expenses: Contact institution. *Financial support:* Research assistantships, teaching assistantships, Federal Work-Study, institutionally sponsored loans, scholarships/grants, traineeships, and unspecified assistantships available. Financial award application deadline: 3/2. In 2006, 28 degrees awarded. *Degree program information:* Part-time programs available. Offers biochemistry (MS); biology (MS); chemistry (MS); geology/geosciences (MS); mathematics (MS); mathematics and science education (MS); microbiology (MS); natural sciences and mathematics (MS); physics (MS). *Application deadline:* For fall admission, 7/1 for domestic students; for spring admission, 12/1 for domestic students. Applications are processed on a rolling basis. *Application fee:* $55. Electronic applications accepted. *Application Contact:* Dr. Henry Fung, Associate Dean for Curriculum and Instruction, 562-985-7898, Fax: 562-985-2315, E-mail: hcfung@csulb.edu. *Dean,* Dr. Laura Kingsford, 562-985-4707, Fax: 562-985-2315, E-mail: lking@csulb.edu.

College of the Arts Students: 121 full-time (76 women), 80 part-time (49 women); includes 30 minority (3 African Americans, 1 American Indian/Alaska Native, 11 Asian Americans or Pacific Islanders, 15 Hispanic Americans), 12 international. Average age 36. 189 applicants, 42% accepted, 59 enrolled. *Faculty:* 94 full-time, 96 part-time/adjunct. Expenses: Contact institution. *Financial support:* Research assistantships, teaching assistantships, Federal Work-Study, institutionally sponsored loans, scholarships/grants, and traineeships available. Financial award application deadline: 3/2. In 2006, 46 degrees awarded. *Degree program information:* Part-time programs available. Offers art (MA, MFA); arts (MA, MFA, MM); dance (performance) (MFA); music (MA); music (performing) (MM); theatre arts (professional performance/design) (MFA); theatre arts/drama (MA). *Application deadline:* For fall admission, 7/1 for domestic students; for spring admission, 12/1 for domestic students. Applications are processed on a rolling basis. *Application fee:* $55. Electronic applications accepted. *Application Contact:* Dr. Holly Harbinger, Associate Dean, 562-985-4364, Fax: 562-985-7883, E-mail: harbinge@csulb.edu. *Dean,* Dr. Donald Para, 562-985-4364, Fax: 562-985-7883, E-mail: para@csulb.edu.

CALIFORNIA STATE UNIVERSITY, LOS ANGELES, Los Angeles, CA 90032-8530

General Information State-supported, coed, comprehensive institution. CGS member. *Enrollment:* 20,565 graduate, professional, and undergraduate students; 1,476 full-time matriculated graduate/professional students (1,017 women), 3,365 part-time matriculated graduate/professional students (2,228 women). *Enrollment by degree level:* 4,841 master's. *Graduate faculty:* 291 full-time (138 women), 147 part-time/adjunct (67 women). Tuition, nonresident: part-time $226 per unit. *Graduate housing:* Room and/or apartments available to single students; on-campus housing not available to married students. Typical cost: $7,866 (including board). Housing application deadline: 7/2. *Student services:* Campus employment opportunities, career counseling, child daycare facilities, disabled student services, free psychological counseling, international student services, multicultural affairs office, writing training. *Library facilities:* John F. Kennedy Memorial Library. *Online resources:* library catalog, web page. *Collection:* 1.2 million titles, 31,366 serial subscriptions, 2,545 audiovisual materials.

Computer facilities: 1,500 computers available on campus for general student use. A campuswide network can be accessed from off campus. Internet access is available. *Web address:* http://www.calstatela.edu/.

General Application Contact: Dr. Jose L. Galvan, Dean of Graduate Studies, 323-343-3820, Fax: 323-343-5653, E-mail: jgalvan@cslanet.calstatela.edu.

GRADUATE UNITS

Graduate Studies Students: 1,476 full-time (1,017 women), 3,365 part-time (2,228 women); includes 2,851 minority (314 African Americans, 25 American Indian/Alaska Native, 902 Asian Americans or Pacific Islanders, 1,610 Hispanic Americans), 367 international. Average age 34. 3,038 applicants, 75% accepted, 770 enrolled. *Faculty:* 291 full-time (138 women), 147 part-time/adjunct (67 women). Expenses: Contact institution. *Financial support:* Fellowships, teaching assistantships, career-related internships or fieldwork and Federal Work-Study available. Support available to part-time students. Financial award application deadline: 3/1.

California State University, Los Angeles (continued)

In 2006, 1188 degrees awarded. *Degree program information:* Part-time and evening/weekend programs available. *Application deadline:* For fall admission, 6/30 for domestic students. Applications are processed on a rolling basis. *Application fee:* $55. *Dean of Graduate Studies,* Dr. Jose L. Galvan, 323-343-3820, Fax: 323-343-5653, E-mail: jgalvan@cslanet.calstatela.edu.

Charter College of Education Students: 591 full-time (423 women), 1,290 part-time (946 women); includes 1,161 minority (113 African Americans, 9 American Indian/Alaska Native, 274 Asian Americans or Pacific Islanders, 765 Hispanic Americans), 71 international. *Faculty:* 63 full-time (41 women), 42 part-time/adjunct (25 women). Expenses: Contact institution. *Financial support:* Career-related internships or fieldwork and Federal Work-Study available. Support available to part-time students. Financial award application deadline: 3/1. In 2006, 531 degrees awarded. *Degree program information:* Part-time and evening/weekend programs available. Offers applied and advanced studies in education (MA); applied behavior analysis (MS); community college counseling (MS); computer education (MA); counseling (MS); education (MA, MS); elementary teaching (MA); instructional technology (MA); psychological foundations (MA); reading (MA); rehabilitation counseling (MS); school counseling and school psychology (MS); secondary teaching (MA); social foundations (MA); special education (MA); teaching English to speakers of other languages (MA). *Application deadline:* For fall admission, 6/30 for domestic students; for spring admission, 2/1 for domestic students. Applications are processed on a rolling basis. *Application fee:* $55. *Dean,* Dr. Mary Falvey, 323-343-4300, Fax: 323-343-4318.

College of Arts and Letters Students: 137 full-time (87 women), 414 part-time (256 women); includes 272 minority (40 African Americans, 1 American Indian/Alaska Native, 57 Asian Americans or Pacific Islanders, 174 Hispanic Americans), 40 international. *Faculty:* 65 full-time (30 women), 49 part-time/adjunct (16 women). Expenses: Contact institution. *Financial support:* Career-related internships or fieldwork and Federal Work-Study available. Support available to part-time students. Financial award application deadline: 3/1. In 2006, 95 degrees awarded. *Degree program information:* Part-time and evening/weekend programs available. Offers art (MA); arts and letters (MA, MFA, MM); English (MA); fine arts (MFA); French (MA); music composition (MM); music education (MA); musicology (MA); performance (MM); philosophy (MA); Spanish (MA); speech communication (MA); theater arts (MA). *Application deadline:* For fall admission, 6/30 for domestic students; for spring admission, 2/1 for domestic students. Applications are processed on a rolling basis. *Application fee:* $55. *Dean,* Dr. Terry Allison, 323-343-4001, Fax: 323-343-6440.

College of Business and Economics Students: 124 full-time (77 women), 282 part-time (144 women); includes 217 minority (22 African Americans, 8 American Indian/Alaska Native, 141 Asian Americans or Pacific Islanders, 46 Hispanic Americans), 80 international. *Faculty:* 21 full-time (2 women), 6 part-time/adjunct (2 women). Expenses: Contact institution. *Financial support:* Fellowships, career-related internships or fieldwork and Federal Work-Study available. Support available to part-time students. Financial award application deadline: 3/1. In 2006, 122 degrees awarded. *Degree program information:* Part-time and evening/weekend programs available. Offers accountancy (MS); accounting (MBA); analytical quantitative economics (MA); business and economics (MA, MBA, MS); business economics (MA, MBA, MS); business information systems (MBA); economics (MA); finance and banking (MBA, MS); finance and law (MBA, MS); health care management (MS); information systems (MBA, MS); international business (MBA, MS); management (MBA, MS); management information systems (MS); marketing (MBA, MS); office management (MBA). *Application deadline:* For fall admission, 6/30 for domestic students; for spring admission, 11/30 for domestic students. Applications are processed on a rolling basis. *Application fee:* $55. *Acting Dean,* Dr. Dong-Woo Lee, 323-343-2800, Fax: 323-343-2813.

College of Engineering, Computer Science, and Technology Students: 57 full-time (10 women), 223 part-time (57 women); includes 138 minority (15 African Americans, 84 Asian Americans or Pacific Islanders, 39 Hispanic Americans), 85 international. *Faculty:* 28 full-time (9 women), 1 part-time/adjunct (0 women). Expenses: Contact institution. *Financial support:* Federal Work-Study available. Support available to part-time students. Financial award application deadline: 3/1. In 2006, 79 degrees awarded. *Degree program information:* Part-time and evening/weekend programs available. Offers civil engineering (MS); computer science (MS); electrical engineering (MS); engineering, computer science, and technology (MS); mechanical engineering (MS). *Application deadline:* For fall admission, 6/30 for domestic students; for spring admission, 2/1 for domestic students. Applications are processed on a rolling basis. *Application fee:* $55. *Dean,* Dr. Keith Moo-Young, 323-343-4500, Fax: 323-343-4555.

College of Health and Human Services Students: 318 full-time (267 women), 560 part-time (473 women); includes 555 minority (66 African Americans, 2 American Indian/Alaska Native, 201 Asian Americans or Pacific Islanders, 286 Hispanic Americans), 32 international. *Faculty:* 51 full-time (34 women), 24 part-time/adjunct (15 women). Expenses: Contact institution. *Financial support:* Career-related internships or fieldwork and Federal Work-Study available. Support available to part-time students. Financial award application deadline: 3/1. In 2006, 219 degrees awarded. *Degree program information:* Part-time and evening/weekend programs available. Offers child development (MA); criminal justice (MS); criminalistics (MS); health and human services (MA, MS, MSW); health science (MA); kinesiology (MA); nursing (MS); nutritional science (MS); physical education (MA); physical education and kinesiology (MA); social work (MSW); speech and hearing (MA); speech-language pathology (MA). *Application deadline:* For fall admission, 6/30 for domestic students; for spring admission, 2/1 for domestic students. Applications are processed on a rolling basis. *Application fee:* $55. *Dean,* Dr. Beatrice Yorker, 323-343-4600, Fax: 323-343-5598.

College of Natural and Social Sciences Students: 249 full-time (153 women), 596 part-time (352 women); includes 508 minority (58 African Americans, 5 American Indian/Alaska Native, 145 Asian Americans or Pacific Islanders, 300 Hispanic Americans), 59 international. *Faculty:* 63 full-time (22 women), 25 part-time/adjunct (9 women). Expenses: Contact institution. *Financial support:* Teaching assistantships, career-related internships or fieldwork and Federal Work-Study available. Support available to part-time students. Financial award application deadline: 3/1. In 2006, 142 degrees awarded. *Degree program information:* Part-time and evening/weekend programs available. Offers analytical chemistry (MS); anthropology (MA); biochemistry (MS); biology (MS); chemistry (MS); geography (MA); geological sciences (MS); history (MA); inorganic chemistry (MS); Latin American studies (MA); mathematics (MS); Mexican-American studies (MA); natural and social sciences (MA, MS); organic chemistry (MS); physical chemistry (MS); physics (MS); political science (MA); psychology (MA, MS); public administration (MS); sociology (MA). *Application deadline:* For fall admission, 6/30 for domestic students; for spring admission, 2/1 for domestic students. Applications are processed on a rolling basis. *Application fee:* $55. *Dean,* Dr. Desdemona Cardoza, 323-343-2000, Fax: 323-343-2011.

CALIFORNIA STATE UNIVERSITY, MONTEREY BAY, Seaside, CA 93955-8001

General Information State-supported, coed, comprehensive institution. *Graduate housing:* Rooms and/or apartments available on a first-come, first-served basis to single and married students.

GRADUATE UNITS

College of Professional Studies Offers professional studies (MA).

Institute for Advanced Studies in Education *Degree program information:* Part-time and evening/weekend programs available. Offers education (MA). Electronic applications accepted.

Institute for Community Collaborative Studies *Degree program information:* Part-time programs available. Offers public policy (MA). Electronic applications accepted.

College of Science, Media Arts and Technology Offers marine science (MS); science, media arts and technology (MS, MSMIT).

School of Information Technology and Communication Design *Degree program information:* Part-time and evening/weekend programs available. Offers management and information technology (MSMIT). Electronic applications accepted.

CALIFORNIA STATE UNIVERSITY, NORTHRIDGE, Northridge, CA 91330

General Information State-supported, coed, comprehensive institution. CGS member. *Enrollment:* 34,560 graduate, professional, and undergraduate students; 1,693 full-time matriculated graduate/professional students (1,179 women), 2,855 part-time matriculated graduate/professional students (1,778 women). *Enrollment by degree level:* 4,548 master's. *Graduate faculty:* 732 full-time (318 women), 1,028 part-time/adjunct (553 women). Tuition, nonresident: full-time $8,136; part-time $4,068 per year. *Required fees:* $3,624; $1,161 per term. *Graduate housing:* Room and/or apartments available to single students; on-campus housing not available to married students. Typical cost: $5,155 per year ($8,105 including board). *Student services:* Campus employment opportunities, campus safety program, career counseling, child daycare facilities, disabled student services, free psychological counseling, international student services, low-cost health insurance, multicultural affairs office, teacher training. *Library facilities:* Oviatt Library. *Online resources:* library catalog, web page. *Collection:* 1.4 million titles, 1,779 serial subscriptions, 10,046 audiovisual materials. *Research affiliation:* Hughes Aircraft Corporation (engineering), Jet Propulsion Laboratory (engineering), Warner Center Institute (child care), Northridge Hospital (biology), Haagen Company (archaeology), California Institute of Technology (science).

Computer facilities: A campuswide network can be accessed from off campus. Internet access and online class registration are available. *Web address:* http://www.csun.edu/.

General Application Contact: Dr. Mack Johnson, Associate Vice President, 818-677-2138.

GRADUATE UNITS

Graduate Studies Students: 1,693 full-time (1,179 women), 2,855 part-time (1,778 women); includes 1,730 minority (257 African Americans, 22 American Indian/Alaska Native, 425 Asian Americans or Pacific Islanders, 1,026 Hispanic Americans), 312 international. Average age 34. 2,806 applicants, 60% accepted, 1064 enrolled. *Faculty:* 732 full-time (318 women), 1,028 part-time/adjunct (553 women). Expenses: Contact institution. *Financial support:* Fellowships, research assistantships, teaching assistantships, career-related internships or fieldwork, Federal Work-Study, institutionally sponsored loans, scholarships/grants, tuition waivers (partial), and unspecified assistantships available. Support available to part-time students. Financial award applicants required to submit FAFSA. In 2006, 1398 degrees awarded. *Degree program information:* Part-time and evening/weekend programs available. Offers interdisciplinary studies (MA, MS). *Application deadline:* For fall admission, 3/31 for domestic students; for spring admission, 10/31 for domestic students. Applications are processed on a rolling basis. *Application fee:* $55. *Application Contact:* 818-677-3755. *Associate Vice President,* Dr. Mack Johnson, 818-677-2138.

College of Arts, Media, and Communication Students: 95 full-time (61 women), 172 part-time (113 women); includes 62 minority (12 African Americans, 3 American Indian/Alaska Native, 19 Asian Americans or Pacific Islanders, 28 Hispanic Americans), 26 international. Average age 34. 239 applicants, 49% accepted, 81 enrolled. *Faculty:* 97 full-time (44 women), 165 part-time/adjunct (75 women). Expenses: Contact institution. *Financial support:* Teaching assistantships, career-related internships or fieldwork, Federal Work-Study, and unspecified assistantships available. Support available to part-time students. Financial award application deadline: 3/1. In 2006, 52 degrees awarded. *Degree program information:* Part-time and evening/weekend programs available. Offers art education (MA); art history (MA); arts, media, and communication (MA, MFA, MM); communication studies (MA); composition (MM); conducting (MM); mass communication (MA); music education (MA); performance (MM); screenwriting (MA); studio art (MA, MFA); theater (MA); visual communication (MA, MFA). *Application deadline:* For fall admission, 11/30 for domestic students. *Application fee:* $55. *Interim Dean,* Prof. David Moon, 818-677-2246, E-mail: art.dept@csun.edu.

College of Business and Economics Students: 52 full-time (26 women), 181 part-time (67 women); includes 61 minority (5 African Americans, 35 Asian Americans or Pacific Islanders, 21 Hispanic Americans), 28 international. Average age 33. 198 applicants, 33% accepted, 49 enrolled. *Faculty:* 97 full-time (26 women), 61 part-time/adjunct (17 women). Expenses: Contact institution. *Financial support:* Teaching assistantships, Federal Work-Study available. Support available to part-time students. Financial award application deadline: 3/1. In 2006, 72 degrees awarded. *Degree program information:* Part-time programs available. Offers business and economics (MBA). *Application deadline:* For fall admission, 11/30 for domestic students. *Application fee:* $55. *Application Contact:* Dr. Deborah Cours, Director of Graduate Programs, 818-677-2467. *Interim Dean,* Dr. William Jennings, 818-677-2455.

College of Education Students: 657 full-time (524 women), 1,393 part-time (1,011 women); includes 968 minority (154 African Americans, 10 American Indian/Alaska Native, 163 Asian Americans or Pacific Islanders, 641 Hispanic Americans), 31 international. Average age 36. 648 applicants, 74% accepted, 361 enrolled. *Faculty:* 92 full-time (58 women), 279 part-time/adjunct (189 women). Expenses: Contact institution. *Financial support:* Fellowships, career-related internships or fieldwork, Federal Work-Study, institutionally sponsored loans, scholarships/grants, and tuition waivers (partial) available. Support available to part-time students. Financial award application deadline: 3/1. In 2006, 586 degrees awarded. *Degree program information:* Part-time and evening/weekend programs available. Offers counseling (MS); early childhood special education (MA); education (MA); education of the deaf and hard of hearing (MA); educational administration (MA); educational psychology (MA Ed); educational therapy (MA); elementary education (MA); genetic counseling (MS); mild/moderate disabilities (MA); moderate/severe disabilities (MA); secondary education (MA). *Application deadline:* For fall admission, 11/30 for domestic students. *Application fee:* $55. *Dean,* Dr. Philip J. Rusche, 818-677-2590.

College of Engineering and Computer Science Students: 171 full-time (37 women), 287 part-time (56 women); includes 148 minority (13 African Americans, 83 Asian Americans or Pacific Islanders, 52 Hispanic Americans), 134 international. Average age 30. 491 applicants, 64% accepted, 136 enrolled. *Faculty:* 60 full-time (11 women), 56 part-time/adjunct (9 women). Expenses: Contact institution. *Financial support:* Teaching assistantships, career-related internships or fieldwork and Federal Work-Study available. Support available to part-time students. Financial award application deadline: 3/1. In 2006, 188 degrees awarded. *Degree program information:* Part-time and evening/weekend programs available. Offers computer science (MS); electrical engineering (MS); engineering (MS); engineering and computer science (MS); engineering management (MS); manufacturing systems engineering (MS); materials engineering (MS); mechanical engineering (MS). *Application deadline:* For fall admission, 11/30 for domestic students. *Application fee:* $55. *Dean,* Dr. S.K. Ramesh, 818-677-4501.

College of Health and Human Development Students: 325 full-time (268 women), 245 part-time (191 women); includes 173 minority (38 African Americans, 2 American Indian/Alaska Native, 66 Asian Americans or Pacific Islanders, 67 Hispanic Americans), 36 international. Average age 31. 469 applicants, 50% accepted, 169 enrolled. *Faculty:* 91 full-time (54 women), 131 part-time/adjunct (83 women). Expenses: Contact institution. *Financial support:* Teaching assistantships, career-related internships or fieldwork, Federal Work-Study, and institutionally sponsored loans available. Support available to part-time students. Financial award application deadline: 3/1. In 2006, 206 degrees awarded. *Degree program information:* Part-time and evening/weekend programs available. Offers communication disorders and sciences (MS); family and consumer sciences (MS); health administration (MS); health and human development (MPH, MPT, MS); health education (MPH); industrial hygiene (MS); kinesiology (MS); physical therapy (MPT); recreation administration (MS). *Application deadline:* For fall admission, 11/30 for domestic students. *Application fee:* $55. *Dean,* Dr. Helen M. Castillo, 818-677-3001.

College of Humanities Students: 81 full-time (55 women), 206 part-time (146 women); includes 106 minority (4 African Americans, 1 American Indian/Alaska Native, 11 Asian Americans or Pacific Islanders, 90 Hispanic Americans), 14 international. Average age 33. 130 applicants, 66% accepted, 60 enrolled. *Faculty:* 76 full-time (40 women), 120 part-time/adjunct (78 women). Expenses: Contact institution. *Financial support:* Teaching assistantships, Federal Work-Study available. Support available to part-time students. Financial award application deadline: 3/1. In 2006, 54 degrees awarded. *Degree program information:* Part-time and evening/weekend programs available. Offers Chicana and Chicano studies (MA); creative writing (MA); humanities (MA); linguistics (MA); literature (MA); rhetoric and composition theory (MA); Spanish (MA). *Application deadline:* For fall admission, 11/30 for domestic students. *Application fee:* $55. *Dean,* Dr. Elizabeth Say, 818-677-3301.

College of Science and Mathematics Students: 90 full-time (57 women), 175 part-time (83 women); includes 70 minority (6 African Americans, 3 American Indian/Alaska Native, 22 Asian Americans or Pacific Islanders, 39 Hispanic Americans), 26 international. Average age 31. 185 applicants, 62% accepted, 89 enrolled. *Faculty:* 109 full-time (34 women), 101 part-time/adjunct (47 women). Expenses: Contact institution. *Financial support:* Research assistantships, teaching assistantships, Federal Work-Study, institutionally sponsored loans, tuition waivers (partial), and unspecified assistantships available. Support available to part-time students. Financial award applicants required to submit FAFSA. In 2006, 62 degrees awarded. *Degree program information:* Part-time and evening/weekend programs available. Offers applied mathematics (MS); biochemistry (MS); biology (MS); chemistry (MS); genetic counseling (MS); geology (MS); mathematics (MS); mathematics for educational careers (MS); physics (MS); science and mathematics (MS). *Application fee:* $55. *Dean,* Dr. Jerry Stinner, 818-677-2004.

College of Social and Behavioral Sciences Students: 209 full-time (143 women), 174 part-time (98 women); includes 126 minority (13 African Americans, 2 American Indian/Alaska Native, 24 Asian Americans or Pacific Islanders, 87 Hispanic Americans), 16 international. Average age 32. 437 applicants, 61% accepted, 112 enrolled. *Faculty:* 110 full-time (51 women), 115 part-time/adjunct (55 women). Expenses: Contact institution. *Financial support:* Teaching assistantships, career-related internships or fieldwork, Federal Work-Study, and institutionally sponsored loans available. Support available to part-time students. Financial award application deadline: 3/1. In 2006, 165 degrees awarded. *Degree program information:* Part-time and evening/weekend programs available. Offers anthropology (MA); geography (MA); history (MA); political science (MA); psychology (MA); public administration (MPA); social and behavioral sciences (MA, MPA, MSW); social work (MSW); sociology (MA). *Application deadline:* For fall admission, 11/30 for domestic students. *Application fee:* $55. *Dean,* Dr. Stella Z. Theodoulou, 818-677-3317.

CALIFORNIA STATE UNIVERSITY, SACRAMENTO, Sacramento, CA 95819-6048

General Information State-supported, coed, comprehensive institution. CGS member. *Enrollment:* 28,529 graduate, professional, and undergraduate students; 1,694 full-time matriculated graduate/professional students (1,186 women), 1,784 part-time matriculated graduate/professional students (1,132 women). *Graduate housing:* Room and/or apartments available on a first-come, first-served basis to single students; on-campus housing not available to married students. *Student services:* Campus employment opportunities, career counseling, child daycare facilities, disabled student services, free psychological counseling, grant writing training, international student services, low-cost health insurance, multicultural affairs office, teacher training, writing training. *Library facilities:* California State University, Sacramento Library. *Online resources:* library catalog, web page, access to other libraries' catalogs. *Collection:* 1.3 million titles, 2,918 serial subscriptions, 23,880 audiovisual materials.

Computer facilities: 700 computers available on campus for general student use. A campuswide network can be accessed from student residence rooms and from off campus. Internet access and online class registration are available. *Web address:* http://www.csus.edu/.

General Application Contact: Dr. Chevelle Newsome, Associate Dean of Graduate Admissions, 916-278-6470, Fax: 916-278-5669, E-mail: gradctr@csus.edu.

GRADUATE UNITS

Graduate Studies Students: 1,694 full-time (1,186 women), 1,784 part-time (1,132 women); includes 1,050 minority (195 African Americans, 30 American Indian/Alaska Native, 393 Asian Americans or Pacific Islanders, 432 Hispanic Americans), 223 international. Average age 32. 4,160 applicants, 66% accepted, 1667 enrolled. Expenses: Contact institution. *Financial support:* Research assistantships, teaching assistantships, career-related internships or fieldwork and Federal Work-Study available. Support available to part-time students. Financial award application deadline: 3/1. *Degree program information:* Part-time and evening/weekend programs available. Offers special majors (MA, MS). *Application deadline:* Applications are processed on a rolling basis. *Application fee:* $55. Electronic applications accepted. *Application Contact:* Rose Marie Fisher, Graduate Services Coordinator, 916-278-6470, Fax: 916-278-5669, E-mail: gradctr@csus.edu. *Associate Dean,* Dr. Chevelle Newsome, 916-248-6470, Fax: 916-278-5669, E-mail: cnewsome@csus.edu.

College of Arts and Letters Students: 197 full-time (126 women), 295 part-time (193 women); includes 115 minority (17 African Americans, 6 American Indian/Alaska Native, 29 Asian Americans or Pacific Islanders, 63 Hispanic Americans), 9 international. Average age 34. 397 applicants, 72% accepted, 182 enrolled. Expenses: Contact institution. *Financial support:* Research assistantships, teaching assistantships, career-related internships or fieldwork and Federal Work-Study available. Support available to part-time students. Financial award application deadline: 3/1. *Degree program information:* Part-time and evening/weekend programs available. Offers arts and letters (MA, MM); communication studies (MA); creative writing (MA); foreign languages (MA); French (MA); German (MA); music (MM); public history (MA); Spanish (MA); studio art (MA); teaching English to speakers of other languages (MA); theater arts (MA); theatre and dance (MA). *Application deadline:* Applications are processed on a rolling basis. *Application fee:* $55. Electronic applications accepted. *Dean,* Jeffrey Mason, 916-278-7674, Fax: 916-278-4588.

College of Business Administration Students: 64 full-time (38 women), 150 part-time (55 women); includes 48 minority (2 African Americans, 1 American Indian/Alaska Native, 27 Asian Americans or Pacific Islanders, 18 Hispanic Americans), 19 international. Average age 30. 373 applicants, 69% accepted, 42 enrolled. Expenses: Contact institution. *Financial support:* Research assistantships, teaching assistantships, career-related internships or fieldwork and Federal Work-Study available. Support available to part-time students. Financial award application deadline: 3/1. *Degree program information:* Part-time and evening/weekend programs available. Offers accountancy (MS); business administration (MBA); human resources (MBA); management information science (MS); urban land development (MBA). *Application deadline:* Applications are processed on a rolling basis. *Application fee:* $55. Electronic applications accepted. *Dean,* Dr. Sanjay Varshney, 916-278-6942, Fax: 916-278-5793.

College of Education Students: 542 full-time (435 women), 561 part-time (463 women); includes 384 minority (89 African Americans, 8 American Indian/Alaska Native, 92 Asian Americans or Pacific Islanders, 195 Hispanic Americans), 12 international. Average age 35. 1,254 applicants, 83% accepted, 764 enrolled. Expenses: Contact institution. *Financial support:* Research assistantships, teaching assistantships, career-related internships or fieldwork and Federal Work-Study available. Support available to part-time students. Financial award application deadline: 3/1. *Degree program information:* Part-time programs available. Offers bilingual/cross-cultural education (MA); career counseling (MS); curriculum and instruction (MA); early childhood education (MA); education (MA, MS); educational administration (MA); generic counseling (MS); guidance (MA); reading education (MA); school counseling (MS); school psychology (MS); special education (MA); vocational rehabilitation (MS). *Application deadline:* Applications are processed on a rolling basis. *Application fee:* $55. Electronic applications accepted. *Dean,* Dr. Vanessa Sheared, 916-278-6639, Fax: 916-278-5904.

College of Engineering and Computer Science Students: 170 full-time (39 women), 193 part-time (42 women); includes 97 minority (12 African Americans, 1 American Indian/Alaska Native, 72 Asian Americans or Pacific Islanders, 12 Hispanic Americans), 164 international. Average age 27. 574 applicants, 51% accepted, 136 enrolled. Expenses: Contact institution. *Financial support:* Research assistantships, teaching assistantships, career-related internships or fieldwork and Federal Work-Study available. Support available to part-time students. Financial award application deadline: 3/1. *Degree program information:* Part-time and evening/weekend programs available. Offers civil engineering (MS); computer systems (MS); electrical engineering (MS); engineering and computer science (MS); mechanical engineering (MS); software engineering (MS). *Application deadline:* Applications are processed on a rolling basis. *Application fee:* $55. Electronic applications accepted. *Dean,* Dr. Emir Jose Macari, 916-278-6366, Fax: 916-278-5949.

College of Health and Human Services Students: 561 full-time (451 women), 229 part-time (156 women); includes 271 minority (56 African Americans, 7 American Indian/Alaska Native, 110 Asian Americans or Pacific Islanders, 98 Hispanic Americans), 8 international. Average age 32. 915 applicants, 52% accepted, 309 enrolled. Expenses: Contact institution. *Financial support:* Research assistantships, teaching assistantships, career-related internships or fieldwork and Federal Work-Study available. Support available to part-time students. Financial award application deadline: 3/1. *Degree program information:* Part-time programs available. Offers audiology (MS); criminal justice (MS); family and children's services (MSW); health and human services (MS, MSW); health care (MSW); mental health (MSW); nursing (MS); physical education (MS); recreation administration (MS); social justice and corrections (MSW); speech pathology (MS). *Application deadline:* Applications are processed on a rolling basis. *Application fee:* $55. Electronic applications accepted. *Dean,* Dr. Marilyn Hopkins, 916-278-5867, Fax: 916-278-7421.

College of Natural Sciences and Mathematics Students: 35 full-time (19 women), 101 part-time (53 women); includes 33 minority (2 African Americans, 1 American Indian/Alaska Native, 22 Asian Americans or Pacific Islanders, 8 Hispanic Americans), 6 international. Average age 30. 214 applicants, 56% accepted, 63 enrolled. Expenses: Contact institution. *Financial support:* Research assistantships, teaching assistantships, career-related internships or fieldwork and Federal Work-Study available. Support available to part-time students. Financial award application deadline: 3/1. *Degree program information:* Part-time programs available. Offers biological sciences (MA, MS); chemistry (MS); immunohematology (MS); marine science (MS); mathematics and statistics (MA); natural sciences and mathematics (MA, MS). *Application deadline:* Applications are processed on a rolling basis. *Application fee:* $55. Electronic applications accepted. *Dean,* Laurel Hefferman, 916-278-4655, Fax: 916-278-5787.

College of Social Sciences and Interdisciplinary Studies Students: 115 full-time (74 women), 240 part-time (157 women); includes 95 minority (15 African Americans, 5 American Indian/Alaska Native, 37 Asian Americans or Pacific Islanders, 38 Hispanic Americans), 4 international. Average age 31. 347 applicants, 59% accepted, 128 enrolled. Expenses: Contact institution. *Financial support:* Teaching assistantships, career-related internships or fieldwork and Federal Work-Study available. Support available to part-time students. Financial award application deadline: 3/1. *Degree program information:* Part-time programs available. Offers anthropology (MA); counseling psychology (MA); government (MA); international affairs (MA); public policy and administration (MPPA); social sciences and interdisciplinary studies (MA, MPPA); sociology (MA). *Application deadline:* Applications are processed on a rolling basis. *Application fee:* $55. Electronic applications accepted. *Dean,* Otis Scott, 916-278-6504, Fax: 916-278-4678.

CALIFORNIA STATE UNIVERSITY, SAN BERNARDINO, San Bernardino, CA 92407-2397

General Information State-supported, coed, comprehensive institution. CGS member. *Enrollment:* 16,479 graduate, professional, and undergraduate students; 1,527 full-time matriculated graduate/professional students (1,028 women), 738 part-time matriculated graduate/professional students (477 women). *Enrollment by degree level:* 2,265 master's. *Graduate faculty:* 431 full-time, 516 part-time/adjunct. *Graduate housing:* Room and/or apartments available on a first-come, first-served basis to single students. Housing application deadline: 8/1. *Student services:* Campus employment opportunities, campus safety program, career counseling, child daycare facilities, disabled student services, exercise/wellness program, free psychological counseling, international student services, low-cost health insurance, multicultural affairs office, teacher training. *Library facilities:* Pfau Library. *Online resources:* library catalog, web page, access to other libraries' catalogs. *Collection:* 731,259 titles, 2,028 serial subscriptions.

Computer facilities: 1,300 computers available on campus for general student use. A campuswide network can be accessed from student residence rooms and from off campus. Internet access and online class registration are available. *Web address:* http://www.csusb.edu/.

General Application Contact: Olivia Rosas, Director of Admissions, 909-537-5188, Fax: 909-537-7034, E-mail: orosas@csusb.edu.

GRADUATE UNITS

Graduate Studies Students: 1,527 full-time (1,028 women), 738 part-time (477 women); includes 953 minority (271 African Americans, 22 American Indian/Alaska Native, 122 Asian Americans or Pacific Islanders, 538 Hispanic Americans), 167 international. Average age 31. 1,468 applicants, 66% accepted, 461 enrolled. *Faculty:* 431 full-time, 516 part-time/adjunct. Expenses: Contact institution. *Financial support:* Fellowships, research assistantships, teaching assistantships, career-related internships or fieldwork, Federal Work-Study, institutionally sponsored loans, scholarships/grants, and unspecified assistantships available. Support available to part-time students. In 2006, 693 degrees awarded. *Degree program information:* Part-time and evening/weekend programs available. Offers interdisciplinary studies (MA). *Application fee:* $55. *Application Contact:* Olivia Rosas, Director of Admissions, 909-537-5188, Fax: 909-537-7034, E-mail: orosas@csusb.edu. *Dean of Graduate Studies,* Dr. Sandra Kamusikiri, 909-537-5058, Fax: 909-537-7028, E-mail: skamusik@csusb.edu.

College of Arts and Letters Students: 96 full-time (69 women), 116 part-time (87 women); includes 85 minority (21 African Americans, 2 American Indian/Alaska Native, 5 Asian Americans or Pacific Islanders, 57 Hispanic Americans), 11 international. Average age 32. 148 applicants, 61% accepted, 27 enrolled. *Faculty:* 95 full-time, 115 part-time/adjunct. Expenses: Contact institution. *Financial support:* Research assistantships, teaching assistantships, career-related internships or fieldwork, Federal Work-Study, institutionally sponsored loans, and writing center tutorships available. Support available to part-time students. Financial award application deadline: 3/1. In 2006, 50 degrees awarded. *Degree program information:* Part-time and evening/weekend programs available. Offers art (MA); arts and letters (MA); communication studies (MA); English composition (MA); Spanish (MA); theatre arts (MA). *Application deadline:* For fall admission, 8/31 priority date for domestic students. *Application fee:* $55. *Dean,* Dr. Eri F. Yasuhara, 909-537-5800, Fax: 909-537-5926, E-mail: eyasuha@csusb.edu.

College of Business and Public Administration Students: 297 full-time (137 women), 100 part-time (45 women); includes 136 minority (36 African Americans, 4 American Indian/Alaska Native, 35 Asian Americans or Pacific Islanders, 61 Hispanic Americans), 118 international. Average age 28. 365 applicants, 69% accepted, 98 enrolled. *Faculty:* 56 full-time, 44 part-time/adjunct. Expenses: Contact institution. *Financial support:* Career-related internships or fieldwork, Federal Work-Study, and institutionally sponsored loans available. Support available to part-time students. Financial award application deadline:3/1. In 2006, 119 degrees awarded. *Degree program information:* Part-time and evening/weekend programs available. Offers business administration (MBA); business and public administration (MBA, MPA); public administration (MPA). *Application deadline:* For fall admission, 8/31 priority date for domestic students. Applications are processed on a rolling basis. *Application fee:* $55. *Dean,* Dr. Karen Dill-Bowerman, 909-537-5700, Fax: 909-537-7026, E-mail: karenb@csusb.edu.

College of Education Students: 692 full-time (515 women), 345 part-time (245 women); includes 479 minority (145 African Americans, 12 American Indian/Alaska Native, 45 Asian Americans or Pacific Islanders, 277 Hispanic Americans), 17 international. Average age 33. 450 applicants, 82% accepted, 147 enrolled. *Faculty:* 69 full-time, 145 part-time/adjunct. Expenses: Contact institution. *Financial support:* Career-related internships or fieldwork and Federal Work-Study available. Support available to part-time students. In 2006, 349 degrees awarded. *Degree program information:* Part-time and evening/weekend programs available. Offers bilingual/cross-cultural education (MA); counseling and guidance (MS); curriculum and instruction (MA); educational administration (MA); educational psychology and counseling (MA, MS); elementary education (MA); English as a second language (MA); environmental education (MA); history and English for secondary teachers (MA); instructional technology (MA); reading (MA); rehabilitation counseling (MA); secondary education (MA); special education (MA); special education and rehabilitation counseling (MA); teaching of

California State University, San Bernardino (continued)

science (MA); vocational and career education (MA). *Application deadline:* For fall admission, 8/31 priority date for domestic students. *Application fee:* $55. *Dean,* Dr. Patricia Arlin, 909-537-5600, Fax: 909-537-7011, E-mail: parlin@csusb.edu.

College of Natural Sciences Students: 96 full-time (56 women), 86 part-time (42 women); includes 67 minority (18 African Americans, 1 American Indian/Alaska Native, 20 Asian Americans or Pacific Islanders, 28 Hispanic Americans), 20 international. Average age 30. 112 applicants, 61% accepted, 32 enrolled. *Faculty:* 108 full-time, 106 part-time/adjunct. Expenses: Contact institution. *Financial support:* Fellowships, research assistantships, teaching assistantships, career-related internships or fieldwork and Federal Work-Study available. In 2006, 54 degrees awarded. *Degree program information:* Part-time programs available. Offers biology (MS); computer science (MS); environmental sciences and chemistry (MS); health science (MS); health services administration (MS); kinesiology (MA Ed); mathematics (MA, MAT); natural sciences (MA, MA Ed, MAT, MS); nursing (MS). *Application fee:* $55. *Dean,* Dr. B. Robert Carlson, 909-537-5300, Fax: 909-537-7005, E-mail: carlson@csusb.edu.

College of Social and Behavioral Sciences Students: 336 full-time (242 women), 79 part-time (52 women); includes 184 minority (51 African Americans, 3 American Indian/Alaska Native, 17 Asian Americans or Pacific Islanders, 113 Hispanic Americans), 6 international. Average age 28. 392 applicants, 49% accepted, 134 enrolled. *Faculty:* 101 full-time, 78 part-time/adjunct. Expenses: Contact institution. *Financial support:* Fellowships, research assistantships, teaching assistantships, career-related internships or fieldwork, Federal Work-Study, institutionally sponsored loans, and unspecified assistantships available. Support available to part-time students. In 2006, 109 degrees awarded. *Degree program information:* Part-time and evening/weekend programs available. Offers clinical/counseling psychology (MS); criminal justice (MA); general experimental psychology (MA); human development (MA); industrial organizational psychology (MS); national security studies (MA); social and behavioral sciences (MA, MS, MSW); social sciences (MA); social work (MSW). *Chair,* Dr. John Conley, 909-537-5500, Fax: 909-537-7107, E-mail: jconley@csusb.edu.

CALIFORNIA STATE UNIVERSITY, SAN MARCOS, San Marcos, CA 92096-0001

General Information State-supported, coed, comprehensive institution. CGS member. *Enrollment:* 6,956 graduate, professional, and undergraduate students; 172 full-time matriculated graduate/professional students (106 women), 468 part-time matriculated graduate/professional students (346 women). *Enrollment by degree level:* 640 master's. *Graduate faculty:* 104 full-time (60 women), 143 part-time/adjunct (85 women). Tuition, nonresident: part-time $339 per unit. *Required fees:* $1,186 per term. *Graduate housing:* Room and/or apartments available on a first-come, first-served basis to single students; on-campus housing not available to married students. Housing application deadline: 10/1. *Student services:* Campus employment opportunities, campus safety program, career counseling, child daycare facilities, disabled student services, exercise/wellness program, free psychological counseling, international student services, low-cost health insurance, multicultural affairs office, teacher training, writing training. *Library facilities:* Kellogg Library. *Online resources:* library catalog, web page, access to other libraries' catalogs. *Collection:* 233,445 titles, 2,043 serial subscriptions.

Computer facilities: 1,300 computers available on campus for general student use. A campuswide network can be accessed from student residence rooms and from off campus. Internet access and online class registration are available. *Web address:* http://www.csusm.edu/.

General Application Contact: Admissions, 760-750-4848, Fax: 760-750-3248, E-mail: apply@csusm.edu.

GRADUATE UNITS

College of Arts and Sciences Students: 71 full-time (45 women), 107 part-time (66 women); includes 57 minority (5 African Americans, 1 American Indian/Alaska Native, 11 Asian Americans or Pacific Islanders, 40 Hispanic Americans), 8 international. Average age 34. 167 applicants, 48% accepted, 48 enrolled. *Faculty:* 48 full-time (29 women), 62 part-time/adjunct (42 women). Expenses: Contact institution. *Financial support:* In 2006–07, 1 fellowship, 11 research assistantships, 8 teaching assistantships with tuition reimbursements were awarded; career-related internships or fieldwork, Federal Work-Study, institutionally sponsored loans, scholarships/grants, traineeships, and unspecified assistantships also available. Support available to part-time students. In 2006, 39 degrees awarded. *Degree program information:* Part-time and evening/weekend programs available. Offers arts and sciences (MA, MS); biological sciences (MS); computer science (MS); literature and writing studies (MA); mathematics (MS); psychology (MA); sociological practice (MA); Spanish (MA). *Application deadline:* For fall admission, 11/30 priority date for domestic students; for spring admission, 8/31 priority date for domestic students. Applications are processed on a rolling basis. *Application fee:* $55. Electronic applications accepted. *Dean,* Dr. Vicki Golich, 760-750-4195, E-mail: vgolich@csusm.edu.

College of Business Administration Students: 65 full-time (27 women), 17 part-time (5 women); includes 17 minority (1 African American, 10 Asian Americans or Pacific Islanders, 6 Hispanic Americans), 4 international. Average age 28. 44 applicants, 30% accepted, 10 enrolled. *Faculty:* 26 full-time (7 women), 28 part-time/adjunct (7 women). Expenses: Contact institution. *Financial support:* In 2006–07, 35 students received support; research assistantships, teaching assistantships, Federal Work-Study available. Support available to part-time students. Financial award applicants required to submit FAFSA. In 2006, 47 degrees awarded. *Degree program information:* Evening/weekend programs available. Offers business management (MBA); government management (MBA). *Application deadline:* For fall admission, 4/30 priority date for domestic students. Applications are processed on a rolling basis. *Application fee:* $55. *Application Contact:* Keith Butler, Operations Manager, 760-750-4266, E-mail: kbutler@csusm.edu. *Dean,* Dennis Guseman, 760-750-4239.

College of Education Students: 36 full-time (34 women), 344 part-time (275 women); includes 87 minority (7 African Americans, 5 American Indian/Alaska Native, 18 Asian Americans or Pacific Islanders, 57 Hispanic Americans), 1 international. Average age 32. 156 applicants, 78% accepted, 43 enrolled. *Faculty:* 30 full-time (24 women), 53 part-time/adjunct (36 women). Expenses: Contact institution. *Financial support:* Fellowships, teaching assistantships, career-related internships or fieldwork and Federal Work-Study available. Support available to part-time students. Financial award applicants required to submit FAFSA. In 2006, 89 degrees awarded. *Degree program information:* Part-time and evening/weekend programs available. Offers education (MA). *Application deadline:* For fall admission, 2/1 priority date for domestic students. Applications are processed on a rolling basis. *Application fee:* $55. *Application Contact:* Beverly Mahdavi, Graduate Admissions Coordinator, 760-750-4281, Fax: 760-750-3538, E-mail: bmahdavi@csusm.edu. *Dean,* Dr. Mark Baldwin, 760-750-4306, Fax: 760-750-4323, E-mail: baldwin@csusm.edu.

CALIFORNIA STATE UNIVERSITY, STANISLAUS, Turlock, CA 95382

General Information State-supported, coed, comprehensive institution. CGS member. *Graduate housing:* Room and/or apartments available on a first-come, first-served basis to single students; on-campus housing not available to married students. Housing application deadline: 8/1. *Research affiliation:* American Council on Education (public policy think tank), E & J Gallo Winery (product development, operations reserach), Kaiser Foundation Research Institute (health services), Valley Mountain Regional Center (serves people with developmental disabilities).

GRADUATE UNITS

College of Arts, Letters, and Sciences *Degree program information:* Part-time and evening/weekend programs available. Offers arts, letters, and sciences (MA, MPA, MS, MSW); behavior analysis psychology (MS); criminal justice (MA); English (MA); general psychology (MA); history (MA); marine sciences (MS); public administration (MPA); social work (MSW). Electronic applications accepted.

College of Business Administration *Degree program information:* Part-time and evening/weekend programs available. Offers business administration (MBA); international finance (MSBA).

College of Education *Degree program information:* Part-time and evening/weekend programs available. Offers curriculum and instruction (MA Ed); education (MA Ed).

CALIFORNIA UNIVERSITY OF PENNSYLVANIA, California, PA 15419-1394

General Information State-supported, coed, comprehensive institution. CGS member. *Enrollment:* 7,720 graduate, professional, and undergraduate students; 800 full-time matriculated graduate/professional students (461 women), 621 part-time matriculated graduate/professional students (387 women). *Enrollment by degree level:* 1,421 master's. *Graduate faculty:* 135 full-time (63 women), 29 part-time/adjunct (7 women). Tuition, state resident: full-time $6,048; part-time $336 per credit. Tuition, nonresident: full-time $9,678; part-time $538 per credit. *Required fees:* $1,854; $263 per credit. Full-time tuition and fees vary according to course load, campus/location and program. *Graduate housing:* Room and/or apartments available on a first-come, first-served basis to single students; on-campus housing not available to married students. Typical cost: $8,345 per year ($8,314 including board). Room and board charges vary according to board plan, campus/location and housing facility selected. *Student services:* Campus employment opportunities, campus safety program, career counseling, child daycare facilities, disabled student services, exercise/wellness program, free psychological counseling, grant writing training, international student services, low-cost health insurance, teacher training, writing training. *Library facilities:* Manderino Library. *Online resources:* library catalog, web page, access to other libraries' catalogs. *Collection:* 437,160 titles, 881 serial subscriptions. *Research affiliation:* The Center for Rural Pennsylvania (agriculture), The Technology Collaborative (robotics), International Technical Education Association (curricular development), NCAA (tobacco use), Gettysburg Travel Council (travel and tourism), NASA (space grant consortium).

Computer facilities: 1,220 computers available on campus for general student use. A campuswide network can be accessed from student residence rooms. Internet access and online class registration are available. *Web address:* http://www.cup.edu/.

General Application Contact: Suzanne C. Powers, Director of Graduate Admissions and Recruitment, 724-938-4029, Fax: 724-938-5712, E-mail: powers_s@cup.edu.

GRADUATE UNITS

School of Graduate Studies and Research Students: 800 full-time (461 women), 621 part-time (387 women); includes 124 minority (79 African Americans, 3 American Indian/Alaska Native, 20 Asian Americans or Pacific Islanders, 22 Hispanic Americans). Average age 31. 477 applicants. *Faculty:* 135 full-time (63 women), 29 part-time/adjunct (7 women). Expenses: Contact institution. *Financial support:* Career-related internships or fieldwork, scholarships/grants, traineeships, tuition waivers (partial), and unspecified assistantships available. Financial award applicants required to submit FAFSA. In 2006, 553 degrees awarded. *Degree program information:* Part-time and evening/weekend programs available. Postbaccalaureate distance learning degree programs offered (no on-campus study). Offers legal studies (MS). *Application deadline:* For fall admission, 8/1 priority date for domestic and international students; for winter admission, 12/1 priority date for domestic and international students; for spring admission, 5/1 priority date for domestic and international students. Applications are processed on a rolling basis. *Application fee:* $25. Electronic applications accepted. *Application Contact:* Suzanne C. Powers, Director of Graduate Admissions and Recruitment, 724-938-4029, Fax: 724-938-5712, E-mail: powers_s@cup.edu. *Dean,* Dr. Ronald W. Wagner, 724-938-4187, Fax: 724-938-5712, E-mail: wagner_r@cup.edu.

College of Liberal Arts Students: 32 full-time (16 women), 49 part-time (45 women); includes 5 minority (4 African Americans, 1 Hispanic American). Average age 30. *Faculty:* 11 full-time (4 women). Expenses: Contact institution. *Financial support:* Career-related internships or fieldwork, scholarships/grants, traineeships, and unspecified assistantships available. In 2006, 22 degrees awarded. *Degree program information:* Part-time and evening/weekend programs available. Offers liberal arts (MA); social science—criminal justice (MA). *Application deadline:* For fall admission, 8/1 priority date for domestic and international students; for winter admission, 12/1 priority date for domestic and international students; for spring admission, 5/1 priority date for domestic and international students. Applications are processed on a rolling basis. *Application fee:* $25. Electronic applications accepted. *Interim Dean,* Dr. Laura Ann Tuennerman, 724-938-4058, E-mail: tuennerman@cup.edu.

School of Education Students: 606 full-time (351 women), 471 part-time (313 women); includes 88 minority (50 African Americans, 3 American Indian/Alaska Native, 19 Asian Americans or Pacific Islanders, 16 Hispanic Americans). *Faculty:* 103 full-time (56 women), 12 part-time/adjunct (5 women). Expenses: Contact institution. *Financial support:* Career-related internships or fieldwork, scholarships/grants, traineeships, and unspecified assistantships available. Financial award applicants required to submit FAFSA. *Degree program information:* Part-time and evening/weekend programs available. Postbaccalaureate distance learning degree programs offered (minimal on-campus study). Offers athletic training (MS); communication disorders (MS); education (M Ed, MAT, MS, MSW); exercise science and health promotion (MS); fitness and wellness (MS); guidance and counseling (M Ed, MS); mentally and/or physically handicapped education (M Ed); performance enhancement and injury prevention (MS); reading specialist (M Ed); rehabilitation sciences (MS); school administration (M Ed); school psychology (MS); secondary education (MAT); social work (MSW); sport management (MS); sport psychology (MS); technology education (M Ed). *Application deadline:* For fall admission, 8/1 priority date for domestic and international students; for winter admission, 12/1 priority date for domestic and international students; for spring admission, 5/1 priority date for domestic and international students. Applications are processed on a rolling basis. *Application fee:* $25. Electronic applications accepted. *Dean,* Geraldine Jones, 724-938-4125, E-mail: jones_gm@cup.edu.

School of Science and Technology Students: 130 full-time (63 women), 118 part-time (50 women); includes 31 minority (25 African Americans, 1 Asian American or Pacific Islander, 5 Hispanic Americans). *Faculty:* 21 full-time (3 women), 5 part-time/adjunct (2 women). Expenses: Contact institution. *Financial support:* Career-related internships or fieldwork, scholarships/grants, traineeships, and unspecified assistantships available. *Degree program information:* Part-time and evening/weekend programs available. Postbaccalaureate distance learning degree programs offered. Offers business administration (MSBA); multimedia technology (MS); science and technology (MS, MSBA). *Application deadline:* For fall admission, 8/1 priority date for domestic and international students; for winter admission, 12/1 priority date for domestic and international students; for spring admission, 5/1 priority date for domestic and international students. Applications are processed on a rolling basis. *Application fee:* $25. Electronic applications accepted. *Dean,* Dr. Leonard Colelli, 724-938-4169, Fax: 724-938-5743, E-mail: colelli@cup.edu.

CALIFORNIA WESTERN SCHOOL OF LAW, San Diego, CA 92101-3090

General Information Independent, coed, graduate-only institution. *Graduate housing:* On-campus housing not available.

GRADUATE UNITS

Graduate and Professional Programs *Degree program information:* Part-time programs available. Offers law (JD, LL M). Electronic applications accepted.

CALUMET COLLEGE OF SAINT JOSEPH, Whiting, IN 46394-2195

General Information Independent-religious, coed, comprehensive institution.

GRADUATE UNITS

Program in Law Enforcement Administration

CALVARY BIBLE COLLEGE AND THEOLOGICAL SEMINARY, Kansas City, MO 64147-1341

General Information Independent-religious, coed, comprehensive institution. *Enrollment:* 329 graduate, professional, and undergraduate students; 25 full-time matriculated graduate/professional students (7 women), 37 part-time matriculated graduate/professional students (10 women). *Enrollment by degree level:* 11 first professional, 51 master's. *Graduate faculty:* 5 full-time (0 women), 1 (woman) part-time/adjunct. *Tuition:* Part-time $270 per credit hour. *Graduate housing:* Rooms and/or apartments available on a first-come, first-served basis to single and married students. Typical cost: $2,472 per year for single students; $3,200 per year for married students. *Student services:* Campus employment opportunities, disabled student services, writing training. *Library facilities:* Hilda Kroeker Library. *Online resources:* library catalog, web page. *Collection:* 59,234 titles, 285 serial subscriptions, 338 audiovisual materials.

Computer facilities: 23 computers available on campus for general student use. A campuswide network can be accessed from student residence rooms. Internet access is available. *Web address:* http://www.calvary.edu/.

General Application Contact: Robert Reinsch, Director of Admissions, 800-326-3960 Ext. 1320, Fax: 816-331-4474.

GRADUATE UNITS

Calvary Theological Seminary Students: 25 full-time (7 women), 37 part-time (10 women); includes 13 minority (8 African Americans, 3 Asian Americans or Pacific Islanders, 2 Hispanic Americans), 2 international. Average age 37. *Faculty:* 5 full-time (0 women), 1 (woman) part-time/adjunct. Expenses: Contact institution. *Financial support:* In 2006–07, 13 students received support. Scholarships/grants available. Financial award application deadline: 11/5. In 2006, 2 M Divs, 5 master's awarded. *Degree program information:* Part-time and evening/weekend programs available. Offers Bible and theology (MS); biblical counseling (MA); biblical studies (MA); Christian ministry (MA); Christian studies (MS); Christian theology (MA); New Testament (MA); Old Testament (MA); pastoral studies (M Div). *Application deadline:* For fall admission, 7/15 priority date for domestic and international students; for spring admission, 12/1 priority date for domestic and international students. *Application fee:* $35. *Application Contact:* Robert Reinsch, Director of Admissions, 800-326-3960 Ext. 1320, Fax: 816-331-4474. *Academic Dean,* Dr. Thomas Baurain, 816-322-0110 Ext. 1504, Fax: 816-331-4474.

CALVIN COLLEGE, Grand Rapids, MI 49546-4388

General Information Independent-religious, coed, comprehensive institution. *Enrollment:* 4,187 graduate, professional, and undergraduate students; 6 full-time matriculated graduate/professional students (5 women), 87 part-time matriculated graduate/professional students (66 women). *Enrollment by degree level:* 93 master's. *Graduate faculty:* 2 full-time (both women), 6 part-time/adjunct (2 women). *Tuition:* Part-time $420 per credit hour. *Graduate housing:* Rooms and/or apartments available on a first-come, first-served basis to single and married students. Typical cost: $3,830 per year ($7,040 including board) for single students; $3,270 per year for married students. Housing application deadline: 5/1. *Student services:* Campus employment opportunities, campus safety program, career counseling, disabled student services, exercise/wellness program, free psychological counseling, international student services, low-cost health insurance, multicultural affairs office, writing training. *Library facilities:* Hekman Library plus 1 other. *Online resources:* library catalog, web page. *Collection:* 824,806 titles, 14,464 serial subscriptions, 26,191 audiovisual materials.

Computer facilities: Computer purchase and lease plans are available. 700 computers available on campus for general student use. A campuswide network can be accessed from student residence rooms and from off campus. Internet access and online class registration are available. *Web address:* http://www.calvin.edu/.

General Application Contact: Deb Abbott, Administrative Assistant, 616-526-6105, Fax: 616-526-6505, E-mail: dka2@calvin.edu.

GRADUATE UNITS

Graduate Programs in Education Students: 6 full-time (5 women), 87 part-time (66 women); includes 9 minority (3 African Americans, 1 American Indian/Alaska Native, 4 Asian Americans or Pacific Islanders, 1 Hispanic American). Average age 29. 26 applicants, 100% accepted. *Faculty:* 2 full-time (both women), 6 part-time/adjunct (2 women). Expenses: Contact institution. *Financial support:* In 2006–07, 19 students received support. Federal Work-Study, scholarships/grants, and tuition waivers (full and partial) available. Support available to part-time students. Financial award application deadline: 4/3. In 2006, 14 degrees awarded. *Degree program information:* Part-time programs available. Offers curriculum and instruction (M Ed); educational leadership (M Ed); learning disabilities (M Ed); literacy (M Ed). *Application deadline:* For fall admission, 8/1 priority date for domestic students, 5/1 priority date for international students; for spring admission, 1/1 priority date for domestic students, 11/1 priority date for international students. Applications are processed on a rolling basis. *Application fee:* $0. Electronic applications accepted. *Application Contact:* Deb Abbott, Administrative Assistant, 616-526-6105, Fax: 616-526-6505, E-mail: dka2@calvin.edu. *Associate Dean for Teacher Education,* Dr. Susan S. Hasseler, 616-526-6597, Fax: 616-526-6505, E-mail: shassele@calvin.edu.

CALVIN THEOLOGICAL SEMINARY, Grand Rapids, MI 49546-4387

General Information Independent-religious, coed, graduate-only institution. *Enrollment by degree level:* 147 first professional, 120 master's, 33 doctoral. *Graduate faculty:* 28 full-time (1 woman), 8 part-time/adjunct (2 women). *Tuition:* Full-time $9,766; part-time $217 per hour. *Graduate housing:* Rooms and/or apartments available on a first-come, first-served basis to single and married students. Typical cost: $2,520 per year for single students; $6,840 per year for married students. Housing application deadline: 4/1. *Student services:* Campus employment opportunities, campus safety program, career counseling, free psychological counseling, international student services, low-cost health insurance. *Library facilities:* Hekman Library. *Online resources:* library catalog, web page. *Collection:* 1 million titles, 2,700 serial subscriptions, 24,000 audiovisual materials.

Computer facilities: 58 computers available on campus for general student use. A campuswide network can be accessed from student residence rooms and from off campus. Internet access and online class registration are available. *Web address:* http://www.calvinseminary.edu/.

General Application Contact: Rev. Gregory Janke, Director of Admissions, 616-957-7035, Fax: 616-957-8621, E-mail: gjanke@calvinseminary.edu.

GRADUATE UNITS

Graduate and Professional Programs Students: 236 full-time (35 women), 64 part-time (15 women); includes 27 minority (7 African Americans, 15 Asian Americans or Pacific Islanders, 5 Hispanic Americans), 93 international. Average age 31. 174 applicants, 77% accepted, 99 enrolled. *Faculty:* 22 full-time (1 woman), 8 part-time/adjunct (2 women). Expenses: Contact institution. *Financial support:* In 2006–07, 187 students received support, including 4 fellowships with full tuition reimbursements available (averaging $8,405 per year), 4 teaching assistantships with full tuition reimbursements available (averaging $5,760 per year); career-related internships or fieldwork, institutionally sponsored loans, scholarships/grants, and tuition waivers (full) also available. Support available to part-time students. Financial award application deadline: 3/1; financial award applicants required to submit FAFSA. In 2006, 23 M Divs, 42 master's, 2 doctorates awarded. *Degree program information:* Part-time programs available. Offers divinity (M Div); educational ministry (MA); historical theology (PhD); missions: church growth (MA); philosophical and moral theology (PhD); systematic theology (PhD); theological studies (MTS); theology (Th M). *Application deadline:* For fall admission, 3/1 priority date for domestic and international students. Applications are processed on a rolling basis. *Application fee:* $25. *Application Contact:* Rev. Gregory Janke, Director of Admissions, 616-957-7035, Fax: 616-957-8621, E-mail: gjanke@calvinseminary.edu. *Head,* Dr. Cornelius Plantinga, 616-957-6024, Fax: 616-957-6536, E-mail: sempres@calvinseminary.edu.

CAMBRIDGE COLLEGE, Cambridge, MA 02138-5304

General Information Independent, coed, comprehensive institution. *Enrollment:* 4,670 graduate, professional, and undergraduate students; 1,857 full-time matriculated graduate/professional students (1,368 women), 1,945 part-time matriculated graduate/professional students (1,501 women). *Enrollment by degree level:* 3,351 master's, 9 doctoral, 442 other advanced degrees. *Graduate faculty:* 24 full-time (10 women), 759 part-time/adjunct (468 women). *Tuition:* Full-time $10,935; part-time $405 per credit hour. One-time fee: $130 full-time. Tuition and fees vary according to degree level and program. *Graduate housing:* On-campus housing not available. *Student services:* Campus employment opportunities, career counseling, disabled student services, international student services, writing training. *Library facilities:* Cambridge College Online Library. *Online resources:* web page. *Collection:* 30,000 titles, 21 serial subscriptions.

Computer facilities: Computer purchase and lease plans are available. A campuswide network can be accessed. Internet access and online class registration are available. *Web address:* http://www.cambridgecollege.edu/.

General Application Contact: Farah Favanbaksh, Senior Director of Admissions, 617-868-1000 Ext. 1124, Fax: 617-349-3561, E-mail: admit@cambridgecollege.edu.

GRADUATE UNITS

Program in Counseling Psychology Students: 385 full-time (297 women), 346 part-time (283 women); includes 309 minority (242 African Americans, 1 American Indian/Alaska Native, 6 Asian Americans or Pacific Islanders, 60 Hispanic Americans), 10 international. Average age 37. 232 applicants, 98% accepted, 206 enrolled. *Faculty:* 6 full-time (1 woman), 54 part-time/adjunct (30 women). Expenses: Contact institution. *Financial support:* Career-related internships or fieldwork and Federal Work-Study available. Financial award applicants required to submit FAFSA. In 2006, 233 master's, 6 other advanced degrees awarded. *Degree program information:* Part-time and evening/weekend programs available. Offers counseling psychology (M Ed, CAGS). *Application deadline:* Applications are processed on a rolling basis. *Application fee:* $30. *Application Contact:* Wendy D. Shattuck, Director of Graduate Admissions, 617-868-1000 Ext. 144, Fax: 617-349-3561, E-mail: admit@cambridgecollege.edu. *Director,* Dr. Niti Seth, 617-873-0208, Fax: 617-349-3545.

Program in Education Students: 963 full-time (758 women), 1,500 part-time (1,182 women); includes 1,168 minority (780 African Americans, 8 American Indian/Alaska Native, 21 Asian Americans or Pacific Islanders, 359 Hispanic Americans), 8 international. Average age 36. 492 applicants, 91% accepted, 371 enrolled. *Faculty:* 10 full-time (4 women), 309 part-time/adjunct (211 women). Expenses: Contact institution. *Financial support:* Teaching assistantships, career-related internships or fieldwork and Federal Work-Study available. Financial award applicants required to submit FAFSA. In 2006, 1,063 master's, 287 other advanced degrees awarded. *Degree program information:* Part-time and evening/weekend programs available. Offers education (CAGS); education leadership (Ed D); education/integrated studies (M Ed). *Application deadline:* For fall admission, 10/3 priority date for domestic students; for spring admission, 2/13 priority date for domestic students. Applications are processed on a rolling basis. *Application fee:* $30. *Application Contact:* Wendy D. Shattuck, Director of Graduate Admissions, 617-868-1000 Ext. 144, Fax: 617-349-3561, E-mail: admit@cambridgecollege.edu. *Dean,* Dr. Anthony DeMatteo, 617-873-0219, Fax: 617-349-3545.

Program in Management Students: 362 full-time (207 women), 219 part-time (135 women); includes 203 minority (131 African Americans, 2 American Indian/Alaska Native, 22 Asian Americans or Pacific Islanders, 48 Hispanic Americans), 80 international. Average age 39. 160 applicants, 96% accepted, 126 enrolled. *Faculty:* 4 full-time (all women), 305 part-time/adjunct (167 women). Expenses: Contact institution. *Financial support:* Teaching assistantships, career-related internships or fieldwork and Federal Work-Study available. Financial award applicants required to submit FAFSA. In 2006, 165 degrees awarded. *Degree program information:* Part-time and evening/weekend programs available. Offers e-commerce (M Mgt); management (M Mgt). *Application deadline:* Applications are processed on a rolling basis. *Application fee:* $30. *Application Contact:* Michael Travaghini, Director of Graduate Admissions, 617-868-1000 Ext. 1162, Fax: 617-349-3561, E-mail: admit@cambridgecollege.edu. *Associate Dean,* Dr. Bill Hancock, 617-873-0281, Fax: 617-349-3545.

CAMERON UNIVERSITY, Lawton, OK 73505-6377

General Information State-supported, coed, comprehensive institution. CGS member. *Enrollment:* 5,734 graduate, professional, and undergraduate students; 139 full-time matriculated graduate/professional students (94 women), 254 part-time matriculated graduate/professional students (179 women). *Enrollment by degree level:* 393 master's. *Graduate faculty:* 47 full-time (20 women), 14 part-time/adjunct (6 women). Tuition, state resident: full-time $2,479; part-time $138 per credit hour. Tuition, nonresident: full-time $5,976; part-time $332 per credit hour. Tuition and fees vary according to campus/location. *Graduate housing:* Room and/or apartments available on a first-come, first-served basis to single students; on-campus housing not available to married students. *Student services:* Campus employment opportunities, campus safety program, disabled student services, exercise/wellness program, grant writing training, international student services, multicultural affairs office, teacher training, writing training. *Library facilities:* Cameron University Library. *Online resources:* library catalog, web page. *Collection:* 262,835 titles, 4,272 serial subscriptions, 2,868 audiovisual materials. *Research affiliation:* Telos-Ok (simulations), Army Research Institute (human factors), Advanced Systems Technology, Inc. (informational systems), Dynamics Research Corporation (multimedia systems), Eagle Systems, Inc. (multimedia systems), Halliburton (energy systems).

Computer facilities: 350 computers available on campus for general student use. A campuswide network can be accessed from student residence rooms and from off campus. Internet access, online courses, e-mail accounts, student information system are available. *Web address:* http://www.cameron.edu/.

General Application Contact: Teresa Enriquez, Graduate Admissions/Enrollment Coordinator, 580-581-2987, E-mail: teresae@cameron.edu.

GRADUATE UNITS

Office of Graduate Studies Students: 139 full-time (94 women), 254 part-time (179 women); includes 128 minority (77 African Americans, 23 American Indian/Alaska Native, 10 Asian Americans or Pacific Islanders, 18 Hispanic Americans). Average age 35. 229 applicants, 79% accepted. *Faculty:* 47 full-time (20 women), 14 part-time/adjunct (6 women). Expenses: Contact institution. *Financial support:* In 2006–07, 290 students received support, including 8 fellowships (averaging $2,000 per year), 6 research assistantships (averaging $3,600 per year), 1 teaching assistantship (averaging $1,280 per year); career-related internships or fieldwork, Federal Work-Study, scholarships/grants, tuition waivers (partial), and unspecified assistantships also available. Support available to part-time students. Financial award application deadline: 4/15; financial award applicants required to submit FAFSA. In 2006, 93 degrees awarded. *Degree program information:* Part-time and evening/weekend programs available. Postbaccalaureate distance learning degree programs offered (no on-campus study). Offers behavioral sciences (MS); business administration (MBA); education (M Ed); educational leadership (MS); entrepreneurial studies (MS); teaching (MAT). *Application deadline:* Applications are processed on a rolling basis. *Application fee:* $15 ($35 for international students). Electronic applications accepted. *Application Contact:* Teresa Enriquez, Graduate Admissions/Enrollment Coordinator, 580-581-2987, E-mail: teresae@cameron.edu. *Assistant V.P. for Academic Affairs and Graduate Coordinator,* Dr. Lance Janda, 580-581-2987, Fax: 580-581-5532, E-mail: lancej@cameron.edu.

CAMPBELLSVILLE UNIVERSITY, Campbellsville, KY 42718-2799

General Information Independent-religious, coed, comprehensive institution. *Enrollment:* 2,376 graduate, professional, and undergraduate students; 505 full-time matriculated graduate/professional students (309 women), 71 part-time matriculated graduate/professional students (29 women). *Enrollment by degree level:* 576 master's. *Graduate faculty:* 47 full-time (21 women), 25 part-time/adjunct (9 women). *Tuition:* Full-time $6,570; part-time $365 per hour. Tuition and fees vary according to program. *Graduate housing:* Rooms and/or apartments available on a first-come, first-served basis to single and married students. Typical cost: $5,932 (including board) for single students. Housing application deadline: 6/30. *Student*

Campbellsville University (continued)

services: Campus safety program, career counseling, exercise/wellness program, international student services, teacher training, writing training. *Library facilities:* Montgomery Library plus 2 others. *Online resources:* library catalog, web page. *Collection:* 172,000 titles, 12,777 serial subscriptions.

Computer facilities: 148 computers available on campus for general student use. Internet access is available. *Web address:* http://www.campbellsville.edu/.

General Application Contact: Karla Deaton, Assistant Director of Admissions, 270-789-5078, Fax: 270-789-5071, E-mail: krdeaton@campbellsville.edu.

GRADUATE UNITS

Carver School of Social Work Students: 15 full-time (12 women); includes 2 minority (both African Americans) 15 applicants, 67% accepted, 10 enrolled. *Faculty:* 6 full-time (3 women), 2 part-time/adjunct (0 women). Expenses: Contact institution. *Financial support:* Applicants required to submit FAFSA. *Degree program information:* Evening/weekend programs available. Offers social work). *Application fee:* $25. Electronic applications accepted. *Program Director,* Dr. Darlene F. Eastridge, 270-789-5178, Fax: 270-789-5542, E-mail: dfeastridge@campbellsville.edu.

College of Arts and Sciences Students: 21 full-time (14 women); includes 6 minority (4 Asian Americans or Pacific Islanders, 2 Hispanic Americans). Average age 27. 11 applicants, 100% accepted, 11 enrolled. *Faculty:* 21 full-time (14 women). Expenses: Contact institution. *Financial support:* In 2006–07, 10 students received support. Institutionally sponsored loans and unspecified assistantships available. Financial award application deadline: 6/1; financial award applicants required to submit FAFSA. In 2006, 5 degrees awarded. *Degree program information:* Part-time programs available. Offers social science (MA). *Application deadline:* Applications are processed on a rolling basis. *Application fee:* $25. Electronic applications accepted. *Application Contact:* Karla Deaton, Assistant Director of Admissions, 270-789-5078, Fax: 270-789-5071, E-mail: krdeaton@campbellsville.edu. *Dean,* Dr. Mary Wilgus, 270-789-5394.

School of Business and Economics Students: 34 full-time (16 women), 17 part-time (10 women), 7 international. Average age 28. 40 applicants, 60% accepted, 23 enrolled. *Faculty:* 2 full-time (0 women), 5 part-time/adjunct (1 woman). Expenses: Contact institution. *Financial support:* In 2006–07, 11 students received support. Tuition waivers (full) and unspecified assistantships available. Financial award application deadline: 6/1; financial award applicants required to submit FAFSA. In 2006, 34 degrees awarded. *Degree program information:* Part-time and evening/weekend programs available. Offers business administration (MBA). *Application deadline:* For fall admission, 9/14 priority date for domestic and international students; for winter admission, 1/18 priority date for domestic and international students; for spring admission, 4/4 priority date for domestic and international students. Applications are processed on a rolling basis. *Application fee:* $25. Electronic applications accepted. *Application Contact:* Karla Deaton, Assistant Director of Admissions, 270-789-5078, Fax: 270-789-5071, E-mail: krdeaton@campbellsville.edu. *Dean,* Dr. Patricia H. Cowherd, 270-789-5553, Fax: 270-789-5066, E-mail: phcowherd@campbellsville.edu.

School of Education Students: 365 full-time (230 women); includes 20 minority (14 African Americans, 1 Asian American or Pacific Islander, 5 Hispanic Americans), 1 international. Average age 31. 80 applicants, 99% accepted, 76 enrolled. *Faculty:* 5 full-time (2 women), 12 part-time/adjunct (7 women). Expenses: Contact institution. *Financial support:* In 2006–07, 250 students received support. Institutionally sponsored loans, scholarships/grants, and unspecified assistantships available. Support available to part-time students. Financial award application deadline: 6/1; financial award applicants required to submit FAFSA. In 2006, 110 degrees awarded. *Degree program information:* Part-time and evening/weekend programs available. Postbaccalaureate distance learning degree programs offered (minimal on-campus study). Offers curriculum and instruction (MAE); special education (MASE). *Application deadline:* For fall admission, 6/1 priority date for domestic students, 5/1 priority date for international students; for spring admission, 11/1 priority date for domestic students, 10/1 priority date for international students. Applications are processed on a rolling basis. *Application fee:* $0. Electronic applications accepted. *Application Contact:* Karla Deaton, Assistant Director of Admissions, 270-789-5078, Fax: 270-789-5071, E-mail: redeaton@campbellsville.edu. *Dean,* Dr. Brenda A. Priddy, 270-789-5344, Fax: 270-789-5206, E-mail: bapriddy@campbellsville.edu.

School of Music Students: 50 full-time (32 women), 29 part-time (16 women); includes 30 minority (all Asian Americans or Pacific Islanders), 36 international. Average age 31. 29 applicants, 97% accepted, 27 enrolled. *Faculty:* 8 full-time (2 women), 3 part-time/adjunct (1 woman). Expenses: Contact institution. *Financial support:* In 2006–07, 24 students received support, including 1 fellowship (averaging $4,300 per year); institutionally sponsored loans and scholarships/grants also available. Support available to part-time students. Financial award application deadline: 6/1; financial award applicants required to submit FAFSA. In 2006, 12 degrees awarded. *Degree program information:* Part-time programs available. Offers church music (MM); music (MA); music education (MM). *Application deadline:* For fall admission, 6/1 priority date for domestic students, 5/1 priority date for international students; for spring admission, 11/1 priority date for domestic students, 10/1 priority date for international students. Applications are processed on a rolling basis. *Application fee:* $25. Electronic applications accepted. *Application Contact:* Karla Deaton, Assistant Director of Admissions, 270-789-5078, Fax: 270-789-5071, E-mail: krdeaton@campbellsville.edu. *Dean,* Dr. J. Robert Gaddis, 270-789-5269, Fax: 270-789-5524, E-mail: jrgaddis@campbellsville.edu.

School of Theology Students: 20 full-time (5 women), 25 part-time (3 women); includes 9 minority (7 African Americans, 1 Asian American or Pacific Islander, 1 Hispanic American). Average age 29. 25 applicants, 76% accepted, 12 enrolled. *Faculty:* 5 full-time (0 women), 3 part-time/adjunct (0 women). Expenses: Contact institution. *Financial support:* In 2006–07, 26 students received support, including 2 fellowships (averaging $1,500 per year); institutionally sponsored loans and scholarships/grants also available. Financial award application deadline: 6/1; financial award applicants required to submit FAFSA. In 2006, 4 degrees awarded. *Degree program information:* Part-time programs available. Offers theology (M Th). *Application deadline:* For fall admission, 8/25 priority date for domestic students; for spring admission, 1/25 for domestic students. Applications are processed on a rolling basis. *Application fee:* $25. Electronic applications accepted. *Application Contact:* Karla Deaton, Assistant Director of Admissions, 270-789-5078, Fax: 270-789-5071, E-mail: krdeaton@campbellsville.edu. *Dean,* Dr. John E. Hurtgen, 270-789-5077, Fax: 270-789-5050, E-mail: jehurtgen@campbellsville.edu.

CAMPBELL UNIVERSITY, Buies Creek, NC 27506

General Information Independent-religious, coed, university. *Enrollment:* 6,033 graduate, professional, and undergraduate students; 1,002 full-time matriculated graduate/professional students (559 women), 606 part-time matriculated graduate/professional students (376 women). *Enrollment by degree level:* 1,004 first professional, 604 master's. *Graduate faculty:* 99 full-time (32 women), 51 part-time/adjunct (14 women). *Tuition:* Part-time $380 per semester hour. *Graduate housing:* Rooms and/or apartments available on a first-come, first-served basis to single and married students. Housing application deadline: 6/2. *Student services:* Campus employment opportunities, campus safety program, career counseling, disabled student services, exercise/wellness program, international student services, low-cost health insurance. *Library facilities:* Carrie Rich Memorial Library plus 2 others. *Online resources:* library catalog, web page, access to other libraries' catalogs. *Collection:* 231,298 titles, 17,268 serial subscriptions.

Computer facilities: 256 computers available on campus for general student use. A campuswide network can be accessed from student residence rooms and from off campus. Internet access is available. *Web address:* http://www.campbell.edu/.

General Application Contact: James S. Farthing, Director of Graduate Admissions for Business and Education, 910-893-1200 Ext. 1318, Fax: 910-814-4718, E-mail: farthing@campbell.edu.

GRADUATE UNITS

Graduate and Professional Programs Students: 1,002 full-time (559 women), 606 part-time (376 women); includes 137 minority (107 African Americans, 15 American Indian/Alaska Native, 15 Hispanic Americans), 47 international. Average age 28. 3,268 applicants, 19% accepted, 402 enrolled. *Faculty:* 112 full-time (34 women), 168 part-time/adjunct (66 women). Expenses: Contact institution. *Financial support:* In 2006–07, 1,179 students received support, including 15 teaching assistantships (averaging $4,000 per year); fellowships, research assistantships, career-related internships or fieldwork, Federal Work-Study, institutionally sponsored loans, scholarships/grants, tuition waivers (partial), and unspecified assistantships also available. Support available to part-time students. Financial award application deadline: 3/15; financial award applicants required to submit FAFSA. In 2006, 371 degrees awarded. *Degree program information:* Part-time and evening/weekend programs available. *Application deadline:* Applications are processed on a rolling basis. *Application fee:* $65. *Application Contact:* James S. Farthing, Director of Graduate Admissions for Business and Education, 910-893-1200 Ext. 1318, Fax: 910-814-4718, E-mail: farthing@campbell.edu. *Vice President for Academic Affairs and Provost,* Dr. M. Dwaine Greene, 910-893-1211, Fax: 910-893-1243, E-mail: greene@campbell.edu.

Divinity School Students: 148 full-time (55 women), 82 part-time (41 women); includes 40 minority (35 African Americans, 1 American Indian/Alaska Native, 4 Hispanic Americans), 2 international. Average age 38. 74 applicants, 81% accepted, 48 enrolled. *Faculty:* 9 full-time (1 woman), 10 part-time/adjunct (3 women). Expenses: Contact institution. *Financial support:* In 2006–07, 193 students received support, including 143 fellowships (averaging $800 per year); scholarships/grants and unspecified assistantships also available. Support available to part-time students. Financial award application deadline: 5/1. In 2006, 27 degrees awarded. Offers Christian education (MA); divinity (M Div); ministry (D Min). *Application deadline:* For fall admission, 7/1 for domestic students; for spring admission, 11/15 for domestic students. Applications are processed on a rolling basis. *Application fee:* $20. *Application Contact:* Kelly M. Jones, Director of Admissions, 910-893-1830, Fax: 910-893-1835, E-mail: kjones@campbell.edu. *Dean,* Dr. Michael Glenn Cogdill, 910-893-1830, Fax: 910-893-1835, E-mail: cogdill@campbell.edu.

Lundy-Fetterman School of Business Students: 49 full-time (18 women), 158 part-time (67 women); includes 5 minority (4 African Americans, 1 Hispanic American), 5 international. Average age 29. 90 applicants, 69% accepted, 50 enrolled. *Faculty:* 11 full-time (1 woman), 4 part-time/adjunct (0 women). Expenses: Contact institution. *Financial support:* In 2006–07, 3 teaching assistantships (averaging $4,000 per year) were awarded; fellowships, research assistantships, career-related internships or fieldwork, Federal Work-Study, institutionally sponsored loans, scholarships/grants, and unspecified assistantships also available. Support available to part-time students. Financial award application deadline: 3/15. In 2006, 135 degrees awarded. *Degree program information:* Part-time and evening/weekend programs available. Offers business (MBA, MTIM). *Application deadline:* Applications are processed on a rolling basis. *Application fee:* $65. *Application Contact:* James S. Farthing, Director of Graduate Admissions for Business and Education, 910-893-1200 Ext. 1318, Fax: 910-814-4718, E-mail: farthing@campbell.edu. *Dean,* Dr. Ben Hawkins, 910-893-1380, Fax: 910-814-4352, E-mail: hawkinsb@campbell.edu.

Norman Adrian Wiggins School of Law Students: 343 full-time (165 women); includes 12 minority (7 African Americans, 3 American Indian/Alaska Native, 2 Hispanic Americans), 5 international. Average age 26. 1,032 applicants, 26% accepted, 122 enrolled. *Faculty:* 23 full-time (5 women), 23 part-time/adjunct (4 women). Expenses: Contact institution. *Financial support:* In 2006–07, 326 students received support, including 15 research assistantships (averaging $960 per year), 15 teaching assistantships (averaging $4,000 per year); career-related internships or fieldwork, Federal Work-Study, institutionally sponsored loans, and scholarships/grants also available. Financial award application deadline: 4/15; financial award applicants required to submit FAFSA. In 2006, 99 degrees awarded. Offers law (JD). *Application deadline:* For fall admission, 3/31 priority date for domestic students. Applications are processed on a rolling basis. *Application fee:* $50. Electronic applications accepted. *Application Contact:* Lewis Hutchison, Assistant Dean for Admissions, 910-893-1754, Fax: 910-893-1780, E-mail: hutchison@law.campbell.edu. *Dean,* Melissa A. Essary, 910-893-1750, Fax: 910-893-1780, E-mail: essary@law.campbell.edu.

School of Education Students: 27 full-time (25 women), 183 part-time (146 women); includes 30 minority (24 African Americans, 3 American Indian/Alaska Native, 3 Hispanic Americans), 1 international. Average age 31. 112 applicants, 74% accepted, 74 enrolled. *Faculty:* 14 full-time (9 women), 12 part-time/adjunct (7 women). Expenses: Contact institution. *Financial support:* In 2006–07, 67 students received support. Career-related internships or fieldwork and Federal Work-Study available. Financial award application deadline: 4/15; financial award applicants required to submit FAFSA. In 2006, 65 degrees awarded. *Degree program information:* Part-time and evening/weekend programs available. Offers administration (MSA); community counseling (MA); elementary education (M Ed); English education (M Ed); interdisciplinary studies (M Ed); mathematics education (M Ed); middle grades education (M Ed); physical education (M Ed); school counseling (M Ed); secondary education (M Ed); social science education (M Ed). *Application deadline:* For fall admission, 8/1 priority date for domestic students; for spring admission, 1/2 priority date for domestic students. Applications are processed on a rolling basis. *Application fee:* $65. *Application Contact:* James S. Farthing, Director of Graduate Admissions for Business and Education, 910-893-1200 Ext. 1318, Fax: 910-814-4718, E-mail: farthing@campbell.edu. *Dean,* Dr. Karen P. Nery, 910-893-1630, Fax: 910-893-1999, E-mail: nery@campbell.edu.

School of Pharmacy Students: 435 full-time (296 women), 183 part-time (122 women); includes 50 minority (37 African Americans, 8 American Indian/Alaska Native, 5 Hispanic Americans), 34 international. Average age 23. 1,960 applicants, 7% accepted, 108 enrolled. *Faculty:* 55 full-time (18 women), 119 part-time/adjunct (52 women). Expenses: Contact institution. *Financial support:* In 2006–07, 350 students received support, including 4 research assistantships (averaging $3,000 per year), 3 teaching assistantships (averaging $4,000 per year); career-related internships or fieldwork, Federal Work-Study, and scholarships/grants also available. Financial award application deadline: 3/15; financial award applicants required to submit FAFSA. In 2006, 89 Pharm Ds, 8 master's awarded. *Degree program information:* Part-time and evening/weekend programs available. Offers clinical research (MS); pharmaceutical science (MS); pharmacy (Pharm D). *Application deadline:* For fall admission, 3/1 for domestic and international students. Applications are processed on a rolling basis. *Application fee:* $25. Electronic applications accepted. *Application Contact:* Dr. Mark Moore, Assistant Dean of Admissions and Student Affairs, 910-893-1690, Fax: 910-893-1937, E-mail: pharmacy@campbell.edu. *Dean,* Dr. Ronald W. Maddox, 910-893-1200 Ext. 1685, Fax: 910-893-1697, E-mail: pharmacy@camel.campbell.edu.

CANADIAN COLLEGE OF NATUROPATHIC MEDICINE, Toronto, ON M2K 1E2, Canada

General Information Independent, coed, primarily women, graduate-only institution. *Enrollment by degree level:* 489 doctoral. *Graduate faculty:* 32 full-time, 85 part-time/adjunct. *Graduate tuition:* Tuition and fees charges are reported in Canadian dollars. *Tuition:* Full-time $17,239 Canadian dollars; part-time $271 Canadian dollars per credit. *Required fees:* $430 Canadian dollars. One-time fee: $50 Canadian dollars full-time. Tuition and fees vary according to course load. *Graduate housing:* Room and/or apartments available on a first-come, first-served basis to single students; on-campus housing not available to married students. Typical cost: $3,080 Canadian dollars per year. *Student services:* Campus employment opportunities, campus safety program, career counseling, disabled student services, exercise/wellness program, free psychological counseling, international student services, low-cost health insurance. *Library facilities:* Learning Resource Centre. *Online resources:* library catalog, web page, access to other libraries' catalogs. *Collection:* 7,000 titles, 120 serial subscriptions, 1,800 audiovisual materials. *Research affiliation:* Sunnybrook and Women's College Hospital, Toronto General Hospital, Mayo Clinic, Sherbourne Health Center, Sick Children's Hospital.

Computer facilities: 40 computers available on campus for general student use. A campuswide network can be accessed. Internet access is available. *Web address:* http://www.ccnm.edu/.

General Application Contact: Student Services and Admissions Office, 416-498-1225 Ext. 245, Fax: 416-498-3197, E-mail: info@ccnm.edu.

GRADUATE UNITS

Doctoral Program in Naturopathic Medicine Students: 454 full-time (333 women), 35 part-time (29 women). Average age 27. 163 applicants, 87% accepted, 105 enrolled. *Faculty:* 32 full-time, 85 part-time/adjunct. Expenses: Contact institution. *Financial support:* In 2006–07, 280 students received support, including 3 research assistantships, 2 teaching assistantships; career-related internships or fieldwork, scholarships/grants, and health care benefits also available. Support available to part-time students. Financial award application deadline: 7/31. In 2006, 130 degrees awarded. Offers naturopathic medicine (ND). *Application deadline:* For fall admission, 1/31 priority date for domestic and international students; for winter admission, 5/30 priority date for domestic and international students; for spring admission, 11/30 priority date for domestic and international students. Applications are processed on a rolling basis. *Application fee:* $150. *Application Contact:* Student Services, 416-498-1225 Ext. 245, Fax: 416-498-3197, E-mail: info@ccnm.edu. *President/CEO,* Bob Bernhardt, 416-498-1255, Fax: 416-498-3197, E-mail: bbernhardt@ccnm.edu.

CANADIAN MEMORIAL CHIROPRACTIC COLLEGE, Toronto, ON M2H 3J1, Canada

General Information Independent, coed, graduate-only institution. *Graduate housing:* On-campus housing not available. *Research affiliation:* University of Waterloo, University of Calgary, University of Toronto.

GRADUATE UNITS

Certificate Programs Offers chiropractic clinical sciences (Certificate); chiropractic radiology (Certificate); chiropractic sports sciences (Certificate).

Professional Program Offers chiropractic (DC).

CANADIAN SOUTHERN BAPTIST SEMINARY, Cochrane, AB T4C 2G1, Canada

General Information Independent-religious, coed, graduate-only institution. *Enrollment by degree level:* 44 master's. *Graduate faculty:* 8 full-time (0 women), 3 part-time/adjunct (1 woman). *Tuition:* Full-time $4,760; part-time $170 per credit hour. *Graduate housing:* Rooms and/or apartments available on a first-come, first-served basis to single and married students. Housing application deadline: 6/30. *Student services:* Campus employment opportunities, free psychological counseling. *Library facilities:* Keith C. Willis Library. *Online resources:* library catalog, access to other libraries' catalogs. *Collection:* 27,399 titles, 235 serial subscriptions, 2 audiovisual materials.

Computer facilities: 12 computers available on campus for general student use. A campuswide network can be accessed from off campus. Internet access is available. *Web address:* http://www.csbs.edu/.

GRADUATE UNITS

Graduate Programs Students: 26 full-time (3 women), 18 part-time (8 women); includes 12 minority (1 American Indian/Alaska Native, 10 Asian Americans or Pacific Islanders, 1 Hispanic American), 12 international. Average age 30. 11 applicants, 100% accepted, 10 enrolled. *Faculty:* 8 full-time (0 women), 3 part-time/adjunct (1 woman). Expenses: Contact institution. In 2006, 13 degrees awarded. *Degree program information:* Part-time programs available. Offers ministry (M Div); religious education (MRE). *Application deadline:* For fall admission, 7/1 priority date for domestic and international students; for winter admission, 11/15 priority date for domestic and international students. Applications are processed on a rolling basis. *Application fee:* $50. *Application Contact:* Kathleen McNaughton, Registrar, E-mail: registrar@csbs.ca.

CANISIUS COLLEGE, Buffalo, NY 14208-1098

General Information Independent-religious, coed, comprehensive institution. *Enrollment:* 4,850 graduate, professional, and undergraduate students; 684 full-time matriculated graduate/professional students (417 women), 705 part-time matriculated graduate/professional students (431 women). *Enrollment by degree level:* 1,389 master's. *Graduate faculty:* 77 full-time (25 women), 127 part-time/adjunct (68 women). *Tuition:* Part-time $645 per credit hour. *Required fees:* $19 per credit hour. Tuition and fees vary according to program. *Graduate housing:* Room and/or apartments available on a first-come, first-served basis to single students; on-campus housing not available to married students. Typical cost: $6,880 per year. Housing application deadline: 5/1. *Student services:* Campus employment opportunities, campus safety program, career counseling, disabled student services, exercise/wellness program, free psychological counseling, international student services, multicultural affairs office, teacher training. *Library facilities:* Andrew L. Bouwhuis Library plus 1 other. *Online resources:* library catalog, web page, access to other libraries' catalogs. *Collection:* 379,498 titles, 24,000 serial subscriptions, 9,596 audiovisual materials.

Computer facilities: Computer purchase and lease plans are available. 348 computers available on campus for general student use. A campuswide network can be accessed from student residence rooms and from off campus. Internet access and online class registration, online accounts are available. *Web address:* http://www.canisius.edu/.

General Application Contact: Ann Marie Muscovic, Director of Admissions, 716-888-2200, Fax: 716-888-3230, E-mail: admissions@canisius.edu.

GRADUATE UNITS

Graduate Division Students: 684 full-time (417 women), 705 part-time (431 women); includes 107 minority (72 African Americans, 2 American Indian/Alaska Native, 15 Asian Americans or Pacific Islanders, 18 Hispanic Americans), 240 international. Average age 29. *Faculty:* 77 full-time (25 women), 127 part-time/adjunct (68 women). Expenses: Contact institution. *Financial support:* Research assistantships, teaching assistantships, career-related internships or fieldwork, Federal Work-Study, institutionally sponsored loans, tuition waivers (partial), and unspecified assistantships available. Support available to part-time students. Financial award applicants required to submit FAFSA. In 2006, 616 degrees awarded. *Degree program information:* Part-time and evening/weekend programs available. *Application deadline:* Applications are processed on a rolling basis. *Application fee:* $25. Electronic applications accepted. *Application Contact:* Ann Marie Muscovic, Director of Admissions, 716-888-2200, Fax: 716-888-3230, E-mail: admissions@canisius.edu. *Vice President for Academic Affairs,* Dr. Herbert J. Nelson, 716-888-2120 Ext. 109, Fax: 716-888-2125, E-mail: nelson@canisius.edu.

College of Arts and Sciences Students: 12 full-time (10 women), 32 part-time (22 women); includes 5 minority (4 African Americans, 1 Asian American or Pacific Islander). Average age 31. *Faculty:* 9 full-time (3 women), 14 part-time/adjunct (6 women). Expenses: Contact institution. *Financial support:* Research assistantships with tuition reimbursements available. Financial award applicants required to submit FAFSA. In 2006, 8 degrees awarded. *Degree program information:* Part-time and evening/weekend programs available. Offers arts and sciences (MS); communication and leadership (MS). *Application deadline:* For fall admission, 7/15 priority date for domestic students; for spring admission, 4/15 priority date for domestic students. Applications are processed on a rolling basis. *Application fee:* $25. Electronic applications accepted. *Application Contact:* Dr. Rosanne L. Hartman, Director, Communication and Leadership, 716-888-2589, Fax: 716-888-3118, E-mail: hartmanr@canisius.edu. *Dean,* Dr. Paula McNutt, 716-888-2130, E-mail: mcnutt@canisius.edu.

Richard J. Wehle School of Business Students: 92 full-time (28 women), 197 part-time (90 women); includes 28 minority (17 African Americans, 6 Asian Americans or Pacific Islanders, 5 Hispanic Americans), 23 international. Average age 29. *Faculty:* 38 full-time (6 women), 13 part-time/adjunct (4 women). Expenses: Contact institution. *Financial support:* Research assistantships with partial tuition reimbursements, career-related internships or fieldwork, institutionally sponsored loans, scholarships/grants, and unspecified assistantships available. Support available to part-time students. Financial award application deadline: 6/15; financial award applicants required to submit FAFSA. In 2006, 106 degrees awarded. *Degree program information:* Part-time and evening/weekend programs available. Offers accounting (MBA); business (MBA, MBAPA); business administration (MBA); professional accounting (MBAPA). *Application deadline:* For fall admission, 7/1 priority date for domestic students; for spring admission, 11/1 priority date for domestic students. Applications are processed on a rolling basis. *Application fee:* $25. Electronic applications accepted. *Application Contact:* Laura McEwen, Director, Graduate Business Programs, 716-888-2142, Fax: 716-888-2145, E-mail: mcewenl@canisius.edu. *Dean,* Dr. Antone Alber, 716-888-2160, Fax: 716-888-2145, E-mail: gradubus@canisius.edu.

School of Education and Human Services Students: 580 full-time (379 women), 476 part-time (319 women); includes 74 minority (51 African Americans, 2 American Indian/Alaska Native, 8 Asian Americans or Pacific Islanders, 13 Hispanic Americans), 217 international. Average age 29. *Faculty:* 30 full-time (16 women), 121 part-time/adjunct (62 women). Expenses: Contact institution. *Financial support:* Career-related internships or fieldwork, institutionally sponsored loans, scholarships/grants, health care benefits, tuition waivers (partial), and unspecified assistantships available. Financial award applicants required to submit FAFSA. In 2006, 502 degrees awarded. *Degree program information:* Part-time and evening/weekend programs available. Offers business education (MS); childhood education (MS); college student personnel (MS); community mental health counseling (MS); counseling and human services (MS); differentiated instruction (MS Ed); early childhood education (MS); education administration (MS); education and human services (MS, MS Ed); education of the deaf and hard of hearing (MS); general education (MS Ed); health and human performance (MS); literacy education (MS Ed); physical education (MS); physical education—birth to 12 (MS); reading education (MS Ed); school and agency counseling (MS); secondary education (MS); special education (MS); sport administration (MS). *Application deadline:* Applications are processed on a rolling basis. *Application fee:* $25. Electronic applications accepted. *Application Contact:* James D. Bagwell, Director of Graduate Recruitment and Admissions, 716-888-2544, Fax: 716-888-3290, E-mail: bagwellj@canisius.edu. *Dean,* Dr. Margaret C. McCarthy, 716-888-2548, Fax: 716-888-3290.

CAPE BRETON UNIVERSITY, Sydney, NS B1P 6L2, Canada

General Information Province-supported, coed, comprehensive institution. *Graduate housing:* Room and/or apartments available on a first-come, first-served basis to single students; on-campus housing not available to married students. Housing application deadline: 3/31. *Research affiliation:* Advanced Glazing, Limited (transparent insulation), Atlantic Geomatics (computer networking and software development), Dynagen Industrial Mine Technology (mining industry equipment), Fortress Louisbourg National Historic Park (museum/heritage projects), Sable Offshore Energy, Inc. (petroleum resources), Hyperspectral Data International Ltd. (marine remote sensing).

GRADUATE UNITS

School of Business Offers community economic development (MBA).

School of Education, Health, and Wellness *Degree program information:* Part-time and evening/weekend programs available. Postbaccalaureate distance learning degree programs offered (no on-campus study). Offers educational counseling (Diploma); educational studies-arts education (Certificate); educational technology (Diploma). Electronic applications accepted.

CAPELLA UNIVERSITY, Minneapolis, MN 55402

General Information Proprietary, coed, upper-level institution. CGS member.

GRADUATE UNITS

Harold Abel School of Psychology *Degree program information:* Part-time and evening/weekend programs available. Postbaccalaureate distance learning degree programs offered (minimal on-campus study). Offers clinical psychology (MS); counseling psychology (MS); educational psychology (MS, PhD); general psychology (MS, PhD); industrial/organizational psychology (MS, PhD); school psychology (MS, Certificate); sport psychology (MS). Electronic applications accepted.

School of Business and Technology *Degree program information:* Part-time and evening/weekend programs available. Postbaccalaureate distance learning degree programs offered (minimal on-campus study). Offers accounting (MBA); business (Certificate); finance (MBA); general business (MBA); health care management (MBA); information technology (MS, Certificate); information technology management (MBA); marketing (MBA); organization and management (MBA, MS, PhD); project management (MBA). Electronic applications accepted.

CAPITAL BIBLE SEMINARY, Lanham, MD 20706-3599

General Information Independent-religious, coed, graduate-only institution. *Enrollment by degree level:* 116 first professional, 235 master's, 20 other advanced degrees. *Graduate faculty:* 12 full-time (0 women), 11 part-time/adjunct (0 women). *Graduate housing:* Rooms and/or apartments available on a first-come, first-served basis to single and married students. Housing application deadline: 7/15. *Student services:* Campus employment opportunities, career counseling, free psychological counseling, international student services. *Library facilities:* Oyer Memorial Library. *Online resources:* library catalog, web page, access to other libraries' catalogs. *Collection:* 87,222 titles, 185 serial subscriptions.

Computer facilities: 20 computers available on campus for general student use. A campuswide network can be accessed. Internet access and online class registration are available. *Web address:* http://www.bible.edu/.

General Application Contact: Prem Suppogu, Director of Admissions, 877-793-7227, Fax: 240-387-1324, E-mail: psuppogu@bible.edu.

GRADUATE UNITS

Graduate and Professional Programs Students: 98 full-time (32 women), 276 part-time (114 women); includes 215 minority (169 African Americans, 39 Asian Americans or Pacific Islanders, 7 Hispanic Americans), 12 international. Average age 41. 105 applicants, 95% accepted, 84 enrolled. *Faculty:* 11 full-time (0 women), 12 part-time/adjunct (0 women). Expenses: Contact institution. *Financial support:* In 2006–07, 181 students received support. Career-related internships or fieldwork available. In 2006, 7 M Divs, 29 master's, 3 other advanced degrees awarded. *Degree program information:* Part-time and evening/weekend programs available. Offers biblical studies (MA, Certificate); Christian counseling (MA); Christian counseling and discipleship (Certificate); ministry leadership (MA); theology (M Div, Th M). *Application deadline:* For fall admission, 7/30 priority date for domestic students; for spring admission, 12/1 priority date for domestic students. Applications are processed on a rolling basis. *Application fee:* $30. *Application Contact:* Prem Suppogu, Director of Admissions, 877-793-7227, Fax: 240-387-1324, E-mail: psuppogu@bible.edu. *Academic Dean,* Dr. George M. Harton, 301-552-1400, Fax: 301-614-1024, E-mail: gharton@bible.edu.

CAPITAL UNIVERSITY, Columbus, OH 43209-2394

General Information Independent-religious, coed, comprehensive institution. *Enrollment:* 3,825 graduate, professional, and undergraduate students; 573 full-time matriculated graduate/professional students (268 women), 436 part-time matriculated graduate/professional students (216 women). *Enrollment by degree level:* 717 first professional, 292 master's. *Graduate faculty:* 17 full-time (12 women), 16 part-time/adjunct (10 women). *Tuition:* Part-time $920 per credit. Part-time tuition and fees vary according to program. *Graduate housing:* On-campus housing not available. *Student services:* Campus employment opportunities, campus safety program, career counseling, free psychological counseling, international student services. *Library facilities:* Blackmore Library. *Online resources:* library catalog, web page. *Collection:* 196,000 titles, 7,055 serial subscriptions, 16,000 audiovisual materials.

Computer facilities: 100 computers available on campus for general student use. A campuswide network can be accessed from student residence rooms and from off campus. Internet access is available. *Web address:* http://www.capital.edu/.

General Application Contact: Dr. Jill D Steuer, Professor and Director of the MSN Program, 614-236-6393, Fax: 614-236-6157, E-mail: jsteuer@capital.edu.

GRADUATE UNITS

Conservatory of Music Students: 73 full-time (63 women), 2 part-time (both women); includes 3 minority (1 African American, 1 American Indian/Alaska Native, 1 Asian American or Pacific Islander), 4 international. Average age 30. *Faculty:* 6 full-time (1 woman), 14

Capital University (continued)

part-time/adjunct (8 women). Expenses: Contact institution. *Financial support:* Scholarships/grants and tuition waivers (partial) available. In 2006, 17 degrees awarded. *Degree program information:* Part-time programs available. Offers music education (MM). Program offered only in summer. *Application deadline:* 3/15 priority date for domestic and international students. Applications are processed on a rolling basis. *Application fee:* $25. Electronic applications accepted. *Application Contact:* Dr. Sandra Mathias, Director, Kod[00e1]ly Institute/Graduate Coordinator, 614-236-6267, Fax: 614-236-6935, E-mail: smathias@capital.edu. *Dean,* Dr. William B. Dederer, 614-236-6474, Fax: 614-236-6935.

Law School *Degree program information:* Part-time and evening/weekend programs available. Offers business (LL M); business and taxation (LL M); law (JD, LL M, MT); taxation (LL M, MT). Electronic applications accepted.

School of Management Average age 29. *Faculty:* 17 full-time (7 women), 23 part-time/adjunct (1 woman). Expenses: Contact institution. *Financial support:* In 2006–07, 2 students received support, including 2 fellowships (averaging $1,000 per year); scholarships/grants and tuition waivers (full) also available. Support available to part-time students. Financial award application deadline: 8/1; financial award applicants required to submit FAFSA. *Degree program information:* Part-time and evening/weekend programs available. Offers management (MBA). *Application deadline:* For fall admission, 8/1 priority date for domestic students; for winter admission, 12/1 priority date for domestic students; for spring admission, 4/1 priority date for domestic students. Applications are processed on a rolling basis. *Application fee:* $25. Electronic applications accepted. *Application Contact:* Trudy Riesser, Director, MBA Enrollment Services, 614-236-6538, Fax: 614-236-6540, E-mail: trieser@capital.edu. *Interim Dean,* Dr. Keirsten Moore, 614-236-6670, Fax: 614-296-6540.

School of Nursing Students: 16 full-time (15 women), 72 part-time (67 women); includes 5 minority (4 African Americans, 1 Asian American or Pacific Islander), 8 international. Average age 41. 20 applicants, 90% accepted, 18 enrolled. *Faculty:* 11 full-time (all women), 2 part-time/adjunct (both women). Expenses: Contact institution. *Financial support:* In 2006–07, 2 students received support. Career-related internships or fieldwork and traineeships available. Financial award applicants required to submit FAFSA. In 2006, 14 degrees awarded. *Degree program information:* Part-time and evening/weekend programs available. Offers administration (MSN); legal studies (MSN); theological studies (MSN). *Application deadline:* For fall admission, 3/30 priority date for domestic and international students; for spring admission, 9/30 priority date for domestic and international students. Applications are processed on a rolling basis. *Application fee:* $25. *Application Contact:* Dr. Jill D Steuer, Professor and Director of the MSN Program, 614-236-6393, Fax: 614-236-6157, E-mail: jsteuer@capital.edu. *Dean and Professor,* Dr. Elaine F. Haynes, 614-236-6703, Fax: 614-236-6157, E-mail: ehaynes@capital.edu.

CAPITOL COLLEGE, Laurel, MD 20708-9759

General Information Independent, coed, comprehensive institution. *Graduate housing:* On-campus housing not available.

GRADUATE UNITS

Graduate Programs *Degree program information:* Part-time and evening/weekend programs available. Postbaccalaureate distance learning degree programs offered (no on-campus study). Offers business administration (MBA); computer science (MS); electrical engineering (MS); information and telecommunications systems management (MS); information architecture (MS); network security (MS). Electronic applications accepted.

CARDEAN UNIVERSITY, Chicago, IL 60606-7204

General Information Proprietary, coed, graduate-only institution.

GRADUATE UNITS

MBA Program *Degree program information:* Part-time and evening/weekend programs available. Postbaccalaureate distance learning degree programs offered (no on-campus study). Offers accounting and information systems (MBA); e-commerce (MBA); finance (MBA); global management (MBA); health care administration (MBA); human resources management (MBA); leadership (MBA); management of information systems (MBA); management of technology (MBA); marketing (MBA); professional accounting (MBA); project management (MBA); risk management (MBA); strategy and economics (MBA).

CARDINAL STRITCH UNIVERSITY, Milwaukee, WI 53217-3985

General Information Independent-religious, coed, comprehensive institution. *Graduate housing:* Room and/or apartments available on a first-come, first-served basis to single students; on-campus housing not available to married students.

GRADUATE UNITS

College of Arts and Sciences *Degree program information:* Part-time and evening/weekend programs available. Offers arts and sciences (MA, MM); clinical psychology (MA); history (MA); lay ministries (MA); ministry (MA); piano (MM); religious studies (MA); visual studies (MA).

College of Business and Management *Degree program information:* Part-time and evening/weekend programs available. Offers business and management (MBA, MSM). Programs also offered in Madison, WI and Minneapolis-St. Paul, MN.

College of Education *Degree program information:* Part-time and evening/weekend programs available. Offers education (ME); educational leadership (MS); instructional technology (ME, MS); leadership for the advancement of learning and service (Ed D, PhD); literacy/English as a second language (MA); reading/language arts (MA); reading/learning disability (MA); special education (MA); teaching (MAT); urban education (MA).

College of Nursing *Degree program information:* Part-time and evening/weekend programs available. Offers nursing (MSN). Electronic applications accepted.

CAREY THEOLOGICAL COLLEGE, Vancouver, BC V6T 1J6, Canada

General Information Independent-religious, coed, graduate-only institution. *Graduate faculty:* 8 full-time (2 women). *Graduate tuition:* Tuition charges are reported in Canadian dollars. *Tuition:* Part-time $240 Canadian dollars per credit. Tuition and fees vary according to program. *Graduate housing:* Rooms and/or apartments available on a first-come, first-served basis to single students and available to married students. Typical cost: $7,980 Canadian dollars (including board) for single students; $7,920 Canadian dollars per year for married students. Room and board charges vary according to housing facility selected. Housing application deadline: 5/31. *Library facilities:* Regent Carey Library plus 3 others. *Online resources:* library catalog, web page, access to other libraries' catalogs. *Collection:* 13,432 serial subscriptions, 8,168 audiovisual materials. *Web address:* http://www.careycentre.com/.

General Application Contact: Myrna Sears, Registrar, 604-224-4308, Fax: 604-224-5014, E-mail: msears@careytheologicalcollege.ca.

GRADUATE UNITS

Graduate Programs Students: 1 full-time (0 women), 464 part-time (207 women). *Faculty:* 8 full-time (2 women). Expenses: Contact institution. In 2006, 12 master's, 5 doctorates awarded. *Degree program information:* Part-time programs available. Offers theology (MPM, D Min). *Application fee:* $50. *Application Contact:* Myrna Sears, Registrar, 604-224-4308, Fax: 604-224-5014, E-mail: msears@careytheologicalcollege.ca. *Academic Vice President,* Dr. Barbara Mutch, 604-224-4308, Fax: 604-224-5014, E-mail: barmutch@careytheologicalcollege.ca.

CARIBBEAN UNIVERSITY, Bayamón, PR 00960-0493

General Information Independent, coed, comprehensive institution.

GRADUATE UNITS

Graduate School

CARLETON UNIVERSITY, Ottawa, ON K1S 5B6, Canada

General Information Province-supported, coed, university. *Enrollment:* 2,859 full-time matriculated graduate/professional students (1,327 women), 297 part-time matriculated graduate/professional students (144 women). *Enrollment by degree level:* 2,074 master's, 1,057 doctoral. *Graduate faculty:* 779. *Graduate housing:* Room and/or apartments guaranteed to single students; on-campus housing not available to married students. Housing application deadline: 5/31. *Student services:* Campus employment opportunities, campus safety program, career counseling, child daycare facilities, disabled student services, exercise/wellness program, free psychological counseling, international student services, low-cost health insurance, writing training. *Library facilities:* MacOdrum Library. *Online resources:* library catalog, web page, access to other libraries' catalogs. *Collection:* 1.9 million titles, 15,824 serial subscriptions, 2,661 audiovisual materials.

Computer facilities: Computer purchase and lease plans are available. 550 computers available on campus for general student use. A campuswide network can be accessed from student residence rooms and from off campus. Internet access and online class registration are available. *Web address:* http://www.carleton.ca/.

General Application Contact: Information Contact, 613-520-2600 Ext. 2525, Fax: 613-520-4049, E-mail: graduate_studies@carleton.ca.

GRADUATE UNITS

Faculty of Graduate Studies Students: 2,859 full-time (1,327 women), 297 part-time (144 women). *Faculty:* 779. Expenses: Contact institution. *Financial support:* In 2006–07, 1,026 fellowships (averaging $3,552 per year), 397 research assistantships (averaging $4,879 per year), 746 teaching assistantships (averaging $8,819 per year) were awarded; career-related internships or fieldwork, institutionally sponsored loans, scholarships/grants, and unspecified assistantships also available. In 2006, 790 master's, 76 doctorates awarded. *Degree program information:* Part-time and evening/weekend programs available. Offers business (MBA, PhD); business administration (MBA); management (PhD). *Application deadline:* Applications are processed on a rolling basis. *Application fee:* $75. Electronic applications accepted. *Application Contact:* Office of Graduate Studies and Research, E-mail: graduate_studies@carleton.ca. *Dean,* John Shepherd, 613-520-2600 Ext. 2518, Fax: 613-520-4049, E-mail: graduate_studies@carleton.ca.

Faculty of Arts and Social Sciences Students: 689 full-time (441 women), 59 part-time (37 women). *Faculty:* 298. Expenses: Contact institution. *Financial support:* In 2006–07, 159 fellowships (averaging $3,672 per year), 54 research assistantships (averaging $2,460 per year), 208 teaching assistantships (averaging $8,819 per year) were awarded; institutionally sponsored loans, scholarships/grants, and unspecified assistantships also available. In 2006, 160 master's, 33 doctorates awarded. *Degree program information:* Part-time and evening/weekend programs available. Offers anthropology (MA); applied language studies (MA); art history: art and its institutions (MA); arts and social sciences (M Sc, MA, PhD); Canadian studies (MA, PhD); cognitive science (PhD); cultural mediations (PhD); English (MA, PhD); film studies (MA); French (MA); geography (M Sc, MA, PhD); history (MA, PhD); neuroscience (M Sc); philosophy (MA); psychology (MA, PhD); sociology (MA, PhD). *Application deadline:* Applications are processed on a rolling basis. *Application fee:* $75. *Dean,* John Osborne, 613-520-2600 Ext. 2355, Fax: 613-520-4481.

Faculty of Engineering and Design Students: 702 full-time (177 women), 72 part-time (13 women). *Faculty:* 126. Expenses: Contact institution. *Financial support:* In 2006–07, 146 fellowships (averaging $2,285 per year), 179 research assistantships (averaging $5,467 per year), 166 teaching assistantships (averaging $8,819 per year) were awarded; career-related internships or fieldwork, institutionally sponsored loans, scholarships/grants, and unspecified assistantships also available. In 2006, 162 master's, 15 doctorates awarded. Offers aerospace engineering (M Eng, MA Sc, PhD); civil and environmental engineering (M Eng, MA Sc, PhD); design studies (M Arch); electrical engineering (M Eng, MA Sc, PhD); engineering and design (M Arch, M Eng, M Sc, MA Sc, PhD); information and systems science (M Sc); materials engineering (M Eng, MA Sc); mechanical engineering (M Eng, MA Sc, PhD); telecommunications technology management (M Eng). *Application deadline:* Applications are processed on a rolling basis. *Application fee:* $75. *Application Contact:* Cate Palmer, Graduate Studies Administrator, 613-520-2600 Ext. 5659, Fax: 613-520-5682, E-mail: cate_palmer@carleton.ca. *Dean,* Rafik Goubran, 613-520-2600 Ext. 5790, Fax: 613-520-7481.

Faculty of Public Affairs and Management Students: 826 full-time (470 women), 116 part-time (73 women). *Faculty:* 180. Expenses: Contact institution. *Financial support:* In 2006–07, 192 fellowships (averaging $4,054 per year), 53 research assistantships (averaging $3,082 per year), 247 teaching assistantships (averaging $8,819 per year) were awarded; career-related internships or fieldwork, institutionally sponsored loans, scholarships/grants, traineeships, and unspecified assistantships also available. In 2006, 326 master's, 14 doctorates awarded. *Degree program information:* Part-time programs available. Offers communication (MA, PhD); conflict resolution (Certificate); economics (MA, PhD); European and European Union studies (MA); human integration studies (Diploma); international affairs (MA, PhD); journalism (MJ); legal studies (MA); political economy (MA); political science (MA, PhD); public administration (MA, DPA); public affairs and management (MA, MJ, MSW, DPA, PhD, Diploma); public policy (PhD); Russian, Eurasian and transition studies (MA); social work (MSW). *Application deadline:* Applications are processed on a rolling basis. *Application fee:* $75 Canadian dollars. *Dean,* Katherine Graham, 613-520-2600 Ext. 3741, Fax: 613-520-3742.

Faculty of Science Students: 397 full-time (152 women), 30 part-time (13 women). *Faculty:* 132. Expenses: Contact institution. *Financial support:* In 2006–07, 115 fellowships (averaging $2,806 per year), 106 research assistantships (averaging $5,586 per year), 122 teaching assistantships (averaging $8,819 per year) were awarded; career-related internships or fieldwork, institutionally sponsored loans, scholarships/grants, and unspecified assistantships also available. In 2006, 87 master's, 22 doctorates awarded. *Degree program information:* Part-time and evening/weekend programs available. Offers biology (M Sc, PhD); chemistry (M Sc, PhD); computer science (MCS, PhD); earth science (M Sc, PhD); information and system science (M Sc); information and systems science (M Sc); mathematics (M Sc, PhD); physics (M Sc, PhD); science (M Sc, MCS, PhD). *Application deadline:* Applications are processed on a rolling basis. *Application fee:* $75 Canadian dollars. *Dean,* George Katsushi Iwama, 613-520-2600 Ext. 4388, Fax: 613-520-4389.

CARLOS ALBIZU UNIVERSITY, San Juan, PR 00901

General Information Independent, coed, upper-level institution. *Enrollment:* 603 full-time matriculated graduate/professional students (515 women), 99 part-time matriculated graduate/professional students (77 women). *Enrollment by degree level:* 81 master's, 575 doctoral. *Graduate faculty:* 22 full-time (13 women), 61 part-time/adjunct (33 women). *Graduate housing:* On-campus housing not available. *Student services:* Career counseling, disabled student services, free psychological counseling, teacher training. *Web address:* http://www.albizu.edu/.

General Application Contact: Carlos Rodríguez, Director of Students Affairs, 787-725-6500 Ext. 21, Fax: 787-721-7187, E-mail: crodriguez@prip.ccas.edu.

GRADUATE UNITS

Graduate Programs in Psychology Students: 603 full-time (515 women), 99 part-time (77 women); all minorities (all Hispanic Americans) Average age 28. 168 applicants, 77% accepted, 124 enrolled. *Faculty:* 22 full-time (13 women), 61 part-time/adjunct (33 women). Expenses: Contact institution. *Financial support:* In 2006–07, 15 research assistantships, 15 teaching assistantships were awarded; career-related internships or fieldwork, Federal Work-Study, institutionally sponsored loans, scholarships/grants, traineeships, and tuition waivers (partial) also available. Support available to part-time students. Financial award application deadline: 4/21; financial award applicants required to submit FAFSA. In 2006, 66 master's, 81 doctorates awarded. *Degree program information:* Part-time and evening/weekend programs available. Offers clinical psychology (MS, PhD, Psy D); general psychology (PhD); industrial/organizational psychology (MS, PhD); speech and language pathology (MS). *Application deadline:* For fall admission, 7/19 for domestic and international students; for winter admission, 11/15 for domestic and international students; for spring admission, 4/21 for domestic and international students. *Application fee:* $75. *Application Contact:* Dr. Jaime Veray,

Special Assistant to Chancellor, 787-725-6500 Ext. 35, Fax: 787-721-7187, E-mail: jveray@albizu.edu. *Chancellor*, Dr. Lourdes Garcia, 787-725-6500 Ext. 34, E-mail: lgarcia@albizu.edu.

CARLOS ALBIZU UNIVERSITY, MIAMI CAMPUS, Miami, FL 33172-2209

General Information Independent, coed, primarily women, comprehensive institution. *Graduate housing:* On-campus housing not available.

GRADUATE UNITS

Graduate Programs *Degree program information:* Part-time and evening/weekend programs available. Offers clinical psychology (Psy D); entrepreneurship (MBA); exceptional student education (MS); industrial/organizational psychology (MS); marriage and family therapy (MS); mental health counseling (MS); nonprofit management (MBA); organizational management (MBA); psychology (MS); school counseling (MS); teaching English as a second language (MS).

CARLOW UNIVERSITY, Pittsburgh, PA 15213-3165

General Information Independent-religious, coed, primarily women, comprehensive institution. *Graduate housing:* Room and/or apartments available on a first-come, first-served basis to single students; on-campus housing not available to married students.

GRADUATE UNITS

Humanities Division *Degree program information:* Part-time and evening/weekend programs available. Offers creative writing (MFA).

School for Social Change *Degree program information:* Part-time and evening/weekend programs available. Offers management of non-profit organization (MS); organizational influence (MS); professional counseling (MSPC); training and development (MS). Electronic applications accepted.

School of Education *Degree program information:* Part-time and evening/weekend programs available. Offers art education (M Ed); early childhood education (M Ed); early childhood supervision (M Ed); education with certificate options (M Ed); educational leadership (M Ed); educational praxis (MA); elementary education (M Ed); instructional technology specialist (M Ed); secondary education (M Ed); special education (M Ed). Electronic applications accepted.

School of Management *Degree program information:* Part-time and evening/weekend programs available. Offers management and technology (MS). Electronic applications accepted.

School of Nursing *Degree program information:* Part-time and evening/weekend programs available. Postbaccalaureate distance learning degree programs offered (minimal on-campus study). Offers home health advanced practice nursing (MSN, PMC); nursing case management/leadership (MSN); nursing leadership (MSN). Electronic applications accepted.

CARNEGIE MELLON UNIVERSITY, Pittsburgh, PA 15213-3891

General Information Independent, coed, university. CGS member. *Graduate housing:* On-campus housing not available. *Research affiliation:* National Census Data Research Center (public policy), Robotics Engineering Consortium (computer science and engineering), Software Engineering Institute (computer science and engineering), Carnegie Bosch Institute for Applied Studies in International Management (business and management), Pittsburgh Supercomputer Center.

GRADUATE UNITS

Carnegie Institute of Technology *Degree program information:* Part-time and evening/weekend programs available. Offers advanced infrastructure systems (MS, PhD); architecture-engineering construction management (MS); bioengineering (MS, PhD); biomedical engineering (MS, PhD); chemical engineering (M Ch E, MS, PhD); civil and environmental engineering (MS, PhD); civil and environmental engineering/engineering and public policy (PhD); civil engineering (MS, PhD); colloids, polymers and surfaces (MS); computational science and engineering (MS, PhD); computer-aided engineering (MS, PhD); computer-aided engineering and management (MS, PhD); electrical and computer engineering (MS, PhD); engineering (MS, PhD); engineering and public policy (PhD); environmental engineering (MS, PhD); environmental management and science (MS, PhD); materials science and engineering (MS, PhD); mechanical engineering (ME, MS, PhD); product development (MPD); technology (M Ch E, ME, MPD, MS, PhD).

Information Networking Institute *Degree program information:* Part-time programs available. Offers information networking (MS); information security technology and management (MS).

Center for the Neural Basis of Cognition Offers neural basis of cognition (PhD).

College of Fine Arts *Degree program information:* Part-time programs available. Offers art (MFA); fine arts (M Des, M Sc, MAM, MET, MFA, MM, MPD, MSA, PhD). Electronic applications accepted.

School of Architecture Offers architecture (MSA); building performance and diagnostics (M Sc, PhD); computational design (M Sc, PhD).

School of Design Offers communication planning and information design (M Des); design (PhD); design theory (PhD); interaction design (M Des); new product development (PhD); product development (MPD); typography and information design (PhD).

School of Drama Offers design (MFA); directing (MFA); dramatic writing (MFA); performance technology and management (MFA).

School of Music *Degree program information:* Part-time programs available. Offers composition (MM); conducting (MM); music education (MM); performance (MM).

College of Humanities and Social Sciences *Degree program information:* Part-time programs available. Offers behavioral decision theory (PhD); cognitive neuroscience (PhD); cognitive psychology (PhD); communication planning and design (M Des); computer-assisted language learning (MCALL); design (MAPW); developmental psychology (PhD); English (MA); history (MA, MS); history and policy (MA, PhD); humanities and social sciences (M Des, MA, MAPW, MCALL, MS, PhD); literary and cultural studies (MA, PhD); logic and computation (MS); logic, computation and methodology (PhD); mathematical finance (PhD); organization science (PhD); philosophy (MA); professional writing (MAPW); research (MAPW); rhetoric (MA, PhD); rhetorical theory (MAPW); science writing (MAPW); second language acquisition (PhD); social and cultural history (PhD); social and decision science (PhD); social/personality/health psychology (PhD); statistics (MS, PhD); technical (MAPW). Electronic applications accepted.

Center for Innovation in Learning Offers instructional science (PhD).

H. John Heinz III School of Public Policy and Management *Degree program information:* Part-time and evening/weekend programs available. Offers arts management (MAM); entertainment industry management (MEIM); health care policy and management (MSHCPM); information security policy and management (MSISPM); information systems management (MISM); medical management (MMM); public management (MPM); public policy analysis (PhD); public policy and management (MAM, MEIM, MIS, MISM, MMM, MPM, MS, MSED, MSHCPM, MSISPM, PhD); sustainable economic development (MIS). Electronic applications accepted.

Joint CMU-Pitt PhD Program in Computational Biology Offers computational biology (PhD).

Mellon College of Science *Degree program information:* Part-time programs available. Offers algorithms, combinatorics, and optimization (PhD); biochemistry (PhD); biophysics (PhD); cell biology (PhD); chemical instrumentation (MS); chemistry (MS, PhD); colloids, polymers and surfaces (MS); computational biology (MS, PhD); developmental biology (PhD); genetics (PhD); mathematical finance (PhD); mathematical sciences (MS, DA, PhD); molecular biology (PhD); neurobiology (PhD); physics (PhD); polymer science (MS); pure and applied logic (PhD); science (MS, DA, PhD). Electronic applications accepted.

School of Computer Science Offers algorithms, combinatorics, and optimization (PhD); computer science (PhD); entertainment technology (MET); human-computer interaction (MHCI, PhD); knowledge discovery and data mining (MS); pure and applied logic (PhD); software engineering (MSE, PhD).

Language Technologies Institute Offers language technologies (MLT, PhD).

Robotics Institute Offers robotics (MS, PhD).

Tepper School of Business *Degree program information:* Part-time programs available. Offers accounting (PhD); algorithms, combinatorics, and optimization (MS, PhD); business management and software engineering (MBMSE); civil engineering and industrial management (MS); computational finance (MSCF); economics (MS, PhD); electronic commerce (MS); environmental engineering and management (MEEM); finance (PhD); financial economics (PhD); industrial administration (MBA, PhD); information systems (PhD); management of manufacturing and automation (MOM, PhD); manufacturing (MOM); marketing (PhD); mathematical finance (PhD); operations research (PhD); organizational behavior and theory (PhD); political economy (PhD); production and operations management (PhD); public policy and management (MS, MSED); software engineering and business management (MS).

CARROLL COLLEGE, Waukesha, WI 53186-5593

General Information Independent-religious, coed, comprehensive institution. *Enrollment:* 3,292 graduate, professional, and undergraduate students; 47 full-time matriculated graduate/professional students (39 women), 152 part-time matriculated graduate/professional students (114 women). *Enrollment by degree level:* 199 master's. *Graduate faculty:* 15 full-time (6 women), 12 part-time/adjunct (9 women). *Tuition:* Part-time $325 per credit. Part-time tuition and fees vary according to program. *Graduate housing:* On-campus housing not available. *Student services:* Campus employment opportunities, campus safety program, career counseling, disabled student services, exercise/wellness program, free psychological counseling, international student services, multicultural affairs office. *Library facilities:* Todd Wehr Memorial Library. *Online resources:* library catalog, web page, access to other libraries' catalogs. *Collection:* 150,000 titles, 18,000 serial subscriptions, 1,025 audiovisual materials.

Computer facilities: 250 computers available on campus for general student use. A campuswide network can be accessed from student residence rooms and from off campus. Internet access and online class registration are available. *Web address:* http://www.cc.edu/.

General Application Contact: Jennifer L. Wells-Sperry, Director of Graduate Admission, 262-524-7357, Fax: 262-650-4851, E-mail: jwells@cc.edu.

GRADUATE UNITS

Graduate Program in Education Average age 36. 80 applicants, 65% accepted, 20 enrolled. *Faculty:* 7 full-time (4 women), 10 part-time/adjunct (8 women). Expenses: Contact institution. *Financial support:* In 2006–07, 18 students received support; fellowships available. Support available to part-time students. Financial award application deadline: 3/15; financial award applicants required to submit FAFSA. In 2006, 30 degrees awarded. *Degree program information:* Part-time and evening/weekend programs available. Offers education (M Ed); learning and teaching (M Ed). *Application deadline:* For fall admission, 8/15 priority date for domestic students. Applications are processed on a rolling basis. *Application fee:* $0. Electronic applications accepted. *Application Contact:* Tina M. Wood, Non-Traditional Admission, 262-524-7518, Fax: 262-650-4851, E-mail: twood@cc.edu. *Director*, Dr. Mary Ann Wisniewski, 262-951-3944, Fax: 262-524-7139, E-mail: mwisniew@cc.edu.

Program in Physical Therapy Students: 47 full-time (39 women); includes 1 minority (Hispanic American) Average age 25. 48 applicants, 69% accepted, 32 enrolled. *Faculty:* 5 full-time (2 women), 1 part-time/adjunct (0 women). Expenses: Contact institution. *Financial support:* In 2006–07, 35 students received support, including fellowships (averaging $3,000 per year). Support available to part-time students. Financial award application deadline: 3/15; financial award applicants required to submit FAFSA. Offers physical therapy (MPT, DPT). *Application deadline:* For fall admission, 7/14 for domestic students. Applications are processed on a rolling basis. *Application fee:* $25. *Application Contact:* Jennifer L. Wells-Sperry, Director of Graduate Admission, 262-524-7357, Fax: 262-951-3037, E-mail: jwells@cc.edu. *Dean, Natural and Health Sciences*, Dr. Jane F. Hopp, 262-524-7294, E-mail: jhopp@cc.edu.

Program in Software Engineering Average age 35. 17 applicants, 59% accepted, 6 enrolled. *Faculty:* 4 full-time (0 women). Expenses: Contact institution. *Financial support:* In 2006–07, 2 students received support. Institutionally sponsored loans available. Support available to part-time students. In 2006, 6 degrees awarded. *Degree program information:* Part-time and evening/weekend programs available. Offers software engineering (MSE). *Application deadline:* For fall admission, 9/15 priority date for domestic students. Applications are processed on a rolling basis. *Application fee:* $0. Electronic applications accepted. *Application Contact:* Jennifer L. Wells-Sperry, Associate Director of Admission, 262-524-7357, Fax: 262-951-3037, E-mail: jwells@cc.edu. *Associate Professor of Computer Science and Program Director*, Dr. Chenglie Hu, 262-524-7170, E-mail: gli@cc.edu.

CARSON-NEWMAN COLLEGE, Jefferson City, TN 37760

General Information Independent-religious, coed, comprehensive institution. *Enrollment:* 1,949 graduate, professional, and undergraduate students; 98 full-time matriculated graduate/professional students (78 women), 52 part-time matriculated graduate/professional students (40 women). *Enrollment by degree level:* 150 master's. *Graduate faculty:* 7 full-time (4 women), 20 part-time/adjunct (12 women). *Tuition:* Part-time $270 per credit hour. *Graduate housing:* Rooms and/or apartments available to single and married students. Housing application deadline: 7/15. *Student services:* Campus employment opportunities, career counseling, free psychological counseling, international student services, low-cost health insurance. *Library facilities:* Stephens-Burnett Library plus 1 other. *Online resources:* library catalog, web page. *Collection:* 218,371 titles, 3,966 serial subscriptions.

Computer facilities: 200 computers available on campus for general student use. A campuswide network can be accessed from student residence rooms and from off campus. Internet access is available. *Web address:* http://www.cn.edu/.

General Application Contact: Graduate Admissions and Services Adviser, 865-473-3468, Fax: 865-472-3475.

GRADUATE UNITS

Department of Nursing Students: 21 full-time (18 women), 11 part-time (all women); includes 1 African American. Average age 32. *Faculty:* 2 full-time (both women), 10 part-time/adjunct (9 women). Expenses: Contact institution. In 2006, 6 degrees awarded. Offers family nurse practitioner (MSN). *Application deadline:* For fall admission, 7/15 priority date for domestic students. Applications are processed on a rolling basis. *Application fee:* $50. *Dean and Chair*, Dr. Patricia Kraft, 865-471-3426.

Graduate Program in Education Students: 77 full-time (60 women), 41 part-time (29 women); includes 2 minority (both African Americans), 27 international. Average age 32. 65 applicants, 97% accepted. *Faculty:* 5 full-time (2 women), 10 part-time/adjunct (3 women). Expenses: Contact institution. *Financial support:* In 2006–07, 86 students received support. Federal Work-Study and unspecified assistantships available. Financial award application deadline: 4/1; financial award applicants required to submit FAFSA. In 2006, 64 degrees awarded. *Degree program information:* Part-time and evening/weekend programs available. Offers curriculum and instruction (M Ed); elementary education (MAT); school counseling (M Ed); secondary education (MAT); teaching English as a second language (MATESL). *Application deadline:* For fall admission, 7/15 priority date for domestic students. Applications are processed on a rolling basis. *Application fee:* $25 ($50 for international students). *Application Contact:* Graduate Admissions and Services Adviser, 865-471-3460, Fax: 865-471-3875. *Chair*, Dr. Jean Love, 865-471-3461.

CARTHAGE COLLEGE, Kenosha, WI 53140

General Information Independent-religious, coed, comprehensive institution. *Graduate housing:* On-campus housing not available.

GRADUATE UNITS

Division of Teacher Education *Degree program information:* Part-time and evening/weekend programs available. Offers classroom guidance and counseling (M Ed); creative arts (M Ed); gifted and talented children (M Ed); language arts (M Ed); modern language

Carthage College (continued)

(M Ed); natural sciences (M Ed); reading (M Ed, Certificate); social sciences (M Ed); teacher leadership (M Ed).

CASE WESTERN RESERVE UNIVERSITY, Cleveland, OH 44106

General Information Independent, coed, university. CGS member. *Enrollment:* 9,592 graduate, professional, and undergraduate students; 3,756 full-time matriculated graduate/professional students (1,749 women), 1,486 part-time matriculated graduate/professional students (787 women). *Enrollment by degree level:* 1,560 first professional, 2,216 master's, 1,466 doctoral. *Graduate faculty:* 1,992 full-time (640 women). *Graduate housing:* On-campus housing not available. *Student services:* Campus employment opportunities, campus safety program, career counseling, disabled student services, exercise/wellness program, free psychological counseling, grant writing training, international student services, low-cost health insurance, multicultural affairs office, teacher training, writing training. *Library facilities:* University Library plus 6 others. *Online resources:* library catalog, web page, access to other libraries' catalogs. *Collection:* 2.5 million titles, 20,265 serial subscriptions, 56,916 audiovisual materials. *Research affiliation:* University Hospitals of Cleveland (biomedical science), Cleveland Hearing and Speech Center (speech-language pathology and audiology), Dow Chemical Company (polymers), Rockwell Automation (sensors), Universities Space Research Association (space exploration), Cleveland Clinic Foundation (biomedical science).

Computer facilities: Computer purchase and lease plans are available. 280 computers available on campus for general student use. A campuswide network can be accessed from student residence rooms and from off campus. Internet access and online class registration, software library, online reference databases, electronic books and journals are available. *Web address:* http://www.case.edu/.

General Application Contact: Susan M. Benedict, Assistant Dean of Graduate Studies, 216-368-4390, Fax: 216-368-4250, E-mail: jgez@po.cwru.edu.

GRADUATE UNITS

Frances Payne Bolton School of Nursing Students: 187 full-time (157 women), 458 part-time (422 women); includes 86 minority (38 African Americans, 1 American Indian/Alaska Native, 34 Asian Americans or Pacific Islanders, 13 Hispanic Americans), 40 international. 390 applicants, 58% accepted, 132 enrolled. *Faculty:* 58 full-time (53 women), 10 part-time/adjunct (9 women). Expenses: Contact institution. *Financial support:* In 2006–07, 5 research assistantships, 7 teaching assistantships were awarded; fellowships, Federal Work-Study, institutionally sponsored loans, scholarships/grants, and tuition waivers (partial) also available. Support available to part-time students. Financial award application deadline: 6/30; financial award applicants required to submit FAFSA. In 2006, 75 master's, 57 doctorates awarded. *Degree program information:* Part-time programs available. Postbaccalaureate distance learning degree programs offered (minimal on-campus study). Offers acute care cardiovascular nursing (MSN); acute care nurse practitioner (MSN, DNP); acute care/flight nurse (MSN); adult nurse practitioner (MSN, DNP); community health nursing (MSN); family nurse practitioner (MSN, DNP); gerontological nurse practitioner (MSN, DNP); graduate entry/prelicensure option (DNP); medical-surgical nursing (MSN, DNP); midwifery/family nursing (DNP); neonatal nurse practitioner (MSN, DNP); nurse anesthesia (MSN); nurse midwifery (MSN); nurse practitioner (MSN); nursing (MSN, DNP, PhD); nursing informatics (MSN); pediatric nurse practitioner (MSN, DNP); post-licensure option (DNP); psychiatric mental health nurse practitioner (DNP); psychiatric-mental health nurse practitioner (MSN); women's health nurse practitioner (MSN, DNP). *Application deadline:* Applications are processed on a rolling basis. *Application fee:* $75. *Application Contact:* Peter Taylor, Recruitment and Retention Specialist, 216-368-0349, Fax: 216-368-0124, E-mail: peter.taylor@case.edu. *Dean,* Dr. May L. Wykle, 216-368-2545.

Mandel School of Applied Social Sciences *Degree program information:* Evening/weekend programs available. Offers social administration (MSSA); social welfare (PhD).

School of Dental Medicine Students: 341 full-time (104 women), 2 part-time (both women); includes 68 minority (10 African Americans, 1 American Indian/Alaska Native, 52 Asian Americans or Pacific Islanders, 5 Hispanic Americans), 15 international. Average age 28. 3,423 applicants, 8% accepted, 92 enrolled. *Faculty:* 49 full-time (14 women), 230 part-time/adjunct (50 women). Expenses: Contact institution. *Financial support:* In 2006–07, 276 students received support. Federal Work-Study, institutionally sponsored loans, scholarships/grants, and health care benefits available. Financial award application deadline: 4/30; financial award applicants required to submit FAFSA. In 2006, 71 first professional degrees, 14 master's awarded. Offers advanced general dentistry (Certificate); dental medicine (DMD, MSD, Certificate); dentistry (DMD, MSD, Certificate); endodontics (MSD, Certificate); oral surgery (Certificate); orthodontics (MSD, Certificate); pedodontics (MSD, Certificate); periodontics (MSD, Certificate). *Application deadline:* For fall admission, 1/1 for domestic and international students. Applications are processed on a rolling basis. *Application fee:* $45. Electronic applications accepted. *Application Contact:* David A. Dalsky, Director of Admissions, 216-368-2460, Fax: 216-368-3204, E-mail: david.dalsky@case.edu. *Dean,* Dr. Jerold S. Goldberg, 216-368-3266, Fax: 216-368-3204, E-mail: jsg@case.edu.

School of Graduate Studies Students: 1,604 full-time (753 women), 404 part-time (192 women). Average age 27. 3,539 applicants, 27% accepted, 453 enrolled. *Faculty:* 1,992 full-time (640 women). Expenses: Contact institution. *Financial support:* Fellowships, research assistantships, teaching assistantships, career-related internships or fieldwork, Federal Work-Study, institutionally sponsored loans, and tuition waivers (full and partial) available. Support available to part-time students. In 2006, 347 master's, 180 doctorates awarded. *Degree program information:* Part-time and evening/weekend programs available. Offers acting (MFA); analytical chemistry (MS, PhD); anthropology (MA, PhD); applied mathematics (MS, PhD); art education (MA); art history (MA, PhD); art history and museum studies (MA, PhD); astronomy (MS, PhD); bioethics (MA, PhD); biology (MS, PhD); clinical psychology (PhD); comparative literature (MA); contemporary dance (MFA); early music (D Mus A); English and American literature (MA, PhD); experimental psychology (PhD); French (MA, PhD); geological sciences (MS, PhD); gerontology (Certificate); history (MA, PhD); inorganic chemistry (MS, PhD); mathematics (MS, PhD); mental retardation (PhD); music (MA, PhD); music education (MA, PhD); organic chemistry (MS, PhD); physical chemistry (MS, PhD); physics (MS, PhD); political science (MA, PhD); sociology (PhD); speech-language pathology (MA, PhD); statistics (MS, PhD); theater (MFA); world literature (MA). *Application fee:* $50. *Application Contact:* Susan M. Benedict, Department Assistant, 216-368-4402, Fax: 216-368-4250, E-mail: smb25@cwru.edu. *Dean,* Dr. Charles E. Rozek, 216-368-4400, Fax: 216-368-4250, E-mail: charles.rozak@case.edu.

The Case School of Engineering Students: 384 full-time, 250 part-time. *Faculty:* 118 full-time (13 women). Expenses: Contact institution. *Financial support:* Fellowships with full and partial tuition reimbursements, research assistantships with full and partial tuition reimbursements, teaching assistantships, career-related internships or fieldwork, Federal Work-Study, and institutionally sponsored loans available. Support available to part-time students. Financial award applicants required to submit FAFSA. In 2006, 134 master's, 65 doctorates awarded. *Degree program information:* Part-time and evening/weekend programs available. Postbaccalaureate distance learning degree programs offered. Offers aerospace engineering (MS, PhD); biomedical engineering (MS, PhD); ceramics and materials science (MS); chemical engineering (MS, PhD); civil engineering (MS, PhD); computer engineering (MS, PhD); computing and information science (MS, PhD); electrical engineering (MS, PhD); engineering (ME, MEM, MS, PhD); engineering mechanics (MS); fluid and thermal engineering sciences (MS, PhD); integration of management and engineering (MEM); macromolecular science (MS, PhD); materials science and engineering (MS, PhD); mechanical engineering (MS, PhD); systems and control engineering (MS, PhD). *Application deadline:* Applications are processed on a rolling basis. *Application fee:* $50. Electronic applications accepted. *Associate Dean,* John Blackwell, 216-368-4436, Fax: 216-368-6939, E-mail: cseinfo@case.edu.

School of Law Students: 670 full-time (273 women), 3 part-time (all women); includes 113 minority (29 African Americans, 2 American Indian/Alaska Native, 73 Asian Americans or Pacific Islanders, 9 Hispanic Americans), 7 international. Average age 25. 2,653 applicants, 28% accepted, 228 enrolled. *Faculty:* 52 full-time (16 women), 130 part-time/adjunct (43 women). Expenses: Contact institution. *Financial support:* In 2006–07, 560 students received support. Career-related internships or fieldwork, Federal Work-Study, and scholarships/grants available. Support available to part-time students. Financial award application deadline: 3/15; financial award applicants required to submit FAFSA. In 2006, 241 JDs, 34 master's awarded. *Degree program information:* Part-time programs available. Offers law (JD); U.S. legal studies (LL M). *Application deadline:* For fall admission, 2/1 priority date for domestic students, 4/1 priority date for international students. Applications are processed on a rolling basis. *Application fee:* $40. Electronic applications accepted. *Application Contact:* Alyson Alber, Interim Assistant Dean for Admissions, 216-368-3600, Fax: 216-368-1042, E-mail: lawadmissions@case.edu. *Dean,* Gary J. Simson, 216-368-3283.

School of Medicine Students: 457 full-time (253 women), 265 part-time (162 women); includes 109 minority (33 African Americans, 3 American Indian/Alaska Native, 63 Asian Americans or Pacific Islanders, 10 Hispanic Americans), 198 international. Average age 28. 1,437 applicants, 38% accepted, 282 enrolled. Expenses: Contact institution. *Financial support:* Fellowships, research assistantships, teaching assistantships, career-related internships or fieldwork, Federal Work-Study, institutionally sponsored loans, and tuition waivers (full and partial) available. Support available to part-time students. In 2006, 132 master's, 59 doctorates awarded. *Degree program information:* Part-time programs available. Offers clinical research (MS); medicine (MD, MPH, MS, PhD). *Application deadline:* Applications are processed on a rolling basis. *Application fee:* $50. *Application Contact:* Susan M. Benedict, Graduate Admissions Coordinator, 216-368-4390, Fax: 216-368-4250, E-mail: smb25@case.edu. *Dean,* Dr. Pamela Davis, 216-368-2825.

Graduate Programs in Medicine Students: 563 full-time (311 women), 125 part-time (82 women); includes 104 minority (28 African Americans, 3 American Indian/Alaska Native, 63 Asian Americans or Pacific Islanders, 10 Hispanic Americans), 182 international. Average age 28. 1,170 applicants, 26% accepted, 150 enrolled. Expenses: Contact institution. *Financial support:* Fellowships, research assistantships, teaching assistantships, career-related internships or fieldwork, Federal Work-Study, institutionally sponsored loans, tuition waivers (full and partial), and unspecified assistantships available. Support available to part-time students. In 2006, 126 master's, 48 doctorates awarded. *Degree program information:* Part-time programs available. Offers anesthesiology (MS); applied anatomy (MS); biochemical research (MS); biochemistry (MS, PhD); biological anthropology (MS, PhD); biomedical sciences (PhD); biostatistics (MS, PhD); cell biology (MS, PhD); cell physiology (PhD); cellular biology (MS, PhD); developmental biology (PhD); dietetics (MS); epidemiology (MS, PhD); genetic and molecular epidemiology (MS, PhD); genetic counseling (MS); health policy (MS, PhD); human, molecular, and developmental genetics and genomics (PhD); immunology (MS, PhD); medicine (MPH, MS, PhD); microbiology (PhD); molecular biology (PhD); molecular/cellular biophysics (PhD); neurobiology (PhD); neuroscience (PhD); nutrition (MS, PhD); pathology (MS, PhD); pharmacology (MS, PhD); physiology and biophysics (PhD); physiology and biotechnology (MS); public health (MPH); public health nutrition (MS); systems physiology (PhD). *Application deadline:* For fall admission, 3/1 priority date for domestic students, 2/1 priority date for international students; for spring admission, 11/1 priority date for domestic students, 10/1 priority date for international students. Applications are processed on a rolling basis. *Application fee:* $50. Electronic applications accepted. *Application Contact:* Susan M. Benedict, Graduate Admissions Coordinator, 216-368-4390, Fax: 216-368-4250, E-mail: smb25@case.edu. *Dean,* Dr. Charles E. Rozek, 216-368-4400, Fax: 216-368-4250, E-mail: charles.rozak@case.edu.

Weatherhead School of Management Students: 500 full-time (174 women), 425 part-time (174 women); includes 136 minority (71 African Americans, 1 American Indian/Alaska Native, 48 Asian Americans or Pacific Islanders, 16 Hispanic Americans), 154 international. Average age 28. 741 applicants, 79% accepted, 361 enrolled. *Faculty:* 75 full-time (16 women), 35 part-time/adjunct (10 women). Expenses: Contact institution. *Financial support:* Fellowships with full and partial tuition reimbursements, career-related internships or fieldwork, Federal Work-Study, institutionally sponsored loans, scholarships/grants, tuition waivers (full and partial), and unspecified assistantships available. Financial award application deadline: 5/1; financial award applicants required to submit FAFSA. In 2006, 377 master's, 27 doctorates, 24 other advanced degrees awarded. *Degree program information:* Part-time and evening/weekend programs available. Offers accountancy (M Acc, PhD); banking and finance (MBA); business administration (EMBA, MBA); economics (MBA); information systems (MBA); labor and human resource policy (MBA); management (MS, MSM, EDM); management for liberal arts graduates (MSM); management policy (MBA); marketing (MBA); operations research (MSM, PhD); organizational behavior and analysis (MBA, MPOD, MS); positive organization development and change (MPOD); supply chain (MSM). *Dean,* Mohan Reddy, 216-368-2038, Fax: 216-368-2845, E-mail: mxr8@po.cwru.edu.

Mandel Center for Nonprofit Organizations Students: 37 full-time (29 women), 29 part-time (23 women); includes 18 minority (9 African Americans, 1 American Indian/Alaska Native, 5 Asian Americans or Pacific Islanders, 3 Hispanic Americans). Average age 31. 22 applicants, 86% accepted, 14 enrolled. *Faculty:* 6 full-time (1 woman), 5 part-time/adjunct (2 women). Expenses: Contact institution. *Financial support:* In 2006–07, 39 students received support, including 1 fellowship with full and partial tuition reimbursement available; career-related internships or fieldwork, Federal Work-Study, and scholarships/grants also available. Financial award application deadline: 5/1; financial award applicants required to submit FAFSA. In 2006, 15 degrees awarded. *Degree program information:* Part-time and evening/weekend programs available. Offers nonprofit organizations (MNO, CNM). *Application deadline:* For fall admission, 6/1 priority date for domestic students; for spring admission, 11/15 priority date for domestic students. Applications are processed on a rolling basis. *Application fee:* $25. *Application Contact:* Carol K. Willen, Director of Graduate Programs, 216-368-8566, Fax: 216-368-4793, E-mail: ckw3@po.cwru.edu. *Director,* Susan Lajoie Eagan, 216-368-2275, Fax: 216-368-8592, E-mail: susan.eagan@case.edu.

CASTLETON STATE COLLEGE, Castleton, VT 05735

General Information State-supported, coed, comprehensive institution. *Graduate housing:* Room and/or apartments available on a first-come, first-served basis to single students; on-campus housing not available to married students. Housing application deadline: 5/19.

GRADUATE UNITS

Division of Graduate Studies *Degree program information:* Part-time and evening/weekend programs available. Offers curriculum and instruction (MA Ed); educational leadership (MA Ed, CAGS); forensic psychology (MA); language arts and reading (MA Ed, CAGS); special education (MA Ed, CAGS).

CATAWBA COLLEGE, Salisbury, NC 28144-2488

General Information Independent-religious, coed, comprehensive institution. *Enrollment:* 1,269 graduate, professional, and undergraduate students; 35 part-time matriculated graduate/professional students (all women). *Enrollment by degree level:* 35 master's. *Graduate faculty:* 4 full-time (3 women), 3 part-time/adjunct (2 women). *Tuition:* Part-time $130 per credit hour. *Graduate housing:* On-campus housing not available. *Student services:* Campus safety program, career counseling, teacher training. *Library facilities:* Corriher-Linn-Black Memorial Library plus 1 other. *Online resources:* library catalog, access to other libraries' catalogs. *Collection:* 112,447 titles, 604 serial subscriptions.

Computer facilities: 97 computers available on campus for general student use. A campuswide network can be accessed from student residence rooms and from off campus. Internet access is available. *Web address:* http://www.catawba.edu/.

General Application Contact: Dr. Lou W. Kasias, Director, Graduate Program, 704-637-4462, Fax: 704-637-4732, E-mail: lakasias@catawba.edu.

GRADUATE UNITS

Program in Education *Faculty:* 3 full-time (2 women), 2 part-time/adjunct (1 woman). Expenses: Contact institution. *Financial support:* Scholarships/grants available. In 2006, 3 degrees awarded. *Degree program information:* Part-time and evening/weekend programs available. Offers elementary education (M Ed). *Application deadline:* For fall admission, 8/1 priority date for domestic students; for winter admission, 12/1 priority date for domestic students; for spring admission, 5/1 priority date for domestic students. Applications are processed on a rolling basis. *Application fee:* $0. *Application Contact:* Dr. Lou W. Kasias, Director, Graduate

Program, 704-637-4462, Fax: 704-637-4732, E-mail: lakasias@catawba.edu. *Chair, Department of Teacher Education,* Dr. James K. Stringfield, 704-637-4461, Fax: 704-637-4732, E-mail: jstringf@catawba.edu.

THE CATHOLIC DISTANCE UNIVERSITY, Hamilton, VA 20158

General Information Independent-religious, coed, graduate-only institution. *Graduate housing:* On-campus housing not available.

GRADUATE UNITS

Graduate Programs *Degree program information:* Part-time and evening/weekend programs available. Postbaccalaureate distance learning degree programs offered (no on-campus study). Offers religious studies (MRS); theology (MA).

CATHOLIC THEOLOGICAL UNION AT CHICAGO, Chicago, IL 60615-5698

General Information Independent-religious, coed, graduate-only institution. *Graduate housing:* Rooms and/or apartments available on a first-come, first-served basis to single and married students. Housing application deadline: 7/1.

GRADUATE UNITS

Graduate and Professional Programs *Degree program information:* Part-time and evening/weekend programs available. Offers biblical spirituality (Certificate); cross-cultural ministries (D Min); cross-cultural missions (Certificate); divinity (M Div); liturgical studies (Certificate); liturgy (D Min); pastoral studies (MAPS, Certificate); spiritual formation (Certificate); spirituality (D Min); theology (MA).

THE CATHOLIC UNIVERSITY OF AMERICA, Washington, DC 20064

General Information Independent-religious, coed, university. CGS member. *Enrollment:* 6,148 graduate, professional, and undergraduate students; 1,335 full-time matriculated graduate/professional students (658 women), 1,584 part-time matriculated graduate/professional students (830 women). *Enrollment by degree level:* 963 first professional, 1,152 master's, 804 doctoral. *Graduate faculty:* 344 full-time (129 women), 347 part-time/adjunct (154 women). *Tuition:* Full-time $27,700; part-time $1,045 per credit hour. *Required fees:* $1,290. Part-time tuition and fees vary according to campus/location and program. *Graduate housing:* Room and/or apartments available on a first-come, first-served basis to single students; on-campus housing not available to married students. Typical cost: $6,224 per year. Room charges vary according to board plan. *Student services:* Campus employment opportunities, campus safety program, career counseling, disabled student services, exercise/wellness program, free psychological counseling, international student services, low-cost health insurance, multicultural affairs office, teacher training, writing training. *Library facilities:* Mullen Library plus 7 others. *Online resources:* library catalog, web page, access to other libraries' catalogs. *Collection:* 1.6 million titles, 10,448 serial subscriptions, 40,697 audiovisual materials. *Research affiliation:* Northrup Grumman (Structural Monitoring), ZT3, Inc. (Materials Science), Hardie Industries (Chemical Analysis), Johns Hopkins University—Applied Physics Laboratory (Medical Imaging), PulseCare, Inc. (Cancer Therapies), Energy Solutions (Federal Services; Waste Remediation).

Computer facilities: Computer purchase and lease plans are available. 450 computers available on campus for general student use. A campuswide network can be accessed from student residence rooms and from off campus. Internet access and online class registration, internet 2, video streaming, online voting, pedagogical software are available. *Web address:* http://www.cua.edu/.

General Application Contact: Christine Mica, Director, University Admissions, 202-319-5305, Fax: 202-319-6533, E-mail: cua-admissions@cua.edu.

GRADUATE UNITS

The Benjamin T. Rome School of Music Students: 56 full-time (37 women), 81 part-time (54 women); includes 24 minority (10 African Americans, 10 Asian Americans or Pacific Islanders, 4 Hispanic Americans), 25 international. Average age 33. 118 applicants, 64% accepted, 35 enrolled. *Faculty:* 14 full-time (4 women), 24 part-time/adjunct (10 women). Expenses: Contact institution. *Financial support:* Fellowships, research assistantships, teaching assistantships, career-related internships or fieldwork, Federal Work-Study, scholarships/grants, tuition waivers (full and partial), and unspecified assistantships available. Support available to part-time students. Financial award application deadline: 2/1; financial award applicants required to submit FAFSA. In 2006, 15 master's, 10 doctorates awarded. *Degree program information:* Part-time programs available. Offers accompanying and chamber music (MM); chamber music (DMA); composition (MM, DMA); instrumental conducting (MM, DMA); liturgical music (M Lit M, DMA); music (M Lit M, MA, MM, MMSM, DMA, PhD); music education (MM, DMA); musicology (MA, PhD); orchestral instruments (MM, DMA); performance (MM, DMA); piano pedagogy (MM, DMA); vocal accompanying (DMA); vocal pedagogy (MM); vocal performance (MM); voice pedagogy and performance (DMA). *Application deadline:* For fall admission, 2/1 priority date for domestic students; for spring admission, 11/15 priority date for domestic students. Applications are processed on a rolling basis. *Application fee:* $55. Electronic applications accepted. *Application Contact:* Christine Mica, Director, University Admissions, 202-319-5305, Fax: 202-319-6533, E-mail: cua-admissions@cua.edu. *Dean,* Murry Sidlin, 202-319-5414, Fax: 202-319-6280, E-mail: cua-music@cua.edu.

Columbus School of Law *Degree program information:* Part-time and evening/weekend programs available. Offers law (JD). Electronic applications accepted.

National Catholic School of Social Service Students: 101 full-time (87 women), 136 part-time (112 women); includes 36 minority (26 African Americans, 4 Asian Americans or Pacific Islanders, 6 Hispanic Americans), 6 international. Average age 34. 178 applicants, 80% accepted, 94 enrolled. *Faculty:* 17 full-time (15 women), 22 part-time/adjunct (19 women). Expenses: Contact institution. *Financial support:* Fellowships, career-related internships or fieldwork, Federal Work-Study, scholarships/grants, and unspecified assistantships available. Support available to part-time students. Financial award application deadline: 2/1; financial award applicants required to submit FAFSA. In 2006, 71 master's, 4 doctorates awarded. *Degree program information:* Part-time programs available. Offers social service (MSW, PhD). *Application deadline:* For fall admission, 2/1 priority date for domestic students; for spring admission, 11/15 priority date for domestic students. Applications are processed on a rolling basis. *Application fee:* $55. Electronic applications accepted. *Application Contact:* Christine Mica, Director, University Admissions, 202-319-5305, Fax: 202-319-6533, E-mail: cua-admissions@cua.edu. *Dean,* Dr. James R. Zabora, 202-319-5454, Fax: 202-319-5093, E-mail: zabora@cua.edu.

School of Architecture and Planning Students: 84 full-time (39 women), 21 part-time (6 women); includes 20 minority (6 African Americans, 7 Asian Americans or Pacific Islanders, 7 Hispanic Americans), 6 international. Average age 27. 127 applicants, 90% accepted, 52 enrolled. *Faculty:* 16 full-time (3 women), 25 part-time/adjunct (7 women). Expenses: Contact institution. *Financial support:* Teaching assistantships, Federal Work-Study, scholarships/grants, tuition waivers (partial), and unspecified assistantships available. Financial award application deadline: 2/1; financial award applicants required to submit FAFSA. In 2006, 36 degrees awarded. *Degree program information:* Part-time programs available. Offers architecture and planning (M Arch, M Arch Studies). *Application deadline:* For fall admission, 2/1 priority date for domestic students; for spring admission, 11/15 priority date for domestic students. Applications are processed on a rolling basis. *Application fee:* $55. Electronic applications accepted. *Application Contact:* Christine Mica, Director, University Admissions, 202-319-5305, Fax: 202-319-6533, E-mail: cua-admissions@cua.edu. *Dean,* Randall Ott, 202-319-5784, Fax: 202-319-5188, E-mail: ott@cua.edu.

School of Arts and Sciences Students: 177 full-time (97 women), 392 part-time (205 women); includes 82 minority (39 African Americans, 14 Asian Americans or Pacific Islanders, 29 Hispanic Americans), 58 international. Average age 33. 723 applicants, 53% accepted, 150 enrolled. *Faculty:* 146 full-time (54 women), 102 part-time/adjunct (56 women). Expenses: Contact institution. *Financial support:* Fellowships, research assistantships, teaching assistantships, career-related internships or fieldwork, Federal Work-Study, institutionally sponsored loans, scholarships/grants, tuition waivers (full and partial), and unspecified assistantships available. Support available to part-time students. Financial award application deadline: 2/1; financial award applicants required to submit FAFSA. In 2006, 89 master's, 35 doctorates awarded. *Degree program information:* Part-time and evening/weekend programs available. Offers acting, directing, and playwriting (MFA); administration, curriculum, and policy studies (MA); American government (MA, PhD); anthropology (MA, PhD); applied experimental psychology (MA, PhD); arts and sciences (MA, MFA, MS, MTS, PhD, Certificate); Byzantine studies (MA, Certificate); Catholic school leadership (MA); cell and microbial biology (MS, PhD); chemistry (MS); classics (MA); clinical laboratory science (MS, PhD); clinical psychology (PhD); comparative literature (MA, PhD); congressional studies (MA); counselor education (MA); early Christian studies (MA, PhD, Certificate); educational administration (PhD); educational psychology (PhD); English as a second language (MA); English language and literature (MA, PhD); French (MA, PhD); general psychology (MA, PhD); Greek and Latin (PhD); history (MA, PhD); human development (PhD); human factors (MA); international affairs (MA); international political economics (MA); Irish studies (MA); Italian (MA); Latin (MA); learning and instruction (MA); medieval studies (MA, PhD, Certificate); physics (MS, PhD); policy studies (PhD); political theory (MA, PhD); rhetoric (MA, PhD); Romance languages and literatures (MA, PhD); Semitic and Egyptian languages and literature (MA, PhD); sociology (MA, PhD); Spanish (MA, PhD); teacher education (MA); theatre history and criticism (MA); world politics (MA, PhD). *Application deadline:* For fall admission, 2/1 priority date for domestic students; for spring admission, 11/15 priority date for domestic students. Applications are processed on a rolling basis. *Application fee:* $55. Electronic applications accepted. *Application Contact:* Christine Mica, Director, University Admissions, 202-319-5305, Fax: 202-319-6533, E-mail: cua-admissions@cua.edu. *Dean,* Dr. Lawrence R. Poos, 202-319-5114, Fax: 202-319-6076, E-mail: poos@cua.edu.

School of Canon Law Students: 30 full-time (3 women), 27 part-time (7 women); includes 6 minority (2 African Americans, 1 Asian American or Pacific Islander, 3 Hispanic Americans), 9 international. Average age 42. 42 applicants, 81% accepted, 22 enrolled. *Faculty:* 6 full-time (1 woman). Expenses: Contact institution. *Financial support:* Fellowships, research assistantships, teaching assistantships, career-related internships or fieldwork, Federal Work-Study, scholarships/grants, tuition waivers (full and partial), and unspecified assistantships available. Support available to part-time students. Financial award application deadline: 2/1; financial award applicants required to submit FAFSA. Offers canon law (JCD, JCL). *Application deadline:* For fall admission, 2/1 priority date for domestic students; for spring admission, 11/15 priority date for domestic students. Applications are processed on a rolling basis. *Application fee:* $55. Electronic applications accepted. *Dean,* Rev. Msgr. Brian Ferme, 202-319-5492, Fax: 202-319-4187, E-mail: ferme@cua.edu.

School of Engineering Students: 33 full-time (10 women), 98 part-time (25 women); includes 22 minority (8 African Americans, 1 American Indian/Alaska Native, 7 Asian Americans or Pacific Islanders, 6 Hispanic Americans), 31 international. Average age 33. 170 applicants, 61% accepted, 37 enrolled. *Faculty:* 25 full-time (2 women), 18 part-time/adjunct (2 women). Expenses: Contact institution. *Financial support:* Fellowships, research assistantships, teaching assistantships, career-related internships or fieldwork, Federal Work-Study, scholarships/grants, tuition waivers (full and partial), and unspecified assistantships available. Support available to part-time students. Financial award application deadline: 2/1; financial award applicants required to submit FAFSA. In 2006, 37 master's, 3 doctorates awarded. *Degree program information:* Part-time and evening/weekend programs available. Offers biomedical engineering (MBE, MS Engr, D Engr, PhD); civil engineering (MCE, D Engr, PhD); construction management (MCE, MS Engr, PhD); design (D Engr, PhD); design and robotics (MME, D Engr, PhD); electrical engineering and computer science (MEE, MS Engr, MSCS, D Engr, PhD); engineering (MBE, MCE, MEE, MME, MS Engr, MSCS, D Engr, PhD); engineering management (MS Engr); environmental engineering (MCE, MS Engr); fluid mechanics and thermal science (MME, D Engr, PhD); geotechnical engineering (MCE); mechanical design (MME); ocean and structural acoustics (MME, MS Engr, PhD); structures and structural mechanics (MCE). *Application deadline:* For fall admission, 2/1 priority date for domestic students; for spring admission, 11/15 priority date for domestic students. Applications are processed on a rolling basis. *Application fee:* $55. Electronic applications accepted. *Application Contact:* Christine Mica, Director, University Admissions, 202-319-5305, Fax: 202-319-6533, E-mail: cua-admissions@cua.edu. *Dean,* Dr. Charles C. Nguyen, 202-319-5160, Fax: 202-319-4499, E-mail: nguyen@cua.edu.

School of Library and Information Science Students: 36 full-time (33 women), 207 part-time (166 women); includes 26 minority (17 African Americans, 2 Asian Americans or Pacific Islanders, 7 Hispanic Americans), 3 international. Average age 35. 155 applicants, 86% accepted, 64 enrolled. *Faculty:* 7 full-time (5 women), 19 part-time/adjunct (9 women). Expenses: Contact institution. *Financial support:* Fellowships, research assistantships, career-related internships or fieldwork, Federal Work-Study, scholarships/grants, tuition waivers (full and partial), and unspecified assistantships available. Support available to part-time students. Financial award application deadline: 2/1; financial award applicants required to submit FAFSA. In 2006, 80 degrees awarded. *Degree program information:* Part-time and evening/weekend programs available. Postbaccalaureate distance learning degree programs offered (minimal on-campus study). Offers library and information science (MSLS). *Application deadline:* For fall admission, 2/1 priority date for domestic students; for spring admission, 11/15 priority date for domestic students. Applications are processed on a rolling basis. *Application fee:* $55. Electronic applications accepted. *Dean,* Dr. Martha L. Hale, 202-319-5085, Fax: 202-319-5574, E-mail: halem@cua.edu.

School of Nursing Students: 27 full-time (25 women), 58 part-time (57 women); includes 31 minority (20 African Americans, 6 Asian Americans or Pacific Islanders, 5 Hispanic Americans), 6 international. Average age 43. 38 applicants, 76% accepted, 15 enrolled. *Faculty:* 17 full-time (all women), 19 part-time/adjunct (18 women). Expenses: Contact institution. *Financial support:* Research assistantships, teaching assistantships, career-related internships or fieldwork, Federal Work-Study, scholarships/grants, tuition waivers (full and partial), and unspecified assistantships available. Support available to part-time students. Financial award application deadline: 2/1; financial award applicants required to submit FAFSA. In 2006, 15 master's, 7 doctorates awarded. *Degree program information:* Part-time programs available. Offers advanced practice nursing (MSN); clinical nursing (DN Sc). *Application deadline:* For fall admission, 2/1 priority date for domestic students; for spring admission, 11/15 priority date for domestic students. Applications are processed on a rolling basis. *Application fee:* $55. Electronic applications accepted. *Dean,* Dr. Nalini Jairath, 202-319-5403, Fax: 202-319-6485, E-mail: jairath@cua.edu.

School of Philosophy Students: 41 full-time (6 women), 77 part-time (16 women); includes 1 minority (Asian American or Pacific Islander), 16 international. Average age 33. 89 applicants, 58% accepted, 28 enrolled. *Faculty:* 16 full-time (3 women), 22 part-time/adjunct (5 women). Expenses: Contact institution. *Financial support:* Fellowships, career-related internships or fieldwork, Federal Work-Study, scholarships/grants, tuition waivers (full and partial), and unspecified assistantships available. Support available to part-time students. Financial award application deadline: 2/1; financial award applicants required to submit FAFSA. In 2006, 19 master's, 5 doctorates awarded. *Degree program information:* Part-time programs available. Offers philosophy (MA, PhD, Ph L). *Application deadline:* For fall admission, 2/1 priority date for domestic students; for spring admission, 11/15 priority date for domestic students. Applications are processed on a rolling basis. *Application fee:* $55. Electronic applications accepted. *Dean,* Rev. Kurt Pritzl, OP, 202-319-5259, Fax: 202-319-4731, E-mail: pritzl@cua.edu.

School of Theology and Religious Studies Students: 161 full-time (19 women), 168 part-time (48 women); includes 27 minority (11 African Americans, 10 Asian Americans or Pacific Islanders, 6 Hispanic Americans), 64 international. Average age 34. 246 applicants, 81% accepted, 95 enrolled. *Faculty:* 40 full-time (6 women), 8 part-time/adjunct (3 women). Expenses: Contact institution. *Financial support:* Fellowships, research assistantships, teaching assistantships, career-related internships or fieldwork, Federal Work-Study, scholarships/grants, tuition waivers (full and partial), and unspecified assistantships available. Support available to part-time students. Financial award application deadline: 2/1; financial award applicants required to submit FAFSA. In 2006, 9 M Divs, 17 master's, 13 doctorates awarded. *Degree program information:* Part-time programs available. Offers religious studies (M Div, STB, MA, MRE, D Min, PhD, STD, STL). *Application deadline:* For fall admission, 2/1 priority date for domestic students; for spring admission, 11/15 priority date for domestic students.

The Catholic University of America (continued)

Applications are processed on a rolling basis. *Application fee:* $55. Electronic applications accepted. *Dean,* Msgr. Kevin W. Irwin, 202-319-5683, Fax: 202-319-4967, E-mail: irwin@cua.edu.

CEDAR CREST COLLEGE, Allentown, PA 18104-6196

General Information Independent-religious, women only, comprehensive institution.

GRADUATE UNITS

Department of Education Offers education (M Ed).

Program in Forensic Science Offers forensic science (MS).

CEDARVILLE UNIVERSITY, Cedarville, OH 45314-0601

General Information Independent-religious, coed, comprehensive institution. *Enrollment:* 3,112 graduate, professional, and undergraduate students; 36 part-time matriculated graduate/professional students (24 women). *Enrollment by degree level:* 36 master's. *Graduate faculty:* 13 part-time/adjunct (2 women). *Tuition:* Part-time $298 per hour. *Graduate housing:* Room and/or apartments available on a first-come, first-served basis to single students; on-campus housing not available to married students. Housing application deadline: 5/1. *Student services:* Campus safety program, career counseling, exercise/wellness program, free psychological counseling. *Library facilities:* Centennial Library. *Online resources:* library catalog, web page, access to other libraries' catalogs. *Collection:* 170,561 titles, 6,400 serial subscriptions, 15,868 audiovisual materials.

Computer facilities: Computer purchase and lease plans are available. 30 computers available on campus for general student use. A campuswide network can be accessed from student residence rooms and from off campus. Internet access and online class registration, software packages are available. *Web address:* http://www.cedarville.edu/.

General Application Contact: Roscoe Smith, Admissions Director, 937-766-7700, Fax: 937-766-7575, E-mail: smithr@cedarville.edu.

GRADUATE UNITS

Graduate Programs Average age 33. 16 applicants, 94% accepted, 15 enrolled. *Faculty:* 13 part-time/adjunct (2 women). Expenses: Contact institution. *Financial support:* Scholarships/grants available. Support available to part-time students. Financial award applicants required to submit FAFSA. In 2006, 3 degrees awarded. *Degree program information:* Part-time and evening/weekend programs available. *Application deadline:* Applications are processed on a rolling basis. *Application fee:* $30. Electronic applications accepted. *Application Contact:* Roscoe Smith, Admissions Director, 937-766-7700, Fax: 937-766-7575, E-mail: smithr@cedarville.edu. *Director of Graduate Recruitment,* Bruce Traeger, 888-CEDARVILLE, Fax: 937-66-7575, E-mail: traegerb@cedarville.edu.

CENTENARY COLLEGE, Hackettstown, NJ 07840-2100

General Information Independent-religious, coed, comprehensive institution. *Graduate housing:* Room and/or apartments available on a first-come, first-served basis to single students; on-campus housing not available to married students. Housing application deadline: 6/1.

GRADUATE UNITS

Program in Business Administration *Degree program information:* Part-time and evening/weekend programs available. Postbaccalaureate distance learning degree programs offered (minimal on-campus study). Offers business administration (MBA).

Program in Counseling Psychology *Degree program information:* Part-time and evening/weekend programs available. Postbaccalaureate distance learning degree programs offered (minimal on-campus study). Offers counseling (MA); counseling psychology (MA).

Program in Education *Degree program information:* Part-time and evening/weekend programs available. Postbaccalaureate distance learning degree programs offered (minimal on-campus study). Offers instructional leadership (MA); special education (MA).

Program in Professional Accounting *Degree program information:* Part-time and evening/weekend programs available. Postbaccalaureate distance learning degree programs offered (minimal on-campus study). Offers professional accounting (MS).

CENTENARY COLLEGE OF LOUISIANA, Shreveport, LA 71104

General Information Independent-religious, coed, comprehensive institution. *Graduate housing:* Rooms and/or apartments available on a first-come, first-served basis to single students and available to married students.

GRADUATE UNITS

Graduate Programs *Degree program information:* Part-time and evening/weekend programs available. Offers administration (M Ed); elementary education (MAT); secondary education (MAT); supervision of instruction (M Ed).

Frost School of Business *Degree program information:* Part-time and evening/weekend programs available. Offers business (MBA).

CENTRAL BAPTIST THEOLOGICAL SEMINARY, Shawnee, KS 66226

General Information Independent-religious, coed, graduate-only institution. *Enrollment by degree level:* 79 first professional, 14 master's, 6 other advanced degrees. *Graduate faculty:* 3 full-time (0 women), 10 part-time/adjunct (4 women). *Tuition:* Part-time $330 per credit hour. *Required fees:* $150 per semester. *Graduate housing:* On-campus housing not available. *Student services:* Campus employment opportunities, career counseling, low-cost health insurance. *Library facilities:* Pratt-Journeycake Library. *Online resources:* library catalog, access to other libraries' catalogs. *Collection:* 104,621 titles, 337 serial subscriptions, 2,716 audiovisual materials.

Computer facilities: 13 computers available on campus for general student use. A campuswide network can be accessed. Internet access is available. *Web address:* http://www.cbts.edu/.

General Application Contact: Steve Guinn, Director of Enrollment Services, 913-667-5707, Fax: 913-371-8110, E-mail: sguinn@cbts.edu.

GRADUATE UNITS

Graduate and Professional Programs Students: 54 full-time (25 women), 45 part-time (24 women); includes 32 minority (26 African Americans, 4 American Indian/Alaska Native, 1 Asian American or Pacific Islander, 1 Hispanic American), 2 international. Average age 42. 46 applicants, 48% accepted, 21 enrolled. *Faculty:* 3 full-time (0 women), 10 part-time/adjunct (4 women). Expenses: Contact institution. *Financial support:* In 2006–07, 33 students received support. Career-related internships or fieldwork, scholarships/grants, and tuition waivers (full and partial) available. Support available to part-time students. Financial award application deadline: 6/21; financial award applicants required to submit FAFSA. In 2006, 18 M Divs, 4 master's awarded. *Degree program information:* Part-time programs available. Offers Christian spirituality (MA); missional church studies (MA); theological studies (MA); theology (M Div, Diploma). *Application deadline:* For fall admission, 8/3 priority date for domestic students; for winter admission, 12/7 priority date for domestic students; for spring admission, 1/4 priority date for domestic students. Applications are processed on a rolling basis. *Application fee:* $0. Electronic applications accepted. *Application Contact:* Steve Guinn, Director of Enrollment Services, 913-667-5707, Fax: 913-371-8110, E-mail: sguinn@cbts.edu. *Dean and Vice President for Administration,* Dr. L. Dean Allen, 913-667-5712, Fax: 913-371-8110, E-mail: dallen@cbts.edu.

CENTRAL CONNECTICUT STATE UNIVERSITY, New Britain, CT 06050-4010

General Information State-supported, coed, comprehensive institution. CGS member. *Enrollment:* 12,144 graduate, professional, and undergraduate students; 536 full-time matriculated graduate/professional students (351 women), 1,595 part-time matriculated graduate/professional students (1,047 women). *Enrollment by degree level:* 1,622 master's, 42 doctoral, 467 other advanced degrees. *Graduate faculty:* 332 full-time (140 women), 415 part-time/adjunct (197 women). *Tuition, area resident:* Full-time $3,970; part-time $380 per credit. Tuition, state resident: full-time $5,955; part-time $380 per credit. Tuition, nonresident: full-time $11,061; part-time $380 per credit. *Required fees:* $3,189. One-time fee: $62 part-time. Tuition and fees vary according to degree level and program. *Graduate housing:* Room and/or apartments available on a first-come, first-served basis to single students; on-campus housing not available to married students. Typical cost: $4,492 per year ($7,890 including board). Housing application deadline: 4/1. *Student services:* Campus employment opportunities, campus safety program, career counseling, child daycare facilities, disabled student services, exercise/wellness program, free psychological counseling, international student services, low-cost health insurance, multicultural affairs office, teacher training, writing training. *Library facilities:* Burritt Library plus 1 other. *Online resources:* library catalog, web page, access to other libraries' catalogs. *Collection:* 688,604 titles, 2,705 serial subscriptions, 8,169 audiovisual materials.

Computer facilities: 880 computers available on campus for general student use. A campuswide network can be accessed from student residence rooms and from off campus. Internet access is available. *Web address:* http://www.ccsu.edu/.

General Application Contact: Patricia Gardner, Graduate Admissions, 860-832-2350, Fax: 860-832-2362, E-mail: graduateadmissions@mail.ccsu.edu.

GRADUATE UNITS

School of Graduate Studies Students: 536 full-time (351 women), 1,595 part-time (1,047 women); includes 229 minority (84 African Americans, 6 American Indian/Alaska Native, 48 Asian Americans or Pacific Islanders, 91 Hispanic Americans), 70 international. Average age 33. 1,266 applicants, 64% accepted, 531 enrolled. *Faculty:* 332 full-time (140 women), 415 part-time/adjunct (197 women). Expenses: Contact institution. *Financial support:* In 2006–07, 102 students received support, including 51 research assistantships (averaging $4,800 per year); career-related internships or fieldwork, Federal Work-Study, scholarships/grants, and unspecified assistantships also available. Support available to part-time students. Financial award application deadline: 3/1; financial award applicants required to submit FAFSA. In 2006, 669 master's, 18 doctorates, 100 other advanced degrees awarded. *Degree program information:* Part-time and evening/weekend programs available. *Application deadline:* For fall admission, 7/1 for domestic students; for spring admission, 12/1 for domestic students. Applications are processed on a rolling basis. *Application fee:* $50. Electronic applications accepted. *Application Contact:* Diane Abraham, Graduate Admissions, 860-832-2350, Fax: 860-832-2362, E-mail: graduateadmissions@mail.ccsu.edu. *Graduate Admissions,* Patricia Gardner, 860-832-2350, Fax: 860-832-2362, E-mail: graduateadmissions@mail.ccsu.edu.

School of Arts and Sciences Students: 269 full-time (166 women), 502 part-time (291 women); includes 90 minority (24 African Americans, 2 American Indian/Alaska Native, 30 Asian Americans or Pacific Islanders, 34 Hispanic Americans), 43 international. Average age 33. 525 applicants, 65% accepted, 205 enrolled. *Faculty:* 217 full-time (91 women), 297 part-time/adjunct (136 women). Expenses: Contact institution. *Financial support:* In 2006–07, 61 students received support, including 27 research assistantships (averaging $4,800 per year); career-related internships or fieldwork, Federal Work-Study, scholarships/grants, and unspecified assistantships also available. Support available to part-time students. Financial award application deadline: 3/1; financial award applicants required to submit FAFSA. In 2006, 186 master's, 23 other advanced degrees awarded. *Degree program information:* Part-time and evening/weekend programs available. Offers anesthesia (MS); art education (MS, Certificate); arts and sciences (MA, MS, Certificate); biological sciences (MA, MS); biology (Certificate); community psychology (MA); computer information technology (MS); criminal justice (MS); earth science (MS); English (MA, Certificate); French (MA); general health (MS); general psychology (MA); geography (MS); graphic information design (MA); health psychology (MA); history (MA, Certificate); international studies (MS); Italian (Certificate); mathematics (MA, MS, Certificate); modern language (MA, Certificate); music education (MS, Certificate); natural sciences (MS); organizational communication (MS); physics (MS); public history (MA); Spanish (MA, MS, Certificate); Spanish language and Hispanic culture (MA); teaching English to speakers of other languages (Certificate). *Application deadline:* For fall admission, 7/1 for domestic students; for spring admission, 12/1 for domestic students. Applications are processed on a rolling basis. *Application fee:* $50. Electronic applications accepted. *Application Contact:* Dr. Paul Altieri, Assistant to the Dean, 860-832-2600. *Dean,* Dr. Susan Pease, 860-832-2600.

School of Business Students: 19 full-time (14 women), 53 part-time (24 women); includes 5 minority (2 African Americans, 1 Asian American or Pacific Islander, 2 Hispanic Americans), 7 international. Average age 32. 29 applicants, 28% accepted, 6 enrolled. *Faculty:* 12 full-time (3 women), 8 part-time/adjunct (2 women). Expenses: Contact institution. *Financial support:* In 2006–07, 2 students received support, including 1 research assistantship (averaging $4,800 per year); career-related internships or fieldwork, Federal Work-Study, scholarships/grants, and unspecified assistantships also available. Support available to part-time students. Financial award application deadline: 3/1; financial award applicants required to submit FAFSA. In 2006, 29 master's, 1 other advanced degree awarded. *Degree program information:* Part-time and evening/weekend programs available. Offers business (MBA, MS, Certificate); business education (MS, Certificate); international business administration (MBA). *Application deadline:* For fall admission, 7/1 for domestic students; for spring admission, 12/1 for domestic students. Applications are processed on a rolling basis. *Application fee:* $50. Electronic applications accepted. *Acting Dean,* Dr. Christopher Galligan, 860-832-3205.

School of Education and Professional Studies Students: 212 full-time (163 women), 927 part-time (709 women); includes 106 minority (49 African Americans, 3 American Indian/Alaska Native, 6 Asian Americans or Pacific Islanders, 48 Hispanic Americans), 9 international. Average age 33. 635 applicants, 62% accepted, 283 enrolled. *Faculty:* 63 full-time (38 women), 76 part-time/adjunct (53 women). Expenses: Contact institution. *Financial support:* In 2006–07, 32 students received support, including 19 research assistantships (averaging $4,800 per year); career-related internships or fieldwork, Federal Work-Study, scholarships/grants, and unspecified assistantships also available. Support available to part-time students. Financial award application deadline: 3/1; financial award applicants required to submit FAFSA. In 2006, 404 master's, 18 doctorates, 75 other advanced degrees awarded. *Degree program information:* Part-time and evening/weekend programs available. Offers early childhood education (MS); education and professional studies (MS, Ed D, Certificate, Sixth Year Certificate); educational foundations policy/secondary education (MS); educational leadership (MS, Ed D, Sixth Year Certificate); educational technology and media (MS); elementary education (MS, Certificate); marriage and family therapy (MS); physical education (MS, Certificate); professional counseling (MS, Certificate); reading (MS, Sixth Year Certificate); school counseling (MS); special education for special educators (MS); special education for teachers certified in areas other than education (MS); student development in higher education (MS). *Application deadline:* For fall admission, 7/1 for domestic students; for spring admission, 12/1 for domestic students. Applications are processed on a rolling basis. *Application fee:* $50. Electronic applications accepted. *Acting Dean,* Dr. Mitchell Sakofs, 860-832-2100.

School of Technology Students: 36 full-time (8 women), 113 part-time (23 women); includes 28 minority (9 African Americans, 1 American Indian/Alaska Native, 11 Asian Americans or Pacific Islanders, 7 Hispanic Americans), 11 international. Average age 34. 77 applicants, 79% accepted, 37 enrolled. *Faculty:* 40 full-time (8 women), 34 part-time/adjunct (6 women). Expenses: Contact institution. *Financial support:* In 2006–07, 7 students received support, including 4 research assistantships (averaging $4,800 per year); career-related internships or fieldwork, Federal Work-Study, scholarships/grants, and unspecified assistantships also available. Support available to part-time students. Financial award application deadline: 3/1; financial award applicants required to submit FAFSA. In 2006, 50 master's, 1 other advanced degree awarded. *Degree program information:* Part-time and evening/weekend programs available. Offers biomolecular sciences (MA); engineering technology (MS); technology (MA, MS, Certificate); technology education (MS, Certificate); technology management (MS). *Application deadline:* For fall admission, 7/1 for domestic students; for spring admission, 12/1 for domestic students. Applications are processed on a rolling basis.

Application fee: $50. Electronic applications accepted. *Application Contact:* Dr. Olusegun Odesina, Information Contact, 860-832-1800. *Dean,* Dr. Zdzislaw Kremens, 860-832-1800.

CENTRAL EUROPEAN UNIVERSITY, H-1051 Budapest, Hungary

General Information Independent, coed, graduate-only institution. CGS member. *Enrollment by degree level:* 619 master's, 394 doctoral. *Graduate faculty:* 95 full-time (30 women), 64 part-time/adjunct (13 women). *Graduate housing:* Room and/or apartments available to single students; on-campus housing not available to married students. *Student services:* Campus employment opportunities, campus safety program, career counseling, disabled student services, free psychological counseling, grant writing training, international student services, low-cost health insurance, multicultural affairs office, writing training. *Library facilities:* Central European University Library. *Online resources:* library catalog, web page, access to other libraries' catalogs. *Collection:* 190,000 titles, 1,650 serial subscriptions, 600 audiovisual materials. *Research affiliation:* Institute of Human Sciences Vienna (social sciences), Open Society Institute, NY.

Computer facilities: 500 computers available on campus for general student use. A campuswide network can be accessed from student residence rooms and from off campus. Internet access and online class registration, laptop area, PC in dormitory rooms are available. *Web address:* http://www.ceu.hu/.

General Application Contact: Zsuzsanna Jaszberenyi, Admissions Officer, 361-327-3009, Fax: 361-327-3211, E-mail: admissions@ceu.hu.

GRADUATE UNITS

CEU Business School Students: 47 full-time (18 women), 158 part-time (22 women). Average age 32. 450 applicants, 43% accepted, 160 enrolled. *Faculty:* 15 full-time (3 women), 30 part-time/adjunct (9 women). Expenses: Contact institution. *Financial support:* In 2006–07, 4 students received support, including research assistantships with partial tuition reimbursements available (averaging $3,800 per year); tuition waivers (partial) and GMAT-based tuition fee discounts also available. In 2006, 77 degrees awarded. *Degree program information:* Part-time and evening/weekend programs available. Offers finance (MBA); general management (MBA); information technology (M Sc); information technology management (MBA); management (EMBA); marketing (MBA); real estate management (MBA). *Application deadline:* For fall admission, 5/22 priority date for domestic students, 5/22 for international students; for winter admission, 11/13 priority date for domestic students, 11/13 for international students. Applications are processed on a rolling basis. *Application fee:* $0. Electronic applications accepted. *Application Contact:* Tunde Hegedus, MBA Program Manager, 36-18875060, Fax: 36-18875133, E-mail: mba@ceubusiness.com. *Dean and Managing Director,* Dr. Paul Garrison, 36-18875050, Fax: 36-18875001, E-mail: garrisonp@ceubusiness.com.

Graduate Studies Students: 968 full-time (481 women), 45 part-time (10 women). Average age 25. 2,500 applicants, 31% accepted, 550 enrolled. *Faculty:* 95 full-time (30 women), 64 part-time/adjunct (13 women). Expenses: Contact institution. *Financial support:* In 2006–07, 582 students received support, including 480 fellowships with full and partial tuition reimbursements available (averaging $5,000 per year); career-related internships or fieldwork, institutionally sponsored loans, scholarships/grants, and tuition waivers (full and partial) also available. Financial award application deadline: 1/6. In 2006, 389 master's, 25 doctorates awarded. Offers comparative constitutional law (LL M); economic and legal studies (LL M, MA); environmental sciences and policy (MS, PhD); history (MA, PhD); human rights (LL M, MA); international business law (LL M); legal studies (SJD). *Application deadline:* For fall admission, 1/15 priority date for domestic and international students. Electronic applications accepted. *Application Contact:* Zsuzsanna Jaszberenyi, Admissions Officer, 361-324-3009, Fax: 367-327-3211, E-mail: admissions@ceu.hu. *Provost,* Dr. Howard Michael Robinson, 361-327-3003, Fax: 361-327-3211, E-mail: robinson@ceu.hu.

School of Social Sciences and Humanities Students: 680 full-time (326 women). Average age 26. 2,500 applicants, 31% accepted, 550 enrolled. *Faculty:* 75 full-time (25 women), 46 part-time/adjunct (10 women). Expenses: Contact institution. *Financial support:* In 2006–07, 402 students received support, including 350 fellowships with full and partial tuition reimbursements available (averaging $5,000 per year); career-related internships or fieldwork, institutionally sponsored loans, and scholarships/grants also available. Financial award application deadline: 1/5. Offers economics (MA, PhD); gender studies (MA, PhD); international relations and European studies (MA, PhD); mathematics and its applications (MS, PhD); medieval studies (MA, PhD); nationalism studies (MA, PhD); philosophy (MA, PhD); political science (MA, PhD); public policy (MA, PhD); sociology and social anthropology (MA, PhD). *Application deadline:* For fall admission, 1/15 priority date for domestic and international students. *Application fee:* $0. Electronic applications accepted. *Application Contact:* Zsuzsanna Jaszberenyi, Admissions Officer, 361-327-3009, Fax: 361-327-3211, E-mail: admissions@ceu.hu. *Provost,* Dr. Howard Michael Robinson, 361-327-3003, Fax: 361-327-3211, E-mail: robinson@ceu.hu.

CENTRAL METHODIST UNIVERSITY, Fayette, MO 65248-1198

General Information Independent-religious, coed, comprehensive institution. *Graduate housing:* Rooms and/or apartments available on a first-come, first-served basis to single and married students. Housing application deadline: 5/1.

GRADUATE UNITS

College of Graduate and Extended Studies *Degree program information:* Part-time and evening/weekend programs available. Postbaccalaureate distance learning degree programs offered (no on-campus study). Electronic applications accepted.

CENTRAL MICHIGAN UNIVERSITY, Mount Pleasant, MI 48859

General Information State-supported, coed, university. CGS member. *Graduate housing:* Rooms and/or apartments available on a first-come, first-served basis to single and married students. *Research affiliation:* Dow Chemical (chemistry), Dow Corning (chemistry), Dendritic Nanotechnologies Inc (chemistry/physics), IBM (information technology), SAP (information technology).

GRADUATE UNITS

Central Michigan University Off-Campus Programs Average age 38. *Faculty:* 1,122 part-time/adjunct. Expenses: Contact institution. *Financial support:* In 2006–07, 3,820 students received support. Scholarships/grants available. Support available to part-time students. Financial award application deadline: 6/11; financial award applicants required to submit FAFSA. In 2006, 1,704 master's, 75 doctorates, 73 other advanced degrees awarded. *Degree program information:* Part-time and evening/weekend programs available. Postbaccalaureate distance learning degree programs offered (no on-campus study). Offers acquisitions administration (MSA, Certificate); counseling (MA); education (MA); educational administration (Ed S); educational administration and community leadership (Ed D); educational technology (MA); general administration (MSA, Certificate); health administration (DHA); health services administration (MSA, Certificate); human resources administration (MSA, Certificate); humanities (MA); information resource management (MSA, Certificate); international administration (MSA, Certificate); leadership (MSA, Certificate); public administration (MSA, Certificate); reading and literacy (MA); school principalship (MA); software engineering administration (MSA, Certificate); sport administration (MA); vehicle design and manufacturing administration (MSA, Certificate). *Application deadline:* Applications are processed on a rolling basis. *Application fee:* $50. Electronic applications accepted. *Application Contact:* Off-Campus Programs Call Center, 877-268-4636, Fax: 989-774-2461, E-mail: cmuoffcampus@cmich.edu. *Vice President and Executive Director,* Dr. Merodie Hancock, 989-774-3865, Fax: 989-774-3542.

College of Graduate Studies *Degree program information:* Part-time and evening/weekend programs available. Postbaccalaureate distance learning degree programs offered (no on-campus study). Offers acquisitions administration (MSA); general administration (MSA); health services administration (MSA); hospitality and tourism administration (MSA); human resources administration (MSA); information resource management (MSA); international administration (MSA); leadership (MSA); long-term care administration (MSA); organizational communication (MSA); public administration (MSA); recreation and park administration (MSA); sport administration (MSA).

College of Business Administration *Degree program information:* Part-time programs available. Offers accounting (MBA); business administration (MA, MBA, MBE, MS); business education (MBE); economics (MA); finance and law (MBA); information systems (MS); management (MBA); marketing and hospitality services administration (MBA).

College of Communication and Fine Arts Offers art (MA, MFA); broadcast and cinematic arts (MA); communication and fine arts (MA, MFA, MM); interpersonal and public communication (MA); music education and supervision (MM); music performance (MM); oral interpretation (MA); theatre (MA).

College of Education and Human Services Offers community leadership (MA); counseling (MA); education and human services (MA, MS, Ed D, Ed S); educational administration (MA, Ed S); educational leadership (Ed D); educational technology (MA); elementary education (MA); human development and family studies (MA); library, media, and technology (MA); middle level education (MA); nutrition and dietetics (MS); professional counseling (MA); reading improvement (MA); recreation and park administration (MA); school counseling (MA); school principalship (MA); secondary education (MA); special education (MA); teaching senior high (MA); therapeutic recreation (MA).

College of Humanities and Social and Behavioral Sciences *Degree program information:* Evening/weekend programs available. Offers applied experimental psychology (PhD); clinical psychology (PhD); composition and communication (MA); creative writing (MA); English language and literature (MA); general, applied, and experimental psychology (MS, PhD); general/experimental psychology (MS); history (MA, PhD); humanities and social and behavioral sciences (MA, MPA, MS, PhD, S Psy S); industrial/organizational psychology (MA, PhD); political science (MA); public administration (MPA); public management (MPA); school psychology (PhD, S Psy S); social and criminal justice (MA); sociology (MA); Spanish (MA); state and local government (MPA); teaching English to speakers of other languages (MA).

College of Science and Technology *Degree program information:* Part-time programs available. Offers biology (MS); chemistry (MS); computer science (MS); conservation biology (MS); industrial education (MA); industrial management and technology (MA); mathematics (MA, MAT, PhD); physics (MS); science and technology (MA, MAT, MS, PhD); teaching chemistry (MA).

The Herbert H. and Grace A. Dow College of Health Professions Offers athletic administration (MA); audiology (Au D); coaching (MA); exercise science (MA); health professions (MA, MS, Au D, DPT); health promotion and program management (MA); physical therapy (DPT); physician assistant (MS); speech and language pathology (MA); sport administration (MA); teaching (MA).

Interdisciplinary Programs Offers humanities (MA); interdisciplinary studies (MA, MSA).

CENTRAL STATE UNIVERSITY, Wilberforce, OH 45384

General Information State-supported, coed, comprehensive institution. *Graduate housing:* Room and/or apartments available on a first-come, first-served basis to single students; on-campus housing not available to married students. Housing application deadline: 6/15.

GRADUATE UNITS

Program in Education *Degree program information:* Part-time and evening/weekend programs available. Offers educational technology (M Ed); leadership (M Ed); literacy (M Ed).

CENTRAL WASHINGTON UNIVERSITY, Ellensburg, WA 98926

General Information State-supported, coed, comprehensive institution. CGS member. *Enrollment:* 10,688 graduate, professional, and undergraduate students; 276 full-time matriculated graduate/professional students (149 women), 182 part-time matriculated graduate/professional students (110 women). *Enrollment by degree level:* 458 master's. *Graduate faculty:* 302 full-time (105 women). Tuition, state resident: full-time $6,312. Tuition, nonresident: full-time $14,112. Tuition and fees vary according to course load and degree level. *Graduate housing:* Rooms and/or apartments available on a first-come, first-served basis to single and married students. Typical cost: $4,950 per year ($7,025 including board) for single students; $5,400 per year ($7,730 including board) for married students. *Student services:* Campus employment opportunities, campus safety program, career counseling, child daycare facilities, disabled student services, exercise/wellness program, free psychological counseling, grant writing training, international student services, low-cost health insurance, multicultural affairs office, teacher training, writing training. *Library facilities:* Central Washington University Library. *Online resources:* library catalog, web page, access to other libraries' catalogs. *Collection:* 434,424 titles, 1,469 serial subscriptions. *Research affiliation:* East-West Center (Pacific area studies), Associated Western Universities (science and engineering), JPL.

Computer facilities: 720 computers available on campus for general student use. A campuswide network can be accessed from student residence rooms and from off campus. Internet access is available. *Web address:* http://www.cwu.edu/.

General Application Contact: Justine Eason, Admissions Program Coordinator, 509-963-3103, Fax: 509-963-1799, E-mail: masters@cwu.edu.

GRADUATE UNITS

Graduate Studies, Research and Continuing Education Students: 276 full-time (149 women), 182 part-time (110 women); includes 61 minority (8 African Americans, 25 American Indian/Alaska Native, 11 Asian Americans or Pacific Islanders, 17 Hispanic Americans), 8 international. 351 applicants, 54% accepted, 127 enrolled. *Faculty:* 302 full-time (105 women). Expenses: Contact institution. *Financial support:* In 2006–07, 48 research assistantships with partial tuition reimbursements (averaging $8,100 per year), 102 teaching assistantships with partial tuition reimbursements (averaging $8,100 per year) were awarded; career-related internships or fieldwork, Federal Work-Study, scholarships/grants, health care benefits, and unspecified assistantships also available. Financial award application deadline: 3/1; financial award applicants required to submit FAFSA. In 2006, 191 degrees awarded. *Degree program information:* Part-time and evening/weekend programs available. Offers individual studies (M Ed, MA, MS). *Application deadline:* For fall admission, 4/1 priority date for domestic students; for winter admission, 10/1 priority date for domestic students; for spring admission, 1/1 priority date for domestic students. Applications are processed on a rolling basis. *Application fee:* $50. Electronic applications accepted. *Application Contact:* Justine Eason, Admissions Program Coordinator, 509-963-3103, Fax: 509-963-1799, E-mail: masters@cwu.edu. *Associate Vice President for Graduate Studies, Research and Continuing Education,* Dr. Wayne S. Quirk, 509-963-3101, Fax: 509-963-1799, E-mail: masters@cwu.edu.

College of Arts and Humanities Students: 68 full-time (28 women), 30 part-time (20 women); includes 9 minority (1 African American, 2 American Indian/Alaska Native, 3 Asian Americans or Pacific Islanders, 3 Hispanic Americans). 89 applicants, 45% accepted, 39 enrolled. *Faculty:* 71 full-time (24 women). Expenses: Contact institution. *Financial support:* In 2006–07, 3 research assistantships with partial tuition reimbursements (averaging $8,100 per year), 40 teaching assistantships with partial tuition reimbursements (averaging $8,100 per year) were awarded; career-related internships or fieldwork, Federal Work-Study, scholarships/grants, health care benefits, and unspecified assistantships also available. Financial award application deadline: 3/1; financial award applicants required to submit FAFSA. In 2006, 42 degrees awarded. *Degree program information:* Part-time programs available. Offers art (MA, MFA); arts and humanities (MA, MFA, MM); English (MA); history (MA); music (MM); teaching English as a second language (MA); theatre production (MA). *Application deadline:* For fall admission, 4/1 for domestic students; for winter admission, 10/1 priority date for domestic students; for spring admission, 1/1 priority date for domestic students. Applications are processed on a rolling basis. *Application fee:* $50. Electronic applications accepted. *Application Contact:* Justine Eason, Admissions Program Coordinator, 509-963-3103, Fax: 509-963-1799, E-mail: masters@cwu.edu. *Dean,* Dr. Marji Morgan, 509-963-1858.

College of Business Students: 20 full-time (11 women), 5 part-time (3 women); includes 4 minority (all Asian Americans or Pacific Islanders) 25 applicants, 72% accepted, 16 enrolled. *Faculty:* 8 full-time (3 women). Expenses: Contact institution. *Financial support:* In 2006–07, 2 research assistantships with partial tuition reimbursements (averaging $8,100 per year) were awarded; Federal Work-Study, health care benefits, and unspecified assistantships also available. In 2006, 16 degrees awarded. *Degree program information:* Part-time

Central Washington University (continued)

programs available. Offers accounting (MPA); business (MPA). *Application deadline:* For fall admission, 4/1 priority date for domestic students; for winter admission, 10/1 for domestic students; for spring admission, 1/1 for domestic students. Applications are processed on a rolling basis. *Application fee:* $50. Electronic applications accepted. *Application Contact:* Justine Eason, Admissions Program Coordinator, 509-963-3103, Fax: 509-963-1799, E-mail: masters@cwu.edu. *Dean,* Dr. Roy Savoian, 509-963-1955.

College of Education and Professional Studies Students: 34 full-time (21 women), 109 part-time (66 women); includes 22 minority (5 African Americans, 7 American Indian/Alaska Native, 4 Asian Americans or Pacific Islanders, 6 Hispanic Americans). 73 applicants, 66% accepted, 37 enrolled. *Faculty:* 78 full-time (28 women). Expenses: Contact institution. *Financial support:* In 2006–07, 2 research assistantships with partial tuition reimbursements (averaging $8,100 per year), 10 teaching assistantships with partial tuition reimbursements (averaging $8,100 per year) were awarded; career-related internships or fieldwork, Federal Work-Study, health care benefits, and unspecified assistantships also available. Financial award application deadline: 3/1; financial award applicants required to submit FAFSA. In 2006, 82 degrees awarded. *Degree program information:* Part-time programs available. Offers education and professional studies (M Ed, MS); educational administration (M Ed); engineering technology (MS); family and consumer sciences education (MS); family studies (MS); health, physical education and nutrition (MS); master teacher (M Ed); nutrition (MS); reading education (M Ed); special education (M Ed). *Application deadline:* For fall admission, 4/1 priority date for domestic students; for winter admission, 10/1 for domestic students; for spring admission, 1/1 for domestic students. Applications are processed on a rolling basis. *Application fee:* $50. Electronic applications accepted. *Application Contact:* Justine Eason, Admissions Program Coordinator, 509-963-3103, Fax: 509-963-1799, E-mail: masters@cwu.edu. *Dean,* Dr. Rebecca Bowers, 509-963-1411, Fax: 509-963-1049.

College of the Sciences Students: 144 full-time (84 women), 18 part-time (5 women); includes 27 minority (16 American Indian/Alaska Native, 5 Asian Americans or Pacific Islanders, 6 Hispanic Americans). 168 applicants, 42% accepted, 68 enrolled. *Faculty:* 92 full-time (29 women). Expenses: Contact institution. *Financial support:* In 2006–07, research assistantships with partial tuition reimbursements (averaging $8,100 per year), teaching assistantships with partial tuition reimbursements (averaging $8,100 per year) were awarded; career-related internships or fieldwork, Federal Work-Study, health care benefits, and unspecified assistantships also available. Financial award application deadline: 3/1; financial award applicants required to submit FAFSA. In 2006, 63 degrees awarded. *Degree program information:* Part-time and evening/weekend programs available. Offers biological sciences (MS); chemistry (MS); experimental psychology (MS); geological sciences (MS); mathematics (MAT); mental health counseling (MS); resource management (MS); school counseling (M Ed); school psychology (M Ed); sciences (M Ed, MAT, MS). *Application deadline:* For fall admission, 4/1 priority date for domestic students. Applications are processed on a rolling basis. *Application fee:* $50. Electronic applications accepted. *Application Contact:* Justine Eason, Admissions Program Coordinator, 509-963-3103, Fax: 509-963-1799, E-mail: masters@cwu.edu. *Dean,* Dr. Meghan Miller, 509-963-1866.

Announcement: CWU's mission is to enable graduate students to competently confront the complexities of modern global society and to prepare them for successful careers as well as for independent, lifelong learning. CWU provides quality graduate programs in selected fields, taught by faculty members dedicated to excellence in teaching and research. Classes are small, and the opportunity to work closely with professors is a hallmark of CWU, as is hands-on research activity. The University is located in an attractive and safe community on the eastern slopes of the Cascade Mountains, 2 hours from Seattle by car.

See Close-Up on page 829.

CENTRAL YESHIVA TOMCHEI TMIMIM-LUBAVITCH, Brooklyn, NY 11230

General Information Independent-religious, men only, comprehensive institution.

GRADUATE UNITS

Graduate Programs

CENTRO DE ESTUDIOS AVANZADOS DE PUERTO RICO Y EL CARIBE, Old San Juan, PR 00902-3970

General Information Independent, coed, graduate-only institution. *Graduate housing:* On-campus housing not available. *Research affiliation:* Museo de las Americas, Museo Hombre Dominicano (Santo Domingo), Archivo General, Museo Universidad del Turabo.

GRADUATE UNITS

Graduate Program in Puerto Rican and Caribbean Studies *Degree program information:* Part-time and evening/weekend programs available. Offers Puerto Rican and Caribbean history (MA, PhD); Puerto Rican and Caribbean literature (MA, PhD); Puerto Rican studies (MA).

CHADRON STATE COLLEGE, Chadron, NE 69337

General Information State-supported, coed, comprehensive institution. *Graduate housing:* Rooms and/or apartments available on a first-come, first-served basis to single and married students. Housing application deadline: 6/1.

GRADUATE UNITS

School of Professional and Graduate Studies *Degree program information:* Part-time and evening/weekend programs available. Postbaccalaureate distance learning degree programs offered (minimal on-campus study). Offers business (MA Ed); business and economics (MBA); community counseling (MA Ed); educational administration (MS Ed, Sp Ed); elementary education (MS Ed); history (MA Ed); language and literature (MA Ed); secondary administration (MS Ed); secondary education (MS Ed). Electronic applications accepted.

CHAMINADE UNIVERSITY OF HONOLULU, Honolulu, HI 96816-1578

General Information Independent-religious, coed, comprehensive institution. *Enrollment:* 465 full-time matriculated graduate/professional students (337 women), 239 part-time matriculated graduate/professional students (174 women). *Enrollment by degree level:* 704 master's. *Graduate faculty:* 30. *Tuition:* Part-time $465 per credit. *Graduate housing:* On-campus housing not available. *Student services:* Campus safety program, career counseling, child daycare facilities, free psychological counseling, international student services, teacher training, writing training. *Library facilities:* Sullivan Library. *Online resources:* library catalog, web page. *Collection:* 78,000 titles, 6,730 serial subscriptions, 566 audiovisual materials.

Computer facilities: 90 computers available on campus for general student use. A campuswide network can be accessed from student residence rooms and from off campus. Internet access is available. *Web address:* http://www.chaminade.edu/.

General Application Contact: Dr. Michael Fassiotto, Assistant to the Provost, 808-739-4674, Fax: 808-739-8329, E-mail: mfassiot@chaminade.edu.

GRADUATE UNITS

Graduate Services Students: 465 full-time (337 women), 239 part-time (174 women); includes 510 minority (39 African Americans, 5 American Indian/Alaska Native, 430 Asian Americans or Pacific Islanders, 36 Hispanic Americans), 5 international. Average age 31. 293 applicants, 58% accepted. *Faculty:* 24 full-time (12 women), 45 part-time/adjunct (32 women). Expenses: Contact institution. *Financial support:* In 2006–07, 414 students received support. Career-related internships or fieldwork, Federal Work-Study, institutionally sponsored loans, and tuition waivers (partial) available. Support available to part-time students. Financial award application deadline: 3/1. In 2006, 258 degrees awarded. *Degree program information:* Part-time and evening/weekend programs available. Offers business administration (MBA); counseling psychology (MSCP); criminal justice administration (MSCJA); forensic science (MSFS); pastoral leadership (MPL); pastoral theology (MPT); social science via peace education (M Ed). *Application deadline:* For fall admission, 9/1 priority date for domestic and international students; for winter admission, 11/1 priority date for domestic and international students; for spring admission, 3/1 priority date for domestic and international students. Applications are processed on a rolling basis. *Application fee:* $50. Electronic applications accepted. *Assistant to the Provost,* Dr. Michael Fassiotto, 808-739-4674, Fax: 808-739-8329, E-mail: mfassiot@chaminade.edu.

CHAMPLAIN COLLEGE, Burlington, VT 05402-0670

General Information Independent, coed, comprehensive institution.

GRADUATE UNITS

Program in Managing Innovation and Information Technology *Degree program information:* Part-time programs available. Postbaccalaureate distance learning degree programs offered (no on-campus study). Offers management of technology (MS). Electronic applications accepted.

CHAPMAN UNIVERSITY, Orange, CA 92866

General Information Independent-religious, coed, comprehensive institution. *Enrollment:* 5,908 graduate, professional, and undergraduate students; 1,142 full-time matriculated graduate/professional students (640 women), 565 part-time matriculated graduate/professional students (345 women). *Enrollment by degree level:* 565 first professional, 1,014 master's, 121 doctoral, 7 other advanced degrees. *Graduate faculty:* 132 full-time (53 women), 116 part-time/adjunct (44 women). *Graduate housing:* Rooms and/or apartments available on a first-come, first-served basis to single and married students. Housing application deadline: 6/1. *Student services:* Campus employment opportunities, campus safety program, career counseling, child daycare facilities, disabled student services, exercise/wellness program, free psychological counseling, international student services, low-cost health insurance, teacher training. *Library facilities:* Leatherby Libraries plus 1 other. *Online resources:* library catalog, web page. *Collection:* 220,759 titles, 1,731 serial subscriptions.

Computer facilities: Computer purchase and lease plans are available. 453 computers available on campus for general student use. A campuswide network can be accessed from student residence rooms and from off campus. Internet access and online class registration are available. *Web address:* http://www.chapman.edu/.

General Application Contact: Saundra Hoover, Director of Graduate Admissions, 714-997-6786, Fax: 714-997-6713, E-mail: shoover@chapman.edu.

GRADUATE UNITS

Graduate Studies Students: 1,178 full-time (627 women), 513 part-time (331 women); includes 363 minority (28 African Americans, 7 American Indian/Alaska Native, 180 Asian Americans or Pacific Islanders, 148 Hispanic Americans), 75 international. Average age 28. 3,423 applicants, 40% accepted, 562 enrolled. *Faculty:* 160 full-time (63 women), 77 part-time/adjunct (26 women). Expenses: Contact institution. *Financial support:* In 2006–07, 1,212 students received support, including 215 fellowships (averaging $3,747 per year); Federal Work-Study also available. Financial award application deadline: 6/30; financial award applicants required to submit FAFSA. In 2006, 181 first professional degrees, 365 master's, 34 doctorates, 2 other advanced degrees awarded. *Degree program information:* Part-time and evening/weekend programs available. *Application deadline:* Applications are processed on a rolling basis. *Application fee:* $55. Electronic applications accepted. *Application Contact:* Saundra Hoover, Director of Graduate Admissions, 714-997-6786, Fax: 714-997-6713, E-mail: shoover@chapman.edu. *Associate Provost,* Dr. Raymond Sfeir, 714-997-6733, Fax: 714-628-7358, E-mail: sfeir@chapman.edu.

Dodge College of Film and Media Arts Students: 238 full-time (85 women), 23 part-time (6 women); includes 37 minority (13 African Americans, 2 American Indian/Alaska Native, 9 Asian Americans or Pacific Islanders, 13 Hispanic Americans), 31 international. Average age 27. 316 applicants, 55% accepted, 102 enrolled. *Faculty:* 33 full-time (5 women), 13 part-time/adjunct (2 women). Expenses: Contact institution. *Financial support:* In 2006–07, 172 students received support, including 98 fellowships (averaging $4,852 per year); Federal Work-Study also available. Financial award application deadline: 6/30; financial award applicants required to submit FAFSA. In 2006, 75 degrees awarded. *Degree program information:* Part-time and evening/weekend programs available. Offers film and media arts (MA, MFA); film and television producing (MFA); film production (MFA); film studies (MA); screenwriting (MFA). *Application deadline:* For fall admission, 2/1 priority date for domestic students. *Application fee:* $55. Electronic applications accepted. *Application Contact:* Joseph Slowensky, Director, 714-744-7882, E-mail: jslowens@chapman.edu. *Dean,* Robert Bassett, 714-997-6765, E-mail: bassett@chapman.edu.

The George L. Argyros School of Business and Economics Students: 96 full-time (34 women), 113 part-time (54 women); includes 55 minority (3 African Americans, 38 Asian Americans or Pacific Islanders, 14 Hispanic Americans), 23 international. Average age 31. 150 applicants, 67% accepted, 64 enrolled. *Faculty:* 33 full-time (10 women), 4 part-time/adjunct (2 women). Expenses: Contact institution. *Financial support:* In 2006–07, 116 students received support, including 29 fellowships (averaging $5,529 per year); Federal Work-Study also available. Financial award application deadline: 6/30; financial award applicants required to submit FAFSA. In 2006, 68 master's, 2 other advanced degrees awarded. *Degree program information:* Part-time and evening/weekend programs available. Offers business and economics (Exec MBA, MBA, MSHRM, Certificate); human resources and management (MSHRM); human resources management (Certificate). *Application deadline:* For fall admission, 5/1 priority date for domestic and international students; for spring admission, 12/30 priority date for domestic and international students. *Application fee:* $55. Electronic applications accepted. *Application Contact:* Debra Gonda, Associate Dean, 714-997-6894, E-mail: gonda@chapman.edu. *Dean,* Dr. Arthur Kraft, 714-997-6684.

School of Education Students: 174 full-time (142 women), 194 part-time (151 women); includes 101 minority (6 African Americans, 2 American Indian/Alaska Native, 27 Asian Americans or Pacific Islanders, 66 Hispanic Americans), 2 international. Average age 29. 202 applicants, 55% accepted, 83 enrolled. *Faculty:* 16 full-time (11 women), 25 part-time/adjunct (14 women). Expenses: Contact institution. *Financial support:* In 2006–07, 328 students received support, including 41 fellowships (averaging $1,927 per year); Federal Work-Study also available. Financial award application deadline: 6/30; financial award applicants required to submit FAFSA. In 2006, 150 degrees awarded. *Degree program information:* Part-time and evening/weekend programs available. Offers cultural and curricular studies (PhD); curriculum and instruction (MA); disability studies (PhD); education (MA, PhD, Ed S); educational leadership and administration (MA); educational psychology (MA); reading education (MA); school counseling (MA); school psychology (Ed S); special education (MA); teaching: elementary education (MA); teaching: secondary education (MA). *Application deadline:* Applications are processed on a rolling basis. *Application fee:* $55. Electronic applications accepted. *Application Contact:* Rika Judd, Graduate Admission Counselor, 714-997-6786, Fax: 714-997-6713, E-mail: rjudd@chapman.edu. *Dean,* Dr. Donald Cardinal, 714-997-6781, E-mail: cardinal@chapman.edu.

School of Law Students: 509 full-time (235 women), 75 part-time (36 women); includes 134 minority (5 African Americans, 3 American Indian/Alaska Native, 90 Asian Americans or Pacific Islanders, 36 Hispanic Americans), 7 international. Average age 26. 2,385 applicants, 33% accepted, 197 enrolled. *Faculty:* 36 full-time (15 women), 30 part-time/adjunct (5 women). Expenses: Contact institution. *Financial support:* In 2006–07, 492 students received support; fellowships, Federal Work-Study available. Financial award application deadline: 6/30; financial award applicants required to submit FAFSA. In 2006, 181 JDs, 15 master's awarded. *Degree program information:* Part-time and evening/weekend programs available. Offers law (JD); taxation (LL M). *Application deadline:* Applications are processed on a rolling basis. *Application fee:* $60. Electronic applications accepted. *Application Contact:* Demetrius L. Greer, Office of Admissions, 888-242-1913, E-mail: greer@chapman.edu. *Dean,* Dr. Parham Williams, 714-628-2500.

Wilkinson College of Letters and Sciences Students: 180 full-time (138 women), 109 part-time (85 women); includes 39 minority (1 African American, 19 Asian Americans or Pacific Islanders, 19 Hispanic Americans), 12 international. Average age 27. 370 applicants, 55% accepted, 116 enrolled. *Faculty:* 42 full-time (22 women), 2 part-time/adjunct (both women). Expenses: Contact institution. *Financial support:* In 2006–07, 67 students received support, including 47 fellowships (averaging $1,933 per year). In 2006, 57 master's, 34 doctorates awarded. Offers creative writing (MFA); food science and nutrition (MS); letters and sciences (MA, MFA, MS, DPT); literature (MA); marriage and family therapy (MA); physical therapy (DPT). *Application fee:* $55. *Dean,* Dr. Roberta Lessor, 714-997-6947, E-mail: lessor@chapman.edu.

See Close-Up on page 831.

CHARLES R. DREW UNIVERSITY OF MEDICINE AND SCIENCE, Los Angeles, CA 90059

General Information Independent, coed, comprehensive institution. *Graduate housing:* On-campus housing not available.

GRADUATE UNITS

College of Allied Health

Professional Program in Medicine Offers medicine (MD).

CHARLESTON SOUTHERN UNIVERSITY, Charleston, SC 29423-8087

General Information Independent-religious, coed, comprehensive institution. *Graduate housing:* On-campus housing not available. *Research affiliation:* Metro Charleston Chamber of Commerce (economic forecasting), Waccamaw Regional Planning and Development Council (economic forecasting), Santee Lynches Council of Governments (economic forecasting).

GRADUATE UNITS

Program in Business *Degree program information:* Part-time and evening/weekend programs available. Offers accounting (MBA); finance (MBA); health care administration (MBA); information systems (MBA); organizational development (MBA).

Program in Criminal Justice *Degree program information:* Part-time and evening/weekend programs available. Offers criminal justice (MSCJ).

Programs in Education *Degree program information:* Part-time and evening/weekend programs available. Offers administration and supervision (M Ed); elementary education (M Ed); English (MAT); science (MAT); secondary education (M Ed); social studies (MAT).

CHATHAM UNIVERSITY, Pittsburgh, PA 15232-2826

General Information Independent, Undergraduate: women only; graduate: coed, comprehensive institution. *Enrollment:* 1,590 graduate, professional, and undergraduate students; 513 full-time matriculated graduate/professional students (421 women), 272 part-time matriculated graduate/professional students (213 women). *Enrollment by degree level:* 724 master's, 52 doctoral, 9 other advanced degrees. *Graduate faculty:* 27 full-time, 54 part-time/adjunct. *Graduate housing:* Rooms and/or apartments available on a first-come, first-served basis to single and married students. *Student services:* Campus employment opportunities, campus safety program, career counseling, exercise/wellness program, free psychological counseling, international student services, low-cost health insurance, teacher training, writing training. *Library facilities:* Jennie King Mellon Library. *Online resources:* library catalog, web page, access to other libraries' catalogs. *Collection:* 87,907 titles, 783 serial subscriptions, 789 audiovisual materials.

Computer facilities: Computer purchase and lease plans are available. 265 computers available on campus for general student use. A campuswide network can be accessed from student residence rooms and from off campus. Internet access and online class registration, computer-aided instruction are available. *Web address:* http://www.chatham.edu/.

General Application Contact: Information Contact, 412-365-1825, Fax: 412-365-1609, E-mail: admissions@chatham.edu.

GRADUATE UNITS

Program in Business Administration Students: 21 full-time (19 women), 18 part-time (15 women). Average age 34. 33 applicants, 73% accepted, 19 enrolled. Expenses: Contact institution. *Financial support:* Career-related internships or fieldwork available. Financial award applicants required to submit FAFSA. In 2006, 31 degrees awarded. *Degree program information:* Part-time and evening/weekend programs available. Offers business administration (MBA); healthcare professional (MBA). *Application deadline:* Applications are processed on a rolling basis. *Application fee:* $45. Electronic applications accepted. *Application Contact:* 412-365-1825, Fax: 412-365-1609, E-mail: admissions@chatham.edu. *Director,* Dr. Mary Reibe, 412-365-1157, Fax: 412-365-1505, E-mail: reibe@chatham.edu.

Program in Counseling Psychology Students: 110 full-time (94 women), 78 part-time (68 women). Average age 30. 103 applicants, 79% accepted, 67 enrolled. Expenses: Contact institution. *Financial support:* Career-related internships or fieldwork available. Financial award applicants required to submit FAFSA. In 2006, 55 degrees awarded. *Degree program information:* Part-time and evening/weekend programs available. Offers counseling psychology (MSCP). *Application deadline:* Applications are processed on a rolling basis. *Application fee:* $45. Electronic applications accepted. *Application Contact:* 412-365-1825, Fax: 412-365-1609, E-mail: admissions@chatham.edu. *Director,* Dr. Mary Beth Mannarino, 412-365-1196, Fax: 412-365-1505, E-mail: mmannarino@chatham.edu.

Program in Education Students: 60 full-time (43 women), 23 part-time (22 women). Average age 29. 48 applicants, 77% accepted, 32 enrolled. Expenses: Contact institution. *Financial support:* Career-related internships or fieldwork available. Financial award applicants required to submit FAFSA. In 2006, 59 degrees awarded. Offers early childhood education (MAT); elementary education (MAT); English—secondary (MAT); environmental education (K-12) (MAT); secondary art (MAT); secondary biology education (MAT); secondary chemistry education (MAT); secondary English education (MAT); secondary math education (MAT); secondary physics education (MAT); secondary social studies education (MAT); special education (MAT). *Application deadline:* For fall admission, 5/1 priority date for domestic and international students; for winter admission, 10/1 priority date for domestic and international students. Applications are processed on a rolling basis. *Application fee:* $45. Electronic applications accepted. *Application Contact:* 412-365-1825, Fax: 412-365-1609, E-mail: admissions@chatham.edu. *Director,* Dr. Wendy Weiner, 412-365-1146, Fax: 412-365-1505, E-mail: wweiner@chatham.edu.

Program in Landscape Architecture Students: 15 full-time (10 women), 9 part-time (5 women). Average age 36. 11 applicants, 82% accepted, 7 enrolled. Expenses: Contact institution. *Financial support:* Career-related internships or fieldwork available. Financial award applicants required to submit FAFSA. In 2006, 1 degree awarded. *Degree program information:* Part-time and evening/weekend programs available. Offers landscape architecture (ML Arch); landscape studies (MA). *Application deadline:* Applications are processed on a rolling basis. *Application fee:* $45. Electronic applications accepted. *Application Contact:* 412-365-1825, Fax: 412-365-1609, E-mail: admissions@chatham.edu. *Director,* Lisa Kunst Vavaro, 412-365-1882, E-mail: lvavro@chatham.edu.

Program in Physical Therapy Students: 66 full-time (48 women), 37 part-time (14 women). Average age 29. 86 applicants, 67% accepted, 44 enrolled. Expenses: Contact institution. *Financial support:* Career-related internships or fieldwork available. Financial award applicants required to submit FAFSA. In 2006, 28 degrees awarded. *Degree program information:* Part-time and evening/weekend programs available. Offers physical therapy (DPT, TDPT). *Application deadline:* For fall admission, 1/5 priority date for domestic students. Applications are processed on a rolling basis. *Application fee:* $45. Electronic applications accepted. *Application Contact:* 412-365-1825, Fax: 412-365-1609, E-mail: admissions@chatham.edu. *Director,* Dr. Patricia Downey, 412-365-1199, Fax: 412-365-1505, E-mail: downey@chatham.edu.

Program in Physician Assistant Studies Students: 97 full-time (86 women), 1 (woman) part-time. Average age 25. 295 applicants, 19% accepted, 55 enrolled. Expenses: Contact institution. *Financial support:* Career-related internships or fieldwork available. Financial award applicants required to submit FAFSA. In 2006, 42 degrees awarded. Offers physician assistant studies (MPAS). *Application deadline:* For fall admission, 1/15 priority date for domestic students. Applications are processed on a rolling basis. *Application fee:* $45. Electronic applications accepted. *Application Contact:* 412-365-1825, Fax: 412-365-1609, E-mail: admissions@chatham.edu. *Director,* Luis Ramos, 412-365-1314, Fax: 412-365-1213, E-mail: lramos@chatham.edu.

Program in Writing Students: 43 full-time (34 women), 26 part-time (23 women). Average age 33. 51 applicants, 86% accepted, 34 enrolled. Expenses: Contact institution. *Financial support:* Career-related internships or fieldwork available. Financial award applicants required to submit FAFSA. In 2006, 23 degrees awarded. *Degree program information:* Part-time and evening/weekend programs available. Postbaccalaureate distance learning degree programs offered. Offers creative writing (MFA); fiction (MFA); non-fiction (MFA); poetry (MFA); professional writing (MAPW); writing for children/adolescent audience (MFA). *Application deadline:* For fall admission, 5/1 priority date for domestic and international students; for winter admission, 10/1 priority date for domestic and international students. Applications are processed on a rolling basis. *Application fee:* $45. Electronic applications accepted. *Application Contact:* 412-365-1825, Fax: 412-365-1609, E-mail: admissions@chatham.edu. *Director,* Dr. Sheryl St. Germain, 412-365-1190, Fax: 412-365-1505, E-mail: sstgermain@chatham.edu.

CHESTNUT HILL COLLEGE, Philadelphia, PA 19118-2693

General Information Independent-religious, coed, primarily women, comprehensive institution. *Enrollment:* 1,918 graduate, professional, and undergraduate students; 162 full-time matriculated graduate/professional students (131 women), 547 part-time matriculated graduate/professional students (455 women). *Enrollment by degree level:* 523 master's, 94 doctoral, 92 other advanced degrees. *Graduate faculty:* 9 full-time (3 women), 75 part-time/adjunct (42 women). *Tuition:* Part-time $470 per credit hour. *Required fees:* $30 per semester. Tuition and fees vary according to degree level. *Graduate housing:* On-campus housing not available. *Student services:* Campus employment opportunities, campus safety program, career counseling, exercise/wellness program, free psychological counseling, international student services, low-cost health insurance, writing training. *Library facilities:* Logue Library. *Online resources:* library catalog, web page, access to other libraries' catalogs. *Collection:* 128,489 titles, 484 serial subscriptions.

Computer facilities: Computer purchase and lease plans are available. 101 computers available on campus for general student use. A campuswide network can be accessed from student residence rooms. Internet access, e-mail are available. *Web address:* http://www.chc.edu/.

General Application Contact: Sr. Ann Harkin, SSJ, Administrative Assistant, 215-248-7170, Fax: 215-248-7161, E-mail: harkina@chc.edu.

GRADUATE UNITS

School of Graduate Studies Students: 162 full-time (131 women), 547 part-time (455 women); includes 125 minority (96 African Americans, 16 Asian Americans or Pacific Islanders, 13 Hispanic Americans), 4 international. Average age 29. *Faculty:* 9 full-time (3 women), 75 part-time/adjunct (42 women). Expenses: Contact institution. *Financial support:* Institutionally sponsored loans available. Financial award application deadline: 7/15; financial award applicants required to submit FAFSA. In 2006, 128 master's, 15 doctorates awarded. *Degree program information:* Part-time and evening/weekend programs available. Postbaccalaureate distance learning degree programs offered (minimal on-campus study). Offers administration of human services (MS); adult and aging services (CAS); applied spirituality (CAS); clinical pastoral education (CAS); clinical psychology (Psy D); counseling psychology and human services (MA, MS, CAS); e-communication (CAS); early childhood education (M Ed); education and technology (CAS); educational leadership (M Ed); elementary education (M Ed); holistic spirituality (MA); holistic spirituality and healthcare (MA); holistic spirituality and spiritual direction (MA); holistic spirituality/health care (CAS); instructional design (CAS); instructional technology specialist (CAS); instructional technology/instruction design (MS); instructional technology/leadership and technology (MS); instructional technology/technology and education (MS); leadership and technology (CAS); leadership development (CAS); multimedia design (CAS); online learning (CAS); restructured environments (CAS); secondary education (M Ed); spirituality (CAS); supervision of spiritual directors (CAS); video (CAS). *Application deadline:* For fall admission, 7/17 priority date for domestic students, 7/17 for international students; for spring admission, 12/15 priority date for domestic students, 12/15 for international students. Applications are processed on a rolling basis. *Application fee:* $50. *Application Contact:* Jayne Mashett, Director of Graduate Admissions, 215-248-7020, Fax: 215-248-7161, E-mail: mashettj@chc.edu. *Dean of the School of Graduate Studies,* Dr. Joyce Huth Munro, 215-248-7120, Fax: 215-248-7161, E-mail: munroj@chc.edu.

See Close-Up on page 833.

CHEYNEY UNIVERSITY OF PENNSYLVANIA, Cheyney, PA 19319-0200

General Information State-supported, coed, comprehensive institution. *Graduate housing:* On-campus housing not available.

GRADUATE UNITS

School of Education *Degree program information:* Part-time and evening/weekend programs available. Offers adult and continuing education (MS); early childhood education (Certificate); education (M Ed, MAT, MS, Certificate); educational administration and supervision (M Ed, Certificate); educational administration of adult and continuing education (M Ed, MS); elementary and secondary principalship (Certificate); elementary education (M Ed, MAT); mathematics education (Certificate); special education (M Ed, MS). Electronic applications accepted.

THE CHICAGO SCHOOL OF PROFESSIONAL PSYCHOLOGY, Chicago, IL 60610

General Information Independent, coed, primarily women, graduate-only institution. CGS member. *Graduate housing:* On-campus housing not available.

GRADUATE UNITS

Graduate School *Degree program information:* Part-time programs available. Offers applied behavior analysis (MA, Certificate); business psychology (Psy D); clinical psychology (Psy D); counseling (MA); forensic psychology (MA); industrial and organizational psychology (MA); school psychology (Ed S). Electronic applications accepted.

CHICAGO STATE UNIVERSITY, Chicago, IL 60628

General Information State-supported, coed, comprehensive institution. *Graduate housing:* Room and/or apartments available on a first-come, first-served basis to single students; on-campus housing not available to married students.

GRADUATE UNITS

School of Graduate and Professional Studies *Degree program information:* Part-time and evening/weekend programs available. Electronic applications accepted.

College of Arts and Sciences *Degree program information:* Part-time and evening/weekend programs available. Offers arts and sciences (MA, MFA, MS, MSW); biological sciences (MS); computer science (MS); counseling (MA); creative writing (MFA); criminal justice (MS); English (MA); geography and economic development (MA); history, philosophy, and political science (MA); mathematics (MS); social work (MSW).

College of Education *Degree program information:* Part-time programs available. Offers bilingual education (M Ed); curriculum and instruction (MS Ed); early childhood education (MAT, MS Ed); education (M Ed, MA, MAT, MS Ed, Ed D); educational leadership (MA, Ed D); elementary education (MAT); general administration (MA); higher education administration (MA); instructional foundations (MS Ed); library information and media studies (MS Ed); middle school education (MAT); physical education (MS Ed); reading (MS Ed); secondary education (MAT); special education (M Ed); teaching of reading (MS Ed); technology and education (MS Ed).

CHICAGO THEOLOGICAL SEMINARY, Chicago, IL 60637-1507

General Information Independent-religious, coed, graduate-only institution. *Enrollment by degree level:* 94 first professional, 36 master's, 101 doctoral. *Graduate faculty:* 12 full-time (4 women). *Tuition:* Full-time $9,920; part-time $1,240 per course. Tuition and fees vary according to program. *Graduate housing:* On-campus housing not available. *Student services:* Campus employment opportunities, career counseling, international student services, writing training. *Library facilities:* Hammond Library. *Collection:* 110,000 titles, 130 serial subscriptions, 500 audiovisual materials.

Computer facilities: 8 computers available on campus for general student use. A campuswide network can be accessed from student residence rooms and from off campus. Internet access is available. *Web address:* http://www.ctschicago.edu/.

General Application Contact: Rev. Alison Buttrick Patton, Director of Admissions, Recruitment and Financial Aid, 773-322-0229, Fax: 773-752-1903, E-mail: apatton@ctschicago.edu.

GRADUATE UNITS

Graduate and Professional Programs Students: 78 full-time (34 women), 153 part-time (76 women); includes 76 minority (65 African Americans, 8 Asian Americans or Pacific Islanders, 3 Hispanic Americans), 30 international. 94 applicants, 84% accepted, 53 enrolled. *Faculty:* 12 full-time (4 women). Expenses: Contact institution. *Financial support:* In 2006–07, 94 students received support, including 15 fellowships (averaging $15,000 per year); institutionally sponsored loans and scholarships/grants also available. Support available to part-time students. Financial award application deadline: 3/1; financial award applicants required to submit FAFSA. In 2006, 20 M Divs, 4 master's, 13 doctorates awarded. *Degree program information:* Part-time programs available. Offers clinical pastoral education (D Min); Jewish-Christian studies (PhD); pastoral counseling (D Min); preaching (D Min); religious studies (MA); spiritual leadership (D Min); theology (M Div); theology and the human sciences (PhD). *Application deadline:* For fall admission, 3/1 priority date for domestic and international students; for spring admission, 11/1 for domestic and international students. Applications are processed on a rolling basis. *Application fee:* $50. *Application Contact:* Rev. Alison Buttrick Patton, Director of Admissions, Recruitment and Financial Aid, 773-322-0229, Fax: 773-752-1903, E-mail: apatton@ctschicago.edu. *Dean,* Dr. Dow Edgerton, 773-752-5757, Fax: 773-752-5925, E-mail: dedgerton@ctschicago.edu.

CHRISTENDOM COLLEGE, Front Royal, VA 22630-5103

General Information Independent-religious, coed, comprehensive institution. *Graduate housing:* On-campus housing not available.

GRADUATE UNITS

Notre Dame Graduate School *Degree program information:* Part-time and evening/weekend programs available. Offers theological studies (MA). Electronic applications accepted.

CHRISTIAN BROTHERS UNIVERSITY, Memphis, TN 38104-5581

General Information Independent-religious, coed, comprehensive institution. *Enrollment:* 1,776 graduate, professional, and undergraduate students; 60 full-time matriculated graduate/professional students (39 women), 261 part-time matriculated graduate/professional students (158 women). *Enrollment by degree level:* 321 master's. *Graduate faculty:* 19 full-time (8 women), 13 part-time/adjunct (6 women). *Graduate housing:* On-campus housing not available. *Student services:* Campus safety program, career counseling, free psychological counseling, low-cost health insurance. *Library facilities:* Plough Memorial Library and Media Center. *Online resources:* library catalog, web page, access to other libraries' catalogs. *Collection:* 107,000 titles, 437 serial subscriptions.

Computer facilities: 300 computers available on campus for general student use. A campuswide network can be accessed from student residence rooms and from off campus. Internet access and online class registration, online class listings, e-mail, course assignments are available. *Web address:* http://www.cbu.edu/.

General Application Contact: Tonna R. Bruce, Dean, Graduate and Professional Studies Programs, 901-321-3296, E-mail: tbruce@cbu.edu.

GRADUATE UNITS

Graduate Programs Students: 60 full-time (39 women), 261 part-time (158 women); includes 106 minority (96 African Americans, 6 Asian Americans or Pacific Islanders, 4 Hispanic Americans), 8 international. Average age 34. *Faculty:* 19 full-time (8 women), 13 part-time/adjunct (6 women). Expenses: Contact institution. *Financial support:* Institutionally sponsored loans available. Support available to part-time students. In 2006, 144 degrees awarded. *Degree program information:* Part-time and evening/weekend programs available. *Application deadline:* Applications are processed on a rolling basis. *Application fee:* $25. *Information Contact,* 901-321-3200.

School of Arts Students: 47 full-time (38 women), 134 part-time (104 women); includes 70 minority (68 African Americans, 1 Asian American or Pacific Islander, 1 Hispanic American), 3 international. Average age 35. *Faculty:* 6 full-time (4 women), 11 part-time/adjunct (5 women). Expenses: Contact institution. *Financial support:* Institutionally sponsored loans available. Support available to part-time students. In 2006, 57 degrees awarded. *Degree program information:* Part-time and evening/weekend programs available. Offers Catholic studies (MACS); curriculum and instruction (M Ed); educational leadership (MSEL); teacher-leadership (M Ed); teaching (MAT). *Application deadline:* Applications are processed on a rolling basis. *Application fee:* $25. *Application Contact:* Dr. Talana L. Vogel, Director, 901-321-4101, Fax: 901-321-3408, E-mail: tvogel@cbu.edu. *Dean,* Dr. Marins Carriere, 901-321-3366, E-mail: mcarrier@cbu.edu.

School of Business Students: 13 full-time (1 woman), 88 part-time (38 women); includes 21 minority (18 African Americans, 2 Asian Americans or Pacific Islanders, 1 Hispanic American), 4 international. Average age 33. *Faculty:* 8 full-time (3 women), 1 part-time/adjunct (0 women). Expenses: Contact institution. *Financial support:* Institutionally sponsored loans available. Support available to part-time students. In 2006, 69 degrees awarded. *Degree program information:* Part-time and evening/weekend programs available. Offers business (MBA); executive leadership (MAEL); financial planning (Certificate); project management (Certificate). *Application deadline:* Applications are processed on a rolling basis. *Application fee:* $25. *Application Contact:* Dr. Bevalee B. Pray, Director, Graduate Business Programs, 901-321-3319, Fax: 901-321-3494. *Dean,* Dr. Mike R. Ryan, 901-321-3316.

School of Engineering Average age 35. *Faculty:* 5 full-time (1 woman), 1 (woman) part-time/adjunct. Expenses: Contact institution. *Financial support:* Institutionally sponsored loans available. In 2006, 18 degrees awarded. *Degree program information:* Part-time and evening/weekend programs available. Postbaccalaureate distance learning degree programs offered (no on-campus study). Offers engineering (MEM, MSEM). *Application fee:* $25. *Application Contact:* Dr. Neal Jackson, Director, 901-321-3283, Fax: 901-321-3494, E-mail: njackson@cbu.edu. *Dean,* Dr. Eric B Welch, 901-321-3405.

CHRISTIAN THEOLOGICAL SEMINARY, Indianapolis, IN 46208-3301

General Information Independent-religious, coed, graduate-only institution. *Graduate housing:* Rooms and/or apartments available on a first-come, first-served basis to single and married students. Housing application deadline: 5/1.

GRADUATE UNITS

Graduate and Professional Programs *Degree program information:* Part-time programs available. Offers marriage and family (MA); pastoral care and counseling (D Min); practical theology (D Min); psychotherapy and faith (MA); sacred theology (STM); specialized ministries (MA); theological studies (MTS); theology (M Div). Electronic applications accepted.

CHRISTIE'S EDUCATION, New York, NY 10036

General Information Proprietary, coed, primarily women, graduate-only institution. *Enrollment by degree level:* 35 master's, 1 other advanced degree. *Graduate faculty:* 6. *Tuition:* Full-time $36,815. One-time fee: $3,055 full-time. *Graduate housing:* On-campus housing not available. *Library facilities:* Christie's Education Library. *Online resources:* library catalog.

Computer facilities: 11 computers available on campus for general student use. Internet access is available. *Web address:* http://www.christies.com/education/ny_overview.asp.

General Application Contact: Margaret Conklin, Registrar/Bursar, 212-355-1501 Ext. 302, Fax: 212-355-7370, E-mail: mconklin@christies.edu.

GRADUATE UNITS

Program in Modern Art, Connoisseurship, and the History of the Art Market Students: 35 full-time. *Faculty:* 5 full-time (4 women). Expenses: Contact institution. *Financial support:* In 2006–07, 3 research assistantships (averaging $7,000 per year) were awarded. In 2006, 32 master's awarded. Offers modern art, connoisseurship, and the history of the art market (MA). *Application deadline:* For fall admission, 1/15 priority date for domestic and international students. Applications are processed on a rolling basis. *Application fee:* $75. *Application Contact:* Margaret Conklin, Registrar/Bursar, 212-355-1501 Ext. 302, Fax: 212-355-7370, E-mail: mconklin@christies.edu. *Director of Studies,* Dr. Véronique Chagnon-Burke, 212-355-2545, Fax: 212-355-7370, E-mail: vchagnonburke@christies.edu.

CHRISTOPHER NEWPORT UNIVERSITY, Newport News, VA 23606-2998

General Information State-supported, coed, comprehensive institution. *Graduate housing:* On-campus housing not available. *Research affiliation:* Langley Research Center, Center for Distance Learning (flow visualization), Thomas Jefferson National Acceleration Facility (instrument and nuclear physics), Applied Research Center (biology, engineering, physics), JDH Technologies (computer software), National Science Foundation (science).

GRADUATE UNITS

Graduate Studies *Degree program information:* Part-time and evening/weekend programs available. Offers applied physics and computer science (MS); art (PK-12) (MAT); biology (6-12) (MAT); computer science (6-12) (MAT); elementary (PK-6) (MAT); English (6-12) (MAT); environmental science (MS); French (PK-12) (MAT); history (6-12) (MAT); history and social science (MAT); mathematics (6-12) (MAT); music (PK-12) (MAT); physics (6-12) (MAT); Spanish (PK-12) (MAT); theater (PK-12) (MAT). Electronic applications accepted.

CHRIST THE KING SEMINARY, East Aurora, NY 14052

General Information Independent-religious, coed, graduate-only institution. *Graduate housing:* On-campus housing not available.

GRADUATE UNITS

Graduate and Professional Programs *Degree program information:* Part-time and evening/weekend programs available. Offers divinity (M Div); pastoral ministry (MA); pastoral studies (Certificate); theology (MA).

CHURCH DIVINITY SCHOOL OF THE PACIFIC, Berkeley, CA 94709-1217

General Information Independent-religious, coed, graduate-only institution. *Graduate housing:* Rooms and/or apartments available on a first-come, first-served basis to single and married students. Housing application deadline: 5/1.

GRADUATE UNITS

Graduate and Professional Programs *Degree program information:* Part-time programs available. Offers theology (M Div, MA, MTS, D Min, Certificate). Electronic applications accepted.

CHURCH OF GOD THEOLOGICAL SEMINARY, Cleveland, TN 37320-3330

General Information Independent-religious, coed, graduate-only institution. *Graduate housing:* Rooms and/or apartments available to single and married students.

GRADUATE UNITS

Graduate and Professional Programs *Degree program information:* Part-time programs available. Offers church ministries (MA); discipleship and Christian formations (MA); theology (M Div).

CINCINNATI CHRISTIAN UNIVERSITY, Cincinnati, OH 45204-3200

General Information Independent-religious, coed, comprehensive institution. *Graduate housing:* On-campus housing not available.

GRADUATE UNITS

Graduate School *Degree program information:* Part-time programs available. Offers biblical studies (MA); church history (MA); counseling (MAC); divinity (M Div); ministry (M Min); practical ministries (MA); theological studies (MA). Electronic applications accepted.

THE CITADEL, THE MILITARY COLLEGE OF SOUTH CAROLINA, Charleston, SC 29409

General Information State-supported, coed, comprehensive institution. *Enrollment:* 3,386 graduate, professional, and undergraduate students; 157 full-time matriculated graduate/professional students (108 women), 631 part-time matriculated graduate/professional students (346 women). *Enrollment by degree level:* 715 master's, 73 other advanced degrees. *Graduate faculty:* 62 full-time (17 women), 19 part-time/adjunct (4 women). Tuition, state resident: part-time $259 per credit hour. Tuition, nonresident: part-time $482 per credit hour. *Graduate housing:* On-campus housing not available. *Student services:* Campus employment opportunities, career counseling, free psychological counseling, international student services, multicultural affairs office, teacher training, writing training. *Library facilities:* Daniel Library. *Online resources:* library catalog, web page, access to other libraries' catalogs. *Collection:* 233,745 titles, 583 serial subscriptions.

Computer facilities: 350 computers available on campus for general student use. A campuswide network can be accessed from student residence rooms and from off campus. Internet access and online class registration are available. *Web address:* http://www.citadel.edu.

General Application Contact: Dr. Raymond S. Jones, Associate Dean, College of Graduate and Professional Studies, 843-953-5089, Fax: 843-953-7630, E-mail: ray.jones@citadel.edu.

GRADUATE UNITS

College of Graduate and Professional Studies Students: 157 full-time (108 women), 631 part-time (346 women); includes 122 minority (101 African Americans, 3 American Indian/Alaska Native, 13 Asian Americans or Pacific Islanders, 5 Hispanic Americans), 8 international. Average age 29. *Faculty:* 62 full-time (17 women), 19 part-time/adjunct (4 women). Expenses: Contact institution. *Financial support:* Fellowships, research assistantships, teaching assistantships, career-related internships or fieldwork and unspecified assistantships available. Support available to part-time students. Financial award application deadline: 7/1; financial award applicants required to submit FAFSA. In 2006, 219 master's, 18 other advanced degrees awarded. *Degree program information:* Part-time and evening/weekend programs available. Offers biology (MA); computer and information science (MS); English (MA); health, exercise, and sports science (MS); history (MA); physical education (MAT); psychology (MA); social science (MA). *Application deadline:* For fall admission, 8/1 priority date for domestic students. Applications are processed on a rolling basis. *Application fee:* $30. *Application Contact:* Dr. Raymond S. Jones, Associate Dean, College of Graduate and Professional Studies, 843-953-5089, Fax: 843-953-7630, E-mail: ray.jones@citadel.edu. *Provost/Dean of the College,* Brig. Gen. Harrison S. Carter, 843-953-5007, Fax: 843-953-7118, E-mail: harry.carter@citadel.edu.

School of Business Administration Students: 24 full-time (7 women), 242 part-time (90 women); includes 32 minority (20 African Americans, 2 American Indian/Alaska Native, 8 Asian Americans or Pacific Islanders, 2 Hispanic Americans), 6 international. Average age 29. Expenses: Contact institution. *Financial support:* Fellowships available. Financial award application deadline: 7/1; financial award applicants required to submit FAFSA. In 2006, 49 degrees awarded. *Degree program information:* Part-time and evening/weekend programs available. Offers business administration (MBA). *Application deadline:* Applications are processed on a rolling basis. *Application fee:* $30. *Application Contact:* Dr. Raymond S. Jones, Associate Dean, College of Graduate and Professional Studies, 843-953-5089, Fax: 843-953-7630, E-mail: ray.jones@citadel.edu. *Head,* Dr. Earl Walker, 843-953-7466, E-mail: earl.walker@citadel.edu.

School of Education Students: 89 full-time (70 women), 281 part-time (190 women); includes 75 minority (70 African Americans, 4 Asian Americans or Pacific Islanders, 1 Hispanic American), 2 international. Average age 30. Expenses: Contact institution. *Financial support:* Fellowships available. Financial award application deadline: 7/1; financial award applicants required to submit FAFSA. In 2006, 119 master's, 18 other advanced degrees awarded. *Degree program information:* Part-time and evening/weekend programs available. Offers education (M Ed, MA, MAT, Ed S); educational administration (M Ed, Ed S); guidance and counseling (M Ed); reading (M Ed); school psychology (MA, Ed S); secondary education (MAT). *Application deadline:* For fall admission, 6/1 for domestic students; for spring admission, 3/1 for domestic students. Applications are processed on a rolling basis. *Application fee:* $30. *Application Contact:* Dr. Raymond S. Jones, Associate Dean, College of Graduate and Professional Studies, 843-953-5089, Fax: 843-953-7630, E-mail: ray.jones@citadel.edu. *Head,* Dr. Tony Johnson, 843-953-5097, Fax: 843-953-7258, E-mail: tony.johnson@citadel.edu.

CITY COLLEGE OF THE CITY UNIVERSITY OF NEW YORK, New York, NY 10031-9198

General Information State and locally supported, coed, university. *Enrollment:* 13,244 graduate, professional, and undergraduate students; 246 full-time matriculated graduate/professional students (115 women), 2,684 part-time matriculated graduate/professional students (1,550 women). *Graduate faculty:* 491 full-time (145 women), 475 part-time/adjunct (240 women). *Graduate housing:* On-campus housing not available. *Student services:* Career counseling, child daycare facilities, free psychological counseling. *Library facilities:* Morris Raphael Cohen Library plus 3 others. *Online resources:* library catalog, web page, access to other libraries' catalogs. *Collection:* 1.4 million titles, 31,000 serial subscriptions, 26,380 audiovisual materials. *Research affiliation:* Museum of Natural History, Hospital for Joint Diseases (biomedical engineering), Lucent Laboratories (engineering), New York Center for Biological Structure.

Computer facilities: 3,000 computers available on campus for general student use. A campuswide network can be accessed from off campus. Internet access is available. *Web address:* http://www.ccny.cuny.edu/.

General Application Contact: Information Contact, 212-650-6977, Fax: 212-650-6417, E-mail: gradadm@ccny.cuny.edu.

GRADUATE UNITS

Graduate School Students: 246 full-time (115 women), 2,684 part-time (1,550 women); includes 1,972 minority (745 African Americans, 1 American Indian/Alaska Native, 402 Asian Americans or Pacific Islanders, 824 Hispanic Americans), 507 international. Expenses: Contact institution. *Financial support:* Fellowships, research assistantships, teaching assistantships, career-related internships or fieldwork, Federal Work-Study, institutionally sponsored loans, and tuition waivers (full and partial) available. Support available to part-time students. In 2006, 707 master's, 5 other advanced degrees awarded. *Degree program information:* Part-time and evening/weekend programs available. *Application fee:* $125. *Application Contact:* 212-650-6977, Fax: 212-650-6417, E-mail: gradadm@ccny.cuny.edu.

College of Liberal Arts and Science Expenses: Contact institution. *Financial support:* Fellowships, research assistantships, teaching assistantships, career-related internships or fieldwork, Federal Work-Study, institutionally sponsored loans, and tuition waivers (full and partial) available. Support available to part-time students. *Degree program information:* Part-time and evening/weekend programs available. Offers advertising design (MFA); art history (MA); art history and museum studies (MA); biochemistry (MA, PhD); biology (MA, PhD); ceramic design (MFA); chemistry (MA, PhD); clinical psychology (PhD); creative writing (MFA); earth and environmental science (PhD); earth systems science (MA); economics (MA); English and American literature (MA); experimental cognition (PhD); fine arts (MFA); general psychology (MA); history (MA); humanities and arts (MA, MFA); international relations (MA); language and literacy (MA); liberal arts and science (MA, MFA, PhD); mathematics (MA); media arts production (MFA); mental health counseling (MA); museum studies (MA); music (MA); painting (MFA); physics (MA, PhD); printmaking (MFA); science (MA, PhD); sculpture (MFA); social science (MA, PhD); sociology (MA); Spanish (MA); wood and metal design (MFA). *Application deadline:* For fall admission, 5/1 for domestic students; for spring admission, 11/1 for domestic students. *Application fee:* $125. *Application Contact:* 212-650-6977, Fax: 212-650-6417, E-mail: gradadm@ccny.cuny.edu.

School of Architecture and Environmental Studies Students: 55. 93 applicants, 63% accepted, 30 enrolled. Expenses: Contact institution. *Financial support:* Fellowships, career-related internships or fieldwork and Federal Work-Study available. Support available to part-time students. *Degree program information:* Part-time programs available. Offers architecture (M Arch, PD); landscape architecture (PD); urban design (MUP). *Application fee:* $125. *Application Contact:* Sarah Morales, Advisor, 212-650-8748, E-mail: archgrad@ccny.cuny.edu. *Dean,* George Ranalli, 212-650-7284, Fax: 212-650-6566, E-mail: granalli@acis32.admin.ccny.cuny.edu.

School of Education Students: 1,325. 576 applicants, 94% accepted, 460 enrolled. Expenses: Contact institution. *Financial support:* Fellowships, research assistantships, teaching assistantships, career-related internships or fieldwork, Federal Work-Study, and tuition waivers (full and partial) available. Support available to part-time students. In 2006, 451 degrees awarded. *Degree program information:* Part-time and evening/weekend programs available. Offers administration and supervision (MS, AC); adolescent mathematics education (MA, AC); bilingual education (MS); childhood education (MS); education (MA, MS, AC); English education (MA); middle school mathematics education (MS); science education (MA); social studies education (AC); teaching students with disabilities (MA). *Application deadline:* For fall admission, 3/15 for domestic students; for spring admission, 10/15 for domestic students. *Application fee:* $125. *Application Contact:* Stacia Pusey, Graduate Admissions Adviser-Education, 212-650-5345, E-mail: spusey@ccny.cuny.edu. *Dean,* Dr. Alfred Posamentier, 212-650-5354.

School of Engineering Students: 400. 290 applicants, 57% accepted, 122 enrolled. Expenses: Contact institution. *Financial support:* In 2006–07, 150 students received support, including fellowships with partial tuition reimbursements available (averaging $20,000 per year), research assistantships with full tuition reimbursements available (averaging $20,000 per year), teaching assistantships (averaging $12,000 per year); Federal Work-Study, institutionally sponsored loans, and tuition waivers (full and partial) also available. Support available to part-time students. Financial award applicants required to submit CSS PROFILE or FAFSA. *Degree program information:* Part-time programs available. Offers biomedical engineering (ME, PhD); chemical engineering (ME, MS, PhD); civil engineering (ME, MS, PhD); computer sciences (MS, PhD); electrical engineering (ME, MS, PhD); engineering (ME, MS, PhD); mechanical engineering (ME, MS, PhD). *Application deadline:* For fall admission, 5/1 for domestic and international students; for spring admission, 11/1 for domestic and international students. Applications are processed on a rolling basis. *Application fee:* $125. *Application Contact:* 212-650-6977, Fax: 212-650-6417, E-mail: gradadm@ccny.cuny.edu. *Associate Dean for Graduate Studies,* Dr. Muntaz G. Kassir, 212-650-8030, Fax: 212-650-8024, E-mail: kassir@ccny.cuny.edu.

See Close-Up on page 835.

CITY OF HOPE NATIONAL MEDICAL CENTER/BECKMAN RESEARCH INSTITUTE, Duarte, CA 91010

General Information Independent, coed, graduate-only institution. *Enrollment by degree level:* 55 doctoral. *Graduate faculty:* 81 full-time (21 women). *Graduate housing:* Rooms and/or apartments available on a first-come, first-served basis to single and married students. Typical cost: $3,000 per year for single students; $3,000 per year for married students. Housing application deadline: 7/14. *Student services:* Campus employment opportunities, campus safety program, career counseling, free psychological counseling, grant writing training, international student services, low-cost health insurance, writing training. *Library facilities:* Graff Medical and Scientific Library. *Online resources:* library catalog, web page, access to other libraries' catalogs. *Collection:* 88,724 titles, 930 serial subscriptions.

Computer facilities: 100 computers available on campus for general student use. A campuswide network can be accessed from student residence rooms and from off campus. Internet access, on-line application are available. *Web address:* http://www.cityofhope.org/gradschool/.

General Application Contact: Dr. Steven J. Novak, Director for Administration, 626-256-8775, Fax: 626-301-8105, E-mail: snovak@coh.org.

GRADUATE UNITS

City of Hope Graduate School of Biological Sciences Students: 55 full-time (28 women). Average age 24. 135 applicants, 16% accepted, 14 enrolled. *Faculty:* 81 full-time (21 women). Expenses: Contact institution. *Financial support:* In 2006–07, 8 fellowships (averaging $26,000 per year), 1 research assistantship (averaging $26,000 per year) were awarded; health care benefits and tuition waivers (full) also available. Financial award application deadline: 2/1. In 2006, 39 degrees awarded. Offers biological sciences (PhD). *Application deadline:* For spring admission, 2/1 priority date for domestic and international students. *Application fee:* $0. *Application Contact:* Dr. Steven J. Novak, Director for Administration, 626-256-8775, Fax: 626-301-8105, E-mail: snovak@coh.org. *Dean,* Dr. John J. Rossi, 626-256-8775, Fax: 626-301-8105, E-mail: jrossi@coh.org.

CITY UNIVERSITY, Bellevue, WA 98005

General Information Independent, coed, comprehensive institution. *Graduate housing:* On-campus housing not available.

GRADUATE UNITS

Graduate Division *Degree program information:* Part-time and evening/weekend programs available. Postbaccalaureate distance learning degree programs offered (no on-campus study). Electronic applications accepted.

Gordon Albright School of Education *Degree program information:* Part-time and evening/weekend programs available. Postbaccalaureate distance learning degree programs offered (no on-campus study). Offers curriculum and instruction (M Ed); educational leadership (M Ed); educational leadership: principal certification (M Ed, Certificate); educational leadership: principal/program administrator certification (Certificate); educational leadership: program administrator certification (M Ed, Certificate); guidance and counseling (M Ed, Certificate); integrated arts and performance learning (M Ed); professional certification-teachers (Certificate); reading (Certificate); reading and literacy (M Ed); reading. literacy, and ESL/ELL (M Ed); teacher certification (MIT); technology, curriculum and instruction (M Ed). Electronic applications accepted.

School of Arts and Sciences *Degree program information:* Part-time and evening/weekend programs available. Postbaccalaureate distance learning degree programs offered (no on-campus study). Offers counseling psychology (MA). Electronic applications accepted.

School of Management *Degree program information:* Part-time and evening/weekend programs available. Postbaccalaureate distance learning degree programs offered (no on-campus study). Offers accounting (MBA); C++ programming (Certificate); computer systems—C++ programming (MS); computer systems—individualized study (MS); computer systems—web programming in e-commerce (MS); computer systems-web development (MS); financial management (MBA, Certificate); general management (MBA, MPA, Certificate); general management-Europe (MBA); human resource management (MPA); individualized study (MBA); information systems (MBA, Certificate); management—general management (MA); management—human resource management (MA); management—individualized study (MA); marketing (MBA, Certificate); personal financial planning (MBA, Certificate); project management (MBA, MS, Certificate); technology management (MS, Certificate); web development (Certificate); web programming in e-commerce (Certificate). Electronic applications accepted.

See Close-Up on page 837.

CITY UNIVERSITY OF NEW YORK SCHOOL OF LAW AT QUEENS COLLEGE, Flushing, NY 11367-1358

General Information State and locally supported, coed, graduate-only institution. *Enrollment by degree level:* 421 first professional. *Graduate faculty:* 27 full-time (14 women), 16 part-time/adjunct (10 women). Tuition, state resident: full-time $8,900. Tuition, nonresident: full-time $14,800. *Required fees:* $1,662. *Graduate housing:* On-campus housing not available. *Student services:* Campus employment opportunities, career counseling, child daycare facilities, disabled student services, free psychological counseling, low-cost health insurance, writing training. *Library facilities:* City University of New York School of Law Library. *Online resources:* library catalog, web page, access to other libraries' catalogs. *Collection:* 104,827 titles, 3,077 serial subscriptions, 12 audiovisual materials.

Computer facilities: 103 computers available on campus for general student use. A campuswide network can be accessed from off campus. Internet access, email are available. *Web address:* http://www.law.cuny.edu/.

General Application Contact: Yvonne Cherena-Pacheco, Assistant Dean for Enrollment Management and Director of Admissions, 718-340-4210, Fax: 718-340-4435, E-mail: admissions@mail.law.cuny.edu.

GRADUATE UNITS

Professional Program Students: 417 full-time (274 women), 4 part-time (3 women); includes 131 minority (30 African Americans, 1 American Indian/Alaska Native, 66 Asian Americans or Pacific Islanders, 34 Hispanic Americans), 17 international. Average age 27. 2,457 applicants, 23% accepted, 144 enrolled. *Faculty:* 27 full-time (14 women), 16 part-time/adjunct (10 women). Expenses: Contact institution. *Financial support:* In 2006–07, 124 students received support, including 20 fellowships (averaging $8,900 per year), 35 research assistantships (averaging $3,000 per year), 3 teaching assistantships (averaging $1,920 per year); career-related internships or fieldwork, Federal Work-Study, scholarships/grants, and tuition waivers (partial) also available. Financial award application deadline: 5/1; financial award applicants required to submit FAFSA. In 2006, 128 degrees awarded. Offers law (JD). *Application deadline:* For fall admission, 3/15 priority date for domestic students. Applications are processed on a rolling basis. *Application fee:* $50. Electronic applications accepted. *Application Contact:* Yvonne Cherena-Pacheco, Assistant Dean for Enrollment Management and Director of Admissions, 718-340-4210, Fax: 718-340-4435, E-mail: admissions@mail.law.cuny.edu. *Professor of Law,* Michelle J. Anderson, 718-340-4201, Fax: 718-340-4482.

CLAFLIN UNIVERSITY, Orangeburg, SC 29115

General Information Independent-religious, coed, comprehensive institution. *Library facilities:* H. V. Manning Library plus 1 other. *Online resources:* library catalog. *Collection:* 160,006 titles, 461 serial subscriptions, 1,619 audiovisual materials.

Computer facilities: 500 computers available on campus for general student use. A campuswide network can be accessed from student residence rooms and from off campus. Internet access is available. *Web address:* http://www.claflin.edu/.

General Application Contact: Michael Zeigler, Director of Admissions, 803-535-5747, Fax: 803-535-5385, E-mail: mzeigler@claflin.edu.

GRADUATE UNITS

Graduate Programs Expenses: Contact institution. *Application fee:* $40 ($55 for international students).

CLAREMONT GRADUATE UNIVERSITY, Claremont, CA 91711-6160

General Information Independent, coed, graduate-only institution. CGS member. *Enrollment by degree level:* 765 master's, 1,250 doctoral, 30 other advanced degrees. *Graduate faculty:* 91 full-time (35 women), 81 part-time/adjunct (30 women). *Graduate housing:* Rooms and/or apartments available on a first-come, first-served basis to single and married students. *Student services:* Campus employment opportunities, campus safety program, career counseling, free psychological counseling, international student services, low-cost health insurance, multicultural affairs office, teacher training, writing training. *Library facilities:* Honnold Library plus 3 others. *Online resources:* library catalog, web page, access to other libraries' catalogs. *Collection:* 2.5 million titles. *Research affiliation:* Rancho Santa Ana Botanic Garden (botany/native plants), Claremont School of Theology (religion).

Computer facilities: 90 computers available on campus for general student use. Internet access and online class registration are available. *Web address:* http://www.cgu.edu/.

General Application Contact: Brenda Wright, Assistant Director of Admissions, 909-627-0434, Fax: 909-607-7285, E-mail: admiss@cgu.edu.

GRADUATE UNITS

Graduate Programs Students: 1,638 full-time (810 women), 407 part-time (234 women); includes 547 minority (110 African Americans, 9 American Indian/Alaska Native, 204 Asian Americans or Pacific Islanders, 224 Hispanic Americans), 323 international. Average age 35. *Faculty:* 91 full-time (35 women), 81 part-time/adjunct (30 women). Expenses: Contact institution. *Financial support:* Fellowships, research assistantships, teaching assistantships, career-related internships or fieldwork, Federal Work-Study, institutionally sponsored loans, scholarships/grants, and tuition waivers (full and partial) available. Support available to part-time students. Financial award application deadline: 2/15; financial award applicants required to submit FAFSA. In 2006, 375 master's, 101 doctorates, 32 other advanced degrees awarded. *Degree program information:* Part-time programs available. Offers applied women's studies (MA); botany (MS, PhD); financial engineering (MS, MSFE, PhD). *Application deadline:* For fall admission, 2/15 priority date for domestic students. Applications are processed on a rolling basis. *Application fee:* $50. Electronic applications accepted. *Provost and Vice President for Academic Affairs,* Yi Feng, 909-626-8694, Fax: 909-621-8450, E-mail: yi.feng@cgu.edu.

Peter F. Drucker and Masatoshi Ito Graduate School of Management Students: 159 full-time (57 women), 75 part-time (28 women); includes 64 minority (10 African Americans, 1 American Indian/Alaska Native, 31 Asian Americans or Pacific Islanders, 22 Hispanic Americans), 51 international. Average age 37. *Faculty:* 13 full-time (3 women), 4 part-time/adjunct (1 woman). Expenses: Contact institution. *Financial support:* Fellowships, research assistantships, teaching assistantships, career-related internships or fieldwork, Federal Work-Study, and institutionally sponsored loans available. Support available to part-time students. Financial award application deadline: 2/15; financial award applicants required to submit FAFSA. In 2006, 85 master's, 2 doctorates, 22 other advanced degrees awarded. *Degree program information:* Part-time programs available. Offers advanced management (MS); executive management (EMBA, MA, MS, PhD, Certificate); leadership (Certificate); management (MA, MBA, PhD, Certificate); strategy (Certificate). *Application deadline:* For fall admission, 2/15 priority date for domestic students. Applications are processed on a rolling basis. Electronic applications accepted. *Henry Y. Hwang Dean and Professor of Management,* Ira A. Jackson, 909-607-9209, Fax: 909-621-8543, E-mail: ira.jackson@cgu.edu.

School of Arts and Humanities Students: 366 full-time (194 women), 50 part-time (31 women); includes 85 minority (12 African Americans, 4 American Indian/Alaska Native, 33 Asian Americans or Pacific Islanders, 36 Hispanic Americans), 27 international. Average age 36. *Faculty:* 18 full-time (7 women), 32 part-time/adjunct (14 women). Expenses: Contact institution. *Financial support:* Fellowships, research assistantships, teaching assistantships, Federal Work-Study and institutionally sponsored loans available. Support available to part-time students. Financial award application deadline: 2/15; financial award applicants required to submit FAFSA. In 2006, 54 master's, 14 doctorates, 1 other advanced degree awarded. *Degree program information:* Part-time programs available. Offers Africana history (Certificate); Africana studies (Certificate); American studies (MA, PhD); archival studies (MA); arts and cultural management (MA); arts and humanities (M Phil, MA, MFA, DCM, DMA, PhD, Certificate); church music (MA, DCM); composition (MA, DMA); critical theory (MA, PhD); cultural studies (MA, PhD); digital media (MA, MFA); drawing (MA, MFA); early modern studies (MA, PhD); English (M Phil, MA, PhD); European studies (MA, PhD); installation (MA, MFA); literary theory (PhD); literature (MA, PhD); literature and creative writing (MA); literature and film (MA); musicology (MA, PhD); new genre (MA, MFA); oral history (MA, PhD); painting (MA, MFA); performance (MA, MFA, DMA); philosophy (MA, PhD); photography (MA, MFA); sculpture (MA, MFA). *Application deadline:* For fall admission, 2/15 priority date for domestic students. Applications are processed on a rolling basis. Electronic applications accepted. *Application Contact:* Lindsay Stadler, Admissions Coordinator, 909-607-8612, Fax: 909-607-1221, E-mail: humanities@cgu.edu. *Dean,* Patricia Easton, 909-607-9440, Fax: 909-607-1221, E-mail: patricia.easton@cgu.edu.

School of Behavioral and Organizational Sciences Students: 198 full-time (144 women), 26 part-time (20 women); includes 73 minority (19 African Americans, 1 American Indian/Alaska Native, 33 Asian Americans or Pacific Islanders, 20 Hispanic Americans), 18 international. Average age 29. *Faculty:* 12 full-time (6 women), 8 part-time/adjunct (1 woman). Expenses: Contact institution. *Financial support:* Fellowships, research assistantships, teaching assistantships, career-related internships or fieldwork, Federal Work-Study, and tuition waivers (full and partial) available. Support available to part-time students. Financial award application deadline: 2/15; financial award applicants required to submit FAFSA. In 2006, 49 master's, 14 doctorates, 9 other advanced degrees awarded. *Degree program information:* Part-time programs available. Offers advanced study in evaluation (Certificate); behavioral and organizational sciences (MA, MS, PhD, Certificate); cognitive psychology (MA, PhD); developmental psychology (MA, PhD); evaluation and applied methods (MA, PhD); human resources design (MS); organizational behavior (MA, PhD); social psychology (MA, PhD). *Application deadline:* For fall admission, 2/15 priority date for domestic students. Applications are processed on a rolling basis. Electronic applications accepted. *Application Contact:* Paul Thomas, Program Coordinator, 909-621-8084, Fax: 909-621-8905, E-mail: paul.thomas@cgu.edu. *Dean,* Stewart Donaldson, 909-607-9001, E-mail: stewart.donaldson@cgu.edu.

School of Educational Studies Students: 236 full-time (155 women), 168 part-time (117 women); includes 177 minority (34 African Americans, 2 American Indian/Alaska Native, 43 Asian Americans or Pacific Islanders, 98 Hispanic Americans), 7 international. Average age 38. *Faculty:* 15 full-time (9 women), 11 part-time/adjunct (9 women). Expenses: Contact institution. *Financial support:* Fellowships, research assistantships, Federal Work-Study and institutionally sponsored loans available. Support available to part-time students. Financial award application deadline: 2/15; financial award applicants required to submit FAFSA. In 2006, 90 master's, 20 doctorates awarded. *Degree program information:* Part-time programs available. Offers Africana education (Certificate); education policy issues (MA, PhD); higher education (PhD); higher education administration (MA); human development (MA, PhD); public school administration (MA, PhD); teacher education (MA, PhD); teaching and learning (MA, PhD); urban education administration (MA, PhD). *Application deadline:* For fall admission, 2/15 priority date for domestic students. Applications are processed on a rolling basis. Electronic applications accepted. *Application Contact:* Cece Gaddy, Administrative Director, 909-621-8317, Fax: 909-621-8734, E-mail: cece.gaddy@cgu.edu. *Dean,* Philip H. Dreyer, 909-621-8075, Fax: 909-621-8734, E-mail: philip.dreyer@cgu.edu.

School of Information Systems and Technology Students: 68 full-time (22 women), 44 part-time (16 women); includes 32 minority (3 African Americans, 21 Asian Americans or Pacific Islanders, 8 Hispanic Americans), 28 international. Average age 37. *Faculty:* 5 full-time (1 woman), 4 part-time/adjunct (0 women). Expenses: Contact institution. *Financial support:* Fellowships, research assistantships, teaching assistantships, Federal Work-Study and institutionally sponsored loans available. Support available to part-time students. Financial award application deadline: 2/15; financial award applicants required to submit FAFSA. In 2006, 13 master's, 7 doctorates awarded. *Degree program information:* Part-time programs available. Offers electronic commerce (MS, PhD); information systems (Certificate); knowledge management (MS, PhD); systems development (MS, PhD); telecommunications and networking (MS, PhD). *Application deadline:* For fall admission, 2/15 priority date for domestic students. Applications are processed on a rolling basis. Electronic applications accepted. *Application Contact:* Go Yoshida, Director of Recruitment/Admissions, 909-621-3140, Fax: 909-621-8564, E-mail: go.yoshida@cgu.edu. *Dean,* Lorne Olfman, 909-607-3035, Fax: 909-621-8564, E-mail: lorne.olfman@cgu.edu.

School of Mathematical Sciences Students: 51 full-time (7 women), 10 part-time (3 women); includes 12 minority (2 African Americans, 5 Asian Americans or Pacific Islanders, 5 Hispanic Americans), 18 international. Average age 37. *Faculty:* 3 full-time (0 women), 4 part-time/adjunct (1 woman). Expenses: Contact institution. *Financial support:* Fellowships, research assistantships, career-related internships or fieldwork, Federal Work-Study, institutionally sponsored loans, and tuition waivers (full and partial) available. Support available to part-time students. Financial award application deadline: 2/15; financial award applicants required to submit FAFSA. In 2006, 7 master's, 5 doctorates awarded. *Degree program information:* Part-time programs available. Offers computational and systems biology (PhD); computational science (PhD); engineering mathematics (PhD); operations research and statistics (MA, MS); physical applied mathematics (MA, MS); pure mathematics (MA, MS); scientific computing (MA, MS); systems and control theory (MA, MS). *Application deadline:* For fall admission, 2/15 priority date for domestic students. Applications are processed on a rolling basis. Electronic applications accepted. *Application Contact:* Susan Townzen, Program Coordinator, 909-621-8080, Fax: 909-607-8261, E-mail: susan.n.townzen@cgu.edu. *Dean,* John Angus, 909-621-8080, Fax: 909-607-8261, E-mail: john.angus@cgu.edu.

School of Politics and Economics Students: 281 full-time (100 women), 24 part-time (14 women); includes 53 minority (13 African Americans, 17 Asian Americans or Pacific Islanders, 23 Hispanic Americans), 110 international. Average age 34. *Faculty:* 14 full-time (3 women), 11 part-time/adjunct (2 women). Expenses: Contact institution. *Financial support:* Fellowships, research assistantships, teaching assistantships, career-related internships or fieldwork, Federal Work-Study, and institutionally sponsored loans available. Support available to part-time students. Financial award application deadline: 2/15; financial award applicants required to submit FAFSA. In 2006, 47 master's, 22 doctorates awarded. *Degree program information:* Part-time programs available. Offers American politics (MA, PhD); business and financial economics (MA, PhD); comparative politics (PhD); economic development (Certificate); economics (PhD); international economic policy and management (MA, PhD); international political economy (MA); international studies (MA); political economy and public policy (MA, PhD); political philosophy (PhD); political science (PhD); politics and economics (MA, PhD, Certificate); politics, economics and business (MA); public policy (MA, PhD); world politics (PhD). *Application deadline:* For fall admission, 2/15 priority date for domestic students. Applications are processed on a rolling basis. Electronic applications accepted. *Application Contact:* Rita Clemons, Admissions Coordinator, 909-621-8699, Fax: 909-621-8545, E-mail: rita.clemons@cgu.edu. *Dean,* Thomas Willett, 909-601-8787, Fax: 909-621-8545, E-mail: thomas.willett@cgu.edu.

School of Religion Students: 212 full-time (92 women), 8 part-time (3 women); includes 41 minority (16 African Americans, 1 American Indian/Alaska Native, 14 Asian Americans or Pacific Islanders, 10 Hispanic Americans), 33 international. Average age 38. *Faculty:* 5 full-time (2 women), 7 part-time/adjunct (2 women). Expenses: Contact institution. *Financial support:* Fellowships, research assistantships, teaching assistantships, Federal Work-Study and institutionally sponsored loans available. Support available to part-time students. Financial award application deadline: 2/15; financial award applicants required to submit FAFSA. In 2006, 11 master's, 14 doctorates awarded. *Degree program information:* Part-time programs available. Offers Hebrew Bible (MA, PhD); history of Christianity and religion in North America (MA, PhD); New Testament (MA, PhD); philosophy of religion and theology (MA, PhD); theology, ethics and culture (MA, PhD); women's studies in religion (MA, PhD). *Application deadline:* For fall admission, 2/15 priority date for domestic students. Applications are processed on a rolling basis. Electronic applications accepted. *Application Contact:* Patrick Horn, Associate Dean, 909-607-8411, Fax: 909-607-9587, E-mail: patrick.horn@cgu.edu. *Dean,* Karen Torjesen, 909-607-3214, Fax: 909-621-9587, E-mail: karen.torjesen@cgu.edu.

CLAREMONT SCHOOL OF THEOLOGY, Claremont, CA 91711-3199

General Information Independent-religious, coed, graduate-only institution. *Enrollment by degree level:* 112 first professional, 71 master's, 45 doctoral, 26 other advanced degrees. *Graduate faculty:* 18 full-time (7 women), 27 part-time/adjunct (12 women). *Tuition:* Part-time $520 per unit. *Required fees:* $190 per semester. Tuition and fees vary according to degree level. *Graduate housing:* Rooms and/or apartments guaranteed to single and married students. Typical cost: $5,985 per year for single students; $9,504 per year for married students. Housing application deadline: 6/1. *Student services:* Campus employment opportunities, career counseling, international student services, low-cost health insurance, writing training. *Library facilities:* Claremont School of Theology Library. *Online resources:* library catalog, web page, access to other libraries' catalogs. *Collection:* 198,406 titles, 628 serial subscriptions, 644 audiovisual materials. *Research affiliation:* Moore Multicultural Resource and Research Center, Institute for Antiquity and Christianity, Center for Process Studies, National United Methodist Native American Center, Center for Pacific and Asian-American Ministries, Ancient Biblical Manuscript Center.

Computer facilities: 20 computers available on campus for general student use. A campuswide network can be accessed. Internet access is available. *Web address:* http://www.cst.edu/.

General Application Contact: Director of Admissions, 866-274-6500, Fax: 909-447-6389, E-mail: admission@cst.edu.

GRADUATE UNITS

Graduate and Professional Programs Students: 88 full-time (44 women), 166 part-time (82 women); includes 77 minority (28 African Americans, 3 American Indian/Alaska Native, 40 Asian Americans or Pacific Islanders, 6 Hispanic Americans), 34 international. Average age 39. 151 applicants, 68% accepted, 55 enrolled. *Faculty:* 18 full-time (7 women), 27 part-time/adjunct (12 women). Expenses: Contact institution. *Financial support:* In 2006–07, 180 students received support, including 10 research assistantships (averaging $1,200 per year), 8 teaching assistantships (averaging $2,000 per year); career-related internships or fieldwork, Federal Work-Study, institutionally sponsored loans, scholarships/grants, and tuition waivers (full and partial) also available. Support available to part-time students. Financial award application deadline: 4/1; financial award applicants required to submit FAFSA. In 2006, 29 M Divs, 24 master's, 14 doctorates awarded. *Degree program information:* Part-time programs available. Offers divinity (M Div); ministry (D Min); practical theology (PhD); religion and theology (MA); religious education (MARE). *Application deadline:* For fall admission, 5/1 for domestic students, 4/1 for international students; for winter admission, 11/1 for domestic and international students; for spring admission, 11/1 priority date for domestic students, 11/1 for international students. Applications are processed on a rolling basis. *Application fee:* $50. Electronic applications accepted. *Application Contact:* Director of Admissions, 866-274-6500, E-mail: admission@cst.edu. *Vice President for Academic Affairs and Dean,* Susan L. Nelson, 909-447-2520, Fax: 909-447-6274, E-mail: snelson@cst.edu.

CLARION UNIVERSITY OF PENNSYLVANIA, Clarion, PA 16214

General Information State-supported, coed, comprehensive institution. CGS member. *Enrollment:* 6,591 graduate, professional, and undergraduate students; 538 matriculated graduate/professional students. *Graduate faculty:* 71. Tuition, state resident: part-time $336 per credit. Tuition, nonresident: part-time $538 per credit. *Graduate housing:* Room and/or apartments available on a first-come, first-served basis to single students; on-campus housing not available to married students. *Student services:* Campus employment opportunities, campus safety program, career counseling, child daycare facilities, disabled student services, free psychological counseling, international student services, low-cost health insurance. *Library* *facilities:* Carlson Library. *Online resources:* library catalog, web page, access to other libraries' catalogs. *Collection:* 442,871 titles, 20,264 serial subscriptions, 7,122 audiovisual materials.

Computer facilities: 400 computers available on campus for general student use. A campuswide network can be accessed from student residence rooms and from off campus. Internet access and online class registration are available. *Web address:* http://www.clarion.edu/.

General Application Contact: Dr. Brenda Sanders Dédé, Assistant Vice President for Academic Affairs, 814-393-2337, Fax: 814-393-2030, E-mail: bdede@clarion.edu.

GRADUATE UNITS

Office of Research and Graduate Studies Students: 521. Expenses: Contact institution. *Financial support:* Research assistantships with full and partial tuition reimbursements, career-related internships or fieldwork available. Support available to part-time students. Financial award application deadline: 5/1. *Degree program information:* Part-time and evening/weekend programs available. *Assistant Vice President for Academic Affairs,* Dr. Brenda Sanders Dédé, 814-393-2337, Fax: 814-393-2030, E-mail: bdede@clarion.edu.

College of Arts and Sciences Students: 35 full-time (20 women), 9 part-time (8 women); includes 4 minority (all African Americans), 3 international. 39 applicants, 64% accepted. Expenses: Contact institution. *Financial support:* In 2006–07, 15 research assistantships with full tuition reimbursements were awarded. Support available to part-time students. Financial award application deadline: 3/1. In 2006, 16 degrees awarded. *Degree program information:* Part-time programs available. Offers arts and sciences (MA, MS); biology (MS); English (MA); mass media arts, journalism, and communication studies (MS). *Application deadline:* For fall admission, 4/15 priority date for international students; for spring admission, 12/1 priority date for domestic students, 9/15 priority date for international students. Applications are processed on a rolling basis. *Application fee:* $30. Electronic applications accepted. *Interim Dean,* Dr. Stephen R. Johnson, 814-393-2225.

College of Business Administration Students: 27 full-time (9 women), 14 part-time (8 women); includes 3 minority (2 African Americans, 1 Hispanic American), 9 international. 53 applicants, 43% accepted. *Faculty:* 23 full-time (2 women). Expenses: Contact institution. *Financial support:* In 2006–07, 16 research assistantships with partial tuition reimbursements (averaging $2,001 per year) were awarded; career-related internships or fieldwork also available. Support available to part-time students. Financial award application deadline: 3/1. In 2006, 20 degrees awarded. *Degree program information:* Part-time and evening/weekend programs available. Offers business administration (MBA). *Application deadline:* For fall admission, 8/1 priority date for domestic students, 4/15 priority date for international students; for spring admission, 12/1 priority date for domestic students, 9/15 priority date for international students. Applications are processed on a rolling basis. *Application fee:* $30. Electronic applications accepted. *Application Contact:* Dr. Soga Ewedemi, MBA Director, 814-393-2605, Fax: 814-393-1910, E-mail: sewedemi@clarion.edu. *Interim Dean,* Dr. James Pesek, 814-393-2600, Fax: 814-393-1910, E-mail: jpesek@clarion.edu.

College of Education and Human Services Students: 387. Expenses: Contact institution. *Financial support:* Research assistantships with full and partial tuition reimbursements, career-related internships or fieldwork available. Support available to part-time students. Financial award application deadline: 3/1. *Degree program information:* Part-time programs available. Offers communication sciences and disorders (MS); curriculum and instruction (M Ed); early childhood (M Ed); education (M Ed); education and human services (M Ed, MS, MSLS, CAS); English (M Ed); history (M Ed); library science (MSLS, CAS); literacy (M Ed); reading (M Ed); rehabilitative sciences (MS); science (M Ed); science education (M Ed); special education (MS); technology (M Ed). *Application deadline:* Applications are processed on a rolling basis. *Interim Dean,* Dr. Nancy Sayre, 814-393-2146, Fax: 814-393-2446, E-mail: nsayre@clarion.edu.

School of Nursing Students: 1 (woman) full-time, 53 part-time (44 women); includes 1 minority (African American) 44 applicants, 82% accepted. *Faculty:* 4 full-time (all women). Expenses: Contact institution. *Financial support:* In 2006–07, 1 research assistantship with full tuition reimbursement (averaging $4,002 per year) was awarded. Financial award application deadline: 3/1. In 2006, 25 degrees awarded. Offers nursing (MSN). *Application deadline:* For fall admission, 6/1 for domestic students, 4/15 priority date for international students; for spring admission, 11/1 for domestic students, 9/15 priority date for international students. *Application fee:* $30. *Acting Director,* Joyce Keenan, 814-676-6591 Ext. 1257, Fax: 814-676-0251, E-mail: jkeenan@clarion.edu.

See Close-Up on page 839.

CLARK ATLANTA UNIVERSITY, Atlanta, GA 30314

General Information Independent-religious, coed, university. CGS member. *Graduate housing:* Room and/or apartments available to single students; on-campus housing not available to married students. Housing application deadline: 6/1.

GRADUATE UNITS

School of Arts and Sciences *Degree program information:* Part-time programs available. Offers African-American studies (MA); Africana women's studies (MA, DA); applied mathematics (MS); arts and sciences (MA, MPA, MS, DA, PhD); biology (MS, PhD); computer and information science (MS); computer science (MS); criminal justice (MA); economics (MA); English (MA); history (MA); humanities (DA); inorganic chemistry (MS, PhD); organic chemistry (MS, PhD); physical chemistry (MS, PhD); physics (MS); political science (MA, PhD); public administration (MPA); Romance languages (MA); science education (DA); sociology (MA).

School of Business Administration *Degree program information:* Part-time programs available. Offers business administration (MBA); decision science (MBA); finance (MBA); marketing (MBA).

School of Education *Degree program information:* Part-time and evening/weekend programs available. Offers counseling (MA, PhD); curriculum (MA, Ed S); education (MA, Ed D, PhD, Ed S); education psychology (MA); educational leadership (MA, Ed D, Ed S); exceptional student education (MA, Ed S).

School of International Affairs and Development Offers international affairs and development (PhD); international business and development (MA); international development administration (MA); international development education and planning (MA); international relations (MA); regional studies (MA).

School of Social Work *Degree program information:* Part-time programs available. Offers social work (MSW, PhD).

CLARKE COLLEGE, Dubuque, IA 52001-3198

General Information Independent-religious, coed, comprehensive institution. *Graduate housing:* On-campus housing not available.

GRADUATE UNITS

Department of Nursing and Health *Degree program information:* Part-time programs available. Offers administration of nursing systems (MSN); advanced practice nursing (MSN); education (MSN); family nurse practitioner (MSN, PMC). Electronic applications accepted.

Physical Therapy Program Offers physical therapy (MSPT). Freshman-entry master's degree program; entry to the MSPT is determined after junior year of the BS program.

Program in Education *Degree program information:* Part-time and evening/weekend programs available. Postbaccalaureate distance learning degree programs offered (minimal on-campus study). Offers early childhood/special education (MA); educational administration: elementary and secondary (MA); educational media: elementary and secondary (MA); multi-categorical resource K–12 (MA); multidisciplinary studies (MA); reading: elementary (MA); technology in education (MA). Electronic applications accepted.

Program in Management *Degree program information:* Part-time and evening/weekend programs available. Offers management (MS). Electronic applications accepted.

CLARKSON COLLEGE, Omaha, NE 68131-2739

General Information Independent, coed, primarily women, comprehensive institution. *Graduate housing:* Room and/or apartments available on a first-come, first-served basis to single students; on-campus housing not available to married students. Housing application deadline: 8/1.

GRADUATE UNITS

Graduate Programs *Degree program information:* Part-time and evening/weekend programs available. Postbaccalaureate distance learning degree programs offered (minimal on-campus study). Offers administration (MSN); education (MSN); family nurse practitioner (MSN). Electronic applications accepted.

CLARKSON UNIVERSITY, Potsdam, NY 13699

General Information Independent, coed, university. *Enrollment:* 2,964 graduate, professional, and undergraduate students; 377 full-time matriculated graduate/professional students (89 women), 37 part-time matriculated graduate/professional students (16 women). *Enrollment by degree level:* 10 first professional, 260 master's, 134 doctoral. *Graduate faculty:* 117 full-time (20 women), 10 part-time/adjunct (5 women). *Tuition:* Full-time $22,776; part-time $949 per credit. *Required fees:* $215. *Graduate housing:* On-campus housing not available. *Student services:* Campus employment opportunities, campus safety program, career counseling, disabled student services, free psychological counseling, international student services, low-cost health insurance, multicultural affairs office. *Library facilities:* Andrew S. Schuler Educational Resources Center plus 1 other. *Online resources:* library catalog, web page. *Collection:* 269,059 titles, 1,778 serial subscriptions, 2,128 audiovisual materials.

Computer facilities: Computer purchase and lease plans are available. 400 computers available on campus for general student use. A campuswide network can be accessed from student residence rooms and from off campus. Internet access and online class registration are available. *Web address:* http://www.clarkson.edu/.

General Application Contact: Donna Brockway, Graduate Admissions International Advisor/Assistant to the Provost, 315-268-6447, Fax: 315-268-7994, E-mail: brockway@clarkson.edu.

GRADUATE UNITS

Graduate School Students: 377 full-time (89 women), 37 part-time (16 women); includes 6 minority (2 African Americans, 3 Asian Americans or Pacific Islanders, 1 Hispanic American), 182 international. Average age 25. 724 applicants, 58% accepted, 169 enrolled. *Faculty:* 117 full-time (20 women), 10 part-time/adjunct (5 women). Expenses: Contact institution. *Financial support:* In 2006–07, 348 students received support, including 2 fellowships with tuition reimbursements available (averaging $25,000 per year), 114 research assistantships with tuition reimbursements available (averaging $19,500 per year), 66 teaching assistantships with tuition reimbursements available (averaging $19,500 per year); scholarships/grants and tuition waivers (partial) also available. Financial award applicants required to submit FAFSA. In 2006, 150 master's, 28 doctorates awarded. *Degree program information:* Part-time and evening/weekend programs available. *Application deadline:* For fall admission, 5/15 priority date for domestic students; for spring admission, 10/15 priority date for domestic students. Applications are processed on a rolling basis. *Application fee:* $25 ($35 for international students). Electronic applications accepted. *Application Contact:* Donna Brockway, Graduate Admissions International Advisor/Assistant to the Provost, 315-268-6447, Fax: 315-268-7994, E-mail: brockway@clarkson.edu.

Center for Health Science Students: 26 full-time (19 women), 2 part-time (1 woman). Average age 26. 17 applicants, 82% accepted, 12 enrolled. *Faculty:* 6 full-time (4 women), 2 part-time/adjunct (both women). Expenses: Contact institution. In 2006, 5 degrees awarded. *Degree program information:* Part-time programs available. Offers basic science (MS); health science (MPT, MS, DPT); physical therapy (MPT, DPT). *Application deadline:* For fall admission, 5/15 priority date for domestic students; for spring admission, 10/15 priority date for domestic students. Applications are processed on a rolling basis. *Application fee:* $25 ($35 for international students). Electronic applications accepted. *Associate Dean of Health Sciences,* Dr. Scott Minor, 315-268-3786, Fax: 315-268-1539, E-mail: sminor@clarkson.edu.

School of Arts and Sciences Students: 90 full-time (17 women), 5 part-time (3 women); includes 1 African American, 2 Asian Americans or Pacific Islanders, 55 international. Average age 27. 180 applicants, 56% accepted, 25 enrolled. *Faculty:* 37 full-time (5 women), 4 part-time/adjunct (2 women). Expenses: Contact institution. *Financial support:* In 2006–07, 85 students received support, including 1 fellowship (averaging $25,000 per year), 21 research assistantships (averaging $19,500 per year), 35 teaching assistantships (averaging $19,500 per year); scholarships/grants and tuition waivers (partial) also available. In 2006, 29 master's, 5 doctorates awarded. *Degree program information:* Part-time programs available. Offers analytical chemistry (MS, PhD); arts and sciences (MS, PhD); computer science (MS); information technology (MS); inorganic chemistry (MS, PhD); mathematics (MS, PhD); organic chemistry (MS, PhD); physical chemistry (MS, PhD); physics (MS, PhD). *Application deadline:* For fall admission, 5/15 priority date for domestic students; for spring admission, 10/15 priority date for domestic students. Applications are processed on a rolling basis. *Application fee:* $25 ($35 for international students). Electronic applications accepted. *Application Contact:* Donna Brockway, Graduate Admissions International Advisor/Assistant to the Provost, 315-268-6447, Fax: 315-268-7994, E-mail: brockway@clarkson.edu. *Dean,* Dr. Dick Pratt, 315-268-2365, Fax: 315-268-3989, E-mail: jpratt@clarkson.edu.

School of Business Students: 58 full-time (17 women), 29 part-time (12 women), 14 international. Average age 28. 167 applicants, 59% accepted, 66 enrolled. *Faculty:* 13 full-time (2 women). Expenses: Contact institution. *Financial support:* In 2006–07, 56 students received support. Tuition waivers (full) available. In 2006, 71 degrees awarded. *Degree program information:* Part-time and evening/weekend programs available. Offers business (MBA, MS); business administration (MBA); engineering and global operations management (MS); human resource management (MS); management information systems (MS); manufacturing management (MS). *Application deadline:* For fall admission, 5/15 priority date for domestic students; for spring admission, 10/15 priority date for domestic students. Applications are processed on a rolling basis. *Application fee:* $25 ($35 for international students). Electronic applications accepted. *Application Contact:* Dr. Farzad Mahmoodi, Graduate Director, 315-268-4281, Fax: 315-268-3810, E-mail: mahmoodi@clarkson.edu. *Director,* Dr. Farzad Mahmoodi, 315-268-4281, Fax: 315-268-3810, E-mail: mahmoodi@clarkson.edu.

School of Engineering Students: 203 full-time (36 women); includes 2 minority (1 African American, 1 Asian American or Pacific Islander), 113 international. Average age 30. 360 applicants, 57% accepted. *Faculty:* 61 full-time (9 women), 4 part-time/adjunct (1 woman). Expenses: Contact institution. *Financial support:* In 2006–07, 179 students received support, including 1 fellowship (averaging $25,000 per year), 93 research assistantships (averaging $19,500 per year), 31 teaching assistantships (averaging $19,500 per year); scholarships/grants and tuition waivers (partial) also available. In 2006, 45 master's, 23 doctorates awarded. *Degree program information:* Part-time programs available. Offers chemical and biomolecular engineering (ME, MS, PhD); civil and environmental engineering (PhD); civil engineering (ME, MS); computer engineering (ME, MS); electrical and computer engineering (PhD); electrical engineering (ME, MS); engineering (ME, MS, PhD); environmental science and engineering (MS, PhD); interdisciplinary engineering science (MS, PhD); mechanical engineering (ME, MS, PhD). *Application deadline:* For fall admission, 5/15 priority date for domestic students; for spring admission, 10/15 priority date for domestic students. Applications are processed on a rolling basis. *Application fee:* $25 ($35 for international students). Electronic applications accepted. *Application Contact:* Donna Brockway, Graduate Admissions International Advisor/Assistant to the Provost, 315-268-6447, Fax: 315-268-7994, E-mail: brockway@clarkson.edu. *Dean,* Dr. Goodarz Ahmadi, 315-268-4494, Fax: 315-268-2322, E-mail: ahmadi@clarkson.edu.

CLARK UNIVERSITY, Worcester, MA 01610-1477

General Information Independent, coed, university. CGS member. *Enrollment:* 3,071 graduate, professional, and undergraduate students; 568 full-time matriculated graduate/professional

Clark University (continued)

students (344 women), 203 part-time matriculated graduate/professional students (96 women). *Enrollment by degree level:* 570 master's, 198 doctoral, 3 other advanced degrees. *Graduate faculty:* 179 full-time (70 women), 131 part-time/adjunct (60 women). *Graduate housing:* Rooms and/or apartments available on a first-come, first-served basis to single and married students. *Student services:* Campus employment opportunities, career counseling, international student services, low-cost health insurance. *Library facilities:* Robert Hutchings Goddard Library plus 4 others. *Online resources:* library catalog, web page, access to other libraries' catalogs. *Collection:* 289,658 titles, 1,383 serial subscriptions. *Research affiliation:* Worcester Foundation for Experimental Biology, Worcester Area Computation Center, Massachusetts Biotechnology Research Institute.

Computer facilities: 200 computers available on campus for general student use. A campuswide network can be accessed from student residence rooms and from off campus. Internet access, online course support are available. *Web address:* http://www.clarku.edu/.

General Application Contact: Denise Robertson, Graduate School Coordinator, 508-793-7676, Fax: 508-793-8834, E-mail: gradadmissions@clarku.edu.

GRADUATE UNITS

Graduate School Students: 568 full-time (344 women), 203 part-time (96 women); includes 43 minority (13 African Americans, 2 American Indian/Alaska Native, 14 Asian Americans or Pacific Islanders, 14 Hispanic Americans), 310 international. Average age 30. 1,156 applicants, 57% accepted, 300 enrolled. *Faculty:* 179 full-time (70 women), 131 part-time/adjunct (60 women). Expenses: Contact institution. *Financial support:* In 2006–07, 5 fellowships with full and partial tuition reimbursements (averaging $12,500 per year), 60 research assistantships with full and partial tuition reimbursements (averaging $12,500 per year), 110 teaching assistantships with full and partial tuition reimbursements (averaging $12,500 per year) were awarded; career-related internships or fieldwork, Federal Work-Study, institutionally sponsored loans, scholarships/grants, and tuition waivers (full and partial) also available. Support available to part-time students. In 2006, 331 master's, 33 doctorates awarded. *Degree program information:* Part-time and evening/weekend programs available. Offers biology (MA, PhD); chemistry (MA, PhD); clinical psychology (PhD); community development and planning (MA); developmental psychology (PhD); economics (PhD); education (MA Ed); English (MA); environmental science and policy (MA); geographic information science (MA); geographic information science for development and environment (MA); geography (PhD); history (MA, CAGS); holocaust history (PhD); international development and social change (MA); physics (MA, PhD); social-personality psychology (PhD). *Application deadline:* Applications are processed on a rolling basis. *Application fee:* $50. Electronic applications accepted. *Application Contact:* Denise Robertson, Graduate School Coordinator, 508-793-7676, Fax: 508-793-8834, E-mail: gradadmissions@clarku.edu. *Director,* Dr. Nancy Budwig, 508-793-7274.

College of Professional and Continuing Education Students: 32 full-time (25 women), 57 part-time (35 women); includes 10 minority (7 African Americans, 1 American Indian/Alaska Native, 1 Asian American or Pacific Islander, 1 Hispanic American), 7 international. Average age 34. 30 applicants, 97% accepted, 27 enrolled. *Faculty:* 44 part-time/adjunct (16 women). Expenses: Contact institution. *Financial support:* Career-related internships or fieldwork available. Support available to part-time students. In 2006, 63 degrees awarded. *Degree program information:* Part-time and evening/weekend programs available. Offers information technology (MIT); liberal studies (MALA); professional and continuing education (MALA, MIT, MPA, MSPC, CAGS, Certificate); professional communication (MSPC); public administration (MPA, Certificate). *Application deadline:* Applications are processed on a rolling basis. *Application fee:* $50. Electronic applications accepted. *Application Contact:* Julia Parent, Director of Marketing, Communications, and Admissions, 508-793-7217, Fax: 508-793-7232, E-mail: jparent@clarku.edu. *Director,* Dr. Thomas Massey, 508-793-7217.

Graduate School of Management Students: 161 full-time (88 women), 125 part-time (47 women); includes 20 minority (4 African Americans, 9 Asian Americans or Pacific Islanders, 7 Hispanic Americans), 157 international. Average age 29. 342 applicants, 81% accepted, 110 enrolled. *Faculty:* 18 full-time (6 women), 11 part-time/adjunct (5 women). Expenses: Contact institution. *Financial support:* In 2006–07, 12 research assistantships with partial tuition reimbursements (averaging $6,000 per year), 12 teaching assistantships with partial tuition reimbursements (averaging $6,000 per year) were awarded; fellowships, career-related internships or fieldwork, Federal Work-Study, institutionally sponsored loans, and tuition waivers (partial) also available. Support available to part-time students. Financial award application deadline: 5/31. In 2006, 122 degrees awarded. *Degree program information:* Part-time and evening/weekend programs available. Offers accounting (MBA); finance (MBA); global business (MBA); health care management (MBA); management (MBA); management of information technology (MBA); marketing (MBA). *Application deadline:* For fall admission, 6/1 priority date for domestic students; for spring admission, 12/1 priority date for domestic students. Applications are processed on a rolling basis. *Application fee:* $50. Electronic applications accepted. *Application Contact:* Patricia Tollo, Admissions Director, 508-793-7406, Fax: 508-793-8822, E-mail: clarkmba@clarku.edu. *Dean,* Dr. Edward Ottensmeyer, 508-793-7406, Fax: 508-793-8822.

See Close-Up on page 841.

CLAYTON STATE UNIVERSITY, Morrow, GA 30260-0285

General Information State-supported, coed, comprehensive institution.

GRADUATE UNITS

School of Graduate Studies Offers business administration (MBA); health administration (MHA); liberal studies (MALS); nursing (MSN).

CLEARY UNIVERSITY, Ann Arbor, MI 48105-2659

General Information Independent, coed, comprehensive institution. *Enrollment:* 691 graduate, professional, and undergraduate students; 8 full-time matriculated graduate/professional students (4 women), 57 part-time matriculated graduate/professional students (33 women). *Enrollment by degree level:* 65 master's. *Graduate faculty:* 4 full-time (2 women), 16 part-time/adjunct (7 women). *Tuition:* Full-time $11,900; part-time $425 per credit hour. *Graduate housing:* On-campus housing not available. *Student services:* Campus employment opportunities, career counseling, writing training. *Library facilities:* Cleary University Library plus 1 other. *Online resources:* library catalog, web page. *Collection:* 10,000 titles, 330 audiovisual materials.

Computer facilities: 60 computers available on campus for general student use. A campuswide network can be accessed from off campus. Internet access is available. *Web address:* http://www.cleary.edu/.

General Application Contact: Carrie Bonofiglio, Director of Student Recruiting, 800-589-1979 Ext. 2213, Fax: 517-552-7805, E-mail: cbono@cleary.edu.

GRADUATE UNITS

Online Program in Business Administration Students: 8 full-time (4 women), 57 part-time (33 women); includes 10 minority (7 African Americans, 1 American Indian/Alaska Native, 2 Asian Americans or Pacific Islanders), 1 international. Average age 34. 39 applicants, 85% accepted, 28 enrolled. *Faculty:* 4 full-time (2 women), 16 part-time/adjunct (7 women). Expenses: Contact institution. *Financial support:* In 2006–07, 14 students received support, including 14 fellowships; Federal Work-Study and scholarships/grants also available. Support available to part-time students. Financial award application deadline: 8/15; financial award applicants required to submit FAFSA. In 2006, 13 degrees awarded. *Degree program information:* Part-time and evening/weekend programs available. Postbaccalaureate distance learning degree programs offered (no on-campus study). Offers business (MBA). *Application deadline:* For fall admission, 8/15 for domestic students, 7/15 for international students; for spring admission, 4/2 for domestic students, 1/2 for international students. Applications are processed on a rolling basis. *Application fee:* $50. Electronic applications accepted. *Application Contact:* Carrie Bonofiglio, Director of Student Recruiting, 800-589-1979, Fax: 517-552-7805, E-mail: cbono@cleary.edu. *Provost and Vice President Academic Affairs,* Dr. Vincent Linder, 800-686-1883, Fax: 734-332-4646, E-mail: vlinder@cleary.edu.

Program in Business Administration Students: 8 full-time (4 women), 57 part-time (33 women); includes 10 minority (7 African Americans, 1 American Indian/Alaska Native, 2 Asian Americans or Pacific Islanders), 1 international. Average age 34. 39 applicants, 85% accepted, 28 enrolled. *Faculty:* 4 full-time (2 women), 16 part-time/adjunct (7 women). Expenses: Contact institution. *Financial support:* In 2006–07, 14 students received support, including 14 fellowships; Federal Work-Study and scholarships/grants also available. Support available to part-time students. Financial award application deadline: 8/15; financial award applicants required to submit FAFSA. In 2006, 13 degrees awarded. *Degree program information:* Part-time and evening/weekend programs available. Postbaccalaureate distance learning degree programs offered (minimal on-campus study). Offers accounting (MBA); management (MBA). *Application deadline:* For fall admission, 8/15 for domestic students, 7/15 for international students; for spring admission, 4/2 for domestic and international students. Applications are processed on a rolling basis. *Application fee:* $50. Electronic applications accepted. *Application Contact:* Carrie Bonofiglio, Director of Student Recruiting, 800-589-1979 Ext. 2213, Fax: 517-552-7805, E-mail: cbono@cleary.edu. *Provost and Vice President Academic Affairs,* Dr. Vincent Linder, 800-686-1883, Fax: 734-332-4646, E-mail: vlinder@cleary.edu.

CLEMSON UNIVERSITY, Clemson, SC 29634

General Information State-supported, coed, university. CGS member. *Enrollment:* 17,165 graduate, professional, and undergraduate students; 2,009 full-time matriculated graduate/professional students (849 women), 837 part-time matriculated graduate/professional students (452 women). *Enrollment by degree level:* 1,838 master's, 1,008 doctoral. *Graduate faculty:* 1,056 full-time (299 women), 90 part-time/adjunct (28 women). Tuition, state resident: full-time $8,812; part-time $450 per hour. Tuition, nonresident: full-time $18,036; part-time $760 per hour. *Required fees:* $474; $5 per term. *Graduate housing:* Rooms and/or apartments available on a first-come, first-served basis to single and married students. Housing application deadline: 1/30. *Student services:* Campus safety program, career counseling, disabled student services, exercise/wellness program, free psychological counseling, grant writing training, international student services, low-cost health insurance. *Library facilities:* Robert Muldrow Cooper Library plus 1 other. *Online resources:* library catalog, web page. *Collection:* 1.2 million titles, 5,587 serial subscriptions. *Research affiliation:* Oak Ridge National Laboratory, South Carolina Universities Research and Education Foundation (energy), Greenville Hospital System (biological sciences), National Textile Center (textile and fiber technology), Savannah National Research Lab (energy).

Computer facilities: Computer purchase and lease plans are available. 1,250 computers available on campus for general student use. A campuswide network can be accessed from student residence rooms and from off campus. Internet access and online class registration, wireless network are available. *Web address:* http://www.clemson.edu/.

General Application Contact: Information Contact, 861-656-3195, E-mail: gradapp@clemson.edu.

GRADUATE UNITS

Graduate School Students: 2,009 full-time (849 women), 837 part-time (452 women); includes 215 minority (141 African Americans, 12 American Indian/Alaska Native, 28 Asian Americans or Pacific Islanders, 34 Hispanic Americans), 661 international. Average age 24. 2,779 applicants, 49% accepted, 676 enrolled. *Faculty:* 1,056 full-time (299 women), 90 part-time/adjunct (28 women). Expenses: Contact institution. *Financial support:* Fellowships, research assistantships, teaching assistantships, career-related internships or fieldwork, Federal Work-Study, institutionally sponsored loans, scholarships/grants, tuition waivers (full and partial), and unspecified assistantships available. Support available to part-time students. Financial award applicants required to submit FAFSA. In 2006, 851 master's, 139 doctorates, 17 other advanced degrees awarded. *Degree program information:* Part-time and evening/weekend programs available. Postbaccalaureate distance learning degree programs offered. Offers interdisciplinary studies (PhD, Certificate); policy studies (PhD, Certificate). *Application deadline:* For fall admission, 7/15 for international students; for spring admission, 9/15 for international students. Applications are processed on a rolling basis. *Application fee:* $50. Electronic applications accepted. *Application Contact:* Dr. Steve Creager, Interim Associate Dean, 864-656-4172, Fax: 864-656-5344, E-mail: screage@clemson.edu. *Dean,* Dr. J. Bruce Rafert, 864-656-4172, Fax: 864-656-5344, E-mail: jbruce@mail.clemson.edu.

College of Agriculture, Forestry and Life Sciences Students: 324 full-time (157 women), 69 part-time (25 women); includes 14 minority (9 African Americans, 1 American Indian/Alaska Native, 1 Asian American or Pacific Islander, 3 Hispanic Americans), 114 international. 334 applicants, 36% accepted, 73 enrolled. *Faculty:* 221 full-time (48 women), 12 part-time/adjunct (3 women). Expenses: Contact institution. *Financial support:* Fellowships, research assistantships, teaching assistantships, career-related internships or fieldwork, Federal Work-Study, institutionally sponsored loans, scholarships/grants, and unspecified assistantships available. Financial award applicants required to submit FAFSA. In 2006, 72 master's, 41 doctorates awarded. *Degree program information:* Part-time programs available. Offers agricultural education (M Ag Ed); agriculture, forestry and life sciences (M Ag Ed, MFR, MS, PhD); animal and veterinary sciences (MS, PhD); applied economics and statistics (MS); biochemistry and molecular biology (MS, PhD); biological sciences (MS, PhD); biosystems engineering (MS, PhD); environmental toxicology (MS, PhD); food technology (PhD); food, nutrition, and culinary science (MS); forest resources (MFR, MS, PhD); genetics (MS, PhD); microbiology (MS, PhD); packaging science (MS); plant and environmental sciences (MS, PhD); wildlife and fisheries biology (MS, PhD); zoology (PhD). *Application deadline:* For fall admission, 4/15 for international students; for spring admission, 9/15 for international students. Applications are processed on a rolling basis. *Application fee:* $50. Electronic applications accepted. *Dean,* Dr. Alan Sams, 864-656-7592, Fax: 864-656-1286.

College of Architecture, Arts, and Humanities Students: 315 full-time (149 women), 57 part-time (28 women); includes 32 minority (20 African Americans, 2 American Indian/Alaska Native, 8 Asian Americans or Pacific Islanders, 2 Hispanic Americans), 16 international. 433 applicants, 54% accepted, 137 enrolled. *Faculty:* 189 full-time (68 women), 20 part-time/adjunct (6 women). Expenses: Contact institution. *Financial support:* Fellowships, research assistantships, teaching assistantships, career-related internships or fieldwork, Federal Work-Study, scholarships/grants, and unspecified assistantships available. Financial award applicants required to submit FAFSA. In 2006, 129 degrees awarded. *Degree program information:* Part-time programs available. Offers architecture (M Arch, MS); architecture, arts, and humanities (M Arch, MA, MCRP, MCSM, MFA, MLA, MRED, MS, PhD); city and regional planning (MCRP); construction science and management (MCSM); developmental planning (MCRP); digital production arts (MFA); English (MA); environmental design and planning (PhD); historic preservation (MS); history (MA); landscape architecture (MLA); professional communication (MA); real estate development (MRED); rhetorics, communication and information design (PhD); visual arts (MFA). *Application deadline:* For fall admission, 4/15 for international students; for spring admission, 9/15 for international students. Applications are processed on a rolling basis. *Application fee:* $50. Electronic applications accepted. *Dean,* Dr. Janice Schach, 864-656-3085, Fax: 864-656-0204.

College of Business and Behavioral Science Students: 204 full-time (92 women), 146 part-time (46 women); includes 25 minority (14 African Americans, 2 American Indian/Alaska Native, 4 Asian Americans or Pacific Islanders, 5 Hispanic Americans), 43 international. 543 applicants, 39% accepted, 117 enrolled. *Faculty:* 158 full-time (42 women), 15 part-time/adjunct (1 woman). Expenses: Contact institution. *Financial support:* Fellowships, research assistantships, teaching assistantships, career-related internships or fieldwork, Federal Work-Study, institutionally sponsored loans, and unspecified assistantships available. Support available to part-time students. Financial award applicants required to submit FAFSA. In 2006, 141 master's, 8 doctorates awarded. *Degree program information:* Part-time and evening/weekend programs available. Offers accountancy and legal studies (MP Acc); applied economics (PhD); applied psychology (MS); applied sociology (MS); business administration (MBA); business and behavioral science (M E Com, MA, MBA, MP Acc, MPA, MRED, MS, PhD); economics (MA); electronic commerce (M E Com); graphic communications (MS); human factors psychology (PhD); industrial/organizational psychology (PhD); management (MS, PhD); marketing (MS); public administration (MPA);

real estate development (MRED). *Application deadline:* For fall admission, 4/15 for international students; for spring admission, 9/15 for international students. Applications are processed on a rolling basis. *Application fee:* $50. *Interim Dean,* Dr. David Grigsby, 864-656-3177.

College of Engineering and Science Students: 866 full-time (235 women), 121 part-time (30 women); includes 58 minority (31 African Americans, 3 American Indian/Alaska Native, 17 Asian Americans or Pacific Islanders, 7 Hispanic Americans), 463 international. 1,906 applicants, 48% accepted, 264 enrolled. *Faculty:* 356 full-time (56 women), 20 part-time/adjunct (5 women). Expenses: Contact institution. *Financial support:* Fellowships, research assistantships, teaching assistantships, career-related internships or fieldwork, institutionally sponsored loans, and unspecified assistantships available. Support available to part-time students. Financial award applicants required to submit FAFSA. In 2006, 274 master's, 68 doctorates awarded. *Degree program information:* Part-time programs available. Offers applied and pure mathematics (MS, PhD); astronomy and astrophysics (MS, PhD); atmospheric physics (MS, PhD); automotive engineering (MS, PhD); bioengineering (MS, PhD); biophysics (MS, PhD); biosystems engineering (MS, PhD); chemical engineering (MS, PhD); chemistry (MS, PhD); civil engineering (MS, PhD); computational mathematics (MS, PhD); computer engineering (MS, PhD); computer science (MS, PhD); electrical engineering (M Engr, MS, PhD); engineering and science (M Engr, MS, PhD); environmental engineering and science (M Engr, MS, PhD); environmental health physics (MS); hydrogeology (MS); industrial engineering (MS, PhD); materials science and engineering (MS, PhD); mechanical engineering (MS, PhD); operations research (MS, PhD); physics (MS, PhD); polymer and fiber science (MS, PhD); statistics (MS, PhD); the environment (MS). *Application fee:* $50. Electronic applications accepted. *Application Contact:* Dr. R. Larry Dooley, Chair, 864-656-3051, Fax: 864-656-4466, E-mail: dooley@eng.clemson.edu. *Dean,* Dr. Esin Gulari, 864-656-3202.

College of Health, Education, and Human Development Students: 300 full-time (216 women), 444 part-time (323 women); includes 86 minority (67 African Americans, 4 American Indian/Alaska Native, 4 Asian Americans or Pacific Islanders, 11 Hispanic Americans), 25 international. 361 applicants, 54% accepted, 142 enrolled. *Faculty:* 118 full-time (75 women), 21 part-time/adjunct (11 women). Expenses: Contact institution. *Financial support:* Fellowships, research assistantships, teaching assistantships, career-related internships or fieldwork, Federal Work-Study, tuition waivers (full and partial), and unspecified assistantships available. Support available to part-time students. Financial award applicants required to submit FAFSA. In 2006, 235 master's, 22 doctorates, 17 other advanced degrees awarded. *Degree program information:* Part-time and evening/weekend programs available. Postbaccalaureate distance learning degree programs offered. Offers administration and supervision (M Ed, Ed S); community counseling (M Ed); counselor education (M Ed); curriculum and instruction (PhD); educational leadership (M Ed, PhD); elementary education (M Ed); English (M Ed); health, education, and human development (M Ed, MAT, MHRD, MPRTM, MS, PhD, Ed S); human resource development (MHRD); mathematics (M Ed); middle grades education (MAT); natural sciences (M Ed); nursing (MS); parks, recreation, and tourism management (MPRTM, MS, PhD); reading (M Ed); school counseling (M Ed); secondary education (M Ed); special education (M Ed); student affairs (M Ed); youth development (MS). *Application deadline:* Applications are processed on a rolling basis. *Application fee:* $50. Electronic applications accepted. *Dean,* Dr. Larry Allen, 864-656-7640, Fax: 864-656-5488.

Institute on Family and Neighborhood Life 17 applicants, 35% accepted, 5 enrolled. Expenses: Contact institution. Offers family and neighborhood life (PhD); international and community studies (PhD). *Head,* Dr. Sue Limber, 964-656-6271.

See Close-Up on page 843.

CLEVELAND CHIROPRACTIC COLLEGE-KANSAS CITY CAMPUS, Kansas City, MO 64131-1181

General Information Independent, coed, upper-level institution. *Enrollment:* 479 graduate, professional, and undergraduate students; 386 full-time matriculated graduate/professional students (127 women), 7 part-time matriculated graduate/professional students (2 women). *Enrollment by degree level:* 393 first professional. *Graduate faculty:* 37 full-time (6 women), 13 part-time/adjunct (3 women). *Graduate housing:* On-campus housing not available. *Student services:* Campus employment opportunities, campus safety program, career counseling, disabled student services, international student services. *Library facilities:* Ruth R. Cleveland Memorial Library. *Online resources:* library catalog, web page. *Collection:* 15,000 titles, 6,100 serial subscriptions, 12,300 audiovisual materials.

Computer facilities: 14 computers available on campus for general student use. A campuswide network can be accessed. Internet access, educational software are available. *Web address:* http://www.cleveland.edu/.

General Application Contact: Melissa Denton, Director of Admissions, 816-501-0161, Fax: 816-501-0205, E-mail: melissa.denton@cleveland.edu.

GRADUATE UNITS

Professional Program Students: 386 full-time (127 women), 7 part-time (2 women); includes 39 minority (10 African Americans, 5 American Indian/Alaska Native, 13 Asian Americans or Pacific Islanders, 11 Hispanic Americans), 6 international. Average age 33. 271 applicants, 51% accepted, 71 enrolled. *Faculty:* 37 full-time (6 women), 13 part-time/adjunct (3 women). Expenses: Contact institution. *Financial support:* Federal Work-Study, institutionally sponsored loans, and scholarships/grants available. Financial award application deadline: 3/1; financial award applicants required to submit FAFSA. In 2006, 114 degrees awarded. *Degree program information:* Part-time programs available. Offers chiropractic (DC). *Application deadline:* For fall admission, 7/1 priority date for domestic and international students; for winter admission, 11/1 priority date for domestic and international students; for spring admission, 3/1 priority date for domestic and international students. Applications are processed on a rolling basis. *Application fee:* $50. Electronic applications accepted. *Application Contact:* Melissa Denton, Director of Admissions, 816-501-0161, Fax: 816-501-0205, E-mail: melissa.denton@cleveland.edu. *Academic Dean,* Dr. Paul Barlett, 816-501-0254.

CLEVELAND CHIROPRACTIC COLLEGE-LOS ANGELES CAMPUS, Los Angeles, CA 90004-2196

General Information Independent, coed, upper-level institution. *Enrollment:* 379 graduate, professional, and undergraduate students; 261 full-time matriculated graduate/professional students (100 women), 15 part-time matriculated graduate/professional students (5 women). *Enrollment by degree level:* 276 first professional. *Graduate faculty:* 26 full-time (9 women), 9 part-time/adjunct (2 women). *Tuition:* Part-time $274 per contact hour. *Required fees:* $145 per term. *Graduate housing:* On-campus housing not available. *Student services:* Campus employment opportunities, campus safety program, career counseling, free psychological counseling, international student services. *Library facilities:* Carl Cleveland Jr. plus 1 other. *Online resources:* library catalog, web page, access to other libraries' catalogs. *Collection:* 23,937 titles, 152 serial subscriptions, 2,323 audiovisual materials.

Computer facilities: A campuswide network can be accessed from off campus. Internet access is available. *Web address:* http://www.clevelandchiropractic.edu/.

General Application Contact: Theresa Moore, Director of Admission, 800-466-CCLA, Fax: 323-906-2094, E-mail: theresa.moore@cleveland.edu.

GRADUATE UNITS

Professional Program Students: 261 full-time (100 women), 15 part-time (5 women); includes 92 minority (9 African Americans, 1 American Indian/Alaska Native, 59 Asian Americans or Pacific Islanders, 23 Hispanic Americans), 15 international. Average age 29. 306 applicants, 15% accepted, 33 enrolled. *Faculty:* 26 full-time (9 women), 9 part-time/adjunct (2 women). Expenses: Contact institution. *Financial support:* Fellowships, research assistantships with partial tuition reimbursements, teaching assistantships with partial tuition reimbursements, Federal Work-Study, scholarships/grants, and tuition waivers (partial) available. Financial award application deadline: 5/1; financial award applicants required to submit FAFSA. In 2006, 75 degrees awarded. Offers chiropractic medicine (DC). *Application deadline:* For fall admission, 8/1 for domestic and international students; for spring admission, 12/1 for domestic and international students. Applications are processed on a rolling basis. *Application fee:* $50. Electronic applications accepted. *Application Contact:* Theresa Moore, Director of Admission, 800-466-CCLA, Fax: 323-906-2094, E-mail: theresa.moore@cleveland.edu. *Vice President for Academic Affairs,* Dr. Ruth Sandefur, 816-501-0100, Fax: 323-660-5387.

THE CLEVELAND INSTITUTE OF ART, Cleveland, OH 44106-1700

General Information Independent, coed, comprehensive institution.

GRADUATE UNITS

Program in Medical Illustration

CLEVELAND INSTITUTE OF MUSIC, Cleveland, OH 44106-1776

General Information Independent, coed, comprehensive institution. *Graduate housing:* Room and/or apartments available on a first-come, first-served basis to single students; on-campus housing not available to married students. Housing application deadline: 5/30.

GRADUATE UNITS

Graduate Programs Offers performance (MM, DMA, AD, CPS). Electronic applications accepted.

CLEVELAND STATE UNIVERSITY, Cleveland, OH 44115

General Information State-supported, coed, university. CGS member. *Enrollment:* 15,483 graduate, professional, and undergraduate students; 1,728 full-time matriculated graduate/professional students (996 women), 4,216 part-time matriculated graduate/professional students (2,652 women). *Graduate faculty:* 637. *Graduate housing:* Room and/or apartments available on a first-come, first-served basis to single students; on-campus housing not available to married students. Housing application deadline: 7/15. *Student services:* Campus employment opportunities, campus safety program, career counseling, child daycare facilities, disabled student services, exercise/wellness program, free psychological counseling, grant writing training, international student services, low-cost health insurance, teacher training. *Library facilities:* University Library plus 1 other. *Online resources:* library catalog, web page, access to other libraries' catalogs. *Collection:* 847,731 titles, 7,826 serial subscriptions, 143,894 audiovisual materials. *Research affiliation:* Cleveland Clinic Foundation, Metro Health System.

Computer facilities: Computer purchase and lease plans are available. 600 computers available on campus for general student use. A campuswide network can be accessed. Internet access and online class registration are available. *Web address:* http://www.csuohio.edu/.

General Application Contact: Giannina Pianalto, Director of Graduate Admissions, 216-523-7572, Fax: 216-687-9214, E-mail: g.pianalto@csuohio.edu.

GRADUATE UNITS

Cleveland-Marshall College of Law Students: 436 full-time (214 women), 312 part-time (150 women); includes 92 minority (45 African Americans, 4 American Indian/Alaska Native, 25 Asian Americans or Pacific Islanders, 18 Hispanic Americans), 12 international. Average age 28. 1,814 applicants, 31% accepted, 247 enrolled. *Faculty:* 42 full-time (17 women), 25 part-time/adjunct (7 women). Expenses: Contact institution. *Financial support:* In 2006–07, 205 students received support, including 4 teaching assistantships with partial tuition reimbursements available (averaging $2,400 per year); career-related internships or fieldwork, Federal Work-Study, institutionally sponsored loans, scholarships/grants, tuition waivers (full and partial), and unspecified assistantships also available. Support available to part-time students. Financial award application deadline: 5/1; financial award applicants required to submit FAFSA. In 2006, 197 degrees awarded. *Degree program information:* Part-time and evening/weekend programs available. Offers law (JD, LL M). *Application deadline:* For fall admission, 5/1 for domestic and international students. Applications are processed on a rolling basis. *Application fee:* $35. Electronic applications accepted. *Application Contact:* Christopher Lucak, Assistant Dean for Admissions, 216-687-4692, Fax: 216-687-6881, E-mail: christopher.lucak@law.csuohio.edu. *Dean,* Geoffrey S. Mearns, 216-687-2300, Fax: 216-687-6881, E-mail: geoffrey.mearns@law.csuohio.edu.

College of Graduate Studies Students: 2 full-time (both women), 205 part-time (160 women); includes 34 minority (29 African Americans, 3 Asian Americans or Pacific Islanders, 2 Hispanic Americans), 1 international. Average age 32. 5,113 applicants, 51% accepted. *Faculty:* 412 full-time (134 women), 178 part-time/adjunct (33 women). Expenses: Contact institution. *Financial support:* In 2006–07, research assistantships with full and partial tuition reimbursements (averaging $3,480 per year), teaching assistantships with full and partial tuition reimbursements (averaging $3,480 per year) were awarded; career-related internships or fieldwork, scholarships/grants, tuition waivers (full and partial), and unspecified assistantships also available. In 2006, 1,278 master's, 37 doctorates, 17 other advanced degrees awarded. *Degree program information:* Part-time and evening/weekend programs available. Postbaccalaureate distance learning degree programs offered (minimal on-campus study). *Application deadline:* For fall admission, 7/15 priority date for domestic students, 6/1 priority date for international students; for spring admission, 12/1 priority date for domestic students, 11/1 priority date for international students. Applications are processed on a rolling basis. *Application fee:* $30. Electronic applications accepted. *Interim Vice Provost for Research/Interim Dean,* Dr. Leo W. Jeffres, 216-687-3595, Fax: 216-687-9214, E-mail: jeffres.dean@csuohio.edu.

College of Education and Human Services Students: 240 full-time (182 women), 1,742 part-time (1,365 women); includes 445 minority (390 African Americans, 1 American Indian/Alaska Native, 13 Asian Americans or Pacific Islanders, 41 Hispanic Americans), 16 international. Average age 34. 1,676 applicants, 40% accepted, 405 enrolled. *Faculty:* 63 full-time (38 women), 16 part-time/adjunct (5 women). Expenses: Contact institution. *Financial support:* In 2006–07, 42 students received support, including 13 research assistantships with full tuition reimbursements available (averaging $6,960 per year), 2 teaching assistantships with full tuition reimbursements available (averaging $7,800 per year); career-related internships or fieldwork, Federal Work-Study, scholarships/grants, tuition waivers (partial), and unspecified assistantships also available. Support available to part-time students. Financial award application deadline: 8/1; financial award applicants required to submit FAFSA. In 2006, 497 master's, 9 doctorates, 27 other advanced degrees awarded. *Degree program information:* Part-time and evening/weekend programs available. Postbaccalaureate distance learning degree programs offered (minimal on-campus study). Offers adult learning and development (M Ed); art education (M Ed); clinical nursing leader (MSN); community agency counseling (M Ed); community health education (M Ed); counseling (PhD); counseling and pupil personnel administration (Ed S); counseling psychology (PhD); early childhood education (M Ed); education and human services (M Ed, MSN, PhD, Ed S); educational administration (Ed S); educational administration and supervision (M Ed); exercise science (M Ed); foreign language education (M Ed); forensic nursing (MSN); human performance (M Ed); leadership and lifelong learning (PhD); learning and development (PhD); mathematics and science education (M Ed); middle childhood education (M Ed); physical education pedagogy (M Ed); policy studies (PhD); population health nursing (MSN); school administration (PhD); school counseling (M Ed); school health education (M Ed); special education (M Ed); sport and exercise psychology (M Ed); sports management (M Ed); teaching English to speakers of other languages (M Ed). *Application deadline:* For fall admission, 7/18 priority date for domestic students, 5/15 for international students; for spring admission, 12/5 priority date for domestic students, 11/1 for international students. Applications are processed on a rolling basis. *Application fee:* $30. Electronic applications accepted. *Dean,* Dr. James A. McLoughlin, 216-687-3737, Fax: 216-687-5415, E-mail: j.mcloughlin@csuohio.edu.

College of Liberal Arts and Social Sciences Students: 239 full-time (178 women), 316 part-time (234 women); includes 139 minority (120 African Americans, 1 American Indian/Alaska Native, 7 Asian Americans or Pacific Islanders, 11 Hispanic Americans), 18 international. Average age 31. 637 applicants, 57% accepted, 221 enrolled. *Faculty:* 126 full-time (48 women), 17 part-time/adjunct (8 women). Expenses: Contact institution. *Financial support:* In 2006–07, 99 research assistantships with full and partial tuition reimbursements (averaging $4,172 per year), 67 teaching assistantships with full and partial tuition reimburse-

Cleveland State University (continued)

ments (averaging $4,657 per year) were awarded; fellowships, career-related internships or fieldwork, Federal Work-Study, institutionally sponsored loans, tuition waivers (full and partial), and unspecified assistantships also available. Support available to part-time students. In 2006, 121 degrees awarded. *Degree program information:* Part-time and evening/weekend programs available. Offers applied communication theory and methodology (MA); art education (M Ed); art history (MA); bioethics (MA, Certificate); composition (MM); creative writing (MFA); culture, communication and health care (Certificate); economics (MA); English (MA); history (MA); liberal arts and social sciences (M Ed, MA, MFA, MM, MSW, Certificate); museum studies (MA); music education (MM); performance (MM); philosophy (MA); social studies (MA); social work (MSW); sociology (MA); Spanish (MA). *Application deadline:* For fall admission, 7/15 priority date for domestic students; for spring admission, 12/2 priority date for domestic students. Applications are processed on a rolling basis. *Application fee:* $30. Electronic applications accepted. *Application Contact:* Giannina Pianalto, Director of Graduate Admissions, 216-523-7572, Fax: 216-687-9214, E-mail: g.pianalto@csuohio.edu. *Dean,* Dr. Gregory M. Sadlek, 216-687-3660.

College of Science Students: 276 full-time (199 women), 243 part-time (150 women). Average age 31. 450 applicants, 48% accepted, 113 enrolled. *Faculty:* 89 full-time (22 women), 65 part-time/adjunct (11 women). Expenses: Contact institution. In 2006, 106 master's, 8 doctorates, 9 other advanced degrees awarded. *Degree program information:* Part-time and evening/weekend programs available. Offers analytical chemistry (MS); applied optics (MS); biology (MS); clinical chemistry (MS); clinical psychology (MA); clinical/bioanalytical chemistry (PhD); condensed matter physics (MS); consumer/industrial research (MA); diversity management (MA); environmental chemistry (MS); environmental science (MS); experimental research psychology (MA); health sciences (MS); inorganic chemistry (MS); mathematics (MA, MS); medical physics (MS); occupational therapy (MOT); organic chemistry (MS); physical chemistry (MS); physical therapy (DPT); regulatory biology (PhD); school psychology (Psy S); science (MA, MOT, MS, DPT, PhD, Psy S); speech pathology and audiology (MA). *Application deadline:* For fall admission, 7/15 priority date for domestic and international students. Applications are processed on a rolling basis. *Application fee:* $30. *Dean,* Dr. Bette R. Bonder, 216-687-5580, E-mail: b.bonder@csuohio.edu.

Fenn College of Engineering Students: 100 full-time (30 women), 307 part-time (75 women); includes 28 minority (12 African Americans, 1 American Indian/Alaska Native, 14 Asian Americans or Pacific Islanders, 1 Hispanic American), 260 international. Average age 27. 422 applicants, 69% accepted, 246 enrolled. *Faculty:* 47 full-time (5 women), 51 part-time/adjunct (8 women). Expenses: Contact institution. *Financial support:* In 2006–07, 1 fellowship with full tuition reimbursement, 120 research assistantships with full and partial tuition reimbursements (averaging $8,694 per year), 20 teaching assistantships with full and partial tuition reimbursements (averaging $8,082 per year) were awarded; career-related internships or fieldwork, Federal Work-Study, institutionally sponsored loans, tuition waivers (full and partial), and unspecified assistantships also available. Support available to part-time students. Financial award application deadline: 3/30. In 2006, 133 master's, 10 doctorates awarded. *Degree program information:* Part-time and evening/weekend programs available. Offers applied biomedical engineering (D Eng); chemical engineering (MS, D Eng); civil engineering (MS, D Eng); electrical engineering (MS, D Eng); engineering (MS, D Eng); engineering mechanics (MS); environmental engineering (MS); industrial engineering (MS, D Eng); mechanical engineering (MS, D Eng); software engineering (MS). *Application deadline:* For fall admission, 7/18 priority date for domestic students; for spring admission, 12/5 for domestic students. Applications are processed on a rolling basis. *Application fee:* $30. Electronic applications accepted. *Dean,* Dr. Paul Bellini, 216-687-2555, Fax: 216-687-9280.

Maxine Goodman Levin College of Urban Affairs Students: 79 full-time (33 women), 264 part-time (155 women); includes 99 minority (84 African Americans, 5 Asian Americans or Pacific Islanders, 10 Hispanic Americans), 24 international. Average age 35. 289 applicants, 63% accepted, 115 enrolled. *Faculty:* 25 full-time (10 women), 11 part-time/adjunct (3 women). Expenses: Contact institution. *Financial support:* In 2006–07, 30 research assistantships with full and partial tuition reimbursements (averaging $7,200 per year), 2 teaching assistantships with full and partial tuition reimbursements (averaging $7,800 per year) were awarded; career-related internships or fieldwork, Federal Work-Study, institutionally sponsored loans, tuition waivers (full and partial), and unspecified assistantships also available. Support available to part-time students. Financial award application deadline:3/1. In 2006, 92 master's, 5 doctorates, 8 other advanced degrees awarded. *Degree program information:* Part-time and evening/weekend programs available. Offers environmental studies (MAES); geographic information systems (Certificate); local and urban management (Certificate); non-profit management (Certificate); nonprofit administration and leadership (MNAL); public administration (MPA); urban affairs (MAES, MNAL, MPA, MS, MUPDD, PhD, Certificate); urban economic development (Certificate); urban planning, design, and development (MUPDD); urban real estate development and finance (Certificate); urban studies (MS); urban studies and public affairs (PhD). *Application deadline:* For fall admission, 7/15 priority date for domestic students. Applications are processed on a rolling basis. *Application fee:* $30. *Application Contact:* Graduate Programs Coordinator, 216-523-7522, Fax: 216-687-5398, E-mail: gradprog@urban.csuohio.edu. *Dean,* Dr. Mark S. Rosentraub, 216-687-2135, E-mail: mrosentraub@urban.csuohio.edu.

Nance College of Business Administration Students: 356 full-time (158 women), 827 part-time (363 women); includes 152 minority (94 African Americans, 3 American Indian/Alaska Native, 42 Asian Americans or Pacific Islanders, 13 Hispanic Americans), 213 international. Average age 31. 1,186 applicants, 59% accepted, 346 enrolled. *Faculty:* 62 full-time (10 women), 15 part-time/adjunct (1 woman). Expenses: Contact institution. *Financial support:* In 2006–07, 45 research assistantships with full tuition reimbursements (averaging $6,960 per year), 1 teaching assistantship with full tuition reimbursement (averaging $7,800 per year) were awarded; career-related internships or fieldwork, Federal Work-Study, tuition waivers (full), and unspecified assistantships also available. Financial award application deadline: 5/17; financial award applicants required to submit FAFSA. In 2006, 431 master's, 3 doctorates, 2 other advanced degrees awarded. *Degree program information:* Part-time and evening/weekend programs available. Offers business administration (DBA); business statistics (MBA); computer information science (MS); data-driven marketing planning (Graduate Certificate); e-commerce (MBA); finance (MBA, DBA); financial accounting/audit (MAC); global business (Graduate Certificate); health care administration (MBA); information systems (DBA); labor relations and human resources (MLRHR); marketing (MBA, DBA); operations management (MBA); production/operations management (DBA); taxation (MAC). *Application deadline:* For fall admission, 7/15 priority date for domestic students, 5/15 for international students; for spring admission, 12/15 priority date for domestic students, 11/1 for international students. Applications are processed on a rolling basis. *Application fee:* $30. Electronic applications accepted. *Application Contact:* Dr. W. Benoy Joseph, Associate Dean, 216-687-2019, Fax: 216-687-9354, E-mail: w.joseph@csuohio.edu. *Dean,* Dr. Robert F. Scherer, 216-687-3786, Fax: 216-687-9354, E-mail: r.scherer@csuohio.edu.

COASTAL CAROLINA UNIVERSITY, Conway, SC 29528-6054

General Information State-supported, coed, comprehensive institution. *Enrollment:* 8,049 graduate, professional, and undergraduate students; 83 full-time matriculated graduate/professional students (46 women), 76 part-time matriculated graduate/professional students (50 women). *Enrollment by degree level:* 159 master's. *Graduate faculty:* 26 full-time (10 women), 16 part-time/adjunct (10 women). Tuition, state resident: full-time $7,920; part-time $330 per credit hour. Tuition, nonresident: full-time $9,600; part-time $400 per credit hour. *Required fees:* $80; $40 per term. *Graduate housing:* On-campus housing not available. *Student services:* Campus safety program, career counseling, disabled student services, free psychological counseling, international student services, multicultural affairs office. *Library facilities:* Kimbel Library. *Online resources:* library catalog, web page, access to other libraries' catalogs. *Collection:* 149,990 titles, 14,771 serial subscriptions, 4,712 audiovisual materials.

Computer facilities: 600 computers available on campus for general student use. A campuswide network can be accessed from student residence rooms and from off campus. Internet access and online class registration, online grades are available. *Web address:* http://www.coastal.edu/.

General Application Contact: Dr. Judy W. Vogt, Vice President, Enrollment Services, 843-349-2037, Fax: 843-349-2127, E-mail: jvogt@coastal.edu.

GRADUATE UNITS

College of Education Students: 48 full-time (31 women), 45 part-time (33 women); includes 8 minority (6 African Americans, 2 Asian Americans or Pacific Islanders). Average age 30. *Faculty:* 8 full-time (4 women), 16 part-time/adjunct (10 women). Expenses: Contact institution. *Financial support:* Fellowships, research assistantships, unspecified assistantships available. Support available to part-time students. Financial award application deadline: 4/1; financial award applicants required to submit FAFSA. In 2006, 70 degrees awarded. *Degree program information:* Part-time and evening/weekend programs available. Offers early childhood education (M Ed); education (MAT); elementary education (M Ed); secondary education (M Ed). *Application deadline:* For fall admission, 8/15 priority date for domestic students. Applications are processed on a rolling basis. *Application fee:* $45. Electronic applications accepted. *Application Contact:* Dr. Judy W. Vogt, Vice President, Enrollment Services, 843-349-2037, Fax: 843-349-2127, E-mail: jvogt@coastal.edu. *Dean,* Dr. Gilbert H. Hunt, 843-349-2607, Fax: 843-349-2332, E-mail: hunt@coastal.edu.

College of Natural and Applied Sciences Students: 22 full-time (12 women), 11 part-time (5 women). Average age 27. *Faculty:* 13 full-time (2 women). Expenses: Contact institution. *Financial support:* Fellowships, research assistantships, unspecified assistantships available. Support available to part-time students. Financial award application deadline: 4/1; financial award applicants required to submit FAFSA. In 2006, 4 degrees awarded. *Degree program information:* Part-time and evening/weekend programs available. Offers coastal marine and wetland studies (MS). *Application deadline:* For fall admission, 8/15 priority date for domestic students. Applications are processed on a rolling basis. *Application fee:* $45. Electronic applications accepted. *Application Contact:* Dr. Judy W. Vogt, Vice President, Enrollment Services, 843-349-2037, Fax: 843-349-2127, E-mail: jvogt@coastal.edu. *Interim Dean,* Dr. Joan F. Piroch, 843-349-2271, Fax: 843-349-2545, E-mail: pirochj@coastal.edu.

Wall College of Business Administration Students: 13 full-time (3 women), 20 part-time (12 women); includes 3 minority (1 African American, 1 Asian American or Pacific Islander, 1 Hispanic American), 2 international. Average age 29. *Faculty:* 5 full-time (4 women). Expenses: Contact institution. *Financial support:* Application deadline: 4/1; Offers business administration (MBA). *Application deadline:* For fall admission, 8/15 for domestic students. Applications are processed on a rolling basis. *Application fee:* $45. Electronic applications accepted. *Application Contact:* Dr. Judy W. Vogt, Vice President, Enrollment Services, 843-349-2037, Fax: 843-349-2127, E-mail: jvogt@coastal.edu. *Director,* John O. Lox, 843-349-2469, E-mail: jlox@coastal.edu.

COE COLLEGE, Cedar Rapids, IA 52402-5092

General Information Independent-religious, coed, comprehensive institution. *Graduate housing:* On-campus housing not available.

GRADUATE UNITS

Department of Education *Degree program information:* Part-time programs available. Offers education (MAT).

COLD SPRING HARBOR LABORATORY, WATSON SCHOOL OF BIOLOGICAL SCIENCES, Cold Spring Harbor, NY 11724

General Information Independent, coed, graduate-only institution. *Graduate housing:* Room and/or apartments guaranteed to single students; on-campus housing not available to married students.

GRADUATE UNITS

Graduate Program Offers biological sciences (PhD).

COLEMAN COLLEGE, San Diego, CA 92123

General Information Independent, coed, comprehensive institution. *Graduate housing:* On-campus housing not available.

GRADUATE UNITS

Program in Business and Technology Management *Degree program information:* Evening/weekend programs available. Postbaccalaureate distance learning degree programs offered (no on-campus study). Offers business and technology management (MS).

Program in Information Technology *Degree program information:* Evening/weekend programs available. Offers information technology (MSIT).

COLGATE ROCHESTER CROZER DIVINITY SCHOOL, Rochester, NY 14620-2530

General Information Independent-religious, coed, graduate-only institution. *Enrollment by degree level:* 80 first professional, 7 master's, 32 doctoral, 5 other advanced degrees. *Graduate faculty:* 8 full-time (5 women), 16 part-time/adjunct (8 women). *Tuition:* Part-time $458 per credit hour. *Required fees:* $17 per course. *Graduate housing:* Rooms and/or apartments available on a first-come, first-served basis to single and married students. Housing application deadline: 7/1. *Student services:* Campus employment opportunities, career counseling, disabled student services. *Library facilities:* Ambrose Swasey Collection plus 1 other. *Online resources:* library catalog, web page, access to other libraries' catalogs. *Collection:* 17,305 titles, 115 serial subscriptions, 723 audiovisual materials.

Computer facilities: 11 computers available on campus for general student use. A campuswide network can be accessed from student residence rooms and from off campus. Internet access and online class registration are available. *Web address:* http://www.crcds.edu/.

General Application Contact: Rev. Melissa M. Morral, Vice President for Enrollment Services, 585-340-9500, Fax: 585-340-9644, E-mail: mmorral@crcds.edu.

GRADUATE UNITS

Graduate and Professional Programs Students: 81 full-time, 43 part-time; includes 27 minority (22 African Americans, 5 Hispanic Americans), 5 international. Average age 43. 47 applicants, 87% accepted, 35 enrolled. *Faculty:* 8 full-time (5 women), 16 part-time/adjunct (8 women). Expenses: Contact institution. *Financial support:* In 2006–07, 44 students received support. Career-related internships or fieldwork, scholarships/grants, and tuition waivers (full and partial) available. Support available to part-time students. Financial award application deadline: 9/1; financial award applicants required to submit FAFSA. In 2006, 17 M Divs, 9 master's, 3 doctorates awarded. *Degree program information:* Part-time and evening/weekend programs available. Offers theology (M Div, MA, D Min, Certificate). *Application deadline:* For fall admission, 7/1 priority date for domestic students, 3/1 for international students; for spring admission, 12/1 priority date for domestic students. Applications are processed on a rolling basis. *Application fee:* $35. *Application Contact:* Rev. Melissa M. Morral, Vice President for Enrollment Services, 585-340-9500, Fax: 585-340-9644, E-mail: mmorral@crcds.edu. *President,* Dr. Eugene C. Bay, 585-271-1320 Ext. 680, Fax: 585-271-8013, E-mail: gbay@crcds.edu.

COLGATE UNIVERSITY, Hamilton, NY 13346-1386

General Information Independent, coed, comprehensive institution. *Enrollment:* 2,788 graduate, professional, and undergraduate students; 3 full-time matriculated graduate/professional students (all women), 3 part-time matriculated graduate/professional students (all women). *Enrollment by degree level:* 6 master's. *Graduate faculty:* 10 full-time (5 women). *Tuition:* Part-time $3,866 per course. *Graduate housing:* Room and/or apartments available to single students; on-campus housing not available to married students. *Student services:* Campus safety program, career counseling, disabled student services, exercise/wellness program, free psychological counseling, low-cost health insurance, teacher training, writing training. *Library facilities:* Everett Needham Case Library plus 1 other. *Online resources:* library catalog, web page, access to other libraries' catalogs. *Collection:* 1.2 million titles, 29,632 serial subscriptions, 16,184 audiovisual materials.

Computer facilities: Computer purchase and lease plans are available. 192 computers available on campus for general student use. A campuswide network can be accessed from student residence rooms and from off campus. Internet access and online class registration, software applications are available. *Web address:* http://www.colgate.edu/.

General Application Contact: Margaret Maurer, Associate Dean of the Faculty and Director of Graduate Studies, 315-228-7720, Fax: 315-228-7831, E-mail: mmaurer@mail.colgate.edu.

GRADUATE UNITS

Graduate Programs Students: 5 full-time (2 women), 1 part-time; includes 2 minority (both African Americans) Average age 23. 7 applicants, 57% accepted, 4 enrolled. *Faculty:* 10 full-time (5 women). Expenses: Contact institution. *Financial support:* In 2006–07, 3 students received support; research assistantships, career-related internships or fieldwork, Federal Work-Study, institutionally sponsored loans, tuition waivers (partial), and unspecified assistantships available. Support available to part-time students. Financial award applicants required to submit FAFSA. In 2006, 3 degrees awarded. *Degree program information:* Part-time programs available. Offers secondary education (MAT). *Application deadline:* For fall admission, 3/15 priority date for domestic students; for spring admission, 9/1 for domestic students. Applications are processed on a rolling basis. *Application fee:* $50. *Associate Dean of the Faculty and Director of Graduate Studies,* Margaret Maurer, 315-228-7720, Fax: 315-228-7831, E-mail: mmaurer@mail.colgate.edu.

COLLÈGE DOMINICAIN DE PHILOSOPHIE ET DE THÉOLOGIE, Ottawa, ON K1R 7G3, Canada

General Information Independent-religious, coed, comprehensive institution. *Enrollment:* 232 graduate, professional, and undergraduate students; 44 full-time matriculated graduate/professional students (7 women), 4 part-time matriculated graduate/professional students (1 woman). *Enrollment by degree level:* 29 master's, 19 doctoral. *Graduate faculty:* 15 full-time (2 women), 16 part-time/adjunct (2 women). *Tuition:* Full-time $3,180; part-time $125 per credit. *Graduate housing:* Room and/or apartments available on a first-come, first-served basis to single students; on-campus housing not available to married students. Typical cost: $5,400 (including board). *Student services:* Campus safety program. *Library facilities:* Bibliothèque du College Dominicain. *Online resources:* library catalog. *Collection:* 125,000 titles, 500 serial subscriptions.

Computer facilities: 4 computers available on campus for general student use. Internet access and online class registration are available. *Web address:* http://www.collegedominicain.ca/.

General Application Contact: Francis Peddle, Master of Studies, 613-233-3696 Ext. 325, Fax: 613-233-6064, E-mail: francis.peddle@collegedominicain.ca.

GRADUATE UNITS

Graduate Programs Students: 44 full-time (7 women), 4 part-time (1 woman); includes 13 minority (5 African Americans, 3 Asian Americans or Pacific Islanders, 5 Hispanic Americans), 8 international. 3 applicants, 100% accepted. *Faculty:* 15 full-time (2 women), 16 part-time/adjunct (2 women). Expenses: Contact institution. In 2006, 6 master's, 3 doctorates awarded. *Degree program information:* Part-time and evening/weekend programs available. Offers pastoral theology (M Prof Past, M Th Past); philosophy (MA Ph, PhD); theology (M Th, MA Th, PhD, Th D, L Th). *Application deadline:* For fall admission, 8/1 priority date for domestic and international students; for winter admission, 12/1 priority date for domestic and international students; for spring admission, 4/1 priority date for domestic and international students. Applications are processed on a rolling basis. *Application fee:* $35. *Application Contact:* Francis Peddle, Master of Studies, 613-233-3696 Ext. 325, Fax: 613-233-6064, E-mail: francis.peddle@collegedominicain.ca.

COLLEGE FOR FINANCIAL PLANNING, Greenwood Village, CO 80111

General Information Proprietary, coed, primarily men, graduate-only institution. *Enrollment by degree level:* 1,088 master's. *Graduate faculty:* 4 full-time (0 women), 6 part-time/adjunct (1 woman). *Tuition:* Full-time $4,275. One-time fee: $75 full-time. *Graduate housing:* On-campus housing not available. *Library facilities:* Apollo University Library. *Online resources:* web page. *Collection:* 17 million titles.

Computer facilities: A campuswide network can be accessed from off campus. Internet access is available. *Web address:* http://www.cfp.edu/.

General Application Contact: JuliAnna Sanchez, Senior Director of Enrollment, 303-220-4992, Fax: 303-220-1810, E-mail: julianna.sanchez@apollogrp.edu.

GRADUATE UNITS

Program in Financial Planning Average age 41. 250 applicants, 96% accepted. *Faculty:* 4 full-time (0 women), 6 part-time/adjunct (1 woman). Expenses: Contact institution. In 2006, 95 degrees awarded. *Degree program information:* Part-time and evening/weekend programs available. Postbaccalaureate distance learning degree programs offered (no on-campus study). Offers finance (MS); financial analysis (MS); personal financial planning (MS). *Application deadline:* Applications are processed on a rolling basis. *Application fee:* $75. Electronic applications accepted. *Application Contact:* JuliAnna Sanchez, Senior Director of Enrollment, 303-220-4992, Fax: 303-220-1810, E-mail: julianna.sanchez@apollogrp.edu. *Vice President, Academic Affairs,* Dr. Jesse B. Arman, 303-220-4823, Fax: 303-220-4811, E-mail: jesse.arman@apollogrp.edu.

COLLEGE MISERICORDIA, Dallas, PA 18612-1098

General Information Independent-religious, coed, comprehensive institution. *Enrollment:* 2,358 graduate, professional, and undergraduate students; 62 full-time matriculated graduate/professional students (50 women), 261 part-time matriculated graduate/professional students (189 women). *Enrollment by degree level:* 256 master's, 67 doctoral. *Graduate faculty:* 17 full-time (9 women), 32 part-time/adjunct (19 women). *Tuition:* Full-time $19,800; part-time $495 per credit. *Required fees:* $1,060. *Graduate housing:* On-campus housing not available. *Student services:* Campus employment opportunities, campus safety program, career counseling, disabled student services, free psychological counseling, international student services, low-cost health insurance, multicultural affairs office, writing training. *Library facilities:* Mary Kintz Bevevino Library. *Online resources:* library catalog, web page, access to other libraries' catalogs. *Collection:* 75,777 titles, 995 serial subscriptions, 3,322 audiovisual materials.

Computer facilities: Computer purchase and lease plans are available. 75 computers available on campus for general student use. A campuswide network can be accessed from student residence rooms and from off campus. Internet access and online class registration are available. *Web address:* http://www.misericordia.edu/.

General Application Contact: Larree Brown, Coordinator of Part-Time Undergraduate and Graduate Programs, 570-674-6451, Fax: 570-674-6232, E-mail: lbrown@misericordia.edu.

GRADUATE UNITS

College of Health Sciences Students: 62 full-time (50 women), 109 part-time (86 women); includes 3 minority (2 African Americans, 1 Hispanic American). *Faculty:* 15 full-time (9 women), 11 part-time/adjunct (9 women). Expenses: Contact institution. *Financial support:* Teaching assistantships, career-related internships or fieldwork, Federal Work-Study, scholarships/grants, traineeships, and tuition waivers (partial) available. Support available to part-time students. Financial award application deadline: 6/30; financial award applicants required to submit FAFSA. In 2006, 80 degrees awarded. *Degree program information:* Part-time and evening/weekend programs available. Offers health sciences (MSN, MSOT, MSPT, MSSLP, DPT); nursing (MSN); occupational therapy (MSOT); physical therapy (MSPT, DPT); speech-language pathology (MSSLP). *Application deadline:* Applications are processed on a rolling basis. *Application fee:* $25. Electronic applications accepted. *Application Contact:* Larree Brown, Coordinator of Part-Time Undergraduate and Graduate Programs, 570-674-6451, Fax: 570-674-6232, E-mail: lbrown@misericordia.edu. *Interim Dean of Health Sciences,* Dr. Ellen McLaughlin, 570-674-6399, E-mail: emclaugh@misericordia.edu.

College of Professional Studies and Social Sciences Average age 36. 36 applicants, 89% accepted, 32 enrolled. *Faculty:* 2 full-time (0 women), 21 part-time/adjunct (10 women). Expenses: Contact institution. *Financial support:* Career-related internships or fieldwork and scholarships/grants available. Support available to part-time students. Financial award application deadline: 6/30; financial award applicants required to submit FAFSA. In 2006, 25 degrees awarded. *Degree program information:* Part-time and evening/weekend programs available. Offers education/curriculum (MS); organizational management (MS). *Application deadline:* For fall admission, 8/1 priority date for domestic students. Applications are processed on a rolling basis. *Application fee:* $25. Electronic applications accepted. *Application Contact:* Larree Brown, Coordinator of Part-Time Undergraduate and Graduate Programs, 570-674-6451, Fax: 570-674-6232, E-mail: lbrown@misericordia.edu. *Dean of Adult and Continuing Education,* Tom O'Neill, 570-674-6331, E-mail: toneill@misericordia.edu.

COLLEGE OF CHARLESTON, Charleston, SC 29424-0001

General Information State-supported, coed, comprehensive institution. *Graduate housing:* On-campus housing not available. *Research affiliation:* South Carolina Marine Resources Division (marine biology), NASA, Oak Ridge Associated Universities (science).

GRADUATE UNITS

Graduate School *Degree program information:* Part-time and evening/weekend programs available.

School of Business and Economics Offers accountancy (MS); business and economics (MS). Electronic applications accepted.

School of Education *Degree program information:* Part-time and evening/weekend programs available. Offers early childhood education (M Ed, MAT); education (M Ed, MAT, Certificate); elementary education (M Ed, MAT); English to speakers of other languages (Certificate); languages (M Ed); science and mathematics for teachers (M Ed); special education (M Ed). Electronic applications accepted.

School of Humanities and Social Sciences *Degree program information:* Part-time and evening/weekend programs available. Offers bilingual legal interpreting (MA, Certificate); English (MA); history (MA); humanities and social sciences (MA, MPA, Certificate); organizational and corporate communication (Certificate); public administration (MPA). Electronic applications accepted.

School of Sciences and Mathematics Offers computer and information sciences (MS); environmental studies (MS); marine biology (MS); mathematics (MS, Certificate); sciences and mathematics (MS, Certificate). Electronic applications accepted.

COLLEGE OF EMMANUEL AND ST. CHAD, Saskatoon, SK S7N 0W6, Canada

General Information Independent-religious, coed, comprehensive institution. *Graduate housing:* Room and/or apartments available on a first-come, first-served basis to single students; on-campus housing not available to married students. Housing application deadline: 6/15.

GRADUATE UNITS

Bachelor of Theology Program *Degree program information:* Part-time programs available. Postbaccalaureate distance learning degree programs offered (minimal on-campus study). Offers theology (B Th).

Graduate Programs *Degree program information:* Part-time programs available. Offers theology (M Div, MTS, STM).

COLLEGE OF MOUNT ST. JOSEPH, Cincinnati, OH 45233-1670

General Information Independent-religious, coed, comprehensive institution. *Enrollment:* 2,259 graduate, professional, and undergraduate students; 146 full-time matriculated graduate/professional students (112 women), 197 part-time matriculated graduate/professional students (157 women). *Enrollment by degree level:* 321 master's, 22 doctoral. *Graduate faculty:* 46 full-time (31 women), 16 part-time/adjunct (9 women). *Tuition:* Part-time $440 per hour. Tuition and fees vary according to program. *Graduate housing:* Room and/or apartments available on a first-come, first-served basis to single students; on-campus housing not available to married students. Housing application deadline: 3/31. *Student services:* Campus employment opportunities, campus safety program, career counseling, child daycare facilities, disabled student services, exercise/wellness program, free psychological counseling, grant writing training, international student services, low-cost health insurance, multicultural affairs office, teacher training, writing training. *Library facilities:* Archbishop Alter Library. *Online resources:* library catalog, web page, access to other libraries' catalogs. *Collection:* 97,172 titles, 9,000 serial subscriptions, 1,818 audiovisual materials.

Computer facilities: Computer purchase and lease plans are available. 278 computers available on campus for general student use. A campuswide network can be accessed from student residence rooms and from off campus. Internet access and online class registration, computer-aided instruction are available. *Web address:* http://www.msj.edu/.

General Application Contact: Marilyn Hoskins, Assistant Director of Admissions for Graduate Recruitment, 513-244-4723, Fax: 513-244-4629, E-mail: marilyn_hoskins@mail.msg.edu.

GRADUATE UNITS

Graduate Education Program Students: 68 full-time (54 women), 115 part-time (96 women); includes 21 minority (16 African Americans, 2 American Indian/Alaska Native, 1 Asian American or Pacific Islander, 2 Hispanic Americans). Average age 34. 91 applicants, 98% accepted, 62 enrolled. *Faculty:* 22 full-time (14 women), 11 part-time/adjunct (6 women). Expenses: Contact institution. *Financial support:* In 2006–07, 3 students received support. Career-related internships or fieldwork and scholarships/grants available. Support available to part-time students. Financial award application deadline: 6/1; financial award applicants required to submit FAFSA. In 2006, 61 degrees awarded. *Degree program information:* Part-time and evening/weekend programs available. Postbaccalaureate distance learning degree programs offered (minimal on-campus study). Offers adolescent young adult education (MA); art (MA); inclusive early childhood education (MA); instructional leadership (MA); middle childhood education (MA); multicultural special education (MA); music (MA); reading (MA). *Application deadline:* Applications are processed on a rolling basis. *Application fee:* $50. Electronic applications accepted. *Application Contact:* Marilyn Hoskins, Assistant Director of Admissions for Graduate Recruitment, 513-244-4723, Fax: 513-244-4629, E-mail: marilyn_hoskins@mail.msg.edu. *Chair,* Dr. Mifrando Obach, 513-244-3263, Fax: 513-244-4867, E-mail: mifrando_obach@mail.msj.edu.

Graduate Program in Religious Studies Students: 1 (woman) full-time, 32 part-time (28 women); includes 4 minority (3 African Americans, 1 Hispanic American). Average age 48. 3 applicants, 100% accepted, 2 enrolled. *Faculty:* 4 full-time (2 women), 3 part-time/adjunct (1 woman). Expenses: Contact institution. *Financial support:* In 2006–07, 20 students received support. Career-related internships or fieldwork and scholarships/grants available. Support available to part-time students. Financial award application deadline: 6/1; financial award applicants required to submit FAFSA. In 2006, 3 degrees awarded. *Degree program information:* Part-time and evening/weekend programs available. Offers spiritual and pastoral care (MA). *Application deadline:* Applications are processed on a rolling basis. *Application fee:* $50. Electronic applications accepted. *Application Contact:* Marilyn Hoskins, Assistant Director of Admissions for Graduate Recruitment, 513-244-4723, Fax: 513-244-4629, E-mail: marilyn_hoskins@mail.msg.edu. *Chair,* Dr. John Trokan, 513-244-4272, Fax: 513-244-4222, E-mail: john_trokan@mail.msj.edu.

Master of Nursing Program Students: 24 full-time (19 women); includes 7 minority (all African Americans), 1 international. Average age 32. 40 applicants, 88% accepted, 24 enrolled. *Faculty:* 6 full-time (5 women), 1 (woman) part-time/adjunct. Expenses: Contact institution. *Financial support:* Career-related internships or fieldwork available. Financial award application deadline: 6/1; financial award applicants required to submit FAFSA. In 2006, 24 degrees awarded. Offers nursing (MN). *Application deadline:* Applications are processed on a rolling basis. *Application fee:* $50. Electronic applications accepted. *Application Contact:* Marilyn Hoskins, Assistant Director of Admissions for Graduate Recruitment, 513-244-4723,

College of Mount St. Joseph (continued)

Fax: 513-244-4629, E-mail: marilyn_hoskins@mail.msg.edu. *Chair, Health Sciences Department*, Dr. Darla Vale, 513-244-4322, Fax: 513-451-2547, E-mail: darla_vale@mail.msj.edu.

Multidisciplinary Program in Organizational Leadership Students: 1 full-time (0 women), 43 part-time (28 women); includes 6 minority (all African Americans) Average age 40. 11 applicants, 100% accepted, 10 enrolled. *Faculty:* 6 full-time (2 women). Expenses: Contact institution. *Financial support:* Application deadline: 6/1; In 2006, 9 degrees awarded. *Degree program information:* Part-time and evening/weekend programs available. Offers organizational leadership (MS). *Application deadline:* Applications are processed on a rolling basis. *Application fee:* $50. Electronic applications accepted. *Application Contact:* Marilyn Hoskins, Assistant Director of Admissions for Graduate Recruitment, 513-244-4723, Fax: 513-244-4629, E-mail: marilyn_hoskins@mail.msg.edu. *Chair*, Dr. Jim Brodzinski, 513-244-4917, Fax: 513-244-4270, E-mail: jim_brodzinski@mail.msj.edu.

Physical Therapy Program Students: 52 full-time (38 women), 6 part-time (4 women), 2 international. Average age 24. 46 applicants, 85% accepted, 23 enrolled. *Faculty:* 8 full-time (all women), 1 (woman) part-time/adjunct. Expenses: Contact institution. *Financial support:* In 2006–07, 24 students received support. Career-related internships or fieldwork, Federal Work-Study, and scholarships/grants available. Support available to part-time students. Financial award application deadline: 6/1; financial award applicants required to submit FAFSA. In 2006, 24 degrees awarded. Offers physical therapy (MPT, DPT). *Application deadline:* For spring admission, 9/1 priority date for domestic and international students. *Application fee:* $50. Electronic applications accepted. *Application Contact:* Marilyn Hoskins, Assistant Director of Admissions for Graduate Recruitment, 513-244-4723, Fax: 513-244-4629, E-mail: marilyn_hoskins@mail.msg.edu. *Chair, Health Sciences Department*, Dr. Darla Vale, 513-244-4322, Fax: 513-451-2547, E-mail: darla_vale@mail.msj.edu.

See Close-Up on page 845.

COLLEGE OF MOUNT SAINT VINCENT, Riverdale, NY 10471-1093

General Information Independent, coed, comprehensive institution. *Enrollment:* 1,812 graduate, professional, and undergraduate students; 37 full-time matriculated graduate/professional students (27 women), 328 part-time matriculated graduate/professional students (273 women). *Enrollment by degree level:* 365 master's. *Graduate faculty:* 20 full-time (17 women), 25 part-time/adjunct (19 women). *Graduate housing:* On-campus housing not available. *Student services:* Campus employment opportunities, campus safety program, career counseling, disabled student services, exercise/wellness program, free psychological counseling, international student services, low-cost health insurance, multicultural affairs office, teacher training, writing training. *Library facilities:* Elizabeth Seton Library. *Online resources:* library catalog, web page, access to other libraries' catalogs. *Collection:* 104,158 titles.

Computer facilities: 184 computers available on campus for general student use. A campuswide network can be accessed from student residence rooms and from off campus. Internet access and online class registration, e-mail are available. *Web address:* http://www.mountsaintvincent.edu/.

General Application Contact: Dr. Edward H. Meyer, Dean, School of Professional and Continuing Studies, 718-405-3373, Fax: 718-405-3764, E-mail: edward.meyer@mountsaintvincent.edu.

GRADUATE UNITS

School of Professional and Continuing Studies Expenses: Contact institution. Offers adult nurse practitioner (MSN, PMC); family nurse practitioner (MSN, PMC); instructional technology and global perspectives (Certificate); middle level education (Certificate); multicultural studies (Certificate); nurse educator (PMC); nursing administration (MSN); nursing for the adult and aged (MSN); urban and multicultural education (MS Ed). *Dean, School of Professional and Continuing Studies*, Dr. Edward H. Meyer, 718-405-3373, Fax: 718-405-3764, E-mail: edward.meyer@mountsaintvincent.edu.

THE COLLEGE OF NEW JERSEY, Ewing, NJ 08628

General Information State-supported, coed, comprehensive institution. CGS member. *Enrollment:* 6,934 graduate, professional, and undergraduate students; 111 full-time matriculated graduate/professional students (86 women), 729 part-time matriculated graduate/professional students (585 women). *Enrollment by degree level:* 840 master's. *Graduate housing:* On-campus housing not available. *Student services:* Campus employment opportunities, career counseling, child daycare facilities, disabled student services, exercise/wellness program, free psychological counseling, international student services, low-cost health insurance. *Library facilities:* New Library. *Online resources:* library catalog, web page. *Collection:* 662,152 titles, 429,632 serial subscriptions, 13,886 audiovisual materials.

Computer facilities: 800 computers available on campus for general student use. A campuswide network can be accessed from student residence rooms and from off campus. Internet access and online class registration are available. *Web address:* http://www.tcnj.edu/.

General Application Contact: Susan L. Hydro, Office of Graduate Studies, Assistant Dean, 609-771-2300, Fax: 609-637-5105, E-mail: graduate@tcnj.edu.

GRADUATE UNITS

Graduate Division Students: 111 full-time (86 women), 729 part-time (585 women); includes 109 minority (47 African Americans, 1 American Indian/Alaska Native, 34 Asian Americans or Pacific Islanders, 27 Hispanic Americans). 608 applicants, 75% accepted. Expenses: Contact institution. *Financial support:* In 2006–07, 36 research assistantships with partial tuition reimbursements were awarded; career-related internships or fieldwork, Federal Work-Study, and unspecified assistantships also available. Support available to part-time students. Financial award application deadline: 5/1; financial award applicants required to submit FAFSA. In 2006, 377 master's, 24 other advanced degrees awarded. *Degree program information:* Part-time and evening/weekend programs available. Offers overseas education (M Ed, Certificate). *Application deadline:* For fall admission, 4/15 for domestic students; for spring admission, 10/15 for domestic students. *Application fee:* $60. Electronic applications accepted. *Application Contact:* Susan L. Hydro, Office of Graduate Studies, Assistant Dean, 609-771-2300, Fax: 609-637-5105, E-mail: graduate@tcnj.edu.

School of Culture and Society Students: 1 (woman) full-time, 43 part-time (31 women); includes 2 minority (1 African American, 1 Asian American or Pacific Islander). 21 applicants, 95% accepted. Expenses: Contact institution. *Financial support:* Unspecified assistantships available. Financial award application deadline: 5/1; financial award applicants required to submit FAFSA. In 2006, 14 degrees awarded. *Degree program information:* Part-time and evening/weekend programs available. Offers applied Spanish studies (MA); culture and society (MA); English (MA). *Application deadline:* For fall admission, 4/15 for domestic students; for spring admission, 10/15 for domestic students. *Application fee:* $60. Electronic applications accepted. *Application Contact:* Susan L. Hydro, Office of Graduate Studies, Assistant Dean, 609-771-2300, Fax: 609-637-5105, E-mail: graduate@tcnj.edu. *Dean*, Dr. Susan Albertine, 609-771-3434, Fax: 609-637-5173.

School of Education Students: 93 full-time (68 women), 619 part-time (489 women); includes 95 minority (42 African Americans, 1 American Indian/Alaska Native, 31 Asian Americans or Pacific Islanders, 21 Hispanic Americans). 581 applicants, 74% accepted. Expenses: Contact institution. *Financial support:* Unspecified assistantships available. Financial award application deadline: 5/1; financial award applicants required to submit FAFSA. In 2006, 353 master's, 24 other advanced degrees awarded. *Degree program information:* Part-time and evening/weekend programs available. Offers community counseling: human services (MA); community counseling: substance abuse and addiction (MA, Certificate); developmental reading (M Ed); education (M Ed, MA, MAT, MS, Certificate, Ed S); educational leadership (M Ed, Certificate); educational technology (MS); elementary education (M Ed, MAT); elementary teaching (MAT); English as a second language (M Ed); marriage and family therapy (Ed S); reading certification (Certificate); school counseling (MA); school personnel licensure: preschool-grade 3 (M Ed, MAT); secondary education (MAT); special education (M Ed, MAT); special education with learning disabilities (Certificate); speech pathology (MA); teaching English as a second language (M Ed, Certificate). *Application deadline:* For fall admission, 4/15 for domestic students; for spring admission, 10/15 for domestic students. *Application fee:* $60. Electronic applications accepted. *Application Contact:* Susan L. Hydro, Office of Graduate Studies, Assistant Dean, 609-771-2300, Fax: 609-637-5105, E-mail: graduate@tcnj.edu. *Dean*, Dr. William Behre, 609-771-2100, Fax: 609-637-5117.

School of Nursing, Health and Exercise Science 6 applicants, 100% accepted. *Faculty:* 3. Expenses: Contact institution. *Financial support:* Unspecified assistantships available. Financial award application deadline: 5/1; financial award applicants required to submit FAFSA. In 2006, 10 degrees awarded. *Degree program information:* Part-time and evening/weekend programs available. Offers health (MAT); health education (M Ed, MAT); nursing (MSN, Certificate); nursing, health and exercise science (M Ed, MAT, MSN, Certificate); physical education (M Ed, MAT). *Application deadline:* For fall admission, 3/15 for domestic students. *Application fee:* $60. Electronic applications accepted. *Application Contact:* Susan L. Hydro, Office of Graduate Studies, Assistant Dean, 609-771-2300, Fax: 609-637-5105, E-mail: graduate@tcnj.edu. *Dean*, Dr. Susan Bakewell-Sachs, 609-771-2541, Fax: 609-637-5159.

See Close-Up on page 847.

THE COLLEGE OF NEW ROCHELLE, New Rochelle, NY 10805-2308

General Information Independent, coed, primarily women, comprehensive institution. CGS member. *Enrollment:* 2,341 graduate, professional, and undergraduate students; 206 full-time matriculated graduate/professional students (182 women), 1,168 part-time matriculated graduate/professional students (1,012 women). *Enrollment by degree level:* 1,370 master's, 4 other advanced degrees. *Graduate faculty:* 25 full-time (16 women), 74 part-time/adjunct (52 women). *Tuition:* Part-time $575 per credit. *Required fees:* $90 per term. *Graduate housing:* Room and/or apartments available on a first-come, first-served basis to single students; on-campus housing not available to married students. Typical cost: $4,000 (including board). Housing application deadline: 8/1. *Student services:* Campus employment opportunities, campus safety program, career counseling, disabled student services, free psychological counseling, international student services, low-cost health insurance, teacher training. *Library facilities:* Gill Library. *Online resources:* library catalog, access to other libraries' catalogs. *Collection:* 220,000 titles, 1,450 serial subscriptions.

Computer facilities: Computer purchase and lease plans are available. 120 computers available on campus for general student use. A campuswide network can be accessed from off campus. Internet access and online class registration are available. *Web address:* http://cnr.edu/.

General Application Contact: Dr. Guy Lometti, Dean of the Graduate School, 914-654-5320, Fax: 914-654-5593, E-mail: glometti@cnv.edu.

GRADUATE UNITS

Graduate School Students: 206 full-time (182 women), 1,168 part-time (1,012 women); includes 272 minority (175 African Americans, 12 American Indian/Alaska Native, 18 Asian Americans or Pacific Islanders, 67 Hispanic Americans), 6 international. Average age 35. *Faculty:* 25 full-time (16 women), 74 part-time/adjunct (52 women). Expenses: Contact institution. *Financial support:* In 2006–07, 188 students received support, including 9 research assistantships with tuition reimbursements available; career-related internships or fieldwork, Federal Work-Study, scholarships/grants, traineeships, tuition waivers (partial), and unspecified assistantships also available. Support available to part-time students. In 2006, 450 master's, 15 other advanced degrees awarded. *Degree program information:* Part-time and evening/weekend programs available. Offers acute care nurse practitioner (MS, Certificate); clinical specialist in holistic nursing (MS, Certificate); family nurse practitioner (MS, Certificate); nursing and health care management (MS); nursing education (Certificate). *Application deadline:* Applications are processed on a rolling basis. *Application fee:* $35. *Dean of the Graduate School*, Dr. Guy Lometti, 914-654-5320, Fax: 914-654-5593, E-mail: glometti@cnv.edu.

Division of Art and Communication Studies Students: 44 full-time (42 women), 100 part-time (87 women); includes 21 minority (16 African Americans, 1 Asian American or Pacific Islander, 4 Hispanic Americans), 2 international. Average age 33. *Faculty:* 4 full-time (2 women), 24 part-time/adjunct (18 women). Expenses: Contact institution. *Financial support:* In 2006–07, 3 research assistantships with tuition reimbursements were awarded; career-related internships or fieldwork, scholarships/grants, tuition waivers (partial), and unspecified assistantships also available. Support available to part-time students. In 2006, 48 degrees awarded. *Degree program information:* Part-time and evening/weekend programs available. Offers art education (MA); art museum education (Certificate); art therapy (MS); communication studies (MS, Certificate); fine art (MS); graphic art (MS); studio art (MS). *Application deadline:* For fall admission, 8/1 priority date for domestic students. Applications are processed on a rolling basis. *Application fee:* $35. *Head*, Dr. John Patton, 914-654-5208, Fax: 914-654-5593.

Division of Education Students: 70 full-time (64 women), 765 part-time (659 women); includes 119 minority (66 African Americans, 9 American Indian/Alaska Native, 5 Asian Americans or Pacific Islanders, 39 Hispanic Americans), 1 international. Average age 33. *Faculty:* 11 full-time (8 women), 29 part-time/adjunct (20 women). Expenses: Contact institution. *Financial support:* In 2006–07, 4 research assistantships with tuition reimbursements were awarded; career-related internships or fieldwork, scholarships/grants, and unspecified assistantships also available. Support available to part-time students. In 2006, 301 master's, 15 other advanced degrees awarded. *Degree program information:* Part-time and evening/weekend programs available. Offers bilingual education (Certificate); creative teaching and learning (MS Ed, Certificate); elementary education/early childhood education (MS Ed); literacy education (MS Ed); school administration and supervision (MS Ed, Certificate, PD); special education (MS Ed); speech-language pathology (MS); teaching English as a second language (MS Ed); teaching English as a second language and multilingual/multicultural education (MS Ed, Certificate). *Application deadline:* For fall admission, 8/1 priority date for domestic students; for spring admission, 4/6 for domestic students. Applications are processed on a rolling basis. *Application fee:* $35. *Acting Division Head*, Dr. Marie Ribarich, 914-654-5333, Fax: 914-654-5593, E-mail: mribarich@cnr.edu.

Division of Human Services Students: 92 full-time (76 women), 190 part-time (160 women); includes 85 minority (63 African Americans, 3 American Indian/Alaska Native, 19 Hispanic Americans), 2 international. Average age 36. *Faculty:* 9 full-time (4 women), 16 part-time/adjunct (8 women). Expenses: Contact institution. *Financial support:* In 2006–07, 2 research assistantships with tuition reimbursements were awarded; career-related internships or fieldwork, scholarships/grants, and unspecified assistantships also available. In 2006, 72 degrees awarded. *Degree program information:* Part-time and evening/weekend programs available. Offers career development (MS, Certificate); community-school psychology (MS); gerontology (MS, Certificate); guidance and counseling (MS); mental health counseling (Certificate). *Application deadline:* For fall admission, 8/1 priority date for domestic students. Applications are processed on a rolling basis. *Application fee:* $35. *Head*, Dr. Marie Ribarich, 914-654-5561, Fax: 914-654-5593, E-mail: mribarich@cnr.edu.

See Close-Up on page 849.

COLLEGE OF NOTRE DAME OF MARYLAND, Baltimore, MD 21210-2476

General Information Independent-religious, Undergraduate: women only; graduate: coed, comprehensive institution. *Enrollment:* 111 full-time matriculated graduate/professional students (96 women), 1,502 part-time matriculated graduate/professional students (1,217 women). *Enrollment by degree level:* 1,613 master's. *Graduate faculty:* 40 full-time (25 women), 125 part-time/adjunct (100 women). *Graduate housing:* On-campus housing not available. *Student services:* Campus safety program, career counseling, disabled student services, international student services, teacher training, writing training. *Library facilities:* Loyola/Notre Dame Library. *Online resources:* library catalog, web page, access to other libraries' catalogs. *Collection:* 400,000 titles, 1,800 serial subscriptions, 27,000 audiovisual materials.

Computer facilities: Computer purchase and lease plans are available. 80 computers available on campus for general student use. A campuswide network can be accessed from student residence rooms and from off campus. Internet access, online classroom assignments and information are available. *Web address:* http://www.ndm.edu/.

General Application Contact: Erica D. Jones, Graduate Admissions Coordinator, 410-532-5317, Fax: 410-532-5333, E-mail: gradadm@ndm.edu.

GRADUATE UNITS

Graduate Studies Students: 111 full-time (96 women), 1,502 part-time (1,217 women). Average age 35. *Faculty:* 37 full-time (22 women), 83 part-time/adjunct (53 women). Expenses: Contact institution. *Financial support:* Career-related internships or fieldwork and institutionally sponsored loans available. Support available to part-time students. Financial award application deadline: 6/30; financial award applicants required to submit FAFSA. In 2006, 303 degrees awarded. *Degree program information:* Part-time and evening/weekend programs available. Offers contemporary communication (MA); instructional leadership for changing populations (PhD); leadership in teaching (MA); liberal studies (MA); management (MA); nonprofit management (MA); teaching (MA); teaching English to speakers of other languages (MA). *Application deadline:* For fall admission, 7/5 for domestic students; for winter admission, 11/5 for domestic students; for spring admission, 12/5 for domestic students. Applications are processed on a rolling basis. *Application fee:* $40. Electronic applications accepted. *Application Contact:* Erica D. Jones, Graduate Admissions Coordinator, 410-532-5317, Fax: 410-532-5333, E-mail: gradadm@ndm.edu. *Dean of Graduate Studies,* Dr. Carolyn Boulger Karlson, 410-532-5316, Fax: 410-532-5333, E-mail: mmahoney@ndm.edu.

COLLEGE OF ST. CATHERINE, St. Paul, MN 55105-1789

General Information Independent-religious, Undergraduate: women only; graduate: coed, comprehensive institution. *Graduate housing:* Rooms and/or apartments available on a first-come, first-served basis to single and married students. Housing application deadline: 5/1.

GRADUATE UNITS

Graduate Programs *Degree program information:* Part-time and evening/weekend programs available. Postbaccalaureate distance learning degree programs offered (no on-campus study). Offers education (MA); holistic health studies (MA); library and information science (MA); nursing (MA); occupational therapy (MA); organizational leadership (MA); physical therapy (MPT, DPT); social work (MSW); theology (MA).

COLLEGE OF ST. CATHERINE–MINNEAPOLIS, Minneapolis, MN 55454-1494

General Information Independent-religious, coed, primarily women, comprehensive institution.

GRADUATE UNITS

Graduate Programs

COLLEGE OF SAINT ELIZABETH, Morristown, NJ 07960-6989

General Information Independent-religious, Undergraduate: women only; graduate: coed, comprehensive institution. *Enrollment:* 1,982 graduate, professional, and undergraduate students; 119 full-time matriculated graduate/professional students (97 women), 580 part-time matriculated graduate/professional students (506 women). *Enrollment by degree level:* 468 master's, 231 other advanced degrees. *Graduate faculty:* 23 full-time (11 women), 37 part-time/adjunct (23 women). *Graduate housing:* Room and/or apartments available on a first-come, first-served basis to single students; on-campus housing not available to married students. Housing application deadline: 5/10. *Student services:* Campus employment opportunities, campus safety program, career counseling, disabled student services, international student services, low-cost health insurance, teacher training. *Library facilities:* Mahoney Library. *Online resources:* library catalog, web page, access to other libraries' catalogs. *Collection:* 109,352 titles, 561 serial subscriptions, 2,418 audiovisual materials. *Research affiliation:* National Institute of Mental Health (mental health service), National Figure Skating Association (sports nutrition), Cornell University and University of Texas Houston (food biotechnology (attitude research)).

Computer facilities: 152 computers available on campus for general student use. A campuswide network can be accessed from student residence rooms and from off campus. Internet access is available. *Web address:* http://www.cse.edu/.

General Application Contact: Michael Szarek, Director of Enrollment Management, 973-290-4112, Fax: 973-290-4167, E-mail: mszarek@cse.edu.

GRADUATE UNITS

Department of Business Administration and Economics Students: 25 full-time (16 women), 57 part-time (50 women); includes 22 minority (12 African Americans, 2 Asian Americans or Pacific Islanders, 8 Hispanic Americans), 4 international. Average age 36. *Faculty:* 3 full-time (1 woman), 6 part-time/adjunct (5 women). Expenses: Contact institution. *Financial support:* Career-related internships or fieldwork, tuition waivers (partial), and unspecified assistantships available. Support available to part-time students. Financial award application deadline: 3/15; financial award applicants required to submit FAFSA. In 2006, 65 degrees awarded. *Degree program information:* Part-time and evening/weekend programs available. Offers management (MS). *Application deadline:* Applications are processed on a rolling basis. *Application fee:* $35. Electronic applications accepted. *Application Contact:* Michael Szarek, Director of Enrollment Management, 973-290-4112, Fax: 973-290-4167, E-mail: mszarek@cse.edu. *Director of the Graduate Program in Management,* Dr. Kathleen Reddick, 973-290-4041, Fax: 973-290-4177, E-mail: kreddick@cse.edu.

Department of Education Students: 69 full-time (58 women), 354 part-time (303 women); includes 21 minority (10 African Americans, 4 Asian Americans or Pacific Islanders, 7 Hispanic Americans). Average age 36. *Faculty:* 8 full-time (3 women), 14 part-time/adjunct (8 women). Expenses: Contact institution. *Financial support:* Career-related internships or fieldwork, Federal Work-Study, tuition waivers (partial), and unspecified assistantships available. Support available to part-time students. Financial award application deadline: 3/15; financial award applicants required to submit FAFSA. In 2006, 82 master's, 31 other advanced degrees awarded. *Degree program information:* Part-time and evening/weekend programs available. Offers accelerated certification for teachers (Certificate); assistive technology (Certificate); education: human services leadership (MA); educational technology (MA). *Application deadline:* For fall admission, 6/30 priority date for domestic students; for spring admission, 11/30 for domestic students. Applications are processed on a rolling basis. *Application fee:* $35. Electronic applications accepted. *Application Contact:* Michael Szarek, Director of Enrollment Management, 973-290-4112, Fax: 973-290-4167, E-mail: mszarek@cse.edu. *Director of Graduate Education Programs,* Dr. Alan H. Markowitz, 973-290-4374, Fax: 973-290-4389, E-mail: amarkowitz@cse.edu.

Department of Foods and Nutrition Students: 16 full-time (15 women), 24 part-time (all women); includes 5 minority (2 African Americans, 2 Asian Americans or Pacific Islanders, 1 Hispanic American). Average age 35. *Faculty:* 3 full-time (all women), 3 part-time/adjunct (all women). Expenses: Contact institution. *Financial support:* Federal Work-Study, tuition waivers (partial), and unspecified assistantships available. Support available to part-time students. Financial award application deadline: 3/15; financial award applicants required to submit FAFSA. In 2006, 7 master's, 10 Certificates awarded. *Degree program information:* Part-time and evening/weekend programs available. Offers dietetic internship (Certificate); nutrition (MS). *Application deadline:* Applications are processed on a rolling basis. *Application fee:* $35. Electronic applications accepted. *Application Contact:* Michael Szarek, Director of Enrollment Management, 973-290-4112, Fax: 973-290-4167, E-mail: mszarek@cse.edu. *Director of the Graduate Program in Nutrition,* Dr. Anne Boresma, 973-290-4065, Fax: 973-290-4167, E-mail: nutrition@cse.edu.

Department of Health Professions and Related Sciences Average age 41. *Faculty:* 1 (woman) full-time, 3 part-time/adjunct (1 woman). Expenses: Contact institution. *Financial support:* Career-related internships or fieldwork, tuition waivers (partial), and unspecified assistantships available. Support available to part-time students. Financial award application deadline: 3/15; financial award applicants required to submit FAFSA. In 2006, 7 degrees awarded. *Degree program information:* Part-time and evening/weekend programs available. Offers health care management (MS). *Application deadline:* Applications are processed on a rolling basis. *Application fee:* $35. Electronic applications accepted. *Application Contact:* Michael Szarek, Director of Enrollment Management, 973-290-4112, Fax: 973-290-4167, E-mail: mszarek@cse.edu. *Director of the Graduate Program in Health Care Management,* Linda Hunter, 973-290-4040, Fax: 973-290-4167, E-mail: lhunter@cse.edu.

Department of Psychology Students: 5 full-time (all women), 46 part-time (43 women); includes 12 minority (6 African Americans, 1 Asian American or Pacific Islander, 5 Hispanic Americans), 2 international. Average age 35. *Faculty:* 5 full-time (2 women), 8 part-time/adjunct (5 women). Expenses: Contact institution. *Financial support:* Career-related internships or fieldwork, tuition waivers (partial), and unspecified assistantships available. Support available to part-time students. Financial award application deadline: 3/15; financial award applicants required to submit FAFSA. In 2006, 2 degrees awarded. *Degree program information:* Part-time and evening/weekend programs available. Offers counseling psychology (MA); student affairs in higher education (Certificate). *Application deadline:* For fall admission, 4/14 priority date for domestic students; for spring admission, 11/15 for domestic students. Applications are processed on a rolling basis. *Application fee:* $35. Electronic applications accepted. *Application Contact:* Michael Szarek, Director of Enrollment Management, 973-290-4112, Fax: 973-290-4167, E-mail: mszarek@cse.edu. *Director of the Graduate Program in Counseling Psychology,* Dr. Valerie Scott, 973-290-4102, Fax: 973-290-4676, E-mail: vscott@cse.edu.

Department of Theology Students: 2 full-time (both women), 17 part-time (14 women); includes 1 minority (African American) Average age 49. *Faculty:* 3 full-time (1 woman), 3 part-time/adjunct (1 woman). Expenses: Contact institution. *Financial support:* Tuition waivers (partial) and unspecified assistantships available. Support available to part-time students. Financial award applicants required to submit FAFSA. In 2006, 5 degrees awarded. *Degree program information:* Part-time and evening/weekend programs available. Offers theology (MA). *Application deadline:* For fall admission, 3/1 priority date for domestic students; for spring admission, 9/1 for domestic students. Applications are processed on a rolling basis. *Application fee:* $35. Electronic applications accepted. *Application Contact:* Michael Szarek, Director of Enrollment Management, 973-290-4112, Fax: 973-290-4167, E-mail: mszarek@cse.edu. *Director of the Graduate Program in Theology,* Sr. Kathleen Flanagan, 973-290-4336, Fax: 973-290-4312, E-mail: kflanagan@cse.edu.

COLLEGE OF ST. JOSEPH, Rutland, VT 05701-3899

General Information Independent-religious, coed, comprehensive institution. *Enrollment:* 509 graduate, professional, and undergraduate students; 54 full-time matriculated graduate/professional students (41 women), 169 part-time matriculated graduate/professional students (128 women). *Enrollment by degree level:* 223 master's. *Graduate faculty:* 13 full-time (4 women), 21 part-time/adjunct (11 women). *Tuition:* Full-time $10,990; part-time $300 per credit. Part-time tuition and fees vary according to program. *Graduate housing:* Room and/or apartments available on a first-come, first-served basis to single students; on-campus housing not available to married students. Typical cost: $7,150 (including board). Housing application deadline: 5/1. *Student services:* Career counseling, free psychological counseling, international student services, low-cost health insurance. *Library facilities:* Giorgetti Library. *Online resources:* library catalog, access to other libraries' catalogs. *Collection:* 75,000 titles, 3,000 serial subscriptions.

Computer facilities: Computer purchase and lease plans are available. 30 computers available on campus for general student use. A campuswide network can be accessed from student residence rooms and from off campus. Internet access is available. *Web address:* http://www.csj.edu/.

General Application Contact: Tracy Gallipo, Director of Admissions, 802-773-5900 Ext. 3262, Fax: 802-773-5900, E-mail: tracygallipo@csj.edu.

GRADUATE UNITS

Graduate Program Students: 54 full-time (41 women), 169 part-time (128 women); includes 1 minority (Hispanic American), 2 international. Average age 34. 79 applicants, 89% accepted, 62 enrolled. *Faculty:* 13 full-time (4 women), 21 part-time/adjunct (11 women). Expenses: Contact institution. *Financial support:* In 2006–07, 4 students received support. Career-related internships or fieldwork, Federal Work-Study, tuition waivers (partial), and unspecified assistantships available. Support available to part-time students. Financial award application deadline: 3/1. In 2006, 64 degrees awarded. *Degree program information:* Part-time and evening/weekend programs available. *Application deadline:* Applications are processed on a rolling basis. *Application fee:* $35. *Application Contact:* Tracy Gallipo, Director of Admissions, 802-773-5900 Ext. 3262, Fax: 802-773-5900, E-mail: tracygallipo@csj.edu. *Vice President of Academic and Student Affairs,* Dr. Gary M. Lawler, 802-776-5214, Fax: 802-776-5258, E-mail: glawler@csj.edu.

Division of Business Students: 2 full-time (1 woman), 17 part-time (8 women), 1 international. Average age 38. 12 applicants, 83% accepted, 9 enrolled. *Faculty:* 2 full-time (0 women), 4 part-time/adjunct (0 women). Expenses: Contact institution. *Financial support:* In 2006–07, 1 student received support, including 1 teaching assistantship with full tuition reimbursement available (averaging $3,000 per year); Federal Work-Study and unspecified assistantships also available. Support available to part-time students. Financial award application deadline: 3/1. In 2006, 3 degrees awarded. *Degree program information:* Part-time and evening/weekend programs available. Offers business administration (MBA). *Application deadline:* Applications are processed on a rolling basis. *Application fee:* $35. *Application Contact:* Tracy Gallipo, Director of Admissions, 802-773-5900 Ext. 3262, Fax: 802-773-5900, E-mail: tracygallipo@csj.edu. *Chair,* Robert Foley, 802-773-5900 Ext. 3248, Fax: 802-776-5258, E-mail: rfoley@csj.edu.

Division of Education Students: 32 full-time, 55 part-time. Average age 33. 47 applicants, 89% accepted, 39 enrolled. *Faculty:* 3 full-time (2 women), 8 part-time/adjunct (5 women). Expenses: Contact institution. *Financial support:* Career-related internships or fieldwork, Federal Work-Study, and unspecified assistantships available. Support available to part-time students. Financial award application deadline: 3/1. In 2006, 46 degrees awarded. *Degree program information:* Part-time and evening/weekend programs available. Offers elementary education (M Ed); English (M Ed); general education (M Ed); mathematics (M Ed); reading (M Ed); secondary education (M Ed); social studies (M Ed); special education (M Ed). *Application deadline:* Applications are processed on a rolling basis. *Application fee:* $35. *Application Contact:* Tracy Gallipo, Director of Admissions, 802-773-5900 Ext. 3262, Fax: 802-773-5900, E-mail: tracygallipo@csj.edu. *Chair,* Dr. Kapi Reith, 802-773-5900 Ext. 3243, Fax: 802-773-5900, E-mail: kreith@csj.edu.

Division of Psychology and Human Services Students: 20 full-time, 51 part-time, 1 international. Average age 35. 20 applicants, 90% accepted, 14 enrolled. *Faculty:* 4 full-time (1 woman), 8 part-time/adjunct (5 women). Expenses: Contact institution. *Financial support:* In 2006–07, 3 students received support, including teaching assistantships with tuition reimbursements available (averaging $3,000 per year); career-related internships or fieldwork, Federal Work-Study, and unspecified assistantships also available. Support available to part-time students. Financial award application deadline: 3/1. In 2006, 11 degrees awarded. *Degree program information:* Part-time and evening/weekend programs available. Offers clinical mental health counseling (MS); clinical psychology (MS); community counseling (MS); school guidance counseling (MS); substance abuse counseling (MS). *Application deadline:* Applications are processed on a rolling basis. *Application fee:* $35. *Application Contact:* Tracy Gallipo, Director of Admissions, 802-773-5900 Ext. 3262, Fax: 802-773-5900, E-mail: tracygallipo@csj.edu. *Chair,* Dr. Craig Knapp, 802-773-5900 Ext. 3219, Fax: 802-776-5258, E-mail: cknapp@csj.edu.

THE COLLEGE OF SAINT ROSE, Albany, NY 12203-1419

General Information Independent, coed, comprehensive institution. CGS member. *Graduate housing:* On-campus housing not available.

GRADUATE UNITS

Graduate Studies *Degree program information:* Part-time and evening/weekend programs available. Electronic applications accepted.

School of Arts and Humanities *Degree program information:* Part-time and evening/weekend programs available. Offers art education (MS Ed, Certificate); arts and humanities (MA, MS Ed, Adv C, Certificate); English (MA); history/political science (MA); music (MA); music education (MS Ed, Adv C, Certificate); public communications (MA).

The College of Saint Rose (continued)

School of Business *Degree program information:* Part-time and evening/weekend programs available. Offers accounting (MS); business (MBA, MS, Certificate); business administration (MBA); not-for-profit management (Certificate). Electronic applications accepted.

School of Education *Degree program information:* Part-time and evening/weekend programs available. Offers applied technology education (MS Ed); bilingual pupil personnel services (Certificate); business and marketing (MS Ed); childhood education (MS Ed); college student personnel (MS Ed); college student services administration (MS Ed); communication disorders (MS Ed); community counseling (MS Ed); counseling (MS Ed); early childhood education (MS Ed); education (MS, MS Ed, Adv C, Certificate); educational administration and supervision (MS Ed, Certificate); educational leadership and administration (MS Ed); educational psychology (MS Ed); ELA—school building leader (Certificate); ELA—school district leader (Certificate); elementary education (K-6) (MS Ed); literacy: birth-grade 6 (MS Ed); literacy: grades 5-12 (MS Ed); reading (Certificate); school administrator and supervisor (Certificate); school counseling (MS Ed); school psychology (MS, Adv C); secondary education (MS Ed, Certificate); special education (MS Ed); teacher education (MS Ed, Certificate). Electronic applications accepted.

School of Mathematics and Sciences *Degree program information:* Part-time and evening/weekend programs available. Offers computer information systems (MS); mathematics and sciences (MS). Electronic applications accepted.

See Close-Up on page 851.

THE COLLEGE OF ST. SCHOLASTICA, Duluth, MN 55811-4199

General Information Independent-religious, coed, comprehensive institution. *Enrollment:* 3,304 graduate, professional, and undergraduate students; 291 full-time matriculated graduate/professional students (233 women), 281 part-time matriculated graduate/professional students (203 women). *Graduate faculty:* 44 full-time (29 women), 56 part-time/adjunct (33 women). *Graduate housing:* Room and/or apartments available on a first-come, first-served basis to single students; on-campus housing not available to married students. Housing application deadline: 5/15. *Student services:* Campus employment opportunities, campus safety program, career counseling, disabled student services, exercise/wellness program, free psychological counseling, international student services, low-cost health insurance, multicultural affairs office, writing training. *Library facilities:* College of St. Scholastica Library. *Online resources:* library catalog, web page, access to other libraries' catalogs. *Collection:* 130,353 titles, 21,656 serial subscriptions, 5,418 audiovisual materials.

Computer facilities: 129 computers available on campus for general student use. A campuswide network can be accessed from student residence rooms and from off campus. Internet access and online class registration, student account information and transcripts online are available. *Web address:* http://www.css.edu/.

General Application Contact: Tonya J. Roth, Graduate Recruitment Counselor, 218-723-6285, Fax: 218-733-2275, E-mail: gradstudies@css.edu.

GRADUATE UNITS

Graduate Studies Students: 337 full-time (270 women), 310 part-time (225 women); includes 46 minority (16 African Americans, 9 American Indian/Alaska Native, 14 Asian Americans or Pacific Islanders, 7 Hispanic Americans), 3 international. Average age 34. 407 applicants, 80% accepted, 241 enrolled. *Faculty:* 44 full-time (29 women), 56 part-time/adjunct (33 women). Expenses: Contact institution. *Financial support:* In 2006–07, 468 students received support, including 14 teaching assistantships (averaging $1,457 per year); scholarships/grants and traineeships also available. Support available to part-time students. Financial award applicants required to submit FAFSA. In 2006, 157 degrees awarded. *Degree program information:* Part-time and evening/weekend programs available. Postbaccalaureate distance learning degree programs offered (minimal on-campus study). Offers computer information systems (MA); curriculum and instruction (M Ed); educational media and technology (M Ed); exercise physiology (MA); health information management (MA, Certificate); management (MA); nursing (MA, PMC); occupational therapy (MA); physical therapy (DPT); teaching (M Ed, Certificate). *Application deadline:* For fall admission, 8/1 priority date for domestic students, 8/1 for international students; for winter admission, 11/15 priority date for domestic students; for spring admission, 11/15 priority date for domestic students, 11/15 for international students. Applications are processed on a rolling basis. *Application fee:* $50. Electronic applications accepted. *Application Contact:* Tonya J. Roth, Graduate Recruitment Counselor, 218-723-6285, Fax: 218-733-2275, E-mail: gradstudies@css.edu. *Vice President of Graduate and Extended Studies,* Dr. Collette Garrity, 651-298-1015, Fax: 651-298-8532, E-mail: cgarrity@css.edu.

COLLEGE OF SANTA FE, Santa Fe, NM 87505-7634

General Information Independent, coed, comprehensive institution. *Graduate housing:* Room and/or apartments available on a first-come, first-served basis to single students; on-campus housing not available to married students.

GRADUATE UNITS

Department of Business Administration *Degree program information:* Part-time and evening/weekend programs available. Offers finance (MBA); human resources (MBA). Program also available at Albuquerque campus.

Department of Education *Degree program information:* Part-time and evening/weekend programs available. Offers at-risk youth (MA); curriculum and instruction (MA); multicultural special education (MA).

COLLEGE OF STATEN ISLAND OF THE CITY UNIVERSITY OF NEW YORK, Staten Island, NY 10314-6600

General Information State and locally supported, coed, comprehensive institution. *Enrollment:* 12,313 graduate, professional, and undergraduate students; 96 full-time matriculated graduate/professional students (66 women), 875 part-time matriculated graduate/professional students (659 women). *Enrollment by degree level:* 920 master's, 51 other advanced degrees. *Graduate faculty:* 59 full-time (32 women), 21 part-time/adjunct (11 women). Tuition, state resident: full-time $6,400; part-time $270 per credit. Tuition, nonresident: part-time $500 per credit. *Required fees:* $53 per semester. *Graduate housing:* On-campus housing not available. *Student services:* Campus employment opportunities, campus safety program, career counseling, child daycare facilities, disabled student services, exercise/wellness program, free psychological counseling, international student services, low-cost health insurance, multicultural affairs office, teacher training, writing training. *Library facilities:* College of Staten Island Library. *Online resources:* library catalog, web page, access to other libraries' catalogs. *Collection:* 229,000 titles, 25,000 serial subscriptions, 4,100 audiovisual materials. *Research affiliation:* Kent Optronics (LCD displays), Dynavax Technologies (biopharmaceutical chemistry), Paul Corporation (smart multicomponent polymer networks), DeGussa Corporation (ink products).

Computer facilities: 1,100 computers available on campus for general student use. A campuswide network can be accessed from off campus. Internet access and online class registration are available. *Web address:* http://www.csi.cuny.edu/.

General Application Contact: Emmanuel Esperance, Deputy Director of Office of Recruitment and Admissions, 718-982-2190, Fax: 718-982-2500, E-mail: admissions@mail.csi.cuny.edu.

GRADUATE UNITS

Graduate Programs Students: 96 full-time (66 women), 875 part-time (659 women); includes 153 minority (54 African Americans, 2 American Indian/Alaska Native, 39 Asian Americans or Pacific Islanders, 58 Hispanic Americans), 55 international. Average age 31. 387 applicants, 84% accepted, 254 enrolled. *Faculty:* 59 full-time (32 women), 21 part-time/adjunct (11 women). Expenses: Contact institution. *Financial support:* In 2006–07, 5 students received support. Applicants required to submit FAFSA. In 2006, 281 master's, 27 other advanced degrees awarded. Offers adolescence education (MS Ed); adult health nursing (MS, 6th Year Certificate); biology (MS); business management (MS); childhood education (MS Ed); cinema and media studies (MA); computer science (MS); English (MA); gerontological nursing (MS, 6th Year Certificate); history (MA); leadership in education (6th Year Certificate); liberal studies (MA); special education (MS Ed). *Application fee:* $125. *Application Contact:* Emmanuel Esperance, Deputy Director of Office of Recruitment and Admissions, 718-982-2259, Fax: 718-982-2500, E-mail: admissions@mail.csi.cuny.edu. *Senior Vice President for Academic Affairs and Provost,* Dr. David Podell, 718-982-2440, Fax: 718-982-2442, E-mail: podell@mail.csi.cuny.edu.

Center for Developmental Neuroscience and Developmental Disabilities Students: 2 full-time (0 women), 20 part-time (12 women); includes 8 minority (3 African Americans, 2 Asian Americans or Pacific Islanders, 3 Hispanic Americans), 2 international. 17 applicants, 88% accepted, 12 enrolled. *Faculty:* 1 full-time, 3 part-time/adjunct. Expenses: Contact institution. *Financial support:* Fellowships with partial tuition reimbursements available. Financial award applicants required to submit FAFSA. In 2006, 1 degree awarded. *Degree program information:* Part-time and evening/weekend programs available. Postbaccalaureate distance learning degree programs offered. Offers neuroscience, mental retardation and developmental disabilities (MS). *Application deadline:* Applications are processed on a rolling basis. *Application fee:* $125. *Application Contact:* Emmanuel Esperance, Deputy Director of Office of Recruitment and Admissions, 718-982-2190, Fax: 718-982-2500, E-mail: admissions@mail.csi.cuny.edu. *Coordinator,* Dr. Probal Banerjee, 718-982-3938, Fax: 718-982-3944, E-mail: banerjee@mail.csi.cuny.edu.

Center for Environmental Science Average age 34. 8 applicants, 88% accepted, 4 enrolled. *Faculty:* 5 full-time (1 woman), 1 part-time/adjunct (0 women). Expenses: Contact institution. *Financial support:* In 2006–07, 1 student received support, including 1 fellowship with partial tuition reimbursement available (averaging $10,000 per year). Financial award applicants required to submit FAFSA. In 2006, 1 degree awarded. *Degree program information:* Part-time and evening/weekend programs available. Offers environmental science (MS). *Application deadline:* Applications are processed on a rolling basis. *Application fee:* $125. *Application Contact:* Emmanuel Esperance, Deputy director of Office of Recruitment and Admissions, 718-982-2259, Fax: 718-982-2500, E-mail: admissions@mail.csi.cuny.edu. *Director,* Dr. Alfred Levine, 718-982-3920, Fax: 718-982-3923, E-mail: envirscimasters@mail.csi.cuny.edu.

See Close-Up on page 853.

COLLEGE OF THE ATLANTIC, Bar Harbor, ME 04609-1198

General Information Independent, coed, comprehensive institution. *Graduate housing:* Room and/or apartments available to single students; on-campus housing not available to married students. Housing application deadline: 6/1. *Research affiliation:* Acadia National Park, National Park Service (research management, environmental education), Mount Desert Island Biological Laboratory, Jackson Laboratory (genetics), Society for Human Ecology (ecological decision making in society).

GRADUATE UNITS

Program in Human Ecology Offers human ecology (M Phil).

COLLEGE OF THE HUMANITIES AND SCIENCES, HARRISON MIDDLETON UNIVERSITY, Tempe, AZ 85282

General Information Independent, coed, comprehensive institution. *Enrollment by degree level:* 33 master's, 5 doctoral. *Graduate faculty:* 17 full-time (7 women), 5 part-time/adjunct (2 women). *Tuition:* Part-time $275 per credit hour. *Student services:* Teacher training. *Web address:* http://www.chumsci.edu/.

General Application Contact: Kathleen Mirabile, Vice-President, Provost, 877-248-6724, Fax: 800-762-1622, E-mail: kmirabile@chumsci.edu.

GRADUATE UNITS

Graduate Program Students: 38 full-time (9 women). *Faculty:* 17 full-time (7 women), 5 part-time/adjunct (2 women). Expenses: Contact institution. In 2006, 10 degrees awarded. *Degree program information:* Part-time and evening/weekend programs available. Postbaccalaureate distance learning degree programs offered (no on-campus study). *Application fee:* $50. *Application Contact:* Kathleen Mirabile, Vice-President, Provost, 877-248-6724, Fax: 800-762-1622, E-mail: kmirabile@chumsci.edu.

COLLEGE OF THE SOUTHWEST, Hobbs, NM 88240-9129

General Information Independent, coed, comprehensive institution. *Enrollment:* 741 graduate, professional, and undergraduate students; 41 full-time matriculated graduate/professional students (28 women), 43 part-time matriculated graduate/professional students (35 women). *Enrollment by degree level:* 84 master's. *Graduate faculty:* 2 full-time (both women), 6 part-time/adjunct (1 woman). *Tuition:* Part-time $375 per credit hour. *Graduate housing:* On-campus housing not available. *Student services:* Campus employment opportunities, teacher training. *Library facilities:* Scarborough Memorial Library plus 1 other. *Online resources:* library catalog, access to other libraries' catalogs. *Collection:* 76,217 titles, 287 serial subscriptions.

Computer facilities: 35 computers available on campus for general student use. A campuswide network can be accessed from student residence rooms. Internet access is available. *Web address:* http://www.csw.edu/.

General Application Contact: Steve Hill, Dean/Recruiting, 505-392-6561 Ext. 1010, Fax: 505-392-6006, E-mail: shill@csw.edu.

GRADUATE UNITS

School of Education Students: 41 full-time (28 women), 43 part-time (35 women); includes 24 minority (1 African American, 1 American Indian/Alaska Native, 1 Asian American or Pacific Islander, 21 Hispanic Americans), 1 international. Average age 38. 119 applicants, 29% accepted, 34 enrolled. *Faculty:* 2 full-time (both women), 6 part-time/adjunct (1 woman). Expenses: Contact institution. *Financial support:* In 2006–07, 58 students received support, including 1 research assistantship; Federal Work-Study, scholarships/grants, and tuition waivers (partial) also available. Support available to part-time students. Financial award application deadline: 4/1; financial award applicants required to submit FAFSA. In 2006, 26 degrees awarded. *Degree program information:* Part-time and evening/weekend programs available. Postbaccalaureate distance learning degree programs offered. Offers curriculum and instruction (MS); educational administration (MS); educational counseling (MS); educational diagnostician (MS). *Application deadline:* For fall admission, 3/1 priority date for domestic students; for spring admission, 10/1 for domestic students. Applications are processed on a rolling basis. *Application fee:* $50. *Application Contact:* Kerrie Mitchell, Coordinator of Financial Aid and Admissions Operations, 505-392-6563 Ext. 1048, Fax: 505-392-6006, E-mail: kmitchell@csw.edu. *Dean,* Dr. Dennis Atherton, 505-392-6561 Ext. 1069, Fax: 505-392-6006, E-mail: datherton@csw.edu.

THE COLLEGE OF WILLIAM AND MARY, Williamsburg, VA 23187-8795

General Information State-supported, coed, university. CGS member. *Enrollment:* 7,709 graduate, professional, and undergraduate students; 1,494 full-time matriculated graduate/professional students (727 women), 383 part-time matriculated graduate/professional students (197 women). *Enrollment by degree level:* 630 first professional, 801 master's, 446 doctoral. *Graduate faculty:* 594 full-time (212 women), 164 part-time/adjunct (83 women). Tuition, state resident: full-time $6,100; part-time $260 per credit. Tuition, nonresident: full-time $18,790; part-time $725 per credit. *Required fees:* $3,314. Tuition and fees vary according to program. *Graduate housing:* Rooms and/or apartments available on a first-come, first-served basis to single and married students. Typical cost: $4,210 per year ($6,932 including board) for single students; $4,210 per year ($6,932 including board) for married students. Housing application deadline: 2/13. *Student services:* Campus employment opportunities, campus safety program, career counseling, child daycare facilities, disabled student services, exercise/wellness program, free psychological counseling, grant writing training, international student services, low-cost health insurance, multicultural affairs office, teacher training. *Library facilities:* Swem Library plus 9 others. *Online resources:* library catalog, web page. *Collection:* 2.1 million titles, 36,877 serial subscriptions, 33,708 audiovisual materials. *Research affiliation:* Thomas Jefferson National Accelerator Center (nuclear physics), Colonial Williamsburg (archaeology, history),

Luna Innovations, Inc. (nanotechnology, defense-related technology, applied science), Center for Excellence in Aging and Geriatric Health (public policy, kinesiology), Incogen, Inc. (computer science, applied science, bioinformatics).

Computer facilities: 225 computers available on campus for general student use. A campuswide network can be accessed from student residence rooms and from off campus. Internet access and online class registration are available. *Web address:* http://www.wm.edu/.

General Application Contact: Dr. Laurie Sanderson, Dean of Research and Graduate Studies, 757-221-2468, E-mail: slsand@um.edu.

GRADUATE UNITS

Faculty of Arts and Sciences Students: 358 full-time (167 women), 65 part-time (33 women); includes 38 minority (23 African Americans, 2 American Indian/Alaska Native, 10 Asian Americans or Pacific Islanders, 3 Hispanic Americans), 67 international. Average age 28. 794 applicants, 32% accepted, 114 enrolled. *Faculty:* 415 full-time (159 women), 104 part-time/adjunct (51 women). Expenses: Contact institution. *Financial support:* Fellowships, research assistantships, teaching assistantships, career-related internships or fieldwork, Federal Work-Study, and institutionally sponsored loans available. Financial award applicants required to submit FAFSA. In 2006, 144 master's, 41 doctorates awarded. *Degree program information:* Part-time programs available. Offers American studies (MA, PhD); anthropology (MA, PhD); applied science (MS, PhD); arts and sciences (MA, MPP, MS, PhD, Psy D); biology (MS); chemistry (MA, MS); clinical psychology (Psy D); computational operations research (MS); computer science (MS, PhD); general experimental psychology (MA); history (MA, PhD); physics (MS, PhD); public policy (MPP). *Application deadline:* For fall admission, 1/15 for domestic and international students. *Application fee:* $30. *Application Contact:* Wanda Carter, Administrator of Graduate Student Services, 757-221-2467, Fax: 757-221-4874, E-mail: wdcart@wm.edu. *Dean of Research and Graduate Studies,* Dr. Laurie Sanderson, 757-221-2468, E-mail: slsand@um.edu.

Mason School of Business Students: 202 full-time (61 women), 138 part-time (25 women); includes 17 African Americans, 11 Asian Americans or Pacific Islanders, 1 Hispanic American, 58 international. Average age 32. 208 applicants, 52% accepted, 58 enrolled. *Faculty:* 57 full-time (15 women), 4 part-time/adjunct (0 women). Expenses: Contact institution. *Financial support:* In 2006–07, 137 students received support, including 44 research assistantships with partial tuition reimbursements available (averaging $4,000 per year); career-related internships or fieldwork, scholarships/grants, and unspecified assistantships also available. Financial award application deadline: 3/1; financial award applicants required to submit FAFSA. In 2006, 167 degrees awarded. *Degree program information:* Part-time and evening/weekend programs available. Offers accounting (M Acc); business administration (MBA). *Application deadline:* For fall admission, 4/1 priority date for domestic students. Applications are processed on a rolling basis. *Application fee:* $100. Electronic applications accepted. *Application Contact:* Kathy Pattison, Director of Admissions, 757-221-2898, Fax: 757-221-2958, E-mail: kpattison@business.wm.edu. *Dean,* Dr. Lawrence Pulley, 757-221-2891, Fax: 757-221-2937, E-mail: larry.pulley@mason.wm.edu.

School of Education Students: 245 full-time (205 women), 227 part-time (184 women); includes 55 minority (44 African Americans, 2 American Indian/Alaska Native, 6 Asian Americans or Pacific Islanders, 3 Hispanic Americans), 7 international. Average age 31. 480 applicants, 57% accepted, 155 enrolled. *Faculty:* 36 full-time (17 women), 17 part-time/adjunct (15 women). Expenses: Contact institution. *Financial support:* In 2006–07, 206 students received support, including 1 fellowship with full tuition reimbursement available (averaging $20,000 per year), 124 research assistantships with full and partial tuition reimbursements available (averaging $10,800 per year); teaching assistantships, career-related internships or fieldwork, Federal Work-Study, institutionally sponsored loans, scholarships/grants, and unspecified assistantships also available. Financial award application deadline: 2/1; financial award applicants required to submit FAFSA. In 2006, 132 master's, 24 doctorates, 12 other advanced degrees awarded. *Degree program information:* Part-time and evening/weekend programs available. Offers community and addictions counseling (M Ed); community counseling (M Ed); curriculum and educational technology (Ed D, PhD); curriculum leadership (Ed D, PhD); education (M Ed, MA Ed, Ed D, PhD, Ed S); educational counseling (Ed D, PhD); educational leadership (M Ed); educational policy, planning, and leadership (Ed D, PhD); elementary education (MA Ed); family counseling (M Ed); gifted education (MA Ed); gifted education administration (M Ed); reading education (MA Ed); school counseling (M Ed); school psychology (M Ed, Ed S); secondary education (MA Ed); special education (MA Ed). *Application deadline:* For fall admission, 2/1 for domestic and international students; for spring admission, 10/1 for domestic and international students. *Application fee:* $30. *Application Contact:* Dorothy Osborne, Director of Admissions, 757-221-2317, E-mail: dsosbo@wm.edu. *Dean,* Dr. Virginia McLaughlin, 757-221-2317, E-mail: vamcla@wm.edu.

School of Marine Science Students: 113 full-time (56 women), 12 part-time (7 women); includes 11 minority (6 African Americans, 2 Asian Americans or Pacific Islanders, 3 Hispanic Americans), 16 international. Average age 29. 103 applicants, 35% accepted, 14 enrolled. *Faculty:* 54 full-time (10 women), 2 part-time/adjunct (1 woman). Expenses: Contact institution. *Financial support:* In 2006–07, fellowships with full tuition reimbursements (averaging $17,200 per year), research assistantships (averaging $16,400 per year) were awarded; teaching assistantships, career-related internships or fieldwork, Federal Work-Study, health care benefits, and unspecified assistantships also available. Support available to part-time students. Financial award application deadline: 6/15; financial award applicants required to submit FAFSA. In 2006, 16 master's, 13 doctorates awarded. Offers marine science (MS, PhD). *Application deadline:* For fall admission, 1/15 for domestic and international students. *Application fee:* $50. *Application Contact:* Sue N. Presson, Graduate School Registrar, 804-684-4106, Fax: 804-684-7881, E-mail: snpres@vims.edu. *Dean and Director,* Dr. John T. Wells, 804-684-7102, Fax: 804-684-7009, E-mail: wells@vims.wm.edu.

School of Marine Science/Virginia Institute of Marine Science Students: 109 full-time (55 women), 7 part-time (2 women); includes 12 minority (8 African Americans, 1 American Indian/Alaska Native, 1 Asian American or Pacific Islander, 2 Hispanic Americans), 14 international. Average age 27. 103 applicants, 35% accepted, 19 enrolled. *Faculty:* 52 full-time (10 women), 5 part-time/adjunct (2 women). Expenses: Contact institution. *Financial support:* Fellowships with full tuition reimbursements, research assistantships with full tuition reimbursements, teaching assistantships with full tuition reimbursements, career-related internships or fieldwork, Federal Work-Study, scholarships/grants, health care benefits, and unspecified assistantships available. Support available to part-time students. Financial award application deadline: 6/15; financial award applicants required to submit FAFSA. In 2006, 10 master's, 12 doctorates awarded. Offers marine science (MS, PhD). *Application deadline:* For fall admission, 1/15 for domestic and international students. *Application fee:* $50. Electronic applications accepted. *Application Contact:* Sue N. Presson, Graduate School Registrar, 804-684-4106, Fax: 804-684-7881, E-mail: snpres@vims.edu. *Dean and Director,* Dr. John T. Wells, 804-684-7102, Fax: 804-684-7009, E-mail: wells@vims.wm.edu.

William & Mary Law School Students: 620 full-time (281 women), 3 part-time (all women); includes 87 minority (49 African Americans, 1 American Indian/Alaska Native, 29 Asian Americans or Pacific Islanders, 8 Hispanic Americans), 4 international. Average age 26. 4,209 applicants, 24% accepted, 204 enrolled. *Faculty:* 32 full-time (10 women), 30 part-time/adjunct (11 women). Expenses: Contact institution. *Financial support:* In 2006–07, 338 students received support, including 222 research assistantships with partial tuition reimbursements available (averaging $4,000 per year), 26 teaching assistantships (averaging $4,900 per year); career-related internships or fieldwork, Federal Work-Study, institutionally sponsored loans, and scholarships/grants also available. Financial award application deadline: 2/15; financial award applicants required to submit FAFSA. In 2006, 206 JDs, 11 master's awarded. Offers law (JD, LL M). *Application deadline:* For fall admission, 3/1 priority date for domestic and international students. *Application fee:* $50. Electronic applications accepted. *Application Contact:* Faye F. Shealy, Associate Dean for Admission, 757-221-3785, Fax: 757-221-3261, E-mail: ffshea@wm.edu. *Dean,* W. Taylor Reveley, 757-221-3800, Fax: 757-221-3261, E-mail: taylor@wm.edu.

See Close-Up on page 855.

COLLÈGE UNIVERSITAIRE DE SAINT-BONIFACE, Saint-Boniface, MB R2H 0H7, Canada

General Information Independent-religious, comprehensive institution.

GRADUATE UNITS

Department of Education Offers education (M Ed).

Program in Canadian Studies Offers Canadian studies (MA).

COLORADO CHRISTIAN UNIVERSITY, Lakewood, CO 80226

General Information Independent-religious, coed, comprehensive institution. *Graduate housing:* On-campus housing not available.

GRADUATE UNITS

Program in Business Administration *Degree program information:* Part-time and evening/weekend programs available. Postbaccalaureate distance learning degree programs offered (minimal on-campus study). Offers business administration (MBA). Electronic applications accepted.

Program in Counseling *Degree program information:* Part-time and evening/weekend programs available. Offers counseling (MA). Electronic applications accepted.

Program in Curriculum and Instruction *Degree program information:* Part-time and evening/weekend programs available. Offers curriculum and instruction (MA). Electronic applications accepted.

THE COLORADO COLLEGE, Colorado Springs, CO 80903-3294

General Information Independent, coed, comprehensive institution. *Enrollment:* 1,998 graduate, professional, and undergraduate students; 27 full-time matriculated graduate/professional students (19 women). *Enrollment by degree level:* 27 master's. *Graduate faculty:* 4 full-time (2 women), 15 part-time/adjunct (10 women). *Tuition:* Full-time $23,567. One-time fee: $1,485 full-time. *Graduate housing:* On-campus housing not available. *Student services:* Campus safety program, career counseling, child daycare facilities, disabled student services, exercise/wellness program, free psychological counseling, grant writing training, international student services, low-cost health insurance, multicultural affairs office, teacher training, writing training. *Library facilities:* Tutt Library plus 2 others. *Online resources:* library catalog, web page, access to other libraries' catalogs. *Collection:* 532,793 titles, 4,649 serial subscriptions, 22,830 audiovisual materials.

Computer facilities: Computer purchase and lease plans are available. 208 computers available on campus for general student use. A campuswide network can be accessed from student residence rooms and from off campus. Internet access and online class registration are available. *Web address:* http://www.coloradocollege.edu/.

General Application Contact: Marsha E. Unruh, Director of Education Career Services, 719-389-6472, Fax: 719-389-6473, E-mail: munruh@coloradocollege.edu.

GRADUATE UNITS

Department of Education Students: 27 full-time (19 women); includes 3 minority (1 African American, 1 Asian American or Pacific Islander, 1 Hispanic American). Average age 27. 49 applicants, 86% accepted, 27 enrolled. *Faculty:* 4 full-time (2 women), 15 part-time/adjunct (10 women). Expenses: Contact institution. *Financial support:* In 2006–07, 24 students received support, including 24 teaching assistantships (averaging $16,000 per year); career-related internships or fieldwork, institutionally sponsored loans, health care benefits, and tuition waivers (partial) also available. Financial award application deadline: 2/15; financial award applicants required to submit CSS PROFILE or FAFSA. In 2006, 36 degrees awarded. Offers art teaching (MAT); elementary education (MAT); elementary school teaching (MAT); English teaching (MAT); foreign language teaching (MAT); mathematics teaching (MAT); music teaching (MAT); science teaching (MAT); secondary education (MAT); social studies teaching (MAT). *Application deadline:* For fall admission, 2/1 for domestic and international students. *Application fee:* $50. *Application Contact:* Marsha E. Unruh, Director of Education Career Services, 719-389-6472, Fax: 719-389-6473, E-mail: munruh@coloradocollege.edu. *Chair,* Charlotte Mendoza, 719-389-6474, Fax: 719-389-6473, E-mail: cmendoza@coloradocollege.edu.

Programs for Experienced Teachers Students: 78; includes 2 minority (both Hispanic Americans) Average age 31. *Faculty:* 18 part-time/adjunct (8 women). Expenses: Contact institution. *Financial support:* Institutionally sponsored loans and half-tuition waivers to teachers with a contract available. In 2006, 28 degrees awarded. *Degree program information:* Part-time programs available. Offers American Southwest studies for all teachers (MAT); arts and humanities for secondary school teachers and administrators (MAT); integrated natural science for all teachers (MAT); liberal arts for elementary school teachers and administrators (MAT). Programs offered during summer only. *Application deadline:* Applications are processed on a rolling basis. *Application fee:* $50. *Application Contact:* Ann H. Van Horn, Assistant Dean of Summer Session, 719-389-6656, Fax: 719-389-6955, E-mail: avanhorn@coloradocollege.edu. *Dean of Summer Programs,* Dr. Libby Rittenberg, 719-389-6657, Fax: 719-389-6955.

COLORADO SCHOOL OF MINES, Golden, CO 80401-1887

General Information State-supported, coed, university. CGS member. *Enrollment:* 4,056 graduate, professional, and undergraduate students; 636 full-time matriculated graduate/professional students (164 women), 140 part-time matriculated graduate/professional students (34 women). *Enrollment by degree level:* 476 master's, 295 doctoral, 5 other advanced degrees. *Graduate faculty:* 253 full-time (41 women), 155 part-time/adjunct (21 women). Tuition, state resident: full-time $8,064; part-time $523 per credit. Tuition, nonresident: full-time $20,340; part-time $1,338 per credit. *Required fees:* $983; $492 per semester. *Graduate housing:* Rooms and/or apartments available on a first-come, first-served basis to single and married students. *Student services:* Campus employment opportunities, campus safety program, career counseling, disabled student services, exercise/wellness program, free psychological counseling, international student services, low-cost health insurance, teacher training, writing training. *Library facilities:* Arthur Lakes Library. *Online resources:* library catalog, web page, access to other libraries' catalogs. *Collection:* 150,000 titles, 4,883 serial subscriptions.

Computer facilities: 400 computers available on campus for general student use. A campuswide network can be accessed from student residence rooms and from off campus. Internet access and online class registration are available. *Web address:* http://www.mines.edu/.

General Application Contact: Kay Leaman, Graduate Admissions Coordinator, 303-273-3249, Fax: 303-273-3244, E-mail: grad-app@mines.edu.

GRADUATE UNITS

Graduate School Students: 636 full-time (164 women), 140 part-time (34 women); includes 55 minority (7 African Americans, 5 American Indian/Alaska Native, 21 Asian Americans or Pacific Islanders, 22 Hispanic Americans), 131 international. 792 applicants, 71% accepted, 267 enrolled. *Faculty:* 253 full-time (41 women), 155 part-time/adjunct (21 women). Expenses: Contact institution. *Financial support:* In 2006–07, 42 fellowships with full tuition reimbursements (averaging $9,600 per year), 192 research assistantships with full tuition reimbursements (averaging $9,600 per year), 158 teaching assistantships with full tuition reimbursements (averaging $9,600 per year) were awarded; career-related internships or fieldwork, Federal Work-Study, institutionally sponsored loans, scholarships/grants, health care benefits, and unspecified assistantships also available. Financial award applicants required to submit FAFSA. In 2006, 211 master's, 45 doctorates awarded. *Degree program information:* Part-time programs available. Offers applied chemistry (PhD); applied physics (PhD); chemical engineering (MS, PhD); chemistry (MS, PhD); engineering geology (Diploma); exploration geosciences (Diploma); geochemistry (MS, PhD); geological engineering (ME, MS, PhD, Diploma); geology (MS, PhD); geophysical engineering (ME, MS, PhD); geophysics (MS, PhD, Diploma); hydrogeology (Diploma); international political economy (Graduate Certificate); liberal arts and international studies (MIPER); materials science (MS, PhD); mathematical and computer sciences (MS, PhD); metallurgical and materials engineering (ME, MS, PhD); mining engineer-

Colorado School of Mines (continued)

ing (ME, MS, PhD); petroleum engineering (ME, MS, PhD); physics (MS); science and technology policy (Graduate Certificate). *Application deadline:* For fall admission, 1/1 priority date for domestic and international students; for spring admission, 9/1 priority date for domestic and international students. *Application fee:* $50 ($70 for international students). Electronic applications accepted. *Application Contact:* Kay Leaman, Graduate Admissions Coordinator, 303-273-3249, Fax: 303-273-3244, E-mail: grad-app@mines.edu. *Dean of Graduate Studies,* Dr. Tom M. Boyd, 303-273-3020, Fax: 303-273-3244, E-mail: tboyd@mines.edu.

Division of Economics and Business Students: 59 full-time (18 women), 17 part-time (2 women); includes 9 minority (4 Asian Americans or Pacific Islanders, 5 Hispanic Americans), 16 international. 109 applicants, 79% accepted, 32 enrolled. *Faculty:* 13 full-time (5 women), 4 part-time/adjunct (0 women). Expenses: Contact institution. *Financial support:* In 2006–07, 18 students received support, including 7 fellowships with full tuition reimbursements available (averaging $9,600 per year), research assistantships with full tuition reimbursements available (averaging $9,600 per year), 13 teaching assistantships with full tuition reimbursements available (averaging $9,600 per year); scholarships/grants, health care benefits, and unspecified assistantships also available. Financial award applicants required to submit FAFSA. In 2006, 37 master's, 3 doctorates awarded. *Degree program information:* Part-time programs available. Offers engineering and technology management (MS); mineral economics (MS, PhD). *Application deadline:* For fall admission, 1/1 priority date for domestic and international students; for spring admission, 9/1 priority date for domestic and international students. *Application fee:* $50 ($70 for international students). Electronic applications accepted. *Application Contact:* Kathleen A. Feighny, Program Manager, 303-273-3979, Fax: 303-273-3416, E-mail: kfeighny@mines.edu. *Head,* Dr. Roderick G. Eggert, 303-273-3981, Fax: 303-273-3416, E-mail: reggert@mines.edu.

Division of Engineering Students: 87 full-time (21 women), 36 part-time (5 women); includes 9 minority (7 Asian Americans or Pacific Islanders, 2 Hispanic Americans), 8 international. 98 applicants, 89% accepted, 46 enrolled. *Faculty:* 39 full-time (7 women), 35 part-time/adjunct (2 women). Expenses: Contact institution. *Financial support:* In 2006–07, 2 fellowships with full tuition reimbursements (averaging $9,600 per year), 21 research assistantships with full tuition reimbursements (averaging $9,600 per year), 26 teaching assistantships with full tuition reimbursements (averaging $9,600 per year) were awarded; scholarships/grants, health care benefits, and unspecified assistantships also available. Financial award applicants required to submit FAFSA. In 2006, 28 master's, 1 doctorate awarded. *Degree program information:* Part-time programs available. Offers engineering systems (ME, MS, PhD). *Application deadline:* For fall admission, 1/1 priority date for domestic and international students; for spring admission, 9/1 priority date for domestic and international students. *Application fee:* $50 ($70 for international students). Electronic applications accepted. *Application Contact:* Jody Lowther, Information Contact, 303-384-2394, Fax: 303-273-3602, E-mail: jlowther@mines.edu. *Head,* Dr. Terence Parker, 303-273-3657, Fax: 303-273-3602, E-mail: tparker@mines.edu.

Division of Environmental Science and Engineering Students: 43 full-time (24 women), 29 part-time (11 women); includes 6 minority (2 Asian Americans or Pacific Islanders, 4 Hispanic Americans), 7 international. 68 applicants, 75% accepted, 28 enrolled. *Faculty:* 19 full-time (3 women), 13 part-time/adjunct (4 women). Expenses: Contact institution. *Financial support:* In 2006–07, 3 fellowships with full tuition reimbursements (averaging $9,600 per year), 19 research assistantships with full tuition reimbursements (averaging $9,600 per year), 8 teaching assistantships with full tuition reimbursements (averaging $9,600 per year) were awarded; scholarships/grants, health care benefits, and unspecified assistantships also available. Financial award applicants required to submit FAFSA. In 2006, 30 master's, 3 doctorates awarded. *Degree program information:* Part-time programs available. Offers environmental science and engineering (MS, PhD). *Application deadline:* For fall admission, 1/1 priority date for domestic and international students; for spring admission, 9/1 priority date for domestic and international students. *Application fee:* $50 ($70 for international students). Electronic applications accepted. *Application Contact:* Tim VanHaverbeke, Research Faculty, 303-273-3467, Fax: 303-273-3413, E-mail: tvanhave@mines.edu. *Director,* Dr. Robert Seigrist, 303-273-3473, Fax: 303-273-3413, E-mail: rseigris@mines.edu.

See Close-Up on page 857.

THE COLORADO SCHOOL OF PROFESSIONAL PSYCHOLOGY, Colorado Springs, CO 80903

General Information Independent, coed, graduate-only institution.

GRADUATE UNITS

Graduate Programs

COLORADO SCHOOL OF TRADITIONAL CHINESE MEDICINE, Denver, CO 80206-2127

General Information Independent, coed, graduate-only institution. *Enrollment by degree level:* 116 master's. *Graduate faculty:* 36 part-time/adjunct (11 women). *Tuition:* Full-time $13,275. *Required fees:* $495. Tuition and fees vary according to course load. *Graduate housing:* On-campus housing not available. *Collection:* 7,400 titles, 80 audiovisual materials.

Computer facilities: 3 computers available on campus for general student use. Internet access, wireless Internet are available. *Web address:* http://www.cstcm.edu/.

General Application Contact: Vladimir Dibrigida, Administrative Director, 303-996-6663, Fax: 303-388-8165, E-mail: director@cstcm.edu.

GRADUATE UNITS

Graduate Programs Students: 80 full-time (56 women), 36 part-time (29 women); includes 20 minority (1 African American, 9 Asian Americans or Pacific Islanders, 10 Hispanic Americans), 4 international. 28 applicants, 100% accepted. *Faculty:* 36 part-time/adjunct (11 women). Expenses: Contact institution. *Financial support:* In 2006–07, 86 students received support. Applicants required to submit FAFSA. In 2006, 22 degrees awarded. *Degree program information:* Part-time and evening/weekend programs available. *Application deadline:* Applications are processed on a rolling basis. *Application fee:* $50 ($100 for international students). *Application Contact:* Kari L. Abarca, Registrar, 303-329-6355 Ext. 12, Fax: 303-388-8165, E-mail: registrar@cstcm.edu. *Administrative Director,* Vladimir Dibrigida, 303-996-6663, Fax: 303-388-8165, E-mail: director@cstcm.edu.

COLORADO STATE UNIVERSITY, Fort Collins, CO 80523-0015

General Information State-supported, coed, university. CGS member. *Enrollment:* 26,723 graduate, professional, and undergraduate students; 2,411 full-time matriculated graduate/professional students (1,462 women), 3,029 part-time matriculated graduate/professional students (1,374 women). *Enrollment by degree level:* 534 first professional, 3,446 master's, 1,460 doctoral. *Graduate faculty:* 879 full-time (250 women), 37 part-time/adjunct (5 women). Tuition, state resident: full-time $4,248; part-time $236 per credit. Tuition, nonresident: full-time $15,642; part-time $869 per credit. *Required fees:* $66 per credit. Tuition and fees vary according to program. *Graduate housing:* Rooms and/or apartments available on a first-come, first-served basis to single and married students. Typical cost: $1,156 per year for single students. Room charges vary according to housing facility selected. *Student services:* Campus employment opportunities, campus safety program, career counseling, child daycare facilities, disabled student services, exercise/wellness program, free psychological counseling, international student services, low-cost health insurance, multicultural affairs office, teacher training, writing training. *Library facilities:* William E. Morgan Library plus 3 others. *Online resources:* library catalog, web page, access to other libraries' catalogs. *Collection:* 2.1 million titles, 31,372 serial subscriptions, 5,932 audiovisual materials. *Research affiliation:* National Centers for Atmospheric Research, National Wildlife Research Center (interactions of wild animals and society), National Center for Genetic Resources Preservation (genetic resources of crops), Department of Commerce/NOAA Joint Institutes (meteorological satellite imagery), Natural Resources Research Center / Agencies of the USDA and Interior (infectious disease).

Computer facilities: 2,095 computers available on campus for general student use. A campuswide network can be accessed from student residence rooms and from off campus. Internet access is available. *Web address:* http://www.colostate.edu/.

General Application Contact: Sandra Dailey, Graduate School, 970-491-6817, Fax: 970-491-2194, E-mail: gschool@grad.colostate.edu.

GRADUATE UNITS

College of Veterinary Medicine and Biomedical Sciences Students: 685 full-time (514 women), 165 part-time (94 women); includes 91 minority (3 African Americans, 8 American Indian/Alaska Native, 42 Asian Americans or Pacific Islanders, 38 Hispanic Americans), 40 international. Average age 28. 1,604 applicants, 15% accepted, 218 enrolled. *Faculty:* 140 full-time (41 women), 5 part-time/adjunct (1 woman). Expenses: Contact institution. *Financial support:* In 2006–07, 18 fellowships with full tuition reimbursements (averaging $20,000 per year), 79 research assistantships with full tuition reimbursements (averaging $18,000 per year), 20 teaching assistantships with partial tuition reimbursements (averaging $18,000 per year) were awarded; institutionally sponsored loans, scholarships/grants, and tuition waivers (partial) also available. Financial award applicants required to submit FAFSA. In 2006, 138 DVMs, 69 master's, 21 doctorates awarded. Offers biomedical sciences (MS, PhD); clinical sciences (MS, PhD); environmental health (MS, PhD); microbiology (MS, PhD); pathology (PhD); radiological health sciences (MS, PhD); veterinary medicine (DVM); veterinary medicine and biomedical sciences (DVM, MS, PhD). *Application deadline:* For fall admission, 3/1 priority date for domestic and international students; for spring admission, 10/1 priority date for domestic and international students. *Application fee:* $50. Electronic applications accepted. *Application Contact:* Dr. Terry Nett, Associate Dean for Research and Graduate Education, 970-491-7053, Fax: 970-491-2250, E-mail: terry.nett@colostate.edu. *Dean,* Dr. Lance Perryman, 970-491-7051, Fax: 970-491-2250, E-mail: lance.perryman@colostate.edu.

Graduate School Students: 1,726 full-time (948 women), 2,864 part-time (1,280 women); includes 440 minority (74 African Americans, 54 American Indian/Alaska Native, 135 Asian Americans or Pacific Islanders, 177 Hispanic Americans), 531 international. Average age 32. 4,236 applicants, 44% accepted, 1100 enrolled. *Faculty:* 738 full-time (208 women), 33 part-time/adjunct (5 women). Expenses: Contact institution. *Financial support:* Fellowships, research assistantships, teaching assistantships, career-related internships or fieldwork, Federal Work-Study, institutionally sponsored loans, traineeships, and tuition waivers (full and partial) available. Support available to part-time students. In 2006, 1,032 master's, 163 doctorates awarded. *Degree program information:* Part-time programs available. Postbaccalaureate distance learning degree programs offered (no on-campus study). Offers cell and molecular biology (MS, PhD); ecology (MS, PhD); molecular, cellular and integrative neurosciences (PhD). *Application fee:* $50. Electronic applications accepted. *Application Contact:* Sandra Dailey, Graduate School, 970-491-6817, Fax: 970-491-2194, E-mail: gschool@grad.colostate.edu. *Vice Provost for Graduate Studies,* Peter K. Dorhout, 970-491-6817, Fax: 970-491-2194, E-mail: peter.dorhout@colostate.edu.

College of Agricultural Sciences Students: 120 full-time (63 women), 95 part-time (44 women); includes 13 minority (1 African American, 3 American Indian/Alaska Native, 2 Asian Americans or Pacific Islanders, 7 Hispanic Americans), 27 international. Average age 31. 158 applicants, 47% accepted, 43 enrolled. *Faculty:* 85 full-time (12 women), 5 part-time/adjunct (0 women). Expenses: Contact institution. *Financial support:* Fellowships, research assistantships, teaching assistantships, career-related internships or fieldwork, Federal Work-Study, institutionally sponsored loans, and traineeships available. Support available to part-time students. In 2006, 48 master's, 11 doctorates awarded. *Degree program information:* Part-time programs available. Postbaccalaureate distance learning degree programs offered. Offers agricultural and resource economics (MS, PhD); agricultural sciences (M Agr, MS, PhD); animal sciences (MS, PhD); entomology (MS, PhD); floriculture (MS, PhD); plant pathology and weed science (MS, PhD); soil and crop sciences (MS, PhD). *Application deadline:* For fall admission, 4/1 priority date for domestic and international students; for spring admission, 9/1 priority date for domestic and international students. Applications are processed on a rolling basis. *Application fee:* $50. Electronic applications accepted. *Application Contact:* Pam Schell, Administrative Assistant, 970-491-2410, Fax: 970-491-4895, E-mail: pam.schell@colostate.edu. *Dean,* Marc Johnson, 970-491-6274, Fax: 970-491-4895, E-mail: m.johnson@colostate.edu.

College of Applied Human Sciences Students: 495 full-time (388 women), 634 part-time (402 women); includes 124 minority (34 African Americans, 9 American Indian/Alaska Native, 26 Asian Americans or Pacific Islanders, 55 Hispanic Americans), 39 international. Average age 34. 905 applicants, 49% accepted, 299 enrolled. *Faculty:* 98 full-time (46 women), 3 part-time/adjunct (all women). Expenses: Contact institution. *Financial support:* Fellowships with full and partial tuition reimbursements, research assistantships with full tuition reimbursements, teaching assistantships with full and partial tuition reimbursements, career-related internships or fieldwork, Federal Work-Study, institutionally sponsored loans, scholarships/grants, traineeships, and tuition waivers (full and partial) available. Support available to part-time students. In 2006, 336 master's, 40 doctorates awarded. *Degree program information:* Part-time programs available. Postbaccalaureate distance learning degree programs offered. Offers applied human sciences (M Ed, MS, MSW, PhD); construction management (MS); design and merchandising (MS); education and human resource studies (M Ed, PhD); food science and human nutrition (MS, PhD); health and exercise science (MS); human bioenergetics (PhD); human development and family studies (MS); occupational therapy (MS); social work (MSW); student affairs in higher education (MS). *Application deadline:* For fall admission, 1/31 priority date for domestic and international students. *Application fee:* $50. Electronic applications accepted. *Application Contact:* Thomas Mazzarisi, Assistant to Dean, 970-491-5236, Fax: 970-491-7859, E-mail: mazzarisi@cahs.colostate.edu. *Dean,* April C. Mason, 977-491-5841, Fax: 970-491-7859, E-mail: april.mson@colostate.edu.

College of Business Students: 43 full-time (19 women), 486 part-time (135 women); includes 70 minority (17 African Americans, 9 American Indian/Alaska Native, 27 Asian Americans or Pacific Islanders, 17 Hispanic Americans), 32 international. Average age 36. 324 applicants, 83% accepted, 222 enrolled. *Faculty:* 48 full-time (11 women), 1 part-time/adjunct (0 women). Expenses: Contact institution. *Financial support:* In 2006–07, 13 fellowships (averaging $1,500 per year), 27 research assistantships with full and partial tuition reimbursements (averaging $3,900 per year) were awarded; teaching assistantships with full and partial tuition reimbursements, career-related internships or fieldwork, Federal Work-Study, and unspecified assistantships also available. Financial award application deadline: 6/1. In 2006, 195 degrees awarded. *Degree program information:* Part-time and evening/weekend programs available. Postbaccalaureate distance learning degree programs offered. Offers accounting (M Acc); business (M Acc, MBA, MS, MSBA); business administration (MBA); computer information systems (MSBA). *Application deadline:* For fall admission, 7/15 for domestic students, 4/1 for international students; for spring admission, 11/15 for domestic students, 10/1 for international students. Applications are processed on a rolling basis. *Application fee:* $50. Electronic applications accepted. *Application Contact:* Rachel Stoll, Admissions Coordinator, 970-491-3704, Fax: 970-491-3481, E-mail: rachel.stoll@colostate.edu. *Associate Dean,* Dr. John Hoxmeier, 970-491-2142, Fax: 970-491-0596, E-mail: john.hoxmeier@colostate.edu.

College of Engineering Students: 242 full-time (70 women), 352 part-time (71 women); includes 45 minority (7 African Americans, 3 American Indian/Alaska Native, 18 Asian Americans or Pacific Islanders, 17 Hispanic Americans), 176 international. Average age 30. 860 applicants, 40% accepted, 121 enrolled. *Faculty:* 80 full-time (5 women), 9 part-time/adjunct (1 woman). Expenses: Contact institution. *Financial support:* In 2006–07, 28 fellowships with full tuition reimbursements (averaging $7,800 per year), 211 research assistantships with full tuition reimbursements (averaging $19,200 per year), 66 teaching assistantships with full tuition reimbursements (averaging $9,600 per year) were awarded; career-related internships or fieldwork, Federal Work-Study, institutionally sponsored loans, scholarships/grants, traineeships, and unspecified assistantships also available. In 2006, 117 master's, 27 doctorates awarded. *Degree program information:* Part-time programs available. Offers atmospheric science (MS, PhD); chemical engineering (MS, PhD); civil engineering (ME, MS, PhD); electrical engineering (MEE, MS, PhD); engineering (ME); mechanical engineering (ME, MS, PhD). *Application deadline:* For fall admission, 2/1 priority date for domestic and international students; for spring admission, 10/1 priority date for domestic and international students. Applications are processed on a rolling basis. *Application fee:* $50. Electronic applications accepted. *Application Contact:* Dr. Tom Siller, Associate Dean, 970-491-1058, Fax: 970-491-3827, E-mail: tjs@engr.colostate.edu. *Interim Dean,* Dr. Sandra L. Woods, 970-491-3366, Fax: 970-491-5569, E-mail: sandra.woods@colostate.edu.

College of Liberal Arts Students: 317 full-time (184 women), 256 part-time (151 women); includes 42 minority (1 African American, 6 American Indian/Alaska Native, 9 Asian Americans or Pacific Islanders, 26 Hispanic Americans), 61 international. Average age 31. 626 applicants, 53% accepted, 164 enrolled. *Faculty:* 209 full-time (83 women), 8 part-time/adjunct (1 woman). Expenses: Contact institution. *Financial support:* In 2006–07, fellowships (averaging $56,000 per year), teaching assistantships with full and partial tuition reimbursements (averaging $13,200 per year) were awarded; career-related internships or fieldwork, Federal Work-Study, institutionally sponsored loans, and traineeships also available. Support available to part-time students. In 2006, 163 master's, 10 doctorates awarded. *Degree program information:* Part-time programs available. Offers anthropology (MA); art (MFA); creative writing (MFA); economics (MA, PhD); English (MA); foreign languages and literatures (MA); history (MA); liberal arts (MA, MFA, MM, MS, PhD); music (MM); philosophy (MA); political science (MA, PhD); sociology (MA, PhD); speech communication (MA); technical communication (MS). *Application deadline:* Applications are processed on a rolling basis. *Application fee:* $50. Electronic applications accepted. *Dean,* Ann Gill, 970-491-5421, Fax: 970-491-0528.

College of Natural Sciences Students: 338 full-time (148 women), 344 part-time (108 women); includes 72 minority (9 African Americans, 15 American Indian/Alaska Native, 23 Asian Americans or Pacific Islanders, 25 Hispanic Americans), 148 international. Average age 30. 1,038 applicants, 28% accepted, 161 enrolled. *Faculty:* 159 full-time (39 women), 7 part-time/adjunct (0 women). Expenses: Contact institution. *Financial support:* In 2006–07, 36 fellowships, 147 research assistantships, 237 teaching assistantships were awarded; career-related internships or fieldwork, Federal Work-Study, institutionally sponsored loans, traineeships, and tuition waivers (partial) also available. Support available to part-time students. Financial award applicants required to submit FAFSA. In 2006, 102 master's, 55 doctorates awarded. *Degree program information:* Part-time programs available. Offers biochemistry (MS, PhD); botany (MS, PhD); chemistry (MS, PhD); computer science (MCS, MS, PhD); mathematics (MS, PhD); natural sciences (MCS, MS, PhD); physics (MS, PhD); psychology (MS, PhD); statistics (MS, PhD); zoology (MS, PhD). *Application deadline:* For fall admission, 4/15 priority date for domestic students, 3/15 priority date for international students; for spring admission, 9/15 priority date for domestic students, 8/15 priority date for international students. Applications are processed on a rolling basis. *Application fee:* $50. Electronic applications accepted. *Application Contact:* Dr. Don Mykles, Associate Dean for Graduate Education, 970-491-6864, Fax: 970-491-6639, E-mail: donald.mykles@colostate.edu. *Dean,* Rick Miranda, 970-491-6864, Fax: 970-491-6639, E-mail: rick.miranda@colostate.edu.

Warner College of Natural Resources Students: 108 full-time (46 women), 144 part-time (58 women); includes 13 minority (1 African American, 4 American Indian/Alaska Native, 1 Asian American or Pacific Islander, 7 Hispanic Americans), 20 international. Average age 32. 193 applicants, 40% accepted, 56 enrolled. *Faculty:* 57 full-time (12 women). Expenses: Contact institution. *Financial support:* In 2006–07, 11 fellowships (averaging $27,000 per year), 54 research assistantships (averaging $16,500 per year), 36 teaching assistantships with tuition reimbursements (averaging $11,187 per year) were awarded; career-related internships or fieldwork, Federal Work-Study, institutionally sponsored loans, and traineeships also available. Support available to part-time students. In 2006, 55 master's, 8 doctorates awarded. *Degree program information:* Part-time programs available. Offers earth sciences (PhD); fishery and wildlife biology (MFWB, MS, PhD); forest sciences (MS, PhD); geosciences (MS); human dimensions of natural resources (MS, PhD); natural resources (MFWB, MNRS, MS, PhD); natural resources stewardship (MNRS); rangeland ecology (MS, PhD); watershed science (MS). *Application deadline:* Applications are processed on a rolling basis. *Application fee:* $50. Electronic applications accepted. *Application Contact:* Crystal L. Lancaster, Coordinator, 970-491-6675, E-mail: crystal.lancaster@colostate.edu. *Dean,* Dr. Joseph T. O'Leary, 970-491-6675, Fax: 970-491-0279.

COLORADO STATE UNIVERSITY-PUEBLO, Pueblo, CO 81001-4901

General Information State-supported, coed, comprehensive institution. *Enrollment:* 6,205 graduate, professional, and undergraduate students; 73 full-time matriculated graduate/professional students (30 women), 78 part-time matriculated graduate/professional students (40 women). *Enrollment by degree level:* 151 master's. *Graduate faculty:* 33 full-time (11 women), 5 part-time/adjunct (1 woman). Tuition, state resident: full-time $2,771; part-time $124 per credit hour. Tuition, nonresident: full-time $10,697; part-time $564 per credit hour. *Required fees:* $729; $41 per credit hour. *Graduate housing:* Room and/or apartments available on a first-come, first-served basis to single students; on-campus housing not available to married students. Typical cost: $2,960 per year ($5,810 including board). Housing application deadline: 8/1. *Student services:* Campus employment opportunities, campus safety program, career counseling, child daycare facilities, disabled student services, exercise/wellness program, free psychological counseling, grant writing training, international student services, low-cost health insurance, writing training. *Library facilities:* Colorado State University-Pueblo Library. *Online resources:* library catalog, web page, access to other libraries' catalogs. *Collection:* 265,062 titles, 8,404 serial subscriptions, 12,902 audiovisual materials.

Computer facilities: 521 computers available on campus for general student use. A campuswide network can be accessed from student residence rooms and from off campus. Internet access is available. *Web address:* http://www.colostate-pueblo.edu/.

General Application Contact: Jennifer Jensen, Associate Director of Admissions, 719-549-2434, Fax: 719-549-2419, E-mail: jensenj@colostate-pueblo.edu.

GRADUATE UNITS

College of Education, Engineering and Professional Studies Students: 6 full-time (2 women), 21 part-time (6 women); includes 2 minority (both Hispanic Americans), 16 international. Average age 26. 20 applicants, 85% accepted, 12 enrolled. *Faculty:* 4 full-time (1 woman), 2 part-time/adjunct (0 women). Expenses: Contact institution. *Financial support:* In 2006–07, 20 students received support, including 7 teaching assistantships with partial tuition reimbursements available (averaging $6,429 per year); Federal Work-Study, scholarships/grants, tuition waivers (partial), and unspecified assistantships also available. Financial award application deadline: 4/1. In 2006, 14 degrees awarded. *Degree program information:* Part-time and evening/weekend programs available. Offers industrial and systems engineering (MS). *Application deadline:* For fall admission, 8/1 priority date for domestic students; for spring admission, 1/1 priority date for domestic students. Applications are processed on a rolling basis. *Application fee:* $35. Electronic applications accepted. *Application Contact:* Dr. Edward Keith Sinkhorn, Graduate Coordinator, 719-549-2778, Fax: 719-549-2512, E-mail: keith.sinkhorn@colostate-pueblo.edu. *Dean,* Dr. Hector R. Carrasco, 719-549-2696, Fax: 719-549-2519, E-mail: carrasco@colostate-pueblo.edu.

College of Science and Mathematics Students: 22 full-time (12 women), 9 part-time (6 women); includes 9 minority (5 Asian Americans or Pacific Islanders, 4 Hispanic Americans). 13 applicants, 100% accepted, 13 enrolled. *Faculty:* 17 full-time (6 women), 2 part-time/adjunct (1 woman). Expenses: Contact institution. *Financial support:* In 2006–07, 6 students received support, including 6 teaching assistantships with partial tuition reimbursements available (averaging $9,000 per year); fellowships, research assistantships, career-related internships or fieldwork, scholarships/grants, tuition waivers (partial), and unspecified assistantships also available. Financial award application deadline: 6/1; financial award applicants required to submit FAFSA. In 2006, 5 degrees awarded. *Degree program information:* Part-time and evening/weekend programs available. Offers applied natural science (MS). *Application deadline:* For fall admission, 6/15 priority date for domestic and international students; for spring admission, 10/15 priority date for domestic and international students. Applications are processed on a rolling basis. *Application fee:* $35. *Application Contact:* Dr. Melvin Druelinger, Director, MSANS Program, 719-549-2325, Fax: 719-549-2071, E-mail: mel.druelinger@colostate-pueblo.edu. *Dean,* Dr. Kristina Proctor, 719-549-2340, Fax: 719-549-2732, E-mail: kristina.proctor@colostate-pueblo.edu.

Malik and Seeme Hasan School of Business Students: 26 full-time (6 women), 51 part-time (25 women); includes 18 minority (2 African Americans, 1 Asian American or Pacific Islander, 15 Hispanic Americans), 22 international. Average age 28. 59 applicants, 78% accepted, 38 enrolled. *Faculty:* 9 full-time (2 women), 1 part-time/adjunct (0 women). Expenses: Contact institution. *Financial support:* In 2006–07, 8 research assistantships (averaging $3,220 per year) were awarded; unspecified assistantships also available. Financial award applicants required to submit FAFSA. In 2006, 21 degrees awarded. *Degree program information:* Part-time and evening/weekend programs available. Offers business (MBA). *Application deadline:* For fall admission, 8/18 priority date for domestic students, 7/1 for international students; for spring admission, 1/12 priority date for domestic students, 11/1 for international students. Applications are processed on a rolling basis. *Application fee:* $35. *Application Contact:* Karen Hughes, Administrative Assistant II, 719-549-2101, Fax: 719-549-2409, E-mail: karen.hughes@colostate-pueblo.edu. *Dean,* Dr. Rex D. Fuller, 719-549-2142, Fax: 719-549-2909, E-mail: rex.fuller@colostate-pueblo.edu.

COLORADO TECHNICAL UNIVERSITY—COLORADO SPRINGS, Colorado Springs, CO 80907-3896

General Information Proprietary, coed, comprehensive institution. *Graduate housing:* On-campus housing not available.

GRADUATE UNITS

Graduate Studies *Degree program information:* Part-time and evening/weekend programs available. Offers accounting (MBA); business administration (MBA); business management (MSM); business technology (MSM); communication systems (MSEE); computer engineering (MSCE); computer science (DCS); computer systems security (MSCS); criminal justice (MSM); database management (MSM); electronic systems (MSEE); human resources management (MSM); information systems security (MSM); information technology (MSM); logistics/supply chain management (MSM); management (DM); organizational leadership (MSM); project management (MSM); software engineering (MSCS); software project management (MSCS); systems engineering (MS); technology management (MBA).

COLORADO TECHNICAL UNIVERSITY—DENVER, Greenwood Village, CO 80111

General Information Proprietary, coed, comprehensive institution. *Graduate housing:* On-campus housing not available.

GRADUATE UNITS

Program in Computer Engineering Offers computer engineering (MS).

Program in Computer Science *Degree program information:* Part-time and evening/weekend programs available. Offers computer systems security (MSCS); software engineering (MSCS); software project management (MSCS).

Program in Electrical Engineering Offers electrical engineering (MS).

Program in Information Science Offers information systems security (MSM).

Program in Systems Engineering Offers systems engineering (MS).

Programs in Business Administration and Management *Degree program information:* Part-time and evening/weekend programs available. Offers accounting (MBA); business administration (MBA); business administration and management (EMBA); business technology (MSM); database management (MSM); human resource management (MBA); information technology (MSM); project management (MSM); technology management (MBA).

COLORADO TECHNICAL UNIVERSITY—SIOUX FALLS, Sioux Falls, SD 57108

General Information Proprietary, coed, comprehensive institution. *Graduate housing:* On-campus housing not available.

GRADUATE UNITS

Program in Computing Offers computer systems security (MSCS); software engineering (MSCS).

Program in Criminal Justice Offers criminal justice (MSM).

Programs in Business Administration and Management *Degree program information:* Evening/weekend programs available. Offers business administration (MBA); business management (MSM); health science management (MSM); human resources management (MSM); information technology (MSM); organizational leadership (MSM); project management (MBA); technology management (MBA).

COLUMBIA COLLEGE, Columbia, MO 65216-0002

General Information Independent-religious, coed, comprehensive institution. *Enrollment:* 1,186 graduate, professional, and undergraduate students; 300 full-time matriculated graduate/professional students (173 women). *Enrollment by degree level:* 300 master's. *Graduate faculty:* 14 full-time (6 women), 40 part-time/adjunct (9 women). *Tuition:* Part-time $270 per credit hour. *Graduate housing:* On-campus housing not available. *Student services:* Career counseling, exercise/wellness program, free psychological counseling, teacher training. *Library facilities:* Stafford Library. *Online resources:* library catalog, web page, access to other libraries' catalogs. *Collection:* 62,265 titles, 382 serial subscriptions.

Computer facilities: Computer purchase and lease plans are available. 137 computers available on campus for general student use. A campuswide network can be accessed from student residence rooms and from off campus. Internet access is available. *Web address:* http://www.ccis.edu/.

General Application Contact: Regina Morin, Director of Admissions, 573-875-7354, Fax: 573-875-7506, E-mail: rmmorin@ccis.edu.

GRADUATE UNITS

Program in Business Administration Students: 196 full-time (98 women); includes 47 minority (36 African Americans, 4 American Indian/Alaska Native, 3 Asian Americans or Pacific Islanders, 4 Hispanic Americans), 5 international. Average age 37. 61 applicants, 72% accepted, 35 enrolled. *Faculty:* 6 full-time (1 woman), 31 part-time/adjunct (7 women). Expenses: Contact institution. *Financial support:* Federal Work-Study and scholarships/grants available. Support available to part-time students. Financial award application deadline: 3/15; financial award applicants required to submit FAFSA. In 2006, 63 degrees awarded. *Degree program information:* Part-time and evening/weekend programs available. Offers business administration (MBA). *Application deadline:* For fall admission, 8/1 priority date for domestic and international students; for winter admission, 1/1 priority date for domestic and international students. Applications are processed on a rolling basis. *Application fee:* $55. *Application Contact:* Regina Morin, Director of Admissions, 573-875-7354, Fax: 573-875-7506, E-mail: rmmorin@ccis.edu. *Chair,* Dr. Ken Middleton, 573-875-7535, Fax: 573-875-7209, E-mail: kamiddleton@email.ccis.edu.

Program in Criminal Justice Students: 27 full-time (14 women); includes 3 minority (all African Americans) Average age 39. 14 applicants, 57% accepted, 6 enrolled. *Faculty:* 3 full-time (0 women), 4 part-time/adjunct (0 women). Expenses: Contact institution. *Financial support:* Career-related internships or fieldwork, institutionally sponsored loans, and scholarships/grants available. Support available to part-time students. Financial award applicants required to submit FAFSA. In 2006, 14 degrees awarded. *Degree program information:* Part-time and evening/weekend programs available. Offers criminal justice (MSCJ). *Application deadline:* For fall admission, 8/1 priority date for domestic and international students; for winter admission, 12/15 priority date for international students; for spring admission, 12/15 priority date for domestic students. Applications are processed on a rolling basis. *Application fee:* $55. *Application Contact:* Regina Morin, Director of Admissions, 573-875-7354, Fax: 573-875-7506, E-mail: rmmorin@ccis.edu. *Chair,* Barry Longford, 573-875-7484, Fax: 573-875-7209, E-mail: mlyman@ccis.edu.

Program in Teaching Students: 77 full-time (61 women); includes 6 minority (4 African Americans, 1 Asian American or Pacific Islander, 1 Hispanic American), 1 international.

Columbia College (continued)

Average age 33. 25 applicants, 80% accepted, 19 enrolled. *Faculty:* 5 full-time (all women), 5 part-time/adjunct (2 women). Expenses: Contact institution. *Financial support:* Career-related internships or fieldwork, Federal Work-Study, and institutionally sponsored loans available. Support available to part-time students. Financial award application deadline: 3/15; financial award applicants required to submit FAFSA. In 2006, 20 degrees awarded. *Degree program information:* Part-time and evening/weekend programs available. Offers teaching (MAT). *Application deadline:* For fall admission, 8/1 priority date for domestic and international students; for winter admission, 12/15 priority date for domestic and international students. Applications are processed on a rolling basis. *Application fee:* $55. *Application Contact:* Regina Morin, Director of Admissions, 573-875-7354, Fax: 573-875-7506, E-mail: rmmorin@ccis.edu. *Chair,* Dr. Judy Brown, 573-875-7590, Fax: 573-875-7209.

COLUMBIA COLLEGE, Columbia, SC 29203-5998

General Information Independent-religious, Undergraduate: women only; graduate: coed, comprehensive institution. *Enrollment:* 1,446 graduate, professional, and undergraduate students; 234 full-time matriculated graduate/professional students (219 women), 69 part-time matriculated graduate/professional students (64 women). *Enrollment by degree level:* 303 master's. *Graduate faculty:* 5 full-time (3 women), 28 part-time/adjunct (17 women). *Tuition:* Part-time $300 per credit. *Graduate housing:* On-campus housing not available. *Student services:* Campus safety program, career counseling. *Library facilities:* J. Drake Edens Library plus 1 other. *Online resources:* library catalog, web page, access to other libraries' catalogs. *Collection:* 146,135 titles, 28,391 serial subscriptions, 7,804 audiovisual materials.

Computer facilities: 150 computers available on campus for general student use. A campuswide network can be accessed. Internet access and online class registration, e-mail, data storage are available. *Web address:* http://www.columbiacollegesc.edu/.

General Application Contact: Carolyn Emeneker, Director of Graduate School and Evening College Admissions, 803-786-3766, Fax: 803-786-3674, E-mail: emeneker@colacoll.edu.

GRADUATE UNITS

Graduate Programs Students: 234 full-time (219 women), 69 part-time (64 women); includes 102 minority (99 African Americans, 1 Asian American or Pacific Islander, 2 Hispanic Americans), 1 international. Average age 33. 235 applicants, 84% accepted, 172 enrolled. *Faculty:* 5 full-time (3 women), 28 part-time/adjunct (17 women). Expenses: Contact institution. *Financial support:* Available to part-time students. Application deadline: 7/1; In 2006, 299 degrees awarded. *Degree program information:* Part-time and evening/weekend programs available. Postbaccalaureate distance learning degree programs offered (minimal on-campus study). Offers divergent learning (M Ed); human behavior and conflict management (MA); interpersonal relations/conflict management (Certificate); organizational behavior/conflict management (Certificate). *Application deadline:* For fall admission, 8/22 priority date for domestic students, 8/22 for international students. Applications are processed on a rolling basis. *Application fee:* $50. Electronic applications accepted. *Application Contact:* Carolyn Emeneker, Director of Graduate School and Evening College Admissions, 803-786-3766, Fax: 803-786-3674, E-mail: emeneker@colacoll.edu. *Provost and Vice President for Academic Affairs,* Dr. Laurie B. Hopkins, 803-786-3669, Fax: 803-754-3178, E-mail: lhopkins@colacoll.edu.

COLUMBIA COLLEGE CHICAGO, Chicago, IL 60605-1996

General Information Independent, coed, comprehensive institution. *Graduate housing:* Room and/or apartments available on a first-come, first-served basis to single students; on-campus housing not available to married students.

GRADUATE UNITS

Graduate School *Degree program information:* Part-time and evening/weekend programs available. Offers architectural studies (MFA); arts, entertainment, and media management (MA); creative writing (MFA); dance/movement therapy (MA, Certificate); elementary (MAT); English (MAT); film and video (MFA); interdisciplinary arts (MA, MAT); interdisciplinary book and paper arts (MFA); interior design (MFA); multicultural education (MA); photography (MA, MFA); poetry (MFA); public affairs journalism (MA); teaching of writing (MA); urban teaching (MA).

COLUMBIA INTERNATIONAL UNIVERSITY, Columbia, SC 29230-3122

General Information Independent-religious, coed, comprehensive institution. *Enrollment:* 959 graduate, professional, and undergraduate students; 232 full-time matriculated graduate/professional students (103 women), 311 part-time matriculated graduate/professional students (120 women). *Enrollment by degree level:* 156 first professional, 262 master's, 93 doctoral, 32 other advanced degrees. *Graduate faculty:* 24 full-time (4 women), 10 part-time/adjunct (4 women). *Tuition:* Part-time $400 per semester hour. Tuition and fees vary according to course load and program. *Graduate housing:* Room and/or apartments available on a first-come, first-served basis to single students; on-campus housing not available to married students. Housing application deadline: 8/27. *Student services:* Campus employment opportunities, campus safety program, career counseling, child daycare facilities, disabled student services, international student services, low-cost health insurance, teacher training. *Library facilities:* G. Allen Fleece Library. *Online resources:* library catalog. *Collection:* 144,388 titles, 47,758 serial subscriptions, 18,983 audiovisual materials.

Computer facilities: 42 computers available on campus for general student use. A campuswide network can be accessed. Internet access and online class registration are available. *Web address:* http://www.ciu.edu/.

General Application Contact: Michelle MacGregor, Director of Admissions, 800-777-2227 Ext. 5335, Fax: 803-786-4209, E-mail: yescbs@ciu.edu.

GRADUATE UNITS

Columbia Biblical Seminary and School of Missions Students: 180 full-time (59 women), 218 part-time (61 women); includes 81 minority (58 African Americans, 1 American Indian/Alaska Native, 18 Asian Americans or Pacific Islanders, 4 Hispanic Americans), 22 international. Average age 36. 277 applicants, 81% accepted, 117 enrolled. *Faculty:* 14 full-time (1 woman), 9 part-time/adjunct (1 woman). Expenses: Contact institution. *Financial support:* In 2006–07, 120 students received support. Career-related internships or fieldwork, Federal Work-Study, institutionally sponsored loans, and scholarships/grants available. Financial award application deadline: 3/15; financial award applicants required to submit FAFSA. In 2006, 20 M Divs, 54 master's, 3 doctorates, 15 other advanced degrees awarded. *Degree program information:* Part-time and evening/weekend programs available. Offers academic ministries (M Div); bible exposition (M Div, MABE); biblical studies (Certificate); counseling ministries (Certificate); divinity (M Div); educational ministries (M Div, MAEM, Certificate); intercultural studies (M Div, MAIS, Certificate); leadership (D Min); leadership for evangelism/mobilization (MALM); member care (D Min); ministry (Certificate); missions (D Min); pastoral counseling and spiritual formation (M Div, MAPS); preaching (D Min); theology (MA). *Application deadline:* For fall admission, 8/1 priority date for domestic and international students; for winter admission, 12/15 priority date for domestic and international students; for spring admission, 1/15 priority date for domestic and international students. Applications are processed on a rolling basis. *Application fee:* $45. Electronic applications accepted. *Application Contact:* Michelle MacGregor, Director of Admissions, 800-777-2227 Ext. 5335, Fax: 803-786-4209, E-mail: yescbs@ciu.edu. *Dean,* Dr. Junias Venugopal, 803-754-4100 Ext. 5330, Fax: 803-786-4209, E-mail: jvenugopal@ciu.edu.

Columbia Graduate School Students: 52 full-time (44 women), 93 part-time (59 women); includes 17 minority (11 African Americans, 2 Asian Americans or Pacific Islanders, 4 Hispanic Americans), 10 international. Average age 35. 107 applicants, 56% accepted, 41 enrolled. *Faculty:* 11 full-time (4 women), 7 part-time/adjunct (5 women). Expenses: Contact institution. *Financial support:* In 2006–07, 35 students received support. Career-related internships or fieldwork, Federal Work-Study, institutionally sponsored loans, and scholarships/grants available. Financial award application deadline: 3/17; financial award applicants required to submit FAFSA. In 2006, 62 degrees awarded. *Degree program information:* Part-time and evening/weekend programs available. Offers Bible teaching (MABT); Christian higher education leadership (Ed D); Christian school educational leadership (Ed D); counseling (MACN); curriculum and instruction (M Ed); early childhood and elementary education (MAT); educational administration (M Ed); teaching English as a foreign language (Certificate); teaching English as a foreign language and intercultural studies (MATF). *Application deadline:* For fall admission, 8/1 priority date for domestic and international students; for winter admission, 12/15 priority date for domestic and international students; for spring admission, 1/15 priority date for domestic and international students. Applications are processed on a rolling basis. *Application fee:* $45. Electronic applications accepted. *Application Contact:* Michelle MacGregor, Director of Admissions, 800-777-2227 Ext. 5335, Fax: 803-786-4209, E-mail: yescbs@ciu.edu. *Dean,* Dr. Milton Uecker, 803-807-5319, Fax: 803-786-4209, E-mail: muecker@ciu.edu.

COLUMBIA SOUTHERN UNIVERSITY, Orange Beach, AL 36561

General Information Proprietary, coed, comprehensive institution. *Graduate housing:* On-campus housing not available.

GRADUATE UNITS

MBA Program *Degree program information:* Part-time and evening/weekend programs available. Postbaccalaureate distance learning degree programs offered (no on-campus study). Offers electronic business and technology (MBA); healthcare management (MBA); human resources management (MBA); international management (MBA); marketing (MBA); project management (MBA); public administration (MBA); sport management (MBA). Electronic applications accepted.

Program in Occupational Safety and Health *Degree program information:* Part-time and evening/weekend programs available. Postbaccalaureate distance learning degree programs offered (no on-campus study). Offers environmental management (MS). Electronic applications accepted.

COLUMBIA THEOLOGICAL SEMINARY, Decatur, GA 30031-0520

General Information Independent-religious, coed, graduate-only institution. *Graduate housing:* Rooms and/or apartments available on a first-come, first-served basis to single students and available to married students. Housing application deadline: 4/30.

GRADUATE UNITS

Graduate and Professional Programs Offers theology (M Div, MATS, Th M, D Min, Th D).

COLUMBIA UNION COLLEGE, Takoma Park, MD 20912-7796

General Information Independent-religious, coed, comprehensive institution.

GRADUATE UNITS

Information and Telecommunications Management Program

MBA Program

COLUMBIA UNIVERSITY, New York, NY 10027

General Information Independent, coed, university. CGS member. *Enrollment by degree level:* 7,537 first professional, 4,937 master's, 2,415 doctoral, 110 other advanced degrees. *Graduate faculty:* 3,462 full-time (1,317 women), 1,027 part-time/adjunct (395 women). *Graduate housing:* Rooms and/or apartments available on a first-come, first-served basis to single and married students. Housing application deadline: 8/4. *Student services:* Campus employment opportunities, campus safety program, career counseling, disabled student services, exercise/wellness program, free psychological counseling, international student services, low-cost health insurance, multicultural affairs office, writing training. *Research affiliation:* Goddard Space Flight Center, Marine Biological Laboratory, American Museum of Natural History, New York Botanical Gardens, Brookhaven National Laboratory, Long Island Biological Laboratory. *Web address:* http://www.columbia.edu/.

General Application Contact: Information Contact, 212-854-1754.

GRADUATE UNITS

College of Physicians and Surgeons *Degree program information:* Part-time programs available. Offers medicine (MD, M Phil, MA, MS, DN Sc, DPT, Ed D, PhD, Adv C); movement science (Ed D); occupational therapy (professional) (MS); occupational therapy administration or education (post-professional) (MS); physical therapy (DPT).

Graduate School of Arts and Sciences at the College of Physicians and Surgeons Offers anatomy (M Phil, MA, PhD); anatomy and cell biology (PhD); biochemistry and molecular biophysics (M Phil, PhD); biomedical informatics (M Phil, MA, PhD); biomedical sciences (M Phil, MA, PhD); biophysics (PhD); cellular, molecular and biophysical studies (M Phil, MA, PhD); genetics (M Phil, MA, PhD); medicine (M Phil, MA, PhD); neurobiology and behavior (M Phil, PhD); pathobiology (M Phil, MA, PhD); pharmacology (M Phil, MA, PhD); pharmacology-toxicology (M Phil, MA, PhD); physiology and cellular biophysics (M Phil, MA, PhD). Only candidates for the PhD are admitted.

Institute of Human Nutrition Students: 37 full-time (29 women), 64 part-time (38 women); includes 31 minority (4 African Americans, 26 Asian Americans or Pacific Islanders, 1 Hispanic American), 15 international. Average age 23. 191 applicants, 44% accepted, 69 enrolled. *Faculty:* 34 full-time (12 women). Expenses: Contact institution. *Financial support:* In 2006–07, 46 students received support, including 10 fellowships (averaging $27,336 per year), 17 research assistantships (averaging $27,336 per year); Federal Work-Study, institutionally sponsored loans, and traineeships also available. Support available to part-time students. Financial award application deadline: 1/4; financial award applicants required to submit FAFSA. In 2006, 41 master's, 6 doctorates awarded. *Degree program information:* Part-time and evening/weekend programs available. Offers nutrition (MS, PhD). *Application deadline:* For fall admission, 4/15 priority date for domestic and international students; for spring admission, 11/15 priority date for domestic and international students. Applications are processed on a rolling basis. *Application fee:* $95. *Application Contact:* Dr. Sharon R. Akabas, Co-Director, MS in Nutrition, 212-305-4808, Fax: 212-305-3079, E-mail: sa109@columbia.edu. *Director,* Dr. Richard J. Deckelbaum, 212-305-4808, Fax: 212-305-3079, E-mail: nutrition@columbia.edu.

Fu Foundation School of Engineering and Applied Science Students: 904 full-time (202 women), 431 part-time (82 women); includes 142 minority (11 African Americans, 1 American Indian/Alaska Native, 113 Asian Americans or Pacific Islanders, 17 Hispanic Americans), 741 international. Average age 25. 3,460 applicants, 38% accepted, 483 enrolled. *Faculty:* 150 full-time (15 women), 87 part-time/adjunct (8 women). Expenses: Contact institution. *Financial support:* In 2006–07, 55 fellowships with full and partial tuition reimbursements (averaging $25,435 per year), 350 research assistantships with full tuition reimbursements (averaging $25,067 per year), 118 teaching assistantships with full and partial tuition reimbursements (averaging $22,559 per year) were awarded; career-related internships or fieldwork, Federal Work-Study, scholarships/grants, traineeships, health care benefits, tuition waivers (partial), and unspecified assistantships also available. Support available to part-time students. Financial award application deadline: 12/15; financial award applicants required to submit FAFSA. In 2006, 431 master's, 85 doctorates, 2 other advanced degrees awarded. *Degree program information:* Part-time programs available. Postbaccalaureate distance learning degree programs offered (no on-campus study). Offers applied mathematics (MS, PhD); applied physics (MS, Eng Sc D, PhD); applied physics and applied mathematics (Engr); biomedical engineering (MS, Eng Sc D, PhD); chemical engineering (MS, Eng Sc D, PhD); civil engineering (MS, Eng Sc D, PhD, Engr); computer engineering (MS); computer science (MS, Eng Sc D, PhD, Engr); construction engineering and management (MS); earth and environmental engineering (MS, Eng Sc D, PhD); electrical engineering (MS, Eng Sc D, PhD, Engr); engineering and applied science (MS, Eng Sc D, PhD, Engr); engineering management systems (MS); engineering mechanics (MS, Eng Sc D, PhD, Engr); financial engineering (MS); industrial engineering (MS, Eng Sc D, PhD, Engr); materials science and engineering (MS, Eng Sc D, PhD); mechanical engineering (MS, Eng Sc D, PhD, Engr); medical physics (MS); metallurgical engineering (Engr); mining engineering (Engr); operations research (MS, Eng Sc D, PhD); solid state science and engineering (MS, Eng Sc D, PhD). *Application deadline:* For fall admission, 12/15 priority date for domestic and international students; for spring admission, 10/1 priority date for domestic and international students. Applications are processed on a rolling basis. *Application fee:* $45. Electronic applications accepted. *Applica-*

tion Contact: Jocelyn Morales, Admissions Officer, 212-854-6901, Fax: 212-854-5900, E-mail: jm2388@columbia.edu. *Dean,* Zvi Galil, 212-854-2993, Fax: 212-854-5900, E-mail: seasgradmit@columbia.edu.

Graduate School of Architecture, Planning, and Preservation Offers advanced architectural design (MS); architecture (M Arch, PhD); architecture and urban design (MS); architecture, planning, and preservation (M Arch, MS, PhD); historic preservation (MS); real estate development (MS); urban planning (MS, PhD). PhD offered through the Graduate School of Arts and Sciences.

Graduate School of Arts and Sciences Students: 2,827 full-time (1,352 women), 422 part-time (233 women); includes 378 minority (76 African Americans, 5 American Indian/Alaska Native, 219 Asian Americans or Pacific Islanders, 78 Hispanic Americans), 947 international. Average age 32. 6,307 applicants, 28% accepted. *Faculty:* 508 full-time, 158 part-time/adjunct. Expenses: Contact institution. *Financial support:* Fellowships, research assistantships, teaching assistantships, career-related internships or fieldwork, Federal Work-Study, and institutionally sponsored loans available. Support available to part-time students. Financial award application deadline: 12/15; financial award applicants required to submit FAFSA. In 2006, 392 master's, 360 doctorates awarded. *Degree program information:* Part-time and evening/weekend programs available. Offers African-American studies (MA); American studies (MA); arts and sciences (M Phil, MA, DMA, PhD, Certificate); climate and society (MA); conservation biology (MA); East Asian regional studies (MA); East Asian studies (MA); French cultural studies (MA); human rights studies (MA); Islamic culture studies (MA); Jewish studies (MA); medieval studies (MA); modern European studies (MA); quantitative methods in the social sciences (MA); Russian, Eurasian and East European regional studies (MA); South Asian studies (MA); sustainable development (PhD); theatre (M Phil, MA, PhD); Yiddish studies (MA). *Application fee:* $85. *Application Contact:* Robert Furno, Assistant Dean for Admissions, 212-854-4738, Fax: 212-854-2863, E-mail: ref8@columbia.edu. *Dean,* Dr. Henry C. Pinkham, 212-854-2861, Fax: 212-854-4912, E-mail: hcp3@columbia.edu.

Division of Humanities Students: 1,056 full-time (615 women), 127 part-time (78 women); includes 133 minority (25 African Americans, 72 Asian Americans or Pacific Islanders, 36 Hispanic Americans), 204 international. Average age 33. 1,988 applicants, 30% accepted. Expenses: Contact institution. *Financial support:* Fellowships, teaching assistantships, Federal Work-Study and institutionally sponsored loans available. Support available to part-time students. Financial award application deadline: 1/5; financial award applicants required to submit FAFSA. In 2006, 136 master's, 89 doctorates awarded. *Degree program information:* Part-time programs available. Offers archaeology (M Phil, MA, PhD); art history and archaeology (M Phil, MA, PhD); classics (M Phil, MA, PhD); comparative literature (M Phil, MA, PhD); East Asian languages and cultures (M Phil, MA, PhD); English literature (M Phil, MA, PhD); French and Romance philology (M Phil, PhD); Germanic languages (M Phil, MA, PhD); Hebrew language and literature (M Phil, MA, PhD); humanities (M Phil, MA, DMA, PhD); Italian (M Phil, MA, PhD); Jewish studies (M Phil, MA, PhD); literature-writing (M Phil, MA, PhD); Middle Eastern languages and cultures (M Phil, MA, PhD); modern art (MA); music (M Phil, MA, DMA, PhD); Oriental studies (M Phil, MA, PhD); philosophy (M Phil, MA, PhD); religion (M Phil, MA, PhD); Romance languages (MA); Russian literature (M Phil, MA, PhD); Slavic languages (M Phil, MA, PhD); South Asian languages and cultures (M Phil, MA, PhD); Spanish and Portuguese (M Phil, MA, PhD). *Application fee:* $85. *Application Contact:* Robert Furno, Assistant Dean for Admissions, 212-854-4738, Fax: 212-854-2863, E-mail: ref8@columbia.edu.

Division of Natural Sciences Students: 473 full-time (157 women), 69 part-time (21 women); includes 46 minority (7 African Americans, 1 American Indian/Alaska Native, 31 Asian Americans or Pacific Islanders, 7 Hispanic Americans), 269 international. Average age 31. 1,388 applicants, 22% accepted. Expenses: Contact institution. *Financial support:* Fellowships, research assistantships, teaching assistantships, career-related internships or fieldwork, Federal Work-Study, and institutionally sponsored loans available. Support available to part-time students. Financial award application deadline: 1/5; financial award applicants required to submit FAFSA. In 2006, 91 master's, 76 doctorates awarded. *Degree program information:* Part-time programs available. Offers astronomy (M Phil, MA, PhD); atmospheric and planetary science (M Phil, PhD); biological sciences (M Phil, MA, PhD); chemical physics (M Phil, PhD); conservation biology (Certificate); ecology and evolutionary biology (PhD); environmental policy (Certificate); experimental psychology (M Phil, MA, PhD); geochemistry (M Phil, MA, PhD); geodetic sciences (M Phil, MA, PhD); geophysics (M Phil, MA, PhD); inorganic chemistry (M Phil, MA, PhD); mathematics (M Phil, MA, PhD); natural sciences (M Phil, MA, PhD, Certificate); oceanography (M Phil, MA, PhD); organic chemistry (M Phil, MA, PhD); philosophical foundations of physics (MA); physics (M Phil, PhD); psychobiology (M Phil, MA, PhD); social psychology (M Phil, MA, PhD); statistics (M Phil, MA, PhD). *Application fee:* $85.

Division of Social Sciences Students: 894 full-time (386 women), 93 part-time (49 women); includes 105 minority (33 African Americans, 4 American Indian/Alaska Native, 45 Asian Americans or Pacific Islanders, 23 Hispanic Americans), 305 international. Average age 32. 1,668 applicants, 37% accepted. Expenses: Contact institution. *Financial support:* Fellowships, teaching assistantships, Federal Work-Study and institutionally sponsored loans available. Support available to part-time students. Financial award application deadline: 1/5; financial award applicants required to submit FAFSA. In 2006, 108 master's, 84 doctorates awarded. *Degree program information:* Part-time programs available. Offers American history (M Phil, MA, PhD); anthropology (M Phil, MA, PhD); economics (M Phil, MA, PhD); history (M Phil, MA, PhD); political science (M Phil, MA, PhD); social sciences (M Phil, MA, PhD); sociology (M Phil, MA, PhD). *Application fee:* $85. *Application Contact:* Robert Furno, Assistant Dean for Admissions, 212-854-4738, Fax: 212-854-2863, E-mail: ref8@columbia.edu.

Graduate School of Business Students: 1,869 full-time (596 women). *Faculty:* 118 full-time (14 women), 106 part-time/adjunct (18 women). Expenses: Contact institution. *Financial support:* Fellowships, research assistantships, teaching assistantships, career-related internships or fieldwork, Federal Work-Study, institutionally sponsored loans, and scholarships/grants available. Financial award applicants required to submit FAFSA. In 2006, 1,046 master's, 15 doctorates awarded. Offers accounting (MBA); business (PhD); business administration (EMBA, MBA); decision, risk, and operations (MBA); entrepreneurship (MBA); finance and economics (MBA); global business administration (EMBA); human resource management (MBA); international business (MBA); management (MBA); marketing (MBA); media (MBA); real estate (MBA); social enterprise (MBA). *Application deadline:* Applications are processed on a rolling basis. Electronic applications accepted. *Application Contact:* Linda B. Meehan, Assistant Dean of Admissions, 212-854-1961, Fax: 212-662-6754, E-mail: apply@claven.gsb.columbia.edu. *Dean,* Prof. Robert Glenn Hubbard, 212-854-0629, Fax: 212-932-0545, E-mail: rghl@columbia.edu.

Graduate School of Journalism *Degree program information:* Part-time programs available. Offers journalism (MS, PhD).

Mailman School of Public Health Students: 635 full-time (431 women), 317 part-time (271 women); includes 311 minority (105 African Americans, 2 American Indian/Alaska Native, 139 Asian Americans or Pacific Islanders, 65 Hispanic Americans), 108 international. Average age 28. 1,718 applicants, 60% accepted, 414 enrolled. *Faculty:* 165 full-time (83 women), 230 part-time/adjunct. Expenses: Contact institution. *Financial support:* In 2006–07, 512 students received support; fellowships, research assistantships, teaching assistantships, career-related internships or fieldwork, Federal Work-Study, and traineeships available. Support available to part-time students. Financial award application deadline: 2/1; financial award applicants required to submit FAFSA. In 2006, 321 master's, 16 doctorates awarded. *Degree program information:* Part-time and evening/weekend programs available. Offers biostatistics (MPH, MS, Dr PH, PhD); environmental health sciences (MPH, Dr PH, PhD); epidemiology (MPH, MS, Dr PH, PhD); health policy and management (Exec MPH, MPH); population and family health (MPH); public health (MPH, Dr PH); sociomedical sciences (MPH, Dr PH, PhD). PhD offered in cooperation with the Graduate School of Arts and Sciences. *Application deadline:* For fall admission, 2/1 for domestic and international students; for spring admission, 10/1 for domestic and international students. Applications are processed on a rolling basis. *Application fee:* $60. Electronic applications accepted. *Application Contact:* June Saunders, Associate Director of Admissions, 212-305-3927, Fax: 212-342-4861, E-mail: ph-admit@columbia.edu. *Dean,* Dr. Allan Rosenfield, 212-305-3927.

School of Continuing Education Students: 9 full-time (3 women), 352 part-time (190 women); includes 89 minority (21 African Americans, 41 Asian Americans or Pacific Islanders, 27 Hispanic Americans), 34 international. *Faculty:* 4 full-time (1 woman), 34 part-time/adjunct (13 women). Expenses: Contact institution. Offers actuarial science (MS); construction administration (MS); fundraising management (MS); information and archive management (MS); landscape design (MS); strategic communications (MS); technology management (Exec MS). *Application deadline:* For fall admission, 7/13 for domestic and international students; for spring admission, 10/15 for domestic students, 11/10 for international students. Electronic applications accepted.

College of Dental Medicine Offers advanced education in general dentistry (Certificate); biomedical informatics (MA, PhD); dental and oral surgery (DDS); dental medicine (DDS, MA, MS, PhD, Certificate); endodontics (Certificate); orthodontics (MS, Certificate); periodontics (MS, Certificate); prosthodontics (MS, Certificate); science education (MA).

School of International and Public Affairs Students: 936 full-time (554 women). Average age 27. 2,223 applicants, 47% accepted, 465 enrolled. *Faculty:* 73 full-time (17 women), 247 part-time/adjunct (94 women). Expenses: Contact institution. *Financial support:* In 2006–07, 281 students received support, including 230 fellowships (averaging $14,537 per year), 51 teaching assistantships (averaging $25,602 per year); research assistantships, career-related internships or fieldwork, Federal Work-Study, and institutionally sponsored loans also available. Financial award application deadline: 1/4; financial award applicants required to submit FAFSA. In 2006, 617 degrees awarded. Offers environmental science and policy (MPA); international affairs (MIA); international and public affairs (MIA, MPA, Certificate); public policy and administration (MPA). *Application deadline:* For fall admission, 1/4 for domestic and international students; for spring admission, 10/1 for domestic and international students. *Application fee:* $85. Electronic applications accepted. *Application Contact:* Matt Clemons, Director of Admissions and Financial Aid, 212-854-6216, Fax: 212-854-3010, E-mail: mc2793@columbia.edu. *Dean,* Dr. John Coatsworth, 212-854-4646, Fax: 212-864-4847, E-mail: jhc2125@columbia.edu.

The East Central Europe Center Expenses: Contact institution. *Financial support:* In 2006–07, 1 research assistantship was awarded; fellowships, career-related internships or fieldwork and Federal Work-Study also available. Financial award application deadline: 1/15. Offers East Central European studies (Certificate). Students must be enrolled in a separate graduate degree program at Columbia University. *Application deadline:* For fall admission, 1/4 for domestic students; for spring admission, 10/1 for domestic students. *Application fee:* $85. Electronic applications accepted. *Application Contact:* Matt Clemons, Director of Admissions and Financial Aid, 212-854-6216, Fax: 212-854-3010, E-mail: mc2793@columbia.edu. *Director,* Dr. John Micgiel, 212-854-4008, Fax: 212-854-8577, E-mail: jsm6@columbia.edu.

The Harriman Institute Expenses: Contact institution. *Financial support:* Fellowships, career-related internships or fieldwork and Federal Work-Study available. Financial award application deadline: 1/15. *Degree program information:* Part-time programs available. Offers Russian, Eurasian, and Eastern European studies (Certificate). Students must be enrolled in a separate graduate degree program at Columbia University. *Application deadline:* For fall admission, 1/4 for domestic students; for spring admission, 10/1 for domestic students. *Application fee:* $85. Electronic applications accepted. *Application Contact:* Matt Clemons, Director of Admissions and Financial Aid, 212-854-6216, Fax: 212-854-3010, E-mail: mc2793@columbia.edu. *Director,* Dr. Catherine Theimer Nepomnyashchy, 212-854-6213, Fax: 212-666-3481, E-mail: cn29@columbia.edu.

Institute for the Study of Europe Expenses: Contact institution. *Financial support:* Application deadline: 1/15. Offers European studies (Certificate). Students must be enrolled in a separate graduate degree program at Columbia University. *Application deadline:* For fall admission, 1/4 for domestic students; for spring admission, 10/1 for domestic students. *Application fee:* $85. Electronic applications accepted. *Application Contact:* Matt Clemons, Director of Admissions and Financial Aid, 212-854-6216, Fax: 212-854-3010, E-mail: mc2793@columbia.edu. *Director,* Dr. Volker Berghahn, 212-854-4618, Fax: 212-854-8577.

Institute of African Studies Expenses: Contact institution. *Financial support:* Application deadline: 1/15. Offers African studies (Certificate). Students must be enrolled in a separate graduate degree program at Columbia University. *Application deadline:* For fall admission, 1/4 priority date for domestic students; for spring admission, 10/1 priority date for domestic students. *Application fee:* $85. Electronic applications accepted. *Application Contact:* Matt Clemons, Director of Admissions and Financial Aid, 212-854-6216, Fax: 212-854-3010, E-mail: mc2793@columbia.edu. *Director,* Mamadou Diouf, 212-854-4633, Fax: 212-854-4639.

Institute of Latin American Studies Expenses: Contact institution. *Financial support:* Application deadline: 1/15. Offers Latin American studies (Certificate). Students must also be enrolled in a separate graduate degree program at Columbia University. *Application deadline:* For fall admission, 1/4 priority date for domestic students; for spring admission, 10/1 priority date for domestic students. *Application fee:* $85. Electronic applications accepted. *Application Contact:* Matt Clemons, Director of Admissions and Financial Aid, 212-854-6216, Fax: 212-854-3010, E-mail: mc2793@columbia.edu.

Middle East Institute Expenses: Contact institution. *Financial support:* Application deadline: 1/5. Offers Middle East studies (Certificate). Students must also be enrolled in a separate graduate degree program at Columbia University. *Application deadline:* For fall admission, 1/4 priority date for domestic students; for spring admission, 10/1 priority date for domestic students. *Application fee:* $85. Electronic applications accepted. *Application Contact:* Matt Clemons, Director of Admissions and Financial Aid, 212-854-6216, Fax: 212-854-3010, E-mail: mc2793@columbia.edu. *Director,* Dr. Rashidi Khalidi, 212-854-2584, Fax: 212-854-1413, E-mail: sipa_admission@columbia.edu.

Southern Asian Institute Expenses: Contact institution. *Financial support:* Application deadline: 1/15. Offers Southern Asian studies (Certificate). Students must be enrolled in a separate graduate degree program at Columbia University. *Application deadline:* For fall admission, 1/4 for domestic students; for spring admission, 10/1 for domestic students. *Application fee:* $85. Electronic applications accepted. *Application Contact:* Matt Clemons, Director of Admissions and Financial Aid, 212-854-6216, Fax: 212-854-3010, E-mail: mc2793@columbia.edu. *Director,* Dr. Vidya Dehejia, 212-854-3616, Fax: 212-854-6987, E-mail: sipa_admission@columbia.edu.

Weatherhead East Asian Institute Expenses: Contact institution. *Financial support:* Application deadline: 1/15. Offers Asian studies (Certificate). Students must be enrolled in a separate graduate degree program at Columbia University. *Application deadline:* For fall admission, 1/4 for domestic students; for spring admission, 10/1 for domestic students. *Application fee:* $85. Electronic applications accepted. *Application Contact:* Matt Clemons, Director of Admissions and Financial Aid, 212-854-6216, Fax: 212-854-3010, E-mail: mc2793@columbia.edu. *Director,* Myron Cohen, 212-854-7912, E-mail: sipa_admission@columbia.edu.

School of Law Offers law (JD, LL M, JSD). Electronic applications accepted.

School of Nursing Students: 173 full-time (159 women), 248 part-time (233 women); includes 82 minority (22 African Americans, 1 American Indian/Alaska Native, 35 Asian Americans or Pacific Islanders, 24 Hispanic Americans). Average age 31. 248 applicants, 100% accepted, 101 enrolled. *Faculty:* 80. Expenses: Contact institution. *Financial support:* Research assistantships, teaching assistantships, Federal Work-Study and institutionally sponsored loans available. Support available to part-time students. Financial award applicants required to submit FAFSA. In 2006, 175 master's, 11 doctorates, 7 other advanced degrees awarded. *Degree program information:* Part-time programs available. Offers acute care nurse practitioner (MS, Adv C); adult nurse practitioner (MS, Adv C); family nurse practitioner (MS, Adv C); geriatric nurse practitioner (MS, Adv C); neonatal nurse practitioner (MS, Adv C); nurse anesthesia (MS, Adv C); nurse midwifery (MS); nursing (MS, DN Sc, DrNP, Adv C); nursing practice (DrNP); nursing science (DN Sc); oncology nursing (MS, Adv C); pediatric nurse practitioner (MS, Adv C); psychiatric mental health nursing (MS, Adv C); women's health nurse practitioner (Adv C). *Application deadline:* Applications are processed on a rolling basis. Electronic applications accepted. *Application Contact:* Judy Wolfe, Director of Admissions, 800-899-8895, E-mail: nursing@columbia.edu. *Dean,* Dr. Mary O'Neil Mundinger, 212-305-3582.

Columbia University (continued)

School of Social Work Students: 850. Average age 26. 1,104 applicants, 425 enrolled. *Faculty:* 50 full-time. Expenses: Contact institution. *Financial support:* Fellowships, research assistantships, teaching assistantships with partial tuition reimbursements, career-related internships or fieldwork, Federal Work-Study, institutionally sponsored loans, scholarships/grants, health care benefits, and unspecified assistantships available. Support available to part-time students. Financial award application deadline: 2/15; financial award applicants required to submit CSS PROFILE or FAFSA. In 2006, 437 master's, 17 doctorates awarded. Offers social work (MSSW, PhD). PhD offered through the Graduate School of Arts and Sciences. *Application deadline:* For fall admission, 3/1 priority date for domestic students; for winter admission, 11/15 priority date for domestic students. Applications are processed on a rolling basis. *Application fee:* $65. Electronic applications accepted. *Application Contact:* Debbie Lesperance, Director of Admissions, 212-851-2211, Fax: 212-851-2305, E-mail: dl635@columbia.edu. *Dean,* Dr. Jeanette Takamura.

School of the Arts Students: 745 full-time; includes 177 minority (38 African Americans, 4 American Indian/Alaska Native, 87 Asian Americans or Pacific Islanders, 48 Hispanic Americans). Average age 27. 2,543 applicants, 13% accepted, 243 enrolled. *Faculty:* 46 full-time (15 women), 153 part-time/adjunct (61 women). Expenses: Contact institution. *Financial support:* In 2006–07, 367 fellowships (averaging $5,876 per year), 36 research assistantships (averaging $19,579 per year), 26 teaching assistantships with full and partial tuition reimbursements (averaging $6,540 per year) were awarded; career-related internships or fieldwork, Federal Work-Study, institutionally sponsored loans, scholarships/grants, health care benefits, tuition waivers (partial), and unspecified assistantships also available. Financial award applicants required to submit FAFSA. In 2006, 207 degrees awarded. Offers arts (MFA); digital media (MFA); directing (MFA); fiction (MFA); new genres (MFA); nonfiction (MFA); painting (MFA); photography (MFA); poetry (MFA); printmaking (MFA); producing (MFA); screen writing (MFA); sculpture (MFA). *Application fee:* $120. Electronic applications accepted. *Application Contact:* Jamie Sosnow, Director of Admissions, 212-854-2134, Fax: 212-854-1309, E-mail: admissions-arts@columbia.edu. *Acting Dean,* Dan Kleinman, 212-854-2875.

Theatre Arts Division Students: 158 full-time (95 women); includes 37 minority (13 African Americans, 13 Asian Americans or Pacific Islanders, 11 Hispanic Americans). Average age 27. 356 applicants, 22% accepted, 59 enrolled. *Faculty:* 10 full-time (5 women), 30 part-time/adjunct (13 women). Expenses: Contact institution. *Financial support:* In 2006–07, 87 fellowships (averaging $6,067 per year), 8 research assistantships (averaging $33,399 per year) were awarded; career-related internships or fieldwork, Federal Work-Study, scholarships/grants, tuition waivers (partial), and unspecified assistantships also available. Financial award applicants required to submit FAFSA. In 2006, 52 degrees awarded. Offers acting (MFA); directing (MFA); dramaturgy (MFA); playwriting (MFA); stage management (MFA); theater management (MFA). *Application deadline:* For fall admission, 1/1 for domestic and international students. *Application fee:* $120. Electronic applications accepted. *Application Contact:* Director of Admissions, 212-854-2134, E-mail: admissions-arts@columbia.edu. *Chair,* Steven Chaikelson, 212-854-3408, Fax: 212-554-3344, E-mail: theatre@columbia.edu.

COLUMBUS STATE UNIVERSITY, Columbus, GA 31907-5645

General Information State-supported, coed, comprehensive institution. *Enrollment:* 7,597 graduate, professional, and undergraduate students; 291 full-time matriculated graduate/professional students (172 women), 524 part-time matriculated graduate/professional students (264 women). *Enrollment by degree level:* 757 master's, 58 other advanced degrees. *Graduate faculty:* 58 full-time (27 women), 19 part-time/adjunct (9 women). Tuition, state resident: part-time $127 per semester hour. Tuition, nonresident: part-time $508 per semester hour. *Required fees:* $264 per semester. Tuition and fees vary according to course load. *Graduate housing:* Room and/or apartments available on a first-come, first-served basis to single students; on-campus housing not available to married students. Housing application deadline: 7/1. *Student services:* Campus employment opportunities, campus safety program, career counseling, disabled student services, exercise/wellness program, free psychological counseling, international student services, low-cost health insurance, multicultural affairs office, teacher training. *Library facilities:* Simon Schwob Memorial Library. *Online resources:* library catalog, web page, access to other libraries' catalogs. *Collection:* 387,026 titles, 1,400 serial subscriptions, 10,864 audiovisual materials.

Computer facilities: 300 computers available on campus for general student use. A campuswide network can be accessed from student residence rooms and from off campus. Internet access and online class registration are available. *Web address:* http://www.colstate.edu/.

General Application Contact: Katie Thornton, Graduate Admissions Specialist, 706-568-2035, Fax: 706-568-2462, E-mail: thornton_katie@colstate.edu.

GRADUATE UNITS

Graduate Studies Students: 291 full-time (172 women), 524 part-time (264 women); includes 250 minority (217 African Americans, 2 American Indian/Alaska Native, 18 Asian Americans or Pacific Islanders, 13 Hispanic Americans), 13 international. Average age 36. 308 applicants, 62% accepted, 150 enrolled. *Faculty:* 58 full-time (27 women), 19 part-time/adjunct (9 women). Expenses: Contact institution. *Financial support:* In 2006–07, 321 students received support, including 56 research assistantships with partial tuition reimbursements available (averaging $3,000 per year); career-related internships or fieldwork, Federal Work-Study, institutionally sponsored loans, scholarships/grants, tuition waivers (partial), and unspecified assistantships also available. Support available to part-time students. Financial award application deadline: 5/1; financial award applicants required to submit FAFSA. In 2006, 303 master's, 47 other advanced degrees awarded. *Degree program information:* Part-time and evening/weekend programs available. Postbaccalaureate distance learning degree programs offered (minimal on-campus study). *Application deadline:* For fall admission, 5/1 priority date for domestic students, 5/1 for international students; for spring admission, 11/1 for domestic and international students. Applications are processed on a rolling basis. *Application fee:* $25. Electronic applications accepted. *Application Contact:* Katie Thornton, Graduate Admissions Specialist, 706-568-2035, Fax: 706-568-2462, E-mail: thornton_katie@colstate.edu. *Vice President for Academic Affairs,* Dr. George E. Stanton, 706-568-2061, Fax: 706-569-3168, E-mail: stanton_george@colstate.edu.

College of Arts and Letters Students: 112 full-time (55 women), 254 part-time (99 women); includes 140 minority (129 African Americans, 2 American Indian/Alaska Native, 3 Asian Americans or Pacific Islanders, 6 Hispanic Americans), 3 international. Average age 36. 113 applicants, 79% accepted, 71 enrolled. *Faculty:* 13 full-time (6 women), 9 part-time/adjunct (4 women). Expenses: Contact institution. *Financial support:* In 2006–07, 104 students received support, including 18 research assistantships with partial tuition reimbursements available (averaging $3,000 per year); career-related internships or fieldwork, Federal Work-Study, institutionally sponsored loans, scholarships/grants, tuition waivers (partial), and unspecified assistantships also available. Support available to part-time students. Financial award application deadline: 5/1; financial award applicants required to submit FAFSA. In 2006, 140 degrees awarded. *Degree program information:* Part-time and evening/weekend programs available. Postbaccalaureate distance learning degree programs offered (minimal on-campus study). Offers art education (M Ed); arts and letters (M Ed, MM, MPA); music education (MM); public administration (MPA). *Application deadline:* For fall admission, 5/1 priority date for domestic students, 5/1 for international students; for spring admission, 11/1 for domestic and international students. Applications are processed on a rolling basis. *Application fee:* $25. Electronic applications accepted. *Application Contact:* Katie Thornton, Graduate Admissions Specialist, 706-568-2035, Fax: 706-568-2462, E-mail: thornton_katie@colstate.edu. *Acting Dean,* Dr. James Patrick McHenry, 706-568-2055, Fax: 706-569-3123, E-mail: mchenry_james@colstate.edu.

College of Education Students: 148 full-time (106 women), 175 part-time (127 women); includes 78 minority (69 African Americans, 4 Asian Americans or Pacific Islanders, 5 Hispanic Americans), 1 international. Average age 36. 117 applicants, 47% accepted, 39 enrolled. *Faculty:* 26 full-time (12 women), 10 part-time/adjunct (5 women). Expenses: Contact institution. *Financial support:* In 2006–07, 185 students received support, including 26 research assistantships with partial tuition reimbursements available (averaging $3,000 per year); career-related internships or fieldwork, Federal Work-Study, institutionally sponsored loans, scholarships/grants, tuition waivers (partial), and unspecified assistantships also available. Support available to part-time students. Financial award application deadline: 5/1; financial award applicants required to submit FAFSA. In 2006, 108 master's, 47 Ed Ss awarded. *Degree program information:* Part-time and evening/weekend programs available. Postbaccalaureate distance learning degree programs offered (minimal on-campus study). Offers community counseling (MS); early childhood education (M Ed, Ed S); education (M Ed, MS, Ed S); educational leadership (M Ed, Ed S); instructional technology (MS); middle grades education (M Ed, Ed S); physical education (M Ed); school counseling (M Ed, Ed S); secondary education (M Ed, Ed S); special education (Ed S). *Application deadline:* For fall admission, 5/1 priority date for domestic students, 5/1 for international students; for spring admission, 11/11 for domestic students, 11/1 for international students. Applications are processed on a rolling basis. *Application fee:* $25. Electronic applications accepted. *Application Contact:* Katie Thornton, Graduate Admissions Specialist, 706-568-2035, Fax: 706-568-2462, E-mail: thornton_katie@colstate.edu. *Dean,* Dr. David Rock, 706-568-2212, Fax: 706-569-3134, E-mail: rock_david@colstate.edu.

College of Science Students: 19 full-time (6 women), 63 part-time (21 women); includes 18 minority (12 African Americans, 6 Asian Americans or Pacific Islanders), 7 international. Average age 36. 40 applicants, 80% accepted, 26 enrolled. *Faculty:* 15 full-time (7 women). Expenses: Contact institution. *Financial support:* In 2006–07, 19 students received support, including 10 research assistantships with partial tuition reimbursements available (averaging $3,000 per year); career-related internships or fieldwork, Federal Work-Study, institutionally sponsored loans, scholarships/grants, tuition waivers (partial), and unspecified assistantships also available. Support available to part-time students. Financial award application deadline: 5/1; financial award applicants required to submit FAFSA. In 2006, 22 degrees awarded. *Degree program information:* Part-time and evening/weekend programs available. Postbaccalaureate distance learning degree programs offered (no on-campus study). Offers applied computer science (MS); environmental science (MS); science (MS). *Application deadline:* For fall admission, 5/1 priority date for domestic students, 5/1 for international students; for spring admission, 11/1 for domestic and international students. Applications are processed on a rolling basis. Electronic applications accepted. *Application Contact:* Katie Thornton, Graduate Admissions Specialist, 706-568-2035, Fax: 706-568-2462, E-mail: thornton_katie@colstate.edu. *Acting Dean,* Dr. Glenn Stokes, 706-568-2056, E-mail: stokes_glenn@colstate.edu.

D. Abbott Turner College of Business Students: 12 full-time (5 women), 32 part-time (17 women); includes 14 minority (7 African Americans, 5 Asian Americans or Pacific Islanders, 2 Hispanic Americans), 2 international. Average age 36. 36 applicants, 42% accepted, 14 enrolled. *Faculty:* 4 full-time (2 women). Expenses: Contact institution. *Financial support:* In 2006–07, 13 students received support, including 2 research assistantships (averaging $3,000 per year). Financial award application deadline: 5/1. In 2006, 33 degrees awarded. Offers business administration (MBA). *Application deadline:* For fall admission, 5/1 priority date for domestic students, 5/1 for international students; for spring admission, 11/1 for domestic and international students. Applications are processed on a rolling basis. *Application fee:* $25. Electronic applications accepted. *Dean,* Dr. Linda U. Hadley, 706-568-2044, Fax: 706-568-2184, E-mail: hadley_linda@colstate.edu.

CONCORDIA LUTHERAN SEMINARY, Edmonton, AB T5B 4E3, Canada

General Information Independent-religious, coed, primarily men, graduate-only institution. *Enrollment by degree level:* 13 first professional, 1 master's, 7 other advanced degrees. *Graduate faculty:* 4 full-time (0 women), 5 part-time/adjunct (0 women). *Graduate tuition:* Tuition and fees charges are reported in Canadian dollars. *Tuition:* Full-time $6,600 Canadian dollars; part-time $200 Canadian dollars per credit. *Required fees:* $25 Canadian dollars per semester. One-time fee: $425 Canadian dollars full-time. *Graduate housing:* On-campus housing not available. *Student services:* Campus employment opportunities. *Library facilities:* Concordia Lutheran Seminary Library. *Online resources:* library catalog, access to other libraries' catalogs. *Collection:* 26,714 titles, 262 serial subscriptions, 727 audiovisual materials.

Computer facilities: 1 computer available on campus for general student use. Internet access is available. *Web address:* http://www.concordiasem.ab.ca/.

General Application Contact: Jeffrey Nachtigall, Director of Admissions, 780-474-1468, Fax: 780-479-5067, E-mail: admissions@concordiasem.ab.ca.

GRADUATE UNITS

Graduate and Professional Programs Students: 13 full-time (0 women), 8 part-time (1 woman); includes 2 minority (both Asian Americans or Pacific Islanders) Average age 31. 3 applicants, 67% accepted, 2 enrolled. *Faculty:* 4 full-time (0 women), 5 part-time/adjunct (0 women). Expenses: Contact institution. *Financial support:* In 2006–07, 21 students received support. Scholarships/grants available. Financial award application deadline: 8/30. In 2006, 3 M Divs, 1 master's awarded. *Degree program information:* Part-time programs available. Offers theology (M Div, MTS). *Application deadline:* For fall admission, 4/1 priority date for domestic students; for winter admission, 10/30 priority date for domestic students. *Application fee:* $30 ($100 for international students). *Application Contact:* Dr. Vernon A. Raaflaub, Director of Admissions, 780-474-1468, Fax: 780-479-3067, E-mail: admissions@concordiasem.ab.ca. *Academic Dean,* Dr. Edward G. Kettner, 780-474-1468, Fax: 780-479-3067, E-mail: ekettner@concordiasem.ab.ca.

CONCORDIA SEMINARY, St. Louis, MO 63105-3199

General Information Independent-religious, coed, primarily men, graduate-only institution. *Graduate housing:* Rooms and/or apartments guaranteed to single students and available to married students. Housing application deadline: 3/4. *Research affiliation:* Center for Reformation Research, Concordia Historical Institute.

GRADUATE UNITS

Graduate Programs Offers theology (M Div, MA, STM, D Min, PhD, Certificate).

CONCORDIA THEOLOGICAL SEMINARY, Fort Wayne, IN 46825-4996

General Information Independent-religious, coed, primarily men, graduate-only institution. *Graduate housing:* Room and/or apartments available to single students; on-campus housing not available to married students.

GRADUATE UNITS

Graduate and Professional Programs *Degree program information:* Part-time programs available. Offers theology (M Div, MA, STM, D Min, D Miss).

CONCORDIA UNIVERSITY, Irvine, CA 92612-3299

General Information Independent-religious, coed, comprehensive institution. *Enrollment:* 2,317 graduate, professional, and undergraduate students; 328 full-time matriculated graduate/professional students (220 women), 556 part-time matriculated graduate/professional students (417 women). *Enrollment by degree level:* 821 master's, 63 other advanced degrees. *Graduate faculty:* 31 full-time, 22 part-time/adjunct. *Graduate housing:* On-campus housing not available. *Student services:* Campus safety program, career counseling, disabled student services, exercise/wellness program, free psychological counseling, international student services, multicultural affairs office, teacher training, writing training. *Library facilities:* Concordia University Library. *Online resources:* library catalog, web page, access to other libraries' catalogs. *Collection:* 80,300 titles, 7,144 serial subscriptions, 1,365 audiovisual materials.

Computer facilities: 42 computers available on campus for general student use. A campuswide network can be accessed from student residence rooms and from off campus. Internet access is available. *Web address:* http://www.cui.edu/.

General Application Contact: Information Contact, 800-229-1200.

GRADUATE UNITS

School of Arts and Sciences Students: 51 full-time (13 women); includes 7 minority (1 African American, 1 Asian American or Pacific Islander, 5 Hispanic Americans), 1 international. *Faculty:* 3 full-time, 4 part-time/adjunct. Expenses: Contact institution. Offers coaching and athletic administration (MA). *Application deadline:* Applications are processed on a rolling basis. *Application fee:* $50 ($300 for international students). *Application Contact:* Roberto Marquez, Coordinator of Graduate Enrollment, 949-854-8002 Ext. 1133, Fax: 949-854-6854, E-mail: roberto.marquez@cui.edu. *Dean,* Dr. Kenneth Mangels, 949-854-8002 Ext. 1350, Fax: 949-854-6854, E-mail: kenneth.mangels@cui.edu.

School of Business and Professional Studies Students: 86 full-time (41 women), 15 part-time (9 women); includes 23 minority (3 African Americans, 16 Asian Americans or Pacific Islanders, 4 Hispanic Americans), 10 international. Average age 32. *Faculty:* 4 full-time, 8 part-time/adjunct. Expenses: Contact institution. *Financial support:* Applicants required to submit FAFSA. In 2006, 14 degrees awarded. *Degree program information:* Part-time programs available. Offers entrepreneurial business administration (MBA); international studies (MA). *Application deadline:* For fall admission, 7/1 for domestic students; for spring admission, 12/1 for domestic students. Applications are processed on a rolling basis. *Application Contact:* Roberto Marquez, Coordinator of Graduate Enrollment, 949-854-8002 Ext. 1133, Fax: 949-854-6894, E-mail: roberto.marquez@cui.edu. *Dean,* Dr. Timothy Peters, 949-854-8002 Ext. 1333, Fax: 949-854-6864, E-mail: tim.peters@cui.edu.

School of Education Students: 228 full-time (185 women), 465 part-time (378 women); includes 145 minority (8 African Americans, 6 American Indian/Alaska Native, 38 Asian Americans or Pacific Islanders, 93 Hispanic Americans), 2 international. Average age 32. *Faculty:* 13 full-time (6 women), 5 part-time/adjunct (3 women). Expenses: Contact institution. *Financial support:* Application deadline: 3/2; In 2006, 75 degrees awarded. *Degree program information:* Part-time and evening/weekend programs available. Postbaccalaureate distance learning degree programs offered (minimal on-campus study). Offers curriculum and instruction (MA); education (M Ed); educational administration and administrative services credential (MA). *Application deadline:* For fall admission, 7/15 priority date for domestic students, 7/15 for international students; for spring admission, 11/30 priority date for domestic students, 11/30 for international students. Applications are processed on a rolling basis. *Application fee:* $50 ($300 for international students). *Application Contact:* Lindsay Anderson, Director of Graduate Enrollment, 949-854-8002 Ext. 1133, Fax: 949-854-6894, E-mail: lindsay.anderson@cui.edu. *Dean,* Dr. Joseph Bordeaux, 949-854-8002 Ext. 1345, Fax: 949-854-6878, E-mail: joseph.bordeaux@cui.edu.

School of Theology Students: 27 full-time (5 women), 6 part-time; includes 3 minority (2 Asian Americans or Pacific Islanders, 1 Hispanic American), 11 international. Average age 32. *Faculty:* 11 full-time, 5 part-time/adjunct. Expenses: Contact institution. *Financial support:* In 2006–07, 1 research assistantship with full tuition reimbursement was awarded; tuition waivers (partial) also available. In 2006, 7 degrees awarded. *Degree program information:* Part-time programs available. Offers theology (MA). *Application deadline:* For fall admission, 7/1 priority date for domestic students; for spring admission, 11/30 priority date for domestic students. *Application fee:* $100 ($300 for international students). *Dean,* Rev. Dr. James V. Bachman, 949-854-8002 Ext. 1751, Fax: 949-854-6854, E-mail: james.bachman@cui.edu.

CONCORDIA UNIVERSITY, Montréal, QC H3G 1M8, Canada

General Information Province-supported, coed, university. *Enrollment:* 32,033 graduate, professional, and undergraduate students; 3,508 full-time matriculated graduate/professional students (1,417 women), 1,403 part-time matriculated graduate/professional students (750 women). *Enrollment by degree level:* 3,272 master's, 821 doctoral, 758 other advanced degrees. *Graduate faculty:* 732. *Graduate housing:* Room and/or apartments available on a first-come, first-served basis to single students; on-campus housing not available to married students. *Student services:* Campus employment opportunities, campus safety program, career counseling, child daycare facilities, disabled student services, exercise/wellness program, free psychological counseling, grant writing training, international student services, multicultural affairs office, writing training. *Library facilities:* Webster Library plus 2 others. *Online resources:* library catalog, web page, access to other libraries' catalogs. *Collection:* 3 million titles, 6,000 serial subscriptions. *Research affiliation:* Blue Metropolis Literary Series (English), Canadian Journalism Project (journalism), Canadian Rural Revitalization Foundation (sociology), Centre de recherche en plasturgie et composites (CREPEC) (mechanical and industrial engineering), Centre de recherche informatique de Montréal (CRIM) (computer science), Center d'experise et de services en application multimédia (multimedia).

Computer facilities: Computer purchase and lease plans are available. 350 computers available on campus for general student use. A campuswide network can be accessed from student residence rooms and from off campus. Internet access and online class registration, specialized software applications are available. *Web address:* http://www.concordia.ca/.

General Application Contact: Dr. Elizabeth Saccà, Dean of Graduate Studies, 514-848-2424 Ext. 3803, Fax: 514-848-2812, E-mail: sgscu@vax2.concordia.ca.

GRADUATE UNITS

School of Graduate Studies Students: 3,508 full-time (1,417 women), 1,403 part-time (750 women). 5,893 applicants, 49% accepted, 1538 enrolled. Expenses: Contact institution. *Financial support:* Fellowships, research assistantships, teaching assistantships, career-related internships or fieldwork, and institutionally sponsored loans available. In 2006, 1,074 master's, 65 doctorates, 236 other advanced degrees awarded. *Degree program information:* Part-time and evening/weekend programs available. Offers individualized research (M Sc, MA, PhD). *Application fee:* $50. *Dean of Graduate Studies,* Dr. Elizabeth Saccà, 514-848-2424 Ext. 3803, Fax: 514-848-2812, E-mail: sgscu@vax2.concordia.ca.

Faculty of Arts and Science Students: 1,116 full-time (683 women), 606 part-time (405 women). 2,259 applicants, 44% accepted, 595 enrolled. Expenses: Contact institution. *Financial support:* Fellowships, research assistantships, teaching assistantships, career-related internships or fieldwork, institutionally sponsored loans, and scholarships/grants available. In 2006, 317 master's, 25 doctorates, 127 other advanced degrees awarded. Offers écriture (Certificate); adult education (Diploma); anglais-français en langue et techniques de localisation (Certificate); applied linguistics (MA); arts and science (M Sc, MA, MTM, PhD, Certificate, Diploma); biology (M Sc, PhD); biotechnology and genomics (Diploma); chemistry (M Sc, PhD); child study (MA); communication (PhD); communication studies (Diploma); community economic development (Diploma); creative writing (MA); economics (MA, PhD, Diploma); educational studies (MA); educational technology (MA, PhD); English (MA); environmental impact assessment (Diploma); exercise science (M Sc); geography, urban and environmental studies (M Sc); history (MA, PhD); history and philosophy of religion (MA); human systems intervention (MA); humanities (PhD); instructional technology (Diploma); journalism (Diploma); Judaic studies (MA); littératures francophones et résonances médiatiques (MA); mathematics (M Sc, MA, PhD); media studies (MA); philosophy (MA); physics (M Sc, PhD); political science (PhD); psychology (clinical) (MA, PhD, Certificate); psychology (general) (MA, PhD); public policy and public administration (MA); religion (PhD); social and cultural anthropology (MA); sociology (MA); teaching English as a second language (Certificate); teaching of mathematics (MTM); theological studies (MA); traductologie (MA); translation (Diploma). *Application fee:* $50. *Dean,* Dr. David Graham, 514-848-2424 Ext. 2081, Fax: 514-848-2877.

Faculty of Engineering and Computer Science Students: 1,590 full-time (314 women), 228 part-time (45 women). 2,012 applicants, 55% accepted, 452 enrolled. Expenses: Contact institution. In 2006, 481 master's, 28 doctorates, 28 other advanced degrees awarded. Offers 3D graphics and game development (Certificate); aerospace engineering (M Eng); building engineering (M Eng, MA Sc, PhD, Certificate); civil engineering (M Eng, MA Sc, PhD); composites (M Eng); computer science (M App Comp Sc, M Comp Sc, PhD, Diploma); electrical and computer engineering (M Eng, MA Sc, PhD); engineering and computer science (M App Comp Sc, M Comp Sc, M Eng, MA Sc, PhD, Certificate, Diploma); environmental engineering (Certificate); industrial engineering (M Eng, MA Sc); information systems security (M Eng, MA Sc); mechanical engineering (M Eng, MA Sc, PhD, Certificate); quality systems engineering (M Eng, MA Sc); service engineering and network management (Certificate); software engineering (MA Sc); software systems for industrial engineering (Certificate). *Application fee:* $50. *Dean,* Dr. Nabil Esmail, 514-848-2424 Ext. 3062, Fax: 514-848-4509.

Faculty of Fine Arts Students: 268 full-time (189 women), 111 part-time (88 women). 636 applicants, 33% accepted, 148 enrolled. Expenses: Contact institution. *Financial support:* Fellowships, research assistantships, teaching assistantships, career-related internships or fieldwork available. In 2006, 89 master's, 5 doctorates, 19 other advanced degrees awarded. *Degree program information:* Part-time programs available. Offers advanced music performance studies (Diploma); art education (MA, PhD); art history (MA, PhD); creative arts therapies (MA); digital technologies in design art practice (Certificate); film studies (MA); fine arts (MA, MFA, PhD, Certificate, Diploma); studio arts (MFA). *Application fee:* $50. *Dean,* Prof. Catherine Wild, 514-848-2424 Ext. 4614, Fax: 514-848-4599.

John Molson School of Business Students: 447 full-time (174 women), 448 part-time (206 women). 925 applicants, 59% accepted, 319 enrolled. Expenses: Contact institution. *Financial support:* Fellowships, career-related internships or fieldwork available. In 2006, 183 master's, 6 doctorates, 62 other advanced degrees awarded. *Degree program information:* Part-time and evening/weekend programs available. Offers administration (M Sc, Diploma); aviation management (Certificate, Diploma); business administration (MBA, UA Undergraduate Associate, PhD); chartered accountancy (Diploma); community organizational development (Certificate); event management and fundraising (Certificate); executive business administration (EMBA); investment management (Diploma); investment management option (MBA); management accounting (Certificate); management of healthcare organizations (Certificate); sport administration (Diploma). *Application fee:* $50. *Application Contact:* Dr. Michel Magnan, Associate Dean, Graduate Programs, 514-848-2424 Ext. 4145, Fax: 514-848-4208. *Dean,* Dr. Jerry Tomberlin, 514-848-2424 Ext. 2700, Fax: 514-848-4502.

See Close-Up on page 859.

CONCORDIA UNIVERSITY, River Forest, IL 60305-1499

General Information Independent-religious, coed, comprehensive institution. CGS member. *Graduate housing:* Rooms and/or apartments available on a first-come, first-served basis to single and married students.

GRADUATE UNITS

College of Arts and Sciences Offers church music (MCM); community counseling (MA); gerontology (MA); human services (MA); liberal studies (MA); music (MA); psychology (MA); religion (MA).

College of Education Offers Christian education (MA); curriculum and instruction (MA); early childhood education (MA, Ed D); educational leadership (Ed D); reading education (MA); school administration (MA, CAS); school counseling (MA, CAS); teaching (MAT); urban teaching (MA).

CONCORDIA UNIVERSITY, Ann Arbor, MI 48105-2797

General Information Independent-religious, coed, comprehensive institution. *Enrollment:* 736 graduate, professional, and undergraduate students; 399 full-time matriculated graduate/professional students (290 women), 8 part-time matriculated graduate/professional students (4 women). *Enrollment by degree level:* 407 master's. *Tuition:* Full-time $7,020; part-time $390 per credit. Tuition and fees vary according to program. *Graduate housing:* On-campus housing not available. *Library facilities:* Zimmerman Library. *Online resources:* library catalog, web page, access to other libraries' catalogs. *Collection:* 117,000 titles, 660 serial subscriptions, 1,400 audiovisual materials.

Computer facilities: 60 computers available on campus for general student use. A campuswide network can be accessed from student residence rooms and from off campus. Internet access is available. *Web address:* http://www.cuaa.edu/.

General Application Contact: Jean Christensen, Associate Director of Graduate Admission, 734-995-7521, Fax: 734-995-4610, E-mail: christj@cuaa.edu.

GRADUATE UNITS

Graduate Programs Students: 399 full-time (290 women), 8 part-time (4 women); includes 112 minority (97 African Americans, 3 American Indian/Alaska Native, 8 Asian Americans or Pacific Islanders, 4 Hispanic Americans). Average age 39. 542 applicants, 69% accepted, 349 enrolled. *Faculty:* 6 full-time (3 women), 56 part-time/adjunct (27 women). Expenses: Contact institution. *Financial support:* In 2006–07, 263 students received support. Applicants required to submit FAFSA. *Degree program information:* Part-time and evening/weekend programs available. *Application deadline:* For fall admission, 9/7 priority date for domestic students, 8/15 priority date for international students; for winter admission, 1/18 priority date for domestic students, 12/15 priority date for international students; for spring admission, 5/10 priority date for domestic students, 4/15 priority date for international students. Applications are processed on a rolling basis. *Application fee:* $100.

CONCORDIA UNIVERSITY, Seward, NE 68434-1599

General Information Independent-religious, coed, comprehensive institution. *Graduate housing:* Rooms and/or apartments available on a first-come, first-served basis to single and married students.

GRADUATE UNITS

Graduate Programs in Education *Degree program information:* Part-time and evening/weekend programs available. Offers curriculum and instruction (M Ed); early childhood education (M Ed); education (M Ed, MPE, MS); educational administration (M Ed); family life ministry (MS); literacy education (M Ed); parish education (MPE). Electronic applications accepted.

CONCORDIA UNIVERSITY, Portland, OR 97211-6099

General Information Independent-religious, coed, comprehensive institution. *Graduate housing:* Room and/or apartments available on a first-come, first-served basis to single students; on-campus housing not available to married students. Housing application deadline: 8/1.

GRADUATE UNITS

College of Education *Degree program information:* Part-time programs available. Postbaccalaureate distance learning degree programs offered (no on-campus study). Offers curriculum and instruction (elementary) (M Ed); educational administration (M Ed); elementary education (MAT); secondary education (MAT). Electronic applications accepted.

School of Management *Degree program information:* Evening/weekend programs available. Offers management (MBA).

CONCORDIA UNIVERSITY AT AUSTIN, Austin, TX 78705-2799

General Information Independent-religious, coed, comprehensive institution.

GRADUATE UNITS

College of Education *Degree program information:* Part-time and evening/weekend programs available. Offers education (M Ed).

CONCORDIA UNIVERSITY, ST. PAUL, St. Paul, MN 55104-5494

General Information Independent-religious, coed, comprehensive institution. *Enrollment:* 2,046 graduate, professional, and undergraduate students; 287 full-time matriculated graduate/professional students (209 women), 51 part-time matriculated graduate/professional students (34 women). *Enrollment by degree level:* 313 master's, 25 other advanced degrees. *Graduate faculty:* 23 full-time (9 women), 37 part-time/adjunct (16 women). *Graduate housing:* On-campus housing not available. *Student services:* Campus employment opportunities, campus safety program, career counseling, child daycare facilities, disabled student services, exercise/wellness program, free psychological counseling, international student services, low-cost health insurance, multicultural affairs office, writing training. *Library facilities:* Library Technology Center. *Online resources:* library catalog, web page, access to other libraries' catalogs. *Collection:* 113,256 titles, 336 serial subscriptions, 3,171 audiovisual materials.

Concordia University, St. Paul (continued)

Computer facilities: Computer purchase and lease plans are available. 1,000 computers available on campus for general student use. A campuswide network can be accessed from student residence rooms and from off campus. Internet access is available. *Web address:* http://www.csp.edu/.

General Application Contact: Kimberly Craig, Director of Graduate and Cohort Admission, 651-603-6223, Fax: 651-603-6320, E-mail: craig@csp.edu.

GRADUATE UNITS

College of Business and Organizational Leadership Students: 186 full-time (114 women); includes 26 minority (16 African Americans, 8 Asian Americans or Pacific Islanders, 2 Hispanic Americans), 1 international. Average age 33. *Faculty:* 11 full-time (2 women), 18 part-time/adjunct (6 women). Expenses: Contact institution. *Financial support:* Federal Work-Study and scholarships/grants available. Financial award applicants required to submit FAFSA. In 2006, 92 degrees awarded. *Degree program information:* Evening/weekend programs available. Postbaccalaureate distance learning degree programs offered (minimal on-campus study). Offers business and organizational leadership (MBA); criminal justice (MAHS); human resources (MAOM); organizational management (MAOM). *Application deadline:* Applications are processed on a rolling basis. *Application fee:* $50. Electronic applications accepted. *Application Contact:* Kimberly Craig, Director of Graduate and Cohort Admission, 651-603-6223, Fax: 651-603-6320, E-mail: craig@csp.edu. *Dean,* Dr. Robert DeGregorio, 651-641-8845, Fax: 651-641-8807, E-mail: degregorio@csp.edu.

College of Education Students: 101 full-time (95 women), 10 part-time (9 women); includes 29 minority (21 African Americans, 1 American Indian/Alaska Native, 6 Asian Americans or Pacific Islanders, 1 Hispanic American). Average age 34. *Faculty:* 8 full-time (7 women), 12 part-time/adjunct (7 women). Expenses: Contact institution. In 2006, 59 master's, 8 other advanced degrees awarded. *Degree program information:* Evening/weekend programs available. Postbaccalaureate distance learning degree programs offered (minimal on-campus study). Offers differentiated instruction (MA Ed); early childhood (MA Ed); family life education (MAHS); special education (Certificate). *Application deadline:* Applications are processed on a rolling basis. *Application fee:* $50. Electronic applications accepted. *Application Contact:* Kimberly Craig, Director of Graduate and Cohort Admission, 651-603-6223, Fax: 651-603-6320, E-mail: craig@csp.edu. *Dean,* Prof. Lonn Maly, 651-641-8278, Fax: 651-641-8807, E-mail: maly@csp.edu.

College of Vocation and Ministry Average age 35. *Faculty:* 4 full-time (0 women), 7 part-time/adjunct (3 women). Expenses: Contact institution. *Financial support:* Federal Work-Study and scholarships/grants available. Financial award applicants required to submit FAFSA. In 2006, 8 master's, 2 other advanced degrees awarded. *Degree program information:* Part-time and evening/weekend programs available. Postbaccalaureate distance learning degree programs offered (minimal on-campus study). Offers Christian education (Certificate); Christian outreach (MA). *Application deadline:* Applications are processed on a rolling basis. *Application fee:* $50. Electronic applications accepted. *Application Contact:* Kimberly Craig, Director of Graduate and Cohort Admission, 651-603-6223, Fax: 651-603-6320, E-mail: craig@csp.edu. *Dean,* Dr. Steven Arnold, 651-641-8213, E-mail: sarnold@csp.edu.

CONCORDIA UNIVERSITY WISCONSIN, Mequon, WI 53097-2402

General Information Independent-religious, coed, comprehensive institution. *Enrollment:* 5,574 graduate, professional, and undergraduate students; 1,112 full-time matriculated graduate/professional students, 680 part-time matriculated graduate/professional students. *Enrollment by degree level:* 1,336 master's, 122 doctoral, 334 other advanced degrees. *Graduate faculty:* 47 full-time, 81 part-time/adjunct. *Graduate housing:* Room and/or apartments available to single students; on-campus housing not available to married students. Housing application deadline: 8/1. *Student services:* Campus employment opportunities, campus safety program, career counseling, disabled student services, exercise/wellness program, free psychological counseling, international student services, low-cost health insurance, writing training. *Library facilities:* Rinker Memorial Library plus 1 other. *Online resources:* library catalog, access to other libraries' catalogs. *Collection:* 79,341 titles, 4,440 serial subscriptions, 4,352 audiovisual materials.

Computer facilities: 100 computers available on campus for general student use. A campuswide network can be accessed from student residence rooms and from off campus. Internet access is available. *Web address:* http://www.cuw.edu/.

General Application Contact: Mary Eberhardt, Graduate Admissions, 262-243-4551, Fax: 262-243-4428, E-mail: mary.eberhardt@cuw.edu.

GRADUATE UNITS

Graduate Programs Students: 1,792 (1,218 women); includes 254 minority (77 African Americans, 4 American Indian/Alaska Native, 144 Asian Americans or Pacific Islanders, 29 Hispanic Americans) 61 international. Average age 36. 151 applicants, 87% accepted. *Faculty:* 47 full-time, 81 part-time/adjunct. Expenses: Contact institution. *Financial support:* Career-related internships or fieldwork and tuition waivers (partial) available. Financial award application deadline: 8/1. In 2006, 245 master's, 20 doctorates awarded. *Degree program information:* Part-time and evening/weekend programs available. Postbaccalaureate distance learning degree programs offered (minimal on-campus study). Offers art education (MS Ed); arts and sciences (MCM); business and legal studies (MBA, MSSPA); church music (MCM); curriculum and instruction (MS Ed); early childhood (MS Ed); educational administration (MS Ed); environmental education (MS Ed); family nurse practitioner (MSN); family studies (MS Ed); finance (MBA); geriatric nurse practitioner (MSN); health and human services (MOT, MSN, MSPT, MSRS, DPT); health care administration (MBA); human resource management (MBA); international business (MBA); international business-English/Chinese (MBA); management (MBA); management information services (MBA); managerial communications (MBA); marketing (MBA); nurse educator (MSN); occupational therapy (MOT); physical therapy (MSPT, DPT); professional counseling (MPC); public administration (MBA); reading (MS Ed); rehabilitation science (MSRS); risk management (MBA); school counseling (MS Ed); special education (MS Ed); student personnel administration (MSSPA). *Application deadline:* For fall admission, 8/1 priority date for domestic students; for winter admission, 12/1 priority date for domestic students; for spring admission, 1/1 priority date for domestic students. Applications are processed on a rolling basis. *Application fee:* $35. Electronic applications accepted. *Application Contact:* Mary Eberhardt, Graduate Admissions, 262-243-4551, Fax: 262-243-4428, E-mail: mary.eberhardt@cuw.edu. *Dean of Graduate Studies,* Dr. Marsha K. Konz, 262-243-4253, Fax: 262-243-4428, E-mail: marsha.konz@cuw.edu.

CONCORD LAW SCHOOL, Los Angeles, CA 90024

General Information Proprietary, coed, graduate-only institution.

GRADUATE UNITS

Program in Law *Degree program information:* Part-time and evening/weekend programs available. Postbaccalaureate distance learning degree programs offered (no on-campus study). Offers law (EJD, JD). Electronic applications accepted.

CONNECTICUT COLLEGE, New London, CT 06320-4196

General Information Independent, coed, comprehensive institution. *Graduate housing:* On-campus housing not available. *Research affiliation:* Hartford Hospital (neurophysiology).

GRADUATE UNITS

Graduate School *Degree program information:* Part-time programs available. Offers botany (MA, MAT); chemistry (MAT); dance (MFA); elementary education (MAT); English (MA, MAT); French and Italian (MA, MAT); German (MAT); Hispanic studies (MA); Latin (MAT); mathematics (MAT); music (MA, MAT); physics (MAT); psychology (MA); Russian studies (MAT); secondary education (MAT); zoology (MA, MAT).

CONSERVATORIO DE MUSICA, San Juan, PR 00918-2199

General Information Public, coed, comprehensive institution. *Enrollment:* 15 full-time matriculated graduate/professional students (4 women), 19 part-time matriculated graduate/professional students (4 women). *Enrollment by degree level:* 32 master's, 2 other advanced degrees. *Graduate faculty:* 2 full-time (0 women), 1 part-time/adjunct (0 women). *Student services:* Campus safety program, low-cost health insurance.

General Application Contact: Eutimia Santiago, Director of Admissions, 787-751-0160 Ext. 275, Fax: 787-754-6284, E-mail: admisiones@cmpr.edu.

GRADUATE UNITS

Program in Musical Performance Students: 2 full-time (1 woman); both minorities (both Hispanic Americans) 6 applicants, 33% accepted, 2 enrolled. *Faculty:* 2 full-time (1 woman). Expenses: Contact institution. *Financial support:* Fellowships, research assistantships, teaching assistantships, scholarships/grants available. Financial award application deadline: 7/31; financial award applicants required to submit FAFSA. Offers instrumental performance (Diploma); vocal performance (Diploma). *Application deadline:* For fall admission, 3/28 for domestic and international students; for winter admission, 10/27 for domestic and international students. *Application fee:* $100. *Application Contact:* Eutimia Santiago, Admission Director, 787-751-0160 Ext. 275, Fax: 787-754-6284, E-mail: esantiago@cmpr.gobierno.pr. *Academic Dean,* Melanie Santana, 787-751-0160 Ext. 254, Fax: 787-753-7187, E-mail: msantana@cmpr.gobierno.pr.

Program in Music Education Students: 19 full-time (4 women), 13 part-time (3 women); all minorities (all Hispanic Americans) 8 applicants, 100% accepted, 7 enrolled. *Faculty:* 2 full-time (0 women), 1 part-time/adjunct (0 women). Expenses: Contact institution. *Financial support:* Fellowships, research assistantships, teaching assistantships, scholarships/grants available. Financial award application deadline: 7/31; financial award applicants required to submit FAFSA. Offers music education (MM Ed). *Application deadline:* For fall admission, 3/24 for domestic and international students; for winter admission, 10/27 for domestic and international students. *Application fee:* $100. *Application Contact:* Eutimia Santiago, Director of Admissions, 787-751-0160 Ext. 275, Fax: 787-754-6284, E-mail: admisiones@cmpr.edu.

CONVERSE COLLEGE, Spartanburg, SC 29302-0006

General Information Independent, Undergraduate: women only; graduate: coed, comprehensive institution. *Enrollment:* 1,977 graduate, professional, and undergraduate students; 156 full-time matriculated graduate/professional students (136 women), 1,069 part-time matriculated graduate/professional students (847 women). *Graduate faculty:* 35 full-time (16 women), 17 part-time/adjunct (8 women). *Tuition:* Part-time $305 per credit hour. *Required fees:* $20 per term. *Graduate housing:* On-campus housing not available. *Student services:* Campus employment opportunities, campus safety program, career counseling, international student services, teacher training. *Library facilities:* Mickel Library. *Online resources:* library catalog, web page, access to other libraries' catalogs. *Collection:* 150,817 titles, 19,808 serial subscriptions, 20,515 audiovisual materials.

Computer facilities: 72 computers available on campus for general student use. A campuswide network can be accessed from student residence rooms and from off campus. Internet access and online class registration are available. *Web address:* http://www.converse.edu/.

General Application Contact: Thomas M. Faulkenberry, Dr., 864-596-9082, Fax: 864-596-9221, E-mail: tom.faulkenberry@converse.edu.

GRADUATE UNITS

Carroll McDaniel Petrie School of Music Students: 13 full-time (10 women), 7 part-time (3 women); includes 5 minority (all African Americans), 3 international. Average age 30. 14 applicants, 86% accepted, 7 enrolled. *Faculty:* 21 full-time (11 women), 13 part-time/adjunct (6 women). Expenses: Contact institution. *Financial support:* In 2006–07, 8 students received support, including 8 teaching assistantships with full and partial tuition reimbursements available (averaging $3,125 per year); fellowships, career-related internships or fieldwork, Federal Work-Study, institutionally sponsored loans, and unspecified assistantships also available. Support available to part-time students. Financial award application deadline: 4/15. In 2006, 9 degrees awarded. *Degree program information:* Part-time and evening/weekend programs available. Offers instrumental performance (M Mus); music education (M Mus); piano pedagogy (M Mus); vocal performance (M Mus). *Application deadline:* For spring admission, 3/1 priority date for domestic and international students. Applications are processed on a rolling basis. *Application fee:* $35. Electronic applications accepted. *Application Contact:* Dr. Patricia S. Foy, Interim Assistant Dean/Director of Graduate Studies in Music, 864-596-9021, Fax: 864-596-9167, E-mail: pattifoy@converse.edu. *Interim Dean,* Dr. Scott M. Robbins, Sr., 864-596-9021, Fax: 864-596-9167, E-mail: scott.robbins@converse.edu.

School of Education and Graduate Studies Students: 156 full-time (136 women), 1,069 part-time (847 women). Average age 35. 115 applicants, 88% accepted. *Faculty:* 13 full-time (8 women), 23 part-time/adjunct (16 women). Expenses: Contact institution. *Financial support:* In 2006–07, 500 students received support; research assistantships, career-related internships or fieldwork and scholarships/grants available. Support available to part-time students. Financial award applicants required to submit FAFSA. In 2006, 186 master's, 26 other advanced degrees awarded. *Degree program information:* Part-time and evening/weekend programs available. Offers administration and supervision (Ed S); art education (M Ed); biology (MAT); chemistry (MAT); curriculum and instruction (Ed S); early childhood education (MAT); education (Ed S); elementary education (M Ed, MAT); English (M Ed, MAT, MLA); gifted education (M Ed); history (MLA); leadership (M Ed); learning disabilities (MAT); liberal arts (MLA); marriage and family therapy (Ed S); mathematics (M Ed, MAT); mental disabilities (MAT); natural sciences (M Ed); political science (MLA); secondary education (M Ed, MAT); social sciences (M Ed, MAT); special education (M Ed, MAT). *Application deadline:* For fall admission, 8/1 for domestic and international students; for winter admission, 11/15 for domestic and international students; for spring admission, 1/15 for domestic and international students. Applications are processed on a rolling basis. *Application fee:* $40. Electronic applications accepted. *Dean of the School of Education and Graduate Studies,* Thomas M. Faulkenberry, 864-596-9082, Fax: 864-596-9221, E-mail: tom.faulkenberry@converse.edu.

CONWAY SCHOOL OF LANDSCAPE DESIGN, Conway, MA 01341-0179

General Information Independent, coed, graduate-only institution. *Graduate housing:* On-campus housing not available.

GRADUATE UNITS

Graduate Program in Landscape Design Offers landscape design/environmental planning (MA).

COOPER UNION FOR THE ADVANCEMENT OF SCIENCE AND ART, New York, NY 10003-7120

General Information Independent, coed, comprehensive institution. *Enrollment:* 968 graduate, professional, and undergraduate students; 41 full-time matriculated graduate/professional students (4 women), 7 part-time matriculated graduate/professional students. *Enrollment by degree level:* 48 master's. *Graduate faculty:* 14 full-time (1 woman), 1 part-time/adjunct (0 women). *Graduate tuition:* All students receive a full-tuition scholarship. *Graduate housing:* On-campus housing not available. *Student services:* Campus employment opportunities, campus safety program, career counseling, international student services, writing training. *Library facilities:* Cooper Union Library. *Online resources:* library catalog, web page, access to other libraries' catalogs. *Collection:* 103,289 titles, 4,254 serial subscriptions, 1,247 audiovisual materials. *Research affiliation:* Zimmer, Pfizer, Con Edison, Lucent, Howard Hughes Medical Institute, Transpo.

Computer facilities: 400 computers available on campus for general student use. A campuswide network can be accessed from student residence rooms and from off campus. Internet access is available. *Web address:* http://www.cooper.edu/.

General Application Contact: Student Contact, 212-353-4120, E-mail: admissions@cooper.edu.

GRADUATE UNITS

Albert Nerken School of Engineering Students: 41 full-time (4 women), 7 part-time; includes 19 minority (2 African Americans, 12 Asian Americans or Pacific Islanders, 5 Hispanic

Americans), 10 international. 44 applicants, 82% accepted, 28 enrolled. *Faculty:* 14 full-time (1 woman), 1 part-time/adjunct (0 women). Expenses: Contact institution. *Financial support:* In 2006–07, 48 students received support, including 3 fellowships with tuition reimbursements available (averaging $16,600 per year); career-related internships or fieldwork, Federal Work-Study, scholarships/grants, and tuition waivers (full) also available. Support available to part-time students. Financial award application deadline: 6/1; financial award applicants required to submit CSS PROFILE or FAFSA. In 2006, 24 degrees awarded. *Degree program information:* Part-time programs available. Offers chemical engineering (ME); civil engineering (ME); electrical engineering (ME); mechanical engineering (ME). *Application deadline:* For fall admission, 5/1 for domestic and international students. Applications are processed on a rolling basis. *Application fee:* $65. *Dean of Engineering*, Eleanor Baum, 212-353-4285, E-mail: baum@cooper.edu.

COPPIN STATE UNIVERSITY, Baltimore, MD 21216-3698

General Information State-supported, coed, comprehensive institution. CGS member. *Enrollment:* 177 full-time matriculated graduate/professional students (142 women), 207 part-time matriculated graduate/professional students (152 women). *Enrollment by degree level:* 384 master's. *Graduate faculty:* 35 full-time (22 women), 28 part-time/adjunct (15 women). *Graduate housing:* On-campus housing not available. *Student services:* Campus employment opportunities, campus safety program, career counseling, disabled student services, exercise/wellness program, free psychological counseling, international student services, low-cost health insurance, teacher training, writing training. *Library facilities:* Parlett L. Moore Library. *Online resources:* library catalog. *Collection:* 134,983 titles, 665 serial subscriptions.

Computer facilities: 130 computers available on campus for general student use. A campuswide network can be accessed from off campus. Internet access is available. *Web address:* http://www.coppin.edu/.

General Application Contact: Dr. Mary Owens, Dean, Graduate Studies and Research Evaluation, 410-951-3090, Fax: 410-951-3092, E-mail: mowens@coppin.edu.

GRADUATE UNITS

Division of Graduate Studies Students: 177 full-time (142 women), 207 part-time (152 women); includes 342 minority (341 African Americans, 1 American Indian/Alaska Native), 12 international. Average age 38. 175 applicants, 77% accepted, 111 enrolled. *Faculty:* 35 full-time (22 women), 28 part-time/adjunct (15 women). Expenses: Contact institution. *Financial support:* In 2006–07, 51 students received support. Career-related internships or fieldwork, Federal Work-Study, institutionally sponsored loans, and scholarships/grants available. Support available to part-time students. Financial award application deadline: 6/30; financial award applicants required to submit FAFSA. In 2006, 85 degrees awarded. *Degree program information:* Part-time and evening/weekend programs available. Postbaccalaureate distance learning degree programs offered. *Application deadline:* For fall admission, 8/15 priority date for domestic and international students; for spring admission, 12/15 priority date for domestic and international students. Applications are processed on a rolling basis. *Application fee:* $45. *Dean, Graduate Studies and Research Evaluation*, Dr. Mary Owens, 410-951-3090, Fax: 410-951-3092, E-mail: mowens@coppin.edu.

Division of Arts and Sciences Students: 118 full-time (94 women), 76 part-time (56 women); includes 185 minority (184 African Americans, 1 American Indian/Alaska Native), 6 international. Average age 38. 58 applicants, 76% accepted, 32 enrolled. *Faculty:* 13 full-time (5 women), 15 part-time/adjunct (7 women). Expenses: Contact institution. *Financial support:* Career-related internships or fieldwork, Federal Work-Study, institutionally sponsored loans, and scholarships/grants available. Support available to part-time students. Financial award application deadline: 6/30; financial award applicants required to submit FAFSA. In 2006, 49 degrees awarded. *Degree program information:* Part-time and evening/weekend programs available. Offers alcohol and substance abuse counseling (MS); arts and sciences (M Ed, MS); criminal justice (MS); human services administration (MS); rehabilitation counseling (M Ed). *Application deadline:* For fall admission, 8/15 priority date for domestic and international students; for spring admission, 12/15 priority date for domestic and international students. Applications are processed on a rolling basis. *Application fee:* $45. *Dean*, Dr. Clyde Mathura, 410-951-3020, E-mail: cmathura@coppin.edu.

Division of Education Students: 34 full-time (25 women), 126 part-time (91 women); includes 131 minority (all African Americans), 4 international. Average age 37. 97 applicants, 76% accepted, 66 enrolled. *Faculty:* 18 full-time (13 women), 8 part-time/adjunct (4 women). Expenses: Contact institution. *Financial support:* Career-related internships or fieldwork, Federal Work-Study, institutionally sponsored loans, and scholarships/grants available. Support available to part-time students. Financial award application deadline: 6/30; financial award applicants required to submit FAFSA. In 2006, 21 degrees awarded. *Degree program information:* Part-time and evening/weekend programs available. Postbaccalaureate distance learning degree programs offered. Offers adult and general education (MS); curriculum and instruction (M Ed, MA, MS); reading education (MS); special education (M Ed); teacher education (MA); teaching (MA). *Application deadline:* For fall admission, 8/15 priority date for domestic students; for spring admission, 12/15 priority date for domestic students. Applications are processed on a rolling basis. *Application fee:* $45. *Chair*, Dr. Julius Chapman, 410-951-3082, Fax: 410-951-3089, E-mail: jchapman@coppin.edu.

Helene Fuld School of Nursing Students: 25 full-time (23 women), 5 part-time (all women); includes 26 minority (all African Americans), 2 international. Average age 36. 20 applicants, 85% accepted, 13 enrolled. *Faculty:* 4 full-time (all women), 5 part-time/adjunct (4 women). Expenses: Contact institution. *Financial support:* Career-related internships or fieldwork, Federal Work-Study, institutionally sponsored loans, and scholarships/grants available. Support available to part-time students. Financial award application deadline: 6/30; financial award applicants required to submit FAFSA. In 2006, 15 degrees awarded. *Degree program information:* Part-time and evening/weekend programs available. Offers family nurse practitioner (PMC); nursing (MSN). *Application deadline:* For fall admission, 5/30 for domestic students. Applications are processed on a rolling basis. *Application fee:* $45. *Dean*, Dr. Marcella Copes, 410-951-3991, Fax: 410-462-3032, E-mail: mcopes@coppin.edu.

CORCORAN COLLEGE OF ART AND DESIGN, Washington, DC 20006-4804

General Information Independent, coed, comprehensive institution. *Enrollment:* 592 graduate, professional, and undergraduate students; 33 full-time matriculated graduate/professional students (32 women), 14 part-time matriculated graduate/professional students (13 women). *Enrollment by degree level:* 47 master's. *Graduate housing:* Rooms and/or apartments available on a first-come, first-served basis to single and married students. Typical cost: $2,400 per year ($11,700 including board) for single students; $2,400 per year ($11,700 including board) for married students. Housing application deadline: 5/15. *Student services:* Campus employment opportunities, career counseling, grant writing training, international student services, teacher training, writing training. *Library facilities:* Corcoran School of Art Library plus 1 other. *Online resources:* library catalog. *Collection:* 29,413 titles, 167 serial subscriptions.

Computer facilities: 117 computers available on campus for general student use. Internet access, online course and grade information, wireless network in classes are available. *Web address:* http://www.corcoran.edu/.

General Application Contact: Elizabeth S. Paladino, Director of Admission, 202-639-1814, Fax: 202-639-1830.

GRADUATE UNITS

Graduate Programs Students: 77 full-time (72 women), 48 part-time (44 women); includes 11 minority (7 African Americans, 2 Asian Americans or Pacific Islanders, 2 Hispanic Americans), 10 international. Average age 31. 103 applicants, 78% accepted, 49 enrolled. Expenses: Contact institution. *Financial support:* In 2006–07, 10 fellowships (averaging $3,000 per year) were awarded; career-related internships or fieldwork and Federal Work-Study also available. Financial award applicants required to submit FAFSA. In 2006, 2 degrees awarded. *Degree program information:* Part-time programs available. *Application deadline:* For fall and spring admission, 3/15 priority date for domestic and international students. Applications are processed on a rolling basis. *Application fee:* $75.

CORNELL UNIVERSITY, Ithaca, NY 14853-0001

General Information Independent, coed, university. CGS member. *Enrollment:* 19,639 graduate, professional, and undergraduate students; 6,077 full-time matriculated graduate/professional students (2,533 women). *Enrollment by degree level:* 896 first professional, 2,344 master's, 2,684 doctoral. *Graduate faculty:* 1,548 full-time (391 women), 85 part-time/adjunct (17 women). *Tuition:* Full-time $32,800. Full-time tuition and fees vary according to program. *Graduate housing:* Rooms and/or apartments available on a first-come, first-served basis to single and married students. Typical cost: $10,776 (including board) for single students; $10,776 (including board) for married students. Room and board charges vary according to board plan and housing facility selected. *Student services:* Campus employment opportunities, campus safety program, career counseling, disabled student services, exercise/wellness program, free psychological counseling, grant writing training, international student services, low-cost health insurance, teacher training, writing training. *Library facilities:* Olin Library plus 17 others. *Online resources:* library catalog, web page. *Collection:* 7.2 million titles, 64,760 serial subscriptions, 427,798 audiovisual materials. *Research affiliation:* Boyce Thompson Institute for Plant Research, Fermi National Accelerator Laboratory, Brookhaven National Laboratory.

Computer facilities: Computer purchase and lease plans are available. 3,000 computers available on campus for general student use. A campuswide network can be accessed from student residence rooms and from off campus. Internet access and online class registration are available. *Web address:* http://www.cornell.edu/.

General Application Contact: Graduate School Application Requests, Caldwell Hall, 607-255-4884, E-mail: gradadmissions@cornell.edu.

GRADUATE UNITS

College of Veterinary Medicine Students: 479 full-time (355 women); includes 94 minority (24 African Americans, 1 American Indian/Alaska Native, 31 Asian Americans or Pacific Islanders, 38 Hispanic Americans), 67 international. Average age 26. 853 applicants, 12% accepted, 84 enrolled. *Faculty:* 156 full-time (48 women). Expenses: Contact institution. *Financial support:* In 2006–07, 452 students received support, including 30 fellowships (averaging $27,162 per year), 119 research assistantships with tuition reimbursements available (averaging $27,162 per year); Federal Work-Study, institutionally sponsored loans, scholarships/grants, and unspecified assistantships also available. Financial award application deadline: 2/1; financial award applicants required to submit CSS PROFILE or FAFSA. In 2006, 85 DVMs, 15 doctorates awarded. Offers comparative biomedical science (PhD); immunology (PhD); pharmacology (PhD); physiology (PhD); veterinary medicine (DVM); zoology (PhD). *Application deadline:* For fall admission, 10/1 for domestic and international students. *Application fee:* $40. Electronic applications accepted. *Application Contact:* Jennifer A. Mailey, Director of Admissions, 607-253-3700, Fax: 607-253-3709, E-mail: jam333@cornell.edu. *Dean*, Dr. Donald F. Smith, 607-253-3771.

Cornell Law School Students: 632 full-time (307 women). Average age 25. 5,131 applicants. *Faculty:* 57 full-time (16 women), 51 part-time/adjunct (12 women). Expenses: Contact institution. *Financial support:* In 2006–07, 250 students received support. Career-related internships or fieldwork, Federal Work-Study, and scholarships/grants available. Financial award application deadline: 3/15; financial award applicants required to submit FAFSA. In 2006, 192 JDs, 56 master's awarded. Offers law (JD, LL M). JD/MLLP offered jointly with Humboldt University, Berlin; JD/DESS offered jointly with Institut d[0092][00c9]tudes Politiques de Paris ('Sciences Po") and Paris I. *Application deadline:* For fall admission, 2/1 for domestic students. Applications are processed on a rolling basis. *Application fee:* $70. Electronic applications accepted. *Application Contact:* Richard D. Geiger, Associate Dean, 607-255-5141, Fax: 607-255-7193, E-mail: rdg9@cornell.edu. *Dean*, Stewart J. Schawb, 607-255-3527.

Graduate School Students: 5,181 full-time (1,994 women); includes 687 minority (125 African Americans, 11 American Indian/Alaska Native, 393 Asian Americans or Pacific Islanders, 158 Hispanic Americans), 2,105 international. Average age 24. 13,271 applicants, 25% accepted, 1405 enrolled. *Faculty:* 1,548 full-time (391 women), 85 part-time/adjunct (17 women). Expenses: Contact institution. *Financial support:* In 2006–07, 3,448 students received support, including 1,018 fellowships with full tuition reimbursements available, 1,224 research assistantships with full tuition reimbursements available, 1,206 teaching assistantships with full tuition reimbursements available; career-related internships or fieldwork, institutionally sponsored loans, scholarships/grants, traineeships, tuition waivers (full and partial), and unspecified assistantships also available. Financial award applicants required to submit FAFSA. In 2006, 1,247 master's, 498 doctorates awarded. Offers acarology (MS, PhD); advanced composites and structures (M Eng); advanced materials processing (M Eng, MS, PhD); aerospace engineering (M Eng, MS, PhD); African history (MA, PhD); African studies (MPS); African-American literature (PhD); African-American studies (MPS); agricultural economics (MPS, MS, PhD); agricultural education (MAT); agriculture and life sciences (M Eng, MAT, MFS, MLA, MPS, MS, PhD); agronomy (MS, PhD); algorithms (M Eng, PhD); American art (PhD); American history (MA, PhD); American literature after 1865 (PhD); American literature to 1865 (PhD); American politics (PhD); American studies (PhD); analytical chemistry (PhD); ancient art and archaeology (PhD); ancient history (MA, PhD); ancient Near Eastern studies (MA, PhD); ancient philosophy (PhD); animal breeding (MS, PhD); animal cytology (MS, PhD); animal genetics (MS, PhD); animal nutrition (MPS, MS, PhD); animal science (MPS, MS, PhD); apiculture (MS, PhD); apparel design (MA, MPS); applied economics (PhD); applied entomology (MS, PhD); applied linguistics (MA, PhD); applied logic and automated reasoning (M Eng, PhD); applied mathematics (PhD); applied mathematics and computational methods (M Eng, MS, PhD); applied physics (PhD); applied probability and statistics (PhD); applied research in human-environment relations (MS); applied statistics (MPS); aquatic entomology (MS, PhD); aquatic science (MPS, MS, PhD); Arabic and Islamic studies (MA, PhD); archaeological anthropology (PhD); artificial intelligence (M Eng, PhD); arts and sciences (MA, MFA, MPA, MPS, MS, DMA, PhD); Asian art (PhD); Asian religions (MA, PhD); astronomy (PhD); astrophysics (PhD); atmospheric science (MS, PhD); baroque art (PhD); basic analytical economics (PhD); behavioral biology (PhD); behavioral physiology (MS, PhD); biblical studies (MA, PhD); bio-organic chemistry (PhD); biochemical engineering (M Eng, MS, PhD); biochemistry (PhD); biological anthropology (PhD); biological control (MS, PhD); biological engineering (M Eng, MPS, MS, PhD); biology (7-12) (MAT); biomechanical engineering (M Eng, MS, PhD); biomedical engineering (M Eng, MS, PhD); biometry (MS, PhD); biophysical chemistry (PhD); biophysics (PhD); biopsychology (PhD); cardiovascular and respiratory physiology (MS, PhD); cell biology (PhD); cellular and molecular medicine (MS, PhD); cellular and molecular toxicology (MS, PhD); cellular immunology (MS, PhD); chemical biology (PhD); chemical physics (PhD); chemical reaction engineering (M Eng, MS, PhD); chemistry (7-12) (MAT); Chinese linguistics (MA, PhD); Chinese philology (MA, PhD); classical and statistical thermodynamics (M Eng, MS, PhD); classical archaeology (PhD); classical Chinese literature (MA, PhD); classical Japanese literature (MA, PhD); classical myth (PhD); classical rhetoric (PhD); cognition (PhD); collective bargaining, labor law and labor history (MILR, MPS, MS, PhD); colonial and postcolonial literature (PhD); combustion (M Eng, MS, PhD); communication (MPS, MS, PhD); communication research methods (MS, PhD); community and regional society (MS); community and regional sociology (MPS, PhD); community development process (MPS); community nutrition (MPS, MS, PhD); comparative and functional anatomy (MS, PhD); comparative biomedical sciences (MS, PhD); comparative literature (PhD); comparative politics (PhD); composition (DMA); computer engineering (M Eng, PhD); computer graphics (M Eng, PhD); computer science (M Eng, PhD); computer vision (M Eng, PhD); concurrency and distributed computing (M Eng, PhD); consumer policy (PhD); controlled environment agriculture (MPS, PhD); controlled environment horticulture (MS); creative writing (MFA); cultural studies (PhD); curriculum and instruction (MPS, MS, PhD); cytology (MS, PhD); dairy science (MPS, MS, PhD); decision theory (MS, PhD); development policy (MPS); developmental and reproductive biology (MS, PhD); developmental biology (MS, PhD); developmental psychology (PhD); drama and the theatre (PhD); dramatic literature (PhD); dynamics and space mechanics (MS, PhD); early modern European history (MA, PhD); earth science (7-12) (MAT); East Asian linguistics (MA, PhD); East Asian studies (MA); ecological and environmental plant pathology (MPS, MS, PhD); ecology (MS, PhD); econometrics and economic statistics (PhD); economic and social statistics (MILR, MS, PhD); economic development (MPS); economic development and planning (PhD); economic geology (M Eng, MS, PhD); economic theory (PhD); economy and society (MA, PhD);

Cornell University (continued)

ecotoxicology and environmental chemistry (MS, PhD); electrical engineering (M Eng, PhD); electrical systems (M Eng, PhD); electrophysics (M Eng, PhD); endocrinology (MS, PhD); energy (M Eng, MPS, MS, PhD); energy and power systems (M Eng, MS, PhD); engineering (M Eng, MS, PhD); engineering geology (M Eng, MS, PhD); engineering management (M Eng, MS, PhD); engineering physics (M Eng); engineering statistics (MS, PhD); English history (MA, PhD); English linguistics (MA, PhD); English poetry (PhD); English Renaissance to 1660 (PhD); environmental and comparative physiology (MS, PhD); environmental archaeology (MA); environmental engineering (M Eng, MPS, MS, PhD); environmental fluid mechanics and hydrology (M Eng, MS, PhD); environmental geophysics (M Eng, MS, PhD); environmental information science (MS, PhD); environmental management (MPS); environmental systems engineering (M Eng, MS, PhD); epidemiological plant pathology (MPS, MS, PhD); evaluation (PhD); evolutionary biology (PhD); experimental design (MS, PhD); experimental physics (MS, PhD); extension, and adult education (MPS, MS, PhD); facilities planning and management (MS); family and social welfare policy (PhD); fiber science (MS, PhD); field crop science (MS, PhD); fishery science (MPS, MS, PhD); fluid dynamics, rheology and biorheology (M Eng, MS, PhD); fluid mechanics (M Eng, MS, PhD); food chemistry (MPS, MS, PhD); food engineering (MPS, MS, PhD); food microbiology (MPS, MS, PhD); food processing engineering (M Eng, MPS, MS, PhD); food processing waste technology (MPS, MS, PhD); food science (MFS, MPS, MS, PhD); forest science (MPS, MS, PhD); French history (MA, PhD); French linguistics (PhD); French literature (PhD); gastrointestinal and metabolic physiology (MS, PhD); gender and life course (MA, PhD); general geology (M Eng, MS, PhD); general linguistics (MA, PhD); general space sciences (PhD); genetics (PhD); geobiology (M Eng, MS, PhD); geochemistry and isotope geology (M Eng, MS, PhD); geohydrology (M Eng, MS, PhD); geomorphology (M Eng, MS, PhD); geophysics (M Eng, MS, PhD); geotechnical engineering (M Eng, MS, PhD); geotectonics (M Eng, MS, PhD); German area studies (MA, PhD); German history (MA, PhD); German intellectual history (MA, PhD); Germanic linguistics (MA, PhD); Germanic literature (MA, PhD); Greek and Latin language and linguistics (PhD); Greek language and literature (PhD); greenhouse crops (MPS, MS, PhD); health administration (MHA); health management and policy (PhD); heat and mass transfer (M Eng, MS, PhD); heat transfer (M Eng, MS, PhD); Hebrew and Judaic studies (MA, PhD); Hispanic literature (PhD); histology (MS, PhD); historical archaeology (MA); history and philosophy of science and technology (MA, PhD); history of science (MA, PhD); horticultural business management (MPS, MS, PhD); horticultural physiology (MPS, MS, PhD); hospitality management (MMH); hotel administration (MS, PhD); housing and design (MS); human computer interaction (PhD); human development and family studies (PhD); human ecology (MA, MHA, MPS, MS, PhD); human experimental psychology (PhD); human factors and ergonomics (MS); human nutrition (MPS, MS, PhD); human resource studies (MILR, MPS, MS, PhD); human-environment relations (MS); immunochemistry (MS, PhD); immunogenetics (MS, PhD); immunopathology (MS, PhD); Indo-European linguistics (MA, PhD); industrial and labor relations problems (MILR, MPS, MS, PhD); industrial organization and control (PhD); infection and immunity (MS, PhD); infectious diseases (MS, PhD); information organization and retrieval (M Eng, PhD); information systems (PhD); infrared astronomy (PhD); inorganic chemistry (PhD); insect behavior (MS, PhD); insect biochemistry (MS, PhD); insect ecology (MS, PhD); insect genetics (MS, PhD); insect morphology (MS, PhD); insect pathology (MS, PhD); insect physiology (MS, PhD); insect systematics (MS, PhD); insect toxicology and insecticide chemistry (MS, PhD); integrated pest management (MS, PhD); interior design (MA, MPS); international agriculture (M Eng, MPS, MS, PhD); international agriculture and development (MPS); international and comparative labor (MILR, MPS, MS, PhD); international communication (MS, PhD); international economics (PhD); international food science (MPS, MS, PhD); international nutrition (MPS, MS, PhD); international planning (MPS); international population (MPS); international relations (PhD); Italian linguistics (PhD); Italian literature (PhD); Japanese linguistics (MA, PhD); kinetics and catalysis (M Eng, MS, PhD); Korean literature (MA, PhD); labor economics (MILR, MPS, MS, PhD); landscape architecture (MLA); landscape horticulture (MPS, MS, PhD); Latin American archaeology (MA); Latin American history (MA, PhD); Latin language and literature (PhD); lesbian, bisexual, and gay literature studies (PhD); literary criticism and theory (PhD); local government organizations and operations (MPS); local roads (M Eng, MPS, MS, PhD); machine systems (M Eng, MPS, MS, PhD); manufacturing systems engineering (PhD); marine geology (MS, PhD); materials and manufacturing engineering (M Eng, MS, PhD); materials chemistry (PhD); materials engineering (M Eng, PhD); materials science (M Eng, PhD); mathematical programming (PhD); mathematical statistics (MS, PhD); mathematics (PhD); mathematics (7-12) (MAT); mechanical systems and design (M Eng, MS, PhD); mechanics of materials (MS, PhD); medical and veterinary entomology (MS, PhD); medieval and Renaissance Latin literature (PhD); medieval archaeology (MA, PhD); medieval art (PhD); medieval Chinese history (MA, PhD); medieval history (MA, PhD); medieval literature (PhD); medieval music (PhD); medieval philology and linguistics (PhD); medieval philosophy (PhD); Mediterranean and Near Eastern archaeology (MA); membrane and epithelial physiology (MS, PhD); methodology (MA, PhD); methods of social research (MPS, MS, PhD); microbiology (PhD); mineralogy (M Eng, MS, PhD); modern art (PhD); modern Chinese history (MA, PhD); modern Chinese literature (MA, PhD); modern European history (MA, PhD); modern Japanese history (MA, PhD); modern Japanese literature (MA, PhD); molecular and cell biology (PhD); molecular and cellular physiology (MS, PhD); molecular biology (PhD); molecular plant pathology (MPS, MS, PhD); monetary and macroeconomics (PhD); multiphase flows (M Eng, MS, PhD); musicology (PhD); mycology (MPS, MS, PhD); neural and sensory physiology (MS, PhD); neurobiology (PhD); nineteenth century (PhD); nuclear engineering (M Eng, MS, PhD); nuclear science (MS, PhD); nursery crops (MPS, MS, PhD); nutrition of horticultural crops (MPS, MS, PhD); nutritional and food toxicology (MS, PhD); nutritional biochemistry (MPS, MS, PhD); Old and Middle English (PhD); old Norse (MA, PhD); operating systems (M Eng, PhD); operations research and industrial engineering (M Eng); organic chemistry (PhD); organizational behavior (MILR, MPS, MS, PhD); organizations (MA, PhD); organometallic chemistry (PhD); paleobotany (MS, PhD); paleontology (M Eng, MS, PhD); parallel computing (M Eng, PhD); performance practice (DMA); personality and social psychology (PhD); petroleum geology (M Eng, MS, PhD); petrology (M Eng, MS, PhD); pharmacology (MS, PhD); philosophy (PhD); phonetics (MA, PhD); phonological theory (MA, PhD); physical chemistry (PhD); physics (MS, PhD); physics (7-12) (MAT); physiological genomics (MS, PhD); physiology of reproduction (MPS, MS, PhD); planetary geology (M Eng, MS, PhD); planetary studies (PhD); plant breeding (MPS, MS, PhD); plant cell biology (MS, PhD); plant disease epidemiology (MPS, MS, PhD); plant ecology (MS, PhD); plant genetics (MPS, MS, PhD); plant molecular biology (MS, PhD); plant morphology, anatomy and biomechanics (MS, PhD); plant pathology (MPS, MS, PhD); plant physiology (MS, PhD); plant propagation (MPS, MS, PhD); plant protection (MPS); policy analysis (MA, PhD); political methodology (PhD); political sociology/social movements (MA, PhD); political thought (PhD); polymer chemistry (PhD); polymer science (MS, PhD); polymers (M Eng, MS, PhD); pomology (MPS, MS, PhD); population and development (MPS, MS, PhD); population medicine and epidemiology (MS); population medicine and epidemiology sciences (PhD); Precambrian geology (M Eng, MS, PhD); premodern Islamic history (MA, PhD); premodern Japanese history (MA, PhD); probability (MS, PhD); program development and planning (MPS); programming environments (M Eng, PhD); programming languages and methodology (M Eng, PhD); prose fiction (PhD); public affairs (MPA); public finance (PhD); public garden management (MPS, MS, PhD); public policy (MPA, PhD); Quaternary geology (M Eng, MS, PhD); racial and ethnic relations (MA, PhD); radio astronomy (PhD); radiophysics (PhD); remote sensing (M Eng, MS, PhD); Renaissance art (PhD); Renaissance history (MA, PhD); reproductive physiology (MS, PhD); resource economics (MPS, MS, PhD); resource policy and management (MPS, MS, PhD); Restoration and eighteenth century (PhD); restoration ecology (MPS, MS, PhD); risk assessment, management and public policy (MS, PhD); robotics (M Eng, PhD); rock mechanics (M Eng, MS, PhD); Romance linguistics (MA, PhD); rural and environmental sociology (MPS, MS, PhD); Russian history (MA, PhD); sampling (MS, PhD); science and environmental communication (MS, PhD); science and technology policy (MPS); scientific computing (M Eng, PhD); second language acquisition (MA, PhD); sedimentology (M Eng, MS, PhD); seismology (M Eng, MS, PhD); semantics (MA, PhD); sensory evaluation (MPS, MS, PhD); Slavic linguistics (MA, PhD); social aspects of information (PhD); social networks (MA, PhD); social psychology (MA, PhD); social psychology of communication (MS, PhD); social stratification (MA, PhD); social studies of science and technology (MA, PhD); sociocultural anthropology (PhD); sociolinguistics (MA, PhD); soil and water engineering (M Eng, MPS, MS, PhD); soil science (MS, PhD); solid mechanics (MS, PhD); South Asian linguistics (MA, PhD); South Asian studies (MA); Southeast Asian art (PhD); Southeast Asian history (MA, PhD); Southeast Asian linguistics (MA, PhD); Southeast Asian studies (MA); Spanish linguistics (PhD); state, economy and society (MS); state, economy, and society (MPS, PhD); statistical computing (MS, PhD); statistics (MPS, MS, PhD); stochastic processes (MS, PhD); Stone Age archaeology (MA); stratigraphy (M Eng, MS, PhD); structural and functional biology (MS, PhD); structural engineering (M Eng, MS, PhD); structural geology (M Eng, MS, PhD); structural mechanics (M Eng, MS); structures and environment (M Eng, MPS, MS, PhD); surface science (M Eng, MS, PhD); syntactic theory (MA, PhD); systematic botany (MS, PhD); systems engineering (M Eng); taxonomy of ornamental plants (MPS, MS, PhD); textile science (MS, PhD); theatre history (PhD); theatre theory and aesthetics (PhD); theoretical astrophysics (PhD); theoretical chemistry (PhD); theoretical physics (MS, PhD); theory and criticism (PhD); theory of computation (M Eng, PhD); theory of music (MA); transportation engineering (MS, PhD); transportation systems engineering (M Eng); turfgrass science (MPS, MS, PhD); twentieth century (PhD); urban horticulture (MPS, MS, PhD); uses and effects of communication (MS, PhD); vegetable crops (MPS, MS, PhD); water resource systems (M Eng, MS, PhD); weed science (MPS, MS, PhD); wildlife science (MPS, MS, PhD); women's literature (PhD). *Application deadline:* For fall admission, 1/15 for domestic and international students; for spring admission, 11/1 for domestic and international students. *Application fee:* $70. Electronic applications accepted. *Application Contact:* Graduate School Application Requests, 607-255-5816, E-mail: gradadmissions@cornell.edu. *Dean*, Dr. Alison G. Power, 607-255-5417.

Field of Environmental Management Expenses: Contact institution. Offers environmental management (MPS). *Application Contact:* Tad McGalliard, Education Coordinator, 607-255-9996, Fax: 607-255-0238, E-mail: tnm2@cornell.edu.

Graduate Field in the Law School Students: 73 full-time (38 women); includes 7 minority (4 Asian Americans or Pacific Islanders, 3 Hispanic Americans), 41 international. Average age 29. 856 applicants, 32% accepted, 61 enrolled. *Faculty:* 37 full-time (9 women). Expenses: Contact institution. *Financial support:* In 2006–07, 8 students received support, including 8 fellowships with full tuition reimbursements available; research assistantships with full tuition reimbursements available, teaching assistantships with full tuition reimbursements available, institutionally sponsored loans, scholarships/grants, health care benefits, tuition waivers (full and partial), and unspecified assistantships also available. Financial award applicants required to submit FAFSA. In 2006, 64 master's, 5 doctorates awarded. Offers law (LL M, JSD). *Application deadline:* For fall admission, 5/1 for domestic students. *Application fee:* $60. Electronic applications accepted. *Application Contact:* Graduate Field Assistant, 607-255-5141, E-mail: gradlaw@law.mail.cornell.edu. *Director of Graduate Studies*, 607-255-5141.

Graduate Field of Management Students: 38 full-time (14 women); includes 2 minority (both Asian Americans or Pacific Islanders), 20 international. Average age 31. 457 applicants, 5% accepted, 8 enrolled. *Faculty:* 57 full-time (11 women). Expenses: Contact institution. *Financial support:* In 2006–07, 37 students received support, including 2 fellowships with full tuition reimbursements available, 31 research assistantships with full tuition reimbursements available, 4 teaching assistantships with full tuition reimbursements available; institutionally sponsored loans, scholarships/grants, health care benefits, tuition waivers (full and partial), and unspecified assistantships also available. Financial award applicants required to submit FAFSA. In 2006, 4 doctorates awarded. Offers accounting (PhD); behavioral decision theory (PhD); finance (PhD); marketing (PhD); organizational behavior (PhD); production and operations management (PhD). *Application deadline:* For fall admission, 1/3 for domestic students. *Application fee:* $60. Electronic applications accepted. *Application Contact:* Graduate Field Assistant, 607-255-9431, E-mail: js_phd@cornell.edu. *Director of Graduate Studies*, 607-255-3669.

Graduate Fields of Architecture, Art and Planning Students: 269 full-time (138 women); includes 35 minority (12 African Americans, 15 Asian Americans or Pacific Islanders, 8 Hispanic Americans), 100 international. Average age 29. 612 applicants, 29% accepted, 89 enrolled. *Faculty:* 108 full-time (22 women). Expenses: Contact institution. *Financial support:* In 2006–07, 136 students received support, including 30 fellowships with full tuition reimbursements available, 48 research assistantships with full tuition reimbursements available, 58 teaching assistantships with full tuition reimbursements available; institutionally sponsored loans, scholarships/grants, health care benefits, tuition waivers (full and partial), and unspecified assistantships also available. Financial award applicants required to submit FAFSA. In 2006, 75 master's, 6 doctorates awarded. Offers architectural design (M Arch); architectural science (MS); architecture, art and planning (M Arch, MA, MFA, MPSRE, MRP, MS, PhD); building technology and environmental science (MS); city and regional planning (MRP, PhD); computer graphics (MS); creative visual arts (MFA); environmental planning and design (MRP, PhD); environmental studies (MA, MS, PhD); historic preservation planning (MA); history of architecture (MA, PhD); history of urban development (MA, PhD); international development planning (MRP, PhD); international spatial problems (MA, MS, PhD); location theory (MA, MS, PhD); multiregional economic analysis (MA, MS, PhD); peace science (MA, MS, PhD); planning methods (MA, MS, PhD); planning theory and systems analysis (MRP, PhD); real estate (MPSRE); regional economics and development planning (MRP, PhD); regional science (MRP, PhD); social and health systems planning (MRP, PhD); theory and criticism of architecture (M Arch); urban and regional economics (MA, MS, PhD); urban and regional theory (MRP, PhD); urban design (M Arch); urban planning history (MRP, PhD). *Application fee:* $60. Electronic applications accepted. *Application Contact:* Graduate School Application Requests, Caldwell Hall, 607-255-5820.

Johnson Graduate School of Management Students: 827 full-time (194 women); includes 147 minority (26 African Americans, 1 American Indian/Alaska Native, 98 Asian Americans or Pacific Islanders, 22 Hispanic Americans), 266 international. Average age 27. 2,043 applicants, 453 enrolled. *Faculty:* 53 full-time (12 women), 3 part-time/adjunct (0 women). Expenses: Contact institution. *Financial support:* Fellowships, research assistantships, career-related internships or fieldwork, Federal Work-Study, institutionally sponsored loans, and tuition waivers (full and partial) available. Financial award application deadline: 2/15; financial award applicants required to submit FAFSA. In 2006, 346 degrees awarded. Offers management (MBA). *Application deadline:* For fall admission, 4/1 for domestic students, 1/1 for international students. *Application fee:* $180. *Application Contact:* 800-847-2082, Fax: 607-254-8886, E-mail: mba@johnson.cornell.edu. *Dean*, Robert J. Swieringa, 607-255-6418.

CORNELL UNIVERSITY, JOAN AND SANFORD I. WEILL MEDICAL COLLEGE AND GRADUATE SCHOOL OF MEDICAL SCIENCES, New York, NY 10021-4896

General Information Independent, coed, graduate-only institution. *Enrollment by degree level:* 405 first professional, 17 master's, 324 doctoral, 67 other advanced degrees. *Graduate faculty:* 2,226 full-time (798 women), 2,049 part-time/adjunct (583 women). *Tuition:* Full-time $33,775. *Required fees:* $1,050. *Graduate housing:* Rooms and/or apartments guaranteed to single students and available to married students. *Student services:* Campus employment opportunities, campus safety program, career counseling, grant writing training, international student services, low-cost health insurance, multicultural affairs office. *Library facilities:* Samuel J. Wood Library and C.V. Starr Biomedical Information Center. *Online resources:* library catalog, web page, access to other libraries' catalogs. *Collection:* 171,933 titles, 4,234 serial subscriptions, 2,354 audiovisual materials. *Research affiliation:* Burke Medical Research Institute (neurology), Strong Cancer Prevention Center (cancer prevention).

Computer facilities: 173 computers available on campus for general student use. A campuswide network can be accessed from student residence rooms and from off campus. Internet access is available. *Web address:* http://www.med.cornell.edu/.

General Application Contact: Liliana Montano, Assistant Dean of Admissions, 212-746-1067, Fax: 212-746-8052, E-mail: cumc-admissions@med.cornell.edu.

GRADUATE UNITS

Weill Graduate School of Medical Sciences Students: 385 full-time (177 women); includes 47 minority (10 African Americans, 24 Asian Americans or Pacific Islanders, 13 Hispanic

Americans), 230 international. Average age 22. 600 applicants. *Faculty:* 246 full-time (64 women). Expenses: Contact institution. *Financial support:* In 2006–07, 4 fellowships (averaging $20,772 per year) were awarded; scholarships/grants, health care benefits, tuition waivers (full), and stipends also available. In 2006, 8 master's, 31 doctorates awarded. Offers biochemistry, cell and molecular biology (PhD); chemical biology and computational biology (PhD); clinical epidemiology and health services research (MS); immunology (MS, PhD); medical sciences (MS, PhD); neuroscience (PhD); pharmacology (PhD); physiology, biophysics and systems biology (PhD). *Application fee:* $60. Electronic applications accepted. *Dean,* Dr. David P. Hajjar, 212-746-6900, E-mail: dphajjar@med.cornell.edu.

Weill Medical College Students: 408 full-time (206 women); includes 177 minority (41 African Americans, 5 American Indian/Alaska Native, 100 Asian Americans or Pacific Islanders, 31 Hispanic Americans), 5 international. Average age 27. 5,235 applicants, 5% accepted, 101 enrolled. *Faculty:* 277 full-time (57 women). Expenses: Contact institution. *Financial support:* In 2006–07, 278 students received support. Federal Work-Study, institutionally sponsored loans, and scholarships/grants available. Financial award application deadline: 9/1; financial award applicants required to submit FAFSA. In 2006, 101 first professional degrees, 8 master's, 41 doctorates awarded. Offers medicine (MD, MS, PhD). *Application deadline:* For fall admission, 10/15 for domestic students. *Application fee:* $75. Electronic applications accepted. *Application Contact:* Liliana Montano, Assistant Dean of Admissions, 212-746-1067, Fax: 212-746-8052, E-mail: cumc-admissions@med.cornell.edu. *Dean,* Dr. Antonio Gotto, 212-746-6005, Fax: 212-746-8424, E-mail: dean@med.cornell.edu.

CORNERSTONE UNIVERSITY, Grand Rapids, MI 49525-5897

General Information Independent-religious, coed, comprehensive institution. *Graduate housing:* Rooms and/or apartments available on a first-come, first-served basis to single and married students.

GRADUATE UNITS

Graduate Programs *Degree program information:* Part-time programs available. Postbaccalaureate distance learning degree programs offered. Offers business administration (MBA); education (MA Ed); management (MSM); teaching English to speakers of other languages (MA, Graduate Certificate). Programs also offered at Holland, Kalamazoo, and Troy, MI campuses. Electronic applications accepted.

COVENANT COLLEGE, Lookout Mountain, GA 30750

General Information Independent-religious, coed, comprehensive institution. *Enrollment by degree level:* 64 master's. *Graduate faculty:* 4 full-time (1 woman), 9 part-time/adjunct (1 woman). *Tuition:* Part-time $410 per credit. *Graduate housing:* Room and/or apartments available on a first-come, first-served basis to single students; on-campus housing not available to married students. Housing application deadline: 5/1. *Student services:* Career counseling. *Library facilities:* Kresge Memorial Library. *Online resources:* library catalog, web page, access to other libraries' catalogs. *Collection:* 85,000 titles, 12,000 serial subscriptions, 4,500 audiovisual materials.

Computer facilities: 135 computers available on campus for general student use. A campuswide network can be accessed from student residence rooms and from off campus. Internet access and online class registration, online student information system are available. *Web address:* http://www.covenant.edu/.

General Application Contact: Rebecca Dodson, Associate Director, Program in Education, 706-419-1406, Fax: 706-820-0672, E-mail: rdodson@covenant.edu.

GRADUATE UNITS

Program in Education Students: 46 full-time (29 women), 18 part-time (11 women); includes 4 minority (3 African Americans, 1 Hispanic American), 2 international. Average age 37. 30 applicants, 97% accepted, 20 enrolled. *Faculty:* 4 full-time (1 woman), 9 part-time/adjunct (1 woman). Expenses: Contact institution. *Financial support:* In 2006–07, 33 students received support. Institutionally sponsored loans, scholarships/grants, and tuition waivers (partial) available. Support available to part-time students. Financial award application deadline: 3/1; financial award applicants required to submit FAFSA. In 2006, 23 degrees awarded. *Degree program information:* Part-time programs available. Offers education (M Ed). *Application deadline:* For fall admission, 3/31 priority date for domestic students. Applications are processed on a rolling basis. *Application fee:* $35. *Application Contact:* Rebecca Dodson, Associate Director, Program in Education, 706-419-1406, Fax: 706-820-0672, E-mail: rdodson@covenant.edu. *Director,* Dr. Jim Drexler, 706-419-1408.

COVENANT THEOLOGICAL SEMINARY, St. Louis, MO 63141-8697

General Information Independent-religious, coed, graduate-only institution. *Enrollment by degree level:* 344 first professional, 321 master's, 48 doctoral, 36 other advanced degrees. *Graduate faculty:* 21 full-time (0 women), 20 part-time/adjunct (5 women). *Tuition:* Full-time $9,000; part-time $360 per credit hour. *Graduate housing:* Rooms and/or apartments available on a first-come, first-served basis to single and married students. Typical cost: $3,660 per year for single students; $8,100 per year for married students. Room charges vary according to campus/location and housing facility selected. *Student services:* Campus employment opportunities, career counseling, disabled student services, free psychological counseling, international student services, writing training. *Library facilities:* J. Oliver Buswell Jr. Library. *Online resources:* library catalog, web page, access to other libraries' catalogs. *Collection:* 75,756 titles, 355 serial subscriptions, 3,378 audiovisual materials.

Computer facilities: 20 computers available on campus for general student use. A campuswide network can be accessed from off campus. Internet access and online class registration are available. *Web address:* http://www.covenantseminary.edu/.

General Application Contact: Rev. Brad Anderson, Senior Director of Enrollment, 314-434-4044, Fax: 314-434-4819, E-mail: admissions@coventseminary.edu.

GRADUATE UNITS

Graduate and Professional Programs Students: 342 full-time (73 women), 457 part-time (133 women); includes 117 minority (55 African Americans, 54 Asian Americans or Pacific Islanders, 8 Hispanic Americans), 20 international. Average age 36. 275 applicants, 82% accepted, 163 enrolled. *Faculty:* 21 full-time (0 women), 20 part-time/adjunct (5 women). Expenses: Contact institution. *Financial support:* In 2006–07, 588 students received support. Career-related internships or fieldwork, institutionally sponsored loans, scholarships/grants, and tuition waivers (full and partial) available. Support available to part-time students. Financial award application deadline: 4/17; financial award applicants required to submit FAFSA. In 2006, 59 first professional degrees, 43 master's, 12 doctorates, 7 other advanced degrees awarded. *Degree program information:* Part-time and evening/weekend programs available. Postbaccalaureate distance learning degree programs offered (minimal on-campus study). Offers theology (M Div, MA, MAC, MAEM, Th M, D Min, Certificate). *Application deadline:* Applications are processed on a rolling basis. *Application fee:* $50. Electronic applications accepted. *Application Contact:* Rev. Brad Anderson, Senior Director of Enrollment, 314-434-4044, Fax: 314-434-4819, E-mail: admissions@coventseminary.edu. *Vice President for Academics,* Dr. Sean Lucas, 314-434-4044.

CRANBROOK ACADEMY OF ART, Bloomfield Hills, MI 48303-0801

General Information Independent, coed, graduate-only institution. *Graduate housing:* Room and/or apartments available on a first-come, first-served basis to single students; on-campus housing not available to married students. Housing application deadline: 2/1.

GRADUATE UNITS

Graduate School Offers architecture (M Arch); ceramics (MFA); design (MFA); fiber arts (MFA); metalsmithing (MFA); painting (MFA); photography (MFA); printmaking (MFA); sculpture (MFA).

CREIGHTON UNIVERSITY, Omaha, NE 68178-0001

General Information Independent-religious, coed, university. CGS member. *Enrollment:* 6,981 graduate, professional, and undergraduate students; 2,417 full-time matriculated graduate/professional students (1,296 women), 489 part-time matriculated graduate/professional students (268 women). *Enrollment by degree level:* 2,351 first professional, 471 master's, 47 doctoral, 37 other advanced degrees. *Tuition:* Part-time $595 per credit hour. *Required fees:* $38 per semester. *Graduate housing:* Rooms and/or apartments available on a first-come, first-served basis to single and married students. Housing application deadline: 5/1. *Student services:* Campus employment opportunities, campus safety program, career counseling, child daycare facilities, disabled student services, exercise/wellness program, free psychological counseling, international student services, low-cost health insurance, multicultural affairs office, teacher training. *Library facilities:* Reinert Alumni Memorial Library plus 2 others. *Online resources:* library catalog, web page, access to other libraries' catalogs. *Collection:* 466,556 titles, 27,144 serial subscriptions, 9,502 audiovisual materials. *Research affiliation:* Creighton University Medical Center, Children's Memorial Hospital, Boys Town Institute for Communication Disorders in Children, Omaha Veterans Administration Hospital, Global Weather Central.

Computer facilities: Computer purchase and lease plans are available. 505 computers available on campus for general student use. A campuswide network can be accessed from student residence rooms and from off campus. Internet access and online class registration, online grade information, financial aid information are available. *Web address:* http://www.creighton.edu/.

General Application Contact: LuAnn M. Schwery, Coordinator of Graduate Programs, 402-280-2870, Fax: 402-280-5762, E-mail: lschwery@creighton.edu.

GRADUATE UNITS

Graduate School Students: 2,417 full-time (1,296 women), 489 part-time (268 women); includes 72 minority (32 African Americans, 3 American Indian/Alaska Native, 16 Asian Americans or Pacific Islanders, 21 Hispanic Americans), 72 international. Average age 30. 392 applicants, 62% accepted. *Faculty:* 280. Expenses: Contact institution. *Financial support:* In 2006–07, research assistantships with tuition reimbursements (averaging $15,700 per year), teaching assistantships with tuition reimbursements (averaging $15,700 per year) were awarded; career-related internships or fieldwork, institutionally sponsored loans, and tuition waivers (partial) also available. Support available to part-time students. Financial award applicants required to submit FAFSA. In 2006, 211 master's awarded. *Degree program information:* Part-time and evening/weekend programs available. *Application deadline:* For fall admission, 3/1 priority date for domestic and international students. Applications are processed on a rolling basis. *Application fee:* $40. Electronic applications accepted. *Application Contact:* LuAnn M. Schwery, Coordinator of Graduate Programs, 402-280-2870, Fax: 402-280-5762, E-mail: lschwery@creighton.edu. *Dean,* Dr. Gail M. Jenson, 402-280-2870, Fax: 402-280-5762, E-mail: gjenson@creighton.edu.

College of Arts and Sciences Students: 51 full-time (27 women), 159 part-time (94 women); includes 17 minority (7 African Americans, 1 American Indian/Alaska Native, 3 Asian Americans or Pacific Islanders, 6 Hispanic Americans), 9 international. 126 applicants, 73% accepted. Expenses: Contact institution. *Financial support:* In 2006–07, teaching assistantships (averaging $10,000 per year); tuition waivers (partial) also available. In 2006, 56 degrees awarded. *Degree program information:* Part-time and evening/weekend programs available. Offers arts and sciences (M Ed, MA, MLS, MS); atmospheric sciences (MS); Christian spirituality (MA); education (M Ed); educational leadership (MS); English (MA); guidance and counseling (MS); international relations (MA); liberal studies (MLS); ministry (MA); physics (MS); special populations in education (MS); theology (MA). *Application deadline:* For fall admission, 3/1 for domestic and international students. Applications are processed on a rolling basis. *Application fee:* $40. Electronic applications accepted. *Application Contact:* Dr. Gail M. Jenson, Dean, 402-280-2870, Fax: 402-280-5762, E-mail: gjenson@creighton.edu. *Interim Dean,* Dr. Robert E, Kennedy, 402-280-2431, E-mail: rekrek@creighton.edu.

Eugene C. Eppley College of Business Administration Students: 26 full-time (9 women), 124 part-time (27 women); includes 17 minority (9 African Americans, 5 Asian Americans or Pacific Islanders, 3 Hispanic Americans), 19 international. Average age 27. 46 applicants, 100% accepted, 27 enrolled. *Faculty:* 13 full-time (3 women), 5 part-time/adjunct (3 women). Expenses: Contact institution. *Financial support:* In 2006–07, 8 research assistantships with full tuition reimbursements (averaging $8,400 per year) were awarded; career-related internships or fieldwork, tuition waivers (partial), and unspecified assistantships also available. Financial award application deadline: 3/1. In 2006, 65 degrees awarded. *Degree program information:* Part-time and evening/weekend programs available. Offers business administration (MBA); information technology (MS); securities and portfolio management (MSAPM). *Application deadline:* For fall admission, 3/1 priority date for domestic students, 3/1 for international students; for spring admission, 10/1 priority date for domestic students, 10/1 for international students. Applications are processed on a rolling basis. *Application fee:* $40. Electronic applications accepted. *Application Contact:* Gail Hafer, Coordinator, 402-280-2829, Fax: 402-280-2172, E-mail: ghafer@creighton.edu. *Director,* Dr. Ravi Nath, 402-280-2439.

School of Dentistry Offers dentistry (DDS).

School of Law Students: 452 full-time (195 women), 16 part-time (7 women); includes 46 minority (10 African Americans, 3 American Indian/Alaska Native, 15 Asian Americans or Pacific Islanders, 18 Hispanic Americans), 1 international. Average age 24. 1,334 applicants, 40% accepted, 161 enrolled. *Faculty:* 26 full-time (6 women), 32 part-time/adjunct (8 women). Expenses: Contact institution. *Financial support:* In 2006–07, 419 students received support. Career-related internships or fieldwork, institutionally sponsored loans, scholarships/grants, and unspecified assistantships available. Support available to part-time students. Financial award application deadline: 7/1; financial award applicants required to submit FAFSA. In 2006, 148 degrees awarded. *Degree program information:* Part-time programs available. Offers law (JD, MS); negotiation and dispute resolution (MS). *Application deadline:* For fall admission, 5/1 priority date for domestic students. Applications are processed on a rolling basis. *Application fee:* $45. Electronic applications accepted. *Application Contact:* Andrea D. Bashara, Assistant Dean, 402-280-2872, Fax: 402-280-3161, E-mail: bashara@creighton.edu. *Dean,* Patrick J. Borchers, 402-280-2874, Fax: 402-280-3161.

School of Medicine Students: 498 full-time (234 women); includes 82 minority (13 African Americans, 10 American Indian/Alaska Native, 29 Asian Americans or Pacific Islanders, 30 Hispanic Americans), 2 international. Average age 25. 4,884 applicants, 6% accepted, 126 enrolled. *Faculty:* 290 full-time (98 women), 24 part-time/adjunct (11 women). Expenses: Contact institution. *Financial support:* In 2006–07, 478 students received support; fellowships with full tuition reimbursements available, research assistantships with tuition reimbursements available, teaching assistantships with tuition reimbursements available, career-related internships or fieldwork, Federal Work-Study, institutionally sponsored loans, and tuition waivers (full and partial) available. Support available to part-time students. Financial award application deadline: 4/1. In 2006, 102 MDs, 13 master's, 115 doctorates awarded. Offers biomedical sciences (MS, PhD); clinical anatomy (MS); medical microbiology and immunology (MS, PhD); medicine (MD, MS, PhD); pharmaceutical sciences (MS); pharmacology (MS, PhD). *Application deadline:* For fall admission, 11/1 for domestic and international students. Applications are processed on a rolling basis. Electronic applications accepted. *Dean,* Dr. Cam E. Enarson, 402-280-2600, Fax: 402-280-2599.

School of Nursing Students: 35 full-time (31 women), 35 part-time (32 women); includes 4 minority (1 African American, 1 Asian American or Pacific Islander, 2 Hispanic Americans). Average age 35. 33 applicants, 91% accepted, 27 enrolled. *Faculty:* 16 full-time (all women), 1 (woman) part-time/adjunct. Expenses: Contact institution. *Financial support:* Career-related internships or fieldwork, Federal Work-Study, institutionally sponsored loans, and traineeships available. Financial award applicants required to submit FAFSA. In 2006, 24 degrees awarded. *Degree program information:* Part-time programs available. Postbaccalaureate distance learning degree programs offered (minimal on-campus study). Offers nursing (MS). *Application deadline:* For fall admission, 3/15 priority date for domestic and international students; for spring admission, 10/15 priority date for domestic and international students. Applications are processed on a rolling basis. *Application fee:* $40. Electronic

Creighton University (continued)

applications accepted. *Application Contact:* Dr. Mary Kunes-Connell, Associate Dean for Academic and Clinical Affairs, 402-280-2024, Fax: 402-280-2045, E-mail: mkc@creighton.edu. *Dean,* Dr. Eleanor V. Howell, 402-280-2004, Fax: 402-280-2045, E-mail: howell@creighton.edu.

School of Pharmacy and Health Professions Postbaccalaureate distance learning degree programs offered (no on-campus study). Offers occupational therapy (OTD); pharmaceutical sciences (MS); pharmacy (Pharm D); pharmacy and health professions (Pharm D, MS, DPT, OTD); physical therapy (DPT). Electronic applications accepted.

THE CRISWELL COLLEGE, Dallas, TX 75246-1537

General Information Independent-religious, coed, comprehensive institution. *Graduate housing:* On-campus housing not available.

GRADUATE UNITS

Graduate School of the Bible *Degree program information:* Part-time programs available. Offers biblical studies (M Div, MA); Christian leadership (MA); ministry (MA); New Testament (MA); Old Testament (MA); theological studies (MA); theology (MA). Electronic applications accepted.

CROWN COLLEGE, St. Bonifacius, MN 55375-9001

General Information Independent-religious, coed, comprehensive institution. *Graduate housing:* Room and/or apartments available on a first-come, first-served basis to married students; on-campus housing not available to single students. Housing application deadline: 7/1.

GRADUATE UNITS

Graduate Studies *Degree program information:* Part-time and evening/weekend programs available. Offers educational leadership (MA); intercultural leadership (MA); ministry leadership (MA); organizational leadership (MA).

CUMBERLAND UNIVERSITY, Lebanon, TN 37087-3408

General Information Independent, coed, comprehensive institution. *Enrollment:* 1,345 graduate, professional, and undergraduate students; 33 full-time matriculated graduate/professional students (23 women), 275 part-time matriculated graduate/professional students (188 women). *Enrollment by degree level:* 308 master's. *Graduate faculty:* 11 full-time (4 women), 14 part-time/adjunct (5 women). *Tuition:* Full-time $10,890; part-time $605 per credit. *Graduate housing:* Room and/or apartments available on a first-come, first-served basis to single students; on-campus housing not available to married students. Typical cost: $2,410 per year ($5,400 including board). *Student services:* Campus employment opportunities, career counseling, disabled student services, international student services, low-cost health insurance. *Library facilities:* Doris and Harry Vise Library. *Online resources:* library catalog, web page, access to other libraries' catalogs. *Collection:* 50,000 titles, 130 serial subscriptions.

Computer facilities: 150 computers available on campus for general student use. A campuswide network can be accessed from student residence rooms and from off campus. Internet access is available. *Web address:* http://www.cumberland.edu/.

General Application Contact: Eddie Pawlawski, Vice President for Enrollment Management, 615-444-2562 Ext. 1225, Fax: 615-444-2569, E-mail: epawlawski@cumberland.edu.

GRADUATE UNITS

Program in Business Administration Students: 8 full-time (6 women), 14 part-time (6 women); includes 4 minority (2 African Americans, 1 Asian American or Pacific Islander, 1 Hispanic American), 4 international. Average age 32. 8 applicants, 100% accepted, 2 enrolled. *Faculty:* 4 full-time (1 woman). Expenses: Contact institution. *Financial support:* Career-related internships or fieldwork, institutionally sponsored loans, and scholarships/grants available. Support available to part-time students. Financial award application deadline: 8/1; financial award applicants required to submit FAFSA. In 2006, 5 degrees awarded. *Degree program information:* Part-time and evening/weekend programs available. Offers business administration (MBA). *Application deadline:* Applications are processed on a rolling basis. *Application fee:* $50. *Dean of the Labry School of Business,* Dr. Paul Stumb, 615-444-2562 Ext. 1210, Fax: 615-444-2569, E-mail: pstumb@cumberland.edu.

Program in Education Students: 25 full-time (16 women), 154 part-time (114 women); includes 21 minority (18 African Americans, 1 American Indian/Alaska Native, 1 Asian American or Pacific Islander, 1 Hispanic American). Average age 33. 23 applicants, 100% accepted, 14 enrolled. *Faculty:* 4 full-time (3 women), 8 part-time/adjunct (2 women). Expenses: Contact institution. *Financial support:* Career-related internships or fieldwork, institutionally sponsored loans, and scholarships/grants available. Support available to part-time students. Financial award application deadline: 8/1; financial award applicants required to submit FAFSA. In 2006, 195 degrees awarded. *Degree program information:* Part-time and evening/weekend programs available. Postbaccalaureate distance learning degree programs offered (no on-campus study). Offers education (MAE). *Application fee:* $50. *Application Contact:* Debbie F. Whitaker, Coordinator, 615-444-2562 Ext. 1217, Fax: 615-444-2569, E-mail: dwhitaker@cumberland.edu. *Dean, School of Education,* Dr. Kenneth C. Collier, 615-444-2562 Ext. 1170, Fax: 877-217-5284, E-mail: ccollier@cumberland.edu.

Program in Organizational Leadership and Human Relations Management Students: 2 full-time (1 woman), 14 part-time (4 women); includes 3 minority (all African Americans), 5 international. Average age 31. 4 applicants, 75% accepted, 3 enrolled. *Faculty:* 1 full-time (0 women), 3 part-time/adjunct (1 woman). Expenses: Contact institution. *Financial support:* Scholarships/grants, tuition waivers (partial), and unspecified assistantships available. Financial award application deadline: 8/1; financial award applicants required to submit FAFSA. In 2006, 6 degrees awarded. *Degree program information:* Part-time and evening/weekend programs available. Offers organizational leadership and human relations management (MS). *Application deadline:* For fall admission, 8/1 priority date for domestic students. *Application fee:* $50. *Associate Professor, Criminal Justice,* Dr. William R. Cheatham, 615-444-2562 Ext. 1276, Fax: 615-444-2569, E-mail: rcheatham@cumberland.edu.

Program in Public Service Administration Average age 37. 47 applicants, 94% accepted, 43 enrolled. *Faculty:* 2 full-time (0 women), 3 part-time/adjunct (2 women). Expenses: Contact institution. *Financial support:* Scholarships/grants and unspecified assistantships available. Financial award application deadline: 8/1; financial award applicants required to submit FAFSA. In 2006, 35 degrees awarded. *Degree program information:* Part-time and evening/weekend programs available. Offers public service administration (MS). *Application fee:* $50. *Application Contact:* Karen Hobson, Assistant to Executive Vice President and Dean, 615-444-2562 Ext. 1139, Fax: 615-444-2569, E-mail: khobson@cumberland.edu. *Professor,* Dr. C. William McKee, 615-444-2562 Ext. 1111, Fax: 615-444-2569, E-mail: bmckee@cumberland.edu.

CURRY COLLEGE, Milton, MA 02186-9984

General Information Independent, coed, comprehensive institution. *Enrollment:* 3,073 graduate, professional, and undergraduate students; 375 part-time matriculated graduate/professional students (186 women). *Enrollment by degree level:* 375 master's. *Graduate faculty:* 17 full-time (9 women), 17 part-time/adjunct (8 women). *Graduate housing:* On-campus housing not available. *Student services:* Campus safety program, career counseling, disabled student services, free psychological counseling, grant writing training, international student services, low-cost health insurance, teacher training, writing training. *Library facilities:* Levin Library plus 1 other. *Online resources:* library catalog, web page, access to other libraries' catalogs. *Collection:* 90,000 titles, 675 serial subscriptions. *Research affiliation:* Public School Systems, Literacy Centers/GED Programs.

Computer facilities: 120 computers available on campus for general student use. A campuswide network can be accessed from student residence rooms and from off campus. Internet access, library online catalog and research databases are available. *Web address:* http://www.curry.edu/.

General Application Contact: John Bresnahan, Director of Graduate Enrollment and Student Services, 617-333-2243, Fax: 617-333-2045, E-mail: jbresnah0104@curry.edu.

GRADUATE UNITS

Division of Continuing Education and Graduate Studies *Faculty:* 17 full-time (9 women), 17 part-time/adjunct (8 women). Expenses: Contact institution. Offers adult education (Certificate); business administration (MBA); criminal justice (MA); educational administration (M Ed); educational therapy (Certificate); elementary education (M Ed); foundations (non-license) (M Ed); learning disabilities across the lifespan (Certificate); reading (M Ed, Certificate); special education (M Ed).

THE CURTIS INSTITUTE OF MUSIC, Philadelphia, PA 19103-6107

General Information Independent, coed, comprehensive institution. *Graduate housing:* On-campus housing not available.

GRADUATE UNITS

Graduate Studies Offers opera (MM).

DAEMEN COLLEGE, Amherst, NY 14226-3592

General Information Independent, coed, comprehensive institution. *Enrollment:* 2,414 graduate, professional, and undergraduate students; 418 full-time matriculated graduate/professional students (330 women), 348 part-time matriculated graduate/professional students (292 women). *Enrollment by degree level:* 52 first professional, 617 master's, 36 other advanced degrees. *Graduate faculty:* 20 full-time (11 women), 64 part-time/adjunct (50 women). *Tuition:* Full-time $11,700; part-time $650 per credit hour. *Required fees:* $15 per credit hour. Tuition and fees vary according to course load. *Graduate housing:* Room and/or apartments available on a first-come, first-served basis to single students; on-campus housing not available to married students. Typical cost: $4,325 (including board). Room and board charges vary according to board plan. Housing application deadline: 7/15. *Student services:* Campus employment opportunities, campus safety program, career counseling, disabled student services, low-cost health insurance, teacher training. *Library facilities:* Marian Library plus 1 other. *Online resources:* library catalog, web page, access to other libraries' catalogs. *Collection:* 127,232 titles, 889 serial subscriptions, 10,584 audiovisual materials.

Computer facilities: 99 computers available on campus for general student use. A campuswide network can be accessed from student residence rooms and from off campus. Internet access is available. *Web address:* http://www.daemen.edu/.

General Application Contact: Karl Shallowhorn, Associate Director of Graduate Admissions, 716-839-8225, Fax: 716-839-8229, E-mail: kshallow@daemen.edu.

GRADUATE UNITS

Department of Accounting and Information Systems Students: 1 (woman) full-time, 3 part-time (1 woman). Average age 32. 5 applicants, 80% accepted, 4 enrolled. *Faculty:* 1 full-time (0 women), 2 part-time/adjunct (0 women). Expenses: Contact institution. *Financial support:* Federal Work-Study and institutionally sponsored loans available. Financial award application deadline: 2/15; financial award applicants required to submit FAFSA. In 2006, 5 degrees awarded. *Degree program information:* Part-time and evening/weekend programs available. Offers global business (MS). *Application deadline:* For fall admission, 3/1 priority date for domestic and international students; for spring admission, 10/1 priority date for domestic and international students. Applications are processed on a rolling basis. *Application fee:* $25. Electronic applications accepted. *Application Contact:* Karl Shallowhorn, Associate Director of Graduate Admissions, 716-839-8225, Fax: 716-839-8229, E-mail: kshallow@daemen.edu. *Chair,* Dr. Linda J. Kuechler, 716-839-8398, Fax: 716-839-8261, E-mail: lkuechle@daemen.edu.

Department of Nursing Students: 13 full-time (12 women), 63 part-time (59 women); includes 12 minority (10 African Americans, 1 Asian American or Pacific Islander, 1 Hispanic American), 3 international. Average age 41. 36 applicants, 58% accepted, 18 enrolled. *Faculty:* 2 full-time (both women), 2 part-time/adjunct (both women). Expenses: Contact institution. *Financial support:* Institutionally sponsored loans and scholarships/grants available. Financial award application deadline: 2/15; financial award applicants required to submit FAFSA. In 2006, 9 degrees awarded. *Degree program information:* Part-time programs available. Offers adult nurse practitioner (MS, Certificate); nursing executive leadership (MS); palliative care nursing (MS, Certificate). *Application deadline:* For fall admission, 3/1 priority date for domestic and international students; for spring admission, 10/1 priority date for domestic and international students. Applications are processed on a rolling basis. *Application fee:* $25. Electronic applications accepted. *Application Contact:* Karl Shallowhorn, Associate Director of Graduate Admissions, 716-839-8225, Fax: 716-839-8229, E-mail: kshallow@daemen.edu. *Chair,* Dr. Mary Lou Rusin, 716-839-8387, Fax: 716-839-8403, E-mail: mrusin@daemen.edu.

Department of Physical Therapy Students: 52 full-time (40 women), 36 part-time (22 women); includes 6 minority (1 African American, 3 Asian Americans or Pacific Islanders, 2 Hispanic Americans), 6 international. Average age 31. 64 applicants, 55% accepted, 29 enrolled. *Faculty:* 8 full-time (5 women), 3 part-time/adjunct (1 woman). Expenses: Contact institution. *Financial support:* In 2006–07, 16 students received support; teaching assistantships, Federal Work-Study, institutionally sponsored loans, and scholarships/grants available. Support available to part-time students. Financial award application deadline: 2/15; financial award applicants required to submit FAFSA. *Degree program information:* Part-time programs available. Offers physical therapy (DPT, TDPT). *Application deadline:* For fall admission, 3/1 priority date for domestic and international students; for spring admission, 10/1 priority date for domestic and international students. Applications are processed on a rolling basis. *Application fee:* $25. Electronic applications accepted. *Application Contact:* Karl Shallowhorn, Associate Director of Graduate Admissions, 716-839-8225, Fax: 716-839-8229, E-mail: kshallow@daemen.edu. *Chair,* Dr. Sharon L. Held, 716-839-8344, Fax: 716-839-8537, E-mail: sheld@daemen.edu.

Education Department Students: 283 full-time (224 women), 238 part-time (202 women); includes 1 minority (African American), 192 international. Average age 33. 314 applicants, 71% accepted, 184 enrolled. *Faculty:* 5 full-time (4 women), 53 part-time/adjunct (45 women). Expenses: Contact institution. *Financial support:* In 2006–07, 48 students received support. Federal Work-Study, institutionally sponsored loans, traineeships, and tuition waivers (partial) available. Support available to part-time students. Financial award application deadline: 2/15; financial award applicants required to submit FAFSA. In 2006, 284 degrees awarded. *Degree program information:* Part-time programs available. Offers adolescence education (MS); childhood education (MS); childhood special education (MS). *Application deadline:* For fall admission, 3/1 priority date for domestic and international students; for spring admission, 10/1 priority date for domestic and international students. Applications are processed on a rolling basis. *Application fee:* $25. Electronic applications accepted. *Application Contact:* Karl Shallowhorn, Associate Director of Graduate Admissions, 716-839-8225, Fax: 716-839-8229, E-mail: kshallow@daemen.edu. *Chair,* Dr. Mary H. Fox, 716-839-8530, Fax: 716-839-8516, E-mail: mfox@daemen.edu.

Physician Assistant Department Students: 62 full-time (49 women); includes 4 minority (2 African Americans, 1 Asian American or Pacific Islander, 1 Hispanic American). Average age 26. 185 applicants, 19% accepted, 8 enrolled. *Faculty:* 3 full-time (0 women). Expenses: Contact institution. *Financial support:* Federal Work-Study and institutionally sponsored loans available. Financial award application deadline: 2/15; financial award applicants required to submit FAFSA. In 2006, 21 degrees awarded. Offers physician assistant (MS). *Application deadline:* For fall admission, 3/1 priority date for domestic and international students; for spring admission, 10/1 priority date for domestic and international students. Applications are processed on a rolling basis. *Application fee:* $25. Electronic applications accepted. *Application Contact:* Karl Shallowhorn, Associate Director of Graduate Admissions, 716-839-8225, Fax: 716-839-8229, E-mail: kshallow@daemen.edu. *Director,* Gregg L. Shutts, 716-839-8316, Fax: 716-839-8252, E-mail: shutts@daemen.edu.

Program in Executive Leadership and Change Students: 7 full-time (4 women), 8 part-time (all women); includes 1 minority (African American) Average age 39. 9 applicants, 100% accepted, 5 enrolled. *Faculty:* 1 full-time (0 women), 4 part-time/adjunct (2 women). Expenses: Contact institution. *Financial support:* Federal Work-Study and institutionally sponsored loans available. Financial award application deadline: 2/15; financial award applicants required to submit FAFSA. In 2006, 9 degrees awarded. *Degree program information:* Part-time and evening/weekend programs available. Offers executive leadership and change (MS). *Applica-*

tion deadline: For fall admission, 3/1 priority date for domestic and international students; for spring admission, 10/1 priority date for domestic and international students. Applications are processed on a rolling basis. *Application fee:* $25. Electronic applications accepted. *Application Contact:* Karl Shallowhorn, Associate Director of Graduate Admissions, 716-839-8225, Fax: 716-839-8229, E-mail: kshallow@daemen.edu. *Executive Director,* Dr. John S. Frederick, 716-839-8342, Fax: 716-839-8261, E-mail: jfrederi@daemen.edu.

DAKOTA STATE UNIVERSITY, Madison, SD 57042-1799

General Information State-supported, coed, comprehensive institution. *Enrollment:* 2,392 graduate, professional, and undergraduate students; 21 full-time matriculated graduate/professional students (2 women), 151 part-time matriculated graduate/professional students (56 women). *Enrollment by degree level:* 159 master's, 13 doctoral. *Graduate faculty:* 45 full-time (12 women), 7 part-time/adjunct (2 women). Tuition, state resident: part-time $120 per credit hour. Tuition, nonresident: part-time $355 per credit hour. *Required fees:* $89 per credit hour. Tuition and fees vary according to course load, campus/location, program and reciprocity agreements. *Graduate housing:* Room and/or apartments available on a first-come, first-served basis to single students; on-campus housing not available to married students. Typical cost: $1,924 per year ($3,927 including board). Room and board charges vary according to board plan and housing facility selected. *Student services:* Campus employment opportunities, campus safety program, career counseling, disabled student services, exercise/wellness program, free psychological counseling, grant writing training, international student services, low-cost health insurance, multicultural affairs office, writing training. *Library facilities:* Karl E. Mundt Library plus 1 other. *Online resources:* library catalog, web page, access to other libraries' catalogs. *Collection:* 95,819 titles, 350 serial subscriptions. *Research affiliation:* SBS-Secure Banking Solutions, LLC (information security), American Respiratory Care Foundation (respiratory care research).

Computer facilities: Computer purchase and lease plans are available. 398 computers available on campus for general student use. A campuswide network can be accessed from student residence rooms and from off campus. Internet access and online class registration, wireless computing initiative placed 860 devices in the hands of full-time freshmen and sophomores are available. *Web address:* http://www.dsu.edu/.

General Application Contact: Jennifer Maher, Program Assistant II, 605-256-5799, Fax: 605-256-5093, E-mail: jennifer.maher@dsu.edu.

GRADUATE UNITS

College of Business and Information Systems Students: 21 full-time (0 women), 95 part-time (20 women); includes 10 minority (1 African American, 1 American Indian/Alaska Native, 8 Asian Americans or Pacific Islanders), 34 international. Average age 33. 53 applicants, 96% accepted, 38 enrolled. *Faculty:* 18 full-time (0 women). Expenses: Contact institution. *Financial support:* In 2006–07, 27 students received support, including 14 research assistantships with partial tuition reimbursements available (averaging $4,812 per year), 2 teaching assistantships with partial tuition reimbursements available (averaging $30,000 per year); fellowships, Federal Work-Study, scholarships/grants, unspecified assistantships, and administrative assistantships also available. Support available to part-time students. Financial award applicants required to submit FAFSA. In 2006, 47 degrees awarded. *Degree program information:* Part-time and evening/weekend programs available. Postbaccalaureate distance learning degree programs offered (minimal on-campus study). Offers business and information systems (MSIA, MSIS, D Sc IS). *Application deadline:* For fall admission, 8/1 for domestic students, 6/1 for international students; for spring admission, 12/1 for domestic students, 10/1 for international students. Applications are processed on a rolling basis. *Application fee:* $35 ($85 for international students). Electronic applications accepted. *Application Contact:* Jennifer Maher, Program Assistant II, Office of Graduate Studies and Research, 605-256-5799, Fax: 605-256-5093, E-mail: jennifer.maher@dsu.edu. *Dean,* Dr. Tom Halverson, 605-256-5165, Fax: 605-256-5060, E-mail: tom.halverson@dsu.edu.

College of Education Average age 36. 40 applicants, 95% accepted, 34 enrolled. *Faculty:* 6 full-time (1 woman), 3 part-time/adjunct (1 woman). Expenses: Contact institution. *Financial support:* In 2006–07, 17 students received support, including 1 research assistantship (averaging $4,812 per year); teaching assistantships, Federal Work-Study, scholarships/grants, tuition waivers (partial), unspecified assistantships, and administrative assistantships also available. Support available to part-time students. Financial award applicants required to submit FAFSA. In 2006, 9 degrees awarded. *Degree program information:* Part-time programs available. Postbaccalaureate distance learning degree programs offered (minimal on-campus study). Offers instructional technology (MSET). *Application deadline:* For fall admission, 8/1 for domestic students, 6/1 for international students. Applications are processed on a rolling basis. *Application fee:* $35 ($85 for international students). Electronic applications accepted. *Application Contact:* Jennifer Maher, Program Assistant II, Office of Studies and Research, 605-256-5799, Fax: 605-256-5093, E-mail: jennifer.maher@dsu.edu. *Dean (Interim),* Dr. Judy Dittman, 605-256-5177, Fax: 605-256-7300, E-mail: judy.dittman@dsu.edu.

DAKOTA WESLEYAN UNIVERSITY, Mitchell, SD 57301-4398

General Information Independent-religious, coed, comprehensive institution.

GRADUATE UNITS

Graduate Program

DALHOUSIE UNIVERSITY, Halifax, NS B3H 4R2, Canada

General Information Province-supported, coed, university. *Graduate housing:* Rooms and/or apartments available on a first-come, first-served basis to single and married students. Housing application deadline: 7/15.

GRADUATE UNITS

Faculty of Architecture Offers architecture (M Arch, MEDS, MURP); urban and rural planning (MURP).

Faculty of Dentistry Offers dental hygiene (Diploma); dentistry (DDS); prosthodontics (MS).

Faculty of Graduate Studies *Degree program information:* Part-time programs available. Postbaccalaureate distance learning degree programs offered. Offers anatomy and neurobiology (M Sc, PhD); community health and epidemiology (M Sc); interdisciplinary studies (PhD); marine affairs (MMM); medicine (M Sc, PhD); microbiology and immunology (M Sc, PhD); neuroscience (M Sc, PhD); pathology (M Sc); pharmacology (M Sc, PhD); physiology and biophysics (M Sc, PhD).

College of Arts and Science *Degree program information:* Part-time programs available. Offers arts and science (M Sc, MA, MDE, PhD); arts and social science (M Sc, MA, MDE, PhD); biology (M Sc, PhD); chemistry (M Sc, PhD); classics (MA, PhD); clinical psychology (PhD); earth sciences (M Sc, PhD); economics (MA, MDE, PhD); English (MA, PhD); French (MA, PhD); German (MA); history (MA, PhD); international development studies (MA); mathematics (M Sc, PhD); oceanography (M Sc, PhD); philosophy (MA, PhD); physics (M Sc, PhD); political science (MA, PhD); psychology (M Sc, PhD); psychology/neuroscience (M Sc, PhD); science (M Sc, MA, MDE, PhD); social anthropology (MA); sociology (MA, PhD); statistics (M Sc, PhD); women's studies (MA).

Faculty of Computer Science Offers computer science (MC Sc, PhD); electronic commerce (MEC).

Faculty of Engineering Offers biological engineering (M Eng, MA Sc, PhD); biomedical engineering (MA Sc); chemical engineering (M Eng, MA Sc, PhD); civil engineering (M Eng, MA Sc, PhD); electrical and computer engineering (M Eng, MA Sc, PhD); engineering (M Eng, M Sc, MA Sc, PhD); engineering mathematics (M Sc, PhD); food science and technology (M Sc, PhD); industrial engineering (M Eng, MA Sc, PhD); internet working (M Eng); mechanical engineering (M Eng, MA Sc, PhD); metallurgical engineering (M Eng, MA Sc, PhD); mining (M Eng, MA Sc, PhD).

Faculty of Health Professions *Degree program information:* Part-time programs available. Postbaccalaureate distance learning degree programs offered. Offers health and human performance (M Sc, MA); health education (MA); health professions (M Sc, MA, MHSA, MN, MSW, PhD); health services administration (MHSA); human communication disorders (M Sc); kinesiology (M Sc); leisure studies (MA); nursing (MN); occupational therapy (M Sc); pharmacy (M Sc, PhD); social work (MSW).

Faculty of Law *Degree program information:* Part-time programs available. Offers law (LL M, JSD).

Faculty of Management *Degree program information:* Part-time programs available. Offers business administration (MBA); information technology (MBA); library and information studies (MLIS); management (MBA, MES, MLIS, MPA, Diploma); public administration (MPA); resource and environmental studies (MES).

Henson College of Public Affairs and Continuing Education Offers information technology education (MITE).

Nova Scotia Agricultural College *Degree program information:* Part-time programs available. Offers agriculture (M Sc).

Faculty of Medicine *Degree program information:* Part-time programs available. Offers biochemistry and molecular biology (M Sc, PhD); medicine (MD, M Sc, PhD).

DALLAS BAPTIST UNIVERSITY, Dallas, TX 75211-9299

General Information Independent-religious, coed, comprehensive institution. *Enrollment:* 5,153 graduate, professional, and undergraduate students; 474 full-time matriculated graduate/professional students (289 women), 1,069 part-time matriculated graduate/professional students (709 women). *Enrollment by degree level:* 1,456 master's, 87 doctoral. *Graduate faculty:* 49 full-time (21 women), 112 part-time/adjunct (46 women). *Tuition:* Full-time $8,370; part-time $465 per credit hour. *Required fees:* $465 per credit hour. *Graduate housing:* Rooms and/or apartments available on a first-come, first-served basis to single and married students. Typical cost: $1,380 per year for single students; $1,380 per year for married students. *Student services:* Campus employment opportunities, campus safety program, career counseling, disabled student services, free psychological counseling, international student services, low-cost health insurance, writing training. *Library facilities:* Vance Memorial Library. *Online resources:* library catalog, web page, access to other libraries' catalogs. *Collection:* 266,502 titles, 402 serial subscriptions, 4,099 audiovisual materials.

Computer facilities: Computer purchase and lease plans are available. 182 computers available on campus for general student use. A campuswide network can be accessed from student residence rooms and from off campus. Internet access and online class registration are available. *Web address:* http://www.dbu.edu/.

General Application Contact: Kit P. Montgomery, Director of Graduate Programs, 214-333-5242, Fax: 214-333-5579, E-mail: graduate@dbu.edu.

GRADUATE UNITS

College of Adult Education Students: 41 full-time, 98 part-time. 87 applicants, 47% accepted, 32 enrolled. *Faculty:* 49 full-time (21 women), 112 part-time/adjunct (46 women). Expenses: Contact institution. *Financial support:* Federal Work-Study, institutionally sponsored loans, scholarships/grants, and tuition waivers (full and partial) available. Support available to part-time students. In 2006, 53 degrees awarded. *Degree program information:* Part-time and evening/weekend programs available. Offers accounting (MA); adult education (MA, MLA); arts (MLA); business (MA); Christian ministry (MLA); church leadership (MA); corporate management (MA); counseling (MA); criminal justice (MA); English (MLA); English as a second language (MA, MLA); finance (MA); fine arts (MLA); higher education (MA); history (MLA); leadership studies (MA); management (MA); management information systems (MA); marketing (MA); missions (MA, MLA); political science (MLA). *Application deadline:* Applications are processed on a rolling basis. *Application fee:* $25. Electronic applications accepted. *Application Contact:* Kit P. Montgomery, Director of Graduate Programs, 214-333-5242, Fax: 214-333-5579, E-mail: graduate@dbu.edu. *Acting Dean,* Dr. Donovan Fredrickson, 214-333-5242, Fax: 214-333-5323, E-mail: graduate@dbu.edu.

College of Humanities and Social Sciences Students: 150 (126 women). *Faculty:* 49 full-time (21 women), 112 part-time/adjunct (46 women). Expenses: Contact institution. *Financial support:* Career-related internships or fieldwork, Federal Work-Study, institutionally sponsored loans, scholarships/grants, and tuition waivers (full and partial) available. Support available to part-time students. Financial award applicants required to submit FAFSA. In 2006, 40 degrees awarded. *Degree program information:* Part-time and evening/weekend programs available. Offers counseling (MA); humanities and social sciences (MA). *Application deadline:* Applications are processed on a rolling basis. *Application fee:* $25. Electronic applications accepted. *Application Contact:* Kit P. Montgomery, Director of Graduate Programs, 214-333-5242, Fax: 214-333-5579, E-mail: graduate@dbu.edu. *Dean,* Dr. Michael Williams, 214-333-5234, Fax: 214-333-6819, E-mail: graduate@dbu.edu.

Dorothy M. Bush College of Education Students: 67 full-time, 269 part-time. 128 applicants, 77% accepted, 56 enrolled. *Faculty:* 49 full-time (21 women), 112 part-time/adjunct (46 women). Expenses: Contact institution. *Financial support:* Federal Work-Study, institutionally sponsored loans, scholarships/grants, and tuition waivers (full and partial) available. Support available to part-time students. In 2006, 107 degrees awarded. *Degree program information:* Part-time and evening/weekend programs available. Offers early childhood education (M Ed); education (M Ed, MAT); education in curriculum and instruction (M Ed); educational leadership (M Ed); elementary reading education (M Ed); general elementary education (M Ed); reading and ESL (M Ed); reading specialist (M Ed); school counseling (M Ed); teaching (MAT). *Application deadline:* Applications are processed on a rolling basis. *Application fee:* $25. Electronic applications accepted. *Application Contact:* Kit P. Montgomery, Director of Graduate Programs, 214-333-5242, Fax: 214-333-5579, E-mail: graduate@dbu.edu. *Dean,* Dr. Charles Carona, 214-333-5200, Fax: 214-333-5551, E-mail: graduate@dbu.edu.

Graduate School of Business Students: 149 full-time, 512 part-time. 313 applicants, 41% accepted, 129 enrolled. *Faculty:* 49 full-time (21 women), 112 part-time/adjunct (46 women). Expenses: Contact institution. *Financial support:* Career-related internships or fieldwork, Federal Work-Study, institutionally sponsored loans, scholarships/grants, and tuition waivers (full and partial) available. Support available to part-time students. In 2006, 201 degrees awarded. *Degree program information:* Part-time and evening/weekend programs available. Postbaccalaureate distance learning degree programs offered (no on-campus study). Offers accounting (MBA); business (MA, MBA); business communication (MA, MBA); conflict resolution management (MA, MBA); e-business (MBA); entrepreneurship (MBA); finance (MBA); general management (MA); health care management (MA, MBA); human resource management (MA); international business (MBA); management (MBA); management information systems (MBA); marketing (MBA); project management (MBA); technology and engineering management (MBA). *Application deadline:* Applications are processed on a rolling basis. *Application fee:* $25. Electronic applications accepted. *Application Contact:* Kit P. Montgomery, Director of Graduate Programs, 214-333-5242, Fax: 214-333-5579, E-mail: graduate@dbu.edu. *Dean,* Dr. Charlene Conner, 214-333-5244, Fax: 214-333-5293, E-mail: graduate@dbu.edu.

School of Leadership and Christian Education Students: 68 full-time, 100 part-time. *Faculty:* 49 full-time (21 women), 112 part-time/adjunct (46 women). Expenses: Contact institution. *Financial support:* Federal Work-Study, institutionally sponsored loans, scholarships/grants, and tuition waivers (full and partial) available. Support available to part-time students. In 2006, 27 degrees awarded. *Degree program information:* Part-time and evening/weekend programs available. Offers adult ministry (MA); Baptist student ministry (MA); business ministry (MA); children's ministry (MA); Christian education: childhood ministry (MA); Christian education: student ministry (MA); collegiate ministry (MA); counseling ministry (MA); education ministry (MA); general ministry (MA); global leadership (MA); higher education (M Ed); leadership and Christian education (M Ed, MA); ministry with students (MA); missions ministry (MA); worship leadership (MA); worship ministry (MA); youth ministry (MA). *Application deadline:* Applications are processed on a rolling basis. *Application fee:* $25. Electronic applications accepted. *Application Contact:* Kit P. Montgomery, Director of Graduate Programs, 214-333-5242, Fax: 214-333-5579, E-mail: graduate@dbu.edu. *Dean,* Dr. Rick Gregory, 214-333-5162, Fax: 214-333-5164, E-mail: graduate@dbu.edu.

DALLAS THEOLOGICAL SEMINARY, Dallas, TX 75204-6499

General Information Independent, coed, graduate-only institution. *Graduate housing:* Rooms and/or apartments available on a first-come, first-served basis to single and married students.

Dallas Theological Seminary (continued)

GRADUATE UNITS

Graduate Programs *Degree program information:* Part-time and evening/weekend programs available. Offers academic ministries (Th M); Bible translation (Th M); biblical and theological studies (CGS); biblical counseling (MA); biblical exegesis and linguistics (MA); biblical studies (MA, PhD); Christian education (MA, D Min); cross-cultural ministries (MA, Th M); educational leadership (Th M); evangelism and discipleship (Th M); interdisciplinary studies (Th M); media arts in ministry (Th M); ministry (D Min); parachurch ministries (Th M); pastoral ministries (Th M); sacred theology (STM); theological studies (PhD); women's ministry (Th M). MA (biblical exegesis and linguistics) offered jointly with the Summer Institute of Linguistics; extension branches located in Chattanooga (TN), Houston (TX), Philadelphia (PA), San Antonio (TX), and the Tampa Bay area (FL). Electronic applications accepted.

DANIEL WEBSTER COLLEGE, Nashua, NH 03063-1300

General Information Independent, coed, comprehensive institution.

GRADUATE UNITS

MBA Program Postbaccalaureate distance learning degree programs offered. Offers applied management (MBA).

MBA Program for Aviation Professionals Postbaccalaureate distance learning degree programs offered. Offers business administration for aviation professionals (MBA).

DANIEL WEBSTER COLLEGE–PORTSMOUTH CAMPUS, Portsmouth, NH 03801

General Information Independent, coed, comprehensive institution.

GRADUATE UNITS

MBA Program Offers applied management (MBA).

MBA Program for Aviation Professionals Offers applied management (MBA).

DARKEI NOAM RABBINICAL COLLEGE, Brooklyn, NY 11210

General Information Independent-religious, men only, comprehensive institution.

GRADUATE UNITS

Graduate Programs

DARTMOUTH COLLEGE, Hanover, NH 03755

General Information Independent, coed, university. CGS member. *Enrollment:* 5,753 graduate, professional, and undergraduate students; 1,573 full-time matriculated graduate/professional students (619 women), 95 part-time matriculated graduate/professional students (51 women). *Enrollment by degree level:* 312 first professional, 798 master's, 470 doctoral, 44 other advanced degrees. *Graduate faculty:* 320 full-time (84 women), 39 part-time/adjunct (19 women). *Tuition:* Full-time $33,297. *Graduate housing:* Rooms and/or apartments available to single and married students. Housing application deadline: 5/15. *Student services:* Campus safety program, career counseling, disabled student services, free psychological counseling, international student services, low-cost health insurance, teacher training, writing training. *Library facilities:* Baker-Berry Library plus 10 others. *Online resources:* library catalog, web page, access to other libraries' catalogs. *Research affiliation:* Cold Regions Research Engineering Laboratory.

Computer facilities: 200 computers available on campus for general student use. A campuswide network can be accessed from student residence rooms and from off campus. Internet access and online class registration are available. *Web address:* http://www.dartmouth.edu/.

General Application Contact: Gary Hutchins, Assistant Dean/School of Arts and Sciences, 603-646-2107, Fax: 603-646-3488, E-mail: g.hutchins@dartmouth.edu.

GRADUATE UNITS

Dartmouth Medical School Offers biochemistry (PhD); cancer biology and molecular therapeutics (PhD); medicine (MD, PhD); molecular pharmacology, toxicology and experimental therapeutics (PhD); neuroscience (PhD); systems biology (PhD); vascular biology (PhD).

Program in Immunology Offers immunology (PhD).

Program in Microbiology and Molecular Pathogenesis Offers microbiology and molecular pathogenesis (PhD).

School of Arts and Sciences Students: 584 full-time (268 women), 88 part-time (48 women); includes 65 minority (10 African Americans, 4 American Indian/Alaska Native, 35 Asian Americans or Pacific Islanders, 16 Hispanic Americans), 162 international. Average age 29. 1,437 applicants, 25% accepted, 182 enrolled. *Faculty:* 230 full-time (64 women), 37 part-time/adjunct (19 women). Expenses: Contact institution. *Financial support:* In 2006–07, 442 students received support, including fellowships with full tuition reimbursements available (averaging $21,600 per year), research assistantships with full tuition reimbursements available (averaging $21,600 per year), teaching assistantships with full tuition reimbursements available (averaging $21,600 per year); career-related internships or fieldwork, Federal Work-Study, institutionally sponsored loans, scholarships/grants, traineeships, tuition waivers (full and partial), and unspecified assistantships also available. Support available to part-time students. Financial award applicants required to submit CSS PROFILE. In 2006, 135 master's, 52 doctorates awarded. Offers arts and sciences (AM, MALS, MPH, MS, PhD); biology of integrated systems (PhD); cancer biology and molecular therapeutics (PhD); chemistry (PhD); cognitive neuroscience (PhD); comparative literature (AM); computer science (MS, PhD); earth sciences (MS, PhD); ecology and evolutionary biology (PhD); electro-acoustic music (AM); genetics (PhD); liberal studies (MALS); mathematics (PhD); microbiology and immunology (PhD); molecular and cellular biology (PhD); molecular pharmacology, toxicology and experimental therapeutics (PhD); neuroscience (PhD); pharmacology and toxicology (PhD); physics and astronomy (MS, PhD); physiology (PhD); psychology (PhD); vascular biology (PhD). Electronic applications accepted. *Application Contact:* Gary Hutchins, Assistant Dean/School of Arts and Sciences, 603-646-2107, Fax: 603-646-3488, E-mail: g.hutchins@dartmouth.edu. *Dean of Graduate Studies,* Dr. Charles Barlowe, 603-646-2106, Fax: 603-646-3488, E-mail: charles.k.barlowe@dartmouth.edu.

Center for the Evaluative Clinical Sciences Students: 35 full-time (20 women), 27 part-time (15 women); includes 6 minority (5 Asian Americans or Pacific Islanders, 1 Hispanic American), 4 international. Average age 36. 68 applicants, 69% accepted, 22 enrolled. *Faculty:* 26 full-time (12 women), 10 part-time/adjunct (9 women). Expenses: Contact institution. *Financial support:* In 2006–07, fellowships with tuition reimbursements (averaging $21,000 per year); research assistantships, teaching assistantships with tuition reimbursements, institutionally sponsored loans and scholarships/grants also available. Financial award application deadline: 6/1; financial award applicants required to submit FAFSA. In 2006, 10 master's, 3 doctorates awarded. *Degree program information:* Part-time programs available. Offers evaluative clinical sciences (MS, PhD); public health (MPH). *Application deadline:* For fall admission, 1/15 for domestic students. Applications are processed on a rolling basis. *Application fee:* $50. *Application Contact:* Susan M. Benson, Academic Programs Director, 603-650-1782, Fax: 603-650-1900, E-mail: ecs@dartmouth.edu. *Director,* Dr. Gerald T. O'Connor, 603-650-1782.

The Neuroscience Center Expenses: Contact institution. Offers neuroscience (PhD). Degrees awarded through participating programs. *Application Contact:* Information Contact, 603-650-8561, Fax: 603-650-8449, E-mail: NeuroscienceCenter@dartmouth.edu.

Thayer School of Engineering Students: 125 full-time (34 women), 2 part-time; includes 12 minority (1 African American, 8 Asian Americans or Pacific Islanders, 3 Hispanic Americans), 49 international. Average age 24. 335 applicants, 42% accepted, 94 enrolled. *Faculty:* 42 full-time (5 women), 31 part-time/adjunct (3 women). Expenses: Contact institution. *Financial support:* In 2006–07, 19 fellowships with full tuition reimbursements (averaging $19,320 per year), 80 research assistantships with full tuition reimbursements (averaging $19,320 per year), 29 teaching assistantships with partial tuition reimbursements (averaging $9,600 per year) were awarded; career-related internships or fieldwork, institutionally sponsored loans, scholarships/grants, and tuition waivers (full and partial) also available. Financial award application deadline: 2/15; financial award applicants required to submit CSS PROFILE. In 2006, 49 master's, 8 doctorates awarded. Offers biomedical engineering (MS, PhD); biotechnology and biochemical engineering (MS, PhD); computer engineering (MS, PhD); electrical engineering (MS, PhD); engineering (MEM, MS, PhD); engineering management (MEM); engineering physics (MS, PhD); manufacturing systems (MS, PhD); materials sciences and engineering (MS, PhD); mechanical engineering (MS, PhD). *Application deadline:* For fall admission, 1/1 priority date for domestic and international students. Applications are processed on a rolling basis. *Application fee:* $45. Electronic applications accepted. *Application Contact:* Candace S. Potter, Graduate Admissions Administrator, 603-646-3844, Fax: 603-646-1620, E-mail: candace.potter@dartmouth.edu. *Dean,* Dr. Joseph J. Helbie, 603-646-2238, Fax: 603-646-2580, E-mail: joseph.j.helbie@dartmouth.edu.

Tuck School of Business at Dartmouth Students: 490 full-time (156 women); includes 71 minority (15 African Americans, 2 American Indian/Alaska Native, 38 Asian Americans or Pacific Islanders, 16 Hispanic Americans), 154 international. Average age 28. 2,276 applicants, 20% accepted, 248 enrolled. *Faculty:* 45 full-time (12 women), 15 part-time/adjunct (5 women). Expenses: Contact institution. *Financial support:* In 2006–07, 395 students received support. Career-related internships or fieldwork, institutionally sponsored loans, scholarships/grants, and health care benefits available. Financial award application deadline: 4/17; financial award applicants required to submit FAFSA. In 2006, 258 degrees awarded. Offers business (MBA). *Application deadline:* For fall admission, 10/12 for domestic and international students; for winter admission, 1/11 for domestic and international students; for spring admission, 4/5 for domestic and international students. *Application fee:* $220. Electronic applications accepted. *Application Contact:* Dawna Clarke, Director of Admissions, 603-646-3162, Fax: 603-646-1441, E-mail: tuck.admissions@dartmouth.edu. *Dean,* Paul Danos, 603-646-2460, Fax: 603-646-1308, E-mail: tuck.public.relations@dartmouth.edu.

See Close-Up on page 861.

DAVENPORT UNIVERSITY, Dearborn, MI 48126-3799

General Information Independent, coed, comprehensive institution. *Graduate housing:* On-campus housing not available.

GRADUATE UNITS

Sneden Graduate School *Degree program information:* Part-time and evening/weekend programs available. Postbaccalaureate distance learning degree programs offered (no on-campus study). Offers accounting (MBA); e-business (MBA); finance (MBA); global business (MBA); health care management (MBA); human resources management (MBA); management (MBA); marketing (MBA).

DAVENPORT UNIVERSITY, Grand Rapids, MI 49503

General Information Independent, coed, comprehensive institution. *Graduate housing:* Room and/or apartments available on a first-come, first-served basis to single students; on-campus housing not available to married students. *Research affiliation:* Human Synergistic Center for Applied Research, Inc. (leadership, organizational culture, strategy).

GRADUATE UNITS

Sneden Graduate School *Degree program information:* Evening/weekend programs available. Offers business (MBA). Electronic applications accepted.

DAVENPORT UNIVERSITY, Warren, MI 48092-5209

General Information Independent, coed, comprehensive institution.

GRADUATE UNITS

Sneden Graduate School Offers accounting (MBA); commerce (MBA); finance (MBA); health care management (MBA); human resources management (MBA); management (MBA).

DEFIANCE COLLEGE, Defiance, OH 43512-1610

General Information Independent-religious, coed, comprehensive institution. *Graduate housing:* On-campus housing not available.

GRADUATE UNITS

Program in Business and Organizational Leadership *Degree program information:* Part-time and evening/weekend programs available. Offers business and organizational leadership (MBOL).

Program in Education *Degree program information:* Part-time programs available. Offers education (MA).

DELAWARE STATE UNIVERSITY, Dover, DE 19901-2277

General Information State-supported, coed, comprehensive institution. *Graduate housing:* On-campus housing not available.

GRADUATE UNITS

Graduate Programs *Degree program information:* Part-time and evening/weekend programs available. Offers applied chemistry (MS); biology (MS); biology education (MS); business administration (MBA); chemistry (MS); curriculum and instruction (MA); education (MA); mathematics (MS); physics (MS); physics teaching (MS); science education (MA); social work (MSW); special education (MA).

DELAWARE VALLEY COLLEGE, Doylestown, PA 18901-2697

General Information Independent, coed, comprehensive institution. *Enrollment:* 2,035 graduate, professional, and undergraduate students; 110 part-time matriculated graduate/professional students (71 women). *Enrollment by degree level:* 110 master's. *Graduate faculty:* 15 part-time/adjunct (5 women). *Graduate housing:* On-campus housing not available. *Student services:* Disabled student services. *Library facilities:* Joseph Krauskopf Memorial Library. *Online resources:* library catalog, web page, access to other libraries' catalogs. *Collection:* 56,347 titles, 728 serial subscriptions.

Computer facilities: 210 computers available on campus for general student use. A campuswide network can be accessed. Internet access and online class registration are available. *Web address:* http://www.devalcol.edu/.

General Application Contact: Dr. Robert W. Valente, Director of Educational Leadership, 215-489-4833, Fax: 215-489-4832, E-mail: robert.valente@devalcol.edu.

GRADUATE UNITS

Program in Educational Leadership Average age 36. 5 applicants, 80% accepted, 4 enrolled. *Faculty:* 15 part-time/adjunct (5 women). Expenses: Contact institution. In 2006, 20 degrees awarded. *Degree program information:* Part-time and evening/weekend programs available. Offers educational leadership (MS). *Application deadline:* For fall admission, 9/7 for domestic students; for spring admission, 1/24 for domestic students. Applications are processed on a rolling basis. *Application fee:* $50. *Director of Educational Leadership,* Dr. Robert W. Valente, 215-489-4833, Fax: 215-489-4832, E-mail: robert.valente@devalcol.edu.

Program in Food and Agribusiness Offers food and agribusiness).

DELL'ARTE SCHOOL OF PHYSICAL THEATRE, Blue Lake, CA 95525

General Information Independent, coed, graduate-only institution.

GRADUATE UNITS

MFA Program Offers ensemble based physical theatre (MFA).

DELTA STATE UNIVERSITY, Cleveland, MS 38733-0001

General Information State-supported, coed, comprehensive institution. *Enrollment:* 4,217 graduate, professional, and undergraduate students; 211 full-time matriculated graduate/professional students (156 women), 519 part-time matriculated graduate/professional students (405 women). *Enrollment by degree level:* 624 master's, 42 doctoral, 64 other advanced degrees.

Graduate faculty: 59 full-time (18 women), 74 part-time/adjunct (35 women). *Graduate housing:* Rooms and/or apartments available on a first-come, first-served basis to single and married students. Housing application deadline: 6/1. *Student services:* Campus employment opportunities, campus safety program, career counseling, child daycare facilities, disabled student services, exercise/wellness program, free psychological counseling, international student services, low-cost health insurance, multicultural affairs office. *Library facilities:* Roberts-LaForge Library plus 1 other. *Online resources:* library catalog, web page. *Collection:* 360,286 titles, 1,258 serial subscriptions, 19,302 audiovisual materials.

Computer facilities: 293 computers available on campus for general student use. A campuswide network can be accessed from student residence rooms and from off campus. Internet access and online class registration, e-mail are available. *Web address:* http://www.deltastate.edu/.

General Application Contact: Dr. Tyrone Jackson, Assistant Dean of Graduate and Continuing Studies, 662-846-4875, Fax: 662-846-4313, E-mail: grad-info@deltastate.edu.

GRADUATE UNITS

Graduate Programs Students: 211 full-time (156 women), 519 part-time (405 women); includes 440 minority (430 African Americans, 1 American Indian/Alaska Native, 6 Asian Americans or Pacific Islanders, 3 Hispanic Americans). Average age 33. 611 applicants, 55% accepted. *Faculty:* 59 full-time (18 women), 74 part-time/adjunct (35 women). Expenses: Contact institution. *Financial support:* Fellowships, research assistantships, career-related internships or fieldwork, Federal Work-Study, institutionally sponsored loans, and unspecified assistantships available. Support available to part-time students. Financial award application deadline: 6/1. In 2006, 187 master's, 3 doctorates, 19 other advanced degrees awarded. *Degree program information:* Part-time and evening/weekend programs available. Postbaccalaureate distance learning degree programs offered (minimal on-campus study). *Application deadline:* For fall admission, 8/1 priority date for domestic students; for spring admission, 12/1 priority date for domestic students. Applications are processed on a rolling basis. *Application fee:* $15. Electronic applications accepted. *Application Contact:* Dr. Tyrone Jackson, Assistant Dean of Graduate and Continuing Studies, 662-846-4875, Fax: 662-846-4313, E-mail: grad-info@deltastate.edu. *Provost and Vice President for Academic Affairs,* Dr. John Thornell, 662-846-4010, Fax: 662-846-4015, E-mail: thornell@deltastate.edu.

College of Arts and Sciences Students: 19 full-time (15 women), 21 part-time (16 women); includes 23 minority (22 African Americans, 1 Hispanic American). Average age 29. *Faculty:* 31 full-time (8 women), 41 part-time/adjunct (15 women). Expenses: Contact institution. *Financial support:* Fellowships, research assistantships, career-related internships or fieldwork, Federal Work-Study, institutionally sponsored loans, and unspecified assistantships available. Support available to part-time students. Financial award application deadline: 6/1. In 2006, 33 degrees awarded. *Degree program information:* Part-time programs available. Offers arts and sciences (M Ed, MSCD, MSCJ, MSNS); biological and physical sciences (MSNS); community development (MSCD); criminal justice (MSCJ); English education (M Ed); history education (M Ed); mathematics education (M Ed); social science secondary education (M Ed). *Application deadline:* For fall admission, 8/1 priority date for domestic students; for spring admission, 12/1 priority date for domestic students. Applications are processed on a rolling basis. *Application fee:* $0. *Dean,* Collier Parker, 662-846-4100, Fax: 662-846-4016, E-mail: cparker@deltastate.edu.

College of Business Students: 37 full-time (20 women), 47 part-time (20 women); includes 31 minority (27 African Americans, 1 American Indian/Alaska Native, 3 Asian Americans or Pacific Islanders). Average age 28. *Faculty:* 9 full-time (1 woman), 8 part-time/adjunct (3 women). Expenses: Contact institution. *Financial support:* Research assistantships, career-related internships or fieldwork, Federal Work-Study, and institutionally sponsored loans available. Support available to part-time students. Financial award application deadline:6/1. In 2006, 42 degrees awarded. *Degree program information:* Part-time and evening/weekend programs available. Postbaccalaureate distance learning degree programs offered (minimal on-campus study). Offers accountancy (MPA); business (MBA, MCA, MPA); commercial aviation (MCA); management (MBA); marketing (MBA). *Application deadline:* For fall admission, 8/1 priority date for domestic students; for spring admission, 12/1 priority date for domestic students. Applications are processed on a rolling basis. *Application fee:* $0. *Application Contact:* Carla Johnson, Coordinator, College of Business Graduate Programs, 662-846-4234, Fax: 662-846-4215, E-mail: cjohnson@deltastate.edu. *Dean,* Dr. Billy Moore, 662-846-4200, Fax: 662-846-4215, E-mail: bcmoore@deltastate.edu.

College of Education Students: 107 full-time (75 women), 334 part-time (280 women); includes 306 minority (302 African Americans, 2 Asian Americans or Pacific Islanders, 2 Hispanic Americans). Average age 32. *Faculty:* 16 full-time (6 women), 23 part-time/adjunct (15 women). Expenses: Contact institution. *Financial support:* Research assistantships, career-related internships or fieldwork, Federal Work-Study, and institutionally sponsored loans available. Support available to part-time students. Financial award application deadline: 6/1. In 2006, 97 master's, 3 doctorates, 18 other advanced degrees awarded. *Degree program information:* Part-time and evening/weekend programs available. Offers administration and supervision (M Ed); administrative and supervision (Ed S); counseling (M Ed); education (M Ed, MAT, Ed D, Ed S); educational administration and supervision (Ed S); educational leadership (M Ed); elementary education (M Ed, MAT, Ed S); physical education and recreation (M Ed); secondary education (Ed S); special education (M Ed); teaching (Ed D). *Application deadline:* For fall admission, 8/1 priority date for domestic students; for spring admission, 12/1 priority date for domestic students. Applications are processed on a rolling basis. *Application fee:* $0. *Dean,* Dr. Matthew Buckley, 662-846-4400, Fax: 662-846-4402.

School of Nursing Students: 35 full-time (all women), 26 part-time (23 women); includes 20 minority (all African Americans) Average age 41. *Faculty:* 3 full-time (all women), 2 part-time/adjunct (1 woman). Expenses: Contact institution. *Financial support:* Research assistantships, career-related internships or fieldwork, Federal Work-Study, and institutionally sponsored loans available. Financial award application deadline: 6/1. In 2006, 15 degrees awarded. *Degree program information:* Part-time programs available. Offers nursing (MSN). *Application deadline:* For fall admission, 8/1 priority date for domestic students; for spring admission, 12/1 priority date for domestic students. Applications are processed on a rolling basis. *Application fee:* $0. Electronic applications accepted. *Dean,* Dr. Lizabeth Carlson, 662-846-4268, Fax: 662-846-4267, E-mail: lcarlson@deltastate.edu.

DENVER SEMINARY, Denver, CO 80250-0100

General Information Independent-religious, coed, graduate-only institution. *Graduate housing:* Rooms and/or apartments available on a first-come, first-served basis to single and married students. Housing application deadline: 6/1.

GRADUATE UNITS

Graduate and Professional Programs *Degree program information:* Part-time and evening/weekend programs available. Postbaccalaureate distance learning degree programs offered (minimal on-campus study). Offers biblical studies (MA); Christian studies (MA, Certificate); church and para church leadership (D Min); counseling licensure (MA); counseling ministry (MA); leadership (MA, Certificate); marriage and family counseling (D Min); pastoral ministry (D Min); philosophy of religion (MA); spiritual guidance (Certificate); theology (M Div, Certificate); youth and family ministry (MA). Electronic applications accepted.

DEPAUL UNIVERSITY, Chicago, IL 60604-2287

General Information Independent-religious, coed, university. *Enrollment:* 23,149 graduate, professional, and undergraduate students; 15,971 full-time matriculated graduate/professional students (8,766 women), 7,177 part-time matriculated graduate/professional students (3,886 women). *Enrollment by degree level:* 1,179 first professional, 6,823 master's, 247 doctoral, 96 other advanced degrees. *Graduate faculty:* 390 full-time (156 women), 251 part-time/adjunct (98 women). *Graduate housing:* On-campus housing not available. *Student services:* Campus employment opportunities, campus safety program, career counseling, disabled student services, exercise/wellness program, free psychological counseling, international student services, low-cost health insurance, multicultural affairs office, writing training. *Library facilities:* John T. Richardson Library plus 2 others. *Online resources:* library catalog, web page, access to other libraries' catalogs. *Collection:* 897,564 titles, 28,514 serial subscriptions, 27,242 audiovisual materials. *Research affiliation:* International Institute of Higher Studies in the Criminal Sciences (law), Metro Chicago Information Center (public services), Civic Federation (public services).

Computer facilities: 1,361 computers available on campus for general student use. A campuswide network can be accessed from student residence rooms and from off campus. Internet access and online class registration are available. *Web address:* http://www.depaul.edu/.

General Application Contact: Information Contact, 312-362-6709.

GRADUATE UNITS

Charles H. Kellstadt Graduate School of Business Students: 969 full-time (356 women), 837 part-time (335 women); includes 247 minority (53 African Americans, 4 American Indian/Alaska Native, 136 Asian Americans or Pacific Islanders, 54 Hispanic Americans), 153 international. Average age 28. 750 applicants, 84% accepted, 367 enrolled. *Faculty:* 134 full-time (32 women), 158 part-time/adjunct (36 women). Expenses: Contact institution. *Financial support:* In 2006–07, 701 students received support. Career-related internships or fieldwork, Federal Work-Study, institutionally sponsored loans, scholarships/grants, tuition waivers (full and partial), and unspecified assistantships available. Support available to part-time students. Financial award application deadline: 4/1. In 2006, 624 degrees awarded. *Degree program information:* Part-time and evening/weekend programs available. Offers applied economics (MBA); behavioral finance (MBA); brand management (MBA); business (M Acc, MA, MBA, MS, MSA, MSF, MSHR, MSMA, MST); computational finance (MS); customer relationship management (MBA); economics (MA); entrepreneurship (MBA); finance (MBA, MSF); financial analysis (MBA); financial management and control (MBA); health sector management (MBA); human resource management (MBA, MSHR); integrated marketing communication (MBA); international business (MBA); international marketing and finance (MBA); leadership/change management (MBA); management planning and strategy (MBA); managerial finance (MBA); marketing analysis (MSMA); marketing and management (MBA); marketing strategy and analysis (MBA); marketing strategy and planning (MBA); new product management (MBA); operations management (MBA); real estate (MS); real estate finance and investment (MBA); sales leadership (MBA); strategy, execution and valuation (MBA). *Application deadline:* For fall admission, 7/1 for domestic students, 6/1 for international students; for winter admission, 10/1 for domestic students, 9/1 for international students; for spring admission, 2/1 for domestic students, 1/1 for international students. Applications are processed on a rolling basis. *Application fee:* $60. Electronic applications accepted. *Application Contact:* Christopher E. Kinsella, Director of Cohort MBA Programs, 312-362-8810, Fax: 312-362-6677, E-mail: kgsb@depaul.edu. *Assistant Dean and Director,* Robert T. Ryan, 312-362-8810, Fax: 312-362-6677, E-mail: rryan1@depaul.edu.

School of Accountancy and Management Information Systems Students: 127 full-time (53 women), 209 part-time (101 women); includes 53 minority (13 African Americans, 3 American Indian/Alaska Native, 28 Asian Americans or Pacific Islanders, 9 Hispanic Americans), 56 international. Average age 30. *Faculty:* 30 full-time (9 women), 54 part-time/adjunct (7 women). Expenses: Contact institution. *Financial support:* In 2006–07, 7 research assistantships with full tuition reimbursements (averaging $4,100 per year) were awarded; institutionally sponsored loans also available. Financial award application deadline: 4/2. In 2006, 141 degrees awarded. *Degree program information:* Part-time and evening/weekend programs available. Offers accountancy (M Acc, MSA); business information technology (MS); e-business (MBA, MS); financial management and control (MBA); management accounting (MBA); management information systems (MBA); taxation (MST). *Application deadline:* For fall admission, 7/1 for domestic students; for winter admission, 10/1 for domestic students; for spring admission, 2/1 for domestic students. Applications are processed on a rolling basis. *Application fee:* $60. *Application Contact:* Christopher E. Kinsella, Director of Cohort MBA Programs, 312-362-8810, Fax: 312-362-6677, E-mail: kgsb@depaul.edu.

College of Law Students: 943 full-time (468 women), 236 part-time (119 women); includes 222 minority (72 African Americans, 3 American Indian/Alaska Native, 72 Asian Americans or Pacific Islanders, 75 Hispanic Americans), 16 international. Average age 27. 5,028 applicants, 28% accepted, 330 enrolled. *Faculty:* 45 full-time (18 women), 54 part-time/adjunct (16 women). Expenses: Contact institution. *Financial support:* In 2006–07, 527 students received support, including 38 fellowships with tuition reimbursements available, 98 research assistantships (averaging $1,200 per year), 16 teaching assistantships (averaging $2,000 per year); career-related internships or fieldwork, Federal Work-Study, scholarships/grants, and tuition waivers (full and partial) also available. Support available to part-time students. Financial award application deadline: 3/1; financial award applicants required to submit FAFSA. In 2006, 311 degrees awarded. *Degree program information:* Part-time programs available. Offers law (JD, LL M). *Application deadline:* For fall admission, 3/1 for domestic students. Applications are processed on a rolling basis. *Application fee:* $60. Electronic applications accepted. *Application Contact:* Michael S Burns, Director of Law Admission and Assistant Dean, 312-362-6831, Fax: 312-362-5280, E-mail: lawinfo@depaul.edu. *Dean,* Glen Weissenberger, 312-362-8088, E-mail: gweissen@depaul.edu.

College of Liberal Arts and Sciences Students: 735 full-time (503 women), 753 part-time (512 women); includes 307 minority (154 African Americans, 4 American Indian/Alaska Native, 68 Asian Americans or Pacific Islanders, 81 Hispanic Americans), 55 international. Average age 31. 1,560 applicants, 47% accepted. *Faculty:* 219 full-time (91 women), 134 part-time/adjunct (52 women). Expenses: Contact institution. *Financial support:* In 2006–07, 60 fellowships with full and partial tuition reimbursements, 12 research assistantships with full and partial tuition reimbursements (averaging $2,500 per year) were awarded; teaching assistantships, career-related internships or fieldwork, Federal Work-Study, institutionally sponsored loans, scholarships/grants, traineeships, tuition waivers (full and partial), and unspecified assistantships also available. Support available to part-time students. Financial award applicants required to submit FAFSA. In 2006, 381 master's, 11 doctorates awarded. *Degree program information:* Part-time and evening/weekend programs available. Offers advanced practice nursing (MS); applied mathematics (MS); applied physics (MS); applied statistics (MS, Certificate); biochemistry (MS); biological sciences (MA, MS); chemistry (MS); clinical psychology (MA, PhD); English (MA); experimental psychology (MA, PhD); general psychology (MS); history (MA); industrial/organizational psychology (MA, PhD); interdisciplinary studies (MA, MS); liberal arts and sciences (MA, MBA, MS, PhD, Certificate); liberal studies (MA); masters entry into nursing practice (MS); mathematics education (MA); multicultural communication (MA); nurse anesthesia (MS); organizational communication (MA); philosophy (MA, PhD); polymer chemistry and coatings technology (MS); sociology (MA); writing (MA). *Application deadline:* Applications are processed on a rolling basis. *Application fee:* $25. Electronic applications accepted. *Application Contact:* Director of Graduate Admissions, 312-362-8300, Fax: 312-362-5749, E-mail: admitdpu@depaul.edu. *Dean,* Michael Mezey, 773-325-7300, Fax: 773-325-7304, E-mail: mmezey@depaul.edu.

School for New Learning Students: 16 full-time (9 women), 139 part-time (96 women); includes 75 minority (42 African Americans, 1 American Indian/Alaska Native, 25 Asian Americans or Pacific Islanders, 7 Hispanic Americans), 1 international. Average age 42. 30 applicants, 80% accepted. *Faculty:* 8 full-time (2 women), 9 part-time/adjunct (5 women). Expenses: Contact institution. *Financial support:* In 2006–07, 7 students received support. Scholarships/grants and tuition waivers (partial) available. Financial award applicants required to submit FAFSA. In 2006, 20 master's awarded. *Degree program information:* Part-time and evening/weekend programs available. Offers applied technology (MS); educating adults (MA); integrated professional studies (MA). *Application deadline:* For fall admission, 9/1 priority date for domestic students; for spring admission, 3/1 priority date for domestic students. Applications are processed on a rolling basis. *Application fee:* $25. Electronic applications accepted. *Application Contact:* Berni Thomas, Assistant Director, 312-362-5744, Fax: 312-362-8809, E-mail: bthoma10@depaul.edu. *Program Director,* Dr. Barbara Radner, 312-362-5515, Fax: 312-362-8809, E-mail: bradner@depaul.edu.

School of Computer Science, Telecommunications, and Information Systems Students: 1,002 full-time (246 women), 995 part-time (263 women); includes 475 minority (185 African Americans, 3 American Indian/Alaska Native, 207 Asian Americans or Pacific Islanders, 80 Hispanic Americans), 329 international. Average age 31. 830 applicants, 80% accepted, 400 enrolled. *Faculty:* 80 full-time (13 women), 133 part-time/adjunct (29 women). Expenses:

DePaul University (continued)

Contact institution. *Financial support:* In 2006–07, 63 teaching assistantships with full and partial tuition reimbursements (averaging $9,085 per year) were awarded; fellowships, research assistantships, Federal Work-Study, tuition waivers (full and partial), and unspecified assistantships also available. Support available to part-time students. Financial award application deadline: 4/1; financial award applicants required to submit FAFSA. In 2006, 514 master's, 4 doctorates awarded. *Degree program information:* Part-time and evening/weekend programs available. Postbaccalaureate distance learning degree programs offered (no on-campus study). Offers business information technology (MS); computational finance (MS); computer graphics and animation (MS); computer science (MS, PhD); computer, information and network security (MS); digital cinema (MFA, MS); e-commerce technology (MS); human-computer interaction (MS); information systems (MS); information technology (MA); instructional technology systems (MS); software engineering (MS); telecommunication systems (MS). *Application deadline:* For fall admission, 8/1 priority date for domestic and international students; for winter admission, 11/15 priority date for domestic and international students; for spring admission, 3/1 priority date for domestic and international students. Applications are processed on a rolling basis. *Application fee:* $25. Electronic applications accepted. *Application Contact:* Maureen Garvey, Information Contact, 312-362-8714, Fax: 312-362-5327, E-mail: mgarvey@cti.depaul.edu. *Dean,* Dr. David Miller, 312-362-8381, Fax: 312-362-5185.

School of Education Students: 1,371 full-time (1,103 women), 474 part-time (362 women); includes 435 minority (144 African Americans, 7 American Indian/Alaska Native, 89 Asian Americans or Pacific Islanders, 195 Hispanic Americans), 11 international. Average age 30. 993 applicants, 80% accepted, 617 enrolled. *Faculty:* 61 full-time (40 women), 76 part-time/adjunct (46 women). Expenses: Contact institution. *Financial support:* In 2006–07, 16 research assistantships with tuition reimbursements (averaging $4,370 per year), 1 teaching assistantship (averaging $6,000 per year) were awarded; career-related internships or fieldwork also available. In 2006, 324 master's, 7 doctorates awarded. *Degree program information:* Part-time and evening/weekend programs available. Offers bilingual and bicultural education (M Ed, MA); curriculum studies (M Ed, MA, Ed D); education (Ed D); educational leadership (M Ed, MA, Ed D); human development and learning (MA); human services and counseling (M Ed, MA); reading and learning disabilities (M Ed, MA); social culture studies in education and development (M Ed, MA); teaching and learning (early childhood, elementary and secondary) (M Ed); teaching and learning (early childhood, elementary, and secondary) (MA). *Application fee:* $25. Electronic applications accepted. *Application Contact:* Dr. John Bollwark, Data Project Manager, 773-325-7582, Fax: 773-325-7713, E-mail: jbollwar@depaul.edu. *Dean,* Dr. Clara Jennings, 773-325-7581, Fax: 773-325-7728, E-mail: cjennings@depaul.edu.

School of Music Students: 9 full-time (1 woman), 18 part-time (3 women); includes 1 minority (African American), 1 international. Average age 27. 175 applicants, 46% accepted. *Faculty:* 11 full-time (2 women), 50 part-time/adjunct (14 women). Expenses: Contact institution. *Financial support:* In 2006–07, 4 fellowships with partial tuition reimbursements were awarded; teaching assistantships, career-related internships or fieldwork, Federal Work-Study, scholarships/grants, and tuition waivers also available. Support available to part-time students. Financial award application deadline: 1/15. In 2006, 40 master's, 5 other advanced degrees awarded. *Degree program information:* Part-time and evening/weekend programs available. Offers applied music (performance) (MM, Certificate); jazz studies (MM); music composition (MM); music education (MM). *Application deadline:* For fall admission, 1/15 priority date for domestic and international students. Applications are processed on a rolling basis. Electronic applications accepted. *Application Contact:* Ross Beacraft, Director of Admissions, 773-325-7444, Fax: 773-325-7429, E-mail: rbeacraft@depaul.edu. *Dean,* Dr. Donald E. Casey, 773-325-7256.

School of Public Service Students: 195 full-time (146 women), 132 part-time (89 women); includes 114 minority (58 African Americans, 1 American Indian/Alaska Native, 27 Asian Americans or Pacific Islanders, 28 Hispanic Americans). 140 applicants, 96% accepted, 96 enrolled. *Faculty:* 11 full-time (2 women), 19 part-time/adjunct (16 women). Expenses: Contact institution. *Financial support:* In 2006–07, 28 students received support, including 3 research assistantships with full tuition reimbursements available (averaging $7,000 per year); career-related internships or fieldwork, Federal Work-Study, institutionally sponsored loans, scholarships/grants, and tuition waivers (partial) also available. Support available to part-time students. Financial award application deadline: 7/1; financial award applicants required to submit FAFSA. In 2006, 89 degrees awarded. *Degree program information:* Part-time and evening/weekend programs available. Postbaccalaureate distance learning degree programs offered (minimal on-campus study). Offers financial administration management (Certificate); health administration (Certificate); health law and policy (MS); international public services (MS); metropolitan planning (Certificate); public administration (MS); public service management (MS); public services (Certificate). *Application deadline:* Applications are processed on a rolling basis. *Application fee:* $25. Electronic applications accepted. *Application Contact:* Megan B. Balderston, Director of Admissions and Marketing, 312-362-5565, Fax: 312-362-5506, E-mail: pubserv@depaul.edu. *Director,* Dr. J. Patrick Murphy, 312-362-5608, Fax: 312-362-5506, E-mail: jpmurphy@depaul.edu.

The Theatre School Students: 35 full-time (18 women); includes 5 minority (4 African Americans, 1 Hispanic American). Average age 28. 208 applicants, 11% accepted, 14 enrolled. *Faculty:* 28 full-time (15 women), 42 part-time/adjunct (17 women). Expenses: Contact institution. *Financial support:* In 2006–07, 26 fellowships (averaging $9,820 per year) were awarded; career-related internships or fieldwork, Federal Work-Study, and institutionally sponsored loans also available. Financial award application deadline: 2/15; financial award applicants required to submit FAFSA. In 2006, 9 degrees awarded. Offers acting (MFA, Certificate); directing (MFA). *Application deadline:* For fall admission, 1/15 priority date for domestic and international students. *Application fee:* $35. Electronic applications accepted. *Application Contact:* Jason Beck, Director of Admissions, 773-325-7999, Fax: 773-325-7920, E-mail: jbeck1@depaul.edu. *Chair,* John Culbert, 773-325-7917 Ext. 7954, Fax: 773-325-7920, E-mail: jculbert@depaul.edu.

DESALES UNIVERSITY, Center Valley, PA 18034-9568

General Information Independent-religious, coed, comprehensive institution. *Enrollment:* 2,936 graduate, professional, and undergraduate students; 58 full-time matriculated graduate/professional students, 752 part-time matriculated graduate/professional students. *Enrollment by degree level:* 810 master's. *Graduate housing:* On-campus housing not available. *Student services:* Career counseling. *Library facilities:* Trexler Library. *Online resources:* library catalog, web page, access to other libraries' catalogs. *Collection:* 151,999 titles, 12,000 serial subscriptions, 4,926 audiovisual materials.

Computer facilities: Computer purchase and lease plans are available. 200 computers available on campus for general student use. A campuswide network can be accessed from student residence rooms and from off campus. Internet access is available. *Web address:* http://www.desales.edu.

General Application Contact: Rev. Peter J. Leonard, Dean of Graduate Education, 610-282-1100 Ext. 1289, Fax: 610-282-0525, E-mail: peter.leonard@desales.edu.

GRADUATE UNITS

Graduate Division Students: 58 full-time, 752 part-time. Expenses: Contact institution. *Financial support:* Career-related internships or fieldwork available. Support available to part-time students. Financial award applicants required to submit FAFSA. In 2006, 180 degrees awarded. *Degree program information:* Part-time and evening/weekend programs available. Offers academic standards and information (Certificate); adult advanced practice nurse specialist (MSN); bilingual/ESL studies (Certificate); biology (M Ed); business administration (MBA); chemistry (M Ed); computers in education (K-12) (M Ed); computers in education (K-8) (M Ed); criminal justice (MACJ); English (M Ed); family nurse practitioner (MSN); information systems (MSIS); instructional technology specialist (Certificate); mathematics (M Ed); nurse educator (MSN); physician assistant studies (MSPAS); special education (M Ed, Certificate); TESOL (M Ed). *Application deadline:* Applications are processed on a rolling basis. *Dean of Graduate Education,* Rev. Peter J. Leonard, 610-282-1100 Ext. 1289, Fax: 610-282-0525, E-mail: peter.leonard@desales.edu.

DES MOINES UNIVERSITY, Des Moines, IA 50312-4104

General Information Independent, coed, graduate-only institution. *Enrollment:* 1,252 full-time matriculated graduate/professional students (635 women), 20 part-time matriculated graduate/professional students (17 women). *Enrollment by degree level:* 1,098 first professional, 174 master's. *Graduate faculty:* 68 full-time (28 women), 22 part-time/adjunct (6 women). *Graduate housing:* On-campus housing not available. *Student services:* Campus employment opportunities, campus safety program, career counseling, exercise/wellness program, free psychological counseling, international student services, low-cost health insurance, multicultural affairs office. *Library facilities:* University Library. *Online resources:* library catalog, web page, access to other libraries' catalogs. *Collection:* 58,039 titles, 581 serial subscriptions, 5,074 audiovisual materials.

Computer facilities: A campuswide network can be accessed from off campus. Internet access, online classes are available. *Web address:* http://www.dmu.edu/.

General Application Contact: Margie Gehringer, Director of Enrollment Management, 515-271-7498, Fax: 515-271-7190, E-mail: margie.gehringer@dmu.edu.

GRADUATE UNITS

College of Health Sciences *Faculty:* 14 full-time (7 women), 5 part-time/adjunct (3 women). Expenses: Contact institution. *Financial support:* In 2006–07, 53 students received support. Career-related internships or fieldwork, institutionally sponsored loans, scholarships/grants, and university employment available. Support available to part-time students. Financial award application deadline: 4/15; financial award applicants required to submit FAFSA. *Degree program information:* Part-time and evening/weekend programs available. Postbaccalaureate distance learning degree programs offered (minimal on-campus study). Offers health sciences (MHA, MPH, MS, DPT); healthcare administration (MHA); physical therapy (DPT); physician assistant (MS); public health (MPH). *Dean,* Jodi Cahalan, 515-271-1415, E-mail: jodi.cahalan@dmu.edu.

College of Osteopathic Medicine Students: 814 full-time (383 women); includes 72 minority (8 African Americans, 1 American Indian/Alaska Native, 48 Asian Americans or Pacific Islanders, 15 Hispanic Americans), 12 international. Average age 25. 1,637 applicants, 25% accepted, 215 enrolled. *Faculty:* 40 full-time (16 women), 22 part-time/adjunct (4 women). Expenses: Contact institution. *Financial support:* In 2006–07, 102 students received support, including 9 fellowships with tuition reimbursements available (averaging $6,000 per year); institutionally sponsored loans, scholarships/grants, and university employment also available. Support available to part-time students. Financial award application deadline: 7/15; financial award applicants required to submit FAFSA. In 2006, 198 degrees awarded. Offers osteopathic medicine (DO). *Application deadline:* For fall admission, 2/1 for domestic students, 2/1 priority date for international students. Applications are processed on a rolling basis. *Application fee:* $50. Electronic applications accepted. *Application Contact:* Jamie Rehmann, Director of Admissions, 515-271-1451, Fax: 515-271-7163, E-mail: doadmit@dmu.edu. *Dean,* Dr. Kendall Reed, 515-271-1515, Fax: 515-271-1532, E-mail: kendall.reed@dmu.edu.

College of Podiatric Medicine and Surgery Students: 181 full-time (51 women); includes 16 minority (4 African Americans, 4 American Indian/Alaska Native, 6 Asian Americans or Pacific Islanders, 2 Hispanic Americans), 4 international. Average age 24. 317 applicants, 28% accepted, 61 enrolled. *Faculty:* 5 full-time (1 woman), 1 part-time/adjunct (0 women). Expenses: Contact institution. *Financial support:* In 2006–07, 82 students received support. Institutionally sponsored loans, scholarships/grants, and university employment available. Support available to part-time students. Financial award application deadline: 7/15; financial award applicants required to submit FAFSA. In 2006, 31 degrees awarded. Offers podiatric medicine and surgery (DPM). *Application deadline:* For fall admission, 4/15 priority date for domestic and international students. Applications are processed on a rolling basis. *Application fee:* $0. Electronic applications accepted. *Application Contact:* Meghan Good, Admissions Coordinator, 515-271-7497, E-mail: cpmsadmit@dmu.edu. *Dean,* Dr. Robert Yoho, 515-271-1464, Fax: 515-271-1521, E-mail: robert.yoho@dmu.edu.

DEVRY UNIVERSITY, Houston, TX 77041

General Information Proprietary, coed, comprehensive institution.

GRADUATE UNITS

Keller Graduate School of Management Offers management (MBA, MISM, MPA, MPM).

DEVRY UNIVERSITY, Tampa, FL 33607-5901

General Information Proprietary, coed, comprehensive institution.

GRADUATE UNITS

Keller Graduate School of Management Offers management (MAFM, MBA, MHRM, MISM, MNCM, MPA, MPM).

DEVRY UNIVERSITY, Chicago, IL 60618-5994

General Information Proprietary, coed, comprehensive institution.

GRADUATE UNITS

Keller Graduate School of Management

DEVRY UNIVERSITY, Orlando, FL 32839

General Information Proprietary, coed, comprehensive institution.

GRADUATE UNITS

Keller Graduate School of Management Offers management (MAFM, MBA, MHRM, MISM, MNCM, MPA, MPM).

DEVRY UNIVERSITY, Bellevue, WA 98004-5519

General Information Proprietary, coed, comprehensive institution.

GRADUATE UNITS

Keller Graduate School of Management Offers management (MAFM, MBA, MHRM, MISM, MNCM, MPA, MPM).

DEVRY UNIVERSITY, Mesa, AZ 85210-2011

General Information Proprietary, coed, comprehensive institution.

GRADUATE UNITS

Keller Graduate School of Management Offers management (MAFM, MBA, MHRM, MISM, MNCM, MPA, MPM).

DEVRY UNIVERSITY, Phoenix, AZ 85021-2995

General Information Proprietary, coed, comprehensive institution.

GRADUATE UNITS

Keller Graduate School of Management Offers management (MAFM, MBA, MHRM, MISM, MNCM, MPA, MPM).

DEVRY UNIVERSITY, Scottsdale, AZ 85258-5140

General Information Proprietary, coed, graduate-only institution.

GRADUATE UNITS

Keller Graduate School of Management Offers management (MAFM, MBA, MHRM, MISM, MNCM, MPA, MPM).

DEVRY UNIVERSITY, Elk Grove, CA 95758

General Information Proprietary, coed, comprehensive institution.

GRADUATE UNITS

Keller Graduate School of Management Offers management (MAFM, MBA, MHRM, MISM, MNCM, MPA, MPM).

DEVRY UNIVERSITY, Fremont, CA 94555

General Information Proprietary, coed, comprehensive institution.

GRADUATE UNITS

Keller Graduate School of Management Offers management (MAFM, MBA, MHRM, MISM, MNCM, MPA, MPM).

DEVRY UNIVERSITY, Irvine, CA 92612-1682

General Information Proprietary, coed, comprehensive institution.

GRADUATE UNITS

Keller Graduate School of Management Offers management (MAFM, MBA, MHRM, MISM, MNCM, MPA, MPM).

DEVRY UNIVERSITY, Long Beach, CA 90806

General Information Proprietary, coed, comprehensive institution.

GRADUATE UNITS

Keller Graduate School of Management Offers management (MAFM, MBA, MHRM, MISM, MNCM, MPA, MPM).

DEVRY UNIVERSITY, Pomona, CA 91768-2642

General Information Proprietary, coed, comprehensive institution.

GRADUATE UNITS

Keller Graduate School of Management Offers management (MAFM, MBA, MHRM, MISM, MNCM, MPA, MPM).

DEVRY UNIVERSITY, San Diego, CA 92108-1633

General Information Proprietary, coed, comprehensive institution.

GRADUATE UNITS

Keller Graduate School of Management Offers management (MAFM, MBA, MHRM, MISM, MNCM, MPA, MPM).

DEVRY UNIVERSITY, San Francisco, CA 94105-2472

General Information Proprietary, coed, comprehensive institution.

GRADUATE UNITS

Keller Graduate School of Management Offers management (MAFM, MBA, MHRM, MISM, MNCM, MPA, MPM).

DEVRY UNIVERSITY, West Hills, CA 91304

General Information Proprietary, coed, comprehensive institution.

GRADUATE UNITS

Keller Graduate School of Management Offers management (MAFM, MBA, MHRM, MISM, MNCM, MPA, MPM).

DEVRY UNIVERSITY, Kansas City, MO 64105-2112

General Information Proprietary, coed, comprehensive institution.

GRADUATE UNITS

Keller Graduate School of Management Offers management (MAFM, MBA, MHRM, MISM, MNCM, MPA, MPM).

DEVRY UNIVERSITY, Broomfield, CO 80021-2588

General Information Proprietary, coed, comprehensive institution.

GRADUATE UNITS

Keller Graduate School of Management

DEVRY UNIVERSITY, Colorado Springs, CO 80910

General Information Proprietary, coed, comprehensive institution.

GRADUATE UNITS

Keller Graduate School of Management Offers management (MAFM, MBA, MHRM, MISM, MNCM, MPA, MPM).

DEVRY UNIVERSITY, Atlanta, GA 30305-1543

General Information Proprietary, coed, comprehensive institution.

GRADUATE UNITS

Keller Graduate School of Management Offers management (MAFM, MBA, MHRM, MISM, MNCM, MPA, MPM).

DEVRY UNIVERSITY, Miami, FL 33131-5351

General Information Proprietary, coed, comprehensive institution.

GRADUATE UNITS

Keller Graduate School of Management Offers management (MAFM, MBA, MHRM, MISM, MNCM, MPA, MPM).

DEVRY UNIVERSITY, Miramar, FL 33027-4150

General Information Proprietary, coed, comprehensive institution.

GRADUATE UNITS

Keller Graduate School of Management Offers management (MAFM, MBA, MHRM, MISM, MNCM, MPA, MPM).

DEVRY UNIVERSITY, Alpharetta, GA 30004

General Information Proprietary, coed, comprehensive institution.

GRADUATE UNITS

Keller Graduate School of Management Offers management (MAFM, MBA, MHRM, MISM, MNCM, MPA, MPM).

DEVRY UNIVERSITY, Decatur, GA 30030-2198

General Information Proprietary, coed, comprehensive institution.

GRADUATE UNITS

Keller Graduate School of Management Offers management (MAFM, MBA, MHRM, MISM, MNCM, MPA, MPM).

DEVRY UNIVERSITY, Duluth, GA 30096-7671

General Information Proprietary, coed, comprehensive institution.

GRADUATE UNITS

Keller Graduate School of Management Offers management (MAFM, MBA, MHRM, MISM, MNCM, MPA, MPM).

DEVRY UNIVERSITY, Elgin, IL 60123-9341

General Information Proprietary, coed, comprehensive institution.

GRADUATE UNITS

Keller Graduate School of Management Offers management (MAFM, MBA, MHRM, MISM, MNCM, MPA, MPM).

DEVRY UNIVERSITY, Gurnee, IL 60031-9126

General Information Proprietary, coed, comprehensive institution.

GRADUATE UNITS

Keller Graduate School of Management Offers management (MAFM, MBA, MHRM, MISM, MNCM, MPA, MPM).

DEVRY UNIVERSITY, Lincolnshire, IL 60069-4460

General Information Proprietary, coed, graduate-only institution.

GRADUATE UNITS

Keller Graduate School of Management Offers management (MAFM, MBA, MHRM, MISM, MNCM, MPA, MPM).

DEVRY UNIVERSITY, Naperville, IL 60563-2361

General Information Proprietary, coed, comprehensive institution.

GRADUATE UNITS

Keller Graduate School of Management Offers management (MAFM, MBA, MHRM, MISM, MNCM, MPA, MPM).

DEVRY UNIVERSITY, Oakbrook Terrace, IL 60181

General Information Proprietary, coed, comprehensive institution. *Graduate housing:* On-campus housing not available.

GRADUATE UNITS

Keller Graduate School of Management *Degree program information:* Part-time and evening/weekend programs available. Postbaccalaureate distance learning degree programs offered (no on-campus study). Offers accounting and financial management (MAFM); business administration (MBA); human resources management (MHRM); information systems management (MISM); network and communications management (MNCM); project management (MPM); public administration (MPA); telecommunications management (MTM). Electronic applications accepted.

DEVRY UNIVERSITY, Schaumburg, IL 60173-5009

General Information Proprietary, coed, graduate-only institution.

GRADUATE UNITS

Keller Graduate School of Management Offers management (MAFM, MBA, MHRM, MISM, MNCM, MPA, MPM).

DEVRY UNIVERSITY, Tinley Park, IL 60477

General Information Proprietary, coed, comprehensive institution.

GRADUATE UNITS

Keller Graduate School of Management Offers management (MAFM, MBA, MHRM, MISM, MNCM, MPA, MPM).

DEVRY UNIVERSITY, Indianapolis, IN 46240-2158

General Information Proprietary, coed, comprehensive institution.

GRADUATE UNITS

Keller Graduate School of Management Offers management (MAFM, MBA, MHRM, MISM, MNCM, MPA, MPM).

DEVRY UNIVERSITY, Merrillville, IN 46410-5673

General Information Proprietary, coed, comprehensive institution.

GRADUATE UNITS

Keller Graduate School of Management Offers management (MAFM, MBA, MHRM, MISM, MNCM, MPA, MPM).

DEVRY UNIVERSITY, Bethesda, MD 20814-3304

General Information Proprietary, coed, comprehensive institution.

GRADUATE UNITS

Keller Graduate School of Management Offers management (MAFM, MBA, MHRM, MISM, MNCM, MPA, MPM, Graduate Certificate).

DEVRY UNIVERSITY, St. Louis, MO 63146-4020

General Information Proprietary, coed, comprehensive institution.

GRADUATE UNITS

Keller Graduate School of Management Offers management (MAFM, MBA, MHRM, MISM, MNCM, MPA, MPM).

DEVRY UNIVERSITY, Henderson, NV 89074-7120

General Information Proprietary, coed, comprehensive institution.

GRADUATE UNITS

Keller Graduate School of Management Offers management (MAFM, MBA, MHRM, MISM, MNCM, MPA, MPM).

DEVRY UNIVERSITY, Charlotte, NC 28211-3627

General Information Proprietary, coed, comprehensive institution.

GRADUATE UNITS

Keller Graduate School of Management Offers management (MAFM, MBA, MHRM, MISM, MNCM, MPA, MPM).

DEVRY UNIVERSITY, Cleveland, OH 44114-2301

General Information Proprietary, coed, comprehensive institution.

GRADUATE UNITS

Keller Graduate School of Management Offers management (MAFM, MBA, MHRM, MISM, MNCM, MPA, MPM).

DEVRY UNIVERSITY, Columbus, OH 43209-2705

General Information Proprietary, coed, comprehensive institution.

GRADUATE UNITS

Keller Graduate School of Management Offers management (MAFM, MBA, MHRM, MISM, MNCM, MPA, MPM).

DEVRY UNIVERSITY, Seven Hills, OH 44131-6907

General Information Proprietary, coed, comprehensive institution.

GRADUATE UNITS

Keller Graduate School of Management Offers management (MAFM, MBA, MHRM, MISM, MNCM, MPA, MPM).

DEVRY UNIVERSITY, Portland, OR 97225-6651

General Information Proprietary, coed, comprehensive institution.

GRADUATE UNITS

Keller Graduate School of Management Offers management (MAFM, MBA, MHRM, MISM, MNCM, MPA, MPM).

DEVRY UNIVERSITY, Chesterbrook, PA 19087-5612

General Information Proprietary, coed, comprehensive institution.

GRADUATE UNITS

Keller Graduate School of Management Offers management (MAFM, MBA, MHRM, MISM, MNCM, MPA, MPM).

DEVRY UNIVERSITY, Fort Washington, PA 19034

General Information Proprietary, coed, comprehensive institution.

GRADUATE UNITS

Keller Graduate School of Management Offers management (MAFM, MBA, MHRM, MISM, MNCM, MPA, MPM).

DEVRY UNIVERSITY, Pittsburgh, PA 15222-9123

General Information Proprietary, coed, comprehensive institution.

GRADUATE UNITS

Keller Graduate School of Management Offers management (MAFM, MBA, MHRM, MISM, MNCM, MPA, MPM).

DEVRY UNIVERSITY, Irving, TX 75063-2439

General Information Proprietary, coed, comprehensive institution.

GRADUATE UNITS

Keller Graduate School of Management Offers management (MAFM, MBA, MHRM, MISM, MNCM, MPA, MPM).

DEVRY UNIVERSITY, Plano, TX 75075-8435

General Information Proprietary, coed, comprehensive institution.

GRADUATE UNITS

Keller Graduate School of Management Offers management (MAFM, MBA, MHRM, MISM, MNCM, MPA, MPM).

DEVRY UNIVERSITY, Arlington, VA 22202

General Information Proprietary, coed, comprehensive institution.

GRADUATE UNITS

Keller Graduate School of Management Offers management (MAFM, MBA, MHRM, MISM, MNCM, MPA, MPM).

DEVRY UNIVERSITY, McLean, VA 22102-3832

General Information Proprietary, coed, comprehensive institution.

GRADUATE UNITS

Keller Graduate School of Management Offers management (MAFM, MBA, MHRM, MISM, MNCM, MPA, MPM).

DEVRY UNIVERSITY, Federal Way, WA 98001

General Information Proprietary, coed, comprehensive institution.

GRADUATE UNITS

Keller Graduate School of Management Offers management (MAFM, MBA, MHRM, MISM, MNCM, MPA, MPM).

DEVRY UNIVERSITY, Milwaukee, WI 53202-4107

General Information Proprietary, coed, comprehensive institution.

GRADUATE UNITS

Keller Graduate School of Management Offers management (MAFM, MBA, MHRM, MISM, MNCM, MPA, MPM).

DEVRY UNIVERSITY, Waukesha, WI 53186-4047

General Information Proprietary, coed, comprehensive institution.

GRADUATE UNITS

Keller Graduate School of Management Offers management (MAFM, MBA, MHRM, MISM, MNCM, MPA, MPM).

DIGIPEN INSTITUTE OF TECHNOLOGY, Redmond, WA 98052

General Information Proprietary, coed, comprehensive institution. *Library facilities:* DigiPen Library plus 1 other. *Online resources:* library catalog. *Collection:* 2,117 titles, 52 serial subscriptions, 277 audiovisual materials. *Web address:* http://www.digipen.edu/.

General Application Contact: Office of Admissions, 866-478-5236, Fax: 425-558-0378, E-mail: admissions@digipen.edu.

DOANE COLLEGE, Crete, NE 68333-2430

General Information Independent-religious, coed, comprehensive institution. *Graduate housing:* On-campus housing not available.

GRADUATE UNITS

Program in Counseling *Degree program information:* Evening/weekend programs available. Offers counseling (MAC).

Program in Education *Degree program information:* Part-time and evening/weekend programs available. Offers curriculum and instruction (M Ed); educational leadership (M Ed). Electronic applications accepted.

Program in Management *Degree program information:* Part-time and evening/weekend programs available. Offers management (MA).

DOMINICAN COLLEGE, Orangeburg, NY 10962-1210

General Information Independent, coed, comprehensive institution. *Enrollment:* 1,856 graduate, professional, and undergraduate students; 48 full-time matriculated graduate/professional students (31 women), 105 part-time matriculated graduate/professional students (85 women). *Enrollment by degree level:* 153 master's. *Graduate faculty:* 12 full-time (11 women), 27 part-time/adjunct (21 women). *Graduate housing:* Room and/or apartments available on a first-come, first-served basis to single students; on-campus housing not available to married students. Typical cost: $4,490 (including board). *Student services:* Campus employment opportunities, career counseling, disabled student services, free psychological counseling, teacher training, writing training. *Library facilities:* Pius X Hall plus 1 other. *Online resources:* library catalog, access to other libraries' catalogs. *Collection:* 103,350 titles, 650 serial subscriptions.

Computer facilities: 38 computers available on campus for general student use. A campuswide network can be accessed from student residence rooms. Internet access is available. *Web address:* http://www.dc.edu/.

General Application Contact: Joyce Elbe, Director of Admissions, 845-848-7896 Ext. 15, Fax: 845-365-3150, E-mail: admissions@dc.edu.

GRADUATE UNITS

Division of Allied Health Expenses: Contact institution. Offers allied health (MS, DPT); occupational therapy (MS); physical therapy (MS, DPT). *Division Director,* Sr. Beryl Herdt, 845-848-6000, Fax: 845-398-4893, E-mail: beryl.herdt@dc.edu.

Division of Nursing Expenses: Contact institution. Offers family nurse practitioner (MSN); nursing (MSN). *Division Director, Nursing,* Dr. Maureen Creegan, 845-848-6027, Fax: 845-398-4891, E-mail: maureen.creegan@dc.edu.

Division of Teacher Education Expenses: Contact institution. Offers teacher education (MS Ed); teacher of students with disabilities (MS Ed); teacher of visually impaired (MS Ed). *Division Director, Teacher Education,* Dr. Roger Tesi, 845-848-4082, Fax: 845-359-7802, E-mail: roger.tesi@dc.edu.

See Close-Up on page 863.

DOMINICAN HOUSE OF STUDIES, PONTIFICAL FACULTY OF THE IMMACULATE CONCEPTION, Washington, DC 20017-1585

General Information Independent-religious, coed, primarily men, graduate-only institution. *Enrollment by degree level:* 38 first professional, 5 master's, 25 other advanced degrees. *Graduate faculty:* 12 full-time (1 woman), 9 part-time/adjunct (2 women). *Tuition:* Full-time $5,400; part-time $450 per credit. *Required fees:* $50 per term. *Graduate housing:* On-campus housing not available. *Student services:* Career counseling. *Library facilities:* Dominican College Library. *Online resources:* web page. *Collection:* 78,000 titles, 450 serial subscriptions, 440 audiovisual materials. *Research affiliation:* Washington Theological Consortium (academic pheotogy).

Computer facilities: 8 computers available on campus for general student use. A campuswide network can be accessed. Internet access is available. *Web address:* http://www.dhs.edu/.

General Application Contact: Gabriel O'Donnell, Associate Dean, 202-529-5300, Fax: 202-636-1700, E-mail: dean@dhs.edu.

GRADUATE UNITS

Graduate and Professional Programs in Theology Students: 58 full-time (2 women), 9 part-time (4 women); includes 4 minority (1 African American, 2 Asian Americans or Pacific Islanders, 1 Hispanic American), 21 international. Average age 32. *Faculty:* 12 full-time (1 woman), 9 part-time/adjunct (2 women). Expenses: Contact institution. *Financial support:* In 2006–07, 1 student received support. Career-related internships or fieldwork and scholarships/grants available. Financial award application deadline: 4/1. In 2006, 9 M Divs, 9 master's, 3 other advanced degrees awarded. *Degree program information:* Part-time programs available. Offers theology (M Div, MA, STL). *Application deadline:* For fall admission, 7/1 priority date for domestic students, 7/1 for international students; for spring admission, 12/1 for domestic and international students. Applications are processed on a rolling basis. *Application fee:* $50. *Application Contact:* Tobias John Nathe, Registrar, 202-529-5300 Ext. 122, Fax: 202-636-1700, E-mail: registrar@dhs.edu. *Associate Dean,* Gabriel O'Donnell, 202-529-5300, Fax: 202-636-1700, E-mail: dean@dhs.edu.

DOMINICAN SCHOOL OF PHILOSOPHY AND THEOLOGY, Berkeley, CA 94708

General Information Independent-religious, coed, upper-level institution. *Graduate housing:* Rooms and/or apartments available on a first-come, first-served basis to single and married students. Housing application deadline: 5/1.

GRADUATE UNITS

Graduate Programs *Degree program information:* Part-time programs available. Offers philosophy (MA); theology (M Div, Certificate). Electronic applications accepted.

DOMINICAN UNIVERSITY, River Forest, IL 60305-1099

General Information Independent-religious, coed, comprehensive institution. *Enrollment:* 3,292 graduate, professional, and undergraduate students; 449 full-time matriculated graduate/professional students (261 women), 1,381 part-time matriculated graduate/professional students (1,065 women). *Enrollment by degree level:* 1,830 master's. *Graduate faculty:* 49 full-time (30 women), 114 part-time/adjunct (61 women). *Tuition:* Full-time $12,420; part-time $690 per credit hour. *Required fees:* $10 per course. Tuition and fees vary according to campus/location and program. *Graduate housing:* Room and/or apartments available on a first-come, first-served basis to single students; on-campus housing not available to married students. Typical cost: $7,450 (including board). Housing application deadline: 7/1. *Student services:* Campus employment opportunities, campus safety program, career counseling, child daycare facilities, free psychological counseling, international student services, low-cost health insurance, multicultural affairs office, teacher training, writing training. *Library facilities:* Rebecca Crown Library. *Online resources:* library catalog, web page, access to other libraries' catalogs. *Collection:* 255,840 titles, 14,089 serial subscriptions, 4,635 audiovisual materials.

Computer facilities: 212 computers available on campus for general student use. A campuswide network can be accessed from student residence rooms and from off campus. Internet access and online class registration, e-mail are available. *Web address:* http://www.dom.edu/.

General Application Contact: Pam Johnson, Vice President of Enrollment Management, 708-524-6544, E-mail: pjohnson@dom.edu.

GRADUATE UNITS

Edward A. and Lois L. Brennan School of Business Students: 171 full-time (46 women), 193 part-time (84 women); includes 26 minority (11 African Americans, 3 Asian Americans or Pacific Islanders, 12 Hispanic Americans), 173 international. Average age 30. 133 applicants, 98% accepted, 106 enrolled. *Faculty:* 12 full-time (4 women), 32 part-time/adjunct (9 women). Expenses: Contact institution. *Financial support:* Career-related internships or fieldwork, tuition waivers (partial), and unspecified assistantships available. Support available to part-time students. Financial award applicants required to submit FAFSA. In 2006, 118 degrees awarded. *Degree program information:* Part-time and evening/weekend programs available. Offers accounting (MSA); business administration (MBA); computer information systems (MSCIS); management information systems (MSMIS); organization management (MSOM). *Application deadline:* Applications are processed on a rolling basis. *Application fee:* $25. Electronic applications accepted. *Application Contact:* Linda Puvogel, Assistant Dean for Graduate Business Programs, 708-524-6507, Fax: 708-524-6939, E-mail: lpuvogel@dom.edu. *Dean,* Dr. Molly Burke, 708-524-6810, Fax: 708-524-6939, E-mail: burkemq@dom.edu.

Graduate School of Library and Information Science Students: 137 full-time (101 women), 588 part-time (484 women); includes 43 minority (11 African Americans, 1 American Indian/Alaska Native, 12 Asian Americans or Pacific Islanders, 19 Hispanic Americans), 5 international. Average age 36. 179 applicants, 99% accepted, 127 enrolled. *Faculty:* 15 full-time (10 women), 28 part-time/adjunct (19 women). Expenses: Contact institution. *Financial support:* Fellowships, research assistantships, career-related internships or fieldwork, Federal Work-Study, scholarships/grants, and tuition waivers (partial) available. Support available to part-time students. Financial award application deadline: 4/15; financial award applicants required to submit FAFSA. In 2006, 269 degrees awarded. *Degree program information:* Part-time and evening/weekend programs available. Postbaccalaureate distance learning degree programs offered (minimal on-campus study). Offers library and information science (MLIS, CSS). *Application deadline:* For fall admission, 6/1 priority date for domestic students; for winter admission, 3/1 priority date for domestic students; for spring admission, 10/1 priority date for domestic students. Applications are processed on a rolling basis. *Application fee:* $25. *Application Contact:* Tracie Hall, Assistant Dean, 708-524-6848, Fax: 708-524-6657, E-mail: thall@dom.edu. *Dean,* Susan Roman, 708-524-6986, Fax: 708-524-6657, E-mail: sroman@dom.edu.

Graduate School of Social Work Students: 75 full-time (68 women), 69 part-time (58 women); includes 20 minority (10 African Americans, 2 Asian Americans or Pacific Islanders, 8 Hispanic Americans), 3 international. Average age 31. 118 applicants, 98% accepted, 57 enrolled. *Faculty:* 5 full-time (2 women), 14 part-time/adjunct (8 women). Expenses: Contact institution. *Financial support:* Career-related internships or fieldwork and scholarships/grants available. In 2006, 53 degrees awarded. Offers social work (MSW). *Application deadline:* Applications are processed on a rolling basis. *Application fee:* $25. *Application Contact:* Felicia Towsend, Director of Admissions, 708-771-5298, Fax: 708-366-3446, E-mail: ftownsend@dom.edu. *Dean,* Dr. Mark Rodgers, 708-366-3316, E-mail: mrodgers@dom.edu.

Institute for Adult Learning Students: 1 full-time (0 women), 17 part-time (14 women); includes 8 minority (5 African Americans, 3 Hispanic Americans). Average age 41. *Faculty:* 5 part-time/adjunct (3 women). Expenses: Contact institution. In 2006, 10 degrees awarded. *Degree program information:* Part-time and evening/weekend programs available. Offers adult learning (MSOL). *Application deadline:* Applications are processed on a rolling basis. *Application fee:* $25. *Application Contact:* Lauren Kelleher, Associate Director of Marketing, 708-714-9003, Fax: 708-714-9126, E-mail: lkellehe@dom.edu. *Executive Director,* Bryan J. Watkins, 708-714-9001, E-mail: bwatkins@dom.edu.

School of Education Students: 65 full-time (46 women), 514 part-time (425 women); includes 78 minority (23 African Americans, 16 Asian Americans or Pacific Islanders, 39 Hispanic Americans), 2 international. Average age 34. 130 applicants, 89% accepted, 100 enrolled. *Faculty:* 17 full-time (14 women), 37 part-time/adjunct (24 women). Expenses: Contact institution. *Financial support:* In 2006–07, 63 students received support. Career-related internships or fieldwork, scholarships/grants, and tuition waivers (partial) available. Support available to part-time students. Financial award application deadline: 8/15; financial award applicants required to submit FAFSA. In 2006, 203 degrees awarded. *Degree program information:* Part-time and evening/weekend programs available. Postbaccalaureate distance learning degree programs offered. Offers curriculum and instruction (MA Ed); early childhood education (MS); education (MAT); educational administration (MA); literacy (MS); special education (MS). *Application deadline:* Applications are processed on a rolling basis. *Application fee:* $25. *Application Contact:* Keven Hansen, Coordinator of Admissions and Recruitment, 708-524-6921, Fax: 708-524-6665, E-mail: educate@dom.edu. *Dean,* Sr. Colleen McNicholas, 708-524-6830, Fax: 708-524-6665, E-mail: educate@dom.edu.

DOMINICAN UNIVERSITY OF CALIFORNIA, San Rafael, CA 94901-2298

General Information Independent-religious, coed, comprehensive institution. *Graduate housing:* Room and/or apartments available on a first-come, first-served basis to single students; on-campus housing not available to married students.

GRADUATE UNITS

Graduate Programs *Degree program information:* Part-time and evening/weekend programs available. Electronic applications accepted.

School of Arts and Sciences *Degree program information:* Part-time and evening/weekend programs available. Offers arts and sciences (MA, MS); counseling psychology (MS); geriatric and nurse educator (MS); humanities (MA); integrated health practices (MS); occupational therapy (MS). Electronic applications accepted.

School of Business, Education and Leadership *Degree program information:* Part-time and evening/weekend programs available. Offers business and international studies (MAM, MBA); business, education and leadership (MAM, MBA, MS, Credential); curriculum and instruction (MS); education (MS, Credential); global strategic management (MBA); management (MAM); multiple subject teaching (Credential); single subject teaching (Credential); special education (Credential); strategic leadership (MBA). Programs also offered in Ukiah, CA. Electronic applications accepted.

DONGGUK ROYAL UNIVERSITY, Los Angeles, CA 90020

General Information Independent, coed, graduate-only institution. *Graduate housing:* On-campus housing not available.

GRADUATE UNITS

Program in Oriental Medicine *Degree program information:* Part-time and evening/weekend programs available. Offers Oriental medicine (MS).

DORDT COLLEGE, Sioux Center, IA 51250-1697

General Information Independent-religious, coed, comprehensive institution. *Enrollment:* 1,261 graduate, professional, and undergraduate students; 30 part-time matriculated graduate/professional students (15 women). *Enrollment by degree level:* 30 master's. *Graduate faculty:* 4 full-time (2 women), 5 part-time/adjunct (2 women). *Graduate housing:* Rooms and/or apartments available to single and married students. *Student services:* Career counseling, teacher training. *Library facilities:* Dordt College Library plus 1 other. *Online resources:* library catalog, web page, access to other libraries' catalogs. *Collection:* 160,000 titles, 6,597 serial subscriptions.

Computer facilities: 250 computers available on campus for general student use. A campuswide network can be accessed from student residence rooms and from off campus. Internet access and online class registration are available. *Web address:* http://www.dordt.edu/.

General Application Contact: Dr. Pat Kornelis, Director of Graduate Education, 712-722-6235, Fax: 712-722-1198, E-mail: pkornelis@dordt.edu.

GRADUATE UNITS

Program in Education 6 applicants, 100% accepted. *Faculty:* 5 full-time (2 women), 3 part-time/adjunct (2 women). Expenses: Contact institution. In 2006, 7 degrees awarded. *Degree program information:* Part-time programs available. Postbaccalaureate distance learning degree programs offered (minimal on-campus study). Offers education (M Ed). *Application deadline:* For spring admission, 6/1 priority date for domestic and international students. Applications are processed on a rolling basis. *Application fee:* $25. Electronic applications accepted. *Application Contact:* Kay DeBoom, Secretary of Graduate Education, 800-343-6738, Fax: 712-722-1198, E-mail: m_ed@dordt.edu. *Director of Graduate Education,* Dr. Pat Kornelis, 712-722-6235, Fax: 712-722-1198, E-mail: pkornelis@dordt.edu.

DOWLING COLLEGE, Oakdale, NY 11769-1999

General Information Independent, coed, comprehensive institution. *Enrollment:* 5,546 graduate, professional, and undergraduate students; 831 full-time matriculated graduate/professional students (527 women), 1,663 part-time matriculated graduate/professional students (1,112 women). *Enrollment by degree level:* 2,408 master's, 86 doctoral. *Graduate faculty:* 117 full-time (43 women), 290 part-time/adjunct (146 women). *Tuition:* Full-time $16,008; part-time $667 per credit. Tuition and fees vary according to course load. *Graduate housing:* Room and/or apartments available on a first-come, first-served basis to single students; on-campus housing not available to married students. Typical cost: $5,748 per year ($8,988 including board). Housing application deadline: 9/1. *Student services:* Campus employment opportunities, campus safety program, career counseling, disabled student services, international student services, low-cost health insurance. *Library facilities:* Dowling College Library. *Online resources:* library catalog. *Collection:* 119,360 titles, 3,131 serial subscriptions.

Computer facilities: 118 computers available on campus for general student use. A campuswide network can be accessed. Internet access and online class registration are available. *Web address:* http://www.dowling.edu/.

General Application Contact: Franks S. Pizzardi, Director of Admissions Operations, 631-244-3227, Fax: 631-244-1059, E-mail: pizzardf@dowling.edu.

GRADUATE UNITS

Graduate Programs in Education Students: 496 full-time (364 women), 1,083 part-time (827 women); includes 119 minority (37 African Americans, 20 Asian Americans or Pacific Islanders, 62 Hispanic Americans), 2 international. Average age 38. 618 applicants, 86% accepted, 300 enrolled. *Faculty:* 29 full-time (13 women), 91 part-time/adjunct (60 women). Expenses: Contact institution. *Financial support:* In 2006–07, 358 students received support, including 20 research assistantships with tuition reimbursements available (averaging $3,150 per year); career-related internships or fieldwork, Federal Work-Study, scholarships/grants, tuition waivers (partial), and unspecified assistantships also available. Support available to part-time students. Financial award application deadline: 6/30; financial award applicants required to submit FAFSA. In 2006, 641 master's, 25 doctorates awarded. *Degree program information:* Part-time and evening/weekend programs available. Postbaccalaureate distance learning degree programs offered. Offers educational administration (Ed D, PD); human development and learning (MS Ed); literacy (MS Ed); literacy/special education (MS Ed); secondary education (MS Ed); special education (MS Ed). *Application deadline:* For fall admission, 9/1 priority date for domestic students; for winter admission, 1/1 priority date for domestic students; for spring admission, 2/1 priority date for domestic students. Applications are processed on a rolling basis. *Application fee:* $25. Electronic applications accepted. *Application Contact:* Franks S. Pizzardi, Director of Admissions Operations, 631-244-3227, Fax: 631-244-1059, E-mail: pizzardf@dowling.edu. *Associate Provost,* Dr. Clyde Payne, 631-244-3404, Fax: 631-589-6644, E-mail: paynec@dowling.edu.

Programs in Arts and Sciences Students: 5 full-time (3 women), 14 part-time (12 women), 1 international. Average age 26. 15 applicants, 80% accepted, 5 enrolled. Expenses: Contact institution. *Financial support:* In 2006–07, 2 research assistantships (averaging $3,150 per year) were awarded; Federal Work-Study, scholarships/grants, and unspecified assistantships also available. Support available to part-time students. Financial award application deadline: 6/30; financial award applicants required to submit FAFSA. In 2006, 2 degrees awarded. *Degree program information:* Part-time and evening/weekend programs available. Offers integrated math and science (MS); liberal studies (MA). *Application deadline:* For fall admission, 9/1 priority date for domestic students; for winter admission, 1/1 priority date for domestic students; for spring admission, 2/1 priority date for domestic students. Applications are processed on a rolling basis. *Application fee:* $25. Electronic applications accepted. *Provost,* Dr. Linda Ardito, 631-244-3232, Fax: 631-244-1033, E-mail: arditol@dowling.edu.

School of Business Students: 239 full-time (105 women), 566 part-time (273 women); includes 132 African Americans, 55 Asian Americans or Pacific Islanders, 48 Hispanic Americans, 3 international. Average age 31. 414 applicants, 82% accepted, 166 enrolled. Expenses: Contact institution. *Financial support:* In 2006–07, 126 students received support, including 30 research assistantships (averaging $3,150 per year); career-related internships or fieldwork, Federal Work-Study, scholarships/grants, and unspecified assistantships also available. Support available to part-time students. Financial award application deadline: 6/30; financial award applicants required to submit FAFSA. In 2006, 471 master's, 1 other advanced degree awarded. *Degree program information:* Part-time and evening/weekend programs available. Offers aviation management (MBA, Certificate); banking and finance (MBA, Certificate); general management (MBA); public management (MBA, Certificate); total quality management (MBA, Certificate). *Application deadline:* For fall admission, 9/1 priority date for domestic students; for winter admission, 1/1 priority date for domestic students; for spring admission, 2/1 priority date for domestic students. Applications are processed on a rolling basis. *Application fee:* $25. Electronic applications accepted. *Application Contact:* Franks S. Pizzardi, Director of Admissions Operations, 631-244-3227, Fax: 631-244-1059, E-mail: pizzardf@dowling.edu. *Dean of the School of Business,* Dr. Elana Zolfo, 631-244-3190, Fax: 631-244-1018, E-mail: zdfoe@dowling.edu.

DRAKE UNIVERSITY, Des Moines, IA 50311-4516

General Information Independent, coed, university. *Enrollment:* 5,366 graduate, professional, and undergraduate students; 977 full-time matriculated graduate/professional students (579 women), 1,143 part-time matriculated graduate/professional students (755 women). *Enrollment by degree level:* 976 first professional, 1,089 master's, 17 doctoral, 38 other advanced degrees. *Graduate faculty:* 32 full-time (14 women), 58 part-time/adjunct (25 women). *Graduate housing:* Room and/or apartments available on a first-come, first-served basis to single students; on-campus housing not available to married students. Housing application deadline: 8/1. *Student services:* Campus employment opportunities, campus safety program, career counseling, disabled student services, exercise/wellness program, free psychological counseling, international student services, low-cost health insurance, teacher training, writing training. *Library facilities:* Cowles Library plus 1 other. *Online resources:* library catalog, web page, access to other libraries' catalogs. *Collection:* 511,168 titles, 31,500 serial subscriptions, 2,163 audiovisual materials. *Research affiliation:* Iowa Department of Education (education), National Science Foundation (arts and sciences), U.S. Department of Education (education), USDA (agriculture), Albertson's Inc. (pharmacy), NASA Through Iowa State University (arts and sciences).

Computer facilities: Computer purchase and lease plans are available. 1,000 computers available on campus for general student use. A campuswide network can be accessed from student residence rooms and from off campus. Internet access is available. *Web address:* http://www.drake.edu/.

General Application Contact: Ann J. Martin, Graduate Coordinator, 515-271-2034, Fax: 515-271-2831, E-mail: ann.martin@drake.edu.

GRADUATE UNITS

College of Business and Public Administration Students: 9 full-time (5 women), 451 part-time (242 women); includes 32 minority (11 African Americans, 1 American Indian/Alaska Native, 13 Asian Americans or Pacific Islanders, 7 Hispanic Americans), 36 international. Average age 24. 297 applicants, 68% accepted, 112 enrolled. *Faculty:* 3 full-time (0 women), 7 part-time/adjunct (1 woman). Expenses: Contact institution. *Financial support:* Fellowships with tuition reimbursements, teaching assistantships, career-related internships or fieldwork and institutionally sponsored loans available. Support available to part-time students. Financial award application deadline: 3/1; financial award applicants required to submit FAFSA. In 2006, 201 degrees awarded. *Degree program information:* Part-time and evening/weekend programs available. Offers business and public administration (M Acc, MBA, MFM, MPA). *Application deadline:* For fall admission, 8/15 priority date for domestic students; for winter admission, 12/20 priority date for domestic students; for spring admission, 12/1 priority date for domestic students. Applications are processed on a rolling basis. *Application fee:* $25. Electronic applications accepted. *Application Contact:* Danette Kenne, Director of Graduate Programs, 515-271-2188, Fax: 515-271-4518, E-mail: cbpa.gradprograms@drake.edu. *Dean,* Dr. Charles Edwards, 515-271-2871, Fax: 515-271-4518, E-mail: charles.edwards@drake.edu.

College of Pharmacy and Health Sciences Students: 496 full-time (350 women), 2 part-time (both women); includes 79 minority (7 African Americans, 68 Asian Americans or Pacific Islanders, 4 Hispanic Americans), 7 international. Average age 24. 1,442 applicants, 33% accepted. *Faculty:* 19 full-time (11 women), 4 part-time/adjunct (3 women). Expenses: Contact institution. *Financial support:* In 2006–07, 10 teaching assistantships (averaging $3,200 per year) were awarded; career-related internships or fieldwork, Federal Work-Study, institutionally sponsored loans, and scholarships/grants also available. Support available to part-time students. Financial award application deadline: 3/1; financial award applicants required to submit FAFSA. In 2006, 105 degrees awarded. Offers pharmacy (Pharm D); pharmacy and health sciences (Pharm D). *Application deadline:* For fall admission, 2/1 priority date for domestic students. *Application fee:* $135. Electronic applications accepted. *Application Contact:* Dr. Renae J. Chesnut, Associate Dean for Student Affairs, 515-271-3018, Fax: 515-271-4171, E-mail: renae.chesnut@drake.edu. *Dean,* Dr. Raylene Rospond, 515-271-1814, Fax: 515-271-4171, E-mail: raylene.rospond@drake.edu.

Law School Students: 432 full-time (203 women), 6 part-time (5 women); includes 43 minority (21 African Americans, 7 American Indian/Alaska Native, 3 Asian Americans or Pacific Islanders, 12 Hispanic Americans), 7 international. Average age 25. 1,106 applicants, 46% accepted. *Faculty:* 17 part-time/adjunct (5 women). Expenses: Contact institution. *Financial support:* In 2006–07, 20 research assistantships (averaging $757 per year), 6 teaching assistantships (averaging $2,142 per year) were awarded; career-related internships or fieldwork, Federal Work-Study, institutionally sponsored loans, scholarships/grants, and tuition waivers (full and partial) also available. Support available to part-time students. Financial award application deadline: 3/1; financial award applicants required to submit FAFSA. In 2006, 158 degrees awarded. Offers law (JD). *Application deadline:* For fall admission, 4/1 priority date for domestic and international students. Applications are processed on a rolling basis. *Application fee:* $40. Electronic applications accepted. *Application Contact:* J. Kara Blanchard, Director of Admission and Financial Aid, 515-271-2953, Fax: 515-271-2530, E-mail: kara.blanchard@drake.edu. *Dean,* David Walker, 515-271-1805, Fax: 515-271-4118, E-mail: david.walker@drake.edu.

School of Education Students: 29 full-time (18 women), 575 part-time (422 women); includes 16 African Americans, 5 Asian Americans or Pacific Islanders, 4 Hispanic Americans, 4 international. 498 applicants, 39% accepted, 175 enrolled. *Faculty:* 10 full-time (3 women), 28 part-time/adjunct (16 women). Expenses: Contact institution. *Financial support:* In 2006–07, 14 research assistantships were awarded; career-related internships or fieldwork and unspecified assistantships also available. Support available to part-time students. In 2006, 219 master's, 7 doctorates, 14 other advanced degrees awarded. *Degree program information:* Part-time and evening/weekend programs available. Offers adult development (MS); adult learning and performance development (MS); art (MAT); biology (MAT); business (MAT);

Drake University (continued)

chemistry (MAT); community agency counseling (MSE); counseling (MSE); education (MAT, MS, MSE, MST, Ed D, Ed S); education leadership (MSE, Ed D, Ed S); effective teaching, learning and leadership (MSE); elementary education (MST); English (MAT); general science (MAT); guidance counseling (MSE); history-American (MAT); history-world (MAT); journalism (MAT); mathematics (MAT); physical science (MAT); physics (MAT); rehabilitation (MS); rehabilitation administration (MS); rehabilitation counseling (MS); rehabilitation placement (MS); secondary education (MAT); sociology (MAT); special education (MSE); speech (MAT); speech communication (MAT); teacher education (MSE); theatre (MAT). *Application deadline:* For fall admission, 7/1 priority date for domestic students, 6/1 priority date for international students; for spring admission, 11/1 priority date for domestic students, 10/1 priority date for international students. Applications are processed on a rolling basis. *Application fee:* $25. Electronic applications accepted. *Application Contact:* Ann J. Martin, Graduate Coordinator, 515-271-2034, Fax: 515-271-2831, E-mail: ann.martin@drake.edu. *Dean,* Dr. Janet McMahill, 515-271-3829, E-mail: janet.mcmahill@drake.edu.

See Close-Up on page 865.

DREW UNIVERSITY, Madison, NJ 07940-1493

General Information Independent-religious, coed, university. CGS member. *Graduate housing:* Rooms and/or apartments available on a first-come, first-served basis to single and married students. Housing application deadline: 7/1. *Research affiliation:* Center for Research Libraries (humanities), Dana Rise Institute (science), Raritan Bay Medical Center (medical humanities), Society for the History of Authorship, Readership and Publishing (book history), Methodist Archives (religion).

GRADUATE UNITS

Caspersen School of Graduate Studies *Degree program information:* Part-time and evening/weekend programs available. Offers anthropology of religion (MA, PhD); Christian social ethics (MA, PhD); English literature (MA, PhD); historical studies (MA, PhD); holocaust and genocide studies (Certificate); interdisciplinary studies (M Litt, D Litt); liturgical studies (MA, PhD); medical humanities (MMH, DMH, CMH); Methodist studies (PhD); modern history and literature (MA, PhD); philosophy of religion (MA, PhD); psychology and religion (MA, PhD); religion in ancient Israel (MA, PhD); sociology of religion (MA, PhD); systematic theology (MA, PhD); the New Testament and early Christianity (MA, PhD); theological ethics (MA, PhD); Wesleyan and Methodist studies (MA, PhD); women's studies (MA).

The Theological School *Degree program information:* Part-time programs available. Postbaccalaureate distance learning degree programs offered (minimal on-campus study). Offers theology (M Div, MTS, STM, D Min, Certificate). Electronic applications accepted.

See Close-Up on page 867.

DREXEL UNIVERSITY, Philadelphia, PA 19104-2875

General Information Independent, coed, university. CGS member. *Graduate housing:* On-campus housing not available.

GRADUATE UNITS

College of Arts and Sciences *Degree program information:* Part-time and evening/weekend programs available. Offers arts and sciences (MA, MS, PhD); biological science (MS, PhD); chemistry (MS, PhD); clinical psychology (MA, MS, PhD); communication (MS); environmental policy (MS); environmental science (MS, PhD); food science (MS); forensic psychology (PhD); health psychology (PhD); law-psychology (PhD); mathematics (MS, PhD); neuropsychology (PhD); nutrition and food sciences (MS, PhD); nutrition science (PhD); physics (MS, PhD); publication management (MS); science, technology and society (MS). Electronic applications accepted.

College of Engineering *Degree program information:* Part-time and evening/weekend programs available. Offers biochemical engineering (MS); chemical engineering (MS, PhD); civil engineering (MS, PhD); computer engineering (MS); computer science (MS, PhD); electrical and computer engineering (PhD); electrical engineering (MSEE, PhD); engineering (MS, MSEE, MSSE, PhD); engineering geology (MS); engineering management (MS, PhD); environmental engineering (MS, PhD); manufacturing engineering (MS, PhD); materials engineering (MS, PhD); mechanical engineering and mechanics (MS, PhD); software engineering (MSSE); telecommunications engineering (MSEE). Electronic applications accepted.

College of Information Science and Technology *Degree program information:* Part-time and evening/weekend programs available. Postbaccalaureate distance learning degree programs offered (no on-campus study). Offers information science and technology (PhD); information studies (PhD, CAS); information systems (MSIS); library and information science (MS). Electronic applications accepted.

College of Media Arts and Design *Degree program information:* Part-time and evening/weekend programs available. Offers architecture (M Arch); arts administration (MS); design (MS); fashion design (MS); interior design (MS); media arts (MS); performing arts (MS). Electronic applications accepted.

College of Medicine *Degree program information:* Part-time programs available. Offers medicine (MD, MBS, MLAS, MMS, MS, PhD, Certificate). Electronic applications accepted.

Biomedical Graduate Programs *Degree program information:* Part-time programs available. Offers biochemistry (MS, PhD); biomedical sciences (MBS, MLAS, MMS, MS, PhD, Certificate); laboratory animal science (MLAS); medical science (MBS, MMS, Certificate); microbiology and immunology (MS, PhD); molecular and cell biology (MS, PhD); molecular and human genetics (MS, PhD); molecular pathobiology (PhD); neuroscience (PhD); pharmacology and physiology (MS, PhD); radiation (MS); radiation biology (MS); radiation physics (PhD); radiation science (PhD); radiopharmaceutical science (MS, PhD). Electronic applications accepted.

College of Nursing and Health Professions *Degree program information:* Part-time and evening/weekend programs available. Offers advanced physician assistant studies (MHS); art therapy (MA); couples and family therapy (PhD); dance/movement therapy (MA); emergency and public safety services (MS); family therapy (MFT); hand/upper quarter rehabilitation (MHS, MS, PhD); movement science (MHS, MS, PhD); music therapy (MA); nurse anesthesia (MSN); nursing (MSN); nursing and health professions (MA, MFT, MHS, MS, MSN, DPT, PhD, Certificate); orthopedics (MHS, MS, PhD); pediatrics (MHS, MS, PhD); physical therapy (DPT, Certificate). Electronic applications accepted.

LeBow College of Business *Degree program information:* Part-time and evening/weekend programs available. Offers accounting (MS); business administration (MBA, PhD, APC); business and administration (MBA, MS, PhD, APC); decision sciences (MS); finance (MS); marketing (MS); taxation (MS). Electronic applications accepted.

School of Biomedical Engineering, Science and Health Systems Offers biomedical engineering (MS, PhD); biomedical science (MS, PhD); biostatistics (MS); clinical/rehabilitation engineering (MS). Electronic applications accepted.

School of Education *Degree program information:* Part-time and evening/weekend programs available. Postbaccalaureate distance learning degree programs offered. Offers educational administration (MS); educational administration and collaborative learning (MS); educational leadership and learning technology (PhD); global and international education (MS); graduate intern teaching (Certificate); higher education (MS); instructional technology (Spt); post-bachelor's teaching (Certificate); school principal (Certificate); school superintendent (Certificate); science of instruction (MS); teaching English as a second language (Certificate); teaching, learning and curriculum (MS). Electronic applications accepted.

School of Journalism Offers journalism (MA).

School of Public Health Offers public health (MPH). Electronic applications accepted.

See Close-Up on page 869.

DRURY UNIVERSITY, Springfield, MO 65802

General Information Independent, coed, comprehensive institution. *Graduate housing:* Rooms and/or apartments available on a first-come, first-served basis to single students and available to married students. *Research affiliation:* Yale University (child development).

GRADUATE UNITS

Breech School of Business Administration *Degree program information:* Part-time and evening/weekend programs available. Offers business administration (MBA); business and international management (MBA). Electronic applications accepted.

Graduate Programs in Education *Degree program information:* Part-time and evening/weekend programs available. Offers elementary education (M Ed); gifted education (M Ed); human services (M Ed); middle school teaching (M Ed); physical education (M Ed); secondary education (M Ed).

Program in Communication *Degree program information:* Part-time and evening/weekend programs available. Offers communication (MA).

Program in Criminology/Criminal Justice *Degree program information:* Part-time and evening/weekend programs available. Offers criminal justice (MS); criminology (MA). Electronic applications accepted.

DUKE UNIVERSITY, Durham, NC 27708-0586

General Information Independent-religious, coed, university. CGS member. *Enrollment:* 13,373 graduate, professional, and undergraduate students; 6,365 full-time matriculated graduate/professional students (2,900 women), 273 part-time matriculated graduate/professional students (208 women). *Enrollment by degree level:* 1,910 first professional, 2,329 master's, 2,341 doctoral, 58 other advanced degrees. *Graduate faculty:* 2,342. *Graduate housing:* Rooms and/or apartments available on a first-come, first-served basis to single students and available to married students. Typical cost: $5,730 per year for single students; $11,460 per year for married students. *Student services:* Campus employment opportunities, campus safety program, career counseling, disabled student services, free psychological counseling, international student services, low-cost health insurance, multicultural affairs office, teacher training, writing training. *Library facilities:* Perkins Library plus 14 others. *Online resources:* library catalog, web page, access to other libraries' catalogs. *Collection:* 5.6 million titles, 31,892 serial subscriptions, 59,547 audiovisual materials. *Research affiliation:* Highlands Biological Station, U.S. Forest Sciences Laboratory, Organization for Tropical Studies.

Computer facilities: Computer purchase and lease plans are available. 600 computers available on campus for general student use. A campuswide network can be accessed from student residence rooms and from off campus. Internet access and online class registration are available. *Web address:* http://www.duke.edu/.

General Application Contact: Bertie S. Belvin, Associate Dean for Academic Services, 919-684-3913, E-mail: grad-admissions@duke.edu.

GRADUATE UNITS

Divinity School *Degree program information:* Part-time programs available. Offers theology (M Div, MCM, MTS, Th M). Electronic applications accepted.

Fuqua School of Business Students: 1,517 full-time (341 women); includes 625 minority (56 African Americans, 9 American Indian/Alaska Native, 491 Asian Americans or Pacific Islanders, 69 Hispanic Americans), 199 international. Average age 32. 3,228 applicants, 45% accepted, 787 enrolled. *Faculty:* 110 full-time (23 women), 31 part-time/adjunct (3 women). Expenses: Contact institution. *Financial support:* In 2006–07, 824 students received support, including 254 fellowships (averaging $14,200 per year); research assistantships, teaching assistantships, career-related internships or fieldwork, Federal Work-Study, institutionally sponsored loans, and scholarships/grants also available. Financial award application deadline: 3/1; financial award applicants required to submit FAFSA. In 2006, 685 degrees awarded. *Degree program information:* Evening/weekend programs available. Postbaccalaureate distance learning degree programs offered. Offers business (EMBA, GEMBA, MBA, MMS, WEMBA, PhD, Certificate); cross continent executive business administration (EMBA); EMBA held with Frankford University (EMBA); global executive business administration (GEMBA); health sector management (Certificate); weekend executive business administration (WEMBA). *Application deadline:* For fall admission, 10/1 for domestic students; for winter admission, 1/3 for domestic students; for spring admission, 3/3 for domestic students. *Application fee:* $185. Electronic applications accepted. *Application Contact:* Liz Riley Hargrove, Assistant Dean and Director of Admissions, 919-660-7705, Fax: 919-681-8026, E-mail: admissions-info@fuqua.duke.edu. *Dean,* Blair H. Sheppard, 919-660-8020, Fax: 919-684-8742, E-mail: blair.sheppard@duke.edu.

Graduate School Students: 2,810 (1,366 women); includes 347 minority (132 African Americans, 8 American Indian/Alaska Native, 129 Asian Americans or Pacific Islanders, 78 Hispanic Americans) 886 international. 7,471 applicants, 20% accepted, 671 enrolled. *Faculty:* 1,627 full-time. Expenses: Contact institution. *Financial support:* In 2006–07, 1,980 students received support, including fellowships with full tuition reimbursements available (averaging $18,250 per year), research assistantships with full tuition reimbursements available (averaging $25,000 per year), teaching assistantships with full tuition reimbursements available (averaging $10,000 per year); career-related internships or fieldwork, Federal Work-Study, institutionally sponsored loans, scholarships/grants, traineeships, and unspecified assistantships also available. Support available to part-time students. Financial award application deadline: 4/15; financial award applicants required to submit FAFSA. In 2006, 344 master's, 292 doctorates awarded. *Degree program information:* Part-time and evening/weekend programs available. Offers art and art history (PhD); biological and biologically inspired materials (PhD, Certificate); biological chemistry (PhD, Certificate); biological psychology (PhD); biology (PhD); business administration (PhD); cell biology (PhD); cellular and molecular biology (PhD); chemistry (PhD); classical studies (PhD); clinical psychology (PhD); cognitive neuroscience (PhD, Certificate); cognitive psychology (PhD); computational biology and bioinformatics (PhD); computer science (MS, PhD); crystallography of macromolecules (PhD); developmental biology (PhD, Certificate); developmental psychology (PhD); East Asian studies (AM, Certificate); ecology (PhD, Certificate); economics (AM, PhD); English (PhD); enzyme mechanisms (PhD); experimental psychology (PhD); French (PhD); genetics and genomics (PhD); German studies (PhD); gross anatomy and physical anthropology (PhD); health psychology (PhD); history (AM, PhD); human social development (PhD); humanities (AM); immunology (PhD); integrated toxicology and environmental health (PhD, Certificate); Latin American studies (PhD); liberal studies (AM); lipid biochemistry (PhD); literature (PhD); mathematics (PhD); medical physics (MS, PhD); medieval and Renaissance studies (Certificate); membrane structure and function (PhD); molecular cancer biology (PhD); molecular genetics (PhD); molecular genetics and microbiology (PhD); music composition (AM, PhD); musicology (AM, PhD); natural resource economics/policy (AM, PhD); natural resource science/ecology (AM, PhD); natural resource systems science (AM, PhD); neuroanatomy (PhD); neurobiology (PhD); neurochemistry (PhD); nucleic acid structure and function (PhD); pathology (PhD); performance practice (AM, PhD); pharmacology (PhD); philosophy (AM, PhD); physical anthropology (PhD); physics (PhD); political science (AM, PhD); protein structure and function (PhD); religion (MA, PhD); Slavic languages and literatures (AM); social/cultural anthropology (PhD); sociology (AM, PhD); Spanish (PhD); structural biology and biophysics (Certificate); teaching (MAT); women's studies (Certificate). *Application deadline:* For fall admission, 12/15 priority date for domestic and international students; for winter admission, 12/15 for domestic and international students; for spring admission, 11/1 for domestic and international students. *Application fee:* $75. Electronic applications accepted. *Application Contact:* Bertie S. Belvin, Associate Dean for Academic Services, 919-684-3913, E-mail: grad-admissions@duke.edu. *Dean,* Jo Rae Wright, 919-681-3267.

Center for Demographic Studies Expenses: Contact institution. *Financial support:* Application deadline: 12/31. Offers demographic studies (PhD). *Application deadline:* For fall admission, 12/31 for domestic students. *Application fee:* $75. *Director,* Dr. Kenneth C. Land, 919-668-2702, Fax: 919-684-3861, E-mail: kland@soc.duke.edu.

Division of Earth and Ocean Sciences Students: 23 full-time (10 women); includes 1 minority (Asian American or Pacific Islander), 4 international. 44 applicants, 23% accepted, 4 enrolled. *Faculty:* 18 full-time. Expenses: Contact institution. *Financial support:* Fellowships, research assistantships, teaching assistantships, Federal Work-Study available. Financial award application deadline: 12/31. In 2006, 1 master's, 4 doctorates awarded. *Degree program information:* Part-time programs available. Offers earth and ocean sciences (MS, PhD). *Application deadline:* For fall admission, 12/15 priority date for domestic and international students; for spring admission, 11/1 for domestic students. *Application fee:* $75. Electronic applications accepted. *Director of Graduate Studies,* Alan Boudreau, 919-684-5646, Fax: 919-684-5833, E-mail: dcgooch@duke.edu.

Institute of Statistics and Decision Sciences Students: 33 full-time (12 women), 19 international. 122 applicants, 10% accepted, 6 enrolled. *Faculty:* 17 full-time. Expenses: Contact institution. *Financial support:* Fellowships, research assistantships, teaching assistantships available. Financial award application deadline: 12/31. In 2006, 7 doctorates awarded. *Degree program information:* Part-time programs available. Offers statistics and decision sciences (PhD). *Application deadline:* For fall admission, 12/15 priority date for domestic and international students. *Application fee:* $75. Electronic applications accepted. *Director of Graduate Studies,* Alan Gelfand, 919-684-8029, Fax: 919-684-8594, E-mail: dgs@stat.duke.edu.

Pratt School of Engineering Expenses: Contact institution. *Financial support:* Fellowships, research assistantships, teaching assistantships, Federal Work-Study available. Financial award application deadline: 12/31. *Degree program information:* Part-time programs available. Offers biomedical engineering (MS, PhD); civil and environmental engineering (MS, PhD); electrical and computer engineering (MS, PhD); engineering (MEM, MS, PhD); engineering management (MEM); environmental engineering (MS, PhD); materials science (MS, PhD); mechanical engineering (MS, PhD). *Dean,* Dr. Kristina M. Johnson, 919-660-5389, Fax: 919-684-4860.

Terry Sanford Institute of Public Policy Students: 100 full-time (64 women); includes 8 minority (4 African Americans, 2 Asian Americans or Pacific Islanders, 2 Hispanic Americans), 16 international. 308 applicants, 49% accepted, 52 enrolled. *Faculty:* 60 full-time. Expenses: Contact institution. *Financial support:* Fellowships, research assistantships, teaching assistantships, career-related internships or fieldwork and Federal Work-Study available. Financial award application deadline: 12/31. In 2006, 58 degrees awarded. Offers international development policy (AM, Certificate); public policy (AM, MPP, PhD, Certificate). *Application deadline:* For fall admission, 12/15 priority date for domestic students, 12/15 for international students. *Application fee:* $75. Electronic applications accepted. *Application Contact:* Chuck Pringle, Information Contact, 919-613-9205, E-mail: mppadmit@duke.edu. *Director,* Fritz Mayer, 919-613-9205, Fax: 919-684-3702, E-mail: mppadmit@duke.edu.

Nicholas School of the Environment and Earth Sciences Students: 257 full-time (162 women). Average age 26. *Faculty:* 58 full-time (14 women), 61 part-time/adjunct (21 women). Expenses: Contact institution. *Financial support:* In 2006–07, 143 fellowships (averaging $10,000 per year), 48 research assistantships (averaging $2,800 per year) were awarded; career-related internships or fieldwork, Federal Work-Study, institutionally sponsored loans, scholarships/grants, and unspecified assistantships also available. Financial award application deadline: 2/1; financial award applicants required to submit FAFSA. In 2006, 115 degrees awarded. *Degree program information:* Part-time programs available. Offers coastal environmental management (MEM); DEL-environmental leadership (MEM); energy and environment (MEM); environmental economics and policy (MEM); environmental health and security (MEM); forest resource management (MF); global environmental change (MEM); resource ecology (MEM); water and air resources (MEM). *Application deadline:* For fall admission, 2/1 for domestic and international students; for spring admission, 10/15 for domestic and international students. Applications are processed on a rolling basis. *Application fee:* $75. Electronic applications accepted. *Application Contact:* Cynthia Peters, Assistant Dean for Enrollment Services, 919-613-8070, Fax: 919-613-8719, E-mail: admissions@nicholas.duke.edu. *Dean,* Dr. William Schlesinger, 919-613-8004, Fax: 919-613-8719.

School of Law Students: 630 full-time (273 women); includes 149 minority (64 African Americans, 2 American Indian/Alaska Native, 60 Asian Americans or Pacific Islanders, 23 Hispanic Americans), 6 international. Average age 26. 4,341 applicants, 23% accepted, 205 enrolled. *Faculty:* 50 full-time (14 women), 43 part-time/adjunct (18 women). Expenses: Contact institution. *Financial support:* In 2006–07, 370 students received support. Federal Work-Study, institutionally sponsored loans, and scholarships/grants available. Financial award application deadline: 4/15; financial award applicants required to submit FAFSA. In 2006, 220 JDs, 96 master's awarded. Offers law (JD, LL M, MLS, SJD). LL M and SJD offered only to international students. *Application deadline:* For fall admission, 2/15 for domestic students. Applications are processed on a rolling basis. *Application fee:* $70. Electronic applications accepted. *Associate Dean, Admissions and Financial Aid,* William J. Hoye, 919-613-7020, Fax: 919-613-7257, E-mail: hoye@law.duke.edu.

School of Medicine Students: 740 full-time (446 women), 94 part-time (52 women); includes 239 minority (86 African Americans, 11 American Indian/Alaska Native, 123 Asian Americans or Pacific Islanders, 19 Hispanic Americans), 24 international. Expenses: Contact institution. *Financial support:* In 2006–07, 585 students received support. Institutionally sponsored loans and scholarships/grants available. Financial award application deadline: 5/1; financial award applicants required to submit CSS PROFILE or FAFSA. In 2006, 85 master's, 141 doctorates awarded. *Degree program information:* Part-time programs available. Offers clinical leadership program (MHS); clinical research (MHS); medicine (MD, MHS, DPT); pathologists' assistant (MHS); physician assistant (MHS). *Application Contact:* Dr. Brenda Armstrong, Director of Admissions, 919-684-2985, Fax: 919-684-8893, E-mail: mcdadm@mc.duke.edu. *Vice Dean of Medical Education,* Dr. Edward Buckley, 919-668-3381, Fax: 919-660-7040, E-mail: buckl002@mc.duke.edu.

Physical Therapy Division Students: 144 full-time (125 women); includes 14 minority (4 African Americans, 1 American Indian/Alaska Native, 7 Asian Americans or Pacific Islanders, 2 Hispanic Americans). 180 applicants, 36% accepted, 63 enrolled. *Faculty:* 5 full-time (0 women), 2 part-time/adjunct (0 women). Expenses: Contact institution. *Financial support:* In 2006–07, 120 students received support. Federal Work-Study, institutionally sponsored loans, and scholarships/grants available. Financial award application deadline: 5/1; financial award applicants required to submit FAFSA. In 2006, 32 degrees awarded. Offers physical therapy (DPT). *Application deadline:* For fall admission, 12/1 priority date for domestic and international students. Applications are processed on a rolling basis. *Application fee:* $75. Electronic applications accepted. *Application Contact:* Anita Aiken, Admissions Coordinator, 919-668-5206, Fax: 919-688-3024, E-mail: anita.aiken@duke.edu. *Professor of the Practice/Division Chief,* Dr. Jan K. Richardson, 919-684-6020, Fax: 919-668-3024, E-mail: richa052@mc.duke.edu.

School of Nursing Students: 178 full-time (162 women), 140 part-time (132 women); includes 48 minority (17 African Americans, 3 American Indian/Alaska Native, 20 Asian Americans or Pacific Islanders, 8 Hispanic Americans). Average age 36. 99 applicants, 92% accepted, 91 enrolled. *Faculty:* 45 full-time (41 women), 169 part-time/adjunct (150 women). Expenses: Contact institution. *Financial support:* In 2006–07, 258 students received support. Career-related internships or fieldwork, institutionally sponsored loans, scholarships/grants, traineeships, and tuition waivers (partial) available. Support available to part-time students. Financial award application deadline: 4/1; financial award applicants required to submit FAFSA. In 2006, 122 master's, 17 other advanced degrees awarded. *Degree program information:* Part-time programs available. Postbaccalaureate distance learning degree programs offered (minimal on-campus study). Offers adult acute care (Certificate); adult cardiovascular (Certificate); adult oncology/HIV (Certificate); adult primary care (Certificate); clinical nurse specialist (MSN); clinical research management (MSN, Certificate); family (Certificate); gerontology (Certificate); health and nursing ministries (MSN, Certificate); health systems leadership and outcomes (Certificate); leadership in community based long term care (MSN, Certificate); neonatal (Certificate); neonatal/pediatric in rural health (MSN, Certificate); nurse anesthetist (MSN, Certificate); nurse practitioner (MSN); nursing (PhD); nursing and healthcare leadership (MSN); nursing education (MSN); nursing informatics (MSN, Certificate); pediatric (Certificate); pediatric acute care (Certificate). *Application deadline:* For fall admission, 7/2 priority date for domestic and international students; for spring admission, 11/15 priority date for domestic and international students. Applications are processed on a rolling basis. *Application fee:* $50. *Application Contact:* Bebe T. Mills, Director of Admissions, 919-684-9151, Fax: 919-668-4693, E-mail: mills031@mc.duke.edu. *Dean/Vice Chancellor for Nursing Affairs,* Dr. Catherine L. Gilliss, 919-684-9444, Fax: 919-684-9414, E-mail: gilli025@mc.duke.edu.

DUQUESNE UNIVERSITY, Pittsburgh, PA 15282-0001

General Information Independent-religious, coed, university. CGS member. *Enrollment:* 10,110 graduate, professional, and undergraduate students; 3,129 full-time matriculated graduate/professional students (1,808 women), 1,303 part-time matriculated graduate/professional students (776 women). *Enrollment by degree level:* 1,353 first professional, 3,079 master's. *Graduate faculty:* 379. *Tuition:* Part-time $723 per credit. *Required fees:* $71 per credit. Tuition and fees vary according to degree level and program. *Graduate housing:* Rooms and/or apartments available on a first-come, first-served basis to single students and available to married students. Typical cost: $4,526 per year ($8,296 including board) for single students; $10,200 per year for married students. Housing application deadline: 8/22. *Student services:* Campus employment opportunities, campus safety program, career counseling, child daycare facilities, disabled student services, exercise/wellness program, free psychological counseling, international student services, low-cost health insurance, multicultural affairs office, teacher training, writing training. *Library facilities:* Gumberg Library plus 1 other. *Online resources:* library catalog, web page, access to other libraries' catalogs. *Collection:* 703,981 titles, 20,020 serial subscriptions, 3,196 audiovisual materials.

Computer facilities: 800 computers available on campus for general student use. A campuswide network can be accessed from student residence rooms and from off campus. Internet access and online class registration are available. *Web address:* http://www.duq.edu/.

General Application Contact: Dr. Ralph L. Pearson, Provost and Academic Vice President, 412-396-6054, E-mail: rlpearson@duq.edu.

GRADUATE UNITS

Bayer School of Natural and Environmental Sciences Students: 122 full-time (74 women), 41 part-time (16 women); includes 9 minority (5 African Americans, 2 Asian Americans or Pacific Islanders, 2 Hispanic Americans), 22 international. Average age 27. 107 applicants, 59% accepted, 34 enrolled. *Faculty:* 40 full-time (14 women), 20 part-time/adjunct (1 woman). Expenses: Contact institution. *Financial support:* In 2006–07, 3 fellowships with full tuition reimbursements (averaging $15,535 per year), 14 research assistantships with full tuition reimbursements (averaging $19,415 per year), 59 teaching assistantships with full tuition reimbursements (averaging $19,415 per year) were awarded; career-related internships or fieldwork, Federal Work-Study, scholarships/grants, tuition waivers (partial), and unspecified assistantships also available. Support available to part-time students. Financial award application deadline: 5/1; financial award applicants required to submit FAFSA. In 2006, 44 master's, 6 doctorates, 2 other advanced degrees awarded. *Degree program information:* Part-time and evening/weekend programs available. Postbaccalaureate distance learning degree programs offered (minimal on-campus study). Offers biochemistry (MS, PhD); biological sciences (MS, PhD); chemistry (MS, PhD); environmental management (MEM, Certificate); environmental science (Certificate); environmental science and management (MS); forensic science and the law (MS); natural and environmental sciences (MEM, MS, PhD, Certificate). *Application deadline:* For fall admission, 2/15 priority date for domestic and international students; for spring admission, 10/1 priority date for domestic and international students. Applications are processed on a rolling basis. *Application fee:* $40 for international students. *Application Contact:* Carolina Martine, Graduate Academic Advisor, 412-396-6339, Fax: 412-396-4881, E-mail: gradinfo@duq.edu. *Dean,* Dr. David W. Seybert, 412-396-4877, Fax: 412-396-4881, E-mail: seybert@duq.edu.

Graduate School of Liberal Arts Students: 461 full-time (236 women), 240 part-time (141 women); includes 13 minority (9 African Americans, 1 Asian American or Pacific Islander, 3 Hispanic Americans), 66 international. Average age 30. 506 applicants, 59% accepted, 186 enrolled. *Faculty:* 112 full-time (36 women), 72 part-time/adjunct (35 women). Expenses: Contact institution. *Financial support:* In 2006–07, 32 research assistantships with full tuition reimbursements (averaging $8,000 per year), 71 teaching assistantships with full tuition reimbursements (averaging $10,000 per year) were awarded; fellowships with full tuition reimbursements, career-related internships or fieldwork, Federal Work-Study, institutionally sponsored loans, scholarships/grants, and tuition waivers (full and partial) also available. Support available to part-time students. Financial award application deadline: 5/1. In 2006, 139 master's, 36 doctorates awarded. *Degree program information:* Part-time and evening/weekend programs available. Postbaccalaureate distance learning degree programs offered. Offers archival, museum, and editing studies (MA); clinical psychology (PhD); communication (MA); computational mathematics (MA, MS); English (MA, PhD); health care ethics (MA, DHCE, PhD, Certificate); history (MA); liberal arts (M Phil, MA, MS, DHCE, PhD, Certificate); liberal studies (M Phil, MA); multimedia technology (MS, Certificate); pastoral ministry (MA); philosophy (MA, PhD); religious education (MA); rhetoric (PhD); systematic theology (PhD); theology (MA). *Application deadline:* Applications are processed on a rolling basis. *Application fee:* $50. *Application Contact:* Linda L. Rendulic, Assistant to the Dean, 412-396-6400, Fax: 412-396-5265, E-mail: rendulic@duq.edu. *Dean,* Dr. Francesco C. Cesareo, 412-396-6400.

Graduate Center for Social and Public Policy Students: 21 full-time (11 women), 14 part-time (10 women); includes 1 minority (African American), 5 international. Average age 27. 30 applicants, 63% accepted, 12 enrolled. *Faculty:* 15 full-time (3 women), 1 (woman) part-time/adjunct. Expenses: Contact institution. *Financial support:* In 2006–07, 20 students received support, including 12 research assistantships with full and partial tuition reimbursements available (averaging $9,000 per year), 4 teaching assistantships with full and partial tuition reimbursements available (averaging $9,000 per year); career-related internships or fieldwork, institutionally sponsored loans, scholarships/grants, tuition waivers (full and partial), and unspecified assistantships also available. Support available to part-time students. Financial award application deadline: 5/1. In 2006, 15 degrees awarded. *Degree program information:* Part-time and evening/weekend programs available. Offers conflict resolution and peace studies (Certificate); social and public policy (MA, Certificate). Programs are a collaboration between the Departments of Political Science and Sociology. *Application deadline:* For fall admission, 4/30 priority date for domestic and international students; for spring admission, 10/31 priority date for domestic and international students. Applications are processed on a rolling basis. *Application fee:* $50. *Director,* Dr. Joseph Yenerall, 412-396-6485, Fax: 412-396-5265, E-mail: socialpolicy@duq.edu.

John F. Donahue Graduate School of Business Students: 110 full-time (49 women), 233 part-time (86 women); includes 26 minority (15 African Americans, 1 American Indian/Alaska Native, 1 Asian American or Pacific Islander, 9 Hispanic Americans), 31 international. Average age 31. 174 applicants, 69% accepted, 75 enrolled. *Faculty:* 50 full-time (5 women), 20 part-time/adjunct (5 women). Expenses: Contact institution. *Financial support:* In 2006–07, 31 students received support, including 27 research assistantships with partial tuition reimbursements available; career-related internships or fieldwork and unspecified assistantships also available. Support available to part-time students. Financial award application deadline: 7/1; financial award applicants required to submit FAFSA. In 2006, 146 degrees awarded. *Degree program information:* Part-time and evening/weekend programs available. Offers business administration (MBA); taxation (MS). *Application deadline:* For fall admission, 6/1 priority date for domestic students, 6/1 for international students; for spring admission, 11/1 for domestic and international students. Applications are processed on a rolling basis. *Application fee:* $50. Electronic applications accepted. *Application Contact:* Dr. Patricia Moore, Assistant Director, 412-396-6276, Fax: 412-396-1726, E-mail: moorep@duq.edu. *Dean,* Alan R. Miciak, 412-396-5848, Fax: 412-396-5304, E-mail: miciak@duq.edu.

John G. Rangos, Sr. School of Health Sciences Students: 261 full-time (229 women), 16 part-time (8 women); includes 11 minority (6 African Americans, 1 American Indian/Alaska Native, 2 Asian Americans or Pacific Islanders, 2 Hispanic Americans), 3 international. Average age 23. 150 applicants, 55% accepted, 41 enrolled. *Faculty:* 35 full-time (22 women), 24 part-time/adjunct (12 women). Expenses: Contact institution. *Financial support:* Federal Work-Study available. In 2006, 66 master's, 13 doctorates awarded. Offers health management systems (MHMS); occupational therapy (MS); physical therapy (DPT); physician assistant (MPA); speech–language pathology (MS). *Application deadline:* For fall admission, 12/1 priority date for domestic students; for winter admission, 5/1 priority date for domestic students. *Application fee:* $50. Electronic applications accepted. *Application Contact:*

Duquesne University (continued)

Christopher R. Hilf, Recruiter/Academic Advisor, 412-396-5653, Fax: 412-396-5554, E-mail: hilfc@duq.edu. *Dean*, Dr. Gregory H. Frazer, 412-396-5303, Fax: 412-396-5554, E-mail: frazer@duq.edu.

Mary Pappert School of Music Students: 64 full-time (20 women), 10 part-time, 19 international. Average age 23. 76 applicants, 92% accepted, 37 enrolled. *Faculty:* 26 full-time (9 women), 74 part-time/adjunct (13 women). Expenses: Contact institution. *Financial support:* In 2006–07, 50 fellowships with full and partial tuition reimbursements were awarded; career-related internships or fieldwork, Federal Work-Study, institutionally sponsored loans, and tuition waivers (full and partial) also available. Support available to part-time students. Financial award application deadline: 4/1. In 2006, 43 master's, 5 other advanced degrees awarded. *Degree program information:* Part-time programs available. Postbaccalaureate distance learning degree programs offered (minimal on-campus study). Offers music composition (MM); music education (MM); music performance (MM, AD); music technology (MM); music theory (MM); sacred music (MM). *Application deadline:* For fall admission, 8/1 priority date for domestic students; for spring admission, 12/1 for domestic students. Applications are processed on a rolling basis. *Application fee:* $50. *Application Contact:* Peggy Eiseman, Administrative Assistant of Admissions, 412-396-5064, Fax: 412-396-5479, E-mail: eiseman@duq.edu. *Dean*, Dr. Edward W. Kocher, 412-396-6082, Fax: 412-396-1524, E-mail: kocher@duq.edu.

School of Education Students: 864; includes 52 minority (36 African Americans, 10 Asian Americans or Pacific Islanders, 6 Hispanic Americans), 8 international. Average age 30. 286 applicants, 80% accepted, 179 enrolled. *Faculty:* 57 full-time (30 women), 40 part-time/adjunct (19 women). Expenses: Contact institution. *Financial support:* In 2006–07, 458 students received support, including 12 research assistantships with full and partial tuition reimbursements available (averaging $5,200 per year), 7 teaching assistantships with full and partial tuition reimbursements available; career-related internships or fieldwork, Federal Work-Study, institutionally sponsored loans, and tuition waivers (partial) also available. Support available to part-time students. In 2006, 282 master's, 30 doctorates, 8 other advanced degrees awarded. *Degree program information:* Part-time and evening/weekend programs available. Offers child psychology (MS Ed); community counseling (MS Ed); counselor education (MS Ed, Ed D); counselor education and supervision (Ed D); early childhood education (MS Ed); education (MS Ed, Ed D, PhD, CAGS); educational leaders (Ed D); educational studies (MS Ed); elementary education (MS Ed); English as a second language (MS Ed); instructional leadership excellence (Ed D); instructional technology (MS Ed, Ed D); marriage and family therapy (MS Ed); reading and language arts (MS Ed); school administration (MS Ed); school administration and supervision (MS Ed); school counseling (MS Ed); school psychology (MS Ed, PhD, CAGS); school supervision (MS Ed); secondary education (MS Ed); special education (MS Ed). *Application deadline:* For fall admission, 8/1 for domestic and international students; for spring admission, 12/1 for domestic and international students. Applications are processed on a rolling basis. *Application fee:* $50. *Application Contact:* Scott Rhodes, Director of Student and Academic Services, 412-396-5193, E-mail: rhodesst@duq.edu. *Dean*, Dr. Olga Welch, 412-396-6102, Fax: 412-396-5585.

School of Law Students: 462 full-time (205 women), 186 part-time (92 women). Average age 23. *Faculty:* 24 full-time (5 women), 44 part-time/adjunct (13 women). Expenses: Contact institution. *Financial support:* In 2006–07, 267 students received support; research assistantships, teaching assistantships, career-related internships or fieldwork, Federal Work-Study, scholarships/grants, tuition waivers (partial), and grant-in-aid awards available. Support available to part-time students. Financial award application deadline: 5/31. In 2006, 168 degrees awarded. *Degree program information:* Part-time and evening/weekend programs available. Offers law (JD, LL M). *Application deadline:* For fall admission, 4/1 for domestic students. Applications are processed on a rolling basis. *Application fee:* $50. *Application Contact:* Joseph P. Campion, Director, Admissions/Law School, 412-396-6296, Fax: 412-396-1073, E-mail: campion@duq.edu. *Dean*, Donald J. Guter, 412-396-6280, Fax: 412-396-1073, E-mail: guterd@duq.edu.

School of Leadership and Professional Advancement Postbaccalaureate distance learning degree programs offered. Offers community leadership (MS); leadership and business ethics (MS); leadership and information technology (MS); leadership and liberal studies (MA); sports leadership (MS).

School of Nursing Students: 98 full-time (91 women), 123 part-time (116 women); includes 16 minority (7 African Americans, 4 American Indian/Alaska Native, 2 Asian Americans or Pacific Islanders, 3 Hispanic Americans). 95 applicants, 67% accepted, 59 enrolled. *Faculty:* 14 full-time (13 women), 5 part-time/adjunct (4 women). Expenses: Contact institution. *Financial support:* In 2006–07, 19 students received support, including 10 research assistantships with partial tuition reimbursements available (averaging $1,600 per year), 4 teaching assistantships with partial tuition reimbursements available (averaging $1,600 per year); institutionally sponsored loans, scholarships/grants, traineeships, tuition waivers (partial), and unspecified assistantships also available. Financial award application deadline: 8/20; financial award applicants required to submit FAFSA. In 2006, 20 master's, 10 doctorates, 11 other advanced degrees awarded. *Degree program information:* Part-time and evening/weekend programs available. Postbaccalaureate distance learning degree programs offered (minimal on-campus study). Offers acute care nursing (Post-Master's Certificate); acute care nursing specialist (MSN); family nurse practitioner (MSN, Post-Master's Certificate); forensic nursing (MSN, Post-Master's Certificate); nursing (MSN, PhD, Post-Master's Certificate); nursing administration (MSN, Post-Master's Certificate); nursing education (MSN, Post-Master's Certificate); psychiatric/mental health nursing (MSN, Post-Master's Certificate). *Application deadline:* For fall admission, 4/1 for domestic and international students; for spring admission, 11/1 for domestic and international students. *Application fee:* $50. *Application Contact:* Susan Hardner, Nurse Recruiter, 412-396-4945, Fax: 412-396-6346, E-mail: nursing@duq.edu. *Dean/Professor*, Dr. Eileen Zungolo, 412-396-6554, Fax: 412-396-5974, E-mail: zungolo@duq.edu.

School of Pharmacy Students: 1,119 full-time (718 women), 31 part-time (16 women); includes 40 minority (15 African Americans, 23 Asian Americans or Pacific Islanders, 2 Hispanic Americans), 60 international. *Faculty:* 36 full-time (11 women), 8 part-time/adjunct (0 women). Expenses: Contact institution. *Financial support:* In 2006–07, 1 fellowship, 4 research assistantships with full tuition reimbursements, 47 teaching assistantships with full tuition reimbursements were awarded; career-related internships or fieldwork, Federal Work-Study, institutionally sponsored loans, and scholarships/grants also available. Support available to part-time students. Financial award applicants required to submit FAFSA. In 2006, 112 Pharm Ds, 1 master's, 2 doctorates awarded. *Degree program information:* Part-time programs available. Postbaccalaureate distance learning degree programs offered (minimal on-campus study). Offers pharmacy (Pharm D, MS, PhD). *Application fee:* $50. *Dean*, Dr. J. Douglas Bricker, 412-396-6380.

Graduate School of Pharmaceutical Sciences Students: 51 full-time (22 women), 17 part-time (7 women); includes 2 minority (both African Americans), 47 international. 220 applicants, 6% accepted, 11 enrolled. *Faculty:* 19 full-time (4 women). Expenses: Contact institution. *Financial support:* In 2006–07, 51 students received support, including 4 research assistantships with full tuition reimbursements available, 47 teaching assistantships with full tuition reimbursements available; career-related internships or fieldwork, Federal Work-Study, institutionally sponsored loans, scholarships/grants, and unspecified assistantships also available. Support available to part-time students. Financial award applicants required to submit FAFSA. In 2006, 1 master's, 2 doctorates awarded. *Degree program information:* Part-time programs available. Offers medicinal chemistry (MS, PhD); pharmaceutical administration (MS); pharmaceutics (MS, PhD); pharmacology/toxicology (MS, PhD). *Application deadline:* For fall admission, 2/1 priority date for domestic students. Applications are processed on a rolling basis. *Application fee:* $50. *Application Contact:* Information Contact, 412-396-1172, E-mail: gsps-adm@duq.edu. *Head*, Dr. James K. Drennen, 412-396-5520.

See Close-Up on page 871.

D'YOUVILLE COLLEGE, Buffalo, NY 14201-1084

General Information Independent, coed, comprehensive institution. *Enrollment:* 3,024 graduate, professional, and undergraduate students; 1,048 full-time matriculated graduate/professional students (760 women), 610 part-time matriculated graduate/professional students (464 women). *Enrollment by degree level:* 44 first professional, 1,142 master's, 63 doctoral, 409 other advanced degrees. *Graduate faculty:* 100 full-time (66 women), 78 part-time/adjunct (47 women). *Graduate housing:* Rooms and/or apartments available on a first-come, first-served basis to single and married students. Housing application deadline: 8/1. *Student services:* Campus employment opportunities, campus safety program, career counseling, disabled student services, exercise/wellness program, free psychological counseling, grant writing training, international student services, low-cost health insurance, multicultural affairs office, writing training. *Library facilities:* D'Youville College Library. *Online resources:* library catalog, web page, access to other libraries' catalogs. *Collection:* 122,057 titles, 665 serial subscriptions.

Computer facilities: Computer purchase and lease plans are available. 72 computers available on campus for general student use. A campuswide network can be accessed from student residence rooms and from off campus. Internet access and online class registration are available. *Web address:* http://www.dyc.edu/.

General Application Contact: Linda Fisher, Graduate Admissions Director, 716-829-8400, Fax: 716-829-7900, E-mail: graduateadmissions@dyc.edu.

GRADUATE UNITS

Department of Business Students: 47 full-time (34 women), 17 part-time (8 women); includes 15 minority (10 African Americans, 5 Hispanic Americans), 16 international. Average age 28. 63 applicants, 52% accepted, 17 enrolled. *Faculty:* 9 full-time (2 women), 10 part-time/adjunct (4 women). Expenses: Contact institution. *Financial support:* In 2006–07, 1 research assistantship with partial tuition reimbursement (averaging $3,000 per year) was awarded; career-related internships or fieldwork, Federal Work-Study, and scholarships/grants also available. Support available to part-time students. Financial award application deadline: 3/1; financial award applicants required to submit FAFSA. In 2006, 15 degrees awarded. *Degree program information:* Part-time and evening/weekend programs available. Offers international business (MS). *Application deadline:* For fall admission, 5/1 priority date for international students; for spring admission, 9/1 priority date for international students. Applications are processed on a rolling basis. *Application fee:* $25. Electronic applications accepted. *Application Contact:* Linda Fisher, Graduate Admissions Director, 716-829-8400, Fax: 716-829-7900, E-mail: graduateadmissions@dyc.edu. *Chair*, Dr. Kushnood Haq, 716-829-8123, Fax: 716-829-7760.

Department of Dietetics Students: 43 full-time (40 women), 15 part-time (13 women); includes 3 minority (2 African Americans, 1 Hispanic American), 5 international. Average age 26. 55 applicants, 67% accepted, 16 enrolled. *Faculty:* 3 full-time (2 women), 4 part-time/adjunct (all women). Expenses: Contact institution. In 2006, 3 degrees awarded. Offers dietetics (MS). Five-year program that begins at freshman entry. *Application deadline:* For fall admission, 5/1 priority date for international students; for spring admission, 9/1 priority date for international students. Applications are processed on a rolling basis. *Application fee:* $25. Electronic applications accepted. *Application Contact:* Ronald Dannecker, Director of Admissions, 716-829-7600, Fax: 716-829-7900, E-mail: admiss@dyc.edu. *Chair*, Dr. Edward Weiss, 716-829-7832, Fax: 716-829-8137.

Department of Education Students: 613 full-time (434 women), 303 part-time (223 women); includes 26 minority (14 African Americans, 1 American Indian/Alaska Native, 2 Asian Americans or Pacific Islanders, 9 Hispanic Americans), 727 international. Average age 28. 1,092 applicants. *Faculty:* 31 full-time (18 women), 38 part-time/adjunct (25 women). Expenses: Contact institution. *Financial support:* In 2006–07, 1 research assistantship with partial tuition reimbursement (averaging $3,000 per year) was awarded; career-related internships or fieldwork and scholarships/grants also available. Support available to part-time students. Financial award application deadline: 3/1; financial award applicants required to submit FAFSA. In 2006, 328 master's, 401 other advanced degrees awarded. *Degree program information:* Part-time and evening/weekend programs available. Offers elementary education (MS Ed, Teaching Certificate); secondary education (MS Ed, Teaching Certificate); special education (MS Ed). *Application deadline:* For fall admission, 5/1 priority date for international students; for spring admission, 9/1 priority date for international students. Applications are processed on a rolling basis. *Application fee:* $25. Electronic applications accepted. *Application Contact:* Linda Fisher, Graduate Admissions Director, 716-829-8400, Fax: 716-829-7900, E-mail: graduateadmissions@dyc.edu. *Chair*, Dr. David Gorlewski, 716-829-8140, Fax: 716-829-7660.

Department of Health Services Administration Students: 12 full-time (7 women), 54 part-time (38 women); includes 8 minority (all African Americans), 17 international. Average age 37. 40 applicants, 70% accepted, 17 enrolled. *Faculty:* 4 full-time (3 women), 3 part-time/adjunct (1 woman). Expenses: Contact institution. *Financial support:* In 2006–07, 1 research assistantship with partial tuition reimbursement (averaging $3,000 per year) was awarded; career-related internships or fieldwork, Federal Work-Study, and scholarships/grants also available. Support available to part-time students. Financial award application deadline: 3/1; financial award applicants required to submit FAFSA. In 2006, 7 master's, 1 other advanced degree awarded. *Degree program information:* Part-time and evening/weekend programs available. Offers clinical research associate (Certificate); health services administration (MS, Certificate); long term care administration (Certificate). *Application deadline:* For fall admission, 5/1 priority date for international students; for spring admission, 9/1 priority date for international students. Applications are processed on a rolling basis. *Application fee:* $25. Electronic applications accepted. *Application Contact:* Linda Fisher, Graduate Admissions Director, 716-829-8400, Fax: 716-829-7900, E-mail: graduateadmissions@dyc.edu. *Chair*, Dr. Walter Iwanenko, 716-829-7612, Fax: 716-829-8184.

Department of Holistic Health Studies Students: 31 full-time (16 women), 6 international. Average age 25. 47 applicants, 55% accepted, 14 enrolled. *Faculty:* 2 full-time (0 women), 6 part-time/adjunct (4 women). Expenses: Contact institution. Offers chiropractic (DC). *Application fee:* $25. *Application Contact:* Linda Fisher, Graduate Admissions Director, 716-829-8400, Fax: 716-829-7900, E-mail: graduateadmissions@dyc.edu. *Chair of Holistic Health Studies*, Dr. Paul Hageman, 716-829-7606 Ext. 7793, Fax: 716-829-7893, E-mail: hagemanp@dyc.edu.

Department of Nursing Students: 77 full-time (72 women), 101 part-time (95 women); includes 17 minority (12 African Americans, 1 American Indian/Alaska Native, 4 Hispanic Americans), 89 international. Average age 36. 177 applicants, 58% accepted, 37 enrolled. *Faculty:* 26 full-time (all women), 7 part-time/adjunct (6 women). Expenses: Contact institution. *Financial support:* In 2006–07, 1 research assistantship with partial tuition reimbursement (averaging $3,000 per year) was awarded; Federal Work-Study and scholarships/grants also available. Support available to part-time students. Financial award application deadline: 3/1; financial award applicants required to submit FAFSA. In 2006, 41 master's, 2 other advanced degrees awarded. *Degree program information:* Part-time and evening/weekend programs available. Offers community health nursing/education (MSN); community health nursing/high risk parents and children (MSN); community health nursing/management (MSN); family nurse practitioner (MS); nursing and health-related professions (Certificate); nursing with clinical focus choice (MSN). *Application deadline:* For fall admission, 5/1 priority date for international students; for spring admission, 9/1 priority date for international students. Applications are processed on a rolling basis. *Application fee:* $25. Electronic applications accepted. *Application Contact:* Linda Fisher, Graduate Admissions Director, 716-829-8400, Fax: 716-829-7900, E-mail: graduateadmissions@dyc.edu. *Chair*, Dr. Verna Kieffer, 716-829-7613, Fax: 716-829-8159.

Department of Physical Therapy Students: 73 full-time (37 women), 16 part-time (6 women); includes 7 minority (2 African Americans, 3 Asian Americans or Pacific Islanders, 2 Hispanic Americans), 58 international. Average age 27. 27 applicants, 37% accepted, 7 enrolled. *Faculty:* 9 full-time (5 women), 5 part-time/adjunct (1 woman). Expenses: Contact institution. *Financial support:* Federal Work-Study and scholarships/grants available. Support available to part-time students. Financial award application deadline: 3/1; financial award applicants required to submit FAFSA. In 2006, 59 master's awarded. *Degree program information:* Part-time programs available. Offers advanced orthopedic physical therapy (Certificate); manual physical therapy (Certificate); physical therapy (MPT, MS, DPT). *Application deadline:* For fall admission, 5/1 priority date for international students; for spring admission, 9/1 priority date for international students. Applications are processed on a rolling basis. *Application fee:* $25. Electronic applications accepted. *Application Contact:* Linda Fisher, Graduate Admissions Director, 716-829-8400, Fax: 716-829-7900, E-mail: graduateadmissions@dyc.edu. *Chair,* Dr. Lynn Rivers, 716-829-7708 Ext. 7708, Fax: 716-829-8137, E-mail: riversl@dyc.edu.

Occupational Therapy Department Students: 75 full-time (66 women), 38 part-time (33 women); includes 5 minority (2 African Americans, 2 American Indian/Alaska Native, 1 Hispanic American), 30 international. Average age 25. 88 applicants, 53% accepted, 20 enrolled. *Faculty:* 7 full-time (all women), 3 part-time/adjunct (2 women). Expenses: Contact institution. In 2006, 19 degrees awarded. Offers occupational therapy (MS). *Application deadline:* For fall admission, 5/1 priority date for international students; for spring admission, 9/1 priority date for international students. Applications are processed on a rolling basis. *Application fee:* $25. Electronic applications accepted. *Application Contact:* Linda Fisher, Graduate Admissions Director, 716-829-8400, Fax: 716-829-7900, E-mail: graduateadmissions@dyc.edu. *Chair,* Dr. Merlene Gingher, 716-829-7624, Fax: 716-829-8137.

See Close-Up on page 873.

EARLHAM COLLEGE, Richmond, IN 47374-4095

General Information Independent-religious, coed, comprehensive institution. *Graduate housing:* On-campus housing not available.

GRADUATE UNITS

Graduate Programs Offers education (M Ed, MAT).

EARLHAM SCHOOL OF RELIGION, Richmond, IN 47374-5360

General Information Independent-religious, coed, graduate-only institution. *Graduate faculty:* 8 full-time (3 women), 3 part-time/adjunct (1 woman). *Tuition:* Full-time $8,370; part-time $310 per credit. *Graduate housing:* On-campus housing not available. *Student services:* Campus employment opportunities, career counseling, exercise/wellness program, international student services, low-cost health insurance. *Library facilities:* Lilly Library plus 2 others. *Online resources:* library catalog, web page, access to other libraries' catalogs. *Collection:* 406,699 titles, 24,708 serial subscriptions, 56,384 audiovisual materials.

Computer facilities: 125 computers available on campus for general student use. A campuswide network can be accessed from student residence rooms and from off campus. Internet access and online class registration are available. *Web address:* http://www.esr.earlham.edu/.

General Application Contact: Susan G. Axtell, Director of Admissions, 800-432-1377, Fax: 765-983-1688, E-mail: axtelsu@earlham.edu.

GRADUATE UNITS

Graduate Programs Students: 69 full-time (46 women). Average age 42. 29 applicants, 76% accepted, 22 enrolled. *Faculty:* 8 full-time (3 women), 3 part-time/adjunct (1 woman). Expenses: Contact institution. *Financial support:* Scholarships/grants and tuition waivers (full and partial) available. Financial award application deadline: 4/15; financial award applicants required to submit FAFSA. In 2006, 10 M Divs, 1 master's awarded. *Degree program information:* Part-time programs available. Postbaccalaureate distance learning degree programs offered (minimal on-campus study). Offers religion (MA); theology (M Div, M Min). *Application deadline:* For fall admission, 7/31 priority date for domestic students; for winter admission, 12/12 priority date for domestic students. Applications are processed on a rolling basis. *Application fee:* $35. Electronic applications accepted. *Application Contact:* Susan G. Axtell, Director of Admissions, 800-432-1377, Fax: 765-983-1688, E-mail: axtelsu@earlham.edu. *Dean,* Jay W. Marshall, 800-432-1377, Fax: 765-983-1688, E-mail: marshja@earlham.edu.

EAST CAROLINA UNIVERSITY, Greenville, NC 27858-4353

General Information State-supported, coed, university. CGS member. *Enrollment:* 24,351 graduate, professional, and undergraduate students; 2,058 full-time matriculated graduate/professional students (1,332 women), 2,347 part-time matriculated graduate/professional students (1,655 women). *Enrollment by degree level:* 290 first professional, 3,703 master's, 379 doctoral, 33 other advanced degrees. *Graduate faculty:* 586 full-time (201 women), 67 part-time/adjunct (34 women). *Graduate housing:* Room and/or apartments available on a first-come, first-served basis to single students; on-campus housing not available to married students. Typical cost: $3,790 per year ($6,940 including board). Room and board charges vary according to board plan and housing facility selected. Housing application deadline: 5/1. *Student services:* Campus employment opportunities, campus safety program, career counseling, disabled student services, exercise/wellness program, free psychological counseling, grant writing training, international student services, low-cost health insurance, multicultural affairs office, teacher training, writing training. *Library facilities:* J. Y. Joyner Library plus 1 other. *Online resources:* library catalog, web page, access to other libraries' catalogs. *Collection:* 2 million titles, 252,699 serial subscriptions.

Computer facilities: Computer purchase and lease plans are available. 1,692 computers available on campus for general student use. A campuswide network can be accessed from student residence rooms and from off campus. Internet access and online class registration are available. *Web address:* http://www.ecu.edu/.

General Application Contact: Dr. Patrick Pellicane, Dean of Graduate School, 252-328-6012, Fax: 252-328-6071, E-mail: gradschool@ecu.edu.

GRADUATE UNITS

Brody School of Medicine Students: 353 full-time (183 women), 57 part-time (38 women); includes 113 minority (67 African Americans, 10 American Indian/Alaska Native, 32 Asian Americans or Pacific Islanders, 4 Hispanic Americans), 13 international. Average age 26. 996 applicants, 17% accepted. *Faculty:* 53 full-time (5 women), 1 part-time/adjunct (0 women). Expenses: Contact institution. *Financial support:* Fellowships with partial tuition reimbursements, institutionally sponsored loans available. Financial award application deadline: 6/1. In 2006, 69 MDs, 16 master's, 9 doctorates awarded. Offers anatomy and cell biology (PhD); biochemistry and molecular biology (PhD); medicine (MD, MPH, PhD); microbiology and immunology (PhD); Pathology (PhD); pharmacology (PhD); physiology (PhD); public health (MPH). *Application fee:* $50. *Application Contact:* Sheila E Lee, Director of Admissions, 252-744-9346, Fax: 252-744-3260, E-mail: leesh@ecu.edu. *Interim Dean,* Dr. Phyllis Horns, 252-744-2201, Fax: 252-744-9003, E-mail: hornsp@ecu.edu.

Graduate School Students: 1,705 full-time (1,149 women), 2,290 part-time (1,617 women); includes 615 minority (494 African Americans, 27 American Indian/Alaska Native, 55 Asian Americans or Pacific Islanders, 39 Hispanic Americans), 88 international. Average age 31. 1,541 applicants, 74% accepted, 825 enrolled. Expenses: Contact institution. *Financial support:* Fellowships with partial tuition reimbursements, research assistantships with partial tuition reimbursements, teaching assistantships with partial tuition reimbursements, career-related internships or fieldwork, Federal Work-Study, scholarships/grants, traineeships, and unspecified assistantships available. Support available to part-time students. Financial award application deadline: 6/1; financial award applicants required to submit FAFSA. In 2006, 1,343 master's, 43 doctorates, 20 other advanced degrees awarded. *Degree program information:* Part-time and evening/weekend programs available. Postbaccalaureate distance learning degree programs offered (no on-campus study). Offers coastal resources management (PhD). *Application deadline:* Applications are processed on a rolling basis. *Application fee:* $60. *Application Contact:* Gail Pinkham, Graduate School Admissions, E-mail: pinkhamg@ecu.edu. *Dean of Graduate School,* Dr. Patrick Pellicane, 252-328-6073, Fax: 252-328-6071, E-mail: gradschool@ecu.edu.

College of Business Students: 265 full-time (117 women), 312 part-time (143 women); includes 87 minority (63 African Americans, 6 American Indian/Alaska Native, 12 Asian Americans or Pacific Islanders, 6 Hispanic Americans), 18 international. Average age 28. 179 applicants, 18% accepted, 28 enrolled. *Faculty:* 73 full-time (14 women). Expenses: Contact institution. *Financial support:* Research assistantships with partial tuition reimbursements, teaching assistantships with partial tuition reimbursements, Federal Work-Study available. Support available to part-time students. Financial award application deadline:6/1. In 2006, 185 degrees awarded. *Degree program information:* Part-time and evening/weekend programs available. Offers accounting (MS); business (MBA, MS, MSA); management (MBA). *Application deadline:* For fall admission, 6/1 priority date for domestic students. Applications are processed on a rolling basis. *Application fee:* $50. *Application Contact:* Len Rhodes, Asst. Dean, 252-328-6012, Fax: 252-328-6071, E-mail: gradbus@ecu.edu. *Dean,* Dr. Frederick D. Niswander, 252-328-6970, Fax: 252-328-6664, E-mail: niswanderr@ecu.edu.

College of Education Students: 223 full-time (186 women), 999 part-time (831 women); includes 196 minority (172 African Americans, 7 American Indian/Alaska Native, 11 Asian Americans or Pacific Islanders, 6 Hispanic Americans), 3 international. Average age 35. 234 applicants, 30% accepted, 61 enrolled. *Faculty:* 72 full-time (38 women), 9 part-time/adjunct (7 women). Expenses: Contact institution. *Financial support:* Research assistantships with partial tuition reimbursements, teaching assistantships with partial tuition reimbursements, Federal Work-Study available. Support available to part-time students. Financial award application deadline: 6/1. In 2006, 444 master's, 24 doctorates, 9 other advanced degrees awarded. *Degree program information:* Part-time and evening/weekend programs available. Postbaccalaureate distance learning degree programs offered (no on-campus study). Offers adult education (MA Ed); behavior/emotional disabilities (MA Ed); counselor education (MS, Ed S); education (MA, MA Ed, MLS, MS, MSA, Ed D, CAS, Ed S); educational administration and supervision (Ed S); educational leadership (Ed D); elementary education (MA Ed); English education (MA Ed); higher education administration (Ed D); information technologies (MS); instruction technology specialist (MA Ed); learning disabilities (MA Ed); library science (MLS, CAS); low incidence disabilities (MA Ed); mathematics (MA Ed); mental retardation (MA Ed); middle grade education (MA Ed); reading education (MA Ed); school administration (MSA); science education (MA, MA Ed); social studies education (MA Ed); supervision (MA Ed); vocation education (MA Ed). *Application deadline:* For fall admission, 6/1 priority date for domestic students. Applications are processed on a rolling basis. *Application fee:* $50. *Application Contact:* Dean of Graduate School, 252-328-6012, Fax: 252-328-6071, E-mail: gradschool@ecu.edu. *Interim Dean,* Dr. John Swope, 252-328-1000, Fax: 252-328-4219, E-mail: swopej@ecu.edu.

College of Fine Arts and Communication Students: 93 full-time (55 women), 44 part-time (29 women); includes 16 minority (8 African Americans, 6 Asian Americans or Pacific Islanders, 2 Hispanic Americans), 4 international. Average age 29. 49 applicants, 8% accepted, 4 enrolled. *Faculty:* 73 full-time (24 women). Expenses: Contact institution. In 2006, 36 degrees awarded. Offers art and design (MA, MA Ed, MFA); fine arts and communication (MA, MA Ed, MFA, MM); health communication (MA); music education (MM); music therapy (MM); performance (MM); theory and composition (MM). *Application fee:* $50. *Application Contact:* Dean of Graduate School, 252-328-6012, Fax: 252-328-6071, E-mail: gradschool@ecu.edu. *Dean,* Jeffery Elwell, 252-328-1282, E-mail: elwellj@ecu.edu.

College of Health and Human Performance Students: 124 full-time (62 women), 114 part-time (65 women); includes 41 minority (37 African Americans, 2 American Indian/Alaska Native, 1 Asian American or Pacific Islander, 1 Hispanic American), 3 international. Average age 27. 33 applicants, 18% accepted, 4 enrolled. *Faculty:* 48 full-time (12 women). Expenses: Contact institution. *Financial support:* Research assistantships, teaching assistantships, Federal Work-Study available. Support available to part-time students. Financial award application deadline: 6/1. In 2006, 79 master's, 1 doctorate awarded. *Degree program information:* Part-time and evening/weekend programs available. Offers bioenergetics (PhD); environmental health (MS); exercise and sport science (MA, MA Ed); health and human performance (MA, MA Ed, MS, PhD); health education (MA, MA Ed); recreation and leisure services administration (MS); therapeutic recreation administration (MS). *Application deadline:* For fall admission, 6/1 priority date for domestic students. Applications are processed on a rolling basis. *Application fee:* $50. *Application Contact:* Dr. Sharon Knight, Director of Graduate Studies, 252-328-4637, Fax: 252-328-4655, E-mail: knights@ecu.edu. *Dean,* Dr. Glen Gilbert, 252-328-4630, Fax: 252-328-4655.

College of Human Ecology Students: 179 full-time (153 women), 118 part-time (90 women); includes 87 minority (76 African Americans, 2 American Indian/Alaska Native, 3 Asian Americans or Pacific Islanders, 6 Hispanic Americans), 1 international. Average age 31. 99 applicants, 14% accepted, 13 enrolled. *Faculty:* 46 full-time (24 women). Expenses: Contact institution. *Financial support:* Fellowships, research assistantships, teaching assistantships, career-related internships or fieldwork and Federal Work-Study available. Support available to part-time students. Financial award application deadline: 6/1. In 2006, 139 degrees awarded. *Degree program information:* Part-time programs available. Offers child development and family relations (MS); criminal justice (MS); human ecology (MS, MSW); marriage and family therapy (MS); nutrition (MS); social work (MSW). *Application deadline:* Applications are processed on a rolling basis. *Application fee:* $50. *Application Contact:* Dean of Graduate School, 252-328-6012, Fax: 252-328-6071, E-mail: gradschool@ecu.edu. *Dean,* Dr. Karla Hughes, 252-328-6891, Fax: 252-328-4276, E-mail: hughesk@ecu.edu.

College of Technology and Computer Science Students: 35 full-time (9 women), 121 part-time (29 women); includes 34 minority (25 African Americans, 1 American Indian/Alaska Native, 3 Asian Americans or Pacific Islanders, 5 Hispanic Americans), 11 international. Average age 33. 78 applicants, 35% accepted, 17 enrolled. *Faculty:* 34 full-time (4 women). Expenses: Contact institution. *Financial support:* Fellowships, research assistantships, teaching assistantships, Federal Work-Study available. Support available to part-time students. Financial award application deadline: 6/1. In 2006, 75 degrees awarded. *Degree program information:* Part-time programs available. Offers computer network professional (Certificate); computer science (MS); industrial technology (MS); information assurance (Certificate); occupational safety (MS); technology and computer science (MS, PhD, Certificate); technology management (PhD); Website developer (Certificate). *Application deadline:* For fall admission, 6/1 priority date for domestic students. Applications are processed on a rolling basis. *Application fee:* $50. *Application Contact:* Dean of Graduate School, 252-328-6012, Fax: 252-328-6071, E-mail: gradschool@ecu.edu. *Dean,* Dr. Ralph Rogers, 252-328-9604, Fax: 252-328-4250, E-mail: rogersm@ecu.edu.

School of Allied Health Sciences Students: 347 full-time (273 women), 55 part-time (49 women); includes 41 minority (25 African Americans, 3 American Indian/Alaska Native, 7 Asian Americans or Pacific Islanders, 6 Hispanic Americans), 4 international. Average age 27. 275 applicants, 14% accepted, 18 enrolled. *Faculty:* 58 full-time (29 women). Expenses: Contact institution. *Financial support:* Research assistantships with partial tuition reimbursements, teaching assistantships with partial tuition reimbursements, career-related internships or fieldwork, Federal Work-Study, and scholarships/grants available. Support available to part-time students. Financial award application deadline: 6/1; financial award applicants required to submit FAFSA. In 2006, 131 master's, 11 doctorates awarded. *Degree program information:* Part-time and evening/weekend programs available. Postbaccalaureate distance learning degree programs offered (no on-campus study). Offers allied health sciences (MPT, MS, MSOT, DPT, PhD); communication sciences and disorders (PhD); occupational therapy (MSOT); physical therapy (MPT, DPT); physician assistant studies (MS); rehabilitation counseling (MS); speech, language and auditory pathology (MS); substance abuse and clinical counseling (MS); vocational evaluation (MS). *Application fee:* $50. *Application Contact:* Dean of Graduate School, 252-328-6012, Fax: 252-328-6071, E-mail: gradschool@ecu.edu. *Dean,* Dr. Stephen Thomas, 252-744-6010, E-mail: thomass@ecu.edu.

School of Nursing Students: 122 full-time (112 women), 254 part-time (230 women); includes 47 minority (39 African Americans, 3 American Indian/Alaska Native, 3 Asian Americans or Pacific Islanders, 2 Hispanic Americans), 2 international. Average age 36. 79 applicants, 27% accepted, 20 enrolled. *Faculty:* 31 full-time (27 women). Expenses: Contact institution. *Financial support:* Research assistantships with partial tuition reimbursements, teaching assistantships with partial tuition reimbursements, Federal Work-Study available. Support available to part-time students. Financial award application deadline: 6/1. In 2006, 56 master's, 4 doctorates awarded. *Degree program information:* Part-time programs available. Offers nursing (MSN, PhD). *Application deadline:* For fall admission, 6/1 priority date for domestic students. Applications are processed on a rolling basis. *Application fee:* $50. *Application Contact:* Dean of Graduate School, 252-328-6012, Fax: 252-328-6071, E-mail: gradschool@ecu.edu. *Interim Dean,* Dr. Sylvia Brown, 252-744-6427, Fax: 252-328-4300.

Thomas Harriot College of Arts and Sciences Students: 317 full-time (182 women), 273 part-time (151 women); includes 65 minority (49 African Americans, 3 American Indian/Alaska Native, 9 Asian Americans or Pacific Islanders, 4 Hispanic Americans), 42

East Carolina University (continued)

international. Average age 29. 219 applicants, 42% accepted, 38 enrolled. *Faculty:* 305 full-time (80 women), 14 part-time/adjunct (3 women). Expenses: Contact institution. *Financial support:* Fellowships with partial tuition reimbursements, research assistantships with partial tuition reimbursements, teaching assistantships with partial tuition reimbursements, career-related internships or fieldwork, Federal Work-Study, scholarships/grants, traineeships, and unspecified assistantships available. Support available to part-time students. Financial award application deadline: 6/1. In 2006, 198 master's, 7 doctorates awarded. *Degree program information:* Part-time and evening/weekend programs available. Offers American history (MA); anthropology (MA); applied and biomedical physics (MS); applied mathematics (MA); applied resource economics (MS); arts and sciences (MA, MA Ed, MPA, MS, PhD); biology (MS); chemistry (MS); clinical psychology (MA); English (MA); European history (MA); general psychology (MA); geography (MA); geology (MS); health psychology (PhD); international studies (MA); maritime history (MA); mathematics (MA); medical physics (MS); molecular biology/biotechnology (MS); physics (PhD); public administration (MPA); sociology (MA). *Application deadline:* Applications are processed on a rolling basis. *Application fee:* $50. *Application Contact:* Dean of Graduate School, 252-328-6012, Fax: 252-328-6071, E-mail: gradschool@ecu.edu. *Dean,* Dr. Alan White, 252-328-6249, E-mail: whitea@ecu.edu.

See Close-Up on page 875.

EAST CENTRAL UNIVERSITY, Ada, OK 74820-6899

General Information State-supported, coed, comprehensive institution. CGS member. *Enrollment:* 4,506 graduate, professional, and undergraduate students; 186 full-time matriculated graduate/professional students (142 women), 536 part-time matriculated graduate/professional students (418 women). *Enrollment by degree level:* 722 master's. *Graduate faculty:* 48. *Graduate housing:* Rooms and/or apartments available on a first-come, first-served basis to single students and available to married students. *Student services:* Campus employment opportunities, career counseling, child daycare facilities, international student services. *Library facilities:* Linscheid Library. *Online resources:* library catalog, web page. *Collection:* 182,126 titles, 25,076 serial subscriptions, 906 audiovisual materials.

Computer facilities: 500 computers available on campus for general student use. A campuswide network can be accessed. Internet access is available. *Web address:* http://www.ecok.edu/.

General Application Contact: Dr. B. Richard Wetherill, Interim Dean, 580-310-5709 Ext. 709, Fax: 580-332-8691, E-mail: rwethell@mailclerk.ecok.edu.

GRADUATE UNITS

School of Graduate Studies Students: 186 full-time (142 women), 536 part-time (418 women); includes 174 minority (30 African Americans, 131 American Indian/Alaska Native, 3 Asian Americans or Pacific Islanders, 10 Hispanic Americans). Average age 36. *Faculty:* 48. Expenses: Contact institution. *Financial support:* Fellowships, teaching assistantships, career-related internships or fieldwork, Federal Work-Study, institutionally sponsored loans, and tuition waivers (partial) available. Support available to part-time students. In 2006, 277 degrees awarded. *Degree program information:* Part-time and evening/weekend programs available. Offers administration (MSHR); counseling (MSHR); criminal justice (MSHR); education (M Ed); psychology (MSPS); rehabilitation counseling (MSHR). *Application deadline:* Applications are processed on a rolling basis. *Application fee:* $0 ($50 for international students). *Application Contact:* Juanita L. Pratt, Secretary, 580-310-5708, Fax: 580-332-8691, E-mail: jpratt@ecok.edu. *Interim Dean,* Dr. B. Richard Wetherill, 580-310-5455, Fax: 580-332-8691, E-mail: rwethell@@mailclerk.ecok.edu.

EASTERN CONNECTICUT STATE UNIVERSITY, Willimantic, CT 06226-2295

General Information State-supported, coed, comprehensive institution. *Enrollment:* 5,239 graduate, professional, and undergraduate students; 84 full-time matriculated graduate/professional students (56 women), 352 part-time matriculated graduate/professional students (265 women). *Enrollment by degree level:* 436 master's. *Graduate faculty:* 19 full-time (10 women), 16 part-time/adjunct (7 women). Tuition, state resident: full-time $3,970. Tuition, nonresident: full-time $11,061; part-time $336 per credit. *Required fees:* $35 per credit. *Graduate housing:* On-campus housing not available. *Student services:* Campus employment opportunities, campus safety program, career counseling, child daycare facilities, disabled student services, free psychological counseling, international student services, low-cost health insurance, multicultural affairs office, teacher training. *Library facilities:* J. Eugene Smith Library. *Online resources:* library catalog, web page, access to other libraries' catalogs. *Collection:* 239,218 titles, 1,729 serial subscriptions. *Research affiliation:* Department of Education (early childhood education, mathematics and science education).

Computer facilities: 637 computers available on campus for general student use. A campuswide network can be accessed from student residence rooms and from off campus. Internet access and online class registration are available. *Web address:* http://www.easternct.edu.

General Application Contact: Dr. Tuesday L. Cooper, Associate Dean, 860-465-4543, Fax: 860-465-4538, E-mail: coopert@easternct.edu.

GRADUATE UNITS

School of Education and Professional Studies/Graduate Division Students: 60 full-time (45 women), 239 part-time (174 women); includes 23 minority (11 African Americans, 4 Asian Americans or Pacific Islanders, 8 Hispanic Americans). Average age 35. 50 applicants, 80% accepted, 31 enrolled. *Faculty:* 19 full-time (10 women), 16 part-time/adjunct (7 women). Expenses: Contact institution. *Financial support:* Teaching assistantships, career-related internships or fieldwork, scholarships/grants, and unspecified assistantships available. Support available to part-time students. Financial award application deadline: 3/15. In 2006, 102 degrees awarded. *Degree program information:* Part-time and evening/weekend programs available. Offers early childhood education (MS); education and professional studies (MS); educational technology (MS); elementary education (MS); organizational management (MS); reading and language arts (MS); science education (MS); secondary education (MS). *Application deadline:* For fall admission, 7/6 priority date for domestic and international students; for spring admission, 11/3 priority date for domestic and international students. Applications are processed on a rolling basis. *Application fee:* $50. *Application Contact:* Dr. Tuesday L. Cooper, Associate Dean, 860-465-4543, Fax: 860-465-4538, E-mail: coopert@easternct.edu. *Dean,* Dr. Patricia A. Kleine, 860-465-5293, Fax: 860-465-4538, E-mail: kleinep@easternct.edu.

Announcement: The School of Education/Professional Studies and Graduate Division offers Master of Science degrees in the following areas: early childhood education, educational technology (online), elementary education, reading/language arts, science education, secondary education, and organizational management. Eastern also offers graduate certification programs in early childhood education, elementary education, and secondary education.

EASTERN ILLINOIS UNIVERSITY, Charleston, IL 61920-3099

General Information State-supported, coed, comprehensive institution. CGS member. *Enrollment:* 12,349 graduate, professional, and undergraduate students; 611 full-time matriculated graduate/professional students, 1,143 part-time matriculated graduate/professional students. *Graduate faculty:* 448. Tuition, state resident: part-time $169 per semester hour. Tuition, nonresident: part-time $508 per semester hour. *Required fees:* $60 per semester hour. *Graduate housing:* Rooms and/or apartments available to single and married students. *Student services:* Campus employment opportunities, campus safety program, career counseling, disabled student services, exercise/wellness program, free psychological counseling, international student services, low-cost health insurance, multicultural affairs office, teacher training, writing training. *Library facilities:* Booth Library. *Online resources:* library catalog, web page, access to other libraries' catalogs. *Collection:* 1 million titles, 14,714 serial subscriptions, 14,129 audiovisual materials.

Computer facilities: Computer purchase and lease plans are available. 798 computers available on campus for general student use. A campuswide network can be accessed from student residence rooms and from off campus. Internet access and online class registration are available. *Web address:* http://www.eiu.edu/.

General Application Contact: Rodney Ranes, Director of Graduate Admissions, 217-581-7489, Fax: 217-581-6020, E-mail: rsranes@eiu.edu.

GRADUATE UNITS

Graduate School Students: 674 full-time, 1,083 part-time. Average age 25. 950 applicants, 89% accepted. *Faculty:* 362 full-time (102 women). Expenses: Contact institution. *Financial support:* In 2006–07, 150 research assistantships with tuition reimbursements (averaging $7,200 per year), 150 teaching assistantships with tuition reimbursements (averaging $7,200 per year) were awarded; career-related internships or fieldwork, Federal Work-Study, institutionally sponsored loans, and unspecified assistantships also available. Support available to part-time students. In 2006, 532 master's, 50 other advanced degrees awarded. *Degree program information:* Part-time and evening/weekend programs available. *Application deadline:* Applications are processed on a rolling basis. *Application fee:* $30. Electronic applications accepted. *Application Contact:* Rodney Ranes, Director of Graduate Admissions, 217-581-7489, Fax: 217-581-6020, E-mail: rsranes@eiu.edu. *Dean,* Dr. Robert M. Augustine, 217-581-2220, Fax: 217-581-6020, E-mail: rmaugustine@eiu.edu.

College of Arts and Humanities Expenses: Contact institution. *Financial support:* In 2006–07, research assistantships with tuition reimbursements (averaging $7,200 per year), teaching assistantships with tuition reimbursements (averaging $7,200 per year) were awarded; career-related internships or fieldwork and Federal Work-Study also available. Support available to part-time students. In 2006, 40 degrees awarded. *Degree program information:* Part-time programs available. Offers art (MA); art education (MA); arts and humanities (MA); communication studies (MA); English (MA); historical administration (MA); history (MA); music (MA). *Application deadline:* For fall admission, 7/31 priority date for domestic students. Applications are processed on a rolling basis. *Application fee:* $30. *Dean,* James Johnson, 217-581-2917.

College of Education and Professional Studies *Faculty:* 38 full-time (20 women). Expenses: Contact institution. *Financial support:* In 2006–07, 12 research assistantships with tuition reimbursements (averaging $7,200 per year), 13 teaching assistantships with tuition reimbursements (averaging $7,200 per year) were awarded; career-related internships or fieldwork and Federal Work-Study also available. Support available to part-time students. In 2006, 294 master's, 45 other advanced degrees awarded. *Degree program information:* Part-time and evening/weekend programs available. Offers college student affairs (MS); community counseling (MS); education and professional studies (MS, MS Ed, Ed S); educational administration (MS Ed, Ed S); elementary education (MS Ed); physical education (MS); school counseling (MS); special education (MS Ed). *Application deadline:* For fall admission, 7/31 priority date for domestic students. Applications are processed on a rolling basis. *Application fee:* $30. *Dean,* Dr. Diane Jackman, 217-581-2524, Fax: 217-581-2518, E-mail: dhjackman@eiu.edu.

College of Sciences *Faculty:* 193 full-time (40 women). Expenses: Contact institution. *Financial support:* In 2006–07, research assistantships with tuition reimbursements (averaging $7,200 per year), teaching assistantships with tuition reimbursements (averaging $7,200 per year) were awarded; career-related internships or fieldwork and Federal Work-Study also available. Support available to part-time students. In 2006, 83 master's, 11 other advanced degrees awarded. *Degree program information:* Part-time programs available. Offers biological sciences (MS); chemistry (MS); clinical psychology (MA); communication disorders and sciences (MS); economics (MA); mathematics (MA); mathematics and computer science (MA); mathematics education (MA); natural sciences (MS); political science (MA); psychology (MA, SSP); school psychology (SSP). *Application deadline:* For fall admission, 7/31 priority date for domestic students. Applications are processed on a rolling basis. *Application fee:* $30. *Dean,* Dr. Mary Ann Hanner, 217-581-3328, Fax: 217-581-7110, E-mail: mahanner@eiu.edu.

Lumpkin College of Business and Applied Sciences *Faculty:* 44 full-time (14 women). Expenses: Contact institution. *Financial support:* In 2006–07, 10 research assistantships with tuition reimbursements (averaging $7,200 per year), 20 teaching assistantships with tuition reimbursements (averaging $7,200 per year) were awarded; career-related internships or fieldwork, Federal Work-Study, institutionally sponsored loans, and unspecified assistantships also available. Support available to part-time students. In 2006, 147 master's, 22 other advanced degrees awarded. *Degree program information:* Part-time and evening/weekend programs available. Offers accountancy (Certificate); business and applied sciences (MA, MBA, MS, Certificate); computer technology (Certificate); dietetics (MS); family and consumer sciences (MS); general management (MBA); gerontology (MA); quality systems (Certificate); technology (MS); technology security (Certificate); work performance improvement (Certificate). *Application deadline:* Applications are processed on a rolling basis. *Application fee:* $30. *Dean,* Dr. Diane Hoadley, 217-581-3526, E-mail: dhoadley@eiu.edu.

See Close-Up on page 877.

EASTERN KENTUCKY UNIVERSITY, Richmond, KY 40475-3102

General Information State-supported, coed, comprehensive institution. CGS member. *Enrollment:* 15,763 graduate, professional, and undergraduate students; 618 full-time matriculated graduate/professional students (413 women), 1,522 part-time matriculated graduate/professional students (1,051 women). *Enrollment by degree level:* 2,130 master's, 10 other advanced degrees. *Graduate faculty:* 218 full-time (109 women), 40 part-time/adjunct (24 women). Tuition, state resident: full-time $5,610. Tuition, nonresident: full-time $15,910. *Graduate housing:* Rooms and/or apartments guaranteed to single students and available to married students. *Student services:* Campus employment opportunities, campus safety program, career counseling, disabled student services, free psychological counseling, international student services, low-cost health insurance, multicultural affairs office. *Library facilities:* John Grant Crabbe Library plus 2 others. *Online resources:* library catalog, web page. *Collection:* 799,496 titles, 2,901 serial subscriptions, 14,021 audiovisual materials.

Computer facilities: Computer purchase and lease plans are available. 1,200 computers available on campus for general student use. A campuswide network can be accessed from student residence rooms and from off campus. Internet access and online class registration are available. *Web address:* http://www.eku.edu/.

General Application Contact: Dr. Gerald Pogatshnik, Dean, 859-622-1742, Fax: 859-622-2975, E-mail: jerry.pogatshnik@eku.edu.

GRADUATE UNITS

The Graduate School Students: 618 full-time (413 women), 1,522 part-time (1,051 women); includes 99 minority (72 African Americans, 5 American Indian/Alaska Native, 12 Asian Americans or Pacific Islanders, 10 Hispanic Americans), 75 international. Average age 31. 1,248 applicants, 72% accepted, 570 enrolled. *Faculty:* 218 full-time (109 women), 40 part-time/adjunct (24 women). Expenses: Contact institution. *Financial support:* In 2006–07, 275 students received support, including research assistantships (averaging $6,500 per year), teaching assistantships (averaging $6,500 per year); fellowships, career-related internships or fieldwork, Federal Work-Study, institutionally sponsored loans, and scholarships/grants also available. Support available to part-time students. Financial award applicants required to submit FAFSA. In 2006, 825 master's, 10 other advanced degrees awarded. *Degree program information:* Part-time and evening/weekend programs available. Postbaccalaureate distance learning degree programs offered. *Application deadline:* For fall admission, 6/1 for international students; for spring admission, 10/15 for international students. Applications are processed on a rolling basis. *Application fee:* $35. Electronic applications accepted. *Application Contact:* Sandy Willis, Data Specialist, 859-622-8971. *Dean,* Dr. Gerald Pogatshnik, 859-622-1742, Fax: 859-622-2975, E-mail: jerry.pogatshnik@eku.edu.

College of Arts and Sciences Students: 193 full-time (99 women), 129 part-time (65 women); includes 20 minority (11 African Americans, 2 American Indian/Alaska Native, 7 Asian Americans or Pacific Islanders), 35 international. Average age 28. 481 applicants, 38% accepted. *Faculty:* 83 full-time (32 women), 4 part-time/adjunct (3 women). Expenses: Contact institution. *Financial support:* In 2006–07, research assistantships (averaging $6,500 per year), teaching assistantships (averaging $6,500 per year) were awarded; career-related internships or fieldwork, Federal Work-Study, and institutionally sponsored loans also available. Support available to part-time students. In 2006, 100 degrees awarded. *Degree program information:* Part-time and evening/weekend programs available. Offers arts and sciences (MA, MFA, MM, MPA, MS, PhD, Psy S); biological sciences (MS); chemistry (MS); choral conducting (MM); clinical psychology (MS); community development (MPA); community health administration (MPA); creative writing (MFA); ecology (MS); English (MA); general public administration (MPA); geology (MS, PhD); history (MA); industrial/organizational psychology (MS); mathematical sciences (MS); performance (MM); political science (MA); school psychology (Psy S); theory/composition (MM). *Application fee:* $35. *Dean,* Dr. Andrew Schoomaster, 859-622-1405.

College of Business and Technology Students: 15 full-time (7 women), 92 part-time (39 women); includes 7 minority (3 African Americans, 2 Asian Americans or Pacific Islanders, 2 Hispanic Americans), 13 international. Average age 33. 144 applicants, 31% accepted, 26 enrolled. *Faculty:* 16 full-time (5 women). Expenses: Contact institution. *Financial support:* In 2006–07, research assistantships (averaging $6,500 per year), teaching assistantships (averaging $6,500 per year) were awarded; Federal Work-Study also available. Support available to part-time students. In 2006, 21 degrees awarded. *Degree program information:* Part-time programs available. Offers business administration (MBA); business and technology (MBA, MS); industrial education (MS); industrial technology (MS); occupational training and development (MS); technical administration (MS); technology education (MS). *Application fee:* $35. *Dean,* Dr. Robert Rogow, 859-622-1409, Fax: 859-622-1413, E-mail: mba@eku.edu.

College of Education Students: 171 full-time (134 women), 969 part-time (751 women); includes 36 minority (26 African Americans, 3 American Indian/Alaska Native, 1 Asian American or Pacific Islander, 6 Hispanic Americans), 1 international. Average age 33. 1,186 applicants, 36% accepted, 346 enrolled. *Faculty:* 53 full-time (30 women), 32 part-time/adjunct (20 women). Expenses: Contact institution. *Financial support:* In 2006–07, research assistantships (averaging $6,500 per year), teaching assistantships (averaging $6,500 per year) were awarded; fellowships, career-related internships or fieldwork, Federal Work-Study, and scholarships/grants also available. Support available to part-time students. In 2006, 462 degrees awarded. *Degree program information:* Part-time programs available. Postbaccalaureate distance learning degree programs offered (minimal on-campus study). Offers agricultural education (MA Ed); allied health sciences education (MA Ed); art education (MA Ed); biological sciences education (MA Ed); business education (MA Ed); chemistry education (MA Ed); communication disorders (MA Ed); earth science education (MA Ed); education (MA, MA Ed); elementary education general (MA Ed); English education (MA Ed); general science education (MA Ed); geography education (MA Ed); history education (MA Ed); home economics education (MA Ed); human services (MA); industrial education (MA Ed); instructional leadership (MA Ed); mathematical sciences education (MA Ed); mental health counseling (MA); music education (MA Ed); physical education (MA Ed); physics education (MA Ed); political science education (MA Ed); psychology education (MA Ed); reading (MA Ed); school counseling (MA Ed); school health education (MA Ed); secondary and higher education (MA Ed); sociology education (MA Ed); special education (MA Ed). *Application fee:* $35. *Application Contact:* 859 622 1828, Fax: 859 622 1831. *Dean,* Dr. William Phillips, 859-622-1175, Fax: 859-622-1831.

College of Health Sciences Students: 175 full-time (137 women), 138 part-time (98 women); includes 20 minority (16 African Americans, 2 Asian Americans or Pacific Islanders, 2 Hispanic Americans), 23 international. Average age 30. 179 applicants, 72% accepted, 79 enrolled. *Faculty:* 48 full-time (39 women), 2 part-time/adjunct (0 women). Expenses: Contact institution. *Financial support:* Career-related internships or fieldwork and institutionally sponsored loans available. Financial award applicants required to submit CSS PROFILE. *Degree program information:* Part-time programs available. Offers chemical abuse and dependency (MPH); community health (MPH); community nutrition (MS); environmental health science (MPH); health sciences (MPH, MS, MSN); occupational therapy (MS); physical education (MS); recreation and park administration (MS); rural community health care (MSN); rural health family nurse practitioner (MSN); sports administration (MS). *Application fee:* $30. *Dean,* Dr. David D. Gale, 859-622-1523, Fax: 859-622-1140, E-mail: david.gale@eku.edu.

College of Justice and Safety Students: 57 full-time (35 women), 106 part-time (30 women); includes 11 minority (all African Americans), 2 international. Average age 32. 2,000 applicants, 3% accepted, 27 enrolled. *Faculty:* 18 full-time (3 women), 2 part-time/adjunct (1 woman). Expenses: Contact institution. *Financial support:* In 2006–07, research assistantships (averaging $6,500 per year), teaching assistantships (averaging $6,500 per year) were awarded; career-related internships or fieldwork and Federal Work-Study also available. Support available to part-time students. In 2006, 42 degrees awarded. *Degree program information:* Part-time programs available. Offers correctional and juvenile justice studies (MS); criminal justice (MS); criminal justice education (MS); justice and safety (MS); loss prevention and safety (MS); police studies (MS). *Application fee:* $35. *Dean,* Dr. Allen Ault, 859-622-3565, Fax: 859-622-6561, E-mail: allen.ault@eku.edu.

EASTERN MENNONITE UNIVERSITY, Harrisonburg, VA 22802-2462

General Information Independent-religious, coed, comprehensive institution. *Enrollment:* 1,324 graduate, professional, and undergraduate students; 111 full-time matriculated graduate/professional students (49 women), 280 part-time matriculated graduate/professional students (213 women). *Enrollment by degree level:* 59 first professional, 332 master's. *Graduate faculty:* 29 full-time (13 women), 43 part-time/adjunct (21 women). *Graduate housing:* Rooms and/or apartments available on a first-come, first-served basis to single and married students. Housing application deadline: 4/15. *Student services:* Campus employment opportunities, career counseling, disabled student services, exercise/wellness program, free psychological counseling, international student services, low-cost health insurance, multicultural affairs office, teacher training, writing training. *Library facilities:* Sadie Hartzler Library. *Online resources:* library catalog, web page. *Collection:* 169,785 titles, 1,033 serial subscriptions.

Computer facilities: 110 computers available on campus for general student use. A campuswide network can be accessed from student residence rooms and from off campus. Internet access is available. *Web address:* http://www.emu.edu/.

General Application Contact: Don A. Yoder, Director of Seminary and Graduate Admissions, 540-432-4257, Fax: 540-432-4598, E-mail: yoderda@emu.edu.

GRADUATE UNITS

Eastern Mennonite Seminary Students: 54 full-time (22 women), 26 part-time (15 women); includes 2 minority (1 Asian American or Pacific Islander, 1 Hispanic American), 5 international. Average age 39. 43 applicants, 100% accepted, 33 enrolled. *Faculty:* 10 full-time (3 women), 7 part-time/adjunct (1 woman). Expenses: Contact institution. *Financial support:* In 2006–07, 43 students received support. Application deadline: 6/30; In 2006, 29 M Divs, 1 master's awarded. *Degree program information:* Part-time programs available. Offers church leadership (MA); divinity (M Div); ministry studies (Certificate); online theological studies (Certificate); religion (MA); theological studies (Certificate). *Application deadline:* For fall admission, 6/15 priority date for domestic and international students; for winter admission, 11/15 priority date for domestic and international students; for spring admission, 3/15 priority date for domestic and international students. Applications are processed on a rolling basis. *Application fee:* $25. *Application Contact:* Don A. Yoder, Director of Seminary and Graduate Admissions, 540-432-4257, Fax: 540-432-4598, E-mail: yoderda@emu.edu. *Seminary Dean,* Dr. Ervin R. Stutzman, 540-432-4261, Fax: 540-432-4444, E-mail: stutzerv@emu.edu.

Program in Business Administration Average age 34. 13 applicants, 100% accepted, 13 enrolled. *Faculty:* 4 full-time (0 women), 6 part-time/adjunct (2 women). Expenses: Contact institution. *Financial support:* Application deadline: 6/30; In 2006, 6 degrees awarded. *Degree program information:* Part-time and evening/weekend programs available. Offers business administration (MBA). *Application deadline:* Applications are processed on a rolling basis. *Application fee:* $25. *Application Contact:* Patricia S. Eckard, Office Coordinator, Business and Economics, 540-432-4150, Fax: 540-432-4071, E-mail: eckardp@emu.edu. *Director MBA Program,* Allon H. Lefever, 540-432-4545, Fax: 540-432-4071, E-mail: allon.lefever@emu.edu.

Program in Conflict Transformation Students: 44 full-time (19 women), 11 part-time (6 women); includes 2 minority (both African Americans), 34 international. Average age 35. 40 applicants, 100% accepted, 25 enrolled. *Faculty:* 6 full-time (3 women), 3 part-time/adjunct (0 women). Expenses: Contact institution. *Financial support:* In 2006–07, 4 students received support. Scholarships/grants available. Financial award application deadline: 6/30; financial award applicants required to submit FAFSA. In 2006, 34 master's, 7 other advanced degrees awarded. *Degree program information:* Part-time programs available. Offers conflict transformation (MA, Graduate Certificate). *Application deadline:* For fall admission, 2/15 priority date for domestic and international students. Applications are processed on a rolling basis. *Application fee:* $25. Electronic applications accepted. *Application Contact:* Janelle Myers-Benner, Administrative Assistant, 540-432-4986, Fax: 540-432-4449, E-mail: bennerj@emu.edu. *Academic Director,* Dr. David Brubaker, 540-432-4423, Fax: 540-432-4449, E-mail: david.brubaker@emu.edu.

Program in Counseling Students: 31 full-time (26 women), 12 part-time (8 women); includes 2 minority (1 African American, 1 Asian American or Pacific Islander). Average age 33. 45 applicants, 64% accepted, 21 enrolled. *Faculty:* 5 full-time (3 women), 1 part-time/adjunct (0 women). Expenses: Contact institution. *Financial support:* In 2006–07, 7 students received support. Scholarships/grants available. Financial award application deadline: 6/30; financial award applicants required to submit FAFSA. In 2006, 16 degrees awarded. *Degree program information:* Part-time programs available. Offers counseling (MA). *Application deadline:* For fall admission, 3/1 for domestic students. *Application fee:* $25. *Application Contact:* Brenda C. Fairweather, Administrative Assistant for Masters in Counseling Program, 540-432-4243, Fax: 540-432-4444, E-mail: fairweat@emu.edu. *Professor of Counselor Education,* Dr. P. David Glanzer, 540-432-4244, Fax: 540-432-4444, E-mail: glanzerd@emu.edu.

Program in Education Average age 34. 51 applicants, 100% accepted, 51 enrolled. *Faculty:* 5 full-time (4 women), 27 part-time/adjunct (17 women). Expenses: Contact institution. *Financial support:* Federal Work-Study and scholarships/grants available. Financial award application deadline: 6/30; financial award applicants required to submit FAFSA. In 2006, 22 degrees awarded. *Degree program information:* Part-time programs available. Offers education (MA). *Application deadline:* Applications are processed on a rolling basis. *Application fee:* $25. *Application Contact:* Yvonne Martin, Education Secretary, 540-432-4350, Fax: 540-432-4071, E-mail: yvonne.martin@emu.edu. *Director,* Dr. Donovan D. Steiner, 540-432-4144, Fax: 540-432-4071, E-mail: steinerd@emu.edu.

EASTERN MICHIGAN UNIVERSITY, Ypsilanti, MI 48197

General Information State-supported, coed, comprehensive institution. CGS member. *Enrollment:* 22,821 graduate, professional, and undergraduate students; 836 full-time matriculated graduate/professional students (543 women), 2,989 part-time matriculated graduate/professional students (1,913 women). *Enrollment by degree level:* 3,596 master's, 161 doctoral, 68 other advanced degrees. *Graduate faculty:* 636 full-time (301 women). Tuition, state resident: part-time $341 per credit hour. Tuition, nonresident: full-time $16,104; part-time $671 per credit hour. *Required fees:* $816; $34 per credit hour. $40 per term. One-time fee: $82 full-time. Tuition and fees vary according to course level, course load, degree level and reciprocity agreements. *Graduate housing:* Rooms and/or apartments available on a first-come, first-served basis to single and married students. *Student services:* Campus employment opportunities, campus safety program, career counseling, child daycare facilities, disabled student services, exercise/wellness program, free psychological counseling, grant writing training, international student services, low-cost health insurance, multicultural affairs office, teacher training, writing training. *Library facilities:* Bruce T. Halle Library. *Online resources:* library catalog, web page, access to other libraries' catalogs. *Collection:* 658,648 titles, 4,457 serial subscriptions, 11,524 audiovisual materials. *Research affiliation:* University of Southern Mississippi (Coatings research), Tianjin Normal University (Geographic information systems), University of Michigan (Nursing, public health), University of London School of Oriental and African Studies (Linguistics).

Computer facilities: Computer purchase and lease plans are available. 1,500 computers available on campus for general student use. A campuswide network can be accessed from student residence rooms and from off campus. Internet access is available. *Web address:* http://www.emich.edu/.

General Application Contact: Graduate Admissions, 734-487-3400, Fax: 734-487-6559, E-mail: graduate_admissions@emich.edu.

GRADUATE UNITS

Graduate School Students: 836 full-time (543 women), 2,989 part-time (1,913 women); includes 633 minority (428 African Americans, 21 American Indian/Alaska Native, 118 Asian Americans or Pacific Islanders, 66 Hispanic Americans), 480 international. Average age 32. 3,130 applicants, 65% accepted, 1146 enrolled. *Faculty:* 636 full-time (301 women). Expenses: Contact institution. *Financial support:* In 2006–07, 2,346 students received support, including 150 fellowships (averaging $2,000 per year), 10 research assistantships with full tuition reimbursements available (averaging $8,500 per year), 40 teaching assistantships with full tuition reimbursements available (averaging $8,000 per year); career-related internships or fieldwork, Federal Work-Study, institutionally sponsored loans, scholarships/grants, tuition waivers (partial), and unspecified assistantships also available. Support available to part-time students. Financial award applicants required to submit FAFSA. In 2006, 1,137 master's, 11 doctorates, 14 other advanced degrees awarded. *Degree program information:* Part-time and evening/weekend programs available. Postbaccalaureate distance learning degree programs offered (minimal on-campus study). *Application deadline:* For fall admission, 5/15 priority date for domestic students, 5/1 priority date for international students; for winter admission, 10/15 priority date for domestic students, 10/1 priority date for international students; for spring admission, 3/15 priority date for domestic students, 3/1 priority date for international students. Applications are processed on a rolling basis. *Application fee:* $35. Electronic applications accepted. *Application Contact:* Graduate Admissions, 734-487-3400, Fax: 734-487-6559, E-mail: graduate.admissions@emich.edu. *Interim Dean,* Dr. Deborah deLaski-Smith, 734-487-0042, Fax: 734-487-0050, E-mail: deb.delaski-smith@emich.edu.

College of Arts and Sciences Students: 275 full-time (164 women), 836 part-time (499 women); includes 168 minority (103 African Americans, 9 American Indian/Alaska Native, 35 Asian Americans or Pacific Islanders, 21 Hispanic Americans), 158 international. Average age 31. *Faculty:* 363 full-time (149 women). Expenses: Contact institution. *Financial support:* Fellowships, research assistantships with full tuition reimbursements, teaching assistantships with full tuition reimbursements, career-related internships or fieldwork, Federal Work-Study, institutionally sponsored loans, and tuition waivers (partial) available. Support available to part-time students. Financial award applicants required to submit FAFSA. In 2006, 336 degrees awarded. *Degree program information:* Part-time and evening/weekend programs available. Offers applied economics (MA); art (MA); art education (MA); arts administration (MA); arts and sciences (MA, MFA, MLS, MPA, MS, PhD, Graduate Certificate); bioinformatics (MS); biology (MS); chemistry (MS); children's literature (MA); clinical psychology (MS, PhD); clinical/behavioral psychology (MS); communication (MA); computer science (MA); creative writing (MA); criminology and criminal justice (MA); development, trade and planning (MA); drama/theatre for the young (MA, MFA); economics (MA); English linguistics (MA); foreign languages (MA); French (MA); general science (MS); geography and geology (MS); German (MA); German for business practices (Graduate Certificate); health economics (MA); Hispanic language and cultures (Graduate Certificate); historic preservation (MS); history (MA); individualized studies program (MLS); international economics and development (MA); interpretation/performance studies (MA); language and international trade (MA); literature (MA); mathematics (MA); mathematics education (MA); music (MA); music education (MA); music performance (MA); music theory-literature (MA); physics (MS); physics education (MS); piano pedagogy (MA); public administration (MPA); social science (MA, MLS); social science and American culture (MLS); sociology (MA); Spanish (MA); Spanish (bilingual-bicultural education) (MA); statistics (MA); studio art (MA, MFA); teaching English to speakers of other languages (MA, Graduate Certificate); theatre (MA); women's and gender studies (MA, MLS); written communication (MA). *Application deadline:* For fall admission, 5/15 priority date for domestic students, 5/1 priority date for international students; for winter admission, 10/15 priority date for

Eastern Michigan University (continued)

domestic students, 10/1 priority date for international students; for spring admission, 3/15 priority date for domestic students, 3/1 priority date for international students. Applications are processed on a rolling basis. *Application fee:* $35. *Interim Dean,* Dr. Hartmut Hoft, 734-487-4344, Fax: 734-485-9592, E-mail: hartmat.hoft@emich.edu.

College of Business Students: 205 full-time (107 women), 323 part-time (169 women); includes 88 minority (35 African Americans, 46 Asian Americans or Pacific Islanders, 7 Hispanic Americans), 173 international. Average age 29. *Faculty:* 58 full-time (16 women). Expenses: Contact institution. *Financial support:* Fellowships, research assistantships with full tuition reimbursements, teaching assistantships with full tuition reimbursements, career-related internships or fieldwork, Federal Work-Study, institutionally sponsored loans, traineeships, tuition waivers (partial), and unspecified assistantships available. Support available to part-time students. Financial award applicants required to submit FAFSA. In 2006, 223 degrees awarded. *Degree program information:* Part-time and evening/weekend programs available. Postbaccalaureate distance learning degree programs offered (minimal on-campus study). Offers accounting (MSA); accounting and taxation (MBA); accounting, financial, and operational control (MBA); business (MBA, MSA, MSHROD, MSIS); business administration (MBA); computer information systems (MBA); computer-based information systems (MSIS); e-business (MBA); enterprise business intelligence (MBA); entrepreneurship (MBA); finance (MBA); human resources (MBA); human resources management and organizational development (MSHROD); information systems (MBA); internal auditing (MBA); international business (MBA); management of human resources (MBA); management organizational development (MBA); nonprofit management (MBA); production and operations management (MBA); strategic quality management (MBA); supply chain management (MBA). *Application deadline:* For fall admission, 5/15 priority date for domestic students, 5/1 priority date for international students; for winter admission, 10/15 priority date for domestic students, 10/1 priority date for international students; for spring admission, 3/15 priority date for domestic students, 3/1 priority date for international students. Applications are processed on a rolling basis. *Application fee:* $35. *Application Contact:* Dawn Gaymer, Assistant Dean, Graduate Business Programs, 734-487-4444, Fax: 734-483-1316, E-mail: dawn.malone@emich.edu. *Dean,* Dr. David Mielke, 734-487-4140, Fax: 734-487-7099, E-mail: dmielke@emich.edu.

College of Education Students: 173 full-time (148 women), 1,140 part-time (866 women); includes 184 minority (144 African Americans, 5 American Indian/Alaska Native, 11 Asian Americans or Pacific Islanders, 24 Hispanic Americans), 19 international. Average age 34. *Faculty:* 90 full-time (67 women). Expenses: Contact institution. *Financial support:* Fellowships, research assistantships with full tuition reimbursements, teaching assistantships with full tuition reimbursements, career-related internships or fieldwork, Federal Work-Study, institutionally sponsored loans, scholarships/grants, tuition waivers (partial), and unspecified assistantships available. Support available to part-time students. Financial award applicants required to submit FAFSA. In 2006, 317 master's, 11 doctorates, 14 other advanced degrees awarded. *Degree program information:* Part-time and evening/weekend programs available. Postbaccalaureate distance learning degree programs offered (minimal on-campus study). Offers college counseling (MA); community counseling (MA); counseling (MA, Post Master's Certificate); early childhood education (MA); education (MA, Ed D, Post Master's Certificate, SPA); educational leadership (Ed D); educational media and technology (MA); educational psychology (MA); elementary education (MA); higher education general administration (MA); higher education student affairs (MA); interdisciplinary cultural studies (MA); K–12 curriculum (MA); K-12 administration (MA); leadership (MA, Ed D, SPA); middle school education (MA); reading (MA); school counseling (MA); school counselor (MA); school counselor licensure (Post Master's Certificate); secondary school teaching (MA); social foundations (MA); special education (MA, SPA); speech and language pathology (MA); teaching for diversity (MA). *Application deadline:* For fall admission, 5/15 priority date for domestic students, 5/1 priority date for international students; for winter admission, 10/15 priority date for domestic students, 10/1 priority date for international students; for spring admission, 3/15 priority date for domestic students, 3/1 priority date for international students. Applications are processed on a rolling basis. *Application fee:* $35. *Dean,* Dr. Vernon C. Polite, 734-487-1414, Fax: 734-484-6471, E-mail: vpolite@emich.edu.

College of Health and Human Services Students: 123 full-time (107 women), 321 part-time (250 women); includes 122 minority (95 African Americans, 2 American Indian/Alaska Native, 16 Asian Americans or Pacific Islanders, 9 Hispanic Americans), 13 international. Average age 33. *Faculty:* 70 full-time (52 women). Expenses: Contact institution. *Financial support:* Fellowships, research assistantships with full tuition reimbursements, teaching assistantships with full tuition reimbursements, career-related internships or fieldwork, Federal Work-Study, institutionally sponsored loans, scholarships/grants, tuition waivers (partial), and unspecified assistantships available. Support available to part-time students. Financial award applicants required to submit FAFSA. In 2006, 155 degrees awarded. *Degree program information:* Part-time and evening/weekend programs available. Postbaccalaureate distance learning degree programs offered (minimal on-campus study). Offers Alzheimer's education (Graduate Certificate); clinical research administration (MS); dietetics/nutrition (MS); gerontology (Graduate Certificate); health and human services (MOT, MS, MSN, MSW, Advanced Certificate, Graduate Certificate); health and physical education (MS); nursing (MSN); nursing education (Advanced Certificate); occupational therapy (MOT, MS); orthotics and prosthetics (MS); social work (MSW); sports management (MS); sports medicine (MS). *Application deadline:* For fall admission, 5/15 priority date for domestic students, 5/1 priority date for international students; for winter admission, 10/15 priority date for domestic students, 10/1 priority date for international students; for spring admission, 3/15 priority date for domestic students, 3/1 priority date for international students. Applications are processed on a rolling basis. *Application fee:* $35. *Dean,* Dr. Jeanne Thomas, 734-487-0077, Fax: 734-487-8536, E-mail: jeanne.thomas@emich.edu.

College of Technology Students: 60 full-time (17 women), 350 part-time (112 women); includes 66 minority (48 African Americans, 5 American Indian/Alaska Native, 10 Asian Americans or Pacific Islanders, 3 Hispanic Americans), 117 international. Average age 35. *Faculty:* 55 full-time (17 women). Expenses: Contact institution. *Financial support:* Fellowships, research assistantships with full tuition reimbursements, teaching assistantships with full tuition reimbursements, career-related internships or fieldwork, Federal Work-Study, institutionally sponsored loans, scholarships/grants, tuition waivers (partial), and unspecified assistantships available. Support available to part-time students. Financial award applicants required to submit FAFSA. In 2006, 105 degrees awarded. *Degree program information:* Part-time and evening/weekend programs available. Postbaccalaureate distance learning degree programs offered (minimal on-campus study). Offers apparel, textile merchandising (MS); career, technical and workforce education (MS); computer aided engineering (MS); construction management (MS); engineering management (MS); hotel and restaurant management (MS); information security (MLS, Graduate Certificate); interior design (MS); liberal studies in technology (MLS); polymers and coatings technology (MS); quality and quality management (MS); technology (MLS, MS, PhD, Graduate Certificate). *Application deadline:* For fall admission, 5/15 priority date for domestic students, 5/1 priority date for international students; for winter admission, 10/15 priority date for domestic students, 10/1 priority date for international students; for spring admission, 3/15 priority date for domestic students, 3/1 priority date for international students. Applications are processed on a rolling basis. *Application fee:* $35. *Interim Dean,* Dr. Morell Boone, 734-487-0354, Fax: 734-487-0843, E-mail: mboone@emich.edu.

See Close-Up on page 879.

EASTERN NAZARENE COLLEGE, Quincy, MA 02170-2999

General Information Independent-religious, coed, comprehensive institution. *Enrollment:* 1,212 graduate, professional, and undergraduate students; 50 full-time matriculated graduate/professional students (30 women), 120 part-time matriculated graduate/professional students (80 women). *Enrollment by degree level:* 170 master's. *Graduate faculty:* 8 full-time (3 women), 8 part-time/adjunct (5 women). *Graduate housing:* Rooms and/or apartments available to single students and available on a first-come, first-served basis to married students. *Student services:* Campus safety program, career counseling, exercise/wellness program, low-cost health insurance, multicultural affairs office, teacher training. *Library facilities:* Nease Library. *Online resources:* library catalog. *Collection:* 117,540 titles, 466 serial subscriptions.

Computer facilities: 98 computers available on campus for general student use. A campuswide network can be accessed from student residence rooms and from off campus. Internet access is available. *Web address:* http://www.enc.edu/.

General Application Contact: Christine Galbraith, Graduate Studies Recruiter, 617-774-6703, Fax: 617-984-4901, E-mail: christine.galbraith@enc.edu.

GRADUATE UNITS

Adult and Graduate Studies Students: 50 full-time (30 women), 120 part-time (80 women). Average age 30. 26 applicants, 100% accepted. *Faculty:* 8 full-time (3 women), 8 part-time/adjunct (5 women). Expenses: Contact institution. *Financial support:* Career-related internships or fieldwork and scholarships/grants available. Support available to part-time students. Financial award applicants required to submit FAFSA. In 2006, 26 degrees awarded. *Degree program information:* Part-time and evening/weekend programs available. Offers marriage and family therapy (MS). *Application deadline:* Applications are processed on a rolling basis. *Application fee:* $35. *Application Contact:* Christine Galbraith, Graduate Studies Recruiter, 617-774-6703, Fax: 617-984-4901, E-mail: christine.galbraith@enc.edu. *Director of Adult and Graduate Studies,* John G. Moran, 617-774-6704, Fax: 617-984-4901.

Division of Education Students: 135. Average age 35. 20 applicants, 100% accepted. *Faculty:* 9 full-time (5 women), 11 part-time/adjunct (5 women). Expenses: Contact institution. *Financial support:* Career-related internships or fieldwork available. Support available to part-time students. Financial award applicants required to submit FAFSA. In 2006, 2 degrees awarded. *Degree program information:* Part-time and evening/weekend programs available. Offers early childhood education (M Ed, Certificate); elementary education (M Ed, Certificate); English as a second language (M Ed, Certificate); instructional enrichment and development (M Ed, Certificate); middle school education (M Ed, Certificate); moderate special needs education (M Ed, Certificate); principal (Certificate); program development and supervision (M Ed, Certificate); secondary education (M Ed, Certificate); special education administrator (Certificate); supervisor (Certificate); teacher of reading (M Ed, Certificate). M Ed and Certificate also available through weekend program for administration, special needs, and reading only. *Application deadline:* Applications are processed on a rolling basis. *Application fee:* $35. *Application Contact:* Christine Galbraith, Graduate Studies Recruiter, 617-774-6703, Fax: 617-984-4901, E-mail: christine.galbraith@enc.edu. *Chair,* Dr. Lorne Ranstrom, 617-745-3528, E-mail: randstrol@enc.edu.

EASTERN NEW MEXICO UNIVERSITY, Portales, NM 88130

General Information State-supported, coed, comprehensive institution. CGS member. *Enrollment:* 4,033 graduate, professional, and undergraduate students; 35 full-time matriculated graduate/professional students (18 women), 477 part-time matriculated graduate/professional students (332 women). *Enrollment by degree level:* 512 master's. *Graduate faculty:* 76 full-time (29 women), 8 part-time/adjunct (7 women). Tuition, state resident: full-time $2,478; part-time $103 per credit hour. Tuition, nonresident: full-time $8,034; part-time $335 per credit hour. *Required fees:* $35 per credit hour. *Graduate housing:* Rooms and/or apartments available on a first-come, first-served basis to single and married students. Typical cost: $2,178 per year ($4,568 including board) for single students. *Student services:* Campus employment opportunities, career counseling, child daycare facilities, disabled student services, free psychological counseling, international student services, low-cost health insurance, multicultural affairs office. *Library facilities:* Golden Library. *Online resources:* library catalog, web page, access to other libraries' catalogs. *Collection:* 305,108 titles, 7,621 serial subscriptions.

Computer facilities: 493 computers available on campus for general student use. A campuswide network can be accessed from student residence rooms and from off campus. Internet access and online class registration are available. *Web address:* http://www.enmu.edu/.

General Application Contact: Dr. Phillip Shelley, Dean, Graduate School, 505-562-2147, Fax: 505-562-2168, E-mail: phillip.shelley@enmu.edu.

GRADUATE UNITS

Graduate School Students: 35 full-time (18 women), 477 part-time (332 women); includes 146 minority (19 African Americans, 16 American Indian/Alaska Native, 7 Asian Americans or Pacific Islanders, 104 Hispanic Americans), 12 international. Average age 35. 322 applicants, 69% accepted. *Faculty:* 76 full-time (29 women), 8 part-time/adjunct (7 women). Expenses: Contact institution. *Financial support:* In 2006–07, 3 fellowships (averaging $1,025 per year), 65 research assistantships (averaging $8,200 per year), 56 teaching assistantships (averaging $8,200 per year) were awarded; career-related internships or fieldwork and Federal Work-Study also available. Support available to part-time students. Financial award application deadline: 3/1. In 2006, 131 degrees awarded. *Degree program information:* Part-time and evening/weekend programs available. Postbaccalaureate distance learning degree programs offered (minimal on-campus study). *Application deadline:* For fall admission, 8/20 priority date for domestic students. Applications are processed on a rolling basis. *Application fee:* $0. Electronic applications accepted. *Dean,* Dr. Phillip Shelley, 505-562-2147, Fax: 505-562-2168, E-mail: phillip.shelley@enmu.edu.

College of Business Students: 6 full-time (3 women), 45 part-time (26 women); includes 16 minority (3 African Americans, 4 Asian Americans or Pacific Islanders, 9 Hispanic Americans), 1 international. Average age 34. 45 applicants, 76% accepted. *Faculty:* 8 full-time (1 woman). Expenses: Contact institution. *Financial support:* In 2006–07, 7 research assistantships (averaging $8,200 per year), teaching assistantships (averaging $8,200 per year) were awarded; fellowships, Federal Work-Study also available. Support available to part-time students. Financial award application deadline: 3/1. In 2006, 9 degrees awarded. *Degree program information:* Part-time and evening/weekend programs available. Postbaccalaureate distance learning degree programs offered (minimal on-campus study). Offers business (MBA). *Application deadline:* For fall admission, 8/20 priority date for domestic students. Applications are processed on a rolling basis. *Application fee:* $0. Electronic applications accepted. *Application Contact:* Dr. John Stockmeyer, Graduate Coordinator, 505-562-2352, E-mail: john.stockmeyer@enmu.edu. *Dean,* Dr. John Groesbeck, 505-562-2343, E-mail: john.groesbeck@enmu.edu.

College of Education and Technology Students: 13 full-time (5 women), 295 part-time (218 women); includes 88 minority (10 African Americans, 12 American Indian/Alaska Native, 66 Hispanic Americans), 1 international. Average age 37. 186 applicants, 62% accepted. *Faculty:* 30 full-time (18 women), 5 part-time/adjunct (all women). Expenses: Contact institution. *Financial support:* In 2006–07, fellowships (averaging $1,025 per year), 19 research assistantships (averaging $8,200 per year), 15 teaching assistantships (averaging $8,200 per year) were awarded; career-related internships or fieldwork and Federal Work-Study also available. Support available to part-time students. Financial award application deadline: 3/1. In 2006, 80 degrees awarded. *Degree program information:* Part-time and evening/weekend programs available. Postbaccalaureate distance learning degree programs offered (minimal on-campus study). Offers counseling (MA); curriculum and instruction (M Ed); education (M Ed); education and technology (M Ed, M Sp Ed, MA, MS); physical education (MS); school counseling (M Ed); special education (M Ed, M Sp Ed). *Application deadline:* For fall admission, 8/20 priority date for domestic students. Applications are processed on a rolling basis. *Application fee:* $0. Electronic applications accepted. *Dean,* Dr. Jerry Harmon, 505-562-2443, E-mail: jerry.harmon@enmu.edu.

College of Liberal Arts and Sciences Students: 16 full-time (10 women), 137 part-time (88 women); includes 42 minority (6 African Americans, 4 American Indian/Alaska Native, 3 Asian Americans or Pacific Islanders, 29 Hispanic Americans), 10 international. Average age 31. 91 applicants, 79% accepted. *Faculty:* 41 full-time (12 women), 2 part-time/adjunct (1 woman). Expenses: Contact institution. *Financial support:* In 2006–07, 3 fellowships (averaging $1,025 per year), 39 research assistantships (averaging $8,200 per year), 41 teaching assistantships (averaging $8,200 per year) were awarded; career-related internships or fieldwork and Federal Work-Study also available. Support available to part-time students. Financial award application deadline: 3/1. In 2006, 42 degrees awarded. *Degree program information:* Part-time and evening/weekend programs available. Postbaccalaureate distance learning degree programs offered. Offers anthropology (MA); biology (MS); chemistry (MS); communicative arts and sciences (MA); English (MA); liberal arts and sciences (MA, MS); mathematical sciences (MA); speech pathology and audiology (MS). *Application deadline:* For fall admission, 8/20 priority date for domestic students. Applications are processed on a rolling basis. *Application fee:* $0. Electronic applications accepted. *Dean,* Dr. Mary Ayala, 505-562-2421, E-mail: mary.ayala@enmu.edu.

EASTERN OREGON UNIVERSITY, La Grande, OR 97850-2899

General Information State-supported, coed, comprehensive institution. *Graduate housing:* Rooms and/or apartments available to single and married students.

GRADUATE UNITS

School of Education and Business *Degree program information:* Part-time programs available. Postbaccalaureate distance learning degree programs offered (minimal on-campus study). Offers education (MS); education and business (MS, MTE); elementary education (MTE); secondary education (MTE).

EASTERN UNIVERSITY, St. Davids, PA 19087-3696

General Information Independent-religious, coed, comprehensive institution. *Graduate housing:* On-campus housing not available.

GRADUATE UNITS

Graduate Business Programs *Degree program information:* Part-time and evening/weekend programs available. Offers business administration (MBA); economic development (MBA, MS); nonprofit management (MBA, MS).

Graduate Education Programs *Degree program information:* Part-time programs available. Offers English as a second or foreign language (Certificate); multicultural education (M Ed); school health services (M Ed).

Office of Interdisciplinary Programs Offers organizational leadership (PhD).

Palmer Theological Seminary *Degree program information:* Part-time and evening/weekend programs available. Offers marriage and family (D Min); renewal of the church for mission (D Min); theology (M Div, MTS, D Min).

Programs in Counseling Offers community/clinical counseling (MA); educational counseling (MA, MS); marriage and family (MA); school counseling (MA); school psychology (MS); student development (MA).

EASTERN VIRGINIA MEDICAL SCHOOL, Norfolk, VA 23501-1980

General Information Independent, coed, graduate-only institution. *Graduate faculty:* 320 full-time (121 women), 1,255 part-time/adjunct (312 women). *Graduate housing:* Rooms and/or apartments available to single and married students. *Student services:* Campus employment opportunities, campus safety program, career counseling, low-cost health insurance. *Library facilities:* Edward E. Brickell Medical Sciences Library. *Online resources:* library catalog, web page. *Collection:* 94,000 titles, 783 serial subscriptions.

Computer facilities: 70 computers available on campus for general student use. A campuswide network can be accessed. Internet access is available. *Web address:* http://www.evms.edu/.

General Application Contact: Jeffrey A. Johnson, Executive Director of Operations and Compliance, 757-446-6196, Fax: 757-446-6179, E-mail: johnsoja@evms.edu.

GRADUATE UNITS

Art Therapy Program Offers art therapy (MS).

Doctoral Program in Biomedical Sciences Students: 24 full-time (18 women); includes 15 minority (2 African Americans, 13 Asian Americans or Pacific Islanders). 10 applicants, 40% accepted, 2 enrolled. *Faculty:* 58. Expenses: Contact institution. *Financial support:* Research assistantships, career-related internships or fieldwork available. In 2006, 4 degrees awarded. Offers biomedical sciences (PhD). *Application deadline:* For fall admission, 2/1 for domestic students. Applications are processed on a rolling basis. *Application fee:* $50. *Director,* Dr. Timothy Bos, 757-446-5677, Fax: 757-624-2255, E-mail: bosj@evms.edu.

Master of Physician Assistant Program Students: 97. 403 applicants, 14% accepted, 51 enrolled. *Faculty:* 7 full-time (3 women). Expenses: Contact institution. *Financial support:* In 2006–07, 97 students received support. Applicants required to submit FAFSA. In 2006, 33 degrees awarded. Offers physician assistant (MPA). *Application deadline:* For winter admission, 6/1 for domestic students. Applications are processed on a rolling basis. *Application fee:* $50. Electronic applications accepted. *Application Contact:* Rose Mwayungu, Director of Health Professions Enrollment, 757-446-7158, Fax: 757-446-8915, E-mail: mwayunra@evms.edu. *Director,* Dr. Thomas Parish, 757-446-7126, Fax: 757-446-7403, E-mail: parishtg@evms.edu.

Master of Public Health Program Students: 51. 71 applicants, 70% accepted, 30 enrolled. *Faculty:* 5 full-time (3 women), 6 part-time/adjunct (3 women). Expenses: Contact institution. *Financial support:* In 2006–07, 33 students received support. Career-related internships or fieldwork and institutionally sponsored loans available. Financial award application deadline: 5/1; financial award applicants required to submit FAFSA. In 2006, 19 degrees awarded. *Degree program information:* Evening/weekend programs available. Postbaccalaureate distance learning degree programs offered (minimal on-campus study). Offers public health (MPH). *Application deadline:* For fall admission, 5/3 priority date for domestic students, 4/30 for international students. *Application fee:* $50 ($100 for international students). *Application Contact:* Paula M. Swartz, Administrative Support Coordinator, 757-446-6120, Fax: 757-446-6121, E-mail: swartzpm@evms.edu. *Director,* Dr. David O. Matson, 757-466-6120, Fax: 757-446-6121, E-mail: matsondo@evms.edu.

Master's Program in Biomedical Sciences (Clinical Embryology and Andrology) Students: 40; includes 14 minority (1 African American, 10 Asian Americans or Pacific Islanders, 3 Hispanic Americans). 44 applicants, 64% accepted, 22 enrolled. *Faculty:* 16. Expenses: Contact institution. *Financial support:* In 2006–07, 10 students received support. In 2006, 20 degrees awarded. Offers biomedical sciences (MS). *Application deadline:* For winter admission, 12/1 for domestic and international students. Applications are processed on a rolling basis. *Application fee:* $50. *Application Contact:* Nancy Garcia, Administrator, 757-446-8935, Fax: 757-446-5905, E-mail: garcianw@evms.edu. *Director,* Dr. Jacob Mayer, 757-446-5049, Fax: 757-446-5905.

Master's Program in Biomedical Sciences / (Medical Master's) Students: 20 full-time (6 women); includes 6 minority (1 African American, 5 Asian Americans or Pacific Islanders). 190 applicants, 19% accepted, 20 enrolled. *Faculty:* 25. Expenses: Contact institution. *Financial support:* Federal Work-Study and institutionally sponsored loans available. In 2006, 19 degrees awarded. Offers biomedical sciences (MS). *Application deadline:* For fall admission, 4/1 for domestic students. *Application fee:* $50. *Application Contact:* Nicole L. Priest, Administrator, 757-446-8480, Fax: 757-446-8449, E-mail: priestnl@evms.edu. *Director,* Dr. Donald Meyer, 757-446-5615, Fax: 757-446-8449, E-mail: meyerdc@evms.edu.

Master's Program in Biomedical Sciences (Research Track) Students: 2. 6 applicants, 67% accepted, 0 enrolled. *Faculty:* 57. Expenses: Contact institution. In 2006, 2 degrees awarded. Offers biomedical sciences (MS). *Application deadline:* For spring admission, 4/1 for domestic students. Applications are processed on a rolling basis. *Application fee:* $50. *Director,* Dr. Timothy Bos, 757-446-5677, Fax: 757-624-2255, E-mail: bosj@evms.edu.

Ophthalmic Technology Program Students: 8 full-time (7 women); includes 3 minority (1 African American, 2 Asian Americans or Pacific Islanders). 8 applicants, 50% accepted, 4 enrolled. *Faculty:* 1 full-time. Expenses: Contact institution. In 2006, 3 degrees awarded. Offers ophthalmic technology (Certificate). *Director,* Lori J. Williams, 757-388-3747, E-mail: optech@evms.edu.

Professional Program in Medicine Students: 437. Expenses: Contact institution. *Financial support:* In 2006–07, 397 students received support. Federal Work-Study and institutionally sponsored loans available. Financial award application deadline: 3/15; financial award applicants required to submit CSS PROFILE or FAFSA. In 2006, 94 degrees awarded. Offers medicine (MD). *Application deadline:* For fall admission, 11/15 priority date for domestic students. Applications are processed on a rolling basis. *Application fee:* $95. *Application Contact:* Susan Castora, Director of Admissions, 757-446-5812, Fax: 757-446-5896, E-mail: castorsl@evms.edu. *Associate Dean for Academic Affairs,* Dr. Michael J. Solhaug, 757-446-5805, Fax: 757-446-5896, E-mail: solhaumj@evms.edu.

Surgical Assistant Program Students: 24 full-time (18 women); includes 6 minority (4 African Americans, 1 Asian American or Pacific Islander, 1 Hispanic American). 23 applicants, 57% accepted, 12 enrolled. *Faculty:* 8. Expenses: Contact institution. *Financial support:* In 2006–07, 18 students received support. Offers surgical assistant (Certificate, Graduate Certificate). *Application deadline:* For winter admission, 3/20 for domestic students. Applications are processed on a rolling basis. *Application fee:* $50. *Application Contact:* Nancy Stromann, Program Coordinator, 757-446-6100, Fax: 757-446-6179, E-mail: stromand@evms.edu. *Program Director,* R. Clinton Crews, 757-446-8961, Fax: 757-446-6179, E-mail: crewsrc@evms.edu.

The Virginia Consortium Program in Clinical Psychology Students: 49 full-time (37 women); includes 14 minority (9 African Americans, 3 Asian Americans or Pacific Islanders, 2 Hispanic Americans). 163 applicants, 10% accepted, 10 enrolled. *Faculty:* 33. Expenses: Contact institution. In 2006, 10 degrees awarded. Offers clinical psychology (Psy D). *Application deadline:* For fall admission, 1/15 for domestic students. *Application fee:* $40. *Application Contact:* Eileen O'Neill, Administrative Coordinator, 757-368-1820, Fax: 757-446-8401, E-mail: exoneill@odu.edu. *Director,* Dr. Michael L. Stutts, 757-446-8400, Fax: 757-446-8401, E-mail: stuttsml@evms.edu.

EASTERN WASHINGTON UNIVERSITY, Cheney, WA 99004-2431

General Information State-supported, coed, comprehensive institution. CGS member. *Graduate housing:* Rooms and/or apartments available on a first-come, first-served basis to single and married students. Housing application deadline: 5/1.

GRADUATE UNITS

Graduate Studies *Degree program information:* Part-time and evening/weekend programs available. Offers interdisciplinary studies (MA, MS).

College of Arts and Letters *Degree program information:* Part-time programs available. Offers arts and letters (M Ed, MA, MFA); composition (MA); creative writing (MFA); English (MA); French education (M Ed); instrumental/vocal performance (MA); music education (MA); music history and literature (MA).

College of Business and Public Administration *Degree program information:* Part-time and evening/weekend programs available. Offers business administration (MBA); business and public administration (MBA, MPA, MURP); public administration (MPA); urban and regional planning (MURP).

College of Education and Human Development *Degree program information:* Part-time programs available. Offers adult education (M Ed); college instruction (MA, MS); college instruction in physical education (MS); counseling psychology (MS); curriculum and instruction (M Ed); early childhood education (M Ed); education and human development (M Ed, MA, MS); educational leadership (M Ed); elementary teaching (M Ed); foundations of education (M Ed); instructional media and technology (M Ed); literacy specialist (M Ed); physical education (MS); school counseling (MS); school library media administration (M Ed); school psychology (MS); science education (M Ed); social science education (M Ed); special education (M Ed); supervising (clinic) teaching (M Ed).

College of Science, Mathematics and Technology *Degree program information:* Part-time programs available. Offers biology (MS); communication disorders (MS); computer science (M Ed, MS); mathematics (MS); occupational therapy (MOT); physical therapy (DPT); science, mathematics and technology (M Ed, MOT, MS, DPT).

College of Social and Behavioral Sciences *Degree program information:* Part-time and evening/weekend programs available. Offers communication studies (MS); history (MA); psychology (MS); school psychology (MS); social and behavioral sciences (MA, MS).

Intercollegiate College of Nursing Offers nursing (MN).

School of Social Work and Human Services *Degree program information:* Part-time programs available. Offers social work and human services (MSW).

EAST STROUDSBURG UNIVERSITY OF PENNSYLVANIA, East Stroudsburg, PA 18301-2999

General Information State-supported, coed, comprehensive institution. *Enrollment:* 7,013 graduate, professional, and undergraduate students; 287 full-time matriculated graduate/professional students (182 women), 546 part-time matriculated graduate/professional students (408 women). *Enrollment by degree level:* 833 master's. *Graduate faculty:* 87 full-time (35 women), 28 part-time/adjunct (17 women). Tuition, state resident: full-time $6,048; part-time $336 per credit. Tuition, nonresident: full-time $9,678; part-time $538 per credit. *Required fees:* $1,353; $67 per credit. One-time fee: $37 part-time. *Graduate housing:* Room and/or apartments available on a first-come, first-served basis to single students; on-campus housing not available to married students. Typical cost: $3,506 per year ($5,302 including board). Room and board charges vary according to board plan and housing facility selected. Housing application deadline: 5/1. *Student services:* Campus employment opportunities, campus safety program, career counseling, child daycare facilities, disabled student services, exercise/wellness program, free psychological counseling, international student services, low-cost health insurance. *Library facilities:* Kemp Library. *Online resources:* library catalog, web page, access to other libraries' catalogs. *Collection:* 449,107 titles, 1,175 serial subscriptions.

Computer facilities: 500 computers available on campus for general student use. A campuswide network can be accessed from student residence rooms and from off campus. Internet access and online class registration are available. *Web address:* http://www3.esu.edu/.

General Application Contact: Dr. Henry Gardner, Associate Provost for Enrollment Management, 570-422-2870, Fax: 570-422-2843, E-mail: hgardner@po-box.esu.edu.

GRADUATE UNITS

Graduate School Students: 287 full-time (182 women), 546 part-time (408 women); includes 56 minority (26 African Americans, 30 Hispanic Americans), 20 international. Average age 31. *Faculty:* 87 full-time (35 women), 28 part-time/adjunct (17 women). Expenses: Contact institution. *Financial support:* In 2006–07, 138 research assistantships with full and partial tuition reimbursements were awarded; career-related internships or fieldwork, Federal Work-Study, and institutionally sponsored loans also available. Financial award application deadline: 3/1; financial award applicants required to submit FAFSA. In 2006, 287 degrees awarded. *Degree program information:* Part-time and evening/weekend programs available. *Application deadline:* For fall admission, 7/31 priority date for domestic students, 5/1 priority date for international students; for spring admission, 11/30 for domestic students, 10/1 for international students. Applications are processed on a rolling basis. *Application fee:* $50. *Application Contact:* Dr. Henry Gardner, Associate Provost for Enrollment Management, 570-422-2870, Fax: 570-422-2843, E-mail: hgardner@po-box.esu.edu. *Interim Dean: Graduate Schools Faculty Research,* Dr. Alberto Cardelle, 570-422-3536, Fax: 570-422-3711, E-mail: acardelle@po-box.esu.edu.

School of Arts and Sciences Students: 67 full-time (25 women), 78 part-time (39 women); includes 13 minority (8 African Americans, 5 Hispanic Americans), 8 international. Average age 31. *Faculty:* 29 full-time (6 women). Expenses: Contact institution. *Financial support:* In 2006–07, 40 research assistantships with full and partial tuition reimbursements were awarded; career-related internships or fieldwork, Federal Work-Study, and institutionally sponsored loans also available. Financial award application deadline: 3/1; financial award applicants required to submit FAFSA. In 2006, 41 degrees awarded. *Degree program information:* Part-time and evening/weekend programs available. Offers arts and sciences (M Ed, MA, MS); biology (M Ed, MS); computer science (MS); history (M Ed, MA); political science (M Ed, MA). *Application deadline:* For fall admission, 7/31 for domestic students, 5/1 priority date for international students; for spring admission, 11/30 for domestic students, 10/1 for international students. Applications are processed on a rolling basis. *Application fee:* $50. *Dean,* Dr. Peter Hawkes, 570-422-3494, Fax: 570-422-3506, E-mail: phawkes@po-box.esu.edu.

East Stroudsburg University of Pennsylvania (continued)

School of Health Sciences and Human Performance Students: 113 full-time (80 women), 61 part-time (33 women); includes 19 minority (9 African Americans, 1 American Indian/Alaska Native, 3 Asian Americans or Pacific Islanders, 6 Hispanic Americans), 9 international. Average age 29. *Faculty:* 24 full-time (11 women), 4 part-time/adjunct (3 women). Expenses: Contact institution. *Financial support:* In 2006–07, 65 research assistantships with full and partial tuition reimbursements were awarded; career-related internships or fieldwork, Federal Work-Study, and institutionally sponsored loans also available. Financial award application deadline: 3/1; financial award applicants required to submit FAFSA. In 2006, 95 degrees awarded. *Degree program information:* Part-time and evening/weekend programs available. Offers cardiac rehabilitation and exercise science (MS); community health education (MPH); health and physical education (M Ed); health education (MS); health sciences and human performance (M Ed, MPH, MS); management and leadership (MS); speech pathology and audiology (MS); sports management (MS). *Application deadline:* For fall admission, 7/31 priority date for domestic students, 5/1 priority date for international students; for spring admission, 11/30 for domestic students, 10/1 for international students. Applications are processed on a rolling basis. *Application fee:* $50. *Dean,* Dr. Mark Kilker, 570-422-3425, Fax: 570-422-3347, E-mail: mkilker@po-box.esu.edu.

School of Professional Studies Students: 107 full-time (77 women), 407 part-time (336 women); includes 32 minority (9 African Americans, 1 American Indian/Alaska Native, 3 Asian Americans or Pacific Islanders, 19 Hispanic Americans), 3 international. Average age 32. *Faculty:* 34 full-time (18 women), 24 part-time/adjunct (14 women). Expenses: Contact institution. *Financial support:* In 2006–07, 33 research assistantships with full and partial tuition reimbursements were awarded; career-related internships or fieldwork, Federal Work-Study, and institutionally sponsored loans also available. Financial award application deadline: 3/1; financial award applicants required to submit FAFSA. In 2006, 151 degrees awarded. *Degree program information:* Part-time and evening/weekend programs available. Offers elementary education (M Ed); instructional technology (M Ed); management and leadership (MS); professional and secondary education (M Ed); reading (M Ed); special education (M Ed). *Application deadline:* For fall admission, 7/31 priority date for domestic students, 5/1 priority date for international students; for spring admission, 11/30 for domestic students, 10/1 for international students. Applications are processed on a rolling basis. *Application fee:* $50. *Interim Dean,* Dr. Pamela Kramer, 570-422-3377, Fax: 570-422-3506, E-mail: pkramer@po-box.esu.edu.

See Close-Up on page 881.

EAST TENNESSEE STATE UNIVERSITY, Johnson City, TN 37614

General Information State-supported, coed, university. CGS member. *Graduate housing:* Rooms and/or apartments available on a first-come, first-served basis to single and married students. Housing application deadline: 7/1. *Research affiliation:* Oak Ridge National Laboratory (biomedical physical science), Eastman Chemical Corporation (biomedical science), Tennessee Mouse Genome Consortium (biomedical science), Tennessee Biotechnology Association (biotechnology), Siemens (scientific and biomedical manufacturing), Marshall Space Flight Center (general).

GRADUATE UNITS

James H. Quillen College of Medicine *Degree program information:* Part-time programs available. Offers anatomy (MS, PhD); biochemistry (MS, PhD); biophysics (MS, PhD); medicine (MD, MS, PhD); microbiology (MS, PhD); pharmacology (MS, PhD); physiology (MS, PhD).

School of Graduate Studies *Degree program information:* Part-time and evening/weekend programs available.

College of Arts and Sciences *Degree program information:* Part-time and evening/weekend programs available. Offers applied sociology (MA); art education (MA); art history (MA); arts and sciences (MA, MFA, MS, MSW); biology (MS); chemistry (MS); clinical psychology (MA); communication (MA); criminal justice and criminology (MA); English (MA); general psychology (MA); general sociology (MA); history (MA); mathematics (MS); microbiology (MS); social work (MSW); studio art (MA, MFA).

College of Business and Technology *Degree program information:* Part-time and evening/weekend programs available. Offers accountancy (M Acc); business administration (MBA, Certificate); business and technology (M Acc, MBA, MCM, MPM, MS, Certificate); city management (MCM); clinical nutrition (MS); community development (MPM); computer science (MS); digital media (MS); engineering technology (MS); general administration (MPM); health care management (Certificate); industrial arts/technology education (MS); information systems science (MS); municipal service management (MPM); software engineering (MS); urban and regional economic development (MPM); urban and regional planning (MPM).

College of Education *Degree program information:* Part-time and evening/weekend programs available. Offers 7-12 (MAT); administrative endorsement (M Ed, Ed D, Ed S); advanced practitioner (M Ed); classroom leadership (Ed D); classroom technology (M Ed); community agency counseling (M Ed, MA); comprehensive concentration (M Ed); counseling (M Ed, MA); early childhood education (M Ed, MA); early childhood general (M Ed); early childhood special education (M Ed); early childhood teaching (M Ed); education (M Ed, MA, MAT, Ed D, Ed S); educational communication (M Ed); educational leadership (M Ed, Ed D, Ed S); educational media/educational technology (M Ed); elementary and secondary (school counseling) (M Ed, MA); elementary education (M Ed, MAT); exercise physiology (MA); fitness leadership (MA); K-12 (MAT); marriage and family therapy (M Ed, MA); modified concentration (M Ed); physical education (M Ed, MA); post secondary and private sector leadership (Ed D); reading and storytelling (M Ed, MA); reading education (M Ed, MA); school leadership (Ed D); school library media (M Ed); school system leadership (Ed S); secondary education (M Ed, MAT); sports management (MA); sports sciences (MA); teacher leadership (Ed S).

College of Nursing *Degree program information:* Part-time programs available. Offers advanced nursing practice (Post Master's Certificate); health care management (Certificate); nursing (MSN, DSN).

College of Public and Allied Health *Degree program information:* Part-time and evening/weekend programs available. Offers audiology (MS, Au D); communicative disorders (MS); community health (MPH); environmental health (MSEH); epidemiology (Certificate); gerontology (Certificate); health care management (Certificate); physical therapy (DPT); public and allied health (MPH, MS, MSEH, Au D, DPT, Certificate); public health (MPH); public health administration (MPH); special education audiology pre-K-12 (MS); special education speech pathology pre-K-12 (MS); speech pathology (MS).

Division of Cross-Disciplinary Studies Offers liberal studies (MALS).

See Close-Up on page 883.

EAST WEST COLLEGE OF NATURAL MEDICINE, Sarasota, FL 34234

General Information Proprietary, coed, graduate-only institution.

GRADUATE UNITS

Graduate Programs

ÉCOLE POLYTECHNIQUE DE MONTRÉAL, Montréal, QC H3C 3A7, Canada

General Information Province-supported, coed, graduate-only institution. *Graduate housing:* Room and/or apartments available to single students; on-campus housing not available to married students. Housing application deadline: 2/1. *Research affiliation:* Energy Research Institute (Quebec), CRIM (computer sciences and engineering), Center for Research on Computation and its Applications (computer science), Center for InterUniversity Research and Analysis on Organization (organizations analysis), Centre Québécois de Valorisation des Biotechnologies (biotechnological process engineering), Metropolitan Gas (natural gas).

GRADUATE UNITS

Graduate Programs *Degree program information:* Part-time and evening/weekend programs available. Offers advanced materials (M Eng, M Sc A, PhD); aerothermics (M Eng, M Sc A, PhD); applied mechanics (M Eng, M Sc A, PhD); automation (M Eng, M Sc A, PhD); chemical engineering (M Eng, M Sc A, PhD, DESS); chemical metallurgy (M Eng, M Sc A, PhD); computer science (M Eng, M Sc A, PhD); electrotechnology (M Eng, M Sc A, PhD); environmental engineering (M Eng, M Sc A, PhD); ergonomy (M Eng, M Sc A, DESS); geotechnical engineering (M Eng, M Sc A, PhD); hydraulics engineering (M Eng, M Sc A, PhD); mathematical method in CA engineering (M Eng, M Sc A, PhD); microelectronics (M Eng, M Sc A, PhD); microwave technology (M Eng, M Sc A, PhD); mining engineering and geological engineering (M Eng, M Sc A, PhD); operational research (M Eng, M Sc A, PhD); optical engineering (M Eng, M Sc A, PhD); physical metallurgy (M Eng, M Sc A, PhD); production (M Eng, M Sc A); solid-state physics and engineering (M Eng, M Sc A, PhD); structural engineering (M Eng, M Sc A, PhD); technology management (M Eng, M Sc A); tool design (M Eng, M Sc A, PhD); transportation engineering (M Eng, M Sc A, PhD).

Institute of Biomedical Engineering *Degree program information:* Part-time programs available. Offers biomedical engineering (M Eng, M Sc A, PhD, DESS).

Institute of Nuclear Engineering Offers nuclear engineering (M Eng, PhD, DESS); nuclear engineering, socio-economics of energy (M Sc A).

ECUMENICAL THEOLOGICAL SEMINARY, Detroit, MI 48201

General Information Independent-religious, coed, graduate-only institution. *Graduate housing:* On-campus housing not available.

GRADUATE UNITS

Professional Program Offers theology (M Div).

Program in Ministry Offers ministry (D Min).

EDEN THEOLOGICAL SEMINARY, St. Louis, MO 63119-3192

General Information Independent-religious, coed, graduate-only institution. *Graduate housing:* Rooms and/or apartments available on a first-come, first-served basis to single and married students. Housing application deadline: 7/30.

GRADUATE UNITS

Graduate and Professional Programs Offers theology (M Div, MAPS, MTS, D Min). Electronic applications accepted.

EDGEWOOD COLLEGE, Madison, WI 53711-1997

General Information Independent-religious, coed, comprehensive institution. *Enrollment:* 2,565 graduate, professional, and undergraduate students; 68 full-time matriculated graduate/professional students (45 women), 493 part-time matriculated graduate/professional students (326 women). *Enrollment by degree level:* 497 master's, 64 doctoral. *Graduate faculty:* 121. *Graduate housing:* Room and/or apartments available on a first-come, first-served basis to single students; on-campus housing not available to married students. Housing application deadline: 8/31. *Student services:* Campus employment opportunities, career counseling, free psychological counseling, international student services, low-cost health insurance, multicultural affairs office, writing training. *Library facilities:* Oscar Rennebohm Library. *Online resources:* library catalog, web page, access to other libraries' catalogs. *Collection:* 90,253 titles, 447 serial subscriptions, 4,359 audiovisual materials.

Computer facilities: Computer purchase and lease plans are available. 140 computers available on campus for general student use. A campuswide network can be accessed from student residence rooms and from off campus. Internet access and online class registration are available. *Web address:* http://www.edgewood.edu/.

General Application Contact: Paula O'Malley, Director for Admissions and Recruitment, 608-663-2217, Fax: 608-663-2214, E-mail: pomalley@edgewood.edu.

GRADUATE UNITS

Program in Business Students: 19 full-time (9 women), 156 part-time (78 women); includes 12 minority (3 African Americans, 5 Asian Americans or Pacific Islanders, 4 Hispanic Americans), 4 international. Average age 33. Expenses: Contact institution. *Financial support:* Career-related internships or fieldwork available. In 2006, 72 degrees awarded. *Degree program information:* Part-time and evening/weekend programs available. Offers business (MBA). *Application deadline:* For fall admission, 8/24 for domestic students, 8/1 for international students; for spring admission, 1/10 for domestic students, 10/1 for international students. Applications are processed on a rolling basis. *Application fee:* $25. Electronic applications accepted. *Application Contact:* Paula O'Malley, Graduate Student Admissions Counselor, 608-663-2282, Fax: 608-663-3291, E-mail: gradprograms@edgewood.edu. *Chair,* Dr. Gary Schroeder, 608-663-3374, Fax: 608-663-3291, E-mail: gschroeder@edgewood.edu.

Program in Education Students: 30 full-time (21 women), 180 part-time (117 women); includes 7 minority (5 African Americans, 2 Asian Americans or Pacific Islanders), 2 international. Average age 38. Expenses: Contact institution. In 2006, 25 master's, 20 doctorates awarded. *Degree program information:* Part-time and evening/weekend programs available. Offers director of instruction (Certificate); director of special education and pupil services (Certificate); education (MA Ed); educational administration (MA); educational leadership (Ed D); emotional disturbances (MA, Certificate); learning disabilities (MA, Certificate); learning disabilities and emotional disturbances (MA, Certificate); school business administration (Certificate); school principalship K-12 (Certificate). *Application deadline:* For fall admission, 8/24 for domestic students, 8/1 for international students; for spring admission, 1/10 for domestic students, 10/1 for international students. Applications are processed on a rolling basis. *Application fee:* $25. Electronic applications accepted. *Application Contact:* Paula O'Malley, Graduate Student Admissions Counselor, 608-663-2282, Fax: 608-663-3291, E-mail: gradprograms@edgewood.edu. *Chair,* Dr. Joseph Schmiedicke, 608-663-2293, Fax: 608-663-3291, E-mail: schmied@edgewood.edu.

Program in Marriage and Family Therapy Students: 16 full-time (12 women), 22 part-time (18 women); includes 4 minority (1 Asian American or Pacific Islander, 3 Hispanic Americans), 1 international. Average age 32. Expenses: Contact institution. In 2006, 13 degrees awarded. *Degree program information:* Part-time and evening/weekend programs available. Offers marriage and family therapy (MS). *Application deadline:* For fall admission, 3/1 for domestic students. *Application fee:* $25. Electronic applications accepted. *Application Contact:* Paula O'Malley, Graduate Student Admissions Counselor, 608-663-2282, Fax: 608-663-3291, E-mail: gradprograms@edgewood.edu. *Director,* Dr. Peter Fabian, 608-663-2233, Fax: 608-663-3291, E-mail: fabian@edgewood.edu.

Program in Nursing Students: 1 (woman) full-time, 35 part-time (30 women), 1 international. Average age 41. Expenses: Contact institution. In 2006, 11 degrees awarded. Offers nursing (MS). *Application deadline:* For fall admission, 8/24 priority date for domestic students, 8/1 for international students; for spring admission, 1/10 priority date for domestic students, 10/1 for international students. Applications are processed on a rolling basis. *Application fee:* $25. Electronic applications accepted. *Application Contact:* Paula O'Malley, Graduate Student Admissions Counselor, 608-663-2282, Fax: 608-663-3291, E-mail: gradprograms@edgewood.edu. *Chair,* Dr. Margaret Noreuil, 608-663-2820, Fax: 608-663-3291, E-mail: mnoreuil@edgewood.edu.

Program in Religious Studies Students: 1 (woman) full-time, 9 part-time (7 women); includes 2 minority (1 African American, 1 Hispanic American). Average age 48. Expenses: Contact institution. *Financial support:* Career-related internships or fieldwork, institutionally sponsored loans, scholarships/grants, and tuition waivers (partial) available. Support available to part-time students. In 2006, 2 degrees awarded. *Degree program information:* Part-time and evening/weekend programs available. Offers religious studies (MA). *Application deadline:* For fall admission, 8/24 for domestic students, 8/1 for international students; for spring admission, 1/10 for domestic students, 10/1 for international students. Applications are processed on a rolling basis. *Application fee:* $25. Electronic applications accepted. *Application Contact:* Paula O'Malley, Graduate Student Admissions Counselor, 608-663-2282, Fax: 608-663-3291, E-mail: gradprograms@edgewood.edu. *Chairperson,* Dr. John Leonard, 608-663-2823, Fax: 608-663-3291, E-mail: jleonard@edgewood.edu.

EDINBORO UNIVERSITY OF PENNSYLVANIA, Edinboro, PA 16444

General Information State-supported, coed, comprehensive institution. *Enrollment:* 7,579 graduate, professional, and undergraduate students; 483 full-time matriculated graduate/professional students (331 women), 653 part-time matriculated graduate/professional students (491 women). *Enrollment by degree level:* 863 master's, 103 other advanced degrees. *Graduate faculty:* 89 full-time (43 women). Tuition, state resident: full-time $6,048; part-time $336 per credit. Tuition, nonresident: full-time $9,678; part-time $538 per credit. *Required fees:* $1,849; $42 per credit. *Graduate housing:* Room and/or apartments available on a first-come, first-served basis to single students; on-campus housing not available to married students. Typical cost: $3,600 per year ($5,718 including board). Housing application deadline: 7/1. *Student services:* Campus employment opportunities, campus safety program, career counseling, disabled student services, exercise/wellness program, free psychological counseling, international student services, low-cost health insurance, multicultural affairs office, teacher training. *Library facilities:* Baron-Forness Library plus 1 other. *Online resources:* library catalog, web page, access to other libraries' catalogs. *Collection:* 493,114 titles, 1,409 serial subscriptions, 13,805 audiovisual materials. *Research affiliation:* Keystone University Research Corporation (applied social research), Precision Manufacturing Institute (manufacturing technology).

Computer facilities: Computer purchase and lease plans are available. 818 computers available on campus for general student use. A campuswide network can be accessed from student residence rooms and from off campus. Internet access and online class registration, e-mail, software are available. *Web address:* http://www.edinboro.edu/.

General Application Contact: Dr. R. Scott Baldwin, Dean of Graduate Studies and Research, 814-732-2856, Fax: 814-732-2611, E-mail: sbaldwin@edinboro.edu.

GRADUATE UNITS

Graduate Studies and Research Students: 424 full-time (294 women), 490 part-time (377 women); includes 38 minority (24 African Americans, 3 American Indian/Alaska Native, 4 Asian Americans or Pacific Islanders, 7 Hispanic Americans), 18 international. Average age 31. 756 applicants, 78% accepted, 429 enrolled. *Faculty:* 89 full-time (43 women). Expenses: Contact institution. *Financial support:* In 2006–07, 137 research assistantships with full and partial tuition reimbursements (averaging $3,850 per year) were awarded; career-related internships or fieldwork, Federal Work-Study, institutionally sponsored loans, scholarships/grants, and unspecified assistantships also available. Support available to part-time students. Financial award application deadline: 2/15; financial award applicants required to submit FAFSA. In 2006, 294 master's, 61 other advanced degrees awarded. *Degree program information:* Part-time and evening/weekend programs available. *Application deadline:* Applications are processed on a rolling basis. *Application fee:* $30. Electronic applications accepted. *Dean,* Dr. R. Scott Baldwin, 814-732-2752, Fax: 814-732-2268, E-mail: sbaldwin@edinboro.edu.

School of Education Students: 233 full-time (174 women), 398 part-time (308 women); includes 20 minority (14 African Americans, 1 American Indian/Alaska Native, 2 Asian Americans or Pacific Islanders, 3 Hispanic Americans). Average age 31. *Faculty:* 39 full-time (26 women). Expenses: Contact institution. *Financial support:* In 2006–07, 66 research assistantships with full and partial tuition reimbursements (averaging $3,850 per year) were awarded; career-related internships or fieldwork, Federal Work-Study, institutionally sponsored loans, scholarships/grants, and unspecified assistantships also available. Support available to part-time students. Financial award application deadline: 2/15; financial award applicants required to submit FAFSA. In 2006, 203 master's, 47 other advanced degrees awarded. *Degree program information:* Part-time and evening/weekend programs available. Offers behavior management (Certificate); character education (M Ed, Certificate); community counseling (MA); counseling (MA); early childhood education (M Ed); education (M Ed, MA, Certificate); educational leadership (M Ed); educational psychology (M Ed); elementary education (M Ed); elementary guidance (MA); elementary school administration (M Ed); letter of eligibility (Certificate); reading (M Ed, Certificate); reading specialist (Certificate); rehabilitation counseling (MA); secondary education (M Ed); secondary guidance (MA); secondary school administration (M Ed); special education (M Ed); student personnel services (MA). Certificates issued by a state agency. *Application deadline:* Applications are processed on a rolling basis. *Application fee:* $30. Electronic applications accepted. *Application Contact:* Dr. R. Scott Baldwin, Dean, 814-732-2752, Fax: 814-732-2268, E-mail: sbaldwin@edinboro.edu. *Interim Dean,* Dr. Kenneth Adams, 814-732-2752, Fax: 814-732-2268, E-mail: kadams@edinboro.edu.

School of Liberal Arts Students: 175 full-time (113 women), 50 part-time (37 women); includes 18 minority (10 African Americans, 2 American Indian/Alaska Native, 2 Asian Americans or Pacific Islanders, 4 Hispanic Americans), 12 international. Average age 30. *Faculty:* 37 full-time (15 women). Expenses: Contact institution. *Financial support:* In 2006–07, 58 research assistantships with full and partial tuition reimbursements (averaging $3,850 per year) were awarded; career-related internships or fieldwork, Federal Work-Study, institutionally sponsored loans, scholarships/grants, and unspecified assistantships also available. Support available to part-time students. Financial award application deadline: 2/15; financial award applicants required to submit FAFSA. In 2006, 87 degrees awarded. *Degree program information:* Part-time and evening/weekend programs available. Offers art (MA); ceramics (MFA); clinical psychology (MA); communications and media studies (MA); fine arts (MFA); jewelry/metalsmithing (MFA); liberal arts (MA, MFA, MSW); painting (MFA); printmaking (MFA); sculpture (MFA); social sciences (MA); social work (MSW); speech language pathology (MA). *Application deadline:* Applications are processed on a rolling basis. *Application fee:* $30. Electronic applications accepted. *Application Contact:* Dr. R. Scott Baldwin, Dean, 814-732-2752, Fax: 814-732-2268, E-mail: sbaldwin@edinboro.edu. *Dean,* Dr. Terry L. Smith, 814-732-2477, Fax: 814-732-2629, E-mail: tlsmith@edinboro.edu.

School of Science, Management and Technology Students: 16 full-time (7 women), 42 part-time (32 women), 6 international. Average age 35. *Faculty:* 13 full-time (2 women). Expenses: Contact institution. *Financial support:* In 2006–07, 12 research assistantships with full and partial tuition reimbursements (averaging $3,850 per year) were awarded; career-related internships or fieldwork, Federal Work-Study, scholarships/grants, and unspecified assistantships also available. Support available to part-time students. Financial award application deadline: 2/15; financial award applicants required to submit FAFSA. In 2006, 4 master's, 1 other advanced degree awarded. *Degree program information:* Part-time and evening/weekend programs available. Offers biology (MS); family nurse practitioner (MSN); information technology (MS, Certificate); science, management and technology (MS, MSN, Certificate). *Application deadline:* Applications are processed on a rolling basis. *Application fee:* $30. Electronic applications accepted. *Application Contact:* Dr. R. Scott Baldwin, Dean, 814-732-2752, Fax: 814-732-2268, E-mail: sbaldwin@edinboro.edu. *Dean,* Dr. Eric Randall, 814-732-2400, Fax: 814-732-2422, E-mail: erandall@edinboro.edu.

EDWARD VIA VIRGINIA COLLEGE OF OSTEOPATHIC MEDICINE, Blacksburg, VA 24060

General Information Independent, coed, graduate-only institution.

GRADUATE UNITS

Graduate Program

ELIZABETH CITY STATE UNIVERSITY, Elizabeth City, NC 27909-7806

General Information State-supported, coed, comprehensive institution.

GRADUATE UNITS

Program in Elementary Education Offers elementary education (M Ed).

ELIZABETHTOWN COLLEGE, Elizabethtown, PA 17022-2298

General Information Independent-religious, coed, comprehensive institution.

GRADUATE UNITS

Department of Occupational Therapy

ELMHURST COLLEGE, Elmhurst, IL 60126-3296

General Information Independent-religious, coed, comprehensive institution. *Enrollment:* 3,107 graduate, professional, and undergraduate students; 266 part-time matriculated graduate/professional students (153 women). *Enrollment by degree level:* 266 master's. *Graduate faculty:* 21 full-time (9 women), 19 part-time/adjunct (6 women). *Tuition:* Part-time $781 per hour. *Required fees:* $75 per hour. Part-time tuition and fees vary according to course load and student level. *Graduate housing:* Rooms and/or apartments available on a first-come, first-served basis to single and married students. Typical cost: $6,490 per year for single students; $10,380 per year for married students. Room charges vary according to housing facility selected. Housing application deadline: 4/1. *Student services:* Campus employment opportunities, campus safety program, career counseling, child daycare facilities, disabled student services, exercise/wellness program, free psychological counseling, international student services, low-cost health insurance, multicultural affairs office, teacher training, writing training. *Library facilities:* Buehler Library. *Online resources:* library catalog, web page, access to other libraries' catalogs. *Collection:* 222,441 titles, 2,010 serial subscriptions.

Computer facilities: 345 computers available on campus for general student use. A campuswide network can be accessed from student residence rooms and from off campus. Internet access and online class registration are available. *Web address:* http://www.elmhurst.edu/.

General Application Contact: Elizabeth D. Kuebler, Director of Adult and Graduate Admission, 630-617-3069, Fax: 630-617-5501, E-mail: betsyk@elmhurst.edu.

GRADUATE UNITS

Graduate Programs Average age 30. 225 applicants, 81% accepted, 129 enrolled. *Faculty:* 21 full-time (9 women), 19 part-time/adjunct (6 women). Expenses: Contact institution. *Financial support:* In 2006–07, 85 students received support. Federal Work-Study and scholarships/grants available. Support available to part-time students. Financial award application deadline: 6/1; financial award applicants required to submit FAFSA. In 2006, 75 degrees awarded. *Degree program information:* Part-time and evening/weekend programs available. Offers business administration (MBA); computer network systems (MS); early childhood special education (M Ed); English studies (MA); industrial/organizational psychology (MA); nursing (MSN); professional accountancy (MPA); supply chain management (MS); teacher leadership (M Ed). *Application deadline:* For fall admission, 5/1 priority date for domestic and international students. Applications are processed on a rolling basis. *Application fee:* $25. Electronic applications accepted. *Application Contact:* Elizabeth D. Kuebler, Director of Adult and Graduate Admission, 630-617-3069, Fax: 630-617-5501, E-mail: betsyk@elmhurst.edu. *Dean of Graduate Studies,* Dr. John E. Bohnert, 630-617-3069, Fax: 630-617-5501, E-mail: gradadm@elmhurst.edu.

ELMS COLLEGE, Chicopee, MA 01013-2839

General Information Independent-religious, coed, primarily women, comprehensive institution. *Enrollment:* 10 full-time matriculated graduate/professional students (8 women), 142 part-time matriculated graduate/professional students (118 women). *Enrollment by degree level:* 124 doctoral, 28 other advanced degrees. *Graduate faculty:* 17 full-time (13 women), 11 part-time/adjunct (7 women). *Tuition:* Full-time $9,180; part-time $510 per credit. Tuition and fees vary according to course load. *Graduate housing:* On-campus housing not available. *Student services:* Career counseling, low-cost health insurance. *Library facilities:* Alumnae Library. *Online resources:* library catalog. *Collection:* 111,379 titles, 529 serial subscriptions, 2,948 audiovisual materials.

Computer facilities: 70 computers available on campus for general student use. A campuswide network can be accessed from student residence rooms and from off campus. Internet access is available. *Web address:* http://www.elms.edu/.

General Application Contact: Joseph P. Wagner, Director of Admission Office, 413-594-2761 Ext. 238, Fax: 413-594-2781, E-mail: wagnerj@elms.edu.

GRADUATE UNITS

Division of Education Students: 8 full-time (6 women), 97 part-time (89 women); includes 4 minority (2 Asian Americans or Pacific Islanders, 2 Hispanic Americans). Average age 36. 48 applicants, 90% accepted, 40 enrolled. *Faculty:* 9 full-time (6 women), 4 part-time/adjunct (2 women). Expenses: Contact institution. *Financial support:* In 2006–07, 3 teaching assistantships with partial tuition reimbursements were awarded; tuition waivers (partial) also available. Support available to part-time students. Financial award application deadline: 4/15; financial award applicants required to submit FAFSA. In 2006, 37 master's, 8 other advanced degrees awarded. *Degree program information:* Part-time and evening/weekend programs available. Offers early childhood education (MAT); education (M Ed, CAGS); elementary education (MAT); English as a second language (MAT); reading (MAT); secondary education (MAT); special education (MAT). *Application deadline:* For fall admission, 7/1 priority date for domestic students; for spring admission, 11/1 priority date for domestic students. Applications are processed on a rolling basis. *Application fee:* $30. *Director,* Dr. Mary Janeczek, 413-594-2761, Fax: 413-592-4871, E-mail: janeczeke@elms.edu.

Program in Communication Sciences and Disorders Average age 35. 4 applicants, 100% accepted, 3 enrolled. *Faculty:* 1 (woman) full-time, 5 part-time/adjunct (3 women). Expenses: Contact institution. *Financial support:* Application deadline: 4/15. In 2006, 2 degrees awarded. *Degree program information:* Part-time programs available. Offers communication sciences and disorders (CAGS). *Application deadline:* For fall admission, 7/1 priority date for domestic students; for spring admission, 11/1 priority date for domestic students. *Application fee:* $30. *Chair-CSD Department,* Dr. Kathryn James, 413-265-2253, E-mail: jamesk@elms.edu.

Religious Studies Department Average age 35. 7 applicants, 86% accepted, 6 enrolled. *Faculty:* 2 full-time (1 woman), 2 part-time/adjunct (0 women). Expenses: Contact institution. *Financial support:* Tuition waivers (partial) available. Financial award application deadline: 4/15; financial award applicants required to submit FAFSA. In 2006, 5 degrees awarded. *Degree program information:* Part-time and evening/weekend programs available. Offers religious studies (MAAT). *Application deadline:* For fall admission, 7/1 priority date for domestic students; for spring admission, 11/1 priority date for domestic students. Applications are processed on a rolling basis. *Application fee:* $30. *Director of MALA/MAAT Programs,* Dr. Martin Pion, 413-594-2761 Ext. 389, Fax: 413-594-3951, E-mail: pionm@elms.edu.

ELON UNIVERSITY, Elon, NC 27244-2010

General Information Independent-religious, coed, comprehensive institution. CGS member. *Enrollment:* 5,230 graduate, professional, and undergraduate students; 235 full-time matriculated graduate/professional students (135 women), 146 part-time matriculated graduate/professional students (72 women). *Enrollment by degree level:* 232 first professional, 149 master's. *Graduate faculty:* 56 full-time (26 women), 17 part-time/adjunct (12 women). *Graduate housing:* On-campus housing not available. *Student services:* Campus employment opportunities, campus safety program, career counseling, disabled student services, exercise/wellness program, free psychological counseling, international student services, low-cost health insurance, multicultural affairs office, teacher training, writing training. *Library facilities:* Carol Grotnes Belk. *Online resources:* library catalog, web page, access to other libraries' catalogs. *Collection:* 250,119 titles, 4,955 serial subscriptions, 17,297 audiovisual materials.

Computer facilities: Computer purchase and lease plans are available. 575 computers available on campus for general student use. A campuswide network can be accessed from student residence rooms and from off campus. Internet access and online class registration, e-mail are available. *Web address:* http://www.elon.edu/.

General Application Contact: Art Fadde, Director of Graduate Admissions, 800-334-8448 Ext. 3, Fax: 336-278-7699, E-mail: afadde@elon.edu.

GRADUATE UNITS

Program in Business Administration Students: 3 full-time (1 woman), 101 part-time (32 women); includes 13 minority (all African Americans), 2 international. Average age 31. 90

Elon University (continued)

applicants, 74% accepted, 55 enrolled. *Faculty:* 26 full-time (6 women), 3 part-time/adjunct (1 woman). Expenses: Contact institution. *Financial support:* In 2006–07, 5 students received support, including 2 fellowships (averaging $8,112 per year); Federal Work-Study and scholarships/grants also available. Support available to part-time students. Financial award application deadline: 3/15; financial award applicants required to submit FAFSA. In 2006, 25 degrees awarded. *Degree program information:* Part-time and evening/weekend programs available. Offers business administration (MBA). *Application deadline:* For fall admission, 8/1 priority date for domestic students; for spring admission, 2/1 priority date for domestic students. Applications are processed on a rolling basis. *Application fee:* $50. Electronic applications accepted. *Application Contact:* Art Fadde, Director of Graduate Admissions, 800-334-8448 Ext. 3, Fax: 336-278-7699, E-mail: afadde@elon.edu. *Director,* Dr. Scott Buechler, 336-278-6000, Fax: 336-278-5952.

Program in Education Average age 31. 62 applicants, 69% accepted, 30 enrolled. *Faculty:* 11 full-time (8 women), 5 part-time/adjunct (all women). Expenses: Contact institution. *Financial support:* In 2006–07, 2 students received support, including 2 fellowships (averaging $2,635 per year); Federal Work-Study and scholarships/grants also available. Support available to part-time students. Financial award application deadline: 6/1; financial award applicants required to submit FAFSA. In 2006, 30 degrees awarded. *Degree program information:* Part-time programs available. Offers elementary education (M Ed); gifted education (M Ed); special education (M Ed). *Application deadline:* For winter admission, 6/1 priority date for domestic students. Applications are processed on a rolling basis. *Application fee:* $50. Electronic applications accepted. *Application Contact:* Art Fadde, Director of Graduate Admissions, 800-334-8448 Ext. 3, Fax: 336-278-7699, E-mail: afadde@elon.edu. *Director,* Dr. Judith B. Howard, 336-278-5885, Fax: 336-278-5919, E-mail: howardj@elon.edu.

Program in Physical Therapy Students: 117 full-time (81 women); includes 8 minority (5 African Americans, 1 Asian American or Pacific Islander, 2 Hispanic Americans). Average age 23. 188 applicants, 28% accepted, 38 enrolled. *Faculty:* 12 full-time (9 women), 9 part-time/adjunct (6 women). Expenses: Contact institution. *Financial support:* In 2006–07, 8 students received support. Federal Work-Study and scholarships/grants available. Support available to part-time students. Financial award application deadline: 10/1; financial award applicants required to submit FAFSA. In 2006, 37 degrees awarded. Offers physical therapy (DPT). *Application deadline:* For winter admission, 12/1 priority date for domestic students. Applications are processed on a rolling basis. *Application fee:* $50. Electronic applications accepted. *Application Contact:* Art Fadde, Director of Graduate Admissions, 800-334-8448 Ext. 3, Fax: 336-278-7699, E-mail: afadde@elon.edu. *Chair,* Dr. Elizabeth A. Rogers, 336-278-6400, Fax: 336-278-6414, E-mail: rogers@elon.edu.

EMBRY-RIDDLE AERONAUTICAL UNIVERSITY, Prescott, AZ 86301-3720

General Information Independent, coed, comprehensive institution. *Enrollment:* 1,674 graduate, professional, and undergraduate students; 28 full-time matriculated graduate/professional students (5 women), 13 part-time matriculated graduate/professional students (4 women). *Enrollment by degree level:* 41 master's. *Graduate faculty:* 5 full-time (1 woman). *Tuition:* Part-time $1,020 per credit. *Graduate housing:* Rooms and/or apartments available on a first-come, first-served basis to single and married students. Typical cost: $4,390 per year ($6,360 including board) for single students; $4,390 per year ($6,360 including board) for married students. Housing application deadline: 6/30. *Student services:* Campus employment opportunities, campus safety program, career counseling, disabled student services, free psychological counseling, international student services, low-cost health insurance. *Library facilities:* ERAU Prescott Library. *Research affiliation:* Safeware Corporation (paradrogue aerodynamics phase I: modeling and analysis for mid-air), Honeywell Engines & Systems (human factors evaluation of Honeywell enhanced ground proximity).

Computer facilities: 365 computers available on campus for general student use. A campuswide network can be accessed from student residence rooms and from off campus. Internet access and online class registration are available. *Web address:* http://www.embryriddle.edu/.

General Application Contact: Deborah Pfingston, Graduate Admissions Coordinator, 928-777-6993, Fax: 928-777-6958, E-mail: deborah.pfingtson@erau.edu.

GRADUATE UNITS

Program in Safety Science Students: 28 full-time (5 women), 13 part-time (4 women); includes 6 minority (3 African Americans, 3 Hispanic Americans), 8 international. Average age 30. 22 applicants, 91% accepted, 15 enrolled. *Faculty:* 5 full-time (1 woman). Expenses: Contact institution. *Financial support:* In 2006–07, 22 students received support, including 8 research assistantships with full tuition reimbursements available (averaging $2,838 per year); career-related internships or fieldwork, Federal Work-Study, and unspecified assistantships also available. Support available to part-time students. Financial award application deadline: 4/15; financial award applicants required to submit FAFSA. In 2006, 11 degrees awarded. Offers safety science (MSSS). *Application deadline:* For fall admission, 8/1 priority date for domestic students; for spring admission, 12/1 priority date for domestic students. Applications are processed on a rolling basis. *Application fee:* $50. Electronic applications accepted. *Application Contact:* Deborah Pfingston, Graduate Admissions Coordinator, 928-777-6993, Fax: 928-777-6958, E-mail: deborahpfingston@erau.edu. *Chair, Safety Science Department,* Dr. Gary Northam, 928-777-3964, Fax: 928-777-6958.

EMBRY-RIDDLE AERONAUTICAL UNIVERSITY, Daytona Beach, FL 32114-3900

General Information Independent, coed, comprehensive institution. *Enrollment:* 4,863 graduate, professional, and undergraduate students; 283 full-time matriculated graduate/professional students (71 women), 107 part-time matriculated graduate/professional students (27 women). *Enrollment by degree level:* 390 master's. *Graduate faculty:* 46 full-time (6 women), 4 part-time/adjunct (1 woman). *Tuition:* Full-time $12,240; part-time $1,020 per credit. *Graduate housing:* Rooms and/or apartments available on a first-come, first-served basis to single and married students. Typical cost: $4,390 per year ($6,360 including board) for single students; $4,390 per year ($6,360 including board) for married students. Housing application deadline: 6/30. *Student services:* Campus employment opportunities, campus safety program, career counseling, disabled student services, free psychological counseling, international student services, low-cost health insurance. *Library facilities:* Jack R. Hunt Memorial Library. *Online resources:* library catalog, web page. *Collection:* 138,327 titles, 741 serial subscriptions, 7,030 audiovisual materials. *Research affiliation:* Jet Set (mesospheric dynamics), JetBlue (enriched quality of instruction), Gulfstream Aerospace (design and delivery of courses), Lockheed Martin (transportation and security), Boeing (passenger behavior and modeling for enplane/deplane efficiency), Chilean Nat'l Directorate of Airports (assessment and operational analysis of airspace and locations for new airports in the central zone of Chile).

Computer facilities: 884 computers available on campus for general student use. A campuswide network can be accessed from student residence rooms and from off campus. Internet access and online class registration are available. *Web address:* http://www.embryriddle.edu/.

General Application Contact: Tom Shea, Director, International and Graduate Admissions, 800-388-3728, Fax: 386-226-7070, E-mail: graduate.admissions@erau.edu.

GRADUATE UNITS

Daytona Beach Campus Graduate Program Students: 283 full-time (71 women), 107 part-time (27 women); includes 51 minority (14 African Americans, 3 American Indian/Alaska Native, 10 Asian Americans or Pacific Islanders, 24 Hispanic Americans), 96 international. Average age 28. 250 applicants, 68% accepted, 53 enrolled. *Faculty:* 46 full-time (6 women), 4 part-time/adjunct (1 woman). Expenses: Contact institution. *Financial support:* In 2006–07, 221 students received support, including 49 research assistantships with full and partial tuition reimbursements available (averaging $6,542 per year), 36 teaching assistantships with full and partial tuition reimbursements available (averaging $6,542 per year); career-related internships or fieldwork, Federal Work-Study, and unspecified assistantships also available. Support available to part-time students. Financial award application deadline: 4/15; financial award applicants required to submit FAFSA. In 2006, 123 degrees awarded. *Degree program information:* Part-time and evening/weekend programs available. Offers aeronautics (MBAA, MS, MS Sp C, MSA, MSAE, MSE, MSHFS); aerospace engineering (MSAE); applied aviation sciences (MSA); business administration in aviation (MBAA); engineering physics (space science) (MS); human factors engineering (MSHFS); software engineering (MSE); space science (MS Sp C); systems engineering (MSHFS). *Application deadline:* For fall admission, 8/1 priority date for domestic students; for spring admission, 12/1 priority date for domestic students. Applications are processed on a rolling basis. *Application fee:* $50. Electronic applications accepted. *Application Contact:* Tom Shea, Director, International and Graduate Admissions, 800-388-3728, Fax: 386-226-7070, E-mail: graduate.admissions@erau.edu. *Chancellor,* Dr. Thomas Connolly, 386-226-6494, Fax: 386-226-7111.

EMBRY-RIDDLE AERONAUTICAL UNIVERSITY WORLDWIDE, Daytona Beach, FL 32114-3900

General Information Independent, coed, comprehensive institution. *Enrollment:* 16,826 graduate, professional, and undergraduate students; 1,857 full-time matriculated graduate/professional students (310 women), 2,118 part-time matriculated graduate/professional students (343 women). *Enrollment by degree level:* 3,975 master's. *Graduate faculty:* 69 full-time (15 women), 326 part-time/adjunct (38 women). *Tuition:* Full-time $7,800; part-time $325 per credit. *Graduate housing:* On-campus housing not available. *Student services:* Career counseling, international student services. *Library facilities:* Jack R. Hunt Memorial Library. *Online resources:* library catalog, web page. *Collection:* 138,237 titles, 741 serial subscriptions, 7,030 audiovisual materials. *Web address:* http://www.embryriddle.edu/.

General Application Contact: Pam Thomas, Director of Enrollment Management, 386-226-6910, Fax: 386-226-6984, E-mail: ecinfo@erau.edu.

GRADUATE UNITS

Worldwide Headquarters Students: 1,857 full-time (310 women), 2,118 part-time (343 women); includes 707 minority (267 African Americans, 44 American Indian/Alaska Native, 139 Asian Americans or Pacific Islanders, 257 Hispanic Americans), 41 international. Average age 35. 978 applicants, 77% accepted, 653 enrolled. *Faculty:* 69 full-time (15 women), 326 part-time/adjunct (38 women). Expenses: Contact institution. *Financial support:* In 2006–07, 101 students received support. Available to part-time students. Applicants required to submit FAFSA. In 2006, 850 degrees awarded. *Degree program information:* Part-time and evening/weekend programs available. Postbaccalaureate distance learning degree programs offered (minimal on-campus study). Offers aeronautics (MAS); management (MSM); technical management (MSTM). *Application deadline:* Applications are processed on a rolling basis. *Application fee:* $50. Electronic applications accepted. *Application Contact:* Pam Thomas, Director of Enrollment Management, 386-226-6910, Fax: 386-226-6984, E-mail: ecinfo@erau.edu. *Chancellor,* Dr. Martin A. Smith, 386-226-6961, Fax: 386-226-6984, E-mail: martin.smith@erau.edu.

EMERSON COLLEGE, Boston, MA 02116-4624

General Information Independent, coed, comprehensive institution. CGS member. *Graduate housing:* On-campus housing not available.

GRADUATE UNITS

Graduate Studies *Degree program information:* Part-time and evening/weekend programs available. Electronic applications accepted.

School of Communication *Degree program information:* Part-time and evening/weekend programs available. Offers broadcast journalism (MA); communication (MA, MS); communication management (MA); communication sciences and disorders (MS); global marketing communication and advertising (MA); health communication (MA); integrated journalism (MA); integrated marketing communication (MA); print/multimedia journalism (MA); print/multimedia journalism, broadcast journalism, integrated journalism (MA); speech-language pathology (MS). Electronic applications accepted.

School of the Arts *Degree program information:* Part-time programs available. Offers arts (MA, MFA); audio production (MA); audio, television/video, and new media production (MA); creative writing (MFA); new media production (MA); publishing and writing (MA); television/video production (MA); theatre education (MA). Electronic applications accepted.

EMMANUEL COLLEGE, Boston, MA 02115

General Information Independent-religious, coed, comprehensive institution. *Enrollment:* 2,340 graduate, professional, and undergraduate students; 5 full-time matriculated graduate/professional students (all women), 179 part-time matriculated graduate/professional students (142 women). *Enrollment by degree level:* 166 master's, 18 other advanced degrees. *Graduate faculty:* 5 full-time (4 women), 30 part-time/adjunct (9 women). *Tuition:* Full-time $5,256. *Graduate housing:* On-campus housing not available. *Student services:* Campus safety program, career counseling, disabled student services, free psychological counseling, international student services, low-cost health insurance, multicultural affairs office, teacher training, writing training. *Library facilities:* Cardinal Cushing Library. *Online resources:* library catalog, web page, access to other libraries' catalogs.

Computer facilities: 115 computers available on campus for general student use. A campuswide network can be accessed from student residence rooms and from off campus. Internet access, software applications are available. *Web address:* http://www.emmanuel.edu/.

General Application Contact: Brian Minchello, Associate Director, Graduate and Professional Programs, 617-735-9928, Fax: 617-735-9708, E-mail: gpp@emmanuel.edu.

GRADUATE UNITS

Graduate Programs Students: 5 full-time (all women), 179 part-time (142 women); includes 46 minority (33 African Americans, 4 Asian Americans or Pacific Islanders, 9 Hispanic Americans), 1 international. Average age 33. 121 applicants, 36% accepted, 42 enrolled. *Faculty:* 5 full-time (4 women), 30 part-time/adjunct (9 women). Expenses: Contact institution. In 2006, 69 master's, 5 other advanced degrees awarded. *Degree program information:* Part-time and evening/weekend programs available. Offers educational leadership (CAGS); elementary education (MAT); human resource management (MS, Certificate); management (MSM); school administration (M Ed); secondary education (MAT). *Application deadline:* For fall admission, 8/15 priority date for domestic students; for spring admission, 12/8 priority date for domestic students. Applications are processed on a rolling basis. *Application fee:* $50. Electronic applications accepted. *Application Contact:* Brian Minchello, Associate Director, Graduate and Professional Programs, 617-735-9928, Fax: 617-735-9708, E-mail: gpp@emmanuel.edu. *Director of Operations-Graduate and Professional Programs,* Ellen Sweeney, 617-264-7704, Fax: 617-735-9708, E-mail: sweeneye@emmanuel.edu.

EMMANUEL SCHOOL OF RELIGION, Johnson City, TN 37601-9438

General Information Independent-religious, coed, primarily men, graduate-only institution. *Graduate faculty:* 12 full-time (1 woman), 3 part-time/adjunct (1 woman). *Tuition:* Part-time $300 per hour. *Graduate housing:* Rooms and/or apartments available on a first-come, first-served basis to single and married students. Housing application deadline: 8/1. *Student services:* Campus employment opportunities, career counseling, low-cost health insurance. *Library facilities:* Main library plus 1 other. *Online resources:* library catalog, web page. *Collection:* 127,000 titles, 733 serial subscriptions. *Research affiliation:* Disciples of Christ Historical Society, American Schools of Oriental Research (ancient Near East).

Computer facilities: 20 computers available on campus for general student use. A campuswide network can be accessed from off campus. Internet access is available. *Web address:* http://www.esr.edu/.

General Application Contact: David Fulks, Director of Admissions, 423-461-1536, Fax: 423-926-6198, E-mail: fulksd@esr.edu.

GRADUATE UNITS

Graduate and Professional Programs Students: 107 full-time (21 women), 41 part-time (14 women); includes 2 minority (both African Americans), 8 international. Average age 32. 50

applicants, 94% accepted. *Faculty:* 12 full-time (1 woman), 3 part-time/adjunct (1 woman). Expenses: Contact institution. *Financial support:* In 2006–07, 100 students received support, including teaching assistantships (averaging $3,600 per year); career-related internships or fieldwork, Federal Work-Study, institutionally sponsored loans, scholarships/grants, and tuition waivers (partial) also available. Support available to part-time students. Financial award application deadline: 4/1. In 2006, 18 M Divs, 7 master's, 2 doctorates awarded. *Degree program information:* Part-time programs available. Offers religion (M Div, MAR, D Min). *Application deadline:* For fall admission, 8/1 priority date for domestic students. Applications are processed on a rolling basis. *Application fee:* $25. *Application Contact:* David Fulks, Director of Admissions, 423-461-1536, Fax: 423-926-6198, E-mail: fulksd@esr.edu. *Dean and Professor of New Testament,* Dr. Robert F. Hull, 423-461-1524, Fax: 423-926-6198, E-mail: hullr@esr.edu.

EMORY & HENRY COLLEGE, Emory, VA 24327-0947

General Information Independent-religious, coed, comprehensive institution. *Enrollment:* 1,051 graduate, professional, and undergraduate students; 1 full-time matriculated graduate/professional student, 54 part-time matriculated graduate/professional students (45 women). *Enrollment by degree level:* 55 master's. *Graduate faculty:* 10 part-time/adjunct (2 women). *Student services:* Teacher training. *Library facilities:* Kelly Library. *Online resources:* library catalog, web page, access to other libraries' catalogs. *Collection:* 343,443 titles, 9,959 serial subscriptions, 7,164 audiovisual materials.

Computer facilities: 250 computers available on campus for general student use. A campuswide network can be accessed from student residence rooms and from off campus. Internet access is available. *Web address:* http://www.ehc.edu/.

General Application Contact: Dr. Jack Roper, Director of Graduate Studies, 276-944-6188, Fax: 276-944-5223, E-mail: jroper@ehc.edu.

GRADUATE UNITS

Graduate Programs Students: 1 full-time (0 women), 54 part-time (45 women). Average age 37. 53 applicants, 100% accepted, 53 enrolled. *Faculty:* 4 part-time/adjunct (2 women). Expenses: Contact institution. *Financial support:* Applicants required to submit FAFSA. In 2006, 62 degrees awarded. *Degree program information:* Part-time and evening/weekend programs available. *Application deadline:* Applications are processed on a rolling basis. *Application fee:* $30. *Director of Graduate Studies,* Dr. Jack Roper, 276-944-6188, Fax: 276-944-5223, E-mail: jroper@ehc.edu.

EMORY UNIVERSITY, Atlanta, GA 30322-1100

General Information Independent-religious, coed, university. CGS member. *Enrollment:* 12,338 graduate, professional, and undergraduate students; 4,877 full-time matriculated graduate/professional students (2,799 women), 815 part-time matriculated graduate/professional students (483 women). *Enrollment by degree level:* 1,533 first professional, 2,053 master's, 1,759 doctoral, 11 other advanced degrees. *Graduate faculty:* 2,760 full-time (966 women), 374 part-time/adjunct (214 women). *Tuition:* Full-time $30,246. *Graduate housing:* Rooms and/or apartments available on a first-come, first-served basis to single and married students. Typical cost: $6,624 per year ($10,201 including board) for single students. *Student services:* Campus employment opportunities, campus safety program, career counseling, child daycare facilities, disabled student services, exercise/wellness program, free psychological counseling, grant writing training, international student services, low-cost health insurance, multicultural affairs office, teacher training, writing training. *Library facilities:* Robert W. Woodruff Library plus 7 others. *Online resources:* library catalog, web page, access to other libraries' catalogs. *Collection:* 3.2 million titles, 51,500 serial subscriptions, 54,000 audiovisual materials. *Research affiliation:* Highlands Biological Station, Centers for Disease Control, Georgia Mental Health Institute, Oak Ridge Associated Universities (energy, health and environment), Emory and Georgia Technical Biomedical Research Center, Georgia Research Consortium.

Computer facilities: Computer purchase and lease plans are available. 600 computers available on campus for general student use. A campuswide network can be accessed from student residence rooms and from off campus. Internet access and online class registration are available. *Web address:* http://www.emory.edu/.

General Application Contact: Kharen Fulton, Director of Admissions, 404-727-0184, Fax: 404-727-4990, E-mail: gradkef@emory.edu.

GRADUATE UNITS

Candler School of Theology *Degree program information:* Part-time programs available. Offers theology (M Div, MTS, Th M, Th D).

Graduate School of Arts and Sciences Offers anthropology (PhD); art history (PhD); arts and sciences (M Ed, MA, MAT, MM, MPH, MS, MSM, MSPH, PhD, Certificate, DAST); biophysics (PhD); biostatistics (MPH, MSPH, PhD); chemistry (PhD); choral conducting (MM, MSM); clinical psychology (PhD); clinical research (MS); cognition and development (PhD); comparative literature (PhD, Certificate); computer science (MS); condensed matter physics (PhD); economics (PhD); English (Certificate); film studies (Certificate); French (PhD, Certificate); French and educational studies (PhD); history (PhD); Jewish studies (MA); mathematics (PhD); Middle Eastern studies (PhD); neuroscience and animal behavior (PhD); non-linear physics (PhD); nursing (PhD); organ performance (MM, MSM); philosophy (Certificate); political science (PhD); psychoanalytic studies (PhD); public health informatics (MSPH); radiological physics (PhD); religion (PhD); sociology (MA, PhD); soft condensed matter physics (PhD); solid-state physics (PhD); Spanish (PhD, Certificate); statistical physics (PhD); women studies (Certificate); women's studies (Certificate). Electronic applications accepted.

Division of Biological and Biomedical Sciences Students: 405 full-time (267 women); includes 82 minority (41 African Americans, 1 American Indian/Alaska Native, 24 Asian Americans or Pacific Islanders, 16 Hispanic Americans), 56 international. Average age 27. 668 applicants, 25% accepted, 78 enrolled. *Faculty:* 315 full-time (68 women). Expenses: Contact institution. *Financial support:* In 2006–07, 171 students received support, including 171 fellowships (averaging $23,500 per year); institutionally sponsored loans, health care benefits, and tuition waivers (full) also available. In 2006, 51 doctorates awarded. Offers biochemistry, cell and developmental biology (PhD); biological and biomedical sciences (PhD); genetics and molecular biology (PhD); immunology and molecular pathogenesis (PhD); microbiology and molecular genetics (PhD); molecular and systems pharmacology (PhD); neuroscience (PhD); nutrition and health sciences (PhD); population biology, ecology and evolution (PhD). *Application deadline:* For fall admission, 1/3 for domestic and international students. *Application fee:* $50. Electronic applications accepted. *Application Contact:* Kathy Smith, Director of Recruitment and Admissions, 404-727-2545, Fax: 404-727-3322, E-mail: kathy.smith@emory.edu. *Acting Director,* Dr. Keith Wilkinson, 404-727-2545, Fax: 404-727-3322.

Division of Educational Studies Offers educational studies (MA, PhD, DAST); middle grades teaching (M Ed, MAT); secondary teaching (M Ed, MAT). Electronic applications accepted.

Division of Religion Offers religion (PhD). Electronic applications accepted.

Graduate Institute of Liberal Arts Offers liberal arts (PhD). Electronic applications accepted.

Nell Hodgson Woodruff School of Nursing *Degree program information:* Part-time programs available. Offers adult and elder health advanced practice nursing (MSN); emergency nurse practitioner (MSN); family nurse practitioner (MSN); family nurse-midwife (MSN); leadership in healthcare (MSN); nurse midwifery (MSN); nursing administration (MSN); pediatric advanced nursing practice (MSN); public health nursing (MSN); women's health nurse practitioner (MSN). Electronic applications accepted.

Roberto C. Goizueta Business School Students: 504 full-time (139 women), 230 part-time (69 women); includes 141 minority (56 African Americans, 65 Asian Americans or Pacific Islanders, 20 Hispanic Americans), 188 international. Average age 30. 989 applicants, 34% accepted, 149 enrolled. *Faculty:* 84 full-time (23 women), 10 part-time/adjunct (1 woman). Expenses: Contact institution. *Financial support:* In 2006–07, 462 students received support, including 50 research assistantships (averaging $8,840 per year), 50 teaching assistantships (averaging $8,840 per year); fellowships with full tuition reimbursements available, career-related internships or fieldwork, Federal Work-Study, institutionally sponsored loans, and scholarships/grants also available. Support available to part-time students. Financial award application deadline: 4/1; financial award applicants required to submit FAFSA. In 2006, 361 master's, 1 doctorate awarded. *Degree program information:* Part-time and evening/weekend programs available. Postbaccalaureate distance learning degree programs offered (minimal on-campus study). Offers business (EMBA, MBA, WEMBA, PhD). *Application deadline:* For fall admission, 3/15 priority date for domestic students, 2/1 priority date for international students; for winter admission, 10/1 priority date for domestic students; for spring admission, 3/1 priority date for domestic students. Applications are processed on a rolling basis. *Application fee:* $140. Electronic applications accepted. *Application Contact:* Julie Barefoot, Associate Dean, 404-727-6311, Fax: 404-727-4612, E-mail: admissions@bus.emory.edu. *Dean,* Lawrence Benveniste, 404-727-6377, Fax: 404-727-0868, E-mail: larry_benveniste@bus.emory.edu.

Rollins School of Public Health Students: 557 full-time (461 women), 148 part-time (102 women); includes 251 minority (156 African Americans, 3 American Indian/Alaska Native, 63 Asian Americans or Pacific Islanders, 29 Hispanic Americans), 68 international. Average age 27. 1,000 applicants, 71% accepted, 324 enrolled. *Faculty:* 160 full-time (75 women), 200 part-time/adjunct (66 women). Expenses: Contact institution. *Financial support:* In 2006–07, 350 students received support; fellowships with full and partial tuition reimbursements available, research assistantships, teaching assistantships, career-related internships or fieldwork, Federal Work-Study, institutionally sponsored loans, scholarships/grants, traineeships, and health care benefits available. Support available to part-time students. Financial award application deadline: 1/5; financial award applicants required to submit FAFSA. In 2006, 300 degrees awarded. *Degree program information:* Part-time and evening/weekend programs available. Postbaccalaureate distance learning degree programs offered (minimal on-campus study). Offers applied epidemiology (MPH); behavioral sciences and health education (MPH, PhD); biostatistics (MPH, MSPH, PhD); environmental and occupational health (MPH, MSPH); epidemiology (MPH, MSPH, PhD); global environmental health (MPH); health policy (MPH); health services management (MPH); health services research and health policy (PhD); healthcare outcomes (MPH); prevention option (MPH); public health (MPH, MSPH, PhD); public health informatics (MSPH); public nutrition (MSPH, PhD). *Application deadline:* For fall admission, 1/5 priority date for domestic and international students. *Application fee:* $75. Electronic applications accepted. *Application Contact:* Kara Brown Robinson, Director of Admissions and Recruitment, 404-727-3317, Fax: 404-727-3996, E-mail: admit@sph.emory.edu. *Executive Associate Dean for Academic Affairs,* Dr. Richard Levinson, 404-727-3956, Fax: 404-712-9853, E-mail: admit@sph.emory.edu.

School of Law Students: 674 full-time (323 women); includes 177 minority (62 African Americans, 72 Asian Americans or Pacific Islanders, 43 Hispanic Americans), 16 international. Average age 24. 3,591 applicants, 29% accepted, 207 enrolled. *Faculty:* 57 full-time (22 women), 26 part-time/adjunct (4 women). Expenses: Contact institution. *Financial support:* In 2006–07, 604 students received support, including 15 fellowships with full tuition reimbursements available (averaging $3,000 per year), 48 research assistantships (averaging $8,580 per year); career-related internships or fieldwork, Federal Work-Study, institutionally sponsored loans, scholarships/grants, and tuition waivers (full and partial) also available. Financial award application deadline: 3/1; financial award applicants required to submit FAFSA. In 2006, 221 JDs, 12 other advanced degrees awarded. Offers law (JD, LL M, Certificate). *Application deadline:* For fall admission, 3/1 for domestic and international students. Applications are processed on a rolling basis. *Application fee:* $70. Electronic applications accepted. *Application Contact:* Lynell A. Cadray, Assistant Dean for Admissions, 404-727-6802, Fax: 404-727-2477, E-mail: lcadray@law.emory.edu. *Dean,* David F. Partlett, 404-712-8815, Fax: 404-727-0866, E-mail: david.partlett@emory.edu.

School of Medicine Students: 777 full-time (451 women), 6 part-time (5 women); includes 199 minority (69 African Americans, 5 American Indian/Alaska Native, 105 Asian Americans or Pacific Islanders, 20 Hispanic Americans), 12 international. 5,204 applicants, 10% accepted, 246 enrolled. *Faculty:* 1,804 full-time (573 women), 1,131 part-time/adjunct (358 women). Expenses: Contact institution. *Financial support:* In 2006–07, 655 students received support. Career-related internships or fieldwork, institutionally sponsored loans, and scholarships/grants available. Financial award application deadline: 4/1; financial award applicants required to submit CSS PROFILE or FAFSA. In 2006, 110 first professional degrees, 80 master's, 21 doctorates awarded. Offers anesthesiology (MM Sc); anesthesiology/patient monitoring systems (MM Sc); medicine (MD, MM Sc, DPT); ophthalmic technology (MM Sc); physical therapy (DPT); physician assistant (MM Sc). *Application deadline:* Applications are processed on a rolling basis. Electronic applications accepted. *Application Contact:* Dr. Ira K. Schwartz, Associate Dean of Student Affairs/Director of Admissions, 404-727-5660, Fax: 404-727-5456, E-mail: medadmissions@emory.edu. *Executive Associate Dean, Medical Education and Student Affairs,* Dr. John William Eley, 404-727-5655, Fax: 404-727-0045, E-mail: jeley@emory.edu.

See Close-Up on page 885.

EMPEROR'S COLLEGE OF TRADITIONAL ORIENTAL MEDICINE, Santa Monica, CA 90403

General Information Private, coed, graduate-only institution. *Graduate housing:* On-campus housing not available. *Research affiliation:* Lotus Herbs (herbs), LA Free Clinic (herbs), UCLA Ashe Center (student health).

GRADUATE UNITS

Graduate Programs *Degree program information:* Part-time and evening/weekend programs available. Offers oriental medicine (MTOM, DAOM).

EMPORIA STATE UNIVERSITY, Emporia, KS 66801-5087

General Information State-supported, coed, comprehensive institution. CGS member. *Enrollment:* 6,473 graduate, professional, and undergraduate students; 252 full-time matriculated graduate/professional students (146 women), 1,382 part-time matriculated graduate/professional students (1,008 women). *Enrollment by degree level:* 1,614 master's, 20 doctoral. *Graduate faculty:* 215 full-time (79 women), 22 part-time/adjunct (18 women). Tuition, state resident: full-time $3,438; part-time $143 per credit hour. Tuition, nonresident: full-time $10,398; part-time $433 per credit hour. *Required fees:* $724; $44 per credit hour. *Graduate housing:* Rooms and/or apartments available on a first-come, first-served basis to single and married students. Typical cost: $2,552 per year ($5,170 including board) for single students; $5,130 per year ($7,748 including board) for married students. Housing application deadline: 8/25. *Student services:* Campus employment opportunities, campus safety program, career counseling, child daycare facilities, disabled student services, exercise/wellness program, free psychological counseling, grant writing training, international student services, low-cost health insurance, multicultural affairs office, teacher training, writing training. *Library facilities:* William Allen White Library. *Online resources:* library catalog, web page, access to other libraries' catalogs. *Collection:* 2.4 million titles, 15,645 serial subscriptions, 8,551 audiovisual materials.

Computer facilities: 410 computers available on campus for general student use. A campuswide network can be accessed from student residence rooms and from off campus. Internet access and online class registration, various software packages are available. *Web address:* http://www.emporia.edu/.

General Application Contact: Mary Sewell, Admissions Coordinator, 800-950-GRAD, Fax: 620-341-5909, E-mail: msewell@emporia.edu.

GRADUATE UNITS

School of Graduate Studies Students: 252 full-time (146 women), 1,382 part-time (1,008 women); includes 72 minority (27 African Americans, 5 American Indian/Alaska Native, 11 Asian Americans or Pacific Islanders, 29 Hispanic Americans), 63 international. Average age 34. 376 applicants, 85% accepted, 246 enrolled. *Faculty:* 215 full-time (79 women), 22 part-time/adjunct (18 women). Expenses: Contact institution. *Financial support:* In 2006–07, 18 research assistantships with full tuition reimbursements (averaging $6,752 per year), 86 teaching assistantships with full tuition reimbursements (averaging $6,752 per year) were awarded; fellowships, career-related internships or fieldwork, Federal Work-Study, institutionally sponsored loans, scholarships/grants, health care benefits, and unspecified assistant-

Emporia State University (continued)

ships also available. Financial award application deadline: 3/15; financial award applicants required to submit FAFSA. In 2006, 489 master's, 1 doctorate, 14 other advanced degrees awarded. *Degree program information:* Part-time and evening/weekend programs available. Postbaccalaureate distance learning degree programs offered (no on-campus study). *Application deadline:* Applications are processed on a rolling basis. *Application fee:* $30 ($75 for international students). Electronic applications accepted. *Application Contact:* Mary Sewell, Admissions Coordinator, 800-950-GRAD, Fax: 620-341-5909, E-mail: msewell@emporia.edu. *Interim Dean,* Dr. Gerrit Bleeker, 620-341-5403, Fax: 620-341-5909, E-mail: gbleeker@emporia.edu.

College of Liberal Arts and Sciences Students: 34 full-time (20 women), 95 part-time (44 women); includes 8 minority (2 African Americans, 1 American Indian/Alaska Native, 1 Asian American or Pacific Islander, 4 Hispanic Americans), 12 international. 46 applicants, 91% accepted, 30 enrolled. *Faculty:* 101 full-time (29 women), 18 part-time/adjunct (15 women). Expenses: Contact institution. *Financial support:* In 2006–07, 7 research assistantships with full tuition reimbursements (averaging $6,752 per year), 43 teaching assistantships with full tuition reimbursements (averaging $6,752 per year) were awarded; fellowships, career-related internships or fieldwork, Federal Work-Study, institutionally sponsored loans, health care benefits, and unspecified assistantships also available. Financial award application deadline: 3/15; financial award applicants required to submit FAFSA. In 2006, 37 master's, 3 other advanced degrees awarded. *Degree program information:* Part-time programs available. Offers American history (MAT); anthropology (MAT); botany (MS); earth science (MS); economics (MAT); English (MA); environmental biology (MS); general biology (MS); geography (MAT); geospatial analysis (Postbaccalaureate Certificate); history (MA); liberal arts and sciences (MA, MAT, MM, MS, Postbaccalaureate Certificate); mathematics (MS); microbial and cellular biology (MS); music education (MM); performance (MM); physical science (MS); political science (MAT); social sciences (MAT); social studies education (MAT); sociology (MAT); teaching English to speakers of other languages (MA); world history (MAT); zoology (MS). *Application deadline:* For fall admission, 8/15 priority date for domestic students. Applications are processed on a rolling basis. *Application fee:* $30 ($75 for international students). Electronic applications accepted. *Dean,* Dr. Rodney Sobieski, 620-341-5278, Fax: 620-341-5681, E-mail: rsobiesk@emporia.edu.

School of Business Students: 66 full-time (24 women), 53 part-time (39 women); includes 4 minority (3 African Americans, 1 Asian American or Pacific Islander), 33 international. 32 applicants, 100% accepted, 26 enrolled. *Faculty:* 30 full-time (4 women). Expenses: Contact institution. *Financial support:* In 2006–07, 7 research assistantships with full tuition reimbursements (averaging $6,752 per year), 4 teaching assistantships with full tuition reimbursements (averaging $6,752 per year) were awarded; fellowships, career-related internships or fieldwork, Federal Work-Study, institutionally sponsored loans, health care benefits, and unspecified assistantships also available. Financial award application deadline: 3/15; financial award applicants required to submit FAFSA. In 2006, 58 degrees awarded. *Degree program information:* Part-time programs available. Postbaccalaureate distance learning degree programs offered (minimal on-campus study). Offers business (MBA, MSBE); business administration (MBA); business education (MSBE). *Application deadline:* For fall admission, 8/15 priority date for domestic students. Applications are processed on a rolling basis. *Application fee:* $30 ($75 for international students). Electronic applications accepted. *Application Contact:* Dr. Donald Miller, Director, MBA Program, 620-341-5456, Fax: 620-341-6523, E-mail: dmiller1@emporia.edu. *Dean,* Dr. Robert Hite, 620-341-5274, Fax: 620-341-5892, E-mail: rhite@emporia.edu.

School of Library and Information Management Students: 9 full-time (4 women), 304 part-time (245 women); includes 11 minority (3 African Americans, 3 Asian Americans or Pacific Islanders, 5 Hispanic Americans), 5 international. 46 applicants, 74% accepted, 26 enrolled. *Faculty:* 10 full-time (8 women). Expenses: Contact institution. *Financial support:* In 2006–07, 2 research assistantships (averaging $6,752 per year), 10 teaching assistantships with full tuition reimbursements (averaging $6,752 per year) were awarded; Federal Work-Study, institutionally sponsored loans, and unspecified assistantships also available. Financial award application deadline: 3/15; financial award applicants required to submit FAFSA. In 2006, 123 master's, 1 doctorate, 4 other advanced degrees awarded. *Degree program information:* Part-time and evening/weekend programs available. Postbaccalaureate distance learning degree programs offered (minimal on-campus study). Offers archives studies (Certificate); legal information management (MLM, Certificate); library and information management (MLS, PhD, Certificate). *Application deadline:* For fall admission, 8/15 priority date for domestic students. *Application fee:* $30 ($75 for international students). *Application Contact:* Daniel Roland, Assistant to the Dean, 620-341-5064, Fax: 620-341-5233, E-mail: rolandda@emporia.edu. *Interim Dean,* Dr. Robert Grover, 620-341-5203, Fax: 620-341-5233, E-mail: rgrover@emporia.edu.

The Teachers College Students: 143 full-time (98 women), 930 part-time (680 women); includes 49 minority (19 African Americans, 4 American Indian/Alaska Native, 6 Asian Americans or Pacific Islanders, 20 Hispanic Americans), 13 international. 252 applicants, 84% accepted, 164 enrolled. *Faculty:* 74 full-time (38 women), 4 part-time/adjunct (3 women). Expenses: Contact institution. *Financial support:* In 2006–07, 3 research assistantships with full tuition reimbursements (averaging $6,752 per year), 29 teaching assistantships with full tuition reimbursements (averaging $6,752 per year) were awarded; fellowships, career-related internships or fieldwork, Federal Work-Study, institutionally sponsored loans, health care benefits, and unspecified assistantships also available. Financial award application deadline: 3/15; financial award applicants required to submit FAFSA. In 2006, 281 master's, 7 other advanced degrees awarded. *Degree program information:* Part-time programs available. Postbaccalaureate distance learning degree programs offered. Offers art therapy (MS); behavior disorders (MS); clinical psychology (MS); counselor education (MS); curriculum and instruction (MS); early childhood education (MS); education (MS, Ed S); educational administration (MS); general psychology (MS); gifted, talented, and creative (MS); industrial/organizational psychology (MS); instructional design and technology (MS); interrelated special education (MS); learning disabilities (MS); master teacher (MS); mental health counseling (MS); mental retardation (MS); physical education (MS); psychology (MS); rehabilitation counseling (MS); school counseling (MS); school psychology (MS, Ed S); special education (MS). *Application deadline:* Applications are processed on a rolling basis. *Application fee:* $30 ($75 for international students). Electronic applications accepted. *Dean,* Dr. Teresa Mehring, 620-341-5367, Fax: 620-341-5785, E-mail: tmehring@emporia.edu.

See Close-Up on page 887.

ENDICOTT COLLEGE, Beverly, MA 01915-2096

General Information Independent, coed, comprehensive institution. *Enrollment by degree level:* 370 master's. *Graduate faculty:* 3 full-time (2 women), 128 part-time/adjunct (56 women). *Tuition:* Part-time $279 per credit. Tuition and fees vary according to program. *Graduate housing:* On-campus housing not available. *Student services:* Campus employment opportunities, campus safety program, career counseling, child daycare facilities, disabled student services, exercise/wellness program, grant writing training, international student services, low-cost health insurance, multicultural affairs office, teacher training, writing training. *Library facilities:* Endicott College Library. *Online resources:* library catalog, web page, access to other libraries' catalogs. *Collection:* 121,000 titles, 3,500 serial subscriptions. *Research affiliation:* Peabody Essex Museum (history), North Shore Consortium (special needs).

Computer facilities: 150 computers available on campus for general student use. A campuswide network can be accessed from student residence rooms and from off campus. Internet access and online class registration, e-mail are available. *Web address:* http://www.endicott.edu/.

General Application Contact: Dr. Paul A. Squarcia, Vice President and Dean of Graduate and Professional Studies, 978-232-2084, Fax: 978-232-3000, E-mail: psquarci@endicott.edu.

GRADUATE UNITS

Van Loan School of Graduate and Professional Studies Students: 86 full-time (57 women), 284 part-time (176 women). Average age 35. *Faculty:* 3 full-time (2 women), 128 part-time/adjunct (56 women). Expenses: Contact institution. *Financial support:* Career-related internships or fieldwork, Federal Work-Study, institutionally sponsored loans, and tuition waivers (partial) available. *Degree program information:* Part-time and evening/weekend programs available. Postbaccalaureate distance learning degree programs offered (minimal on-campus study). Offers arts and learning (M Ed); business administration (MBA); hospitality organizational training and management (M Ed); initial and professional licensure (M Ed); integrative learning (M Ed); international education (M Ed); organizational management (M Ed); sport management (M Ed). *Application deadline:* Applications are processed on a rolling basis. *Application fee:* $50. *Vice President and Dean of Graduate and Professional Studies,* Dr. Paul A. Squarcia, 978-232-2084, Fax: 978-232-3000, E-mail: psquarci@endicott.edu.

EPISCOPAL DIVINITY SCHOOL, Cambridge, MA 02138-3494

General Information Independent-religious, coed, graduate-only institution. *Graduate housing:* Rooms and/or apartments available on a first-come, first-served basis to single and married students. Housing application deadline: 7/31. *Research affiliation:* Boston Theological Institute.

GRADUATE UNITS

Graduate and Professional Programs *Degree program information:* Part-time programs available.

EPISCOPAL THEOLOGICAL SEMINARY OF THE SOUTHWEST, Austin, TX 78768-2247

General Information Independent-religious, coed, graduate-only institution. *Enrollment by degree level:* 58 first professional, 41 master's, 1 other advanced degree. *Graduate faculty:* 12 full-time (3 women), 28 part-time/adjunct (12 women). *Tuition:* Full-time $13,150; part-time $390 per credit hour. *Required fees:* $20 per year. Tuition and fees vary according to program. *Graduate housing:* Rooms and/or apartments available on a first-come, first-served basis to single students and available to married students. Typical cost: $5,100 per year ($5,586 including board) for single students; $10,200 per year ($10,686 including board) for married students. Housing application deadline: 8/1. *Student services:* Campus employment opportunities, international student services, low-cost health insurance, writing training. *Library facilities:* Episcopal Theological Seminary of the Southwest Booher Library plus 1 other. *Online resources:* library catalog, web page, access to other libraries' catalogs. *Collection:* 109,452 titles, 275 serial subscriptions, 2,163 audiovisual materials.

Computer facilities: 8 computers available on campus for general student use. A campuswide network can be accessed. Internet access is available. *Web address:* http://www.etss.edu/.

General Application Contact: Joseph Liro, Director of Admissions, 512-472-4133 Ext. 375, Fax: 512-472-3098, E-mail: jliro@etss.edu.

GRADUATE UNITS

Graduate and Professional Programs Students: 67 full-time (37 women), 37 part-time (28 women); includes 7 minority (6 African Americans, 1 Hispanic American), 1 international. Average age 44. 37 applicants, 95% accepted, 26 enrolled. *Faculty:* 12 full-time (3 women), 28 part-time/adjunct (12 women). Expenses: Contact institution. *Financial support:* Career-related internships or fieldwork and scholarships/grants available. Support available to part-time students. Financial award application deadline: 6/17. In 2006, 23 M Divs, 14 master's, 1 other advanced degree awarded. *Degree program information:* Part-time and evening/weekend programs available. Offers Anglican studies (Advanced Diploma); chaplaincy (MAPM); counseling (MAC); discipleship (MAPM); divinity (M Div); religion (MAR); spiritual formation (MAPM); theological studies (Advanced Diploma). *Application deadline:* For fall admission, 6/17 for domestic students; for spring admission, 11/2 for domestic students. Applications are processed on a rolling basis. *Application fee:* $50. *Application Contact:* Joseph Liro, Director of Admissions, 512-472-4133 Ext. 307, Fax: 512-472-3098, E-mail: jliro@etss.edu. *Dean and President,* Very Rev. Douglas Travis, 512-472-4133 Ext. 307, Fax: 512-472-3098, E-mail: dtravis@etss.edu.

ERIKSON INSTITUTE, Chicago, IL 60611-5627

General Information Independent, coed, primarily women, graduate-only institution.

GRADUATE UNITS

Academic Programs *Degree program information:* Part-time and evening/weekend programs available. Offers administration (Certificate); bilingual/ESL (Certificate); child development (MS); early childhood education (MS); infant mental health (Certificate); infant studies (Certificate).

ERSKINE THEOLOGICAL SEMINARY, Due West, SC 29639-0668

General Information Independent-religious, coed, graduate-only institution. *Graduate housing:* Room and/or apartments available on a first-come, first-served basis to single students; on-campus housing not available to married students. Housing application deadline: 6/1.

GRADUATE UNITS

Graduate and Professional Programs *Degree program information:* Part-time and evening/weekend programs available. Offers theology (M Div, MACE, MACM, MAPM, MATS, MCM, D Min). Electronic applications accepted.

EVANGELICAL SEMINARY OF PUERTO RICO, San Juan, PR 00925-2207

General Information Independent-religious, coed, graduate-only institution. *Graduate housing:* Rooms and/or apartments available on a first-come, first-served basis to single and married students. Housing application deadline: 12/15.

GRADUATE UNITS

Graduate and Professional Programs *Degree program information:* Part-time programs available. Offers theology (M Div, MAR, D Min).

EVANGELICAL THEOLOGICAL SEMINARY, Myerstown, PA 17067-1212

General Information Independent-religious, coed, graduate-only institution. *Enrollment by degree level:* 75 first professional, 76 master's, 26 other advanced degrees. *Graduate faculty:* 6 full-time (1 woman), 17 part-time/adjunct (4 women). *Tuition:* Full-time $9,720; part-time $405 per credit. *Required fees:* $25 per term. *Graduate housing:* Rooms and/or apartments available on a first-come, first-served basis to single and married students. Typical cost: $3,300 per year for single students; $5,700 per year for married students. Housing application deadline: 6/1. *Student services:* Campus employment opportunities, career counseling, international student services, low-cost health insurance, writing training. *Library facilities:* Rostad Library. *Online resources:* library catalog, web page, access to other libraries' catalogs. *Collection:* 80,000 titles, 650 serial subscriptions, 670 audiovisual materials.

Computer facilities: 17 computers available on campus for general student use. A campuswide network can be accessed from student residence rooms and from off campus. Internet access, library searching, course selection are available. *Web address:* http://www.evangelical.edu/.

General Application Contact: Tom M. Maiello, Dean of Admissions, 800-532-5775 Ext. 109, Fax: 717-866-4667, E-mail: admissions@evangelical.edu.

GRADUATE UNITS

Graduate and Professional Programs Students: 22 full-time (6 women), 155 part-time (63 women). Average age 36. 44 applicants, 91% accepted, 36 enrolled. *Faculty:* 6 full-time (1 woman), 17 part-time/adjunct (4 women). Expenses: Contact institution. *Financial support:* Career-related internships or fieldwork, scholarships/grants, and tuition waivers (full) available. Support available to part-time students. Financial award application deadline: 6/1; financial award applicants required to submit FAFSA. In 2006, 9 M Divs, 7 master's awarded. *Degree program information:* Part-time programs available. Offers divinity (M Div); marriage and family therapy (MA); ministry (Certificate); religion (MA). *Application deadline:* For fall admission, 6/1 priority date for domestic students, 4/1 priority date for international students; for spring admission, 11/1 priority date for domestic students, 9/1 priority date for international students. Applications are processed on a rolling basis. *Application fee:* $35. *Application Contact:* Tom M. Maiello, Dean of Admissions, 800-532-5775 Ext. 109, Fax: 717-866-4667, E-mail: admissions@evangelical.edu. *Vice President, Academic Affairs,* Rev. Dr. John V. Tornfelt, 717-866-5775 Ext. 140, Fax: 717-866-4667, E-mail: jtornfelt@evangelical.edu.

EVANGEL UNIVERSITY, Springfield, MO 65802-2191

General Information Independent-religious, coed, comprehensive institution. *Enrollment:* 1,721 graduate, professional, and undergraduate students; 35 full-time matriculated graduate/professional students (20 women), 46 part-time matriculated graduate/professional students (38 women). *Enrollment by degree level:* 81 master's. *Graduate faculty:* 13 full-time (7 women), 12 part-time/adjunct (8 women). *Graduate housing:* Rooms and/or apartments available on a first-come, first-served basis to single and married students. Housing application deadline:5/1. *Student services:* Campus employment opportunities, campus safety program, career counseling, disabled student services, exercise/wellness program, free psychological counseling, international student services, multicultural affairs office, teacher training, writing training. *Library facilities:* Claude Kendrick Library. *Online resources:* library catalog, access to other libraries' catalogs. *Collection:* 100,691 titles, 1,060 serial subscriptions.

Computer facilities: 136 computers available on campus for general student use. *Web address:* http://www.evangel.edu/.

General Application Contact: Charity H. Fahlstrom, Director of Graduate and Professional Studies Admissions, 417-865-2811 Ext. 1227, Fax: 417-575-5484.

GRADUATE UNITS

Department of Education Students: 2 full-time (both women), 17 part-time (14 women); includes 2 minority (1 Asian American or Pacific Islander, 1 Hispanic American). Average age 26. 10 applicants, 100% accepted, 10 enrolled. *Faculty:* 4 full-time (2 women), 6 part-time/adjunct (5 women). Expenses: Contact institution. *Financial support:* In 2006–07, 6 students received support. Career-related internships or fieldwork, institutionally sponsored loans, and scholarships/grants available. Support available to part-time students. Financial award application deadline: 3/1; financial award applicants required to submit FAFSA. In 2006, 13 degrees awarded. *Degree program information:* Part-time and evening/weekend programs available. Offers educational leadership (M Ed); reading education (M Ed); secondary teaching (M Ed); teaching (MA). *Application deadline:* For fall admission, 7/15 priority date for domestic students; for spring admission, 11/15 priority date for domestic students. Applications are processed on a rolling basis. *Application fee:* $25. *Application Contact:* Charity H. Fahlstrom, Director of Graduate and Professional Studies Admissions, 417-865-2811 Ext. 1227, Fax: 417-575-5484. *Chair,* Dr. Jeff Hittenberger, 417-865-2815 Ext. 8559, E-mail: hittenbergerj@evangel.edu.

Department of Psychology Students: 9 full-time (7 women), 10 part-time (8 women); includes 1 minority (African American) Average age 25. 14 applicants, 71% accepted, 10 enrolled. *Faculty:* 5 full-time (3 women), 3 part-time/adjunct (1 woman). Expenses: Contact institution. *Financial support:* In 2006–07, 12 students received support; research assistantships with partial tuition reimbursements available, teaching assistantships with partial tuition reimbursements available, career-related internships or fieldwork, institutionally sponsored loans, scholarships/grants, and unspecified assistantships available. Support available to part-time students. Financial award application deadline: 3/1; financial award applicants required to submit FAFSA. In 2006, 16 degrees awarded. *Degree program information:* Part-time and evening/weekend programs available. Offers clinical psychology (MS); counseling psychology (MS). *Application deadline:* For fall admission, 2/1 priority date for domestic students; for spring admission, 10/15 priority date for domestic students. Applications are processed on a rolling basis. *Application fee:* $25. *Application Contact:* Charity H. Fahlstrom, Director of Graduate and Professional Studies Admissions, 417-865-2811 Ext. 1227, Fax: 417-575-5484. *Chair,* Dr. Grant Jones, 417-865-2815 Ext. 8619, E-mail: jonesg@evangel.edu.

Organizational Leadership Program Students: 20 full-time (8 women), 1 part-time; includes 1 minority (Hispanic American) Average age 35. 11 applicants, 100% accepted, 9 enrolled. *Faculty:* 4 full-time (2 women), 3 part-time/adjunct (2 women). Expenses: Contact institution. *Financial support:* In 2006–07, 12 students received support. Career-related internships or fieldwork, institutionally sponsored loans, and scholarships/grants available. Support available to part-time students. Financial award application deadline: 3/1; financial award applicants required to submit FAFSA. *Degree program information:* Part-time and evening/weekend programs available. Offers organizational leadership (MOL). *Application deadline:* For fall admission, 7/15 priority date for domestic and international students; for spring admission, 11/15 priority date for domestic and international students. Applications are processed on a rolling basis. *Application fee:* $25. *Application Contact:* Charity H. Fahlstrom, Director of Graduate and Professional Studies Admissions, 417-865-2811 Ext. 1227, Fax: 417-575-5484. *Director of Graduate Studies,* Dr. Jeff Fulks, 417-865-2811 Ext. 8616, Fax: 417-575-5484, E-mail: fulksj@evangel.edu.

EVERGLADES UNIVERSITY, Boca Raton, FL 33431

General Information Independent, coed, comprehensive institution.

GRADUATE UNITS

Graduate Programs Offers aviation science (MSA); business administration (MBA); information technology (MIT). Electronic applications accepted.

THE EVERGREEN STATE COLLEGE, Olympia, WA 98505

General Information State-supported, coed, comprehensive institution. *Enrollment:* 4,416 graduate, professional, and undergraduate students; 128 full-time matriculated graduate/professional students (84 women), 164 part-time matriculated graduate/professional students (104 women). *Enrollment by degree level:* 292 master's. *Graduate faculty:* 18 full-time (10 women), 7 part-time/adjunct (2 women). Tuition, state resident: full-time $6,546; part-time $218 per credit. Tuition, nonresident: full-time $19,982; part-time $666 per credit. Tuition and fees vary according to course load. *Graduate housing:* Rooms and/or apartments available on a first-come, first-served basis to single and married students. Typical cost: $7,140 (including board) for single students; $7,140 (including board) for married students. Room and board charges vary according to board plan and housing facility selected. Housing application deadline: 6/1. *Student services:* Campus employment opportunities, campus safety program, career counseling, child daycare facilities, disabled student services, exercise/wellness program, free psychological counseling, grant writing training, international student services, multicultural affairs office, teacher training, writing training. *Library facilities:* Daniel J. Evans Library. *Online resources:* library catalog, web page, access to other libraries' catalogs. *Collection:* 471,406 titles, 12,579 serial subscriptions, 89,195 audiovisual materials. *Research affiliation:* Washington State Institute for Public Policy.

Computer facilities: 300 computers available on campus for general student use. A campuswide network can be accessed from student residence rooms and from off campus. Internet access and online class registration are available. *Web address:* http://www.evergreen.edu/.

General Application Contact: J. T. Austin, Graduate Studies Office, 360-867-6707, Fax: 360-867-5430, E-mail: graduatestudies@evergreen.edu.

GRADUATE UNITS

Graduate Programs Students: 128 full-time (84 women), 164 part-time (104 women); includes 50 minority (10 African Americans, 26 American Indian/Alaska Native, 10 Asian Americans or Pacific Islanders, 4 Hispanic Americans), 2 international. Average age 33. 194 applicants, 91% accepted, 124 enrolled. *Faculty:* 18 full-time (10 women), 7 part-time/adjunct (2 women). Expenses: Contact institution. *Financial support:* Fellowships with partial tuition reimbursements, research assistantships with partial tuition reimbursements, career-related internships or fieldwork, Federal Work-Study, scholarships/grants, tuition waivers (full and partial), and unspecified assistantships available. Support available to part-time students. Financial award application deadline: 3/15; financial award applicants required to submit FAFSA. In 2006, 92 degrees awarded. *Degree program information:* Part-time and evening/weekend programs available. Offers environmental studies (MES); public administration (MPA); teaching (MIT). *Application deadline:* For fall admission, 2/15 priority date for domestic and international students. Applications are processed on a rolling basis. *Application fee:* $50. Electronic applications accepted. *Application Contact:* J. T. Austin, Graduate Studies Office, 360-867-6707, Fax: 360-867-5430, E-mail: graduatestudies@evergreen.edu. *Vice President and Provost,* Dr. Don Bantz, 360-867-6400, Fax: 360-867-6745, E-mail: bantzd@evergreen.edu.

EXCELSIOR COLLEGE, Albany, NY 12203-5159

General Information Independent, coed, comprehensive institution. *Enrollment:* 30,680 graduate, professional, and undergraduate students; 186 full-time matriculated graduate/professional students (102 women), 430 part-time matriculated graduate/professional students (254 women). *Enrollment by degree level:* 579 master's, 37 other advanced degrees. *Graduate faculty:* 15 full-time (6 women), 94 part-time/adjunct (68 women). *Tuition:* Part-time $365 per credit hour. *Student services:* Disabled student services, writing training. *Library facilities:* Excelsior College Virtual Library. *Online resources:* web page.

Computer facilities: A campuswide network can be accessed from off campus. Online class registration is available. *Web address:* http://www.excelsior.edu/.

General Application Contact: Admissions Counselor, 518-464-8500, Fax: 518-464-8777, E-mail: admissions@excelsior.edu.

GRADUATE UNITS

School of Business and Technology Average age 45. *Faculty:* 10 part-time/adjunct (5 women). Expenses: Contact institution. *Degree program information:* Part-time and evening/weekend programs available. Postbaccalaureate distance learning degree programs offered (no on-campus study). Offers business and technology (MBA). *Application deadline:* Applications are processed on a rolling basis. *Application fee:* $100. *Application Contact:* Admissions, 888-647-2388 Ext. 133, Fax: 518-464-8777, E-mail: admissions@excelsior.edu. *Dean,* Dr. Harpal S. Dhillon, 518-464-8500, Fax: 518-464-8777, E-mail: hdhillon@excelsior.edu.

School of Health Sciences Average age 47. *Faculty:* 1 (woman) full-time, 28 part-time/adjunct (24 women). Expenses: Contact institution. *Financial support:* In 2006–07, 1 student received support. Scholarships/grants available. Support available to part-time students. *Degree program information:* Part-time and evening/weekend programs available. Postbaccalaureate distance learning degree programs offered (no on-campus study). Offers healthcare informatics (Certificate); hospice and palliative care (Certificate); nursing management (Certificate). *Application deadline:* Applications are processed on a rolling basis. *Application fee:* $100. Electronic applications accepted. *Application Contact:* Laura Goff, Student Service Coordinator, 518-464-8500, Fax: 518-464-8777, E-mail: lgoff@excelsior.edu. *Director,* Deborah Sopczyk, 518-464-8500, Fax: 518-464-8777, E-mail: informatics@excelsior.edu.

School of Liberal Arts Students: 170 full-time (90 women), 180 part-time (80 women); includes 180 minority (60 African Americans, 20 American Indian/Alaska Native, 20 Asian Americans or Pacific Islanders, 80 Hispanic Americans), 20 international. Average age 49. 150 applicants, 67% accepted. *Faculty:* 11 full-time (2 women), 35 part-time/adjunct (20 women). Expenses: Contact institution. *Financial support:* In 2006–07, 2 fellowships (averaging $2,000 per year) were awarded; career-related internships or fieldwork, scholarships/grants, and traineeships also available. In 2006, 45 degrees awarded. *Degree program information:* Part-time and evening/weekend programs available. Postbaccalaureate distance learning degree programs offered (no on-campus study). Offers liberal studies (MA). *Application deadline:* Applications are processed on a rolling basis. *Application fee:* $100. Electronic applications accepted. *Application Contact:* Susan Carlson, Administrative Assistant to the Director, 518-464-8500 Ext. 1323, Fax: 518-464-8777, E-mail: mls@excelsior.edu. *Director/Associate Dean,* Dr. Susan Smith Nash, 518-464-8500, Fax: 518-464-8777, E-mail: mlsadmin@excelsior.edu.

School of Nursing Students: 16 full-time (12 women), 116 part-time (96 women); includes 20 minority (11 African Americans, 1 American Indian/Alaska Native, 5 Asian Americans or Pacific Islanders, 3 Hispanic Americans). Average age 45. 53 applicants, 92% accepted, 48 enrolled. *Faculty:* 3 full-time (all women), 21 part-time/adjunct (19 women). Expenses: Contact institution. *Financial support:* In 2006–07, 20 students received support. Scholarships/grants and traineeships available. Support available to part-time students. Financial award application deadline: 8/26. In 2006, 8 degrees awarded. *Degree program information:* Part-time and evening/weekend programs available. Postbaccalaureate distance learning degree programs offered (no on-campus study). Offers clinical systems management (MS); nursing (MS). *Application deadline:* Applications are processed on a rolling basis. *Application fee:* $100. Electronic applications accepted. *Application Contact:* Christine McIlwraith, Graduate Advisor, 518-464-8500, Fax: 518-464-8777, E-mail: nursingmasters@excelsior.edu. *Director, Graduate Program in Nursing/Associate Dean,* Dr. Patricia Ann Edwards, 518-464-8500, Fax: 518-464-8777, E-mail: msn@excelsior.edu.

FACULTAD DE DERECHO EUGENIO MARÍA DE HOSTOS, Mayagüez, PR 00681

General Information Independent, graduate-only institution.

GRADUATE UNITS

School of Law Offers law (JD).

FAIRFIELD UNIVERSITY, Fairfield, CT 06824-5195

General Information Independent-religious, coed, comprehensive institution. *Enrollment:* 5,091 graduate, professional, and undergraduate students; 270 full-time matriculated graduate/professional students (180 women), 813 part-time matriculated graduate/professional students (514 women). *Enrollment by degree level:* 1,083 master's. *Graduate faculty:* 78 full-time (43 women), 49 part-time/adjunct (18 women). *Graduate housing:* On-campus housing not available. *Student services:* Campus employment opportunities, campus safety program, career counseling, disabled student services, exercise/wellness program, free psychological counseling, international student services, multicultural affairs office, teacher training. *Library facilities:* Dimenna-Nyselius Library. *Online resources:* library catalog, web page. *Collection:* 347,244 titles, 1,614 serial subscriptions, 10,757 audiovisual materials.

Computer facilities: Computer purchase and lease plans are available. 150 computers available on campus for general student use. A campuswide network can be accessed from student residence rooms and from off campus. Internet access and online class registration are available. *Web address:* http://www.fairfield.edu/.

General Application Contact: Marianne Gumpper, Director of Graduate and Continuing Studies Admissions, 203-254-4184, Fax: 203-254-4073, E-mail: gradadmis@mail.fairfield.edu.

GRADUATE UNITS

Charles F. Dolan School of Business Students: 65 full-time (31 women), 125 part-time (54 women); includes 4 Asian Americans or Pacific Islanders, 4 Hispanic Americans, 22 international. Average age 27. 99 applicants, 45% accepted, 38 enrolled. *Faculty:* 43 full-time (17 women), 2 part-time/adjunct (1 woman). Expenses: Contact institution. *Financial support:* Unspecified assistantships available. In 2006, 78 degrees awarded. *Degree program information:* Part-time and evening/weekend programs available. Offers accounting (MBA, MS, CAS); finance (MBA, MS, CAS); general management (MBA); human resource management (MBA, CAS); information systems and operations (MBA); information systems and operations management (CAS); international business (MBA, CAS); marketing (MBA, CAS); taxation (MBA, MS, CAS). *Application deadline:* For fall admission, 8/15 priority date for domestic students, 5/15 priority date for international students; for spring admission, 11/15 priority date for domestic students, 10/15 priority date for international students. Applications are processed on a rolling basis. *Application fee:* $55. Electronic applications accepted. *Application Contact:* Marianne Gumpper, Director of Graduate and Continuing Studies Admissions, 203-254-4184, Fax: 203-254-4073, E-mail: gradadmis@mail.fairfield.edu. *Dean,* Dr. Norman A. Solomon, 203-254-4000 Ext. 4070, Fax: 203-254-4105, E-mail: nsolomon@mail.fairfield.edu.

College of Arts and Sciences Students: 6 full-time (4 women), 88 part-time (52 women); includes 5 minority (2 African Americans, 1 American Indian/Alaska Native, 1 Asian American

Fairfield University (continued)

or Pacific Islander, 1 Hispanic American). Average age 41. 34 applicants, 76% accepted, 18 enrolled. *Faculty:* 40 full-time (15 women), 3 part-time/adjunct (0 women). Expenses: Contact institution. *Financial support:* Tuition waivers (partial) and unspecified assistantships available. Financial award applicants required to submit FAFSA. In 2006, 25 degrees awarded. *Degree program information:* Part-time and evening/weekend programs available. Offers American studies (MA); arts and sciences (MA, MS); mathematics and quantitative methods (MS). *Application deadline:* For fall admission, 7/1 for domestic students, 6/15 priority date for international students; for spring admission, 12/1 for domestic students, 10/15 priority date for international students. Applications are processed on a rolling basis. *Application fee:* $55. *Application Contact:* Marianne Gumpper, Director of Graduate and Continuing Studies Admissions, 203-254-4184, Fax: 203-254-4073, E-mail: gradadmis@mail.fairfield.edu. *Dean,* Dr. Timothy L. Snyder, 203-254-4000 Ext. 2221, Fax: 203-254-4119, E-mail: tsnyder@mail.fairfield.edu.

Graduate School of Education and Allied Professions Students: 172 full-time (139 women), 416 part-time (342 women); includes 54 minority (16 African Americans, 2 American Indian/Alaska Native, 9 Asian Americans or Pacific Islanders, 27 Hispanic Americans), 7 international. Average age 30. 204 applicants, 46% accepted, 70 enrolled. *Faculty:* 17 full-time (14 women), 25 part-time/adjunct (14 women). Expenses: Contact institution. *Financial support:* In 2006–07, 10 research assistantships were awarded; career-related internships or fieldwork and tuition waivers (partial) also available. Financial award applicants required to submit FAFSA. In 2006, 144 master's, 26 other advanced degrees awarded. *Degree program information:* Part-time and evening/weekend programs available. Postbaccalaureate distance learning degree programs offered. Offers applied psychology (MA); community counseling (MA); computers in education (MA, CAS); counselor education (CAS); education and allied professions (MA, CAS); educational media (MA, CAS); elementary education (MA); marriage and family therapy (MA); school counseling (MA); school media specialist (MA, CAS); school psychology (MA, CAS); secondary education (MA); special education (MA, CAS); teaching and foundations (MA, CAS); TESOL, foreign language and bilingual/multicultural education (MA, CAS). *Application deadline:* Applications are processed on a rolling basis. *Application fee:* $55. Electronic applications accepted. *Application Contact:* Marianne Gumpper, Director of Graduate and Continuing Studies Admissions, 203-254-4184, Fax: 203-254-4073, E-mail: gradadmis@mail.fairfield.edu. *Dean,* Dr. Susan D. Franzosa, 203-254-4000 Ext. 4250, Fax: 203-254-4241, E-mail: sfranzosa@mail.fairfield.edu.

School of Engineering Students: 24 full-time (3 women), 132 part-time (22 women). 54 applicants, 59% accepted, 21 enrolled. *Faculty:* 5 full-time (0 women), 18 part-time/adjunct (1 woman). Expenses: Contact institution. *Financial support:* Career-related internships or fieldwork available. Financial award applicants required to submit FAFSA. In 2006, 56 degrees awarded. *Degree program information:* Part-time and evening/weekend programs available. Offers electrical and computer engineering (MS); management of technology (MS); mechanical engineering (MS); software engineering (MS). *Application deadline:* For fall admission, 8/15 priority date for domestic students, 5/15 priority date for international students; for spring admission, 12/15 priority date for domestic students, 10/15 priority date for international students. Applications are processed on a rolling basis. *Application fee:* $55. *Application Contact:* Marianne Gumpper, Director of Graduate and Continuing Studies Admissions, 203-254-4184, Fax: 203-254-4073, E-mail: gradadmis@mail.fairfield.edu. *Dean,* Dr. Evangelos Hadjimichael, 203-254-4000 Ext. 4147, Fax: 203-254-4013, E-mail: ehadjimichael@mail.fairfield.edu.

School of Nursing Students: 3 full-time (all women), 39 part-time (all women); includes 5 minority (2 African Americans, 3 Asian Americans or Pacific Islanders). Average age 42. 23 applicants, 30% accepted, 3 enrolled. *Faculty:* 13 full-time (12 women), 2 part-time/adjunct (both women). Expenses: Contact institution. *Financial support:* Traineeships available. Financial award applicants required to submit FAFSA. In 2006, 9 degrees awarded. *Degree program information:* Part-time programs available. Offers adult nurse practitioner (MSN, PMC); family nurse practitioner (MSN, PMC); healthcare management (MSN); nurse anesthesia (MSN); psychiatric nurse practitioner (MSN, PMC). *Application deadline:* For fall admission, 4/1 priority date for domestic students, 6/15 priority date for international students; for spring admission, 11/1 priority date for domestic students, 10/15 priority date for international students. Applications are processed on a rolling basis. *Application fee:* $55. *Application Contact:* Marianne Gumpper, Director of Graduate and Continuing Studies Admissions, 203-254-4184, Fax: 203-254-4073, E-mail: gradadmis@mail.fairfield.edu. *Dean,* Dr. Jeanne M. Novotny, 203-254-4000 Ext. 2701, Fax: 203-254-4126, E-mail: jnovotny@mail.fairfield.edu.

FAIRLEIGH DICKINSON UNIVERSITY, COLLEGE AT FLORHAM, Madison, NJ 07940-1099

General Information Independent, coed, comprehensive institution. *Enrollment:* 3,562 graduate, professional, and undergraduate students; 349 full-time matriculated graduate/professional students (200 women), 556 part-time matriculated graduate/professional students (297 women). *Enrollment by degree level:* 892 master's, 13 other advanced degrees. *Graduate faculty:* 116 full-time, 189 part-time/adjunct. *Library facilities:* College of Florham Library. *Online resources:* library catalog. *Collection:* 227,700 titles, 1,230 serial subscriptions, 690 audiovisual materials.

Computer facilities: 300 computers available on campus for general student use. A campuswide network can be accessed from student residence rooms and from off campus. *Web address:* http://www.fdu.edu/.

General Application Contact: Thomas M. Shea, University Director of International and Graduate Admissions, 973-443-8905, Fax: 973-443-8088, E-mail: grad@fdu.edu.

GRADUATE UNITS

Anthony J. Petrocelli College of Continuing Studies Students: 8 full-time (4 women), 30 part-time (14 women), 2 international. Average age 31. 22 applicants, 100% accepted, 22 enrolled. Expenses: Contact institution. In 2006, 16 degrees awarded. Offers continuing studies (MAS, MPA, MS). *Application deadline:* Applications are processed on a rolling basis. *Application fee:* $40.

International School of Hospitality and Tourism Management Students: 7 full-time (3 women), 26 part-time (12 women), 1 international. Average age 32. 19 applicants, 100% accepted, 19 enrolled. Expenses: Contact institution. In 2006, 11 degrees awarded. Offers hospitality management studies (MS). *Application deadline:* Applications are processed on a rolling basis. *Application fee:* $40.

Public Administration Institute Students: 1 (woman) full-time, 2 part-time (both women), 1 international. Average age 25. 2 applicants, 100% accepted, 2 enrolled. Expenses: Contact institution. In 2006, 4 degrees awarded. Offers public administration (MPA). *Application fee:* $40.

School of Administrative Science Average age 25. 1 applicant, 100% accepted, 1 enrolled. Expenses: Contact institution. In 2006, 1 degree awarded. Offers administrative science (MAS). *Application fee:* $40.

Maxwell Becton College of Arts and Sciences Students: 162 full-time (96 women), 155 part-time (103 women), 48 international. Average age 31. 300 applicants, 68% accepted, 98 enrolled. Expenses: Contact institution. In 2006, 99 degrees awarded. Offers arts and sciences (MA, MFA, MS, Certificate); biology (MS); chemistry (MS); clinical/counseling psychology (MA); corporate and organizational communication (MA); creative writing (MFA); industrial/organizational psychology (MA); organizational behavior (MA, Certificate); organizational leadership (Certificate). *Application deadline:* Applications are processed on a rolling basis. *Application fee:* $40.

Silberman College of Business Students: 117 full-time (48 women), 313 part-time (139 women), 23 international. Average age 31. 201 applicants, 70% accepted, 106 enrolled. Expenses: Contact institution. In 2006, 144 degrees awarded. *Degree program information:* Part-time and evening/weekend programs available. Offers accounting (MS); business (MBA, MS, Certificate); business administration (MBA); entrepreneurial studies (MBA, Certificate); evolving technology (Certificate); finance (MBA, Certificate); international business (MBA, Certificate); international taxation (Certificate); management (MBA, Certificate); marketing (MBA, Certificate); taxation (MS, Certificate). *Application deadline:* Applications are processed on a rolling basis. *Application fee:* $40. *Dean,* Dr. David Steele, 201-692-7200, Fax: 201-692-7199, E-mail: steele@fdu.edu.

Center for Healthcare Management Studies Students: 8 full-time (3 women), 23 part-time (8 women), 2 international. Average age 31. 12 applicants, 67% accepted, 8 enrolled. Expenses: Contact institution. In 2006, 9 degrees awarded. Offers healthcare management studies (MBA, Certificate); pharmaceutical studies (MBA, Certificate). *Application fee:* $40.

Center for Human Resource Management Studies Students: 6 full-time (3 women), 13 part-time (11 women), 1 international. Average age 29. 13 applicants, 62% accepted, 4 enrolled. Expenses: Contact institution. In 2006, 8 degrees awarded. Offers human resource management (MBA); human resource management studies (MBA). *Application fee:* $40.

University College: Arts, Sciences, and Professional Studies Students: 62 full-time (52 women), 58 part-time (41 women). Average age 29. 77 applicants, 83% accepted, 58 enrolled. Expenses: Contact institution. In 2006, 86 degrees awarded. Offers arts, sciences, and professional studies (MA, MAT, Certificate). *Application deadline:* Applications are processed on a rolling basis. *Application fee:* $40.

Peter Sammartino School of Education Students: 62 full-time (52 women), 58 part-time (41 women). Average age 29. 77 applicants, 83% accepted, 58 enrolled. Expenses: Contact institution. In 2006, 86 degrees awarded. Offers education for certified teachers (MA, Certificate); educational leadership (MA); instructional technology (Certificate); literacy/reading (Certificate); teaching (MAT). *Application deadline:* Applications are processed on a rolling basis. *Application fee:* $40.

See Close-Up on page 889.

FAIRLEIGH DICKINSON UNIVERSITY, METROPOLITAN CAMPUS, Teaneck, NJ 07666-1914

General Information Independent, coed, comprehensive institution. *Enrollment:* 8,491 graduate, professional, and undergraduate students; 937 full-time matriculated graduate/professional students (456 women), 1,622 part-time matriculated graduate/professional students (965 women). *Enrollment by degree level:* 2,199 master's, 132 doctoral, 228 other advanced degrees. *Graduate faculty:* 185 full-time, 440 part-time/adjunct. *Library facilities:* Weiner Library plus 3 others. *Online resources:* library catalog, web page. *Collection:* 371,900 titles, 1,690 serial subscriptions, 3,100 audiovisual materials.

Computer facilities: 210 computers available on campus for general student use. A campuswide network can be accessed from student residence rooms and from off campus. *Web address:* http://www.fdu.edu/.

General Application Contact: Thomas Shea, University Director of International and Graduate Admissions, 201-692-2554, Fax: 201-692-2560, E-mail: globaleducation@fdu.edu.

GRADUATE UNITS

Anthony J. Petrocelli College of Continuing Studies Students: 154 full-time (75 women), 677 part-time (300 women), 85 international. Average age 38. 393 applicants, 91% accepted, 208 enrolled. Expenses: Contact institution. In 2006, 265 degrees awarded. Offers continuing studies (MAS, MPA, MS, Certificate). *Application deadline:* Applications are processed on a rolling basis. *Application fee:* $40. *Dean,* Kenneth T. Vehrkens, 201-692-2000.

International School of Hospitality and Tourism Management Students: 8 full-time (5 women), 17 part-time (10 women), 7 international. Average age 35. 13 applicants, 10 enrolled. Expenses: Contact institution. In 2006, 10 degrees awarded. Offers hospitality management studies (MS). *Application deadline:* Applications are processed on a rolling basis. *Application fee:* $40. *Director,* Dr. Richard Wisch, 201-692-2000.

Public Administration Institute Students: 82 full-time (39 women), 95 part-time (51 women), 48 international. Average age 35. 147 applicants, 87% accepted, 55 enrolled. Expenses: Contact institution. In 2006, 35 degrees awarded. Offers public administration (MPA, Certificate); public non-profit management (Certificate). *Application deadline:* Applications are processed on a rolling basis. *Application fee:* $40. *Director,* Dr. William Roberts, 201-692-2000.

School of Administrative Science Students: 64 full-time (31 women), 565 part-time (239 women), 30 international. Average age 39. 233 applicants, 94% accepted, 143 enrolled. Expenses: Contact institution. In 2006, 220 degrees awarded. Offers administrative science (MAS, Certificate). *Application deadline:* Applications are processed on a rolling basis. *Application fee:* $40. *Director/Executive Associate Dean,* Ronald Calissi, 201-692-2000.

Maxwell Becton College of Arts and Sciences Expenses: Contact institution. Offers arts and sciences (MA); corporate communications (MA). *Application fee:* $40.

Silberman College of Business Students: 217 full-time (95 women), 152 part-time (74 women), 143 international. Average age 31. 360 applicants, 61% accepted, 109 enrolled. Expenses: Contact institution. In 2006, 209 degrees awarded. Offers accounting (MS, Certificate); business (MBA, MS, Certificate); business administration (MBA); entrepreneurial studies (MBA, Certificate); finance (MBA, Certificate); international business (MBA); management (MBA, Certificate); management information systems (Certificate); marketing (MBA, Certificate); taxation (MS). *Application deadline:* Applications are processed on a rolling basis. *Application fee:* $40. *Dean,* Dr. Robert Greenfield, 201-692-2000.

Center for Healthcare Management Studies Students: 17 full-time (9 women), 19 part-time (10 women), 6 international. Average age 33. 17 applicants, 47% accepted, 1 enrolled. Expenses: Contact institution. In 2006, 29 degrees awarded. Offers chemical studies (Certificate); management for health system executives (MBA); pharmaceutical studies (MBA, Certificate). *Application deadline:* Applications are processed on a rolling basis. *Application fee:* $40. *Director,* Dr. Peter Caliguari, 201-692-2000.

Center for Human Resources Management Studies Students: 44 full-time (12 women), 24 part-time (9 women), 5 international. Average age 37. 48 applicants, 88% accepted, 25 enrolled. Expenses: Contact institution. In 2006, 26 degrees awarded. Offers executive education (MBA); human resource management (Certificate). *Application deadline:* Applications are processed on a rolling basis. *Application fee:* $40.

University College: Arts, Sciences, and Professional Studies Students: 566 full-time (286 women), 793 part-time (591 women), 352 international. Average age 33. 1,400 applicants, 70% accepted, 362 enrolled. Expenses: Contact institution. In 2006, 348 master's, 13 doctorates awarded. Offers art and media studies (MA); arts, sciences, and professional studies (MA, MAT, MS, MSEE, MSN, PhD, Psy D, Certificate); English and literature (MA); media and communications (MA); systems science (MS). *Application deadline:* Applications are processed on a rolling basis. *Application fee:* $40. *Dean,* Dr. John Snyder, 201-692-2000.

Henry P. Becton School of Nursing and Allied Health Average age 43. 34 applicants, 82% accepted, 19 enrolled. Expenses: Contact institution. In 2006, 11 degrees awarded. Offers medical technology (MS); nursing (MSN, Certificate). *Application deadline:* Applications are processed on a rolling basis. *Application fee:* $40. *Director,* Dr. Minerva Guttman, 201-692-2000.

Peter Sammartino School of Education Students: 70 full-time (54 women), 515 part-time (424 women), 14 international. Average age 36. 290 applicants, 92% accepted, 130 enrolled. Expenses: Contact institution. In 2006, 106 degrees awarded. *Degree program information:* Part-time programs available. Offers dyslexia specialist (Certificate); education for certified teachers (MA); educational leadership (MA); instructional technology (Certificate); learning disabilities (MA); literacy/reading (Certificate); multilingual education (MA); teacher of the handicapped (Certificate); teaching (MAT). *Application deadline:* Applications are processed on a rolling basis. *Application fee:* $40. *Director,* Dr. Vicki Cohen, 201-692-2525, Fax: 201-692-2603, E-mail: vicki_cohen@fdu.edu.

School of Computer Sciences and Engineering Students: 266 full-time (69 women), 106 part-time (47 women), 304 international. Average age 26. 792 applicants, 62% accepted, 126 enrolled. Expenses: Contact institution. In 2006, 166 degrees awarded. Offers computer engineering (MS); computer science (MS); e-commerce (MS); electrical engineering (MSEE); management information systems (MS); mathematical foundation (MS). *Application deadline:* Applications are processed on a rolling basis. *Application fee:* $40. *Director,* Dr. Alfredo Tan, 201-692-2000.

School of History, Political and International Studies Students: 7 full-time (3 women), 5 part-time (3 women), 3 international. Average age 27. 17 applicants, 71% accepted, 3 enrolled. Expenses: Contact institution. In 2006, 3 degrees awarded. Offers history (MA); international studies (MA); political science (MA). *Application deadline:* Applications are processed on a rolling basis. *Application fee:* $40. *Director,* Dr. Faramarz S. Fatemi, 201-692-2272, Fax: 201-692-9096, E-mail: fatemi@fdu.edu.

School of Natural Sciences Students: 37 full-time (24 women), 35 part-time (22 women), 25 international. Average age 28. 117 applicants, 55% accepted, 24 enrolled. Expenses: Contact institution. In 2006, 28 degrees awarded. Offers biology (MS); chemistry (MS); science (MA). *Application deadline:* Applications are processed on a rolling basis. *Application fee:* $40. *Director,* Dr. Irwin Isquith, 201-692-2000.

School of Psychology Students: 178 full-time (131 women), 56 part-time (25 women), 5 international. Average age 34. 136 applicants, 75% accepted, 53 enrolled. Expenses: Contact institution. In 2006, 31 master's, 13 doctorates awarded. Offers clinical psychology (PhD); clinical psychopharmacology (MA); general-theoretical psychology (MA, Certificate); school psychology (MA, Psy D). *Application deadline:* Applications are processed on a rolling basis. *Application fee:* $40. *Director,* Dr. Christopher Capuano, 201-692-2000.

See Close-Up on page 889.

FAIRMONT STATE UNIVERSITY, Fairmont, WV 26554

General Information State-supported, coed, comprehensive institution.

GRADUATE UNITS

Graduate Studies Offers business administration (MBA); criminal justice (MS); education (MAT); human and community service administration (MS); leadership studies (M Ed); nursing administration (MS); nursing education (MS); online learning (M Ed); professional studies (M Ed); reading (M Ed); special education (M Ed).

FAITH BAPTIST BIBLE COLLEGE AND THEOLOGICAL SEMINARY, Ankeny, IA 50021

General Information Independent-religious, coed, comprehensive institution. *Enrollment:* 404 graduate, professional, and undergraduate students; 43 full-time matriculated graduate/professional students (4 women), 38 part-time matriculated graduate/professional students (2 women). *Enrollment by degree level:* 42 first professional, 39 master's. *Graduate faculty:* 4 full-time (0 women), 7 part-time/adjunct (0 women). *Tuition:* Full-time $9,788; part-time $375 per credit. One-time fee: $50 full-time. Tuition and fees vary according to class time and course load. *Graduate housing:* Rooms and/or apartments available on a first-come, first-served basis to single and married students. Typical cost: $2,190 per year ($4,794 including board) for single students. Housing application deadline: 8/1. *Student services:* Campus employment opportunities, career counseling, free psychological counseling, international student services, low-cost health insurance. *Library facilities:* Patten Hall. *Online resources:* library catalog, web page. *Collection:* 63,840 titles, 395 serial subscriptions, 6,563 audiovisual materials.

Computer facilities: 50 computers available on campus for general student use. A campuswide network can be accessed from student residence rooms and from off campus. Internet access and online class registration are available. *Web address:* http://www.faith.edu/.

General Application Contact: Tim Nilius, Vice President of Enrollment, 888-FAITH4U, Fax: 515-964-1638, E-mail: niliust@faith.edu.

GRADUATE UNITS

Graduate Program Students: 63 full-time (4 women), 18 part-time (2 women); includes 2 minority (1 Asian American or Pacific Islander, 1 Hispanic American), 1 international. Average age 29. 33 applicants, 94% accepted, 25 enrolled. *Faculty:* 4 full-time (0 women), 7 part-time/adjunct (0 women). Expenses: Contact institution. *Financial support:* In 2006–07, 70 students received support. Career-related internships or fieldwork and scholarships/grants available. Support available to part-time students. Financial award application deadline: 3/1; financial award applicants required to submit FAFSA. In 2006, 10 first professional degrees, 19 master's awarded. *Degree program information:* Part-time programs available. Offers biblical studies (MA); pastoral studies (M Div); pastoral training (MA); religion (MA); theological studies (MA). *Application deadline:* For fall admission, 8/1 priority date for domestic students, 8/1 for international students; for spring admission, 12/15 for domestic and international students. Applications are processed on a rolling basis. *Application fee:* $25. *Application Contact:* Tim Nilius, Vice President of Enrollment, 888-FAITH4U, Fax: 515-964-1638, E-mail: niliust@faith.edu. *Vice President of Academic Services, Seminary,* Dr. John Hartog, 515-964-0601 Ext. 278, Fax: 515-964-1638, E-mail: hartogj3@faith.edu.

FAITH EVANGELICAL LUTHERAN SEMINARY, Tacoma, WA 98407

General Information Independent-religious, coed, graduate-only institution.

GRADUATE UNITS

Graduate and Professional Programs *Degree program information:* Part-time and evening/weekend programs available. Postbaccalaureate distance learning degree programs offered (minimal on-campus study). Offers theology (B Th, M Div, MCM, MTS, D Min).

FASHION INSTITUTE OF TECHNOLOGY, New York, NY 10001-5992

General Information State and locally supported, coed, primarily women, comprehensive institution. *Enrollment:* 10,010 graduate, professional, and undergraduate students; 97 full-time matriculated graduate/professional students (78 women), 88 part-time matriculated graduate/professional students (73 women). *Enrollment by degree level:* 185 master's. *Graduate faculty:* 7 full-time (5 women), 27 part-time/adjunct (22 women). Tuition, state resident: full-time $6,900; part-time $288 per credit. Tuition, nonresident: full-time $10,920; part-time $455 per credit. *Required fees:* $420; $30 per term. *Graduate housing:* Room and/or apartments available on a first-come, first-served basis to single students; on-campus housing not available to married students. Typical cost: $9,545 per year ($12,935 including board). *Student services:* Career counseling, disabled student services, exercise/wellness program, free psychological counseling, international student services. *Library facilities:* Gladys Marcus Library. *Online resources:* library catalog, web page, access to other libraries' catalogs. *Collection:* 240,712 titles, 3,378 serial subscriptions, 134,534 audiovisual materials.

Computer facilities: 300 computers available on campus for general student use. A campuswide network can be accessed from student residence rooms and from off campus. Internet access and online class registration are available. *Web address:* http://www.fitnyc.edu/.

General Application Contact: Dr. Steven Zucker, Dean, School of Graduate Studies, 212-217-5714, Fax: 212-217-5156, E-mail: gradinfo@fitnyc.edu.

GRADUATE UNITS

School of Graduate Studies Students: 97 full-time (78 women), 86 part-time (71 women); includes 17 minority (3 African Americans, 8 Asian Americans or Pacific Islanders, 6 Hispanic Americans), 30 international. Average age 32. 338 applicants, 37% accepted, 76 enrolled. *Faculty:* 3 full-time (2 women), 20 part-time/adjunct (17 women). Expenses: Contact institution. *Financial support:* In 2006–07, 46 students received support. Federal Work-Study and scholarships/grants available. Financial award applicants required to submit FAFSA. In 2006, 50 master's awarded. Offers art market: principles and practices (MA); cosmetics and fragrance marketing and management (MPS); exhibition design (MA); fashion and textile studies: history, theory, and museum practice (MA); global fashion management (MPS); illustration (MA). *Application deadline:* For fall admission, 2/15 priority date for domestic and international students. Applications are processed on a rolling basis. *Application fee:* $25. *Application Contact:* Umilta Allsop, Administrative Assistant, 212-217-5716, Fax: 212-217-5156, E-mail: umilta_allsop@fitnyc.edu. *Dean, School of Graduate Studies,* Dr. Steven Zucker, 212-217-5714, Fax: 212-217-5156, E-mail: gradinfo@fitnyc.edu.

FAULKNER UNIVERSITY, Montgomery, AL 36109-3398

General Information Independent-religious, coed, comprehensive institution. *Enrollment:* 2,625 graduate, professional, and undergraduate students; 182 full-time matriculated graduate/professional students (69 women), 92 part-time matriculated graduate/professional students (42 women). *Enrollment by degree level:* 274 first professional. *Graduate faculty:* 25 full-time (9 women), 4 part-time/adjunct (3 women). *Graduate housing:* On-campus housing not available. *Student services:* Campus employment opportunities, career counseling, disabled student services, writing training. *Library facilities:* Gus Nichols Library plus 1 other. *Online resources:* library catalog, web page, access to other libraries' catalogs. *Collection:* 170,577 titles, 3,233 serial subscriptions, 2,300 audiovisual materials.

Computer facilities: 185 computers available on campus for general student use. A campuswide network can be accessed from student residence rooms and from off campus. Internet access, e-mail, student account access are available. *Web address:* http://www.faulkner.edu/.

General Application Contact: Andrew R Matthews, Assistant Dean for Student Services, 334-386-7910, Fax: 334-386-7908, E-mail: amatthews@faulkner.edu.

GRADUATE UNITS

Thomas Goode Jones School of Law Students: 182 full-time (69 women), 92 part-time (42 women); includes 28 minority (20 African Americans, 3 American Indian/Alaska Native, 3 Asian Americans or Pacific Islanders, 2 Hispanic Americans). Average age 28. 316 applicants, 58% accepted, 106 enrolled. *Faculty:* 25 full-time (9 women), 4 part-time/adjunct (3 women). Expenses: Contact institution. *Financial support:* In 2006–07, 78 students received support. Career-related internships or fieldwork, scholarships/grants, and tuition waivers (full and partial) available. Support available to part-time students. Financial award application deadline: 5/1; financial award applicants required to submit FAFSA. In 2006, 54 degrees awarded. *Degree program information:* Part-time and evening/weekend programs available. Offers law (JD). *Application deadline:* For fall admission, 5/1 for domestic students. Applications are processed on a rolling basis. *Application fee:* $25. Electronic applications accepted. *Application Contact:* Andrew R Matthews, Assistant Dean for Student Services, 334-386-7910, Fax: 334-386-7908, E-mail: amatthews@faulkner.edu. *Dean,* Charles I. Nelson, 334-386-7220, Fax: 334-386-7545, E-mail: cnelson@faulkner.edu.

FAYETTEVILLE STATE UNIVERSITY, Fayetteville, NC 28301-4298

General Information State-supported, coed, comprehensive institution. CGS member. *Enrollment:* 6,301 graduate, professional, and undergraduate students; 165 full-time matriculated graduate/professional students (133 women), 219 part-time matriculated graduate/professional students (173 women). *Enrollment by degree level:* 339 master's, 45 doctoral. *Graduate faculty:* 135 full-time (64 women), 6 part-time/adjunct (3 women). Tuition, state resident: full-time $2,118. Tuition, nonresident: full-time $11,708. *Required fees:* $1,099. Tuition and fees vary according to course load. *Graduate housing:* On-campus housing not available. *Student services:* Career counseling, child daycare facilities, free psychological counseling, low-cost health insurance. *Library facilities:* Charles W. Chestnut Library. *Online resources:* library catalog, web page, access to other libraries' catalogs. *Collection:* 334,089 titles, 2,735 serial subscriptions, 17,458 audiovisual materials. *Research affiliation:* Research Triangle Park.

Computer facilities: 355 computers available on campus for general student use. A campuswide network can be accessed from student residence rooms and from off campus. Internet access and online class registration, access to student information are available. *Web address:* http://www.uncfsu.edu/.

General Application Contact: Charles Darlington, Director of Admissions, 910-672-1371, Fax: 910-672-1414, E-mail: cdarlington@uncfsu.edu.

GRADUATE UNITS

Graduate School Expenses: Contact institution. *Financial support:* Institutionally sponsored loans available. Support available to part-time students. *Degree program information:* Part-time and evening/weekend programs available. Offers biology (MA Ed, MS); criminal justice (MA); educational leadership (Ed D); elementary education (MA Ed); English (MA); history (MA, MA Ed); mathematics (MA Ed, MS); middle grades (MA Ed); political science (MA, MA Ed); psychology (MA); reading (MA Ed); school administration (MSA); social work (MSW); sociology (MA Ed); special education (MA Ed). *Application deadline:* For fall admission, 8/1 for domestic students; for spring admission, 12/15 for domestic students. Applications are processed on a rolling basis. *Application fee:* $25.

FELICIAN COLLEGE, Lodi, NJ 07644-2117

General Information Independent-religious, coed, comprehensive institution. *Enrollment:* 1,992 graduate, professional, and undergraduate students; 75 matriculated graduate/professional students. *Enrollment by degree level:* 63 master's, 12 other advanced degrees. *Tuition:* Part-time $675 per credit. Tuition and fees vary according to program. *Graduate housing:* Room and/or apartments available on a first-come, first-served basis to single students; on-campus housing not available to married students. *Student services:* Campus employment opportunities, child daycare facilities, disabled student services, exercise/wellness program, free psychological counseling, international student services, low-cost health insurance, teacher training, writing training. *Library facilities:* Felician College Library. *Online resources:* library catalog, web page. *Collection:* 101,040 titles, 563 serial subscriptions, 3,991 audiovisual materials.

Computer facilities: 100 computers available on campus for general student use. A campuswide network can be accessed from student residence rooms and from off campus. Internet access is available. *Web address:* http://www.felician.edu/.

General Application Contact: Wendy Lin-Cook, Director of Adult and Graduate Admission, 201-559-6077, Fax: 201-559-6138, E-mail: adultandgraduate@felician.edu.

GRADUATE UNITS

Program in Advanced Practice Nursing 29 applicants, 90% accepted, 24 enrolled. Expenses: Contact institution. *Financial support:* In 2006–07, 10 students received support. Traineeships available. Financial award applicants required to submit FAFSA. *Degree program information:* Part-time and evening/weekend programs available. Postbaccalaureate distance learning degree programs offered (no on-campus study). Offers adult nurse practitioner (MSN, PMC); family nurse practitioner (MSN, PMC); school nurse/teacher of health education (Certificate). *Application deadline:* Applications are processed on a rolling basis. *Application fee:* $40. *Application Contact:* Wendy Lin-Cook, Director of Adult and Graduate Admission, 201-559-6077, Fax: 201-559-6138, E-mail: adultandgraduate@felician.edu. *Dean, Division of Health Sciences,* Dr. Muriel Shore, 201-559-6030, E-mail: shorem@inet.felician.edu.

Program in Business Students: 47. 28 applicants, 89% accepted, 24 enrolled. Expenses: Contact institution. *Degree program information:* Part-time and evening/weekend programs available. Offers innovation and entrepreneurship (MBA). *Application deadline:* Applications are processed on a rolling basis. *Application fee:* $40. *Application Contact:* Dominic DiGioacching, Associate Director of Adult and Graduate Admission, 201-559-6097, Fax: 201-559-6138, E-mail: digioacchinod@felician.edu. *Dean, Division of Business and Management Services,* Dr. William Morgan, 201-559-6140, E-mail: morganw@felician.edu.

Program in Education 18 applicants, 50% accepted, 9 enrolled. Expenses: Contact institution. *Financial support:* Federal Work-Study available. *Degree program information:* Part-time and evening/weekend programs available. Offers elementary education (MA); supervisory (MA); teacher for students with disabilities (MA). *Application deadline:* Applications are processed on a rolling basis. *Application fee:* $40. *Application Contact:* Wendy Lin-Cook, Director of Adult and Graduate Admission, 201-559-6077, Fax: 201-559-6138, E-mail: adultandgraduate@felician.edu. *Associate Dean,* Dr. Julie Goods, 201-559-3529, E-mail: goodj@felician.edu.

Program in Religious Education 24 applicants, 79% accepted, 18 enrolled. Expenses: Contact institution. *Financial support:* Scholarships/grants and tuition waivers (partial) available. *Degree program information:* Part-time and evening/weekend programs available. Postbaccalaureate distance learning degree programs offered (no on-campus study). Offers religious education (MA, Certificate, PMC). *Application deadline:* Applications are processed

Felician College (continued)

on a rolling basis. *Application fee:* $40. *Application Contact:* Wendy Lin-Cook, Director of Adult and Graduate Admission, 201-559-6077, Fax: 201-559-6138, E-mail: adultandgraduate@felician.edu. *Director,* Dr. Dolores M. Henchy, 201-559-6053, Fax: 973-472-8936, E-mail: henchyd@inet.felician.edu.

FERRIS STATE UNIVERSITY, Big Rapids, MI 49307

General Information State-supported, coed, comprehensive institution. *Enrollment:* 12,575 graduate, professional, and undergraduate students; 739 full-time matriculated graduate/professional students (424 women), 427 part-time matriculated graduate/professional students (266 women). *Enrollment by degree level:* 648 first professional, 518 master's. *Graduate faculty:* 84 full-time (40 women), 127 part-time/adjunct (59 women). Tuition, state resident: part-time $355 per credit hour. Tuition, nonresident: part-time $687 per credit hour. *Graduate housing:* Rooms and/or apartments available on a first-come, first-served basis to single and married students. *Student services:* Campus employment opportunities, campus safety program, career counseling, child daycare facilities, disabled student services, free psychological counseling, international student services, low-cost health insurance, multicultural affairs office, teacher training. *Library facilities:* FLITE: Ferris Library for Information, Technology and Education. *Online resources:* library catalog, web page, access to other libraries' catalogs. *Collection:* 354,173 titles, 1,049 serial subscriptions. *Research affiliation:* Research Technology Institute (materials science, manufacturing sciences), Vistakon–Johnson & Johnson (optometry), Allergan-Hydron (optometry), Bausch & Lomb (optometry), Ciba Vision Care (optometry).

Computer facilities: Computer purchase and lease plans are available. 2,373 computers available on campus for general student use. A campuswide network can be accessed from student residence rooms and from off campus. Internet access and online class registration are available. *Web address:* http://www.ferris.edu/.

General Application Contact: Craig Westman, Interim Dean Enrollment Services/Director Admissions and Records, 231-591-2100, Fax: 231-591-3944, E-mail: admissions@ferris.edu.

GRADUATE UNITS

College of Allied Health Sciences Expenses: Contact institution. Offers allied health sciences (MS).

School of Nursing Average age 39. 22 applicants, 100% accepted, 22 enrolled. *Faculty:* 2 full-time (1 woman). Expenses: Contact institution. *Financial support:* In 2006–07, 3 students received support. Scholarships/grants available. In 2006, 2 degrees awarded. *Degree program information:* Part-time and evening/weekend programs available. Postbaccalaureate distance learning degree programs offered (minimal on-campus study). Offers nursing (MS); nursing administration (MS); nursing education (MS); nursing informatics (MS). *Application deadline:* For fall admission, 8/26 for domestic students; for winter admission, 12/16 for domestic students. Applications are processed on a rolling basis. *Application fee:* $30. Electronic applications accepted. *Director,* Dr. Julie A. Coon, 231-591-2267, Fax: 231-591-2325, E-mail: coonj@ferris.edu.

College of Business Students: 35 full-time (12 women), 60 part-time (24 women); includes 5 minority (3 African Americans, 1 American Indian/Alaska Native, 1 Asian American or Pacific Islander), 13 international. Average age 34. 90 applicants, 72% accepted, 29 enrolled. *Faculty:* 5 full-time (2 women), 2 part-time/adjunct (both women). Expenses: Contact institution. *Financial support:* In 2006–07, 40 research assistantships, 10 teaching assistantships were awarded; career-related internships or fieldwork, Federal Work-Study, and unspecified assistantships also available. Support available to part-time students. Financial award applicants required to submit FAFSA. In 2006, 40 degrees awarded. *Degree program information:* Part-time and evening/weekend programs available. Offers application development (MSISM); database administration (MSISM); e-business (MSISM); information systems (MBA); networking (MSISM); quality management (MBA); security (MSISM). *Application deadline:* For fall admission, 7/1 priority date for domestic students, 6/15 for international students; for winter admission, 11/1 priority date for domestic students, 10/15 for international students; for spring admission, 3/1 priority date for domestic students, 2/15 for international students. Applications are processed on a rolling basis. Electronic applications accepted. *Application Contact:* Shannon Yost, Department Secretary, 231-591-2168, Fax: 231-591-2973, E-mail: yosts@ferris.edu. *Department Chair,* Dr. Bill Boras, 231-591-2168, Fax: 231-591-2973, E-mail: cbgp@ferris.edu.

College of Education and Human Services Students: 49 full-time (33 women), 301 part-time (193 women); includes 48 minority (37 African Americans, 2 American Indian/Alaska Native, 2 Asian Americans or Pacific Islanders, 7 Hispanic Americans), 1 international. Average age 36. *Faculty:* 19 full-time (11 women), 27 part-time/adjunct (19 women). Expenses: Contact institution. *Financial support:* In 2006–07, 8 students received support, including research assistantships with full tuition reimbursements available (averaging $3,960 per year), 1 teaching assistantship with partial tuition reimbursement available (averaging $3,800 per year); career-related internships or fieldwork and tuition waivers (full and partial) also available. Support available to part-time students. In 2006, 113 degrees awarded. *Degree program information:* Part-time and evening/weekend programs available. Postbaccalaureate distance learning degree programs offered. Offers education and human services (M Ed, MS, MSCTE). *Application deadline:* For fall admission, 8/31 for domestic students; for winter admission, 12/10 for domestic students. Applications are processed on a rolling basis. *Application fee:* $30. *Dean,* Michelle Johnston, 231-591-3646, Fax: 231-592-3792, E-mail: michelle_johnston@ferris.edu.

School of Criminal Justice Students: 11 full-time (6 women), 47 part-time (29 women); includes 18 minority (15 African Americans, 1 American Indian/Alaska Native, 2 Hispanic Americans). Average age 34. 24 applicants, 96% accepted, 20 enrolled. *Faculty:* 5 full-time (1 woman). Expenses: Contact institution. *Financial support:* In 2006–07, 4 students received support, including research assistantships (averaging $3,960 per year); career-related internships or fieldwork also available. In 2006, 19 degrees awarded. *Degree program information:* Part-time programs available. Offers criminal justice administration (MS). *Application deadline:* For fall admission, 8/23 priority date for domestic students; for winter admission, 12/10 priority date for domestic students. Applications are processed on a rolling basis. *Application fee:* $30. Electronic applications accepted. *Application Contact:* Dr. Nancy L. Hogan, Assistant Professor, 231-591-2664, Fax: 231-591-3792, E-mail: nancy_hogan@ferris.edu. *Director,* Dr. Frank Crowe, 231-591-2840, Fax: 231-591-3792, E-mail: crowef@ferris.edu.

School of Education Students: 38 full-time (27 women), 254 part-time (164 women); includes 30 minority (22 African Americans, 1 American Indian/Alaska Native, 2 Asian Americans or Pacific Islanders, 5 Hispanic Americans), 1 international. Average age 37. 171 applicants, 99% accepted. *Faculty:* 13 full-time (9 women), 26 part-time/adjunct (19 women). Expenses: Contact institution. *Financial support:* Career-related internships or fieldwork and tuition waivers (full and partial) available. Support available to part-time students. Financial award applicants required to submit FAFSA. In 2006, 92 degrees awarded. *Degree program information:* Part-time and evening/weekend programs available. Postbaccalaureate distance learning degree programs offered (no on-campus study). Offers administration (MSCTE); curriculum and instruction (M Ed); education technology (MSCTE); instructor (MSCTE); post-secondary administration (MSCTE); training and development (MSCTE). *Application deadline:* For fall admission, 6/1 priority date for domestic students; for winter admission, 12/10 priority date for domestic students. Applications are processed on a rolling basis. *Application fee:* $30. *Application Contact:* Sigrid Robertson, Secretary, 231-591-3511, Fax: 231-591-2041, E-mail: robertss@ferris.edu. *Interim Director,* 231-591-5362, Fax: 231-591-2041.

College of Pharmacy Students: 495 full-time (278 women), 20 part-time (11 women); includes 60 minority (10 African Americans, 3 American Indian/Alaska Native, 44 Asian Americans or Pacific Islanders, 3 Hispanic Americans), 34 international. Average age 28. 734 applicants, 20% accepted. *Faculty:* 38 full-time (22 women), 6 part-time/adjunct (5 women). Expenses: Contact institution. *Financial support:* Institutionally sponsored loans and scholarships/grants available. Financial award applicants required to submit FAFSA. In 2006, 118 degrees awarded. Offers pharmacy (Pharm D). *Application deadline:* For fall admission, 1/31 for domestic students. *Application fee:* $0. *Application Contact:* Dr. Rodney A. Larson, Assistant Dean, 231-591-3780, Fax: 231-591-3829, E-mail: larsonr@ferris.edu. *Dean,* Dr. Ian Mathison, 231-591-2254, Fax: 231-591-3829, E-mail: mathisol@ferris.edu.

Kendall College of Art and Design Students: 27 full-time (15 women), 12 part-time (6 women); includes 2 minority (1 African American, 1 Asian American or Pacific Islander). Average age 33. 21 applicants, 71% accepted, 13 enrolled. Expenses: Contact institution. *Financial support:* In 2006–07, 30 students received support, including 5 fellowships (averaging $6,464 per year), 25 teaching assistantships (averaging $4,500 per year); scholarships/grants and unspecified assistantships also available. Financial award application deadline:3/1. In 2006, 18 degrees awarded. Offers art and design (MFA). *Application deadline:* For fall admission, 3/1 for domestic and international students; for winter admission, 11/1 for domestic and international students. Applications are processed on a rolling basis. *Application fee:* $30. *Application Contact:* Sandra Britton, Director of Enrollment Management, 616-451-2787, Fax: 616-836-9689, E-mail: brittons@ferris.edu. *President,* Dr. Oliver H. Evans, 616-451-2787.

Michigan College of Optometry Students: 133 full-time (86 women); includes 10 minority (3 African Americans, 7 Asian Americans or Pacific Islanders), 5 international. Average age 27. 255 applicants, 14% accepted. *Faculty:* 20 full-time (4 women), 92 part-time/adjunct (33 women). Expenses: Contact institution. *Financial support:* In 2006–07, 122 students received support. Career-related internships or fieldwork, Federal Work-Study, and scholarships/grants available. Financial award application deadline: 3/15; financial award applicants required to submit FAFSA. In 2006, 34 degrees awarded. Offers optometry (OD). *Application deadline:* For fall admission, 2/1 for domestic and international students. Applications are processed on a rolling basis. *Application fee:* $30. Electronic applications accepted. *Application Contact:* Dr. Nancy Peterson-Klein, Associate Dean, 231-591-3703, Fax: 231-591-2394, E-mail: peterson@ferris.edu. *Dean,* Dr. Kevin L. Alexander, 231-591-3706, Fax: 231-591-2394, E-mail: alexandk@ferris.edu.

FIELDING GRADUATE UNIVERSITY, Santa Barbara, CA 93105-3538

General Information Independent, coed, graduate-only institution. CGS member. *Enrollment by degree level:* 195 master's, 1,224 doctoral, 107 other advanced degrees. *Graduate faculty:* 80 full-time (38 women), 68 part-time/adjunct (29 women). *Tuition:* Full-time $18,630; part-time $395 per credit. Tuition and fees vary according to course load and program. *Graduate housing:* On-campus housing not available. *Student services:* Disabled student services, international student services. *Library facilities:* Fielding Graduate University Library Services. *Online resources:* web page. *Collection:* 1,765 titles, 9,751 serial subscriptions.

Computer facilities: A campuswide network can be accessed from off campus. Internet access and online class registration are available. *Web address:* http://www.fielding.edu/.

General Application Contact: Admission Office, 800-340-1099, E-mail: admission@fielding.edu.

GRADUATE UNITS

Graduate Programs Students: 1,419 full-time (1,001 women), 107 part-time (69 women); includes 392 minority (216 African Americans, 21 American Indian/Alaska Native, 62 Asian Americans or Pacific Islanders, 93 Hispanic Americans), 23 international. Average age 46. 524 applicants, 65% accepted, 245 enrolled. *Faculty:* 80 full-time (38 women), 68 part-time/adjunct (29 women). Expenses: Contact institution. *Financial support:* In 2006–07, 1,035 students received support, including 3 teaching assistantships (averaging $2,700 per year); career-related internships or fieldwork, institutionally sponsored loans, scholarships/grants, and tuition waivers (partial) also available. Financial award application deadline: 3/1; financial award applicants required to submit FAFSA. In 2006, 190 master's, 119 doctorates, 35 other advanced degrees awarded. *Degree program information:* Evening/weekend programs available. Postbaccalaureate distance learning degree programs offered (minimal on-campus study). *Application deadline:* For fall admission, 2/15 for domestic and international students; for spring admission, 8/15 for domestic and international students. *Application fee:* $75. Electronic applications accepted. *Application Contact:* Kathy Wells, Admission Assistant, 800-340-1099, Fax: 805-687-9793, E-mail: kwells@fielding.edu. *President,* Dr. Judith Kuipers, 805-898-2903, Fax: 805-687-4590, E-mail: jkuipers@fielding.edu.

School of Educational Leadership and Change Students: 383 full-time (276 women); includes 162 minority (105 African Americans, 13 American Indian/Alaska Native, 21 Asian Americans or Pacific Islanders, 23 Hispanic Americans). Average age 48. 104 applicants, 96% accepted, 70 enrolled. *Faculty:* 18 full-time (10 women), 30 part-time/adjunct (14 women). Expenses: Contact institution. *Financial support:* In 2006–07, 330 students received support. Institutionally sponsored loans, scholarships/grants, and tuition waivers (partial) available. Financial award application deadline: 3/1; financial award applicants required to submit FAFSA. In 2006, 39 master's, 29 doctorates awarded. Offers collaborative educational leadership (MA); educational leadership (Ed D). *Application deadline:* For fall admission, 7/1 priority date for domestic students; for spring admission, 12/31 priority date for domestic students. Applications are processed on a rolling basis. *Application fee:* $75. Electronic applications accepted. *Application Contact:* David Brule, Admission Counselor, 800-340-1099, Fax: 805-687-9793, E-mail: dbrule@fielding.edu. *Dean,* Dr. Judy Witt, 805-898-2940, E-mail: jwitt@fielding.edu.

School of Human and Organization Development Students: 526 full-time (353 women), 8 part-time (5 women); includes 119 minority (70 African Americans, 3 American Indian/Alaska Native, 22 Asian Americans or Pacific Islanders, 24 Hispanic Americans), 13 international. Average age 47. 148 applicants, 90% accepted, 97 enrolled. *Faculty:* 26 full-time (11 women), 21 part-time/adjunct (5 women). Expenses: Contact institution. *Financial support:* In 2006–07, 291 students received support, including 3 teaching assistantships (averaging $2,700 per year); career-related internships or fieldwork, institutionally sponsored loans, and scholarships/grants also available. Financial award application deadline: 3/1; financial award applicants required to submit FAFSA. In 2006, 90 master's, 55 doctorates, 3 other advanced degrees awarded. *Degree program information:* Evening/weekend programs available. Offers human and organizational systems (PhD); human development (PhD); integral studies (Certificate); organization management and development (MA). *Application deadline:* For fall admission, 3/1 for domestic and international students; for spring admission, 9/1 for domestic and international students. *Application fee:* $75. Electronic applications accepted. *Application Contact:* Carmen Kuchera, Admission Counselor, 800-340-1099, Fax: 805-687-9793, E-mail: ckuchera@fielding.edu. *Dean,* Dr. Charles McClintock, 805-898-2930, Fax: 805-687-4590, E-mail: cmcclintock@fielding.edu.

School of Psychology Students: 510 full-time (372 women), 99 part-time (64 women); includes 111 minority (41 African Americans, 5 American Indian/Alaska Native, 19 Asian Americans or Pacific Islanders, 46 Hispanic Americans), 10 international. Average age 45. 272 applicants, 40% accepted, 78 enrolled. *Faculty:* 36 full-time (17 women), 17 part-time/adjunct (10 women). Expenses: Contact institution. *Financial support:* In 2006–07, 414 students received support. Career-related internships or fieldwork and scholarships/grants available. Financial award application deadline: 3/1; financial award applicants required to submit FAFSA. In 2006, 35 doctorates, 32 other advanced degrees awarded. *Degree program information:* Evening/weekend programs available. Offers clinical psychology (PhD); clinical psychology respecialization (Post-Doctoral Certificate); media psychology (PhD); neuropsychology (Post-Doctoral Certificate). *Application deadline:* For fall admission, 2/22 for domestic students; for spring admission, 8/24 for domestic students. *Application fee:* $75. Electronic applications accepted. *Application Contact:* Addie Merrill, Admission Counselor, 800-340-1099, Fax: 805-687-9793, E-mail: amerrill@fielding.edu. *Dean,* Dr. Ronald Giannetti, 805-898-2909, E-mail: rongian@fielding.edu.

FISK UNIVERSITY, Nashville, TN 37208-3051

General Information Independent-religious, coed, comprehensive institution. *Graduate housing:* Rooms and/or apartments available on a first-come, first-served basis to single and married students. Housing application deadline: 4/6. *Research affiliation:* Oak Ridge Associated Universities (chemical physics).

GRADUATE UNITS

Graduate Programs *Degree program information:* Part-time programs available. Offers biology (MA); chemistry (MA); clinical psychology (MA); general sociology (MA); physics (MA); psychology (MA).

FITCHBURG STATE COLLEGE, Fitchburg, MA 01420-2697

General Information State-supported, coed, comprehensive institution. CGS member. *Enrollment:* 5,508 graduate, professional, and undergraduate students; 200 full-time matriculated graduate/professional students (144 women), 721 part-time matriculated graduate/professional students (544 women). *Enrollment by degree level:* 823 master's, 98 other advanced degrees. Tuition, state resident: part-time $150 per credit. Tuition, nonresident: part-time $150 per credit. *Required fees:* $90 per credit. *Graduate housing:* On-campus housing not available. *Student services:* Campus employment opportunities, campus safety program, career counseling, child daycare facilities, disabled student services, exercise/wellness program, free psychological counseling, international student services, low-cost health insurance, multicultural affairs office, teacher training, writing training. *Library facilities:* Hammond Library. *Online resources:* library catalog, web page, access to other libraries' catalogs. *Collection:* 242,418 titles, 2,208 serial subscriptions, 1,845 audiovisual materials.

Computer facilities: 135 computers available on campus for general student use. A campuswide network can be accessed from student residence rooms and from off campus. Internet access and online class registration are available. *Web address:* http://www.fsc.edu/.

General Application Contact: Director of Admissions, 978-665-3144, Fax: 978-665-4540, E-mail: admissions@fsc.edu.

GRADUATE UNITS

Division of Graduate and Continuing Education Students: 167 full-time (106 women), 686 part-time (527 women); includes 15 African Americans, 8 Asian Americans or Pacific Islanders, 13 Hispanic Americans, 47 international. Average age 35. 397 applicants, 96% accepted, 270 enrolled. Expenses: Contact institution. *Financial support:* In 2006–07, research assistantships with partial tuition reimbursements (averaging $5,500 per year); Federal Work-Study, scholarships/grants, and unspecified assistantships also available. Support available to part-time students. Financial award application deadline: 3/1; financial award applicants required to submit FAFSA. In 2006, 484 master's, 53 other advanced degrees awarded. *Degree program information:* Part-time and evening/weekend programs available. Offers accounting (MBA); applied communications (MS, Certificate); arts education (M Ed); biology and teaching biology (MA, MAT); computer science (MS); criminal justice (MS); early childhood education (M Ed); educational technology (Certificate); elementary education (M Ed); elementary school guidance counseling (MS); English and teaching English (secondary level) (MA, MAT); fine arts director (Certificate); forensic nursing (MS, Certificate); general studies education (M Ed); guided studies (M Ed); higher education administration (CAGS); history and teaching history (secondary level) (MA, MAT); human resource management (MBA); interdisciplinary studies (CAGS); library media (MS); management (MBA); marriage and family therapy (Certificate); media technology (MS); mental health counseling (MS); middle school education (M Ed); non-licensure (M Ed, CAGS); occupational education (M Ed); professional mentoring for teachers (Certificate); reading specialist (M Ed); school principal (M Ed, CAGS); science education (M Ed); secondary education (M Ed); secondary school guidance counseling (MS); supervisor director (M Ed, CAGS); teaching students with moderate disabilities (M Ed); teaching students with severe disabilities (M Ed); technical and professional writing (MS); technology education (M Ed); technology leader (M Ed, CAGS). *Application deadline:* Applications are processed on a rolling basis. *Application fee:* $25 ($50 for international students). *Application Contact:* Director of Admissions, 978-665-3144, Fax: 978-665-4540, E-mail: admissions@fsc.edu. *Dean, Graduate and Continuing Education,* Catherine Canney, 978-665-3182, Fax: 978-665-3658, E-mail: gce@fsc.edu.

FIVE BRANCHES INSTITUTE: COLLEGE OF TRADITIONAL CHINESE MEDICINE, Santa Cruz, CA 95062

General Information Independent, coed, graduate-only institution. *Graduate housing:* On-campus housing not available.

GRADUATE UNITS

Program in Traditional Chinese Medicine Offers traditional Chinese medicine (MTCM). Electronic applications accepted.

FIVE TOWNS COLLEGE, Dix Hills, NY 11746-6055

General Information Independent, coed, comprehensive institution. *Enrollment:* 1,254 graduate, professional, and undergraduate students; 25 full-time matriculated graduate/professional students (19 women), 48 part-time matriculated graduate/professional students (30 women). *Enrollment by degree level:* 58 master's, 15 doctoral. *Graduate faculty:* 3 full-time (all women), 12 part-time/adjunct (2 women). *Graduate housing:* On-campus housing not available. *Student services:* Campus employment opportunities, campus safety program, career counseling, international student services, low-cost health insurance, teacher training, writing training. *Library facilities:* Five Towns College Library. *Online resources:* library catalog, access to other libraries' catalogs. *Collection:* 40,000 titles, 565 serial subscriptions.

Computer facilities: Computer purchase and lease plans are available. 110 computers available on campus for general student use. A campuswide network can be accessed. Internet access is available. *Web address:* http://www.fivetowns.edu/.

General Application Contact: Jerry Cohen, Dean of Enrollment, 631-424-7000, Fax: 631-656-2172, E-mail: admissions@ftc.edu.

GRADUATE UNITS

Department of Music Students: 25 full-time (19 women), 48 part-time (30 women); includes 10 minority (4 African Americans, 4 Asian Americans or Pacific Islanders, 2 Hispanic Americans). Average age 35. 82 applicants, 100% accepted. *Faculty:* 13 full-time (all women), 12 part-time/adjunct (2 women). Expenses: Contact institution. *Financial support:* Fellowships with tuition reimbursements, tuition waivers (partial) available. Financial award applicants required to submit FAFSA. In 2006, 20 degrees awarded. *Degree program information:* Part-time programs available. Offers jazz/commercial music (MM); music (DMA); music education (MM). *Application deadline:* Applications are processed on a rolling basis. *Application fee:* $50. *Application Contact:* Jerry Cohen, Dean of Enrollment, 631-656-2121, Fax: 631-656-2172, E-mail: admissions@ftc.edu. *Dean of Graduate Studies,* Dr. Jill Miller-Thorn, 631-656-2100, Fax: 631-656-2172, E-mail: jmillerthorn@ftc.edu.

Program in Childhood Education Students: 2 full-time (both women), 5 part-time (4 women); includes 1 minority (African American) Average age 38. 34 applicants, 82% accepted. *Faculty:* 2 full-time (both women), 5 part-time/adjunct (4 women). Expenses: Contact institution. In 2006, 4 degrees awarded. *Degree program information:* Part-time and evening/weekend programs available. Offers childhood education (MS Ed). *Application fee:* $50. *Director of Childhood Education,* Patricia Schmidt, 631-424-7020, Fax: 631-656-2172.

FLORIDA AGRICULTURAL AND MECHANICAL UNIVERSITY, Tallahassee, FL 32307-3200

General Information State-supported, coed, university. CGS member. *Graduate housing:* Rooms and/or apartments available on a first-come, first-served basis to single and married students. Housing application deadline: 6/1. *Research affiliation:* The Boeing Company (aerospace science), Minority Health Professions Foundation (health science), Pfizer, Inc.

GRADUATE UNITS

College of Law Offers law (JD).

Division of Graduate Studies, Research, and Continuing Education *Degree program information:* Part-time and evening/weekend programs available.

College of Arts and Sciences *Degree program information:* Part-time programs available. Offers African American history (MASS); arts and sciences (MASS, MS, MSW, PhD); biology (MS); chemistry (MS); community psychology (MS); criminal justice (MASS); economics (MASS); history (MASS); history and political sciences (MASS, MSW); physics (MS, PhD); political science (MASS); public administration (MASS); public management (MASS); school psychology (MS); social work (MASS); sociology (MASS); software engineering (MS).

College of Education *Degree program information:* Part-time and evening/weekend programs available. Offers administration and supervision (M Ed, MS Ed, PhD); adult education (M Ed, MS Ed); biology (M Ed); business education (MBE); chemistry (MS Ed); early childhood and elementary education (M Ed, MS Ed); education (M Ed, MBE, MS Ed, PhD); educational leadership (PhD); English (MS Ed); guidance and counseling (M Ed, MS Ed); health, physical education, and recreation (M Ed, MS Ed); history (MS Ed); industrial education (M Ed, MS Ed); math (MS Ed); physics (MS Ed).

College of Engineering Science, Technology, and Agriculture Offers agribusiness (MS); animal science (MS); engineering science, technology, and agriculture (MS); engineering technology (MS); entomology (MS); food science (MS); international programs (MS); plant science (MS).

College of Pharmacy and Pharmaceutical Sciences Offers environmental toxicology (PhD); medicinal chemistry (MS, PhD); pharmaceutics (MS, PhD); pharmacology/toxicology (MS, PhD); pharmacy administration (MS); pharmacy and pharmaceutical sciences (Pharm D, MPH, MS, Ex Doc, PhD); public health (MPH).

FAMU-FSU College of Engineering Offers biomedical engineering (MS, PhD); chemical engineering (MS, PhD); civil engineering (MS, PhD); electrical engineering (MS, PhD); engineering (MS, PhD); environmental engineering (MS, PhD); industrial engineering (MS, PhD); mechanical engineering (MS, PhD). College administered jointly by Florida State University.

School of Allied Health Sciences Offers health administration (MS); physical therapy (MPT).

School of Architecture *Degree program information:* Part-time programs available. Offers architectural studies (MS Arch); architecture (professional) (M Arch); landscape architecture (MLA).

School of Business and Industry Offers accounting (MBA); finance (MBA); management information systems (MBA); marketing (MBA).

School of Journalism Media and Graphic Arts Offers journalism (MS).

School of Nursing Offers nursing (MS).

Environmental Sciences Institute Students: 24 full-time (19 women), 10 part-time (8 women); includes 30 minority (26 African Americans, 2 Asian Americans or Pacific Islanders, 2 Hispanic Americans), 2 international. Average age 22. 14 applicants, 36% accepted, 4 enrolled. *Faculty:* 8 full-time (1 woman), 1 (woman) part-time/adjunct. Expenses: Contact institution. *Financial support:* In 2006–07, 10 fellowships with full and partial tuition reimbursements, 16 research assistantships were awarded; career-related internships or fieldwork, institutionally sponsored loans, scholarships/grants, and unspecified assistantships also available. Financial award applicants required to submit FAFSA. In 2006, 3 master's, 2 doctorates awarded. Offers environmental sciences (MS, PhD). *Application deadline:* For fall admission, 4/1 priority date for domestic and international students; for spring admission, 11/1 priority date for domestic and international students. *Application fee:* $20. *Application Contact:* Ora S. Mukes, Coordinator Academic Support Services, 850-561-2641, Fax: 805-412-5504, E-mail: ora.mukes@famu.org. *Director,* Dr. Henry Neal Williams, 850-599-3550, Fax: 850-599-8183, E-mail: henryneal.williams@famu.ed.

FLORIDA ATLANTIC UNIVERSITY, Boca Raton, FL 33431-0991

General Information State-supported, coed, university. CGS member. *Enrollment:* 25,385 graduate, professional, and undergraduate students; 1,500 full-time matriculated graduate/professional students (909 women), 1,976 part-time matriculated graduate/professional students (1,291 women). *Enrollment by degree level:* 2,782 master's, 658 doctoral, 36 other advanced degrees. *Graduate faculty:* 1,023 full-time (452 women), 548 part-time/adjunct (257 women). *Tuition, area resident:* Full-time $4,394. Tuition, nonresident: full-time $16,441. *Graduate housing:* Room and/or apartments available on a first-come, first-served basis to single students; on-campus housing not available to married students. Typical cost: $8,280 (including board). Housing application deadline: 5/1. *Student services:* Campus employment opportunities, campus safety program, career counseling, disabled student services, exercise/wellness program, free psychological counseling, international student services, low-cost health insurance, multicultural affairs office, teacher training. *Library facilities:* S. E. Wimberly Library plus 2 others. *Online resources:* library catalog, web page, access to other libraries' catalogs. *Collection:* 1.3 million titles, 12,811 serial subscriptions. *Research affiliation:* Company of Biologists, LTD, Shell Oil Co. (engineering), Children's Services Council (urban redevelopment), Motorola Corporation (engineering), Harbor Branch Oceanographic Institution (marine resources characterization), Smithsonian Marine Station (marine resources characterization).

Computer facilities: 822 computers available on campus for general student use. A campuswide network can be accessed from student residence rooms and from off campus. Internet access and online class registration are available. *Web address:* http://www.fau.edu/.

General Application Contact: Joann Arlington, Graduate Studies-Admissions, 561-297-3624, Fax: 561-297-2117, E-mail: arlingto@fau.edu.

GRADUATE UNITS

Charles E. Schmidt College of Science Students: 296 full-time (167 women), 106 part-time (61 women); includes 68 minority (14 African Americans, 1 American Indian/Alaska Native, 14 Asian Americans or Pacific Islanders, 39 Hispanic Americans), 100 international. Average age 31. 297 applicants, 34% accepted, 66 enrolled. *Faculty:* 110 full-time (15 women), 3 part-time/adjunct (0 women). Expenses: Contact institution. *Financial support:* In 2006–07, 20 research assistantships with partial tuition reimbursements (averaging $15,000 per year), 149 teaching assistantships with partial tuition reimbursements (averaging $15,000 per year) were awarded; fellowships with partial tuition reimbursements, career-related internships or fieldwork, Federal Work-Study, institutionally sponsored loans, scholarships/grants, tuition waivers (partial), and unspecified assistantships also available. In 2006, 95 master's, 21 doctorates awarded. *Degree program information:* Part-time programs available. Offers applied mathematics and statistics (MS); biological sciences (MS, MST); chemistry and biochemistry (MS, MST, PhD); environmental sciences (MS); geography (MA, MAT); geology (MS); mathematics (MS, MST, PhD); physics (MS, MST, PhD); psychology (MA, PhD); science (MA, MAT, MS, MST, PhD). *Application deadline:* For fall admission, 6/1 for domestic students, 2/15 for international students; for spring admission, 11/1 for domestic students, 8/15 for international students. Applications are processed on a rolling basis. *Application fee:* $30. Electronic applications accepted. *Application Contact:* Dr. Leslie Terry, Associate Dean of Student Services, 561-297-3700, Fax: 561-297-3388. *Dean,* Dr. Gary Perry, 561-297-3035, Fax: 561-297-3792.

Center for Complex Systems and Brain Sciences Students: 20 full-time (7 women), 3 part-time; includes 2 minority (1 American Indian/Alaska Native, 1 Hispanic American), 9 international. Average age 31. 19 applicants, 21% accepted, 4 enrolled. *Faculty:* 15 full-time (1 woman). Expenses: Contact institution. *Financial support:* In 2006–07, 2 fellowships with full tuition reimbursements (averaging $16,060 per year), 5 research assistantships with partial tuition reimbursements (averaging $16,060 per year), 9 teaching assistantships with partial tuition reimbursements (averaging $16,060 per year) were awarded; Federal Work-Study, traineeships, and unspecified assistantships also available. In 2006, 5 degrees awarded. Offers complex systems and brain sciences (PhD). *Application deadline:* For fall admission, 2/15 priority date for domestic and international students; for spring admission, 11/1 for domestic students, 8/15 for international students. *Application fee:* $30. *Application Contact:* Dr. Betty Tuller, Associate Director, 561-297-2227, Fax: 561-297-3634, E-mail: tuller@ccs.fau.edu. *Director,* Dr. J. A. Scott Kelso, 561-297-2230, Fax: 561-297-3634, E-mail: kelso@ccs.fau.edu.

College of Architecture, Urban and Public Affairs Students: 107 full-time (81 women), 186 part-time (126 women); includes 81 minority (41 African Americans, 5 Asian Americans or Pacific Islanders, 35 Hispanic Americans), 5 international. Average age 34. 253 applicants, 51% accepted, 82 enrolled. *Faculty:* 35 full-time (15 women), 14 part-time/adjunct (4 women). Expenses: Contact institution. *Financial support:* In 2006–07, 27 students received support,

Florida Atlantic University (continued)

including 3 fellowships with partial tuition reimbursements available (averaging $11,250 per year), 4 research assistantships with partial tuition reimbursements available (averaging $16,000 per year), 12 teaching assistantships with partial tuition reimbursements available (averaging $16,000 per year); career-related internships or fieldwork, Federal Work-Study, and institutionally sponsored loans also available. Support available to part-time students. Financial award application deadline: 4/1. In 2006, 92 master's, 3 doctorates awarded. *Degree program information:* Part-time and evening/weekend programs available. Offers architecture, urban and public affairs (MCJ, MNM, MPA, MSW, MURP, PhD); criminology and criminal justice (MCJ); urban and regional planning (MURP). *Application deadline:* For fall admission, 4/15 for domestic students, 2/15 for international students; for spring admission, 11/1 for domestic students, 8/15 for international students. Applications are processed on a rolling basis. *Application fee:* $30. *Application Contact:* Todd Hedrick, Academic Advisor, 954-762-5662, E-mail: thedrick@fau.edu. *Dean,* Dr. Rosalyn Carter, 954-762-5660, Fax: 954-762-5673, E-mail: rcarter@fau.edu.

School of Public Administration Students: 26 full-time (13 women), 63 part-time (34 women); includes 26 minority (16 African Americans, 1 American Indian/Alaska Native, 2 Asian Americans or Pacific Islanders, 7 Hispanic Americans), 4 international. Average age 35. 62 applicants, 50% accepted, 21 enrolled. *Faculty:* 12 full-time (5 women), 6 part-time/adjunct (2 women). Expenses: Contact institution. *Financial support:* In 2006–07, 15 students received support, including 3 fellowships with full tuition reimbursements available (averaging $16,000 per year), 1 research assistantship with partial tuition reimbursement available (averaging $3,750 per year), 11 teaching assistantships with partial tuition reimbursements available (averaging $12,000 per year); career-related internships or fieldwork, Federal Work-Study, institutionally sponsored loans, and tuition waivers (partial) also available. Support available to part-time students. Financial award application deadline: 4/1. In 2006, 20 master's, 3 doctorates awarded. *Degree program information:* Part-time and evening/weekend programs available. Offers nonprofit management (MNM); public administration (MNM, MPA, PhD). *Application deadline:* For fall admission, 4/1 priority date for domestic students; for spring admission, 11/1 for domestic students. Applications are processed on a rolling basis. *Application fee:* $30. *Application Contact:* Todd Hedrick, Academic Advisor, 954-762-5662, E-mail: thedrick@fau.edu. *Director,* Dr. Hugh T. Miller, 954-762-5650, Fax: 954-762-5693, E-mail: hmiller@fau.edu.

School of Social Work Students: 55 full-time (51 women), 72 part-time (63 women); includes 38 minority (15 African Americans, 1 Asian American or Pacific Islander, 22 Hispanic Americans), 1 international. Average age 34. 128 applicants, 52% accepted, 43 enrolled. *Faculty:* 15 full-time (8 women), 10 part-time/adjunct (7 women). Expenses: Contact institution. *Financial support:* In 2006–07, 2 research assistantships with tuition reimbursements (averaging $7,000 per year) were awarded; fellowships with tuition reimbursements, career-related internships or fieldwork, Federal Work-Study, institutionally sponsored loans, and tuition waivers (partial) also available. Financial award application deadline: 4/1. In 2006, 50 degrees awarded. *Degree program information:* Part-time and evening/weekend programs available. Offers social work (MSW). *Application deadline:* For fall admission, 6/1 priority date for domestic students; for spring admission, 10/20 priority date for domestic students. Applications are processed on a rolling basis. *Application fee:* $30. *Application Contact:* Dr. Elwood Hamlin, Professor, 501-297-3234, E-mail: ehamlin@fau.edu. *Director,* Dr. Michele Hawkins, 561-297-3234, Fax: 561-297-2866, E-mail: mhawkins@fau.edu.

College of Biomedical Science Students: 44 full-time (28 women), 12 part-time (6 women); includes 28 minority (10 African Americans, 5 Asian Americans or Pacific Islanders, 13 Hispanic Americans), 11 international. Average age 27. 51 applicants, 65% accepted, 27 enrolled. *Faculty:* 30 full-time (9 women). Expenses: Contact institution. *Financial support:* Research assistantships available. In 2006, 19 degrees awarded. Offers biomedical science (MS, PhD). *Application deadline:* For fall admission, 6/1 for domestic students, 2/15 for international students; for spring admission, 11/1 for domestic students, 8/15 for international students. *Application fee:* $30. *Application Contact:* Kathy Jurewicz, Program Assistant, 561-297-2216, E-mail: kjurewicz@fau.edu. *Dean,* Dr. Michael Friedland, 561-297-2219.

College of Business Students: 287 full-time (128 women), 608 part-time (320 women); includes 236 minority (78 African Americans, 2 American Indian/Alaska Native, 54 Asian Americans or Pacific Islanders, 102 Hispanic Americans), 71 international. Average age 32. 593 applicants, 56% accepted, 244 enrolled. *Faculty:* 120 full-time (37 women), 31 part-time/adjunct (7 women). Expenses: Contact institution. *Financial support:* In 2006–07, 46 students received support, including 9 research assistantships with partial tuition reimbursements available (averaging $18,000 per year), 30 teaching assistantships with full tuition reimbursements available (averaging $18,000 per year); fellowships with partial tuition reimbursements available, career-related internships or fieldwork, Federal Work-Study, institutionally sponsored loans, tuition waivers (full and partial), and unspecified assistantships also available. Support available to part-time students. Financial award application deadline: 3/1. In 2006, 290 master's awarded. *Degree program information:* Part-time and evening/weekend programs available. Postbaccalaureate distance learning degree programs offered (minimal on-campus study). Offers business (Exec MBA, M Ac, M Tax, MBA, MHA, MS, MST); business administration (Exec MBA, MBA); economics (MS, MST); finance (MS); health administration (MHA). *Application deadline:* For fall admission, 7/11 priority date for domestic students, 2/15 priority date for international students; for winter admission, 11/1 priority date for domestic students, 8/15 priority date for international students; for spring admission, 4/1 priority date for domestic students, 1/15 priority date for international students. Applications are processed on a rolling basis. *Application fee:* $30. *Application Contact:* Fredrick G. Taylor, Graduate Adviser, 561-297-2768, Fax: 561-297-1315, E-mail: mba@fau.edu. *Dean,* Dr. Dennis Coates, 561-297-3630, Fax: 561-297-3686, E-mail: coates@fau.edu.

School of Accounting Students: 54 full-time (29 women), 204 part-time (111 women); includes 69 minority (24 African Americans, 13 Asian Americans or Pacific Islanders, 32 Hispanic Americans), 9 international. Average age 33. 132 applicants, 59% accepted, 56 enrolled. *Faculty:* 19 full-time (6 women). Expenses: Contact institution. *Financial support:* In 2006–07, 1 student received support, including 1 research assistantship with partial tuition reimbursement available (averaging $6,000 per year), teaching assistantships (averaging $12,000 per year); fellowships, career-related internships or fieldwork, Federal Work-Study, institutionally sponsored loans, scholarships/grants, and tuition waivers (partial) also available. Support available to part-time students. Financial award application deadline: 3/1. In 2006, 78 degrees awarded. *Degree program information:* Part-time and evening/weekend programs available. Postbaccalaureate distance learning degree programs offered (minimal on-campus study). Offers accounting (M Ac, M Tax); taxation (M Tax). *Application deadline:* For fall admission, 2/1 priority date for domestic students, 2/15 priority date for international students; for winter admission, 11/1 priority date for domestic students, 8/15 priority date for international students; for spring admission, 4/1 priority date for domestic students, 1/15 priority date for international students. Applications are processed on a rolling basis. *Application fee:* $30. *Application Contact:* Fredrick G. Taylor, Graduate Adviser, 561-297-2768, Fax: 561-297-1315, E-mail: mba@fau.edu. *Director,* Dr. Carl Borgia, 561-297-3636, Fax: 561-297-7023, E-mail: borgiac@fau.edu.

College of Education Students: 279 full-time (224 women), 532 part-time (418 women); includes 220 minority (109 African Americans, 2 American Indian/Alaska Native, 18 Asian Americans or Pacific Islanders, 91 Hispanic Americans), 14 international. Average age 35. 504 applicants, 54% accepted, 194 enrolled. *Faculty:* 67 full-time (37 women), 36 part-time/adjunct (18 women). Expenses: Contact institution. *Financial support:* In 2006–07, 29 students received support, including 17 research assistantships with partial tuition reimbursements available (averaging $7,500 per year), 12 teaching assistantships with partial tuition reimbursements available (averaging $7,500 per year); fellowships with partial tuition reimbursements available, career-related internships or fieldwork, Federal Work-Study, and unspecified assistantships also available. In 2006, 264 master's, 22 doctorates, 20 other advanced degrees awarded. *Degree program information:* Part-time and evening/weekend programs available. Offers adult/community education (M Ed, PhD, Ed S); art teacher education (M Ed); counselor education (M Ed); curriculum and instruction (M Ed, Ed D, Ed S); education (M Ed, MS, MSF, Ed D, PhD, Ed S); educational leadership (M Ed, PhD, Ed S); educational psychology (MSF); educational research (MSF); educational technology (MSF); elementary education (M Ed); emotional handicaps (M Ed); exceptional student education (M Ed, Ed D); exercise science and health promotion (M Ed, MS); family counseling (Ed S); foundations of education (M Ed); foundations-educational research (M Ed); foundations-educational technology (M Ed); higher education management (M Ed, PhD); learning disabilities (M Ed); mental health counseling (M Ed, Ed S); mental retardation (M Ed); multicultural education (MSF); reading teacher education (M Ed); rehabilitation counseling (M Ed); school counseling (Ed S); special education (Ed D); speech-language pathology (MS); varying exceptionalities (M Ed). *Application deadline:* Applications are processed on a rolling basis. *Application fee:* $30. Electronic applications accepted. *Application Contact:* Dr. Eliah Watlington, Associate Dean, Office for Academic and Student Services, 561-297-3574, Fax: 261-297-2991, E-mail: ewatlinge@fau.edu. *Dean,* Dr. Gregory Aloia, 561-297-3564, E-mail: galoia@fau.edu.

College of Engineering Students: 151 full-time (38 women), 121 part-time (39 women); includes 70 minority (12 African Americans, 30 Asian Americans or Pacific Islanders, 28 Hispanic Americans), 105 international. Average age 31. 165 applicants, 52% accepted, 55 enrolled. *Faculty:* 70 full-time (4 women), 5 part-time/adjunct (0 women). Expenses: Contact institution. *Financial support:* In 2006–07, research assistantships with partial tuition reimbursements (averaging $15,000 per year), teaching assistantships with partial tuition reimbursements (averaging $15,000 per year) were awarded; fellowships, career-related internships or fieldwork, Federal Work-Study, and unspecified assistantships also available. Support available to part-time students. Financial award applicants required to submit FAFSA. In 2006, 86 master's, 9 doctorates awarded. *Degree program information:* Part-time and evening/weekend programs available. Postbaccalaureate distance learning degree programs offered (minimal on-campus study). Offers civil engineering (MS); computer engineering (MS, PhD); computer science (MS, PhD); electrical engineering (MS, PhD); engineering (MS, PhD); mechanical engineering (MS, PhD); ocean engineering (MS, PhD). *Application deadline:* Applications are processed on a rolling basis. *Application fee:* $30. *Application Contact:* Sharon Schlossberg, Information Contact, 561-297-2680, E-mail: sschloss@fau.edu. *Dean,* Dr. Karl Stevens, 561-297-3400, Fax: 561-297-2659, E-mail: stevens@fau.edu.

College of Nursing Students: 76 full-time (72 women), 213 part-time (197 women); includes 107 minority (63 African Americans, 15 Asian Americans or Pacific Islanders, 29 Hispanic Americans), 4 international. Average age 40. 134 applicants, 60% accepted, 72 enrolled. *Faculty:* 20 full-time (19 women), 13 part-time/adjunct (10 women). Expenses: Contact institution. *Financial support:* In 2006–07, 62 students received support, including 11 research assistantships with partial tuition reimbursements available, 6 teaching assistantships with partial tuition reimbursements available; career-related internships or fieldwork, Federal Work-Study, institutionally sponsored loans, scholarships/grants, and traineeships also available. Support available to part-time students. In 2006, 81 master's, 4 doctorates awarded. *Degree program information:* Part-time programs available. Offers nursing (MS, DNS, Post Master's Certificate). *Application deadline:* For fall admission, 6/2 for domestic students; for spring admission, 10/20 for domestic students. Applications are processed on a rolling basis. *Application fee:* $30. *Application Contact:* Dr. Lynne M. Dunphy, Graduate Coordinator, 561-297-3261, Fax: 561-297-0088, E-mail: ldunphy@fau.edu. *Dean,* Dr. Anne Boykin, 561-297-3206, Fax: 561-297-3687, E-mail: boykina@acc.fau.edu.

Dorothy F. Schmidt College of Arts and Letters Students: 260 full-time (171 women), 198 part-time (124 women); includes 104 minority (38 African Americans, 2 American Indian/Alaska Native, 10 Asian Americans or Pacific Islanders, 54 Hispanic Americans), 32 international. Average age 35. 316 applicants, 62% accepted, 152 enrolled. *Faculty:* 110 full-time (35 women). Expenses: Contact institution. *Financial support:* In 2006–07, 5 fellowships with partial tuition reimbursements (averaging $12,000 per year), 100 teaching assistantships (averaging $7,500 per year) were awarded; research assistantships, career-related internships or fieldwork, Federal Work-Study, institutionally sponsored loans, and tuition waivers (partial) also available. Support available to part-time students. In 2006, 114 master's, 2 doctorates awarded. *Degree program information:* Part-time programs available. Offers American literature (MA); anthropology (MA, MAT); art education (MAT); arts and letters (MA, MAT, MFA, MLBLST, PhD, Certificate); ceramics (MFA); communication (MA); comparative literature (MA); comparative studies (PhD); creative writing (MFA); English literature (MA); fantasy and science fiction (MA); French (MA); German (MA); history (MA); liberal studies (MLBLST); multicultural literature (MA); music (MA); painting (MFA); political science (MA, MAT); sociology (MA, MAT); Spanish (MA); teaching French (MAT); teaching German (MAT); teaching Spanish (MAT); theatre (MFA). *Application deadline:* For fall admission, 6/1 priority date for domestic students. Applications are processed on a rolling basis. *Application fee:* $30. Electronic applications accepted. *Application Contact:* Dr. Ken Keaton, Associate Dean, 561-297-3802, Fax: 561-297-2744, E-mail: keaton@fau.edu. *Interim Dean,* Dr. Sandra Norman, 561-297-3803.

Women's Studies Center Students: 5 full-time (all women), 3 part-time (all women), 1 international. Average age 29. 8 applicants, 63% accepted, 3 enrolled. *Faculty:* 4 full-time (all women), 1 (woman) part-time/adjunct. Expenses: Contact institution. *Financial support:* In 2006–07, fellowships with full and partial tuition reimbursements (averaging $750 per year), teaching assistantships with full and partial tuition reimbursements (averaging $6,012 per year) were awarded; career-related internships or fieldwork, Federal Work-Study, institutionally sponsored loans, scholarships/grants, and unspecified assistantships also available. Support available to part-time students. In 2006, 2 degrees awarded. Offers women's studies (MA, Certificate). *Application deadline:* Applications are processed on a rolling basis. *Application fee:* $30. *Application Contact:* Dr. Jane Caputi, Professor, 954-297-3865, Fax: 561-297-2127, E-mail: jcaputi@fau.edu. *Director,* Dr. Marsha Rose, 561-297-3865, Fax: 561-297-2127.

FLORIDA ATLANTIC UNIVERSITY, JUPITER CAMPUS, Jupiter, FL 33458

General Information State-supported, coed, comprehensive institution.

GRADUATE UNITS

College of Architecture, Urban and Public Affairs Offers architecture, urban and public affairs (MPA, MSW).

College of Business Offers business (MBA).

College of Education Offers exceptional student education (M Ed); reading (M Ed).

FLORIDA COASTAL SCHOOL OF LAW, Jacksonville, FL 32256

General Information Proprietary, coed, graduate-only institution. *Enrollment by degree level:* 1,040 first professional. *Graduate faculty:* 58 full-time (36 women), 34 part-time/adjunct (8 women). *Tuition:* Full-time $25,388; part-time $10,355 per term. *Required fees:* $630 per term. *Student services:* Campus employment opportunities, campus safety program, career counseling, disabled student services, grant writing training, international student services, low-cost health insurance, multicultural affairs office, teacher training, writing training. *Library facilities:* Law Library. *Online resources:* library catalog, web page, access to other libraries' catalogs. *Collection:* 220,381 titles, 2,844 serial subscriptions, 158 audiovisual materials.

Computer facilities: 76 computers available on campus for general student use. A campuswide network can be accessed from off campus. Internet access and online class registration, online grades are available. *Web address:* http://www.fcsl.edu/.

General Application Contact: Admissions Office, 904-680-7710, Fax: 904-680-7692, E-mail: admissions@fcsl.edu.

GRADUATE UNITS

Professional Program Students: 824 full-time (379 women), 216 part-time (108 women); includes 233 minority (95 African Americans, 15 American Indian/Alaska Native, 53 Asian Americans or Pacific Islanders, 70 Hispanic Americans), 7 international. Average age 26. 4,940 applicants, 48% accepted, 553 enrolled. *Faculty:* 58 full-time (36 women), 34 part-time/adjunct (8 women). Expenses: Contact institution. *Financial support:* In 2006–07, 513 students received support, including 14 research assistantships (averaging $2,000 per year), 12 teaching assistantships (averaging $2,000 per year); scholarships/grants and tuition waivers (full and partial) also available. Support available to part-time students. Financial award applicants required to submit FAFSA. In 2006, 219 degrees awarded. *Degree program information:* Part-time programs available. Offers law (JD). *Application deadline:* Applications are processed on a rolling basis. *Application fee:* $50. Electronic applications accepted. *Application Contact:* 904-680-7710, Fax: 904-680-7776, E-mail: admissions@fcsl.edu. *Dean,* Peter Goplerud, E-mail: pgoplerud@fcsl.edu.

FLORIDA COLLEGE OF INTEGRATIVE MEDICINE, Orlando, FL 32809

General Information Proprietary, coed, graduate-only institution. *Enrollment by degree level:* 110 master's. *Graduate faculty:* 3 full-time (2 women), 7 part-time/adjunct (4 women). *Tuition:* Full-time $11,500. *Required fees:* $500. *Graduate housing:* On-campus housing not available. *Student services:* Career counseling, exercise/wellness program, international student services. *Library facilities:* Florida College of Integrative Medicine Library. *Online resources:* web page. *Collection:* 2,000 titles, 48 serial subscriptions, 200 audiovisual materials.

Computer facilities: 4 computers available on campus for general student use. A campuswide network can be accessed. Internet access is available. *Web address:* http://www.fcim.edu/.

General Application Contact: Jon Diament, Admissions Officer, 407-888-8689 Ext. 15, Fax: 407-888-8211, E-mail: jdiament@fcim.edu.

GRADUATE UNITS

Graduate Program Students: 110 full-time (80 women); includes 29 minority (3 African Americans, 16 Asian Americans or Pacific Islanders, 10 Hispanic Americans), 3 international. Average age 32. 35 applicants, 77% accepted. *Faculty:* 3 full-time (2 women), 7 part-time/adjunct (4 women). Expenses: Contact institution. *Financial support:* Application deadline: 6/15; In 2006, 16 degrees awarded. *Degree program information:* Evening/weekend programs available. Offers Oriental medicine (MSOM). *Application deadline:* For fall admission, 6/15 priority date for domestic students; for spring admission, 12/15 priority date for domestic students. Applications are processed on a rolling basis. *Application fee:* $50. Electronic applications accepted. *Application Contact:* Jon Diament, Admissions Officer, 407-888-8689 Ext. 15, Fax: 407-888-8211, E-mail: jdiament@fcim.edu. *Academic Dean,* Dr. Lin Chai, 407-888-8689, Fax: 407-888-8211, E-mail: lchai@tcim.edu.

FLORIDA GULF COAST UNIVERSITY, Fort Myers, FL 33965-6565

General Information State-supported, coed, comprehensive institution. *Enrollment:* 8,292 graduate, professional, and undergraduate students; 247 full-time matriculated graduate/professional students (184 women), 550 part-time matriculated graduate/professional students (378 women). *Enrollment by degree level:* 797 master's. *Graduate faculty:* 278 full-time (136 women), 194 part-time/adjunct (87 women). Tuition, state resident: full-time $4,326. Tuition, nonresident: full-time $18,523. *Required fees:* $1,211. One-time fee: $5 full-time. *Graduate housing:* Room and/or apartments available on a first-come, first-served basis to single students; on-campus housing not available to married students. Typical cost: $4,710 per year ($7,740 including board). Housing application deadline: 2/15. *Student services:* Campus employment opportunities, campus safety program, career counseling, child daycare facilities, disabled student services, exercise/wellness program, free psychological counseling, international student services, low-cost health insurance, multicultural affairs office, teacher training. *Library facilities:* Library Services. *Online resources:* library catalog, web page, access to other libraries' catalogs. *Collection:* 312,132 titles, 7,119 serial subscriptions, 10,078 audiovisual materials.

Computer facilities: 323 computers available on campus for general student use. A campuswide network can be accessed from student residence rooms and from off campus. Internet access and online class registration, online admissions and advising are available. *Web address:* http://www.fgcu.edu/.

General Application Contact: Michael Sayarese, Director of Graduate Studies, 239-590-7988, Fax: 239-590-7843, E-mail: graduate@fgcu.edu.

GRADUATE UNITS

College of Arts and Sciences Students: 37 full-time (25 women), 20 part-time (13 women); includes 4 minority (1 African American, 3 Hispanic Americans). Average age 33. 45 applicants, 76% accepted, 26 enrolled. *Faculty:* 124 full-time (51 women), 102 part-time/adjunct (40 women). Expenses: Contact institution. In 2006, 2 degrees awarded. *Degree program information:* Part-time programs available. Offers arts and sciences (MA, MS); English (MA); environmental science (MS). *Application deadline:* For fall admission, 7/1 priority date for domestic students; for spring admission, 11/15 for domestic students. Applications are processed on a rolling basis. *Application fee:* $30. Electronic applications accepted. *Application Contact:* Mikele Meether, Adviser, 239-590-7204, Fax: 239-590-7200, E-mail: mmeether@fgcu.edu. *Dean,* Dr. Donna Price Henry, 239-590-7231, Fax: 239-590-7200, E-mail: dhenry@fgcu.edu.

College of Business Students: 120 full-time (58 women), 61 part-time (36 women); includes 31 minority (7 African Americans, 4 Asian Americans or Pacific Islanders, 20 Hispanic Americans), 9 international. Average age 31. 108 applicants, 83% accepted, 67 enrolled. *Faculty:* 51 full-time (14 women), 18 part-time/adjunct (0 women). Expenses: Contact institution. In 2006, 55 degrees awarded. *Degree program information:* Part-time and evening/weekend programs available. Offers accounting and taxation (MS); business (MBA, MS); business administration (MBA); computer and information systems (MS). *Application deadline:* For fall admission, 7/1 priority date for domestic students; for spring admission, 11/1 for domestic students. Applications are processed on a rolling basis. *Application fee:* $30. Electronic applications accepted. *Application Contact:* Carol Burnette, Associate Dean, 239-590-7350, Fax: 239-590-7330, E-mail: burnette@fgcu.edu. *Dean,* Dr. Richard Pegnetter, 239-590-7310, Fax: 239-590-7330, E-mail: epegnett@fgcu.edu.

College of Education Students: 229 full-time (179 women), 66 part-time (50 women); includes 31 minority (5 African Americans, 1 American Indian/Alaska Native, 2 Asian Americans or Pacific Islanders, 23 Hispanic Americans), 2 international. Average age 36. 143 applicants, 85% accepted, 95 enrolled. *Faculty:* 31 full-time (21 women), 30 part-time/adjunct (24 women). Expenses: Contact institution. In 2006, 89 degrees awarded. *Degree program information:* Part-time and evening/weekend programs available. Postbaccalaureate distance learning degree programs offered (minimal on-campus study). Offers behavior disorders (MA); biology (MAT); counselor education (M Ed, MA); education (M Ed, MA, MAT); educational leadership (M Ed); educational technology (M Ed, MA); elementary education (M Ed, MA); English (MAT); mathematics (MAT); mental retardation (MA); reading education (M Ed); social sciences (MAT); specific learning disabilities (MA); varying exceptionalities (MA). *Application deadline:* For fall admission, 7/1 priority date for domestic students; for spring admission, 10/15 for domestic students. Applications are processed on a rolling basis. *Application fee:* $30. Electronic applications accepted. *Application Contact:* Edward Beckett, Adviser/Counselor, 239-590-7759, Fax: 239-590-7801, E-mail: ebeckett@fgcu.edu. *Dean,* Dr. Marci Greene, 239-590-7781, Fax: 239-590-7801, E-mail: mgreene@fgcu.edu.

College of Health Professions Students: 114 full-time (82 women), 44 part-time (39 women); includes 24 minority (5 African Americans, 2 American Indian/Alaska Native, 4 Asian Americans or Pacific Islanders, 13 Hispanic Americans). Average age 34. 87 applicants, 79% accepted, 46 enrolled. *Faculty:* 42 full-time (35 women), 21 part-time/adjunct (14 women). Expenses: Contact institution. *Financial support:* Career-related internships or fieldwork, Federal Work-Study, and institutionally sponsored loans available. In 2006, 56 degrees awarded. *Degree program information:* Part-time and evening/weekend programs available. Postbaccalaureate distance learning degree programs offered (minimal on-campus study). Offers geriatric recreational therapy (MS); health professions (MS, MSN); health sciences (MS); occupational therapy (MS); physical therapy (MS). *Application deadline:* Applications are processed on a rolling basis. *Application fee:* $30. Electronic applications accepted. *Application Contact:* Lynn O'Hare, Administrative Assistant, 239-590-7451, Fax: 239-590-7474, E-mail: lohare@fgcu.edu. *Dean,* Dr. Denise Heinemann, 239-590-7511, Fax: 239-590-7474.

School of Nursing Students: 50 full-time (35 women), 10 part-time (all women); includes 9 minority (3 African Americans, 2 American Indian/Alaska Native, 3 Asian Americans or Pacific Islanders, 1 Hispanic American). Average age 36. 16 applicants, 88% accepted, 12 enrolled. *Faculty:* 42 full-time (35 women), 21 part-time/adjunct (14 women). Expenses: Contact institution. In 2006, 41 degrees awarded. *Degree program information:* Part-time programs available. Offers nursing (MSN). *Application deadline:* For fall admission, 4/15 priority date for domestic students; for spring admission, 8/1 for domestic students. Applications are processed on a rolling basis. *Application fee:* $30. Electronic applications accepted. *Interim Director,* Dr. Peg Gray-Vickrey, 239-590-1094, Fax: 239-590-7474, E-mail: mgrayvic@fgcu.edu.

College of Public and Social Services Students: 61 full-time (41 women), 47 part-time (39 women); includes 19 minority (5 African Americans, 1 American Indian/Alaska Native, 3 Asian Americans or Pacific Islanders, 10 Hispanic Americans). Average age 33. 74 applicants, 91% accepted, 56 enrolled. *Faculty:* 29 full-time (14 women), 15 part-time/adjunct (5 women). Expenses: Contact institution. *Financial support:* Research assistantships, career-related internships or fieldwork and tuition waivers (full and partial) available. Support available to part-time students. In 2006, 32 degrees awarded. *Degree program information:* Part-time and evening/weekend programs available. Offers criminal justice (MPA); environmental policy (MPA); general public administration (MPA); management (MPA); public and social services (MPA, MSW); social work (MSW). *Application deadline:* Applications are processed on a rolling basis. *Application fee:* $30. Electronic applications accepted. *Assistant Director,* Dr. Barbara Stites, 239-590-7602, Fax: 239-590-7846.

FLORIDA INSTITUTE OF TECHNOLOGY, Melbourne, FL 32901-6975

General Information Independent, coed, university. *Enrollment:* 4,741 graduate, professional, and undergraduate students; 627 full-time matriculated graduate/professional students (291 women), 1,687 part-time matriculated graduate/professional students (621 women). *Enrollment by degree level:* 2,039 master's, 275 doctoral. *Graduate faculty:* 155 full-time (24 women), 149 part-time/adjunct (19 women). *Tuition:* Part-time $900 per credit. *Graduate housing:* Room and/or apartments available on a first-come, first-served basis to single students; on-campus housing not available to married students. Typical cost: $4,200 per year ($7,400 including board). Room and board charges vary according to board plan and housing facility selected. *Student services:* Campus employment opportunities, career counseling, disabled student services, exercise/wellness program, free psychological counseling, international student services, low-cost health insurance, teacher training, writing training. *Library facilities:* Evans Library. *Online resources:* library catalog, web page, access to other libraries' catalogs. *Collection:* 290,582 titles, 18,051 serial subscriptions, 5,964 audiovisual materials. *Research affiliation:* Lockheed Martin Corporation (biological sciences), Microsoft Corporation (simulation software development), General Electric-Harris (software testing), Boeing Corporation (digital signal processing aeronautics), Arthur D. Little, Inc/U.S. Navy (oceanography/trace metal studies), IBM (software technology, information assurance).

Computer facilities: 400 computers available on campus for general student use. A campuswide network can be accessed from student residence rooms and from off campus. Internet access and online class registration are available. *Web address:* http://www.fit.edu/.

General Application Contact: Carolyn P. Farrior, Director of Graduate Admissions, 321-674-7118, Fax: 321-723-9468, E-mail: cfarrior@fit.edu.

GRADUATE UNITS

Graduate Programs Students: 627 full-time (291 women), 1,687 part-time (621 women); includes 483 minority (281 African Americans, 10 American Indian/Alaska Native, 85 Asian Americans or Pacific Islanders, 107 Hispanic Americans), 281 international. Average age 33. 2,046 applicants, 59% accepted, 563 enrolled. *Faculty:* 155 full-time (24 women), 149 part-time/adjunct (19 women). Expenses: Contact institution. *Financial support:* In 2006–07, 189 students received support, including 7 fellowships with full and partial tuition reimbursements available (averaging $9,110 per year), 71 research assistantships with full and partial tuition reimbursements available (averaging $15,599 per year), 111 teaching assistantships with full and partial tuition reimbursements available (averaging $14,997 per year); career-related internships or fieldwork, institutionally sponsored loans, tuition waivers (partial), unspecified assistantships, and tuition remissions also available. Support available to part-time students. Financial award application deadline: 3/1; financial award applicants required to submit FAFSA. In 2006, 743 master's, 41 doctorates, 1 other advanced degree awarded. *Degree program information:* Part-time and evening/weekend programs available. Postbaccalaureate distance learning degree programs offered (no on-campus study). *Application deadline:* Applications are processed on a rolling basis. *Application fee:* $50. Electronic applications accepted. *Application Contact:* Carolyn P. Farrior, Director of Graduate Admissions, 321-674-7118, Fax: 321-723-9468, E-mail: cfarrior@fit.edu. *Director Graduate Programs,* Antionet Mortara, 321-674-8137, Fax: 321-674-7052, E-mail: amortara@fit.edu.

College of Aeronautics Students: 16 full-time (6 women), 8 part-time (1 woman); includes 5 minority (1 African American, 4 Hispanic Americans), 7 international. Average age 25. 23 applicants, 61% accepted, 4 enrolled. *Faculty:* 9 full-time (0 women), 2 part-time/adjunct (1 woman). Expenses: Contact institution. *Financial support:* Career-related internships or fieldwork, institutionally sponsored loans, unspecified assistantships, and tuition remissions available. Financial award application deadline: 3/1. In 2006, 7 degrees awarded. *Degree program information:* Part-time and evening/weekend programs available. Offers airport development and management (MSA); applied aviation safety (MSA); aviation human factors (MS). *Application deadline:* For fall admission, 8/1 for domestic students; for spring admission, 12/1 for domestic students. Applications are processed on a rolling basis. *Application fee:* $50. Electronic applications accepted. *Application Contact:* Carolyn P. Farrior, Director of Graduate Admissions, 321-674-7118, Fax: 321-723-9468, E-mail: cfarrior@fit.edu. *Dean,* Dr. Ken Stackpoole, 321-674-8971, Fax: 321-674-7368, E-mail: kenstackpoole@fit.edu.

College of Business Students: 19 full-time (7 women), 64 part-time (21 women); includes 7 minority (3 African Americans, 1 American Indian/Alaska Native, 2 Asian Americans or Pacific Islanders, 1 Hispanic American), 10 international. Average age 30. 58 applicants, 64% accepted, 15 enrolled. *Faculty:* 12 full-time (6 women), 2 part-time/adjunct (0 women). Expenses: Contact institution. *Financial support:* Institutionally sponsored loans, unspecified assistantships, and tuition remissions available. Financial award application deadline: 3/1; financial award applicants required to submit FAFSA. In 2006, 16 degrees awarded. *Degree program information:* Part-time and evening/weekend programs available. Offers business (EMBA, MBA). *Application deadline:* Applications are processed on a rolling basis. *Application fee:* $50. Electronic applications accepted. *Application Contact:* Carolyn P. Farrior, Director of Graduate Admissions, 321-674-7118, Fax: 321-723-9468, E-mail: cfarrior@fit.edu. *Interim Dean,* Dr. Robert H. Fronk, 321-674-7327, Fax: 321-674-8896, E-mail: fronk@fit.edu.

College of Engineering Students: 204 full-time (46 women), 283 part-time (55 women); includes 40 minority (7 African Americans, 17 Asian Americans or Pacific Islanders, 16 Hispanic Americans), 167 international. Average age 31. 737 applicants, 57% accepted, 103 enrolled. *Faculty:* 65 full-time (3 women), 6 part-time/adjunct (0 women). Expenses: Contact institution. *Financial support:* In 2006–07, 94 students received support, including 7 fellowships with full and partial tuition reimbursements available (averaging $9,110 per year), 40 research assistantships with full and partial tuition reimbursements available (averaging $8,404 per year), 47 teaching assistantships with full and partial tuition reimbursements available (averaging $11,705 per year); career-related internships or fieldwork, institutionally sponsored loans, and tuition remissions also available. Financial award application deadline: 3/1; financial award applicants required to submit FAFSA. In 2006, 147 master's, 8 doctorates awarded. *Degree program information:* Part-time and evening/weekend programs available. Offers aerospace engineering (MS, PhD); biological oceanography (MS); chemical engineering (MS, PhD); chemical oceanography (MS); civil engineering (MS, PhD); coastal zone management (MS); computer engineering (MS, PhD); computer science (MS, PhD); electrical engineering (MS, PhD); engineering (MS, PhD); engineering management (MS); environmental resource management (MS); environmental science (MS, PhD); geological oceanography (MS); mechanical engineering (MS, PhD); meteorology (MS); ocean engineering (MS, PhD); oceanography (MS, PhD); physical oceanography (MS); software engineering (MS); systems engineering (MS). *Application deadline:* Applications are processed on a rolling basis. *Application fee:* $50. Electronic applications accepted. *Application Contact:* Carolyn P. Farrior, Director of Graduate Admissions, 321-674-7118, Fax: 321-723-9468, E-mail: cfarrior@fit.edu. *Dean,* Dr. Thomas Waite, 321-674-8020, Fax: 321-674-7270, E-mail: twaite@fit.edu.

Florida Institute of Technology (continued)

College of Psychology and Liberal Arts Students: 192 full-time (147 women), 12 part-time (7 women); includes 29 minority (12 African Americans, 4 Asian Americans or Pacific Islanders, 13 Hispanic Americans), 14 international. Average age 27. 308 applicants, 61% accepted, 70 enrolled. *Faculty:* 19 full-time (8 women), 6 part-time/adjunct (0 women). Expenses: Contact institution. *Financial support:* In 2006–07, 7 students received support, including 2 research assistantships with full and partial tuition reimbursements available (averaging $4,526 per year), 5 teaching assistantships with full and partial tuition reimbursements available (averaging $7,202 per year); tuition remissions also available. Financial award application deadline: 3/1. In 2006, 38 master's, 17 doctorates awarded. *Degree program information:* Part-time programs available. Offers applied behavior analysis (MS); clinical psychology (Psy D); communication (MS); humanities and communication (MS); industrial/organizational psychology (MS, PhD); psychology (MS, PhD, Psy D). *Application deadline:* For fall admission, 3/15 for domestic students. Applications are processed on a rolling basis. *Application fee:* $50. Electronic applications accepted. *Application Contact:* Carolyn P. Farrior, Director of Graduate Admissions, 321-674-7118, Fax: 321-723-9468, E-mail: cfarrior@fit.edu. *Dean,* Dr. Mary Beth Kenkel, 321-674-8142, Fax: 321-674-7105, E-mail: mkenkel@fit.edu.

College of Science Students: 118 full-time (51 women), 62 part-time (30 women); includes 18 minority (6 African Americans, 4 Asian Americans or Pacific Islanders, 8 Hispanic Americans), 55 international. Average age 31. 300 applicants, 47% accepted, 54 enrolled. *Faculty:* 39 full-time (3 women), 4 part-time/adjunct (1 woman). Expenses: Contact institution. *Financial support:* In 2006–07, 88 students received support, including 29 research assistantships with full and partial tuition reimbursements available (averaging $26,287 per year), 59 teaching assistantships with full and partial tuition reimbursements available (averaging $18,281 per year); fellowships with full and partial tuition reimbursements available, career-related internships or fieldwork and tuition remissions also available. Financial award application deadline: 3/1; financial award applicants required to submit FAFSA. In 2006, 30 master's, 16 doctorates, 1 other advanced degree awarded. *Degree program information:* Part-time and evening/weekend programs available. Offers applied mathematics (MS, PhD); biological sciences (PhD); biotechnology (MS); cell and molecular biology (MS, PhD); chemistry (MS, PhD); computer education (MS); ecology (MS); elementary science education (M Ed); environmental education (MS); marine biology (MS); mathematics education (MS, Ed D, PhD, Ed S); operations research (MS, PhD); physics (MS, PhD); science (M Ed, MAT, MS, Ed D, PhD, Ed S); science and mathematics education (MAT); science education (MS, Ed D, PhD, Ed S); space sciences (MS, PhD). *Application deadline:* Applications are processed on a rolling basis. *Application fee:* $50. Electronic applications accepted. *Application Contact:* Carolyn P. Farrior, Director of Graduate Admissions, 321-674-7118, Fax: 321-723-9468, E-mail: cfarrior@fit.edu. *Dean,* Dr. Gordon L. Nelson, 321-674-7260, Fax: 321-674-8864, E-mail: nelson@fit.edu.

University College Students: 78 full-time (34 women), 1,258 part-time (507 women); includes 384 minority (252 African Americans, 9 American Indian/Alaska Native, 58 Asian Americans or Pacific Islanders, 65 Hispanic Americans), 28 international. Average age 36. 629 applicants, 65% accepted, 320 enrolled. *Faculty:* 11 full-time (4 women), 129 part-time/adjunct (17 women). Expenses: Contact institution. *Financial support:* Institutionally sponsored loans available. Financial award application deadline: 3/1; financial award applicants required to submit FAFSA. In 2006, 505 degrees awarded. *Degree program information:* Part-time and evening/weekend programs available. Postbaccalaureate distance learning degree programs offered (no on-campus study). Offers acquisition and contract management (MS, PMBA); aerospace engineering (MS); business administration (PMBA); computer information systems (MS); computer science (MS); e-business (PMBA); electrical engineering (MS); engineering management (MS); human resource management (PMBA); human resources management (MS); information systems (PMBA); logistics management (MS); management (MS); materiel acquisition management (MS); mechanical engineering (MS); operations research (MS); project management (MS); public administration (MPA); software engineering (MS); space systems (MS); space systems management (MS); systems management (MS). *Application deadline:* Applications are processed on a rolling basis. *Application fee:* $50. Electronic applications accepted. *Application Contact:* Carolyn P. Farrior, Director of Graduate Admissions, 321-674-7118, Fax: 321-723-9468, E-mail: cfarrior@fit.edu. *Dean,* Dr. Clifford Bragdon, 321-674-8821, Fax: 321-951-7694, E-mail: cbragdon@fit.edu.

See Close-Ups on pages 891 and 893.

FLORIDA INTERNATIONAL UNIVERSITY, Miami, FL 33199

General Information State-supported, coed, university. CGS member. *Enrollment:* 37,997 graduate, professional, and undergraduate students; 3,330 full-time matriculated graduate/professional students (1,882 women), 2,415 part-time matriculated graduate/professional students (1,495 women). *Enrollment by degree level:* 383 first professional, 4,330 master's, 1,032 doctoral. *Graduate faculty:* 759 full-time (259 women), 11 part-time/adjunct (5 women). Tuition, state resident: part-time $249 per credit hour. Tuition, nonresident: part-time $753 per credit hour. Tuition and fees vary according to program. *Graduate housing:* Rooms and/or apartments available on a first-come, first-served basis to single and married students. *Student services:* Campus employment opportunities, campus safety program, career counseling, child daycare facilities, disabled student services, free psychological counseling, international student services, low-cost health insurance, multicultural affairs office. *Library facilities:* University Park Library plus 2 others. *Online resources:* library catalog, web page, access to other libraries' catalogs. *Collection:* 2 million titles, 40,813 serial subscriptions, 159,978 audiovisual materials. *Research affiliation:* American Heart Association (biomedical engineering), Boeing Company (engineering), Innovia, LLCa (biomedical engineering), Lockheed Martin (engineering), Lennar Homes (architecture), Montgomery Watson (engineering).

Computer facilities: 600 computers available on campus for general student use. A campuswide network can be accessed from student residence rooms and from off campus. Internet access and online class registration are available. *Web address:* http://www.fiu.edu/.

General Application Contact: Nanette Rojas, Coordinator of Graduate Admissions, 305-348-7442, Fax: 305-348-7441, E-mail: gradadm@fiu.edu.

GRADUATE UNITS

Alvah H. Chapman, Jr. Graduate School of Business Students: 571 full-time (267 women), 329 part-time (148 women); includes 520 minority (67 African Americans, 47 Asian Americans or Pacific Islanders, 406 Hispanic Americans), 223 international. 1,140 applicants, 36% accepted, 276 enrolled. *Faculty:* 95 full-time (29 women), 2 part-time/adjunct (0 women). Expenses: Contact institution. *Financial support:* Fellowships, research assistantships, teaching assistantships, Federal Work-Study available. In 2006, 473 master's, 4 doctorates awarded. *Degree program information:* Part-time and evening/weekend programs available. Offers business administration (M Acc, MBA, MIB, MS, MSF, MST, PhD); decision sciences and information systems (PhD); finance (MSF); international business (MIB). *Application deadline:* For fall admission, 4/1 priority date for domestic students; for spring admission, 10/1 for domestic students. Applications are processed on a rolling basis. *Application fee:* $25. *Executive Dean,* Dr. Joyce J. Elam, 305-348-2751, Fax: 305-348-3278, E-mail: elamj@fiu.edu.

School of Accounting Students: 45 full-time (24 women), 57 part-time (30 women); includes 77 minority (8 African Americans, 2 Asian Americans or Pacific Islanders, 67 Hispanic Americans), 5 international. Average age 30. 157 applicants, 29% accepted, 42 enrolled. *Faculty:* 17 full-time (6 women). Expenses: Contact institution. In 2006, 93 degrees awarded. *Degree program information:* Part-time and evening/weekend programs available. Offers accounting (M Acc); taxation (MST). *Application deadline:* For fall admission, 4/1 priority date for domestic students; for spring admission, 10/1 for domestic students. Applications are processed on a rolling basis. *Application fee:* $25. *Acting Director,* Dr. Christos Koulamas, 305-348-2830, Fax: 305-348-4126, E-mail: christos.koulamas@fiu.edu.

College of Architecture and the Arts Students: 166 full-time (84 women), 37 part-time (22 women); includes 121 minority (17 African Americans, 6 Asian Americans or Pacific Islanders, 98 Hispanic Americans), 23 international. Average age 31. 126 applicants, 55% accepted, 53 enrolled. *Faculty:* 67 full-time (23 women). Expenses: Contact institution. In 2006, 62 degrees awarded. *Degree program information:* Part-time and evening/weekend programs available. Offers architecture (MS); art and art history (MFA); landscape architecture (MS); music (MM, MS). *Application deadline:* For fall admission, 4/1 priority date for domestic students; for spring admission, 10/1 for domestic students. Applications are processed on a rolling basis. *Application fee:* $25. *Dean,* Juan A. Bueno, 305-348-3176, Fax: 305-348-6716, E-mail: buenoj@fiu.edu.

School of Art and Art History Students: 166 full-time (84 women), 37 part-time (22 women); includes 121 minority (17 African Americans, 6 Asian Americans or Pacific Islanders, 98 Hispanic Americans), 23 international. 17 applicants, 29% accepted, 5 enrolled. *Faculty:* 14 full-time (6 women). Expenses: Contact institution. Offers visual arts (MFA). *Application fee:* $25. *Director,* Dr. Juan Martinez, 305-348-2897, Fax: 305-348-6544, E-mail: juan.martinez@fiu.edu.

College of Arts and Sciences Students: 596 full-time (334 women), 377 part-time (231 women); includes 445 minority (69 African Americans, 36 Asian Americans or Pacific Islanders, 340 Hispanic Americans), 179 international. Average age 33. 919 applicants, 38% accepted, 217 enrolled. *Faculty:* 341 full-time (111 women), 9 part-time/adjunct (5 women). Expenses: Contact institution. *Financial support:* Fellowships, research assistantships, teaching assistantships, career-related internships or fieldwork, Federal Work-Study, institutionally sponsored loans, and tuition waivers (full and partial) available. Support available to part-time students. Financial award application deadline: 4/1. In 2006, 163 master's, 36 doctorates awarded. *Degree program information:* Part-time and evening/weekend programs available. Offers African-new world studies (MA); arts and sciences (MA, MFA, MM, MS, PhD); biological management (MS); biology (MS, PhD); chemistry (MS, PhD); comparative sociology (MA); creative writing (MFA); developmental psychology (PhD); earth sciences (MS, PhD); economics (MA, PhD); energy (MS); English (MA); forensic science (MS); general psychology (MS); history (MA, PhD); international relations (PhD); international studies (MA); Latin American and Caribbean studies (MA); liberal studies (MA); linguistics (MA); mathematical sciences (MS); physics (MS, PhD); political science (MS, PhD); pollution (MS); psychology (MS); religious studies (MA); sociology (PhD); Spanish (MA, PhD); statistics (MS). *Application deadline:* Applications are processed on a rolling basis. *Application fee:* $25. *Interim Dean,* Dr. Mark Szuchman, 305-348-2864, Fax: 305-348-4172, E-mail: mark.szuchman@fiu.edu.

School of Music Students: 35 full-time (15 women), 14 part-time (11 women); includes 23 minority (5 African Americans, 1 Asian American or Pacific Islander, 17 Hispanic Americans), 12 international. Average age 31. 34 applicants, 50% accepted, 17 enrolled. *Faculty:* 22 full-time (3 women). Expenses: Contact institution. In 2006, 19 degrees awarded. *Degree program information:* Part-time and evening/weekend programs available. Offers music (MM); music education (MS). *Application fee:* $25. *Director,* Dr. Joseph Rohm, 305-348-3354, Fax: 305-348-4073, E-mail: joseph.rohm@fiu.edu.

College of Education Students: 307 full-time (223 women), 613 part-time (493 women); includes 655 minority (202 African Americans, 21 Asian Americans or Pacific Islanders, 432 Hispanic Americans). Average age 33. 492 applicants, 53% accepted, 252 enrolled. *Faculty:* 62 full-time (34 women), 41 part-time/adjunct (11 women). Expenses: Contact institution. *Financial support:* In 2006–07, 4 research assistantships, 25 teaching assistantships were awarded; fellowships, career-related internships or fieldwork, Federal Work-Study, institutionally sponsored loans, and tuition waivers (full and partial) also available. Support available to part-time students. In 2006, 272 master's, 17 doctorates, 25 other advanced degrees awarded. *Degree program information:* Part-time and evening/weekend programs available. Offers adult education (MS); adult education in human resource development (Ed D); advanced athletic injury training/sports medicine (MS); advanced teacher preparation (MS); art education (MAT, MS, Ed D); conflict resolution and consensus building (Certificate); counselor education (MS); curriculum and instruction (Ed S); curriculum development (MS); curriculum studies (PhD); early childhood education (MS, Ed D); education (MA, MAT, MS, Ed D, PhD, Certificate, Ed S); educational administration and supervision (Ed D); educational leadership (MS, Certificate, Ed S); elementary education (MS, Ed D); English education (MAT, MS, Ed D); exceptional student education (MS, Ed D); exercise and sports science (MS); foreign language education (Certificate); foreign language education—teaching English to speakers of other languages (TESOL) (Certificate); foreign language education- teaching English to speakers of other languages (TESOL) (MS); French education—initial teacher preparation (MAT); higher education (Ed D); higher education administration (MS); human resource development (MS); international and intercultural development education (Ed D); international and intercultural developmental education (MS); language, literacy and culture (PhD); learning technologies (MS, Ed D, PhD); leisure services (MS); mathematics education (MAT, MS, Ed D, PhD); mental health counseling (MS); modern language education/bilingual education (MS, Ed D); parks and recreation management (MS); physical education (MS); reading education (MS, Ed D); rehabilitation counseling (MS); school counseling (MS); school psychology (Ed S); science education (MAT, MS, Ed D, PhD); social studies education (MAT, MS, Ed D); Spanish education—initial teacher preparation (MAT); special education (MS); sports management (MS); strength and conditioning (MS); teaching English (MS); therapeutic recreation (MS); urban education (MS). *Application deadline:* For fall admission, 6/1 priority date for domestic students, 4/1 for international students; for winter admission, 10/1 priority date for domestic students, 9/1 for international students; for spring admission, 3/1 priority date for domestic students, 2/1 for international students. Applications are processed on a rolling basis. *Application fee:* $30. Electronic applications accepted. *Application Contact:* Marisa Salazar, Student Recruiter, 305-348-3002, Fax: 305-348-3227, E-mail: marisa.salazar@fiu.edu. *Unit Head,* Dr. Luis Miron, 305-348-3202, Fax: 305-348-3205, E-mail: luis.miron@fiu.edu.

College of Engineering and Computing Students: 452 full-time (127 women), 359 part-time (104 women); includes 362 minority (64 African Americans, 1 American Indian/Alaska Native, 45 Asian Americans or Pacific Islanders, 252 Hispanic Americans), 354 international. Average age 32. 636 applicants, 58% accepted, 138 enrolled. *Faculty:* 100 full-time (13 women), 1 part-time/adjunct (0 women). Expenses: Contact institution. *Financial support:* Fellowships, research assistantships, teaching assistantships, career-related internships or fieldwork, Federal Work-Study, and institutionally sponsored loans available. In 2006, 210 master's, 18 doctorates awarded. *Degree program information:* Part-time and evening/weekend programs available. Offers biomedical engineering (MS, PhD); civil engineering (MS, PhD); computer engineering (MS); construction management (MS); electrical engineering (MS, PhD); engineering and computing (MS, PhD); environmental and urban systems (MS); environmental engineering (MS); industrial engineering (MS, PhD); mechanical and materials engineering (MS, PhD); telecommunications and networking (MS). *Application deadline:* For fall admission, 4/1 priority date for domestic students; for spring admission, 10/1 for domestic students. Applications are processed on a rolling basis. *Application fee:* $25. *Executive Dean,* Dr. Vish Prasad, 305-348-6050, Fax: 305-348-1401, E-mail: prasad@fiu.edu.

School of Computing and Information Sciences Students: 78 full-time (25 women), 40 part-time (5 women); includes 46 minority (11 Asian Americans or Pacific Islanders, 35 Hispanic Americans), 58 international. Average age 30. 110 applicants, 53% accepted, 15 enrolled. *Faculty:* 26 full-time (3 women), 1 part-time/adjunct (0 women). Expenses: Contact institution. *Financial support:* Application deadline: 4/1. In 2006, 25 master's, 6 doctorates awarded. *Degree program information:* Part-time and evening/weekend programs available. Offers computing and information sciences (MS, PhD). *Application deadline:* For fall admission, 4/1 priority date for domestic students; for spring admission, 10/1 for domestic students. Applications are processed on a rolling basis. *Application fee:* $25. *Director,* Dr. Yi Deng, 305-348-2744, Fax: 305-348-3549, E-mail: yi.deng@fiu.edu.

College of Law Students: 370 full-time (172 women), 13 part-time (4 women); includes 217 minority (38 African Americans, 2 American Indian/Alaska Native, 8 Asian Americans or Pacific Islanders, 169 Hispanic Americans), 1 international. 1,323 applicants, 19% accepted, 155 enrolled. *Faculty:* 23 full-time (9 women), 1 part-time/adjunct (0 women). Expenses: Contact institution. In 2006, 82 degrees awarded. Offers law (JD). *Application fee:* $25. *Dean,* Dr. Leonard Strickman, 305-348-1118, Fax: 305-348-1159, E-mail: leonard.strickman@fiu.edu.

College of Nursing and Health Sciences Students: 376 full-time (286 women), 174 part-time (142 women); includes 382 minority (92 African Americans, 3 American Indian/Alaska Native, 32 Asian Americans or Pacific Islanders, 255 Hispanic Americans), 9 international. Average age 36. 846 applicants, 57% accepted, 283 enrolled. *Faculty:* 46 full-time (36 women), 2 part-time/adjunct (1 woman). Expenses: Contact institution. *Financial support:* Fellowships, research assistantships, career-related internships or fieldwork, Federal Work-Study, and institutionally sponsored loans available. In 2006, 155 degrees awarded. *Degree program information:* Part-time and evening/weekend programs available. Offers communication sciences and disorders (MS); health sciences (MS); health services administration (MHSA); nursing and health sciences (MHSA, MS, MSN, PhD); occupational therapy (MS); physical therapy (MS). *Application deadline:* For fall admission, 4/1 priority date for domestic students; for spring admission, 10/1 for domestic students. Applications are processed on a rolling basis. *Application fee:* $25. *Acting Executive Dean,* Dr. Ray Thomlison, 305-348-5840, Fax: 305-348-5253, E-mail: ray.thomlison@fiu.edu.

School of Nursing Students: 119 full-time (79 women), 109 part-time (83 women); includes 152 minority (45 African Americans, 19 Asian Americans or Pacific Islanders, 88 Hispanic Americans). Average age 38. 157 applicants, 28% accepted, 31 enrolled. *Faculty:* 30 full-time (25 women), 2 part-time/adjunct (1 woman). Expenses: Contact institution. In 2006, 69 degrees awarded. *Degree program information:* Part-time programs available. Offers nursing (MSN, PhD). *Application deadline:* For fall admission, 4/1 priority date for domestic students; for spring admission, 10/1 for domestic students. Applications are processed on a rolling basis. *Application fee:* $25. *Dean,* Dr. Divina Grossman, 305-919-5301, Fax: 305-919-5395, E-mail: divina.grossman@fiu.edu.

College of Social Work, Justice and Public Affairs Students: 217 full-time (165 women), 246 part-time (174 women); includes 373 minority (144 African Americans, 7 Asian Americans or Pacific Islanders, 222 Hispanic Americans), 9 international. Average age 33. 133 applicants, 68% accepted, 56 enrolled. *Faculty:* 29 full-time (10 women), 1 (woman) part-time/adjunct. Expenses: Contact institution. *Financial support:* In 2006–07, 2 fellowships were awarded; career-related internships or fieldwork, Federal Work-Study, and institutionally sponsored loans also available. In 2006, 173 master's, 4 doctorates awarded. *Degree program information:* Part-time and evening/weekend programs available. Offers social work, justice and public affairs (MPA, MS, MSW, PhD). *Application deadline:* For fall admission, 4/1 priority date for domestic students; for spring admission, 10/1 for domestic students. Applications are processed on a rolling basis. *Application fee:* $25. *Director,* Dr. Ray Thomlison, 305-348-5890, Fax: 305-348-5848, E-mail: ray.thomlison@fiu.edu.

School of Criminal Justice Students: 30 full-time (20 women), 33 part-time (21 women); includes 49 minority (24 African Americans, 25 Hispanic Americans). Average age 34. 47 applicants, 57% accepted, 17 enrolled. *Faculty:* 8 full-time (3 women). Expenses: Contact institution. In 2006, 30 degrees awarded. *Degree program information:* Part-time and evening/weekend programs available. Offers criminal justice (MS). *Application deadline:* For fall admission, 4/1 priority date for domestic students; for spring admission, 10/1 for domestic students. Applications are processed on a rolling basis. *Application fee:* $25. *Head,* Dr. Lisa Stolzenberg, 305-348-5890, Fax: 305-348-2503, E-mail: lisa.stolzenberg@fiu.edu.

School of Public Administration Students: 62 full-time (38 women), 115 part-time (74 women); includes 146 minority (56 African Americans, 2 Asian Americans or Pacific Islanders, 88 Hispanic Americans), 7 international. Average age 35. 86 applicants, 74% accepted, 39 enrolled. *Faculty:* 9 full-time (2 women). Expenses: Contact institution. *Financial support:* In 2006–07, 2 fellowships were awarded; career-related internships or fieldwork, Federal Work-Study, and institutionally sponsored loans also available. In 2006, 55 master's, 1 doctorate awarded. *Degree program information:* Part-time and evening/weekend programs available. Offers public administration (MPA, PhD). *Application deadline:* For fall admission, 4/1 priority date for domestic students; for spring admission, 10/1 for domestic students. Applications are processed on a rolling basis. *Application fee:* $25. *Director,* Dr. Meredith Newman, 305-348-5890, Fax: 305-348-5848, E-mail: meredith.newman@fiu.edu.

School of Social Work Students: 125 full-time (107 women), 98 part-time (79 women); includes 178 minority (64 African Americans, 5 Asian Americans or Pacific Islanders, 109 Hispanic Americans), 2 international. Average age 38. 131 applicants, 66% accepted, 58 enrolled. *Faculty:* 12 full-time (5 women), 1 (woman) part-time/adjunct. Expenses: Contact institution. In 2006, 88 master's, 3 doctorates awarded. *Degree program information:* Part-time and evening/weekend programs available. Offers social work (MSW, PhD). *Application deadline:* For fall admission, 4/1 priority date for domestic students; for spring admission, 10/1 for domestic students. Applications are processed on a rolling basis. *Application fee:* $25. *Acting Dean,* Dr. Gary Lowe, 305-348-7196, Fax: 305-348-5848, E-mail: gary.lowe@fiu.edu.

School of Hospitality Management Students: 92 full-time (63 women), 49 part-time (25 women); includes 41 minority (14 African Americans, 5 Asian Americans or Pacific Islanders, 22 Hispanic Americans), 68 international. Average age 29. 82 applicants, 71% accepted, 27 enrolled. *Faculty:* 18 full-time (5 women), 2 part-time/adjunct (0 women). Expenses: Contact institution. In 2006, 62 degrees awarded. Offers hotel and food service management (MS). *Application fee:* $25. *Dean,* Dr. Joseph West, 305-919-4500, Fax: 305-919-4555, E-mail: jwest@fiu.edu.

School of Journalism and Mass Communication Students: 70 full-time (51 women), 46 part-time (42 women); includes 76 minority (11 African Americans, 4 Asian Americans or Pacific Islanders, 61 Hispanic Americans), 16 international. Average age 32. 119 applicants, 50% accepted, 38 enrolled. *Faculty:* 16 full-time (10 women), 1 (woman) part-time/adjunct. Expenses: Contact institution. *Financial support:* Application deadline: 4/1. In 2006, 48 degrees awarded. *Degree program information:* Part-time and evening/weekend programs available. Offers mass communication (MS). *Application deadline:* For fall admission, 4/1 priority date for domestic students; for spring admission, 10/1 for domestic students. Applications are processed on a rolling basis. *Application fee:* $25. *Dean,* Dr. Lillian Kopenhaver, 305-919-5625, Fax: 305-919-5203, E-mail: kopenha@fiu.edu.

School of Public Health Students: 150 full-time (113 women), 156 part-time (122 women); includes 195 minority (77 African Americans, 24 Asian Americans or Pacific Islanders, 94 Hispanic Americans), 34 international. 219 applicants, 61% accepted, 58 enrolled. *Faculty:* 30 full-time (19 women). Expenses: Contact institution. In 2006, 56 master's, 1 doctorate awarded. Offers dietetics and nutrition (MS, PhD); public health (MHSA, MPH, MS, PhD). *Application fee:* $25. *Dean,* Dr. Michele Ciccazzo, 305-348-4903, Fax: 305-3484901, E-mail: michele.ciccazzo@fiu.edu.

See Close-Up on page 895.

FLORIDA METROPOLITAN UNIVERSITY–BRANDON CAMPUS, Tampa, FL 33619

General Information Proprietary, coed, comprehensive institution. *Enrollment:* 972 graduate, professional, and undergraduate students; 8 full-time matriculated graduate/professional students (6 women), 44 part-time matriculated graduate/professional students (27 women). *Enrollment by degree level:* 52 master's. *Graduate faculty:* 1 (woman) full-time, 5 part-time/adjunct (2 women). *Tuition:* Full-time $14,016; part-time $438 per credit. *Required fees:* $60 per quarter. *Graduate housing:* On-campus housing not available. *Student services:* Campus employment opportunities. *Library facilities:* Florida Metropolitan Unversity Library. *Online resources:* library catalog, web page. *Collection:* 4,589 titles, 48 serial subscriptions, 270 audiovisual materials.

Computer facilities: 81 computers available on campus for general student use. A campuswide network can be accessed. Internet access is available. *Web address:* http://www.fmu.edu/.

General Application Contact: Shandretta Pointer, Admissions Office, 813-621-0041 Ext. 106, Fax: 813-628-0919, E-mail: spointer@cci.edu.

GRADUATE UNITS

Program in Business Administration Students: 6 full-time (4 women), 32 part-time (18 women); includes 14 minority (7 African Americans, 7 Hispanic Americans). Average age 34. *Faculty:* 1 (woman) full-time, 4 part-time/adjunct (2 women). Expenses: Contact institution. *Financial support:* Federal Work-Study, institutionally sponsored loans, and scholarships/grants available. In 2006, 28 degrees awarded. *Degree program information:* Part-time and evening/weekend programs available. Postbaccalaureate distance learning degree programs offered (minimal on-campus study). Offers business administration (MBA). *Application deadline:* Applications are processed on a rolling basis. *Application fee:* $25. *Application Contact:* Shandretta Pointer, Admissions Office, 813-621-0041 Ext. 106, Fax: 813-628-0919, E-mail: spointer@cci.edu. *Chair,* James Jehs, 813-621-0041 Ext. 140, Fax: 813-623-5769.

Program in Criminal Justice Students: 2 full-time (both women), 12 part-time (9 women); includes 7 minority (6 African Americans, 1 Hispanic American). Average age 38. *Faculty:* 1 part-time/adjunct (0 women). Expenses: Contact institution. *Financial support:* Federal Work-Study, institutionally sponsored loans, and scholarships/grants available. In 2006, 11 degrees awarded. *Degree program information:* Part-time and evening/weekend programs available. Postbaccalaureate distance learning degree programs offered (minimal on-campus study). Offers criminal justice (MS). *Application deadline:* Applications are processed on a rolling basis. *Application fee:* $25. *Application Contact:* Shandretta Pointer, Admissions Office, 813-621-0041 Ext. 106, Fax: 813-628-0919, E-mail: spointer@cci.edu. *Chair,* Tom Parks, 813-621-0041, Fax: 813-623-5769.

FLORIDA METROPOLITAN UNIVERSITY–JACKSONVILLE CAMPUS, Jacksonville, FL 32256

General Information Proprietary, coed, comprehensive institution.

GRADUATE UNITS

Graduate Programs

FLORIDA METROPOLITAN UNIVERSITY–LAKELAND CAMPUS, Lakeland, FL 33801

General Information Proprietary, coed, comprehensive institution.

GRADUATE UNITS

Program in Criminal Justice Offers criminal justice (MS).

FLORIDA METROPOLITAN UNIVERSITY–MELBOURNE CAMPUS, Melbourne, FL 32935-6657

General Information Proprietary, coed, comprehensive institution.

GRADUATE UNITS

Program in Business Administration Offers business administration (MBA).

FLORIDA METROPOLITAN UNIVERSITY–NORTH ORLANDO CAMPUS, Orlando, FL 32810-5674

General Information Proprietary, coed, comprehensive institution. *Graduate housing:* On-campus housing not available.

GRADUATE UNITS

Division of Business Administration *Degree program information:* Part-time and evening/weekend programs available. Offers business administration (MBA).

FLORIDA METROPOLITAN UNIVERSITY–PINELLAS CAMPUS, Clearwater, FL 33759

General Information Proprietary, coed, comprehensive institution.

GRADUATE UNITS

Graduate School of Business Offers business (MBA).

FLORIDA METROPOLITAN UNIVERSITY–POMPANO BEACH CAMPUS, Pompano Beach, FL 33062

General Information Proprietary, coed, comprehensive institution. *Graduate housing:* On-campus housing not available.

GRADUATE UNITS

Program in Criminal Justice Offers criminal justice (MS).

School of Business *Degree program information:* Part-time and evening/weekend programs available. Offers business (MBA).

FLORIDA METROPOLITAN UNIVERSITY–SOUTH ORLANDO CAMPUS, Orlando, FL 32819

General Information Proprietary, coed, comprehensive institution. *Graduate housing:* On-campus housing not available.

GRADUATE UNITS

Program in Business Administration Offers accounting (MBA); general management (MBA); human resources (MBA); international management (MBA).

FLORIDA METROPOLITAN UNIVERSITY–TAMPA CAMPUS, Tampa, FL 33614-5899

General Information Proprietary, coed, comprehensive institution. *Graduate housing:* On-campus housing not available.

GRADUATE UNITS

Department of Business Administration *Degree program information:* Part-time and evening/weekend programs available. Offers accounting (MBA); human resources (MBA); international business (MBA).

FLORIDA SOUTHERN COLLEGE, Lakeland, FL 33801-5698

General Information Independent-religious, coed, comprehensive institution. *Enrollment:* 1,873 graduate, professional, and undergraduate students; 124 part-time matriculated graduate/professional students (95 women). *Enrollment by degree level:* 124 master's. *Graduate faculty:* 22 full-time (9 women), 4 part-time/adjunct (3 women). *Tuition:* Part-time $250 per credit hour. *Required fees:* $10 per term. Tuition and fees vary according to program. *Graduate housing:* On-campus housing not available. *Student services:* Campus employment opportunities, campus safety program, career counseling, disabled student services, exercise/wellness program, free psychological counseling, international student services, multicultural affairs office, teacher training. *Library facilities:* E. T. Roux Library. *Online resources:* library catalog, web page, access to other libraries' catalogs. *Collection:* 182,765 titles, 939 serial subscriptions, 15,567 audiovisual materials.

Computer facilities: Computer purchase and lease plans are available. 250 computers available on campus for general student use. A campuswide network can be accessed from student residence rooms and from off campus. Internet access and online class registration, campus portal are available. *Web address:* http://www.flsouthern.edu/.

General Application Contact: Craig Story, Evening Program Director, 863-680-6276, Fax: 863-680-4205, E-mail: cstory@flsouthern.edu.

GRADUATE UNITS

Program in Business Administration Average age 31. 15 applicants, 80% accepted, 8 enrolled. *Faculty:* 12 full-time (2 women). Expenses: Contact institution. *Financial support:* In 2006–07, 9 students received support. Scholarships/grants available. Support available to part-time students. Financial award applicants required to submit FAFSA. In 2006, 9 degrees awarded. *Degree program information:* Part-time and evening/weekend programs available. Offers accounting (MBA); business administration (MBA); international business (MBA). *Application deadline:* For fall admission, 8/1 for domestic students; for spring admission, 12/1 for domestic students. Applications are processed on a rolling basis. *Application fee:* $30. *Application Contact:* Craig Story, Evening Program Director, 863-680-6276, Fax: 863-680-4205, E-mail: cstory@flsouthern.edu. *Program Coordinator,* Dr. Larry Ross, 863-680-4285, Fax: 863-680-4355, E-mail: lross@flsouthern.edu.

Florida Southern College (continued)

Program in Nursing Average age 43. 16 applicants, 75% accepted, 11 enrolled. *Faculty:* 5 full-time (all women). Expenses: Contact institution. *Financial support:* In 2006–07, 10 students received support. Scholarships/grants and traineeships available. Support available to part-time students. In 2006, 11 degrees awarded. *Degree program information:* Part-time and evening/weekend programs available. Offers nursing (MSN). *Application deadline:* For fall admission, 6/1 for domestic students; for spring admission, 11/1 for domestic students. Applications are processed on a rolling basis. *Application fee:* $30. *Application Contact:* Craig Story, Evening Program Director, 863-680-6276, Fax: 863-680-4205, E-mail: cstory@flsouthern.edu. *Program Coordinator*, Dr. Mavra E. Kear, 863-680-4310, Fax: 863-680-3872, E-mail: mkear@flsouthern.edu.

Programs in Teaching Average age 32. 20 applicants, 80% accepted, 12 enrolled. *Faculty:* 5 full-time (2 women), 6 part-time/adjunct (3 women). Expenses: Contact institution. *Financial support:* In 2006–07, 24 students received support. Scholarships/grants available. Support available to part-time students. Financial award applicants required to submit FAFSA. In 2006, 25 degrees awarded. *Degree program information:* Part-time and evening/weekend programs available. Offers teaching (MAT); teaching and learning (M Ed). *Application deadline:* For fall admission, 8/1 for domestic students; for spring admission, 12/1 for domestic students. Applications are processed on a rolling basis. *Application fee:* $30. *Application Contact:* Craig Story, Evening Program Director, 863-680-6276, Fax: 863-680-4205, E-mail: cstory@flsouthern.edu. *Program Coordinator*, Dr. Charles B. Watts, 863-680-4958, Fax: 863-680-4102, E-mail: cwatts@flsouthern.edu.

FLORIDA STATE UNIVERSITY, Tallahassee, FL 32306

General Information State-supported, coed, university. CGS member. *Enrollment:* 39,973 graduate, professional, and undergraduate students; 5,429 full-time matriculated graduate/professional students (2,854 women), 2,745 part-time matriculated graduate/professional students (1,722 women). *Enrollment by degree level:* 1,041 first professional, 4,499 master's, 2,555 doctoral, 79 other advanced degrees. *Graduate faculty:* 1,159 full-time (385 women), 119 part-time/adjunct (56 women). Tuition, state resident: full-time $5,822; part-time $243 per credit hour. Tuition, nonresident: full-time $20,976; part-time $874 per credit hour. Tuition and fees vary according to program. *Graduate housing:* Rooms and/or apartments available to single and married students. *Student services:* Campus employment opportunities, campus safety program, career counseling, child daycare facilities, disabled student services, exercise/wellness program, free psychological counseling, grant writing training, international student services, low-cost health insurance, multicultural affairs office, teacher training, writing training. *Library facilities:* Robert Manning Strozier Library plus 8 others. *Online resources:* library catalog, web page, access to other libraries' catalogs. *Collection:* 2.9 million titles, 58,093 serial subscriptions, 251,340 audiovisual materials. *Research affiliation:* National Center for Atmospheric Research, Fermi National Accelerator Laboratory, Southeastern Archaeological Studies, Center for the Study of Southern Culture and Religion.

Computer facilities: Computer purchase and lease plans are available. 3,771 computers available on campus for general student use. A campuswide network can be accessed from student residence rooms and from off campus. Internet access and online class registration, course home pages, course search, online fee payment are available. *Web address:* http://www.fsu.edu/.

General Application Contact: Melanie Booker, Associate Director for Graduate Admissions, 850-644-3420, Fax: 850-644-0197, E-mail: mbooker@admin.fsu.edu.

GRADUATE UNITS

College of Law Students: 765 full-time (305 women); includes 143 minority (43 African Americans, 6 American Indian/Alaska Native, 33 Asian Americans or Pacific Islanders, 61 Hispanic Americans), 12 international. Average age 23. 3,313 applicants, 24% accepted, 196 enrolled. *Faculty:* 46 full-time (18 women), 14 part-time/adjunct (4 women). Expenses: Contact institution. *Financial support:* In 2006–07, 260 fellowships (averaging $1,500 per year), 58 research assistantships (averaging $3,300 per year), 6 teaching assistantships (averaging $2,069 per year) were awarded; scholarships/grants also available. Financial award application deadline: 4/1; financial award applicants required to submit FAFSA. In 2006, 244 degrees awarded. Offers law (JD). *Application deadline:* For fall admission, 3/15 priority date for domestic students. Applications are processed on a rolling basis. *Application fee:* $30. Electronic applications accepted. *Application Contact:* Sharon J. Booker, Director of Admissions and Records, 850-644-3787, Fax: 850-644-7284, E-mail: admissions@law.fsu.edu. *Dean*, Donald J. Weidner, 850-644-3400, Fax: 850-644-5487, E-mail: dweidner@law.fsu.edu.

College of Medicine Students: 284 full-time (165 women); includes 106 minority (36 African Americans, 2 American Indian/Alaska Native, 35 Asian Americans or Pacific Islanders, 33 Hispanic Americans). Average age 25. 1,849 applicants, 10% accepted, 100 enrolled. *Faculty:* 105 full-time (32 women), 568 part-time/adjunct (122 women). Expenses: Contact institution. *Financial support:* In 2006–07, 156 students received support, including 2 fellowships (averaging $5,000 per year); scholarships/grants also available. Financial award application deadline: 7/1; financial award applicants required to submit FAFSA. In 2006, 36 degrees awarded. Offers biomedical sciences (PhD); medicine (MD). *Application deadline:* For fall admission, 12/15 for domestic students. Applications are processed on a rolling basis. *Application fee:* $30. Electronic applications accepted. *Application Contact:* Admissions Coordinator, 850-644-7904, Fax: 850-645-2846, E-mail: medadmissions@med.fsu.edu. *Dean*, Dr. J. Ocie Harris, 850-644-1855, Fax: 850-645-1420, E-mail: ocie.harris@med.fsu.edu.

Graduate Studies Students: 4,388 full-time (2,379 women), 2,739 part-time (1,721 women); includes 1,362 minority (701 African Americans, 40 American Indian/Alaska Native, 215 Asian Americans or Pacific Islanders, 406 Hispanic Americans), 908 international. Average age 31. *Faculty:* 1,118 full-time (367 women), 106 part-time/adjunct (52 women). Expenses: Contact institution. *Financial support:* Fellowships, research assistantships, teaching assistantships, career-related internships or fieldwork, Federal Work-Study, institutionally sponsored loans, scholarships/grants, traineeships, and unspecified assistantships available. Support available to part-time students. Financial award applicants required to submit FAFSA. In 2006, 1,897 master's, 363 doctorates awarded. *Degree program information:* Part-time and evening/weekend programs available. *Application deadline:* For fall admission, 7/1 for domestic students, 5/1 for international students. *Application fee:* $30. Electronic applications accepted. *Application Contact:* Melanie Booker, Associate Director for Graduate Admissions, 850-644-3420, Fax: 850-644-0197, E-mail: mbooker@admin.fsu.edu. *Dean, Graduate Studies*, Dr. Nancy Marcus, 850-644-3500, Fax: 850-644-2969, E-mail: nmarcus@mailer.fsu.edu.

College of Arts and Sciences Students: 1,495 full-time (639 women), 265 part-time (136 women); includes 227 minority (75 African Americans, 7 American Indian/Alaska Native, 58 Asian Americans or Pacific Islanders, 87 Hispanic Americans), 371 international. Average age 31. *Faculty:* 448 full-time (101 women), 13 part-time/adjunct (4 women). Expenses: Contact institution. *Financial support:* Fellowships, research assistantships, teaching assistantships, career-related internships or fieldwork, Federal Work-Study, institutionally sponsored loans, scholarships/grants, traineeships, tuition waivers (full), and unspecified assistantships available. Support available to part-time students. In 2006, 285 master's, 140 doctorates awarded. *Degree program information:* Part-time programs available. Offers American and Florida studies (MA, Certificate); analytical chemistry (MS, PhD); anthropology (MA, MS, PhD); applied behavior analysis (MS); applied mathematics (MS, PhD); applied statistics (MS); arts and sciences (MA, MFA, MS, PhD, Certificate); biochemistry (MS, PhD); biochemistry, molecular and cell biology (PhD); biomedical mathematics (MS, PhD); biostatistics (MS, PhD); cell biology (MS, PhD); chemical physics (MS, PhD); classical archaeology (MA); classical civilization (MA, PhD); classics (MA); clinical psychology (PhD); cognitive psychology (PhD); computational structural biology (PhD); computer science (MA, MS, PhD); creative writing (MFA); developmental biology (MS, PhD); developmental psychology (PhD); ecology (MS, PhD); evolutionary biology (MS, PhD); financial mathematics (MS, PhD); French (MA, PhD); genetics (MS, PhD); geological sciences (MS, PhD); geophysical fluid dynamics (PhD); German (MA); Greek (MA); Greek and Latin (MA); historical administration (MA); history (MA, PhD); history and philosophy of science (MA); humanities (PhD); immunology (MS, PhD); information security (MS); inorganic chemistry (MS, PhD); interdisciplinary humanities (MA, PhD); Italian (MA); Italian studies (MA); Latin (MA); literature (MA, PhD); marine biology (MS, PhD); mathematical statistics (MS, PhD); meteorology (MS, PhD); microbiology (MS, PhD); molecular biology (MS, PhD); molecular biophysics (PhD); neuroscience (PhD); oceanography (MS, PhD); organic chemistry (MS, PhD); philosophy (MA, PhD); physical chemistry (MS, PhD); physics (MS, PhD); plant sciences (MS, PhD); pure mathematics (MS, PhD); religion (MA, PhD); rhetoric and composition (MA, PhD); Slavic languages and literatures (MA); Slavic languages/Russian (MA); social psychology (PhD); software engineering (MA, MS); Spanish (MA, PhD). *Application fee:* $30. *Application Contact:* Ginger Martin, Academic Coordinator, 850-644-1081, Fax: 850-644-9656, E-mail: vmartin@mailer.fsu.edu. *Dean*, Dr. Joseph Travis, 850-644-1081.

College of Business Students: 145 full-time (62 women), 444 part-time (143 women); includes 147 minority (58 African Americans, 3 American Indian/Alaska Native, 45 Asian Americans or Pacific Islanders, 41 Hispanic Americans). Average age 29. 789 applicants, 50% accepted, 321 enrolled. *Faculty:* 107 full-time (26 women), 21 part-time/adjunct (2 women). Expenses: Contact institution. *Financial support:* In 2006–07, 126 students received support, including 40 fellowships with partial tuition reimbursements available (averaging $4,600 per year), 37 research assistantships with partial tuition reimbursements available (averaging $4,600 per year), 49 teaching assistantships with partial tuition reimbursements available (averaging $10,500 per year); unspecified assistantships also available. Financial award application deadline: 1/1. In 2006, 263 master's, 19 doctorates awarded. *Degree program information:* Part-time and evening/weekend programs available. Postbaccalaureate distance learning degree programs offered (no on-campus study). Offers accounting (M Acc); business administration (MBA, PhD); insurance (MSM); management information systems (MS). *Application deadline:* For fall admission, 5/1 for domestic and international students; for spring admission, 10/1 for domestic students, 9/1 for international students. Applications are processed on a rolling basis. *Application fee:* $30. Electronic applications accepted. *Application Contact:* Lisa Beverly, Coordinator, Graduate Programs Admissions, 850-644-6458, Fax: 850-644-0588, E-mail: lbeverly@cob.fsu.edu. *Dean*, Dr. Caryn Beck-Duolley, 850-644-3090, Fax: 850-644-0915.

College of Communication Students: 172 full-time (141 women), 108 part-time (62 women); includes 102 minority (41 African Americans, 1 American Indian/Alaska Native, 37 Asian Americans or Pacific Islanders, 23 Hispanic Americans), 4 international. Average age 27. 361 applicants, 46% accepted, 99 enrolled. *Faculty:* 43 full-time (21 women), 9 part-time/adjunct (7 women). Expenses: Contact institution. *Financial support:* In 2006–07, 101 students received support, including 2 fellowships with full tuition reimbursements available (averaging $16,300 per year), 29 research assistantships with full and partial tuition reimbursements available, 56 teaching assistantships with full and partial tuition reimbursements available; career-related internships or fieldwork, Federal Work-Study, institutionally sponsored loans, tuition waivers (partial), and unspecified assistantships also available. Support available to part-time students. Financial award applicants required to submit FAFSA. In 2006, 102 master's, 13 doctorates awarded. *Degree program information:* Part-time programs available. Offers communication (Adv M, MA, MS, PhD); communication sciences and disorders (Adv M, MS, PhD); integrated marketing communication (MA, MS); mass communication (MA, MS, PhD); media and communication studies (MA, MS); speech communication (PhD). *Application deadline:* For fall admission, 2/1 priority date for domestic students, 2/1 for international students; for winter admission, 11/1 priority date for domestic students. Applications are processed on a rolling basis. *Application fee:* $30. Electronic applications accepted. *Dean*, Dr. John K. Mayo, 850-644-9698, Fax: 850-644-0611.

College of Criminology and Criminal Justice Students: 84 full-time (56 women), 37 part-time (25 women); includes 23 minority (11 African Americans, 2 American Indian/Alaska Native, 4 Asian Americans or Pacific Islanders, 6 Hispanic Americans). Average age 25. 104 applicants, 60% accepted, 32 enrolled. *Faculty:* 21 full-time (5 women). Expenses: Contact institution. *Financial support:* In 2006–07, 29 research assistantships with full tuition reimbursements (averaging $11,000 per year) were awarded; fellowships with full tuition reimbursements, institutionally sponsored loans, scholarships/grants, tuition waivers (partial), and unspecified assistantships also available. Financial award application deadline: 2/15; financial award applicants required to submit FAFSA. In 2006, 37 master's, 4 doctorates awarded. *Degree program information:* Part-time and evening/weekend programs available. Postbaccalaureate distance learning degree programs offered (no on-campus study). Offers criminology and criminal justice (MA, MSC, PhD). *Application deadline:* For fall admission, 7/1 for domestic students, 3/1 for international students. Applications are processed on a rolling basis. *Application fee:* $30. Electronic applications accepted. *Application Contact:* Margarita Frankeberger, Graduate Student Coordinator, 850-644-7373, Fax: 850-645-1454, E-mail: mfrankeb@mailer.fsu.edu. *Dean*, Dr. Thomas Blomberg, 850-644-7380, Fax: 850-644-9614.

College of Education Students: 1,247; includes 355 minority (164 African Americans, 3 American Indian/Alaska Native, 125 Asian Americans or Pacific Islanders, 63 Hispanic Americans). 1,114 applicants, 52% accepted, 335 enrolled. *Faculty:* 94 full-time (55 women), 34 part-time/adjunct (16 women). Expenses: Contact institution. *Financial support:* In 2006–07, 13 fellowships, 207 research assistantships, 205 teaching assistantships were awarded; career-related internships or fieldwork and traineeships also available. Financial award applicants required to submit FAFSA. In 2006, 330 master's, 58 doctorates, 37 other advanced degrees awarded. *Degree program information:* Part-time and evening/weekend programs available. Postbaccalaureate distance learning degree programs offered. Offers adult education and human resource development (MS, Ed D, PhD, Ed S); counseling/school psychology (PhD); early childhood education (MS, Ed D, PhD, Ed S); education (MS, Ed D, PhD, Ed S); educational administration/leadership (MS, Ed D, PhD, Ed S); educational leadership/administration (MS, Ed D, PhD, Ed S); educational psychology (MS, PhD); elementary education (MS, Ed D, PhD, Ed S); emotional disturbance/learning disabilities (MS); English education (MS, PhD, Ed S); health education (MS); higher education (MS, Ed D, PhD, Ed S); history and philosophy of education (MS, PhD, Ed S); institutional research (MS, Ed D, PhD, Ed S); instructional systems (MS, PhD, Ed S); international and intercultural education (MS, PhD, Ed S); learning and cognition (MS, PhD); mathematics education (MS, PhD, Ed S); measurement and statistics (MS, PhD); mental retardation (MS); multilingual-multicultural education (MS, PhD, Ed S); open and distance learning (MS); physical education (MS, Ed D, PhD, Ed S); policy planning and analysis (MS, Ed D, PhD, Ed S); program evaluation (MS, PhD); psychological services (MS, PhD, Ed S); reading education/language arts (MS, Ed D, PhD, Ed S); recreation management (MS); rehabilitation counseling (MS, PhD, Ed S); school psychology (MS, Ed S); science education (MS, PhD, Ed S); social science education (MS, Ed D, PhD, Ed S); social, history and philosophy of education (MS, PhD, Ed S); special education (MS, PhD, Ed S); sport management (MS, Ed D, PhD, Ed S); sports psychology (MS, PhD); visual disabilities (MS). *Application deadline:* For fall admission, 7/1 priority date for domestic students; for spring admission, 11/1 for domestic students. Applications are processed on a rolling basis. *Application fee:* $30. Electronic applications accepted. *Application Contact:* Gwendolyn Harris Johnson, Graduate Coordinator, Office of Academic Services, 850-644-3760, Fax: 850-644-6868, E-mail: johnson@coe.fsu.edu. *Dean*, Dr. Marcy P Driscoll, 850-644-6885, Fax: 850-644-2725, E-mail: driscoll@coe.fsu.edu.

College of Human Sciences Students: 116 full-time (93 women), 70 part-time (56 women); includes 47 minority (31 African Americans, 5 Asian Americans or Pacific Islanders, 11 Hispanic Americans), 23 international. 161 applicants, 63% accepted, 50 enrolled. *Faculty:* 43 full-time (31 women). Expenses: Contact institution. *Financial support:* In 2006–07, 94 students received support, including 4 fellowships with partial tuition reimbursements available (averaging $10,000 per year), 14 research assistantships with partial tuition reimbursements available (averaging $8,000 per year), 60 teaching assistantships with partial tuition reimbursements available (averaging $8,000 per year); career-related internships or fieldwork, Federal Work-Study, institutionally sponsored loans, scholarships/grants, and unspecified assistantships also available. Financial award application deadline: 1/15; financial award applicants required to submit FAFSA. In 2006, 41 master's, 12 doctorates awarded. *Degree program information:* Part-time programs available. Offers apparel product development (MS); apparel/textile product development (PhD); child development (MS, PhD); creative design (MS); exercise science (PhD); family relations (MS, PhD); global product development (MS); human sciences (MS, PhD); marriage and family therapy (PhD); nutrition and food science (PhD); nutrition and food sciences (MS); professional merchandising

(MS); retail merchandising (MS, PhD); textiles (MS). *Application deadline:* For fall admission, 7/1 for domestic students, 5/1 for international students; for spring admission, 11/1 for domestic students, 12/1 for international students. Applications are processed on a rolling basis. *Application fee:* $30. Electronic applications accepted. *Application Contact:* Jennifer Boyles, Coordinator of Academic Support Services, 850-644-7221, Fax: 850-644-0700, E-mail: jaboyles@fsu.edu. *Dean,* Dr. Billie J. Collier, 850-644-1281, Fax: 850-644-0700, E-mail: bcollier@fsu.edu.

College of Information Students: 47 full-time (31 women), 746 part-time (541 women); includes 151 minority (76 African Americans, 4 American Indian/Alaska Native, 23 Asian Americans or Pacific Islanders, 48 Hispanic Americans), 47 international. Average age 35. 502 applicants, 75% accepted, 263 enrolled. *Faculty:* 29 full-time (14 women), 8 part-time/adjunct (4 women). Expenses: Contact institution. *Financial support:* In 2006–07, 209 students received support, including 13 fellowships with full tuition reimbursements available, 102 research assistantships with full tuition reimbursements available, 94 teaching assistantships with full tuition reimbursements available; career-related internships or fieldwork, Federal Work-Study, scholarships/grants, and unspecified assistantships also available. Financial award application deadline: 3/1; financial award applicants required to submit FAFSA. In 2006, 202 master's, 5 doctorates, 4 other advanced degrees awarded. *Degree program information:* Part-time and evening/weekend programs available. Postbaccalaureate distance learning degree programs offered (no on-campus study). Offers library and information studies (MS, PhD, Specialist). *Application deadline:* For fall admission, 6/1 priority date for domestic students, 6/1 for international students. Applications are processed on a rolling basis. *Application fee:* $30. Electronic applications accepted. *Application Contact:* Delores Bryant, Graduate Program Assistant, 850-644-5775, Fax: 850-644-9763, E-mail: grad@ci.fsu.edu. *Dean,* Dr. Lawrence Dennis, 850-644-2216, Fax: 850-644-9763, E-mail: ldennis@ci.fsu.edu.

College of Motion Picture, Television, and Recording Arts Students: 56 full-time (19 women); includes 20 minority (6 African Americans, 11 Asian Americans or Pacific Islanders, 3 Hispanic Americans), 9 international. Average age 27. 207 applicants, 14% accepted, 30 enrolled. *Faculty:* 11 full-time (3 women). Expenses: Contact institution. *Financial support:* In 2006–07, 1 fellowship with partial tuition reimbursement (averaging $6,300 per year), 12 teaching assistantships with partial tuition reimbursements (averaging $4,100 per year) were awarded; Federal Work-Study and unspecified assistantships also available. Financial award application deadline: 1/1; financial award applicants required to submit FAFSA. In 2006, 28 degrees awarded. Offers production (MFA); screen and play writing (MFA). *Application deadline:* For fall admission, 12/15 for domestic and international students. *Application fee:* $30. *Application Contact:* Cynthia Lugo, Program Assistant, 850-644-8524, Fax: 850-644-2626, E-mail: clugo@film.fsu.edu. *Dean,* Frank Patterson, 850-644-0453, Fax: 850-644-2626.

College of Music Students: 406 full-time (211 women); includes 98 minority (28 African Americans, 38 Asian Americans or Pacific Islanders, 32 Hispanic Americans). Average age 26. 525 applicants, 38% accepted, 145 enrolled. *Faculty:* 88 full-time, 13 part-time/adjunct. Expenses: Contact institution. *Financial support:* In 2006–07, 225 students received support, including 3 fellowships with full tuition reimbursements available (averaging $15,000 per year), 9 research assistantships with full tuition reimbursements available (averaging $3,000 per year), 173 teaching assistantships with full tuition reimbursements available (averaging $3,000 per year); career-related internships or fieldwork, Federal Work-Study, and tuition waivers (partial) also available. Support available to part-time students. Financial award application deadline: 2/28; financial award applicants required to submit FAFSA. In 2006, 102 master's, 41 doctorates awarded. Offers accompanying (MM); arts administration (MA); choral conducting (MM); composition (MM, DM); ethnomusicology (MM); instrumental accompanying (MM); instrumental conducting (MM); jazz studies (MM); music education (MM Ed, Ed D, PhD); music theory (MM, PhD); music therapy (MM); musicology (MM, PhD); opera (MM); performance (MM, DM); piano pedagogy (MM); vocal accompanying (MM). *Application deadline:* For fall admission, 7/1 for domestic students, 5/2 for international students; for spring admission, 11/3 for domestic students, 9/1 for international students. Applications are processed on a rolling basis. *Application fee:* $30. Electronic applications accepted. *Application Contact:* Dr. Seth Beckman, Assistant Dean for Academic Affairs/Director of Graduate Studies, 850-644-5848, Fax: 850-644-2033, E-mail: sbeckman@mailer.fsu.edu. *Dean,* Don Gibson, 850-644-4361, Fax: 850-644-2033.

College of Nursing Students: 10 full-time (all women), 75 part-time (69 women); includes 16 minority (10 African Americans, 2 Asian Americans or Pacific Islanders, 4 Hispanic Americans). Average age 39. 43 applicants, 81% accepted, 32 enrolled. *Faculty:* 10 full-time (9 women), 1 part-time/adjunct (0 women). Expenses: Contact institution. *Financial support:* In 2006–07, 25 students received support, including 1 fellowship with partial tuition reimbursement available (averaging $6,300 per year), 3 research assistantships with partial tuition reimbursements available (averaging $3,000 per year), 13 teaching assistantships with partial tuition reimbursements available (averaging $3,000 per year); career-related internships or fieldwork, Federal Work-Study, institutionally sponsored loans, traineeships, and tuition waivers (partial) also available. Financial award application deadline: 4/15; financial award applicants required to submit FAFSA. In 2006, 13 master's, 9 other advanced degrees awarded. *Degree program information:* Part-time programs available. Postbaccalaureate distance learning degree programs offered (no on-campus study). Offers family nurse practitioner (MSN, Certificate); nurse educator (MSN, Certificate); pediatric nurse practitioner (MSN, Certificate). *Application deadline:* For fall admission, 7/1 for domestic students; for spring admission, 10/15 for domestic students. Applications are processed on a rolling basis. *Application fee:* $30. Electronic applications accepted. *Application Contact:* Eddie Page, Graduate Program Coordinator, 850-644-5638, Fax: 850-645-7321, E-mail: epage@fsu.edu. *Dean,* Dr. Katherine P. Mason, 850-644-5417, Fax: 850-644-7660, E-mail: kmason@mailer.fsu.edu.

College of Social Sciences Students: 376 full-time (165 women), 282 part-time (156 women); includes 138 minority (92 African Americans, 1 American Indian/Alaska Native, 7 Asian Americans or Pacific Islanders, 38 Hispanic Americans), 78 international. Average age 27. 811 applicants, 69% accepted, 241 enrolled. *Faculty:* 129 full-time (32 women), 12 part-time/adjunct (4 women). Expenses: Contact institution. *Financial support:* In 2006–07, 196 students received support, including 16 fellowships with full and partial tuition reimbursements available (averaging $16,421 per year), 79 research assistantships with full and partial tuition reimbursements available (averaging $10,318 per year), 85 teaching assistantships with tuition reimbursements available (averaging $12,775 per year); career-related internships or fieldwork, Federal Work-Study, institutionally sponsored loans, scholarships/grants, health care benefits, tuition waivers (full and partial), and unspecified assistantships also available. Support available to part-time students. Financial award application deadline: 1/15; financial award applicants required to submit FAFSA. In 2006, 195 master's, 32 doctorates awarded. *Degree program information:* Part-time and evening/weekend programs available. Offers Asian studies (MA); demography and population health (MS, Certificate); economics (MS, PhD); geographic information systems (MS); geography (MA, MS, PhD); international affairs (MA, MS); political science (MA, MS, PhD); public administration and policy (MPA, PhD, Certificate); Russian and East European studies (MA); social health sciences (MHPR, MPA, MPH, MS); social science (MA, MS); social sciences (MA, MHPR, MPA, MPH, MS, MSP, PhD, Certificate); sociology (MA, MS, PhD); urban and regional planning (MSP, PhD). *Application deadline:* For fall admission, 6/1 priority date for domestic students, 7/1 priority date for international students; for spring admission, 10/15 priority date for domestic students, 9/1 priority date for international students. Applications are processed on a rolling basis. *Application fee:* $30. Electronic applications accepted. *Dean,* Dr. David W. Rasmussen, 850-644-5488, Fax: 850-645-4923, E-mail: drasmuss@coss.fsu.edu.

College of Social Work Students: 241 full-time (208 women), 138 part-time (114 women); includes 86 minority (55 African Americans, 3 American Indian/Alaska Native, 6 Asian Americans or Pacific Islanders, 22 Hispanic Americans). Average age 30. 343 applicants, 62% accepted, 138 enrolled. *Faculty:* 33 full-time (19 women), 28 part-time/adjunct (24 women). Expenses: Contact institution. *Financial support:* In 2006–07, 79 students received support, including 9 fellowships with partial tuition reimbursements available, 35 research assistantships with partial tuition reimbursements available (averaging $3,500 per year), 21 teaching assistantships with full tuition reimbursements available (averaging $15,000 per year); career-related internships or fieldwork, Federal Work-Study, institutionally sponsored loans, scholarships/grants, traineeships, health care benefits, and unspecified assistantships also available. Support available to part-time students. Financial award application deadline: 3/1; financial award applicants required to submit FAFSA. In 2006, 151 master's, 7 doctorates awarded. *Degree program information:* Part-time and evening/weekend programs available. Postbaccalaureate distance learning degree programs offered (no on-campus study). Offers clinical social work (MSW); social policy and administration (MSW); social work (PhD). *Application deadline:* For fall admission, 6/1 priority date for domestic students; for winter admission, 3/1 priority date for domestic students; for spring admission, 11/1 priority date for domestic students. Applications are processed on a rolling basis. Electronic applications accepted. *Application Contact:* Vicky Verano, Director of Recruitment and Admissions, 800-378-9550, Fax: 850-644-9750, E-mail: vveranoc@mailer.fsu.edu. *Dean,* Dr. C. Aaron McNeece, 850-644-4752, Fax: 850-644-9750.

College of Visual Arts, Theatre and Dance Students: 289 full-time (214 women), 101 part-time (70 women); includes 69 minority (33 African Americans, 2 American Indian/Alaska Native, 23 Asian Americans or Pacific Islanders, 11 Hispanic Americans), 5 international. Average age 27. 266 applicants, 60% accepted, 113 enrolled. *Faculty:* 89 full-time (43 women), 10 part-time/adjunct (all women). Expenses: Contact institution. *Financial support:* In 2006–07, 4 fellowships with partial tuition reimbursements (averaging $18,000 per year), 90 research assistantships with partial tuition reimbursements (averaging $4,957 per year), 78 teaching assistantships with partial tuition reimbursements (averaging $8,001 per year) were awarded; career-related internships or fieldwork, Federal Work-Study, institutionally sponsored loans, scholarships/grants, and unspecified assistantships also available. Support available to part-time students. Financial award applicants required to submit FAFSA. In 2006, 92 master's, 14 doctorates, 16 other advanced degrees awarded. *Degree program information:* Part-time programs available. Offers American dance studies (MA); art education (MA, MS, Ed D, PhD, Ed S); art history (MA, PhD); dance (MFA); interior design (MA, MFA, MS); museum studies (Certificate); studio and related studies (MA); studio art (MFA); visual arts, theatre and dance (MA, MFA, MS, Ed D, PhD, Certificate, Ed S). *Application deadline:* Applications are processed on a rolling basis. *Application fee:* $30. Electronic applications accepted. *Dean,* Dr. Sally E. McRorie, 850-664-5244, Fax: 850-644-2604, E-mail: smcrorie@mailer.fsu.edu.

FAMU-FSU College of Engineering Students: 271 full-time (58 women); includes 179 minority (57 African Americans, 104 Asian Americans or Pacific Islanders, 18 Hispanic Americans). Average age 29. 285 applicants, 49% accepted, 66 enrolled. *Faculty:* 82 full-time (10 women), 12 part-time/adjunct (1 woman). Expenses: Contact institution. *Financial support:* In 2006–07, 3 fellowships with full tuition reimbursements (averaging $18,000 per year), 162 research assistantships with full tuition reimbursements, 60 teaching assistantships with full tuition reimbursements were awarded; career-related internships or fieldwork, institutionally sponsored loans, scholarships/grants, tuition waivers (full), and unspecified assistantships also available. Financial award application deadline: 6/15. In 2006, 47 master's, 22 doctorates awarded. *Degree program information:* Part-time programs available. Postbaccalaureate distance learning degree programs offered (minimal on-campus study). Offers biomedical engineering (MS, PhD); chemical engineering (MS, PhD); civil and environmental engineering (MS, PhD); electrical engineering (MS, PhD); engineering (MS, PhD); industrial engineering (MS, PhD); mechanical engineering (MS, PhD). *Application deadline:* For fall admission, 7/1 for domestic students, 5/1 for international students; for spring admission, 11/1 for domestic students, 9/1 for international students. Applications are processed on a rolling basis. *Application fee:* $30. *Dean and Professor,* Dr. Ching-Jen Chen, 850-410-6439, Fax: 850-410-6546, E-mail: cjchen@eng.fsu.edu.

School of Theatre Students: 98 full-time (53 women), 12 part-time (4 women); includes 12 minority (6 African Americans, 1 American Indian/Alaska Native, 1 Asian American or Pacific Islander, 4 Hispanic Americans). Average age 25. 88 applicants, 42% accepted, 22 enrolled. *Faculty:* 21 full-time (9 women). Expenses: Contact institution. *Financial support:* In 2006–07, 1 fellowship with full tuition reimbursement (averaging $18,000 per year), 31 research assistantships with full tuition reimbursements (averaging $8,300 per year), 57 teaching assistantships with full tuition reimbursements (averaging $8,900 per year) were awarded; career-related internships or fieldwork, Federal Work-Study, institutionally sponsored loans, scholarships/grants, health care benefits, and unspecified assistantships also available. Financial award application deadline: 1/1; financial award applicants required to submit FAFSA. In 2006, 29 master's, 1 doctorate awarded. Offers acting (MFA); directing (MFA); lighting, costume, and scenic design (MFA); technical production (MFA); theater management (MFA); theatre (MA, MS, PhD). *Application deadline:* For fall admission, 1/1 priority date for domestic and international students. Applications are processed on a rolling basis. *Application fee:* $30. *Application Contact:* Barbara Thomas, Program Assistant, 850-644-7234, Fax: 850-644-7246, E-mail: bgthomas@admin.fsu.edu. *Director,* Cameron Jackson, 850-644-7257, Fax: 850-644-7408, E-mail: ccjackson@admin.fsu.edu.

See Close-Up on page 897.

FONTBONNE UNIVERSITY, St. Louis, MO 63105-3098

General Information Independent-religious, coed, comprehensive institution. *Enrollment:* 2,924 graduate, professional, and undergraduate students; 446 full-time matriculated graduate/professional students (310 women), 360 part-time matriculated graduate/professional students (273 women). *Enrollment by degree level:* 806 master's. *Graduate faculty:* 27 full-time (15 women), 120 part-time/adjunct (55 women). *Tuition:* Full-time $4,890; part-time $489 per credit. *Required fees:* $160; $76 per credit. Full-time tuition and fees vary according to course load and program. *Graduate housing:* Room and/or apartments available on a first-come, first-served basis to single students; on-campus housing not available to married students. Typical cost: $6,970 (including board). Room and board charges vary according to board plan and housing facility selected. Housing application deadline: 3/8. *Student services:* Career counseling, disabled student services, free psychological counseling, international student services, multicultural affairs office. *Library facilities:* Fontbonne Library. *Online resources:* library catalog, web page, access to other libraries' catalogs. *Collection:* 88,063 titles, 19,532 serial subscriptions, 3,084 audiovisual materials.

Computer facilities: 120 computers available on campus for general student use. A campuswide network can be accessed from student residence rooms and from off campus. Internet access and online class registration are available. *Web address:* http://www.fontbonne.edu/.

General Application Contact: Peggy Musen, Associate Dean of Enrollment Management and Director of Admissions, 314-889-1400, Fax: 314-889-1451, E-mail: pmusen@fontbonne.edu.

GRADUATE UNITS

Graduate Programs Students: 446 full-time (310 women), 360 part-time (273 women); includes 318 minority (305 African Americans, 3 American Indian/Alaska Native, 5 Asian Americans or Pacific Islanders, 5 Hispanic Americans), 44 international. Average age 35. *Faculty:* 27 full-time (15 women), 120 part-time/adjunct (55 women). Expenses: Contact institution. *Financial support:* Fellowships with full tuition reimbursements, teaching assistantships with partial tuition reimbursements available. Support available to part-time students. Financial award application deadline: 4/1; financial award applicants required to submit FAFSA. In 2006, 312 degrees awarded. *Degree program information:* Part-time and evening/weekend programs available. Offers accounting (MS); art (MA); business administration (MBA); computer education (MS); early intervention in deaf education (MA); education (MA); family and consumer sciences (MA); fine arts (MFA); options in business administration (MBA); options in management (MM); speech-language pathology (MS); taxation (MST); theater education (MA). *Application deadline:* For fall admission, 8/15 priority date for domestic students; for spring admission, 12/15 for domestic students. Applications are processed on a rolling basis. *Application fee:* $25. Electronic applications accepted. *Vice President and Dean for Academic and Student Affairs,* Dr. Nancy Blattner, 314-889-1401, Fax: 314-889-1451, E-mail: nblattner@fontbonne.edu.

FORDHAM UNIVERSITY, New York, NY 10458

General Information Independent-religious, coed, university. CGS member. *Enrollment:* 14,732 graduate, professional, and undergraduate students; 3,298 full-time matriculated

Fordham University (continued)

graduate/professional students (2,020 women), 3,838 part-time matriculated graduate/professional students (2,407 women). *Graduate faculty:* 502 full-time, 416 part-time/adjunct. *Graduate housing:* Room and/or apartments available on a first-come, first-served basis to single students; on-campus housing not available to married students. Housing application deadline: 4/10. *Student services:* Campus employment opportunities, campus safety program, career counseling, disabled student services, free psychological counseling, international student services, low-cost health insurance, teacher training, writing training. *Library facilities:* Walsh Library plus 3 others. *Online resources:* library catalog, web page, access to other libraries' catalogs. *Collection:* 2.4 million titles, 32,300 serial subscriptions, 32,621 audiovisual materials. *Research affiliation:* Memorial Sloan-Kettering Cancer Center, Wildlife Conservation Society, New York Ocean Science Library, New York Botanical Gardens, Folger Shakespeare Library, Equator Initiative /UNDP.

Computer facilities: Computer purchase and lease plans are available. 1,400 computers available on campus for general student use. A campuswide network can be accessed from student residence rooms and from off campus. Internet access and online class registration are available. *Web address:* http://www.fordham.edu/.

General Application Contact: Charlene Dundie, Director of Graduate Admissions, 718-817-4420, Fax: 718-817-3566, E-mail: dundie@fordham.edu.

GRADUATE UNITS

Graduate School of Arts and Sciences Students: 392 full-time (209 women), 462 part-time (229 women); includes 99 minority (37 African Americans, 2 American Indian/Alaska Native, 25 Asian Americans or Pacific Islanders, 35 Hispanic Americans), 134 international. Average age 30. 1,432 applicants, 39% accepted, 258 enrolled. *Faculty:* 249 full-time (81 women), 6 part-time/adjunct. Expenses: Contact institution. *Financial support:* In 2006–07, 25 fellowships with full and partial tuition reimbursements (averaging $18,070 per year), 180 research assistantships with full and partial tuition reimbursements (averaging $15,648 per year), 101 teaching assistantships with full and partial tuition reimbursements (averaging $13,439 per year) were awarded; career-related internships or fieldwork, Federal Work-Study, institutionally sponsored loans, scholarships/grants, health care benefits, tuition waivers (full and partial), and unspecified assistantships also available. Support available to part-time students. Financial award application deadline: 1/4; financial award applicants required to submit FAFSA. In 2006, 200 master's, 63 doctorates, 15 other advanced degrees awarded. *Degree program information:* Part-time and evening/weekend programs available. Offers applied developmental psychology (PhD); arts and sciences (MA, MS, PhD, Certificate); biological sciences (MS, PhD); classical Greek and Latin literature (MA); classics (PhD); clinical psychology (PhD); computer science (MS); economics (MA, PhD); elections and campaign management (MA); English language and literature (MA, PhD); health care ethics (Certificate); history (MA, PhD); humanities and sciences (MA); international political economy and development (MA, Certificate); Latin American and Latino studies (Certificate); philosophical resources (MA); philosophy (MA, PhD); psychometrics (PhD); public communications (MA); sociology (MA, PhD); theology (MA, PhD). *Application deadline:* For fall admission, 1/4 priority date for domestic and international students; for spring admission, 10/31 for domestic and international students. *Application fee:* $65. Electronic applications accepted. *Application Contact:* Charlene Dundie, Director of Graduate Admissions, 718-817-4420, Fax: 718-817-3566, E-mail: dundie@fordham.edu. *Dean,* Dr. Nancy A. Busch, 718-817-4400, Fax: 718-817-4474, E-mail: busch@fordham.edu.

Center for Medieval Studies Students: 5 full-time (4 women), 7 part-time (6 women), 1 international. Average age 28. 19 applicants, 84% accepted, 9 enrolled. Expenses: Contact institution. *Financial support:* In 2006–07, 3 students received support, including 3 research assistantships with tuition reimbursements available (averaging $14,900 per year); fellowships with tuition reimbursements available, institutionally sponsored loans, tuition waivers (full and partial), and unspecified assistantships also available. Financial award application deadline: 1/4; financial award applicants required to submit FAFSA. In 2006, 8 degrees awarded. *Degree program information:* Part-time and evening/weekend programs available. Offers medieval studies (MA, Certificate). *Application deadline:* For fall admission, 1/4 priority date for domestic students; for spring admission, 11/1 for domestic students. *Application fee:* $65. Electronic applications accepted. *Application Contact:* Charlene Dundie, Director of Graduate Admissions, 718-817-4420, Fax: 718-817-3566, E-mail: dundie@fordham.edu. *Director,* Dr. Maryanne Kowaleski, 718-817-4655, E-mail: kowaleski@fordham.edu.

Graduate School of Business Students: 345 full-time (132 women), 1,183 part-time (448 women); includes 238 minority (59 African Americans, 1 American Indian/Alaska Native, 116 Asian Americans or Pacific Islanders, 62 Hispanic Americans), 77 international. 1,081 applicants, 65% accepted, 422 enrolled. *Faculty:* 87 full-time, 41 part-time/adjunct. Expenses: Contact institution. *Financial support:* In 2006–07, 7 fellowships (averaging $27,000 per year), 128 research assistantships were awarded; career-related internships or fieldwork, institutionally sponsored loans, scholarships/grants, and unspecified assistantships also available. Support available to part-time students. Financial award application deadline: 5/1; financial award applicants required to submit FAFSA. In 2006, 454 degrees awarded. *Degree program information:* Part-time and evening/weekend programs available. Offers accounting (MBA); communications and media management (MBA); finance (MBA, MS); information systems (MBA, MS); management systems (MBA); marketing (MBA); media management (MS); taxation (MS). *Application deadline:* For fall admission, 6/1 priority date for domestic students, 5/1 priority date for international students; for winter admission, 11/1 priority date for domestic students, 10/1 priority date for international students; for spring admission, 3/1 priority date for domestic students, 2/1 priority date for international students. Applications are processed on a rolling basis. *Application fee:* $65. Electronic applications accepted. *Application Contact:* Frank Fletcher, Director of Admissions and Financial Aid, 212-636-6200, Fax: 212-636-7076, E-mail: admissionsgb@fordham.edu. *Dean,* Dr. Howard Tuckman, 212-636-6165, Fax: 212-307-1779, E-mail: tuckman@fordham.edu.

Graduate School of Education Students: 187 full-time (142 women), 1,164 part-time (883 women); includes 368 minority (136 African Americans, 1 American Indian/Alaska Native, 69 Asian Americans or Pacific Islanders, 162 Hispanic Americans), 5 international. Average age 34. 1,283 applicants, 73% accepted, 506 enrolled. *Faculty:* 48 full-time (32 women), 81 part-time/adjunct (54 women). Expenses: Contact institution. *Financial support:* In 2006–07, 557 students received support, including 131 fellowships with partial tuition reimbursements available (averaging $3,500 per year), 91 research assistantships with partial tuition reimbursements available (averaging $8,250 per year); career-related internships or fieldwork, Federal Work-Study, and scholarships/grants also available. Support available to part-time students. Financial award applicants required to submit FAFSA. In 2006, 573 master's, 45 doctorates, 6 other advanced degrees awarded. *Degree program information:* Part-time and evening/weekend programs available. Offers education (MAT, MS, MSE, MST, Ed D, PhD, Adv C). *Application fee:* $65. *Application Contact:* Dr. Joseph Korevec, Director of Admissions and Financial Aid, 212-636-6400, Fax: 212-636-7826, E-mail: korevec@fordham.edu. *Dean,* Dr. James Hennessy, 212-636-6400, E-mail: hennessy@fordham.edu.

Division of Curriculum and Teaching Students: 68 full-time (51 women), 663 part-time (612 women); includes 200 minority (74 African Americans, 1 American Indian/Alaska Native, 37 Asian Americans or Pacific Islanders, 88 Hispanic Americans), 3 international. Average age 32. 636 applicants, 86% accepted, 322 enrolled. *Faculty:* 22 full-time (18 women), 38 part-time/adjunct (28 women). Expenses: Contact institution. *Financial support:* Applicants required to submit FAFSA. In 2006, 351 master's, 8 doctorates awarded. Offers adult education (MS, MSE); bilingual teacher education (MSE); curriculum and teaching (MSE); early childhood education (MSE); elementary education (MST); language, literacy, and learning (PhD); reading education (MSE, Adv C); secondary education (MAT, MSE); special education (MSE, Adv C); teaching English as a second language (MSE). *Application fee:* $65. *Chairperson,* Dr. Terry Osborn, 212-636-6450.

Division of Educational Leadership, Administration and Policy Students: 1 full-time (0 women), 229 part-time (174 women); includes 62 minority (23 African Americans, 12 Asian Americans or Pacific Islanders, 27 Hispanic Americans), 1 international. Average age 39. 144 applicants, 73% accepted, 82 enrolled. *Faculty:* 8 full-time (3 women), 20 part-time/adjunct (12 women). Expenses: Contact institution. *Financial support:* Career-related internships or fieldwork available. Financial award applicants required to submit FAFSA. In 2006, 105 master's, 19 doctorates awarded. Offers administration and supervision (MSE, Adv C); administration and supervision for church leaders (PhD); educational administration and supervision (Ed D, PhD); human resource program administration (MS). *Application fee:* $65. *Chairperson,* Dr. Gerald Cattaro, 212-636-6441.

Division of Psychological and Educational Services Students: 118 full-time (90 women), 272 part-time (206 women); includes 106 minority (39 African Americans, 20 Asian Americans or Pacific Islanders, 47 Hispanic Americans), 1 international. Average age 30. 503 applicants, 58% accepted, 102 enrolled. *Faculty:* 18 full-time (11 women), 23 part-time/adjunct (14 women). Expenses: Contact institution. *Financial support:* Applicants required to submit FAFSA. In 2006, 117 master's, 18 doctorates, 6 other advanced degrees awarded. Offers counseling and personnel services (MSE, Adv C); counseling psychology (PhD); educational psychology (MSE, PhD); school psychology (PhD); urban and urban bilingual school psychology (Adv C). *Application fee:* $65. *Chairman,* Dr. Mitch Rabinowitz, 212-636-6461.

Graduate School of Religion and Religious Education Students: 70 full-time (28 women), 121 part-time (50 women); includes 29 minority (5 African Americans, 7 Asian Americans or Pacific Islanders, 17 Hispanic Americans), 75 international. Average age 37. 78 applicants, 96% accepted, 53 enrolled. *Faculty:* 9 full-time (3 women), 10 part-time/adjunct (3 women). Expenses: Contact institution. *Financial support:* In 2006–07, 140 students received support, including 3 research assistantships with full tuition reimbursements available (averaging $4,400 per year); scholarships/grants, unspecified assistantships, and university work-study also available. Support available to part-time students. Financial award application deadline: 2/1. In 2006, 38 master's, 8 doctorates, 3 other advanced degrees awarded. *Degree program information:* Part-time programs available. Offers pastoral counseling and spiritual care (MA); pastoral ministry/spirituality/pastoral counseling (D Min); religion and religious education (MA); religious education (MS, PhD, PD); spiritual direction (Certificate). *Application deadline:* For fall admission, 7/1 priority date for domestic students, 5/1 priority date for international students; for spring admission, 12/1 priority date for domestic students, 10/1 priority date for international students. Applications are processed on a rolling basis. *Application fee:* $65. Electronic applications accepted. *Application Contact:* Dr. Robert Binder, Associate Dean, 718-817-4808, Fax: 718-817-3352, E-mail: binder@fordham.edu. *Dean,* Rev. Anthony J. Ciorra, 718-817-4804, Fax: 718-817-3352, E-mail: ciorra@fordham.edu.

Graduate School of Social Service Students: 972 full-time (866 women), 373 part-time (326 women); includes 506 minority (280 African Americans, 28 Asian Americans or Pacific Islanders, 198 Hispanic Americans). Average age 32. 1,701 applicants, 61% accepted, 694 enrolled. *Faculty:* 50 full-time (38 women), 85 part-time/adjunct (61 women). Expenses: Contact institution. *Financial support:* In 2006–07, 838 students received support, including 39 research assistantships with partial tuition reimbursements available (averaging $1,980 per year); fellowships with partial tuition reimbursements available, career-related internships or fieldwork, scholarships/grants, tuition waivers (partial), and unspecified assistantships also available. Support available to part-time students. Financial award application deadline: 9/1; financial award applicants required to submit FAFSA. In 2006, 539 degrees awarded. *Degree program information:* Part-time and evening/weekend programs available. Offers social work (MSW, PhD). *Application deadline:* For fall admission, 6/1 priority date for domestic students; for spring admission, 12/1 priority date for domestic students. Applications are processed on a rolling basis. *Application fee:* $50. *Application Contact:* Elaine Gerald, Assistant Dean, 212-636-6600, Fax: 212-636-6613, E-mail: gssadmission@fordham.edu. *Dean,* Dr. Peter B. Vaughan, 212-636-6616.

School of Law Students: 1,259 full-time (592 women), 373 part-time (165 women). 7,080 applicants, 26% accepted, 564 enrolled. *Faculty:* 78 full-time (30 women), 128 part-time/adjunct (44 women). Expenses: Contact institution. *Financial support:* In 2006–07, 1,143 students received support. Career-related internships or fieldwork, institutionally sponsored loans, and scholarships/grants available. Support available to part-time students. Financial award application deadline: 4/1; financial award applicants required to submit CSS PROFILE or FAFSA. In 2006, 477 JDs, 65 master's awarded. *Degree program information:* Part-time and evening/weekend programs available. Offers banking, corporate and finance law (LL M); intellectual property and information law (LL M); international business and trade law (LL M); law (JD). *Application deadline:* For fall admission, 3/1 for domestic students. Applications are processed on a rolling basis. *Application fee:* $65. Electronic applications accepted. *Application Contact:* Stephen G. Brown, Assistant Dean for Admissions and Financial Aid, 212-636-6810, E-mail: lawadmissins@law.fordham.edu. *Dean,* William Michael Treanor, 212-636-6875, Fax: 212-636-6921, E-mail: wtreanor@law.fordham.edu.

See Close-Up on page 899.

FOREST INSTITUTE OF PROFESSIONAL PSYCHOLOGY, Springfield, MO 65807

General Information Independent, coed, graduate-only institution. *Graduate housing:* Rooms and/or apartments available on a first-come, first-served basis to single and married students.

GRADUATE UNITS

Graduate Programs Offers clinical psychology (Psy D); marriage and family therapy (PGC); psychology (MA). Electronic applications accepted.

FORT HAYS STATE UNIVERSITY, Hays, KS 67601-4099

General Information State-supported, coed, comprehensive institution. CGS member. *Enrollment:* 7,403 graduate, professional, and undergraduate students; 186 full-time matriculated graduate/professional students (114 women), 651 part-time matriculated graduate/professional students (397 women). *Graduate faculty:* 127 full-time (31 women). *Graduate housing:* Rooms and/or apartments available to single and married students. Housing application deadline: 8/1. *Student services:* Campus employment opportunities, career counseling, child daycare facilities, disabled student services, exercise/wellness program, free psychological counseling, grant writing training, international student services, low-cost health insurance. *Library facilities:* Forsyth Library. *Online resources:* library catalog, web page, access to other libraries' catalogs. *Collection:* 624,637 titles, 1,689 serial subscriptions.

Computer facilities: Computer purchase and lease plans are available. 813 computers available on campus for general student use. A campuswide network can be accessed from student residence rooms and from off campus. Internet access is available. *Web address:* http://www.fhsu.edu/.

General Application Contact: Dr. Steven Trout, Interim Dean, 785-628-4236, Fax: 785-628-4479, E-mail: strout@fhsu.edu.

GRADUATE UNITS

Graduate School Students: 229 full-time (147 women), 608 part-time (380 women); includes 120 minority (19 African Americans, 7 American Indian/Alaska Native, 75 Asian Americans or Pacific Islanders, 19 Hispanic Americans). Average age 34. 476 applicants, 69% accepted. *Faculty:* 127 full-time (31 women). Expenses: Contact institution. *Financial support:* Research assistantships, teaching assistantships, career-related internships or fieldwork, Federal Work-Study, institutionally sponsored loans, and tuition waivers (full and partial) available. Support available to part-time students. In 2006, 281 master's, 6 other advanced degrees awarded. *Degree program information:* Part-time programs available. *Application deadline:* Applications are processed on a rolling basis. *Application fee:* $35. Electronic applications accepted. *Interim Dean,* Dr. Steven Trout, 785-628-4236, Fax: 785-628-4479, E-mail: strout@fhsu.edu.

College of Arts and Sciences Students: 126 full-time (82 women), 290 part-time (145 women); includes 89 minority (16 African Americans, 4 American Indian/Alaska Native, 58 Asian Americans or Pacific Islanders, 11 Hispanic Americans). Average age 31. 274 applicants, 67% accepted. *Faculty:* 54 full-time (10 women). Expenses: Contact institution. *Financial support:* Research assistantships, teaching assistantships, career-related internships or fieldwork, institutionally sponsored loans, and tuition waivers (full and partial) available. Support available to part-time students. In 2006, 130 master's, 6 other advanced degrees awarded. *Degree program information:* Part-time programs available. Offers arts and sciences (MA, MFA, MLS, MS, Ed S); communication (MS); English (MA); geology (MS); history (MA); liberal studies (MLS); psychology (MS); school psychology (Ed S); studio art (MFA). *Application deadline:* Applications are processed on a rolling basis.

Application fee: $35. Electronic applications accepted. *Dean*, Dr. Paul Faber, 785-628-4234, E-mail: pfaber@fhsu.edu.

College of Business and Leadership Students: 14 full-time (6 women), 8 part-time (3 women); includes 10 minority (all Asian Americans or Pacific Islanders) Average age 31. 39 applicants, 59% accepted. *Faculty:* 19 full-time (1 woman). Expenses: Contact institution. *Financial support:* In 2006–07, 5 teaching assistantships (averaging $5,000 per year) were awarded; research assistantships, career-related internships or fieldwork, institutionally sponsored loans, and tuition waivers (full) also available. Support available to part-time students. In 2006, 18 degrees awarded. *Degree program information:* Part-time programs available. Offers accounting (MBA); business and leadership (MBA); management (MBA). *Application deadline:* For fall admission, 7/1 priority date for domestic students. Applications are processed on a rolling basis. *Application fee:* $35. Electronic applications accepted. *Dean*, Dr. Steve Williams, 785-628-5339, E-mail: swilliams@fhsu.edu.

College of Education and Technology Students: 25 full-time (17 women), 219 part-time (163 women); includes 16 minority (1 African American, 3 American Indian/Alaska Native, 6 Asian Americans or Pacific Islanders, 6 Hispanic Americans). Average age 36. 83 applicants, 76% accepted. *Faculty:* 23 full-time (9 women). Expenses: Contact institution. *Financial support:* Research assistantships, teaching assistantships, career-related internships or fieldwork, institutionally sponsored loans, and tuition waivers (full) available. Support available to part-time students. In 2006, 87 degrees awarded. *Degree program information:* Part-time programs available. Offers counseling (MS); education (MSE); education and technology (MS, MSE, Ed S); educational administration (MS, Ed S); elementary education (MS); instructional technology (MS); secondary education (MS); special education (MS). *Application deadline:* For fall admission, 7/1 priority date for domestic students. Applications are processed on a rolling basis. *Application fee:* $35. Electronic applications accepted. *Dean*, Dr. Deb Mercer, 785-628-5866, E-mail: dmercer@fhsu.edu.

College of Health and Life Sciences Students: 64 full-time (42 women), 91 part-time (69 women); includes 5 minority (2 African Americans, 1 Asian American or Pacific Islander, 2 Hispanic Americans). Average age 29. 80 applicants, 75% accepted. *Faculty:* 31 full-time (11 women). Expenses: Contact institution. *Financial support:* Research assistantships, teaching assistantships, tuition waivers (full) available. In 2006, 46 degrees awarded. *Degree program information:* Part-time programs available. Offers biology (MS); health and human performance (MS); health and life sciences (MS, MSN); nursing (MSN); speech-language pathology (MS). *Application deadline:* Applications are processed on a rolling basis. *Application fee:* $35. Electronic applications accepted. *Dean*, Dr. Jeff Briggs, 785-628-4200, E-mail: jbriggs@fhsu.edu.

FORT VALLEY STATE UNIVERSITY, Fort Valley, GA 31030-4313

General Information State-supported, coed, comprehensive institution. *Graduate housing:* Room and/or apartments available on a first-come, first-served basis to single students; on-campus housing not available to married students. Housing application deadline: 7/21.

GRADUATE UNITS

College of Graduate Studies and Extended Education *Degree program information:* Part-time programs available. Offers animal science (MS); early childhood education (MS); environmental health (MPH); guidance and counseling (MS, Ed S); mental health counseling (MS); middle grades education (MS); vocational rehabilitation counseling (MS).

FRAMINGHAM STATE COLLEGE, Framingham, MA 01701-9101

General Information State-supported, coed, comprehensive institution. *Enrollment:* 5,861 graduate, professional, and undergraduate students; 1,404 matriculated graduate/professional students. *Enrollment by degree level:* 1,404 master's. *Graduate faculty:* 25 full-time, 50 part-time/adjunct. *Graduate housing:* On-campus housing not available. *Student services:* Career counseling, child daycare facilities, disabled student services, free psychological counseling, grant writing training, low-cost health insurance, multicultural affairs office, teacher training, writing training. *Library facilities:* Whittemore Library. *Online resources:* library catalog, web page. *Collection:* 165,219 titles, 409 serial subscriptions, 3,313 audiovisual materials.

Computer facilities: Computer purchase and lease plans are available. 575 computers available on campus for general student use. A campuswide network can be accessed from student residence rooms and from off campus. Internet access and online class registration, TELNET are available. *Web address:* http://www.framingham.edu/.

General Application Contact: Dr. Janet Castleman, Dean of Graduate and Continuing Education, E-mail: jcastleman@frc.mass.edu.

GRADUATE UNITS

Division of Graduate and Continuing Education Students: 1,404. *Faculty:* 25 full-time, 50 part-time/adjunct. Expenses: Contact institution. In 2006, 299 degrees awarded. *Degree program information:* Part-time and evening/weekend programs available. Offers art (M Ed); biology (M Ed); business administration (MA); counseling psychology (MA); curriculum and instructional technology (M Ed); dietetics (MS); early childhood education (M Ed); educational leadership (MA); elementary education (M Ed); English (M Ed); food science and nutrition science (MS); health care administration (MA); history (M Ed); human nutrition: education and media technologies (MS); human resource management (MA); literacy and language (M Ed); mathematics (M Ed); public administration (MA); Spanish (M Ed); special education (M Ed); teaching of English as a second language (M Ed). *Application deadline:* Applications are processed on a rolling basis. *Application Contact:* 508-626-4550, Fax: 508-626-4030, E-mail: dgce@frc.mass.edu. *Dean of Graduate and Continuing Education*, Dr. Janet Castleman, E-mail: jcastleman@frc.mass.edu.

FRANCISCAN SCHOOL OF THEOLOGY, Berkeley, CA 94709-1294

General Information Independent-religious, coed, graduate-only institution. *Graduate faculty:* 7 full-time (3 women), 10 part-time/adjunct (0 women). *Tuition:* Full-time $11,400; part-time $600 per unit. *Graduate housing:* Rooms and/or apartments available on a first-come, first-served basis to single and married students. Housing application deadline: 5/15. *Student services:* Career counseling, international student services, low-cost health insurance, multicultural affairs office. *Library facilities:* Graduate Theological Union Library. *Online resources:* library catalog, web page. *Collection:* 452,333 titles, 1,547 serial subscriptions, 9,642 audiovisual materials.

Computer facilities: 7 computers available on campus for general student use. A campuswide network can be accessed from off campus. Internet access is available. *Web address:* http://www.fst.edu/.

General Application Contact: Pat Morgan, Recruitment Director, 510-848-5232 Ext. 15, Fax: 510-549-9466, E-mail: info@fst.edu.

GRADUATE UNITS

Graduate and Professional Programs Students: 49 full-time (26 women), 23 part-time (15 women); includes 17 minority (1 African American, 7 Asian Americans or Pacific Islanders, 9 Hispanic Americans), 5 international. Average age 43. *Faculty:* 7 full-time (3 women), 10 part-time/adjunct (0 women). Expenses: Contact institution. *Financial support:* In 2006–07, 40 students received support. Career-related internships or fieldwork, scholarships/grants, and tuition waivers (full and partial) available. Financial award application deadline: 5/1; financial award applicants required to submit FAFSA. In 2006, 13 M Divs, 20 master's awarded. *Degree program information:* Part-time programs available. Offers theology (M Div, MA, MAMC, MTS). *Application deadline:* For fall admission, 4/1 priority date for domestic and international students; for spring admission, 10/1 priority date for domestic and international students. Applications are processed on a rolling basis. *Application fee:* $40. *Application Contact:* Pat Morgan, Recruitment Director, 510-848-5232 Ext. 15, Fax: 510-549-9466, E-mail: info@fst.edu. *President*, Dr. Mario DiCicco, 510-848-5232, Fax: 510-549-9466, E-mail: mariod@aol.com.

FRANCISCAN UNIVERSITY OF STEUBENVILLE, Steubenville, OH 43952-1763

General Information Independent-religious, coed, comprehensive institution. *Graduate housing:* On-campus housing not available.

GRADUATE UNITS

Graduate Programs *Degree program information:* Part-time and evening/weekend programs available. Postbaccalaureate distance learning degree programs offered (minimal on-campus study). Offers administration (MS Ed); business (MBA); counseling (MA); nursing (MSN); philosophy (MA); teaching (MS Ed); theology and Christian ministry (MA).

FRANCIS MARION UNIVERSITY, Florence, SC 29501-0547

General Information State-supported, coed, comprehensive institution. *Enrollment:* 4,075 graduate, professional, and undergraduate students; 33 full-time matriculated graduate/professional students (27 women), 235 part-time matriculated graduate/professional students (192 women). *Enrollment by degree level:* 268 master's. *Graduate faculty:* 117 full-time (33 women), 8 part-time/adjunct (5 women). Tuition, state resident: full-time $6,527; part-time $326 per credit hour. Tuition, nonresident: full-time $13,054; part-time $653 per credit hour. *Required fees:* $185; $5 per credit hour. $45 per term. *Graduate housing:* Room and/or apartments available on a first-come, first-served basis to single students; on-campus housing not available to married students. Typical cost: $2,960 per year ($5,430 including board). Housing application deadline: 8/1. *Student services:* Campus employment opportunities, campus safety program, career counseling, disabled student services, free psychological counseling, international student services, low-cost health insurance, multicultural affairs office, teacher training. *Library facilities:* James A. Rogers Library plus 1 other. *Online resources:* library catalog, web page, access to other libraries' catalogs. *Collection:* 396,204 titles, 1,504 serial subscriptions, 9,297 audiovisual materials.

Computer facilities: 551 computers available on campus for general student use. A campuswide network can be accessed from student residence rooms and from off campus. Internet access and online class registration, Blackboard are available. *Web address:* http://www.fmarion.edu/.

General Application Contact: Rannie Gamble, Administrative Manager, 843-661-1286, Fax: 843-661-4688, E-mail: rgamble@fmarion.edu.

GRADUATE UNITS

Graduate Programs Students: 33 full-time (27 women), 235 part-time (192 women); includes 67 minority (64 African Americans, 1 Asian American or Pacific Islander, 2 Hispanic Americans), 3 international. Average age 32. 322 applicants, 100% accepted, 187 enrolled. *Faculty:* 117 full-time (33 women), 8 part-time/adjunct (5 women). Expenses: Contact institution. *Financial support:* In 2006–07, 7 research assistantships (averaging $6,000 per year), 3 teaching assistantships (averaging $8,000 per year) were awarded; career-related internships or fieldwork and unspecified assistantships also available. Support available to part-time students. Financial award application deadline: 3/1; financial award applicants required to submit FAFSA. In 2006, 122 degrees awarded. *Degree program information:* Part-time and evening/weekend programs available. Offers applied clinical psychology (MS); applied community psychology (MS); school psychology (MS). *Application deadline:* For fall admission, 4/15 priority date for domestic students; for spring admission, 10/15 priority date for domestic students. Applications are processed on a rolling basis. *Application fee:* $30. *Provost's Office*, 843-661-1284, Fax: 843-661-4688.

School of Business Students: 7 full-time (5 women), 49 part-time (24 women); includes 11 minority (8 African Americans, 1 Asian American or Pacific Islander, 2 Hispanic Americans), 1 international. Average age 31. 32 applicants, 100% accepted, 13 enrolled. *Faculty:* 16 full-time (2 women). Expenses: Contact institution. *Financial support:* In 2006–07, 2 research assistantships (averaging $3,000 per year) were awarded; unspecified assistantships also available. Support available to part-time students. Financial award application deadline: 3/1; financial award applicants required to submit FAFSA. In 2006, 18 degrees awarded. *Degree program information:* Part-time and evening/weekend programs available. Offers business (MBA); health management (MBA). *Application deadline:* For fall admission, 4/15 priority date for domestic students; for spring admission, 10/15 priority date for domestic students. Applications are processed on a rolling basis. *Application fee:* $30. *Dean*, Dr. M. Barry O'Brien, 843-661-1419, Fax: 843-661-1432, E-mail: mbobrien@fmarion.edu.

School of Education Students: 11 full-time (8 women), 158 part-time (141 women); includes 54 minority (all African Americans), 1 international. Average age 34. 248 applicants, 100% accepted. *Faculty:* 19 full-time (11 women), 1 part-time/adjunct (0 women). Expenses: Contact institution. *Financial support:* In 2006–07, 3 research assistantships (averaging $6,000 per year) were awarded; unspecified assistantships also available. Support available to part-time students. Financial award application deadline: 3/1; financial award applicants required to submit FAFSA. In 2006, 91 degrees awarded. *Degree program information:* Part-time programs available. Offers early childhood education (M Ed); elementary education (M Ed); learning disabilities (M Ed, MAT); remedial education (M Ed); secondary education (M Ed). *Application deadline:* For fall admission, 4/15 priority date for domestic students; for spring admission, 10/15 priority date for domestic students. Applications are processed on a rolling basis. *Application fee:* $30. *Dean*, Dr. James R. Faulkenberry, 843-661-1460, Fax: 843-661-4647.

FRANKLIN PIERCE LAW CENTER, Concord, NH 03301-4197

General Information Independent, coed, graduate-only institution. *Graduate housing:* On-campus housing not available. *Research affiliation:* Patent, Trademark, and Copyright Research Foundation, Institute for Health Law and Ethics, Academy of Applied Science.

GRADUATE UNITS

Professional Program Offers intellectual property (Diploma); intellectual property, commerce and technology (LL M, MIP); law (JD). Diploma awarded as part of Intellectual Property Summer Institute. Electronic applications accepted.

FRANKLIN PIERCE UNIVERSITY, Rindge, NH 03461-0060

General Information Independent, coed, comprehensive institution. *Graduate housing:* On-campus housing not available.

GRADUATE UNITS

Graduate Studies *Degree program information:* Part-time and evening/weekend programs available. Offers information technology management (MS); leadership (MBA); physical therapy (MS). Electronic applications accepted.

FRANKLIN UNIVERSITY, Columbus, OH 43215-5399

General Information Independent, coed, comprehensive institution. *Enrollment:* 608 full-time matriculated graduate/professional students (310 women), 143 part-time matriculated graduate/professional students (62 women). *Enrollment by degree level:* 751 master's. *Graduate faculty:* 6 full-time (1 woman), 55 part-time/adjunct (17 women). *Tuition:* Full-time $7,110; part-time $395 per credit hour. Tuition and fees vary according to campus/location and program. *Graduate housing:* On-campus housing not available. *Student services:* Campus employment opportunities, disabled student services, international student services, writing training. *Library facilities:* Franklin University Library. *Online resources:* library catalog, web page, access to other libraries' catalogs. *Collection:* 27,547 titles, 15,290 serial subscriptions, 246 audiovisual materials.

Computer facilities: 341 computers available on campus for general student use. A campuswide network can be accessed. Internet access and online class registration are available. *Web address:* http://www.franklin.edu/.

General Application Contact: Graduate Services Office, 614-797-4700, Fax: 614-221-7723, E-mail: gradschl@franklin.edu.

GRADUATE UNITS

Computer Science Program Students: 40 full-time (9 women), 39 part-time (8 women); includes 23 minority (8 African Americans, 13 Asian Americans or Pacific Islanders, 2 Hispanic

Franklin University (continued)

Americans), 26 international. Average age 33. *Faculty:* 1 full-time (0 women), 6 part-time/adjunct (0 women). Expenses: Contact institution. *Financial support:* In 2006–07, 19 students received support. Application deadline: 6/15; In 2006, 9 degrees awarded. *Degree program information:* Part-time and evening/weekend programs available. Offers computer science (MS). *Application deadline:* For fall admission, 8/15 priority date for domestic students; for winter admission, 12/20 priority date for domestic students; for spring admission, 4/4 priority date for domestic students. Applications are processed on a rolling basis. *Application fee:* $30. Electronic applications accepted. *Application Contact:* 614-797-4700, Fax: 614-221-7723, E-mail: gradschl@franklin.edu. *Program Chair,* Dr. Ron Hartung, 614-947-6139, Fax: 614-224-4025, E-mail: hartung@franklin.edu.

Graduate School of Business Students: 483 full-time (242 women), 91 part-time (47 women); includes 176 minority (119 African Americans, 44 Asian Americans or Pacific Islanders, 13 Hispanic Americans), 30 international. Average age 35. *Faculty:* 3 full-time (0 women), 33 part-time/adjunct (12 women). Expenses: Contact institution. *Financial support:* In 2006–07, 267 students received support. Institutionally sponsored loans available. Financial award application deadline: 6/30; financial award applicants required to submit FAFSA. In 2006, 125 degrees awarded. *Degree program information:* Part-time and evening/weekend programs available. Postbaccalaureate distance learning degree programs offered (minimal on-campus study). Offers business (MBA). *Application deadline:* For fall admission, 8/1 priority date for domestic students; for winter admission, 1/2 priority date for domestic students; for spring admission, 4/4 priority date for domestic students. Applications are processed on a rolling basis. *Application fee:* $30. Electronic applications accepted. *Application Contact:* Graduate Services Office, 614-797-4700, Fax: 614-221-7723, E-mail: gradschl@franklin.edu. *Program Chair,* Dr. Terry Boyd, 614-947-6140, Fax: 614-224-4025.

Marketing and Communications Program Students: 83 full-time (58 women), 13 part-time (10 women); includes 23 minority (21 African Americans, 2 Asian Americans or Pacific Islanders), 7 international. Average age 34. *Faculty:* 1 full-time (0 women), 7 part-time/adjunct (1 woman). Expenses: Contact institution. *Financial support:* In 2006–07, 50 students received support. Application deadline: 6/30. In 2006, 20 degrees awarded. *Degree program information:* Part-time and evening/weekend programs available. Offers marketing and communications (MS). *Application deadline:* For fall admission, 8/15 priority date for domestic students; for winter admission, 12/20 priority date for domestic students; for spring admission, 4/4 priority date for domestic students. Applications are processed on a rolling basis. *Application fee:* $30. Electronic applications accepted. *Application Contact:* Graduate Services Office, 614-797-4700, Fax: 614-224-7723, E-mail: gradschl@franklin.edu. *Program Chair,* Dr. Doug Ross, 614-947-6149.

FRANK LLOYD WRIGHT SCHOOL OF ARCHITECTURE, Scottsdale, AZ 85261-4430

General Information Independent, coed, graduate-only institution. *Graduate housing:* Rooms and/or apartments guaranteed to single students and available on a first-come, first-served basis to married students.

GRADUATE UNITS

Graduate Program Offers architecture (M Arch). Summer session held in Spring Green, WI.

FREDERICK S. PARDEE RAND GRADUATE SCHOOL, Santa Monica, CA 90407-2138

General Information Independent, coed, graduate-only institution. *Enrollment by degree level:* 96 doctoral. *Graduate faculty:* 1 full-time (0 women), 142 part-time/adjunct (38 women). *Graduate housing:* On-campus housing not available. *Student services:* Campus employment opportunities, career counseling, free psychological counseling, grant writing training, international student services, low-cost health insurance, writing training. *Library facilities:* RAND Corporation Library. *Collection:* 240,000 titles, 9,300 serial subscriptions, 1,290 audiovisual materials. *Research affiliation:* RAND (not for profit research).

Computer facilities: 96 computers available on campus for general student use. A campuswide network can be accessed from student residence rooms and from off campus. Internet access and online class registration are available. *Web address:* http://www.prgs.edu/.

General Application Contact: Dr. Alex Duke, Assistant Dean, 310-393-0411 Ext. 6201, Fax: 310-451-6978, E-mail: alex_duke@prgs.edu.

GRADUATE UNITS

Program in Policy Analysis Students: 96 full-time (35 women); includes 10 minority (1 African American, 7 Asian Americans or Pacific Islanders, 2 Hispanic Americans), 43 international. Average age 28. 126 applicants, 24% accepted, 22 enrolled. *Faculty:* 1 full-time (0 women), 140 part-time/adjunct (36 women). Expenses: Contact institution. *Financial support:* In 2006–07, 96 fellowships, 96 research assistantships, 24 teaching assistantships (averaging $1,500 per year) were awarded; career-related internships or fieldwork also available. In 2006, 19 doctorates awarded. Offers policy analysis (PhD). *Application deadline:* For fall admission, 1/10 priority date for domestic and international students. *Application fee:* $50. Electronic applications accepted. *Application Contact:* Dr. Alex Duke, Assistant Dean, 310-393-0411 Ext. 6201, Fax: 310-451-6978, E-mail: alex_duke@prgs.edu. *Dean,* Dr. John D. Graham, 310-393-0411 Ext. 7075, Fax: 310-451-6978, E-mail: john_graham@prgs.edu.

FREED-HARDEMAN UNIVERSITY, Henderson, TN 38340-2399

General Information Independent-religious, coed, comprehensive institution. *Enrollment:* 1,969 graduate, professional, and undergraduate students; 97 full-time matriculated graduate/professional students (59 women), 399 part-time matriculated graduate/professional students (274 women). *Enrollment by degree level:* 15 first professional, 422 master's, 59 other advanced degrees. *Graduate faculty:* 22 full-time (5 women), 10 part-time/adjunct (5 women). *Tuition:* Part-time $334 per credit hour. *Required fees:* $10 per credit hour. *Graduate housing:* Room and/or apartments available on a first-come, first-served basis to single students; on-campus housing not available to married students. Typical cost: $3,700 per year ($6,820 including board). Housing application deadline: 8/22. *Student services:* Campus employment opportunities, campus safety program, career counseling, child daycare facilities, disabled student services, exercise/wellness program, free psychological counseling, grant writing training, international student services, teacher training. *Library facilities:* Loden-Daniel Library. *Online resources:* library catalog, web page. *Collection:* 154,689 titles, 1,715 serial subscriptions, 42,735 audiovisual materials.

Computer facilities: Computer purchase and lease plans are available. 250 computers available on campus for general student use. A campuswide network can be accessed from student residence rooms and from off campus. Internet access and online class registration are available. *Web address:* http://www.fhu.edu/.

General Application Contact: Dr. Samuel T. Jones, Vice President for Academics, 731-989-6004, Fax: 731-989-6945, E-mail: sjones@fhu.edu.

GRADUATE UNITS

Program in Business Administration Students: 10 full-time (2 women), 8 part-time (3 women). Average age 30. Expenses: Contact institution. Offers business administration (MBA). *Application fee:* $32. *Director of Graduate Studies, School of Business,* Dr. Tom Deberry, 731-989-6659, E-mail: tdelberry@fhu.edu.

Program in Counseling Students: 23 full-time (17 women), 44 part-time (28 women); includes 17 minority (15 African Americans, 1 Asian American or Pacific Islander, 1 Hispanic American). Average age 31. *Faculty:* 8 full-time (2 women), 4 part-time/adjunct (3 women). Expenses: Contact institution. *Financial support:* Career-related internships or fieldwork, Federal Work-Study, tuition waivers (partial), and unspecified assistantships available. Support available to part-time students. Financial award application deadline: 8/1; financial award applicants required to submit FAFSA. In 2006, 25 degrees awarded. *Degree program information:* Part-time and evening/weekend programs available. Offers counseling (MS). *Application deadline:* For fall admission, 8/1 priority date for domestic students; for spring admission, 12/1 for domestic students. Applications are processed on a rolling basis. *Application fee:* $32. *Graduate Director,* Dr. Mike Cravens, 731-989-6666, Fax: 731-989-6065, E-mail: mcravens@fhu.edu.

Program in Education Students: 51 full-time (40 women), 286 part-time (235 women); includes 203 minority (202 African Americans, 1 Asian American or Pacific Islander), 2 international. Average age 34. *Faculty:* 9 full-time (3 women), 6 part-time/adjunct (4 women). Expenses: Contact institution. *Financial support:* Career-related internships or fieldwork, Federal Work-Study, tuition waivers (partial), and unspecified assistantships available. Support available to part-time students. Financial award application deadline: 8/1; financial award applicants required to submit FAFSA. In 2006, 78 master's, 24 other advanced degrees awarded. *Degree program information:* Part-time and evening/weekend programs available. Offers curriculum and instruction (M Ed); school counseling (M Ed); school leadership (Ed S). *Application deadline:* For fall admission, 8/1 for domestic students; for spring admission, 12/1 for domestic students. Applications are processed on a rolling basis. *Application fee:* $32. *Graduate Director,* Dr. Elizabeth Saunders, 731-989-6082, Fax: 731-989-6065, E-mail: esaunders@fhu.edu.

School of Biblical Studies Students: 13 full-time (0 women), 52 part-time (1 woman); includes 5 minority (3 African Americans, 1 American Indian/Alaska Native, 1 Hispanic American), 2 international. Average age 29. *Faculty:* 5 full-time (0 women), 1 part-time/adjunct (0 women). Expenses: Contact institution. *Financial support:* Career-related internships or fieldwork, Federal Work-Study, tuition waivers (partial), and unspecified assistantships available. Support available to part-time students. Financial award application deadline: 8/1; financial award applicants required to submit FAFSA. In 2006, 20 degrees awarded. *Degree program information:* Part-time programs available. Offers biblical studies (M Div, M Min, MA); divinity (M Div); ministry (M Min); New Testament (MA). *Application deadline:* For fall admission, 8/1 priority date for domestic students; for spring admission, 12/1 for domestic students. Applications are processed on a rolling basis. *Application fee:* $32. *Director of Graduate Studies,* Dr. Earl Edwards, 731-989-6626, Fax: 731-989-6059, E-mail: eedwards@fhu.edu.

FRESNO PACIFIC UNIVERSITY, Fresno, CA 93702-4709

General Information Independent-religious, coed, comprehensive institution. *Enrollment:* 2,324 graduate, professional, and undergraduate students; 161 full-time matriculated graduate/professional students (117 women), 577 part-time matriculated graduate/professional students (416 women). *Enrollment by degree level:* 510 master's. *Graduate faculty:* 16 full-time (6 women), 22 part-time/adjunct (9 women). *Tuition:* Full-time $7,470; part-time $415 per credit. *Graduate housing:* On-campus housing not available. *Student services:* Campus employment opportunities, career counseling, grant writing training, international student services, teacher training. *Library facilities:* Hiebert Library. *Online resources:* library catalog, web page, access to other libraries' catalogs. *Collection:* 196,000 titles, 16,000 serial subscriptions.

Computer facilities: 72 computers available on campus for general student use. A campuswide network can be accessed from student residence rooms and from off campus. Internet access is available. *Web address:* http://www.fresno.edu/.

General Application Contact: Vivian Galba, Admissions Coordinator, 559-453-3667, Fax: 559-453-2100, E-mail: vgalba@fresno.edu.

GRADUATE UNITS

Graduate Programs Students: 101 full-time (76 women), 409 part-time (287 women); includes 158 minority (20 African Americans, 5 American Indian/Alaska Native, 16 Asian Americans or Pacific Islanders, 117 Hispanic Americans), 12 international. Average age 38. 103 applicants, 76% accepted, 7 enrolled. *Faculty:* 16 full-time (6 women), 22 part-time/adjunct (9 women). Expenses: Contact institution. *Financial support:* In 2006–07, 276 students received support. Career-related internships or fieldwork, scholarships/grants, and tuition waivers (full and partial) available. Support available to part-time students. Financial award applicants required to submit FAFSA. In 2006, 165 degrees awarded. *Degree program information:* Part-time and evening/weekend programs available. Offers individualized study (MA); kinesiology (MA); leadership and organizational studies (MA); peacemaking and conflict studies (MA); teaching English to speakers of other languages (MA). *Application deadline:* For fall admission, 7/15 priority date for domestic and international students; for spring admission, 11/15 priority date for domestic and international students. Applications are processed on a rolling basis. *Application fee:* $90. Electronic applications accepted.

Programs in Education Students: 73 full-time (59 women), 399 part-time (295 women); includes 136 minority (9 African Americans, 5 American Indian/Alaska Native, 12 Asian Americans or Pacific Islanders, 110 Hispanic Americans), 2 international. Average age 39. 124 applicants, 73% accepted, 10 enrolled. *Faculty:* 12 full-time (5 women), 19 part-time/adjunct (9 women). Expenses: Contact institution. *Financial support:* In 2006–07, 260 students received support. Career-related internships or fieldwork, scholarships/grants, and tuition waivers (full and partial) available. Support available to part-time students. Financial award applicants required to submit FAFSA. In 2006, 128 degrees awarded. *Degree program information:* Part-time and evening/weekend programs available. Offers administration (MA Ed); administrative services (MA Ed); bilingual/cross-cultural education (MA Ed); curriculum and teaching (MA Ed); educational technology (MA Ed); foundations, curriculum and teaching (MA Ed); integrated mathematics/science education (MA Ed); language development (MA Ed); language, literacy, and culture (MA Ed); mathematics education (MA Ed); mathematics/science/computer education (MA Ed); middle school mathematics (MA Ed); mild/moderate (MA Ed); moderate/severe (MA Ed); multilingual contexts (MA Ed); physical and health impairments (MA Ed); pupil personnel services (MA Ed); reading (MA Ed); reading/English as a second language (MA Ed); reading/language arts (MA Ed); school counseling (MA Ed); school library and information technology (MA Ed); school psychology (MA Ed); secondary school mathematics (MA Ed); special education (MA Ed). *Application deadline:* For fall admission, 7/15 for domestic and international students; for spring admission, 11/15 for domestic and international students. Applications are processed on a rolling basis. *Application fee:* $90. Electronic applications accepted.

FRIENDS UNIVERSITY, Wichita, KS 67213

General Information Independent, coed, comprehensive institution. *Enrollment:* 650 full-time matriculated graduate/professional students. *Graduate faculty:* 19 full-time (7 women). *Graduate housing:* Rooms and/or apartments available on a first-come, first-served basis to single and married students. Housing application deadline: 8/1. *Student services:* Campus employment opportunities, campus safety program, career counseling, disabled student services, free psychological counseling, international student services, writing training. *Library facilities:* Edmund Stanley Library plus 3 others. *Online resources:* library catalog. *Collection:* 105,989 titles, 857 serial subscriptions.

Computer facilities: 190 computers available on campus for general student use. A campuswide network can be accessed from student residence rooms and from off campus. *Web address:* http://www.friends.edu/.

General Application Contact: Craig Davis, Director of Graduate Admissions, 800-794-6945 Ext. 5573, Fax: 316-295-5050, E-mail: cdavis@friends.edu.

GRADUATE UNITS

Graduate School Students: 650 full-time. *Faculty:* 21 full-time (9 women). Expenses: Contact institution. *Financial support:* Applicants required to submit FAFSA. In 2006, 260 degrees awarded. *Degree program information:* Evening/weekend programs available. Postbaccalaureate distance learning degree programs offered (minimal on-campus study). *Application deadline:* For fall admission, 6/1 priority date for domestic students, 5/1 priority date for international students; for spring admission, 11/1 priority date for domestic students, 10/1 priority date for international students. Applications are processed on a rolling basis. *Application fee:* $45 ($65 for international students). Electronic applications accepted. *Application Contact:* Craig Davis, Director of Graduate Admissions, 800-794-6945 Ext. 5573, Fax: 316-295-5050, E-mail: cdavis@friends.edu. *Dean,* Dr. Al Saber, 800-794-6945 Ext. 5859, Fax: 316-295-5040, E-mail: asaber@friends.edu.

Division of Business, Technology, and Leadership Students: 360 full-time. *Faculty:* 8 full-time, 13 part-time/adjunct. Expenses: Contact institution. In 2006, 157 degrees awarded. *Degree program information:* Evening/weekend programs available. Offers business administration (MBA); business law (MBL); business, technology, and leadership (EMBA, MBA, MBL, MHCL, MMIS, MSM, MSOD, MSPM); executive business administration (EMBA); health care leadership (MHCL); management (MSM); management information systems (MMIS); organization development (MSOD); service/production management (MSPM). *Application deadline:* For fall admission, 8/15 priority date for domestic students; for spring admission, 11/1 priority date for domestic students. Applications are processed on a rolling basis. *Application fee:* $45 ($65 for international students). Electronic applications accepted. *Application Contact:* Craig Davis, Director of Graduate Admissions, 800-794-6945 Ext. 5573, Fax: 316-295-5050, E-mail: cdavis@friends.edu. *Division Chair,* Dr. William Wunder, 800-794-6945 Ext. 5591, Fax: 316-295-5040.

Division of Science, Arts, and Education *Faculty:* 9 full-time (4 women), 27 part-time/adjunct. Expenses: Contact institution. In 2006, 107 degrees awarded. *Degree program information:* Evening/weekend programs available. Postbaccalaureate distance learning degree programs offered (minimal on-campus study). Offers Christian ministry (MACM); elementary education (MAT); environmental studies (MSES); family therapy (MSFT); liberal studies (MALS); school leadership (MSL); science, arts, and education (MACM, MALS, MAT, MSES, MSFT, MSL); secondary education (MAT). *Application deadline:* For fall admission, 3/15 priority date for domestic and international students. Applications are processed on a rolling basis. *Application fee:* $45 ($65 for international students). Electronic applications accepted. *Application Contact:* Craig Davis, Director of Graduate Admissions, 800-794-6945 Ext. 5573, Fax: 316-295-5050, E-mail: cdavis@friends.edu. *Division Chair,* Dr. Dan Lord, 800-794-6945 Ext. 5617, E-mail: dlord@friends.edu.

FRONTIER SCHOOL OF MIDWIFERY AND FAMILY NURSING, Hyden, KY 41749

General Information Independent, coed, primarily women, graduate-only institution.

GRADUATE UNITS

Graduate Programs

FROSTBURG STATE UNIVERSITY, Frostburg, MD 21532-1099

General Information State-supported, coed, comprehensive institution. *Graduate housing:* Room and/or apartments available to single students; on-campus housing not available to married students. Housing application deadline: 6/1.

GRADUATE UNITS

Graduate School *Degree program information:* Part-time and evening/weekend programs available. Electronic applications accepted.

College of Business *Degree program information:* Part-time and evening/weekend programs available. Offers business (MBA); business administration (MBA). Electronic applications accepted.

College of Education *Degree program information:* Part-time and evening/weekend programs available. Offers curriculum and instruction (M Ed); education (M Ed, MAT, MS); educational administration and supervision (M Ed); educational technology (M Ed); elementary (M Ed); elementary education (M Ed); elementary teaching (MAT); human performance (MS); interdisciplinary education (M Ed); parks and recreational management (MS); reading (M Ed); school counseling (M Ed); secondary (M Ed); secondary education (M Ed); secondary teaching (MAT); special education (M Ed). Electronic applications accepted.

College of Liberal Arts and Sciences *Degree program information:* Part-time and evening/weekend programs available. Offers applied computer science (MS); applied ecology and conservation biology (MS); counseling psychology (MS); fisheries and wildlife management (MS); liberal arts and sciences (MS). Electronic applications accepted.

FULLER THEOLOGICAL SEMINARY, Pasadena, CA 91182

General Information Independent-religious, coed, graduate-only institution. *Graduate housing:* Rooms and/or apartments available on a first-come, first-served basis to single students and available to married students.

GRADUATE UNITS

Graduate School of Psychology Offers clinical psychology (PhD, Psy D); marital/family therapy (MS); psychology (MA, MS).

Graduate School of Theology *Degree program information:* Part-time and evening/weekend programs available. Offers theology (M Div, MACL, MAT, Th M, D Min, PhD). M Div offered jointly with Denver Conservative Baptist Seminary.

Graduate School of World Mission *Degree program information:* Part-time and evening/weekend programs available. Offers global ministries (D Min); intercultural studies (MA, Th M, PhD); missiology (D Miss, PhD); world mission (MA, Th M, D Min, D Miss, PhD).

FURMAN UNIVERSITY, Greenville, SC 29613

General Information Independent, coed, comprehensive institution. *Enrollment:* 3,010 graduate, professional, and undergraduate students; 115 full-time matriculated graduate/professional students (89 women), 76 part-time matriculated graduate/professional students (61 women). *Enrollment by degree level:* 191 master's. *Graduate faculty:* 26 full-time (15 women), 19 part-time/adjunct (15 women). *Tuition:* Part-time $347 per credit. *Graduate housing:* On-campus housing not available. *Student services:* Campus employment opportunities, campus safety program, career counseling, disabled student services, exercise/wellness program, free psychological counseling, international student services, multicultural affairs office, teacher training. *Library facilities:* James Buchanan Duke Library plus 2 others. *Online resources:* library catalog, web page, access to other libraries' catalogs. *Collection:* 453,211 titles, 2,052 serial subscriptions.

Computer facilities: 340 computers available on campus for general student use. A campuswide network can be accessed from student residence rooms and from off campus. Internet access and online class registration are available. *Web address:* http://www.furman.edu/.

General Application Contact: Troy M. Terry, Director of Graduate Studies, 864-294-2213, Fax: 864-294-3579, E-mail: troy.terry@furman.edu.

GRADUATE UNITS

Graduate Division Students: 115 full-time (89 women), 76 part-time (61 women); includes 27 minority (23 African Americans, 4 Hispanic Americans). Average age 32. 40 applicants, 100% accepted, 40 enrolled. *Faculty:* 26 full-time (15 women), 19 part-time/adjunct (15 women). Expenses: Contact institution. *Financial support:* In 2006–07, 102 students received support, including 5 fellowships (averaging $4,350 per year); career-related internships or fieldwork, scholarships/grants, and unspecified assistantships also available. Financial award application deadline: 1/15; financial award applicants required to submit FAFSA. In 2006, 116 degrees awarded. *Degree program information:* Part-time and evening/weekend programs available. Offers chemistry (MS); early childhood education (MA); elementary education (MA); English as a second language (MA); middle school education (MA); reading (MA); school administration (MA); special education (MA). *Application deadline:* For fall admission, 8/1 priority date for domestic and international students; for winter admission, 12/1 priority date for domestic and international students; for spring admission, 2/1 priority date for domestic and international students. Applications are processed on a rolling basis. *Application fee:* $50. *Application Contact:* Phyllis Bray, Department Assistant, 864-294-2213, Fax: 864-294-3579, E-mail: phyllis.bray@furman.edu. *Director of Graduate Studies,* Troy M. Terry, 864-294-2213, Fax: 864-294-3579, E-mail: troy.terry@furman.edu.

GALLAUDET UNIVERSITY, Washington, DC 20002-3625

General Information Independent, coed, university. CGS member. *Graduate housing:* Rooms and/or apartments available on a first-come, first-served basis to single students and available to married students. Housing application deadline: 4/1. *Research affiliation:* George Washington University (minority involvement in science), Georgia State University (vocabulary development in deaf children), Medical College of Virginia (genetics and deafness), University of Maryland College Park (audiology and speech science), University of Wisconsin (telecommunications access for deaf and hard of hearing people), Delmarva Foundation for Medical Care (cultural competence for health service providers).

GRADUATE UNITS

The Graduate School *Degree program information:* Part-time programs available.

College of Arts and Sciences Offers arts and sciences (MA, MSW, PhD, Psy S); clinical psychology (PhD); developmental psychology (MA); school psychology (MA, Psy S); social work (MSW).

School of Communication *Degree program information:* Part-time programs available. Offers audiology (Au D); communication (MA, MS, Au D); interpretation (MA); linguistics (MA); speech and language pathology (MS).

School of Education and Human Services Offers administration (MS); administration and supervision (PhD, Ed S); community counseling (MA); early childhood education (MA, Ed S); education and human services (MA, MS, PhD, Certificate, Ed S); education of deaf and hard of hearing students and multihandicapped deaf and hard of hearing students (MA, Ed S); elementary education (MA, Ed S); individualized program of study (PhD); instructional supervision (Ed S); integrating technology in the classroom (Certificate); leadership training (MS); leisure services administration (MS); mental health counseling (MA); parent/infant specialty (MA, Ed S); school counseling (MA); secondary education (MA, Ed S); special education administration (PhD).

GANNON UNIVERSITY, Erie, PA 16541-0001

General Information Independent-religious, coed, comprehensive institution. *Enrollment:* 3,815 graduate, professional, and undergraduate students; 410 full-time matriculated graduate/professional students (207 women), 680 part-time matriculated graduate/professional students (446 women). *Enrollment by degree level:* 882 master's, 123 doctoral, 85 other advanced degrees. *Graduate faculty:* 67 full-time (32 women), 51 part-time/adjunct (17 women). *Tuition:* Full-time $12,240; part-time $680 per credit. *Required fees:* $496; $16 per credit. Tuition and fees vary according to course load, degree level, campus/location and program. *Graduate housing:* On-campus housing not available. *Student services:* Campus employment opportunities, campus safety program, career counseling, disabled student services, exercise/wellness program, free psychological counseling, international student services, low-cost health insurance, multicultural affairs office. *Library facilities:* Nash Library plus 1 other. *Online resources:* library catalog, web page. *Collection:* 270,590 titles, 14,301 serial subscriptions, 3,523 audiovisual materials. *Research affiliation:* Nanologic (energy), Hamot Medical Center (biology and physical therapy), G. E. Rail and Rail Power (electrical and mechanical engineering/computer and information science), Shriners Hospital (occupational therapy), Erie Public Schools (occupational therapy), Achievement Center (occupational therapy).

Computer facilities: 175 computers available on campus for general student use. A campuswide network can be accessed from student residence rooms and from off campus. Internet access and online class registration are available. *Web address:* http://www.gannon.edu/.

General Application Contact: Debra Meszaros, Director of Graduate Recruitment, 814-871-5819, Fax: 814-871-5827, E-mail: cfal@gannon.edu.

GRADUATE UNITS

School of Graduate Studies Students: 410 full-time (207 women), 680 part-time (446 women); includes 31 minority (21 African Americans, 2 American Indian/Alaska Native, 3 Asian Americans or Pacific Islanders, 5 Hispanic Americans), 178 international. Average age 29. 1,229 applicants, 73% accepted, 316 enrolled. *Faculty:* 67 full-time (32 women), 51 part-time/adjunct (17 women). Expenses: Contact institution. *Financial support:* In 2006–07, 39 fellowships (averaging $3,816 per year), 5 teaching assistantships (averaging $5,666 per year) were awarded; career-related internships or fieldwork, Federal Work-Study, scholarships/grants, traineeships, tuition waivers (partial), unspecified assistantships, and administrative assistantships also available. Support available to part-time students. Financial award application deadline: 7/1; financial award applicants required to submit FAFSA. In 2006, 409 master's, 17 doctorates, 10 other advanced degrees awarded. *Degree program information:* Part-time and evening/weekend programs available. *Application deadline:* Applications are processed on a rolling basis. *Application fee:* $25. *Application Contact:* Debra Meszaros, Director of Graduate Recruitment, 814-871-5819, Fax: 814-871-5827, E-mail: cfal@gannon.edu. *Dean,* Michael J. O'Neill, 814-871-7339, E-mail: oneill001@gannon.edu.

College of Humanities, Business, and Education Students: 108 full-time (62 women), 586 part-time (392 women); includes 29 minority (20 African Americans, 1 American Indian/Alaska Native, 3 Asian Americans or Pacific Islanders, 5 Hispanic Americans), 23 international. Average age 31. 352 applicants, 81% accepted, 172 enrolled. *Faculty:* 29 full-time (11 women), 38 part-time/adjunct (13 women). Expenses: Contact institution. *Financial support:* In 2006–07, 15 fellowships (averaging $3,425 per year), 5 teaching assistantships (averaging $5,666 per year) were awarded; career-related internships or fieldwork, Federal Work-Study, scholarships/grants, traineeships, unspecified assistantships, and administrative assistantships also available. Support available to part-time students. Financial award application deadline: 7/1; financial award applicants required to submit FAFSA. In 2006, 282 master's, 1 doctorate, 8 other advanced degrees awarded. *Degree program information:* Part-time and evening/weekend programs available. Offers accounting (Certificate); advanced counselor studies (Certificate); business (MBA, MPA, Certificate); business administration (MBA); community counseling (MS, Certificate); counseling psychology (PhD); curriculum and instruction (M Ed); early intervention (MS, Certificate); education (M Ed, MS, Certificate); educational computing technology (M Ed); educational leadership (M Ed); English (MA); English as a second language (Certificate); finance (Certificate); gerontology (Certificate); human resources management (Certificate); humanities (MA, MS, PhD, Certificate); humanities, business, and education (M Ed, MA, MBA, MPA, MS, PhD, Certificate); instructional technology specialist (Certificate); investments (Certificate); marketing (Certificate); organizational leadership (Certificate); pastoral studies (MA, Certificate); principal certification (Certificate); public administration (MPA, Certificate); reading (M Ed, Certificate); risk management (Certificate); school counselor preparation (Certificate); superintendent letter of eligibility certification (Certificate). *Application deadline:* Applications are processed on a rolling basis. *Application fee:* $25. *Application Contact:* Debra Meszaros, Director of Graduate Recruitment, 814-871-5819, Fax: 814-871-5827, E-mail: cfal@gannon.edu. *Dean,* Dr. Timothy Downs, 814-871-7549, Fax: 814-871-7652, E-mail: downs001@gannon.edu.

College of Sciences, Engineering, and Health Sciences Students: 302 full-time (145 women), 94 part-time (54 women); includes 2 minority (1 African American, 1 American Indian/Alaska Native), 155 international. Average age 26. 877 applicants, 70% accepted, 144 enrolled. *Faculty:* 38 full-time (21 women), 13 part-time/adjunct (4 women). Expenses: Contact institution. *Financial support:* In 2006–07, 14 fellowships (averaging $2,888 per year) were awarded; career-related internships or fieldwork, Federal Work-Study, scholarships/grants, traineeships, and unspecified assistantships also available. Support available to part-time students. Financial award application deadline: 7/1; financial award applicants required to submit FAFSA. In 2006, 127 master's, 16 doctorates, 2 other advanced degrees awarded. *Degree program information:* Part-time and evening/weekend programs available. Offers anesthesia (MSN); business administration (MSN); case management (MSN); computer and information science (MSCIS); electrical engineering (MSEE); embedded software engineering (MSES); engineering and computer science (MSCIS, MSE, MSEE, MSES, MSME); engineering management (MSE); environmental and occupational science and health (Certificate); environmental health and engineering (MS); environmental studies (MS); health sciences (MPAS, MS, MSN, DPT, Certificate); mechanical engineering (MSME); medical-surgical nursing (MSN); natural and environmental sciences (M Ed); nurse anesthesia (Certificate); nursing rural practitioner (MSN); occupational therapy (MS); physical therapy (DPT); physician assistant (MPAS); sciences (M Ed, MS, Certificate); sciences, engineering, and health sciences (M Ed, MPAS, MS, MSCIS, MSE, MSEE, MSES, MSME, MSN, DPT, Certificate). *Application fee:* $25. *Application Contact:* Debra Meszaros, Director of Graduate Recruitment, 814-871-5819, Fax: 814-871-5827, E-mail: cfal@gannon.edu. *Dean,* Dr. Carolynn Masters, 814-871-7605, E-mail: masters004@gannon.edu.

GARDNER-WEBB UNIVERSITY, Boiling Springs, NC 28017

General Information Independent-religious, coed, comprehensive institution. *Enrollment:* 3,840 graduate, professional, and undergraduate students; 203 full-time matriculated graduate/professional students (77 women), 1,008 part-time matriculated graduate/professional students (635 women). *Enrollment by degree level:* 1,157 master's, 54 doctoral. *Graduate faculty:* 46 full-time (20 women), 13 part-time/adjunct (5 women). *Tuition:* Full-time $3,144; part-time $262 per hour. *Graduate housing:* Room and/or apartments available on a first-come, first-served basis to single students; on-campus housing not available to married students. *Student services:* Campus employment opportunities, campus safety program, career counseling, disabled student services, exercise/wellness program, free psychological counseling, international student services, low-cost health insurance, teacher training, writing training. *Library facilities:* Dover Memorial Library. *Online resources:* library catalog, web page. *Collection:* 236,000 titles, 15,000 serial subscriptions, 10,400 audiovisual materials.

Computer facilities: 150 computers available on campus for general student use. A campuswide network can be accessed from student residence rooms and from off campus. Internet access and online class registration are available. *Web address:* http://www.gardner-webb.edu/.

General Application Contact: Dr. Gayle B. Price, Dean, Graduate School, 704-406-4723, Fax: 704-406-4329, E-mail: gradschool@gardner-webb.edu.

GRADUATE UNITS

Graduate School Students: 203 full-time (77 women), 1,008 part-time (635 women); includes 306 minority (273 African Americans, 1 American Indian/Alaska Native, 10 Asian Americans or Pacific Islanders, 22 Hispanic Americans), 1 international. Average age 29. 275 applicants, 91% accepted, 237 enrolled. *Faculty:* 29 full-time (11 women), 8 part-time/adjunct (3 women). Expenses: Contact institution. *Financial support:* Fellowships, Federal Work-Study, institutionally sponsored loans, and unspecified assistantships available. Support available to part-time students. In 2006, 390 master's, 8 doctorates awarded. *Degree program information:* Part-time and evening/weekend programs available. Offers curriculum and instruction (Ed D); educational leadership (Ed D); elementary education (MA); English (MA); English education (MA); middle grades education (MA); nursing (MSN, PMC); school administration (MA, Ed D); sport science and pedagogy (MA). *Application deadline:* Applications are processed on a rolling basis. *Application fee:* $25. Electronic applications accepted. *Dean,* Dr. Gayle B. Price, 704-406-4723, Fax: 704-406-4329, E-mail: gradschool@gardner-webb.edu.

Graduate School of Business Students: 55 full-time (29 women), 362 part-time (193 women); includes 103 minority (86 African Americans, 6 Asian Americans or Pacific Islanders, 11 Hispanic Americans), 1 international. Average age 33. 147 applicants, 80% accepted, 117 enrolled. *Faculty:* 12 full-time (1 woman), 6 part-time/adjunct (1 woman). Expenses: Contact institution. *Financial support:* In 2006–07, 23 students received support. Unspecified assistantships available. Support available to part-time students. Financial award applicants required to submit FAFSA. In 2006, 138 degrees awarded. *Degree program information:* Part-time and evening/weekend programs available. Postbaccalaureate distance learning degree programs offered (no on-campus study). Offers business (IMBA, M Acc, MBA). *Application deadline:* For fall admission, 8/29 for domestic students; for spring admission, 1/13 for domestic students. Applications are processed on a rolling basis. *Application fee:* $25. Electronic applications accepted. *Application Contact:* Kristen J. Setzer, Director of Admissions, 800-457-4622, Fax: 704-434-3895, E-mail: ksetzer@gardner-webb.edu. *Director,* Dr. Anthony Negbenebor, 704-406-4622, Fax: 704-406-3895, E-mail: anegbenebor@gardner-webb.edu.

School of Psychology Students: 3 full-time (all women), 83 part-time (70 women); includes 15 minority (12 African Americans, 1 Asian American or Pacific Islander, 2 Hispanic Americans). Average age 32. *Faculty:* 5 full-time (4 women). Expenses: Contact institution. *Financial support:* Unspecified assistantships available. In 2006, 17 degrees awarded. *Degree program information:* Part-time and evening/weekend programs available. Offers mental health counseling (MA); school counseling (MA). *Application deadline:* For fall admission, 7/1 priority date for domestic students. Applications are processed on a rolling basis. *Application fee:* $25. Electronic applications accepted. *Chair,* Dr. David Carscaddon, 704-406-4437, Fax: 704-406-4329, E-mail: dcarscaddon@gardner-webb.edu.

M. Christopher White School of Divinity Students: 106 full-time (29 women), 58 part-time (12 women); includes 29 minority (27 African Americans, 2 Hispanic Americans). Average age 34. 69 applicants, 97% accepted, 59 enrolled. *Faculty:* 9 full-time (2 women), 7 part-time/adjunct (1 woman). Expenses: Contact institution. *Financial support:* Fellowships, institutionally sponsored loans and unspecified assistantships available. Support available to part-time students. Financial award application deadline: 5/15. In 2006, 33 master's, 5 doctorates awarded. *Degree program information:* Part-time programs available. Offers business administration (MA); Christian education (M Div); English (MA); ministry (D Min); missiology (M Div); pastoral care and counseling (M Div); pastoral ministry (M Div). *Application deadline:* For fall admission, 8/1 priority date for domestic students; for spring admission, 12/15 priority date for domestic students. Applications are processed on a rolling basis. *Application fee:* $25. *Application Contact:* Dr. Toby Ziglar, Director of Admissions, 704-406-3205, Fax: 704-406-3935, E-mail: tziglar@gardner-webb.edu. *Dean,* Dr. Robert W. Canoy, 704-406-4400, Fax: 704-406-3935, E-mail: rcanoy@gardner-webb.edu.

GARRETT-EVANGELICAL THEOLOGICAL SEMINARY, Evanston, IL 60201-3298

General Information Independent-religious, coed, graduate-only institution. *Graduate housing:* Rooms and/or apartments guaranteed to single students and available to married students. Housing application deadline: 4/1.

GRADUATE UNITS

Graduate and Professional Programs *Degree program information:* Part-time programs available. Offers Bible and culture (PhD); Christian education (MA); Christian education and congregational studies (PhD); contemporary theology and culture (PhD); divinity (M Div); ethics, church, and society (MA); liturgical studies (PhD); ministry (D Min); music ministry (MA); pastoral care and counseling (MA); pastoral theology, personality, and culture (PhD); spiritual formation and evangelism (MA); theological studies (MTS). Electronic applications accepted.

GENERAL THEOLOGICAL SEMINARY, New York, NY 10011-4977

General Information Independent-religious, coed, graduate-only institution. *Graduate housing:* Rooms and/or apartments available to single and married students. Housing application deadline: 6/1.

GRADUATE UNITS

Graduate and Professional Programs *Degree program information:* Part-time and evening/weekend programs available. Offers Anglican studies (STM, Th D); divinity (M Div); spiritual direction (MASD, STM); theology (MA).

GENEVA COLLEGE, Beaver Falls, PA 15010-3599

General Information Independent-religious, coed, comprehensive institution. *Graduate housing:* On-campus housing not available.

GRADUATE UNITS

Program in Business Administration *Degree program information:* Part-time and evening/weekend programs available. Offers business administration (MBA). Electronic applications accepted.

Program in Counseling *Degree program information:* Part-time and evening/weekend programs available. Offers marriage and family (MA); mental health (MA); school counseling (MA). Electronic applications accepted.

Program in Higher Education *Degree program information:* Part-time and evening/weekend programs available. Postbaccalaureate distance learning degree programs offered (minimal on-campus study). Offers campus ministry (MA); college teaching (MA); educational leadership (MA); student affairs administration (MA). Electronic applications accepted.

Program in Organizational Leadership *Degree program information:* Evening/weekend programs available. Offers organizational leadership (MS). Electronic applications accepted.

Program in Special Education *Degree program information:* Part-time and evening/weekend programs available. Offers special education (M Ed). Electronic applications accepted.

GEORGE FOX UNIVERSITY, Newberg, OR 97132-2697

General Information Independent-religious, coed, university. *Enrollment:* 3,252 graduate, professional, and undergraduate students; 444 full-time matriculated graduate/professional students (289 women), 944 part-time matriculated graduate/professional students (513 women). *Enrollment by degree level:* 60 first professional, 899 master's, 245 doctoral, 184 other advanced degrees. *Graduate faculty:* 80 full-time (38 women), 82 part-time/adjunct (40 women). *Graduate housing:* On-campus housing not available. *Student services:* Campus employment opportunities, career counseling, disabled student services, free psychological counseling, international student services, multicultural affairs office, teacher training. *Library facilities:* Murdock Learning Resource Center. *Online resources:* library catalog, web page, access to other libraries' catalogs. *Collection:* 208,048 titles, 3,900 serial subscriptions, 6,335 audiovisual materials.

Computer facilities: 1,300 computers available on campus for general student use. A campuswide network can be accessed from student residence rooms and from off campus. Internet access and online class registration are available. *Web address:* http://www.georgefox.edu/.

General Application Contact: Brandon Connelly, Director of Admission for Graduate Programs, 503-554-6121, Fax: 503-554-3110, E-mail: bconnelly@georgefox.edu.

GRADUATE UNITS

George Fox Evangelical Seminary Students: 71 full-time (17 women), 190 part-time (63 women); includes 25 minority (7 African Americans, 12 Asian Americans or Pacific Islanders, 6 Hispanic Americans), 2 international. Average age 42. 82 applicants, 94% accepted, 70 enrolled. *Faculty:* 7 full-time (2 women), 14 part-time/adjunct (5 women). Expenses: Contact institution. *Financial support:* In 2006–07, 8 research assistantships, 8 teaching assistantships were awarded; career-related internships or fieldwork and scholarships/grants also available. Support available to part-time students. Financial award application deadline: 5/1; financial award applicants required to submit FAFSA. In 2006, 10 M Divs, 20 master's, 17 doctorates, 4 other advanced degrees awarded. *Degree program information:* Part-time programs available. Offers divinity (M Div); ministry (D Min); ministry leadership (MA); spiritual formation (MA); spiritual formation and discipleship (Certificate); theological studies (MA). *Application deadline:* For fall admission, 7/1 for domestic and international students; for spring admission, 10/15 for domestic and international students. Applications are processed on a rolling basis. *Application fee:* $40. Electronic applications accepted. *Application Contact:* Sheila Bartlett, Admissions Counselor, 800-631-0921, Fax: 503-554-6111, E-mail: sbartlett@georgefox.edu. *Dean,* Dr. Jules Glanzer, 503-554-6152, E-mail: jglanzer@georgefox.edu.

Graduate Department of Clinical Psychology Students: 92 full-time (53 women), 9 part-time (3 women); includes 10 minority (1 African American, 2 American Indian/Alaska Native, 5 Asian Americans or Pacific Islanders, 2 Hispanic Americans), 1 international. Average age 29. 48 applicants, 52% accepted, 22 enrolled. *Faculty:* 12 full-time (4 women), 5 part-time/adjunct (1 woman). Expenses: Contact institution. *Financial support:* Teaching assistantships, career-related internships or fieldwork available. Financial award applicants required to submit FAFSA. In 2006, 20 master's, 14 doctorates awarded. Offers clinical psychology (Psy D); psychology (MA). *Application deadline:* For fall admission, 1/1 for domestic and international students. *Application fee:* $40. Electronic applications accepted. *Application Contact:* Adina McConaughey, Admission Counselor, 800-631-0921, Fax: 503-554-2263, E-mail: amcconaughey@georgefox.edu. *Director,* Dr. Wayne Adams, 800-765-4369 Ext. 2760, E-mail: wadams@georgefox.edu.

Program in Organizational Leadership Students: 1 (woman) full-time, 22 part-time (9 women); includes 1 minority (Asian American or Pacific Islander), 1 international. Average age 38. 14 applicants, 86% accepted, 11 enrolled. *Faculty:* 3 full-time (2 women), 2 part-time/adjunct (0 women). Expenses: Contact institution. In 2006, 9 degrees awarded. *Degree program information:* Part-time and evening/weekend programs available. Offers organizational leadership (MAOL). Offered only in Boise, ID. *Application deadline:* For fall admission, 7/1 for domestic students. Applications are processed on a rolling basis. *Application fee:* $40. Electronic applications accepted. *Application Contact:* Kris Thompson, Admissions Counselor, 208-375-3900, E-mail: kthompson@georgefox.edu. *Director,* Dr. Mary Olson, 208-375-3900, Fax: 208-375-3564, E-mail: molson@georgefox.edu.

School of Education Students: 157 full-time (125 women), 312 part-time (225 women); includes 15 minority (2 African Americans, 3 American Indian/Alaska Native, 3 Asian Americans or Pacific Islanders, 7 Hispanic Americans), 3 international. Average age 36. 165 applicants, 76% accepted, 106 enrolled. *Faculty:* 34 full-time (18 women), 27 part-time/adjunct (19 women). Expenses: Contact institution. *Financial support:* Career-related internships or fieldwork available. Financial award applicants required to submit FAFSA. In 2006, 208 master's, 11 doctorates, 1 other advanced degree awarded. *Degree program information:* Evening/weekend programs available. Postbaccalaureate distance learning degree programs offered (minimal on-campus study). Offers counseling (MA, MS, Certificate); educational foundations and leadership (M Ed, Ed D); marriage and family therapy (MA, Certificate); school counseling (MA); school psychology (MS, Certificate); teaching (MAT); trauma (Certificate). *Application deadline:* For fall admission, 2/1 for domestic students. Applications are processed on a rolling basis. *Application fee:* $40. Electronic applications accepted. *Application Contact:* Beth Molzahn, Admissions Counselor, 800-631-0921, Fax: 503-554-3856, E-mail: bmolzahn@georgefox.edu. *Dean,* Dr. James Worthington, 503-554-2871, E-mail: jworthington@georgefox.edu.

School of Management Students: 1 full-time (0 women), 239 part-time (79 women); includes 24 minority (4 African Americans, 2 American Indian/Alaska Native, 11 Asian Americans or Pacific Islanders, 7 Hispanic Americans), 1 international. Average age 36. 79 applicants, 76% accepted, 49 enrolled. *Faculty:* 11 full-time (4 women), 7 part-time/adjunct (1 woman). Expenses: Contact institution. *Financial support:* Applicants required to submit FAFSA. In 2006, 99 degrees awarded. *Degree program information:* Part-time and evening/weekend programs available. Offers management (MBA, DM). *Application deadline:* For fall admission, 7/1 for domestic students; for spring admission, 10/15 for domestic students. Applications are processed on a rolling basis. *Application fee:* $40. Electronic applications accepted. *Application Contact:* Amber Russell, Admissions Counselor, 800-631-0921, Fax: 503-554-3856, E-mail: arussell@georgefox.edu. *Acting Dean,* Dr. Dirk Barran, 800-631-0921, E-mail: dbarram@georgefox.edu.

See Close-Up on page 901.

GEORGE MASON UNIVERSITY, Fairfax, VA 22030

General Information State-supported, coed, university. CGS member. *Enrollment:* 29,889 graduate, professional, and undergraduate students; 2,308 full-time matriculated graduate/professional students (1,223 women), 7,015 part-time matriculated graduate/professional students (3,940 women). *Enrollment by degree level:* 752 first professional, 6,571 master's, 1,776 doctoral, 224 other advanced degrees. *Graduate faculty:* 1,108 full-time (431 women), 920 part-time/adjunct (466 women). Tuition, state resident: full-time $5,724; part-time $238 per credit. Tuition, nonresident: full-time $16,896; part-time $704 per credit. *Required fees:* $1,656; $69 per credit. *Graduate housing:* Room and/or apartments available to single students; on-campus housing not available to married students. Housing application deadline: 6/1. *Student services:* Campus employment opportunities, campus safety program, career counseling, child daycare facilities, disabled student services, exercise/wellness program, free psychological counseling, grant writing training, international student services, low-cost health insurance, multicultural affairs office, writing training. *Library facilities:* Fenwick Library plus 1 other. *Online resources:* library catalog, web page, access to other libraries' catalogs. *Collection:* 1.5 million titles, 27,708 serial subscriptions, 27,344 audiovisual materials. *Research* *affiliation:* Medical Sciences Research Institute, Science Applications Internation Corporation (science, technology), Bellcore (software), Chi Associates (biotechnology).

Computer facilities: 1,500 computers available on campus for general student use. A campuswide network can be accessed from student residence rooms and from off campus. Internet access, telephone registration are available. *Web address:* http://www.gmu.edu/.

General Application Contact: Dan Robb, Director of Graduate Admissions, 703-993-4201, Fax: 703-993-2392.

GRADUATE UNITS

College of Health and Human Services Students: 98 full-time (81 women), 301 part-time (260 women); includes 121 minority (60 African Americans, 45 Asian Americans or Pacific Islanders, 16 Hispanic Americans), 27 international. Average age 39. 326 applicants, 61% accepted, 121 enrolled. *Faculty:* 69 full-time (55 women), 75 part-time/adjunct (66 women). Expenses: Contact institution. *Financial support:* Fellowships, research assistantships, teaching assistantships, tuition waivers (partial) available. Support available to part-time students. Financial award application deadline: 3/1; financial award applicants required to submit FAFSA. In 2006, 89 master's, 7 doctorates, 11 other advanced degrees awarded. Offers advanced clinical nursing (MSN); nurse practitioner (MSN); nursing (MSN, PhD); nursing administration (MSN); nursing education (Certificate); nursing educator (MSN); social work (MSW). *Application deadline:* For fall admission, 5/1 for domestic students; for spring admission, 11/1 for domestic students. *Application fee:* $60 ($75 for international students). Electronic applications accepted. *Application Contact:* Dr. James D. Vail, Associate Dean, Graduate Programs and Research, 703-993-1947, Fax: 703-993-1942, E-mail: nursinfo@gmu.edu. *Dean,* Dr. Shirley S. Travis, 703-993-1918.

College of Humanities and Social Sciences Students: 441 full-time (263 women), 1,212 part-time (731 women); includes 232 minority (81 African Americans, 8 American Indian/Alaska Native, 68 Asian Americans or Pacific Islanders, 75 Hispanic Americans), 115 international. Average age 32. 2,005 applicants, 50% accepted, 517 enrolled. *Faculty:* 345 full-time (143 women), 288 part-time/adjunct (152 women). Expenses: Contact institution. *Financial support:* Fellowships, research assistantships, teaching assistantships, career-related internships or fieldwork and Federal Work-Study available. Support available to part-time students. Financial award application deadline: 3/1; financial award applicants required to submit FAFSA. In 2006, 255 master's, 57 doctorates awarded. *Degree program information:* Part-time and evening/weekend programs available. Offers clinical psychology (PhD); communications (MA); creative writing (MFA); cultural studies (PhD); developmental psychology (PhD); economics (MA, PhD); English (MA); English literature (MA); experimental neuropsychology (MA); foreign languages (MA); history (MA, PhD); human factors engineering psychology (MA, PhD); humanities and social sciences (MA, MAIS, MFA, MPA, MS, MSW, DA Ed, PhD, Certificate); industrial/organizational psychology (MA, PhD); interdisciplinary studies (MAIS); liberal studies (MAIS); life-span development psychology (MA); linguistics (MA); professional writing and editing (MA); public administration (MPA); school psychology (MA); social work (MSW); sociology (MA); teaching writing and literature (MA). Electronic applications accepted. *Application Contact:* Susan Swett, Director of Graduate Admissions, 703-993-2423, Fax: 703-993-8714, E-mail: sswett@gmu.edu. *Chair,* Jack Censer, 703-993-8715, Fax: 703-993-8714, E-mail: jcenser@gmu.edu.

The National Center for Community College Education Students: 4 full-time (3 women), 73 part-time (44 women); includes 22 minority (14 African Americans, 5 Asian Americans or Pacific Islanders, 3 Hispanic Americans). Average age 48. 18 applicants, 67% accepted, 6 enrolled. *Faculty:* 3 part-time/adjunct (2 women). Expenses: Contact institution. *Financial support:* Fellowships available. Support available to part-time students. Financial award application deadline: 3/1; financial award applicants required to submit FAFSA. In 2006, 8 doctorates, 3 other advanced degrees awarded. Offers community college education (DA Ed, Certificate). *Application deadline:* For fall admission, 5/1 for domestic students; for spring admission, 11/1 for domestic students. *Application fee:* $60 ($75 for international students). Electronic applications accepted. *Interim Director,* Nance Lucas, 703-993-2310, Fax: 703-993-2307.

College of Science Students: 142 full-time (60 women), 649 part-time (267 women). Average age 34. 238 applicants, 84% accepted. *Faculty:* 122 full-time (39 women), 62 part-time/adjunct (22 women). Expenses: Contact institution. *Financial support:* In 2006–07, 22 fellowships with tuition reimbursements (averaging $2,800 per year), 56 research assistantships with full tuition reimbursements (averaging $13,000 per year) were awarded; teaching assistantships, career-related internships or fieldwork, Federal Work-Study, institutionally sponsored loans, and tuition waivers (partial) also available. Financial award application deadline: 2/1; financial award applicants required to submit FAFSA. In 2006, 173 master's, 66 doctorates, 29 Certificates awarded. *Degree program information:* Part-time and evening/weekend programs available. Offers applied and engineering physics (MS); biodefense (MS, PhD); bioinformatics and computational biology (MS, PhD, Certificate); biology (MS, PhD); chemistry (MS); chemistry and biochemistry (MS); climate dynamics (PhD); computational and data sciences (MS, PhD, Certificate); computational social science (PhD); computational techniques and applications (Certificate); earth systems and geoinformation sciences (PhD, Certificate); earth systems geoinformation science (MS); environmental science and policy (MS, PhD); geographic and cartographic sciences (MS); geography (MS); mathematical sciences (MS, PhD); mathematics (MS, PhD); nanotechnology and nanoscience (Certificate); neuroscience (PhD); physical sciences (PhD); physics and astronomy (MS); remote sensing and earth image processing (Certificate). *Application deadline:* For fall admission, 3/1 priority date for domestic students, 2/1 for international students; for spring admission, 11/1 priority date for domestic students. Applications are processed on a rolling basis. *Application fee:* $60. Electronic applications accepted. *Application Contact:* Dr. Peter A. Becker, Associate Dean for Graduate Programs, 703-993-3619, Fax: 703-993-9034, E-mail: pbecker@gmu.edu. *Director,* Dr. Vikas E. Chandhoke, 703-993-3622, Fax: 703-993-1993, E-mail: cosinfo@gmu.edu.

College of Visual and Performing Arts Students: 63 full-time (48 women), 93 part-time (66 women); includes 30 minority (16 African Americans, 9 Asian Americans or Pacific Islanders, 5 Hispanic Americans), 9 international. Average age 31. 137 applicants, 50% accepted, 47 enrolled. *Faculty:* 46 full-time (24 women), 63 part-time/adjunct (40 women). Expenses: Contact institution. *Financial support:* Fellowships, teaching assistantships, career-related internships or fieldwork, Federal Work-Study, and institutionally sponsored loans available. Support available to part-time students. Financial award application deadline: 3/1; financial award applicants required to submit FAFSA. In 2006, 37 degrees awarded. Offers dance (MFA); music (MA); music education (MA); visual and performing arts (MA, MFA); visual technologies (MA). *Application deadline:* For fall admission, 5/1 for domestic students; for spring admission, 11/1 for domestic students. *Application fee:* $60 ($75 for international students). Electronic applications accepted. *Application Contact:* Dr. Scott M. Martin, Director, 703-993-4574, Fax: 703-993-8798, E-mail: avt@gmu.edu. *Dean,* William Reeder, 703-993-8877, Fax: 703-993-8883.

Graduate School of Education Students: 309 full-time (257 women), 2,160 part-time (1,735 women); includes 407 minority (209 African Americans, 3 American Indian/Alaska Native, 92 Asian Americans or Pacific Islanders, 103 Hispanic Americans), 52 international. Average age 35. 1,396 applicants, 68% accepted, 779 enrolled. *Faculty:* 108 full-time (70 women), 193 part-time/adjunct (140 women). Expenses: Contact institution. *Financial support:* Fellowships, research assistantships, teaching assistantships, career-related internships or fieldwork and Federal Work-Study available. Support available to part-time students. Financial award application deadline: 3/1; financial award applicants required to submit FAFSA. In 2006, 904 master's, 26 doctorates awarded. *Degree program information:* Part-time and evening/weekend programs available. Offers bilingual/multicultural/English as a second language education (M Ed); counseling and development (M Ed); early childhood education (M Ed); education (M Ed, MA, MS, PhD); education leadership (M Ed); exercise, fitness and health promotion (MS); initiatives in educational transformation (MA); instructional technology (M Ed); middle education (M Ed); reading (M Ed); secondary education (M Ed); special education (M Ed). *Application deadline:* For fall admission, 5/1 for domestic students; for spring admission, 11/1 for domestic students. *Application fee:* $60 ($75 for international students). Electronic applications accepted. *Application Contact:* Dr. Mark Goor, Information Contact, 703-993-4648, E-mail: gseinfo@gmu.edu. *Dean,* Jeffrey Gorrell, 703-993-2004, E-mail: gseinfo@gmu.edu.

Institute for Conflict Analysis and Resolution Students: 76 full-time (46 women), 174 part-time (113 women); includes 47 minority (26 African Americans, 1 American Indian/Alaska Native, 12 Asian Americans or Pacific Islanders, 8 Hispanic Americans), 56 international. Average age 36. 285 applicants, 46% accepted, 88 enrolled. *Faculty:* 19 full-time (7 women), 8 part-time/adjunct (5 women). Expenses: Contact institution. *Financial support:* Fellowships, research assistantships, teaching assistantships, career-related internships or fieldwork available. Support available to part-time students. Financial award application deadline: 3/1; financial award applicants required to submit FAFSA. In 2006, 51 master's, 121 doctorates awarded. *Degree program information:* Part-time programs available. Offers conflict analysis and resolution (MS, PhD). *Application deadline:* For fall admission, 3/1 for domestic students; for spring admission, 11/1 for domestic students. *Application fee:* $60 ($75 for international students). Electronic applications accepted. *Director,* Dr. Sara Cobb, 703-993-1300, Fax: 703-993-1302, E-mail: icarinfo@gmu.edu.

School of Law *Degree program information:* Part-time and evening/weekend programs available. Offers intellectual property (LL M); law (JD); law and economics (LL M). Electronic applications accepted.

School of Management Students: 105 full-time (45 women), 269 part-time (96 women); includes 78 minority (16 African Americans, 2 American Indian/Alaska Native, 50 Asian Americans or Pacific Islanders, 10 Hispanic Americans), 41 international. Average age 35. 370 applicants, 49% accepted, 127 enrolled. *Faculty:* 34 part-time/adjunct (11 women). Expenses: Contact institution. *Financial support:* Fellowships, research assistantships, teaching assistantships, career-related internships or fieldwork and Federal Work-Study available. Support available to part-time students. Financial award application deadline: 3/1; financial award applicants required to submit FAFSA. In 2006, 200 degrees awarded. *Degree program information:* Part-time and evening/weekend programs available. Offers bio-science management (MS); business administration (EMBA, MBA); management (EMBA, MBA, MS); technology management (MS). *Application deadline:* For fall admission, 5/1 for domestic students; for spring admission, 11/1 for domestic students. Applications are processed on a rolling basis. *Application fee:* $60 ($75 for international students). Electronic applications accepted. *Application Contact:* Dr. Andres Fortino, Director, 703-993-1872, Fax: 703-993-1867, E-mail: masonmba@som.gmu.edu. *Dean,* Richard Klimoski, 703-993-1807, E-mail: rklimosk@gmu.edu.

School of Public Policy Students: 262 full-time (133 women), 627 part-time (312 women); includes 188 minority (77 African Americans, 2 American Indian/Alaska Native, 56 Asian Americans or Pacific Islanders, 53 Hispanic Americans), 105 international. Average age 31. 692 applicants, 68% accepted, 255 enrolled. *Faculty:* 48 full-time (8 women), 41 part-time/adjunct (6 women). Expenses: Contact institution. *Financial support:* In 2006–07, 27 research assistantships with full tuition reimbursements (averaging $16,000 per year) were awarded; career-related internships or fieldwork, Federal Work-Study, scholarships/grants, tuition waivers (partial), and unspecified assistantships also available. Support available to part-time students. Financial award application deadline: 3/1; financial award applicants required to submit FAFSA. In 2006, 233 master's, 14 doctorates awarded. *Degree program information:* Part-time and evening/weekend programs available. Offers international commerce and policy (MA); organization development and knowledge management (MNPS); peace operations (MNPS); public policy (MA, MNPS, MPP, PhD); transportation policy, operations and logistics (MA). *Application deadline:* Applications are processed on a rolling basis. *Application fee:* $60. Electronic applications accepted. *Application Contact:* Leslie Metzger Levin, Director of Graduate Admissions, 703-993-8099, Fax: 703-993-4876, E-mail: lmetzger@gmu.edu. *Dean,* Dr. Kingsley Haynes, 703-993-8200, Fax: 703-993-2284, E-mail: khaynes@gmu.edu.

Volgenau School of Information Technology and Engineering Students: 294 full-time (68 women), 1,230 part-time (239 women); includes 347 minority (71 African Americans, 2 American Indian/Alaska Native, 236 Asian Americans or Pacific Islanders, 38 Hispanic Americans), 497 international. Average age 31. 1,236 applicants, 63% accepted, 342 enrolled. *Faculty:* 123 full-time (29 women), 107 part-time/adjunct (15 women). Expenses: Contact institution. *Financial support:* Fellowships, research assistantships, teaching assistantships, career-related internships or fieldwork, Federal Work-Study, institutionally sponsored loans, and unspecified assistantships available. Support available to part-time students. Financial award application deadline: 3/1; financial award applicants required to submit FAFSA. In 2006, 438 master's, 22 doctorates awarded. *Degree program information:* Part-time and evening/weekend programs available. Offers civil and infrastructure engineering (MS); computer science (MS, PhD); electrical and computer engineering (PhD); electrical engineering (MS); federal statistics (Certificate); information systems (MS); information technology (MS, PhD, Engr); information technology and engineering (MS, PhD, Certificate, Engr); operations research and management science (MS); software systems engineering (MS); statistical science (MS, PhD); systems engineering (MS); telecommunication (MS). *Application deadline:* For fall admission, 5/1 for domestic students; for spring admission, 11/1 for domestic students. *Application fee:* $75. Electronic applications accepted. *Application Contact:* Dr. Stephen G. Nash, Associate Dean, 703-993-1505, Fax: 703-993-1734, E-mail: itegrad@gmu.edu. *Dean,* Lloyd Griffiths, 703-993-1500, Fax: 703-993-1734, E-mail: lgriffiths@gmu.edu.

GEORGE MEANY CENTER FOR LABOR STUDIES-THE NATIONAL LABOR COLLEGE, Silver Spring, MD 20903

General Information Independent, coed, comprehensive institution.

GRADUATE UNITS

Graduate Studies

GEORGETOWN COLLEGE, Georgetown, KY 40324-1696

General Information Independent-religious, coed, comprehensive institution. *Graduate housing:* Room and/or apartments available to single students; on-campus housing not available to married students.

GRADUATE UNITS

Department of Education *Degree program information:* Part-time programs available. Offers education (MA Ed).

GEORGETOWN UNIVERSITY, Washington, DC 20057

General Information Independent-religious, coed, university. CGS member. *Graduate housing:* On-campus housing not available.

GRADUATE UNITS

Graduate School of Arts and Sciences Offers American government (MA, PhD); analytical chemistry (MS, PhD); Arab studies (MA, Certificate); Arabic language, literature, and linguistics (MS, PhD); arts and sciences (MA, MALS, MAT, MBA, MPP, MS, PhD, Certificate); bilingual education (Certificate); biochemistry (MS, PhD); biology (MS, PhD); British and American literature (MA); chemical physics (MS, PhD); communication, culture, and technology (MA); comparative government (PhD); conflict resolution (MA); demography (MA); economics (PhD); German (MS, PhD); history (MA, PhD); inorganic chemistry (MS, PhD); international relations (PhD); linguistics (MS, PhD); national security studies (MA); organic chemistry (MS, PhD); philosophy (MA, PhD); physical chemistry (MS, PhD); political theory (PhD); psychology (PhD); Russian and East European studies (MA); Spanish (MS, PhD); teaching English as a second language (MAT, Certificate); teaching English as a second language and bilingual education (MAT); theoretical chemistry (MS, PhD).

BMW Center for German and European Studies Offers German and European studies (MA).

Center for Latin American Studies Offers Latin American studies (MA).

Edmund A. Walsh School of Foreign Service Offers foreign service (MS).

The Georgetown Public Policy Institute Offers public policy (MPP).

McDonough School of Business Offers business administration (MBA).

Programs in Biomedical Sciences Offers biochemistry and molecular biology (PhD); biohazardous threat agents and emerging infectious diseases (MS); biomedical sciences (MS, PhD); biostatistics and epidemiology (MS); cell biology (PhD); general microbiology and immunology (MS); global infectious diseases (PhD); health physics (MS); microbiology

Georgetown University (continued)

and immunology research (PhD); neuroscience (PhD); pathology (MS, PhD); pharmacology (PhD); physiology and biophysics (MS, PhD); radiobiology (MS); science policy and advocacy (MS).

School for Summer and Continuing Education Offers summer and continuing education (MALS).

School of Nursing and Health Studies Offers nursing (MS).

Law Center *Degree program information:* Part-time and evening/weekend programs available. Offers advocacy (LL M); common law studies (LL M); general (LL M); international and comparative law (LL M); labor and employment law (LL M); law (JD, SJD); securities regulation (LL M); taxation (LL M).

National Institutes of Health Sponsored Programs Offers biomedical sciences (MS, PhD).

School of Medicine Offers medicine (MD).

THE GEORGE WASHINGTON UNIVERSITY, Washington, DC 20052

General Information Independent, coed, university. CGS member. *Graduate housing:* On-campus housing not available. *Research affiliation:* NASA–Langley Research Center (aeroacoustics, aeronautics, astronautics), National Institutes of Health (biostatistics), Smithsonian Institution, Library of Congress, Goddard Space Flight Center (radar modeling analysis, space systems technologies), Children's Hospital National Medical Center.

GRADUATE UNITS

College of Professional Studies Offers healthcare corporate compliance (Graduate Certificate); molecular biotechnology (MPS); paralegal studies (MPS, Graduate Certificate); professional service firm management (MPS); publishing (MPS).

Graduate School of Political Management Offers legislative affairs (MA); PAC and political management (Certificate); political management (MA). Electronic applications accepted.

Columbian College of Arts and Sciences *Degree program information:* Part-time and evening/weekend programs available. Offers American studies (MA, PhD); analytical chemistry (MS, PhD); anthropology (MA); applied mathematics (MA, MS); applied social psychology (PhD); art history (MA, PhD); art therapy (MA, Certificate); arts and sciences (MA, MFA, MFS, MPA, MPP, MS, MSFS, PhD, Psy D, Certificate, Graduate Certificate); biochemistry (PhD); biological sciences (MS, PhD); biostatistics (MS, PhD); ceramics (MFA); classical acting (MFA); clinical psychology (PhD); cognitive neuropsychology (PhD); crime scene investigation (MFS); criminal justice (MA); design (MFA); economics (MA, PhD); English (MA, PhD); epidemiology (MS, PhD); folklife (MA); forensic chemistry (MFS, MSFS); forensic molecular biology (MFS, MSFS); forensic sciences (MFS, MSFS); forensic toxicology (MFS, MSFS); genomics, proteomics, and bioinformatics (MS); geography (MA); geology (MS, PhD); geosciences (MS, PhD); high-technology crime investigation (MFS); Hinduism and Islam (MA); historic preservation (MA); history (MA, PhD); hominid paleobiology (MS, PhD); human resource management (MA); human sciences (PhD); industrial and engineering statistics (MS); industrial-organizational psychology (PhD); inorganic chemistry (MS, PhD); interior design (MFA); leadership and coaching (Certificate); material culture (MA); materials science (MS, PhD); museum studies (MA, Certificate); museum training (MA); organic chemistry (MS, PhD); organizational management (MA); painting (MFA); photography (MFA); physical chemistry (MS, PhD); physics (MA, PhD); political science (MA, PhD); printmaking (MFA); professional psychology (Psy D); pure mathematics (MA, PhD); sculpture (MFA); security management (MFS); sociology (MA); speech pathology (MA); statistics (MS, PhD); survey design and data analysis (Graduate Certificate); theater design (MFA); women's studies (MA, Certificate). Electronic applications accepted.

Institute for Biomedical Sciences *Degree program information:* Part-time and evening/weekend programs available. Offers biochemistry and molecular biology (PhD); genetics (MS, PhD); microbiology and immunology (PhD); molecular and cellular oncology (PhD); molecular medicine (PhD); neuroscience (PhD); neurosciences (PhD); pharmacology (PhD); pharmacology and physiology (PhD). Electronic applications accepted.

School of Media and Public Affairs Offers media and public affairs (MA). Electronic applications accepted.

School of Public Policy and Public Administration *Degree program information:* Part-time and evening/weekend programs available. Offers budget and public finance (MPA); environmental and resource policy (MA); federal policy, politics, and management (MPA); international development management (MPA); managing public organizations (MPA); managing state and local governments and urban policy (MPA); nonprofit management (MPA); philosophy and social policy (MA); policy analysis and evaluation (MPA); public administration (MPA); public policy (MA, MPP); public policy and administration (PhD); public policy and public administration (MPA); women's studies (MA). Electronic applications accepted.

Elliott School of International Affairs *Degree program information:* Part-time and evening/weekend programs available. Offers Asian studies (MA); European and Eurasian studies (MA); international affairs (MA, MIPP, MIS); international development studies (MA); international policy and practice (MIPP, MIS); international trade and investment policy (MA); Latin American and hemispheric studies (MA); science, technology, and public policy (MA); security policy studies (MA). Electronic applications accepted.

Graduate School of Education and Human Development *Degree program information:* Part-time and evening/weekend programs available. Postbaccalaureate distance learning degree programs offered (no on-campus study). Offers counseling (PhD, Ed S); counseling: school, community and rehabilitation (MA Ed); curriculum and instruction (MA Ed, Ed D, Ed S); early childhood special education (MA Ed); education and human development (M Ed, MA Ed, MAT, Ed D, PhD, Certificate, Ed S); education policy (Ed D); education policy studies (MA Ed); educational administration (Ed D); educational administration and policy studies (Ed D); educational human development (MA Ed); educational leadership and administration (MA Ed, Ed S); educational technology leadership (MA Ed); elementary education (M Ed); higher education administration (MA Ed, Ed D, Ed S); human resource development (MA Ed, Ed D, Ed S); infant special education (MA Ed); international education (MA Ed); museum education (MAT); secondary education (M Ed); special education (Ed D, Ed S); special education of seriously emotionally disturbed students (MA Ed); transitional special education (MA Ed, Certificate). Electronic applications accepted.

Law School *Degree program information:* Part-time and evening/weekend programs available. Offers law (JD, LL M, SJD).

National Institutes of Health Sponsored Programs Offers biomedical sciences (PhD).

School of Business *Degree program information:* Part-time and evening/weekend programs available. Offers accountancy (M Accy, MBA, PhD); business (M Accy, MBA, MS, MSF, MSIST, MTA, PMBA, PhD, Professional Certificate); business economics and public policy (MBA); event and meeting management (MTA); event management (Professional Certificate); finance (MSF, PhD); finance and investments (MBA); human resources management (MBA); information systems (MSIST); information systems development (MSIST); information systems management (MBA); information systems project management (MSIST); international business (MBA, PhD); international hotel management (MTA); logistics, operations, and materials management (MBA); management and organization (PhD); management decision making (MBA, PhD); management information systems (MSIST); management of science, technology, and innovation (MBA); marketing (MBA, PhD); organizational behavior and development (MBA); project management (MS); real estate development (MBA); sports management (MTA); strategic management and public policy (PhD); sustainable destination management (MTA); tourism administration (MTA); tourism and hospitality management (MBA); tourism destination management (Professional Certificate). PMBA program also offered in Alexandria and Ashburn, VA. Electronic applications accepted.

School of Engineering and Applied Science *Degree program information:* Part-time and evening/weekend programs available. Offers civil and environmental engineering (MS, D Sc, App Sc, Engr); computer science (MS, D Sc, App Sc, Engr); electrical and computer engineering (MS, D Sc); engineering and applied science (MEM, MS, D Sc, App Sc, Engr); engineering management and systems engineering (MEM, MS, D Sc, App Sc, Engr); mechanical and aerospace engineering (MS, D Sc, App Sc, Engr); telecommunication and computers (MS).

School of Medicine and Health Sciences Offers adult nurse practitioner (MSN, Post Master's Certificate); advanced family nurse practitioner (Post Master's Certificate); clinical practice management (MSHS); clinical research administration (MSHS); clinical research administration for nurses (MSN); emergency services management (MSHS); end-of-life care (MSHS, MSN); family nurse practitioner (MSN); immunohematology (MSHS); medicine (MD); medicine and health sciences (MD, MSHS, MSN, DPT, Post Master's Certificate); nursing leadership and management (MSN); oral biology (MSHS); physical therapy (DPT); physician assistant (MSHS).

School of Public Health and Health Services *Degree program information:* Part-time and evening/weekend programs available. Offers biostatistics (MPH); community-oriented primary care (MPH); environmental and occupational health (Dr PH); epidemiology (MPH); exercise science (MS); health behavior (Dr PH); health information systems (MPH); health management and leadership (MHSA); health policy (MHSA, Dr PH); health promotion (MPH); health services administration (Specialist); international health policy and programs (MPH); international health promotion (MPH); maternal and child health (MPH); microbiology and emerging infectious diseases (MSPH); public health and emergency management (Certificate); public health and health services (MHSA, MPH, MS, MSPH, Dr PH, Certificate, Specialist); public health management (MPH).

GEORGIA CAMPUS–PHILADELPHIA COLLEGE OF OSTEOPATHIC MEDICINE, Suwanee, GA 30024

General Information Independent, coed, graduate-only institution.

GRADUATE UNITS

Program in Biomedical Sciences Offers biomedical sciences (MS, Certificate).

Program in Osteopathic Medicine Offers osteopathic medicine (DO).

GEORGIA COLLEGE & STATE UNIVERSITY, Milledgeville, GA 31061

General Information State-supported, coed, comprehensive institution. *Enrollment:* 6,041 graduate, professional, and undergraduate students; 390 full-time matriculated graduate/professional students (254 women), 510 part-time matriculated graduate/professional students (327 women). *Enrollment by degree level:* 900 master's. *Graduate faculty:* 298 full-time (157 women). Tuition, state resident: full-time $3,222; part-time $179 per credit hour. Tuition, nonresident: full-time $12,870; part-time $715 per credit hour. Tuition and fees vary according to course load. *Graduate housing:* Room and/or apartments available on a first-come, first-served basis to single students; on-campus housing not available to married students. Typical cost: $7,116 (including board). Room and board charges vary according to board plan, campus/location and housing facility selected. *Student services:* Campus employment opportunities, campus safety program, career counseling, disabled student services, exercise/wellness program, free psychological counseling, grant writing training, international student services, multicultural affairs office, teacher training. *Library facilities:* Ina Dillard Russell Library. *Online resources:* library catalog, web page, access to other libraries' catalogs. *Collection:* 175,299 titles, 22,955 serial subscriptions, 5,306 audiovisual materials.

Computer facilities: 500 computers available on campus for general student use. A campuswide network can be accessed from student residence rooms and from off campus. Internet access and online class registration are available. *Web address:* http://www.gcsu.edu/.

General Application Contact: Leah Donna Douglas, Research and Graduate Services, Research Coordinator, 478-445-6278, Fax: 478-445-6271, E-mail: donna.douglas@gcsu.edu.

GRADUATE UNITS

Graduate School Students: 390 full-time (254 women), 510 part-time (327 women); includes 191 minority (162 African Americans, 3 American Indian/Alaska Native, 13 Asian Americans or Pacific Islanders, 13 Hispanic Americans), 37 international. Average age 34. 842 applicants, 59% accepted. *Faculty:* 298 full-time (157 women). Expenses: Contact institution. *Financial support:* In 2006–07, 110 research assistantships with tuition reimbursements were awarded; career-related internships or fieldwork, Federal Work-Study, and unspecified assistantships also available. Support available to part-time students. Financial award application deadline: 3/1; financial award applicants required to submit FAFSA. In 2006, 383 master's, 63 other advanced degrees awarded. *Degree program information:* Part-time and evening/weekend programs available. Postbaccalaureate distance learning degree programs offered (no on-campus study). *Application deadline:* For fall admission, 7/15 priority date for domestic students. Applications are processed on a rolling basis. *Application fee:* $25. Electronic applications accepted. *Application Contact:* Rebecca Miles, Graduate Admissions Specialist, 478-445-6289, Fax: 478-445-1914. *Associate Vice President of the Extended University, Research and Graduate Services,* Dr. Mark Pelton, 478-445-2753, Fax: 478-445-6271, E-mail: mark.pelton@gcsu.edu.

The J. Whitney Bunting School of Business Students: 44 full-time (19 women), 139 part-time (71 women); includes 28 minority (19 African Americans, 6 Asian Americans or Pacific Islanders, 3 Hispanic Americans), 17 international. Average age 30. 135 applicants, 56% accepted, 42 enrolled. *Faculty:* 43 full-time (18 women). Expenses: Contact institution. *Financial support:* In 2006–07, 24 research assistantships with tuition reimbursements were awarded; career-related internships or fieldwork, Federal Work-Study, and unspecified assistantships also available. Support available to part-time students. Financial award application deadline: 3/1; financial award applicants required to submit FAFSA. In 2006, 76 degrees awarded. *Degree program information:* Part-time and evening/weekend programs available. Postbaccalaureate distance learning degree programs offered (no on-campus study). Offers accountancy (MACCT); business (MBA); information systems (MIS). *Application deadline:* For fall admission, 7/1 priority date for domestic students; for spring admission, 11/15 priority date for domestic students. Applications are processed on a rolling basis. *Application fee:* $25. Electronic applications accepted. *Application Contact:* Lynn Hanson, Director of Graduate Programs in Business, 478-445-5115, E-mail: lynn.hanson@gcsu.edu. *Dean,* Dr. Faye Gilbert, 478-445-5497, E-mail: faye.gilbert@gcsu.edu.

School of Education Students: 219 full-time (166 women), 126 part-time (101 women); includes 79 minority (70 African Americans, 3 American Indian/Alaska Native, 1 Asian American or Pacific Islander, 5 Hispanic Americans), 3 international. Average age 35. 323 applicants, 52% accepted, 84 enrolled. *Faculty:* 44 full-time (30 women). Expenses: Contact institution. *Financial support:* In 2006–07, 11 research assistantships were awarded; career-related internships or fieldwork, Federal Work-Study, and unspecified assistantships also available. Support available to part-time students. Financial award application deadline: 3/1; financial award applicants required to submit FAFSA. In 2006, 152 master's, 46 other advanced degrees awarded. *Degree program information:* Part-time programs available. Offers administration and supervision (M Ed, Ed S); behavior disorders (M Ed); early childhood education (M Ed, Ed S); education (M Ed, MAT, Ed S); English education (M Ed); instructional technology (M Ed); interrelated teaching (M Ed); learning disabilities (M Ed); mathematics education (M Ed); mental retardation (M Ed); middle grades education (M Ed, Ed S); natural science education (M Ed, Ed S); secondary education (MAT); social science education (M Ed, Ed S); special education (M Ed). *Application deadline:* For fall admission, 7/1 priority date for domestic students. Applications are processed on a rolling basis. *Application fee:* $25. Electronic applications accepted. *Application Contact:* Dr. W. Bee Crews, Coordinator of Graduate Programs, 478-445-4056, E-mail: b.crews@gcsu.edu. *Dean,* Dr. Linda Irwin-Devitis, 478-445-4546, E-mail: linda.irwin-devitis@gcsu.edu.

School of Health Sciences Students: 26 full-time (18 women), 59 part-time (51 women); includes 18 minority (16 African Americans, 1 Asian American or Pacific Islander, 1 Hispanic American), 4 international. Average age 33. 77 applicants, 61% accepted, 24 enrolled. *Faculty:* 35 full-time (28 women). Expenses: Contact institution. *Financial support:* In 2006–07, 14 research assistantships with tuition reimbursements (averaging $3,800 per year) were awarded; career-related internships or fieldwork, Federal Work-Study, and unspecified assistantships also available. Support available to part-time students. Financial award application deadline: 3/1; financial award applicants required to submit FAFSA. In 2006, 18 degrees awarded. Offers health and physical education (M Ed, Ed S); kinesiology (M Ed, Ed S); music therapy (MMT); nursing (MSN). *Application deadline:* For fall admission, 7/1 priority date for domestic students. Applications are processed on a rolling basis. *Application fee:* $25. Electronic applications accepted. *Dean*, Dr. Sandra Gangstead, 478-445-4092.

School of Liberal Arts and Sciences Students: 89 full-time (48 women), 124 part-time (74 women); includes 57 minority (51 African Americans, 2 American Indian/Alaska Native, 2 Asian Americans or Pacific Islanders, 2 Hispanic Americans), 2 international. 185 applicants, 61% accepted, 82 enrolled. *Faculty:* 165 full-time (73 women). Expenses: Contact institution. *Financial support:* In 2006–07, 61 research assistantships with tuition reimbursements were awarded; career-related internships or fieldwork, Federal Work-Study, and unspecified assistantships also available. Support available to part-time students. Financial award application deadline: 3/1; financial award applicants required to submit FAFSA. In 2006, 99 degrees awarded. *Degree program information:* Part-time programs available. Offers biology (MS); creative writing (MFA); criminal justice (MS); English (MA); history (MA); liberal arts and sciences (MA, MFA, MPA, MS, MSA, MSLS); logistics (MSA, MSLS); logistics management (MSA); logistics systems (MSLS); public administration and public affairs (MPA, MS). *Application deadline:* For fall admission, 7/1 priority date for domestic students. Applications are processed on a rolling basis. *Application fee:* $25. Electronic applications accepted. *Dean*, Dr. Beth Rushing, 478-445-4441, E-mail: beth.rushing@gcsu.edu.

GEORGIA INSTITUTE OF TECHNOLOGY, Atlanta, GA 30332-0001

General Information State-supported, coed, university. CGS member. *Graduate housing:* Rooms and/or apartments available on a first-come, first-served basis to single and married students. Housing application deadline: 5/1. *Research affiliation:* Oak Ridge National Laboratory (energy, health, environment), Yerkes Regional Primate Research Center (biomedicine, physiology and behavior), Skidaway Institute of Oceanography (marine geology), Southeastern Universities Research Association (high-energy physics), Emory University Medical School (biomedical engineering), Zoo Atlanta (environmental design, environmental psychology).

GRADUATE UNITS

Graduate Studies and Research *Degree program information:* Part-time and evening/weekend programs available. Postbaccalaureate distance learning degree programs offered. Offers algorithms, combinatorics, and optimization (PhD); statistics (MS Stat). Electronic applications accepted.

College of Architecture Offers architecture (PhD); economic development (MCRP); environmental planning and management (MCRP); geographic information systems (MCRP); integrated facility management (MS); integrated project delivery systems (MS); land development (MCRP); land use planning (MCRP); transportation (MCRP); urban design (MCRP). Electronic applications accepted.

College of Computing *Degree program information:* Part-time programs available. Offers algorithms, combinatorics, and optimization (PhD); computer science (MS, MSCS, PhD); human computer interaction (MSHCI).

College of Engineering *Degree program information:* Part-time programs available. Postbaccalaureate distance learning degree programs offered. Offers aerospace engineering (MS, MSAE, PhD); algorithms, combinatorics, and optimization (PhD); bioengineering (MS Bio E, PhD); biomedical engineering (MS Bio E); chemical engineering (MS Ch E, PhD); civil engineering (MS, MSCE, PhD); electrical and computer engineering (MS, MSEE, PhD); engineering (MS, MS Bio E, MS Ch E, MS Env E, MS Poly, MS Stat, MSAE, MSCE, MSEE, MSESM, MSHS, MSIE, MSME, MSNE, MSOR, PhD, Certificate); engineering science and mechanics (MS, MSESM, PhD); environmental engineering (MS, MS Env E, PhD); health systems (MSHS); industrial and systems engineering (MS, MS Stat, MSIE, PhD); industrial engineering (MS, MSIE); materials science and engineering (MS, PhD); mechanical engineering (MS, MS Bio E, MSME, PhD); medical physics (MS); nuclear and radiological engineering (MSNE, PhD); nuclear and radiological engineering and medical physics (MS, MSNE, PhD); operations research (MSOR); paper science and engineering (MS, PhD); polymer, textile and fiber engineering (MS, PhD); polymers (MS Poly); statistics (MS Stat). Electronic applications accepted.

College of Management Offers accounting (MBA, PhD); e-commerce (Certificate); engineering entrepreneurship (MBA); entrepreneurship (Certificate); finance (MBA, PhD); information technology management (MBA, PhD); international business (MBA, Certificate); management (MBA, MS, MSMOT, PhD, Certificate); management of technology (Certificate); marketing (MBA, PhD); operations management (MBA, PhD); organizational behavior (MBA, PhD); quantitative and computational finance (MS); strategic management (MBA, PhD). Electronic applications accepted.

College of Sciences *Degree program information:* Part-time programs available. Offers algorithms, combinatorics, and optimization (PhD); applied biology (MS, PhD); applied mathematics (MS); atmospheric chemistry and air pollution (MS, PhD); atmospheric dynamics and climate (MS, PhD); bioinformatics (MS, PhD); biology (MS); chemistry and biochemistry (MS, MS Chem, PhD); geochemistry (MS, PhD); human computer interaction (MSHCI); hydrologic cycle (MS, PhD); mathematics (PhD); ocean sciences (MS, PhD); physics (MS, PhD); prosthetics and orthotics (MS); psychology (MS, MS Psy, PhD); quantitative and computational finance (MS); sciences (MS, MS Chem, MS Phys, MS Psy, MS Stat, MSA Phy, MSHCI, PhD); solid-earth and environmental geophysics (MS, PhD); statistics (MS Stat). Electronic applications accepted.

Ivan Allen College of Policy and International Affairs *Degree program information:* Part-time and evening/weekend programs available. Offers economics (MS); history of technology (MSHT, PhD); human computer interaction (MSHCI); information design and technology (MSIDT); international affairs (MS Int A); policy and international affairs (MS, MS Int A, MS Pub P, MSHCI, MSHT, MSIDT, PhD); public policy (MS Pub P, PhD). Electronic applications accepted.

GEORGIAN COURT UNIVERSITY, Lakewood, NJ 08701-2697

General Information Independent-religious, Undergraduate: women only; graduate: coed, comprehensive institution. *Enrollment:* 3,047 graduate, professional, and undergraduate students; 199 full-time matriculated graduate/professional students (170 women), 880 part-time matriculated graduate/professional students (722 women). *Enrollment by degree level:* 829 master's, 250 other advanced degrees. *Graduate faculty:* 54 full-time (29 women), 54 part-time/adjunct (28 women). *Graduate housing:* On-campus housing not available. *Student services:* Campus employment opportunities, career counseling, disabled student services, exercise/wellness program, free psychological counseling, low-cost health insurance, teacher training. *Library facilities:* The Sister Mary Joseph Cunningham Library. *Online resources:* library catalog, web page. *Collection:* 145,413 titles, 1,123 serial subscriptions.

Computer facilities: 180 computers available on campus for general student use. A campuswide network can be accessed from student residence rooms. Internet access is available. *Web address:* http://www.georgian.edu/.

General Application Contact: Eugene Soltys, Director of Graduate Admissions, 732-987-2760 Ext. 2760, Fax: 732-987-2000, E-mail: admissions@georgian.edu.

GRADUATE UNITS

School of Arts and Humanities Average age 50. 7 applicants, 86% accepted, 4 enrolled. *Faculty:* 3 full-time (1 woman). Expenses: Contact institution. *Financial support:* Scholarships/grants, health care benefits, and unspecified assistantships available. Financial award application deadline: 4/15; financial award applicants required to submit FAFSA. In 2006, 10 degrees awarded. *Degree program information:* Part-time and evening/weekend programs available. Offers theology (MA, Certificate). *Application deadline:* For fall admission, 8/1 priority date for domestic students, 4/1 for international students; for spring admission, 1/1 priority date for domestic students, 7/1 for international students. Applications are processed on a rolling basis. *Application fee:* $40. Electronic applications accepted. *Application Contact:* Eugene Soltys, Director of Graduate Admissions, 732-987-2760 Ext. 2760, Fax: 732-987-2000, E-mail: admissions@georgian.edu. *Dean*, Dr. Linda James, 732-987-2617.

School of Business Students: 36 full-time (29 women), 130 part-time (93 women); includes 27 minority (9 African Americans, 7 Asian Americans or Pacific Islanders, 11 Hispanic Americans), 5 international. Average age 34. 55 applicants, 95% accepted, 40 enrolled. *Faculty:* 8 full-time (4 women), 8 part-time/adjunct (3 women). Expenses: Contact institution. *Financial support:* Scholarships/grants, health care benefits, and unspecified assistantships available. Financial award application deadline: 4/15; financial award applicants required to submit FAFSA. In 2006, 61 degrees awarded. *Degree program information:* Part-time and evening/weekend programs available. Offers business (MBA). *Application deadline:* For fall admission, 8/1 priority date for domestic students, 4/1 for international students; for spring admission, 1/1 priority date for domestic students, 7/1 for international students. Applications are processed on a rolling basis. *Application fee:* $40. Electronic applications accepted. *Application Contact:* Eugene Soltys, Director of Graduate Admissions, 732-987-2760 Ext. 2760, Fax: 732-987-2000, E-mail: admissions@georgian.edu. *Dean*, Dr. Siamack Shoisi, 732-987-2724.

School of Education Students: 128 full-time (110 women), 594 part-time (495 women); includes 56 minority (17 African Americans, 8 Asian Americans or Pacific Islanders, 31 Hispanic Americans), 1 international. Average age 34. 676 applicants, 80% accepted, 312 enrolled. *Faculty:* 25 full-time (14 women), 41 part-time/adjunct (23 women). Expenses: Contact institution. *Financial support:* In 2006–07, 183 students received support. Scholarships/grants, health care benefits, and unspecified assistantships available. Financial award application deadline: 4/15; financial award applicants required to submit FAFSA. In 2006, 130 master's, 4 other advanced degrees awarded. *Degree program information:* Part-time and evening/weekend programs available. Offers administration, supervision, and curriculum planning (MA); early intervention studies (Certificate); education (MA); instructional technology (MA, Certificate); special education (MA); substance awareness coordinator (Certificate). *Application deadline:* For fall admission, 8/1 priority date for domestic students, 4/1 for international students; for spring admission, 1/1 priority date for domestic students, 7/1 for international students. Applications are processed on a rolling basis. *Application fee:* $40. Electronic applications accepted. *Application Contact:* Eugene Soltys, Director of Graduate Admissions, 732-987-2760 Ext. 2760, Fax: 732-987-2000, E-mail: admissions@georgian.edu. *Dean*, Sr. Mary Gurley, OSF, 732-987-2525, E-mail: garleym@gergian.edu.

School of Sciences and Mathematics Students: 35 full-time (31 women), 109 part-time (94 women); includes 13 minority (7 African Americans, 1 American Indian/Alaska Native, 3 Asian Americans or Pacific Islanders, 2 Hispanic Americans), 1 international. Average age 36. 80 applicants, 71% accepted, 44 enrolled. *Faculty:* 17 full-time (10 women), 6 part-time/adjunct (3 women). Expenses: Contact institution. *Financial support:* Scholarships/grants, health care benefits, and unspecified assistantships available. Financial award application deadline: 4/15; financial award applicants required to submit FAFSA. In 2006, 33 master's, 11 other advanced degrees awarded. *Degree program information:* Part-time and evening/weekend programs available. Offers biology (MS); counseling psychology (MA); holistic health (Certificate); holistic health studies (MA); mathematics (MA); professional counselor (Certificate); school psychology (Certificate). *Application deadline:* For fall admission, 8/1 priority date for domestic students, 4/1 for international students; for spring admission, 1/1 priority date for domestic students, 7/1 for international students. Applications are processed on a rolling basis. *Application fee:* $40. Electronic applications accepted. *Application Contact:* Eugene Soltys, Director of Graduate Admissions, 732-987-2760 Ext. 2760, Fax: 732-987-2000, E-mail: admissions@georgian.edu. *Dean*, Dr. Linda James, 732-987-2617.

GEORGIA SOUTHERN UNIVERSITY, Statesboro, GA 30460

General Information State-supported, coed, comprehensive institution. CGS member. *Enrollment:* 16,425 graduate, professional, and undergraduate students; 583 full-time matriculated graduate/professional students (367 women), 1,195 part-time matriculated graduate/professional students (898 women). *Enrollment by degree level:* 1,107 master's, 476 doctoral, 195 other advanced degrees. *Graduate faculty:* 427 full-time (169 women), 27 part-time/adjunct (17 women). *Graduate housing:* Room and/or apartments available on a first-come, first-served basis to single students; on-campus housing not available to married students. Typical cost: $4,052 per year ($6,500 including board). Housing application deadline: 5/1. *Student services:* Campus employment opportunities, campus safety program, career counseling, disabled student services, exercise/wellness program, free psychological counseling, grant writing training, international student services, low-cost health insurance. *Library facilities:* Henderson Library. *Online resources:* library catalog, web page, access to other libraries' catalogs. *Collection:* 588,997 titles, 2,690 serial subscriptions, 29,118 audiovisual materials. *Research affiliation:* Skidaway Institute of Oceanography (marine sciences), St. Catherine's Island Foundation (marine science, life sciences), Space Telescope Science Institute (astronomy, physics), Mount Desert Island Biological Laboratory (marine biology), Oak Ridge National Laboratory (physical sciences).

Computer facilities: 1,675 computers available on campus for general student use. A campuswide network can be accessed from student residence rooms and from off campus. Internet access and online class registration are available. *Web address:* http://www.georgiasouthern.edu/.

General Application Contact: Office of Graduate Admissions, 912-681-5384, Fax: 912-681-0740, E-mail: gradadmissions@georgiasouthern.edu.

GRADUATE UNITS

Jack N. Averitt College of Graduate Studies Students: 583 full-time (367 women), 1,195 part-time (898 women); includes 423 minority (377 African Americans, 6 American Indian/Alaska Native, 20 Asian Americans or Pacific Islanders, 20 Hispanic Americans), 61 international. Average age 33. 614 applicants, 80% accepted, 349 enrolled. *Faculty:* 427 full-time (169 women), 27 part-time/adjunct (17 women). Expenses: Contact institution. *Financial support:* In 2006–07, 945 students received support, including 192 research assistantships with partial tuition reimbursements available (averaging $5,500 per year), teaching assistantships with partial tuition reimbursements available (averaging $5,500 per year); career-related internships or fieldwork, Federal Work-Study, scholarships/grants, traineeships, tuition waivers (partial), unspecified assistantships, and doctoral stipends also available. Support available to part-time students. Financial award application deadline: 4/15; financial award applicants required to submit FAFSA. In 2006, 436 master's, 27 doctorates, 66 other advanced degrees awarded. *Degree program information:* Part-time programs available. *Application deadline:* For fall admission, 3/1 priority date for domestic students, 3/1 for international students; for spring admission, 10/1 priority date for domestic students, 10/1 for international students. Applications are processed on a rolling basis. *Application fee:* $50. Electronic applications accepted. *Application Contact:* 912-681-5384, Fax: 912-681-0740, E-mail: gradadmissions@georgiasouthern.edu. *Interim Dean of Graduate Studies and Research*, Dr. Saundra Nettles, 912-681-0581, Fax: 912-681-0605, E-mail: snettles@georgiasouthern.edu.

Allen E. Paulson College of Science and Technology Students: 43 full-time (22 women), 32 part-time (16 women); includes 11 minority (7 African Americans, 1 American Indian/Alaska Native, 1 Asian American or Pacific Islander, 2 Hispanic Americans), 9 international. Average age 29. 36 applicants, 75% accepted, 19 enrolled. *Faculty:* 84 full-time (19 women). Expenses: Contact institution. *Financial support:* In 2006–07, 52 students received support, including 38 research assistantships with partial tuition reimbursements available (averaging $5,500 per year), teaching assistantships with partial tuition reimbursements available (averaging $5,500 per year); career-related internships or fieldwork, Federal Work-Study, scholarships/grants, tuition waivers (partial), and unspecified assistantships also available. Support available to part-time students. Financial award application deadline: 4/15; financial award applicants required to submit FAFSA. In 2006, 23 degrees awarded. *Degree program information:* Part-time programs available. Offers biology (MS); mathematics (MS); mechanical and electrical engineering (M Tech); science and technology (M Tech, MS). *Application deadline:* For fall admission, 3/1 priority date for domestic students, 3/1 for international students; for spring admission, 10/1 priority date for domestic students, 10/1 for international students. Applications are processed on a rolling basis. *Application fee:* $50. Electronic applications accepted. *Application Contact:* 912-681-5384, Fax: 912-681-0740, E-mail: gradadmissions@@georgiasouthern.edu. *Dean*, Dr. Bret Danilowicz, 912-681-5111, Fax: 912-681-0836, E-mail: bdanilowicz@georgiasouthern.edu.

College of Business Administration Students: 125 full-time (60 women), 122 part-time (53 women); includes 54 minority (43 African Americans, 2 American Indian/Alaska Native, 7

Georgia Southern University (continued)

Asian Americans or Pacific Islanders, 2 Hispanic Americans), 33 international. Average age 28. 130 applicants, 77% accepted, 75 enrolled. *Faculty:* 62 full-time (15 women). Expenses: Contact institution. *Financial support:* In 2006–07, 145 students received support, including 23 research assistantships with partial tuition reimbursements available (averaging $5,500 per year), teaching assistantships with partial tuition reimbursements available (averaging $5,500 per year); career-related internships or fieldwork, Federal Work-Study, scholarships/grants, tuition waivers (partial), and unspecified assistantships also available. Support available to part-time students. Financial award application deadline: 4/15; financial award applicants required to submit FAFSA. In 2006, 122 degrees awarded. *Degree program information:* Part-time and evening/weekend programs available. Offers accounting (M Acc); business administration (M Acc, MBA). *Application deadline:* For fall admission, 3/1 priority date for domestic students, 3/1 for international students; for spring admission, 10/1 priority date for domestic students, 10/1 for international students. Applications are processed on a rolling basis. *Application fee:* $50. Electronic applications accepted. *Application Contact:* 912-681-5384, Fax: 912-681-0740, E-mail: gradadmissions@georgiasouthern.edu. *Dean,* Dr. Ron Shiffler, 912-681-5106, Fax: 912-681-0292, E-mail: shiffler@georgiasouthern.edu.

College of Education Students: 207 full-time (168 women), 907 part-time (734 women); includes 284 minority (269 African Americans, 3 American Indian/Alaska Native, 4 Asian Americans or Pacific Islanders, 8 Hispanic Americans), 2 international. Average age 36. 241 applicants, 85% accepted, 134 enrolled. *Faculty:* 60 full-time (37 women), 19 part-time/adjunct (13 women). Expenses: Contact institution. *Financial support:* In 2006–07, 483 students received support, including 26 research assistantships with partial tuition reimbursements available (averaging $5,500 per year), teaching assistantships with partial tuition reimbursements available (averaging $5,500 per year); career-related internships or fieldwork, Federal Work-Study, scholarships/grants, tuition waivers (partial), unspecified assistantships, and doctoral stipends also available. Support available to part-time students. Financial award application deadline: 4/15; financial award applicants required to submit FAFSA. In 2006, 172 master's, 27 doctorates, 66 Ed Ss awarded. *Degree program information:* Part-time programs available. Offers art education (M Ed, MAT); business education (M Ed, MAT); counselor education (M Ed, Ed S); curriculum studies (Ed D); early childhood education (M Ed); education (M Ed, MAT, Ed D, Ed S); educational administration (Ed D); educational leadership (M Ed, Ed S); English education (M Ed, MAT); French education (M Ed); health and physical education (M Ed); higher education (M Ed); instructional technology (M Ed); mathematics education (M Ed, MAT); middle grades education (M Ed, MAT); reading education (M Ed); school psychology (M Ed, Ed S); science education (M Ed, MAT); social science education (M Ed, MAT); Spanish education (MAT); special education (M Ed, MAT); teaching and learning (Ed S); technology education (M Ed). *Application deadline:* For fall admission, 3/1 priority date for domestic students, 3/1 for international students; for spring admission, 10/1 priority date for domestic students, 10/1 for international students. Applications are processed on a rolling basis. *Application fee:* $50. Electronic applications accepted. *Application Contact:* 912-681-5384, Fax: 912-681-0740, E-mail: gradadmissions@georgiasouthern.edu. *Dean,* Dr. Lucindia Chance, 912-681-5648, Fax: 912-681-5093, E-mail: lchance@georgiasouthern.edu.

College of Health and Human Sciences Students: 70 full-time (36 women), 51 part-time (43 women); includes 17 minority (14 African Americans, 2 Asian Americans or Pacific Islanders, 1 Hispanic American), 5 international. Average age 28. 76 applicants, 80% accepted, 46 enrolled. *Faculty:* 41 full-time (24 women). Expenses: Contact institution. *Financial support:* In 2006–07, 100 students received support, including 57 research assistantships with partial tuition reimbursements available (averaging $5,500 per year), teaching assistantships with tuition reimbursements available (averaging $5,500 per year); career-related internships or fieldwork, Federal Work-Study, scholarships/grants, traineeships, tuition waivers (partial), and unspecified assistantships also available. Support available to part-time students. Financial award application deadline: 4/15; financial award applicants required to submit FAFSA. In 2006, 47 degrees awarded. *Degree program information:* Part-time and evening/weekend programs available. Offers health and human sciences (MS, MSN, Certificate); health and kinesiology (MS); recreation administration (MS); rural community health nurse practitioner (MSN); rural community health nurse specialist (Certificate); rural family nurse practitioner (MSN, Certificate); sport management (MS); women's health nurse practitioner (MSN, Certificate). *Application deadline:* For fall admission, 3/1 priority date for domestic students, 3/1 for international students; for spring admission, 10/1 priority date for domestic students, 10/1 for international students. Applications are processed on a rolling basis. *Application fee:* $50. Electronic applications accepted. *Application Contact:* 912-681-5384, Fax: 912-681-0740, E-mail: gradadmissions@georgiasouthern.edu. *Dean,* Dr. Frederick Whitt, 912-681-5322, Fax: 912-681-5349, E-mail: fwhitt@georgiasouthern.edu.

College of Liberal Arts and Social Sciences Students: 107 full-time (61 women), 74 part-time (46 women); includes 45 minority (34 African Americans, 4 Asian Americans or Pacific Islanders, 7 Hispanic Americans), 2 international. Average age 30. 103 applicants, 80% accepted, 65 enrolled. *Faculty:* 142 full-time (61 women), 6 part-time/adjunct (4 women). Expenses: Contact institution. *Financial support:* In 2006–07, 134 students received support, including 46 research assistantships with partial tuition reimbursements available (averaging $5,500 per year), teaching assistantships with partial tuition reimbursements available (averaging $5,500 per year); career-related internships or fieldwork, Federal Work-Study, scholarships/grants, tuition waivers (partial), and unspecified assistantships also available. Support available to part-time students. Financial award application deadline: 4/15; financial award applicants required to submit FAFSA. In 2006, 61 degrees awarded. *Degree program information:* Part-time programs available. Offers English (MA); fine arts (MFA); foreign languages (MA); history (MA); liberal arts and social sciences (MA, MFA, MM, MPA, MS); music (MM); psychology (MS); public administration (MPA); sociology (MA). *Application deadline:* For fall admission, 3/1 priority date for domestic students, 3/1 for international students; for spring admission, 10/1 priority date for domestic students, 10/1 for international students. Applications are processed on a rolling basis. *Application fee:* $50. Electronic applications accepted. *Application Contact:* 912-681-5384, Fax: 912-681-0740, E-mail: gradadmissions@georgiasouthern.edu. *Dean,* Dr. Jane Rhoades Hudak, 912-681-5434, Fax: 912-681-5346, E-mail: jhudak@georgiasouthern.edu.

Jiann-Ping Hsu College of Public Health Students: 31 full-time (20 women), 9 part-time (6 women); includes 13 minority (11 African Americans, 2 Asian Americans or Pacific Islanders), 10 international. Average age 28. 28 applicants, 57% accepted, 10 enrolled. *Faculty:* 12 full-time (5 women). Expenses: Contact institution. *Financial support:* In 2006–07, 31 students received support, including research assistantships with partial tuition reimbursements available (averaging $5,500 per year), teaching assistantships with partial tuition reimbursements available (averaging $5,500 per year); career-related internships or fieldwork, Federal Work-Study, scholarships/grants, tuition waivers (partial), and unspecified assistantships also available. Support available to part-time students. Financial award application deadline: 4/15; financial award applicants required to submit FAFSA. In 2006, 11 degrees awarded. *Degree program information:* Part-time programs available. Offers health services administration (MHSA); public health (MHSA, MPH). *Application deadline:* For fall admission, 3/1 priority date for domestic students, 3/1 for international students; for spring admission, 10/1 priority date for domestic students, 10/1 for international students. Applications are processed on a rolling basis. *Application fee:* $50. Electronic applications accepted. *Application Contact:* 912-681-5384, Fax: 912-681-0740, E-mail: gradadmissions@georgiasouthern.edu. *Dean,* Dr. Charlie Hardy, 912-681-5653, Fax: 912-681-0381, E-mail: chardy@georgiasouthern.edu.

GEORGIA SOUTHWESTERN STATE UNIVERSITY, Americus, GA 31709-4693

General Information State-supported, coed, comprehensive institution. *Graduate housing:* Room and/or apartments available on a first-come, first-served basis to single students; on-campus housing not available to married students. Housing application deadline: 8/1.

GRADUATE UNITS

Graduate Studies *Degree program information:* Part-time programs available. Electronic applications accepted.

School of Business Administration Offers business administration (MBA). Electronic applications accepted.

School of Computer and Information Sciences *Degree program information:* Part-time programs available. Offers computer information systems (MS); computer science (MS). Electronic applications accepted.

School of Education Offers early childhood education (M Ed, Ed S); health and physical education (M Ed); middle grades education (M Ed, Ed S); reading (M Ed); secondary education (M Ed); special education (M Ed). Electronic applications accepted.

GEORGIA STATE UNIVERSITY, Atlanta, GA 30303-3083

General Information State-supported, coed, university. CGS member. *Enrollment:* 26,134 graduate, professional, and undergraduate students; 4,045 full-time matriculated graduate/professional students (2,474 women), 2,967 part-time matriculated graduate/professional students (1,730 women). *Enrollment by degree level:* 661 first professional, 4,250 master's, 1,486 doctoral, 615 other advanced degrees. *Graduate faculty:* 762 full-time (313 women). *Graduate housing:* Rooms and/or apartments available on a first-come, first-served basis to single and married students. *Student services:* Campus employment opportunities, campus safety program, career counseling, child daycare facilities, exercise/wellness program, free psychological counseling, international student services. *Library facilities:* Pullen Library plus 1 other. *Online resources:* library catalog, web page, access to other libraries' catalogs. *Collection:* 1.5 million titles, 7,788 serial subscriptions, 22,551 audiovisual materials. *Research affiliation:* Oak Ridge National Laboratory (environmental policy), Research Atlanta Inc. (policy studies), Cerro Tololo Interamerican Observatory (astronomy), Argonne National Laboratory, Advanced Photon Source (crystallography).

Computer facilities: Computer purchase and lease plans are available. 775 computers available on campus for general student use. A campuswide network can be accessed from student residence rooms and from off campus. Internet access and online class registration are available. *Web address:* http://www.gsu.edu/.

General Application Contact: Daniel Niccum, Associate Director, 404-651-2365, Fax: 404-651-4811, E-mail: admissions@gsu.edu.

GRADUATE UNITS

Andrew Young School of Policy Studies Students: 226 full-time (107 women), 119 part-time (75 women); includes 118 minority (102 African Americans, 2 Asian Americans or Pacific Islanders, 14 Hispanic Americans), 42 international. Average age 33. 476 applicants, 41% accepted, 93 enrolled. *Faculty:* 55 full-time (16 women). Expenses: Contact institution. *Financial support:* In 2006–07, research assistantships with full tuition reimbursements (averaging $17,000 per year), teaching assistantships with full tuition reimbursements (averaging $17,000 per year) were awarded; fellowships, career-related internships or fieldwork, Federal Work-Study, institutionally sponsored loans, scholarships/grants, and tuition waivers (partial) also available. Support available to part-time students. Financial award applicants required to submit FAFSA. In 2006, 97 master's, 19 doctorates awarded. *Degree program information:* Part-time and evening/weekend programs available. Offers economics (MA, PhD); policy studies (MA, MPA, MS, PhD); public administration (MPA); public policy (PhD); urban policy studies (MS). *Application deadline:* For fall admission, 4/1 for domestic and international students; for spring admission, 10/1 for domestic and international students. Applications are processed on a rolling basis. *Application fee:* $50. Electronic applications accepted. *Application Contact:* Sue Fagan, Office of Academic Assistance Director, 404-651-3504, Fax: 404-651-3536, E-mail: suefagan@gsu.edu. *Dean,* Dr. Roy Bahl, 404-651-3993, Fax: 404-651-3996.

College of Arts and Sciences Students: 1,815 (1,076 women); includes 614 minority (229 African Americans, 5 American Indian/Alaska Native, 317 Asian Americans or Pacific Islanders, 63 Hispanic Americans) 39 international. 2,188 applicants, 36% accepted, 500 enrolled. *Faculty:* 423 full-time (256 women). Expenses: Contact institution. *Financial support:* Fellowships, research assistantships with full tuition reimbursements, teaching assistantships with full tuition reimbursements, career-related internships or fieldwork, Federal Work-Study, institutionally sponsored loans, tuition waivers (full and partial), and unspecified assistantships available. Support available to part-time students. Financial award applicants required to submit FAFSA. In 2006, 420 master's, 73 doctorates awarded. *Degree program information:* Part-time and evening/weekend programs available. Offers anthropology (MA); applied and environmental microbiology (MS, PhD); applied linguistics (MA, PhD); arts and sciences (M Mu, MA, MA Ed, MAT, MFA, MHP, MS, PhD, Certificate); astronomy (PhD); cellular and molecular biology and physiology (MS, PhD); chemistry (MS, PhD); computer science (MS, PhD); creative writing (MA, MFA, PhD); English (MA, PhD); fiction (MFA); film/video/digital imaging (MA); French (MA, Certificate); geographic information systems (Certificate); geography (MA); geology (MS); German (MA, Certificate); gerontology (MA); heritage preservation (MHP); history (MA, PhD); human communication and social influence (MA); hydrogeology (Certificate); literary studies and composition (MA, PhD); mass communication (MA); mathematics (MAT, MS); molecular genetics and biochemistry (MS, PhD); moving image studies (PhD); neurobiology and behavior (MS, PhD); philosophy (MA); physics (MS, PhD); poetry (MFA); political science (MA, PhD); psychology (MA, PhD); public communication (PhD); religious studies (MA); rhetoric (MA, PhD); sociology (MA, PhD); Spanish (MA, Certificate); translation and interpretation (Certificate). *Application deadline:* For fall admission, 8/1 for domestic students; for winter admission, 10/1 for domestic students; for spring admission, 12/1 for domestic students. Applications are processed on a rolling basis. *Application fee:* $50. Electronic applications accepted. *Application Contact:* Shelly-Ann Williams, Manager, Graduate and Scheduling Services, 404-651-2297, Fax: 404-651-0275, E-mail: swilliams@gsu.edu. *Dean,* Dr. Lauren B. Adamson, 404-651-2294, Fax: 404-651-1549, E-mail: ladamson@gsu.edu.

Ernest G. Welch School of Art and Design Students: 60 full-time (43 women), 30 part-time (27 women); includes 17 minority (10 African Americans, 6 Asian Americans or Pacific Islanders, 1 Hispanic American). 77 applicants, 47% accepted, 25 enrolled. *Faculty:* 32 full-time (20 women), 6 part-time/adjunct (4 women). Expenses: Contact institution. *Financial support:* In 2006–07, 46 research assistantships with full tuition reimbursements (averaging $4,800 per year) were awarded; teaching assistantships with full tuition reimbursements, career-related internships or fieldwork, Federal Work-Study, institutionally sponsored loans, and unspecified assistantships also available. In 2006, 22 degrees awarded. Offers art and design (MA, MA Ed, MFA); art education (MA Ed); art history (MA); studio art (MFA). *Application deadline:* For fall admission, 1/6 for domestic and international students. *Application fee:* $50. Electronic applications accepted. *Application Contact:* Prof. Nancy Floyd, Director of Graduate Studies, 404-651-0488, Fax: 404-651-1779, E-mail: artgrad@gsu.edu. *Director,* Prof. Cheryl Goldsleger, 404-651-0485, Fax: 404-651-1779, E-mail: artcgg@langate.gsu.edu.

School of Music Students: 55 full-time (20 women), 25 part-time (12 women); includes 20 minority (15 African Americans, 5 Asian Americans or Pacific Islanders). 74 applicants, 72% accepted, 32 enrolled. *Faculty:* 29 full-time (7 women), 19 part-time/adjunct (7 women). Expenses: Contact institution. *Financial support:* In 2006–07, 37 students received support, including 1 fellowship with full tuition reimbursement available (averaging $5,000 per year), 30 research assistantships with full tuition reimbursements available (averaging $6,000 per year), 3 teaching assistantships with full tuition reimbursements available (averaging $12,000 per year); career-related internships or fieldwork, Federal Work-Study, institutionally sponsored loans, tuition waivers (full), and unspecified assistantships also available. Support available to part-time students. Financial award application deadline: 4/15; financial award applicants required to submit FAFSA. In 2006, 33 degrees awarded. *Degree program information:* Part-time and evening/weekend programs available. Offers music (M Mu). *Application deadline:* For fall admission, 4/15 for domestic students, 3/15 for international students; for spring admission, 10/15 for domestic students, 9/15 for international students. Applications are processed on a rolling basis. *Application fee:* $50. Electronic applications accepted. *Application Contact:* Dr. David Myers, Associate Director, 404-651-3676, Fax: 404-651-1583, E-mail: dmyers@gsu.edu. *Director,* Dr. John Haberlen, 404-651-3676, Fax: 404-651-1583, E-mail: jhaberlen@gsu.edu.

Women's Studies Institute Students: 5 full-time, 5 part-time; includes 7 minority (all African Americans) 27 applicants, 56% accepted. *Faculty:* 5 full-time (all women). Expenses: Contact institution. *Financial support:* In 2006–07, 1 fellowship with tuition reimbursement (averaging $3,500 per year), 1 research assistantship with tuition reimbursement (averaging $6,000 per year), teaching assistantships with tuition reimbursements (averaging $6,000 per year) were awarded; career-related internships or fieldwork, Federal Work-Study, institutionally sponsored loans, health care benefits, tuition waivers (partial), and unspecified assistantships also available. Support available to part-time students. Financial award application deadline: 2/15; financial award applicants required to submit FAFSA. In 2006, 4 degrees awarded. *Degree program information:* Part-time programs available. Offers women's studies (MA). *Application deadline:* For fall admission, 8/1 for domestic students; for spring admission, 12/1 for domestic students. Applications are processed on a rolling basis. *Application fee:* $25. Electronic applications accepted. *Application Contact:* Dr. Layli Phillips, Director of Graduate Studies, 404-651-2524, Fax: 404-651-1398, E-mail: layli@gsu.edu. *Director,* Dr. Susan Talburt, 404-463-0857, Fax: 404-651-1398, E-mail: stalburt@gsu.edu.

College of Education Students: 665 full-time (548 women), 904 part-time (707 women); includes 346 minority (286 African Americans, 14 American Indian/Alaska Native, 25 Asian Americans or Pacific Islanders, 21 Hispanic Americans), 47 international. Average age 33. 809 applicants, 67% accepted. *Faculty:* 121 full-time (74 women), 74 part-time/adjunct (54 women). Expenses: Contact institution. *Financial support:* In 2006–07, 194 research assistantships, 28 teaching assistantships were awarded; fellowships, career-related internships or fieldwork, Federal Work-Study, institutionally sponsored loans, and tuition waivers (partial) also available. Support available to part-time students. In 2006, 421 master's, 49 doctorates, 100 other advanced degrees awarded. *Degree program information:* Part-time and evening/weekend programs available. Offers art education (Ed S); behavior and learning disabilities (M Ed); communication disorders (M Ed); counseling psychology (PhD); counselor education and practice (PhD); early childhood education (M Ed, PhD, Ed S); education (M Ed, MLM, MS, PhD, Ed S); education of students with exceptionalities (PhD); educational leadership (M Ed, PhD, Ed S); educational psychology (MS, PhD); educational research (MS, PhD); English education (M Ed, Ed S); exercise science (MS); health and physical education (M Ed); instructional technology (MS, PhD, Ed S); library media technology (MLM, PhD, Ed S); library science/media (MLM, MS, PhD, Ed S); mathematics education (M Ed, PhD, Ed S); middle childhood education (M Ed, Ed S); multiple and severe disabilities (M Ed); music education (PhD); professional counseling (MS, PhD, Ed S); reading instruction (M Ed, PhD, Ed S); reading, language and literacy (M Ed); reading, language, and literacy (PhD, Ed S); rehabilitation counseling (MS); research, measurements and statistics (PhD); school counseling (M Ed, Ed S); school psychology (M Ed, PhD, Ed S); science education (M Ed, PhD, Ed S); secondary education (M Ed, PhD, Ed S); social foundations of education (MS, PhD); social studies education (M Ed, PhD, Ed S); sport science (PhD); sports administration (MS); sports medicine (MS); teaching English as a second language (M Ed). *Application fee:* $25. *Dean,* Dr. Ron P. Colarusso, 404-651-2310.

College of Health and Human Sciences Students: 334 full-time (278 women), 197 part-time (183 women); includes 166 minority (129 African Americans, 37 Asian Americans or Pacific Islanders), 26 international. Average age 33. 621 applicants, 41% accepted, 160 enrolled. *Faculty:* 122. Expenses: Contact institution. *Financial support:* In 2006–07, 180 research assistantships with full and partial tuition reimbursements (averaging $3,048 per year) were awarded; fellowships with full tuition reimbursements, teaching assistantships with full tuition reimbursements, career-related internships or fieldwork, Federal Work-Study, institutionally sponsored loans, traineeships, tuition waivers (partial), and unspecified assistantships also available. Support available to part-time students. Financial award application deadline: 4/1; financial award applicants required to submit FAFSA. In 2006, 152 master's, 6 doctorates awarded. *Degree program information:* Part-time and evening/weekend programs available. Offers criminal justice (MS); health and human sciences (MPH, MS, MSW, DPT, PhD, Certificate). *Application fee:* $50. Electronic applications accepted. *Application Contact:* 404-651-3064, Fax: 404-651-4871, E-mail: chhs-oaa@gsu.edu. *Dean,* Dr. Susan Kelley, 404-651-3030, E-mail: skelly@gsu.edu.

Institute of Public Health Students: 45 full-time (29 women), 39 part-time (34 women). 146 applicants, 37% accepted, 21 enrolled. *Faculty:* 7 full-time (2 women), 1 part-time/adjunct (0 women). Expenses: Contact institution. *Financial support:* In 2006–07, research assistantships with full and partial tuition reimbursements (averaging $3,108 per year); Federal Work-Study, scholarships/grants, tuition waivers (partial), and unspecified assistantships also available. Support available to part-time students. In 2006, 13 master's, 1 other advanced degree awarded. *Degree program information:* Part-time and evening/weekend programs available. Offers public health (MPH, Certificate). *Application deadline:* For fall admission, 3/1 for domestic students; for spring admission, 10/1 for domestic students. *Application fee:* $50. *Application Contact:* Denise Gouveia, Application Contact, 404-651-3064, Fax: 404-651-4571, E-mail: dgouveia@gsu.edu. *Director,* Michael P Eriksen, 404-651-4133, E-mail: meriksen@gsu.edu.

School of Health Professions Expenses: Contact institution. Offers health professions (MS, DPT, Certificate); nutrition (MS, Certificate); physical therapy (DPT). *Director,* Dr. Lynda Goodfellow, 404-651-3091, E-mail: ltgoodfellow@gsu.edu.

School of Nursing Students: 72 full-time (66 women), 128 part-time (123 women); includes 75 minority (61 African Americans, 9 Asian Americans or Pacific Islanders, 5 Hispanic Americans), 2 international. Average age 37. 70 applicants, 54% accepted, 30 enrolled. *Faculty:* 35 full-time (all women), 1 (woman) part-time/adjunct. Expenses: Contact institution. *Financial support:* In 2006–07, research assistantships with full and partial tuition reimbursements (averaging $3,108 per year); fellowships with full tuition reimbursements, teaching assistantships, Federal Work-Study, institutionally sponsored loans, scholarships/grants, traineeships, and tuition waivers (partial) also available. Support available to part-time students. Financial award application deadline: 4/1; financial award applicants required to submit FAFSA. In 2006, 39 master's, 6 doctorates awarded. *Degree program information:* Part-time and evening/weekend programs available. Offers adult health (MS); child health (MS); family nurse practitioner (MS); health promotion, protection and restoration (PhD); nursing (Certificate); perinatal/women's health (MS); psychiatric/mental health (MS). *Application deadline:* For fall admission, 3/1 priority date for domestic students; for spring admission, 10/1 priority date for domestic students. Applications are processed on a rolling basis. *Application fee:* $50. Electronic applications accepted. *Application Contact:* Barbara Smith, Admissions Counselor II, 404-651-3834, Fax: 404-651-4871, E-mail: bbsmith@gsu.edu. *Director,* Dr. Barbara Woodring, 404-651-3040.

School of Social Work Students: 50 full-time (46 women), 5 part-time (4 women); includes 19 minority (16 African Americans, 3 Asian Americans or Pacific Islanders), 2 international. Average age 32. 83 applicants, 55% accepted, 21 enrolled. *Faculty:* 16 full-time (11 women), 2 part-time/adjunct (1 woman). Expenses: Contact institution. *Financial support:* In 2006–07, research assistantships with full and partial tuition reimbursements (averaging $3,108 per year); Federal Work-Study, scholarships/grants, tuition waivers (partial), and unspecified assistantships also available. Support available to part-time students. Financial award application deadline: 4/1; financial award applicants required to submit FAFSA. In 2006, 32 degrees awarded. *Degree program information:* Part-time programs available. Offers community partnerships (MSW). *Application deadline:* For fall admission, 2/1 priority date for domestic students. Applications are processed on a rolling basis. *Application fee:* $50. Electronic applications accepted. *Application Contact:* Renanda Dear, Director, Student and Community Services, 404-651-3526, Fax: 404-651-1863, E-mail: rwood@gsu.edu. *Director,* Dr. Nancy Kropf, 404-651-3526.

College of Law Students: 453 full-time (226 women), 210 part-time (89 women); includes 128 minority (73 African Americans, 3 American Indian/Alaska Native, 33 Asian Americans or Pacific Islanders, 19 Hispanic Americans). Average age 28. 2,910 applicants, 21% accepted, 213 enrolled. *Faculty:* 46 full-time (21 women), 49 part-time/adjunct (17 women). Expenses: Contact institution. *Financial support:* In 2006–07, 127 research assistantships with full and partial tuition reimbursements (averaging $1,000 per year) were awarded; career-related internships or fieldwork, Federal Work-Study, institutionally sponsored loans, scholarships/grants, tuition waivers (partial), and unspecified assistantships also available. Support available to part-time students. Financial award application deadline: 4/1; financial award applicants required to submit FAFSA. In 2006, 181 degrees awarded. *Degree program information:* Part-time and evening/weekend programs available. Offers law (JD). *Application deadline:* For fall admission, 3/15 for domestic students, 3/15 priority date for international students. Applications are processed on a rolling basis. *Application fee:* $50. Electronic applications accepted. *Application Contact:* Dr. Cheryl Jester Jackson, Director of Admissions, 404-651-2048, Fax: 404-651-1244, E-mail: cjgeorge@gsulaw.gsu.edu. *Dean,* Dr. Steven J. Kaminshine, 404-651-2035, Fax: 404-651-2570, E-mail: skaminshine@gsu.edu.

J. Mack Robinson College of Business Students: 727 full-time (313 women), 1,014 part-time (333 women); includes 378 minority (198 African Americans, 3 American Indian/Alaska Native, 139 Asian Americans or Pacific Islanders, 38 Hispanic Americans), 271 international. Average age 31. 1,004 applicants, 55% accepted, 403 enrolled. *Faculty:* 174 full-time (53 women), 6 part-time/adjunct (3 women). Expenses: Contact institution. *Financial support:* Fellowships, research assistantships, teaching assistantships, career-related internships or fieldwork and tuition waivers (partial) available. Support available to part-time students. Financial award applicants required to submit FAFSA. In 2006, 602 master's, 22 doctorates awarded. *Degree program information:* Part-time and evening/weekend programs available. Offers accounting/information systems (MBA); actuarial science (MAS, MBA); business (EMBA, MAS, MBA, MHA, MIB, MPA, MS, MSHA, MSIS, MSRE, MTX, PMBA, PhD, Certificate); business analysis (MBA, MS); computer information systems (MBA, MSIS, PhD); enterprise risk management (MBA); entrepreneurship (MBA); finance (MBA, MS, PhD); general business (MBA); general business administration (EMBA, PMBA); human resources management (MBA, MS); information systems consulting (MBA); information systems risk management (MBA); international business and information technology (MBA); international entrepreneurship (MBA); management (MBA, PhD); marketing (MBA, MS, PhD); operations management (MBA, MS, PhD); organization change (MS); personal financial planning (MS, Certificate); real estate (MBA, MSRE, PhD, Certificate); risk management and insurance (MBA, MS, PhD). *Application deadline:* For fall admission, 5/1 for domestic students, 2/1 for international students; for spring admission, 10/15 for domestic students, 5/1 for international students. Applications are processed on a rolling basis. *Application fee:* $50. Electronic applications accepted. *Application Contact:* Dr. Diane M. Fennig, Director of Master's Admissions and Advisement, 404-463-4568, Fax: 404-651-2721. *Dean,* Dr. H. Fenwick Huss, 404-651-2600, Fax: 404-651-2804.

Institute of Health Administration Students: 27 full-time (13 women), 38 part-time (18 women); includes 12 minority (6 African Americans, 6 Asian Americans or Pacific Islanders), 5 international. Average age 30. 20 applicants, 45% accepted, 6 enrolled. *Faculty:* 5 full-time (2 women). Expenses: Contact institution. *Financial support:* Career-related internships or fieldwork and tuition waivers (partial) available. Support available to part-time students. Financial award applicants required to submit FAFSA. In 2006, 21 degrees awarded. Offers health administration (MBA, MHA, MSHA). *Application deadline:* For fall admission, 5/1 for domestic students, 2/1 for international students; for spring admission, 10/15 for domestic students, 5/1 for international students. Applications are processed on a rolling basis. *Application fee:* $50. Electronic applications accepted. *Director,* Dr. Andrew T. Sumner, 404-651-2637, Fax: 404-651-1230.

Institute of International Business Students: 35 full-time (14 women), 63 part-time (27 women); includes 23 minority (12 African Americans, 6 Asian Americans or Pacific Islanders, 5 Hispanic Americans), 13 international. Average age 31. 30 applicants, 67% accepted, 14 enrolled. *Faculty:* 6 full-time (2 women). Expenses: Contact institution. *Financial support:* Fellowships, research assistantships, teaching assistantships, career-related internships or fieldwork and tuition waivers (partial) available. Support available to part-time students. Financial award application deadline: 5/1; financial award applicants required to submit FAFSA. In 2006, 49 degrees awarded. *Degree program information:* Part-time and evening/weekend programs available. Offers international business (MBA, MIB). *Application deadline:* For fall admission, 5/1 for domestic students, 2/1 for international students; for spring admission, 10/15 for domestic students, 5/1 for international students. Applications are processed on a rolling basis. *Application fee:* $50. Electronic applications accepted. *Director,* Dr. Joan Gabel, 404-651-3877, Fax: 404-651-3498.

School of Accountancy Students: 77 full-time (50 women), 99 part-time (46 women); includes 33 minority (12 African Americans, 1 American Indian/Alaska Native, 17 Asian Americans or Pacific Islanders, 3 Hispanic Americans), 21 international. Average age 31. 125 applicants, 50% accepted, 41 enrolled. *Faculty:* 12 full-time (2 women), 5 part-time/adjunct (1 woman). Expenses: Contact institution. *Financial support:* Fellowships, research assistantships, teaching assistantships, career-related internships or fieldwork and tuition waivers (partial) available. Support available to part-time students. Financial award applicants required to submit FAFSA. In 2006, 58 master's, 2 doctorates awarded. *Degree program information:* Part-time and evening/weekend programs available. Offers accountancy (MBA, MPA, MTX, PhD, Certificate); taxation (MTX). *Application deadline:* For fall admission, 5/1 for domestic students, 2/1 for international students; for spring admission, 10/15 for domestic students, 5/1 for international students. Applications are processed on a rolling basis. *Application fee:* $50. Electronic applications accepted. *Application Contact:* Graduate Student and Alumni Services, 404-463-4568, Fax: 404-651-2721, E-mail: mastersadmissions@gsu.edu. *Interim Director,* Dr. Galen R. Sevcik, 404-643-9334, Fax: 404-651-1033, E-mail: gsevcik@gsu.edu.

W. T. Beebe Institute of Personnel and Employee Relations Students: 5 full-time (2 women), 21 part-time (19 women); includes 4 minority (3 African Americans, 1 Asian American or Pacific Islander), 2 international. Average age 32. 8 applicants, 75% accepted, 6 enrolled. Expenses: Contact institution. *Financial support:* Fellowships, research assistantships, teaching assistantships, career-related internships or fieldwork and tuition waivers (partial) available. Support available to part-time students. Financial award applicants required to submit FAFSA. In 2006, 13 master's, 1 doctorate awarded. *Degree program information:* Part-time and evening/weekend programs available. Offers personnel and employee relations (MBA, MS, PhD). *Application deadline:* For fall admission, 5/1 for domestic students, 2/1 for international students; for spring admission, 10/15 for domestic students, 5/1 for international students. Applications are processed on a rolling basis. *Application fee:* $50. *Application Contact:* Graduate Student and Alumni Services, 404-463-4568, Fax: 404-651-2721, E-mail: mastersadmissions@gsu.edu. *Director,* Dr. Todd J. Maurer, 404-651-2884, Fax: 404-651-1700.

GERSTNER SLOAN-KETTERING GRADUATE SCHOOL OF BIOMEDICAL SCIENCES, New York, NY 10021

General Information Independent, coed, graduate-only institution.

GRADUATE UNITS

Program in Cancer Biology Offers cancer biology (PhD).

GLION INSTITUTE OF HIGHER EDUCATION, CH-1823 Glion-sur-Montreux, Switzerland

General Information Proprietary, coed, comprehensive institution.

GRADUATE UNITS

Graduate Programs

GLOBAL UNIVERSITY OF THE ASSEMBLIES OF GOD, Springfield, MO 65804

General Information Independent-religious, coed, comprehensive institution. *Graduate housing:* On-campus housing not available.

GRADUATE UNITS

School of Graduate Studies *Degree program information:* Part-time and evening/weekend programs available. Postbaccalaureate distance learning degree programs offered (no on-campus study). Offers biblical studies (MA); divinity (M Div); ministerial studies (MA). Electronic applications accepted.

GODDARD COLLEGE, Plainfield, VT 05667-9432

General Information Independent, coed, comprehensive institution. *Enrollment:* 415 full-time matriculated graduate/professional students (306 women). *Enrollment by degree level:* 415 master's. *Graduate faculty:* 2 full-time (1 woman), 72 part-time/adjunct (53 women).

Goddard College (continued)

Tuition: Full-time $12,506; part-time $10,392 per year. *Required fees:* $998; $499 per term. *Graduate housing:* On-campus housing not available. *Student services:* Disabled student services. *Library facilities:* Eliot Pratt Center. *Online resources:* library catalog, web page. *Collection:* 70,000 titles, 17 serial subscriptions, 300 audiovisual materials.

Computer facilities: 27 computers available on campus for general student use. A campuswide network can be accessed from student residence rooms and from off campus. Internet access, library services are available. *Web address:* http://www.goddard.edu/.

General Application Contact: Brenda J. Hawkins, Director of Admissions, 800-906-8311 Ext. 240, Fax: 802-454-1029, E-mail: brenda.hawkins@goddard.edu.

GRADUATE UNITS

Graduate Program Students: 415 full-time (306 women); includes 47 minority (25 African Americans, 8 American Indian/Alaska Native, 6 Asian Americans or Pacific Islanders, 8 Hispanic Americans). Average age 40. 243 applicants, 91% accepted, 158 enrolled. *Faculty:* 2 full-time (1 woman), 72 part-time/adjunct (53 women). Expenses: Contact institution. *Financial support:* In 2006–07, 395 students received support. Federal Work-Study and tuition waivers (full) available. Financial award applicants required to submit FAFSA. In 2006, 122 degrees awarded. Postbaccalaureate distance learning degree programs offered (minimal on-campus study). Offers consciousness studies (MA); environmental studies (MA); health arts and sciences (MA); interdisciplinary arts (MFA); organizational development (MA); psychology and counseling (MA); socially responsible business and sustainable communities (MA); teacher education (MA); transformative language arts (MA); writing (MFA). *Application deadline:* Applications are processed on a rolling basis. *Application fee:* $40. Electronic applications accepted. *Application Contact:* Brenda J. Hawkins, Director of Admissions, 800-906-8311 Ext. 240, Fax: 802-454-1029, E-mail: brenda.hawkins@goddard.edu. *Director,* Dr. Susan Fleming, 802-454-8311 Ext. 270, Fax: 802-454-8017, E-mail: susan.fleming@goddard.edu.

GOLDEN GATE BAPTIST THEOLOGICAL SEMINARY, Mill Valley, CA 94941-3197

General Information Independent-religious, coed, graduate-only institution. *Graduate housing:* Rooms and/or apartments available on a first-come, first-served basis to single and married students. Housing application deadline: 6/15.

GRADUATE UNITS

Graduate and Professional Programs *Degree program information:* Part-time and evening/weekend programs available. Offers divinity (M Div); early childhood education (Certificate); education leadership (MAEL, Diploma); ministry (D Min); theological studies (MTS); theology (Th M); youth ministry (Certificate). Electronic applications accepted.

GOLDEN GATE UNIVERSITY, San Francisco, CA 94105-2968

General Information Independent, coed, university. *Enrollment:* 1,166 full-time matriculated graduate/professional students (658 women), 1,963 part-time matriculated graduate/professional students (1,019 women). *Enrollment by degree level:* 940 first professional, 2,149 master's, 40 doctoral. *Graduate faculty:* 97 full-time, 398 part-time/adjunct. *Graduate housing:* On-campus housing not available. *Student services:* Campus employment opportunities, career counseling, international student services, low-cost health insurance. *Library facilities:* Golden Gate University Library plus 1 other. *Online resources:* library catalog, access to other libraries' catalogs. *Collection:* 79,204 titles, 3,335 serial subscriptions.

Computer facilities: Computer purchase and lease plans are available. 52 computers available on campus for general student use. A campuswide network can be accessed. Internet access and online class registration are available. *Web address:* http://www.ggu.edu/.

General Application Contact: Angela Williams, Enrollment Services, 415-442-7800, Fax: 415-442-7807, E-mail: info@ggu.edu.

GRADUATE UNITS

Ageno School of Business Students: 355 full-time (192 women), 977 part-time (465 women); includes 447 minority (85 African Americans, 5 American Indian/Alaska Native, 274 Asian Americans or Pacific Islanders, 83 Hispanic Americans), 226 international. Average age 34. 548 applicants, 74% accepted, 201 enrolled. Expenses: Contact institution. *Financial support:* Career-related internships or fieldwork, Federal Work-Study, and institutionally sponsored loans available. Support available to part-time students. Financial award applicants required to submit FAFSA. In 2006, 545 master's, 21 doctorates awarded. *Degree program information:* Part-time and evening/weekend programs available. Offers accounting (M Ac, MBA); business administration (EMBA, MBA, DBA); finance (MBA, MS, Certificate); financial planning (MS, Certificate); human resource management (MBA, MS); human resources management (Certificate); information technology (MBA); information technology management (MS, Certificate); integrated marketing and communications (MS, Certificate); international business (MBA); management (MBA); marketing (MBA, MS, Certificate); operations management (Certificate); psychology (MA, Certificate); public relations (MS, Certificate). *Application deadline:* Applications are processed on a rolling basis. *Application fee:* $55 ($90 for international students). *Application Contact:* Enrollment Services, 415-442-7800, Fax: 415-442-7807, E-mail: info@ggu.edu. *Dean,* Terry Connelly, 415-442-6519, Fax: 415-442-5369.

School of Law Students: 733 full-time (415 women), 345 part-time (196 women); includes 276 minority (47 African Americans, 4 American Indian/Alaska Native, 168 Asian Americans or Pacific Islanders, 57 Hispanic Americans), 74 international. Average age 28. 2,761 applicants, 49% accepted, 222 enrolled. *Faculty:* 49 full-time (22 women), 68 part-time/adjunct (31 women). Expenses: Contact institution. *Financial support:* In 2006–07, 331 students received support, including 3 fellowships (averaging $36,000 per year), 60 research assistantships (averaging $2,400 per year), 30 teaching assistantships (averaging $2,400 per year); career-related internships or fieldwork, Federal Work-Study, institutionally sponsored loans, scholarships/grants, tuition waivers (full and partial), and unspecified assistantships also available. Support available to part-time students. Financial award application deadline: 3/1; financial award applicants required to submit FAFSA. In 2006, 168 JDs, 113 master's, 3 doctorates awarded. *Degree program information:* Part-time and evening/weekend programs available. Offers environmental law (LL M); intellectual property law (LL M); international legal studies (LL M, SJD); law (JD); taxation (LL M); U.S. legal studies (LL M). *Application deadline:* For fall admission, 4/1 for domestic students, 4/15 for international students; for spring admission, 11/15 for international students. Applications are processed on a rolling basis. *Application fee:* $60. Electronic applications accepted. *Application Contact:* Sherolyn Hurst, Director of Admissions, 415-442-6630, Fax: 415-442-6631, E-mail: lawadmit@ggu.edu. *Dean,* Frederic White, 415-442-6600, Fax: 415-442-6609.

School of Taxation Students: 54 full-time (29 women), 630 part-time (358 women); includes 211 minority (21 African Americans, 1 American Indian/Alaska Native, 159 Asian Americans or Pacific Islanders, 30 Hispanic Americans), 37 international. Average age 36. 281 applicants, 86% accepted, 149 enrolled. Expenses: Contact institution. *Financial support:* Career-related internships or fieldwork, Federal Work-Study, and institutionally sponsored loans available. Support available to part-time students. Financial award applicants required to submit FAFSA. In 2006, 215 degrees awarded. *Degree program information:* Part-time and evening/weekend programs available. Offers taxation (MS, Certificate). *Application deadline:* For fall admission, 7/1 priority date for domestic students. Applications are processed on a rolling basis. *Application fee:* $55 ($90 for international students). *Application Contact:* Enrollment Services, 415-442-7800, Fax: 415-442-7807, E-mail: info@ggu.edu. *Dean,* Mary Canning, 415-442-7885.

GOLDEY-BEACOM COLLEGE, Wilmington, DE 19808-1999

General Information Independent, coed, comprehensive institution. *Graduate housing:* Room and/or apartments available on a first-come, first-served basis to single students; on-campus housing not available to married students.

GRADUATE UNITS

Graduate Program *Degree program information:* Part-time and evening/weekend programs available. Offers business administration (MBA); financial management (MBA); human resource management (MBA); information technology (MBA); management (MM); marketing management (MBA). Electronic applications accepted.

GONZAGA UNIVERSITY, Spokane, WA 99258

General Information Independent-religious, coed, comprehensive institution. *Enrollment:* 6,610 graduate, professional, and undergraduate students; 888 full-time matriculated graduate/professional students (431 women), 1,443 part-time matriculated graduate/professional students (842 women). *Enrollment by degree level:* 555 first professional, 1,656 master's, 120 doctoral. *Graduate faculty:* 155 full-time (45 women), 45 part-time/adjunct (15 women). *Tuition:* Full-time $10,620; part-time $590 per credit. *Graduate housing:* Rooms and/or apartments available on a first-come, first-served basis to single and married students. Typical cost: $3,560 per year ($7,220 including board) for single students. Room and board charges vary according to board plan. *Student services:* Campus employment opportunities, career counseling, disabled student services, free psychological counseling, grant writing training, international student services, low-cost health insurance, multicultural affairs office, writing training. *Library facilities:* Ralph E. and Helen Higgins Foley Center plus 1 other. *Online resources:* library catalog, web page, access to other libraries' catalogs. *Collection:* 305,517 titles, 32,106 serial subscriptions.

Computer facilities: Computer purchase and lease plans are available. 350 computers available on campus for general student use. A campuswide network can be accessed from student residence rooms and from off campus. Internet access and online class registration are available. *Web address:* http://www.gonzaga.edu/.

General Application Contact: Julie McCulloh, Dean of Admissions, 509-323-6592, Fax: 509-323-5780, E-mail: mcculloh@gu.gonzaga.edu.

GRADUATE UNITS

College of Arts and Sciences Students: 8 full-time (2 women), 44 part-time (19 women); includes 1 Hispanic American, 2 international. Average age 41. 36 applicants, 72% accepted. *Faculty:* 44 full-time (5 women). Expenses: Contact institution. *Financial support:* Fellowships, teaching assistantships, Federal Work-Study available. Support available to part-time students. Financial award application deadline: 3/1. In 2006, 19 degrees awarded. *Degree program information:* Part-time programs available. Offers arts and sciences (MA); pastoral ministry (MA); philosophy (MA); religious studies (MA); spirituality (MA). *Application deadline:* For fall admission, 7/20 priority date for domestic students; for spring admission, 11/1 for domestic students. Applications are processed on a rolling basis. *Application fee:* $40. *Dean,* Dr. Robert Prusch, 509-328-4220 Ext. 5522.

Program in Teaching English as a Second Language Students: 2 full-time (1 woman), 12 part-time (11 women); includes 1 minority (Asian American or Pacific Islander), 5 international. Average age 35. 12 applicants, 83% accepted. Expenses: Contact institution. In 2006, 9 degrees awarded. Offers teaching English as a second language (MATESL). *Application deadline:* Applications are processed on a rolling basis. *Application fee:* $40. Electronic applications accepted. *Chairperson,* Dr. Mary Jeannot, 509-324-6559.

School of Business Administration Students: 67 full-time (25 women), 134 part-time (51 women); includes 25 minority (1 African American, 14 American Indian/Alaska Native, 5 Asian Americans or Pacific Islanders, 5 Hispanic Americans), 10 international. Average age 31. *Faculty:* 24 full-time (1 woman). Expenses: Contact institution. *Financial support:* Teaching assistantships, Federal Work-Study available. Support available to part-time students. Financial award application deadline: 3/1. In 2006, 88 degrees awarded. *Degree program information:* Part-time and evening/weekend programs available. Offers business administration (M Acc, MBA). *Application deadline:* For fall admission, 7/20 priority date for domestic students; for spring admission, 11/1 for domestic students. Applications are processed on a rolling basis. *Application fee:* $40. *Dean,* Dr. Clarence H. Barnes, 509-328-4220 Ext. 5502.

School of Education Students: 68 full-time (48 women), 540 part-time (338 women); includes 42 minority (7 African Americans, 19 American Indian/Alaska Native, 6 Asian Americans or Pacific Islanders, 10 Hispanic Americans), 3 international. Average age 36. Expenses: Contact institution. *Financial support:* Teaching assistantships, Federal Work-Study and tuition waivers (full and partial) available. Support available to part-time students. Financial award application deadline: 3/1. In 2006, 216 degrees awarded. *Degree program information:* Part-time and evening/weekend programs available. Offers administration and curriculum (MAA); anesthesiology education (M Anesth Ed); counseling psychology (MAC, MAP); education (M Anesth Ed, MA Ed Ad, MAA, MAC, MAP, MASPAA, MES, MIT, MTA); educational administration (MA Ed Ad); initial teaching (MIT); special education (MES); sports and athletic administration (MASPAA); teaching at-risk students (MAT). *Application fee:* $40. *Dean,* Dr. Shirley Williams, 509-328-4220 Ext. 3503, Fax: 509-324-5812.

School of Law Students: 544 full-time (240 women), 11 part-time (8 women); includes 46 minority (1 African American, 11 American Indian/Alaska Native, 25 Asian Americans or Pacific Islanders, 9 Hispanic Americans), 3 international. Average age 27. *Faculty:* 30 full-time (12 women), 35 part-time/adjunct (7 women). Expenses: Contact institution. *Financial support:* In 2006–07, 425 students received support. Career-related internships or fieldwork, Federal Work-Study, institutionally sponsored loans, and scholarships/grants available. Support available to part-time students. Financial award application deadline: 3/15; financial award applicants required to submit FAFSA. In 2006, 187 degrees awarded. *Degree program information:* Part-time programs available. Offers law (JD). *Application deadline:* For fall admission, 4/1 priority date for domestic students. Applications are processed on a rolling basis. *Application fee:* $40. *Application Contact:* Susan Lee, Director of Admissions, 509-323-5532, Fax: 509-323-3857, E-mail: admissions@lawschool.gonzaga.edu. *Dean,* Earl Martin, 509-328-4220 Ext. 3700.

School of Professional Studies Students: 196 full-time (114 women), 674 part-time (402 women); includes 133 minority (39 African Americans, 14 American Indian/Alaska Native, 44 Asian Americans or Pacific Islanders, 36 Hispanic Americans), 7 international. Average age 39. 249 applicants, 51% accepted. *Faculty:* 20 full-time (6 women). Expenses: Contact institution. *Financial support:* Application deadline: 3/1. In 2006, 112 master's, 16 doctorates awarded. Offers communication and leadership studies (MA); leadership studies (PhD); nursing (MSN); organizational leadership (MOL). *Application deadline:* For fall admission, 7/20 priority date for domestic students; for spring admission, 11/1 for domestic students. Applications are processed on a rolling basis. *Application fee:* $40. *Dean,* Dr. Mary McFarland, 509-328-4220 Ext. 3542.

GOODING INSTITUTE OF NURSE ANESTHESIA, Panama City, FL 32401

General Information County-supported, coed, graduate-only institution. *Graduate housing:* On-campus housing not available.

GRADUATE UNITS

Program in Nurse Anesthesia Offers nurse anesthesia (MS).

GORDON COLLEGE, Wenham, MA 01984-1899

General Information Independent-religious, coed, comprehensive institution. *Enrollment:* 1,660 graduate, professional, and undergraduate students; 2 full-time matriculated graduate/professional students (both women), 131 part-time matriculated graduate/professional students (107 women). *Enrollment by degree level:* 133 master's. *Graduate faculty:* 5 full-time (4 women), 9 part-time/adjunct (5 women). *Graduate housing:* On-campus housing not available. *Student services:* Campus employment opportunities, career counseling, disabled student services, free psychological counseling, low-cost health insurance, teacher training. *Library facilities:* Jenks Learning Resource Center. *Online resources:* library catalog, access to other libraries' catalogs. *Collection:* 142,688 titles, 8,555 serial subscriptions.

Computer facilities: 141 computers available on campus for general student use. A campuswide network can be accessed from student residence rooms and from off campus. Internet access and online class registration are available. *Web address:* http://www.gordon.edu/.

General Application Contact: E. Jean Bilsbury, Program Coordinator, 978-867-4322, Fax: 978-867-4663, E-mail: jean.bilsbury@gordon.edu.

GRADUATE UNITS

Graduate Education Students: 2 full-time (both women), 131 part-time (107 women); includes 2 minority (both Asian Americans or Pacific Islanders) Average age 28. 133 applicants, 100% accepted, 133 enrolled. *Faculty:* 5 full-time (4 women), 9 part-time/adjunct (5 women). Expenses: Contact institution. In 2006, 12 degrees awarded. *Degree program information:* Part-time and evening/weekend programs available. Offers education (M Ed, MAT); music education (MME). *Application deadline:* Applications are processed on a rolling basis. *Application fee:* $50. *Application Contact:* E. Jean Bilsbury, Program Coordinator, 978-867-4322, Fax: 978-867-4663, E-mail: jean.bilsbury@gordon.edu. *Dean of Graduate Studies,* Dr. Malcolm L. Patterson, 978-867-4355, Fax: 978-867-4663, E-mail: malcolm.patterson@gordon.edu.

GORDON-CONWELL THEOLOGICAL SEMINARY, South Hamilton, MA 01982-2395

General Information Independent-religious, coed, graduate-only institution. *Graduate housing:* Rooms and/or apartments available to single and married students. Housing application deadline: 4/1.

GRADUATE UNITS

Graduate and Professional Programs *Degree program information:* Part-time and evening/weekend programs available. Offers Christian education (MACE); church history (MACH); counseling (MACO); ministry (D Min); missions/evangelism (MAME); New Testament (MANT); Old Testament (MAOT); religion (MAR); theology (M Div, MATH, Th M).

GOUCHER COLLEGE, Baltimore, MD 21204-2794

General Information Independent, coed, comprehensive institution. *Enrollment:* 2,310 graduate, professional, and undergraduate students; 141 full-time matriculated graduate/professional students (111 women), 644 part-time matriculated graduate/professional students (516 women). *Graduate faculty:* 7 full-time (3 women), 142 part-time/adjunct (99 women). *Graduate housing:* On-campus housing not available. *Student services:* Career counseling, low-cost health insurance. *Library facilities:* Julia Rogers Library. *Online resources:* library catalog, web page. *Collection:* 305,486 titles, 27,416 serial subscriptions, 5,511 audiovisual materials. *Research affiliation:* Sheppard-Pratt Hospital (education).

Computer facilities: Computer purchase and lease plans are available. 150 computers available on campus for general student use. A campuswide network can be accessed from student residence rooms and from off campus. Internet access, transcripts, course schedules, financial aid information, billing, ePortfolios are available. *Web address:* http://www.goucher.edu/.

General Application Contact: Dr. Frederick Mauk, Associate Dean for Graduate and Professional Studies, 410-337-6242, Fax: 410-337-6085, E-mail: fmauk@goucher.edu.

GRADUATE UNITS

Historic Preservation Program Students: 2 full-time (1 woman), 37 part-time (23 women). Average age 42. *Faculty:* 18 part-time/adjunct (6 women). Expenses: Contact institution. *Financial support:* Career-related internships or fieldwork available. Support available to part-time students. Financial award application deadline: 1/31; financial award applicants required to submit FAFSA. In 2006, 6 degrees awarded. *Degree program information:* Part-time and evening/weekend programs available. Postbaccalaureate distance learning degree programs offered (minimal on-campus study). Offers historic preservation (MA). *Application deadline:* For fall admission, 2/15 for domestic students. *Application fee:* $50. *Director,* Richard Wagner, 410-337-6200, Fax: 410-337-6085, E-mail: rwagner@goucher.edu.

Program in Arts Administration Students: 24 full-time (19 women), 17 part-time (12 women); includes 2 minority (both Hispanic Americans), 1 international. Average age 36. *Faculty:* 16 part-time/adjunct (14 women). Expenses: Contact institution. *Financial support:* Institutionally sponsored loans available. Financial award application deadline: 3/15. In 2006, 10 degrees awarded. *Degree program information:* Part-time programs available. Postbaccalaureate distance learning degree programs offered (minimal on-campus study). Offers arts administration (MA). *Application deadline:* For fall admission, 3/15 for domestic students. *Application fee:* $50. *Director,* Dr. Jean Brody, 410-337-6200, Fax: 410-337-6085, E-mail: jbrody@goucher.edu.

Program in Creative Nonfiction Students: 51 full-time (43 women), 1 international. Average age 40. *Faculty:* 9 part-time/adjunct (4 women). Expenses: Contact institution. *Financial support:* Career-related internships or fieldwork and institutionally sponsored loans available. Financial award application deadline: 2/15; financial award applicants required to submit FAFSA. In 2006, 23 degrees awarded. *Degree program information:* Part-time and evening/weekend programs available. Postbaccalaureate distance learning degree programs offered (minimal on-campus study). Offers creative nonfiction (MFA). *Application deadline:* For fall admission, 3/5 for domestic students. *Application fee:* $50. *Director,* Patsy Sims, 410-337-6200, Fax: 410-337-6085, E-mail: psims@goucher.edu.

Program in Post-Baccalaureate Premedical Studies Students: 24 full-time (15 women); includes 7 minority (5 African Americans, 1 Asian American or Pacific Islander, 1 Hispanic American). Average age 24. *Faculty:* 7 full-time (3 women), 1 part-time/adjunct (0 women). Expenses: Contact institution. *Financial support:* Institutionally sponsored loans and scholarships/grants available. Financial award application deadline: 3/1; financial award applicants required to submit FAFSA. Offers premedical studies (Certificate). *Application deadline:* Applications are processed on a rolling basis. *Application fee:* $50. *Director,* Liza Thompson, 800-414-3437, Fax: 410-337-6461, E-mail: lthompso@goucher.edu.

Programs in Education Students: 40 full-time (33 women), 590 part-time (481 women); includes 86 minority (75 African Americans, 1 American Indian/Alaska Native, 5 Asian Americans or Pacific Islanders, 5 Hispanic Americans), 1 international. Average age 34. 40 applicants, 88% accepted, 25 enrolled. *Faculty:* 98 part-time/adjunct (75 women). Expenses: Contact institution. *Financial support:* In 2006–07, 3 research assistantships with tuition reimbursements (averaging $4,500 per year) were awarded; career-related internships or fieldwork and need-based awards also available. Support available to part-time students. Financial award application deadline: 8/15; financial award applicants required to submit FAFSA. In 2006, 54 degrees awarded. *Degree program information:* Part-time and evening/weekend programs available. Offers education (M Ed, MAT). *Application deadline:* For fall admission, 9/1 priority date for domestic students; for spring admission, 1/15 for domestic students. Applications are processed on a rolling basis. *Application fee:* $25. *Application Contact:* Megan Cornett, Associate Director, Administrative Student Services, 410-337-6200, Fax: 410-337-6394, E-mail: mcornett@goucher.edu. *Director,* Dr. Phyllis Sunshine, 410-337-6047, Fax: 410-337-6394, E-mail: psunshin@goucher.edu.

GOVERNORS STATE UNIVERSITY, University Park, IL 60466-0975

General Information State-supported, coed, upper-level institution. *Enrollment:* 203 full-time matriculated graduate/professional students (143 women), 2,558 part-time matriculated graduate/professional students (1,930 women). *Enrollment by degree level:* 2,739 master's, 22 doctoral. *Graduate faculty:* 185 full-time (78 women), 27 part-time/adjunct (13 women). Tuition, state resident: full-time $4,104; part-time $171 per hour. Tuition, nonresident: part-time $513 per hour. *Graduate housing:* On-campus housing not available. *Student services:* Campus employment opportunities, campus safety program, career counseling, child daycare facilities, disabled student services, exercise/wellness program, free psychological counseling, international student services, low-cost health insurance, teacher training. *Library facilities:* University Library. *Online resources:* library catalog, web page. *Collection:* 260,000 titles, 2,200 serial subscriptions, 2,700 audiovisual materials.

Computer facilities: 165 computers available on campus for general student use. A campuswide network can be accessed from off campus. *Web address:* http://www.govst.edu/.

General Application Contact: Dr. William T. Craig, Associate Director of Admission, 708-534-4492, Fax: 708-534-1640, E-mail: b-craig@govst.edu.

GRADUATE UNITS

College of Arts and Sciences Students: 396 (230 women). Average age 29. 412 applicants, 58% accepted, 211 enrolled. *Faculty:* 48 full-time (18 women), 12 part-time/adjunct (5 women). Expenses: Contact institution. *Financial support:* In 2006–07, 11 research assistantships were awarded; career-related internships or fieldwork, Federal Work-Study, institutionally sponsored loans, and scholarships/grants also available. Support available to part-time students. Financial award application deadline: 5/1. *Degree program information:* Part-time and evening/weekend programs available. Offers analytical chemistry (MS); art (MA); arts and sciences (MA, MS); communication studies (MA); computer science (MS); English (MA); environmental biology (MS); instructional and training technology (MA); media communication (MA); political and justice studies (MA). *Application deadline:* For fall admission, 7/15 priority date for domestic students; for spring admission, 11/10 priority date for domestic students. Applications are processed on a rolling basis. *Application fee:* $25. *Interim Dean,* Dr. Eric V. Martin, 708-534-4101.

College of Business and Public Administration Students: 72 full-time, 296 part-time. Average age 33. 310 applicants, 61% accepted, 155 enrolled. *Faculty:* 34 full-time (9 women), 11 part-time/adjunct (4 women). Expenses: Contact institution. *Financial support:* Fellowships, research assistantships, career-related internships or fieldwork, Federal Work-Study, institutionally sponsored loans, scholarships/grants, and tuition waivers (full and partial) available. Support available to part-time students. Financial award application deadline: 5/1. In 2006, 62 degrees awarded. *Degree program information:* Part-time and evening/weekend programs available. Offers accounting (MS); business administration (MBA); business and public administration (MBA, MPA, MS); management information systems (MS); public administration (MPA). *Application deadline:* For fall admission, 7/15 priority date for domestic students; for spring admission, 11/10 for domestic students. Applications are processed on a rolling basis. *Application fee:* $25. *Application Contact:* Dortha Brown, Adviser, 708-534-4391. *Dean,* Dr. William Nowlin, 708-534-4930.

College of Education Students: 128 full-time, 881 part-time. Average age 36. 604 applicants, 73% accepted, 387 enrolled. *Faculty:* 36 full-time (15 women), 14 part-time/adjunct (8 women). Expenses: Contact institution. *Financial support:* Career-related internships or fieldwork, Federal Work-Study, institutionally sponsored loans, tuition waivers (full and partial), and unspecified assistantships available. Support available to part-time students. Financial award application deadline: 5/1. *Degree program information:* Part-time and evening/weekend programs available. Offers counseling (MA); early childhood education (MA); education (MA); educational administration and supervision (MA); multi-categorical special education (MA); psychology (MA); reading (MA). *Application deadline:* For fall admission, 7/15 priority date for domestic students; for spring admission, 11/10 for domestic students. Applications are processed on a rolling basis. *Application fee:* $25. *Application Contact:* John Powers, Adviser, 708-534-6363. *Dean,* Dr. Steven C. Russell, 708-534-4050.

College of Health Professions Students: 187 full-time, 384 part-time. Average age 33. 355 applicants, 78% accepted, 202 enrolled. *Faculty:* 28 full-time (11 women), 13 part-time/adjunct (5 women). Expenses: Contact institution. *Financial support:* Research assistantships, career-related internships or fieldwork, Federal Work-Study, institutionally sponsored loans, scholarships/grants, and tuition waivers (full and partial) available. Support available to part-time students. Financial award application deadline: 5/1. In 2006, 119 degrees awarded. *Degree program information:* Part-time and evening/weekend programs available. Offers addictions studies (MHS); communication disorders (MHS); health administration (MHA); health professions (MHA, MHS, MOT, MPT, MSN, MSW, DPT); nursing (MSN); occupational therapy (MOT); physical therapy (MPT, DPT); social work (MSW). *Application deadline:* Applications are processed on a rolling basis. *Application fee:* $25. *Dean,* Dr. Linda Samson, 708-534-4388.

GRACE COLLEGE, Winona Lake, IN 46590-1294

General Information Independent-religious, coed, comprehensive institution. *Graduate housing:* On-campus housing not available.

GRADUATE UNITS

Graduate School Offers clinical counseling (MA); interpersonal relations (MA).

GRACELAND UNIVERSITY, Lamoni, IA 50140

General Information Independent-religious, coed, comprehensive institution. *Enrollment:* 2,116 graduate, professional, and undergraduate students; 696 full-time matriculated graduate/professional students (543 women), 157 part-time matriculated graduate/professional students (122 women). *Enrollment by degree level:* 853 master's. *Graduate faculty:* 18 full-time (16 women), 39 part-time/adjunct (23 women). *Graduate housing:* On-campus housing not available. *Student services:* Campus safety program, career counseling, free psychological counseling, teacher training. *Library facilities:* Frederick Madison Smith Library. *Online resources:* library catalog, web page, access to other libraries' catalogs. *Collection:* 193,172 titles, 780 serial subscriptions, 3,428 audiovisual materials.

Computer facilities: 106 computers available on campus for general student use. A campuswide network can be accessed from student residence rooms and from off campus. Internet access and online class registration are available. *Web address:* http://www.graceland.edu/.

General Application Contact: John D. Koehler, Manager of Recruiting, 816-833-0524 Ext. 4804, Fax: 816-833-2990, E-mail: jkoehler@graceland.edu.

GRADUATE UNITS

Community of Christ Seminary Students: 17 full-time (3 women), 34 part-time (20 women); includes 3 minority (2 American Indian/Alaska Native, 1 Hispanic American), 4 international. Average age 47. 24 applicants, 75% accepted, 17 enrolled. *Faculty:* 1 (woman) full-time, 14 part-time/adjunct (4 women). Expenses: Contact institution. *Financial support:* In 2006–07, 1 student received support. Scholarships/grants available. Financial award application deadline: 12/15; financial award applicants required to submit FAFSA. In 2006, 17 degrees awarded. *Degree program information:* Part-time programs available. Postbaccalaureate distance learning degree programs offered (minimal on-campus study). Offers Christian ministry (MACM); religion (MAR). *Application deadline:* For fall admission, 8/15 priority date for domestic students; for winter admission, 10/15 priority date for domestic students; for spring admission, 4/15 priority date for domestic students. Applications are processed on a rolling basis. *Application fee:* $50. *Application Contact:* Tere E. Naylor, Administrative Assistant, 816-833-0524 Ext. 4903, Fax: 816-833-2990, E-mail: tnaylor@graceland.edu. *Dean,* Dr. Don H. Compier, 800-833-0524 Ext. 4900, Fax: 816-833-2990, E-mail: dcompier@graceland.edu.

School of Education Students: 585 full-time (447 women). Average age 36. 240 applicants, 99% accepted, 213 enrolled. *Faculty:* 6 full-time (4 women), 20 part-time/adjunct (14 women). Expenses: Contact institution. *Financial support:* In 2006–07, 451 students received support. Institutionally sponsored loans and scholarships/grants available. Financial award application deadline: 12/15; financial award applicants required to submit FAFSA. In 2006, 229 degrees awarded. *Degree program information:* Part-time and evening/weekend programs available. Postbaccalaureate distance learning degree programs offered (minimal on-campus study). Offers education (M Ed). *Application deadline:* For spring admission, 1/15 priority date for domestic students. *Application fee:* $50. Electronic applications accepted. *Application Contact:* Tom Kotz, Associate Dean, 641-784-5313 Ext. 4520, E-mail: kotz@graceland.edu. *Dean,* Dr. William L. Armstrong, 641-784-5000 Ext. 5254, E-mail: billa@graceland.edu.

School of Nursing Students: 94 full-time (93 women), 123 part-time (102 women); includes 16 minority (10 African Americans, 4 Asian Americans or Pacific Islanders, 2 Hispanic Americans). Average age 44. 123 applicants, 90% accepted, 105 enrolled. *Faculty:* 11 full-time (all women), 5 part-time/adjunct (all women). Expenses: Contact institution. *Financial support:* In 2006–07, 3 students received support. Institutionally sponsored loans and traineeships available. Support available to part-time students. Financial award applicants required to submit FAFSA. In 2006, 42 master's, 2 other advanced degrees awarded. *Degree program information:* Part-time programs available. Postbaccalaureate distance learning degree programs offered (minimal on-campus study). Offers family nurse practitioner (MSN, PMC); health care administration (MSN, PMC); nurse educator (MSN, PMC). *Application deadline:* For fall admission, 6/1 priority date for domestic students; for winter admission, 10/1 priority

Graceland University (continued)

date for domestic students; for spring admission, 3/1 priority date for domestic students. Applications are processed on a rolling basis. *Application fee:* $50. Electronic applications accepted. *Application Contact:* John D. Koehler, Manager of Recruiting, 816-833-0524 Ext. 4804, Fax: 816-833-2990, E-mail: jkoehler@graceland.edu. *Dean,* Dr. Kathryn A Ballou, 800-833-0524 Ext. 4201, Fax: 816-833-2990, E-mail: kaballou@graceland.edu.

GRACE THEOLOGICAL SEMINARY, Winona Lake, IN 46590-9907

General Information Independent-religious, coed, primarily men, graduate-only institution. *Graduate housing:* On-campus housing not available.

GRADUATE UNITS

Graduate and Professional Programs *Degree program information:* Part-time programs available. Postbaccalaureate distance learning degree programs offered (no on-campus study). Offers biblical studies (Certificate, Diploma); counseling (M Div); ministry (MA); missions (M Div, MA); theology (M Div, MA, D Min). Electronic applications accepted.

GRACE UNIVERSITY, Omaha, NE 68108

General Information Independent-religious, coed, comprehensive institution. *Graduate housing:* Rooms and/or apartments available on a first-come, first-served basis to single and married students.

GRADUATE UNITS

College of Graduate Studies *Degree program information:* Part-time and evening/weekend programs available. Offers biblical studies (MA); counseling (MA). Electronic applications accepted.

GRADUATE INSTITUTE OF APPLIED LINGUISTICS, Dallas, TX 75236

General Information Independent, coed, graduate-only institution. *Enrollment by degree level:* 35 master's, 60 other advanced degrees. *Graduate faculty:* 9 full-time (2 women), 22 part-time/adjunct (5 women). *Tuition:* Part-time $340 per credit. Full-time tuition and fees vary according to program. *Student services:* International student services, teacher training. *Library facilities:* GIAL Library. *Online resources:* library catalog, web page. *Collection:* 40,000 titles, 106 serial subscriptions, 12 audiovisual materials.

Computer facilities: 22 computers available on campus for general student use. A campuswide network can be accessed. Internet access is available. *Web address:* http://www.gial.edu/.

General Application Contact: Grace M. Fuqua, Admissions Officer, 972-708-7343, Fax: 972-708-7396, E-mail: admissions@gial.edu.

GRADUATE UNITS

Graduate Programs Students: 41 full-time (19 women), 54 part-time (30 women); includes 6 minority (4 Asian Americans or Pacific Islanders, 2 Hispanic Americans). Average age 32. 56 applicants, 98% accepted. Expenses: Contact institution. *Financial support:* In 2006–07, 51 students received support. Scholarships/grants and tuition waivers (partial) available. Financial award application deadline: 11/20. In 2006, 20 degrees awarded. *Degree program information:* Part-time programs available. Offers applied linguistics (MA, Certificate); language development (MA). *Application deadline:* Applications are processed on a rolling basis. *Application fee:* $20. Electronic applications accepted. *Application Contact:* Grace M. Fuqua, Admissions Officer, 972-708-7343, Fax: 972-708-7396, E-mail: admissions@gial.edu.

GRADUATE SCHOOL AND UNIVERSITY CENTER OF THE CITY UNIVERSITY OF NEW YORK, New York, NY 10016-4039

General Information State and locally supported, coed, graduate-only institution. CGS member. *Graduate faculty:* 1,471 full-time (318 women). *Graduate housing:* Rooms and/or apartments available to single and married students. Housing application deadline: 5/1. *Student services:* Career counseling, free psychological counseling, low-cost health insurance. *Library facilities:* Mina Rees Library. *Collection:* 204,000 titles, 1,680 serial subscriptions. *Research affiliation:* American Museum of Natural History (anthropology), Roche Institute of Molecular Biology (biological sciences), New York Botanical Gardens (biological sciences). *Web address:* http://www.gc.cuny.edu/.

General Application Contact: Les Gribben, Director of Admissions, 212-817-7470, Fax: 212-817-1624, E-mail: lgribben@gc.cuny.edu.

GRADUATE UNITS

Graduate Studies Students: 4,012 full-time (2,257 women), 352 part-time (189 women); includes 683 minority (225 African Americans, 7 American Indian/Alaska Native, 157 Asian Americans or Pacific Islanders, 294 Hispanic Americans), 1,085 international. Average age 34. 3,385 applicants, 41% accepted, 753 enrolled. *Faculty:* 1,471 full-time (318 women). Expenses: Contact institution. *Financial support:* In 2006–07, 2,212 fellowships, 156 research assistantships, 224 teaching assistantships were awarded; career-related internships or fieldwork, Federal Work-Study, institutionally sponsored loans, and tuition waivers (full and partial) also available. Financial award application deadline: 2/1; financial award applicants required to submit FAFSA. In 2006, 59 master's, 320 doctorates awarded. Offers accounting (PhD); anthropological linguistics (PhD); archaeology (PhD); architecture (PhD); basic applied neurocognition (PhD); behavioral science (PhD); biochemistry (PhD); biology (PhD); biomedical engineering (PhD); biopsychology (PhD); chemical engineering (PhD); chemistry (PhD); civil engineering (PhD); classical studies (MA, PhD); clinical psychology (PhD); comparative literature (MA, PhD); computer science (PhD); criminal justice (PhD); cultural anthropology (PhD); developmental psychology (PhD); earth and environmental sciences (PhD); economics (PhD); educational psychology (PhD); electrical engineering (PhD); English (PhD); environmental psychology (PhD); experimental psychology (PhD); finance (PhD); French (PhD); Germanic languages and literatures (MA, PhD); graphic arts (PhD); Hispanic and Luso-Brazilian literatures (PhD); history (PhD); industrial psychology (PhD); learning processes (PhD); liberal studies (MA); linguistics (MA, PhD); management planning systems (PhD); mathematics (PhD); mechanical engineering (PhD); music (DMA, PhD); neuropsychology (PhD); painting (PhD); philosophy (MA, PhD); photography (PhD); physical anthropology (PhD); physics (PhD); political science (MA, PhD); psychology (PhD); sculpture (PhD); social personality (PhD); social welfare (DSW, PhD); sociology (PhD); speech and hearing sciences (PhD); theatre (PhD); urban education (PhD). *Application fee:* $125. Electronic applications accepted. *Application Contact:* Les Gribben, Director of Admissions, 212-817-7470, Fax: 212-817-1624, E-mail: lgribben@gc.cuny.edu. *Acting Provost and Senior Vice President for Academic Affairs,* Dr. Linda Edwards, 212-817-7200, Fax: 212-817-1612, E-mail: provost@gc.cuny.edu.

Interdisciplinary Studies Expenses: Contact institution. *Financial support:* Application deadline: 2/1. Offers language in social context (PhD); medieval studies (PhD); public policy (MA, PhD); urban studies (MA, PhD); women's studies (MA, PhD). *Application deadline:* For fall admission, 2/1 for domestic students. *Application fee:* $40. *Chairman,* 212-642-2430.

GRADUATE THEOLOGICAL UNION, Berkeley, CA 94709-1212

General Information Independent-religious, coed, graduate-only institution. *Enrollment by degree level:* 149 master's, 225 doctoral, 8 other advanced degrees. *Graduate faculty:* 65 full-time (21 women), 39 part-time/adjunct (15 women). *Graduate housing:* Rooms and/or apartments available on a first-come, first-served basis to single and married students. Housing application deadline: 6/1. *Student services:* Campus employment opportunities, disabled student services, international student services, low-cost health insurance, teacher training, writing training. *Library facilities:* Flora Lamson Hewlett Library. *Online resources:* library catalog, web page, access to other libraries' catalogs. *Collection:* 461,683 titles, 1,556 serial subscriptions, 7,990 audiovisual materials.

Computer facilities: 40 computers available on campus for general student use. A campuswide network can be accessed from student residence rooms and from off campus. Internet access is available. *Web address:* http://www.gtu.edu/.

General Application Contact: Dr. Kathleen Kook, Assistant Dean for Admissions, 800-826-4488, Fax: 510-649-1730, E-mail: gtuadm@gtu.edu.

GRADUATE UNITS

Graduate Programs Students: 327 full-time (151 women), 55 part-time (34 women); includes 14 African Americans, 19 Asian Americans or Pacific Islanders, 9 Hispanic Americans, 87 international. Average age 40. *Faculty:* 65 full-time (21 women), 39 part-time/adjunct (15 women). Expenses: Contact institution. *Financial support:* In 2006–07, 108 fellowships (averaging $10,555 per year), 3 research assistantships (averaging $4,000 per year), 22 teaching assistantships (averaging $4,000 per year) were awarded; Federal Work-Study, scholarships/grants, and tuition waivers (partial) also available. Support available to part-time students. Financial award application deadline: 2/1; financial award applicants required to submit FAFSA. In 2006, 40 master's, 25 doctorates awarded. Offers art and religion (MA, PhD); biblical languages (MA); biblical studies (Old and New Testament) (MA, PhD, Th D); Buddhist studies (MA); Christian spirituality (MA, PhD); cultural and historical studies of religions (MA, PhD); ethics and social theory (PhD); history (MA, PhD, Th D); homiletics (MA, PhD, Th D); interdisciplinary studies (PhD, Th D); Jewish studies (MA, PhD, Certificate); liturgical studies (MA, PhD, Th D); Near Eastern religions (PhD); Orthodox Christian studies (MA); religion and psychology (MA, PhD); religion and society/ethics and social theory (MA); systematic and philosophical theology (MA, PhD, Th D). *Application deadline:* For fall admission, 12/15 for domestic and international students; for winter admission, 2/15 for domestic and international students; for spring admission, 9/30 for domestic and international students. *Application fee:* $40. Electronic applications accepted. *Application Contact:* Dr. Kathleen Kook, Assistant Dean for Admissions, 800-826-4488, Fax: 510-649-1730, E-mail: gtuadm@gtu.edu. *Dean,* Dr. Arthur G. Holder, 510-649-2440, Fax: 510-649-1417, E-mail: aholder@gtu.edu.

GRAMBLING STATE UNIVERSITY, Grambling, LA 71245

General Information State-supported, coed, university. CGS member. *Enrollment:* 5,065 graduate, professional, and undergraduate students; 314 full-time matriculated graduate/professional students (228 women), 148 part-time matriculated graduate/professional students (111 women). *Enrollment by degree level:* 387 master's, 57 doctoral, 18 other advanced degrees. *Graduate faculty:* 45 full-time (24 women), 14 part-time/adjunct (5 women). Tuition, state resident: full-time $2,232; part-time $124 per credit hour. Tuition, nonresident: full-time $7,582; part-time $124 per credit hour. *Required fees:* $1,127. *Graduate housing:* Rooms and/or apartments available to single and married students. Typical cost: $2,242 per year ($3,714 including board) for single students; $4,242 (including board) for married students. Housing application deadline: 7/15. *Student services:* Campus employment opportunities, career counseling, child daycare facilities, low-cost health insurance. *Library facilities:* A. C. Lewis Memorial Library. *Online resources:* library catalog, web page, access to other libraries' catalogs. *Collection:* 275,048 titles, 1,600 serial subscriptions, 5,760 audiovisual materials. *Research affiliation:* US Environmental Protection Agency (human health and environment), NASA (aeronautics research), National Science Foundation (science and engineering).

Computer facilities: Computer purchase and lease plans are available. 250 computers available on campus for general student use. A campuswide network can be accessed from student residence rooms and from off campus. Internet access is available. *Web address:* http://www.gram.edu/.

General Application Contact: Jacklen Greer-Hill, Administrative Assistant, School of Graduate Studies and Research, 318-274-2158, Fax: 318-274-7373, E-mail: greerj@alpha0.gram.edu.

GRADUATE UNITS

School of Graduate Studies and Research Students: 314 full-time (228 women), 148 part-time (111 women); includes 388 minority (385 African Americans, 3 Asian Americans or Pacific Islanders), 9 international. Average age 33. 183 applicants, 85% accepted, 113 enrolled. *Faculty:* 45 full-time (24 women), 14 part-time/adjunct (5 women). Expenses: Contact institution. *Financial support:* In 2006–07, 370 students received support, including 55 research assistantships (averaging $3,720 per year); fellowships, teaching assistantships, career-related internships or fieldwork, Federal Work-Study, institutionally sponsored loans, scholarships/grants, tuition waivers (full and partial), and unspecified assistantships also available. Support available to part-time students. Financial award application deadline: 5/31; financial award applicants required to submit FAFSA. In 2006, 165 master's, 4 doctorates awarded. *Degree program information:* Part-time and evening/weekend programs available. Postbaccalaureate distance learning degree programs offered. *Application deadline:* For fall admission, 7/1 for domestic students; for spring admission, 12/1 for domestic students. Applications are processed on a rolling basis. *Application fee:* $20 ($30 for international students). *Application Contact:* Jacklen Greer-Hill, Administrative Assistant, School of Graduate Studies and Research, 318-274-2158, Fax: 318-274-7373, E-mail: greerj@alpha0.gram.edu. *Dean,* Dr. Janet Guyden, 318-274-7374, Fax: 318-274-7373, E-mail: guydenj@gram.edu.

College of Arts and Sciences Students: 98 full-time (68 women), 34 part-time (23 women); includes 128 minority (all African Americans), 4 international. Average age 30. *Faculty:* 6 full-time (2 women), 3 part-time/adjunct (2 women). Expenses: Contact institution. *Financial support:* In 2006–07, 103 students received support, including 15 research assistantships (averaging $3,920 per year); institutionally sponsored loans and unspecified assistantships also available. Financial award application deadline: 5/31; financial award applicants required to submit FAFSA. In 2006, 58 degrees awarded. *Degree program information:* Part-time programs available. Offers arts and sciences (MAT, MPA); public administration (MPA); social sciences (MAT). *Application deadline:* For fall admission, 7/1 for domestic students; for spring admission, 12/1 for domestic students. *Application fee:* $20 ($30 for international students). *Dean,* Dr. Connie Walton, 318-274-6202, Fax: 318-274-6041, E-mail: waltonc@gram.edu.

College of Education Students: 64 full-time (33 women), 72 part-time (56 women); includes 112 minority (110 African Americans, 2 Asian Americans or Pacific Islanders), 2 international. Average age 36. *Faculty:* 21 full-time (10 women), 2 part-time/adjunct (0 women). Expenses: Contact institution. *Financial support:* In 2006–07, 100 students received support, including 12 research assistantships (averaging $5,333 per year); teaching assistantships, career-related internships or fieldwork, institutionally sponsored loans, and unspecified assistantships also available. Financial award application deadline: 5/31; financial award applicants required to submit FAFSA. In 2006, 32 master's, 4 doctorates awarded. *Degree program information:* Part-time and evening/weekend programs available. Postbaccalaureate distance learning degree programs offered (minimal on-campus study). Offers curriculum and instruction (Ed D); developmental education (Ed D); education (M Ed, MS, Ed D); educational leadership (M Ed, Ed D); elementary/early childhood education (MS); special education (M Ed); sports administration (MS). *Application deadline:* For fall admission, 7/1 for domestic students; for spring admission, 12/1 for domestic students. Applications are processed on a rolling basis. *Application fee:* $20 ($30 for international students). *Dean,* Dr. Sean Warner, 318-274-3235, Fax: 318-274-2799, E-mail: warners@gram.edu.

College of Professional Studies Students: 152 full-time (127 women), 42 part-time (32 women); includes 148 minority (147 African Americans, 1 Asian American or Pacific Islander), 3 international. Average age 32. *Faculty:* 16 full-time (8 women), 7 part-time/adjunct (2 women). Expenses: Contact institution. *Financial support:* In 2006–07, 137 students received support, including 19 research assistantships (averaging $3,342 per year); teaching assistantships, institutionally sponsored loans and unspecified assistantships also available. Financial award application deadline: 5/31; financial award applicants required to submit FAFSA. In 2006, 75 degrees awarded. *Degree program information:* Part-time programs available. Offers criminal justice (MS); family nurse practitioner (MSN, PMC); mass communication (MA); nurse educator (MSN); social work (MSW). *Application deadline:* For fall admission, 7/1 for domestic students; for spring admission, 12/1 for domestic students. Applications are processed on a rolling basis. *Application fee:* $20 ($30 for international students). *Acting Dean,* Dr. Marianne Fisher-Giorlando, 318-274-3234, Fax: 318-273-6041, E-mail: giorlando@gram.edu.

GRAND CANYON UNIVERSITY, Phoenix, AZ 85017-1097

General Information Independent-religious, coed, comprehensive institution. *Graduate housing:* Rooms and/or apartments available on a first-come, first-served basis to single and married students. Housing application deadline: 3/15.

GRADUATE UNITS

College of Business *Degree program information:* Part-time and evening/weekend programs available. Offers business (MBA).

College of Education *Degree program information:* Part-time and evening/weekend programs available. Postbaccalaureate distance learning degree programs offered (no on-campus study). Offers elementary education (M Ed, MA); reading education (MA); secondary education (M Ed); teaching (MAT); teaching English as a second language (MA).

GRAND RAPIDS THEOLOGICAL SEMINARY OF CORNERSTONE UNIVERSITY, Grand Rapids, MI 49525-5897

General Information Independent-religious, coed, graduate-only institution. *Graduate housing:* Rooms and/or apartments available on a first-come, first-served basis to single and married students. Housing application deadline: 6/1.

GRADUATE UNITS

Graduate Programs *Degree program information:* Part-time programs available. Postbaccalaureate distance learning degree programs offered (minimal on-campus study). Offers biblical counseling (MA); chaplaincy (M Div); Christian education (M Div, MA); intercultural studies (MA); missions (M Div); New Testament (MA, Th M); Old Testament (MA, Th M); pastoral studies (M Div); systematic theology (MA); theology (Th M). Electronic applications accepted.

GRAND VALLEY STATE UNIVERSITY, Allendale, MI 49401-9403

General Information State-supported, coed, comprehensive institution. CGS member. *Enrollment:* 23,295 graduate, professional, and undergraduate students; 792 full-time matriculated graduate/professional students (558 women), 2,381 part-time matriculated graduate/professional students (1,620 women). *Enrollment by degree level:* 3,060 master's, 113 doctoral. *Graduate faculty:* 261 full-time (115 women), 89 part-time/adjunct (39 women). Tuition, state resident: full-time $5,850; part-time $325 per credit. Tuition, nonresident: full-time $10,800; part-time $600 per credit. Tuition and fees vary according to course load. *Graduate housing:* Rooms and/or apartments available on a first-come, first-served basis to single and married students. Typical cost: $2,500 per year ($3,600 including board) for single students; $2,820 per year for married students. Room and board charges vary according to board plan, campus/location and housing facility selected. Housing application deadline: 2/1. *Student services:* Campus employment opportunities, campus safety program, career counseling, child daycare facilities, disabled student services, exercise/wellness program, free psychological counseling, grant writing training, international student services, low-cost health insurance, multicultural affairs office, teacher training, writing training. *Library facilities:* James H. Zumberge Library plus 2 others. *Online resources:* library catalog, web page. *Collection:* 634,000 titles, 5,000 serial subscriptions. *Research affiliation:* Progressive AE (water quality), Elkins Innovations (Life Sciences).

Computer facilities: 2,600 computers available on campus for general student use. A campuswide network can be accessed from student residence rooms and from off campus. Internet access and online class registration, transcript, degree audit, credit card payments, grades are available. *Web address:* http://www.gvsu.edu/.

General Application Contact: Tracey James-Heer, Associate Director for Graduate Recruitment, 616-331-2025, Fax: 616-486-6476, E-mail: james-ht@gvsu.edu.

GRADUATE UNITS

College of Community and Public Service Students: 195 full-time (148 women), 414 part-time (324 women); includes 100 minority (60 African Americans, 11 American Indian/Alaska Native, 10 Asian Americans or Pacific Islanders, 19 Hispanic Americans). Average age 32. 254 applicants, 81% accepted, 143 enrolled. *Faculty:* 44 full-time (22 women), 15 part-time/adjunct (8 women). Expenses: Contact institution. *Financial support:* In 2006–07, 20 students received support, including research assistantships with full and partial tuition reimbursements available (averaging $8,000 per year); fellowships, teaching assistantships, career-related internships or fieldwork, Federal Work-Study, institutionally sponsored loans, scholarships/grants, and unspecified assistantships also available. Financial award application deadline: 5/1. In 2006, 161 degrees awarded. *Degree program information:* Part-time and evening/weekend programs available. Postbaccalaureate distance learning degree programs offered (no on-campus study). Offers community and public service (MHA, MPA, MS, MSW). *Application deadline:* For fall admission, 5/1 priority date for domestic students; for winter admission, 11/1 priority date for domestic students; for spring admission, 4/10 priority date for domestic students. Applications are processed on a rolling basis. *Application fee:* $30. Electronic applications accepted. *Dean,* Dr. Rodney Mulder, 616-331-6550, Fax: 616-771-6550.

School of Criminal Justice Students: 13 full-time (8 women), 19 part-time (15 women); includes 4 minority (3 African Americans, 1 Hispanic American). Average age 29. 21 applicants, 90% accepted, 12 enrolled. *Faculty:* 13 full-time (5 women), 13 part-time/adjunct (5 women). Expenses: Contact institution. *Financial support:* In 2006–07, 5 students received support, including 5 research assistantships with full tuition reimbursements available (averaging $8,000 per year); career-related internships or fieldwork, Federal Work-Study, and scholarships/grants also available. Financial award application deadline: 5/1. In 2006, 6 degrees awarded. *Degree program information:* Part-time and evening/weekend programs available. Postbaccalaureate distance learning degree programs offered (no on-campus study). Offers criminal justice (MS). *Application deadline:* For fall admission, 7/30 priority date for domestic students; for winter admission, 12/10 priority date for domestic students; for spring admission, 4/10 priority date for domestic students. *Application fee:* $30. *Application Contact:* Dr. Debra Ross, 616-331-7150, Fax: 616-331-7155, E-mail: rossd@gvsu.edu. *Director,* Dr. Jonathan White, 616-331-7243, Fax: 616-331-7155, E-mail: whitej@gvsu.edu.

School of Public and Nonprofit Administration Students: 58 full-time (31 women), 144 part-time (88 women); includes 36 minority (21 African Americans, 2 American Indian/Alaska Native, 8 Asian Americans or Pacific Islanders, 5 Hispanic Americans). Average age 32. 102 applicants, 89% accepted, 61 enrolled. *Faculty:* 12 full-time (5 women), 7 part-time/adjunct (3 women). Expenses: Contact institution. *Financial support:* In 2006–07, 28 students received support, including 28 research assistantships with partial tuition reimbursements available (averaging $6,000 per year); career-related internships or fieldwork, Federal Work-Study, scholarships/grants, and unspecified assistantships also available. Financial award application deadline: 5/1. In 2006, 45 degrees awarded. *Degree program information:* Part-time and evening/weekend programs available. Offers health administration (MHA); public and nonprofit administration (MHA, MPA). *Application deadline:* For fall admission, 5/1 priority date for domestic students; for winter admission, 11/1 priority date for domestic students. Applications are processed on a rolling basis. *Application fee:* $30. Electronic applications accepted. *Director,* Dr. Mark Hoffman, 616-331-6575, Fax: 616-331-7120, E-mail: hoffman@gvsu.edu.

School of Social Work Students: 124 full-time (109 women), 251 part-time (221 women); includes 60 minority (36 African Americans, 9 American Indian/Alaska Native, 2 Asian Americans or Pacific Islanders, 13 Hispanic Americans). Average age 33. 131 applicants, 74% accepted, 70 enrolled. *Faculty:* 20 full-time (13 women), 13 part-time/adjunct (9 women). Expenses: Contact institution. *Financial support:* In 2006–07, 22 students received support, including 22 research assistantships with full and partial tuition reimbursements available (averaging $6,000 per year); career-related internships or fieldwork, Federal Work-Study, institutionally sponsored loans, and unspecified assistantships also available. In 2006, 110 degrees awarded. *Degree program information:* Part-time programs available. Offers social work (MSW). *Application deadline:* For fall admission, 5/1 priority date for domestic students; for winter admission, 10/1 priority date for domestic students; for spring admission, 3/15 priority date for domestic students. Applications are processed on a rolling basis. *Application fee:* $30. Electronic applications accepted. *Application Contact:* Prof. Lois Smith Owens, Chair, Admissions, 616-331-6577, E-mail: owensl@gvsu.edu. *Director,* Dr. Elaine Schott, 616-331-6550, Fax: 616-771-6570, E-mail: schottl@gusu.edu.

College of Education Students: 203 full-time (150 women), 1,388 part-time (1,052 women); includes 86 minority (46 African Americans, 10 American Indian/Alaska Native, 7 Asian Americans or Pacific Islanders, 23 Hispanic Americans). Average age 33. 399 applicants, 93% accepted, 272 enrolled. *Faculty:* 80 full-time (39 women), 40 part-time/adjunct (21 women). Expenses: Contact institution. *Financial support:* In 2006–07, 46 research assistantships with full and partial tuition reimbursements (averaging $8,000 per year) were awarded; career-related internships or fieldwork, Federal Work-Study, scholarships/grants, and unspecified assistantships also available. In 2006, 462 degrees awarded. *Degree program information:* Part-time and evening/weekend programs available. Postbaccalaureate distance learning degree programs offered (minimal on-campus study). Offers adult and higher education (M Ed); early childhood developmental delay (M Ed); early childhood education (M Ed); education (M Ed); education of the gifted and talented (M Ed); educational leadership (M Ed); educational technology (M Ed); elementary education (M Ed); emotional impairment (M Ed); learning disabilities (M Ed); middle and high school education (M Ed); reading and language arts (M Ed); school counseling (M Ed); special education endorsements (M Ed); student affairs leadership (M Ed); teaching English to speakers of other languages (M Ed). *Application deadline:* Applications are processed on a rolling basis. *Application fee:* $30. Electronic applications accepted. *Application Contact:* Dr. Douglas Busman, Admissions Office, 616-331-2025, Fax: 616-331-2000, E-mail: busmando@gvsu.edu. *Dean,* Dr. Elaine C. Collins, 616-331-6821, Fax: 616-331-6515, E-mail: collinse@gvsu.edu.

College of Health Professions Students: 234 full-time (187 women), 18 part-time (17 women); includes 18 minority (5 African Americans, 1 American Indian/Alaska Native, 7 Asian Americans or Pacific Islanders, 5 Hispanic Americans). Average age 25. 250 applicants, 45% accepted, 95 enrolled. *Faculty:* 25 full-time (14 women), 3 part-time/adjunct (2 women). Expenses: Contact institution. *Financial support:* In 2006–07, 11 research assistantships with full tuition reimbursements (averaging $8,000 per year) were awarded; career-related internships or fieldwork, Federal Work-Study, institutionally sponsored loans, and scholarships/grants also available. Financial award application deadline: 2/15. In 2006, 74 degrees awarded. Offers health professions (MPAS, MS, DPT); occupational therapy (MS); physical therapy (MS, DPT); physician assistant studies (MPAS). *Application deadline:* For winter admission, 1/15 priority date for domestic and international students. Applications are processed on a rolling basis. Electronic applications accepted. *Application Contact:* Darlene Zwart, Student Services Coordinator, 616-331-3958, E-mail: zwartda@gvsu.edu. *Dean,* Dr. Jane Toot, 616-331-3356, Fax: 616-331-3350, E-mail: tootj@gvsu.edu.

College of Liberal Arts and Sciences Students: 45 full-time (26 women), 96 part-time (56 women); includes 17 minority (8 African Americans, 1 American Indian/Alaska Native, 4 Asian Americans or Pacific Islanders, 4 Hispanic Americans). Average age 32. 94 applicants, 77% accepted, 48 enrolled. *Faculty:* 36 full-time (15 women), 3 part-time/adjunct (0 women). Expenses: Contact institution. *Financial support:* In 2006–07, 22 research assistantships with full and partial tuition reimbursements (averaging $8,000 per year), teaching assistantships with full and partial tuition reimbursements (averaging $8,000 per year) were awarded; fellowships, career-related internships or fieldwork, Federal Work-Study, institutionally sponsored loans, scholarships/grants, and unspecified assistantships also available. In 2006, 26 degrees awarded. *Degree program information:* Part-time and evening/weekend programs available. Offers biology (MS); biomedical sciences (MHS); biostatistics (MS); cell and molecular biology (MS); English (MA); liberal arts and sciences (MA, MHS, MS). *Application fee:* $30. Electronic applications accepted. *Dean,* Dr. Frederick Antczak, 616-331-2261.

School of Communications Students: 13 full-time (10 women), 39 part-time (21 women); includes 9 minority (6 African Americans, 1 American Indian/Alaska Native, 1 Asian American or Pacific Islander, 1 Hispanic American). Average age 33. 20 applicants, 85% accepted, 9 enrolled. *Faculty:* 4 full-time (0 women), 2 part-time/adjunct (0 women). Expenses: Contact institution. *Financial support:* In 2006–07, 1 student received support, including 1 research assistantship with tuition reimbursement available (averaging $8,000 per year); career-related internships or fieldwork, Federal Work-Study, and institutionally sponsored loans also available. Support available to part-time students. Financial award application deadline: 4/15. In 2006, 18 degrees awarded. *Degree program information:* Part-time and evening/weekend programs available. Offers communications (MS). *Application deadline:* For fall admission, 8/15 priority date for domestic students; for winter admission, 12/15 priority date for domestic students; for spring admission, 4/15 priority date for domestic students. Applications are processed on a rolling basis. *Application fee:* $30. Electronic applications accepted. *Application Contact:* Dr. William Michael Pritchard, Information Contact, 616-331-3668, Fax: 616-331-2700, E-mail: pritchmi@gvsu.edu. *Director,* Dr. Alex Nesterenko, 616-331-3668, Fax: 616-895-2700, E-mail: nesterea@gvsu.edu.

Kirkhof College of Nursing Students: 3 full-time (all women), 46 part-time (42 women); includes 4 minority (1 African American, 1 Asian American or Pacific Islander, 2 Hispanic Americans). Average age 35. 15 applicants, 67% accepted, 8 enrolled. *Faculty:* 17 full-time (all women), 1 (woman) part-time/adjunct. Expenses: Contact institution. *Financial support:* In 2006–07, 7 research assistantships with full and partial tuition reimbursements (averaging $8,000 per year) were awarded; career-related internships or fieldwork, Federal Work-Study, institutionally sponsored loans, and traineeships also available. Financial award application deadline: 2/15. In 2006, 20 degrees awarded. *Degree program information:* Part-time programs available. Offers advanced practice (MSN); case management (MSN); nursing administration (MSN); nursing education (MSN). *Application deadline:* For fall admission, 3/15 priority date for domestic students. Applications are processed on a rolling basis. *Application fee:* $30. Electronic applications accepted. *Application Contact:* Dr. Jean Martin, Director of Graduate Programs, 616-331-7167, Fax: 616-331-7362, E-mail: martinj@gvsu.edu. *Dean,* Dr. Phyllis Gendler, 616-331-7161, Fax: 616-331-7362, E-mail: gendlerp@gvsu.edu.

Padnos College of Engineering and Computing Students: 32 full-time (9 women), 95 part-time (15 women); includes 4 African Americans, 9 Asian Americans or Pacific Islanders, 1 Hispanic American. Average age 29. 106 applicants, 74% accepted, 46 enrolled. *Faculty:* 22 full-time (0 women), 2 part-time/adjunct (0 women). Expenses: Contact institution. *Financial support:* In 2006–07, 5 research assistantships with full and partial tuition reimbursements (averaging $8,000 per year) were awarded; unspecified assistantships also available. In 2006, 17 degrees awarded. *Degree program information:* Part-time programs available. Offers engineering and computing (MS, MSE); medical and bioinformatics (MS). *Application deadline:* For fall admission, 2/1 for domestic students. Applications are processed on a rolling basis. *Application fee:* $30. Electronic applications accepted. *Dean,* Dr. Paul Plotkowski, 616-331-6260, Fax: 616-331-7215, E-mail: plotkowp@gvsu.edu.

School of Computing and Information Systems Students: 13 full-time (6 women), 57 part-time (14 women); includes 9 minority (2 African Americans, 7 Asian Americans or Pacific Islanders). Average age 32. 26 applicants, 96% accepted, 13 enrolled. *Faculty:* 12 full-time (0 women). Expenses: Contact institution. *Financial support:* In 2006–07, 2 research assistantships with full and partial tuition reimbursements (averaging $8,000 per year) were awarded. In 2006, 33 degrees awarded. *Degree program information:* Part-time and evening/weekend programs available. Offers computer information systems (MS). *Application deadline:* For fall admission, 6/1 for international students; for winter admission, 9/1 for international students. Applications are processed on a rolling basis. *Application fee:* $30. Electronic applications accepted. *Application Contact:* D. Robert Adams, CIS Graduate Program Chair, 616-331-3885, Fax: 616-331-2106, E-mail: adams@cis.gvsu.edu. *Director,* Paul Leidig, 616-331-2038, Fax: 616-331-2106, E-mail: leidigp@gvsu.edu.

School of Engineering Students: 17 full-time (4 women), 42 part-time (6 women); includes 4 minority (1 African American, 3 Asian Americans or Pacific Islanders). Average age 28. 57 applicants, 82% accepted, 24 enrolled. *Faculty:* 14 full-time (0 women). Expenses: Contact institution. *Financial support:* In 2006–07, 6 students received support, including 3 research assistantships with full tuition reimbursements available (averaging $11,000 per year), 3 teaching assistantships with full tuition reimbursements available (averaging $8,000 per year); career-related internships or fieldwork, Federal Work-Study, institutionally sponsored loans, scholarships/grants, and unspecified assistantships also available. In 2006, 4 degrees awarded. *Degree program information:* Part-time and evening/weekend programs available. Offers electrical and computer engineering (MSE); manufacturing engineering (MSE);

Grand Valley State University (continued)

manufacturing operations (MSE); mechanical engineering (MSE); product design and manufacturing engineering (MSE). *Application deadline:* Applications are processed on a rolling basis. *Application fee:* $30. Electronic applications accepted. *Application Contact:* Dr. Charlie Standridge, Graduate Director, 616-331-6759, E-mail: standric@gvsu.edu. *Director*, Dr. Jeff Ray, 616-331-6762, Fax: 616-331-7215, E-mail: rayj@gvsu.edu.

Seidman College of Business Students: 80 full-time (35 women), 327 part-time (117 women); includes 20 minority (5 African Americans, 1 American Indian/Alaska Native, 11 Asian Americans or Pacific Islanders, 3 Hispanic Americans), 20 international. Average age 30. 125 applicants, 83% accepted, 83 enrolled. *Faculty:* 25 full-time (3 women), 13 part-time/adjunct (1 woman). Expenses: Contact institution. *Financial support:* In 2006–07, 104 students received support, including 27 research assistantships with full and partial tuition reimbursements available (averaging $4,889 per year); fellowships, Federal Work-Study, institutionally sponsored loans, and unspecified assistantships also available. Support available to part-time students. Financial award application deadline: 2/15; financial award applicants required to submit FAFSA. In 2006, 99 degrees awarded. *Degree program information:* Part-time and evening/weekend programs available. Offers accounting (MSA); business (MBA, MSA, MST); business administration (MBA); taxation (MST). *Application deadline:* For fall admission, 8/1 priority date for domestic students, 5/1 priority date for international students; for winter admission, 12/1 priority date for domestic students, 11/1 priority date for international students; for spring admission, 4/1 priority date for domestic students, 3/1 priority date for international students. Applications are processed on a rolling basis. *Application fee:* $30. Electronic applications accepted. *Application Contact:* Claudia J. Bajema, Director, Graduate Business Programs, 616-331-7387, Fax: 616-331-7389, E-mail: bajemac@gvsu.edu. *Dean*, Dr. H. James Williams, 616-331-7385, Fax: 616-331-7380, E-mail: williahj@gvsu.edu.

See Close-Up on page 903.

GRANTHAM UNIVERSITY, Kansas City, MO 64153

General Information Proprietary, coed, comprehensive institution. *Enrollment:* 9,500 graduate, professional, and undergraduate students; 549 matriculated graduate/professional students. *Enrollment by degree level:* 549 master's. *Student services:* International student services.

Computer facilities: Internet access and online class registration are available. *Web address:* http://www.grantham.edu/.

General Application Contact: DeAnn Wandler, Director of Admissions, 800-955-2527, Fax: 816-595-5757, E-mail: admissions@grantham.edu.

GRADUATE UNITS

College of Computer Science and Engineering Technology Students: 177 full-time. Average age 36. Expenses: Contact institution. *Financial support:* Institutionally sponsored loans and scholarships/grants available. *Degree program information:* Part-time and evening/weekend programs available. Postbaccalaureate distance learning degree programs offered (no on-campus study). Offers information management technology (MS); information technology (MS); project management (MS). *Application deadline:* Applications are processed on a rolling basis. *Application fee:* $0. Electronic applications accepted. *Application Contact:* DeAnn Wandler, Director of Admissions, 800-955-2527, Fax: 816-595-5757, E-mail: admissions@grantham.edu.

Mark Skousen School of Business Students: 372 full-time. Average age 36. *Faculty:* 30. Expenses: Contact institution. *Financial support:* Institutionally sponsored loans and scholarships/grants available. *Degree program information:* Part-time and evening/weekend programs available. Postbaccalaureate distance learning degree programs offered (no on-campus study). Offers information management (MBA); project management (MBA). *Application deadline:* Applications are processed on a rolling basis. *Application fee:* $0. Electronic applications accepted. *Application Contact:* DeAnn Wandler, Director of Admissions, 800-955-2527, Fax: 816-595-5757, E-mail: admissions@grantham.edu.

GRATZ COLLEGE, Melrose Park, PA 19027

General Information Independent-religious, coed, comprehensive institution. *Graduate housing:* On-campus housing not available.

GRADUATE UNITS

Graduate Programs *Degree program information:* Part-time and evening/weekend programs available. Postbaccalaureate distance learning degree programs offered (minimal on-campus study). Offers classical studies (MA); education (MA); Israel studies (Certificate); Jewish communal studies (MA, Certificate); Jewish education (MA, Certificate); Jewish music (MA, Certificate); Jewish studies (MA); Judaica librarianship (Certificate); modern studies (MA).

GREEN MOUNTAIN COLLEGE, Poultney, VT 05764-1199

General Information Independent, coed, comprehensive institution. *Enrollment:* 759 graduate, professional, and undergraduate students; 30 full-time matriculated graduate/professional students (18 women). *Enrollment by degree level:* 30 master's. *Graduate faculty:* 23 full-time (6 women), 5 part-time/adjunct (1 woman). *Tuition:* Part-time $550 per credit. Tuition and fees vary according to program. *Student services:* Career counseling, grant writing training. *Library facilities:* Griswold Library. *Online resources:* library catalog, web page, access to other libraries' catalogs. *Collection:* 95,140 titles, 296 serial subscriptions, 672 audiovisual materials.

Computer facilities: 80 computers available on campus for general student use. A campuswide network can be accessed from student residence rooms and from off campus. Internet access and online class registration, personal network folders, electronic course folders are available. *Web address:* http://www.greenmtn.edu/.

General Application Contact: Susan Whiting, Administrative Assistant, 802-287-8319, E-mail: masters@greenmtn.edu.

GRADUATE UNITS

Program in Business Administration Students: 13 full-time (10 women). Average age 35. 20 applicants, 70% accepted, 13 enrolled. *Faculty:* 8 full-time (1 woman), 3 part-time/adjunct (1 woman). Expenses: Contact institution. *Financial support:* In 2006–07, 3 students received support. Postbaccalaureate distance learning degree programs offered (no on-campus study). Offers business administration (MBA). Distance learning only. *Application deadline:* Applications are processed on a rolling basis. *Application fee:* $30. Electronic applications accepted. *Application Contact:* Susan Whiting, Administrative Assistant, 802-287-8319, E-mail: mba@greenmtn.edu. *Director of MBA*, Dr. William H. Prado, 802-287-8241, E-mail: pradow@greenmtn.edu.

Program in Environmental Studies Students: 18 full-time (8 women). 80 applicants, 30% accepted, 18 enrolled. *Faculty:* 15 full-time (5 women), 2 part-time/adjunct (0 women). Expenses: Contact institution. *Financial support:* In 2006–07, 1 student received support. *Degree program information:* Part-time and evening/weekend programs available. Postbaccalaureate distance learning degree programs offered (no on-campus study). Offers environmental studies (MS). Distance learning only. *Application deadline:* Applications are processed on a rolling basis. *Application fee:* $30. Electronic applications accepted. *Application Contact:* Susan Whiting, Administrative Assistant, 802-287-8319, E-mail: masters@greenmtn.edu. *Program Director*, Dr. Laird Christensen, 802-287-8344, E-mail: christensenl@greenmtn.edu.

See Close-Up on page 905.

GREENSBORO COLLEGE, Greensboro, NC 27401-1875

General Information Independent-religious, coed, comprehensive institution. *Enrollment:* 1 (woman) full-time matriculated graduate/professional student, 30 part-time matriculated graduate/professional students (26 women). *Enrollment by degree level:* 31 master's. *Graduate faculty:* 8 full-time (7 women). *Tuition:* Part-time $275 per credit hour. *Required fees:* $30 per semester. *Graduate housing:* Rooms and/or apartments guaranteed to single and married students. Housing application deadline: 6/1. *Student services:* Career counseling, free psychological counseling, international student services, teacher training, writing training. *Library facilities:* James Addison Jones Library. *Online resources:* library catalog, web page, access to other libraries' catalogs. *Collection:* 108,350 titles, 290 serial subscriptions, 2,686 audiovisual materials.

Computer facilities: 120 computers available on campus for general student use. A campuswide network can be accessed from student residence rooms and from off campus. Internet access, online course support are available. *Web address:* http://www.gborocollege.edu/.

General Application Contact: Dr. Rebecca Blomgren, Dean of Graduate and Professional Studies, 336-272-7102, Fax: 336-271-6634, E-mail: blomgrenr@gborocollege.edu.

GRADUATE UNITS

Program in Education Students: 2 full-time (both women), 16 part-time (all women); includes 2 minority (1 African American, 1 Hispanic American). 5 applicants, 40% accepted, 2 enrolled. *Faculty:* 4 full-time (3 women). Expenses: Contact institution. *Financial support:* In 2006–07, 12 students received support. Scholarships/grants available. Support available to part-time students. In 2006, 12 degrees awarded. *Degree program information:* Part-time and evening/weekend programs available. Offers elementary education (M Ed); special education (M Ed). *Application deadline:* For fall admission, 3/15 for domestic students. Applications are processed on a rolling basis. *Application fee:* $35. Electronic applications accepted. *Dean of Graduate and Professional Studies*, Dr. Rebecca Blomgren, 336-272-7102, Fax: 336-271-6634, E-mail: blomgrenr@gborocollege.edu.

Program in Teaching English to Speakers of Other Languages Average age 35. 4 applicants, 75% accepted, 2 enrolled. *Faculty:* 3 full-time (2 women). Expenses: Contact institution. *Financial support:* In 2006–07, 11 students received support. Scholarships/grants available. Support available to part-time students. Financial award applicants required to submit FAFSA. In 2006, 14 degrees awarded. *Degree program information:* Part-time and evening/weekend programs available. Offers teaching English to speakers of other languages (MA). *Application deadline:* For fall admission, 3/15 for domestic students. Applications are processed on a rolling basis. *Application fee:* $35. Electronic applications accepted. *Application Contact:* Office of Graduate and Professional Studies, 336-272-7102, E-mail: adults@gborocollege.edu. *Graduate and Professional Studies*, Dr. Rebecca Blomgren, 336-272-7102, Fax: 336-271-6634, E-mail: blomgrenc@gborocollege.edu.

GREENVILLE COLLEGE, Greenville, IL 62246-0159

General Information Independent-religious, coed, comprehensive institution. *Graduate housing:* On-campus housing not available.

GRADUATE UNITS

Program in Education Offers education (MAT); elementary education (MAE); secondary education (MAE). Electronic applications accepted.

Program in Leadership and Ministry *Degree program information:* Part-time programs available. Offers leadership and ministry (MA). Electronic applications accepted.

GWYNEDD-MERCY COLLEGE, Gwynedd Valley, PA 19437-0901

General Information Independent-religious, coed, comprehensive institution. *Enrollment:* 2,727 graduate, professional, and undergraduate students; 100 full-time matriculated graduate/professional students (72 women), 492 part-time matriculated graduate/professional students (400 women). *Enrollment by degree level:* 592 master's. *Graduate faculty:* 13 full-time (9 women), 26 part-time/adjunct (13 women). *Tuition:* Part-time $525 per credit hour. *Graduate housing:* On-campus housing not available. *Student services:* Campus employment opportunities, career counseling, international student services, low-cost health insurance, teacher training. *Library facilities:* Lourdes Library plus 1 other. *Online resources:* library catalog, web page, access to other libraries' catalogs. *Collection:* 101,552 titles, 667 serial subscriptions, 11,107 audiovisual materials.

Computer facilities: Computer purchase and lease plans are available. 97 computers available on campus for general student use. A campuswide network can be accessed from student residence rooms and from off campus. Internet access is available. *Web address:* http://www.gmc.edu/.

General Application Contact: Information Contact, 800-342-5462, Fax: 215-641-5556.

GRADUATE UNITS

School of Business and Computer Information Sciences Offers business and computer information sciences (MSM).

School of Education Students: 92 full-time (66 women), 464 part-time (374 women); includes 52 minority (49 African Americans, 3 Hispanic Americans), 1 international. Average age 34. *Faculty:* 9 full-time (5 women), 37 part-time/adjunct (17 women). Expenses: Contact institution. *Financial support:* In 2006–07, 2 research assistantships were awarded; career-related internships or fieldwork, Federal Work-Study, tuition waivers (full and partial), and unspecified assistantships also available. Financial award applicants required to submit FAFSA. In 2006, 160 degrees awarded. *Degree program information:* Part-time and evening/weekend programs available. Offers educational administration (MS); master teacher (MS); reading (MS); school counseling (MS); special education (MS). *Application deadline:* Applications are processed on a rolling basis. *Application fee:* $25. *Application Contact:* Marian Watkins, Graduate Program Coordinator, 215-641-5561, Fax: 215-542-4695, E-mail: watkins.m@gmc.edu. *Dean*, Dr. Lorraine Cavaliere, EdD, 215-641-5549, Fax: 215-542-4695, E-mail: cavaliere.l@gmc.edu.

School of Nursing Students: 7 full-time (5 women), 38 part-time (35 women); includes 3 minority (1 African American, 1 Asian American or Pacific Islander, 1 Hispanic American). Average age 41. 18 applicants, 89% accepted, 11 enrolled. *Faculty:* 5 full-time (all women), 3 part-time/adjunct (2 women). Expenses: Contact institution. *Financial support:* In 2006–07, 21 students received support. Scholarships/grants, traineeships, and unspecified assistantships available. Financial award application deadline: 8/30. In 2006, 5 degrees awarded. Offers clinical nurse specialist (MSN); nurse practitioner (MSN). *Application deadline:* For fall admission, 8/1 priority date for domestic students; for winter admission, 12/1 priority date for domestic students. Applications are processed on a rolling basis. *Application fee:* $25. Electronic applications accepted. *Application Contact:* Dr. Barbara A. Jones, Director, 215-646-7300 Ext. 407, Fax: 215-641-5564, E-mail: jones.b@gmc.edu. *Dean*, Dr. Andrea D. Hollingsworth, 215-646-7300 Ext. 539, Fax: 215-641-5517, E-mail: hollingsworth.a@gmc.edu.

HAMLINE UNIVERSITY, St. Paul, MN 55104-1284

General Information Independent-religious, coed, comprehensive institution. *Enrollment:* 4,575 graduate, professional, and undergraduate students; 1,158 full-time matriculated graduate/professional students (655 women), 1,144 part-time matriculated graduate/professional students (873 women). *Enrollment by degree level:* 725 first professional, 1,499 master's, 62 doctoral, 16 other advanced degrees. *Graduate faculty:* 78 full-time (44 women), 185 part-time/adjunct (119 women). *Tuition:* Full-time $5,104; part-time $319 per credit. One-time fee: $175. Tuition and fees vary according to course load, degree level and program. *Graduate housing:* Rooms and/or apartments available on a first-come, first-served basis to single and married students. Typical cost: $7,906 per year ($9,306 including board) for single students; $8,238 per year ($9,638 including board) for married students. Room and board charges vary according to board plan and housing facility selected. Housing application deadline: 5/1. *Student services:* Campus employment opportunities, campus safety program, career counseling, disabled student services, free psychological counseling, international student services, low-cost health insurance, multicultural affairs office, teacher training, writing training. *Library facilities:* Bush Library plus 1 other. *Online resources:* library catalog, web page, access to other libraries' catalogs. *Collection:* 228,973 titles, 1,681 serial subscriptions, 4,886 audiovisual materials. *Research affiliation:* Minnesota Women Elected Officials.

Computer facilities: 130 computers available on campus for general student use. A campuswide network can be accessed from student residence rooms and from off campus. Internet access and online class registration are available. *Web address:* http://www.hamline.edu/.

General Application Contact: Rae A. Lenway, Director Graduate Recruitment and Admission, 651-523-2592, Fax: 651-523-3058, E-mail: rlenway01@hamline.edu.

GRADUATE UNITS

Graduate School of Education Students: 224 full-time (165 women), 836 part-time (659 women); includes 60 minority (16 African Americans, 5 American Indian/Alaska Native, 30 Asian Americans or Pacific Islanders, 9 Hispanic Americans), 10 international. Average age 35. 332 applicants, 90% accepted, 254 enrolled. *Faculty:* 22 full-time (15 women), 74 part-time/adjunct (55 women). Expenses: Contact institution. *Financial support:* Federal Work-Study available. Financial award applicants required to submit FAFSA. In 2006, 156 master's, 9 doctorates awarded. *Degree program information:* Part-time and evening/weekend programs available. Offers education (MA Ed, MAESL, MAT, Ed D). *Application deadline:* For fall admission, 6/15 priority date for domestic students; for spring admission, 6/1 priority date for domestic students. Applications are processed on a rolling basis. *Application fee:* $30. *Application Contact:* Director, Graduate Admission, 651-523-2900, Fax: 651-523-2458, E-mail: gradprog@hamline.edu. *Interim Dean,* Mary K. Boyd, 651-523-2900, Fax: 651-523-2458, E-mail: mmurrayboyd01@hamline.edu.

Graduate School of Liberal Studies Students: 32 full-time (23 women), 156 part-time (119 women); includes 7 minority (3 African Americans, 1 American Indian/Alaska Native, 1 Asian American or Pacific Islander, 2 Hispanic Americans), 4 international. Average age 37. 72 applicants, 64% accepted, 39 enrolled. *Faculty:* 5 full-time (4 women), 9 part-time/adjunct (6 women). Expenses: Contact institution. *Financial support:* Federal Work-Study available. Financial award applicants required to submit FAFSA. In 2006, 42 degrees awarded. *Degree program information:* Part-time and evening/weekend programs available. Offers liberal studies (MALS, MFA, CALS). *Application deadline:* For fall admission, 3/1 priority date for domestic students; for spring admission, 9/1 priority date for domestic students. Applications are processed on a rolling basis. *Application fee:* $30. Electronic applications accepted. *Application Contact:* Rae A. Lenway, Director Graduate Recruitment and Admission, 651-523-2592, Fax: 3-2458, E-mail: rlenway01@hamline.edu. *Dean,* Mary Francóis Rockcastle, 651-523-2901, Fax: 651-523-2490, E-mail: mrockcastle@hamline.edu.

Graduate School of Management Students: 184 full-time (101 women), 145 part-time (87 women); includes 29 minority (14 African Americans, 2 American Indian/Alaska Native, 9 Asian Americans or Pacific Islanders, 4 Hispanic Americans), 65 international. Average age 33. 145 applicants, 72% accepted, 86 enrolled. *Faculty:* 10 full-time (5 women), 29 part-time/adjunct (13 women). Expenses: Contact institution. *Financial support:* Federal Work-Study available. Financial award applicants required to submit FAFSA. In 2006, 92 master's awarded. *Degree program information:* Part-time and evening/weekend programs available. Offers management (MAM); nonprofit management (MANM); public administration (MAPA). *Application deadline:* For fall admission, 3/30 priority date for domestic students. Applications are processed on a rolling basis. *Application fee:* $30. Electronic applications accepted. *Application Contact:* Rae A. Lenway, Director Graduate Recruitment and Admission, 651-523-2592, Fax: 458, E-mail: rlenway01@hamline.edu. *Dean,* Julian Schuster, 651-523-2335, Fax: 651-523-3098, E-mail: jschuster01@hamline.edu.

School of Law Students: 498 full-time (257 women), 218 part-time (112 women); includes 91 minority (22 African Americans, 4 American Indian/Alaska Native, 36 Asian Americans or Pacific Islanders, 29 Hispanic Americans), 7 international. Average age 28. 1,510 applicants, 47% accepted, 250 enrolled. *Faculty:* 44 full-time (20 women), 55 part-time/adjunct (21 women). Expenses: Contact institution. *Financial support:* In 2006–07, 669 students received support, including 20 fellowships with full and partial tuition reimbursements available (averaging $3,000 per year); career-related internships or fieldwork, Federal Work-Study, and scholarships/grants also available. Support available to part-time students. Financial award applicants required to submit FAFSA. In 2006, 184 first professional degrees, 9 master's awarded. *Degree program information:* Part-time and evening/weekend programs available. Offers law (JD, LL M). *Application deadline:* For fall admission, 5/1 priority date for domestic students. Applications are processed on a rolling basis. *Application fee:* $40. Electronic applications accepted. *Application Contact:* Robin C. Ingli, Director of Admissions, 800-388-3688, Fax: 651-523-3064, E-mail: ringli@hamline.edu. *Dean,* Jon M. Garon, 651-523-2968, Fax: 651-523-2435, E-mail: jgaron@hamline.edu.

HAMPTON UNIVERSITY, Hampton, VA 23668

General Information Independent, coed, university. CGS member. *Graduate housing:* Rooms and/or apartments available to single and married students. Housing application deadline: 6/1. *Research affiliation:* NASA–Langley Research Center (physical sciences), Southeastern Universities Research Association (science), Continuous Electron Beam Accelerator Facility (science).

GRADUATE UNITS

Graduate College *Degree program information:* Part-time and evening/weekend programs available. Offers applied mathematics (MS); biological sciences (MA, MS); business (MBA); chemistry (MS); college student development (MA); communicative sciences and disorders (MA); community agency counseling (MA); computer science (MS); counseling (MA); elementary education (MA); museum studies (MA); nursing (MS); physical therapy (DPT); physics (MS, PhD); special education (MA); teaching (MT).

See Close-Up on page 907.

HARDING UNIVERSITY, Searcy, AR 72149-0001

General Information Independent-religious, coed, comprehensive institution. *Enrollment:* 6,085 graduate, professional, and undergraduate students; 305 full-time matriculated graduate/professional students (217 women), 564 part-time matriculated graduate/professional students (370 women). *Enrollment by degree level:* 869 master's. *Graduate faculty:* 16 full-time (3 women), 87 part-time/adjunct (36 women). *Tuition:* Part-time $455 per semester hour. *Required fees:* $20 per semester hour. Tuition and fees vary according to course load. *Graduate housing:* Rooms and/or apartments available on a first-come, first-served basis to single and married students. Housing application deadline: 3/30. *Student services:* Campus employment opportunities, campus safety program, career counseling, disabled student services, exercise/wellness program, free psychological counseling, international student services, writing training. *Library facilities:* Brackett Library plus 1 other. *Online resources:* library catalog, web page, access to other libraries' catalogs. *Collection:* 230,499 titles, 16,582 serial subscriptions, 9,153 audiovisual materials.

Computer facilities: 327 computers available on campus for general student use. A campuswide network can be accessed from student residence rooms and from off campus. Internet access and online class registration are available. *Web address:* http://www.harding.edu/.

General Application Contact: Dr. Larry Long, Vice President, Academic Affairs, 501-279-4335, Fax: 501-279-5192, E-mail: vpaa@harding.edu.

GRADUATE UNITS

College of Bible and Religion Students: 24 full-time (14 women), 23 part-time (1 woman); includes 1 minority (African American), 1 international. Average age 31. 39 applicants, 62% accepted, 21 enrolled. *Faculty:* 4 full-time (0 women), 12 part-time/adjunct (2 women). Expenses: Contact institution. *Financial support:* Career-related internships or fieldwork, Federal Work-Study, institutionally sponsored loans, and scholarships/grants available. Financial award application deadline: 4/1. In 2006, 13 degrees awarded. *Degree program information:* Part-time programs available. Offers Bible and religion (M Min, MS); marriage and family therapy (MS); mental health counseling (MS); ministry (M Min). *Application fee:* $25. *Dean,* Bruce McLarty, 501-279-4449, Fax: 501-279-4042, E-mail: bmclarty@harding.edu.

College of Business Administration Students: 88 full-time (50 women), 72 part-time (28 women); includes 14 minority (10 African Americans, 2 American Indian/Alaska Native, 2 Hispanic Americans), 44 international. Average age 28. 70 applicants, 100% accepted, 55 enrolled. *Faculty:* 27 part-time/adjunct (3 women). Expenses: Contact institution. *Financial support:* Unspecified assistantships available. Financial award application deadline: 7/30; financial award applicants required to submit FAFSA. In 2006, 39 degrees awarded. *Degree program information:* Part-time and evening/weekend programs available. Postbaccalaureate distance learning degree programs offered (no on-campus study). Offers business administration (MBA). *Application deadline:* For fall admission, 8/1 priority date for domestic and international students; for spring admission, 12/1 priority date for domestic and international students. *Application fee:* $35. Electronic applications accepted. *Application Contact:* Suzanne Guymon, Marketing Manager, 501-279-5726, Fax: 501-279-4805, E-mail: sguymon1@harding.edu. *Director of Graduate Studies,* Allen Figley, 501-279-5790, Fax: 501-279-4805, E-mail: afigley@harding.edu.

College of Education Students: 153 full-time (123 women), 469 part-time (341 women); includes 72 minority (63 African Americans, 4 American Indian/Alaska Native, 1 Asian American or Pacific Islander, 4 Hispanic Americans), 9 international. Average age 35. 175 applicants, 90% accepted, 147 enrolled. *Faculty:* 8 full-time (2 women), 45 part-time/adjunct (30 women). Expenses: Contact institution. *Financial support:* Scholarships/grants and unspecified assistantships available. Support available to part-time students. In 2006, 241 degrees awarded. *Degree program information:* Part-time programs available. Offers advanced studies in teaching and learning (M Ed); art (MSE); behavioral science (MSE); Bible and religion (MSE); counseling (MS, Ed S); early childhood education (M Ed); early childhood special education (M Ed, MSE); education (MSE); educational leadership (M Ed, Ed S); elementary education (M Ed); English (MSE); family and consumer science (MSE); French (MSE); history/social science (MSE); kinesiology (MSE); math (MSE); physical science (MSE); reading (M Ed); secondary education (M Ed); Spanish (MSE); special education licensure (M Ed); teaching (MAT). *Application deadline:* For fall admission, 8/1 for domestic and international students; for spring admission, 1/1 for domestic and international students. Applications are processed on a rolling basis. *Application fee:* $35. *Chair,* Pat Bashaw, 501-279-4183, Fax: 501-279-4051, E-mail: pbashaw@harding.edu.

HARDING UNIVERSITY GRADUATE SCHOOL OF RELIGION, Memphis, TN 38117-5499

General Information Independent-religious, coed, primarily men, graduate-only institution. *Enrollment by degree level:* 84 first professional, 71 master's, 19 doctoral. *Graduate faculty:* 8 full-time (0 women), 12 part-time/adjunct (1 woman). *Tuition:* Part-time $455 per semester hour. *Required fees:* $20 per semester hour. $14 per term. *Graduate housing:* Rooms and/or apartments available to single and married students. *Student services:* Career counseling, low-cost health insurance. *Library facilities:* L. M. Graves Memorial Library. *Online resources:* library catalog, web page, access to other libraries' catalogs. *Collection:* 136,000 titles, 595 serial subscriptions, 2,638 audiovisual materials.

Computer facilities: 15 computers available on campus for general student use. Internet access and online class registration are available. *Web address:* http://www.hugsr.edu/.

General Application Contact: Mark K. Parker, Director of Admissions, 901-761-1356, Fax: 901-761-1358, E-mail: mparker@hugsr.edu.

GRADUATE UNITS

Graduate Programs Students: 45 full-time (9 women), 129 part-time (18 women); includes 26 minority (23 African Americans, 2 Asian Americans or Pacific Islanders, 1 Hispanic American), 2 international. Average age 35. 49 applicants, 71% accepted, 26 enrolled. *Faculty:* 8 full-time (0 women), 12 part-time/adjunct (1 woman). Expenses: Contact institution. *Financial support:* In 2006–07, 168 students received support, including 7 fellowships with partial tuition reimbursements available (averaging $3,000 per year), 4 research assistantships with partial tuition reimbursements available (averaging $3,000 per year); career-related internships or fieldwork, institutionally sponsored loans, scholarships/grants, tuition waivers (partial), and unspecified assistantships also available. Support available to part-time students. Financial award application deadline: 3/1; financial award applicants required to submit FAFSA. In 2006, 13 first professional degrees, 20 master's, 3 doctorates awarded. *Degree program information:* Part-time programs available. Postbaccalaureate distance learning degree programs offered (minimal on-campus study). *Application deadline:* For fall admission, 12/7 priority date for domestic students; for spring admission, 5/3 priority date for domestic students. Applications are processed on a rolling basis. *Application fee:* $40. Electronic applications accepted. *Application Contact:* Mark K. Parker, Director of Admissions, 901-761-1356, Fax: 901-761-1358, E-mail: mparker@hugsr.edu. *Vice President and Dean,* Dr. Evertt W. Huffard, 901-761-1352, Fax: 901-761-1358, E-mail: dean@hugsr.edu.

HARDIN-SIMMONS UNIVERSITY, Abilene, TX 79698-0001

General Information Independent-religious, coed, comprehensive institution. *Enrollment:* 2,372 graduate, professional, and undergraduate students; 204 full-time matriculated graduate/professional students (106 women), 187 part-time matriculated graduate/professional students (98 women). *Enrollment by degree level:* 96 first professional, 218 master's, 77 doctoral. *Graduate faculty:* 74 full-time (28 women), 17 part-time/adjunct (5 women). *Tuition:* Full-time $9,090; part-time $505 per hour. *Required fees:* $490; $66 per semester. One-time fee: $50. Tuition and fees vary according to course load and degree level. *Graduate housing:* Rooms and/or apartments available on a first-come, first-served basis to single and married students. Typical cost: $2,365 per year ($4,580 including board) for single students; $2,365 per year ($4,580 including board) for married students. Room and board charges vary according to board plan and housing facility selected. *Student services:* Campus employment opportunities, career counseling, free psychological counseling. *Library facilities:* Richardson Library plus 1 other. *Online resources:* library catalog, web page, access to other libraries' catalogs. *Collection:* 245,587 titles, 36,225 serial subscriptions, 10,767 audiovisual materials.

Computer facilities: 224 computers available on campus for general student use. A campuswide network can be accessed from student residence rooms and from off campus. Internet access is available. *Web address:* http://www.hsutx.edu/.

General Application Contact: Dr. Gary Stanlake, Dean of Graduate Studies, 325-670-1298, Fax: 325-670-1564, E-mail: gradoff@hsutx.edu.

GRADUATE UNITS

The Acton MBA in Entrepreneurship Expenses: Contact institution. Offers entrepreneurship (MBA). *Application deadline:* For fall admission, 3/15 priority date for domestic students. *Application fee:* $50. *Application Contact:* Jessica Blanchard, Director of Recruiting, 512-703-1231, E-mail: jblanchard@actonmba.org.

Graduate School Students: 204 full-time (106 women), 187 part-time (98 women); includes 33 minority (6 African Americans, 2 American Indian/Alaska Native, 5 Asian Americans or Pacific Islanders, 20 Hispanic Americans), 2 international. Average age 31. 129 applicants, 98% accepted, 105 enrolled. *Faculty:* 74 full-time (28 women), 17 part-time/adjunct (5 women). Expenses: Contact institution. *Financial support:* In 2006–07, 290 students received support, including 54 fellowships (averaging $1,126 per year); career-related internships or fieldwork, scholarships/grants, unspecified assistantships, and recreation assistantships, coaching assistantships also available. Support available to part-time students. Financial award application deadline: 6/30; financial award applicants required to submit FAFSA. In 2006, 16 first professional degrees, 89 master's awarded. *Degree program information:* Part-time programs available. Offers English (MA); family psychology (MA); history (MA); liberal arts (MA); religion (MA); theology (MA). *Application deadline:* For fall admission, 8/15 priority date for domestic students; for spring admission, 1/5 priority date for domestic students. Applications are processed on a rolling basis. *Application fee:* $50 ($100 for international students). *Dean of Graduate Studies,* Dr. Gary Stanlake, 325-670-1298, Fax: 325-670-1564, E-mail: gradoff@hsutx.edu.

Holland School of Sciences and Mathematics Students: 5 full-time (4 women), 5 part-time (2 women), 1 international. Average age 38. 2 applicants, 100% accepted, 2 enrolled. *Faculty:* 4 full-time (1 woman). Expenses: Contact institution. *Financial support:* In 2006–07, 10 students received support, including 1 fellowship (averaging $1,200 per year); career-related internships or fieldwork and scholarships/grants also available. Support available to part-time students. Financial award application deadline: 6/30; financial award applicants required to submit FAFSA. In 2006, 4 degrees awarded. *Degree program information:* Part-time programs available. Offers environmental management (MS); physical therapy (DPT); sciences and mathematics (MS, DPT). *Application deadline:* For fall admission, 8/15 priority date for domestic students; for spring admission, 1/5 priority date

Hardin-Simmons University (continued)

for domestic students. Applications are processed on a rolling basis. *Application fee:* $50 ($100 for international students). *Application Contact:* Dr. Gary Stanlake, Dean of Graduate Studies, 325-670-1298, Fax: 325-670-1564, E-mail: gradoff@hsutx.edu. *Dean,* Dr. Christopher McNair, 325-670-1401, Fax: 325-670-1385, E-mail: cmcnair@hsutx.edu.

Irvin School of Education Students: 34 full-time (23 women), 74 part-time (56 women); includes 17 minority (5 African Americans, 2 Asian Americans or Pacific Islanders, 10 Hispanic Americans). Average age 32. 47 applicants, 100% accepted, 38 enrolled. *Faculty:* 9 full-time (4 women), 4 part-time/adjunct (1 woman). Expenses: Contact institution. *Financial support:* In 2006–07, 101 students received support, including 29 fellowships (averaging $1,062 per year); career-related internships or fieldwork, scholarships/grants, unspecified assistantships, and coaching assistantships also available. Support available to part-time students. Financial award application deadline: 6/30; financial award applicants required to submit FAFSA. In 2006, 55 degrees awarded. *Degree program information:* Part-time programs available. Offers advanced physical education (M Ed); counseling and human development (M Ed); education (M Ed); gifted education (M Ed); reading specialist (M Ed); sports and recreation management (M Ed). *Application deadline:* For fall admission, 8/15 priority date for domestic students; for spring admission, 1/5 priority date for domestic students. Applications are processed on a rolling basis. *Application fee:* $50 ($100 for international students). *Application Contact:* Dr. Gary Stanlake, Dean of Graduate Studies, 325-670-1298, Fax: 325-670-1564, E-mail: gradoff@hsutx.edu. *Dean,* Dr. Pam Williford, 325-670-1347, Fax: 325-670-5859, E-mail: pwilliford@hsutx.edu.

Kelley College of Business Students: 4 full-time (1 woman), 18 part-time (8 women); includes 1 minority (American Indian/Alaska Native). Average age 34. 13 applicants, 85% accepted, 8 enrolled. *Faculty:* 7 full-time (1 woman), 1 part-time/adjunct (0 women). Expenses: Contact institution. *Financial support:* In 2006–07, 22 students received support; fellowships, scholarships/grants available. Support available to part-time students. Financial award application deadline: 6/30; financial award applicants required to submit FAFSA. In 2006, 5 degrees awarded. *Degree program information:* Part-time and evening/weekend programs available. Offers business (MBA). *Application deadline:* For fall admission, 8/15 priority date for domestic students; for spring admission, 1/5 priority date for domestic students. Applications are processed on a rolling basis. *Application fee:* $50 ($100 for international students). *Application Contact:* Dr. Gary Stanlake, Dean of Graduate Studies, 325-670-1298, Fax: 325-670-1564, E-mail: gradoff@hsutx.edu. *Director,* Dr. Charles Walts, 325-670-1293, Fax: 325-670-1523, E-mail: cwalts@hsutx.edu.

Logsdon Seminary Students: 62 full-time (12 women), 55 part-time (10 women); includes 8 minority (1 American Indian/Alaska Native, 1 Asian American or Pacific Islander, 6 Hispanic Americans), 1 international. Average age 32. 43 applicants, 100% accepted, 40 enrolled. *Faculty:* 11 full-time (1 woman), 7 part-time/adjunct (1 woman). Expenses: Contact institution. *Financial support:* In 2006–07, 97 students received support, including 7 fellowships (averaging $1,200 per year); scholarships/grants also available. Support available to part-time students. Financial award application deadline: 6/30; financial award applicants required to submit FAFSA. In 2006, 16 first professional degrees, 4 master's awarded. *Degree program information:* Part-time and evening/weekend programs available. Offers family ministry (MA); theology (M Div). *Application deadline:* For fall admission, 8/15 priority date for domestic students; for spring admission, 1/5 priority date for domestic students. Applications are processed on a rolling basis. *Application fee:* $50 ($100 for international students). *Application Contact:* Dr. Gary Stanlake, Dean of Graduate Studies, 325-670-1298, Fax: 325-670-1564, E-mail: gradoff@hsutx.edu. *Dean,* Dr. Thomas Brisco, 325-670-1266, Fax: 325-670-1406, E-mail: tbrisco@hsutx.edu.

School of Music Students: 6 full-time (1 woman), 2 part-time. Average age 27. 3 applicants, 100% accepted, 1 enrolled. *Faculty:* 12 full-time (6 women). Expenses: Contact institution. *Financial support:* In 2006–07, 5 fellowships (averaging $1,200 per year) were awarded; career-related internships or fieldwork and scholarships/grants also available. Support available to part-time students. Financial award application deadline: 6/30; financial award applicants required to submit FAFSA. In 2006, 2 degrees awarded. *Degree program information:* Part-time programs available. Offers church music (MM); music education (MM); music performance (MM); theory-composition (MM). *Application deadline:* For fall admission, 8/15 priority date for domestic students; for spring admission, 1/5 priority date for domestic students. Applications are processed on a rolling basis. *Application fee:* $50 ($100 for international students). *Application Contact:* Dr. Gary Stanlake, Dean of Graduate Studies, 325-670-1298, Fax: 325-670-1564, E-mail: gradoff@hsutx.edu. *Director,* Dr. Leigh Anne Hunsaker, 325-670-1391, Fax: 325-670-5873, E-mail: hunsaker@hsutx.edu.

School of Nursing Students: 1 full-time (0 women), 8 part-time (6 women). Average age 39. 5 applicants, 100% accepted, 3 enrolled. *Faculty:* 5 full-time (all women). Expenses: Contact institution. *Financial support:* In 2006–07, 8 students received support. Career-related internships or fieldwork and scholarships/grants available. Support available to part-time students. Financial award application deadline: 6/30; financial award applicants required to submit FAFSA. In 2006, 2 degrees awarded. *Degree program information:* Part-time programs available. Offers advanced healthcare delivery (MSN); family nurse practitioner (MSN). *Application deadline:* For fall admission, 8/15 priority date for domestic students; for spring admission, 1/5 priority date for domestic students. Applications are processed on a rolling basis. *Application fee:* $50 ($100 for international students). *Application Contact:* Dr. Gary Stanlake, Dean of Graduate Studies, 325-670-1298, Fax: 325-670-1564, E-mail: gradoff@hsutx.edu. *Dean,* Dr. Janet Noles, 325-672-2441, Fax: 325-670-1564, E-mail: jnoles@hsutx.edu.

HARRISBURG UNIVERSITY OF SCIENCE AND TECHNOLOGY, Harrisburg, PA 17101

General Information Independent, coed, comprehensive institution.

GRADUATE UNITS

Graduate Studies Offers computer and information science (Graduate Certificate); information technology project management (MA).

HARTFORD SEMINARY, Hartford, CT 06105-2279

General Information Independent-religious, coed, graduate-only institution. *Graduate faculty:* 31. *Tuition:* Part-time $1,460 per course. *Graduate housing:* On-campus housing not available. *Student services:* Campus employment opportunities, career counseling, international student services, writing training. *Online resources:* library catalog, web page. *Collection:* 72,000 titles, 310 serial subscriptions, 280 audiovisual materials.

Computer facilities: 7 computers available on campus for general student use. A campuswide network can be accessed from off campus. Internet access is available. *Web address:* http://www.hartsem.edu/.

General Application Contact: Marcia Pavao, Administrative Assistant, Admissions, 860-509-9512, Fax: 860-509-9509, E-mail: pavao@hartsem.edu.

GRADUATE UNITS

Graduate Programs Students: 34 full-time (16 women), 139 part-time (80 women); includes 40 minority (30 African Americans, 7 Asian Americans or Pacific Islanders, 3 Hispanic Americans), 22 international. *Faculty:* 12 full-time (5 women), 19 part-time/adjunct (7 women). Expenses: Contact institution. *Financial support:* In 2006–07, 33 students received support. Scholarships/grants and tuition waivers (partial) available. Support available to part-time students. Financial award application deadline: 6/1. *Degree program information:* Part-time and evening/weekend programs available. Postbaccalaureate distance learning degree programs offered (no on-campus study). Offers black ministry (Certificate); Islamic studies (MA); ministerios Hispanos (Certificate); ministry (D Min); religious studies (MA); women's leadership institute (Certificate). *Application deadline:* For fall admission, 7/15 priority date for domestic students, 8/10 priority date for international students; for winter admission, 12/1 priority date for domestic and international students; for spring admission, 4/5 priority date for domestic students, 5/1 priority date for international students. Applications are processed on a rolling basis. *Application fee:* $40. *Application Contact:* Dr. Vanessa Avery-Wall, Admissions and Student Support Manager, 860-509-9552, Fax: 860-509-9509, E-mail: vaw@hartsem.edu. *Interim Dean,* Dr. Efrain Agosto, 860-509-9554, E-mail: eagosto@hartsem.edu.

HARVARD UNIVERSITY, Cambridge, MA 02138

General Information Independent, coed, university. CGS member. *Enrollment:* 19,538 graduate, professional, and undergraduate students; 12,034 full-time matriculated graduate/professional students (5,674 women), 980 part-time matriculated graduate/professional students (506 women). *Enrollment by degree level:* 2,813 first professional, 5,364 master's, 4,424 doctoral, 413 other advanced degrees. *Graduate faculty:* 2,497. *Tuition:* Full-time $30,275. Full-time tuition and fees vary according to program and student level. *Graduate housing:* Rooms and/or apartments available to single and married students. Housing application deadline: 5/1. *Student services:* Campus employment opportunities, campus safety program, career counseling, child daycare facilities, disabled student services, exercise/wellness program, free psychological counseling, grant writing training, international student services, low-cost health insurance, multicultural affairs office, teacher training, writing training. *Library facilities:* Widener Library. *Research affiliation:* Woods Hole Oceanographic Institution (biology).

Computer facilities: A campuswide network can be accessed from student residence rooms and from off campus. Internet access is available. *Web address:* http://www.harvard.edu/.

General Application Contact: Admissions Office, 617-495-1814, E-mail: gfas@fas.harvard.edu.

GRADUATE UNITS

Business School Offers business (MBA, DBA, PhD); business administration (DBA); business economics (PhD); health policy management (PhD); information and technology management (PhD); organizational behavior (PhD).

Divinity School Students: 439 full-time (232 women); includes 71 minority (21 African Americans, 5 American Indian/Alaska Native, 28 Asian Americans or Pacific Islanders, 17 Hispanic Americans), 36 international. Average age 26. 581 applicants, 49% accepted, 178 enrolled. *Faculty:* 37 full-time (12 women), 39 part-time/adjunct (16 women). Expenses: Contact institution. *Financial support:* In 2006–07, 406 students received support, including 382 fellowships with tuition reimbursements available (averaging $16,763 per year); teaching assistantships, career-related internships or fieldwork, Federal Work-Study, and scholarships/grants also available. Support available to part-time students. Financial award application deadline: 2/1; financial award applicants required to submit FAFSA. In 2006, 42 M Divs, 108 master's, 9 doctorates awarded. Offers divinity (M Div, MTS, Th M, PhD, Th D). *Application deadline:* For fall admission, 1/11 priority date for domestic and international students. *Application fee:* $75. Electronic applications accepted. *Application Contact:* Maritza Hernandez, Director of Admissions and Financial Aid, 617-495-5796, Fax: 617-495-0345, E-mail: mhernandez@hds.harvard.edu. *Dean,* William A. Graham, 917-495-4513, Fax: 617-496-8026.

Extension School Students: 101 full-time (56 women), 564 part-time (278 women); includes 167 minority (35 African Americans, 1 American Indian/Alaska Native, 84 Asian Americans or Pacific Islanders, 47 Hispanic Americans). Average age 36. *Faculty:* 236 part-time/adjunct. Expenses: Contact institution. *Financial support:* In 2006–07, 268 students received support. Scholarships/grants available. Support available to part-time students. Financial award application deadline: 8/6; financial award applicants required to submit FAFSA. In 2006, 112 master's, 184 other advanced degrees awarded. *Degree program information:* Part-time and evening/weekend programs available. Offers applied sciences (CAS); biotechnology (ALM); educational technologies (ALM); educational technology (CET); English for graduate and professional studies (DGP); environmental management (ALM, CEM); information technology (ALM); journalism (ALM); liberal arts (ALM); management (ALM, CM); mathematics for teaching (ALM); museum studies (ALM); premedical studies (Diploma); publication and communication (CPC). *Application deadline:* Applications are processed on a rolling basis. *Application fee:* $75. *Application Contact:* Program Director, 617-495-4024, Fax: 617-495-9176. *Dean,* Michael Shinagel.

Graduate School of Arts and Sciences Students: 3,695 (1,700 women); includes 549 minority (128 African Americans, 14 American Indian/Alaska Native, 287 Asian Americans or Pacific Islanders, 120 Hispanic Americans). 9,237 applicants, 13% accepted, 731 enrolled. *Faculty:* 1,179 full-time (275 women). Expenses: Contact institution. *Financial support:* Fellowships, research assistantships, teaching assistantships, career-related internships or fieldwork, Federal Work-Study, institutionally sponsored loans, scholarships/grants, and tuition waivers (full) available. In 2006, 296 master's, 441 doctorates awarded. Offers African and African American studies (PhD); African history (PhD); Akkadian and Sumerian (AM, PhD); American history (PhD); ancient art (PhD); ancient Near Eastern art (PhD); ancient, medieval, early modern, and modern Europe (PhD); anthropology and Middle Eastern studies (PhD); Arabic (AM, PhD); archaeology (PhD); architecture (PhD); Armenian (AM, PhD); arts and sciences (AM, ME, MFS, SM, PhD); astronomy (PhD); astrophysics (PhD); baroque art (PhD); biblical history (AM, PhD); biochemical chemistry (PhD); biological anthropology (PhD); biological sciences in dental medicine (PhD); biological sciences in public health (PhD); biology (PhD); biophysics (PhD); business economics (PhD); Byzantine art (PhD); Byzantine Greek (PhD); chemical biology (PhD); chemical physics (PhD); Chinese (PhD); Chinese studies (AM); classical archaeology (PhD); classical art (PhD); classical philology (PhD); classical philosophy (PhD); comparative literature (PhD); composition (AM, PhD); critical theory (PhD); descriptive linguistics (PhD); diplomatic history (PhD); earth and planetary sciences (AM, PhD); East Asian history (PhD); economic and social history (PhD); economics (PhD); economics and Middle Eastern studies (PhD); eighteenth-century literature (PhD); experimental physics (PhD); fine arts and Middle Eastern studies (PhD); forest science (MFS); French (AM, PhD); German (PhD); health policy (PhD); Hebrew (AM, PhD); historical linguistics (PhD); history and Middle Eastern studies (PhD); history of American civilization (PhD); history of science (AM, PhD); Indian art (PhD); Indian philosophy (AM, PhD); Indo-Muslim culture (AM, PhD); information, technology and management (PhD); Inner Asian and Altaic studies (PhD); inorganic chemistry (PhD); intellectual history (PhD); Iranian (AM, PhD); Irish (PhD); Islamic art (PhD); Italian (AM, PhD); Japanese (PhD); Japanese and Chinese art (PhD); Japanese studies (AM); Jewish history and literature (AM, PhD); Korean (PhD); Korean studies (AM); landscape architecture (PhD); Latin American history (PhD); legal anthropology (AM); literature: nineteenth-century to the present (PhD); mathematics (PhD); medical anthropology (AM); medical engineering/medical physics (PhD); medieval art (PhD); medieval Latin (PhD); medieval literature and language (PhD); modern art (PhD); modern British and American literature (PhD); molecular and cellular biology (PhD); Mongolian (PhD); Mongolian studies (AM); musicology (AM); musicology and ethnomusicology (PhD); Near Eastern history (PhD); neurobiology (PhD); oceanic history (PhD); oral literature (PhD); organic chemistry (PhD); organizational behavior (PhD); Pali (AM, PhD); Persian (AM, PhD); philosophy (PhD); physical chemistry (PhD); Polish (PhD); political economy and government (PhD); political science (PhD); Portuguese (AM, PhD); psychology (PhD); public policy (PhD); regional studies–Middle East (AM); regional studies-Russia, Eastern Europe, and Central Asia (AM); Renaissance and modern architecture (PhD); Renaissance art (PhD); Renaissance literature (PhD); Russian (PhD); Sanskrit (AM, PhD); Scandinavian (PhD); Semitic philology (AM, PhD); Serbo-Croatian (PhD); Slavic philology (PhD); social anthropology (AM, PhD); social change and development (AM); social policy (PhD); social psychology (PhD); sociology (PhD); Spanish (AM, PhD); statistics (AM, PhD); study of religion (PhD); Syro-Palestinian archaeology (AM, PhD); systems biology (PhD); theoretical linguistics (PhD); theoretical physics (PhD); theory (AM, PhD); Tibetan (AM, PhD); Turkish (AM, PhD); Ukrainian (PhD); urban planning (PhD); Urdu (AM, PhD); Vietnamese (PhD); Vietnamese studies (AM); Welsh (PhD). *Application fee:* $90. Electronic applications accepted. *Application Contact:* Office of Admissions and Financial Aid, 617-495-5315. *Dean,* Dr. Theda Skocpol, 617-496-1464.

Division of Medical Sciences Students: 433 full-time (210 women). Expenses: Contact institution. *Financial support:* Fellowships, research assistantships, teaching assistantships, institutionally sponsored loans and tuition waivers (full) available. Financial award application deadline: 1/1. In 2006, 83 doctorates awarded. Offers biological chemistry and molecular pharmacology (PhD); cell biology (PhD); genetics (PhD); microbiology and molecular genetics (PhD); pathology (PhD). *Application fee:* $60. *Administrator,* Leah Wade Simons, 617-432-2029.

School of Engineering and Applied Sciences Students: 337 full-time (80 women), 8 part-time (1 woman); includes 55 minority (8 African Americans, 3 American Indian/Alaska Native, 37 Asian Americans or Pacific Islanders, 7 Hispanic Americans), 148 international. 1,291 applicants, 14% accepted, 114 enrolled. *Faculty:* 79 full-time (6 women), 12 part-time/adjunct (3 women). Expenses: Contact institution. *Financial support:* In 2006–07, 75 fellowships with full tuition reimbursements (averaging $19,980 per year), 209 research assistantships (averaging $32,988 per year), 129 teaching assistantships (averaging $5,243 per year) were awarded; Federal Work-Study, institutionally sponsored loans, traineeships, and health care benefits also available. In 2006, 60 master's, 33 doctorates awarded. *Degree program information:* Part-time programs available. Offers applied mathematics (ME, SM, PhD); applied physics (ME, SM, PhD); computer science (ME, SM, PhD); engineering science (ME); engineering sciences (SM, PhD). *Application deadline:* For fall admission, 12/15 priority date for domestic and international students; for winter admission, 1/2 for domestic and international students. *Application fee:* $95. Electronic applications accepted. *Application Contact:* Office of Admissions and Financial Aid, 617-495-5315, E-mail: admissions@seas.harvard.edu. *Dean,* Ventatesh Narayanamurti, 617-495-5829, Fax: 617-495-5264, E-mail: venky@deas.harvard.edu.

Graduate School of Design Students: 605 full-time (301 women); includes 126 minority (8 African Americans, 3 American Indian/Alaska Native, 93 Asian Americans or Pacific Islanders, 22 Hispanic Americans), 193 international. Average age 29. 1,323 applicants, 24% accepted. *Faculty:* 35 full-time (9 women), 120 part-time/adjunct (35 women). Expenses: Contact institution. *Financial support:* Fellowships, research assistantships, teaching assistantships, Federal Work-Study available. Support available to part-time students. Financial award application deadline: 2/11; financial award applicants required to submit CSS PROFILE or FAFSA. In 2006, 194 master's, 12 doctorates awarded. Offers architecture (M Arch); design (M Arch, M Des S, MAUD, MLA, MLAUD, MUP, Dr DES); design studies (M Des S); landscape architecture (MLA); urban planning (MUP); urban planning and design (MAUD, MLAUD). *Application fee:* $75. Electronic applications accepted. *Application Contact:* Gail Gustafson, Director of Admissions, 617-495-5453, Fax: 617-495-8949, E-mail: ggustafson@gsd.harvard.edu. *Dean,* Alan Altshuler, 617-495-4237.

Graduate School of Education Students: 846 full-time (628 women), 125 part-time (96 women); includes 232 minority (87 African Americans, 6 American Indian/Alaska Native, 96 Asian Americans or Pacific Islanders, 43 Hispanic Americans), 116 international. Average age 31. 1,705 applicants, 47% accepted, 633 enrolled. *Faculty:* 58 full-time (25 women), 40 part-time/adjunct (22 women). Expenses: Contact institution. *Financial support:* In 2006–07, 613 students received support, including 194 fellowships with full and partial tuition reimbursements available (averaging $12,008 per year), 47 research assistantships (averaging $9,340 per year), 153 teaching assistantships (averaging $7,710 per year); career-related internships or fieldwork, Federal Work-Study, institutionally sponsored loans, scholarships/grants, health care benefits, tuition waivers (full and partial), and unspecified assistantships also available. Support available to part-time students. Financial award application deadline: 2/2; financial award applicants required to submit FAFSA. In 2006, 591 master's, 70 doctorates awarded. *Degree program information:* Part-time programs available. Offers arts in education (Ed M); culture, communities and education (Ed D); education (Ed M, Ed D); education policy (Ed D); education policy and management (Ed M); education policy, leadership and instructional practice (Ed D); higher education (Ed M, Ed D); human development and education (Ed D); human development and psychology (Ed M); international education policy (Ed M); language and literacy (Ed M); learning and teaching (Ed M); mid-career mathematics and science (teaching certificate) (Ed M); mind brain and education (Ed M); quantitative policy analysis in education (Ed D); risk and prevention (Ed M); school leadership (Ed M); special studies (Ed M); teaching and curriculum (teaching certificate) (Ed M); technology innovation and education (Ed M); urban superintendency (Ed D). *Application deadline:* For fall admission, 1/2 for domestic and international students. *Application fee:* $85. Electronic applications accepted. *Application Contact:* Information Contact, 617-495-3414, Fax: 617-496-3577, E-mail: gseadmissions@harvard.edu. *Dean,* Dr. Kathleen McCartney, 617-495-3401.

Harvard Medical School Students: 771 (385 women); includes 363 minority (91 African Americans, 12 American Indian/Alaska Native, 195 Asian Americans or Pacific Islanders, 65 Hispanic Americans) 44 international. Average age 24. 4,598 applicants, 5% accepted, 165 enrolled. *Faculty:* 7,393 full-time, 2,816 part-time/adjunct. Expenses: Contact institution. *Financial support:* In 2006–07, 517 students received support; fellowships, research assistantships, teaching assistantships, Federal Work-Study, institutionally sponsored loans, and scholarships/grants available. Financial award application deadline: 4/15; financial award applicants required to submit CSS PROFILE or FAFSA. In 2006, 147 degrees awarded. Offers medicine (MD, M Eng, SM, PhD, Sc D). *Application deadline:* For fall admission, 10/15 for domestic students. *Application fee:* $85. Electronic applications accepted. *Application Contact:* 617-432-1550, Fax: 617-432-3307, E-mail: admissions_office@hms.harvard.edu. *Dean of the Faculty of Medicine,* Dr. Joseph B. Martin, 617-432-1501.

Division of Health Sciences and Technology Students: 427 full-time (131 women); includes 156 minority (10 African Americans, 1 American Indian/Alaska Native, 127 Asian Americans or Pacific Islanders, 18 Hispanic Americans), 60 international. Average age 28. 949 applicants, 10% accepted, 71 enrolled. *Faculty:* 66 full-time (6 women), 213 part-time/adjunct (34 women). Expenses: Contact institution. *Financial support:* In 2006–07, 110 fellowships with full tuition reimbursements (averaging $57,760 per year), 96 research assistantships with full tuition reimbursements (averaging $42,730 per year), 6 teaching assistantships with full tuition reimbursements (averaging $59,488 per year) were awarded; Federal Work-Study, institutionally sponsored loans, scholarships/grants, traineeships, and health care benefits also available. Support available to part-time students. Financial award application deadline: 12/15; financial award applicants required to submit FAFSA. In 2006, 26 first professional degrees, 24 master's, 26 doctorates awarded. Offers biomedical engineering (M Eng); biomedical enterprise (SM); biomedical informatics (SM); health sciences and technology (MD, M Eng, SM, PhD, Sc D); medical engineering (PhD); medical engineering/medical physics (Sc D); medical physics (PhD); medical sciences (MD); speech and hearing bioscience and technology (PhD, Sc D). *Application deadline:* For fall admission, 12/15 for domestic students. *Application fee:* $70.

John F. Kennedy School of Government Students: 614 full-time (233 women); includes 109 minority (32 African Americans, 6 American Indian/Alaska Native, 40 Asian Americans or Pacific Islanders, 31 Hispanic Americans), 273 international. Average age 31. 2,471 applicants, 40% accepted, 614 enrolled. *Faculty:* 70. Expenses: Contact institution. *Financial support:* Fellowships, research assistantships, teaching assistantships, career-related internships or fieldwork, Federal Work-Study, institutionally sponsored loans, scholarships/grants, and unspecified assistantships available. Support available to part-time students. Financial award applicants required to submit CSS PROFILE or FAFSA. Offers government (MPA, MPAID, MPP, MPPUP, PhD); political economy and government (PhD); public administration (MPA); public administration and international development (MPAID); public policy (MPP, PhD); public policy and urban planning (MPPUP). *Application fee:* $80. Electronic applications accepted. *Application Contact:* 617-495-1155, Fax: 617-496-1165, E-mail: ksg_admissions@harvard.edu. *Dean,* Dr. David Ellwood.

Law School Offers law (JD, LL M, SJD).

School of Dental Medicine Offers advanced general dentistry (Certificate); dental medicine (DMD, M Med Sc, D Med Sc, Certificate); dental public health (Certificate); endodontics (Certificate); general practice residency (Certificate); oral biology (M Med Sc, D Med Sc); oral pathology (Certificate); oral surgery (Certificate); orthodontics (Certificate); pediatric dentistry (Certificate); periodontics (Certificate); prosthodontics (Certificate).

School of Public Health *Degree program information:* Part-time programs available. Offers biostatistics (SM, PhD); clinical effectiveness (MPH); environmental health (MOH, SM, DPH, PhD, SD); epidemiology (SM, DPH, SD); exposure, epidemiology and risk (SM, SD); family and community health (MPH); genetics and complex diseases (PhD); health care management and policy (MPH); health policy (PhD); health policy and management (SM, SD); immunology and infectious diseases (PhD, SD); international health (MPH); nutrition (DPH, PhD, SD); nutritional epidemiology (DPH, SD); occupational and environmental health (MPH); occupational health (MOH, SM, DPH, SD); physiology (PhD, SD); population and international health (SM, DPH, SD); public health (MOH, MPH, SM, DPH, PhD, SD); public health nutrition (DPH, SD); quantitative methods (MPH); society, human development and health (SM, DPH, SD). Electronic applications accepted.

See Close-Up on page 909.

HASTINGS COLLEGE, Hastings, NE 68901-7696

General Information Independent-religious, coed, comprehensive institution. *Graduate housing:* On-campus housing not available.

GRADUATE UNITS

Program in Teacher Education *Degree program information:* Part-time programs available. Offers teacher education (MAT). Electronic applications accepted.

HAWAI'I PACIFIC UNIVERSITY, Honolulu, HI 96813

General Information Independent, coed, comprehensive institution. *Enrollment:* 8,080 graduate, professional, and undergraduate students; 708 full-time matriculated graduate/professional students (384 women), 516 part-time matriculated graduate/professional students (249 women). *Enrollment by degree level:* 1,224 master's. *Graduate faculty:* 77 full-time, 38 part-time/adjunct. *Tuition:* Full-time $10,080; part-time $560 per credit. *Graduate housing:* Room and/or apartments available on a first-come, first-served basis to single students; on-campus housing not available to married students. Typical cost: $9,840 (including board). *Student services:* Campus employment opportunities, campus safety program, career counseling, international student services, low-cost health insurance. *Library facilities:* Meader Library plus 2 others. *Online resources:* library catalog, web page, access to other libraries' catalogs. *Collection:* 162,000 titles, 12,000 serial subscriptions, 8,700 audiovisual materials. *Research affiliation:* Oceanic Institute (marine science).

Computer facilities: Computer purchase and lease plans are available. 590 computers available on campus for general student use. A campuswide network can be accessed from student residence rooms and from off campus. Internet access and online class registration are available. *Web address:* http://www.hpu.edu/.

General Application Contact: Danny Lam, Assistant Director of Graduate Admissions, 808-544-1135, Fax: 808-544-0280, E-mail: graduate@hpu.edu.

GRADUATE UNITS

College of Business Administration Students: 320 full-time (150 women), 205 part-time (95 women); includes 168 minority (17 African Americans, 7 American Indian/Alaska Native, 137 Asian Americans or Pacific Islanders, 7 Hispanic Americans), 232 international. Average age 31. 279 applicants, 67% accepted, 166 enrolled. *Faculty:* 40 full-time (16 women), 30 part-time/adjunct (10 women). Expenses: Contact institution. *Financial support:* In 2006–07, 118 students received support; research assistantships, career-related internships or fieldwork, Federal Work-Study, scholarships/grants, and unspecified assistantships available. Support available to part-time students. Financial award application deadline: 3/1; financial award applicants required to submit FAFSA. In 2006, 172 degrees awarded. *Degree program information:* Part-time and evening/weekend programs available. Offers accounting/CPA (MBA); communication (MBA); e-business (MBA); economics (MBA); finance (MBA); human resource management (MBA); information systems (MBA); international business (MBA); management (MBA); marketing (MBA); organizational change (MBA); travel industry management (MBA). *Application deadline:* For fall admission, 2/15 priority date for domestic students; for spring admission, 10/15 priority date for domestic students. Applications are processed on a rolling basis. *Application fee:* $50. Electronic applications accepted. *Application Contact:* Danny Lam, Assistant Director of Graduate Admissions, 808-544-1135, Fax: 808-544-0280, E-mail: graduate@hpu.edu. *Dean,* Dr. Charles Steilen, 808-544-9301, Fax: 808-544-0283, E-mail: csteilen@hpu.edu.

College of Communication Students: 99 full-time (73 women), 41 part-time (32 women); includes 36 minority (4 African Americans, 3 American Indian/Alaska Native, 27 Asian Americans or Pacific Islanders, 2 Hispanic Americans), 64 international. Average age 34. 101 applicants, 71% accepted, 50 enrolled. *Faculty:* 6 full-time (3 women), 6 part-time/adjunct (4 women). Expenses: Contact institution. *Financial support:* In 2006–07, 46 students received support. Career-related internships or fieldwork, Federal Work-Study, scholarships/grants, and unspecified assistantships available. Support available to part-time students. Financial award application deadline: 3/1; financial award applicants required to submit FAFSA. In 2006, 40 degrees awarded. *Degree program information:* Part-time and evening/weekend programs available. Offers communication (MA). *Application deadline:* For fall admission, 2/15 priority date for domestic students; for spring admission, 10/15 priority date for domestic students. Applications are processed on a rolling basis. *Application fee:* $50. Electronic applications accepted. *Application Contact:* Danny Lam, Assistant Director of Graduate Admissions, 808-544-1135, Fax: 808-544-0280, E-mail: graduate@hpu.edu. *Dean,* Dr. James Whitfield, 808-544-0824, Fax: 808-544-0835, E-mail: jwhitfield@hpu.edu.

College of International Studies Students: 41 full-time (25 women), 19 part-time (13 women); includes 18 minority (3 African Americans, 15 Asian Americans or Pacific Islanders), 29 international. Average age 32. 31 applicants, 55% accepted, 15 enrolled. *Faculty:* 6 full-time (4 women), 2 part-time/adjunct (both women). Expenses: Contact institution. *Financial support:* In 2006–07, 16 students received support. Career-related internships or fieldwork, Federal Work-Study, scholarships/grants, and unspecified assistantships available. Support available to part-time students. Financial award application deadline: 3/1; financial award applicants required to submit FAFSA. In 2006, 26 degrees awarded. *Degree program information:* Part-time and evening/weekend programs available. Offers teaching English as a second language (MA). *Application deadline:* For fall admission, 2/15 priority date for domestic students; for spring admission, 10/15 priority date for domestic students. Applications are processed on a rolling basis. *Application fee:* $50. Electronic applications accepted. *Application Contact:* Danny Lam, Assistant Director of Graduate Admissions, 808-544-1135, Fax: 808-544-0280, E-mail: graduate@hpu.edu. *Dean,* Dr. Carlos Juarez, 808-566-2493, Fax: 808-544-0834, E-mail: cjuarez@hpu.edu.

College of Liberal Arts Students: 86 full-time (45 women), 49 part-time (18 women); includes 47 minority (7 African Americans, 5 American Indian/Alaska Native, 31 Asian Americans or Pacific Islanders, 4 Hispanic Americans), 11 international. Average age 35. 134 applicants, 69% accepted, 46 enrolled. *Faculty:* 3 full-time (0 women), 5 part-time/adjunct (1 woman). Expenses: Contact institution. *Financial support:* In 2006–07, 60 students received support. Career-related internships or fieldwork, Federal Work-Study, scholarships/grants, and unspecified assistantships available. Support available to part-time students. Financial award application deadline: 3/1; financial award applicants required to submit FAFSA. In 2006, 3 degrees awarded. *Degree program information:* Part-time and evening/weekend programs available. Offers diplomacy and military studies (MA); social work (MA). *Application deadline:* For fall admission, 2/15 priority date for domestic students; for spring admission, 10/15 priority date for domestic students. Applications are processed on a rolling basis. *Application fee:* $50. Electronic applications accepted. *Application Contact:* Danny Lam, Assistant Director of Graduate Admissions, 808-544-1135, Fax: 808-544-0280, E-mail: graduate@hpu.edu. *Associate Vice President and Dean,* Dr. Leslie Correa, 808-544-0228, Fax: 808-544-1424, E-mail: lcorrea@hpu.edu.

College of Natural Sciences Expenses: Contact institution. *Financial support:* Federal Work-Study, scholarships/grants, and unspecified assistantships available. Support available to part-time students. Offers marine science (MS). *Application deadline:* Applications are processed on a rolling basis. *Application fee:* $50. Electronic applications accepted. *Application Contact:* Danny Lam, Assistant Director of Graduate Admissions, 808-544-1135, Fax: 808-544-0280, E-mail: graduate@hpu.edu. *Vice President, Research/Dean,* Dr. Alissa Arp, 808-236-3553, Fax: 808-236-5880, E-mail: aarp@hpu.edu.

College of Professional Studies Students: 118 full-time (56 women), 149 part-time (57 women); includes 101 minority (15 African Americans, 5 American Indian/Alaska Native, 70 Asian Americans or Pacific Islanders, 11 Hispanic Americans), 87 international. Average age 32. 188 applicants, 58% accepted, 67 enrolled. *Faculty:* 15 full-time (2 women), 7 part-time/adjunct (2 women). Expenses: Contact institution. *Financial support:* In 2006–07, 54 students received support. Career-related internships or fieldwork, Federal Work-Study, scholarships/grants, and unspecified assistantships available. Support available to part-time students.

Hawai'i Pacific University (continued)

Financial award application deadline: 3/1; financial award applicants required to submit FAFSA. In 2006, 65 degrees awarded. *Degree program information:* Part-time and evening/weekend programs available. Offers global leadership and sustainable development (MA); human resource management (MA); information systems (MSIS); organizational change (MA). *Application deadline:* For fall admission, 2/15 priority date for domestic students; for spring admission, 10/15 priority date for domestic students. Applications are processed on a rolling basis. *Application fee:* $50. Electronic applications accepted. *Application Contact:* Danny Lam, Assistant Director of Graduate Admissions, 808-544-1135, Fax: 808-544-0280, E-mail: graduate@hpu.edu. *Dean,* Dr. Gordon Jones, 808-544-1181, Fax: 808-544-0247, E-mail: gjones@hpu.edu.

Program in Secondary Education Students: 24 full-time (13 women), 28 part-time (13 women); includes 25 minority (1 American Indian/Alaska Native, 22 Asian Americans or Pacific Islanders, 2 Hispanic Americans), 1 international. Average age 28. 46 applicants, 65% accepted, 22 enrolled. *Faculty:* 12 full-time (6 women). Expenses: Contact institution. *Financial support:* In 2006–07, 31 students received support. Career-related internships or fieldwork, Federal Work-Study, scholarships/grants, and unspecified assistantships available. Support available to part-time students. Financial award application deadline: 3/1. Offers secondary education (M Ed). *Application deadline:* For fall admission, 2/15 priority date for domestic students; for spring admission, 10/15 priority date for domestic students. Applications are processed on a rolling basis. *Application fee:* $50. Electronic applications accepted. *Application Contact:* Danny Lam, Assistant Director of Graduate Admissions, 808-544-1135, Fax: 808-544-0280, E-mail: graduate@hpu.edu. *Director, Teacher Education Program,* Dr. Valentina Abordonado, 808-544-1143, Fax: 808-544-0841, E-mail: vabordonado@hpu.edu.

School of Nursing Students: 26 full-time (23 women), 10 part-time (all women); includes 18 minority (2 African Americans, 1 American Indian/Alaska Native, 13 Asian Americans or Pacific Islanders, 2 Hispanic Americans). Average age 35. 22 applicants, 77% accepted, 13 enrolled. *Faculty:* 11 full-time (all women), 1 part-time/adjunct (0 women). Expenses: Contact institution. *Financial support:* In 2006–07, 20 students received support. Career-related internships or fieldwork, Federal Work-Study, scholarships/grants, and traineeships available. Support available to part-time students. Financial award application deadline: 3/1; financial award applicants required to submit FAFSA. In 2006, 10 degrees awarded. *Degree program information:* Part-time and evening/weekend programs available. Offers community clinical nurse specialist (MSN); community clinical nurse specialist educator option (MSN); family nurse practitioner (MSN). *Application deadline:* Applications are processed on a rolling basis. *Application fee:* $50. Electronic applications accepted. *Application Contact:* Danny Lam, Assistant Director of Graduate Admissions, 808-544-1135, Fax: 808-544-0280, E-mail: graduate@hpu.edu. *Interim Dean,* Dr. Patricia Langotsuka, 808-236-5812, Fax: 808-236-5818, E-mail: potsuka@hpu.edu.

See Close-Up on page 911.

HAWAI'I THEOLOGICAL SEMINARY, Honolulu, HI 96817

General Information Independent-religious, coed, upper-level institution. *Graduate housing:* On-campus housing not available.

GRADUATE UNITS

Graduate Studies *Degree program information:* Part-time and evening/weekend programs available. Offers religion (MAR); theology (M Div).

HAZELDEN GRADUATE SCHOOL OF ADDICTION STUDIES, Center City, MN 55012

General Information Independent, coed, graduate-only institution.

HEBREW COLLEGE, Newton Centre, MA 02459

General Information Independent-religious, coed, comprehensive institution. *Enrollment:* 74 full-time matriculated graduate/professional students (40 women), 173 part-time matriculated graduate/professional students (137 women). *Enrollment by degree level:* 103 master's, 128 other advanced degrees. *Graduate faculty:* 6 full-time (1 woman), 19 part-time/adjunct (7 women). *Graduate housing:* On-campus housing not available. *Student services:* Career counseling, international student services, low-cost health insurance, teacher training. *Library facilities:* Rae and Joseph Gann Library. *Online resources:* web page. *Collection:* 125,000 titles, 280 serial subscriptions.

Computer facilities: 10 computers available on campus for general student use. Internet access is available. *Web address:* http://www.hebrewcollege.edu/.

General Application Contact: Kate Nachman, Director of Admissions, 617-559-8610, Fax: 617-559-8601, E-mail: admissions@hebrewcollege.edu.

GRADUATE UNITS

Cantor Educator Program Students: 15 full-time (10 women), 1 part-time. 10 applicants, 60% accepted, 5 enrolled. Expenses: Contact institution. *Financial support:* In 2006–07, fellowships (averaging $5,000 per year); tuition waivers (partial) also available. Support available to part-time students. Financial award application deadline: 4/15; financial award applicants required to submit FAFSA. Offers cantor educator (MJ Ed). *Application deadline:* For fall admission, 12/15 priority date for domestic and international students; for winter admission, 2/15 priority date for domestic and international students; for spring admission, 5/30 priority date for domestic and international students. *Application fee:* $50. *Application Contact:* Kate Nachman, Director of Admissions, 617-559-8610, Fax: 617-559-8601, E-mail: admissions@hebrewcollege.edu. *Dean,* Dr. Scott Sokol, 617-559-8600.

Program in Jewish Studies Students: 39 (24 women). Average age 30. 26 applicants, 69% accepted, 14 enrolled. *Faculty:* 6 full-time (1 woman), 19 part-time/adjunct (7 women). Expenses: Contact institution. *Financial support:* In 2006–07, fellowships (averaging $5,000 per year); tuition waivers (partial) also available. Support available to part-time students. Financial award application deadline: 4/15; financial award applicants required to submit FAFSA. *Degree program information:* Part-time and evening/weekend programs available. Postbaccalaureate distance learning degree programs offered (minimal on-campus study). Offers Jewish liturgical music (Certificate); Jewish music education (Certificate); Jewish studies (MA). *Application deadline:* For fall admission, 12/15 priority date for domestic and international students; for winter admission, 2/15 priority date for domestic and international students; for spring admission, 5/30 priority date for domestic and international students. Applications are processed on a rolling basis. *Application fee:* $50. *Application Contact:* Kate Nachman, Director of Admissions, 617-559-8610, Fax: 617-559-8601, E-mail: admissions@hebrewcollege.edu. *Provost,* Dr. Barry Mesch, 617-559-8600, Fax: 617-559-8601, E-mail: bmesch@hebrewcollege.edu.

Rabbinical School Students: 48 full-time (28 women). 33 applicants, 48% accepted, 11 enrolled. Expenses: Contact institution. *Financial support:* In 2006–07, fellowships (averaging $10,000 per year); career-related internships or fieldwork, scholarships/grants, and tuition waivers (partial) also available. Financial award applicants required to submit FAFSA. *Application deadline:* For fall admission, 12/15 priority date for domestic students; for winter admission, 2/1 priority date for domestic students. *Application fee:* $60. *Application Contact:* Kate Nachman, Director of Admissions, 617-559-8610, Fax: 617-559-8601, E-mail: admissions@hebrewcollege.edu. *Dean,* Rabbi Sharon Cohen Anisfeld, 617-559-8600.

Shoolman Graduate School of Education Students: 51 (42 women). Average age 37. 33 applicants, 79% accepted, 19 enrolled. *Faculty:* 6 full-time (1 woman), 19 part-time/adjunct (7 women). Expenses: Contact institution. *Financial support:* Fellowships, career-related internships or fieldwork and tuition waivers (partial) available. Support available to part-time students. Financial award application deadline: 4/15; financial award applicants required to submit FAFSA. In 2006, 5 degrees awarded. *Degree program information:* Part-time and evening/weekend programs available. Postbaccalaureate distance learning degree programs offered. Offers early childhood Jewish education (Certificate); Jewish day school education (Certificate); Jewish education (MJ Ed); Jewish family education (Certificate); Jewish special education (Certificate); Jewish youth education, informal education and camping (Certificate). *Application deadline:* For fall admission, 12/15 priority date for domestic and international students; for winter admission, 2/15 priority date for domestic and international students; for spring admission, 5/30 priority date for domestic and international students. *Application fee:* $50. *Application Contact:* Kate Nachman, Director of Admissions, 617-559-8610, Fax: 617-559-8601, E-mail: admissions@hebrewcollege.edu. *Provost,* Dr. Barry Mesch, 617-559-8600, Fax: 617-559-8601, E-mail: bmesch@hebrewcollege.edu.

See Close-Up on page 913.

HEBREW THEOLOGICAL COLLEGE, Skokie, IL 60077-3263

General Information Independent-religious, men only, comprehensive institution.

GRADUATE UNITS

Department of Talmud and Rabbinics Offers Talmud and rabbinics (Rabbi).

HEBREW UNION COLLEGE–JEWISH INSTITUTE OF RELIGION, Los Angeles, CA 90007-3796

General Information Independent-religious, coed, graduate-only institution. *Enrollment by degree level:* 59 first professional, 44 master's, 2 doctoral. *Graduate faculty:* 20 full-time (10 women), 27 part-time/adjunct (13 women). *Tuition:* Full-time $16,000; part-time $680 per unit. One-time fee: $100 full-time. *Graduate housing:* On-campus housing not available. *Student services:* Campus employment opportunities, career counseling, grant writing training, international student services, low-cost health insurance. *Library facilities:* Frances-Henry Library plus 1 other. *Online resources:* library catalog, web page, access to other libraries' catalogs. *Collection:* 115,000 titles, 850 serial subscriptions, 2,000 audiovisual materials.

Computer facilities: 12 computers available on campus for general student use. A campuswide network can be accessed from off campus. Internet access is available. *Web address:* http://www.huc.edu/.

General Application Contact: Director of Admissions and Recruitment, 213-749-3424 Ext. 4221, Fax: 213-747-6128.

GRADUATE UNITS

Edgar F. Magnin School of Graduate Studies Students: 2 full-time (1 woman), 2 part-time, 1 international. Average age 39. Expenses: Contact institution. *Financial support:* In 2006–07, 2 students received support, including teaching assistantships (averaging $12,000 per year); fellowships, career-related internships or fieldwork, scholarships/grants, and unspecified assistantships also available. Financial award application deadline: 3/2; financial award applicants required to submit FAFSA. In 2006, 3 degrees awarded. *Degree program information:* Part-time programs available. Offers religion (MAJS, DHL, DHS). *Application deadline:* For fall admission, 4/1 for domestic and international students. Applications are processed on a rolling basis. *Application fee:* $50. *Application Contact:* Director of Admissions and Recruitment, 213-749-3424 Ext. 4221, Fax: 213-747-6128. *Director,* Dr. Sharon Gillerman, 213-749-3424 Ext. 4241, Fax: 213-747-6128, E-mail: sgillerman@huc.edu.

Rhea Hirsch School of Education Students: 21 full-time (15 women), 1 international. Average age 29. 11 applicants, 100% accepted, 11 enrolled. *Faculty:* 3 full-time (2 women), 7 part-time/adjunct (5 women). Expenses: Contact institution. *Financial support:* Career-related internships or fieldwork and scholarships/grants available. Support available to part-time students. Financial award application deadline: 3/2; financial award applicants required to submit FAFSA. In 2006, 6 master's, 5 other advanced degrees awarded. Offers day school teaching (Certificate); Jewish education (MAJE, PhD). *Application deadline:* For fall admission, 2/1 for domestic and international students. *Application fee:* $50. *Application Contact:* Director of Admissions and Recruitment, 213-749-3424 Ext. 4221, Fax: 213-7476128. *Director,* Dr. Michael Zeldin, 213-749-3424 Ext. 4216, Fax: 213-747-6128, E-mail: mzeldin@huc.edu.

School of Jewish Communal Service Students: 25 full-time (19 women), 1 (woman) part-time, 2 international. Average age 25. 11 applicants, 100% accepted, 7 enrolled. *Faculty:* 3 full-time (2 women), 9 part-time/adjunct (3 women). Expenses: Contact institution. *Financial support:* Career-related internships or fieldwork and scholarships/grants available. Financial award application deadline: 3/2; financial award applicants required to submit FAFSA. In 2006, 9 master's, 9 other advanced degrees awarded. Offers Jewish communal service (MAJCS, Certificate). *Application deadline:* For fall admission, 2/1 for domestic and international students. *Application fee:* $50. *Application Contact:* Director of Admissions and Recruitment, 213-749-3424 Ext. 4221, Fax: 213-747-6128. *Interim Director,* Macla Abraham, 213-749-3424 Ext. 4218, Fax: 213-747-6128, E-mail: mabraham@huc.edu.

School of Rabbinical Studies Students: 57 full-time (41 women), 2 part-time (both women), 2 international. Average age 32. 55 applicants, 73% accepted, 38 enrolled. *Faculty:* 11 full-time (5 women), 12 part-time/adjunct (4 women). Expenses: Contact institution. *Financial support:* Career-related internships or fieldwork and scholarships/grants available. Financial award application deadline: 3/15; financial award applicants required to submit FAFSA. In 2006, 14 MAHLs awarded. Offers rabbinical studies (MAHL). *Application deadline:* For fall admission, 12/31 for domestic and international students. *Application fee:* $75. *Application Contact:* Director of Admissions and Recruitment, 213-749-3424 Ext. 4221, Fax: 213-747-6128. *Director,* Rabbi Richard Levy, 213-749-3424 Ext. 4203, Fax: 213-747-6128, E-mail: rlevy@huc.edu.

HEBREW UNION COLLEGE–JEWISH INSTITUTE OF RELIGION, New York, NY 10012-1186

General Information Independent-religious, coed, graduate-only institution. *Enrollment by degree level:* 78 first professional, 64 master's, 32 doctoral. *Graduate faculty:* 21 full-time (9 women), 34 part-time/adjunct (12 women). *Tuition:* Full-time $16,000; part-time $680 per credit. *Required fees:* $35. One-time fee: $75 full-time. *Graduate housing:* On-campus housing not available. *Student services:* Campus employment opportunities, career counseling. *Library facilities:* Klau Library plus 1 other. *Online resources:* library catalog, web page, access to other libraries' catalogs. *Collection:* 142,500 titles, 247 serial subscriptions.

Computer facilities: 4 computers available on campus for general student use. A campuswide network can be accessed from off campus. Internet access is available. *Web address:* http://www.huc.edu/.

General Application Contact: Rabbi Faith Joy Dantowitz, Regional Director of Recruitment and Admissions, 212-674-5300 Ext. 2207, Fax: 212-388-1720, E-mail: fdantowitz@huc.edu.

GRADUATE UNITS

Rabbinical School Students: 78 full-time (45 women), 3 international. Average age 33. *Faculty:* 21 full-time (9 women), 20 part-time/adjunct (7 women). Expenses: Contact institution. *Financial support:* Career-related internships or fieldwork and scholarships/grants available. Financial award application deadline: 6/1; financial award applicants required to submit CSS PROFILE or FAFSA. In 2006, 20 MAHLs awarded. Offers rabbinical studies (MAHL). *Application deadline:* For fall admission, 10/28 priority date for domestic students. *Application fee:* $75. *Application Contact:* Rabbi Faith Joy Dantowitz, Director of Recruitment and Admissions, 212-674-5300 Ext. 2207, Fax: 212-388-1720, E-mail: fdantowitz@huc.edu. *Associate Dean,* Rabbi Shirley Idelson, 212-674-5300 Ext. 2217, Fax: 212-388-1720, E-mail: sidelson@huc.edu.

School of Education Students: 8 full-time (6 women), 16 part-time (10 women), 3 international. Average age 32. *Faculty:* 21 full-time (9 women), 10 part-time/adjunct (4 women). Expenses: Contact institution. *Financial support:* Career-related internships or fieldwork and scholarships/grants available. Financial award application deadline: 6/1; financial award applicants required to submit FAFSA. In 2006, 5 degrees awarded. *Degree program information:* Part-time programs available. Offers education (MARE). *Application deadline:* Applications are processed on a rolling basis. *Application fee:* $35. *Application Contact:* Merline Denis, Administrative Assistant, 212-824-2252, Fax: 212-388-1720, E-mail: mdenis@huc.edu. *Director,* Jo Kay, 212-674-5300 Ext. 2213, Fax: 212-388-1720, E-mail: jkay@huc.edu.

School of Graduate Studies Students: 21 full-time (13 women), 37 part-time (16 women); includes 4 minority (3 African Americans, 1 Asian American or Pacific Islander), 4 international. Average age 40. *Faculty:* 21 full-time (9 women), 28 part-time/adjunct (8 women). Expenses: Contact institution. *Financial support:* Applicants required to submit FAFSA. In 2006, 4 degrees awarded. *Degree program information:* Part-time programs available. Offers Hebrew letters (DHL); Judaic studies (MAJS); pastoral counseling (D Min). *Application fee:* $50. *Application Contact:* Merline Denis, Administrative Assistant, 212-824-2252, Fax: 212-388-1720, E-mail: mdenis@huc.edu. *Director,* Dr. Carol Ochs, 212-674-2252, Fax: 212-388-1720, E-mail: cochs@earthlink.net.

School of Sacred Music Students: 39 full-time (30 women), 3 international. Average age 26. *Faculty:* 21 full-time (9 women), 17 part-time/adjunct (7 women). Expenses: Contact institution. *Financial support:* Fellowships, career-related internships or fieldwork and scholarships/grants available. Financial award application deadline: 5/1; financial award applicants required to submit FAFSA. Offers sacred music (MSM). *Application Contact:* Rabbi Faith Joy Dantowitz, Director of Recruitment and Admissions, 212-674-5300 Ext. 2207, Fax: 212-388-1720, E-mail: fdantowitz@huc.edu. *Director,* Cantor Bruce Ruben, 212-674-5300 Ext. 2225, Fax: 212-388-1720.

HEBREW UNION COLLEGE–JEWISH INSTITUTE OF RELIGION, Cincinnati, OH 45220-2488

General Information Independent-religious, coed, graduate-only institution. CGS member. *Enrollment by degree level:* 68 first professional, 1 master's, 65 doctoral. *Graduate faculty:* 21 full-time (2 women), 4 part-time/adjunct (2 women). *Tuition:* Full-time $16,000. *Graduate housing:* Room and/or apartments available on a first-come, first-served basis to single students. Typical cost: $3,000 per year. Housing application deadline: 7/31. *Student services:* Campus employment opportunities, campus safety program, career counseling, child daycare facilities, low-cost health insurance. *Library facilities:* Klau Library. *Online resources:* library catalog, web page. *Collection:* 464,789 titles, 2,595 serial subscriptions, 14,800 audiovisual materials. *Research affiliation:* Union for Reform Judaism (Jewish education, survey and analysis of reform education), Oriental Institute (neo-Babylonian texts).

Computer facilities: 10 computers available on campus for general student use. A campuswide network can be accessed from off campus. Internet access, CD-ROM databases are available. *Web address:* http://www.huc.edu/.

General Application Contact: John Braunstein, Associate Provost for Enrollment and Planning, 212-824-2857, Fax: 212-533-0124, E-mail: jbraunstein@huc.edu.

GRADUATE UNITS

Rabbinic School Students: 62 full-time (35 women), 6 part-time (4 women); includes 1 minority (African American), 3 international. Average age 30. 69 applicants, 68% accepted, 41 enrolled. *Faculty:* 18 full-time (3 women), 4 part-time/adjunct (1 woman). Expenses: Contact institution. *Financial support:* In 2006–07, 55 students received support, including 1 teaching assistantship (averaging $2,000 per year); career-related internships or fieldwork, institutionally sponsored loans, and scholarships/grants also available. Financial award application deadline: 9/1; financial award applicants required to submit FAFSA. In 2006, 8 MAHLs awarded. Offers rabbinic studies (MAHL). *Application deadline:* For fall admission, 11/1 priority date for domestic students. *Application fee:* $75. *Application Contact:* John Braunstein, Associate Provost for Enrollment and Planning, 212-824-2857, Fax: 212-533-0124, E-mail: jbraunstein@huc.edu. *Director of Rabbinic School,* Rabbi Kenneth A. Kanter, 513-221-1875 Ext. 3238, Fax: 513-221-0321, E-mail: kanter@huc.edu.

School of Graduate Studies Students: 43 full-time (8 women), 23 part-time (4 women); includes 1 minority (African American), 5 international. Average age 35. 25 applicants, 12% accepted, 3 enrolled. *Faculty:* 18 full-time (2 women), 1 part-time/adjunct (0 women). Expenses: Contact institution. *Financial support:* In 2006–07, 17 fellowships with full and partial tuition reimbursements (averaging $9,000 per year), 3 teaching assistantships with full and partial tuition reimbursements (averaging $2,000 per year) were awarded; institutionally sponsored loans, scholarships/grants, and tuition waivers (full and partial) also available. Financial award application deadline: 2/15; financial award applicants required to submit FAFSA. In 2006, 6 master's, 3 doctorates awarded. *Degree program information:* Part-time programs available. Offers Bible and the ancient Near East (M Phil, MA, PhD); Hebrew letters (DHL); history of biblical interpretation (M Phil, MA, PhD); Jewish and Christian studies in the Greco-Roman period (M Phil, PhD); Jewish and cognate studies (M Phil); Judaic and cognate studies (MA, PhD); modern Jewish history (M Phil, MA, PhD); philosophy and Jewish religious thought (M Phil, MA, PhD); rabbinics (M Phil, MA, PhD). *Application deadline:* For fall admission, 2/15 for domestic and international students. *Application fee:* $35. *Director,* Dr. Adam Kamesar, 513-221-1875, Fax: 513-221-0321, E-mail: akamesar@huc.edu.

HEC MONTREAL, Montréal, QC H3T 2A7, Canada

General Information Province-supported, coed, comprehensive institution. *Enrollment:* 12,035 graduate, professional, and undergraduate students; 1,359 full-time matriculated graduate/professional students (616 women), 1,142 part-time matriculated graduate/professional students (570 women). *Enrollment by degree level:* 1,098 master's, 165 doctoral, 1,238 other advanced degrees. *Graduate faculty:* 258 full-time (74 women), 361 part-time/adjunct (110 women). *Graduate tuition:* Tuition and fees charges are reported in Canadian dollars. Tuition, Canadian resident: part-time $56 Canadian dollars per credit. *Required fees:* $30 Canadian dollars per semester. *Graduate housing:* Rooms and/or apartments available on a first-come, first-served basis to single and married students. Typical cost: $29,550 Canadian dollars per year for single students; $50,916 Canadian dollars per year for married students. *Student services:* Campus employment opportunities, career counseling, child daycare facilities, disabled student services, free psychological counseling, international student services, multicultural affairs office. *Library facilities:* Myriam et J.-Robert Ouimet Library plus 1 other. *Online resources:* library catalog, web page, access to other libraries' catalogs. *Collection:* 345,143 titles, 5,557 serial subscriptions. *Research affiliation:* Centre Francophone de Recherche en Informatisation des Organisations (information systems), Ad Opt (operational research), Hydro Quebec (finance), Center for InterUniversity Research and Analysis on Organizations (economics and finance), CGI (information systems).

Computer facilities: 250 computers available on campus for general student use. A campuswide network can be accessed from off campus. Internet access and online class registration are available. *Web address:* http://www.hec.ca/.

General Application Contact: Manon Vaillant, Registrar, 514-340-6110, Fax: 514-340-5640, E-mail: registraire.info@hec.ca.

GRADUATE UNITS

School of Business Administration Students: 1,359 full-time (616 women), 1,142 part-time (570 women). Average age 29. 3,882 applicants, 63% accepted, 1833 enrolled. *Faculty:* 258 full-time (74 women), 361 part-time/adjunct (110 women). Expenses: Contact institution. *Financial support:* Research assistantships, teaching assistantships, scholarships/grants available. In 2006, 436 master's, 9 doctorates, 302 Diplomas awarded. *Degree program information:* Part-time and evening/weekend programs available. Offers administration (LL M, M Sc, PhD, Diploma); applied economics (M Sc); applied financial economics (M Sc); business administration (LL M, M Sc, MBA, PhD, Diploma); business administration and management (MBA); business intelligence (M Sc); controllership (M Sc); e-business (Diploma); electronic commerce (M Sc); finance (M Sc); financial engineering (M Sc); human resources management (M Sc); information systems (M Sc); international business (M Sc); international management (M Sc); logistics (M Sc); management (M Sc, Diploma); management and sustainable development (Diploma); management of cultural organizations (Diploma); marketing (M Sc); marketing communication (Diploma); private wealth management (Diploma); production and operations management (M Sc); public accountancy (Diploma); supply chain management (Diploma); taxation (LL M, Diploma). Most courses are given in French. *Application fee:* $60 Canadian dollars. Electronic applications accepted. *Application Contact:* Manon Vaillant, Registrar, 514-340-6110, Fax: 514-340-5640, E-mail: registraire.info@hec.ca. *Director,* Dr. Michel Patry, 514-340-6110, Fax: 514-340-5640.

HEIDELBERG COLLEGE, Tiffin, OH 44883-2462

General Information Independent-religious, coed, comprehensive institution. *Enrollment:* 1,569 graduate, professional, and undergraduate students; 50 full-time matriculated graduate/professional students (28 women), 202 part-time matriculated graduate/professional students (148 women). *Enrollment by degree level:* 252 master's. *Graduate faculty:* 4 full-time (1 woman), 11 part-time/adjunct (6 women). *Tuition:* Part-time $345 per hour. Tuition and fees vary according to program. *Graduate housing:* On-campus housing not available. *Student services:* Campus employment opportunities, career counseling, exercise/wellness program, free psychological counseling, international student services, multicultural affairs office, teacher training. *Library facilities:* Beeghly Library. *Online resources:* library catalog, web page, access to other libraries' catalogs. *Collection:* 268,702 titles, 513 serial subscriptions.

Computer facilities: 125 computers available on campus for general student use. A campuswide network can be accessed from student residence rooms and from off campus. Internet access and online class registration are available. *Web address:* http://www.heidelberg.edu/.

General Application Contact: Dr. G. Michael Pratt, Graduate Studies Office, 419-448-2288, Fax: 419-448-2072, E-mail: mpratt@heidelberg.edu.

GRADUATE UNITS

Program in Business Students: 26 full-time (12 women), 36 part-time (24 women); includes 5 minority (4 African Americans, 1 Asian American or Pacific Islander), 1 international. 23 applicants, 100% accepted, 17 enrolled. *Faculty:* 1 full-time (0 women), 2 part-time/adjunct (1 woman). Expenses: Contact institution. *Financial support:* In 2006–07, 17 students received support. Federal Work-Study available. Support available to part-time students. Financial award applicants required to submit FAFSA. In 2006, 5 degrees awarded. *Degree program information:* Part-time and evening/weekend programs available. Offers business (MBA). *Application deadline:* Applications are processed on a rolling basis. *Application fee:* $25. *Application Contact:* Dr. G. Michael Pratt, Graduate Studies Office, 419-448-2288, Fax: 419-448-2072, E-mail: mpratt@heidelberg.edu. *Director of Graduate Studies in Business,* Dr. Henry G. Rennie, 419-448-2221, Fax: 419-448-2072, E-mail: hrennie@nike.heidelberg.edu.

Program in Counseling Students: 15 full-time (12 women), 61 part-time (51 women); includes 9 minority (6 African Americans, 1 American Indian/Alaska Native, 2 Hispanic Americans). 26 applicants, 88% accepted, 23 enrolled. *Faculty:* 3 full-time (1 woman), 6 part-time/adjunct (3 women). Expenses: Contact institution. *Financial support:* In 2006–07, 51 students received support, including 1 teaching assistantship; Federal Work-Study also available. Support available to part-time students. Financial award applicants required to submit FAFSA. In 2006, 15 degrees awarded. *Degree program information:* Part-time and evening/weekend programs available. Offers counseling (MA). *Application deadline:* Applications are processed on a rolling basis. *Application fee:* $25. *Application Contact:* Dr. G. Michael Pratt, Graduate Studies Office, 419-448-2288, Fax: 419-448-2072, E-mail: mpratt@heidelberg.edu. *Director of Graduate Studies in Counseling,* Dr. Jo-Ann Lipford Sanders, 419-448-2312, Fax: 419-448-2072, E-mail: jsanders@heidelberg.edu.

Program in Education Students: 9 full-time (4 women), 105 part-time (72 women); includes 10 minority (4 African Americans, 5 Asian Americans or Pacific Islanders, 1 Hispanic American). 24 applicants, 83% accepted, 19 enrolled. *Faculty:* 3 part-time/adjunct (2 women). Expenses: Contact institution. *Financial support:* In 2006–07, 20 students received support. Federal Work-Study available. Support available to part-time students. Financial award applicants required to submit FAFSA. In 2006, 34 degrees awarded. *Degree program information:* Part-time and evening/weekend programs available. Offers education (MA). *Application deadline:* Applications are processed on a rolling basis. *Application fee:* $25. *Application Contact:* Dr. G. Michael Pratt, Graduate Studies Office, 419-448-2288, Fax: 419-448-2072, E-mail: mpratt@heidelberg.edu. *Director of Graduate Studies in Education,* Dr. Jim Getz, 419-448-2068, Fax: 419-448-2072, E-mail: jgetz@heidelberg.edu.

HENDERSON STATE UNIVERSITY, Arkadelphia, AR 71999-0001

General Information State-supported, coed, comprehensive institution. *Enrollment:* 3,664 graduate, professional, and undergraduate students; 132 full-time matriculated graduate/professional students (80 women), 314 part-time matriculated graduate/professional students (236 women). *Enrollment by degree level:* 425 master's, 21 other advanced degrees. *Graduate faculty:* 57 full-time (17 women), 9 part-time/adjunct (4 women). Tuition, state resident: full-time $3,294; part-time $183 per credit hour. Tuition, nonresident: full-time $6,588; part-time $366 per credit hour. *Required fees:* $176 per term. *Graduate housing:* Room and/or apartments available on a first-come, first-served basis to single students; on-campus housing not available to married students. Typical cost: $4,286 (including board). *Student services:* Campus employment opportunities, career counseling, disabled student services, free psychological counseling, international student services. *Library facilities:* Huie Library. *Online resources:* library catalog, web page, access to other libraries' catalogs.

Computer facilities: 125 computers available on campus for general student use. A campuswide network can be accessed from student residence rooms and from off campus. *Web address:* http://www.hsu.edu.

General Application Contact: Dr. Marck L. Beggs, Graduate Dean, 870-230-5126, Fax: 870-230-5479, E-mail: beggsm@hsu.edu.

GRADUATE UNITS

Graduate Studies Students: 132 full-time (80 women), 314 part-time (236 women); includes 55 minority (52 African Americans, 1 American Indian/Alaska Native, 2 Hispanic Americans), 42 international. Average age 33. 353 applicants, 29% accepted, 66 enrolled. *Faculty:* 57 full-time (17 women), 9 part-time/adjunct (4 women). Expenses: Contact institution. *Financial support:* In 2006–07, 16 teaching assistantships with full tuition reimbursements (averaging $4,000 per year) were awarded; Federal Work-Study and institutionally sponsored loans also available. Support available to part-time students. Financial award application deadline: 7/31; financial award applicants required to submit FAFSA. In 2006, 86 master's, 6 other advanced degrees awarded. *Degree program information:* Part-time programs available. *Application deadline:* For fall admission, 5/1 priority date for domestic students, 5/1 for international students; for winter admission, 10/1 for international students; for spring admission, 12/1 priority date for domestic students, 4/1 for international students. Applications are processed on a rolling basis. *Application fee:* $0 ($30 for international students). *Application Contact:* Erin Lafont, Administrative Assistant I, 870-230-5126, Fax: 870-230-5479, E-mail: lafonte@hsu.edu. *Graduate Dean,* Dr. Marck L. Beggs, 870-230-5126, Fax: 870-230-5479, E-mail: beggsm@hsu.edu.

Ellis College of Arts and Sciences Students: 15 full-time (9 women), 29 part-time (16 women); includes 7 minority (all African Americans), 4 international. Average age 32. *Faculty:* 10 full-time (4 women). Expenses: Contact institution. *Financial support:* In 2006–07, 1 teaching assistantship with tuition reimbursement (averaging $4,000 per year) was awarded; Federal Work-Study and institutionally sponsored loans also available. Support available to part-time students. Financial award application deadline: 7/31; financial award applicants required to submit FAFSA. In 2006, 8 degrees awarded. *Degree program information:* Part-time programs available. Offers arts and sciences (MLA). *Application deadline:* For fall admission, 5/1 priority date for domestic students, 5/1 for international students; for winter admission, 10/1 for international students; for spring admission, 12/1 priority date for domestic students, 4/1 for international students. Applications are processed on a rolling basis. *Application fee:* $0 ($30 for international students). *Application Contact:* Dr. Marck L. Beggs, Graduate Dean, 870-230-5126, Fax: 870-230-5479, E-mail: beggsm@hsu.edu. *Dean,* Dr. Maralyn Sommer, 870-230-5404, Fax: 870-230-5144, E-mail: sommerm@hsu.edu.

School of Business Administration Students: 28 full-time (11 women), 13 part-time (10 women); includes 11 minority (10 African Americans, 1 American Indian/Alaska Native), 4 international. Average age 27. *Faculty:* 10 full-time (1 woman). Expenses: Contact institution. *Financial support:* In 2006–07, 7 teaching assistantships with tuition reimbursements (averaging $4,000 per year) were awarded; research assistantships, Federal Work-Study and institutionally sponsored loans also available. Support available to part-time students. Financial award application deadline: 7/31. In 2006, 20 degrees awarded. *Degree program information:* Part-time programs available. Offers business administration (MBA). *Application deadline:* For fall admission, 5/1 priority date for domestic students, 5/1 for international students; for winter admission, 10/1 for international students; for spring admission, 12/1 priority date for domestic students, 4/1 for international students. Applications are processed on a rolling basis. *Application fee:* $0 ($30 for international students). *Application Contact:* Dr. Marck L. Beggs, Graduate Dean, 870-230-5126, Fax: 870-230-5479,

Henderson State University (continued)

E-mail: beggsm@hsu.edu. *Dean,* Dr. Paul Huo, 870-230-5310, Fax: 870-230-5286, E-mail: huoy@hsu.edu.

School of Education Students: 89 full-time (60 women), 272 part-time (210 women); includes 37 minority (35 African Americans, 2 Hispanic Americans), 34 international. Average age 36. *Faculty:* 37 full-time (12 women), 9 part-time/adjunct (4 women). Expenses: Contact institution. *Financial support:* In 2006–07, 7 teaching assistantships with full tuition reimbursements (averaging $4,000 per year) were awarded; research assistantships, Federal Work-Study and institutionally sponsored loans also available. Support available to part-time students. Financial award application deadline: 7/31. In 2006, 64 degrees awarded. *Degree program information:* Part-time programs available. Offers community counseling (MS); early childhood (P-4) (MSE); early childhood special education (MSE); education (MAT); educational leadership (Ed S); elementary school counseling (MSE); English (MSE); English as a second language (MSE, CP); instructional specialist (MSE); math (MSE); middle school (MSE); reading (MSE); recreation (MS); school administration (MSE); secondary school counseling (MSE); social science (MSE); sports administration (MS). *Application deadline:* For fall admission, 5/1 priority date for domestic students, 5/1 for international students; for winter admission, 10/1 for international students; for spring admission, 12/1 priority date for domestic students, 4/1 for international students. Applications are processed on a rolling basis. *Application fee:* $0 ($30 for international students). *Application Contact:* Dr. Marck L. Beggs, Graduate Dean, 870-230-5126, Fax: 870-230-5479, E-mail: beggsm@hsu.edu. *Dean,* Dr. Judy Harrison, 870-230-5358, Fax: 870-230-5455, E-mail: harrisj@hsu.edu.

HENDRIX COLLEGE, Conway, AR 72032-3080

General Information Independent-religious, coed, comprehensive institution. *Enrollment:* 1,095 graduate, professional, and undergraduate students; 8 full-time matriculated graduate/professional students (6 women). *Enrollment by degree level:* 8 master's. *Graduate faculty:* 5 full-time (1 woman), 1 part-time/adjunct (0 women). *Tuition:* Full-time $18,742. *Graduate housing:* Room and/or apartments available on a first-come, first-served basis to single students. Typical cost: $3,008 per year ($6,738 including board). Housing application deadline: 6/1. *Student services:* Campus employment opportunities, career counseling, disabled student services, exercise/wellness program, multicultural affairs office, writing training. *Library facilities:* Olin C. and Marjorie H. Bailey Library. *Online resources:* library catalog, web page. *Collection:* 219,843 titles, 37,162 serial subscriptions, 2,161 audiovisual materials.

Computer facilities: 75 computers available on campus for general student use. A campuswide network can be accessed from student residence rooms and from off campus. Internet access and online class registration are available. *Web address:* http://www.hendrix.edu/.

General Application Contact: Prof. Stephen W. Kerr, Professor of Economics and Business, 501-329-6811, Fax: 501-450-1400, E-mail: kerr@hendrix.edu.

GRADUATE UNITS

Program in Accounting Students: 8 full-time (6 women). Average age 22. 8 applicants, 100% accepted, 8 enrolled. *Faculty:* 5 full-time (1 woman), 1 part-time/adjunct (0 women). Expenses: Contact institution. *Financial support:* In 2006–07, 5 students received support, including 1 teaching assistantship with partial tuition reimbursement available (averaging $600 per year); career-related internships or fieldwork, Federal Work-Study, scholarships/grants, and tuition waivers (partial) also available. Financial award application deadline: 2/1; financial award applicants required to submit FAFSA. In 2006, 10 degrees awarded. *Degree program information:* Part-time programs available. Offers accounting (MA). *Application deadline:* For fall admission, 2/1 priority date for domestic and international students. Applications are processed on a rolling basis. *Application fee:* $50. *Professor of Economics and Business,* Prof. Stephen W. Kerr, 501-329-6811, Fax: 501-450-1400, E-mail: kerr@hendrix.edu.

HERITAGE BAPTIST COLLEGE AND HERITAGE THEOLOGICAL SEMINARY, Cambridge, ON N3C 3T2, Canada

General Information Independent-religious, coed, comprehensive institution.

GRADUATE UNITS

Program in Theological Studies Offers divinity (MA); theological studies (MA, Certificate).

HERITAGE CHRISTIAN UNIVERSITY, Florence, AL 35630

General Information Independent-religious, coed, primarily men, comprehensive institution.

GRADUATE UNITS

Graduate Programs Offers counseling (MM); Greek (MA); ministry (MM); New Testament (MA).

HERITAGE UNIVERSITY, Toppenish, WA 98948-9599

General Information Independent, coed, comprehensive institution. *Enrollment:* 328 full-time matriculated graduate/professional students (232 women), 146 part-time matriculated graduate/professional students (96 women). *Enrollment by degree level:* 474 master's. *Graduate faculty:* 21 full-time (13 women), 67 part-time/adjunct (35 women). *Graduate housing:* On-campus housing not available. *Student services:* Campus employment opportunities, campus safety program, career counseling, child daycare facilities, disabled student services, exercise/wellness program, free psychological counseling, grant writing training, multicultural affairs office, teacher training, writing training. *Library facilities:* Library and Resource Center. *Online resources:* library catalog, web page, access to other libraries' catalogs. *Collection:* 47,500 titles, 15,000 serial subscriptions, 400 audiovisual materials.

Computer facilities: 158 computers available on campus for general student use. A campuswide network can be accessed from off campus. Internet access is available. *Web address:* http://www.heritage.edu/.

General Application Contact: Kathy Otto, Coordinator of Administrative Services, 509-865-8635, Fax: 509-865-8629, E-mail: otto_k@heritage.edu.

GRADUATE UNITS

Graduate Programs in Education Students: 328 full-time (232 women), 146 part-time (96 women); includes 135 minority (11 African Americans, 11 American Indian/Alaska Native, 12 Asian Americans or Pacific Islanders, 101 Hispanic Americans). Average age 38. 245 applicants, 76% accepted, 134 enrolled. *Faculty:* 21 full-time (13 women), 67 part-time/adjunct (35 women). Expenses: Contact institution. *Financial support:* Career-related internships or fieldwork, Federal Work-Study, institutionally sponsored loans, and tuition waivers (partial) available. Support available to part-time students. Financial award application deadline: 2/10; financial award applicants required to submit FAFSA. In 2006, 254 degrees awarded. *Degree program information:* Part-time and evening/weekend programs available. Offers bilingual education/ESL (M Ed); biology (M Ed); counseling (M Ed); educational administration (M Ed); English and literature (M Ed); professional studies (M Ed); reading/literacy (M Ed); special education (M Ed); teaching (MIT). *Application deadline:* For fall admission, 3/15 priority date for domestic and international students; for spring admission, 2/1 priority date for domestic and international students. Applications are processed on a rolling basis. *Application fee:* $50 ($100 for international students). *Application Contact:* Kathy Otto, Coordinator of Administrative Services, 509-865-8635, Fax: 509-865-8629, E-mail: otto_k@heritage.edu. *Dean of the College of Education and Psychology,* Jim Borst, 509-865-8652, Fax: 509-865-8629, E-mail: borst_j@heritage.edu.

HIGH POINT UNIVERSITY, High Point, NC 27262-3598

General Information Independent-religious, coed, comprehensive institution. CGS member. *Enrollment:* 2,811 graduate, professional, and undergraduate students; 49 full-time matriculated graduate/professional students (29 women), 202 part-time matriculated graduate/professional students (130 women). *Enrollment by degree level:* 251 master's. *Graduate faculty:* 31 full-time (11 women), 1 part-time/adjunct (0 women). *Tuition:* Full-time $9,270; part-time $1,545 per course. *Graduate housing:* Rooms and/or apartments available on a first-come, first-served basis to single and married students. Housing application deadline: 5/31. *Student services:* Campus safety program, career counseling, disabled student services, exercise/wellness program, free psychological counseling, low-cost health insurance. *Library facilities:* Herman and Louise Smith Library. *Online resources:* library catalog, web page, access to other libraries' catalogs. *Collection:* 204,141 titles, 23,767 serial subscriptions, 7,988 audiovisual materials.

Computer facilities: 176 computers available on campus for general student use. A campuswide network can be accessed from student residence rooms and from off campus. Internet access is available. *Web address:* http://www.highpoint.edu/.

General Application Contact: Dr. Alberta Haynes Herron, Dean of Norcross Graduate School, 336-841-9198, Fax: 336-888-6378, E-mail: aherron@highpoint.edu.

GRADUATE UNITS

Norcross Graduate School Students: 49 full-time (29 women), 202 part-time (130 women); includes 72 minority (66 African Americans, 1 American Indian/Alaska Native, 2 Asian Americans or Pacific Islanders, 3 Hispanic Americans), 11 international. Average age 33. 171 applicants, 71% accepted, 94 enrolled. *Faculty:* 31 full-time (11 women), 1 part-time/adjunct (0 women). Expenses: Contact institution. *Financial support:* In 2006–07, 190 students received support. Federal Work-Study, scholarships/grants, and unspecified assistantships available. Support available to part-time students. Financial award application deadline: 3/1; financial award applicants required to submit FAFSA. In 2006, 95 degrees awarded. *Degree program information:* Part-time and evening/weekend programs available. Offers business administration (MBA); educational leadership (M Ed); elementary education (M Ed); history (MA); nonprofit organizations (MPA); special education (M Ed); sport studies (MS). *Application deadline:* For fall admission, 4/15 priority date for domestic and international students; for spring admission, 10/15 priority date for domestic and international students. Applications are processed on a rolling basis. *Application fee:* $50. Electronic applications accepted. *Application Contact:* Dr. Alberta Haynes Herron, Dean of Norcross Graduate School, 336-841-9198, Fax: 336-888-6378, E-mail: aherron@highpoint.edu.

HILLSDALE FREE WILL BAPTIST COLLEGE, Moore, OK 73160-1208

General Information Independent-religious, coed, comprehensive institution. *Graduate housing:* Room and/or apartments available on a first-come, first-served basis to single students.

GRADUATE UNITS

Department of Bible Studies *Degree program information:* Part-time and evening/weekend programs available. Offers ministry (MA).

HODGES UNIVERSITY, Naples, FL 34119

General Information Independent, coed, comprehensive institution. *Enrollment:* 1,640 graduate, professional, and undergraduate students; 35 full-time matriculated graduate/professional students (22 women), 156 part-time matriculated graduate/professional students (100 women). *Graduate faculty:* 17 full-time (4 women). *Library facilities:* Information Resource Center plus 1 other. *Online resources:* library catalog, web page, access to other libraries' catalogs. *Collection:* 29,711 titles, 230 serial subscriptions.

Computer facilities: 500 computers available on campus for general student use. A campuswide network can be accessed. Internet access is available. *Web address:* http://www.internationalcollege.edu/.

General Application Contact: Terry McMahan, President, 239-513-1122, Fax: 239-598-6253, E-mail: tmcmahan@internationalcollege.edu.

GRADUATE UNITS

Graduate Programs Students: 35 full-time (22 women), 156 part-time (100 women); includes 52 minority (24 African Americans, 1 American Indian/Alaska Native, 4 Asian Americans or Pacific Islanders, 23 Hispanic Americans). Average age 32. *Faculty:* 17 full-time (4 women). Expenses: Contact institution. *Financial support:* Federal Work-Study and scholarships/grants available. Financial award applicants required to submit FAFSA. In 2006, 101 degrees awarded. *Degree program information:* Part-time and evening/weekend programs available. Postbaccalaureate distance learning degree programs offered (no on-campus study). *Application fee:* $50. Electronic applications accepted. *Application Contact:* Rita Lampus, Vice President of Student Enrollment Management, 239-513-1122, Fax: 239-598-6253, E-mail: rlampus@internationalcollege.edu. *President,* Terry McMahan, 239-513-1122, Fax: 239-598-6253, E-mail: tmcmahan@internationalcollege.edu.

HOFSTRA UNIVERSITY, Hempstead, NY 11549

General Information Independent, coed, university. CGS member. *Enrollment:* 12,550 graduate, professional, and undergraduate students; 2,094 full-time matriculated graduate/professional students (1,273 women), 1,766 part-time matriculated graduate/professional students (1,118 women). *Enrollment by degree level:* 1,127 first professional, 2,373 master's, 254 doctoral, 106 other advanced degrees. *Graduate faculty:* 246 full-time (103 women), 183 part-time/adjunct (84 women). *Tuition:* Full-time $13,320; part-time $740 per credit. *Required fees:* $930; $155 per term. *Graduate housing:* Rooms and/or apartments available on a first-come, first-served basis to single and married students. Typical cost: $9,000 per year ($11,000 including board) for single students. Room and board charges vary according to board plan and housing facility selected. *Student services:* Campus employment opportunities, campus safety program, career counseling, child daycare facilities, disabled student services, exercise/wellness program, free psychological counseling, grant writing training, international student services, low-cost health insurance, multicultural affairs office, teacher training, writing training. *Library facilities:* Axinn Library plus 1 other. *Online resources:* library catalog, web page, access to other libraries' catalogs. *Collection:* 1.2 million titles, 9,950 serial subscriptions, 14,730 audiovisual materials.

Computer facilities: Computer purchase and lease plans are available. 1,175 computers available on campus for general student use. A campuswide network can be accessed from student residence rooms and from off campus. Internet access and online class registration are available. *Web address:* http://www.hofstra.edu/.

General Application Contact: Carol Drummer, Dean of Graduate Admissions, 516-463-4876, Fax: 516-463-4664, E-mail: gradstudent@hofstra.edu.

GRADUATE UNITS

College of Liberal Arts and Sciences Students: 297 full-time (226 women), 136 part-time (80 women); includes 59 minority (17 African Americans, 16 Asian Americans or Pacific Islanders, 26 Hispanic Americans), 5 international. Average age 27. 755 applicants, 44% accepted, 143 enrolled. *Faculty:* 77 full-time (28 women), 35 part-time/adjunct (15 women). Expenses: Contact institution. *Financial support:* In 2006–07, 228 students received support, including 126 fellowships with tuition reimbursements available (averaging $4,758 per year), 18 research assistantships with full and partial tuition reimbursements available (averaging $6,325 per year); career-related internships or fieldwork, Federal Work-Study, scholarships/grants, tuition waivers (full and partial), unspecified assistantships, and creative writing awards also available. Support available to part-time students. Financial award applicants required to submit FAFSA. In 2006, 121 master's, 39 doctorates, 8 other advanced degrees awarded. *Degree program information:* Part-time and evening/weekend programs available. Offers applied linguistics (MA); applied mathematics (MS); applied organizational psychology (PhD); audiology (MA, Au D); biology (MA, MS); clinical and school psychology (MA, PhD); comparative arts and culture (MA); computer science (MA, MS); engineering management (MS); English (literature) (MA); English and creative writing (MA); industrial/organizational psychology (MA); liberal arts and sciences (MA, MS, Au D, PhD, Psy D, CAS); mathematics (MA); school and community psychology (MS); school-community psychology (Psy D, CAS); Spanish (MA); speech-language pathology (MA). *Application deadline:* Applications are processed on a rolling basis. *Application fee:* $60. Electronic applications accepted. *Application Contact:* Carol Drummer, Dean of Graduate Admissions, 516-463-4876, Fax: 516-463-4664, E-mail: gradstudent@hofstra.edu. *Dean,* Dr. Bernard J. Firestone, 516-463-5411, Fax: 516-463-4861, E-mail: lasbjf@hofstra.edu.

Frank G. Zarb School of Business Students: 194 full-time (72 women), 451 part-time (198 women); includes 126 minority (43 African Americans, 58 Asian Americans or Pacific Islanders, 25 Hispanic Americans), 54 international. Average age 31. 429 applicants, 85% accepted, 217 enrolled. *Faculty:* 42 full-time (8 women), 8 part-time/adjunct (1 woman). Expenses: Contact institution. *Financial support:* In 2006–07, 110 students received support, including 79 fellowships with tuition reimbursements available (averaging $6,259 per year), 11 research assistantships with full and partial tuition reimbursements available (averaging $4,866 per year); career-related internships or fieldwork, Federal Work-Study, scholarships/grants, health care benefits, tuition waivers (full and partial), and unspecified assistantships also available. Support available to part-time students. Financial award applicants required to submit FAFSA. In 2006, 176 master's, 3 other advanced degrees awarded. *Degree program information:* Part-time and evening/weekend programs available. Offers accounting (MBA, MS); business (EMBA, MBA, MS, Advanced Certificate); business administration (EMBA); business computer information systems (MBA); computer information systems (MS); finance (MBA, MS); health services management (MBA); human resource management (MS, Advanced Certificate); international business (MBA, MS, Advanced Certificate); management (EMBA, MBA); marketing (MBA, MS, Advanced Certificate); marketing research (MS); quality management (MBA); quantitative finance (MS); taxation (MBA, MS). *Application deadline:* Applications are processed on a rolling basis. *Application fee:* $60. Electronic applications accepted. *Application Contact:* Carol Drummer, Dean of Graduate Admissions, 516-463-4876, Fax: 516-463-4664, E-mail: gradstudent@hofstra.edu. *Dean,* Salvatore F. Sodano, 516-463-5685, Fax: 516-463-5268, E-mail: bizsfs@hofstra.edu.

New College Average age 33. 2 applicants, 100% accepted. Expenses: Contact institution. *Financial support:* Fellowships with tuition reimbursements, research assistantships with full and partial tuition reimbursements, tuition waivers (full and partial) and unspecified assistantships available. Financial award applicants required to submit FAFSA. *Degree program information:* Part-time and evening/weekend programs available. Offers interdisciplinary studies (MA). *Application deadline:* Applications are processed on a rolling basis. *Application fee:* $60. Electronic applications accepted. *Application Contact:* Carol Drummer, Dean of Graduate Admissions, 516-463-4876, Fax: 516-463-4664, E-mail: gradstudent@hofstra.edu. *Vice Dean,* Dr. Barry Nass, 516-463-5820, Fax: 516-463-4832, E-mail: barry.n.nass@hofstra.edu.

School of Communication Students: 10 full-time (8 women), 18 part-time (11 women); includes 2 minority (both African Americans), 2 international. Average age 29. 35 applicants, 94% accepted, 15 enrolled. *Faculty:* 7 full-time (4 women), 1 part-time/adjunct (0 women). Expenses: Contact institution. *Financial support:* In 2006–07, 22 students received support, including 1 fellowship with tuition reimbursement available (averaging $3,000 per year), 6 research assistantships with full and partial tuition reimbursements available (averaging $6,546 per year); scholarships/grants, tuition waivers (full and partial), and unspecified assistantships also available. Support available to part-time students. Financial award applicants required to submit FAFSA. In 2006, 4 degrees awarded. *Degree program information:* Part-time and evening/weekend programs available. Offers audio, video, and film (MFA); communication (MA, MFA); journalism (MA); speech communication, rhetoric, and performance studies (MA). *Application deadline:* Applications are processed on a rolling basis. *Application fee:* $60. Electronic applications accepted. *Application Contact:* Carol Drummer, Dean of Graduate Admissions, 516-463-4876, Fax: 516-463-4664, E-mail: gradstudent@hofstra.edu. *Dean,* Dr. Sybil A. DelGaudio, 516-463-5431, Fax: 516-463-4866, E-mail: avfsdg@hofstra.edu.

School of Education and Allied Human Services Students: 702 full-time (551 women), 900 part-time (700 women); includes 131 minority (11 African Americans, 1 American Indian/Alaska Native, 35 Asian Americans or Pacific Islanders, 84 Hispanic Americans), 21 international. Average age 29. 1,094 applicants, 84% accepted, 545 enrolled. *Faculty:* 62 full-time (45 women), 94 part-time/adjunct (60 women). Expenses: Contact institution. *Financial support:* In 2006–07, 593 students received support, including 104 fellowships with tuition reimbursements available (averaging $3,571 per year), 42 research assistantships with full and partial tuition reimbursements available (averaging $5,859 per year); career-related internships or fieldwork, Federal Work-Study, institutionally sponsored loans, scholarships/grants, traineeships, health care benefits, tuition waivers (full and partial), unspecified assistantships, and tuition vouchers for cooperating teachers also available. Support available to part-time students. Financial award applicants required to submit FAFSA. In 2006, 641 master's, 10 doctorates, 62 other advanced degrees awarded. *Degree program information:* Part-time and evening/weekend programs available. Postbaccalaureate distance learning degree programs offered. Offers addiction studies (CAS); advanced literacy studies (birth-6) (PD); advanced literacy studies (grades 5–12) (PD); bilingual education (MA); bilingual extension education (CAS); business education (MS Ed); counseling (MA, MS Ed, Advanced Certificate, PD); creative arts therapy (MA, MS Ed); creative arts therapy and special education (birth-grade 2) (MS Ed); creative arts therapy and special education (grades 1-12) (MS Ed); divorce mediation (CAS); early childhood and childhood education (MS Ed); early childhood education (MA, MS Ed); early childhood special education (MS Ed, Advanced Certificate); education and allied human services (MA, MHA, MS, MS Ed, Ed D, PhD, Advanced Certificate, CAS, PD); educational administration (MS Ed, CAS); educational administration and policy studies (MS Ed); educational and policy leadership (Ed D); educational leadership (CAS); elementary education (MA, MS Ed); elementary education-math/science/technology (MA); English education (MA, MS Ed); family therapy (CAS); fine arts education (MA, MS Ed); foreign language education (MA, MS Ed); foundations of education (MA, CAS); French (MA, MS Ed); German (MA, MS Ed); gerontology (MS, Advanced Certificate); gifted education (Advanced Certificate); health administration (MHA); health education (MS); inclusive early childhood special education (MS Ed); inclusive elementary special education (MS Ed); inclusive secondary special education (MS Ed); intensive program in fine arts or music (Advanced Certificate); intensive program in secondary education (CAS); literacy studies (MA, MS Ed, Ed D, PhD, CAS, PD); literacy studies (birth–grade 6) (MS Ed, CAS); literacy studies (birth-grade 6) and special education (birth-grade 2) (MS Ed); literacy studies (birth-grade 6) and special education (grades 1-6) (MS Ed); literacy studies (grades 5–12) (MS Ed, CAS); literacy studies and special education (MS Ed); marriage and family therapy (MA, CAS, PD); mathematics education (MA, MS Ed); mental health counseling (MA); middle level education (CAS); middle school extension (grades 5-6) (CAS); middle school extension (grades 7-9) (CAS); music education (MA, MS Ed); physical education (MS); program evaluation (MS Ed); rehabilitation administration (PD); rehabilitation counseling (MS Ed, PD); rehabilitation counseling in mental health (MS Ed); Russian (MA, MS Ed); school counselor (MS Ed); school counselor-bilingual extension (Advanced Certificate); school district business leader (CAS); science education (MA, MS Ed, CAS); science education (biology, chemistry, geology, physics, earth science) (MA); science education (biology, chemistry, physics, earth science, geology) (MS Ed); secondary education (intensive program) (CAS); social studies education (MA, MS Ed); Spanish (MA, MS Ed); special education (MA, MS Ed, Advanced Certificate, PD); special education assessment and diagnosis (Advanced Certificate); teaching of writing (birth–grade 6) (MA); teaching of writing (grades 5–12) (MA); teaching students with severe/multiple disabilities (Advanced Certificate); TESL/bilingual education (MA, MS Ed, CAS); TESOL (MS Ed, CAS); wind conducting (MA). *Application deadline:* Applications are processed on a rolling basis. *Application fee:* $60. Electronic applications accepted. *Application Contact:* Carol Drummer, Dean of Graduate Admissions, 516-463-4876, Fax: 516-463-4664, E-mail: gradstudent@hofstra.edu. *Interim Dean,* Dr. Maureen O. Murphy, 516-463-6775, E-mail: catmom@hofstra.edu.

School of Law Students: 891 full-time (416 women), 257 part-time (127 women); includes 245 minority (87 African Americans, 2 American Indian/Alaska Native, 92 Asian Americans or Pacific Islanders, 64 Hispanic Americans), 22 international. Average age 26. 4,810 applicants, 43% accepted, 461 enrolled. *Faculty:* 58 full-time (21 women), 37 part-time/adjunct (7 women). Expenses: Contact institution. *Financial support:* In 2006–07, 591 students received support, including 483 fellowships with tuition reimbursements available (averaging $14,864 per year), 1 research assistantship with full and partial tuition reimbursement available (averaging $3,825 per year); Federal Work-Study, scholarships/grants, health care benefits, and unspecified assistantships also available. Financial award applicants required to submit FAFSA. In 2006, 300 JDs, 10 master's awarded. *Degree program information:* Part-time and evening/weekend programs available. Offers American legal studies (LL M); family law (LL M); international law (LL M); law (JD). *Application deadline:* For fall admission, 4/15 priority date for domestic and international students. Applications are processed on a rolling basis. *Application fee:* $60. Electronic applications accepted. *Application Contact:* Noreen A. O'Brien, Director of Law School Enrollment- Operations, 516-463-5243, Fax: 516-463-6264, E-mail: lawadmissions@hofstra.edu. *Interim Dean,* Nora V. Demleitner, 516-463-6190, Fax: 516-463-6091, E-mail: lawnvd@hofstra.edu.

See Close-Up on page 915.

HOLLINS UNIVERSITY, Roanoke, VA 24020-1603

General Information Independent, Undergraduate: women only; graduate: coed, comprehensive institution. *Enrollment:* 1,061 graduate, professional, and undergraduate students; 179 full-time matriculated graduate/professional students (136 women), 148 part-time matriculated graduate/professional students (119 women). *Enrollment by degree level:* 318 master's, 9 other advanced degrees. *Graduate faculty:* 23 full-time (9 women), 33 part-time/adjunct (17 women). *Graduate housing:* Room and/or apartments available on a first-come, first-served basis to single students; on-campus housing not available to married students. Housing application deadline: 8/1. *Student services:* Campus safety program, career counseling, disabled student services, international student services, low-cost health insurance, multicultural affairs office, teacher training, writing training. *Library facilities:* Wyndham Robertson Library plus 1 other. *Online resources:* library catalog, web page, access to other libraries' catalogs. *Collection:* 232,507 titles, 43,004 serial subscriptions, 7,493 audiovisual materials.

Computer facilities: 100 computers available on campus for general student use. A campuswide network can be accessed from student residence rooms and from off campus. Internet access, applications software are available. *Web address:* http://www.hollins.edu/.

General Application Contact: Cathy S. Koon, Manager of Graduate Services, 540-362-6326, Fax: 540-362-6288, E-mail: ckoon@hollins.edu.

GRADUATE UNITS

Graduate Programs Students: 179 full-time (136 women), 148 part-time (119 women); includes 41 minority (26 African Americans, 2 American Indian/Alaska Native, 5 Asian Americans or Pacific Islanders, 8 Hispanic Americans). Average age 33. 371 applicants, 47% accepted, 121 enrolled. *Faculty:* 23 full-time (9 women), 33 part-time/adjunct (17 women). Expenses: Contact institution. *Financial support:* In 2006–07, 216 students received support, including 35 fellowships (averaging $8,963 per year), 8 teaching assistantships (averaging $6,000 per year); Federal Work-Study and scholarships/grants also available. Support available to part-time students. Financial award application deadline: 7/15; financial award applicants required to submit FAFSA. In 2006, 100 degrees awarded. *Degree program information:* Part-time and evening/weekend programs available. Offers children's literature (MA, MFA); creative writing (MFA); dance (MFA); humanities (MALS); interdisciplinary studies (MALS); liberal studies (CAS); playwriting (MFA); screenwriting and film studies (MA, MFA); social science (MALS); teaching (MAT); visual and performing arts (MALS). *Application deadline:* For fall admission, 1/6 priority date for domestic and international students. Applications are processed on a rolling basis. *Application fee:* $40. Electronic applications accepted. *Application Contact:* Cathy S. Koon, Manager of Graduate Services, 540-362-6326, Fax: 540-362-6288, E-mail: ckoon@hollins.edu. *Provost,* Dr. Wayne Markert, 540-362-6491, Fax: 540-362-6288.

See Close-Up on page 917.

HOLMES INSTITUTE, Burbank, CA 91505

General Information Independent-religious, coed, graduate-only institution. *Graduate faculty:* 50. *Web address:* http://www.holmesinstitute.org/.

GRADUATE UNITS

Graduate Program *Faculty:* 50. Expenses: Contact institution.

HOLY APOSTLES COLLEGE AND SEMINARY, Cromwell, CT 06416-2005

General Information Independent-religious, coed, comprehensive institution. *Enrollment:* 270 graduate, professional, and undergraduate students; 61 full-time matriculated graduate/professional students (1 woman), 132 part-time matriculated graduate/professional students (48 women). *Enrollment by degree level:* 52 first professional, 129 master's, 11 other advanced degrees. *Graduate faculty:* 10 full-time (2 women), 13 part-time/adjunct (4 women). *Tuition:* Part-time $250 per credit. *Graduate housing:* On-campus housing not available. *Student services:* Free psychological counseling, writing training. *Library facilities:* Holy Apostles College and Seminary Library. *Online resources:* library catalog, web page, access to other libraries' catalogs. *Collection:* 85,000 titles, 250 serial subscriptions, 400 audiovisual materials.

Computer facilities: 6 computers available on campus for general student use. Internet access is available. *Web address:* http://www.holyapostles.edu/.

General Application Contact: Dr. Cynthia Toolin, Registrar, 860-632-3033, Fax: 860-632-3075, E-mail: registrar@holyapostles.edu.

GRADUATE UNITS

Department of Theology Students: 61 full-time (1 woman), 147 part-time (56 women); includes 21 minority (4 Asian Americans or Pacific Islanders, 17 Hispanic Americans), 14 international. Average age 44. *Faculty:* 10 full-time (2 women), 13 part-time/adjunct (4 women). Expenses: Contact institution. *Financial support:* In 2006–07, 25 students received support. Career-related internships or fieldwork and scholarships/grants available. Support available to part-time students. Financial award applicants required to submit FAFSA. In 2006, 9 M Divs, 28 master's, 3 other advanced degrees awarded. *Degree program information:* Part-time and evening/weekend programs available. Postbaccalaureate distance learning degree programs offered (no on-campus study). Offers bioethics (MA, Certificate, Post Master's Certificate); church history (MA, Certificate, Post Master's Certificate); dogmatic theology (MA, Certificate, Post Master's Certificate); liturgical music (MA, Certificate, Post Master's Certificate); liturgy (MA, Certificate, Post Master's Certificate); moral theology (MA, Certificate, Post Master's Certificate); philosophical theology (MA, Certificate, Post Master's Certificate); religious education (MA, Certificate, Post Master's Certificate); sacred scripture (MA, Post Master's Certificate); sacred scriptures (Certificate); theology (M Div). *Application deadline:* For fall admission, 8/15 priority date for domestic and international students; for spring admission, 1/15 priority date for domestic and international students. Applications are processed on a rolling basis. *Application fee:* $25. Electronic applications accepted. *Application Contact:* Rev. Douglas L. Mosey, President and Rector, 860-632-3012, Fax: 860-632-0176, E-mail: rector@holyapostles.edu. *Academic Dean,* Rev. Maurice Sheehan, OFM, 860-632-3001, Fax: 860-632-3075.

HOLY CROSS GREEK ORTHODOX SCHOOL OF THEOLOGY, Brookline, MA 02445-7496

General Information Independent-religious, coed, primarily men, graduate-only institution. *Graduate housing:* Rooms and/or apartments available on a first-come, first-served basis to single and married students.

GRADUATE UNITS

Theological Programs *Degree program information:* Part-time programs available. Offers theology (M Div, MTS, Th M).

HOLY FAMILY UNIVERSITY, Philadelphia, PA 19114-2094

General Information Independent-religious, coed, comprehensive institution. *Graduate housing:* On-campus housing not available.

GRADUATE UNITS

Graduate School *Degree program information:* Part-time and evening/weekend programs available. Electronic applications accepted.

School of Arts and Sciences *Degree program information:* Part-time and evening/weekend programs available. Offers counseling psychology (MS).

Holy Family University (continued)

School of Business *Degree program information:* Part-time and evening/weekend programs available. Offers human resources management (MS); information systems management (MS).

School of Education *Degree program information:* Part-time and evening/weekend programs available. Offers education (M Ed); elementary education (M Ed); reading specialist (M Ed); secondary education (M Ed).

School of Nursing *Degree program information:* Part-time and evening/weekend programs available. Offers nursing (MSN).

HOLY NAMES UNIVERSITY, Oakland, CA 94619-1699

General Information Independent-religious, coed, primarily women, comprehensive institution. *Enrollment:* 1,048 graduate, professional, and undergraduate students; 176 full-time matriculated graduate/professional students (152 women), 249 part-time matriculated graduate/professional students (188 women). *Enrollment by degree level:* 319 master's, 106 other advanced degrees. *Graduate faculty:* 12 full-time (10 women), 50 part-time/adjunct (35 women). *Tuition:* Full-time $10,800; part-time $600 per unit. *Required fees:* $240; $120 per term. *Graduate housing:* Room and/or apartments available on a first-come, first-served basis to single students; on-campus housing not available to married students. Typical cost: $7,500 (including board). Room and board charges vary according to board plan. Housing application deadline: 8/15. *Student services:* Campus employment opportunities, campus safety program, career counseling, free psychological counseling, international student services, low-cost health insurance. *Library facilities:* Cushing Library. *Online resources:* web page. *Collection:* 109,297 titles, 8,003 serial subscriptions, 5,078 audiovisual materials.

Computer facilities: 86 computers available on campus for general student use. A campuswide network can be accessed from student residence rooms and from off campus. Internet access is available. *Web address:* http://www.hnu.edu/.

General Application Contact: Gary Murdough, Graduate Admissions Office, 510-436-1351, Fax: 510-436-1325, E-mail: admissions@hnu.edu.

GRADUATE UNITS

Graduate Division Students: 176 full-time (152 women), 249 part-time (188 women); includes 186 minority (118 African Americans, 2 American Indian/Alaska Native, 40 Asian Americans or Pacific Islanders, 26 Hispanic Americans), 17 international. Average age 41. 219 applicants, 76% accepted, 142 enrolled. *Faculty:* 12 full-time (10 women), 50 part-time/adjunct (35 women). Expenses: Contact institution. *Financial support:* In 2006–07, 193 students received support. Scholarships/grants available. Support available to part-time students. Financial award application deadline: 3/2; financial award applicants required to submit FAFSA. In 2006, 60 master's, 37 other advanced degrees awarded. *Degree program information:* Part-time and evening/weekend programs available. Offers advanced curriculum studies (M Ed); community health nursing/case manager (MS); counseling psychology (MA); educational therapy (M Ed); family nurse practitioner (MS); Kodály music education (Certificate); management (MBA); mild/moderate disabilities (Ed S); multiple subject credential (M Ed); music education with a Kodály emphasis (MM); pastoral counseling (MA, Certificate); pastoral ministries (MA); performance (MM); piano pedagogy (MM); piano pedagogy with Suzuki emphasis (Certificate); single subject credential (M Ed); special education (M Ed); teaching English as a second language (M Ed, Certificate); urban education (M Ed). *Application deadline:* For fall admission, 8/1 priority date for domestic students; for spring admission, 12/1 priority date for domestic students. Applications are processed on a rolling basis. *Application fee:* $50. Electronic applications accepted. *Application Contact:* Gary Murdough, Graduate Admissions Office, 510-436-1351, Fax: 510-436-1325, E-mail: admissions@hnu.edu. *Vice President for Academic Affairs,* Dr. Lizbeth Martin, 510-436-1040, Fax: 510-436-1199, E-mail: martin@hnu.edu.

Sophia Center: Spirituality for the New Millennium Students: 12 full-time (10 women), 33 part-time (26 women); includes 6 minority (4 African Americans, 2 Hispanic Americans), 5 international. Average age 53. 20 applicants, 100% accepted, 20 enrolled. *Faculty:* 1 full-time (0 women), 12 part-time/adjunct (7 women). Expenses: Contact institution. *Financial support:* In 2006–07, 15 students received support. Available to part-time students. Application deadline: 3/2; In 2006, 17 master's, 1 other advanced degree awarded. Offers creation spirituality (Certificate); culture and creation spirituality (MA). *Application deadline:* For fall admission, 8/1 priority date for domestic students; for spring admission, 12/1 priority date for domestic students. Applications are processed on a rolling basis. *Application fee:* $50. *Application Contact:* 800-430-1351, Fax: 510-436-1325, E-mail: admissions@hnu.edu. *Program Director,* Dr. James Conlon, 510-436-1046.

HOOD COLLEGE, Frederick, MD 21701-8575

General Information Independent, coed, comprehensive institution. CGS member. *Enrollment:* 2,248 graduate, professional, and undergraduate students; 63 full-time matriculated graduate/professional students (38 women), 891 part-time matriculated graduate/professional students (657 women). *Enrollment by degree level:* 778 master's, 176 other advanced degrees. *Graduate faculty:* 31 full-time (11 women), 67 part-time/adjunct (27 women). *Tuition:* Part-time $350 per credit. *Required fees:* $20 per semester. *Graduate housing:* On-campus housing not available. *Student services:* Campus employment opportunities, campus safety program, career counseling, disabled student services, international student services, multicultural affairs office, teacher training. *Library facilities:* Beneficial-Hodson Library and Information Technology Center. *Online resources:* library catalog, web page, access to other libraries' catalogs. *Collection:* 206,800 titles, 28,377 serial subscriptions, 5,899 audiovisual materials.

Computer facilities: 277 computers available on campus for general student use. A campuswide network can be accessed from student residence rooms and from off campus. Internet access and online class registration are available. *Web address:* http://www.hood.edu/.

General Application Contact: Dr. Kathleen C. Bands, Associate Dean of Graduate School, 301-696-3811, Fax: 301-696-3597, E-mail: gofurther@hood.edu.

GRADUATE UNITS

Graduate School Students: 63 full-time (38 women), 891 part-time (657 women); includes 88 minority (51 African Americans, 24 Asian Americans or Pacific Islanders, 13 Hispanic Americans), 30 international. Average age 34. 315 applicants, 98% accepted, 216 enrolled. *Faculty:* 31 full-time (11 women), 67 part-time/adjunct (27 women). Expenses: Contact institution. *Financial support:* Research assistantships, career-related internships or fieldwork and unspecified assistantships available. Financial award applicants required to submit FAFSA. In 2006, 176 master's, 37 other advanced degrees awarded. *Degree program information:* Part-time and evening/weekend programs available. Offers administration and management (MBA); biomedical science (MS); ceramic arts (MFA, Certificate); computer and information sciences (MS); computer science (MS); curriculum and instruction (MS); educational leadership (MS); environmental biology (MS); foreign language proficiency (Certificate); human sciences (MA); humanities (MA); management of information technology (MS); reading specialization (MS); secondary mathematics education (Certificate); teaching the struggling reader (Certificate); thanatology (MA, Certificate). *Application deadline:* Applications are processed on a rolling basis. Electronic applications accepted. *Application Contact:* Dr. Kathleen C. Bands, Associate Dean of Graduate School, 301-696-3811, Fax: 301-696-3597, E-mail: gofurther@hood.edu. *Dean of the Graduate School,* Dr. Frank Sweeney, 301-696-3600, Fax: 301-696-3597, E-mail: sweeney@hood.edu.

HOOD THEOLOGICAL SEMINARY, Salisbury, NC 28144

General Information Independent-religious, coed, graduate-only institution. *Enrollment by degree level:* 201 first professional, 20 master's, 43 doctoral. *Graduate faculty:* 8 full-time (2 women), 8 part-time/adjunct (3 women). *Graduate housing:* Rooms and/or apartments guaranteed to single students and available on a first-come, first-served basis to married students. Typical cost: $3,600 (including board) for single students. Housing application deadline: 8/15. *Student services:* Campus employment opportunities, writing training. *Library facilities:* Hood Seminary Library. *Online resources:* library catalog, access to other libraries' catalogs. *Collection:* 30,677 titles, 346 serial subscriptions, 237 audiovisual materials.

Computer facilities: 7 computers available on campus for general student use. A campuswide network can be accessed from student residence rooms. Internet access is available. *Web address:* http://www.hoodseminary.edu/.

General Application Contact: Director of Admissions, 704-636-6455, Fax: 704-636-7699, E-mail: admissions@hoodseminary.edu.

GRADUATE UNITS

Graduate and Professional Programs Students: 231 full-time (94 women), 33 part-time (12 women); includes 175 minority (173 African Americans, 2 American Indian/Alaska Native). Average age 47. 98 applicants, 89% accepted. *Faculty:* 8 full-time (2 women), 8 part-time/adjunct (3 women). Expenses: Contact institution. *Financial support:* In 2006–07, 164 students received support. Scholarships/grants and resident assistantships available. Financial award application deadline: 6/30; financial award applicants required to submit FAFSA. In 2006, 29 M Divs, 4 master's, 9 doctorates awarded. *Degree program information:* Evening/weekend programs available. Offers theology (M Div, MTS, D Min). *Application deadline:* For fall admission, 7/15 priority date for domestic students; for spring admission, 12/1 for domestic students. *Application fee:* $30. *Application Contact:* Director of Admissions, 704-636-6455, Fax: 704-636-7699, E-mail: admissions@hoodseminary.edu. *President,* Dr. Albert J. D. Aymer, 704-636-6823, Fax: 704-636-7699, E-mail: president@hoodseminary.edu.

HOPE INTERNATIONAL UNIVERSITY, Fullerton, CA 92831-3138

General Information Independent-religious, coed, comprehensive institution. *Enrollment:* 903 graduate, professional, and undergraduate students; 126 full-time matriculated graduate/professional students (92 women), 146 part-time matriculated graduate/professional students (80 women). *Enrollment by degree level:* 272 master's. *Graduate faculty:* 6 full-time (1 woman), 37 part-time/adjunct (15 women). *Graduate housing:* Room and/or apartments available on a first-come, first-served basis to single students; on-campus housing not available to married students. Housing application deadline: 7/15. *Student services:* Campus employment opportunities, career counseling, free psychological counseling, international student services, low-cost health insurance, multicultural affairs office, teacher training. *Library facilities:* Darling Library. *Online resources:* library catalog, access to other libraries' catalogs. *Collection:* 100,000 titles, 500 serial subscriptions.

Computer facilities: 44 computers available on campus for general student use. A campuswide network can be accessed from off campus. Internet access is available. *Web address:* http://www.hiu.edu/.

General Application Contact: Teresa Smith, Director of Graduate and Adult Admissions, 714-879-3901, Fax: 714-681-7450.

GRADUATE UNITS

School of Graduate Studies Students: 126 full-time (92 women), 146 part-time (80 women); includes 90 minority (31 African Americans, 1 American Indian/Alaska Native, 34 Asian Americans or Pacific Islanders, 24 Hispanic Americans), 4 international. Average age 29. 260 applicants, 69% accepted, 170 enrolled. *Faculty:* 7 full-time (1 woman), 36 part-time/adjunct (15 women). Expenses: Contact institution. *Financial support:* In 2006–07, 75 students received support, including 75 fellowships (averaging $1,679 per year); scholarships/grants and tuition waivers (partial) also available. Support available to part-time students. Financial award applicants required to submit FAFSA. In 2006, 76 degrees awarded. *Degree program information:* Part-time and evening/weekend programs available. Postbaccalaureate distance learning degree programs offered (minimal on-campus study). Offers church music (MA, MCM); congregational leadership (MA); counseling (MA); education (ME); intercultural studies/urban ministries (MA); international development (MBA, MSM); marriage and family therapy (MFT); marriage, family, and child counseling (MA); nonprofit management (MBA); psychology (MA). *Application deadline:* Applications are processed on a rolling basis. *Application fee:* $75. Electronic applications accepted. *Application Contact:* Teresa Smith, Director of Graduate and Adult Admissions, 714-879-3901, Fax: 714-681-7450. *Dean,* Dr. Alan Rabe, 718-879-3901 Ext. 2288, Fax: 714-681-7450, E-mail: arabe@hiu.edu.

HOUGHTON COLLEGE, Houghton, NY 14744

General Information Independent-religious, coed, comprehensive institution.

GRADUATE UNITS

Greatbatch School of Music Offers music (MA, MMus).

HOUSTON BAPTIST UNIVERSITY, Houston, TX 77074-3298

General Information Independent-religious, coed, comprehensive institution. *Graduate housing:* Room and/or apartments available on a first-come, first-served basis to single students; on-campus housing not available to married students.

GRADUATE UNITS

College of Arts and Humanities *Degree program information:* Part-time and evening/weekend programs available. Offers arts and humanities (MATS, MLA); liberal arts (MLA); theological studies (MATS).

College of Business and Economics *Degree program information:* Part-time and evening/weekend programs available. Offers accounting (MACCT); business administration (MBA, MSM); business and economics (MACCT, MBA, MSHA, MSHRM, MSM); health administration (MSHA); human resources management (MSHRM).

College of Education and Behavioral Sciences *Degree program information:* Part-time and evening/weekend programs available. Offers bilingual education (M Ed); Christian counseling (MACC); counselor education (M Ed); curriculum and instruction (M Ed); education and behavioral sciences (M Ed, MACC, MAP); educational administration (M Ed); educational diagnostician (M Ed); psychology (MAP); reading education (M Ed).

HOUSTON GRADUATE SCHOOL OF THEOLOGY, Houston, TX 77092

General Information Independent-religious, coed, graduate-only institution. *Graduate housing:* On-campus housing not available.

GRADUATE UNITS

Graduate School *Degree program information:* Part-time and evening/weekend programs available. Offers counseling (MA); pastoral ministry (M Div, D Min); theology (MA).

HOWARD UNIVERSITY, Washington, DC 20059-0002

General Information Independent, coed, university. CGS member. *Graduate housing:* Rooms and/or apartments available on a first-come, first-served basis to single and married students. Housing application deadline: 4/1. *Research affiliation:* Ewing Marion Kauffman Foundation (science education).

GRADUATE UNITS

College of Dentistry Offers advanced education program general dentistry (Certificate); dentistry (DDS); general dentistry (Certificate); oral and maxillofacial surgery (Certificate); orthodontics (Certificate); pediatric dentistry (Certificate).

College of Engineering, Architecture, and Computer Sciences *Degree program information:* Part-time programs available. Offers engineering, architecture, and computer sciences (M Eng, MCS, MS, PhD). Electronic applications accepted.

School of Engineering and Computer Science *Degree program information:* Part-time programs available. Offers chemical engineering (MS); civil engineering (M Eng); electrical engineering (M Eng, PhD); engineering and computer science (M Eng, MCS, MS, PhD); mechanical engineering (M Eng, PhD); systems and computer science (MCS). Electronic applications accepted.

College of Medicine Offers biochemistry and molecular biology (PhD); biotechnology (MS); medicine (MD, MS, PhD); microbiology (PhD); pharmacology (MS, PhD).

College of Pharmacy, Nursing and Allied Health Sciences Students: 399 full-time (254 women), 13 part-time (all women); includes 342 minority (251 African Americans, 2 American

Indian/Alaska Native, 79 Asian Americans or Pacific Islanders, 10 Hispanic Americans), 34 international. *Faculty:* 31 full-time (16 women), 396 part-time/adjunct (217 women). Expenses: Contact institution. *Financial support:* Research assistantships, teaching assistantships, career-related internships or fieldwork, Federal Work-Study, institutionally sponsored loans, and scholarships/grants available. Support available to part-time students. Financial award applicants required to submit FAFSA. In 2006, 23 first professional degrees, 9 master's, 1 other advanced degree awarded. *Degree program information:* Part-time programs available. Offers pharmacy, nursing and allied health sciences (Pharm D, MSN, Certificate). *Application fee:* $45. Electronic applications accepted. *Interim Dean,* Dr. Beatrice Adderley-Kelly, 202-806-5431, Fax: 202-234-1375, E-mail: bkelly@howard.edu.

Division of Nursing Students: 23 full-time (20 women), 5 part-time (all women); includes 26 minority (23 African Americans, 1 American Indian/Alaska Native, 1 Asian American or Pacific Islander, 1 Hispanic American). Average age 36. 15 applicants, 73% accepted. *Faculty:* 3 full-time (all women), 6 part-time/adjunct (all women). Expenses: Contact institution. *Financial support:* In 2006–07, teaching assistantships (averaging $16,000 per year); career-related internships or fieldwork, institutionally sponsored loans, and scholarships/grants also available. Financial award application deadline: 4/1. In 2006, 1 master's, 1 other advanced degree awarded. *Degree program information:* Part-time programs available. Offers nurse practitioner (Certificate); primary family health nursing (MSN). *Application deadline:* For fall admission, 4/1 priority date for domestic students; for spring admission, 11/1 for domestic students. Applications are processed on a rolling basis. *Application fee:* $45. *Application Contact:* Dr. Mamie C. Montague, Chair, Graduate Program, 202-806-7460, Fax: 202-806-5958, E-mail: mmontague@howard.edu. *Associate Dean (Interim),* Dr. Mamie C. Montague, 202-806-7456, Fax: 202-806-5958, E-mail: mmontague@howard.edu.

School of Pharmacy Students: 368 full-time (228 women); includes 301 minority (213 African Americans, 1 American Indian/Alaska Native, 78 Asian Americans or Pacific Islanders, 9 Hispanic Americans), 32 international. Average age 25. 1,517 applicants, 4% accepted, 49 enrolled. *Faculty:* 26 full-time (12 women), 390 part-time/adjunct (211 women). Expenses: Contact institution. *Financial support:* In 2006–07, 351 students received support, including 3 fellowships (averaging $52,000 per year), 6 teaching assistantships (averaging $6,000 per year); career-related internships or fieldwork, Federal Work-Study, institutionally sponsored loans, and scholarships/grants also available. Financial award application deadline: 2/15; financial award applicants required to submit FAFSA. In 2006, 82 Pharm Ds awarded. Postbaccalaureate distance learning degree programs offered (minimal on-campus study). Offers pharmacy (Pharm D). *Application deadline:* For fall admission, 12/1 for domestic and international students. Applications are processed on a rolling basis. *Application fee:* $45. Electronic applications accepted. *Application Contact:* Dr. Joseph R. Ofosu, Assistant Dean for Student Services, 202-806-6530, Fax: 202-806-4636, E-mail: jofosu@howard.edu. *Associate Dean (Interim),* Dr. Clarence E. Curry, 202-806-6530, Fax: 202-806-4636, E-mail: cecurry@howard.edu.

Graduate School Expenses: Contact institution. *Financial support:* Fellowships, research assistantships, teaching assistantships, career-related internships or fieldwork, Federal Work-Study, institutionally sponsored loans, and scholarships/grants available. Financial award applicants required to submit FAFSA. *Degree program information:* Part-time and evening/weekend programs available. Offers African diaspora (MA, PhD); African history (MA, PhD); African studies (MA, PhD); analytical chemistry (MS, PhD); anatomy (MS, PhD); applied mathematics (MS, PhD); atmospheric (MS, PhD); atmospheric sciences (MS, PhD); biochemistry (MS, PhD); biology (MS, PhD); biophysics (PhD); clinical psychology (PhD); developmental psychology (PhD); economics (MA, PhD); English (MA, PhD); environmental (MS, PhD); exercise physiology (MS); experimental psychology (PhD); French (MA); health education (MS); inorganic chemistry (MS, PhD); Latin America and the Caribbean (MA, PhD); mathematics (MS, PhD); neuropsychology (PhD); nutrition (MS, PhD); organic chemistry (MS, PhD); personality psychology (PhD); philosophy (MA); physical chemistry (MS, PhD); physics (MS, PhD); physiology (PhD); political science (MA, PhD); psychology (MS); public administration (MAPA); public affairs (MA); public history (MA); social psychology (PhD); sociology (MA, PhD); Spanish (MA); sports studies (MS); United States history (MA, PhD); urban recreation (MS). *Application deadline:* For spring admission, 11/1 for domestic students. *Application fee:* $45. Electronic applications accepted. *Application Contact:* Director of Admissions, 202-806-6200. *Dean,* Dr. Orlando L. Taylor, 202-806-6800, Fax: 202-462-4053.

Division of Fine Arts *Degree program information:* Part-time programs available. Offers 3D reality (sculpture and ceramics) (MFA); applied music (MM); art history (MA); design (MFA); electronic studio (MFA); fine arts (MFA); history of art and visual culture (MA); instrument (MM Ed); jazz studies (MM); organ (MM Ed); painting (MFA); photography (MFA); piano (MM Ed); voice (MM Ed).

School of Business *Degree program information:* Part-time and evening/weekend programs available. Postbaccalaureate distance learning degree programs offered (no on-campus study). Offers accounting (MBA); business (MBA); entrepreneurship (MBA); finance (MBA); information systems (MBA); international business (MBA); marketing (MBA); supply chain management (MBA).

School of Communications *Degree program information:* Part-time and evening/weekend programs available. Offers communication sciences (PhD); communications (MA, MFA, MS, PhD); film (MFA); intercultural communication (MA, PhD); organizational communication (MA, PhD); speech pathology (MS). Electronic applications accepted.

Division of Mass Communication and Media Studies *Degree program information:* Part-time and evening/weekend programs available. Offers mass communication (MA, PhD); media studies (MA, PhD). Electronic applications accepted.

School of Divinity *Degree program information:* Part-time and evening/weekend programs available. Offers theology (M Div, MARS, D Min). Electronic applications accepted.

School of Education Students: 136 full-time (102 women), 132 part-time (94 women); includes 211 minority (206 African Americans, 4 Asian Americans or Pacific Islanders, 1 Hispanic American), 7 international. Average age 27. 297 applicants, 59% accepted, 114 enrolled. *Faculty:* 34 full-time (18 women), 5 part-time/adjunct (4 women). Expenses: Contact institution. *Financial support:* In 2006–07, 34 students received support, including 12 fellowships with full tuition reimbursements available (averaging $14,000 per year), 15 research assistantships (averaging $10,000 per year), 7 teaching assistantships with full tuition reimbursements available (averaging $13,000 per year); career-related internships or fieldwork, Federal Work-Study, institutionally sponsored loans, scholarships/grants, tuition waivers (full and partial), and unspecified assistantships also available. Financial award application deadline: 4/1; financial award applicants required to submit FAFSA. In 2006, 53 master's, 10 doctorates awarded. *Degree program information:* Part-time and evening/weekend programs available. Offers counseling and guidance (M Ed, MA, CAGS); counseling psychology (M Ed, MA, PhD, CAGS); early childhood education (M Ed, MA, MAT, CAGS); education (M Ed, MA, MAT, MS, Ed D, PhD, CAGS); educational administration (M Ed, MA, Ed D, CAGS); educational administration and policy (Ed D); educational psychology (M Ed, MA, Ed D, PhD, CAGS); elementary education (M Ed); human development (MS); reading (M Ed, MA, MAT, CAGS); school psychology (M Ed, MA, Ed D, PhD, CAGS); secondary education (M Ed, MA, MAT, CAGS); special education (M Ed, MA, CAGS). *Application deadline:* For fall admission, 4/1 priority date for domestic students. Applications are processed on a rolling basis. *Application fee:* $45. *Application Contact:* Dr. Marilyn M. Irving, Associate Dean, 202-806-7340, Fax: 202-806-5302, E-mail: mirving@howard.edu. Dr. Leslie T. Fenwick.

School of Law Offers law (JD, LL M). Electronic applications accepted.

School of Social Work *Degree program information:* Part-time programs available. Offers social work (MSW, PhD).

HULT INTERNATIONAL BUSINESS SCHOOL, Cambridge, MA 02141

General Information Independent, coed, primarily men, graduate-only institution. *Enrollment by degree level:* 129 master's. *Graduate faculty:* 4 full-time (2 women), 28 part-time/adjunct (4 women). *Tuition:* Full-time $39,250. *Graduate housing:* On-campus housing not available. *Student services:* Campus employment opportunities, career counseling, disabled student services, international student services, low-cost health insurance, multicultural affairs office, writing training. *Library facilities:* O'Neill Library plus 7 others. *Online resources:* library catalog, web page, access to other libraries' catalogs. *Collection:* 2 million titles, 17,500 serial subscriptions.

Computer facilities: 8 computers available on campus for general student use. A campuswide network can be accessed from student residence rooms and from off campus. Internet access, Extranet are available. *Web address:* http://www.hult.edu/.

General Application Contact: Ashley M. Ludovicy, Recruiting Coordinator, 617-746-1990, Fax: 617-746-1991, E-mail: admissions@hult.edu.

GRADUATE UNITS

Graduate Program Students: 129 full-time (37 women); includes 51 minority (3 African Americans, 30 Asian Americans or Pacific Islanders, 18 Hispanic Americans), 59 international. Average age 30. 532 applicants, 46% accepted, 129 enrolled. *Faculty:* 4 full-time (2 women), 28 part-time/adjunct (4 women). Expenses: Contact institution. *Financial support:* In 2006–07, 125 students received support, including 8 fellowships with tuition reimbursements available (averaging $4,000 per year); institutionally sponsored loans, scholarships/grants, and tuition waivers (partial) also available. Financial award application deadline: 6/1; financial award applicants required to submit FAFSA. In 2006, 107 degrees awarded. Offers management (MBA). *Application deadline:* For fall admission, 6/1 priority date for domestic and international students; for winter admission, 11/1 priority date for domestic and international students; for spring admission, 12/1 priority date for domestic and international students. Applications are processed on a rolling basis. *Application fee:* $150. Electronic applications accepted. *Application Contact:* Ashley M. Ludovicy, Recruiting Coordinator, 617-746-1990, Fax: 617-746-1991, E-mail: admissions@hult.edu.

HUMBOLDT STATE UNIVERSITY, Arcata, CA 95521-8299

General Information State-supported, coed, comprehensive institution. CGS member. *Enrollment:* 7,435 graduate, professional, and undergraduate students; 322 full-time matriculated graduate/professional students (201 women), 125 part-time matriculated graduate/professional students (74 women). *Enrollment by degree level:* 447 master's. *Graduate faculty:* 288 full-time (109 women), 263 part-time/adjunct (153 women). *Graduate housing:* Room and/or apartments available on a first-come, first-served basis to single students; on-campus housing not available to married students. Housing application deadline: 2/1. *Student services:* Campus employment opportunities, campus safety program, career counseling, child daycare facilities, disabled student services, free psychological counseling, low-cost health insurance, multicultural affairs office. *Library facilities:* Humboldt State University Library. *Online resources:* library catalog, web page, access to other libraries' catalogs. *Collection:* 1 million titles, 1,737 serial subscriptions, 20,962 audiovisual materials. *Research affiliation:* California Cooperative Fisheries Research Unit, Redwood Sciences Laboratory of the Pacific Southwest Forest and Range Experiment Station, U.S. Fish and Wildlife Service–Wildlife Field Station, National Sea Grant, McIntire-Stennis (forestry).

Computer facilities: 778 computers available on campus for general student use. A campuswide network can be accessed from student residence rooms and from off campus. Internet access and online class registration are available. *Web address:* http://www.humboldt.edu/.

General Application Contact: Carla Douglas, Research and Graduate Studies, 707-826-3949, E-mail: cpd1@humboldt.edu.

GRADUATE UNITS

Graduate Studies Students: 322 full-time (201 women), 125 part-time (74 women); includes 60 minority (10 African Americans, 11 American Indian/Alaska Native, 12 Asian Americans or Pacific Islanders, 27 Hispanic Americans), 11 international. Average age 32. 385 applicants, 49% accepted, 132 enrolled. Expenses: Contact institution. *Financial support:* Fellowships, research assistantships, teaching assistantships, career-related internships or fieldwork, Federal Work-Study, and institutionally sponsored loans available. Support available to part-time students. Financial award application deadline: 3/1; financial award applicants required to submit FAFSA. In 2006, 154 degrees awarded. *Degree program information:* Part-time and evening/weekend programs available. *Application deadline:* Applications are processed on a rolling basis. *Application fee:* $55. Electronic applications accepted. *Application Contact:* Carla Douglas, Administrative Support Coordinator, 707-826-3949, Fax: 707-826-3939, E-mail: cpd1@humboldt.edu. *Interim Dean,* Dr. Chris Hopper, 707-826-3949, Fax: 707-826-3939, E-mail: cah3@humboldt.edu.

College of Arts, Humanities, and Social Sciences Students: 72 full-time (44 women), 20 part-time (11 women); includes 13 minority (4 African Americans, 2 American Indian/Alaska Native, 1 Asian American or Pacific Islander, 6 Hispanic Americans), 1 international. Average age 32. 59 applicants, 64% accepted, 23 enrolled. Expenses: Contact institution. *Financial support:* Fellowships, teaching assistantships, career-related internships or fieldwork, Federal Work-Study, and institutionally sponsored loans available. Support available to part-time students. Financial award application deadline: 3/1; financial award applicants required to submit FAFSA. In 2006, 47 degrees awarded. Offers arts, humanities, and social sciences (MA, MFA, MSW); English (MA); environment and community (MA); sociology (MA); theatre, film and dance (MA). *Application deadline:* Applications are processed on a rolling basis. *Application fee:* $55. Electronic applications accepted. *Dean,* Dr. Robert Snyder, 707-826-4491, Fax: 707-826-4498, E-mail: ras1@humboldt.edu.

College of Natural Resources and Sciences Students: 165 full-time (94 women), 66 part-time (31 women); includes 21 minority (3 American Indian/Alaska Native, 4 Asian Americans or Pacific Islanders, 14 Hispanic Americans), 6 international. Average age 31. 204 applicants, 37% accepted, 56 enrolled. *Faculty:* 148 full-time (34 women), 66 part-time/adjunct (32 women). Expenses: Contact institution. *Financial support:* Fellowships, career-related internships or fieldwork and Federal Work-Study available. Support available to part-time students. Financial award application deadline: 3/1; financial award applicants required to submit FAFSA. In 2006, 51 degrees awarded. *Degree program information:* Part-time programs available. Offers biological sciences (MA); environmental systems (MS); natural resources (MS); natural resources and sciences (MA, MS); psychology (MA). *Application deadline:* Applications are processed on a rolling basis. *Application fee:* $55. *Dean,* Dr. Jim Howard, 707-826-3256, Fax: 707-826-3562, E-mail: howard@humboldt.edu.

College of Professional Studies Students: 85 full-time (63 women), 39 part-time (32 women); includes 26 minority (6 African Americans, 6 American Indian/Alaska Native, 7 Asian Americans or Pacific Islanders, 7 Hispanic Americans), 4 international. Average age 35. 122 applicants, 62% accepted, 53 enrolled. Expenses: Contact institution. *Financial support:* Fellowships, teaching assistantships, career-related internships or fieldwork, Federal Work-Study, and institutionally sponsored loans available. Support available to part-time students. Financial award application deadline: 3/1; financial award applicants required to submit FAFSA. In 2006, 52 degrees awarded. *Degree program information:* Part-time and evening/weekend programs available. Offers athletic training education (MS); business (MBA); education (MA); exercise science/wellness management (MS); pre-physical therapy (MS); social work (MSW); teaching/coaching (MS). *Application deadline:* Applications are processed on a rolling basis. *Application fee:* $55. *Dean,* Dr. Susan Higgins, 707-826-3961, Fax: 707-826-3963, E-mail: shiggins@humboldt.edu.

HUMPHREYS COLLEGE, Stockton, CA 95207-3896

General Information Independent, coed, comprehensive institution. *Enrollment:* 75 part-time matriculated graduate/professional students (43 women). *Enrollment by degree level:* 75 first professional. *Graduate faculty:* 2 full-time (1 woman), 23 part-time/adjunct (5 women). *Tuition:* Part-time $315 per unit. *Graduate housing:* Room and/or apartments available on a first-come, first-served basis to single students; on-campus housing not available to married students. *Student services:* Campus employment opportunities, career counseling, child daycare facilities. *Library facilities:* Humphreys College Library plus 1 other. *Collection:* 20,500 titles, 115 serial subscriptions.

Computer facilities: 40 computers available on campus for general student use. Internet access is available. *Web address:* http://www.humphreys.edu/.

General Application Contact: Santa Lopez-Minatre, Admission Counselor, 209-478-0800 Ext. 202, Fax: 209-478-8721, E-mail: slopez@humphreys.edu.

Humphreys College (continued)

GRADUATE UNITS

Laurence Drivon School of Law Average age 36. 101 applicants, 41% accepted, 32 enrolled. *Faculty:* 2 full-time (1 woman), 23 part-time/adjunct (5 women). Expenses: Contact institution. *Financial support:* In 2006–07, 62 students received support. Federal Work-Study available. Support available to part-time students. Financial award application deadline: 7/1; financial award applicants required to submit FAFSA. In 2006, 7 degrees awarded. Offers law (JD). *Application deadline:* For fall admission, 7/1 priority date for domestic students. Applications are processed on a rolling basis. *Application fee:* $35. Electronic applications accepted. *Application Contact:* Santa Lopez-Minatre, Admission Counselor, 209-478-0800 Ext. 202, Fax: 209-478-8721, E-mail: slopez@humphreys.edu. *Dean,* Leo Patrick Piggott, 209-478-0800 Ext. 243, Fax: 209-235-2889.

HUNTER COLLEGE OF THE CITY UNIVERSITY OF NEW YORK, New York, NY 10021-5085

General Information State and locally supported, coed, comprehensive institution. *Enrollment:* 20,899 graduate, professional, and undergraduate students; 946 full-time matriculated graduate/professional students (769 women), 3,249 part-time matriculated graduate/professional students (2,522 women). *Enrollment by degree level:* 4,062 master's, 133 other advanced degrees. *Graduate faculty:* 313 full-time (166 women), 198 part-time/adjunct (122 women). Tuition, state resident: part-time $270 per credit. Tuition, nonresident: part-time $500 per credit. *Required fees:* $45 per semester. *Graduate housing:* Room and/or apartments available on a first-come, first-served basis to single students; on-campus housing not available to married students. Typical cost: $5,083 per year. *Student services:* Campus employment opportunities, campus safety program, career counseling, child daycare facilities, disabled student services, exercise/wellness program, free psychological counseling, international student services, teacher training, writing training. *Library facilities:* Hunter College Library. *Online resources:* library catalog, web page, access to other libraries' catalogs. *Collection:* 789,718 titles, 4,282 serial subscriptions. *Research affiliation:* Bellevue Hospital Center, The Mount Sinai Medical Center, New York Hospital, Cornell University Medical Center.

Computer facilities: 750 computers available on campus for general student use. A campuswide network can be accessed. Internet access is available. *Web address:* http://www.hunter.cuny.edu/.

General Application Contact: William Zlata, Director for Graduate Admissions, 212-772-4482, Fax: 212-650-3336, E-mail: admissions@hunter.cuny.edu.

GRADUATE UNITS

Graduate School Students: 946 full-time (769 women), 3,249 part-time (2,522 women); includes 1,003 minority (378 African Americans, 4 American Indian/Alaska Native, 226 Asian Americans or Pacific Islanders, 395 Hispanic Americans). Average age 33. 4,439 applicants, 4171 enrolled. *Faculty:* 313 full-time (166 women), 198 part-time/adjunct (122 women). Expenses: Contact institution. *Financial support:* Fellowships with full and partial tuition reimbursements, research assistantships with partial tuition reimbursements, teaching assistantships, career-related internships or fieldwork, Federal Work-Study, institutionally sponsored loans, scholarships/grants, traineeships, tuition waivers (full and partial), unspecified assistantships, and lesson stipends available. Support available to part-time students. Financial award applicants required to submit FAFSA. In 2006, 1,254 master's, 57 other advanced degrees awarded. *Degree program information:* Part-time and evening/weekend programs available. *Application fee:* $125. *Application Contact:* Michael Goldstein, Assistant Director for Graduate Admissions, 212-772-4288, Fax: 212-650-3336, E-mail: admissions@hunter.cuny.edu. *Director of Admissions,* William Zlata, 212-772-4288, Fax: 212-650-3336, E-mail: bill.zlata@hunter.cuny.edu.

School of Arts and Sciences Students: 146 full-time (88 women), 920 part-time (598 women); includes 159 minority (29 African Americans, 1 American Indian/Alaska Native, 64 Asian Americans or Pacific Islanders, 65 Hispanic Americans), 55 international. Average age 32. 1,427 applicants, 37% accepted, 327 enrolled. *Faculty:* 133 full-time (47 women), 22 part-time/adjunct (11 women). Expenses: Contact institution. *Financial support:* Fellowships, research assistantships, teaching assistantships, career-related internships or fieldwork, Federal Work-Study, institutionally sponsored loans, scholarships/grants, tuition waivers (full and partial), unspecified assistantships, and lesson stipends available. Support available to part-time students. In 2006, 323 degrees awarded. *Degree program information:* Part-time and evening/weekend programs available. Offers accounting (MS); analytical geography (MA); anthropology (MA); applied and evaluative psychology (MA); applied mathematics (MA); applied social research (MS); art history (MA); arts and sciences (MA, MFA, MS, MUP, PhD, Certificate); biochemistry (MA); biological sciences (MA, PhD); biopsychology and comparative psychology (MA); British and American literature (MA); creative writing (MFA); earth system science (MA); economics (MA); English education (MA); environmental and social issues (MA); fine arts (MFA); French (MA); French education (MA); geographic information science (Certificate); geographic information systems (MA); history (MA); integrated media arts (MA, MFA); Italian (MA); Italian education (MA); mathematics for secondary education (MA); music (MA); music education (MA); physics (MA, PhD); pure mathematics (MA); social research (MS); social, cognitive, and developmental psychology (MA); Spanish (MA); Spanish education (MA); studio art (MFA); teaching earth science (MA); teaching Latin (MA); theatre (MA); urban affairs (MS); urban planning (MUP). *Application deadline:* For fall admission, 2/1 for domestic and international students; for spring admission, 11/1 for domestic students, 9/1 for international students. *Application fee:* $125. *Application Contact:* William Zlata, Director for Graduate Admissions, 212-772-4482, Fax: 212-650-3336, E-mail: admissions@hunter.cuny.edu. *Acting Dean,* Dr. Judith Friedlander, 212-772-5121, Fax: 212-772-5138, E-mail: judith.friedlander@hunter.cuny.edu.

School of Education Students: 204 full-time (183 women), 1,625 part-time (1,360 women); includes 333 minority (85 African Americans, 2 American Indian/Alaska Native, 86 Asian Americans or Pacific Islanders, 160 Hispanic Americans). Average age 31. 1,177 applicants, 52% accepted, 408 enrolled. *Faculty:* 112 full-time (64 women), 126 part-time/adjunct (77 women). Expenses: Contact institution. *Financial support:* Fellowships, career-related internships or fieldwork, Federal Work-Study, institutionally sponsored loans, and tuition waivers (full and partial) available. Support available to part-time students. In 2006, 439 master's, 55 other advanced degrees awarded. Offers bilingual education (MS); biology education (MA); blind or visually impaired (MS Ed); chemistry education (MA); corrective reading (K–12) (MS Ed); deaf or hard of hearing (MS Ed); early childhood education (MS); earth science (MA); education (MA, MS, MS Ed, AC); educational supervision and administration (AC); elementary education (MS); English education (MA); French education (MA); Italian education (MA); literacy education (MS); mathematics education (MA); music education (MA); physics education (MA); rehabilitation counseling (MS Ed); school counseling (MS Ed); school counseling with bilingual extension (MS Ed); school counselor (MS Ed); severe/multiple disabilities (MS Ed); social studies education (MA); Spanish education (MA); special education (MS Ed); teaching English as a second language (MA). *Application deadline:* For fall admission, 4/1 for domestic students, 2/1 for international students; for spring admission, 11/1 for domestic students, 9/1 for international students. Applications are processed on a rolling basis. *Application fee:* $125. *Application Contact:* William Zlata, Director for Graduate Admissions, 212-772-4482, Fax: 212-650-3336, E-mail: admissions@hunter.cuny.edu. *Dean,* Dr. David Steiner, 212-772-4622, E-mail: david.steiner@hunter.cuny.edu.

School of Social Work Students: 460 full-time (384 women), 374 part-time (286 women); includes 187 minority (88 African Americans, 18 Asian Americans or Pacific Islanders, 81 Hispanic Americans). Average age 35. 1,115 applicants, 37% accepted, 372 enrolled. *Faculty:* 32 full-time (21 women), 37 part-time/adjunct (23 women). Expenses: Contact institution. *Financial support:* In 2006–07, 120 fellowships (averaging $1,000 per year) were awarded; career-related internships or fieldwork, Federal Work-Study, and tuition waivers (partial) also available. Support available to part-time students. In 2006, 275 degrees awarded. Offers social work (MSW, DSW). *Application deadline:* For fall admission, 1/15 for domestic and international students. Applications are processed on a rolling basis. *Application fee:* $125. *Application Contact:* Raymond Montero, Coordinator of Admissions, 212-452-7005, E-mail: grad.socworkadvisor@hunter.cuny.edu. *Dean,* Dr. Jacqueline B. Mondros, 212-452-7085.

Schools of the Health Professions Students: 155 full-time (120 women), 322 part-time (268 women). Average age 33. 517 applicants, 38% accepted, 98 enrolled. *Faculty:* 45 full-time (41 women), 26 part-time/adjunct (22 women). Expenses: Contact institution. *Financial support:* Federal Work-Study and tuition waivers (partial) available. Support available to part-time students. In 2006, 217 degrees awarded. *Degree program information:* Part-time and evening/weekend programs available. Offers adult nurse practitioner (MS); audiology (MS); community health nursing (MS); community health nursing/community health education); environmental and occupational health sciences (MS); gerontological nurse practitioner (MS); health professions (MPH, MPT, MS, AC); maternal child-health nursing (MS); medical/surgical nursing (MS); nursing (MS, AC); pediatric nurse practitioner (MS, AC); physical therapy (MPT); psychiatric nursing (MS); public health (MPH); speech language pathology (MS); teacher of speech and hearing handicapped (MS). *Application deadline:* For fall admission, 4/1 for domestic students, 2/1 for international students; for spring admission, 11/1 for domestic students, 9/1 for international students. *Application fee:* $125. *Dean,* Lauren N. Sherwen, 212-481-4314.

HUNTINGTON COLLEGE OF HEALTH SCIENCES, Knoxville, TN 37919-7736

General Information Proprietary, coed, comprehensive institution.

GRADUATE UNITS

Program in Nutrition Offers nutrition (MS).

HUNTINGTON UNIVERSITY, Huntington, IN 46750-1299

General Information Independent-religious, coed, comprehensive institution. *Enrollment:* 1,084 graduate, professional, and undergraduate students; 9 full-time matriculated graduate/professional students (5 women), 67 part-time matriculated graduate/professional students (14 women). *Enrollment by degree level:* 76 master's. *Graduate faculty:* 4 full-time (0 women), 16 part-time/adjunct (4 women). *Graduate housing:* On-campus housing not available. *Student services:* Campus employment opportunities, career counseling, free psychological counseling, low-cost health insurance, writing training. *Library facilities:* Richlyn Library plus 1 other. *Online resources:* web page. *Collection:* 166,122 titles. *Research affiliation:* Link Institute (youth ministry).

Computer facilities: 190 computers available on campus for general student use. A campuswide network can be accessed from student residence rooms and from off campus. Internet access is available. *Web address:* http://www.huntington.edu/.

General Application Contact: Jennifer L Dakin, GSCM Admissions and Marketing Coordinator, 260-359-4129, Fax: 260-359-4126, E-mail: jdakin@huntington.edu.

GRADUATE UNITS

Graduate School of Christian Ministries Students: 9 full-time (5 women), 67 part-time (14 women); includes 2 minority (both African Americans), 2 international. Average age 39. 27 applicants, 89% accepted, 24 enrolled. *Faculty:* 4 full-time (0 women), 16 part-time/adjunct (4 women). Expenses: Contact institution. *Financial support:* In 2006–07, 51 students received support. Scholarships/grants and health care benefits available. Support available to part-time students. In 2006, 4 degrees awarded. *Degree program information:* Part-time programs available. Postbaccalaureate distance learning degree programs offered (minimal on-campus study). Offers counseling ministries (MA); discipling ministries (MA); pastoral ministries (MA); youth ministry leadership (MA). *Application deadline:* For fall admission, 8/1 priority date for domestic students, 8/1 for international students; for winter admission, 12/1 priority date for domestic students, 12/1 for international students; for spring admission, 3/1 priority date for domestic students, 3/1 for international students. Applications are processed on a rolling basis. *Application fee:* $20. Electronic applications accepted. *Application Contact:* Jennifer L Dakin, GSCM Admissions and Marketing Coordinator, 260-359-4129, Fax: 260-359-4126, E-mail: jdakin@huntington.edu. *Dean for Christian Ministries,* Dr. Ray Seilhamer, 260-359-4128, Fax: 260-359-4126, E-mail: rseilhamer@huntington.edu.

HURON UNIVERSITY USA IN LONDON, London WC1B 4JP, United Kingdom

General Information Independent, coed, comprehensive institution. *Graduate housing:* Room and/or apartments available on a first-come, first-served basis to single students; on-campus housing not available to married students. Housing application deadline: 7/9.

GRADUATE UNITS

Graduate Programs Offers advertising (MA); conflict resolution (MA); diplomacy (MA); entrepreneurship (MBA); finance (MS); international business (MBA); international finance (MBA); international public law (MA); international relations (MA); marketing (MA, MBA); Middle East international security (MA); politics (MA); public relations (MA); security studies (MA); terrorism (MA); U.S. foreign policy (MA).

HUSSON COLLEGE, Bangor, ME 04401-2999

General Information Independent, coed, comprehensive institution. *Graduate housing:* Room and/or apartments available on a first-come, first-served basis to single students; on-campus housing not available to married students. Housing application deadline: 6/1.

GRADUATE UNITS

Graduate Studies Division *Degree program information:* Part-time and evening/weekend programs available. Offers business (MSB); family nurse practitioner (MSN); nursing (MSN); physical therapy (MSPT); psychiatric nursing (MSN).

ICR GRADUATE SCHOOL, Santee, CA 92071

General Information Independent-religious, coed, graduate-only institution. *Enrollment by degree level:* 12 master's. *Graduate faculty:* 5 full-time (1 woman), 1 part-time/adjunct (0 women). *Tuition:* Part-time $200 per semester hour. *Graduate housing:* On-campus housing not available. *Student services:* Campus employment opportunities, campus safety program, career counseling. *Collection:* 25,000 titles, 109 serial subscriptions.

Computer facilities: 8 computers available on campus for general student use. Internet access is available. *Web address:* http://www.icr.edu/.

General Application Contact: Dr. Jack Kriege, Registrar, 619-448-0900 Ext. 6016, Fax: 619-448-3469, E-mail: jkriege@icr.org.

GRADUATE UNITS

Graduate Programs Students: 6 full-time (2 women), 6 part-time (3 women). Average age 45. *Faculty:* 5 full-time (1 woman), 1 part-time/adjunct (0 women). Expenses: Contact institution. In 2006, 4 degrees awarded. *Degree program information:* Part-time programs available. Offers astro/geophysics (MS); biology (MS); geology (MS); science education (MS). *Application deadline:* Applications are processed on a rolling basis. *Application fee:* $30. *Application Contact:* Dr. Jack Kriege, Registrar, 619-448-0900 Ext. 6016, Fax: 619-448-3469, E-mail: jkriege@icr.org. *Dean,* Dr. Kenneth B. Cumming, 619-448-0900, Fax: 619-448-3469.

IDAHO STATE UNIVERSITY, Pocatello, ID 83209

General Information State-supported, coed, university. CGS member. *Enrollment:* 12,679 graduate, professional, and undergraduate students; 1,081 full-time matriculated graduate/professional students (545 women), 958 part-time matriculated graduate/professional students (523 women). *Enrollment by degree level:* 244 first professional, 1,420 master's, 375 doctoral. *Graduate faculty:* 232 full-time (65 women), 10 part-time/adjunct (6 women). Tuition, state resident: part-time $251 per credit. Tuition, nonresident: part-time $366 per credit. Tuition and fees vary according to degree level, program and reciprocity agreements. *Graduate housing:* Rooms and/or apartments available on a first-come, first-served basis to single and married students. Typical cost: $4,200 per year ($6,900 including board) for single students; $5,400 per year ($8,100 including board) for married students. Room and board charges vary according to board plan and housing facility selected. Housing application deadline: 5/1.

Student services: Campus employment opportunities, campus safety program, career counseling, child daycare facilities, disabled student services, exercise/wellness program, free psychological counseling, grant writing training, international student services, low-cost health insurance, multicultural affairs office, teacher training, writing training. *Library facilities:* Eli M. Oboler Library. *Online resources:* library catalog, web page. *Collection:* 1.2 million titles, 444 serial subscriptions, 2,204 audiovisual materials. *Research affiliation:* Environmental Science and Research Foundation (waste management, ecology), Bechtel BWXT ID, LLC (environmental management, nuclear sciences), J. R. Simplot Company, Idaho (plant sciences, environmental studies), Inland Northwest Research Alliance (science), AMI Semiconductor (computer sciences, environmental management), S. M. Stoller Corporation (ecology, waste management).

Computer facilities: 562 computers available on campus for general student use. A campuswide network can be accessed from student residence rooms and from off campus. Internet access and online class registration are available. *Web address:* http://www.isu.edu/.

General Application Contact: Dr. Thomas Jackson, Dean, 208-282-2390, Fax: 208-282-4847, E-mail: tjackson@isu.edu.

GRADUATE UNITS

Office of Graduate Studies Students: 1,081 full-time (545 women), 958 part-time (523 women); includes 91 minority (5 African Americans, 13 American Indian/Alaska Native, 37 Asian Americans or Pacific Islanders, 36 Hispanic Americans), 153 international. Average age 35. *Faculty:* 266 full-time (81 women), 7 part-time/adjunct (4 women). Expenses: Contact institution. *Financial support:* In 2006–07, 26 fellowships with full and partial tuition reimbursements (averaging $12,164 per year), 84 research assistantships with full and partial tuition reimbursements (averaging $11,303 per year), 217 teaching assistantships with full and partial tuition reimbursements (averaging $8,694 per year) were awarded; career-related internships or fieldwork, Federal Work-Study, institutionally sponsored loans, scholarships/grants, traineeships, and tuition waivers (full and partial) also available. Support available to part-time students. Financial award application deadline: 1/1. In 2006, 63 first professional degrees, 340 master's, 56 doctorates, 13 other advanced degrees awarded. *Degree program information:* Part-time and evening/weekend programs available. Offers general interdisciplinary (M Ed, MA, MNS); waste management and environmental science (MS). *Application deadline:* For fall admission, 7/1 for domestic students, 6/1 for international students; for spring admission, 12/1 for domestic students, 11/1 for international students. Applications are processed on a rolling basis. *Application fee:* $55. *Application Contact:* Ellen Combs, Graduate School Technical Records Specialist, 208-282-2150, Fax: 208-282-4847. *Dean,* Dr. Thomas Jackson, 208-282-2390, Fax: 208-282-4847, E-mail: tjackson@isu.edu.

College of Arts and Sciences Students: 277 full-time (139 women), 176 part-time (84 women); includes 15 minority (4 American Indian/Alaska Native, 1 Asian American or Pacific Islander, 10 Hispanic Americans), 51 international. Average age 35. *Faculty:* 156 full-time (42 women), 4 part-time/adjunct (2 women). Expenses: Contact institution. *Financial support:* In 2006–07, 26 fellowships with full and partial tuition reimbursements (averaging $12,164 per year), 67 research assistantships with full and partial tuition reimbursements (averaging $11,303 per year), 101 teaching assistantships with full and partial tuition reimbursements (averaging $8,694 per year) were awarded; career-related internships or fieldwork, Federal Work-Study, institutionally sponsored loans, scholarships/grants, traineeships, and tuition waivers (full and partial) also available. Support available to part-time students. Financial award application deadline: 1/1. In 2006, 81 master's, 12 doctorates, 4 other advanced degrees awarded. *Degree program information:* Part-time programs available. Offers anthropology (MA, MS); art and pre-architecture (MFA); arts and sciences (MA, MFA, MNS, MPA, MS, DA, PhD, Post-Master's Certificate, Postbaccalaureate Certificate); biology (MNS, MS, DA, PhD); chemistry (MNS, MS); clinical laboratory science (MS); clinical psychology (PhD); English (MA, DA, Post-Master's Certificate); geographic information science (MS); geology (MNS, MS); geophysics/hydrology (MS); geotechnology (Postbaccalaureate Certificate); historical resources management (MA); mathematics (MS, DA); mathematics for secondary teachers (MA); microbiology (MS); physics (MNS, MS, PhD); political science (MA, DA); psychology (MS); public administration (MPA); sociology (MA); speech communication (MA); theatre (MA). *Application deadline:* For fall admission, 7/1 for domestic students, 6/1 for international students; for spring admission, 12/1 for domestic students, 11/1 for international students. Applications are processed on a rolling basis. *Application fee:* $55. *Application Contact:* Ellen Combs, Graduate School Technical Records Specialist, 208-282-2150, Fax: 208-282-4847. *Dean,* Dr. John Kijinski, 208-282-3204, E-mail: kijijhon@isu.edu.

College of Business Students: 55 full-time (11 women), 73 part-time (16 women); includes 3 minority (1 African American, 1 Asian American or Pacific Islander, 1 Hispanic American), 14 international. Average age 31. *Faculty:* 26 full-time (4 women). Expenses: Contact institution. *Financial support:* In 2006–07, 9 teaching assistantships with full and partial tuition reimbursements (averaging $8,694 per year) were awarded; career-related internships or fieldwork, Federal Work-Study, traineeships, tuition waivers (full and partial), and unspecified assistantships also available. Support available to part-time students. Financial award application deadline: 1/1. In 2006, 45 degrees awarded. *Degree program information:* Part-time and evening/weekend programs available. Postbaccalaureate distance learning degree programs offered (minimal on-campus study). Offers business administration (MBA, Postbaccalaureate Certificate); computer information systems (MS, Postbaccalaureate Certificate). *Application deadline:* For fall admission, 7/1 for domestic students, 6/1 for international students; for spring admission, 12/1 for domestic students, 11/1 for international students. Applications are processed on a rolling basis. *Application fee:* $55. *Dean,* Dr. William Stratton, 208-282-3585, Fax: 208-282-4367.

College of Education Students: 76 full-time (40 women), 330 part-time (184 women); includes 18 minority (3 African Americans, 4 American Indian/Alaska Native, 6 Asian Americans or Pacific Islanders, 5 Hispanic Americans), 21 international. Average age 40. *Faculty:* 23 full-time (11 women). Expenses: Contact institution. *Financial support:* In 2006–07, 21 teaching assistantships with full and partial tuition reimbursements (averaging $8,694 per year) were awarded; career-related internships or fieldwork, Federal Work-Study, institutionally sponsored loans, scholarships/grants, tuition waivers (full and partial), and unspecified assistantships also available. Support available to part-time students. Financial award application deadline: 1/1. In 2006, 59 master's, 17 doctorates, 2 other advanced degrees awarded. *Degree program information:* Part-time and evening/weekend programs available. Postbaccalaureate distance learning degree programs offered (no on-campus study). Offers child and family studies (M Ed); curriculum leadership (M Ed); education (M Ed); educational administration (M Ed, 6th Year Certificate, Ed S); educational foundations (5th Year Certificate); educational leadership (Ed D); elementary education (M Ed); human exceptionality (M Ed); instructional design (PhD); instructional technology (M Ed); physical education (MPE); school psychology (Ed S); special education (Ed S). *Application deadline:* For fall admission, 7/1 for domestic students, 6/1 for international students; for spring admission, 12/1 for domestic students, 11/1 for international students. Applications are processed on a rolling basis. *Application fee:* $55. *Application Contact:* Dr. Peter Denner, Director, Office of Standards and Assessment, 208-282-2783, Fax: 208-282-4697, E-mail: dennpete@isu.edu. *Dean,* Dr. Deborah Hedeen, 208-282-3259, Fax: 208-282-4697, E-mail: hededebo@isu.edu.

College of Engineering Students: 41 full-time (5 women), 44 part-time (11 women); includes 6 minority (3 Asian Americans or Pacific Islanders, 3 Hispanic Americans), 33 international. Average age 35. *Faculty:* 12 full-time (1 woman), 1 part-time/adjunct (0 women). Expenses: Contact institution. *Financial support:* In 2006–07, 7 research assistantships with full and partial tuition reimbursements (averaging $11,303 per year), 5 teaching assistantships with full and partial tuition reimbursements (averaging $8,694 per year) were awarded; Federal Work-Study, institutionally sponsored loans, and tuition waivers (full and partial) also available. Support available to part-time students. Financial award application deadline:1/1. In 2006, 18 master's, 3 doctorates, 2 other advanced degrees awarded. *Degree program information:* Part-time programs available. Offers civil engineering (MS); engineering and applied science (PhD); engineering structures and mechanics (MS); environmental engineering (MS); measurement and control engineering (MS); mechanical engineering (MS); nuclear science and engineering (MS, PhD, Postbaccalaureate Certificate). *Application deadline:* For fall admission, 7/1 for domestic students, 6/1 for international students; for spring admission, 12/1 for domestic students, 11/1 for international students. Applications are processed on a rolling basis. *Application fee:* $55. *Application Contact:* Ellen Combs, Graduate School Technical Records Specialist, 208-282-2150, Fax: 208-282-4847. *Dean,* Dr. Richard Jacobsen, 208-282-2902, Fax: 208-282-4538.

College of Pharmacy Students: 247 full-time (106 women), 20 part-time (11 women); includes 21 minority (1 American Indian/Alaska Native, 16 Asian Americans or Pacific Islanders, 4 Hispanic Americans), 19 international. Average age 28. *Faculty:* 15 full-time (3 women). Expenses: Contact institution. *Financial support:* In 2006–07, 8 research assistantships with full and partial tuition reimbursements (averaging $11,303 per year), 5 teaching assistantships with full and partial tuition reimbursements (averaging $8,694 per year) were awarded; fellowships, career-related internships or fieldwork, Federal Work-Study, scholarships/grants, traineeships, tuition waivers (full and partial), and unspecified assistantships also available. Support available to part-time students. Financial award application deadline: 1/1. In 2006, 63 first professional degrees, 1 master's, 3 doctorates awarded. *Degree program information:* Part-time programs available. Postbaccalaureate distance learning degree programs offered (minimal on-campus study). Offers biopharmaceutical analysis (PhD); biopharmaceutics (PhD); pharmaceutical chemistry (MS); pharmaceutical science (PhD); pharmaceutics (MS); pharmacognosy (MS); pharmacokinetics (PhD); pharmacology (MS, PhD); pharmacy (Pharm D); pharmacy administration (MS, PhD). *Application deadline:* For fall admission, 7/1 for domestic students, 6/1 for international students; for spring admission, 12/1 for domestic students, 11/1 for international students. Applications are processed on a rolling basis. *Application fee:* $55. *Application Contact:* Ellen Combs, Graduate School Technical Records Specialist, 208-282-2150, Fax: 208-282-4847. *Dean,* Dr. Joseph Steiner, 208-282-2175, Fax: 208-282-4482.

College of Technology Students: 23 full-time (13 women), 53 part-time (23 women); includes 5 minority (2 American Indian/Alaska Native, 1 Asian American or Pacific Islander, 2 Hispanic Americans), 1 international. Average age 42. *Faculty:* 3 full-time (1 woman). Expenses: Contact institution. *Financial support:* In 2006–07, 2 teaching assistantships with full and partial tuition reimbursements (averaging $8,694 per year) were awarded; career-related internships or fieldwork, Federal Work-Study, scholarships/grants, tuition waivers (full and partial), and unspecified assistantships also available. Support available to part-time students. Financial award application deadline: 1/1. In 2006, 7 degrees awarded. *Degree program information:* Part-time and evening/weekend programs available. Postbaccalaureate distance learning degree programs offered (minimal on-campus study). Offers technology (MTD); training and development (MTD). *Application deadline:* For fall admission, 7/1 for domestic students, 6/1 for international students; for spring admission, 12/1 for domestic students, 11/1 for international students. Applications are processed on a rolling basis. *Application fee:* $55. *Application Contact:* Debra K. Ronneburg, Director of Admissions/Student Services, 208-282-2622, Fax: 208-282-5195, E-mail: ctech@isu.edu. *Interim Dean,* Dr. Marilyn Davis, 208-282-2507, Fax: 208-282-4641, E-mail: mdavis@isu.edu.

Kasiska College of Health Professions Students: 355 full-time (227 women), 157 part-time (116 women); includes 20 minority (1 African American, 1 American Indian/Alaska Native, 8 Asian Americans or Pacific Islanders, 10 Hispanic Americans), 14 international. Average age 33. *Faculty:* 29 full-time (17 women), 1 (woman) part-time/adjunct. Expenses: Contact institution. *Financial support:* In 2006–07, 2 research assistantships with full and partial tuition reimbursements (averaging $11,303 per year), 26 teaching assistantships with full and partial tuition reimbursements (averaging $8,694 per year) were awarded; career-related internships or fieldwork, institutionally sponsored loans, scholarships/grants, traineeships, tuition waivers (full and partial), and unspecified assistantships also available. Support available to part-time students. Financial award application deadline: 1/1. In 2006, 128 master's, 21 doctorates, 5 other advanced degrees awarded. *Degree program information:* Part-time programs available. Offers advanced general dentistry (Post-Doctoral Certificate); audiology (MS, Au D); counseling (M Coun, Ed S, Postbaccalaureate Certificate); counselor education and counseling (PhD); deaf education (MS); dental hygiene (MS); dietetics (Certificate); family medicine (Post-Master's Certificate); health education (MHE); health professions (M Coun, MHE, MOT, MPAS, MPH, MS, Au D, DPT, PhD, Certificate, Ed S, Post-Doctoral Certificate, Post-Master's Certificate, Postbaccalaureate Certificate); nursing (MS, Post-Master's Certificate); occupational therapy (MOT); physical therapy (DPT); physician assistant studies (MPAS); public health (MPH); speech language pathology (MS). *Application deadline:* For fall admission, 7/1 for domestic students, 6/1 for international students; for spring admission, 12/1 for domestic students, 11/1 for international students. Applications are processed on a rolling basis. *Application fee:* $55. *Application Contact:* Ellen Combs, Graduate School Technical Records Specialist, 208-282-2150, Fax: 208-282-4847. *Dean,* Dr. Linda Hatzenbuehler, 208-282-3287, Fax: 208-282-4000, E-mail: hatzlind@isu.edu.

ILIFF SCHOOL OF THEOLOGY, Denver, CO 80210-4798

General Information Independent-religious, coed, graduate-only institution. *Graduate housing:* Rooms and/or apartments available on a first-come, first-served basis to single and married students.

GRADUATE UNITS

Graduate and Professional Programs *Degree program information:* Part-time and evening/weekend programs available. Offers biblical studies (MA); church history (MA); religion (MA); religion and social change (MA); specialized ministry (MASM); theology (M Div, MTS, D Min, PhD); theology/ethics (MA). Electronic applications accepted.

ILLINOIS COLLEGE OF OPTOMETRY, Chicago, IL 60616-3878

General Information Independent, coed, graduate-only institution. *Enrollment by degree level:* 604 first professional. *Graduate faculty:* 44 full-time (24 women), 37 part-time/adjunct (24 women). *Tuition:* Full-time $27,495. *Graduate housing:* Rooms and/or apartments guaranteed to single students and available on a first-come, first-served basis to married students. Typical cost: $8,217 (including board) for single students; $11,220 per year for married students. Housing application deadline: 6/1. *Student services:* Campus employment opportunities, campus safety program, career counseling, disabled student services, exercise/wellness program, free psychological counseling, international student services, low-cost health insurance. *Library facilities:* Carl F. Shepard Library. *Online resources:* library catalog, web page, access to other libraries' catalogs. *Collection:* 32,070 titles, 213 serial subscriptions, 660 audiovisual materials. *Research affiliation:* University of Chicago (vision science), Rush University (cataract development), Ocular Science (contact lenses), University of Illinois at Chicago (neuropharmacology), Vision Service Plan (pediatric optometry), Ciba Vision (contact lenses).

Computer facilities: 44 computers available on campus for general student use. A campuswide network can be accessed from student residence rooms. Internet access is available. *Web address:* http://www.ico.edu/.

General Application Contact: Teisha Johnson, Director of Admissions, 312-949-7400, Fax: 312-949-7680, E-mail: tjohnson@ico.edu.

GRADUATE UNITS

Professional Program Students: 604 full-time (399 women); includes 170 minority (12 African Americans, 5 American Indian/Alaska Native, 140 Asian Americans or Pacific Islanders, 13 Hispanic Americans), 94 international. Average age 24. 936 applicants, 31% accepted, 155 enrolled. *Faculty:* 44 full-time (24 women), 37 part-time/adjunct (24 women). Expenses: Contact institution. *Financial support:* In 2006–07, 525 students received support. Federal Work-Study and scholarships/grants available. Support available to part-time students. Financial award application deadline: 4/15; financial award applicants required to submit FAFSA. In 2006, 162 degrees awarded. Offers optometry (OD). *Application deadline:* For fall admission, 3/15 for domestic and international students. Applications are processed on a rolling basis. *Application fee:* $75. Electronic applications accepted. *Application Contact:* Teisha Johnson, Director of Admissions, 312-949-7400, Fax: 312-949-7680, E-mail: tjohnson@ico.edu. *President,* Dr. Arol Augsburger, 312-949-7705, Fax: 312-949-7670, E-mail: aaugsburger@eyecare.ico.edu.

ILLINOIS INSTITUTE OF TECHNOLOGY, Chicago, IL 60616-3793

General Information Independent, coed, university. CGS member. *Enrollment:* 6,795 graduate, professional, and undergraduate students; 2,725 full-time matriculated graduate/professional students (1,035 women), 1,525 part-time matriculated graduate/professional students (521 women). *Enrollment by degree level:* 1,041 first professional, 2,560 master's, 567 doctoral, 82 other advanced degrees. *Graduate faculty:* 353 full-time (77 women), 286 part-time/adjunct (67 women). *Tuition:* Full-time $13,086; part-time $727 per credit. *Required fees:* $7 per credit. $235 per term. Tuition and fees vary according to class time, course level, course load, program and student level. *Graduate housing:* Rooms and/or apartments available on a first-come, first-served basis to single and married students. Typical cost: $4,212 per year ($8,250 including board) for single students; $11,262 per year for married students. Room and board charges vary according to board plan, campus/location and housing facility selected. Housing application deadline: 6/1. *Student services:* Campus employment opportunities, campus safety program, career counseling, disabled student services, free psychological counseling, grant writing training, international student services, low-cost health insurance, multicultural affairs office, teacher training, writing training. *Library facilities:* Paul V. Galvin Library plus 5 others. *Online resources:* library catalog, web page, access to other libraries' catalogs. *Collection:* 1.1 million titles, 21,498 serial subscriptions, 3,266 audiovisual materials.

Computer facilities: Computer purchase and lease plans are available. 650 computers available on campus for general student use. A campuswide network can be accessed from student residence rooms and from off campus. Internet access and online class registration are available. *Web address:* http://www.iit.edu/.

General Application Contact: Morgan Frederick, Office of Graduate Admissions, 866-472-3448, Fax: 312-567-3138, E-mail: inquiry.grad@iit.edu.

GRADUATE UNITS

Chicago-Kent College of Law Students: 827 full-time (395 women), 302 part-time (130 women); includes 221 minority (61 African Americans, 4 American Indian/Alaska Native, 95 Asian Americans or Pacific Islanders, 61 Hispanic Americans), 70 international. Average age 27. 3,510 applicants, 31% accepted, 307 enrolled. *Faculty:* 61 full-time (20 women), 132 part-time/adjunct (34 women). Expenses: Contact institution. *Financial support:* In 2006–07, 573 students received support. Career-related internships or fieldwork, institutionally sponsored loans, scholarships/grants, and tuition waivers (full) available. Support available to part-time students. Financial award application deadline: 3/15; financial award applicants required to submit FAFSA. In 2006, 283 JDs, 28 master's awarded. *Degree program information:* Part-time and evening/weekend programs available. Offers family law (LL M); financial services (LL M); international intellectual property (LL M); international law (LL M); law (JD); taxation (LL M). *Application deadline:* For fall admission, 3/1 priority date for domestic and international students. Applications are processed on a rolling basis. *Application fee:* $60. Electronic applications accepted. *Application Contact:* Nicole Vilches, Assistant Dean, 312-906-5020, Fax: 312-906-5274, E-mail: admit@kentlaw.edu. *Dean,* Harold J. Krent, 312-906-5010, Fax: 312-906-5335, E-mail: hkrent@kentlaw.edu.

Graduate College Students: 1,613 full-time (528 women), 1,052 part-time (352 women); includes 325 minority (112 African Americans, 4 American Indian/Alaska Native, 143 Asian Americans or Pacific Islanders, 66 Hispanic Americans), 1,551 international. Average age 28. 5,669 applicants, 59% accepted, 937 enrolled. *Faculty:* 262 full-time (51 women), 170 part-time/adjunct (43 women). Expenses: Contact institution. *Financial support:* Fellowships with full and partial tuition reimbursements, research assistantships with full and partial tuition reimbursements, teaching assistantships with full and partial tuition reimbursements, career-related internships or fieldwork, Federal Work-Study, institutionally sponsored loans, scholarships/grants, traineeships, health care benefits, tuition waivers (full and partial), and unspecified assistantships available. Support available to part-time students. Financial award applicants required to submit FAFSA. In 2006, 739 master's, 61 doctorates awarded. *Degree program information:* Part-time and evening/weekend programs available. Postbaccalaureate distance learning degree programs offered (no on-campus study). *Application deadline:* Applications are processed on a rolling basis. *Application fee:* $40. Electronic applications accepted. *Application Contact:* Morgan Frederick, Assistant Director of Graduate Communications, 866-472-3448, Fax: 312-567-3138, E-mail: inquiry.grad@iit.edu. *Dean/Vice Provost,* Dr. Ali Cinar, 312-567-3637, Fax: 312-567-7517, E-mail: gradstu@iit.edu.

Armour College of Engineering Students: 627 full-time (132 women), 428 part-time (83 women); includes 81 minority (22 African Americans, 43 Asian Americans or Pacific Islanders, 16 Hispanic Americans), 769 international. Average age 26. 2,841 applicants, 58% accepted, 390 enrolled. *Faculty:* 84 full-time (6 women), 30 part-time/adjunct (1 woman). Expenses: Contact institution. *Financial support:* In 2006–07, 12 fellowships with tuition reimbursements, 120 research assistantships with tuition reimbursements, 80 teaching assistantships with tuition reimbursements were awarded; career-related internships or fieldwork, Federal Work-Study, institutionally sponsored loans, scholarships/grants, traineeships, health care benefits, tuition waivers (partial), and unspecified assistantships also available. Support available to part-time students. Financial award applicants required to submit FAFSA. In 2006, 283 master's, 26 doctorates awarded. *Degree program information:* Part-time and evening/weekend programs available. Postbaccalaureate distance learning degree programs offered (no on-campus study). Offers architectural engineering (M Arch E); biological engineering (MBE); biomedical engineering (PhD); biomedical imaging and signals (MS); chemical engineering (M Ch E, MS, PhD); civil engineering (MS, PhD); computer engineering (MS, PhD); computer/electrical engineering (MS); construction engineering and management (MCEM); electrical and computer engineering (MECE); electrical engineering (MS, PhD); electricity markets (MEM); engineering (M Arch E, M Ch E, M Env E, M Geoenv E, M Trans E, MBE, MCEM, MECE, MEM, MFPE, MGE, MGE, MMAE, MME, MMME, MNE, MPW, MS, MSE, MTSE, PhD); environmental engineering (M Env E, MS, PhD); food process engineering (MFPE); food processing engineering (MS); gas engineering (MGE); geoenvironmental engineering (M Geoenv E); geotechnical engineering (MGE); manufacturing engineering (MME, MS); materials science and engineering (MMME, MS, PhD); mechanical and aerospace engineering (MMAE, MS, PhD); network engineering (MNE); power engineering (MS); public works (MPW); structural engineering (MSE); telecommunications and software engineering (MTSE); transportation engineering (M Trans E); VLSI and microelectronics (MS). *Application deadline:* For fall admission, 5/1 for domestic and international students; for spring admission, 10/15 for domestic and international students. Applications are processed on a rolling basis. *Application fee:* $40. Electronic applications accepted. *Application Contact:* Morgan Frederick, Assistant Director of Graduate Communications, 866-472-3448, Fax: 312-567-3138, E-mail: inquiry.grad@iit.edu. *Dean,* Dr. Hamid Arastoopour, 312-567-3009, Fax: 312-567-7961, E-mail: arastoopour@iit.edu.

Center for Professional Development Students: 117 full-time (28 women), 79 part-time (23 women); includes 37 minority (11 African Americans, 22 Asian Americans or Pacific Islanders, 4 Hispanic Americans), 115 international. Average age 29. 229 applicants, 77% accepted, 82 enrolled. *Faculty:* 18 part-time/adjunct (1 woman). Expenses: Contact institution. *Financial support:* Career-related internships or fieldwork, Federal Work-Study, institutionally sponsored loans, scholarships/grants, traineeships, health care benefits, tuition waivers (partial), and unspecified assistantships available. Support available to part-time students. In 2006, 45 master's awarded. *Degree program information:* Part-time and evening/weekend programs available. Postbaccalaureate distance learning degree programs offered (no on-campus study). Offers industrial technology and operations (MITO); information technology and management (MITM). *Application deadline:* For fall admission, 5/1 for domestic and international students; for spring admission, 10/15 for domestic and international students. Applications are processed on a rolling basis. *Application fee:* $40. Electronic applications accepted. *Application Contact:* Barbara C. Kozi, Administrator, 630-682-6040, Fax: 630-682-6010, E-mail: kozi@iit.edu. *Director,* C. Robert Carlson, 630-682-6002, Fax: 630-682-6010, E-mail: carlson@iit.edu.

College of Architecture Students: 172 full-time (72 women), 34 part-time (9 women); includes 24 minority (4 African Americans, 9 Asian Americans or Pacific Islanders, 11 Hispanic Americans), 82 international. Average age 28. 338 applicants, 73% accepted, 73 enrolled. *Faculty:* 38 full-time (7 women), 49 part-time/adjunct (14 women). Expenses: Contact institution. *Financial support:* In 2006–07, 56 teaching assistantships were awarded; fellowships, career-related internships or fieldwork, Federal Work-Study, institutionally sponsored loans, scholarships/grants, and health care benefits also available. Support available to part-time students. Financial award applicants required to submit FAFSA. In 2006, 43 master's, 2 doctorates awarded. *Degree program information:* Part-time programs available. Offers architecture (M Ar, PhD). *Application deadline:* For fall admission, 1/15 for domestic and international students. Applications are processed on a rolling basis. *Application fee:* $40. Electronic applications accepted. *Application Contact:* Shannon Kennedy, Coordinator for Academic Affairs, 312-567-3231, Fax: 312-567-5820, E-mail: kennedys@iit.edu. *Dean,* Donna V. Robertson, 312-567-3230, Fax: 312-567-5820, E-mail: robertson@iit.edu.

College of Science and Letters Students: 487 full-time (165 women), 415 part-time (176 women); includes 123 minority (55 African Americans, 3 American Indian/Alaska Native, 44 Asian Americans or Pacific Islanders, 21 Hispanic Americans), 517 international. Average age 29. 1,850 applicants, 59% accepted, 307 enrolled. *Faculty:* 118 full-time (29 women), 49 part-time/adjunct (18 women). Expenses: Contact institution. *Financial support:* Fellowships with tuition reimbursements, research assistantships with tuition reimbursements, teaching assistantships with tuition reimbursements, career-related internships or fieldwork, Federal Work-Study, institutionally sponsored loans, scholarships/grants, traineeships, health care benefits, and unspecified assistantships available. Support available to part-time students. Financial award applicants required to submit FAFSA. In 2006, 281 master's, 22 doctorates awarded. *Degree program information:* Part-time and evening/weekend programs available. Postbaccalaureate distance learning degree programs offered (no on-campus study). Offers analytical chemistry (M Ch, MS, PhD); applied mathematics (MS, PhD); biology (MBS, MS, PhD); chemistry (M Ch, M Chem, MS, PhD); computer science (MCS, MS, PhD); food safety and technology (MS); health physics (MHP); information architecture (MS); materials and chemical synthesis (M Ch); mathematical finance (MMF); mathematics education (MME, MS, PhD); molecular biochemistry and biophysics (MS, PhD); nonprofit management (MPA); physics (MHP, MS, PhD); public administration (MPA); public safety and crisis management (MPA); science and letters (M Ch, M Chem, MBS, MCS, MHP, MME, MMF, MPA, MS, MSE, MST, MTSE, PhD); science education (MS, MSE, PhD); teaching (MST); technical communication (PhD); technical communication and information design (MS); telecommunications and software engineering (MTSE). *Application deadline:* For fall admission, 5/1 for domestic and international students; for spring admission, 10/5 for domestic and international students. Applications are processed on a rolling basis. *Application fee:* $40. Electronic applications accepted. *Application Contact:* Morgan Frederick, Assistant Director of Graduate Communications, 866-472-3448, Fax: 312-567-3138, E-mail: inquiry.grad@iit.edu. *Dean,* Dr. Fred R. McMorris, 312-567-8981, Fax: 312-567-3135, E-mail: mcmorris@iit.edu.

Institute of Design Students: 99 full-time (47 women), 25 part-time (9 women); includes 17 minority (2 African Americans, 12 Asian Americans or Pacific Islanders, 3 Hispanic Americans), 43 international. Average age 31. 121 applicants, 73% accepted, 53 enrolled. *Faculty:* 8 full-time (1 woman), 16 part-time/adjunct (3 women). Expenses: Contact institution. *Financial support:* In 2006–07, 18 fellowships (averaging $5,100 per year), 4 research assistantships (averaging $10,000 per year), 10 teaching assistantships (averaging $1,000 per year) were awarded; career-related internships or fieldwork, Federal Work-Study, institutionally sponsored loans, scholarships/grants, health care benefits, and unspecified assistantships also available. Support available to part-time students. Financial award applicants required to submit FAFSA. In 2006, 42 degrees awarded. Offers design (M Des, MSDM, PhD). *Application deadline:* For fall admission, 2/15 priority date for domestic students, 2/15 for international students; for spring admission, 9/15 priority date for domestic students, 9/15 for international students. *Application fee:* $50. *Director of Admissions and Retention,* Rachel Smothers, 312-808-4906, Fax: 312-808-4901, E-mail: rachels@iit.edu.

Institute of Psychology Students: 111 full-time (84 women), 71 part-time (52 women); includes 43 minority (18 African Americans, 1 American Indian/Alaska Native, 13 Asian Americans or Pacific Islanders, 11 Hispanic Americans), 25 international. Average age 29. 290 applicants, 37% accepted, 32 enrolled. *Faculty:* 14 full-time (8 women), 8 part-time/adjunct (6 women). Expenses: Contact institution. *Financial support:* In 2006–07, 107 fellowships with partial tuition reimbursements (averaging $1,038 per year), 3 research assistantships with partial tuition reimbursements (averaging $2,100 per year), 41 teaching assistantships with partial tuition reimbursements (averaging $2,345 per year) were awarded; career-related internships or fieldwork, Federal Work-Study, institutionally sponsored loans, scholarships/grants, traineeships, health care benefits, and unspecified assistantships also available. Support available to part-time students. Financial award applicants required to submit FAFSA. In 2006, 45 master's, 11 doctorates awarded. *Degree program information:* Evening/weekend programs available. Offers clinical psychology (PhD); industrial/organizational psychology (PhD); personnel/human resource development (MS); psychology (MS); rehabilitation counseling (MS); rehabilitation counseling education (PhD). *Application deadline:* For fall admission, 1/15 for domestic and international students. *Application fee:* $40. Electronic applications accepted. *Application Contact:* Application Contact, 312-567-3500, Fax: 312-567-3493, E-mail: psychology@iit.edu. *Director,* Dr. M. Ellen Mitchell, 312-567-3501, Fax: 312-567-3493, E-mail: mitchelle@iit.edu.

Stuart School of Business Students: 285 full-time (112 women), 171 part-time (39 women); includes 44 minority (8 African Americans, 32 Asian Americans or Pacific Islanders, 4 Hispanic Americans), 288 international. Average age 29. 759 applicants, 76% accepted, 189 enrolled. *Faculty:* 24 full-time (2 women), 42 part-time/adjunct (4 women). Expenses: Contact institution. *Financial support:* Fellowships, career-related internships or fieldwork, Federal Work-Study, institutionally sponsored loans, scholarships/grants, traineeships, health care benefits, and unspecified assistantships available. Support available to part-time students. Financial award applicants required to submit FAFSA. In 2006, 154 master's, 2 doctorates awarded. *Degree program information:* Part-time and evening/weekend programs available. Offers business (MBA, MMF, MS, PhD); entrepreneurship (MBA); environmental management (MS); finance (MS); financial management (MBA); financial markets (MBA); healthcare management (MBA); information technology management (MBA); international business (MBA); management science (MBA); marketing (MBA); marketing communication (MS); mathematical finance (MMF); operations, quality, and technology management (MBA); strategic management of organizations (MBA); sustainable enterprise (MBA). *Application deadline:* For fall admission, 8/15 priority date for domestic students, 7/1 for international students; for winter admission, 11/1 priority date for domestic students, 10/1 for international students; for spring admission, 1/1 priority date for domestic students, 1/1 for international students. Applications are processed on a rolling basis. *Application fee:* $75. Electronic applications accepted. *Application Contact:* Brian Jansen, Director of Graduate Admissions, 312-906-6521, Fax: 312-906-6549, E-mail: admission@stuart.iit.edu. *Dean,* Dr. Harvey Kahalas, 312-906-6547, Fax: 312-906-6549, E-mail: kahalas@stuart.iit.edu.

ILLINOIS STATE UNIVERSITY, Normal, IL 61790-2200

General Information State-supported, coed, university. CGS member. *Enrollment:* 20,521 graduate, professional, and undergraduate students; 1,083 full-time matriculated graduate/professional students (656 women), 1,210 part-time matriculated graduate/professional students (805 women). *Enrollment by degree level:* 1,814 master's, 433 doctoral, 46 other advanced degrees. *Graduate faculty:* 616 full-time (238 women), 15 part-time/adjunct (5 women). Tuition, state resident: full-time $3,330; part-time $185 per credit hour. Tuition, nonresident: full-time $6,948; part-time $438 per credit hour. *Required fees:* $1,259; $52 per credit hour. *Graduate housing:* Rooms and/or apartments available to single and married students. Typical cost: $2,948 per year ($3,200 including board) for single students. Room and board charges vary according to board plan and housing facility selected. Housing application deadline: 4/1. *Student services:* Campus employment opportunities, campus safety program, career counseling, child daycare facilities, disabled student services, exercise/wellness program, free psychological counseling, international student services, low-cost health insurance, multicultural affairs office, teacher training. *Library facilities:* Milner Library. *Online resources:* library catalog, web page, access to other libraries' catalogs. *Collection:* 1.6 million titles, 14,166 serial subscriptions.

Computer facilities: 1,869 computers available on campus for general student use. A campuswide network can be accessed from student residence rooms and from off campus. Internet access is available. *Web address:* http://www.ilstu.edu/.

General Application Contact: Dr. Gary McGinnis, Associate Vice President of Research, Graduate Studies and International Education, 309-438-2583, Fax: 309-438-7912, E-mail: gradinfo@ilstu.edu.

GRADUATE UNITS

Graduate School Students: 1,083 full-time (656 women), 1,210 part-time (805 women); includes 227 minority (103 African Americans, 7 American Indian/Alaska Native, 51 Asian Americans or Pacific Islanders, 66 Hispanic Americans), 294 international. 1,660 applicants, 54% accepted. *Faculty:* 616 full-time (238 women), 15 part-time/adjunct (5 women). Expenses: Contact institution. *Financial support:* In 2006–07, 353 research assistantships, 313 teaching assistantships were awarded; fellowships, career-related internships or fieldwork, Federal Work-Study, institutionally sponsored loans, tuition waivers (full and partial), and unspecified assistantships also available. Support available to part-time students. Financial award application deadline: 4/1. In 2006, 754 master's, 52 doctorates, 10 other advanced degrees awarded. *Degree program information:* Part-time programs available. *Application deadline:* Applications are processed on a rolling basis. *Application fee:* $40. *Associate Vice President of Research, Graduate Studies and International Education,* Dr. Gary McGinnis, 309-438-2583, Fax: 309-438-9712, E-mail: gradinfo@ilstu.edu.

College of Applied Science and Technology Students: 182 full-time (96 women), 114 part-time (55 women); includes 30 minority (12 African Americans, 1 American Indian/Alaska Native, 9 Asian Americans or Pacific Islanders, 8 Hispanic Americans), 63 international. 262 applicants, 71% accepted. *Faculty:* 78 full-time (27 women). Expenses: Contact institution. *Financial support:* In 2006–07, 17 research assistantships, 16 teaching assistantships were awarded; fellowships, career-related internships or fieldwork, Federal Work-Study, institutionally sponsored loans, tuition waivers (full and partial), and unspecified assistantships also available. Support available to part-time students. Financial award application deadline: 4/1. In 2006, 135 degrees awarded. *Degree program information:* Part-time programs available. Offers agribusiness (MS); applied science and technology (MA, MS); criminal justice sciences (MA, MS); family and consumer sciences (MA, MS); health education (MS); information technology (MS); physical education (MS); technology (MS). *Application deadline:* Applications are processed on a rolling basis. *Application fee:* $40. *Dean,* Dr. J. Robert Rossman, 309-438-7602.

College of Arts and Sciences Students: 595 full-time (381 women), 321 part-time (213 women); includes 97 minority (36 African Americans, 4 American Indian/Alaska Native, 14 Asian Americans or Pacific Islanders, 43 Hispanic Americans), 153 international. 1,023 applicants, 44% accepted. *Faculty:* 292 full-time (116 women), 9 part-time/adjunct (2 women). Expenses: Contact institution. *Financial support:* In 2006–07, 101 research assistantships, 159 teaching assistantships were awarded; career-related internships or fieldwork, Federal Work-Study, institutionally sponsored loans, tuition waivers (full and partial), and unspecified assistantships also available. Support available to part-time students. Financial award application deadline: 4/1. In 2006, 266 master's, 18 doctorates, 4 other advanced degrees awarded. *Degree program information:* Part-time programs available. Offers animal behavior (MS); arts and sciences (MA, MS, MSW, PhD, SSP); bacteriology (MS); biochemistry (MS); biological sciences (MS); biology (PhD); biophysics (MS); biotechnology (MS); botany (MS, PhD); cell biology (MS); chemistry (MS); communication (MA, MS); conservation biology (MS); developmental biology (MS); ecology (MS, PhD); economics (MA, MS); English (MA, MS, PhD); English studies (PhD); entomology (MS); evolutionary biology (MS); French (MA); French and German (MA); French and Spanish (MA); genetics (MS, PhD); geohydrology (MS); German (MA); German and Spanish (MA); historical archaeology (MA, MS); history (MA, MS); immunology (MS); mathematics (MA, MS); mathematics education (PhD); microbiology (MS, PhD); molecular biology (MS); molecular genetics (MS); neurobiology (MS); neuroscience (MS); parasitology (MS); physiology (MS, PhD); plant biology (MS); plant molecular biology (MS); plant sciences (MS); politics and government (MA, MS); psychology (MA, MS); school psychology (PhD, SSP); social work (MSW); sociology (MA, MS); Spanish (MA); speech pathology and audiology (MA, MS); structural biology (MS); writing (MA, MS); zoology (MS, PhD). *Application deadline:* Applications are processed on a rolling basis. *Application fee:* $40. *Dean,* Dr. Gary Olson, 309-438-5669.

College of Business Students: 101 full-time (36 women), 113 part-time (41 women); includes 16 minority (3 African Americans, 11 Asian Americans or Pacific Islanders, 2 Hispanic Americans), 37 international. 109 applicants, 72% accepted. *Faculty:* 37 full-time (9 women), 1 part-time/adjunct (0 women). Expenses: Contact institution. *Financial support:* In 2006–07, 62 research assistantships, 4 teaching assistantships were awarded; career-related internships or fieldwork, Federal Work-Study, institutionally sponsored loans, and tuition waivers (full and partial) also available. Support available to part-time students. Financial award application deadline: 4/1. In 2006, 103 degrees awarded. *Degree program information:* Part-time programs available. Offers accounting (MPA, MS); business (MBA, MPA, MS); business administration (MBA). *Application deadline:* Applications are processed on a rolling basis. *Application fee:* $40. *Dean,* Dr. Dixie Mills, 309-438-2251.

College of Education Students: 71 full-time (49 women), 612 part-time (456 women); includes 69 minority (47 African Americans, 2 American Indian/Alaska Native, 11 Asian Americans or Pacific Islanders, 9 Hispanic Americans), 15 international. 119 applicants, 89% accepted. *Faculty:* 58 full-time (31 women), 3 part-time/adjunct (1 woman). Expenses: Contact institution. *Financial support:* In 2006–07, 52 research assistantships, 6 teaching assistantships were awarded; career-related internships or fieldwork, Federal Work-Study, institutionally sponsored loans, tuition waivers (full and partial), and unspecified assistantships also available. Support available to part-time students. Financial award application deadline: 4/1. In 2006, 186 master's, 34 doctorates awarded. *Degree program information:* Part-time programs available. Offers curriculum and instruction (MS, MS Ed, Ed D); education (MS, MS Ed, Ed D, PhD); educational administration and foundations (MS, MS Ed, Ed D, PhD); educational policies (Ed D); guidance and counseling (MS, MS Ed); postsecondary education (Ed D); reading (MS Ed); special education (MS, MS Ed, Ed D); supervision (Ed D). *Application deadline:* Applications are processed on a rolling basis. *Application fee:* $40. *Dean,* Dr. Deborah Curtis, 309-438-5415.

College of Fine Arts Students: 117 full-time (78 women), 29 part-time (22 women); includes 12 minority (4 African Americans, 4 Asian Americans or Pacific Islanders, 4 Hispanic Americans), 25 international. 136 applicants, 45% accepted. *Faculty:* 84 full-time (36 women). Expenses: Contact institution. *Financial support:* In 2006–07, 17 research assistantships, 79 teaching assistantships were awarded; career-related internships or fieldwork, Federal Work-Study, institutionally sponsored loans, tuition waivers (full and partial), and unspecified assistantships also available. Support available to part-time students. Financial award application deadline: 4/1. In 2006, 51 degrees awarded. *Degree program information:* Part-time programs available. Offers art history (MA, MS); arts technology (MS); ceramics (MFA, MS); drawing (MFA, MS); fibers (MFA, MS); fine arts (MA, MFA, MM, MM Ed, MS); glass (MFA, MS); graphic design (MFA, MS); metals (MFA, MS); music (MM, MM Ed); painting (MFA, MS); photography (MFA, MS); printmaking (MFA, MS); sculpture (MFA, MS); theatre (MA, MFA, MS). *Application deadline:* Applications are processed on a rolling basis. *Application fee:* $40. *Dean,* Dr. Lonny Gordon, 309-438-8321.

Mennonite College of Nursing Students: 17 full-time (16 women), 21 part-time (18 women); includes 3 minority (1 African American, 2 Asian Americans or Pacific Islanders), 1 international. 11 applicants, 100% accepted. *Faculty:* 7 full-time (all women). Expenses: Contact institution. *Financial support:* In 2006–07, 4 research assistantships (averaging $6,694 per year) were awarded. In 2006, 13 master's, 1 other advanced degree awarded. Offers family nurse practitioner (PMC); nursing (MSN). *Application fee:* $40. *Dean,* Nancy Ridenour, 309-438-7400, Fax: 309-438-2620.

See Close-Up on page 919.

IMCA–INTERNATIONAL MANAGEMENT CENTRES ASSOCIATION, Buckingham MK18 1BP, United Kingdom

General Information Independent, graduate-only institution.

GRADUATE UNITS

Programs in Business Administration Postbaccalaureate distance learning degree programs offered (no on-campus study). Offers business administration (M Phil, MBA, D Phil, DBA).

IMMACULATA UNIVERSITY, Immaculata, PA 19345

General Information Independent-religious, coed, primarily women, comprehensive institution. *Enrollment:* 4,067 graduate, professional, and undergraduate students; 102 full-time matriculated graduate/professional students (81 women), 875 part-time matriculated graduate/professional students (672 women). *Graduate faculty:* 44. *Graduate housing:* On-campus housing not available. *Student services:* Campus employment opportunities, campus safety program, career counseling, disabled student services, exercise/wellness program, international student services, low-cost health insurance, writing training. *Library facilities:* Gabriele Library. *Online resources:* library catalog, web page. *Collection:* 143,145 titles, 604 serial subscriptions, 3,422 audiovisual materials.

Computer facilities: 254 computers available on campus for general student use. A campuswide network can be accessed from student residence rooms. Internet access is available. *Web address:* http://www.immaculata.edu/.

General Application Contact: Sandra A. Rollison, Director of Graduate Admission, 610-647-4400 Ext. 3215, Fax: 610-993-8550, E-mail: srollison@immaculata.edu.

GRADUATE UNITS

College of Graduate Studies Students: 102 full-time (81 women), 875 part-time (672 women); includes 44 minority (31 African Americans, 8 Asian Americans or Pacific Islanders, 5 Hispanic Americans), 3 international. Average age 33. 324 applicants, 62% accepted, 132 enrolled. *Faculty:* 44. Expenses: Contact institution. *Financial support:* Career-related internships or fieldwork, Federal Work-Study, and scholarships/grants available. Support available to part-time students. Financial award application deadline: 5/1; financial award applicants required to submit FAFSA. In 2006, 113 master's, 44 doctorates awarded. *Degree program information:* Part-time and evening/weekend programs available. Offers clinical psychology (Psy D); counseling psychology (MA, Certificate); cultural and linguistic diversity (MA); educational leadership and administration (MA, Ed D); elementary education (Certificate); intermediate unit director (Certificate); music therapy (MA); nursing (MSN); nutrition education (MA); nutrition education/approved pre-professional practice program (MA); organization studies (MA); school principal (Certificate); school psychology (Psy D); school superintendent (Certificate); secondary education (Certificate); special education (Certificate). *Application deadline:* Applications are processed on a rolling basis. *Application fee:* $35. *Application Contact:* Sandra A. Rollison, Director of Graduate Admission, 610-647-4400 Ext. 3215, Fax: 610-993-8550, E-mail: srollison@immaculata.edu. *Dean,* Sr. Ann M. Heath, 610-647-4400 Ext. 3211, Fax: 610-993-8550.

See Close-Up on page 921.

INDIANA STATE UNIVERSITY, Terre Haute, IN 47809-1401

General Information State-supported, coed, university. CGS member. *Enrollment:* 10,568 graduate, professional, and undergraduate students; 767 full-time matriculated graduate/professional students (424 women), 1,264 part-time matriculated graduate/professional students (751 women). *Graduate faculty:* 269 full-time (85 women), 101 part-time/adjunct (46 women). Tuition, state resident: part-time $278 per credit. Tuition, nonresident: part-time $552 per credit. *Graduate housing:* Rooms and/or apartments available on a first-come, first-served basis to single and married students. *Student services:* Campus employment opportunities, campus safety program, career counseling, child daycare facilities, disabled student services, exercise/wellness program, free psychological counseling, grant writing training, international student services, low-cost health insurance, teacher training, writing training. *Library facilities:* Cunningham Memorial Library plus 1 other. *Online resources:* library catalog, web page, access to other libraries' catalogs. *Collection:* 1.3 million titles, 43,464 serial subscriptions, 32,843 audiovisual materials. *Research affiliation:* NASA–Stennis Space Center (remote sensing), Indiana University School of Medicine (microbiology), Walther Cancer Institute (psychosocial impacts of cancer).

Computer facilities: 450 computers available on campus for general student use. A campuswide network can be accessed from student residence rooms and from off campus. Internet access is available. *Web address:* http://web.indstate.edu/.

General Application Contact: Dr. Jolynn Kuhlman, Interim Dean, School of Graduate Studies, 800-444-GRAD, Fax: 812-237-8060, E-mail: grdstudy@amber.indstate.edu.

GRADUATE UNITS

School of Graduate Studies Students: 767 full-time (424 women), 1,264 part-time (751 women); includes 254 minority (159 African Americans, 10 American Indian/Alaska Native, 48 Asian Americans or Pacific Islanders, 37 Hispanic Americans), 296 international. Average age 33. 1,530 applicants, 73% accepted, 526 enrolled. *Faculty:* 269 full-time (85 women), 101 part-time/adjunct (46 women). Expenses: Contact institution. *Financial support:* In 2006–07, 325 research assistantships with partial tuition reimbursements (averaging $6,787 per year), 119 teaching assistantships with partial tuition reimbursements (averaging $6,247 per year) were awarded; fellowships with partial tuition reimbursements, career-related internships or fieldwork, Federal Work-Study, institutionally sponsored loans, scholarships/grants, tuition waivers (full and partial), and unspecified assistantships also available. Support available to part-time students. Financial award application deadline: 3/1; financial award applicants required to submit FAFSA. In 2006, 499 master's, 70 doctorates, 24 other advanced degrees awarded. *Degree program information:* Part-time and evening/weekend programs available. Postbaccalaureate distance learning degree programs offered (no on-campus study). Offers technology management (PhD). *Application deadline:* For fall admission, 6/1 priority date for domestic students; for spring admission, 11/1 priority date for domestic students. Applications are processed on a rolling basis. *Application fee:* $35. Electronic applications accepted. *Interim Dean,* Dr. Jolynn Kuhlman, 800-444-4723, Fax: 812-237-8060.

College of Arts and Sciences Students: 301 full-time (164 women), 258 part-time (133 women); includes 66 minority (33 African Americans, 2 American Indian/Alaska Native, 20 Asian Americans or Pacific Islanders, 11 Hispanic Americans), 110 international. Average age 30. 606 applicants, 63% accepted, 179 enrolled. *Faculty:* 136 full-time (44 women), 44 part-time/adjunct (14 women). Expenses: Contact institution. *Financial support:* In 2006–07, 9 research assistantships with partial tuition reimbursements, 126 teaching assistantships with partial tuition reimbursements (averaging $6,720 per year) were awarded; fellowships with partial tuition reimbursements, career-related internships or fieldwork, Federal Work-Study, institutionally sponsored loans, scholarships/grants, and tuition waivers (partial) also available. Support available to part-time students. Financial award application deadline: 3/1; financial award applicants required to submit FAFSA. In 2006, 133 master's, 18 doctorates awarded. *Degree program information:* Part-time and evening/weekend programs available. Offers arts and sciences (MA, MFA, MM, MPA, MS, PhD, Psy D, CAS); ceramics (MA, MFA); child development and family life (MS); clinical psychology (Psy D); clothing and textiles (MS); communication studies (MA, MS); computer science (MS); criminology (MA, MS); dietetics (MS); drawing (MA, MFA); earth sciences (MA, MS); ecology (PhD); economic geography (PhD); English (MA, MS); European history (MA, MS); family and consumer sciences education (MS); French (MA, MS); general psychology (MA, MS); geography (MA); geology (MS); graphic design (MA, MFA); history of labor and reform movements in the U.S. (MA); life sciences (MS); linguistics/teaching English as a second language (MA, MS); mathematics (MS); mathematics and computer science (MA); microbiology (PhD); music performance (MM); non-west history (MA, MS); nutrition and foods (MS); painting (MA, MFA); photography (MA, MFA); physical geography (PhD); physiology (PhD); political science (MA, MS); printmaking (MA, MFA); public administration (MPA); radio, television and film (MA, MS); science education (MS); sculpture (MA, MFA); Spanish (MA, MS); sports medicine (PhD); TESL/TEFL (CAS); theatre (MA, MS); U.S. history (MA, MS). *Application deadline:* For spring admission, 11/1 priority date for domestic students. Applications are processed on a rolling basis. *Application fee:* $35. Electronic applications accepted. *Interim Dean,* Dr. Thomas Sauer, 812-237-2788.

College of Business Students: 32 full-time (13 women), 19 part-time (9 women); includes 5 minority (2 African Americans, 3 Asian Americans or Pacific Islanders), 17 international. Average age 27. 92 applicants, 74% accepted, 15 enrolled. *Faculty:* 18 full-time (7 women), 6 part-time/adjunct (0 women). Expenses: Contact institution. *Financial support:* In 2006–07, 14 research assistantships with partial tuition reimbursements (averaging $6,300 per year) were awarded; career-related internships or fieldwork and tuition waivers (partial)

Indiana State University (continued)

also available. Financial award application deadline: 3/1; financial award applicants required to submit FAFSA. In 2006, 36 degrees awarded. *Degree program information:* Part-time and evening/weekend programs available. Offers business (MBA). *Application deadline:* For fall admission, 7/1 priority date for domestic students; for spring admission, 11/1 priority date for domestic students. Applications are processed on a rolling basis. *Application fee:* $35. Electronic applications accepted. *Dean,* Dr. Ronald Green, 812-237-2000.

College of Education Students: 229 full-time (157 women), 521 part-time (368 women); includes 74 minority (51 African Americans, 4 American Indian/Alaska Native, 7 Asian Americans or Pacific Islanders, 12 Hispanic Americans), 45 international. Average age 35. 385 applicants, 71% accepted, 140 enrolled. *Faculty:* 38 full-time (16 women), 23 part-time/adjunct (16 women). Expenses: Contact institution. *Financial support:* In 2006–07, 61 teaching assistantships with partial tuition reimbursements (averaging $5,793 per year) were awarded; fellowships with partial tuition reimbursements, research assistantships with partial tuition reimbursements, career-related internships or fieldwork, Federal Work-Study, institutionally sponsored loans, and tuition waivers (partial) also available. Support available to part-time students. Financial award application deadline: 3/1; financial award applicants required to submit FAFSA. In 2006, 155 master's, 44 doctorates, 24 other advanced degrees awarded. *Degree program information:* Part-time and evening/weekend programs available. Offers counseling psychology (MS, PhD); counselor education (PhD); curriculum and instruction (M Ed, PhD); early childhood education (M Ed); education (M Ed, MA, MS, PhD, Ed S); educational administration (PhD, Ed S); educational technology (MS); elementary education (M Ed); literacy (M Ed); marriage and family counseling (MS); school administration and supervision (M Ed); school counseling (M Ed); school psychology (M Ed, PhD, Ed S); speech-language pathology (MA, MS); student affairs administration (PhD); student affairs and higher education (MS). *Application deadline:* Applications are processed on a rolling basis. *Application fee:* $35. Electronic applications accepted. *Dean,* Dr. Bradley Balch, 812-237-2919.

College of Health and Human Performance Students: 61 full-time (23 women), 61 part-time (16 women); includes 9 African Americans, 1 American Indian/Alaska Native, 2 Hispanic Americans, 35 international. Average age 28. 71 applicants, 89% accepted, 32 enrolled. *Faculty:* 25 full-time (11 women), 2 part-time/adjunct (0 women). Expenses: Contact institution. *Financial support:* In 2006–07, 25 research assistantships with partial tuition reimbursements (averaging $6,174 per year) were awarded; teaching assistantships with partial tuition reimbursements, tuition waivers (full) and unspecified assistantships also available. Financial award application deadline: 3/1; financial award applicants required to submit FAFSA. In 2006, 46 degrees awarded. Offers adult fitness (MA, MS); athletic training (MS); coaching (MA, MS); community health promotion (MA, MS); exercise science (MA, MS); health and human performance (MA, MS); master teacher (MA, MS); occupational safety management (MA, MS); recreation and sport management (MA, MS); school health and safety (MA, MS). *Application deadline:* For fall admission, 7/1 priority date for domestic students; for spring admission, 11/1 priority date for domestic students. Applications are processed on a rolling basis. *Application fee:* $35. Electronic applications accepted. *Interim Dean,* Dr. Douglas Timmons, 812-237-2471.

College of Nursing Students: 37 full-time (34 women), 123 part-time (111 women); includes 25 minority (14 African Americans, 2 American Indian/Alaska Native, 4 Asian Americans or Pacific Islanders, 5 Hispanic Americans), 2 international. Average age 38. 101 applicants, 97% accepted, 76 enrolled. *Faculty:* 6 full-time (all women), 5 part-time/adjunct (all women). Expenses: Contact institution. *Financial support:* In 2006–07, 3 research assistantships with partial tuition reimbursements (averaging $6,300 per year) were awarded; teaching assistantships with partial tuition reimbursements, career-related internships or fieldwork and Federal Work-Study also available. Support available to part-time students. Financial award application deadline: 3/1; financial award applicants required to submit FAFSA. In 2006, 10 degrees awarded. *Degree program information:* Part-time programs available. Offers nursing (MS). *Application deadline:* For fall admission, 7/1 priority date for domestic students; for spring admission, 11/1 priority date for domestic students. Applications are processed on a rolling basis. *Application fee:* $35. Electronic applications accepted. *Interim Dean,* Dr. Esther Acree, 812-237-3683.

College of Technology Students: 102 full-time (29 women), 244 part-time (89 women); includes 65 minority (45 African Americans, 14 Asian Americans or Pacific Islanders, 6 Hispanic Americans), 86 international. Average age 34. 222 applicants, 88% accepted, 81 enrolled. *Faculty:* 63 full-time (4 women), 2 part-time/adjunct (1 woman). Expenses: Contact institution. *Financial support:* In 2006–07, 23 research assistantships with partial tuition reimbursements (averaging $7,300 per year) were awarded; fellowships with partial tuition reimbursements, teaching assistantships with partial tuition reimbursements, Federal Work-Study and institutionally sponsored loans also available. Financial award application deadline: 3/1; financial award applicants required to submit FAFSA. In 2006, 99 master's, 8 doctorates awarded. Offers career and technical education (MS); electronics and computer technology (MS); human resource development (MS); industrial technology (MS); technology (MS, PhD); technology education (MS). *Application deadline:* For fall admission, 7/1 priority date for domestic students; for spring admission, 11/1 priority date for domestic students. Applications are processed on a rolling basis. *Application fee:* $35. Electronic applications accepted. *Dean,* Dr. W. Tad Foster, 812-237-3166.

See Close-Up on page 923.

INDIANA TECH, Fort Wayne, IN 46803-1297

General Information Independent, coed, comprehensive institution. *Graduate housing:* On-campus housing not available.

GRADUATE UNITS

Program in Business Administration *Degree program information:* Part-time and evening/weekend programs available. Offers accounting (MBA); human resources (MBA); management (MBA); marketing (MBA). Electronic applications accepted.

Program in Management *Degree program information:* Part-time and evening/weekend programs available. Offers management (MSM). Electronic applications accepted.

Program in Science *Degree program information:* Part-time and evening/weekend programs available. Offers science (MSE). Electronic applications accepted.

INDIANA UNIVERSITY BLOOMINGTON, Bloomington, IN 47405-7000

General Information State-supported, coed, university. CGS member. *Enrollment:* 38,247 graduate, professional, and undergraduate students; 5,381 full-time matriculated graduate/professional students (2,683 women), 2,567 part-time matriculated graduate/professional students (1,378 women). *Enrollment by degree level:* 937 first professional, 3,436 master's, 3,396 doctoral, 178 other advanced degrees. *Graduate faculty:* 1,080 full-time (328 women), 4 part-time/adjunct (2 women). Tuition, state resident: full-time $5,791; part-time $241 per credit hour. Tuition, nonresident: full-time $16,866; part-time $703 per credit hour. *Graduate housing:* Rooms and/or apartments available to single and married students. *Student services:* Campus employment opportunities, campus safety program, career counseling, child daycare facilities, disabled student services, exercise/wellness program, free psychological counseling, international student services, low-cost health insurance, multicultural affairs office, writing training. *Library facilities:* Indiana University Library plus 32 others. *Online resources:* library catalog, web page, access to other libraries' catalogs. *Collection:* 6.5 million titles, 60,019 serial subscriptions.

Computer facilities: 2,262 computers available on campus for general student use. A campuswide network can be accessed from student residence rooms and from off campus. Internet access and online class registration, various software packages are available. *Web address:* http://www.iub.edu/.

General Application Contact: Information Contact, 812-855-0661, Fax: 812-855-5102, E-mail: iuadmit@indiana.edu.

GRADUATE UNITS

Graduate School Students: 2,221 full-time (1,130 women), 1,729 part-time (894 women); includes 401 minority (148 African Americans, 22 American Indian/Alaska Native, 107 Asian Americans or Pacific Islanders, 124 Hispanic Americans), 1,129 international. Average age 30. Expenses: Contact institution. *Financial support:* Fellowships with full and partial tuition reimbursements, research assistantships, teaching assistantships, career-related internships or fieldwork, Federal Work-Study, institutionally sponsored loans, and tuition waivers (full and partial) available. Support available to part-time students. In 2006, 432 master's, 326 doctorates awarded. *Degree program information:* Part-time programs available. *Application deadline:* For fall admission, 1/15 priority date for domestic students, 12/15 for international students; for spring admission, 9/1 for domestic and international students. *Application fee:* $50 ($60 for international students). Electronic applications accepted. *Application Contact:* Graduate School, 812-855-8853, E-mail: grdschl@indiana.edu.

College of Arts and Sciences Students: 1,591 full-time (808 women), 1,120 part-time (572 women); includes 269 minority (90 African Americans, 17 American Indian/Alaska Native, 68 Asian Americans or Pacific Islanders, 94 Hispanic Americans), 675 international. Average age 29. *Faculty:* 644 full-time (197 women), 1 (woman) part-time/adjunct. Expenses: Contact institution. *Financial support:* In 2006–07, fellowships with full and partial tuition reimbursements (averaging $9,825 per year); research assistantships, teaching assistantships, career-related internships or fieldwork, Federal Work-Study, institutionally sponsored loans, and tuition waivers (full and partial) also available. Support available to part-time students. In 2006, 373 master's, 186 doctorates awarded. *Degree program information:* Part-time programs available. Offers acting (MFA); African American and African diaspora studies (MA); African languages and linguistics (PhD); analytical chemistry (PhD); anthropology (MA, PhD); applied mathematics–numerical analysis (MA, PhD); arts and sciences (MA, MAT, MFA, MS, Au D, PhD, Certificate); astronomy (MA, PhD); astrophysics (PhD); audiology (Au D); auditory sciences (PhD); biogeochemistry (MS, PhD); biological chemistry (PhD); biology and behavior (PhD); biology teaching (MAT); Central Eurasian studies (MA, PhD); chemistry (MAT); Chinese (MA, PhD); classical studies (MA, MAT, PhD); clinical science (PhD); cognitive psychology (PhD); communication and culture (MA, PhD); comparative literature (MA, MAT, PhD); composition, literacy, and culture (PhD); computational linguistics (MA); computer science (MS, PhD); creative writing (MA, MFA); crime (MA, PhD); criminal justice (MA, PhD); cross-cultural perspectives of crime and justice (MA, PhD); design and technology (MFA); developmental psychology (PhD); directing (MFA); East Asian languages and cultures (PhD); East Asian studies (MA); economic geology (MS, PhD); economics (MA, PhD); evolution, ecology, and behavior (MA, PhD); fine arts (MA, MFA, PhD); folklore (MA, PhD); French (MA, PhD); genetics (PhD); geobiology (MS, PhD); geography (MA, MAT, MS, PhD); geophysics, structural geology and tectonics (MS, PhD); German literature and studies (PhD); German studies (MA, PhD); Hispanic linguistics (MA, PhD); Hispanic literature (MA); history (MA, MAT, PhD); history and philosophy of science (MA, PhD); history of art (MA, PhD); hydrogeology (MS, PhD); inorganic chemistry (PhD); Italian (MA, PhD); Japanese (MA, PhD); journalism (MA, MAT); language (MA); language pedagogy (MA); language sciences (PhD); Latin American and Caribbean studies (MA); law and society (MA, PhD); linguistics (PhD); literature (MA, PhD); Luso-Brazilian literature (MA); Luso-Brazilian studies (PhD); mass communication (PhD); mass communications (PhD); mathematics education (MAT); medieval German studies (PhD); microbiology (MA, PhD); mineralogy (MS, PhD); molecular, cellular, and developmental biology (PhD); Near Eastern languages and cultures (MA, PhD); philosophy (MA, PhD); physical chemistry (PhD); physics (MAT, MS, PhD); plant sciences (MA, PhD); playwriting (MFA); political science (MA, PhD); probability-statistics (MA, PhD); psychological and brain sciences (MA); religious studies (MA, PhD); Russian and East European studies (MA, Certificate); Slavic languages and literatures (MA, MAT, PhD); social psychology (PhD); sociology (MA, PhD); Spanish literatures (PhD); speech and voice sciences (PhD); speech-language pathology (MA); stratigraphy and sedimentology (MS, PhD); teaching German (MAT); teaching Spanish (MAT); telecommunications (MA, MS); theatre and drama (MAT); theatre history (MA, PhD); theory (MA, PhD); West European studies (MA); writing (MA); zoology (MA, PhD). PhD offered through the University Graduate School. *Application deadline:* For fall admission, 1/15 priority date for domestic students, 12/15 for international students; for spring admission, 9/1 for domestic and international students. *Application fee:* $50 ($60 for international students). Electronic applications accepted. *Dean,* Bennett Bertenthal, 812-855-1646.

Jacobs School of Music Students: 619 full-time (332 women), 270 part-time (140 women); includes 90 minority (20 African Americans, 3 American Indian/Alaska Native, 49 Asian Americans or Pacific Islanders, 18 Hispanic Americans), 273 international. Average age 28. *Faculty:* 35 full-time (13 women). Expenses: Contact institution. *Financial support:* Fellowships with full and partial tuition reimbursements, research assistantships, teaching assistantships with full tuition reimbursements, Federal Work-Study, institutionally sponsored loans, scholarships/grants, tuition waivers (full and partial), and unspecified assistantships available. Support available to part-time students. Financial award application deadline: 3/1; financial award applicants required to submit FAFSA. In 2006, 172 master's, 45 doctorates, 50 other advanced degrees awarded. Offers church music (DM); music (MA, MM, MME, MS, DM, DME, PhD, AD, Performance Diploma, Spec); music literature and performance (DM); performance (MM); performance and church music (MM). *Application deadline:* For fall admission, 12/1 for domestic and international students; for spring admission, 9/1 for domestic and international students. *Application fee:* $100 ($110 for international students). *Dean,* Gwyn Richards, 812-855-2435, E-mail: jln@indiana.edu.

Kelley School of Business Students: 634 full-time (173 women), 35 part-time (13 women); includes 88 minority (20 African Americans, 55 Asian Americans or Pacific Islanders, 13 Hispanic Americans), 256 international. Average age 27. *Faculty:* 87 full-time (15 women). Expenses: Contact institution. *Financial support:* Fellowships with full and partial tuition reimbursements, research assistantships, teaching assistantships, career-related internships or fieldwork, Federal Work-Study, institutionally sponsored loans, tuition waivers (full and partial), and unspecified assistantships available. Support available to part-time students. Financial award application deadline: 3/1; financial award applicants required to submit FAFSA. In 2006, 350 master's, 18 doctorates awarded. Offers business (MBA, MPA, MS, DBA, PhD); business economics and public policy (PhD). PhD offered through the University Graduate School. *Application deadline:* For fall admission, 1/15 priority date for domestic students, 12/1 priority date for international students; for winter admission, 3/1 priority date for domestic students; for spring admission, 4/15 for domestic students, 9/1 for international students. *Application fee:* $50 ($60 for international students). Electronic applications accepted. *Application Contact:* Director of Admissions and Financial Aid, 812-855-8006, Fax: 812-855-9039. *Dean,* Daniel Smith, 812-855-8100, Fax: 812-855-8679, E-mail: business@indiana.edu.

School of Education Students: 471 full-time (322 women), 603 part-time (384 women); includes 120 minority (61 African Americans, 2 American Indian/Alaska Native, 24 Asian Americans or Pacific Islanders, 33 Hispanic Americans), 221 international. Average age 33. 1,837 applicants, 39% accepted, 354 enrolled. *Faculty:* 102 full-time (43 women), 112 part-time/adjunct (45 women). Expenses: Contact institution. *Financial support:* In 2006–07, 122 fellowships with full and partial tuition reimbursements (averaging $18,000 per year), 91 research assistantships with tuition reimbursements (averaging $11,400 per year), 148 teaching assistantships with tuition reimbursements (averaging $13,600 per year) were awarded; Federal Work-Study, scholarships/grants, tuition waivers (full and partial), and unspecified assistantships also available. Financial award application deadline: 3/1. In 2006, 323 master's, 96 doctorates, 5 other advanced degrees awarded. *Degree program information:* Part-time programs available. Postbaccalaureate distance learning degree programs offered. Offers art education (MS, Ed D, PhD); counseling (MS, PhD, Ed S); counseling psychology (PhD); counselor education (MS, Ed S); curriculum studies (Ed D, PhD); education (MS, Ed D, PhD, Ed S); education policy studies (PhD); educational leadership (MS, Ed D, PhD, Ed S); educational psychology (MS, PhD); elementary education (MS, Ed D, PhD, Ed S); higher education (MS, Ed D, PhD); history and philosophy of education (MS); history of education (PhD); instructional systems technology (MS, PhD, Ed S); international and comparative education (MS, PhD); language education (MS, Ed D, PhD, Ed S); learning and developmental sciences (MS, PhD); mathematics education (MS, Ed D, PhD); philosophy of education (PhD); school psychology (PhD, Ed S); science education (MS, Ed D, PhD); secondary education (MS, Ed D, PhD); social studies education (MS, PhD); special education (MS, Ed D, PhD, Ed S); student affairs administration (MS). PhD offered through the University Graduate School. *Application deadline:* For fall admission, 1/15 priority date for domestic students, 12/1 priority date for international students; for spring admission, 11/1 priority date for domestic students, 9/1 priority date for international students. Applications are processed on a rolling basis. *Application fee:* $50 ($65 for international students). Electronic applications accepted. *Application Contact:* Elizabeth Tilghman, Admissions Coordinator, 812-856-8552, Fax: 812-856-8505, E-mail: etilghma@indiana.edu. *Dean,* Dr. Gerardo Gonzalez, 812-856-8001, Fax: 812-856-8088, E-mail: gonzalez@indiana.edu.

School of Health, Physical Education and Recreation Students: 199 full-time (105 women), 134 part-time (72 women); includes 40 minority (31 African Americans, 2 American Indian/Alaska Native, 5 Asian Americans or Pacific Islanders, 2 Hispanic Americans), 54 international. Average age 29. *Faculty:* 53 full-time (19 women), 1 (woman) part-time/adjunct. Expenses: Contact institution. *Financial support:* In 2006–07, 115 students received support; fellowships with full and partial tuition reimbursements available, research assistantships with tuition reimbursements available, teaching assistantships with tuition reimbursements available, career-related internships or fieldwork, Federal Work-Study, institutionally sponsored loans, scholarships/grants, and tuition waivers (full and partial) available. Support available to part-time students. Financial award application deadline: 3/1. In 2006, 124 master's, 17 doctorates awarded. *Degree program information:* Part-time programs available. Postbaccalaureate distance learning degree programs offered (no on-campus study). Offers adapted physical education (MS); applied sport science (MS); athletic training (MS); biomechanics (MS); clinical exercise physiology (MS); ergonomics (MS); exercise physiology (MS); health behavior (PhD); health promotion (MS); health, physical education and recreation (MPH, MS, PhD, PE Dir, Re Dir); human development/family studies (MS); human performance (MS, PhD, PE Dir); leisure behavior (PhD); motor control (MS); nutrition science (MS); outdoor recreation management (MS); park and recreation administration (MS); public health (MPH); recreation (Re Dir); recreational sports administration (MS); safety management (MS); school and college health education (MS); sport management (MS); therapeutic recreation (MS). PhD offered through the University Graduate School. *Application deadline:* For fall admission, 3/1 for domestic students, 1/1 for international students; for spring admission, 11/1 for domestic students, 9/1 for international students. *Application fee:* $50 ($60 for international students). *Dean,* David Gallahue, 812-855-1561, Fax: 812-855-4983, E-mail: hper@indiana.edu.

School of Informatics Students: 97 full-time (35 women), 10 part-time (1 woman); includes 7 minority (4 African Americans, 1 Asian American or Pacific Islander, 2 Hispanic Americans), 54 international. Average age 27. *Faculty:* 33 full-time (3 women). Expenses: Contact institution. *Financial support:* Fellowships with full and partial tuition reimbursements, research assistantships, teaching assistantships, Federal Work-Study, institutionally sponsored loans, scholarships/grants, and tuition waivers (full and partial) available. Support available to part-time students. In 2006, 36 degrees awarded. Offers bioinformatics (MS); chemical informatics (MS); health informatics (MS); human computer interaction (MS); informatics (PhD); laboratory informatics (MS); media arts and science (MS); music informatics (MS). *Application deadline:* For fall admission, 1/17 for domestic students, 1/15 for international students; for spring admission, 4/15 for domestic students, 9/1 for international students. *Application fee:* $50 ($60 for international students). Electronic applications accepted. *Application Contact:* Martin Siegel, Associate Dean for Graduate Studies and Research, 812-856-1103, E-mail: msiegel@indiana.edu. *Dean,* J. Michael Dunn, 812-856-5754, Fax: 812-856-4764, E-mail: informat@indiana.edu.

School of Law Students: 654 full-time (274 women), 74 part-time (29 women); includes 95 minority (39 African Americans, 35 Asian Americans or Pacific Islanders, 21 Hispanic Americans), 101 international. Average age 26. 2,718 applicants, 39% accepted, 211 enrolled. *Faculty:* 59 full-time (19 women), 15 part-time/adjunct (4 women). Expenses: Contact institution. *Financial support:* In 2006–07, 581 students received support, including 477 fellowships (averaging $7,982 per year), 99 research assistantships (averaging $811 per year), 5 teaching assistantships (averaging $3,000 per year); career-related internships or fieldwork, Federal Work-Study, institutionally sponsored loans, scholarships/grants, health care benefits, and unspecified assistantships also available. Financial award application deadline: 3/1; financial award applicants required to submit FAFSA. In 2006, 211 first professional degrees, 62 master's, 3 doctorates awarded. Offers comparative law (MCL); juridical science (SJD); law (JD, LL M); law and social sciences (PhD); legal studies (Certificate). *Application deadline:* For fall admission, 3/1 priority date for domestic and international students. Applications are processed on a rolling basis. *Application fee:* $35 ($60 for international students). Electronic applications accepted. *Application Contact:* Patricia S. Clark, Director of Admissions, 812-855-2704, Fax: 812-855-0555, E-mail: psclark@indiana.edu. *Dean,* Lauren K. Robel, 812-855-8885, Fax: 812-855-7057, E-mail: lrobel@indiana.edu.

School of Library and Information Science Students: 211 full-time (152 women), 120 part-time (81 women); includes 28 minority (9 African Americans, 1 American Indian/Alaska Native, 7 Asian Americans or Pacific Islanders, 11 Hispanic Americans), 31 international. Average age 30. *Faculty:* 12 full-time (7 women). Expenses: Contact institution. *Financial support:* Fellowships with full and partial tuition reimbursements, Federal Work-Study, institutionally sponsored loans, and scholarships/grants available. Support available to part-time students. In 2006, 165 master's, 1 doctorate awarded. *Degree program information:* Part-time programs available. Offers library and information science (MIS, MLS, PhD, Sp LIS). PhD offered through the University Graduate School. *Application deadline:* For fall admission, 5/15 priority date for domestic students, 12/1 priority date for international students; for spring admission, 3/15 priority date for domestic students, 9/1 priority date for international students. Applications are processed on a rolling basis. *Application fee:* $50 ($60 for international students). Electronic applications accepted. *Application Contact:* Rhonda Spencer, Information Contact, 812-855-2018, Fax: 812-855-6166. *Dean,* Debora Shaw, 812-855-2018, Fax: 812-855-6166.

School of Optometry Students: 323 full-time (195 women), 15 part-time (12 women); includes 37 minority (12 African Americans, 18 Asian Americans or Pacific Islanders, 7 Hispanic Americans), 31 international. Average age 25. 371 applicants, 37% accepted, 75 enrolled. *Faculty:* 22 full-time (4 women). Expenses: Contact institution. *Financial support:* In 2006–07, 15 fellowships with full tuition reimbursements (averaging $20,000 per year), 2 research assistantships with full tuition reimbursements were awarded; Federal Work-Study, institutionally sponsored loans, and scholarships/grants also available. Support available to part-time students. Financial award application deadline: 12/1; financial award applicants required to submit FAFSA. In 2006, 67 ODs, 1 doctorate awarded. Offers optometry (OD, MS, PhD). PhD offered through the University Graduate School. *Application deadline:* For fall admission, 1/15 for domestic students; for winter admission, 2/1 for domestic and international students; for spring admission, 9/1 for domestic students. *Application fee:* $50 ($60 for international students). *Application Contact:* Andrea Waldbieser, Associate Director, Student Administration/Student Services, 812-855-1292, Fax: 812-855-4389. *Dean,* Dr. Gerald E. Lowther, 812-855-4440, Fax: 812-855-8664, E-mail: glowther@indiana.edu.

School of Public and Environmental Affairs Students: 303 full-time (165 women), 30 part-time (18 women); includes 36 minority (20 African Americans, 1 American Indian/Alaska Native, 6 Asian Americans or Pacific Islanders, 9 Hispanic Americans), 49 international. Average age 27. 410 applicants, 91% accepted, 182 enrolled. Expenses: Contact institution. *Financial support:* In 2006–07, 2 fellowships with full tuition reimbursements (averaging $10,000 per year), research assistantships with partial tuition reimbursements (averaging $5,000 per year), teaching assistantships with partial tuition reimbursements (averaging $5,000 per year) were awarded; Federal Work-Study, scholarships/grants, tuition waivers (partial), unspecified assistantships, and service corps program also available. Financial award application deadline: 2/1; financial award applicants required to submit FAFSA. In 2006, 160 master's, 6 doctorates, 10 other advanced degrees awarded. *Degree program information:* Part-time programs available. Offers environmental science (MSES, PhD); nonprofit management (Certificate); public affairs (MPA, PhD); public and environmental affairs (MA, MPA, MSES, PhD, Certificate); public management (Certificate); public policy (PhD). *Application deadline:* For fall admission, 2/1 priority date for domestic students, 12/1 priority date for international students; for spring admission, 5/1 for domestic and international students. *Application fee:* $50 ($60 for international students). Electronic applications accepted. *Application Contact:* Jennifer Forney, Director, Graduate Student Services, 812-855-9485, E-mail: jjforney@indiana.edu. *Interim Dean,* Charles Kurt Zorn, 812-855-5058, Fax: 812-855-6234, E-mail: zorn@indiana.edu.

INDIANA UNIVERSITY KOKOMO, Kokomo, IN 46904-9003

General Information State-supported, coed, comprehensive institution. *Enrollment:* 2,734 graduate, professional, and undergraduate students; 8 full-time matriculated graduate/professional students (1 woman), 54 part-time matriculated graduate/professional students (27 women). *Enrollment by degree level:* 59 master's, 3 other advanced degrees. *Graduate faculty:* 22 full-time (8 women). Tuition, state resident: full-time $4,391; part-time $183 per hour. Tuition, nonresident: full-time $10,043; part-time $418 per hour. Tuition and fees vary according to course load, campus/location and program. *Graduate housing:* On-campus housing not available. *Student services:* Career counseling, child daycare facilities, disabled student services, multicultural affairs office, teacher training. *Library facilities:* Main library plus 1 other. *Collection:* 132,424 titles, 1,513 serial subscriptions.

Computer facilities: 120 computers available on campus for general student use. Internet access is available. *Web address:* http://www.iuk.edu/.

General Application Contact: Admissions Office, 765-455-9357.

GRADUATE UNITS

Division of Education Average age 32. *Faculty:* 1 full-time (0 women). Expenses: Contact institution. *Financial support:* Minority teacher scholarships available. In 2006, 3 degrees awarded. *Degree program information:* Part-time and evening/weekend programs available. Offers elementary education (MS); secondary education (MS). *Application deadline:* For fall admission, 8/1 for domestic students; for spring admission, 12/1 for domestic students. Applications are processed on a rolling basis. *Application fee:* $40 ($50 for international students). *Application Contact:* Charlotte Miller, Coordinator Educational/Student Resources, 765-455-9367, Fax: 765-455-9503, E-mail: cmiller@iuk.edu. *Dean,* D. Antonio Cantu, 765-455-9287, Fax: 765-455-9503.

School of Arts and Sciences Students: 1 full-time (0 women), 10 part-time (5 women); includes 2 minority (1 African American, 1 Hispanic American). Average age 42. 2 applicants, 50% accepted, 1 enrolled. *Faculty:* 32 full-time (10 women). Expenses: Contact institution. In 2006, 4 degrees awarded. Offers liberal studies (MALS). *Application deadline:* For fall admission, 4/15 priority date for domestic students; for spring admission, 10/15 priority date for domestic students. Applications are processed on a rolling basis. *Application fee:* $40. *Application Contact:* Dr. Terri Bourus, Director of Master of Liberal Arts Program, 765-455-9372, Fax: 765-455-9566, E-mail: tbourus@iuk.edu. *Dean,* Dr. Susan Sclame-Giesecke, 765-455-9258, Fax: 765-455-9566, E-mail: sgieseck@iuk.edu.

School of Business Students: 7 full-time (1 woman), 38 part-time (18 women); includes 4 minority (2 African Americans, 1 Asian American or Pacific Islander, 1 Hispanic American), 4 international. Average age 34. 27 applicants, 81% accepted, 22 enrolled. *Faculty:* 14 full-time (6 women). Expenses: Contact institution. *Financial support:* In 2006–07, 2 students received support; fellowships, research assistantships, teaching assistantships, career-related internships or fieldwork and tuition waivers (partial) available. In 2006, 19 degrees awarded. *Degree program information:* Part-time and evening/weekend programs available. Offers business administration (MBA). *Application deadline:* For fall admission, 8/1 priority date for domestic and international students; for spring admission, 12/15 priority date for domestic and international students. Applications are processed on a rolling basis. *Application fee:* $40 ($60 for international students). *Application Contact:* Dr. Linda Ficht, Director of MBA Program, 765-455-9275, Fax: 765-455-9348, E-mail: lficht@iuk.edu. *Dean,* Dr. Niranjan Pati, 756-455-9275, Fax: 756-455-9348, E-mail: npati@iuk.edu.

School of Public and Environmental Affairs Average age 39. Expenses: Contact institution. In 2006, 3 degrees awarded. Offers public management (Graduate Certificate). *Application deadline:* For fall admission, 8/1 priority date for domestic students; for spring admission, 12/9 priority date for domestic students. *Application fee:* $40 ($50 for international students). *Assistant Dean,* Dr. Robert Dibie, 765-455-9417, Fax: 765-455-9537, E-mail: iuadmis@iuk.edu.

INDIANA UNIVERSITY NORTHWEST, Gary, IN 46408-1197

General Information State-supported, coed, comprehensive institution. *Enrollment:* 4,819 graduate, professional, and undergraduate students; 59 full-time matriculated graduate/professional students (49 women), 342 part-time matriculated graduate/professional students (252 women). *Enrollment by degree level:* 328 master's, 73 other advanced degrees. *Graduate faculty:* 44 full-time (15 women). Tuition, state resident: full-time $4,332; part-time $181 per credit hour. Tuition, nonresident: full-time $10,081; part-time $420 per credit hour. Tuition and fees vary according to course load, campus/location and program. *Graduate housing:* On-campus housing not available. *Student services:* Campus employment opportunities, campus safety program, career counseling, child daycare facilities, free psychological counseling, international student services, low-cost health insurance. *Library facilities:* IUN Library. *Online resources:* library catalog, web page, access to other libraries' catalogs. *Collection:* 251,508 titles, 1,541 serial subscriptions.

Computer facilities: 250 computers available on campus for general student use. A campuswide network can be accessed from off campus. Internet access and online class registration are available. *Web address:* http://www.iun.edu/.

General Application Contact: Admissions Counselor, 219-980-6760, Fax: 219-980-7103.

GRADUATE UNITS

Division of Social Work Students: 29 full-time (27 women), 88 part-time (73 women); includes 54 minority (46 African Americans, 1 American Indian/Alaska Native, 2 Asian Americans or Pacific Islanders, 5 Hispanic Americans), 1 international. Average age 34. *Faculty:* 1 full-time (0 women). Expenses: Contact institution. *Financial support:* In 2006–07, 43 students received support. Career-related internships or fieldwork, Federal Work-Study, tuition waivers (partial), and tuition remissions available. Support available to part-time students. Financial award application deadline: 6/1; financial award applicants required to submit FAFSA. *Degree program information:* Part-time and evening/weekend programs available. Offers social work (MSW). *Application deadline:* For fall admission, 2/1 for domestic students. *Application fee:* $25. *Application Contact:* Kellie Branch, Assistant to the Director, 219-980-7111. *Director,* Dr. Denise Travis, 219-980-7111, Fax: 219-981-4264, E-mail: dtravis@iun.edu.

School of Business and Economics Students: 11 full-time (7 women), 72 part-time (38 women); includes 19 minority (10 African Americans, 1 Asian American or Pacific Islander, 8 Hispanic Americans). Average age 32. *Faculty:* 5 full-time (0 women). Expenses: Contact institution. *Financial support:* In 2006–07, 9 students received support. Federal Work-Study, institutionally sponsored loans, and unspecified assistantships available. Support available to part-time students. Financial award application deadline: 7/15. In 2006, 39 degrees awarded. *Degree program information:* Part-time and evening/weekend programs available. Offers accountancy (M Acc); accounting (Certificate); business administration (MBA). *Application deadline:* For fall admission, 7/15 priority date for domestic students; for spring admission, 11/15 for domestic students. Applications are processed on a rolling basis. *Application fee:* $25. *Application Contact:* John Gibson, Director of Graduate Program, 219-980-6500, Fax: 219-980-6916, E-mail: jagibson@iun.edu. *Dean,* Anna Rominger, 219-980-6636, Fax: 219-980-6916, E-mail: iunbiz@iun.edu.

School of Education Students: 3 full-time (all women), 64 part-time (49 women); includes 26 minority (23 African Americans, 3 Hispanic Americans). Average age 40. *Faculty:* 5 full-time (2 women). Expenses: Contact institution. In 2006, 36 degrees awarded. *Degree program information:* Part-time and evening/weekend programs available. Offers elementary education (MS Ed); secondary education (MS Ed). *Application deadline:* For fall admission, 7/15 priority date for domestic students; for spring admission, 11/15 for domestic students. *Application fee:* $25. *Dean,* Dr. Stanley E. Wigle, 219-980-6510, Fax: 219-981-4208, E-mail: amsanche@iun.edu.

School of Public and Environmental Affairs Students: 16 full-time (12 women), 118 part-time (92 women); includes 89 minority (76 African Americans, 1 Asian American or Pacific Islander, 12 Hispanic Americans). Average age 39. *Faculty:* 5 full-time (3 women). Expenses: Contact institution. *Financial support:* Career-related internships or fieldwork,

Indiana University Northwest (continued)

Federal Work-Study, and tuition waivers (partial) available. Support available to part-time students. Financial award application deadline: 3/1. In 2006, 30 master's, 31 other advanced degrees awarded. *Degree program information:* Part-time programs available. Offers criminal justice (MPA); environmental affairs (Certificate); health services administration (MPA); human services administration (MPA); nonprofit management (Certificate); public administration (MPA); public management (MPA, Certificate). *Application deadline:* For fall admission, 8/15 priority date for domestic students. Applications are processed on a rolling basis. *Application fee:* $25. *Application Contact:* Sandra Hall Smith, Secretary, 219-980-6695, Fax: 219-980-6737, E-mail: shsmith@iun.edu. *Interim Assistant Dean/Division Director,* Karen Evans, 219-980-6695, Fax: 219-980-6737.

INDIANA UNIVERSITY OF PENNSYLVANIA, Indiana, PA 15705-1087

General Information State-supported, coed, university. CGS member. *Enrollment:* 14,248 graduate, professional, and undergraduate students; 1,100 full-time matriculated graduate/professional students (677 women), 1,172 part-time matriculated graduate/professional students (761 women). *Enrollment by degree level:* 1,641 master's, 631 doctoral. *Graduate faculty:* 278 full-time (114 women), 14 part-time/adjunct (9 women). Tuition, state resident: full-time $6,048; part-time $336 per credit. Tuition, nonresident: full-time $9,678; part-time $538 per credit. *Required fees:* $1,069; $148 per year. *Graduate housing:* Room and/or apartments available on a first-come, first-served basis to single students; on-campus housing not available to married students. Typical cost: $3,150 per year ($5,160 including board). Housing application deadline: 4/15. *Student services:* Campus employment opportunities, campus safety program, career counseling, disabled student services, free psychological counseling, international student services, low-cost health insurance, multicultural affairs office. *Library facilities:* Stapleton Library. *Online resources:* library catalog, web page, access to other libraries' catalogs. *Collection:* 852,531 titles, 16,290 serial subscriptions.

Computer facilities: Computer purchase and lease plans are available. 3,500 computers available on campus for general student use. A campuswide network can be accessed from student residence rooms and from off campus. Internet access and online class registration are available. *Web address:* http://www.iup.edu/.

General Application Contact: Donna Griffith, Assistant Dean, 724-357-2222, Fax: 724-357-4862, E-mail: graduate-admissions@iup.edu.

GRADUATE UNITS

School of Graduate Studies and Research Students: 1,100 full-time (677 women), 1,172 part-time (761 women); includes 139 minority (94 African Americans, 2 American Indian/Alaska Native, 26 Asian Americans or Pacific Islanders, 17 Hispanic Americans), 331 international. Average age 32. 2,668 applicants, 58% accepted. *Faculty:* 278 full-time (114 women), 14 part-time/adjunct (9 women). Expenses: Contact institution. *Financial support:* In 2006–07, 13 fellowships with full tuition reimbursements (averaging $5,000 per year), 273 research assistantships with full and partial tuition reimbursements (averaging $5,500 per year), 30 teaching assistantships with partial tuition reimbursements (averaging $17,001 per year) were awarded; career-related internships or fieldwork, Federal Work-Study, scholarships/grants, and tuition waivers (full) also available. Support available to part-time students. Financial award application deadline: 3/15; financial award applicants required to submit FAFSA. In 2006, 559 master's, 89 doctorates, 11 other advanced degrees awarded. *Degree program information:* Part-time and evening/weekend programs available. *Application deadline:* Applications are processed on a rolling basis. *Application fee:* $30. *Application Contact:* Donna Griffith, Assistant Dean, 724-357-2222, Fax: 724-357-4862, E-mail: graduate-admissions@iup.edu. *Dean,* Dr. Alicia Linzey, 724-357-2222, Fax: 724-357-4862, E-mail: avlinzey@iup.edu.

College of Education and Educational Technology Students: 286 full-time (211 women), 604 part-time (438 women); includes 56 minority (48 African Americans, 4 Asian Americans or Pacific Islanders, 4 Hispanic Americans), 15 international. Average age 33. 1,114 applicants, 61% accepted. *Faculty:* 59 full-time (31 women), 9 part-time/adjunct (6 women). Expenses: Contact institution. *Financial support:* In 2006–07, 14 fellowships (averaging $1,000 per year), 102 research assistantships (averaging $4,990 per year), 6 teaching assistantships with partial tuition reimbursements (averaging $17,001 per year) were awarded; career-related internships or fieldwork and Federal Work-Study also available. Support available to part-time students. Financial award application deadline: 3/15; financial award applicants required to submit FAFSA. In 2006, 210 master's, 25 doctorates, 11 other advanced degrees awarded. *Degree program information:* Part-time and evening/weekend programs available. Offers administration and leadership studies (D Ed); adult education and communication technology (MA); communications technology (MA); community counseling (MA); counselor education (M Ed); curriculum and instruction (M Ed, D Ed); early childhood education (M Ed); education (M Ed, Certificate); education and educational technology (M Ed, MA, MS, D Ed, Certificate); education of exceptional persons (M Ed); educational psychology (M Ed, Certificate); literacy (M Ed); principal (Certificate); reading (M Ed); school psychology (D Ed, Certificate); speech-language pathology (MS); student affairs in higher education (MA). *Application deadline:* Applications are processed on a rolling basis. *Application fee:* $30. *Application Contact:* Dr. Edward Nardi, Interim Associate Dean, 724-357-2480, Fax: 724-357-5595, E-mail: ewnardi@iup.edu. *Dean,* Dr. Mary Ann Rafoth, 724-357-2480, Fax: 724-357-5595.

College of Fine Arts Students: 25 full-time (15 women), 12 part-time (6 women), 5 international. Average age 29. 56 applicants, 46% accepted. *Faculty:* 23 full-time (7 women), 2 part-time/adjunct (1 woman). Expenses: Contact institution. *Financial support:* In 2006–07, 2 fellowships (averaging $375 per year), 32 research assistantships with full and partial tuition reimbursements (averaging $1,500 per year) were awarded; career-related internships or fieldwork and Federal Work-Study also available. Support available to part-time students. Financial award application deadline: 3/15; financial award applicants required to submit FAFSA. In 2006, 10 degrees awarded. *Degree program information:* Part-time programs available. Offers art (MA, MFA); fine arts (MA, MFA); music (MA); music education (MA); music history and literature (MA); music theory and composition (MA); performance (MA). *Application deadline:* For fall admission, 7/1 priority date for domestic students; for spring admission, 11/1 for domestic students. Applications are processed on a rolling basis. *Application fee:* $30. *Application Contact:* Dr. Douglas Bish, Associate Dean, 724-357-2397, E-mail: dbish@iup.edu. *Dean,* Michael Hood, 724-357-2397, E-mail: mhood@iup.edu.

College of Health and Human Services Students: 105 full-time (69 women), 157 part-time (103 women); includes 8 minority (6 African Americans, 2 Asian Americans or Pacific Islanders), 19 international. Average age 33. 243 applicants, 67% accepted. *Faculty:* 22 full-time (12 women), 2 part-time/adjunct (both women). Expenses: Contact institution. *Financial support:* In 2006–07, 39 research assistantships with full and partial tuition reimbursements (averaging $4,990 per year) were awarded; career-related internships or fieldwork and Federal Work-Study also available. Support available to part-time students. Financial award application deadline: 3/15; financial award applicants required to submit FAFSA. In 2006, 99 degrees awarded. *Degree program information:* Part-time and evening/weekend programs available. Offers aquatics administration and facilities management (MS); exercise science (MS); food and nutrition (MS); health and human services (MA, MS, Certificate); industrial and labor relations (MA); nursing (MS); safety sciences (MS, Certificate); sport management (MS); sport science (MS). *Application deadline:* For fall admission, 7/1 priority date for domestic students; for spring admission, 11/1 for domestic students. Applications are processed on a rolling basis. *Application fee:* $30. *Application Contact:* Dr. Jacqueline Beck, Associate Dean, 724-357-2560, E-mail: jbeck@iup.edu. *Dean,* Dr. Carleen Zoni, 724-357-2555, E-mail: cczoni@iup.edu.

College of Humanities and Social Sciences Students: 441 full-time (258 women), 192 part-time (120 women); includes 52 minority (35 African Americans, 1 American Indian/Alaska Native, 9 Asian Americans or Pacific Islanders, 7 Hispanic Americans), 111 international. Average age 34. 615 applicants, 52% accepted. *Faculty:* 91 full-time (41 women). Expenses: Contact institution. *Financial support:* In 2006–07, 9 fellowships (averaging $1,000 per year), 95 research assistantships (averaging $4,990 per year), 4 teaching assistantships (averaging $17,001 per year) were awarded; career-related internships or fieldwork, Federal Work-Study, and tuition waivers (full) also available. Support available to part-time students. Financial award application deadline: 3/15; financial award applicants required to submit FAFSA. In 2006, 107 master's, 57 doctorates awarded. *Degree program information:* Part-time and evening/weekend programs available. Offers administration and leadership studies (PhD); composition and teaching English to speakers of other languages (MA, MAT, PhD); criminology (MA, PhD); generalist (MA); geography (MA, MS); history (MA); humanities and social sciences (MA, MAT, MS, PhD); literature (MA); literature and criticism (MA, PhD); public affairs (MA); rhetoric and linguistics (PhD); sociology (MA); teaching English (MAT); teaching English to speakers of other languages (MA). *Application deadline:* For fall admission, 7/1 priority date for domestic students; for spring admission, 11/1 for domestic students. Applications are processed on a rolling basis. *Application fee:* $30. *Dean,* Dr. Yaw Asamoah, 724-357-5764.

College of Natural Sciences and Mathematics Students: 104 full-time (71 women), 27 part-time (18 women); includes 6 minority (1 African American, 2 Asian Americans or Pacific Islanders, 3 Hispanic Americans), 12 international. Average age 29. 231 applicants, 23% accepted. *Faculty:* 50 full-time (15 women). Expenses: Contact institution. *Financial support:* In 2006–07, 5 fellowships (averaging $500 per year), 71 research assistantships with full and partial tuition reimbursements (averaging $4,990 per year), 2 teaching assistantships (averaging $17,001 per year) were awarded; career-related internships or fieldwork, Federal Work-Study, and outside grants and professional employment also available. Support available to part-time students. Financial award application deadline: 3/15; financial award applicants required to submit FAFSA. In 2006, 36 master's, 7 doctorates awarded. *Degree program information:* Part-time programs available. Offers applied mathematics (MS); biology (MS); chemistry (MA, MS); clinical psychology (Psy D); elementary and middle school mathematics education (M Ed); mathematics education (M Ed); natural sciences and mathematics (M Ed, MA, MS, Psy D); physics (MA, MS); psychology (MA). *Application deadline:* Applications are processed on a rolling basis. *Application fee:* $30. *Application Contact:* Dr. Jacqueline Gorman, Dean's Associate, 724-357-2609, E-mail: jgorman@iup.edu. *Interim Dean,* Dr. Gerald Buriok, 724-357-2609.

Eberly College of Business and Information Technology Students: 129 full-time (50 women), 146 part-time (50 women); includes 11 minority (2 African Americans, 6 Asian Americans or Pacific Islanders, 3 Hispanic Americans), 168 international. Average age 27. 316 applicants, 66% accepted. *Faculty:* 33 full-time (8 women), 1 part-time/adjunct (0 women). Expenses: Contact institution. *Financial support:* In 2006–07, 1 fellowship (averaging $250 per year), 68 research assistantships with full and partial tuition reimbursements (averaging $1,372 per year) were awarded; career-related internships or fieldwork and Federal Work-Study also available. Support available to part-time students. Financial award application deadline: 3/15; financial award applicants required to submit FAFSA. In 2006, 95 degrees awarded. *Degree program information:* Part-time and evening/weekend programs available. Offers business (M Ed, MBA); business administration (MBA); business/workforce development (M Ed). *Application deadline:* For fall admission, 7/1 priority date for domestic students; for spring admission, 11/1 for domestic students. Applications are processed on a rolling basis. *Application fee:* $30. *Dean,* Dr. Robert Camp, 724-357-4783, E-mail: bobcamp@iup.edu.

See Close-Up on page 925.

INDIANA UNIVERSITY–PURDUE UNIVERSITY FORT WAYNE, Fort Wayne, IN 46805-1499

General Information State-supported, coed, comprehensive institution. CGS member. *Enrollment:* 11,672 graduate, professional, and undergraduate students; 93 full-time matriculated graduate/professional students (49 women), 539 part-time matriculated graduate/professional students (323 women). *Enrollment by degree level:* 632 master's. *Graduate faculty:* 178 full-time (63 women), 3 part-time/adjunct (1 woman). Tuition, state resident: full-time $4,039; part-time $224 per credit. Tuition, nonresident: full-time $9,220; part-time $512 per credit. *Required fees:* $429; $24 per credit. Tuition and fees vary according to course load. *Graduate housing:* Room and/or apartments available on a first-come, first-served basis to single students; on-campus housing not available to married students. Typical cost: $4,940 per year. *Student services:* Campus employment opportunities, campus safety program, career counseling, child daycare facilities, disabled student services, exercise/wellness program, free psychological counseling, international student services, low-cost health insurance, multicultural affairs office, teacher training, writing training. *Library facilities:* Helmke Library. *Online resources:* library catalog, web page, access to other libraries' catalogs. *Collection:* 478,091 titles, 24,872 serial subscriptions, 6,527 audiovisual materials. *Research affiliation:* Indiana Family Health Council Inc. (health and human services), The Lilly Endowment Inc. (education (research and external support)), The Foellinger Foundation (continuing studies), Vulcan Construction Materials LP (archaeology), Church & Dwight (dental health), Center for Field Studies, Earthwatch (biology).

Computer facilities: 285 computers available on campus for general student use. A campuswide network can be accessed from off campus. Internet access and online class registration, students academic records are available. *Web address:* http://www.ipfw.edu/.

General Application Contact: Susan Humphreys, Graduate Applications Coordinator, 260-481-6145, Fax: 260-481-6880, E-mail: ask@ipfw.edu.

GRADUATE UNITS

College of Arts and Sciences Students: 45 full-time (26 women), 83 part-time (48 women); includes 15 minority (8 African Americans, 2 American Indian/Alaska Native, 1 Asian American or Pacific Islander, 4 Hispanic Americans), 4 international. Average age 32. 58 applicants, 95% accepted, 48 enrolled. *Faculty:* 96 full-time (30 women), 2 part-time/adjunct (1 woman). Expenses: Contact institution. *Financial support:* In 2006–07, 9 research assistantships with partial tuition reimbursements (averaging $11,950 per year), 42 teaching assistantships with partial tuition reimbursements (averaging $11,950 per year) were awarded; career-related internships or fieldwork, institutionally sponsored loans, and scholarships/grants also available. Support available to part-time students. Financial award application deadline: 3/1; financial award applicants required to submit FAFSA. In 2006, 50 master's, 3 other advanced degrees awarded. *Degree program information:* Part-time and evening/weekend programs available. Offers applied mathematics (MS); applied statistics (Certificate); arts and sciences (MA, MAT, MLS, MS, Certificate); biology (MS); English (MA, MAT); liberal studies (MLS); mathematics (MS); operations research (MS); professional communication (MA, MS); sociological practice (MA); TENL (teaching English as a new language) (Certificate). *Application deadline:* For fall admission, 2/15 for domestic students; for spring admission, 9/1 for domestic students. Applications are processed on a rolling basis. *Application fee:* $30. *Dean,* Dr. Marc Lipman, 260-481-6160, Fax: 260-481-6985, E-mail: lipmanm@ipfw.edu.

College of Engineering, Technology, and Computer Science Students: 3 full-time (1 woman), 20 part-time (6 women); includes 2 minority (1 African American, 1 Asian American or Pacific Islander), 2 international. Average age 35. 9 applicants, 100% accepted, 6 enrolled. *Faculty:* 10 full-time (0 women), 1 part-time/adjunct (0 women). Expenses: Contact institution. *Financial support:* In 2006–07, 1 teaching assistantship with partial tuition reimbursement (averaging $11,950 per year) was awarded; career-related internships or fieldwork, scholarships/grants, and unspecified assistantships also available. Support available to part-time students. Financial award application deadline: 3/1; financial award applicants required to submit FAFSA. In 2006, 4 degrees awarded. *Degree program information:* Part-time programs available. Offers applied computer science (MS); engineering, technology, and computer science (MS). *Application deadline:* For fall admission, 8/1 priority date for domestic students; for spring admission, 11/1 for domestic students. Applications are processed on a rolling basis. *Application fee:* $55. *Application Contact:* Dr. Kenneth Modesitt, Interim Chair of Computer Science, 260-481-6803, Fax: 260-481-5734, E-mail: modesitk@ipfw.edu. *Dean,* Dr. Gerard Voland, 260-481-6839, Fax: 260-481-5734, E-mail: volandg@ipfw.edu.

Division of Public and Environmental Affairs Students: 5 full-time (3 women), 40 part-time (25 women); includes 6 minority (4 African Americans, 1 American Indian/Alaska Native, 1 Asian American or Pacific Islander). Average age 34. 12 applicants, 92% accepted, 10 enrolled. *Faculty:* 8 full-time (2 women). Expenses: Contact institution. *Financial support:* In 2006–07, 1 teaching assistantship with partial tuition reimbursement (averaging $11,950 per year) was awarded; career-related internships or fieldwork and scholarships/grants also available. Support available to part-time students. Financial award application deadline: 3/1; financial award applicants required to submit FAFSA. In 2006, 14 degrees awarded. *Degree program information:* Part-time programs available. Offers public affairs (MPA); public management (MPM, Certificate). *Application deadline:* For fall admission, 8/1 priority date for domestic students; for spring admission, 12/1 for domestic students. Applications are processed on a rolling basis. *Application fee:* $30. *Interim Assistant Dean and Director,* Dr. Geralyn Miller, 260-481-6350, Fax: 260-481-6346, E-mail: millergm@ipfw.edu.

School of Business and Management Sciences Students: 32 full-time (13 women), 114 part-time (39 women); includes 8 minority (2 African Americans, 5 Asian Americans or Pacific Islanders, 1 Hispanic American), 14 international. Average age 30. 64 applicants, 78% accepted, 49 enrolled. *Faculty:* 31 full-time (8 women). Expenses: Contact institution. *Financial support:* In 2006–07, 11 teaching assistantships with partial tuition reimbursements (averaging $11,950 per year) were awarded; scholarships/grants and unspecified assistantships also available. Support available to part-time students. Financial award application deadline: 3/1; financial award applicants required to submit FAFSA. In 2006, 39 degrees awarded. *Degree program information:* Part-time programs available. Offers business administration (MBA). *Application deadline:* For fall admission, 7/1 for domestic students, 5/1 for international students; for spring admission, 11/1 for domestic students, 10/1 for international students. Applications are processed on a rolling basis. *Application fee:* $30. *Application Contact:* Dr. Zoher Shipchandler, Interim Director Graduate Programs, 260-481-6474, Fax: 260-481-6879, E-mail: shipchan@ipfw.edu. *Dean,* Dr. John L. Wellington, 260-481-6461, Fax: 260-481-6879, E-mail: wellingj@ipfw.edu.

School of Education Students: 7 full-time (5 women), 268 part-time (193 women); includes 26 minority (16 African Americans, 1 Asian American or Pacific Islander, 9 Hispanic Americans), 1 international. Average age 37. 131 applicants, 87% accepted, 97 enrolled. *Faculty:* 24 full-time (14 women). Expenses: Contact institution. *Financial support:* In 2006–07, 1 teaching assistantship with partial tuition reimbursement (averaging $11,950 per year) was awarded; scholarships/grants also available. Support available to part-time students. Financial award application deadline: 3/1; financial award applicants required to submit FAFSA. In 2006, 104 degrees awarded. *Degree program information:* Part-time programs available. Offers counselor education (MS Ed); education (MS Ed); educational administration (MS Ed); elementary education (MS Ed); secondary education (MS Ed). *Application deadline:* For fall admission, 7/1 priority date for domestic students; for spring admission, 12/1 for domestic students. Applications are processed on a rolling basis. *Application fee:* $30. *Application Contact:* Vicky L. Schmidt, Graduate Recorder, 260-481-6450, Fax: 260-481-5408, E-mail: schmidt@ipfw.edu. *Dean,* Dr. Barry Kanpol, 260-481-4146, Fax: 260-481-5408, E-mail: kanpolb@ipfw.edu.

School of Health Sciences Average age 47. 9 applicants, 100% accepted, 5 enrolled. *Faculty:* 9 full-time (all women). Expenses: Contact institution. *Financial support:* Scholarships/grants available. Support available to part-time students. Financial award application deadline: 3/1; financial award applicants required to submit FAFSA. In 2006, 2 degrees awarded. *Degree program information:* Part-time programs available. Offers health sciences (MS, Certificate); nursing administration (MS, Certificate). *Application deadline:* For fall admission, 8/1 priority date for domestic students; for spring admission, 12/1 for domestic students. Applications are processed on a rolling basis. *Application fee:* $55. Electronic applications accepted. *Application Contact:* Dr. Carol Sternberger, Chair, 260-481-6816, Fax: 260-481-5707, E-mail: sternber@ipfw.edu. *Dean,* Dr. Linda Finke, 260-481-6967, Fax: 260-481-5701, E-mail: finkel@ipfw.edu.

INDIANA UNIVERSITY–PURDUE UNIVERSITY INDIANAPOLIS, Indianapolis, IN 46202-2896

General Information State-supported, coed, university. *Enrollment:* 29,764 graduate, professional, and undergraduate students; 3,735 full-time matriculated graduate/professional students (2,024 women), 3,989 part-time matriculated graduate/professional students (2,224 women). *Enrollment by degree level:* 2,580 first professional, 4,512 master's, 451 doctoral, 172 other advanced degrees. *Graduate faculty:* 599 full-time (195 women), 2 part-time/adjunct (1 woman). Tuition, state resident: full-time $5,437; part-time $227 per credit hour. Tuition, nonresident: full-time $15,694; part-time $654 per credit hour. *Required fees:* $620. Tuition and fees vary according to course load, campus/location and program. *Graduate housing:* Rooms and/or apartments available on a first-come, first-served basis to single and married students. *Student services:* Campus employment opportunities, campus safety program, career counseling, child daycare facilities, disabled student services, exercise/wellness program, free psychological counseling, international student services, low-cost health insurance, multicultural affairs office, writing training. *Library facilities:* University Library plus 5 others. *Online resources:* library catalog, web page, access to other libraries' catalogs. *Collection:* 1.5 million titles, 14,673 serial subscriptions.

Computer facilities: 500 computers available on campus for general student use. A campuswide network can be accessed from student residence rooms and from off campus. Internet access and online class registration are available. *Web address:* http://www.iupui.edu/.

General Application Contact: Dr. Sherry Queener, Director, Graduate Studies and Associate Dean, 317-274-1577, Fax: 317-278-2380.

GRADUATE UNITS

Department of Economics Students: 7 full-time (4 women), 14 part-time (5 women), 11 international. Average age 29. 57 applicants, 23% accepted, 11 enrolled. *Faculty:* 14 full-time (3 women). Expenses: Contact institution. *Financial support:* In 2006–07, 3 fellowships with partial tuition reimbursements (averaging $14,000 per year), 5 research assistantships with partial tuition reimbursements (averaging $11,000 per year) were awarded; career-related internships or fieldwork and health care benefits also available. In 2006, 7 degrees awarded. Offers economics (MA). *Application deadline:* For fall admission, 2/1 priority date for domestic and international students. *Application fee:* $35 ($50 for international students). *Application Contact:* Natalie Harvey, Information Contact, 317-274-4756, Fax: 317-274-0097. *Chair,* Paul Carlin, 317-278-9230, E-mail: pcarlin@iupui.edu.

Department of English Students: 6 full-time (3 women), 32 part-time (13 women); includes 2 minority (1 African American, 1 Hispanic American), 3 international. Average age 32. *Faculty:* 20 full-time (8 women). Expenses: Contact institution. *Financial support:* Fellowships, research assistantships, career-related internships or fieldwork available. In 2006, 10 degrees awarded. Offers English (MA); teaching English (MA). *Application fee:* $50 ($60 for international students). *Chair,* Susanmarie Harrington, 317-2788-1153.

Department of History Students: 7 full-time (all women), 29 part-time (16 women); includes 2 minority (1 African American, 1 Hispanic American). Average age 30. *Faculty:* 14 full-time (6 women). Expenses: Contact institution. *Financial support:* Fellowships with full tuition reimbursements, research assistantships with full tuition reimbursements, teaching assistantships with full tuition reimbursements, career-related internships or fieldwork available. In 2006, 11 degrees awarded. *Degree program information:* Part-time and evening/weekend programs available. Offers history (MA); public history (MA). *Application deadline:* For fall admission, 2/1 priority date for domestic students. Applications are processed on a rolling basis. *Application fee:* $50 ($60 for international students). *Application Contact:* Mary Gelzleichter, Graduate Secretary, 317-274-5840, Fax: 317-278-7800, E-mail: mgelzlei@liupui.edu. *Chair,* Robert Barrows, 317-274-2457.

Herron School of Art and Design Students: 2 full-time (both women), 11 part-time (7 women); includes 1 minority (Hispanic American) Average age 37. *Faculty:* 2 full-time (both women). Expenses: Contact institution. *Financial support:* Career-related internships or fieldwork, Federal Work-Study, institutionally sponsored loans, scholarships/grants, and tuition waivers (partial) available. Support available to part-time students. In 2006, 1 degree awarded. *Degree program information:* Part-time and evening/weekend programs available. Offers art education (MAE); furniture design (MFA); printmaking (MFA); sculpture (MFA); visual communication (MFA). *Application deadline:* For fall admission, 6/1 priority date for domestic students, 3/15 priority date for international students; for spring admission, 11/1 priority date for domestic students, 10/15 priority date for international students. Applications are processed on a rolling basis. *Application fee:* $50 ($60 for international students). Electronic applications accepted. *Application Contact:* Herron Student Services Office, 317-378-9400, E-mail: herrart@iupui.edu. *Dean,* Valerie Eickmeier, 317-278-9470, Fax: 317-278-9471, E-mail: herron@iupui.edu.

Indiana University School of Medicine Students: 1,295 full-time (608 women), 191 part-time (126 women); includes 242 minority (95 African Americans, 5 American Indian/Alaska Native, 101 Asian Americans or Pacific Islanders, 41 Hispanic Americans), 80 international. Average age 26. *Faculty:* 270 full-time (56 women). Expenses: Contact institution. *Financial support:* Fellowships with full and partial tuition reimbursements, research assistantships with full and partial tuition reimbursements, teaching assistantships with full tuition reimbursements, Federal Work-Study, institutionally sponsored loans, scholarships/grants, tuition waivers (full and partial), and stipends available. Support available to part-time students. In 2006, 258 MDs, 43 master's awarded. Offers anatomy and cell biology (MS, PhD); biochemistry and molecular biology (PhD); genetic counseling (MS); medical and molecular genetics (MS, PhD); medicine (MD, MPH, MS, DPT, PhD); microbiology and immunology (MS, PhD); pathology and laboratory medicine (MS, PhD); pharmacology (MS, PhD); public health (MPH); toxicology (MS, PhD). *Application deadline:* For fall admission, 8/1 priority date for domestic students. Applications are processed on a rolling basis. *Application fee:* $50 ($60 for international students). *Application Contact:* Robert M. Stump, Director of Admissions, 317-274-3772, E-mail: inmedadm@iupui.edu. *Dean,* Dr. D. Craig Brater, 317-274-5000, Fax: 317-278-5211.

School of Health and Rehabilitation Sciences Students: 180 full-time (149 women), 35 part-time (21 women); includes 17 minority (6 African Americans, 7 Asian Americans or Pacific Islanders, 4 Hispanic Americans), 3 international. Average age 27. *Faculty:* 8 full-time (5 women). Expenses: Contact institution. *Financial support:* Fellowships, research assistantships, teaching assistantships, Federal Work-Study, institutionally sponsored loans, and scholarships/grants available. Support available to part-time students. Financial award applicants required to submit FAFSA. In 2006, 9 master's, 32 doctorates awarded. *Degree program information:* Part-time and evening/weekend programs available. Offers health sciences education (MS); nutrition and dietetics (MS); occupational therapy (MS); physical therapy (DPT). *Application deadline:* For fall admission, 1/15 priority date for domestic students; for spring admission, 10/15 for domestic students. *Application fee:* $50 ($60 for international students). *Dean of the School of Allied Health Sciences,* Dr. Mark S. Sothmann, 317-274-4702, E-mail: msothman@iupui.edu.

Kelley School of Business Students: 116 full-time (47 women), 932 part-time (226 women); includes 140 minority (42 African Americans, 3 American Indian/Alaska Native, 81 Asian Americans or Pacific Islanders, 14 Hispanic Americans), 135 international. Average age 32. *Faculty:* 20 full-time (4 women), 1 part-time/adjunct (0 women). Expenses: Contact institution. *Financial support:* Fellowships, Federal Work-Study, institutionally sponsored loans, and scholarships/grants available. Support available to part-time students. Financial award application deadline: 3/1; financial award applicants required to submit FAFSA. In 2006, 400 degrees awarded. *Degree program information:* Part-time and evening/weekend programs available. Postbaccalaureate distance learning degree programs offered (minimal on-campus study). Offers business (MBA, MPA). *Application deadline:* For fall admission, 4/15 priority date for domestic and international students; for spring admission, 11/1 priority date for domestic and international students. *Application fee:* $50 ($55 for international students). Electronic applications accepted. *Application Contact:* Julie L. Moore, Recorder/Admission Coordinator, 317-274-4895, Fax: 317-274-2483, E-mail: mbaindy@iupui.edu. *Associate Dean, Indianapolis Programs,* Roger W. Schmenner, 317-274-2481, Fax: 317-274-2483, E-mail: busugrad@iupui.edu.

School of Dentistry Students: 452 full-time (176 women), 60 part-time (27 women); includes 69 minority (10 African Americans, 3 American Indian/Alaska Native, 42 Asian Americans or Pacific Islanders, 14 Hispanic Americans), 45 international. Average age 27. *Faculty:* 16 full-time (2 women). Expenses: Contact institution. *Financial support:* In 2006–07, 43 students received support; fellowships, research assistantships, teaching assistantships, Federal Work-Study, institutionally sponsored loans, and scholarships/grants available. Financial award application deadline: 3/1; financial award applicants required to submit FAFSA. In 2006, 98 DDSs, 30 master's, 2 doctorates awarded. Offers dentistry (DDS, MS, MSD, PhD, Certificate). *Application deadline:* For fall admission, 10/1 for domestic students, 10/1 priority date for international students; for spring admission, 2/1 for domestic and international students. *Application fee:* $50 ($60 for international students). *Application Contact:* Robert Kasberg, Associate Dean for Student Affairs and Director of Admissions, 317-274-8173, Fax: 317-274-2419, E-mail: blerner@iupui.edu. *Dean,* Lawrence I. Goldblatt, 317-274-7461.

School of Education Students: 77 full-time (66 women), 430 part-time (334 women); includes 46 minority (29 African Americans, 1 American Indian/Alaska Native, 7 Asian Americans or Pacific Islanders, 9 Hispanic Americans), 7 international. Average age 32. *Faculty:* 13 full-time (7 women). Expenses: Contact institution. *Financial support:* Fellowships, research assistantships with partial tuition reimbursements, teaching assistantships, Federal Work-Study, institutionally sponsored loans, scholarships/grants, and tuition waivers (partial) available. Support available to part-time students. In 2006, 162 degrees awarded. *Degree program information:* Part-time and evening/weekend programs available. Offers education (MS, Certificate). *Application deadline:* For fall admission, 3/1 priority date for domestic students; for spring admission, 11/1 for domestic students. *Application fee:* $50 ($55 for international students). *Application Contact:* Marsha Schuler, Graduate Advisor, 317-274-6801, Fax: 317-274-6864, E-mail: edugrad@iupui.edu. *Executive Associate Dean,* Dr. Khaula Murtadha, 317-274-6801, Fax: 317-274-6864.

School of Engineering and Technology Students: 37 full-time (7 women), 66 part-time (12 women); includes 10 minority (6 African Americans, 4 Asian Americans or Pacific Islanders), 51 international. Average age 27. *Faculty:* 2 full-time (1 woman). Expenses: Contact institution. *Financial support:* In 2006–07, 16 students received support; fellowships with tuition reimbursements available, research assistantships with full and partial tuition reimbursements available, teaching assistantships, Federal Work-Study, institutionally sponsored loans, and tuition waivers (full and partial) available. Support available to part-time students. Financial award application deadline: 3/1. In 2006, 53 master's, 6 other advanced degrees awarded. *Degree program information:* Part-time and evening/weekend programs available. Offers biomedical engineering (MS, MS Bm E, PhD); computer-aided mechanical engineering (Certificate); electrical and computer engineering (MS, MSECE, PhD); engineering (interdisciplinary) (MSE); engineering and technology (MS, MS Bm E, MSE, MSECE, MSME, PhD, Certificate); mechanical engineering (MSME, PhD). *Application deadline:* For fall admission, 5/1 for domestic students. *Application fee:* $50 ($60 for international students). *Application Contact:* Valerie Diemer, Graduate Program, 317-278-4960, Fax: 317-278-1671, E-mail: grad@engr.iupui.edu. *Dean,* Dr. H. Oner Yurtseven, 317-274-0802, Fax: 317-274-4567.

School of Informatics Students: 40 full-time (16 women), 84 part-time (39 women); includes 21 minority (10 African Americans, 8 Asian Americans or Pacific Islanders, 3 Hispanic Americans), 25 international. Average age 35. *Faculty:* 3 full-time (0 women). Expenses: Contact institution. *Financial support:* Teaching assistantships, career-related internships or fieldwork, Federal Work-Study, institutionally sponsored loans, and scholarships/grants available. Support available to part-time students. In 2006, 39 degrees awarded. *Degree program information:* Part-time and evening/weekend programs available. Offers informatics (PhD); media arts and science (MS). *Application deadline:* For fall admission, 3/15 for domestic students; for spring admission, 11/15 for domestic students. *Application fee:* $50 ($60 for international students). *Executive Associate Dean,* Darrell L. Bailey, 317-278-4636, Fax: 317-278-7769.

School of Law Students: 728 full-time (365 women), 290 part-time (130 women); includes 633 minority (60 African Americans, 1 American Indian/Alaska Native, 23 Asian Americans or Pacific Islanders, 549 Hispanic Americans), 73 international. Average age 28. *Faculty:* 1 (woman) full-time. Expenses: Contact institution. *Financial support:* Research assistantships with full and partial tuition reimbursements, Federal Work-Study, institutionally sponsored loans, and scholarships/grants available. Support available to part-time students. Financial award applicants required to submit FAFSA. In 2006, 250 JDs, 36 master's awarded. Offers law (JD, LL M, SJD). *Application deadline:* For fall admission, 11/30 priority date for domestic students. *Application fee:* $50 ($60 for international students). *Application Contact:* Patricia

Indiana University–Purdue University Indianapolis (continued)

Kinney, Director of Admissions, 317-274-2459, Fax: 317-278-4780, E-mail: pkkinney@iupui.edu. *Interim Dean*, Susanah M. Mead, 317-274-8523.

School of Liberal Arts Students: 105 full-time (72 women), 234 part-time (141 women); includes 39 minority (24 African Americans, 4 American Indian/Alaska Native, 4 Asian Americans or Pacific Islanders, 7 Hispanic Americans), 18 international. Average age 32. Expenses: Contact institution. Offers American philosophy (Certificate); bioethics (Certificate); liberal arts (MA, PhD, Certificate); philosophy (MA, PhD); political science (MA, Certificate); sociology (MA). *Application Contact:* Director of Research and Graduate Programs, 317-274-8305. *Dean, School of Liberal Arts*, Robert W. White, 317-274-8448.

School of Library and Information Science Students: 52 full-time (42 women), 237 part-time (198 women); includes 20 minority (14 African Americans, 3 Asian Americans or Pacific Islanders, 3 Hispanic Americans), 1 international. Average age 36. *Faculty:* 3 full-time (2 women). Expenses: Contact institution. *Financial support:* Career-related internships or fieldwork, Federal Work-Study, institutionally sponsored loans, and scholarships/grants available. Support available to part-time students. In 2006, 97 degrees awarded. *Degree program information:* Part-time and evening/weekend programs available. Offers library and information science (MLS). *Application deadline:* For fall admission, 7/15 priority date for domestic students; for spring admission, 11/15 priority date for domestic students. Applications are processed on a rolling basis. *Application fee:* $50 ($60 for international students). *Executive Associate Dean*, Dr. Daniel Collison, 317-278-2375, Fax: 317-278-1807, E-mail: slisindy@iupui.edu.

School of Music Students: 10 full-time (5 women), 21 part-time (6 women); includes 4 minority (all African Americans), 1 international. Expenses: Contact institution. *Financial support:* Teaching assistantships with full tuition reimbursements, Federal Work-Study, institutionally sponsored loans, and scholarships/grants available. Support available to part-time students. Financial award application deadline: 11/15. In 2006, 13 master's awarded. *Degree program information:* Part-time and evening/weekend programs available. Post-baccalaureate distance learning degree programs offered. Offers music technology (MS). *Application deadline:* For fall admission, 4/15 priority date for domestic students, 3/15 for international students; for spring admission, 11/15 priority date for domestic students, 11/15 for international students. Applications are processed on a rolling basis. *Application fee:* $50 ($60 for international students). *Director*, G. David Peters, 317-278-2594.

School of Nursing Students: 52 full-time (51 women), 415 part-time (396 women); includes 27 minority (16 African Americans, 3 Asian Americans or Pacific Islanders, 8 Hispanic Americans), 4 international. Average age 38. *Faculty:* 45 full-time (44 women), 1 (woman) part-time/adjunct. Expenses: Contact institution. *Financial support:* In 2006–07, 93 students received support; fellowships with full tuition reimbursements available, research assistantships with full tuition reimbursements available, teaching assistantships with full tuition reimbursements available, Federal Work-Study, institutionally sponsored loans, scholarships/grants, and tuition waivers (full) available. Support available to part-time students. Financial award application deadline: 5/1. In 2006, 106 master's, 3 doctorates awarded. *Degree program information:* Part-time programs available. Offers acute care nurse practitioner (MSN); adult clinical nurse specialist (MSN); adult health clinical nurse specialist (MSN); adult health nursing (MSN); adult nurse practitioner (MSN); adult psychiatric/mental health nursing (MSN); child psychiatric/mental health nursing (MSN); community health nursing (MSN); family nurse practitioner (MSN); neonatal nurse practitioner (MSN); nursing science (PhD); pediatric clinical nurse specialist (MSN); women's health nurse practitioner (MSN). *Application deadline:* For fall admission, 2/15 for domestic students; for spring admission, 9/15 for domestic students. *Application fee:* $50 ($60 for international students). *Application Contact:* Martez Plummer, Assistant Dean for Student Affairs, 317-274-2806, E-mail: mplummer@iupui.edu. *Associate Dean for Graduate Programs*, 317-274-2806, E-mail: nursing@iupui.edu.

School of Physical Education and Tourism Management Students: 8 full-time (6 women), 8 part-time (3 women); includes 3 minority (1 African American, 2 Asian Americans or Pacific Islanders), 1 international. Average age 30. *Faculty:* 4 full-time (2 women). Expenses: Contact institution. *Financial support:* Career-related internships or fieldwork, Federal Work-Study, institutionally sponsored loans, and scholarships/grants available. Support available to part-time students. In 2006, 5 degrees awarded. Offers physical education and tourism management (MS). *Dean*, P. Nicholas Kellum, 317-274-0606, Fax: 317-278-2041, E-mail: pkellum@iupui.edu.

School of Public and Environmental Affairs Students: 83 full-time (56 women), 290 part-time (129 women); includes 50 minority (26 African Americans, 2 American Indian/Alaska Native, 17 Asian Americans or Pacific Islanders, 5 Hispanic Americans), 6 international. Average age 35. *Faculty:* 17 full-time (6 women). Expenses: Contact institution. *Financial support:* Fellowships with full and partial tuition reimbursements, research assistantships with full and partial tuition reimbursements, career-related internships or fieldwork, Federal Work-Study, institutionally sponsored loans, and scholarships/grants available. Support available to part-time students. Financial award application deadline: 3/1. In 2006, 77 master's awarded. *Degree program information:* Part-time and evening/weekend programs available. Offers criminal justice (MPA); environmental management (MPA); health administration (MHA); nonprofit management (MPA); policy analysis (MPA); public affairs (MPA); public management (MPA). *Application deadline:* For fall admission, 7/15 priority date for domestic students; for spring admission, 11/15 for domestic students. Applications are processed on a rolling basis. *Application fee:* $50 ($60 for international students). *Application Contact:* 317-274-4656, Fax: 317-274-5153, E-mail: speainfo@speanet.iupui.edu. *Associate Dean*, Dr. Greg Lindsey, 317-274-4656, Fax: 317-274-5153.

School of Science Students: 184 full-time (97 women), 197 part-time (95 women); includes 55 minority (13 African Americans, 3 American Indian/Alaska Native, 30 Asian Americans or Pacific Islanders, 9 Hispanic Americans), 72 international. Average age 28. *Faculty:* 56 full-time (7 women). Expenses: Contact institution. *Financial support:* Fellowships with full and partial tuition reimbursements, research assistantships with full and partial tuition reimbursements, teaching assistantships with full and partial tuition reimbursements, career-related internships or fieldwork, Federal Work-Study, institutionally sponsored loans, scholarships/grants, tuition waivers (full and partial), and co-op positions available. Support available to part-time students. Financial award applicants required to submit FAFSA. *Degree program information:* Part-time and evening/weekend programs available. Offers applied mathematics (MS, PhD); applied statistics (MS); biology (MS, PhD); chemistry (MS, PhD); clinical rehabilitation psychology (MS, PhD); computer science (MS, PhD); geology (MS); industrial/organizational psychology (MS); math education (MS); mathematics (MS, PhD); physics (MS, PhD); psychobiology of addictions (PhD); science (MS, PhD). *Application fee:* $50 ($60 for international students). Electronic applications accepted. *Dean, School of Science*, William Bosran, 317-274-0625, Fax: 317-274-0628, E-mail: science@iupui.edu.

School of Social Work Students: 291 full-time (250 women), 294 part-time (251 women); includes 85 minority (66 African Americans, 2 American Indian/Alaska Native, 6 Asian Americans or Pacific Islanders, 11 Hispanic Americans), 5 international. Average age 32. *Faculty:* 16 full-time (7 women). Expenses: Contact institution. *Financial support:* In 2006–07, 27 students received support; fellowships with full tuition reimbursements available, research assistantships with partial tuition reimbursements available, teaching assistantships, Federal Work-Study, institutionally sponsored loans, scholarships/grants, and tuition waivers (partial) available. Support available to part-time students. Financial award applicants required to submit FAFSA. In 2006, 250 master's, 2 doctorates awarded. *Degree program information:* Part-time and evening/weekend programs available. Offers social work (MSW, PhD, Certificate). *Application fee:* $50 ($60 for international students). *Application Contact:* Sherry Gass, Student Services Secretary, 317-274-6727, Fax: 317-274-8630, E-mail: stgass@iupui.edu. *Dean*, Michael Patchner, 317-274-8362, Fax: 317-274-8630, E-mail: patchner@iupui.edu.

INDIANA UNIVERSITY SCHOOL OF LAW-INDIANAPOLIS, Indianapolis, IN 46202-3225

General Information State-supported, coed, graduate-only institution. *Enrollment by degree level:* 945 first professional, 71 master's, 2 doctoral. *Graduate faculty:* 52 full-time (21 women), 54 part-time/adjunct (16 women). Tuition, state resident: full-time $12,408; part-time $414 per credit hour. Tuition, nonresident: full-time $27,404; part-time $913 per credit hour. Tuition and fees vary according to course load and program. *Graduate housing:* Rooms and/or apartments available on a first-come, first-served basis to single and married students. *Student services:* Campus employment opportunities, campus safety program, career counseling, child daycare facilities, disabled student services, exercise/wellness program, free psychological counseling, international student services, low-cost health insurance, multicultural affairs office, teacher training, writing training. *Library facilities:* Ruth Lilly Law Library plus 4 others. *Online resources:* library catalog, web page, access to other libraries' catalogs. *Collection:* 357,083 titles, 3,098 serial subscriptions, 429 audiovisual materials.

Computer facilities: 95 computers available on campus for general student use. A campuswide network can be accessed from student residence rooms and from off campus. Internet access and online class registration are available. *Web address:* http://www.iulaw.indy.indiana.edu/.

General Application Contact: Patricia K. Kinney, Director of Admissions, 317-274-2459, Fax: 317-278-4780, E-mail: pkkinney@iupui.edu.

GRADUATE UNITS

School of Law Students: 728 full-time (365 women), 290 part-time (130 women); includes 113 minority (60 African Americans, 1 American Indian/Alaska Native, 23 Asian Americans or Pacific Islanders, 29 Hispanic Americans), 73 international. Average age 28. 1,820 applicants, 26% accepted, 286 enrolled. *Faculty:* 52 full-time (21 women), 54 part-time/adjunct (16 women). Expenses: Contact institution. *Financial support:* In 2006–07, 682 students received support, including 149 fellowships with partial tuition reimbursements available (averaging $4,520 per year); career-related internships or fieldwork, Federal Work-Study, and scholarships/grants also available. Support available to part-time students. Financial award application deadline: 6/30; financial award applicants required to submit FAFSA. In 2006, 250 first professional degrees, 36 master's awarded. *Degree program information:* Part-time and evening/weekend programs available. Offers American law for foreign lawyers (LL M); health law, policy and bioethics (LL M); intellectual property law (LL M); international and comparative law (LL M); international human rights law (LL M); law (JD). *Application deadline:* For fall admission, 3/1 priority date for domestic and international students. Applications are processed on a rolling basis. *Application fee:* $50 ($60 for international students). Electronic applications accepted. *Application Contact:* Patricia K. Kinney, Director of Admissions, 317-274-2459, Fax: 317-278-4780, E-mail: pkkinney@iupui.edu. *Dean, School of Law*, Susanah M. Mead, 317-274-2581, Fax: 317-274-3955.

INDIANA UNIVERSITY SOUTH BEND, South Bend, IN 46634-7111

General Information State-supported, coed, comprehensive institution. *Enrollment:* 7,420 graduate, professional, and undergraduate students; 196 full-time matriculated graduate/professional students (130 women), 538 part-time matriculated graduate/professional students (364 women). *Enrollment by degree level:* 724 master's, 10 other advanced degrees. *Graduate faculty:* 60 full-time (26 women). Tuition, state resident: full-time $4,450; part-time $185 per credit hour. Tuition, nonresident: full-time $10,954; part-time $456 per credit hour. Tuition and fees vary according to course load, campus/location and program. *Graduate housing:* On-campus housing not available. *Student services:* Campus employment opportunities, campus safety program, career counseling, child daycare facilities, disabled student services, exercise/wellness program, free psychological counseling, international student services, low-cost health insurance. *Library facilities:* Franklin D. Schurz Library plus 1 other. *Collection:* 300,202 titles, 1,937 serial subscriptions.

Computer facilities: 200 computers available on campus for general student use. Internet access is available. *Web address:* http://www.iusb.edu/.

General Application Contact: Admissions Counselor, 574-520-4839, Fax: 574-520-4834, E-mail: graduate@iusb.edu.

GRADUATE UNITS

College of Liberal Arts and Sciences Students: 15 full-time (8 women), 73 part-time (43 women); includes 14 minority (7 African Americans, 2 American Indian/Alaska Native, 2 Asian Americans or Pacific Islanders, 3 Hispanic Americans), 8 international. Average age 38. 36 applicants, 94% accepted, 26 enrolled. *Faculty:* 79 full-time (33 women). Expenses: Contact institution. *Financial support:* In 2006–07, 5 students received support, including 5 teaching assistantships (averaging $4,000 per year); Federal Work-Study also available. Support available to part-time students. In 2006, 9 degrees awarded. *Degree program information:* Part-time and evening/weekend programs available. Offers applied mathematics and computer science (MS); English (MA); liberal studies (MLS). *Application deadline:* For fall admission, 7/31 priority date for domestic students, 7/1 priority date for international students; for spring admission, 3/31 priority date for domestic students, 11/1 priority date for international students. Applications are processed on a rolling basis. *Application fee:* $45 ($55 for international students). *Application Contact:* Gil L. Martin, Graduate Admissions and Recruitment Officer, 574-520-4585, Fax: 574-520-5549, E-mail: marting@iusb.edu. *Dean*, Dr. Lynn R. Williams, 574-520-4322, Fax: 574-520-4528, E-mail: lwilliam@iusb.edu.

School of Business and Economics Students: 69 full-time (39 women), 118 part-time (43 women); includes 13 minority (5 African Americans, 4 Asian Americans or Pacific Islanders, 4 Hispanic Americans), 55 international. Average age 31. 49 applicants, 100% accepted, 47 enrolled. *Faculty:* 17 full-time (2 women), 3 part-time/adjunct (1 woman). Expenses: Contact institution. *Financial support:* Federal Work-Study and institutionally sponsored loans available. Support available to part-time students. Financial award applicants required to submit FAFSA. In 2006, 51 degrees awarded. *Degree program information:* Part-time and evening/weekend programs available. Offers accounting (MSA); business administration (MBA); management of information technologies (MS). *Application deadline:* For fall admission, 7/1 priority date for domestic and international students; for spring admission, 11/1 priority date for domestic and international students. Applications are processed on a rolling basis. *Application fee:* $45 ($55 for international students). *Application Contact:* Sharon Peterson, Secretary—Graduate Business, 574-520-4138, Fax: 574-520-4866, E-mail: speterso@iusb.edu. *Assistant Dean, Director of Graduate Studies*, Dr. P. N. Saksena, 574-520-4456, Fax: 574-520-4866, E-mail: psakena@iusb.edu.

School of Education Students: 58 full-time (38 women), 237 part-time (186 women); includes 33 minority (22 African Americans, 1 American Indian/Alaska Native, 6 Asian Americans or Pacific Islanders, 4 Hispanic Americans), 5 international. Average age 35. 127 applicants, 100% accepted, 61 enrolled. *Faculty:* 21 full-time (11 women), 9 part-time/adjunct (3 women). Expenses: Contact institution. *Financial support:* Career-related internships or fieldwork available. Support available to part-time students. Financial award application deadline: 3/1; financial award applicants required to submit FAFSA. In 2006, 141 degrees awarded. *Degree program information:* Part-time and evening/weekend programs available. Offers counseling and human services (MS Ed); elementary education (MS Ed); secondary education (MS Ed); special education (MS Ed). *Application deadline:* For fall admission, 7/1 for domestic students; for spring admission, 11/1 for domestic students. Applications are processed on a rolling basis. *Application fee:* $45. Electronic applications accepted. *Application Contact:* Gil L. Martin, Graduate Admissions and Recruitment Officer, 574-520-4585, Fax: 574-520-5549, E-mail: marting@iusb.edu. *Professor and Dean, School of Education*, Dr. Michael Horvath, 574-520-4339, Fax: 574-520-4550.

School of Public and Environmental Affairs Students: 11 full-time (7 women), 36 part-time (29 women); includes 8 minority (5 African Americans, 1 Asian American or Pacific Islander, 2 Hispanic Americans), 3 international. Average age 34. *Faculty:* 4 full-time (1 woman). Expenses: Contact institution. *Financial support:* Fellowships, research assistantships, career-related internships or fieldwork, Federal Work-Study, and institutionally sponsored loans available. Support available to part-time students. Financial award application deadline: 3/1; financial award applicants required to submit FAFSA. In 2006, 27 degrees awarded. *Degree program information:* Part-time and evening/weekend programs available. Offers health systems administration and policy (MPA); health systems management (Certificate); nonprofit management (Certificate); public and community services administration and policy (MPA); public management (Certificate); urban affairs (Certificate). *Application deadline:* For fall admission,

7/1 priority date for domestic students; for spring admission, 11/1 for domestic students. Applications are processed on a rolling basis. *Dean,* Leda M. Hall, 574-520-4803.

School of Social Work Students: 35 full-time (33 women), 69 part-time (60 women); includes 14 minority (8 African Americans, 1 American Indian/Alaska Native, 1 Asian American or Pacific Islander, 4 Hispanic Americans), 1 international. Average age 35. *Faculty:* 4 full-time (2 women). Expenses: Contact institution. *Financial support:* Career-related internships or fieldwork and Federal Work-Study available. Support available to part-time students. Financial award application deadline: 3/1; financial award applicants required to submit FAFSA. *Degree program information:* Part-time and evening/weekend programs available. Offers social work (MSW). *Application deadline:* For fall admission, 2/1 priority date for domestic students. *Application fee:* $40. *Program Director,* Dr. Paul R. Newcomb, 574-520-4880, Fax: 574-520-4876, E-mail: msn@iusb.edu.

School of the Arts Students: 8 full-time (5 women), 5 part-time (3 women); includes 1 minority (Asian American or Pacific Islander), 11 international. Average age 30. *Faculty:* 1 full-time (0 women). Expenses: Contact institution. *Financial support:* Fellowships, teaching assistantships, Federal Work-Study available. Support available to part-time students. Financial award application deadline: 3/1; financial award applicants required to submit FAFSA. In 2006, 4 master's awarded. *Degree program information:* Part-time programs available. Offers music (MM). *Application deadline:* For fall admission, 7/1 priority date for domestic students; for spring admission, 11/1 for domestic students. Applications are processed on a rolling basis. *Dean,* Dr. Thomas Miller, 574-520-4301, Fax: 574-520-4317, E-mail: messelst@iusb.edu.

INDIANA UNIVERSITY SOUTHEAST, New Albany, IN 47150-6405

General Information State-supported, coed, comprehensive institution. *Enrollment:* 6,183 graduate, professional, and undergraduate students; 18 full-time matriculated graduate/professional students (10 women), 568 part-time matriculated graduate/professional students (358 women). *Enrollment by degree level:* 586 master's. *Graduate faculty:* 63 full-time (22 women). Tuition, state resident: full-time $4,458; part-time $186 per credit hour. Tuition, nonresident: full-time $10,196; part-time $425 per credit hour. Tuition and fees vary according to course load, campus/location and program. *Graduate housing:* On-campus housing not available. *Student services:* Campus employment opportunities, campus safety program, career counseling, child daycare facilities, disabled student services, free psychological counseling, low-cost health insurance, multicultural affairs office. *Library facilities:* Main library plus 1 other. *Collection:* 215,429 titles, 962 serial subscriptions.

Computer facilities: 200 computers available on campus for general student use. A campuswide network can be accessed from off campus. Internet access is available. *Web address:* http://www.ius.edu/.

General Application Contact: Admissions Counselor, 812-941-2212, Fax: 812-941-2595, E-mail: admissions@ius.edu.

GRADUATE UNITS

Program in Liberal Studies Students: 3 full-time (2 women), 28 part-time (18 women); includes 4 minority (all African Americans) Average age 39. Expenses: Contact institution. In 2006, 2 degrees awarded. Offers liberal studies (MLS). *Application fee:* $35. *Application Contact:* Debra Voyles, Administrative Assistant, 812-941-2604, E-mail: davoyles@ius.edu. *Director,* Dr. Sandra S. French, 812-941-2393, E-mail: sfrench@ius.edu.

School of Business Students: 10 full-time (4 women), 201 part-time (65 women); includes 12 minority (2 African Americans, 8 Asian Americans or Pacific Islanders, 2 Hispanic Americans), 5 international. Average age 31. *Faculty:* 11 full-time (2 women). Expenses: Contact institution. In 2006, 60 degrees awarded. Offers accounting (Certificate); business administration (MBA); economics (Certificate); finance (Certificate); general business (Certificate); information and operations management (Certificate); management and marketing (Certificate); strategic finance (MS). *Application fee:* $35. *Application Contact:* Dr. Jay White, Director of Graduate Business Programs, 812-941-2364, Fax: 812-941-2581, E-mail: jwhite04@ius.edu. *Dean,* Chris Bjornson, 812-941-2362, Fax: 812-941-2672.

School of Education Students: 5 full-time (4 women), 339 part-time (275 women); includes 19 minority (17 African Americans, 1 Asian American or Pacific Islander, 1 Hispanic American). Average age 32. Expenses: Contact institution. *Financial support:* In 2006–07, 29 students received support. Career-related internships or fieldwork, Federal Work-Study, and institutionally sponsored loans available. Support available to part-time students. Financial award applicants required to submit FAFSA. In 2006, 176 degrees awarded. *Degree program information:* Part-time and evening/weekend programs available. Offers counselor education (MS Ed); elementary education (MS Ed); secondary education (MS Ed). *Application deadline:* Applications are processed on a rolling basis. *Application fee:* $30. *Dean,* Dr. Gloria Murray, 812-941-2385, Fax: 812-941-2667, E-mail: soeinfo@ius.edu.

INDIANA WESLEYAN UNIVERSITY, Marion, IN 46953-4974

General Information Independent-religious, coed, comprehensive institution. *Enrollment:* 4,461 full-time matriculated graduate/professional students (2,836 women), 156 part-time matriculated graduate/professional students (92 women). *Enrollment by degree level:* 4,540 master's, 77 doctoral. *Graduate faculty:* 30 full-time (14 women). *Tuition:* Full-time $16,000; part-time $400 per credit. *Required fees:* $3,000. Tuition and fees vary according to degree level, campus/location and program. *Graduate housing:* Room and/or apartments available on a first-come, first-served basis to single students; on-campus housing not available to married students. Housing application deadline: 4/10. *Student services:* Exercise/wellness program, international student services, teacher training. *Library facilities:* Jackson Library. *Online resources:* library catalog, web page, access to other libraries' catalogs. *Collection:* 141,236 titles, 76,011 serial subscriptions, 11,321 audiovisual materials.

Computer facilities: A campuswide network can be accessed from student residence rooms. Internet access is available. *Web address:* http://www.indwes.edu/.

General Application Contact: Dr. Jim Freemyer, Director of Graduate Education, 765-677-2278, Fax: 765-677-2023, E-mail: jfreemyer@indwes.edu.

GRADUATE UNITS

College of Adult and Professional Studies Students: 2,629 full-time. Average age 35. *Faculty:* 21 full-time (6 women), 294 part-time/adjunct (85 women). Expenses: Contact institution. *Financial support:* Available to part-time students. Applicants required to submit FAFSA. In 2006, 1353 degrees awarded. *Degree program information:* Evening/weekend programs available. Postbaccalaureate distance learning degree programs offered (minimal on-campus study). Offers accounting (MBA); adult and professional studies (M Ed, MBA, MS); applied management (MBA); curriculum and instruction (M Ed); health care management (MBA); management (MS). *Application deadline:* Applications are processed on a rolling basis. *Application fee:* $25. Electronic applications accepted. *Application Contact:* Kris Douglas, Marketing Manager, 800-234-5327, Fax: 765-674-8028, E-mail: kris.douglas@apollogrp.org. *Dean,* Dr. Tom Griffin, 765-677-2348, E-mail: tom.griffin@indwes.edu.

College of Graduate Studies Students: 552 full-time (383 women), 79 part-time (53 women). *Faculty:* 13 full-time (6 women), 87 part-time/adjunct. Expenses: Contact institution. *Financial support:* In 2006–07, 15 fellowships were awarded; career-related internships or fieldwork, Federal Work-Study, scholarships/grants, and traineeships also available. Support available to part-time students. In 2006, 127 degrees awarded. *Degree program information:* Part-time and evening/weekend programs available. Postbaccalaureate distance learning degree programs offered. Offers community counseling (MS); marriage and family counseling (MS); ministerial education (MA); ministry (MA); organizational leadership (Ed D); school counseling (MS). *Application deadline:* Applications are processed on a rolling basis. *Application fee:* $25. Electronic applications accepted. *Application Contact:* David McMillan, Assistant Director of Enrollment Management, 765-677-2688, E-mail: david.mcmillan@indwes.edu. *Dean,* Dr. Jim Fuller, 765-677-2352, Fax: 765-677-2380.

Division of Nursing Students: 312 full-time (296 women), 8 part-time (4 women); includes 45 minority (41 African Americans, 2 Asian Americans or Pacific Islanders, 2 Hispanic Americans). Average age 40. *Faculty:* 2 full-time (both women), 6 part-time/adjunct (3 women). Expenses: Contact institution. *Financial support:* In 2006–07, 15 fellowships were awarded; career-related internships or fieldwork, scholarships/grants, and traineeships also available. Support available to part-time students. Financial award application deadline: 3/15. In 2006, 87 degrees awarded. *Degree program information:* Part-time and evening/weekend programs available. Offers community health nursing (MS); nursing (Post Master's Certificate); nursing administration (MS); nursing education (MS); primary care nursing (MS). *Application deadline:* For fall admission, 7/31 priority date for domestic students; for winter admission, 11/15 priority date for domestic students; for spring admission, 4/15 priority date for domestic students. Electronic applications accepted. *Application Contact:* David McMillan, Assistant Director of Enrollment Management, 765-677-2688, E-mail: david.mcmillan@indwes.edu. *Director,* Pam Giles, 765-677-1716, E-mail: gradnurse@indwes.edu.

INSTITUTE FOR CHRISTIAN STUDIES, Toronto, ON M5T 1R4, Canada

General Information Independent-religious, coed, graduate-only institution. *Graduate housing:* On-campus housing not available.

GRADUATE UNITS

Graduate Programs *Degree program information:* Part-time programs available. Postbaccalaureate distance learning degree programs offered (minimal on-campus study). Offers education (M Phil F, PhD); history of philosophy (M Phil F, PhD); philosophical aesthetics (M Phil F, PhD); philosophy of religion (M Phil F, PhD); political theory (M Phil F, PhD); systematic philosophy (M Phil F, PhD); theology (M Phil F, PhD); worldview studies (MWS).

INSTITUTE FOR CLINICAL SOCIAL WORK, Chicago, IL 60601

General Information Independent, coed, primarily women, graduate-only institution. CGS member. *Graduate housing:* On-campus housing not available.

GRADUATE UNITS

Graduate Programs *Degree program information:* Part-time programs available. Offers clinical social work (PhD).

INSTITUTE OF CLINICAL ACUPUNCTURE AND ORIENTAL MEDICINE, Honolulu, HI 96813

General Information Proprietary, coed, graduate-only institution.

GRADUATE UNITS

Program in Oriental Medicine Offers Oriental medicine (MSOM).

INSTITUTE OF PUBLIC ADMINISTRATION, Dublin 4, Ireland

General Information Proprietary, coed, comprehensive institution.

GRADUATE UNITS

Programs in Public Administration Offers healthcare management (MA); local government management (MA); public management (MA, Diploma).

INSTITUTE OF TRANSPERSONAL PSYCHOLOGY, Palo Alto, CA 94303

General Information Independent, coed, graduate-only institution. *Enrollment by degree level:* 165 master's, 287 doctoral. *Graduate faculty:* 22 full-time (10 women), 44 part-time/adjunct (28 women). *Graduate housing:* On-campus housing not available. *Student services:* Campus employment opportunities, international student services. *Library facilities:* Institute of Transpersonal Psychology Library. *Online resources:* library catalog, web page, access to other libraries' catalogs. *Collection:* 15,000 titles, 170 serial subscriptions.

Computer facilities: 10 computers available on campus for general student use. A campuswide network can be accessed. Internet access is available. *Web address:* http://www.itp.edu/.

General Application Contact: Lyn Carr, Admissions Office, 650-493-4430 Ext. 216, Fax: 650-493-6835, E-mail: itpinfo@itp.edu.

GRADUATE UNITS

Global Programs Students: 177 full-time (144 women); includes 24 minority (7 African Americans, 1 American Indian/Alaska Native, 7 Asian Americans or Pacific Islanders, 9 Hispanic Americans), 33 international. Average age 43. 112 applicants, 88% accepted, 80 enrolled. *Faculty:* 8 full-time (4 women), 26 part-time/adjunct (19 women). Expenses: Contact institution. *Financial support:* In 2006–07, 68 students received support. Federal Work-Study and scholarships/grants available. Support available to part-time students. Financial award application deadline: 6/30; financial award applicants required to submit FAFSA. In 2006, 28 master's, 4 doctorates awarded. Postbaccalaureate distance learning degree programs offered (minimal on-campus study). Offers psychology (PhD); transpersonal psychology (MTP); transpersonal studies (MA, Certificate). *Application deadline:* Applications are processed on a rolling basis. *Application fee:* $55. *Application Contact:* Hana Schneider, Admissions Assistant, 650-493-4430 Ext. 240, Fax: 650-493-6835, E-mail: itpinfo@itp.edu. *Academic Vice President,* Dr. Paul Roy, 650-493-4430 Ext. 243, Fax: 650-493-6835, E-mail: proy@itp.edu.

Residential Programs Students: 285 (217 women); includes 28 minority (4 African Americans, 2 American Indian/Alaska Native, 10 Asian Americans or Pacific Islanders, 12 Hispanic Americans) 14 international. Average age 38. 132 applicants, 80% accepted, 79 enrolled. *Faculty:* 17 full-time (9 women), 31 part-time/adjunct (18 women). Expenses: Contact institution. *Financial support:* In 2006–07, 178 students received support; teaching assistantships, career-related internships or fieldwork, Federal Work-Study, and scholarships/grants available. Support available to part-time students. Financial award application deadline: 7/1; financial award applicants required to submit FAFSA. In 2006, 32 master's, 22 doctorates awarded. *Degree program information:* Part-time and evening/weekend programs available. Offers clinical psychology (PhD); counseling psychology (MA); transpersonal psychology (MA, PhD). *Application deadline:* For fall admission, 2/15 priority date for domestic students. Applications are processed on a rolling basis. *Application fee:* $55. *Application Contact:* 650-493-4430 Ext. 16, Fax: 650-493-6835, E-mail: itpinfo@itp.edu. *Ph.D. Chair,* Dr. Chris Dryer, 650-493-4430, Fax: 650-493-6835.

THE INSTITUTE OF WORLD POLITICS, Washington, DC 20036

General Information Independent, coed, graduate-only institution. *Graduate housing:* On-campus housing not available.

GRADUATE UNITS

Graduate Programs in Statecraft and National Security Affairs *Degree program information:* Part-time and evening/weekend programs available. Offers American foreign policy (Certificate); comparative political culture (Certificate); democracy building (Certificate); intelligence (Certificate); international politics (Certificate); national security affairs (Certificate); public diplomacy and political warfare (Certificate); statecraft and national security affairs (MA); statecraft and world politics (MA). Electronic applications accepted.

INSTITUT FRANCO-EUROPÉEN DE CHIROPRATIQUE, F-94200 Ivry-sur-Seine, France

General Information Independent, coed, graduate-only institution.

GRADUATE UNITS

Professional Program Offers chiropractic (DC).

INSTITUTO CENTROAMERICANO DE ADMINISTRACIÓN DE EMPRESAS, La Garita, Alajuela, Costa Rica

General Information Independent, coed, graduate-only institution. *Graduate housing:* Rooms and/or apartments available to single and married students. *Research affiliation:* Tropical Agricultural Research and Higher Education Center (agribusiness), Harvard Institute for International Development (macroeconomics and environment), Earth University (agri-

Instituto Centroamericano de Administración de Empresas (continued)

business), Inter-American Institute for Cooperation on Agriculture (agribusiness), David Rockefeller Center for Latin American Studies (competitiveness), Zamarono (agribusiness).

GRADUATE UNITS

Graduate Programs Offers agribusiness (MIAM); business administration (EMBA); entrepreneurial economics (MBA); industry and technology (MBA); sustainable development (MBA). Electronic applications accepted.

INSTITUTO TECNOLÓGICO Y DE ESTUDIOS SUPERIORES DE MONTERREY, CAMPUS CENTRAL DE VERACRUZ, 94500 Córdoba, Veracruz, Mexico

General Information Independent, coed, comprehensive institution.

GRADUATE UNITS

Graduate Programs *Degree program information:* Part-time and evening/weekend programs available. Postbaccalaureate distance learning degree programs offered (minimal on-campus study). Electronic applications accepted.

INSTITUTO TECNOLÓGICO Y DE ESTUDIOS SUPERIORES DE MONTERREY, CAMPUS CHIAPAS, 29000 Tuxtla Gutiérrez, Chiapas, Mexico

General Information Independent, coed, comprehensive institution.

INSTITUTO TECNOLÓGICO Y DE ESTUDIOS SUPERIORES DE MONTERREY, CAMPUS CHIHUAHUA, 31300 Chihuahua, Chihuahua, Mexico

General Information Independent, coed, comprehensive institution.

GRADUATE UNITS

Graduate Programs Offers computer systems engineering (Ingeniero); electrical engineering (Ingeniero); electromechanical engineering (Ingeniero); electronic engineering (Ingeniero); engineering administration (MEA); industrial engineering (MIE, Ingeniero); international trade (MIT); mechanical engineering (Ingeniero).

INSTITUTO TECNOLÓGICO Y DE ESTUDIOS SUPERIORES DE MONTERREY, CAMPUS CIUDAD DE MÉXICO, 14380 Ciudad de Mexico, DF, Mexico

General Information Independent, coed, comprehensive institution. *Graduate housing:* On-campus housing not available. *Research affiliation:* McGill University (management), Concordia University (business and management), Eli Lilly S.A. de C.U. (technological development), Ford Motor Company (industrial organization), German Research Center on Artificial Intelligence (informatics), Brent University (telecommunications).

GRADUATE UNITS

Division of Business *Degree program information:* Part-time and evening/weekend programs available. Postbaccalaureate distance learning degree programs offered (minimal on-campus study). Offers business administration (EMBA, MBA, PhD); economy (MBA); finance (MBA).

Division of Engineering and Architecture *Degree program information:* Part-time and evening/weekend programs available. Postbaccalaureate distance learning degree programs offered (minimal on-campus study). Offers management (MA); telecommunications (MA).

Division of Humanities and Social Sciences *Degree program information:* Part-time and evening/weekend programs available. Offers humanities and social sciences (LL B).

Virtual University Division *Degree program information:* Part-time and evening/weekend programs available. Postbaccalaureate distance learning degree programs offered (minimal on-campus study).

INSTITUTO TECNOLÓGICO Y DE ESTUDIOS SUPERIORES DE MONTERREY, CAMPUS CIUDAD JUÁREZ, 32320 Ciudad Juárez, Chihuahua, Mexico

General Information Independent, coed, comprehensive institution.

GRADUATE UNITS

Program in Administration of Information Technology Offers administration of information technology (MAIT).

Program in Business Administration Offers business administration (MBA).

Program in Education Offers education (M Ed).

Program in Financial Administration Offers financial administration (MFA).

Program in Industrial Engineering Offers industrial engineering (MIE).

Program in Quality Management Offers quality management (MQM).

Program in Telecommunications Offers telecommunications (MTEL).

INSTITUTO TECNOLÓGICO Y DE ESTUDIOS SUPERIORES DE MONTERREY, CAMPUS CIUDAD OBREGÓN, 85000 Ciudad Obregón, Sonora, Mexico

General Information Independent, coed, comprehensive institution.

GRADUATE UNITS

Program in Administration Offers administration (MA).

Program in Administration of Information Technology Offers administration of information technology (MATI).

Program in Administration of Telecommunications Offers administration of telecommunications (MAT).

Program in Engineering Offers engineering (ME).

Program in Finance Offers finance (MF).

Program in International Relations Offers international relations (MIR).

Program in Marketing Technology Offers marketing technology (MMT).

Programs in Education Offers cognitive development (ME); communications (ME); mathematics (ME).

INSTITUTO TECNOLÓGICO Y DE ESTUDIOS SUPERIORES DE MONTERREY, CAMPUS COLIMA, 28010 Colima, Colima, Mexico

General Information Independent, coed, comprehensive institution.

INSTITUTO TECNOLÓGICO Y DE ESTUDIOS SUPERIORES DE MONTERREY, CAMPUS CUERNAVACA, 62000 Temixco, Morelos, Mexico

General Information Independent, coed, comprehensive institution.

GRADUATE UNITS

Programs in Business Administration Offers finance (MA); human resources management (MA); international business (MA); marketing (MA).

Programs in Information Science Offers administration of information technology (MATI); computer science (MCC, DCC); information technology (MTI).

INSTITUTO TECNOLÓGICO Y DE ESTUDIOS SUPERIORES DE MONTERREY, CAMPUS ESTADO DE MÉXICO, Estado de Mexico 52926, Mexico

General Information Independent, coed, comprehensive institution. *Graduate housing:* On-campus housing not available. *Research affiliation:* Transportadora San Marcos, S.A. de C.V. (quality control), Microsoft (Visual Studio.Net) (computer science), Trinity (new products), Texas Instruments (semiconductors), Sony Electronics (new products), Kaltex (quality control).

GRADUATE UNITS

Professional and Graduate Division *Degree program information:* Part-time programs available. Postbaccalaureate distance learning degree programs offered (minimal on-campus study). Offers administration of information technologies (MITA); architecture (M Arch); business administration (GMBA, MBA); computer sciences (MCS, PhD); education (M Ed); educational institution administration (MAD); educational technology and innovation (PhD); electronic commerce (MEC); environmental systems (MS); finance (MAF); humanistic studies (MHS); information sciences and knowledge management (MISKM); information systems (MS); manufacturing systems (MS); marketing (MEM); quality systems and productivity (MS); science and materials engineering (PhD); telecommunications management (MTM).

INSTITUTO TECNOLÓGICO Y DE ESTUDIOS SUPERIORES DE MONTERREY, CAMPUS GUADALAJARA, 45140 Zapopan, Jalisco, Mexico

General Information Independent, coed, comprehensive institution. *Graduate housing:* Rooms and/or apartments available to single and married students. Housing application deadline: 8/30.

GRADUATE UNITS

Program in Business Administration *Degree program information:* Part-time and evening/weekend programs available. Postbaccalaureate distance learning degree programs offered. Offers business administration (MBA).

Program in Finance Offers finance (MF).

INSTITUTO TECNOLÓGICO Y DE ESTUDIOS SUPERIORES DE MONTERREY, CAMPUS HIDALGO, 42090 Pachuca, Hidalgo, Mexico

General Information Independent, coed, comprehensive institution.

INSTITUTO TECNOLÓGICO Y DE ESTUDIOS SUPERIORES DE MONTERREY, CAMPUS IRAPUATO, 36660 Irapuato, Guanajuato, Mexico

General Information Independent, coed, comprehensive institution.

GRADUATE UNITS

Graduate Programs Offers administration (MBA); administration of information technology (MAIT); administration of telecommunications (MAT); architecture (M Arch); computer science (MCS); education (M Ed); educational administration (MEA); educational innovation and technology (DEIT); educational technology (MET); electronic commerce (MBA); environmental administration and planning (MEAP); environmental systems (MES); finances (MBA); humanistic studies (MHS); international management for Latin American executives (MIMLAE); library and information science (MLIS); manufacturing quality management (MMQM); marketing research (MBA).

INSTITUTO TECNOLÓGICO Y DE ESTUDIOS SUPERIORES DE MONTERREY, CAMPUS LAGUNA, 27250 Torreón, Coahuila, Mexico

General Information Independent, coed, comprehensive institution. *Graduate housing:* On-campus housing not available.

GRADUATE UNITS

Graduate School *Degree program information:* Part-time programs available. Offers business administration (MBA); industrial engineering (MIE); management information systems (MS).

INSTITUTO TECNOLÓGICO Y DE ESTUDIOS SUPERIORES DE MONTERREY, CAMPUS LEÓN, 37120 León, Guanajuato, Mexico

General Information Independent, coed, comprehensive institution.

GRADUATE UNITS

Program in Business Administration *Degree program information:* Part-time programs available. Offers business administration (MBA).

INSTITUTO TECNOLÓGICO Y DE ESTUDIOS SUPERIORES DE MONTERREY, CAMPUS MAZATLÁN, 82000 Mazatlán, Sinaloa, Mexico

General Information Independent, coed, comprehensive institution.

INSTITUTO TECNOLÓGICO Y DE ESTUDIOS SUPERIORES DE MONTERREY, CAMPUS MONTERREY, 64849 Monterrey, Nuevo León, Mexico

General Information Independent, coed, university. *Graduate housing:* Room and/or apartments available to single students; on-campus housing not available to married students. *Research affiliation:* IBM de México (computer science), Southwest Research Institute (environment), Hylsa (steel), Vitro (glass products), Cydsa (petrochemicals), Cemex (cement).

GRADUATE UNITS

Graduate and Research Division *Degree program information:* Part-time and evening/weekend programs available. Offers agricultural parasitology (PhD); agricultural sciences (MS); applied statistics (M Eng); artificial intelligence (PhD); automation engineering (M Eng); biotechnology (MS); chemical engineering (M Eng); chemistry (MS, PhD); civil engineering (M Eng); communications (MS); computer science (MS); education (MA); electrical engineering (M Eng); electronic engineering (M Eng); environmental engineering (M Eng); farming productivity (MS); food processing engineering (MS); industrial engineering (M Eng, PhD); informatics (PhD); information systems (MS); information technology (MS); manufacturing engineering (M Eng); mechanical engineering (M Eng); phytopathology (MS); systems and quality engineering (M Eng).

Graduate School of Business Administration and Leadership *Degree program information:* Part-time programs available. Offers business administration (MA, MBA); finance (M Sc); international business (M Sc); management (PhD); management and leadership (M Sc, MA, MBA, PhD); marketing (M Sc).

INSTITUTO TECNOLÓGICO Y DE ESTUDIOS SUPERIORES DE MONTERREY, CAMPUS QUERÉTARO, 76130 Querétaro, Querétaro, Mexico

General Information Independent, coed, comprehensive institution. *Graduate housing:* Room and/or apartments guaranteed to single students; on-campus housing not available to married students. Housing application deadline: 6/15. *Research affiliation:* Transmisiones y Equipos Mecanicos (manufacturing designing).

GRADUATE UNITS

School of Business Offers business (MBA).

INSTITUTO TECNOLÓGICO Y DE ESTUDIOS SUPERIORES DE MONTERREY, CAMPUS SALTILLO, 25270 Saltillo, Coahuila, Mexico

General Information Independent, coed, comprehensive institution.

INSTITUTO TECNOLÓGICO Y DE ESTUDIOS SUPERIORES DE MONTERREY, CAMPUS SAN LUIS POTOSÍ, 78140 San Luis Potosí, SLP, Mexico

General Information Independent, coed, comprehensive institution.

INSTITUTO TECNOLÓGICO Y DE ESTUDIOS SUPERIORES DE MONTERREY, CAMPUS SINALOA, 80800 Culiacán, Sinaloa, Mexico

General Information Independent, coed, comprehensive institution.

INSTITUTO TECNOLÓGICO Y DE ESTUDIOS SUPERIORES DE MONTERREY, CAMPUS SONORA NORTE, 83000 Hermosillo, Sonora, Mexico

General Information Independent, coed, comprehensive institution. *Graduate housing:* On-campus housing not available. *Research affiliation:* National Council for Science and Technology (engineering).

GRADUATE UNITS

Program in Business Offers business (MA).

Program in Education Offers education (MA).

Program in Technological Information Management Offers technological information management (MA).

INSTITUTO TECNOLÓGICO Y DE ESTUDIOS SUPERIORES DE MONTERREY, CAMPUS TAMPICO, 89120 Altimira, Tamaulipas, Mexico

General Information Independent, coed, comprehensive institution.

INSTITUTO TECNOLÓGICO Y DE ESTUDIOS SUPERIORES DE MONTERREY, CAMPUS TOLUCA, 50252 Toluca, Estado de Mexico, Mexico

General Information Independent, coed, comprehensive institution.

GRADUATE UNITS

Graduate Programs *Degree program information:* Part-time and evening/weekend programs available.

INSTITUTO TECNOLÓGICO Y DE ESTUDIOS SUPERIORES DE MONTERREY, CAMPUS ZACATECAS, 98000 Zacatecas, Zacatecas, Mexico

General Information Independent, coed, comprehensive institution.

INTER AMERICAN UNIVERSITY OF PUERTO RICO, AGUADILLA CAMPUS, Aguadilla, PR 00605

General Information Independent, coed, comprehensive institution.

GRADUATE UNITS

Graduate School *Degree program information:* Part-time and evening/weekend programs available. Electronic applications accepted.

INTER AMERICAN UNIVERSITY OF PUERTO RICO, ARECIBO CAMPUS, Arecibo, PR 00614-4050

General Information Independent, coed, comprehensive institution.

GRADUATE UNITS

Program in Anesthesia Offers anesthesia (MS).

Program in Nursing Offers community nursing (MS); primary care nursing (MS).

Programs in Education Offers administration and educational supervision (MA Ed); counseling and guidance (MA Ed).

INTER AMERICAN UNIVERSITY OF PUERTO RICO, BARRANQUITAS CAMPUS, Barranquitas, PR 00794

General Information Independent, coed, comprehensive institution. *Graduate housing:* Rooms and/or apartments available to single and married students.

GRADUATE UNITS

Program in Education Offers educational administration and supervision (MA); elementary education (MA). Electronic applications accepted.

INTER AMERICAN UNIVERSITY OF PUERTO RICO, BAYAMÓN CAMPUS, Bayamón, PR 00957

General Information Independent, coed, comprehensive institution. *Enrollment:* 5,045 graduate, professional, and undergraduate students; 11 full-time matriculated graduate/professional students (10 women), 50 part-time matriculated graduate/professional students (24 women). *Enrollment by degree level:* 61 master's. *Graduate faculty:* 7 full-time (1 woman), 2 part-time/adjunct (1 woman). *Tuition:* Part-time $175 per credit. *Required fees:* $231 per semester. *Graduate housing:* On-campus housing not available. *Student services:* Child daycare facilities, exercise/wellness program, free psychological counseling. *Library facilities:* Centro de Acceso a la Informacion plus 1 other. *Online resources:* library catalog, web page, access to other libraries' catalogs. *Collection:* 55,695 titles, 196 serial subscriptions.

Computer facilities: Computer purchase and lease plans are available. 700 computers available on campus for general student use. A campuswide network can be accessed from student residence rooms and from off campus. Internet access and online class registration are available. *Web address:* http://bc.inter.edu/.

General Application Contact: Carlos Alicea, Director of Admissions, 787-279-1200, Fax: 787-279-2205, E-mail: calicea@bc.inter.edu.

GRADUATE UNITS

Graduate School Students: 11 full-time (10 women), 50 part-time (24 women); all Hispanic Americans *Faculty:* 7 full-time (1 woman), 2 part-time/adjunct (1 woman). Expenses: Contact institution. *Degree program information:* Part-time and evening/weekend programs available. *Application deadline:* For fall admission, 7/1 for domestic students. *Application fee:* $31. *Application Contact:* Carlos Alicea, Director of Admission, 787-279-1912 Ext. 2017, Fax: 787-279-2205, E-mail: calicea@bc.inter.edu. *Chancellor,* Prof. Juan F. Martinez, 787-279-1912 Ext. 2295, Fax: 787-279-2205, E-mail: jmartinez@bc.inter.edu.

INTER AMERICAN UNIVERSITY OF PUERTO RICO, GUAYAMA CAMPUS, Guayama, PR 00785

General Information Independent, coed, comprehensive institution.

GRADUATE UNITS

Department of Education and Social Sciences Offers early childhood education (MA).

INTER AMERICAN UNIVERSITY OF PUERTO RICO, METROPOLITAN CAMPUS, San Juan, PR 00919-1293

General Information Independent, coed, comprehensive institution. CGS member. *Graduate housing:* On-campus housing not available. *Research affiliation:* Innovation Technology (electronics).

GRADUATE UNITS

Faculty of Education *Degree program information:* Part-time and evening/weekend programs available. Offers administration and supervision (MA); education (Ed D); elementary education (MA); guidance and counseling (MA); health and physical education (MA); higher education (MA Ed); occupational education (MA); special education (MA Ed); teaching of science (MA Ed); vocational evaluation (MA). Electronic applications accepted.

Faculty of Liberal Arts *Degree program information:* Part-time and evening/weekend programs available. Offers humanistic studies (MA, PhD); Spanish (MA); teaching English as a second language (MA); theological studies (PhD). Electronic applications accepted.

Faculty of Science and Technology *Degree program information:* Part-time and evening/weekend programs available. Offers administration of laboratories (MS); educational computing (MA); medical technology (MS); micromolecular biology (MS); open information systems (MS). Electronic applications accepted.

Faculty of Economics and Administrative Sciences *Degree program information:* Part-time and evening/weekend programs available. Offers accounting (MBA); business and management development (PhD); business education (MA); finance (MBA); human resources (MBA); industrial management (MBA); labor relations (MA); marketing (MBA). Electronic applications accepted.

School of Criminal Justice *Degree program information:* Part-time and evening/weekend programs available. Offers criminal justice (MA). Electronic applications accepted.

School of Psychology Offers psychology (MA). Electronic applications accepted.

School of Social Work *Degree program information:* Evening/weekend programs available. Offers clinical services (MSW); social administration (MSW). Electronic applications accepted.

INTER AMERICAN UNIVERSITY OF PUERTO RICO, PONCE CAMPUS, Mercedita, PR 00715-1602

General Information Independent, coed, comprehensive institution.

GRADUATE UNITS

Graduate School

INTER AMERICAN UNIVERSITY OF PUERTO RICO, SAN GERMÁN CAMPUS, San Germán, PR 00683-5008

General Information Independent, coed, university. *Enrollment:* 5,960 graduate, professional, and undergraduate students; 471 full-time matriculated graduate/professional students, 581 part-time matriculated graduate/professional students. *Enrollment by degree level:* 928 master's, 124 doctoral. *Graduate faculty:* 55 full-time, 48 part-time/adjunct. *Tuition:* Part-time $175 per credit. *Required fees:* $238 per semester. Tuition and fees vary according to degree level. *Graduate housing:* Room and/or apartments available on a first-come, first-served basis to single students; on-campus housing not available to married students. Typical cost: $900 per year ($2,400 including board). Room and board charges vary according to board plan and housing facility selected. Housing application deadline: 6/15. *Student services:* Campus employment opportunities, campus safety program, career counseling, child daycare facilities, disabled student services, free psychological counseling, international student services, low-cost health insurance. *Library facilities:* Juan Cancio Ortiz Library. *Online resources:* library catalog, web page, access to other libraries' catalogs. *Collection:* 155,745 titles, 3,242 serial subscriptions, 2,165 audiovisual materials.

Computer facilities: 1,400 computers available on campus for general student use. A campuswide network can be accessed. Internet access and online class registration are available. *Web address:* http://www.sg.inter.edu/.

General Application Contact: Dr. Carlos E. Irizarry, Director of Graduate Studies Center, 787-264-1912 Ext. 7357, Fax: 787-892-6350, E-mail: carlos.irizarry@sg.inter.edu.

GRADUATE UNITS

Graduate Studies Center Students: 471 full-time, 581 part-time. Average age 31. 461 applicants, 77% accepted, 342 enrolled. *Faculty:* 55 full-time, 48 part-time/adjunct. Expenses: Contact institution. *Financial support:* Fellowships, research assistantships, teaching assistantships, Federal Work-Study and unspecified assistantships available. In 2006, 269 master's, 2 doctorates awarded. *Degree program information:* Part-time and evening/weekend programs available. Offers accounting (MBA); administration and supervision (MA); applied mathematics (MA); art (MFA); business education (MA); ceramics (MFA); counseling psychology (MA, PhD); drawing (MFA); elementary education (MA); environmental sciences (MS); finance (MBA); guidance and counseling (MA); human resources (MBA, PhD); industrial relations (MBA); international business (PhD); interregional and international business (PhD); labor relations (PhD); library and information sciences (MLS); management information systems (MBA); marketing (MBA); music education (MA); painting (MFA); photography (MFA); physical education and scientific analysis of human body movement (MA); printmaking (MFA); quality organizational design (MBA); school psychology (MS, PhD); science education (MA); sculpture (MFA); special education (MA); teaching English as a second language (MA). *Application deadline:* For fall admission, 4/30 priority date for domestic students; for spring admission, 11/15 for domestic students. Applications are processed on a rolling basis. *Application fee:* $31. *Director of Graduate Studies Center,* Dr. Carlos E. Irizarry, 787-264-1912 Ext. 7357, Fax: 787-892-6350, E-mail: carlos.irizarry@sg.inter.edu.

INTER AMERICAN UNIVERSITY OF PUERTO RICO SCHOOL OF LAW, San Juan, PR 00936-8351

General Information Independent, coed, graduate-only institution.

GRADUATE UNITS

Professional Program *Degree program information:* Part-time and evening/weekend programs available. Offers law (JD).

INTER AMERICAN UNIVERSITY OF PUERTO RICO SCHOOL OF OPTOMETRY, San Juan, PR 00919

General Information Independent, coed, graduate-only institution. *Graduate housing:* On-campus housing not available.

GRADUATE UNITS

Professional Program Offers optometry (OD). Electronic applications accepted.

INTERDENOMINATIONAL THEOLOGICAL CENTER, Atlanta, GA 30314-4112

General Information Independent-religious, coed, graduate-only institution. *Graduate faculty:* 22 full-time (9 women), 20 part-time/adjunct (10 women). *Tuition:* Full-time $8,282; part-time $424 per credit. *Required fees:* $240. Tuition and fees vary according to student's religious affiliation. *Graduate housing:* Rooms and/or apartments available on a first-come, first-served basis to single students and available to married students. Typical cost: $3,766 per year for single students; $3,766 per year for married students. Housing application deadline: 8/1. *Student services:* Campus employment opportunities, campus safety program, exercise/wellness program, free psychological counseling, international student services, low-cost health insurance. *Library facilities:* Robert W. Woodruff Library. *Online resources:* library catalog, web page, access to other libraries' catalogs. *Collection:* 353,745 titles, 1,739 serial subscriptions. *Research affiliation:* Emory University Library, Candler School of Theology Library, Columbia Theological Seminary Library, Atlanta University Center, Inc.

Interdenominational Theological Center (continued)

Computer facilities: 50 computers available on campus for general student use. A campuswide network can be accessed. Internet access and online class registration are available. *Web address:* http://www.itc.edu/.

General Application Contact: Walter Cabassa, Office of Admission and Recruitment, 404-527-7792, E-mail: wcabassa@itc.edu.

GRADUATE UNITS

Graduate and Professional Programs Students: 279 full-time (122 women), 187 part-time (84 women); includes 432 minority (429 African Americans, 3 Hispanic Americans), 19 international. Average age 40. 152 applicants, 80% accepted, 101 enrolled. *Faculty:* 22 full-time (9 women), 20 part-time/adjunct (10 women). Expenses: Contact institution. *Financial support:* In 2006–07, 375 students received support, including 4 research assistantships; career-related internships or fieldwork and Federal Work-Study also available. Support available to part-time students. Financial award application deadline: 6/15; financial award applicants required to submit FAFSA. In 2006, 81 M Divs, 8 master's, 5 doctorates awarded. *Degree program information:* Part-time and evening/weekend programs available. Postbaccalaureate distance learning degree programs offered (minimal on-campus study). Offers theology (M Div, MACE, MACM, D Min, Th D). *Application deadline:* For fall admission, 7/1 for domestic students; for spring admission, 11/15 for domestic students. Applications are processed on a rolling basis. *Application fee:* $50. *Application Contact:* Walter Cabassa, Office of Admission and Recruitment, 404-527-7792, E-mail: wcabassa@itc.edu. *President,* Dr. Michael A. Battle, 404-527-7702, Fax: 404-527-7770, E-mail: mbattle@itc.edu.

INTERNATIONAL BAPTIST COLLEGE, Tempe, AZ 85282

General Information Independent-religious, coed, comprehensive institution. *Enrollment:* 5 full-time matriculated graduate/professional students, 18 part-time matriculated graduate/professional students (2 women). *Graduate faculty:* 2 full-time (0 women), 9 part-time/adjunct (0 women). *Graduate housing:* Room and/or apartments available on a first-come, first-served basis to single students; on-campus housing not available to married students. *Student services:* Campus employment opportunities, career counseling, child daycare facilities, international student services, writing training.

Computer facilities: 6 computers available on campus for general student use. *Web address:* http://www.tri-citybaptist.org/ibc/.

General Application Contact: Jeff Caupp, Graduate School Administration, 480-838-7070, Fax: 480-838-5432.

GRADUATE UNITS

Program in Biblical Studies Students: 1 full-time (0 women), 5 part-time. *Faculty:* 2 full-time (0 women). Expenses: Contact institution. *Financial support:* Scholarships/grants available. Offers Biblical studies (MA). *Application deadline:* Applications are processed on a rolling basis. *Application fee:* $25. *Graduate School Administration,* Jeff Caupp, 480-838-7070, Fax: 480-838-5432.

Program in Ministry *Faculty:* 1 full-time (0 women), 5 part-time/adjunct (0 women). Expenses: Contact institution. *Financial support:* Scholarships/grants available. Offers ministry (M Min, D Min). *Application deadline:* Applications are processed on a rolling basis. *Application fee:* $25. *Application Contact:* Jeff Caupp, Graduate School Administration, 480-838-7070, Fax: 480-838-5432. *Chairman of the Board,* Dr. Michael Sproul.

INTERNATIONAL COLLEGE OF THE CAYMAN ISLANDS, Newlands, Grand Cayman, Cayman Islands

General Information Independent, coed, comprehensive institution. *Graduate housing:* Room and/or apartments available on a first-come, first-served basis to single students; on-campus housing not available to married students.

GRADUATE UNITS

Graduate Program in Management *Degree program information:* Part-time and evening/weekend programs available. Offers business administration (MBA); management (MS).

INTERNATIONAL TECHNOLOGICAL UNIVERSITY, Santa Clara, CA 95050

General Information Independent, coed, upper-level institution. *Research affiliation:* Linux Works, Inc. (software), @Channel (software), New Trends Technology, Inc. (hardware), Pico Turbo, Inc. (hardware).

GRADUATE UNITS

MBA Program *Degree program information:* Part-time and evening/weekend programs available. Offers business administration (MBA).

Program in Computer Engineering Offers computer engineering (MSCE).

Program in Electrical Engineering *Degree program information:* Part-time and evening/weekend programs available. Offers electrical engineering (MSEE).

Program in Software Engineering Offers software engineering (MSSE).

INTERNATIONAL UNIVERSITY IN GENEVA, CH-1215 Geneva 15, Switzerland

General Information Private, coed, comprehensive institution. *Graduate housing:* Room and/or apartments available to single students; on-campus housing not available to married students.

GRADUATE UNITS

MBA Program *Degree program information:* Part-time and evening/weekend programs available. Offers e-commerce (MBA); human relations (MBA); international business (Exec MBA, MBA); marketing (MBA); organizational development (MBA); telecommunications (MBA). Electronic applications accepted.

Program in Media and Communication Offers media and communication (MA).

THE INTERNATIONAL UNIVERSITY OF MONACO, MC-98000 Principality of Monaco, Monaco

General Information Independent, coed, comprehensive institution. *Graduate housing:* Rooms and/or apartments guaranteed to single and married students. *Research affiliation:* Alpstar (hedge funds).

GRADUATE UNITS

Graduate Programs *Degree program information:* Part-time programs available. Offers entrepreneurship (EMBA, MBA); financial engineering (M Sc); international marketing (EMBA, MBA); luxury goods and services (EMBA, M Sc, MBA); wealth and asset management (EMBA, MBA). Electronic applications accepted.

IONA COLLEGE, New Rochelle, NY 10801-1890

General Information Independent-religious, coed, comprehensive institution. *Enrollment:* 4,242 graduate, professional, and undergraduate students; 172 full-time matriculated graduate/professional students (129 women), 603 part-time matriculated graduate/professional students (382 women). *Enrollment by degree level:* 771 master's, 4 other advanced degrees. *Graduate faculty:* 114 full-time (33 women), 68 part-time/adjunct (33 women). *Tuition:* Part-time $665 per credit. *Required fees:* $150 per term. *Graduate housing:* On-campus housing not available. *Student services:* Campus employment opportunities, campus safety program, career counseling, disabled student services, exercise/wellness program, free psychological counseling, international student services, multicultural affairs office. *Library facilities:* Ryan Library plus 2 others. *Online resources:* library catalog, web page, access to other libraries' catalogs. *Collection:* 281,876 titles, 752 serial subscriptions, 3,379 audiovisual materials. *Research affiliation:* IBM (teacher preparation).

Computer facilities: Computer purchase and lease plans are available. 500 computers available on campus for general student use. A campuswide network can be accessed from student residence rooms and from off campus. Internet access and online class registration are available. *Web address:* http://www.iona.edu/.

General Application Contact: Thomas Weede, Director of Admissions, 914-633-2120, Fax: 914-633-2642, E-mail: tweede@iona.edu.

GRADUATE UNITS

Hagan School of Business Students: 34 full-time (18 women), 232 part-time (110 women); includes 27 minority (15 African Americans, 7 Asian Americans or Pacific Islanders, 5 Hispanic Americans), 10 international. Average age 31. 96 applicants, 84% accepted, 68 enrolled. *Faculty:* 27 full-time (5 women), 12 part-time/adjunct (2 women). Expenses: Contact institution. *Financial support:* In 2006–07, 2 fellowships with tuition reimbursements (averaging $7,000 per year) were awarded; Federal Work-Study, scholarships/grants, tuition waivers (partial), and unspecified assistantships also available. Support available to part-time students. In 2006, 118 master's, 40 other advanced degrees awarded. *Degree program information:* Part-time and evening/weekend programs available. Offers business (MBA, PMC); financial management (MBA, PMC); human resource management (MBA, PMC); information and decision technology management (MBA, PMC); international business (PMC); management (MBA, PMC); marketing (MBA). *Application deadline:* For fall admission, 8/15 priority date for domestic students, 8/1 for international students; for winter admission, 11/15 priority date for domestic students, 11/1 for international students; for spring admission, 2/15 priority date for domestic students, 2/1 for international students. Applications are processed on a rolling basis. *Application fee:* $50. Electronic applications accepted. *Application Contact:* Veronica Jarek-Prinz, Graduate Admissions, 914-633-2289, Fax: 914-633-2012, E-mail: vjarekprinz@iona.edu. *Dean,* Dr. Vincent Calluzo, 914-633-2256, E-mail: vcalluzo@iona.edu.

School of Arts and Science Students: 138 full-time (111 women), 371 part-time (272 women); includes 99 minority (48 African Americans, 1 American Indian/Alaska Native, 4 Asian Americans or Pacific Islanders, 46 Hispanic Americans), 9 international. Average age 31. 410 applicants, 67% accepted, 124 enrolled. *Faculty:* 87 full-time (28 women), 56 part-time/adjunct (31 women). Expenses: Contact institution. *Financial support:* Career-related internships or fieldwork, tuition waivers (partial), and unspecified assistantships available. Support available to part-time students. In 2006, 189 master's, 4 other advanced degrees awarded. *Degree program information:* Part-time and evening/weekend programs available. Offers arts and science (MA, MS, MS Ed, MST, Certificate); biology education (MS Ed, MST); computer science (MS); criminal justice (MS); educational leadership (MS Ed); educational technology (MS, Certificate); English (MA); English education (MS Ed, MST); experimental psychology (MA); family counseling (MS, Certificate); health service administration (MS, Certificate); history (MA); industrial-organizational psychology (MA); journalism (MS); mathematics education (MS Ed, MST); mental health counseling (MA); multicultural education (MS Ed); pastoral counseling (MS); psychology (MA); public relations (MA); school psychology (MA); social studies education (MS Ed, MST); Spanish (MA); Spanish education (MS Ed, MST); teaching education (MST); telecommunications (MS, Certificate). *Application deadline:* For fall admission, 8/1 priority date for domestic students, 5/1 priority date for international students; for winter admission, 12/1 priority date for domestic students, 8/1 priority date for international students; for spring admission, 1/1 priority date for domestic students, 9/1 priority date for international students. Applications are processed on a rolling basis. *Application fee:* $50. Electronic applications accepted. *Application Contact:* Veronica Jarek-Prinz, Graduate Admissions, 914-633-2289, Fax: 914-633-2012, E-mail: vjarekprinz@iona.edu. *Dean,* Dr. Alexander R. Eodice, 914-633-2112, Fax: 914-633-2023, E-mail: aeodice@iona.edu.

See Close-Up on page 927.

IOWA STATE UNIVERSITY OF SCIENCE AND TECHNOLOGY, Ames, IA 50011

General Information State-supported, coed, university. CGS member. *Enrollment:* 25,462 graduate, professional, and undergraduate students; 2,761 full-time matriculated graduate/professional students (1,155 women), 1,207 part-time matriculated graduate/professional students (561 women). *Enrollment by degree level:* 1,984 master's, 1,937 doctoral, 47 other advanced degrees. *Graduate faculty:* 1,384 full-time, 163 part-time/adjunct. Tuition, state resident: full-time $5,936; part-time $330 per credit. Tuition, nonresident: full-time $16,350; part-time $330 per credit. *Graduate housing:* Rooms and/or apartments available on a first-come, first-served basis to single and married students. Housing application deadline: 6/15. *Student services:* Campus employment opportunities, campus safety program, career counseling, child daycare facilities, disabled student services, exercise/wellness program, free psychological counseling, international student services, low-cost health insurance, multicultural affairs office, teacher training. *Library facilities:* University Library plus 1 other. *Online resources:* library catalog, web page, access to other libraries' catalogs. *Collection:* 2.5 million titles, 52,533 serial subscriptions. *Research affiliation:* U.S. Department of Energy–Ames Laboratory, North Central Regional Center for Rural Development, National Soil Tilth Laboratory, National Animal Disease Center, National Veterinary Services Laboratories.

Computer facilities: Computer purchase and lease plans are available. 2,400 computers available on campus for general student use. A campuswide network can be accessed from student residence rooms and from off campus. Internet access and online class registration, e-mail, network services are available. *Web address:* http://www.iastate.edu/.

General Application Contact: Information Contact, 515-294-5836, Fax: 515-294-2592, E-mail: grad_admissions@iastate.edu.

GRADUATE UNITS

College of Veterinary Medicine Students: 499 full-time (356 women), 25 part-time (16 women); includes 14 minority (3 African Americans, 5 Asian Americans or Pacific Islanders, 6 Hispanic Americans), 32 international. *Faculty:* 106 full-time, 20 part-time/adjunct. Expenses: Contact institution. *Financial support:* In 2006–07, 41 research assistantships with full and partial tuition reimbursements (averaging $15,668 per year), 8 teaching assistantships with full and partial tuition reimbursements (averaging $15,018 per year) were awarded; fellowships, career-related internships or fieldwork, Federal Work-Study, institutionally sponsored loans, scholarships/grants, health care benefits, and unspecified assistantships also available. In 2006, 7 master's, 11 doctorates awarded. *Degree program information:* Part-time programs available. Offers biomedical sciences (MS, PhD); veterinary clinical sciences (MS); veterinary diagnostic and production animal medicine (MS); veterinary medicine (DVM, MS, PhD); veterinary microbiology (MS, PhD); veterinary microbiology and preventive medicine (MS, PhD); veterinary pathology (MS, PhD); veterinary preventative medicine (MS). Electronic applications accepted. *Dean,* Dr. John Thomson, 515-294-1250.

Graduate College Students: 2,761 full-time (1,155 women), 1,207 part-time (561 women); includes 267 minority (119 African Americans, 11 American Indian/Alaska Native, 75 Asian Americans or Pacific Islanders, 62 Hispanic Americans), 1,437 international. 4,641 applicants, 41% accepted, 1274 enrolled. *Faculty:* 1,384 full-time, 163 part-time/adjunct. Expenses: Contact institution. *Financial support:* In 2006–07, 1,722 research assistantships with full and partial tuition reimbursements (averaging $15,603 per year), 700 teaching assistantships with full and partial tuition reimbursements (averaging $14,912 per year) were awarded; fellowships, career-related internships or fieldwork, Federal Work-Study, institutionally sponsored loans, scholarships/grants, traineeships, health care benefits, and unspecified assistantships also available. Support available to part-time students. In 2006, 894 master's, 281 doctorates awarded. *Degree program information:* Part-time and evening/weekend programs available. Postbaccalaureate distance learning degree programs offered (minimal on-campus study). Offers bioinformatics and computational biology (PhD); biorenewable resources and technology (MS, PhD); ecology and evolutionary biology (MS, PhD); environmental sciences (MS, PhD); genetics (MS, PhD); human-computer interaction (MS, PhD); immunobiology (MS, PhD); information assurance (MS); interdisciplinary graduate studies (MA, MS); interdisciplinary studies (MA, MBA, MS, PhD); microbiology (MS, PhD); molecular, cellular, and developmental biology (MS, PhD); neuroscience (MS, PhD); nutritional sciences (MS, PhD); plant physiology (MS, PhD); sustainable agriculture (MS, PhD); toxicology (MS, PhD); transportation (MS). *Application deadline:* Applications are processed on a rolling basis. *Application fee:* $30 ($70 for international students). Electronic applications accepted. *Associate Provost for Academic*

Progress and Dean of the Graduate College, Dr. David K. Holger, 515-294-7184, E-mail: grad_admissions@iastate.edu.

College of Agriculture Students: 424 full-time (189 women), 171 part-time (56 women); includes 34 minority (16 African Americans, 9 Asian Americans or Pacific Islanders, 9 Hispanic Americans), 204 international. 329 applicants, 40% accepted, 99 enrolled. *Faculty:* 224 full-time, 36 part-time/adjunct. Expenses: Contact institution. *Financial support:* In 2006–07, 371 research assistantships with full and partial tuition reimbursements (averaging $17,906 per year), 36 teaching assistantships with full and partial tuition reimbursements (averaging $17,451 per year) were awarded; fellowships, Federal Work-Study, scholarships/grants, health care benefits, and unspecified assistantships also available. Support available to part-time students. In 2006, 125 master's, 52 doctorates awarded. *Degree program information:* Part-time programs available. Postbaccalaureate distance learning degree programs offered (no on-campus study). Offers agricultural education and studies (MS, PhD); agricultural meteorology (MS, PhD); agriculture (M Ag, MS, PhD); agronomy (MS); animal breeding and genetics (MS, PhD); animal ecology (MS, PhD); animal physiology (MS); animal psychology (PhD); animal science (MS, PhD); biochemistry (MS, PhD); biophysics (MS, PhD); crop production and physiology (MS, PhD); entomology (MS, PhD); forestry (MS, PhD); genetics (MS, PhD); horticulture (MS, PhD); industrial education and technology (MS, PhD); meat science (MS, PhD); molecular, cellular, and developmental biology (MS, PhD); plant breeding (MS, PhD); plant pathology (MS, PhD); soil science (MS, PhD); toxicology (MS, PhD). *Application deadline:* Applications are processed on a rolling basis. *Application fee:* $50 ($70 for international students). Electronic applications accepted. *Dean*, Dr. Wendy Wintersteen, 515-294-2518, Fax: 515-294-6800.

College of Business Students: 156 full-time (73 women), 121 part-time (51 women); includes 13 minority (1 African American, 7 Asian Americans or Pacific Islanders, 5 Hispanic Americans), 51 international. 247 applicants, 57% accepted, 104 enrolled. *Faculty:* 64 full-time, 2 part-time/adjunct. Expenses: Contact institution. *Financial support:* In 2006–07, 54 research assistantships with full and partial tuition reimbursements (averaging $17,059 per year), 5 teaching assistantships with full and partial tuition reimbursements (averaging $17,232 per year) were awarded; fellowships, scholarships/grants, health care benefits, and unspecified assistantships also available. In 2006, 130 degrees awarded. Offers accounting (M Acc); business (M Acc, MBA, MS); business administration (MBA, MS); information systems (MS). *Application fee:* $30 ($70 for international students). Electronic applications accepted. *Dean*, Dr. Labh S Hira, 515-294-2422, E-mail: busgrad@iastate.edu.

College of Design Students: 110 full-time (51 women), 39 part-time (23 women); includes 13 minority (5 African Americans, 5 Asian Americans or Pacific Islanders, 3 Hispanic Americans), 35 international. Average age 32. 137 applicants, 55% accepted, 39 enrolled. *Faculty:* 84 full-time, 7 part-time/adjunct. Expenses: Contact institution. *Financial support:* In 2006–07, 42 research assistantships with full and partial tuition reimbursements (averaging $17,592 per year), 36 teaching assistantships with full and partial tuition reimbursements (averaging $17,649 per year) were awarded; career-related internships or fieldwork, Federal Work-Study, institutionally sponsored loans, tuition waivers (partial), and unspecified assistantships also available. Support available to part-time students. Financial award applicants required to submit FAFSA. In 2006, 51 degrees awarded. *Degree program information:* Part-time programs available. Offers architectural studies (MSAS); architecture (M Arch); art and design (MA); art education (MA); community and regional planning (MCRP); design (M Arch, MA, MCRP, MFA, MLA, MS, MSAS); graphic design (MFA); integrated visual arts (MFA); interior design (MFA); landscape architecture (MLA); transportation (MS). *Application deadline:* Applications are processed on a rolling basis. *Application fee:* $30 ($70 for international students). Electronic applications accepted. *Dean*, Mark Engelbrecht, 515-294-7427, Fax: 515-294-9755, E-mail: mengelbr@iastate.edu.

College of Engineering Students: 608 full-time (128 women), 225 part-time (34 women); includes 49 minority (14 African Americans, 1 American Indian/Alaska Native, 22 Asian Americans or Pacific Islanders, 12 Hispanic Americans), 438 international. 1,300 applicants, 23% accepted, 171 enrolled. *Faculty:* 220 full-time, 21 part-time/adjunct. Expenses: Contact institution. *Financial support:* In 2006–07, 479 research assistantships with full and partial tuition reimbursements (averaging $19,254 per year), 96 teaching assistantships with full and partial tuition reimbursements (averaging $19,058 per year) were awarded; fellowships, Federal Work-Study, scholarships/grants, health care benefits, and unspecified assistantships also available. Support available to part-time students. In 2006, 191 master's, 73 doctorates awarded. *Degree program information:* Part-time programs available. Offers aerospace engineering (M Eng, MS, PhD); agricultural and biosystems engineering (M Eng, MS, PhD); chemical and biological engineering (M Eng, MS, PhD); civil engineering (MS, PhD); computer engineering (MS, PhD); electrical engineering (MS, PhD); engineering (M Eng, MS, PhD); engineering mechanics (M Eng, MS, PhD); industrial engineering (MS, PhD); materials science and engineering (MS, PhD); mechanical engineering (MS, PhD); operations research (MS); systems engineering (M Eng). *Application fee:* $30 ($70 for international students). Electronic applications accepted. *Dean*, Dr. Mark J Kushner, 515-294-9988, E-mail: mjk@iastate.edu.

College of Human Sciences Students: 284 full-time (208 women), 372 part-time (252 women); includes 69 minority (39 African Americans, 5 American Indian/Alaska Native, 10 Asian Americans or Pacific Islanders, 15 Hispanic Americans), 88 international. 405 applicants, 60% accepted, 136 enrolled. *Faculty:* 138 full-time, 34 part-time/adjunct. Expenses: Contact institution. *Financial support:* In 2006–07, 191 research assistantships with full and partial tuition reimbursements (averaging $17,007 per year), 57 teaching assistantships with full and partial tuition reimbursements (averaging $17,642 per year) were awarded; fellowships, career-related internships or fieldwork, Federal Work-Study, scholarships/grants, health care benefits, and unspecified assistantships also available. Support available to part-time students. In 2006, 164 master's, 45 doctorates awarded. *Degree program information:* Part-time programs available. Offers counselor education (M Ed, MS); curriculum and instructional technology (M Ed, MS, PhD); education (M Ed); educational administration (M Ed, MS); educational leadership (PhD); elementary education (M Ed, MS); exercise and sport science (MS); family and consumer sciences (MFCS); family and consumer sciences education and studies (M Ed, MS, PhD); food science and technology (MS, PhD); foodservice and lodging management (MFCS, MS, PhD); health and human performance (PhD); higher education (M Ed, MS); historical, philosophical, and comparative studies in education (M Ed, MS); human development and family studies (MFCS, MS, PhD); human sciences (M Ed, MFCS, MS, PhD); marriage and family therapy (PhD); nutrition (MS, PhD); organizational learning and human resource development (M Ed, MS); research and evaluation (MS); special education (M Ed, MS); textiles and clothing (MFCS, MS, PhD). *Application fee:* $30 ($70 for international students). Electronic applications accepted. *Dean*, Dr. Cheryl Acterberg, 515-294-7000.

College of Liberal Arts and Sciences Students: 988 full-time (403 women), 210 part-time (106 women); includes 54 minority (25 African Americans, 4 American Indian/Alaska Native, 17 Asian Americans or Pacific Islanders, 8 Hispanic Americans), 539 international. 1,378 applicants, 39% accepted, 297 enrolled. *Faculty:* 442 full-time, 38 part-time/adjunct. Expenses: Contact institution. *Financial support:* In 2006–07, 442 research assistantships with full and partial tuition reimbursements (averaging $17,640 per year), 450 teaching assistantships with full and partial tuition reimbursements (averaging $17,770 per year) were awarded; fellowships, Federal Work-Study, institutionally sponsored loans, scholarships/grants, health care benefits, and unspecified assistantships also available. Support available to part-time students. In 2006, 201 master's, 96 doctorates awarded. *Degree program information:* Part-time programs available. Offers agricultural economics (MS, PhD); agricultural history and rural studies (PhD); anthropology (MA); applied mathematics (MS, PhD); applied physics (MS, PhD); astrophysics (MS, PhD); chemistry (MS, PhD); cognitive psychology (PhD); computer science (MS, PhD); condensed matter physics (MS, PhD); counseling psychology (PhD); earth science (MS, PhD); ecology, evolution, and organismal biology (MS, PhD); economics (MS, PhD); English (MA); general psychology (MS); genetics, developmental and cell biology (MS, PhD); geology (MS, PhD); high energy physics (MS, PhD); history (MA); history of technology and science (MA, PhD); journalism and mass communication (MS); liberal arts and sciences (MA, MPA, MS, MSM, PhD); mathematics (MS, PhD); meteorology (MS, PhD); nuclear physics (MS, PhD); physics (MS, PhD); political science (MA); public administration (MPA); rhetoric and professional communication (PhD); rural sociology (MS, PhD); school mathematics (MSM); social psychology (PhD); sociology (MS, PhD); statistics (MS, PhD); water resources (MS, PhD). *Application fee:* $30 ($70 for international students). Electronic applications accepted. *Dean*, Dr. Michael Whiteford, 515-294-3220, Fax: 515-294-1303.

See Close-Up on page 929.

ITHACA COLLEGE, Ithaca, NY 14850-7020

General Information Independent, coed, comprehensive institution. CGS member. *Enrollment:* 6,409 graduate, professional, and undergraduate students; 339 full-time matriculated graduate/professional students (251 women), 33 part-time matriculated graduate/professional students (19 women). *Enrollment by degree level:* 310 master's, 62 doctoral. *Graduate faculty:* 153 full-time (62 women), 10 part-time/adjunct (9 women). *Tuition:* Full-time $16,650; part-time $555 per credit hour. *Graduate housing:* On-campus housing not available. *Student services:* Campus employment opportunities, campus safety program, career counseling, disabled student services, exercise/wellness program, free psychological counseling, international student services, low-cost health insurance, multicultural affairs office, writing training. *Library facilities:* Ithaca College Library. *Online resources:* library catalog, web page, access to other libraries' catalogs. *Collection:* 363,648 titles, 44,327 serial subscriptions, 29,734 audiovisual materials. *Research affiliation:* Ithaca Talent Agency/Suzuki Institute (strings, piano), Biotechnology Institute of St. Stephen's University (Hungary) (biotechnology), Ornithology Laboratory of Cornell University (biology), University of Limerick, Ireland: The Irish World Music Center (strings, voice, dance, musicology).

Computer facilities: Computer purchase and lease plans are available. 640 computers available on campus for general student use. A campuswide network can be accessed from student residence rooms and from off campus. Internet access and online class registration are available. *Web address:* http://www.ithaca.edu/.

General Application Contact: Dr. Gregory Woodward, Dean of Graduate Studies, 607-274-3527, Fax: 607-274-1263, E-mail: gradstudies@ithaca.edu.

GRADUATE UNITS

Graduate Studies Students: 339 full-time (251 women), 33 part-time (19 women); includes 18 minority (4 African Americans, 7 Asian Americans or Pacific Islanders, 7 Hispanic Americans), 20 international. Average age 24. 378 applicants, 43% accepted. *Faculty:* 153 full-time (62 women), 10 part-time/adjunct (9 women). Expenses: Contact institution. *Financial support:* In 2006–07, 309 students received support, including 83 teaching assistantships (averaging $7,905 per year); career-related internships or fieldwork, Federal Work-Study, institutionally sponsored loans, scholarships/grants, and unspecified assistantships also available. Support available to part-time students. Financial award applicants required to submit FAFSA. In 2006, 180 master's, 47 doctorates awarded. *Degree program information:* Part-time programs available. Offers biology 7-12 (MAT); chemistry 7-12 (MAT); English 7-12 (MAT); French 7-12 (MAT); humanities and sciences (MAT); math 7-12 (MAT); physics 7-12 (MAT); social studies 7-12 (MAT); Spanish (MAT). *Application deadline:* Applications are processed on a rolling basis. *Application fee:* $40. Electronic applications accepted. *Dean of Graduate Studies*, Dr. Gregory Woodward, 607-274-3527, Fax: 607-274-1263, E-mail: gradstudies@ithaca.edu.

Roy H. Park School of Communications Students: 29 full-time (23 women), 4 part-time (2 women); includes 4 minority (2 African Americans, 1 Asian American or Pacific Islander, 1 Hispanic American), 11 international. Average age 28. 28 applicants, 89% accepted, 17 enrolled. *Faculty:* 9 full-time (4 women). Expenses: Contact institution. *Financial support:* In 2006–07, 28 students received support, including 17 teaching assistantships (averaging $8,131 per year); career-related internships or fieldwork, Federal Work-Study, institutionally sponsored loans, scholarships/grants, and unspecified assistantships also available. Support available to part-time students. Financial award application deadline: 3/1; financial award applicants required to submit FAFSA. In 2006, 14 master's awarded. *Degree program information:* Part-time programs available. Offers communications (MS). *Application deadline:* For fall admission, 7/5 for domestic students; for spring admission, 12/1 for domestic students. Applications are processed on a rolling basis. *Application fee:* $40. *Dean*, Dianne Lynch, 607-274-1021.

School of Business Students: 21 full-time (11 women), 7 part-time (2 women); includes 2 minority (1 African American, 1 Hispanic American). Average age 25. 41 applicants, 63% accepted, 22 enrolled. *Faculty:* 23 full-time (6 women). Expenses: Contact institution. *Financial support:* In 2006–07, 23 students received support, including 11 fellowships (averaging $4,091 per year); Federal Work-Study, institutionally sponsored loans, and scholarships/grants also available. Support available to part-time students. Financial award application deadline: 4/15; financial award applicants required to submit FAFSA. In 2006, 10 master's awarded. *Degree program information:* Part-time programs available. Offers accountancy (MBA); business (MBA); business administration (MBA). *Application deadline:* For fall admission, 8/1 for domestic students; for spring admission, 12/1 for domestic students. Applications are processed on a rolling basis. *Application fee:* $40. *Dean*, Dr. Susan West Engelkemeyer, 607-274-3117, Fax: 607-274-1152, E-mail: sengelkemyer@ithaca.edu.

School of Health Sciences and Human Performance Students: 242 full-time (196 women), 13 part-time (8 women); includes 10 minority (1 African American, 6 Asian Americans or Pacific Islanders, 3 Hispanic Americans), 7 international. Average age 24. 185 applicants, 42% accepted. *Faculty:* 48 full-time (26 women), 8 part-time/adjunct (all women). Expenses: Contact institution. *Financial support:* In 2006–07, 219 students received support, including 60 teaching assistantships (averaging $8,124 per year); career-related internships or fieldwork, Federal Work-Study, institutionally sponsored loans, scholarships/grants, and unspecified assistantships also available. Support available to part-time students. Financial award applicants required to submit FAFSA. In 2006, 116 master's, 47 doctorates awarded. *Degree program information:* Part-time programs available. Offers exercise and sport sciences (MS); health education (MS); health sciences and human performance (MS, DPT); occupational therapy (MS); physical education (MS); physical therapy (DPT); speech pathology (MS); sport management (MS); teacher of the speech and hearing handicapped (MS). *Application fee:* $40. *Dean*, Dr. Steven Siconolfi, 607-274-3237, Fax: 607-274-1137, E-mail: ssiconolfi@ithaca.edu.

School of Music Students: 39 full-time (19 women), 7 part-time (5 women); includes 1 minority (Hispanic American), 2 international. Average age 25. 112 applicants, 29% accepted, 27 enrolled. *Faculty:* 59 full-time (21 women), 1 part-time/adjunct (0 women). Expenses: Contact institution. *Financial support:* In 2006–07, 39 students received support, including 29 teaching assistantships (averaging $8,767 per year); career-related internships or fieldwork, Federal Work-Study, institutionally sponsored loans, scholarships/grants, and unspecified assistantships also available. Support available to part-time students. Financial award applicants required to submit FAFSA. In 2006, 37 degrees awarded. *Degree program information:* Part-time programs available. Offers composition (MM); conducting (MM); music (MM, MS); music education (MM, MS); performance (MM); Suzuki pedagogy (MM). *Application deadline:* For fall admission, 3/1 for domestic students; for spring admission, 12/1 for domestic students. Applications are processed on a rolling basis. *Application fee:* $40. *Dean*, Dr. Arthur Ostrander, 607-274-3343, Fax: 607-274-1727.

See Close-Up on page 931.

ITT TECHNICAL INSTITUTE, Indianapolis, IN 46268-1119

General Information Proprietary, coed.

GRADUATE UNITS

Online MBA Program Offers business (MBA).

JACKSON STATE UNIVERSITY, Jackson, MS 39217

General Information State-supported, coed, university. CGS member. *Enrollment:* 8,256 graduate, professional, and undergraduate students; 525 full-time matriculated graduate/professional students (349 women), 579 part-time matriculated graduate/professional students (374 women). *Graduate faculty:* 213 full-time (83 women), 15 part-time/adjunct (6 women). *Graduate housing:* Room and/or apartments available on a first-come, first-served basis to

Jackson State University (continued)

single students; on-campus housing not available to married students. Housing application deadline: 7/15. *Student services:* Campus employment opportunities, campus safety program, career counseling, child daycare facilities, disabled student services, exercise/wellness program, grant writing training, international student services, multicultural affairs office, teacher training, writing training. *Library facilities:* H. T. Sampson Library plus 1 other. *Online resources:* library catalog. *Collection:* 236,933 titles, 3,409 serial subscriptions, 4,285 audiovisual materials. *Research affiliation:* Lawrence A. Berkeley Laboratories (biology, chemistry), U.S. Department of Energy (biology), National Science Foundation (biology, chemistry), U.S. Environmental Protection Agency, Oak Ridge Associated Universities (science), Raytheon Systems Company (computer science).

Computer facilities: A campuswide network can be accessed from off campus. Internet access is available. *Web address:* http://www.jsums.edu/.

General Application Contact: Dr. Dorris R. Robinson-Gardner, Dean of the Graduate School, 601-979-2455, Fax: 601-979-4325, E-mail: dgardner@ccaix.jsums.edu.

GRADUATE UNITS

Graduate School Students: 525 full-time (349 women), 579 part-time (374 women); includes 906 minority (884 African Americans, 3 American Indian/Alaska Native, 18 Asian Americans or Pacific Islanders, 1 Hispanic American), 83 international. Average age 30. *Faculty:* 213 full-time (83 women), 15 part-time/adjunct (6 women). Expenses: Contact institution. *Financial support:* Fellowships, research assistantships, teaching assistantships, career-related internships or fieldwork, Federal Work-Study, institutionally sponsored loans, scholarships/grants, tuition waivers (full and partial), and unspecified assistantships available. Support available to part-time students. Financial award application deadline: 3/1; financial award applicants required to submit FAFSA. In 2006, 289 master's, 29 doctorates, 13 other advanced degrees awarded. *Degree program information:* Part-time and evening/weekend programs available. Postbaccalaureate distance learning degree programs offered (minimal on-campus study). *Application deadline:* Applications are processed on a rolling basis. *Application fee:* $20. *Application Contact:* Curtis Gore, Director of Graduate Admissions, 601-979-2455, Fax: 601-974-4325, E-mail: cgore@ccaix.jsums.edu. *Dean,* Dr. Dorris R. Robinson-Gardner, 601-968-2455, Fax: 601-974-6196, E-mail: dgardner@ccaix.jsums.edu.

College of Public Service Students: 10 full-time (all women); includes 6 minority (all African Americans) Expenses: Contact institution. *Financial support:* In 2006–07, 5 students received support. Career-related internships or fieldwork, Federal Work-Study, scholarships/grants, tuition waivers (full), and unspecified assistantships available. Support available to part-time students. Financial award application deadline: 3/1; financial award applicants required to submit FAFSA. Offers communicative disorders (MS); public service (MS). *Application deadline:* For fall admission, 3/1 for domestic students; for spring admission, 10/1 for domestic students. *Application fee:* $20. *Application Contact:* Curtis Gore, Director of Graduate Admissions, 601-979-2455, Fax: 601-974-4325, E-mail: cgore@ccaix.jsums.edu. *Dean,* Dr. Gwednolyn Prater, 601-979-8836, Fax: 601-979-8837, E-mail: deanofcps@jsums.edu.

School of Business Students: 57 full-time (36 women), 55 part-time (39 women); includes 88 minority (86 African Americans, 2 Asian Americans or Pacific Islanders), 13 international. *Faculty:* 20 full-time (8 women). Expenses: Contact institution. *Financial support:* Fellowships, research assistantships, teaching assistantships, career-related internships or fieldwork, Federal Work-Study, scholarships/grants, tuition waivers (full and partial), and unspecified assistantships available. Support available to part-time students. Financial award application deadline: 3/1; financial award applicants required to submit FAFSA. In 2006, 66 degrees awarded. *Degree program information:* Part-time and evening/weekend programs available. Offers accounting (MPA); business (MBA, MPA, PhD); business administration (MBA). *Application deadline:* For fall admission, 3/1 priority date for domestic students. Applications are processed on a rolling basis. *Application fee:* $20. *Application Contact:* Curtis Gore, Director of Graduate Admissions, 601-979-2455, Fax: 601-974-4325, E-mail: cgore@ccaix.jsums.edu. *Dean,* Dr. Glenda B. Glover, 601-979-2411, Fax: 601-979-2690, E-mail: gglover@ccaix.jsums.edu.

School of Education Students: 131 full-time (92 women), 187 part-time (130 women); includes 289 minority (all African Americans), 2 international. *Faculty:* 50 full-time (26 women), 11 part-time/adjunct (4 women). Expenses: Contact institution. *Financial support:* Career-related internships or fieldwork, Federal Work-Study, scholarships/grants, and unspecified assistantships available. Support available to part-time students. Financial award application deadline: 3/1; financial award applicants required to submit FAFSA. In 2006, 111 master's, 18 doctorates, 13 other advanced degrees awarded. *Degree program information:* Part-time and evening/weekend programs available. Offers community and agency counseling (MS); early childhood education (MS Ed, Ed D); education (MS, MS Ed, Ed D, PhD, Ed S); education administration (Ed S); educational administration (MS Ed, PhD); elementary education (MS Ed, Ed S); guidance and counseling (MS, MS Ed, Ed S); health, physical education and recreation (MS Ed); rehabilitative counseling (MS Ed); rehabilitative counseling service (MS Ed); secondary education (MS Ed, Ed S); special education (MS Ed, Ed S). *Application deadline:* For fall admission, 3/1 priority date for domestic students; for spring admission, 10/1 for domestic students. Applications are processed on a rolling basis. *Application fee:* $20. *Application Contact:* Curtis Gore, Director of Graduate Admissions, 601-979-2455, Fax: 601-974-4325, E-mail: cgore@ccaix.jsums.edu. *Interim Dean,* Dr. Daniel Watkins, 601-979-2433, E-mail: daniel.watkins@jsums.edu.

School of Liberal Arts Students: 112 full-time (69 women), 125 part-time (88 women); includes 206 minority (205 African Americans, 1 American Indian/Alaska Native), 8 international. *Faculty:* 79 full-time (35 women), 2 part-time/adjunct (1 woman). Expenses: Contact institution. *Financial support:* Fellowships, research assistantships, teaching assistantships, career-related internships or fieldwork, Federal Work-Study, scholarships/grants, tuition waivers (full and partial), and unspecified assistantships available. Support available to part-time students. Financial award application deadline: 3/1; financial award applicants required to submit FAFSA. In 2006, 54 master's, 4 doctorates awarded. *Degree program information:* Part-time and evening/weekend programs available. Offers clinical psychology (PhD); criminology and justice service (MA); English (MA); history (MA); liberal arts (MA, MAT, MM Ed, MPPA, MS, PhD); mass communications (MS); music education (MM Ed); political science (MA); public policy and administration (MPPA, PhD); sociology (MA); teaching English (MAT); urban and regional planning (MS). *Application deadline:* For fall admission, 3/1 priority date for domestic students. Applications are processed on a rolling basis. *Application fee:* $20. *Application Contact:* Curtis Gore, Director of Graduate Admissions, 601-979-2455, Fax: 601-974-4325, E-mail: cgore@ccaix.jsums.edu. *Dean,* Dr. Dollye M. E. Robinson, 601-979-2422, E-mail: dollye.robinson@jsums.edu.

School of Science and Technology Students: 110 full-time (56 women), 92 part-time (36 women); includes 142 minority (125 African Americans, 1 American Indian/Alaska Native, 15 Asian Americans or Pacific Islanders, 1 Hispanic American), 50 international. *Faculty:* 59 full-time (10 women), 2 part-time/adjunct (1 woman). Expenses: Contact institution. *Financial support:* Career-related internships or fieldwork, Federal Work-Study, scholarships/grants, and unspecified assistantships available. Support available to part-time students. Financial award application deadline: 3/1; financial award applicants required to submit FAFSA. In 2006, 46 master's, 7 doctorates awarded. *Degree program information:* Part-time and evening/weekend programs available. Offers biology education (MST); chemistry (MS, PhD); computer science (MS); environmental science (MS, PhD); hazardous materials management (MS); industrial arts education (MS Ed); mathematics (MS); mathematics education (MST); science and technology (MS, MS Ed, MST, PhD); science education (MST). *Application deadline:* For fall admission, 3/1 priority date for domestic students; for spring admission, 10/1 for domestic students. Applications are processed on a rolling basis. *Application fee:* $20. *Application Contact:* Curtis Gore, Director of Graduate Admissions, 601-979-2455, Fax: 601-974-4325, E-mail: cgore@ccaix.jsums.edu. *Interim Dean,* Dr. Mark G. Hardy, 601-979-253, E-mail: mark.g.hardy@jsums.edu.

School of Social Work Students: 86 full-time (72 women), 25 part-time (21 women); includes 83 minority (82 African Americans, 1 American Indian/Alaska Native), 1 international. *Faculty:* 5 full-time (4 women). Expenses: Contact institution. *Financial support:* In 2006–07, 20 students received support. Career-related internships or fieldwork, Federal Work-Study, scholarships/grants, tuition waivers, and unspecified assistantships available. Support available to part-time students. Financial award application deadline: 3/1; financial award applicants required to submit FAFSA. In 2006, 12 degrees awarded. *Degree program information:* Evening/weekend programs available. Offers social work (MSW, PhD). *Application deadline:* For fall admission, 2/1 for domestic students. *Application fee:* $20. *Application Contact:* Curtis Gore, Director of Graduate Admissions, 601-979-2455, Fax: 601-974-4325, E-mail: cgore@ccaix.jsums.edu. *Dean,* Dr. Gwednolyn Prater, 601-979-8836, Fax: 601-979-8837, E-mail: deanofcps@jsums.edu.

JACKSONVILLE STATE UNIVERSITY, Jacksonville, AL 36265-1602

General Information State-supported, coed, comprehensive institution. *Enrollment:* 8,957 graduate, professional, and undergraduate students; 365 full-time matriculated graduate/professional students (257 women), 1,281 part-time matriculated graduate/professional students (828 women). *Enrollment by degree level:* 1,320 master's, 326 other advanced degrees. *Graduate faculty:* 109 full-time (69 women), 22 part-time/adjunct (15 women). Tuition, state resident: full-time $5,400; part-time $225 per credit hour. Tuition, nonresident: full-time $10,800; part-time $450 per credit hour. One-time fee: $20 full-time. *Graduate housing:* Rooms and/or apartments available on a first-come, first-served basis to single students and available to married students. Typical cost: $1,950 per year ($3,764 including board) for single students; $1,950 per year ($3,764 including board) for married students. *Student services:* Campus employment opportunities, campus safety program, career counseling, child daycare facilities, disabled student services, exercise/wellness program, free psychological counseling, international student services, multicultural affairs office. *Library facilities:* Houston Cole Library. *Online resources:* library catalog, web page, access to other libraries' catalogs. *Collection:* 685,991 titles, 14,376 serial subscriptions.

Computer facilities: 330 computers available on campus for general student use. A campuswide network can be accessed from student residence rooms and from off campus. *Web address:* http://www.jsu.edu/.

General Application Contact: Dr. William D. Carr, Dean of the College of Graduate Studies and Continuing Education, 256-782-5329, Fax: 256-782-5321, E-mail: graduate@jsu.edu.

GRADUATE UNITS

College of Graduate Studies and Continuing Education Students: 365 full-time (257 women), 1,281 part-time (828 women); includes 371 minority (337 African Americans, 12 American Indian/Alaska Native, 10 Asian Americans or Pacific Islanders, 12 Hispanic Americans), 9 international. *Faculty:* 109 full-time (69 women), 22 part-time/adjunct (15 women). Expenses: Contact institution. *Financial support:* In 2006–07, 26 research assistantships, 28 teaching assistantships were awarded. Support available to part-time students. Financial award application deadline: 4/1; financial award applicants required to submit FAFSA. In 2006, 511 master's, 135 other advanced degrees awarded. *Degree program information:* Part-time and evening/weekend programs available. Offers liberal studies (MA). *Application deadline:* Applications are processed on a rolling basis. *Application fee:* $20. *Application Contact:* Dr. Jean Pugliese, Associate Dean, 256-782-8278, Fax: 256-782-5321, E-mail: graduate@jsu.edu. *Dean,* Dr. William D. Carr, 256-782-5329, Fax: 256-782-5321, E-mail: bcarr@jsu.edu.

College of Arts and Sciences Students: 116 full-time (83 women), 336 part-time (144 women); includes 107 minority (95 African Americans, 3 American Indian/Alaska Native, 3 Asian Americans or Pacific Islanders, 6 Hispanic Americans), 2 international. *Faculty:* 61 full-time (12 women), 4 part-time/adjunct (0 women). Expenses: Contact institution. *Financial support:* In 2006–07, 4 research assistantships, 22 teaching assistantships were awarded. Support available to part-time students. Financial award application deadline: 4/1; financial award applicants required to submit FAFSA. In 2006, 124 degrees awarded. *Degree program information:* Part-time and evening/weekend programs available. Offers arts and sciences (MA, MPA, MS); biology (MS); computer systems and software design (MS); criminal justice (MS); emergency management (MS); English (MA); history (MA); mathematics (MS); music (MA); political science (MPA); psychology (MS). *Application deadline:* Applications are processed on a rolling basis. *Application fee:* $20. *Application Contact:* 256-782-5329, Fax: 256-782-5321, E-mail: graduate@jsu.edu. *Dean,* Dr. Earl Wade, 256-782-5649.

College of Commerce and Business Administration Students: 10 full-time (7 women), 55 part-time (25 women); includes 15 minority (7 African Americans, 1 American Indian/Alaska Native, 5 Asian Americans or Pacific Islanders, 2 Hispanic Americans), 3 international. *Faculty:* 11 full-time (4 women). Expenses: Contact institution. *Financial support:* In 2006–07, 4 research assistantships were awarded. Support available to part-time students. Financial award application deadline: 4/1. In 2006, 20 degrees awarded. *Degree program information:* Part-time and evening/weekend programs available. Offers commerce and business administration (MBA). *Application deadline:* Applications are processed on a rolling basis. *Application fee:* $20. *Application Contact:* 256-782-5329. *Dean,* Dr. William Fielding, 256-782-5508.

College of Education and Professional Studies Students: 237 full-time (165 women), 782 part-time (574 women); includes 235 minority (222 African Americans, 8 American Indian/Alaska Native, 1 Asian American or Pacific Islander, 4 Hispanic Americans), 4 international. *Faculty:* 36 full-time (23 women), 18 part-time/adjunct (7 women). Expenses: Contact institution. *Financial support:* In 2006–07, 18 research assistantships were awarded. Support available to part-time students. Financial award application deadline: 4/1. In 2006, 357 master's, 135 other advanced degrees awarded. *Degree program information:* Part-time and evening/weekend programs available. Offers early childhood education (MS Ed); education (Ed S); education and professional studies (MS, MS Ed, Ed S); educational administration (MS Ed, Ed S); elementary education (MS Ed); guidance and counseling (MS); health and physical education (MS Ed); instructional media (MS Ed); reading specialist (MS Ed); secondary education (MS Ed); special education (MS Ed). *Application deadline:* Applications are processed on a rolling basis. *Application fee:* $20. *Application Contact:* 256-782-5329. *Dean,* Dr. Cynthia Harper, 256-782-8213.

College of Nursing *Faculty:* 2 full-time (both women). Expenses: Contact institution. *Financial support:* In 2006–07, 3 teaching assistantships with tuition reimbursements were awarded. Financial award application deadline: 4/1. In 2006, 10 degrees awarded. Offers nursing (MSN). *Application deadline:* Applications are processed on a rolling basis. *Application fee:* $20. Electronic applications accepted. *Dean,* Dr. Sarah Latham, 256-782-5431.

JACKSONVILLE UNIVERSITY, Jacksonville, FL 32211-3394

General Information Independent, coed, comprehensive institution. *Graduate housing:* Room and/or apartments available on a first-come, first-served basis to single students; on-campus housing not available to married students. Housing application deadline: 8/1.

GRADUATE UNITS

College of Arts and Sciences *Degree program information:* Part-time and evening/weekend programs available. Offers arts and sciences (MAT, MSN, Certificate).

School of Education *Degree program information:* Part-time and evening/weekend programs available. Offers computer sciences (MAT); early childhood education (Certificate); elementary education (MAT); integrated learning with educational technology (MAT); mathematics education (MAT); music education (MAT); reading education (MAT); second career as a teacher (Certificate); second careers as a teacher (Certificate).

School of Nursing *Degree program information:* Part-time programs available. Offers nursing (MSN).

School of Orthodontics Offers orthodontics (Certificate).

Davis College of Business *Degree program information:* Part-time and evening/weekend programs available. Offers business (Exec MBA, MBA); business administration (Exec MBA, MBA).

JAMES MADISON UNIVERSITY, Harrisonburg, VA 22807

General Information State-supported, coed, comprehensive institution. CGS member. *Enrollment:* 17,393 graduate, professional, and undergraduate students; 762 full-time matriculated graduate/professional students (546 women), 376 part-time matriculated graduate/professional students (169 women). *Enrollment by degree level:* 1,029 master's, 78 doctoral, 31 other advanced degrees. *Graduate faculty:* 228 full-time (100 women), 60 part-time/adjunct (31 women). Tuition, state resident: full-time $6,336; part-time $264 per credit hour. Tuition, nonresident: full-time $17,832; part-time $743 per credit hour. *Graduate housing:* Room and/or apartments available on a first-come, first-served basis to single students; on-campus housing not available to married students. Typical cost: $4,508 per year. Housing application deadline: 5/1. *Student services:* Campus employment opportunities, campus safety program, career counseling, disabled student services, free psychological counseling, international student services, multicultural affairs office, teacher training. *Library facilities:* Carrier Library plus 2 others. *Online resources:* library catalog, web page. *Collection:* 659,136 titles, 15,909 serial subscriptions, 37,198 audiovisual materials.

Computer facilities: Computer purchase and lease plans are available. 600 computers available on campus for general student use. A campuswide network can be accessed from student residence rooms and from off campus. Internet access and online class registration are available. *Web address:* http://www.jmu.edu/.

General Application Contact: Dr. Reid Linn, Dean, College of Graduate and Outreach Programs, 540-568-6131, Fax: 540-568-7860, E-mail: grad_programs@jmu.edu.

GRADUATE UNITS

College of Graduate and Outreach Programs Students: 762 full-time (546 women), 376 part-time (169 women); includes 84 minority (37 African Americans, 3 American Indian/Alaska Native, 32 Asian Americans or Pacific Islanders, 12 Hispanic Americans), 26 international. Average age 27. 805 applicants, 56% accepted, 286 enrolled. *Faculty:* 228 full-time (100 women), 60 part-time/adjunct (31 women). Expenses: Contact institution. *Financial support:* In 2006–07, 305 students received support, including 30 teaching assistantships with full tuition reimbursements available (averaging $8,167 per year); career-related internships or fieldwork, Federal Work-Study, and unspecified assistantships also available. Financial award application deadline: 3/1; financial award applicants required to submit FAFSA. In 2006, 498 master's, 10 doctorates, 18 other advanced degrees awarded. *Degree program information:* Part-time and evening/weekend programs available. Postbaccalaureate distance learning degree programs offered (no on-campus study). *Application deadline:* For fall admission, 5/1 priority date for domestic students; for spring admission, 9/1 priority date for domestic students. Applications are processed on a rolling basis. *Application fee:* $55. Electronic applications accepted. *Application Contact:* Lynette M. Bible, Director of Graduate Admissions, 540-568-6395, Fax: 540-568-7860, E-mail: biblelm@jmu.edu. *Dean, College of Graduate and Outreach Programs,* Dr. Reid Linn, 540-568-6131, Fax: 540-568-7860, E-mail: grad_programs@jmu.edu.

College of Arts and Letters Students: 64 full-time (30 women), 40 part-time (22 women); includes 7 minority (5 African Americans, 1 American Indian/Alaska Native, 1 Asian American or Pacific Islander), 2 international. Average age 27. 79 applicants, 84% accepted, 42 enrolled. *Faculty:* 31 full-time (12 women), 3 part-time/adjunct (1 woman). Expenses: Contact institution. *Financial support:* In 2006–07, 36 students received support, including 6 teaching assistantships with full tuition reimbursements available (averaging $8,167 per year); Federal Work-Study and unspecified assistantships also available. Financial award application deadline: 3/1; financial award applicants required to submit FAFSA. In 2006, 23 degrees awarded. *Degree program information:* Part-time programs available. Offers arts and letters (MA, MPA, MS); English (MA); history (MA); public administration (MPA); technical and scientific communication (MA, MS). *Application deadline:* For fall admission, 4/1 priority date for domestic students; for spring admission, 9/1 priority date for domestic students. Applications are processed on a rolling basis. *Application fee:* $55. Electronic applications accepted. *Dean,* Dr. David K. Jeffrey, 540-568-6334.

College of Business Students: 71 full-time (29 women), 92 part-time (29 women); includes 20 minority (5 African Americans, 1 American Indian/Alaska Native, 14 Asian Americans or Pacific Islanders), 5 international. Average age 27. 57 applicants, 67% accepted, 27 enrolled. *Faculty:* 23 full-time (7 women). Expenses: Contact institution. *Financial support:* In 2006–07, 25 students received support. Federal Work-Study and unspecified assistantships available. Financial award application deadline: 3/1; financial award applicants required to submit FAFSA. In 2006, 68 degrees awarded. *Degree program information:* Part-time and evening/weekend programs available. Postbaccalaureate distance learning degree programs offered (no on-campus study). Offers accounting (MS); business (MBA, MS); business administration (MBA). *Application deadline:* For fall admission, 5/1 priority date for domestic students; for spring admission, 9/1 priority date for domestic students. Applications are processed on a rolling basis. *Application fee:* $55. Electronic applications accepted. *Dean,* Dr. Robert D. Reid, 540-568-3254.

College of Education Students: 204 full-time (168 women), 43 part-time (26 women); includes 9 minority (4 African Americans, 1 American Indian/Alaska Native, 2 Asian Americans or Pacific Islanders, 2 Hispanic Americans). Average age 27. 81 applicants, 98% accepted, 57 enrolled. *Faculty:* 34 full-time (26 women), 28 part-time/adjunct (17 women). Expenses: Contact institution. *Financial support:* In 2006–07, 26 students received support. Career-related internships or fieldwork, Federal Work-Study, and unspecified assistantships available. Financial award application deadline: 3/1; financial award applicants required to submit FAFSA. In 2006, 216 degrees awarded. *Degree program information:* Part-time and evening/weekend programs available. Offers adult education/human resource development (MS Ed); early childhood education (MAT); education (M Ed, MAT, MS Ed); educational leadership (M Ed); exceptional education (M Ed); middle education (MAT); reading education (M Ed); secondary education (MAT). *Application deadline:* For fall admission, 5/1 priority date for domestic students; for spring admission, 9/1 priority date for domestic students. Applications are processed on a rolling basis. *Application fee:* $55. Electronic applications accepted. *Dean,* Dr. Phillip M. Wishon, 540-568-6572.

College of Integrated Science and Technology Students: 391 full-time (303 women), 182 part-time (80 women); includes 47 minority (23 African Americans, 14 Asian Americans or Pacific Islanders, 10 Hispanic Americans), 18 international. Average age 27. 543 applicants, 44% accepted, 146 enrolled. *Faculty:* 99 full-time (43 women), 21 part-time/adjunct (11 women). Expenses: Contact institution. *Financial support:* In 2006–07, 190 students received support, including 18 teaching assistantships with full tuition reimbursements available (averaging $8,167 per year); Federal Work-Study and unspecified assistantships also available. Financial award application deadline: 3/1; financial award applicants required to submit FAFSA. In 2006, 175 master's, 10 doctorates, 18 other advanced degrees awarded. *Degree program information:* Part-time programs available. Postbaccalaureate distance learning degree programs offered (no on-campus study). Offers assessment and measurement (PhD); audiology (Au D, PhD); clinical audiology (PhD); college student personnel administration (M Ed); combined-integrated clinical and school psychology (Psy D); community counseling psychology (MA, Ed S); computer science (MS); health education (MS, MS Ed); integrated science and technology (M Ed, MA, MOT, MPAS, MS, MS Ed, MSN, Au D, PhD, Psy D, Ed S); kinesiology (MS); nursing (MSN); occupational therapy (MOT); physician assistant studies (MPAS); psychological sciences (MA); school counseling (M Ed, Ed S); school psychology (M Ed, MA, Ed S); speech-language pathology (MS, PhD). *Application deadline:* For fall admission, 2/1 priority date for domestic students; for spring admission, 9/1 priority date for domestic students. Applications are processed on a rolling basis. *Application fee:* $55. Electronic applications accepted. *Dean,* Dr. A. Jerry Benson, 540-568-3283.

College of Science and Mathematics Students: 11 full-time (6 women), 8 part-time (5 women), 1 international. Average age 27. 24 applicants, 42% accepted, 7 enrolled. *Faculty:* 15 full-time (3 women), 1 part-time/adjunct (0 women). Expenses: Contact institution. *Financial support:* In 2006–07, 9 students received support. Federal Work-Study and unspecified assistantships available. Financial award application deadline: 3/1; financial award applicants required to submit FAFSA. In 2006, 7 degrees awarded. *Degree program information:* Part-time programs available. Offers biology (MS); mathematics and statistics (M Ed); science and mathematics (M Ed, MS). *Application deadline:* For fall admission, 2/15 priority date for domestic students; for spring admission, 9/1 priority date for domestic students. Applications are processed on a rolling basis. *Application fee:* $55. Electronic applications accepted. *Dean,* Dr. David F. Brakke, 540-568-3508.

College of Visual and Performing Arts Students: 21 full-time (10 women), 11 part-time (7 women); includes 1 minority (Asian American or Pacific Islander) Average age 27. 21 applicants, 62% accepted, 7 enrolled. *Faculty:* 26 full-time (9 women), 7 part-time/adjunct (2 women). Expenses: Contact institution. *Financial support:* In 2006–07, 19 students received support, including 6 teaching assistantships with full tuition reimbursements available (averaging $8,167 per year). Financial award application deadline: 3/1; financial award applicants required to submit FAFSA. In 2006, 9 degrees awarded. *Degree program information:* Part-time programs available. Offers art education (MA); art history (MA); ceramics (MFA); conducting (MM); drawing/painting (MFA); metal/jewelry (MFA); music education (MM); performance (MM); photography (MFA); printmaking (MFA); sculpture (MFA); studio art (MA); theory-composition (MM); visual and performing arts (MA, MFA, MM); weaving/fibers (MFA). *Application deadline:* For fall admission, 2/15 priority date for domestic students; for spring admission, 9/1 priority date for domestic students. *Application fee:* $55. *Interim Dean,* Dr. Marilou Johnson, 540-568-7073.

JEFFERSON COLLEGE OF HEALTH SCIENCES, Roanoke, VA 24031-3186

General Information Independent, coed, comprehensive institution.

GRADUATE UNITS

Program in Nursing Offers nursing education (MSN); nursing management (MSN).

JESUIT SCHOOL OF THEOLOGY AT BERKELEY, Berkeley, CA 94709-1193

General Information Independent-religious, coed, graduate-only institution. *Graduate housing:* Room and/or apartments available to single students; on-campus housing not available to married students.

GRADUATE UNITS

Programs in Theology *Degree program information:* Part-time programs available. Offers theology (M Div, MA, MABL, MTS, Th M, STD, STL).

THE JEWISH THEOLOGICAL SEMINARY, New York, NY 10027-4649

General Information Independent-religious, coed, university. *Enrollment:* 625 graduate, professional, and undergraduate students; 319 full-time matriculated graduate/professional students (159 women), 88 part-time matriculated graduate/professional students (48 women). *Enrollment by degree level:* 184 first professional, 129 master's, 94 doctoral. *Graduate faculty:* 62 full-time (19 women), 59 part-time/adjunct (28 women). *Tuition:* Full-time $18,880; part-time $900 per credit. *Required fees:* $250; $125 per semester. Tuition and fees vary according to program. *Graduate housing:* Rooms and/or apartments available on a first-come, first-served basis to single and married students. Typical cost: $8,730 per year for single students; $12,060 per year for married students. Room charges vary according to housing facility selected. Housing application deadline: 5/15. *Student services:* Campus employment opportunities, career counseling, free psychological counseling, low-cost health insurance. *Library facilities:* Library of the Jewish Theological Seminary. *Online resources:* library catalog, web page, access to other libraries' catalogs. *Collection:* 380,000 titles, 720 serial subscriptions, 5,250 audiovisual materials.

Computer facilities: 50 computers available on campus for general student use. A campuswide network can be accessed from student residence rooms and from off campus. Internet access is available. *Web address:* http://www.jtsa.edu/.

General Application Contact: Student Contact, 212-678-8000.

GRADUATE UNITS

The Graduate School Students: 104 full-time (54 women), 36 part-time (18 women); includes 1 minority (Asian American or Pacific Islander), 1 international. Average age 28. 76 applicants, 62% accepted, 26 enrolled. *Faculty:* 62 full-time (19 women), 59 part-time/adjunct (28 women). Expenses: Contact institution. *Financial support:* Fellowships, career-related internships or fieldwork and tuition waivers (full and partial) available. Support available to part-time students. Financial award application deadline: 3/1; financial award applicants required to submit FAFSA. In 2006, 31 master's, 6 doctorates awarded. *Degree program information:* Part-time programs available. Offers ancient Judaism (MA, DHL, PhD); Bible (MA, DHL, PhD); Jewish education (PhD); Jewish history (MA, DHL, PhD); Jewish literature (MA, DHL, PhD); Jewish philosophy (MA, DHL, PhD); liturgy (MA, DHL, PhD); medieval Jewish studies (MA, DHL, PhD); Midrash (MA, DHL, PhD); modern Jewish studies (MA, DHL, PhD); Talmud and rabbinics (MA, DHL, PhD). *Application deadline:* For fall admission, 1/15 priority date for domestic students. Applications are processed on a rolling basis. *Application fee:* $50. *Application Contact:* Alayne Manas, Assistant Director, Graduate School of Admissions, 212-678-8032, Fax: 212-678-8947, E-mail: almanas@jtsa.edu. *Dean,* Dr. Stephen Garfinkel, 212-678-8024, Fax: 212-678-8947, E-mail: gradschool@jtsa.edu.

H. L. Miller Cantorial School and College of Jewish Music Students: 42 full-time (20 women), 2 part-time. Average age 32. 13 applicants, 62% accepted, 8 enrolled. *Faculty:* 62 full-time (19 women), 59 part-time/adjunct (28 women). Expenses: Contact institution. *Financial support:* Career-related internships or fieldwork available. Support available to part-time students. Financial award application deadline: 3/1; financial award applicants required to submit FAFSA. In 2006, 6 degrees awarded. Offers Jewish music (MSM). *Application deadline:* For fall admission, 1/1 priority date for domestic students. Applications are processed on a rolling basis. *Application fee:* $50. *Application Contact:* Cheryl Goldwasser, Executive Assistant, 212-678-8037, Fax: 212-678-8947, E-mail: shgoldwasser@jtsa.edu. *Dean,* Hazzan Henry Rosenblum, 212-678-8036, Fax: 212-678-8947, E-mail: herosenblum@jtsa.edu.

The Rabbinical School Students: 118 full-time (41 women), 22 part-time (10 women); includes 1 minority (Hispanic American) Average age 29. 48 applicants, 63% accepted, 20 enrolled. *Faculty:* 62 full-time (19 women), 59 part-time/adjunct (28 women). Expenses: Contact institution. *Financial support:* Career-related internships or fieldwork available. Support available to part-time students. Financial award application deadline: 3/1; financial award applicants required to submit FAFSA. In 2006, 8 master's, 19 other advanced degrees awarded. Offers theology (MA, Rabbi). *Application deadline:* For fall admission, 12/31 for domestic students. Applications are processed on a rolling basis. *Application fee:* $65. *Application Contact:* Rabbi Charles Savenor, Associate Dean of the Rabbinical School, 212-678-8818, Fax: 212-678-8947, E-mail: chsavenor@jtsa.edu. *Dean,* Rabbi William Lebeau, 212-678-8067, Fax: 212-678-8947, E-mail: wilebeau@jtsa.edu.

William Davidson Graduate School of Jewish Education Students: 83 full-time (56 women), 42 part-time (23 women); includes 2 minority (both Hispanic Americans) Average age 33. 56 applicants, 80% accepted, 32 enrolled. *Faculty:* 62 full-time (19 women), 59 part-time/adjunct (28 women). Expenses: Contact institution. *Financial support:* Fellowships, career-related internships or fieldwork available. Financial award application deadline: 3/1. In 2006, 6 master's, 1 doctorate awarded. *Degree program information:* Part-time programs available. Postbaccalaureate distance learning degree programs offered (minimal on-campus study). Offers Jewish education (MA, Ed D). Offered in conjunction with Rabbinical School; H. L. Miller Cantorial School and College of Jewish Music; Teacher's College, Columbia University; and Union Theological Seminary. *Application deadline:* For fall admission, 2/1 priority date for domestic students. Applications are processed on a rolling basis. *Application fee:* $50. *Application Contact:* Jamie Beth Schindler, Director of Admissions, 212-678-8866, Fax: 212-749-9085, E-mail: jaschindler@jtsa.edu. *Dean,* Dr. Steven Brown, 212-678-8030, Fax: 212-749-9085, E-mail: stbrown@jtsa.edu.

JEWISH UNIVERSITY OF AMERICA, Skokie, IL 60077-3248

General Information Independent-religious, men only, graduate-only institution. *Graduate housing:* On-campus housing not available.

GRADUATE UNITS

Graduate School *Degree program information:* Part-time and evening/weekend programs available. Offers Jewish education (MJ Ed, DJ Ed).

Jewish University of America (continued)

Abrams Institute of Pastoral Counseling Offers counseling (MA); pastoral counseling (MPC, DPC).

Graduate Research Division *Degree program information:* Part-time programs available. Offers Bible (MHL, DHL); Hebrew (MHL, DHL); history (MHL, DHL); Jewish studies (MHL, DHL); philosophy (MHL, DHL); rabbinics (MHL, DHL).

JOHN BROWN UNIVERSITY, Siloam Springs, AR 72761-2121

General Information Independent-religious, coed, comprehensive institution. *Graduate housing:* Rooms and/or apartments available on a first-come, first-served basis to single and married students.

GRADUATE UNITS

Department of Business Administration *Degree program information:* Part-time and evening/weekend programs available. Offers business administration (MBA); leadership and ethics (MS). Electronic applications accepted.

Program in Counseling *Degree program information:* Part-time and evening/weekend programs available. Offers community counseling (MS); marriage and family therapy (MS); school counseling (MS). Electronic applications accepted.

Program in Ministry *Degree program information:* Part-time and evening/weekend programs available. Offers ministry (MA). Electronic applications accepted.

JOHN CARROLL UNIVERSITY, University Heights, OH 44118-4581

General Information Independent-religious, coed, comprehensive institution. CGS member. *Enrollment:* 188 full-time matriculated graduate/professional students (128 women), 515 part-time matriculated graduate/professional students (323 women). *Enrollment by degree level:* 703 master's. *Graduate faculty:* 140 full-time (41 women), 42 part-time/adjunct (23 women). *Tuition:* Full-time $9,675; part-time $645 per credit hour. Tuition and fees vary according to program. *Graduate housing:* On-campus housing not available. *Student services:* Career counseling, disabled student services, exercise/wellness program, free psychological counseling, international student services, multicultural affairs office, writing training. *Library facilities:* Grasselli Library. *Online resources:* library catalog, web page, access to other libraries' catalogs. *Collection:* 620,000 titles, 2,198 serial subscriptions, 5,820 audiovisual materials.

Computer facilities: 210 computers available on campus for general student use. A campuswide network can be accessed from student residence rooms and from off campus. Internet access and online class registration are available. *Web address:* http://www.jcu.edu/.

General Application Contact: Jennifer Tucker, Records Management Assistant, 216-397-1925, Fax: 216-397-1835, E-mail: jtucker@jcu.edu.

GRADUATE UNITS

Graduate School Students: 188 full-time (128 women), 515 part-time (323 women); includes 52 minority (47 African Americans, 2 Asian Americans or Pacific Islanders, 3 Hispanic Americans), 5 international. Average age 32. 336 applicants, 69% accepted, 163 enrolled. *Faculty:* 140 full-time (41 women), 42 part-time/adjunct (23 women). Expenses: Contact institution. *Financial support:* In 2006–07, 128 students received support, including 56 teaching assistantships with full tuition reimbursements available (averaging $8,700 per year); career-related internships or fieldwork, institutionally sponsored loans, scholarships/grants, tuition waivers (partial), and unspecified assistantships also available. Support available to part-time students. Financial award applicants required to submit FAFSA. In 2006, 294 degrees awarded. *Degree program information:* Part-time and evening/weekend programs available. Offers administration (M Ed, MA); biology (MA, MS); clinical counseling (Certificate); communications management (MA); community counseling (MA); educational and school psychology (M Ed, MA); English (MA); history (MA); humanities (MA); integrated science (MA); mathematics (MA, MS); nonprofit administration (MA); professional teacher education (M Ed, MA); religious studies (MA); school based adolescent-young adult education (M Ed); school based early childhood education (M Ed); school based middle childhood education (M Ed); school based multi-age education (M Ed); school counseling (M Ed, MA). *Application deadline:* Applications are processed on a rolling basis. *Application fee:* $25 ($35 for international students). *Application Contact:* Jennifer Tucker, Records Management Assistant, 216-397-1925, Fax: 216-397-1835, E-mail: jtucker@jcu.edu. *Dean,* Dr. Mary E. Beadle, 216-397-4204, Fax: 216-397-3009, E-mail: mbeadle@jcu.edu.

John M. and Mary Jo Boler School of Business Students: 31 full-time (13 women), 171 part-time (72 women); includes 14 minority (12 African Americans, 1 Asian American or Pacific Islander, 1 Hispanic American). Average age 29. 62 applicants, 81% accepted, 36 enrolled. *Faculty:* 33 full-time (6 women), 2 part-time/adjunct (0 women). Expenses: Contact institution. *Financial support:* In 2006–07, 6 research assistantships with full tuition reimbursements (averaging $8,000 per year) were awarded; scholarships/grants and unspecified assistantships also available. Financial award application deadline: 3/15; financial award applicants required to submit FAFSA. In 2006, 91 degrees awarded. *Degree program information:* Part-time and evening/weekend programs available. Offers accountancy (MS); business (MBA). *Application deadline:* Applications are processed on a rolling basis. *Application fee:* $25 ($35 for international students). *Application Contact:* Gayle T. Bruno-Gannon, Assistant to the Dean, 216-397-1970, Fax: 216-397-1728, E-mail: ggannon@jcu.edu. *Associate Dean,* Dr. Karen Schuele, 216-397-4606, Fax: 216-397-1728, E-mail: kschuele@jcu.edu.

JOHN F. KENNEDY UNIVERSITY, Pleasant Hill, CA 94523-4817

General Information Independent, coed, comprehensive institution. *Graduate housing:* On-campus housing not available.

GRADUATE UNITS

Graduate School of Holistic Studies *Degree program information:* Part-time and evening/weekend programs available. Offers consciousness studies (MA); counseling psychology (MA); dream studies (Certificate); holistic health education (MA); holistic studies (MA, MFA, Certificate); integral psychology (MA, Certificate); life coaching (Certificate); studio arts (MFA); transformative arts (MA).

Graduate School of Professional Psychology *Degree program information:* Part-time and evening/weekend programs available. Offers counseling psychology (MA); organizational psychology (MA, Certificate); professional psychology (MA, Psy D, Certificate); psychology (Psy D); sport psychology (MA).

School of Education and Liberal Arts *Degree program information:* Part-time and evening/weekend programs available. Offers education (MAT); education and liberal arts (MA, MAT, Certificate); museum studies (MA, Certificate).

School of Law *Degree program information:* Part-time and evening/weekend programs available. Offers law (JD).

School of Management *Degree program information:* Part-time and evening/weekend programs available. Offers business administration (MBA); career coaching (Certificate); career development (MA, Certificate); management (MA, MBA, Certificate); organizational leadership (Certificate).

JOHN JAY COLLEGE OF CRIMINAL JUSTICE OF THE CITY UNIVERSITY OF NEW YORK, New York, NY 10019-1093

General Information State and locally supported, coed, comprehensive institution. *Graduate housing:* On-campus housing not available. *Research affiliation:* Criminal Justice Center, Criminal Justice Research and Evaluation Center, Center on Violence and Human Survival, Center for Dispute Resolution, The Fire Science Institute, The Institute For Criminal Justice Ethics.

GRADUATE UNITS

Graduate Studies *Degree program information:* Part-time and evening/weekend programs available. Offers criminal justice (MA, PhD); criminology and deviance (PhD); forensic computing (MS); forensic psychology (PhD); forensic science (PhD); law and philosophy (PhD); organizational behavior (PhD); protection management (MS); public administration (MPA); public policy (PhD).

JOHN MARSHALL LAW SCHOOL, Chicago, IL 60604-3968

General Information Independent, coed, graduate-only institution. *Enrollment by degree level:* 1,414 first professional, 164 master's. *Graduate faculty:* 64 full-time (23 women), 113 part-time/adjunct (29 women). *Graduate housing:* On-campus housing not available. *Student services:* Campus employment opportunities, campus safety program, career counseling, disabled student services, free psychological counseling, international student services, low-cost health insurance, multicultural affairs office, writing training. *Library facilities:* The John Marshall Law School Library. *Online resources:* library catalog, web page, access to other libraries' catalogs. *Collection:* 239,403 titles, 5,514 serial subscriptions, 2,582 audiovisual materials.

Computer facilities: 118 computers available on campus for general student use. A campuswide network can be accessed from off campus. Internet access and online class registration are available. *Web address:* http://www.jmls.edu/.

General Application Contact: William B. Powers, Associate Dean of Admission and Student Affairs, 800-537-4280, Fax: 312-427-5136, E-mail: admission@jmls.edu.

GRADUATE UNITS

Graduate and Professional Programs Students: 1,157 full-time (479 women), 421 part-time (187 women); includes 253 minority (76 African Americans, 10 American Indian/Alaska Native, 101 Asian Americans or Pacific Islanders, 66 Hispanic Americans), 48 international. Average age 27. 3,169 applicants, 37% accepted, 333 enrolled. *Faculty:* 64 full-time (23 women), 113 part-time/adjunct (29 women). Expenses: Contact institution. *Financial support:* In 2006–07, 1,339 students received support. Scholarships/grants and tuition waivers (full and partial) available. Support available to part-time students. Financial award application deadline: 6/1; financial award applicants required to submit FAFSA. In 2006, 347 JDs, 69 master's awarded. *Degree program information:* Part-time and evening/weekend programs available. Offers comparative legal studies (LL M); employee benefits (LL M, MS); information technology (LL M, MS); intellectual property (LL M); international business and trade (LL M); law (JD); real estate (LL M, MS); taxation (LL M, MS). *Application deadline:* For fall admission, 3/1 priority date for domestic and international students; for spring admission, 10/15 priority date for domestic and international students. Applications are processed on a rolling basis. *Application fee:* $60. Electronic applications accepted. *Application Contact:* William B. Powers, Associate Dean of Admission and Student Affairs, 800-537-4280, Fax: 312-427-5136, E-mail: admission@jmls.edu. *Dean,* John Corkery, 312-427-2737.

THE JOHNS HOPKINS UNIVERSITY, Baltimore, MD 21218-2699

General Information Independent, coed, university. CGS member. *Enrollment:* 6,140 full-time matriculated graduate/professional students (3,269 women), 8,060 part-time matriculated graduate/professional students (4,091 women). *Enrollment by degree level:* 482 first professional, 9,568 master's, 2,543 doctoral, 1,607 other advanced degrees. *Graduate faculty:* 3,430 full-time (1,243 women), 217 part-time/adjunct (96 women). *Tuition:* Full-time $32,976. Tuition and fees vary according to degree level and program. *Graduate housing:* On-campus housing not available. *Student services:* Campus employment opportunities, campus safety program, career counseling, disabled student services, exercise/wellness program, free psychological counseling, international student services, low-cost health insurance, multicultural affairs office, teacher training, writing training. *Library facilities:* Milton S. Eisenhower Library plus 6 others. *Online resources:* library catalog, web page, access to other libraries' catalogs. *Collection:* 3.5 million titles, 30,023 serial subscriptions. *Research affiliation:* Space Telescope Science Institute (astronomy), Howard Hughes Medical Institute (biomedical sciences), Bristol-Myers Squibb (human nutrition), SmithKline Beecham (asthma and allergy), Carnegie Institution of Washington (biological sciences), General Electric (medical technology).

Computer facilities: 140 computers available on campus for general student use. A campuswide network can be accessed from student residence rooms and from off campus. Internet access and online class registration are available. *Web address:* http://www.jhu.edu/.

General Application Contact: Graduate Admissions Office, 410-516-8174.

GRADUATE UNITS

Bloomberg School of Public Health Students: 1,197 full-time (872 women), 454 part-time (279 women); includes 388 minority (107 African Americans, 5 American Indian/Alaska Native, 218 Asian Americans or Pacific Islanders, 58 Hispanic Americans), 388 international. Average age 29. 3,047 applicants, 52% accepted, 755 enrolled. *Faculty:* 517 full-time (253 women), 572 part-time/adjunct (222 women). Expenses: Contact institution. *Financial support:* In 2006–07, 1,650 students received support, including 38 fellowships (averaging $34,333 per year), 59 research assistantships (averaging $23,525 per year), 11 teaching assistantships (averaging $3,126 per year); career-related internships or fieldwork, Federal Work-Study, institutionally sponsored loans, scholarships/grants, traineeships, health care benefits, and stipends also available. Support available to part-time students. Financial award application deadline: 3/15; financial award applicants required to submit FAFSA. In 2006, 507 master's, 123 doctorates awarded. *Degree program information:* Part-time and evening/weekend programs available. Postbaccalaureate distance learning degree programs offered (minimal on-campus study). Offers behavioral sciences and health education (MHS); biochemistry and molecular biology (MHS, Sc M, PhD); bioinformatics (MHS); biostatistics (MHS, Sc M, PhD); cancer epidemiology (MHS, Sc M, PhD, Sc D); cardiovascular disease epidemiology (MHS, Sc M, PhD, Sc D); child and adolescent health and development (Dr PH, PhD); children's mental health services (PhD); clinical epidemiology (MHS, Sc M, PhD, Sc D); clinical investigation (MHS, Sc M, PhD); clinical trials (PhD, Sc D); demography (MHS); disease prevention and control (MHS, PhD); drug dependence epidemiology (PhD); environmental health engineering (PhD); environmental health sciences (MHS, Dr PH); epidemiology (Dr PH); epidemiology (general) (MHS, Sc M, PhD, Sc D); epidemiology of aging (MHS, Sc M, PhD, Sc D); genetic counseling (Sc M); health and public policy (PhD); health care management and leadership (Dr PH); health finance and management (MHS); health policy (MHS); health services research (PhD); health systems (MHS, PhD); human genetics/genetic epidemiology (MHS, Sc M, PhD, Sc D); human nutrition (MHS, PhD); infectious disease epidemiology (MHS, Sc M, PhD, Sc D); international health (Dr PH); mental health (MHS); molecular imaging (PhD); molecular microbiology and immunology (MHS, Sc M, PhD); occupational and environmental health (PhD); occupational and environmental hygiene (MHS); occupational/environmental epidemiology (MHS, Sc M, PhD, Sc D); physiology (PhD); population and health (Dr PH, PhD); population, family and reproductive health (MHS); psychiatric epidemiology (PhD); public health (MHS, MPH, Sc M, Dr PH, PhD, Sc D); reproductive, perinatal women's health (Dr PH, PhD); social and behavioral interventions (MHS, PhD); social and behavioral sciences (PhD, Sc D); toxicology (PhD). *Application deadline:* Applications are processed on a rolling basis. *Application fee:* $45. Electronic applications accepted. *Application Contact:* Jennifer L. Kerilla, Associate Director of Admissions: Communications, Recruitment and Special Projects, 410-955-3543, Fax: 410-955-0464, E-mail: jkerilla@jhsph.edu. *Dean,* Dr. Michael J. Klag, 410-955-3540, Fax: 410-955-0121, E-mail: mklag@jhsph.edu.

Carey Business School Students: 363 full-time (166 women), 1,463 part-time (614 women); includes 362 minority (187 African Americans, 5 American Indian/Alaska Native, 131 Asian Americans or Pacific Islanders, 39 Hispanic Americans), 20 international. Average age 33. 1,634 applicants, 70% accepted, 936 enrolled. *Faculty:* 20 full-time (4 women), 226 part-time/adjunct (43 women). Expenses: Contact institution. *Financial support:* In 2006–07, 412 students received support. Scholarships/grants available. Support available to part-time students. Financial award application deadline: 6/1; financial award applicants required to submit FAFSA. In 2006, 587 master's, 174 other advanced degrees awarded. *Degree program information:* Part-time and evening/weekend programs available. Postbaccalaureate distance learning degree programs offered (minimal on-campus study). Offers business administration

(MBA); business of health (MBA, Certificate); business of medicine (Certificate); business of nursing (Certificate); competitive intelligence (Certificate); finance (MS, Certificate); financial management (Certificate); information and telecommunication systems (Certificate); information security management (Certificate); information technology (MS, Certificate); information technology and telecommunication systems for business (MS); investments (Certificate); leadership and management in the life sciences (MBA, Certificate); leadership development (Certificate); management (MS, Certificate); marketing (MS); medical services management (MBA); organization development and strategic human resources (MS); real estate (MS); senior living and health care real estate (Certificate); skilled facilitator (Certificate). *Application deadline:* For fall admission, 5/1 for international students; for spring admission, 10/15 for international students. Applications are processed on a rolling basis. *Application fee:* $60. *Application Contact:* Robin Reed, Senior Academic Coordinator, 800-gotojhu, Fax: 410-872-1251, E-mail: onestop.admissions@jhu.edu. *Interim Dean,* Dr. Pamela Cranston, 410-516-4892, Fax: 410-516-0734, E-mail: pcranston@jhu.edu.

Engineering and Applied Science Programs for Professionals *Faculty:* 226 part-time/adjunct (27 women). Expenses: Contact institution. In 2006, 637 degrees awarded. Offers applied and computational mathematics (MS); applied biomedical engineering (MS); applied physics (MS); bioinformatics (MS); chemical and biomolecular engineering (M Ch E); civil engineering (MCE); computer science (MS); electrical and computer engineering (MS); engineering and applied science (M Ch E, M Mat SE, MCE, MEE, MME, MS, MSE, Certificate, Post-Master's Certificate); environmental engineering (MS); environmental engineering and science (MEE, MS, Certificate); environmental planning and management (MS); information systems and technology (MS); materials science and engineering (M Mat SE, MSE); mechanical engineering (MME); systems engineering (MS, Certificate, Post-Master's Certificate); technical innovation and new ventures (Graduate Certificate); technical management (MS, Post-Master's Certificate); telecommunications and networking (MS). *Application deadline:* Applications are processed on a rolling basis. *Application fee:* $70. Electronic applications accepted. *Application Contact:* Toni M. Riley, Director, Student Services, 410-540-2960, Fax: 410-579-8049, E-mail: triley4@jhu.edu. *Associate Dean,* Dr. Allan Bjerkaas, 410-540-2960, Fax: 410-579-8049, E-mail: bjerkaas@jhu.edu.

G. W. C. Whiting School of Engineering Students: 722 full-time (205 women), 35 part-time (8 women); includes 83 minority (11 African Americans, 1 American Indian/Alaska Native, 53 Asian Americans or Pacific Islanders, 18 Hispanic Americans), 370 international. Average age 27. 3,005 applicants, 20% accepted, 262 enrolled. *Faculty:* 159 full-time (20 women), 73 part-time/adjunct (9 women). Expenses: Contact institution. *Financial support:* In 2006–07, 93 fellowships with full and partial tuition reimbursements (averaging $20,889 per year), 381 research assistantships with full tuition reimbursements (averaging $22,312 per year), 84 teaching assistantships with full and partial tuition reimbursements (averaging $21,179 per year) were awarded; Federal Work-Study, institutionally sponsored loans, scholarships/grants, health care benefits, tuition waivers (full and partial), and unspecified assistantships also available. Support available to part-time students. Financial award applicants required to submit FAFSA. In 2006, 174 master's, 66 doctorates awarded. *Degree program information:* Part-time and evening/weekend programs available. Offers biomedical engineering (MSE, PhD); chemical and biomolecular engineering (MSE, PhD); civil engineering (MCE, MSE, PhD); computer science (MSE, PhD); discrete mathematics (MA, MSE, PhD); electrical and computer engineering (MSE, PhD); engineering (M Ch E, M Mat SE, MA, MCE, MEE, MME, MS, MSE, PhD, Certificate, Post-Master's Certificate); geography and environmental engineering (MA, MS, MSE, PhD); materials science and engineering (M Mat SE, MSE, PhD); mechanical engineering (MSE, PhD); operations research/optimization/decision science (MA, MSE, PhD); statistics/probability/stochastic processes (MA, MSE, PhD). Electronic applications accepted. *Application Contact:* Gail O'Connor, Coordinator of Graduate Admissions, 410-516-8174, Fax: 410-516-0780, E-mail: graduateadmissions@jhu.edu. *Interim Dean,* Dr. Nicholas P. Jones, 410-516-8350 Ext. 3, Fax: 410-516-8627.

Information Security Institute Students: 29 full-time (7 women), 6 part-time; includes 5 minority (1 African American, 3 Asian Americans or Pacific Islanders, 1 Hispanic American), 6 international. Average age 25. 69 applicants, 45% accepted, 21 enrolled. *Faculty:* 4 part-time/adjunct (0 women). Expenses: Contact institution. *Financial support:* In 2006–07, 28 students received support, including 18 fellowships with full tuition reimbursements available (averaging $12,978 per year), 2 teaching assistantships with tuition reimbursements available (averaging $11,997 per year); career-related internships or fieldwork, Federal Work-Study, institutionally sponsored loans, scholarships/grants, traineeships, health care benefits, tuition waivers (partial), and unspecified assistantships also available. In 2006, 24 degrees awarded. *Degree program information:* Part-time programs available. Offers security informatics (MS). *Application deadline:* For fall admission, 7/15 priority date for domestic students, 3/15 for international students. Applications are processed on a rolling basis. *Application fee:* $0. Electronic applications accepted. *Application Contact:* Deborah K. Higgins, Graduate Coordinator, 410-516-8521, Fax: 410-516-3301, E-mail: dhiggins@jhu.edu. *Director,* Dr. Gerald M. Masson, 410-516-7013, Fax: 410-516-3301, E-mail: masson@jhu.edu.

National Institutes of Health Sponsored Programs Offers biology (PhD); cell, molecular, and developmental biology and biophysics). Electronic applications accepted.

Paul H. Nitze School of Advanced International Studies Offers emerging markets (Certificate); interdisciplinary studies (MA, PhD); international public policy (MIPP); international studies (Certificate). Electronic applications accepted.

Peabody Conservatory of Music Students: 308 full-time (186 women), 16 part-time (9 women); includes 34 minority (7 African Americans, 21 Asian Americans or Pacific Islanders, 6 Hispanic Americans), 156 international. Average age 25. 716 applicants, 50% accepted, 163 enrolled. *Faculty:* 70 full-time (18 women), 63 part-time/adjunct (22 women). Expenses: Contact institution. *Financial support:* In 2006–07, 259 students received support, including 51 teaching assistantships (averaging $20,288 per year); Federal Work-Study, scholarships/grants, and unspecified assistantships also available. Financial award application deadline: 3/1; financial award applicants required to submit FAFSA. In 2006, 107 master's, 9 doctorates, 32 other advanced degrees awarded. Offers music (MA, MM, DMA, AD, GPD). *Application deadline:* For fall admission, 12/1 for domestic students. *Application fee:* $100. *Application Contact:* David Lane, Director of Admissions, 800-368-2521, Fax: 410-659-8102, E-mail: admissions@peabody.jhu.edu. *Director,* Jeffrey Sharkey, 410-659-8100 Ext. 3060, Fax: 410-659-8131.

School of Medicine Students: 1,263 full-time (615 women), 1 (woman) part-time; includes 409 minority (97 African Americans, 5 American Indian/Alaska Native, 259 Asian Americans or Pacific Islanders, 48 Hispanic Americans), 270 international. 5,344 applicants, 10% accepted, 261 enrolled. *Faculty:* 2,448 full-time (872 women), 1,249 part-time/adjunct (378 women). Expenses: Contact institution. *Financial support:* In 2006–07, fellowships with full tuition reimbursements (averaging $23,000 per year); research assistantships, teaching assistantships, career-related internships or fieldwork, Federal Work-Study, institutionally sponsored loans, and tuition waivers (full) also available. In 2006, 102 MDs, 10 master's, 90 doctorates awarded. Offers medicine (MD, MA, MS, PhD). *Application deadline:* Applications are processed on a rolling basis. *Application fee:* $75. Electronic applications accepted. *Application Contact:* Dr. James Weiss, Associate Dean of Admissions, 410-955-3182. *Dean of Medical Faculty and Chief Executive Officer,* Dr. Edward D. Miller, 410-955-3180.

Division of Health Sciences Informatics Students: 11 full-time (5 women); includes 6 minority (4 African Americans, 2 Asian Americans or Pacific Islanders). 11 applicants, 45% accepted, 5 enrolled. *Faculty:* 40 part-time/adjunct (10 women). Expenses: Contact institution. *Financial support:* In 2006–07, 11 fellowships with full tuition reimbursements (averaging $42,750 per year) were awarded; career-related internships or fieldwork and health care benefits also available. In 2006, 1 degree awarded. Offers health sciences informatics (MS). *Application deadline:* For spring admission, 2/15 priority date for domestic students. *Application fee:* $75. Electronic applications accepted. *Application Contact:* Senior Academic Program Coordinator, 443-287-6083, Fax: 410-614-2064. *Director, Training Program,* Dr. Harold P. Lehmann, 410-502-2569, Fax: 410-614-2064, E-mail: lehmann@jhmi.edu.

Graduate Programs in Medicine Students: 781 full-time (385 women), 1 (woman) part-time; includes 179 minority (51 African Americans, 2 American Indian/Alaska Native, 105 Asian Americans or Pacific Islanders, 21 Hispanic Americans), 257 international. 1,195 applicants, 22% accepted, 141 enrolled. *Faculty:* 237 full-time (72 women), 33 part-time/adjunct (11 women). Expenses: Contact institution. *Financial support:* In 2006–07, fellowships with full tuition reimbursements (averaging $23,000 per year); research assistantships, teaching assistantships with tuition reimbursements, career-related internships or fieldwork, Federal Work-Study, institutionally sponsored loans, and tuition waivers (full) also available. Financial award applicants required to submit FAFSA. In 2006, 10 master's, 90 doctorates awarded. Offers biochemistry, cellular and molecular biology (PhD); biological chemistry (PhD); biophysics and biophysical chemistry (MS, PhD); cellular and molecular medicine (PhD); cellular and molecular physiology (PhD); functional anatomy and evolution (PhD); human genetics and molecular biology (PhD); immunology (PhD); medical and biological illustration (MA); medicine (MA, MS, PhD); neuroscience (PhD); pathobiology (PhD); pharmacology and molecular sciences (PhD); physiology (PhD). *Application deadline:* For fall admission, 1/10 priority date for domestic and international students. Applications are processed on a rolling basis. *Application fee:* $75. Electronic applications accepted. *Associate Dean for Graduate Programs,* Dr. Peter Maloney, 410-614-3385.

School of Nursing Students: 79 full-time (74 women), 174 part-time (166 women); includes 71 minority (18 African Americans, 5 American Indian/Alaska Native, 42 Asian Americans or Pacific Islanders, 6 Hispanic Americans), 1 international. Average age 30. 287 applicants, 84% accepted, 105 enrolled. *Faculty:* 33 full-time (26 women), 7 part-time/adjunct (6 women). Expenses: Contact institution. *Financial support:* In 2006–07, 37 students received support, including 6 fellowships with partial tuition reimbursements available (averaging $23,272 per year); research assistantships with full tuition reimbursements available, teaching assistantships with full tuition reimbursements available, career-related internships or fieldwork, Federal Work-Study, institutionally sponsored loans, scholarships/grants, traineeships, and tuition waivers (partial) also available. Support available to part-time students. Financial award application deadline: 3/15; financial award applicants required to submit FAFSA. In 2006, 47 master's, 3 doctorates awarded. *Degree program information:* Part-time programs available. Offers adult acute/critical care (MSN, Certificate); adult and pediatric primary care (MSN); adult or pediatric primary care (Certificate); clinical nurse specialist (MSN); clinical nurse specialist and health systems management (MSN); family primary care (MSN, Certificate); health systems management (MSN); nursing (MSN, PhD, Certificate); public health nursing (MSN). *Application deadline:* For fall admission, 3/1 priority date for domestic and international students; for winter admission, 7/1 priority date for domestic and international students; for spring admission, 7/1 priority date for domestic and international students. Applications are processed on a rolling basis. *Application fee:* $75. *Application Contact:* Mary O'Rourke, Director of Admissions/Student Services, 410-955-7548, Fax: 410-614-7086, E-mail: orourke@son.jhmi.edu. *Dean,* Dr. Martha N. Hill, 410-955-7544, Fax: 410-955-4890, E-mail: mnhill@son.jhmi.edu.

School of Education Students: 345 full-time (275 women), 1,397 part-time (1,125 women); includes 311 minority (229 African Americans, 6 American Indian/Alaska Native, 54 Asian Americans or Pacific Islanders, 22 Hispanic Americans), 11 international. Average age 31. 1,499 applicants, 77% accepted, 1046 enrolled. *Faculty:* 37 full-time (24 women), 174 part-time/adjunct (104 women). Expenses: Contact institution. *Financial support:* In 2006–07, 667 students received support. Scholarships/grants available. Support available to part-time students. Financial award application deadline: 6/1; financial award applicants required to submit FAFSA. In 2006, 538 master's, 1 doctorate, 215 other advanced degrees awarded. *Degree program information:* Part-time and evening/weekend programs available. Postbaccalaureate distance learning degree programs offered (minimal on-campus study). Offers addictions counseling (Certificate); adult learning (Certificate); advanced methods for differential instruction and inclusive education (Certificate); assistive technology for communication and social interaction (Certificate); business leadership for independent schools (Certificate); clinical community counseling (Certificate); counseling (MS, CAGS); counseling at-risk youth (Certificate); early intervention/preschool special education specialist (Certificate); earth/space science (Certificate); education (MAT, MS, Ed D, CAGS, Certificate); education of students with autism and other pervasive developmental disorders (Certificate); educational leadership for independent schools (Certificate); educational studies (MS); effective teaching of reading (Certificate); elementary education (MAT); English for speakers of other languages (MAT); ESL instruction (Certificate); gifted education (Certificate); leadership for school, family and community collaboration (Certificate); management (MS); organizational counseling (Certificate); reading (MS); school administration and supervision (MS, Certificate); secondary education (MAT); special education (MS, Ed D, CAGS); spiritual and existential counseling and therapy (Certificate); teacher development and leadership (Ed D); teacher leadership (Certificate); technology for educators (MS); urban education (Certificate). *Application deadline:* For fall admission, 5/1 for international students; for spring admission, 10/15 for international students. Applications are processed on a rolling basis. *Application fee:* $60. *Application Contact:* Carol Herrman, Admissions Coordinator, 410-872-1234, Fax: 410-872-1251, E-mail: onestop.admissions@jhu.edu. *Dean,* Dr. Ralph Fessler, 410-516-7820, Fax: 410-516-6697, E-mail: fess@jhu.edu.

Zanvyl Krieger School of Arts and Sciences Students: 979 full-time (446 women), 9 part-time (2 women); includes 79 minority (14 African Americans, 3 American Indian/Alaska Native, 37 Asian Americans or Pacific Islanders, 25 Hispanic Americans), 315 international. Average age 26. 2,956 applicants, 17% accepted, 266 enrolled. *Faculty:* 339 full-time (101 women), 114 part-time/adjunct (32 women). Expenses: Contact institution. *Financial support:* In 2006–07, 206 fellowships with full and partial tuition reimbursements (averaging $24,740 per year), 151 research assistantships with full and partial tuition reimbursements (averaging $11,328 per year), 355 teaching assistantships with full and partial tuition reimbursements (averaging $14,204 per year) were awarded; career-related internships or fieldwork, Federal Work-Study, institutionally sponsored loans, scholarships/grants, health care benefits, tuition waivers (full and partial), and unspecified assistantships also available. Support available to part-time students. Financial award applicants required to submit FAFSA. In 2006, 160 master's, 126 doctorates awarded. Offers anthropology (PhD); applied economics (MA); arts and sciences (MA, MFA, MS, PhD); astronomy (PhD); bioinformatics (MS); biology (PhD); biophysics (MA, PhD); bioscience regulatory affairs (MS); biotechnology (MS); chemistry (PhD); chemistry-biology (PhD); classics (PhD); cognitive science (PhD); communication in contemporary society (MA); earth and planetary sciences (MA, PhD); economics (PhD); English and American literature (PhD); environmental sciences and policy (MS); fiction writing (MFA); French (PhD); German (PhD); government (MA, Certificate); history (PhD); history of art (MA, PhD); history of science and technology (MA, PhD); homeland security (Certificate); Italian (PhD); liberal arts (MA, Certificate); mathematics (PhD); Near Eastern studies (PhD); philosophy (MA, PhD); physics (PhD); poetry (MFA); political science (MA, PhD); psychological and brain sciences (PhD); science writing (MA); sociology (PhD); Spanish (PhD); writing (MA). *Application fee:* $75. *Application Contact:* Gail O'Connor, Coordinator of Graduate Admissions, 410-516-8174, Fax: 410-516-0780, E-mail: graduateadmissions@jhu.edu. *Dean,* Dr. Adam Falk, 410-516-8212, Fax: 410-516-6017.

Humanities Center Students: 23 full-time (12 women), 1 part-time; includes 2 minority (both Asian Americans or Pacific Islanders), 6 international. Average age 24. 61 applicants, 8% accepted, 5 enrolled. *Faculty:* 5 full-time (2 women), 4 part-time/adjunct (3 women). Expenses: Contact institution. *Financial support:* In 2006–07, 20 students received support, including 4 fellowships with full tuition reimbursements available (averaging $14,000 per year), 1 research assistantship with full tuition reimbursement available (averaging $14,000 per year), 7 teaching assistantships with full tuition reimbursements available (averaging $14,000 per year); Federal Work-Study, institutionally sponsored loans, and tuition waivers (full) also available. Financial award application deadline: 3/14; financial award applicants required to submit FAFSA. In 2006, 1 degree awarded. *Degree program information:* Part-time programs available. Offers humanities (PhD). *Application deadline:* For fall admission, 1/15 for domestic students. *Application fee:* $60. Electronic applications accepted. *Application Contact:* Marva Philip, Administrator, 410-516-7619, Fax: 410-516-4897, E-mail: mphilip@jhunix.hcf.jhu.edu. *Chair,* Ruth Leys, 410-516-7368, Fax: 410-516-4897, E-mail: leys@jhu.edu.

Institute for Public Policy Students: 61 full-time (43 women); includes 6 minority (3 African Americans, 1 American Indian/Alaska Native, 2 Asian Americans or Pacific Islanders), 9 international. Average age 25. 141 applicants, 50% accepted, 35 enrolled. *Faculty:* 8 full-time (4 women), 4 part-time/adjunct (2 women). Expenses: Contact institution. *Financial support:* Career-related internships or fieldwork, Federal Work-Study, and unspecified

The Johns Hopkins University (continued)

assistantships available. Financial award application deadline: 4/15; financial award applicants required to submit FAFSA. In 2006, 24 degrees awarded. Offers public policy (MA). *Application deadline:* For fall admission, 2/1 for domestic and international students. *Application fee:* $60. Electronic applications accepted. *Application Contact:* Jennifer Arndt, Assistant Director, 410-516-7174, Fax: 410-516-4624, E-mail: jarndt@jhu.edu. *Director,* Dr. Sandra J. Newman, 410-516-7180, Fax: 410-516-4624, E-mail: sjn@jhu.edu.

See Close-Up on page 933.

JOHNSON & WALES UNIVERSITY, Providence, RI 02903-3703

General Information Independent, coed, comprehensive institution. *Enrollment:* 10,310 graduate, professional, and undergraduate students; 805 full-time matriculated graduate/professional students (417 women), 156 part-time matriculated graduate/professional students (91 women). *Enrollment by degree level:* 9 first professional, 857 master's, 95 doctoral. *Graduate faculty:* 17 full-time (5 women), 14 part-time/adjunct (3 women). *Graduate housing:* Room and/or apartments available to single students; on-campus housing not available to married students. *Student services:* Campus employment opportunities, campus safety program, career counseling, free psychological counseling, international student services, low-cost health insurance. *Library facilities:* Johnson & Wales University Library plus 1 other. *Online resources:* library catalog, web page, access to other libraries' catalogs. *Collection:* 104,327 titles, 415 serial subscriptions, 3,687 audiovisual materials. *Research affiliation:* Consortium of Rhode Island Academic and Research Libraries, Association of Institutional Research.

Computer facilities: 400 computers available on campus for general student use. A campuswide network can be accessed from student residence rooms and from off campus. Internet access and online class registration are available. *Web address:* http://www.jwu.edu/.

General Application Contact: Dr. Allan G. Freedman, Director of Graduate Admissions, 401-598-1015, Fax: 401-598-1286, E-mail: gradadm@jwu.edu.

GRADUATE UNITS

The Alan Shawn Feinstein Graduate School Students: 805 full-time (417 women), 156 part-time (91 women); includes 36 African Americans, 17 Asian Americans or Pacific Islanders, 10 Hispanic Americans, 444 international. 613 applicants, 73% accepted, 309 enrolled. *Faculty:* 17 full-time (5 women), 14 part-time/adjunct (3 women). Expenses: Contact institution. *Financial support:* Career-related internships or fieldwork, institutionally sponsored loans, tuition waivers (partial), and unspecified assistantships available. Support available to part-time students. Financial award application deadline: 5/1. In 2006, 335 master's, 17 doctorates awarded. *Degree program information:* Part-time and evening/weekend programs available. Offers accounting (MBA); business education and secondary special education (MAT); educational leadership (Ed D); elementary education and special education (MAT); event leadership (MBA); financial management (MBA); food service education and secondary special education (MAT); international trade (MBA); marketing (MBA); organizational leadership (MBA). *Application deadline:* Applications are processed on a rolling basis. *Application fee:* $0. *Application Contact:* Dr. Allan G. Freedman, Director of Graduate Admissions, 401-598-1015, Fax: 401-598-1286, E-mail: gradadm@jwu.edu. *Dean,* Dr. Frank Pontarelli, 401-598-1333, Fax: 401-598-1125.

See Close-Up on page 935.

JOHNSON BIBLE COLLEGE, Knoxville, TN 37998-1001

General Information Independent-religious, coed, comprehensive institution. *Enrollment:* 17 full-time matriculated graduate/professional students (12 women), 114 part-time matriculated graduate/professional students (29 women). *Enrollment by degree level:* 131 master's. *Graduate faculty:* 5 full-time (1 woman), 12 part-time/adjunct (3 women). *Tuition:* Full-time $6,100. *Required fees:* $730. *Graduate housing:* Rooms and/or apartments available on a first-come, first-served basis to single students and available to married students. Housing application deadline: 8/1. *Student services:* Campus employment opportunities, career counseling, child daycare facilities, free psychological counseling, low-cost health insurance. *Library facilities:* Glass Memorial Library plus 1 other. *Online resources:* library catalog, web page. *Collection:* 104,808 titles, 397 serial subscriptions, 13,057 audiovisual materials.

Computer facilities: 34 computers available on campus for general student use. A campuswide network can be accessed from student residence rooms and from off campus. Internet access is available. *Web address:* http://www.jbc.edu/.

General Application Contact: Richard Beam, Vice President of Academics, 865-251-2358, Fax: 865-251-2337, E-mail: rbeam@jbc.edu.

GRADUATE UNITS

Department of Marriage and Family Therapy Students: 12 full-time (9 women), 9 part-time (8 women); includes 2 minority (1 African American, 1 Asian American or Pacific Islander). Average age 30. 10 applicants, 80% accepted, 8 enrolled. *Faculty:* 3 full-time (0 women), 1 part-time/adjunct (0 women). Expenses: Contact institution. *Financial support:* In 2006–07, 11 students received support. Scholarships/grants available. Financial award application deadline: 8/1; financial award applicants required to submit FAFSA. In 2006, 34 degrees awarded. Offers marriage and family therapy/professional counseling (MA). *Application deadline:* For fall admission, 3/1 for domestic students. *Application fee:* $50. *Application Contact:* Anita Rankin, Office Coordinator, 865-251-3402, Fax: 865-251-2435. *Chair,* Dr. Rick Townsend, 865-573-4517, Fax: 865-251-2435, E-mail: rtownsen@jbc.edu.

Program in New Testament Students: 2 full-time (0 women), 89 part-time (8 women). Average age 38. *Faculty:* 1 full-time (0 women), 5 part-time/adjunct (0 women). Expenses: Contact institution. *Financial support:* Career-related internships or fieldwork and institutionally sponsored loans available. Financial award application deadline: 8/1. In 2006, 6 degrees awarded. *Degree program information:* Part-time and evening/weekend programs available. Postbaccalaureate distance learning degree programs offered (no on-campus study). Offers preaching (MA); research (MA). *Application deadline:* For fall admission, 6/1 priority date for domestic students; for spring admission, 11/15 for domestic students. Applications are processed on a rolling basis. *Application fee:* $50. *Application Contact:* Marsha Ketchen, Application Contact, 800-669-7884, Fax: 865-251-2285, E-mail: mketchen@jbc.edu. *Director of Distance Learning,* Dr. John Ketchen, 800-669-7889, Fax: 865-251-2285, E-mail: jketchen@jbc.edu.

Teacher Education Program Students: 12 full-time (all women), 13 part-time (10 women), 1 international. Average age 30. 18 applicants, 100% accepted, 18 enrolled. *Faculty:* 1 (woman) full-time, 7 part-time/adjunct (3 women). Expenses: Contact institution. *Financial support:* Career-related internships or fieldwork available. Support available to part-time students. Financial award application deadline: 5/1; financial award applicants required to submit FAFSA. In 2006, 18 degrees awarded. *Degree program information:* Part-time programs available. Offers Bible and educational technology (MA); holistic education (MA). *Application deadline:* For fall admission, 7/1 priority date for domestic and international students; for spring admission, 12/1 priority date for domestic and international students. Applications are processed on a rolling basis. *Application fee:* $50. *Graduate Program Coordinator,* Dr. Chris Templar, 865-251-2348, Fax: 865-251-3438, E-mail: ctemplar@jbc.edu.

JOHNSON STATE COLLEGE, Johnson, VT 05656-9405

General Information State-supported, coed, comprehensive institution. *Enrollment:* 1,866 graduate, professional, and undergraduate students; 71 full-time matriculated graduate/professional students (51 women), 168 part-time matriculated graduate/professional students (112 women). *Enrollment by degree level:* 230 master's, 9 other advanced degrees. *Graduate faculty:* 13 full-time (8 women), 12 part-time/adjunct (10 women). *Graduate housing:* Rooms and/or apartments available on a first-come, first-served basis to single and married students. Housing application deadline: 6/1. *Student services:* Child daycare facilities, low-cost health insurance. *Library facilities:* Library and Learning Center. *Online resources:* library catalog, access to other libraries' catalogs. *Collection:* 100,053 titles, 522 serial subscriptions.

Computer facilities: 131 computers available on campus for general student use. A campuswide network can be accessed from student residence rooms and from off campus. Internet access is available. *Web address:* http://www.johnsonstatecollege.edu/.

General Application Contact: Catherine H. Higley, Administrative Assistant for Graduate Programs, 800-635-2356 Ext. 1244, Fax: 802-635-1248, E-mail: higleyc@jsc.vsc.edu.

GRADUATE UNITS

Graduate Program in Education Students: 5 full-time (all women), 67 part-time (51 women). *Faculty:* 5 full-time (3 women), 6 part-time/adjunct (5 women). Expenses: Contact institution. *Financial support:* Career-related internships or fieldwork, Federal Work-Study, institutionally sponsored loans, and unspecified assistantships available. Support available to part-time students. Financial award application deadline: 3/1; financial award applicants required to submit FAFSA. *Degree program information:* Part-time programs available. Offers applied behavior analysis (MA Ed); children's mental health (MA Ed); curriculum and instruction (MA Ed); developmental disabilities (MA Ed); education of the gifted (MA Ed); reading education (MA Ed); science education (MA Ed); secondary education (MA Ed, CAGS); special education (MA Ed); teaching all secondary students (MA Ed, CAGS). *Application deadline:* For fall admission, 7/15 priority date for domestic students, 4/15 priority date for international students; for spring admission, 11/1 priority date for domestic students, 8/15 priority date for international students. Applications are processed on a rolling basis. *Application fee:* $35. *Application Contact:* Catherine H. Higley, Administrative Assistant for Graduate Programs, 800-635-2356 Ext. 1244, Fax: 802-635-1248, E-mail: higleyc@jsc.vsc.edu.

Program in Counseling Students: 54 full-time (42 women), 49 part-time (39 women). *Faculty:* 5 full-time (3 women), 6 part-time/adjunct (5 women). Expenses: Contact institution. *Financial support:* Career-related internships or fieldwork, Federal Work-Study, institutionally sponsored loans, and unspecified assistantships available. Support available to part-time students. Financial award application deadline: 3/1; financial award applicants required to submit FAFSA. *Degree program information:* Part-time programs available. Offers counseling (MA). *Application deadline:* For fall admission, 4/1 priority date for domestic students, 4/15 priority date for international students; for spring admission, 11/1 priority date for domestic students, 8/15 priority date for international students. Applications are processed on a rolling basis. *Application fee:* $35. *Application Contact:* Catherine H. Higley, Administrative Assistant for Graduate Programs, 800-635-2356 Ext. 1244, Fax: 802-635-1248, E-mail: higleyc@jsc.vsc.edu.

Program in Fine Arts Students: 6 full-time (4 women), 20 part-time (18 women). *Faculty:* 3 full-time (2 women). Expenses: Contact institution. *Financial support:* Federal Work-Study and unspecified assistantships available. Support available to part-time students. Financial award application deadline: 3/1; financial award applicants required to submit FAFSA. *Degree program information:* Part-time programs available. Postbaccalaureate distance learning degree programs offered (minimal on-campus study). Offers drawing (MFA); painting (MFA); sculpture (MFA). *Application deadline:* For fall admission, 2/15 for domestic and international students. *Application fee:* $35. *Application Contact:* Catherine H. Higley, Administrative Assistant for Graduate Programs, 800-635-2356 Ext. 1244, Fax: 802-635-1248, E-mail: higleyc@jsc.vsc.edu.

JOINT MILITARY INTELLIGENCE COLLEGE, Washington, DC 20340-5100

General Information Federally supported, coed, graduate-only institution. *Graduate housing:* On-campus housing not available.

GRADUATE UNITS

School of Intelligence Studies *Degree program information:* Part-time and evening/weekend programs available. Offers intelligence studies (MSSI, Certificate). Open only to federal government employees.

JONES INTERNATIONAL UNIVERSITY, Centennial, CO 80112

General Information Proprietary, coed, comprehensive institution. *Graduate housing:* On-campus housing not available.

GRADUATE UNITS

Graduate School of Business Administration *Degree program information:* Part-time and evening/weekend programs available. Postbaccalaureate distance learning degree programs offered (no on-campus study). Offers accounting (MBA); business communication (MABC); entrepreneurship (MABC, MBA); finance (MBA); global enterprise management (MBA); health care management (MBA); information security management (MBA); information technology management (MBA); leadership and influence (MABC); leading the customer-driven organization (MABC); negotiation and conflict management (MBA); project management (MABC, MBA). Program only offered online. Electronic applications accepted.

Graduate School of Education *Degree program information:* Part-time and evening/weekend programs available. Postbaccalaureate distance learning degree programs offered (no on-campus study). Offers adult education (M Ed); corporate training and knowledge management (M Ed); curriculum and instruction (M Ed); e-learning technology and design (M Ed); educational leadership and administration (M Ed); educational leadership and administration: principal and administrator licensure (M Ed); elementary curriculum instruction and assessment (M Ed); higher education leadership and administration (M Ed); K-12 instructional technology (M Ed); K-12 instructional technology: teacher licensure (M Ed); secondary curriculum instruction and assessment (M Ed); technology and design (M Ed). Electronic applications accepted.

THE JUDGE ADVOCATE GENERAL'S SCHOOL, U.S. ARMY, Charlottesville, VA 22903-1781

General Information Federally supported, coed, primarily men, graduate-only institution. *Graduate housing:* On-campus housing not available.

GRADUATE UNITS

Graduate Programs Offers military law (LL M). Only active duty military lawyers attend this school.

JUDSON COLLEGE, Elgin, IL 60123-1498

General Information Independent-religious, coed, comprehensive institution.

GRADUATE UNITS

Graduate Programs

THE JUILLIARD SCHOOL, New York, NY 10023-6588

General Information Independent, coed, comprehensive institution. *Graduate housing:* Room and/or apartments available on a first-come, first-served basis to single students; on-campus housing not available to married students. Housing application deadline: 5/1.

GRADUATE UNITS

Program in Music Offers music (MM, DMA, Artist Diploma, Diploma). Electronic applications accepted.

KANSAS CITY UNIVERSITY OF MEDICINE AND BIOSCIENCES, Kansas City, MO 64106-1453

General Information Independent, coed, graduate-only institution. *Enrollment by degree level:* 960 first professional, 28 master's. *Graduate faculty:* 43 full-time (14 women), 2 part-time/adjunct (0 women). *Graduate housing:* On-campus housing not available. *Student services:* Campus employment opportunities, campus safety program, career counseling, free psychological counseling. *Library facilities:* Kansas City University of Medicine and Biosciences Library. *Online resources:* library catalog, web page, access to other libraries' catalogs. *Collection:* 82,302 titles, 892 serial subscriptions, 7,710 audiovisual materials. *Research affiliation:* Boehringer Ingelheim (HIV), Mylanta-Bertek (hypertension), Covance (hypertension), Novartis (COPD).

Computer facilities: 98 computers available on campus for general student use. A campuswide network can be accessed from student residence rooms. Internet access and online class registration are available. *Web address:* http://www.kcumb.edu/.

General Application Contact: Phil D. Byrne, Vice President of Admissions, 816-283-2392, Fax: 816-460-0506, E-mail: pbyrne@kcumb.edu.

GRADUATE UNITS

College of Osteopathic Medicine Students: 960 full-time (480 women). Average age 25. 2,800 applicants, 17% accepted, 268 enrolled. *Faculty:* 44 full-time (13 women), 13 part-time/adjunct (7 women). Expenses: Contact institution. *Financial support:* In 2006–07, 54 students received support, including 2 fellowships with full tuition reimbursements available; career-related internships or fieldwork, institutionally sponsored loans, and scholarships/grants also available. Financial award application deadline: 4/1; financial award applicants required to submit FAFSA. In 2006, 203 DOs awarded. Offers osteopathic medicine (DO). *Application deadline:* For fall admission, 4/1 for domestic students. Applications are processed on a rolling basis. *Application fee:* $50. *Application Contact:* Phil D. Byrne, Vice President of Admissions, 816-283-2392, Fax: 816-460-0506, E-mail: pbyrne@kcumb.edu. *Vice President for Academic Affairs/Dean,* Dr. Sandra K. Willsie, 816-283-2308, Fax: 816-283-2347, E-mail: swillsie@kcumb.edu.

KANSAS STATE UNIVERSITY, Manhattan, KS 66506

General Information State-supported, coed, university. CGS member. *Enrollment:* 23,141 graduate, professional, and undergraduate students; 2,120 full-time matriculated graduate/professional students (991 women), 1,672 part-time matriculated graduate/professional students (1,171 women). *Graduate faculty:* 906 full-time (231 women), 207 part-time/adjunct (48 women). Tuition, state resident: full-time $6,352; part-time $240 per credit hour. Tuition, nonresident: full-time $14,296; part-time $571 per credit hour. *Required fees:* $585. *Graduate housing:* Rooms and/or apartments available on a first-come, first-served basis to single and married students. Housing application deadline: 2/1. *Student services:* Campus employment opportunities, campus safety program, career counseling, child daycare facilities, disabled student services, exercise/wellness program, free psychological counseling, grant writing training, international student services, low-cost health insurance, multicultural affairs office, teacher training. *Library facilities:* Hale Library plus 3 others. *Online resources:* library catalog, web page, access to other libraries' catalogs. *Collection:* 1.6 million titles, 1,365 serial subscriptions. *Research affiliation:* U.S. Grain Marketing Research Laboratory, NASA-Research Center, Midwest Research Institute, VISTEON.

Computer facilities: 326 computers available on campus for general student use. A campuswide network can be accessed from student residence rooms and from off campus. Internet access and online class registration are available. *Web address:* http://www.ksu.edu/.

General Application Contact: Dr. James Guikema, Associate Dean, 785-532-7927, Fax: 785-532-2983, E-mail: guikema@gradresearch.grad.ksu.edu.

GRADUATE UNITS

College of Veterinary Medicine Students: 472 full-time (314 women), 20 part-time (12 women); includes 18 minority (1 African American, 2 American Indian/Alaska Native, 5 Asian Americans or Pacific Islanders, 10 Hispanic Americans), 30 international. *Faculty:* 62 full-time (15 women), 17 part-time/adjunct (6 women). Expenses: Contact institution. *Financial support:* Research assistantships, teaching assistantships, Federal Work-Study, institutionally sponsored loans, and scholarships/grants available. Financial award application deadline: 3/1; financial award applicants required to submit FAFSA. In 2006, 106 DVMs, 4 master's, 8 doctorates awarded. Offers anatomy and physiology (MS, PhD); biomedical science (MS); clinical sciences (MS); diagnostic medicine/pathobiology (MS, PhD); physiology (PhD); veterinary medicine (DVM, MS, PhD). *Application deadline:* For fall admission, 2/1 priority date for domestic students. Applications are processed on a rolling basis. *Application fee:* $30 ($55 for international students). Electronic applications accepted. *Application Contact:* Gail Eyestone, Administrative Assistant, 785-532-4005, Fax: 785-532-5884, E-mail: geyestone@vet.ksu.edu. *Dean,* Ralph Richardson, 785-532-4005, Fax: 785-532-5884, E-mail: dean@vet.ksu.edu.

Graduate School Students: 2,120 full-time (991 women), 1,672 part-time (1,171 women); includes 347 minority (170 African Americans, 45 American Indian/Alaska Native, 61 Asian Americans or Pacific Islanders, 71 Hispanic Americans), 703 international. Average age 26. 2,082 applicants, 53% accepted, 502 enrolled. *Faculty:* 904 full-time (229 women), 207 part-time/adjunct (48 women). Expenses: Contact institution. *Financial support:* In 2006–07, 654 research assistantships (averaging $14,974 per year), 467 teaching assistantships with full tuition reimbursements (averaging $10,752 per year) were awarded; fellowships, career-related internships or fieldwork, Federal Work-Study, institutionally sponsored loans, scholarships/grants, and tuition waivers (full and partial) also available. Support available to part-time students. Financial award application deadline: 3/1; financial award applicants required to submit FAFSA. In 2006, 724 master's, 160 doctorates awarded. *Degree program information:* Part-time and evening/weekend programs available. Postbaccalaureate distance learning degree programs offered (minimal on-campus study). Offers food science (MS, PhD); genetics (MS, PhD). *Application deadline:* Applications are processed on a rolling basis. *Application fee:* $30 ($55 for international students). Electronic applications accepted. *Application Contact:* Dr. Carol W Shanklin, Associate Dean, 785-532-6191, Fax: 785-532-5944, E-mail: shanklin@ksu.edu. *Dean,* Ron Trewyn, 785-532-5110.

College of Agriculture Students: 216 full-time (98 women), 109 part-time (49 women); includes 20 minority (10 African Americans, 2 American Indian/Alaska Native, 4 Asian Americans or Pacific Islanders, 4 Hispanic Americans), 92 international. 187 applicants, 50% accepted, 52 enrolled. *Faculty:* 168 full-time (24 women), 56 part-time/adjunct (6 women). Expenses: Contact institution. *Financial support:* In 2006–07, 205 research assistantships (averaging $15,691 per year), 25 teaching assistantships (averaging $9,657 per year) were awarded; fellowships, career-related internships or fieldwork, Federal Work-Study, institutionally sponsored loans, scholarships/grants, and tuition waivers (partial) also available. Support available to part-time students. Financial award application deadline: 3/1; financial award applicants required to submit FAFSA. In 2006, 42 master's, 36 doctorates awarded. *Degree program information:* Part-time programs available. Postbaccalaureate distance learning degree programs offered (minimal on-campus study). Offers agricultural economics (MAB, MS, PhD); agriculture (MAB, MS, PhD); animal breeding and genetics (MS, PhD); crop science (MS, PhD); entomology (MS, PhD); grain science and industry (MS, PhD); horticulture (MS, PhD); meat science (MS, PhD); monogastric nutrition (MS, PhD); physiology (MS, PhD); plant pathology (MS, PhD); range management (MS, PhD); ruminant nutrition (MS, PhD); soil science (MS, PhD); weed science (MS, PhD). *Application deadline:* For fall admission, 2/1 for domestic students; for spring admission, 10/1 for domestic students. *Application fee:* $30 ($55 for international students). Electronic applications accepted. *Dean,* Fred Cholick, 785-532-7137, Fax: 785-532-6563, E-mail: fcholick@ksu.edu.

College of Architecture, Planning and Design Students: 93 full-time (33 women), 8 part-time (5 women); includes 4 minority (3 African Americans, 1 American Indian/Alaska Native), 10 international. 40 applicants, 83% accepted, 28 enrolled. *Faculty:* 46 full-time (12 women), 4 part-time/adjunct (3 women). Expenses: Contact institution. *Financial support:* In 2006–07, 2 research assistantships (averaging $5,969 per year), 13 teaching assistantships with full tuition reimbursements (averaging $8,077 per year) were awarded; fellowships, career-related internships or fieldwork, Federal Work-Study, institutionally sponsored loans, and scholarships/grants also available. Support available to part-time students. Financial award application deadline: 3/1; financial award applicants required to submit FAFSA. In 2006, 18 degrees awarded. *Degree program information:* Part-time and evening/weekend programs available. Postbaccalaureate distance learning degree programs offered (minimal on-campus study). Offers architecture (M Arch); architecture, planning and design (M Arch, MLA, MRCP); landscape architecture (MLA); regional and community planning (MRCP). *Application deadline:* For fall admission, 2/1 for domestic students, 2/1 priority date for international students; for spring admission, 8/1 for domestic students, 8/1 priority date for international students. Applications are processed on a rolling basis. *Application fee:* $70 ($80 for international students). Electronic applications accepted. *Dean,* Dennis Law, 785-532-5950, Fax: 785-532-6722, E-mail: delaw@ksu.edu.

College of Arts and Sciences Students: 739 full-time (334 women), 164 part-time (77 women); includes 69 minority (23 African Americans, 5 American Indian/Alaska Native, 26 Asian Americans or Pacific Islanders, 15 Hispanic Americans), 269 international. 795 applicants, 50% accepted, 257 enrolled. *Faculty:* 326 full-time (84 women), 50 part-time/adjunct (12 women). Expenses: Contact institution. *Financial support:* In 2006–07, 170 research assistantships (averaging $14,865 per year), 360 teaching assistantships with full tuition reimbursements (averaging $10,926 per year) were awarded; fellowships, career-related internships or fieldwork, Federal Work-Study, institutionally sponsored loans, scholarships/grants, and tuition waivers also available. Support available to part-time students. Financial award application deadline: 3/1; financial award applicants required to submit FAFSA. In 2006, 204 master's, 42 doctorates awarded. *Degree program information:* Part-time programs available. Postbaccalaureate distance learning degree programs offered (minimal on-campus study). Offers analytical chemistry (MS); art (MFA); arts and sciences (MA, MFA, MM, MPA, MS, PhD); biochemistry (MS, PhD); biological chemistry (MS); biology (MS, PhD); chemistry (PhD); economics (MA, PhD); English (MA); French (MA); geography (MA, PhD); geology (MS); German (MA); history (MA, PhD); inorganic chemistry (MS); international service (MA); kinesiology (MS); mass communications (MS); materials chemistry (MS); mathematics (MS, PhD); microbiology (PhD); music education (MM); music education/band conducting (MM); music history and literature (MM); organic chemistry (MS); performance (MM); performance with pedagogy emphasis (MM); physical chemistry (MS); physics (MS, PhD); political science (MA); psychology (MS, PhD); public administration (MPA); rhetoric/communication (MA); sociology (MA, PhD); Spanish (MA); statistics (MS, PhD); theatre (MA); theory and composition (MM). *Application deadline:* Applications are processed on a rolling basis. *Application fee:* $30 ($55 for international students). Electronic applications accepted. *Dean,* Stephen White, 785-532-6900, Fax: 785-532-7004, E-mail: sewhite@ksu.edu.

College of Business Administration Students: 128 full-time (55 women), 19 part-time (16 women); includes 16 minority (9 African Americans, 1 American Indian/Alaska Native, 6 Asian Americans or Pacific Islanders), 30 international. 57 applicants, 82% accepted, 40 enrolled. *Faculty:* 31 full-time (4 women). Expenses: Contact institution. *Financial support:* In 2006–07, 7 research assistantships with partial tuition reimbursements (averaging $3,780 per year), 16 teaching assistantships with partial tuition reimbursements (averaging $5,105 per year) were awarded; fellowships, Federal Work-Study, institutionally sponsored loans, and scholarships/grants also available. Support available to part-time students. Financial award application deadline: 3/1; financial award applicants required to submit FAFSA. In 2006, 79 degrees awarded. *Degree program information:* Part-time programs available. Offers accounting (M Acc); business administration (M Acc, MBA). *Application deadline:* For fall admission, 7/1 for domestic students, 2/1 for international students; for spring admission, 12/1 for domestic students, 8/1 for international students. Applications are processed on a rolling basis. *Application fee:* $50 ($60 for international students). *Application Contact:* Lynn S. Waugh, Information Contact, 785-532-7190, Fax: 785-532-7024, E-mail: lwaugh@ksu.edu. *Interim Dean,* Yar M. Ebadi, 785-532-7227, Fax: 785-532-7024, E-mail: ebadi@ksu.edu.

College of Education Students: 278 full-time (189 women), 401 part-time (293 women); includes 70 minority (32 African Americans, 4 American Indian/Alaska Native, 11 Asian Americans or Pacific Islanders, 23 Hispanic Americans), 21 international. Average age 25. 155 applicants, 68% accepted, 82 enrolled. *Faculty:* 58 full-time (26 women), 10 part-time/adjunct (2 women). Expenses: Contact institution. *Financial support:* In 2006–07, 19 research assistantships (averaging $11,223 per year), 16 teaching assistantships with full tuition reimbursements (averaging $12,145 per year) were awarded; fellowships, career-related internships or fieldwork, Federal Work-Study, institutionally sponsored loans, and scholarships/grants also available. Support available to part-time students. Financial award application deadline: 3/1; financial award applicants required to submit FAFSA. In 2006, 135 master's, 34 doctorates awarded. *Degree program information:* Part-time and evening/weekend programs available. Postbaccalaureate distance learning degree programs offered. Offers adult and continuing education (MS, Ed D); counseling and student development-college student personnel work (MS); counseling and student development-school counseling (MS); counselor education and supervisors (PhD); curriculum and instruction (MS, Ed D, PhD); education (MS, Ed D, PhD); educational administration (MS, Ed D); school counseling (Ed D); special education (MS, Ed D); student affairs in higher education (PhD). *Application deadline:* For fall admission, 3/1 priority date for domestic students, 2/1 priority date for international students; for spring admission, 10/1 priority date for domestic students, 8/1 priority date for international students. Applications are processed on a rolling basis. *Application fee:* $30 ($55 for international students). Electronic applications accepted. *Application Contact:* Dr. Paul R. Burden, Head, 785-532-5595, Fax: 785-532-7304, E-mail: burden@ksu.edu. *Dean,* Michael Holen, 785-532-5525, Fax: 785-532-7304, E-mail: mholen@ksu.edu.

College of Engineering Students: 262 full-time (55 women), 113 part-time (19 women); includes 18 minority (6 African Americans, 1 American Indian/Alaska Native, 7 Asian Americans or Pacific Islanders, 4 Hispanic Americans), 189 international. 500 applicants, 57% accepted, 125 enrolled. *Faculty:* 107 full-time (9 women), 31 part-time/adjunct (3 women). Expenses: Contact institution. *Financial support:* In 2006–07, 140 research assistantships (averaging $14,807 per year), 30 teaching assistantships (averaging $13,010 per year) were awarded; fellowships, career-related internships or fieldwork, Federal Work-Study, institutionally sponsored loans, and scholarships/grants also available. Support available to part-time students. Financial award application deadline: 3/1; financial award applicants required to submit FAFSA. In 2006, 114 master's, 16 doctorates awarded. *Degree program information:* Part-time programs available. Postbaccalaureate distance learning degree programs offered (minimal on-campus study). Offers architectural engineering (MS); bioengineering (MS, PhD); biological and agricultural engineering (MS); chemical engineering (MS); civil engineering (MS); communications systems (MS, PhD); computer engineering (MS, PhD); computer science (MS, PhD); control systems (MS, PhD); electromagnetics (MS, PhD); engineering (PhD); engineering management (MEM); industrial engineering (MS, PhD); instrumentation (MS, PhD); mechanical engineering (MS); nuclear engineering (MS); operations research (MS); power systems (MS, PhD); signal processing (MS, PhD); software engineering (MSE); solid-state electronics (MS, PhD). *Application deadline:* For fall admission, 2/1 priority date for domestic and international students; for spring admission, 8/1 priority date for domestic and international students. Applications are processed on a rolling basis. *Application fee:* $30 ($55 for international students). Electronic applications accepted. *Application Contact:* Maureen Lockhart, Administrative Assistant, 785-532-5441, Fax: 785-532-7810, E-mail: maureen@ksu.edu. *Dean,* Richard Gallagher, 785-532-5590, Fax: 785-532-7810, E-mail: rrgllghr@ksu.edu.

College of Human Ecology Students: 240 full-time (165 women), 83 part-time (60 women); includes 48 minority (33 African Americans, 3 American Indian/Alaska Native, 7 Asian Americans or Pacific Islanders, 5 Hispanic Americans), 35 international. 239 applicants, 62% accepted, 72 enrolled. *Faculty:* 46 full-time (30 women), 15 part-time/adjunct (8 women). Expenses: Contact institution. *Financial support:* In 2006–07, 27 research assistantships (averaging $13,778 per year), 11 teaching assistantships with full and partial tuition reimbursements (averaging $10,082 per year) were awarded; fellowships with partial tuition reimbursements, career-related internships or fieldwork, Federal Work-Study, institutionally sponsored loans, scholarships/grants, and tuition waivers (full) also available. Support available to part-time students. Financial award application deadline: 3/1; financial award applicants required to submit FAFSA. In 2006, 58 master's, 18 doctorates awarded. *Degree program information:* Part-time programs available. Postbaccalaureate distance learning degree programs offered. Offers apparel and textiles (MS, PhD); dietetics and administration (MS); family life education and consultation (PhD); family studies and human services (MS); food science (MS, PhD); food service and hospitality management (MS); food service, hospitality management, and administrative dietetics (PhD); human ecology (MS, PhD); human nutrition (MS, PhD); institutional management (PhD); lifespan and human development (PhD); marriage and family therapy (PhD); public health (MS). *Application deadline:* For fall admission, 2/1 priority date for domestic and international students; for spring admission, 9/1 for domestic students, 9/1 priority date for international students. *Application fee:* $30 ($55 for international students). Electronic applications accepted. *Application Contact:* Patricia Haas, Administrative Specialist, 785-532-5500, Fax: 785-

Kansas State University (continued)

532-5504, E-mail: haas@humec.ksu.edu. *Interim Dean,* Dr. Virginia Moxley, 785-532-5500, Fax: 785-532-5504, E-mail: moxley@ksu.edu.

See Close-Up on page 937.

KANSAS WESLEYAN UNIVERSITY, Salina, KS 67401-6196

General Information Independent-religious, coed, comprehensive institution. *Graduate housing:* Rooms and/or apartments available to single and married students.

GRADUATE UNITS

Program in Business Administration *Degree program information:* Part-time and evening/weekend programs available. Offers business administration (MBA).

KEAN UNIVERSITY, Union, NJ 07083

General Information State-supported, coed, comprehensive institution. CGS member. *Enrollment:* 13,050 graduate, professional, and undergraduate students; 626 full-time matriculated graduate/professional students (483 women), 1,592 part-time matriculated graduate/professional students (1,229 women). *Enrollment by degree level:* 2,152 master's, 66 other advanced degrees. *Graduate faculty:* 215 full-time (110 women). Tuition, state resident: full-time $8,856; part-time $369 per credit. Tuition, nonresident: full-time $11,256; part-time $469 per credit. *Graduate housing:* On-campus housing not available. *Student services:* Campus employment opportunities, campus safety program, career counseling, child daycare facilities, disabled student services, exercise/wellness program, free psychological counseling, grant writing training, international student services, low-cost health insurance, multicultural affairs office, teacher training, writing training. *Library facilities:* Nancy Thompson Library. *Online resources:* library catalog, web page. *Collection:* 321,261 titles, 2,790 serial subscriptions, 6,651 audiovisual materials. *Research affiliation:* National Bureau of Economic Research (Alcoholic Advertising and Youth: An Econometric Approach), New Jersey Institute of Technology (Partitioning to Support Auditing and Extending the UMLS), Shodor Foundation (Intelligent Internet Search Engines for Science Research and Education), University of Medicine and Dentistry of New Jersey (Biochemistry, Molecular Biology and Neuroscience), Institute of Vertebrate Paleontology and Paleoanthropology, China (Paleoanthropology), Robert Wood Johnson Foundation (The Effect of Tobacco Control Policy).

Computer facilities: Computer purchase and lease plans are available. 2,000 computers available on campus for general student use. A campuswide network can be accessed from student residence rooms and from off campus. Internet access and online class registration are available. *Web address:* http://www.kean.edu/.

General Application Contact: Joanne Morris, Director of Graduate Admissions, 908-737-3355, Fax: 908-737-3354, E-mail: grad-adm@kean.edu.

GRADUATE UNITS

College of Business and Public Administration Students: 107 full-time (68 women), 160 part-time (94 women); includes 155 minority (93 African Americans, 28 Asian Americans or Pacific Islanders, 34 Hispanic Americans), 26 international. Average age 32. 109 applicants, 84% accepted, 61 enrolled. *Faculty:* 16 full-time (6 women). Expenses: Contact institution. *Financial support:* In 2006–07, 23 research assistantships with full tuition reimbursements (averaging $3,217 per year) were awarded; career-related internships or fieldwork, institutionally sponsored loans, and unspecified assistantships also available. In 2006, 92 degrees awarded. *Degree program information:* Part-time and evening/weekend programs available. Offers accounting (MS); business and public administration (MPA, MS); criminal justice (MPA); environmental management (MPA); health services administration (MPA); non-profit management (MPA); public administration (MPA). *Application deadline:* For fall admission, 5/1 for domestic students; for spring admission, 11/1 for domestic students. *Application fee:* $60 ($150 for international students). Electronic applications accepted. *Application Contact:* Joanne Morris, Director of Graduate Admissions, 908-737-3355, Fax: 908-737-3354, E-mail: grad-adm@kean.edu. *Dean,* Dr. Alfred Ntoko, 908-737-4120, Fax: 908-737-4125, E-mail: antoko@kean.edu.

College of Education Students: 203 full-time (170 women), 1,123 part-time (924 women); includes 330 minority (147 African Americans, 29 Asian Americans or Pacific Islanders, 154 Hispanic Americans), 7 international. Average age 33. 719 applicants, 80% accepted, 407 enrolled. *Faculty:* 84 full-time (55 women). Expenses: Contact institution. *Financial support:* In 2006–07, 34 research assistantships with full tuition reimbursements (averaging $3,217 per year) were awarded; career-related internships or fieldwork and unspecified assistantships also available. In 2006, 390 degrees awarded. *Degree program information:* Part-time programs available. Offers administration in early childhood and family studies (MA); adult literacy (MA); advanced curriculum and teaching (MA); alcohol and drug abuse counseling (MA); basic skills (MA); bilingual/bicultural education (MA); business and industry counseling (MA, PMC); classroom instruction (MA); community/agency counseling (MA); developmental disabilities (MA); early childhood education (MA); earth science (MA); education (MA, MS, PMC); education for family living (MA); educational media specialist (MA); educational technology (MA); elementary education (MA); emotionally disturbed and socially maladjusted (MA); exercise science (MS); learning disabilities (MA); mathematics/science/computer education (MA); pre-school handicapped (MA); principals and supervisors (MA); reading specialization (MA); school business administration (MA); school counseling (MA); speech language pathology (MA); supervisors (MA); teaching (MA); teaching English as a second language (MA). *Application deadline:* For fall admission, 5/1 for domestic students; for spring admission, 11/1 for domestic students. *Application fee:* $60 ($150 for international students). Electronic applications accepted. *Application Contact:* Joanne Morris, Director of Graduate Admissions, 908-737-3355, Fax: 908-737-3354, E-mail: grad-adm@kean.edu. *Dean,* Dr. Frank Esposito, 908-737-3750, Fax: 908-737-3760, E-mail: fesposito@kean.edu.

College of Humanities and Social Sciences Students: 164 full-time (131 women), 81 part-time (63 women); includes 83 minority (53 African Americans, 5 Asian Americans or Pacific Islanders, 25 Hispanic Americans), 6 international. Average age 29. 302 applicants, 70% accepted, 96 enrolled. *Faculty:* 43 full-time (22 women). Expenses: Contact institution. *Financial support:* In 2006–07, 20 research assistantships with full tuition reimbursements (averaging $3,217 per year) were awarded; career-related internships or fieldwork, institutionally sponsored loans, scholarships/grants, and unspecified assistantships also available. In 2006, 103 master's, 15 other advanced degrees awarded. *Degree program information:* Part-time and evening/weekend programs available. Offers advanced standing (MSW); behavioral sciences (MA); business and industry counseling (MA); communication studies (MA); educational psychology (MA); human behavior and organizational psychology (MA); humanities and social sciences (MA, MSW, Diploma); marriage and family therapy (Diploma); political science (MA); psychological services (MA); school psychology (Diploma); social work (MSW). *Application deadline:* For fall admission, 5/1 for domestic students; for spring admission, 11/1 for domestic students. *Application fee:* $60 ($150 for international students). Electronic applications accepted. *Application Contact:* Joanne Morris, Director of Graduate Admissions, 908-737-3355, Fax: 908-737-3354, E-mail: grad-adm@kean.edu. *Dean,* Dr. Kenneth Dollarhide, 908-737-0430, Fax: 908-737-3914, E-mail: kdollarh@kean.edu.

College of Natural, Applied and Health Sciences Students: 70 full-time (61 women), 95 part-time (74 women); includes 73 minority (44 African Americans, 18 Asian Americans or Pacific Islanders, 11 Hispanic Americans), 2 international. Average age 36. 128 applicants, 69% accepted, 49 enrolled. *Faculty:* 34 full-time (16 women). Expenses: Contact institution. *Financial support:* In 2006–07, 14 research assistantships with full tuition reimbursements (averaging $3,217 per year) were awarded; unspecified assistantships also available. In 2006, 48 degrees awarded. *Degree program information:* Part-time and evening/weekend programs available. Offers clinical management (MSN); community health (MSN); computer applications (MA); computing, statistics and mathematics (MS); natural, applied and health sciences (MA, MS, MSN); nursing and public administration); occupational therapy (MS); supervision of math education (MA); teaching of math (MA). *Application deadline:* For fall admission, 5/1 for domestic students; for spring admission, 11/1 for domestic students. *Application fee:* $60 ($150 for international students). Electronic applications accepted. *Application Contact:* Joanne Morris, Director of Graduate Admissions, 908-737-3355, Fax: 908-737-3354, E-mail: grad-adm@kean.edu. *Dean,* Dr. Xiaobo Yu, 908-737-3600, Fax: 908-737-3606, E-mail: xyu@kean.edu.

Nathan Weiss Graduate College Students: 45 full-time (27 women), 57 part-time (31 women); includes 41 minority (15 African Americans, 8 Asian Americans or Pacific Islanders, 18 Hispanic Americans), 20 international. Average age 32. 58 applicants, 95% accepted, 26 enrolled. *Faculty:* 8 full-time (2 women). Expenses: Contact institution. *Financial support:* In 2006–07, 23 research assistantships with full tuition reimbursements (averaging $3,217 per year) were awarded. In 2006, 25 degrees awarded. *Degree program information:* Part-time and evening/weekend programs available. Offers biotechnology (MS); global management (MBA); holocaust and genocide studies (MA); management information systems (MSMIS). *Application deadline:* For fall admission, 5/1 for domestic students. *Application fee:* $60 ($150 for international students). Electronic applications accepted. *Application Contact:* Joanne Morris, Director of Graduate Admissions, 908-737-3355, Fax: 908-737-3354, E-mail: grad-adm@kean.edu. *Dean,* Dr. Kristie Reilly, 908-737-3440, Fax: 908-737-3444, E-mail: kreilly@kean.edu.

School of Visual and Performing Arts Students: 37 full-time (26 women), 76 part-time (43 women); includes 31 minority (16 African Americans, 4 Asian Americans or Pacific Islanders, 11 Hispanic Americans), 6 international. Average age 35. 51 applicants, 88% accepted, 30 enrolled. *Faculty:* 30 full-time (9 women). Expenses: Contact institution. *Financial support:* In 2006–07, 6 research assistantships with full tuition reimbursements (averaging $3,217 per year) were awarded. In 2006, 29 degrees awarded. Offers certification (MA); graphic communication technology management (MS); liberal studies (MA); studio/research (MA); supervision (MA); visual and performing arts (MA, MS). *Application deadline:* For fall admission, 5/1 for domestic students; for spring admission, 11/1 for domestic students. *Application fee:* $60 ($150 for international students). *Application Contact:* Joanne Morris, Director of Graduate Admissions, 908-737-3355, Fax: 908-737-3354, E-mail: grad-adm@kean.edu. *Dean,* Dr. Carole Shaffer-Koros, 908-737-4376, Fax: 908-737-4377, E-mail: ckoros@kean.edu.

See Close-Up on page 939.

KECK GRADUATE INSTITUTE OF APPLIED LIFE SCIENCES, Claremont, CA 91711

General Information Independent, coed, graduate-only institution.

GRADUATE UNITS

Bioscience Program Offers bioscience (MBS). Electronic applications accepted.

KEENE STATE COLLEGE, Keene, NH 03435

General Information State-supported, coed, comprehensive institution. *Enrollment:* 4,940 graduate, professional, and undergraduate students; 47 full-time matriculated graduate/professional students (35 women), 84 part-time matriculated graduate/professional students (61 women). *Enrollment by degree level:* 131 master's. *Graduate faculty:* 10 full-time (6 women), 7 part-time/adjunct (5 women). *Tuition, area resident:* Part-time $265 per credit. Tuition, state resident: full-time $5,780; part-time $290 per credit. Tuition, nonresident: full-time $13,050. *Required fees:* $80 per credit. Part-time tuition and fees vary according to course load. *Graduate housing:* Rooms and/or apartments available on a first-come, first-served basis to single and married students. Typical cost: $4,700 per year ($7,026 including board) for single students; $5,734 per year for married students. Room and board charges vary according to board plan and housing facility selected. Housing application deadline: 5/1. *Student services:* Campus employment opportunities, campus safety program, career counseling, child daycare facilities, disabled student services, exercise/wellness program, free psychological counseling, international student services, low-cost health insurance, multicultural affairs office, teacher training, writing training. *Library facilities:* Mason Library. *Online resources:* library catalog, web page, access to other libraries' catalogs. *Collection:* 324,176 titles, 1,486 serial subscriptions, 8,160 audiovisual materials.

Computer facilities: Computer purchase and lease plans are available. 500 computers available on campus for general student use. A campuswide network can be accessed from student residence rooms and from off campus. Internet access, e-mail, personal Web pages are available. *Web address:* http://www.keene.edu/.

General Application Contact: Peggy Richmond, Director of Admissions, 603-358-2276, Fax: 603-358-2767, E-mail: admissions@keene.edu.

GRADUATE UNITS

Division of Graduate and Professional Studies Expenses: Contact institution. *Financial support:* Research assistantships, career-related internships or fieldwork, Federal Work-Study, institutionally sponsored loans, and unspecified assistantships available. Support available to part-time students. Financial award application deadline: 3/1; financial award applicants required to submit FAFSA. In 2006, 48 master's, 13 other advanced degrees awarded. *Degree program information:* Part-time and evening/weekend programs available. Offers curriculum and instruction (M Ed); educational administration (M Ed); educational leadership (PMC); school counselor (M Ed, PMC); special education (M Ed, PMC). *Application Contact:* Peggy Richmond, Director of Admissions, 603-358-2276, Fax: 603-358-2767, E-mail: admissions@keene.edu. *Dean,* Dr. John Couture, 603-358-2220, E-mail: jcouture@keene.edu.

KEHILATH YAKOV RABBINICAL SEMINARY, Brooklyn, NY 11211-7207

General Information Independent-religious, men only, comprehensive institution.

GRADUATE UNITS

Graduate Programs

KELLER GRADUATE SCHOOL OF MANAGEMENT, Long Island City, NY 11101-3051

General Information Proprietary, coed, graduate-only institution.

GRADUATE UNITS

Keller Graduate School of Management Offers management (MBA, MISM).

KELLER GRADUATE SCHOOL OF MANAGEMENT, New York, NY 10036-4041

General Information Proprietary, coed, graduate-only institution.

GRADUATE UNITS

Keller Graduate School of Management Offers management (MBA, MISM).

KENNESAW STATE UNIVERSITY, Kennesaw, GA 30144-5591

General Information State-supported, coed, comprehensive institution. CGS member. *Enrollment:* 19,854 graduate, professional, and undergraduate students; 625 full-time matriculated graduate/professional students (420 women), 1,283 part-time matriculated graduate/professional students (735 women). *Enrollment by degree level:* 1,908 master's. *Graduate faculty:* 221 full-time (88 women), 34 part-time/adjunct (12 women). Tuition, state resident: full-time $3,044; part-time $127 per semester hour. Tuition, nonresident: full-time $12,172; part-time $508 per semester hour. *Required fees:* $353 per semester. Full-time tuition and fees vary according to campus/location and program. *Graduate housing:* Room and/or apartments available on a first-come, first-served basis to single students; on-campus housing not available to married students. *Student services:* Campus employment opportunities, campus safety program, career counseling, disabled student services, exercise/wellness program, free psychological counseling, international student services, low-cost health insurance, multicultural affairs office, teacher training, writing training. *Library facilities:* Horace W. Sturgis Library. *Online resources:* library catalog, web page, access to other libraries' catalogs. *Collection:* 630,614 titles, 4,410 serial subscriptions, 10,000 audiovisual materials.

Computer facilities: 1,087 computers available on campus for general student use. A campuswide network can be accessed from student residence rooms and from off campus. Internet access and online class registration are available. *Web address:* http://www.kennesaw.edu/.

General Application Contact: Vilma Marquez, Admissions Counselor, 770-420-4377, Fax: 770-423-6885, E-mail: ksugrad@kennesaw.edu.

GRADUATE UNITS

College of Health and Human Services Students: 96 full-time (92 women), 13 part-time (11 women); includes 28 minority (23 African Americans, 3 Asian Americans or Pacific Islanders, 2 Hispanic Americans), 1 international. Average age 36. 169 applicants, 53% accepted, 78 enrolled. *Faculty:* 7 full-time (6 women), 15 part-time/adjunct (10 women). Expenses: Contact institution. *Financial support:* In 2006–07, 2 research assistantships with full tuition reimbursements (averaging $15,000 per year) were awarded; Federal Work-Study also available. Support available to part-time students. Financial award application deadline: 6/15; financial award applicants required to submit FAFSA. In 2006, 42 degrees awarded. *Degree program information:* Part-time and evening/weekend programs available. Offers advanced care management and leadership (MSN); health and human services (MSN, MSW); primary care nurse practitioner (MSN); social work (MSW). *Application deadline:* For fall admission, 5/31 for domestic students. *Application fee:* $50. Electronic applications accepted. *Application Contact:* Vilma Marquez, Admissions Counselor, 770-420-4377, Fax: 770-423-6885, E-mail: ksugrad@kennesaw.edu. *Dean,* Dr. Richard Sowell, 770-423-6565, Fax: 770-423-6627, E-mail: rsowell@kennesaw.edu.

College of Humanities and Social Sciences Students: 106 full-time (80 women), 114 part-time (83 women); includes 50 minority (47 African Americans, 1 Asian American or Pacific Islander, 2 Hispanic Americans), 10 international. Average age 33. 117 applicants, 85% accepted, 75 enrolled. *Faculty:* 35 full-time (19 women), 6 part-time/adjunct (2 women). Expenses: Contact institution. *Financial support:* In 2006–07, 2 research assistantships with full tuition reimbursements (averaging $15,000 per year) were awarded; Federal Work-Study and unspecified assistantships also available. Support available to part-time students. Financial award application deadline: 6/15; financial award applicants required to submit FAFSA. In 2006, 123 degrees awarded. *Degree program information:* Part-time and evening/weekend programs available. Offers conflict management (MSCM); humanities and social sciences (MAPW, MPA, MSCM); professional writing (MAPW); public administration (MPA). *Application deadline:* For fall admission, 7/15 priority date for domestic students; for spring admission, 10/15 priority date for domestic students. Applications are processed on a rolling basis. *Application fee:* $50. Electronic applications accepted. *Application Contact:* Vilma Marquez, Admissions Counselor, 770-420-4377, Fax: 770-423-6885, E-mail: ksugrad@kennesaw.edu. *Dean,* Dr. Richard Vengroff, 770-423-6124, E-mail: rvengrof@kennesaw.edu.

College of Science and Mathematics Students: 44 full-time (12 women), 105 part-time (33 women); includes 32 minority (17 African Americans, 11 Asian Americans or Pacific Islanders, 4 Hispanic Americans), 26 international. Average age 36. 93 applicants, 84% accepted, 58 enrolled. *Faculty:* 22 full-time (3 women), 1 (woman) part-time/adjunct. Expenses: Contact institution. *Financial support:* In 2006–07, 2 research assistantships with full tuition reimbursements (averaging $15,000 per year) were awarded; Federal Work-Study and unspecified assistantships also available. Support available to part-time students. Financial award application deadline: 6/15; financial award applicants required to submit FAFSA. In 2006, 54 degrees awarded. *Degree program information:* Part-time programs available. Offers applied computer science (MSaCS); applied statistics (MSAS); information systems (MSIS); science and mathematics (MSAS, MSIS, MSaCS). *Application deadline:* For fall admission, 7/15 for domestic students; for spring admission, 10/15 for domestic students. Applications are processed on a rolling basis. *Application fee:* $50. Electronic applications accepted. *Application Contact:* Vilma Marquez, Admissions Counselor, 770-420-4377, Fax: 770-423-6885, E-mail: ksugrad@kennesaw.edu. *Dean,* Dr. Laurence I. Peterson, 770-423-6160, Fax: 770-423-6530, E-mail: lpeterso@kennesaw.edu.

Leland and Clarice C. Bagwell College of Education Students: 175 full-time (160 women), 505 part-time (383 women); includes 103 minority (88 African Americans, 5 Asian Americans or Pacific Islanders, 10 Hispanic Americans), 22 international. Average age 35. 174 applicants, 97% accepted, 149 enrolled. *Faculty:* 60 full-time (38 women), 12 part-time/adjunct (4 women). Expenses: Contact institution. *Financial support:* Federal Work-Study available. Support available to part-time students. Financial award application deadline: 6/15; financial award applicants required to submit FAFSA. In 2006, 283 degrees awarded. *Degree program information:* Part-time programs available. Offers adolescent education (M Ed); early childhood education (M Ed); education (M Ed, MAT, Ed D, Ed S); educational leadership (M Ed); leadership for learning (Ed D, Ed S); special education (M Ed); teaching (MAT). *Application deadline:* For fall admission, 7/15 priority date for domestic students; for spring admission, 10/15 priority date for domestic students. *Application fee:* $50. Electronic applications accepted. *Application Contact:* Alisha O'Brien, Administrative Coordinator, 770-423-6043, Fax: 770-420-4435, E-mail: aobrien@kennesaw.edu. *Interim Dean,* Dr. Frank Butler, 770-423-6117, Fax: 770-423-6567.

Michael J. Coles College of Business Students: 204 full-time (76 women), 546 part-time (225 women); includes 156 minority (84 African Americans, 5 American Indian/Alaska Native, 49 Asian Americans or Pacific Islanders, 18 Hispanic Americans), 76 international. Average age 33. 365 applicants, 81% accepted, 251 enrolled. *Faculty:* 62 full-time (21 women), 9 part-time/adjunct (2 women). Expenses: Contact institution. *Financial support:* Federal Work-Study available. Support available to part-time students. Financial award application deadline: 6/15; financial award applicants required to submit FAFSA. In 2006, 217 degrees awarded. *Degree program information:* Part-time and evening/weekend programs available. Offers accounting (M Acc); business (M Acc, MBA); business administration (MBA). *Application deadline:* For fall admission, 7/15 priority date for domestic students; for spring admission, 10/15 priority date for domestic students. Applications are processed on a rolling basis. *Application fee:* $50. Electronic applications accepted. *Application Contact:* Vilma Marquez, Admissions Counselor, 770-420-4377, Fax: 770-423-6885, E-mail: ksugrad@kennesaw.edu. *Dean,* Dr. Timothy Mescon, 770-423-6425, Fax: 770-423-6141, E-mail: tmescon@coles2.kennesaw.edu.

KENRICK-GLENNON SEMINARY, St. Louis, MO 63119-4330

General Information Independent-religious, men only, graduate-only institution. *Graduate housing:* Room and/or apartments available to single students; on-campus housing not available to married students.

GRADUATE UNITS

Graduate and Professional Programs Offers theology (M Div, MA, Certificate).

KENT STATE UNIVERSITY, Kent, OH 44242-0001

General Information State-supported, coed, university. CGS member. *Graduate housing:* Rooms and/or apartments available on a first-come, first-served basis to single students and available to married students.

GRADUATE UNITS

College of Architecture and Environmental Design *Degree program information:* Part-time programs available. Offers architecture (M Arch); architecture and environmental design (Certificate). Electronic applications accepted.

College of Arts and Sciences *Degree program information:* Part-time programs available. Offers analytical chemistry (MS, PhD); anthropology (MA); applied mathematics (MA, MS, PhD); arts and sciences (MA, MFA, MLS, MPA, MS, PhD); biochemistry (MS, PhD); botany (MS); chemical physics (MS, PhD); chemistry (MA, MS, PhD); clinical psychology (MA, PhD); comparative literature (MA); computer science (MA, MS, PhD); creative writing (MFA); ecology (MS, PhD); English for teachers (MA); experimental psychology (MA, PhD); French (MA); geography (MA, PhD); geology (MS, PhD); German (MA); history (MA, PhD); inorganic chemistry (MS, PhD); Japanese (MA); justice studies (MA); Latin (MA); liberal studies (MLS); literature (PhD); literature and writing (MA); organic chemistry (MS, PhD); philosophy (MA); physical chemistry (MS, PhD); physics (MA, MS, PhD); physiology (MS, PhD); political science (MA); public administration (MPA); public policy (PhD); pure mathematics (MA, MS, PhD); rhetoric and composition (PhD); Russian (MA); sociology (MA, PhD); Spanish (MA); teaching English as a second language (MA); translation (MA). Electronic applications accepted.

College of Communication and Information Offers communication and information (MA, MFA, MLS, MS, PhD).

School of Communication Studies Offers communication studies (MA, PhD). Electronic applications accepted.

School of Journalism and Mass Communication *Degree program information:* Part-time programs available. Offers journalism and mass communication (MA). Electronic applications accepted.

School of Library and Information Science Offers information architecture and knowledge management (MS); library and information science (MLS, MS).

School of Visual Communication Design *Degree program information:* Part-time programs available. Offers visual communication design (MA, MFA).

College of Fine and Professional Arts Offers fine and professional arts (MA, MFA, MLS, MM, MPH, MS, Au D, PhD, Certificate). Electronic applications accepted.

Hugh A. Glauser School of Music Offers composition (MA); conducting (MM); ethnomusicology (MA); music education (MM, PhD); musicology (MA); musicology-ethnomusicology (PhD); performance (MM); theory (MA); theory and composition (PhD). Electronic applications accepted.

School of Art Offers art education (MA); art history (MA); crafts (MA, MFA); fine arts (MA, MFA). Electronic applications accepted.

School of Theatre and Dance *Degree program information:* Part-time programs available. Offers acting (MFA); design and technology (MFA); theatre (MA, MFA). Electronic applications accepted.

College of Nursing *Degree program information:* Part-time programs available. Offers clinical nursing (MSN); nursing (PhD); nursing administration (MSN); nursing education (MSN); parent-child nursing (MSN). Electronic applications accepted.

Graduate School of Education, Health, and Human Services Students: 769 full-time (616 women), 964 part-time (757 women); includes 158 minority (125 African Americans, 5 American Indian/Alaska Native, 11 Asian Americans or Pacific Islanders, 17 Hispanic Americans), 76 international. 670 applicants, 63% accepted. *Faculty:* 115 full-time (67 women), 87 part-time/adjunct (71 women). Expenses: Contact institution. *Financial support:* In 2006–07, 21 fellowships with full tuition reimbursements (averaging $8,497 per year), 124 research assistantships with full tuition reimbursements were awarded; teaching assistantships with full tuition reimbursements, career-related internships or fieldwork, Federal Work-Study, institutionally sponsored loans, scholarships/grants, health care benefits, and unspecified assistantships also available. Support available to part-time students. Financial award application deadline: 4/1; financial award applicants required to submit FAFSA. In 2006, 422 master's, 31 doctorates, 25 other advanced degrees awarded. *Degree program information:* Part-time and evening/weekend programs available. Postbaccalaureate distance learning degree programs offered (no on-campus study). Offers athletic training (MA); career technical teacher education (M Ed, MA, Ed S); community counseling (M Ed, MA); computer technology (M Ed, MA); counseling (Ed S); counseling and human development services (PhD); cultural foundations (M Ed, MA, PhD); curriculum and instruction (M Ed, MA, PhD, Ed S); deaf education (M Ed, MA); early childhood education (M Ed, MA, MAT); education, health, and human services (M Ed, MA, MAT, MPH, MS, Au D, PhD, Ed S); educational administration (PhD, Ed S); educational interpreter (M Ed, MA); educational psychology (M Ed, MA, PhD); evaluation and measurement (M Ed, MA, PhD); exercise physiology (MA, PhD); general special education (M Ed, MA); gifted (M Ed, MA); health education and promotion (M Ed, MA, PhD); higher education administration and student personnel (M Ed, MA); instructional technology (M Ed, MA); instructional technology general (M Ed, MA); intervention specialist (M Ed, MA); junior high/middle school (M Ed, MA); K-12 leadership (M Ed, MA, PhD, Ed S); library media (M Ed, MA); math specialization (M Ed, MA); mild/moderate (M Ed, MA); moderate/intensive (M Ed, MA); physical teacher education (MA); public health (MPH); reading (M Ed, MA); rehabilitation counseling (M Ed, MA, Ed S); school counseling (M Ed, MA); school psychology (M Ed, PhD, Ed S); secondary education (MAT); special education (PhD, Ed S); sport and recreation management (MA); sports studies (MA); transition to work (M Ed, MA). *Application deadline:* Applications are processed on a rolling basis. *Application fee:* $30. Electronic applications accepted. *Application Contact:* Nancy Miller, Office of Student Services, Academic Program Coordinator, 330-672-2576, Fax: 330-672-9162, E-mail: nmiller1@kent.edu. *Dean,* Dr. David A. England, 330-672-2808, Fax: 330-672-3407, E-mail: denglan1@kent.edu.

School of Exercise, Leisure and Sport Students: 52 full-time (27 women), 37 part-time (15 women); includes 12 minority (11 African Americans, 1 Hispanic American), 4 international. 52 applicants, 69% accepted. *Faculty:* 26 full-time (13 women). Expenses: Contact institution. *Financial support:* Fellowships with full tuition reimbursements, research assistantships with full tuition reimbursements, teaching assistantships with full tuition reimbursements, career-related internships or fieldwork, Federal Work-Study, institutionally sponsored loans, and tuition waivers (full) available. Financial award application deadline: 3/15. In 2006, 9 degrees awarded. Offers exercise, leisure and sport (MA, PhD). *Application deadline:* For fall admission, 7/18 for domestic students; for spring admission, 11/29 for domestic students. Applications are processed on a rolling basis. *Application fee:* $30. Electronic applications accepted. *Application Contact:* Aaron L. Mulroony, Graduate Coordinator, 330-672-2857, Fax: 330-672-4106, E-mail: amulroon@kent.edu. *Interim Director,* Wayne Munson, 330-672-2012, Fax: 330-672-4106, E-mail: wmunson@kent.edu.

School of Family and Consumer Studies Students: 20 full-time (18 women), 19 part-time (18 women); includes 4 minority (2 African Americans, 2 Asian Americans or Pacific Islanders), 1 international. Average age 33. 18 applicants, 67% accepted. *Faculty:* 21 full-time (14 women). Expenses: Contact institution. *Financial support:* In 2006–07, 4 students received support, including 4 research assistantships with full tuition reimbursements available (averaging $7,210 per year); Federal Work-Study, scholarships/grants, and unspecified assistantships also available. Financial award application deadline: 2/1; financial award applicants required to submit FAFSA. In 2006, 2 degrees awarded. *Degree program information:* Part-time programs available. Offers dietetic internship (MS); family and consumer studies (MA, MS); gerontology (MA); human development and family studies (MA); nutrition (MS). *Application deadline:* Applications are processed on a rolling basis. *Application fee:* $30. Electronic applications accepted. *Application Contact:* Dr. Maureen Blankemeyer, Graduate Coordinator, 330-672-9397, Fax: 330-672-2194, E-mail: mblankem@kent.edu. *Director,* Dr. Mary Dellmann-Jenkins, 330-672-2197, Fax: 330-672-2194, E-mail: mdellman@kent.edu.

School of Speech Pathology and Audiology Students: 110 full-time (105 women), 7 part-time (all women); includes 7 minority (3 African Americans, 1 American Indian/Alaska Native, 1 Asian American or Pacific Islander, 2 Hispanic Americans), 5 international. Average age 23. 136 applicants, 32% accepted. *Faculty:* 19 full-time (13 women). Expenses: Contact institution. *Financial support:* Fellowships with full tuition reimbursements, research assistantships with full tuition reimbursements, teaching assistantships with full tuition reimbursements, career-related internships or fieldwork, Federal Work-Study, scholarships/grants, and tuition waivers (full) available. Financial award application deadline: 3/1. In 2006, 8 master's, 2 doctorates awarded. Offers audiology (Au D, PhD); speech pathology and audiology (MA, Au D, PhD). *Application deadline:* For fall admission, 3/1 for domestic students; for spring admission, 10/15 for domestic students. Applications are processed on a rolling basis. *Application fee:* $30. Electronic applications accepted. *Application Contact:* Dr. Robert S. Pierce, Coordinator for Graduate Studies, 330-672-2672, Fax: 330-672-2643, E-mail: rpierce@kent.edu. *Director,* Dr. Lynne B. Rowan, 330-672-2672, Fax: 330-672-2643, E-mail: lrowan@kent.edu.

Graduate School of Management Students: 261 full-time (119 women), 158 part-time (78 women); includes 21 minority (6 African Americans, 1 American Indian/Alaska Native, 13 Asian Americans or Pacific Islanders, 1 Hispanic American), 79 international. Average age 29. 399 applicants, 78% accepted, 171 enrolled. *Faculty:* 58 full-time (12 women). Expenses: Contact institution. *Financial support:* In 2006–07, 96 students received support, including 60 research assistantships with full tuition reimbursements available (averaging $4,875 per year), 36 teaching assistantships with full tuition reimbursements available (averaging $15,000 per year); fellowships with full tuition reimbursements available, career-related internships or

Kent State University (continued)
fieldwork, Federal Work-Study, scholarships/grants, and tuition waivers (full) also available. Financial award applicants required to submit FAFSA. In 2006, 158 master's, 8 doctorates awarded. *Degree program information:* Part-time and evening/weekend programs available. Offers accounting (MS, PhD); business administration (MBA); economics (MA); finance (PhD); financial engineering (MSFE); management (MA, MBA, MS, MSFE, PhD); management systems (PhD); marketing (PhD). *Application fee:* $30. Electronic applications accepted. *Application Contact:* Louise M. Ditchey, Director, 330-672-2282, Fax: 330-672-7303, E-mail: gradbus@bsa3.kent.edu. *Associate Dean,* Dr. Frederick W. Schroath, 330-672-2282, Fax: 330-672-7303, E-mail: fschroat@kent.edu.

Program in Biological Anthropology Offers biological anthropology (PhD). Offered in cooperation with Northeastern Ohio Universities College of Medicine.

School of Biomedical Sciences Offers biomedical sciences (MS, PhD); cellular and molecular biology (MS, PhD); neuroscience (MS, PhD); pharmacology (MS, PhD); physiology (MS, PhD). Offered in cooperation with Northeastern Ohio Universities College of Medicine.

School of Technology *Degree program information:* Part-time programs available. Postbaccalaureate distance learning degree programs offered. Offers technology (M Tech, MA). Electronic applications accepted.

KENT STATE UNIVERSITY, GEAUGA CAMPUS, Burton, OH 44021-9500

General Information State-supported, coed.

KENTUCKY CHRISTIAN UNIVERSITY, Grayson, KY 41143-2205

General Information Independent-religious, coed, comprehensive institution. *Enrollment:* 556 graduate, professional, and undergraduate students; 1 (woman) full-time matriculated graduate/professional student, 17 part-time matriculated graduate/professional students (2 women). *Enrollment by degree level:* 18 master's. *Graduate faculty:* 9 part-time/adjunct (0 women). *Tuition:* Part-time $225 per credit hour. *Graduate housing:* Rooms and/or apartments available on a first-come, first-served basis to single and married students. Typical cost: $2,312 (including board) for single students; $4,200 per year for married students. *Student services:* Exercise/wellness program, international student services, low-cost health insurance. *Library facilities:* Young Library. *Online resources:* library catalog, web page. *Collection:* 103,323 titles, 395 serial subscriptions.

Computer facilities: 50 computers available on campus for general student use. A campuswide network can be accessed from student residence rooms and from off campus. Internet access is available. *Web address:* http://www.kcu.edu/.

General Application Contact: Jane Shick, Academic Office Manager, 877-811-6391, Fax: 606-474-3189, E-mail: gradstudies@kcu.edu.

GRADUATE UNITS

Graduate School Students: 1 (woman) full-time, 17 part-time (2 women), 5 international. Average age 35. 11 applicants, 55% accepted, 6 enrolled. *Faculty:* 9 part-time/adjunct (0 women). Expenses: Contact institution. *Financial support:* Teaching assistantships with full tuition reimbursements, scholarships/grants and unspecified assistantships available. Support available to part-time students. In 2006, 2 degrees awarded. *Degree program information:* Part-time programs available. Offers Christian leadership (MA); New Testament (MA). *Application deadline:* Applications are processed on a rolling basis. *Application fee:* $35. Electronic applications accepted. *Application Contact:* Jane Shick, Academic Office Manager, 877-811-6391, Fax: 606-474-3189, E-mail: gradstudies@kcu.edu. *Graduate Dean,* Dr. David Fiensy, 606-474-3263, Fax: 606-474-3189, E-mail: dfiensy@kcu.edu.

KENTUCKY STATE UNIVERSITY, Frankfort, KY 40601

General Information State-related, coed, comprehensive institution. *Enrollment:* 2,500 graduate, professional, and undergraduate students; 54 full-time matriculated graduate/professional students (29 women), 105 part-time matriculated graduate/professional students (53 women). *Enrollment by degree level:* 154 master's, 5 other advanced degrees. *Graduate faculty:* 21 full-time (3 women). Tuition, state resident: part-time $285 per credit. Tuition, nonresident: part-time $685 per credit. *Required fees:* $35 per credit. *Graduate housing:* Room and/or apartments available on a first-come, first-served basis to single students; on-campus housing not available to married students. Typical cost: $3,234 per year ($6,274 including board). Room and board charges vary according to housing facility selected. Housing application deadline: 7/1. *Student services:* Campus employment opportunities, career counseling, child daycare facilities, disabled student services, free psychological counseling, grant writing training, international student services, low-cost health insurance, multicultural affairs office. *Library facilities:* Blazer Library. *Online resources:* library catalog. *Collection:* 457,728 titles, 809 serial subscriptions, 4,863 audiovisual materials.

Computer facilities: 230 computers available on campus for general student use. A campuswide network can be accessed from off campus. Internet access, e-mail are available. *Web address:* http://www.kysu.edu/.

General Application Contact: James Burrell, Director of Admission, 502-597-6322, Fax: 502-597-5814, E-mail: james.burrell@kysu.edu.

GRADUATE UNITS

College of Mathematics, Sciences, Technology and Health Students: 10 full-time (3 women), 31 part-time (11 women); includes 23 minority (13 African Americans, 10 Asian Americans or Pacific Islanders). Average age 31. 47 applicants, 47% accepted, 13 enrolled. *Faculty:* 10 full-time (1 woman). Expenses: Contact institution. *Financial support:* In 2006–07, 21 research assistantships (averaging $6,882 per year) were awarded; fellowships, teaching assistantships also available. Financial award application deadline: 4/15; financial award applicants required to submit FAFSA. In 2006, 5 degrees awarded. *Degree program information:* Part-time programs available. Offers aquaculture (MS); computer science (MSCST). *Application deadline:* For fall admission, 7/1 priority date for domestic students, 4/1 priority date for international students; for spring admission, 11/15 priority date for domestic students, 8/15 priority date for international students. Applications are processed on a rolling basis. *Application fee:* $30 ($100 for international students). Electronic applications accepted. *Application Contact:* James Burrell, Director of Admission, 502-597-6322, Fax: 502-597-5814, E-mail: james.burrell@kysu.edu. *Dean,* Dr. Charles Bennett, 502-597-6926, E-mail: charles.bennett@kysu.edu.

College of Professional Studies Students: 44 full-time (26 women), 69 part-time (40 women); includes 67 minority (64 African Americans, 1 Asian American or Pacific Islander, 2 Hispanic Americans), 1 international. Average age 32. 70 applicants, 74% accepted, 41 enrolled. *Faculty:* 11 full-time (2 women). Expenses: Contact institution. *Financial support:* In 2006–07, 4 research assistantships (averaging $613 per year) were awarded. Financial award application deadline: 4/15; financial award applicants required to submit FAFSA. In 2006, 26 degrees awarded. *Degree program information:* Part-time and evening/weekend programs available. Offers business (MBA); public administration (MPA); special education (MA). *Application deadline:* For fall admission, 7/1 priority date for domestic students, 4/1 priority date for international students; for spring admission, 11/15 priority date for domestic students, 8/15 priority date for international students. Applications are processed on a rolling basis. *Application fee:* $30 ($100 for international students). Electronic applications accepted. *Application Contact:* James Burrell, Director of Admission, 502-597-6322, Fax: 502-597-5814, E-mail: james.burrell@kysu.edu. *Dean,* Dr. Gashaw Lake, E-mail: gashaw.lake@kysu.edu.

KETTERING UNIVERSITY, Flint, MI 48504-4898

General Information Independent, coed, comprehensive institution. *Enrollment:* 2,809 graduate, professional, and undergraduate students; 13 full-time matriculated graduate/professional students (4 women), 506 part-time matriculated graduate/professional students (131 women). *Enrollment by degree level:* 519 master's. *Graduate faculty:* 19 full-time (5 women), 8 part-time/adjunct (1 woman). *Tuition:* Part-time $629 per credit. *Graduate housing:* Room and/or apartments available on a first-come, first-served basis to single students; on-campus housing not available to married students. Typical cost: $5,283 per year ($8,418 including board). Housing application deadline: 7/15. *Student services:* Campus employment opportunities, disabled student services, exercise/wellness program, free psychological counseling, international student services, low-cost health insurance, multicultural affairs office. *Library facilities:* Kettering University Library plus 1 other. *Online resources:* library catalog, web page, access to other libraries' catalogs. *Collection:* 122,360 titles, 525 serial subscriptions, 1,280 audiovisual materials.

Computer facilities: 300 computers available on campus for general student use. A campuswide network can be accessed from student residence rooms and from off campus. Internet access and online class registration are available. *Web address:* http://www.kettering.edu/.

General Application Contact: Allison Fleming, Graduate Admissions Assistant, 810-762-7953, Fax: 810-762-9935, E-mail: afleming@kettering.edu.

GRADUATE UNITS

Graduate School Students: 13 full-time (4 women), 506 part-time (131 women); includes 121 minority (57 African Americans, 1 American Indian/Alaska Native, 13 Asian Americans or Pacific Islanders, 50 Hispanic Americans), 9 international. Average age 32. 178 applicants, 81% accepted, 100 enrolled. *Faculty:* 27 full-time (7 women), 2 part-time/adjunct (0 women). Expenses: Contact institution. *Financial support:* In 2006–07, fellowships with full tuition reimbursements (averaging $13,000 per year), research assistantships with full tuition reimbursements (averaging $13,000 per year), teaching assistantships with full tuition reimbursements (averaging $13,000 per year) were awarded; Federal Work-Study, scholarships/grants, and tuition waivers (partial) also available. Support available to part-time students. Financial award application deadline: 7/15; financial award applicants required to submit CSS PROFILE or FAFSA. In 2006, 185 degrees awarded. *Degree program information:* Part-time and evening/weekend programs available. Postbaccalaureate distance learning degree programs offered (no on-campus study). Offers automotive systems (MS Eng); business administration (MBA); computer aided engineering simulation (MS Eng); electrical and computer engineering (MS Eng); engineering management (MSEM); information technology (MSIT); manufacturing management (MSMM); manufacturing operations (MSMO); manufacturing systems engineering (MS Eng); mechanical cognate (MS Eng); mechanical design (MS Eng); operations management (MSOM). *Application deadline:* For fall admission, 8/15 for domestic students, 4/1 priority date for international students; for winter admission, 11/15 for domestic students; for spring admission, 2/15 for domestic students. Applications are processed on a rolling basis. *Application fee:* $0. Electronic applications accepted. *Application Contact:* Allison Fleming, Graduate Admissions Assistant, 810-762-7953, Fax: 810-762-9935, E-mail: afleming@kettering.edu. *Vice President of Graduate Studies and Corporate Connections,* Dr. Tony Hain, 810-762-9616, Fax: 810-762-9935, E-mail: thain@kettering.edu.

KEUKA COLLEGE, Keuka Park, NY 14478-0098

General Information Independent-religious, coed, comprehensive institution. *Enrollment:* 1,521 graduate, professional, and undergraduate students; 58 full-time matriculated graduate/professional students (39 women), 100 part-time matriculated graduate/professional students (54 women). *Enrollment by degree level:* 158 master's. *Graduate faculty:* 6 full-time (4 women), 25 part-time/adjunct (7 women). *Tuition:* Part-time $520 per credit. Part-time tuition and fees vary according to program. *Graduate housing:* On-campus housing not available. *Student services:* Career counseling, disabled student services, grant writing training, teacher training, writing training. *Library facilities:* Lightner Library. *Online resources:* library catalog. *Collection:* 112,541 titles, 384 serial subscriptions, 3,551 audiovisual materials.

Computer facilities: 105 computers available on campus for general student use. A campuswide network can be accessed from student residence rooms and from off campus. Internet access is available. *Web address:* http://www.keuka.edu/.

General Application Contact: Claudine Ninestine, Director of Admissions, 315-279-5413, Fax: 315-279-5386, E-mail: admissions@mail.keuka.edu.

GRADUATE UNITS

Program in Childhood Education 36 applicants, 100% accepted. *Faculty:* 4 part-time/adjunct (3 women). Expenses: Contact institution. In 2006, 49 degrees awarded. *Degree program information:* Part-time and evening/weekend programs available. Offers childhood education (MS). *Application deadline:* For fall admission, 8/15 priority date for domestic students; for winter admission, 12/15 priority date for domestic students; for spring admission, 4/15 priority date for domestic students. Applications are processed on a rolling basis. *Application fee:* $30. *Director of Graduate Program in Education,* Dr. Diane Burke, 315-279-5688.

Program in Management Students: 46 full-time (29 women), 56 part-time (33 women); includes 9 minority (4 African Americans, 1 American Indian/Alaska Native, 2 Asian Americans or Pacific Islanders, 2 Hispanic Americans). 47 applicants, 100% accepted, 47 enrolled. *Faculty:* 3 full-time (1 woman), 16 part-time/adjunct (3 women). Expenses: Contact institution. In 2006, 41 degrees awarded. *Degree program information:* Evening/weekend programs available. Offers management (MS). *Application deadline:* For fall admission, 8/15 priority date for domestic students; for winter admission, 12/15 priority date for domestic students; for spring admission, 4/15 priority date for domestic students. Applications are processed on a rolling basis. *Application fee:* $30. *Chair, Division of Business and Management,* Gary M. Smith, 315-279-5352, E-mail: gsmith@mail.keuka.edu.

Program in Occupational Therapy Students: 12 full-time (10 women). Average age 23. 12 applicants, 100% accepted. *Faculty:* 5 full-time (3 women). Expenses: Contact institution. In 2006, 16 degrees awarded. Offers occupational therapy (MS). *Application deadline:* For fall admission, 8/15 priority date for domestic students; for winter admission, 12/15 priority date for domestic students; for spring admission, 4/15 priority date for domestic students. Applications are processed on a rolling basis. *Application fee:* $30. *Associate Professor and Chair,* Dr. Vicki Smith, 315-279-5666, Fax: 315-279-5439, E-mail: vlsmith@mail.keuka.edu.

KING COLLEGE, Bristol, TN 37620-2699

General Information Independent-religious, coed, comprehensive institution. *Graduate housing:* Room and/or apartments available on a first-come, first-served basis to single students; on-campus housing not available to married students.

GRADUATE UNITS

School of Business and Economics *Degree program information:* Part-time and evening/weekend programs available. Postbaccalaureate distance learning degree programs offered (no on-campus study). Offers business and economics (MBA). Electronic applications accepted.

KING'S COLLEGE, Wilkes-Barre, PA 18711-0801

General Information Independent-religious, coed, comprehensive institution. *Enrollment:* 2,386 graduate, professional, and undergraduate students; 64 full-time matriculated graduate/professional students (55 women), 219 part-time matriculated graduate/professional students (175 women). *Enrollment by degree level:* 283 master's. *Graduate faculty:* 14 full-time (8 women), 16 part-time/adjunct (10 women). *Tuition:* Full-time $26,598; part-time $625 per credit. *Required fees:* $900. *Graduate housing:* On-campus housing not available. *Student services:* Career counseling, free psychological counseling, multicultural affairs office. *Library facilities:* D. Leonard Corgan Library. *Online resources:* library catalog, web page, access to other libraries' catalogs. *Collection:* 176,537 titles, 15,808 serial subscriptions, 2,835 audiovisual materials.

Computer facilities: Computer purchase and lease plans are available. 318 computers available on campus for general student use. A campuswide network can be accessed from student residence rooms and from off campus. Internet access is available. *Web address:* http://www.kings.edu/.

General Application Contact: Dr. Elizabeth S. Lott, Director of Graduate Programs, 570-208-5991, Fax: 570-825-9049, E-mail: eslott@kings.edu.

GRADUATE UNITS

Program in Physician Assistant Studies Students: 64 full-time (55 women); includes 4 minority (3 African Americans, 1 Hispanic American), 1 international. Average age 25. 265

applicants, 24% accepted, 41 enrolled. *Faculty:* 6 full-time (5 women), 6 part-time/adjunct (4 women). Expenses: Contact institution. In 2006, 34 degrees awarded. Offers physician assistant studies (MSPAS). *Application deadline:* For fall admission, 11/1 priority date for domestic and international students. *Application fee:* $30. Electronic applications accepted. *Director of Graduate Programs*, Dr. Elizabeth S. Lott, 570-208-5991, Fax: 570-825-9049, E-mail: eslott@kings.edu.

Program in Reading Average age 27. *Faculty:* 3 full-time (2 women), 9 part-time/adjunct (6 women). Expenses: Contact institution. In 2006, 16 degrees awarded. *Degree program information:* Part-time and evening/weekend programs available. Offers reading (M Ed). *Application deadline:* Applications are processed on a rolling basis. *Application fee:* $35. *Director of Graduate Programs*, Dr. Elizabeth S. Lott, 570-208-5991, Fax: 570-825-9049, E-mail: eslott@kings.edu.

William G. McGowan School of Business Average age 35. *Faculty:* 4 full-time (1 woman), 1 part-time/adjunct (0 women). Expenses: Contact institution. In 2006, 6 degrees awarded. *Degree program information:* Part-time and evening/weekend programs available. Offers health care administration (MS). *Application deadline:* For fall admission, 7/31 priority date for domestic students; for spring admission, 12/1 priority date for domestic students. Applications are processed on a rolling basis. *Application fee:* $35. *Application Contact:* Dr. Elizabeth S. Lott, Director of Graduate Programs, 570-208-5991, Fax: 570-825-9049, E-mail: eslott@kings.edu. *Director*, Dr. John J. Ryan, 570-208-5932, Fax: 570-826-5989, E-mail: jjryan@kings.edu.

KNOWLEDGE SYSTEMS INSTITUTE, Skokie, IL 60076

General Information Independent, coed, graduate-only institution. *Graduate housing:* Rooms and/or apartments available on a first-come, first-served basis to single and married students. Housing application deadline: 7/15.

GRADUATE UNITS

Program in Computer and Information Sciences *Degree program information:* Part-time and evening/weekend programs available. Postbaccalaureate distance learning degree programs offered (minimal on-campus study). Offers computer and information sciences (MS). Electronic applications accepted.

KNOX COLLEGE, Toronto, ON M5S 2E6, Canada

General Information Independent-religious, coed, graduate-only institution. *Enrollment by degree level:* 79 first professional, 15 master's, 26 doctoral. *Graduate faculty:* 6 full-time (2 women), 4 part-time/adjunct (0 women). *Graduate housing:* Room and/or apartments available on a first-come, first-served basis to single students; on-campus housing not available to married students. Housing application deadline: 5/31. *Student services:* International student services, writing training. *Library facilities:* Caven Library plus 7 others. *Online resources:* library catalog, access to other libraries' catalogs. *Collection:* 69,251 titles, 321 serial subscriptions.

Computer facilities: 10 computers available on campus for general student use. A campuswide network can be accessed from student residence rooms and from off campus. Internet access and online class registration are available. *Web address:* http://www.utoronto.ca/knox/.

General Application Contact: Ruth McCarten, Registrar, 416-978-4501, Fax: 416-971-2133, E-mail: knox.registrar@utoronto.ca.

GRADUATE UNITS

College of Theology Students: 67 full-time (24 women), 53 part-time (28 women); includes 60 minority (1 African American, 59 Asian Americans or Pacific Islanders). Average age 39. 36 applicants, 67% accepted, 19 enrolled. *Faculty:* 6 full-time (2 women), 4 part-time/adjunct (0 women). Expenses: Contact institution. *Financial support:* In 2006–07, 35 students received support, including 4 teaching assistantships (averaging $5,000 per year); career-related internships or fieldwork, institutionally sponsored loans, scholarships/grants, and tuition waivers (partial) also available. Financial award application deadline: 5/15. In 2006, 21 master's, 2 doctorates awarded. *Degree program information:* Part-time programs available. Offers theology (M Div, MRE, MTS, Th M, D Min, Th D). Applicants for D Min, Th M, and Th D must apply to Toronto School of Theology. *Application deadline:* For fall admission, 5/31 for domestic and international students; for winter admission, 10/31 for domestic and international students; for spring admission, 4/2 for domestic and international students. *Application fee:* $100. *Application Contact:* Ruth McCarten, Registrar, 416-978-4501, Fax: 416-971-2133, E-mail: knox.registrar@utoronto.ca. *Director, Academic Programs*, Rev. Beth McCutcheon, 416-978-2791, Fax: 416-971-2133, E-mail: mb.mccutcheon@utoronto.ca.

KNOX THEOLOGICAL SEMINARY, Fort Lauderdale, FL 33308

General Information Independent-religious, coed, primarily men, graduate-only institution. *Enrollment by degree level:* 48 first professional, 68 master's, 17 doctoral, 12 other advanced degrees. *Graduate faculty:* 4 full-time (0 women), 3 part-time/adjunct (0 women). *Graduate housing:* On-campus housing not available. *Student services:* Campus employment opportunities, career counseling. *Library facilities:* Knox Seminary Library. *Collection:* 32,000 titles, 100 serial subscriptions, 2,000 audiovisual materials.

Computer facilities: 9 computers available on campus for general student use. A campuswide network can be accessed from off campus. Internet access is available. *Web address:* http://www.knoxseminary.edu/.

General Application Contact: Jim Dietz, Director of Student Services, 800-344-5669, Fax: 954-351-3343, E-mail: jdietz@knoxseminary.edu.

GRADUATE UNITS

Graduate Programs Students: 41 full-time (5 women), 104 part-time (30 women). *Faculty:* 4 full-time (0 women), 3 part-time/adjunct (0 women). Expenses: Contact institution. *Financial support:* Scholarships/grants available. Support available to part-time students. In 2006, 11 first professional degrees, 5 master's, 5 doctorates awarded. *Degree program information:* Part-time and evening/weekend programs available. Offers Biblical studies (CBS); divinity (M Div); evangelism (ME); ministry (D Min); New and Old Testament (MBT). *Application deadline:* For fall admission, 6/1 priority date for domestic and international students; for winter admission, 12/1 priority date for domestic and international students; for spring admission, 1/1 priority date for domestic and international students. Applications are processed on a rolling basis. *Application fee:* $50. *Application Contact:* Jim Dietz, Director of Student Services, 800-344-5669, Fax: 954-351-3343, E-mail: jdietz@knoxseminary.edu.

KOL YAAKOV TORAH CENTER, Monsey, NY 10952-2954

General Information Independent-religious, men only, comprehensive institution. *Graduate housing:* Room and/or apartments available to single students; on-campus housing not available to married students.

GRADUATE UNITS

Graduate Program *Degree program information:* Part-time and evening/weekend programs available.

KUTZTOWN UNIVERSITY OF PENNSYLVANIA, Kutztown, PA 19530-0730

General Information State-supported, coed, comprehensive institution. CGS member. *Enrollment:* 10,193 graduate, professional, and undergraduate students; 291 full-time matriculated graduate/professional students (185 women), 590 part-time matriculated graduate/professional students (421 women). *Enrollment by degree level:* 728 master's, 153 other advanced degrees. *Graduate faculty:* 71 full-time (30 women), 6 part-time/adjunct (4 women). Tuition, state resident: full-time $6,048; part-time $336 per credit. Tuition, nonresident: full-time $9,678; part-time $538 per credit. *Graduate housing:* On-campus housing not available. *Student services:* Campus employment opportunities, campus safety program, career counseling, child daycare facilities, disabled student services, exercise/wellness program, free psychological counseling, international student services, low-cost health insurance, multicultural affairs office. *Library facilities:* Rohrbach Library. *Online resources:* library catalog, web page, access to other libraries' catalogs. *Collection:* 500,484 titles, 15,600 serial subscriptions.

Computer facilities: 650 computers available on campus for general student use. A campuswide network can be accessed from student residence rooms and from off campus. Internet access and online class registration are available. *Web address:* http://www.kutztown.edu/.

General Application Contact: Dr. Regis Bernhardt, Interim Dean of Graduate Studies, 610-683-4253, Fax: 610-683-4255, E-mail: graduate@kutztown.edu.

GRADUATE UNITS

College of Graduate Studies and Extended Learning Students: 291 full-time (185 women), 590 part-time (421 women); includes 51 minority (20 African Americans, 5 American Indian/Alaska Native, 7 Asian Americans or Pacific Islanders, 19 Hispanic Americans), 20 international. Average age 31. 768 applicants, 78% accepted, 202 enrolled. *Faculty:* 71 full-time (30 women), 6 part-time/adjunct (4 women). Expenses: Contact institution. *Financial support:* In 2006–07, 25 research assistantships with full tuition reimbursements (averaging $5,000 per year) were awarded; career-related internships or fieldwork, Federal Work-Study, and unspecified assistantships also available. Financial award application deadline: 3/15; financial award applicants required to submit FAFSA. In 2006, 200 degrees awarded. *Degree program information:* Part-time and evening/weekend programs available. Offers agency counseling (MA); counselor education (M Ed); marital and family therapy (MA); student affairs in higher education (M Ed). *Application deadline:* Applications are processed on a rolling basis. *Application fee:* $35. Electronic applications accepted. *Interim Dean of Graduate Studies*, Dr. Regis Bernhardt, 610-683-4253, Fax: 610-683-4255, E-mail: graduate@kutztown.edu.

College of Business Students: 22 full-time (10 women), 73 part-time (24 women); includes 9 minority (4 African Americans, 3 Asian Americans or Pacific Islanders, 2 Hispanic Americans), 7 international. Average age 32. 48 applicants, 27% accepted, 11 enrolled. *Faculty:* 12 full-time (2 women). Expenses: Contact institution. *Financial support:* In 2006–07, research assistantships with full tuition reimbursements (averaging $5,000 per year); career-related internships or fieldwork, Federal Work-Study, and unspecified assistantships also available. Financial award application deadline: 3/15; financial award applicants required to submit FAFSA. In 2006, 32 degrees awarded. *Degree program information:* Part-time and evening/weekend programs available. Offers business (MBA); business administration (MBA). *Application deadline:* Applications are processed on a rolling basis. *Application fee:* $35. *Interim Dean*, Dr. Fidelis M. Ikem, 610-683-4575, Fax: 610-683-4573, E-mail: ikem@kutztown.edu.

College of Education Students: 120 full-time (68 women), 297 part-time (230 women); includes 12 minority (3 African Americans, 1 American Indian/Alaska Native, 3 Asian Americans or Pacific Islanders, 5 Hispanic Americans), 3 international. Average age 32. 259 applicants, 84% accepted, 117 enrolled. *Faculty:* 20 full-time (12 women), 2 part-time/adjunct (both women). Expenses: Contact institution. *Financial support:* In 2006–07, research assistantships with full tuition reimbursements (averaging $5,000 per year); career-related internships or fieldwork, Federal Work-Study, and unspecified assistantships also available. Financial award application deadline: 3/15; financial award applicants required to submit FAFSA. In 2006, 70 degrees awarded. *Degree program information:* Part-time and evening/weekend programs available. Offers biology (M Ed); curriculum and instruction (M Ed); early childhood education (Certificate); education (M Ed, MLS, Certificate); elementary education (M Ed, Certificate); English (M Ed); instructional technology (M Ed, Certificate); library science (MLS, Certificate); mathematics (M Ed); reading (M Ed); secondary education (Certificate); social studies (M Ed); special education (Certificate). *Application deadline:* Applications are processed on a rolling basis. *Application fee:* $35. Electronic applications accepted.

College of Liberal Arts and Sciences Students: 57 full-time (39 women), 70 part-time (46 women); includes 20 minority (9 African Americans, 4 American Indian/Alaska Native, 1 Asian American or Pacific Islander, 6 Hispanic Americans), 9 international. Average age 32. 105 applicants, 64% accepted, 38 enrolled. *Faculty:* 16 full-time (4 women). Expenses: Contact institution. *Financial support:* In 2006–07, research assistantships with full tuition reimbursements (averaging $5,000 per year); career-related internships or fieldwork, Federal Work-Study, and unspecified assistantships also available. Financial award application deadline: 3/15; financial award applicants required to submit FAFSA. In 2006, 43 degrees awarded. *Degree program information:* Part-time and evening/weekend programs available. Offers computer science (MS); electronic media (MS); English (MA); liberal arts and sciences (MA, MPA, MS, MSW, Certificate); public administration (MPA); school nursing (Certificate); social work (MSW). *Application deadline:* Applications are processed on a rolling basis. *Application fee:* $35. Electronic applications accepted. *Dean*, Dr. Bashar Hanna, 610-683-4305, Fax: 610-683-4633, E-mail: hanna@kutztown.edu.

College of Visual and Performing Arts Students: 30 full-time (21 women), 41 part-time (36 women), 1 international. Average age 30. 42 applicants, 83% accepted, 19 enrolled. *Faculty:* 18 full-time (9 women), 4 part-time/adjunct (2 women). Expenses: Contact institution. *Financial support:* In 2006–07, research assistantships with full tuition reimbursements (averaging $5,000 per year); career-related internships or fieldwork, Federal Work-Study, and unspecified assistantships also available. Financial award application deadline: 3/15; financial award applicants required to submit FAFSA. In 2006, 13 degrees awarded. *Degree program information:* Part-time programs available. Offers art education (M Ed, Certificate); music education (Certificate); visual and performing arts (M Ed, Certificate). *Application deadline:* Applications are processed on a rolling basis. *Application fee:* $35. Electronic applications accepted. *Dean*, Dr. William Mowder, 610-683-4500, Fax: 610-683-4547, E-mail: mowder@kutztown.edu.

See Close-Up on page 941.

LAGRANGE COLLEGE, LaGrange, GA 30240-2999

General Information Independent-religious, coed, comprehensive institution. *Graduate housing:* Room and/or apartments available to single students; on-campus housing not available to married students.

GRADUATE UNITS

Graduate Programs *Degree program information:* Part-time and evening/weekend programs available. Offers art education (MAT); curriculum and instruction (M Ed); music education (MAT); secondary education (MAT). Electronic applications accepted.

LAKE ERIE COLLEGE, Painesville, OH 44077-3389

General Information Independent, coed, comprehensive institution. *Enrollment:* 332 part-time matriculated graduate/professional students (249 women). *Enrollment by degree level:* 332 master's. *Graduate faculty:* 10 full-time (3 women), 8 part-time/adjunct (2 women). *Tuition:* Part-time $595 per credit hour. *Required fees:* $45 per credit hour. *Graduate housing:* On-campus housing not available. *Student services:* Campus employment opportunities, campus safety program, career counseling, disabled student services, exercise/wellness program, free psychological counseling, international student services, teacher training. *Library facilities:* Lincoln Library plus 2 others. *Online resources:* library catalog, web page. *Collection:* 87,000 titles, 6,050 serial subscriptions, 2,000 audiovisual materials.

Computer facilities: 104 computers available on campus for general student use. A campuswide network can be accessed from student residence rooms and from off campus. Internet access and online class registration are available. *Web address:* http://www.lec.edu/.

General Application Contact: Information Contact, 440-575-7050, Fax: 440-375-7005, E-mail: admissions@lec.edu.

GRADUATE UNITS

Division of Education Average age 37. 9 applicants, 89% accepted, 5 enrolled. *Faculty:* 4 full-time (1 woman), 4 part-time/adjunct (1 woman). Expenses: Contact institution. *Financial support:* Applicants required to submit FAFSA. In 2006, 20 degrees awarded. *Degree program information:* Part-time and evening/weekend programs available. Offers curriculum and instruction (MS Ed); education (MS Ed); educational leadership (MS Ed); reading (MS Ed). *Application deadline:* For fall admission, 8/1 priority date for domestic students, 6/1 for international students; for spring admission, 12/15 for domestic students, 10/1 for international students.

Lake Erie College (continued)

Applications are processed on a rolling basis. *Application fee:* $25 ($50 for international students). Electronic applications accepted. *Application Contact:* 440-375-7050, Fax: 440-375-7005, E-mail: admissions@lec.edu. *Associate Dean*, Dr. Richard Bonde, 440-375-7156, Fax: 440-375-7005, E-mail: rbonde@lec.edu.

Division of Management Studies Average age 33. 40 applicants, 98% accepted, 29 enrolled. *Faculty:* 6 full-time (2 women), 4 part-time/adjunct (1 woman). Expenses: Contact institution. *Financial support:* Career-related internships or fieldwork available. Financial award applicants required to submit FAFSA. In 2006, 22 degrees awarded. *Degree program information:* Part-time and evening/weekend programs available. Offers general management (MBA); management healthcare administration (MBA). *Application deadline:* For fall admission, 8/1 priority date for domestic students, 6/1 for international students; for spring admission, 12/15 for domestic students, 10/1 for international students. Applications are processed on a rolling basis. *Application fee:* $25 ($50 for international students). Electronic applications accepted. *Application Contact:* Admissions Office, 440-375-7050, Fax: 440-375-7005, E-mail: admissions@lec.edu. *Associate Dean*, Prof. Robert Trebar, 440-375-7115, Fax: 440-375-7005, E-mail: rtrebar@lec.edu.

LAKE ERIE COLLEGE OF OSTEOPATHIC MEDICINE, Erie, PA 16509-1025

General Information Independent, coed, graduate-only institution. *Enrollment by degree level:* 1,239 first professional, 16 master's. *Graduate faculty:* 61 full-time (9 women), 1,293 part-time/adjunct (257 women). *Tuition:* Full-time $25,000. *Required fees:* $1,095. *Graduate housing:* On-campus housing not available. *Student services:* Campus safety program, career counseling, exercise/wellness program, free psychological counseling, international student services, low-cost health insurance. *Library facilities:* LECOM Learning Resource Center. *Online resources:* library catalog, web page, access to other libraries' catalogs. *Collection:* 9,800 titles, 211 serial subscriptions, 810 audiovisual materials. *Research affiliation:* West Virginia University (neurology), Neuro Structural Research Laboratories (neurology), Cornelli Consulting (CORCON, Italy) (neurology), University of Maryland (neurology), Duke University (neurology).

Computer facilities: 24 computers available on campus for general student use. A campuswide network can be accessed from off campus. Internet access is available. *Web address:* http://www.lecom.edu.

General Application Contact: Amy Rowe, Admissions Coordinator, 814-866-6641, Fax: 814-866-8123, E-mail: arowe@lecom.edu.

GRADUATE UNITS

Professional Programs Students: 1,355 full-time (700 women); includes 261 minority (57 African Americans, 3 American Indian/Alaska Native, 171 Asian Americans or Pacific Islanders, 30 Hispanic Americans). Average age 25. 4,526 applicants, 15% accepted, 366 enrolled. *Faculty:* 85 full-time (20 women), 84 part-time/adjunct (19 women). Expenses: Contact institution. *Financial support:* In 2006–07, 1,238 students received support. Institutionally sponsored loans and scholarships/grants available. Financial award application deadline: 6/30; financial award applicants required to submit FAFSA. In 2006, 198 DOs, 88 other advanced degrees awarded. Offers biomedical sciences (Postbaccalaureate Certificate); medical education (MS); osteopathic medicine (DO); pharmacy (Pharm D). *Application deadline:* For fall admission, 3/1 for domestic students. Applications are processed on a rolling basis. *Application fee:* $50. Electronic applications accepted. *Application Contact:* Amy Rowe, Admissions Coordinator, 814-866-6641, Fax: 814-866-8123, E-mail: arowe@lecom.edu. *Provost Dean Vice President of Academic Affairs*, Dr. Silvia M. Ferretti, 814-866-6641, Fax: 814-866-8123.

LAKE FOREST COLLEGE, Lake Forest, IL 60045-2399

General Information Independent, coed, comprehensive institution. *Enrollment:* 1,448 graduate, professional, and undergraduate students; 2 full-time matriculated graduate/professional students (1 woman), 40 part-time matriculated graduate/professional students (22 women). *Enrollment by degree level:* 42 master's. *Graduate faculty:* 15 full-time (7 women). *Tuition:* Full-time $14,400. *Graduate housing:* On-campus housing not available. *Student services:* Writing training. *Library facilities:* Donnelley and Lee Library. *Online resources:* library catalog, web page, access to other libraries' catalogs. *Collection:* 263,918 titles, 1,798 serial subscriptions, 5,800 audiovisual materials.

Computer facilities: Computer purchase and lease plans are available. 120 computers available on campus for general student use. A campuswide network can be accessed from student residence rooms and from off campus. Internet access, file storage are available. *Web address:* http://www.lakeforest.edu/.

General Application Contact: Prof. Carol Gayle, Associate Director, Graduate Program in Liberal Studies, 847-735-5083, Fax: 847-735-6291, E-mail: gayle@lfc.edu.

GRADUATE UNITS

Graduate Program in Liberal Studies Students: 2 full-time (1 woman), 40 part-time (22 women); includes 3 minority (1 African American, 2 Asian Americans or Pacific Islanders). Average age 40. 26 applicants, 62% accepted, 10 enrolled. *Faculty:* 15 full-time (7 women). Expenses: Contact institution. *Financial support:* In 2006–07, 9 students received support. Tuition waivers (partial) and grants for full-time teachers available. Financial award application deadline: 8/15; financial award applicants required to submit FAFSA. In 2006, 7 degrees awarded. *Degree program information:* Part-time and evening/weekend programs available. Offers liberal studies (MLS). *Application deadline:* For fall admission, 7/1 priority date for domestic students; for spring admission, 12/1 priority date for domestic students. Applications are processed on a rolling basis. *Application fee:* $20. Electronic applications accepted. *Application Contact:* Prof. Carol Gayle, Associate Director, Graduate Program in Liberal Studies, 847-735-5083, Fax: 847-735-6291, E-mail: gayle@lfc.edu. *Director*, Prof. D. L. LeMahieu, 847-735-5133, Fax: 847-735-6291, E-mail: lemahieu@lfc.edu.

LAKE FOREST GRADUATE SCHOOL OF MANAGEMENT, Lake Forest, IL 60045

General Information Independent, coed, graduate-only institution. *Enrollment by degree level:* 797 master's. *Graduate faculty:* 160 part-time/adjunct (36 women). *Tuition:* Part-time $2,475 per course. *Graduate housing:* On-campus housing not available. *Library facilities:* First Search and OCLC. *Online resources:* library catalog.

Computer facilities: 12 computers available on campus for general student use. A campuswide network can be accessed. Internet access is available. *Web address:* http://www.lakeforestmba.edu/.

General Application Contact: Angel Baldassano, Senior Admissions Manager, 800-737-4MBA, Fax: 847-295-3656, E-mail: admiss@lfgsm.edu.

GRADUATE UNITS

MBA Program Average age 38. 206 applicants, 97% accepted, 174 enrolled. *Faculty:* 160 part-time/adjunct (36 women). Expenses: Contact institution. *Financial support:* In 2006–07, 202 students received support. Scholarships/grants available. Support available to part-time students. Financial award applicants required to submit FAFSA. In 2006, 262 degrees awarded. *Degree program information:* Part-time and evening/weekend programs available. Offers management (MBA). *Application deadline:* For fall admission, 8/13 priority date for domestic students; for spring admission, 1/15 priority date for domestic students. Applications are processed on a rolling basis. *Application fee:* $0. Electronic applications accepted. *Application Contact:* Angel Baldassano, Senior Admissions Manager, 800-737-4MBA, Fax: 847-295-3656, E-mail: admiss@lfgsm.edu. *Vice President and Academic Dean*, Arlene Mayzel, 847-574-5198, Fax: 847-574-5199, E-mail: amayzel@lfgsm.edu.

LAKEHEAD UNIVERSITY, Thunder Bay, ON P7B 5E1, Canada

General Information Province-supported, coed, comprehensive institution. *Graduate housing:* Rooms and/or apartments available to single students and available on a first-come, first-served basis to married students. Housing application deadline: 3/10. *Research affiliation:* Bowater Inc. (chemistry), Thunder Bay Regional Cancer Centre (psychosocial oncology), Centre for Northern Forest Ecosystem Research (biology, forestry, tourism), Bowater Inc. (engineering), Placer Dome (biology), Falcon bridge (biology).

GRADUATE UNITS

Graduate Studies *Degree program information:* Part-time and evening/weekend programs available. Offers clinical psychology (MA, PhD); experimental psychology (MA); geology (M Sc); history (MA); native Canadian philosophy (MA); physics (M Sc); specialization gerontology (M Ed, M Sc, MA, MSW); women's studies (M Ed, MA, MSW).

Faculty of Education *Degree program information:* Part-time and evening/weekend programs available. Offers curriculum development (M Ed); education administration (M Ed); educational studies (PhD).

Faculty of Engineering *Degree program information:* Part-time programs available. Offers control engineering (M Sc Engr).

Faculty of Forestry *Degree program information:* Part-time programs available. Offers forestry (M Sc F, MF).

Faculty of Social Sciences and Humanities *Degree program information:* Part-time and evening/weekend programs available. Offers arts and science (M Sc, MA, MSW, PhD); biology (M Sc); chemistry (M Sc); economics (MA); English (MA); sociology (MA).

School of Kinesiology *Degree program information:* Part-time programs available. Offers applied sport science and coaching (M Sc, MA).

School of Mathematical Sciences *Degree program information:* Part-time and evening/weekend programs available. Offers computer science (M Sc, MA); mathematics and statistics (M Sc, MA).

School of Social Work *Degree program information:* Part-time programs available. Offers social work (MSW).

LAKELAND COLLEGE, Sheboygan, WI 53082-0359

General Information Independent-religious, coed, comprehensive institution. *Graduate housing:* On-campus housing not available.

GRADUATE UNITS

Graduate Studies Division *Degree program information:* Part-time and evening/weekend programs available. Offers business administration (MBA); education (M Ed); theology (MAT).

LAMAR UNIVERSITY, Beaumont, TX 77710

General Information State-supported, coed, university. CGS member. *Enrollment:* 609 full-time matriculated graduate/professional students (241 women), 378 part-time matriculated graduate/professional students (205 women). *Enrollment by degree level:* 877 master's, 110 doctoral. *Graduate faculty:* 178 full-time (64 women), 24 part-time/adjunct (11 women). Tuition, nonresident: part-time $33 per hour. *Required fees:* $43 per hour. $110 per semester. *Graduate housing:* Room and/or apartments available to single students; on-campus housing not available to married students. Typical cost: $1,898 per year ($5,888 including board). Housing application deadline: 9/1. *Student services:* Campus employment opportunities, campus safety program, career counseling, child daycare facilities, disabled student services, exercise/wellness program, free psychological counseling, grant writing training, international student services, low-cost health insurance, multicultural affairs office, teacher training, writing training. *Library facilities:* Mary and John Gray Library. *Online resources:* library catalog, web page. *Collection:* 698,285 titles, 2,900 serial subscriptions, 6,572 audiovisual materials. *Research affiliation:* BASF, National Council of Research Administrators, Grants Resource Center.

Computer facilities: 120 computers available on campus for general student use. A campuswide network can be accessed from student residence rooms and from off campus. *Web address:* http://www.lamar.edu/.

General Application Contact: Sandy Drane, Coordinator of Graduate Admissions, 409-880-8356, Fax: 409-880-8414, E-mail: gradmissions@hal.lamar.edu.

GRADUATE UNITS

College of Graduate Studies Students: 609 full-time (241 women), 378 part-time (205 women); includes 127 minority (84 African Americans, 2 American Indian/Alaska Native, 14 Asian Americans or Pacific Islanders, 27 Hispanic Americans), 433 international. Average age 30. 1,859 applicants, 34% accepted, 287 enrolled. *Faculty:* 178 full-time (64 women), 24 part-time/adjunct (11 women). Expenses: Contact institution. *Financial support:* Fellowships with partial tuition reimbursements, research assistantships, teaching assistantships, career-related internships or fieldwork, Federal Work-Study, institutionally sponsored loans, scholarships/grants, and tuition waivers (partial) available. Support available to part-time students. Financial award application deadline: 4/1; financial award applicants required to submit FAFSA. In 2006, 348 master's, 8 doctorates awarded. *Degree program information:* Part-time and evening/weekend programs available. *Application deadline:* For fall admission, 5/15 for domestic students; for spring admission, 10/1 for domestic students. Applications are processed on a rolling basis. *Application fee:* $25 ($50 for international students). *Application Contact:* Sandy Drane, Coordinator of Graduate Admissions, 409-880-8356, Fax: 409-880-8414, E-mail: gradmissions@hal.lamar.edu. *Assistant Dean*, Dr. James W. Westgate, 409-880-7978, E-mail: westgate@hal.lamar.edu.

College of Arts and Sciences Students: 152 full-time (55 women), 74 part-time (28 women); includes 13 minority (8 African Americans, 5 Hispanic Americans), 132 international. Average age 28. 546 applicants, 36% accepted, 79 enrolled. *Faculty:* 60 full-time (18 women), 3 part-time/adjunct (0 women). Expenses: Contact institution. *Financial support:* Fellowships, research assistantships, teaching assistantships with tuition reimbursements, career-related internships or fieldwork, Federal Work-Study, institutionally sponsored loans, scholarships/grants, and tuition waivers (partial) available. Support available to part-time students. Financial award application deadline: 4/1. In 2006, 63 degrees awarded. *Degree program information:* Part-time and evening/weekend programs available. Offers applied criminology (MS); arts and sciences (MA, MPA, MS, MSN); biology (MS); chemistry (MS); community/clinical psychology (MS); computer science (MS); English (MA); history (MA); industrial/organizational psychology (MS); mathematics (MS); nursing administration online (MSN); nursing education online (MSN); public administration (MPA). *Application deadline:* For fall admission, 8/1 priority date for domestic students; for spring admission, 12/1 priority date for domestic students. Applications are processed on a rolling basis. *Application fee:* $25 ($50 for international students). *Application Contact:* Dr. James W. Westgate, Assistant Dean, 409-880-7978, E-mail: westgate@hal.lamar.edu. *Dean*, Dr. Brenda S. Nichols, 409-880-8508, Fax: 409-880-8007.

College of Business Students: 55 full-time (27 women), 45 part-time (20 women); includes 17 minority (9 African Americans, 4 Asian Americans or Pacific Islanders, 4 Hispanic Americans), 14 international. Average age 29. 131 applicants, 34% accepted, 29 enrolled. *Faculty:* 20 full-time (8 women), 2 part-time/adjunct (1 woman). Expenses: Contact institution. *Financial support:* In 2006–07, 12 students received support, including 4 research assistantships with partial tuition reimbursements available; fellowships with tuition reimbursements available, career-related internships or fieldwork, Federal Work-Study, institutionally sponsored loans, scholarships/grants, and tuition waivers (partial) also available. Support available to part-time students. Financial award application deadline: 4/1; financial award applicants required to submit FAFSA. In 2006, 29 degrees awarded. *Degree program information:* Part-time and evening/weekend programs available. Offers accounting (MBA); experiential business and Entrepreneurship (MBA); financial management (MBA); healthcare administration (MBA); information systems (MBA); management (MBA). *Application deadline:* For fall admission, 3/15 priority date for domestic students; for spring admission, 10/1 priority date for domestic students. Applications are processed on a rolling basis. *Application fee:* $25 ($50 for international students). *Application Contact:* Dr. Brad Mayer, Professor and Associate Dean, 409-880-2383, Fax: 409-880-8605, E-mail: bradley.mayer@lamar.edu. *Dean*, Dr. Enrique R. Venta, 409-880-8604, Fax: 409-880-8088, E-mail: henry.venta@lamar.edu.

College of Education and Human Development Students: 88 full-time (60 women), 149 part-time (113 women); includes 53 minority (41 African Americans, 1 American Indian/Alaska Native, 5 Asian Americans or Pacific Islanders, 6 Hispanic Americans), 4 international. Average age 36. 397 applicants, 36% accepted, 54 enrolled. *Faculty:* 28 full-time (18 women), 14 part-time/adjunct (8 women). Expenses: Contact institution. *Financial support:* Fellowships, research assistantships, teaching assistantships, career-related internships or fieldwork, Federal Work-Study, institutionally sponsored loans, and scholarships/grants available. Support available to part-time students. Financial award application deadline:4/1. In 2006, 80 degrees awarded. *Degree program information:* Part-time and evening/weekend programs available. Postbaccalaureate distance learning degree programs offered. Offers counseling and development (M Ed, Certificate); education (Ed D); education administration (M Ed); education and human development (M Ed, MS, DE, Ed D, Certificate); educational leadership (DE); family and consumer science (MS); kinesiology (MS); principal (Certificate); school superintendent (Certificate); supervision (M Ed); technology application (Certificate); vocational home economics (Certificate). *Application deadline:* For fall admission, 8/1 for domestic students; for spring admission, 12/1 for domestic students. Applications are processed on a rolling basis. *Application fee:* $25 ($50 for international students). *Application Contact:* Dr. Lula Henry, Director of Professional Service, 409-880-8218. *Dean,* Dr. H. Lowery-Moore, 409-880-8661.

College of Engineering Students: 232 full-time (29 women), 74 part-time (20 women); includes 12 minority (7 African Americans, 4 Asian Americans or Pacific Islanders, 1 Hispanic American), 280 international. Average age 25. 656 applicants, 34% accepted, 93 enrolled. *Faculty:* 36 full-time (4 women), 1 part-time/adjunct (0 women). Expenses: Contact institution. *Financial support:* In 2006–07, fellowships with partial tuition reimbursements (averaging $6,000 per year), research assistantships with partial tuition reimbursements (averaging $7,500 per year), teaching assistantships with partial tuition reimbursements (averaging $7,500 per year) were awarded; career-related internships or fieldwork, Federal Work-Study, institutionally sponsored loans, scholarships/grants, tuition waivers (full and partial), and laboratory assistantships, graders also available. Support available to part-time students. Financial award application deadline: 4/1. In 2006, 149 master's, 7 doctorates awarded. *Degree program information:* Part-time and evening/weekend programs available. Offers chemical engineering (ME, MES, DE, PhD); civil engineering (ME, MES, DE); electrical engineering (ME, MES, DE); engineering (ME, MEM, MES, MS, DE, PhD); engineering management (MEM); environmental engineering (MS); environmental studies (MS); industrial engineering (ME, MES, DE); mechanical engineering (ME, MES, DE). *Application deadline:* For fall admission, 5/15 priority date for domestic students; for spring admission, 10/1 priority date for domestic students. Applications are processed on a rolling basis. *Application fee:* $25 ($50 for international students). *Application Contact:* Sandy Drane, Coordinator of Graduate Admissions, 409-880-8356, Fax: 409-880-8414, E-mail: gradmissions@hal.lamar.edu. *Chair,* Dr. Jack Hopper, 409-880-8784, Fax: 409-880-2197, E-mail: che_dept@hal.lamar.edu.

College of Fine Arts and Communication Students: 82 full-time (70 women), 36 part-time (24 women); includes 32 minority (19 African Americans, 1 American Indian/Alaska Native, 1 Asian American or Pacific Islander, 11 Hispanic Americans), 3 international. Average age 31. 129 applicants, 29% accepted, 32 enrolled. *Faculty:* 30 full-time (16 women), 4 part-time/adjunct (2 women). Expenses: Contact institution. *Financial support:* Fellowships, research assistantships, teaching assistantships, career-related internships or fieldwork, Federal Work-Study, institutionally sponsored loans, and tuition waivers (partial) available. Support available to part-time students. Financial award application deadline: 4/1. In 2006, 27 master's, 1 doctorate awarded. *Degree program information:* Part-time and evening/weekend programs available. Offers art history (MA); audiology (MS, Au D); deaf studies/deaf education (MS, Ed D); fine arts and communication (MA, MM, MM Ed, MS, Au D, Ed D); music education (MM Ed); music performance (MM); photography (MA); speech language pathology (MS); studio art (MA); theatre (MS); visual design (MA). *Application deadline:* For fall admission, 8/1 for domestic students; for spring admission, 12/1 for domestic students. Applications are processed on a rolling basis. *Application fee:* $25 ($50 for international students). *Application Contact:* Debbie Piper, Coordinator of Graduate Admissions, 409-880-8356, Fax: 409-880-8414, E-mail: gradmissions@hal.lamar.edu. *Dean,* Dr. Russ A. Schultz, 409-880-8137, Fax: 409-880-2286, E-mail: russ.schultz@lamar.edu.

See Close-Up on page 943.

LANCASTER BIBLE COLLEGE, Lancaster, PA 17608-3403

General Information Independent-religious, coed, comprehensive institution. *Enrollment:* 958 graduate, professional, and undergraduate students; 55 full-time matriculated graduate/professional students (28 women), 117 part-time matriculated graduate/professional students (55 women). *Enrollment by degree level:* 172 master's. *Graduate faculty:* 8 full-time (1 woman), 5 part-time/adjunct (1 woman). *Tuition:* Full-time $4,620; part-time $385 per credit. *Graduate housing:* On-campus housing not available. *Student services:* Campus employment opportunities, career counseling, international student services. *Library facilities:* Lancaster Bible College Library. *Online resources:* library catalog, access to other libraries' catalogs. *Collection:* 132,599 titles, 6,852 serial subscriptions.

Computer facilities: 50 computers available on campus for general student use. A campuswide network can be accessed from student residence rooms. Internet access is available. *Web address:* http://www.lbc.edu/.

General Application Contact: Dr. Ray A. Naugle, Dean of Graduate Education, 717-560-8297, Fax: 717-560-8236, E-mail: rnaugle@lbc.edu.

GRADUATE UNITS

Graduate School Students: 55 full-time (28 women), 117 part-time (55 women); includes 21 minority (15 African Americans, 5 Asian Americans or Pacific Islanders, 1 Hispanic American). Average age 36. *Faculty:* 8 full-time (1 woman), 5 part-time/adjunct (1 woman). Expenses: Contact institution. *Financial support:* In 2006–07, 31 students received support, including 2 teaching assistantships (averaging $1,800 per year); scholarships/grants and unspecified assistantships also available. Support available to part-time students. Financial award application deadline: 6/1; financial award applicants required to submit FAFSA. In 2006, 16 degrees awarded. *Degree program information:* Part-time and evening/weekend programs available. Offers Bible (MA); consulting resource teacher (M Ed); counseling (MA); ministry (MA); school counseling (M Ed). *Application deadline:* Applications are processed on a rolling basis. *Application fee:* $25. *Application Contact:* Emily Higgins, Student Application Contact, 717-560-8297, E-mail: ehiggins@lbc.edu. *Dean of Graduate Education,* Dr. Ray A. Naugle, 717-560-8297, Fax: 717-560-8236, E-mail: rnaugle@lbc.edu.

LANCASTER THEOLOGICAL SEMINARY, Lancaster, PA 17603-2812

General Information Independent-religious, coed, graduate-only institution. *Enrollment by degree level:* 101 first professional, 17 master's, 35 doctoral, 11 other advanced degrees. *Graduate faculty:* 12 full-time (3 women), 19 part-time/adjunct (8 women). *Tuition:* Full-time $10,750; part-time $400 per credit. *Graduate housing:* Rooms and/or apartments available on a first-come, first-served basis to single and married students. Housing application deadline: 8/1. *Student services:* Campus employment opportunities, disabled student services, international student services. *Library facilities:* Philip Schaff Library. *Online resources:* library catalog. *Collection:* 122,000 titles, 385 serial subscriptions.

Computer facilities: 12 computers available on campus for general student use. A campuswide network can be accessed. Internet access and online class registration are available. *Web address:* http://www.lancasterseminary.edu/.

General Application Contact: Rev. Ava Blackwell, Director of Admissions and Financial Aid, 717-290-8737, Fax: 717-393-0423, E-mail: ablackwell@lancasterseminary.edu.

GRADUATE UNITS

Graduate and Professional Programs Students: 112 full-time (83 women), 52 part-time (39 women); includes 23 minority (21 African Americans, 2 Hispanic Americans). Average age 44. 54 applicants, 96% accepted, 49 enrolled. *Faculty:* 12 full-time (3 women), 19 part-time/adjunct (8 women). Expenses: Contact institution. *Financial support:* In 2006–07, 76 students received support. Career-related internships or fieldwork, scholarships/grants, and tuition waivers (partial) available. Financial award application deadline: 4/15; financial award applicants required to submit FAFSA. In 2006, 33 M Divs, 7 master's awarded. Offers biblical studies (M Div, MAR); church life and work (M Div, MAR); historical studies (M Div, MAR); integrated ministry studies (M Div, MAR); lay leadership (Certificate); theological studies (M Div, MAR); theology (D Min). *Application deadline:* For fall admission, 4/1 priority date for domestic students, 1/1 for international students; for spring admission, 11/15 priority date for domestic students. Applications are processed on a rolling basis. *Application fee:* $50. *Application Contact:* Rev. Ava Blackwell, Director of Admissions and Financial Aid, 717-290-8737, Fax: 717-393-0423, E-mail: ablackwell@lancasterseminary.edu. *Vice President of Academic Affairs and Dean of the Seminary,* Dr. Edwin D. Aponte, 717-393-0654, Fax: 717-393-0423, E-mail: eaponte@lancasterseminary.edu.

LANDER UNIVERSITY, Greenwood, SC 29649-2099

General Information State-supported, coed, comprehensive institution. *Enrollment:* 2,682 graduate, professional, and undergraduate students; 11 full-time matriculated graduate/professional students (8 women), 29 part-time matriculated graduate/professional students (25 women). *Enrollment by degree level:* 40 master's. *Graduate faculty:* 6 full-time (3 women), 4 part-time/adjunct (all women). Tuition, state resident: full-time $7,824; part-time $326 per credit hour. Tuition, nonresident: full-time $14,932; part-time $622 per credit hour. *Required fees:* $550. *Graduate housing:* Room and/or apartments available on a first-come, first-served basis to single students; on-campus housing not available to married students. Typical cost: $5,755 (including board). Room and board charges vary according to board plan. *Student services:* Campus employment opportunities, campus safety program, career counseling, disabled student services, free psychological counseling, international student services, low-cost health insurance, multicultural affairs office, teacher training. *Library facilities:* Jackson Library. *Online resources:* library catalog, web page. *Collection:* 186,690 titles, 657 serial subscriptions.

Computer facilities: Computer purchase and lease plans are available. 125 computers available on campus for general student use. A campuswide network can be accessed from student residence rooms and from off campus. Internet access and online class registration are available. *Web address:* http://www.lander.edu/.

General Application Contact: Dr. Linda Neely, Director of Graduate Studies, 864-388-8352, Fax: 864-388-8144, E-mail: lneely@lander.edu.

GRADUATE UNITS

School of Education Students: 11 full-time (8 women), 29 part-time (25 women); includes 5 minority (all African Americans) Average age 34. *Faculty:* 6 full-time (3 women), 4 part-time/adjunct (all women). Expenses: Contact institution. *Financial support:* Federal Work-Study available. Support available to part-time students. Financial award application deadline: 4/15; financial award applicants required to submit FAFSA. In 2006, 41 degrees awarded. *Degree program information:* Part-time programs available. Offers elementary education (M Ed); teaching (MAT). *Application deadline:* Applications are processed on a rolling basis. *Application fee:* $35. Electronic applications accepted. *Application Contact:* Dr. Linda Neely, Director of Graduate Studies, 864-388-8268, Fax: 864-388-8144, E-mail: lneely@lander.edu. *Dean,* Dr. Sandra Lemoine, 864-388-8225, Fax: 864-388-8890.

LANGSTON UNIVERSITY, Langston, OK 73050-0907

General Information State-supported, coed, comprehensive institution. CGS member. *Graduate housing:* Rooms and/or apartments available on a first-come, first-served basis to single and married students.

GRADUATE UNITS

School of Education and Behavioral Sciences *Degree program information:* Part-time programs available. Offers bilingual/multicultural (M Ed); elementary education (M Ed); English as a second language (M Ed); rehabilitation counseling (M Sc); urban education (M Ed).

School of Physical Therapy Offers physical therapy (DPT).

LA ROCHE COLLEGE, Pittsburgh, PA 15237-5898

General Information Independent-religious, coed, comprehensive institution. *Enrollment:* 1,533 graduate, professional, and undergraduate students; 70 full-time matriculated graduate/professional students (41 women), 97 part-time matriculated graduate/professional students (77 women). *Enrollment by degree level:* 150 master's, 17 other advanced degrees. *Graduate faculty:* 5 full-time (3 women), 11 part-time/adjunct (3 women). *Tuition:* Full-time $9,900; part-time $550 per credit. *Required fees:* $14 per credit. *Graduate housing:* On-campus housing not available. *Student services:* Campus employment opportunities, career counseling, disabled student services, free psychological counseling, international student services, low-cost health insurance, multicultural affairs office. *Library facilities:* John J. Wright Library. *Online resources:* library catalog, web page. *Collection:* 108,432 titles, 601 serial subscriptions.

Computer facilities: 200 computers available on campus for general student use. A campuswide network can be accessed from student residence rooms and from off campus. Internet access and online class registration are available. *Web address:* http://www.laroche.edu/.

General Application Contact: Hope Schiffgens, Director of Admissions for Graduate and Continuing Education, 412-536-1266, Fax: 412-536-1283, E-mail: schombh1@laroche.edu.

GRADUATE UNITS

School of Graduate Studies Students: 70 full-time (41 women), 97 part-time (77 women); includes 4 minority (2 African Americans, 1 Asian American or Pacific Islander, 1 Hispanic American), 5 international. Average age 35. 44 applicants, 98% accepted, 40 enrolled. *Faculty:* 5 full-time (3 women), 11 part-time/adjunct (3 women). Expenses: Contact institution. *Financial support:* Unspecified assistantships available. Financial award application deadline: 3/31; financial award applicants required to submit FAFSA. In 2006, 62 degrees awarded. *Degree program information:* Part-time and evening/weekend programs available. Offers family nurse practitioner (MSN); human resources management (MS, Certificate); nurse anesthesia (MS); nursing management (MSN). *Application deadline:* Applications are processed on a rolling basis. *Application fee:* $50. Electronic applications accepted. *Application Contact:* Hope Schiffgens, Director of Admissions for Graduate and Continuing Education, 412-536-1266, Fax: 412-536-1283, E-mail: schombh1@laroche.edu. *Vice President for Academic Affairs and Graduate Dean,* Dr. Howard Ishiyama, 412-536-1282, Fax: 412-536-1290, E-mail: ishiyah1@laroche.edu.

LA SALLE UNIVERSITY, Philadelphia, PA 19141-1199

General Information Independent-religious, coed, comprehensive institution. *Graduate housing:* Room and/or apartments available on a first-come, first-served basis to single students; on-campus housing not available to married students. Housing application deadline: 7/1.

GRADUATE UNITS

School of Arts and Sciences *Degree program information:* Part-time and evening/weekend programs available. Offers arts and sciences (MA, MS, Psy D); bilingual/bicultural studies (Spanish) (MA); Central and Eastern European studies (MA); clinical psychology (Psy D); clinical-counseling psychology (MA); computer information science (MS); education (MA); family psychology (Psy D); history (MA); information technology leadership (MS); pastoral studies (MA); professional communication (MA); rehabilitation psychology (Psy D); religion (MA); theological studies (MA).

School of Business *Degree program information:* Part-time and evening/weekend programs available. Offers business administration (MBA, MS, Certificate). Electronic applications accepted.

School of Nursing and Health Sciences *Degree program information:* Part-time programs available. Postbaccalaureate distance learning degree programs offered (minimal on-campus study). Offers adult health and illness, clinical nurse specialist (MSN); gerontology (Certificate); nursing administration (MSN); nursing education (Certificate); nursing informatics (Certificate); primary care of adults-nurse practitioner (MSN); public health nursing (MSN); school nursing (Certificate); speech-language-hearing science (MS); wound, ostomy and continence nursing (Certificate); wound, ostomy, and continence nursing (MSN).

LASELL COLLEGE, Newton, MA 02466-2709

General Information Independent, coed, comprehensive institution. *Graduate housing:* On-campus housing not available. *Research affiliation:* Lasell Village (elder care), The Rosemary B. Fuss Center for Research on Aging and Intergenerational Studies (elder care).

GRADUATE UNITS

Program in Management *Degree program information:* Part-time and evening/weekend programs available. Offers elder care administration (MS); elder care marketing (MS); management (MS); marketing (MS). Electronic applications accepted.

LA SIERRA UNIVERSITY, Riverside, CA 92515

General Information Independent-religious, coed, comprehensive institution. CGS member. *Graduate housing:* Rooms and/or apartments available on a first-come, first-served basis to single students and available to married students.

GRADUATE UNITS

College of Arts and Sciences *Degree program information:* Part-time programs available. Offers arts and sciences (MA); English (MA).

School of Business and Management Offers business administration and management (MBA); executive business administration (EMBA); leadership, values, and ethics for business and management (Certificate).

School of Education *Degree program information:* Part-time and evening/weekend programs available. Offers administration and leadership (MA, Ed D, Ed S); counseling (MA); curriculum and instruction (MA, Ed D, Ed S); education (MA, Ed D, Ed S); educational psychology (Ed S); school psychology (Ed S); special education (MA).

School of Religion *Degree program information:* Part-time programs available. Offers religion (MA); religious education (MA); religious studies (MA).

LAURA AND ALVIN SIEGAL COLLEGE OF JUDAIC STUDIES, Beachwood, OH 44122-7116

General Information Independent, coed, comprehensive institution. *Graduate housing:* On-campus housing not available.

GRADUATE UNITS

Graduate Programs *Degree program information:* Part-time and evening/weekend programs available. Postbaccalaureate distance learning degree programs offered (no on-campus study). Offers humanities (MA); Jewish education (MAJS); Judaic studies (MAJS); religious education (MAJS).

LAURENTIAN UNIVERSITY, Sudbury, ON P3E 2C6, Canada

General Information Province-supported, coed, comprehensive institution. *Graduate housing:* Rooms and/or apartments available on a first-come, first-served basis to single and married students.

GRADUATE UNITS

School of Graduate Studies and Research *Degree program information:* Part-time and evening/weekend programs available. Offers applied physics (M Sc); biology (M Sc); chemistry and biochemistry (M Sc); geology (M Sc); history (MA); human development (M Sc, MA); humanities: interpretation and values (MA); sociology (MA).

School of Commerce and Administration *Degree program information:* Part-time and evening/weekend programs available. Offers commerce and administration (MBA).

School of Engineering *Degree program information:* Part-time programs available. Offers metallurgy (MA Sc); mineral resource engineering (MA Sc); mineral resources engineering (M Eng).

School of Social Work *Degree program information:* Part-time programs available. Offers social service (MSS). Open only to French-speaking students.

LAWRENCE TECHNOLOGICAL UNIVERSITY, Southfield, MI 48075-1058

General Information Independent, coed, university. *Enrollment:* 4,049 graduate, professional, and undergraduate students; 79 full-time matriculated graduate/professional students (28 women), 1,223 part-time matriculated graduate/professional students (397 women). *Enrollment by degree level:* 1,214 master's, 88 doctoral. *Graduate faculty:* 43 full-time (13 women), 97 part-time/adjunct (15 women). *Graduate housing:* Rooms and/or apartments available on a first-come, first-served basis to single and married students. Housing application deadline: 5/1. *Student services:* Campus employment opportunities, career counseling, exercise/wellness program, international student services, low-cost health insurance, writing training. *Library facilities:* Lawrence Technological University Library plus 1 other. *Online resources:* library catalog, web page, access to other libraries' catalogs. *Collection:* 128,000 titles, 750 serial subscriptions, 136 audiovisual materials. *Research affiliation:* William Beaumont Hospital (biomedical engineering), Chrysler Challenge Fund (automotive), Mitsubishi Chemical Corporation (carbon fiber reinforced polymer tendons and rods), Tokyo Rope Manufacturer (carbon fiber composites cables), Kistler Instrument Corp. (automotive test instrumentation products), AM General (carbon fiber composites).

Computer facilities: Computer purchase and lease plans are available. 60 computers available on campus for general student use. A campuswide network can be accessed from student residence rooms and from off campus. Internet access and online class registration, degree audit, black board, SCT Banner (student information) are available. *Web address:* http://www.ltu.edu/.

General Application Contact: Jane Rohrback, Director of Admissions, 248-204-3160, Fax: 248-204-3188, E-mail: admissions@ltu.edu.

GRADUATE UNITS

College of Architecture and Design Students: 20 full-time (7 women), 102 part-time (54 women); includes 23 minority (11 African Americans, 9 Asian Americans or Pacific Islanders, 3 Hispanic Americans), 2 international. Average age 28. 65 applicants, 77% accepted, 29 enrolled. *Faculty:* 11 full-time (4 women), 17 part-time/adjunct (2 women). Expenses: Contact institution. *Financial support:* Application deadline: 3/1; In 2006, 44 degrees awarded. *Degree program information:* Part-time and evening/weekend programs available. Offers architecture (M Arch); interior design (MID). *Application deadline:* For fall admission, 8/1 priority date for domestic students; for winter admission, 12/1 priority date for domestic students; for spring admission, 2/1 for domestic students. Applications are processed on a rolling basis. *Application fee:* $50. Electronic applications accepted. *Application Contact:* Jane Rohrback, Director of Admissions, 248-204-3160, Fax: 248-204-3188, E-mail: admissions@ltu.edu. *Dean of the College of Architecture and Design,* Glen LeRoy, 248-204-2800, Fax: 248-204-2900, E-mail: archdean@ltu.edu.

College of Arts and Sciences Students: 5 full-time (0 women), 100 part-time (59 women); includes 21 minority (8 African Americans, 13 Asian Americans or Pacific Islanders), 2 international. Average age 33. 87 applicants, 87% accepted, 39 enrolled. *Faculty:* 9 full-time (3 women), 8 part-time/adjunct (0 women). Expenses: Contact institution. *Financial support:* Application deadline: 3/1; In 2006, 42 degrees awarded. *Degree program information:* Part-time and evening/weekend programs available. Offers computer science (MS); educational technology (MET); science education (MSE); technical communication (MS). *Application deadline:* For fall admission, 8/1 priority date for domestic students; for winter admission, 12/1 priority date for domestic students; for spring admission, 5/1 for domestic students. Applications are processed on a rolling basis. *Application fee:* $50. Electronic applications accepted. *Application Contact:* Jane Rohrback, Director of Admissions, 248-204-3160, Fax: 248-204-3188, E-mail: admissions@ltu.edu. *Interim Dean,* Dr. Hsiao-Ping Moore, 248-204-3500, Fax: 248-204-3518, E-mail: scidean@ltu.edu.

College of Engineering Students: 7 full-time (1 woman), 319 part-time (49 women); includes 70 minority (21 African Americans, 41 Asian Americans or Pacific Islanders, 8 Hispanic Americans), 8 international. Average age 29. 212 applicants, 79% accepted, 102 enrolled. *Faculty:* 12 full-time (2 women), 11 part-time/adjunct (0 women). Expenses: Contact institution. *Financial support:* Institutionally sponsored loans available. Support available to part-time students. Financial award application deadline: 3/1; financial award applicants required to submit FAFSA. In 2006, 67 degrees awarded. *Degree program information:* Part-time and evening/weekend programs available. Offers automotive engineering (MAE); civil engineering (MCE); construction engineering management (MS); electrical and computer engineering (MS); engineering management (ME); manufacturing systems (MEMS, DE); mechanical engineering (MS); mechatronic systems engineering (MS). *Application deadline:* For fall admission, 8/1 priority date for domestic students; for winter admission, 12/1 priority date for domestic students; for spring admission, 5/1 for domestic students. Applications are processed on a rolling basis. *Application fee:* $50. Electronic applications accepted. *Application Contact:* Jane Rohrback, Director of Admissions, 248-204-3160, Fax: 248-204-3188, E-mail: admissions@ltu.edu. *Dean,* Dr. Laird Johnston, 248-204-2500, Fax: 248-204-2509, E-mail: lejohnston@ltu.edu.

College of Management Students: 47 full-time (20 women), 702 part-time (235 women); includes 285 minority (98 African Americans, 178 Asian Americans or Pacific Islanders, 9 Hispanic Americans), 15 international. Average age 34. 337 applicants, 90% accepted, 192 enrolled. *Faculty:* 11 full-time (4 women), 61 part-time/adjunct (13 women). Expenses: Contact institution. *Financial support:* Institutionally sponsored loans available. Support available to part-time students. Financial award application deadline: 3/1; financial award applicants required to submit FAFSA. In 2006, 281 degrees awarded. *Degree program information:* Part-time and evening/weekend programs available. Offers business administration (MBA, DBA); information systems (MS); information technology (DM); operations management (MS). *Application deadline:* For fall admission, 8/1 priority date for domestic students; for winter admission, 12/1 priority date for domestic students; for spring admission, 5/1 for domestic students. Applications are processed on a rolling basis. *Application fee:* $50. Electronic applications accepted. *Application Contact:* Jane Rohrback, Director of Admissions, 248-204-3160, Fax: 248-204-3188, E-mail: admissions@ltu.edu. *Dean,* Dr. Lou DeGennaro, 248-204-3050, E-mail: degennaro@ltu.edu.

LEADERSHIP INSTITUTE OF SEATTLE, Kenmore, WA 98028-4966

General Information Independent, coed, graduate-only institution. *Enrollment by degree level:* 140 master's. *Graduate faculty:* 10 full-time (6 women), 5 part-time/adjunct (2 women). *Tuition:* Full-time $14,560. *Required fees:* $3,700. *Graduate housing:* On-campus housing not available. *Student services:* Campus employment opportunities, career counseling, disabled student services, free psychological counseling, international student services, low-cost health insurance, writing training. *Library facilities:* Pino-Emory Library plus 1 other. *Online resources:* library catalog, access to other libraries' catalogs. *Collection:* 4,000 titles, 15 serial subscriptions, 250 audiovisual materials.

Computer facilities: 20 computers available on campus for general student use. Internet access is available. *Web address:* http://www.lios.org/.

General Application Contact: Scott Harris, Director, Academic Admissions, 425-939-8124, Fax: 425-939-8110, E-mail: sharris@lios.org.

GRADUATE UNITS

School of Applied Behavioral Science Students: 140 full-time (114 women); includes 18 minority (4 African Americans, 2 American Indian/Alaska Native, 8 Asian Americans or Pacific Islanders, 4 Hispanic Americans), 6 international. Average age 37. 105 applicants, 97% accepted, 90 enrolled. *Faculty:* 10 full-time (6 women), 5 part-time/adjunct (2 women). Expenses: Contact institution. *Financial support:* In 2006–07, 101 students received support. Career-related internships or fieldwork and scholarships/grants available. Financial award applicants required to submit FAFSA. In 2006, 70 degrees awarded. Offers consulting and coaching in organizations (MA); systems counseling (MA). *Application deadline:* For fall admission, 7/20 priority date for domestic and international students; for winter admission, 11/9 priority date for domestic and international students. Applications are processed on a rolling basis. *Application fee:* $65. *Application Contact:* Scott Harris, Director, Academic Admissions, 425-939-8124, Fax: 425-939-8110, E-mail: sharris@lios.org. *Dean,* Daniel D. Leahy, 425-939-8100, Fax: 425-939-8110, E-mail: dleahy@lios.org.

LEBANESE AMERICAN UNIVERSITY, Beirut, Lebanon

General Information Private, comprehensive institution.

GRADUATE UNITS

School of Arts and Sciences Offers computer science (MS); international affairs (MA).

School of Business Offers business (MBA).

School of Pharmacy Offers pharmacy (Pharm D).

LEBANON VALLEY COLLEGE, Annville, PA 17003-1400

General Information Independent-religious, coed, comprehensive institution. *Enrollment:* 1,961 graduate, professional, and undergraduate students; 28 full-time matriculated graduate/professional students (21 women), 90 part-time matriculated graduate/professional students (55 women). *Enrollment by degree level:* 90 master's, 28 other advanced degrees. *Tuition:* Full-time $28,280; part-time $390 per credit. *Required fees:* $575. *Graduate housing:* On-campus housing not available. *Student services:* Career counseling, disabled student services. *Library facilities:* Bishop Library. *Online resources:* library catalog, web page, access to other libraries' catalogs. *Collection:* 187,289 titles, 820 serial subscriptions, 12,632 audiovisual materials.

Computer facilities: 227 computers available on campus for general student use. A campuswide network can be accessed from student residence rooms and from off campus. Internet access and online class registration are available. *Web address:* http://www.lvc.edu/.

General Application Contact: Elaine D. Feather, Director of Graduate Studies and Continuing Education, 717-867-6213, Fax: 717-867-6018, E-mail: feather@lvc.edu.

GRADUATE UNITS

Graduate Studies and Continuing Education Average age 34. *Faculty:* 4 full-time (1 woman), 12 part-time/adjunct (4 women). Expenses: Contact institution. *Financial support:* Application deadline: 5/1; In 2006, 41 degrees awarded. *Degree program information:* Part-time and evening/weekend programs available. Offers business administration (MBA); music education (MME); science education (MSE). *Application deadline:* Applications are processed on a rolling basis. *Application fee:* $30. Electronic applications accepted. *Director of Graduate Studies and Continuing Education,* Elaine D. Feather, 717-867-6213, Fax: 717-867-6018, E-mail: feather@lvc.edu.

LEE UNIVERSITY, Cleveland, TN 37320-3450

General Information Independent-religious, coed, comprehensive institution. *Enrollment:* 4,012 graduate, professional, and undergraduate students; 153 full-time matriculated graduate/professional students (104 women), 135 part-time matriculated graduate/professional students (83 women). *Enrollment by degree level:* 288 master's. *Graduate faculty:* 72 full-time (18 women), 3 part-time/adjunct (0 women). *Tuition:* Part-time $412 per credit. *Required fees:* $10 per semester. Tuition and fees vary according to course load. *Graduate housing:* Rooms and/or apartments available on a first-come, first-served basis to single and married students. Typical cost: $2,788 per year ($5,252 including board) for single students; $4,023 per year ($6,487 including board) for married students. Room and board charges vary according to board plan and housing facility selected. *Student services:* Campus employment opportunities, campus safety program, career counseling, disabled student services, exercise/wellness program, free psychological counseling, international student services, teacher training, writing training. *Library facilities:* William G. Squires Library plus 3 others. *Online resources:* library catalog, web page, access to other libraries' catalogs. *Collection:* 151,905 titles, 10,000 serial subscriptions, 5,448 audiovisual materials.

Computer facilities: Computer purchase and lease plans are available. A campuswide network can be accessed from off campus. Internet access and online class registration are available. *Web address:* http://www.leeuniversity.edu/.

General Application Contact: Vicki Glasscock, Graduate Admissions Director, 423-614-8059, E-mail: vglasscock@leeuniversity.edu.

GRADUATE UNITS

Program in Behavioral Sciences Students: 76 full-time (63 women), 13 part-time (12 women); includes 32 minority (2 African Americans, 25 American Indian/Alaska Native, 1 Asian American or Pacific Islander, 4 Hispanic Americans), 3 international. 51 applicants, 73% accepted, 23 enrolled. *Faculty:* 12 full-time (3 women), 2 part-time/adjunct (0 women). Expenses: Contact institution. *Financial support:* Career-related internships or fieldwork, Federal Work-Study, and institutionally sponsored loans available. In 2006, 23 degrees awarded. Offers mental health counseling (MS); school counseling (MS). *Application deadline:* For fall admission, 4/1 priority date for domestic and international students; for spring admission, 10/1 for domestic and international students. Applications are processed on a rolling basis. *Application fee:* $25. *Application Contact:* Vicki Glasscock, Graduate Admissions Director, 423-614-8059, E-mail: vglasscock@leeuniversity.edu. *Director*, Dr. Doyle Goff, 423-614-8126, Fax: 423-614-8129, E-mail: drgoff@leeuniversity.edu.

Program in Education Students: 103 full-time (66 women), 22 part-time (15 women); includes 43 minority (5 African Americans, 36 American Indian/Alaska Native, 2 Hispanic Americans), 3 international. 49 applicants, 100% accepted, 28 enrolled. *Faculty:* 25 full-time (11 women). Expenses: Contact institution. *Financial support:* Career-related internships or fieldwork, Federal Work-Study, and institutionally sponsored loans available. In 2006, 75 degrees awarded. Offers classroom teaching (M Ed); educational leadership (M Ed); elementary/secondary education (MAT); special education (elementary) (M Ed); special education (secondary) (M Ed, MAT); special education (severe disabilities) (M Ed). *Application deadline:* For fall admission, 4/1 for domestic students; for spring admission, 10/1 for domestic students. Applications are processed on a rolling basis. *Application fee:* $25. *Application Contact:* Vicki Glasscock, Graduate Admissions Director, 423-614-8059, E-mail: vglasscock@leeuniversity.edu. *Director*, Dr. Gary Riggins, 423-614-8193.

Program in Music Students: 26 full-time (12 women), 3 part-time (all women); includes 12 minority (1 African American, 10 American Indian/Alaska Native, 1 Hispanic American), 4 international. 24 applicants, 71% accepted, 9 enrolled. *Faculty:* 21 full-time (4 women), 1 part-time/adjunct (0 women). Expenses: Contact institution. *Financial support:* In 2006–07, 13 teaching assistantships (averaging $2,275 per year) were awarded; career-related internships or fieldwork, Federal Work-Study, institutionally sponsored loans, and scholarships/grants also available. Financial award application deadline: 4/15; financial award applicants required to submit FAFSA. In 2006, 2 degrees awarded. *Degree program information:* Part-time programs available. Offers church music (MCM); music education (MME); performance (MMMP). *Application deadline:* For fall admission, 4/1 for domestic students; for spring admission, 10/1 for domestic students. Applications are processed on a rolling basis. *Application fee:* $25. *Application Contact:* Vicki Glasscock, Graduate Admissions Director, 423-614-8059, E-mail: vglasscock@leeuniversity.edu. *Director*, Dr. Jim W. Burns, 423-614-8240, Fax: 423-614-8242, E-mail: gradmusic@leeuniversity.edu.

Program in Religion Students: 39 full-time (15 women), 6 part-time; includes 7 minority (1 African American, 4 American Indian/Alaska Native, 1 Asian American or Pacific Islander, 1 Hispanic American), 4 international. 21 applicants, 81% accepted, 13 enrolled. *Faculty:* 14 full-time (0 women). Expenses: Contact institution. *Financial support:* Career-related internships or fieldwork, Federal Work-Study, and institutionally sponsored loans available. In 2006, 5 degrees awarded. Offers biblical studies (MA); theological studies (MA); youth and family ministry (MA). *Application deadline:* For fall admission, 4/1 for domestic students; for spring admission, 10/1 for domestic students. *Application fee:* $25. *Application Contact:* Vicki Glasscock, Graduate Admissions Director, 423-614-8059, E-mail: vglasscock@leeuniversity.edu. *Director*, Dr. Michael Fuller, 423-614-8338, E-mail: mfuller@leeuniversity.edu.

LEHIGH UNIVERSITY, Bethlehem, PA 18015-3094

General Information Independent, coed, university. CGS member. *Enrollment:* 6,858 graduate, professional, and undergraduate students; 928 full-time matriculated graduate/professional students (402 women), 1,024 part-time matriculated graduate/professional students (495 women). *Enrollment by degree level:* 1,254 master's, 698 doctoral. *Graduate faculty:* 370 full-time (85 women), 100 part-time/adjunct (24 women). *Graduate housing:* Rooms and/or apartments available on a first-come, first-served basis to single and married students. *Student services:* Campus employment opportunities, campus safety program, career counseling, child daycare facilities, exercise/wellness program, free psychological counseling, international student services, low-cost health insurance, multicultural affairs office, teacher training, writing training. *Library facilities:* E. W. Fairchild-Martindale Library plus 1 other. *Online resources:* library catalog, web page, access to other libraries' catalogs. *Collection:* 1.2 million titles, 6,271 serial subscriptions.

Computer facilities: 572 computers available on campus for general student use. A campuswide network can be accessed from student residence rooms and from off campus. Internet access and online class registration are available. *Web address:* http://www.lehigh.edu/.

General Application Contact: Information Contact, 610-758-3000.

GRADUATE UNITS

College of Arts and Sciences Students: 282 full-time (147 women), 216 part-time (105 women); includes 29 minority (8 African Americans, 1 American Indian/Alaska Native, 11 Asian Americans or Pacific Islanders, 9 Hispanic Americans), 65 international. 534 applicants, 56% accepted, 161 enrolled. *Faculty:* 159 full-time (43 women), 26 part-time/adjunct (12 women). Expenses: Contact institution. *Financial support:* In 2006–07, 10 fellowships with full tuition reimbursements (averaging $16,000 per year), 21 research assistantships with full tuition reimbursements, 119 teaching assistantships with full tuition reimbursements (averaging $13,500 per year) were awarded; career-related internships or fieldwork, Federal Work-Study, institutionally sponsored loans, scholarships/grants, tuition waivers (full and partial), and unspecified assistantships also available. Support available to part-time students. Financial award application deadline: 1/15. In 2006, 128 master's, 27 doctorates awarded. *Degree program information:* Part-time programs available. Postbaccalaureate distance learning degree programs offered (no on-campus study). Offers American studies (MA); applied mathematics (MS, PhD); arts and sciences (MA, MS, PhD); biochemistry (PhD); chemistry (MS, PhD); clinical chemistry (MS); earth and environmental sciences (MS, PhD); English (MA, PhD); history (MA, PhD); human cognition and development (MS, PhD); integrative biology (PhD); mathematics (MS, PhD); molecular biology (MS, PhD); pharmaceutical chemistry (MS, PhD); photonics (MS); physics (MS, PhD); political science (MA); polymer science (MS, PhD); polymer science and engineering (MS, PhD); sociology (MA); statistics (MS). *Application deadline:* For fall admission, 7/15 for domestic students; for spring admission, 12/30 for domestic students. Applications are processed on a rolling basis. *Application fee:* $50. Electronic applications accepted. *Application Contact:* Mary Ann Haller, Coordinator, 610-758-4280, Fax: 610-758-6232, E-mail: mh0h@lehigh.edu. *Dean*, Dr. Anne S. Meltzer, 610-758-3300, Fax: 610-758-3677, E-mail: asm3@lehigh.edu.

College of Business and Economics Students: 87 full-time (25 women), 219 part-time (60 women); includes 34 minority (9 African Americans, 22 Asian Americans or Pacific Islanders, 3 Hispanic Americans), 56 international. 371 applicants, 69% accepted, 151 enrolled. *Faculty:* 64 full-time (14 women), 12 part-time/adjunct (0 women). Expenses: Contact institution. *Financial support:* In 2006–07, 2 fellowships with full tuition reimbursements (averaging $13,200 per year), 8 research assistantships with full and partial tuition reimbursements (averaging $1,000 per year), 13 teaching assistantships with full tuition reimbursements (averaging $13,200 per year) were awarded; career-related internships or fieldwork, scholarships/grants, health care benefits, tuition waivers (full and partial), and unspecified assistantships also available. Support available to part-time students. Financial award application deadline: 1/15. In 2006, 103 master's, 2 doctorates awarded. *Degree program information:* Part-time and evening/weekend programs available. Postbaccalaureate distance learning degree programs offered (minimal on-campus study). Offers accounting (MS); accounting and information analysis (MS); analytical finance (MS); business administration (MBA); economics (MS, PhD); entrepreneurship (Certificate); finance (MS); health and bio-pharmaceutical economics (MS); organizational leadership (Certificate); project management (Certificate); supply chain management (Certificate). *Application deadline:* For fall admission, 7/15 for domestic students, 5/1 for international students; for spring admission, 12/1 for domestic and international students. Applications are processed on a rolling basis. *Application fee:* $60. Electronic applications accepted. *Application Contact:* Mary- Theresa Taglang, Director of Graduate Programs, 610-758-5285, Fax: 610-758-5283, E-mail: mtt4@lehigh.edu. *Graduate Business Programs*, Michael G. Kolchin, 610-758-4450, Fax: 610-758-5283, E-mail: mgk1@lehigh.edu.

College of Education Students: 164 full-time (137 women), 428 part-time (296 women); includes 40 minority (19 African Americans, 1 American Indian/Alaska Native, 11 Asian Americans or Pacific Islanders, 9 Hispanic Americans), 50 international. 389 applicants, 50% accepted, 89 enrolled. *Faculty:* 29 full-time (16 women), 17 part-time/adjunct (9 women). Expenses: Contact institution. *Financial support:* Fellowships with full and partial tuition reimbursements, research assistantships with full and partial tuition reimbursements, teaching assistantships with full and partial tuition reimbursements, career-related internships or fieldwork, Federal Work-Study, institutionally sponsored loans, scholarships/grants, tuition waivers (full and partial), and unspecified assistantships available. Financial award application deadline: 1/31. In 2006, 180 master's, 10 doctorates awarded. *Degree program information:* Part-time and evening/weekend programs available. Postbaccalaureate distance learning degree programs offered (minimal on-campus study). Offers academic intervention (M Ed); counseling and human services (M Ed); counseling psychology (M Ed, PhD, Certificate); education (M Ed, MA, MS, Ed D, PhD, Certificate, Ed S); educational leadership (M Ed, Ed D, Certificate); educational technology (Ed D, PhD, Certificate); elementary education (M Ed); instructional technology (MS); international counseling (M Ed, Certificate); learning sciences and technology (PhD); project management (Certificate); school counseling (M Ed); school psychology (PhD, Ed S); secondary education (M Ed, MA); special education (M Ed, PhD, Certificate); technology use in schools (Certificate); technology–based teacher education (M Ed, PhD); technology-based teacher education (MA). *Application fee:* $60. Electronic applications accepted. *Application Contact:* Donna M. Johnson, Executive Secretary, 610-758-3231, Fax: 610-758-6223, E-mail: dmj4@lehigh.edu. *Dean*, Dr. Sally A. White, 610-758-3221, Fax: 610-758-6223, E-mail: saw8@lehigh.edu.

P.C. Rossin College of Engineering and Applied Science Students: 394 full-time (93 women), 156 part-time (33 women); includes 33 minority (10 African Americans, 1 American Indian/Alaska Native, 13 Asian Americans or Pacific Islanders, 9 Hispanic Americans), 293 international. Average age 24. 880 applicants, 73% accepted, 151 enrolled. *Faculty:* 124 full-time (13 women), 4 part-time/adjunct (0 women). Expenses: Contact institution. *Financial support:* In 2006–07, 47 fellowships with full and partial tuition reimbursements (averaging $19,200 per year), 221 research assistantships with full and partial tuition reimbursements (averaging $18,780 per year), 44 teaching assistantships with full and partial tuition reimbursements (averaging $18,780 per year) were awarded; career-related internships or fieldwork, Federal Work-Study, institutionally sponsored loans, scholarships/grants, and tuition waivers (full and partial) also available. Support available to part-time students. Financial award application deadline: 1/15. In 2006, 132 master's, 36 doctorates awarded. *Degree program information:* Part-time and evening/weekend programs available. Postbaccalaureate distance learning degree programs offered (no on-campus study). Offers analytical finance (MS); chemical engineering (M Eng, MS, PhD); civil and environmental engineering (M Eng, MS, PhD); computational engineering and mechanics (MS, PhD); computer engineering (MS, PhD); computer science (MS, PhD); electrical engineering (M Eng, MS, PhD); engineering and applied science (M Eng, MS, PhD); industrial engineering (M Eng, MS, PhD); information and systems engineering (M Eng, MS); management science (MS); manufacturing systems engineering (MS); materials science and engineering (M Eng, MS, PhD); mechanical engineering (M Eng, MS, PhD); photonics (MS); polymer science/engineering (MS, PhD); quality engineering (MS); wireless network engineering (MS). *Application deadline:* For fall admission, 7/15 for domestic students; for spring admission, 12/1 for domestic students. Applications are processed on a rolling basis. *Application fee:* $65. Electronic applications accepted. *Application Contact:* Amy L. Josar, Administrative Coordinator of Graduate Studies and Research, 610-758-6310, Fax: 610-758-5623, E-mail: ineas@lehigh.edu. *Associate Dean of Graduate Studies and Research*, Dr. John P. Coulter, 610-758-6310, Fax: 610-758-5623, E-mail: john.coulter@lehigh.edu.

Center for Polymer Science and Engineering Students: 4 full-time (2 women), 10 part-time (4 women). Average age 30. 41 applicants, 54% accepted. Expenses: Contact institution. *Financial support:* In 2006–07, fellowships (averaging $17,667 per year), research assistantships (averaging $17,667 per year), teaching assistantships (averaging $17,667 per year) were awarded. Financial award application deadline: 1/15. In 2006, 7 master's, 1 doctorate awarded. *Degree program information:* Part-time and evening/weekend programs available. Postbaccalaureate distance learning degree programs offered (no on-campus study). Offers polymer science and engineering (M Eng, MS, PhD). Programs are interdisciplinary. *Application deadline:* For fall admission, 7/15 for domestic students, 1/15 for international students; for spring admission, 12/1 for domestic and international students. Applications are processed on a rolling basis. *Application fee:* $65. Electronic applications accepted. *Application Contact:* James E. Roberts, Chair, Polymer Education Committee, 610-758-4841, Fax: 610-758-6536, E-mail: jer1@lehigh.edu. *Director*, Dr. Raymond A. Pearson, 610-758-3590, Fax: 610-758-3526, E-mail: rp02@lehigh.edu.

LEHMAN COLLEGE OF THE CITY UNIVERSITY OF NEW YORK, Bronx, NY 10468-1589

General Information State and locally supported, coed, comprehensive institution. *Graduate housing:* On-campus housing not available. *Research affiliation:* New York Botanical Gardens, Montefiore Hospital and Medical Center.

GRADUATE UNITS

Division of Arts and Humanities *Degree program information:* Part-time and evening/weekend programs available. Offers art (MA, MFA); arts and humanities (MA, MAT, MFA); English (MA); history (MA); music (MAT); Spanish (MA); speech-language pathology and audiology (MA).

Division of Education *Degree program information:* Part-time and evening/weekend programs available. Offers bilingual special education (MS Ed); business education (MS Ed); early childhood education (MS Ed); early special education (MS Ed); education (MA, MS Ed); elementary education (MS Ed); emotional handicaps (MS Ed); English education (MS Ed); guidance and counseling (MS Ed); learning disabilities (MS Ed); mathematics 7–12 (MS Ed); mental retardation (MS Ed); music education (MS Ed); reading teacher (MS Ed); science education (MS Ed); social studies 7–12 (MA); teachers of special education (MS Ed); teaching English to speakers of other languages (MS Ed).

Division of Natural and Social Sciences *Degree program information:* Part-time and evening/weekend programs available. Offers accounting (MS); adult health nursing (MS); biology (MA); clinical nutrition (MS); community nutrition (MS); computer science (MS); dietetic internship (MS); health education and promotion (MA); health N–12 teacher (MS Ed); mathematics (MA); natural and social sciences (MA, MS, MS Ed, PhD); nursing of older adults (MS); nutrition (MS); parent-child nursing (MS); pediatric nurse practitioner (MS); plant sciences (PhD); recreation (MA, MS Ed); recreation education (MA, MS Ed).

LE MOYNE COLLEGE, Syracuse, NY 13214

General Information Independent-religious, coed, comprehensive institution. *Enrollment:* 3,536 graduate, professional, and undergraduate students; 153 full-time matriculated graduate/professional students (121 women), 423 part-time matriculated graduate/professional students (304 women). *Enrollment by degree level:* 576 master's. *Graduate faculty:* 38 full-time (15 women), 42 part-time/adjunct (23 women). *Tuition:* Full-time $9,846; part-time $547 per credit hour. Tuition and fees vary according to program. *Graduate housing:* On-campus housing not available. *Student services:* Campus employment opportunities, campus safety program, career counseling, disabled student services, free psychological counseling, international student services, low-cost health insurance, multicultural affairs office, teacher training. *Library facilities:* Noreen Reale Falcone Library. *Online resources:* library catalog, web page, access to other libraries' catalogs. *Collection:* 280,245 titles, 35,430 serial subscriptions, 12,387 audiovisual materials.

Le Moyne College (continued)

Computer facilities: 325 computers available on campus for general student use. A campuswide network can be accessed from student residence rooms and from off campus. Internet access and online class registration, ECHO (campus-wide portal) are available. *Web address:* http://www.lemoyne.edu/.

General Application Contact: Kristen P. Trapasso, Director of Graduate Admission, 315-445-4265, Fax: 315-445-6027, E-mail: trapaskp@lemoyne.edu.

GRADUATE UNITS

Department of Education Students: 63 full-time (55 women), 324 part-time (259 women); includes 21 minority (13 African Americans, 1 American Indian/Alaska Native, 3 Asian Americans or Pacific Islanders, 4 Hispanic Americans), 1 international. Average age 31. 105 applicants, 100% accepted, 105 enrolled. *Faculty:* 12 full-time (6 women), 31 part-time/adjunct (18 women). Expenses: Contact institution. *Financial support:* In 2006–07, 247 students received support. Unspecified assistantships available. Support available to part-time students. Financial award applicants required to submit FAFSA. In 2006, 266 degrees awarded. *Degree program information:* Part-time and evening/weekend programs available. Offers education (MS Ed, MST). *Application deadline:* Applications are processed on a rolling basis. *Application fee:* $50. *Chair, Education Department and Director of Graduate Education,* Dr. Cathy Leogrande, 315-445-4376, Fax: 315-445-4744, E-mail: leogracc@lemoyne.edu.

Department of Physician Assistant Studies Students: 87 full-time (64 women), 1 part-time; includes 15 minority (4 African Americans, 7 Asian Americans or Pacific Islanders, 4 Hispanic Americans). Average age 28. 236 applicants, 21% accepted, 37 enrolled. *Faculty:* 7 full-time (5 women), 8 part-time/adjunct (3 women). Expenses: Contact institution. *Financial support:* In 2006–07, 83 students received support. Applicants required to submit FAFSA. In 2006, 20 degrees awarded. Offers physician assistant studies (MS). *Application deadline:* For fall admission, 10/1 for domestic and international students. Electronic applications accepted. *Application Contact:* Kristen P. Trapasso, Director of Graduate Admission, 315-445-4265, Fax: 315-445-6027, E-mail: trapaskp@lemoyne.edu. *Professor and Chair of Department of Physician Assistant Studies,* Dr. Linda G. Allison, 315-445-4745, Fax: 315-445-4602, E-mail: allisolg@lemoyne.edu.

Division of Management Students: 3 full-time (2 women), 98 part-time (45 women); includes 7 minority (4 African Americans, 1 American Indian/Alaska Native, 2 Asian Americans or Pacific Islanders). Average age 33. 80 applicants, 85% accepted, 68 enrolled. *Faculty:* 18 full-time (3 women), 1 part-time/adjunct (0 women). Expenses: Contact institution. *Financial support:* In 2006–07, 27 students received support. Scholarships/grants and unspecified assistantships available. Support available to part-time students. Financial award applicants required to submit FAFSA. In 2006, 38 degrees awarded. *Degree program information:* Part-time and evening/weekend programs available. Offers management (MBA). *Application deadline:* Applications are processed on a rolling basis. *Application fee:* $0. *Application Contact:* Kristen P. Trapasso, Director of Graduate Admission, 315-445-4265, Fax: 315-445-6027, E-mail: trapaskp@lemoyne.edu. *Director of MBA Program,* Dr. George Kulick, 315-445-4786, Fax: 315-445-4787, E-mail: kulick@lemoyne.edu.

LENOIR-RHYNE COLLEGE, Hickory, NC 28603

General Information Independent-religious, coed, comprehensive institution. *Graduate housing:* On-campus housing not available.

GRADUATE UNITS

Graduate Programs *Degree program information:* Part-time and evening/weekend programs available. Electronic applications accepted.

Charles M. Snipes School of Business *Degree program information:* Part-time and evening/weekend programs available. Offers business (MBA). Electronic applications accepted.

School of Education *Degree program information:* Part-time and evening/weekend programs available. Offers birth through kindergarten education (MA); elementary education (MA); literacy education K-12 (MA). Electronic applications accepted.

School of Social and Behavioral Sciences *Degree program information:* Part-time and evening/weekend programs available. Offers community/agency counseling (MA); school counseling (MA). Electronic applications accepted.

LESLEY UNIVERSITY, Cambridge, MA 02138-2790

General Information Independent, coed, comprehensive institution. CGS member. *Enrollment:* 6,539 graduate, professional, and undergraduate students; 1,028 full-time matriculated graduate/professional students (909 women), 4,996 part-time matriculated graduate/professional students (4,405 women). *Enrollment by degree level:* 5,280 master's, 78 doctoral, 666 other advanced degrees. *Graduate faculty:* 103 full-time (83 women), 403 part-time/adjunct (276 women). *Graduate housing:* On-campus housing not available. *Student services:* Campus employment opportunities, campus safety program, career counseling, disabled student services, free psychological counseling, international student services, teacher training, writing training. *Library facilities:* Eleanor DeWolfe Ludcke Library plus 2 others. *Online resources:* library catalog, web page, access to other libraries' catalogs. *Collection:* 118,729 titles, 1,150 serial subscriptions, 49,943 audiovisual materials. *Research affiliation:* TERC (education research and development).

Computer facilities: Computer purchase and lease plans are available. 175 computers available on campus for general student use. A campuswide network can be accessed from student residence rooms and from off campus. Internet access and online class registration are available. *Web address:* http://www.lesley.edu/.

General Application Contact: Kristen Card, Associate Director of On-Campus Admissions, 617-349-8734, Fax: 617-349-8313, E-mail: kmcard@lesley.edu.

GRADUATE UNITS

Graduate School of Arts and Social Sciences Students: 721 full-time (648 women), 2,074 part-time (1,897 women); includes 182 minority (104 African Americans, 12 American Indian/Alaska Native, 14 Asian Americans or Pacific Islanders, 52 Hispanic Americans), 66 international. Average age 37. 1,005 applicants, 92% accepted, 717 enrolled. *Faculty:* 49 full-time (41 women), 185 part-time/adjunct (137 women). Expenses: Contact institution. *Financial support:* In 2006–07, 64 students received support, including research assistantships (averaging $3,400 per year), 1 teaching assistantship (averaging $7,298 per year); career-related internships or fieldwork, Federal Work-Study, scholarships/grants, and unspecified assistantships also available. Support available to part-time students. Financial award application deadline: 4/15; financial award applicants required to submit FAFSA. In 2006, 1,179 master's, 2 doctorates, 1 other advanced degree awarded. *Degree program information:* Part-time and evening/weekend programs available. Postbaccalaureate distance learning degree programs offered (minimal on-campus study). Offers clinical mental health counseling (MA); counseling psychology (MA, CAGS); creative arts in learning (CAGS); creative writing (MFA); ecological teaching and learning (MS); environmental education (MS); expressive therapies (MA, PhD, CAGS); independent studies (CAGS); independent study (MA); individualized studies (MA); integrative holistic health (MA); intercultural relations (MA, CAGS); interdisciplinary studies (MA); professional counseling (MA); school counseling (MA); visual arts (MFA); women's studies (MA). *Application deadline:* Applications are processed on a rolling basis. *Application fee:* $50. Electronic applications accepted. *Application Contact:* Christina Murray, Senior Assistant Director, On-Campus Admissions, 617-349-8827, Fax: 617-349-8313, E-mail: cmurray3@lesley.edu. *Dean,* Dr. Julia Halevy, 617-349-8317, Fax: 617-349-8366, E-mail: jhalevy@lesley.edu.

Division of Expressive Therapies Students: 241 full-time (227 women), 126 part-time (119 women); includes 9 minority (1 African American, 1 American Indian/Alaska Native, 1 Asian American or Pacific Islander, 6 Hispanic Americans), 35 international. Average age 32. 220 applicants, 86% accepted, 153 enrolled. *Faculty:* 9 full-time (8 women), 32 part-time/adjunct (27 women). Expenses: Contact institution. *Financial support:* In 2006–07, 24 students received support, including 1 teaching assistantship (averaging $7,298 per year); Federal Work-Study, scholarships/grants, and unspecified assistantships also available. Support available to part-time students. Financial award application deadline: 4/15; financial award applicants required to submit FAFSA. In 2006, 102 master's, 2 doctorates awarded. Offers art (MA); dance (MA); expressive therapies (MA, PhD, CAGS); music (MA). *Application deadline:* Applications are processed on a rolling basis. *Application fee:* $50. *Application Contact:* Gilda Resmini-Walsh, Assistant Director, Advising and Student Services, 617-349-8444, E-mail: gresmini@lesley.edu. *Director,* Julia Byers, 617-349-8121, E-mail: jbyers@lesley.edu.

School of Education Students: 242 full-time (222 women), 2,903 part-time (2,495 women); includes 279 minority (179 African Americans, 7 American Indian/Alaska Native, 25 Asian Americans or Pacific Islanders, 68 Hispanic Americans), 10 international. Average age 36. 1,186 applicants, 96% accepted, 792 enrolled. *Faculty:* 47 full-time (39 women), 208 part-time/adjunct (135 women). Expenses: Contact institution. *Financial support:* In 2006–07, 26 students received support, including research assistantships (averaging $3,400 per year), teaching assistantships (averaging $3,400 per year); career-related internships or fieldwork, Federal Work-Study, scholarships/grants, and unspecified assistantships also available. Support available to part-time students. Financial award application deadline: 4/15; financial award applicants required to submit FAFSA. In 2006, 1,724 master's, 6 doctorates, 17 other advanced degrees awarded. *Degree program information:* Part-time and evening/weekend programs available. Postbaccalaureate distance learning degree programs offered (no on-campus study). Offers curriculum and instruction (M Ed, CAGS); early childhood education (M Ed); educational studies (PhD); elementary education (M Ed); individually designed (M Ed); middle school education (M Ed); moderate special needs (M Ed); reading (M Ed, CAGS); science in education (M Ed); severe special needs (M Ed); special needs (CAGS); technology in education (M Ed, CAGS). *Application deadline:* Applications are processed on a rolling basis. *Application fee:* $50. Electronic applications accepted. *Application Contact:* Kristen Card, Associate Director of On-Campus Admissions, 617-349-8734, Fax: 617-349-8313, E-mail: kmcard@lesley.edu. *Dean,* Dr. Mario Borunda, 617-349-8375, Fax: 617-349-8607, E-mail: mborunda@lesley.edu.

LETOURNEAU UNIVERSITY, Longview, TX 75607-7001

General Information Independent-religious, coed, comprehensive institution. *Enrollment:* 3,975 graduate, professional, and undergraduate students; 217 full-time matriculated graduate/professional students (135 women), 123 part-time matriculated graduate/professional students (71 women). *Enrollment by degree level:* 340 master's. *Graduate faculty:* 7 full-time (0 women), 29 part-time/adjunct (7 women). *Tuition:* Full-time $10,043; part-time $510 per credit hour. *Required fees:* $975; $50 per credit hour. One-time fee: $75 full-time. *Graduate housing:* Room and/or apartments available on a first-come, first-served basis to married students; on-campus housing not available to single students. *Student services:* Teacher training. *Library facilities:* Margaret Estes Resource Center. *Collection:* 84,779 titles, 383 serial subscriptions, 3,144 audiovisual materials.

Computer facilities: Computer purchase and lease plans are available. 191 computers available on campus for general student use. A campuswide network can be accessed from student residence rooms and from off campus. Internet access and online class registration are available. *Web address:* http://www.letu.edu/.

General Application Contact: Chris Fontaine, Assistant VP for Enrollment Management and Market Research, 903-233-3250, Fax: 903-233-3227, E-mail: chrisfontaine@letu.edu.

GRADUATE UNITS

Graduate and Professional Studies Students: 217 full-time (135 women), 123 part-time (71 women); includes 165 minority (124 African Americans, 8 American Indian/Alaska Native, 7 Asian Americans or Pacific Islanders, 26 Hispanic Americans), 2 international. Average age 37. 394 applicants, 90% accepted, 337 enrolled. *Faculty:* 7 full-time (0 women), 29 part-time/adjunct (7 women). Expenses: Contact institution. *Financial support:* Applicants required to submit FAFSA. In 2006, 182 degrees awarded. *Degree program information:* Part-time and evening/weekend programs available. Postbaccalaureate distance learning degree programs offered (no on-campus study). Offers business administration (MBA); educational leadership (MBA). *Application deadline:* Applications are processed on a rolling basis. *Application fee:* $50. Electronic applications accepted. *Application Contact:* Chris Fontaine, Assistant VP for Enrollment Management and Market Research, 903-233-3250, Fax: 903-233-3227, E-mail: chrisfontaine@letu.edu. *Associate Vice President for the school of Graduate and Professional Studies,* Dr. Scott Ray, 903-233-3250, Fax: 903-233-3227, E-mail: scottray@letu.edu.

LEWIS & CLARK COLLEGE, Portland, OR 97219-7899

General Information Independent, coed, comprehensive institution. *Enrollment:* 3,641 graduate, professional, and undergraduate students; 234 full-time matriculated graduate/professional students (182 women), 257 part-time matriculated graduate/professional students (199 women). *Enrollment by degree level:* 413 master's, 40 doctoral, 38 other advanced degrees. *Graduate faculty:* 39 full-time (27 women), 66 part-time/adjunct (40 women). *Tuition:* Part-time $610 per semester hour. *Graduate housing:* On-campus housing not available. *Student services:* Campus employment opportunities, campus safety program, career counseling, disabled student services, free psychological counseling, international student services, low-cost health insurance, multicultural affairs office, writing training. *Library facilities:* Aubrey Watzek Library plus 1 other. *Online resources:* library catalog, web page, access to other libraries' catalogs. *Collection:* 227,609 titles, 7,477 serial subscriptions, 11,586 audiovisual materials.

Computer facilities: Computer purchase and lease plans are available. 158 computers available on campus for general student use. A campuswide network can be accessed from student residence rooms and from off campus. Internet access and online class registration are available. *Web address:* http://www.lclark.edu/.

General Application Contact: Helen L. Hayes, Administrative Specialist, Graduate Office of Admissions, 503-768-6200, Fax: 503-768-6205, E-mail: gseadmit@lclark.edu.

GRADUATE UNITS

Graduate School of Education and Counseling Students: 234 full-time (182 women), 257 part-time (199 women); includes 52 minority (8 African Americans, 9 American Indian/Alaska Native, 16 Asian Americans or Pacific Islanders, 19 Hispanic Americans), 2 international. Average age 33. 429 applicants, 86% accepted, 237 enrolled. *Faculty:* 39 full-time (27 women), 66 part-time/adjunct (40 women). Expenses: Contact institution. *Financial support:* In 2006–07, 353 students received support. Career-related internships or fieldwork, Federal Work-Study, institutionally sponsored loans, scholarships/grants, health care benefits, and tuition waivers (partial) available. Support available to part-time students. Financial award applicants required to submit FAFSA. In 2006, 226 master's, 15 other advanced degrees awarded. *Degree program information:* Part-time and evening/weekend programs available. Offers addictions treatment (MA); counseling psychology (MA, MS); early childhood/elementary education (MAT); education (MAT); education and counseling (M Ed, MA, MAT, MS, Ed D, Ed S); educational leadership (M Ed, Ed D); marriage and family therapy (MA); middle level/high school education (MAT); psychological and cultural studies (MA); school counseling (M Ed); school psychology (MS, Ed S); special education (M Ed). *Application fee:* $50. Electronic applications accepted. *Application Contact:* Becky Haas, Director of Admissions, 503-768-6200, Fax: 503-768-6205, E-mail: gseadmit@lclark.edu. *Dean,* Dr. Peter W. Cookson, 503-768-6004, Fax: 503-768-6005, E-mail: graddean@lclark.edu.

Lewis & Clark School of Law Students: 543 full-time (256 women), 185 part-time (84 women); includes 134 minority (16 African Americans, 10 American Indian/Alaska Native, 70 Asian Americans or Pacific Islanders, 38 Hispanic Americans), 13 international. Average age 28. 2,273 applicants, 40% accepted, 225 enrolled. *Faculty:* 46 full-time (20 women), 27 part-time/adjunct (13 women). Expenses: Contact institution. *Financial support:* In 2006–07, 674 students received support, including 44 research assistantships (averaging $1,250 per year), 26 teaching assistantships (averaging $1,788 per year); fellowships, career-related internships or fieldwork, Federal Work-Study, scholarships/grants, and tuition waivers (partial) also available. Support available to part-time students. Financial award application deadline: 3/1; financial award applicants required to submit FAFSA. In 2006, 232 JDs, 8 master's awarded. *Degree program information:* Part-time and evening/weekend programs available. Offers environmental and natural resources law (LL M); law (JD). *Application deadline:* For fall admission, 3/1 priority date for domestic students, 1/15 priority date for international students. Applications are processed on a rolling basis. *Application fee:* $50. Electronic applications accepted. *Application Contact:* 503-768-6613, Fax: 503-768-6793, E-mail: lawadmss@lclark.edu. *Dean, School of Law,* Robert H. Klonoff, 503-768-6602, Fax: 503-768-6671.

LEWIS UNIVERSITY, Romeoville, IL 60446

General Information Independent-religious, coed, comprehensive institution. *Graduate housing:* Room and/or apartments available on a first-come, first-served basis to single students; on-campus housing not available to married students. Housing application deadline: 7/1.

GRADUATE UNITS

College of Arts and Sciences *Degree program information:* Part-time and evening/weekend programs available. Offers administration/education (MA); arts and sciences (M Ed, MA, MA Ed, MAE, MPSA, MS, CAS); child and adolescent counseling (MA); criminal/social justice (MS); curriculum and instruction (MA Ed); education (M Ed, MAE); educational leadership (MA Ed); general administrative program (CAS); higher education/student services (MA); instructional leadership (MA Ed); mental health counseling (MA); organizational management (MA); public administration (MA); school counseling and guidance (MA); special education (MA); superintendent endorsement program (CAS); training and development (MA). Electronic applications accepted.

College of Business *Degree program information:* Part-time and evening/weekend programs available. Offers business (MBA). Electronic applications accepted.

Graduate School of Management *Degree program information:* Part-time programs available. Offers accounting (MBA); e-business (MBA); finance (MBA); healthcare management (MBA); human resources management (MBA); international business (MBA); management information systems (MBA); marketing (MBA); technology and operations management (MBA).

College of Nursing and Health Professions *Degree program information:* Part-time and evening/weekend programs available. Offers case management (MSN); nursing administration (MSN); nursing and health professions (MSN); nursing education (MSN). Electronic applications accepted.

LEXINGTON THEOLOGICAL SEMINARY, Lexington, KY 40508-3218

General Information Independent-religious, coed, graduate-only institution. *Graduate housing:* Rooms and/or apartments available on a first-come, first-served basis to single and married students. Housing application deadline: 6/15.

GRADUATE UNITS

Graduate and Professional Programs *Degree program information:* Part-time and evening/weekend programs available. Offers theology (M Div, MA, MAPS, D Min).

LIBERTY UNIVERSITY, Lynchburg, VA 24502

General Information Independent-religious, coed, comprehensive institution. *Enrollment:* 17,606 graduate, professional, and undergraduate students; 1,137 full-time matriculated graduate/professional students (408 women), 2,935 part-time matriculated graduate/professional students (1,270 women). *Enrollment by degree level:* 670 first professional, 3,172 master's, 204 doctoral, 26 other advanced degrees. *Graduate faculty:* 56 full-time (9 women), 91 part-time/adjunct (20 women). *Graduate housing:* Room and/or apartments guaranteed to single students; on-campus housing not available to married students. Typical cost: $5,400 (including board). Room and board charges vary according to housing facility selected. *Student services:* Campus employment opportunities, career counseling, free psychological counseling, international student services, multicultural affairs office. *Library facilities:* A. Pierre Guillermin Integrated Learning Resource Center plus 1 other. *Online resources:* library catalog, web page. *Collection:* 260,295 titles, 46,176 serial subscriptions, 6,455 audiovisual materials.

Computer facilities: Computer purchase and lease plans are available. 406 computers available on campus for general student use. A campuswide network can be accessed from student residence rooms and from off campus. Internet access and online class registration are available. *Web address:* http://www.liberty.edu/.

General Application Contact: Kyle A Falce, Director of Graduate Admissions, 800-424-9596, Fax: 800-628-7977, E-mail: gradadmissions@liberty.edu.

GRADUATE UNITS

College of Arts and Sciences Students: 205 full-time (146 women), 947 part-time (718 women); includes 302 minority (255 African Americans, 5 American Indian/Alaska Native, 11 Asian Americans or Pacific Islanders, 31 Hispanic Americans), 34 international. Average age 36. 1,480 applicants, 88% accepted, 553 enrolled. *Faculty:* 13 full-time (2 women), 54 part-time/adjunct (15 women). Expenses: Contact institution. *Financial support:* In 2006–07, 817 students received support, including 9 teaching assistantships with tuition reimbursements available; Federal Work-Study also available. In 2006, 201 master's, 5 doctorates awarded. *Degree program information:* Part-time programs available. Postbaccalaureate distance learning degree programs offered (minimal on-campus study). Offers counseling (MA); nursing (MSN); pastoral care and counseling (PhD); professional counseling (PhD). *Application deadline:* For fall admission, 6/1 priority date for domestic students; for spring admission, 11/1 priority date for domestic students. Applications are processed on a rolling basis. *Application fee:* $35. Electronic applications accepted. *Application Contact:* Kyle A Falce, Director of Graduate Admissions, 800-424-9596, Fax: 800-628-7977, E-mail: gradadmissions@liberty.edu. *Dean,* Dr. Ronald E. Hawkins, 434-592-4030, Fax: 434-522-0416, E-mail: rehawkin@liberty.edu.

Liberty Theological Seminary and Graduate School Students: 517 full-time (80 women), 1,027 part-time (164 women); includes 269 minority (183 African Americans, 8 American Indian/Alaska Native, 27 Asian Americans or Pacific Islanders, 51 Hispanic Americans), 116 international. Average age 37. 1,433 applicants, 84% accepted, 620 enrolled. *Faculty:* 17 full-time (0 women), 34 part-time/adjunct (0 women). Expenses: Contact institution. *Financial support:* In 2006–07, 844 students received support, including 5 teaching assistantships with tuition reimbursements available; career-related internships or fieldwork and Federal Work-Study also available. In 2006, 48 M Divs, 201 master's, 20 doctorates awarded. *Degree program information:* Part-time programs available. Postbaccalaureate distance learning degree programs offered (minimal on-campus study). Offers religious studies (M Div, MA, MAR, MRE, D Min); theology (Th M). *Application deadline:* For fall admission, 6/1 priority date for domestic students; for spring admission, 11/1 for domestic students. Applications are processed on a rolling basis. *Application fee:* $35. Electronic applications accepted. *Application Contact:* Kyle A Falce, Director of Graduate Admissions, 800-424-9596, Fax: 800-628-7977, E-mail: gradadmissions@liberty.edu. *Dean,* Dr. Ergun Caner, 434-582-2099, Fax: 434-522-0415, E-mail: ecaner@liberty.edu.

School of Business Students: 206 full-time (88 women), 644 part-time (202 women); includes 197 minority (154 African Americans, 4 American Indian/Alaska Native, 18 Asian Americans or Pacific Islanders, 21 Hispanic Americans), 22 international. Average age 34. 712 applicants, 92% accepted, 334 enrolled. *Faculty:* 9 full-time (0 women), 6 part-time/adjunct (3 women). Expenses: Contact institution. *Financial support:* In 2006–07, 625 students received support. In 2006, 265 degrees awarded. *Degree program information:* Part-time programs available. Postbaccalaureate distance learning degree programs offered (minimal on-campus study). Offers business (MBA). *Application deadline:* For fall admission, 6/1 for domestic students; for spring admission, 11/1 for domestic students. Applications are processed on a rolling basis. *Application fee:* $35. Electronic applications accepted. *Application Contact:* Kyle A Falce, Director of Graduate Admissions, 800-424-9596, Fax: 800-628-7977, E-mail: gradadmissions@liberty.edu. *Dean,* Dr. Bruce K. Bell, 434-592-3863, Fax: 434-582-2366, E-mail: bkbell@liberty.edu.

School of Communications Students: 19 full-time (13 women), 7 part-time (5 women); includes 3 minority (all African Americans), 7 international. Average age 26. 20 applicants, 70% accepted, 11 enrolled. *Faculty:* 7 full-time (2 women). Expenses: Contact institution. *Financial support:* In 2006–07, 25 students received support. Federal Work-Study and unspecified assistantships available. In 2006, 9 degrees awarded. *Degree program information:* Part-time programs available. Offers communications (MA). *Application deadline:* For fall admission, 6/1 priority date for domestic students; for spring admission, 11/1 priority date for domestic students. *Application fee:* $35. Electronic applications accepted. *Application Contact:* Kyle A Falce, Director of Graduate Admissions, 800-424-9596, Fax: 800-628-7977, E-mail: gradadmissions@liberty.edu. *Dean,* Dr. William G. Gribbin, 434-582-2466, E-mail: wgribbin@liberty.edu.

School of Education Students: 33 full-time (22 women), 308 part-time (180 women); includes 22 minority (12 African Americans, 2 American Indian/Alaska Native, 2 Asian Americans or Pacific Islanders, 6 Hispanic Americans), 5 international. Average age 39. 434 applicants, 77% accepted, 111 enrolled. *Faculty:* 8 full-time (3 women), 7 part-time/adjunct (3 women). Expenses: Contact institution. *Financial support:* In 2006–07, 226 students received support. Federal Work-Study and tuition waivers (partial) available. In 2006, 39 master's, 12 doctorates, 16 other advanced degrees awarded. *Degree program information:* Part-time programs available. Postbaccalaureate distance learning degree programs offered (minimal on-campus study). Offers administration and supervision (M Ed); curriculum and instruction (M Ed); early childhood education (M Ed); education specialist (Ed S); educational leadership (Ed D); elementary education (M Ed); gifted education (M Ed); reading specialist (M Ed); school counseling (M Ed); secondary education (M Ed); special education (M Ed). *Application deadline:* For fall admission, 6/1 priority date for domestic students; for spring admission, 11/1 for domestic students. Applications are processed on a rolling basis. *Application fee:* $35. Electronic applications accepted. *Application Contact:* Kyle A Falce, Director of Graduate Admissions, 800-424-9596, Fax: 800-628-7977, E-mail: gradadmissions@liberty.edu. *Dean,* Dr. Karen L. Parker, 434-582-2195, Fax: 434-582-2468, E-mail: kparker@liberty.edu.

School of Law Students: 157 full-time (59 women), 2 part-time (1 woman); includes 15 minority (9 African Americans, 1 American Indian/Alaska Native, 3 Asian Americans or Pacific Islanders, 2 Hispanic Americans), 3 international. Average age 28. 226 applicants, 47% accepted, 73 enrolled. *Faculty:* 14 full-time (4 women), 4 part-time/adjunct (1 woman). Expenses: Contact institution. *Financial support:* In 2006–07, 157 students received support. Offers law (JD). *Application deadline:* For fall admission, 6/1 for domestic students. *Application fee:* $50. Electronic applications accepted. *Application Contact:* Michelle Crawford Rickert, Assistant Dean, Admissions for the School of Law, 434-592-5471, Fax: 434-522-0404, E-mail: mcrawfordrickert@liberty.edu. *Dean,* Mathew D. Staver, 434-592-5300, Fax: 434-522-0404, E-mail: law@liberty.edu.

LIFE CHIROPRACTIC COLLEGE WEST, Hayward, CA 94545

General Information Independent, coed, graduate-only institution. *Graduate housing:* On-campus housing not available. *Research affiliation:* Orthopedic System, Inc., Foundation for Chiropractic Education and Research, Foundation for the Advancement of Chiropractic Tenets, San Francisco Spine Center.

GRADUATE UNITS

Professional Program Offers chiropractic (DC).

LIFE UNIVERSITY, Marietta, GA 30060-2903

General Information Independent, coed, comprehensive institution. *Enrollment:* 1,662 graduate, professional, and undergraduate students; 1,089 full-time matriculated graduate/professional students (391 women), 78 part-time matriculated graduate/professional students (25 women). *Enrollment by degree level:* 1,135 first professional, 32 master's. *Graduate faculty:* 100 full-time (36 women), 28 part-time/adjunct (15 women). *Graduate housing:* Rooms and/or apartments available on a first-come, first-served basis to single and married students. Typical cost: $12,000 (including board) for single students. *Student services:* Campus employment opportunities, campus safety program, career counseling, disabled student services, exercise/wellness program, free psychological counseling, international student services. *Library facilities:* Library & Learning Services plus 1 other. *Online resources:* library catalog, web page. *Collection:* 56,199 titles, 22,816 serial subscriptions, 8,533 audiovisual materials.

Computer facilities: 118 computers available on campus for general student use. A campuswide network can be accessed from student residence rooms and from off campus. Internet access and online class registration are available. *Web address:* http://www.life.edu/.

General Application Contact: Dr. Deborah Heairlston, Director of Enrollment Services, 800-543-3202, Fax: 770-426-2895, E-mail: drdeb@life.edu.

GRADUATE UNITS

College of Arts and Sciences Students: 1,089 full-time (391 women), 78 part-time (25 women); includes 171 minority (94 African Americans, 5 American Indian/Alaska Native, 33 Asian Americans or Pacific Islanders, 39 Hispanic Americans). Average age 28. 656 applicants, 47% accepted, 181 enrolled. *Faculty:* 100 full-time (36 women), 28 part-time/adjunct (15 women). Expenses: Contact institution. *Financial support:* Research assistantships, Federal Work-Study, institutionally sponsored loans, scholarships/grants, and tuition waivers (partial) available. Support available to part-time students. Financial award application deadline: 9/1; financial award applicants required to submit FAFSA. In 2006, 9 degrees awarded. *Degree program information:* Part-time programs available. Offers chiropractic sport science (MS); exercise and sport science (MS); sport coaching (MS); sport health science (MS); sport injury management (MS). *Application deadline:* Applications are processed on a rolling basis. *Application fee:* $50. Electronic applications accepted. *Application Contact:* Dr. Deborah Heairlston, Director of New Student Development, 770-426-2884, Fax: 770-426-2895, E-mail: drdeb@life.edu. *Academic Dean,* Dr. Jerry Hardee, 770-426-2697, Fax: 770-426-2790, E-mail: jhardee@life.edu.

College of Chiropractic *Degree program information:* Part-time programs available. Offers chiropractic (DC). Electronic applications accepted.

LINCOLN CHRISTIAN SEMINARY, Lincoln, IL 62656-2167

General Information Independent-religious, coed, graduate-only institution. *Graduate housing:* Rooms and/or apartments available on a first-come, first-served basis to single and married students.

GRADUATE UNITS

Graduate and Professional Programs *Degree program information:* Part-time programs available. Offers Bible and theology (MA); Bible translation (MA); counseling ministry (MA); divinity (M Div); leadership ministry (MA). MA in Bible translation offered jointly with Pioneer Bible Translators (Dallas, TX).

LINCOLN MEMORIAL UNIVERSITY, Harrogate, TN 37752-1901

General Information Independent, coed, comprehensive institution. *Enrollment:* 2,981 graduate, professional, and undergraduate students; 235 full-time matriculated graduate/professional students (177 women), 1,352 part-time matriculated graduate/professional students (1,013 women). *Enrollment by degree level:* 701 master's, 886 other advanced degrees. *Graduate faculty:* 33 full-time (17 women), 11 part-time/adjunct (6 women). *Graduate housing:* Rooms and/or apartments available on a first-come, first-served basis to single and married students. Housing application deadline: 8/1. *Student services:* Career counseling, child daycare facilities, international student services, teacher training. *Library facilities:* Carnegie Library plus 1 other. *Online resources:* library catalog, web page. *Collection:* 174,737 titles, 20,982 serial subscriptions, 2,402 audiovisual materials.

Computer facilities: 150 computers available on campus for general student use. A campuswide network can be accessed from student residence rooms. Internet access is available. *Web address:* http://www.lmunet.edu/.

General Application Contact: Barbara McCune, Senior Assistant, Graduate Office, 423-869-6374, Fax: 423-869-6261, E-mail: graduate@lmunet.edu.

GRADUATE UNITS

School of Business Students: 18 full-time (8 women), 37 part-time (18 women); includes 2 minority (both African Americans), 6 international. 72 applicants, 88% accepted. *Faculty:* 4 full-time (0 women). Expenses: Contact institution. *Financial support:* Career-related internships or fieldwork and unspecified assistantships available. Support available to part-time

Lincoln Memorial University (continued)

students. Financial award application deadline: 4/1; financial award applicants required to submit FAFSA. In 2006, 22 degrees awarded. *Degree program information:* Part-time and evening/weekend programs available. Offers business (MBA). *Application deadline:* For fall admission, 8/10 priority date for domestic students. Applications are processed on a rolling basis. *Application fee:* $25. *Application Contact:* Robin Lamb, Office Assistant, Graduate Studies, 423-869-6254, Fax: 423-869-6269, E-mail: robin.lamb@lmunet.edu. *Dean,* Dr. Bill Hamby, 423-869-7085, Fax: 423-869-6269, E-mail: bill.hamby@lmunet.edu.

School of Education Students: 207 full-time (159 women), 1,315 part-time (995 women); includes 106 minority (93 African Americans, 1 American Indian/Alaska Native, 1 Asian American or Pacific Islander, 11 Hispanic Americans), 2 international. 1,397 applicants, 98% accepted. *Faculty:* 25 full-time (13 women), 11 part-time/adjunct (6 women). Expenses: Contact institution. *Financial support:* Career-related internships or fieldwork and unspecified assistantships available. Support available to part-time students. Financial award application deadline: 4/1; financial award applicants required to submit FAFSA. In 2006, 194 master's, 778 other advanced degrees awarded. *Degree program information:* Part-time and evening/weekend programs available. Offers administration and supervision (M Ed, Ed S); counseling and guidance (M Ed); curriculum and instruction (M Ed, Ed S). *Application deadline:* For fall admission, 8/10 priority date for domestic students. *Application fee:* $25. *Application Contact:* Barbara McCune, Senior Assistant, Graduate Office, 423-869-6374, Fax: 423-869-6261, E-mail: graduate@lmunet.edu. *Dean, School of Graduate Studies,* Dr. Fred Bedelle, 423-869-6223, Fax: 423-869-6261, E-mail: graduate@inetlmu.lmunet.edu.

School of Nursing and Allied Health Students: 10 full-time (all women); includes 1 minority (African American) *Faculty:* 4 full-time (all women). Expenses: Contact institution. Offers nursing (MSN). *Dean,* Dr. Mary Modorin, 423-869-6319, Fax: 423-869-6244, E-mail: maryanne.moderin@lmunet.edu.

LINCOLN UNIVERSITY, Oakland, CA 94612

General Information Independent, coed, comprehensive institution. *Graduate housing:* On-campus housing not available.

GRADUATE UNITS

Business Administration Program Offers business administration (MBA). Electronic applications accepted.

LINCOLN UNIVERSITY, Jefferson City, MO 65102

General Information State-supported, coed, comprehensive institution. *Enrollment:* 3,224 graduate, professional, and undergraduate students; 68 full-time matriculated graduate/professional students (50 women), 102 part-time matriculated graduate/professional students (75 women). *Enrollment by degree level:* 170 master's. *Graduate faculty:* 1 (woman) full-time, 28 part-time/adjunct (10 women). Tuition, state resident: part-time $189 per credit hour. Tuition, nonresident: part-time $351 per credit hour. *Required fees:* $15 per credit hour. $20 per semester. *Graduate housing:* Room and/or apartments available on a first-come, first-served basis to single students; on-campus housing not available to married students. Typical cost: $2,050 per year ($3,990 including board). Room and board charges vary according to board plan. Housing application deadline: 7/1. *Student services:* Campus employment opportunities, campus safety program, career counseling, disabled student services, free psychological counseling, international student services, low-cost health insurance. *Library facilities:* Inman Page Library. *Online resources:* library catalog, web page, access to other libraries' catalogs. *Collection:* 204,948 titles, 368 serial subscriptions, 5,497 audiovisual materials.

Computer facilities: Computer purchase and lease plans are available. 141 computers available on campus for general student use. A campuswide network can be accessed. Internet access and online class registration are available. *Web address:* http://www.lincolnu.edu/.

General Application Contact: Dr. Linda S. Bickel, Dean of the School of Graduate Studies and Continuing Education, 573-681-5247, Fax: 573-681-5106, E-mail: gradschool@lincolnu.edu.

GRADUATE UNITS

School of Graduate Studies and Continuing Education Students: 68 full-time (50 women), 102 part-time (75 women); includes 39 minority (35 African Americans, 2 American Indian/Alaska Native, 2 Asian Americans or Pacific Islanders), 29 international. Average age 33. 48 applicants, 98% accepted, 29 enrolled. *Faculty:* 1 (woman) full-time, 28 part-time/adjunct (10 women). Expenses: Contact institution. *Financial support:* Federal Work-Study and scholarships/grants available. Financial award application deadline: 4/1; financial award applicants required to submit FAFSA. In 2006, 70 master's, 3 other advanced degrees awarded. *Degree program information:* Part-time and evening/weekend programs available. *Application deadline:* For fall admission, 7/1 priority date for domestic and international students; for spring admission, 12/1 priority date for domestic and international students. Applications are processed on a rolling basis. *Application fee:* $17. *Application Contact:* Irasema Steck, Administrative Assistant, 573-681-5247, Fax: 573-681-5106, E-mail: gradschool@lincolnu.edu. *Dean of the School of Graduate Studies and Continuing Education,* Dr. Linda S. Bickel, 573-681-5247, Fax: 573-681-5106, E-mail: gradschool@lincolnu.edu.

College of Business and Professional Studies Students: 39 full-time (26 women), 23 part-time (14 women); includes 18 minority (17 African Americans, 1 American Indian/Alaska Native), 24 international. Average age 31. 28 applicants, 96% accepted, 14 enrolled. *Faculty:* 7 part-time/adjunct (2 women). Expenses: Contact institution. *Financial support:* Federal Work-Study and scholarships/grants available. Financial award application deadline: 4/1; financial award applicants required to submit FAFSA. In 2006, 31 degrees awarded. *Degree program information:* Part-time and evening/weekend programs available. Offers business administration (MBA); business and professional studies (MBA). *Application deadline:* For fall admission, 7/1 priority date for domestic and international students; for spring admission, 12/1 priority date for domestic and international students. Applications are processed on a rolling basis. *Application fee:* $17. *Dean,* Dr. Felix M. Edoho, 573-681-5489, Fax: 573-681-5488, E-mail: edohof@lincolnu.edu.

College of Liberal Arts, Education and Journalism Students: 29 full-time (24 women), 79 part-time (61 women); includes 21 minority (18 African Americans, 1 American Indian/Alaska Native, 2 Asian Americans or Pacific Islanders), 5 international. Average age 34. 20 applicants, 100% accepted, 15 enrolled. *Faculty:* 1 (woman) full-time, 21 part-time/adjunct (8 women). Expenses: Contact institution. *Financial support:* Federal Work-Study and scholarships/grants available. Financial award application deadline: 4/1; financial award applicants required to submit FAFSA. In 2006, 39 master's, 3 other advanced degrees awarded. *Degree program information:* Part-time and evening/weekend programs available. Offers educational leadership (Ed S); guidance and counseling (M Ed); history (MA); liberal arts, education and journalism (M Ed, MA, Ed S); school administration and supervision (M Ed); school teaching (M Ed); social science (MA); sociology (MA); sociology/criminal justice (MA). *Application deadline:* For fall admission, 7/1 priority date for domestic and international students; for spring admission, 12/1 priority date for domestic and international students. Applications are processed on a rolling basis. *Application fee:* $17. *Dean,* Dr. Patrick Henry, 573-681-5300, Fax: 573-681-5144, E-mail: henryp@lincolnu.edu.

LINCOLN UNIVERSITY, Lincoln University, PA 19352

General Information State-related, coed, comprehensive institution. *Graduate housing:* On-campus housing not available.

GRADUATE UNITS

Graduate Program in Human Services *Degree program information:* Evening/weekend programs available. Offers human services (M Hum Svcs).

LINDENWOOD UNIVERSITY, St. Charles, MO 63301-1695

General Information Independent-religious, coed, comprehensive institution. *Enrollment:* 9,525 graduate, professional, and undergraduate students; 1,374 full-time matriculated graduate/professional students (895 women), 2,083 part-time matriculated graduate/professional students (1,572 women). *Enrollment by degree level:* 3,247 master's, 62 doctoral, 139 other advanced degrees. *Graduate faculty:* 67 full-time (23 women), 48 part-time/adjunct (22 women). *Tuition:* Part-time $340 per credit hour. Tuition and fees vary according to course level, course load, degree level and program. *Graduate housing:* Rooms and/or apartments available on a first-come, first-served basis to single students and available to married students. Housing application deadline: 8/30. *Student services:* Campus employment opportunities, career counseling, disabled student services, international student services, teacher training, writing training. *Library facilities:* Butler Library. *Online resources:* library catalog, web page, access to other libraries' catalogs. *Collection:* 122,358 titles, 28,732 serial subscriptions, 1,342 audiovisual materials.

Computer facilities: Computer purchase and lease plans are available. 160 computers available on campus for general student use. A campuswide network can be accessed from student residence rooms and from off campus. Internet access, WEBCT are available. *Web address:* http://www.lindenwood.edu/.

General Application Contact: Brett Barger, Dean, Adult, Corporate and Graduate Admissions, 636-949-4934, Fax: 636-949-4109, E-mail: adultadmissions@lindenwood.edu.

GRADUATE UNITS

Graduate Programs Students: 1,374 full-time (895 women), 2,083 part-time (1,572 women); includes 751 minority (688 African Americans, 14 American Indian/Alaska Native, 20 Asian Americans or Pacific Islanders, 29 Hispanic Americans), 97 international. Average age 34. *Faculty:* 67 full-time (23 women), 48 part-time/adjunct (22 women). Expenses: Contact institution. *Financial support:* Career-related internships or fieldwork, Federal Work-Study, institutionally sponsored loans, tuition waivers (partial), and unspecified assistantships available. Financial award application deadline: 6/30; financial award applicants required to submit FAFSA. In 2006, 1,206 master's, 18 other advanced degrees awarded. *Degree program information:* Part-time and evening/weekend programs available. Offers administration (MSA); business administration (MBA); communications (MA); criminal justice and administration (MS); gerontology (MA); health management (MS); human resource management (MS); management (MSA); marketing (MSA); writing (MFA). *Application deadline:* For fall admission, 8/30 priority date for domestic and international students; for winter admission, 12/30 priority date for domestic and international students; for spring admission, 12/30 priority date for domestic and international students. Applications are processed on a rolling basis. *Application fee:* $30 ($100 for international students). Electronic applications accepted. *Application Contact:* Brett Barger, Dean, Adult, Corporate and Graduate Admissions, 636-949-4934, Fax: 636-949-4109, E-mail: adultadmissions@lindenwood.edu. *Vice President of Academic Affairs,* Dr. John Weitzel, 636-949-4708, Fax: 636-949-4992, E-mail: jweitzel@lindenwood.edu.

Division of Education Students: 569 full-time (446 women), 1,869 part-time (1,433 women); includes 526 minority (494 African Americans, 8 American Indian/Alaska Native, 9 Asian Americans or Pacific Islanders, 15 Hispanic Americans), 8 international. Average age 35. *Faculty:* 15 full-time (6 women), 16 part-time/adjunct (11 women). Expenses: Contact institution. *Financial support:* Career-related internships or fieldwork, institutionally sponsored loans, and tuition waivers (partial) available. Financial award application deadline: 6/30; financial award applicants required to submit FAFSA. In 2006, 747 master's, 19 other advanced degrees awarded. *Degree program information:* Part-time and evening/weekend programs available. Offers education (MA); educational administration (MA, Ed D, Ed S); instructional leadership (Ed D, Ed S); library media (MA); professional and school counseling (MA); professional counseling (MA); school counseling (MA); teaching (MA). *Application deadline:* For fall admission, 8/30 priority date for domestic and international students; for spring admission, 12/30 priority date for domestic and international students. Applications are processed on a rolling basis. *Application fee:* $30 ($100 for international students). Electronic applications accepted. *Application Contact:* Brett Barger, Dean, Adult, Corporate and Graduate Admissions, 636-949-4934, Fax: 636-949-4109, E-mail: adultadmissions@lindenwood.edu. *Dean of Education,* Dr. John Dougherty, 636-949-4937, E-mail: jdougherty@lindenwood.edu.

Division of Fine and Performing Arts Students: 30 full-time (17 women), 20 part-time (14 women); includes 5 minority (4 African Americans, 1 American Indian/Alaska Native), 6 international. Average age 33. *Faculty:* 18 full-time (7 women). Expenses: Contact institution. *Financial support:* Career-related internships or fieldwork, institutionally sponsored loans, tuition waivers (partial), and unspecified assistantships available. Financial award application deadline: 6/30; financial award applicants required to submit FAFSA. In 2006, 18 degrees awarded. *Degree program information:* Part-time programs available. Offers arts management (MA); communication arts (MA); studio art (MFA); theatre arts (MA, MFA); theatre arts management (MFA). *Application deadline:* For fall admission, 8/30 priority date for domestic and international students; for spring admission, 12/30 priority date for domestic and international students. Applications are processed on a rolling basis. *Application fee:* $30 ($100 for international students). *Application Contact:* Brett Barger, Dean, Adult, Corporate and Graduate Admissions, 636-949-4934, Fax: 636-949-4109, E-mail: adultadmissions@lindenwood.edu. *Dean of Fine Arts,* Marsha Parker, 636-949-4906, Fax: 636-949-4910, E-mail: mparker@lindenwood.edu.

Division of Management Students: 177 full-time (78 women), 138 part-time (67 women); includes 43 minority (27 African Americans, 4 American Indian/Alaska Native, 6 Asian Americans or Pacific Islanders, 6 Hispanic Americans), 73 international. Average age 30. *Faculty:* 38 full-time (15 women), 20 part-time/adjunct (5 women). Expenses: Contact institution. *Financial support:* Career-related internships or fieldwork, Federal Work-Study, institutionally sponsored loans, and tuition waivers (partial) available. Financial award application deadline: 6/30; financial award applicants required to submit FAFSA. In 2006, 159 degrees awarded. *Degree program information:* Part-time and evening/weekend programs available. Offers accounting (MBA, MS); business administration (MBA); entrepreneurial studies (MBA); finance (MBA, MS); human resource management (MBA); human resources (MS); international business (MBA, MS); management (MBA, MS); management information systems (MBA, MS); managing business to business (MA); managing human resources (MA); managing international business (MA); managing investment management (MA); managing leadership (MA); managing marketing (MA); managing organizational behavior (MA); managing sales (MA); managing, training and development (MA); marketing (MBA, MS); nonprofit administration (MA); public management (MBA, MS); sport management (MA). *Application deadline:* For fall admission, 7/30 priority date for domestic students, 9/30 priority date for international students; for winter admission, 12/30 priority date for domestic and international students; for spring admission, 3/30 priority date for domestic and international students. Applications are processed on a rolling basis. *Application fee:* $30 ($100 for international students). Electronic applications accepted. *Application Contact:* Brett Barger, Dean Adult, Corporate and Graduate Admissions, 636-949-4366, Fax: 636-949-4109, E-mail: bbarger@lindenwood.edu. *Dean,* Ed Morris, 636-949-4832, Fax: 636-949-4910, E-mail: emorris@lindenwood.edu.

LINDSEY WILSON COLLEGE, Columbia, KY 42728-1298

General Information Independent-religious, coed, comprehensive institution. *Graduate housing:* Rooms and/or apartments available on a first-come, first-served basis to single and married students.

GRADUATE UNITS

School of Professional Counseling *Degree program information:* Part-time and evening/weekend programs available. Offers counseling and human development (M Ed).

LIPSCOMB UNIVERSITY, Nashville, TN 37204-3951

General Information Independent-religious, coed, comprehensive institution. *Enrollment:* 2,563 graduate, professional, and undergraduate students; 128 full-time matriculated graduate/professional students (67 women), 146 part-time matriculated graduate/professional students (55 women). *Enrollment by degree level:* 30 first professional, 244 master's. *Graduate faculty:* 21 full-time (4 women), 13 part-time/adjunct (6 women). *Tuition:* Part-time $560 per semester hour. Tuition and fees vary according to program. *Graduate housing:* Rooms and/or apartments available on a first-come, first-served basis to single and married students. Housing application deadline: 7/15. *Student services:* Campus employment opportunities, career counseling, disabled student services, exercise/wellness program, free psychological counseling, international student services, multicultural affairs office, teacher training. *Library facilities:* Beaman Library plus 1 other. *Online resources:* library catalog, web page, access to other libraries' catalogs. *Collection:* 253,398 titles, 850 serial subscriptions.

Computer facilities: 245 computers available on campus for general student use. A campuswide network can be accessed from student residence rooms and from off campus. Internet access and online class registration are available. *Web address:* http://www.lipscomb.edu/.

General Application Contact: Dr. Randy Bouldin, Associate Provost for Graduate Studies, 615-966-5711, Fax: 615-966-7619, E-mail: randy.bouldin@lipscomb.edu.

GRADUATE UNITS

Hazelip School of Theology Students: 15 full-time (2 women), 66 part-time (10 women); includes 6 minority (all African Americans), 2 international. Average age 32. 30 applicants, 80% accepted, 21 enrolled. *Faculty:* 8 full-time (0 women), 7 part-time/adjunct (0 women). Expenses: Contact institution. *Financial support:* Scholarships/grants available. Support available to part-time students. Financial award application deadline: 3/1; financial award applicants required to submit FAFSA. In 2006, 18 degrees awarded. *Degree program information:* Part-time and evening/weekend programs available. Offers biblical studies (MA); Christian studies (MA); divinity (M Div); ministry (MA); New Testament (MA); Old Testament (MA); theological studies (MTS); theology (MA). *Application deadline:* For fall admission, 8/14 priority date for domestic students; for spring admission, 12/31 for domestic students. Applications are processed on a rolling basis. *Application fee:* $0 ($75 for international students). Electronic applications accepted. *Application Contact:* Audrey Everson, Information Contact, 615-966-6051, Fax: 615-966-6052, E-mail: audrey.everson@lipscomb.edu. *Director*, Dr. Mark Black, 615-966-1000 Ext. 5799, Fax: 615-966-1808, E-mail: mark.black@lipscomb.edu.

MBA Program Students: 18 full-time (6 women), 50 part-time (23 women); includes 5 minority (4 African Americans, 1 American Indian/Alaska Native), 2 international. Average age 30. 48 applicants, 73% accepted, 27 enrolled. *Faculty:* 11 full-time (3 women), 6 part-time/adjunct (0 women). Expenses: Contact institution. *Financial support:* In 2006–07, 25 students received support. Career-related internships or fieldwork, Federal Work-Study, scholarships/grants, tuition waivers (partial), and unspecified assistantships available. Support available to part-time students. Financial award application deadline: 7/1; financial award applicants required to submit FAFSA. In 2006, 30 degrees awarded. *Degree program information:* Part-time and evening/weekend programs available. Offers accounting (MBA); business administration (general) (MBA); conflict management (MBA); financial services (MBA); healthcare management (MBA); leadership (MBA); nonprofit management (MBA). *Application deadline:* For fall admission, 7/1 for domestic students, 2/1 for international students; for winter admission, 12/1 for domestic students, 6/1 for international students. Applications are processed on a rolling basis. *Application fee:* $50 ($75 for international students). Electronic applications accepted. *Application Contact:* Jackie Cash, MBA Assistant, 615-966-1833, Fax: 615-966-1818, E-mail: jackie.cash@lipscomb.edu. *Associate Dean of Graduate Business Studies*, Dr. Steven K. Yoho, 615-966-1833, Fax: 615-966-1818, E-mail: steven.yoho@lipscomb.edu.

Program in Education Students: 95 full-time (59 women), 30 part-time (22 women); includes 14 minority (13 African Americans, 1 Asian American or Pacific Islander). Average age 32. *Faculty:* 3 full-time (1 woman), 9 part-time/adjunct (6 women). Expenses: Contact institution. *Financial support:* In 2006–07, 67 students received support. Federal Work-Study, tuition waivers (full), and unspecified assistantships available. Support available to part-time students. Financial award applicants required to submit FAFSA. In 2006, 25 degrees awarded. *Degree program information:* Part-time and evening/weekend programs available. Offers instructional leadership (M Ed); learning and teaching (MALT); school administration and supervision (M Ed); special education instruction, K-12 (MASE). *Application deadline:* For fall admission, 8/29 priority date for domestic students; for spring admission, 1/16 priority date for domestic students. Applications are processed on a rolling basis. *Application fee:* $60. *Application Contact:* Jackie Sanders, Administrative Assistant, 615-966-1000 Ext. 6081, Fax: 615-966-7628, E-mail: jackie.sanders@lipscomb.edu. *Director*, Dr. Junior High, 615-966-1000 Ext. 6067, Fax: 615-966-7628, E-mail: junior.high@lipscomb.edu.

LOCK HAVEN UNIVERSITY OF PENNSYLVANIA, Lock Haven, PA 17745-2390

General Information State-supported, coed, comprehensive institution. *Graduate housing:* Room and/or apartments available on a first-come, first-served basis to single students; on-campus housing not available to married students. Housing application deadline: 6/1.

GRADUATE UNITS

Office of Graduate Studies *Degree program information:* Part-time and evening/weekend programs available. Postbaccalaureate distance learning degree programs offered. Offers alternative education (M Ed); liberal arts (MLA); physician assistant in rural primary care (MHS); teaching and learning (M Ed). Electronic applications accepted.

LOGAN UNIVERSITY-COLLEGE OF CHIROPRACTIC, Chesterfield, MO 63006-1065

General Information Independent, coed, upper-level institution. *Enrollment:* 1,098 graduate, professional, and undergraduate students; 921 full-time matriculated graduate/professional students (294 women), 54 part-time matriculated graduate/professional students (22 women). *Enrollment by degree level:* 923 first professional, 2 master's. *Graduate faculty:* 53 full-time (16 women), 52 part-time/adjunct (26 women). *Tuition:* Full-time $12,800; part-time $400 per credit hour. *Required fees:* $270. *Graduate housing:* On-campus housing not available. *Student services:* Campus employment opportunities, career counseling, disabled student services, exercise/wellness program, free psychological counseling, international student services, low-cost health insurance, multicultural affairs office. *Library facilities:* Learning Resources Center. *Online resources:* library catalog, web page, access to other libraries' catalogs. *Collection:* 14,001 titles, 163 serial subscriptions, 2,366 audiovisual materials. *Research affiliation:* Foot Levelers (Orthotics), Biofreeze (topical analgesic), NanoGreen (nutrition), ProAdjuster (chiropractic), Graston (rehabilitation), Spine force (rehabilitation).

Computer facilities: 75 computers available on campus for general student use. A campuswide network can be accessed. Internet access is available. *Web address:* http://www.logan.edu/.

General Application Contact: Cindy Sutton, Associate Director, Admissions, 636-227-2100 Ext. 1756, Fax: 636-207-2425, E-mail: loganadm@logan.edu.

GRADUATE UNITS

Chiropractic Program Students: 921 full-time (294 women), 52 part-time (21 women); includes 76 minority (30 African Americans, 4 American Indian/Alaska Native, 19 Asian Americans or Pacific Islanders, 23 Hispanic Americans), 40 international. Average age 27. 240 applicants, 96% accepted, 147 enrolled. *Faculty:* 53 full-time (16 women), 52 part-time/adjunct (26 women). Expenses: Contact institution. *Financial support:* In 2006–07, 100 students received support. Federal Work-Study and scholarships/grants available. Support available to part-time students. Financial award applicants required to submit FAFSA. In 2006, 229 degrees awarded. Offers chiropractic (DC). *Application deadline:* For fall admission, 7/15 priority date for domestic and international students; for winter admission, 11/15 priority date for domestic and international students; for spring admission, 3/15 priority date for domestic students, 3/15 for international students. Applications are processed on a rolling basis. *Application fee:* $50. Electronic applications accepted. *Application Contact:* Cindy Sutton, Associate Director, Admissions, 636-227-2100 Ext. 1756, Fax: 636-207-2425, E-mail: loganadm@logan.edu. *Associate Vice President, Academic Affairs*, Dr. Carl Saubert, 636-227-2100, Fax: 636-207-2431, E-mail: carl.saubert@logan.edu.

LOGOS EVANGELICAL SEMINARY, El Monte, CA 91731

General Information Independent-religious, coed, graduate-only institution. *Enrollment by degree level:* 52 master's, 35 doctoral, 40 other advanced degrees. *Graduate faculty:* 10 full-time (2 women), 7 part-time/adjunct (1 woman). *Tuition:* Full-time $7,680; part-time $240 per unit. Full-time tuition and fees vary according to course level, degree level and program. *Graduate housing:* Room and/or apartments available on a first-come, first-served basis to single students. Typical cost: $420 per year; $535 per year for married students. Room charges vary according to housing facility selected. *Student services:* Campus employment opportunities, career counseling, exercise/wellness program, international student services, low-cost health insurance. *Library facilities:* Logos Evangelical Seminary Library. *Online resources:* web page. *Collection:* 46,500 titles, 140 serial subscriptions, 2,750 audiovisual materials.

Computer facilities: 16 computers available on campus for general student use. A campuswide network can be accessed. Internet access is available. *Web address:* http://www.logos-seminary.edu/.

General Application Contact: Jane Peng, Administrative Coordinator of Academic Affairs, 626-571-5110 Ext. 26, Fax: 626-307-6487, E-mail: janepeng@les.edu.

GRADUATE UNITS

Graduate Programs Students: 72 full-time (30 women), 55 part-time (34 women); includes 126 minority (all Asian Americans or Pacific Islanders) Average age 44. 34 applicants, 71% accepted, 21 enrolled. *Faculty:* 10 full-time (2 women), 7 part-time/adjunct (1 woman). Expenses: Contact institution. *Financial support:* Application deadline: 3/1. In 2006, 14 first professional degrees, 3 master's, 5 doctorates awarded. *Degree program information:* Part-time programs available. *Application deadline:* For fall admission, 7/15 priority date for domestic students, 5/15 priority date for international students; for winter admission, 9/10 priority date for domestic and international students; for spring admission, 12/15 priority date for domestic students, 10/15 priority date for international students. *Application fee:* $25 ($50 for international students). *Application Contact:* Becky Perng, Admission Officer, 626-571-5110 Ext. 12, E-mail: admission@les.edu. *Academic Dean*, Dr. Ekron Chen, 626-571-5110, E-mail: ekron@les.edu.

LOMA LINDA UNIVERSITY, Loma Linda, CA 92350

General Information Independent-religious, coed, upper-level institution. CGS member. *Graduate housing:* Room and/or apartments available on a first-come, first-served basis to single students; on-campus housing not available to married students. *Research affiliation:* City of Hope Hospital (cancer research).

GRADUATE UNITS

Department of Graduate Nursing *Degree program information:* Part-time programs available. Offers adult and aging family nursing (MS); growing family nursing (MS); nursing administration (MS, Certificate).

Faculty of Religion Offers biomedical and clinical ethics (MA, Certificate); clinical ministry (MA, Certificate); religion (MA, Certificate); religion and science (MA).

School of Allied Health Professions Offers allied health professions (MHIS, MPT, MS, DPT); health information systems (MHIS); physical therapy (MPT, DPT); physician assistant (MS); speech-language pathology and audiology (MS).

School of Dentistry Offers dentistry (DDS, MS, Certificate); endodontics (MS, Certificate); implant dentistry (MS, Certificate); oral and maxillofacial surgery (MS, Certificate); orthodontics (MS, Certificate); periodontics (MS).

School of Medicine Offers biochemistry/microbiology (MS, PhD); medicine (MD, MS, PhD); pathology and human anatomy (MS, PhD); physiology/pharmacology (MS, PhD).

School of Public Health *Degree program information:* Part-time programs available. Offers environmental and occupational health (MPH, MSPH); epidemiology and biostatistics (MPH, MSPH); global health (MPH); health administration (MHA, MPH); health promotion and education (MPH, Dr PH); public health (MHA, MPH, MSPH, Dr PH); public health nutrition (MPH, Dr PH).

School of Science and Technology Offers biological and earth sciences (MS, PhD); counseling and family science (MA, MS, DMFT, PhD, Certificate); psychology (PhD, Psy D); science and technology (MA, MS, MSW, DMFT, PhD, Psy D, Certificate); social policy and research (PhD); social work (MSW).

LONG ISLAND UNIVERSITY, BRENTWOOD CAMPUS, Brentwood, NY 11717

General Information Independent, coed, upper-level institution. *Graduate housing:* On-campus housing not available.

GRADUATE UNITS

School of Education *Degree program information:* Part-time and evening/weekend programs available. Offers elementary education (MS); reading (MS); school counseling (MS); school district administration and supervision (MS); special education (MS).

School of Public Service *Degree program information:* Part-time and evening/weekend programs available. Offers criminal justice (MS).

LONG ISLAND UNIVERSITY, BROOKLYN CAMPUS, Brooklyn, NY 11201-8423

General Information Independent, coed, university. *Graduate housing:* Rooms and/or apartments available to single and married students. Housing application deadline: 9/1.

GRADUATE UNITS

Arnold and Marie Schwartz College of Pharmacy and Health Sciences Students: 326 (125 women); includes 293 minority (35 African Americans, 1 American Indian/Alaska Native, 255 Asian Americans or Pacific Islanders, 2 Hispanic Americans). Average age 25. *Faculty:* 53 full-time (22 women), 25 part-time/adjunct (6 women). Expenses: Contact institution. *Financial support:* In 2006–07, 5 fellowships with full tuition reimbursements (averaging $13,500 per year), 30 teaching assistantships with full and partial tuition reimbursements (averaging $6,000 per year) were awarded; Federal Work-Study and institutionally sponsored loans also available. Support available to part-time students. Financial award applicants required to submit FAFSA. In 2006, 54 master's, 2 doctorates awarded. *Degree program information:* Part-time and evening/weekend programs available. Offers cosmetic science (MS); drug regulatory affairs (MS); industrial pharmacy (MS); pharmaceutical sciences (MS, PhD); pharmaceutics (PhD); pharmacology/toxicology (MS); pharmacy administration (MS); pharmacy and health sciences (MS, PhD); social and administrative sciences (MS). *Application deadline:* Applications are processed on a rolling basis. *Application fee:* $30. *Application Contact:* Edward Dettling, Director of Graduate Admissions, 718-488-1011, Fax: 718-797-2399, E-mail: admissions@brooklyn.liu.edu. *Dean*, Dr. Stephen M. Gross, 718-488-1004, Fax: 718-488-0628, E-mail: sgross@liu.edu.

Richard L. Conolly College of Liberal Arts and Sciences *Degree program information:* Part-time and evening/weekend programs available. Offers biology (MS); chemistry (MS); clinical psychology (PhD); economics (MA); English literature (MA); history (MS); liberal arts and sciences (MA, MS, PhD, Certificate); media arts (MA); political science (MA); professional and creative writing (MA); psychology (MA); speech-language pathology (MS); teaching of writing (MA); United Nations studies (Certificate); urban studies (MA). Electronic applications accepted.

School of Business, Public Administration and Information Sciences *Degree program information:* Part-time and evening/weekend programs available. Offers accounting (MS); business administration (MBA); business, public administration and information sciences (MBA, MPA, MS); computer science (MS); human resources management (MS); public administration (MPA); taxation (MS). Electronic applications accepted.

School of Education *Degree program information:* Part-time and evening/weekend programs available. Offers bilingual education (MS Ed); computers in education (MS); counseling and development (MS, MS Ed, Certificate); education (MS, MS Ed, Certificate); elementary education (MS Ed); leadership and policy (MS); mathematics education (MS Ed); reading (MS Ed); school psychology (MS Ed); secondary education (MS Ed); special education (MS Ed); teaching English to speakers of other languages (MS Ed). Electronic applications accepted.

Long Island University, Brooklyn Campus (continued)

School of Health Professions *Degree program information:* Part-time and evening/weekend programs available. Offers adapted physical education (MS); athletic training and sports sciences (MS); community mental health (MS); exercise physiology (MS); family health (MS); health management (MS); health professions (MS, DPT, TDPT); health sciences (MS); physical therapy (DPT, TDPT). Electronic applications accepted.

School of Nursing Offers adult nurse practitioner (MS, Certificate); nurse executive (MS); nursing (MS, Certificate). Electronic applications accepted.

LONG ISLAND UNIVERSITY, C.W. POST CAMPUS, Brookville, NY 11548-1300

General Information Independent, coed, comprehensive institution. *Graduate housing:* Room and/or apartments available on a first-come, first-served basis to single students; on-campus housing not available to married students. Housing application deadline: 6/1.

GRADUATE UNITS

College of Information and Computer Science *Degree program information:* Part-time and evening/weekend programs available. Postbaccalaureate distance learning degree programs offered. Offers information and computer science (MS, PhD, Certificate); information systems (MS); information technology education (MS); management engineering (MS). Electronic applications accepted.

Palmer School of Library and Information Science *Degree program information:* Part-time and evening/weekend programs available. Postbaccalaureate distance learning degree programs offered (minimal on-campus study). Offers archives and records management (Certificate); information studies (PhD); library and information science (MS); library media specialist (MS); public library management (Certificate). Electronic applications accepted.

College of Liberal Arts and Sciences *Degree program information:* Part-time and evening/weekend programs available. Offers applied behavior analysis (Advanced Certificate); applied mathematics (MS); biology (MS); biology education (MS); clinical psychology (Psy D); English (MA); English for adolescence education (MS); environmental management (MS); environmental science (MS); experimental psychology (MA, Advanced Certificate); history (MA); interdisciplinary studies (MA, MS); liberal arts and sciences (MA, MS, Psy D, Advanced Certificate); mathematics education (MS); mathematics for secondary school teachers (MS); political science/international studies (MA); Spanish (MA); Spanish education (MS). Electronic applications accepted.

College of Management *Degree program information:* Part-time and evening/weekend programs available. Offers management (MBA, MPA, MS, Certificate). Electronic applications accepted.

School of Business *Degree program information:* Part-time and evening/weekend programs available. Offers accounting and taxation (Certificate); business administration (Certificate); finance (MBA, Certificate); general business administration (MBA); international business (MBA, Certificate); management (MBA, Certificate); management information systems (MBA, Certificate); marketing (MBA, Certificate). Electronic applications accepted.

School of Professional Accountancy *Degree program information:* Part-time and evening/weekend programs available. Offers accounting (MS); taxation (MS). Electronic applications accepted.

School of Public Service *Degree program information:* Part-time and evening/weekend programs available. Offers criminal justice (MS); fraud examination (MS); gerontology (Certificate); health care administration (MPA); health care administration/gerontology (MPA); nonprofit management (MPA, Certificate); public administration (MPA); public service (MPA, MS, Certificate); security administration (MS). Electronic applications accepted.

School of Education *Degree program information:* Part-time and evening/weekend programs available. Offers adolescence education (MS); adolescence education: biology (MS); adolescence education: earth science (MS); adolescence education: English (MS); adolescence education: mathematics (MS); adolescence education: social studies (MS); adolescence education: Spanish (MS); art education (MS); bilingual education (MS); childhood education (MS); childhood education/literacy (MS); childhood education/special education (MS); computers in education (MS); early childhood education (MS); education (MA, MS, MS Ed, PD); literacy (MS Ed); mental health counseling (MS); middle childhood education (MS); music education (MS); school administration and supervision (MS Ed); school business administration (PD); school counseling (MS); school district administration (PD); special education (MS Ed); speech language pathology (MA); teaching English to speakers of other languages (MS). Electronic applications accepted.

School of Health Professions and Nursing *Degree program information:* Part-time and evening/weekend programs available. Postbaccalaureate distance learning degree programs offered. Offers cardiovascular perfusion (MS, Certificate); clinical laboratory management (MS); clinical nurse specialist (MS); dietetic internship (Certificate); family nurse practitioner (MS, Certificate); health professions and nursing (MS, Certificate); hematology (MS); immunology (MS); medical biology (MS); medical chemistry (MS); medical microbiology (MS); nutrition (MS). Electronic applications accepted.

School of Visual and Performing Arts *Degree program information:* Part-time and evening/weekend programs available. Offers art (MA); art education (MS); clinical art therapy (MA); fine art and design (MFA); interactive multimedia arts (MA); music (MA); music education (MS); theatre (MA); visual and performing arts (MA, MFA, MS). Electronic applications accepted.

See Close-Up on page 945.

LONG ISLAND UNIVERSITY, ROCKLAND GRADUATE CAMPUS, Orangeburg, NY 10962

General Information Independent, coed, graduate-only institution. *Graduate housing:* On-campus housing not available.

GRADUATE UNITS

Graduate School *Degree program information:* Part-time and evening/weekend programs available. Offers business administration (MBA, Post Master's Certificate); childhood education (MS); childhood literacy (MS); childhood special education (MS); cosmetical dermatological sciences (MS); financial management (MPA); gerontology (Advanced Certificate); health administration (MPA); health services management (MPA); industrial pharmacy (MS); literacy (MS Ed); long term care administration (MPA); medical practice management (MPA); mental health counseling (MS); nonprofit management (MPA, Advanced Certificate); school building leader (MS Ed, Advanced Certificate); school counselor (MS); school district business leader (Advanced Certificate); school district leader (Advanced Certificate); special education (MS Ed).

LONG ISLAND UNIVERSITY, SOUTHAMPTON GRADUATE CAMPUS, Southampton, NY 11968-4198

General Information Independent, coed, primarily women, graduate-only institution. *Enrollment:* 40 full-time matriculated graduate/professional students, 111 part-time matriculated graduate/professional students. *Enrollment by degree level:* 128 master's, 23 other advanced degrees. *Graduate faculty:* 6 full-time (2 women), 11 part-time/adjunct (5 women). *Tuition:* Part-time $790 per credit. *Required fees:* $220 per semester. *Student services:* Campus employment opportunities, campus safety program, career counseling, international student services, low-cost health insurance. *Library facilities:* Southampton Graduate Campus Library. *Online resources:* library catalog, web page. *Collection:* 155,000 titles, 155 serial subscriptions, 655 audiovisual materials.

Computer facilities: 48 computers available on campus for general student use. A campuswide network can be accessed from off campus. Internet access is available. *Web address:* http://www.southampton.liu.edu/.

General Application Contact: Joyce Tuttle, Director of Graduate Admissions and Program Administration, 631-287-8010, Fax: 631-287-8253, E-mail: joyce.tuttle@liu.edu.

GRADUATE UNITS

Education Division Students: 21 full-time (15 women), 79 part-time (59 women). Average age 31. 111 applicants. *Faculty:* 4 full-time (3 women), 9 part-time/adjunct (5 women). Expenses: Contact institution. *Financial support:* In 2006–07, 96 students received support. Scholarships/grants and tuition waivers (partial) available. Support available to part-time students. Financial award applicants required to submit FAFSA. In 2006, 25 degrees awarded. *Degree program information:* Part-time and evening/weekend programs available. Offers childhood education (MS Ed); education (MS Ed); elementary education (MS Ed); literacy education (MS Ed); teaching students with disabilities (MS Ed). *Application deadline:* For fall admission, 6/21 priority date for domestic students, 4/15 priority date for international students; for winter admission, 12/1 priority date for domestic students, 10/1 priority date for international students; for spring admission, 12/30 priority date for domestic students, 10/30 priority date for international students. Applications are processed on a rolling basis. *Application fee:* $30. Electronic applications accepted. *Application Contact:* Joyce Tuttle, Director of Graduate Admissions and Program Administration, 631-287-8010, Fax: 631-287-8253, E-mail: joyce.tuttle@liu.edu. *Director,* Dr. R. Lawrence McCann, 631-287-8211, E-mail: admissions@southampton.liu.edu.

Homeland Security Management Institute Students: 4 full-time (2 women), 61 part-time (10 women). 88 applicants, 81% accepted, 65 enrolled. *Faculty:* 2 full-time (0 women), 4 part-time/adjunct (1 woman). Expenses: Contact institution. *Financial support:* Career-related internships or fieldwork and scholarships/grants available. Support available to part-time students. Offers homeland security management (MS, Advanced Certificate). *Application deadline:* For fall admission, 5/30 priority date for domestic students; for winter admission, 11/30 priority date for domestic students; for spring admission, 11/30 priority date for domestic students. *Application fee:* $30. *Application Contact:* Joyce Tuttle, Director of Graduate Admissions and Program Administration, 631-287-8010, Fax: 631-287-8253, E-mail: joyce.tuttle@liu.edu. *Unit Head,* Dr. Vincent E. Henry, 631-287-8010, Fax: 631-287-8130, E-mail: vincent.henry@liu.edu.

LONG ISLAND UNIVERSITY, WESTCHESTER GRADUATE CAMPUS, Purchase, NY 10577

General Information Independent, coed, graduate-only institution. *Enrollment by degree level:* 331 master's. *Graduate faculty:* 7 full-time, 34 part-time/adjunct. *Tuition:* Part-time $790 per credit. *Student services:* Campus employment opportunities, international student services, low-cost health insurance, writing training. *Library facilities:* Long Island University Library System. *Online resources:* library catalog, web page. *Collection:* 267,566 titles, 179,984 serial subscriptions, 8,105 audiovisual materials.

Computer facilities: 40 computers available on campus for general student use. A campuswide network can be accessed from off campus. Internet access and online class registration are available. *Web address:* http://www.liu.edu/westchester/.

General Application Contact: Ellen Brief, Coordinator of Admissions, Marketing, Student Services and Public Relations, 914-831-2701, Fax: 914-251-5959, E-mail: westchester@liu.edu.

GRADUATE UNITS

Program in Business Administration 13 applicants, 77% accepted, 7 enrolled. *Faculty:* 1 full-time (0 women), 7 part-time/adjunct (3 women). Expenses: Contact institution. *Financial support:* In 2006–07, 4 students received support. Scholarships/grants, tuition waivers (partial), and unspecified assistantships available. Financial award applicants required to submit FAFSA. In 2006, 18 degrees awarded. *Degree program information:* Part-time and evening/weekend programs available. Offers business administration (MBA). *Application deadline:* Applications are processed on a rolling basis. *Application fee:* $30. *Application Contact:* Ellen Brief, Coordinator of Admissions, Marketing, Student Services and Public Relations, 914-831-2701, Fax: 914-251-5959, E-mail: ellen.brief@liu.edu. *Program Director,* Dr. Lynn Johnson, 914-831-2711, Fax: 914-251-5959, E-mail: lynn.johnson@liu.edu.

Program in Education-School Counselor and School Psychology Students: 84 (72 women). 40 applicants, 73% accepted, 21 enrolled. *Faculty:* 2 full-time (both women), 12 part-time/adjunct (8 women). Expenses: Contact institution. *Financial support:* In 2006–07, 22 students received support. Scholarships/grants, tuition waivers (partial), and unspecified assistantships available. In 2006, 21 degrees awarded. *Degree program information:* Part-time and evening/weekend programs available. Offers school counselor (MS Ed); school psychologist (MS Ed). *Application deadline:* Applications are processed on a rolling basis. *Application fee:* $30. *Application Contact:* Ellen Brief, Coordinator of Admissions, Marketing, Student Services and Public Relations, 914-831-2701, Fax: 914-251-5959, E-mail: westchester@liu.edu. *Director,* Prof. Beth Weiner, 914-831-2717, Fax: 914-251-5959, E-mail: beth.weiner@liu.edu.

Program in Library and Information Science Students: 110 (88 women). 22 applicants, 91% accepted, 18 enrolled. *Faculty:* 1 (woman) full-time, 19 part-time/adjunct (11 women). Expenses: Contact institution. *Financial support:* In 2006–07, 24 students received support. Scholarships/grants, tuition waivers, and unspecified assistantships available. In 2006, 35 degrees awarded. *Degree program information:* Part-time and evening/weekend programs available. Offers library and information science (MS). *Application deadline:* Applications are processed on a rolling basis. *Application fee:* $30. *Application Contact:* Ellen Brief, Coordinator of Admissions, Marketing, Student Services and Public Relations, 914-831-2701, Fax: 914-251-5959, E-mail: ellen.brief@liu.edu. *Coordinator,* Trudy Katz, 914-831-2712, E-mail: trudy.katz@liu.edu.

Programs in Education-Teaching 50 applicants, 92% accepted, 42 enrolled. *Faculty:* 4 full-time, 32 part-time/adjunct. Expenses: Contact institution. *Financial support:* In 2006–07, 38 students received support. Scholarships/grants, tuition waivers (partial), and unspecified assistantships available. In 2006, 72 degrees awarded. *Degree program information:* Part-time and evening/weekend programs available. Offers early childhood education (MS Ed); elementary education (MS Ed); literacy education (MS Ed); second language, TESOL, bilingual education (MS Ed); special education and secondary education (MS Ed). *Application deadline:* Applications are processed on a rolling basis. *Application fee:* $30. *Application Contact:* Ellen Brief, Coordinator of Admissions, Marketing, Student Services and Public Relations, 914-831-2701, Fax: 914-251-5959, E-mail: ellen.brief@liu.edu. *Academic Dean, Associate Provost,* Dr. Sylvia Blake, 914-831-2704, Fax: 914-251-5959, E-mail: sylvia.blake@liu.edu.

Program in Second Language, TESOL, Bilingual Education 4 applicants, 100% accepted, 4 enrolled. *Faculty:* 1 (woman) full-time, 5 part-time/adjunct (4 women). Expenses: Contact institution. *Financial support:* Scholarships/grants, tuition waivers (partial), and unspecified assistantships available. In 2006, 3 degrees awarded. *Degree program information:* Part-time and evening/weekend programs available. Offers second language, TESOL, bilingual education (MS Ed). *Application deadline:* Applications are processed on a rolling basis. *Application Contact:* Ellen Brief, Coordinator of Admissions, Marketing, Student Services and Public Relations, 914-831-2701, Fax: 914-251-5959, E-mail: ellen.brief@liu.edu. *Director,* Dr. Helaine Marshall, 914-831-2713, Fax: 914-251-5959, E-mail: helaine.marshall@liu.edu.

See Close-Up on page 947.

LONGWOOD UNIVERSITY, Farmville, VA 23909

General Information State-supported, coed, comprehensive institution. CGS member. *Graduate housing:* On-campus housing not available.

GRADUATE UNITS

Office of Graduate Studies *Degree program information:* Part-time and evening/weekend programs available. Offers 6-12 initial teaching/licensure (MA); creative writing (MA); criminal justice (MS); English education and writing (MA); literature (MA).

College of Business and Economics Offers retail management (MBA).

College of Education and Human Services *Degree program information:* Part-time and evening/weekend programs available. Offers communication sciences and disorders (MS); community and college counseling (MS); curriculum and instruction specialist-elementary

(MS); curriculum and instruction specialist-secondary (MS); educational leadership (MS); guidance and counseling (MS); literacy and culture (MS); school library media (MS).

LONGY SCHOOL OF MUSIC, Cambridge, MA 02138

General Information Independent, coed, graduate-only institution. *Enrollment by degree level:* 121 master's, 37 other advanced degrees. *Graduate faculty:* 88 part-time/adjunct (42 women). *Tuition:* Full-time $22,750; part-time $1,290 per credit. *Required fees:* $400; $400 per year. *Graduate housing:* On-campus housing not available. *Student services:* Campus employment opportunities, career counseling, international student services, low-cost health insurance. *Library facilities:* Bakalar Library. *Online resources:* library catalog, access to other libraries' catalogs. *Collection:* 14,500 titles, 35 serial subscriptions, 8,900 audiovisual materials.

Computer facilities: 6 computers available on campus for general student use. A campuswide network can be accessed. Internet access is available. *Web address:* http://www.longy.edu/.

General Application Contact: Heather McCowen, Associate Dean of Admissions and Student Services, 617-876-0956 Ext. 521, Fax: 617-876-9326, E-mail: music@longy.edu.

GRADUATE UNITS

Conservatory at Longy Students: 118 full-time (85 women), 40 part-time (26 women); includes 15 minority (8 African Americans, 6 Asian Americans or Pacific Islanders, 1 Hispanic American), 42 international. Average age 28. 129 applicants, 82% accepted, 60 enrolled. *Faculty:* 88 part-time/adjunct (42 women). Expenses: Contact institution. *Financial support:* In 2006–07, 122 students received support, including 8 teaching assistantships (averaging $1,890 per year); scholarships/grants and unspecified assistantships also available. Financial award application deadline: 3/1; financial award applicants required to submit FAFSA. In 2006, 33 master's, 18 other advanced degrees awarded. *Degree program information:* Part-time programs available. Offers chamber ensemble (Artist Diploma); collaborative piano (MM, Artist Diploma, GPD); composition (MM); Dalcroze eurhythmics (MM); early music (MM, Artist Diploma, GPD); instrumental performance (MM, Artist Diploma, GPD); modern American music (MM, GPD); opera performance (MM, GPD); organ performance (MM, Artist Diploma, GPD); piano performance (MM, Artist Diploma, GPD); vocal performance (MM, Artist Diploma, GPD). *Application deadline:* For fall admission, 1/15 priority date for domestic and international students; for spring admission, 12/1 for domestic and international students. Applications are processed on a rolling basis. *Application fee:* $90. *Application Contact:* Heather McCowen, Director of Admissions, 617-876-0956 Ext. 521, Fax: 617-876-9326, E-mail: music@longy.edu. *President,* Dr. Karen Zorn, 617-876-0956, Fax: 617-876-9326, E-mail: music@longy.edu.

LORAS COLLEGE, Dubuque, IA 52004-0178

General Information Independent-religious, coed, comprehensive institution. *Enrollment:* 1,673 graduate, professional, and undergraduate students; 8 full-time matriculated graduate/professional students (4 women), 74 part-time matriculated graduate/professional students (50 women). *Enrollment by degree level:* 82 master's. *Graduate faculty:* 12 full-time (4 women), 5 part-time/adjunct (3 women). *Tuition:* Full-time $7,650; part-time $425 per credit. *Graduate housing:* On-campus housing not available. *Student services:* Campus employment opportunities, career counseling, disabled student services, free psychological counseling, multicultural affairs office. *Library facilities:* Academic Resource Center. *Online resources:* library catalog, web page, access to other libraries' catalogs. *Collection:* 351,550 titles, 554 serial subscriptions.

Computer facilities: Computer purchase and lease plans are available. 20 computers available on campus for general student use. A campuswide network can be accessed from student residence rooms and from off campus. Internet access and online class registration are available. *Web address:* http://www.loras.edu/.

General Application Contact: Michelle Rice, Graduate Admissions Counselor, 563-588-7166, E-mail: michelle.rice@loras.edu.

GRADUATE UNITS

Graduate Division Students: 8 full-time (4 women), 74 part-time (50 women), 1 international. Average age 34. 27 applicants, 81% accepted, 13 enrolled. *Faculty:* 12 full-time (4 women), 5 part-time/adjunct (3 women). Expenses: Contact institution. *Financial support:* Applicants required to submit FAFSA. In 2006, 33 degrees awarded. *Degree program information:* Part-time and evening/weekend programs available. Offers applied psychology (MA); educational leadership (MA); instructional strategist I K-6 and 7-12 (MA); ministry (MA); theology (MA). *Application deadline:* Applications are processed on a rolling basis. *Application fee:* $25. *Application Contact:* Michelle Rice, Graduate Admissions Counselor, 563-588-7166, E-mail: michelle.rice@loras.edu. *Director,* Dr. Cheryl Jacobsen, 563-588-7107, E-mail: cheryl.jacobsen@loras.edu.

LOUISIANA STATE UNIVERSITY AND AGRICULTURAL AND MECHANICAL COLLEGE, Baton Rouge, LA 70803

General Information State-supported, coed, university. CGS member. *Enrollment:* 29,925 graduate, professional, and undergraduate students; 3,326 full-time matriculated graduate/professional students (1,738 women), 1,129 part-time matriculated graduate/professional students (650 women). *Enrollment by degree level:* 368 first professional, 2,217 master's, 1,870 doctoral. *Graduate faculty:* 1,214 full-time (284 women), 22 part-time/adjunct (8 women). *Graduate housing:* Rooms and/or apartments available on a first-come, first-served basis to single and married students. Housing application deadline: 3/15. *Student services:* Campus employment opportunities, campus safety program, career counseling, child daycare facilities, disabled student services, exercise/wellness program, free psychological counseling, grant writing training, international student services, low-cost health insurance, multicultural affairs office, teacher training, writing training. *Library facilities:* Troy H. Middleton Library plus 7 others. *Online resources:* library catalog, web page, access to other libraries' catalogs. *Collection:* 1.4 million titles, 58,918 serial subscriptions. *Research affiliation:* Laser Interferometer Gravitational Wave Observatory, Inter-University Consortium for Political and Social Research, Coalition for Academic Scientific Computing, Organization for Tropical Studies, Arctic Research Consortium of the U. S., Albert Einstein Institute.

Computer facilities: 7,000 computers available on campus for general student use. A campuswide network can be accessed from student residence rooms and from off campus. Internet access and online class registration, e-mail, wireless, grades, payroll, storage, e-portfolio are available. *Web address:* http://www.lsu.edu/.

General Application Contact: Reneé Renegar, Office of Graduate Admissions, 225-578-1641, Fax: 225-578-1370, E-mail: rreneg1@lsu.edu.

GRADUATE UNITS

Graduate School Average age 31. 3,047 applicants, 46% accepted. *Faculty:* 1,214 full-time (284 women), 22 part-time/adjunct (8 women). Expenses: Contact institution. *Financial support:* In 2006–07, 2,142 students received support, including 183 fellowships with full tuition reimbursements available (averaging $24,658 per year), 965 research assistantships with partial tuition reimbursements available (averaging $16,130 per year), 990 teaching assistantships with partial tuition reimbursements available (averaging $13,804 per year); career-related internships or fieldwork, Federal Work-Study, institutionally sponsored loans, scholarships/grants, traineeships, tuition waivers (full and partial), and unspecified assistantships also available. Support available to part-time students. Financial award application deadline: 1/15; financial award applicants required to submit FAFSA. In 2006, 1,013 master's, 266 doctorates, 8 other advanced degrees awarded. *Degree program information:* Part-time and evening/weekend programs available. Postbaccalaureate distance learning degree programs offered. *Application deadline:* For fall admission, 5/15 priority date for domestic students, 5/15 for international students; for winter admission, 10/15 priority date for domestic students; for spring admission, 10/15 for domestic and international students. Applications are processed on a rolling basis. *Application fee:* $25. Electronic applications accepted. *Application Contact:* Marie Hamilton, Assistant Dean, 225-578-3885, Fax: 225-578-1370, E-mail: mhamil3@lsu.edu. *Associate Dean,* Dr. Stacia Haynie, 225-578-3885, Fax: 225-578-1370, E-mail: pohayn@lsu.edu.

College of Agriculture Students: 300 full-time (154 women), 148 part-time (88 women); includes 45 minority (30 African Americans, 2 American Indian/Alaska Native, 5 Asian Americans or Pacific Islanders, 8 Hispanic Americans), 138 international. Average age 32. 178 applicants, 46% accepted, 37 enrolled. *Faculty:* 184 full-time (25 women). Expenses: Contact institution. *Financial support:* In 2006–07, 258 students received support, including 9 fellowships with full tuition reimbursements available (averaging $27,106 per year), 186 research assistantships with partial tuition reimbursements available (averaging $15,768 per year), 52 teaching assistantships with partial tuition reimbursements available (averaging $11,004 per year); career-related internships or fieldwork, Federal Work-Study, institutionally sponsored loans, tuition waivers (full), and unspecified assistantships also available. Support available to part-time students. Financial award applicants required to submit FAFSA. In 2006, 98 master's, 37 doctorates awarded. *Degree program information:* Part-time programs available. Offers agricultural economics and agribusiness (MS, PhD); agriculture (M App St, MS, MSBAE, PhD); agronomy (MS, PhD); animal sciences (MS, PhD); applied statistics (M App St); biological and agricultural engineering (MSBAE); comprehensive vocational education (MS, PhD); engineering science (MS, PhD); entomology (MS, PhD); extension and international education (MS, PhD); fisheries (MS); food science (MS, PhD); forestry (MS, PhD); horticulture (MS, PhD); human ecology (MS, PhD); industrial education (MS); plant health (MS, PhD); vocational agriculture education (MS, PhD); vocational business education (MS); vocational home economics education (MS); wildlife (MS); wildlife and fisheries science (PhD). *Application deadline:* For fall admission, 5/15 for domestic and international students; for spring admission, 10/15 for domestic and international students. Applications are processed on a rolling basis. *Application fee:* $25. Electronic applications accepted. *Application Contact:* Paula Beecher, Recruiting Coordinator, 225-578-2468, E-mail: pbeeche@lsu.edu. *Dean,* Dr. Kenneth Koonce, 225-578-2362, Fax: 225-578-2526, E-mail: kkoonce@lsu.edu.

College of Art and Design Students: 103 full-time (55 women), 7 part-time (4 women); includes 10 minority (5 African Americans, 3 Asian Americans or Pacific Islanders, 2 Hispanic Americans), 14 international. Average age 31. 117 applicants, 48% accepted, 27 enrolled. *Faculty:* 56 full-time (13 women). Expenses: Contact institution. *Financial support:* In 2006–07, 53 students received support, including 38 teaching assistantships with partial tuition reimbursements available (averaging $6,813 per year); fellowships, research assistantships with partial tuition reimbursements available, career-related internships or fieldwork, Federal Work-Study, institutionally sponsored loans, scholarships/grants, tuition waivers (full and partial), and unspecified assistantships also available. Support available to part-time students. Financial award applicants required to submit FAFSA. In 2006, 29 degrees awarded. *Degree program information:* Part-time programs available. Offers architecture (M Arch); art and design (M Arch, MA, MFA, MLA); art history (MA); ceramics (MFA); graphic design (MFA); landscape architecture (MLA); painting and drawing (MFA); photography (MFA); printmaking (MFA); sculpture (MFA); studio art (MFA). *Application deadline:* For fall admission, 1/25 priority date for domestic students, 5/15 for international students; for spring admission, 10/15 for international students. Applications are processed on a rolling basis. *Application fee:* $25. Electronic applications accepted. *Application Contact:* Theresa Mooney, Academic Counselor, 225-578-5400, Fax: 225-578-1445, E-mail: deacon1@lsu.edu. *Dean,* David Cronrath, 225-578-5400, Fax: 225-578-5040, E-mail: dc1@lsu.edu.

College of Arts and Sciences Students: 583 full-time (323 women), 169 part-time (85 women); includes 80 minority (47 African Americans, 4 American Indian/Alaska Native, 13 Asian Americans or Pacific Islanders, 16 Hispanic Americans), 109 international. Average age 30. 701 applicants, 37% accepted, 105 enrolled. *Faculty:* 295 full-time (86 women), 6 part-time/adjunct (4 women). Expenses: Contact institution. *Financial support:* In 2006–07, 20 fellowships with full tuition reimbursements, 69 research assistantships with full and partial tuition reimbursements (averaging $16,796 per year), 341 teaching assistantships with full and partial tuition reimbursements (averaging $13,313 per year) were awarded; career-related internships or fieldwork, Federal Work-Study, institutionally sponsored loans, scholarships/grants, traineeships, tuition waivers (full), and unspecified assistantships also available. Support available to part-time students. Financial award applicants required to submit FAFSA. In 2006, 134 master's, 60 doctorates awarded. *Degree program information:* Part-time and evening/weekend programs available. Offers anthropology (MA); arts and sciences (MA, MALA, MFA, MS, PhD); biological psychology (MA, PhD); clinical psychology (MA, PhD); cognitive psychology (MA, PhD); communication sciences and disorders (MA, PhD); communication studies (MA, PhD); comparative literature (MA, PhD); creative writing (MFA); developmental psychology (MA, PhD); English (MA, PhD); French literature and linguistics (MA, PhD); geography (MA, MS, PhD); history (MA, PhD); industrial/organizational psychology (MA, PhD); liberal arts (MALA); linguistics (MA, PhD); mathematics (MS, PhD); philosophy (MA); political science (MA, PhD); school psychology (MA, PhD); sociology (MA, PhD); Spanish (MA). *Application deadline:* For fall admission, 5/15 priority date for domestic students, 5/15 for international students; for spring admission, 10/15 priority date for domestic students, 10/15 for international students. *Application fee:* $25. Electronic applications accepted. *Application Contact:* Dr. Robin Roberts, Associate Dean, 225-578-8273, Fax: 225-587-6447, E-mail: rrobert@lsu.edu. *Dean,* Dr. Guillermo Ferreya, 225-578-8273, Fax: 225-578-6447, E-mail: dnferr@lsu.edu.

College of Basic Sciences Students: 489 full-time (174 women), 67 part-time (32 women); includes 76 minority (60 African Americans, 1 American Indian/Alaska Native, 12 Asian Americans or Pacific Islanders, 3 Hispanic Americans), 244 international. Average age 30. 457 applicants, 33% accepted, 70 enrolled. *Faculty:* 184 full-time (28 women), 5 part-time/adjunct (2 women). Expenses: Contact institution. *Financial support:* In 2006–07, 440 students received support, including fellowships with full and partial tuition reimbursements available (averaging $28,424 per year), 204 research assistantships with full and partial tuition reimbursements available (averaging $20,176 per year), 219 teaching assistantships with full and partial tuition reimbursements available (averaging $17,357 per year); career-related internships or fieldwork, Federal Work-Study, institutionally sponsored loans, tuition waivers (full and partial), and unspecified assistantships also available. Support available to part-time students. Financial award applicants required to submit FAFSA. In 2006, 50 master's, 47 doctorates awarded. *Degree program information:* Part-time programs available. Offers astronomy (PhD); astrophysics (PhD); basic sciences (MNS, MS, MSSS, PhD); biochemistry (MS, PhD); biological science (MS, PhD); chemistry (MS, PhD); computer science (MSSS, PhD); geology and geophysics (MS, PhD); natural sciences (MNS); physics (MS, PhD); systems science (MSSS). *Application deadline:* For fall admission, 5/15 for international students; for spring admission, 10/15 for international students. Applications are processed on a rolling basis. *Application fee:* $25. Electronic applications accepted. *Application Contact:* Dr. Fred Rainey, Associate Dean, 225-578-4200, Fax: 225-578-8826, E-mail: frainey@lsu.edu. *Dean,* Dr. Kevin Carman, 225-578-8859, Fax: 225-578-8826, E-mail: bascdean@lsu.edu.

College of Education Students: 194 full-time (135 women), 210 part-time (155 women); includes 75 minority (59 African Americans, 3 American Indian/Alaska Native, 6 Asian Americans or Pacific Islanders, 7 Hispanic Americans), 21 international. Average age 34. 159 applicants, 55% accepted, 18 enrolled. *Faculty:* 53 full-time (29 women). Expenses: Contact institution. *Financial support:* In 2006–07, 117 students received support, including fellowships (averaging $24,345 per year), 26 research assistantships with partial tuition reimbursements available (averaging $9,904 per year), 50 teaching assistantships with partial tuition reimbursements available (averaging $12,622 per year); career-related internships or fieldwork, Federal Work-Study, institutionally sponsored loans, tuition waivers (partial), and unspecified assistantships also available. Support available to part-time students. Financial award applicants required to submit FAFSA. In 2006, 120 master's, 31 doctorates, 7 other advanced degrees awarded. *Degree program information:* Part-time and evening/weekend programs available. Offers counseling (M Ed, MA, Ed S); education (M Ed, MA, MS, PhD, Ed S); educational administration (M Ed, MA, PhD, Ed S); educational technology (MA); elementary education (M Ed); higher education (PhD); kinesiology (MS, PhD); research methodology (PhD); secondary education (M Ed). *Application deadline:* For fall admission, 1/25 priority date for domestic students, 5/15 for international students; for spring admission, 10/15 for international students. Applications are processed on a rolling basis. *Application fee:* $25. Electronic applications accepted. *Application Contact:* Dr.

Louisiana State University and Agricultural and Mechanical College (continued)

Patricia Exner, Associate Dean, 225-578-2208, Fax: 225-578-2267, E-mail: pexner@lsu.edu. *Dean*, Dr. Jayne Fleener, 225-578-1258, Fax: 225-578-2267, E-mail: fleener@lsu.edu.

College of Engineering Students: 385 full-time (84 women), 81 part-time (18 women); includes 23 minority (11 African Americans, 1 American Indian/Alaska Native, 2 Asian Americans or Pacific Islanders, 9 Hispanic Americans), 346 international. Average age 29. 490 applicants, 50% accepted, 91 enrolled. *Faculty:* 128 full-time (7 women), 2 part-time/adjunct (0 women). Expenses: Contact institution. *Financial support:* In 2006–07, 324 students received support, including fellowships with full and partial tuition reimbursements available (averaging $21,934 per year), 232 research assistantships with full and partial tuition reimbursements available (averaging $15,749 per year), 89 teaching assistantships with full and partial tuition reimbursements available (averaging $11,514 per year); career-related internships or fieldwork, Federal Work-Study, institutionally sponsored loans, scholarships/grants, tuition waivers (full and partial), and unspecified assistantships also available. Financial award applicants required to submit FAFSA. In 2006, 111 master's, 30 doctorates awarded. *Degree program information:* Part-time and evening/weekend programs available. Offers chemical engineering (MS Ch E, PhD); electrical and computer engineering (MSEE, PhD); engineering (MS Ch E, MS Pet E, MSCE, MSEE, MSES, MSIE, MSME, PhD); engineering science (MSES, PhD); environmental engineering (MSCE, PhD); geotechnical engineering (MSCE, PhD); industrial engineering (MSIE); mechanical engineering (MSME, PhD); petroleum engineering (MS Pet E, PhD); structural engineering and mechanics (MSCE, PhD); transportation engineering (MSCE, PhD); water resources (MSCE, PhD). *Application deadline:* For fall admission, 1/25 priority date for domestic students, 5/15 for international students; for spring admission, 10/15 for international students. Applications are processed on a rolling basis. *Application fee:* $25. Electronic applications accepted. *Application Contact:* Dr. W. David Constant, Associate Dean for Research and Graduate Studies, 225-578-9165, Fax: 225-578-9162, E-mail: hscons@lsu.edu. *Dean*, Dr. Zaki Bassiouni, 225-578-5701, Fax: 225-578-9162, E-mail: pezab@lsu.edu.

College of Music and Dramatic Arts Students: 152 full-time (86 women), 38 part-time (22 women); includes 24 minority (11 African Americans, 8 Asian Americans or Pacific Islanders, 5 Hispanic Americans), 33 international. Average age 31. 151 applicants, 55% accepted, 49 enrolled. *Faculty:* 63 full-time (23 women), 3 part-time/adjunct (2 women). Expenses: Contact institution. *Financial support:* In 2006–07, 7 fellowships with full and partial tuition reimbursements (averaging $28,687 per year), 2 research assistantships with full and partial tuition reimbursements (averaging $8,250 per year), 103 teaching assistantships with full and partial tuition reimbursements (averaging $9,933 per year) were awarded; Federal Work-Study, scholarships/grants, tuition waivers (full and partial), and unspecified assistantships also available. Support available to part-time students. Financial award applicants required to submit FAFSA. In 2006, 38 master's, 21 doctorates awarded. *Degree program information:* Part-time programs available. Offers acting (MFA); directing (MFA); music (MM, DMA, PhD); music and dramatic arts (MFA, MM, DMA, PhD); music education (PhD); theatre (PhD); theatre design/technology (MFA). *Application deadline:* For fall admission, 3/15 priority date for domestic students, 5/15 for international students; for spring admission, 10/15 for international students. Applications are processed on a rolling basis. *Application fee:* $25. *Interim Dean*, Dr. Sara Lyn Baird, 225-578-3261, Fax: 225-578-2562.

E. J. Ourso College of Business Students: 360 full-time (138 women), 191 part-time (81 women); includes 63 minority (41 African Americans, 3 American Indian/Alaska Native, 8 Asian Americans or Pacific Islanders, 11 Hispanic Americans), 82 international. Average age 29. 496 applicants, 54% accepted. *Faculty:* 84 full-time (14 women), 2 part-time/adjunct (0 women). Expenses: Contact institution. *Financial support:* In 2006–07, 193 students received support, including 6 fellowships (averaging $39,449 per year), 88 research assistantships with full and partial tuition reimbursements available (averaging $11,156 per year), 59 teaching assistantships with full and partial tuition reimbursements available (averaging $11,388 per year); career-related internships or fieldwork, Federal Work-Study, institutionally sponsored loans, scholarships/grants, and unspecified assistantships also available. Support available to part-time students. Financial award applicants required to submit FAFSA. In 2006, 250 master's, 14 doctorates awarded. *Degree program information:* Part-time and evening/weekend programs available. Offers accounting (MS, PhD); business (EMBA, MBA, MPA, MS, PMBA, PhD); business administration (PhD); economics (MS, PhD); finance (MS); information systems and decision sciences (MS, PhD); public administration (MPA). *Application deadline:* For fall admission, 1/25 priority date for domestic students, 5/15 for international students; for spring admission, 10/15 for international students. Applications are processed on a rolling basis. *Application fee:* $25. Electronic applications accepted. *Interim Dean*, Dr. William R. Lane, 225-578-5297, Fax: 225-578-5256, E-mail: filane@lsu.edu.

Manship School of Mass Communication Students: 40 full-time (29 women), 21 part-time (15 women); includes 5 minority (all African Americans), 15 international. Average age 31. 64 applicants, 52% accepted, 9 enrolled. *Faculty:* 23 full-time (13 women). Expenses: Contact institution. *Financial support:* In 2006–07, 36 students received support, including 1 fellowship (averaging $12,776 per year), 29 research assistantships with full and partial tuition reimbursements available (averaging $15,713 per year), 5 teaching assistantships with full and partial tuition reimbursements available (averaging $17,400 per year); career-related internships or fieldwork, Federal Work-Study, institutionally sponsored loans, scholarships/grants, tuition waivers (full and partial), and unspecified assistantships also available. Support available to part-time students. Financial award application deadline: 3/1; financial award applicants required to submit FAFSA. In 2006, 18 master's, 5 doctorates awarded. *Degree program information:* Part-time programs available. Postbaccalaureate distance learning degree programs offered (minimal on-campus study). Offers mass communication (MMC, PhD). *Application deadline:* For fall admission, 1/25 priority date for domestic students, 5/15 for international students; for spring admission, 10/15 for international students. Applications are processed on a rolling basis. *Application fee:* $25. Electronic applications accepted. *Application Contact:* Dr. Margaret DeFleur, Associate Dean of Graduate Studies and Research, 225-578-9294, Fax: 225-578-2125, E-mail: defleur@lsu.edu. *Dean*, Dr. John Maxwell Hamilton, 225-578-2002, Fax: 225-578-2125, E-mail: jhamilt@lsu.edu.

School of Library and Information Science Students: 63 full-time (47 women), 101 part-time (90 women); includes 19 minority (13 African Americans, 5 American Indian/Alaska Native, 1 Asian American or Pacific Islander), 6 international. Average age 36. 48 applicants, 73% accepted, 17 enrolled. *Faculty:* 11 full-time (9 women). Expenses: Contact institution. *Financial support:* In 2006–07, 33 students received support, including 10 research assistantships with partial tuition reimbursements available (averaging $8,878 per year), 14 teaching assistantships with partial tuition reimbursements available (averaging $10,730 per year); fellowships, career-related internships or fieldwork, Federal Work-Study, institutionally sponsored loans, scholarships/grants, and unspecified assistantships also available. Support available to part-time students. Financial award applicants required to submit FAFSA. In 2006, 63 master's awarded. *Degree program information:* Evening/weekend programs available. Offers library and information science (MLIS, CAS). *Application deadline:* For fall admission, 1/25 priority date for domestic students, 5/15 for international students; for spring admission, 10/15 for international students. Applications are processed on a rolling basis. *Application fee:* $25. Electronic applications accepted. *Dean*, Dr. Beth M. Paskoff, 225-578-3158, Fax: 225-578-4581, E-mail: lspask@lsu.edu.

School of Social Work Students: 174 full-time (162 women), 48 part-time (37 women); includes 57 minority (51 African Americans, 3 American Indian/Alaska Native, 1 Asian American or Pacific Islander, 2 Hispanic Americans), 3 international. Average age 31. 116 applicants, 73% accepted, 34 enrolled. *Faculty:* 12 full-time (8 women). Expenses: Contact institution. *Financial support:* In 2006–07, 26 students received support, including 4 research assistantships with partial tuition reimbursements available (averaging $10,750 per year), 13 teaching assistantships with partial tuition reimbursements available (averaging $9,717 per year); fellowships, career-related internships or fieldwork, Federal Work-Study, scholarships/grants, and unspecified assistantships also available. Support available to part-time students. Financial award applicants required to submit FAFSA. In 2006, 75 master's, 2 doctorates awarded. *Degree program information:* Part-time programs available. Offers social work (MSW, PhD). *Application deadline:* For fall admission, 3/1 for domestic students, 5/15 for international students; for spring admission, 10/15 for international students. *Application fee:* $25. Electronic applications accepted. *Application Contact:* Denise Chiasson Breaux, Director of Student Services, 225-578-1234, Fax: 225-578-1357, E-mail: dchiass@lsu.edu. *Dean*, Dr. Pamela Ann Monroe, 225-578-5875, E-mail: pmonroe@lsu.edu.

School of the Coast and Environment Students: 72 full-time (41 women), 31 part-time (14 women); includes 5 minority (3 African Americans, 1 American Indian/Alaska Native, 1 Hispanic American), 18 international. Average age 31. 43 applicants, 47% accepted, 14 enrolled. *Faculty:* 39 full-time (4 women), 2 part-time/adjunct (0 women). Expenses: Contact institution. *Financial support:* In 2006–07, 8 fellowships with full tuition reimbursements (averaging $31,489 per year), 48 research assistantships with full and partial tuition reimbursements (averaging $16,308 per year), 5 teaching assistantships with full and partial tuition reimbursements (averaging $12,950 per year) were awarded; career-related internships or fieldwork, Federal Work-Study, institutionally sponsored loans, and unspecified assistantships also available. Financial award applicants required to submit FAFSA. In 2006, 18 master's, 8 doctorates awarded. *Degree program information:* Part-time programs available. Offers environmental planning and management (MS); environmental toxicology (MS); oceanography and coastal sciences (MS, PhD); the coast and environment (MS, PhD). *Application deadline:* For fall admission, 1/25 priority date for domestic students, 5/15 for international students; for spring admission, 10/15 for international students. Applications are processed on a rolling basis. *Application fee:* $25. Electronic applications accepted. *Dean*, Dr. Ed Laws, 225-578-6316, Fax: 225-578-5328.

Paul M. Hebert Law Center Students: 578 full-time (286 women); includes 57 minority (42 African Americans, 2 American Indian/Alaska Native, 7 Asian Americans or Pacific Islanders, 6 Hispanic Americans), 1 international. Average age 26. 1,353 applicants, 35% accepted, 204 enrolled. *Faculty:* 45 full-time (13 women), 51 part-time/adjunct (6 women). Expenses: Contact institution. *Financial support:* In 2006–07, 5 fellowships with tuition reimbursements were awarded; scholarships/grants and tuition waivers (full and partial) also available. Financial award applicants required to submit FAFSA. Offers law (JD, LL M, MCL). *Application deadline:* For fall admission, 3/1 priority date for domestic students, 2/1 priority date for international students. Applications are processed on a rolling basis. *Application fee:* $25. Electronic applications accepted. *Application Contact:* Michele Forbes, Director of Student Affairs and Registrar, 225-578-8646, Fax: 225-578-8647, E-mail: michele.forbes@law.lsu.edu. *Chancellor*, John J. Costonis, 225-578-8491, Fax: 225-578-8202, E-mail: john.costonis@law.lsu.edu.

School of Veterinary Medicine Students: 43 full-time (22 women), 17 part-time (9 women); includes 2 minority (1 American Indian/Alaska Native, 1 Hispanic American), 22 international. Average age 32. 27 applicants, 48% accepted, 7 enrolled. *Faculty:* 83 full-time (25 women), 2 part-time/adjunct (0 women). Expenses: Contact institution. *Financial support:* In 2006–07, fellowships with full tuition reimbursements (averaging $20,729 per year), 38 research assistantships with full and partial tuition reimbursements (averaging $22,618 per year) were awarded; teaching assistantships with full and partial tuition reimbursements, career-related internships or fieldwork, Federal Work-Study, institutionally sponsored loans, scholarships/grants, tuition waivers (full and partial), and unspecified assistantships also available. Financial award applicants required to submit FAFSA. In 2006, 3 master's, 5 doctorates awarded. Offers comparative biomedical sciences (MS, PhD); pathobiological sciences (MS, PhD); veterinary clinical sciences (MS, PhD); veterinary medicine (DVM, MS, PhD). *Application deadline:* For fall admission, 3/1 priority date for domestic students, 5/15 for international students; for spring admission, 10/15 for international students. Applications are processed on a rolling basis. *Application fee:* $25. Electronic applications accepted. *Dean*, Dr. Peter Haynes, 225-578-9903, Fax: 225-578-9916, E-mail: pfhaynes@vetmed.lsu.edu.

LOUISIANA STATE UNIVERSITY HEALTH SCIENCES CENTER, New Orleans, LA 70112-2223

General Information State-supported, coed, university. CGS member. *Enrollment:* 1,775 full-time matriculated graduate/professional students (856 women), 196 part-time matriculated graduate/professional students (169 women). *Enrollment by degree level:* 1,315 first professional, 321 master's, 213 doctoral, 39 other advanced degrees. *Graduate faculty:* 1,680. Tuition, state resident: full-time $5,868; part-time $722 per credit. Tuition, nonresident: full-time $8,993; part-time $1,104 per credit. *Graduate housing:* Rooms and/or apartments available to single and married students. Housing application deadline: 6/1. *Student services:* Campus safety program, free psychological counseling, low-cost health insurance. *Library facilities:* John P. Ische Library plus 2 others. *Online resources:* library catalog, web page, access to other libraries' catalogs. *Collection:* 232,617 titles, 2,359 serial subscriptions, 3,200 audiovisual materials.

Computer facilities: Computer purchase and lease plans are available. 100 computers available on campus for general student use. A campuswide network can be accessed from student residence rooms and from off campus. Internet access is available. *Web address:* http://www.lsuhsc.edu/no/.

General Application Contact: Jack Dale Hines, Coordinator of the School of Graduate Studies, 504-568-2211, Fax: 504-568-5588, E-mail: jhines@lsuhsc.edu.

GRADUATE UNITS

School of Allied Health Professions *Degree program information:* Part-time and evening/weekend programs available. Offers allied health professions (MCD, MHS, MOT, MPT); audiology (MCD); clinical concepts (MHS); education (MHS); management administration (MHS); physical therapy (MPT); rehabilitation counseling (MHS); speech pathology (MCD).

School of Dentistry Offers dentistry (DDS).

School of Graduate Studies in New Orleans Students: 119 full-time (63 women), 3 part-time (2 women); includes 22 minority (12 African Americans, 1 Asian American or Pacific Islander, 9 Hispanic Americans), 30 international. Average age 26. 59 applicants, 22% accepted. *Faculty:* 138 full-time (27 women), 29 part-time/adjunct (8 women). Expenses: Contact institution. *Financial support:* In 2006–07, 2 fellowships with full tuition reimbursements (averaging $20,000 per year), 28 research assistantships with full tuition reimbursements (averaging $20,000 per year), 27 teaching assistantships with full tuition reimbursements (averaging $20,000 per year) were awarded; Federal Work-Study, scholarships/grants, and tuition waivers (full) also available. In 2006, 11 master's, 5 doctorates awarded. *Degree program information:* Part-time and evening/weekend programs available. Offers biometry (MPH, MS); cell biology and anatomy (MS, PhD); human genetics (MS, PhD); medicine (MPH, MS, PhD); microbiology and immunology (MS, PhD); neuroscience (MS, PhD); pathology (MS, PhD); pharmacology and experimental therapeutics (MS, PhD); physiology (MS, PhD); public health and preventive medicine (MPH). *Application deadline:* For fall admission, 4/1 for domestic and international students; for spring admission, 10/1 for domestic and international students. Applications are processed on a rolling basis. *Application fee:* $30. *Application Contact:* Jack Dale Hines, Coordinator of the School of Graduate Studies, 504-568-2211, Fax: 504-568-5588, E-mail: jhines@lsuhsc.edu. *Head*, Dr. Joseph M. Moerschbaecher, 504-568-4740, Fax: 504-568-2361.

School of Medicine in New Orleans Offers medicine (MD, MPH). Open only to Louisiana residents. Electronic applications accepted.

School of Nursing *Degree program information:* Part-time programs available. Offers adult health and illness (MN); adult health and nursing (DNS); neonatal nurse practitioner (MN); nursing (MN); nursing service administration (MN, DNS); parent-child health nursing (MN); primary care nurse practitioner (MN); psychiatric/community mental health nursing (MN, DNS); public health/community health nursing (MN, DNS).

LOUISIANA STATE UNIVERSITY HEALTH SCIENCES CENTER AT SHREVEPORT, Shreveport, LA 71130-3932

General Information State-supported, coed, university.

GRADUATE UNITS

Department of Biochemistry and Molecular Biology Offers biochemistry and molecular biology (MS, PhD).

Department of Cellular Biology and Anatomy Offers cellular biology and anatomy (MS, PhD).

Department of Microbiology and Immunology Offers microbiology and immunology (MS, PhD).

Department of Molecular and Cellular Physiology Offers physiology (MS, PhD).

Department of Pharmacology, Toxicology and Neuroscience Offers pharmacology (PhD).

School of Medicine Offers medicine (MD).

LOUISIANA STATE UNIVERSITY IN SHREVEPORT, Shreveport, LA 71115-2399

General Information State-supported, coed, comprehensive institution. *Enrollment:* 4,023 graduate, professional, and undergraduate students; 102 full-time matriculated graduate/professional students (75 women), 301 part-time matriculated graduate/professional students (220 women). *Enrollment by degree level:* 386 master's, 17 other advanced degrees. *Graduate faculty:* 91 full-time (31 women), 9 part-time/adjunct (7 women). *Graduate housing:* Rooms and/or apartments available on a first-come, first-served basis to single and married students. *Student services:* Campus employment opportunities, career counseling, disabled student services, exercise/wellness program, free psychological counseling, teacher training. *Library facilities:* Noel Memorial Library. *Online resources:* library catalog, web page, access to other libraries' catalogs. *Collection:* 279,821 titles, 1,190 serial subscriptions. *Research affiliation:* Cotton, Inc. (plant physiology), Biomedical Research Institute, Louisiana Manufacturing Science Center (robotics), Department of Agriculture (crop science), Micromanufacturing Institute (manufacturing technology).

Computer facilities: Computer purchase and lease plans are available. A campuswide network can be accessed from off campus. Internet access is available. *Web address:* http://www.lsus.edu/.

General Application Contact: Dr. Patricia Doerr, Dean of Graduate Studies, 318-797-5247, Fax: 318-798-4120, E-mail: pdoerr@lsus.edu.

GRADUATE UNITS

College of Business Administration *Degree program information:* Part-time and evening/weekend programs available. Offers healthcare (MBA).

College of Education and Human Development Students: 12 full-time (10 women), 165 part-time (137 women); includes 50 minority (48 African Americans, 1 Asian American or Pacific Islander, 1 Hispanic American). Average age 33. *Faculty:* 15 full-time (9 women), 6 part-time/adjunct (5 women). Expenses: Contact institution. *Financial support:* In 2006–07, 2 research assistantships with partial tuition reimbursements were awarded; teaching assistantships, career-related internships or fieldwork and Federal Work-Study also available. Support available to part-time students. Financial award applicants required to submit FAFSA. In 2006, 50 master's, 6 other advanced degrees awarded. *Degree program information:* Part-time and evening/weekend programs available. Offers counseling psychology (MS); education (M Ed); education and human development (M Ed, MS, SSP); school psychology (SSP). *Application deadline:* For fall admission, 8/18 priority date for domestic students; for spring admission, 11/30 priority date for domestic students. Applications are processed on a rolling basis. *Application fee:* $10. *Application Contact:* Dr. Ruth Ray, Coordinator of Graduate Programs in Education, 318-797-5036, Fax: 318-798-4144, E-mail: rray@pilot.lsus.edu. *Chair,* Dr. David B. Gustavson, 318-797-5032, Fax: 318-798-4144, E-mail: dgustavs@pilot.lsus.edu.

College of Liberal Arts Students: 24 full-time (20 women), 93 part-time (70 women); includes 33 minority (27 African Americans, 2 Asian Americans or Pacific Islanders, 4 Hispanic Americans). Average age 27. 50 applicants, 100% accepted. *Faculty:* 26 full-time (9 women), 17 part-time/adjunct (9 women). Expenses: Contact institution. *Financial support:* In 2006–07, 51 students received support, including 7 research assistantships with full tuition reimbursements available (averaging $8,000 per year); Federal Work-Study also available. Support available to part-time students. In 2006, 21 degrees awarded. *Degree program information:* Part-time and evening/weekend programs available. Postbaccalaureate distance learning degree programs offered. Offers health administration (MHA); human services administration (MS); liberal arts (MA, MHA, MS). *Application deadline:* For fall admission, 8/5 priority date for domestic students; for spring admission, 11/15 priority date for domestic students. Applications are processed on a rolling basis. *Application fee:* $10 ($20 for international students). *Dean,* Dr. Larry Anderson, 318-797-5371, Fax: 318-797-5358, E-mail: landerso@pilot.lsus.edu.

College of Sciences Students: 11 full-time (5 women), 9 part-time (4 women); includes 7 minority (3 African Americans, 4 Asian Americans or Pacific Islanders). Average age 32. 12 applicants, 100% accepted, 10 enrolled. *Faculty:* 7 full-time (2 women), 3 part-time/adjunct (1 woman). Expenses: Contact institution. *Financial support:* In 2006–07, teaching assistantships with partial tuition reimbursements (averaging $1,600 per year); scholarships/grants also available. Financial award application deadline: 3/1. In 2006, 1 degree awarded. *Degree program information:* Part-time and evening/weekend programs available. Offers systems technology (MSST). *Application deadline:* For fall admission, 8/5 priority date for domestic students, 6/1 priority date for international students; for spring admission, 12/15 for domestic students, 10/1 priority date for international students. Applications are processed on a rolling basis. *Application fee:* $10 ($20 for international students). *Application Contact:* Mickey Diez, Director of Admissions and Registrar, 318-797-5000, E-mail: mdiez@lsus.edu. *Chair, Computer Science Department,* Dr. John Sigle, 318-797-5093, Fax: 318-795-2419, E-mail: jsigle@lsus.edu.

LOUISIANA TECH UNIVERSITY, Ruston, LA 71272

General Information State-supported, coed, university. *Graduate housing:* Rooms and/or apartments guaranteed to single students and available on a first-come, first-served basis to married students. Housing application deadline: 7/15.

GRADUATE UNITS

Graduate School *Degree program information:* Part-time programs available.

College of Administration and Business *Degree program information:* Part-time programs available. Offers administration and business (MBA, MPA, DBA); business administration (MBA, DBA); business economics (MBA, DBA); finance (MBA, DBA); management (MBA, DBA); marketing (MBA, DBA); professional accountancy (MBA, MPA, DBA).

College of Applied and Natural Sciences *Degree program information:* Part-time programs available. Offers applied and natural sciences (MS); biological sciences (MS); dietetics (MS); human ecology (MS).

College of Education *Degree program information:* Part-time programs available. Offers counseling (MA); counseling psychology (PhD); curriculum and instruction (MS, Ed D); education (M Ed, MA, MS, Ed D, PhD); educational leadership (Ed D); health and exercise science (MS); industrial/organizational psychology (MA); secondary education (M Ed); special education (MA).

College of Engineering and Science *Degree program information:* Part-time programs available. Offers applied computational analysis and modeling (PhD); biomedical engineering (MS, PhD); chemical engineering (MS, PhD); chemistry (MS); civil engineering (MS, PhD); computer science (MS); electrical engineering (MS, PhD); engineering (PhD); engineering and science (MS, PhD); industrial engineering (MS, PhD); manufacturing systems engineering (MS); mathematics and statistics (MS); mechanical engineering (MS, PhD); operations research (MS); physics (MS).

College of Liberal Arts *Degree program information:* Part-time programs available. Offers art and graphic design (MFA); English (MA); history (MA); interior design (MFA); liberal arts (MA, MFA); photography (MFA); speech (MA); speech pathology and audiology (MA); studio art (MFA).

LOUISVILLE PRESBYTERIAN THEOLOGICAL SEMINARY, Louisville, KY 40205-1798

General Information Independent-religious, coed, graduate-only institution. *Enrollment by degree level:* 99 first professional, 64 master's, 54 doctoral. *Graduate faculty:* 19 full-time (9 women), 30 part-time/adjunct (11 women). *Tuition:* Full-time $9,300; part-time $310 per credit. *Required fees:* $227. Tuition and fees vary according to course load and degree level. *Graduate housing:* Rooms and/or apartments available on a first-come, first-served basis to single and married students. Typical cost: $3,780 per year ($4,880 including board) for single students; $4,203 per year ($6,203 including board) for married students. Housing application deadline: 4/15. *Student services:* Campus employment opportunities, career counseling, disabled student services, free psychological counseling, international student services, low-cost health insurance, writing training. *Library facilities:* Ernest White Library. *Online resources:* library catalog, web page, access to other libraries' catalogs. *Collection:* 163,716 titles, 660 serial subscriptions, 7,000 audiovisual materials. *Research affiliation:* Louisville Institute (American religion).

Computer facilities: 13 computers available on campus for general student use. A campuswide network can be accessed from student residence rooms. Internet access is available. *Web address:* http://www.lpts.edu/.

General Application Contact: Kerry Rice, Director of Admissions, 502-895-3411 Ext. 371, Fax: 502-895-1096, E-mail: krice@lpts.edu.

GRADUATE UNITS

Graduate and Professional Programs Students: 125 full-time (72 women), 92 part-time (49 women); includes 30 minority (21 African Americans, 2 American Indian/Alaska Native, 2 Asian Americans or Pacific Islanders, 5 Hispanic Americans), 8 international. Average age 41. 131 applicants, 79% accepted, 68 enrolled. *Faculty:* 19 full-time (9 women), 30 part-time/adjunct (11 women). Expenses: Contact institution. *Financial support:* Career-related internships or fieldwork, Federal Work-Study, institutionally sponsored loans, and scholarships/grants available. Financial award application deadline: 4/15; financial award applicants required to submit CSS PROFILE or FAFSA. In 2006, 27 M Divs, 16 master's, 3 doctorates awarded. *Degree program information:* Part-time programs available. Offers Bible (MAR); divinity (M Div); ministry (D Min); religious thought (MAR); theology (Th M). *Application deadline:* For fall admission, 6/1 priority date for domestic and international students; for spring admission, 11/15 priority date for domestic and international students. Applications are processed on a rolling basis. *Application fee:* $60. Electronic applications accepted. *Application Contact:* Kerry Rice, Director of Admissions, 502-895-3411 Ext. 371, Fax: 502-895-1096, E-mail: krice@lpts.edu. *Dean,* Dr. David Hester, 502-895-3411 Ext. 294, Fax: 502-895-1096, E-mail: dhester@lpts.edu.

LOURDES COLLEGE, Sylvania, OH 43560-2898

General Information Independent-religious, coed, comprehensive institution. *Graduate housing:* On-campus housing not available.

GRADUATE UNITS

School of Graduate and Professional Studies *Degree program information:* Evening/weekend programs available. Offers endorsement in computer technology (M Ed); organizational leadership (MOL).

LOYOLA COLLEGE IN MARYLAND, Baltimore, MD 21210-2699

General Information Independent-religious, coed, comprehensive institution. *Enrollment:* 6,035 graduate, professional, and undergraduate students; 704 full-time matriculated graduate/professional students (474 women), 1,732 part-time matriculated graduate/professional students (1,039 women). *Enrollment by degree level:* 2,295 master's, 83 doctoral, 58 other advanced degrees. *Graduate faculty:* 94 full-time (45 women), 105 part-time/adjunct (42 women). *Graduate housing:* On-campus housing not available. *Student services:* Campus employment opportunities, campus safety program, career counseling, disabled student services, exercise/wellness program, international student services, low-cost health insurance, multicultural affairs office. *Library facilities:* Loyola/Notre Dame Library. *Online resources:* library catalog, web page, access to other libraries' catalogs. *Collection:* 293,639 titles, 2,126 serial subscriptions.

Computer facilities: 292 computers available on campus for general student use. A campuswide network can be accessed from student residence rooms and from off campus. Internet access is available. *Web address:* http://www.loyola.edu/.

General Application Contact: Scott Greatorex, Director, Graduate Admissions, 410-617-5020, Fax: 410-617-2002, E-mail: graduate@loyola.edu.

GRADUATE UNITS

Graduate Programs Students: 704 full-time (474 women), 1,732 part-time (1,039 women); includes 379 minority (261 African Americans, 2 American Indian/Alaska Native, 69 Asian Americans or Pacific Islanders, 47 Hispanic Americans), 76 international. Average age 33. *Faculty:* 94 full-time (45 women), 105 part-time/adjunct (42 women). Expenses: Contact institution. *Financial support:* Research assistantships, career-related internships or fieldwork, scholarships/grants, and college/university gift aid from institutional funds available. Financial award applicants required to submit FAFSA. In 2006, 814 master's, 22 doctorates, 12 other advanced degrees awarded. *Degree program information:* Part-time and evening/weekend programs available. *Application deadline:* For fall admission, 8/20 priority date for domestic students. Applications are processed on a rolling basis. *Application fee:* $50. *Application Contact:* Scott Greatorex, Director, Graduate Admissions, 410-617-5020, Fax: 410-617-2002, E-mail: graduate@loyola.edu. *President,* Rev. Brian Linnane, 410-617-2201.

College of Arts and Sciences Students: 497 full-time (404 women), 933 part-time (708 women); includes 253 minority (196 African Americans, 1 American Indian/Alaska Native, 27 Asian Americans or Pacific Islanders, 29 Hispanic Americans), 52 international. Average age 33. *Faculty:* 64 full-time (38 women), 88 part-time/adjunct (40 women). Expenses: Contact institution. *Financial support:* Research assistantships, career-related internships or fieldwork available. Financial award applicants required to submit FAFSA. In 2006, 518 master's, 22 doctorates, 12 other advanced degrees awarded. *Degree program information:* Part-time and evening/weekend programs available. Offers administration and supervision (M Ed, MA, CAS); arts and sciences (M Ed, MA, MES, MMS, MS, PhD, Psy D, CAS); clinical psychology (MS, Psy D, CAS); computer science (MS); counseling psychology (MS, CAS); curriculum and instruction (M Ed, MA, CAS); educational technology (M Ed); employee assistance and substance abuse (CAS); engineering science (MES, MS); guidance and counseling (M Ed, MA, CAS); liberal studies (MMS); Montessori education (M Ed, CAS); pastoral counseling (MS, PhD, CAS); reading (M Ed, CAS); software engineering (MS); special education (M Ed, CAS); speech-language pathology and audiology (MS, CAS); spiritual and pastoral care (MA). *Application deadline:* Applications are processed on a rolling basis. *Application fee:* $50. *Application Contact:* Scott Greatorex, Director, Graduate Admissions, 410-617-5020, Fax: 410-617-2002, E-mail: graduate@loyola.edu. *Dean,* Dr. James Buckley, 410-617-2563, E-mail: jbuckley@loyola.edu.

Sellinger School of Business and Management Students: 207 full-time (70 women), 799 part-time (331 women); includes 126 minority (65 African Americans, 1 American Indian/Alaska Native, 42 Asian Americans or Pacific Islanders, 18 Hispanic Americans), 24 international. Average age 32. *Faculty:* 30 full-time (7 women), 17 part-time/adjunct (2 women). Expenses: Contact institution. *Financial support:* Research assistantships, career-related internships or fieldwork available. Financial award applicants required to submit FAFSA. In 2006, 296 degrees awarded. *Degree program information:* Part-time and evening/weekend programs available. Offers business and management (MBA, MSF, XMBA); decision sciences (MBA); economics (MBA); executive business administration (MBA, XMBA); finance (MBA); marketing/management (MBA). *Application deadline:* For fall admission, 8/15 priority date for domestic students; for spring admission, 11/20 priority date for domestic students. Applications are processed on a rolling basis. *Application fee:* $50. *Application Contact:* Scott Greatorex, Director, Graduate Admissions, 410-617-5743 Ext. 2407, Fax: 410-617-2002, E-mail: mba@loyola.edu. *Associate Dean,* John Moran, 410-617-2457, E-mail: jmoran@loyola.edu.

LOYOLA MARYMOUNT UNIVERSITY, Los Angeles, CA 90045-2659

General Information Independent-religious, coed, comprehensive institution. CGS member. *Enrollment:* 8,903 graduate, professional, and undergraduate students; 2,385 full-time matriculated graduate/professional students (1,353 women), 841 part-time matriculated graduate/professional students (479 women). *Enrollment by degree level:* 1,327 first professional, 1,860 master's, 39 doctoral. *Graduate faculty:* 461 full-time (169 women), 436 part-time/adjunct (251 women). *Graduate housing:* Room and/or apartments available on a first-come, first-served basis to single students; on-campus housing not available to married students. Typical cost: $9,000 per year. *Student services:* Campus employment opportunities, career counseling, child daycare facilities, disabled student services, exercise/wellness program, free psychological counseling, international student services, low-cost health insurance, multicultural affairs office, teacher training. *Library facilities:* Charles von der Ahe Library plus 1 other. *Online resources:* library catalog, web page, access to other libraries' catalogs. *Collection:* 495,920 titles, 10,057 serial subscriptions.

Computer facilities: Computer purchase and lease plans are available. 300 computers available on campus for general student use. A campuswide network can be accessed from student residence rooms and from off campus. Internet access is available. *Web address:* http://www.lmu.edu/.

General Application Contact: Chake H. Kouyoumjian, Director, Graduate Admissions, 310-338-2721, Fax: 310-338-6086, E-mail: ckouyoum@lmu.edu.

GRADUATE UNITS

Graduate Division Students: 2,385 full-time (1,353 women), 841 part-time (479 women); includes 1,377 minority (208 African Americans, 16 American Indian/Alaska Native, 545 Asian Americans or Pacific Islanders, 608 Hispanic Americans), 80 international. Average age 25. 1,484 applicants, 78% accepted, 756 enrolled. *Faculty:* 388 full-time (142 women), 444 part-time/adjunct (239 women). Expenses: Contact institution. *Financial support:* In 2006–07, 1,162 students received support, including research assistantships (averaging $12,370 per year); fellowships, career-related internships or fieldwork, Federal Work-Study, scholarships/grants, unspecified assistantships, and staff assistantships, teaching associateships also available. Support available to part-time students. Financial award application deadline: 6/1; financial award applicants required to submit FAFSA. In 2006, 647 degrees awarded. *Degree program information:* Part-time and evening/weekend programs available. Offers marital and family therapy (MA). *Application deadline:* Applications are processed on a rolling basis. *Application fee:* $50. Electronic applications accepted. *Application Contact:* Chake H. Kouyoumjian, Director, Graduate Admissions, 310-338-2721, Fax: 310-338-6086, E-mail: ckouyoum@lmu.edu. *Academic Vice President and Chair of Graduate Council,* Dr. Ernest Rose, 310-338-2733, Fax: 310-338-1841, E-mail: erose@lmu.edu.

College of Business Administration Students: 284 full-time (103 women), 48 part-time (24 women); includes 119 minority (24 African Americans, 1 American Indian/Alaska Native, 54 Asian Americans or Pacific Islanders, 40 Hispanic Americans), 29 international. Average age 25. 291 applicants, 69% accepted, 129 enrolled. *Faculty:* 54 full-time (10 women), 25 part-time/adjunct (2 women). Expenses: Contact institution. *Financial support:* In 2006–07, 122 students received support, including 9 research assistantships (averaging $12,370 per year); Federal Work-Study and scholarships/grants also available. Support available to part-time students. Financial award application deadline: 6/1; financial award applicants required to submit FAFSA. In 2006, 162 degrees awarded. *Degree program information:* Part-time and evening/weekend programs available. Offers business administration (MBA). *Application deadline:* Applications are processed on a rolling basis. *Application fee:* $50. Electronic applications accepted. *Application Contact:* Dr. Rachelle Katz, Associate Dean and Director of MBA Program, 310-338-2848, E-mail: rkatz@lmu.edu. *Dean,* Dr. John T. Wholihan, 310-338-7504, Fax: 310-338-2899.

College of Liberal Arts Students: 89 full-time (47 women), 106 part-time (62 women); includes 61 minority (12 African Americans, 15 Asian Americans or Pacific Islanders, 34 Hispanic Americans), 10 international. Average age 25. 161 applicants, 73% accepted, 70 enrolled. *Faculty:* 149 full-time (57 women), 86 part-time/adjunct (47 women). Expenses: Contact institution. *Financial support:* In 2006–07, 10 research assistantships (averaging $12,370 per year) were awarded; fellowships, Federal Work-Study, scholarships/grants, and unspecified assistantships also available. Support available to part-time students. Financial award application deadline: 6/1; financial award applicants required to submit FAFSA. In 2006, 40 degrees awarded. *Degree program information:* Part-time and evening/weekend programs available. Offers bioethics (MA); creative writing (MA); liberal arts (MA); literature (MA); pastoral theology (MA); philosophy (MA); theology (MA). *Application fee:* $50. Electronic applications accepted. *Dean,* Dr. Michael Engh, 310-338-2716, Fax: 310-338-2704, E-mail: mengh@lmu.edu.

College of Science and Engineering Students: 70 full-time (20 women), 63 part-time (19 women); includes 75 minority (16 African Americans, 2 American Indian/Alaska Native, 29 Asian Americans or Pacific Islanders, 28 Hispanic Americans), 10 international. Average age 32. 101 applicants, 54% accepted, 48 enrolled. *Faculty:* 78 full-time (19 women), 35 part-time/adjunct (11 women). Expenses: Contact institution. *Financial support:* In 2006–07, 21 students received support, including 3 research assistantships (averaging $12,370 per year); Federal Work-Study, scholarships/grants, unspecified assistantships, and instructorships also available. Support available to part-time students. Financial award application deadline: 6/1; financial award applicants required to submit FAFSA. In 2006, 33 degrees awarded. *Degree program information:* Part-time and evening/weekend programs available. Offers civil engineering (MS, MSE); computer science (MS); electrical engineering (MSE); engineering and production management (MS); environmental science (MS); mathematics (MAT); mechanical engineering (MSE); science and engineering (MAT, MS, MSE, Certificate); systems engineering (MS, Certificate). *Application fee:* $50. Electronic applications accepted. *Application Contact:* Dr. Richard S. Plumb, Dean, 310-338-2834, Fax: 310-338-7399, E-mail: rplumb@lmu.edu. *Dean,* Dr. Richard S. Plumb, 310-338-2834, Fax: 310-338-7399, E-mail: rplumb@lmu.edu.

School of Education Students: 840 full-time (646 women), 269 part-time (201 women); includes 554 minority (94 African Americans, 6 American Indian/Alaska Native, 116 Asian Americans or Pacific Islanders, 338 Hispanic Americans), 16 international. Average age 29. 668 applicants, 69% accepted, 418 enrolled. *Faculty:* 30 full-time (20 women), 138 part-time/adjunct (104 women). Expenses: Contact institution. *Financial support:* In 2006–07, 753 students received support, including 18 research assistantships (averaging $12,370 per year); Federal Work-Study and scholarships/grants also available. Support available to part-time students. Financial award application deadline: 6/1; financial award applicants required to submit FAFSA. In 2006, 340 degrees awarded. *Degree program information:* Part-time and evening/weekend programs available. Offers bilingual and bicultural education (MA); Catholic inclusive education (MA); Catholic school administration (MA); child/adolescent literacy (MA); counseling (MA); education (M Ed, MA, Ed D); educational leadership in social justice (Ed D); elementary education (MA); general education (M Ed); literacy/language arts (M Ed); school administration (M Ed); school psychology (MA); secondary education (MA); special education (MA); special education specialist in mild and moderate disabilities (MA). *Application deadline:* For fall admission, 7/15 for domestic students; for spring admission, 11/15 for domestic students. *Application fee:* $50. Electronic applications accepted. *Dean,* Dr. Shane Martin, 310-338-2863, Fax: 310-338-1976, E-mail: smartin@lmu.edu.

School of Film and Television Students: 70 full-time (24 women), 18 part-time (8 women); includes 29 minority (13 African Americans, 8 Asian Americans or Pacific Islanders, 8 Hispanic Americans), 9 international. Average age 27. 126 applicants, 22% accepted, 14 enrolled. *Faculty:* 27 full-time (8 women), 39 part-time/adjunct (12 women). Expenses: Contact institution. *Financial support:* In 2006–07, 72 students received support, including 13 research assistantships (averaging $12,370 per year); teaching assistantships, career-related internships or fieldwork and scholarships/grants also available. Support available to part-time students. Financial award application deadline: 6/1; financial award applicants required to submit FAFSA. In 2006, 43 degrees awarded. Offers film and television (MFA); film production (MFA); screen writing (MFA); television production (MFA). *Application deadline:* For fall admission, 3/15 for domestic students. *Application fee:* $50. Electronic applications accepted. *Application Contact:* Dr. Eric Xavier, Graduate Director, 310-338-2779, Fax: 310-338-3030, E-mail: exavier@lmu.edu. *Dean,* Teri Schwartz, 310-338-3089, Fax: 310-338-3089, E-mail: tschwartz@lmu.edu.

Loyola Law School Students: 1,022 full-time, 343 part-time; includes 233 minority (55 African Americans, 8 American Indian/Alaska Native, 42 Asian Americans or Pacific Islanders, 128 Hispanic Americans), 20 international. Average age 23. 4,537 applicants, 30% accepted, 423 enrolled. *Faculty:* 65 full-time (26 women), 61 part-time/adjunct (27 women). Expenses: Contact institution. *Financial support:* In 2006–07, 246 students received support; research assistantships, Federal Work-Study and scholarships/grants available. Financial award application deadline: 3/15; financial award applicants required to submit FAFSA. In 2006, 419 JDs, 15 master's awarded. *Degree program information:* Part-time and evening/weekend programs available. Offers American law and international practice (LL M); law (JD); taxation (LL M). *Application deadline:* For fall admission, 2/1 priority date for domestic and international students. Applications are processed on a rolling basis. *Application fee:* $65. Electronic applications accepted. *Application Contact:* Janell Lundy Roberts, Assistant Dean, Admissions, 213-736-1074, Fax: 213-736-6523, E-mail: admissions@lls.edu. *Dean,* David W. Burcham, 213-736-1028, Fax: 213-487-6736, E-mail: david.burcham@lls.edu.

See Close-Up on page 949.

LOYOLA UNIVERSITY CHICAGO, Chicago, IL 60611-2196

General Information Independent-religious, coed, university. CGS member. *Enrollment:* 15,194 graduate, professional, and undergraduate students; 2,886 full-time matriculated graduate/professional students (1,684 women), 1,981 part-time matriculated graduate/professional students (1,181 women). *Graduate faculty:* 1,274 full-time (501 women), 913 part-time/adjunct (300 women). *Graduate housing:* Room and/or apartments available on a first-come, first-served basis to single students; on-campus housing not available to married students. *Student services:* Campus employment opportunities, campus safety program, career counseling, disabled student services, free psychological counseling, international student services, low-cost health insurance, teacher training. *Library facilities:* Cudahy Library plus 2 others. *Online resources:* library catalog, web page. *Collection:* 1.4 million titles, 136,663 serial subscriptions, 16,486 audiovisual materials. *Research affiliation:* Erikson Institute for Early Education.

Computer facilities: 318 computers available on campus for general student use. A campuswide network can be accessed from student residence rooms and from off campus. Internet access is available. *Web address:* http://www.luc.edu/.

General Application Contact: Janice K. Atkinson, Director, Graduate and Professional Enrollment Management, 312-915-8902, Fax: 312-915-8905, E-mail: gradapp@luc.edu.

GRADUATE UNITS

Graduate School Students: 1,075 full-time (639 women), 383 part-time (231 women); includes 220 minority (88 African Americans, 2 American Indian/Alaska Native, 70 Asian Americans or Pacific Islanders, 60 Hispanic Americans), 156 international. 3,656 applicants, 61% accepted, 1180 enrolled. *Faculty:* 481 full-time (222 women). Expenses: Contact institution. *Financial support:* In 2006–07, 270 students received support, including 30 fellowships with full tuition reimbursements available (averaging $16,000 per year), 85 research assistantships with full tuition reimbursements available (averaging $18,000 per year), 85 teaching assistantships with full tuition reimbursements available (averaging $14,000 per year); career-related internships or fieldwork, Federal Work-Study, institutionally sponsored loans, scholarships/grants, and unspecified assistantships also available. Support available to part-time students. Financial award application deadline: 2/1; financial award applicants required to submit FAFSA. In 2006, 218 master's, 81 doctorates awarded. *Degree program information:* Part-time and evening/weekend programs available. Postbaccalaureate distance learning degree programs offered (no on-campus study). Offers American politics and policy (MA, PhD); applied human perception and performance (MS); applied social psychology (MA, PhD); applied sociology (MA); biochemistry (MS, PhD); biology (MA, MS); cell and molecular physiology (MS, PhD); cell biology, neurobiology and anatomy (MS, PhD); chemistry (MS, PhD); clinical psychology (PhD); criminal justice (MA); developmental psychology (PhD); English (MA, PhD); history (MA, PhD); immunology (MS, PhD); information technology (MS); international studies (MA, PhD); mathematics (MS); microbiology (MS, PhD); molecular biology (PhD); neuroscience (MS, PhD); pharmacology and experimental therapeutics (MS, PhD); philosophy (MA, PhD); political theory and philosophy (MA, PhD); public library (MA); scientific technical computing (MS); sociology (MA, PhD); software technology (MS); Spanish (MA); theology (MA, PhD); virology (MS, PhD). *Application deadline:* Applications are processed on a rolling basis. *Application fee:* $40. Electronic applications accepted. *Application Contact:* Ron Martin, Assistant Director of Enrollment Management, 312-915-8950, Fax: 312-915-8905, E-mail: gradapp@luc.edu. *Dean,* Dr. Samuel Attoh, 773-508-3459, Fax: 773-508-2460, E-mail: sattoh@luc.edu.

Marcella Niehoff School of Nursing Students: 60 full-time (54 women), 227 part-time (213 women); includes 48 minority (13 African Americans, 23 Asian Americans or Pacific Islanders, 12 Hispanic Americans), 1 international. Average age 32. 31 applicants, 45% accepted. *Faculty:* 26 full-time (25 women), 58 part-time/adjunct (50 women). Expenses: Contact institution. *Financial support:* In 2006–07, 10 students received support, including 1 fellowship with tuition reimbursement available, 4 research assistantships with tuition reimbursements available, 1 teaching assistantship with tuition reimbursement available; career-related internships or fieldwork, Federal Work-Study, institutionally sponsored loans, traineeships, and unspecified assistantships also available. Support available to part-time students. Financial award applicants required to submit FAFSA. In 2006, 33 master's, 8 doctorates awarded. *Degree program information:* Part-time and evening/weekend programs available. Offers acute care clinical nurse specialist (MSN); acute care nurse practitioner (MSN); adult clinical nurse specialist (MSN); adult nurse practitioner (MSN); cardiovascular health and disease management clinical nurse specialist (MSN); emergency nurse practitioner (MSN); family nurse practitioner (MSN); health systems management (MSN); nursing (PhD); oncology clinical nurse specialist (MSN); population-based infection control and environmental safety (MSN); women's health nurse practitioner (MSN). *Application deadline:* For fall admission, 8/1 priority date for domestic and international students; for spring admission, 12/1 priority date for domestic and international students. Applications are processed on a rolling basis. *Application fee:* $40. Electronic applications accepted. *Application Contact:* Dr. Vicki A. Keough, Associate Professor, 708-216-3582, Fax: 708-216-9555, E-mail: vkeough@luc.edu. *Dean,* Dr. Ida Androwich, 773-508-3255, E-mail: iandrow@luc.edu.

Graduate School of Business Students: 180 full-time (94 women), 546 part-time (262 women); includes 153 minority (44 African Americans, 73 Asian Americans or Pacific Islanders, 36 Hispanic Americans). Average age 27. 717 applicants, 72% accepted, 314 enrolled. *Faculty:* 64 full-time (14 women). Expenses: Contact institution. *Financial support:* In 2006–07, 25 students received support, including 14 research assistantships with partial tuition reimbursements available (averaging $5,000 per year); career-related internships or fieldwork, Federal Work-Study, and institutionally sponsored loans also available. Support available to part-time students. Financial award application deadline: 3/10; financial award applicants required to submit FAFSA. In 2006, 329 degrees awarded. *Degree program information:* Part-time and evening/weekend programs available. Offers accountancy (MS, MSA); business administration (MBA); healthcare management (MBA); human resources and employee relations (MS, MSHR); information systems and operations management (MS); information systems management (MS); integrated marketing communications (MS); marketing (MS, MSIMC); strategic financial services (MBA). *Application deadline:* For fall admission, 7/1 for domestic and international students; for winter admission, 9/1 for domestic and international students; for spring admission, 1/3 for domestic and international students. Applications are processed on a rolling basis. *Application fee:* $50. Electronic applications accepted. *Application Contact:* Olivia Heath, Enrollment Advisor, 312-915-8908, Fax: 312-915-7207, E-mail: oheath@luc.edu. *Associate Dean,* Dr. Mary Ann McGrath, 312-915-7107, Fax: 312-915-6136, E-mail: mmcgrat@luc.edu.

Institute of Human Resources and Employee Relations Students: 12 full-time (7 women), 65 part-time (53 women); includes 24 minority (8 African Americans, 11 Asian Americans or Pacific Islanders, 5 Hispanic Americans). *Faculty:* 6 full-time (3 women), 1 part-time/

adjunct (0 women). Expenses: Contact institution. *Financial support:* In 2006–07, 3 research assistantships were awarded; career-related internships or fieldwork and Federal Work-Study also available. Support available to part-time students. Financial award applicants required to submit FAFSA. In 2006, 34 degrees awarded. *Degree program information:* Part-time programs available. Offers human resources (MS); human resources and employee relations (MS, MSHR). *Application deadline:* For fall admission, 7/1 for domestic and international students; for winter admission, 9/1 for domestic and international students; for spring admission, 1/3 for domestic and international students. Applications are processed on a rolling basis. *Application fee:* $50. *Application Contact:* Olivia Heath, Enrollment Advisor, 312-915-8908, Fax: 312-915-7207, E-mail: oheath@luc.edu. *Chair,* Dr. Arup Varma, 312-915-6595, Fax: 312-915-6231, E-mail: avarma@luc.edu.

Institute of Pastoral Studies Students: 106 full-time (57 women), 118 part-time (82 women); includes 20 minority (13 African Americans, 1 Asian American or Pacific Islander, 6 Hispanic Americans), 15 international. Average age 42. 93 applicants, 91% accepted, 72 enrolled. *Faculty:* 6 full-time (1 woman), 33 part-time/adjunct (16 women). Expenses: Contact institution. *Financial support:* In 2006–07, 84 students received support. Career-related internships or fieldwork, Federal Work-Study, institutionally sponsored loans, scholarships/grants, and tuition waivers (partial) available. Support available to part-time students. Financial award application deadline: 3/1; financial award applicants required to submit FAFSA. In 2006, 29 degrees awarded. *Degree program information:* Part-time and evening/weekend programs available. Offers divinity (M Div); pastoral counseling (MA, Certificate); pastoral studies (MA); religious education (Certificate); social justice (MA); spiritual direction (Certificate); spirituality (MA). *Application deadline:* Applications are processed on a rolling basis. *Application fee:* $50. Electronic applications accepted. *Application Contact:* Randy Gibbons, Administrative Assistant, 312-915-7450, Fax: 312-915-7410, E-mail: rgibbon@luc.edu. *Director,* Dr. Robert A. Ludwig, 312-915-7467, Fax: 312-915-7410, E-mail: rludwig@luc.edu.

School of Education Students: 366 full-time (300 women), 681 part-time (482 women). Average age 36. 717 applicants, 57% accepted, 217 enrolled. *Faculty:* 41 full-time (29 women), 68 part-time/adjunct (44 women). Expenses: Contact institution. *Financial support:* In 2006–07, fellowships with full tuition reimbursements (averaging $11,000 per year), 15 research assistantships with full tuition reimbursements (averaging $8,500 per year), teaching assistantships with full tuition reimbursements (averaging $11,000 per year) were awarded; career-related internships or fieldwork, Federal Work-Study, institutionally sponsored loans, scholarships/grants, tuition waivers (partial), and unspecified assistantships also available. Support available to part-time students. Financial award application deadline: 2/15; financial award applicants required to submit FAFSA. In 2006, 258 master's, 95 doctorates, 21 other advanced degrees awarded. *Degree program information:* Part-time and evening/weekend programs available. Offers administration and supervision (M Ed, Ed D, Certificate); community counseling (M Ed, MA); counseling psychology (PhD); cultural and educational policy studies (M Ed, MA, Ed D, PhD); curriculum and instruction (M Ed, Ed D); education (M Ed, MA, Ed D, PhD, Certificate, Ed S); educational psychology (M Ed); elementary education (M Ed); higher education (M Ed, PhD); instructional leadership (M Ed); reading specialist (M Ed); research methods (M Ed, MA, PhD); school counseling (M Ed, Certificate); school psychology (M Ed, PhD, Ed S); school technology (M Ed); science education (M Ed); secondary education (M Ed); special education (M Ed). *Application deadline:* For fall admission, 7/1 for domestic and international students; for spring admission, 11/1 for domestic and international students. Applications are processed on a rolling basis. *Application fee:* $50. Electronic applications accepted. *Application Contact:* Marie Rosin-Dittmar, Information Contact, 312-915-6800, E-mail: schleduc@luc.edu. *Dean,* Dr. David Prasse, 312-915-6992, Fax: 312-915-6630, E-mail: dprasse@luc.edu.

School of Law Students: 607 full-time (318 women), 252 part-time (123 women); includes 137 minority (39 African Americans, 2 American Indian/Alaska Native, 62 Asian Americans or Pacific Islanders, 34 Hispanic Americans), 12 international. Average age 26. 4,469 applicants, 22% accepted, 295 enrolled. *Faculty:* 41 full-time (15 women), 97 part-time/adjunct (53 women). Expenses: Contact institution. *Financial support:* In 2006–07, 494 students received support; fellowships, research assistantships, Federal Work-Study, institutionally sponsored loans, scholarships/grants, tuition waivers (partial), and unspecified assistantships available. Support available to part-time students. Financial award application deadline: 3/1; financial award applicants required to submit FAFSA. In 2006, 264 JDs, 37 master's awarded. *Degree program information:* Part-time programs available. Offers business law (LL M, MJ); child and family law (LL M, MJ); health law (LL M, MJ, D Law, SJD); law (JD). *Application deadline:* For fall admission, 4/1 for domestic and international students. Applications are processed on a rolling basis. *Application fee:* $50. Electronic applications accepted. *Application Contact:* Pamela A. Bloomquist, Assistant Dean, Law Admission and Financial Assistance, 312-915-7170, Fax: 312-915-7906, E-mail: law-admissions@luc.edu. *Dean,* David N. Yellen, 312-815-7120.

School of Social Work *Degree program information:* Part-time programs available. Offers social work (MSW, PhD). Electronic applications accepted.

Stritch School of Medicine Students: 552 full-time (276 women); includes 114 minority (16 African Americans, 5 American Indian/Alaska Native, 80 Asian Americans or Pacific Islanders, 13 Hispanic Americans). Average age 24. 4,707 applicants, 6% accepted, 140 enrolled. *Faculty:* 641 full-time (220 women), 715 part-time/adjunct (187 women). Expenses: Contact institution. *Financial support:* In 2006–07, 513 students received support. Institutionally sponsored loans and scholarships/grants available. Financial award application deadline: 3/30; financial award applicants required to submit FAFSA. In 2006, 130 MDs awarded. Offers medicine (MD). *Application deadline:* For fall admission, 11/15 for domestic students. Applications are processed on a rolling basis. *Application fee:* $70. *Application Contact:* LaDonna E. Norstrom, Assistant Dean for Admissions, 708-216-3229. *Dean,* Dr. John M. Lee, 708-216-3223, Fax: 708-216-4305.

See Close-Up on page 951.

LOYOLA UNIVERSITY NEW ORLEANS, New Orleans, LA 70118-6195

General Information Independent-religious, coed, comprehensive institution. *Graduate housing:* Room and/or apartments available on a first-come, first-served basis to single students; on-campus housing not available to married students. Housing application deadline: 8/1. *Research affiliation:* New Orleans Museum of Art (communications, history, visual arts).

GRADUATE UNITS

City College Offers criminal justice (MCJ); family nurse practitioner (MSN); health care systems management (MSN).

Loyola Institute for Ministry *Degree program information:* Part-time and evening/weekend programs available. Postbaccalaureate distance learning degree programs offered (no on-campus study). Offers pastoral studies (MPS); religious education (MRE); theology and ministry (Certificate).

College of Arts and Sciences *Degree program information:* Part-time and evening/weekend programs available. Offers arts and sciences (MA, MS); counseling (MS); elementary education (MS); mass communication (MA); reading education (MS); religious studies (MA); secondary education (MS). Electronic applications accepted.

College of Music *Degree program information:* Part-time programs available. Offers music (MM, MME, MMT). Electronic applications accepted.

Joseph A. Butt, S.J., College of Business Administration *Degree program information:* Part-time and evening/weekend programs available. Postbaccalaureate distance learning degree programs offered. Offers business administration (MBA). Electronic applications accepted.

School of Law *Degree program information:* Part-time and evening/weekend programs available. Offers law (JD). Electronic applications accepted.

LUBBOCK CHRISTIAN UNIVERSITY, Lubbock, TX 79407-2099

General Information Independent-religious, coed, comprehensive institution. *Graduate housing:* Rooms and/or apartments available to single and married students. Housing application deadline: 8/15.

GRADUATE UNITS

Graduate Biblical Studies *Degree program information:* Part-time programs available. Offers Bible and ministry (MS); biblical interpretation (MA).

LUTHERAN SCHOOL OF THEOLOGY AT CHICAGO, Chicago, IL 60615-5199

General Information Independent-religious, coed, graduate-only institution. *Graduate faculty:* 22 full-time, 15 part-time/adjunct. *Tuition:* Full-time $10,350; part-time $1,150 per course. *Graduate housing:* Rooms and/or apartments available to single and married students. *Student services:* Career counseling, international student services, low-cost health insurance. *Library facilities:* Jesuit-Krauss-McCormick Library. *Collection:* 334,388 titles. *Research affiliation:* Zygon Center for Religion and Science, Chicago Center for Public Ministry. *Web address:* http://www.lstc.edu/.

General Application Contact: Dorothy C. Dominiak, Director of Admissions and Financial Aid, 773-256-0726, Fax: 773-256-0782, E-mail: ddominia@lstc.edu.

GRADUATE UNITS

Graduate and Professional Programs Students: 199 full-time, 184 part-time. *Faculty:* 22 full-time, 15 part-time/adjunct. Expenses: Contact institution. *Financial support:* Career-related internships or fieldwork and scholarships/grants available. Support available to part-time students. *Degree program information:* Part-time programs available. Offers ministry (D Min); ministry, pastoral care, and counseling (D Min PCC); theological studies (MA, PhD); theology (M Div, Th M). *Application deadline:* Applications are processed on a rolling basis. *Application fee:* $25. *Application Contact:* Dorothy C. Dominiak, Assistant Director of Admissions and Financial Aid, 773-256-0726, Fax: 773-256-0782, E-mail: ddominia@lstc.edu. *Dean,* Dr. Kathleen Billman, 773-256-0721, Fax: 773-256-0782, E-mail: kbillman@lstc.edu.

LUTHERAN THEOLOGICAL SEMINARY, Saskatoon, SK S7N 0X3, Canada

General Information Independent-religious, coed, graduate-only institution. *Graduate housing:* Room and/or apartments available to single students; on-campus housing not available to married students. Housing application deadline: 4/30.

GRADUATE UNITS

Graduate and Professional Programs *Degree program information:* Part-time programs available. Offers history (MTS, STM); New Testament (MTS, STM); Old Testament (MTS, STM); pastoral counseling (MTS, STM); systematics (MTS, STM).

LUTHERAN THEOLOGICAL SEMINARY AT GETTYSBURG, Gettysburg, PA 17325-1795

General Information Independent-religious, coed, graduate-only institution. *Graduate housing:* Rooms and/or apartments available on a first-come, first-served basis to single and married students. Housing application deadline: 4/1.

GRADUATE UNITS

Graduate and Professional Programs *Degree program information:* Part-time programs available. Postbaccalaureate distance learning degree programs offered (no on-campus study). Offers divinity (M Div); ministerial studies (MAMS); outdoor ministry (MAR); parish ministry (D Min); theology (STM). Electronic applications accepted.

THE LUTHERAN THEOLOGICAL SEMINARY AT PHILADELPHIA, Philadelphia, PA 19119-1794

General Information Independent-religious, coed, graduate-only institution. *Graduate housing:* Rooms and/or apartments available on a first-come, first-served basis to single and married students. Housing application deadline: 4/15.

GRADUATE UNITS

Graduate School *Degree program information:* Part-time and evening/weekend programs available. Offers divinity (M Div); ministry (D Min); religion (MAR); social ministry (Certificate); theology (STM, Th D). Electronic applications accepted.

LUTHERAN THEOLOGICAL SOUTHERN SEMINARY, Columbia, SC 29203

General Information Independent-religious, coed, graduate-only institution. *Graduate housing:* Rooms and/or apartments available on a first-come, first-served basis to single and married students. Housing application deadline: 5/1.

GRADUATE UNITS

Graduate and Professional Programs *Degree program information:* Part-time programs available. Offers theology (M Div, MAR, STM, D Min).

LUTHER RICE UNIVERSITY, Lithonia, GA 30038-2454

General Information Independent-religious, coed, comprehensive institution. *Graduate housing:* On-campus housing not available.

GRADUATE UNITS

Graduate Programs *Degree program information:* Part-time programs available. Postbaccalaureate distance learning degree programs offered (no on-campus study). Offers Bible/theology (M Div); Christian education (M Div); Christian studies (MA); church ministry (D Min); counseling (M Div); discipleship counseling (MA); ministry (M Div, MA); missions/evangelism (M Div).

LUTHER SEMINARY, St. Paul, MN 55108-1445

General Information Independent-religious, coed, graduate-only institution. *Enrollment by degree level:* 410 first professional, 160 master's, 180 doctoral. *Graduate faculty:* 39 full-time (6 women), 13 part-time/adjunct (4 women). *Graduate housing:* Rooms and/or apartments available on a first-come, first-served basis to single and married students. *Student services:* Campus employment opportunities, campus safety program, career counseling, child daycare facilities, free psychological counseling, international student services, low-cost health insurance. *Library facilities:* Luther Seminary Library. *Online resources:* library catalog. *Collection:* 229,738 titles, 778 serial subscriptions, 1,106 audiovisual materials.

Computer facilities: 22 computers available on campus for general student use. A campuswide network can be accessed from student residence rooms and from off campus. Internet access is available. *Web address:* http://www.luthersem.edu/.

General Application Contact: Ron Olson, Director of Admissions, 612-641-3521, Fax: 612-641-3497, E-mail: rdolson@luthersem.edu.

GRADUATE UNITS

Graduate and Professional Programs Students: 633 full-time, 186 part-time, 48 international. Average age 34. 277 applicants, 96% accepted. *Faculty:* 39 full-time (6 women), 13 part-time/adjunct (4 women). Expenses: Contact institution. *Financial support:* In 2006–07, 450 students received support. Career-related internships or fieldwork, Federal Work-Study, institutionally sponsored loans, and scholarships/grants available. Support available to part-time students. Financial award application deadline: 6/1; financial award applicants required to submit FAFSA. In 2006, 93 M Divs, 49 master's, 8 doctorates awarded. *Degree program information:* Part-time programs available. Offers theology (M Div, M Th, MA, MSM, D Min, PhD). *Application deadline:* For fall admission, 7/1 priority date for domestic students. Applications are processed on a rolling basis. *Application fee:* $50. Electronic applications accepted. *Application Contact:* Ron Olson, Director of Admissions, 612-641-3521, Fax: 612-641-3497, E-mail: rdolson@luthersem.edu. *Dean of Academic Affairs,* Dr. David Lose, 651-641-3471, Fax: 651-641-1609, E-mail: dlose@luthersem.edu.

LYNCHBURG COLLEGE, Lynchburg, VA 24501-3199

General Information Independent-religious, coed, comprehensive institution. *Enrollment:* 2,398 graduate, professional, and undergraduate students; 92 full-time matriculated graduate/professional students (73 women), 192 part-time matriculated graduate/professional students (142 women). *Enrollment by degree level:* 284 master's. *Graduate faculty:* 30 full-time (17 women), 9 part-time/adjunct (1 woman). *Tuition:* Full-time $6,300; part-time $350 per credit. *Required fees:* $100. *Graduate housing:* Room and/or apartments available on a first-come, first-served basis to single students; on-campus housing not available to married students. Typical cost: $6,200 (including board). Housing application deadline: 8/1. *Student services:* Campus employment opportunities, career counseling, disabled student services, exercise/wellness program, free psychological counseling, grant writing training, international student services, multicultural affairs office, teacher training, writing training. *Library facilities:* Knight-Capron Library. *Online resources:* library catalog, web page. *Collection:* 225,000 titles, 518 serial subscriptions, 6,212 audiovisual materials.

Computer facilities: 217 computers available on campus for general student use. A campuswide network can be accessed from student residence rooms. Internet access is available. *Web address:* http://www.lynchburg.edu/.

General Application Contact: Dr. Edward Polloway, Vice President for Graduate and Community Advancement, 434-544-8655, E-mail: polloway@lynchburg.edu.

GRADUATE UNITS

Graduate Studies Students: 92 full-time (73 women), 192 part-time (142 women); includes 30 minority (20 African Americans, 2 American Indian/Alaska Native, 1 Asian American or Pacific Islander, 7 Hispanic Americans), 27 international. Average age 34. 112 applicants, 59% accepted, 51 enrolled. *Faculty:* 30 full-time (17 women), 9 part-time/adjunct (1 woman). Expenses: Contact institution. *Financial support:* Fellowships, teaching assistantships, career-related internships or fieldwork, Federal Work-Study, scholarships/grants, and unspecified assistantships available. In 2006, 92 degrees awarded. *Degree program information:* Part-time and evening/weekend programs available. *Application deadline:* For fall admission, 7/31 for domestic students, 6/1 for international students; for spring admission, 11/30 for domestic students, 10/1 for international students. *Application fee:* $30. Electronic applications accepted. *Vice President for Graduate and Community Advancement*, Dr. Edward Polloway, 434-544-8655, E-mail: polloway@lynchburg.edu.

School of Business and Economics Students: 14 full-time (6 women), 34 part-time (18 women); includes 5 minority (2 African Americans, 1 American Indian/Alaska Native, 2 Hispanic Americans). Average age 34. 22 applicants, 55% accepted, 11 enrolled. *Faculty:* 6 full-time (1 woman), 1 part-time/adjunct (0 women). Expenses: Contact institution. *Financial support:* Fellowships, teaching assistantships, Federal Work-Study, institutionally sponsored loans, and scholarships/grants available. Financial award applicants required to submit FAFSA. In 2006, 9 degrees awarded. *Degree program information:* Part-time and evening/weekend programs available. Offers business (MBA). *Application deadline:* For fall admission, 7/31 for domestic students, 6/1 for international students; for spring admission, 11/30 for domestic students, 10/1 for international students. *Application fee:* $30. *Application Contact:* Dr. Sally Selden, MBA Program Director, 434-544-8266. *Dean*, Dr. Dan Messerschmidt, 434-522-8417.

School of Education and Human Development Students: 78 full-time (67 women), 158 part-time (124 women); includes 25 minority (18 African Americans, 1 American Indian/Alaska Native, 1 Asian American or Pacific Islander, 5 Hispanic Americans), 27 international. Average age 34. 90 applicants, 60% accepted, 40 enrolled. *Faculty:* 24 full-time (16 women), 8 part-time/adjunct (1 woman). Expenses: Contact institution. *Financial support:* Career-related internships or fieldwork, scholarships/grants, and unspecified assistantships available. Financial award applicants required to submit FAFSA. In 2006, 83 degrees awarded. *Degree program information:* Part-time and evening/weekend programs available. Offers community counseling (M Ed); counselor education (M Ed); early childhood special education (M Ed); educational leadership (M Ed); English education (M Ed); mental retardation (M Ed); school counseling (M Ed); science education (M Ed); severely/profoundly handicapped education (M Ed); special education (M Ed); teaching and learning (M Ed); teaching children with learning disabilities (M Ed); teaching the emotionally disturbed (M Ed). *Application deadline:* For fall admission, 7/31 for domestic students, 6/1 for international students; for spring admission, 11/30 for domestic students, 10/1 for international students. *Application fee:* $30. *Dean*, Dr. Jan Stenette, 434-544-8662.

LYNDON STATE COLLEGE, Lyndonville, VT 05851-0919

General Information State-supported, coed, comprehensive institution. *Graduate housing:* On-campus housing not available.

GRADUATE UNITS

Graduate Programs in Education *Degree program information:* Part-time and evening/weekend programs available. Offers curriculum and instruction (M Ed); education (M Ed); natural sciences (MST); reading specialist (M Ed); science education (MST); special education (M Ed); teaching and counseling (M Ed).

LYNN UNIVERSITY, Boca Raton, FL 33431-5598

General Information Independent, coed, comprehensive institution. *Enrollment:* 2,715 graduate, professional, and undergraduate students; 143 full-time matriculated graduate/professional students (76 women), 272 part-time matriculated graduate/professional students (144 women). *Enrollment by degree level:* 292 master's, 123 doctoral. *Graduate faculty:* 36 full-time (16 women), 33 part-time/adjunct (10 women). *Tuition:* Full-time $26,200. *Required fees:* $1,500. Tuition and fees vary according to class time, course load and degree level. *Graduate housing:* Room and/or apartments available on a first-come, first-served basis to single students; on-campus housing not available to married students. Typical cost: $9,650 (including board). *Student services:* Campus employment opportunities, campus safety program, career counseling, exercise/wellness program, free psychological counseling, international student services, low-cost health insurance, multicultural affairs office. *Library facilities:* Eugene M. and Christine E. Lynn Library. *Online resources:* library catalog, access to other libraries' catalogs. *Collection:* 173,000 titles, 455 serial subscriptions, 13,500 audiovisual materials.

Computer facilities: 150 computers available on campus for general student use. A campuswide network can be accessed from student residence rooms and from off campus. Internet access and online class registration are available. *Web address:* http://www.lynn.edu/.

General Application Contact: Dr. Larissa Baia, Assistant Director of Graduate Admissions, 561-237-7916 Ext. 7845, Fax: 561-237-7100, E-mail: admissionspm@lynn.edu.

GRADUATE UNITS

College of Arts and Sciences Students: 20 full-time (10 women), 18 part-time (8 women); includes 7 minority (4 African Americans, 1 Asian American or Pacific Islander, 2 Hispanic Americans), 2 international. Average age 35. 19 applicants, 100% accepted, 16 enrolled. *Faculty:* 7 full-time (3 women), 3 part-time/adjunct (0 women). Expenses: Contact institution. *Financial support:* In 2006–07, 34 students received support. Career-related internships or fieldwork, Federal Work-Study, institutionally sponsored loans, scholarships/grants, tuition waivers (full and partial), and unspecified assistantships available. Support available to part-time students. Financial award application deadline: 8/1; financial award applicants required to submit FAFSA. In 2006, 25 degrees awarded. *Degree program information:* Part-time and evening/weekend programs available. Postbaccalaureate distance learning degree programs offered. Offers applied psychology (MS); criminal justice administration (MS); emergency planning and administration (MS, Certificate). *Application fee:* $50. *Application Contact:* Dr. Larissa Baia, Assistant Director of Graduate Admissions, 561-237-7916, Fax: 561-237-7100, E-mail: admissionpm@lynn.edu. *Dean*, Dr. Pamela J. Monaco, 561-237-7290, Fax: 561-236-7216, E-mail: pmonaco@lynn.edu.

College of Business and Management Students: 71 full-time (37 women), 113 part-time (47 women); includes 35 minority (13 African Americans, 6 Asian Americans or Pacific Islanders, 16 Hispanic Americans), 55 international. Average age 32. 114 applicants, 88% accepted, 71 enrolled. *Faculty:* 13 full-time (5 women), 7 part-time/adjunct (3 women). Expenses: Contact institution. *Financial support:* In 2006–07, 160 students received support. Career-related internships or fieldwork, Federal Work-Study, institutionally sponsored loans, scholarships/grants, tuition waivers (full and partial), and unspecified assistantships available. Support available to part-time students. Financial award application deadline: 8/1; financial award applicants required to submit FAFSA. In 2006, 83 master's, 9 doctorates awarded. *Degree program information:* Part-time and evening/weekend programs available. Postbaccalaureate distance learning degree programs offered. Offers aviation management (MBA); financial valuation and investment management (MBA); global leadership (PhD); hospitality management (MBA); international business (MBA); marketing (MBA); mass communication and media management (MBA); sports and athletics administration (MBA). *Application deadline:* Applications are processed on a rolling basis. *Application fee:* $50. Electronic applications accepted. *Application Contact:* Dr. Larissa Baia, Assistant Director of Graduate Admissions, 561-237-7916, Fax: 561-237-7100, E-mail: admissionpm@lynn.edu. *Dean*, Dr. Russell Boisjoly, 561-237-7458, Fax: 561-237-7014, E-mail: rboisjoly@lynn.edu.

Conservatory of Music Students: 17 full-time (3 women), 25 part-time (10 women); includes 1 minority (African American), 29 international. Average age 25. 28 applicants, 86% accepted, 23 enrolled. *Faculty:* 8 full-time (3 women), 15 part-time/adjunct (3 women). Expenses: Contact institution. *Financial support:* In 2006–07, 6 students received support. Federal Work-Study, institutionally sponsored loans, scholarships/grants, and unspecified assistantships available. Support available to part-time students. Financial award application deadline: 8/1; financial award applicants required to submit FAFSA. In 2006, 6 degrees awarded. *Degree program information:* Part-time and evening/weekend programs available. Offers music performance (MM); professional performance (Certificate). *Application deadline:* For fall admission, 3/31 priority date for domestic and international students; for spring admission, 12/1 priority date for domestic and international students. Applications are processed on a rolling basis. *Application fee:* $50. *Application Contact:* Dr. Larissa Baia, Assistant Director Graduate Admissions, 561-237-7916, Fax: 561-237-7100, E-mail: admissionpm@lynn.edu. *Dean*, Dr. Jon Robertson, 561-237-7702, Fax: 561-237-9002, E-mail: jrobertson@lynn.edu.

Donald and Helen Ross College of Education Students: 29 full-time (22 women), 88 part-time (61 women); includes 30 minority (18 African Americans, 1 Asian American or Pacific Islander, 11 Hispanic Americans), 10 international. Average age 36. 48 applicants, 79% accepted, 33 enrolled. *Faculty:* 5 full-time (3 women), 8 part-time/adjunct (4 women). Expenses: Contact institution. *Financial support:* Career-related internships or fieldwork, Federal Work-Study, institutionally sponsored loans, scholarships/grants, tuition waivers (partial), and unspecified assistantships available. Support available to part-time students. Financial award application deadline: 8/1; financial award applicants required to submit FAFSA. In 2006, 69 master's, 6 doctorates awarded. *Degree program information:* Part-time and evening/weekend programs available. Offers exceptional student education (M Ed); global leadership (PhD). *Application deadline:* Applications are processed on a rolling basis. *Application fee:* $50. Electronic applications accepted. *Application Contact:* Dr. Larissa Baia, Assistant Director of Graduate Admissions, 561-237-7916, Fax: 561-237-7100, E-mail: lbaia@lynn.edu. *Dean*, Dr. Patrick Hartwick, 561-237-7441, Fax: 561-237-7792, E-mail: phartwick@lynn.edu.

Eugene M. and Christine E. Lynn College of International Communication Students: 6 full-time (4 women), 5 part-time (4 women); includes 1 minority (Hispanic American), 3 international. Average age 28. 8 applicants, 63% accepted, 3 enrolled. *Faculty:* 3 full-time (2 women). Expenses: Contact institution. *Financial support:* In 2006–07, 10 students received support. Career-related internships or fieldwork, Federal Work-Study, institutionally sponsored loans, scholarships/grants, tuition waivers (partial), and unspecified assistantships available. Support available to part-time students. Financial award application deadline: 8/1; financial award applicants required to submit FAFSA. In 2006, 7 degrees awarded. *Degree program information:* Part-time and evening/weekend programs available. Offers mass communication (MS). *Application fee:* $50. *Application Contact:* Dr. Larissa Baia, Assistant Director Graduate Admissions, 561-237-7916, Fax: 561-237-7100, E-mail: admissionpm@lynn.edu. *Dean*, Dr. David L. Jaffe, 561-237-7098, Fax: 561-237-7097, E-mail: djaffee@lynn.edu.

MACHZIKEI HADATH RABBINICAL COLLEGE, Brooklyn, NY 11204-1805

General Information Independent-religious, men only, comprehensive institution. *Graduate housing:* Room and/or apartments available to single students; on-campus housing not available to married students.

GRADUATE UNITS

Graduate Programs

MADONNA UNIVERSITY, Livonia, MI 48150-1173

General Information Independent-religious, coed, comprehensive institution. *Enrollment:* 4,156 graduate, professional, and undergraduate students; 104 full-time matriculated graduate/professional students (76 women), 790 part-time matriculated graduate/professional students (600 women). *Enrollment by degree level:* 894 master's. *Graduate faculty:* 40 full-time (20 women), 39 part-time/adjunct (12 women). *Graduate housing:* Room and/or apartments available on a first-come, first-served basis to single students; on-campus housing not available to married students. Housing application deadline: 4/29. *Student services:* Campus safety program, career counseling, child daycare facilities, disabled student services, international student services, low-cost health insurance, multicultural affairs office, writing training. *Library facilities:* Madonna University Library. *Online resources:* library catalog, web page, access to other libraries' catalogs. *Collection:* 199,144 titles, 1,679 serial subscriptions, 938 audiovisual materials.

Computer facilities: Computer purchase and lease plans are available. 175 computers available on campus for general student use. A campuswide network can be accessed from student residence rooms and from off campus. Internet access and online class registration, wireless network are available. *Web address:* http://www.madonna.edu.

General Application Contact: Sandra Kellums, Coordinator of Graduate Admissions and Records, 734-432-5667, Fax: 734-432-5862, E-mail: skellum@madonna.edu.

GRADUATE UNITS

Department of English Students: 21 full-time (19 women); includes 8 minority (2 African Americans, 2 American Indian/Alaska Native, 2 Asian Americans or Pacific Islanders, 2 Hispanic Americans), 2 international. Average age 38. 16 applicants, 56% accepted. *Faculty:* 3 full-time (2 women), 1 (woman) part-time/adjunct. Expenses: Contact institution. *Financial support:* Institutionally sponsored loans available. Support available to part-time students. Financial award application deadline: 3/1; financial award applicants required to submit FAFSA. In 2006, 13 degrees awarded. *Degree program information:* Part-time and evening/weekend programs available. Offers teaching English to speakers of other languages (MATESOL). *Application deadline:* For fall admission, 8/1 priority date for domestic students; for winter admission, 12/1 priority date for domestic students; for spring admission, 4/1 priority date for domestic students. Applications are processed on a rolling basis. *Application fee:* $25 ($200 for international students). Electronic applications accepted. *Application Contact:* Sandra Kellums, Coordinator of Graduate Admissions and Records, 734-432-5667, Fax: 734-432-5862, E-mail: skellum@madonna.edu. *Director*, Dr. Andrew Domzalski, 734-432-5420, E-mail: adomzalski@madonna.edu.

Department of Psychology Students: 20 full-time (19 women), 19 part-time (15 women); includes 8 minority (2 African Americans, 4 Asian Americans or Pacific Islanders, 2 Hispanic Americans), 1 international. Average age 34. 16 applicants, 56% accepted. *Faculty:* 3 full-time (1 woman), 8 part-time/adjunct (4 women). Expenses: Contact institution. *Financial support:* Institutionally sponsored loans available. Support available to part-time students. In 2006, 13 degrees awarded. *Degree program information:* Part-time and evening/weekend programs available. Offers clinical psychology (MSCP). *Application deadline:* For fall admission, 3/1 for domestic students. *Application fee:* $25 ($200 for international students). Electronic applications accepted. *Application Contact:* Sandra Kellums, Coordinator of Graduate Admissions and Records, 734-432-5667, Fax: 734-432-5862, E-mail: skellum@madonna.edu. *Chairperson*, Dr. Robert Cohen, 734-432-5736, E-mail: rcohen@madonna.edu.

Program in Health Services Average age 38. 2 applicants, 50% accepted. *Faculty:* 2 full-time (both women), 5 part-time/adjunct (0 women). Expenses: Contact institution. *Financial support:* Institutionally sponsored loans and scholarships/grants available. Support available to part-time students. In 2006, 2 degrees awarded. *Degree program information:* Part-time programs available. Offers health services (MSHS). *Application deadline:* For fall admission, 8/1 priority date for domestic students; for winter admission, 12/1 priority date for domestic students; for spring admission, 4/1 priority date for domestic students. Applications are processed on a rolling basis. *Application fee:* $25 ($200 for international students). Electronic applications accepted. *Application Contact:* Sandra Kellums, Coordinator of Graduate Admissions and Records, 734-432-5667, Fax: 734-432-5862, E-mail: skellum@madonna.edu. *Dean,* Dr. Ted Biermann, 734-432-5515, E-mail: tbiermann@madonna.edu.

Program in Hospice *Degree program information:* Part-time and evening/weekend programs available. Offers hospice (MSH). Electronic applications accepted.

Program in Liberal Studies Students: 1 (woman) full-time, 3 part-time (all women); includes 1 minority (African American) Average age 43. Expenses: Contact institution. In 2006, 1 degree awarded. Offers liberal studies (MALS). *Application fee:* $25 ($200 for international students). *Director,* Dr. Dwight Lang, 734-432-5569, E-mail: dlang@madonna.edu.

Program in Nursing Students: 12 full-time (all women), 82 part-time (80 women); includes 9 minority (5 African Americans, 3 Asian Americans or Pacific Islanders, 1 Hispanic American), 3 international. Average age 40. 20 applicants, 50% accepted. *Faculty:* 3 full-time (all women). Expenses: Contact institution. *Financial support:* Career-related internships or fieldwork, Federal Work-Study, institutionally sponsored loans, and scholarships/grants available. Support available to part-time students. In 2006, 10 degrees awarded. *Degree program information:* Part-time programs available. Offers adult health: chronic health conditions (MSN); adult nurse practitioner (MSN); nursing administration (MSN). *Application deadline:* For fall admission, 8/1 priority date for domestic students; for winter admission, 12/1 priority date for domestic students; for spring admission, 4/1 priority date for domestic students. Applications are processed on a rolling basis. *Application fee:* $25 ($200 for international students). Electronic applications accepted. *Application Contact:* Sandra Kellums, Coordinator of Graduate Admissions and Records, 734-432-5667, Fax: 734-432-5862, E-mail: skellum@madonna.edu. *Chairperson,* Dr. Nancy O'Connor, 734-432-5461, Fax: 734-432-5463, E-mail: noconnor@madonna.edu.

Program in Religious Studies Average age 44. 4 applicants, 100% accepted. *Faculty:* 5 full-time (2 women), 5 part-time/adjunct (0 women). Expenses: Contact institution. In 2006, 3 degrees awarded. Offers pastoral ministry (MA). *Application fee:* $25 ($200 for international students).

Programs in Education Students: 2 full-time (both women), 154 part-time (134 women); includes 10 minority (6 African Americans, 1 Asian American or Pacific Islander, 3 Hispanic Americans), 2 international. Average age 36. 20 applicants, 85% accepted. *Faculty:* 11 full-time (7 women), 8 part-time/adjunct (2 women). Expenses: Contact institution. *Financial support:* Career-related internships or fieldwork, Federal Work-Study, institutionally sponsored loans, and scholarships/grants available. Support available to part-time students. In 2006, 133 degrees awarded. *Degree program information:* Part-time and evening/weekend programs available. Offers Catholic school leadership (MSA); educational leadership (MSA); learning disabilities (MAT); literacy education (MAT); teaching and learning (MAT). *Application deadline:* For fall admission, 8/1 priority date for domestic students; for winter admission, 12/1 priority date for domestic students; for spring admission, 4/1 priority date for domestic students. Applications are processed on a rolling basis. *Application fee:* $25 ($200 for international students). Electronic applications accepted. *Application Contact:* Sandra Kellums, Coordinator of Graduate Admissions and Records, 734-432-5667, Fax: 734-432-5862, E-mail: skellum@madonna.edu. *Dean,* Dr. Robert Kimball, 734-432-5652, E-mail: rkimball@madonna.edu.

School of Business Students: 34 full-time (21 women), 214 part-time (107 women); includes 26 minority (7 African Americans, 7 American Indian/Alaska Native, 4 Asian Americans or Pacific Islanders, 8 Hispanic Americans), 88 international. Average age 36. 60 applicants, 60% accepted. *Faculty:* 12 full-time (3 women), 14 part-time/adjunct (3 women). Expenses: Contact institution. *Financial support:* Career-related internships or fieldwork, institutionally sponsored loans, and scholarships/grants available. Support available to part-time students. In 2006, 41 degrees awarded. *Degree program information:* Part-time and evening/weekend programs available. Postbaccalaureate distance learning degree programs offered (minimal on-campus study). Offers business administration (MBA); international business (MSBA); leadership studies (MSBA); leadership studies in criminal justice (MSBA); quality and operations management (MSBA). *Application deadline:* For fall admission, 8/1 priority date for domestic students; for winter admission, 12/1 priority date for domestic students; for spring admission, 4/1 priority date for domestic students. Applications are processed on a rolling basis. *Application fee:* $25 ($200 for international students). Electronic applications accepted. *Application Contact:* Sandra Kellums, Coordinator of Graduate Admissions and Records, 734-432-5667, Fax: 734-432-5862, E-mail: skellum@madonna.edu. *Dean,* Dr. Stuart Arends, 734-432-5366, Fax: 734-432-5364, E-mail: sarends@madonna.edu.

MAHARISHI UNIVERSITY OF MANAGEMENT, Fairfield, IA 52557

General Information Independent, coed, university. *Graduate housing:* Rooms and/or apartments guaranteed to single students and available on a first-come, first-served basis to married students. Housing application deadline: 8/1.

GRADUATE UNITS

Graduate Studies *Degree program information:* Evening/weekend programs available. Postbaccalaureate distance learning degree programs offered (minimal on-campus study). Offers business administration (MBA, PhD); computer science (MS); Maharishi consciousness-based health care (MS, PhD); Maharishi Vedic science (MA, PhD); teaching elementary education (MA); teaching secondary education (MA). Electronic applications accepted.

MAINE COLLEGE OF ART, Portland, ME 04101-3987

General Information Independent, coed, comprehensive institution. *Enrollment:* 409 graduate, professional, and undergraduate students; 27 full-time matriculated graduate/professional students (13 women). *Enrollment by degree level:* 27 master's. *Graduate faculty:* 3 full-time (1 woman), 25 part-time/adjunct (12 women). *Tuition:* Full-time $24,670. *Graduate housing:* Room and/or apartments available to single students; on-campus housing not available to married students. *Student services:* Career counseling, teacher training, writing training. *Library facilities:* Joanne Waxman Library at the Maine College of Art. *Online resources:* library catalog, web page, access to other libraries' catalogs. *Collection:* 24,609 titles, 100 serial subscriptions.

Computer facilities: Computer purchase and lease plans are available. 57 computers available on campus for general student use. A campuswide network can be accessed. Internet access is available. *Web address:* http://www.meca.edu/.

General Application Contact: Rachel A. Katz, Operations Coordinator, 207-775-5154 Ext. 30, Fax: 207-775-5087, E-mail: rkatz@meca.edu.

GRADUATE UNITS

Program in Studio Arts Students: 27 full-time (13 women). Average age 34. 58 applicants, 43% accepted. *Faculty:* 3 full-time (1 woman), 25 part-time/adjunct (12 women). Expenses: Contact institution. *Financial support:* Application deadline: 3/1; In 2006, 14 degrees awarded. Offers studio arts (MFA). *Application deadline:* For fall admission, 2/1 priority date for domestic students. Applications are processed on a rolling basis. *Application fee:* $40 ($60 for international students). Electronic applications accepted. *Application Contact:* Rachel A. Katz, Operations Coordinator, 207-775-5154 Ext. 30, Fax: 207-775-5087, E-mail: rkatz@meca.edu. *Director,* Katarina Weslien, 207-775-5154 Ext. 57, Fax: 207-775-5087, E-mail: kweslien@meca.edu.

MAINE MARITIME ACADEMY, Castine, ME 04420

General Information State-supported, coed, primarily men, comprehensive institution. *Graduate housing:* Rooms and/or apartments available on a first-come, first-served basis to single and married students. Housing application deadline: 3/15.

GRADUATE UNITS

Department of Graduate Studies *Degree program information:* Part-time and evening/weekend programs available. Postbaccalaureate distance learning degree programs offered (no on-campus study). Offers global supply chain management (MS, Certificate, Diploma); international business (MS, Certificate, Diploma); maritime management (MS, Certificate, Diploma). Electronic applications accepted.

MALASPINA UNIVERSITY-COLLEGE, Nanaimo, BC V9R 5S5, Canada

General Information Province-supported, coed, comprehensive institution. *Graduate housing:* Room and/or apartments available on a first-come, first-served basis to single students; on-campus housing not available to married students. Housing application deadline: 3/5.

GRADUATE UNITS

Program in Business Administration *Degree program information:* Part-time and evening/weekend programs available. Offers business administration (EMBA, IMBA, MBA). Program offered jointly with University of Hertfordshire. Electronic applications accepted.

MALONE COLLEGE, Canton, OH 44709-3897

General Information Independent-religious, coed, comprehensive institution. *Enrollment:* 2,296 graduate, professional, and undergraduate students; 35 full-time matriculated graduate/professional students (28 women), 299 part-time matriculated graduate/professional students (212 women). *Enrollment by degree level:* 334 master's. *Graduate faculty:* 35 full-time (16 women), 36 part-time/adjunct (22 women). *Tuition:* Part-time $399 per credit hour. *Graduate housing:* On-campus housing not available. *Student services:* Career counseling, writing training. *Library facilities:* Everett L. Cattell Library. *Online resources:* library catalog, web page, access to other libraries' catalogs. *Collection:* 245,530 titles, 6,869 serial subscriptions, 13,354 audiovisual materials.

Computer facilities: 200 computers available on campus for general student use. A campuswide network can be accessed from student residence rooms and from off campus. Internet access is available. *Web address:* http://www.malone.edu/.

General Application Contact: Dr. David Kleffman, Recruiter, 330-471-8447, Fax: 330-471-8343, E-mail: dkleffman@malone.edu.

MANHATTAN COLLEGE, Riverdale, NY 10471

General Information Independent-religious, coed, comprehensive institution. *Enrollment:* 3,357 graduate, professional, and undergraduate students; 97 full-time matriculated graduate/professional students (52 women), 341 part-time matriculated graduate/professional students (207 women). *Enrollment by degree level:* 438 master's. *Graduate faculty:* 53 full-time (12 women), 49 part-time/adjunct (18 women). *Graduate housing:* On-campus housing not available. *Student services:* Career counseling, disabled student services, free psychological counseling, low-cost health insurance. *Library facilities:* O'Malley Library plus 1 other. *Online resources:* library catalog, web page, access to other libraries' catalogs. *Collection:* 211,376 titles, 1,190 serial subscriptions.

Computer facilities: 375 computers available on campus for general student use. A campuswide network can be accessed from student residence rooms and from off campus. Internet access and online class registration are available. *Web address:* http://www.manhattan.edu/.

General Application Contact: Dr. Weldon Jackson, Provost, 718-862-7303, Fax: 718-862-8014, E-mail: weldon.jackson@manhattan.edu.

GRADUATE UNITS

Graduate Division Students: 122 full-time (89 women), 327 part-time (181 women). Average age 31. 304 applicants, 86% accepted. *Faculty:* 88. Expenses: Contact institution. *Financial support:* Fellowships, research assistantships, teaching assistantships, career-related internships or fieldwork, Federal Work-Study, scholarships/grants, tuition waivers (full and partial), and laboratory assistantships available. Support available to part-time students. Financial award application deadline: 2/1. In 2006, 150 master's, 15 other advanced degrees awarded. *Degree program information:* Part-time and evening/weekend programs available. *Application deadline:* For fall admission, 8/10 priority date for domestic and international students; for winter admission, 1/7 priority date for domestic and international students; for spring admission, 1/7 priority date for domestic and international students. Applications are processed on a rolling basis. *Application fee:* $50. *Application Contact:* Weldon Jackson. *Provost,* Dr. Weldon Jackson, 718-862-7303, Fax: 718-862-8014, E-mail: weldon.jackson@manhattan.edu.

School of Education Students: 44 full-time (38 women), 198 part-time (167 women). Average age 30. 172 applicants, 77% accepted, 118 enrolled. *Faculty:* 14 full-time (8 women), 24 part-time/adjunct (17 women). Expenses: Contact institution. *Financial support:* Federal Work-Study, scholarships/grants, tuition waivers (partial), and unspecified assistantships available. Financial award application deadline: 2/1. In 2006, 70 master's awarded. *Degree program information:* Part-time and evening/weekend programs available. Offers 5 year dual childhood/special education (MS Ed); counseling (MA, Diploma); dual childhood/special education (MS Ed); school building leadership (MS Ed, Diploma); special education (MS Ed). *Application deadline:* For fall admission, 8/10 priority date for domestic students; for spring admission, 1/7 priority date for domestic students. Applications are processed on a rolling basis. *Application fee:* $50. *Application Contact:* Weldon Jackson. *Dean,* Dr. William Merriman, 718-862-7373, Fax: 718-862-8011.

School of Engineering Students: 53 full-time (14 women), 143 part-time (40 women). Average age 28. 89 applicants, 83% accepted, 62 enrolled. *Faculty:* 39 full-time (4 women), 25 part-time/adjunct (1 woman). Expenses: Contact institution. *Financial support:* In 2006–07, 43 students received support; fellowships with partial tuition reimbursements available, research assistantships with partial tuition reimbursements available, teaching assistantships with partial tuition reimbursements available, career-related internships or fieldwork, Federal Work-Study, scholarships/grants, and laboratory assistantships available. Support available to part-time students. Financial award application deadline: 2/1. In 2006, 61 degrees awarded. *Degree program information:* Part-time and evening/weekend programs available. Offers chemical engineering (MS); civil engineering (MS); computer engineering (MS); electrical engineering (MS); environmental engineering (ME, MS); mechanical engineering (MS). *Application deadline:* For fall admission, 8/10 priority date for domestic students; for spring admission, 1/7 for domestic students. Applications are processed on a rolling basis. *Application fee:* $50. *Application Contact:* Information Contact, 718-862-7281, Fax: 718-863-8015, E-mail: deanengr@manhattan.edu. *Dean,* Dr. Richard H. Heist, 718-862-7281, Fax: 718-862-8015, E-mail: deanengr@manhattan.edu.

MANHATTAN SCHOOL OF MUSIC, New York, NY 10027-4698

General Information Independent, coed, comprehensive institution. *Graduate housing:* Room and/or apartments available on a first-come, first-served basis to single students; on-campus housing not available to married students. Housing application deadline: 5/1.

GRADUATE UNITS

Graduate Programs Offers composition (MM, DMA); jazz (MM, DMA); music performance (MM, DMA); orchestral performance (MM). Electronic applications accepted.

Professional Studies Certificate Program Offers instrumental music (CPS); vocal music (CPS). Electronic applications accepted.

MANHATTANVILLE COLLEGE, Purchase, NY 10577-2132

General Information Independent, coed, comprehensive institution. *Enrollment:* 2,974 graduate, professional, and undergraduate students; 309 full-time matriculated graduate/professional students (225 women), 689 part-time matriculated graduate/professional students (483 women). *Enrollment by degree level:* 998 master's. *Graduate housing:* Rooms and/or apartments available on a first-come, first-served basis to single students and available to married students. Housing application deadline: 7/1. *Student services:* Campus employment opportunities, campus safety program, career counseling, disabled student services, free psychologi-

Manhattanville College (continued)

cal counseling, international student services, multicultural affairs office. *Library facilities:* Manhattanville College Library. *Online resources:* library catalog, web page, access to other libraries' catalogs. *Collection:* 239,202 titles, 27,838 serial subscriptions.

Computer facilities: Computer purchase and lease plans are available. 200 computers available on campus for general student use. A campuswide network can be accessed from student residence rooms and from off campus. Internet access and online class registration are available. *Web address:* http://www.manhattanville.edu/.

General Application Contact: Graduate Admissions, 914-694-3425, Fax: 914-694-3488, E-mail: gps@mville.edu.

GRADUATE UNITS

Graduate Programs Students: 309 full-time (225 women), 669 part-time (463 women); includes 86 minority (34 African Americans, 6 Asian Americans or Pacific Islanders, 46 Hispanic Americans), 15 international. Expenses: Contact institution. *Financial support:* Career-related internships or fieldwork, institutionally sponsored loans, tuition waivers (partial), and unspecified assistantships available. Support available to part-time students. Financial award applicants required to submit FAFSA. In 2006, 333 degrees awarded. *Degree program information:* Part-time and evening/weekend programs available. Offers integrated marketing communications (MS); international management (MS); leadership and strategic management (MS); liberal studies (MA); management communications (MS); organization development and human resources management (MS); sports business management (MS); writing (MA). *Application deadline:* Applications are processed on a rolling basis. *Application fee:* $55. *Interim Provost,* Dr. Scott F. Stoddert, 914-323-5262.

School of Education Students: 294 full-time (219 women), 474 part-time (337 women); includes 65 minority (20 African Americans, 6 Asian Americans or Pacific Islanders, 39 Hispanic Americans), 6 international. Expenses: Contact institution. *Financial support:* Career-related internships or fieldwork and institutionally sponsored loans available. Support available to part-time students. In 2006, 267 degrees awarded. *Degree program information:* Part-time and evening/weekend programs available. Offers biology (MAT); biology and special education (MPS); chemistry (MAT); chemistry and special education (MPS); child and early childhood education (MAT); childhood and early childhood education (MAT); childhood and special education (MPS); childhood education (MAT); early childhood education (birth-grade 2) (MAT); education (MAT, MPS); educational leadership (MPS); English (MAT); English and special education (MPS); literacy (MPS); literacy (birth-grade 6) (MPS); literacy (birth-grade 6) and special education (grades 1-6) (MPS); literacy and special education (MPS); math (MAT); math and special education (MPS); music education (MAT); physical education and sport pedagogy (MAT); second language (MAT); social studies (MAT); social studies and special education (MPS); special education (MPS); special education (birth-grade 2) (MPS); special education (birth-grade 6) (MPS); special education childhood (MPS); teaching English as a second language (MPS). *Application deadline:* Applications are processed on a rolling basis. *Application fee:* $55. Electronic applications accepted. *Application Contact:* Alyce Ware Poli, Director of Admissions, 914-323-5142, Fax: 914-694-1732, E-mail: edschool@mville.edu. *Dean,* Dr. Shelley Wepner, 914-323-5192, Fax: 914-694-2386, E-mail: wepners@mville.edu.

See Close-Up on page 953.

MANSFIELD UNIVERSITY OF PENNSYLVANIA, Mansfield, PA 16933

General Information State-supported, coed, comprehensive institution. *Enrollment:* 3,360 graduate, professional, and undergraduate students; 70 full-time matriculated graduate/professional students (60 women), 354 part-time matriculated graduate/professional students (305 women). *Enrollment by degree level:* 424 master's. *Graduate faculty:* 42 full-time (19 women), 13 part-time/adjunct (11 women). Tuition, state resident: part-time $336 per credit. Tuition, nonresident: part-time $538 per credit. Tuition and fees vary according to course load and reciprocity agreements. *Graduate housing:* Room and/or apartments available on a first-come, first-served basis to single students; on-campus housing not available to married students. *Student services:* Campus employment opportunities, campus safety program, career counseling, child daycare facilities, disabled student services, exercise/wellness program, free psychological counseling, grant writing training, international student services, low-cost health insurance, multicultural affairs office, teacher training. *Library facilities:* North Hall Library. *Online resources:* library catalog, web page, access to other libraries' catalogs. *Collection:* 246,141 titles, 2,948 serial subscriptions, 26,742 audiovisual materials.

Computer facilities: Computer purchase and lease plans are available. 550 computers available on campus for general student use. A campuswide network can be accessed from student residence rooms and from off campus. Internet access and online class registration are available. *Web address:* http://www.mansfield.edu/.

General Application Contact: Judi Brayer, Assistant Director of Enrollment Management/ Graduate Admissions, 570-662-4818, Fax: 570-662-4121, E-mail: jbrayer@mansfield.edu.

GRADUATE UNITS

Graduate Studies Students: 67 full-time (58 women), 321 part-time (277 women); includes 35 minority (23 African Americans, 3 American Indian/Alaska Native, 3 Asian Americans or Pacific Islanders, 6 Hispanic Americans), 1 international. Average age 35. 544 applicants, 56% accepted, 188 enrolled. *Faculty:* 26 full-time (15 women), 22 part-time/adjunct (18 women). Expenses: Contact institution. *Financial support:* In 2006–07, 41 students received support. Career-related internships or fieldwork and unspecified assistantships available. Support available to part-time students. Financial award application deadline: 5/1; financial award applicants required to submit FAFSA. In 2006, 90 degrees awarded. *Degree program information:* Part-time and evening/weekend programs available. Postbaccalaureate distance learning degree programs offered (no on-campus study). Offers art education (M Ed); band conducting (MA); choral conducting (MA); elementary education (M Ed); library science (M Ed); nursing (MSN); performance (MA); secondary education (MS). *Application deadline:* For fall admission, 8/1 priority date for domestic students, 6/1 for international students. Applications are processed on a rolling basis. *Application fee:* $25. Electronic applications accepted. *Application Contact:* Judi Brayer, Assistant Director of Enrollment Management/ Graduate Admissions, 570-662-4818, Fax: 570-662-4121, E-mail: jbrayer@mansfield.edu. *Interim Associate Provost,* Dr. Denise Seigart, 570-662-4807, Fax: 570-662-4115, E-mail: dseigart@mansfield.edu.

MAPLE SPRINGS BAPTIST BIBLE COLLEGE AND SEMINARY, Capitol Heights, MD 20743

General Information Independent-religious, coed, comprehensive institution. *Graduate housing:* On-campus housing not available.

GRADUATE UNITS

Graduate and Professional Programs Offers biblical studies (MA, Certificate); Christian counseling (MA); church administration (MA); divinity (M Div); ministry (D Min); religious education (MA).

MARANATHA BAPTIST BIBLE COLLEGE, Watertown, WI 53094

General Information Independent-religious, coed, comprehensive institution. *Enrollment:* 876 graduate, professional, and undergraduate students; 15 full-time matriculated graduate/professional students (4 women), 39 part-time matriculated graduate/professional students (5 women). *Enrollment by degree level:* 54 master's. *Graduate faculty:* 5 full-time (0 women), 2 part-time/adjunct (0 women). *Tuition:* Full-time $3,120; part-time $195 per credit. *Required fees:* $280; $18 per credit. One-time fee: $175 full-time. *Graduate housing:* On-campus housing not available. *Student services:* Campus employment opportunities. *Library facilities:* Cedarholm Library and Resource Center. *Online resources:* library catalog, access to other libraries' catalogs. *Collection:* 122,251 titles, 502 serial subscriptions.

Computer facilities: 61 computers available on campus for general student use. A campuswide network can be accessed from student residence rooms and from off campus. Internet access is available. *Web address:* http://www.mbbc.edu/.

General Application Contact: Dr. Jim Harrison, Director of Admissions, 920-206-2327, Fax: 920-261-9109, E-mail: admissions@mbbc.edu.

GRADUATE UNITS

Program in Biblical Counseling Students: 6 full-time (4 women), 2 part-time (both women). Average age 26. 6 applicants, 100% accepted, 6 enrolled. *Faculty:* 5 full-time (0 women), 2 part-time/adjunct (0 women). Expenses: Contact institution. *Financial support:* In 2006–07, 3 students received support. Scholarships/grants and tuition waivers (full and partial) available. Support available to part-time students. In 2006, 1 degree awarded. *Degree program information:* Part-time programs available. Postbaccalaureate distance learning degree programs offered. Offers biblical counseling (MA). *Application deadline:* Applications are processed on a rolling basis. *Application fee:* $50. *Application Contact:* Dr. Jim Harrison, Director of Admissions, 920-206-2327, Fax: 920-261-9109, E-mail: admissions@mbbc.edu. *Interim President,* Dr. Larry Oats, 920-206-2324, Fax: 920-261-9109, E-mail: loats@mbbc.edu.

Program in Biblical Studies Students: 9 full-time (0 women), 29 part-time; includes 1 minority (African American) Average age 27. 36 applicants, 47% accepted, 17 enrolled. *Faculty:* 5 full-time (0 women), 2 part-time/adjunct (0 women). Expenses: Contact institution. *Financial support:* In 2006–07, 3 students received support. Scholarships/grants and tuition waivers (full and partial) available. Support available to part-time students. In 2006, 7 degrees awarded. *Degree program information:* Part-time programs available. Postbaccalaureate distance learning degree programs offered (minimal on-campus study). Offers biblical studies (MA). *Application deadline:* Applications are processed on a rolling basis. *Application fee:* $40. *Application Contact:* Dr. Jim Harrison, Director of Admissions, 920-206-2327, Fax: 920-261-9109, E-mail: admissions@mbbc.edu. *Interim President,* Dr. Larry Oats, 920-206-2324, Fax: 920-261-9109, E-mail: loats@mbbc.edu.

Program in Cross-Cultural Studies Average age 25. *Faculty:* 5 full-time (0 women), 2 part-time/adjunct (0 women). Expenses: Contact institution. *Financial support:* Scholarships/ grants and tuition waivers (full and partial) available. Support available to part-time students. *Degree program information:* Part-time programs available. Postbaccalaureate distance learning degree programs offered. Offers cross-cultural studies (MA). *Application deadline:* Applications are processed on a rolling basis. *Application fee:* $50. *Application Contact:* Dr. Jim Harrison, Director of Admissions, 920-206-2327, Fax: 920-261-9109, E-mail: admissions@mbbc.edu. *Interim President,* Dr. Larry Oats, 920-206-2324, Fax: 920-261-9109, E-mail: loats@mbbc.edu.

Program in Theology Students: 2 full-time (0 women). Average age 27. *Faculty:* 5 full-time (0 women), 2 part-time/adjunct (0 women). Expenses: Contact institution. Offers theology (MA). *Application Contact:* Dr. Jim Harrison, Director of Admissions, 920-206-2327, Fax: 920-261-9109, E-mail: admissions@mbbc.edu. *Interim President,* Dr. Larry Oats, 920-206-2324, Fax: 920-261-9109, E-mail: loats@mbbc.edu.

MARIAN COLLEGE, Indianapolis, IN 46222-1997

General Information Independent-religious, coed, comprehensive institution.

GRADUATE UNITS

Department of Education Offers education (MAT).

MARIAN COLLEGE OF FOND DU LAC, Fond du Lac, WI 54935-4699

General Information Independent-religious, coed, comprehensive institution. *Enrollment:* 3,040 graduate, professional, and undergraduate students; 44 full-time matriculated graduate/professional students (29 women), 870 part-time matriculated graduate/professional students (582 women). *Enrollment by degree level:* 860 master's, 54 doctoral. *Graduate faculty:* 19 full-time (7 women), 40 part-time/adjunct (22 women). *Tuition:* Part-time $310 per credit. Tuition and fees vary according to degree level and program. *Graduate housing:* On-campus housing not available. *Student services:* Campus employment opportunities, campus safety program, career counseling, child daycare facilities, disabled student services, exercise/ wellness program, free psychological counseling, multicultural affairs office, teacher training, writing training. *Library facilities:* Cardinal Meyer Library. *Online resources:* library catalog, web page, access to other libraries' catalogs. *Collection:* 94,217 titles, 952 serial subscriptions, 1,320 audiovisual materials.

Computer facilities: 225 computers available on campus for general student use. A campuswide network can be accessed from student residence rooms. Internet access and online class registration are available. *Web address:* http://www.mariancollege.edu/.

General Application Contact: Sheryl Ayala, Vice President for Academic Affairs, 920-923-7604.

GRADUATE UNITS

Business Division Students: 1 full-time (0 women), 95 part-time (55 women); includes 7 minority (5 African Americans, 1 American Indian/Alaska Native, 1 Hispanic American). Average age 38. 44 applicants, 100% accepted, 44 enrolled. *Faculty:* 6 part-time/adjunct (0 women). Expenses: Contact institution. *Financial support:* In 2006–07, 23 students received support. Institutionally sponsored loans available. Support available to part-time students. Financial award application deadline: 3/1; financial award applicants required to submit FAFSA. In 2006, 33 degrees awarded. *Degree program information:* Part-time and evening/weekend programs available. Offers organizational leadership and quality (MS). *Application deadline:* Applications are processed on a rolling basis. *Application fee:* $25. Electronic applications accepted. *Application Contact:* Tracy Qualman, Director of Marketing and Admission, 920-923-7159, Fax: 920-923-7167, E-mail: tqualmann@mariancollege.edu. *Dean of Lifelong Learning,* David McPhail, 920-923-8760, Fax: 920-923-7167, E-mail: dmcphail@mariancollege.edu.

School of Education Students: 30 full-time (16 women), 759 part-time (511 women); includes 37 minority (10 African Americans, 9 American Indian/Alaska Native, 6 Asian Americans or Pacific Islanders, 12 Hispanic Americans), 2 international. Average age 33. 96 applicants, 100% accepted, 96 enrolled. *Faculty:* 15 full-time (5 women), 32 part-time/adjunct (20 women). Expenses: Contact institution. *Financial support:* In 2006–07, 197 students received support. Federal Work-Study and institutionally sponsored loans available. Support available to part-time students. Financial award application deadline: 3/1; financial award applicants required to submit FAFSA. In 2006, 200 degrees awarded. *Degree program information:* Part-time programs available. Offers educational leadership (MA, PhD); teacher development (MA). *Application deadline:* Applications are processed on a rolling basis. *Application fee:* $50. *Application Contact:* Robert Bohnsack, Graduate Education Admissions, 920-923-8100, Fax: 920-923-7154, E-mail: bbohnsack@mariancollege.edu. *Dean, School of Education,* Dr. Kathryn Polmanteer, 920-923-8099, Fax: 920-923-7663, E-mail: knpolmanteer94@mariancollege.edu.

School of Nursing Students: 13 full-time (all women), 15 part-time (all women); includes 1 minority (American Indian/Alaska Native). Average age 37. 9 applicants, 100% accepted, 9 enrolled. *Faculty:* 4 full-time (3 women), 4 part-time/adjunct (2 women). Expenses: Contact institution. *Financial support:* In 2006–07, 19 students received support. Institutionally sponsored loans and scholarships/grants available. Support available to part-time students. Financial award application deadline: 3/1; financial award applicants required to submit FAFSA. In 2006, 16 degrees awarded. *Degree program information:* Part-time and evening/weekend programs available. Offers adult nurse practitioner (MSN); nurse educator (MSN). *Application deadline:* Applications are processed on a rolling basis. *Application fee:* $50. Electronic applications accepted. *Application Contact:* Dr. Lea Monahan, Director, 920-923-7608, Fax: 920-923-8770, E-mail: lmonahan@mariancollege.edu. *Dean, School of Nursing,* Dr. James C. McCann, 920-923-8094, Fax: 920-923-8770, E-mail: jcmccann70@mariancollege.edu.

MARIETTA COLLEGE, Marietta, OH 45750-4000

General Information Independent, coed, comprehensive institution. *Enrollment:* 1,530 graduate, professional, and undergraduate students; 73 full-time matriculated graduate/professional students (50 women), 45 part-time matriculated graduate/professional students (30 women). *Enrollment by degree level:* 118 master's. *Graduate faculty:* 15 full-time (8 women), 4 part-time/adjunct (1 woman). *Graduate housing:* On-campus housing not available. *Student services:* Campus safety program, career counseling, disabled student services, free psychological counseling, international student services, teacher training, writing training. *Library facilities:* Dawes Memorial Library. *Online resources:* library catalog, web page, access to other libraries' catalogs. *Collection:* 246,706 titles, 28,188 serial subscriptions, 6,147 audiovisual materials.

Computer facilities: 200 computers available on campus for general student use. A campuswide network can be accessed from student residence rooms and from off campus. Internet access is available. *Web address:* http://www.marietta.edu/.

General Application Contact: Cathy J. Brown, Director of Graduate and Continuing Studies, 740-376-4740, Fax: 740-376-4423, E-mail: ce@marietta.edu.

GRADUATE UNITS

Program in Corporate Media Students: 15 full-time (11 women), 3 part-time (1 woman). *Faculty:* 5 full-time (4 women), 2 part-time/adjunct (0 women). Expenses: Contact institution. Offers corporate media (MCM). *Application Contact:* Cathy J. Brown, Director of Graduate and Continuing Studies, 740-376-4740, Fax: 740-376-4423, E-mail: ce@marietta.edu. *Chair,* Dr. Liane Gray-Starner, 740-376-4680, E-mail: graystal@marietta.edu.

Program in Education Students: 4 full-time (3 women), 31 part-time (23 women). Average age 35. *Faculty:* 2 full-time (1 woman), 2 part-time/adjunct (1 woman). Expenses: Contact institution. *Financial support:* Available to part-time students. *Degree program information:* Part-time and evening/weekend programs available. Offers education (MA). *Application deadline:* For fall admission, 8/23 priority date for domestic students. *Application fee:* $25. *Chair,* Dr. Dorothy Erb, 740-376-4761.

Program in Physician Assistant Studies Students: 43 full-time (28 women), 1 (woman) part-time. Average age 25. *Faculty:* 3 full-time (2 women), 1 part-time/adjunct (0 women). Expenses: Contact institution. Offers physician assistant studies (MS). *Director,* Dr. Gloria M. Stewart, 740-370-4458.

Program in Psychology Students: 10 full-time (7 women), 6 part-time (5 women). *Faculty:* 3 full-time (1 woman). Expenses: Contact institution. Offers psychology (MAP). *Chair,* Dr. Mark E. Sibicky, 740-376-4762, E-mail: sibickym@marietta.edu.

MARIST COLLEGE, Poughkeepsie, NY 12601-1387

General Information Independent, coed, comprehensive institution. *Enrollment:* 5,877 graduate, professional, and undergraduate students; 168 full-time matriculated graduate/professional students (102 women), 686 part-time matriculated graduate/professional students (352 women). *Enrollment by degree level:* 839 master's, 15 other advanced degrees. *Graduate faculty:* 57 full-time (24 women), 36 part-time/adjunct (20 women). *Tuition:* Full-time $11,340; part-time $630 per credit. *Required fees:* $60; $30 per semester. *Graduate housing:* On-campus housing not available. *Student services:* Campus employment opportunities, campus safety program, career counseling, disabled student services, free psychological counseling, international student services, low-cost health insurance. *Library facilities:* James A. Cannavino Library. *Online resources:* library catalog, web page, access to other libraries' catalogs. *Collection:* 197,209 titles, 22,755 serial subscriptions, 5,488 audiovisual materials. *Research affiliation:* Hudson River Psychiatric Center, St. Francis Hospital, Dutchess County Community Mental Health Center, Center for Advanced Brain Imaging Psychology, NYSTAR (New York State Office of Technology and Academic Research), HVTDC (Hudson Valley Technology Development Corp.).

Computer facilities: Computer purchase and lease plans are available. 585 computers available on campus for general student use. A campuswide network can be accessed from student residence rooms and from off campus. Internet access and online class registration are available. *Web address:* http://www.marist.edu/.

General Application Contact: Anu R. Ailawadhi, Director of Graduate Admissions, 845-575-3800, Fax: 845-575-3166, E-mail: graduate@marist.edu.

GRADUATE UNITS

Graduate Programs Students: 168 full-time (102 women), 686 part-time (352 women); includes 107 minority (45 African Americans, 3 American Indian/Alaska Native, 27 Asian Americans or Pacific Islanders, 32 Hispanic Americans), 53 international. Average age 33. 383 applicants, 82% accepted, 225 enrolled. *Faculty:* 57 full-time (24 women), 36 part-time/adjunct (20 women). Expenses: Contact institution. *Financial support:* In 2006–07, 327 students received support. Career-related internships or fieldwork, scholarships/grants, and unspecified assistantships available. Support available to part-time students. Financial award application deadline: 8/15; financial award applicants required to submit FAFSA. In 2006, 287 master's, 9 other advanced degrees awarded. *Degree program information:* Part-time and evening/weekend programs available. Postbaccalaureate distance learning degree programs offered (minimal on-campus study). *Application deadline:* For fall admission, 8/1 for domestic students, 6/1 for international students; for spring admission, 12/1 for domestic students, 10/15 for international students. Applications are processed on a rolling basis. *Application fee:* $50. Electronic applications accepted. *Application Contact:* Anu R. Ailawadhi, Director of Graduate Admissions, 845-575-3800, Fax: 845-575-3166, E-mail: graduate@marist.edu. *Academic Vice President,* Dr. Artin Arslanian, 845-575-3000 Ext. 2629, E-mail: artin.arslanian@marist.edu.

School of Communication and the Arts Students: 5 full-time (4 women), 46 part-time (37 women); includes 1 minority (Asian American or Pacific Islander), 1 international. Average age 34. 61 applicants, 75% accepted, 35 enrolled. *Faculty:* 3 full-time (2 women), 1 part-time/adjunct (0 women). Expenses: Contact institution. *Financial support:* In 2006–07, 23 students received support; research assistantships, scholarships/grants available. Support available to part-time students. Financial award application deadline: 8/15; financial award applicants required to submit FAFSA. *Degree program information:* Part-time programs available. Postbaccalaureate distance learning degree programs offered (minimal on-campus study). Offers organizational communication and leadership (MA). *Application deadline:* For fall admission, 8/1 for domestic students, 6/1 for international students; for spring admission, 11/15 for international students. Applications are processed on a rolling basis. *Application fee:* $50. Electronic applications accepted. *Assistant Dean,* Dr. Subir Sengupta, 845-575-2678, E-mail: subir.sengupta@marist.edu.

School of Computer Science and Mathematics Students: 41 full-time (6 women), 70 part-time (21 women); includes 25 minority (10 African Americans, 3 American Indian/Alaska Native, 8 Asian Americans or Pacific Islanders, 4 Hispanic Americans), 38 international. Average age 31. 50 applicants, 92% accepted, 33 enrolled. *Faculty:* 14 full-time (5 women). Expenses: Contact institution. *Financial support:* In 2006–07, 23 students received support. Scholarships/grants available. Support available to part-time students. Financial award application deadline: 8/15; financial award applicants required to submit FAFSA. In 2006, 48 master's, 3 other advanced degrees awarded. *Degree program information:* Part-time and evening/weekend programs available. Postbaccalaureate distance learning degree programs offered (minimal on-campus study). Offers information systems (MS, Adv C); software development (MS); technology management (MS). *Application deadline:* For fall admission, 8/1 for domestic students, 6/1 for international students; for spring admission, 12/15 for domestic students, 10/15 for international students. Applications are processed on a rolling basis. *Application fee:* $50. Electronic applications accepted. *Application Contact:* Anu R. Ailawadhi, Director of Graduate Admissions, 845-575-3800, Fax: 845-575-3166, E-mail: graduate@marist.edu. *Dean,* Dr. Roger Norton, 845-575-3000, E-mail: roger.norton@marist.edu.

School of Management Students: 24 full-time (11 women), 429 part-time (190 women); includes 60 minority (26 African Americans, 16 Asian Americans or Pacific Islanders, 18 Hispanic Americans), 9 international. Average age 35. 142 applicants, 86% accepted, 87 enrolled. *Faculty:* 18 full-time (8 women), 10 part-time/adjunct (5 women). Expenses: Contact institution. *Financial support:* In 2006–07, 131 students received support. Scholarships/grants available. Support available to part-time students. Financial award application deadline: 8/15; financial award applicants required to submit FAFSA. In 2006, 134 master's, 2 other advanced degrees awarded. *Degree program information:* Part-time and evening/weekend programs available. Postbaccalaureate distance learning degree programs offered (no on-campus study). Offers business administration (MBA, Adv C); executive leadership (Adv C); public administration (MPA); technology management (MS). *Application deadline:* For fall admission, 7/1 for domestic students, 6/1 for international students; for spring admission, 12/15 for domestic students, 10/15 for international students. Applications are processed on a rolling basis. *Application fee:* $50. Electronic applications accepted. *Application Contact:* Anu R. Ailawadhi, Director of Graduate Admissions, 845-575-3800, Fax: 845-575-3166, E-mail: graduate@marist.edu. *Interim Dean,* Dr. Elmore R. Alexander, 845-575-3225, E-mail: elmore.alexander@marist.edu.

School of Social and Behavioral Sciences Students: 98 full-time (81 women), 120 part-time (98 women); includes 21 minority (9 African Americans, 2 Asian Americans or Pacific Islanders, 10 Hispanic Americans), 4 international. Average age 30. 105 applicants, 72% accepted, 52 enrolled. *Faculty:* 21 full-time (9 women), 25 part-time/adjunct (14 women). Expenses: Contact institution. *Financial support:* In 2006–07, 146 students received support. Career-related internships or fieldwork, scholarships/grants, and unspecified assistantships available. Support available to part-time students. Financial award application deadline: 8/15; financial award applicants required to submit FAFSA. In 2006, 105 master's, 4 other advanced degrees awarded. *Degree program information:* Part-time and evening/weekend programs available. Offers counseling psychology (MA); education (M Ed); education psychology (MA); school psychology (MA, Adv C). *Application deadline:* For fall admission, 8/1 for domestic students, 6/1 for international students; for spring admission, 12/1 for domestic students, 10/15 for international students. Applications are processed on a rolling basis. *Application fee:* $50. Electronic applications accepted. *Application Contact:* Anu R. Ailawadhi, Director of Graduate Admissions, 845-575-3800, Fax: 845-575-3166, E-mail: graduate@marist.edu. *Dean,* Margaret Calista, 845-575-3000 Ext. 2960, E-mail: margaret.calista@marist.edu.

MARLBORO COLLEGE, Marlboro, VT 05344

General Information Independent, coed, comprehensive institution. *Enrollment:* 400 graduate, professional, and undergraduate students; 15 full-time matriculated graduate/professional students (10 women), 34 part-time matriculated graduate/professional students (19 women). *Enrollment by degree level:* 49 master's. *Graduate faculty:* 2 full-time (0 women), 20 part-time/adjunct (10 women). *Tuition:* Full-time $18,900; part-time $630 per credit. Tuition and fees vary according to program. *Graduate housing:* On-campus housing not available. *Student services:* Career counseling, free psychological counseling, low-cost health insurance, teacher training. *Library facilities:* Rice Memorial Library. *Online resources:* library catalog, web page, access to other libraries' catalogs. *Collection:* 71,000 titles, 275 serial subscriptions.

Computer facilities: 47 computers available on campus for general student use. A campuswide network can be accessed from student residence rooms and from off campus. Internet access is available. *Web address:* http://www.marlboro.edu/.

General Application Contact: Bethany Catron, Director of Admissions, 802-258-9209, Fax: 802-258-9201, E-mail: bcatron@gradcenter.marlboro.edu.

GRADUATE UNITS

Graduate Center Students: 15 full-time (10 women), 34 part-time (19 women); includes 7 minority (1 African American, 4 American Indian/Alaska Native, 2 Hispanic Americans). Average age 45. *Faculty:* 2 full-time (0 women), 20 part-time/adjunct (10 women). Expenses: Contact institution. *Financial support:* Applicants required to submit FAFSA. In 2006, 25 degrees awarded. *Degree program information:* Part-time and evening/weekend programs available. Postbaccalaureate distance learning degree programs offered (minimal on-campus study). Offers information technologies (MS); Internet engineering (MS); management (MS); managing for sustainability (MBA); teaching with Internet technologies (MAT). *Application deadline:* Applications are processed on a rolling basis. *Application fee:* $0. Electronic applications accepted. *Application Contact:* Bethany Catron, Director of Admissions, 802-258-9209, Fax: 802-258-9201, E-mail: bcatron@gradcenter.marlboro.edu. *Academic Director,* Kevin Bell, 802-258-9203, Fax: 802-258-9201, E-mail: kbell@gradcenter.marlboro.edu.

MARQUETTE UNIVERSITY, Milwaukee, WI 53201-1881

General Information Independent-religious, coed, university. CGS member. *Enrollment:* 11,548 graduate, professional, and undergraduate students; 2,004 full-time matriculated graduate/professional students (1,017 women), 1,329 part-time matriculated graduate/professional students (666 women). *Enrollment by degree level:* 1,012 first professional, 1,623 master's, 646 doctoral, 52 other advanced degrees. *Graduate faculty:* 606 full-time (234 women), 438 part-time/adjunct (180 women). *Graduate housing:* Rooms and/or apartments available on a first-come, first-served basis to single and married students. *Student services:* Campus employment opportunities, campus safety program, career counseling, child daycare facilities, disabled student services, exercise/wellness program, free psychological counseling, grant writing training, international student services, low-cost health insurance, multicultural affairs office, teacher training, writing training. *Library facilities:* Raynor Memorial Libraries plus 1 other. *Online resources:* library catalog, web page, access to other libraries' catalogs. *Collection:* 1.5 million titles, 23,039 serial subscriptions. *Research affiliation:* American Educational Research Association, Argonne National Laboratory, Milwaukee Museum, NASA.

Computer facilities: Computer purchase and lease plans are available. 1,200 computers available on campus for general student use. A campuswide network can be accessed from student residence rooms and from off campus. Internet access is available. *Web address:* http://www.marquette.edu/.

General Application Contact: Erin Fox, Assistant Director for Recruitment, 414-288-5319, Fax: 414-288-1902, E-mail: erin.fox@marquette.edu.

GRADUATE UNITS

Graduate School Students: 1,086 full-time (588 women), 1,171 part-time (585 women); includes 202 minority (56 African Americans, 11 American Indian/Alaska Native, 69 Asian Americans or Pacific Islanders, 66 Hispanic Americans), 283 international. Average age 31. 2,202 applicants, 67% accepted, 875 enrolled. *Faculty:* 519 full-time (202 women), 289 part-time/adjunct (150 women). Expenses: Contact institution. *Financial support:* Fellowships, research assistantships with full tuition reimbursements, teaching assistantships with full tuition reimbursements, career-related internships or fieldwork, Federal Work-Study, institutionally sponsored loans, scholarships/grants, and tuition waivers (full and partial) available. Support available to part-time students. Financial award application deadline: 2/15. In 2006, 610 master's, 126 doctorates awarded. *Degree program information:* Part-time and evening/weekend programs available. Offers interdisciplinary studies (PhD); public service (MAPS). *Application deadline:* Applications are processed on a rolling basis. *Application fee:* $40. Electronic applications accepted. *Application Contact:* Erin Fox, Assistant Director for Recruitment, 414-288-5319, Fax: 414-288-1902, E-mail: erin.fox@marquette.edu. *Vice Provost for Research/Dean,* Dr. William Wiener, 414-288-1532, Fax: 414-288-1578.

College of Arts and Sciences Students: 412 full-time (174 women), 187 part-time (84 women); includes 45 minority (8 African Americans, 2 American Indian/Alaska Native, 15 Asian Americans or Pacific Islanders, 20 Hispanic Americans), 118 international. Average age 32. 625 applicants, 57% accepted, 162 enrolled. *Faculty:* 276 full-time (99 women), 79 part-time/adjunct (36 women). Expenses: Contact institution. *Financial support:* In 2006–07, 9 fellowships, 48 research assistantships, 196 teaching assistantships were awarded; career-related internships or fieldwork, Federal Work-Study, institutionally sponsored loans, scholarships/grants, and tuition waivers (full and partial) also available. Support available to part-time students. Financial award application deadline: 2/15. In 2006, 85 master's, 41 doctorates awarded. *Degree program information:* Part-time programs available. Offers algebra (PhD); American literature (PhD); analytical chemistry (MS, PhD); ancient philosophy (MA, PhD); arts and sciences (MA, MAT, MS, PhD); bio-mathematical modeling (PhD); bioanalytical chemistry (MS, PhD); bioinformatics (MS); biophysical chemistry (MS, PhD); British and American literature (MA); British empiricism and analytic philosophy (MA, PhD); British literature (PhD); cell biology (MS, PhD); chemical physics (MS, PhD); Christian philosophy (MA, PhD); clinical psychology (MS); computers (MS); computing (MS); developmental biology (MS, PhD); early modern European philosophy (MA, PhD); ecology (MS, PhD); endocrinology (MS, PhD); ethics (MA, PhD); European history (MA, PhD); evolutionary biology (MS, PhD); genetics (MS, PhD); German philosophy (MA, PhD); historical theology (MA, PhD); inorganic chemistry (MS, PhD); international affairs (MA);

Marquette University (continued)

mathematics (MS); mathematics education (MS); medieval history (MA); medieval philosophy (MA, PhD); microbiology (MS, PhD); molecular biology (MS, PhD); muscle and exercise physiology (MS, PhD); neurobiology (MS, PhD); organic chemistry (MS, PhD); phenomenology and existentialism (MA, PhD); philosophy of religion (MA, PhD); physical chemistry (MS, PhD); political science (MA); psychology (PhD); religious studies (PhD); Renaissance and Reformation (MA); reproductive physiology (MS, PhD); social and applied philosophy (MA); Spanish (MA, MAT); statistics (MS); systematic theology (MA, PhD); theology (MA); theology and society (PhD); United States (MA, PhD). *Application fee:* $40. *Application Contact:* Erin Fox, Assistant Director for Recruitment, 414-288-5319, Fax: 414-288-1902, E-mail: erin.fox@marquette.edu. *Dean,* Dr. Michael A. McKinney, 414-288-7472.

College of Business Administration Students: 126 full-time (53 women), 445 part-time (148 women); includes 54 minority (8 African Americans, 4 American Indian/Alaska Native, 35 Asian Americans or Pacific Islanders, 7 Hispanic Americans), 46 international. Average age 31. 451 applicants, 77% accepted, 258 enrolled. *Faculty:* 64 full-time (18 women), 27 part-time/adjunct (7 women). Expenses: Contact institution. *Financial support:* In 2006–07, 4 research assistantships, 13 teaching assistantships were awarded; Federal Work-Study, institutionally sponsored loans, scholarships/grants, and tuition waivers (full and partial) also available. Support available to part-time students. Financial award application deadline: 2/15. In 2006, 231 degrees awarded. *Degree program information:* Part-time and evening/weekend programs available. Offers accounting (MSA); business administration (MBA, MSA, MSAE, MSHR); business economics (MSAE); financial economics (MSAE); human resources (MSHR); international economics (MSAE). *Application fee:* $40. *Dean,* Dr. David Shrock, 414-288-7141, Fax: 414-288-1578.

College of Communication Students: 29 full-time (19 women), 23 part-time (11 women); includes 5 minority (1 African American, 3 Asian Americans or Pacific Islanders, 1 Hispanic American), 11 international. Average age 29. 119 applicants, 54% accepted, 29 enrolled. *Faculty:* 33 full-time (17 women), 43 part-time/adjunct (25 women). Expenses: Contact institution. *Financial support:* In 2006–07, 6 research assistantships, 12 teaching assistantships were awarded; career-related internships or fieldwork, Federal Work-Study, institutionally sponsored loans, scholarships/grants, and tuition waivers (full and partial) also available. Support available to part-time students. Financial award application deadline: 2/15. In 2006, 17 degrees awarded. *Degree program information:* Part-time and evening/weekend programs available. Offers advertising and public relations (MA); broadcasting and electronic communications (MA); communications studies (MA); journalism (MA); mass communications (MA); religious communications (MA); science, health and environmental communications (MA). *Application fee:* $40. *Dean,* Dr. Ana Garner, 414-288-3588, Fax: 414-288-1578.

College of Engineering Students: 124 full-time (36 women), 120 part-time (27 women); includes 17 minority (4 African Americans, 1 American Indian/Alaska Native, 5 Asian Americans or Pacific Islanders, 7 Hispanic Americans), 88 international. Average age 29. 331 applicants, 77% accepted, 98 enrolled. *Faculty:* 61 full-time (8 women), 17 part-time/adjunct (2 women). Expenses: Contact institution. *Financial support:* In 2006–07, 115 students received support, including 30 fellowships with tuition reimbursements available (averaging $16,866 per year), 53 research assistantships with tuition reimbursements available (averaging $14,861 per year), 32 teaching assistantships with tuition reimbursements available (averaging $13,790 per year); Federal Work-Study, institutionally sponsored loans, scholarships/grants, and tuition waivers (full and partial) also available. Support available to part-time students. Financial award application deadline: 2/15. In 2006, 66 master's, 8 doctorates awarded. *Degree program information:* Part-time and evening/weekend programs available. Offers bioinstrumentation/computers (MS, PhD); biomechanics/biomaterials (MS, PhD); computing (MS); construction and public works management (MS, PhD); electrical engineering (MS, PhD); engineering (MS, PhD); engineering management (MS); environmental/water resources engineering (MS, PhD); functional imaging (PhD); healthcare technologies management (MS); mechanical engineering (MS, PhD); structural/geotechnical engineering (MS, PhD); systems physiology (MS, PhD); transportation planning and engineering (MS, PhD). *Application deadline:* Applications are processed on a rolling basis. *Application fee:* $40. Electronic applications accepted. *Application Contact:* Craig Pierce, Director of Admissions, 414-288-7137, Fax: 414-288-1902, E-mail: mugs@vms.csd.mu.edu. *Dean,* Dr. Stan V. Jaskolski, 414-288-6591, Fax: 414-288-7082, E-mail: stan.jaskolski@marquette.edu.

College of Health Sciences Students: 148 full-time (121 women), 24 part-time (22 women); includes 19 minority (2 African Americans, 3 Asian Americans or Pacific Islanders, 14 Hispanic Americans), 1 international. Average age 25. *Faculty:* 27 full-time (16 women), 26 part-time/adjunct (16 women). Expenses: Contact institution. In 2006, 61 master's, 68 doctorates awarded. Offers health sciences (MS, DPT); physical therapy (DPT); physician assistant studies (MS); speech-language pathology (MS). *Dean,* Dr. Jack C. Brooks, 414-288-5053, E-mail: jack.brooks@mu.edu.

College of Nursing Students: 104 full-time (98 women), 122 part-time (114 women); includes 18 minority (5 African Americans, 2 American Indian/Alaska Native, 4 Asian Americans or Pacific Islanders, 7 Hispanic Americans), 2 international. Average age 34. 122 applicants, 79% accepted, 73 enrolled. *Faculty:* 29 full-time (27 women), 39 part-time/adjunct (37 women). Expenses: Contact institution. *Financial support:* In 2006–07, 6 research assistantships, 1 teaching assistantship were awarded; career-related internships or fieldwork, Federal Work-Study, institutionally sponsored loans, scholarships/grants, and tuition waivers (full and partial) also available. Support available to part-time students. Financial award application deadline: 2/15. In 2006, 46 degrees awarded. *Degree program information:* Part-time and evening/weekend programs available. Offers adult nurse practitioner (Certificate); advanced practice nursing (MSN); gerontological nurse practitioner (Certificate); neonatal nurse practitioner (Certificate); nurse-midwifery (Certificate); nursing (PhD); pediatric nurse practitioner (Certificate). *Application fee:* $40. *Application Contact:* Dr. Judy Miller, Director of Graduate Studies, 414-288-3810, Fax: 414-288-1578. *Dean,* Dr. Lea Acord, 414-288-3812, Fax: 414-288-1578.

School of Education Students: 81 full-time (64 women), 142 part-time (104 women); includes 14 minority (7 African Americans, 2 Asian Americans or Pacific Islanders, 5 Hispanic Americans), 5 international. Average age 37. 310 applicants, 59% accepted, 152 enrolled. *Faculty:* 20 full-time (12 women), 27 part-time/adjunct (14 women). Expenses: Contact institution. *Financial support:* In 2006–07, 5 research assistantships, 5 teaching assistantships were awarded; Federal Work-Study, institutionally sponsored loans, scholarships/grants, and tuition waivers (full and partial) also available. Support available to part-time students. Financial award application deadline: 2/15. In 2006, 47 master's, 6 doctorates awarded. *Degree program information:* Part-time programs available. Offers education (MA, Ed D, PhD, Spec). *Application fee:* $40. *Application Contact:* Dr. Joan Whipp, Assistant Dean, 414-288-1421, Fax: 414-288-5333. *Dean,* Dr. Bill Henk, 414-288-7376.

Law School Students: 499 full-time (200 women), 190 part-time (94 women); includes 63 minority (15 African Americans, 5 American Indian/Alaska Native, 19 Asian Americans or Pacific Islanders, 24 Hispanic Americans), 5 international. Average age 25. 1,908 applicants, 40% accepted, 222 enrolled. *Faculty:* 42 full-time (19 women), 71 part-time/adjunct (23 women). Expenses: Contact institution. *Financial support:* In 2006–07, 302 students received support. Career-related internships or fieldwork, Federal Work-Study, and scholarships/grants available. Support available to part-time students. Financial award application deadline: 3/1; financial award applicants required to submit FAFSA. In 2006, 201 degrees awarded. *Degree program information:* Part-time and evening/weekend programs available. Offers law (JD). *Application deadline:* For fall admission, 4/1 for domestic students. Applications are processed on a rolling basis. *Application fee:* $50. Electronic applications accepted. *Application Contact:* Sean Reilly, Assistant Dean for Admissions, 414-288-6767, Fax: 414-288-0676, E-mail: sean.reilly@marquette.edu. *Dean,* Joseph D. Kearney, 414-288-7090, Fax: 414-288-6403, E-mail: joseph.kearney@marquette.edu.

School of Dentistry Offers advanced training in general dentistry (MS); dental biomaterials (MS); dentistry (DDS, MS); endodontics (MS); orthodontics (MS); prosthodontics (MS).

MARSHALL UNIVERSITY, Huntington, WV 25755

General Information State-supported, coed, university. CGS member. *Enrollment:* 13,936 graduate, professional, and undergraduate students; 1,600 full-time matriculated graduate/professional students (993 women), 1,917 part-time matriculated graduate/professional students (1,416 women). *Enrollment by degree level:* 221 first professional, 3,070 master's, 158 doctoral, 68 other advanced degrees. *Graduate faculty:* 359 full-time (156 women), 147 part-time/adjunct (101 women). *Graduate housing:* Rooms and/or apartments available on a first-come, first-served basis to single and married students. Typical cost: $3,618 per year ($6,492 including board) for single students; $3,156 per year ($5,932 including board) for married students. *Student services:* Campus employment opportunities, campus safety program, career counseling, child daycare facilities, disabled student services, exercise/wellness program, free psychological counseling, grant writing training, international student services, low-cost health insurance, multicultural affairs office, teacher training, writing training. *Library facilities:* John Deaver Drinko Library plus 2 others. *Online resources:* library catalog, web page. *Collection:* 1.6 million titles, 22,591 serial subscriptions, 209,391 audiovisual materials. *Research affiliation:* Wyeth Ayerst Pharmaceutical (clinical pharmaceutical study), Dominion Power (field research), Greenbrier County Commission (field research), Kanawha Valley Local Port District (field research), Bayer Corporation (field research).

Computer facilities: 1,854 computers available on campus for general student use. A campuswide network can be accessed from student residence rooms and from off campus. Internet access and online class registration are available. *Web address:* http://www.marshall.edu/.

General Application Contact: Information Contact, 304-746-1900, Fax: 304-746-1902, E-mail: services@marshall.edu.

GRADUATE UNITS

Academic Affairs Division Students: 1,600 full-time (993 women), 1,917 part-time (1,416 women); includes 136 minority (91 African Americans, 14 American Indian/Alaska Native, 17 Asian Americans or Pacific Islanders, 14 Hispanic Americans), 157 international. Average age 33. *Faculty:* 359 full-time (156 women), 147 part-time/adjunct (101 women). Expenses: Contact institution. *Financial support:* Fellowships, research assistantships, teaching assistantships, career-related internships or fieldwork, Federal Work-Study, tuition waivers (full and partial), and unspecified assistantships available. Support available to part-time students. In 2006, 821 master's, 9 doctorates, 29 other advanced degrees awarded. *Degree program information:* Part-time and evening/weekend programs available. Offers forensic science (MS). *Application deadline:* Applications are processed on a rolling basis. *Application fee:* $40 ($100 for international students). *Application Contact:* Information Contact, 304-746-1900, Fax: 304-746-1902, E-mail: services@marshall.edu. *Provost and Senior Vice President for Academic Affairs,* Dr. Sarah Denman, 304-696-5442, E-mail: denmans@marshall.edu.

College of Education and Human Services Students: 602 full-time (433 women), 1,304 part-time (1,038 women); includes 92 minority (69 African Americans, 6 American Indian/Alaska Native, 7 Asian Americans or Pacific Islanders, 10 Hispanic Americans), 66 international. Average age 35. *Faculty:* 33 full-time (18 women), 7 part-time/adjunct (4 women). Expenses: Contact institution. *Financial support:* Career-related internships or fieldwork, Federal Work-Study, tuition waivers (full and partial), and unspecified assistantships available. Support available to part-time students. In 2006, 462 master's, 9 doctorates, 29 other advanced degrees awarded. *Degree program information:* Evening/weekend programs available. Offers adult and technical education (MS); counseling (MA, Ed S); early childhood education (MA); education (MAT); education and human services (MA, MAT, MS, Ed D, Ed S); education and professional development (MA, Ed D, Ed S); elementary education (MA); exercise science (MS); exercise science, sports and recreation (MS); family and consumer sciences (MA); human development and allied technology (MA, MS); leadership studies (MA, Ed D, Ed S); reading education (MA, Ed S); school psychology (Ed S); secondary education (MA); special education (MA); sport administration (MS). *Application deadline:* Applications are processed on a rolling basis. *Application fee:* $40 ($100 for international students). *Application Contact:* Information Contact, 304-746-1900, Fax: 304-746-1902, E-mail: services@marshall.edu. *Executive Dean,* Dr. Rosalyn Anstine Templeton, 304-696-3131, E-mail: templetonr@marshall.edu.

College of Fine Arts Students: 16 full-time (9 women), 17 part-time (12 women); includes 1 minority (African American), 2 international. Average age 31. *Faculty:* 26 full-time (10 women), 2 part-time/adjunct (1 woman). Expenses: Contact institution. In 2006, 12 degrees awarded. *Degree program information:* Evening/weekend programs available. Offers art (MA); fine arts (MA); music (MA). *Application fee:* $40. *Application Contact:* Information Contact, 304-746-1900, Fax: 304-746-1902, E-mail: services@marshall.edu. *Dean,* Dr. Donald Van Horn, 304-696-2964, E-mail: vanhorn@marshall.edu.

College of Health Professions Students: 64 full-time (62 women), 103 part-time (100 women). Average age 33. *Faculty:* 28 full-time (27 women), 2 part-time/adjunct (1 woman). Expenses: Contact institution. In 2006, 50 degrees awarded. Offers communication disorders (MA); dietetics (MS); health professions (MA, MS, MSN); nursing (MSN). *Application fee:* $40. *Application Contact:* Information Contact, 304-746-1900, Fax: 304-746-1902, E-mail: services@marshall.edu. *Dean,* Dr. Shortie McKinney, 304-696-5270, E-mail: mckinnes@marshall.edu.

College of Information, Technology and Engineering Students: 38 full-time (11 women), 110 part-time (25 women); includes 6 minority (4 African Americans, 1 American Indian/Alaska Native, 1 Asian American or Pacific Islander), 14 international. Average age 33. *Faculty:* 20 full-time (2 women), 1 part-time/adjunct (0 women). Expenses: Contact institution. *Financial support:* Fellowships, tuition waivers (full) available. Support available to part-time students. Financial award application deadline: 8/1; financial award applicants required to submit FAFSA. In 2006, 60 degrees awarded. *Degree program information:* Part-time and evening/weekend programs available. Offers engineering and computer science (MSE); environmental science (MS); environmental science and safety technology (MS); information systems (MS); information systems and technology management (MS); information, technology and engineering (MS, MSE); safety (MS); technology management (MS). *Application fee:* $40. *Application Contact:* Information Contact, 304-746-1900, Fax: 304-746-1902, E-mail: services@marshall.edu. *Interim Dean,* Dr. Tony Szwilski, 304-696-5457, E-mail: szwilski@marshall.edu.

College of Liberal Arts Students: 242 full-time (150 women), 91 part-time (57 women); includes 16 minority (8 African Americans, 3 American Indian/Alaska Native, 3 Asian Americans or Pacific Islanders, 2 Hispanic Americans), 20 international. Average age 29. *Faculty:* 107 full-time (46 women), 7 part-time/adjunct (5 women). Expenses: Contact institution. *Financial support:* Fellowships, teaching assistantships with tuition reimbursements available. In 2006, 91 degrees awarded. *Degree program information:* Evening/weekend programs available. Offers clinical psychology (MA); communication studies (MA); criminal justice (MS); English (MA); general psychology (MA); geography (MA, MS); history (MA); humanities (MA); industrial and organizational psychology (MA); liberal arts (MA, MS, Psy D); political science (MA); psychology (Psy D); sociology and anthropology (MA). *Application fee:* $40. *Application Contact:* Information Contact, 304-746-1900, Fax: 304-746-1902, E-mail: services@marshall.edu. *Dean,* Dr. Christina Murphy, 304-696-2731, E-mail: murphyc@marshall.edu.

College of Science Students: 73 full-time (29 women), 17 part-time (7 women); includes 10 minority (3 African Americans, 2 American Indian/Alaska Native, 4 Asian Americans or Pacific Islanders, 1 Hispanic American), 17 international. Average age 27. *Faculty:* 47 full-time (14 women), 2 part-time/adjunct (1 woman). Expenses: Contact institution. *Financial support:* Career-related internships or fieldwork available. In 2006, 28 degrees awarded. Offers biological science (MA, MS); chemistry (MS); mathematics (MA, MS); physical science (MS); science (MA, MS). *Application fee:* $40. *Application Contact:* Information Contact, 304-746-1900, Fax: 304-746-1902, E-mail: services@marshall.edu. *Dean,* Dr. Andrew Rogerson, 304-696-3518, E-mail: rogersona@marshall.edu.

Lewis College of Business Students: 155 full-time (93 women), 70 part-time (35 women); includes 10 minority (5 African Americans, 2 American Indian/Alaska Native, 2 Asian Americans or Pacific Islanders, 1 Hispanic American), 35 international. Average age 29. *Faculty:* 48 full-time (14 women), 2 part-time/adjunct (0 women). Expenses: Contact institution. *Financial support:* Career-related internships or fieldwork and tuition waivers (full) available. Support available to part-time students. Financial award applicants required to submit FAFSA. In 2006, 108 degrees awarded. *Degree program information:* Part-time and evening/weekend programs available. Offers business (MBA, MS); business administration (MBA); health care administration (MS); human resource management (MS); management (MBA, MS). *Application deadline:* Applications are processed on a rolling basis. *Application fee:* $40. *Application Contact:* Information Contact, 304-746-1900, Fax: 304-746-1902, E-mail: services@marshall.edu. *Dean*, Dr. Paul Uselding, 304-696-3319, Fax: 304-696-4344, E-mail: uselding@marshall.edu.

School of Journalism and Mass Communications Students: 14 full-time (10 women), 1 part-time; includes 1 minority (African American), 3 international. Average age 25. *Faculty:* 8 full-time (4 women). Expenses: Contact institution. In 2006, 10 degrees awarded. Offers journalism and mass communications (MAJ). *Application fee:* $40. *Application Contact:* Information Contact, 304-746-1900, Fax: 304-746-1902, E-mail: services@marshall.edu. *Dean*, Dr. Corley F. Dennison, 304-696-2809, E-mail: dennisoc@marshall.edu.

Joan C. Edwards School of Medicine Students: 266 full-time (115 women), 2 part-time (1 woman); includes 34 minority (8 African Americans, 1 American Indian/Alaska Native, 23 Asian Americans or Pacific Islanders, 2 Hispanic Americans), 8 international. Average age 26. 1,620 applicants, 9% accepted, 80 enrolled. *Faculty:* 194 full-time (55 women), 40 part-time/adjunct (15 women). Expenses: Contact institution. *Financial support:* In 2006–07, 220 students received support, including 26 research assistantships with tuition reimbursements available (averaging $21,700 per year); career-related internships or fieldwork, Federal Work-Study, institutionally sponsored loans, scholarships/grants, and unspecified assistantships also available. Support available to part-time students. Financial award application deadline: 5/1; financial award applicants required to submit FAFSA. In 2006, 42 MDs, 5 doctorates awarded. Offers biomedical sciences (MS, PhD); medicine (MD, MS, PhD). *Application deadline:* For fall admission, 12/1 for domestic students. Applications are processed on a rolling basis. *Application Contact:* Cynthia A. Warren, Assistant Dean for Admissions and Student Affairs, 304-691-1738, Fax: 304-691-1744, E-mail: warren@marshall.edu. *Dean and Vice President*, Dr. Charles H. McKown, 304-691-1700, Fax: 304-691-1726.

See Close-Up on page 955.

MARS HILL GRADUATE SCHOOL, Bothell, WA 98021

General Information Independent-religious, coed, graduate-only institution.

GRADUATE UNITS

Graduate Programs

MARTIN UNIVERSITY, Indianapolis, IN 46218-3867

General Information Independent, coed, comprehensive institution. *Graduate housing:* On-campus housing not available.

GRADUATE UNITS

Division of Psychology *Degree program information:* Part-time and evening/weekend programs available. Offers community psychology (MS).

Graduate School of Urban Ministry *Degree program information:* Part-time and evening/weekend programs available. Offers urban ministry studies (MA).

MARY BALDWIN COLLEGE, Staunton, VA 24401-3610

General Information Independent, coed, primarily women, comprehensive institution. *Enrollment:* 1,755 graduate, professional, and undergraduate students; 104 full-time matriculated graduate/professional students (76 women), 101 part-time matriculated graduate/professional students (85 women). *Enrollment by degree level:* 205 master's. *Graduate faculty:* 5 full-time (3 women), 38 part-time/adjunct (20 women). *Graduate housing:* On-campus housing not available. *Student services:* Campus employment opportunities, campus safety program, career counseling, disabled student services, international student services, low-cost health insurance, multicultural affairs office, teacher training, writing training. *Library facilities:* Grafton Library. *Online resources:* library catalog, web page, access to other libraries' catalogs. *Collection:* 152,862 titles, 17,715 serial subscriptions, 6,991 audiovisual materials.

Computer facilities: 227 computers available on campus for general student use. A campuswide network can be accessed from student residence rooms and from off campus. Internet access and online class registration are available. *Web address:* http://www.mbc.edu/.

General Application Contact: Lisa Branson, Executive Director of Admissions and Financial Aid, 540-887-7260, E-mail: lbranson@mbc.edu.

GRADUATE UNITS

Graduate Studies Average age 30. Expenses: Contact institution. *Financial support:* In 2006–07, 148 students received support, including 4 research assistantships with partial tuition reimbursements available; career-related internships or fieldwork and scholarships/grants also available. Support available to part-time students. Financial award application deadline: 5/15; financial award applicants required to submit FAFSA. In 2006, 69 degrees awarded. *Degree program information:* Part-time and evening/weekend programs available. Postbaccalaureate distance learning degree programs offered (minimal on-campus study). Offers acting (M Litt); directing (M Litt); elementary education (MAT); middle grades education (MAT); Shakespeare and Renaissance literature in performance (M Litt, MFA); teaching (M Litt, MAT). *Application deadline:* Applications are processed on a rolling basis. *Application fee:* $35. *Application Contact:* Dr. Julie Fox, Assistant Director of Operations, 540-887-7237, E-mail: jfox@mbc.edu.

MARYGROVE COLLEGE, Detroit, MI 48221-2599

General Information Independent-religious, coed, primarily women, comprehensive institution. *Graduate housing:* Room and/or apartments available to single students; on-campus housing not available to married students.

GRADUATE UNITS

Graduate Division *Degree program information:* Part-time and evening/weekend programs available. Postbaccalaureate distance learning degree programs offered (no on-campus study). Offers educational leadership (MA); modern language translation (MA); pastoral ministry (MA); social justice (MA). Electronic applications accepted.

Education Unit *Degree program information:* Part-time and evening/weekend programs available. Postbaccalaureate distance learning degree programs offered (no on-campus study). Offers adult learning (MA); art of teaching (MAT); griot (M Ed); reading education (M Ed); sage (M Ed).

Human Resource Management Unit Offers human resource management (MA).

MARYLAND INSTITUTE COLLEGE OF ART, Baltimore, MD 21217

General Information Independent, coed, comprehensive institution. *Enrollment:* 1,866 graduate, professional, and undergraduate students; 146 full-time matriculated graduate/professional students (90 women), 80 part-time matriculated graduate/professional students (62 women). *Enrollment by degree level:* 207 master's, 19 other advanced degrees. *Graduate faculty:* 21 full-time (13 women), 20 part-time/adjunct (14 women). *Tuition:* Full-time $27,840; part-time $1,160 per credit. *Required fees:* $830; $415 per term. *Graduate housing:* Room and/or apartments available on a first-come, first-served basis to single students; on-campus housing not available to married students. Typical cost: $5,625 per year ($7,685 including board). Housing application deadline: 5/1. *Student services:* Campus employment opportunities, campus safety program, career counseling, disabled student services, exercise/wellness program, free psychological counseling, grant writing training, international student services, low-cost health insurance, multicultural affairs office, teacher training, writing training. *Library facilities:* Decker Library plus 1 other. *Online resources:* library catalog, web page, access to other libraries' catalogs. *Collection:* 76,500 titles, 315 serial subscriptions, 4,800 audiovisual materials.

Computer facilities: 305 computers available on campus for general student use. A campuswide network can be accessed from student residence rooms and from off campus. Internet access, e-mail, campus Portal, online gallery space, network storage space, personal websites are available. *Web address:* http://www.mica.edu/.

General Application Contact: Scott G. Kelly, Associate Dean of Graduate Admission, 410-225-2256, Fax: 410-225-2408, E-mail: graduate@mica.edu.

GRADUATE UNITS

Graduate Studies Students: 146 full-time (90 women), 80 part-time (62 women); includes 35 minority (11 African Americans, 2 American Indian/Alaska Native, 12 Asian Americans or Pacific Islanders, 10 Hispanic Americans), 14 international. Average age 29. *Faculty:* 21 full-time (13 women), 20 part-time/adjunct (14 women). Expenses: Contact institution. *Financial support:* In 2006–07, 209 students received support, including 14 fellowships (averaging $13,920 per year), 76 teaching assistantships (averaging $1,800 per year); career-related internships or fieldwork and scholarships/grants also available. Financial award application deadline: 3/1; financial award applicants required to submit FAFSA. In 2006, 100 master's, 24 other advanced degrees awarded. *Degree program information:* Part-time programs available. Offers art education (MA, MAT); community arts (MA); digital arts (MA); fine arts (Certificate); graphic design (MFA); photography (MFA); studio art (MFA). *Application deadline:* For fall admission, 2/15 for domestic and international students. *Application fee:* $50. *Application Contact:* Scott G. Kelly, Associate Dean of Graduate Admission, 410-225-2256, Fax: 410-225-2408, E-mail: graduate@mica.edu. *Dean*, Dr. Leslie King-Hammond, 410-225-2534, Fax: 410-225-2408, E-mail: graduate@mica.edu.

Hoffberger School of Painting Students: 14 full-time (4 women); includes 3 minority (1 African American, 2 Hispanic Americans). Average age 28. *Faculty:* 1 (woman) full-time, 1 part-time/adjunct (0 women). Expenses: Contact institution. *Financial support:* In 2006–07, 14 students received support, including fellowships (averaging $13,920 per year), teaching assistantships (averaging $1,800 per year); career-related internships or fieldwork and scholarships/grants also available. Financial award application deadline: 3/1; financial award applicants required to submit FAFSA. In 2006, 6 degrees awarded. Offers painting (MFA). *Application deadline:* For fall admission, 2/15 for domestic and international students. *Application fee:* $50. *Application Contact:* Scott G. Kelly, Associate Dean of Graduate Admission, 410-225-2256, Fax: 410-225-2408, E-mail: graduate@mica.edu. *Director*, Grace Hartigan, 410-225-2534, Fax: 410-225-2408, E-mail: graduate@mica.edu.

Mount Royal Graduate School of Art Students: 27 full-time (17 women); includes 3 minority (1 African American, 1 Asian American or Pacific Islander, 1 Hispanic American), 3 international. Average age 28. *Faculty:* 1 (woman) full-time, 3 part-time/adjunct (1 woman). Expenses: Contact institution. *Financial support:* In 2006–07, 27 students received support, including 2 fellowships (averaging $13,920 per year), 25 teaching assistantships (averaging $1,800 per year); career-related internships or fieldwork and scholarships/grants also available. Financial award application deadline: 3/1; financial award applicants required to submit FAFSA. In 2006, 12 degrees awarded. Offers painting (MFA). *Application deadline:* For fall admission, 2/15 for domestic and international students. *Application fee:* $50. *Application Contact:* Scott G. Kelly, Associate Dean of Graduate Admission, 410-225-2256, Fax: 410-225-2408, E-mail: graduate@mica.edu. *Director*, Frances Barth, 410-225-2534, Fax: 410-225-2408, E-mail: graduate@mica.edu.

Rinehart Graduate School of Sculpture Students: 10 full-time (4 women); includes 1 minority (Hispanic American) Average age 28. *Faculty:* 2 full-time (1 woman). Expenses: Contact institution. *Financial support:* In 2006–07, 10 students received support, including 2 fellowships (averaging $13,920 per year), 8 teaching assistantships (averaging $1,800 per year); career-related internships or fieldwork and scholarships/grants also available. Financial award application deadline: 3/1; financial award applicants required to submit FAFSA. In 2006, 6 degrees awarded. Offers sculpture (MFA). *Application deadline:* For fall admission, 2/15 for domestic and international students. *Application fee:* $50. *Application Contact:* Scott G. Kelly, Associate Dean of Graduate Admission, 410-225-2256, Fax: 410-225-2408, E-mail: graduate@mica.edu. *Director*, Maren Hassinger, 410-225-2271, Fax: 410-225-2408.

MARYLHURST UNIVERSITY, Marylhurst, OR 97036-0261

General Information Independent-religious, coed, comprehensive institution. *Enrollment:* 1,249 graduate, professional, and undergraduate students; 86 full-time matriculated graduate/professional students (70 women), 306 part-time matriculated graduate/professional students (185 women). *Enrollment by degree level:* 31 first professional, 361 master's. *Graduate faculty:* 6 full-time (2 women), 36 part-time/adjunct (14 women). *Tuition:* Part-time $395 per credit. *Required fees:* $8 per credit. *Graduate housing:* On-campus housing not available. *Student services:* Career counseling, disabled student services, international student services, low-cost health insurance, writing training. *Library facilities:* Shoen Library. *Online resources:* library catalog, web page, access to other libraries' catalogs.

Computer facilities: 40 computers available on campus for general student use. A campuswide network can be accessed. Internet access and online class registration are available. *Web address:* http://www.marylhurst.edu/.

General Application Contact: Information Contact, 503-636-8141 Ext. 6268, Fax: 503-635-6585, E-mail: admissions@marylhurst.edu.

GRADUATE UNITS

Department of Art Therapy Counseling Students: 47 full-time (43 women), 7 part-time (all women). Average age 32. *Faculty:* 2 full-time (both women), 7 part-time/adjunct (6 women). Expenses: Contact institution. *Financial support:* Federal Work-Study and scholarships/grants available. Support available to part-time students. Financial award applicants required to submit FAFSA. In 2006, 19 degrees awarded. *Degree program information:* Part-time and evening/weekend programs available. Offers art therapy (PGC); art therapy counseling (MA); counseling (PGC). *Application deadline:* For fall admission, 2/15 priority date for domestic and international students. Applications are processed on a rolling basis. *Application fee:* $40 ($50 for international students). *Application Contact:* Kathleen Schneff, Admissions Specialist, 800-634-9982 Ext. 3322, Fax: 503-635-6585, E-mail: admissions@marylhurst.edu. *Chairperson*, Christine Turner, 503-699-6244 Ext. 3381, Fax: 503-636-1957, E-mail: cturner@marylhurst.edu.

Department of Business Administration Students: 14 full-time (8 women), 215 part-time (107 women); includes 13 minority (3 African Americans, 1 American Indian/Alaska Native, 7 Asian Americans or Pacific Islanders, 2 Hispanic Americans), 11 international. Average age 37. *Faculty:* 2 full-time (0 women), 18 part-time/adjunct (6 women). Expenses: Contact institution. *Financial support:* Federal Work-Study and scholarships/grants available. Support available to part-time students. Financial award applicants required to submit FAFSA. In 2006, 69 degrees awarded. *Degree program information:* Part-time and evening/weekend programs available. Postbaccalaureate distance learning degree programs offered (no on-campus study). Offers business administration (MBA). *Application deadline:* Applications are processed on a rolling basis. *Application fee:* $40 ($50 for international students). Electronic applications accepted. *Application Contact:* Kathleen Schneff, Admissions Specialist, 800-634-9982 Ext. 3322, Fax: 503-635-6585, E-mail: admissions@marylhurst.edu. *Director of Business Programming*, Bob Hanks, 503-675-3961, Fax: 503-697-5597, E-mail: mba@marylhurst.edu.

Department of Interdisciplinary Studies Students: 3 full-time (2 women), 43 part-time (36 women); includes 2 minority (1 Asian American or Pacific Islander, 1 Hispanic American), 1 international. Average age 46. *Faculty:* 2 full-time (both women), 4 part-time/adjunct (0 women). Expenses: Contact institution. *Financial support:* Federal Work-Study and scholarships/grants available. Support available to part-time students. Financial award applicants required to submit FAFSA. In 2006, 21 degrees awarded. *Degree program information:* Part-time and evening/weekend programs available. Offers interdisciplinary studies (MA). *Application deadline:* Applications are processed on a rolling basis. *Application fee:* $40 ($50 for international students). Electronic applications accepted. *Application Contact:* Kathleen Schneff, Admissions Specialist, 800-634-9982 Ext. 3322, Fax: 503-635-6585, E-mail: admissions@marylhurst.edu. *Chair*, Dr. Debrah B. Bokowski, 503-636-8141 Ext. 3338, Fax: 503-697-5597, E-mail: dbokowski@marylhurst.edu.

Department of Religious StudiesûApplied Theology Program Students: 4 full-time (2 women), 28 part-time (25 women); includes 2 minority (1 Asian American or Pacific Islander, 1 Hispanic American). Average age 47. *Faculty:* 1 full-time (0 women), 7 part-time/adjunct (4 women). Expenses: Contact institution. *Financial support:* Fellowships, research assistantships, teaching assistantships, Federal Work-Study and scholarships/grants available. Sup-

Marylhurst University (continued)

port available to part-time students. Financial award applicants required to submit FAFSA. In 2006, 7 degrees awarded. *Degree program information:* Part-time and evening/weekend programs available. Offers applied theology (MAAT). *Application deadline:* For fall admission, 6/30 priority date for domestic students; for winter admission, 11/30 priority date for domestic students; for spring admission, 3/30 priority date for domestic students. Applications are processed on a rolling basis. *Application fee:* $40 ($50 for international students). Electronic applications accepted. *Application Contact:* Kathleen Schneff, Admissions Specialist, 800-634-9982 Ext. 3322, Fax: 503-635-6585, E-mail: admissions@marylhurst.edu. *Chair,* Dr. Jerry Roussell, 503-699-6305, Fax: 503-697-5597, E-mail: jroussell@marylhurst.edu.

Department of Religious StudiesûDivinity Program Students: 18 full-time (15 women), 13 part-time (10 women). Average age 47. *Faculty:* 1 full-time (0 women), 7 part-time/adjunct (4 women). Expenses: Contact institution. *Financial support:* Fellowships, research assistantships, teaching assistantships, Federal Work-Study and scholarships/grants available. Support available to part-time students. In 2006, 2 degrees awarded. *Degree program information:* Part-time and evening/weekend programs available. Offers divinity (M Div). *Application deadline:* For fall admission, 6/30 for domestic students; for winter admission, 11/30 for domestic students; for spring admission, 3/30 for domestic students. Applications are processed on a rolling basis. *Application fee:* $40 ($50 for international students). Electronic applications accepted. *Application Contact:* Kathleen Schneff, Admissions Specialist, 800-634-9982 Ext. 3322, Fax: 503-635-6585, E-mail: admissions@marylhurst.edu. *Chair,* Dr. Jerry Roussell, 503-699-6305, Fax: 503-697-5597, E-mail: jroussell@marylhurst.edu.

MARYMOUNT UNIVERSITY, Arlington, VA 22207-4299

General Information Independent-religious, coed, comprehensive institution. *Enrollment:* 3,604 graduate, professional, and undergraduate students; 437 full-time matriculated graduate/professional students (355 women), 861 part-time matriculated graduate/professional students (617 women). *Enrollment by degree level:* 1,020 master's, 127 doctoral, 91 other advanced degrees. *Graduate faculty:* 69 full-time (48 women), 62 part-time/adjunct (33 women). *Tuition:* Full-time $11,160; part-time $620 per credit. *Required fees:* $113; $630 per credit. *Graduate housing:* On-campus housing not available. *Student services:* Campus employment opportunities, campus safety program, career counseling, disabled student services, free psychological counseling, international student services, low-cost health insurance, teacher training. *Library facilities:* Emerson C. Reinsch Library plus 1 other. *Online resources:* library catalog, web page, access to other libraries' catalogs. *Collection:* 187,097 titles, 1,048 serial subscriptions.

Computer facilities: Computer purchase and lease plans are available. 177 computers available on campus for general student use. A campuswide network can be accessed from off campus. Internet access and online class registration are available. *Web address:* http://www.marymount.edu/.

General Application Contact: Francesca Reed, Coordinator, Graduate Admissions, 703-284-5901, Fax: 703-527-3815, E-mail: grad.admissions@marymount.edu.

GRADUATE UNITS

Corporate Outreach Program Average age 38. 16 applicants, 100% accepted, 13 enrolled. *Faculty:* 1 (woman) part-time/adjunct. Expenses: Contact institution. In 2006, 14 degrees awarded. *Degree program information:* Part-time and evening/weekend programs available. *Application deadline:* Applications are processed on a rolling basis. *Application fee:* $40. Electronic applications accepted. *Director,* Dr. Stuart Werner, 703-284-5962, E-mail: stuart.werner@marymount.edu.

School of Arts and Sciences Students: 33 full-time (29 women), 63 part-time (52 women); includes 24 minority (17 African Americans, 1 American Indian/Alaska Native, 5 Asian Americans or Pacific Islanders, 1 Hispanic American), 9 international. Average age 31. 61 applicants, 98% accepted, 29 enrolled. *Faculty:* 10 full-time (8 women), 2 part-time/adjunct (0 women). Expenses: Contact institution. *Financial support:* Research assistantships with full and partial tuition reimbursements, career-related internships or fieldwork, scholarships/grants, and unspecified assistantships available. Support available to part-time students. Financial award applicants required to submit FAFSA. In 2006, 37 degrees awarded. *Degree program information:* Part-time and evening/weekend programs available. Offers arts and sciences (MA, MS, Certificate); computer science (MS, Certificate); computer security and information assurance (Certificate); forensic computing (Certificate); humanities (MA); humanities: teaching licensure in secondary English (MA); interior design (MA); literature and languages (MA). *Application deadline:* Applications are processed on a rolling basis. *Application fee:* $40. Electronic applications accepted. *Dean,* Dr. Teresa Reed, 703-284-1560, Fax: 703-284-3859, E-mail: teresa.reed@marymount.edu.

School of Business Administration Students: 75 full-time (42 women), 306 part-time (167 women); includes 132 minority (79 African Americans, 2 American Indian/Alaska Native, 24 Asian Americans or Pacific Islanders, 27 Hispanic Americans), 43 international. Average age 32. 156 applicants, 96% accepted, 78 enrolled. *Faculty:* 23 full-time (12 women), 12 part-time/adjunct (4 women). Expenses: Contact institution. *Financial support:* Research assistantships with full tuition reimbursements, career-related internships or fieldwork, scholarships/grants, and unspecified assistantships available. Support available to part-time students. Financial award applicants required to submit FAFSA. In 2006, 160 master's, 16 other advanced degrees awarded. *Degree program information:* Part-time and evening/weekend programs available. Offers advanced leadership (Certificate); business administration (MA, MBA, MS, Certificate); health care informatics (Certificate); health care management (MS); human resource management (MA, Certificate); information systems (MS, Certificate); information systems program management (Certificate); instructional design (Certificate); leading and managing change (Certificate); legal administration (MA); management (MS); management studies (Certificate); organization development (Certificate); paralegal studies (Certificate); project management (Certificate). *Application deadline:* Applications are processed on a rolling basis. *Application fee:* $40. Electronic applications accepted. *Dean,* James Ryerson, 703-284-5965, Fax: 703-527-3830, E-mail: james.ryerson@marymount.edu.

School of Education and Human Services Students: 256 full-time (222 women), 276 part-time (234 women); includes 80 minority (40 African Americans, 5 American Indian/Alaska Native, 18 Asian Americans or Pacific Islanders, 17 Hispanic Americans), 9 international. Average age 31. 376 applicants, 71% accepted, 164 enrolled. *Faculty:* 21 full-time (15 women), 18 part-time/adjunct (10 women). Expenses: Contact institution. *Financial support:* Research assistantships with full tuition reimbursements, career-related internships or fieldwork, scholarships/grants, and unspecified assistantships available. Support available to part-time students. Financial award applicants required to submit FAFSA. In 2006, 248 master's, 4 other advanced degrees awarded. *Degree program information:* Part-time and evening/weekend programs available. Postbaccalaureate distance learning degree programs offered (minimal on-campus study). Offers alternative teacher licensure (Certificate); Catholic school leadership (M Ed, Certificate); community counseling (MA, Certificate); community counseling and forensic psychology); education and human services (M Ed, MA, Certificate); elementary education (M Ed); English as a second language (M Ed); forensic psychology); learning disabilities (M Ed); pastoral and spiritual care (MA); pastoral counseling (MA, Certificate); professional studies (M Ed); school counseling (MA); secondary education (M Ed). *Application deadline:* Applications are processed on a rolling basis. *Application fee:* $40. Electronic applications accepted. *Dean,* Dr. Wayne Lesko, 703-284-1620, Fax: 703-284-1631, E-mail: wayne.lesko@marymount.edu.

School of Health Professions Students: 64 full-time (55 women), 130 part-time (101 women); includes 56 minority (30 African Americans, 18 Asian Americans or Pacific Islanders, 8 Hispanic Americans), 5 international. Average age 34. 130 applicants, 95% accepted, 78 enrolled. *Faculty:* 15 full-time (13 women), 6 part-time/adjunct (4 women). Expenses: Contact institution. *Financial support:* Research assistantships with full and partial tuition reimbursements, career-related internships or fieldwork, scholarships/grants, and unspecified assistantships available. Support available to part-time students. Financial award applicants required to submit FAFSA. In 2006, 21 master's, 16 doctorates, 2 other advanced degrees awarded. *Degree program information:* Part-time and evening/weekend programs available. Offers family nurse practitioner (MSN, Certificate); health professions (MS, MSN, DPT, Certificate); health promotion management (MS); nursing administration (MSN, Certificate); nursing education (MSN, Certificate); physical therapy (DPT); RN to MSN (MSN). *Application deadline:* Applications are processed on a rolling basis. *Application fee:* $40. Electronic applications accepted. *Dean,* Dr. Tess Cappello, 703-284-1580, Fax: 703-284-3819, E-mail: tess.cappello@marymount.edu.

MARYVILLE UNIVERSITY OF SAINT LOUIS, St. Louis, MO 63141-7299

General Information Independent, coed, comprehensive institution. *Enrollment:* 3,333 graduate, professional, and undergraduate students; 140 full-time matriculated graduate/professional students (108 women), 445 part-time matriculated graduate/professional students (329 women). *Enrollment by degree level:* 500 master's, 85 doctoral. *Graduate faculty:* 84 full-time (55 women), 36 part-time/adjunct (23 women). *Tuition:* Full-time $17,800; part-time $555 per credit. *Required fees:* $55 per semester. Tuition and fees vary according to degree level and program. *Graduate housing:* Room and/or apartments available on a first-come, first-served basis to single students; on-campus housing not available to married students. *Student services:* Campus employment opportunities, campus safety program, career counseling, disabled student services, exercise/wellness program, free psychological counseling, international student services, low-cost health insurance, multicultural affairs office, teacher training, writing training. *Library facilities:* Maryville University Library. *Online resources:* library catalog, web page, access to other libraries' catalogs. *Collection:* 213,053 titles, 14,110 serial subscriptions. *Research affiliation:* Monsanto Fund (early childhood, science, mathematics curriculum development and teacher enrichment), Southwestern Bell Foundation (secondary education curriculum and teacher education).

Computer facilities: 401 computers available on campus for general student use. A campuswide network can be accessed from student residence rooms and from off campus. Internet access, e-mail, specialized software, university catalog, schedules, wireless internet in some areas are available. *Web address:* http://www.maryville.edu/.

General Application Contact: Kelli Anderson, Research Analyst, 314-529-9324, Fax: 314-529-9900, E-mail: kanderson@maryville.edu.

GRADUATE UNITS

The John E. Simon School of Business Students: 34 full-time (23 women), 162 part-time (101 women); includes 9 African Americans, 8 Asian Americans or Pacific Islanders, 2 international. Average age 31. 56 applicants, 96% accepted, 38 enrolled. Expenses: Contact institution. *Financial support:* Career-related internships or fieldwork, Federal Work-Study, tuition waivers (partial), and campus employment available. Financial award application deadline: 7/31; financial award applicants required to submit FAFSA. In 2006, 89 degrees awarded. *Degree program information:* Part-time and evening/weekend programs available. Offers accounting (MBA, PGC); business studies (PGC); e-business (MBA, PGC); management (MBA, PGC); marketing (MBA, PGC). *Application deadline:* Applications are processed on a rolling basis. *Application fee:* $35 ($50 for international students). Electronic applications accepted. *Application Contact:* Kathy Dougherty, Director of MBA Admissions and Enrollment, 314-529-9382, Fax: 314-529-9975, E-mail: business@marville.edu. *Dean,* Dr. Pamela Horwitz, 314-529-9418, Fax: 314-529-9975, E-mail: horwitz@maryville.edu.

School of Education Students: 17 full-time (14 women), 168 part-time (129 women); includes 20 African Americans, 2 Asian Americans or Pacific Islanders, 1 Hispanic American, 2 international. Average age 37. 39 applicants, 95% accepted, 24 enrolled. Expenses: Contact institution. *Financial support:* Career-related internships or fieldwork, Federal Work-Study, tuition waivers (partial), and professional educator discounts available. Financial award application deadline: 7/31; financial award applicants required to submit FAFSA. In 2006, 37 degrees awarded. *Degree program information:* Part-time and evening/weekend programs available. Offers art education (MA Ed); early childhood education (MA Ed); education (Ed D); elementary education (MA Ed); elementary education/English (MA Ed); environmental education (MA Ed); gifted education (MA Ed); middle grades education (MA Ed); reading specialist (MA Ed); secondary education (MA Ed). *Application deadline:* Applications are processed on a rolling basis. *Application fee:* $35 ($50 for international students). Electronic applications accepted. *Application Contact:* Dr. Lillian Curtis, Graduate Admissions Coordinator, 314-529-9542, Fax: 314-529-9921, E-mail: teachered@maryville.edu. *Dean,* Dr. Sam Hausfather, 314-529-9466, Fax: 314-529-9921, E-mail: shausfather@maryville.edu.

School of Health Professions *Faculty:* 17 full-time (14 women), 11 part-time/adjunct (6 women). Expenses: Contact institution. *Financial support:* Career-related internships or fieldwork, Federal Work-Study, and campus employment available. Financial award application deadline: 7/31. *Degree program information:* Part-time and evening/weekend programs available. Offers health professions (MARC, MMT, MOT, MSN, DPT); music therapy (MMT); nursing (MSN); occupational therapy (MOT); physical therapy (DPT); rehabilitation counseling (MARC). *Application deadline:* Applications are processed on a rolling basis. *Application fee:* $35 ($50 for international students). Electronic applications accepted. *Application Contact:* School of Health Professions—Graduate Programs, 314-529-9523, Fax: 314-529-9139, E-mail: hlthprofessions@maryville.edu. *Dean,* Charles Gulas, 314-529-9625, E-mail: hlthprofessions@maryville.edu.

MARYWOOD UNIVERSITY, Scranton, PA 18509-1598

General Information Independent-religious, coed, comprehensive institution. *Enrollment:* 3,180 graduate, professional, and undergraduate students; 516 full-time matriculated graduate/professional students (410 women), 768 part-time matriculated graduate/professional students (596 women). *Enrollment by degree level:* 933 master's, 126 doctoral, 93 other advanced degrees. *Graduate faculty:* 133 full-time (73 women), 177 part-time/adjunct (106 women). *Tuition:* Part-time $672 per credit. Tuition and fees vary according to degree level, campus/location and program. *Graduate housing:* Room and/or apartments available on a first-come, first-served basis to single students; on-campus housing not available to married students. Typical cost: $5,514 per year ($9,690 including board). Housing application deadline: 5/1. *Student services:* Campus employment opportunities, campus safety program, career counseling, child daycare facilities, disabled student services, exercise/wellness program, free psychological counseling, grant writing training, international student services, low-cost health insurance, multicultural affairs office, teacher training, writing training. *Library facilities:* Learning Resources Center plus 1 other. *Online resources:* library catalog, web page, access to other libraries' catalogs. *Collection:* 219,794 titles, 14,656 serial subscriptions, 48,096 audiovisual materials.

Computer facilities: 367 computers available on campus for general student use. A campuswide network can be accessed from student residence rooms and from off campus. Internet access and online class registration are available. *Web address:* http://www.marywood.edu/.

General Application Contact: Dr. Deborah M. Flynn, Coordinator of Graduate Advising (Enrollment Management), 570-348-6211, E-mail: flynn@ac.marywood.edu.

GRADUATE UNITS

Academic Affairs Students: 516 full-time (410 women), 768 part-time (596 women); includes 66 minority (31 African Americans, 2 American Indian/Alaska Native, 12 Asian Americans or Pacific Islanders, 21 Hispanic Americans), 17 international. Average age 33. 1,405 applicants, 57% accepted, 606 enrolled. *Faculty:* 39 full-time (25 women). Expenses: Contact institution. *Financial support:* In 2006–07, 387 students received support, including 36 research assistantships with partial tuition reimbursements available (averaging $8,770 per year); career-related internships or fieldwork, scholarships/grants, tuition waivers (partial), and unspecified assistantships also available. Support available to part-time students. Financial award application deadline: 2/14; financial award applicants required to submit FAFSA. In 2006, 320 master's, 18 doctorates, 1 other advanced degree awarded. *Degree program information:* Part-time and evening/weekend programs available. *Application deadline:* For fall admission, 4/15 priority date for domestic and international students; for spring admission, 11/15 priority date for domestic and international students. Applications are processed on a rolling basis. *Application fee:* $30. Electronic applications accepted. *Application Contact:* Dr. Deborah M. Flynn, Coordinator of Graduate Advising (Enrollment Management), 570-348-6211, E-mail: flynn@ac.marywood.edu. *Vice president for Academic Affairs (Interim),* Dr. Barbara Rose Sadowski, 570-348-6230, Fax: 570-961-4745.

College of Education and Human Development Students: 141 full-time (119 women), 289 part-time (236 women); includes 12 minority (5 African Americans, 1 American Indian/Alaska Native, 3 Asian Americans or Pacific Islanders, 3 Hispanic Americans), 5 international. Average age 32. *Faculty:* 16 full-time (9 women). Expenses: Contact institution. Offers addiction (MA); child/clinical school psychology (MA); clinical psychology (Psy D); clinical services (MA); counseling (Certificate); early childhood intervention (MS); education (M Ed); education and human development (M Ed, MA, MAT, MS, PhD, Psy D, Certificate, Ed S); educational administration (PhD); elementary education (MAT); elementary school counseling (MS); general (MA); general theoretical psychology (MA); health promotion (PhD); higher education administration (MS, PhD); human development—general (PhD); instructional leadership (M Ed, PhD); mental health counseling (MA); pastoral (MA); psychology (MA); reading education (MS); school leadership (MS); school psychology (Ed S); secondary education (MAT); secondary school counseling (MS); social work (PhD); special education (MS); special education administration and supervision (MS); speech-language pathology (MS). *Application fee:* $30. *Dean,* Dr. Mary Anne Fedrick.

College of Health and Human Services Students: 259 full-time (211 women), 191 part-time (161 women); includes 34 minority (17 African Americans, 1 American Indian/Alaska Native, 5 Asian Americans or Pacific Islanders, 11 Hispanic Americans), 5 international. Average age 33. *Faculty:* 20 full-time (13 women). Expenses: Contact institution. Offers clinical physician assistant (MS); criminal justice (MPA); dietetic internships (Certificate); dietetics/internships (Certificate); gerontology (MS, Certificate); health and human services (MHSA, MPA, MS, MSW, PhD, Certificate); health services administration (MHSA); human development (PhD); long-term care management (MHSA); managed care (MHSA); nursing administration (MS); nutrition (MS); physician assistant studies (MS); public administration (MPA); social work (MSW); sports nutrition and exercise science (MS). *Application fee:* $30. *Dean,* Dr. Ronald Bulbulian, 570-340-6001, E-mail: bulbulian@es.marywood.edu.

College of Liberal Arts and Sciences Students: 5 full-time (4 women), 12 part-time (9 women), 1 international. Average age 28. Expenses: Contact institution. Offers biotechnology (MS); criminal justice (MS); liberal arts and sciences (MS). *Application fee:* $30. *Dean,* Dr. Kurt Torell, 570-348-6211, E-mail: ktorell@marywood.edu.

Insalaco College of Creative Arts and Management Students: 58 full-time (38 women), 144 part-time (91 women); includes 13 minority (7 African Americans, 1 Asian American or Pacific Islander, 5 Hispanic Americans), 6 international. Average age 35. Expenses: Contact institution. Offers advertising design (MA, MFA); art education (MA); art therapy (MA, Certificate); ceramics (MA); clay (MA, MFA); communication arts (MA, Certificate); corporate communication (MS, Certificate); creative arts and management (MA, MBA, MFA, MMT, MS, Certificate); e-business (MS, Certificate); fibers (MFA); finance and investments (MBA); general management (MBA); graphic design (MA, MFA); health communication (MS, Certificate); illustration (MA, MFA); information sciences (MS); instructional technology (MS, Certificate); interdisciplinary (MA); interior architecture (MA); library science/information science (MS); library science/information specialist (Certificate); management information systems (MBA, MS); media management (MA); metals (MFA); music education (MA); music therapy (MMT, Certificate); painting (MA, MFA); photography (MA, MFA); printmaking (MA, MFA); production (MA); sculpture (MA); studio art (MA); visual arts (MFA); vocal pedagogy (Certificate); weaving (MA). *Application fee:* $30. *Dean,* Dr. Devorah Namm, 570-348-6211.

MASSACHUSETTS COLLEGE OF ART, Boston, MA 02115-5882

General Information State-supported, coed, comprehensive institution. *Enrollment:* 2,286 graduate, professional, and undergraduate students; 80 full-time matriculated graduate/professional students (47 women), 31 part-time matriculated graduate/professional students (24 women). *Enrollment by degree level:* 111 master's. *Graduate faculty:* 16 full-time (7 women), 18 part-time/adjunct (13 women). Tuition, nonresident: full-time $15,500; part-time $1,550 per unit. *Required fees:* $1,330. *Graduate housing:* On-campus housing not available. *Student services:* Campus employment opportunities, campus safety program, career counseling, free psychological counseling, international student services, low-cost health insurance. *Library facilities:* Morton R. Godine Library. *Collection:* 231,586 titles, 757 serial subscriptions.

Computer facilities: 250 computers available on campus for general student use. A campuswide network can be accessed from off campus. *Web address:* http://www.massart.edu/.

General Application Contact: George Creamer, Director of Graduate Programs, 617-879-7163, Fax: 617-879-7171, E-mail: creamer@massart.edu.

GRADUATE UNITS

Graduate Programs Students: 80 full-time (47 women), 31 part-time (24 women); includes 11 minority (3 African Americans, 5 Asian Americans or Pacific Islanders, 3 Hispanic Americans), 11 international. Average age 34. 384 applicants, 24% accepted, 49 enrolled. *Faculty:* 18 full-time (9 women), 16 part-time/adjunct (10 women). Expenses: Contact institution. *Financial support:* In 2006–07, 43 research assistantships (averaging $1,000 per year), 40 teaching assistantships (averaging $1,200 per year) were awarded; career-related internships or fieldwork, Federal Work-Study, unspecified assistantships, and clerical/technical assistantships also available. Support available to part-time students. Financial award application deadline: 5/1; financial award applicants required to submit FAFSA. In 2006, 46 degrees awarded. *Degree program information:* Part-time programs available. Offers art education (MSAE); ceramics (MFA); design (MFA); fibers (MFA); film (MFA); glass (MFA); media and performing arts (MFA); metals (MFA); painting (MFA); photography (MFA); printmaking (MFA); sculpture (MFA). *Application deadline:* For fall admission, 2/1 for domestic students. Applications are processed on a rolling basis. *Application fee:* $75. *Application Contact:* George Creamer, Director, 617-879-7163, Fax: 617-879-7171, E-mail: creamer@massart.edu. *Director,* George Creamer, 617-879-7163, Fax: 617-879-7171, E-mail: creamer@massart.edu.

MASSACHUSETTS COLLEGE OF LIBERAL ARTS, North Adams, MA 01247-4100

General Information State-supported, coed, comprehensive institution. *Graduate housing:* On-campus housing not available.

GRADUATE UNITS

Program in Education *Degree program information:* Part-time and evening/weekend programs available. Offers curriculum and instruction (M Ed); educational administration (M Ed); reading (M Ed); special education (M Ed).

MASSACHUSETTS COLLEGE OF PHARMACY AND HEALTH SCIENCES, Boston, MA 02115-5896

General Information Independent, coed, university. *Graduate housing:* On-campus housing not available. *Research affiliation:* Center for Analytical Science (analytical medicinal chemistry), Center for Brain Sciences (neuropharmacology).

GRADUATE UNITS

Graduate Studies Offers chemistry (MS, PhD); drug discovery and development (MS); drug regulatory affairs and health policy (MS); pharmaceutics (MS, PhD); pharmacology (MS, PhD); pharmacy and health sciences (MS, PhD); pharmacy systems administration (MS).

MASSACHUSETTS INSTITUTE OF TECHNOLOGY, Cambridge, MA 02139-4307

General Information Independent, coed, university. CGS member. *Enrollment:* 10,253 graduate, professional, and undergraduate students; 5,911 full-time matriculated graduate/professional students (1,760 women), 62 part-time matriculated graduate/professional students (19 women). *Enrollment by degree level:* 2,401 master's, 3,572 doctoral. *Graduate faculty:* 986 full-time (186 women), 12 part-time/adjunct (2 women). *Tuition:* Full-time $33,400; part-time $525 per unit. *Required fees:* $200. Part-time tuition and fees vary according to course load. *Graduate housing:* Rooms and/or apartments available to single and married students. Typical cost: $14,250 (including board) for single students. Room and board charges vary according to board plan and housing facility selected. Housing application deadline: 5/18. *Student services:* Campus employment opportunities, campus safety program, career counseling, child daycare facilities, disabled student services, exercise/wellness program, free psychological counseling, grant writing training, international student services, low-cost health insurance, teacher training, writing training. *Library facilities:* MIT Libraries plus 11 others. *Online resources:* library catalog, web page. *Collection:* 964,656 titles, 22,991 serial subscriptions, 33,005 audiovisual materials. *Research affiliation:* Dupont (bio-technology, materials, chemical and biological sciences), Whitehead Institute (developmental biology), Howard Hughes Medical Institute (biomedical research), Woods Hole Oceanographic Institute (applied ocean science and engineering), Carnegie Institution of Washington (optical astronomy), Idaho National Laboratory (nuclear engineering research).

Computer facilities: Computer purchase and lease plans are available. 1,100 computers available on campus for general student use. A campuswide network can be accessed from student residence rooms and from off campus. Internet access is available. *Web address:* http://web.mit.edu/.

General Application Contact: Stuart Schmill, Interim Director of Admissions, 617-253-2917, Fax: 617-258-8304, E-mail: mitgrad@mit.edu.

GRADUATE UNITS

Operations Research Center Students: 54 full-time (9 women); includes 1 minority (African American), 29 international. Average age 22. 146 applicants, 21% accepted, 18 enrolled. *Faculty:* 47 full-time (5 women). Expenses: Contact institution. *Financial support:* In 2006–07, 13 fellowships (averaging $16,290 per year), 32 research assistantships (averaging $16,290 per year), 9 teaching assistantships (averaging $16,290 per year) were awarded; Federal Work-Study, institutionally sponsored loans, scholarships/grants, and tuition waivers also available. Financial award application deadline: 12/15. In 2006, 7 master's, 8 doctorates awarded. Offers operations research (SM, PhD). *Application deadline:* For fall admission, 12/15 for domestic and international students. *Application fee:* $70. Electronic applications accepted. *Application Contact:* Laura A. Rose, Admissions Coordinator, 617-253-9303, Fax: 617-258-9214, E-mail: lrose@mit.edu. *Co-Director,* Dr. Dimitris J. Bertsimas, 617-253-4223, Fax: 617-258-9214, E-mail: dbertsim@mit.edu.

School of Architecture and Planning Students: 578 full-time (243 women), 1 (woman) part-time; includes 90 minority (16 African Americans, 3 American Indian/Alaska Native, 51 Asian Americans or Pacific Islanders, 20 Hispanic Americans), 200 international. Average age 28. 1,457 applicants, 28% accepted, 254 enrolled. *Faculty:* 75 full-time (23 women), 4 part-time/adjunct (1 woman). Expenses: Contact institution. *Financial support:* In 2006–07, 485 students received support, including 190 fellowships with tuition reimbursements available (averaging $16,616 per year), 186 research assistantships with tuition reimbursements available (averaging $22,263 per year), 47 teaching assistantships with tuition reimbursements available (averaging $18,376 per year); career-related internships or fieldwork, Federal Work-Study, institutionally sponsored loans, scholarships/grants, health care benefits, tuition waivers, and unspecified assistantships also available. In 2006, 182 master's, 43 doctorates awarded. Offers architecture (M Arch, SM Arch S, SM Vis S, SMBT, PhD); architecture and planning (M Arch, MCP, MSRED, SM, SM Arch S, SM Vis S, SMBT, PhD); city planning (MCP); media arts and sciences (SM, PhD); media technology (SM); urban and regional planning (PhD); urban and regional studies (PhD); urban studies and planning (SM). *Application fee:* $70. Electronic applications accepted. *Application Contact:* Graduate Admissions, 617-253-2917, Fax: 617-258-8304, E-mail: mitgrad@mit.edu. *Dean,* Prof. Adèle Naudé Santos, 617-253-4401, Fax: 617-253-9417, E-mail: sap-info@mit.edu.

Center for Real Estate Students: 29 full-time (7 women); includes 2 minority (both Asian Americans or Pacific Islanders), 9 international. Average age 29. *Faculty:* 8 full-time (3 women), 5 part-time/adjunct (0 women). Expenses: Contact institution. *Financial support:* In 2006–07, 8 fellowships were awarded. In 2006, 36 degrees awarded. Offers real estate (MSRED). *Application deadline:* For fall admission, 2/15 for domestic students. *Application fee:* $70. Electronic applications accepted. *Application Contact:* Maria Vieira, Associate Director of Education, 617-253-4373. *Director,* David Geltner, 617-253-5131, Fax: 617-258-6991.

School of Engineering Students: 2,650 full-time (642 women), 12 part-time (2 women); includes 425 minority (49 African Americans, 5 American Indian/Alaska Native, 296 Asian Americans or Pacific Islanders, 75 Hispanic Americans), 1,073 international. Average age 27. 6,460 applicants, 22% accepted, 893 enrolled. *Faculty:* 370 full-time (52 women), 3 part-time/adjunct (0 women). Expenses: Contact institution. *Financial support:* In 2006–07, 510 fellowships with tuition reimbursements (averaging $20,965 per year), 1,539 research assistantships with tuition reimbursements (averaging $22,867 per year), 241 teaching assistantships with tuition reimbursements (averaging $23,883 per year) were awarded; career-related internships or fieldwork, Federal Work-Study, institutionally sponsored loans, scholarships/grants, traineeships, health care benefits, and unspecified assistantships also available. In 2006, 735 master's, 288 doctorates, 10 other advanced degrees awarded. Offers aeroacoustics (PhD, Sc D); aerodynamics (PhD, Sc D); aeroelasticity (PhD, Sc D); aeronautics and astronautics (SM, PhD, Sc D, EAA); aerospace systems (PhD, Sc D); aircraft propulsion (PhD, Sc D); applied biosciences (PhD, Sc D); astrodynamics (PhD, Sc D); bio- and polymeric materials (PhD, Sc D); bioengineering (PhD, Sc D); biological oceanography (PhD, Sc D); biomaterials (PhD, Sc D); biomedical engineering (M Eng, PhD, Sc D); ceramics (PhD, Sc D); chemical engineering (SM, PhD, Sc D); chemical engineering practice (SM, PhD); chemical oceanography (PhD, Sc D); civil and environmental engineering (M Eng, SM, PhD, Sc D, CE); civil and environmental systems (PhD, Sc D); civil engineering (PhD, Sc D); coastal engineering (PhD, Sc D); computation for design and optimization (SM); computational and systems biology (PhD); computational fluid dynamics (PhD, Sc D); computer science (PhD, Sc D, ECS); computer systems (PhD, Sc D); construction engineering and management (PhD, Sc D); dynamics energy conversion (PhD, Sc D); electrical engineering (PhD, Sc D, EE); electrical engineering and computer science (M Eng, SM, PhD, Sc D); electronic materials (PhD, Sc D); electronic, photonic and magnetic materials (PhD, Sc D); emerging, fundamental and computational studies in materials science (Sc D); emerging, fundamental, and computational studies in materials science (PhD); engineering (M Eng, SM, PhD, Sc D, CE, EAA, ECS, EE, Mat E, Mech E, Met E, NE, Naval E); environmental biology (PhD, Sc D); environmental chemistry (PhD, Sc D); environmental engineering (PhD, Sc D); environmental fluid mechanics (PhD, Sc D); estimation and control (PhD, Sc D); flight transportation (PhD, Sc D); fluid mechanics (PhD, Sc D); gas turbine structures (PhD, Sc D); gas turbines (PhD, Sc D); genetic toxicology (PhD, Sc D); geotechnical and geoenvironmental engineering (PhD, Sc D); humans and automation (PhD, Sc D); hydrology (PhD, Sc D); information technology (PhD, Sc D); instrumentation (PhD, Sc D); manufacturing engineering (M Eng); materials engineering (PhD, Sc D, Mat E); materials science (PhD, Sc D); materials science and engineering (M Eng, SM, PhD, Sc D); mechanical engineering (SM, PhD, Sc D, Mech E); metallurgical engineering (Met E); molecular and systems bacterial pathogenesis (PhD, Sc D); molecular and systems toxicology and pharmacology (PhD, Sc D); molecular systems toxicology (PhD, Sc D); naval architecture and marine engineering (SM, PhD, Sc D); navigation and control systems (PhD, Sc D); nuclear science and engineering (SM, PhD, Sc D, NE); ocean engineering (SM, PhD, Sc D, Naval E); oceanographic engineering (SM, PhD, Sc D); physics of fluids (PhD, Sc D); plasma physics (PhD, Sc D); polymers (PhD, Sc D); space propulsion (PhD, Sc D); structural and environmental materials (PhD, Sc D); structural dynamics (PhD, Sc D); structures and materials (PhD, Sc D); structures technology (PhD, Sc D); toxicology (SM, PhD, Sc D); transportation (PhD, Sc D); vehicle design (PhD, Sc D). *Application fee:* $70. Electronic applications accepted. *Application Contact:* Graduate Admissions, 617-253-2917, Fax: 617-258-8304, E-mail: mitgrad@mit.edu. *Dean,* Prof. Thomas L. Magnanti, 617-253-3291, Fax: 617-253-8549.

Engineering Systems Division Students: 254 full-time (55 women), 3 part-time (1 woman); includes 31 minority (6 African Americans, 1 American Indian/Alaska Native, 19 Asian Americans or Pacific Islanders, 5 Hispanic Americans), 84 international. Average age 31. 577 applicants, 37% accepted, 151 enrolled. *Faculty:* 1 full-time (0 women). Expenses: Contact institution. *Financial support:* In 2006–07, 169 students received support, including 27 fellowships with tuition reimbursements available (averaging $10,091 per year), 87 research assistantships with tuition reimbursements available (averaging $20,543 per year), 9 teaching assistantships with tuition reimbursements available (averaging $16,331 per year); career-related internships or fieldwork, Federal Work-Study, institutionally sponsored loans, scholarships/grants, health care benefits, and unspecified assistantships

Massachusetts Institute of Technology (continued)

also available. In 2006, 124 master's, 9 doctorates awarded. Offers engineering and management (SM); engineering systems (SM, PhD); logistics (M Eng); technology and policy (SM); technology, management and policy (PhD). *Application fee:* $70. *Application Contact:* Graduate Admissions, 617-253-1182, E-mail: esdgrad@mit.edu. *Acting Director*, Prof. Joel Moses, 617-253-9756, E-mail: esdinquiries@mit.edu.

School of Humanities, Arts, and Social Sciences Students: 311 full-time (125 women); includes 33 minority (3 African Americans, 2 American Indian/Alaska Native, 19 Asian Americans or Pacific Islanders, 9 Hispanic Americans), 124 international. Average age 28. 1,606 applicants, 9% accepted, 76 enrolled. *Faculty:* 155 full-time (47 women), 1 (woman) part-time/adjunct. Expenses: Contact institution. *Financial support:* In 2006–07, 287 students received support, including 129 fellowships with tuition reimbursements available (averaging $26,448 per year), 55 research assistantships with tuition reimbursements available (averaging $22,958 per year), 61 teaching assistantships with tuition reimbursements available (averaging $29,184 per year); Federal Work-Study, institutionally sponsored loans, scholarships/grants, health care benefits, and unspecified assistantships also available. In 2006, 18 master's, 42 doctorates awarded. Offers comparative media studies (SM); economics (SM, PhD); history, anthropology, and science, technology and society (PhD); humanities, arts, and social sciences (SM, PhD); linguistics (PhD); philosophy (PhD); political science (SM, PhD); science writing (SM). *Application fee:* $70. Electronic applications accepted. *Application Contact:* Graduate Admissions Office, 617-253-2917, Fax: 617-258-8304, E-mail: mitgrad@mit.edu. *Dean*, Prof. Deborah Fitzgerald, 617-253-3450, E-mail: www-shass@mit.edu.

School of Science Students: 1,094 full-time (384 women), 2 part-time (both women); includes 147 minority (18 African Americans, 3 American Indian/Alaska Native, 90 Asian Americans or Pacific Islanders, 36 Hispanic Americans), 349 international. Average age 26. 2,574 applicants, 19% accepted, 233 enrolled. *Faculty:* 271 full-time (39 women), 2 part-time/adjunct (0 women). Expenses: Contact institution. *Financial support:* In 2006–07, 347 fellowships with tuition reimbursements (averaging $22,420 per year), 554 research assistantships with tuition reimbursements (averaging $24,403 per year), 176 teaching assistantships with tuition reimbursements (averaging $25,387 per year) were awarded; Federal Work-Study, institutionally sponsored loans, scholarships/grants, traineeships, health care benefits, and unspecified assistantships also available. In 2006, 25 master's, 181 doctorates awarded. Offers atmospheric chemistry (PhD, Sc D); atmospheric science (SM, PhD, Sc D); biochemistry (PhD); biological chemistry (PhD, Sc D); biological oceanography (PhD); biophysical chemistry and molecular structure (PhD); cell biology (PhD); climate physics and chemistry (PhD, Sc D); cognitive science (PhD); developmental biology (PhD); earth and planetary sciences (SM); genetics/microbiology (PhD); geochemistry (PhD, Sc D); geology (PhD, Sc D); geophysics (PhD, Sc D); immunology (PhD); inorganic chemistry (PhD, Sc D); marine geology and geophysics (SM); mathematics (PhD); neurobiology (PhD); neuroscience (PhD); oceanography (SM); organic chemistry (PhD, Sc D); physical chemistry (PhD, Sc D); physical oceanography (PhD, Sc D); physics (PhD); planetary sciences (PhD, Sc D); science (SM, PhD, Sc D). *Application fee:* $70. Electronic applications accepted. *Application Contact:* Graduate Admissions Office, 617-253-2917, Fax: 617-258-8304, E-mail: mitgrad@mit.edu. *Dean*, Prof. Marc A. Kastner, 617-253-4800, Fax: 617-253-8554, E-mail: mkastner@mit.edu.

Sloan School of Management Students: 781 full-time (242 women); includes 170 minority (15 African Americans, 4 American Indian/Alaska Native, 130 Asian Americans or Pacific Islanders, 21 Hispanic Americans), 234 international. Average age 28. 2,944 applicants, 20% accepted. *Faculty:* 106 full-time (17 women). Expenses: Contact institution. *Financial support:* Fellowships with tuition reimbursements, research assistantships with tuition reimbursements, teaching assistantships with tuition reimbursements, institutionally sponsored loans available. Postbaccalaureate distance learning degree programs offered. Offers management (MBA, MS, SM, PhD). *Application deadline:* For fall admission, 1/10 for domestic and international students. *Application fee:* $230. Electronic applications accepted. *Application Contact:* Rod Garcia, Director of Admissions, MBA Program, 617-253-5434, Fax: 617-253-6405, E-mail: mbaadmissions@sloan.mit.edu. *Dean*, Richard L. Schmalensee, 617-253-2957, Fax: 617-258-6617, E-mail: rschmal@mit.edu.

Whitaker College of Health Sciences and Technology Expenses: Contact institution. *Financial support:* Fellowships with full tuition reimbursements, research assistantships with full tuition reimbursements, teaching assistantships with full tuition reimbursements, Federal Work-Study, institutionally sponsored loans, scholarships/grants, traineeships, and health care benefits available. Support available to part-time students. Financial award application deadline: 12/15. Offers biomedical engineering (M Eng); biomedical enterprise (SM); biomedical informatics (SM); health sciences and technology (MD, M Eng, SM, PhD, Sc D); medical engineering (PhD); medical engineering and medical physics (Sc D); medical physics (PhD); medical sciences (MD); speech and hearing bioscience and technology (PhD, Sc D). *Application deadline:* For fall admission, 12/15 for domestic students. *Application fee:* $70. *Application Contact:* Charlene Placido, Assistant Provost for Research, 617-253-1975, Fax: 617-253-8388, E-mail: placido@mit.edu. *Director*, Dr. Martha L. Gray, E-mail: mgray@mit.edu.

MASSACHUSETTS MARITIME ACADEMY, Buzzards Bay, MA 02532-1803

General Information State-supported, coed, primarily men, comprehensive institution.

GRADUATE UNITS

Program in Facilities Management Offers facilities management (MS).

MASSACHUSETTS SCHOOL OF LAW AT ANDOVER, Andover, MA 01810

General Information Independent, coed, graduate-only institution. *Enrollment by degree level:* 650 first professional. *Graduate faculty:* 20 full-time (10 women), 65 part-time/adjunct (25 women). *Tuition:* Full-time $13,320. One-time fee: $750 full-time. *Graduate housing:* On-campus housing not available. *Student services:* Campus employment opportunities, campus safety program, career counseling, disabled student services, free psychological counseling, low-cost health insurance, multicultural affairs office, writing training. *Library facilities:* Law Library plus 1 other. *Online resources:* library catalog, web page, access to other libraries' catalogs.

Computer facilities: 30 computers available on campus for general student use. A campuswide network can be accessed from student residence rooms and from off campus. Internet access, westlaw/LexisNexis are available. *Web address:* http://www.mslaw.edu/.

General Application Contact: Paula Colby-Clements, Director of Admissions, 978-681-0800, Fax: 978-684-7517, E-mail: pcolby@mslaw.edu.

GRADUATE UNITS

Professional Program Students: 260 full-time (130 women), 390 part-time (195 women). 320 applicants, 63% accepted, 166 enrolled. *Faculty:* 20 full-time (10 women), 65 part-time/adjunct (25 women). Expenses: Contact institution. In 2006, 120 degrees awarded. *Degree program information:* Part-time and evening/weekend programs available. Offers law (JD). *Application deadline:* Applications are processed on a rolling basis. *Application fee:* $40. Electronic applications accepted. *Application Contact:* Paula Colby-Clements, Director of Admissions, 978-681-0800, Fax: 978-684-7517, E-mail: pcolby@mslaw.edu. *Director of Admissions*, Paula Colby-Clements, 978-681-0800, Fax: 978-684-7517, E-mail: pcolby@mslaw.edu.

MASSACHUSETTS SCHOOL OF PROFESSIONAL PSYCHOLOGY, Boston, MA 02132

General Information Independent, coed, primarily women, graduate-only institution. *Graduate housing:* On-campus housing not available.

GRADUATE UNITS

Graduate Programs Offers clinical psychology (Psy D); clinical psychopharmacology (Post-Doctoral MS). Electronic applications accepted.

THE MASTER'S COLLEGE AND SEMINARY, Santa Clarita, CA 91321-1200

General Information Independent-religious, coed, comprehensive institution. *Enrollment:* 1,521 graduate, professional, and undergraduate students; 216 full-time matriculated graduate/professional students, 165 part-time matriculated graduate/professional students. *Enrollment by degree level:* 303 first professional, 17 master's, 34 doctoral, 27 other advanced degrees. *Graduate faculty:* 18 full-time (0 women), 11 part-time/adjunct (0 women). *Tuition:* Full-time $7,840; part-time $285 per credit hour. *Required fees:* $280; $140 per semester. Tuition and fees vary according to degree level and program. *Graduate housing:* On-campus housing not available. *Student services:* Campus employment opportunities, campus safety program, career counseling, international student services, low-cost health insurance, writing training. *Library facilities:* Powell Library plus 1 other. *Online resources:* library catalog, web page, access to other libraries' catalogs. *Collection:* 178,337 titles, 12,867 serial subscriptions, 7,413 audiovisual materials.

Computer facilities: Computer purchase and lease plans are available. 57 computers available on campus for general student use. A campuswide network can be accessed from student residence rooms and from off campus. Internet access and online class registration are available. *Web address:* http://www.masters.edu/.

General Application Contact: Ray Mehringer, Director of Admissions and Placement, 818-792-6488, Fax: 818-909-5725.

GRADUATE UNITS

The Master's Seminary Students: 216 full-time (0 women), 165 part-time; includes 66 minority (9 African Americans, 41 Asian Americans or Pacific Islanders, 16 Hispanic Americans), 28 international. Average age 28. 142 applicants, 81% accepted, 87 enrolled. *Faculty:* 18 full-time (0 women), 11 part-time/adjunct (0 women). Expenses: Contact institution. *Financial support:* In 2006–07, 121 students received support, including 10 teaching assistantships (averaging $4,000 per year); career-related internships or fieldwork, scholarships/grants, and tuition waivers (partial) also available. Support available to part-time students. Financial award application deadline: 6/1; financial award applicants required to submit FAFSA. In 2006, 59 M Divs, 9 master's awarded. *Degree program information:* Part-time programs available. Offers biblical counseling (MABC); New Testament (Th D); Old Testament (Th D); preaching (D Min); theology (M Div, M Th, Th D). *Application deadline:* For fall admission, 6/1 priority date for domestic and international students; for winter admission, 10/1 priority date for domestic and international students; for spring admission, 1/1 for domestic and international students. Applications are processed on a rolling basis. *Application fee:* $30. *Application Contact:* Ray Mehringer, Director of Admissions and Placement, 818-792-6488, Fax: 818-909-5725. *Senior Vice President and Dean*, Dr. Richard L. Mayhue, 818-782-6488 Ext. 5632, E-mail: mayhue@tms.edu.

MAYO GRADUATE SCHOOL, Rochester, MN 55905

General Information Independent, coed, graduate-only institution. *Graduate housing:* On-campus housing not available.

GRADUATE UNITS

Graduate Programs in Biomedical Sciences Offers biochemistry and structural biology (PhD); biomedical engineering (PhD); biomedical sciences (PhD); cell biology and genetics (PhD); immunology (PhD); molecular biology (PhD); molecular neuroscience (PhD); molecular pharmacology and experimental therapeutics (PhD); tumor biology (PhD); virology and gene therapy (PhD). Electronic applications accepted.

MAYO MEDICAL SCHOOL, Rochester, MN 55905

General Information Independent, coed, graduate-only institution. *Graduate housing:* On-campus housing not available.

GRADUATE UNITS

Professional Program Offers medicine (MD). MD offered through the Mayo Foundation's Division of Education. Electronic applications accepted.

MAYO SCHOOL OF HEALTH SCIENCES, Rochester, MN 55905

General Information Independent, coed, graduate-only institution. *Enrollment:* 161 full-time matriculated graduate/professional students (117 women), 4 part-time matriculated graduate/professional students (1 woman). *Graduate faculty:* 6 full-time (1 woman), 4 part-time/adjunct (3 women). *Student services:* Campus employment opportunities, campus safety program, career counseling, child daycare facilities, exercise/wellness program, free psychological counseling, low-cost health insurance, multicultural affairs office. *Library facilities:* Venables Library plus 5 others.

Computer facilities: A campuswide network can be accessed from off campus. Internet access is available. *Web address:* http://www.mayo.edu/mshs/.

General Application Contact: Wendy Hagan, Administrative Secretary, 507-284-3293.

GRADUATE UNITS

Program in Nurse Anesthesia Students: 117 full-time (65 women); includes 10 minority (5 African Americans, 4 Asian Americans or Pacific Islanders, 1 Hispanic American). Average age 30. 83 applicants, 30 enrolled. *Faculty:* 1 (woman) full-time, 2 part-time/adjunct (1 woman). Expenses: Contact institution. *Financial support:* Scholarships/grants, health care benefits, and stipends available. Financial award applicants required to submit FAFSA. In 2006, 30 degrees awarded. Offers nurse anesthesia (MNA). *Application deadline:* For fall admission, 10/15 for domestic students. Applications are processed on a rolling basis. *Application fee:* $50. Electronic applications accepted. *Application Contact:* Val Martin, Administrative Assistant, 507-284-3678, Fax: 507-284-0656. *Director*, Mary E. Marienau, 507-284-3293, Fax: 507-284-0656, E-mail: marienau.mary@mayo.edu.

Program in Physical Therapy Students: 66 full-time (47 women); includes 3 minority (all Asian Americans or Pacific Islanders) Average age 25. 54 applicants, 39% accepted. *Faculty:* 5 full-time (0 women), 2 part-time/adjunct (both women). Expenses: Contact institution. *Financial support:* Scholarships/grants available. Financial award applicants required to submit FAFSA. Offers physical therapy (DPT). *Application deadline:* For winter admission, 1/15 for domestic students. Applications are processed on a rolling basis. *Application fee:* $50. Electronic applications accepted. *Application Contact:* Carol Cooper, Secretary, 507-284-2054, E-mail: cooper.carol@mayo.edu. *Director*, Dr. John Hollman, 507-284-8487.

MCCORMICK THEOLOGICAL SEMINARY, Chicago, IL 60615

General Information Independent-religious, coed, graduate-only institution. *Graduate housing:* Rooms and/or apartments available on a first-come, first-served basis to single and married students. Housing application deadline: 7/1.

GRADUATE UNITS

Graduate and Professional Programs *Degree program information:* Part-time and evening/weekend programs available. Offers ministry (D Min); theological studies (MATS, Certificate); theology (M Div).

MCDANIEL COLLEGE, Westminster, MD 21157-4390

General Information Independent, coed, comprehensive institution. *Graduate housing:* On-campus housing not available.

GRADUATE UNITS

Graduate and Professional Studies *Degree program information:* Part-time and evening/weekend programs available. Offers curriculum and instruction (MS); education of the deaf (MS); educational administration (MS); elementary education (MS); guidance and counseling (MS); human resources development (MS); human services management in special education (MS); liberal studies (MLA); media/library science (MS); physical education (MS); reading education (MS); secondary education (MS); special education (MS).

MCGILL UNIVERSITY, Montréal, QC H3A 2T5, Canada

General Information Province-supported, coed, university. CGS member. *Graduate housing:* Rooms and/or apartments available on a first-come, first-served basis to single students and available to married students. *Research affiliation:* MAPAQ/CORPAQ (agricultural technologies), AstraZeneca (pain research/medicine), Danone/Unilever (human nutrition), General Motors of Canada (automotive materials), Pfizer Inc. (studies in aging), Nortel Networks (telecommunications).

GRADUATE UNITS

Faculty of Graduate and Postdoctoral Studies *Degree program information:* Part-time programs available. Postbaccalaureate distance learning degree programs offered (minimal on-campus study). Electronic applications accepted.

Desautels Faculty of Management *Degree program information:* Part-time programs available. Offers administration (PhD); entrepreneurial studies (MBA); finance (MBA); general management (Post Master's Certificate); information systems (MBA); international business (exchange program) (MBA); international Master's program in practicing management (MM); management (MBA); management for development (MBA); manufacturing management (MMM); marketing (MBA); operations management (MBA); public accountancy (Diploma); strategic management (MBA). Electronic applications accepted.

Faculty of Agricultural and Environmental Sciences *Degree program information:* Part-time programs available. Offers agricultural and environmental sciences (M Sc, M Sc A, PhD, Certificate, Graduate Diploma); agricultural economics (M Sc); animal science (M Sc, M Sc A, PhD); biotechnology (M Sc A, Certificate); computer applications (M Sc, M Sc A, PhD); dietetics (M Sc A, Graduate Diploma); entomology (M Sc, PhD); environmental assessment (M Sc); food engineering (M Sc, M Sc A, PhD); food science and agricultural chemistry (M Sc, PhD); forest science (M Sc, PhD); grain drying (M Sc, M Sc A, PhD); human nutrition (M Sc, M Sc A, PhD); irrigation and drainage (M Sc, M Sc A, PhD); machinery (M Sc, M Sc A, PhD); microbiology (M Sc, PhD); micrometeorology (M Sc, PhD); neotropical environment (M Sc, PhD); parasitology (M Sc, PhD); plant science (M Sc, M Sc A, PhD, Certificate); pollution control (M Sc, M Sc A, PhD); post-harvest technology (M Sc, M Sc A, PhD); soil dynamics (M Sc, M Sc A, PhD); soil science (M Sc, PhD); structure and environment (M Sc, M Sc A, PhD); vegetable and fruit storage (M Sc, M Sc A, PhD); wildlife biology (M Sc, PhD).

Faculty of Arts *Degree program information:* Part-time and evening/weekend programs available. Offers anthropology (MA, PhD); art history and communication studies (MA, PhD); arts (MA, MSW, PhD, Diploma); bioethics (MA); East Asian studies (MA, PhD); economics (MA, PhD); English (MA, PhD); French language and literature (MA, PhD); German studies (MA, PhD); Hispanic studies (MA, PhD); history (MA, PhD); history of medicine (MA); Islamic studies (MA, PhD, Diploma); Italian studies (MA, PhD); Jewish studies (MA, PhD); language acquisition (PhD); linguistics (MA, PhD); medical anthropology (MA); medical sociology (MA); neo-tropical environment (MA); philosophy (PhD); political science (MA, PhD); Russian literature (MA, PhD); social statistics (MA); social work (MSW, PhD, Diploma); sociology (MA, PhD, Diploma). Electronic applications accepted.

Faculty of Dentistry Offers forensic dentistry (Certificate); oral and maxillofacial surgery (M Sc, PhD). Electronic applications accepted.

Faculty of Education *Degree program information:* Part-time and evening/weekend programs available. Offers counseling psychology (MA, PhD); culture and values in education (MA, PhD); curriculum (MA); education (M Ed, M Sc, MA, MLIS, PhD, Certificate, Diploma); educational leadership (Certificate, Diploma); educational psychology (M Ed, MA, PhD); educational studies (PhD); integrated studies in education (M Ed); kinesiology and physical education (M Sc, MA, PhD, Certificate, Diploma); leadership (MA); library and information studies (MLIS, PhD, Certificate, Diploma); school psychology (M Ed, MA, PhD, Diploma); school/applied child psychology and applied developmental psychology (M Ed, MA, PhD, Diploma); second language education (MA, PhD).

Faculty of Engineering *Degree program information:* Part-time and evening/weekend programs available. Offers aerospace (M Eng); affordable homes (M Arch I, Diploma); architectural history and theory (M Arch I); architecture (PhD); chemical engineering (M Eng, PhD); domestic environment (M Arch I); domestic environments (Diploma); electrical and computer engineering (M Eng, PhD); engineering (M Arch I, M Arch II, M Eng, M Sc, MMM, MUP, PhD, Diploma); environmental engineering (M Eng, M Sc, PhD); environmental planning (MUP); fluid mechanics (M Sc); fluid mechanics and hydraulic engineering (M Eng, PhD); housing (MUP); manufacturing management (MMM); materials engineering (M Eng, PhD); mechanical engineering (M Eng, M Sc, PhD); minimum cost housing in developing countries (M Arch I, Diploma); mining engineering (M Eng, M Sc, PhD, Diploma); professional architecture (M Arch II); rehabilitation of urban infrastructure (M Eng, PhD); soil behavior (M Eng, PhD); soil mechanics and foundations (M Eng, PhD); structures and structural mechanics (M Eng, PhD); transportation (MUP); urban planning (PhD); urban planning and design (MUP); water resources (M Sc); water resources engineering (M Eng, PhD). Electronic applications accepted.

Faculty of Law Offers air and space law (LL M, DCL, Certificate); bioethics (LL M); comparative law (LL M, DCL, Certificate); law (LL M, DCL). Applications for LL M with specialization in bioethics are made initially through the Biomedical Ethics Unit in the Faculty of Medicine. Electronic applications accepted.

Faculty of Medicine *Degree program information:* Part-time programs available. Offers anatomy and cell biology (M Sc, PhD); biochemistry (M Sc, PhD); bioethics (M Sc); biomedical engineering (M Eng, PhD); communication science and disorders (M Sc); communication sciences and disorders (PhD); community health (M Sc); environmental health (M Sc); epidemiology and biostatistics (M Sc, PhD, Diploma); experimental medicine (M Sc, PhD); genetic counseling (M Sc); health care evaluation (M Sc); human genetics (M Sc, PhD); medical anthropology (MA, PhD); medical history (MA, PhD); medical radiation physics (M Sc, PhD); medical sociology (MA, PhD); medical statistics (M Sc); medicine (M Eng, M Sc, M Sc A, MA, PhD, Diploma, Graduate Diploma); microbiology and immunology (M Sc, M Sc A, PhD); neurology and neurosurgery (M Sc, PhD); nurse practitioner (Graduate Diploma); nursing (M Sc A, PhD); occupational health (M Sc); otolaryngology (M Sc); pathology (M Sc, PhD); pharmacology and therapeutics (M Sc, PhD); physiology (M Sc, PhD); psychiatry (M Sc); rehabilitation science (M Sc, PhD); speech-language pathology (M Sc A); surgery (M Sc, PhD).

Faculty of Religious Studies Offers religious studies and theology (MA, STM, PhD). Electronic applications accepted.

Faculty of Science *Degree program information:* Part-time programs available. Offers atmospheric science (M Sc, PhD); bioinformatics (M Sc, PhD); biology (M Sc, PhD); chemical biology (M Sc, PhD); chemistry (M Sc, PhD); clinical psychology (PhD); computational science and engineering (M Sc); computer science (M Sc, PhD); earth and planetary sciences (M Sc, PhD); experimental psychology (M Sc, MA, PhD); geography (M Sc, MA, PhD); mathematics and statistics (M Sc, MA, PhD); neo-tropical environment (M Sc, MA, PhD); physical oceanography (M Sc, PhD); physics (M Sc, PhD); science (M Sc, M Sc A, MA, PhD); social statistics (MA).

Schulich School of Music Offers composition (M Mus, D Mus, PhD); music education (MA, PhD); music technology (MA, PhD); musicology (MA, PhD); performance (M Mus); performance studies (D Mus); sound recording (M Mus, PhD); theory (MA, PhD). Electronic applications accepted.

Professional Program in Dentistry Average age 25. *Faculty:* 18 full-time (3 women), 135 part-time/adjunct (24 women). Expenses: Contact institution. In 2006, 34 degrees awarded. Offers dentistry (DMD). *Application deadline:* For fall admission, 11/15 for domestic students; for winter admission, 1/15 for domestic students. Applications are processed on a rolling basis. *Application fee:* $80 Canadian dollars. Electronic applications accepted. *Application Contact:* Patricia Bassett, Graduate Secretary, 514-398-7203 Ext. 00091, Fax: 514-398-2028, E-mail: patricia.bassett@mcgill.ca. *Dean,* Dr. James P. Lund, 514-398-7219, Fax: 514-398-8900, E-mail: james.lund@mcgill.ca.

Professional Program in Medicine Students: 648 full-time (363 women), 65 international. Average age 24. 1,044 applicants, 24% accepted, 172 enrolled. *Faculty:* 824 full-time (334 women), 2,236 part-time/adjunct (906 women). Expenses: Contact institution. *Financial support:* Fellowships, research assistantships, scholarships/grants and health care benefits available. Financial award application deadline: 1/1. Offers medicine). *Application deadline:* For fall admission, 1/15 for domestic students, 11/15 for international students. *Application fee:* $60. Electronic applications accepted. *Application Contact:* Michel Dansereau, Admissions Officer, 514-398-3517, Fax: 514-398-4631, E-mail: michel.dansereau@mcgill.ca. *Director, Admission Office,* France Drolet, 514-398-3517, Fax: 514-398-4631, E-mail: admissions.med@mcgill.ca.

MCKENDREE COLLEGE, Lebanon, IL 62254-1299

General Information Independent-religious, coed, comprehensive institution.

GRADUATE UNITS

Graduate Programs

MCMASTER UNIVERSITY, Hamilton, ON L8S 4M2, Canada

General Information Province-supported, coed, university. *Enrollment:* 2,290 full-time matriculated graduate/professional students, 380 part-time matriculated graduate/professional students. *Graduate faculty:* 615 full-time, 63 part-time/adjunct. *Graduate housing:* Room and/or apartments available to single students; on-campus housing not available to married students. Housing application deadline: 6/30. *Student services:* Campus employment opportunities, campus safety program, career counseling, child daycare facilities, disabled student services, exercise/wellness program, free psychological counseling, international student services, low-cost health insurance, multicultural affairs office, writing training. *Library facilities:* Mills Memorial Library plus 4 others. *Online resources:* library catalog, web page, access to other libraries' catalogs. *Collection:* 1.7 million titles, 11,976 serial subscriptions. *Research affiliation:* Commonwealth Development (telecommunications), Canadian Centre for Inland Waters (chemical and civil engineering).

Computer facilities: 400 computers available on campus for general student use. A campuswide network can be accessed from student residence rooms and from off campus. Internet access is available. *Web address:* http://www.mcmaster.ca/.

General Application Contact: John A. Scime, Graduate Registrar and Secretary, 905-525-9140 Ext. 23684, Fax: 905-521-0689, E-mail: scime@mcmaster.ca.

GRADUATE UNITS

Faculty of Health Sciences Students: 665 full-time, 126 part-time. *Faculty:* 358. Expenses: Contact institution. *Financial support:* Teaching assistantships available. *Degree program information:* Part-time programs available. Postbaccalaureate distance learning degree programs offered (minimal on-campus study). Offers blood and vascular (M Sc, PhD); genetics and cancer (M Sc, PhD); health research methodology (course-based) (M Sc); health research methodology (thesis) (M Sc, PhD); health sciences (M Sc, PhD); immunity and infection (M Sc, PhD); metabolism and nutrition (M Sc, PhD); neurosciences and behavioral sciences (M Sc, PhD); nursing (M Sc, PhD); occupational therapy (M Sc); physiology/pharmacology (M Sc, PhD); physiotherapy (M Sc); rehabilitation science (M Sc, PhD); rehabilitation science (course-based) (M Sc). *Application Contact:* Dr. Carl Richards, Associate Dean, 905-525-9140 Ext. 22983, Fax: 905-546-1129. *Dean/Vice President,* Dr. John G. Kelton, 905-525-9140 Ext. 22100, Fax: 905-546-0800, E-mail: keltonj@mcmaster.ca.

McMaster Divinity College *Degree program information:* Part-time programs available. Offers Biblical studies (MA, MTS, Diploma); biblical studies (M Div); Christian interpretation/history (M Div, MA, MTS, Diploma); Christian ministry (M Div, MA, MTS, Diploma); Christian Studies (Certificate); Christian theology (PhD). Affiliated with the Toronto School of Theology.

School of Graduate Studies Students: 2,475 full-time, 421 part-time. *Faculty:* 609 full-time, 73 part-time/adjunct. Expenses: Contact institution. *Financial support:* In 2006–07, 1,625 fellowships (averaging $5,000 per year), 186 research assistantships (averaging $2,000 per year), 1,409 teaching assistantships (averaging $8,440 per year) were awarded; career-related internships or fieldwork, Federal Work-Study, institutionally sponsored loans, scholarships/grants, and tuition waivers (partial) also available. In 2006, 710 master's, 112 doctorates awarded. *Degree program information:* Part-time programs available. *Application fee:* $90. *Application Contact:* John A. Scime, Graduate Registrar and Secretary, 905-525-9140 Ext. 23684, Fax: 905-521-0689, E-mail: scime@mcmaster.ca. *Dean,* Dr. Fred L. Hall, 905-525-9140 Ext. 23683, Fax: 905-521-0689, E-mail: deangrad@mcmaster.ca.

Faculty of Business Students: 218 full-time, 101 part-time. *Faculty:* 51 full-time. Expenses: Contact institution. *Financial support:* In 2006–07, teaching assistantships (averaging $8,440 per year); fellowships, research assistantships, career-related internships or fieldwork, Federal Work-Study, and scholarships/grants also available. *Degree program information:* Part-time programs available. Offers business (MBA, PhD); human resources and management (MBA, PhD); management science/systems (PhD). *Application deadline:* For fall admission, 6/1 for domestic students. *Application fee:* $90. *Application Contact:* Denise Anderson, Manager, Recruitment and Admissions, 905-525-9140 Ext. 23940, Fax: 905-521-8995, E-mail: anderd@mcmaster.ca. *Dean,* Paul Bates, 905-525-9140 Ext. 24431, Fax: 905-526-0852, E-mail: deanbus@mcmaster.ca.

Faculty of Engineering Students: 581 full-time, 103 part-time. *Faculty:* 144 full-time, 26 part-time/adjunct. Expenses: Contact institution. *Financial support:* In 2006–07, teaching assistantships (averaging $8,440 per year); fellowships, research assistantships, career-related internships or fieldwork, Federal Work-Study, and scholarships/grants also available. *Degree program information:* Part-time programs available. Offers chemical engineering (M Eng, MA Sc, PhD); civil engineering (M Eng, MA Sc, PhD); computer science (M Sc, PhD); electrical engineering (M Eng, MA Sc, PhD); engineering (M Eng, M Sc, MA Sc, PhD); engineering physics (M Eng, MA Sc, PhD); materials engineering (M Eng, MA Sc, PhD); materials science (M Eng, PhD); mechanical engineering (M Eng, MA Sc, PhD); nuclear engineering (PhD); software engineering (M Eng, MA Sc, PhD). *Application deadline:* For fall admission, 3/1 priority date for domestic students. Applications are processed on a rolling basis. *Application fee:* $90. *Dean of the Faculty of Engineering,* Dr. M. Elbestawi, 905-525-9140 Ext. 24900, Fax: 905-528-4952, E-mail: deaneng@mcmaster.ca.

Faculty of Humanities Students: 195 full-time, 7 part-time. *Faculty:* 93 full-time, 1 part-time/adjunct. Expenses: Contact institution. *Financial support:* In 2006–07, teaching assistantships (averaging $8,440 per year); fellowships, research assistantships, career-related internships or fieldwork, Federal Work-Study, institutionally sponsored loans, and scholarships/grants also available. *Degree program information:* Part-time and evening/weekend programs available. Offers classics (MA, PhD); cultural studies and critical theory (MA); English (MA, PhD); French (MA); globalization studies (MA); history (MA, PhD); humanities (MA, PhD); music criticism (MA); philosophy (MA, PhD). *Application deadline:* Applications are processed on a rolling basis. *Application fee:* $90. *Dean,* Dr. Suzanne Crosta, 905-525-9140 Ext. 24603, Fax: 905-528-6733, E-mail: deanhum@mcmaster.ca.

Faculty of Science Students: 457 full-time, 29 part-time. *Faculty:* 240 full-time, 27 part-time/adjunct. Expenses: Contact institution. *Financial support:* In 2006–07, teaching assistantships (averaging $8,440 per year); fellowships, research assistantships, career-related internships or fieldwork, institutionally sponsored loans, scholarships/grants, and tuition waivers (full and partial) also available. *Degree program information:* Part-time and evening/weekend programs available. Offers analytical chemistry (M Sc, PhD); applied statistics (M Sc); astrophysics (PhD); biochemistry and biomedical sciences (M Sc, PhD); biology (M Sc, PhD); chemical physics (M Sc, PhD); chemistry (M Sc, PhD); geochemistry (PhD); geology (M Sc, PhD); health and radiation physics (M Sc); human geography (MA, PhD); inorganic chemistry (M Sc, PhD); mathematics (M Sc, PhD); medical physics (M Sc, PhD); medical statistics (M Sc); organic chemistry (M Sc, PhD); physical chemistry (M Sc, PhD); physical geography (M Sc, PhD); physics (PhD); polymer chemistry (M Sc, PhD); psychology (M Sc, PhD); science (M Sc, MA, PhD); statistical theory (M Sc); statistics (M Sc). *Application deadline:* Applications are processed on a rolling basis. *Application fee:* $90. *Dean,* Dr. John Capone, 905-525-9140 Ext. 22615, Fax: 905-546-9995, E-mail: deansci@mcmaster.ca.

Faculty of Social Sciences Students: 300 full-time, 53 part-time. 687 applicants, 20% accepted. *Faculty:* 132 full-time, 19 part-time/adjunct. Expenses: Contact institution. *Financial support:* In 2006–07, teaching assistantships (averaging $8,440 per year); fellowships, research assistantships, scholarships/grants and tuition waivers (partial) also avail-

McMaster University (continued)

able. *Degree program information:* Part-time and evening/weekend programs available. Offers analysis of social welfare policy (MSW); analysis of social work practice (MSW); anthropology (MA, PhD); economics (MA, PhD); human biodynamics (M Sc, PhD); international relations (PhD); political science (MA); public and the global economy (MA); public policy (PhD); public policy and administration (MA); religious studies (MA, PhD); social sciences (M Sc, MA, MSW, PhD); sociology (MA, PhD); work and society (MA). *Application fee:* $90. *Dean,* Dr. Susan J. Elliott, 905-525-9140 Ext. 26156, Fax: 905-521-8635, E-mail: deansoc@mcmaster.ca.

MCNEESE STATE UNIVERSITY, Lake Charles, LA 70609

General Information State-supported, coed, comprehensive institution. *Enrollment:* 8,343 graduate, professional, and undergraduate students; 323 full-time matriculated graduate/professional students (160 women), 463 part-time matriculated graduate/professional students (355 women). *Enrollment by degree level:* 773 master's, 13 other advanced degrees. *Graduate faculty:* 97 full-time (32 women), 5 part-time/adjunct (4 women). *Tuition, area resident:* Full-time $2,226; part-time $193 per hour. *Required fees:* $919; $106 per hour. *Graduate housing:* Rooms and/or apartments available on a first-come, first-served basis to single and married students. Typical cost: $3,996 (including board) for single students; $6,120 (including board) for married students. Room and board charges vary according to board plan and housing facility selected. Housing application deadline: 8/15. *Student services:* Campus employment opportunities, campus safety program, career counseling, disabled student services, exercise/wellness program, free psychological counseling, international student services, low-cost health insurance, multicultural affairs office. *Library facilities:* Frazer Memorial Library plus 2 others. *Online resources:* library catalog, web page, access to other libraries' catalogs. *Collection:* 332,521 titles, 22,177 serial subscriptions.

Computer facilities: 700 computers available on campus for general student use. A campuswide network can be accessed from student residence rooms and from off campus. Internet access and online class registration are available. *Web address:* http://www.mcneese.edu/.

General Application Contact: Tammie Pettis, Director of Admissions, 337-475-5282, Fax: 337-475-5151, E-mail: info@mcneese.edu.

GRADUATE UNITS

Graduate School Students: 323 full-time (160 women), 463 part-time (355 women); includes 139 minority (115 African Americans, 3 American Indian/Alaska Native, 7 Asian Americans or Pacific Islanders, 14 Hispanic Americans), 144 international. Average age 32. *Faculty:* 97 full-time (32 women), 5 part-time/adjunct (4 women). Expenses: Contact institution. *Financial support:* Fellowships, research assistantships, teaching assistantships, career-related internships or fieldwork, Federal Work-Study, institutionally sponsored loans, and unspecified assistantships available. Support available to part-time students. Financial award application deadline: 5/1. In 2006, 284 master's, 2 other advanced degrees awarded. *Degree program information:* Part-time and evening/weekend programs available. *Application deadline:* For fall admission, 5/15 priority date for domestic students, 5/1 priority date for international students; for spring admission, 10/1 priority date for international students. Applications are processed on a rolling basis. *Application fee:* $20 ($30 for international students). *Interim Dean,* Dr. George F. Mead, 337-475-5394, Fax: 337-475-5397, E-mail: mead@mcneese.edu.

College of Business Students: 38 full-time (14 women), 36 part-time (20 women); includes 7 minority (3 African Americans, 2 Asian Americans or Pacific Islanders, 2 Hispanic Americans), 21 international. *Faculty:* 11 full-time (0 women). Expenses: Contact institution. *Financial support:* Research assistantships, teaching assistantships, Federal Work-Study available. Support available to part-time students. Financial award application deadline:5/1. In 2006, 18 degrees awarded. *Degree program information:* Part-time and evening/weekend programs available. Offers business (MBA); business administration (MBA). *Application deadline:* For fall admission, 5/15 priority date for domestic students. Applications are processed on a rolling basis. *Application fee:* $20 ($30 for international students). *Application Contact:* Dr. Bruce Swindle, Director, 337-475-5576, Fax: 337-475-5986, E-mail: mbaprog@mcneese.edu. *Dean,* Dr. Mitchell Adrian, 337-475-5514, Fax: 337-475-5010, E-mail: madrian@mcneese.edu.

College of Education Students: 122 full-time (89 women), 347 part-time (290 women); includes 110 minority (95 African Americans, 2 American Indian/Alaska Native, 4 Asian Americans or Pacific Islanders, 9 Hispanic Americans), 11 international. *Faculty:* 34 full-time (17 women), 3 part-time/adjunct (2 women). Expenses: Contact institution. *Financial support:* Fellowships, research assistantships, teaching assistantships, Federal Work-Study available. Support available to part-time students. Financial award application deadline: 5/1. In 2006, 163 master's, 2 other advanced degrees awarded. *Degree program information:* Part-time and evening/weekend programs available. Offers counseling psychology (MA); curriculum and instruction (M Ed); early childhood education (M Ed); education (M Ed, MA, MAT, MS, Ed S); educational leadership (M Ed, Ed S); educational technology leadership (M Ed); elementary education (M Ed, MAT); exercise physiology (MS); general psychology (MA); health promotion (MS); instructional technology (MS); school counseling (M Ed); secondary education (M Ed, MAT); special education (mild/moderate) (MAT); teaching (MAT). *Application deadline:* For fall admission, 5/15 priority date for domestic students. Applications are processed on a rolling basis. *Application fee:* $20 ($30 for international students). *Dean,* Dr. Wayne R Fetter, 337-475-5432, Fax: 337-475-5467, E-mail: wfetter@mcneese.edu.

College of Engineering and Technology Students: 63 full-time (13 women), 15 part-time (1 woman); includes 1 minority (Hispanic American), 70 international. *Faculty:* 11 full-time (0 women). Expenses: Contact institution. *Financial support:* Federal Work-Study available. Support available to part-time students. Financial award application deadline: 5/1. In 2006, 47 degrees awarded. *Degree program information:* Part-time and evening/weekend programs available. Offers chemical engineering (M Eng); civil engineering (M Eng); electrical engineering (M Eng); engineering management (M Eng); mechanical engineering (M Eng). *Application deadline:* For fall admission, 5/15 priority date for domestic students. Applications are processed on a rolling basis. *Application fee:* $20 ($30 for international students). *Application Contact:* Dr. Jay O. Uppot, Director of Graduate Studies, 337-475-5874, Fax: 337-475-5286, E-mail: juppot@mcneese.edu. *Dean,* Dr. Nikos Kiritsis, 337-475-5875, Fax: 337-475-5237, E-mail: nikosk@mcneese.edu.

College of Liberal Arts Students: 24 full-time (10 women), 10 part-time (5 women); includes 4 minority (3 African Americans, 1 American Indian/Alaska Native). *Faculty:* 18 full-time (6 women), 1 (woman) part-time/adjunct. Expenses: Contact institution. *Financial support:* Teaching assistantships, Federal Work-Study available. Support available to part-time students. Financial award application deadline: 5/1. In 2006, 17 degrees awarded. *Degree program information:* Part-time and evening/weekend programs available. Offers creative writing (MFA); English (MA); liberal arts (MA, MFA, MM Ed); music education (MM Ed). *Application deadline:* For fall admission, 5/15 priority date for domestic students. Applications are processed on a rolling basis. *Application fee:* $20 ($30 for international students). *Dean,* Dr. Ray Miles, 337-475-5192, Fax: 337-475-5594, E-mail: miles@mcneese.edu.

College of Nursing Students: 16 full-time (11 women), 42 part-time (37 women); includes 7 minority (all African Americans) *Faculty:* 4 full-time (all women), 1 (woman) part-time/adjunct. Expenses: Contact institution. *Financial support:* Application deadline: 5/1. In 2006, 14 degrees awarded. Offers nursing (MSN). *Application deadline:* For fall admission, 5/15 priority date for domestic students. Applications are processed on a rolling basis. *Application fee:* $20 ($30 for international students). *Dean,* Dr. Peggy L. Wolfe, 337-475-5820, Fax: 337-475-5924, E-mail: pwolfe@mcneese.edu.

College of Science Students: 60 full-time (23 women), 13 part-time (2 women); includes 10 minority (7 African Americans, 1 Asian American or Pacific Islander, 2 Hispanic Americans), 42 international. *Faculty:* 19 full-time (5 women). Expenses: Contact institution. *Financial support:* Teaching assistantships, Federal Work-Study available. Support available to part-time students. Financial award application deadline: 5/1. In 2006, 25 degrees awarded. *Degree program information:* Part-time and evening/weekend programs available. Offers agricultural sciences (MS); chemistry (MS); chemistry environmental science education (MS); environmental and chemical sciences (MS); environmental sciences (MS); mathematical science (MS); science (MS). *Application deadline:* For fall admission, 5/15 priority date for domestic students. Applications are processed on a rolling basis. *Application fee:* $20 ($30 for international students). *Dean,* Dr. George F. Mead, 337-475-5785, Fax: 337-475-5249, E-mail: mead@mcneese.edu.

MEADVILLE LOMBARD THEOLOGICAL SCHOOL, Chicago, IL 60637-1602

General Information Independent-religious, coed, graduate-only institution. *Graduate housing:* Rooms and/or apartments available on a first-come, first-served basis to single and married students. Housing application deadline: 4/15.

GRADUATE UNITS

Graduate and Professional Programs *Degree program information:* Part-time programs available. Postbaccalaureate distance learning degree programs offered (minimal on-campus study). Offers divinity (M Div); ministry (D Min); religion (MA).

MEDAILLE COLLEGE, Buffalo, NY 14214-2695

General Information Independent, coed, comprehensive institution. *Enrollment:* 2,971 graduate, professional, and undergraduate students; 1,133 full-time matriculated graduate/professional students (864 women), 131 part-time matriculated graduate/professional students (99 women). *Enrollment by degree level:* 1,264 master's. *Graduate faculty:* 43 full-time (26 women), 117 part-time/adjunct (65 women). *Tuition:* Part-time $580 per credit hour. Full-time tuition and fees vary according to program. *Graduate housing:* Rooms and/or apartments available on a first-come, first-served basis to single and married students. Typical cost: $8,024 (including board) for single students; $8,024 (including board) for married students. Housing application deadline: 8/15. *Student services:* Campus employment opportunities, campus safety program, career counseling, disabled student services, exercise/wellness program, free psychological counseling, low-cost health insurance, multicultural affairs office, teacher training, writing training. *Library facilities:* Medaille College Library. *Online resources:* library catalog, web page, access to other libraries' catalogs. *Collection:* 56,854 titles, 238 serial subscriptions.

Computer facilities: 105 computers available on campus for general student use. A campuswide network can be accessed from student residence rooms and from off campus. Internet access is available. *Web address:* http://www.medaille.edu/.

General Application Contact: Susan Greenwald, Executive Director of Admissions, 716-635-5033 Ext. 2011, Fax: 716-631-1380, E-mail: sgreenwald@medaille.edu.

GRADUATE UNITS

Program in Business Administration—Amherst Students: 228 full-time (136 women); includes 64 minority (49 African Americans, 2 American Indian/Alaska Native, 2 Asian Americans or Pacific Islanders, 11 Hispanic Americans). Average age 36. 135 applicants, 96% accepted, 127 enrolled. *Faculty:* 4 full-time (1 woman), 30 part-time/adjunct (15 women). Expenses: Contact institution. *Financial support:* In 2006–07, 150 students received support. Federal Work-Study available. Financial award applicants required to submit FAFSA. In 2006, 86 degrees awarded. *Degree program information:* Evening/weekend programs available. Offers business administration (MBA); organizational leadership (MA). *Application deadline:* Applications are processed on a rolling basis. *Application fee:* $100. *Application Contact:* Susan Greenwald, Executive Director of Admissions, 716-635-5033 Ext. 2011, Fax: 716-631-1380, E-mail: sgreenwald@medaille.edu. *Associate Dean for Special Programs,* Jennifer Bavifard, 716-631-1061 Ext. 150, Fax: 716-631-1380, E-mail: jbavifar@medaille.edu.

Program in Business Administration—Rochester Students: 46 full-time (32 women); includes 14 minority (9 African Americans, 5 Hispanic Americans). Average age 36. 31 applicants, 87% accepted, 25 enrolled. *Faculty:* 3 full-time (2 women), 53 part-time/adjunct (27 women). Expenses: Contact institution. *Financial support:* In 2006–07, 34 students received support. Federal Work-Study available. Financial award applicants required to submit FAFSA. In 2006, 18 degrees awarded. *Degree program information:* Evening/weekend programs available. Offers business administration (MBA); organizational leadership (MA). *Application deadline:* Applications are processed on a rolling basis. *Application fee:* $100. *Application Contact:* Jane Rowlands, Marketing Support, 585-272-0030, Fax: 585-272-0057, E-mail: jrowlands@medaille.edu. *Branch Campus Director,* Lorraine Beach-Horner, 585-272-0030 Ext. 102, Fax: 585-273-0057, E-mail: lbeach-horner@medaille.edu.

Program in Education Students: 516 full-time (417 women), 334 part-time (276 women); includes 16 minority (13 African Americans, 2 Asian Americans or Pacific Islanders, 1 Hispanic American), 654 international. Average age 27. 725 applicants, 97% accepted, 655 enrolled. *Faculty:* 30 full-time (20 women), 28 part-time/adjunct (18 women). Expenses: Contact institution. *Financial support:* In 2006–07, 390 students received support. Federal Work-Study available. Financial award applicants required to submit FAFSA. In 2006, 229 degrees awarded. *Degree program information:* Part-time and evening/weekend programs available. Offers curriculum and instruction (MS Ed); education preparation (MS Ed); literacy (MS Ed); special education (MS). *Application deadline:* For fall admission, 8/15 priority date for domestic students; for spring admission, 1/15 priority date for domestic students. Applications are processed on a rolling basis. *Application fee:* $35. Electronic applications accepted. *Application Contact:* Susan Greenwald, Executive Director of Admissions, 716-635-5033 Ext. 2011, Fax: 716-631-1380, E-mail: sgreenwald@medaille.edu. *Director of Graduate Programs,* Dr. Robert DiSibio, 716-635-5033 Ext. 2017, Fax: 716-634-2232, E-mail: rdisibio@medaille.edu.

Programs in Psychology Students: 96 full-time (80 women); includes 13 minority (12 African Americans, 1 Hispanic American). Average age 34. 48 applicants, 94% accepted, 43 enrolled. *Faculty:* 6 full-time (3 women), 6 part-time/adjunct (5 women). Expenses: Contact institution. *Financial support:* In 2006–07, 65 students received support. Federal Work-Study available. Financial award applicants required to submit FAFSA. In 2006, 8 degrees awarded. *Degree program information:* Part-time and evening/weekend programs available. Offers mental health counseling (MA); psychology (MA). *Application deadline:* Applications are processed on a rolling basis. *Application fee:* $35. Electronic applications accepted. *Application Contact:* Susan Greenwald, Executive Director of Admissions, 716-635-5033 Ext. 2011, Fax: 716-631-1380, E-mail: sgreenwald@medaille.edu. *Interim Dean of Adult and Graduate Studies,* Dr. Judith Horowitz, 716-880-2229 Ext. 229, Fax: 716-884-0291, E-mail: jhorowitz@medaille.edu.

MEDICAL COLLEGE OF GEORGIA, Augusta, GA 30912

General Information State-supported, coed, upper-level institution. CGS member. *Enrollment:* 2,227 graduate, professional, and undergraduate students; 1,524 full-time matriculated graduate/professional students (827 women), 48 part-time matriculated graduate/professional students (28 women). *Enrollment by degree level:* 953 first professional, 329 master's, 265 doctoral. *Graduate faculty:* 651 full-time (226 women), 139 part-time/adjunct (61 women). Tuition, state resident: full-time $2,293; part-time $192 per credit hour. Tuition, nonresident: full-time $9,169; part-time $765 per credit hour. *Required fees:* $293 per semester. *Graduate housing:* Rooms and/or apartments available on a first-come, first-served basis to single and married students. *Student services:* Campus employment opportunities, campus safety program, career counseling, child daycare facilities, exercise/wellness program, free psychological counseling, international student services, low-cost health insurance, multicultural affairs office. *Library facilities:* Robert B. Greenblatt MD Library. *Online resources:* library catalog, web page, access to other libraries' catalogs. *Collection:* 164,138 titles, 2,429 serial subscriptions. *Research affiliation:* Medical College of Georgia Research Institute, Inc. (biomedical research), Advanced Technology Development Center (biotechnology transfer), Educational Research and Development Association of Georgia Universities (university health and safety), Georgia Research Alliance (science and technology development), Georgia Medical Center Authority (biotechnology and economic development), Georgia Tech Research Corporation (technology development).

Computer facilities: 322 computers available on campus for general student use. A campuswide network can be accessed. Internet access is available. *Web address:* http://www.mcg.edu/.

General Application Contact: Carol S. Nobles, Director of Student Recruitment and Admissions, 706-721-2725, Fax: 706-721-7279, E-mail: cnobles@mail.mcg.edu.

GRADUATE UNITS

School of Allied Health Sciences Students: 271 full-time (219 women); includes 27 African Americans, 8 Asian Americans or Pacific Islanders, 5 Hispanic Americans. Average age 31. 58 applicants, 45% accepted, 21 enrolled. *Faculty:* 34 full-time (12 women). Expenses: Contact institution. *Financial support:* Federal Work-Study available. Support available to part-time students. Financial award application deadline: 5/31; financial award applicants required to submit FAFSA. In 2006, 72 degrees awarded. Postbaccalaureate distance learning degree programs offered. Offers allied health sciences (MHS, MPH, MS, DPT); health information management (MPH, MS); medical illustration (MS); occupational therapy (MHS, MS); physical therapy (MS, DPT). *Application deadline:* For fall admission, 6/15 for domestic students, 1/15 for international students. Applications are processed on a rolling basis. *Application fee:* $30. *Dean/Professor,* Dr. Shelley Mishoe, 706-721-2621, Fax: 706-721-7312, E-mail: smishoe@mail.mcg.edu.

School of Dentistry Students: 63 full-time (21 women); includes 19 minority (4 African Americans, 1 American Indian/Alaska Native, 10 Asian Americans or Pacific Islanders, 4 Hispanic Americans). Average age 25. 267 applicants, 29% accepted, 63 enrolled. *Faculty:* 68 full-time (12 women), 31 part-time/adjunct (3 women). Expenses: Contact institution. *Financial support:* Federal Work-Study and scholarships/grants available. Financial award application deadline: 5/1; financial award applicants required to submit FAFSA. In 2006, 56 degrees awarded. Offers dentistry (DMD). *Application deadline:* For fall admission, 10/15 for domestic students. *Application fee:* $30. Electronic applications accepted. *Application Contact:* Dr. Carole M. Hanes, Associate Dean for Student and Alumni Affairs, 706-721-3587, Fax: 706-721-6276, E-mail: chanes@mcg.edu. *Dean,* Connie Drisko, 706-721-2117, Fax: 706-721-6276, E-mail: cdrisko@mcg.edu.

School of Graduate Studies Students: 264 full-time (170 women), 67 part-time (42 women); includes 59 minority (37 African Americans, 17 Asian Americans or Pacific Islanders, 5 Hispanic Americans), 69 international. Average age 33. 362 applicants, 44% accepted, 88 enrolled. *Faculty:* 210 full-time (67 women), 6 part-time/adjunct (3 women). Expenses: Contact institution. *Financial support:* In 2006–07, 8 fellowships with partial tuition reimbursements (averaging $26,000 per year), 122 research assistantships with partial tuition reimbursements (averaging $23,000 per year) were awarded; teaching assistantships, career-related internships or fieldwork, Federal Work-Study, institutionally sponsored loans, scholarships/grants, traineeships, and unspecified assistantships also available. Support available to part-time students. Financial award application deadline: 5/31; financial award applicants required to submit FAFSA. In 2006, 38 master's, 20 doctorates awarded. *Degree program information:* Part-time programs available. Postbaccalaureate distance learning degree programs offered (no on-campus study). Offers adult nursing (MSN); biochemistry and molecular biology (MS, PhD); biostatistics and bioinformatics (MS); cellular biology and anatomy (MS, PhD); community health nursing (MSN); dental hygiene (MS); medical technology (MS); mental health nursing (MSN); molecular medicine (MS, PhD); neuroscience (MS, PhD); nurse practitioner (MSN); nursing (DNP, PhD); nursing anesthesia (MSN); oral biology and maxillofacial pathology (MS, PhD); parent-child nursing (MSN); pharmacology (MS, PhD); physician assistant (MPA, MS); physiology (MS, PhD); radiologic sciences (MS); respiratory therapy (MS). *Application deadline:* For fall admission, 6/30 for domestic students, 1/15 for international students. Applications are processed on a rolling basis. *Application fee:* $30. *Application Contact:* Carol S. Nobles, Director of Student Recruitment and Admissions, 706-721-2725, Fax: 706-721-7279, E-mail: cnobles@mail.mcg.edu. *Dean,* Dr. Gretchen B. Caughman, 706-721-3278, Fax: 706-721-6829, E-mail: gcaughma@mail.mcg.edu.

Vascular Biology Center Students: 13 full-time (8 women); includes 3 minority (1 African American, 2 Asian Americans or Pacific Islanders), 6 international. Average age 29. *Faculty:* 8 full-time (2 women), 1 (woman) part-time/adjunct. Expenses: Contact institution. *Financial support:* In 2006–07, 1 fellowship with partial tuition reimbursement (averaging $26,000 per year), 10 research assistantships with partial tuition reimbursements (averaging $23,000 per year) were awarded; Federal Work-Study, institutionally sponsored loans, traineeships, and unspecified assistantships also available. Support available to part-time students. Financial award application deadline: 5/31. In 2006, 2 degrees awarded. Offers vascular biology (MS, PhD). *Application deadline:* For fall admission, 1/15 for domestic students. *Application fee:* $30. *Application Contact:* Dr. David Pollock, Program Director, 706-721-8514, Fax: 706-721-8545, E-mail: dpollock@mail.mcg.edu. *Regents Professor and Director,* Dr. John D. Catravas, 706-721-6338, Fax: 706-721-8545, E-mail: jcatrava@mail.mcg.edu.

School of Medicine Offers medicine (MD).

MEDICAL COLLEGE OF WISCONSIN, Milwaukee, WI 53226-0509

General Information Independent, coed, graduate-only institution. CGS member. *Graduate housing:* On-campus housing not available. *Research affiliation:* General Electric Medical Systems (biophysics, radiology).

GRADUATE UNITS

Graduate School of Biomedical Sciences *Degree program information:* Part-time and evening/weekend programs available. Postbaccalaureate distance learning degree programs offered (minimal on-campus study). Offers biochemistry (MS, PhD); bioethics (MA); bioinformatics (MS); biomedical sciences (MA, MPH, MS, PhD); biophysics (PhD); biostatistics (PhD); cell and developmental biology (MS, PhD); epidemiology (MS); functional imaging (PhD); health care technologies (PhD); medical informatics (MS); microbiology and molecular genetics (MS, PhD); pathology (MS, PhD); pharmacology and toxicology (MS, PhD); physiology (MS, PhD).

Medical School *Degree program information:* Part-time programs available. Postbaccalaureate distance learning degree programs offered (no on-campus study). Offers general preventive medicine and public health (MPH); medicine (MD, MPH); occupational medicine (MPH).

MEDICAL UNIVERSITY OF SOUTH CAROLINA, Charleston, SC 29425-0002

General Information State-supported, coed, upper-level institution. CGS member. *Enrollment:* 1,910 full-time matriculated graduate/professional students (1,149 women), 179 part-time matriculated graduate/professional students (142 women). *Enrollment by degree level:* 1,136 first professional, 634 master's, 319 doctoral. *Graduate faculty:* 1,163 full-time (440 women), 170 part-time/adjunct (53 women). *Graduate housing:* On-campus housing not available. *Student services:* Campus employment opportunities, campus safety program, exercise/wellness program, free psychological counseling, grant writing training, international student services, low-cost health insurance, multicultural affairs office, writing training. *Library facilities:* Medical University of South Carolina Library plus 1 other. *Online resources:* library catalog, web page, access to other libraries' catalogs. *Collection:* 225,061 titles, 3,746 serial subscriptions, 1,570 audiovisual materials. *Research affiliation:* GlaxoSmithKline (Sepsis), Sanofic Synthelabo Inc. (Cancer), Astra Pharmaceuticals LP (Renal/Hypertension), Microbia, Inc. (Renal), Amgen, Inc. (Scleroderma).

Computer facilities: 200 computers available on campus for general student use. A campuswide network can be accessed from off campus. Internet access is available. *Web address:* http://www.musc.edu/.

General Application Contact: George W. Ohlandt, Director of Admissions, 843-792-3813, Fax: 843-792-6615, E-mail: ohlandtg@musc.edu.

GRADUATE UNITS

College of Dental Medicine Students: 220 full-time (93 women); includes 32 minority (12 African Americans, 1 American Indian/Alaska Native, 13 Asian Americans or Pacific Islanders, 6 Hispanic Americans). Average age 26. 467 applicants, 13% accepted, 54 enrolled. *Faculty:* 47 full-time (8 women), 25 part-time/adjunct (5 women). Expenses: Contact institution. *Financial support:* In 2006–07, 197 students received support. Federal Work-Study, scholarships/grants, and tuition waivers (partial) available. Support available to part-time students. Financial award application deadline: 3/15; financial award applicants required to submit FAFSA. In 2006, 49 degrees awarded. Offers dental medicine (DMD). *Application deadline:* For fall admission, 2/1 for domestic and international students. *Application fee:* $75. Electronic applications accepted. *Application Contact:* Jill R. Stevens, Graduate Studies Admissions, 843-792-4892, Fax: 843-792-6615, E-mail: stevensj@musc.edu. *Dean,* Dr. John J. Sanders, 843-792-3811, Fax: 843-792-1376, E-mail: sandersjj@musc.edu.

College of Graduate Studies Students: 208 full-time (114 women), 56 part-time (36 women); includes 33 minority (14 African Americans, 1 American Indian/Alaska Native, 11 Asian Americans or Pacific Islanders, 7 Hispanic Americans), 32 international. Average age 28. 355 applicants, 33% accepted, 78 enrolled. *Faculty:* 390 full-time (122 women). Expenses: Contact institution. *Financial support:* In 2006–07, fellowships with partial tuition reimbursements (averaging $21,000 per year); Federal Work-Study and scholarships/grants also available. Support available to part-time students. Financial award application deadline: 3/1; financial award applicants required to submit FAFSA. In 2006, 22 master's, 39 doctorates awarded. Offers biochemistry and molecular biology (MS, PhD); bioinformatics (MS, PhD); biostatistics (MS, PhD); cancer biology (PhD); cell and molecular pharmacology and experimental therapeutics (MS, PhD); cell biology and anatomy (PhD); clinical research (MS); epidemiology (MS, PhD); marine biomedicine (PhD); microbiology and immunology (MS, PhD); neurosciences (MS, PhD); pathology and laboratory medicine (MS, PhD). *Application deadline:* For fall admission, 1/15 priority date for domestic and international students. Applications are processed on a rolling basis. *Application fee:* $0 ($75 for international students). Electronic applications accepted. *Application Contact:* Dr. Cynthia F. Wright, Assistant Dean for Admissions, 843-792-3391, Fax: 843-792-6590, E-mail: wrightcf@musc.edu. *Dean,* Dr. Perry V. Halushka, 843-792-3012, Fax: 843-792-6590, E-mail: halushpv@musc.edu.

College of Health Professions Students: 499 full-time (373 women), 38 part-time (26 women); includes 73 minority (45 African Americans, 2 American Indian/Alaska Native, 12 Asian Americans or Pacific Islanders, 14 Hispanic Americans), 8 international. Average age 28. 637 applicants, 44% accepted, 220 enrolled. *Faculty:* 91 full-time (50 women), 6 part-time/adjunct (1 woman). Expenses: Contact institution. *Financial support:* In 2006–07, 483 students received support. Career-related internships or fieldwork, Federal Work-Study, scholarships/grants, and tuition waivers (partial) available. Support available to part-time students. Financial award application deadline: 3/15; financial award applicants required to submit FAFSA. In 2006, 193 master's, 9 doctorates awarded. *Degree program information:* Part-time programs available. Offers anesthesia for nurses (MS); communication sciences and disorders (MSR); cytology and biosciences (MS); health administration (DHA); health administration-executive (MHA); health administration-residential (MHA); health professions (MHA, MS, MSR, DHA, DPT); occupational therapy (MSR); physical therapy (DPT); physician assistant (MS). *Application fee:* $75. Electronic applications accepted. *Application Contact:* Jennifer R. Bailey, Director of Student Services, 843-792-1601, Fax: 843-792-0253, E-mail: baileyje@musc.edu. *Interim Dean,* Dr. Becki A. Trickey, 843-792-8702, Fax: 843-792-3322, E-mail: trickeyb@musc.edu.

College of Medicine Students: 600 full-time (284 women); includes 121 minority (56 African Americans, 3 American Indian/Alaska Native, 46 Asian Americans or Pacific Islanders, 16 Hispanic Americans), 7 international. Average age 26. 1,501 applicants, 10% accepted, 135 enrolled. *Faculty:* 949 full-time (332 women), 136 part-time/adjunct (45 women). Expenses: Contact institution. *Financial support:* In 2006–07, 487 students received support. Federal Work-Study and scholarships/grants available. Financial award application deadline: 3/15; financial award applicants required to submit FAFSA. In 2006, 135 degrees awarded. Offers medicine (MD). *Application deadline:* For fall admission, 12/1 for domestic and international students. Applications are processed on a rolling basis. *Application fee:* $75. Electronic applications accepted. *Application Contact:* Wanda L. Taylor, Director of Admissions, 843-792-2055, Fax: 843-792-0204, E-mail: taylorwl@musc.edu. *Dean,* Dr. Jerry G. Reves, 843-792-2842, Fax: 843-792-2967, E-mail: revesj@musc.edu.

College of Nursing Students: 67 full-time (56 women), 85 part-time (80 women); includes 21 minority (15 African Americans, 2 American Indian/Alaska Native, 2 Asian Americans or Pacific Islanders, 2 Hispanic Americans). Average age 35. 87 applicants, 84% accepted, 73 enrolled. *Faculty:* 34 full-time (33 women), 2 part-time/adjunct (both women). Expenses: Contact institution. *Financial support:* Federal Work-Study, scholarships/grants, and traineeships available. Support available to part-time students. Financial award application deadline: 3/15; financial award applicants required to submit FAFSA. In 2006, 58 degrees awarded. *Degree program information:* Part-time programs available. Postbaccalaureate distance learning degree programs offered (minimal on-campus study). Offers adult nurse practitioner (MSN); family nurse practitioner (MSN); gerontological nurse practitioner (MSN); neonatal nurse practitioner (MSN); nurse educator (MSN); nurse midwifery (MSN); nursing (MSN, PhD); nursing administration (MSN); pediatric nursing (MSN); psychiatric mental health nurse practitioner (MSN). *Application deadline:* For fall admission, 2/1 for domestic and international students; for spring admission, 9/15 for domestic and international students. *Application fee:* $75. Electronic applications accepted. *Application Contact:* Carolyn F. Page, Director, Student Services, 843-792-3844, Fax: 843-792-9258, E-mail: pagecf@musc.edu. *Dean,* Dr. Gail W. Stuart, 843-792-3941, Fax: 843-792-0504, E-mail: stuartg@musc.edu.

College of Pharmacy Students: 316 full-time (229 women); includes 51 minority (24 African Americans, 2 American Indian/Alaska Native, 19 Asian Americans or Pacific Islanders, 6 Hispanic Americans). Average age 25. 612 applicants, 17% accepted, 81 enrolled. *Faculty:* 42 full-time (17 women), 1 part-time/adjunct (0 women). Expenses: Contact institution. *Financial support:* In 2006–07, 270 students received support. Career-related internships or fieldwork, Federal Work-Study, institutionally sponsored loans, and scholarships/grants available. Financial award application deadline: 8/15; financial award applicants required to submit FAFSA. In 2006, 54 degrees awarded. Offers pharmaceutical sciences (PhD); pharmacy (Pharm D). *Application deadline:* For fall admission, 1/15 for domestic and international students. *Application fee:* $75. Electronic applications accepted. *Interim Dean,* Dr. Arnold W. Karig, 843-792-8452, Fax: 843-792-9081, E-mail: karigaw@musc.edu.

MEHARRY MEDICAL COLLEGE, Nashville, TN 37208-9989

General Information Independent-religious, coed, graduate-only institution. CGS member. *Graduate housing:* Rooms and/or apartments available on a first-come, first-served basis to single and married students.

GRADUATE UNITS

School of Dentistry Offers dentistry (DDS).

School of Graduate Studies *Degree program information:* Part-time and evening/weekend programs available. Offers biochemistry (PhD); biomedical sciences (PhD); general preventive medicine (MSPH); health services administration (MSPH); microbiology (PhD); occupational medicine (MSPH); pharmacology (MS, PhD); physiology (PhD); public health administration (MSPH).

School of Medicine Offers medicine (MD).

MEMORIAL UNIVERSITY OF NEWFOUNDLAND, St. John's, NL A1C 5S7, Canada

General Information Province-supported, coed, university. *Graduate housing:* Rooms and/or apartments available on a first-come, first-served basis to single and married students. *Research affiliation:* Eastern Regional Health Authority (health research).

GRADUATE UNITS

Faculty of Medicine *Degree program information:* Part-time programs available. Postbaccalaureate distance learning degree programs offered (no on-campus study). Offers medicine (MD, M Sc, PhD, Diploma). Electronic applications accepted.

Graduate Programs in Medicine *Degree program information:* Part-time programs available. Offers basic medical sciences (M Sc, PhD); clinical epidemiology (M Sc, PhD, Diploma); community health (M Sc, PhD, Diploma); human genetics (M Sc, PhD); medicine (M Sc, PhD, Diploma). Electronic applications accepted.

School of Graduate Studies *Degree program information:* Part-time and evening/weekend programs available. Postbaccalaureate distance learning degree programs offered (minimal on-campus study). Offers applied social psychology (MASP); aquaculture (M Sc); archaeol-

Memorial University of Newfoundland (continued)

ogy and physical anthropology (MA, PhD); atomic and molecular physics (M Sc, PhD); biochemistry (M Sc, PhD); biology (M Sc, PhD); chemistry (M Sc, PhD); classics (MA); cognitive and behavioral ecology (M Sc, PhD); computational science (M Sc); computational science (cooperative) (M Sc); computer engineering (MA Sc); computer science (M Sc, PhD); condensed matter physics (M Sc, PhD); economics (MA); employment relations (MER); English language and literature (MA, PhD); environmental science (M Env Sc, M Sc); environmental systems engineering and management (MA Sc); ethnomusicology (MA, PhD); experimental psychology (M Sc, PhD); fisheries resource management (MMS, Advanced Diploma); folklore (MA, PhD); food science (M Sc, PhD); French studies (MA); gender (PhD); geography (M Sc, MA, PhD); geology (M Sc, PhD); geophysics (M Sc, PhD); German language and literature (M Phil, MA); history (MA, PhD); humanities (M Phil); instrumental analysis (M Sc); linguistics (MA, PhD); marine biology (M Sc, PhD); maritime sociology (PhD); mathematics (M Sc, PhD); oil and gas studies (MOGS); philosophy (MA); physical oceanography (M Sc, PhD); physics (M Sc); political science (MA); religious studies (MA); social and cultural anthropology (MA, PhD); sociology (M Phil, MA); statistics (M Sc, MAS, PhD); work and development (PhD). Electronic applications accepted.

Faculty of Business Administration *Degree program information:* Part-time programs available. Offers business administration (EMBA, MBA). Electronic applications accepted.

Faculty of Education *Degree program information:* Part-time programs available. Offers counseling psychology (M Ed); curriculum, teaching, and learning studies (M Ed); education (PhD); educational leadership studies (M Ed); information technology (M Ed); post-secondary studies (M Ed, Diploma). Electronic applications accepted.

Faculty of Engineering and Applied Science *Degree program information:* Part-time programs available. Offers civil engineering (M Eng, PhD); electrical and computer engineering (M Eng, PhD); mechanical engineering (M Eng, PhD); ocean and naval architecture engineering (M Eng, PhD). Electronic applications accepted.

School of Human Kinetics and Recreation *Degree program information:* Part-time programs available. Offers administration, curriculum and supervision (MPE); biomechanics/ergonomics (MS Kin); exercise and work physiology (MS Kin); sport psychology (MS Kin). Electronic applications accepted.

School of Music Offers conducting (MMus); performance pedagogy (MMus); performing (MMus). Electronic applications accepted.

School of Nursing *Degree program information:* Part-time programs available. Offers nursing (MN, PMD). Electronic applications accepted.

School of Pharmacy *Degree program information:* Part-time programs available. Offers pharmacy (MSCPharm, PhD). Electronic applications accepted.

School of Social Work *Degree program information:* Part-time and evening/weekend programs available. Offers social work (MSW). Electronic applications accepted.

MEMPHIS COLLEGE OF ART, Memphis, TN 38104-2764

General Information Independent, coed, comprehensive institution. *Enrollment:* 308 graduate, professional, and undergraduate students; 11 full-time matriculated graduate/professional students (6 women), 8 part-time matriculated graduate/professional students (5 women). *Enrollment by degree level:* 19 master's. *Graduate faculty:* 11 full-time (4 women), 3 part-time/adjunct (2 women). *Tuition:* Full-time $21,000; part-time $875 per hour. *Required fees:* $560. Tuition and fees vary according to program. *Graduate housing:* Room and/or apartments available on a first-come, first-served basis to single students; on-campus housing not available to married students. Typical cost: $5,600 per year ($7,600 including board). Room and board charges vary according to housing facility selected. Housing application deadline: 8/15. *Student services:* Campus employment opportunities, campus safety program, career counseling, international student services, teacher training. *Library facilities:* G. Pillow Lewis Library plus 1 other. *Online resources:* web page. *Collection:* 14,500 titles, 108 serial subscriptions, 175 audiovisual materials.

Computer facilities: Computer purchase and lease plans are available. 70 computers available on campus for general student use. Internet access is available. *Web address:* http://www.mca.edu/.

General Application Contact: Annette James Moore, Director of Admissions, 800-727-1088, Fax: 901-272-5158, E-mail: info@mca.edu.

GRADUATE UNITS

Graduate Programs Students: 11 full-time (6 women); includes 2 minority (both Hispanic Americans) Average age 26. 46 applicants, 41% accepted, 11 enrolled. *Faculty:* 11 full-time (4 women), 3 part-time/adjunct (2 women). Expenses: Contact institution. *Financial support:* In 2006–07, 5 teaching assistantships with partial tuition reimbursements (averaging $2,000 per year) were awarded; career-related internships or fieldwork, Federal Work-Study, institutionally sponsored loans, scholarships/grants, tuition waivers (partial), unspecified assistantships, and merit awards also available. Support available to part-time students. Financial award application deadline: 8/1; financial award applicants required to submit FAFSA. In 2006, 6 degrees awarded. *Degree program information:* Part-time programs available. Offers art education (MA, MAT); computer arts (MFA); fiber/surface design (MFA); painting (MFA); papermaking (MFA); photography (MFA); printmaking (MFA); sculpture (MFA); studio art (MFA). *Application deadline:* For fall admission, 3/1 priority date for domestic and international students; for spring admission, 11/1 priority date for domestic and international students. *Application fee:* $50. Electronic applications accepted. *Application Contact:* Annette James Moore, Director of Admissions, 800-727-1088, Fax: 901-272-5158, E-mail: info@mca.edu. *Vice President Academic Affairs,* Ken Strickland, 901-272-5100, Fax: 901-272-5104, E-mail: info@mca.edu.

MEMPHIS THEOLOGICAL SEMINARY, Memphis, TN 38104-4395

General Information Independent-religious, coed, graduate-only institution. *Graduate housing:* Rooms and/or apartments available on a first-come, first-served basis to single and married students. Housing application deadline: 7/15. *Research affiliation:* Lilly Foundation (technology/religion), Wabash Center for Teaching and Learning (theology, religion).

GRADUATE UNITS

Graduate and Professional Programs *Degree program information:* Part-time programs available. Offers theology (M Div, MAR, D Min).

MENNONITE BRETHREN BIBLICAL SEMINARY, Fresno, CA 93727-5097

General Information Independent-religious, coed, graduate-only institution. *Graduate housing:* Rooms and/or apartments available on a first-come, first-served basis to single and married students.

GRADUATE UNITS

School of Theology *Degree program information:* Part-time programs available. Postbaccalaureate distance learning degree programs offered (minimal on-campus study). Offers church ministry (MA); divinity (M Div); intercultural mission (MA); marriage, family, and child counseling (MAMFCC, Diploma); New Testament (MA); Old Testament (MA); theology (MA).

MERCER UNIVERSITY, Macon, GA 31207-0003

General Information Independent-religious, coed, comprehensive institution. *Enrollment:* 5,090 graduate, professional, and undergraduate students; 1,802 full-time matriculated graduate/professional students (1,000 women), 712 part-time matriculated graduate/professional students (454 women). *Enrollment by degree level:* 1,470 first professional, 932 master's, 92 doctoral, 20 other advanced degrees. *Graduate faculty:* 125 full-time (52 women), 27 part-time/adjunct (10 women). *Graduate housing:* Rooms and/or apartments available on a first-come, first-served basis to single and married students. *Student services:* Campus employment opportunities, campus safety program, career counseling, disabled student services, free psychological counseling, international student services, low-cost health insurance. *Library facilities:* Jack Tarver Library plus 3 others. *Online resources:* library catalog, web page. *Collection:* 692,225 titles, 28,163 serial subscriptions, 64,319 audiovisual materials. *Research affiliation:* Central State Hospital of Milledgeville, Georgia (schizophrenia, treatment of psychosis, tumor necrosis), MedCen Foundation (basic clinical investigations).

Computer facilities: 350 computers available on campus for general student use. A campuswide network can be accessed from student residence rooms and from off campus. Internet access and online class registration are available. *Web address:* http://www.mercer.edu/.

General Application Contact: Information Contact, 478-301-2700.

GRADUATE UNITS

Graduate Studies, Cecil B. Day Campus Students: 996 full-time (614 women), 511 part-time (346 women); includes 486 minority (360 African Americans, 7 American Indian/Alaska Native, 94 Asian Americans or Pacific Islanders, 25 Hispanic Americans), 83 international. Average age 31. *Faculty:* 79 full-time (40 women), 22 part-time/adjunct (7 women). Expenses: Contact institution. *Financial support:* Teaching assistantships, career-related internships or fieldwork, Federal Work-Study, and scholarships/grants available. Support available to part-time students. In 2006, 161 M Divs, 237 master's, 5 doctorates, 4 other advanced degrees awarded. *Degree program information:* Part-time and evening/weekend programs available. Postbaccalaureate distance learning degree programs offered (no on-campus study).

College of Pharmacy and Health Sciences Students: 584 full-time (401 women), 27 part-time (22 women); includes 158 minority (69 African Americans, 3 American Indian/Alaska Native, 71 Asian Americans or Pacific Islanders, 15 Hispanic Americans), 33 international. Average age 26. 2,250 applicants, 12% accepted, 155 enrolled. *Faculty:* 21 full-time (13 women), 2 part-time/adjunct (1 woman). Expenses: Contact institution. *Financial support:* In 2006–07, 350 students received support; teaching assistantships with tuition reimbursements available, career-related internships or fieldwork, Federal Work-Study, institutionally sponsored loans, scholarships/grants, and tuition waivers available. Support available to part-time students. Financial award application deadline: 5/1; financial award applicants required to submit FAFSA. In 2006, 128 Pharm Ds, 5 doctorates awarded. Offers medical sciences (MS); pharmacy (Pharm D, PhD). *Application deadline:* For fall admission, 1/1 for domestic students. Applications are processed on a rolling basis. *Application fee:* $25. Electronic applications accepted. *Application Contact:* Dr. James W. Bartling, Associate Dean for Student Affairs and Admissions, 678-547-6232, Fax: 678-547-6063, E-mail: bartling_jw@mercer.edu. *Dean,* Dr. Hewitt W. Matthews, 678-547-6304, Fax: 678-547-6315, E-mail: matthews_h@mercer.edu.

Eugene W. Stetson School of Business and Economics Students: 195 full-time (81 women), 147 part-time (70 women); includes 111 minority (90 African Americans, 2 American Indian/Alaska Native, 14 Asian Americans or Pacific Islanders, 5 Hispanic Americans), 37 international. Average age 32. *Faculty:* 19 full-time (5 women), 6 part-time/adjunct (0 women). Expenses: Contact institution. *Financial support:* Federal Work-Study available. In 2006, 158 degrees awarded. *Degree program information:* Part-time and evening/weekend programs available. Offers business administration (MBA, XMBA). *Application deadline:* For fall admission, 7/1 priority date for domestic students; for spring admission, 11/1 priority date for domestic students. Applications are processed on a rolling basis. *Application fee:* $50 ($100 for international students). Electronic applications accepted. *Assistant Vice President of Admissions,* Karen G. Herlitz, 678-547-6206, Fax: 678-547-6367, E-mail: herlitz.kg@mercer.edu.

Georgia Baptist College of Nursing Students: 8 full-time (all women), 5 part-time (all women); includes 4 minority (all African Americans) Average age 39. 5 applicants, 100% accepted, 4 enrolled. *Faculty:* 13 full-time (12 women). Expenses: Contact institution. *Financial support:* In 2006–07, 13 students received support. Institutionally sponsored loans, scholarships/grants, and traineeships available. Support available to part-time students. Financial award applicants required to submit FAFSA. In 2006, 8 degrees awarded. *Degree program information:* Part-time programs available. Offers nurse education (Certificate); nursing (MSN). *Application deadline:* For fall admission, 7/1 for domestic students, 4/15 for international students; for spring admission, 12/1 for domestic students. Applications are processed on a rolling basis. *Application fee:* $50. *Application Contact:* Lynn Vines, Director of Admissions, 678-547-6700, Fax: 678-547-6794, E-mail: nursing@mercer.edu. *Dean/Professor,* Dr. Susan S. Gunby, 678-547-6799, Fax: 678-547-6796, E-mail: nursing@mercer.edu.

James and Carolyn McAfee School of Theology Students: 156 full-time (82 women), 70 part-time (32 women); includes 72 minority (67 African Americans, 2 Asian Americans or Pacific Islanders, 3 Hispanic Americans), 5 international. Average age 34. 117 applicants, 81% accepted, 49 enrolled. *Faculty:* 12 full-time (3 women), 6 part-time/adjunct (3 women). Expenses: Contact institution. *Financial support:* In 2006–07, 30 students received support. Career-related internships or fieldwork, Federal Work-Study, institutionally sponsored loans, and scholarships/grants available. Support available to part-time students. Financial award applicants required to submit FAFSA. In 2006, 34 degrees awarded. *Degree program information:* Part-time programs available. Offers theology (M Div, D Min). *Application deadline:* Applications are processed on a rolling basis. *Application fee:* $35. *Application Contact:* Ryan A. Clark, Director of Admissions, 678-547-6491, Fax: 678-547-6478, E-mail: clark_ra@mercer.edu. *Dean,* Dr. R. Alan Culpepper, 678-547-6470, Fax: 678-547-6478, E-mail: culpepper_ra@mercer.edu.

Tift College of Education Students: 31 full-time (23 women), 211 part-time (174 women); includes 111 minority (101 African Americans, 2 American Indian/Alaska Native, 6 Asian Americans or Pacific Islanders, 2 Hispanic Americans), 2 international. Average age 33. *Faculty:* 13 full-time (6 women), 7 part-time/adjunct (3 women). Expenses: Contact institution. *Financial support:* Federal Work-Study available. Support available to part-time students. Financial award application deadline: 5/1. In 2006, 57 master's, 4 other advanced degrees awarded. *Degree program information:* Part-time and evening/weekend programs available. Offers early childhood education (M Ed, MAT); educational leadership (M Ed, PhD); middle grades education (M Ed, MAT); reading education (M Ed); secondary education (M Ed, MAT); teacher leadership (Ed S). *Application deadline:* For fall admission, 8/1 for domestic and international students; for spring admission, 12/1 for domestic and international students. Applications are processed on a rolling basis. *Application fee:* $25. *Application Contact:* Dr. Allison Gilmore, Associate Dean for Graduate Teacher Education, 678-547-6330, Fax: 678-547-6055, E-mail: gilmore_a@mercer.edu. *Dean,* Dr. Carl R. Martray, 478-301-5397, Fax: 478-301-2280, E-mail: martray_cr@mercer.edu.

Graduate Studies, Macon Campus Students: 28 full-time (13 women), 182 part-time (89 women); includes 50 minority (37 African Americans, 1 American Indian/Alaska Native, 8 Asian Americans or Pacific Islanders, 4 Hispanic Americans), 11 international. Average age 32. *Faculty:* 43 full-time (12 women), 5 part-time/adjunct (3 women). Expenses: Contact institution. *Financial support:* Career-related internships or fieldwork, Federal Work-Study, and institutionally sponsored loans available. Support available to part-time students. In 2006, 68 degrees awarded. *Degree program information:* Part-time and evening/weekend programs available. *Application Contact:* Director, 912-301-2700.

Eugene W. Stetson School of Business and Economics Students: 9 full-time (5 women), 39 part-time (21 women); includes 8 minority (6 African Americans, 2 Asian Americans or Pacific Islanders), 6 international. Average age 27. 16 applicants, 94% accepted, 15 enrolled. *Faculty:* 9 full-time (3 women). Expenses: Contact institution. In 2006, 18 degrees awarded. *Degree program information:* Part-time and evening/weekend programs available. Offers business and economics (MBA). *Application deadline:* For fall admission, 8/1 for domestic students; for spring admission, 12/1 for domestic students. Applications are processed on a rolling basis. *Application fee:* $50 ($100 for international students). *Application Contact:* Robert Holland, Director, Academic Administrator, 478-301-2835, Fax: 478-301-2635, E-mail: holland_r@mercer.edu. *Dean,* Dr. William S. Mounts, 478-301-2837, Fax: 478-301-2635, E-mail: mounts_ws@mercer.edu.

School of Engineering Students: 5 full-time (0 women), 72 part-time (17 women); includes 17 minority (7 African Americans, 6 Asian Americans or Pacific Islanders, 4 Hispanic Americans), 4 international. Average age 32. *Faculty:* 20 full-time (3 women), 1 part-time/adjunct (0 women). Expenses: Contact institution. *Financial support:* Federal Work-Study available. In 2006, 26 degrees awarded. *Degree program information:* Part-time and evening/weekend programs available. Postbaccalaureate distance learning degree programs offered (no on-campus study). Offers computer engineering (MSE); electrical engineering

(MSE); engineering management (MSE); mechanical engineering (MSE); software engineering (MSE); software systems (MS); technical communications management (MS); technical management (MS). *Application deadline:* For fall admission, 7/1 for domestic students; for spring admission, 11/15 for international students. Applications are processed on a rolling basis. *Application fee:* $35 ($50 for international students). Electronic applications accepted. *Application Contact:* Kathy Olivier, Graduate Program Coordinator, 478-301-5480, Fax: 478-301-5434, E-mail: olivier_kk@mercer.edu. *Dean,* Dr. M. Dayne Aldridge, 478-301-2459, Fax: 478-301-5593, E-mail: aldridge_md@mercer.edu.

School of Music Students: 11 full-time (5 women), 3 part-time (2 women); includes 2 minority (both African Americans), 1 international. Average age 32. *Faculty:* 1 full-time (0 women). Expenses: Contact institution. In 2006, 1 degree awarded. Offers choral conducting (MM); church music (MM); performance (MM). *Application fee:* $50. *Application Contact:* Gina Cook Nelson, Director of Admissions, 478-301-2307, E-mail: nelson_gc@mercer.edu. *Director of Graduate Studies,* John E. Simons, 478-301-4012, E-mail: simons_je@mercer.edu.

Tift College of Education Students: 3 full-time (all women), 68 part-time (49 women); includes 23 minority (22 African Americans, 1 American Indian/Alaska Native). Average age 31. 25 applicants, 68% accepted, 11 enrolled. *Faculty:* 13 full-time (6 women), 4 part-time/adjunct (3 women). Expenses: Contact institution. *Financial support:* Federal Work-Study and institutionally sponsored loans available. Support available to part-time students. Financial award application deadline: 5/1. In 2006, 19 degrees awarded. *Degree program information:* Part-time and evening/weekend programs available. Offers collaborative education (M Ed); educational leadership (M Ed, PhD). *Application deadline:* For fall admission, 8/1 for domestic students; for spring admission, 12/1 for domestic students. Applications are processed on a rolling basis. *Application fee:* $25. *Application Contact:* Dr. Penny Elkins, Associate Dean, 678-547-6556, Fax: 678-547-6389, E-mail: elkins_pl@mercer.edu. *Dean,* Dr. Carl R. Martray, 478-301-5397, Fax: 478-301-2280, E-mail: martray_cr@mercer.edu.

School of Medicine Students: 334 full-time (185 women), 18 part-time (all women); includes 88 minority (53 African Americans, 33 Asian Americans or Pacific Islanders, 2 Hispanic Americans). Expenses: Contact institution. *Financial support:* In 2006–07, 352 students received support. Institutionally sponsored loans available. Financial award application deadline: 4/1; financial award applicants required to submit FAFSA. In 2006, 36 master's awarded. Offers medicine (MD, MFT, MPH, MSA). *Application deadline:* For fall admission, 11/1 for domestic students, 10/1 for international students. Applications are processed on a rolling basis. *Application fee:* $50 ($150 for international students). *Application Contact:* Mary C. Putnam, Enrollment Associate, 478-301-2542, Fax: 478-301-2547, E-mail: putnam_mc@mercer.edu. *Dean,* Dr. Martin Dalton, 478-301-5570, Fax: 478-301-2547.

Walter F. George School of Law Students: 451 full-time (194 women); includes 74 minority (50 African Americans, 2 American Indian/Alaska Native, 12 Asian Americans or Pacific Islanders, 10 Hispanic Americans), 3 international. Average age 24. 1,290 applicants, 35% accepted, 176 enrolled. *Faculty:* 31 full-time (10 women), 34 part-time/adjunct (9 women). Expenses: Contact institution. *Financial support:* In 2006–07, 383 students received support, including 15 fellowships (averaging $3,800 per year), 13 research assistantships (averaging $476 per year); career-related internships or fieldwork, Federal Work-Study, institutionally sponsored loans, scholarships/grants, tuition waivers (partial), and institutional work-study also available. Support available to part-time students. Financial award application deadline: 4/1; financial award applicants required to submit FAFSA. In 2006, 127 degrees awarded. *Degree program information:* Part-time programs available. Offers law (JD). *Application deadline:* For fall admission, 3/15 priority date for domestic students. Applications are processed on a rolling basis. *Application fee:* $50. Electronic applications accepted. *Application Contact:* Susan Martin, Admissions Assistant, 478-301-2605, Fax: 478-301-2989, E-mail: martin_sv@mercer.edu. *Dean,* Daisy H. Floyd, 478-301-2602, Fax: 478-301-2101, E-mail: floyd_dh@mercer.edu.

MERCY COLLEGE, Dobbs Ferry, NY 10522-1189

General Information Independent, coed, comprehensive institution. CGS member. *Enrollment:* 9,120 graduate, professional, and undergraduate students; 1,117 full-time matriculated graduate/professional students (885 women), 2,692 part-time matriculated graduate/professional students (2,039 women). *Enrollment by degree level:* 3,537 master's. *Tuition:* Part-time $595 per credit. *Required fees:* $9 per credit. Tuition and fees vary according to program. *Graduate housing:* Room and/or apartments available on a first-come, first-served basis to single students; on-campus housing not available to married students. *Student services:* Campus employment opportunities, career counseling, disabled student services, free psychological counseling, international student services, teacher training, writing training. *Library facilities:* Mercy College Library. *Online resources:* library catalog, web page. *Collection:* 322,610 titles, 1,765 serial subscriptions.

Computer facilities: 138 computers available on campus for general student use. A campuswide network can be accessed from off campus. Internet access is available. *Web address:* http://www.mercy.edu/.

General Application Contact: Kathleen Jackson, Director of Admissions, 800-Mercy-NY, Fax: 914-674-7382, E-mail: admissions@mercy.edu.

GRADUATE UNITS

Division of Business and Accounting Students: 95 full-time (66 women), 246 part-time (164 women); includes 159 minority (103 African Americans, 8 Asian Americans or Pacific Islanders, 48 Hispanic Americans), 34 international. Average age 36. Expenses: Contact institution. In 2006, 192 degrees awarded. Offers banking (MS); business administration (MBA); direct marketing (MS); human resource management (MS); organizational leadership (MS); securities (MS). *Application deadline:* For fall admission, 2/1 for domestic students. Applications are processed on a rolling basis. *Application fee:* $37. Electronic applications accepted. *Application Contact:* Kathleen Jackson, Director of Admissions, 800-Mercy-NY, Fax: 914-674-7382, E-mail: admissions@mercy.edu. *Director,* Wayne L. Cioffari, 914-674-7481, Fax: 914-674-7488, E-mail: mba@mercy.edu.

Division of Education Students: 572 full-time (467 women), 1,719 part-time (1,287 women); includes 943 minority (470 African Americans, 7 American Indian/Alaska Native, 48 Asian Americans or Pacific Islanders, 418 Hispanic Americans), 6 international. Average age 33. Expenses: Contact institution. *Financial support:* Institutionally sponsored loans, scholarships/grants, and unspecified assistantships available. Support available to part-time students. In 2006, 1090 degrees awarded. Offers adolescence education: grades 7-12 (MS); applied behavior analysis (MS); bilingual education (MS); childhood education: grades 1-6 (MS); early childhood education: birth—grade 2 (MS); education (MS); elementary education (MS); learning technology (MS); middle childhood education: grades 5-9 (MS); reading (MS); school administration and supervision (MS); school building leadership (MS); school business administration (MS); secondary education (MS); special education (MS); students with disabilities: grades 5-9 (MS); students with disabilities: grades 7-12 (MS); teaching English to speakers of other languages (MS); teaching literacy: birth—grade 6 (MS); teaching literacy: grades 5-12 (MS); urban education (MS). *Application deadline:* For fall admission, 2/1 for domestic students. Applications are processed on a rolling basis. *Application fee:* $37. *Application Contact:* Kathleen Jackson, Director of Admissions, 800-Mercy-NY, Fax: 914-674-7382, E-mail: admissions@mercy.edu. *Chairperson,* Dr. William Prattella, 914-674-7555, Fax: 914-674-7352, E-mail: wprattella@mercy.edu.

Division of Health Professions Students: 264 full-time (200 women), 147 part-time (134 women); includes 152 minority (75 African Americans, 26 Asian Americans or Pacific Islanders, 51 Hispanic Americans), 17 international. Average age 33. Expenses: Contact institution. In 2006, 109 degrees awarded. Offers adult nurse practitioner (MS, AC); communication disorders (MS); nursing (MS); nursing administration (MS); nursing education (MS); occupational therapy (MS); physical therapy (MS); physician assistant (MPS, MS). *Application fee:* $62. *Application Contact:* Kathleen Jackson, Director of Admissions, 800-Mercy-NY, Fax: 914-674-7382, E-mail: admissions@mercy.edu. Dr. Pat Chute, 914-674-7746, E-mail: pchute@mercy.edu.

Division of Literature, Language, and Communication Students: 6 full-time (4 women), 42 part-time (29 women); includes 6 minority (3 African Americans, 1 American Indian/Alaska Native, 2 Hispanic Americans). Average age 36. Expenses: Contact institution. *Financial support:* In 2006–07, 1 student received support, including 1 research assistantship with full tuition reimbursement available (averaging $1,200 per year). In 2006, 3 degrees awarded. *Degree program information:* Part-time and evening/weekend programs available. Postbaccalaureate distance learning degree programs offered (minimal on-campus study). Offers English literature (MA). *Application deadline:* Applications are processed on a rolling basis. *Application fee:* $37. *Application Contact:* Kathleen Jackson, Director of Admissions, 800-Mercy-NY, Fax: 914-674-7382, E-mail: admissions@mercy.edu. *Program Director,* Dr. Sean Dugan, 914-674-7356, Fax: 914-962-0931, E-mail: sdugan@mercy.edu.

Division of Mathematics and Computer Information Science Average age 35. Expenses: Contact institution. In 2006, 6 degrees awarded. Offers Internet business systems (MS, Certificate). *Application fee:* $37. *Application Contact:* Kathleen Jackson, Director of Admissions, 800-Mercy-NY, Fax: 914-674-7382, E-mail: admissions@mercy.edu. *Division Chair,* Nagaraj Rao, 914-674-7593, E-mail: nrao@mercy.edu.

Division of Social and Behavioral Sciences Students: 168 full-time (139 women), 280 part-time (237 women); includes 287 minority (131 African Americans, 1 American Indian/Alaska Native, 9 Asian Americans or Pacific Islanders, 146 Hispanic Americans), 1 international. Average age 34. Expenses: Contact institution. In 2006, 97 degrees awarded. Offers alcohol and substance abuse counseling (AC); counseling (MS, AC); family counseling (AC); health services management (MPA, MS, AC, Certificate); marriage and family therapy (MS); mental health counseling (MS); psychology (MS); retirement counseling (AC); school psychology (MS). *Application fee:* $37. *Application Contact:* Kathleen Jackson, Director of Admissions, 800-Mercy-NY, Fax: 914-674-7382, E-mail: admissions@mercy.edu. *Chair,* Diana Juettner, 914-674-7338.

MERCYHURST COLLEGE, Erie, PA 16546

General Information Independent-religious, coed, comprehensive institution. *Graduate housing:* Room and/or apartments available on a first-come, first-served basis to single students; on-campus housing not available to married students. Housing application deadline: 8/15.

GRADUATE UNITS

Graduate Program *Degree program information:* Part-time and evening/weekend programs available. Offers administration of justice (MS); applied intelligence (MS, Certificate); bilingual/bicultural special education (MS); educational leadership (Certificate); forensic and biological anthropology (MS); organizational leadership (MS, Certificate); special education (MS). Electronic applications accepted.

MEREDITH COLLEGE, Raleigh, NC 27607-5298

General Information Independent, Undergraduate: women only; graduate: coed, comprehensive institution. CGS member. *Enrollment:* 2,139 graduate, professional, and undergraduate students; 12 full-time matriculated graduate/professional students (10 women), 126 part-time matriculated graduate/professional students (112 women). *Enrollment by degree level:* 138 master's. *Graduate faculty:* 13 full-time (10 women), 5 part-time/adjunct (2 women). *Graduate housing:* On-campus housing not available. *Student services:* Campus safety program, career counseling, disabled student services, free psychological counseling, international student services. *Library facilities:* Carlyle Campbell Library plus 1 other. *Online resources:* library catalog, web page, access to other libraries' catalogs. *Collection:* 186,100 titles, 669 serial subscriptions.

Computer facilities: Computer purchase and lease plans are available. 140 computers available on campus for general student use. A campuswide network can be accessed from student residence rooms. Internet access and online class registration, wireless connectivity in most buildings; laptop program that provides computer/printer/standard load are available. *Web address:* http://www.meredith.edu/.

General Application Contact: Christie B. Hill, Director of Graduate Admissions, 919-760-8423, Fax: 919-760-2898, E-mail: hillc@meredith.edu.

GRADUATE UNITS

John E. Weems Graduate School Students: 12 full-time (10 women), 101 part-time (88 women); includes 19 minority (10 African Americans, 1 American Indian/Alaska Native, 6 Asian Americans or Pacific Islanders, 2 Hispanic Americans), 3 international. Average age 33. 65 applicants, 66% accepted, 32 enrolled. *Faculty:* 13 full-time (10 women), 5 part-time/adjunct (2 women). Expenses: Contact institution. *Financial support:* Career-related internships or fieldwork, institutionally sponsored loans, scholarships/grants, and tuition waivers (partial) available. Support available to part-time students. Financial award application deadline: 2/15; financial award applicants required to submit FAFSA. In 2006, 37 degrees awarded. *Degree program information:* Part-time and evening/weekend programs available. Offers music (MM); nutrition (MS). *Application deadline:* For fall admission, 7/1 priority date for domestic and international students; for spring admission, 11/1 priority date for domestic and international students. Applications are processed on a rolling basis. *Application fee:* $50. Electronic applications accepted. *Application Contact:* Christie B. Hill, Director of Graduate Admissions, 919-760-8423, Fax: 919-760-2898, E-mail: hillc@meredith.edu. *Director,* Dr. Claire McCullough, 919-760-8423, Fax: 919-760-2898, E-mail: mccullou@meredith.edu.

School of Business Students: 2 full-time (both women), 58 part-time (46 women); includes 15 minority (8 African Americans, 5 Asian Americans or Pacific Islanders, 2 Hispanic Americans). Average age 32. 39 applicants, 59% accepted, 18 enrolled. *Faculty:* 4 full-time (all women), 2 part-time/adjunct (0 women). Expenses: Contact institution. *Financial support:* Career-related internships or fieldwork, institutionally sponsored loans, scholarships/grants, and tuition waivers (partial) available. Support available to part-time students. Financial award application deadline: 2/15; financial award applicants required to submit FAFSA. In 2006, 27 degrees awarded. *Degree program information:* Part-time and evening/weekend programs available. Offers business administration (MBA). *Application deadline:* For fall admission, 7/1 priority date for domestic and international students; for spring admission, 11/1 priority date for domestic and international students. Applications are processed on a rolling basis. *Application fee:* $50. Electronic applications accepted. *Application Contact:* Page Midyette, Coordinator, 919-760-2281, Fax: 919-760-2898, E-mail: midyette@meredith.edu. *Dean,* Dr. Denise Rotundo, 919-760-8471, Fax: 919-760-8470.

School of Education Students: 1 full-time (0 women), 23 part-time (all women); includes 1 minority (African American), 1 international. Average age 34. 12 applicants, 92% accepted, 7 enrolled. *Faculty:* 4 full-time (all women), 1 (woman) part-time/adjunct. Expenses: Contact institution. *Financial support:* Career-related internships or fieldwork, institutionally sponsored loans, and tuition waivers (partial) available. Support available to part-time students. Financial award application deadline: 2/15; financial award applicants required to submit FAFSA. In 2006, 5 degrees awarded. *Degree program information:* Part-time and evening/weekend programs available. Offers education (M Ed). *Application deadline:* For fall admission, 7/1 priority date for domestic students; for spring admission, 11/1 priority date for domestic students. Applications are processed on a rolling basis. *Application fee:* $50. Electronic applications accepted. *Application Contact:* Dr. Ellen Graden, Coordinator, 919-760-8077, Fax: 919-760-2303, E-mail: gradene@meredith.edu. *Graduate Program Manager,* Erin Barrow, 919-760-8316, Fax: 919-760-2303, E-mail: barrower@meredith.edu.

MERRIMACK COLLEGE, North Andover, MA 01845-5800

General Information Independent-religious, coed, comprehensive institution. *Enrollment:* 2,251 graduate, professional, and undergraduate students; 38 part-time matriculated graduate/professional students (34 women). *Enrollment by degree level:* 38 master's. *Graduate faculty:* 4 full-time (2 women), 5 part-time/adjunct (4 women). *Tuition:* Part-time $400 per credit hour. Part-time tuition and fees vary according to course load. *Graduate housing:* On-campus housing not available. *Student services:* Campus safety program, disabled student services, international student services, teacher training. *Library facilities:* McQuade Library. *Online resources:* library catalog, web page, access to other libraries' catalogs. *Collection:* 120,836 titles, 2,066 serial subscriptions, 2,462 audiovisual materials.

Computer facilities: 175 computers available on campus for general student use. A campuswide network can be accessed from student residence rooms. Internet access is available. *Web address:* http://www.merrimack.edu/.

Merrimack College (continued)

General Application Contact: Dr. Claire M. Thornton, Chair, 978-837-5368, Fax: 978-837-5069, E-mail: claire.thornton@merrimack.edu.

GRADUATE UNITS

Department of Education Average age 30. 12 applicants, 100% accepted. *Faculty:* 4 full-time (2 women), 5 part-time/adjunct (4 women). Expenses: Contact institution. *Financial support:* Career-related internships or fieldwork and credit hour discount for teachers in local school districts available. In 2006, 8 degrees awarded. *Degree program information:* Part-time and evening/weekend programs available. Offers education (M Ed). *Application deadline:* For fall admission, 8/15 priority date for domestic students; for spring admission, 1/15 for domestic students. Applications are processed on a rolling basis. *Application fee:* $50. *Chair,* Dr. Claire M. Thornton, 978-837-5368, Fax: 978-837-5069, E-mail: claire.thornton@merrimack.edu.

MESA STATE COLLEGE, Grand Junction, CO 81501-3122

General Information State-supported, coed, comprehensive institution. *Graduate housing:* Room and/or apartments available on a first-come, first-served basis to single students; on-campus housing not available to married students. Housing application deadline: 6/1.

GRADUATE UNITS

School of Business and Professional Studies *Degree program information:* Part-time and evening/weekend programs available. Offers business administration (MBA). Electronic applications accepted.

MESIVTA OF EASTERN PARKWAY RABBINICAL SEMINARY, Brooklyn, NY 11218-5559

General Information Independent-religious, men only, comprehensive institution.

GRADUATE UNITS

Graduate Programs

MESIVTA TIFERETH JERUSALEM OF AMERICA, New York, NY 10002-6301

General Information Independent-religious, men only, comprehensive institution.

GRADUATE UNITS

Graduate Programs

MESIVTA TORAH VODAATH RABBINICAL SEMINARY, Brooklyn, NY 11218-5299

General Information Independent-religious, men only, comprehensive institution.

GRADUATE UNITS

Graduate Programs

METHODIST THEOLOGICAL SCHOOL IN OHIO, Delaware, OH 43015-8004

General Information Independent-religious, coed, graduate-only institution. *Graduate housing:* Rooms and/or apartments available on a first-come, first-served basis to single students and available to married students. Housing application deadline: 8/15.

GRADUATE UNITS

Graduate and Professional Programs *Degree program information:* Part-time programs available. Offers theology (M Div, MACE, MACM, MASM, MTS).

METHODIST UNIVERSITY, Fayetteville, NC 28311-1498

General Information Independent-religious, coed, comprehensive institution.

GRADUATE UNITS

School of Graduate Studies

METROPOLITAN COLLEGE OF NEW YORK, New York, NY 10013-1919

General Information Independent, coed, primarily women, comprehensive institution. *Enrollment:* 1,238 graduate, professional, and undergraduate students; 389 full-time matriculated graduate/professional students (354 women). *Enrollment by degree level:* 389 master's. *Graduate faculty:* 13 full-time (6 women), 46 part-time/adjunct (17 women). *Tuition:* Full-time $9,800; part-time $840 per unit. *Required fees:* $100 per term. *Graduate housing:* On-campus housing not available. *Student services:* Career counseling, free psychological counseling, grant writing training, international student services. *Library facilities:* Main Library. *Online resources:* library catalog, web page, access to other libraries' catalogs. *Collection:* 31,766 titles, 459 audiovisual materials. *Research affiliation:* U.S. Department of Homeland Security (homeland security), U.S. Federal Emergency Management Administration (higher education).

Computer facilities: 130 computers available on campus for general student use. A campuswide network can be accessed from off campus. Internet access is available. *Web address:* http://www.metropolitan.edu/.

General Application Contact: Robert Hernandez, Graduate Admissions Coordinator, 212-343-1234 Ext. 2709, Fax: 212-343-8474, E-mail: rhernandez@mcny.edu.

GRADUATE UNITS

Program in Childhood Education Students: 36 full-time (30 women); includes 23 minority (16 African Americans, 3 Asian Americans or Pacific Islanders, 4 Hispanic Americans), 1 international. Average age 34. 44 applicants, 73% accepted, 17 enrolled. *Faculty:* 7 full-time (5 women), 9 part-time/adjunct (6 women). Expenses: Contact institution. *Financial support:* In 2006–07, 35 students received support. Career-related internships or fieldwork, Federal Work-Study, institutionally sponsored loans, and scholarships/grants available. Financial award application deadline: 8/15; financial award applicants required to submit FAFSA. In 2006, 24 degrees awarded. Offers childhood education (MS). *Application deadline:* For fall admission, 8/1 priority date for domestic students, 7/1 for international students; for winter admission, 11/15 priority date for domestic students, 11/15 for international students; for spring admission, 4/15 priority date for domestic students, 3/15 for international students. *Application fee:* $45. *Application Contact:* Sylvia Cameron, Graduate Admissions Coordinator, 212-343-1234 Ext. 2704, Fax: 212-343-7900, E-mail: scameron@mcny.edu. *Director,* Dr. Patrick Ianniello, 212-343-1234 Ext. 2424, E-mail: pianniello@metropolitan.edu.

Program in General Management Students: 42 full-time (20 women); includes 24 African Americans, 4 Hispanic Americans, 3 international. Average age 36. 42 applicants, 71% accepted, 26 enrolled. *Faculty:* 2 full-time (1 woman), 13 part-time/adjunct (6 women). Expenses: Contact institution. *Financial support:* In 2006–07, 39 students received support. Scholarships/grants available. Financial award application deadline: 8/15; financial award applicants required to submit FAFSA. In 2006, 29 degrees awarded. *Degree program information:* Evening/weekend programs available. Offers general management (MBA). *Application deadline:* For fall admission, 7/15 priority date for domestic students; for winter admission, 11/15 priority date for domestic students; for spring admission, 3/30 priority date for domestic students. Applications are processed on a rolling basis. *Application fee:* $45. Electronic applications accepted. *Application Contact:* Emery Ailes, MBA Recruiter, 212-343-1234, Fax: 212-343-8470. *Dean, Graduate School for Business,* Dr. Robert Gilmore, 212-343-1234 Ext. 2209.

Program in Media Management Students: 39 full-time (25 women); includes 16 minority (11 African Americans, 2 Asian Americans or Pacific Islanders, 3 Hispanic Americans). Average age 30. 70 applicants, 51% accepted, 24 enrolled. *Faculty:* 4 full-time (2 women), 17 part-time/adjunct (4 women). Expenses: Contact institution. *Financial support:* In 2006–07, fellowships with tuition reimbursements (averaging $21,538 per year), research assistantships with partial tuition reimbursements (averaging $7,438 per year) were awarded; career-related internships or fieldwork, scholarships/grants, tuition waivers (partial), and unspecified assistantships also available. Financial award application deadline: 8/15; financial award applicants required to submit FAFSA. In 2006, 25 degrees awarded. *Degree program information:* Evening/weekend programs available. Offers media management (MBA). *Application deadline:* For fall admission, 7/15 priority date for domestic students, 7/1 for international students; for winter admission, 11/10 for domestic students, 10/1 for international students; for spring admission, 3/30 for domestic students, 3/1 for international students. Applications are processed on a rolling basis. *Application fee:* $45. Electronic applications accepted. *Dean, Graduate School for Business,* Dr. Fay Ran, 212-343-1234 Ext. 2209, E-mail: fran@metropolitan.edu.

Program in Public Administration Students: 207 full-time (156 women); includes 183 minority (160 African Americans, 23 Hispanic Americans). Average age 37. 140 applicants, 71% accepted, 98 enrolled. *Faculty:* 5 full-time (1 woman), 26 part-time/adjunct (10 women). Expenses: Contact institution. *Financial support:* In 2006–07, 196 students received support, including 3 fellowships with tuition reimbursements available (averaging $5,700 per year); career-related internships or fieldwork, scholarships/grants, and tuition waivers (partial) also available. Financial award application deadline: 8/15; financial award applicants required to submit FAFSA. In 2006, 138 degrees awarded. *Degree program information:* Evening/weekend programs available. Offers public administration (MPA). *Application deadline:* For fall admission, 7/30 priority date for domestic students, 7/1 for international students; for winter admission, 11/30 priority date for domestic students, 11/1 for international students; for spring admission, 3/30 priority date for domestic students, 3/1 for international students. Applications are processed on a rolling basis. *Application fee:* $45. Electronic applications accepted. *Application Contact:* Robert Hernandez, Graduate Admissions Coordinator, 212-343-1234 Ext. 2709, Fax: 212-343-8474, E-mail: rhernandez@mcny.edu. *Dean, Graduate School for Public Affairs Administration,* Prof. Humphrey Crookendale, 212-343-1234 Ext. 2209, E-mail: hcrookendale@mcny.edu.

METROPOLITAN STATE UNIVERSITY, St. Paul, MN 55106-5000

General Information State-supported, coed, comprehensive institution. *Graduate housing:* On-campus housing not available.

GRADUATE UNITS

College of Arts and Sciences Offers technical communication (MS).

College of Management *Degree program information:* Part-time and evening/weekend programs available. Offers finance (MBA); human resource management (MBA); information management (MMIS); international business (MBA); law enforcement (MPNA); management information systems (MBA); marketing (MBA); nonprofit management (MPNA); organizational studies (MBA); public administration (MPNA); purchasing management (MBA); systems management (MMIS).

School of Nursing *Degree program information:* Part-time programs available. Offers nursing (MSN).

MGH INSTITUTE OF HEALTH PROFESSIONS, Boston, MA 02129

General Information Independent, coed, primarily women, graduate-only institution. *Enrollment by degree level:* 389 master's, 249 doctoral, 55 other advanced degrees. *Graduate faculty:* 61 full-time (52 women), 49 part-time/adjunct (31 women). *Graduate housing:* On-campus housing not available. *Student services:* Campus employment opportunities, campus safety program, career counseling, child daycare facilities, disabled student services, international student services, low-cost health insurance, teacher training, writing training. *Library facilities:* Treadwell Library. *Online resources:* library catalog, web page, access to other libraries' catalogs. *Collection:* 46,590 titles, 737 serial subscriptions, 79 audiovisual materials. *Research affiliation:* Massachusetts General Hospital, Spaulding Rehabilitation Hospital, McLean Psychiatric Hospital, Partners Health Care System, Inc., Brigham and Women's Hospital.

Computer facilities: 50 computers available on campus for general student use. A campuswide network can be accessed from off campus. Internet access and online class registration are available. *Web address:* http://www.mghihp.edu/.

General Application Contact: Maureen Rika Judd, Manager of Admissions, 617-726-6069, Fax: 617-726-8010, E-mail: admissions@mghihp.edu.

GRADUATE UNITS

Graduate Programs Students: 388 full-time (345 women), 305 part-time (240 women); includes 103 minority (27 African Americans, 56 Asian Americans or Pacific Islanders, 20 Hispanic Americans), 1 international. Average age 32. 902 applicants, 53% accepted, 254 enrolled. *Faculty:* 61 full-time (52 women), 49 part-time/adjunct (31 women). Expenses: Contact institution. *Financial support:* In 2006–07, 411 students received support; research assistantships, teaching assistantships, career-related internships or fieldwork, scholarships/grants, traineeships, tuition waivers (partial), and unspecified assistantships available. Support available to part-time students. Financial award application deadline: 3/3; financial award applicants required to submit FAFSA. In 2006, 132 master's, 130 doctorates, 35 other advanced degrees awarded. *Degree program information:* Part-time and evening/weekend programs available. Postbaccalaureate distance learning degree programs offered (no on-campus study). Offers advanced practice nursing (MSN); clinical investigation (MS, Certificate); gerontological nursing (MSN); medical imaging (Certificate); pediatric nursing (MSN); physical therapy (MS, DPT, Certificate); psychiatric nursing (MSN); reading (Certificate); speech-language pathology (MS); teaching and learning for health care education (Certificate); women's health nursing (MSN). *Application deadline:* For fall admission, 1/1 priority date for domestic students, 3/1 for international students; for winter admission, 11/1 priority date for domestic students, 7/1 for international students; for spring admission, 3/1 priority date for domestic students, 11/1 for international students. *Application fee:* $50. Electronic applications accepted. *Application Contact:* Maureen Rika Judd, Manager of Admissions, 617-726-6069, Fax: 617-726-8010, E-mail: admissions@mghihp.edu. *President,* Ann W. Caldwell, 617-726-8002, Fax: 617-726-3716, E-mail: caldwell.ann@mgh.harvard.edu.

MIAMI INTERNATIONAL UNIVERSITY OF ART & DESIGN, Miami, FL 33132-1418

General Information Proprietary, coed, comprehensive institution. *Graduate housing:* Room and/or apartments available on a first-come, first-served basis to single students; on-campus housing not available to married students.

GRADUATE UNITS

Program in Computer Animation *Degree program information:* Evening/weekend programs available. Offers computer animation (MFA). Electronic applications accepted.

Program in Film *Degree program information:* Evening/weekend programs available. Offers film (MFA). Electronic applications accepted.

Program in Graphic Design *Degree program information:* Evening/weekend programs available. Offers graphic design (MFA). Electronic applications accepted.

Program in Interior Design Offers interior design (MFA).

Program in Visual Arts *Degree program information:* Evening/weekend programs available. Offers visual arts (MFA). Electronic applications accepted.

MIAMI UNIVERSITY, Oxford, OH 45056

General Information State-related, coed, university. CGS member. *Graduate housing:* Rooms and/or apartments available on a first-come, first-served basis to single and married students. Housing application deadline: 3/1.

GRADUATE UNITS

Graduate School *Degree program information:* Part-time programs available. Electronic applications accepted.

College of Arts and Sciences *Degree program information:* Part-time programs available. Offers analytical chemistry (MS, PhD); arts and sciences (MA, MAT, MGS, MS, MS Stat, MTSC, PhD); biochemistry (MS, PhD); biological sciences (MAT); botany (MA, MS, PhD); chemical education (MS, PhD); chemistry (MS, PhD); clinical psychology (PhD); comparative religion (MA); composition and rhetoric (MA, PhD); creative writing (MA); criticism (PhD); English and American literature and language (PhD); English education (MAT); experimental psychology (PhD); French (MA); geography (MA); geology (MA, MS, PhD); gerontology (MGS); history (MA, PhD); inorganic chemistry (MS, PhD); library theory (PhD); literature (MA, MAT, PhD); mass communication (MA); mathematics (MA, MAT, MS); mathematics/operations research (MS); microbiology (MS, PhD); organic chemistry (MS, PhD); philosophy (MA); physical chemistry (MS, PhD); physics (MAT, MS); political science (MA, MAT, PhD); social gerontology (PhD); social psychology (PhD); Spanish (MA); speech communication (MA); speech pathology and audiology (MA, MS); statistics (MS Stat); technical and scientific communication (MTSC); zoology (MA, MS, PhD).

Institute of Environmental Sciences *Degree program information:* Part-time programs available. Offers environmental sciences (M En S). Electronic applications accepted.

Richard T. Farmer School of Business Administration *Degree program information:* Part-time programs available. Offers accountancy (M Acc); business administration (MBA); economics (MA); finance (MBA); general management (MBA); management information systems (MBA); marketing (MBA); quality and process improvement (MBA).

School of Education and Allied Professions *Degree program information:* Part-time programs available. Offers adolescent education (MAT); child and family studies (MS); college student personnel services (MS); curriculum and teacher leadership (M Ed); education and allied professions (M Ed, MAT, MS, Ed D, PhD, Ed S); educational administration (Ed D, PhD); educational leadership (M Ed, MS); educational psychology (M Ed); elementary education (M Ed, MAT); elementary mathematics education (M Ed); exercise and health studies (MS); reading education (M Ed); school psychology (MS, Ed S); secondary education (M Ed, MAT); special education (M Ed); sport studies (MS).

School of Engineering and Applied Science Offers computer science (MCS); computer science and systems analysis (MCS); paper science and engineering (MS); software development (Certificate).

School of Fine Arts *Degree program information:* Part-time programs available. Offers architecture (M Arch); art education (MA); fine arts (M Arch, MA, MFA, MM); music education (MM); music performance (MM); studio art (MFA); theatre (MA).

See Close-Up on page 957.

MICHIGAN SCHOOL OF PROFESSIONAL PSYCHOLOGY, Farmington Hills, MI 48334

General Information Independent, coed, graduate-only institution. *Enrollment by degree level:* 35 master's, 85 doctoral. *Graduate faculty:* 4 full-time (2 women), 13 part-time/adjunct (6 women). *Tuition:* Full-time $21,255. *Required fees:* $1,500. Full-time tuition and fees vary according to class time, course level, course load, degree level, program and student level. *Graduate housing:* On-campus housing not available. *Library facilities:* Moustakas Johnson Library. *Online resources:* library catalog, access to other libraries' catalogs. *Collection:* 10,354 titles, 37 serial subscriptions, 185 audiovisual materials.

Computer facilities: 16 computers available on campus for general student use. A campuswide network can be accessed from off campus. Internet access is available. *Web address:* http://www.humanpsych.edu/.

General Application Contact: Linda Potter-Gallant, Admissions Advisor, 248-476-1122, Fax: 248-476-1125, E-mail: lpgallant@mispp.edu.

GRADUATE UNITS

Programs in Humanistic and Clinical Psychology Students: 125 full-time; includes 18 minority (13 African Americans, 5 Asian Americans or Pacific Islanders). Average age 38. 200 applicants, 40% accepted. *Faculty:* 4 full-time (2 women), 13 part-time/adjunct (6 women). Expenses: Contact institution. *Financial support:* In 2006–07, 39 students received support. Application deadline: 6/30; In 2006, 30 master's, 16 doctorates awarded. Offers humanistic and clinical psychology (MA, Psy D). *Application deadline:* For fall admission, 1/15 priority date for domestic students. Applications are processed on a rolling basis. *Application fee:* $75. Electronic applications accepted. *Application Contact:* Linda Potter-Gallant, Admissions Advisor, 248-476-1122, Fax: 248-476-1125, E-mail: lpgallant@mispp.edu. *President,* Dr. Kerry Moustakas, 248-476-1122, Fax: 248-476-1125, E-mail: kmoustakas@mispp.edu.

MICHIGAN STATE UNIVERSITY, East Lansing, MI 48824

General Information State-supported, coed, university. CGS member. *Enrollment:* 45,520 graduate, professional, and undergraduate students; 6,734 full-time matriculated graduate/professional students (3,492 women), 1,695 part-time matriculated graduate/professional students (1,164 women). *Graduate faculty:* 1,944 full-time (611 women), 17 part-time/adjunct (5 women). Tuition, state resident: part-time $346 per credit hour. Tuition, nonresident: part-time $730 per credit hour. Tuition and fees vary according to program. *Graduate housing:* Rooms and/or apartments available on a first-come, first-served basis to single and married students. *Student services:* Campus employment opportunities, campus safety program, career counseling, child daycare facilities, disabled student services, exercise/wellness program, free psychological counseling, grant writing training, international student services, low-cost health insurance, multicultural affairs office, teacher training, writing training. *Library facilities:* Main Library plus 14 others. *Online resources:* library catalog, web page, access to other libraries' catalogs. *Collection:* 4.8 million titles, 37,832 serial subscriptions, 342,873 audiovisual materials. *Research affiliation:* Argonne National Laboratory (high-energy physics and structural biology), Association of Sea Grant Programs (fresh water ecosystems), Fraunhofer Center (manufacturing), Michigan Economic Development Corporation (life sciences, homeland security, automotive technologies), Oak Ridge Associate Universities (scientific research and education), Southern Astrophysical Research (SOAR) Telescope (astronomy).

Computer facilities: Computer purchase and lease plans are available. 2,000 computers available on campus for general student use. A campuswide network can be accessed from student residence rooms and from off campus. Internet access and online class registration are available. *Web address:* http://www.msu.edu/.

General Application Contact: Dr. Karen Klomparens, Dean of the Graduate School and Associate Provost for Graduate Education, 517-432-1236, Fax: 517-353-3768, E-mail: galindo@opb.msu.edu.

GRADUATE UNITS

College of Human Medicine Students: 496 full-time (281 women), 33 part-time (20 women); includes 156 minority (50 African Americans, 2 American Indian/Alaska Native, 65 Asian Americans or Pacific Islanders, 39 Hispanic Americans), 28 international. Average age 27. *Faculty:* 86 full-time (28 women). Expenses: Contact institution. *Financial support:* In 2006–07, 54 fellowships with tuition reimbursements, 38 research assistantships with tuition reimbursements (averaging $14,385 per year), 1 teaching assistantship with tuition reimbursement (averaging $15,120 per year) were awarded; career-related internships or fieldwork, Federal Work-Study, institutionally sponsored loans, scholarships/grants, and unspecified assistantships also available. Support available to part-time students. In 2006, 89 MDs, 8 master's, 3 doctorates awarded. Offers biochemistry and molecular biology (MS, PhD); bioethics, humanities, and society (MA); epidemiology (MS, PhD); human medicine (MD); human medicine/medical scientist training program (MD); microbiology (MS); microbiology and molecular genetics (PhD); pharmacology and toxicology (MS, PhD); physiology (MS, PhD). *Application Contact:* CHM Admissions Officer, 517-353-9620, Fax: 517-432-0021, E-mail: mdadmissions@msu.edu. *Dean,* Dr. Marsha D. Rappley, 517-353-1730, Fax: 517-355-0342, E-mail: rappley@msu.edu.

College of Osteopathic Medicine Students: 703 full-time (377 women), 7 part-time (4 women); includes 133 minority (23 African Americans, 4 American Indian/Alaska Native, 96 Asian Americans or Pacific Islanders, 10 Hispanic Americans), 2 international. Average age 26. *Faculty:* 59 full-time (21 women). Expenses: Contact institution. *Financial support:* In 2006–07, 19 fellowships with tuition reimbursements, 16 research assistantships with tuition reimbursements (averaging $15,638 per year), 1 teaching assistantship with tuition reimbursement (averaging $15,804 per year) were awarded. In 2006, 123 DOs, 1 doctorate awarded. Offers biochemistry and molecular biology (MS, PhD); microbiology (MS); microbiology and molecular genetics (PhD); osteopathic medicine (DO, MS, PhD); pharmacology and toxicology (MS, PhD); pharmacology and toxicology-environmental toxicology (PhD); physiology (MS, PhD). *Dean,* Dr. William D. Strampel, 517-355-9616, Fax: 517-432-2125, E-mail: strampe3@msu.edu.

College of Veterinary Medicine Students: 473 full-time (363 women), 69 part-time (46 women); includes 68 minority (15 African Americans, 6 American Indian/Alaska Native, 27 Asian Americans or Pacific Islanders, 20 Hispanic Americans), 39 international. Average age 27. *Faculty:* 90 full-time (30 women), 3 part-time/adjunct (0 women). Expenses: Contact institution. *Financial support:* In 2006–07, 38 fellowships with tuition reimbursements, 24 research assistantships with tuition reimbursements (averaging $15,680 per year) were awarded. In 2006, 102 DVMs, 12 master's, 10 doctorates awarded. Offers animal science–environmental toxicology (PhD); biochemistry and molecular biology–environmental toxicology (PhD); chemistry–environmental toxicology (PhD); comparative medicine and integrative biology (MS, PhD); crop and soil sciences–environmental toxicology (PhD); environmental engineering–environmental toxicology (PhD); environmental geosciences–environmental toxicology (PhD); fisheries and wildlife–environmental toxicology (PhD); food safety (MS); food safety and toxicology (MS); food science–environmental toxicology (PhD); forestry–environmental toxicology (PhD); industrial microbiology (MS); integrative toxicology (PhD); large animal clinical sciences (MS, PhD); microbiology (MS, PhD); microbiology and molecular genetics (MS, PhD); microbiology–environmental toxicology (PhD); pathobiology and diagnostic investigation (MS, PhD); pathology (MS, PhD); pathology–environmental toxicology (PhD); pharmacology and toxicology–environmental toxicology (PhD); small animal clinical sciences (MS); veterinary medicine (DVM); veterinary medicine/medical scientist training program (DVM); zoology–environmental toxicology (PhD). *Application Contact:* 517-353-9793, Fax: 517-353-3041, E-mail: admiss@cvm.msu.edu. *Dean,* Dr. Christopher Brown, 517-335-6509, Fax: 517-432-1037.

The Graduate School Students: 5,196 full-time (2,543 women), 1,669 part-time (1,149 women); includes 873 minority (405 African Americans, 39 American Indian/Alaska Native, 232 Asian Americans or Pacific Islanders, 197 Hispanic Americans), 2,041 international. Average age 30. 8,578 applicants, 33% accepted. Expenses: Contact institution. *Financial support:* Fellowships with tuition reimbursements, research assistantships with tuition reimbursements, teaching assistantships with tuition reimbursements, career-related internships or fieldwork, Federal Work-Study, institutionally sponsored loans, scholarships/grants, health care benefits, and unspecified assistantships available. Support available to part-time students. Financial award applicants required to submit FAFSA. *Degree program information:* Part-time and evening/weekend programs available. Postbaccalaureate distance learning degree programs offered. *Application deadline:* For fall admission, 12/28 priority date for domestic students. Applications are processed on a rolling basis. *Application fee:* $50. Electronic applications accepted. *Dean of the Graduate School and Associate Provost for Graduate Education,* Dr. Karen Klomparens, 517-355-0301, Fax: 517-353-3355.

College of Agriculture and Natural Resources Students: 499 full-time (250 women), 123 part-time (56 women); includes 54 minority (16 African Americans, 5 American Indian/Alaska Native, 18 Asian Americans or Pacific Islanders, 15 Hispanic Americans), 261 international. Average age 30. 456 applicants, 34% accepted. *Faculty:* 286 full-time (64 women), 1 part-time/adjunct (0 women). Expenses: Contact institution. *Financial support:* In 2006–07, 102 fellowships with tuition reimbursements (averaging $6,547 per year), 345 research assistantships with tuition reimbursements (averaging $13,027 per year), 45 teaching assistantships with tuition reimbursements (averaging $12,503 per year) were awarded; career-related internships or fieldwork, Federal Work-Study, institutionally sponsored loans, scholarships/grants, tuition waivers (partial), and unspecified assistantships also available. Support available to part-time students. In 2006, 126 master's, 64 doctorates awarded. Offers agricultural economics (MS, PhD); agricultural technology and systems management (MS, PhD); agriculture and natural resources (MA, MIPS, MS, MURP, PhD); animal science (MS, PhD); animal science-environmental toxicology (PhD); biosystems engineering (MS, PhD); community, agriculture, recreation, and resource studies (MS, PhD); construction management (MS, PhD); crop and soil sciences (MS, PhD); crop and soil sciences-environmental toxicology (PhD); entomology (MS, PhD); environmental design (MA); fisheries and wildlife (MS, PhD); fisheries and wildlife—environmental toxicology (PhD); food science (MS, PhD); food science—environmental toxicology (PhD); forestry (MS, PhD); forestry-environmental toxicology (PhD); horticulture (MS, PhD); human nutrition (MS, PhD); human nutrition-environmental toxicology (PhD); integrated pest management (MS); interior design and facilities management (MA); international planning studies (MIPS); packaging (MS, PhD); plant breeding and genetics (MS, PhD); plant breeding and genetics-crop and soil sciences (MS, PhD); plant breeding and genetics-forestry (MS, PhD); plant breeding and genetics-horticulture (MS, PhD); plant pathology (MS, PhD); urban and regional planning (MURP). *Application fee:* $50. *Application Contact:* Elva L. Hernandez, Graduate Secretary, 517-355-8588, Fax: 517-353-9896. *Dean,* Dr. Jeffrey D. Armstrong, 517-355-0232, Fax: 517-353-9896, E-mail: armstroj@msu.edu.

College of Arts and Letters Students: 634 full-time (354 women), 115 part-time (71 women); includes 108 minority (48 African Americans, 11 American Indian/Alaska Native, 25 Asian Americans or Pacific Islanders, 24 Hispanic Americans), 227 international. Average age 31. 810 applicants, 42% accepted. *Faculty:* 239 full-time (99 women), 3 part-time/adjunct (1 woman). Expenses: Contact institution. *Financial support:* In 2006–07, 169 fellowships with tuition reimbursements, 85 research assistantships with tuition reimbursements (averaging $12,378 per year), 306 teaching assistantships with tuition reimbursements (averaging $12,343 per year) were awarded. In 2006, 89 master's, 58 doctorates awarded. Offers African-American and African studies (MA, PhD); American studies (MA, PhD); applied Spanish linguistics (MA); arts and letters (MA, MFA, PhD); critical studies in literacy and pedagogy (MA); digital rhetoric and professional writing (MA); English (PhD); French (MA); French language and literature (PhD); German studies (MA, PhD); Hispanic cultural studies (PhD); Hispanic literatures (MA); history (MA, PhD); history-secondary school teaching (MA); linguistics (MA, PhD); literature in English (MA); philosophy (MA, PhD); rhetoric and writing (PhD); second language studies (PhD); studio art (MFA); teaching English to speakers of other languages (MA); theatre (MA, MFA). *Application fee:* $50. Electronic applications accepted. *Application Contact:* Janet Roe-Darden, Assistant for Graduate Studies, 517-355-5360, Fax: 517-432-0129, E-mail: jroe@msu.edu. *Dean,* Dr. Karin A. Warst, 517-355-4597, Fax: 517-355-0159, E-mail: wurst@cal.msu.edu.

College of Communication Arts and Sciences Students: 254 full-time (182 women), 85 part-time (54 women); includes 47 minority (23 African Americans, 15 Asian Americans or Pacific Islanders, 9 Hispanic Americans), 120 international. Average age 28. 592 applicants, 42% accepted. *Faculty:* 72 full-time (28 women). Expenses: Contact institution. *Financial support:* In 2006–07, 31 fellowships with tuition reimbursements, 33 research assistantships with tuition reimbursements (averaging $12,914 per year), 59 teaching assistantships with tuition reimbursements (averaging $12,950 per year) were awarded. In 2006, 115 master's, 13 doctorates awarded. Offers advertising (MA); communication (MA, PhD); communication arts and sciences (MA, MS, PhD); communicative sciences and disorders (MA, PhD); health communication (MA); journalism (MA); media and information studies (PhD); public relations (MA); retailing (MS, PhD); telecommunication, information studies, and media (MA). *Dean,* Dr. Charles T. Salmon, 517-355-3410, Fax: 517-432-1244, E-mail: salmon@msu.edu.

College of Education Students: 627 full-time (417 women), 580 part-time (433 women); includes 162 minority (101 African Americans, 5 American Indian/Alaska Native, 25 Asian Americans or Pacific Islanders, 31 Hispanic Americans), 167 international. Average age 32. 742 applicants, 55% accepted. *Faculty:* 123 full-time (66 women), 1 (woman) part-time/adjunct. Expenses: Contact institution. *Financial support:* In 2006–07, 234 fellowships with tuition reimbursements, 266 research assistantships with tuition reimbursements (averaging $13,686 per year), 176 teaching assistantships with tuition reimbursements (averaging $13,796 per year) were awarded. In 2006, 575 master's, 101 doctorates awarded. Offers counseling (MA); curriculum and teaching (MA); curriculum, teaching and education policy (PhD, Ed S); education (MA, MS, PhD, Ed S); education for professional teachers (MA); educational policy (PhD); educational psychology and educational technology (PhD); educational technology (MA); higher, adult and lifelong education (MA, PhD); K–12

Michigan State University (continued)

educational administration (MA, PhD, Ed S); kinesiology (MS, PhD); literacy instruction (MA); measurement and quantitative methods (PhD); rehabilitation counseling (MA); rehabilitation counselor education (PhD); school psychology (MA, PhD, Ed S); special education (MA, PhD); student affairs administration (MA). Electronic applications accepted. *Dean,* Dr. Carole Ames, 517-355-1734, Fax: 517-353-6393, E-mail: cames@msu.edu.

College of Engineering Students: 510 full-time (104 women), 61 part-time (9 women); includes 63 minority (28 African Americans, 16 Asian Americans or Pacific Islanders, 19 Hispanic Americans), 332 international. Average age 27. 1,363 applicants, 14% accepted. *Faculty:* 142 full-time (15 women), 3 part-time/adjunct (1 woman). Expenses: Contact institution. *Financial support:* In 2006–07, 116 fellowships with tuition reimbursements, 289 research assistantships with tuition reimbursements (averaging $15,548 per year), 132 teaching assistantships with tuition reimbursements (averaging $15,112 per year) were awarded. In 2006, 90 master's, 72 doctorates awarded. *Degree program information:* Part-time programs available. Offers chemical engineering (MS, PhD); civil engineering (MS, PhD); computer science (MS, PhD); electrical engineering (MS, PhD); engineering (MS, PhD); engineering mechanics (MS, PhD); environmental engineering (MS, PhD); environmental engineering-environmental toxicology (PhD); materials science and engineering (MS, PhD); mechanical engineering (MS, PhD). Electronic applications accepted. *Dean,* Dr. Satish Udpa, 517-355-5113, Fax: 517-355-2288, E-mail: udpa@egr.msu.edu.

College of Music Students: 234 full-time (126 women), 51 part-time (31 women); includes 27 minority (5 African Americans, 1 American Indian/Alaska Native, 17 Asian Americans or Pacific Islanders, 4 Hispanic Americans), 107 international. Average age 29. 316 applicants, 44% accepted. *Faculty:* 56 full-time (15 women), 3 part-time/adjunct (1 woman). Expenses: Contact institution. *Financial support:* In 2006–07, 24 fellowships with tuition reimbursements, 21 research assistantships with tuition reimbursements (averaging $12,247 per year), 84 teaching assistantships with tuition reimbursements (averaging $12,181 per year) were awarded. In 2006, 34 master's, 23 doctorates awarded. Offers music (PhD); music composition (M Mus, DMA); music conducting (M Mus, DMA); music education (M Mus); music performance (M Mus, DMA); music theory (M Mus); music therapy (M Mus); musicology (MA); piano pedagogy (M Mus). Electronic applications accepted. *Application Contact:* Anne Simon, Assistant to the Associate Director for Graduate Studies, 517-353-9122, Fax: 517-432-2880, E-mail: gradprograms@music.msu.edu. *Dean,* Prof. James B. Forger, 517-355-4583, Fax: 517-432-2880, E-mail: forger@msu.edu.

College of Natural Science Students: 950 full-time (405 women), 56 part-time (33 women); includes 61 minority (13 African Americans, 4 American Indian/Alaska Native, 25 Asian Americans or Pacific Islanders, 19 Hispanic Americans), 460 international. Average age 28. 1,440 applicants, 23% accepted. *Faculty:* 315 full-time (61 women). Expenses: Contact institution. *Financial support:* In 2006–07, 241 fellowships with tuition reimbursements, 400 research assistantships with tuition reimbursements (averaging $15,234 per year), 384 teaching assistantships with tuition reimbursements (averaging $14,397 per year) were awarded. In 2006, 120 master's, 97 doctorates awarded. Offers applied mathematics (MS, PhD); applied statistics (MS); astrophysics and astronomy (MS, PhD); biochemistry and molecular biology (MS, PhD); biochemistry and molecular biology/environmental toxicology (PhD); biological science (MS); biological, physical and general science for teachers (MAT, MS); biomedical laboratory operations (MS); cell and molecular biology (MS, PhD); cell and molecular biology/environmental toxicology (PhD); chemical physics (PhD); chemistry (MS, PhD); chemistry-environmental toxicology (PhD); clinical laboratory sciences (MS); computational chemistry (MS); ecology, evolutionary biology and behavior (PhD); environmental geosciences (MS, PhD); environmental geosciences-environmental toxicology (PhD); general science (MAT); genetics (MS, PhD); geological sciences (MS, PhD); industrial mathematics (MS); mathematics (MAT, MS, PhD); mathematics education (MS, PhD); natural science (MAT, MS, PhD); neuroscience (MS, PhD); physical science (MS); physics (MS, PhD); plant biology (MS, PhD); plant breeding and genetics—plant biology (MS, PhD); statistics (MS, PhD); zoo and aquarium management (MS); zoology (MS, PhD); zoology-environmental toxicology (PhD). Electronic applications accepted. *Acting Dean,* Dr. Estelle E. McGroarty, 517-355-4473, Fax: 517-432-1054, E-mail: mcgroar1@msu.edu.

College of Nursing Students: 35 full-time (31 women), 156 part-time (146 women); includes 14 minority (8 African Americans, 1 American Indian/Alaska Native, 2 Asian Americans or Pacific Islanders, 3 Hispanic Americans), 1 international. Average age 39. 134 applicants, 70% accepted. *Faculty:* 22 full-time (19 women). Expenses: Contact institution. *Financial support:* In 2006–07, 42 fellowships with tuition reimbursements, 5 research assistantships with tuition reimbursements (averaging $12,839 per year) were awarded. In 2006, 24 master's, 1 doctorate awarded. *Degree program information:* Part-time programs available. Postbaccalaureate distance learning degree programs offered (no on-campus study). Offers nursing (MSN, PhD). *Application deadline:* For fall admission, 11/1 priority date for domestic students. *Application fee:* $50. Electronic applications accepted. *Application Contact:* Tiffany Tewel, Secretary for Student Affairs, 517-353-4827, Fax: 517-353-9553, E-mail: nurse@hc.msu.edu. *Dean,* Dr. Mary Mundt, 517-355-6527, Fax: 517-353-9553, E-mail: mary.mundt@msu.edu.

College of Social Science Students: 771 full-time (479 women), 328 part-time (238 women); includes 199 minority (95 African Americans, 11 American Indian/Alaska Native, 32 Asian Americans or Pacific Islanders, 61 Hispanic Americans), 164 international. Average age 30. 1,673 applicants, 34% accepted. *Faculty:* 312 full-time (118 women), 5 part-time/adjunct (2 women). Expenses: Contact institution. *Financial support:* In 2006–07, 191 fellowships with tuition reimbursements (averaging $6,831 per year), 176 research assistantships with tuition reimbursements (averaging $12,713 per year), 188 teaching assistantships with tuition reimbursements (averaging $12,541 per year) were awarded; career-related internships or fieldwork, Federal Work-Study, institutionally sponsored loans, scholarships/grants, and unspecified assistantships also available. Support available to part-time students. In 2006, 296 master's, 36 doctorates awarded. Offers anthropology (MA, PhD); Chicano/Latino studies (PhD); child development (MA); clinical social work (MSW); community services (MS); criminal justice (MS, PhD); economics (MA, PhD); family and child ecology (PhD); family studies (MA); forensic science (MS); geographic information science (MS); geography (MA, PhD); human resources and labor relations (MLRHR); industrial relations and human resources (PhD); marriage and family therapy (MA); organizational and community practice (MSW); political science (MA, PhD); professional applications in anthropology (MA); psychology (MA, PhD); public policy (MPP); social science (MA, MIPS, MLRHR, MPP, MS, MSW, MURP, PhD); social science—global applications (MA); social work (PhD); sociology (MA, PhD); youth development (MA). *Application fee:* $50. Electronic applications accepted. *Dean,* Dr. Marietta Baba, 517-355-6675, Fax: 517-355-1912, E-mail: mbaba@msu.edu.

Eli Broad Graduate School of Management Students: 782 full-time (255 women), 57 part-time (21 women); includes 121 minority (44 African Americans, 3 American Indian/Alaska Native, 58 Asian Americans or Pacific Islanders, 16 Hispanic Americans), 205 international. Average age 30. 1,124 applicants, 35% accepted. *Faculty:* 106 full-time (20 women), 2 part-time/adjunct (0 women). Expenses: Contact institution. *Financial support:* In 2006–07, 144 fellowships with tuition reimbursements, 115 research assistantships with tuition reimbursements (averaging $12,920 per year), 39 teaching assistantships with tuition reimbursements (averaging $12,641 per year) were awarded. In 2006, 430 master's, 17 doctorates awarded. *Degree program information:* Evening/weekend programs available. Offers accounting (MS); business administration (MBA, PhD); corporate business administration (MBA); finance (MS); food service management (MS); hospitality business (MS); integrative management (MBA); management (MBA, MS, PhD); manufacturing and engineering management (MS); supply chain management (MS). Electronic applications accepted. *Application Contact:* Cynthia Kindel, Executive Assistant, PhD Programs, 517-353-8713, Fax: 517-353-6395, E-mail: kindelc@bus.msu.edu. *Dean,* Dr. Robert B. Duncan, 517-355-8377, Fax: 517-355-6395, E-mail: duncan@bus.msu.edu.

See Close-Up on page 959.

MICHIGAN STATE UNIVERSITY COLLEGE OF LAW, East Lansing, MI 48824-1300

General Information Independent, coed, graduate-only institution. *Graduate housing:* Rooms and/or apartments available on a first-come, first-served basis to single students and available to married students. Housing application deadline: 4/1.

GRADUATE UNITS

Professional Program *Degree program information:* Part-time and evening/weekend programs available. Offers American legal system (LL M); intellectual property (LL M); law (JD). Electronic applications accepted.

MICHIGAN TECHNOLOGICAL UNIVERSITY, Houghton, MI 49931-1295

General Information State-supported, coed, university. CGS member. *Graduate housing:* Rooms and/or apartments available on a first-come, first-served basis to single and married students.

GRADUATE UNITS

Graduate School *Degree program information:* Part-time programs available. Postbaccalaureate distance learning degree programs offered (minimal on-campus study). Electronic applications accepted.

College of Engineering *Degree program information:* Part-time programs available. Postbaccalaureate distance learning degree programs offered (minimal on-campus study). Offers biomedical engineering (PhD); chemical engineering (MS, PhD); civil engineering (ME, MS, PhD); electrical engineering (MS, PhD); engineering (ME, MS, PhD); engineering mechanics (MS); environmental engineering (ME, MS, PhD); environmental engineering science (MS); geological engineering (MS, PhD); geology (MS, PhD); geophysics (MS); materials science and engineering (MS, PhD); mechanical engineering (MS, PhD); mechanical engineering-engineering mechanics (PhD); mining engineering (MS, PhD). Electronic applications accepted.

College of Sciences and Arts *Degree program information:* Part-time programs available. Offers applied science education (MS); biological sciences (MS, PhD); chemistry (MS, PhD); computational science and engineering (PhD); computer science (MS, PhD); engineering physics (PhD); environmental policy (MS); industrial archaeology (MS); industrial heritage and archeology (PhD); mathematical sciences (MS, PhD); physics (MS, PhD); rhetoric and technical communication (MS, PhD); sciences and arts (MS, PhD). Electronic applications accepted.

School of Business and Economics *Degree program information:* Part-time programs available. Offers business administration (MS); business and economics (MS); mineral economics (MS). Electronic applications accepted.

School of Forest Resources and Environmental Science *Degree program information:* Part-time programs available. Offers applied ecology (MS); forest ecology and management (MS); forest molecular genetics and biotechnology (MS, PhD); forest science (PhD); forestry (MF, MS). Electronic applications accepted.

Sustainable Futures Institute *Degree program information:* Part-time programs available. Offers sustainability (Certificate).

See Close-Up on page 961.

MICHIGAN THEOLOGICAL SEMINARY, Plymouth, MI 48170

General Information Independent-religious, coed, graduate-only institution. *Graduate housing:* On-campus housing not available.

GRADUATE UNITS

Graduate Programs *Degree program information:* Part-time and evening/weekend programs available. Offers Christian education (MA); counseling psychology (MA); divinity (M Div); expository communication (D Min); theological studies (MA).

MID-AMERICA BAPTIST THEOLOGICAL SEMINARY, Cordova, TN 38016

General Information Independent-religious, coed, primarily men. *Enrollment:* 327 graduate, professional, and undergraduate students; 222 full-time matriculated graduate/professional students (16 women), 54 part-time matriculated graduate/professional students (11 women). *Enrollment by degree level:* 110 first professional, 68 master's, 98 doctoral. *Graduate faculty:* 34 full-time (11 women), 5 part-time/adjunct (1 woman). *Tuition:* Full-time $3,760; part-time $310 per credit hour. *Graduate housing:* Rooms and/or apartments available on a first-come, first-served basis to single and married students. Typical cost: $5,400 per year for single students; $7,620 per year for married students. *Student services:* Career counseling, low-cost health insurance. *Library facilities:* Ora Byram Allison Memorial Library. *Online resources:* library catalog, web page. *Collection:* 119,000 titles, 931 serial subscriptions.

Computer facilities: 10 computers available on campus for general student use. Internet access is available. *Web address:* http://www.mabts.edu/.

General Application Contact: Tanner Hickman, Admissions Counselor, 901-751-8453, Fax: 901-751-8454, E-mail: thickman@mabts.edu.

GRADUATE UNITS

Graduate and Professional Programs Students: 222 full-time (16 women), 54 part-time (11 women); includes 21 minority (all African Americans), 16 international. Average age 29. *Faculty:* 24 full-time (1 woman), 5 part-time/adjunct (1 woman). Expenses: Contact institution. In 2006, 44 M Divs, 13 master's, 9 doctorates awarded. Offers theology (M Div, MACE, MCE, MM, D Min, PhD). *Application deadline:* For fall admission, 7/20 priority date for domestic students. Applications are processed on a rolling basis. *Application fee:* $25. Electronic applications accepted. *Application Contact:* Tanner Hickman, Admissions Counselor, 901-751-8453, Fax: 901-751-8454, E-mail: thickman@mabts.edu. *President,* Dr. Michael R. Spradlin, 901-751-8453.

MID-AMERICA BAPTIST THEOLOGICAL SEMINARY NORTHEAST BRANCH, Schenectady, NY 12303-3463

General Information Independent-religious, coed, primarily men, graduate-only institution. *Graduate housing:* On-campus housing not available.

GRADUATE UNITS

Program in Theology *Degree program information:* Part-time and evening/weekend programs available. Offers theology (M Div).

MIDAMERICA NAZARENE UNIVERSITY, Olathe, KS 66062-1899

General Information Independent-religious, coed, comprehensive institution. *Graduate housing:* On-campus housing not available.

GRADUATE UNITS

Graduate Studies in Counseling Offers counseling (MAC).

Graduate Studies in Education *Degree program information:* Evening/weekend programs available. Offers curriculum and instruction (M Ed); educational technology (MET); special education (MA).

Graduate Studies in Management *Degree program information:* Evening/weekend programs available. Offers management (MAOA, MBA). Electronic applications accepted.

MID-AMERICA REFORMED SEMINARY, Dyer, IN 46311

General Information Independent-religious, men only, graduate-only institution.

GRADUATE UNITS

Graduate Program

MIDDLEBURY COLLEGE, Middlebury, VT 05753-6002

General Information Independent, coed, comprehensive institution. *Enrollment:* 2,406 graduate, professional, and undergraduate students; 931 full-time matriculated graduate/professional students. *Graduate faculty:* 138 full-time. *Graduate housing:* Room and/or apartments guaranteed to single students; on-campus housing not available to married students. *Student services:* Campus safety program, career counseling, disabled student services, free psychological counseling, international student services, teacher training. *Library facilities:* Main Library plus 3 others. *Online resources:* library catalog, web page, access to other libraries' catalogs. *Collection:* 853,000 titles, 2,908 serial subscriptions, 45,024 audiovisual materials.

Computer facilities: Computer purchase and lease plans are available. 494 computers available on campus for general student use. A campuswide network can be accessed from student residence rooms and from off campus. Internet access and online class registration, help-line, e-mail, personal web pages, file servers are available. *Web address:* http://www.middlebury.edu/.

General Application Contact: Language Schools Office, 802-443-5510, Fax: 802-443-2075.

GRADUATE UNITS

Bread Loaf School of English Students: 501 full-time; includes 29 minority (14 African Americans, 1 American Indian/Alaska Native, 8 Asian Americans or Pacific Islanders, 6 Hispanic Americans). Average age 33. *Faculty:* 56 full-time. Expenses: Contact institution. *Financial support:* In 2006–07, 247 students received support. Scholarships/grants available. Support available to part-time students. In 2006, 85 master's awarded. Offers English (M Litt, MA). Offered during summer only. *Application deadline:* Applications are processed on a rolling basis. *Application fee:* $55. *Director,* Dr. James Maddox, 802-443-5418, Fax: 802-443-2060, E-mail: blse@breadnet.middlebury.edu.

Language Schools Students: 430 full-time (313 women); includes 75 minority (13 African Americans, 1 American Indian/Alaska Native, 15 Asian Americans or Pacific Islanders, 46 Hispanic Americans). Average age 32. 601 applicants, 93% accepted, 428 enrolled. *Faculty:* 82 full-time (37 women). Expenses: Contact institution. *Financial support:* Fellowships, scholarships/grants available. In 2006, 176 master's, 3 doctorates awarded. Offers Chinese (MA); French (MA, DML); German (MA, DML); Italian (MA, DML); language (MA, DML); Russian (MA, DML); Spanish (MA, DML). *Application deadline:* Applications are processed on a rolling basis. *Application fee:* $50. Electronic applications accepted. *Application Contact:* Kara Gennarelli, Language Schools Office, 802-443-5727, Fax: 802-443-2075, E-mail: languages@middlebury.edu. *Dean, Language Schools and Schools Abroad,* Dr. Michael E. Geisler, 802-443-5508, Fax: 802-443-2075.

MIDDLE TENNESSEE SCHOOL OF ANESTHESIA, Madison, TN 37116

General Information Independent, coed, graduate-only institution. *Graduate housing:* On-campus housing not available.

GRADUATE UNITS

Program in Nurse Anesthesia Offers nurse anesthesia (MS).

MIDDLE TENNESSEE STATE UNIVERSITY, Murfreesboro, TN 37132

General Information State-supported, coed, university. CGS member. *Graduate faculty:* 352 full-time (140 women), 10 part-time/adjunct (6 women). *Graduate housing:* Rooms and/or apartments available on a first-come, first-served basis to single and married students. *Student services:* Campus employment opportunities, campus safety program, career counseling, disabled student services, exercise/wellness program, free psychological counseling, international student services, low-cost health insurance, multicultural affairs office. *Library facilities:* James E. Walker Library. *Online resources:* library catalog, web page, access to other libraries' catalogs. *Collection:* 748,888 titles, 4,144 serial subscriptions.

Computer facilities: 2,300 computers available on campus for general student use. A campuswide network can be accessed from student residence rooms and from off campus. Internet access and online class registration are available. *Web address:* http://www.mtsu.edu/.

General Application Contact: Dr. Donald L. Curry, Dean and Vice Provost for Research, 615-898-2840, Fax: 615-904-8020, E-mail: dcurry@mtsu.edu.

GRADUATE UNITS

College of Graduate Studies Average age 30. 1,024 applicants, 89% accepted. *Faculty:* 402 full-time (174 women), 6 part-time/adjunct (2 women). Expenses: Contact institution. *Financial support:* In 2006–07, 192 students received support. Application deadline: 5/1; In 2006, 555 master's, 10 doctorates, 89 other advanced degrees awarded. *Degree program information:* Part-time and evening/weekend programs available. Postbaccalaureate distance learning degree programs offered. *Application deadline:* For fall admission, 8/1 priority date for domestic students. Applications are processed on a rolling basis. *Application fee:* $25. Electronic applications accepted. *Vice Provost for Research/Dean,* Dr. Abdul S. Rao, 615-898-2840, Fax: 615-904-8020, E-mail: arao@mtsu.edu.

College of Basic and Applied Sciences Expenses: Contact institution. *Financial support:* In 2006–07, 59 students received support. Application deadline: 5/1; *Degree program information:* Part-time and evening/weekend programs available. Postbaccalaureate distance learning degree programs offered. Offers aerospace education (M Ed); aviation administration (MS); basic and applied sciences (M Ed, MS, MSN, MST, MVTE, DA); biology (MS); chemistry (MS, DA); computer science (MS); engineering technology and industrial studies (MS, MVTE); mathematics (MS); mathematics education (MST); nursing (MSN). *Application deadline:* For fall admission, 8/1 priority date for domestic students. Applications are processed on a rolling basis. *Application fee:* $25. Electronic applications accepted. *Dean,* Dr. Thomas Cheatham, 615-898-2613, Fax: 615-898-2615.

College of Business Expenses: Contact institution. *Financial support:* In 2006–07, 26 students received support. Application deadline: 5/1; *Degree program information:* Part-time and evening/weekend programs available. Postbaccalaureate distance learning degree programs offered. Offers accounting (MS); business (MA, MBA, MBE, MS, PhD); business education (MBE); computer information systems (MS); economics and finance (MA, PhD); information systems (MS); management and marketing (MBA). *Application deadline:* For fall admission, 8/1 priority date for domestic students. Applications are processed on a rolling basis. *Application fee:* $25. Electronic applications accepted. *Dean,* Dr. James E. Burton, 615-898-2764, Fax: 615-898-4736, E-mail: relam@mtsu.edu.

College of Education and Behavioral Science Expenses: Contact institution. *Financial support:* In 2006–07, 57 students received support. Application deadline: 5/1; *Degree program information:* Part-time and evening/weekend programs available. Postbaccalaureate distance learning degree programs offered. Offers administration and supervision (M Ed, Ed S); child development and family studies (MS); criminal justice administration (MCJ); curriculum and instruction (M Ed, Ed S); dyslexic studies (Graduate Certificate); early childhood education (M Ed); education and behavioral science (M Ed, MA, MCJ, MS, PhD, Ed S, Graduate Certificate); elementary education (M Ed, Ed S); English as a second language (M Ed); exercise science and health promotion (MS); health, physical education, recreation and safety (MS); human performance (PhD); industrial/organizational psychology (MA); middle school education (M Ed); nutrition and food science (MS); physical education (PhD); professional counseling (M Ed, Ed S); psychology (MA); reading (M Ed); school counseling (M Ed); school psychology (Ed S); special education (M Ed). *Application deadline:* For fall admission, 8/1 priority date for domestic students. Applications are processed on a rolling basis. *Application fee:* $25. Electronic applications accepted. *Dean,* Dr. Gloria Bonner, 615-898-2874, Fax: 615-898-2530, E-mail: gbonner@mtsu.edu.

College of Liberal Arts Expenses: Contact institution. *Financial support:* In 2006–07, 74 students received support. Application deadline: 5/1; *Degree program information:* Part-time and evening/weekend programs available. Postbaccalaureate distance learning degree programs offered. Offers English (MA, PhD); foreign languages and literatures (MAT); geosciences (Graduate Certificate); gerontology (Graduate Certificate); health care management (Graduate Certificate); historic preservation (DA); history (MA, DA); liberal arts (MA, MAT, DA, PhD, Graduate Certificate); music (MA); public history (PhD); sociology (MA). *Application deadline:* For fall admission, 8/1 priority date for domestic students. Applications are processed on a rolling basis. *Application fee:* $25. Electronic applications accepted. *Dean,* Dr. John McDaniel, 615-898-2534, Fax: 615-898-5907, E-mail: mcdaniel@mtsu.edu.

College of Mass Communication Students: 16 full-time (2 women), 67 part-time (45 women); includes 27 minority (18 African Americans, 8 Asian Americans or Pacific Islanders, 1 Hispanic American). Average age 28. 23 applicants, 96% accepted. *Faculty:* 17 full-time (2 women), 1 part-time/adjunct (0 women). Expenses: Contact institution. *Financial support:* In 2006–07, 6 students received support. Application deadline: 5/1; In 2006, 13 degrees awarded. *Degree program information:* Part-time and evening/weekend programs available. Postbaccalaureate distance learning degree programs offered. Offers journalism (MS); mass communication (MS); recording arts (MFA). *Application deadline:* For fall admission, 8/1 priority date for domestic students. Applications are processed on a rolling basis. *Application fee:* $25. Electronic applications accepted. *Dean,* Dr. Anantha Babbili, 615-898-2813, Fax: 615-898-5682.

MIDWEST COLLEGE OF ORIENTAL MEDICINE, Racine, WI 53403-9747

General Information Proprietary, coed, graduate-only institution. *Graduate housing:* On-campus housing not available. *Research affiliation:* Guangzhou University of Traditional Chinese Medicine (pharmacology).

GRADUATE UNITS

Graduate Programs *Degree program information:* Part-time and evening/weekend programs available. Offers acupuncture (Certificate); oriental medicine (MSOM).

Graduate Programs-Chicago *Degree program information:* Part-time and evening/weekend programs available.

MIDWESTERN BAPTIST THEOLOGICAL SEMINARY, Kansas City, MO 64118-4697

General Information Independent-religious, coed, graduate-only institution. *Graduate housing:* Rooms and/or apartments guaranteed to single and married students.

GRADUATE UNITS

Graduate and Professional Programs *Degree program information:* Part-time programs available. Postbaccalaureate distance learning degree programs offered (minimal on-campus study). Offers Biblical studies (MA); Christian education (MACE); divinity/ministry (M Div); ministry (D Min); sacred music (MCM). Electronic applications accepted.

MIDWESTERN STATE UNIVERSITY, Wichita Falls, TX 76308

General Information State-supported, coed, comprehensive institution. *Enrollment:* 6,042 graduate, professional, and undergraduate students; 107 full-time matriculated graduate/professional students (68 women), 427 part-time matriculated graduate/professional students (277 women). *Enrollment by degree level:* 534 master's. *Graduate faculty:* 78 full-time (29 women), 13 part-time/adjunct (8 women). *Graduate housing:* Rooms and/or apartments available on a first-come, first-served basis to single and married students. Typical cost: $2,660 per year ($5,220 including board) for single students; $2,520 per year ($5,080 including board) for married students. Room and board charges vary according to board plan and housing facility selected. *Student services:* Campus employment opportunities, career counseling, disabled student services, exercise/wellness program, free psychological counseling, international student services, low-cost health insurance, teacher training. *Library facilities:* Moffett Library. *Online resources:* library catalog, web page, access to other libraries' catalogs. *Collection:* 441,251 titles, 1,246 serial subscriptions, 27,363 audiovisual materials.

Computer facilities: 402 computers available on campus for general student use. A campuswide network can be accessed from student residence rooms and from off campus. Internet access and online class registration are available. *Web address:* http://www.mwsu.edu/.

General Application Contact: Barbara Ramos Merkle, Director of Admissions, 800-842-1922, Fax: 940-397-4672, E-mail: admissions@mwsu.edu.

GRADUATE UNITS

Graduate Studies Students: 107 full-time (68 women), 427 part-time (277 women); includes 69 minority (24 African Americans, 9 American Indian/Alaska Native, 13 Asian Americans or Pacific Islanders, 23 Hispanic Americans), 61 international. Average age 34. 250 applicants, 83% accepted, 101 enrolled. *Faculty:* 78 full-time (29 women), 13 part-time/adjunct (8 women). Expenses: Contact institution. *Financial support:* In 2006–07, 414 students received support, including 106 teaching assistantships with partial tuition reimbursements available (averaging $6,557 per year); career-related internships or fieldwork, Federal Work-Study, institutionally sponsored loans, scholarships/grants, tuition waivers (partial), and unspecified assistantships also available. Support available to part-time students. Financial award application deadline: 5/1; financial award applicants required to submit FAFSA. In 2006, 160 degrees awarded. *Degree program information:* Part-time and evening/weekend programs available. *Application deadline:* For fall admission, 7/1 for domestic students, 4/1 for international students; for spring admission, 11/1 for domestic students, 8/1 for international students. Applications are processed on a rolling basis. *Application fee:* $35 ($50 for international students). Electronic applications accepted. *Application Contact:* Barbara Ramos Merkle, Director of Admissions, 800-842-1922, Fax: 940-397-4672, E-mail: admissions@mwsu.edu. *Dean and Associate Provost,* Dr. Emerson Capps, 940-397-4315, Fax: 940-397-4042, E-mail: emerson.capps@mwsu.edu.

College of Business Administration Students: 21 full-time (12 women), 35 part-time (12 women); includes 6 minority (2 African Americans, 4 Hispanic Americans), 19 international. Average age 30. 19 applicants, 68% accepted, 12 enrolled. *Faculty:* 13 full-time (1 woman). Expenses: Contact institution. *Financial support:* In 2006–07, 34 students received support, including 2 teaching assistantships with partial tuition reimbursements available (averaging $7,766 per year); career-related internships or fieldwork, Federal Work-Study, institutionally sponsored loans, tuition waivers (partial), and unspecified assistantships also available. Support available to part-time students. Financial award application deadline: 5/1; financial award applicants required to submit FAFSA. In 2006, 15 degrees awarded. *Degree program information:* Part-time and evening/weekend programs available. Offers business administration (MBA); health services administration (MBA). *Application deadline:* For fall admission, 7/1 for domestic students, 4/1 for international students; for spring admission, 11/1 for domestic students, 8/1 for international students. Applications are processed on a rolling basis. *Application fee:* $35 ($50 for international students). Electronic applications accepted. *Application Contact:* Dr. David Wierschem, Graduate Coordinator, 940-397-6260, Fax: 940-397-4280, E-mail: david.wierschem@mwsu.edu. *Dean,* Anthony Chelte, 940-397-4088, Fax: 940-397-4280, E-mail: anthony.chelte@mwsu.edu.

College of Education Students: 18 full-time (15 women), 156 part-time (121 women); includes 14 minority (6 African Americans, 1 American Indian/Alaska Native, 1 Asian American or Pacific Islander, 6 Hispanic Americans), 5 international. Average age 36. 47 applicants, 77% accepted, 20 enrolled. *Faculty:* 14 full-time (9 women), 8 part-time/adjunct (6 women). Expenses: Contact institution. *Financial support:* In 2006–07, 116 students received support, including 7 teaching assistantships with partial tuition reimbursements available (averaging $6,412 per year); career-related internships or fieldwork, Federal Work-Study, institutionally sponsored loans, tuition waivers (partial), and unspecified assistantships also available. Support available to part-time students. Financial award application deadline: 5/1; financial award applicants required to submit FAFSA. In 2006, 68 degrees awarded. *Degree program information:* Part-time and evening/weekend programs available. Offers curriculum and instruction (ME); education (M Ed, MA, ME); educational leadership and technology (ME); general counseling (MA); human resource development (MA); reading education (M Ed); school counseling (M Ed); special education (M Ed); training and development (MA). *Application deadline:* For fall admission, 7/1 for domestic

Midwestern State University (continued)

students, 4/1 for international students; for spring admission, 11/1 for domestic students, 8/1 for international students. Applications are processed on a rolling basis. *Application fee:* $35 ($50 for international students). Electronic applications accepted. *Application Contact:* Dr. Ann Estrada, Chair, 940-397-4136, Fax: 940-397-4672, E-mail: ann.estrada@mwsu.edu. *Dean,* Dr. Grant Simpson, 940-397-4564, Fax: 940-397-4694, E-mail: grant.simpson@mwsu.edu.

College of Health Sciences and Human Services Students: 33 full-time (18 women), 164 part-time (107 women); includes 32 minority (11 African Americans, 6 American Indian/Alaska Native, 4 Asian Americans or Pacific Islanders, 11 Hispanic Americans), 19 international. Average age 36. 75 applicants, 81% accepted, 45 enrolled. *Faculty:* 14 full-time (13 women), 9 part-time/adjunct (2 women). Expenses: Contact institution. *Financial support:* In 2006–07, 179 students received support, including 16 teaching assistantships with partial tuition reimbursements available (averaging $7,548 per year); career-related internships or fieldwork, Federal Work-Study, institutionally sponsored loans, scholarships/grants, tuition waivers (partial), and unspecified assistantships also available. Support available to part-time students. Financial award application deadline: 5/1; financial award applicants required to submit FAFSA. In 2006, 45 degrees awarded. *Degree program information:* Part-time and evening/weekend programs available. Offers family nurse practitioner (MSN); health sciences and human services (MHA, MPA, MSK, MSN, MSR); health services administration (MHA, MSN); kinesiology (MSK); nurse educator (MSN); public administration (MPA); public administration (administrative justice) (MPA); public administration (health services administration) with certificate (MPA); public administration (health services) (MPA); radiologic administration (MSR); radiologic education (MSR); radiologic sciences (MSR); radiologist assistant (MSR). *Application deadline:* For fall admission, 7/1 for domestic students, 4/1 for international students; for spring admission, 11/1 for domestic students, 8/1 for international students. Applications are processed on a rolling basis. *Application fee:* $35 ($50 for international students). Electronic applications accepted. *Application Contact:* 800-842-1922, Fax: 940-397-4672, E-mail: admissions@mwsu.edu. *Dean,* Dr. Susan Sportsman, 940-397-4594, Fax: 940-397-4513, E-mail: susan.sportsman@mwsu.edu.

College of Humanities and Social Sciences Students: 27 full-time (19 women), 38 part-time (26 women); includes 9 minority (3 African Americans, 1 American Indian/Alaska Native, 3 Asian Americans or Pacific Islanders, 2 Hispanic Americans), 6 international. Average age 29. 25 applicants, 84% accepted, 17 enrolled. *Faculty:* 21 full-time (4 women), 1 part-time/adjunct (0 women). Expenses: Contact institution. *Financial support:* In 2006–07, 50 students received support, including 45 teaching assistantships with partial tuition reimbursements available (averaging $5,521 per year); career-related internships or fieldwork, Federal Work-Study, institutionally sponsored loans, scholarships/grants, tuition waivers (partial), and unspecified assistantships also available. Support available to part-time students. Financial award application deadline: 5/1; financial award applicants required to submit FAFSA. In 2006, 14 degrees awarded. *Degree program information:* Part-time and evening/weekend programs available. Offers English (MA); history (MA); humanities and social sciences (MA); political science (MA); psychology (MA). *Application deadline:* For fall admission, 7/1 for domestic students, 4/1 for international students; for spring admission, 11/1 for domestic students, 8/1 for international students. Applications are processed on a rolling basis. *Application fee:* $35 ($50 for international students). Electronic applications accepted. *Application Contact:* 800-842-1922, Fax: 940-397-4672, E-mail: admissions@mwsu.edu. *Dean,* Dr. Samuel E. Watson, 940-397-4746, Fax: 940-397-4929, E-mail: samuel.watson@mwsu.edu.

College of Science and Mathematics Students: 8 full-time (4 women), 34 part-time (11 women); includes 8 minority (2 African Americans, 1 American Indian/Alaska Native, 5 Asian Americans or Pacific Islanders), 12 international. Average age 31. 9 applicants, 78% accepted, 7 enrolled. *Faculty:* 10 full-time (2 women), 1 part-time/adjunct (0 women). Expenses: Contact institution. *Financial support:* In 2006–07, 35 students received support, including 25 teaching assistantships with partial tuition reimbursements available (averaging $7,200 per year); career-related internships or fieldwork, Federal Work-Study, institutionally sponsored loans, scholarships/grants, and unspecified assistantships also available. Support available to part-time students. Financial award application deadline: 5/1; financial award applicants required to submit FAFSA. In 2006, 12 degrees awarded. *Degree program information:* Part-time and evening/weekend programs available. Offers biology (MS); computer science (MS). *Application deadline:* For fall admission, 7/1 for domestic students, 4/1 for international students; for spring admission, 11/1 for domestic students, 8/1 for international students. Applications are processed on a rolling basis. *Application fee:* $35 ($50 for international students). Electronic applications accepted. *Application Contact:* Dr. Stewart Carpenter, Graduate Coordinator, Computer Science, 940-397-4279, Fax: 940-397-4442, E-mail: stewart.carpenter@mwsu.edu. *Dean,* Dr. Betty Stewart, 940-397-4198, Fax: 940-397-4299, E-mail: betty.stewart@mwsu.edu.

MIDWESTERN UNIVERSITY, DOWNERS GROVE CAMPUS, Downers Grove, IL 60515-1235

General Information Independent, coed, graduate-only institution. *Enrollment by degree level:* 1,502 first professional, 285 master's, 188 doctoral. *Graduate faculty:* 123 full-time (75 women), 385 part-time/adjunct (92 women). *Graduate housing:* Rooms and/or apartments available on a first-come, first-served basis to single and married students. *Student services:* Campus employment opportunities, campus safety program, career counseling, exercise/wellness program, free psychological counseling, low-cost health insurance. *Library facilities:* Library Technology Center. *Online resources:* library catalog, web page, access to other libraries' catalogs. *Collection:* 82,828 titles, 975 serial subscriptions, 429 audiovisual materials.

Computer facilities: 63 computers available on campus for general student use. A campuswide network can be accessed from student residence rooms and from off campus. Internet access, Black Board Learning Software are available. *Web address:* http://www.midwestern.edu/.

General Application Contact: Michael Laken, Director of Admissions, 630-515-6148, Fax: 630-971-6086, E-mail: admissil@midwestern.edu.

GRADUATE UNITS

Chicago College of Osteopathic Medicine Students: 690 full-time (376 women); includes 188 minority (5 African Americans, 175 Asian Americans or Pacific Islanders, 8 Hispanic Americans), 10 international. Average age 26. 3,197 applicants, 12% accepted, 174 enrolled. *Faculty:* 44 full-time (19 women), 253 part-time/adjunct (54 women). Expenses: Contact institution. *Financial support:* In 2006–07, 568 students received support; fellowships with partial tuition reimbursements available, career-related internships or fieldwork, Federal Work-Study, institutionally sponsored loans, and tuition waivers (full and partial) available. Financial award application deadline: 6/1; financial award applicants required to submit FAFSA. In 2006, 153 degrees awarded. Offers osteopathic medicine (DO). *Application deadline:* For fall admission, 1/1 for domestic students. Applications are processed on a rolling basis. *Application fee:* $50. *Application Contact:* Michael Laken, Director of Admissions, 630-515-6148, Fax: 630-971-6086, E-mail: admissil@midwestern.edu. *Dean,* Dr. Karen J. Nichols, 630-515-6147, E-mail: knicho@midwestern.edu.

Chicago College of Pharmacy Students: 758 full-time (488 women), 54 part-time (35 women); includes 286 minority (23 African Americans, 2 American Indian/Alaska Native, 244 Asian Americans or Pacific Islanders, 17 Hispanic Americans), 13 international. Average age 25. 1,950 applicants, 20% accepted, 215 enrolled. *Faculty:* 45 full-time (33 women), 22 part-time/adjunct (14 women). Expenses: Contact institution. *Financial support:* Federal Work-Study and institutionally sponsored loans available. Support available to part-time students. Financial award applicants required to submit FAFSA. In 2006, 153 degrees awarded. *Degree program information:* Part-time programs available. Postbaccalaureate distance learning degree programs offered (minimal on-campus study). Offers pharmacy (Pharm D). *Application deadline:* For fall admission, 2/3 for domestic students. *Application fee:* $50. *Application Contact:* Michael Laken, Director of Admissions, 630-515-6148, Fax: 630-971-6086, E-mail: admissil@midwestern.edu. *Dean,* Dr. Mary W. L. Lee, 630 515 7311, E-mail: mleexx@midwestern.edu.

College of Health Sciences, Illinois Campus Students: 470 full-time (383 women), 3 part-time (1 woman); includes 69 minority (16 African Americans, 39 Asian Americans or Pacific Islanders, 14 Hispanic Americans), 2 international. Average age 25. 921 applicants, 49% accepted, 203 enrolled. *Faculty:* 33 full-time (23 women), 108 part-time/adjunct (24 women). Expenses: Contact institution. *Financial support:* In 2006–07, 229 students received support. Federal Work-Study, institutionally sponsored loans, and scholarships/grants available. Financial award applicants required to submit FAFSA. In 2006, 74 master's, 23 doctorates awarded. Offers biomedical sciences (MBS); clinical psychology (MA, Psy D); health sciences (MA, MBS, MMS, MOT, DPT, Psy D); occupational therapy (MOT); physical therapy (DPT); physician assistant studies (MMS). *Application deadline:* Applications are processed on a rolling basis. *Application fee:* $50. *Application Contact:* Michael Laken, Director of Admissions, 630-515-6148, Fax: 630-971-6086, E-mail: admissil@midwestern.edu. *Dean,* Dr. Jacquelyn J. Smith, 630-515-6388.

MIDWESTERN UNIVERSITY, GLENDALE CAMPUS, Glendale, AZ 85308

General Information Independent, coed, upper-level institution. *Enrollment:* 1,344 full-time matriculated graduate/professional students (667 women), 21 part-time matriculated graduate/professional students (14 women). *Enrollment by degree level:* 1,058 first professional, 307 master's. *Graduate faculty:* 103 full-time (39 women), 910 part-time/adjunct (161 women). *Graduate housing:* Rooms and/or apartments available on a first-come, first-served basis to single and married students. *Student services:* Exercise/wellness program. *Web address:* http://www.midwestern.edu/.

General Application Contact: James Walters, Director of Admissions, 888-247-9277, Fax: 623-572-3340, E-mail: admissaz@midwestern.edu.

GRADUATE UNITS

College of Health Sciences, Arizona Campus Students: 369 full-time (243 women), 17 part-time (11 women); includes 62 minority (13 African Americans, 4 American Indian/Alaska Native, 26 Asian Americans or Pacific Islanders, 19 Hispanic Americans), 4 international. Average age 28. 806 applicants, 68% accepted, 215 enrolled. *Faculty:* 26 full-time (11 women), 115 part-time/adjunct (36 women). Expenses: Contact institution. *Financial support:* Federal Work-Study available. In 2006, 84 degrees awarded. *Degree program information:* Part-time programs available. Offers bioethics (MA, Certificate); biomedical sciences (MBS); cardiovascular science (MCVS); health professions education (MHPE); health sciences (DPM, MA, MBS, MCVS, MHPE, MMS, MOT, MS, Certificate); nurse anesthesia (MS); occupational therapy (MOT); physician assistant studies (MMS); podiatric medicine (DPM). *Application deadline:* For fall admission, 6/4 for domestic students. Applications are processed on a rolling basis. *Application fee:* $50. *Application Contact:* James Walters, Director of Admissions, 888-247-9277, Fax: 623-572-3340, E-mail: admissaz@midwestern.edu. *Dean,* Dr. Jacquelyn Smith, 623-572-3601, Fax: 623-572-3601.

College of Pharmacy-Glendale Students: 392 full-time (208 women), 3 part-time (2 women); includes 92 minority (3 African Americans, 3 American Indian/Alaska Native, 68 Asian Americans or Pacific Islanders, 18 Hispanic Americans), 5 international. Average age 28. 1,505 applicants, 15% accepted, 130 enrolled. *Faculty:* 22 full-time (12 women), 10 part-time/adjunct (5 women). Expenses: Contact institution. *Financial support:* Applicants required to submit FAFSA. In 2006, 125 degrees awarded. Offers pharmacy (Pharm D). *Application deadline:* For fall admission, 2/1 for domestic students. *Application fee:* $50. *Application Contact:* James Walters, Director of Admissions, 888-247-9277, Fax: 623-572-3340, E-mail: admissaz@midwestern.edu. *Dean,* Dr. Anne Y. F. Lin, 623-572-3501.

MIDWEST UNIVERSITY, Wentzville, MO 63385

General Information Independent-religious, coed, university. *Graduate housing:* Rooms and/or apartments available on a first-come, first-served basis to single and married students. Housing application deadline: 1/21.

GRADUATE UNITS

Graduate Programs *Degree program information:* Part-time programs available. Postbaccalaureate distance learning degree programs offered (minimal on-campus study). Offers church music (MA, D Min); theology (M Div, MA, D Min).

MIDWIVES COLLEGE OF UTAH, Orem, UT 84058

General Information Independent, women only, comprehensive institution.

GRADUATE UNITS

Graduate Program

MILLERSVILLE UNIVERSITY OF PENNSYLVANIA, Millersville, PA 17551-0302

General Information State-supported, coed, comprehensive institution. CGS member. *Enrollment:* 8,194 graduate, professional, and undergraduate students; 127 full-time matriculated graduate/professional students (96 women), 444 part-time matriculated graduate/professional students (304 women). *Enrollment by degree level:* 571 master's. *Graduate faculty:* 216 full-time (108 women), 95 part-time/adjunct (50 women). Tuition, state resident: full-time $6,048; part-time $336 per credit. Tuition, nonresident: full-time $9,678; part-time $538 per credit. *Required fees:* $1,244. Tuition and fees vary according to course load. *Graduate housing:* On-campus housing not available. *Student services:* Campus employment opportunities, campus safety program, career counseling, child daycare facilities, disabled student services, exercise/wellness program, free psychological counseling, international student services, low-cost health insurance, teacher training. *Library facilities:* Helen A. Ganser Library. *Online resources:* library catalog, web page, access to other libraries' catalogs. *Collection:* 515,381 titles, 10,105 serial subscriptions, 13,770 audiovisual materials. *Research affiliation:* Marine Science Consortium.

Computer facilities: Computer purchase and lease plans are available. 510 computers available on campus for general student use. A campuswide network can be accessed from student residence rooms and from off campus. Internet access and online class registration are available. *Web address:* http://www.millersville.edu/.

General Application Contact: Dr. Victor S. DeSantis, Dean of Graduate Studies and Research, 717-872-3099, Fax: 717-871-2022, E-mail: victor.desantis@millersville.edu.

GRADUATE UNITS

Graduate School Students: 127 full-time (96 women), 444 part-time (304 women); includes 29 minority (13 African Americans, 2 American Indian/Alaska Native, 4 Asian Americans or Pacific Islanders, 10 Hispanic Americans), 7 international. Average age 30. 203 applicants, 71% accepted, 108 enrolled. *Faculty:* 216 full-time (108 women), 95 part-time/adjunct (50 women). Expenses: Contact institution. *Financial support:* In 2006–07, 93 students received support, including 93 research assistantships with full and partial tuition reimbursements available (averaging $4,250 per year); career-related internships or fieldwork, Federal Work-Study, institutionally sponsored loans, and unspecified assistantships also available. Support available to part-time students. Financial award application deadline: 3/15; financial award applicants required to submit FAFSA. In 2006, 235 degrees awarded. *Degree program information:* Part-time and evening/weekend programs available. *Application deadline:* For fall admission, 3/1 priority date for domestic and international students; for winter admission, 10/1 priority date for domestic students; for spring admission, 10/1 priority date for domestic students. Applications are processed on a rolling basis. *Application fee:* $35. *Dean of Graduate Studies and Research,* Dr. Victor S. DeSantis, 717-872-3099, Fax: 717-871-2022, E-mail: victor.desantis@millersville.edu.

School of Education Students: 83 full-time (64 women), 316 part-time (222 women); includes 17 minority (9 African Americans, 1 American Indian/Alaska Native, 1 Asian American or Pacific Islander, 6 Hispanic Americans), 3 international. Average age 29. 131 applicants, 65% accepted, 63 enrolled. *Faculty:* 90 full-time (52 women), 43 part-time/adjunct (17 women). Expenses: Contact institution. *Financial support:* In 2006–07, 63 students received support, including 63 research assistantships with full and partial tuition reimbursements available (averaging $4,250 per year); career-related internships or fieldwork, Federal Work-Study, institutionally sponsored loans, and unspecified assistantships also available. Support available to part-time students. Financial award application deadline: 3/15; financial award applicants required to submit FAFSA. In 2006, 177 degrees awarded. *Degree program information:* Part-time and evening/weekend programs available. Offers athletic coaching (M Ed); athletic management (M Ed); clinical psychology (MS); early childhood education (M Ed); education (M Ed, MS); elementary education (M Ed); leadership for teaching and learning (M Ed); psychology (MS); reading/language arts education (M Ed); school counseling (M Ed); school psychology (MS); special education (M Ed); sport management (M Ed); technology education (M Ed). *Application deadline:* For fall admission, 3/1 priority date for domestic students; for spring admission, 10/1 priority date for domestic students. Applications are processed on a rolling basis. *Application fee:* $35. *Application Contact:* Dr. Victor S. DeSantis, Dean of Graduate Studies, 717-872-3099, Fax: 717-871-2022, E-mail: victor.desantis@millersville.edu. *Dean,* Dr. Jane S. Bray, 717-872-3379, Fax: 717-872-3856, E-mail: jane.bray@millersville.edu.

School of Humanities and Social Sciences Students: 38 full-time (29 women), 86 part-time (46 women); includes 9 minority (3 African Americans, 2 Asian Americans or Pacific Islanders, 4 Hispanic Americans), 4 international. Average age 31. 57 applicants, 82% accepted, 31 enrolled. *Faculty:* 81 full-time (40 women), 38 part-time/adjunct (21 women). Expenses: Contact institution. *Financial support:* In 2006–07, 28 students received support, including 28 research assistantships with full tuition reimbursements available (averaging $4,250 per year); career-related internships or fieldwork, Federal Work-Study, institutionally sponsored loans, and unspecified assistantships also available. Support available to part-time students. Financial award application deadline: 3/15; financial award applicants required to submit FAFSA. In 2006, 41 degrees awarded. *Degree program information:* Part-time and evening/weekend programs available. Offers art education (M Ed); business administration (MBA); English (MA); English education (M Ed); French (M Ed, MA); German (M Ed, MA); history (MA); humanities and social sciences (M Ed, MA, MBA, MSW); social work (MSW); Spanish (M Ed, MA). *Application deadline:* For fall admission, 3/1 priority date for domestic students; for winter admission, 10/1 priority date for domestic students; for spring admission, 10/1 priority date for domestic students. Applications are processed on a rolling basis. *Application fee:* $35. *Application Contact:* Dr. Victor S. DeSantis, Dean of Graduate Studies, 717-872-3099, Fax: 717-871-2022, E-mail: victor.desantis@millersville.edu. *Dean,* Dr. John N. Short, 717-872-3553, Fax: 717-871-2003, E-mail: john.short@millersville.edu.

School of Science and Mathematics Students: 6 full-time (3 women), 42 part-time (36 women); includes 3 minority (1 African American, 1 American Indian/Alaska Native, 1 Asian American or Pacific Islander). Average age 37. 6 applicants, 100% accepted, 6 enrolled. *Faculty:* 45 full-time (16 women), 14 part-time/adjunct (12 women). Expenses: Contact institution. *Financial support:* In 2006–07, 2 students received support, including 2 research assistantships with full tuition reimbursements available (averaging $4,250 per year); career-related internships or fieldwork, Federal Work-Study, institutionally sponsored loans, and unspecified assistantships also available. Support available to part-time students. Financial award application deadline: 3/15; financial award applicants required to submit FAFSA. In 2006, 17 degrees awarded. *Degree program information:* Part-time and evening/weekend programs available. Offers biology (MS); mathematics (M Ed); nursing (MSN). *Application deadline:* For fall admission, 3/1 priority date for domestic students, 3/1 for international students; for winter admission, 10/1 priority date for domestic students; for spring admission, 10/1 priority date for domestic students. Applications are processed on a rolling basis. *Application fee:* $35. *Application Contact:* Dr. Victor S. DeSantis, Dean of Graduate Studies, 717-872-3099, Fax: 717-871-2022, E-mail: victor.desantis@millersville.edu. *Dean,* Dr. Edward C. Shane, 717-872-3407, Fax: 717-872-3985.

MILLIGAN COLLEGE, Milligan College, TN 37682

General Information Independent-religious, coed, comprehensive institution. *Enrollment:* 951 graduate, professional, and undergraduate students; 152 full-time matriculated graduate/professional students (99 women), 53 part-time matriculated graduate/professional students (42 women). *Enrollment by degree level:* 202 master's. *Graduate faculty:* 15 full-time (7 women), 8 part-time/adjunct (4 women). *Tuition:* Part-time $305 per hour. Tuition and fees vary according to course load and program. *Graduate housing:* Rooms and/or apartments available on a first-come, first-served basis to single and married students. Housing application deadline: 4/1. *Student services:* Campus employment opportunities, career counseling, disabled student services, free psychological counseling, international student services, teacher training, writing training. *Library facilities:* P. H. Welshimer Memorial Library. *Online resources:* library catalog, web page, access to other libraries' catalogs. *Collection:* 179,619 titles, 10,861 serial subscriptions, 1,865 audiovisual materials.

Computer facilities: Computer purchase and lease plans are available. 122 computers available on campus for general student use. A campuswide network can be accessed from student residence rooms and from off campus. Internet access is available. *Web address:* http://www.milligan.edu/.

General Application Contact: Carrie Davidson, Graduate Admissions Specialist, 423-461-8306, Fax: 423-461-8789, E-mail: cdavidson@milligan.edu.

GRADUATE UNITS

Area of Teacher Education Students: 37 full-time (24 women), 50 part-time (38 women); includes 3 minority (all African Americans), 1 international. 52 applicants, 92% accepted, 41 enrolled. *Faculty:* 6 full-time (5 women), 6 part-time/adjunct (4 women). Expenses: Contact institution. *Financial support:* Career-related internships or fieldwork, institutionally sponsored loans, and scholarships/grants available. Financial award application deadline: 4/15; financial award applicants required to submit FAFSA. In 2006, 46 degrees awarded. *Degree program information:* Part-time programs available. Offers teacher education (M Ed). *Application deadline:* For fall admission, 8/1 priority date for domestic students; for winter admission, 11/15 priority date for domestic students; for spring admission, 4/1 priority date for domestic students. Applications are processed on a rolling basis. *Application fee:* $30. Electronic applications accepted. *Application Contact:* Carrie Davidson, Graduate Admissions Specialist, 423-461-8306, Fax: 423-461-8789, E-mail: cdavidson@milligan.edu. *Director of Teacher Education,* Dr. Lyn C. Howell, 423-461-8484, Fax: 423-461-3103, E-mail: lchowell@milligan.edu.

Program in Occupational Therapy Students: 44 full-time (38 women), 3 part-time (all women). Average age 28. 40 applicants, 80% accepted, 26 enrolled. *Faculty:* 5 full-time (3 women), 2 part-time/adjunct (1 woman). Expenses: Contact institution. *Financial support:* In 2006–07, 1 teaching assistantship (averaging $6,000 per year) was awarded; career-related internships or fieldwork and institutionally sponsored loans also available. Financial award application deadline: 4/15; financial award applicants required to submit FAFSA. In 2006, 21 degrees awarded. Offers occupational therapy (MSOT). *Application deadline:* For spring admission, 4/1 priority date for domestic and international students. Applications are processed on a rolling basis. *Application fee:* $30. Electronic applications accepted. *Application Contact:* Claire Marr, Office Manager and Admissions Representative, 423-975-8010, Fax: 423-975-8019, E-mail: cmarr@milligan.edu. *Program Director and Associate Professor,* Jeff Snodgrass, 423-975-8010, Fax: 423-975-8019, E-mail: jsnodgrass@milligan.edu.

MILLIKIN UNIVERSITY, Decatur, IL 62522-2084

General Information Independent-religious, coed, comprehensive institution.

GRADUATE UNITS

Tabor School of Business Offers business (MBA).

MILLSAPS COLLEGE, Jackson, MS 39210-0001

General Information Independent-religious, coed, comprehensive institution. *Enrollment:* 1,084 graduate, professional, and undergraduate students; 40 full-time matriculated graduate/professional students (21 women), 41 part-time matriculated graduate/professional students (21 women). *Graduate faculty:* 16 full-time (6 women), 1 part-time/adjunct (0 women). *Tuition:* Part-time $816 per hour. *Graduate housing:* Room and/or apartments available to single students; on-campus housing not available to married students. Housing application deadline: 6/1. *Student services:* Campus employment opportunities, campus safety program, career counseling, free psychological counseling, low-cost health insurance. *Library facilities:* Millsaps Wilson Library. *Online resources:* library catalog, web page, access to other libraries' catalogs. *Collection:* 194,797 titles, 16,221 serial subscriptions, 8,554 audiovisual materials.

Computer facilities: Computer purchase and lease plans are available. 120 computers available on campus for general student use. A campuswide network can be accessed from student residence rooms and from off campus. Internet access is available. *Web address:* http://www.millsaps.edu/.

General Application Contact: Dr. Bill Brisler, Associate Director of Graduate Business Admissions, 601-974-1277, Fax: 601-974-1260, E-mail: mbamacc@millsaps.edu.

GRADUATE UNITS

Else School of Management Students: 40 full-time (21 women), 41 part-time (21 women); includes 8 minority (6 African Americans, 1 Asian American or Pacific Islander, 1 Hispanic American), 5 international. Average age 26. 109 applicants, 76% accepted, 45 enrolled. *Faculty:* 16 full-time (6 women), 1 part-time/adjunct (0 women). Expenses: Contact institution. *Financial support:* In 2006–07, research assistantships (averaging $2,500 per year); career-related internships or fieldwork, Federal Work-Study, institutionally sponsored loans, scholarships/grants, and tuition waivers (partial) also available. Support available to part-time students. Financial award application deadline: 7/1; financial award applicants required to submit FAFSA. In 2006, 31 degrees awarded. *Degree program information:* Part-time programs available. Offers accounting (M Acc); business administration (MBA). *Application deadline:* For fall admission, 7/1 priority date for domestic students; for spring admission, 11/15 priority date for domestic students. Applications are processed on a rolling basis. *Application fee:* $25. Electronic applications accepted. *Application Contact:* Dr. Bill Brisler, Associate Director of Graduate Business Admissions, 601-974-1277, Fax: 601-974-1260, E-mail: mbamacc@millsaps.edu. *Dean,* Howard L McMillan, 601-974-1250, Fax: 601-974-1260.

MILLS COLLEGE, Oakland, CA 94613-1000

General Information Independent, Undergraduate: women only; graduate: coed, comprehensive institution. *Enrollment:* 1,410 graduate, professional, and undergraduate students; 430 full-time matriculated graduate/professional students (343 women), 51 part-time matriculated graduate/professional students (45 women). *Enrollment by degree level:* 362 master's, 44 doctoral, 75 other advanced degrees. *Graduate faculty:* 89 full-time (53 women), 94 part-time/adjunct (70 women). *Graduate housing:* Rooms and/or apartments available on a first-come, first-served basis to single and married students. Housing application deadline: 9/1. *Student services:* Campus employment opportunities, campus safety program, career counseling, child daycare facilities, disabled student services, exercise/wellness program, free psychological counseling, international student services, low-cost health insurance, teacher training, writing training. *Library facilities:* F. W. Olin Library plus 1 other. *Online resources:* library catalog, web page, access to other libraries' catalogs. *Collection:* 254,351 titles, 13,211 serial subscriptions, 7,640 audiovisual materials.

Computer facilities: Computer purchase and lease plans are available. 267 computers available on campus for general student use. A campuswide network can be accessed from student residence rooms and from off campus. Internet access is available. *Web address:* http://www.mills.edu/.

General Application Contact: Marianne B. Sheldon, Director of Graduate Studies, 510-430-2355, Fax: 510-430-2159, E-mail: grad-studies@mills.edu.

GRADUATE UNITS

Graduate Studies Students: 432 full-time (344 women), 59 part-time (50 women); includes 147 minority (54 African Americans, 3 American Indian/Alaska Native, 50 Asian Americans or Pacific Islanders, 40 Hispanic Americans), 8 international. Average age 31. 716 applicants, 65% accepted, 243 enrolled. *Faculty:* 89 full-time (53 women), 94 part-time/adjunct (70 women). Expenses: Contact institution. *Financial support:* In 2006–07, 181 fellowships with partial tuition reimbursements (averaging $1,785 per year), 76 teaching assistantships with partial tuition reimbursements (averaging $4,337 per year) were awarded; career-related internships or fieldwork, institutionally sponsored loans, scholarships/grants, and residence awards also available. Support available to part-time students. Financial award application deadline: 2/1; financial award applicants required to submit CSS PROFILE or FAFSA. In 2006, 138 master's, 2 doctorates, 78 other advanced degrees awarded. *Degree program information:* Part-time and evening/weekend programs available. Offers administration (Ed D); ceramics (MFA); child life in health care settings (MA); computer science (Certificate); creative writing (MFA); dance (MA, MFA); early childhood education (MA); education (MA); English (MA, MFA); interdisciplinary computer science (MA); management (MBA); multimedia/art (MFA); multimedia/music (MFA); music (MA, MFA); painting (MFA); photography (MFA); pre-med (Certificate); sculpture (MFA). *Application deadline:* For fall admission, 2/1 for domestic and international students; for spring admission, 11/1 for domestic and international students. Applications are processed on a rolling basis. *Application fee:* $50. *Application Contact:* Randy McGlauthing, Director of Graduate Admissions, 510-430-2355, Fax: 510-430-2159, E-mail: rmcglaut@mills.edu. *Director,* Marianne B. Sheldon, 510-430-2345, Fax: 510-430-2159, E-mail: mshel@mills.edu.

See Close-Up on page 963.

MILWAUKEE SCHOOL OF ENGINEERING, Milwaukee, WI 53202-3109

General Information Independent, coed, comprehensive institution. *Enrollment:* 2,427 graduate, professional, and undergraduate students; 31 full-time matriculated graduate/professional students (12 women), 193 part-time matriculated graduate/professional students (38 women). *Enrollment by degree level:* 224 master's. *Graduate faculty:* 10 full-time (1 woman), 21 part-time/adjunct (4 women). *Tuition:* Part-time $526 per credit. *Graduate housing:* Room and/or apartments available on a first-come, first-served basis to single students; on-campus housing not available to married students. Typical cost: $3,969 per year ($6,189 including board). Housing application deadline: 7/1. *Student services:* Campus employment opportunities, campus safety program, career counseling, disabled student services, exercise/wellness program, free psychological counseling, international student services, low-cost health insurance, multicultural affairs office, writing training. *Library facilities:* Walter Schroeder Library. *Online resources:* library catalog, web page, access to other libraries' catalogs. *Collection:* 72,192 titles, 376 serial subscriptions, 1,421 audiovisual materials. *Research affiliation:* Medical College of Wisconsin (physics), Caterpillar, Inc. (electrohydraulics), The Procter & Gamble Company (rapid tooling), 3DMD (biomolecular modeling), National Fluid Power Association (hydralics and pneumatics).

Computer facilities: Computer purchase and lease plans are available. 125 computers available on campus for general student use. A campuswide network can be accessed from student residence rooms and from off campus. Internet access and online class registration, e-mail are available. *Web address:* http://www.msoe.edu/.

General Application Contact: Julie A. Schuster, Graduate Admissions Counselor, 800-332-6763, Fax: 414-277-7475, E-mail: schuster@msoe.edu.

GRADUATE UNITS

Department of Architectural Engineering and Building Construction Students: 3 full-time (1 woman), 16 part-time (5 women); includes 1 minority (Asian American or Pacific Islander) Average age 23. 18 applicants, 72% accepted, 3 enrolled. *Faculty:* 3 full-time (1 woman), 6 part-time/adjunct (0 women). Expenses: Contact institution. *Financial support:* In 2006–07, 4 students received support, including 2 research assistantships (averaging $12,500 per year); career-related internships or fieldwork also available. Support available to part-time students. Financial award applicants required to submit FAFSA. In 2006, 5 degrees awarded. *Degree program information:* Part-time and evening/weekend programs available. Offers environmental engineering (MS); structural engineering (MS). *Application deadline:* Applications are processed on a rolling basis. *Application fee:* $30. Electronic applications accepted. *Application Contact:* Julie A. Schuster, Graduate Admissions Counselor, 800-332-6763, Fax: 414-

Milwaukee School of Engineering (continued)

277-7475, E-mail: schuster@msoe.edu. *Chair*, Dr. Deborah J. Jackman, 414-277-7472, Fax: 414-277-7479, E-mail: jackman@msoe.edu.

Department of Electrical Engineering and Computer Science Students: 14 full-time (5 women), 28 part-time (2 women); includes 1 minority (African American), 1 international. Average age 29. 66 applicants, 44% accepted, 15 enrolled. *Faculty:* 2 full-time (0 women), 7 part-time/adjunct (2 women). Expenses: Contact institution. *Financial support:* In 2006–07, 16 students received support, including 2 research assistantships (averaging $15,000 per year); career-related internships or fieldwork also available. Support available to part-time students. Financial award applicants required to submit FAFSA. In 2006, 10 degrees awarded. *Degree program information:* Part-time and evening/weekend programs available. Offers engineering (MS); perfusion (MS). *Application deadline:* Applications are processed on a rolling basis. *Application fee:* $30. Electronic applications accepted. *Application Contact:* Julie A. Schuster, Graduate Admissions, 800-332-6763, Fax: 414-277-7475, E-mail: schuster@msoe.edu. *Chairman*, Dr. Owe Petersen, 414-277-7114, Fax: 414-277-7465, E-mail: petersen@msoe.edu.

Rader School of Business Students: 14 full-time (6 women), 149 part-time (31 women); includes 11 minority (7 African Americans, 1 Asian American or Pacific Islander, 3 Hispanic Americans), 5 international. Average age 25. 64 applicants, 61% accepted, 25 enrolled. *Faculty:* 5 full-time (0 women), 8 part-time/adjunct (2 women). Expenses: Contact institution. *Financial support:* In 2006–07, 57 students received support. Career-related internships or fieldwork available. Support available to part-time students. Financial award applicants required to submit FAFSA. In 2006, 41 degrees awarded. *Degree program information:* Part-time and evening/weekend programs available. Offers engineering management (MS); medical informatics (MS). *Application deadline:* Applications are processed on a rolling basis. *Application fee:* $30. Electronic applications accepted. *Application Contact:* Julie A. Schuster, Graduate Admissions, 800-332-6763, Fax: 414-277-7475, E-mail: schuster@msoe.edu. *Chairman, Rader School of Business*, Dr. Steven Bialer, 414-277-7364, Fax: 414-277-7479, E-mail: bialer@msoe.edu.

MINNEAPOLIS COLLEGE OF ART AND DESIGN, Minneapolis, MN 55404-4347

General Information Independent, coed, comprehensive institution. *Enrollment:* 749 graduate, professional, and undergraduate students; 39 full-time matriculated graduate/professional students (26 women), 8 part-time matriculated graduate/professional students (4 women). *Enrollment by degree level:* 33 master's, 14 other advanced degrees. *Graduate faculty:* 32 full-time (12 women). *Tuition:* Full-time $27,000; part-time $900 per credit. *Required fees:* $200. *Graduate housing:* On-campus housing not available. *Student services:* Campus employment opportunities, campus safety program, career counseling, disabled student services, exercise/wellness program, free psychological counseling, grant writing training, international student services, low-cost health insurance, multicultural affairs office, teacher training, writing training. *Library facilities:* Minneapolis College of Art and Design Library. *Online resources:* web page. *Collection:* 47,166 titles, 196 serial subscriptions, 139,245 audiovisual materials.

Computer facilities: 110 computers available on campus for general student use. A campuswide network can be accessed from off campus. Internet access is available. *Web address:* http://www.mcad.edu/.

General Application Contact: William Mullen, Vice President of Enrollment Management, 612-874-3762, Fax: 612-874-3701, E-mail: william_mullen@mcad.edu.

GRADUATE UNITS

Program in Arts Students: 7 full-time (5 women), 7 part-time (3 women). Average age 24. 138 applicants, 26% accepted. Expenses: Contact institution. *Financial support:* Career-related internships or fieldwork available. Financial award applicants required to submit FAFSA. In 2006, 15 degrees awarded. *Degree program information:* Part-time programs available. Offers design (Certificate); fine arts (Certificate); media (Certificate). *Application deadline:* For fall admission, 2/15 for domestic and international students. *Application fee:* $50. Electronic applications accepted. *Application Contact:* William Mullen, Vice President of Enrollment Management, 612-874-3762, Fax: 612-874-3701, E-mail: william_mullen@mcad.edu. *Graduate Director*, Carole Fisher, 612-874-3629, E-mail: carole_fisher@mcad.edu.

Program in Visual Studies Students: 32 full-time (21 women), 1 (woman) part-time; includes 1 minority (American Indian/Alaska Native). Average age 27. 150 applicants, 15% accepted, 12 enrolled. *Faculty:* 23 full-time (7 women), 9 part-time/adjunct (4 women). Expenses: Contact institution. *Financial support:* In 2006–07, 23 students received support. Career-related internships or fieldwork, Federal Work-Study, scholarships/grants, and unspecified assistantships available. Support available to part-time students. Financial award application deadline: 3/5; financial award applicants required to submit FAFSA. In 2006, 7 degrees awarded. *Degree program information:* Part-time programs available. Offers animation (MFA); comic art (MFA); drawing (MFA); filmmaking (MFA); fine arts (MFA); furniture design (MFA); graphic design (MFA); illustration (MFA); interactive media (MFA); painting (MFA); photography (MFA); printmaking (MFA); sculpture (MFA). *Application deadline:* For fall admission, 2/15 for domestic and international students. *Application fee:* $50. Electronic applications accepted. *Application Contact:* William Mullen, Vice President of Enrollment Management, 612-874-3762, Fax: 612-874-3701, E-mail: william_mullen@mcad.edu. *Graduate Director*, Carole Fisher, 612-874-3629, E-mail: carole_fisher@mcad.edu.

MINNESOTA STATE UNIVERSITY MANKATO, Mankato, MN 56001

General Information State-supported, coed, comprehensive institution. CGS member. *Enrollment:* 14,148 graduate, professional, and undergraduate students; 544 full-time matriculated graduate/professional students (319 women), 1,047 part-time matriculated graduate/professional students (644 women). *Enrollment by degree level:* 1,591 master's. *Graduate housing:* Room and/or apartments available on a first-come, first-served basis to single students; on-campus housing not available to married students. *Student services:* Campus employment opportunities, campus safety program, career counseling, child daycare facilities, disabled student services, exercise/wellness program, free psychological counseling, international student services, low-cost health insurance, multicultural affairs office, teacher training. *Library facilities:* Memorial Library. *Online resources:* library catalog, web page. *Collection:* 474,252 titles, 3,400 serial subscriptions.

Computer facilities: 900 computers available on campus for general student use. A campuswide network can be accessed from student residence rooms and from off campus. Internet access and online class registration are available. *Web address:* http://www.mnsu.edu/.

General Application Contact: Information Contact, 507-389-2321, E-mail: grad@mnsu.edu.

GRADUATE UNITS

College of Graduate Studies Students: 544 full-time (319 women), 1,047 part-time (644 women). Average age 32. Expenses: Contact institution. *Financial support:* In 2006–07, research assistantships with full and partial tuition reimbursements (averaging $9,000 per year), teaching assistantships with full and partial tuition reimbursements (averaging $10,800 per year) were awarded; fellowships with full tuition reimbursements, career-related internships or fieldwork, Federal Work-Study, institutionally sponsored loans, scholarships/grants, and unspecified assistantships also available. Support available to part-time students. Financial award application deadline: 3/15; financial award applicants required to submit FAFSA. In 2006, 401 master's, 46 other advanced degrees awarded. *Degree program information:* Part-time programs available. Postbaccalaureate distance learning degree programs offered. Offers multidisciplinary studies (MS). *Application deadline:* For fall admission, 7/1 priority date for domestic students, 5/1 for international students; for spring admission, 11/1 for domestic students, 10/1 for international students. Applications are processed on a rolling basis. *Application fee:* $40. Electronic applications accepted. *Application Contact:* 507-389-2321, E-mail: grad@mnsu.edu. *Interim Dean*, Dr. Anne Blackhurst, 507-389-2321.

College of Allied Health and Nursing Students: 101 full-time (73 women), 127 part-time (82 women). Average age 32. Expenses: Contact institution. *Financial support:* Research assistantships with full tuition reimbursements, teaching assistantships with full tuition reimbursements, career-related internships or fieldwork, Federal Work-Study, institutionally sponsored loans, and unspecified assistantships available. Support available to part-time students. Financial award application deadline: 3/15; financial award applicants required to submit FAFSA. In 2006, 66 degrees awarded. *Degree program information:* Part-time programs available. Offers allied health and nursing (MA, MS, MSN, MT, SP); chemical dependency studies (MS); communication disorders (MS); community health (MS); family nursing (MSN); health science (MS, MT); human performance (MA, MS, MT, SP); managed care (MSN); rehabilitation counseling (MS); school health (MS). *Application deadline:* Applications are processed on a rolling basis. *Application fee:* $40. Electronic applications accepted. *Application Contact:* 507-389-2321, E-mail: grad@mnsu.edu. *Dean*, Dr. Kaye Herth, 507-389-6315.

College of Arts and Humanities Students: 92 full-time (52 women), 129 part-time (85 women). Average age 32. Expenses: Contact institution. *Financial support:* Research assistantships with full tuition reimbursements, teaching assistantships with full tuition reimbursements, career-related internships or fieldwork, Federal Work-Study, institutionally sponsored loans, and unspecified assistantships available. Support available to part-time students. Financial award application deadline: 3/15; financial award applicants required to submit FAFSA. In 2006, 50 degrees awarded. *Degree program information:* Part-time and evening/weekend programs available. Offers art education (MS); arts and humanities (MA, MAT, MFA, MM, MS, MT, Certificate); creative writing (MFA); English (MA, MS); English literature (MA); forensics (MFA); French (MAT, MS); music (MM, MT); Spanish (MAT, MS); speech communication (MA, MS, MT); studio art (MA); teaching art (MAT, MT); teaching English (MS, MT); teaching English as a second language (MA); technical communication (Certificate); theatre and dance (MA, MFA). *Application deadline:* Applications are processed on a rolling basis. *Application fee:* $40. *Application Contact:* 507-389-2321, E-mail: grad@mnsu.edu. *Dean*, Dr. Jane F. Earley, 507-389-1712.

College of Business Students: 8 full-time (3 women), 32 part-time (13 women). Expenses: Contact institution. Offers accounting and business law (MBA); finance (MBA); management (MBA); marketing and international business (MBA). *Application deadline:* For fall admission, 6/1 for domestic students; for spring admission, 10/1 for domestic students. Electronic applications accepted. *Dean*, Scott Johnson, 507-389-5420.

College of Education Students: 154 full-time (110 women), 429 part-time (304 women). Average age 35. Expenses: Contact institution. *Financial support:* Fellowships with partial tuition reimbursements, research assistantships with full tuition reimbursements, teaching assistantships with full tuition reimbursements, career-related internships or fieldwork, Federal Work-Study, institutionally sponsored loans, and unspecified assistantships available. Support available to part-time students. Financial award application deadline: 3/15; financial award applicants required to submit FAFSA. In 2006, 162 master's, 46 other advanced degrees awarded. *Degree program information:* Part-time and evening/weekend programs available. Offers college student affairs (MS); computer services administration (MS); curriculum and instruction (SP); early education for exceptional children (MS); education (MA, MAT, MS, MT, Certificate, SP); educational administration (Certificate); educational leadership (MS); educational studies: elementary and early childhood (MS); elementary school administration (MS, SP); emotional/behavioral disorders (MS, Certificate); experiential education (MS, Certificate, SP); general school administration (MS); higher education administration (MS); learning disabilities (MS, Certificate); library media education (MS, Certificate, SP); marriage and family (Certificate); professional community counseling (MS); professional school counseling (MS); secondary administration (MS, SP); talent development and gifted education (MS, Certificate, SP); teaching and learning (MS, Certificate); vocational-technical administration (MS). *Application deadline:* Applications are processed on a rolling basis. *Application fee:* $40. Electronic applications accepted. *Application Contact:* 507-389-2321, E-mail: grad@mnsu.edu. *Dean*, Dr. Michael Miller, 507-389-5445.

College of Science, Engineering and Technology Students: 43 full-time (13 women), 71 part-time (25 women). Average age 28. Expenses: Contact institution. *Financial support:* Fellowships with full tuition reimbursements, research assistantships with full tuition reimbursements, teaching assistantships with full tuition reimbursements, career-related internships or fieldwork, Federal Work-Study, institutionally sponsored loans, and unspecified assistantships available. Support available to part-time students. Financial award application deadline: 3/15; financial award applicants required to submit FAFSA. In 2006, 37 degrees awarded. *Degree program information:* Part-time programs available. Offers biology (MS); biology education (MS); computer and information sciences (MS, Certificate); computer science (MS, Graduate Certificate); electrical and computer engineering technology (MSE); electrical engineering (MS); environmental science (MS); manufacturing engineering technology (MS); mathematics (MA, MS); mathematics education (MAT, MS); physics (MS); physics and astronomy (MT); science, engineering and technology (MA, MAT, MS, MSE, MT, Certificate, Graduate Certificate); statistics (MS). *Application deadline:* For fall admission, 7/1 priority date for domestic students; for spring admission, 11/1 for domestic students. Applications are processed on a rolling basis. *Application fee:* $40. Electronic applications accepted. *Application Contact:* 507-389-2321, E-mail: grad@mnsu.edu. *Dean*, Dr. John Frey, 507-389-5998.

College of Social and Behavioral Sciences Students: 133 full-time (63 women), 169 part-time (78 women). Average age 27. Expenses: Contact institution. *Financial support:* Fellowships with partial tuition reimbursements, research assistantships with full tuition reimbursements, teaching assistantships with full tuition reimbursements, career-related internships or fieldwork, Federal Work-Study, institutionally sponsored loans, and unspecified assistantships available. Support available to part-time students. Financial award application deadline: 3/15; financial award applicants required to submit FAFSA. In 2006, 75 degrees awarded. *Degree program information:* Part-time programs available. Offers anthropology (MS); clinical psychology (MA); ethnic and multicultural studies (MS); geography (MS); geography education (MT); gerontology (MS, Certificate); history (MA, MS); human services planning and administration (MS); industrial/organizational psychology (MA); local government (Certificate); political science (MA, MS, MT); psychology (MT); public administration (MAPA); social and behavioral sciences (MA, MAPA, MS, MT, Certificate); social studies (MS); sociology (MA); sociology: corrections (MS); teaching history (MS, MT); urban and regional studies (MA); urban planning (Certificate); women's studies (MS, Certificate). *Application deadline:* Applications are processed on a rolling basis. *Application fee:* $40. Electronic applications accepted. *Application Contact:* 507-389-2321, E-mail: grad@mnsu.edu. *Interim Dean*, Dr. William Wagner, 507-389-6307.

MINNESOTA STATE UNIVERSITY MOORHEAD, Moorhead, MN 56563-0002

General Information State-supported, coed, comprehensive institution. *Enrollment:* 81 full-time matriculated graduate/professional students (59 women), 228 part-time matriculated graduate/professional students (168 women). *Enrollment by degree level:* 309 master's. *Graduate faculty:* 129. *Graduate housing:* Room and/or apartments available to single students; on-campus housing not available to married students. Typical cost: $3,866 per year ($5,938 including board). Room and board charges vary according to board plan and housing facility selected. Housing application deadline: 3/1. *Student services:* Campus employment opportunities, campus safety program, career counseling, child daycare facilities, disabled student services, free psychological counseling, grant writing training, international student services, low-cost health insurance, multicultural affairs office, writing training. *Library facilities:* Livingston Lord Library. *Online resources:* library catalog, web page, access to other libraries' catalogs. *Collection:* 367,334 titles, 1,539 serial subscriptions. *Research affiliation:* West Central Minnesota Business Innovation Center.

Computer facilities: 450 computers available on campus for general student use. A campuswide network can be accessed from student residence rooms and from off campus. Internet access and online class registration are available. *Web address:* http://www.mnstate.edu/.

General Application Contact: Karla Wenger, Graduate Studies Office, 218-477-2344, Fax: 218-477-2482, E-mail: wengerk@mnstate.edu.

GRADUATE UNITS

Graduate Studies Students: 81 full-time (59 women), 228 part-time (168 women); includes 10 minority (2 African Americans, 3 American Indian/Alaska Native, 1 Asian American or Pacific Islander, 4 Hispanic Americans), 6 international. Average age 33. 210 applicants, 56% accepted. *Faculty:* 129. Expenses: Contact institution. *Financial support:* Research assistantships, teaching assistantships with partial tuition reimbursements, career-related internships or fieldwork, Federal Work-Study, and unspecified assistantships available. Support available to part-time students. Financial award application deadline: 7/15; financial award applicants required to submit FAFSA. In 2006, 99 degrees awarded. *Degree program information:* Part-time and evening/weekend programs available. Postbaccalaureate distance learning degree programs offered (minimal on-campus study). *Application fee:* $20. Electronic applications accepted. *Application Contact:* Karla Wenger, Graduate Studies Office, 218-236-2344, Fax: 218-236-2482, E-mail: wengerk@mnstate.edu. *Director of Graduate Studies,* Dr. Richard K. Adler, 218-477-2344, E-mail: adlerri@mnstate.edu.

College of Arts and Humanities Students: 15 full-time (3 women), 38 part-time (24 women); includes 1 American Indian/Alaska Native, 1 Asian American or Pacific Islander, 1 Hispanic American. 19 applicants, 79% accepted. *Faculty:* 26 full-time (6 women), 1 part-time/adjunct (0 women). Expenses: Contact institution. *Financial support:* Research assistantships, teaching assistantships with partial tuition reimbursements, Federal Work-Study and unspecified assistantships available. Financial award application deadline: 7/15; financial award applicants required to submit FAFSA. In 2006, 14 degrees awarded. *Degree program information:* Part-time programs available. Offers arts and humanities (MFA, MLA); creative writing (MFA); liberal studies (MLA). *Application deadline:* Applications are processed on a rolling basis. *Application fee:* $20. Electronic applications accepted. *Application Contact:* Karla Wenger, Graduate Studies Office, 218-477-2344, Fax: 218-477-2482, E-mail: wengerk@mnstate.edu. *Dean of Arts and Humanities,* Dr. Kathleen Enz Finken, 218-477-2764, E-mail: enz@mnstate.edu.

College of Education and Human Services Students: 45 full-time (42 women), 167 part-time (130 women); includes 4 minority (2 American Indian/Alaska Native, 2 Hispanic Americans), 4 international. 154 applicants, 56% accepted. *Faculty:* 18 full-time (11 women), 25 part-time/adjunct (13 women). Expenses: Contact institution. *Financial support:* Career-related internships or fieldwork, Federal Work-Study, and unspecified assistantships available. Financial award application deadline: 7/15; financial award applicants required to submit FAFSA. In 2006, 60 degrees awarded. *Degree program information:* Part-time and evening/weekend programs available. Offers counseling and student affairs (MS); curriculum and instruction (MS); educational leadership (MS, Ed S); nursing (MS); reading (MS); special education (MS); speech-language pathology (MS). *Application deadline:* For fall admission, 4/15 priority date for domestic students; for spring admission, 11/1 priority date for domestic students. Applications are processed on a rolling basis. *Application fee:* $20. Electronic applications accepted. *Application Contact:* Karla Wenger, Graduate Studies Office, 218-477-2344, Fax: 218-477-2482, E-mail: wengerk@mnstate.edu. *Dean of Education and Human Services,* Dr. Michael Parsons, 218-477-2096.

College of Social and Natural Sciences Students: 21 full-time (14 women), 23 part-time (14 women); includes 2 African Americans, 1 Hispanic American, 2 international. 37 applicants, 43% accepted. *Faculty:* 18 full-time (9 women), 6 part-time/adjunct (3 women). Expenses: Contact institution. *Financial support:* Research assistantships, career-related internships or fieldwork, Federal Work-Study, and unspecified assistantships available. Financial award application deadline: 7/15; financial award applicants required to submit FAFSA. In 2006, 25 degrees awarded. *Degree program information:* Part-time and evening/weekend programs available. Offers public, human services, and health administration (MS); school psychology (MS, Psy S); social and natural sciences (MS, Psy S). *Application deadline:* Applications are processed on a rolling basis. *Application fee:* $20. Electronic applications accepted. *Application Contact:* Karla Wenger, Graduate Studies Office, 218-477-2344, Fax: 218-477-2482, E-mail: wengerk@mnstate.edu. *Dean,* Dr. Ron Jeppson, 218-477-5892, E-mail: jeppson@mnstate.edu.

MINOT STATE UNIVERSITY, Minot, ND 58707-0002

General Information State-supported, coed, comprehensive institution. *Enrollment:* 3,712 graduate, professional, and undergraduate students; 274 matriculated graduate/professional students (225 women). *Enrollment by degree level:* 274 master's. *Graduate faculty:* 76 full-time (24 women), 47 part-time/adjunct (26 women). *Graduate housing:* Rooms and/or apartments available on a first-come, first-served basis to single and married students. Housing application deadline: 6/30. *Student services:* Campus employment opportunities, campus safety program, career counseling, disabled student services, exercise/wellness program, free psychological counseling, international student services, multicultural affairs office, writing training. *Library facilities:* Gordon B. Olson Library. *Online resources:* library catalog, web page, access to other libraries' catalogs. *Collection:* 428,407 titles, 693 serial subscriptions, 123,173 audiovisual materials.

Computer facilities: 460 computers available on campus for general student use. A campuswide network can be accessed from student residence rooms and from off campus. Internet access and online class registration are available. *Web address:* http://www.minotstateu.edu/.

General Application Contact: Brenda Anderson, Administrative Assistant, 701-858-3250 Ext. 3150, Fax: 701-858-4286, E-mail: olsenren@minotstateu.edu.

GRADUATE UNITS

Graduate School Students: 96 full-time (81 women), 178 part-time (144 women); includes 17 minority (7 African Americans, 4 American Indian/Alaska Native, 2 Asian Americans or Pacific Islanders, 4 Hispanic Americans), 35 international. Average age 30. *Faculty:* 76 full-time (24 women), 47 part-time/adjunct (26 women). Expenses: Contact institution. *Financial support:* In 2006–07, 111 students received support, including 10 research assistantships with partial tuition reimbursements available (averaging $1,000 per year), 10 teaching assistantships with partial tuition reimbursements available; career-related internships or fieldwork, institutionally sponsored loans, scholarships/grants, traineeships, tuition waivers (partial), and unspecified assistantships also available. Support available to part-time students. Financial award application deadline: 4/1; financial award applicants required to submit FAFSA. In 2006, 82 master's, 7 other advanced degrees awarded. Postbaccalaureate distance learning degree programs offered. Offers audiology (MS); criminal justice (MS); education of the deaf (MS); elementary education (M Ed); information systems (MSIS); learning disabilities (MS); management (MS); mathematics (MAT); music education (MME); school psychology (Ed Sp); science (MAT); special education strategist (MS); speech-language pathology (MS). *Application deadline:* Applications are processed on a rolling basis. *Application fee:* $35. *Application Contact:* Brenda Anderson, Administrative Assistant, 701-858-3250, Fax: 701-858-4286, E-mail: brenda.anderson@minotstateu.edu. *Dean,* Dr. Linda Cresap, 701-858-3250, E-mail: linda.cresap@minotstateu.edu.

MIRRER YESHIVA, Brooklyn, NY 11223-2010

General Information Independent-religious, men only, comprehensive institution.

GRADUATE UNITS

Graduate Programs

MISSISSIPPI COLLEGE, Clinton, MS 39058

General Information Independent-religious, coed, comprehensive institution. *Enrollment:* 4,039 graduate, professional, and undergraduate students; 764 full-time matriculated graduate/professional students (351 women), 620 part-time matriculated graduate/professional students (479 women). *Enrollment by degree level:* 528 first professional, 856 master's. *Graduate faculty:* 97 full-time (31 women), 72 part-time/adjunct (32 women). *Tuition:* Full-time $7,290; part-time $405 per hour. *Required fees:* $150 per term. Tuition and fees vary according to campus/location and program. *Graduate housing:* Rooms and/or apartments available on a first-come, first-served basis to single students and available to married students. Typical cost: $3,700 per year ($5,500 including board) for single students. Housing application deadline: 8/15. *Student services:* Campus employment opportunities, career counseling, disabled student services, free psychological counseling, international student services, multicultural affairs office. *Library facilities:* Leland Speed Library plus 1 other. *Online resources:* library catalog, web page, access to other libraries' catalogs. *Collection:* 370,404 titles, 4,742 serial subscriptions, 18,348 audiovisual materials. *Research affiliation:* Gulf Coast Research Laboratory.

Computer facilities: 250 computers available on campus for general student use. A campuswide network can be accessed from student residence rooms and from off campus. Internet access is available. *Web address:* http://www.mc.edu/.

General Application Contact: Dr. Debbie C. Norris, Graduate Dean, 601-925-3260, Fax: 601-925-3889, E-mail: dnorris@mc.edu.

GRADUATE UNITS

Graduate School Students: 242 full-time (141 women), 614 part-time (475 women); includes 348 minority (332 African Americans, 4 American Indian/Alaska Native, 10 Asian Americans or Pacific Islanders, 2 Hispanic Americans), 95 international. Average age 30. *Faculty:* 78 full-time (24 women), 39 part-time/adjunct (20 women). Expenses: Contact institution. *Financial support:* Teaching assistantships, career-related internships or fieldwork, Federal Work-Study, tuition waivers (partial), and unspecified assistantships available. Support available to part-time students. Financial award application deadline: 4/1; financial award applicants required to submit FAFSA. In 2006, 272 master's, 6 other advanced degrees awarded. *Degree program information:* Part-time and evening/weekend programs available. Offers health services administration (MHSA); liberal studies (MLS). *Application deadline:* Applications are processed on a rolling basis. *Application fee:* $25. Electronic applications accepted. *Application Contact:* Cynthia Betz, Secretary, 601-925-3225, Fax: 601-925-3889, E-mail: betz@mc.edu. *Graduate Dean,* Dr. Debbie C. Norris, 601-925-3260, Fax: 601-925-3889, E-mail: dnorris@mc.edu.

College of Arts and Sciences Students: 99 full-time (46 women), 117 part-time (84 women); includes 61 minority (55 African Americans, 1 American Indian/Alaska Native, 4 Asian Americans or Pacific Islanders, 1 Hispanic American), 56 international. Average age 28. *Faculty:* 49 full-time (15 women), 16 part-time/adjunct (7 women). Expenses: Contact institution. *Financial support:* Teaching assistantships, career-related internships or fieldwork, Federal Work-Study, scholarships/grants, tuition waivers (partial), and unspecified assistantships available. Support available to part-time students. Financial award application deadline: 4/1; financial award applicants required to submit FAFSA. In 2006, 53 degrees awarded. *Degree program information:* Part-time and evening/weekend programs available. Offers administration of justice (MSS); applied communication (MSC); applied music performance (MM); art (M Ed, MA, MFA); arts and sciences (M Ed, MA, MCS, MFA, MM, MS, MSC, MSS, Certificate); biological science (M Ed); biology (MCS); biology-biological sciences (MS); biology-medical sciences (MS); chemistry (MCS, MS); Christian studies and the arts (M Ed, MA, MFA, MM, MSC); computer science (M Ed, MS); conducting (MM); English (M Ed, MA); history (M Ed, MA, MSS); humanities and social sciences (M Ed, MA, MS, MSS, Certificate); mathematics (M Ed, MCS, MS); music education (MM); music performance: organ (MM); paralegal studies (Certificate); political science (MSS); public relations and corporate communication (MSC); science and mathematics (M Ed, MCS, MS); social sciences (M Ed, MSS); sociology (MSS); teaching English to speakers of other languages (MA, MS); vocal pedagogy (MM). *Application deadline:* Applications are processed on a rolling basis. *Application fee:* $25. Electronic applications accepted. *Dean,* Dr. Ron Howard, 601-925-3327, Fax: 601-925-3499, E-mail: howard@mc.edu.

School of Business Students: 55 full-time (28 women), 111 part-time (58 women); includes 41 minority (35 African Americans, 6 Asian Americans or Pacific Islanders), 32 international. Average age 29. *Faculty:* 12 full-time (2 women), 1 part-time/adjunct (0 women). Expenses: Contact institution. *Financial support:* Federal Work-Study and unspecified assistantships available. Support available to part-time students. Financial award application deadline: 4/1; financial award applicants required to submit FAFSA. In 2006, 45 master's, 5 other advanced degrees awarded. *Degree program information:* Part-time and evening/weekend programs available. Offers accounting (Certificate); business administration (MBA); business education (M Ed). *Application deadline:* For fall admission, 8/15 priority date for domestic students. Applications are processed on a rolling basis. *Application fee:* $25. Electronic applications accepted. *Dean,* Dr. Marcelo Eduardo, 601-925-3420, E-mail: eduardo@mc.edu.

School of Education Students: 83 full-time (63 women), 345 part-time (300 women); includes 211 minority (207 African Americans, 3 American Indian/Alaska Native, 1 Hispanic American), 5 international. Average age 32. *Faculty:* 15 full-time (7 women), 16 part-time/adjunct (10 women). Expenses: Contact institution. *Financial support:* Teaching assistantships, career-related internships or fieldwork, Federal Work-Study, scholarships/grants, and unspecified assistantships available. Support available to part-time students. Financial award application deadline: 4/1; financial award applicants required to submit FAFSA. In 2006, 155 degrees awarded. *Degree program information:* Part-time and evening/weekend programs available. Offers art (M Ed); biological science (M Ed); business education (M Ed); computer science (M Ed); counseling (Ed S); dyslexia therapy (M Ed); education (M Ed, MS, Ed S); educational leadership (M Ed, Ed S); elementary education (M Ed, Ed S); English (M Ed); higher education administration (MS); marriage and family counseling (MS); mathematics (M Ed); mental health counseling (MS); school counseling (M Ed); secondary education (M Ed); social studies (history) (M Ed); teaching arts (M Ed). *Application deadline:* For fall admission, 8/15 priority date for domestic students. Applications are processed on a rolling basis. *Application fee:* $25. Electronic applications accepted. *Dean,* Dr. Don Locke, 601-925-3250, E-mail: locke@mc.edu.

School of Law Students: 522 full-time (210 women), 6 part-time (4 women); includes 40 minority (34 African Americans, 1 American Indian/Alaska Native, 2 Asian Americans or Pacific Islanders, 3 Hispanic Americans). 1,171 applicants, 41% accepted, 195 enrolled. *Faculty:* 19 full-time (7 women), 33 part-time/adjunct (12 women). Expenses: Contact institution. *Financial support:* In 2006–07, 490 students received support. Federal Work-Study and scholarships/grants available. Financial award applicants required to submit FAFSA. In 2006, 129 degrees awarded. Offers civil law studies (Certificate); law (JD). *Application deadline:* For fall admission, 6/1 priority date for domestic students. Applications are processed on a rolling basis. *Application fee:* $50. Electronic applications accepted. *Application Contact:* Patricia H. Evans, Assistant Dean for Admissions, 601-925-7151, Fax: 601-925-7166, E-mail: pevans@mc.edu. *Dean,* James H. Rosenblatt, 601-925-7101, Fax: 601-925-7115, E-mail: rosenblatt@mc.edu.

MISSISSIPPI STATE UNIVERSITY, Mississippi State, MS 39762

General Information State-supported, coed, university. CGS member. *Enrollment:* 16,206 graduate, professional, and undergraduate students; 1,793 full-time matriculated graduate/professional students (824 women), 1,783 part-time matriculated graduate/professional students (966 women). *Enrollment by degree level:* 264 first professional, 2,198 master's, 1,010 doctoral, 104 other advanced degrees. *Graduate faculty:* 1,071 full-time (352 women), 197 part-time/adjunct (102 women). *International tuition:* $10,882 full-time. Tuition, state resident: full-time $4,550; part-time $253 per hour. Tuition, nonresident: full-time $10,552; part-time $584 per hour. Tuition and fees vary according to course load. *Graduate housing:* Rooms and/or apartments available on a first-come, first-served basis to single students and available to married students. Typical cost: $5,124 per year for single students; $3,924 per year for married students. Housing application deadline: 8/1. *Student services:* Campus employment opportunities, campus safety program, career counseling, child daycare facilities, disabled student services, exercise/wellness program, free psychological counseling, grant writing training, international student services, low-cost health insurance, multicultural affairs office, teacher training, writing training. *Library facilities:* Mitchell Memorial Library plus 2 others. *Online resources:* library catalog, web page, access to other libraries' catalogs. *Collection:* 2.4 million titles, 39,772 serial subscriptions, 324,334 audiovisual materials. *Research affiliation:* Mississippi Research Consortium (interdisciplinary research), NASA John C. Stennis Space Center (interdisciplinary research), Mississippi Mineral Resources Institute (geology–sciences and engineering), Mississippi Research and Technology Park (engineering—interdisciplinary), Oak Ridge Associated Universities (energy related research–interdisciplinary), Southeastern Universities Research Association (interdisciplinary research).

Computer facilities: 2,000 computers available on campus for general student use. A campuswide network can be accessed from student residence rooms and from off campus.

Mississippi State University (continued)

Internet access and online class registration, wireless network with partial campus coverage are available. *Web address:* http://www.msstate.edu/.

General Application Contact: Dr. Phil Bonfanti, Director of Admissions, 662-325-4104, Fax: 662-325-8872, E-mail: admit@msstate.edu.

GRADUATE UNITS

Bagley College of Engineering Students: 340 full-time (71 women), 133 part-time (26 women); includes 50 minority (34 African Americans, 12 Asian Americans or Pacific Islanders, 4 Hispanic Americans), 209 international. Average age 28. 1,462 applicants, 31% accepted, 91 enrolled. *Faculty:* 133 full-time (23 women), 11 part-time/adjunct (1 woman). Expenses: Contact institution. *Financial support:* In 2006–07, 32 teaching assistantships with full tuition reimbursements (averaging $11,378 per year) were awarded; research assistantships with full tuition reimbursements, Federal Work-Study, institutionally sponsored loans, and unspecified assistantships also available. Financial award applicants required to submit FAFSA. In 2006, 84 master's, 16 doctorates awarded. *Degree program information:* Part-time programs available. Postbaccalaureate distance learning degree programs offered (no on-campus study). Offers aerospace engineering (MS); civil engineering (MS, PhD); computer engineering (MS, PhD); computer science (MS, PhD); electrical engineering (MS, PhD); engineering (PhD); engineering mechanics (MS); industrial and systems engineering (MS, PhD); mechanical engineering (MS, PhD). *Application deadline:* For fall admission, 7/1 for domestic students; for spring admission, 11/1 for domestic students. Applications are processed on a rolling basis. *Application fee:* $30. *Application Contact:* Dr. Phil Bonfanti, Director of Admissions, 662-325-4104, Fax: 662-325-8872, E-mail: admit@msstate.edu. *Dean,* Dr. Kirk H. Schulz, 662-325-2270, Fax: 662-325-8573, E-mail: schulz@engr.msstate.edu.

David C. Swalm School of Chemical Engineering Students: 15 full-time (2 women), 1 part-time; includes 4 minority (3 African Americans, 1 Asian American or Pacific Islander), 3 international. Average age 24. 63 applicants, 13% accepted, 8 enrolled. *Faculty:* 14 full-time (4 women), 1 part-time/adjunct (0 women). Expenses: Contact institution. *Financial support:* In 2006–07, 1 teaching assistantship with tuition reimbursement (averaging $13,091 per year) was awarded; research assistantships with full tuition reimbursements, Federal Work-Study, institutionally sponsored loans, and unspecified assistantships also available. Financial award applicants required to submit FAFSA. In 2006, 2 degrees awarded. Offers chemical engineering (MS); engineering (PhD). *Application deadline:* For fall admission, 4/1 priority date for domestic students; for spring admission, 8/1 priority date for domestic students. Applications are processed on a rolling basis. *Application fee:* $30. *Application Contact:* Dr. Phil Bonfanti, Director of Admissions, 662-325-4104, Fax: 662-325-8872, E-mail: admit@msstate.edu. *Director,* Dr. Mark White, 662-325-2480, Fax: 662-325-2482, E-mail: white@che.msstate.edu.

College of Agriculture and Life Sciences Students: 159 full-time (58 women), 87 part-time (48 women); includes 18 minority (14 African Americans, 2 Asian Americans or Pacific Islanders, 2 Hispanic Americans), 75 international. Average age 29. 139 applicants, 38% accepted, 27 enrolled. *Faculty:* 147 full-time (28 women), 14 part-time/adjunct (7 women). Expenses: Contact institution. *Financial support:* In 2006–07, 18 teaching assistantships with full tuition reimbursements (averaging $10,455 per year) were awarded; research assistantships with full tuition reimbursements, career-related internships or fieldwork, Federal Work-Study, institutionally sponsored loans, scholarships/grants, tuition waivers (partial), and unspecified assistantships also available. Financial award applicants required to submit FAFSA. In 2006, 59 master's, 15 doctorates awarded. *Degree program information:* Part-time programs available. Offers agribusiness management (MABM); agricultural economics (PhD); agricultural pest management (MS); agriculture and extension education (MS); agriculture and life sciences (MABM, MLA, MS, PhD); agronomy (MS, PhD); biochemistry (MS); biological engineering (MS); biomedical engineering (MS, PhD); engineering (PhD); entomology (MS, PhD); food science (PhD); food science, nutrition and health promotion (MS); horticulture (MS, PhD); landscape architecture (MLA); molecular biology (PhD); nutrition (MS, PhD); plant pathology (MS, PhD); poultry science (MS); weed science (MS, PhD). *Application deadline:* For fall admission, 7/1 for domestic students; for spring admission, 11/1 for domestic students. Applications are processed on a rolling basis. *Application fee:* $30. *Application Contact:* Dr. Phil Bonfanti, Director of Admissions, 662-325-4104, Fax: 662-325-8872, E-mail: admit@msstate.edu. *Dean and Vice President,* Dr. Vance Watson, 662-325-2110, E-mail: vwatson@dafvm.msstate.edu.

College of Architecture, Art and Design Students: 17 full-time (6 women), 4 part-time (1 woman); includes 5 minority (3 African Americans, 2 Asian Americans or Pacific Islanders), 7 international. Average age 32. 18 applicants, 83% accepted, 7 enrolled. *Faculty:* 40 full-time (18 women), 7 part-time/adjunct (0 women). Expenses: Contact institution. *Financial support:* In 2006–07, 7 students received support; research assistantships with full tuition reimbursements available, career-related internships or fieldwork, Federal Work-Study, institutionally sponsored loans, and unspecified assistantships available. Financial award application deadline: 3/1; financial award applicants required to submit FAFSA. In 2006, 10 degrees awarded. Offers architecture, art and design (MFA, MS); electronic visualization (MFA). *Application deadline:* For fall admission, 3/1 priority date for domestic students. Applications are processed on a rolling basis. *Application fee:* $30. Electronic applications accepted. *Application Contact:* Dr. Phil Bonfanti, Director of Admissions, 662-325-4104, Fax: 662-325-8872, E-mail: admit@msstate.edu. *Dean,* James L. West, 662-325-2202, Fax: 662-325-8872, E-mail: jwest@coa.msstate.edu.

School of Architecture Students: 17 full-time (6 women), 3 part-time (1 woman); includes 5 minority (3 African Americans, 2 Asian Americans or Pacific Islanders), 7 international. Average age 32. *Faculty:* 15 full-time (5 women), 5 part-time/adjunct (0 women). Expenses: Contact institution. In 2006, 9 degrees awarded. Offers architecture (MS). *Application fee:* $30. *Application Contact:* Dr. Phil Bonfanti, Director of Admissions, 662-325-4104, Fax: 662-325-8872, E-mail: admit@msstate.edu. *Director,* Dr. Larry Barrow, 662-325-2541, Fax: 662-325-8872, E-mail: lbarrow@caad.msstate.edu.

College of Arts and Sciences Students: 336 full-time (150 women), 424 part-time (202 women); includes 87 minority (60 African Americans, 5 American Indian/Alaska Native, 9 Asian Americans or Pacific Islanders, 13 Hispanic Americans), 83 international. Average age 33. 474 applicants, 59% accepted, 219 enrolled. *Faculty:* 254 full-time (102 women), 39 part-time/adjunct (19 women). Expenses: Contact institution. *Financial support:* In 2006–07, 226 students received support, including 186 teaching assistantships with full tuition reimbursements available (averaging $10,416 per year); fellowships with full tuition reimbursements available, research assistantships with full tuition reimbursements available, Federal Work-Study, institutionally sponsored loans, scholarships/grants, tuition waivers (partial), and unspecified assistantships also available. Financial award applicants required to submit FAFSA. In 2006, 236 master's, 16 doctorates awarded. *Degree program information:* Part-time and evening/weekend programs available. Offers applied anthropology (MA); arts and sciences (MA, MPPA, MS, PhD); biological sciences (MS, PhD); chemistry (MS, PhD); clinical psychology (MS); cognitive science (PhD); engineering physics (PhD); English (MA); experimental psychology (MS); French (MA); French/German (MA); geosciences (MS); German (MA); history (MA, PhD); mathematical sciences (PhD); mathematics (MS); physics (MS); political science (MA); public policy and administration (MPPA, PhD); sociology (MS, PhD); Spanish (MA); Spanish/French (MA); Spanish/German (MA); statistics (MS). *Application deadline:* For fall admission, 7/1 for domestic students; for spring admission, 11/1 for domestic students. Applications are processed on a rolling basis. *Application fee:* $30. *Application Contact:* Dr. Phil Bonfanti, Director of Admissions, 662-325-4104, Fax: 662-325-8872, E-mail: admit@msstate.edu. *Dean,* Dr. Philip B. Oldham, 662-325-2646, Fax: 662-325-8740, E-mail: poldham@deanas.msstate.edu.

College of Business and Industry Students: 193 full-time (74 women), 163 part-time (55 women); includes 34 minority (28 African Americans, 1 American Indian/Alaska Native, 2 Asian Americans or Pacific Islanders, 3 Hispanic Americans), 43 international. Average age 29. 700 applicants, 33% accepted, 158 enrolled. *Faculty:* 66 full-time (18 women), 18 part-time/adjunct (9 women). Expenses: Contact institution. *Financial support:* In 2006–07, 30 teaching assistantships with full tuition reimbursements (averaging $10,968 per year) were awarded; research assistantships with full tuition reimbursements, career-related internships or fieldwork, Federal Work-Study, institutionally sponsored loans, and unspecified assistantships also available. Financial award applicants required to submit FAFSA. In 2006, 145 master's, 11 doctorates awarded. *Degree program information:* Part-time and evening/weekend programs available. Postbaccalaureate distance learning degree programs offered (no on-campus study). Offers applied economics (PhD); business administration (MBA, PhD); business and industry (MA, MBA, MPA, MSBA, MSIS, MTX, PhD); economics (MA); finance (MSBA); information systems (MSIS); project management (MBA). *Application deadline:* For fall admission, 7/1 for domestic students; for spring admission, 11/1 for domestic students. Applications are processed on a rolling basis. *Application fee:* $30. *Application Contact:* Dr. Phil Bonfanti, Director of Admissions, 662-325-4104, Fax: 662-325-8872, E-mail: admit@msstate.edu. *Interim Dean,* Dr. Dan P. Hollingsworth, 662-325-3580, Fax: 662-325-7360, E-mail: dhollingsworth@cobilan.msstate.edu.

School of Accountancy Students: 47 full-time (20 women), 4 part-time (3 women); includes 4 minority (all African Americans), 7 international. Average age 24. 28 applicants, 75% accepted, 18 enrolled. *Faculty:* 9 full-time (4 women), 4 part-time/adjunct (1 woman). Expenses: Contact institution. *Financial support:* Research assistantships with tuition reimbursements, teaching assistantships with partial tuition reimbursements, career-related internships or fieldwork, Federal Work-Study, institutionally sponsored loans, and unspecified assistantships available. Support available to part-time students. Financial award applicants required to submit FAFSA. In 2006, 26 degrees awarded. Offers accountancy (MPA, MTX). *Application deadline:* For fall admission, 7/1 for domestic students; for spring admission, 11/1 for domestic students. Applications are processed on a rolling basis. *Application fee:* $30. *Application Contact:* Dr. Phil Bonfanti, Director of Admissions, 662-325-4104, Fax: 662-325-8872, E-mail: admit@msstate.edu. *Interim Director,* Dr. Clyde Herring, 662-325-3710, Fax: 662-325-1646, E-mail: cherring@cobilan.msstate.edu.

College of Education Students: 327 full-time (230 women), 627 part-time (469 women); includes 389 minority (375 African Americans, 4 American Indian/Alaska Native, 4 Asian Americans or Pacific Islanders, 6 Hispanic Americans), 14 international. Average age 35. 245 applicants, 70% accepted, 122 enrolled. *Faculty:* 107 full-time (57 women), 38 part-time/adjunct (34 women). Expenses: Contact institution. *Financial support:* In 2006–07, 20 teaching assistantships (averaging $8,056 per year) were awarded; research assistantships, career-related internships or fieldwork, Federal Work-Study, institutionally sponsored loans, scholarships/grants, and unspecified assistantships also available. Financial award applicants required to submit FAFSA. In 2006, 214 master's, 42 doctorates, 34 other advanced degrees awarded. *Degree program information:* Part-time and evening/weekend programs available. Postbaccalaureate distance learning degree programs offered (minimal on-campus study). Offers counselor education (MS, PhD, Ed S); curriculum and instruction (PhD); education (MS, MSIT, Ed D, PhD, Ed S); educational psychology (MS, PhD, Ed S); elementary education (MS, Ed D, PhD, Ed S); exercise science (MS); health education/health promotion (MS); instructional technology (MSIT); secondary education (MS, Ed D, PhD, Ed S); special education (MS, Ed S); sports administration (MS); teaching/coaching (MS); technology (MS, Ed D, PhD, Ed S); workforce education leadership (MS). *Application deadline:* For fall admission, 7/1 for domestic students; for spring admission, 11/1 for domestic students. Applications are processed on a rolling basis. *Application fee:* $30. *Application Contact:* Dr. Phil Bonfanti, Director of Admissions, 662-325-4104, Fax: 662-325-8872, E-mail: admit@msstate.edu. *Dean,* Dr. Richard Blackbourn, 662-325-3717, Fax: 662-325-8784, E-mail: rlb277@msstate.edu.

College of Forest Resources Students: 80 full-time (26 women), 30 part-time (9 women); includes 6 minority (2 African Americans, 1 Asian American or Pacific Islander, 3 Hispanic Americans), 15 international. Average age 29. 26 applicants, 46% accepted, 10 enrolled. *Faculty:* 53 full-time (6 women), 1 part-time/adjunct (0 women). Expenses: Contact institution. *Financial support:* In 2006–07, 3 teaching assistantships with full tuition reimbursements (averaging $11,728 per year) were awarded; research assistantships with full tuition reimbursements, career-related internships or fieldwork, Federal Work-Study, institutionally sponsored loans, and unspecified assistantships also available. Financial award applicants required to submit FAFSA. In 2006, 17 master's, 5 doctorates awarded. *Degree program information:* Part-time programs available. Offers forest products (MS, PhD); forest resources (MS, PhD); forestry (MS); wildlife and fisheries science (MS). *Application deadline:* For fall admission, 7/1 for domestic students; for spring admission, 11/1 for domestic students. Applications are processed on a rolling basis. *Application fee:* $30. Electronic applications accepted. *Application Contact:* Dr. Phil Bonfanti, Director of Admissions, 662-325-4104, Fax: 662-325-8872, E-mail: admit@msstate.edu. *Dean,* Dr. George M. Hopper, 662-325-2696, Fax: 662-325-8726, E-mail: ghopper@cfr.msstate.edu.

College of Veterinary Medicine Offers environmental toxicology (PhD); veterinary medical science (MS, PhD); veterinary medicine (DVM, MS, PhD). Electronic applications accepted.

MISSISSIPPI UNIVERSITY FOR WOMEN, Columbus, MS 39701-9998

General Information State-supported, coed, primarily women, comprehensive institution. *Graduate housing:* Rooms and/or apartments available on a first-come, first-served basis to single and married students.

GRADUATE UNITS

Graduate School *Degree program information:* Part-time programs available.

Division of Education and Human Sciences *Degree program information:* Part-time programs available. Offers gifted studies (M Ed); instructional management (M Ed); speech/language pathology (MS).

Division of Health and Kinesiology Offers health education (MS).

Division of Nursing *Degree program information:* Part-time programs available. Offers nursing (MSN, Certificate).

MISSISSIPPI VALLEY STATE UNIVERSITY, Itta Bena, MS 38941-1400

General Information State-supported, coed, comprehensive institution. *Graduate housing:* Room and/or apartments available to single students; on-campus housing not available to married students. Housing application deadline: 8/1.

GRADUATE UNITS

Department of Criminal Justice and Social Work *Degree program information:* Part-time and evening/weekend programs available. Offers criminal justice (MS). Electronic applications accepted.

Department of Education Offers education (MAT); elementary education (MA).

Department of Natural Science and Environmental Health *Degree program information:* Part-time and evening/weekend programs available. Offers bioinformatics (MS); environmental health (MS).

MISSOURI BAPTIST UNIVERSITY, St. Louis, MO 63141-8660

General Information Independent-religious, coed, comprehensive institution.

MISSOURI STATE UNIVERSITY, Springfield, MO 65804-0094

General Information State-supported, coed, comprehensive institution. CGS member. *Enrollment:* 19,218 graduate, professional, and undergraduate students; 1,136 full-time matriculated graduate/professional students (683 women), 1,159 part-time matriculated graduate/professional students (708 women). *Enrollment by degree level:* 2,201 master's, 49 doctoral, 45 other advanced degrees. *Graduate faculty:* 404 full-time (139 women), 98 part-time/adjunct (23 women). Tuition, state resident: full-time $3,582; part-time $199 per credit hour. Tuition, nonresident: full-time $6,984; part-time $199 per credit hour. *Required fees:* $548. Full-time tuition and fees vary according to course level, course load, program and reciprocity agreements. *Graduate housing:* Rooms and/or apartments available on a first-come, first-served basis to single and married students. Typical cost: $3,257 per year ($5,078 including board) for single students; $5,268 per year ($5,968 including board) for married students. Room and board charges vary according to board plan and housing facility selected. *Student services:* Campus employment opportunities, campus safety program, career counseling, child daycare facilities, disabled student services, exercise/wellness program, free psychological counseling, grant writing training, international student services, low-cost health insurance, multicultural affairs office, teacher training, writing training. *Library facilities:* Meyer Library plus 3 others. *Online resources:* library catalog, web page, access to other libraries' catalogs. *Collection:* 1.7 million titles, 4,238 serial subscriptions, 33,547 audiovisual materials.

Computer facilities: Computer purchase and lease plans are available. 1,800 computers available on campus for general student use. A campuswide network can be accessed from student residence rooms and from off campus. Internet access and online class registration are available. *Web address:* http://www.missouristate.edu/.

General Application Contact: Tobin Bushman, Coordinator of Admissions and Recruitment, 417-836-5331, Fax: 417-836-6888, E-mail: tobinbushman@missouristate.edu.

GRADUATE UNITS

Graduate College Students: 1,136 full-time (683 women), 1,159 part-time (708 women); includes 97 minority (41 African Americans, 21 American Indian/Alaska Native, 17 Asian Americans or Pacific Islanders, 18 Hispanic Americans), 235 international. Average age 30. 1,055 applicants, 63% accepted, 479 enrolled. *Faculty:* 404 full-time (139 women), 98 part-time/adjunct (23 women). Expenses: Contact institution. *Financial support:* In 2006–07, 39 research assistantships with full tuition reimbursements (averaging $8,317 per year), 102 teaching assistantships with full tuition reimbursements (averaging $7,259 per year) were awarded; career-related internships or fieldwork, Federal Work-Study, institutionally sponsored loans, scholarships/grants, tuition waivers (partial), and unspecified assistantships also available. Support available to part-time students. Financial award application deadline: 3/31; financial award applicants required to submit FAFSA. In 2006, 734 master's, 3 doctorates, 17 other advanced degrees awarded. *Degree program information:* Part-time and evening/weekend programs available. Postbaccalaureate distance learning degree programs offered. Offers applied communication (MSAS); criminal justice (MSAS); environmental management (MSAS); project management (MSAS); sports management (MSAS). *Application deadline:* For fall admission, 7/20 priority date for domestic students; for spring admission, 12/20 priority date for domestic students. Applications are processed on a rolling basis. *Application fee:* $35. Electronic applications accepted. *Application Contact:* Tobin Bushman, Coordinator of Admissions and Recruitment, 417-836-5331, Fax: 417-836-6888, E-mail: tobinbushman@missouristate.edu. *Associate Provost,* Frank A. Einhellig, 417-836-5335, Fax: 417-836-6888, E-mail: frankeinhellig@missouristate.edu.

College of Arts and Letters Students: 102 full-time (62 women), 75 part-time (44 women); includes 12 minority (6 African Americans, 2 Asian Americans or Pacific Islanders, 4 Hispanic Americans), 5 international. Average age 29. 83 applicants, 61% accepted, 37 enrolled. *Faculty:* 78 full-time (35 women). Expenses: Contact institution. *Financial support:* In 2006–07, research assistantships with full tuition reimbursements (averaging $8,750 per year), 48 teaching assistantships with full tuition reimbursements (averaging $6,780 per year) were awarded; career-related internships or fieldwork, Federal Work-Study, institutionally sponsored loans, scholarships/grants, and unspecified assistantships also available. Support available to part-time students. Financial award application deadline: 3/31; financial award applicants required to submit FAFSA. In 2006, 64 degrees awarded. *Degree program information:* Part-time and evening/weekend programs available. Offers arts and letters (MA, MM, MS Ed); communication and mass media (MA); English and writing (MA); music (MM); secondary education (MS Ed); theatre (MA). *Application deadline:* For fall admission, 7/20 for domestic students; for spring admission, 12/20 for domestic students. Applications are processed on a rolling basis. *Application fee:* $35. Electronic applications accepted. *Dean,* 417-836-5247, Fax: 417-836-6940.

College of Business Administration Students: 310 full-time (144 women), 218 part-time (83 women); includes 23 minority (12 African Americans, 2 American Indian/Alaska Native, 6 Asian Americans or Pacific Islanders, 3 Hispanic Americans), 127 international. Average age 28. 239 applicants, 58% accepted, 124 enrolled. *Faculty:* 70 full-time (18 women). Expenses: Contact institution. *Financial support:* In 2006–07, 3 research assistantships with full tuition reimbursements (averaging $8,260 per year), 5 teaching assistantships with full tuition reimbursements (averaging $6,780 per year) were awarded; career-related internships or fieldwork, Federal Work-Study, institutionally sponsored loans, scholarships/grants, tuition waivers (partial), and unspecified assistantships also available. Support available to part-time students. Financial award application deadline: 3/31; financial award applicants required to submit FAFSA. In 2006, 205 degrees awarded. *Degree program information:* Part-time and evening/weekend programs available. Postbaccalaureate distance learning degree programs offered (minimal on-campus study). Offers accountancy (M Acc); business administration (M Acc, MBA, MHA, MS, MS Ed); computer information systems (MS); health administration (MHA); secondary education (MS Ed). *Application deadline:* For fall admission, 7/20 priority date for domestic students; for spring admission, 12/20 priority date for domestic students. Applications are processed on a rolling basis. *Application fee:* $35. Electronic applications accepted. *Application Contact:* Dr. Michael Hignite, Director, 417-836-5646, Fax: 417-836-4407, E-mail: mikehignite@missouristate.edu. *Dean,* Dr. Ronald Bottin, 417-836-4408, Fax: 417-836-4407, E-mail: COBA@missouristate.edu.

College of Education Students: 140 full-time (110 women), 506 part-time (387 women); includes 23 minority (10 African Americans, 6 American Indian/Alaska Native, 3 Asian Americans or Pacific Islanders, 4 Hispanic Americans), 2 international. Average age 34. 91 applicants, 80% accepted, 57 enrolled. *Faculty:* 37 full-time (19 women), 6 part-time/adjunct (3 women). Expenses: Contact institution. *Financial support:* In 2006–07, research assistantships with full tuition reimbursements (averaging $6,575 per year), 3 teaching assistantships with full tuition reimbursements (averaging $6,780 per year) were awarded; career-related internships or fieldwork, Federal Work-Study, scholarships/grants, and unspecified assistantships also available. Financial award application deadline: 3/31; financial award applicants required to submit FAFSA. In 2006, 170 master's, 17 other advanced degrees awarded. *Degree program information:* Part-time and evening/weekend programs available. Postbaccalaureate distance learning degree programs offered (minimal on-campus study). Offers counseling (MS); director of special education (Ed S); early childhood and family development (MS); education (MAT, MS, MS Ed, Ed S); educational administration (MS Ed, Ed S); elementary education (MS Ed); elementary principal (Ed S); instructional media technology (MS Ed); reading education (MS Ed); secondary education (MS Ed); secondary principal (Ed S); special education (MS Ed); superintendent (Ed S); teacher education (MAT, MS Ed); teaching (MAT). *Application deadline:* For fall admission, 7/20 priority date for domestic students; for spring admission, 12/20 priority date for domestic students. Applications are processed on a rolling basis. *Application fee:* $35. Electronic applications accepted. *Dean,* Dr. David L. Hough, 417-836-5254, Fax: 417-836-4884, E-mail: coestudentservices@missouristate.edu.

College of Health and Human Services Students: 407 full-time (293 women), 107 part-time (82 women); includes 23 minority (9 African Americans, 8 American Indian/Alaska Native, 1 Asian American or Pacific Islander, 5 Hispanic Americans), 63 international. Average age 29. 410 applicants, 55% accepted, 141 enrolled. *Faculty:* 88 full-time (42 women), 65 part-time/adjunct (16 women). Expenses: Contact institution. *Financial support:* In 2006–07, 15 research assistantships with full tuition reimbursements (averaging $7,520 per year), 17 teaching assistantships with full tuition reimbursements (averaging $6,780 per year) were awarded; career-related internships or fieldwork, Federal Work-Study, institutionally sponsored loans, scholarships/grants, and unspecified assistantships also available. Support available to part-time students. Financial award application deadline: 3/31; financial award applicants required to submit FAFSA. In 2006, 155 master's, 3 doctorates awarded. *Degree program information:* Part-time programs available. Offers audiology (Au D); cell and molecular biology (MS); communication sciences and disorders (MS); health and human services (MPH, MPT, MS, MS Ed, MSN, MSW, Au D); health promotion and wellness management (MS); nurse anesthesia (MS); nursing (MSN); physical therapy (MPT); physician assistant studies (MS); psychology (MS); public health (MPH); secondary education (MS Ed); social work (MSW). *Application fee:* $35. Electronic applications accepted. *Acting Dean,* Dr. Helen Reid, 417-836-4176, Fax: 417-836-6905.

College of Humanities and Public Affairs Students: 95 full-time (43 women), 100 part-time (36 women); includes 9 minority (2 African Americans, 3 American Indian/Alaska Native, 3 Asian Americans or Pacific Islanders, 1 Hispanic American), 15 international. Average age 30. 109 applicants, 84% accepted, 57 enrolled. *Faculty:* 36 full-time (8 women), 20 part-time/adjunct (2 women). Expenses: Contact institution. *Financial support:* In 2006–07, 2 research assistantships with full tuition reimbursements (averaging $9,000 per year), 3 teaching assistantships with full tuition reimbursements (averaging $8,260 per year) were awarded; career-related internships or fieldwork, Federal Work-Study, institutionally sponsored loans, scholarships/grants, tuition waivers (partial), and unspecified assistantships also available. Support available to part-time students. Financial award application deadline: 3/31; financial award applicants required to submit FAFSA. In 2006, 59 degrees awarded. *Degree program information:* Part-time and evening/weekend programs available. Offers defense and strategic studies (MS); history (MA); humanities and public affairs (MA, MIAA, MPA, MS, MS Ed); international affairs and administration (MIAA); public administration (MPA); religious studies (MA); secondary education (MS Ed). *Application deadline:* For fall admission, 7/20 priority date for domestic students; for spring admission, 12/20 priority date for domestic students. Applications are processed on a rolling basis. *Application fee:* $35. Electronic applications accepted. *Dean,* Dr. Lorene H. Stone, 417-836-5529, Fax: 417-836-8472, E-mail: lorenestone@missouristate.edu.

College of Natural and Applied Sciences Students: 73 full-time (27 women), 85 part-time (32 women); includes 5 minority (2 American Indian/Alaska Native, 2 Asian Americans or Pacific Islanders, 1 Hispanic American), 20 international. Average age 29. 101 applicants, 63% accepted, 48 enrolled. *Faculty:* 95 full-time (17 women), 7 part-time/adjunct (2 women). Expenses: Contact institution. *Financial support:* In 2006–07, 18 research assistantships with full tuition reimbursements (averaging $9,000 per year), 26 teaching assistantships with full tuition reimbursements (averaging $8,488 per year) were awarded; career-related internships or fieldwork, Federal Work-Study, scholarships/grants, and unspecified assistantships also available. Support available to part-time students. Financial award application deadline: 3/31; financial award applicants required to submit FAFSA. In 2006, 52 degrees awarded. *Degree program information:* Part-time and evening/weekend programs available. Offers agriculture (MNAS); biology (MNAS, MS); chemistry (MNAS, MS); computer science (MNAS); consumer sciences (MNAS); fruit science (MNAS); geography, geology and planning (MNAS); geospatial sciences (MS); materials science (MS); mathematics (MS); natural and applied sciences (MNAS, MS, MS Ed); physics, astronomy, and materials science (MNAS); plant science (MS); secondary education (MS Ed). *Application deadline:* For fall admission, 7/20 for domestic students; for spring admission, 12/20 for domestic students. Applications are processed on a rolling basis. *Application fee:* $35. Electronic applications accepted. *Dean,* Dr. Tamera Jahnke, 417-836-5249, Fax: 417-836-6934.

See Close-Up on page 965.

MOLLOY COLLEGE, Rockville Centre, NY 11571-5002

General Information Independent, coed, comprehensive institution. *Graduate housing:* On-campus housing not available.

GRADUATE UNITS

Department of Nursing *Degree program information:* Part-time and evening/weekend programs available. Offers adult nurse practitioner (Advanced Certificate); clinical nurse specialist: adult health (Advanced Certificate); family nurse practitioner (Advanced Certificate); nurse practitioner psychiatry (Advanced Certificate); nursing (MS); nursing administration (Advanced Certificate); nursing administration with informatics (Advanced Certificate); nursing education (Advanced Certificate); nursing informatics (Advanced Certificate); pediatric nurse practitioner (Advanced Certificate).

MONMOUTH UNIVERSITY, West Long Branch, NJ 07764-1898

General Information Independent, coed, comprehensive institution. *Enrollment:* 6,399 graduate, professional, and undergraduate students; 468 full-time matriculated graduate/professional students (342 women), 1,284 part-time matriculated graduate/professional students (956 women). *Enrollment by degree level:* 1,752 master's. *Graduate faculty:* 143 full-time (70 women), 53 part-time/adjunct (34 women). *Tuition:* Full-time $12,780; part-time $710 per credit. *Required fees:* $628; $314 per term. *Graduate housing:* On-campus housing not available. *Student services:* Campus employment opportunities, campus safety program, career counseling, disabled student services, exercise/wellness program, free psychological counseling, international student services, low-cost health insurance, multicultural affairs office, writing training. *Library facilities:* Monmouth University Library. *Online resources:* library catalog, web page. *Collection:* 280,000 titles, 25,196 serial subscriptions.

Computer facilities: 673 computers available on campus for general student use. A campuswide network can be accessed from student residence rooms and from off campus. Internet access is available. *Web address:* http://www.monmouth.edu/.

General Application Contact: Kevin Roane, Director, Office of Graduate Admission, 732-571-3452, Fax: 732-263-5123, E-mail: gradadm@monmouth.edu.

GRADUATE UNITS

Graduate School Students: 468 full-time (342 women), 1,284 part-time (956 women); includes 192 minority (89 African Americans, 4 American Indian/Alaska Native, 41 Asian Americans or Pacific Islanders, 58 Hispanic Americans), 57 international. Average age 32. 1,205 applicants, 95% accepted, 504 enrolled. *Faculty:* 143 full-time (70 women), 53 part-time/adjunct (34 women). Expenses: Contact institution. *Financial support:* In 2006–07, 912 fellowships (averaging $1,953 per year), 92 research assistantships (averaging $7,123 per year) were awarded; career-related internships or fieldwork, scholarships/grants, tuition waivers (full and partial), and unspecified assistantships also available. Support available to part-time students. Financial award application deadline: 3/1; financial award applicants required to submit FAFSA. In 2006, 538 degrees awarded. *Degree program information:* Part-time and evening/weekend programs available. Offers community and international development (MSW); computer science (MS); corporate and public communication (MA); criminal justice administration (MA, Certificate); English (MA); history (MA); human resources communication (Certificate); liberal arts (MA); media studies (Certificate); practice with families and children (MSW); professional counseling (PMC); psychological counseling (MA); public policy (MA); public relations (Certificate); software development (Certificate); software engineering (MS, Certificate). *Application deadline:* For fall admission, 7/15 priority date for domestic students, 6/1 for international students; for spring admission, 11/15 priority date for domestic students, 11/1 for international students. Applications are processed on a rolling basis. *Application fee:* $50. Electronic applications accepted. *Application Contact:* Kevin Roane, Director, Office of Graduate Admission, 732-571-3452, Fax: 732-263-5123, E-mail: gradadm@monmouth.edu. *Dean,* Dr. Datta V. Naik, 732-571-7550, Fax: 732-263-5142.

The Marjorie K. Unterberg School of Nursing and Health Studies Students: 5 full-time (4 women), 189 part-time (186 women); includes 26 minority (9 African Americans, 13 Asian Americans or Pacific Islanders, 4 Hispanic Americans). Average age 43. 94 applicants, 100% accepted, 44 enrolled. *Faculty:* 10 full-time (all women), 1 part-time/adjunct (0 women). Expenses: Contact institution. *Financial support:* In 2006–07, 136 fellowships (averaging $1,053 per year), 4 research assistantships (averaging $3,483 per year) were awarded; career-related internships or fieldwork, scholarships/grants, tuition waivers (partial), and unspecified assistantships also available. Support available to part-time students. Financial award application deadline: 3/1; financial award applicants required to submit FAFSA. In 2006, 38 degrees awarded. *Degree program information:* Part-time and evening/weekend programs available. Offers advanced practice nursing (Post-Master's Certificate); nursing (MSN); school nursing (Certificate); substance awareness coordinator (Certificate). *Application deadline:* For fall admission, 7/15 priority date for domestic students, 6/1 for international students; for spring admission, 11/15 priority date for domestic students, 11/1 for international students. Applications are processed on a rolling basis. *Application fee:* $50. Electronic applications accepted. *Application Contact:* Kevin Roane, Director, Office of Graduate Admission, 732-571-3452, Fax: 732-263-5123, E-mail: gradadm@monmouth.edu. *Director,* Dr. Janet Mahoney, 732-571-3443, Fax: 732-263-5131, E-mail: jmahoney@monmouth.edu.

School of Business Administration Students: 36 full-time (18 women), 198 part-time (88 women); includes 22 minority (9 African Americans, 1 American Indian/Alaska Native, 6 Asian Americans or Pacific Islanders, 6 Hispanic Americans), 12 international. Average age 30. 123 applicants, 89% accepted, 54 enrolled. *Faculty:* 30 full-time (11 women), 3 part-time/adjunct (1 woman). Expenses: Contact institution. *Financial support:* In 2006–07, 126

Monmouth University (continued)

fellowships (averaging $1,459 per year), 12 research assistantships (averaging $8,362 per year) were awarded; career-related internships or fieldwork, scholarships/grants, tuition waivers (partial), and unspecified assistantships also available. Support available to part-time students. Financial award application deadline: 3/1; financial award applicants required to submit FAFSA. In 2006, 74 degrees awarded. *Degree program information:* Part-time and evening/weekend programs available. Offers accounting (MBA); business administration (MBA); health care management (MBA, Certificate). *Application deadline:* For fall admission, 7/15 priority date for domestic students, 6/1 for international students; for spring admission, 11/15 priority date for domestic students, 11/1 for international students. Applications are processed on a rolling basis. *Application fee:* $50. Electronic applications accepted. *Application Contact:* Kevin Roane, Director, Office of Graduate Admission, 732-571-3452, Fax: 732-263-5123, E-mail: gradadm@monmouth.edu. *Program Director*, Donald Smith, 732-571-7536, Fax: 732-263-5517, E-mail: dsmith@monmouth.edu.

School of Education Students: 169 full-time (133 women), 426 part-time (374 women); includes 45 minority (21 African Americans, 2 American Indian/Alaska Native, 2 Asian Americans or Pacific Islanders, 20 Hispanic Americans). Average age 31. 355 applicants, 96% accepted, 138 enrolled. *Faculty:* 24 full-time (15 women), 25 part-time/adjunct (17 women). Expenses: Contact institution. *Financial support:* In 2006–07, 221 fellowships (averaging $2,053 per year), 17 research assistantships (averaging $6,527 per year) were awarded; career-related internships or fieldwork, scholarships/grants, tuition waivers (partial), and unspecified assistantships also available. Support available to part-time students. Financial award application deadline: 3/1; financial award applicants required to submit FAFSA. In 2006, 209 degrees awarded. *Degree program information:* Part-time and evening/weekend programs available. Offers educational counseling (MS Ed); elementary education (MAT); learning disabilities-teacher consultant (Certificate); principal studies (MS Ed); reading specialist (MS Ed, Certificate); special education (MS Ed); supervisor (Certificate); teacher of the handicapped (Certificate). *Application deadline:* For fall admission, 7/15 priority date for domestic students; for spring admission, 11/15 priority date for domestic students. Applications are processed on a rolling basis. *Application fee:* $50. Electronic applications accepted. *Application Contact:* Kevin Roane, Director, Office of Graduate Admission, 732-571-3452, Fax: 732-263-5123, E-mail: gradadm@monmouth.edu. *Program Director*, Dr. Lynn Romeo, 732-571-4484, Fax: 732-263-5277, E-mail: lromeo@monmouth.edu.

See Close-Up on page 967.

MONROE COLLEGE, Bronx, NY 10468-5407

General Information Proprietary, coed, comprehensive institution.

GRADUATE UNITS

King School of Business Postbaccalaureate distance learning degree programs offered. Offers business management (MBA). Program also offered in New Rochelle, NY.

MONTANA STATE UNIVERSITY, Bozeman, MT 59717

General Information State-supported, coed, university. CGS member. *Enrollment:* 12,338 graduate, professional, and undergraduate students; 421 full-time matriculated graduate/professional students (179 women), 806 part-time matriculated graduate/professional students (403 women). *Graduate faculty:* 526 full-time (183 women), 212 part-time/adjunct (117 women). Tuition, state resident: full-time $5,113. Tuition, nonresident: full-time $12,501. *Graduate housing:* Rooms and/or apartments available on a first-come, first-served basis to single and married students. Typical cost: $6,450 (including board) for single students. *Student services:* Campus employment opportunities, campus safety program, career counseling, child daycare facilities, disabled student services, exercise/wellness program, free psychological counseling, international student services, low-cost health insurance, multicultural affairs office, teacher training, writing training. *Library facilities:* Renne Library plus 2 others. *Online resources:* library catalog, web page, access to other libraries' catalogs. *Collection:* 712,241 titles, 8,757 serial subscriptions, 9,346 audiovisual materials. *Research affiliation:* ILX Lightwave (laser diodes, electro-optical test equipment), Scientific Materials (laser crystals), Eli Lilly & Company (antifungal technology), LigoCyte Pharmaceuticals, Inc. (pharmaceuticals), Microvision (information transmission system), Phillips Environmental (microbial technology).

Computer facilities: 850 computers available on campus for general student use. A campuswide network can be accessed from student residence rooms and from off campus. Internet access and online class registration, e-mail are available. *Web address:* http://www.montana.edu/.

General Application Contact: Dr. Carl A. Fox, Vice Provost for Graduate Education, 406-994-4145, Fax: 406-994-7433, E-mail: gradstudy@montana.edu.

GRADUATE UNITS

College of Graduate Studies Students: 421 full-time (179 women), 806 part-time (403 women); includes 41 minority (4 African Americans, 12 American Indian/Alaska Native, 14 Asian Americans or Pacific Islanders, 11 Hispanic Americans), 113 international. Average age 30. 970 applicants, 64% accepted, 457 enrolled. *Faculty:* 526 full-time (183 women), 212 part-time/adjunct (117 women). Expenses: Contact institution. *Financial support:* Fellowships with full and partial tuition reimbursements, research assistantships with full and partial tuition reimbursements, teaching assistantships with full and partial tuition reimbursements, career-related internships or fieldwork, Federal Work-Study, institutionally sponsored loans, scholarships/grants, traineeships, tuition waivers (full and partial), and unspecified assistantships available. Support available to part-time students. Financial award application deadline: 3/1; financial award applicants required to submit FAFSA. In 2006, 440 master's, 40 doctorates awarded. *Degree program information:* Part-time programs available. *Application deadline:* For fall admission, 7/15 priority date for domestic students, 5/15 priority date for international students; for spring admission, 12/1 priority date for domestic students, 10/1 priority date for international students. Applications are processed on a rolling basis. *Application fee:* $30. Electronic applications accepted. *Vice Provost for Graduate Education*, Dr. Carl A. Fox, 406-994-4145, Fax: 406-994-7433, E-mail: gradstudy@montana.edu.

College of Agriculture Students: 35 full-time (18 women), 95 part-time (51 women); includes 2 minority (1 Asian American or Pacific Islander, 1 Hispanic American), 19 international. Average age 27. 72 applicants, 58% accepted, 32 enrolled. *Faculty:* 74 full-time (10 women), 11 part-time/adjunct (2 women). Expenses: Contact institution. *Financial support:* Application deadline: 3/1; In 2006, 37 master's, 7 doctorates awarded. *Degree program information:* Part-time programs available. Offers agriculture (MS, PhD); animal and range sciences (MS, PhD); applied economics (MS); land rehabilitation (interdisciplinary) (MS); land resources and environmental sciences (MS, PhD); plant pathology (MS); plant sciences (MS, PhD); veterinary molecular biology (MS, PhD). *Application deadline:* For fall admission, 7/15 priority date for domestic students, 5/15 priority date for international students; for spring admission, 12/1 priority date for domestic students, 10/1 priority date for international students. Applications are processed on a rolling basis. *Application fee:* $30. Electronic applications accepted. *Dean*, Dr. Jeffrey S. Jacobsen, 406-994-7060, Fax: 406-994-3933, E-mail: jefj@montana.edu.

College of Arts and Architecture Students: 99 full-time (34 women), 62 part-time (28 women); includes 5 minority (2 American Indian/Alaska Native, 1 Asian American or Pacific Islander, 2 Hispanic Americans), 8 international. Average age 28. 129 applicants, 55% accepted, 65 enrolled. *Faculty:* 61 full-time (13 women), 28 part-time/adjunct (17 women). Expenses: Contact institution. *Financial support:* Application deadline: 3/1; In 2006, 67 degrees awarded. *Degree program information:* Part-time programs available. Offers architecture (M Arch); art (MFA); arts and architecture (M Arch, MFA); science and natural history filmmaking (MFA). *Application deadline:* For fall admission, 7/15 priority date for domestic students, 5/15 priority date for international students; for spring admission, 12/1 priority date for domestic students, 10/1 priority date for international students. Applications are processed on a rolling basis. *Application fee:* $30. Electronic applications accepted. *Dean, College of Arts and Architecture*, Susan Agre-Kippenhan, 406-994-4405, Fax: 406-994-3680, E-mail: susanak@montana.edu.

College of Business Students: 31 full-time (17 women), 2 part-time (both women); includes 2 minority (1 Asian American or Pacific Islander, 1 Hispanic American), 2 international. Average age 25. 16 applicants, 88% accepted, 13 enrolled. *Faculty:* 29 full-time (9 women), 21 part-time/adjunct (10 women). Expenses: Contact institution. *Financial support:* In 2006–07, 5 teaching assistantships with partial tuition reimbursements (averaging $4,108 per year) were awarded; career-related internships or fieldwork, scholarships/grants, and unspecified assistantships also available. Financial award application deadline: 3/1; financial award applicants required to submit FAFSA. In 2006, 41 degrees awarded. *Degree program information:* Part-time programs available. Offers professional accountancy (MP Ac). *Application deadline:* For fall admission, 7/15 priority date for domestic students, 5/15 priority date for international students; for spring admission, 12/1 priority date for domestic students, 10/1 priority date for international students. Applications are processed on a rolling basis. *Application fee:* $30. Electronic applications accepted. *Dean, College of Business*, Dr. Richard J. Semenik, 406-994-4421, Fax: 406-994-6206, E-mail: semenik@montana.edu.

College of Education, Health, and Human Development Students: 50 full-time (36 women), 165 part-time (107 women); includes 11 minority (3 African Americans, 4 American Indian/Alaska Native, 3 Asian Americans or Pacific Islanders, 1 Hispanic American), 2 international. Average age 36. 79 applicants, 56% accepted, 42 enrolled. *Faculty:* 48 full-time (29 women), 22 part-time/adjunct (17 women). Expenses: Contact institution. *Financial support:* Application deadline: 3/1; In 2006, 84 master's, 9 doctorates awarded. *Degree program information:* Part-time programs available. Offers education (M Ed, Ed D, Ed S); education, health, and human development (M Ed, MS, Ed D, Ed S); health and human development (MS). *Application deadline:* For fall admission, 7/15 priority date for domestic students, 5/15 priority date for international students; for spring admission, 12/1 priority date for domestic students, 10/1 priority date for international students. Applications are processed on a rolling basis. *Application fee:* $30. Electronic applications accepted. *Dean, College of Education, Health and Human Development*, Larry Baker, 406-994-6752, Fax: 406-994-1854, E-mail: lbaker@montana.edu.

College of Engineering Students: 65 full-time (8 women), 82 part-time (13 women); includes 5 minority (2 American Indian/Alaska Native, 3 Asian Americans or Pacific Islanders), 38 international. Average age 27. 145 applicants, 51% accepted, 47 enrolled. *Faculty:* 68 full-time (4 women), 22 part-time/adjunct (3 women). Expenses: Contact institution. *Financial support:* Application deadline: 3/1; In 2006, 60 master's, 8 doctorates awarded. *Degree program information:* Part-time programs available. Offers chemical engineering (MS); civil engineering (MS); computer science (MS, PhD); electrical engineering (MS); engineering (PhD); environmental engineering (MS); industrial and management engineering (MS); land rehabilitation (intercollege) (MS); mechanical engineering (MS). *Application deadline:* For fall admission, 7/15 priority date for domestic students, 5/15 priority date for international students; for spring admission, 12/1 priority date for domestic students, 10/1 priority date for international students. Applications are processed on a rolling basis. *Application fee:* $30. Electronic applications accepted. *Dean, College of Engineering*, Dr. Robert Marley.

College of Letters and Science Students: 116 full-time (46 women), 309 part-time (143 women); includes 15 minority (1 African American, 4 American Indian/Alaska Native, 4 Asian Americans or Pacific Islanders, 6 Hispanic Americans), 44 international. Average age 30. 299 applicants, 48% accepted, 97 enrolled. *Faculty:* 188 full-time (65 women), 82 part-time/adjunct (43 women). Expenses: Contact institution. *Financial support:* Application deadline: 3/1; In 2006, 81 master's, 16 doctorates awarded. *Degree program information:* Part-time programs available. Offers applied psychology (MS); biochemistry (MS, PhD); biological sciences (MS, PhD); chemistry (MS, PhD); earth sciences (MS, PhD); English (MA); fish and wildlife biology (PhD); fish and wildlife management (MS); history (MA, PhD); land rehabilitation (intercollege) (MS); letters and science (MA, MPA, MS, PhD); mathematics (MS, PhD); microbiology (MS, PhD); Native American studies (MA); neuroscience (MS, PhD); physics (MS, PhD); public administration (MPA); statistics (MS, PhD). *Application deadline:* For fall admission, 7/15 priority date for domestic students, 5/15 priority date for international students; for spring admission, 12/1 priority date for domestic students, 10/1 priority date for international students. Applications are processed on a rolling basis. *Application fee:* $30. Electronic applications accepted. *Interim Dean*, Dr. George Tuthill, 406-994-4288, Fax: 406-994-6879.

College of Nursing Students: 24 full-time (20 women), 9 part-time (8 women). Average age 38. 20 applicants, 85% accepted, 12 enrolled. *Faculty:* 58 full-time (53 women), 26 part-time/adjunct (25 women). Expenses: Contact institution. *Financial support:* In 2006–07, 18 students received support, including 4 teaching assistantships with partial tuition reimbursements available (averaging $5,320 per year); institutionally sponsored loans, scholarships/grants, traineeships, tuition waivers (partial), and unspecified assistantships also available. Financial award application deadline: 3/1; financial award applicants required to submit FAFSA. In 2006, 15 degrees awarded. *Degree program information:* Part-time programs available. Postbaccalaureate distance learning degree programs offered (minimal on-campus study). Offers clinical nurse specialist (CNS) (MN, Post-Master's Certificate); family nurse practitioner (MN, Post-Master's Certificate); nursing education (Certificate). *Application deadline:* For fall admission, 7/15 priority date for domestic students, 5/15 priority date for international students; for spring admission, 12/1 priority date for domestic students, 10/1 priority date for international students. Applications are processed on a rolling basis. *Application fee:* $30. Electronic applications accepted. *Dean, College of Nursing*, Dr. Elizabeth Kinion, 406-994-2725, Fax: 406-994-6020, E-mail: ekinion@montana.edu.

MONTANA STATE UNIVERSITY–BILLINGS, Billings, MT 59101-0298

General Information State-supported, coed, comprehensive institution. *Enrollment:* 4,799 graduate, professional, and undergraduate students; 345 full-time matriculated graduate/professional students (252 women). *Enrollment by degree level:* 345 master's. *Graduate faculty:* 60 full-time (24 women). Tuition, state resident: full-time $4,599. Tuition, nonresident: full-time $10,786. *Graduate housing:* Rooms and/or apartments available on a first-come, first-served basis to single and married students. *Student services:* Campus employment opportunities, campus safety program, career counseling, child daycare facilities, disabled student services, exercise/wellness program, free psychological counseling, grant writing training, international student services, low-cost health insurance, multicultural affairs office, teacher training, writing training. *Library facilities:* Montana State University-Billings Library plus 2 others. *Online resources:* library catalog, web page, access to other libraries' catalogs. *Collection:* 488,004 titles, 3,276 serial subscriptions.

Computer facilities: 863 computers available on campus for general student use. A campuswide network can be accessed from student residence rooms and from off campus. Internet access and online class registration, online degree programs are available. *Web address:* http://www.msubillings.edu/.

General Application Contact: David M. Sullivan, Graduate Studies Counselor, 406-657-2053, Fax: 406-657-2299, E-mail: dsullivan@msubillings.edu.

GRADUATE UNITS

College of Allied Health Professions Students: 93. 21 applicants, 100% accepted, 21 enrolled. Expenses: Contact institution. In 2006, 10 degrees awarded. Offers allied health professions (MHA, MS, MSRC); athletic training (MS); health administration (MHA); rehabilitation and human services (MSRC); sport management (MS). *Application fee:* $40. *Application Contact:* David M. Sullivan, Graduate Studies Counselor, 406-657-2053, Fax: 406-657-2299, E-mail: dsullivan@msubillings.edu. *Dean*, Dr. David Garloff, 406-896-5833, E-mail: dgarloff@msubillings.edu.

College of Arts and Sciences Students: 38. 19 applicants, 100% accepted, 19 enrolled. Expenses: Contact institution. *Financial support:* Teaching assistantships with partial tuition reimbursements, career-related internships or fieldwork, Federal Work-Study, institutionally sponsored loans, scholarships/grants, tuition waivers (partial), and unspecified assistantships available. Support available to part-time students. Financial award application deadline: 5/1; financial award applicants required to submit FAFSA. In 2006, 15 degrees awarded. *Degree program information:* Part-time programs available. Postbaccalaureate distance learning degree programs offered. Offers arts and sciences (MPA, MS); psychology (MS); public administration (MPA); public relations (MS). *Application deadline:* Applications are processed on a rolling basis. *Application fee:* $40. *Application Contact:* David M. Sullivan, Graduate Studies Counselor, 406-657-2053, Fax: 406-657-2299, E-mail: dsullivan@msubillings.edu. *Dean,* Dr. Tasneem Khaleel, 406-657-2177, E-mail: tkhaleel@msubillings.edu.

College of Education and Human Services Students: 216. 97 applicants, 100% accepted, 97 enrolled. *Faculty:* 28 full-time (17 women). Expenses: Contact institution. *Financial support:* Teaching assistantships with partial tuition reimbursements, career-related internships or fieldwork, Federal Work-Study, institutionally sponsored loans, scholarships/grants, tuition waivers (partial), and unspecified assistantships available. Support available to part-time students. Financial award application deadline: 5/1; financial award applicants required to submit FAFSA. In 2006, 41 degrees awarded. *Degree program information:* Part-time programs available. Postbaccalaureate distance learning degree programs offered (minimal on-campus study). Offers advanced studies (MS Sp Ed); early childhood education (M Ed); education and human services (M Ed, MS Sp Ed, Certificate); educational technology (M Ed); general curriculum (M Ed); interdisciplinary studies (M Ed); reading (M Ed); school counseling (M Ed); secondary education (M Ed); special education (MS Sp Ed); special education generalist (MS Sp Ed); teaching (Certificate). *Application deadline:* Applications are processed on a rolling basis. *Application fee:* $40. *Application Contact:* David M. Sullivan, Graduate Studies Counselor, 406-657-2053, Fax: 406-657-2299, E-mail: dsullivan@msubillings.edu. *Interim Dean,* Dr. Mary Susan Fishbaugh, 406-657-2285, Fax: 406-657-2299, E-mail: mfishbaugh@msubillings.edu.

MONTANA STATE UNIVERSITY–NORTHERN, Havre, MT 59501-7751

General Information State-supported, coed, comprehensive institution. *Graduate housing:* Rooms and/or apartments available on a first-come, first-served basis to single students and available to married students. Housing application deadline: 8/22.

GRADUATE UNITS

College of Education and Graduate Programs *Degree program information:* Part-time and evening/weekend programs available. Postbaccalaureate distance learning degree programs offered (minimal on-campus study). Offers counselor education (M Ed); learning development (M Ed). Electronic applications accepted.

MONTANA TECH OF THE UNIVERSITY OF MONTANA, Butte, MT 59701-8997

General Information State-supported, coed, comprehensive institution. *Enrollment:* 2,951 graduate, professional, and undergraduate students; 62 full-time matriculated graduate/professional students (25 women), 30 part-time matriculated graduate/professional students (10 women). *Enrollment by degree level:* 92 master's. *Graduate faculty:* 113 full-time (27 women), 65 part-time/adjunct (24 women). Tuition, state resident: part-time $219 per credit. Tuition, nonresident: part-time $480 per credit. *Required fees:* $305 per credit. *Graduate housing:* Rooms and/or apartments guaranteed to single students and available on a first-come, first-served basis to married students. Typical cost: $4,740 (including board) for single students; $4,740 (including board) for married students. Room and board charges vary according to board plan, campus/location and housing facility selected. Housing application deadline: 8/22. *Student services:* Campus employment opportunities, campus safety program, career counseling, exercise/wellness program, free psychological counseling, grant writing training, international student services, low-cost health insurance. *Library facilities:* Montana Tech Library plus 1 other. *Online resources:* library catalog, web page, access to other libraries' catalogs. *Collection:* 165,734 titles, 20,233 serial subscriptions. *Research affiliation:* MSE-TA (electric efficiency), Universal Technical Resource Services (titanium production), Stillwater Mining (minerals production and training), National Center for Health Infocare (health care infomatics).

Computer facilities: 500 computers available on campus for general student use. A campuswide network can be accessed from student residence rooms and from off campus. Internet access and online class registration are available. *Web address:* http://www.mtech.edu/.

General Application Contact: Cindy Dunstan, Administrator, Graduate School, 406-496-4304, Fax: 406-496-4710, E-mail: cdunstan@mtech.edu.

GRADUATE UNITS

Graduate School Students: 62 full-time (25 women), 30 part-time (10 women); includes 7 minority (1 African American, 2 American Indian/Alaska Native, 2 Asian Americans or Pacific Islanders, 2 Hispanic Americans). 84 applicants, 76% accepted, 40 enrolled. *Faculty:* 113 full-time, 65 part-time/adjunct. Expenses: Contact institution. *Financial support:* In 2006–07, 46 students received support, including 6 research assistantships with full tuition reimbursements available (averaging $5,200 per year), 27 teaching assistantships with partial tuition reimbursements available (averaging $8,000 per year); career-related internships or fieldwork, tuition waivers (full and partial), and unspecified assistantships also available. Financial award application deadline: 4/1; financial award applicants required to submit FAFSA. In 2006, 25 master's awarded. *Degree program information:* Part-time and evening/weekend programs available. Postbaccalaureate distance learning degree programs offered (no on-campus study). Offers electrical engineering (MS); engineering (MS); environmental engineering (MS); geochemistry (MS); geological engineering (MS); geology (MS); geophysical engineering (MS); hydrogeological engineering (MS); hydrogeology (MS); industrial hygiene (MS); metallurgical/mineral processing engineering (MS); mining engineering (MS); petroleum engineering (MS); project engineering and management (MPEM); technical communication (MS). *Application deadline:* For fall admission, 4/1 priority date for domestic students, 3/1 priority date for international students; for spring admission, 10/1 priority date for domestic students, 7/1 priority date for international students. Applications are processed on a rolling basis. *Application fee:* $30. Electronic applications accepted. *Application Contact:* Cindy Dunstan, Administrator, Graduate School, 406-496-4304, Fax: 406-496-4710, E-mail: cdunstan@mtech.edu. *Associate Vice Chancellor, Research and Graduate Studies,* Dr. Joseph Figueira, 406-496-4102, Fax: 406-496-4334.

MONTCLAIR STATE UNIVERSITY, Montclair, NJ 07043-1624

General Information State-supported, coed, comprehensive institution. CGS member. *Enrollment:* 16,076 graduate, professional, and undergraduate students; 803 full-time matriculated graduate/professional students (597 women), 2,571 part-time matriculated graduate/professional students (1,877 women). *Enrollment by degree level:* 2,416 master's, 73 doctoral, 885 other advanced degrees. *Graduate faculty:* 491 full-time (218 women), 706 part-time/adjunct (404 women). Tuition, state resident: part-time $450 per credit. Tuition, nonresident: part-time $682 per credit. Tuition and fees vary according to degree level and program. *Graduate housing:* Room and/or apartments available on a first-come, first-served basis to single students. Typical cost: $3,500 per year ($9,880 including board). Room and board charges vary according to board plan, campus/location and housing facility selected. Housing application deadline: 3/1. *Student services:* Campus employment opportunities, campus safety program, career counseling, child daycare facilities, disabled student services, exercise/wellness program, free psychological counseling, international student services, low-cost health insurance, teacher training. *Library facilities:* Sprague Library. *Online resources:* library catalog, web page, access to other libraries' catalogs. *Collection:* 495,462 titles, 3,094 serial subscriptions, 14,184 audiovisual materials. *Research affiliation:* Deafness Research Foundation (heating science), The International Society for Optical Engineering (optics and photonics), Spencer Foundation (education improvement).

Computer facilities: Computer purchase and lease plans are available. 218 computers available on campus for general student use. A campuswide network can be accessed from student residence rooms and from off campus. Internet access and online class registration are available. *Web address:* http://www.montclair.edu/.

General Application Contact: Dr. Kim C. O'Halloran, Associate Dean of the Graduate School, 973-655-5147, Fax: 973-655-7869, E-mail: graduate.school@montclair.edu.

GRADUATE UNITS

The Graduate School Students: 677 full-time (505 women), 1,807 part-time (1,272 women); includes 467 minority (187 African Americans, 2 American Indian/Alaska Native, 91 Asian Americans or Pacific Islanders, 187 Hispanic Americans), 102 international. Average age 33. 1,695 applicants, 42% accepted, 496 enrolled. *Faculty:* 474 full-time (206 women), 694 part-time/adjunct (383 women). Expenses: Contact institution. *Financial support:* In 2006–07, 140 research assistantships with full tuition reimbursements (averaging $7,000 per year) were awarded; Federal Work-Study, scholarships/grants, and unspecified assistantships also available. Support available to part-time students. Financial award application deadline: 3/1; financial award applicants required to submit FAFSA. In 2006, 725 master's, 4 doctorates, 457 other advanced degrees awarded. *Degree program information:* Part-time and evening/weekend programs available. *Application deadline:* For fall admission, 6/1 for international students; for spring admission, 10/1 for international students. Applications are processed on a rolling basis. *Application fee:* $60. Electronic applications accepted. *Application Contact:* Information Contact, 973-655-5147, Fax: 973-655-7869, E-mail: graduate.school@montclair.edu. *Associate Dean of the Graduate School,* Dr. Kim C. O'Halloran, 973-655-5147, Fax: 973-655-7869, E-mail: graduate.school@montclair.edu.

College of Education and Human Services Students: 1,505; includes 269 minority (129 African Americans, 1 American Indian/Alaska Native, 38 Asian Americans or Pacific Islanders, 101 Hispanic Americans), 18 international. Average age 33. 526 applicants, 49% accepted, 190 enrolled. *Faculty:* 93 full-time (64 women), 177 part-time/adjunct (127 women). Expenses: Contact institution. *Financial support:* In 2006–07, 72 research assistantships with full tuition reimbursements (averaging $7,000 per year) were awarded; Federal Work-Study, scholarships/grants, and unspecified assistantships also available. Support available to part-time students. Financial award application deadline: 3/1; financial award applicants required to submit FAFSA. In 2006, 323 master's, 4 doctorates, 92 other advanced degrees awarded. *Degree program information:* Part-time and evening/weekend programs available. Offers administration and supervision (MA); advanced counseling (Certificate); counseling and guidance (MA); critical thinking (M Ed); early childhood /elementary education (M Ed); early childhood education and teaching students in disabilities (MAT); early childhood special education (M Ed, Certificate); education (M Ed); education and human services (M Ed, MA, MAT, MS, Ed D, Certificate); educational technology (M Ed); elementary education with disabilities (MAT); elementary school teacher (Certificate); food safety instructor (Certificate); health and physical education (Certificate); health education (MA); learning disabilities (Certificate); mathematics education (Ed D); nutrition and exercise science (MS, Certificate); nutrition and food science (MS); philosophy for children (M Ed, Ed D, Certificate); physical education (MA, Certificate); reading (MA, Certificate); reading specialist (Certificate); school administrator (Certificate); school business administrator (Certificate); school counselor (Certificate); school library media specialist (Certificate); substance awareness coordinator (Certificate); teaching (MAT, Certificate). *Application deadline:* For fall admission, 6/1 for international students; for spring admission, 10/1 for international students. Applications are processed on a rolling basis. *Application fee:* $60. Electronic applications accepted. *Application Contact:* Dr. Kim C. O'Halloran, Associate Dean of the Graduate School, 973-655-5147, Fax: 973-655-7869, E-mail: graduate.school@montclair.edu. *Dean,* Dr. Ada Beth Cutler, 973-655-5167, E-mail: cutler@mail.montclair.edu.

College of Humanities and Social Sciences Students: 196 full-time (164 women), 492 part-time (381 women); includes 174 minority (72 African Americans, 23 Asian Americans or Pacific Islanders, 79 Hispanic Americans), 16 international. 580 applicants, 37% accepted, 145 enrolled. *Faculty:* 175 full-time (88 women), 241 part-time/adjunct (139 women). Expenses: Contact institution. *Financial support:* In 2006–07, 32 research assistantships with full tuition reimbursements (averaging $7,000 per year) were awarded; Federal Work-Study, scholarships/grants, and unspecified assistantships also available. Support available to part-time students. Financial award application deadline: 3/1; financial award applicants required to submit FAFSA. In 2006, 111 master's, 4 doctorates, 104 other advanced degrees awarded. *Degree program information:* Part-time and evening/weekend programs available. Offers applied linguistics (MA); applied sociology (MA); audiology (Sc D); child advocacy (MA, Certificate); dispute resolution (MA); educational psychology (MA); English (MA); French (MA, Certificate); governance, compliance and regulation (MA); humanities and social sciences (MA, Sc D, Certificate); law office management and technology (MA); paralegal (Certificate); psychology (MA); public child welfare (MA); school psychologist (Certificate); social sciences (MA); Spanish (MA); speech/language pathology (MA); teaching English to speakers of other languages (MA); translating and interpreting Spanish (Certificate). *Application deadline:* For fall admission, 6/1 for international students; for spring admission, 10/1 for international students. Applications are processed on a rolling basis. *Application fee:* $60. Electronic applications accepted. *Application Contact:* Dr. Carla M. Narrett, Dean of the Graduate School, 973-655-5147, Fax: 973-655-7869, E-mail: graduate.school@montclair.edu. *Dean,* Dr. Mary Papazian, 973-655-4314.

College of Science and Mathematics Students: 85 full-time (44 women), 282 part-time (175 women); includes 61 minority (21 African Americans, 20 Asian Americans or Pacific Islanders, 20 Hispanic Americans), 33 international. 202 applicants, 40% accepted, 57 enrolled. *Faculty:* 91 full-time (25 women), 75 part-time/adjunct (29 women). Expenses: Contact institution. *Financial support:* In 2006–07, 36 research assistantships with full tuition reimbursements were awarded; Federal Work-Study, scholarships/grants, and unspecified assistantships also available. Support available to part-time students. Financial award application deadline: 3/1; financial award applicants required to submit FAFSA. In 2006, 68 master's, 25 other advanced degrees awarded. *Degree program information:* Part-time and evening/weekend programs available. Offers applied mathematics (MS); applied statistics (MS); biology (MS); chemistry (MS); CISCO (Certificate); environmental management (MA, D Env M); environmental studies (MS); geoscience (MS, Certificate); informatics (MS); mathematics (MS); molecular biology (Certificate); object oriented computing (Certificate); science and mathematics (MA, MS, D Env M, Certificate); teaching middle grades math (Certificate). *Application deadline:* For fall admission, 6/1 for international students; for spring admission, 10/1 for international students. Applications are processed on a rolling basis. *Application fee:* $60. Electronic applications accepted. *Dean,* Dr. Robert Prezant, 973-655-5108.

School of Business Students: 56 full-time (31 women), 254 part-time (111 women); includes 49 minority (8 African Americans, 1 American Indian/Alaska Native, 24 Asian Americans or Pacific Islanders, 16 Hispanic Americans), 32 international. 238 applicants, 40% accepted, 62 enrolled. *Faculty:* 73 full-time (19 women), 34 part-time/adjunct (13 women). Expenses: Contact institution. *Financial support:* In 2006–07, 28 students received support, including 17 research assistantships with full tuition reimbursements available (averaging $7,000 per year); Federal Work-Study, scholarships/grants, and unspecified assistantships also available. Support available to part-time students. Financial award application deadline: 3/1; financial award applicants required to submit FAFSA. In 2006, 137 degrees awarded. *Degree program information:* Part-time and evening/weekend programs available. Offers accounting (MBA); business (MA, MBA); business economics (MBA); finance (MBA); international business (MBA); management (MBA); management information systems (MBA); marketing (MBA). *Application deadline:* For fall admission, 6/1 for international students; for spring admission, 10/1 for international students. Applications are processed on a rolling basis. *Application fee:* $60. Electronic applications accepted. *Application Contact:* Dr. Carla M. Narrett, Dean of the Graduate School, 973-655-5147, Fax: 973-655-7869, E-mail: graduate.school@montclair.edu. *Dean,* Dr. Alan Oppenheim, 973-655-4303, E-mail: oppenheima@mail.montclair.edu.

School of the Arts Students: 61 full-time (41 women), 112 part-time (79 women); includes 20 minority (10 African Americans, 5 Asian Americans or Pacific Islanders, 5 Hispanic Americans), 13 international. 149 applicants, 46% accepted, 42 enrolled. *Faculty:* 61 full-time (24 women), 179 part-time/adjunct (96 women). Expenses: Contact institution. *Financial support:* In 2006–07, 8 research assistantships with full tuition reimbursements (averaging $7,000 per year) were awarded; Federal Work-Study, scholarships/grants, and unspecified assistantships also available. Support available to part-time students. Financial award application deadline: 3/1; financial award applicants required to submit FAFSA. In 2006, 70 master's, 7 other advanced degrees awarded. *Degree program information:* Part-time and evening/weekend programs available. Offers art education (MA); art history

Montclair State University (continued)

(MA); arts (MA, MFA, AD, Certificate); music (AD); music education (MA); music therapy (MA); organizational communication (MA); performance (MA, Certificate); public relations (MA); speech communication (MA); studio arts (MA, MFA); theatre (MA); theory/composition (MA). *Application deadline:* For fall admission, 2/1 for domestic students, 6/1 for international students; for spring admission, 10/1 for international students. Applications are processed on a rolling basis. *Application fee:* $60. Electronic applications accepted. *Application Contact:* Dr. Carla M. Narrett, Dean of the Graduate School, 973-655-5147, Fax: 973-655-7869, E-mail: graduate.school@montclair.edu. *Dean,* Dr. Geoffrey Newman, 973-655-5104, E-mail: newmang@mail.montclair.edu.

See Close-Up on page 969.

MONTEREY INSTITUTE OF INTERNATIONAL STUDIES, Monterey, CA 93940-2691

General Information Independent, coed, graduate-only institution. *Enrollment:* 632 full-time matriculated graduate/professional students (426 women), 83 part-time matriculated graduate/professional students (56 women). *Enrollment by degree level:* 711 master's, 4 other advanced degrees. *Graduate faculty:* 59 full-time (24 women), 77 part-time/adjunct (45 women). *Tuition:* Full-time $26,500; part-time $1,200 per credit. *Required fees:* $200. *Graduate housing:* On-campus housing not available. *Student services:* Campus employment opportunities, career counseling, disabled student services, exercise/wellness program, international student services, low-cost health insurance, writing training. *Library facilities:* William Tell Coleman Library. *Online resources:* library catalog, web page, access to other libraries' catalogs. *Collection:* 97,000 titles, 575 serial subscriptions.

Computer facilities: 140 computers available on campus for general student use. A campuswide network can be accessed from off campus. Internet access is available. *Web address:* http://www.miis.edu/.

General Application Contact: Admissions Office, 831-647-4123, Fax: 831-647-6405, E-mail: admit@miis.edu.

GRADUATE UNITS

Fisher Graduate School of International Business Students: 68 full-time (31 women), 1 part-time; includes 12 minority (1 African American, 6 Asian Americans or Pacific Islanders, 5 Hispanic Americans), 19 international. Average age 28. 86 applicants, 94% accepted, 41 enrolled. *Faculty:* 7 full-time (1 woman), 3 part-time/adjunct (0 women). Expenses: Contact institution. *Financial support:* In 2006–07, 59 students received support, including 2 research assistantships with partial tuition reimbursements available (averaging $4,000 per year); career-related internships or fieldwork, Federal Work-Study, institutionally sponsored loans, scholarships/grants, tuition waivers (partial), and unspecified assistantships also available. Support available to part-time students. Financial award application deadline: 3/15; financial award applicants required to submit FAFSA. In 2006, 43 degrees awarded. Offers international business (MBA). *Application deadline:* For fall admission, 3/15 priority date for domestic students; for spring admission, 10/1 priority date for domestic students. Applications are processed on a rolling basis. *Application fee:* $50. Electronic applications accepted. *Application Contact:* 831-647-4123, Fax: 831-647-6405, E-mail: admit@miis.edu. *Dean,* Dr. Ernest J. Scalberg, 831-647-4140, Fax: 831-647-6506, E-mail: fgsib@miis.edu.

Graduate School of International Policy Studies Students: 346 full-time (209 women), 9 part-time (4 women); includes 42 minority (6 African Americans, 18 Asian Americans or Pacific Islanders, 18 Hispanic Americans), 70 international. Average age 27. 362 applicants, 99% accepted, 159 enrolled. *Faculty:* 17 full-time (3 women), 16 part-time/adjunct (3 women). Expenses: Contact institution. *Financial support:* In 2006–07, 329 students received support, including 60 research assistantships with partial tuition reimbursements available (averaging $4,000 per year); career-related internships or fieldwork, Federal Work-Study, institutionally sponsored loans, scholarships/grants, and tuition waivers (partial) also available. Support available to part-time students. Financial award application deadline: 3/15; financial award applicants required to submit FAFSA. In 2006, 156 degrees awarded. Offers international environmental policy (MA); international management (MPA); international policy studies (MA, MPA); international trade policy (MA). *Application deadline:* For fall admission, 3/15 priority date for domestic and international students; for spring admission, 10/1 priority date for domestic and international students. Applications are processed on a rolling basis. *Application fee:* $50. Electronic applications accepted. *Application Contact:* 831-647-4123, Fax: 831-647-6405, E-mail: admit@miis.edu. *Dean,* Dr. Edward J. Lawrence, 831-647-4155, Fax: 831-647-4199, E-mail: gsips@miis.edu.

Graduate School of Language and Educational Linguistics Students: 46 full-time (38 women), 72 part-time (51 women); includes 1 African American, 10 Asian Americans or Pacific Islanders, 27 international. Average age 34. 96 applicants, 91% accepted, 43 enrolled. *Faculty:* 18 full-time (9 women), 35 part-time/adjunct (27 women). Expenses: Contact institution. *Financial support:* In 2006–07, 103 students received support, including 8 research assistantships with partial tuition reimbursements available (averaging $4,000 per year); career-related internships or fieldwork, Federal Work-Study, institutionally sponsored loans, scholarships/grants, tuition waivers (partial), and unspecified assistantships also available. Support available to part-time students. Financial award application deadline: 3/15; financial award applicants required to submit FAFSA. In 2006, 38 degrees awarded. Offers language and educational linguistics (MATESOL, MATFL); teaching English to speakers of other languages (MATESOL); teaching foreign language (MATFL). *Application deadline:* For fall admission, 3/15 priority date for domestic students; for spring admission, 10/1 priority date for domestic students. Applications are processed on a rolling basis. *Application fee:* $50. Electronic applications accepted. *Application Contact:* 831-647-4123, Fax: 831-647-6405, E-mail: admit@miis.edu. *Dean,* Dr. Ruth Larimer, 831-647-4185, Fax: 831-647-6650, E-mail: gslel@miis.edu.

Graduate School of Translation and Interpretation Students: 172 full-time (148 women), 1 (woman) part-time; includes 20 minority (6 African Americans, 11 Asian Americans or Pacific Islanders, 3 Hispanic Americans), 100 international. Average age 28. 204 applicants, 63% accepted, 86 enrolled. *Faculty:* 17 full-time (11 women), 23 part-time/adjunct (15 women). Expenses: Contact institution. *Financial support:* In 2006–07, 149 students received support, including 16 research assistantships with partial tuition reimbursements available (averaging $4,000 per year); career-related internships or fieldwork, Federal Work-Study, institutionally sponsored loans, scholarships/grants, tuition waivers (partial), and unspecified assistantships also available. Support available to part-time students. Financial award application deadline: 3/15; financial award applicants required to submit FAFSA. In 2006, 80 degrees awarded. Offers conference interpretation (MA); translation (MA); translation and interpretation (MA); translation and localization management (MA). *Application deadline:* For fall admission, 3/15 priority date for domestic students; for spring admission, 10/1 priority date for domestic students. Applications are processed on a rolling basis. *Application fee:* $50. Electronic applications accepted. *Application Contact:* 831-647-4123, Fax: 831-647-6405, E-mail: admit@miis.edu. *Dean,* Dr. Chuanyun Bao, 831-647-4170, Fax: 831-647-3560, E-mail: gsti@miis.edu.

MONTREAT COLLEGE, Montreat, NC 28757-1267

General Information Independent-religious, coed, comprehensive institution. *Graduate housing:* On-campus housing not available.

GRADUATE UNITS

School of Professional and Adult Studies *Degree program information:* Evening/weekend programs available. Postbaccalaureate distance learning degree programs offered. Offers business administration (MBA); K-6 education (MA Ed).

MOODY BIBLE INSTITUTE, Chicago, IL 60610-3284

General Information Independent-religious, coed, comprehensive institution. *Graduate housing:* Rooms and/or apartments guaranteed to single students and available on a first-come, first-served basis to married students. Housing application deadline: 6/1.

GRADUATE UNITS

Graduate School *Degree program information:* Part-time programs available. Offers biblical studies (MABS, Certificate); intercultural studies (MAIS); ministry (M Div, MA Min, MAUM); spiritual formation (MASF); teaching English to speakers of other languages (Certificate); urban ministry (MAUM).

MORAVIAN COLLEGE, Bethlehem, PA 18018-6650

General Information Independent-religious, coed, comprehensive institution. *Enrollment:* 1,965 graduate, professional, and undergraduate students; 1 (woman) full-time matriculated graduate/professional student, 158 part-time matriculated graduate/professional students (102 women). *Enrollment by degree level:* 159 master's. *Graduate faculty:* 12 full-time (5 women), 16 part-time/adjunct (9 women). *Graduate housing:* On-campus housing not available. *Student services:* Career counseling, disabled student services, international student services, multicultural affairs office, teacher training, writing training. *Library facilities:* Reeves Library. *Online resources:* library catalog, web page, access to other libraries' catalogs. *Collection:* 260,363 titles, 3,274 serial subscriptions, 4,740 audiovisual materials.

Computer facilities: Computer purchase and lease plans are available. 236 computers available on campus for general student use. A campuswide network can be accessed from student residence rooms and from off campus. Internet access is available. *Web address:* http://www.moravian.edu/.

General Application Contact: Dr. William A. Kleintop, Associate Dean for Business and Management Programs, 610-507-1400, Fax: 610-861-1466, E-mail: comenius@moravian.edu.

GRADUATE UNITS

The Comenius Center for Continuing, Professional, and Graduate Studies Students: 1 (woman) full-time, 158 part-time (102 women). *Faculty:* 12 full-time (5 women), 16 part-time/adjunct (9 women). Expenses: Contact institution. In 2006, 37 degrees awarded. *Degree program information:* Part-time and evening/weekend programs available. Offers business and management (MBA); curriculum and instruction (M Ed). *Application deadline:* For fall admission, 7/1 priority date for domestic students; for winter admission, 10/1 priority date for domestic students. Applications are processed on a rolling basis. *Dean, Continuing and Graduate Studies,* Dr. Florence Kimball, 610-861-1400, Fax: 610-861-1466, E-mail: comenius@moravian.edu.

MORAVIAN THEOLOGICAL SEMINARY, Bethlehem, PA 18018-6614

General Information Independent-religious, coed, graduate-only institution. *Graduate housing:* Rooms and/or apartments available to single and married students. Housing application deadline: 2/15.

GRADUATE UNITS

Graduate and Professional Programs *Degree program information:* Part-time programs available. Offers theology (M Div, MAPC, MATS).

MOREHEAD STATE UNIVERSITY, Morehead, KY 40351

General Information State-supported, coed, comprehensive institution. *Enrollment:* 9,025 graduate, professional, and undergraduate students; 344 full-time matriculated graduate/professional students (209 women), 777 part-time matriculated graduate/professional students (534 women). *Enrollment by degree level:* 1,121 master's. *Graduate faculty:* 218 full-time (84 women), 78 part-time/adjunct (38 women). *Graduate housing:* Rooms and/or apartments available on a first-come, first-served basis to single and married students. *Student services:* Campus employment opportunities, campus safety program, career counseling, child daycare facilities, disabled student services, exercise/wellness program, free psychological counseling, grant writing training, international student services, low-cost health insurance, multicultural affairs office, teacher training, writing training. *Library facilities:* Camden Carroll Library. *Online resources:* library catalog, web page. *Collection:* 523,767 titles, 26,817 serial subscriptions, 21,458 audiovisual materials.

Computer facilities: 1,000 computers available on campus for general student use. A campuswide network can be accessed from student residence rooms and from off campus. Internet access and online class registration are available. *Web address:* http://www.moreheadstate.edu/.

General Application Contact: Michelle Barber, Graduate Admissions Counselor, 606-783-2039, Fax: 606-783-5061, E-mail: m.barber@moreheadstate.edu.

GRADUATE UNITS

Graduate Programs Students: 344 full-time (209 women), 777 part-time (534 women); includes 43 minority (26 African Americans, 6 American Indian/Alaska Native, 6 Asian Americans or Pacific Islanders, 5 Hispanic Americans), 26 international. Average age 32. *Faculty:* 218 full-time (84 women), 78 part-time/adjunct (38 women). Expenses: Contact institution. *Financial support:* In 2006–07, 34 research assistantships (averaging $6,000 per year), 99 teaching assistantships (averaging $6,000 per year) were awarded; career-related internships or fieldwork, Federal Work-Study, and unspecified assistantships also available. Financial award application deadline: 4/1; financial award applicants required to submit FAFSA. In 2006, 366 master's, 7 other advanced degrees awarded. *Degree program information:* Part-time and evening/weekend programs available. Postbaccalaureate distance learning degree programs offered (minimal on-campus study). *Application deadline:* For fall admission, 7/1 priority date for domestic and international students; for spring admission, 12/1 priority date for domestic and international students. Applications are processed on a rolling basis. *Application fee:* $0 ($55 for international students). Electronic applications accepted. *Application Contact:* Michelle Barber, Graduate Admissions Counselor, 606-783-2039, Fax: 606-783-5061, E-mail: m.barber@moreheadstate.edu. *Associate Vice President for Graduate and Undergraduate Programs,* Dr. Deborah Abell, 606-783-2004, Fax: 606-783-5061, E-mail: d.abell@moreheadstate.edu.

Caudill College of Humanities Students: 54 full-time (28 women), 40 part-time (28 women); includes 2 minority (1 Asian American or Pacific Islander, 1 Hispanic American), 4 international. Average age 32. *Faculty:* 81 full-time (45 women), 19 part-time/adjunct (11 women). Expenses: Contact institution. *Financial support:* In 2006–07, 35 teaching assistantships (averaging $6,000 per year) were awarded; career-related internships or fieldwork, Federal Work-Study, and unspecified assistantships also available. Financial award application deadline: 4/1; financial award applicants required to submit FAFSA. In 2006, 26 degrees awarded. *Degree program information:* Part-time and evening/weekend programs available. Postbaccalaureate distance learning degree programs offered. Offers art education (MA); communication (MA); criminology (MA); English (MA); general sociology (MA); gerontology (MA); humanities (MA, MM); music education (MM); music performance (MM); studio art (MA). *Application deadline:* For fall admission, 8/1 priority date for domestic and international students; for spring admission, 12/1 priority date for domestic and international students. Applications are processed on a rolling basis. *Application fee:* $0 ($55 for international students). Electronic applications accepted. *Application Contact:* Michelle Barber, Graduate Admissions Counselor, 606-783-2039, Fax: 606-783-5061, E-mail: m.barber@moreheadstate.edu. *Dean,* Dr. Michael Seelig, 606-783-2650, Fax: 606-783-5046, E-mail: m.seelig@moreheadstate.edu.

College of Business Students: 33 full-time (16 women), 149 part-time (84 women); includes 13 minority (8 African Americans, 3 Asian Americans or Pacific Islanders, 2 Hispanic Americans), 3 international. Average age 32. *Faculty:* 13 full-time (2 women), 10 part-time/adjunct (3 women). Expenses: Contact institution. *Financial support:* In 2006–07, 13 teaching assistantships (averaging $6,000 per year) were awarded; career-related internships or fieldwork, Federal Work-Study, and unspecified assistantships also available. Financial award application deadline: 4/1; financial award applicants required to submit FAFSA. In 2006, 57 degrees awarded. *Degree program information:* Part-time and evening/weekend programs available. Postbaccalaureate distance learning degree programs offered (minimal on-campus study). Offers business (MBA, MSIS); information systems (MSIS). *Application deadline:* For fall admission, 8/1 for domestic and international students; for spring admission, 12/1 for domestic and international students. Applications are processed on a rolling basis. *Application fee:* $0 ($55 for international students). Electronic applications accepted.

Application Contact: Michelle Barber, Graduate Admissions Counselor, 606-783-2039, Fax: 606-783-5061, E-mail: m.barber@moreheadstate.edu. *Dean,* Dr. Robert L. Albert, 606-783-2174, Fax: 606-783-5025, E-mail: r.albert@moreheadstate.edu.

College of Education Students: 191 full-time (134 women), 535 part-time (395 women); includes 21 minority (12 African Americans, 5 American Indian/Alaska Native, 1 Asian American or Pacific Islander, 3 Hispanic Americans), 4 international. Average age 32. *Faculty:* 54 full-time (32 women), 37 part-time/adjunct (25 women). Expenses: Contact institution. *Financial support:* In 2006–07, 1 research assistantship (averaging $6,000 per year), 8 teaching assistantships (averaging $6,000 per year) were awarded; career-related internships or fieldwork, Federal Work-Study, and unspecified assistantships also available. Financial award application deadline: 4/1; financial award applicants required to submit FAFSA. In 2006, 280 master's, 4 other advanced degrees awarded. *Degree program information:* Part-time and evening/weekend programs available. Offers adult and higher education (MA, Ed S); counseling (MA Ed, Ed S); curriculum and instruction (Ed S); education (MA, MA Ed, MAT, Ed S); elementary education (MA Ed, MAT); exercise physiology (MA); health and physical education (MA); instructional leadership (Ed S); international education (MA Ed); middle school education (MA Ed, MAT); reading (MA Ed); school administration (MA, Ed S); secondary education (MA Ed, MAT); special education (MA Ed, MAT); sports management (MA). *Application deadline:* For fall admission, 8/1 priority date for domestic and international students; for spring admission, 12/1 priority date for domestic and international students. Applications are processed on a rolling basis. *Application fee:* $0 ($55 for international students). Electronic applications accepted. *Application Contact:* Michelle Barber, Graduate Admissions Counselor, 606-783-2039, Fax: 606-783-5061, E-mail: m.barber@moreheadstate.edu. *Dean,* Dr. Cathy Gunn, 606-783-2040, Fax: 606-783-5029, E-mail: c.gunn@moreheadstate.edu.

College of Science and Technology Students: 58 full-time (30 women), 41 part-time (20 women); includes 6 minority (4 African Americans, 1 American Indian/Alaska Native, 1 Asian American or Pacific Islander), 14 international. Average age 32. *Faculty:* 49 full-time (13 women), 12 part-time/adjunct (1 woman). Expenses: Contact institution. *Financial support:* In 2006–07, 34 research assistantships (averaging $6,000 per year), 11 teaching assistantships (averaging $6,000 per year) were awarded; career-related internships or fieldwork and Federal Work-Study also available. Financial award application deadline: 4/1; financial award applicants required to submit FAFSA. In 2006, 38 degrees awarded. *Degree program information:* Part-time and evening/weekend programs available. Offers biology (MS); career and technical education (MS); clinical psychology (MA); counseling psychology (MA); experimental/general psychology (MA); industrial technology (MS); regional analysis and public policy (MS); science and technology (MA, MS). *Application deadline:* For fall admission, 8/1 priority date for domestic and international students; for spring admission, 12/1 priority date for domestic and international students. Applications are processed on a rolling basis. *Application fee:* $0. Electronic applications accepted. *Application Contact:* Michelle Barber, Graduate Admissions Counselor, 606-783-2039, Fax: 606-783-5061, E-mail: m.barber@moreheadstate.edu. *Dean,* Dr. Gerald DeMoss, 606-783-2158, Fax: 606-783-5039, E-mail: g.demoss@moreheadstate.edu.

Institute for Regional Analysis and Public Policy Students: 8 full-time (1 woman), 12 part-time (7 women); includes 1 minority (African American), 1 international. Average age 32. *Faculty:* 6 full-time (2 women), 5 part-time/adjunct (1 woman). Expenses: Contact institution. *Financial support:* In 2006–07, 4 teaching assistantships (averaging $6,000 per year) were awarded. Offers public administration (MPA). *Application deadline:* For fall admission, 8/1 priority date for domestic and international students; for spring admission, 12/1 priority date for domestic and international students. Applications are processed on a rolling basis. Electronic applications accepted. *Application Contact:* Michelle Barber, Graduate Admissions Counselor, 606-783-2039, Fax: 606-783-5061, E-mail: m.barber@moreheadstate.edu. *Dean,* Dr. David Rudy, 606-783-5419, Fax: 606-783-5092, E-mail: d.rudy@moreheadstate.edu.

MOREHOUSE SCHOOL OF MEDICINE, Atlanta, GA 30310-1495

General Information Independent, coed, graduate-only institution. *Graduate housing:* Room and/or apartments available on a first-come, first-served basis to single students; on-campus housing not available to married students. *Research affiliation:* Parke-Davis (cardiovascular risk factors), Bristol Myers Squibb (pharmacokinetics), Wyeth (helicobacter pylori study), CareStat (renal insufficiency), Merck (hypotension), NitroMel, Inc. (heart failure).

GRADUATE UNITS

Master of Public Health Program *Degree program information:* Part-time programs available. Offers public health (MPH). Electronic applications accepted.

Professional Program Offers medicine (MD). Electronic applications accepted.

Program in Biomedical Sciences Offers biomedical sciences (PhD). Electronic applications accepted.

Program in Clinical Research Offers clinical research (MS).

MORGAN STATE UNIVERSITY, Baltimore, MD 21251

General Information State-supported, coed, university. CGS member. *Enrollment:* 450 full-time matriculated graduate/professional students, 362 part-time matriculated graduate/professional students. *Enrollment by degree level:* 476 master's, 336 doctoral. *Graduate faculty:* 222. Tuition, state resident: part-time $272 per credit. Tuition, nonresident: part-time $478 per credit. *Required fees:* $38 per credit. *Graduate housing:* Rooms and/or apartments available on a first-come, first-served basis to single and married students. *Student services:* Campus employment opportunities, campus safety program, career counseling, child daycare facilities, disabled student services, grant writing training, international student services, low-cost health insurance, teacher training, writing training. *Library facilities:* Morris Soper Library. *Online resources:* library catalog. *Collection:* 333,101 titles, 2,526 serial subscriptions.

Computer facilities: 285 computers available on campus for general student use. A campuswide network can be accessed from student residence rooms and from off campus. Internet access and online class registration, engineering lab supercomputer are available. *Web address:* http://www.morgan.edu/.

General Application Contact: Dr. Maurice C. Taylor, Dean, 443-885-3185, Fax: 443-885-8226, E-mail: mctaylor@moac.morgan.edu.

GRADUATE UNITS

School of Graduate Studies Students: 450 full-time, 362 part-time; includes 544 minority (526 African Americans, 2 American Indian/Alaska Native, 13 Asian Americans or Pacific Islanders, 3 Hispanic Americans), 182 international. 673 applicants, 49% accepted, 201 enrolled. *Faculty:* 172 full-time, 10 part-time/adjunct. Expenses: Contact institution. *Financial support:* In 2006–07, 317 students received support, including fellowships with full tuition reimbursements available (averaging $16,000 per year), research assistantships with full tuition reimbursements available (averaging $10,500 per year), teaching assistantships with full tuition reimbursements available (averaging $10,500 per year); career-related internships or fieldwork, Federal Work-Study, institutionally sponsored loans, scholarships/grants, health care benefits, tuition waivers (full), and unspecified assistantships also available. Support available to part-time students. Financial award application deadline: 2/1. In 2006, 109 master's, 40 doctorates awarded. *Degree program information:* Part-time and evening/weekend programs available. Offers public health and policy (MPH, Dr PH). *Application deadline:* For fall admission, 2/1 priority date for domestic and international students; for spring admission, 10/1 priority date for domestic and international students. Applications are processed on a rolling basis. *Application fee:* $0. *Dean,* Dr. Maurice C. Taylor, 443-885-3185, Fax: 443-885-8226, E-mail: mctaylor@moac.morgan.edu.

Clarence M. Mitchell, Jr. School of Engineering Students: 93. Expenses: Contact institution. *Financial support:* Fellowships, research assistantships, career-related internships or fieldwork, Federal Work-Study, institutionally sponsored loans, scholarships/grants, health care benefits, and unspecified assistantships available. Support available to part-time students. Financial award application deadline: 2/1. In 2006, 18 master's, 5 doctorates awarded. *Degree program information:* Part-time and evening/weekend programs available. Offers civil engineering (M Eng, D Eng); electrical engineering (M Eng, D Eng); industrial engineering (M Eng, D Eng); transportation (MS). *Application deadline:* For fall admission, 2/1 priority date for domestic students; for spring admission, 10/1 priority date for domestic students. Applications are processed on a rolling basis. *Application fee:* $0. *Application Contact:* Dr. Maurice C. Taylor, Dean, 443-885-3185, Fax: 443-885-8226, E-mail: mctaylor@moac.morgan.edu. *Dean,* Dr. Eugene DeLoatch, 443-885-3231.

College of Liberal Arts Students: 126. Expenses: Contact institution. *Financial support:* Fellowships, research assistantships, teaching assistantships, career-related internships or fieldwork, Federal Work-Study, institutionally sponsored loans, scholarships/grants, health care benefits, and unspecified assistantships available. Support available to part-time students. Financial award application deadline: 2/1. In 2006, 17 degrees awarded. *Degree program information:* Part-time programs available. Offers African-American studies (MA); economics (MA); English (MA, PhD); history (MA, PhD); international studies (MA); liberal arts (MA, MS, PhD); music (MA); psychometrics (MS, PhD); sociology (MA, MS); telecommunications management (MS). *Application deadline:* For fall admission, 2/1 priority date for domestic students; for spring admission, 10/1 priority date for domestic students. Applications are processed on a rolling basis. *Application fee:* $0. *Application Contact:* Dr. Maurice C. Taylor, Dean, 443-885-3185, Fax: 443-885-8226, E-mail: mctaylor@moac.morgan.edu. *Dean,* Dr. Burney J. Hollis, 443-885-3090.

Earl G. Graves School of Business and Management Students: 87. *Faculty:* 37 full-time. Expenses: Contact institution. *Financial support:* Fellowships, research assistantships, teaching assistantships available. Financial award application deadline: 2/1. In 2006, 16 master's, 1 doctorate awarded. *Degree program information:* Part-time and evening/weekend programs available. Offers business administration (MBA, PhD); business and management (MBA, PhD). *Application deadline:* For fall admission, 2/1 priority date for domestic students; for spring admission, 10/1 priority date for domestic students. Applications are processed on a rolling basis. *Application fee:* $0. *Application Contact:* Dr. Maurice C. Taylor, Dean, 443-885-3185, Fax: 443-885-8226, E-mail: mctaylor@moac.morgan.edu. *Dean,* Dr. Otis A. Thomas, 443-885-3160, E-mail: athomas@moac.morgan.edu.

Institute of Architecture and Planning Students: 120 (68 women). Average age 29. *Faculty:* 10 full-time (3 women). Expenses: Contact institution. *Financial support:* Fellowships, research assistantships, teaching assistantships, Federal Work-Study and scholarships/grants available. Financial award application deadline: 2/1. In 2006, 22 degrees awarded. Offers architecture (M Arch); city and regional planning (MCRP); landscape architecture (MLA, MSLA). *Application deadline:* For fall admission, 2/1 priority date for domestic students; for spring admission, 10/1 priority date for domestic students. Applications are processed on a rolling basis. *Application fee:* $0. *Application Contact:* Dr. Maurice C. Taylor, Dean, 443-885-3185, Fax: 443-885-8226, E-mail: mctaylor@moac.morgan.edu. *Director,* Dr. Richard E. Lloyd, 443-885-3225.

School of Computer, Mathematical, and Natural Sciences Students: 35. Expenses: Contact institution. *Financial support:* Fellowships, research assistantships, teaching assistantships available. Financial award application deadline: 2/1. In 2006, 2 degrees awarded. Offers bio-environmental science (PhD); bioinformatics (MS); biology (MS); chemistry (MS); computer, mathematical, and natural sciences (MA, MS, PhD); mathematics (MA); physics (MS). *Application deadline:* For fall admission, 2/1 priority date for domestic students; for spring admission, 10/1 priority date for domestic students. Applications are processed on a rolling basis. *Application fee:* $0. *Application Contact:* Dr. Maurice C. Taylor, Dean, 443-885-3185, Fax: 443-885-8226, E-mail: mctaylor@moac.morgan.edu. *Dean,* Dr. Joseph Whittaker, 443-885-4515.

School of Education and Urban Studies Students: 256. *Faculty:* 26. Expenses: Contact institution. *Financial support:* Fellowships, research assistantships, career-related internships or fieldwork, Federal Work-Study, institutionally sponsored loans, scholarships/grants, health care benefits, and unspecified assistantships available. Support available to part-time students. Financial award application deadline: 2/1. In 2006, 10 master's, 25 doctorates awarded. *Degree program information:* Part-time programs available. Offers education and urban studies (MAT, MS, MSW, Ed D, PhD); educational administration and supervision (MS); elementary and middle school education (MS); elementary education (MAT, MS); high school education (MAT); higher education administration (PhD); higher education-community college leadership (Ed D); mathematics education (MS, Ed D); middle school education (MAT); science education (MS, Ed D); social work (MSW, PhD). *Application deadline:* For fall admission, 2/1 priority date for domestic students; for spring admission, 10/1 priority date for domestic students. Applications are processed on a rolling basis. *Application fee:* $0. *Application Contact:* Dr. Maurice C. Taylor, Dean, 443-885-3185, Fax: 443-885-8226, E-mail: mctaylor@moac.morgan.edu. *Dean,* Dr. Patricia L. Welch, 443-885-3385, Fax: 443-885-8240, E-mail: pmorris@moac.morgan.edu.

MORNINGSIDE COLLEGE, Sioux City, IA 51106

General Information Independent-religious, coed, comprehensive institution. *Graduate housing:* Rooms and/or apartments available to single and married students. Housing application deadline: 7/1. *Research affiliation:* Iowa Public Service Company (biology, chemistry, physics).

GRADUATE UNITS

Graduate Division *Degree program information:* Part-time and evening/weekend programs available. Offers elementary education (MAT); reading specialist (MAT); special education (MAT); technology based learning (MAT).

MORRISON UNIVERSITY, Reno, NV 89521

General Information Proprietary, coed, comprehensive institution. *Graduate housing:* On-campus housing not available.

GRADUATE UNITS

Graduate School *Degree program information:* Part-time and evening/weekend programs available. Electronic applications accepted.

MOUNTAIN STATE UNIVERSITY, Beckley, WV 25802-9003

General Information Independent, coed, comprehensive institution. *Enrollment:* 4,420 graduate, professional, and undergraduate students; 468 full-time matriculated graduate/professional students (259 women), 52 part-time matriculated graduate/professional students (32 women). *Enrollment by degree level:* 520 master's. *Graduate faculty:* 21 full-time (9 women), 67 part-time/adjunct (25 women). *Tuition:* Full-time $3,660; part-time $305 per credit. Tuition and fees vary according to course load and program. *Graduate housing:* Room and/or apartments available on a first-come, first-served basis to single students; on-campus housing not available to married students. Typical cost: $2,810 per year ($5,636 including board). Room and board charges vary according to board plan. *Student services:* Campus employment opportunities, campus safety program, career counseling, disabled student services, exercise/wellness program, grant writing training, international student services, multicultural affairs office, writing training. *Library facilities:* Mountain State University Library. *Online resources:* library catalog. *Collection:* 113,361 titles, 155 serial subscriptions, 4,877 audiovisual materials.

Computer facilities: 97 computers available on campus for general student use. A campuswide network can be accessed from student residence rooms and from off campus. Internet access is available. *Web address:* http://www.mountainstate.edu/.

General Application Contact: Dinah Rock, Coordinator of Graduate Academic Services, 304-929-1588, Fax: 304-929-1637, E-mail: drock@mountainstate.edu.

GRADUATE UNITS

Graduate Studies Students: 468 full-time (259 women), 52 part-time (32 women); includes 85 minority (56 African Americans, 5 American Indian/Alaska Native, 9 Asian Americans or Pacific Islanders, 15 Hispanic Americans), 10 international. Average age 35. 592 applicants, 79% accepted, 329 enrolled. *Faculty:* 21 full-time (9 women), 67 part-time/adjunct (25 women). Expenses: Contact institution. *Financial support:* In 2006–07, 2 research assistantships (averaging $1,200 per year) were awarded; career-related internships or fieldwork, Federal

Mountain State University (continued)

Work-Study, scholarships/grants, tuition waivers (partial), and unspecified assistantships also available. Support available to part-time students. Financial award applicants required to submit FAFSA. In 2006, 195 degrees awarded. *Degree program information:* Part-time and evening/weekend programs available. Postbaccalaureate distance learning degree programs offered (no on-campus study). Offers administration/education (MSN); criminal justice administration (MCJA); family nurse practitioner (MSN); health science (MHS); interdisciplinary studies (MA, MS); nurse anesthesia (MSN); physician assistant (MSPA); registered nurse anesthetist (Certificate); strategic leadership (MSSL). *Application deadline:* For fall admission, 5/31 priority date for domestic and international students. Applications are processed on a rolling basis. *Application fee:* $25 ($50 for international students). Electronic applications accepted. *Application Contact:* Dinah Rock, Coordinator of Graduate Academic Services, 304-929-1588, Fax: 304-929-1637, E-mail: drock@mountainstate.edu. *Executive Vice President and Chief Academic Officer,* James G. Silosky, 304-929-1316, Fax: 304-253-3483, E-mail: jsilosky@mountainstate.edu.

MOUNT ALLISON UNIVERSITY, Sackville, NB E4L 1E4, Canada

General Information Province-supported, coed, comprehensive institution. *Enrollment:* 2,240 graduate, professional, and undergraduate students; 16 full-time matriculated graduate/professional students (13 women). *Enrollment by degree level:* 16 master's. *Graduate faculty:* 18 full-time (4 women). *Graduate housing:* Room and/or apartments available to single students; on-campus housing not available to married students. Typical cost: $4,140 per year ($7,300 including board). Room and board charges vary according to board plan. Housing application deadline: 5/15. *Student services:* Campus employment opportunities, campus safety program, child daycare facilities, disabled student services, exercise/wellness program, free psychological counseling, international student services, low-cost health insurance. *Library facilities:* Ralph Pickard Bell Library plus 3 others. *Online resources:* library catalog, web page, access to other libraries' catalogs. *Collection:* 400,000 titles, 1,700 serial subscriptions. *Research affiliation:* Huntsman Marine Science Centre (marine biology), Atlantic Cancer Institute (medical research), Moncton Hospital (medical research).

Computer facilities: 100 computers available on campus for general student use. A campuswide network can be accessed from student residence rooms and from off campus. Internet access and online class registration, online student account/Websis are available. *Web address:* http://www.mta.ca/.

General Application Contact: Dr. Glen Briand, Associate Professor, 506-364-2346, E-mail: gbriand@mta.ca.

GRADUATE UNITS

Department of Biology Students: 12 full-time (9 women). Average age 24. 3 applicants, 100% accepted. *Faculty:* 10 full-time (3 women). Expenses: Contact institution. *Financial support:* In 2006–07, 2 fellowships (averaging $12,000 per year) were awarded. Offers biology (M Sc). *Application Contact:* Dr. Felix Baerlocher, Head, 506-364-2500, E-mail: fbaerlocher@mta.ca. *Head,* Dr. Felix Baerlocher, 506-364-2500, E-mail: fbaerlocher@mta.ca.

Department of Chemistry Students: 4 full-time (all women). 1 applicant, 100% accepted. *Faculty:* 8 full-time (1 woman). Expenses: Contact institution. *Financial support:* Fellowships, research assistantships available. Offers chemistry (M Sc). *Application Contact:* Anna Sheridan-Jonah, Graduate Studies Coordinator, E-mail: asherida@mta.ca. *Head,* Dr. Stephen Duffy, 506-364-2361, E-mail: sduffy@mta.edu.

MOUNT ALOYSIUS COLLEGE, Cresson, PA 16630-1999

General Information Independent-religious, coed, comprehensive institution.

GRADUATE UNITS

Program in Correctional Administration Offers correctional administration (MA).

Program in Health and Human Services Administration Offers health and human services administration (MS).

Program in Psychology Offers psychology (MS).

MOUNT ANGEL SEMINARY, Saint Benedict, OR 97373

General Information Independent-religious, Undergraduate: men only; graduate: coed, comprehensive institution. *Graduate housing:* Room and/or apartments guaranteed to single students; on-campus housing not available to married students.

GRADUATE UNITS

Program in Theology *Degree program information:* Part-time programs available. Offers theology (M Div, MA).

MOUNT CARMEL COLLEGE OF NURSING, Columbus, OH 43222

General Information Independent, coed, primarily women, comprehensive institution. *Graduate housing:* Room and/or apartments available on a first-come, first-served basis to single students; on-campus housing not available to married students.

GRADUATE UNITS

College of Nursing *Degree program information:* Part-time programs available. Offers adult health (MS); nursing education (MS).

MOUNT HOLYOKE COLLEGE, South Hadley, MA 01075

General Information Independent, women only, comprehensive institution.

GRADUATE UNITS

Department of Psychology and Education Offers psychology and education (MA).

MOUNT MARTY COLLEGE, Yankton, SD 57078-3724

General Information Independent-religious, coed, comprehensive institution. *Enrollment:* 1,220 graduate, professional, and undergraduate students; 70 full-time matriculated graduate/professional students (42 women). *Enrollment by degree level:* 70 master's. *Graduate faculty:* 4 full-time (3 women), 1 part-time/adjunct (0 women). *Graduate housing:* On-campus housing not available. *Student services:* Career counseling, free psychological counseling, low-cost health insurance. *Library facilities:* Mount Marty College Library. *Online resources:* library catalog, web page, access to other libraries' catalogs. *Collection:* 76,571 titles, 424 serial subscriptions.

Computer facilities: Computer purchase and lease plans are available. 21 computers available on campus for general student use. A campuswide network can be accessed from student residence rooms and from off campus. Internet access is available. *Web address:* http://www.mtmc.edu/.

General Application Contact: Brandi Tschumper, Vice President of Enrollment, 800-658-4552, Fax: 605-688-1508, E-mail: mmcadmit@mtmc.edu.

GRADUATE UNITS

Graduate Studies Division Students: 70 full-time (42 women); includes 4 minority (2 African Americans, 1 Asian American or Pacific Islander, 1 Hispanic American). 140 applicants, 28% accepted, 39 enrolled. *Faculty:* 4 full-time (3 women), 1 part-time/adjunct (0 women). Expenses: Contact institution. *Financial support:* In 2006–07, 70 students received support. Scholarships/grants available. Financial award application deadline: 8/1; financial award applicants required to submit FAFSA. In 2006, 37 degrees awarded. Offers business administration (MBA); nurse anesthesia (MS); pastoral ministries (MPM). *Application deadline:* For fall admission, 12/1 priority date for domestic students. Applications are processed on a rolling basis. *Application fee:* $35. Electronic applications accepted. *Vice President of Enrollment,* Brandi Tschumper, 800-658-4552, Fax: 605-688-1508, E-mail: mmcadmit@mtmc.edu.

MOUNT MARY COLLEGE, Milwaukee, WI 53222-4597

General Information Independent-religious, Undergraduate: women only; graduate: coed, comprehensive institution. *Enrollment:* 1,732 graduate, professional, and undergraduate students; 97 full-time matriculated graduate/professional students (92 women), 153 part-time matriculated graduate/professional students (143 women). *Enrollment by degree level:* 250 master's. *Graduate faculty:* 12 full-time (11 women), 22 part-time/adjunct (19 women). *Tuition:* Part-time $490 per credit. *Required fees:* $48 per term. Tuition and fees vary according to course load and program. *Graduate housing:* Room and/or apartments available on a first-come, first-served basis to single students; on-campus housing not available to married students. Typical cost: $5,990 (including board). Housing application deadline: 8/1. *Student services:* Campus employment opportunities, campus safety program, career counseling, child daycare facilities, disabled student services, exercise/wellness program, free psychological counseling, international student services, multicultural affairs office, teacher training, writing training. *Library facilities:* Haggerty Library. *Online resources:* library catalog, web page, access to other libraries' catalogs. *Collection:* 103,450 titles, 22,210 serial subscriptions, 8,104 audiovisual materials.

Computer facilities: 170 computers available on campus for general student use. A campuswide network can be accessed from student residence rooms and from off campus. Internet access is available. *Web address:* http://www.mtmary.edu/.

General Application Contact: Dr. Douglas J. Mickelson, Associate Dean for Graduate and Continuing Education, 414-256-1252, Fax: 414-256-0167, E-mail: mickelsd@mtmary.edu.

GRADUATE UNITS

Graduate Programs Students: 97 full-time (92 women), 153 part-time (143 women); includes 29 minority (19 African Americans, 1 Asian American or Pacific Islander, 9 Hispanic Americans). Average age 35. 217 applicants, 56% accepted, 100 enrolled. *Faculty:* 12 full-time (11 women), 22 part-time/adjunct (19 women). Expenses: Contact institution. *Financial support:* In 2006–07, 7 students received support. Career-related internships or fieldwork, Federal Work-Study, and unspecified assistantships available. Support available to part-time students. Financial award application deadline: 5/1; financial award applicants required to submit FAFSA. In 2006, 71 degrees awarded. *Degree program information:* Part-time and evening/weekend programs available. Offers administrative dietetics (MS); art therapy (MS); business administration (MBA); clinical dietetics (MS); community counseling (MS); education (MA); English (MA); nutrition education (MS); occupational therapy (MS); professional development (MA). *Application deadline:* For fall admission, 8/1 priority date for domestic and international students; for spring admission, 12/1 priority date for domestic and international students. Applications are processed on a rolling basis. *Application fee:* $35 ($75 for international students). Electronic applications accepted. *Associate Dean for Graduate and Continuing Education,* Dr. Douglas J. Mickelson, 414-256-1252, Fax: 414-256-0167, E-mail: mickelsd@mtmary.edu.

MOUNT SAINT MARY COLLEGE, Newburgh, NY 12550-3494

General Information Independent, coed, comprehensive institution. *Enrollment:* 2,601 graduate, professional, and undergraduate students; 108 full-time matriculated graduate/professional students (88 women), 439 part-time matriculated graduate/professional students (353 women). *Enrollment by degree level:* 547 master's. *Graduate faculty:* 20 full-time (12 women), 26 part-time/adjunct (20 women). *Tuition:* Full-time $11,880; part-time $660 per credit. *Graduate housing:* On-campus housing not available. *Student services:* Campus employment opportunities, campus safety program, career counseling, free psychological counseling, international student services. *Library facilities:* Curtin Memorial Library plus 1 other. *Online resources:* library catalog, web page, access to other libraries' catalogs. *Collection:* 118,207 titles, 317 serial subscriptions, 5,963 audiovisual materials.

Computer facilities: 336 computers available on campus for general student use. A campuswide network can be accessed from student residence rooms and from off campus. Internet access and online class registration, intranet are available. *Web address:* http://www.msmc.edu/.

General Application Contact: Graduate Coordinator, 845-561-0800, Fax: 845-562-6762.

GRADUATE UNITS

Division of Business Students: 20 full-time (13 women), 43 part-time (24 women); includes 20 minority (12 African Americans, 3 Asian Americans or Pacific Islanders, 5 Hispanic Americans). Average age 33. 23 applicants, 100% accepted, 22 enrolled. *Faculty:* 6 full-time (2 women), 4 part-time/adjunct (1 woman). Expenses: Contact institution. *Financial support:* In 2006–07, 8 students received support. Unspecified assistantships available. Financial award application deadline: 3/15. In 2006, 24 degrees awarded. *Degree program information:* Part-time and evening/weekend programs available. Offers business (MBA); financial planning (MBA). *Application deadline:* Applications are processed on a rolling basis. *Application fee:* $35. *Application Contact:* Janice Banker, Secretary, 845-569-3582, Fax: 845-569-3885, E-mail: banker@msmc.edu. *Coordinator,* David R. Rant, 845-569-3124, Fax: 845-562-6762, E-mail: rant@msmc.edu.

Division of Education Students: 87 full-time (74 women), 368 part-time (303 women); includes 38 minority (12 African Americans, 2 American Indian/Alaska Native, 5 Asian Americans or Pacific Islanders, 19 Hispanic Americans). Average age 31. 164 applicants, 45% accepted, 58 enrolled. *Faculty:* 11 full-time (8 women), 21 part-time/adjunct (18 women). Expenses: Contact institution. *Financial support:* In 2006–07, 30 students received support. Unspecified assistantships available. Financial award application deadline: 3/15. In 2006, 131 degrees awarded. *Degree program information:* Part-time and evening/weekend programs available. Offers adolescence and special education (MS Ed); adolescence education (MS Ed); childhood and special education (MS Ed); childhood education (MS Ed); literacy and special education (MS Ed); literacy/childhood (MS Ed); middle school (5-6) (MS Ed); middle school (7-9) (MS Ed); special education (1-6) (MS Ed); special education (7-12) (MS Ed). *Application deadline:* Applications are processed on a rolling basis. *Application fee:* $35. *Coordinator,* Theresa Lewis, 845-569-3149, Fax: 845-569-3535, E-mail: tlewis@msmc.edu.

Division of Nursing Students: 1 (woman) full-time, 28 part-time (26 women); includes 3 minority (2 African Americans, 1 Asian American or Pacific Islander). Average age 42. 12 applicants, 100% accepted, 10 enrolled. *Faculty:* 3 full-time (2 women), 1 (woman) part-time/adjunct. Expenses: Contact institution. *Financial support:* Unspecified assistantships and nursing lab assistant available. Financial award application deadline: 3/15; financial award applicants required to submit FAFSA. In 2006, 6 degrees awarded. *Degree program information:* Part-time and evening/weekend programs available. Offers adult nurse practitioner (MS); clinical nurse specialist-adult health (MS). *Application deadline:* For fall admission, 6/3 priority date for domestic students; for spring admission, 10/31 priority date for domestic students. Applications are processed on a rolling basis. *Application fee:* $35. *Coordinator,* Dr. Karen Baldwin, 845-569-3512, Fax: 845-562-6762, E-mail: baldwin@msmc.edu.

MOUNT ST. MARY'S COLLEGE, Los Angeles, CA 90049-1599

General Information Independent-religious, coed, primarily women, comprehensive institution. *Enrollment:* 2,384 graduate, professional, and undergraduate students; 245 full-time matriculated graduate/professional students (191 women), 218 part-time matriculated graduate/professional students (173 women). *Enrollment by degree level:* 389 master's, 74 doctoral. *Graduate faculty:* 16 full-time (all women), 23 part-time/adjunct (19 women). *Tuition:* Part-time $630 per unit. *Graduate housing:* On-campus housing not available. *Library facilities:* Charles Williard Coe Memorial Library. *Online resources:* library catalog, web page. *Collection:* 140,000 titles, 750 serial subscriptions.

Computer facilities: 85 computers available on campus for general student use. A campuswide network can be accessed from student residence rooms and from off campus. *Web address:* http://www.msmc.la.edu/.

General Application Contact: Tom Hoener, Director, Graduate Recruitment, 213-477-2800, Fax: 213-477-2519, E-mail: thoener@msmc.la.edu.

GRADUATE UNITS

Graduate Division Students: 245 full-time (191 women), 218 part-time (173 women); includes 228 minority (46 African Americans, 1 American Indian/Alaska Native, 46 Asian Americans or

Pacific Islanders, 135 Hispanic Americans). Average age 34. *Faculty:* 16 full-time (all women), 23 part-time/adjunct (19 women). Expenses: Contact institution. *Financial support:* Career-related internships or fieldwork, Federal Work-Study, institutionally sponsored loans, and tuition waivers (full and partial) available. Support available to part-time students. Financial award application deadline: 3/15; financial award applicants required to submit FAFSA. In 2006, 67 degrees awarded. *Degree program information:* Part-time and evening/weekend programs available. Offers administrative studies (MS); counseling psychology (MS); elementary education (MS); humanities (MA); nursing (MS); physical therapy (DPT); religious studies (MA); secondary education (MS); special education (MS). *Application deadline:* Applications are processed on a rolling basis. *Application Contact:* Tom Hoener, Director, Graduate Recruitment, 213-477-2800, Fax: 213-477-2519, E-mail: thoener@msmc.la.edu.

MOUNT ST. MARY'S UNIVERSITY, Emmitsburg, MD 21727-7799

General Information Independent-religious, coed, comprehensive institution. *Enrollment:* 2,186 graduate, professional, and undergraduate students; 221 full-time matriculated graduate/professional students (52 women), 270 part-time matriculated graduate/professional students (155 women). *Enrollment by degree level:* 101 first professional, 390 master's. *Graduate faculty:* 24 full-time (4 women), 24 part-time/adjunct (6 women). *Tuition:* Part-time $395 per credit hour. *Required fees:* $12 per credit hour. Tuition and fees vary according to program. *Graduate housing:* Room and/or apartments available on a first-come, first-served basis to single students; on-campus housing not available to married students. Typical cost: $4,380 per year ($8,690 including board). *Student services:* Campus employment opportunities, campus safety program, career counseling, disabled student services, exercise/wellness program, free psychological counseling, international student services, low-cost health insurance, multicultural affairs office, teacher training, writing training. *Library facilities:* Phillips Library. *Online resources:* library catalog, web page, access to other libraries' catalogs. *Collection:* 211,201 titles, 905 serial subscriptions, 5,108 audiovisual materials.

Computer facilities: Computer purchase and lease plans are available. 150 computers available on campus for general student use. A campuswide network can be accessed from student residence rooms and from off campus. Internet access and online class registration are available. *Web address:* http://www.msmary.edu/.

General Application Contact: David Rehm, Vice President for Academic Affairs, 301-447-5218, Fax: 301-447-5863, E-mail: rehm@msmary.edu.

GRADUATE UNITS

Graduate Seminary Students: 144 full-time (0 women), 2 part-time; includes 13 minority (2 African Americans, 8 Asian Americans or Pacific Islanders, 3 Hispanic Americans), 19 international. Average age 30. 58 applicants, 88% accepted, 49 enrolled. *Faculty:* 12 full-time (1 woman), 8 part-time/adjunct (2 women). Expenses: Contact institution. *Financial support:* In 2006–07, 48 students received support. Career-related internships or fieldwork and scholarships/grants available. Financial award applicants required to submit FAFSA. In 2006, 24 first professional degrees, 14 master's awarded. Offers theology (M Div, MA). *Application deadline:* Applications are processed on a rolling basis. *Application fee:* $25. *Application Contact:* Paula Smaldone, Seminary Admissions, 301-447-5295, Fax: 301-447-5636, E-mail: psmaldone@msmary.edu. *Vice President/Rector,* Rev. Steven P. Rohlfs, 301-447-5295, Fax: 301-447-5636, E-mail: rohlfs@msmary.edu.

Program in Business Administration Students: 32 full-time (18 women), 197 part-time (99 women); includes 13 minority (6 African Americans, 3 Asian Americans or Pacific Islanders, 4 Hispanic Americans), 6 international. Average age 32. 96 applicants, 99% accepted, 52 enrolled. *Faculty:* 10 full-time (1 woman), 9 part-time/adjunct (1 woman). Expenses: Contact institution. *Financial support:* In 2006–07, 68 students received support. Career-related internships or fieldwork and unspecified assistantships available. Financial award applicants required to submit FAFSA. In 2006, 92 degrees awarded. *Degree program information:* Part-time and evening/weekend programs available. Offers business administration (MBA). *Application deadline:* For fall admission, 8/21 priority date for domestic students; for winter admission, 10/14 priority date for domestic students; for spring admission, 2/24 priority date for domestic students. Applications are processed on a rolling basis. *Application fee:* $35. *Application Contact:* Sandy Kauffman, Administrative Assistant, 301-447-5326, Fax: 301-447-5335, E-mail: kauffman@msmary.edu.

Program in Education Students: 45 full-time (34 women), 70 part-time (55 women); includes 7 minority (4 African Americans, 1 American Indian/Alaska Native, 2 Hispanic Americans), 2 international. Average age 33. *Faculty:* 2 full-time (both women), 7 part-time/adjunct (3 women). Expenses: Contact institution. *Financial support:* In 2006–07, 48 students received support. Career-related internships or fieldwork and unspecified assistantships available. Financial award applicants required to submit FAFSA. In 2006, 25 degrees awarded. *Degree program information:* Part-time and evening/weekend programs available. Offers education (M Ed, MAT). *Application deadline:* For fall admission, 8/15 priority date for domestic students. Applications are processed on a rolling basis. *Application fee:* $35. *Director,* Laura Frazier, 301-447-5371, Fax: 301-447-5250, E-mail: frazier@msmary.edu.

MOUNT SAINT VINCENT UNIVERSITY, Halifax, NS B3M 2J6, Canada

General Information Province-supported, coed, primarily women, comprehensive institution. *Graduate housing:* Room and/or apartments available on a first-come, first-served basis to single students; on-campus housing not available to married students. Housing application deadline: 5/15.

GRADUATE UNITS

Graduate Programs *Degree program information:* Part-time and evening/weekend programs available. Postbaccalaureate distance learning degree programs offered (minimal on-campus study). Offers applied human nutrition (M Sc AHN, MAHN); child and youth study (MA); family studies and gerontology (MA); women's studies (MA). Electronic applications accepted.

Faculty of Education *Degree program information:* Part-time and evening/weekend programs available. Postbaccalaureate distance learning degree programs offered (minimal on-campus study). Offers adult education (M Ed, MA Ed, MA-R); curriculum studies (M Ed, MA Ed, MA-R); education of the blind or visually impaired (M Ed, MA Ed); education of the deaf or hard of hearing (M Ed, MA Ed); education of young adolescents (M Ed, MA Ed, MA-R); educational foundations (M Ed, MA Ed, MA-R); educational psychology (M Ed, MA Ed, MA-R); elementary education (M Ed, MA Ed, MA-R); general studies (M Ed, MA Ed, MA-R); human relations (M Ed, MA Ed); literacy education (M Ed, MA Ed, MA-R); school psychology (MASP); teaching English as a second language (M Ed, MA Ed, MA-R). Electronic applications accepted.

MOUNT SINAI SCHOOL OF MEDICINE OF NEW YORK UNIVERSITY, New York, NY 10029-6504

General Information Independent, coed, graduate-only institution. *Graduate housing:* Rooms and/or apartments guaranteed to single and married students. Housing application deadline: 7/1.

GRADUATE UNITS

Graduate School of Biological Sciences Offers bioethics (MS); biophysics, structural biology and biomathematics (PhD); community medicine (MPH); genetic counseling (MS); genetics and genomic sciences (PhD); mechanisms of disease and therapy (PhD); microbiology (PhD); molecular, cellular, biochemical and developmental sciences (PhD); neurosciences (PhD). Electronic applications accepted.

Medical School Offers medicine (MD).

MOUNT VERNON NAZARENE UNIVERSITY, Mount Vernon, OH 43050-9500

General Information Independent-religious, coed, comprehensive institution. *Graduate housing:* On-campus housing not available.

GRADUATE UNITS

Department of Education *Degree program information:* Part-time and evening/weekend programs available. Offers education (MA Ed); professional educator's license (MA Ed).

Program in Management *Degree program information:* Part-time and evening/weekend programs available. Offers management (MSM).

Program in Ministry *Degree program information:* Part-time and evening/weekend programs available. Offers ministry (M Min).

MULTNOMAH BIBLE COLLEGE AND BIBLICAL SEMINARY, Portland, OR 97220-5898

General Information Independent-religious, coed, comprehensive institution. *Enrollment:* 827 graduate, professional, and undergraduate students; 156 full-time matriculated graduate/professional students (40 women), 85 part-time matriculated graduate/professional students (35 women). *Enrollment by degree level:* 131 first professional, 67 master's, 43 other advanced degrees. *Graduate faculty:* 8 full-time (0 women), 15 part-time/adjunct (4 women). *Graduate housing:* Rooms and/or apartments available on a first-come, first-served basis to single and married students. Typical cost: $2,500 per year ($3,500 including board) for single students. Housing application deadline: 7/1. *Student services:* Campus employment opportunities, career counseling, free psychological counseling, international student services. *Library facilities:* John Mitchell Library. *Online resources:* library catalog, access to other libraries' catalogs. *Collection:* 108,297 titles, 378 serial subscriptions, 1,662 audiovisual materials.

Computer facilities: 42 computers available on campus for general student use. A campuswide network can be accessed from student residence rooms and from off campus. Internet access and online class registration are available. *Web address:* http://www.multnomah.edu/.

General Application Contact: Penny Rader, Seminary Admissions Counselor, 503-251-6485, Fax: 503-254-1268, E-mail: admiss@multnomah.edu.

GRADUATE UNITS

Multnomah Biblical Seminary Students: 156 full-time (40 women), 85 part-time (35 women); includes 37 minority (9 African Americans, 1 American Indian/Alaska Native, 23 Asian Americans or Pacific Islanders, 4 Hispanic Americans), 12 international. Average age 34. 163 applicants, 83% accepted, 102 enrolled. *Faculty:* 8 full-time (0 women), 15 part-time/adjunct (4 women). Expenses: Contact institution. *Financial support:* Career-related internships or fieldwork and scholarships/grants available. Support available to part-time students. Financial award application deadline: 7/15; financial award applicants required to submit FAFSA. In 2006, 18 first professional degrees, 24 master's, 33 other advanced degrees awarded. *Degree program information:* Part-time and evening/weekend programs available. Offers biblical studies (MA, Certificate); divinity (M Div); pastoral studies (MA); theology (M Div, MA, Certificate). *Application deadline:* For fall admission, 7/15 priority date for domestic and international students; for spring admission, 11/15 priority date for domestic and international students. Applications are processed on a rolling basis. *Application fee:* $40. *Application Contact:* Penny Rader, Seminary Admissions Counselor, 503-251-6485, Fax: 503-254-1268, E-mail: admiss@multnomah.edu. *Dean,* Dr. Donald L. Brake, 503-255-0332, Fax: 503-251-6444, E-mail: dbrake@multnomah.edu.

MURRAY STATE UNIVERSITY, Murray, KY 42071

General Information State-supported, coed, comprehensive institution. CGS member. *Enrollment:* 10,298 graduate, professional, and undergraduate students; 538 full-time matriculated graduate/professional students (314 women), 1,151 part-time matriculated graduate/professional students (844 women). *Enrollment by degree level:* 1,689 master's. *Graduate faculty:* 354. *Graduate housing:* Rooms and/or apartments available on a first-come, first-served basis to single and married students. *Student services:* Campus employment opportunities, campus safety program, career counseling, child daycare facilities, disabled student services, exercise/wellness program, free psychological counseling, international student services, low-cost health insurance, multicultural affairs office. *Library facilities:* Waterfield Library plus 1 other. *Online resources:* library catalog, web page, access to other libraries' catalogs. *Collection:* 518,450 titles, 1,381 serial subscriptions, 10,885 audiovisual materials.

Computer facilities: Computer purchase and lease plans are available. 1,800 computers available on campus for general student use. A campuswide network can be accessed from student residence rooms and from off campus. Internet access and online class registration are available. *Web address:* http://www.murraystate.edu/.

General Application Contact: Dr. Sandra J. Jordan, University Coordinator of Graduate Studies, 270-809-3027, Fax: 270-809-3565, E-mail: sandra.jordan@murraystate.edu.

GRADUATE UNITS

College of Business and Public Affairs Students: 208 full-time (96 women), 190 part-time (92 women); includes 40 minority (20 African Americans, 5 Asian Americans or Pacific Islanders, 15 Hispanic Americans), 125 international. 150 applicants, 96% accepted. *Faculty:* 61 full-time (10 women). Expenses: Contact institution. *Financial support:* Research assistantships, teaching assistantships, career-related internships or fieldwork and Federal Work-Study available. Financial award application deadline: 4/1. In 2006, 71 degrees awarded. *Degree program information:* Part-time and evening/weekend programs available. Offers business administration (MBA); business and public affairs (MA, MBA, MPAC, MS); economics (MS); mass communications (MA, MS); organizational communication (MA, MS); professional accountancy (MPAC); telecommunications systems management (MS). *Application deadline:* Applications are processed on a rolling basis. *Application fee:* $25. *Dean,* Dr. Dannie Harrison, 270-809-4183, Fax: 270-809-3482, E-mail: dannie.harrison@murraystate.edu.

College of Education Students: 67 full-time (50 women), 899 part-time (720 women); includes 63 minority (55 African Americans, 2 American Indian/Alaska Native, 2 Asian Americans or Pacific Islanders, 4 Hispanic Americans), 20 international. 196 applicants, 100% accepted. *Faculty:* 41 full-time (15 women). Expenses: Contact institution. *Financial support:* Research assistantships, teaching assistantships, Federal Work-Study available. Financial award application deadline: 4/1. *Degree program information:* Part-time programs available. Offers advanced learning behavior disorders (MA Ed); community and agency counseling (Ed S); early childhood education (MA Ed); education (MA Ed, MS, Ed D, PhD, Ed S); elementary education and reading and writing (MA Ed, Ed S); health, physical education, and recreation (MA); human development and leadership (MS); industrial and technical education (MS); learning disabilities (MA Ed); middle school education (MA Ed, Ed S); moderate/severe disorders (MA Ed); reading and writing (MA Ed); school administration (MA Ed, Ed S); school guidance and counseling (MA Ed, Ed S); secondary education (MA Ed, Ed S); special education (MA Ed). *Application deadline:* Applications are processed on a rolling basis. *Application fee:* $20. *Application Contact:* Dr. Ken Purcell, Coordinator of Graduate Programs, 270-809-6123, Fax: 270-809-2540, E-mail: kp@coe.murraystate.edu. *Dean,* Dr. Russ Wall, 270-809-3829, E-mail: russ.wall@coe.murraystate.edu.

College of Health Sciences and Human Services Students: 96 full-time (65 women), 99 part-time (75 women); includes 3 minority (all African Americans), 4 international. Average age 25. 60 applicants, 97% accepted. *Faculty:* 30 full-time (15 women). Expenses: Contact institution. *Financial support:* Research assistantships, teaching assistantships, Federal Work-Study available. Financial award application deadline: 4/1. *Degree program information:* Part-time programs available. Offers clinical nurse specialist (MSN); environmental science (MS); exercise and leisure studies (MS); family nurse practitioner (MSN); health sciences and human services (MS, MSN); industrial hygiene (MS); nurse anesthesia (MSN); safety management (MS); speech-language pathology (MS). *Application deadline:* Applications are processed on a rolling basis. *Application fee:* $25. *Dean,* Dr. Elizabeth Blodgett, 270-809-3970, Fax: 270-809-5403, E-mail: betty.blodgett@murraystate.edu.

College of Humanities and Fine Arts Students: 58 full-time (38 women), 58 part-time (33 women). 38 applicants, 82% accepted. *Faculty:* 88 full-time (28 women). Expenses: Contact institution. *Financial support:* Research assistantships, teaching assistantships, Federal Work-

Murray State University (continued)

Study available. Financial award application deadline: 4/1. In 2006, 45 degrees awarded. *Degree program information:* Part-time programs available. Offers clinical psychology (MA, MS); creative writing (MFA); English (MA); history (MA); humanities and fine arts (MA, MFA, MME, MPA, MS); music education (MME); psychology (MA, MS); public administration (MPA); public affairs (MPA); teaching English to speakers of other languages (MA). *Application deadline:* Applications are processed on a rolling basis. *Application fee:* $25. *Graduate Coordinator*, Dr. Ted Brown, 270-809-4543.

College of Science, Engineering and Technology Students: 71 full-time (34 women), 46 part-time (14 women); includes 14 minority (8 African Americans, 1 American Indian/Alaska Native, 2 Asian Americans or Pacific Islanders, 3 Hispanic Americans), 42 international. 57 applicants, 100% accepted. *Faculty:* 89 full-time (9 women). Expenses: Contact institution. *Financial support:* In 2006–07, research assistantships with partial tuition reimbursements (averaging $7,000 per year), teaching assistantships with partial tuition reimbursements (averaging $7,000 per year) were awarded; Federal Work-Study also available. Financial award application deadline: 4/1. In 2006, 61 degrees awarded. *Degree program information:* Part-time programs available. Offers biological sciences (MAT, MS, PhD); chemistry (MS); geosciences (MS); management of technology (MS); mathematics (MA, MAT, MS); science, engineering and technology (MA, MAT, MS, PhD); water science (MS). *Application deadline:* Applications are processed on a rolling basis. *Application fee:* $25. *Interim ean*, Dr. Neil V. Weber, 270-809-3391, Fax: 270-809-3631.

School of Agriculture Students: 37 full-time (17 women), 22 part-time (8 women); includes 1 minority (African American), 1 international. Average age 25. 18 applicants, 83% accepted. *Faculty:* 10 full-time (0 women). Expenses: Contact institution. *Financial support:* Research assistantships, teaching assistantships, Federal Work-Study available. Financial award application deadline: 4/1. *Degree program information:* Evening/weekend programs available. Postbaccalaureate distance learning degree programs offered (minimal on-campus study). Offers agriculture (MS); agriculture education (MS). *Application deadline:* Applications are processed on a rolling basis. *Application fee:* $25. *Application Contact:* Dr. Jay A. Morgan, Graduate Coordinator, 270-809-6924, Fax: 270-809-5454, E-mail: jay.morgan@murraystate.edu. *Dean*, Dr. Tony L. Brannon, 270-809-6423, Fax: 270-809-5454, E-mail: tony.brannon@murraystate.edu.

MUSKINGUM COLLEGE, New Concord, OH 43762

General Information Independent-religious, coed, comprehensive institution. *Graduate housing:* On-campus housing not available.

GRADUATE UNITS

Graduate Program in Education *Degree program information:* Part-time programs available. Offers education (MAE).

MYERS UNIVERSITY, Cleveland, OH 44114-4624

General Information Independent, coed, comprehensive institution. *Graduate housing:* On-campus housing not available.

GRADUATE UNITS

Charles R. McDonald School of Business *Degree program information:* Part-time and evening/weekend programs available. Postbaccalaureate distance learning degree programs offered (no on-campus study). Offers business (MBA, MFP, MMG).

NAROPA UNIVERSITY, Boulder, CO 80302-6697

General Information Independent, coed, comprehensive institution. *Enrollment:* 1,136 graduate, professional, and undergraduate students; 391 full-time matriculated graduate/professional students (274 women), 243 part-time matriculated graduate/professional students (175 women). *Enrollment by degree level:* 26 first professional, 608 master's. *Graduate faculty:* 39 full-time (18 women), 80 part-time/adjunct (59 women). *Tuition:* Full-time $15,070; part-time $646 per credit. Tuition and fees vary according to course load. *Graduate housing:* On-campus housing not available. *Student services:* Campus employment opportunities, campus safety program, career counseling, disabled student services, international student services, multicultural affairs office, writing training. *Library facilities:* Allen Ginsberg Library. *Online resources:* library catalog, web page. *Collection:* 27,500 titles, 75 serial subscriptions.

Computer facilities: 48 computers available on campus for general student use. A campuswide network can be accessed. Internet access and online class registration are available. *Web address:* http://www.naropa.edu/.

General Application Contact: Office of Admissions, 303-546-3572, Fax: 303-546-3583, E-mail: admissions@naropa.edu.

GRADUATE UNITS

Graduate Programs Students: 391 full-time (274 women), 243 part-time (175 women); includes 43 minority (7 African Americans, 1 American Indian/Alaska Native, 14 Asian Americans or Pacific Islanders, 21 Hispanic Americans), 42 international. Average age 33. 410 applicants, 74% accepted, 231 enrolled. *Faculty:* 35 full-time (14 women), 83 part-time/adjunct (63 women). Expenses: Contact institution. *Financial support:* In 2006–07, 121 students received support, including 11 research assistantships with partial tuition reimbursements available (averaging $3,000 per year), 6 teaching assistantships with partial tuition reimbursements available (averaging $3,000 per year); career-related internships or fieldwork, Federal Work-Study, scholarships/grants, health care benefits, tuition waivers (partial), and unspecified assistantships also available. Support available to part-time students. Financial award application deadline: 3/1; financial award applicants required to submit FAFSA. In 2006, 9 first professional degrees, 262 master's awarded. *Degree program information:* Part-time and evening/weekend programs available. Offers art therapy (MA); body psychotherapy (MA); contemplative education (MA); contemplative psychotherapy (MA); creative writing (MFA); dance/movement therapy (MA); divinity (M Div); ecopsychology (MA); environmental leadership (MA); Indo-Tibetan Buddhism (MA); Indo-Tibetan Buddhism with language (MA); religious studies (MA); religious studies with language (MA); theater: contemporary performance (MFA); theater: Lecoq-based actor-created theater (MFA); transpersonal counseling psychology (MA); transpersonal psychology (MA); wilderness therapy (MA); writing and poetics (MFA). *Application deadline:* For fall admission, 1/15 priority date for domestic and international students; for spring admission, 10/15 priority date for domestic students. Applications are processed on a rolling basis. *Application fee:* $60. Electronic applications accepted. *Application Contact:* Susan Elizabeth Boyle, Dean of Admissions, 303-546-3572, Fax: 303-546-3583, E-mail: sboyle@naropa.edu. *President*, Thomas B. Coburn, 303-546-3517.

NASHOTAH HOUSE, Nashotah, WI 53058-9793

General Information Independent-religious, coed, primarily men, graduate-only institution. *Graduate housing:* Rooms and/or apartments available on a first-come, first-served basis to single and married students. Housing application deadline: 8/15.

GRADUATE UNITS

School of Theology *Degree program information:* Part-time programs available. Offers theology (M Div, MTS, STM, Certificate).

NATIONAL AMERICAN UNIVERSITY, Rapid City, SD 57701

General Information Proprietary, coed, comprehensive institution. *Graduate housing:* Room and/or apartments available on a first-come, first-served basis to single students. Housing application deadline: 6/1.

GRADUATE UNITS

Graduate Programs *Degree program information:* Part-time and evening/weekend programs available. Postbaccalaureate distance learning degree programs offered. Offers business (MBA, MM). Programs also offered in Wichita, KS; Albuquerque, NM; Bloomington, MN; Brooklyn Center, MN; Colorado Springs, CO; Denver, CO; Independence, MO; Overland Park, KS; Rio Rancho, NM; Roseville, MN; Zona Rosa, MO. Electronic applications accepted.

NATIONAL COLLEGE OF MIDWIFERY, Taos, NM 87571

General Information Independent, women only, comprehensive institution.

GRADUATE UNITS

Graduate Programs *Degree program information:* Part-time and evening/weekend programs available. Postbaccalaureate distance learning degree programs offered (no on-campus study). Offers midwifery (MS, PhD). Electronic applications accepted.

NATIONAL COLLEGE OF NATURAL MEDICINE, Portland, OR 97201

General Information Independent, coed, primarily women, graduate-only institution. *Enrollment by degree level:* 118 master's, 365 doctoral. *Graduate faculty:* 23 full-time (9 women), 74 part-time/adjunct (38 women). *Tuition:* Full-time $19,698; part-time $273 per credit. *Required fees:* $60. One-time fee: $50 full-time. Tuition and fees vary according to program. *Graduate housing:* On-campus housing not available. *Student services:* Campus employment opportunities, campus safety program, career counseling, disabled student services, free psychological counseling, grant writing training, international student services, low-cost health insurance. *Library facilities:* National College of Natural Medicine Library plus 2 others. *Online resources:* library catalog, web page, access to other libraries' catalogs. *Collection:* 13,000 titles, 150 serial subscriptions, 1,000 audiovisual materials. *Research affiliation:* Oregon Health and Science University, Kaiser Center for Health Research, Oregon College of Oriental Medicine.

Computer facilities: 18 computers available on campus for general student use. A campuswide network can be accessed. Internet access, VRS Software Programs, WIFI are available. *Web address:* http://www.ncnm.edu/.

General Application Contact: Rigo Nunez, Graduate Director, 503-552-1664, Fax: 203-499-0027, E-mail: admissions@ncmn.edu.

GRADUATE UNITS

Program in Classical Chinese Medicine Students: 116 full-time (84 women), 2 part-time (both women); includes 14 minority (1 African American, 8 Asian Americans or Pacific Islanders, 5 Hispanic Americans). Average age 29. 61 applicants, 89% accepted, 35 enrolled. *Faculty:* 10 full-time (4 women), 21 part-time/adjunct (7 women). Expenses: Contact institution. *Financial support:* In 2006–07, 77 students received support. Federal Work-Study and scholarships/grants available. Financial award application deadline: 4/30; financial award applicants required to submit FAFSA. In 2006, 33 master's awarded. Offers classical Chinese medicine (MSOM). *Application deadline:* For fall admission, 11/1 priority date for domestic and international students; for winter admission, 2/1 priority date for domestic and international students. Applications are processed on a rolling basis. *Application fee:* $75. *Application Contact:* Kendra Lapp, Admissions Coordinator, 503-552-1660, Fax: 503-499-0027, E-mail: admissions@ncnm.edu. *Dean*, Dr. Laurie Regan, 503-552-1775, Fax: 503-499-0027, E-mail: admissions@ncnm.edu.

Program in Naturopathic Medicine Students: 382 full-time (308 women); includes 44 minority (4 African Americans, 2 American Indian/Alaska Native, 11 Asian Americans or Pacific Islanders, 27 Hispanic Americans), 4 international. Average age 29. 199 applicants, 83% accepted, 97 enrolled. *Faculty:* 13 full-time (5 women), 53 part-time/adjunct (31 women). Expenses: Contact institution. *Financial support:* In 2006–07, 308 students received support. Federal Work-Study and scholarships/grants available. Financial award application deadline: 4/30; financial award applicants required to submit FAFSA. In 2006, 65 degrees awarded. Offers naturopathic medicine (ND). *Application deadline:* For fall admission, 11/1 priority date for domestic and international students; for winter admission, 2/1 priority date for domestic and international students. Applications are processed on a rolling basis. *Application fee:* $75. *Application Contact:* Kendra Lapp, Admissions Coordinator, 503-552-1660, Fax: 503-499-0027, E-mail: admissions@ncnm.edu. *Dean*, Dr. Rita Bettenburg, 503-552-1761, Fax: 503-499-0022, E-mail: rbettenburg@ncnm.edu.

NATIONAL DEFENSE UNIVERSITY, Washington, DC 20319-5066

General Information Federally supported, coed, graduate-only institution. *Enrollment by degree level:* 533 master's. *Graduate faculty:* 145 full-time. *Student services:* Exercise/wellness program, international student services. *Library facilities:* NDU Library plus 1 other. *Online resources:* web page. *Collection:* 500,000 titles.

Computer facilities: 1,500 computers available on campus for general student use. A campuswide network can be accessed from off campus. Internet access is available. *Web address:* http://www.ndu.edu/.

General Application Contact: Dr. Susan Martin Studds, Acting Provost, 202-685-3935, Fax: 202-685-3860, E-mail: studdss@ndu.edu.

GRADUATE UNITS

Industrial College of the Armed Forces Students: 312 full-time. *Faculty:* 87 full-time. Expenses: Contact institution. In 2006, 296 degrees awarded. Offers national resource strategy (MS). Open only to Department of Defense employees and specific federal agencies. *Commandant*, Rear Adm. Gerard M. Mauer, 202-685-4333.

Joint Advanced Warfighting School Students: 36 full-time. Expenses: Contact institution. In 2006, 25 degrees awarded. Offers joint campaign planning and strategy (MS). Open only to Department of Defense employees and specific federal agencies. *Commandant*, Maj. Gen. Byron S. Bagby, 757-443-6301.

National War College Students: 221 full-time. *Faculty:* 62 full-time (10 women). Expenses: Contact institution. In 2006, 200 degrees awarded. Offers national security strategy (MS). Open only to Department of Defense employees and specific federal agencies. *Commandant*, Brig. Gen. Robert P. Steel, 202-685-2128, Fax: 202-685-3993.

THE NATIONAL GRADUATE SCHOOL OF QUALITY MANAGEMENT, Falmouth, MA 02541

General Information Independent, coed, graduate-only institution.

GRADUATE UNITS

Program in Quality Systems Management Offers e-commerce (MS); management (MS); six sigma (MS).

NATIONAL-LOUIS UNIVERSITY, Chicago, IL 60603

General Information Independent, coed, university. *Enrollment:* 1,391 full-time matriculated graduate/professional students (1,042 women), 3,830 part-time matriculated graduate/professional students (3,020 women). *Enrollment by degree level:* 4,623 master's, 273 doctoral, 325 other advanced degrees. *Graduate faculty:* 246 full-time (163 women), 856 part-time/adjunct (574 women). *Tuition:* Full-time $17,685. One-time fee: $40 full-time. *Graduate housing:* Room and/or apartments available on a first-come, first-served basis to single students; on-campus housing not available to married students. *Student services:* Campus employment opportunities, career counseling, disabled student services, international student services, low-cost health insurance, teacher training, writing training. *Library facilities:* NLU Library plus 5 others. *Online resources:* library catalog. *Collection:* 5,043 audiovisual materials.

Computer facilities: A campuswide network can be accessed from off campus. Internet access is available. *Web address:* http://www.nl.edu/.

General Application Contact: Dr. Larry Poselli, Vice President of Enrollment Management, 312-261-3021, Fax: 312-261-3726, E-mail: lposelli@nl.edu.

GRADUATE UNITS

College of Arts and Sciences Students: 69 full-time (59 women), 488 part-time (404 women); includes 197 minority (160 African Americans, 3 American Indian/Alaska Native, 9 Asian Americans or Pacific Islanders, 25 Hispanic Americans), 1 international. Average age 39. 148 applicants, 98% accepted. *Faculty:* 77 full-time (48 women), 554 part-time/adjunct (359 women). Expenses: Contact institution. *Financial support:* Career-related internships or fieldwork, Federal Work-Study, institutionally sponsored loans, scholarships/grants, and tuition waivers available. Support available to part-time students. Financial award applicants required to submit FAFSA. In 2006, 87 master's, 8 other advanced degrees awarded. *Degree program information:* Part-time and evening/weekend programs available. Postbaccalaureate distance learning degree programs offered (minimal on-campus study). Offers addictions counseling (Certificate); addictions treatment (Certificate); arts and sciences (M Ed, MA, MS, Ed D, Certificate); career counseling and development studies (Certificate); community counseling (MS); community wellness and prevention (Certificate); counseling (Certificate); cultural psychology (MA); eating disorders counseling (Certificate); employee assistance programs (MS, Certificate); gerontology administration (Certificate); gerontology counseling (MS, Certificate); health psychology (MA); human development (MA); human services administration (MS, Certificate); long-term care administration (Certificate); organizational psychology (MA); psychology (Certificate); school counseling (MS); written communication (MS). *Application fee:* $40. *Application Contact:* Ken G. Kabira, Senior Vice President and Chief Marketing Officer, 312-261-3021, Fax: 312-261-3726, E-mail: ken.g.kabira@nl.edu. *Coordinator,* Dr. Martha Casazza, 847-475-1100 Ext. 3992, E-mail: mcasazza@nl.edu.

Division of Language and Academic Development Students: 15 full-time (13 women), 48 part-time (39 women); includes 18 minority (14 African Americans, 1 American Indian/Alaska Native, 1 Asian American or Pacific Islander, 2 Hispanic Americans). Average age 46. 24 applicants, 100% accepted. Expenses: Contact institution. *Financial support:* Fellowships, research assistantships, career-related internships or fieldwork, Federal Work-Study, institutionally sponsored loans, scholarships/grants, and tuition waivers available. Support available to part-time students. Financial award application deadline: 4/15; financial award applicants required to submit FAFSA. In 2006, 23 master's, 2 other advanced degrees awarded. *Degree program information:* Part-time programs available. Postbaccalaureate distance learning degree programs offered (minimal on-campus study). Offers adult education (Ed D); adult literacy and developmental studies (M Ed, Certificate); adult, continuing, and literacy education (M Ed, Certificate). *Application fee:* $25. *Application Contact:* David McCulloch, Vice President for University Services, 800-443-5522 Ext. 5127, Fax: 847-465-0593, E-mail: dmcc@wheeling1.nl.edu. *Dean,* Judith Kent, 847-475-1100 Ext. 3416.

College of Management and Business Students: 188 full-time (121 women), 14 part-time (7 women); includes 36 minority (7 African Americans, 1 American Indian/Alaska Native, 9 Asian Americans or Pacific Islanders, 19 Hispanic Americans), 1 international. Average age 36. 107 applicants, 99% accepted. *Faculty:* 26 full-time (9 women), 352 part-time/adjunct (102 women). Expenses: Contact institution. *Financial support:* Federal Work-Study, institutionally sponsored loans, and scholarships/grants available. Support available to part-time students. Financial award applicants required to submit FAFSA. In 2006, 251 degrees awarded. *Degree program information:* Part-time and evening/weekend programs available. Offers business administration (MBA); human resource management and development (MS); management (MS); management and business (MBA, MS). *Application deadline:* Applications are processed on a rolling basis. *Application fee:* $25. *Application Contact:* David McCulloch, Vice President for University Services, 800-443-5522 Ext. 5127, Fax: 847-465-0593, E-mail: dmcc@wheeling1.nl.edu. *Dean,* Dr. Richard Magner, 312-261-3850, E-mail: rmagner@nl.edu.

National College of Education Students: 1,127 full-time (855 women), 2,682 part-time (2,020 women); includes 731 minority (429 African Americans, 8 American Indian/Alaska Native, 77 Asian Americans or Pacific Islanders, 217 Hispanic Americans). Average age 35. 721 applicants, 99% accepted. *Faculty:* 163 full-time (118 women), 588 part-time/adjunct (416 women). Expenses: Contact institution. *Financial support:* Fellowships, research assistantships, teaching assistantships, career-related internships or fieldwork, Federal Work-Study, institutionally sponsored loans, and scholarships/grants available. Support available to part-time students. Financial award applicants required to submit FAFSA. In 2006, 1,503 master's, 13 doctorates, 70 other advanced degrees awarded. *Degree program information:* Part-time and evening/weekend programs available. Offers administration and supervision (M Ed, CAS, Ed S); adult education (Ed D); curriculum and instruction (M Ed, MS Ed, CAS); curriculum and social inquiry (Ed D); early childhood administration (M Ed, CAS); early childhood curriculum and instruction specialist (M Ed, MS Ed, CAS); early childhood education (M Ed, MAT, CAS); education (M Ed, MAT, MS Ed, Ed D, CAS, Ed S); educational leadership (Ed D); educational leadership/superintendent endorsement (Ed D); educational psychology (CAS, Ed S); educational psychology/human learning and development (M Ed, MS Ed); educational psychology/school psychology (Ed D); elementary education (MAT); general special education (M Ed, MAT, CAS); human learning and development (Ed D); interdisciplinary studies in curriculum and instruction (M Ed); language and literacy (M Ed, MS Ed, CAS); learning disabilities (M Ed, CAS); learning disabilities/behavior disorders (M Ed, MAT, CAS); mathematics education (M Ed, MS Ed, CAS); reading and language (Ed D); reading recovery (CAS); reading specialist (M Ed, MS Ed, CAS); school psychology (M Ed, Ed S); science education (M Ed, MS Ed, CAS); secondary education (MAT); technology in education (M Ed, MS Ed, CAS). *Application deadline:* Applications are processed on a rolling basis. *Application fee:* $25. *Application Contact:* David McCulloch, Vice President for University Services, 800-443-5522 Ext. 5127, Fax: 847-465-0593, E-mail: dmcc@wheeling1.nl.edu. *Dean,* Dr. Alison Hilsobeck, 847-475-1100 Ext. 5336.

NATIONAL THEATRE CONSERVATORY, Denver, CO 80204-2157

General Information Independent, coed, graduate-only institution. *Enrollment by degree level:* 23 master's. *Graduate faculty:* 4 full-time (1 woman), 12 part-time/adjunct (2 women). *Graduate housing:* On-campus housing not available. *Student services:* Campus employment opportunities, career counseling, free psychological counseling. *Library facilities:* Jones Library of the National Theatre Conservatory. *Online resources:* library catalog, access to other libraries' catalogs. *Collection:* 34,000 titles, 15 serial subscriptions, 2,105 audiovisual materials.

Computer facilities: 8 computers available on campus for general student use. A campuswide network can be accessed from off campus. Internet access and online class registration are available. *Web address:* http://www.denvercenter.org/.

General Application Contact: Kate R. Amberg, Registrar, 303-446-4855, Fax: 303-623-0693, E-mail: ntc@dcpa.org.

GRADUATE UNITS

Department of Acting Students: 23 full-time (9 women); includes 6 minority (2 African Americans, 4 Hispanic Americans). Average age 26. 451 applicants, 2% accepted, 7 enrolled. *Faculty:* 4 full-time (1 woman), 12 part-time/adjunct (2 women). Expenses: Contact institution. *Financial support:* Career-related internships or fieldwork and scholarships/grants available. In 2006, 8 degrees awarded. Offers acting (MFA, Certificate). *Application deadline:* For fall admission, 1/11 for domestic students. *Application fee:* $60. *Application Contact:* Kate R. Amberg, Registrar, 303-446-4855, Fax: 303-623-0693, E-mail: ntc@dcpa.org. *Director of Education,* Daniel Renner, 303-446-4855, Fax: 303-623-0693, E-mail: renner@dcpa.org.

NATIONAL UNIVERSITY, La Jolla, CA 92037-1011

General Information Independent, coed, comprehensive institution. CGS member. *Enrollment:* 25,992 graduate, professional, and undergraduate students; 6,652 full-time matriculated graduate/professional students (4,423 women), 12,152 part-time matriculated graduate/professional students (7,594 women). *Enrollment by degree level:* 18,804 master's. *Graduate faculty:* 201 full-time (88 women), 2,974 part-time/adjunct (1,455 women). *Tuition:* Full-time $7,722; part-time $286 per unit. One-time fee: $60. *Graduate housing:* On-campus housing not available. *Student services:* Campus employment opportunities, campus safety program, career counseling, disabled student services, international student services, multicultural affairs office, teacher training, writing training. *Library facilities:* Central Library. *Online resources:* library catalog, web page. *Collection:* 250,000 titles, 18,889 serial subscriptions, 17,884 audiovisual materials.

Computer facilities: 2,253 computers available on campus for general student use. A campuswide network can be accessed from off campus. Internet access and online class registration are available. *Web address:* http://www.nu.edu/.

General Application Contact: Dominick Giovanniello, Associate Regional Dean—San Diego, 800-NAT-UNIV, Fax: 858-642-8709, E-mail: dgiovann@nu.edu.

GRADUATE UNITS

Academic Affairs Students: 6,655 full-time (4,423 women), 12,159 part-time (7,594 women); includes 5,539 minority (1,622 African Americans, 117 American Indian/Alaska Native, 1,125 Asian Americans or Pacific Islanders, 2,675 Hispanic Americans), 252 international. Average age 36. 10,349 applicants, 9330 enrolled. *Faculty:* 201 full-time (88 women), 2,974 part-time/adjunct (1,455 women). Expenses: Contact institution. *Financial support:* Career-related internships or fieldwork, institutionally sponsored loans, scholarships/grants, and tuition waivers (partial) available. Support available to part-time students. Financial award application deadline: 6/30; financial award applicants required to submit FAFSA. In 2006, 3118 degrees awarded. *Degree program information:* Part-time and evening/weekend programs available. Postbaccalaureate distance learning degree programs offered (no on-campus study). *Application deadline:* Applications are processed on a rolling basis. *Application fee:* $60 ($65 for international students). Electronic applications accepted. *Application Contact:* Dominick Giovanniello, Associate Regional Dean—San Diego, 800-NAT-UNIV, Fax: 858-642-8709, E-mail: dgiovann@nu.edu. *Senior Vice President of Academic Affairs,* Dr. Thomas M. Green, 858-642-8106, Fax: 858-642-8719, E-mail: acooper@nu.edu.

College of Letters and Sciences Students: 529 full-time (415 women), 573 part-time (423 women); includes 297 minority (126 African Americans, 4 American Indian/Alaska Native, 48 Asian Americans or Pacific Islanders, 119 Hispanic Americans), 8 international. Average age 36. 733 applicants, 619 enrolled. *Faculty:* 50 full-time (21 women), 595 part-time/adjunct (311 women). Expenses: Contact institution. *Financial support:* Career-related internships or fieldwork, institutionally sponsored loans, scholarships/grants, and tuition waivers (partial) available. Support available to part-time students. Financial award application deadline: 6/30; financial award applicants required to submit FAFSA. In 2006, 260 degrees awarded. *Degree program information:* Part-time and evening/weekend programs available. Postbaccalaureate distance learning degree programs offered (no on-campus study). Offers counseling psychology (MA); creative writing (MFA); English (MA); human behavior (MA); industrial organizational psychology (MS); letters and sciences (MA, MFA, MS). *Application deadline:* Applications are processed on a rolling basis. *Application fee:* $60 ($65 for international students). Electronic applications accepted. *Application Contact:* Dominick Giovanniello, Associate Regional Dean—San Diego, 800-NAT-UNIV, Fax: 858-642-8709, E-mail: dgiovann@nu.edu. *Dean,* Dr. Michael Mcanear, 858-642-8430, Fax: 858-642-8715, E-mail: mcanear@nu.edu.

School of Business and Management Students: 808 full-time (422 women), 1,458 part-time (753 women); includes 817 minority (251 African Americans, 12 American Indian/Alaska Native, 262 Asian Americans or Pacific Islanders, 292 Hispanic Americans), 173 international. Average age 35. 1,413 applicants, 1220 enrolled. *Faculty:* 38 full-time (8 women), 528 part-time/adjunct (133 women). Expenses: Contact institution. *Financial support:* Career-related internships or fieldwork, scholarships/grants, and tuition waivers (partial) available. Support available to part-time students. Financial award application deadline: 6/30; financial award applicants required to submit FAFSA. In 2006, 550 degrees awarded. *Degree program information:* Part-time and evening/weekend programs available. Postbaccalaureate distance learning degree programs offered (no on-campus study). Offers business and management (EMBA, MA, MBA, MFS, MS); e-business (MS); finance (MS); finance, accounting, and economics (EMBA, MBA); forensic science (MFS); human resource management and organizational development (MA); management (MA); organizational leadership (MS); taxation (MS). *Application deadline:* Applications are processed on a rolling basis. *Application fee:* $60 ($65 for international students). Electronic applications accepted. *Application Contact:* Dominick Giovanniello, Associate Regional Dean—San Diego, 800-NAT-UNIV, Fax: 858-642-8709, E-mail: dgiovann@nu.edu. *Dean,* Dr. Wali Mondal, 858-642-8439, Fax: 858-642-8406, E-mail: wmondal@nu.edu.

School of Education Students: 5,069 full-time (3,477 women), 9,206 part-time (5,886 women); includes 4,077 minority (1,132 African Americans, 91 American Indian/Alaska Native, 723 Asian Americans or Pacific Islanders, 2,131 Hispanic Americans), 39 international. Average age 36. 7,948 applicants, 7313 enrolled. *Faculty:* 79 full-time (45 women), 1,560 part-time/adjunct (895 women). Expenses: Contact institution. *Financial support:* Career-related internships or fieldwork, institutionally sponsored loans, scholarships/grants, and tuition waivers (partial) available. Support available to part-time students. Financial award application deadline: 6/30. In 2006, 2556 degrees awarded. *Degree program information:* Part-time and evening/weekend programs available. Postbaccalaureate distance learning degree programs offered (no on-campus study). Offers best practices (MA); cross-cultural teaching (M Ed); deaf and hard of hearing education (MS); education (M Ed, MA, MS); educational administration (MS); educational counseling (MS); educational technology (MS); exceptional student education (MS); school psychology (MS); special education (MS); teaching (MA). *Application deadline:* Applications are processed on a rolling basis. *Application fee:* $60 ($65 for international students). Electronic applications accepted. *Application Contact:* Dominick Giovanniello, Associate Regional Dean—San Diego, 800-NAT-UNIV, Fax: 858-642-8709, E-mail: dgiovann@nu.edu. *Dean,* Dr. Gloria Johnston, 858-642-8320, E-mail: gjohnsto@nu.edu.

School of Engineering and Technology Students: 88 full-time (18 women), 117 part-time (29 women); includes 82 minority (21 African Americans, 1 American Indian/Alaska Native, 36 Asian Americans or Pacific Islanders, 24 Hispanic Americans), 26 international. Average age 36. 278 applicants, 199 enrolled. *Faculty:* 14 full-time (1 woman), 165 part-time/adjunct (24 women). Expenses: Contact institution. *Financial support:* Career-related internships or fieldwork, institutionally sponsored loans, scholarships/grants, and tuition waivers (partial) available. Support available to part-time students. Financial award application deadline: 6/30; financial award applicants required to submit FAFSA. In 2006, 76 degrees awarded. *Degree program information:* Part-time and evening/weekend programs available. Postbaccalaureate distance learning degree programs offered (no on-campus study). Offers computer science (MS); database administration (MS); engineering and technology (MS); engineering management (MS); environmental engineering (MS); homeland security and safety engineering (MS); information systems (MS); software engineering (MS); system engineering (MS); technology management (MS); wireless communications (MS). *Application deadline:* Applications are processed on a rolling basis. *Application fee:* $60 ($65 for international students). Electronic applications accepted. *Application Contact:* Dominick Giovanniello, Associate Regional Dean—San Diego, 800-NAT-UNIV, Fax: 858-642-8709, E-mail: dgiovann@nu.edu. *Dean,* Dr. Howard Evans, 858-642-8482, Fax: 858-642-8489, E-mail: hevans@nu.edu.

School of Health and Human Services Students: 6 full-time (5 women), 8 part-time (3 women); includes 6 minority (2 African Americans, 4 Hispanic Americans). Average age 33. 16 applicants, 12 enrolled. *Faculty:* 2 full-time (0 women), 1 (woman) part-time/adjunct. Expenses: Contact institution. *Financial support:* Career-related internships or fieldwork, institutionally sponsored loans, and scholarships/grants available. Support available to part-time students. Financial award application deadline: 6/30; financial award applicants required to submit FAFSA. *Degree program information:* Part-time and evening/weekend programs available. Postbaccalaureate distance learning degree programs offered (no on-campus study). Offers health and human services (MHCA, MS); health care administration (MS). *Application deadline:* Applications are processed on a rolling basis. *Application fee:* $60 ($65 for international students). Electronic applications accepted. *Application Contact:* Dominick Giovanniello, Associate Regional Dean—San Diego, 800-NAT-UNIV, Fax: 858-642-8709, E-mail: dgiovann@nu.edu. *Interim Dean,* Dr. Thomas M. Green, 858-642-8107, Fax: 858-642-8716, E-mail: tgreen@nu.edu.

School of Media and Communication Students: 71 full-time (31 women), 138 part-time (66 women); includes 54 minority (22 African Americans, 1 American Indian/Alaska Native, 13 Asian Americans or Pacific Islanders, 18 Hispanic Americans). Average age 39. 179 applicants, 167 enrolled. *Faculty:* 11 full-time (5 women), 23 part-time/adjunct (8 women). Expenses: Contact institution. *Financial support:* Career-related internships or fieldwork, institutionally sponsored loans, scholarships/grants, and tuition waivers (partial) available. Support available to part-time students. Financial award application deadline: 6/30; financial award applicants required to submit FAFSA. In 2006, 29 degrees awarded. *Degree program information:* Part-time and evening/weekend programs available. Postbaccalaureate distance learning degree programs offered (no on-campus study). Offers digital cinema (MFA); educational and instructional technology (MS); media (MFA, MS); video game production and design (MFA). *Application deadline:* Applications are processed on a rolling basis.

National University (continued)

Application fee: $60 ($65 for international students). Electronic applications accepted. *Application Contact:* Dominick Giovanniello, Associate Regional Dean—San Diego, 800-NAT-UNIV, Fax: 858-642-8709, E-mail: dgiovann@nu.edu. *Dean,* Debra B. Schneiger, 858-642-8424, Fax: 858-642-8743, E-mail: dschneiger@nu.edu.

NATIONAL UNIVERSITY OF HEALTH SCIENCES, Lombard, IL 60148-4583

General Information Independent, coed, graduate-only institution. *Enrollment:* 341 full-time matriculated graduate/professional students (153 women). *Enrollment by degree level:* 341 first professional. *Graduate faculty:* 49 full-time (10 women), 40 part-time/adjunct (15 women). *Tuition:* Full-time $16,187. Full-time tuition and fees vary according to course load. *Graduate housing:* Rooms and/or apartments available on a first-come, first-served basis to single and married students. Typical cost: $5,936 per year for single students; $6,398 per year for married students. Room charges vary according to housing facility selected. *Student services:* Campus employment opportunities, campus safety program, career counseling. *Library facilities:* NUHS—Learning Resource Center. *Online resources:* library catalog. *Collection:* 28,440 titles, 335 serial subscriptions, 2,220 audiovisual materials.

Computer facilities: 72 computers available on campus for general student use. A campuswide network can be accessed. Internet access and online class registration, student email, course documents are available. *Web address:* http://www.nuhs.edu/.

General Application Contact: Victoria Sweeney, Director of Admissions, 800-826-6285 Ext. 6572, Fax: 630-889-6554, E-mail: vsweeney@nuhs.edu.

GRADUATE UNITS

College of Professional Studies Students: 394 full-time (186 women); includes 80 minority (19 African Americans, 47 Asian Americans or Pacific Islanders, 14 Hispanic Americans), 12 international. Average age 27. *Faculty:* 49 full-time (10 women), 40 part-time/adjunct (15 women). Expenses: Contact institution. *Financial support:* Fellowships, research assistantships, teaching assistantships, Federal Work-Study, scholarships/grants, and tuition waivers (partial) available. Support available to part-time students. Financial award applicants required to submit FAFSA. In 2006, 86 DCs, 2 master's awarded. Offers acupuncture (MSAC); chiropractic medicine (DC); naturopathic medicine (ND); Oriental medicine (MSOM). *Application deadline:* For fall admission, 8/22 for domestic and international students; for winter admission, 11/22 for domestic and international students; for spring admission, 4/18 for domestic and international students. Applications are processed on a rolling basis. *Application fee:* $55. Electronic applications accepted. *Application Contact:* Victoria Sweeney, Director of Admissions, 800-826-6285 Ext. 6572, Fax: 630-889-6554, E-mail: v.sweeney@nuhs.edu. *President,* Dr. James F. Winterstein, 630-889-6604, Fax: 630-889-6600, E-mail: jwinterstein@nuhs.edu.

NAVAL POSTGRADUATE SCHOOL, Monterey, CA 93943

General Information Federally supported, coed, graduate-only institution. CGS member. *Graduate housing:* Rooms and/or apartments available to single and married students.

GRADUATE UNITS

Graduate Programs *Degree program information:* Part-time programs available. Postbaccalaureate distance learning degree programs offered (minimal on-campus study). Offers applied mathematics (MS, PhD); applied physics (MS); applied science (MS); computer science (MS, PhD); defense analysis (MS); electrical and computer engineering (MS, PhD, Eng); electrical engineering (MS); engineering acoustics (MS); information sciences (MS); intelligence (MA); international relations (MA); joint information operations (MS); knowledge superiority (MS, Certificate); mechanical and astronautical engineering (MS, D Eng, PhD, Eng); meteorology (MS, PhD); modeling of virtual environments and simulations (MS, PhD); oceanography (MS, PhD); operations research (MS); physical oceanography (MS); physics (MS, PhD); political science (MA); regional security education (MA); security building (MA); security studies (MA); software engineering (MS, PhD); space systems operations (MS); special operations (MS); systems engineering (MS, PhD, Certificate); systems engineering and analysis (MS); systems engineering management (MS). Programs only open to commissioned officers of the United States and friendly nations and selected United States federal civilian employees.

School of Business and Public Policy *Degree program information:* Part-time programs available. Postbaccalaureate distance learning degree programs offered (minimal on-campus study). Offers contract management (MS); defense-focused business administration (MBA); executive business administration (MBA); leadership and human resource development (MS); management (MS); program management (MS); systems engineering management (MS). Program only open to commissioned officers of the United States and friendly nations and selected United States federal civilian employees.

NAVAL WAR COLLEGE, Newport, RI 02841-1207

General Information Federally supported, coed, primarily men, graduate-only institution.

GRADUATE UNITS

Program in National Security and Strategic Studies Offers national security and strategic studies (MA). Program open only to full-time military personnel.

NAZARENE THEOLOGICAL SEMINARY, Kansas City, MO 64131-1263

General Information Independent-religious, coed, graduate-only institution. *Enrollment by degree level:* 232 first professional, 61 master's, 14 doctoral. *Graduate faculty:* 20 full-time (3 women), 12 part-time/adjunct (2 women). *Tuition:* Full-time $8,136; part-time $339 per credit. *Required fees:* $75 per semester. *Graduate housing:* On-campus housing not available. *Student services:* Campus employment opportunities, career counseling, free psychological counseling, international student services, low-cost health insurance. *Library facilities:* William Broadhurst Library. *Online resources:* library catalog, web page, access to other libraries' catalogs. *Collection:* 107,229 titles, 547 serial subscriptions, 2,272 audiovisual materials. *Research affiliation:* University of Missouri-Kansas City (religious studies).

Computer facilities: 10 computers available on campus for general student use. A campuswide network can be accessed from off campus. Internet access is available. *Web address:* http://www.nts.edu/.

General Application Contact: Jay A. Sandbloom, Director of Admissions, 816-333-6254 Ext. 211, Fax: 816-333-6271, E-mail: jasandbloom@nts.edu.

GRADUATE UNITS

Graduate and Professional Programs Students: 166 full-time (46 women), 141 part-time (34 women); includes 23 minority (9 African Americans, 2 American Indian/Alaska Native, 4 Asian Americans or Pacific Islanders, 8 Hispanic Americans), 4 international. Average age 31. 115 applicants, 83% accepted, 78 enrolled. *Faculty:* 20 full-time (3 women), 12 part-time/adjunct (2 women). Expenses: Contact institution. *Financial support:* In 2006–07, 235 students received support, including 15 teaching assistantships (averaging $1,400 per year); institutionally sponsored loans and scholarships/grants also available. Support available to part-time students. Financial award application deadline: 3/1; financial award applicants required to submit FAFSA. In 2006, 37 M Divs, 24 master's, 9 doctorates awarded. *Degree program information:* Part-time programs available. Offers Christian education (MA); intercultural studies (MA); theological studies (MA); theology (M Div, D Min). *Application deadline:* For fall admission, 8/1 priority date for domestic students; for spring admission, 12/1 for domestic students. Applications are processed on a rolling basis. *Application fee:* $25 ($200 for international students). Electronic applications accepted. *Application Contact:* Jay A. Sandbloom, Director of Admissions, 816-333-6254 Ext. 211, Fax: 816-333-6271, E-mail: jasandbloom@nts.edu. *Dean of the Faculty,* Dr. Roger L. Hahn, 816-333-6254 Ext. 220, Fax: 816-333-6271, E-mail: rlhahn@nts.edu.

NAZARETH COLLEGE OF ROCHESTER, Rochester, NY 14618-3790

General Information Independent, coed, comprehensive institution. *Enrollment:* 3,179 graduate, professional, and undergraduate students; 423 full-time matriculated graduate/professional students (360 women), 675 part-time matriculated graduate/professional students (549 women). *Enrollment by degree level:* 1,098 master's. *Graduate faculty:* 93. *Graduate housing:* On-campus housing not available. *Student services:* Campus employment opportunities, campus safety program, career counseling, child daycare facilities, disabled student services, free psychological counseling, international student services, multicultural affairs office, teacher training. *Library facilities:* Lorette Wilmot Library. *Online resources:* library catalog, web page, access to other libraries' catalogs. *Collection:* 283,248 titles, 16,102 serial subscriptions.

Computer facilities: 150 computers available on campus for general student use. A campuswide network can be accessed from student residence rooms and from off campus. Internet access is available. *Web address:* http://www.naz.edu/.

General Application Contact: Judith G. Baker, Director, Graduate Admissions, 585-389-2050, Fax: 585-389-2817, E-mail: gradstudies@naz.edu.

GRADUATE UNITS

Graduate Studies Students: 423 full-time (360 women), 675 part-time (549 women); includes 111 minority (57 African Americans, 11 American Indian/Alaska Native, 19 Asian Americans or Pacific Islanders, 24 Hispanic Americans), 2 international. Average age 33. 614 applicants, 85% accepted, 296 enrolled. *Faculty:* 34 full-time (21 women), 54 part-time/adjunct (39 women). Expenses: Contact institution. *Financial support:* In 2006–07, 40 research assistantships with partial tuition reimbursements were awarded; career-related internships or fieldwork and scholarships/grants also available. Support available to part-time students. Financial award application deadline: 3/1; financial award applicants required to submit FAFSA. In 2006, 443 degrees awarded. *Degree program information:* Part-time and evening/weekend programs available. Postbaccalaureate distance learning degree programs offered. Offers art education (MS Ed); art therapy (MS); business education (MS Ed); communication sciences and disorders (MS); creative arts therapy (MS); educational technology/computer education (MS Ed); gerontological nurse practitioner (MS); human resource management (MS); inclusive education-adolescence level (MS Ed); inclusive education-childhood level (MS Ed); inclusive education-early childhood level (MS Ed); liberal studies (MA); literacy education (MS Ed); management (MS); music education (MS Ed); music therapy (MS); physical therapy (MS, DPT); social work (MSW); teaching English to speakers of other languages (MS Ed). *Application deadline:* For fall admission, 4/1 for domestic students; for spring admission, 10/1 for domestic students. Applications are processed on a rolling basis. *Application fee:* $40. *Application Contact:* Judith G. Baker, Director, Graduate Admissions, 585-389-2050, Fax: 585-389-2817, E-mail: gradstudies@naz.edu. *Associate Vice President for Graduate Studies,* Dr. Kay F. Marshman, 585-389-2815, Fax: 585-389-2817, E-mail: gradstudies@naz.edu.

NEBRASKA METHODIST COLLEGE, Omaha, NE 68114

General Information Independent-religious, coed, primarily women, comprehensive institution. *Enrollment:* 512 graduate, professional, and undergraduate students; 66 full-time matriculated graduate/professional students (65 women). *Enrollment by degree level:* 66 master's. *Graduate faculty:* 9 full-time (all women), 19 part-time/adjunct (9 women). *Tuition:* Part-time $486 per credit hour. *Required fees:* $25 per credit hour. Full-time tuition and fees vary according to program. *Graduate housing:* Room and/or apartments available on a first-come, first-served basis to single students; on-campus housing not available to married students. Housing application deadline: 4/1. *Student services:* Campus employment opportunities, campus safety program, career counseling, disabled student services, exercise/wellness program, free psychological counseling, grant writing training, international student services, low-cost health insurance, teacher training, writing training. *Library facilities:* John Moritz Library plus 1 other. *Online resources:* web page. *Collection:* 8,656 titles, 475 serial subscriptions.

Computer facilities: 45 computers available on campus for general student use. A campuswide network can be accessed. Internet access is available. *Web address:* http://www.methodistcollege.edu/.

General Application Contact: Deann Sterner, Director of Admissions, 402-354-7200, Fax: 402-354-7020, E-mail: admissions@methodistcollege.edu.

GRADUATE UNITS

Program in Health Promotion Management Students: 20 full-time (all women); includes 1 minority (Hispanic American) Average age 34. 19 applicants, 84% accepted, 13 enrolled. *Faculty:* 9 part-time/adjunct (5 women). Expenses: Contact institution. *Financial support:* In 2006–07, 13 students received support; research assistantships with full and partial tuition reimbursements available, scholarships/grants available. Support available to part-time students. Financial award applicants required to submit FAFSA. In 2006, 10 degrees awarded. *Degree program information:* Evening/weekend programs available. Postbaccalaureate distance learning degree programs offered (minimal on-campus study). Offers health promotion management (MS). *Application deadline:* Applications are processed on a rolling basis. *Application fee:* $25. *Application Contact:* Deann Sterner, Director of Admissions, 402-354-7200, Fax: 402-354-7020, E-mail: admissions@methodistcollege.edu. *Program Director,* Sarah Bonney, 402-354-7200, Fax: 402-354-7020.

Program in Nursing Students: 40 full-time (all women); includes 2 minority (1 African American, 1 Asian American or Pacific Islander). Average age 41. 25 applicants, 84% accepted, 17 enrolled. *Faculty:* 7 full-time (all women), 3 part-time/adjunct (all women). Expenses: Contact institution. *Financial support:* In 2006–07, 13 students received support; research assistantships with full and partial tuition reimbursements available, scholarships/grants available. Support available to part-time students. Financial award applicants required to submit FAFSA. In 2006, 14 degrees awarded. *Degree program information:* Evening/weekend programs available. Postbaccalaureate distance learning degree programs offered (minimal on-campus study). Offers nursing (MSN). *Application deadline:* For spring admission, 11/1 for domestic and international students. Applications are processed on a rolling basis. *Application fee:* $25. *Application Contact:* Deann Sterner, Director of Admissions, 402-354-7200, Fax: 402-354-7020, E-mail: admissions@methodistcollege.edu. *Program Chair,* Linda Foley, 402-354-7050, Fax: 402-354-7020, E-mail: linda.foley@methodistcollege.edu.

NEBRASKA WESLEYAN UNIVERSITY, Lincoln, NE 68504-2796

General Information Independent-religious, coed, comprehensive institution. *Enrollment:* 2,068 graduate, professional, and undergraduate students; 57 full-time matriculated graduate/professional students (49 women), 147 part-time matriculated graduate/professional students (111 women). *Enrollment by degree level:* 204 master's. *Graduate faculty:* 8 full-time (5 women), 13 part-time/adjunct (8 women). *Tuition:* Part-time $290 per credit. *Student services:* Disabled student services. *Library facilities:* Cochrane Woods Library. *Online resources:* library catalog, web page, access to other libraries' catalogs. *Collection:* 178,531 titles, 743 serial subscriptions.

Computer facilities: Computer purchase and lease plans are available. 336 computers available on campus for general student use. A campuswide network can be accessed from student residence rooms and from off campus. Internet access and online class registration, online grades are available. *Web address:* http://www.nebrwesleyan.edu/.

General Application Contact: University College Office, 402-465-2329, Fax: 402-465-2179, E-mail: universitycollege@nebrwesleyan.edu.

GRADUATE UNITS

University College Students: 57 full-time (49 women), 147 part-time (111 women); includes 12 minority (2 African Americans, 3 American Indian/Alaska Native, 1 Asian American or Pacific Islander, 6 Hispanic Americans), 1 international. Average age 33. *Faculty:* 8 full-time (5 women), 13 part-time/adjunct (8 women). Expenses: Contact institution. In 2006, 55 degrees awarded. *Degree program information:* Part-time programs available. Offers forensic science (MFS); historical studies (MA); nursing (MSN). *Application fee:* $50. *Provost,* Dr. Georgianne Mastera, 402-465-2110, E-mail: gm@nebrwesleyan.edu.

NER ISRAEL RABBINICAL COLLEGE, Baltimore, MD 21208

General Information Independent-religious, men only, comprehensive institution. *Enrollment:* 177 full-time matriculated graduate/professional students, 19 part-time matriculated graduate/professional students. *Enrollment by degree level:* 116 master's, 55 doctoral, 25 other advanced degrees. *Graduate faculty:* 9 full-time (0 women), 8 part-time/adjunct (0 women). *Tuition:* Full-time $8,000. *Graduate housing:* Rooms and/or apartments guaranteed to single students and available on a first-come, first-served basis to married students. Typical cost: $3,000 per year ($6,000 including board) for single students. *Student services:* Campus employment opportunities, career counseling, international student services, teacher training.

General Application Contact: Rabbi Ezra Neuberger, Information Contact, 410-484-7200, Fax: 410-484-3060.

GRADUATE UNITS

Graduate Programs Students: 177 full-time (0 women), 19 part-time. *Faculty:* 9 full-time (0 women), 8 part-time/adjunct (0 women). Expenses: Contact institution. In 2006, 20 master's, 2 doctorates awarded. *Application deadline:* Applications are processed on a rolling basis. *Application fee:* $50. *Application Contact:* Rabbi Ezra Neuberger, Information Contact, 410-484-7200, Fax: 410-484-3060.

NER ISRAEL YESHIVA COLLEGE OF TORONTO, Thornhill, ON L4J 8A7, Canada

General Information Independent-religious, men only, comprehensive institution.

GRADUATE UNITS

Graduate Programs

NEUMANN COLLEGE, Aston, PA 19014-1298

General Information Independent-religious, coed, comprehensive institution. *Enrollment:* 2,969 graduate, professional, and undergraduate students; 105 full-time matriculated graduate/professional students (69 women), 446 part-time matriculated graduate/professional students (308 women). *Enrollment by degree level:* 551 master's. *Graduate faculty:* 26 full-time (15 women), 23 part-time/adjunct (18 women). *Graduate housing:* On-campus housing not available. *Student services:* Campus employment opportunities, campus safety program, career counseling, child daycare facilities, disabled student services, exercise/wellness program, free psychological counseling, writing training. *Library facilities:* Neumann College Library. *Online resources:* library catalog, web page, access to other libraries' catalogs. *Collection:* 75,000 titles, 400 serial subscriptions, 2,000 audiovisual materials.

Computer facilities: 200 computers available on campus for general student use. A campuswide network can be accessed from student residence rooms and from off campus. Internet access, e-mail are available. *Web address:* http://www.neumann.edu/.

General Application Contact: Louise Bank, Assistant Director of Admissions, Graduate and Evening Programs, 610-558-5604, Fax: 610-459-1370, E-mail: bankl@neumann.edu.

GRADUATE UNITS

Program in Education Students: 21 full-time (16 women), 222 part-time (156 women); includes 20 minority (18 African Americans, 2 Hispanic Americans). Average age 34. 100 applicants, 100% accepted, 75 enrolled. *Faculty:* 5 full-time (1 woman), 2 part-time/adjunct (1 woman). Expenses: Contact institution. *Financial support:* Available to part-time students. Application deadline: 3/15; In 2006, 78 degrees awarded. *Degree program information:* Part-time programs available. Offers education (MS). *Application deadline:* Applications are processed on a rolling basis. *Application fee:* $50. *Application Contact:* Louise Bank, Assistant Director of Admissions, Graduate and Evening Programs, 610-558-5604, Fax: 610-459-1370, E-mail: bankl@neumann.edu. *Coordinator, Division of Education and Human Services,* Dr. Andrew DeSanto, 610-558-5640, Fax: 610-459-1370, E-mail: desantoa@neumann.edu.

Program in Nursing and Health Sciences Students: 1 full-time (0 women), 27 part-time (26 women); includes 2 minority (1 African American, 1 Hispanic American). Average age 44. 10 applicants, 100% accepted, 8 enrolled. *Faculty:* 5 full-time (4 women), 1 part-time/adjunct (0 women). Expenses: Contact institution. *Financial support:* Available to part-time students. Application deadline: 3/15; In 2006, 3 degrees awarded. *Degree program information:* Part-time programs available. Offers nursing (MS). *Application deadline:* Applications are processed on a rolling basis. *Application fee:* $50. *Application Contact:* Louise Bank, Assistant Director of Admissions, Graduate and Evening Programs, 610-558-5604, Fax: 610-459-1370, E-mail: bankl@neumann.edu. *Dean, Division of Nursing and Health Services,* Dr. Kathleen Hoover, 610-558-5561, Fax: 610-459-1370.

Program in Pastoral Counseling Students: 9 full-time (7 women), 92 part-time (71 women); includes 10 minority (8 African Americans, 1 Asian American or Pacific Islander, 1 Hispanic American). Average age 47. 50 applicants, 100% accepted, 45 enrolled. *Faculty:* 4 full-time (3 women), 7 part-time/adjunct (6 women). Expenses: Contact institution. *Financial support:* In 2006–07, 8 students received support. Available to part-time students. Application deadline: 3/15; In 2006, 27 degrees awarded. *Degree program information:* Part-time and evening/weekend programs available. Offers pastoral counseling (MS, CAS); spiritual direction (CSD). *Application deadline:* Applications are processed on a rolling basis. *Application fee:* $50. *Application Contact:* Louise Bank, Assistant Director of Admissions, Graduate and Evening Programs, 610-558-5604, Fax: 610-459-1370, E-mail: bankl@neumann.edu. *Executive Director,* Dr. Leonard DiPaul, 610-558-5572, Fax: 610-459-1370.

Program in Physical Therapy Students: 69 full-time (42 women), 19 part-time (10 women); includes 14 minority (3 African Americans, 6 Asian Americans or Pacific Islanders, 5 Hispanic Americans). Average age 30. 96 applicants, 47% accepted, 35 enrolled. *Faculty:* 5 full-time (3 women), 10 part-time/adjunct (8 women). Expenses: Contact institution. *Financial support:* Available to part-time students. Application deadline: 3/15; In 2006, 19 degrees awarded. *Degree program information:* Evening/weekend programs available. Offers physical therapy (MS, DPT). *Application deadline:* For fall admission, 12/1 for domestic students. *Application fee:* $50. *Application Contact:* Louise Bank, Assistant Director of Admissions, Graduate and Evening Programs, 610-558-5604, Fax: 610-459-1370, E-mail: bankl@neumann.edu. *Director,* Dr. Robert Post, 610-558-5233, Fax: 610-459-1370, E-mail: postr@neumann.edu.

Program in Sports Management Students: 5 full-time (4 women), 21 part-time (8 women); includes 6 minority (all African Americans) Average age 29. 10 applicants, 100% accepted, 8 enrolled. *Faculty:* 5 full-time (2 women). Expenses: Contact institution. *Financial support:* Available to part-time students. Application deadline: 3/15; In 2006, 9 degrees awarded. *Degree program information:* Part-time programs available. Offers sports management (MS). *Application deadline:* Applications are processed on a rolling basis. *Application fee:* $50. *Application Contact:* Louise Bank, Assistant Director of Admissions, Graduate and Evening Programs, 610-558-5604, Fax: 610-459-1370, E-mail: bankl@neumann.edu. *Coordinator,* Dr. Sandra L. Slabik, 610-361-5291, Fax: 610-558-5574, E-mail: slabiks@neumann.edu.

Program in Strategic Leadership Average age 41. 40 applicants, 100% accepted, 35 enrolled. *Faculty:* 1 (woman) full-time, 4 part-time/adjunct (2 women). Expenses: Contact institution. *Financial support:* Available to part-time students. Application deadline: 3/15; In 2006, 55 degrees awarded. Offers strategic leadership (MS). *Application fee:* $50. *Application Contact:* Louise Bank, Assistant Director of Admissions, Graduate and Evening Programs, 610-558-5604, Fax: 610-459-1370, E-mail: bankl@neumann.edu. *Coordinator, Division of Continuing Adult and Professional Studies,* Dr. Judith Stang, 610-361-5292, E-mail: stangj@neumann.edu.

NEW BRUNSWICK THEOLOGICAL SEMINARY, New Brunswick, NJ 08901-1196

General Information Independent-religious, coed, graduate-only institution. *Graduate housing:* Rooms and/or apartments available on a first-come, first-served basis to single students and available to married students.

GRADUATE UNITS

Graduate and Professional Programs *Degree program information:* Part-time and evening/weekend programs available. Offers metro-urban ministry (D Min); theological studies (M Div, MA, D Min). Electronic applications accepted.

NEW COLLEGE OF CALIFORNIA, San Francisco, CA 94102-5206

General Information Independent, coed, comprehensive institution. *Graduate housing:* On-campus housing not available.

GRADUATE UNITS

School of Graduate Psychology *Degree program information:* Evening/weekend programs available. Offers feminist clinical psychology (MA); social-clinical psychology (MA); spiritual/transformatives clinical psychology (MA).

School of Humanities *Degree program information:* Part-time and evening/weekend programs available. Offers humanities and leadership (MA); Irish studies (MA); media studies (MA); poetics (MA, MFA); poetics and writing (MFA); teaching (MAT); women's spirituality (MA); writing and consciousness (MA).

School of Law Students: 70 full-time (45 women), 50 part-time (28 women). Average age 30. 100 applicants, 50% accepted. *Faculty:* 6 full-time (4 women), 18 part-time/adjunct (6 women). Expenses: Contact institution. *Financial support:* Career-related internships or fieldwork, Federal Work-Study, and scholarships/grants available. Support available to part-time students. Financial award application deadline: 3/1; financial award applicants required to submit FAFSA. In 2006, 22 degrees awarded. *Degree program information:* Part-time programs available. Offers law (JD). *Application deadline:* For fall admission, 12/1 priority date for domestic students; for spring admission, 3/1 priority date for domestic students. Applications are processed on a rolling basis. *Application fee:* $55. Electronic applications accepted. *Application Contact:* Sharon Pittman, Associate Dean for Admissions, 415-241-1374, Fax: 415-241-9525, E-mail: lawadmissions@newcollege.edu. *Dean,* Debrenia Madison, 415-241-1325, Fax: 415-241-1353, E-mail: madison@newcollege.edu.

See Close-Up on page 971.

NEW ENGLAND COLLEGE, Henniker, NH 03242-3293

General Information Independent, coed, comprehensive institution. *Graduate housing:* Room and/or apartments available on a first-come, first-served basis to single students; on-campus housing not available to married students. Housing application deadline: 5/1.

GRADUATE UNITS

Program in Community Mental Health Counseling *Degree program information:* Part-time and evening/weekend programs available. Offers human services (MS); mental health counseling (MS).

Program in Creative Writing *Degree program information:* Part-time and evening/weekend programs available. Offers poetry (MFA). Electronic applications accepted.

Program in Education *Degree program information:* Part-time and evening/weekend programs available. Offers literacy and language arts (M Ed); meeting the needs of all learners/special education (M Ed); teacher leadership/school reform (M Ed).

Program in Management *Degree program information:* Part-time and evening/weekend programs available. Offers healthcare administration (MS); nonprofit leadership (MS); organizational leadership (MS). Electronic applications accepted.

Program in Public Policy *Degree program information:* Part-time and evening/weekend programs available. Postbaccalaureate distance learning degree programs offered (no on-campus study). Offers public policy (MA). Electronic applications accepted.

THE NEW ENGLAND COLLEGE OF OPTOMETRY, Boston, MA 02115-1100

General Information Independent, coed, graduate-only institution. *Enrollment by degree level:* 441 first professional. *Graduate faculty:* 44 full-time (21 women), 28 part-time/adjunct (13 women). *Graduate housing:* On-campus housing not available. *Student services:* Campus employment opportunities, career counseling, free psychological counseling, international student services, low-cost health insurance. *Library facilities:* Library. *Online resources:* library catalog, web page. *Collection:* 18,537 titles, 239 serial subscriptions, 12,229 audiovisual materials. *Research affiliation:* Vistakon Johnson and Johnson (contact lens study).

Computer facilities: 31 computers available on campus for general student use. A campuswide network can be accessed from off campus. Internet access is available. *Web address:* http://www.neco.edu/.

General Application Contact: Dr. Taline Farra, Director of Admissions, 617-587-5580, Fax: 617-587-5550, E-mail: farrat@neco.edu.

GRADUATE UNITS

Professional Program Students: 436 full-time (309 women), 5 part-time (4 women); includes 129 minority (12 African Americans, 107 Asian Americans or Pacific Islanders, 10 Hispanic Americans), 77 international. Average age 25. 680 applicants, 110 enrolled. Expenses: Contact institution. *Financial support:* In 2006–07, 4 research assistantships (averaging $5,193 per year) were awarded; career-related internships or fieldwork, Federal Work-Study, institutionally sponsored loans, and scholarships/grants also available. Financial award application deadline: 4/1; financial award applicants required to submit FAFSA. In 2006, 116 degrees awarded. Offers optometry (OD); vision science (MS). *Application deadline:* For fall admission, 3/31 for domestic students. Applications are processed on a rolling basis. *Application fee:* $75. Electronic applications accepted. *Application Contact:* Dr. Taline Farra, Director of Admissions, 617-587-5580, Fax: 617-587-5550, E-mail: farrat@neco.edu.

NEW ENGLAND CONSERVATORY OF MUSIC, Boston, MA 02115-5000

General Information Independent, coed, comprehensive institution. *Graduate housing:* Room and/or apartments available on a first-come, first-served basis to single students. Housing application deadline: 6/15.

GRADUATE UNITS

Graduate Program in Music Offers music (MM, DMA, Diploma).

NEW ENGLAND SCHOOL OF ACUPUNCTURE, Watertown, MA 02472

General Information Independent, coed, graduate-only institution. *Graduate housing:* On-campus housing not available.

GRADUATE UNITS

Program in Acupuncture and Oriental Medicine *Degree program information:* Part-time programs available. Offers acupuncture (M Ac); acupuncture and Oriental medicine (MAOM).

NEW ENGLAND SCHOOL OF LAW, Boston, MA 02116-5687

General Information Independent, coed, graduate-only institution. *Enrollment by degree level:* 1,100 first professional. *Graduate faculty:* 33 full-time (12 women), 83 part-time/adjunct (29 women). *Tuition:* Full-time $25,800; part-time $19,350 per year. One-time fee: $65 full-time. *Graduate housing:* On-campus housing not available. *Student services:* Campus employment opportunities, career counseling, disabled student services, low-cost health insurance, writing training. *Library facilities:* New England School of Law Library. *Online resources:* library catalog, web page, access to other libraries' catalogs. *Collection:* 196,907 titles, 5,586 serial subscriptions, 2,293 audiovisual materials.

Computer facilities: 115 computers available on campus for general student use. A campuswide network can be accessed from off campus. Internet access is available. *Web address:* http://www.nesl.edu/.

New England School of Law (continued)

General Application Contact: Michelle L'Etoile, Director of Admissions, 617-422-7210, Fax: 617-422-7201, E-mail: admit@admin.nesl.edu.

GRADUATE UNITS

Professional Program Students: 719 full-time (398 women), 381 part-time (190 women); includes 127 minority (20 African Americans, 2 American Indian/Alaska Native, 71 Asian Americans or Pacific Islanders, 34 Hispanic Americans). Average age 27. 3,362 applicants, 50% accepted, 393 enrolled. *Faculty:* 33 full-time (12 women), 83 part-time/adjunct (29 women). Expenses: Contact institution. *Financial support:* In 2006–07, 454 students received support. Federal Work-Study, institutionally sponsored loans, scholarships/grants, and tuition waivers (full and partial) available. Support available to part-time students. Financial award application deadline: 4/20; financial award applicants required to submit FAFSA. In 2006, 315 degrees awarded. *Degree program information:* Part-time and evening/weekend programs available. Offers law (JD). *Application deadline:* For fall admission, 3/15 for domestic students. Applications are processed on a rolling basis. *Application fee:* $65. Electronic applications accepted. *Application Contact:* Michelle L'Etoile, Director of Admissions, 617-422-7210, Fax: 617-422-7201, E-mail: admit@admin.nesl.edu. *Dean,* John F. O'Brien, 617-422-7221, Fax: 617-422-7333, E-mail: jobrien@admin.nesl.edu.

NEW JERSEY CITY UNIVERSITY, Jersey City, NJ 07305-1597

General Information State-supported, coed, comprehensive institution. *Enrollment:* 8,523 graduate, professional, and undergraduate students; 47 full-time matriculated graduate/professional students (37 women), 965 part-time matriculated graduate/professional students (668 women). *Enrollment by degree level:* 1,012 master's. *Graduate faculty:* 177. Tuition, state resident: full-time $7,038; part-time $391 per credit. Tuition, nonresident: full-time $12,510; part-time $695 per credit. *Required fees:* $65 per credit. *Graduate housing:* On-campus housing not available. *Student services:* Campus employment opportunities, campus safety program, career counseling, child daycare facilities, disabled student services, free psychological counseling, international student services. *Library facilities:* Congressman Frank J. Guarini Library. *Online resources:* library catalog, web page. *Collection:* 212,786 titles, 1,260 serial subscriptions, 2,234 audiovisual materials.

Computer facilities: 1,400 computers available on campus for general student use. A campuswide network can be accessed from student residence rooms and from off campus. Internet access and online class registration are available. *Web address:* http://www.njcu.edu/.

General Application Contact: Dr. Richard Hendrix, Dean of Graduate Studies, 201-200-3409, Fax: 201-200-3411, E-mail: rhendrix@njcu.edu.

GRADUATE UNITS

Graduate and Continuing Education Students: 47 full-time (37 women), 965 part-time (668 women); includes 229 minority (79 African Americans, 31 Asian Americans or Pacific Islanders, 119 Hispanic Americans), 50 international. Average age 35. 1,440 applicants, 97% accepted, 822 enrolled. *Faculty:* 177. Expenses: Contact institution. *Financial support:* Fellowships, research assistantships, career-related internships or fieldwork and unspecified assistantships available. In 2006, 620 master's, 5 other advanced degrees awarded. *Degree program information:* Part-time and evening/weekend programs available. *Application deadline:* For fall admission, 8/1 priority date for domestic students; for spring admission, 12/1 for domestic students. Applications are processed on a rolling basis. *Application fee:* $0. *Dean of Graduate Studies,* Dr. Richard Hendrix, 201-200-3409, Fax: 201-200-3411, E-mail: r.hendrix@njcu.edu.

College of Arts and Sciences Students: 26 full-time (21 women), 197 part-time (139 women); includes 61 minority (21 African Americans, 8 Asian Americans or Pacific Islanders, 32 Hispanic Americans), 9 international. Average age 33. *Faculty:* 45. Expenses: Contact institution. *Financial support:* Career-related internships or fieldwork and unspecified assistantships available. In 2006, 76 master's, 5 other advanced degrees awarded. *Degree program information:* Part-time and evening/weekend programs available. Offers art (MFA); art education (MA); arts and sciences (MA, MFA, MM, PD); counseling (MA); educational psychology (MA, PD); mathematics education (MA); music education (MA); performance (MM); school psychology (PD); studio art (MFA). *Application deadline:* For fall admission, 8/1 priority date for domestic students; for spring admission, 12/1 for domestic students. Applications are processed on a rolling basis. *Application fee:* $0. *Dean,* Dr. Liza Fiol-Mata, 201-200-3001, E-mail: lfiol@njcu.edu.

College of Education Students: 21 full-time (16 women), 694 part-time (488 women); includes 144 minority (46 African Americans, 19 Asian Americans or Pacific Islanders, 79 Hispanic Americans), 39 international. Average age 35. *Faculty:* 118. Expenses: Contact institution. *Financial support:* Fellowships, research assistantships, career-related internships or fieldwork and unspecified assistantships available. In 2006, 508 degrees awarded. Offers basics and urban studies (MA); bilingual/bicultural education and English as a second language (MA); early childhood education (MA); education (MA, MAT); educational administration and supervision (MA); educational technology (MA); elementary education (MAT); elementary school reading (MA); reading specialist (MA); secondary education (MAT); secondary school reading (MA); special education (MA). *Application deadline:* For fall admission, 8/1 for domestic students; for spring admission, 12/1 for domestic students. *Application fee:* $0. *Acting Dean,* Dr. Ivan Banks, 201-200-2102, E-mail: ibanks@njcu.edu.

College of Professional Studies Students: 2 full-time (1 woman), 110 part-time (65 women); includes 34 minority (15 African Americans, 5 Asian Americans or Pacific Islanders, 14 Hispanic Americans), 6 international. Average age 38. *Faculty:* 22. Expenses: Contact institution. *Financial support:* Career-related internships or fieldwork and unspecified assistantships available. In 2006, 36 degrees awarded. *Degree program information:* Part-time and evening/weekend programs available. Offers accounting (MS); community health education (MS); criminal justice (MS); finance (MS); health administration (MS); holistic nursing (MSN); law enforcement (MS); professional security studies (MS); school health education (MS); urban health (MSN). *Application deadline:* For fall admission, 8/1 priority date for domestic students; for spring admission, 12/1 for domestic students. Applications are processed on a rolling basis. *Application fee:* $0. *Dean,* Dr. Sandra Bloomberg, 201-200-3321, E-mail: sbloomberg@njcu.edu.

NEW JERSEY INSTITUTE OF TECHNOLOGY, Newark, NJ 07102

General Information State-supported, coed, university. CGS member. *Enrollment:* 8,209 graduate, professional, and undergraduate students; 1,569 full-time matriculated graduate/professional students (488 women), 1,260 part-time matriculated graduate/professional students (378 women). *Enrollment by degree level:* 2,149 master's, 433 doctoral, 247 other advanced degrees. *Graduate faculty:* 399 full-time (59 women), 247 part-time/adjunct (42 women). Tuition, state resident: full-time $11,896; part-time $648 per credit. Tuition, nonresident: full-time $16,900; part-time $892 per credit. *Required fees:* $336; $66 per credit. $168 per term. Tuition and fees vary according to course load. *Graduate housing:* Room and/or apartments available on a first-come, first-served basis to single students; on-campus housing not available to married students. Typical cost: $6,330 per year ($9,000 including board). Room and board charges vary according to board plan. Housing application deadline: 3/31. *Student services:* Campus employment opportunities, campus safety program, career counseling, child daycare facilities, disabled student services, exercise/wellness program, international student services, low-cost health insurance, teacher training, writing training. *Library facilities:* Van Houten Library plus 1 other. *Online resources:* library catalog, web page, access to other libraries' catalogs. *Collection:* 160,000 titles, 1,100 serial subscriptions.

Computer facilities: Computer purchase and lease plans are available. 1,938 computers available on campus for general student use. A campuswide network can be accessed from student residence rooms and from off campus. Internet access and online class registration are available. *Web address:* http://www.njit.edu/.

General Application Contact: Kathryn Kelly, Director of Admissions, 973-596-3300, Fax: 973-596-3461, E-mail: admissions@njit.edu.

GRADUATE UNITS

Office of Graduate Studies Students: 1,569 full-time (488 women), 1,260 part-time (378 women); includes 765 minority (183 African Americans, 7 American Indian/Alaska Native, 413 Asian Americans or Pacific Islanders, 162 Hispanic Americans), 1,203 international. Average age 32. 4,529 applicants, 57% accepted, 955 enrolled. *Faculty:* 399 full-time (59 women), 247 part-time/adjunct (42 women). Expenses: Contact institution. *Financial support:* Fellowships with full and partial tuition reimbursements, research assistantships with full and partial tuition reimbursements, teaching assistantships with full and partial tuition reimbursements, career-related internships or fieldwork, Federal Work-Study, institutionally sponsored loans, and unspecified assistantships available. Financial award application deadline: 3/15. In 2006, 912 master's, 75 doctorates, 1 other advanced degree awarded. *Degree program information:* Part-time and evening/weekend programs available. *Application deadline:* For fall admission, 6/5 priority date for domestic students; for spring admission, 10/15 for domestic students. Applications are processed on a rolling basis. *Application fee:* $60. Electronic applications accepted. *Application Contact:* Kathryn Kelly, Director of Admissions, 973-596-3300, Fax: 973-596-3461, E-mail: admissions@njit.edu. *Dean of Graduate Studies,* Dr. Ronald Kane, 973-596-3462, E-mail: ronald.kane@njit.edu.

College of Computing Science Students: 432 full-time (136 women), 274 part-time (62 women); includes 165 minority (22 African Americans, 1 American Indian/Alaska Native, 120 Asian Americans or Pacific Islanders, 22 Hispanic Americans), 383 international. Average age 31. 1,283 applicants, 62% accepted, 268 enrolled. *Faculty:* 52 full-time (4 women), 18 part-time/adjunct (3 women). Expenses: Contact institution. *Financial support:* Fellowships with full and partial tuition reimbursements, research assistantships with full and partial tuition reimbursements, teaching assistantships with full and partial tuition reimbursements, career-related internships or fieldwork, Federal Work-Study, institutionally sponsored loans, and unspecified assistantships available. Financial award application deadline: 3/15. In 2006, 334 master's, 18 doctorates awarded. *Degree program information:* Part-time and evening/weekend programs available. Offers computational biology (MS); computer science (MS, PhD); information systems (MS, PhD); telecommunication (MS). *Application deadline:* For fall admission, 6/5 priority date for domestic students; for spring admission, 10/15 for domestic students. Applications are processed on a rolling basis. *Application fee:* $60. Electronic applications accepted. *Application Contact:* Kathryn Kelly, Director of Admissions, 973-596-3300, Fax: 973-596-3461, E-mail: admissions@njit.edu. *Chairperson,* Dr. Narain Gehani, 973-542-5488, Fax: 973-596-5777, E-mail: narain.gehani@njit.edu.

College of Science and Liberal Arts Students: 159 full-time (60 women), 133 part-time (59 women); includes 73 minority (23 African Americans, 1 American Indian/Alaska Native, 37 Asian Americans or Pacific Islanders, 12 Hispanic Americans), 121 international. Average age 33. 396 applicants, 48% accepted, 96 enrolled. *Faculty:* 152 full-time (27 women), 62 part-time/adjunct (19 women). Expenses: Contact institution. *Financial support:* Fellowships with full tuition reimbursements, research assistantships with full tuition reimbursements, teaching assistantships with full tuition reimbursements available. Financial award application deadline: 3/15. In 2006, 75 master's, 19 doctorates awarded. *Degree program information:* Part-time and evening/weekend programs available. Offers applied mathematics (MS); applied physics (MS, PhD); applied statistics (MS); biology (MS, PhD); chemistry (MS, PhD); computing biology (MS); environmental policy studies (MS, PhD); environmental science (MS, PhD); history (MA, MAT); materials science and engineering (MS, PhD); mathematics science (PhD); occupational safety and industrial hygiene (MS); professional and technical communication (MS); public health (MS); science and liberal arts (MA, MAT, MS, PhD). *Application deadline:* For fall admission, 6/5 priority date for domestic students; for spring admission, 10/15 for domestic students. Applications are processed on a rolling basis. *Application fee:* $60. Electronic applications accepted. *Application Contact:* Kathryn Kelly, Director of Admissions, 973-596-3300, Fax: 973-596-3461, E-mail: admissions@njit.edu. *Acting Dean,* Dr. Fadi P. Deek, 973-596-2997, Fax: 973-596-5777, E-mail: fadi.deek@njit.edu.

Newark College of Engineering Students: 727 full-time (193 women), 462 part-time (117 women); includes 309 minority (79 African Americans, 1 American Indian/Alaska Native, 151 Asian Americans or Pacific Islanders, 78 Hispanic Americans), 577 international. Average age 36. 2,379 applicants, 55% accepted, 452 enrolled. *Faculty:* 144 full-time (14 women), 94 part-time/adjunct (3 women). Expenses: Contact institution. *Financial support:* Fellowships with full and partial tuition reimbursements, research assistantships with full and partial tuition reimbursements, teaching assistantships with full and partial tuition reimbursements available. Financial award application deadline: 3/15. In 2006, 373 master's, 37 doctorates awarded. *Degree program information:* Part-time and evening/weekend programs available. Offers biomedical engineering (MS, PhD); chemical engineering (MS, PhD); civil engineering (MS, PhD); computer engineering (MS, PhD); electrical engineering (MS, PhD); engineering (MS, PhD, Engineer); engineering management (MS); engineering science (MS); environmental engineering (MS, PhD); industrial engineering (MS, PhD); Internet engineering (MS); manufacturing engineering (MS); mechanical engineering (MS, PhD, Engineer); occupational safety and health engineering (MS); pharmaceutical engineering (MS); transportation (MS, PhD). *Application deadline:* For fall admission, 6/5 priority date for domestic students; for spring admission, 10/15 for domestic students. Applications are processed on a rolling basis. *Application fee:* $60. Electronic applications accepted. *Application Contact:* Kathryn Kelly, Director of Admissions, 973-596-3300, Fax: 973-596-3461, E-mail: admissions@njit.edu. *Dean,* Dr. John Schuring, 973-596-5849, E-mail: john.r.schuring@njit.edu.

School of Architecture Students: 102 full-time (56 women), 21 part-time (11 women); includes 24 minority (11 African Americans, 1 American Indian/Alaska Native, 6 Asian Americans or Pacific Islanders, 6 Hispanic Americans), 28 international. Average age 34. 149 applicants, 54% accepted, 42 enrolled. *Faculty:* 27 full-time (6 women), 50 part-time/adjunct (12 women). Expenses: Contact institution. *Financial support:* Fellowships with full and partial tuition reimbursements, research assistantships with full and partial tuition reimbursements, teaching assistantships with full and partial tuition reimbursements, career-related internships or fieldwork, Federal Work-Study, institutionally sponsored loans, and unspecified assistantships available. Financial award application deadline: 3/15. In 2006, 37 degrees awarded. *Degree program information:* Part-time and evening/weekend programs available. Offers architecture (M Arch, MS); infrastructure planning (MIP); urban systems (PhD). *Application deadline:* For fall admission, 6/5 priority date for domestic students; for spring admission, 10/15 for domestic students. Applications are processed on a rolling basis. *Application fee:* $60. Electronic applications accepted. *Application Contact:* Kathryn Kelly, Director of Admissions, 973-596-3300, Fax: 973-596-3461, E-mail: admissions@njit.edu. *Dean,* Urs P. Gauchat, 973-596-3079, E-mail: urs.p.gauchat@njit.edu.

School of Management Students: 133 full-time (40 women), 130 part-time (37 women); includes 106 minority (24 African Americans, 1 American Indian/Alaska Native, 60 Asian Americans or Pacific Islanders, 21 Hispanic Americans), 67 international. Average age 34. 322 applicants, 57% accepted, 97 enrolled. *Faculty:* 24 full-time (8 women), 17 part-time/adjunct (5 women). Expenses: Contact institution. *Financial support:* Fellowships with full and partial tuition reimbursements, research assistantships with full and partial tuition reimbursements, teaching assistantships with full and partial tuition reimbursements, career-related internships or fieldwork, Federal Work-Study, institutionally sponsored loans, and unspecified assistantships available. Financial award application deadline: 3/15. In 2006, 93 master's, 1 doctorate awarded. *Degree program information:* Part-time and evening/weekend programs available. Offers management of business administration (MBA); management of technology (MS, PhD). *Application deadline:* For fall admission, 6/5 priority date for domestic students; for spring admission, 10/15 for domestic students. Applications are processed on a rolling basis. *Application fee:* $60. Electronic applications accepted. *Application Contact:* Kathryn Kelly, Director of Admissions, 973-596-3300, Fax: 973-596-3461, E-mail: admissions@njit.edu. *Dean,* Dr. David L Hawk, 973-596-3019, E-mail: david.l.hawk@njit.edu.

NEW LIFE THEOLOGICAL SEMINARY, Charlotte, NC 28206-7901

General Information Independent-religious, coed, comprehensive institution. *Enrollment by degree level:* 12 master's. *Graduate faculty:* 4 full-time (0 women), 4 part-time/adjunct (1 woman). *Tuition:* Part-time $700 per course. *Student services:* Campus employment opportunities, grant writing training, writing training. *Web address:* http://www.nlts.org/.

General Application Contact: Dr. Phil Newton, Vice President/Chief Admissions Officer/ Admission, 704-334-6882, Fax: 704-334-6885, E-mail: pnewton@nlts.org.

GRADUATE UNITS

Graduate Program Students: 9 full-time (3 women), 3 part-time (all women); includes 5 African Americans, 4 international. 4 applicants, 100% accepted, 4 enrolled. *Faculty:* 4 full-time (0 women), 4 part-time/adjunct (1 woman). Expenses: Contact institution. *Application deadline:* For fall admission, 8/22 for domestic and international students; for spring admission, 1/22 for domestic and international students. *Application fee:* $40 ($140 for international students). Electronic applications accepted.

NEWMAN THEOLOGICAL COLLEGE, Edmonton, AB T6V 1H3, Canada

General Information Independent-religious, coed, comprehensive institution. *Enrollment:* 36 full-time matriculated graduate/professional students (10 women), 127 part-time matriculated graduate/professional students (81 women). *Graduate faculty:* 12 full-time (4 women), 12 part-time/adjunct (4 women). *Tuition:* Full-time $9,000; part-time $900 per term. *Required fees:* $50; $20 per term. One-time fee: $40 full-time. *Graduate housing:* On-campus housing not available. *Student services:* Career counseling. *Library facilities:* Sopchyshyn Library plus 1 other. *Web address:* http://www.newman.edu/.

General Application Contact: Carol Anne Seed, Registrar, 780-447-2993 Ext. 227, Fax: 780-447-2685.

GRADUATE UNITS

Religious Education Program Average age 44. 50 applicants, 80% accepted, 32 enrolled. *Faculty:* 1 full-time (0 women), 5 part-time/adjunct (3 women). Expenses: Contact institution. *Financial support:* Tuition bursaries available. Support available to part-time students. Financial award application deadline: 5/30. In 2006, 4 master's, 8 other advanced degrees awarded. *Degree program information:* Part-time programs available. Postbaccalaureate distance learning degree programs offered (no on-campus study). Offers Catholic school administration (CCSA); religious education (MRE, GDRE). *Application deadline:* For fall admission, 8/30 priority date for domestic students; for winter admission, 12/21 for domestic students; for spring admission, 4/30 for domestic students. *Application fee:* $25. *Application Contact:* Carol Anne Seed, Registrar, 780-447-2993 Ext. 227, Fax: 780-447-2685. *Director,* Dr. Dan Kingdon, 780-447-2993 Ext. 224, Fax: 780-447-2685, E-mail: dan.kingdon@newman.edu.

Theology Program Students: 36 full-time (10 women), 43 part-time (22 women). Average age 43. 25 applicants, 84% accepted, 14 enrolled. *Faculty:* 11 full-time (4 women), 7 part-time/adjunct (1 woman). Expenses: Contact institution. *Financial support:* In 2006–07, 11 students received support. Tuition bursaries available. Support available to part-time students. Financial award application deadline: 5/30. In 2006, 9 M Divs, 3 master's awarded. *Degree program information:* Part-time programs available. Offers theology (M Div, M Th, MTS). *Application deadline:* For fall admission, 8/30 priority date for domestic students; for winter admission, 12/21 for domestic students; for spring admission, 4/30 for domestic students. Applications are processed on a rolling basis. *Application fee:* $25. *Application Contact:* Carol Anne Seed, Registrar, 780-447-2993 Ext. 227, Fax: 780-447-2685. *Acting Dean,* Dr. Bob McKeon, 708-447-2993 Ext. 231, Fax: 780-447-2685, E-mail: bob.mckeon@newman.edu.

NEWMAN UNIVERSITY, Wichita, KS 67213-2097

General Information Independent-religious, coed, comprehensive institution. *Enrollment:* 2,104 graduate, professional, and undergraduate students; 114 full-time matriculated graduate/professional students (78 women), 199 part-time matriculated graduate/professional students (124 women). *Enrollment by degree level:* 313 master's. *Graduate faculty:* 18 full-time (4 women), 13 part-time/adjunct (11 women). *Graduate housing:* Rooms and/or apartments available on a first-come, first-served basis to single and married students. Housing application deadline: 8/1. *Student services:* Campus employment opportunities, campus safety program, career counseling, child daycare facilities, disabled student services, exercise/wellness program, free psychological counseling, international student services, low-cost health insurance, teacher training, writing training. *Library facilities:* Dungan Library and Campus Center plus 1 other. *Online resources:* library catalog, web page, access to other libraries' catalogs. *Collection:* 108,735 titles, 267 serial subscriptions, 1,872 audiovisual materials.

Computer facilities: Computer purchase and lease plans are available. 90 computers available on campus for general student use. A campuswide network can be accessed from student residence rooms and from off campus. Internet access and online class registration are available. *Web address:* http://www.newmanu.edu/.

General Application Contact: Linda Kay Sabala, Director of Graduate Admissions, 316-942-4291 Ext. 2230, Fax: 316-942-4483, E-mail: sabalal@newmanu.edu.

GRADUATE UNITS

School of Business Students: 34 full-time (14 women), 76 part-time (30 women); includes 14 minority (6 African Americans, 1 American Indian/Alaska Native, 3 Asian Americans or Pacific Islanders, 4 Hispanic Americans), 31 international. Average age 31. 74 applicants, 80% accepted, 46 enrolled. *Faculty:* 6 full-time (2 women), 3 part-time/adjunct (1 woman). Expenses: Contact institution. *Financial support:* In 2006–07, 3 students received support. Federal Work-Study and tuition waivers available. Financial award application deadline: 8/15; financial award applicants required to submit FAFSA. In 2006, 76 degrees awarded. *Degree program information:* Part-time programs available. Offers international business (MBA); leadership (MBA); management (MBA); technology (MBA). *Application deadline:* For fall admission, 8/1 priority date for domestic students; for winter admission, 1/1 priority date for domestic students; for spring admission, 1/1 priority date for domestic students. Applications are processed on a rolling basis. *Application fee:* $25 ($40 for international students). Electronic applications accepted. *Application Contact:* Linda Kay Sabala, Director of Graduate Admissions, 316-942-4291 Ext. 2230, Fax: 316-942-4483, E-mail: sabalal@newmanu.edu. *Dean,* Dr. Joe Goetz, 316-942-4291 Ext. 2111, Fax: 316-942-4486, E-mail: goetzj@newmanu.edu.

School of Education Students: 2 full-time (both women), 41 part-time (24 women); includes 3 minority (2 African Americans, 1 American Indian/Alaska Native), 3 international. Average age 35. 25 applicants, 92% accepted, 17 enrolled. *Faculty:* 3 full-time (0 women), 4 part-time/adjunct (all women). Expenses: Contact institution. *Financial support:* In 2006–07, 8 students received support. Federal Work-Study and tuition waivers (full) available. Financial award application deadline: 8/15; financial award applicants required to submit FAFSA. In 2006, 35 degrees awarded. *Degree program information:* Part-time programs available. Postbaccalaureate distance learning degree programs offered (no on-campus study). Offers building leadership (MS Ed); curriculum and instruction (MS Ed). *Application deadline:* For fall admission, 8/15 priority date for domestic students; for spring admission, 1/10 priority date for domestic students. Applications are processed on a rolling basis. *Application fee:* $25 ($40 for international students). Electronic applications accepted. *Application Contact:* Linda Kay Sabala, Director of Graduate Admissions, 316-942-4291 Ext. 2230, Fax: 316-942-4483, E-mail: sabalal@newmanu.edu. *Director,* Dr. Guy Glidden, 316-942-4291 Ext. 2331, Fax: 316-942-4483, E-mail: gliddeng@newmanu.edu.

School of Nursing and Allied Health Students: 24 full-time (13 women), 2 part-time; includes 4 minority (1 African American, 1 Asian American or Pacific Islander, 2 Hispanic Americans). Average age 34. 94 applicants, 15% accepted, 12 enrolled. *Faculty:* 4 full-time (3 women), 1 part-time/adjunct (0 women). Expenses: Contact institution. *Financial support:* Federal Work-Study and tuition waivers (full) available. Financial award application deadline: 8/15; financial award applicants required to submit FAFSA. In 2006, 12 degrees awarded. Offers nurse anesthesia (MS). *Application deadline:* For fall admission, 12/1 for domestic and international students. Applications are processed on a rolling basis. *Application fee:* $25 ($40 for international students). Electronic applications accepted. *Application Contact:* Linda Kay Sabala, Director of Graduate Admissions, 316-942-4291 Ext. 2230, Fax: 316-942-4483, E-mail: sabalal@newmanu.edu. *Director,* Sharon Niemann, 316-942-4291 Ext. 2272, Fax: 316-942-4483, E-mail: niemanns@newmanu.edu.

School of Social Work Students: 54 full-time (49 women), 81 part-time (70 women); includes 31 minority (18 African Americans, 1 American Indian/Alaska Native, 3 Asian Americans or Pacific Islanders, 9 Hispanic Americans), 2 international. Average age 36. 88 applicants, 78% accepted, 55 enrolled. *Faculty:* 7 full-time (2 women), 6 part-time/adjunct (2 women). Expenses: Contact institution. *Financial support:* In 2006–07, 7 students received support. Federal Work-Study, scholarships/grants, and tuition waivers (full) available. Financial award application deadline: 8/15; financial award applicants required to submit FAFSA. In 2006, 41 degrees awarded. Postbaccalaureate distance learning degree programs offered (no on-campus study). Offers social work (MSW). *Application deadline:* For fall admission, 8/15 for domestic students. Applications are processed on a rolling basis. *Application fee:* $25 ($40 for international students). *Application Contact:* Linda Kay Sabala, Director of Graduate Admissions, 316-942-4291 Ext. 2230, Fax: 316-942-4483, E-mail: sabalal@newmanu.edu. *Dean,* Dr. Kevin Brown, 316-942-4291 Ext. 2458, Fax: 316-942-4483.

NEW MEXICO HIGHLANDS UNIVERSITY, Las Vegas, NM 87701

General Information State-supported, coed, comprehensive institution. CGS member. *Enrollment:* 3,750 graduate, professional, and undergraduate students; 542 full-time matriculated graduate/professional students (377 women), 637 part-time matriculated graduate/professional students (439 women). *Enrollment by degree level:* 1,179 master's. *Graduate faculty:* 79 full-time (33 women), 33 part-time/adjunct (18 women). Tuition, state resident: part-time $101 per credit hour. Tuition, nonresident: part-time $101 per credit hour. *Graduate housing:* Rooms and/or apartments guaranteed to single and married students. Typical cost: $2,596 (including board) for single students; $1,790 per year for married students. *Student services:* Career counseling, child daycare facilities, disabled student services, exercise/wellness program, free psychological counseling, international student services, low-cost health insurance, teacher training, writing training. *Library facilities:* Donnelly Library. *Online resources:* library catalog, web page, access to other libraries' catalogs. *Collection:* 386,489 titles, 740 serial subscriptions. *Research affiliation:* Los Alamos National Laboratory (science, math, engineering and technology), Spectra Gases, Inc. (chemistry).

Computer facilities: 500 computers available on campus for general student use. A campuswide network can be accessed from student residence rooms and from off campus. Internet access and online class registration are available. *Web address:* http://www.nmhu.edu/.

General Application Contact: Diane Trujillo, Administrative Assistant Graduate Studies, 505-454-3266, Fax: 505-454-3558, E-mail: dtrujillo@nmhu.edu.

GRADUATE UNITS

Graduate Studies Students: 542 full-time (377 women), 637 part-time (439 women); includes 598 minority (29 African Americans, 89 American Indian/Alaska Native, 11 Asian Americans or Pacific Islanders, 469 Hispanic Americans), 51 international. Average age 37. 635 applicants, 90% accepted, 433 enrolled. *Faculty:* 79 full-time (33 women), 33 part-time/adjunct (18 women). Expenses: Contact institution. *Financial support:* In 2006–07, 546 students received support, including 20 research assistantships with full and partial tuition reimbursements available (averaging $6,500 per year), 71 teaching assistantships with full and partial tuition reimbursements available (averaging $6,500 per year); fellowships, career-related internships or fieldwork, Federal Work-Study, institutionally sponsored loans, scholarships/grants, tuition waivers (full and partial), and unspecified assistantships also available. Support available to part-time students. Financial award application deadline: 3/1. In 2006, 306 degrees awarded. *Degree program information:* Part-time programs available. *Application deadline:* For fall admission, 8/1 priority date for domestic students. Applications are processed on a rolling basis. *Application fee:* $15. *Application Contact:* Diane Trujillo, Administrative Assistant Graduate Studies, 505-454-3266, Fax: 505-454-3558, E-mail: dtrujillo@nmhu.edu. *Interim Vice President for Academic Affairs,* Dr. Gilbert Rivera, 505-426-2250, Fax: 505-454-3558, E-mail: gilbertrivera@nmhu.edu.

College of Arts and Sciences Students: 89 full-time (40 women), 56 part-time (33 women); includes 56 minority (2 African Americans, 2 American Indian/Alaska Native, 1 Asian American or Pacific Islander, 51 Hispanic Americans), 29 international. Average age 32. 108 applicants, 78% accepted, 45 enrolled. *Faculty:* 42 full-time (17 women), 9 part-time/adjunct (5 women). Expenses: Contact institution. *Financial support:* In 2006–07, 73 students received support, including 20 research assistantships with full and partial tuition reimbursements available (averaging $6,500 per year), 47 teaching assistantships with full and partial tuition reimbursements available (averaging $6,500 per year); career-related internships or fieldwork, Federal Work-Study, institutionally sponsored loans, scholarships/grants, tuition waivers (full and partial), and unspecified assistantships also available. Support available to part-time students. Financial award application deadline: 3/1. In 2006, 31 degrees awarded. *Degree program information:* Part-time programs available. Offers administration (MA); anthropology (MA); applied chemistry (MS); applied sociology (MA); arts and sciences (MA, MS); biology (MS); cognitive science (MA, MS); computer graphics (MA, MS); design studies (MA); digital audio and video production (MA); English (MA); Hispanic language and literature (MA); historical and cross-cultural perspective (MA); history and political science (MA); life science (MS); multimedia systems (MA, MS); natural resource management (MS); networking technology (MA, MS); political and governmental processes (MA); psychology (MS). *Application deadline:* For fall admission, 8/1 priority date for domestic students. Applications are processed on a rolling basis. *Application fee:* $15. Electronic applications accepted. *Application Contact:* Diane Trujillo, Administrative Assistant Graduate Studies, 505-454-3266, Fax: 505-454-3558, E-mail: dtrujillo@nmhu.edu. *Dean,* Dr. C.G. (Tino) Mendez, 505-454-3080, Fax: 505-454-3389, E-mail: tmendez@nmhu.edu.

School of Business Students: 57 full-time (39 women), 103 part-time (69 women); includes 97 minority (1 African American, 26 American Indian/Alaska Native, 4 Asian Americans or Pacific Islanders, 66 Hispanic Americans), 17 international. Average age 35. 69 applicants, 84% accepted, 42 enrolled. *Faculty:* 12 full-time (4 women), 1 part-time/adjunct (0 women). Expenses: Contact institution. *Financial support:* In 2006–07, 67 students received support, including 8 teaching assistantships with full and partial tuition reimbursements available (averaging $6,500 per year); career-related internships or fieldwork, Federal Work-Study, institutionally sponsored loans, scholarships/grants, tuition waivers (full and partial), and unspecified assistantships also available. Support available to part-time students. Financial award application deadline: 3/1; financial award applicants required to submit FAFSA. In 2006, 29 degrees awarded. Offers business administration (MBA). *Application deadline:* For fall admission, 8/1 priority date for domestic students. Applications are processed on a rolling basis. *Application fee:* $15. *Application Contact:* Diane Trujillo, Administrative Assistant Graduate Studies, 505-454-3266, Fax: 505-454-3558, E-mail: dtrujillo@nmhu.edu. *Dean,* Dr. William Taylor, 505-454-3344, Fax: 505-454-3354.

School of Education Students: 171 full-time (117 women), 413 part-time (286 women); includes 305 minority (17 African Americans, 30 American Indian/Alaska Native, 4 Asian Americans or Pacific Islanders, 254 Hispanic Americans), 3 international. Average age 40. 111 applicants, 84% accepted, 63 enrolled. *Faculty:* 14 full-time (6 women), 11 part-time/adjunct (9 women). Expenses: Contact institution. *Financial support:* In 2006–07, 205 students received support, including 16 teaching assistantships with full and partial tuition reimbursements available (averaging $6,500 per year); career-related internships or fieldwork, Federal Work-Study, institutionally sponsored loans, scholarships/grants, traineeships, tuition waivers (partial), and unspecified assistantships also available. Support available to part-time students. Financial award application deadline: 3/1; financial award applicants required to submit FAFSA. In 2006, 111 degrees awarded. *Degree program information:* Part-time programs available. Offers education (MA); educational leadership (MA); exercise and sport sciences (MA); guidance and counseling (MA); human performance and sport (MA); special education (MA); sports administration (MA); teacher education (MA). *Application deadline:* For fall admission, 8/1 priority date for domestic students. Applications are processed on a rolling basis. *Application fee:* $15. *Application Contact:* Diane Trujillo, Administrative Assistant Graduate Studies, 505-454-3266, Fax: 505-454-3558, E-mail: dtrujillo@nmhu.edu. *Dean,* Dr. Francisco Hidalgo, 505-454-3357, Fax: 505-454-3384, E-mail: fhidalgo@nmhu.edu.

School of Social Work Students: 225 full-time (181 women), 65 part-time (51 women); includes 140 minority (9 African Americans, 31 American Indian/Alaska Native, 2 Asian

New Mexico Highlands University (continued)

Americans or Pacific Islanders, 98 Hispanic Americans), 2 international. Average age 37. 136 applicants, 94% accepted, 102 enrolled. *Faculty:* 11 full-time (4 women), 12 part-time/adjunct (6 women). Expenses: Contact institution. *Financial support:* In 2006–07, 201 students received support. Career-related internships or fieldwork, Federal Work-Study, institutionally sponsored loans, scholarships/grants, tuition waivers (partial), and unspecified assistantships available. Support available to part-time students. Financial award application deadline: 3/1; financial award applicants required to submit FAFSA. In 2006, 135 degrees awarded. *Degree program information:* Part-time programs available. Offers bilingual/bicultural social work practice (MSW); clinical practice (MSW); community organization (MSW). *Application deadline:* For fall admission, 8/1 priority date for domestic students. Applications are processed on a rolling basis. *Application fee:* $15. *Application Contact:* Diane Trujillo, Administrative Assistant Graduate Studies, 505-454-3266, Fax: 505-454-3558, E-mail: dtrujillo@nmhu.edu. *Dean,* Dr. Alfredo Garcia, 505-891-9053, Fax: 505-454-3290, E-mail: a_garcia@nmhu.edu.

NEW MEXICO INSTITUTE OF MINING AND TECHNOLOGY, Socorro, NM 87801

General Information State-supported, coed, university. *Enrollment:* 1,846 graduate, professional, and undergraduate students; 229 full-time matriculated graduate/professional students (68 women), 127 part-time matriculated graduate/professional students (55 women). *Enrollment by degree level:* 272 master's, 84 doctoral. *Graduate faculty:* 96 full-time (14 women), 36 part-time/adjunct (7 women). Tuition, state resident: full-time $3,593; part-time $200 per credit. Tuition, nonresident: full-time $11,554; part-time $642 per credit. *Required fees:* $419; $16 per credit. $34 per term. Tuition and fees vary according to course load. *Graduate housing:* Rooms and/or apartments available on a first-come, first-served basis to single and married students. Typical cost: $1,905 (including board) for single students; $2,700 per year for married students. Room and board charges vary according to housing facility selected. Housing application deadline: 6/1. *Student services:* Campus employment opportunities, career counseling, child daycare facilities, disabled student services, free psychological counseling, grant writing training, international student services, low-cost health insurance, multicultural affairs office. *Library facilities:* New Mexico Tech Library plus 1 other. *Online resources:* web page. *Collection:* 321,829 titles, 884 serial subscriptions. *Research affiliation:* National Center for Atmospheric Research (atmosphere research), National Radio Astronomy Observatory (astronomy), Joint Center for Materials Research (materials engineering/metallurgy), Gas Technology Institute (natural gas recovery), Optical Surface Technologies LLC (custom optical components).

Computer facilities: 225 computers available on campus for general student use. A campuswide network can be accessed from student residence rooms and from off campus. Internet access and online class registration are available. *Web address:* http://www.nmt.edu/.

General Application Contact: Dr. David B. Johnson, Dean of Graduate Studies, 505-835-5513, Fax: 505-835-5476, E-mail: graduate@nmt.edu.

GRADUATE UNITS

Graduate Studies Students: 250 full-time (72 women), 106 part-time (51 women); includes 37 minority (1 African American, 2 American Indian/Alaska Native, 8 Asian Americans or Pacific Islanders, 26 Hispanic Americans), 119 international. Average age 30. 433 applicants, 45% accepted, 161 enrolled. *Faculty:* 96 full-time (14 women), 36 part-time/adjunct (7 women). Expenses: Contact institution. *Financial support:* In 2006–07, 4 fellowships (averaging $8,360 per year), 145 research assistantships (averaging $13,032 per year), 85 teaching assistantships with full and partial tuition reimbursements (averaging $10,000 per year) were awarded; Federal Work-Study, institutionally sponsored loans, scholarships/grants, and unspecified assistantships also available. Support available to part-time students. Financial award application deadline: 3/1; financial award applicants required to submit CSS PROFILE or FAFSA. In 2006, 104 master's, 19 doctorates awarded. Offers advanced mechanics (MS); applied math (PhD); astrophysics (MS, PhD); atmospheric physics (MS, PhD); biochemistry (MS); biology (MS); chemistry (MS); computer science (MS, PhD); electrical engineering (MS); engineering management (MEM); environmental chemistry (PhD); environmental engineering (MS); explosives engineering (MS); explosives technology and atmospheric chemistry (PhD); geochemistry (MS, PhD); geology (MS, PhD); geology and geochemistry (MS, PhD); geophysics (MS, PhD); hydrology (MS, PhD); instrumentation (MS); materials engineering (MS, PhD); mathematical physics (PhD); mathematics (MS); mining and mineral engineering (MS); operations research (MS); petroleum engineering (MS, PhD); science teaching (MST). *Application deadline:* For fall admission, 3/1 priority date for domestic and international students; for spring admission, 6/1 for domestic and international students. Applications are processed on a rolling basis. *Application fee:* $16. Electronic applications accepted. *Application Contact:* Debbie Wallace, Administrative Secretary, 505-835-5513, Fax: 505-835-5476, E-mail: dwallace@admin.nmt.edu. *Dean,* Dr. David B. Johnson, 505-835-5513, Fax: 505-835-5476, E-mail: graduate@nmt.edu.

See Close-Up on page 973.

NEW MEXICO STATE UNIVERSITY, Las Cruces, NM 88003-8001

General Information State-supported, coed, university. CGS member. *Enrollment:* 16,415 graduate, professional, and undergraduate students; 1,712 full-time matriculated graduate/professional students (901 women), 1,493 part-time matriculated graduate/professional students (911 women). *Enrollment by degree level:* 2,432 master's, 725 doctoral, 48 other advanced degrees. *Graduate faculty:* 495 full-time (168 women), 57 part-time/adjunct (26 women). *Graduate housing:* Rooms and/or apartments available on a first-come, first-served basis to single students and available to married students. Typical cost: $2,350 per year ($5,576 including board) for single students. *Student services:* Campus employment opportunities, campus safety program, career counseling, disabled student services, free psychological counseling, international student services, low-cost health insurance. *Library facilities:* New Mexico State University Library plus 2 others. *Online resources:* library catalog, web page, access to other libraries' catalogs. *Collection:* 1.7 million titles, 2,890 serial subscriptions, 4,332 audiovisual materials. *Research affiliation:* Corporation for Public Broadcasting, General Motors Corporation, Sandia National Laboratory, Cotton Incorporated, Institute for Advanced Study.

Computer facilities: 500 computers available on campus for general student use. A campuswide network can be accessed from student residence rooms and from off campus. Internet access and online class registration are available. *Web address:* http://www.nmsu.edu/.

General Application Contact: Elena Luna, Coordinator, 505-646-3498, Fax: 505-646-7721, E-mail: rosluna@nmsu.edu.

GRADUATE UNITS

Graduate School Students: 1,712 full-time (901 women), 1,493 part-time (911 women); includes 1,057 minority (70 African Americans, 56 American Indian/Alaska Native, 32 Asian Americans or Pacific Islanders, 899 Hispanic Americans), 566 international. Average age 34. 1,907 applicants, 76% accepted. *Faculty:* 495 full-time (168 women), 57 part-time/adjunct (26 women). Expenses: Contact institution. *Financial support:* In 2006–07, 73 fellowships, 241 research assistantships, 526 teaching assistantships were awarded; career-related internships or fieldwork, Federal Work-Study, scholarships/grants, traineeships, health care benefits, and unspecified assistantships also available. Support available to part-time students. In 2006, 835 master's, 79 doctorates, 4 other advanced degrees awarded. *Degree program information:* Part-time and evening/weekend programs available. Postbaccalaureate distance learning degree programs offered (no on-campus study). Offers interdisciplinary studies (MA, MS, PhD); molecular biology (MS, PhD). *Application fee:* $30 ($50 for international students). Electronic applications accepted. *Application Contact:* Elena Luna, Coordinator, 505-646-3498, Fax: 505-646-7721, E-mail: rosluna@nmsu.edu. *Dean,* Dr. Linda Lacey, 505-646-5746, Fax: 505-646-7721, E-mail: lacey@nmsu.edu.

College of Agriculture and Home Economics Students: 165 full-time (80 women), 70 part-time (33 women); includes 56 minority (3 African Americans, 4 American Indian/Alaska Native, 1 Asian American or Pacific Islander, 48 Hispanic Americans), 45 international. Average age 30. 98 applicants, 82% accepted. *Faculty:* 81 full-time (23 women), 7 part-time/adjunct (3 women). Expenses: Contact institution. *Financial support:* In 2006–07, 9 fellowships, 88 research assistantships, 52 teaching assistantships were awarded; career-related internships or fieldwork, Federal Work-Study, and health care benefits also available. Support available to part-time students. Financial award application deadline: 3/1. In 2006, 77 master's, 6 doctorates awarded. *Degree program information:* Part-time and evening/weekend programs available. Offers agribusiness (M Ag, MBA); agricultural biology (MS); agricultural economics (MS); agriculture and extension education (MA); agriculture and home economics (M Ag, MA, MBA, MS, PhD); animal science (M Ag, MS, PhD); economics (MA); family and consumer sciences (MS); general agronomy (MS, PhD); horticulture (MS); range science (M Ag, MS, PhD); wildlife science (MS). *Application deadline:* For fall admission, 7/1 priority date for domestic students; for spring admission, 11/1 for domestic students. Applications are processed on a rolling basis. *Application fee:* $30 ($50 for international students). Electronic applications accepted. *Interim Dean,* Dr. Lowell Catlett, 505-646-1806, Fax: 505-646-5975, E-mail: agdean@nmsu.edu.

College of Arts and Sciences Students: 613 full-time (277 women), 273 part-time (135 women); includes 192 minority (22 African Americans, 11 American Indian/Alaska Native, 9 Asian Americans or Pacific Islanders, 150 Hispanic Americans), 205 international. Average age 31. 700 applicants, 73% accepted. *Faculty:* 217 full-time (77 women), 19 part-time/adjunct (11 women). Expenses: Contact institution. *Financial support:* In 2006–07, 35 fellowships, 95 research assistantships, 235 teaching assistantships were awarded; career-related internships or fieldwork, Federal Work-Study, scholarships/grants, and health care benefits also available. Support available to part-time students. In 2006, 178 master's, 33 doctorates awarded. *Degree program information:* Part-time programs available. Postbaccalaureate distance learning degree programs offered. Offers anthropology (MA); art history (MA); arts and sciences (MA, MAG, MCJ, MFA, MM, MPA, MS, PhD); astronomy (MS, PhD); biology (MS, PhD); ceramics (MA, MFA); chemistry and biochemistry (MS, PhD); communication studies (MA); computer science (MS, PhD); creative writing (MFA); criminal justice (MCJ); design (MA, MFA); drawing (MA, MFA); English (MA); geography (MAG); geological sciences (MS); government (MA, MPA); history (MA); mathematical sciences (MS, PhD); metals (MA, MFA); music (MM); painting (MA, MFA); photography (MA, MFA); physics (MS, PhD); printmaking (MA, MFA); psychology (MA, PhD); rhetoric and professional communication (PhD); sculpture (MA, MFA); sociology (MA); Spanish (MA). *Application fee:* $30 ($50 for international students). Electronic applications accepted. *Dean,* Dr. Waded Cruzado-Salas, 505-646-2001, Fax: 505-646-6096, E-mail: wcruzado@nmsu.edu.

College of Business Students: 144 full-time (64 women), 149 part-time (66 women); includes 109 minority (4 African Americans, 2 American Indian/Alaska Native, 3 Asian Americans or Pacific Islanders, 100 Hispanic Americans), 47 international. Average age 32. 177 applicants, 75% accepted. *Faculty:* 42 full-time (11 women), 4 part-time/adjunct (2 women). Expenses: Contact institution. *Financial support:* In 2006–07, 4 fellowships, 4 research assistantships, 77 teaching assistantships were awarded; career-related internships or fieldwork, Federal Work-Study, institutionally sponsored loans, scholarships/grants, health care benefits, and unspecified assistantships also available. Support available to part-time students. Financial award application deadline: 3/1. In 2006, 79 master's, 4 doctorates awarded. *Degree program information:* Part-time programs available. Offers accounting and information systems (M Acct); business (M Acct, MA, MBA, MS, PhD); business administration (PhD); economics (MA); experimental statistics (MS). *Application deadline:* For fall admission, 7/1 priority date for domestic students; for spring admission, 11/1 for domestic students. Applications are processed on a rolling basis. *Application fee:* $30 ($50 for international students). Electronic applications accepted. *Dean,* Dr. Garrey Carruthers, 505-646-2821, Fax: 505-646-6155, E-mail: garrey@nmsu.edu.

College of Education Students: 358 full-time (276 women), 611 part-time (464 women); includes 434 minority (27 African Americans, 20 American Indian/Alaska Native, 10 Asian Americans or Pacific Islanders, 377 Hispanic Americans), 41 international. Average age 37. 403 applicants, 77% accepted. *Faculty:* 58 full-time (30 women), 12 part-time/adjunct (4 women). Expenses: Contact institution. *Financial support:* In 2006–07, 18 fellowships, 60 teaching assistantships were awarded; research assistantships, career-related internships or fieldwork, Federal Work-Study, and health care benefits also available. Support available to part-time students. Financial award application deadline: 3/1. In 2006, 291 master's, 25 doctorates, 4 other advanced degrees awarded. *Degree program information:* Part-time and evening/weekend programs available. Postbaccalaureate distance learning degree programs offered (minimal on-campus study). Offers counseling and guidance (MA); counseling psychology (PhD); curriculum and instruction (MAT, Ed D, PhD, Ed S); education (MA, MAT, Ed D, PhD, Ed S); educational administration (MA, PhD); educational management and development (Ed D); general education (MA); reading (Ed S); school psychology (Ed S); special education (MA, Ed D, PhD). *Application deadline:* Applications are processed on a rolling basis. *Application fee:* $30 ($50 for international students). Electronic applications accepted. *Dean,* Dr. Robert Moulton, 505-646-3404, Fax: 505-646-6032, E-mail: moulton@nmsu.edu.

College of Engineering Students: 249 full-time (59 women), 156 part-time (28 women); includes 94 minority (3 African Americans, 3 American Indian/Alaska Native, 6 Asian Americans or Pacific Islanders, 82 Hispanic Americans), 206 international. Average age 29. 274 applicants, 78% accepted, 65 enrolled. *Faculty:* 62 full-time (5 women), 4 part-time/adjunct (0 women). Expenses: Contact institution. *Financial support:* In 2006–07, 5 fellowships, 50 research assistantships, 73 teaching assistantships were awarded; career-related internships or fieldwork, Federal Work-Study, and health care benefits also available. Support available to part-time students. Financial award application deadline: 3/1. In 2006, 107 master's, 7 doctorates awarded. *Degree program information:* Part-time programs available. Offers chemical engineering (MS Ch E, PhD); civil engineering (MSCE, PhD); electrical and computer engineering (MSEE, PhD); engineering (MS Ch E, MS Env E, MSCE, MSEE, MSIE, MSME, PhD); environmental engineering (MS Env E); industrial engineering (MSIE, PhD); mechanical engineering (MSME, PhD). *Application deadline:* For fall admission, 7/1 priority date for domestic students; for spring admission, 11/1 for domestic students. Applications are processed on a rolling basis. *Application fee:* $30 ($50 for international students). Electronic applications accepted. *Dean,* Dr. Steven Castillo, 505-646-2914, Fax: 505-646-3549, E-mail: scastill@nmsu.edu.

College of Health and Social Services Students: 156 full-time (131 women), 132 part-time (117 women); includes 118 minority (6 African Americans, 14 American Indian/Alaska Native, 2 Asian Americans or Pacific Islanders, 96 Hispanic Americans), 7 international. Average age 37. 179 applicants, 74% accepted. *Faculty:* 32 full-time (20 women), 11 part-time/adjunct (6 women). Expenses: Contact institution. *Financial support:* In 2006–07, 2 research assistantships, 17 teaching assistantships were awarded; fellowships, career-related internships or fieldwork, Federal Work-Study, scholarships/grants, traineeships, and health care benefits also available. Financial award application deadline: 3/1. In 2006, 99 degrees awarded. *Degree program information:* Part-time and evening/weekend programs available. Postbaccalaureate distance learning degree programs offered. Offers community/public health (MSN); health and social services (MPH, MSN, MSW); health science (MPH); medical-surgical (adult health) (MSN); psychiatric/mental health (MSN); social work (MSW). *Application deadline:* For fall admission, 7/1 priority date for domestic students. Applications are processed on a rolling basis. *Application fee:* $30 ($50 for international students). Electronic applications accepted. *Application Contact:* Dr. Larry K. Olsen, Associate Dean, 505-646-3526, E-mail: lolsen@nmsu.edu. *Dean,* Dr. Jeffrey Brandon, 505-646-3526, Fax: 505-646-6166, E-mail: jbrandon@nmsu.edu.

NEW ORLEANS BAPTIST THEOLOGICAL SEMINARY, New Orleans, LA 70126-4858

General Information Independent-religious, coed, primarily men, comprehensive institution. *Graduate housing:* Rooms and/or apartments available to single and married students.

GRADUATE UNITS

Graduate and Professional Programs *Degree program information:* Evening/weekend programs available. Offers biblical studies (M Div, D Min, PhD); Christian education (M Div,

MACE, D Min, DEM, PhD); church music ministries (MMCM, DMA); pastoral ministries (M Div, MAMFC, D Min, PhD); theological and historical studies (M Div, D Min, PhD); theology (M Div, MACE, MAMFC, MMCM, D Min, DEM, DMA, PhD).

THE NEW SCHOOL: A UNIVERSITY, New York, NY 10011

General Information Independent, coed, university. *Graduate housing:* Rooms and/or apartments available on a first-come, first-served basis to single students and available to married students. Housing application deadline: 5/1. *Student services:* Campus employment opportunities, campus safety program, career counseling, disabled student services, free psychological counseling, grant writing training, international student services, low-cost health insurance, multicultural affairs office, teacher training, writing training. *Web address:* http://www.newschool.edu/.

General Application Contact: Christy Kalan, Director of Enrollment Management, 212-229-5154, E-mail: kalanc@newschool.edu.

GRADUATE UNITS

Mannes College The New School for Music Students: 183 full-time (111 women), 1 part-time; includes 16 minority (1 African American, 12 Asian Americans or Pacific Islanders, 3 Hispanic Americans), 96 international. Average age 25. Expenses: Contact institution. *Financial support:* Fellowships with partial tuition reimbursements, research assistantships with partial tuition reimbursements, teaching assistantships with partial tuition reimbursements, career-related internships or fieldwork, Federal Work-Study, scholarships/grants, and tuition waivers (partial) available. Support available to part-time students. Financial award application deadline: 3/1; financial award applicants required to submit FAFSA. In 2006, 46 master's, 20 other advanced degrees awarded. Offers music performance (MM, PD). *Application deadline:* For fall admission, 12/1 for domestic students. *Application fee:* $100. *Application Contact:* Director of Admissions, 212-580-0210 Ext. 263. *Dean,* Joel Lester, 212-580-0210 Ext. 221.

Milano The New School for Management and Urban Policy Students: 177 full-time (129 women), 305 part-time (228 women); includes 198 minority (100 African Americans, 2 American Indian/Alaska Native, 29 Asian Americans or Pacific Islanders, 67 Hispanic Americans), 32 international. Average age 33. *Faculty:* 20 full-time (5 women), 46 part-time/adjunct (20 women). Expenses: Contact institution. *Financial support:* Fellowships with full and partial tuition reimbursements, research assistantships, career-related internships or fieldwork, Federal Work-Study, scholarships/grants, and tuition waivers (full and partial) available. Support available to part-time students. Financial award application deadline: 3/1; financial award applicants required to submit FAFSA. In 2006, 141 master's, 1 doctorate, 11 Adv Cs awarded. *Degree program information:* Part-time and evening/weekend programs available. Postbaccalaureate distance learning degree programs offered (minimal on-campus study). Offers health services management and policy (MS); human resources management (MS, Adv C); management and urban policy (MS, PhD, Adv C); medical group practice management (Adv C); nonprofit management (MS); organizational change management (MS); public and urban policy (PhD); urban policy analysis and management (MS). *Application deadline:* For fall admission, 9/1 priority date for domestic students. Applications are processed on a rolling basis. *Application fee:* $50. *Application Contact:* Peter King, Director of Admissions, 212-229-5400, Fax: 212-229-5354, E-mail: kingp@newschool.edu. *Dean,* Dr. Fred Hochberg, 212-229-5400 Ext. 1200, Fax: 212-229-8935, E-mail: ednsu@newschool.edu.

The New School for Drama Students: 122 full-time (83 women), 28 part-time (18 women); includes 21 minority (13 African Americans, 2 Asian Americans or Pacific Islanders, 6 Hispanic Americans), 28 international. Average age 27. *Faculty:* 36 part-time/adjunct (16 women). Expenses: Contact institution. *Financial support:* Federal Work-Study and scholarships/grants available. Financial award application deadline: 3/1; financial award applicants required to submit FAFSA. In 2006, 58 degrees awarded. Offers acting (MFA); directing (MFA); playwriting (MFA). *Application deadline:* For fall admission, 1/10 priority date for domestic students. *Application fee:* $50. *Application Contact:* Matthew Kelty, Director of Admissions, 212-229-5150, E-mail: keltym@newschool.edu. *Director,* Robert LuPone, 212-229-5859, E-mail: luponer@newschool.edu.

The New School for General Studies Students: 569 full-time (357 women), 369 part-time (236 women); includes 178 minority (70 African Americans, 1 American Indian/Alaska Native, 55 Asian Americans or Pacific Islanders, 52 Hispanic Americans), 140 international. Average age 30. Expenses: Contact institution. *Financial support:* Fellowships with partial tuition reimbursements, teaching assistantships with partial tuition reimbursements, career-related internships or fieldwork, Federal Work-Study, scholarships/grants, tuition waivers (full and partial), and unspecified assistantships available. Support available to part-time students. Financial award application deadline: 3/1; financial award applicants required to submit FAFSA. In 2006, 326 degrees awarded. *Degree program information:* Part-time and evening/weekend programs available. Postbaccalaureate distance learning degree programs offered (no on-campus study). Offers communication theory (MA); creative writing (MFA); global management, trade, and finance (MA, MS); international development (MA, MS); international media and communication (MA, MS); international politics and diplomacy (MA, MS); media studies (MA); service, civic, and non-profit management (MS); teaching English to speakers of other languages (MA). *Application deadline:* Applications are processed on a rolling basis. *Application fee:* $50. *Application Contact:* Gerianne Brusati, Associate Dean, Admissions and Student Services, 212-229-5630, Fax: 212-989-3887, E-mail: admissions@dialnsa.edu. *Dean,* Dr. Linda Dunne, 212-229-5613, Fax: 212-645-0661, E-mail: dunnel@newschool.edu.

The New School for Social Research Students: 803 full-time (424 women), 280 part-time (162 women); includes 173 minority (55 African Americans, 2 American Indian/Alaska Native, 49 Asian Americans or Pacific Islanders, 67 Hispanic Americans), 310 international. Average age 32. *Faculty:* 66 full-time (24 women), 26 part-time/adjunct (7 women). Expenses: Contact institution. *Financial support:* Fellowships, research assistantships, teaching assistantships, career-related internships or fieldwork, Federal Work-Study, scholarships/grants, and tuition waivers (full and partial) available. Financial award application deadline: 3/1; financial award applicants required to submit FAFSA. In 2006, 165 master's, 55 doctorates awarded. *Degree program information:* Part-time and evening/weekend programs available. Offers anthropology (MA, DS Sc, PhD); clinical psychology (PhD); economics (MA, DS Sc, PhD); general psychology (MA, PhD); global finance (MS); historical studies (MA, PhD); liberal studies (MA); philosophy (MA, DS Sc, PhD); political science (MA, DS Sc, PhD); social research (MA, MS, DS Sc, PhD); sociology (MA, DS Sc, PhD). *Application deadline:* For fall admission, 1/15 priority date for domestic students. Applications are processed on a rolling basis. *Application fee:* $50. *Application Contact:* Henry Watkin, Interim Director of Admissions, 800-523-5411, Fax: 212-989-7102, E-mail: gfadmit@newschool.edu. *Dean,* Dr. Michael Schober, 212-229-5777, E-mail: schober@newschool.edu.

Parsons The New School for Design Students: 352 full-time (218 women), 66 part-time (51 women); includes 64 minority (9 African Americans, 2 American Indian/Alaska Native, 33 Asian Americans or Pacific Islanders, 20 Hispanic Americans), 113 international. Average age 28. Expenses: Contact institution. *Financial support:* Fellowships with partial tuition reimbursements, research assistantships with partial tuition reimbursements, teaching assistantships with partial tuition reimbursements, Federal Work-Study, scholarships/grants, and tuition waivers (partial) available. Financial award application deadline: 3/1; financial award applicants required to submit FAFSA. In 2006, 164 degrees awarded. Offers architecture (M Arch); design (M Arch, MA, MFA); design and technology (MFA); fine arts (MFA); history of decorative arts (MA); lighting design (MFA); photography and related technologies (MFA). *Application deadline:* For fall admission, 3/1 priority date for domestic students. Applications are processed on a rolling basis. *Application fee:* $40. *Application Contact:* Anthony Padilla, Director of Admissions, 212-229-8989 Ext. 4023, Fax: 212-229-8975, E-mail: padillaa@newschool.edu. *Dean,* Tim Marshall, 212-229-8950 Ext. 4201, E-mail: marshalt@newschool.edu.

See Close-Up on page 975.

NEWSCHOOL OF ARCHITECTURE & DESIGN, San Diego, CA 92101-6634

General Information Proprietary, coed, primarily men, comprehensive institution. *Graduate housing:* On-campus housing not available. *Research affiliation:* Center City Development Corporation.

GRADUATE UNITS

Program in Architecture *Degree program information:* Part-time and evening/weekend programs available. Offers architecture (M Arch, MS).

NEW YORK ACADEMY OF ART, New York, NY 10013-2911

General Information Independent, coed, graduate-only institution. *Enrollment by degree level:* 107 master's. *Graduate faculty:* 5 full-time (1 woman), 27 part-time/adjunct (6 women). *Tuition:* Full-time $21,000. *Required fees:* $500. *Graduate housing:* Rooms and/or apartments available on a first-come, first-served basis to single and married students. Housing application deadline: 6/30. *Student services:* Campus employment opportunities, campus safety program, career counseling, grant writing training, international student services, low-cost health insurance, writing training. *Library facilities:* New York Academy of Art Library. *Collection:* 10,000 titles, 60 serial subscriptions, 240 audiovisual materials.

Computer facilities: 4 computers available on campus for general student use. A campuswide network can be accessed. Internet access is available. *Web address:* http://www.nyaa.edu/.

General Application Contact: Andrew Mueller, Director of Admissions/Registration, 212-966-0300, Fax: 212-966-3217, E-mail: andrew@nyaa.edu.

GRADUATE UNITS

Program in Figurative Art Students: 104 full-time (42 women), 3 part-time (2 women); includes 18 minority (2 African Americans, 2 American Indian/Alaska Native, 12 Asian Americans or Pacific Islanders, 2 Hispanic Americans), 16 international. Average age 28. 100 applicants, 87% accepted, 60 enrolled. *Faculty:* 5 full-time (1 woman), 27 part-time/adjunct (6 women). Expenses: Contact institution. *Financial support:* In 2006–07, 3 fellowships (averaging $30,000 per year) were awarded; career-related internships or fieldwork and scholarships/grants also available. Financial award application deadline: 9/1; financial award applicants required to submit FAFSA. In 2006, 50 degrees awarded. Offers figurative art (MFA). *Application deadline:* For fall admission, 4/15 priority date for domestic and international students. Applications are processed on a rolling basis. *Application fee:* $70. *Application Contact:* Andrew Mueller, Director of Admissions/Registration, 212-966-0300, Fax: 212-966-3217, E-mail: andrew@nyaa.edu. *Executive Director,* Wayne A. Linker, 212-966-0300, Fax: 212-966-3217, E-mail: info@nyaa.edu.

NEW YORK CHIROPRACTIC COLLEGE, Seneca Falls, NY 13148-0800

General Information Independent, coed, graduate-only institution. *Enrollment by degree level:* 647 first professional, 139 master's. *Graduate faculty:* 56 full-time (24 women), 27 part-time/adjunct (7 women). *Tuition:* Full-time $14,960. *Required fees:* $680. *Graduate housing:* Rooms and/or apartments available on a first-come, first-served basis to single and married students. Typical cost: $3,750 per year ($6,150 including board) for single students; $4,680 per year ($7,080 including board) for married students. *Student services:* Campus employment opportunities, campus safety program, career counseling, disabled student services, exercise/wellness program, free psychological counseling. *Library facilities:* New York Chiropractic College Library. *Online resources:* library catalog, web page, access to other libraries' catalogs. *Collection:* 35,393 titles, 230 serial subscriptions, 37,710 audiovisual materials. *Research affiliation:* Foot Levelers, Inc. (orthotics research).

Computer facilities: 105 computers available on campus for general student use. A campuswide network can be accessed from student residence rooms and from off campus. Internet access, student email accounts, online grade viewing, Intranet are available. *Web address:* http://www.nycc.edu/.

General Application Contact: Michael Lynch, Director of Admissions, 315-568-3052, Fax: 315-568-3087, E-mail: mlynch@nycc.edu.

GRADUATE UNITS

Professional Program Students: 645 full-time (272 women), 2 part-time (1 woman); includes 76 minority (17 African Americans, 28 Asian Americans or Pacific Islanders, 31 Hispanic Americans), 85 international. Average age 25. 368 applicants, 65% accepted, 191 enrolled. *Faculty:* 48 full-time (19 women), 24 part-time/adjunct (8 women). Expenses: Contact institution. *Financial support:* In 2006–07, 583 students received support, including 5 fellowships with full tuition reimbursements available (averaging $30,000 per year); Federal Work-Study and scholarships/grants also available. Financial award applicants required to submit FAFSA. In 2006, 189 degrees awarded. Offers chiropractic (DC). *Application deadline:* Applications are processed on a rolling basis. *Application fee:* $60. Electronic applications accepted. *Application Contact:* Michael Lynch, Director of Admissions, 315-568-3052, Fax: 315-568-3087, E-mail: mlynch@nycc.edu. *Interim Executive Vice President of Academic Affairs,* Dr. Mike Mestan, 315-568-3864, Fax: 315-568-3087, E-mail: mlynch@nycc.edu.

Program in Acupuncture and Oriental Medicine Students: 59 full-time (47 women), 39 part-time (19 women); includes 10 minority (2 American Indian/Alaska Native, 7 Asian Americans or Pacific Islanders, 1 Hispanic American), 2 international. Average age 34. 39 applicants, 90% accepted, 30 enrolled. *Faculty:* 9 full-time (6 women), 6 part-time/adjunct (3 women). Expenses: Contact institution. *Financial support:* In 2006–07, 88 students received support, including 1 fellowship with tuition reimbursement available (averaging $30,000 per year); Federal Work-Study and scholarships/grants also available. Financial award applicants required to submit FAFSA. In 2006, 28 master's awarded. Offers acupuncture (MS); acupuncture and Oriental medicine (MS). *Application deadline:* Applications are processed on a rolling basis. *Application fee:* $60. Electronic applications accepted. *Application Contact:* Michael Lynch, Director of Admissions, 315-568-3052, Fax: 315-568-3087, E-mail: mlynch@nycc.edu. *Dean of School of Acupuncture and Oriental Medicine,* Marilee Murphy, 315-568-3268, E-mail: mmurphy@nycc.edu.

NEW YORK COLLEGE OF HEALTH PROFESSIONS, Syosset, NY 11791-4413

General Information Independent, coed. *Graduate housing:* On-campus housing not available. *Research affiliation:* North Shore Hospital (acupuncture).

GRADUATE UNITS

Graduate School of Oriental Medicine *Degree program information:* Part-time programs available. Offers acupuncture (MS); Oriental medicine (MS).

NEW YORK COLLEGE OF PODIATRIC MEDICINE, New York, NY 10035

General Information Independent, coed, graduate-only institution. *Graduate housing:* Rooms and/or apartments available on a first-come, first-served basis to single and married students. Typical cost: $9,000 per year for single students. Housing application deadline: 8/15. *Research affiliation:* Cyberlogics (ultrasound use), Novartis (fungal diseases of nail), Prescription Dispensing Laboratories (topical verapamil), Anodyne Corporation (light energy applications).

GRADUATE UNITS

Professional Program Offers podiatric medicine (DPM).

NEW YORK COLLEGE OF TRADITIONAL CHINESE MEDICINE, Mineola, NY 11501

General Information Independent, coed, graduate-only institution.

GRADUATE UNITS

Graduate Programs

NEW YORK FILM ACADEMY, Los Angeles, CA 90068

General Information Independent, coed, graduate-only institution.

GRADUATE UNITS

Program in Filmmaking Offers acting for film (MFA); filmmaking (MFA); producing (MFA); screenwriting (MFA).

NEW YORK INSTITUTE OF TECHNOLOGY, Old Westbury, NY 11568-8000

General Information Independent, coed, university. CGS member. *Enrollment:* 11,404 graduate, professional, and undergraduate students; 2,460 full-time matriculated graduate/professional students (1,163 women), 2,158 part-time matriculated graduate/professional students (986 women). *Enrollment by degree level:* 1,206 first professional, 3,260 master's, 129 doctoral, 23 other advanced degrees. *Graduate faculty:* 256 full-time (81 women), 419 part-time/adjunct (146 women). *Tuition:* Full-time $16,800; part-time $700 per credit. *Graduate housing:* Room and/or apartments available on a first-come, first-served basis to single students; on-campus housing not available to married students. Typical cost: $5,936 per year ($9,636 including board). *Student services:* Campus employment opportunities, career counseling, disabled student services, exercise/wellness program, free psychological counseling, international student services, low-cost health insurance, multicultural affairs office, teacher training, writing training. *Library facilities:* George and Gertrude Wisser Memorial Library plus 4 others. *Online resources:* library catalog, web page. *Collection:* 272,227 titles, 13,827 serial subscriptions.

Computer facilities: 815 computers available on campus for general student use. A campuswide network can be accessed from student residence rooms and from off campus. Internet access, e-mail are available. *Web address:* http://www.nyit.edu/.

General Application Contact: Jacquelyn Nealon, Dean of Admissions and Financial Aid, 516-686-7925, Fax: 516-686-7613, E-mail: jnealon@nyit.edu.

GRADUATE UNITS

Ellis College *Degree program information:* Part-time and evening/weekend programs available. Postbaccalaureate distance learning degree programs offered (no on-campus study). Offers accounting and information systems (MBA); communication arts—advertising and public relations (MA); e-commerce (MBA); finance (MBA); general business studies (MBA); global management (MBA); health care administration (MBA); human resources management (MBA); human resources management and labor relations (MS); instructional technology for educators (MS); instructional technology for professional trainers (MS); leadership (MBA); management of information systems (MBA); management of technology (MBA); marketing (MBA); multimedia (Advanced Certificate); professional accounting (MBA); project management (MBA); risk management (MBA); strategy and economics (MBA). Electronic applications accepted.

Graduate Division Students: 2,460 full-time (1,163 women), 2,158 part-time (986 women); includes 1,101 minority (372 African Americans, 9 American Indian/Alaska Native, 516 Asian Americans or Pacific Islanders, 204 Hispanic Americans), 917 international. Average age 31. 3,454 applicants, 81% accepted, 705 enrolled. *Faculty:* 256 full-time (81 women), 419 part-time/adjunct (146 women). Expenses: Contact institution. *Financial support:* Fellowships with partial tuition reimbursements, research assistantships with partial tuition reimbursements, career-related internships or fieldwork, Federal Work-Study, institutionally sponsored loans, tuition waivers (full and partial), and unspecified assistantships available. Support available to part-time students. Financial award applicants required to submit FAFSA. In 2006, 1,473 master's, 30 doctorates, 13 other advanced degrees awarded. *Degree program information:* Part-time and evening/weekend programs available. Postbaccalaureate distance learning degree programs offered (minimal on-campus study). *Application deadline:* For fall admission, 7/1 priority date for domestic students; for spring admission, 12/1 priority date for domestic students. Applications are processed on a rolling basis. *Application fee:* $50. Electronic applications accepted. *Application Contact:* Jacquelyn Nealon, Dean of Admissions and Financial Aid, 516-686-7925, Fax: 516-686-7613, E-mail: jnealon@nyit.edu. *Director of Academic Affairs,* Dr. Spencer Turkel, 516-686-7413, Fax: 516-686-7631, E-mail: sturkel@nyit.edu.

School of Allied Health and Life Sciences Students: 212 full-time (145 women), 69 part-time (44 women); includes 67 minority (18 African Americans, 31 Asian Americans or Pacific Islanders, 18 Hispanic Americans), 20 international. Average age 29. 356 applicants, 54% accepted, 43 enrolled. Expenses: Contact institution. *Financial support:* Fellowships, research assistantships with partial tuition reimbursements, career-related internships or fieldwork, institutionally sponsored loans, tuition waivers (full and partial), and unspecified assistantships available. Support available to part-time students. Financial award applicants required to submit FAFSA. In 2006, 40 master's, 30 doctorates awarded. *Degree program information:* Part-time and evening/weekend programs available. Postbaccalaureate distance learning degree programs offered. Offers allied health and life sciences (MPS, MS, DPT); clinical nutrition (MS); human relations (MPS); occupational therapy (MS); physical therapy (MS, DPT); physician assistant (MS). *Application deadline:* For fall admission, 7/1 priority date for domestic students; for spring admission, 12/1 priority date for domestic students. Applications are processed on a rolling basis. *Application fee:* $50. Electronic applications accepted. *Application Contact:* Jacquelyn Nealon, Dean of Admissions and Financial Aid, 516-686-7925, Fax: 516-686-7613, E-mail: jnealon@nyit.edu. *Dean,* Dr. Barbara Ross-Lee, 516-686-3722, Fax: 516-686-3830, E-mail: brosslee@nyit.edu.

School of Architecture Students: 10 full-time (5 women), 2 part-time; includes 2 minority (1 Asian American or Pacific Islander, 1 Hispanic American), 7 international. Average age 33. 35 applicants, 49% accepted, 6 enrolled. Expenses: Contact institution. *Financial support:* Research assistantships with partial tuition reimbursements, institutionally sponsored loans and tuition waivers (full and partial) available. Support available to part-time students. Financial award applicants required to submit FAFSA. In 2006, 7 degrees awarded. *Degree program information:* Part-time programs available. Offers urban and regional design (M Arch). *Application deadline:* For fall admission, 7/1 priority date for domestic students; for spring admission, 12/1 priority date for domestic students. Applications are processed on a rolling basis. *Application fee:* $50. Electronic applications accepted. *Application Contact:* Jacquelyn Nealon, Dean of Admissions and Financial Aid, 516-686-7925, Fax: 516-686-7613, E-mail: jnealon@nyit.edu. *Dean,* Judith DiMaio, 516-686-7594, Fax: 516-686-7921, E-mail: jdimaio@nyit.edu.

School of Arts, Sciences, and Communication Students: 149 full-time (93 women), 113 part-time (67 women); includes 55 minority (30 African Americans, 9 Asian Americans or Pacific Islanders, 16 Hispanic Americans), 91 international. Average age 31. 231 applicants, 81% accepted, 111 enrolled. Expenses: Contact institution. *Financial support:* Research assistantships with partial tuition reimbursements, career-related internships or fieldwork, Federal Work-Study, institutionally sponsored loans, tuition waivers (partial), and unspecified assistantships available. Support available to part-time students. Financial award applicants required to submit FAFSA. In 2006, 153 degrees awarded. *Degree program information:* Part-time and evening/weekend programs available. Offers arts, sciences, and communication (MA); communication arts (MA). *Application deadline:* For fall admission, 7/1 priority date for domestic students; for spring admission, 12/1 priority date for domestic students. Applications are processed on a rolling basis. *Application fee:* $50. Electronic applications accepted. *Application Contact:* Jacquelyn Nealon, Dean of Admissions and Financial Aid, 516-686-7925, Fax: 516-686-7613, E-mail: jnealon@nyit.edu. *Dean,* Dr. Roger Yu, 516-686-7700, Fax: 516-626-3655.

School of Education and Professional Services Students: 19 full-time (14 women), 339 part-time (223 women); includes 52 minority (28 African Americans, 1 American Indian/Alaska Native, 3 Asian Americans or Pacific Islanders, 20 Hispanic Americans), 8 international. Average age 34. 371 applicants, 81% accepted, 150 enrolled. Expenses: Contact institution. *Financial support:* Research assistantships with partial tuition reimbursements, career-related internships or fieldwork, institutionally sponsored loans, and tuition waivers (full and partial) available. Support available to part-time students. Financial award applicants required to submit FAFSA. In 2006, 123 master's, 3 other advanced degrees awarded. *Degree program information:* Part-time and evening/weekend programs available. Postbaccalaureate distance learning degree programs offered. Offers distance learning (Advanced Certificate); district leadership and technology (Professional Diploma); education and professional services (MS, Advanced Certificate, Professional Diploma); elementary education (MS); instructional technology (MS); mental health counseling and school counseling (MS); multimedia (Advanced Certificate); school counseling (MS); school leadership and technology (Professional Diploma). *Application deadline:* For fall admission, 7/1 priority date for domestic students; for spring admission, 12/1 priority date for domestic students. Applications are processed on a rolling basis. *Application fee:* $50. Electronic applications accepted. *Application Contact:* Jacquelyn Nealon, Dean of Admissions and Financial Aid, 516-686-7925, Fax: 516-686-7613, E-mail: jnealon@nyit.edu. *Dean,* Dr. Jacqueline Kress, 516-686-7706, Fax: 516-686-7655.

School of Engineering and Technology Students: 501 full-time (105 women), 269 part-time (56 women); includes 78 minority (27 African Americans, 34 Asian Americans or Pacific Islanders, 17 Hispanic Americans), 564 international. Average age 31. 1,161 applicants, 75% accepted, 205 enrolled. Expenses: Contact institution. *Financial support:* Fellowships, research assistantships with partial tuition reimbursements, career-related internships or fieldwork, institutionally sponsored loans, tuition waivers (full and partial), and unspecified assistantships available. Support available to part-time students. Financial award applicants required to submit FAFSA. In 2006, 192 master's, 9 other advanced degrees awarded. *Degree program information:* Part-time and evening/weekend programs available. Postbaccalaureate distance learning degree programs offered. Offers computer science (MS); electrical engineering and computer engineering (MS); energy management (MS); energy technology (Advanced Certificate); engineering and technology (MS, Advanced Certificate); environmental management (Advanced Certificate); environmental technology (MS); facilities management (Advanced Certificate). *Application deadline:* For fall admission, 7/1 priority date for domestic students; for spring admission, 12/1 priority date for domestic students. Applications are processed on a rolling basis. *Application fee:* $50. Electronic applications accepted. *Application Contact:* Jacquelyn Nealon, Dean of Admissions and Financial Aid, 516-686-7925, Fax: 516-686-7613, E-mail: jnealon@nyit.edu. *Dean,* Dr. Heskia Heskiaoff, 516-686-7931, Fax: 516-625-5801.

School of Management Students: 363 full-time (138 women), 1,366 part-time (597 women); includes 322 minority (168 African Americans, 6 American Indian/Alaska Native, 89 Asian Americans or Pacific Islanders, 59 Hispanic Americans), 226 international. Average age 29. 1,419 applicants, 89% accepted, 188 enrolled. Expenses: Contact institution. *Financial support:* Fellowships, research assistantships with partial tuition reimbursements, career-related internships or fieldwork, institutionally sponsored loans, tuition waivers (full and partial), and unspecified assistantships available. Support available to part-time students. Financial award applicants required to submit FAFSA. In 2006, 958 master's, 1 other advanced degree awarded. *Degree program information:* Part-time and evening/weekend programs available. Postbaccalaureate distance learning degree programs offered. Offers accounting (Advanced Certificate); business administration (MBA); finance (Advanced Certificate); human resources administration (Advanced Certificate); human resources management and labor relations (MS); international business (Advanced Certificate); labor relations (Advanced Certificate); management (MBA, MS, Advanced Certificate); management of information systems (Advanced Certificate); marketing (Advanced Certificate). *Application deadline:* For fall admission, 7/1 priority date for domestic students; for spring admission, 12/1 priority date for domestic students. Applications are processed on a rolling basis. *Application fee:* $50. Electronic applications accepted. *Application Contact:* Jacquelyn Nealon, Dean of Admissions and Financial Aid, 516-686-7925, Fax: 516-686-7613, E-mail: jnealon@nyit.edu. *Dean,* Dr. David R. Decker, 516-686-7830, Fax: 516-686-7655.

New York College of Osteopathic Medicine Students: 1,206 full-time (663 women); includes 525 minority (101 African Americans, 2 American Indian/Alaska Native, 349 Asian Americans or Pacific Islanders, 73 Hispanic Americans), 1 international. Average age 27. 2,569 applicants, 24% accepted, 304 enrolled. *Faculty:* 68 full-time (19 women), 35 part-time/adjunct (10 women). Expenses: Contact institution. *Financial support:* In 2006–07, 914 students received support, including fellowships with partial tuition reimbursements available (averaging $17,200 per year); tuition waivers (full and partial) also available. Financial award application deadline: 4/1; financial award applicants required to submit FAFSA. In 2006, 242 degrees awarded. Offers osteopathic medicine (DO). *Application deadline:* For fall admission, 2/1 for domestic students. *Application fee:* $60. *Application Contact:* Michael J. Schaefer, Director of Admissions, 516-686-3747, Fax: 516-686-3831, E-mail: mschaefe@nyit.edu. *Dean,* Dr. Barbara Ross-Lee, 516-686-3722, Fax: 516-686-3830, E-mail: brosslee@nyit.edu.

NEW YORK LAW SCHOOL, New York, NY 10013

General Information Independent, coed, graduate-only institution. *Enrollment by degree level:* 1,510 first professional, 40 master's. *Graduate faculty:* 76 full-time (28 women), 94 part-time/adjunct (36 women). *Tuition:* Full-time $38,535. *Required fees:* $809. Tuition and fees vary according to degree level and student level. *Graduate housing:* Room and/or apartments available on a first-come, first-served basis to single students; on-campus housing not available to married students. Typical cost: $13,650 per year. Room charges vary according to housing facility selected. Housing application deadline: 6/1. *Student services:* Campus employment opportunities, campus safety program, career counseling, disabled student services, free psychological counseling, international student services, low-cost health insurance, writing training. *Library facilities:* Mendik Library. *Online resources:* library catalog, web page, access to other libraries' catalogs. *Collection:* 518,496 titles, 5,379 serial subscriptions.

Computer facilities: 142 computers available on campus for general student use. A campuswide network can be accessed from student residence rooms and from off campus. Internet access and online class registration are available. *Web address:* http://www.nyls.edu/.

General Application Contact: William D. Perez, Assistant Dean for Admissions and Financial Aid, 212-431-2888, Fax: 212-966-1522, E-mail: wperez@nyls.edu.

GRADUATE UNITS

Professional Program Students: 1,168 full-time (629 women), 394 part-time (203 women); includes 355 minority (93 African Americans, 3 American Indian/Alaska Native, 142 Asian Americans or Pacific Islanders, 117 Hispanic Americans), 9 international. Average age 28. 5,557 applicants, 44% accepted, 549 enrolled. *Faculty:* 76 full-time (28 women), 94 part-time/adjunct (36 women). Expenses: Contact institution. *Financial support:* In 2006–07, 679 students received support, including 202 research assistantships (averaging $3,920 per year), 5 teaching assistantships (averaging $1,000 per year); career-related internships or fieldwork, Federal Work-Study, institutionally sponsored loans, and scholarships/grants also available. Support available to part-time students. Financial award application deadline: 4/2; financial award applicants required to submit FAFSA. In 2006, 521 degrees awarded. *Degree program information:* Part-time and evening/weekend programs available. Offers law (JD); tax (LL M). *Application deadline:* For fall admission, 4/1 priority date for domestic and international students. Applications are processed on a rolling basis. *Application fee:* $60. Electronic applications accepted. *Application Contact:* William D. Perez, Assistant Dean for Admissions and Financial Aid, 212-431-2888, Fax: 212-966-1522, E-mail: wperez@nyls.edu. *President and Dean,* Richard A. Matasar, 212-431-2840, Fax: 212-219-3752, E-mail: rmatasar@nyls.edu.

NEW YORK MEDICAL COLLEGE, Valhalla, NY 10595-1691

General Information Independent, coed, graduate-only institution. CGS member. *Graduate housing:* Rooms and/or apartments available on a first-come, first-served basis to single and married students. *Research affiliation:* American Health Foundation.

GRADUATE UNITS

Graduate School of Basic Medical Sciences *Degree program information:* Part-time and evening/weekend programs available. Offers basic medical sciences (MS, PhD); biochemistry and molecular biology (MS, PhD); cell biology and neuroscience (MS, PhD); experimental pathology (MS, PhD); microbiology and immunology (MS, PhD); pharmacology (MS, PhD); physiology (MS, PhD).

Professional Program Students: 774 full-time (395 women); includes 321 minority (18 African Americans, 1 American Indian/Alaska Native, 293 Asian Americans or Pacific Islanders, 9 Hispanic Americans), 3 international. Average age 25. 9,647 applicants, 8% accepted, 194 enrolled. *Faculty:* 1,346 full-time (462 women), 1,672 part-time/adjunct (438 women). Expenses: Contact institution. *Financial support:* In 2006–07, 50 research assistantships with full tuition reimbursements (averaging $22,000 per year) were awarded; Federal Work-Study, institutionally sponsored loans, scholarships/grants, and tuition waivers (full) also available. Support available to part-time students. Financial award application deadline: 4/30; financial award applicants required to submit FAFSA. In 2006, 185 degrees awarded. Offers medicine (MD). *Application deadline:* For fall admission, 12/15 for domestic and international students. Applications are processed on a rolling basis. *Application fee:* $100. Electronic applications accepted. *Application Contact:* Dr. Fern Juster, Admissions Office, 914-594-4507, Fax: 914-594-4613, E-mail: mdadmit@nymc.edu. *Provost and Dean, School of Medicine,* Dr. Ralph A. O'Connell, 914-594-4900, Fax: 914-594-4145.

School of Public Health Students: 143 full-time (114 women), 314 part-time (212 women). Average age 31. 154 applicants, 71% accepted, 37 enrolled. *Faculty:* 42 full-time (22 women), 182 part-time/adjunct (99 women). Expenses: Contact institution. *Financial support:* In 2006–07, 139 students received support; research assistantships with full and partial tuition reimbursements available, teaching assistantships with full and partial tuition reimbursements available, career-related internships or fieldwork, Federal Work-Study, institutionally sponsored loans, health care benefits, tuition waivers (partial), and tuition reimbursements available. Support available to part-time students. Financial award applicants required to submit FAFSA. In 2006, 76 master's, 13 doctorates awarded. *Degree program information:* Part-time and evening/weekend programs available. Offers behavioral sciences and health promotion (MPH); biostatistics (MPH, MS); disability and human development (MPH); environmental health science (MPH); epidemiology (MPH, Dr PH); general public health (MPH); health informatics (MPH); health policy and management (MPH); international health (MPH); maternal and child health (MPH); physical therapy (DPT); public health (MPH, MS, DPT, Dr PH, Graduate Certificate); public health informatics (Graduate Certificate); speech-language pathology (MS). *Application deadline:* For fall admission, 8/1 priority date for domestic students, 5/15 for international students; for spring admission, 12/1 priority date for domestic students, 10/15 for international students. Applications are processed on a rolling basis. *Application fee:* $50 ($100 for international students). Electronic applications accepted. *Application Contact:* Marian F. McGowan, Information Contact, 914-594-4510, Fax: 914-594-4292, E-mail: sph_admissions@nymc.edu. *Dean,* Dr. Robert W. Amler, 914-594-4531, Fax: 914-594-4292, E-mail: robert_amler@nymc.edu.

NEW YORK SCHOOL OF INTERIOR DESIGN, New York, NY 10021-5110

General Information Independent, coed, primarily women, comprehensive institution. *Enrollment:* 736 graduate, professional, and undergraduate students; 18 full-time matriculated graduate/professional students (14 women). *Enrollment by degree level:* 18 master's. *Graduate faculty:* 9 part-time/adjunct (5 women). *Tuition:* Full-time $20,500. *Graduate housing:* On-campus housing not available. *Student services:* Campus employment opportunities, career counseling, international student services, low-cost health insurance. *Library facilities:* NYSID Library. *Online resources:* library catalog, web page, access to other libraries' catalogs. *Collection:* 12,000 titles, 110 serial subscriptions, 50 audiovisual materials. *Research affiliation:* Metropolitan New York Library Council–Research Consortium.

Computer facilities: 135 computers available on campus for general student use. A campuswide network can be accessed from off campus. Internet access is available. *Web address:* http://www.nysid.edu/.

General Application Contact: Scott Ageloff, Dean, 212-472-1500 Ext. 301, Fax: 212-288-6577, E-mail: scott@nysid.edu.

GRADUATE UNITS

Program in Interior Design Students: 18 full-time (14 women), 14 international. Average age 25. 38 applicants, 50% accepted, 10 enrolled. *Faculty:* 9 part-time/adjunct (5 women). Expenses: Contact institution. *Financial support:* In 2006–07, 6 students received support, including 6 fellowships (averaging $10,000 per year); career-related internships or fieldwork, Federal Work-Study, institutionally sponsored loans, and scholarships/grants also available. Financial award application deadline: 5/1; financial award applicants required to submit FAFSA. In 2006, 6 degrees awarded. Offers interior design (MFA). *Application deadline:* For fall admission, 3/15 priority date for domestic and international students. Applications are processed on a rolling basis. *Application fee:* $50 ($75 for international students). Electronic applications accepted. *Application Contact:* David T. Sprouls, Director of Admissions, 212-472-1500 Ext. 202, Fax: 212-472-1867, E-mail: david@nysid.edu. *Dean,* Scott Ageloff, 212-472-1500 Ext. 301, Fax: 212-288-6577, E-mail: scott@nysid.edu.

NEW YORK THEOLOGICAL SEMINARY, New York, NY 10115

General Information Independent-religious, coed, graduate-only institution. *Graduate housing:* On-campus housing not available. *Research affiliation:* Bellevue Hospital Center, Goldwater Memorial Hospital, Institutes of Religion and Health, Lutheran Medical Center, Postgraduate Center for Mental Health.

GRADUATE UNITS

Graduate and Professional Programs *Degree program information:* Part-time programs available. Offers theology (M Div, MPS, MSW, D Min).

NEW YORK UNIVERSITY, New York, NY 10012-1019

General Information Independent, coed, university. CGS member. *Enrollment:* 40,870 graduate, professional, and undergraduate students; 11,599 full-time matriculated graduate/professional students (6,593 women), 8,306 part-time matriculated graduate/professional students (4,713 women). *Enrollment by degree level:* 3,428 first professional, 13,466 master's, 2,039 doctoral, 478 other advanced degrees. *Graduate faculty:* 3,363 full-time (1,267 women), 3,392 part-time/adjunct. *Tuition:* Part-time $1,080 per unit. *Required fees:* $56 per unit. $329 per term. Tuition and fees vary according to program. *Graduate housing:* Rooms and/or apartments available on a first-come, first-served basis to single and married students. *Student services:* Campus employment opportunities, campus safety program, career counseling, disabled student services, exercise/wellness program, free psychological counseling, grant writing training, international student services, low-cost health insurance, multicultural affairs office, teacher training, writing training. *Library facilities:* Elmer H. Bobst Library plus 11 others. *Online resources:* library catalog, web page, access to other libraries' catalogs. *Collection:* 5.2 million titles, 48,958 serial subscriptions. *Research affiliation:* New York Botanical Gardens, Center for American Archaeology, American Museum of Natural History, Inter-University Doctoral Consortium, Metropolitan Museum of Art, Smithsonian Institute.

Computer facilities: Computer purchase and lease plans are available. 4,500 computers available on campus for general student use. A campuswide network can be accessed from student residence rooms and from off campus. Internet access and online class registration are available. *Web address:* http://www.nyu.edu/.

General Application Contact: New York University Information, 212-998-1212.

GRADUATE UNITS

College of Dentistry Students: 1,290 full-time (705 women), 477 part-time (437 women); includes 975 minority (118 African Americans, 2 American Indian/Alaska Native, 780 Asian Americans or Pacific Islanders, 75 Hispanic Americans). Average age 31. 5,551 applicants, 15% accepted, 534 enrolled. *Faculty:* 257 full-time, 663 part-time/adjunct. Expenses: Contact institution. *Financial support:* In 2006–07, 1,151 students received support, including fellowships (averaging $25,000 per year); Federal Work-Study, institutionally sponsored loans, scholarships/grants, and unspecified assistantships also available. Support available to part-time students. Financial award application deadline: 3/1; financial award applicants required to submit FAFSA. In 2006, 308 DDSs, 110 master's, 10 doctorates, 50 other advanced degrees awarded. Offers clinical research (MS); dentistry (DDS, MS, PhD, Advanced Certificate); endodontics (Advanced Certificate); oral and maxillofacial surgery (Advanced Certificate); orthodontics (Advanced Certificate); pediatric dentistry (Advanced Certificate); periodontics (Advanced Certificate); prosthodontics (Advanced Certificate); prosthodontics (implantology) (Advanced Certificate). *Application deadline:* For fall admission, 4/1 priority date for domestic students. Applications are processed on a rolling basis. *Application fee:* $75. *Application Contact:* Dr. Anthony M. Palatta, Assistant Dean for Student Affairs and Admissions, 212-998-9918, Fax: 212-995-4240, E-mail: ap16@nyu.edu. *Interim Dean,* Dr. Richard Vogel, 212-998-9898, Fax: 212-995-4240, E-mail: richard.vogel@nyu.edu.

College of Nursing Students: 16 full-time (all women), 468 part-time (432 women); includes 172 minority (74 African Americans, 77 Asian Americans or Pacific Islanders, 21 Hispanic Americans). 177 applicants, 85% accepted, 123 enrolled. *Faculty:* 30 full-time (all women). Expenses: Contact institution. *Financial support:* In 2006–07, 2 research assistantships with full and partial tuition reimbursements were awarded; fellowships with full and partial tuition reimbursements, career-related internships or fieldwork, Federal Work-Study, institutionally sponsored loans, scholarships/grants, and tuition waivers (partial) also available. Support available to part-time students. Financial award application deadline: 2/1; financial award applicants required to submit FAFSA. In 2006, 100 master's, 10 doctorates, 7 other advanced degrees awarded. *Degree program information:* Part-time and evening/weekend programs available. Offers advanced practice nursing: adult acute care (MS, Advanced Certificate); advanced practice nursing: adult primary care (MS, Advanced Certificate); advanced practice nursing: adult primary care/geriatrics (MS); advanced practice nursing: children with special needs (Advanced Certificate); advanced practice nursing: geriatrics (MS, Advanced Certificate); advanced practice nursing: holistic nursing (MS, Advanced Certificate); advanced practice nursing: home health nursing (Advanced Certificate); advanced practice nursing: mental health (MS); advanced practice nursing: mental health nursing (Advanced Certificate); advanced practice nursing: pediatrics (MS, Advanced Certificate); advanced practice nursing: pediatrics/children with special needs (MS); midwifery (MS, Advanced Certificate); nursing (MS, PhD, Advanced Certificate); nursing administration (MS, Advanced Certificate); nursing education (MS, Advanced Certificate); nursing informatics (MS, Advanced Certificate); palliative care (MS, Advanced Certificate); research and theory development in nursing science (PhD). *Application deadline:* Applications are processed on a rolling basis. *Application fee:* $65. *Application Contact:* Amy Knowles, Assistant Dean for Student Affairs and Admissions, 212-998-5333, Fax: 212-995-4302, E-mail: ak96@nyu.edu. *Dean, College of Nursing,* Dr. Terry Fulmer, 212-998-5303, Fax: 212-995-3143.

Gallatin School of Individualized Study Students: 46 full-time (33 women), 158 part-time (123 women); includes 61 minority (28 African Americans, 1 American Indian/Alaska Native, 16 Asian Americans or Pacific Islanders, 16 Hispanic Americans), 7 international. Average age 30. 216 applicants, 48% accepted, 53 enrolled. *Faculty:* 26 full-time (15 women), 11 part-time/adjunct (4 women). Expenses: Contact institution. *Financial support:* In 2006–07, 120 students received support, including 3 fellowships with partial tuition reimbursements available (averaging $21,000 per year), 1 research assistantship with full tuition reimbursement available (averaging $15,000 per year); career-related internships or fieldwork, Federal Work-Study, institutionally sponsored loans, scholarships/grants, and unspecified assistantships also available. Support available to part-time students. Financial award application deadline: 3/1; financial award applicants required to submit FAFSA. In 2006, 53 degrees awarded. *Degree program information:* Part-time and evening/weekend programs available. Offers individualized study (MA). *Application deadline:* For fall admission, 2/1 priority date for domestic and international students; for spring admission, 11/1 priority date for domestic students, 11/1 for international students. Applications are processed on a rolling basis. *Application fee:* $50. *Application Contact:* Frances R. Levin, Director of Graduate Admissions, 212-998-7370, Fax: 212-995-4150, E-mail: gallatin.gradadmissions@nyu.edu. *Interim Dean,* Dr. Ali Mirsepassi, 212-998-7370.

Graduate School of Arts and Science Students: 2,942 full-time (1,605 women), 1,443 part-time (811 women); includes 650 minority (149 African Americans, 5 American Indian/Alaska Native, 313 Asian Americans or Pacific Islanders, 183 Hispanic Americans), 1,282 international. Average age 29. 10,148 applicants, 29% accepted, 1251 enrolled. *Faculty:* 597 full-time (159 women), 393 part-time/adjunct. Expenses: Contact institution. *Financial support:* In 2006–07, 783 fellowships with tuition reimbursements, 111 research assistantships with tuition reimbursements, 502 teaching assistantships with tuition reimbursements were awarded; career-related internships or fieldwork, Federal Work-Study, institutionally sponsored loans, scholarships/grants, health care benefits, tuition waivers (partial), unspecified assistantships, and instructorships also available. Financial award applicants required to submit FAFSA. In 2006, 907 master's, 222 doctorates awarded. *Degree program information:* Part-time and evening/weekend programs available. Offers African diaspora (PhD); African history (PhD); Africana studies (MA); American studies (MA, PhD); anthropology (MA, PhD); anthropology and French studies (PhD); applied economic analysis (Advanced Certificate); archival management and historical editing (Advanced Certificate); arts and science (MA, MFA, MS, PhD, Advanced Certificate); Atlantic history (PhD); biology (PhD); biomaterials science (MS); biomedical journalism (MS); cancer and molecular biology (PhD); chemistry (MS, PhD); classics (MA, PhD); cognition and perception (PhD); community psychology (PhD); comparative literature (MA, PhD); composition and theory (MA, PhD); computational biology (PhD); computers in biological research (MS); creative writing (MA, MFA); cultural reporting and criticism (MA); developmental genetics (PhD); early music performance (Advanced Certificate); economics (MA, PhD); English and American literature (MA, PhD); environmental health sciences (MS, PhD); ethnomusicology (MA, PhD); French studies and sociology (PhD); French studies/history (PhD); French studies/journalism (MA); general biology (MS); general psychology (MA); German studies and critical thought (MA, PhD); Hebrew and Judaic studies (MA, PhD); Hebrew and Judaic studies/history (PhD); Hebrew and Judaic studies/museum studies (MA); history (MA, PhD); humanities and social thought (MA); immunology and microbiology (PhD); industrial/organizational psychology (MA); Italian (MA, PhD); Italian studies (MA); journalism (MA); Latin American and Caribbean studies/journalism (MA); linguistics (MA, PhD); Middle Eastern history (MA); Middle Eastern studies/history (PhD); molecular genetics (PhD); museum studies (MA, Advanced Certificate); Near Eastern studies/journalism (MA); neurobiology (PhD); oral biology (MS); philosophy (MA, PhD); physics (MS, PhD); plant biology (PhD); poetics and theory (Advanced Certificate); political campaign management (MA); politics (MA, PhD); Portuguese (MA, PhD); psychotherapy and psychoanalysis (Advanced Certificate); public history (Advanced Certificate); recombinant DNA technology (MS); religion (Advanced Certificate); religious studies (MA); Russian literature (MA); science and environmental reporting (Advanced Certificate); Slavic literature (MA); social theory (Advanced Certificate); social/personality psychology (PhD); sociology (MA, PhD); Spanish (PhD); Spanish and Latin American literatures and cultures (MA); Spanish language and translation (MA); world history (MA). *Application fee:* $80. Electronic applications accepted. *Application Contact:* Roberta Popik, Associate Dean of Enrollment, 212-998-8050, Fax: 212-995-4557, E-mail: gsas.admissions@nyu.edu. *Dean,* Catharine R. Stimpson, 212-998-8040.

Center for European Studies Students: 14 full-time (12 women), 1 part-time, 6 international. Average age 25. 24 applicants, 92% accepted, 8 enrolled. *Faculty:* 4 full-time (0 women). Expenses: Contact institution. *Financial support:* Fellowships with tuition reimbursements, teaching assistantships with tuition reimbursements, career-related internships or fieldwork, Federal Work-Study, institutionally sponsored loans, and scholarships/grants available. Financial award application deadline: 1/4; financial award applicants required to submit FAFSA. In 2006, 8 degrees awarded. Offers European studies (MA). *Application deadline:* For fall admission, 1/4 priority date for domestic students. *Application fee:* $80. Electronic applications accepted. *Application Contact:* Jennifer Denbo, Department Graduate Administrator, 212-998-3838, Fax: 212-995-4188. *Director,* Katherine Fleming, 212-998-3838, Fax: 212-995-4188, E-mail: european.studies@nyu.edu.

Center for French Civilization and Culture Students: 106 full-time (74 women), 21 part-time (17 women); includes 13 minority (4 African Americans, 5 Asian Americans or Pacific Islanders, 4 Hispanic Americans), 37 international. Average age 29. 149 applicants, 59% accepted, 46 enrolled. Expenses: Contact institution. *Financial support:* Fellowships with tuition reimbursements, research assistantships with tuition reimbursements, teaching assistantships with tuition reimbursements, Federal Work-Study, institutionally sponsored loans, scholarships/grants, traineeships, unspecified assistantships, and instructorships available. Financial award application deadline: 1/4; financial award applicants required to submit FAFSA. In 2006, 31 master's, 7 doctorates awarded. *Degree program information:* Part-time and evening/weekend programs available. Offers French (PhD); French civilization (PhD); French civilization and culture (MA, PhD, Advanced Certificate); French language and civilization (MA); French literature (MA); French studies (MA, PhD, Advanced Certificate); French studies and anthropology (PhD); French studies and history (PhD); French studies and journalism (MA); French studies and sociology (PhD); Romance languages and literatures (MA). *Application deadline:* For fall admission, 1/4 for domestic students. *Application fee:* $80. *Application Contact:* Brett Underhill, Graduate Secretary, 212-998-8700, Fax: 212-995-3539, E-mail: french.grad@nyu.edu. *Chair,* Judith Miller, 212-998-8700, Fax: 212-995-3539, E-mail: french.grad@nyu.edu.

New York University (continued)

Center for Latin American and Caribbean Studies Students: 30 full-time (20 women), 25 part-time (15 women); includes 21 minority (2 African Americans, 1 American Indian/Alaska Native, 18 Hispanic Americans), 7 international. Average age 28. 67 applicants, 85% accepted, 18 enrolled. *Faculty:* 2 full-time (0 women), 5 part-time/adjunct. Expenses: Contact institution. *Financial support:* Fellowships with tuition reimbursements, teaching assistantships with tuition reimbursements, Federal Work-Study, institutionally sponsored loans, scholarships/grants, health care benefits, and unspecified assistantships available. Financial award application deadline: 1/4; financial award applicants required to submit FAFSA. In 2006, 24 degrees awarded. *Degree program information:* Part-time programs available. Offers Latin American and Caribbean studies (MA). *Application deadline:* For fall admission, 1/4 priority date for domestic students; for spring admission, 11/1 for domestic students. *Application fee:* $80. *Application Contact:* Maritza Colon, Department Administrator, 212-998-8686, Fax: 212-995-4163, E-mail: clacs.info@nyu.edu. *Director,* Tom Abercrombie, 212-998-8686, Fax: 212-995-4163, E-mail: clacs.info@nyu.edu.

Center for Neural Science Students: 39 full-time (18 women); includes 9 minority (2 African Americans, 5 Asian Americans or Pacific Islanders, 2 Hispanic Americans), 7 international. Average age 28. 124 applicants, 17% accepted, 16 enrolled. *Faculty:* 15 full-time (3 women), 4 part-time/adjunct. Expenses: Contact institution. *Financial support:* Fellowships with tuition reimbursements, research assistantships with tuition reimbursements, career-related internships or fieldwork, Federal Work-Study, institutionally sponsored loans, scholarships/grants, health care benefits, and unspecified assistantships available. Financial award application deadline: 1/4; financial award applicants required to submit FAFSA. In 2006, 5 degrees awarded. Offers neural science (PhD). *Application deadline:* For fall admission, 1/4 for domestic students. *Application fee:* $80. *Application Contact:* Lynne Kiorpes, Director of Graduate Studies, 212-998-7780, Fax: 212-995-4011, E-mail: cns@nyu.edu. *Chair,* J. Anthony Movshon, 212-998-7780, Fax: 212-995-4011, E-mail: cns@nyu.edu.

Courant Institute of Mathematical Sciences Students: 351 full-time (72 women), 306 part-time (58 women); includes 84 minority (6 African Americans, 70 Asian Americans or Pacific Islanders, 8 Hispanic Americans), 314 international. Average age 28. 1,446 applicants, 36% accepted, 189 enrolled. *Faculty:* 76 full-time (1 woman). Expenses: Contact institution. *Financial support:* Fellowships with tuition reimbursements, research assistantships with tuition reimbursements, teaching assistantships with tuition reimbursements, career-related internships or fieldwork, Federal Work-Study, institutionally sponsored loans, scholarships/grants, health care benefits, tuition waivers (full and partial), and unspecified assistantships available. Financial award application deadline: 1/4; financial award applicants required to submit FAFSA. In 2006, 156 master's, 27 doctorates awarded. *Degree program information:* Part-time and evening/weekend programs available. Offers atmosphere ocean science and mathematics (PhD); computer science (MS, PhD); information systems (MS); mathematics (MS, PhD); mathematics and statistics/operations research (MS); mathematics in finance (MS); scientific computing (MS). *Application deadline:* For fall admission, 1/4 for domestic students. *Application fee:* $80. *Application Contact:* Tamar Arnon, Application Contact, 212-998-3238, Fax: 212-995-4195, E-mail: admissions@math.nyu.edu. *Director of Graduate Studies,* Fedor Bogomolov, 212-998-3238, Fax: 212-995-4121, E-mail: admissions@math.nyu.edu.

Hagop Kevorkian Center for Near Eastern Studies Students: 63 full-time (36 women), 17 part-time (13 women); includes 9 minority (3 African Americans, 5 Asian Americans or Pacific Islanders, 1 Hispanic American), 17 international. Average age 30. 203 applicants, 20% accepted, 15 enrolled. *Faculty:* 32 full-time (11 women). Expenses: Contact institution. *Financial support:* Fellowships with tuition reimbursements, teaching assistantships with tuition reimbursements, Federal Work-Study and institutionally sponsored loans available. Financial award application deadline: 1/4; financial award applicants required to submit FAFSA. In 2006, 16 master's, 3 doctorates awarded. *Degree program information:* Part-time and evening/weekend programs available. Offers Middle Eastern and Islamic studies (MA, PhD); Middle Eastern and Islamic studies/history (PhD); Near Eastern studies (MA); Near Eastern studies (museum studies) (MA); Near Eastern studies/journalism (MA). *Application deadline:* For fall admission, 1/4 for domestic students. *Application fee:* $80. *Chair,* Timothy Mitchell, 212-998-8877, Fax: 212-995-4144, E-mail: kevorkian.center@nyu.edu.

Institute for Law and Society Students: 19 full-time (15 women), 1 part-time; includes 2 minority (both Asian Americans or Pacific Islanders), 5 international. Average age 32. 52 applicants, 10% accepted, 3 enrolled. *Faculty:* 3 full-time (1 woman). Expenses: Contact institution. *Financial support:* Fellowships with tuition reimbursements, teaching assistantships with tuition reimbursements, career-related internships or fieldwork, Federal Work-Study, institutionally sponsored loans, scholarships/grants, health care benefits, and unspecified assistantships available. Financial award application deadline: 12/15; financial award applicants required to submit FAFSA. In 2006, 2 master's, 2 doctorates awarded. Offers law and society (MA, PhD). *Application deadline:* For fall admission, 12/15 for domestic students. *Application fee:* $80. *Application Contact:* Jo Dixon, Director of Graduate Studies, 212-998-8536, Fax: 212-995-4034, E-mail: law.society@nyu.edu. *Director,* Lewis Kornhauser, 212-998-8536, Fax: 212-995-4034, E-mail: law.society@nyu.edu.

Institute of Fine Arts Students: 212 full-time (166 women), 80 part-time (60 women); includes 34 minority (2 African Americans, 21 Asian Americans or Pacific Islanders, 11 Hispanic Americans), 34 international. Average age 32. 315 applicants, 31% accepted, 54 enrolled. *Faculty:* 19 full-time (5 women). Expenses: Contact institution. *Financial support:* Fellowships with tuition reimbursements, research assistantships with tuition reimbursements, teaching assistantships with tuition reimbursements, career-related internships or fieldwork, Federal Work-Study, institutionally sponsored loans, and tuition waivers (partial) available. Financial award application deadline: 12/15; financial award applicants required to submit FAFSA. In 2006, 21 master's, 17 doctorates awarded. *Degree program information:* Part-time programs available. Offers architectural studies (PhD); art history and archaeology (MA, PhD); classical art and archaeology (PhD); curatorial studies (PhD); East and South Asian art (PhD); Near Eastern art and archaeology (PhD). *Application deadline:* For fall admission, 1/4 for domestic students. *Application fee:* $80. *Application Contact:* Priscilla Saucek, Director of Graduate Studies, 212-992-5800, Fax: 212-992-5807, E-mail: ifa.program@nyu.edu. *Chair,* Mariet Westermann, 212-992-5800, E-mail: ifa.program@nyu.edu.

Leonard N. Stern School of Business *Degree program information:* Part-time and evening/weekend programs available. Offers accounting (MBA, PhD); economics (MBA, PhD); entertainment, media and technology (MBA); finance (MBA, PhD); general marketing (MBA); information systems (MBA, PhD); information, operations and management sciences (MBA, PhD); management and organizations (MBA, PhD, APC); management organizations (MBA); marketing (MBA, PhD); operations management (MBA, PhD); organization theory (PhD); organizational behavior (PhD); product management (MBA); statistics (MBA, PhD); strategy (PhD). Electronic applications accepted.

National Institutes of Health Sponsored Programs Expenses: Contact institution. *Financial support:* Research assistantships with full tuition reimbursements, institutionally sponsored loans and health care benefits available. Offers structural biology (PhD). *Application deadline:* For fall admission, 2/1 for domestic students. *Application fee:* $60.

Robert F. Wagner Graduate School of Public Service Students: 390 full-time (275 women), 426 part-time (309 women); includes 199 minority (62 African Americans, 2 American Indian/Alaska Native, 81 Asian Americans or Pacific Islanders, 54 Hispanic Americans), 75 international. Average age 29. 1,439 applicants, 52% accepted, 261 enrolled. *Faculty:* 29 full-time (15 women), 58 part-time/adjunct (31 women). Expenses: Contact institution. *Financial support:* In 2006–07, 196 fellowships (averaging $9,897 per year), 11 research assistantships with full and partial tuition reimbursements (averaging $15,000 per year) were awarded; career-related internships or fieldwork, Federal Work-Study, institutionally sponsored loans, scholarships/grants, health care benefits, and unspecified assistantships also available. Support available to part-time students. Financial award application deadline: 1/15; financial award applicants required to submit FAFSA. In 2006, 334 master's, 5 doctorates awarded. *Degree program information:* Part-time and evening/weekend programs available. Offers health finance (MPA); health policy analysis (MPA); health policy and management (Advanced Certificate); health services management (MPA); housing (Advanced Certificate); international health (MPA); international public service organizations management (MS); management (MS); public administration (PhD); public and nonprofit management and policy (MPA, Advanced Certificate); public economics (Advanced Certificate); public service (MPA, MS, MUP, PhD, Advanced Certificate); quantitative analysis and computer applications for policy and planning (Advanced Certificate); urban planning (MUP). *Application deadline:* For fall admission, 6/1 for domestic students, 1/15 for international students; for spring admission, 11/15 for domestic students, 10/1 for international students. Applications are processed on a rolling basis. *Application fee:* $70. Electronic applications accepted. *Application Contact:* Bethany Godsoe, Assistant Dean, Enrollment and Student Services, 212-998-7414, Fax: 212-995-4164, E-mail: wagner.admissions@nyu.edu. *Dean,* Prof. Ellen Schall, 212-998-7400, Fax: 212-995-4161.

School of Continuing and Professional Studies Students: 467 full-time (228 women), 1,540 part-time (677 women); includes 470 minority (148 African Americans, 192 Asian Americans or Pacific Islanders, 130 Hispanic Americans), 234 international. Average age 30. 1,316 applicants, 68% accepted, 557 enrolled. *Faculty:* 33 full-time (8 women), 193 part-time/adjunct (44 women). Expenses: Contact institution. *Financial support:* In 2006–07, 1,508 students received support, including fellowships (averaging $1,600 per year); research assistantships, career-related internships or fieldwork, Federal Work-Study, institutionally sponsored loans, scholarships/grants, and tuition waivers (partial) also available. Support available to part-time students. Financial award application deadline: 3/1; financial award applicants required to submit FAFSA. In 2006, 209 master's, 55 other advanced degrees awarded. *Degree program information:* Part-time and evening/weekend programs available. Postbaccalaureate distance learning degree programs offered (no on-campus study). Offers fundraising (MS); graphic communications management and technology (MA). *Application deadline:* For fall admission, 3/15 priority date for domestic and international students; for spring admission, 10/15 priority date for domestic students, 8/15 priority date for international students. Applications are processed on a rolling basis. *Application fee:* $75. Electronic applications accepted. *Application Contact:* Office of Admissions, 212-998-7100, Fax: 212-995-4674. *Dean,* Robert Lapiner, 212-998-7000, Fax: 212-995-4130.

Center for Advanced Digital Applications Students: 65 full-time (25 women), 55 part-time (24 women); includes 31 minority (9 African Americans, 12 Asian Americans or Pacific Islanders, 10 Hispanic Americans), 16 international. Average age 30. 73 applicants, 71% accepted, 40 enrolled. *Faculty:* 2 full-time (1 woman), 26 part-time/adjunct (5 women). Expenses: Contact institution. *Financial support:* In 2006–07, 90 students received support, including fellowships with tuition reimbursements available (averaging $1,547 per year). Financial award application deadline: 3/1; financial award applicants required to submit FAFSA. In 2006, 10 degrees awarded. Offers digital imaging and design (MS). *Application deadline:* For fall admission, 3/15 priority date for domestic and international students; for spring admission, 10/15 priority date for domestic students, 8/15 priority date for international students. Applications are processed on a rolling basis. *Application fee:* $75. *Application Contact:* Kathy Wang, Assistant Director, 212-992-3370, Fax: 212-992-3377, E-mail: cada@nyu.edu. *Director,* Dr. Michael Hosenfeld, 212-992-3370, Fax: 212-992-3377, E-mail: cada@nyu.edu.

Center for Global Affairs Students: 98 full-time (61 women), 113 part-time (75 women); includes 47 minority (17 African Americans, 15 Asian Americans or Pacific Islanders, 15 Hispanic Americans), 26 international. Average age 29. 214 applicants, 64% accepted, 76 enrolled. *Faculty:* 5 full-time (1 woman), 32 part-time/adjunct (16 women). Expenses: Contact institution. *Financial support:* In 2006–07, 149 students received support, including fellowships (averaging $1,570 per year). In 2006, 15 degrees awarded. *Degree program information:* Part-time programs available. Offers global studies (MS). *Application deadline:* For fall admission, 3/15 priority date for domestic and international students; for spring admission, 10/15 priority date for domestic students, 8/15 priority date for international students. Applications are processed on a rolling basis. *Application fee:* $75. *Application Contact:* Mykellan Ledden, Interim Associate Director, 212-992-8380, Fax: 212-995-4597, E-mail: mykellan.ledden@nyu.edu. *Assistant Dean and Director,* Dr. Vera Jelinek, 212-992-8380, Fax: 212-995-4597, E-mail: vj1@nyu.edu.

Center for Management Students: 57 full-time (43 women), 460 part-time (238 women); includes 160 minority (57 African Americans, 66 Asian Americans or Pacific Islanders, 37 Hispanic Americans), 75 international. Average age 32. 331 applicants, 55% accepted, 109 enrolled. *Faculty:* 8 full-time (0 women), 46 part-time/adjunct (15 women). Expenses: Contact institution. *Financial support:* In 2006–07, 134 students received support, including fellowships (averaging $970 per year); career-related internships or fieldwork and scholarships/grants also available. Support available to part-time students. Financial award application deadline: 3/1. In 2006, 23 master's, 9 other advanced degrees awarded. *Degree program information:* Part-time and evening/weekend programs available. Postbaccalaureate distance learning degree programs offered (minimal on-campus study). Offers applied database technologies (MS); benefits and compensation (Advanced Certificate); enterprise and risk management (Advanced Certificate); executive coaching and organizational development (Advanced Certificate); human resource development (MS); human resource management (MS, Advanced Certificate); human resources management and development (MS); information technologies (Advanced Certificate); leadership and knowledge management (MS); management and systems (MS, Advanced Certificate); management in the Internet E-conomy (MS); organizational effectiveness (MS); strategy and leadership (Advanced Certificate); systems management (MS). *Application deadline:* For fall admission, 3/15 priority date for domestic and international students; for spring admission, 10/15 priority date for domestic students, 8/15 priority date for international students. Applications are processed on a rolling basis. *Application fee:* $75. *Application Contact:* Helen Sapp, Assistant Director, 212-992-3600, Fax: 212-992-3676, E-mail: helen.sapp@nyu.edu. *Assistant Dean,* Dr. Anthony Davidson, 212-992-3600, Fax: 212-995-3550, E-mail: ard3@nyu.edu.

Center for Marketing Students: 20 full-time (16 women), 65 part-time (41 women); includes 15 minority (4 African Americans, 7 Asian Americans or Pacific Islanders, 4 Hispanic Americans), 22 international. Average age 30. 95 applicants, 27% accepted, 16 enrolled. *Faculty:* 1 full-time (0 women), 11 part-time/adjunct (3 women). Expenses: Contact institution. *Financial support:* In 2006–07, 80 students received support, including fellowships (averaging $1,547 per year); career-related internships or fieldwork and scholarships/grants also available. Support available to part-time students. Financial award application deadline: 3/1; financial award applicants required to submit FAFSA. In 2006, 11 degrees awarded. *Degree program information:* Part-time programs available. Offers direct and interactive marketing (MS); public relations and corporate communications (MS, Advanced Certificate). *Application deadline:* For fall admission, 3/15 priority date for domestic students, 4/1 priority date for international students; for spring admission, 10/15 priority date for domestic students, 8/15 priority date for international students. Applications are processed on a rolling basis. *Application fee:* $75. *Application Contact:* Fadia Saint-Juste, Program Coordinator, 212-992-3221, Fax: 212-992-3377, E-mail: fs20@nyu.edu. *Director,* Dr. Marjorie Kalter, 212-992-3221, Fax: 212-992-3377, E-mail: mk99@nyu.edu.

Center for Publishing Students: 26 full-time (21 women), 69 part-time (58 women); includes 12 minority (3 African Americans, 3 Asian Americans or Pacific Islanders, 6 Hispanic Americans), 13 international. Average age 28. 66 applicants, 83% accepted, 26 enrolled. *Faculty:* 1 (woman) full-time, 35 part-time/adjunct (21 women). Expenses: Contact institution. *Financial support:* In 2006–07, fellowships (averaging $3,923 per year); career-related internships or fieldwork, Federal Work-Study, institutionally sponsored loans, and scholarships/grants also available. Support available to part-time students. Financial award application deadline: 3/1; financial award applicants required to submit FAFSA. In 2006, 11 degrees awarded. *Degree program information:* Part-time and evening/weekend programs available. Offers publishing (MS). *Application deadline:* For fall admission, 3/15 priority date for domestic and international students; for spring admission, 10/15 priority date for domestic students, 8/15 priority date for international students. Applications are processed on a rolling basis. *Application fee:* $75. *Application Contact:* Alyssa Léal, Associate Director, 212-790-3236, Fax: 212-790-3233, E-mail: alyssa.leal@nyu.edu. *Director,* Andrea L. Chambers, 212-992-3235, Fax: 212-790-3233, E-mail: andrea.chambers@nyu.edu.

Real Estate Institute Students: 111 full-time (28 women), 650 part-time (182 women); includes 145 minority (42 African Americans, 62 Asian Americans or Pacific Islanders, 41 Hispanic Americans), 68 international. Average age 31. 375 applicants, 74% accepted,

184 enrolled. *Faculty:* 11 full-time (2 women), 105 part-time/adjunct (13 women). Expenses: Contact institution. *Financial support:* In 2006–07, 455 students received support, including fellowships (averaging $1,255 per year); career-related internships or fieldwork and scholarships/grants also available. Support available to part-time students. Financial award application deadline: 3/1; financial award applicants required to submit FAFSA. In 2006, 112 master's, 40 other advanced degrees awarded. *Degree program information:* Part-time and evening/weekend programs available. Offers construction management (MS, Advanced Certificate); real estate (MS, Advanced Certificate). *Application deadline:* For fall admission, 3/15 priority date for domestic and international students; for spring admission, 10/15 priority date for domestic students, 8/15 priority date for international students. Applications are processed on a rolling basis. *Application fee:* $75. *Application Contact:* Marcie Burros, Associate Director, 212-992-3335, Fax: 212-992-3686, E-mail: gradadmissions@nyu.edu. *Associate Dean,* D. Kenneth Patton, 212-992-3335, Fax: 212-992-3686, E-mail: dkp2@nyu.edu.

Tisch Center for Hospitality, Tourism and Sports Management Students: 97 full-time (44 women), 131 part-time (63 women); includes 55 minority (14 African Americans, 26 Asian Americans or Pacific Islanders, 15 Hispanic Americans), 31 international. Average age 28. 184 applicants, 63% accepted, 65 enrolled. *Faculty:* 10 full-time (4 women), 51 part-time/adjunct (10 women). Expenses: Contact institution. *Financial support:* In 2006–07, fellowships (averaging $2,121 per year); research assistantships, career-related internships or fieldwork, Federal Work-Study, institutionally sponsored loans, and scholarships/grants also available. Support available to part-time students. Financial award application deadline: 3/1; financial award applicants required to submit FAFSA. In 2006, 36 master's, 6 other advanced degrees awarded. *Degree program information:* Part-time and evening/weekend programs available. Postbaccalaureate distance learning degree programs offered (minimal on-campus study). Offers hospitality industry studies (MS, Advanced Certificate); sports business (MS, Advanced Certificate); tourism and travel management (MS, Advanced Certificate). *Application deadline:* For fall admission, 3/15 priority date for domestic and international students; for spring admission, 10/15 priority date for domestic students, 8/15 priority date for international students. Applications are processed on a rolling basis. *Application fee:* $75. *Associate Dean,* Dr. Lalia Rach, 212-998-9100, Fax: 212-995-4676.

School of Law Students: 1,442 full-time (667 women); includes 345 minority (124 African Americans, 153 Asian Americans or Pacific Islanders, 68 Hispanic Americans), 53 international. 7,571 applicants, 448 enrolled. *Faculty:* 117 full-time (35 women), 64 part-time/adjunct (18 women). Expenses: Contact institution. *Financial support:* Fellowships, research assistantships, teaching assistantships, career-related internships or fieldwork, Federal Work-Study, institutionally sponsored loans, scholarships/grants, tuition waivers (partial), and loan repayment assistance available. Financial award application deadline: 4/15; financial award applicants required to submit FAFSA. In 2006, 465 JDs, 472 master's, 6 doctorates awarded. *Degree program information:* Part-time programs available. Offers law (JD, LL M, JSD); law and business (Advanced Certificate); tax (Advanced Certificate). *Application deadline:* For fall admission, 2/1 for domestic students. *Application fee:* $85. Electronic applications accepted. *Application Contact:* Kenneth J. Kleinrock, Assistant Dean for Admissions, 212-998-6060, Fax: 212-995-4527. *Dean,* Richard L. Revesz, 212-998-6000, Fax: 212-995-3150.

School of Medicine Students: 984 full-time (509 women); includes 334 minority (58 African Americans, 6 American Indian/Alaska Native, 209 Asian Americans or Pacific Islanders, 61 Hispanic Americans), 83 international. Average age 24. 8,162 applicants, 7% accepted, 201 enrolled. *Faculty:* 1,241 full-time (390 women), 318 part-time/adjunct (105 women). Expenses: Contact institution. *Financial support:* In 2006–07, 486 students received support, including 75 research assistantships (averaging $25,000 per year); fellowships with full tuition reimbursements available, teaching assistantships, Federal Work-Study, institutionally sponsored loans, and health care benefits also available. Financial award application deadline: 7/15; financial award applicants required to submit FAFSA. In 2006, 155 MDs, 32 doctorates awarded. Offers clinical investigation (MS); medicine (MD). *Application deadline:* For fall admission, 10/15 for domestic students. Applications are processed on a rolling basis. *Application fee:* $100. *Application Contact:* Dr. Nancy Genieser, Associate Dean, Admissions, 212-263-5290, Fax: 212-263-0720, E-mail: nancy.genieser@nyumc.org. *Dean,* Dr. Robert M. Glickman, 212-263-5370, Fax: 212-263-8622.

Sackler Institute of Graduate Biomedical Sciences Students: 272 full-time (153 women); includes 80 minority (20 African Americans, 2 American Indian/Alaska Native, 41 Asian Americans or Pacific Islanders, 17 Hispanic Americans), 77 international. Average age 28. 739 applicants, 15% accepted, 41 enrolled. *Faculty:* 168 full-time (41 women). Expenses: Contact institution. *Financial support:* In 2006–07, fellowships with tuition reimbursements (averaging $27,000 per year), research assistantships with tuition reimbursements (averaging $27,000 per year), teaching assistantships with tuition reimbursements (averaging $27,000 per year) were awarded; career-related internships or fieldwork, Federal Work-Study, institutionally sponsored loans, scholarships/grants, health care benefits, tuition waivers (full), and unspecified assistantships also available. Financial award application deadline: 2/1; financial award applicants required to submit FAFSA. In 2006, 32 degrees awarded. Offers cellular and molecular biology (PhD); computational biology (PhD); developmental genetics (PhD); immunology (PhD); medical and molecular parasitology (PhD); microbiology (PhD); molecular oncology (PhD); molecular oncology and immunology (PhD); molecular pharmacology and signal transduction (PhD); neuroscience (PhD); neuroscience and physiology (PhD); pathobiology (PhD); pharmacology (PhD); physiology (PhD); structural biology (PhD). *Application deadline:* For fall admission, 1/4 priority date for domestic students. Applications are processed on a rolling basis. *Application fee:* $85. Electronic applications accepted. *Application Contact:* Lisabeth Greene, Program Coordinator, 212-263-5648, Fax: 212-263-7600, E-mail: sackler-info@med.nyu.edu. *Senior Associate Dean for Graduate Studies,* Dr. Joel D. Oppenheim, 212-263-8001, Fax: 212-263-7600.

School of Social Work Students: 631 full-time (558 women), 369 part-time (310 women); includes 291 minority (108 African Americans, 3 American Indian/Alaska Native, 62 Asian Americans or Pacific Islanders, 118 Hispanic Americans), 25 international. Average age 27. 1,341 applicants, 81% accepted, 397 enrolled. *Faculty:* 39 full-time (32 women), 129 part-time/adjunct (94 women). Expenses: Contact institution. *Financial support:* In 2006–07, 650 students received support, including 5 research assistantships with full and partial tuition reimbursements available (averaging $5,000 per year); career-related internships or fieldwork, Federal Work-Study, scholarships/grants, tuition waivers (partial), and unspecified assistantships also available. Support available to part-time students. Financial award application deadline: 3/1; financial award applicants required to submit FAFSA. In 2006, 465 master's, 12 doctorates awarded. *Degree program information:* Part-time and evening/weekend programs available. Offers social work (MSW, PhD). *Application deadline:* For fall admission, 3/1 for domestic students, 3/15 for international students; for spring admission, 11/3 for domestic students, 11/2 for international students. *Application fee:* $50. *Application Contact:* Robert W. Sommo, Assistant Dean for Enrollment Services, 212-998-5910, Fax: 212-995-4171, E-mail: ssw.admissions@nyu.edu. *Dean,* Dr. Suzanne England, 212-998-5959, Fax: 212-995-4172.

Steinhardt School of Culture, Education and Human Development Students: 2,065 full-time (1,661 women), 1,441 part-time (1,136 women); includes 758 minority (244 African Americans, 5 American Indian/Alaska Native, 278 Asian Americans or Pacific Islanders, 231 Hispanic Americans), 492 international. Average age 32. 4,826 applicants, 55% accepted, 1257 enrolled. *Faculty:* 241 full-time (141 women), 717 part-time/adjunct (399 women). Expenses: Contact institution. *Financial support:* In 2006–07, fellowships with full and partial tuition reimbursements (averaging $15,000 per year); research assistantships with full and partial tuition reimbursements, teaching assistantships with full and partial tuition reimbursements, career-related internships or fieldwork, Federal Work-Study, institutionally sponsored loans, scholarships/grants, traineeships, tuition waivers (partial), and unspecified assistantships also available. Support available to part-time students. Financial award application deadline: 2/1; financial award applicants required to submit FAFSA. In 2006, 1,271 master's, 97 doctorates, 11 other advanced degrees awarded. *Degree program information:* Part-time and evening/weekend programs available. Offers advanced occupational therapy (MA); art education (MA, PhD); art therapy (MA); arts and humanities education (MA, PhD); bilingual education (MA, PhD, Advanced Certificate); biology grades 7-12 (MA); business education (MA, Advanced Certificate); business education in higher education (MA); chemistry grades 7-12 (MA); childhood education (MA, PhD, Advanced Certificate); childhood special education (MA); clinical nutrition (MS); community health (MPH); community public health (MPH, PhD); counseling and guidance (MA, Advanced Certificate); counseling for mental health and wellness (MA); counseling psychology (PhD); counselor education (MA, PhD, Advanced Certificate); culture, education and human development (MA, MFA, MM, MPH, MS, DA, DPS, DPT, Ed D, PhD, Advanced Certificate); dance education (MA, Ed D, PhD); drama therapy (MA); early childhood and childhood education (MA, PhD, Advanced Certificate); early childhood education (MA, PhD, Advanced Certificate); early childhood special education (MA); education and Jewish studies (PhD); education policy (MA); educational and developmental psychology (MA, PhD); educational communication and technology (MA, PhD, Advanced Certificate); educational leadership (MA, Ed D, PhD, Advanced Certificate); educational psychology (MA); educational theatre (MA, Ed D, PhD, Advanced Certificate); educational theatre for colleges and communities (MA, PhD); educational theatre with English 7-12 (MA); English education (MA, PhD, Advanced Certificate); environmental conservation education (MA); food management (MA); food studies (MA); food studies and food management (MA, PhD); foods and nutrition (MS); for-profit sector (MA); foreign language education (MA, Advanced Certificate); foreign language education/TESOL (MA); higher education (MA, PhD); higher education administration (PhD); history of education (MA, PhD); international community health (MPH); international education (MA, PhD, Advanced Certificate); literacy education (MA); mathematics education (MA); media ecology/culture and communication (PhD); media, culture, and communication (MA); multilingual/multicultural studies (MA, PhD, Advanced Certificate); music business (MA); music education (MA, Ed D, PhD, Advanced Certificate); music performance and composition (MA, PhD); music technology (MM); music therapy (MA, DA); not-for-profit sector (MA); nutrition and dietetics (MS, PhD); occupational therapy (MA, MS, DPS, PhD); performing arts administration (MA); philosophy of education (MA, PhD); physical therapists pathokinesiology (MA); physical therapy (DPT); physics grades 7-12 (MA); practicing physical therapist (DPT); psychological development (PhD); public health (PhD); public health nutrition (MPH); research in physical therapy (PhD); school psychology (PhD); science education (MA); social and cultural studies of education (MA); social studies education (MA); sociology of education (MA, PhD); special education (MA); speech-language pathology and audiology (MA, PhD); student personnel administration higher education (MA); studio art (MA, MFA); teaching and learning (Ed D, PhD); teaching educational theatre, all grades (MA); teaching English to speakers of other languages (MA, PhD, Advanced Certificate); visual arts administration (MA); visual culture (MA, PhD); visual culture: costume studies (MA); visual culture: theory (MA, PhD); workplace learning (Advanced Certificate). *Application deadline:* For fall admission, 2/1 priority date for domestic students, 2/1 for international students; for spring admission, 12/1 for domestic and international students. Applications are processed on a rolling basis. *Application fee:* $50. *Application Contact:* 212-998-5030, Fax: 212-995-4328, E-mail: steinhardt.gradadmissions@nyu.edu. *Dean,* Dr. Mary Brabeck, 212-998-5000.

Tisch School of the Arts Students: 803 full-time (420 women), 96 part-time (37 women); includes 169 minority (68 African Americans, 6 American Indian/Alaska Native, 61 Asian Americans or Pacific Islanders, 34 Hispanic Americans), 188 international. Average age 29. 2,732 applicants, 22% accepted, 365 enrolled. *Faculty:* 105 full-time, 127 part-time/adjunct. Expenses: Contact institution. *Financial support:* Fellowships, research assistantships, teaching assistantships, career-related internships or fieldwork, Federal Work-Study, institutionally sponsored loans, scholarships/grants, tuition waivers (full and partial), and unspecified assistantships available. Support available to part-time students. Financial award application deadline: 2/1; financial award applicants required to submit CSS PROFILE or FAFSA. In 2006, 286 master's, 15 doctorates awarded. Offers acting (MFA); arts (MA, MFA, MPS, PhD); cinema studies (MA, PhD); dance (MFA); design for stage and film (MFA); dramatic writing (MFA); interactive telecommunications (MPS); moving image archiving and preservation (MA); musical theatre writing (MFA); performance studies (MA, PhD). *Application fee:* $75. Electronic applications accepted. *Application Contact:* Dan Sandford, Director of Graduate Admissions, 212-998-1918, Fax: 212-995-4060, E-mail: tisch.gradadmissions@nyu.edu. *Dean,* Mary Schmidt Campbell, 212-998-1800.

Kanbar Institute of Film and Television Students: 112 full-time (49 women), 57 part-time (20 women); includes 55 minority (24 African Americans, 3 American Indian/Alaska Native, 24 Asian Americans or Pacific Islanders, 4 Hispanic Americans), 27 international. Average age 29. 707 applicants, 8% accepted, 36 enrolled. *Faculty:* 19 full-time, 15 part-time/adjunct. Expenses: Contact institution. *Financial support:* In 2006–07, 60 students received support, including 16 fellowships with full and partial tuition reimbursements available, 6 teaching assistantships with tuition reimbursements available; Federal Work-Study, institutionally sponsored loans, scholarships/grants, tuition waivers (full and partial), and unspecified assistantships also available. Financial award application deadline: 2/15; financial award applicants required to submit FAFSA. In 2006, 30 degrees awarded. Offers film and television (MFA). *Application deadline:* For fall admission, 12/1 for domestic and international students. *Application fee:* $60. Electronic applications accepted. *Application Contact:* Dan Sandford, Director of Graduate Admissions, 212-998-1918, Fax: 212-995-4060, E-mail: tisch.gradadmissions@nyu.edu. *Chair,* John Tintori, 212-998-1780, E-mail: jt42@nyu.edu.

See Close-Up on page 977.

NIAGARA UNIVERSITY, Niagara Falls, Niagara University, NY 14109

General Information Independent-religious, coed, comprehensive institution. *Enrollment:* 3,881 graduate, professional, and undergraduate students; 582 full-time matriculated graduate/professional students (396 women), 332 part-time matriculated graduate/professional students (233 women). *Enrollment by degree level:* 887 master's, 27 other advanced degrees. *Graduate faculty:* 40 full-time (20 women), 30 part-time/adjunct (14 women). *Graduate housing:* Room and/or apartments available to single students; on-campus housing not available to married students. Typical cost: $9,300 (including board). Housing application deadline: 8/1. *Student services:* Campus employment opportunities, campus safety program, career counseling, disabled student services, free psychological counseling, international student services, low-cost health insurance, multicultural affairs office. *Library facilities:* Our Lady of Angels Library. *Online resources:* library catalog. *Collection:* 273,753 titles, 21,001 serial subscriptions. *Research affiliation:* Roswell Park Memorial Institute.

Computer facilities: 150 computers available on campus for general student use. A campuswide network can be accessed from student residence rooms. Internet access and online class registration are available. *Web address:* http://www.niagara.edu/.

General Application Contact: Carlos Tejada, Associate Dean for Graduate Recruitment, 716-286-8769, Fax: 716-286-8170.

GRADUATE UNITS

Graduate Division of Arts and Sciences Students: 27 full-time (15 women), 23 part-time (14 women); includes 7 minority (4 African Americans, 3 Hispanic Americans), 3 international. *Faculty:* 5 full-time (1 woman). Expenses: Contact institution. *Financial support:* Fellowships, career-related internships or fieldwork and Federal Work-Study available. Support available to part-time students. In 2006, 26 degrees awarded. *Degree program information:* Part-time and evening/weekend programs available. Offers criminal justice (MS); criminal justice administration (MS). *Application deadline:* For fall admission, 8/1 for domestic students. Applications are processed on a rolling basis. *Application fee:* $30. *Application Contact:* Dr. Talia Harmon, Director, 716-286-8093, Fax: 716-286-8061, E-mail: tharmon@niagara.edu. *Dean,* Dr. Nancy McGlen, 716-286-8060, Fax: 716-286-8061, E-mail: nmcglen@niagara.edu.

Graduate Division of Business Administration Students: 89 full-time (42 women), 37 part-time (12 women); includes 8 minority (4 African Americans, 1 American Indian/Alaska Native, 2 Asian Americans or Pacific Islanders, 1 Hispanic American), 29 international. Average age 30. 89 applicants, 73% accepted. *Faculty:* 7 full-time (2 women). Expenses: Contact institution. *Financial support:* In 2006–07, 3 fellowships, 2 research assistantships were awarded; career-related internships or fieldwork and Federal Work-Study also available. Support available to part-time students. Financial award application deadline: 8/1; financial award applicants required to submit FAFSA. In 2006, 41 degrees awarded. *Degree program information:* Part-time and evening/weekend programs available. Offers business (MBA);

Niagara University (continued)

commerce (MBA). *Application deadline:* For fall admission, 8/1 for domestic students; for spring admission, 11/1 for domestic students. Applications are processed on a rolling basis. *Application fee:* $30. *Director*, Wick Hannan, 716-286-8178, Fax: 716-286-8206, E-mail: wkh@niagara.edu.

Graduate Division of Education Students: 466 full-time (339 women), 272 part-time (207 women); includes 26 minority (15 African Americans, 7 American Indian/Alaska Native, 4 Hispanic Americans), 278 international. Average age 37. 382 applicants, 75% accepted. *Faculty:* 27 full-time (17 women), 29 part-time/adjunct (14 women). Expenses: Contact institution. *Financial support:* In 2006–07, 2 fellowships, 3 research assistantships were awarded; career-related internships or fieldwork, Federal Work-Study, scholarships/grants, and unspecified assistantships also available. Support available to part-time students. Financial award application deadline: 3/15. In 2006, 405 master's, 14 other advanced degrees awarded. *Degree program information:* Part-time and evening/weekend programs available. Offers administration and supervision (MS Ed, Certificate); elementary education (MS Ed); foundations of teaching (MA, MS Ed); inclusive education (MS Ed); literacy instruction (MS Ed); mental health counseling (MS Ed, Certificate); school business administration (MS Ed, Certificate); school counseling (MS Ed, Certificate); school psychology (MS); secondary education (MS Ed); teacher education (MS Ed). *Application deadline:* For fall admission, 8/1 for domestic students. Applications are processed on a rolling basis. *Application fee:* $30. *Dean*, Dr. Debra A. Colley, 716-286-8560, Fax: 716-286-8561, E-mail: dcolley@niagara.edu.

NICHOLLS STATE UNIVERSITY, Thibodaux, LA 70310

General Information State-supported, coed, comprehensive institution. *Enrollment:* 6,805 graduate, professional, and undergraduate students; 109 full-time matriculated graduate/professional students (67 women), 275 part-time matriculated graduate/professional students (211 women). *Enrollment by degree level:* 371 master's, 13 other advanced degrees. *Graduate faculty:* 66 full-time (24 women), 25 part-time/adjunct (10 women). Tuition, state resident: part-time $450 per hour. Tuition, nonresident: part-time $450 per hour. *Graduate housing:* Rooms and/or apartments available on a first-come, first-served basis to single and married students. Housing application deadline: 4/13. *Student services:* Campus employment opportunities, campus safety program, career counseling, disabled student services, free psychological counseling, international student services, low-cost health insurance. *Library facilities:* Allen J. Ellender Memorial Library plus 3 others. *Online resources:* web page.

Computer facilities: 250 computers available on campus for general student use. A campuswide network can be accessed from student residence rooms and from off campus. Internet access and online class registration are available. *Web address:* http://www.nicholls.edu.

General Application Contact: Dr. Betty A. Kleen, Director, University Graduate Studies, 985-448-4191, Fax: 985-448-4922, E-mail: betty.kleen@nicholls.edu.

GRADUATE UNITS

Graduate Studies Students: 109 full-time (67 women), 275 part-time (211 women); includes 89 minority (77 African Americans, 6 American Indian/Alaska Native, 2 Asian Americans or Pacific Islanders, 4 Hispanic Americans), 19 international. Average age 30. *Faculty:* 66 full-time (24 women), 25 part-time/adjunct (10 women). Expenses: Contact institution. *Financial support:* In 2006–07, 65 research assistantships with full tuition reimbursements (averaging $4,000 per year), 18 teaching assistantships with full tuition reimbursements (averaging $6,000 per year) were awarded; unspecified assistantships also available. Support available to part-time students. In 2006, 138 master's, 7 other advanced degrees awarded. *Degree program information:* Part-time and evening/weekend programs available. Postbaccalaureate distance learning degree programs offered (minimal on-campus study). *Application deadline:* For fall admission, 8/1 priority date for domestic students, 7/1 priority date for international students; for spring admission, 12/1 priority date for domestic students, 11/1 priority date for international students. Applications are processed on a rolling basis. *Application fee:* $20 ($30 for international students). *Director, University Graduate Studies*, Dr. Betty A. Kleen, 985-448-4191, Fax: 985-448-4922, E-mail: betty.kleen@nicholls.edu.

College of Arts and Sciences Students: 20 full-time (8 women), 12 part-time (2 women); includes 1 minority (Hispanic American), 2 international. Average age 27. 22 applicants, 77% accepted, 17 enrolled. *Faculty:* 15 full-time (4 women), 1 part-time/adjunct (0 women). Expenses: Contact institution. *Financial support:* In 2006–07, 19 students received support, including 9 research assistantships with full tuition reimbursements available (averaging $8,000 per year), 5 teaching assistantships with full tuition reimbursements available (averaging $10,000 per year); unspecified assistantships also available. Financial award application deadline: 6/17. In 2006, 6 degrees awarded. *Degree program information:* Part-time and evening/weekend programs available. Offers arts and sciences (MS); community/technical college mathematics (MS); marine and environmental biology (MS). *Application deadline:* For fall admission, 8/1 priority date for domestic students, 7/1 priority date for international students; for spring admission, 12/1 priority date for domestic students, 11/1 priority date for international students. Applications are processed on a rolling basis. *Application fee:* $20 ($30 for international students). Electronic applications accepted. *Dean*, Dr. Badiollah R. Asrabadi, 985-448-4385, Fax: 985-448-4927, E-mail: as-tjm@nicholls.edu.

College of Business Administration Students: 40 full-time (20 women), 62 part-time (34 women); includes 8 minority (7 African Americans, 1 Asian American or Pacific Islander), 15 international. Average age 27. 56 applicants, 98% accepted, 36 enrolled. *Faculty:* 27 full-time (5 women). Expenses: Contact institution. *Financial support:* In 2006–07, 16 students received support, including 16 research assistantships with full tuition reimbursements available (averaging $4,000 per year); unspecified assistantships also available. Financial award application deadline: 6/1. In 2006, 26 degrees awarded. *Degree program information:* Part-time and evening/weekend programs available. Offers business administration (MBA). *Application deadline:* For fall admission, 8/1 priority date for domestic students, 7/1 priority date for international students; for spring admission, 12/1 priority date for domestic students, 11/1 priority date for international students. Applications are processed on a rolling basis. *Application fee:* $20 ($30 for international students). Electronic applications accepted. *Dean*, Dr. Shawn Mauldin, 985-448-4172, Fax: 985-448-4922.

College of Education Students: 49 full-time (39 women), 201 part-time (175 women); includes 80 minority (70 African Americans, 6 American Indian/Alaska Native, 1 Asian American or Pacific Islander, 3 Hispanic Americans), 2 international. Average age 32. *Faculty:* 24 full-time (15 women), 9 part-time/adjunct (6 women). Expenses: Contact institution. *Financial support:* In 2006–07, 10 research assistantships with full tuition reimbursements (averaging $4,000 per year), 8 teaching assistantships with full tuition reimbursements (averaging $6,000 per year) were awarded. Financial award application deadline: 6/17. In 2006, 95 master's, 7 other advanced degrees awarded. *Degree program information:* Part-time and evening/weekend programs available. Offers administration and supervision (M Ed); counselor education (M Ed); curriculum and instruction (M Ed); education (M Ed, MA, SSP); psychological counseling (MA); school psychology (SSP). *Application deadline:* For fall admission, 8/1 priority date for domestic students, 7/1 for international students; for spring admission, 12/1 priority date for domestic students, 11/1 for international students. Applications are processed on a rolling basis. *Application fee:* $20 ($30 for international students). Electronic applications accepted. *Dean*, Dr. Deborah Bordelon, 985-448-4325, E-mail: deborah.bordelon@nicholls.edu.

NICHOLS COLLEGE, Dudley, MA 01571-5000

General Information Independent, coed, comprehensive institution. *Enrollment:* 1,470 graduate, professional, and undergraduate students; 33 full-time matriculated graduate/professional students (16 women), 218 part-time matriculated graduate/professional students (107 women). *Enrollment by degree level:* 251 master's. *Graduate faculty:* 5 full-time (2 women), 20 part-time/adjunct (4 women). *Tuition:* Part-time $495 per credit. *Graduate housing:* On-campus housing not available. *Student services:* Career counseling, free psychological counseling, low-cost health insurance. *Library facilities:* Conant Library plus 1 other. *Online resources:* library catalog, web page. *Collection:* 70,046 titles, 161 serial subscriptions, 1,553 audiovisual materials.

Computer facilities: Computer purchase and lease plans are available. 850 computers available on campus for general student use. A campuswide network can be accessed from student residence rooms and from off campus. Internet access and online class registration are available. *Web address:* http://www.nichols.edu/.

General Application Contact: Rayanne Drouin, Director of Enrollment Services, 508-213-2150, Fax: 508-213-2490, E-mail: rayanne.drouin@nichols.edu.

GRADUATE UNITS

Graduate Program in Business Administration Students: 33 full-time (16 women), 218 part-time (107 women); includes 17 minority (12 African Americans, 1 American Indian/Alaska Native, 1 Asian American or Pacific Islander, 3 Hispanic Americans), 3 international. Average age 34. *Faculty:* 5 full-time (2 women), 20 part-time/adjunct (6 women). Expenses: Contact institution. *Financial support:* Career-related internships or fieldwork available. In 2006, 77 degrees awarded. *Degree program information:* Part-time and evening/weekend programs available. Postbaccalaureate distance learning degree programs offered (no on-campus study). Offers business administration (MBA). *Application deadline:* Applications are processed on a rolling basis. *Application fee:* $25. Electronic applications accepted. *Application Contact:* Rayanne Drouin, Director of Enrollment Services, 508-213-2150, Fax: 508-213-2490, E-mail: rayanne.drouin@nichols.edu. *Dean, Graduate and Professional Studies*, Laurie Albert, 508-213-2440, Fax: 508-213-2490.

THE NIGERIAN BAPTIST THEOLOGICAL SEMINARY, Ogbomoso, Oyo, Nigeria

General Information Independent-religious, coed, primarily men, comprehensive institution. *Graduate housing:* Rooms and/or apartments available to single and married students.

GRADUATE UNITS

Graduate Studies *Degree program information:* Part-time programs available. Offers church music (Diploma); divinity (M Div); theological studies (MATS); theology (M Th).

NIPISSING UNIVERSITY, North Bay, ON P1B 8L7, Canada

General Information Province-supported, coed, comprehensive institution. *Enrollment:* 5,412 graduate, professional, and undergraduate students; 844 full-time matriculated graduate/professional students (611 women), 219 part-time matriculated graduate/professional students (154 women). *Graduate faculty:* 50 full-time (25 women), 11 part-time/adjunct (5 women). *Tuition, area resident:* Part-time $561 per course. *Required fees:* $37 per course. *Graduate housing:* Room and/or apartments available to single students; on-campus housing not available to married students. Typical cost: $4,060 per year. Housing application deadline: 6/13. *Student services:* Campus employment opportunities, campus safety program, career counseling, disabled student services, exercise/wellness program, free psychological counseling, international student services, low-cost health insurance, teacher training. *Library facilities:* Education Centre Library. *Online resources:* library catalog, web page, access to other libraries' catalogs. *Collection:* 187,000 titles, 19,115 serial subscriptions, 5,988 audiovisual materials. *Research affiliation:* Tembec (forestry restoration), Foresty Partnership Trust (forestry restoration), Metals in the Human Environment Research Network (MITHE-RN) (assessing environmental pollutants on aquatic ecosystems), Canada Space Agency (CSA) & MacDonald, Dettwiler and Associates Ltd (MDA)—RADARSAT-2 (remote sensing), Education Quality and Accountability Office (EQAO) (assessing educational quality), Ontario Association of Deans of Education (OADE) (assessing pre-service practicum processes).

Computer facilities: Computer purchase and lease plans are available. 163 computers available on campus for general student use. A campuswide network can be accessed from student residence rooms and from off campus. Internet access and online class registration are available. *Web address:* http://www.nipissingu.ca/.

General Application Contact: Rebecca Roome-Rancourt, Assistant Registrar, Admissions, 705-474-3461 Ext. 4292, Fax: 705-495-1772, E-mail: rebeccar@nipissingu.ca.

GRADUATE UNITS

Faculty of Education Students: 844 full-time (611 women), 219 part-time (154 women). 5,007 applicants, 40% accepted, 842 enrolled. *Faculty:* 50 full-time (25 women), 11 part-time/adjunct (5 women). Expenses: Contact institution. In 2006, 39 master's, 711 other advanced degrees awarded. *Degree program information:* Part-time and evening/weekend programs available. Offers education (M Ed, Certificate). *Application deadline:* For fall admission, 6/15 for domestic students. *Application fee:* $140. *Application Contact:* Rebecca Roome-Rancourt, Assistant Registrar, Admissions, 705-474-3461 Ext. 4292, Fax: 705-495-1772, E-mail: rebeccar@nipissingu.ca. *Dean of Education*, Dr. Ronald Common, 705-474-3461 Ext. 4268, Fax: 705-474-3264, E-mail: ronaldc@nipissingu.ca.

NORFOLK STATE UNIVERSITY, Norfolk, VA 23504

General Information State-supported, coed, comprehensive institution. CGS member. *Graduate housing:* Room and/or apartments available to single students; on-campus housing not available to married students. Housing application deadline: 3/1. *Research affiliation:* Department of Energy NASA, National Science (fundamental and applied research studies), NASA Langley Research Center (NASA interests; aerospace applications; lidan application), National Science Foundation (fundamental and applied research studies), Department of Education (Title III projects; no child left behind initiative), University of Virginia's IGERT (science and engineering interactions with matter), Applied Research Center (technology transfer).

GRADUATE UNITS

School of Graduate Studies *Degree program information:* Part-time programs available. Electronic applications accepted.

School of Education *Degree program information:* Part-time programs available. Offers early childhood education (MAT); education (MA, MAT); pre-elementary education (MA); principal preparation (MA); secondary education (MAT); severe disabilities (MA); teaching (MA); urban education/administration (MA).

School of Liberal Arts *Degree program information:* Part-time programs available. Offers applied sociology (MS); community/clinical psychology (MA); criminal justice (MA); liberal arts (MA, MFA, MM, MS, Psy D); media and communication (MA); music (MM); music education (MM); performance (MM); psychology (Psy D); theory and composition (MM); urban affairs (MA); visual studies (MA, MFA).

School of Science and Technology Offers computer science (MS); electronics engineering (MS); materials science (MS); optical engineering (MS); science and technology (MS).

School of Social Work *Degree program information:* Part-time programs available. Offers social work (MSW, PhD).

NORTH CAROLINA AGRICULTURAL AND TECHNICAL STATE UNIVERSITY, Greensboro, NC 27411

General Information State-supported, coed, university. CGS member. *Graduate housing:* Room and/or apartments available on a first-come, first-served basis to single students; on-campus housing not available to married students. Housing application deadline: 5/8. *Research affiliation:* North Carolina Biotechnology Research Center (biotechnology research), The Boeing Company (aerospace engineering), Northrop Grumman Corporation (high performance computing), Research Triangle Institute (environmental protection, advanced technology), Rockwell Inc. (avionics technology, communications technology), Honeywell (industrial automation control).

GRADUATE UNITS

Graduate School *Degree program information:* Part-time and evening/weekend programs available.

College of Arts and Sciences *Degree program information:* Part-time and evening/weekend programs available. Offers art education (MS); arts and sciences (MA, MS, MSW); biology (MS); chemistry (MS); English (MA); English and Afro-American literature (MA); history education (MS); mathematics education (MS); social science education (MS); sociology and social work (MSW).

College of Engineering *Degree program information:* Part-time programs available. Offers architectural, agricultural, civil and environmental engineering (MSAE, MSCE, MSE); chemical engineering (MSE); computer science (MSCS); electrical engineering (MSEE, PhD); engineering (MSAE, MSCE, MSCS, MSE, MSEE, MSISE, MSME, PhD); industrial and systems engineering (MSISE, PhD); mechanical engineering (MSME, PhD).

School of Agriculture and Environmental and Allied Sciences *Degree program information:* Part-time and evening/weekend programs available. Offers agricultural economics (MS); agricultural education (MS); agriculture and environmental and allied sciences (MS); food and nutrition (MS); plant science (MS).

School of Education *Degree program information:* Part-time and evening/weekend programs available. Offers adult education (MS); biology education (MS); chemistry education (MS); early childhood education (MS); education (MS); educational administration (MS); educational media (MS); elementary education (MS); English education (MS); guidance and counseling (MS); health and physical education (MS); history education (MS); human resources (MS); intermediate education (MS); reading (MS); social science education (MS).

School of Technology *Degree program information:* Part-time and evening/weekend programs available. Offers industrial arts education (MS); industrial technology (MS, MSIT); safety and driver education (MS); technology (MS, MSIT); technology education (MS); vocational-industrial education (MS).

See Close-Up on page 979.

NORTH CAROLINA CENTRAL UNIVERSITY, Durham, NC 27707-3129

General Information State-supported, coed, comprehensive institution. CGS member. *Graduate housing:* Room and/or apartments available to single students; on-campus housing not available to married students. Housing application deadline: 7/1.

GRADUATE UNITS

Division of Academic Affairs *Degree program information:* Part-time and evening/weekend programs available.

College of Arts and Sciences *Degree program information:* Part-time and evening/weekend programs available. Offers arts and sciences (MA, MPA, MS); biology (MS); chemistry (MS); criminal justice (MS); earth sciences (MS); English (MA); general physical education (MS); history (MA); human sciences (MS); mathematics (MS); psychology (MA); public administration (MPA); recreation administration (MS); sociology (MA); special physical education (MS); therapeutic recreation (MS).

School of Business *Degree program information:* Part-time and evening/weekend programs available. Offers business (MBA).

School of Education *Degree program information:* Part-time and evening/weekend programs available. Offers agency counseling (MA); career counseling (MA); development leadership and professional studies (MA); education (M Ed, MA); education of the emotionally handicapped (M Ed); education of the mentally handicapped (M Ed); elementary education (M Ed, MA); instructional media (MA); school counseling (MA); speech pathology and audiology (M Ed).

School of Law *Degree program information:* Part-time and evening/weekend programs available. Offers law (JD, LL B).

School of Library and Information Sciences *Degree program information:* Part-time and evening/weekend programs available. Offers library and information sciences (MIS, MLS).

NORTH CAROLINA SCHOOL OF THE ARTS, Winston-Salem, NC 27127-2188

General Information State-supported, coed, comprehensive institution. *Enrollment:* 845 graduate, professional, and undergraduate students; 96 full-time matriculated graduate/professional students (47 women), 1 part-time matriculated graduate/professional student. *Enrollment by degree level:* 97 master's. *Graduate faculty:* 76. Tuition, state resident: full-time $3,074. Tuition, nonresident: full-time $14,354. *Required fees:* $1,605. *Graduate housing:* Room and/or apartments available on a first-come, first-served basis to single students. Typical cost: $6,139 (including board). Housing application deadline: 5/16. *Student services:* Campus employment opportunities, campus safety program, career counseling, disabled student services, exercise/wellness program, free psychological counseling, grant writing training, international student services, low-cost health insurance, writing training. *Library facilities:* Semans Library plus 1 other. *Online resources:* library catalog, access to other libraries' catalogs. *Collection:* 87,917 titles, 490 serial subscriptions.

Computer facilities: 60 computers available on campus for general student use. A campuswide network can be accessed from student residence rooms and from off campus. Internet access and online class registration are available. *Web address:* http://www.ncarts.edu/.

General Application Contact: Sheeler Lawson, Director of Admissions, 336-770-3290, Fax: 336-770-3370, E-mail: admissions@ncarts.edu.

GRADUATE UNITS

School of Design and Production Students: 69 full-time (39 women); includes 4 minority (all African Americans), 2 international. Average age 25. 86 applicants, 77% accepted, 48 enrolled. *Faculty:* 19 full-time (4 women), 16 part-time/adjunct (6 women). Expenses: Contact institution. *Financial support:* In 2006–07, 59 teaching assistantships with partial tuition reimbursements (averaging $1,500 per year) were awarded; career-related internships or fieldwork, Federal Work-Study, and unspecified assistantships also available. Support available to part-time students. Financial award application deadline: 3/15; financial award applicants required to submit FAFSA. In 2006, 14 degrees awarded. Offers costume design (MFA); costume technology (MFA); film production design (MFA); scene design (MFA); scene painting/properties (MFA); sound design (MFA); technical direction (MFA); wig and make-up design (MFA). *Application deadline:* For fall admission, 4/1 priority date for domestic students. Applications are processed on a rolling basis. *Application fee:* $60 ($100 for international students). Electronic applications accepted. *Application Contact:* Sheeler Lawson, Director of Admissions, 336-770-3290, Fax: 336-770-3370, E-mail: admissions@ncarts.edu. *Dean,* Joseph A. Tilford, 336-770-3214 Ext. 103, Fax: 336-770-3213.

School of Filmmaking Students: 10 full-time (2 women). Average age 25. 3 applicants, 100% accepted, 3 enrolled. *Faculty:* 2 full-time (0 women). Expenses: Contact institution. *Financial support:* In 2006–07, fellowships (averaging $2,000 per year); career-related internships or fieldwork and Federal Work-Study also available. Support available to part-time students. Financial award application deadline: 3/15; financial award applicants required to submit FAFSA. In 2006, 2 degrees awarded. Offers film music composition (MFA). *Application deadline:* For fall admission, 4/1 priority date for domestic students. Applications are processed on a rolling basis. *Application fee:* $60 ($100 for international students). *Application Contact:* Sheeler Lawson, Director of Admissions, 336-770-3290, Fax: 336-770-3370, E-mail: admissions@ncarts.edu. *Interim Dean,* David Elkins, 336-770-1330, Fax: 336-770-1339, E-mail: elkinsd@ncarts.edu.

School of Music Students: 40 full-time (15 women); includes 4 minority (1 American Indian/Alaska Native, 3 Hispanic Americans), 26 international. Average age 25. *Faculty:* 30 full-time (9 women), 11 part-time/adjunct (3 women). Expenses: Contact institution. *Financial support:* In 2006–07, 8 fellowships with partial tuition reimbursements (averaging $2,000 per year), 10 teaching assistantships with partial tuition reimbursements (averaging $3,000 per year) were awarded; career-related internships or fieldwork and Federal Work-Study also available. Support available to part-time students. Financial award application deadline: 3/15; financial award applicants required to submit FAFSA. In 2006, 14 degrees awarded. Offers music performance (MM); orchestral conducting (MM). *Application deadline:* For fall admission, 4/1 priority date for domestic students. Applications are processed on a rolling basis. *Application fee:* $60 ($100 for international students). *Application Contact:* Sheeler Lawson, Director of Admissions, 336-770-3290, Fax: 336-770-3370, E-mail: admissions@ncarts.edu. *Dean,* Dr. Thomas Clark, 336-770-3251, Fax: 336-770-3248, E-mail: clarkt@ncarts.edu.

NORTH CAROLINA STATE UNIVERSITY, Raleigh, NC 27695

General Information State-supported, coed, university. CGS member. *Graduate housing:* Rooms and/or apartments available on a first-come, first-served basis to single and married students. *Research affiliation:* Triangle Universities Nuclear Laboratory, Research Triangle Institute, Highlands Biological Station, National Humanities Center, Microelectronics Center of North Carolina, North Carolina-Japan Center.

GRADUATE UNITS

College of Veterinary Medicine *Degree program information:* Part-time programs available. Offers cell biology and morphology (MS, PhD); epidemiology and population medicine (MS, PhD); immunology (MS, PhD); microbiology and immunology (MS, PhD); pathology (MS, PhD); pharmacology (MS, PhD); specialized veterinary medicine (MS); veterinary medicine (DVM, MS, MSpVM, MVPH, PhD); veterinary public health (MVPH). Electronic applications accepted.

Graduate School *Degree program information:* Part-time and evening/weekend programs available. Postbaccalaureate distance learning degree programs offered. Electronic applications accepted.

College of Agriculture and Life Sciences *Degree program information:* Part-time programs available. Offers agricultural and resource economics (MS); agricultural education (MAEE, MS); agriculture and life sciences (M Tox, MAEE, MB, MBAE, MFG, MFM, MFS, MG, MMB, MN, MP, MS, MZS, PhD); animal science (MS); animal science and poultry science (PhD); biochemistry (MS, PhD); bioinformatics (MB, PhD); biological and agricultural engineering (MBAE, MS, PhD); botany (MS, PhD); crop science (MS, PhD); entomology (MS, PhD); environmental and molecular toxicology (M Tox, MS, PhD); extension education (MAEE, MS); financial mathematics (MFM); food science (MFS, MS, PhD); functional genomics (MFG, MS, PhD); genetics (MG, MS, PhD); horticultural science (MS, PhD); immunology (MS, PhD); microbial biotechnology (MMB); microbiology (MS, PhD); nutrition (MN, MS, PhD); physiology (MP, MS, PhD); plant pathology (MS, PhD); poultry science (MS); soil science (MS, PhD); zoology (MS, MZS, PhD). Electronic applications accepted.

College of Design *Degree program information:* Part-time programs available. Offers architecture (M Arch); art and design (MAD); design (M Arch, MAD, MID, MLA, UA Undergraduate Associate, PhD); graphic design (UA Undergraduate Associate); industrial design (MID); landscape architecture (MLA). Electronic applications accepted.

College of Education *Degree program information:* Part-time programs available. Offers adult and community college education (M Ed, MS, Ed D); agency counseling (M Ed, MS); counselor education (M Ed, MS, PhD); curriculum and instruction (M Ed, MS, PhD); education (M Ed, MS, MSA, Ed D, PhD, Certificate); educational administration and supervision (Ed D); educational research and policy analysis (PhD); higher education administration (M Ed, MS, Ed D); mathematics education (M Ed, MS, PhD); middle grades education (M Ed, MS); school administration (MSA); science education (M Ed, MS, PhD); special education (M Ed, MS); technology education (M Ed, MS, Ed D); training and development (M Ed, MS). Electronic applications accepted.

College of Engineering *Degree program information:* Part-time programs available. Offers aerospace engineering (MS, PhD); biomedical engineering (MS, PhD); chemical engineering (M Ch E, MS, PhD); civil engineering (MCE, MS, PhD); computer engineering (MS, PhD); computer networking (MS); computer science (MC Sc, MS, PhD); electrical engineering (MS, PhD); engineering (M Ch E, M Eng, MC Sc, MCE, MIE, MIMS, MME, MMSE, MNE, MOR, MS, PhD); industrial engineering (MIE, MS, PhD); integrated manufacturing systems engineering (MIMS); materials science and engineering (MMSE, MS, PhD); mechanical engineering (MME, MS, PhD); nuclear engineering (MNE, MS, PhD); operations research (MOR, MS, PhD). Electronic applications accepted.

College of Humanities and Social Sciences *Degree program information:* Part-time and evening/weekend programs available. Offers anthropology (MA); bioarchaeology (MA); creative writing (MFA); cultural anthropology (MA); developmental psychology (PhD); English (MA); environmental anthropology (MA); ergonomics and experimental psychology (PhD); French language and literature (MA); history (MA); humanities and social sciences (M Soc, MA, MAIS, MFA, MPA, MS, PhD); industrial/organizational psychology (PhD); international studies (MAIS); liberal studies (MA); organizational communication (MS); psychology in the public interest (PhD); public administration (MPA, PhD); public history (MA); rural sociology (MS); school psychology (PhD); sociology (M Soc, MS, PhD); Spanish language and literature (MA); technical communication (MS). Electronic applications accepted.

College of Management *Degree program information:* Part-time programs available. Offers accounting (MAC); business administration (MBA); economics (M Econ, MA, PhD); financial management (MBA); information technology management (MBA); marketing management (MBA); product innovation management (MBA); supply chain management (MBA); technology commercialization (MBA). Electronic applications accepted.

College of Natural Resources *Degree program information:* Part-time programs available. Offers fisheries and wildlife sciences (MFWS, MS); forestry (MF, MS, PhD); geographic information systems (MS); maintenance management (MRRA, MS); natural resources (MF, MFWS, MNR, MRRA, MS, MWPS, PhD); parks, recreation and tourism management (PhD); recreation planning (MRRA, MS); recreation resources administration/public administration (MRRA); recreation/park management (MRRA, MS); sports management (MRRA, MS); travel and tourism management (MS); wood and paper science (MS, MWPS, PhD). Electronic applications accepted.

College of Physical and Mathematical Sciences *Degree program information:* Part-time programs available. Offers applied mathematics (MS, PhD); biomathematics (M Biomath, MS, PhD); chemistry (MCH, MS, PhD); ecology (PhD); marine, earth, and atmospheric sciences (MS, PhD); mathematics (MS, PhD); meteorology (MS, PhD); oceanography (MS, PhD); physical and mathematical sciences (M Biomath, M Stat, MCH, MS, PhD); physics (MS, PhD); statistics (M Stat, MS, PhD). Electronic applications accepted.

College of Textiles *Degree program information:* Part-time and evening/weekend programs available. Postbaccalaureate distance learning degree programs offered. Offers fiber and polymer sciences (PhD); textile and apparel technology and management (MS, MT); textile chemistry (MS); textile engineering (MS); textile technology management (PhD); textiles (MS, MT, PhD). Electronic applications accepted.

NORTH CENTRAL COLLEGE, Naperville, IL 60566-7063

General Information Independent-religious, coed, comprehensive institution. *Graduate housing:* Room and/or apartments available on a first-come, first-served basis to single students; on-campus housing not available to married students.

GRADUATE UNITS

Graduate Programs *Degree program information:* Part-time and evening/weekend programs available. Offers business administration (MBA); computer science (MS); education (MA Ed); leadership studies (MLD); liberal studies (MALS); management information systems (MS). Electronic applications accepted.

NORTHCENTRAL UNIVERSITY, Prescott, AZ 86314

General Information Proprietary, coed, comprehensive institution.

NORTH DAKOTA STATE UNIVERSITY, Fargo, ND 58105

General Information State-supported, coed, university. CGS member. *Enrollment:* 12,258 graduate, professional, and undergraduate students; 550 full-time matriculated graduate/professional students (227 women), 1,112 part-time matriculated graduate/professional students (563 women). *Enrollment by degree level:* 1,138 master's, 524 doctoral. *Graduate faculty:* 432 full-time (65 women), 21 part-time/adjunct (6 women). *Graduate housing:* Rooms and/or apartments available on a first-come, first-served basis to single and married students. *Student services:* Career counseling, child daycare facilities, disabled student services, free psychological counseling, international student services, low-cost health insurance, multicultural affairs office. *Library facilities:* North Dakota State University Library plus 3 others. *Online resources:* library catalog, web page, access to other libraries' catalogs. *Collection:*

North Dakota State University (continued)

303,274 titles, 2,499 serial subscriptions, 3,276 audiovisual materials. *Research affiliation:* U.S. Department of Agriculture–Metabolism and Radiation Laboratory.

Computer facilities: 500 computers available on campus for general student use. A campuswide network can be accessed from student residence rooms and from off campus. Internet access is available. *Web address:* http://www.ndsu.edu/.

General Application Contact: Dr. David A. Wittrock, Dean, 701-231-8909, Fax: 701-231-6524.

GRADUATE UNITS

The Graduate School Students: 550 full-time (227 women), 1,112 part-time (563 women); includes 94 minority (15 African Americans, 12 American Indian/Alaska Native, 55 Asian Americans or Pacific Islanders, 12 Hispanic Americans), 406 international. Average age 25. 1,081 applicants, 65% accepted, 399 enrolled. *Faculty:* 432 full-time (65 women), 21 part-time/adjunct (6 women). Expenses: Contact institution. *Financial support:* Fellowships with full tuition reimbursements, research assistantships with full tuition reimbursements, teaching assistantships with full tuition reimbursements, career-related internships or fieldwork, Federal Work-Study, institutionally sponsored loans, scholarships/grants, traineeships, tuition waivers (full and partial), and unspecified assistantships available. Support available to part-time students. Financial award applicants required to submit FAFSA. In 2006, 281 master's, 59 doctorates, 8 other advanced degrees awarded. *Degree program information:* Part-time and evening/weekend programs available. Postbaccalaureate distance learning degree programs offered (minimal on-campus study). Offers agricultural education (M Ed, MS); agricultural extension education (MS); applied mathematics (MS, PhD); applied statistics (MS, Certificate); biochemistry (MS, PhD); biological sciences (MS); botany (MS, PhD); cellular and molecular biology (PhD); chemistry (MS, PhD); child development and family science (MS); clinical psychology (MS); coatings and polymeric materials (MS, PhD); cognitive and visual neuroscience (PhD); computer science (MS, PhD); counseling (M Ed, MS, PhD); couple and family therapy (MS); curriculum and instruction (M Ed, MS); dietetics (MS); education (PhD); educational leadership (M Ed, MS, Ed S); entry level athletic training (MS); environmental and conservation sciences (MS, PhD); environmental science (MS); exercise science (MS); family and consumer sciences education (M Ed, MS); family financial planning (MS); genomics (MS, PhD); gerontology (MS, PhD); health/social psychology (PhD); history education (M Ed, MS); human development (PhD); human development and education (M Ed, MS, PhD, Ed S); mathematics (MS, PhD); mathematics education (M Ed, MS); music education (M Ed, MS); natural resource management (MS, PhD); natural resources (MS, PhD); nutrition science (MS); operations research (MS); pedagogy (M Ed, MS); physical education and athletic administration (M Ed, MS); physics (MS, PhD); psychology (MS); public health (MS); science and mathematics (MS, PhD, Certificate); science education (M Ed, MS); software engineering (MS, PhD, Certificate); sport pedagogy (MS); sports recreation management (MS); statistics (PhD); transportation and logistics (PhD); zoology (MS, PhD). *Application deadline:* For fall admission, 7/31 priority date for domestic students, 5/1 priority date for international students; for spring admission, 12/15 priority date for domestic students, 8/1 priority date for international students. *Application fee:* $45 ($60 for international students). Electronic applications accepted. *Dean,* Dr. David A. Wittrock, 701-231-8909, Fax: 701-231-6524.

College of Agriculture, Food Systems, and Natural Resources Students: 164 (67 women); includes 60 minority (8 African Americans, 46 Asian Americans or Pacific Islanders, 6 Hispanic Americans). *Faculty:* 126. Expenses: Contact institution. *Financial support:* Fellowships with full tuition reimbursements, research assistantships with full tuition reimbursements, teaching assistantships with full tuition reimbursements, career-related internships or fieldwork, Federal Work-Study, and institutionally sponsored loans available. Support available to part-time students. *Degree program information:* Part-time programs available. Offers agribusiness and applied economics (MS); agriculture, food systems, and natural resources (MS, PhD); animal science (MS, PhD); cellular and molecular biology (PhD); cereal science (MS, PhD); crop and weed sciences (MS); entomology (MS, PhD); environment and conservation science (MS, PhD); environmental and conservation science (PhD); environmental conservation science (MS); food safety (MS, PhD); genomics and bioinformatics (MS, PhD); horticulture (MS); international agribusiness (MS); microbiology (MS); molecular pathogenesis (PhD); natural resource management (MS, PhD); plant pathology (MS, PhD); plant sciences (PhD); range sciences (MS, PhD); soil sciences (MS, PhD). *Application deadline:* Applications are processed on a rolling basis. *Application fee:* $45 ($60 for international students). Electronic applications accepted. *Dean,* Dr. Kenneth F. Grafton, 701-231-8790, Fax: 701-231-8520, E-mail: k.grafton@ndsu.edu.

College of Arts, Humanities and Social Sciences Students: 43 full-time (22 women), 138 part-time (98 women). *Faculty:* 77 full-time (26 women). Expenses: Contact institution. *Financial support:* In 2006–07, 3 fellowships with full tuition reimbursements (averaging $12,150 per year), 93 teaching assistantships with full tuition reimbursements (averaging $8,000 per year) were awarded; research assistantships with full tuition reimbursements, career-related internships or fieldwork, Federal Work-Study, institutionally sponsored loans, scholarships/grants, and tuition waivers (full) also available. Support available to part-time students. In 2006, 20 master's, 5 doctorates awarded. *Degree program information:* Part-time and evening/weekend programs available. Offers arts, humanities and social sciences (M Ed, MA, MM, MS, DMA, PhD); communication (PhD); criminal justice (MS, PhD); emergency management (MS, PhD); English (MA, MS); history (MA, MS, PhD); mass communication (MA, MS); music (M Ed, MM, DMA); social science (MA, MS); sociology (MS); speech communication (MA, MS). *Application deadline:* Applications are processed on a rolling basis. *Application fee:* $45 ($60 for international students). *Dean,* Dr. Thomas J. Riley, 701-231-9588, Fax: 701-231-1047, E-mail: thomas.riley@ndsu.edu.

College of Business Administration Students: 21 full-time (9 women), 75 part-time (35 women); includes 4 minority (2 African Americans, 2 Hispanic Americans). Average age 29. 55 applicants, 76% accepted, 38 enrolled. *Faculty:* 25 full-time (5 women). Expenses: Contact institution. *Financial support:* In 2006–07, 14 students received support, including 13 research assistantships, 1 teaching assistantship; institutionally sponsored loans and tuition waivers (partial) also available. Support available to part-time students. Financial award application deadline: 5/15; financial award applicants required to submit FAFSA. In 2006, 32 degrees awarded. *Degree program information:* Part-time and evening/weekend programs available. Offers business administration (MBA). *Application deadline:* For fall admission, 7/15 priority date for domestic students; for spring admission, 11/15 for domestic students. Applications are processed on a rolling basis. *Application fee:* $45 ($60 for international students). *Application Contact:* Paul R. Brown, Director, 701-231-7681, Fax: 701-231-7508, E-mail: paul.brown@ndsu.edu. *Dean,* Dr. Ron Johnson, 701-231-8805.

College of Engineering and Architecture Students: 49 full-time (10 women), 105 part-time (11 women); includes 72 minority (1 African American, 8 American Indian/Alaska Native, 62 Asian Americans or Pacific Islanders, 1 Hispanic American), 47 international. Average age 27. 225 applicants, 47% accepted. *Faculty:* 72 full-time (9 women), 11 part-time/adjunct (0 women). Expenses: Contact institution. *Financial support:* In 2006–07, 150 students received support, including fellowships with full tuition reimbursements available (averaging $15,000 per year), research assistantships with full tuition reimbursements available (averaging $9,000 per year), teaching assistantships with full tuition reimbursements available (averaging $8,000 per year); career-related internships or fieldwork, Federal Work-Study, institutionally sponsored loans, scholarships/grants, and tuition waivers (full) also available. Support available to part-time students. Financial award application deadline: 4/15. In 2006, 32 master's, 5 doctorates awarded. *Degree program information:* Part-time programs available. Offers agricultural and biosystems engineering (MS, PhD); civil engineering (MS, PhD); electrical and computer engineering); engineering (PhD); engineering and architecture (MS, PhD); environmental engineering (MS, PhD); industrial and manufacturing engineering (PhD); industrial engineering and management (MS); manufacturing engineering (MS); mechanical engineering (MS, PhD); natural resource management (MS, PhD); natural resources management (PhD); transportation and logistics (PhD). *Application deadline:* For fall admission, 4/1 priority date for domestic and international students; for spring admission, 10/1 priority date for domestic and international students. Applications are processed on a rolling basis. *Application fee:* $45 ($60 for international students). *Application Contact:* Dr. David A. Wittrock, Dean, 701-231-8909, Fax: 701-231-6524. *Dean,* Dr. Gary R. Smith, 701-231-7525, Fax: 701-231-8957, E-mail: gary.smith@ndsu.edu.

College of Pharmacy, Nursing and Allied Sciences Expenses: Contact institution. *Financial support:* Research assistantships with full tuition reimbursements, career-related internships or fieldwork, Federal Work-Study, institutionally sponsored loans, and scholarships/grants available. Financial award application deadline: 4/1. *Degree program information:* Part-time programs available. Offers nursing (MS, DNP); pharmaceutical sciences (MS, PhD); pharmacy, nursing and allied sciences (MS, DNP, PhD). *Application deadline:* For fall admission, 4/1 for domestic students. Applications are processed on a rolling basis. *Application fee:* $45 ($60 for international students). *Application Contact:* Dr. Jonathan Sheng, Assistant Professor, 701-231-6140, Fax: 701-231-8333, E-mail: jonathan.sheng@ndsu.edu. *Dean,* Dr. Charles D. Peterson, 701-231-7609, Fax: 701-231-7606.

See Close-Up on page 981.

NORTHEASTERN ILLINOIS UNIVERSITY, Chicago, IL 60625-4699

General Information State-supported, coed, comprehensive institution. CGS member. *Enrollment:* 12,056 graduate, professional, and undergraduate students; 340 full-time matriculated graduate/professional students (179 women), 1,454 part-time matriculated graduate/professional students (1,011 women). *Enrollment by degree level:* 1,794 master's. *Graduate faculty:* 259 full-time (110 women), 170 part-time/adjunct (85 women). *Graduate housing:* On-campus housing not available. *Student services:* Campus employment opportunities, campus safety program, career counseling, child daycare facilities, disabled student services, exercise/wellness program, free psychological counseling, grant writing training, international student services, low-cost health insurance, teacher training. *Library facilities:* Ronald Williams Library. *Online resources:* library catalog, web page, access to other libraries' catalogs. *Collection:* 718,536 titles, 2,919 serial subscriptions, 8,222 audiovisual materials. *Research affiliation:* Advocate Health Care Network (health care cost containment), Lutheran General Hospital (clinical cardiology), Advocate Medical Group (health care outcomes research).

Computer facilities: 360 computers available on campus for general student use. A campuswide network can be accessed from off campus. Internet access and online class registration, productivity software are available. *Web address:* http://www.neiu.edu/.

General Application Contact: Dr. Janet P. Fredericks, Dean of the Graduate College, 773-442-6010, Fax: 773-442-6020, E-mail: j-fredericks@neiu.edu.

GRADUATE UNITS

Graduate College Average age 34. 526 applicants, 87% accepted. *Faculty:* 259 full-time (110 women), 173 part-time/adjunct (85 women). Expenses: Contact institution. *Financial support:* In 2006–07, 509 students received support, including 86 research assistantships with full tuition reimbursements available (averaging $6,600 per year); career-related internships or fieldwork, Federal Work-Study, institutionally sponsored loans, and tuition waivers (full and partial) also available. Support available to part-time students. Financial award applicants required to submit FAFSA. In 2006, 515 degrees awarded. *Degree program information:* Part-time and evening/weekend programs available. *Application deadline:* For fall admission, 4/1 priority date for domestic students; for spring admission, 8/15 for domestic students. Applications are processed on a rolling basis. *Application fee:* $25. *Application Contact:* Diane O'Cherony, Administrative Aide, 773-442-6003, Fax: 773-442-6020, E-mail: dsochero@neiu.edu. *Dean of the Graduate College,* Dr. Janet P. Fredericks, 773-442-6010, Fax: 773-442-6020, E-mail: j-fredericks@neiu.edu.

College of Arts and Sciences Students: 118 full-time (33 women), 417 part-time (234 women); includes 140 minority (36 African Americans, 1 American Indian/Alaska Native, 60 Asian Americans or Pacific Islanders, 43 Hispanic Americans), 68 international. Average age 32. 130 applicants, 90% accepted. *Faculty:* 139 full-time (47 women), 65 part-time/adjunct (23 women). Expenses: Contact institution. *Financial support:* In 2006–07, 270 students received support, including 57 research assistantships with full tuition reimbursements available (averaging $6,600 per year); career-related internships or fieldwork, Federal Work-Study, institutionally sponsored loans, and tuition waivers (full and partial) also available. Support available to part-time students. Financial award applicants required to submit FAFSA. In 2006, 114 degrees awarded. *Degree program information:* Part-time and evening/weekend programs available. Offers arts and sciences (MA, MS); biology (MS); chemistry (MS); communication, media and theatre (MA); composition/writing (MA); computer science (MS); earth science (MS); English (MA); geography and environmental studies (MA); gerontology (MA); history (MA); linguistics (MA); literature (MA); mathematics (MA, MS); mathematics for elementary school teachers (MA); music (MA); political science (MA). *Application deadline:* For fall admission, 4/1 priority date for domestic students; for spring admission, 8/15 for domestic students. Applications are processed on a rolling basis. *Application fee:* $25.

College of Business and Management Students: 24 full-time (12 women), 40 part-time (16 women); includes 15 minority (4 African Americans, 8 Asian Americans or Pacific Islanders, 3 Hispanic Americans), 21 international. Average age 31. 23 applicants, 91% accepted. *Faculty:* 24 full-time (3 women), 13 part-time/adjunct (4 women). Expenses: Contact institution. *Financial support:* In 2006–07, 20 students received support, including 8 research assistantships with full tuition reimbursements available (averaging $6,600 per year); career-related internships or fieldwork, Federal Work-Study, institutionally sponsored loans, and tuition waivers (full and partial) also available. Support available to part-time students. In 2006, 13 degrees awarded. *Degree program information:* Part-time and evening/weekend programs available. Offers accounting (MBA); finance (MBA); management (MBA); marketing (MBA). *Application deadline:* For fall admission, 4/1 priority date for domestic students; for spring admission, 8/15 for domestic students. Applications are processed on a rolling basis. *Application fee:* $25.

College of Education Students: 169 full-time (122 women), 976 part-time (751 women); includes 299 minority (125 African Americans, 1 American Indian/Alaska Native, 35 Asian Americans or Pacific Islanders, 138 Hispanic Americans), 11 international. Average age 35. 363 applicants, 86% accepted. *Faculty:* 83 full-time (47 women), 64 part-time/adjunct (40 women). Expenses: Contact institution. *Financial support:* In 2006–07, 219 students received support, including 21 research assistantships with full tuition reimbursements available (averaging $6,600 per year); career-related internships or fieldwork, Federal Work-Study, institutionally sponsored loans, and tuition waivers (full and partial) also available. Support available to part-time students. Financial award applicants required to submit FAFSA. In 2006, 145 degrees awarded. *Degree program information:* Part-time and evening/weekend programs available. Offers bilingual/bicultural education (MAT, MSI); early childhood special education (MA); educating children with behavior disorders (MA); educating individuals with mental retardation (MA); education (MA, MAT, MSI); educational administration and supervision (MA); educational leadership (MA); gifted education (MA); guidance and counseling (MA); human resource development (MA); inner city studies (MA); instruction (MSI); language arts (MAT, MSI); reading (MA); special education (MA); teaching (MAT); teaching children with learning disabilities (MA). *Application deadline:* For fall admission, 4/1 priority date for domestic students; for spring admission, 8/15 for domestic students. Applications are processed on a rolling basis. *Application fee:* $25.

NORTHEASTERN OHIO UNIVERSITIES COLLEGE OF MEDICINE, Rootstown, OH 44272-0095

General Information State-supported, coed, graduate-only institution. *Enrollment by degree level:* 459 first professional. *Graduate faculty:* 278 full-time (76 women), 1,631 part-time/adjunct (316 women). *Graduate housing:* On-campus housing not available. *Student services:* Campus employment opportunities, campus safety program, career counseling, disabled student services, free psychological counseling, low-cost health insurance, multicultural affairs office. *Library facilities:* Oliver Ocasek Regional Medical Information Center. *Online resources:* library catalog, web page, access to other libraries' catalogs. *Collection:* 125,027 titles, 3,948 serial subscriptions, 1,457 audiovisual materials. *Research affiliation:* National Institutes of Health (anatomy, biochemistry, immunology, neurobiology, microbiology), National Science Foundation (anatomy), NASA (microbiology, immunology, biochemistry), Department of Defense (US Army) (physiology, microbiology), Health Resources and Services Administration (human health), Oregon Department of Justice (human health).

Computer facilities: 50 computers available on campus for general student use. A campuswide network can be accessed from student residence rooms and from off campus. Internet access is available. *Web address:* http://www.neoucom.edu/.

General Application Contact: Jill Byers, Director of Admissions, 330-325-6270, E-mail: admission@neoucom.edu.

GRADUATE UNITS

Professional Program Students: 459 full-time (240 women); includes 186 minority (16 African Americans, 3 American Indian/Alaska Native, 158 Asian Americans or Pacific Islanders, 9 Hispanic Americans). Average age 24. 2,031 applicants, 11% accepted, 140 enrolled. *Faculty:* 278 full-time (76 women), 1,631 part-time/adjunct (316 women). Expenses: Contact institution. *Financial support:* In 2006–07, 164 students received support. Institutionally sponsored loans and scholarships/grants available. Financial award application deadline: 4/15; financial award applicants required to submit FAFSA. In 2006, 111 degrees awarded. Offers medicine (MD). *Application deadline:* For fall admission, 10/1 for domestic students. Applications are processed on a rolling basis. *Application fee:* $40. Electronic applications accepted. *Application Contact:* Jill Byers, Director of Admissions, 330-325-6270, E-mail: admission@neoucom.edu. *President and Dean*, Dr. Lois Margaret Nora, 330-325-6255.

NORTHEASTERN SEMINARY AT ROBERTS WESLEYAN COLLEGE, Rochester, NY 14624

General Information Independent-religious, coed, graduate-only institution. *Enrollment by degree level:* 87 first professional, 32 master's, 19 doctoral. *Graduate faculty:* 7 full-time (1 woman), 17 part-time/adjunct (5 women). *Tuition:* Part-time $338 per credit hour. *Graduate housing:* On-campus housing not available. *Student services:* Campus employment opportunities, campus safety program, career counseling, disabled student services, exercise/wellness program, international student services, low-cost health insurance, teacher training, writing training. *Library facilities:* B. Thomas Golisano Library plus 2 others. *Online resources:* library catalog, web page. *Collection:* 128,369 titles, 1,216 serial subscriptions, 4,654 audiovisual materials.

Computer facilities: 104 computers available on campus for general student use. A campuswide network can be accessed from student residence rooms and from off campus. Internet access is available. *Web address:* http://www.nes.edu/.

General Application Contact: Barbara Touchstone, Coordinator of Admissions, 585-594-6802, Fax: 585-594-6801, E-mail: touchstone_barbara@nes.edu.

GRADUATE UNITS

Graduate and Professional Programs Students: 125 full-time (45 women), 13 part-time (5 women); includes 51 minority (40 African Americans, 2 Asian Americans or Pacific Islanders, 9 Hispanic Americans). Average age 43. 37 applicants, 73% accepted, 24 enrolled. *Faculty:* 7 full-time (1 woman), 17 part-time/adjunct (5 women). Expenses: Contact institution. *Financial support:* In 2006–07, 138 students received support, including teaching assistantships with partial tuition reimbursements available (averaging $3,200 per year); career-related internships or fieldwork, institutionally sponsored loans, scholarships/grants, and tuition waivers (partial) also available. Financial award applicants required to submit FAFSA. In 2006, 15 first professional degrees, 15 master's awarded. *Degree program information:* Evening/weekend programs available. Offers ministry (D Min); theological studies (MA); theology (M Div). *Application deadline:* For fall admission, 8/1 priority date for domestic and international students; for spring admission, 3/1 priority date for domestic and international students. Applications are processed on a rolling basis. *Application fee:* $35. Electronic applications accepted. *Application Contact:* Barbara Touchstone, Coordinator of Admissions, 585-594-6802, Fax: 585-594-6801, E-mail: touchstone_barbara@nes.edu. *Dean*, Dr. Wayne G. McCown, 585-594-6800, Fax: 585-594-6801.

NORTHEASTERN STATE UNIVERSITY, Tahlequah, OK 74464-2399

General Information State-supported, coed, comprehensive institution. *Enrollment:* 9,540 graduate, professional, and undergraduate students; 338 full-time matriculated graduate/professional students (238 women), 651 part-time matriculated graduate/professional students (440 women). *Enrollment by degree level:* 103 first professional, 886 master's. *Graduate faculty:* 121 full-time (35 women), 10 part-time/adjunct (5 women). *Graduate housing:* Rooms and/or apartments available to single and married students. Housing application deadline:6/1. *Student services:* Campus employment opportunities, career counseling, disabled student services, free psychological counseling, international student services, low-cost health insurance, multicultural affairs office, teacher training. *Library facilities:* John Vaughn Library. *Online resources:* library catalog, web page. *Collection:* 466,526 titles, 17,570 serial subscriptions, 7,871 audiovisual materials.

Computer facilities: 534 computers available on campus for general student use. A campuswide network can be accessed from student residence rooms and from off campus. Internet access is available. *Web address:* http://www.nsuok.edu/.

General Application Contact: Donna Trout, Graduate Program Coordinator, 918-449-6000 Ext. 6123, Fax: 918-449-6147, E-mail: troutdk@nsuok.edu.

GRADUATE UNITS

College of Optometry Students: 103 full-time (59 women); includes 17 minority (3 African Americans, 10 American Indian/Alaska Native, 3 Asian Americans or Pacific Islanders, 1 Hispanic American). Average age 26. 108 applicants, 33% accepted, 26 enrolled. *Faculty:* 24 full-time (10 women), 10 part-time/adjunct (5 women). Expenses: Contact institution. *Financial support:* In 2006–07, 42 students received support. Federal Work-Study, institutionally sponsored loans, scholarships/grants, tuition waivers (partial), and residencies available. Financial award application deadline: 5/1; financial award applicants required to submit FAFSA. In 2006, 25 degrees awarded. Offers optometry (OD). Applicants must be residents of Oklahoma, Arkansas, Kansas, Colorado, New Mexico, Missouri, Texas, or Nebraska. *Application deadline:* For fall admission, 2/1 for domestic students. Applications are processed on a rolling basis. *Application fee:* $45. *Application Contact:* Natalie Batt, Student and Alumni Affairs, 918-456-5511 Ext. 4036, Fax: 918-458-2104, E-mail: batt@nsuok.edu. *Dean*, Dr. George E. Foster, 918-456-5511 Ext. 4000, Fax: 918-458-2104, E-mail: fosterge@nsuok.edu.

Graduate College Students: 235 full-time (179 women), 651 part-time (440 women); includes 250 minority (43 African Americans, 174 American Indian/Alaska Native, 14 Asian Americans or Pacific Islanders, 19 Hispanic Americans), 9 international. Average age 35. *Faculty:* 121 full-time (35 women), 10 part-time/adjunct (5 women). Expenses: Contact institution. *Financial support:* Research assistantships, teaching assistantships, career-related internships or fieldwork, Federal Work-Study, scholarships/grants, and tuition waivers (partial) available. Financial award application deadline: 3/1. In 2006, 257 degrees awarded. *Degree program information:* Part-time and evening/weekend programs available. *Application deadline:* Applications are processed on a rolling basis. *Application fee:* $0. Electronic applications accepted. *Application Contact:* Margie Railey, Administrative Assistant, 918-456-5511 Ext. 2093, Fax: 918-458-2061, E-mail: railey@nsuok.edu. *Dean*, Dr. Thomas L. Jackson, 918-456-5511 Ext. 2220, Fax: 918-458-2061, E-mail: jacks009@nsuok.edu.

College of Business and Technology Students: 23 full-time (13 women), 134 part-time (66 women); includes 51 minority (8 African Americans, 39 American Indian/Alaska Native, 3 Asian Americans or Pacific Islanders, 1 Hispanic American), 6 international. *Faculty:* 12 full-time (2 women). Expenses: Contact institution. *Financial support:* Teaching assistantships, Federal Work-Study available. Financial award application deadline: 3/1. In 2006, 21 degrees awarded. *Degree program information:* Part-time and evening/weekend programs available. Offers accounting and financial analysis (MS); business administration (MBA); business and technology (MBA, MS); industrial management (MS). *Application deadline:* For fall admission, 6/1 priority date for domestic students. Applications are processed on a rolling basis. *Application fee:* $0 ($25 for international students). *Dean*, Dr. John Schleede, 918-456-5511 Ext. 2910, Fax: 918-458-2337, E-mail: schleede@nsuok.edu.

College of Education Students: 151 full-time (117 women), 422 part-time (319 women); includes 156 minority (28 African Americans, 103 American Indian/Alaska Native, 11 Asian Americans or Pacific Islanders, 14 Hispanic Americans), 2 international. *Faculty:* 26 full-time (11 women). Expenses: Contact institution. *Financial support:* Teaching assistantships, career-related internships or fieldwork and Federal Work-Study available. Financial award application deadline: 3/1. In 2006, 187 degrees awarded. *Degree program information:* Part-time and evening/weekend programs available. Offers collegiate scholarship and services (MS); counseling psychology (MS); early childhood education (M Ed); education (M Ed, MS, MS Ed); health and kinesiology (MS Ed); library media and information technology (MS Ed); mathematics education (M Ed); reading (M Ed); school administration (M Ed); school counseling (M Ed); teaching (M Ed). *Application deadline:* For fall admission, 6/1 priority date for domestic students. Applications are processed on a rolling basis. *Application fee:* $0 ($25 for international students). Electronic applications accepted. *Head*, Dr. Kay Grant, 918-456-5511 Ext. 3700.

College of Liberal Arts Students: 31 full-time (21 women), 80 part-time (45 women); includes 30 minority (4 African Americans, 25 American Indian/Alaska Native, 1 Hispanic American). *Faculty:* 26 full-time (6 women). Expenses: Contact institution. *Financial support:* Teaching assistantships, Federal Work-Study available. Financial award application deadline: 3/1. In 2006, 32 degrees awarded. *Degree program information:* Part-time and evening/weekend programs available. Offers American studies (MA); communication (MA); criminal justice (MS); English (MA); liberal arts (MA, MS). *Application deadline:* For fall admission, 6/1 priority date for domestic students. Applications are processed on a rolling basis. *Application fee:* $0 ($25 for international students). Electronic applications accepted. *Interim Dean*, Dr. Paul Westbrook, 918-456-5511 Ext. 3600, Fax: 918-458-2348, E-mail: westbroo@nsuok.edu.

College of Science and Health Professions Students: 30 full-time (28 women), 15 part-time (10 women); includes 13 minority (3 African Americans, 7 American Indian/Alaska Native, 3 Hispanic Americans), 1 international. Expenses: Contact institution. In 2006, 17 degrees awarded. Offers science and health professions (M Ed, MS); science education (M Ed); speech-language pathology (MS). *Interim Dean*, Dr. Doug Penisten, 918-456-5511 Ext. 3800.

NORTHEASTERN UNIVERSITY, Boston, MA 02115-5096

General Information Independent, coed, university. CGS member. *Enrollment:* 20,605 graduate, professional, and undergraduate students; 3,298 full-time matriculated graduate/professional students (1,773 women), 2,112 part-time matriculated graduate/professional students (1,098 women). *Enrollment by degree level:* 630 first professional, 3,956 master's, 824 doctoral. *Graduate faculty:* 884 full-time (314 women), 424 part-time/adjunct (246 women). *Graduate housing:* Room and/or apartments available on a first-come, first-served basis to single students; on-campus housing not available to married students. *Student services:* Campus employment opportunities, campus safety program, career counseling, child daycare facilities, disabled student services, exercise/wellness program, free psychological counseling, international student services, low-cost health insurance, multicultural affairs office, teacher training. *Library facilities:* Snell Library plus 4 others. *Online resources:* library catalog, web page, access to other libraries' catalogs. *Collection:* 994,122 titles, 6,773 serial subscriptions. *Research affiliation:* BBN Technologies (information technology), Analog Devices, Inc. (electronics), General Electric Company (engineering), Jobs for America's Graduates (labor studies), Cytyc Corporation (medical technology).

Computer facilities: 1,993 computers available on campus for general student use. A campuswide network can be accessed from student residence rooms and from off campus. Internet access and online class registration are available. *Web address:* http://www.northeastern.edu.

General Application Contact: Information Contact, 617-373-2000.

GRADUATE UNITS

Bouvé College of Health Sciences Graduate School Students: 923 full-time (740 women), 256 part-time (202 women). 1,624 applicants, 30% accepted. *Faculty:* 128 full-time (84 women), 83 part-time/adjunct. Expenses: Contact institution. *Financial support:* In 2006–07, 5 research assistantships with full tuition reimbursements (averaging $15,823 per year), 25 teaching assistantships with full tuition reimbursements were awarded; fellowships, career-related internships or fieldwork, Federal Work-Study, tuition waivers (partial), and administrative assistantships also available. Support available to part-time students. Financial award application deadline: 3/1; financial award applicants required to submit FAFSA. In 2006, 247 master's, 16 doctorates, 25 other advanced degrees awarded. *Degree program information:* Part-time and evening/weekend programs available. Offers applied behavior analysis (MS); applied educational psychology (MS); audiology (Au D); biotechnology (PSM); clinical exercise physiology (MS); college student development and counseling (MS); counseling psychology (MS, PhD, CAGS); health sciences (Pharm D, MS, MS Ed, PSM, Au D, PhD, CAGS, CAS); pharmaceutical sciences (PhD); pharmacology (MS); pharmacy (Pharm D); school counseling (MS); school psychology (MS, PhD, CAGS); special needs and intensive special needs (MS Ed); speech-language pathology (MS); toxicology (MS). *Application deadline:* Applications are processed on a rolling basis. *Application fee:* $50. *Application Contact:* Margaret Schnabel, Director of Graduate Admissions, 617-373-2708, Fax: 617-373-4704, E-mail: bouvegrad@neu.edu. *Director*, Suzanne B. Greenberg, 617-373-3195, E-mail: s.greenberg@neu.edu.

School of Health Professions Students: 70 full-time (50 women). Average age 29. 203 applicants, 24% accepted. Expenses: Contact institution. *Financial support:* Federal Work-Study and tuition waivers (partial) available. Support available to part-time students. Financial award application deadline: 3/1; financial award applicants required to submit FAFSA. In 2006, 31 degrees awarded. *Degree program information:* Part-time and evening/weekend programs available. Offers physician assistant (MS). *Application deadline:* For fall admission, 11/1 for domestic students; for spring admission, 3/1 for domestic students. Applications are processed on a rolling basis. *Application fee:* $50. *Application Contact:* Margaret Schnabel, Director of Graduate Admissions, 617-373-2708, Fax: 617-373-4704, E-mail: bouvegrad@neu.edu.

School of Nursing Students: 152 full-time (127 women), 91 part-time (78 women). Average age 38. 300 applicants, 25% accepted. *Faculty:* 30 full-time (29 women), 30 part-time/adjunct. Expenses: Contact institution. *Financial support:* In 2006–07, 34 students received support, including 2 research assistantships with full tuition reimbursements available (averaging $13,546 per year), 7 teaching assistantships with full tuition reimbursements available (averaging $13,546 per year); fellowships, career-related internships or fieldwork, institutionally sponsored loans, tuition waivers (full and partial), and unspecified assistantships also available. Support available to part-time students. Financial award application deadline: 7/1; financial award applicants required to submit FAFSA. In 2006, 58 degrees awarded. *Degree program information:* Part-time programs available. Offers community health nursing (MS, CAS); critical care-acute care nurse practitioner (MS, CAS); critical care-neonatal nurse practitioner (MS, CAS); nurse anesthesia (MS); nursing (MS, PhD, CAS); nursing administration (MS); primary care nursing (MS, CAS); psychiatric-mental health nursing (MS, CAS). *Application deadline:* Applications are processed on a rolling basis. *Application fee:* $50. *Application Contact:* Margaret Schnabel, Director of Graduate Admissions, 617-373-2708, Fax: 617-373-4704, E-mail: bouvegrad@neu.edu. *Dean*, Dr. Nancy Hoffart, 617-373-3649, Fax: 617-373-8675, E-mail: n.hoffart@neu.edu.

College of Arts and Sciences Students: 604 full-time (327 women), 167 part-time (83 women). Average age 26. 1,462 applicants, 21% accepted. *Faculty:* 362 full-time (112 women), 175 part-time/adjunct. Expenses: Contact institution. *Financial support:* Fellowships with tuition reimbursements, research assistantships with tuition reimbursements, teaching assistantships with tuition reimbursements, career-related internships or fieldwork, Federal Work-Study, institutionally sponsored loans, tuition waivers (full and partial), and unspecified assistantships available. Support available to part-time students. Financial award applicants required to submit FAFSA. In 2006, 205 master's, 50 doctorates awarded. *Degree program information:* Part-time and evening/weekend programs available. Offers analytical chemistry (PhD); applied mathematics (MS); arts and sciences (M Arch, MA, MAW, MPA, MS, MSOR, PMS, PSM, PhD, Certificate); bioinformatics (PMS); biology (MS, PhD); biotechnology (MS); chemistry (MS, PhD); cinema studies (Certificate); development administration (MPA); economics (MA, PhD); English (MA, PhD); experimental psychology (MA, PhD); health administration and policy (MPA); history (MA); inorganic chemistry (PhD); law, policy, and society (MS,

Northeastern University (continued)

PhD); marine biology (MS); mathematics (MS, PhD); operations research (MSOR); organic chemistry (PhD); physical chemistry (PhD); physics (MS, PhD); political science (MA); public administration (MPA); public and international affairs (PhD); public history (MA); sociology (MA, PhD); state and local government (MPA); women's studies (Certificate); world history (PhD). *Application deadline:* Applications are processed on a rolling basis. *Application fee:* $50. Electronic applications accepted. *Application Contact:* Graduate School of Arts and Sciences, 617-373-3982, Fax: 617-373-7281. *Associate Dean and Director of the Graduate School*, Dr. Mary Loeffelholz, 617-373-6060, Fax: 617-373-2942.

School of Journalism Students: 19 full-time (12 women), 5 part-time (2 women). Average age 28. 74 applicants, 27% accepted. *Faculty:* 13 full-time (5 women), 4 part-time/adjunct. Expenses: Contact institution. *Financial support:* Career-related internships or fieldwork, Federal Work-Study, institutionally sponsored loans, scholarships/grants, tuition waivers (partial), and unspecified assistantships available. Financial award application deadline: 3/1; financial award applicants required to submit FAFSA. In 2006, 20 degrees awarded. *Degree program information:* Part-time and evening/weekend programs available. Offers journalism (MA). *Application deadline:* For fall admission, 2/1 priority date for domestic students, 5/1 for international students. Applications are processed on a rolling basis. *Application fee:* $50. Electronic applications accepted. *Application Contact:* Carol Medige, Graduate Assistant, 617-373-3236, Fax: 617-373-8773, E-mail: gradjourn@neu.edu. *Graduate Coordinator*, Prof. Stephen Burgard, 617-373-3238, Fax: 617-373-8773, E-mail: s.burgard@neu.edu.

College of Computer and Information Science Students: 196 full-time (38 women), 38 part-time (9 women). Average age 28. 451 applicants, 55% accepted. *Faculty:* 26 full-time (5 women), 5 part-time/adjunct (4 women). Expenses: Contact institution. *Financial support:* In 2006–07, 23 research assistantships with full tuition reimbursements (averaging $16,302 per year), 16 teaching assistantships with full tuition reimbursements (averaging $15,675 per year) were awarded; fellowships, career-related internships or fieldwork, Federal Work-Study, and institutionally sponsored loans also available. Financial award application deadline: 1/15. In 2006, 49 master's, 4 doctorates awarded. *Degree program information:* Part-time and evening/weekend programs available. Offers computer and information science (PhD); computer science (MS); health informatics (MS); information assurance (MS); telecommunication systems management (MS). *Application deadline:* For fall admission, 7/15 for domestic students, 5/1 for international students; for spring admission, 11/30 for domestic students, 9/1 for international students. Applications are processed on a rolling basis. *Application fee:* $50. Electronic applications accepted. *Application Contact:* Dr. Agnes Chan, Associate Dean and Director of Graduate Program, 617-373-2462, Fax: 617-373-5121, E-mail: gradschool@ccs.neu.edu. *Dean*, Dr. Larry A. Finkelstein, 617-373-2462, Fax: 617-373-5121.

College of Criminal Justice Students: 66 full-time (46 women), 12 part-time (5 women). Average age 25. 69 applicants, 43% accepted. *Faculty:* 16 full-time (4 women), 6 part-time/adjunct. Expenses: Contact institution. *Financial support:* In 2006–07, 12 teaching assistantships with full tuition reimbursements (averaging $13,260 per year) were awarded; research assistantships with full and partial tuition reimbursements, career-related internships or fieldwork, Federal Work-Study, and institutionally sponsored loans also available. Support available to part-time students. Financial award application deadline: 3/31; financial award applicants required to submit FAFSA. In 2006, 31 degrees awarded. *Degree program information:* Part-time and evening/weekend programs available. Offers criminal justice (MS, PhD). *Application deadline:* For fall admission, 3/1 for domestic students; for spring admission, 10/1 for domestic students. Applications are processed on a rolling basis. *Application fee:* $50. Electronic applications accepted. *Application Contact:* Laurie A. Mastone, Assistant to the Director, 617-373-2813, Fax: 617-373-8723, E-mail: l.mastone@neu.edu. *Dean*, Jack McDevitt, 617-373-2813, Fax: 617-373-8723.

College of Engineering Students: 554 full-time (137 women), 288 part-time (44 women). Average age 25. 968 applicants, 60% accepted. *Faculty:* 104 full-time (13 women), 27 part-time/adjunct. Expenses: Contact institution. *Financial support:* In 2006–07, 267 students received support, including 11 fellowships with full tuition reimbursements available, 115 research assistantships with full tuition reimbursements available (averaging $15,782 per year), 106 teaching assistantships with full tuition reimbursements available (averaging $15,782 per year); career-related internships or fieldwork, Federal Work-Study, scholarships/grants, tuition waivers (full), and unspecified assistantships also available. Support available to part-time students. Financial award application deadline: 2/15; financial award applicants required to submit FAFSA. In 2006, 220 master's, 27 doctorates awarded. *Degree program information:* Part-time programs available. Offers chemical engineering (MS, PhD); civil and environmental engineering (MS, PhD); computer engineering (PhD); computer systems engineering (MS); electrical engineering (MS, PhD); engineering (MS, PSM, PhD); engineering management (MS); industrial engineering (MS, PhD); information systems (MS); mechanical engineering (MS, PhD); operations research (MS); telecommunication systems management (MS). *Application deadline:* For fall admission, 2/15 priority date for domestic and international students. Applications are processed on a rolling basis. *Application fee:* $50. Electronic applications accepted. *Application Contact:* Stephen L. Gibson, Associate Director, 617-373-2711, Fax: 617-373-2501, E-mail: grad-eng@coe.neu.edu. *Associate Dean of Engineering for Research and Graduate Studies*, Dr. Yaman Yener, 617-373-2711, Fax: 617-373-2501.

Graduate School of Business Administration Students: 224 full-time (88 women), 552 part-time (215 women). Average age 30. 529 applicants, 41% accepted. *Faculty:* 102 full-time (20 women), 34 part-time/adjunct. Expenses: Contact institution. *Financial support:* In 2006–07, 49 teaching assistantships (averaging $12,298 per year) were awarded; fellowships, research assistantships, career-related internships or fieldwork, Federal Work-Study, institutionally sponsored loans, and unspecified assistantships also available. Support available to part-time students. Financial award application deadline: 3/1; financial award applicants required to submit FAFSA. In 2006, 365 degrees awarded. *Degree program information:* Part-time and evening/weekend programs available. Offers business administration (EMBA, MBA, MSF, MST, CAGS); finance (MSF). *Application deadline:* Applications are processed on a rolling basis. *Application fee:* $50. Electronic applications accepted. *Application Contact:* Admissions Coordinator, 617-373-4951. *Director of Graduate Programs*, Kate Klepper, 617-373-5417, Fax: 617-373-8564, E-mail: gsba@cba.neu.edu.

Graduate School of Professional Accounting Students: 61 full-time (31 women), 69 part-time (37 women). Average age 32. 205 applicants, 72% accepted. *Faculty:* 16 full-time (6 women). Expenses: Contact institution. *Financial support:* Career-related internships or fieldwork, Federal Work-Study, institutionally sponsored loans, and scholarships/grants available. Support available to part-time students. Financial award application deadline: 3/1; financial award applicants required to submit FAFSA. In 2006, 80 degrees awarded. Offers professional accounting (MST, CAGS); taxation (MST, CAGS). *Application deadline:* For fall admission, 4/1 for domestic students, 1/15 for international students. Applications are processed on a rolling basis. *Application fee:* $100. Electronic applications accepted. *Director*, Annarita Meeker, 617-373-4621.

School of Architecture 51 applicants, 63% accepted. *Faculty:* 6 full-time (3 women), 17 part-time/adjunct. Expenses: Contact institution. *Financial support:* Federal Work-Study and scholarships/grants available. Support available to part-time students. Financial award application deadline: 3/1; financial award applicants required to submit FAFSA. In 2006, 12 master's awarded. Offers architecture (M Arch). *Application deadline:* For fall admission, 8/1 for domestic students, 5/1 for international students. Applications are processed on a rolling basis. *Application fee:* $50. Electronic applications accepted. *Application Contact:* Danielle Walquist, Administrative Assistant, 617-373-4637, Fax: 617-373-7080, E-mail: gradarch@neu.edu. *Chair*, George Thrush, 617-373-4637, Fax: 617-373-7080, E-mail: thrush@neu.edu.

School of Law Average age 26. 3,354 applicants, 213 enrolled. *Faculty:* 34 full-time (18 women), 15 part-time/adjunct. Expenses: Contact institution. *Financial support:* In 2006–07, 405 students received support, including 39 teaching assistantships (averaging $3,500 per year); fellowships, research assistantships, career-related internships or fieldwork, Federal Work-Study, institutionally sponsored loans, scholarships/grants, and tuition waivers (full and partial) also available. Financial award application deadline: 2/15; financial award applicants required to submit CSS PROFILE or FAFSA. In 2006, 192 degrees awarded. Offers law (JD). *Application deadline:* For fall admission, 3/1 for domestic students. Applications are processed on a rolling basis. *Application fee:* $75. Electronic applications accepted. *Application Contact:* Judy Cote, Information Contact, 617-373-2395, Fax: 617-373-8865, E-mail: lawadmissions@neu.edu. *Dean*, Emily A. Spieler, 617-373-3307, Fax: 617-373-8793, E-mail: e.spieler@neu.edu.

School of Technological Entrepreneurship Students: 11 full-time (3 women), 3 part-time. 26 applicants, 77% accepted. *Faculty:* 6 full-time (0 women), 1 part-time/adjunct (0 women). Expenses: Contact institution. Offers technological entrepreneurship (MS). *Dean*, Paul M. Zavracky, 617-373-2788, Fax: 617-373-7490, E-mail: ste@neu.edu.

See Close-Up on page 983.

NORTHERN ARIZONA UNIVERSITY, Flagstaff, AZ 86011

General Information State-supported, coed, university. CGS member. *Graduate housing:* Rooms and/or apartments available to single and married students. *Research affiliation:* Museum of Northern Arizona, Lowell Observatory, Rocky Mountain Forest and Range Experiment Station, U.S. Naval Observatory, U.S. Geological Survey, W. L. Gore and Associates, Inc.

GRADUATE UNITS

Consortium of Professional Schools and Colleges

College of Health Professions *Degree program information:* Part-time programs available. Offers case management (Certificate); communications sciences and disorders (MS); exercise science (MS); health education and health promotion (MPH); health professions (MPH, MS, MSN, DPT, Certificate); nursing (MSN); physical education (MS); physical therapy (DPT).

School of Forestry *Degree program information:* Part-time programs available. Offers forestry (MF, MSF, PhD).

Graduate College *Degree program information:* Part-time and evening/weekend programs available. Electronic applications accepted.

College of Arts and Letters *Degree program information:* Part-time programs available. Offers applied linguistics (PhD); arts and letters (MA, MAT, MLS, MM, PhD, Certificate); choral conducting (MM); creative writing (MA); English (MA); English education (MA); general English (MA); history (MA, PhD); instrumental conducting (MM); instrumental performance (MM); liberal studies (MLS); literature (MA); modern languages (MAT); music education (MM); music history (MM); rhetoric (MA); teaching English as a second language (MA); teaching English as a second language/applied linguistics (MA, PhD, Certificate); teaching English as a second language/English as a second language (Certificate); theory and composition (MM); vocal performance (MM).

College of Business Administration *Degree program information:* Part-time programs available. Offers general management (MBA); management information systems (MBA).

College of Education *Degree program information:* Part-time and evening/weekend programs available. Offers administration (M Ed); bilingual multicultural education (M Ed); community college (M Ed); counseling (M Ed, MA); counseling psychology (Ed D); curriculum and instruction (Ed D); early childhood education (M Ed); education (M Ed, MA, Ed D, Certificate); educational leadership (Ed D); educational technology (M Ed); elementary education (M Ed); English as a Second Language/Teaching English as a second language (Certificate); learning and instruction (Ed D); school leadership (M Ed); school psychology (Ed D); secondary education (M Ed); special education (M Ed); teaching (M Ed).

College of Engineering and Natural Science Offers applied physics (MS); biology (MS, PhD); biology education (MAT); chemistry (MS); conservation ecology (Certificate); earth science (MAT, MS); engineering (M Eng, MAT, MS, PhD, Certificate); environmental sciences and policy (MS); geology (MS); mathematics (MAT, MS); physical science (MAT); quaternary sciences (MS); statistics (MS).

College of Social and Behavioral Sciences *Degree program information:* Part-time programs available. Offers anthropology (MA); applied communication (MA); applied geographic information science (MS); applied health psychology (MA); applied sociology (MA); archaeology (MA); criminal justice (MS); criminal justice policy and planning (Certificate); general (MA); geographic information systems (Certificate); political science (MA, PhD, Certificate); public administration (MPA); public management (Certificate); public policy (PhD); rural geography (MA); social and behavioral sciences (MA, MPA, MS, PhD, Certificate).

NORTHERN BAPTIST THEOLOGICAL SEMINARY, Lombard, IL 60148-5698

General Information Independent-religious, coed, graduate-only institution. *Enrollment by degree level:* 80 first professional, 88 master's, 65 doctoral. *Graduate faculty:* 7 full-time (1 woman), 29 part-time/adjunct (5 women). *Tuition:* Full-time $14,400; part-time $400 per hour. *Graduate housing:* Rooms and/or apartments available on a first-come, first-served basis to single and married students. Typical cost: $7,500 per year for single students; $8,600 per year for married students. Housing application deadline: 6/30. *Student services:* Free psychological counseling, low-cost health insurance. *Library facilities:* Brimsom-Grow Library. *Online resources:* library catalog, web page, access to other libraries' catalogs. *Collection:* 51,343 titles, 299 serial subscriptions, 1,639 audiovisual materials.

Computer facilities: 18 computers available on campus for general student use. A campuswide network can be accessed from student residence rooms. Internet access is available. *Web address:* http://www.seminary.edu/.

General Application Contact: Charles Dresser, Director of Admissions, 630-620-2191, Fax: 630-620-2190, E-mail: cdresser@seminary.edu.

GRADUATE UNITS

Graduate and Professional Programs Students: 112 full-time (25 women), 121 part-time (47 women); includes 97 minority (71 African Americans, 15 Asian Americans or Pacific Islanders, 11 Hispanic Americans), 4 international. Average age 40. 71 applicants, 90% accepted. *Faculty:* 7 full-time (1 woman), 29 part-time/adjunct (5 women). Expenses: Contact institution. *Financial support:* Career-related internships or fieldwork and scholarships/grants available. Support available to part-time students. Financial award application deadline: 9/1. In 2006, 24 M Divs, 8 master's, 8 doctorates awarded. *Degree program information:* Part-time programs available. Offers Bible (MA); Christian ministries (MACM); divinity (M Div); ethics (MA); history (MA); ministry (D Min); theology (MA); worship/spirituality (MAWS); youth ministry (MAYM). *Application deadline:* For fall admission, 9/1 priority date for domestic students; for winter admission, 12/1 priority date for domestic students; for spring admission, 3/1 priority date for domestic students. Applications are processed on a rolling basis. *Application fee:* $35. Electronic applications accepted. *Application Contact:* Charles Dresser, Director of Admissions, 630-620-2191, Fax: 630-620-2190, E-mail: cdresser@seminary.edu. *Dean*, Dr. Charles Hambrick-Stowe, 630-620-2103, Fax: 630-620-2190.

NORTHERN ILLINOIS UNIVERSITY, De Kalb, IL 60115-2854

General Information State-supported, coed, university. CGS member. *Enrollment:* 25,313 graduate, professional, and undergraduate students; 2,211 full-time matriculated graduate/professional students (1,150 women), 3,159 part-time matriculated graduate/professional students (1,947 women). *Enrollment by degree level:* 315 first professional, 3,902 master's, 973 doctoral, 180 other advanced degrees. *Graduate faculty:* 672 full-time (248 women), 66 part-time/adjunct (17 women). *Graduate housing:* Rooms and/or apartments available on a first-come, first-served basis to single and married students. Typical cost: $4,288 per year ($7,488 including board) for single students. *Student services:* Campus employment opportunities, campus safety program, career counseling, child daycare facilities, disabled student services, exercise/wellness program, free psychological counseling, grant writing training, international student services, low-cost health insurance, teacher training, writing training. *Library facilities:* Founders Memorial Library plus 8 others. *Online resources:* library catalog, web page, access to other libraries' catalogs. *Collection:* 3.1 million titles, 24,696 serial subscriptions. *Research affiliation:* Argonne National Laboratory, Fermi National Accelerator Laboratory, Field Museum of Natural History, Burpee Museum of Natural History.

Computer facilities: 1,200 computers available on campus for general student use. A campuswide network can be accessed from student residence rooms and from off campus. Internet access and online class registration are available. *Web address:* http://www.niu.edu/.

General Application Contact: Dr. Bradley G. Bond, Associate Dean, Graduate School, 815-753-0395, Fax: 815-753-6366, E-mail: gradsch@niu.edu.

GRADUATE UNITS

College of Law Students: 314 full-time (163 women), 1 part-time; includes 62 minority (27 African Americans, 1 American Indian/Alaska Native, 13 Asian Americans or Pacific Islanders, 21 Hispanic Americans). Average age 25. 1,514 applicants, 26% accepted, 105 enrolled. *Faculty:* 22 full-time (11 women). Expenses: Contact institution. *Financial support:* In 2006–07, 10 teaching assistantships were awarded; research assistantships, career-related internships or fieldwork, Federal Work-Study, tuition waivers (full and partial), and unspecified assistantships also available. Support available to part-time students. Financial award application deadline: 3/1; financial award applicants required to submit FAFSA. In 2006, 109 degrees awarded. *Degree program information:* Part-time programs available. Offers law (JD). *Application deadline:* For fall admission, 5/15 priority date for domestic and international students. Applications are processed on a rolling basis. *Application fee:* $35 ($50 for international students). Electronic applications accepted. *Application Contact:* Judith L. Malen, Director of Admissions and Financial Aid, 815-753-1420, E-mail: jmalen@niu.edu. *Dean,* LeRoy Pernell, 815-753-1067, Fax: 815-753-1310, E-mail: lpernell@niu.edu.

Graduate School Students: 2,200 full-time (1,167 women), 3,293 part-time (1,968 women); includes 845 minority (329 African Americans, 15 American Indian/Alaska Native, 258 Asian Americans or Pacific Islanders, 243 Hispanic Americans), 529 international. Average age 33. *Faculty:* 672 full-time (248 women), 66 part-time/adjunct (17 women). Expenses: Contact institution. *Financial support:* In 2006–07, 24 fellowships with full tuition reimbursements, 340 research assistantships with full tuition reimbursements, 986 teaching assistantships with full tuition reimbursements were awarded; career-related internships or fieldwork, Federal Work-Study, scholarships/grants, tuition waivers (full), and unspecified assistantships also available. Support available to part-time students. Financial award applicants required to submit FAFSA. In 2006, 1,567 master's, 80 doctorates, 34 other advanced degrees awarded. *Degree program information:* Part-time and evening/weekend programs available. Postbaccalaureate distance learning degree programs offered (minimal on-campus study). *Application deadline:* For fall admission, 6/1 for domestic students, 5/1 for international students; for spring admission, 11/1 for domestic students, 10/1 for international students. Applications are processed on a rolling basis. *Application fee:* $30. Electronic applications accepted. *Application Contact:* Graduate School Office, 815-753-0395, E-mail: gradsch@niu.edu. *Dean of the Graduate School and Vice President for Research,* Dr. Rathindra N. Bose, 815-753-1883, Fax: 815-753-6366, E-mail: rbose@niu.edu.

College of Business Students: 234 full-time (86 women), 605 part-time (233 women); includes 158 minority (22 African Americans, 2 American Indian/Alaska Native, 102 Asian Americans or Pacific Islanders, 32 Hispanic Americans), 28 international. Average age 31. 395 applicants, 81% accepted, 199 enrolled. *Faculty:* 53 full-time (17 women), 3 part-time/adjunct (0 women). Expenses: Contact institution. *Financial support:* In 2006–07, 3 research assistantships with full tuition reimbursements, 3 teaching assistantships with full tuition reimbursements were awarded; fellowships with full tuition reimbursements, career-related internships or fieldwork, Federal Work-Study, scholarships/grants, tuition waivers (full), and unspecified assistantships also available. Support available to part-time students. Financial award applicants required to submit FAFSA. In 2006, 385 degrees awarded. *Degree program information:* Part-time and evening/weekend programs available. Offers accountancy (MAS, MST); business (MAS, MBA, MS, MST); business administration (MBA); management information systems (MS). *Application deadline:* For fall admission, 6/1 for domestic students, 5/1 for international students; for spring admission, 11/1 for domestic students, 10/1 for international students. Applications are processed on a rolling basis. *Application fee:* $30. Electronic applications accepted. *Application Contact:* Office of Graduate Studies in Business, 815-753-6301. *Dean,* Dr. Denise Schownbachler, 815-753-6225, Fax: 815-753-5305, E-mail: denises@niu.edu.

College of Education Students: 308 full-time (197 women), 1,745 part-time (1,227 women); includes 404 minority (184 African Americans, 4 American Indian/Alaska Native, 43 Asian Americans or Pacific Islanders, 173 Hispanic Americans), 46 international. Average age 37. 569 applicants, 77% accepted, 308 enrolled. *Faculty:* 110 full-time (66 women), 5 part-time/adjunct (3 women). Expenses: Contact institution. *Financial support:* In 2006–07, 7 research assistantships with full tuition reimbursements, 5 teaching assistantships with full tuition reimbursements were awarded; fellowships with full tuition reimbursements, career-related internships or fieldwork, Federal Work-Study, scholarships/grants, tuition waivers (full), and unspecified assistantships also available. Support available to part-time students. Financial award applicants required to submit FAFSA. In 2006, 635 master's, 57 doctorates, 56 other advanced degrees awarded. *Degree program information:* Part-time and evening/weekend programs available. Postbaccalaureate distance learning degree programs offered (minimal on-campus study). Offers adult and higher education (MS Ed, Ed D); counseling (MS Ed, Ed D); curriculum and instruction (MS Ed, Ed D); early childhood education (MS Ed); education (MS, MS Ed, Ed D, Ed S); educational administration (MS Ed, Ed D, Ed S); educational psychology (MS Ed, Ed D); educational research and evaluation (MS); elementary education (MS Ed); foundations of education (MS Ed); instructional technology (MS Ed, Ed D); literacy education (MS Ed); physical education (MS Ed); school business management (MS Ed); special education (MS Ed); sport management (MS). *Application deadline:* For fall admission, 6/1 for domestic students, 5/1 for international students; for spring admission, 11/1 for domestic students, 10/1 for international students. Applications are processed on a rolling basis. *Application fee:* $30. Electronic applications accepted. *Dean,* Dr. Christine Sorensen, 815-753-9056, Fax: 815-753-2100, E-mail: csorensen@niu.edu.

College of Engineering and Engineering Technology Students: 126 full-time (29 women), 80 part-time (18 women); includes 22 minority (8 African Americans, 1 American Indian/Alaska Native, 9 Asian Americans or Pacific Islanders, 4 Hispanic Americans), 125 international. Average age 26. *Faculty:* 36 full-time (2 women), 2 part-time/adjunct (0 women). Expenses: Contact institution. *Financial support:* In 2006–07, 12 research assistantships with full tuition reimbursements, 9 teaching assistantships with full tuition reimbursements were awarded; fellowships with full tuition reimbursements, career-related internships or fieldwork, Federal Work-Study, scholarships/grants, tuition waivers (full), and unspecified assistantships also available. Support available to part-time students. Financial award applicants required to submit FAFSA. In 2006, 75 degrees awarded. *Degree program information:* Part-time and evening/weekend programs available. Offers electrical engineering (MS); engineering and engineering technology (MS); industrial engineering (MS); industrial management (MS); mechanical engineering (MS). *Application deadline:* For fall admission, 6/1 for domestic students, 5/1 for international students; for spring admission, 11/1 for domestic students, 10/1 for international students. Applications are processed on a rolling basis. *Application fee:* $30. Electronic applications accepted. *Acting Dean,* Dr. Promod Vohra, 815-753-1281, Fax: 815-753-1310, E-mail: vohra@ceat.niu.edu.

College of Health and Human Sciences Students: 221 full-time (195 women), 210 part-time (199 women); includes 64 minority (28 African Americans, 1 American Indian/Alaska Native, 18 Asian Americans or Pacific Islanders, 17 Hispanic Americans), 22 international. Average age 31. 497 applicants, 56% accepted, 113 enrolled. *Faculty:* 46 full-time (37 women), 5 part-time/adjunct (3 women). Expenses: Contact institution. *Financial support:* In 2006–07, 3 teaching assistantships with full tuition reimbursements were awarded; fellowships with full tuition reimbursements, research assistantships with full tuition reimbursements, career-related internships or fieldwork, Federal Work-Study, scholarships/grants, tuition waivers (full), and unspecified assistantships also available. Support available to part-time students. Financial award applicants required to submit FAFSA. In 2006, 150 degrees awarded. *Degree program information:* Part-time and evening/weekend programs available. Offers applied family and child studies (MS); communicative disorders (MA, Au D); health and human sciences (MA, MPH, MPT, MS, Au D); nursing (MS); nutrition and dietetics (MS); physical therapy (MPT); public health (MPH). *Application deadline:* For fall admission, 6/1 for domestic students, 5/1 for international students; for spring admission, 11/1 for domestic students, 10/1 for international students. Applications are processed on a rolling basis. *Application fee:* $30. Electronic applications accepted. *Dean,* Dr. Shirley Richmond, 815-753-6155, E-mail: srichmond@niu.edu.

College of Liberal Arts and Sciences Students: 829 full-time (385 women), 451 part-time (224 women); includes 136 minority (43 African Americans, 10 American Indian/Alaska Native, 47 Asian Americans or Pacific Islanders, 36 Hispanic Americans), 215 international. Average age 30. *Faculty:* 342 full-time (99 women), 36 part-time/adjunct (7 women). Expenses: Contact institution. *Financial support:* Fellowships with full tuition reimbursements, research assistantships with full tuition reimbursements, teaching assistantships with full tuition reimbursements, career-related internships or fieldwork, Federal Work-Study, scholarships/grants, tuition waivers (full), and unspecified assistantships available. Support available to part-time students. Financial award applicants required to submit FAFSA. In 2006, 316 master's, 49 doctorates awarded. *Degree program information:* Part-time and evening/weekend programs available. Offers anthropology (MA); biological sciences (MS, PhD); chemistry (MS, PhD); communication studies (MA); computer science (MS); economics (MA, PhD); English (MA, PhD); French (MA); geography (MS); geology (MS, PhD); history (MA, PhD); liberal arts and sciences (MA, MPA, MS, PhD); mathematical sciences (PhD); mathematics (MS); philosophy (MA); physics (MS, PhD); political science (MA, PhD); psychology (MA, PhD); public administration (MPA); sociology (MA); Spanish (MA); statistics (MS). *Application deadline:* For fall admission, 6/1 for domestic students, 5/1 for international students; for spring admission, 11/1 for domestic students, 10/1 for international students. Applications are processed on a rolling basis. *Application fee:* $30. Electronic applications accepted. *Acting Dean,* Dr. Joeseph Grush, 815-753-1061, Fax: 815-753-7950, E-mail: jgrush@niu.edu.

College of Visual and Performing Arts Students: 179 full-time (95 women), 67 part-time (46 women); includes 26 minority (13 African Americans, 8 Asian Americans or Pacific Islanders, 5 Hispanic Americans), 33 international. Average age 31. *Faculty:* 85 full-time (27 women), 15 part-time/adjunct (4 women). Expenses: Contact institution. *Financial support:* Fellowships with full tuition reimbursements, research assistantships with full tuition reimbursements, teaching assistantships with full tuition reimbursements, career-related internships or fieldwork, Federal Work-Study, scholarships/grants, tuition waivers (full), and unspecified assistantships available. Support available to part-time students. Financial award applicants required to submit FAFSA. In 2006, 94 master's, 12 other advanced degrees awarded. *Degree program information:* Part-time and evening/weekend programs available. Offers art (MA, MFA, MS); music (MM, Performer's Certificate); theatre and dance (MFA); visual and performing arts (MA, MFA, MM, MS, Performer's Certificate). *Application deadline:* For fall admission, 5/1 for international students; for spring admission, 10/1 for international students. Applications are processed on a rolling basis. *Application fee:* $30. Electronic applications accepted. *Dean,* Dr. Harold Kafer, 815-753-1138, Fax: 815-753-8372, E-mail: hakafer@niu.edu.

NORTHERN KENTUCKY UNIVERSITY, Highland Heights, KY 41099

General Information State-supported, coed, comprehensive institution. CGS member. *Enrollment:* 14,617 graduate, professional, and undergraduate students; 461 full-time matriculated graduate/professional students (242 women), 1,306 part-time matriculated graduate/professional students (820 women). *Enrollment by degree level:* 523 first professional, 1,206 master's, 38 other advanced degrees. Tuition, state resident: full-time $5,274; part-time $293 per hour. Tuition, nonresident: full-time $10,314; part-time $573 per hour. Tuition and fees vary according to course load, program and reciprocity agreements. *Graduate housing:* Room and/or apartments available on a first-come, first-served basis to single students; on-campus housing not available to married students. Typical cost: $2,320 per year ($3,980 including board). Housing application deadline: 5/1. *Student services:* Campus employment opportunities, campus safety program, career counseling, child daycare facilities, disabled student services, exercise/wellness program, free psychological counseling, international student services, low-cost health insurance, multicultural affairs office. *Library facilities:* Steely Library plus 1 other. *Online resources:* library catalog, web page, access to other libraries' catalogs. *Collection:* 667,064 titles, 1,731 serial subscriptions, 4,406 audiovisual materials.

Computer facilities: 600 computers available on campus for general student use. A campuswide network can be accessed from student residence rooms and from off campus. Internet access and online class registration are available. *Web address:* http://www.nku.edu/.

General Application Contact: Dr. Peg Griffin, Director of Graduate Programs, 859-572-1555, Fax: 859-572-6670, E-mail: gradprog@nku.edu.

GRADUATE UNITS

Office of Graduate Programs Students: 461 full-time (242 women), 1,306 part-time (820 women); includes 123 minority (66 African Americans, 5 American Indian/Alaska Native, 34 Asian Americans or Pacific Islanders, 18 Hispanic Americans), 18 international. Average age 31. 810 applicants, 68% accepted, 459 enrolled. Expenses: Contact institution. *Financial support:* In 2006–07, 561 students received support. Traineeships and unspecified assistantships available. In 2006, 376 degrees awarded. *Degree program information:* Part-time and evening/weekend programs available. Postbaccalaureate distance learning degree programs offered (no on-campus study). *Application deadline:* For fall admission, 8/1 priority date for domestic students, 6/1 for international students; for spring admission, 12/1 priority date for domestic students, 10/1 for international students. Applications are processed on a rolling basis. *Application fee:* $30. Electronic applications accepted. *Application Contact:* Dr. Peg Griffin, Director of Graduate Programs, 859-572-1555, Fax: 859-572-6670, E-mail: gradprog@nku.edu. *Associate Provost for Outreach/Dean of Graduate Studies,* Dr. Carole A. Beere, 859-572-5930, Fax: 859-572-5565, E-mail: beerec@nku.edu.

College of Arts and Sciences Students: 32 full-time (20 women), 160 part-time (96 women); includes 20 minority (17 African Americans, 3 Asian Americans or Pacific Islanders), 3 international. Average age 33. 89 applicants, 61% accepted, 49 enrolled. Expenses: Contact institution. *Financial support:* In 2006–07, 99 students received support. Unspecified assistantships available. In 2006, 34 master's awarded. *Degree program information:* Part-time and evening/weekend programs available. Offers industrial psychology (Certificate); industrial-organizational psychology (MSIO); liberal studies (MALS); non-profit management (Certificate); occupational health psychology (Certificate); organizational psychology (Certificate); public administration (MPA). *Application deadline:* For fall admission, 8/1 for domestic students, 6/1 for international students; for spring admission, 12/1 for domestic students, 10/1 for international students. *Application fee:* $30. *Application Contact:* Dr. Peg Griffin, Director of Graduate Programs, 859-572-1555, Fax: 859-572-6670, E-mail: gradprog@nku.edu. *Dean,* Dr. Kevin Corcoran, 859-572-5494, Fax: 859-572-6185, E-mail: corcorank1@nku.edu.

College of Business Students: 43 full-time (21 women), 273 part-time (118 women); includes 25 minority (17 African Americans, 8 Asian Americans or Pacific Islanders), 11 international. Average age 33. 169 applicants, 61% accepted, 80 enrolled. *Faculty:* 14 full-time (7 women), 7 part-time/adjunct (3 women). Expenses: Contact institution. *Financial support:* In 2006–07, 123 students received support. Unspecified assistantships available. In 2006, 93 degrees awarded. *Degree program information:* Part-time and evening/weekend programs available. Offers accountancy (M Acc); business (M Acc, MA, MBA); business administration (MBA); executive leadership and organizational change (MA). *Application deadline:* For fall admission, 8/1 priority date for domestic students, 6/1 priority date for international students; for spring admission, 12/1 priority date for domestic students, 10/1 priority date for international students. *Application fee:* $30. *Application Contact:* Dr. Gregory Farfsing, Director of MBA Programs, 859-572-6357, Fax: 859-572-6177, E-mail: farfsingg@nku.edu. *Dean,* Michael Carrell, 859-572-5165, Fax: 859-572-6177, E-mail: carrellm@nku.edu.

College of Education and Human Services Students: 44 full-time (33 women), 432 part-time (345 women); includes 14 minority (6 African Americans, 2 American Indian/Alaska Native, 1 Asian American or Pacific Islander, 5 Hispanic Americans). Average age 35. 253 applicants, 62% accepted, 117 enrolled. *Faculty:* 42 full-time (25 women), 8 part-time/adjunct (5 women). Expenses: Contact institution. *Financial support:* In 2006–07, 253 students received support. Unspecified assistantships available. In 2006, 193 degrees awarded.

Northern Kentucky University (continued)

Degree program information: Part-time and evening/weekend programs available. Offers community counseling (MSCC); education (M Ed); instructional leadership (MA); school counseling (MASC); special education (Certificate); teaching (MAT). *Application deadline:* For fall admission, 8/1 priority date for domestic students, 6/1 for international students; for spring admission, 12/1 priority date for domestic students, 10/1 for international students. Applications are processed on a rolling basis. *Application fee:* $30. Electronic applications accepted. *Application Contact:* Dr. Peg Griffin, Director of Graduate Programs, 859-572-1555, Fax: 859-572-6670, E-mail: gradprog@nku.edu. *Dean,* Dr. Elaine McNally Jarchow, 859-572-5229, Fax: 859-572-6623, E-mail: jarchowe1@nku.edu.

College of Informatics Students: 16 full-time (7 women), 70 part-time (26 women); includes 14 minority (3 African Americans, 11 Asian Americans or Pacific Islanders), 4 international. Average age 35. 73 applicants, 64% accepted, 39 enrolled. *Faculty:* 22 full-time (5 women), 4 part-time/adjunct (1 woman). Expenses: Contact institution. *Financial support:* In 2006–07, 38 students received support. Unspecified assistantships available. In 2006, 26 degrees awarded. *Degree program information:* Part-time and evening/weekend programs available. Offers business informatics (MS); communication (MA Comm); computer science (MSCS); corporate information security (Certificate); health informatics (MHI); secure software engineering (Certificate). *Application deadline:* For fall admission, 8/1 priority date for domestic students, 6/1 priority date for international students; for spring admission, 12/1 priority date for domestic students, 10/1 priority date for international students. Applications are processed on a rolling basis. *Application fee:* $30. Electronic applications accepted. *Application Contact:* Dr. Peg Griffin, Director of Graduate Programs, 859-572-1555, Fax: 859-572-6670, E-mail: gradprog@nku.edu. *Dean,* Dr. Douglas Perry, 859-572-5666, Fax: 859-572-6097, E-mail: perrydl@nku.edu.

School of Nursing and Health Professions Students: 25 full-time (24 women), 111 part-time (105 women); includes 6 minority (2 African Americans, 4 Asian Americans or Pacific Islanders). Average age 37. 58 applicants, 83% accepted, 42 enrolled. Expenses: Contact institution. *Financial support:* In 2006–07, 48 students received support. Unspecified assistantships available. In 2006, 30 degrees awarded. *Degree program information:* Part-time and evening/weekend programs available. Postbaccalaureate distance learning degree programs offered (no on-campus study). Offers nurse practitioner advancement (Certificate); nursing (MSN, Post-Master's Certificate). *Application Contact:* Dr. Peg Griffin, Director of Graduate Programs, 859-572-1555, Fax: 859-572-6670, E-mail: gradprog@nku.edu. *Chair, Nursing and Health Professions,* Dr. Margaret M. Anderson, 859-572-5248, Fax: 859-572-1934, E-mail: andersonm@nku.edu.

Salmon P. Chase College of Law Students: 283 full-time (126 women), 241 part-time (109 women); includes 40 minority (19 African Americans, 3 American Indian/Alaska Native, 5 Asian Americans or Pacific Islanders, 13 Hispanic Americans). Average age 27. 1,117 applicants, 31% accepted, 150 enrolled. *Faculty:* 36 full-time (13 women), 24 part-time/adjunct (11 women). Expenses: Contact institution. *Financial support:* In 2006–07, 8 fellowships (averaging $6,000 per year), 20 research assistantships (averaging $1,200 per year) were awarded; career-related internships or fieldwork, Federal Work-Study, scholarships/grants, and unspecified assistantships also available. Support available to part-time students. Financial award application deadline: 3/1; financial award applicants required to submit FAFSA. In 2006, 142 degrees awarded. *Degree program information:* Part-time and evening/weekend programs available. Offers law (JD). *Application deadline:* For fall admission, 4/1 for domestic and international students. Applications are processed on a rolling basis. *Application fee:* $40. Electronic applications accepted. *Application Contact:* Ashley Folger Gray, Director of Admissions, 859-572-5841, Fax: 859-572-6081, E-mail: folger@nku.edu. *Dean,* Dennis R. Honabach, 859-572-6406, Fax: 859-572-6183, E-mail: honabachd1@nku.edu.

NORTHERN MICHIGAN UNIVERSITY, Marquette, MI 49855-5301

General Information State-supported, coed, comprehensive institution. CGS member. *Graduate housing:* Rooms and/or apartments available to single and married students.

GRADUATE UNITS

College of Graduate Studies *Degree program information:* Part-time and evening/weekend programs available. Postbaccalaureate distance learning degree programs offered. Electronic applications accepted.

College of Arts and Sciences *Degree program information:* Part-time programs available. Postbaccalaureate distance learning degree programs offered (minimal on-campus study). Offers administrative services (MA); arts and sciences (MA, MFA, MPA, MS); biochemistry (MS); biology (MS); chemistry (MS); creative writing (MFA); literature (MA); pedagogy (MA); public administration (MPA); writing (MA).

College of Professional Studies *Degree program information:* Part-time programs available. Offers administration and supervision (MA Ed, Ed S); behavioral sciences and human services (MA, MA Ed, MS, MSN, Ed S); communication disorders (MA); criminal justice (MS); elementary education (MA Ed); exercise science (MS); nursing (MSN); psychology (MS); secondary education (MA Ed); special education (MA Ed).

NORTHERN STATE UNIVERSITY, Aberdeen, SD 57401-7198

General Information State-supported, coed, comprehensive institution. *Enrollment:* 2,407 graduate, professional, and undergraduate students; 16 full-time matriculated graduate/professional students (13 women), 137 part-time matriculated graduate/professional students (93 women). *Enrollment by degree level:* 153 master's. *Graduate faculty:* 84 full-time (21 women). *International tuition:* $13,000 full-time. Tuition, state resident: full-time $3,373; part-time $120 per credit. Tuition, nonresident: full-time $9,943; part-time $355 per credit. *Required fees:* $86 per credit. One-time fee: $35 full-time. Tuition and fees vary according to course load, degree level and reciprocity agreements. *Graduate housing:* Room and/or apartments available on a first-come, first-served basis to single students; on-campus housing not available to married students. *Student services:* Campus employment opportunities, campus safety program, career counseling, child daycare facilities, disabled student services, exercise/wellness program, free psychological counseling, international student services, low-cost health insurance, multicultural affairs office, writing training. *Library facilities:* Beulah Williams Library. *Online resources:* library catalog, web page, access to other libraries' catalogs. *Collection:* 192,007 titles, 882 serial subscriptions. *Research affiliation:* AASCU-Grants Resource Center.

Computer facilities: 900 computers available on campus for general student use. A campuswide network can be accessed from student residence rooms and from off campus. Internet access and online class registration are available. *Web address:* http://www.northern.edu/.

General Application Contact: Tammy K. Griffith, Senior Secretary, 605-626-2558, Fax: 605-626-2542, E-mail: griffith@northern.edu.

GRADUATE UNITS

Division of Graduate Studies in Education Students: 16 full-time (13 women), 137 part-time (93 women); includes 7 minority (1 African American, 1 American Indian/Alaska Native, 4 Asian Americans or Pacific Islanders, 1 Hispanic American). Average age 32. *Faculty:* 84 full-time (21 women). Expenses: Contact institution. *Financial support:* In 2006–07, 51 students received support, including 31 teaching assistantships with partial tuition reimbursements available (averaging $4,812 per year); career-related internships or fieldwork, Federal Work-Study, institutionally sponsored loans, scholarships/grants, and unspecified assistantships also available. Support available to part-time students. Financial award application deadline: 3/1; financial award applicants required to submit FAFSA. In 2006, 60 degrees awarded. *Degree program information:* Part-time and evening/weekend programs available. Offers education (MS, MS Ed); educational studies (MS Ed); elementary classroom teaching (MS Ed); elementary school administration (MS Ed); guidance and counseling (MS Ed); health, physical education, and coaching (MS Ed); language and literacy (MS Ed); secondary classroom teaching (MS Ed); secondary school administration (MS Ed); special education (MS Ed). *Application deadline:* For fall admission, 8/15 priority date for domestic students; for spring admission, 12/15 for domestic students. Applications are processed on a rolling basis. *Application fee:* $35. Electronic applications accepted. *Application Contact:* Tammy K. Griffith, Senior Secretary, 605-626-2558, Fax: 605-626-2542, E-mail: griffith@northern.edu. *Director of Graduate Studies,* Dr. Tom Hawley, 605-626-2558, Fax: 605-626-2542, E-mail: thawley@northern.edu.

Center for Statewide E-Learning Students: 1 (woman) full-time, 5 part-time (2 women); includes 1 minority (Hispanic American) Average age 32. *Faculty:* 2 full-time (1 woman), 1 part-time/adjunct (0 women). Expenses: Contact institution. *Financial support:* In 2006–07, 5 teaching assistantships with partial tuition reimbursements (averaging $4,812 per year) were awarded; career-related internships or fieldwork, Federal Work-Study, institutionally sponsored loans, scholarships/grants, and unspecified assistantships also available. Support available to part-time students. Financial award application deadline: 3/1; financial award applicants required to submit FAFSA. In 2006, 3 degrees awarded. *Degree program information:* Part-time and evening/weekend programs available. Offers e-learning design and instruction (MS Ed); e-learning technology and administration (MS). *Application deadline:* For fall admission, 8/15 priority date for domestic students; for spring admission, 12/15 for domestic students. Applications are processed on a rolling basis. *Application fee:* $35. Electronic applications accepted. *Application Contact:* Tammy K. Griffith, Senior Secretary, 605-626-2558, Fax: 605-626-2542, E-mail: griffith@northern.edu.

NORTH GEORGIA COLLEGE & STATE UNIVERSITY, Dahlonega, GA 30597

General Information State-supported, coed, comprehensive institution. *Enrollment:* 4,922 graduate, professional, and undergraduate students; 127 full-time matriculated graduate/professional students (92 women), 439 part-time matriculated graduate/professional students (331 women). *Enrollment by degree level:* 538 master's. *Graduate faculty:* 125 full-time (56 women), 28 part-time/adjunct (17 women). Tuition, state resident: full-time $3,044; part-time $127 per credit hour. Tuition, nonresident: full-time $12,172; part-time $508 per credit hour. *Required fees:* $892; $458 per semester. *Graduate housing:* Room and/or apartments available on a first-come, first-served basis to single students; on-campus housing not available to married students. Typical cost: $2,384 per year ($4,780 including board). Housing application deadline: 1/1. *Student services:* Campus employment opportunities, campus safety program, career counseling, disabled student services, exercise/wellness program, free psychological counseling, international student services, low-cost health insurance, multicultural affairs office, teacher training, writing training. *Library facilities:* Stewart Library. *Online resources:* library catalog, web page, access to other libraries' catalogs. *Collection:* 146,888 titles, 2,548 serial subscriptions, 3,151 audiovisual materials. *Research affiliation:* Northeast Georgia Medical Center, Morehouse School of Medicine, St. Joseph's Hospital, Mettler Electronic Corporation.

Computer facilities: 470 computers available on campus for general student use. A campuswide network can be accessed from student residence rooms and from off campus. Internet access and online class registration are available. *Web address:* http://www.ngcsu.edu/.

General Application Contact: Dr. Donna A. Gessell, Director of Graduate Studies and External Programs, 706-864-1528, Fax: 706-867-2795, E-mail: dgessell@ngcsu.edu.

GRADUATE UNITS

Graduate Studies Students: 127 full-time (92 women), 439 part-time (331 women); includes 23 minority (14 African Americans, 2 American Indian/Alaska Native, 6 Asian Americans or Pacific Islanders, 1 Hispanic American). Average age 34. 215 applicants, 57% accepted, 102 enrolled. *Faculty:* 125 full-time (56 women), 27 part-time/adjunct (16 women). Expenses: Contact institution. *Financial support:* Career-related internships or fieldwork, scholarships/grants, and unspecified assistantships available. Support available to part-time students. Financial award application deadline: 5/1; financial award applicants required to submit FAFSA. In 2006, 185 master's, 21 other advanced degrees awarded. *Degree program information:* Part-time and evening/weekend programs available. Postbaccalaureate distance learning degree programs offered. Offers community counseling (MS); early childhood education (M Ed); educational leadership (Ed S); family nurse practitioner (MSN); middle grades education (M Ed); nursing education (MSN); physical therapy (DPT); public administration (MPA); secondary education (M Ed); special education (M Ed). *Application deadline:* For fall admission, 7/1 priority date for domestic students; for spring admission, 12/10 priority date for domestic students. Applications are processed on a rolling basis. *Application fee:* $25. Electronic applications accepted. *Director of Graduate Studies and External Programs,* Dr. Donna A. Gessell, 706-864-1528, Fax: 706-867-2795, E-mail: dgessell@ngcsu.edu.

NORTH GREENVILLE UNIVERSITY, Tigerville, SC 29688-1892

General Information Independent-religious, coed. *Enrollment:* 1,948 graduate, professional, and undergraduate students; 47 full-time matriculated graduate/professional students (17 women), 35 part-time matriculated graduate/professional students (10 women). *Library facilities:* Hester Memorial Library. *Online resources:* library catalog, web page. *Collection:* 49,000 titles, 536 serial subscriptions, 5,644 audiovisual materials.

Computer facilities: 72 computers available on campus for general student use. A campuswide network can be accessed from student residence rooms and from off campus. Internet access is available. *Web address:* http://www.ngu.edu/.

General Application Contact: Tawana Scott, Director of Graduate Enrollment, 864-877-1598, Fax: 864-877-1653, E-mail: tscott@ngu.edu.

GRADUATE UNITS

T. Walter Brashier Graduate School Students: 47 full-time (17 women), 35 part-time (10 women); includes 9 minority (7 African Americans, 2 Hispanic Americans), 6 international. Average age 32. 120 applicants, 79% accepted, 32 enrolled. Expenses: Contact institution. *Financial support:* In 2006–07, 35 students received support. Federal Work-Study, institutionally sponsored loans, scholarships/grants, and tuition waivers (partial) available. Support available to part-time students. In 2006, 1 degree awarded. *Degree program information:* Part-time and evening/weekend programs available. Offers business administration (MBA); Christian ministry (MCM). *Application deadline:* Applications are processed on a rolling basis. *Application fee:* $30. Electronic applications accepted. *Application Contact:* Tawana Scott, Director of Graduate Enrollment, 864-877-1598, Fax: 864-877-1653, E-mail: tscott@ngu.edu. *Vice President and Dean for Graduate Studies,* Dr. J. Samuel Isgett, 864-877-3052, Fax: 864-877-1653, E-mail: sisgett@ngu.edu.

NORTH PARK THEOLOGICAL SEMINARY, Chicago, IL 60625-4895

General Information Independent-religious, coed, graduate-only institution. *Graduate housing:* Rooms and/or apartments available to single and married students. Housing application deadline: 9/1. *Research affiliation:* Northside Chicago Theological Institute, Covenant Archives and Historical Society, American Theological Library Association.

GRADUATE UNITS

Graduate and Professional Programs *Degree program information:* Part-time programs available. Offers Christian studies (Certificate); preaching (D Min); religious education (MACE); theological studies (MATS); theology (M Div).

NORTH PARK UNIVERSITY, Chicago, IL 60625-4895

General Information Independent-religious, coed, comprehensive institution. *Graduate housing:* Rooms and/or apartments available to single and married students.

GRADUATE UNITS

Center for Management Education *Degree program information:* Part-time and evening/weekend programs available. Offers management education (MBA, MM).

School of Community Development Offers community development (MA).

School of Education Offers education (MA).

School of Nursing *Degree program information:* Part-time and evening/weekend programs available. Offers nursing (MS).

NORTH SHORE–LIJ GRADUATE SCHOOL OF MOLECULAR MEDICINE, Manhasset, NY 11030

General Information Independent, coed, graduate-only institution. *Enrollment by degree level:* 8 doctoral. *Graduate faculty:* 26 full-time (10 women). *Graduate housing:* On-campus housing not available. *Student services:* Campus employment opportunities, campus safety program, child daycare facilities, free psychological counseling, grant writing training, low-cost health insurance. *Library facilities:* North Shore Library plus 3 others. *Online resources:* library catalog. *Collection:* 30,000 titles, 5,800 serial subscriptions. *Research affiliation:* Feinstein Institute for Medical Research (medicine and medical research).

Computer facilities: 20 computers available on campus for general student use. A campuswide network can be accessed from student residence rooms and from off campus. Internet access is available. *Web address:* http://www.northshorelij.com/nonav.cfm?ID=2585.

General Application Contact: Dr. Annette T. Lee, Associate Dean, 516-562-1108, Fax: 516-562-1153, E-mail: anlee@nshs.edu.

GRADUATE UNITS

Graduate Program Students: 8 full-time (2 women); includes 2 minority (1 Asian American or Pacific Islander, 1 Hispanic American). Average age 30. 19 applicants, 26% accepted, 5 enrolled. *Faculty:* 30 full-time (11 women). Expenses: Contact institution. *Financial support:* In 2006–07, 8 students received support, including 8 fellowships with tuition reimbursements available (averaging $50,000 per year); health care benefits and tuition waivers (full) also available. In 2006, 1 degree awarded. Offers molecular medicine (PhD). *Application deadline:* Applications are processed on a rolling basis. *Application fee:* $25. *Application Contact:* Dr. Annette T. Lee, Associate Dean, 516-562-1108, Fax: 516-562-1153, E-mail: anlee@nshs.edu. *Dean,* Dr. Bettie M. Steinberg, 516-562-1159, Fax: 516-562-1022, E-mail: bsteinbe@lij.edu.

NORTHWEST BAPTIST SEMINARY, Tacoma, WA 98407

General Information Independent-religious, coed, primarily men, graduate-only institution. *Graduate housing:* On-campus housing not available.

GRADUATE UNITS

Programs in Theology *Degree program information:* Part-time and evening/weekend programs available. Offers theology (M Div, M Min, MTS, STM, Th M, D Min, Certificate).

NORTHWEST CHRISTIAN COLLEGE, Eugene, OR 97401-3745

General Information Independent-religious, coed, comprehensive institution. *Graduate housing:* Rooms and/or apartments available on a first-come, first-served basis to single students and available to married students.

GRADUATE UNITS

Department of Education and Counseling *Degree program information:* Part-time and evening/weekend programs available. Postbaccalaureate distance learning degree programs offered (minimal on-campus study). Offers school counseling/consulting (MA). Electronic applications accepted.

School of Business and Management *Degree program information:* Part-time and evening/weekend programs available. Offers business and management (MBA).

NORTHWESTERN HEALTH SCIENCES UNIVERSITY, Bloomington, MN 55431-1599

General Information Independent, coed, graduate-only institution. *Graduate housing:* On-campus housing not available. *Research affiliation:* Berman Center for Outcomes and Clinical Research (outcomes and clinical research), Pain Assessment and Rehabilitation Center (pain management), University of Minnesota, School of Medicine (orthopedic surgery).

GRADUATE UNITS

Minnesota College of Acupuncture and Oriental Medicine Offers acupuncture (M Ac); oriental medicine (MOM). Electronic applications accepted.

Northwestern College of Chiropractic Offers chiropractic (DC). Electronic applications accepted.

School of Massage Therapy Offers massage therapy (Professional Certificate).

NORTHWESTERN OKLAHOMA STATE UNIVERSITY, Alva, OK 73717-2799

General Information State-supported, coed, comprehensive institution. *Enrollment:* 2,024 graduate, professional, and undergraduate students; 43 full-time matriculated graduate/professional students (33 women), 111 part-time matriculated graduate/professional students (88 women). *Enrollment by degree level:* 154 master's. *Graduate faculty:* 32 full-time (17 women), 12 part-time/adjunct (7 women). Tuition, state resident: part-time $700 per year. Tuition, nonresident: part-time $1,715 per year. *Graduate housing:* Room and/or apartments available to single students; on-campus housing not available to married students. *Student services:* Campus employment opportunities, career counseling, exercise/wellness program, free psychological counseling, international student services. *Library facilities:* J. W. Martin Library plus 1 other. *Online resources:* library catalog, web page, access to other libraries' catalogs. *Collection:* 344,640 titles, 3,990 serial subscriptions, 3,609 audiovisual materials.

Computer facilities: 131 computers available on campus for general student use. A campuswide network can be accessed from off campus. Internet access and online class registration are available. *Web address:* http://www.nwosu.edu/.

General Application Contact: Dr. Rodney C. Murrow, Associate Dean of Graduate Studies, 580-327-8589, E-mail: rcmurrow@nwosu.edu.

GRADUATE UNITS

School of Professional Studies Students: 43 full-time (33 women), 111 part-time (88 women); includes 10 minority (1 African American, 6 American Indian/Alaska Native, 3 Hispanic Americans), 2 international. Average age 31. 75 applicants, 92% accepted, 57 enrolled. *Faculty:* 32 full-time (17 women), 12 part-time/adjunct (7 women). Expenses: Contact institution. *Financial support:* Federal Work-Study available. Support available to part-time students. Financial award application deadline: 5/1. In 2006, 68 degrees awarded. *Degree program information:* Part-time programs available. Offers adult education management and administration (M Ed); counseling psychology (MCP); curriculum and instruction (M Ed); education: non-certificate option (M Ed); educational leadership (M Ed); elementary education (M Ed); guidance and counseling K–12 (M Ed); reading specialist (M Ed); secondary education (M Ed). *Application deadline:* Applications are processed on a rolling basis. *Application fee:* $15. *Dean,* Dr. James Bowen, 580-327-8455.

NORTHWESTERN POLYTECHNIC UNIVERSITY, Fremont, CA 94539-7482

General Information Independent, coed, comprehensive institution. *Graduate housing:* Room and/or apartments available on a first-come, first-served basis to single students; on-campus housing not available to married students.

GRADUATE UNITS

School of Business and Information Technology *Degree program information:* Part-time and evening/weekend programs available. Offers business and information technology (MBA).

School of Engineering *Degree program information:* Part-time and evening/weekend programs available. Offers computer science (MS); computer systems engineering (MS); electrical engineering (MS).

NORTHWESTERN STATE UNIVERSITY OF LOUISIANA, Natchitoches, LA 71497

General Information State-supported, coed, comprehensive institution. CGS member. *Enrollment:* 9,431 graduate, professional, and undergraduate students; 280 full-time matriculated graduate/professional students (214 women), 698 part-time matriculated graduate/professional students (568 women). *Enrollment by degree level:* 865 master's, 113 other advanced degrees. *Graduate faculty:* 74 full-time (41 women), 29 part-time/adjunct (22 women). *Graduate housing:* Rooms and/or apartments available on a first-come, first-served basis to single and married students. Housing application deadline: 7/30. *Student services:* Campus employment opportunities, campus safety program, career counseling, disabled student services, exercise/wellness program, free psychological counseling, low-cost health insurance. *Library facilities:* Eugene P. Watson Memorial Library. *Online resources:* library catalog, web page, access to other libraries' catalogs. *Collection:* 861,048 titles, 1,403 serial subscriptions, 1,456 audiovisual materials. *Research affiliation:* Federal Records and Archives Services, Central State Hospital, NASA (strategic defense initiative).

Computer facilities: Computer purchase and lease plans are available. 1,132 computers available on campus for general student use. A campuswide network can be accessed from student residence rooms and from off campus. Internet access and online class registration are available. *Web address:* http://www.nsula.edu/.

General Application Contact: Dr. Steven G. Horton, Associate Provost/Dean, Graduate Studies, Research, and Information Systems, 318-357-5851, Fax: 318-357-5019, E-mail: grad_school@nsula.edu.

GRADUATE UNITS

Graduate Studies and Research Students: 280 full-time (214 women), 698 part-time (568 women); includes 286 minority (255 African Americans, 11 American Indian/Alaska Native, 5 Asian Americans or Pacific Islanders, 15 Hispanic Americans), 4 international. Average age 34. *Faculty:* 74 full-time (41 women), 29 part-time/adjunct (22 women). Expenses: Contact institution. *Financial support:* Fellowships, research assistantships with tuition reimbursements, teaching assistantships with tuition reimbursements, career-related internships or fieldwork, Federal Work-Study, and tuition waivers (partial) available. Support available to part-time students. Financial award application deadline: 7/15. In 2006, 223 master's, 20 other advanced degrees awarded. *Degree program information:* Part-time and evening/weekend programs available. Postbaccalaureate distance learning degree programs offered (no on-campus study). Offers clinical psychology (MS); English (MA); health and human performance (MS); heritage resources (MA). *Application deadline:* For fall admission, 8/1 priority date for domestic students; for spring admission, 1/10 for domestic students. Applications are processed on a rolling basis. *Application fee:* $20 ($30 for international students). Electronic applications accepted. *Associate Provost/Dean, Graduate Studies, Research, and Information Systems,* Dr. Steven G. Horton, 318-357-5851, Fax: 318-357-5019, E-mail: grad_school@nsula.edu.

College of Education Students: 139 full-time (117 women), 532 part-time (438 women); includes 220 minority (200 African Americans, 8 American Indian/Alaska Native, 3 Asian Americans or Pacific Islanders, 9 Hispanic Americans). Average age 35. *Faculty:* 23 full-time (13 women), 20 part-time/adjunct (14 women). Expenses: Contact institution. *Financial support:* Career-related internships or fieldwork and Federal Work-Study available. Financial award application deadline: 7/15. In 2006, 183 master's, 11 other advanced degrees awarded. Offers adult and continuing education (M Ed); business and distributive education (M Ed); counseling (M Ed, Ed S); counseling and guidance (M Ed, Ed S); curriculum and instruction (M Ed); early childhood education (M Ed); early childhood education and teaching (M Ed); education (M Ed); education leadership (M Ed); educational leadership (Ed S); educational technology (M Ed, Ed S); educational technology leadership (M Ed); elementary education (MAT); elementary teaching (M Ed, Ed S); English education (M Ed); home economics education (M Ed); mathematics education (M Ed); middle school education (MAT); reading (M Ed, Ed S); science education (M Ed); secondary education (MAT); secondary teaching (M Ed, Ed S); social sciences education (M Ed); special education (M Ed, Ed S); student personnel services (MA); teacher education and professional development, specific levels and methods (M Ed). *Application deadline:* For fall admission, 8/1 priority date for domestic students; for spring admission, 1/10 for domestic students. Applications are processed on a rolling basis. *Application fee:* $20 ($30 for international students). *Application Contact:* Dr. Steven G. Horton, Associate Provost/Dean, Graduate Studies, Research, and Information Systems, 318-357-5851, Fax: 318-357-5019, E-mail: grad_school@nsula.edu. *Chair,* Dr. Vickie Gentry, 318-357-6288, Fax: 318-357-6275, E-mail: education@nsula.edu.

College of Nursing Students: 27 full-time (23 women), 106 part-time (99 women); includes 17 minority (16 African Americans, 1 Hispanic American). Average age 36. *Faculty:* 9 full-time (all women), 5 part-time/adjunct (all women). Expenses: Contact institution. *Financial support:* Career-related internships or fieldwork and Federal Work-Study available. Support available to part-time students. Financial award application deadline: 7/15. In 2006, 27 degrees awarded. *Degree program information:* Part-time programs available. Offers nursing (MSN). *Application deadline:* For fall admission, 8/1 priority date for domestic students; for spring admission, 1/10 for domestic students. Applications are processed on a rolling basis. *Application fee:* $20 ($30 for international students). *Application Contact:* Dr. Steven G. Horton, Associate Provost/Dean, Graduate Studies, Research, and Information Systems, 318-357-5851, Fax: 318-357-5019, E-mail: grad_school@nsula.edu. *Director,* Dr. Norann Planchock, 318-677-3100, Fax: 318-676-7887, E-mail: planchockn@alpha.nsula.edu.

School of Creative and Performing Arts Students: 19 full-time (11 women), 13 part-time (4 women); includes 4 minority (3 African Americans, 1 Hispanic American), 2 international. Average age 33. *Faculty:* 21 full-time (8 women), 2 part-time/adjunct (1 woman). Expenses: Contact institution. *Financial support:* Career-related internships or fieldwork and Federal Work-Study available. Support available to part-time students. Financial award application deadline: 7/15. In 2006, 9 degrees awarded. Offers art (MA); fine and graphic arts (MA); music (MM). *Application deadline:* For fall admission, 8/1 priority date for domestic students; for spring admission, 1/10 for domestic students. Applications are processed on a rolling basis. *Application fee:* $20 ($30 for international students). *Application Contact:* Dr. Steven G. Horton, Associate Provost/Dean, Graduate Studies, Research, and Information Systems, 318-357-5851, Fax: 318-357-5019, E-mail: grad_school@nsula.edu. *Chairman,* William E. Brent, 318-357-4522, Fax: 318-357-5906, E-mail: brent@alpha.nsula.edu.

NORTHWESTERN UNIVERSITY, Evanston, IL 60208

General Information Independent, coed, university. CGS member. *Graduate housing:* Rooms and/or apartments available on a first-come, first-served basis to single students and available to married students. Housing application deadline: 9/1. *Research affiliation:* Amoco Oil Company (materials science and engineering), Dow Chemical Company (materials science and engineering), E. I. du Pont de Nemours and Company (physics), Exxon Chemical Company (chemical engineering), Ford Motor Company (mechanical engineering), Medtronics, Inc. (cardiology).

GRADUATE UNITS

The Graduate School *Degree program information:* Part-time and evening/weekend programs available. Offers African studies (Certificate); biochemistry, molecular biology, and cell biology (PhD); biotechnology (PhD); cell and molecular biology (PhD); clinical investigation (MSCI, Certificate); clinical psychology (PhD); counseling psychology (MA); developmental biology and genetics (PhD); genetic counseling (MS); hormone action and signal transduction (PhD); law and social science (Certificate); liberal studies (MA); literature (MA); management and organizations and sociology (PhD); marital and family therapy (MS); mathematical methods in social science (MS); neuroscience (PhD); public health (MPH); structural biology, biochemistry, and biophysics (PhD). DPT offered through the Medical School; MSC offered through the School of Speech. Electronic applications accepted.

Center for International and Comparative Studies Offers international and comparative studies (Certificate).

Institute for Neuroscience Offers neuroscience (PhD). Admissions and degree offered through The Graduate School.

Northwestern University (continued)

Judd A. and Marjorie Weinberg College of Arts and Sciences *Degree program information:* Part-time and evening/weekend programs available. Offers anthropology (PhD); art history (PhD); arts and sciences (MA, MFA, MS, PhD, Certificate); astrophysics (PhD); brain, behavior and cognition (PhD); chemistry (PhD); clinical psychology (PhD); cognitive psychology (PhD); comparative literary studies (PhD); economics (MA, PhD); eighteenth-century studies (Certificate); English (MA, PhD); French (PhD); French and comparative literature (PhD); geological sciences (MS, PhD); German literature and critical thought (PhD); history (PhD); Italian studies (Certificate); linguistics (MA, PhD); mathematics (PhD); neurobiology and physiology (MS); personality (PhD); philosophy (PhD); physics (MS, PhD); political science (MA, PhD); Slavic languages and literature (PhD); social psychology (PhD); sociology (PhD); statistics (MS, PhD); visual arts (MFA).

Kellogg School of Management *Degree program information:* Part-time and evening/weekend programs available. Offers accounting (PhD); business administration (MBA); finance (PhD); management (MBA, PhD); management and organizations (PhD); managerial economics and strategy (PhD); marketing (PhD). PhD admissions and degree offered through The Graduate School. Electronic applications accepted.

School of Communication *Degree program information:* Part-time programs available. Offers audiology and hearing sciences (MA, PhD); clinical audiology (Au D); communication (MA, MFA, MSC, Au D, PhD); communication studies (MA, PhD); communication systems strategy and management (MSC); directing (MFA); learning disabilities (MA, PhD); managerial communication (MSC); performance studies (MA, PhD); radio/television/film (MA, MFA, PhD); speech and language pathology (MA, PhD); speech and language pathology and learning disabilities (MA); stage design (MFA); theatre (MA); theatre and drama (PhD). MA, MFA, and PhD admissions and degrees offered through The Graduate School; MSC admissions and degrees offered through the School of Speech.

School of Education and Social Policy Students: 159 full-time (102 women), 138 part-time (104 women); includes 48 minority (18 African Americans, 1 American Indian/Alaska Native, 20 Asian Americans or Pacific Islanders, 9 Hispanic Americans), 13 international. Average age 30. 200 applicants, 39% accepted, 61 enrolled. *Faculty:* 37 full-time (13 women), 64 part-time/adjunct (34 women). Expenses: Contact institution. *Financial support:* In 2006–07, 42 fellowships with full tuition reimbursements (averaging $24,096 per year), 20 research assistantships with full tuition reimbursements, 15 teaching assistantships with full tuition reimbursements (averaging $19,740 per year) were awarded; career-related internships or fieldwork, Federal Work-Study, institutionally sponsored loans, scholarships/grants, and tuition waivers (partial) also available. Financial award application deadline: 1/15; financial award applicants required to submit FAFSA. In 2006, 88 master's, 11 doctorates awarded. *Degree program information:* Part-time and evening/weekend programs available. Offers advanced teaching (MS); education (MS); elementary education and policy (MS); higher education administration (MS); human development and social policy (PhD); learning and organizational change (MS); learning sciences (MA, PhD); secondary teaching (MS). MA and PhD admissions and degrees offered through The Graduate School. *Application fee:* $60 ($75 for international students). Electronic applications accepted. *Application Contact:* 847-491-3790, Fax: 847-491-4664, E-mail: sesp@northwestern.edu. *Graduate Student Advisor,* Mark P. Hoffman, 847-491-3790, Fax: 847-491-4664, E-mail: markhoffman@northwestern.edu.

Law School Students: 768 full-time (354 women); includes 266 minority (64 African Americans, 5 American Indian/Alaska Native, 133 Asian Americans or Pacific Islanders, 64 Hispanic Americans), 32 international. Average age 26. 5,015 applicants, 17% accepted, 233 enrolled. *Faculty:* 100 full-time (53 women), 71 part-time/adjunct (17 women). Expenses: Contact institution. *Financial support:* In 2006–07, 254 fellowships (averaging $20,000 per year) were awarded; career-related internships or fieldwork, Federal Work-Study, institutionally sponsored loans, and scholarships/grants also available. Financial award application deadline: 2/15; financial award applicants required to submit FAFSA. In 2006, 265 degrees awarded. Offers executive law (LL M); international law (JD); law (JD, LL M). *Application deadline:* For fall admission, 2/15 for domestic students, 2/1 for international students. Applications are processed on a rolling basis. *Application fee:* $80 ($85 for international students). Electronic applications accepted. *Application Contact:* Johann H. Lee, Assistant Dean of Admissions and Financial Aid, 312-503-8465, Fax: 312-503-0178, E-mail: johann@law.northwestern.edu. *Chair,* David Van Zandt, 847-491-8024, Fax: 847-467-1035.

McCormick School of Engineering and Applied Science *Degree program information:* Part-time and evening/weekend programs available. Offers applied mathematics (MS, PhD); biomedical engineering (MS, PhD); chemical engineering (MS, PhD); computational biology and bioinformatics (MS); computer science (MS, PhD); electrical and computer engineering (MS, PhD); electronic materials (MS, PhD, Certificate); engineering and applied science (MEM, MIT, MME, MMM, MPD, MPM, MS, PhD, Certificate); engineering management (MEM); environmental engineering and science (MS, PhD); fluid mechanics (MS, PhD); geotechnical engineering (MS, PhD); industrial engineering and management science (MS, PhD); information technology (MIT); manufacturing engineering (MME); materials science and engineering (MS, PhD); mechanical engineering (MS, PhD); mechanics of materials and solids (MS, PhD); operations research (MS, PhD); project management (MPM, PhD); solid mechanics (MS, PhD); structural engineering and materials (MS, PhD); theoretical and applied mechanics (MS, PhD); transportation systems analysis and planning (MS, PhD). MS and PhD admissions and degrees offered through The Graduate School. Electronic applications accepted.

Medill School of Journalism Offers advertising/sales promotion (MSIMC); broadcast journalism (MSJ); direct database and e-commerce marketing (MSIMC); general studies (MSIMC); integrated marketing communications (MSIMC); magazine publishing (MSJ); new media (MSJ); public relations (MSIMC); reporting and writing (MSJ). Electronic applications accepted.

Northwestern University Feinberg School of Medicine Students: 695 full-time (347 women); includes 342 minority (44 African Americans, 8 American Indian/Alaska Native, 259 Asian Americans or Pacific Islanders, 31 Hispanic Americans), 25 international. Average age 24. 6,753 applicants, 5% accepted, 174 enrolled. *Faculty:* 1,570 full-time (558 women), 1,790 part-time/adjunct (711 women). Expenses: Contact institution. *Financial support:* Research assistantships, teaching assistantships, career-related internships or fieldwork, institutionally sponsored loans, and scholarships/grants available. Financial award applicants required to submit FAFSA. In 2006, 166 degrees awarded. Offers cancer biology (PhD); cell biology (PhD); clinical investigation (MSCI); developmental biology (PhD); evolutionary biology (PhD); immunology and microbial pathogenesis (PhD); medicine (MD, MS, MSCI, DPT, PhD); molecular biology and genetics (PhD); neurobiology (PhD); pharmacology and toxicology (PhD); physical therapy and human movement sciences (DPT); structural biology and biochemistry (PhD). *Application deadline:* For fall admission, 10/15 for domestic students. Applications are processed on a rolling basis. *Application fee:* $75. Electronic applications accepted. *Application Contact:* Delores G. Brown, Associate Dean for Admissions, 312-503-8206, Fax: 312-503-0550, E-mail: med-admissions@northwestern.edu. *Dean,* Lewis Landsberg, 312-503-0340.

School of Music Offers collaborative arts (DM); conducting (MM, DM); jazz pedagogy (MM); keyboard (MM, DM, CP); music (MM, DM, PhD, CP); music cognition (PhD); music composition (MM, DM); music education (MM, PhD); music technology (MM, PhD); music theory (MM, PhD); musicology (MM, PhD); opera production (MM); performance (MM); piano performance and pedagogy (MM); string performance and pedagogy (MM); strings (MM, DM); strings, winds and percussion (CP); voice (MM, DM, CP); winds and percussion (MM, DM). PhD admissions and degree offered through The Graduate School.

NORTHWEST MISSOURI STATE UNIVERSITY, Maryville, MO 64468-6001

General Information State-supported, coed, comprehensive institution. *Enrollment:* 6,220 graduate, professional, and undergraduate students; 255 full-time matriculated graduate/professional students (110 women), 431 part-time matriculated graduate/professional students (270 women). *Enrollment by degree level:* 649 master's, 37 other advanced degrees. *Graduate faculty:* 134 full-time (47 women). *Graduate housing:* Room and/or apartments available on a first-come, first-served basis to single students; on-campus housing not available to married students. Typical cost: $2,631 per year ($3,861 including board). Housing application deadline: 7/1. *Student services:* Campus employment opportunities, campus safety program, career counseling, disabled student services, free psychological counseling, international student services, low-cost health insurance, multicultural affairs office, writing training. *Library facilities:* B. D. Owens Library plus 1 other. *Online resources:* library catalog, web page, access to other libraries' catalogs. *Collection:* 371,026 titles, 24,054 serial subscriptions, 6,253 audiovisual materials.

Computer facilities: 2,450 computers available on campus for general student use. A campuswide network can be accessed from student residence rooms and from off campus. Internet access is available. *Web address:* http://www.nwmissouri.edu/.

General Application Contact: Dr. Frances Shipley, Dean of Graduate School, 660-562-1145, Fax: 660-562-1096, E-mail: gradsch@nwmissouri.edu.

GRADUATE UNITS

Graduate School Students: 255 full-time (110 women), 431 part-time (270 women); includes 45 minority (26 African Americans, 1 American Indian/Alaska Native, 9 Asian Americans or Pacific Islanders, 9 Hispanic Americans), 95 international. Average age 25. 578 applicants, 61% accepted, 159 enrolled. *Faculty:* 134 full-time (47 women). Expenses: Contact institution. *Financial support:* In 2006–07, 50 research assistantships with full tuition reimbursements (averaging $6,000 per year), 74 teaching assistantships with full tuition reimbursements (averaging $6,000 per year) were awarded; career-related internships or fieldwork, Federal Work-Study, institutionally sponsored loans, scholarships/grants, unspecified assistantships, and administrative assistantships, tutorial assistantships also available. Financial award application deadline: 3/1; financial award applicants required to submit FAFSA. In 2006, 148 master's, 17 other advanced degrees awarded. *Degree program information:* Part-time programs available. *Application deadline:* For fall admission, 7/1 for domestic and international students; for spring admission, 11/15 for domestic and international students. Applications are processed on a rolling basis. *Application fee:* $0 ($50 for international students). Electronic applications accepted. *Application Contact:* Nina Nickerson, Office Manager, 660-562-1145, Fax: 660-562-1096, E-mail: gradsch@mail.nwmissouri.edu. *Dean of Graduate School,* Dr. Frances Shipley, 660-562-1145, Fax: 660-562-1096, E-mail: gradsch@mail.nwmissouri.edu.

College of Arts and Sciences Students: 35 full-time (18 women), 135 part-time (57 women); includes 10 minority (2 American Indian/Alaska Native, 5 Asian Americans or Pacific Islanders, 3 Hispanic Americans). 62 applicants, 69% accepted, 35 enrolled. *Faculty:* 63 full-time (15 women). Expenses: Contact institution. *Financial support:* In 2006–07, 7 research assistantships with full tuition reimbursements (averaging $6,000 per year), 15 teaching assistantships with full tuition reimbursements (averaging $6,000 per year) were awarded; administrative assistantships, tutorial assistantships also available. Financial award application deadline: 3/1; financial award applicants required to submit FAFSA. In 2006, 12 degrees awarded. *Degree program information:* Part-time programs available. Offers arts and sciences (MA, MS, MS Ed); biology (MS); English (MA); English with speech emphasis (MA); geographic information sciences (MS); history (MA); teaching English with speech emphasis (MS Ed); teaching history (MS Ed); teaching mathematics (MS Ed); teaching music (MS Ed). *Application deadline:* For fall admission, 7/1 for domestic and international students; for spring admission, 11/15 for domestic and international students. Applications are processed on a rolling basis. *Application fee:* $0 ($50 for international students). Electronic applications accepted. *Application Contact:* Dr. Frances Shipley, Dean of Graduate School, 660-562-1145, Fax: 660-562-1096, E-mail: gradsch@nwmissouri.edu. *Dean,* Dr. Charles McAdams, 660-562-1197.

College of Education and Human Services Students: 67 full-time (40 women), 237 part-time (172 women); includes 9 minority (6 African Americans, 1 Asian American or Pacific Islander, 2 Hispanic Americans), 1 international. 136 applicants, 52% accepted, 70 enrolled. *Faculty:* 44 full-time (27 women). Expenses: Contact institution. *Financial support:* In 2006–07, 16 research assistantships with full tuition reimbursements (averaging $6,000 per year), 35 teaching assistantships with full tuition reimbursements (averaging $6,000 per year) were awarded; unspecified assistantships also available. Financial award application deadline: 3/1; financial award applicants required to submit FAFSA. In 2006, 83 master's, 17 other advanced degrees awarded. *Degree program information:* Part-time programs available. Offers education and human services (MS, MS Ed, Ed S); educational leadership (MS Ed, Ed S); educational leadership: elementary (MS Ed); educational leadership: secondary (MS Ed); elementary principalship (Ed S); guidance and counseling (MS Ed); health and physical education (MS Ed); reading (MS Ed); recreation (MS); secondary individualized prescribed programs (MS Ed); secondary principalship (Ed S); special education (MS Ed); superintendency (Ed S); teaching secondary (MS Ed); teaching: early childhood (MS Ed); teaching: elementary self contained (MS Ed); teaching: middle school (MS Ed); teaching: science (MS Ed); teaching: secondary (MS Ed). *Application deadline:* For fall admission, 7/1 for domestic and international students; for spring admission, 11/15 for domestic and international students. *Application fee:* $0 ($50 for international students). Electronic applications accepted. *Application Contact:* Dr. Frances Shipley, Dean of Graduate School, 660-562-1145, Fax: 660-562-1096, E-mail: gradsch@nwmissouri.edu. *Dean,* Dr. Max Ruhl, 660-562-1778.

Melvin and Valorie Booth College of Business and Professional Studies Students: 129 full-time (40 women), 39 part-time (28 women); includes 3 minority (2 Asian Americans or Pacific Islanders, 1 Hispanic American), 94 international. 406 applicants, 53% accepted, 64 enrolled. *Faculty:* 28 full-time (6 women). Expenses: Contact institution. *Financial support:* In 2006–07, 16 research assistantships with full tuition reimbursements (averaging $6,000 per year), 10 teaching assistantships with full tuition reimbursements (averaging $6,000 per year) were awarded; career-related internships or fieldwork and administrative assistantships, tutorial assistantships also available. Financial award application deadline: 3/1; financial award applicants required to submit FAFSA. In 2006, 57 degrees awarded. *Degree program information:* Part-time programs available. Offers accounting (MBA); agricultural economics (MBA); agriculture (MS); applied computer science (MS); business administration (MBA); business and professional studies (MBA, MS, MS Ed); health management (MBA); management information systems (MBA); school computer studies (MS); teaching agriculture (MS Ed); teaching instructional technology (MS Ed). *Application deadline:* For fall admission, 7/1 for domestic and international students; for spring admission, 11/15 for domestic and international students. Applications are processed on a rolling basis. *Application fee:* $0 ($50 for international students). Electronic applications accepted. *Application Contact:* Dr. Frances Shipley, Dean of Graduate School, 660-562-1145, Fax: 660-562-1096, E-mail: gradsch@nwmissouri.edu. *Dean,* Dr. Thomas Billesbach, 660-562-1277.

NORTHWEST NAZARENE UNIVERSITY, Nampa, ID 83686-5897

General Information Independent-religious, coed, comprehensive institution. *Enrollment:* 1,749 graduate, professional, and undergraduate students; 453 full-time matriculated graduate/professional students (242 women), 56 part-time matriculated graduate/professional students (35 women). *Enrollment by degree level:* 509 master's. *Graduate faculty:* 42 full-time (15 women), 47 part-time/adjunct (19 women). *Graduate housing:* Rooms and/or apartments available on a first-come, first-served basis to single students and available to married students. Housing application deadline: 4/1. *Student services:* Career counseling, free psychological counseling, multicultural affairs office, teacher training. *Library facilities:* John E. Riley Library. *Online resources:* library catalog, web page, access to other libraries' catalogs. *Collection:* 100,966 titles, 821 serial subscriptions.

Computer facilities: Computer purchase and lease plans are available. 400 computers available on campus for general student use. A campuswide network can be accessed from student residence rooms and from off campus. Internet access, various software packages are available. *Web address:* http://www.nnu.edu/.

General Application Contact: Dr. Mark Maddix, Director, Graduate Studies, 208-467-8817, Fax: 208-467-8252, E-mail: mamaddix@nnu.edu.

GRADUATE UNITS

Graduate Studies Students: 453 full-time (242 women), 56 part-time (35 women); includes 23 minority (3 African Americans, 2 American Indian/Alaska Native, 6 Asian Americans or Pacific Islanders, 12 Hispanic Americans), 6 international. Average age 34. *Faculty:* 42

full-time (15 women), 47 part-time/adjunct (19 women). Expenses: Contact institution. *Financial support:* In 2006–07, 193 students received support. Career-related internships or fieldwork available. In 2006, 135 degrees awarded. *Degree program information:* Part-time and evening/weekend programs available. Offers business administration (MBA); Christian education (MA); community counseling (MS); counselor education (MS); curriculum and instruction (M Ed); educational leadership (M Ed); exceptional child (M Ed); marriage and family counseling (MS); pastoral ministry (MA); reading education (M Ed); religion (M Div, MA); school counseling (M Ed, MS); social work (MSW); spiritual formation (MA); teacher education (M Ed). *Application deadline:* Applications are processed on a rolling basis. *Application fee:* $50. Electronic applications accepted. *Application Contact:* Vicki Funk, Secretary, 208-467-8368, Fax: 208-467-8252, E-mail: vlfunk@nnu.edu. *Director, Graduate Studies,* Dr. Mark Maddix, 208-467-8817, Fax: 208-467-8252, E-mail: mamaddix@nnu.edu.

NORTHWEST UNIVERSITY, Kirkland, WA 98033

General Information Independent-religious, coed, comprehensive institution. *Enrollment:* 1,265 graduate, professional, and undergraduate students; 110 full-time matriculated graduate/professional students (74 women), 14 part-time matriculated graduate/professional students (13 women). *Enrollment by degree level:* 124 master's. *Graduate faculty:* 10 full-time (4 women), 22 part-time/adjunct (11 women). *Tuition:* Full-time $12,938; part-time $691 per credit. *Required fees:* $85 per term. Tuition and fees vary according to course load and program. *Graduate housing:* Rooms and/or apartments available on a first-come, first-served basis to single and married students. Typical cost: $3,100 per year for single students; $5,940 per year for married students. Room charges vary according to board plan and housing facility selected. *Student services:* Campus employment opportunities, campus safety program, career counseling, disabled student services, free psychological counseling, international student services, low-cost health insurance. *Library facilities:* D. V. Hurst Library. *Online resources:* library catalog, web page, access to other libraries' catalogs. *Collection:* 120,226 titles, 11,454 serial subscriptions, 4,216 audiovisual materials.

Computer facilities: 88 computers available on campus for general student use. A campuswide network can be accessed from student residence rooms and from off campus. Internet access and online class registration are available. *Web address:* http://www.northwestu.edu/.

General Application Contact: Darrell Hughes, Director of Graduate and Professional Studies Enrollment, 425-889-7787, Fax: 425-803-3059, E-mail: gpse@northwestu.edu.

NORTHWOOD UNIVERSITY, Midland, MI 48640-2398

General Information Independent, coed, comprehensive institution. *Graduate housing:* Room and/or apartments available on a first-come, first-served basis to single students. Housing application deadline: 8/30. *Research affiliation:* Motor & Equipment Manufacturers Association (automotive), Specialized Equipment Manufacturers Association (automotive), Automotive Aftermarket Industry Association (automotive), Automotive Warehouse Distributors Association (automotive).

GRADUATE UNITS

Richard DeVos Graduate School of Management *Degree program information:* Part-time and evening/weekend programs available. Offers management (EMBA, MBA, MMBA). Electronic applications accepted.

NORWICH UNIVERSITY, Northfield, VT 05663

General Information Independent, coed, comprehensive institution. *Enrollment:* 400 full-time matriculated graduate/professional students (150 women). *Enrollment by degree level:* 400 master's. *Graduate faculty:* 4 full-time (0 women), 152 part-time/adjunct (52 women). *Student services:* Career counseling, disabled student services, teacher training. *Library facilities:* Kreitzberg Library. *Online resources:* library catalog, web page, access to other libraries' catalogs. *Collection:* 280,000 titles, 904 serial subscriptions, 1,501 audiovisual materials.

Computer facilities: 142 computers available on campus for general student use. A campuswide network can be accessed from student residence rooms and from off campus. Internet access is available. *Web address:* http://www.norwich.edu/.

General Application Contact: Jane D. Joslin, Administrative Assistant, 802-485-2730, Fax: 802-485-2533, E-mail: jdaniels@norwich.edu.

GRADUATE UNITS

School of Graduate Studies Expenses: Contact institution. *Financial support:* Scholarships/grants available. Financial award applicants required to submit FAFSA. In 2006, 306 degrees awarded. *Degree program information:* Evening/weekend programs available. Post-baccalaureate distance learning degree programs offered (no on-campus study). Offers business administration (MBA); civil engineering (MCE); education (M Ed); information assurance (MS); international (MA); justice administration (MJA); military history (MA); nursing administration (MSN); organizational leadership (MSOL); public administration (MPA). *Application deadline:* For fall admission, 7/1 for domestic students, 8/1 for international students; for winter admission, 11/1 for domestic and international students; for spring admission, 3/1 for domestic and international students. *Application fee:* $50. Electronic applications accepted. *Director,* Dr. William Clemments, 802-485-2730.

NOTRE DAME COLLEGE, South Euclid, OH 44121-4293

General Information Independent-religious, coed, comprehensive institution. *Graduate housing:* On-campus housing not available.

GRADUATE UNITS

Graduate Studies *Degree program information:* Part-time and evening/weekend programs available. Offers accounting (Certificate); creative critical thinking (M Ed); financial services management (Certificate); information systems (Certificate); learning disabilities (M Ed); management (Certificate); paralegal (Certificate); pastoral ministry (Certificate); reading (M Ed); teacher education (Certificate).

NOTRE DAME DE NAMUR UNIVERSITY, Belmont, CA 94002-1908

General Information Independent-religious, coed, comprehensive institution. *Enrollment:* 1,583 graduate, professional, and undergraduate students; 193 full-time matriculated graduate/professional students (154 women), 533 part-time matriculated graduate/professional students (420 women). *Enrollment by degree level:* 496 master's, 216 other advanced degrees. *Graduate faculty:* 28 full-time (13 women), 63 part-time/adjunct (44 women). *Tuition:* Part-time $655 per credit. *Graduate housing:* Rooms and/or apartments available on a first-come, first-served basis to single and married students. Typical cost: $7,000 per year ($10,350 including board) for single students. Room and board charges vary according to board plan and housing facility selected. Housing application deadline: 7/1. *Student services:* Campus employment opportunities, campus safety program, career counseling, disabled student services, free psychological counseling, international student services, low-cost health insurance, multicultural affairs office, teacher training, writing training. *Library facilities:* Carl Gellert and Celia Berta Gellert Library. *Online resources:* library catalog, web page, access to other libraries' catalogs. *Collection:* 90,702 titles, 15,000 serial subscriptions, 9,122 audiovisual materials.

Computer facilities: 50 computers available on campus for general student use. A campuswide network can be accessed from off campus. Internet access is available. *Web address:* http://www.ndnu.edu.

General Application Contact: Helen Valine, Director of Graduate Admissions, 650-508-3534, Fax: 650-508-3426, E-mail: grad.admit@ndnu.edu.

GRADUATE UNITS

Division of Academic Affairs Students: 193 full-time (154 women), 533 part-time (420 women); includes 192 minority (24 African Americans, 4 American Indian/Alaska Native, 83 Asian Americans or Pacific Islanders, 81 Hispanic Americans), 19 international. Average age 35. 335 applicants, 96% accepted, 287 enrolled. *Faculty:* 28 full-time (13 women), 63 part-time/adjunct (44 women). Expenses: Contact institution. *Financial support:* Career-related internships or fieldwork and scholarships/grants available. Support available to part-time students. Financial award applicants required to submit FAFSA. In 2006, 184 master's, 63 other advanced degrees awarded. *Degree program information:* Part-time and evening/weekend programs available. *Application deadline:* For fall admission, 8/1 priority date for domestic students; for spring admission, 12/1 priority date for domestic students. Applications are processed on a rolling basis. *Application fee:* $50. Electronic applications accepted. *Application Contact:* Helen Valine, Director of Graduate Admissions, 650-508-3534, Fax: 650-508-3426, E-mail: grad.admit@ndnu.edu. *Executive Vice President and Provost,* Dr. Judith Maxwell Greig, 650-508-3494, Fax: 650-508-3495, E-mail: jgreig@ndnu.edu.

School of Arts and Humanities Students: 6 full-time (3 women), 29 part-time (23 women); includes 12 minority (1 African American, 1 American Indian/Alaska Native, 6 Asian Americans or Pacific Islanders, 4 Hispanic Americans), 2 international. Average age 37. 13 applicants, 100% accepted, 11 enrolled. *Faculty:* 8 full-time (4 women), 13 part-time/adjunct (7 women). Expenses: Contact institution. In 2006, 12 degrees awarded. *Degree program information:* Part-time programs available. Offers arts and humanities (MA, MM, Certificate); English (MA); music (MM); pedagogy (MM); performance (MM); teaching English to speakers of other languages (Certificate). *Application deadline:* For fall admission, 8/1 for domestic students; for spring admission, 12/1 for domestic students. *Application fee:* $50. *Application Contact:* Helen Valine, Director of Graduate Admissions, 650-508-3534, Fax: 650-508-3426, E-mail: grad.admit@ndnu.edu. *Interim Dean,* Dr. Gregory B. White, 650-508-3436, Fax: 650-508-3662, E-mail: gwhite@ndnu.edu.

School of Business and Management Students: 26 full-time (13 women), 142 part-time (101 women); includes 62 minority (4 African Americans, 2 American Indian/Alaska Native, 26 Asian Americans or Pacific Islanders, 30 Hispanic Americans), 10 international. Average age 33. 87 applicants, 99% accepted, 70 enrolled. *Faculty:* 8 full-time (1 woman), 8 part-time/adjunct (2 women). Expenses: Contact institution. In 2006, 67 degrees awarded. Offers business administration (MBA); business and management (MBA, MPA, MSM); management (MSM); public administration (MPA). *Application deadline:* For fall admission, 8/1 for domestic students; for spring admission, 12/1 for domestic students. *Application fee:* $50. *Application Contact:* Helen Valine, Director of Graduate Admissions, 650-508-3534, Fax: 650-508-3426, E-mail: grad.admit@ndnu.edu. *Dean,* Dr. George Klemic, 650-508-3601, E-mail: gklemic@ndnu.edu.

School of Education and Leadership Students: 89 full-time (80 women), 225 part-time (180 women); includes 52 minority (9 African Americans, 23 Asian Americans or Pacific Islanders, 20 Hispanic Americans), 1 international. Average age 36. 155 applicants, 98% accepted, 146 enrolled. *Faculty:* 8 full-time (5 women), 18 part-time/adjunct (13 women). Expenses: Contact institution. In 2006, 54 master's, 63 other advanced degrees awarded. *Degree program information:* Part-time programs available. Offers education (MA); education and leadership (MA, MAT, Certificate); education in technology leadership (MA, Certificate); reading (MA, Certificate); special education (MA, Certificate); teaching (MAT). *Application deadline:* For fall admission, 8/1 for domestic students; for spring admission, 12/1 for domestic students. *Application fee:* $50. *Application Contact:* Helen Valine, Director of Graduate Admissions, 650-508-3534, Fax: 650-508-3426, E-mail: grad.admit@ndnu.edu. *Dean,* Dr. Joanne Rossi, 650-508-3613, E-mail: jrossi@ndnu.edu.

School of Sciences Students: 72 full-time (68 women), 123 part-time (106 women); includes 64 minority (10 African Americans, 1 American Indian/Alaska Native, 26 Asian Americans or Pacific Islanders, 27 Hispanic Americans), 6 international. 82 applicants, 88% accepted, 52 enrolled. *Faculty:* 4 full-time (3 women), 14 part-time/adjunct (12 women). Expenses: Contact institution. In 2006, 51 degrees awarded. Offers art therapy psychology (MAAT, MAMFT); chemical dependency (MACP); counseling psychology (MACP); gerontology (MA, Certificate); marital and family therapy (MACP, MAMFT); premedical studies (Certificate); sciences (MA, MAAT, MACP, MAMFT, Certificate). *Application deadline:* For fall admission, 8/1 for domestic students; for spring admission, 12/1 for domestic students. *Application fee:* $50. *Application Contact:* Helen Valine, Director of Graduate Admissions, 650-508-3534, Fax: 650-508-3426, E-mail: grad.admit@ndnu.edu. *Dean,* Dr. Gregory B. White, 650-508-3436, Fax: 650-508-3662, E-mail: gwhite@ndnu.edu.

NOTRE DAME SEMINARY, New Orleans, LA 70118-4391

General Information Independent-religious, coed, primarily men, graduate-only institution.

GRADUATE UNITS

Graduate School of Theology *Degree program information:* Part-time programs available. Offers theology (M Div, MA).

NOVA SCOTIA AGRICULTURAL COLLEGE, Truro, NS B2N 5E3, Canada

General Information Province-supported, coed, comprehensive institution. *Enrollment:* 793 graduate, professional, and undergraduate students; 53 full-time matriculated graduate/professional students (31 women), 16 part-time matriculated graduate/professional students (14 women). *Enrollment by degree level:* 69 master's. *Graduate faculty:* 48 full-time (8 women), 20 part-time/adjunct (0 women). Tuition, province resident: full-time $7,254; part-time $2,418 per year. Tuition and fees vary according to student level. *Graduate housing:* Room and/or apartments available on a first-come, first-served basis to single students; on-campus housing not available to married students. Typical cost: $6,552 per year. Room charges vary according to housing facility selected. Housing application deadline: 6/30. *Student services:* Campus employment opportunities, campus safety program, career counseling, child daycare facilities, exercise/wellness program, free psychological counseling, international student services, teacher training. *Library facilities:* MacRae Library. *Collection:* 23,000 titles, 800 serial subscriptions. *Research affiliation:* Crop Development Institute (crop physiology/horticulture), Atlantic Poultry Research Institute (poultry), Organic Agriculture Centre of Canada (organic agriculture), Performance Genomics, Inc. (animal genomics), Bio-Environmental Engineering Centre (resource and environmental sciences), Atlantic BioVenture Centre (bio-products, bio-resources, value-added).

Computer facilities: 110 computers available on campus for general student use. A campuswide network can be accessed. Internet access and online class registration are available. *Web address:* http://www.nsac.ns.ca/.

General Application Contact: Jill L. Rogers, Manager, Research and Graduate Studies, 902-893-6360, Fax: 902-893-3430, E-mail: jrogers@nsac.ca.

GRADUATE UNITS

Research and Graduate Studies Students: 53 full-time (31 women), 16 part-time (14 women); includes 7 minority (2 African Americans, 5 Asian Americans or Pacific Islanders). Average age 25. *Faculty:* 48 full-time (8 women), 20 part-time/adjunct (0 women). Expenses: Contact institution. *Financial support:* In 2006–07, 45 students received support, including 7 fellowships (averaging $15,000 per year), 10 research assistantships (averaging $15,000 per year), 15 teaching assistantships (averaging $900 per year); career-related internships or fieldwork, scholarships/grants, and unspecified assistantships also available. In 2006, 15 degrees awarded. *Degree program information:* Part-time programs available. Offers agriculture (M Sc). *Application deadline:* For fall admission, 6/1 for domestic students, 4/1 priority date for international students; for winter admission, 10/31 for domestic students, 8/31 priority date for international students; for spring admission, 2/28 for domestic students, 12/31 priority date for international students. Applications are processed on a rolling basis. *Application fee:* $70. *Application Contact:* Marie Law, Administrative Assistant, 902-893-6502, Fax: 902-893-3430, E-mail: mlaw@nsac.ca. *Manager,* Jill L. Rogers, 902-893-6360, Fax: 902-893-3430, E-mail: jrogers@nsac.ca.

NOVA SOUTHEASTERN UNIVERSITY, Fort Lauderdale, FL 33314-7796

General Information Independent, coed, university. CGS member. *Enrollment:* 25,960 graduate, professional, and undergraduate students; 10,055 full-time matriculated graduate/professional students (6,920 women), 10,492 part-time matriculated graduate/professional students (7,612 women). *Enrollment by degree level:* 3,407 first professional, 9,387 master's,

Nova Southeastern University (continued)

6,113 doctoral, 1,341 other advanced degrees. *Graduate housing:* On-campus housing not available. *Student services:* Campus employment opportunities, campus safety program, career counseling, disabled student services, exercise/wellness program, free psychological counseling, international student services, low-cost health insurance, teacher training. *Library facilities:* Alvin Sherman Library, Research, and Information Technology Center plus 4 others. *Online resources:* library catalog, web page, access to other libraries' catalogs. *Collection:* 725,000 titles, 22,295 serial subscriptions, 23,738 audiovisual materials.

Computer facilities: 2,000 computers available on campus for general student use. A campuswide network can be accessed from student residence rooms and from off campus. Internet access and online class registration are available. *Web address:* http://www.nova.edu/.

General Application Contact: Information Contact, 800-541-6682, E-mail: nsuinfo@nsu.nova.edu.

GRADUATE UNITS

Center for Psychological Studies Students: 749 full-time (629 women), 517 part-time (453 women); includes 525 minority (231 African Americans, 3 American Indian/Alaska Native, 33 Asian Americans or Pacific Islanders, 258 Hispanic Americans), 20 international. Average age 34. 1,063 applicants, 39% accepted, 413 enrolled. *Faculty:* 92. Expenses: Contact institution. *Financial support:* In 2006–07, 11 research assistantships, 29 teaching assistantships (averaging $1,000 per year) were awarded; career-related internships or fieldwork, Federal Work-Study, institutionally sponsored loans, scholarships/grants, and unspecified assistantships also available. Support available to part-time students. Financial award application deadline: 4/1. In 2006, 223 master's, 69 doctorates, 27 other advanced degrees awarded. Postbaccalaureate distance learning degree programs offered. Offers clinical pharmacology (MS); clinical psychology (PhD, Psy D, SPS); mental health counseling (MS); psychological studies (MS, PhD, Psy D, Psy S, SPS); school guidance and counseling (MS); school psychology (Psy S). *Application deadline:* Applications are processed on a rolling basis. *Application fee:* $50. Electronic applications accepted. *Application Contact:* Carlos Perez, Enrollment Management, 954-262-5790, Fax: 954-262-3893, E-mail: cpsinfo@cps.nova.edu. *Dean,* Karen Grosby, 954-262-5701, Fax: 954-262-3859, E-mail: grosby@nova.edu.

Fischler School of Education and Human Services Students: 2,474 full-time (1,926 women), 7,291 part-time (5,895 women); includes 5,034 minority (3,835 African Americans, 24 American Indian/Alaska Native, 93 Asian Americans or Pacific Islanders, 1,082 Hispanic Americans), 207 international. Average age 38. 2,813 applicants, 79% accepted. *Faculty:* 131 full-time (78 women), 548 part-time/adjunct (342 women). Expenses: Contact institution. *Financial support:* In 2006–07, 5,072 students received support, including 2 fellowships (averaging $9,375 per year); career-related internships or fieldwork, Federal Work-Study, and tuition waivers (full) also available. Support available to part-time students. Financial award application deadline: 1/7. In 2006, 2,192 master's, 489 doctorates, 425 other advanced degrees awarded. *Degree program information:* Part-time and evening/weekend programs available. Offers adult education (Ed D); athletic administration (MS); child and youth care administration (MS); child and youth studies (Ed D); cognitive and behavioral disabilities (MS); computer science education (Ed S); computer science education (K-12) (MS); computing and information technology (Ed D); curriculum and teaching (Ed S); curriculum, instruction and technology (MS); curriculum, instruction, management and administration (Ed S); early childhood education administration (MS); early childhood special education (MS); early literacy and reading (Ed S); early literacy education (MS); education and human services (MA, MS, Ed D, SLPD, Ed S); education technology (MS); educational leaders (Ed D); educational leadership (Ed D); educational leadership (administration K–12) (MS, Ed S); educational media (Ed S); educational media (K-12) (MS); elementary education (MS, Ed S); English (MS, Ed S); exceptional student education (MS); family support studies (MS); gifted education (MS, Ed S); health care education (Ed D); higher education (Ed D); human serviced administration (Ed D); instructional leadership (Ed D); instructional technology and distance education (MS, Ed D); instructional technology distance education (Ed D); interdisciplinary arts education (MS); management and administration of educational programs (MS); mathematics (MS, Ed S); multicultural early intervention (MS); organizational leadership (Ed D); pre-kindergarten/primary (MS); preschool education (MS); reading (MS, Ed S); science (MS, Ed S); secondary education (MS); social studies (MS, Ed S); Spanish language (MS); special education (Ed D); speech language pathology (Ed D); speech-language pathology (MS, SLPD); substance abuse counseling and education (MS); teaching and learning (MA, MS); teaching English to speakers of other languages (MS, Ed S); technology management and administration (Ed S); urban studies education (MS); varying exceptionalities (Ed S); vocational, occupational and technical education (Ed D). *Application deadline:* For fall admission, 8/11 priority date for domestic and international students; for winter admission, 12/28 priority date for domestic and international students; for spring admission, 4/22 priority date for domestic and international students. Applications are processed on a rolling basis. *Application fee:* $50. Electronic applications accepted. *Application Contact:* Jennifer Quiñones Nottingham, Dean of Student Affairs, 800-986-3223 Ext. 8624, Fax: 954-262-3911, E-mail: jlquinon@nova.edu. *Provost/Dean,* Dr. H. Wells Singleton, 954-262-8730, Fax: 954-262-3912, E-mail: singlew@nova.edu.

Graduate School of Computer and Information Sciences Students: 241 full-time (76 women), 731 part-time (240 women); includes 338 minority (158 African Americans, 2 American Indian/Alaska Native, 62 Asian Americans or Pacific Islanders, 116 Hispanic Americans), 44 international. Average age 41. *Faculty:* 20 full-time (5 women), 21 part-time/adjunct (3 women). Expenses: Contact institution. *Financial support:* Federal Work-Study, scholarships/grants, and unspecified assistantships available. Support available to part-time students. Financial award application deadline: 5/1. In 2006, 152 master's, 46 doctorates awarded. *Degree program information:* Part-time and evening/weekend programs available. Postbaccalaureate distance learning degree programs offered (no on-campus study). Offers computer information systems (MS, PhD); computer science (MS, PhD); computing technology in education (MS, PhD); information security (MS); information systems (PhD); management information systems (MS). *Application deadline:* Applications are processed on a rolling basis. *Application fee:* $50. *Application Contact:* 954-262-2000, Fax: 954-262-3915, E-mail: scisinfo@nova.edu. *Dean,* Dr. Edward Lieblein.

Graduate School of Humanities and Social Sciences Students: 160 full-time (121 women), 359 part-time (291 women); includes 228 minority (148 African Americans, 4 American Indian/Alaska Native, 8 Asian Americans or Pacific Islanders, 68 Hispanic Americans), 35 international. Average age 37. 250 applicants, 89% accepted, 147 enrolled. *Faculty:* 17 full-time (10 women), 13 part-time/adjunct (4 women). Expenses: Contact institution. *Financial support:* In 2006–07, 393 students received support, including 15 research assistantships (averaging $10,000 per year), 3 teaching assistantships (averaging $1,000 per year); career-related internships or fieldwork, Federal Work-Study, scholarships/grants, unspecified assistantships, and clinical assistantships also available. Financial award application deadline: 4/1; financial award applicants required to submit CSS PROFILE. In 2006, 61 master's, 6 doctorates awarded. *Degree program information:* Part-time and evening/weekend programs available. Postbaccalaureate distance learning degree programs offered (minimal on-campus study). Offers college student affairs (MS); college student personnel administration (Certificate); community solutions and partnership (MS); conflict analysis and resolution (MS, PhD); conflict analysis and resolution studies (Certificate); cross-disciplinary studies (MA); family ministry (Certificate); family studies (Certificate); family systems healthcare (Certificate); family therapy (MS, PhD, Certificate); health care conflict resolution (Certificate); humanities and social sciences (MA, MS, DMFT, PhD, Certificate); marriage and family therapy (DMFT); peace studies (Certificate). *Application deadline:* For fall admission, 7/1 priority date for domestic and international students; for winter admission, 11/1 priority date for domestic and international students; for spring admission, 3/1 priority date for domestic and international students. Applications are processed on a rolling basis. *Application fee:* $50. Electronic applications accepted. *Application Contact:* Marcia Arango, Student Recruitment Coordinator, 954-262-3006, Fax: 954-262-3968, E-mail: marango@nsu.nova.edu. *Dean,* Dr. Honggang Yang, 954-262-3016, Fax: 954-262-3968, E-mail: yangh@nova.edu.

Health Professions Division Students: 2,873 full-time (1,768 women), 601 part-time (436 women); includes 1,358 minority (241 African Americans, 17 American Indian/Alaska Native, 485 Asian Americans or Pacific Islanders, 615 Hispanic Americans), 103 international. Expenses: Contact institution. *Financial support:* Fellowships, teaching assistantships, career-related internships or fieldwork, Federal Work-Study, institutionally sponsored loans, scholarships/grants, and unspecified assistantships available. Support available to part-time students. In 2006, 503 first professional degrees, 213 master's, 69 doctorates awarded. Postbaccalaureate distance learning degree programs offered (minimal on-campus study). Offers health professions (DMD, DO, OD, Pharm D, MBS, MH Sc, MMS, MOT, MPH, MS, MSN, Au D, DHSc, DPT, OTD, PhD, TDPT). *Application deadline:* Applications are processed on a rolling basis. *Application fee:* $50. *Chancellor,* Dr. Frederick Lippman, 954-262-1100 Ext. 1507.

College of Allied Health and Nursing Students: 521 full-time (407 women), 379 part-time (278 women); includes 269 minority (119 African Americans, 6 American Indian/Alaska Native, 46 Asian Americans or Pacific Islanders, 98 Hispanic Americans), 14 international. *Faculty:* 43 full-time (25 women), 8 part-time/adjunct (4 women). Expenses: Contact institution. *Financial support:* Teaching assistantships, institutionally sponsored loans and unspecified assistantships available. In 2006, 152 master's, 69 doctorates awarded. Postbaccalaureate distance learning degree programs offered (minimal on-campus study). Offers allied health and nursing (MH Sc, MMS, MOT, MSN, Au D, DHSc, DPT, OTD, PhD, TDPT); audiology (Au D); health science (MH Sc, DHSc); medical science/physician assistant (MMS); nursing (MSN); occupational therapy (MOT, OTD, PhD); physical therapy (DPT, PhD, TDPT). *Application deadline:* Applications are processed on a rolling basis. *Application fee:* $50. *Application Contact:* Marla Frolinger, Admissions Counselor, 954-262-1100, E-mail: marlaf@nova.edu. *Dean,* Dr. Richard Davis, 954-262-1203, E-mail: redavis@nova.edu.

College of Dental Medicine Students: 437 full-time (189 women), 9 part-time (4 women); includes 129 minority (9 African Americans, 4 American Indian/Alaska Native, 55 Asian Americans or Pacific Islanders, 61 Hispanic Americans), 57 international. Average age 24. 2,285 applicants, 8% accepted, 105 enrolled. *Faculty:* 76 full-time (20 women), 175 part-time/adjunct (36 women). Expenses: Contact institution. *Financial support:* In 2006–07, 372 students received support, including 8 teaching assistantships with full tuition reimbursements available; fellowships with full tuition reimbursements available also available. Financial award application deadline: 4/3; financial award applicants required to submit FAFSA. In 2006, 100 degrees awarded. Offers dental medicine (DMD); dentistry (MS). *Application deadline:* For fall admission, 2/1 for domestic students, 2/15 for international students. Applications are processed on a rolling basis. *Application fee:* $50. *Application Contact:* Su-Ann Zarrett, Dental Admissions Counselor, 954-262-1108, Fax: 954-262-2282, E-mail: zarrett@nsu.nova.edu. *Dean,* Dr. Robert A. Uchin, 954-262-7312, Fax: 954-262-1782, E-mail: ruchin@nova.edu.

College of Medical Sciences Students: 30 full-time (18 women), 1 part-time; includes 16 minority (4 African Americans, 3 Asian Americans or Pacific Islanders, 9 Hispanic Americans). Average age 27. 108 applicants, 23% accepted. *Faculty:* 31 full-time (11 women), 2 part-time/adjunct (1 woman). Expenses: Contact institution. *Financial support:* Applicants required to submit FAFSA. Offers biomedical sciences (MBS). *Application deadline:* For spring admission, 4/15 for domestic students. Applications are processed on a rolling basis. *Application fee:* $50. *Application Contact:* Doreen Palmer, Admissions Counselor, 954-262-1111, Fax: 954-262-2282, E-mail: medinfo@nsu.nova.edu. *Dean,* Dr. Harold E. Laubach, 954-262-1303, Fax: 954-262-1802, E-mail: harold@nsu.nova.edu.

College of Optometry Students: 333 full-time (222 women), 106 part-time (73 women); includes 178 minority (24 African Americans, 98 Asian Americans or Pacific Islanders, 56 Hispanic Americans), 9 international. Average age 24. 673 applicants, 77% accepted, 118 enrolled. *Faculty:* 42 full-time (26 women), 14 part-time/adjunct (7 women). Expenses: Contact institution. *Financial support:* Institutionally sponsored loans and scholarships/grants available. Financial award application deadline: 4/1. In 2006, 75 ODs, 3 master's awarded. Postbaccalaureate distance learning degree programs offered (no on-campus study). Offers clinical vision research (MS); optometry (OD). *Application deadline:* For fall admission, 4/1 for domestic and international students. Applications are processed on a rolling basis. *Application fee:* $50. Electronic applications accepted. *Application Contact:* Fran Franconeri, Admissions Counselor, 954-262-1132, Fax: 954-262-2282. *Dean,* Dr. David Loshin, 954-262-1404, Fax: 954-262-1818.

College of Osteopathic Medicine Students: 888 full-time (461 women), 34 part-time (23 women); includes 316 minority (41 African Americans, 5 American Indian/Alaska Native, 152 Asian Americans or Pacific Islanders, 118 Hispanic Americans), 13 international. 2,059 applicants, 16% accepted, 207 enrolled. *Faculty:* 90 full-time (28 women), 757 part-time/adjunct (132 women). Expenses: Contact institution. *Financial support:* In 2006–07, 598 students received support, including 12 fellowships with partial tuition reimbursements available; research assistantships, teaching assistantships, career-related internships or fieldwork, Federal Work-Study, institutionally sponsored loans, and scholarships/grants also available. Financial award application deadline: 6/1; financial award applicants required to submit FAFSA. In 2006, 155 DOs, 21 master's awarded. Offers osteopathic medicine (DO); public health (MPH). *Application deadline:* For fall admission, 1/15 for domestic students. Applications are processed on a rolling basis. *Application fee:* $50. *Application Contact:* John Chaffin, Associate Director of Admissions and Student Affairs, 954-262-1113. *Dean,* Dr. Anthony J. Silavgni, 954-262-1407, E-mail: silvagni@hpd.nova.edu.

College of Pharmacy Students: 593 full-time (419 women), 61 part-time (48 women); includes 383 minority (41 African Americans, 1 American Indian/Alaska Native, 78 Asian Americans or Pacific Islanders, 263 Hispanic Americans), 4 international. Average age 25. 1,177 applicants, 22% accepted, 189 enrolled. *Faculty:* 52 full-time (32 women), 9 part-time/adjunct (3 women). Expenses: Contact institution. *Financial support:* Career-related internships or fieldwork, Federal Work-Study, institutionally sponsored loans, and scholarships/grants available. Financial award application deadline: 4/15; financial award applicants required to submit FAFSA. In 2006, 173 degrees awarded. Postbaccalaureate distance learning degree programs offered (minimal on-campus study). Offers pharmacy (Pharm D). *Application deadline:* For fall admission, 3/1 for domestic students, 2/1 for international students. Applications are processed on a rolling basis. *Application fee:* $50. Electronic applications accepted. *Application Contact:* Tracy Templin, Admissions Counselor, 954-262-1112, Fax: 954-262-2282, E-mail: dpetracy@nsu.nova.edu. *Dean,* Dr. Andrés Malavé, 954-262-1300, Fax: 954-262-2278.

H. Wayne Huizenga School of Business and Entrepreneurship Students: 361 full-time (200 women), 2,726 part-time (1,631 women); includes 1,756 minority (931 African Americans, 8 American Indian/Alaska Native, 133 Asian Americans or Pacific Islanders, 684 Hispanic Americans), 254 international. Average age 38. Expenses: Contact institution. *Financial support:* Career-related internships or fieldwork, Federal Work-Study, institutionally sponsored loans, and scholarships/grants available. Support available to part-time students. In 2006, 881 master's, 77 doctorates awarded. *Degree program information:* Part-time and evening/weekend programs available. Offers accounting (M Acc); business administration (MBA, DBA); human resources management (MSHRM); international business administration (MIBA, DIBA); leadership (MS); public administration (MPA, DPA); real estate development (MBA); taxation (MT). *Application deadline:* For fall admission, 8/15 for domestic students; for spring admission, 2/10 for domestic students. Applications are processed on a rolling basis. *Application fee:* $50. *Application Contact:* Karen Goldberg, Assistant Director, 954-262-5039, Fax: 954-262-3822, E-mail: karen@nova.edu. *Dean,* Dr. Randolph A. Pohlman, 954-262-5005, E-mail: pohlman@huizenga.nova.edu.

Institute Studies Students: 14 full-time (11 women), 238 part-time (200 women); includes 96 minority (56 African Americans, 3 American Indian/Alaska Native, 6 Asian Americans or Pacific Islanders, 31 Hispanic Americans). 41 applicants, 73% accepted, 30 enrolled. *Faculty:* 41 part-time/adjunct (7 women). Expenses: Contact institution. In 2006, 36 degrees awarded. *Degree program information:* Part-time and evening/weekend programs available. Offers counseling (MS); criminal justice (MS). *Application deadline:* For fall admission, 7/8 for domestic and international students; for winter admission, 1/8 for domestic and international students; for spring admission, 3/8 for domestic and international students. Applications are processed on a rolling basis. *Application fee:* $50. Electronic applications accepted. *Application Contact:* Russell Garner, Information Contact/Administrative Assistant, 954-262-7001, E-mail: cji@nova.edu. *Director,* Dr. Tammy Kushner, 954-262-7001, Fax: 954-937-7005, E-mail: kushner@nova.edu.

Oceanographic Center Students: 12 full-time (9 women), 208 part-time (122 women); includes 12 minority (4 African Americans, 1 American Indian/Alaska Native, 3 Asian Americans or Pacific Islanders, 4 Hispanic Americans), 2 international. Average age 30. 82 applicants, 91% accepted, 49 enrolled. *Faculty:* 15 full-time (1 woman), 5 part-time/adjunct (0 women). Expenses: Contact institution. *Financial support:* In 2006–07, 6 research assistantships (averaging $4,000 per year), 3 teaching assistantships (averaging $3,500 per year) were awarded; career-related internships or fieldwork, Federal Work-Study, scholarships/grants, tuition waivers (partial), and unspecified assistantships also available. Support available to part-time students. Financial award applicants required to submit FAFSA. In 2006, 25 master's, 1 doctorate awarded. *Degree program information:* Part-time and evening/weekend programs available. Offers coastal zone management (MS); marine biology (MS, PhD); marine biology and oceanography (PhD); marine environmental science (MS); oceanography (PhD); physical oceanography (MS). *Application deadline:* Applications are processed on a rolling basis. *Application fee:* $50. *Application Contact:* Dr. Richard Spieler, Director of Academic Programs, 954-262-3600, Fax: 954-262-4020, E-mail: spieler@nova.edu. *Dean,* Dr. Richard Dodge, 954-262-3600, Fax: 954-262-4020, E-mail: dodge@nsu.nova.edu.

Shepard Broad Law Center Students: 966 full-time (506 women), 29 part-time (18 women); includes 265 minority (63 African Americans, 3 American Indian/Alaska Native, 27 Asian Americans or Pacific Islanders, 172 Hispanic Americans), 11 international. Average age 27. 2,821 applicants, 34% accepted, 315 enrolled. *Faculty:* 66 full-time (37 women), 53 part-time/adjunct (17 women). Expenses: Contact institution. *Financial support:* In 2006–07, 58 fellowships were awarded; research assistantships, teaching assistantships, Federal Work-Study, scholarships/grants, tuition waivers (full and partial), unspecified assistantships, and mediation programs also available. Support available to part-time students. Financial award application deadline: 4/15; financial award applicants required to submit FAFSA. In 2006, 261 JDs, 24 master's awarded. *Degree program information:* Part-time and evening/weekend programs available. Postbaccalaureate distance learning degree programs offered (minimal on-campus study). Offers education law (MS); employment law (MS); health law (MS); law (JD). *Application deadline:* For fall admission, 3/1 priority date for domestic students. Applications are processed on a rolling basis. *Application fee:* $50. Electronic applications accepted. *Application Contact:* Beth Hall, Assistant Dean of Admissions, 954-262-6121, Fax: 954-262-3844, E-mail: hallb@nsu.law.nova.edu. *Dean,* Joseph D. Harbaugh, 954-262-6105, Fax: 954-262-3834, E-mail: harbaughj@nsu.law.nova.edu.

NSCAD UNIVERSITY, Halifax, NS B3J 3J6, Canada

General Information Province-supported, coed, comprehensive institution. *Enrollment:* 1,038 graduate, professional, and undergraduate students; 15 full-time matriculated graduate/professional students (5 women). *Enrollment by degree level:* 15 master's. *Graduate faculty:* 42 full-time (18 women). *International tuition:* $12,120 full-time. *Tuition, area resident:* Full-time $5,500; part-time $230 per credit. *Graduate housing:* On-campus housing not available. *Student services:* Campus employment opportunities, career counseling, disabled student services, free psychological counseling, international student services, low-cost health insurance, teacher training, writing training. *Library facilities:* Nova Scotia College of Art and Design Library. *Online resources:* library catalog, access to other libraries' catalogs. *Collection:* 32,000 titles, 235 serial subscriptions.

Computer facilities: 60 computers available on campus for general student use. Internet access, CD-ROM databases are available. *Web address:* http://www.nscad.ca/.

General Application Contact: Terrence Bailey, Director, Admissions, 902-494-8188, Fax: 902-425-2987, E-mail: tbailey@nscad.ns.ca.

GRADUATE UNITS

Program in Fine Arts Students: 25 full-time (12 women). Average age 33. 190 applicants, 5% accepted, 8 enrolled. *Faculty:* 42 full-time (18 women). Expenses: Contact institution. *Financial support:* In 2006–07, 10 students received support, including 10 teaching assistantships (averaging $5,000 per year); scholarships/grants also available. Financial award application deadline: 1/15. In 2006, 10 degrees awarded. Offers craft (MFA); design (M Des); fine and media arts (MFA). *Application deadline:* For fall admission, 1/15 for domestic and international students. *Application fee:* $50. *Application Contact:* Terrence Bailey, Director, Admissions, 902-494-8188, Fax: 902-425-2987, E-mail: tbailey@nscad.ns.ca. *Chair,* Bruce Barber, 902-494-8155, Fax: 902-425-2420, E-mail: bbarber@nscad.ns.ca.

NYACK COLLEGE, Nyack, NY 10960-3698

General Information Independent-religious, coed, comprehensive institution. *Graduate housing:* Rooms and/or apartments available on a first-come, first-served basis to single and married students.

GRADUATE UNITS

Graduate and Professional Programs *Degree program information:* Part-time programs available.

School of Business *Degree program information:* Evening/weekend programs available. Offers accounting (MBA); business administration (MBA).

School of Education *Degree program information:* Part-time and evening/weekend programs available. Offers inclusive education (MS).

OAKLAND CITY UNIVERSITY, Oakland City, IN 47660-1099

General Information Independent-religious, coed, comprehensive institution. *Graduate housing:* Room and/or apartments available to single students; on-campus housing not available to married students. Housing application deadline: 7/1.

GRADUATE UNITS

Chapman Seminary *Degree program information:* Part-time programs available. Offers religious studies (M Div, D Min).

School of Adult and Extended Learning *Degree program information:* Part-time and evening/weekend programs available. Offers management (MS Mgt).

School of Education and Technology Offers educational leadership (Ed D); teaching (MA).

OAKLAND UNIVERSITY, Rochester, MI 48309-4401

General Information State-supported, coed, university. CGS member. *Enrollment:* 17,737 graduate, professional, and undergraduate students; 1,319 full-time matriculated graduate/professional students (892 women), 2,479 part-time matriculated graduate/professional students (1,579 women). *Enrollment by degree level:* 3,043 master's, 451 doctoral, 304 other advanced degrees. *Graduate faculty:* 298 full-time (119 women), 83 part-time/adjunct (42 women). Tuition, state resident: full-time $9,936; part-time $414 per credit. Tuition, nonresident: full-time $17,202; part-time $716 per credit. *Graduate housing:* Rooms and/or apartments available on a first-come, first-served basis to single and married students. *Student services:* Campus employment opportunities, campus safety program, career counseling, child daycare facilities, disabled student services, exercise/wellness program, free psychological counseling, international student services, low-cost health insurance, multicultural affairs office. *Library facilities:* Kresge Library plus 1 other. *Online resources:* library catalog, web page, access to other libraries' catalogs. *Collection:* 2.1 million titles, 11,896 serial subscriptions, 18,767 audiovisual materials. *Research affiliation:* Henry Ford Health Systems (medical physics), Beaumont Hospital Corporation (eye research, nursing).

Computer facilities: A campuswide network can be accessed from student residence rooms and from off campus. Internet access and online class registration are available. *Web address:* http://www.oakland.edu/.

General Application Contact: Christina J. Grabowski, Associate Director of Graduate Study and Lifelong Learning, 248-370-3167, Fax: 248-370-4114, E-mail: grabowsk@oakland.edu.

GRADUATE UNITS

Graduate Study and Lifelong Learning Students: 1,319 full-time (892 women), 2,479 part-time (1,579 women); includes 416 minority (201 African Americans, 16 American Indian/Alaska Native, 151 Asian Americans or Pacific Islanders, 48 Hispanic Americans), 296 international. Average age 32. 1,613 applicants, 76% accepted, 905 enrolled. *Faculty:* 216 full-time (77 women), 83 part-time/adjunct (42 women). Expenses: Contact institution. *Financial support:* Fellowships, research assistantships, teaching assistantships, career-related internships or fieldwork, Federal Work-Study, institutionally sponsored loans, and tuition waivers (full) available. Financial award application deadline: 3/1; financial award applicants required to submit FAFSA. In 2006, 930 master's, 62 doctorates, 159 other advanced degrees awarded. *Degree program information:* Part-time and evening/weekend programs available. *Application deadline:* For fall admission, 5/1 for international students; for winter admission, 9/1 for international students. Applications are processed on a rolling basis. *Application fee:* $35. Electronic applications accepted. *Graduate Admissions,* 248-370-3167, Fax: 248-370-4114, E-mail: gradmail@oakland.edu.

College of Arts and Sciences Students: 169 full-time (91 women), 196 part-time (126 women); includes 41 minority (26 African Americans, 2 American Indian/Alaska Native, 8 Asian Americans or Pacific Islanders, 5 Hispanic Americans), 43 international. Average age 33. 183 applicants, 78% accepted, 96 enrolled. *Faculty:* 67 full-time (14 women), 11 part-time/adjunct (4 women). Expenses: Contact institution. *Financial support:* Fellowships, research assistantships, teaching assistantships, career-related internships or fieldwork, Federal Work-Study, institutionally sponsored loans, and tuition waivers (full) available. Financial award application deadline: 3/1; financial award applicants required to submit FAFSA. In 2006, 70 master's, 7 doctorates, 2 other advanced degrees awarded. *Degree program information:* Part-time and evening/weekend programs available. Offers applied mathematical sciences (PhD); applied statistics (MS); arts and sciences (MA, MM, MPA, MS, PhD, Certificate); biological sciences (MA, MS); cellular biology of aging (MS); chemistry (MS); English (MA); health and environmental chemistry (PhD); history (MA); industrial applied mathematics (MS); liberal studies (MA); linguistics (MA); mathematics (MA); medical physics (PhD); music (MM); music education (PhD); physics (MS); public administration (MPA); statistical methods (Certificate); teaching English as a second language (Certificate). *Application deadline:* For fall admission, 7/15 priority date for domestic students, 5/1 for international students; for winter admission, 12/1 priority date for domestic students, 9/1 for international students; for spring admission, 3/15 priority date for domestic students. Applications are processed on a rolling basis. *Application fee:* $35. Electronic applications accepted. *Graduate Admissions,* 248-370-3167, Fax: 248-370-4114, E-mail: gradmail@oakland.edu.

School of Business Administration Students: 84 full-time (31 women), 478 part-time (156 women); includes 83 minority (17 African Americans, 1 American Indian/Alaska Native, 53 Asian Americans or Pacific Islanders, 12 Hispanic Americans), 60 international. Average age 31. 147 applicants, 90% accepted, 85 enrolled. *Faculty:* 30 full-time (5 women), 9 part-time/adjunct (2 women). Expenses: Contact institution. *Financial support:* Career-related internships or fieldwork, Federal Work-Study, institutionally sponsored loans, and tuition waivers (full) available. Financial award application deadline: 3/1; financial award applicants required to submit FAFSA. In 2006, 194 master's, 1 other advanced degree awarded. *Degree program information:* Part-time and evening/weekend programs available. Offers accounting (M Acc, Certificate); business administration (MBA); economics (Certificate); entrepreneurship (Certificate); finance (Certificate); general management (Certificate); human resource management (Certificate); information technology management (MS); international business (Certificate); management information systems (Certificate); marketing (Certificate); production and operations management (Certificate). *Application deadline:* For fall admission, 8/15 priority date for domestic students, 5/1 priority date for international students; for winter admission, 12/1 priority date for domestic students, 9/1 priority date for international students; for spring admission, 4/15 priority date for domestic students. Applications are processed on a rolling basis. *Application fee:* $35. Electronic applications accepted. *Application Contact:* Donna Free, Coordinator, 248-370-3281. *Dean,* Dr. Jonathan Silberman, 248-370-3286, Fax: 248-370-4974.

School of Education and Human Services Students: 624 full-time (540 women), 1,262 part-time (1,060 women); includes 174 minority (124 African Americans, 9 American Indian/Alaska Native, 21 Asian Americans or Pacific Islanders, 20 Hispanic Americans), 14 international. Average age 34. 634 applicants, 88% accepted, 468 enrolled. *Faculty:* 56 full-time (32 women), 44 part-time/adjunct (31 women). Expenses: Contact institution. *Financial support:* Career-related internships or fieldwork, Federal Work-Study, institutionally sponsored loans, and tuition waivers (full) available. Financial award application deadline: 3/1; financial award applicants required to submit FAFSA. In 2006, 454 master's, 18 doctorates, 140 other advanced degrees awarded. *Degree program information:* Part-time and evening/weekend programs available. Offers advanced microcomputer applications (Certificate); counseling (MA, PhD, Certificate); early childhood education (M Ed, PhD, Certificate); early mathematics education (Certificate); education and human services (M Ed, MA, MAT, MTD, PhD, Certificate, Ed S); education studies (M Ed); educational leadership (M Ed, PhD); higher education (Certificate); higher education administration (Certificate); human resource development (MTD); microcomputer applications (Certificate); reading (Certificate); reading and language arts (MAT); reading education (PhD); reading, language arts and literature (Certificate); school administration (Ed S); secondary education (MAT); special education (M Ed, Certificate). *Application deadline:* Applications are processed on a rolling basis. *Application fee:* $35. Electronic applications accepted. *Dean,* Dr. Mary L. Otto, 248-370-3050, Fax: 248-370-4202, E-mail: otto@oakland.edu.

School of Engineering and Computer Science Students: 236 full-time (62 women), 311 part-time (45 women); includes 67 minority (9 African Americans, 3 American Indian/Alaska Native, 50 Asian Americans or Pacific Islanders, 5 Hispanic Americans), 151 international. Average age 31. 226 applicants, 90% accepted, 123 enrolled. *Faculty:* 32 full-time (5 women), 9 part-time/adjunct (0 women). Expenses: Contact institution. *Financial support:* Federal Work-Study, institutionally sponsored loans, and tuition waivers (full) available. Financial award application deadline: 3/1; financial award applicants required to submit FAFSA. In 2006, 165 master's, 10 doctorates awarded. *Degree program information:* Part-time and evening/weekend programs available. Offers computer science (MS); electrical and computer engineering (MS); embedded systems (MS); engineering and computer science (MS, PhD); engineering management (MS); information systems engineering (MS); mechanical engineering (MS, PhD); software engineering (MS); systems engineering (MS, PhD). *Application deadline:* For fall admission, 8/1 priority date for domestic students, 5/1 priority date for international students; for winter admission, 12/1 priority date for domestic students, 9/1 priority date for international students; for spring admission, 4/1 priority date for domestic students. Applications are processed on a rolling basis. *Application fee:* $35. Electronic applications accepted. *Application Contact:* Information Contact, 248-370-2233. *Dean,* Dr. Pieter A. Frick, 248-370-2217, Fax: 248-370-2217, E-mail: frick@oakland.edu.

School of Health Sciences Students: 138 full-time (111 women), 108 part-time (82 women); includes 23 minority (9 African Americans, 12 Asian Americans or Pacific Islanders, 2 Hispanic Americans), 26 international. Average age 28. 238 applicants, 47% accepted, 81 enrolled. *Faculty:* 14 full-time (8 women), 2 part-time/adjunct (1 woman). Expenses: Contact institution. *Financial support:* Fellowships, Federal Work-Study, institutionally sponsored loans, and tuition waivers (full) available. Financial award application deadline: 3/1; financial award applicants required to submit FAFSA. In 2006, 8 master's, 27 doctorates, 15 other advanced degrees awarded. Offers complimentary medicine and wellness (Certificate); exercise science (MS, Certificate); health sciences (MS, MSPT, DPT, Dr Sc PT, Certificate); neurological rehabilitation (Certificate); orthopedic manual physical therapy (Certificate); orthopedic physical therapy (Certificate); pediatric rehabilitation (Certificate); physical therapy (MSPT, DPT, Dr Sc PT); safety management (MS); teaching and learning for rehabilitation professionals (Certificate). *Application deadline:* For fall admission, 10/15 for domestic and international students. Applications are processed on a rolling basis. *Application fee:* $30. Electronic applications accepted. *Dean,* Dr. Kenneth R. Hightower, 248-370-3562, Fax: 248-370-4227, E-mail: hightower@oakland.edu.

School of Nursing Students: 68 full-time (57 women), 124 part-time (110 women); includes 28 minority (16 African Americans, 1 American Indian/Alaska Native, 7 Asian Americans or Pacific Islanders, 4 Hispanic Americans), 2 international. Average age 37. 185 applicants, 43% accepted, 52 enrolled. *Faculty:* 16 full-time (13 women), 1 part-time/adjunct (0 women). Expenses: Contact institution. *Financial support:* Federal Work-Study, institutionally sponsored loans, and tuition waivers (full) available. Financial award application deadline: 3/1; financial award applicants required to submit FAFSA. In 2006, 39 master's, 1 other advanced degree awarded. *Degree program information:* Part-time and evening/weekend programs available. Offers adult gerontological nurse practitioner (MSN, Certificate); adult health (MSN);

Oakland University (continued)

family nurse practitioner (MSN, Certificate); nurse anesthetist (MSN, Certificate); nursing (MSN, DNP, Certificate); nursing education (MSN, Certificate); nursing practice (DNP). *Application fee:* $35. Electronic applications accepted. *Application Contact:* Mary Bray, Graduate Program Coordinator, 248-370-4482. *Dean,* Dr. Linda Thompson, 248-370-4081, Fax: 248-370-4279.

See Close-Up on page 985.

OBERLIN COLLEGE, Oberlin, OH 44074

General Information Independent, coed, comprehensive institution. *Enrollment:* 2,841 graduate, professional, and undergraduate students; 12 full-time matriculated graduate/professional students (8 women). *Enrollment by degree level:* 12 master's. *Graduate faculty:* 80 full-time, 18 part-time/adjunct. *Graduate housing:* Room and/or apartments available on a first-come, first-served basis to single students; on-campus housing not available to married students. Housing application deadline: 6/15. *Student services:* Campus employment opportunities, campus safety program, career counseling, disabled student services, exercise/wellness program, free psychological counseling, international student services, multicultural affairs office, writing training. *Library facilities:* Mudd Center Library plus 3 others. *Online resources:* library catalog, access to other libraries' catalogs. *Collection:* 1.5 million titles, 4,560 serial subscriptions.

Computer facilities: 340 computers available on campus for general student use. A campuswide network can be accessed from student residence rooms and from off campus. Internet access and online class registration are available. *Web address:* http://www.oberlin.edu/.

General Application Contact: Michael Manderen, Director of Conservatory Admissions, 440-775-8413, Fax: 440-775-6972, E-mail: conservatory.admissions@oberlin.edu.

GRADUATE UNITS

Conservatory of Music Students: 12 full-time (8 women). 4 applicants, 50% accepted, 2 enrolled. Expenses: Contact institution. *Financial support:* Career-related internships or fieldwork, Federal Work-Study, and scholarships/grants available. Financial award applicants required to submit CSS PROFILE or FAFSA. In 2006, 2 degrees awarded. Offers music (MM, MM Ed, MMT). *Application deadline:* For fall admission, 12/1 for domestic and international students. *Application fee:* $100. Electronic applications accepted. *Application Contact:* Michael Manderen, Director of Conservatory Admissions, 440-775-8413, Fax: 440-775-6972, E-mail: conservatory.admissions@oberlin.edu. *Dean,* David Stull, 440-775-8200.

OBLATE SCHOOL OF THEOLOGY, San Antonio, TX 78216-6693

General Information Independent-religious, coed, graduate-only institution. *Enrollment by degree level:* 73 first professional, 43 master's, 43 doctoral. *Graduate faculty:* 18 full-time (4 women), 4 part-time/adjunct (1 woman). *Tuition:* Full-time $10,894; part-time $419 per credit. *Required fees:* $105 per semester. One-time fee: $70 full-time. Tuition and fees vary according to course load and degree level. *Graduate housing:* On-campus housing not available. *Student services:* Campus employment opportunities, international student services, writing training. *Library facilities:* Donald E. O'Shaughessey. *Online resources:* library catalog. *Collection:* 90,000 titles, 360 serial subscriptions.

Computer facilities: 10 computers available on campus for general student use. A campuswide network can be accessed from off campus. Internet access is available. *Web address:* http://www.ost.edu/.

General Application Contact: James Oberhausen, Registrar, 210-341-1366 Ext. 212, Fax: 210-341-4519, E-mail: registrar@ost.edu.

GRADUATE UNITS

Graduate and Professional Programs Students: 92 full-time (9 women), 67 part-time (30 women); includes 60 minority (8 African Americans, 4 Asian Americans or Pacific Islanders, 48 Hispanic Americans), 34 international. Average age 39. 30 applicants, 100% accepted, 30 enrolled. *Faculty:* 18 full-time (4 women), 4 part-time/adjunct (1 woman). Expenses: Contact institution. *Financial support:* Available to part-time students. Application deadline: 8/1; In 2006, 13 M Divs, 7 master's, 5 other advanced degrees awarded. *Degree program information:* Part-time programs available. Offers divinity (M Div); Hispanic ministry (D Min); pastoral ministry (MAP Min); pastoral studies (Certificate); spirituality (MA Sp); supervision (D Min); theology (MA Th). *Application deadline:* For fall admission, 6/15 priority date for domestic and international students; for spring admission, 12/30 for domestic and international students. Applications are processed on a rolling basis. *Application fee:* $40. *Application Contact:* James Oberhausen, Director of Admission/Registrar, 210-341-1366 Ext. 212, Fax: 210-341-4519, E-mail: registrar@ost.edu. *Academic Dean,* Sr. Elaine Brothers, 210-341-1366, Fax: 214-341-4519, E-mail: ebrothers@ost.edu.

OCCIDENTAL COLLEGE, Los Angeles, CA 90041-3314

General Information Independent, coed, comprehensive institution. *Enrollment:* 1,825 graduate, professional, and undergraduate students; 9 full-time matriculated graduate/professional students (8 women), 6 part-time matriculated graduate/professional students (3 women). *Enrollment by degree level:* 15 master's. *Graduate faculty:* 150 full-time (68 women). *Tuition:* Part-time $1,367 per unit. *Required fees:* $445 per semester. *Graduate housing:* On-campus housing not available. *Student services:* Campus employment opportunities, campus safety program, career counseling, child daycare facilities, free psychological counseling, low-cost health insurance, multicultural affairs office, teacher training. *Library facilities:* Mary Norton Clapp Library plus 2 others. *Online resources:* library catalog, web page, access to other libraries' catalogs. *Collection:* 497,161 titles, 903 serial subscriptions.

Computer facilities: 300 computers available on campus for general student use. A campuswide network can be accessed from student residence rooms and from off campus. Internet access and online class registration, e-mail, online grade access, wireless network are available. *Web address:* http://www.oxy.edu/.

General Application Contact: Susan Molik, Academic Services Assistant, Graduate Office, 323-259-2921, Fax: 323-341-4988, E-mail: molik@oxy.edu.

GRADUATE UNITS

Graduate Studies Students: 9 full-time (8 women), 6 part-time (3 women); includes 7 minority (2 Asian Americans or Pacific Islanders, 5 Hispanic Americans). Average age 25. 11 applicants, 100% accepted, 9 enrolled. *Faculty:* 150 full-time (68 women). Expenses: Contact institution. *Financial support:* Fellowships, Federal Work-Study, institutionally sponsored loans, and scholarships/grants available. Support available to part-time students. Financial award application deadline: 3/1; financial award applicants required to submit FAFSA. In 2006, 9 degrees awarded. *Degree program information:* Part-time programs available. Offers biology (MA); elementary education (MAT); English and comparative literary studies (MAT); history (MAT); liberal studies (MAT); life science (MAT); mathematics (MAT); physical science (MAT); secondary education (MAT); social science (MAT); Spanish (MAT). *Application deadline:* For fall admission, 3/1 for domestic and international students; for spring admission, 10/1 for domestic and international students. Applications are processed on a rolling basis. *Application fee:* $50. *Application Contact:* Susan Molik, Academic Services Assistant, Graduate Office, 323-259-2921, Fax: 323-341-4988, E-mail: molik@oxy.edu. *Director,* 323-259-2921.

OGI SCHOOL OF SCIENCE & ENGINEERING AT OREGON HEALTH & SCIENCE UNIVERSITY, Beaverton, OR 97006-8921

General Information State-related, coed, graduate-only institution. *Enrollment by degree level:* 171 master's, 95 doctoral, 27 other advanced degrees. *Graduate faculty:* 43 full-time (11 women), 66 part-time/adjunct (16 women). Tuition, nonresident: full-time $22,760; part-time $625 per credit. *Required fees:* $65 per term. *Graduate housing:* On-campus housing not available. *Student services:* Campus employment opportunities, campus safety program, grant writing training, international student services. *Library facilities:* Samuel L. Diack Memorial Library. *Online resources:* library catalog, web page, access to other libraries' catalogs. *Collection:* 262,853 titles, 1,990 serial subscriptions, 1,323 audiovisual materials. *Research affiliation:* Biospeech dnc (center for spoken language), GeoSyntech (environmental and biomolecular systems), Intel (computer science), Calpine Corporation (coastal land), HemCon Inc. (biomedical), Medical Research Foundation (biomedical spoken language, environmental and biomolecular).

Computer facilities: 60 computers available on campus for general student use. A campuswide network can be accessed from off campus. Internet access and online class registration are available. *Web address:* http://www.ogi.edu/.

General Application Contact: Enrollment Manager, 800-685-2423, Fax: 503-748-1285, E-mail: admissions@admin.ogi.edu.

GRADUATE UNITS

Graduate Studies Students: 76 full-time (27 women), 217 part-time (73 women); includes 112 minority (6 African Americans, 2 American Indian/Alaska Native, 94 Asian Americans or Pacific Islanders, 10 Hispanic Americans), 21 international. Average age 34. 125 applicants, 46% accepted, 27 enrolled. *Faculty:* 39 full-time (10 women), 30 part-time/adjunct (2 women). Expenses: Contact institution. *Financial support:* In 2006–07, 200 students received support, including 75 research assistantships with full and partial tuition reimbursements available (averaging $22,000 per year), 22 teaching assistantships with full and partial tuition reimbursements available (averaging $10,000 per year); fellowships with full and partial tuition reimbursements available, career-related internships or fieldwork, Federal Work-Study, scholarships/grants, and tuition waivers (partial) also available. In 2006, 75 master's, 14 doctorates, 11 other advanced degrees awarded. *Degree program information:* Part-time and evening/weekend programs available. Offers biochemistry and molecular biology (MS, PhD); biomedical engineering (MS, PhD); coastal and land margin research (M Sc, PhD); computer science (PhD); computer science and engineering (MS, PhD); electrical engineering (MS, PhD); environmental health systems (MS); environmental information technology (MS, PhD); environmental science and engineering (MS, PhD); health care management (Certificate); management in science and technology (MS, Certificate). *Application deadline:* Applications are processed on a rolling basis. *Application fee:* $65. Electronic applications accepted. *Application Contact:* Enrollment Manager, 800-685-2423, Fax: 503-748-1285, E-mail: admissions@admin.ogi.edu. *Dean,* Dr. Edward W. Thompson, 503-748-1128, Fax: 503-690-1029, E-mail: thompsed@ohsu.edu.

OGLALA LAKOTA COLLEGE, Kyle, SD 57752-0490

General Information State and locally supported, coed, comprehensive institution. *Graduate housing:* On-campus housing not available.

GRADUATE UNITS

Graduate Studies *Degree program information:* Part-time and evening/weekend programs available. Offers educational administration (MA); Lakota leadership and management (MA).

OGLETHORPE UNIVERSITY, Atlanta, GA 30319-2797

General Information Independent, coed, comprehensive institution. *Graduate housing:* On-campus housing not available.

GRADUATE UNITS

Division of Business Administration Offers business administration (MBA).

Division of Education *Degree program information:* Part-time programs available. Offers early childhood education (MAT).

OHIO COLLEGE OF PODIATRIC MEDICINE, Cleveland, OH 44106-3082

General Information Independent, coed, graduate-only institution. *Enrollment by degree level:* 246 first professional. *Graduate faculty:* 15 full-time (4 women), 12 part-time/adjunct (7 women). *Tuition:* Full-time $24,000; part-time $1,200 per credit hour. *Required fees:* $1,420. *Graduate housing:* On-campus housing not available. *Student services:* Campus employment opportunities, campus safety program, career counseling, disabled student services, free psychological counseling, international student services, low-cost health insurance. *Library facilities:* Medical Library. *Online resources:* library catalog, web page. *Collection:* 17,651 titles, 154 serial subscriptions, 689 audiovisual materials.

Computer facilities: 33 computers available on campus for general student use. A campuswide network can be accessed from off campus. Internet access is available. *Web address:* http://www.ocpm.edu/.

General Application Contact: Lois Lott, Dean of Student Affairs, 216-231-3300 Ext. 8130, Fax: 216-231-1005, E-mail: llott@ocpm.edu.

GRADUATE UNITS

Professional Program Students: 309 full-time (156 women), 1 part-time; includes 85 minority (48 African Americans, 2 American Indian/Alaska Native, 27 Asian Americans or Pacific Islanders, 8 Hispanic Americans), 8 international. Average age 26. 365 applicants, 29% accepted, 95 enrolled. *Faculty:* 15 full-time (4 women), 12 part-time/adjunct (7 women). Expenses: Contact institution. *Financial support:* Career-related internships or fieldwork, Federal Work-Study, institutionally sponsored loans, and scholarships/grants available. Financial award application deadline: 5/30; financial award applicants required to submit FAFSA. In 2006, 45 degrees awarded. Offers podiatric medicine (DPM). *Application deadline:* For fall admission, 6/1 priority date for domestic students. Applications are processed on a rolling basis. *Application fee:* $50. Electronic applications accepted. *Application Contact:* Lois Lott, Dean of Student Affairs, 216-231-3300 Ext. 8130, Fax: 216-231-1005, E-mail: llott@ocpm.edu. *President,* Dr. Thomas Melillo, 216-231-3300.

OHIO DOMINICAN UNIVERSITY, Columbus, OH 43219-2099

General Information Independent-religious, coed, comprehensive institution. *Enrollment:* 3,054 graduate, professional, and undergraduate students; 309 full-time matriculated graduate/professional students (156 women), 150 part-time matriculated graduate/professional students (102 women). *Enrollment by degree level:* 459 master's. *Tuition:* Part-time $450 per credit. *Required fees:* $10 per semester. *Graduate housing:* Room and/or apartments available on a first-come, first-served basis to single students; on-campus housing not available to married students. Typical cost: $6,800 (including board). *Student services:* Campus employment opportunities, campus safety program, career counseling, disabled student services, free psychological counseling, international student services, writing training. *Library facilities:* Spangler Library. *Online resources:* library catalog, web page, access to other libraries' catalogs. *Collection:* 104,739 titles, 511 serial subscriptions, 3,470 audiovisual materials.

Computer facilities: 198 computers available on campus for general student use. A campuswide network can be accessed from student residence rooms and from off campus. Internet access and online class registration are available. *Web address:* http://www.ohiodominican.edu/.

General Application Contact: Jill M. Westerfeld, Graduate Admissions Recruiter, 614-251-4725, Fax: 614-251-4634, E-mail: westerfj@ohiodominican.edu.

GRADUATE UNITS

Graduate Programs Students: 309 full-time (156 women), 150 part-time (102 women); includes 97 minority (85 African Americans, 1 American Indian/Alaska Native, 7 Asian Americans or Pacific Islanders, 4 Hispanic Americans), 11 international. Average age 34. Expenses: Contact institution. *Financial support:* Applicants required to submit FAFSA. In 2006, 147 degrees awarded. *Degree program information:* Part-time and evening/weekend programs available. Offers liberal studies (MA); TESOL (MA). *Application deadline:* For fall admission, 8/15 priority date for domestic and international students; for spring admission, 1/13 priority date for domestic and international students. Applications are processed on a rolling basis. *Application fee:* $25. *Application Contact:* Jill M. Westerfeld, Graduate Admissions Recruiter, 614-251-4725, Fax: 614-251-4634, E-mail: westerfj@ohiodominican.edu. *Vice President for Academic Affairs,* Dr. Mary Todd, 614-251-4731, Fax: 614-251-4772, E-mail: toddm@ohiodominican.edu.

Division of Business Students: 249 full-time (110 women), 33 part-time (14 women); includes 80 minority (71 African Americans, 1 American Indian/Alaska Native, 5 Asian Americans or Pacific Islanders, 3 Hispanic Americans), 10 international. Average age 32. Expenses:

Contact institution. *Financial support:* Applicants required to submit FAFSA. In 2006, 132 degrees awarded. *Degree program information:* Part-time and evening/weekend programs available. Offers business (MBA). Program also offered in Dayton, OH. *Application deadline:* For fall admission, 8/15 priority date for domestic and international students; for spring admission, 1/13 priority date for domestic and international students. Applications are processed on a rolling basis. *Application fee:* $25. *Application Contact:* Jill M. Westerfeld, Graduate Admissions Recruiter, 614-251-4725, Fax: 614-251-4634, E-mail: westerfj@ohiodominican.edu. *Director of Graduate Business Programs,* Antonio Emanuel, 614-251-4559, E-mail: emanuela@ohiodominican.edu.

Division of Education Students: 18 full-time (14 women), 69 part-time (56 women); includes 6 minority (4 African Americans, 1 Asian American or Pacific Islander, 1 Hispanic American). Average age 35. Expenses: Contact institution. *Financial support:* Applicants required to submit FAFSA. In 2006, 9 degrees awarded. *Degree program information:* Part-time and evening/weekend programs available. Offers education (M Ed). *Application deadline:* For fall admission, 8/15 priority date for domestic and international students; for spring admission, 1/13 priority date for domestic and international students. Applications are processed on a rolling basis. *Application fee:* $25. *Application Contact:* Jill M. Westerfeld, Graduate Admissions Recruiter, 614-251-4725, Fax: 614-251-4634, E-mail: westerfj@ohiodominican.edu. *Vice President for Academic Affairs,* Dr. Mary Todd, 614-251-4731, Fax: 614-251-4772, E-mail: toddm@ohiodominican.edu.

Division of Theology, Arts and Ideas Students: 10 full-time (6 women), 18 part-time (12 women); includes 2 minority (both African Americans), 1 international. Average age 41. Expenses: Contact institution. *Financial support:* Applicants required to submit FAFSA. In 2006, 3 degrees awarded. *Degree program information:* Part-time and evening/weekend programs available. Offers theology (MA). *Application deadline:* For fall admission, 8/15 priority date for domestic and international students; for spring admission, 1/13 priority date for domestic and international students. Applications are processed on a rolling basis. *Application fee:* $25. *Application Contact:* Jill M. Westerfeld, Graduate Admissions Recruiter, 614-251-4725, Fax: 614-251-4634, E-mail: westerfj@ohiodominican.edu. *Director, MA in Theology,* Dr. Barbara Finan, 614-251-4721, E-mail: finanb@ohiodominican.edu.

OHIO NORTHERN UNIVERSITY, Ada, OH 45810-1599

General Information Independent-religious, coed, comprehensive institution. *Graduate housing:* Room and/or apartments available on a first-come, first-served basis to single students; on-campus housing not available to married students.

GRADUATE UNITS

Claude W. Pettit College of Law Offers law (JD). Electronic applications accepted.

Raabe College of Pharmacy Postbaccalaureate distance learning degree programs offered (no on-campus study). Offers pharmacy (Pharm D). Students enter the program as undergraduates. Electronic applications accepted.

THE OHIO STATE UNIVERSITY, Columbus, OH 43210

General Information State-supported, coed, university. CGS member. *Enrollment:* 51,818 graduate, professional, and undergraduate students; 10,205 full-time matriculated graduate/professional students (5,320 women), 3,134 part-time matriculated graduate/professional students (2,021 women). *Enrollment by degree level:* 3,256 first professional, 4,904 master's, 5,179 doctoral. *Graduate faculty:* 2,876. Tuition, state resident: full-time $9,438. Tuition, nonresident: full-time $22,791. Tuition and fees vary according to course load, campus/location and program. *Graduate housing:* Rooms and/or apartments available to single students and available on a first-come, first-served basis to married students. *Student services:* Campus safety program, career counseling, child daycare facilities, disabled student services, exercise/wellness program, free psychological counseling, grant writing training, international student services, low-cost health insurance, multicultural affairs office, teacher training, writing training. *Library facilities:* Main Library plus 12 others. *Online resources:* library catalog, web page, access to other libraries' catalogs. *Collection:* 5.9 million titles, 43,086 serial subscriptions, 68,454 audiovisual materials. *Research affiliation:* Children's Hospital (pediatrics), Transportation Research Center, Midwest Universities Consortium for International Activities, Science and Technology Campus, Ohio Learning Network (education).

Computer facilities: 800 computers available on campus for general student use. A campuswide network can be accessed from student residence rooms and from off campus. Internet access and online class registration are available. *Web address:* http://www.osu.edu/.

General Application Contact: Information Contact, 614-292-9444, Fax: 614-292-3895, E-mail: domestic.grad@osu.edu.

GRADUATE UNITS

College of Dentistry Students: 506 full-time (179 women), 3 part-time; includes 67 minority (14 African Americans, 1 American Indian/Alaska Native, 47 Asian Americans or Pacific Islanders, 5 Hispanic Americans), 20 international. Average age 26. *Faculty:* 148 full-time (51 women), 150 part-time/adjunct (30 women). Expenses: Contact institution. *Financial support:* In 2006–07, 7 fellowships with tuition reimbursements, 13 research assistantships with tuition reimbursements (averaging $11,000 per year), 78 teaching assistantships with tuition reimbursements (averaging $12,000 per year) were awarded; Federal Work-Study and institutionally sponsored loans also available. Financial award application deadline: 3/1. In 2006, 99 first professional degrees, 25 master's, 4 doctorates awarded. Offers dentistry (DDS, MS, PhD); oral biology (PhD). *Application deadline:* Applications are processed on a rolling basis. Electronic applications accepted. *Application Contact:* Graduate Admissions, 614-292-9444, Fax: 614-292-3985, E-mail: domestic.grad@osu.edu. *Interim Dean,* Dr. Carole Anderson, 614-292-9755, Fax: 614-292-4619, E-mail: anderson.32@osu.edu.

College of Medicine Students: 1,156 full-time (561 women), 140 part-time (106 women); includes 298 minority (70 African Americans, 12 American Indian/Alaska Native, 183 Asian Americans or Pacific Islanders, 33 Hispanic Americans), 36 international. Average age 25. *Faculty:* 999 full-time (254 women), 500 part-time/adjunct (132 women). Expenses: Contact institution. *Financial support:* In 2006–07, 141 students received support; fellowships, research assistantships, teaching assistantships, Federal Work-Study, institutionally sponsored loans, and scholarships/grants available. Support available to part-time students. Financial award application deadline: 3/1; financial award applicants required to submit FAFSA. In 2006, 202 MDs, 93 master's, 12 doctorates awarded. Offers anatomy (MS, PhD); biomedical science (MD, MS, PhD); experimental pathobiology (MS); immunology (PhD); medical genetics (PhD); medical science (PhD); medicine (MD, MOT, MPT, MS, PhD); molecular virology (PhD); molecular virology, immunology and medical genetics (MS, PhD); neuroscience (PhD); pathology assistant (MS); pharmacology (PhD). *Application deadline:* For fall admission, 8/15 priority date for domestic students, 7/1 priority date for international students; for winter admission, 12/1 priority date for domestic students, 11/1 priority date for international students; for spring admission, 3/1 priority date for domestic students, 2/1 priority date for international students. Applications are processed on a rolling basis. Electronic applications accepted. *Application Contact:* 614-292-9444, Fax: 614-292-3895, E-mail: domestic.grad@osu.edu. *Dean,* Dr. Wiley W. Souba, 614-292-2600, Fax: 614-292-1301, E-mail: chip.souba@osumc.edu.

School of Allied Medical Professions Students: 162 full-time (145 women), 126 part-time (101 women); includes 18 minority (7 African Americans, 1 American Indian/Alaska Native, 7 Asian Americans or Pacific Islanders, 3 Hispanic Americans), 10 international. Average age 27. 27 applicants, 74% accepted, 7 enrolled. *Faculty:* 25 full-time (14 women), 2 part-time/adjunct (1 woman). Expenses: Contact institution. *Financial support:* In 2006–07, 14 students received support; fellowships, research assistantships with full tuition reimbursements available, teaching assistantships with full tuition reimbursements available, traineeships and administrative assistantships available. Financial award application deadline:3/1. In 2006, 82 degrees awarded. *Degree program information:* Part-time programs available. Offers allied medicine (MS); circulation technology (MS); occupational therapy (MOT); physical therapy (MPT). *Application deadline:* For fall admission, 8/15 priority date for domestic students, 7/1 priority date for international students; for winter admission, 12/1 priority date for domestic students, 11/1 priority date for international students; for spring admission, 3/1 priority date for domestic students, 2/1 priority date for international students. Applications are processed on a rolling basis. *Application fee:* $40 ($50 for international students). Electronic applications accepted. *Application Contact:* 614-292-9444, Fax: 614-292-3895, E-mail: domestic.grad@osu.edu. *Director,* Deborah S. Larsen, 614-292-5921, Fax: 614-292-0210, E-mail: nichols.3@osu.edu.

College of Optometry Students: 260 full-time (157 women), 5 part-time (4 women); includes 33 minority (8 African Americans, 18 Asian Americans or Pacific Islanders, 7 Hispanic Americans), 6 international. Average age 25. Expenses: Contact institution. *Financial support:* Research assistantships with full tuition reimbursements, teaching assistantships with full tuition reimbursements, Federal Work-Study, institutionally sponsored loans, and scholarships/grants available. Financial award application deadline: 2/1; financial award applicants required to submit FAFSA. Offers optometry (OD, MS, PhD); vision science (MS, PhD). *Application deadline:* For fall admission, 8/15 priority date for domestic students, 7/1 priority date for international students; for winter admission, 12/1 priority date for domestic students, 11/1 priority date for international students; for spring admission, 3/1 priority date for domestic students, 2/1 priority date for international students. Applications are processed on a rolling basis. *Application fee:* $40 ($50 for international students). Electronic applications accepted. *Application Contact:* 614-292-9444, Fax: 614-292-3895, E-mail: domestic.grad@osu.edu. *Dean,* Dr. Melvin D. Shipp, 614-292-3246, Fax: 614-292-7493, E-mail: shipp.25@osu.edu.

College of Pharmacy Students: 546 full-time (370 women), 5 part-time (1 woman); includes 73 minority (20 African Americans, 48 Asian Americans or Pacific Islanders, 5 Hispanic Americans), 64 international. Average age 26. 1,165 applicants, 15% accepted, 142 enrolled. *Faculty:* 42 full-time (6 women), 1 part-time/adjunct (0 women). Expenses: Contact institution. *Financial support:* In 2006–07, 174 students received support, including 6 fellowships with full tuition reimbursements available (averaging $22,500 per year), 48 research assistantships with full tuition reimbursements available (averaging $30,000 per year), 30 teaching assistantships with full tuition reimbursements available (averaging $19,800 per year); career-related internships or fieldwork, Federal Work-Study, institutionally sponsored loans, scholarships/grants, and traineeships also available. In 2006, 111 Pharm Ds, 11 master's, 15 doctorates awarded. *Degree program information:* Part-time programs available. Offers health-system pharmacy administration (MS); medicinal chemistry and pharmacognosy (MS, PhD); pharmaceutical administration (MS, PhD); pharmaceutics (MS, PhD); pharmacology (MS, PhD); pharmacy (Pharm D, MS, PhD); pharmacy practice and administration (MS, PhD). *Application deadline:* For fall admission, 1/1 priority date for domestic students. *Application fee:* $40 ($50 for international students). Electronic applications accepted. *Application Contact:* Kathy I. Brooks, Graduate Program Coordinator, 614-292-6822, Fax: 614-292-2588, E-mail: gadmbrks@dendrite.pharmacy.ohio-state.edu. *Dean,* Dr. Robert W. Brueggemeier, 614-292-5231, Fax: 614-292-2435, E-mail: brueggemeier.1@osu.edu.

School of Public Health Students: 128 full-time (89 women), 95 part-time (65 women); includes 42 minority (19 African Americans, 19 Asian Americans or Pacific Islanders, 4 Hispanic Americans), 14 international. 242 applicants, 71% accepted, 33 enrolled. *Faculty:* 28 full-time (13 women), 9 part-time/adjunct (2 women). Expenses: Contact institution. *Financial support:* In 2006–07, 12 fellowships with full tuition reimbursements (averaging $14,400 per year), 21 research assistantships with full tuition reimbursements (averaging $12,000 per year) were awarded; Federal Work-Study, institutionally sponsored loans, traineeships, and unspecified assistantships also available. Support available to part-time students. Financial award application deadline: 7/1. In 2006, 65 master's, 5 doctorates awarded. *Degree program information:* Part-time and evening/weekend programs available. Offers public health (MHA, MPH, MS, PhD). *Application deadline:* For fall admission, 8/15 priority date for domestic students, 7/1 priority date for international students; for winter admission, 12/1 priority date for domestic students, 11/1 priority date for international students; for spring admission, 3/1 priority date for domestic students, 2/1 priority date for international students. Applications are processed on a rolling basis. *Application fee:* $40 ($50 for international students). Electronic applications accepted. *Application Contact:* 614-292-9444, Fax: 614-292-3895, E-mail: domestic.grad@osu.edu. *Graduate Studies Committee Chair,* Robert J. Caswell, 614-293-4014, Fax: 614-293-3937, E-mail: caswell.1@osu.edu.

College of Veterinary Medicine Students: 651 full-time (503 women), 26 part-time (13 women); includes 35 minority (7 African Americans, 2 American Indian/Alaska Native, 19 Asian Americans or Pacific Islanders, 7 Hispanic Americans), 47 international. Average age 26. *Faculty:* 133. Expenses: Contact institution. In 2006, 133 DVMs, 23 master's, 13 doctorates awarded. Offers anatomy and cellular biology (MS, PhD); pathobiology (MS, PhD); pharmacology (MS, PhD); toxicology (MS, PhD); veterinary clinical sciences (MS, PhD); veterinary medicine (DVM, MS, PhD); veterinary physiology (MS, PhD); veterinary preventive medicine (MS, PhD). *Application deadline:* For fall admission, 8/15 priority date for domestic students, 7/1 priority date for international students; for winter admission, 12/1 priority date for domestic students, 11/1 priority date for international students; for spring admission, 3/1 priority date for domestic students, 2/1 priority date for international students. Applications are processed on a rolling basis. Electronic applications accepted. *Application Contact:* 614-292-9444, Fax: 614-292-3895, E-mail: domestic.grad@osu.edu. *Dean,* Thomas Rosol, 614-688-8749, Fax: 614-292-3544, E-mail: rosol.1@osu.edu.

Graduate School Average age 30. *Faculty:* 2,876. Expenses: Contact institution. *Financial support:* Fellowships, research assistantships, teaching assistantships, career-related internships or fieldwork, Federal Work-Study, institutionally sponsored loans, and unspecified assistantships available. Support available to part-time students. *Degree program information:* Part-time and evening/weekend programs available. Offers textiles and clothing (MS, PhD). *Application deadline:* For fall admission, 8/12 priority date for domestic students, 7/1 priority date for international students; for winter admission, 12/1 priority date for domestic students, 11/1 priority date for international students; for spring admission, 3/1 priority date for domestic students, 2/1 priority date for international students. Applications are processed on a rolling basis. *Application fee:* $40 ($50 for international students). Electronic applications accepted. *Application Contact:* 614-292-9444, Fax: 614-292-3895, E-mail: domestic.grad@osu.edu. *Dean,* Peter S. Osmer, 614-292-6031, Fax: 614-292-3656, E-mail: osmer.1@osu.edu.

College of Biological Sciences Students: 285 full-time (151 women), 167 part-time (91 women); includes 27 minority (8 African Americans, 1 American Indian/Alaska Native, 9 Asian Americans or Pacific Islanders, 9 Hispanic Americans), 208 international. Average age 28. 299 applicants, 58% accepted, 63 enrolled. *Faculty:* 429. Expenses: Contact institution. *Financial support:* Fellowships, research assistantships, teaching assistantships, career-related internships or fieldwork, Federal Work-Study, and institutionally sponsored loans available. Support available to part-time students. In 2006, 53 master's, 39 doctorates awarded. *Degree program information:* Part-time programs available. Offers biochemistry (MS); biological sciences (MS, PhD); biophysics (MS, PhD); cell and developmental biology (MS, PhD); entomology (MS, PhD); environmental science (MS, PhD); evolution, ecology, and organismal biology (MS, PhD); genetics (MS, PhD); microbiology (MS, PhD); molecular biology (MS, PhD); molecular, cellular and developmental biology (MS, PhD); plant biology (MS, PhD). *Application deadline:* For fall admission, 8/15 priority date for domestic students, 7/1 priority date for international students; for winter admission, 12/1 priority date for domestic students, 11/1 priority date for international students; for spring admission, 3/1 priority date for domestic students, 2/1 priority date for international students. Applications are processed on a rolling basis. *Application fee:* $40 ($50 for international students). Electronic applications accepted. *Application Contact:* 614-292-9444, Fax: 614-292-3985, E-mail: domestic.grad@osu.edu. *Dean,* Dr. Joan M. Herbers, 614-292-1627, Fax: 614-292-1538, E-mail: herbers.4@osu.edu.

College of Education and Human Ecology Students: 829 full-time (612 women), 844 part-time (645 women); includes 222 minority (162 African Americans, 5 American Indian/Alaska Native, 32 Asian Americans or Pacific Islanders, 23 Hispanic Americans), 197 international. Average age 33. 868 applicants, 59% accepted, 187 enrolled. *Faculty:* 178. Expenses: Contact institution. *Financial support:* Fellowships with tuition reimbursements, research assistantships with tuition reimbursements, teaching assistantships with tuition reimbursements, career-related internships or fieldwork, Federal Work-Study, institutionally sponsored loans, scholarships/grants, traineeships, health care benefits, and unspecified assistantships available. Support available to part-time students. In 2006, 735 master's, 112 doctorates awarded. Offers education and human ecology (M Ed, MA, MS, PhD); educational policy and leadership (M Ed, MA, PhD); family and consumer sciences educa-

The Ohio State University (continued)

tion (M Ed, MS); family resource management (MS, PhD); food service management (MS, PhD); foods (MS, PhD); higher education and student affairs (MA); hospitality management (MS, PhD); human development and family science (M Ed, MS, PhD); nutrition (MS, PhD); physical activity and educational services (M Ed, MA, PhD); teaching and learning (M Ed, MA, PhD). *Application deadline:* For fall admission, 8/15 priority date for domestic students, 7/1 priority date for international students; for winter admission, 12/1 priority date for domestic students, 11/1 priority date for international students; for spring admission, 3/1 priority date for domestic students, 2/1 priority date for international students. Applications are processed on a rolling basis. *Application fee:* $40 ($50 for international students). Electronic applications accepted. *Application Contact:* 614-292-9444, Fax: 614-292-3895, E-mail: domestic.grad@osu.edu. *Dean,* Dr. David Andrews, 614-292-2801, Fax: 614-292-2581, E-mail: andrews.128@osu.edu.

College of Engineering Students: 1,154 full-time (273 women), 212 part-time (47 women); includes 89 minority (24 African Americans, 3 American Indian/Alaska Native, 48 Asian Americans or Pacific Islanders, 14 Hispanic Americans), 700 international. Average age 27. 1,992 applicants, 38% accepted, 232 enrolled. *Faculty:* 475. Expenses: Contact institution. *Financial support:* Fellowships, research assistantships, teaching assistantships, career-related internships or fieldwork, Federal Work-Study, institutionally sponsored loans, and unspecified assistantships available. Support available to part-time students. In 2006, 327 master's, 137 doctorates awarded. *Degree program information:* Part-time and evening/weekend programs available. Offers aeronautical and astronautical engineering (MS, PhD); architecture (M Arch, M Land Arch, MCRP, PhD); biomedical engineering (MS, PhD); chemical engineering (MS, PhD); city and regional planning (MCRP, PhD); civil engineering (MS, PhD); computer and information science (MS, PhD); electrical engineering (MS, PhD); engineering (M Arch, M Land Arch, MCRP, MS, MWE, PhD); engineering mechanics (MS, PhD); geodetic science and surveying (MS, PhD); industrial and systems engineering (MS, PhD); landscape architecture (M Land Arch); materials science and engineering (MS, PhD); mechanical engineering (MS, PhD); nuclear engineering (MS, PhD); welding engineering (MS, MWE, PhD). *Application deadline:* For fall admission, 8/15 priority date for domestic students, 7/1 priority date for international students; for winter admission, 12/1 priority date for domestic students, 11/1 priority date for international students; for spring admission, 3/1 priority date for domestic students, 2/1 priority date for international students. Applications are processed on a rolling basis. *Application fee:* $40 ($50 for international students). Electronic applications accepted. *Application Contact:* 614-292-9444, Fax: 614-292-3895, E-mail: domestic.grad@osu.edu. *Dean,* Dr. William A. Baeslack, 614-292-2836, Fax: 614-292-9379, E-mail: baeslack.1@osu.edu.

College of Food, Agricultural, and Environmental Sciences Students: 337 full-time (171 women), 67 part-time (43 women); includes 30 minority (12 African Americans, 1 American Indian/Alaska Native, 5 Asian Americans or Pacific Islanders, 12 Hispanic Americans), 162 international. Average age 30. 225 applicants, 73% accepted. *Faculty:* 313. Expenses: Contact institution. *Financial support:* Fellowships, research assistantships, teaching assistantships, career-related internships or fieldwork, Federal Work-Study, institutionally sponsored loans, and unspecified assistantships available. Support available to part-time students. In 2006, 66 master's, 54 doctorates awarded. *Degree program information:* Part-time programs available. Offers agricultural economics and rural sociology (MS, PhD); animal sciences (MS, PhD); environment and natural resources (MS, PhD); food science and nutrition (MS, PhD); food, agricultural, and biological engineering (MS, PhD); food, agricultural, and environmental sciences (M Ed, MS, PhD); horticulture and crop science (MS, PhD); human and community resource development (M Ed, MS, PhD); human dimensions in natural resources (MS, PhD); natural resources (MS, PhD); plant pathology (MS, PhD); rural sociology (MS, PhD); soil science (MS, PhD); vocational education (PhD). *Application deadline:* For fall admission, 8/15 priority date for domestic students, 7/1 priority date for international students; for winter admission, 12/1 priority date for domestic students, 11/1 priority date for international students; for spring admission, 3/1 priority date for domestic students, 2/1 priority date for international students. Applications are processed on a rolling basis. *Application fee:* $40 ($50 for international students). Electronic applications accepted. *Application Contact:* Graduate Admissions, 614-292-9444, Fax: 614-292-3895, E-mail: domestic.grad@osu.edu. *Dean,* Dr. Bobby D. Moser, 614-292-6891, Fax: 614-292-1218, E-mail: moser.2@osu.edu.

College of Humanities Students: 636 full-time (359 women), 66 part-time (43 women); includes 80 minority (42 African Americans, 2 American Indian/Alaska Native, 13 Asian Americans or Pacific Islanders, 23 Hispanic Americans), 139 international. Average age 30. 970 applicants, 34% accepted, 144 enrolled. *Faculty:* 502. Expenses: Contact institution. *Financial support:* Fellowships, research assistantships, teaching assistantships, career-related internships or fieldwork, Federal Work-Study, institutionally sponsored loans, and unspecified assistantships available. Support available to part-time students. In 2006, 151 master's, 51 doctorates awarded. *Degree program information:* Part-time programs available. Offers African-American and African studies (MA); classics (MA); comparative studies (MA, PhD); East Asian languages and literatures (MA, PhD); English (MA, MFA, PhD); French (MA, PhD); Germanic languages and literatures (MA, PhD); Greek and Latin (MA, PhD); history (MA, PhD); humanities (MA, MFA, PhD); Italian (MA); Japanese (MA, PhD); linguistics (MA, PhD); Near Eastern languages and cultures (MA, PhD); philosophy (MA, PhD); Slavic and East European languages and literatures (MA, PhD); Slavic and East European studies (MA); Spanish and Portuguese (MA, PhD); women's studies (MA, PhD). *Application deadline:* For fall admission, 8/15 priority date for domestic students, 11/1 priority date for international students; for winter admission, 12/1 priority date for domestic students, 7/1 priority date for international students; for spring admission, 3/1 priority date for domestic students, 2/1 priority date for international students. Applications are processed on a rolling basis. *Application fee:* $40 ($50 for international students). Electronic applications accepted. *Application Contact:* 614-292-9444, Fax: 614-292-3895, E-mail: domestic.grad@osu.edu. *Dean,* Dr. John W. Roberts, 614-292-1882, Fax: 614-292-8666, E-mail: roberts.420@osu.edu.

College of Mathematical and Physical Sciences Students: 644 full-time (201 women), 81 part-time (28 women); includes 29 minority (5 African Americans, 2 American Indian/Alaska Native, 11 Asian Americans or Pacific Islanders, 11 Hispanic Americans), 312 international. Average age 27. 472 applicants, 61% accepted, 92 enrolled. *Faculty:* 339. Expenses: Contact institution. *Financial support:* Fellowships, research assistantships, teaching assistantships, Federal Work-Study, institutionally sponsored loans, and unspecified assistantships available. Support available to part-time students. In 2006, 105 master's, 83 doctorates awarded. *Degree program information:* Part-time programs available. Offers astronomy (MS, PhD); biostatistics (PhD); chemical physics (MS, PhD); chemistry (MS, PhD); geological sciences (MS, PhD); mathematical and physical sciences (M Appl Stat, MA, MS, PhD); mathematics (MA, MS, PhD); physics (MS, PhD); statistics (M Appl Stat, MS, PhD). *Application deadline:* For fall admission, 8/15 priority date for domestic students, 7/1 priority date for international students; for winter admission, 12/1 priority date for domestic students, 11/1 priority date for international students; for spring admission, 3/1 priority date for domestic students, 2/1 priority date for international students. Applications are processed on a rolling basis. *Application fee:* $40 ($50 for international students). Electronic applications accepted. *Application Contact:* 614-292-9444, Fax: 614-292-3895, E-mail: domestic.grad@osu.edu. *Dean,* Dr. Richard R. Freeman, 614-292-8908, Fax: 614-292-3639, E-mail: freeman.261@osu.edu.

College of Nursing Students: 174 full-time (160 women), 103 part-time (96 women); includes 34 minority (19 African Americans, 5 American Indian/Alaska Native, 8 Asian Americans or Pacific Islanders, 2 Hispanic Americans), 4 international. Average age 32. 203 applicants, 54% accepted, 18 enrolled. *Faculty:* 31. Expenses: Contact institution. *Financial support:* Fellowships, research assistantships, teaching assistantships, Federal Work-Study, institutionally sponsored loans, and unspecified assistantships available. Support available to part-time students. In 2006, 69 master's, 2 doctorates awarded. *Degree program information:* Part-time programs available. Offers nursing (MS, PhD). *Application deadline:* For fall admission, 8/15 priority date for domestic students, 7/1 priority date for international students; for winter admission, 12/1 priority date for domestic students, 11/1 priority date for international students; for spring admission, 3/1 priority date for domestic students, 2/1 priority date for international students. Applications are processed on a rolling basis. *Application fee:* $40 ($50 for international students). Electronic applications accepted. *Application Contact:* 614-292-9444, Fax: 614-292-3895, E-mail: domestic.grad@osu.edu. *Dean,* Dr. Elizabeth R. Lenz, 614-292-8900, Fax: 614-292-4535, E-mail: lenz.23@osu.edu.

College of Social and Behavioral Sciences Students: 678 full-time (378 women), 65 part-time (40 women); includes 85 minority (28 African Americans, 2 American Indian/Alaska Native, 29 Asian Americans or Pacific Islanders, 26 Hispanic Americans), 182 international. Average age 28. 1,404 applicants, 30% accepted, 126 enrolled. *Faculty:* 384. Expenses: Contact institution. *Financial support:* Fellowships, research assistantships, teaching assistantships, Federal Work-Study, institutionally sponsored loans, and unspecified assistantships available. Support available to part-time students. In 2006, 162 master's, 84 doctorates awarded. *Degree program information:* Part-time programs available. Offers anthropology (MA, PhD); atmospheric sciences (MS, PhD); behavioral neuroscience (PhD); clinical psychology (PhD); cognitive psychology (PhD); communication (MA, PhD); developmental psychology (PhD); economics (MA, PhD); geography (MA, PhD); mental retardation and developmental disabilities (PhD); political science (MA, PhD); psychology (MA); quantitative psychology (PhD); social and behavioral science (MA, MS, Au D, PhD); social and behavioral sciences (MA, MS, Au D, PhD); social psychology (PhD); sociology (MA, PhD); speech and hearing science (MA, Au D, PhD). *Application deadline:* For fall admission, 8/15 priority date for domestic students, 7/1 priority date for international students; for winter admission, 12/1 priority date for domestic students, 11/1 priority date for international students; for spring admission, 3/1 priority date for domestic students, 2/1 priority date for international students. Applications are processed on a rolling basis. *Application fee:* $40 ($50 for international students). Electronic applications accepted. *Application Contact:* 614-292-9444, Fax: 614-292-3895, E-mail: domestic.grad@osu.edu. *Dean,* Dr. Paul A. Beck, 614-292-8448, Fax: 614-292-9530, E-mail: beck.9@osu.edu.

College of Social Work Students: 262 full-time (229 women), 188 part-time (158 women); includes 75 minority (59 African Americans, 3 American Indian/Alaska Native, 8 Asian Americans or Pacific Islanders, 5 Hispanic Americans), 9 international. Average age 31. 271 applicants, 86% accepted, 79 enrolled. *Faculty:* 31. Expenses: Contact institution. *Financial support:* Fellowships, research assistantships, teaching assistantships, Federal Work-Study, institutionally sponsored loans, and unspecified assistantships available. Support available to part-time students. In 2006, 170 master's, 2 doctorates awarded. *Degree program information:* Part-time programs available. Offers social work (MSW, PhD). *Application deadline:* For fall admission, 8/15 priority date for domestic students, 7/1 priority date for international students; for winter admission, 12/1 priority date for domestic students, 11/1 priority date for international students; for spring admission, 3/1 priority date for domestic students, 2/1 priority date for international students. Applications are processed on a rolling basis. *Application fee:* $40 ($50 for international students). Electronic applications accepted. *Application Contact:* 614-292-9444, Fax: 614-292-3895, E-mail: domestic.grad@osu.edu. *Dean,* William Meezan, 614-292-5300, Fax: 614-292-6940, E-mail: meezan.1@osu.edu.

College of the Arts Students: 396 full-time (257 women), 153 part-time (113 women); includes 57 minority (30 African Americans, 5 American Indian/Alaska Native, 11 Asian Americans or Pacific Islanders, 11 Hispanic Americans), 87 international. Average age 31. 538 applicants, 52% accepted, 112 enrolled. *Faculty:* 193. Expenses: Contact institution. *Financial support:* Fellowships, research assistantships, teaching assistantships, career-related internships or fieldwork, Federal Work-Study, institutionally sponsored loans, and unspecified assistantships available. Support available to part-time students. Financial award applicants required to submit FAFSA. In 2006, 140 master's, 21 doctorates awarded. *Degree program information:* Part-time programs available. Offers art (MFA); art education (MA, PhD); arts (M Mus, MA, MFA, PhD); arts policy and administration (MA); dance (MA, MFA, PhD); history of art (MA, PhD); industrial, interior, and visual communication design (MA, MFA); music (M Mus, MA, PhD); theatre (MA, MFA, PhD). *Application deadline:* For fall admission, 8/15 priority date for domestic students, 7/1 priority date for international students; for winter admission, 12/1 priority date for domestic students, 11/1 priority date for international students; for spring admission, 3/1 priority date for domestic students, 2/1 priority date for international students. Applications are processed on a rolling basis. *Application fee:* $40 ($50 for international students). Electronic applications accepted. *Application Contact:* 614-292-9444, Fax: 614-292-3895, E-mail: domestic.grad@osu.edu. *Dean,* Karen A. Bell, 614-292-5171, Fax: 614-292-8623, E-mail: bell.1@osu.edu.

Max M. Fisher College of Business Students: 586 full-time (221 women), 271 part-time (100 women); includes 130 minority (25 African Americans, 4 American Indian/Alaska Native, 83 Asian Americans or Pacific Islanders, 18 Hispanic Americans), 207 international. Average age 29. 923 applicants, 58% accepted, 223 enrolled. *Faculty:* 128. Expenses: Contact institution. *Financial support:* Fellowships, research assistantships, teaching assistantships, career-related internships or fieldwork, Federal Work-Study, institutionally sponsored loans, and unspecified assistantships available. Support available to part-time students. In 2006, 434 master's, 9 doctorates awarded. *Degree program information:* Part-time programs available. Offers accounting and management information systems (M Acc, MA, PhD); business (M Acc, MA, MBA, MBLE, MLHR, PhD); business administration (MA, MBA, PhD); business logistics engineering (MBLE); finance (MA, PhD); labor and human resources (MLHR, PhD). *Application deadline:* For fall admission, 8/15 priority date for domestic students, 7/1 priority date for international students; for winter admission, 12/1 priority date for domestic students, 11/1 priority date for international students; for spring admission, 3/1 priority date for domestic students, 2/1 priority date for international students. Applications are processed on a rolling basis. *Application fee:* $40 ($50 for international students). Electronic applications accepted. *Application Contact:* Dr. Karen Wruck, Associate Dean for Graduate Programs, 614-688-5443, E-mail: wruck_1@fisher.osu.edu. *Acting Dean,* Dr. Steve Mangum, 614-292-2668, E-mail: mangum_1@fisher.osu.edu.

John Glenn School of Public Affairs Students: 50 full-time (22 women), 48 part-time (25 women); includes 15 minority (10 African Americans, 4 Asian Americans or Pacific Islanders, 1 Hispanic American), 11 international. Average age 32. 105 applicants, 41% accepted, 10 enrolled. *Faculty:* 14. Expenses: Contact institution. *Financial support:* Fellowships, research assistantships, teaching assistantships, Federal Work-Study, institutionally sponsored loans, and unspecified assistantships available. Support available to part-time students. In 2006, 32 master's, 2 doctorates awarded. *Degree program information:* Part-time programs available. Offers public affairs (MA, MPA, PhD). *Application deadline:* For fall admission, 8/15 priority date for domestic students, 7/1 priority date for international students; for winter admission, 12/1 priority date for domestic students, 11/1 priority date for international students; for spring admission, 3/1 priority date for domestic students, 2/1 priority date for international students. Applications are processed on a rolling basis. *Application fee:* $40 ($50 for international students). Electronic applications accepted. *Application Contact:* 614-292-9444, Fax: 614-292-3895, E-mail: domestic.grad@osu.edu. *Graduate Studies Committee Chair,* Mary K. Marvel, 614-292-8696, Fax: 614-292-4868, E-mail: marvel.1@osu.edu.

Moritz College of Law Students: 672 full-time (282 women), 6 part-time (3 women); includes 133 minority (56 African Americans, 2 American Indian/Alaska Native, 58 Asian Americans or Pacific Islanders, 17 Hispanic Americans), 11 international. Average age 25. *Faculty:* 43 full-time (12 women). Expenses: Contact institution. *Financial support:* In 2006–07, 550 students received support. Career-related internships or fieldwork, Federal Work-Study, institutionally sponsored loans, and scholarships/grants available. Financial award application deadline: 3/1; financial award applicants required to submit FAFSA. In 2006, 258 degrees awarded. Offers law (JD, LL M, MSL). *Application deadline:* For fall admission, 3/1 priority date for domestic students. Applications are processed on a rolling basis. Electronic applications accepted. *Application Contact:* Graduate Studies Committee Chair, 614-292-9444, Fax: 614-292-3895, E-mail: domestic.grad@osu.edu. *Dean,* Nancy H. Rogers, 614-292-5992, Fax: 614-292-1492, E-mail: rogers.23@osu.edu.

THE OHIO STATE UNIVERSITY AT LIMA, Lima, OH 45804

General Information State-supported, coed, comprehensive institution. *Enrollment:* 1,214 graduate, professional, and undergraduate students; 46 full-time matriculated graduate/professional students (37 women), 32 part-time matriculated graduate/professional students (27 women). *Enrollment by degree level:* 74 master's, 4 doctoral. *Graduate faculty:* 10. Tuition, state resident: full-time $8,919. Tuition, nonresident: full-time $22,272. Tuition and fees vary according to course load, campus/location and program. *Student services:* Campus safety program, career counseling, child daycare facilities, disabled student services, exercise/wellness program, free psychological counseling, grant writing training, international student services, low-cost health insurance, multicultural affairs office, teacher training, writing training. *Library facilities:* Ohio State University-Lima Campus Library. *Online resources:* library catalog, access to other libraries' catalogs. *Collection:* 73,180 titles, 508 serial subscriptions, 2,279 audiovisual materials.

Computer facilities: 104 computers available on campus for general student use. *Web address:* http://www.lima.osu.edu/.

General Application Contact: Graduate Admissions, 614-292-9444, Fax: 614-292-3985, E-mail: domestic.grad@osu.edu.

GRADUATE UNITS

Graduate Programs Students: 46 full-time (37 women), 32 part-time (27 women), 1 international. Average age 30. Expenses: Contact institution. *Application deadline:* For fall admission, 8/15 priority date for domestic students, 7/1 priority date for international students; for winter admission, 12/1 priority date for domestic students, 11/1 priority date for international students; for spring admission, 3/1 priority date for domestic students, 2/1 priority date for international students. Applications are processed on a rolling basis. *Application fee:* $40 ($50 for international students). Electronic applications accepted. *Application Contact:* Graduate Admissions, 614-292-9444, Fax: 614-292-3895, E-mail: domestic.grad@osu.edu. *Dean/Director,* Dr. John Snyder, 419-995-8481, E-mail: snyder.4@osu.edu.

THE OHIO STATE UNIVERSITY AT MARION, Marion, OH 43302-5695

General Information State-supported, coed, comprehensive institution. *Enrollment:* 1,538 graduate, professional, and undergraduate students; 63 full-time matriculated graduate/professional students (56 women), 43 part-time matriculated graduate/professional students (41 women). *Enrollment by degree level:* 77 master's, 29 doctoral. *Graduate faculty:* 35. Tuition, state resident: full-time $8,919. Tuition, nonresident: full-time $22,272. Tuition and fees vary according to course load, campus/location and program. *Student services:* Campus safety program, career counseling, child daycare facilities, disabled student services, exercise/wellness program, free psychological counseling, grant writing training, international student services, low-cost health insurance, multicultural affairs office, teacher training, writing training. *Library facilities:* Ohio State University-Marion Campus Library. *Online resources:* library catalog, web page, access to other libraries' catalogs. *Collection:* 40,000 titles, 400 serial subscriptions, 3,800 audiovisual materials.

Computer facilities: 174 computers available on campus for general student use. *Web address:* http://www.marion.ohio-state.edu/.

General Application Contact: Graduate Admissions, 614-292-9444, Fax: 614-292-3985, E-mail: domestic.grad@osu.edu.

GRADUATE UNITS

Graduate Programs Students: 63 full-time (56 women), 43 part-time (41 women); includes 2 minority (both African Americans), 1 international. Average age 32. Expenses: Contact institution. *Application deadline:* For fall admission, 8/15 priority date for domestic students, 7/1 priority date for international students; for winter admission, 12/1 priority date for domestic students, 11/1 priority date for international students; for spring admission, 3/1 priority date for domestic students, 2/1 priority date for international students. Applications are processed on a rolling basis. *Application fee:* $40 ($50 for international students). Electronic applications accepted. *Application Contact:* Graduate Admissions, 614-292-9444, Fax: 614-292-3895, E-mail: domestic.grad@osu.edu. *Dean/Director,* Gregory S. Rose, 740-389-6786 Ext. 6218, E-mail: rose.9@osu.edu.

THE OHIO STATE UNIVERSITY–MANSFIELD CAMPUS, Mansfield, OH 44906-1599

General Information State-supported, coed, comprehensive institution. *Enrollment:* 1,464 graduate, professional, and undergraduate students; 35 full-time matriculated graduate/professional students (32 women), 46 part-time matriculated graduate/professional students (42 women). *Enrollment by degree level:* 56 master's, 25 doctoral. *Graduate faculty:* 8 full-time (4 women). Tuition, state resident: full-time $8,919. Tuition, nonresident: full-time $22,272. Tuition and fees vary according to course load, campus/location and program. *Student services:* Campus employment opportunities, campus safety program, career counseling, child daycare facilities, disabled student services, exercise/wellness program, free psychological counseling, grant writing training, international student services, low-cost health insurance, multicultural affairs office, teacher training, writing training. *Library facilities:* Ohio State University-Mansfield Campus Library. *Online resources:* library catalog, access to other libraries' catalogs. *Collection:* 45,977 titles, 453 serial subscriptions.

Computer facilities: 103 computers available on campus for general student use. *Web address:* http://www.mansfield.osu.edu/.

General Application Contact: Graduate Admissions, 614-292-9444, Fax: 914-292-3895, E-mail: domestic.grad@osu.edu.

GRADUATE UNITS

Graduate Programs Students: 35 full-time (32 women), 46 part-time (42 women); includes 4 minority (all African Americans), 1 international. Average age 32. *Faculty:* 8 full-time (4 women). Expenses: Contact institution. *Financial support:* In 2006–07, 14 students received support, including 3 teaching assistantships with full tuition reimbursements available (averaging $9,000 per year); Federal Work-Study and scholarships/grants also available. Support available to part-time students. Financial award application deadline: 7/1. *Application deadline:* For fall admission, 8/15 priority date for domestic students, 7/1 priority date for international students; for winter admission, 12/1 priority date for domestic students, 11/1 priority date for international students; for spring admission, 3/1 priority date for domestic students, 2/1 priority date for international students. Applications are processed on a rolling basis. *Application fee:* $40 ($50 for international students). Electronic applications accepted. *Application Contact:* Graduate Admissions, 614-292-9444, Fax: 614-292-3895, E-mail: domestic.grad@osu.edu.

THE OHIO STATE UNIVERSITY–NEWARK CAMPUS, Newark, OH 43055-1797

General Information State-supported, coed, comprehensive institution. *Enrollment:* 2,310 graduate, professional, and undergraduate students; 31 full-time matriculated graduate/professional students (25 women), 39 part-time matriculated graduate/professional students (34 women). *Enrollment by degree level:* 67 master's, 3 doctoral. *Graduate faculty:* 12. Tuition, state resident: full-time $8,919. Tuition, nonresident: full-time $22,272. Tuition and fees vary according to course level, campus/location and program. *Student services:* Campus safety program, career counseling, child daycare facilities, disabled student services, exercise/wellness program, free psychological counseling, grant writing training, international student services, low-cost health insurance, multicultural affairs office, teacher training, writing training. *Library facilities:* Ohio State University Newark Campus Library. *Online resources:* library catalog, access to other libraries' catalogs. *Collection:* 49,000 titles, 423 serial subscriptions, 2,680 audiovisual materials.

Computer facilities: 36 computers available on campus for general student use. *Web address:* http://www.newark.osu.edu/.

General Application Contact: Graduate Admissions, 614-292-9444, Fax: 614-292-3985, E-mail: domestic.grad@osu.edu.

GRADUATE UNITS

Graduate Programs Students: 31 full-time (25 women), 39 part-time (34 women); includes 3 minority (1 African American, 1 Asian American or Pacific Islander, 1 Hispanic American), 1 international. Average age 33. Expenses: Contact institution. *Application deadline:* For fall admission, 8/15 priority date for domestic students, 7/1 priority date for international students; for winter admission, 12/1 priority date for domestic students, 11/1 priority date for international students; for spring admission, 3/1 priority date for domestic students, 2/1 priority date for international students. Applications are processed on a rolling basis. *Application fee:* $40 ($50 for international students). Electronic applications accepted. *Application Contact:* Graduate Admissions, 614-292-9444, Fax: 614-292-3985, E-mail: domestic.grad@osu.edu. *Dean/Director,* Dr. William L. MacDonald, 740-366-9333 Ext. 330, E-mail: macdonald.24@osu.edu.

OHIO UNIVERSITY, Athens, OH 45701-2979

General Information State-supported, coed, university. CGS member. *Enrollment:* 20,593 graduate, professional, and undergraduate students; 2,422 full-time matriculated graduate/professional students (1,222 women), 729 part-time matriculated graduate/professional students (414 women). *Enrollment by degree level:* 2,328 master's, 823 doctoral. *Graduate faculty:* 938 full-time (331 women), 340 part-time/adjunct (152 women). *Graduate housing:* Rooms and/or apartments available on a first-come, first-served basis to single and married students. Housing application deadline: 5/1. *Student services:* Campus employment opportunities, campus safety program, career counseling, child daycare facilities, disabled student services, exercise/wellness program, free psychological counseling, international student services, low-cost health insurance, multicultural affairs office. *Library facilities:* Alden Library plus 1 other. *Online resources:* library catalog, web page, access to other libraries' catalogs. *Collection:* 2.7 million titles, 27,606 serial subscriptions, 93,337 audiovisual materials.

Computer facilities: 1,500 computers available on campus for general student use. A campuswide network can be accessed from student residence rooms and from off campus. Internet access and online class registration are available. *Web address:* http://www.ohio.edu/.

General Application Contact: Information Contact, 740-593-2800, Fax: 740-593-4625, E-mail: graduatestudies@ohio.edu.

GRADUATE UNITS

College of Osteopathic Medicine Students: 434 full-time (227 women); includes 104 minority (47 African Americans, 4 American Indian/Alaska Native, 34 Asian Americans or Pacific Islanders, 19 Hispanic Americans). Average age 24. 2,736 applicants, 61% accepted, 108 enrolled. *Faculty:* 77 full-time (23 women), 34 part-time/adjunct (10 women). Expenses: Contact institution. *Financial support:* In 2006–07, 400 students received support, including 10 fellowships with full tuition reimbursements available (averaging $8,600 per year); career-related internships or fieldwork, Federal Work-Study, institutionally sponsored loans, scholarships/grants, and tuition waivers (partial) also available. Financial award application deadline: 4/1; financial award applicants required to submit FAFSA. In 2006, 102 degrees awarded. Offers osteopathic medicine (DO). *Application deadline:* For fall admission, 2/1 for domestic students. Applications are processed on a rolling basis. *Application fee:* $30. Electronic applications accepted. *Application Contact:* Dr. John D. Schriner, Director of Admissions, 740-593-4313, Fax: 740-593-2256, E-mail: admissions@exchange.oucom.ohiou.edu. *Dean,* Dr. John A. Brose, 740-593-2178, Fax: 740-593-0761, E-mail: blue@ohio.edu.

Graduate Studies Students: 2,422 full-time (1,222 women), 729 part-time (414 women); includes 188 minority (108 African Americans, 7 American Indian/Alaska Native, 36 Asian Americans or Pacific Islanders, 37 Hispanic Americans), 914 international. 4,099 applicants, 44% accepted, 901 enrolled. *Faculty:* 938 full-time (331 women), 340 part-time/adjunct (152 women). Expenses: Contact institution. *Financial support:* In 2006–07, 1,992 students received support, including 71 fellowships with full tuition reimbursements available (averaging $10,467 per year), 447 research assistantships with full and partial tuition reimbursements available (averaging $9,433 per year), 491 teaching assistantships with full and partial tuition reimbursements available (averaging $9,977 per year); career-related internships or fieldwork, Federal Work-Study, institutionally sponsored loans, scholarships/grants, traineeships, tuition waivers (full and partial), unspecified assistantships, and associateships, stipends also available. Financial award applicants required to submit FAFSA. In 2006, 980 master's, 147 doctorates awarded. *Degree program information:* Part-time and evening/weekend programs available. Offers interdisciplinary studies (PhD). *Application fee:* $45. Electronic applications accepted. *Application Contact:* Dr. Michael J. Mumper, Graduate Student Services, 740-597-7577, Fax: 740-593-4625, E-mail: mumper@ohio.edu. *Associate Provost for Graduate Studies,* Dr. Michael J. Mumper, 740-593-4372, Fax: 740-593-4625, E-mail: mumper@ohio.edu.

Center for International Studies Students: 132 full-time (80 women), 6 part-time (3 women); includes 9 minority (4 African Americans, 2 Asian Americans or Pacific Islanders, 3 Hispanic Americans), 92 international. 306 applicants, 61% accepted, 88 enrolled. *Faculty:* 95 full-time (27 women), 13 part-time/adjunct (6 women). Expenses: Contact institution. *Financial support:* In 2006–07, 116 students received support, including 14 fellowships with full tuition reimbursements available (averaging $11,000 per year), 40 research assistantships with full and partial tuition reimbursements available (averaging $10,000 per year), 3 teaching assistantships with full and partial tuition reimbursements available (averaging $10,000 per year); career-related internships or fieldwork, Federal Work-Study, institutionally sponsored loans, scholarships/grants, and tuition waivers (full) also available. Financial award application deadline: 1/1. In 2006, 81 degrees awarded. Offers African studies (MA); communications and development studies (MA); development studies (MA); international studies (MA); Latin American studies (MA); Southeast Asian studies (MA). *Application deadline:* For fall admission, 1/1 for domestic and international students. *Application fee:* $45. *Application Contact:* Joan Kraynanski, Administrative Assistant, 740-593-1840, Fax: 740-593-1837, E-mail: kraynans@ohio.edu. *Director,* Dr. Josep Rota, 740-593-1839, Fax: 740-593-1837, E-mail: rota@ohio.edu.

College of Arts and Sciences Students: 574 full-time (307 women), 114 part-time (47 women); includes 39 minority (10 African Americans, 5 American Indian/Alaska Native, 11 Asian Americans or Pacific Islanders, 13 Hispanic Americans), 262 international. 1,064 applicants, 45% accepted, 306 enrolled. *Faculty:* 330 full-time (111 women), 41 part-time/adjunct (15 women). Expenses: Contact institution. *Financial support:* In 2006–07, 417 students received support, including 41 fellowships with full tuition reimbursements available (averaging $15,637 per year), 74 research assistantships with full tuition reimbursements available (averaging $11,552 per year), 277 teaching assistantships with full tuition reimbursements available (averaging $11,586 per year); career-related internships or fieldwork, Federal Work-Study, institutionally sponsored loans, scholarships/grants, traineeships, tuition waivers (full and partial), and unspecified assistantships also available. In 2006, 217 master's, 34 doctorates awarded. *Degree program information:* Part-time programs available. Offers applied economics (MA); applied linguistics/TESOL (MA); arts and sciences (MA, MPA, MS, MSS, MSW, PhD); astronomy (MS, PhD); biological sciences (MS, PhD); cell biology and physiology (MS, PhD); chemistry and biochemistry (MS, PhD); clinical psychology (PhD); ecology and evolutionary biology (MS, PhD); English language and literature (MA, PhD); environmental and plant biology (MS, PhD); environmental geochemistry (MS); environmental geology (MS); environmental studies (MS); environmental/hydrology (MS); exercise physiology and muscle biology (MS, PhD); experimental psychology (PhD); financial economics (MA); French (MA); geography (MA); geology (MS); geology education (MS); geomorphology/surficial processes (MS); geophysics (MS); history (MA, PhD); hydrogeology (MS); mathematics (MS, PhD); microbiology (MS, PhD); molecular and cellular biology (MS, PhD); neuroscience (MS, PhD); organizational psychology (PhD); philosophy (MA); physics (MS, PhD); political science (MA); public administration (MPA); sedimentology (MS); social sciences (MSS); social work (MSW); sociology (MA); Spanish (MA); structure/tectonics (MS). *Application fee:* $45. Electronic applications accepted. *Interim Dean,* Dr. Ben M. Ogles, 740-593-2850, Fax: 740-593-0053, E-mail: ogles@ohio.edu.

College of Business Students: 116 full-time (38 women), 8 part-time (2 women); includes 14 minority (9 African Americans, 4 Asian Americans or Pacific Islanders, 1 Hispanic American), 23 international. 162 applicants, 43% accepted, 37 enrolled. *Faculty:* 44 full-time (15 women), 16 part-time/adjunct (7 women). Expenses: Contact institution. *Financial support:* In 2006–07, 50 students received support, including 20 research assistantships with full and partial tuition reimbursements available (averaging $8,000 per year); career-related internships or fieldwork and institutionally sponsored loans also available. Financial award application deadline: 2/1. In 2006, 94 degrees awarded. *Degree program information:* Part-time and evening/weekend programs available. Offers business (EMBA, MBA); busi-

Ohio University (continued)

ness administration (EMBA, MBA). *Application deadline:* For fall admission, 2/1 priority date for domestic students, 1/15 priority date for international students. *Application fee:* $45. Electronic applications accepted. *Application Contact:* Jan Ross, Assistant Dean, 740-593-2007, Fax: 740-593-1388, E-mail: rossj@ohio.edu. *Director, Executive Education,* Dr. Edward B. Yost, 740-593-2007, Fax: 740-593-1388, E-mail: yost@ohio.edu.

College of Education Students: 257 full-time (174 women), 218 part-time (147 women); includes 29 minority (23 African Americans, 2 Asian Americans or Pacific Islanders, 4 Hispanic Americans), 157 international. 423 applicants, 64% accepted, 192 enrolled. *Faculty:* 44 full-time (25 women), 21 part-time/adjunct (8 women). Expenses: Contact institution. *Financial support:* In 2006–07, 164 students received support, including 100 research assistantships with full tuition reimbursements available (averaging $6,500 per year), 8 teaching assistantships with full tuition reimbursements available (averaging $7,200 per year); Federal Work-Study, institutionally sponsored loans, tuition waivers (full), and unspecified assistantships also available. Financial award application deadline: 3/15. In 2006, 52 master's, 21 doctorates awarded. *Degree program information:* Part-time and evening/weekend programs available. Offers adolescent to young adult education (M Ed); college student personnel (M Ed); community/agency counseling (M Ed); computer education and technology (M Ed); counselor education (PhD); curriculum and instruction (M Ed, PhD); education (M Ed, Ed D, PhD); educational administration (M Ed, Ed D); educational research and evaluation (M Ed, PhD); higher education (M Ed, PhD); instructional technology (PhD); mathematics education (PhD); middle child education (M Ed); reading and language arts (PhD); reading education (M Ed); rehabilitation counseling (M Ed); school counseling (M Ed); social studies education (PhD); special education (M Ed, PhD). *Application deadline:* Applications are processed on a rolling basis. *Application fee:* $45. Electronic applications accepted. *Application Contact:* Floyd J. Doney, Director of Student Affairs, 740-593-4400, Fax: 740-593-9310, E-mail: doney@ohio.edu. *Dean,* Dr. Ren'ee A. Middleton, 740-593-4403, E-mail: middletonr@ohio.edu.

College of Fine Arts Students: 219 full-time (114 women), 32 part-time (23 women); includes 17 minority (7 African Americans, 2 American Indian/Alaska Native, 3 Asian Americans or Pacific Islanders, 5 Hispanic Americans), 80 international. 478 applicants, 22% accepted, 89 enrolled. *Faculty:* 87 full-time (27 women), 17 part-time/adjunct (5 women). Expenses: Contact institution. *Financial support:* In 2006–07, 189 students received support, including 48 research assistantships with full and partial tuition reimbursements available, 89 teaching assistantships with full and partial tuition reimbursements available (averaging $6,695 per year); career-related internships or fieldwork, Federal Work-Study, institutionally sponsored loans, scholarships/grants, tuition waivers (full and partial), and associateships also available. In 2006, 77 master's, 2 doctorates awarded. *Degree program information:* Part-time programs available. Postbaccalaureate distance learning degree programs offered (minimal on-campus study). Offers accompanying (MM); art education (MA); art history (MA); art history/studio (MFA); ceramics (MFA); composition (MM); conducting (MM); film (MFA); film studies (MA); fine arts (MA, MFA, MM, PhD, Certificate); history/literature (MM); interdisciplinary arts (PhD); music education (MM); music therapy (MM); painting (MFA); performance (MM, Certificate); performance/pedagogy (MM); photography (MFA); printmaking (MFA); sculpture (MFA); theater (MA, MFA); theory (MM). *Application fee:* $45. Electronic applications accepted. *Dean,* Charles A. McWeeney, 740-593-1808, Fax: 740-593-0570.

College of Health and Human Services Students: 100 full-time (73 women), 8 part-time (7 women); includes 10 minority (6 African Americans, 3 Asian Americans or Pacific Islanders, 1 Hispanic American), 18 international. 490 applicants, 55% accepted, 101 enrolled. *Faculty:* 55 full-time (27 women), 21 part-time/adjunct (13 women). Expenses: Contact institution. *Financial support:* In 2006–07, 3 fellowships with tuition reimbursements (averaging $3,200 per year), 61 research assistantships with full and partial tuition reimbursements (averaging $7,133 per year), 39 teaching assistantships with full and partial tuition reimbursements (averaging $9,525 per year) were awarded; career-related internships or fieldwork, Federal Work-Study, institutionally sponsored loans, scholarships/grants, tuition waivers (full), unspecified assistantships, and stipends also available. In 2006, 35 master's, 1 doctorate awarded. *Degree program information:* Part-time programs available. Offers athletic training education (MS RSS); audiology (Au D); child development and family life (MSHCS); coaching education (MS); early childhood education (MSHCS); family studies (MSHCS); food and nutrition (MSHCS); health and human services (MA, MFA, MPH, MS, MS RSS, MSA, MSHCS, MSP Ex, Au D, DPT, PhD); health sciences (MHA, MPH); hearing science (PhD); physical therapy (DPT); physiology of exercise (MSP Ex); recreation studies (MS); speech language pathology (MA); speech-language science (PhD); sports administration and facility management (MSA). *Application deadline:* Applications are processed on a rolling basis. *Application fee:* $45. Electronic applications accepted. *Dean,* Dr. Gary Neiman, 740-593-9336, Fax: 740-593-0285, E-mail: neiman@ohio.edu.

Russ College of Engineering and Technology Students: 262 full-time (42 women), 46 part-time (6 women); includes 3 minority (2 African Americans, 1 Asian American or Pacific Islander), 226 international. 427 applicants, 57% accepted, 69 enrolled. *Faculty:* 114 full-time (6 women), 15 part-time/adjunct (3 women). Expenses: Contact institution. *Financial support:* In 2006–07, 30 fellowships with full tuition reimbursements (averaging $16,000 per year), 115 research assistantships with full tuition reimbursements (averaging $14,250 per year), 74 teaching assistantships with full tuition reimbursements (averaging $12,000 per year) were awarded; career-related internships or fieldwork, Federal Work-Study, institutionally sponsored loans, tuition waivers (full and partial), and unspecified assistantships also available. In 2006, 89 master's, 5 doctorates awarded. *Degree program information:* Part-time programs available. Offers biomedical engineering (MS); chemical engineering (MS, PhD); civil (PhD); computer science (MS); construction (MS); electrical engineering (MS, PhD); engineering and technology (MS, PhD); environmental (MS); geotechnical and environmental engineering (MS); industrial (PhD); industrial and manufacturing systems engineering (MS); integrated engineering (PhD); manufacturing engineering (MS); mechanical (PhD); mechanical engineering (MS, PhD); structures (MS); transportation (MS); water resources and structures (MS). *Application deadline:* Applications are processed on a rolling basis. *Application fee:* $45. Electronic applications accepted. *Application Contact:* Information Contact, 740-593-1922, Fax: 740-593-0007. *Dean,* Dr. Dennis Irwin, 740-593-1482, Fax: 740-593-0659, E-mail: irwind@ohio.edu.

Scripps College of Communication Students: 116 full-time (61 women), 36 part-time (20 women); includes 12 minority (6 African Americans, 3 Asian Americans or Pacific Islanders, 3 Hispanic Americans), 72 international. 316 applicants, 39% accepted, 85 enrolled. *Faculty:* 93 full-time (33 women). Expenses: Contact institution. *Financial support:* In 2006–07, 64 students received support, including 7 fellowships (averaging $7,000 per year), 22 research assistantships with full and partial tuition reimbursements available (averaging $8,600 per year), 28 teaching assistantships with full tuition reimbursements available (averaging $14,000 per year); career-related internships or fieldwork, Federal Work-Study, institutionally sponsored loans, and tuition waivers (full and partial) also available. Financial award application deadline: 2/1; financial award applicants required to submit FAFSA. In 2006, 39 master's, 13 doctorates awarded. *Degree program information:* Part-time programs available. Offers communication (MA, MCTP, MS, PhD); communication studies (PhD); information and telecommunication systems (MCTP); journalism (MS, PhD); telecommunications (MA, PhD); visual communication (MA). *Application deadline:* For fall admission, 2/1 priority date for domestic students, 1/1 priority date for international students. Applications are processed on a rolling basis. *Application fee:* $45. Electronic applications accepted. *Application Contact:* Dr. David H. Mould, Associate Dean, 740-593-4885, Fax: 740-593-0459, E-mail: mould@ohio.edu. *Dean,* Dr. Gregory J. Shepherd, 740-593-4883, Fax: 740-593-0459, E-mail: shepherg@ohio.edu.

OHR HAMEIR THEOLOGICAL SEMINARY, Peekskill, NY 10566

General Information Independent-religious, men only, comprehensive institution.

GRADUATE UNITS

Graduate Programs

OKLAHOMA CHRISTIAN UNIVERSITY, Oklahoma City, OK 73136-1100

General Information Independent-religious, coed, comprehensive institution. *Enrollment:* 2,120 graduate, professional, and undergraduate students; 11 full-time matriculated graduate/professional students (3 women), 44 part-time matriculated graduate/professional students (4 women). *Enrollment by degree level:* 21 first professional, 34 master's. *Graduate faculty:* 12 full-time (0 women). *Graduate housing:* Rooms and/or apartments available on a first-come, first-served basis to single and married students. Typical cost: $1,839 (including board) for single students; $4,635 per year for married students. Room and board charges vary according to board plan, campus/location and housing facility selected. *Student services:* Campus employment opportunities, campus safety program, exercise/wellness program, free psychological counseling, international student services, low-cost health insurance, writing training. *Library facilities:* Tom and Ada Beam Library. *Online resources:* library catalog, web page, access to other libraries' catalogs. *Collection:* 125,841 titles, 8,139 serial subscriptions, 6,248 audiovisual materials.

Computer facilities: Computer purchase and lease plans are available. 101 computers available on campus for general student use. A campuswide network can be accessed from student residence rooms and from off campus. Internet access, each student has a laptop computer are available. *Web address:* http://www.oc.edu/.

General Application Contact: Dr. Bob Young, Director, 405-425-5485, Fax: 405-425-5076, E-mail: bob.young@oc.edu.

GRADUATE UNITS

Graduate School of Bible Students: 11 full-time (3 women), 44 part-time (4 women); includes 3 minority (2 African Americans, 1 American Indian/Alaska Native), 3 international. Average age 30. 23 applicants, 100% accepted, 16 enrolled. *Faculty:* 12 full-time (0 women). Expenses: Contact institution. *Financial support:* In 2006–07, 49 students received support. Career-related internships or fieldwork, Federal Work-Study, scholarships/grants, and tuition waivers (partial) available. Support available to part-time students. Financial award application deadline: 3/1. In 2006, 8 degrees awarded. *Degree program information:* Part-time and evening/weekend programs available. Offers family life ministry (MA); ministry (M Div, MA); youth ministry (MA). *Application deadline:* For fall admission, 8/15 priority date for domestic and international students; for spring admission, 1/3 priority date for domestic and international students. Applications are processed on a rolling basis. *Application fee:* $25. Electronic applications accepted. *Application Contact:* Dr. Bob Young, Director, 405-425-5485, Fax: 405-425-5076, E-mail: bob.young@oc.edu. *Chair,* Dr. John Harrison, 405-425-5377, Fax: 405-425-5076, E-mail: john.harrison@oc.edu.

OKLAHOMA CITY UNIVERSITY, Oklahoma City, OK 73106-1402

General Information Independent-religious, coed, comprehensive institution. *Enrollment:* 3,713 graduate, professional, and undergraduate students; 1,224 full-time matriculated graduate/professional students (530 women), 553 part-time matriculated graduate/professional students (246 women). *Enrollment by degree level:* 691 first professional, 1,086 master's. *Graduate faculty:* 186 full-time (77 women), 160 part-time/adjunct (85 women). *Tuition:* Full-time $12,780; part-time $710 per hour. *Required fees:* $89 per hour. *Graduate housing:* Rooms and/or apartments available on a first-come, first-served basis to single and married students. Housing application deadline: 8/15. *Student services:* Campus employment opportunities, campus safety program, career counseling, disabled student services, exercise/wellness program, free psychological counseling, grant writing training, international student services, low-cost health insurance, teacher training, writing training. *Library facilities:* Dulaney Browne Library plus 1 other. *Online resources:* library catalog, web page, access to other libraries' catalogs. *Collection:* 520,953 titles, 14,000 serial subscriptions, 1,611 audiovisual materials.

Computer facilities: 264 computers available on campus for general student use. A campuswide network can be accessed from student residence rooms and from off campus. Internet access and online class registration are available. *Web address:* http://www.okcu.edu/.

General Application Contact: Leslie McKenzie, Director, Graduate Admissions, 800-633-7242, Fax: 405-208-5356, E-mail: gadmissions@okcu.edu.

GRADUATE UNITS

Kramer School of Nursing Students: 7 full-time (all women), 17 part-time (14 women); all minorities (3 African Americans, 3 American Indian/Alaska Native, 1 Asian American or Pacific Islander, 17 Hispanic Americans). Average age 47. 15 applicants, 93% accepted. Expenses: Contact institution. In 2006, 2 degrees awarded. Offers nursing (MSN). *Application Contact:* Dr. Susan Barnes, Director, MSN Program, 405-208-5917, Fax: 405-208-5914, E-mail: sbarnes@okcu.edu. *Dean,* Dr. Marvel L. Williamson, 405-208-5900, Fax: 405-208-5914, E-mail: mwilliamson@okcu.edu.

Margaret E. Petree College of Performing Arts Expenses: Contact institution. Offers costume design (MA); performing arts (MA, MM); technical theater (MA); theater (MA); theater for young audiences (MA). *Application deadline:* For fall admission, 8/22 for domestic students; for spring admission, 1/15 for domestic students. *Application fee:* $30 ($70 for international students). *Application Contact:* Leslie McKenzie, Director, Graduate Admissions, 800-633-7242, Fax: 405-208-5356, E-mail: gadmissions@okcu.edu.

Wanda L. Bass School of Music Students: 55 full-time (31 women), 2 part-time (both women); includes 1 minority (African American), 18 international. Average age 26. 45 applicants, 91% accepted. *Faculty:* 19 full-time (6 women), 25 part-time/adjunct (12 women). Expenses: Contact institution. *Financial support:* Fellowships with partial tuition reimbursements, career-related internships or fieldwork, Federal Work-Study, and institutionally sponsored loans available. Financial award application deadline: 4/1; financial award applicants required to submit FAFSA. In 2006, 11 degrees awarded. *Degree program information:* Part-time programs available. Offers composition (MM); conducting (MM); musical theatre (MM); opera performance (MM); performance (MM). *Application deadline:* For fall admission, 8/22 for domestic students; for spring admission, 1/15 for domestic students. Applications are processed on a rolling basis. *Application fee:* $30 ($70 for international students). *Application Contact:* Leslie Mckenzie, Director Graduate Admissions, 800-633-7242, Fax: 405-208-5356, E-mail: gadmissions@okcu.edu. *Dean,* Mark Parker, 405-208-5474, Fax: 405-208-5971, E-mail: mparker@okcu.edu.

Meinders School of Business Students: 611. Average age 28. *Faculty:* 25 full-time (7 women), 25 part-time/adjunct (5 women). Expenses: Contact institution. *Financial support:* Fellowships with partial tuition reimbursements, career-related internships or fieldwork, Federal Work-Study, institutionally sponsored loans, and tuition waivers (partial) available. Support available to part-time students. Financial award application deadline: 8/1; financial award applicants required to submit FAFSA. *Degree program information:* Part-time and evening/weekend programs available. Offers accounting (MSA); business (MBA, MSA); finance (MBA); health administration (MBA); information technology (MBA); integrated marketing communications (MBA); international business (MBA); marketing (MBA). *Application deadline:* For fall admission, 8/15 priority date for domestic students; for spring admission, 1/15 for domestic students. Applications are processed on a rolling basis. *Application fee:* $30 ($70 for international students). *Application Contact:* Leslie McKenzie, Director, Graduate Admissions, 800-633-7242, Fax: 405-208-5356, E-mail: gadmissions@okcu.edu. *Dean,* Dr. Vince Orza, 405-208-5276, Fax: 405-208-5008, E-mail: vorza@okcu.edu.

Petree College of Arts and Sciences Students: 656. Average age 31. *Faculty:* 40 full-time (14 women), 34 part-time/adjunct (14 women). Expenses: Contact institution. *Financial support:* Fellowships with partial tuition reimbursements, career-related internships or fieldwork, Federal Work-Study, institutionally sponsored loans, and tuition waivers (full and partial) available. Support available to part-time students. Financial award application deadline: 8/1; financial award applicants required to submit FAFSA. In 2006, 131 degrees awarded. *Degree program information:* Part-time and evening/weekend programs available. Offers art (MLA); arts and sciences (M Ed, MA, MCJ, MLA, MS); general studies (MLA); leadership/management (MLA); literature (MLA); mass communications (MLA); philosophy (MLA); writing (MLA). *Application deadline:* For fall admission, 8/22 for domestic students; for spring admission, 1/15 for domestic students. Applications are processed on a rolling basis. *Application fee:* $30 ($70 for international students). *Application Contact:* Leslie McKenzie, Director, Graduate Admissions, 800-633-7242, Fax: 405-208-5356, E-mail: gadmissions@okcu.edu. *Dean,* Dr. David Evans, 405-208-5446, Fax: 405-208-5447, E-mail: devans@okcu.edu.

Division of Computer Science Students: 85 full-time (18 women), 6 part-time; includes 1 minority (Asian American or Pacific Islander), 86 international. Average age 24. *Faculty:* 9 full-time (1 woman), 1 part-time/adjunct (0 women). Expenses: Contact institution. *Financial support:* Fellowships with partial tuition reimbursements, career-related internships or fieldwork, Federal Work-Study, institutionally sponsored loans, and tuition waivers (partial) available. Support available to part-time students. Financial award application deadline: 8/1; financial award applicants required to submit FAFSA. In 2006, 45 degrees awarded. *Degree program information:* Part-time and evening/weekend programs available. Offers computer science (MS). *Application deadline:* For fall admission, 8/22 for domestic students; for spring admission, 1/15 for domestic students. Applications are processed on a rolling basis. *Application fee:* $30 ($70 for international students). *Application Contact:* Leslie McKenzie, Director, Graduate Admissions, 800-633-7242, Fax: 405-208-5356, E-mail: gadmissions@okcu.edu. *Program Director,* Dr. Art Kazmieczak, 405-208-6052, Fax: 405-208-5356, E-mail: akazmieczak@okcu.edu.

Division of Education and Kinesiology Exercise Studies Students: 66 full-time (53 women), 25 part-time (19 women); includes 8 minority (4 African Americans, 3 Asian Americans or Pacific Islanders, 1 Hispanic American), 54 international. Average age 33. 30 applicants, 77% accepted. *Faculty:* 5 full-time (3 women), 14 part-time/adjunct (9 women). Expenses: Contact institution. *Financial support:* Fellowships with partial tuition reimbursements, career-related internships or fieldwork, Federal Work-Study, institutionally sponsored loans, and tuition waivers (full and partial) available. Support available to part-time students. Financial award application deadline: 8/1; financial award applicants required to submit FAFSA. In 2006, 41 degrees awarded. *Degree program information:* Part-time and evening/weekend programs available. Offers applied behavioral studies (M Ed); early childhood education (M Ed); education and kinesiology exercise studies (M Ed, MA); elementary education (M Ed); teaching English to speakers of other languages (MA). *Application deadline:* For fall admission, 8/22 for domestic students; for spring admission, 1/15 for domestic students. Applications are processed on a rolling basis. *Application fee:* $35 ($70 for international students). *Application Contact:* Leslie McKenzie, Director, Graduate Admissions, 800-633-7242, Fax: 405-208-5356, E-mail: gadmissions@okcu.edu. *Chair,* 405-208-5368, Fax: 405-208-5447.

Division of Social Sciences Students: 13 full-time (10 women), 3 part-time (1 woman); includes 3 minority (all African Americans), 2 international. Average age 35. 9 applicants, 89% accepted. *Faculty:* 4 full-time (1 woman), 3 part-time/adjunct (2 women). Expenses: Contact institution. *Financial support:* Fellowships with partial tuition reimbursements, career-related internships or fieldwork available. Financial award application deadline: 8/1; financial award applicants required to submit FAFSA. In 2006, 7 degrees awarded. *Degree program information:* Part-time and evening/weekend programs available. Offers criminal justice (MCJ). *Application deadline:* For fall admission, 8/22 for domestic students; for spring admission, 1/15 for domestic students. Applications are processed on a rolling basis. *Application fee:* $30 ($70 for international students). *Application Contact:* Leslie McKenzie, Director, Graduate Admissions, 800-633-7242, Fax: 405-208-5356, E-mail: gadmissions@okcu.edu. *Director,* Dr. Jody Horn, 405-208-5247, Fax: 405-208-5447, E-mail: jhorn@okcu.edu.

School of Law Students: 472 full-time (192 women), 133 part-time (56 women); includes 107 minority (17 African Americans, 41 American Indian/Alaska Native, 21 Asian Americans or Pacific Islanders, 28 Hispanic Americans), 6 international. *Faculty:* 30 full-time (10 women), 41 part-time/adjunct (12 women). Expenses: Contact institution. *Financial support:* Career-related internships or fieldwork, Federal Work-Study, institutionally sponsored loans, and tuition waivers (partial) available. Support available to part-time students. Financial award application deadline: 8/1; financial award applicants required to submit FAFSA. In 2006, 215 degrees awarded. *Degree program information:* Part-time and evening/weekend programs available. Offers law (JD). *Application deadline:* For fall admission, 6/1 for domestic students. *Application fee:* $50 ($70 for international students). Electronic applications accepted. *Application Contact:* Tamara Martinez-Anderson, Assistant Dean, Law School Admissions, 800-633-7242 Ext. 2, Fax: 405-208-5354, E-mail: tmartinezanderson@okcu.edu. *Dean,* Dr. Larry Hellman, 405-208-5337, Fax: 405-208-6041, E-mail: lhellman@okcu.edu.

Wimberly School of Religion and Graduate Theological Center Students: 4 full-time (1 woman), 2 part-time (both women); includes 2 minority (both African Americans), 2 international. Average age 38. 3 applicants, 67% accepted. *Faculty:* 4 full-time (2 women), 5 part-time/adjunct (2 women). Expenses: Contact institution. *Financial support:* Fellowships with partial tuition reimbursements, career-related internships or fieldwork, Federal Work-Study, institutionally sponsored loans, and tuition waivers (partial) available. Support available to part-time students. Financial award applicants required to submit FAFSA. In 2006, 2 degrees awarded. *Degree program information:* Part-time and evening/weekend programs available. Offers religion and theology (M Rel, MAR). *Application deadline:* For fall admission, 8/22 for domestic students; for spring admission, 1/9 for domestic students. Applications are processed on a rolling basis. *Application fee:* $30 ($70 for international students). *Application Contact:* Leslie Mckenzie, Director, Graduate Admissions, 800-633-7242, Fax: 405-208-5356, E-mail: gadmissions@okcu.edu. *Dean,* Dr. Mark Davies, 405-208-5284, Fax: 405-208-6046, E-mail: mdavies@okcu.edu.

OKLAHOMA STATE UNIVERSITY, Stillwater, OK 74078

General Information State-supported, coed, university. CGS member. *Enrollment:* 23,307 graduate, professional, and undergraduate students; 1,501 full-time matriculated graduate/professional students (700 women), 2,238 part-time matriculated graduate/professional students (1,051 women). *Enrollment by degree level:* 2,411 master's, 1,328 doctoral. *Graduate faculty:* 996 full-time (277 women), 193 part-time/adjunct (85 women). Tuition, state resident: part-time $146 per credit hour. Tuition, nonresident: part-time $516 per credit hour. *Required fees:* $44 per credit hour. Tuition and fees vary according to program. *Graduate housing:* Rooms and/or apartments available on a first-come, first-served basis to single and married students. Typical cost: $3,015 per year ($6,015 including board) for single students; $6,612 per year for married students. Room and board charges vary according to board plan and housing facility selected. *Student services:* Campus employment opportunities, campus safety program, career counseling, disabled student services, exercise/wellness program, free psychological counseling, grant writing training, international student services, low-cost health insurance, multicultural affairs office, teacher training. *Library facilities:* Edmon Low Library plus 3 others. *Online resources:* library catalog, web page, access to other libraries' catalogs. *Collection:* 2.6 million titles, 38,745 serial subscriptions, 19,510 audiovisual materials. *Research affiliation:* Howard Hughes Foundation (biological sciences), Cotton, Inc. (Plant and Soil Sciences), National Cattlemen's Beef Assoc. (animal science), Noble Research Foundation (entomology), American Heart Association (physiological sciences), Fourjay Foundation (psychology).

Computer facilities: 2,456 computers available on campus for general student use. A campuswide network can be accessed from student residence rooms and from off campus. Internet access and online class registration are available. *Web address:* http://osu.okstate.edu/.

General Application Contact: Dr. Gordon Emslie, Dean, 405-744-6368, Fax: 405-744-0355, E-mail: grad_i@okstate.edu.

GRADUATE UNITS

Center for Veterinary Health Sciences Average age 26. *Faculty:* 67 full-time (19 women), 22 part-time/adjunct (16 women). Expenses: Contact institution. *Financial support:* Fellowships, research assistantships, teaching assistantships, career-related internships or fieldwork, Federal Work-Study, and tuition waivers (partial) available. Support available to part-time students. Financial award application deadline: 3/1; financial award applicants required to submit FAFSA. Postbaccalaureate distance learning degree programs offered. Offers veterinary biomedical sciences (MS, PhD); veterinary health sciences (DVM, MS, PhD); veterinary medicine (DVM). *Application deadline:* Applications are processed on a rolling basis. *Application Contact:* Dr. Michael Lorenz, Dean, 405-744-6651, Fax: 405-744-6633, E-mail: michael.lorenz@okstate.edu. *Dean,* Dr. Michael Lorenz, 405-744-6651, Fax: 405-744-6633, E-mail: michael.lorenz@okstate.edu.

College of Agricultural Science and Natural Resources Students: 136 full-time (64 women), 204 part-time (96 women); includes 30 minority (7 African Americans, 14 American Indian/Alaska Native, 5 Asian Americans or Pacific Islanders, 4 Hispanic Americans), 134 international. Average age 30. 335 applicants, 33% accepted, 64 enrolled. *Faculty:* 226 full-time (42 women), 18 part-time/adjunct (3 women). Expenses: Contact institution. *Financial support:* In 2006–07, 218 research assistantships (averaging $14,770 per year), 29 teaching assistantships (averaging $13,168 per year) were awarded; fellowships, career-related internships or fieldwork, Federal Work-Study, scholarships/grants, health care benefits, tuition waivers (partial), and unspecified assistantships also available. Support available to part-time students. Financial award application deadline: 3/1. In 2006, 50 master's, 32 doctorates awarded. *Degree program information:* Part-time programs available. Offers agricultural economics (M Ag, MS, PhD); agricultural education, communications and 4H youth development (M Ag, MS, PhD); agricultural science and natural resources (M Ag, MS, PhD); agronomy (M Ag, MS, PhD); animal breeding and reproduction (PhD); animal nutrition (PhD); animal sciences (M Ag, MS); biochemistry and molecular biology (MS, PhD); biomechanical engineering (MS, PhD); bioprocessing and biotechnology (MS, PhD); crop science (PhD); entomology (PhD); environmental and natural resources (MS, PhD); environmental science (PhD); food processing (MS, PhD); food science (MS, PhD); forestry (M Ag, MS); horticulture (M Ag, MS); plant pathology (PhD); plant science (PhD); soil science (PhD). *Application deadline:* For fall admission, 3/1 priority date for international students; for spring admission, 8/1 priority date for international students. Applications are processed on a rolling basis. *Application fee:* $40 ($75 for international students). Electronic applications accepted. *Dean,* Dr. Robert E. Whitson, 405-744-5398, Fax: 405-744-5339.

College of Arts and Sciences Students: 360 full-time (153 women), 507 part-time (226 women); includes 103 minority (21 African Americans, 42 American Indian/Alaska Native, 20 Asian Americans or Pacific Islanders, 20 Hispanic Americans), 242 international. Average age 31. 1,139 applicants, 37% accepted, 216 enrolled. *Faculty:* 385 full-time (110 women), 48 part-time/adjunct (22 women). Expenses: Contact institution. *Financial support:* In 2006–07, 116 research assistantships (averaging $12,987 per year), 443 teaching assistantships (averaging $13,918 per year) were awarded; fellowships, career-related internships or fieldwork, Federal Work-Study, scholarships/grants, health care benefits, tuition waivers (full and partial), and unspecified assistantships also available. Support available to part-time students. Financial award application deadline: 3/1. In 2006, 162 master's, 44 doctorates awarded. Offers applied history (MA); applied mathematics (MS); arts and sciences (MA, MM, MS, PhD); botany (MS); chemistry (MS, PhD); clinical psychology (PhD); communications sciences and disorders (MS); computer science (MS, PhD); conservation science (MS, PhD); corrections (MS); creative writing (MA, PhD); environmental science (PhD); experimental psychology (PhD); fire and emergency management administration (MS); general psychology (MS); geography (MS, PhD); history (MA, PhD); literature (MA, PhD); mathematics (pure and applied) (PhD); mathematics (pure) (MS); mathematics education (MS, PhD); microbiology and molecular genetics (MS, PhD); pedagogy and performance (MM); philosophy (MA); photonics (MS, PhD); physics (MS, PhD); plant science (PhD); political science (MA); sociology (MS, PhD); statistics (MS, PhD); technical writing (MA, PhD); theatre (MA); zoology (MS, PhD). *Application deadline:* For fall admission, 3/1 priority date for international students; for spring admission, 8/1 priority date for international students. Applications are processed on a rolling basis. *Application fee:* $40 ($75 for international students). Electronic applications accepted. *Dean,* Peter M. A. Sherwood, 405-744-5663, Fax: 405-744-1797.

School of Geology Students: 21 full-time (6 women), 19 part-time (3 women); includes 4 minority (3 American Indian/Alaska Native, 1 Hispanic American), 7 international. Average age 28. 39 applicants, 49% accepted, 12 enrolled. *Faculty:* 11 full-time (3 women). Expenses: Contact institution. *Financial support:* In 2006–07, 14 research assistantships (averaging $9,067 per year), 24 teaching assistantships (averaging $8,414 per year) were awarded; career-related internships or fieldwork, Federal Work-Study, scholarships/grants, health care benefits, tuition waivers (partial), and unspecified assistantships also available. Support available to part-time students. Financial award application deadline: 3/1. In 2006, 7 degrees awarded. Offers geology (MS). *Application deadline:* For fall admission, 6/1 priority date for domestic students, 3/1 priority date for international students; for spring admission, 8/1 priority date for international students. Applications are processed on a rolling basis. *Application fee:* $40 ($75 for international students). Electronic applications accepted. *Head,* Dr. Jay Gregg, 405-744-6358, E-mail: jay.gregg@okstate.edu.

School of Journalism and Broadcasting Students: 10 full-time (5 women), 15 part-time (10 women); includes 2 minority (1 American Indian/Alaska Native, 1 Hispanic American), 2 international. Average age 32. 30 applicants, 27% accepted, 7 enrolled. *Faculty:* 19 full-time (6 women), 4 part-time/adjunct (0 women). Expenses: Contact institution. *Financial support:* In 2006–07, 1 research assistantship (averaging $7,770 per year), 6 teaching assistantships (averaging $8,325 per year) were awarded; career-related internships or fieldwork, Federal Work-Study, scholarships/grants, health care benefits, tuition waivers (partial), and unspecified assistantships also available. Support available to part-time students. Financial award application deadline: 3/1. In 2006, 8 degrees awarded. Offers mass communication (MS). *Application deadline:* For fall admission, 4/15 priority date for domestic students, 3/1 priority date for international students; for spring admission, 11/15 priority date for domestic students, 8/1 priority date for international students. Applications are processed on a rolling basis. *Application fee:* $40 ($75 for international students). Electronic applications accepted. *Director,* Tom Weir, 405-744-6354.

College of Education Students: 257 full-time (186 women), 551 part-time (369 women); includes 152 minority (52 African Americans, 63 American Indian/Alaska Native, 15 Asian Americans or Pacific Islanders, 22 Hispanic Americans), 47 international. Average age 37. 535 applicants, 33% accepted, 141 enrolled. *Faculty:* 98 full-time (55 women), 63 part-time/adjunct (36 women). Expenses: Contact institution. *Financial support:* In 2006–07, 52 research assistantships (averaging $7,658 per year), 90 teaching assistantships (averaging $8,353 per year) were awarded; career-related internships or fieldwork, Federal Work-Study, scholarships/grants, health care benefits, tuition waivers (partial), and unspecified assistantships also available. Support available to part-time students. Financial award application deadline: 3/1. In 2006, 137 master's, 63 doctorates awarded. Offers education (MS, Ed D, PhD, Ed S). *Application deadline:* For fall admission, 3/1 priority date for international students; for spring admission, 8/1 priority date for international students. Applications are processed on a rolling basis. *Application fee:* $40 ($75 for international students). Electronic applications accepted. *Dean,* Dr. Pamela Fry, 405-744-3373.

School of Applied Health and Educational Psychology Students: 189 full-time (137 women), 180 part-time (113 women); includes 75 minority (25 African Americans, 34 American Indian/Alaska Native, 5 Asian Americans or Pacific Islanders, 11 Hispanic Americans), 27 international. Average age 33. 275 applicants, 28% accepted, 64 enrolled. *Faculty:* 37 full-time (17 women), 12 part-time/adjunct (8 women). Expenses: Contact institution. *Financial support:* In 2006–07, 29 research assistantships (averaging $6,452 per year), 64 teaching assistantships (averaging $8,263 per year) were awarded; career-related internships or fieldwork, Federal Work-Study, scholarships/grants, health care benefits, tuition waivers (partial), and unspecified assistantships also available. Support available to part-time students. Financial award application deadline: 3/1. In 2006, 45 master's, 21 doctorates awarded. *Degree program information:* Part-time programs available. Offers applied behavioral studies (MS, Ed D, PhD); counseling and student personnel (MS, PhD); educational psychology (PhD); health (MS, Ed D); leisure sciences (MS, Ed D); physical education (MS, Ed D); physical education and leisure sciences (Ed D); school psychology (Ed S). *Application deadline:* For fall admission, 7/1 priority date for domestic students, 3/1 priority date for international students; for spring admission, 8/1 priority date for international students. Applications are processed on a rolling basis. *Application fee:* $40 ($75 for international students). Electronic applications accepted. *Head,* Dr. John Romans, 405-744-6040.

School of Educational Studies Students: 40 full-time (28 women), 160 part-time (93 women); includes 34 minority (14 African Americans, 11 American Indian/Alaska Native, 5 Asian Americans or Pacific Islanders, 4 Hispanic Americans), 8 international. Average age 40. 124 applicants, 43% accepted, 37 enrolled. *Faculty:* 28 full-time (10 women), 25 part-time/adjunct (6 women). Expenses: Contact institution. *Financial support:* In 2006–07, 13 research assistantships (averaging $8,838 per year), 7 teaching assistantships (averaging $7,586 per year) were awarded; career-related internships or fieldwork, Federal Work-Study, and

Oklahoma State University (continued)

tuition waivers (partial) also available. Support available to part-time students. Financial award application deadline: 3/1. In 2006, 34 master's, 29 doctorates awarded. Offers educational administration (MS); higher education (MS, Ed D); technical education (MS, Ed D); trade and industrial education (MS, Ed D). *Application deadline:* For fall admission, 7/1 priority date for domestic students, 3/1 priority date for international students; for spring admission, 8/1 priority date for international students. Applications are processed on a rolling basis. *Application fee:* $40 ($75 for international students). Electronic applications accepted. *Head,* Dr. Bert Jacobson, 405-744-6275.

School of Teaching and Curriculum Leadership Students: 28 full-time (21 women), 211 part-time (163 women); includes 43 minority (13 African Americans, 18 American Indian/Alaska Native, 5 Asian Americans or Pacific Islanders, 7 Hispanic Americans), 12 international. Average age 40. 136 applicants, 34% accepted, 40 enrolled. *Faculty:* 32 full-time (27 women), 26 part-time/adjunct (22 women). Expenses: Contact institution. *Financial support:* In 2006–07, 10 research assistantships (averaging $9,621 per year), 19 teaching assistantships (averaging $8,939 per year) were awarded; career-related internships or fieldwork, Federal Work-Study, scholarships/grants, health care benefits, tuition waivers (partial), and unspecified assistantships also available. Support available to part-time students. Financial award application deadline: 3/1. In 2006, 58 master's, 13 doctorates awarded. Offers teaching and curriculum leadership (MS, PhD). *Application deadline:* For fall admission, 7/1 priority date for domestic students, 3/1 priority date for international students; for spring admission, 8/1 priority date for international students. Applications are processed on a rolling basis. *Application fee:* $40 ($75 for international students). Electronic applications accepted. *Head,* Dr. Christine Ormsbee, 405-744-7125.

College of Engineering, Architecture and Technology Students: 227 full-time (43 women), 343 part-time (65 women); includes 42 minority (11 African Americans, 17 American Indian/Alaska Native, 6 Asian Americans or Pacific Islanders, 8 Hispanic Americans), 285 international. Average age 30. 956 applicants, 45% accepted, 146 enrolled. *Faculty:* 112 full-time (7 women), 13 part-time/adjunct (0 women). Expenses: Contact institution. *Financial support:* In 2006–07, 174 research assistantships (averaging $10,636 per year), 118 teaching assistantships (averaging $7,696 per year) were awarded; fellowships, career-related internships or fieldwork, Federal Work-Study, scholarships/grants, health care benefits, tuition waivers (partial), and unspecified assistantships also available. Support available to part-time students. Financial award application deadline: 3/1. In 2006, 136 master's, 31 doctorates awarded. Offers engineering, architecture and technology (M Arch, M Arch E, M Bio E, MIEM, MS, PhD). *Application deadline:* For fall admission, 7/1 priority date for domestic students, 3/1 priority date for international students; for spring admission, 8/1 priority date for international students. Applications are processed on a rolling basis. *Application fee:* $40 ($75 for international students). Electronic applications accepted. *Dean,* Dr. Karl N. Reid, 405-744-5140.

School of Architecture Students: 2 full-time (0 women), 1 international. Average age 27. 14 applicants, 29% accepted, 1 enrolled. *Faculty:* 18 full-time (2 women). Expenses: Contact institution. *Financial support:* Teaching assistantships, career-related internships or fieldwork, Federal Work-Study, scholarships/grants, health care benefits, tuition waivers (partial), and unspecified assistantships available. Support available to part-time students. Financial award application deadline: 3/1. In 2006, 1 degree awarded. Offers architectural engineering (M Arch E); architecture (M Arch, M Arch E). *Application deadline:* For fall admission, 2/15 priority date for domestic students, 3/1 priority date for international students; for spring admission, 8/1 priority date for international students. Applications are processed on a rolling basis. *Application fee:* $40 ($75 for international students). Electronic applications accepted. *Head,* Dr. Randy Seitsinger, 405-744-6043.

School of Chemical Engineering Students: 17 full-time (2 women), 14 part-time (3 women); includes 2 minority (both American Indian/Alaska Native), 26 international. Average age 27. 45 applicants, 47% accepted, 11 enrolled. *Faculty:* 11 full-time (2 women), 2 part-time/adjunct (0 women). Expenses: Contact institution. *Financial support:* In 2006–07, 22 research assistantships (averaging $11,602 per year), 13 teaching assistantships (averaging $9,591 per year) were awarded; fellowships, career-related internships or fieldwork, Federal Work-Study, scholarships/grants, health care benefits, tuition waivers (partial), and unspecified assistantships also available. Support available to part-time students. Financial award application deadline: 3/1. In 2006, 8 master's, 5 doctorates awarded. Offers chemical engineering (MS, PhD). *Application deadline:* For fall admission, 7/1 priority date for domestic students, 3/1 priority date for international students; for spring admission, 8/1 priority date for international students. Applications are processed on a rolling basis. *Application fee:* $40 ($75 for international students). Electronic applications accepted. *Head,* Dr. Russell Rhinehart, 405-744-5280.

School of Civil and Environmental Engineering Students: 26 full-time (9 women), 29 part-time (10 women); includes 8 minority (1 African American, 4 American Indian/Alaska Native, 1 Asian American or Pacific Islander, 2 Hispanic Americans), 26 international. Average age 29. 92 applicants, 47% accepted, 14 enrolled. *Faculty:* 17 full-time (1 woman), 1 part-time/adjunct (0 women). Expenses: Contact institution. *Financial support:* In 2006–07, 15 research assistantships (averaging $10,879 per year), 12 teaching assistantships (averaging $10,275 per year) were awarded; career-related internships or fieldwork, Federal Work-Study, and tuition waivers (partial) also available. Support available to part-time students. Financial award application deadline: 3/1. In 2006, 27 master's, 1 doctorate awarded. Offers civil engineering (MS, PhD); environmental engineering (MS, PhD). *Application deadline:* For fall admission, 7/1 priority date for domestic students, 3/1 priority date for international students; for spring admission, 8/1 priority date for international students. Applications are processed on a rolling basis. *Application fee:* $40 ($75 for international students). Electronic applications accepted. *Interim Head,* Dr. John Veenstra, 405-744-5190.

School of Electrical and Computer Engineering Students: 56 full-time (8 women), 77 part-time (9 women); includes 6 minority (1 African American, 2 American Indian/Alaska Native, 1 Asian American or Pacific Islander, 2 Hispanic Americans), 85 international. Average age 29. 370 applicants, 33% accepted, 39 enrolled. *Faculty:* 28 full-time (1 woman), 2 part-time/adjunct (0 women). Expenses: Contact institution. *Financial support:* In 2006–07, 57 research assistantships (averaging $10,595 per year), 23 teaching assistantships (averaging $7,934 per year) were awarded; career-related internships or fieldwork, Federal Work-Study, scholarships/grants, health care benefits, tuition waivers (partial), and unspecified assistantships also available. Support available to part-time students. Financial award application deadline: 3/1. In 2006, 27 master's, 11 doctorates awarded. Offers control systems engineering (MS); electrical and computer engineering (MS, PhD). *Application deadline:* For fall admission, 7/1 priority date for domestic students, 3/1 priority date for international students; for spring admission, 8/1 priority date for international students. Applications are processed on a rolling basis. *Application fee:* $40 ($75 for international students). Electronic applications accepted. *Head,* Dr. Keith Teague, 405-744-5151.

School of Industrial Engineering and Management Students: 59 full-time (14 women), 175 part-time (36 women); includes 24 minority (9 African Americans, 7 American Indian/Alaska Native, 4 Asian Americans or Pacific Islanders, 4 Hispanic Americans), 75 international. Average age 33. 241 applicants, 66% accepted, 57 enrolled. *Faculty:* 11 full-time (1 woman), 3 part-time/adjunct (0 women). Expenses: Contact institution. *Financial support:* In 2006–07, 21 research assistantships (averaging $8,009 per year), 20 teaching assistantships (averaging $6,776 per year) were awarded; career-related internships or fieldwork, Federal Work-Study, scholarships/grants, health care benefits, tuition waivers (partial), and unspecified assistantships also available. Support available to part-time students. Financial award application deadline: 3/1. In 2006, 62 master's, 3 doctorates awarded. Offers engineering and technology management (MS); industrial engineering and management (MIEM, MS, PhD); manufacturing systems engineering (MS). *Application deadline:* For fall admission, 7/1 priority date for domestic students, 3/1 priority date for international students; for spring admission, 8/1 priority date for international students. Applications are processed on a rolling basis. *Application fee:* $40 ($75 for international students). Electronic applications accepted. *Head,* Dr. William J. Kolarik, 405-744-6055.

School of Mechanical and Aerospace Engineering Students: 67 full-time (10 women), 48 part-time (7 women); includes 2 minority (both American Indian/Alaska Native), 72 international. Average age 27. 194 applicants, 43% accepted, 24 enrolled. *Faculty:* 25 full-time (0 women), 4 part-time/adjunct (0 women). Expenses: Contact institution. *Financial support:* In 2006–07, 59 research assistantships (averaging $11,188 per year), 50 teaching assistantships (averaging $6,843 per year) were awarded; career-related internships or fieldwork, Federal Work-Study, scholarships/grants, health care benefits, tuition waivers (partial), and unspecified assistantships also available. Support available to part-time students. Financial award application deadline: 3/1. In 2006, 11 master's, 11 doctorates awarded. Offers mechanical engineering (MS, PhD). *Application deadline:* For fall admission, 7/1 priority date for domestic students, 3/1 priority date for international students; for spring admission, 8/1 priority date for international students. Applications are processed on a rolling basis. *Application fee:* $40 ($75 for international students). Electronic applications accepted. *Head,* Dr. Lawrence L. Hoberock, 405-744-5900.

College of Human Environmental Sciences Students: 116 full-time (96 women), 104 part-time (75 women); includes 24 minority (8 African Americans, 10 American Indian/Alaska Native, 4 Asian Americans or Pacific Islanders, 2 Hispanic Americans), 77 international. Average age 32. 157 applicants, 38% accepted, 38 enrolled. *Faculty:* 72 full-time (47 women), 7 part-time/adjunct (4 women). Expenses: Contact institution. *Financial support:* In 2006–07, 81 research assistantships (averaging $9,990 per year), 37 teaching assistantships (averaging $9,889 per year) were awarded; career-related internships or fieldwork, Federal Work-Study, and tuition waivers (partial) also available. Support available to part-time students. Financial award application deadline: 3/1. In 2006, 56 master's, 9 doctorates awarded. Offers design, housing and merchandising (MS, PhD); human development and family science (MS, PhD); human environmental sciences (MS, PhD); nutritional sciences (MS, PhD). *Application deadline:* For fall admission, 3/1 priority date for international students; for spring admission, 8/1 priority date for international students. Applications are processed on a rolling basis. *Application fee:* $40 ($75 for international students). Electronic applications accepted. *Dean,* Dr. Patricia Knaub, 405-744-9805.

School of Hotel and Restaurant Administration Students: 26 full-time (15 women), 31 part-time (19 women); includes 3 minority (1 African American, 2 Asian Americans or Pacific Islanders), 42 international. Average age 35. 25 applicants, 20% accepted, 0 enrolled. *Faculty:* 10 full-time (2 women), 2 part-time/adjunct (0 women). Expenses: Contact institution. *Financial support:* In 2006–07, 9 research assistantships (averaging $8,181 per year), 8 teaching assistantships (averaging $13,030 per year) were awarded; career-related internships or fieldwork, Federal Work-Study, scholarships/grants, health care benefits, tuition waivers (partial), and unspecified assistantships also available. Support available to part-time students. Financial award application deadline: 3/1. In 2006, 8 master's, 2 doctorates awarded. Offers hotel and restaurant administration (MS, PhD). *Application deadline:* For fall admission, 7/1 priority date for domestic students, 3/1 priority date for international students; for spring admission, 8/1 priority date for international students. Applications are processed on a rolling basis. *Application fee:* $40 ($75 for international students). Electronic applications accepted. *Interim Head,* Dr. Bill Ryan, 405-744-6713.

Graduate College Students: 94 full-time (49 women), 166 part-time (88 women); includes 44 minority (17 African Americans, 19 American Indian/Alaska Native, 3 Asian Americans or Pacific Islanders, 5 Hispanic Americans), 61 international. Average age 32. 762 applicants, 77% accepted, 69 enrolled. *Faculty:* 2 full-time (0 women), 3 part-time/adjunct (1 woman). Expenses: Contact institution. *Financial support:* In 2006–07, 5 research assistantships (averaging $10,254 per year) were awarded; career-related internships or fieldwork, Federal Work-Study, scholarships/grants, tuition waivers (full and partial), and unspecified assistantships also available. Support available to part-time students. Financial award application deadline: 3/1. In 2006, 78 master's, 7 doctorates awarded. *Degree program information:* Part-time programs available. Offers aviation and space science (MS); biophotonics (MS, PhD); environmental sciences (MS, PhD); gerontology (MS); health care administration (MS); international studies (MS); natural and applied sciences (MS); plant science (PhD). *Application deadline:* For fall admission, 3/1 priority date for international students; for spring admission, 8/1 priority date for international students. Applications are processed on a rolling basis. *Application fee:* $40 ($75 for international students). Electronic applications accepted. *Application Contact:* Dr. Craig Satterfield, Director of Student Services, 405-744-6368, Fax: 405-744-0355, E-mail: grad_i@okstate.edu. *Dean,* Dr. Gordon Emslie, 405-744-6368, Fax: 405-744-0355, E-mail: grad_i@okstate.edu.

William S. Spears School of Business Students: 311 full-time (109 women), 363 part-time (132 women); includes 72 minority (17 African Americans, 34 American Indian/Alaska Native, 10 Asian Americans or Pacific Islanders, 11 Hispanic Americans), 178 international. 786 applicants, 44% accepted, 207 enrolled. *Faculty:* 119 full-time (26 women), 23 part-time/adjunct (9 women). Expenses: Contact institution. *Financial support:* In 2006–07, 22 research assistantships (averaging $10,065 per year), 142 teaching assistantships (averaging $8,473 per year) were awarded; career-related internships or fieldwork, Federal Work-Study, scholarships/grants, health care benefits, tuition waivers (partial), and unspecified assistantships also available. Support available to part-time students. Financial award application deadline: 3/1. In 2006, 231 master's, 9 doctorates awarded. Offers business (MBA, MS, MSQFE, PhD); business administration (MBA); economics and legal studies in business (MS, PhD); finance (MBA, MSQFE, PhD); management (MBA, PhD); management information systems (PhD); management information systems/accounting information systems (MS); management science (PhD); marketing (MBA, PhD); operations management (PhD); telecommunications management (MS, PhD). *Application deadline:* For fall admission, 7/1 priority date for domestic students, 3/1 priority date for international students; for spring admission, 8/1 priority date for international students. Applications are processed on a rolling basis. *Application fee:* $40 ($75 for international students). Electronic applications accepted. *Dean,* Dr. Sara M. Freedman, 405-744-5064.

School of Accounting Students: 53 full-time (27 women), 16 part-time (8 women); includes 9 minority (1 African American, 8 American Indian/Alaska Native), 19 international. Average age 28. 79 applicants, 35% accepted, 20 enrolled. *Faculty:* 20 full-time (7 women). Expenses: Contact institution. *Financial support:* In 2006–07, 6 research assistantships (averaging $18,667 per year), 24 teaching assistantships (averaging $7,908 per year) were awarded; career-related internships or fieldwork, Federal Work-Study, scholarships/grants, health care benefits, tuition waivers (partial), and unspecified assistantships also available. Support available to part-time students. Financial award application deadline: 3/1. In 2006, 37 degrees awarded. Offers accounting (MS, PhD). *Application deadline:* For fall admission, 7/1 priority date for domestic students, 3/1 priority date for international students; for spring admission, 8/1 priority date for international students. Applications are processed on a rolling basis. *Application fee:* $40 ($75 for international students). Electronic applications accepted. *Head,* Dr. Don Hansen, 405-744-5123.

OKLAHOMA STATE UNIVERSITY CENTER FOR HEALTH SCIENCES, Tulsa, OK 74107-1898

General Information State-supported, coed, graduate-only institution. *Enrollment by degree level:* 351 first professional, 32 master's, 14 doctoral. *Graduate housing:* On-campus housing not available. *Student services:* Campus safety program, career counseling, disabled student services, free psychological counseling, low-cost health insurance. *Library facilities:* Oklahoma State University Center for Health Sciences Medical Library plus 1 other. *Online resources:* library catalog, web page, access to other libraries' catalogs. *Collection:* 58,594 titles, 12,730 serial subscriptions, 124,110 audiovisual materials. *Research affiliation:* Sun River, Inc. (cognitive rehabilitation), Merck and Company (pharmaceutical sciences), Viropharma (pharmaceutical sciences), Ingenex (pharmaceutical sciences), Proctor & Gamble (pharmaceutical sciences), Glaxo-Smith Kline (pharmaceutical sciences).

Computer facilities: 51 computers available on campus for general student use. A campuswide network can be accessed from off campus. Internet access is available. *Web address:* http://osu.com.okstate.edu/.

General Application Contact: Leah Haines, Associate Director of Admissions and Registrar, 800-677-1972, Fax: 918-561-8243, E-mail: leah.haines@okstate.edu.

GRADUATE UNITS

College of Osteopathic Medicine Students: 351 full-time (166 women); includes 88 minority (17 African Americans, 38 American Indian/Alaska Native, 26 Asian Americans or Pacific

Islanders, 7 Hispanic Americans). Average age 28. 1,454 applicants, 10% accepted, 88 enrolled. Expenses: Contact institution. *Financial support:* In 2006–07, 337 students received support. Federal Work-Study, institutionally sponsored loans, scholarships/grants, and tuition waivers available. Financial award application deadline: 3/31; financial award applicants required to submit FAFSA. In 2006, 92 degrees awarded. Offers osteopathic medicine (DO). *Application deadline:* For fall admission, 2/1 for domestic students. Applications are processed on a rolling basis. *Application fee:* $40. *Application Contact:* Leah Haines, Associate Director of Admissions and Registrar, 800-677-1972, Fax: 918-561-8243, E-mail: leah.haines@okstate.edu. *President and Dean, Center for Health Sciences,* Dr. John J. Fernandes, Fax: 918-561-8243.

Program in Biomedical Sciences Students: 11 full-time (4 women), 10 part-time (8 women); includes 4 minority (all American Indian/Alaska Native), 5 international. Average age 31. 22 applicants, 82% accepted, 18 enrolled. Expenses: Contact institution. *Financial support:* In 2006–07, 9 students received support, including 8 research assistantships with partial tuition reimbursements available (averaging $20,800 per year); scholarships/grants and tuition waivers (partial) also available. Financial award application deadline: 4/10; financial award applicants required to submit FAFSA. In 2006, 1 degree awarded. Offers biomedical sciences (MS, PhD). *Application deadline:* For fall admission, 8/15 priority date for domestic students, 8/15 for international students; for winter admission, 1/3 priority date for domestic students, 1/3 for international students. Applications are processed on a rolling basis. *Application fee:* $40 ($75 for international students). *Application Contact:* Leah Haines, Associate Director of Admissions and Registrar, 800-677-1972, Fax: 918-561-8243, E-mail: leah.haines@okstate.edu. *Director,* Dr. Earl L. Blewett, 918-561-8405, Fax: 918-561-8276.

Program in Forensic Sciences Students: 6 full-time (5 women), 30 part-time (23 women); includes 6 minority (4 African Americans, 1 Asian American or Pacific Islander, 1 Hispanic American). Average age 34. 47 applicants, 26% accepted, 11 enrolled. *Faculty:* 2 full-time (0 women), 14 part-time/adjunct (5 women). Expenses: Contact institution. *Financial support:* In 2006–07, 5 students received support, including 5 research assistantships (averaging $13,200 per year); Federal Work-Study also available. Support available to part-time students. In 2006, 6 degrees awarded. *Degree program information:* Part-time and evening/weekend programs available. Postbaccalaureate distance learning degree programs offered (minimal on-campus study). Offers forensic DNA/molecular biology (MS); forensic examination of questioned documents (MFSA); forensic pathology (MS); forensic psychology (MS); forensic sciences (MFSA); forensic toxicology (MS). *Application deadline:* For fall admission, 3/1 for domestic students, 2/1 priority date for international students; for spring admission, 10/31 for international students. *Application fee:* $40 ($75 for international students). *Application Contact:* Cathy Newsome, Coordinator, 918-699-8608, Fax: 918-561-8414, E-mail: cathy.newsome@okstate.edu. *Director,* Dr. Robert T. Allen, 918-561-1108, Fax: 918-561-8414.

OLD DOMINION UNIVERSITY, Norfolk, VA 23529

General Information State-supported, coed, university. CGS member. *Enrollment:* 21,625 graduate, professional, and undergraduate students; 1,262 full-time matriculated graduate/professional students (802 women), 2,711 part-time matriculated graduate/professional students (1,486 women). *Enrollment by degree level:* 3,096 master's, 839 doctoral, 38 other advanced degrees. *Graduate faculty:* 554 full-time (178 women), 105 part-time/adjunct (61 women). *Tuition, area resident:* Part-time $285 per credit hour. Tuition, nonresident: part-time $715 per credit hour. *Required fees:* $94 per semester. *Graduate housing:* Room and/or apartments available to single students; on-campus housing not available to married students. Typical cost: $3,640 per year ($6,640 including board). Room and board charges vary according to board plan and housing facility selected. Housing application deadline: 5/1. *Student services:* Campus employment opportunities, campus safety program, career counseling, disabled student services, free psychological counseling, grant writing training, international student services, low-cost health insurance, multicultural affairs office, teacher training. *Library facilities:* Douglas and Patricia Perry Library plus 2 others. *Online resources:* library catalog, web page, access to other libraries' catalogs. *Collection:* 968,921 titles, 16,371 serial subscriptions, 52,071 audiovisual materials. *Research affiliation:* Joint Forces Command (modelling, simulation, and technology development), Virginia Commerical Space Flight Authority (aerospace engineering), Mid Atlantic Institue for Space and Technology (aerospace engineering), Virginia Space Grant Consortium (STEM disciplines), Virgina Tidewater Consortium for Higher Education (multidisciplinary).

Computer facilities: 800 computers available on campus for general student use. A campuswide network can be accessed from student residence rooms and from off campus. Internet access and online class registration, online courses are available. *Web address:* http://www.odu.edu/.

General Application Contact: Alice McAdory, Director of Admissions, 757-683-3685, Fax: 757-683-3255, E-mail: gradadmit@odu.edu.

GRADUATE UNITS

College of Arts and Letters Students: 143 full-time (85 women), 188 part-time (133 women); includes 61 minority (45 African Americans, 1 American Indian/Alaska Native, 5 Asian Americans or Pacific Islanders, 10 Hispanic Americans), 20 international. Average age 32. 276 applicants, 66% accepted, 117 enrolled. *Faculty:* 128 full-time (44 women), 4 part-time/adjunct (1 woman). Expenses: Contact institution. *Financial support:* In 2006–07, 214 students received support, including 3 fellowships with full and partial tuition reimbursements available (averaging $15,000 per year), 12 research assistantships with full and partial tuition reimbursements available (averaging $11,000 per year), 24 teaching assistantships with full and partial tuition reimbursements available (averaging $8,500 per year); career-related internships or fieldwork, institutionally sponsored loans, scholarships/grants, tuition waivers (partial), and unspecified assistantships also available. Support available to part-time students. Financial award application deadline: 2/15; financial award applicants required to submit CSS PROFILE or FAFSA. In 2006, 88 master's, 6 doctorates awarded. *Degree program information:* Part-time and evening/weekend programs available. Offers applied linguistics (MA); applied sociology (MA); arts and letters (MA, MFA, MME, PhD); creative writing (MFA); criminology and criminal justice (PhD); English (MA, PhD); history (MA); humanities (MA); international studies (MA, PhD); music education (MME); visual studies (MA, MFA). *Application deadline:* For fall admission, 6/1 priority date for domestic students, 2/15 for international students; for spring admission, 11/1 priority date for domestic students, 10/1 for international students. *Application fee:* $40. Electronic applications accepted. *Application Contact:* Dr. Robert Wojtowicz, Associate Dean, 757-683-6077, Fax: 757-683-5746, E-mail: rwojtowi@odu.edu. *Dean,* Dr. Chandra deSilva, 757-683-3915, Fax: 757-683-3317, E-mail: cdesilva@odu.edu.

College of Business and Public Administration Students: 150 full-time (70 women), 368 part-time (165 women); includes 105 minority (70 African Americans, 1 American Indian/Alaska Native, 26 Asian Americans or Pacific Islanders, 8 Hispanic Americans), 72 international. Average age 32. 368 applicants, 75% accepted. *Faculty:* 71 full-time (17 women), 9 part-time/adjunct (3 women). Expenses: Contact institution. *Financial support:* In 2006–07, 230 students received support, including 12 fellowships with partial tuition reimbursements available (averaging $7,500 per year), 70 research assistantships with full and partial tuition reimbursements available (averaging $7,500 per year), 12 teaching assistantships with full and partial tuition reimbursements available (averaging $10,000 per year); career-related internships or fieldwork, scholarships/grants, tuition waivers (partial), and unspecified assistantships also available. Support available to part-time students. Financial award application deadline: 2/15; financial award applicants required to submit FAFSA. In 2006, 170 master's, 6 doctorates awarded. *Degree program information:* Part-time and evening/weekend programs available. Postbaccalaureate distance learning degree programs offered (no on-campus study). Offers accounting (MS); business administration (MBA, PhD); business and public administration (MA, MBA, MPA, MS, MUS, PhD); economics (MA); finance (PhD); management (PhD); marketing (PhD); policy analysis/program evaluation (MUS); public administration (MPA); public administration and urban policy (PhD); public planning analysis (MUS); urban administration (MUS). *Application deadline:* For fall admission, 6/1 priority date for domestic and international students; for winter admission, 11/1 priority date for domestic and international students. Applications are processed on a rolling basis. *Application fee:* $40. Electronic applications accepted. *Application Contact:* Dr. Ali Ardalan, Associate Dean, 757-683-3520, Fax: 757-683-4076, E-mail: aardalan@odu.edu. *Dean,* Dr. Nancy Bagranoff, 757-683-3520, Fax: 757-683-4076, E-mail: nbagranoff@odu.edu.

College of Engineering and Technology Students: 150 full-time (40 women), 611 part-time (118 women); includes 113 minority (43 African Americans, 2 American Indian/Alaska Native, 38 Asian Americans or Pacific Islanders, 30 Hispanic Americans), 183 international. Average age 31. 453 applicants, 70% accepted, 192 enrolled. *Faculty:* 79 full-time (5 women), 14 part-time/adjunct (3 women). Expenses: Contact institution. *Financial support:* In 2006–07, 9 fellowships with full and partial tuition reimbursements (averaging $14,000 per year), 91 research assistantships with full and partial tuition reimbursements (averaging $14,000 per year), 17 teaching assistantships with full and partial tuition reimbursements (averaging $12,000 per year) were awarded; career-related internships or fieldwork, Federal Work-Study, institutionally sponsored loans, scholarships/grants, tuition waivers (partial), and unspecified assistantships also available. Support available to part-time students. Financial award applicants required to submit FAFSA. In 2006, 279 master's, 17 doctorates awarded. *Degree program information:* Part-time and evening/weekend programs available. Postbaccalaureate distance learning degree programs offered. Offers aerospace engineering (ME, MS, PhD); civil engineering (ME, MS, PhD); computer engineering (ME, MS); design and manufacturing (ME); electrical and computer engineering (PhD); electrical engineering (ME, MS); engineering and technology (ME, MEM, MS, PhD); engineering management (MEM, MS, PhD); environmental engineering (ME, MS, PhD); experimental methods (ME); mechanical engineering (ME, MS, PhD); modeling and simulation (ME, MS, PhD); motorsports (ME); systems engineering (ME). *Application deadline:* For fall admission, 6/1 for domestic students, 2/15 for international students; for spring admission, 1/1 for domestic students, 10/1 for international students. Applications are processed on a rolling basis. *Application fee:* $40. Electronic applications accepted. *Application Contact:* Dr. Linda Vahala, Associate Dean, 757-683-3789, Fax: 757-683-4898, E-mail: lvahala@odu.edu. *Dean,* Dr. Oktay Baysal, 757-683-3789, Fax: 757-683-4898, E-mail: obaysal@odu.edu.

College of Health Sciences Students: 220 full-time (174 women), 224 part-time (175 women); includes 69 minority (46 African Americans, 1 American Indian/Alaska Native, 17 Asian Americans or Pacific Islanders, 5 Hispanic Americans), 14 international. Average age 33. 335 applicants, 73% accepted, 110 enrolled. *Faculty:* 41 full-time (30 women), 10 part-time/adjunct (8 women). Expenses: Contact institution. *Financial support:* In 2006–07, 210 students received support, including 1 fellowship with full tuition reimbursement available (averaging $2,220 per year), 15 research assistantships with tuition reimbursements available (averaging $11,000 per year), 6 teaching assistantships with tuition reimbursements available (averaging $9,000 per year); career-related internships or fieldwork, institutionally sponsored loans, scholarships/grants, traineeships, tuition waivers (partial), and unspecified assistantships also available. Support available to part-time students. Financial award application deadline: 2/15; financial award applicants required to submit FAFSA. In 2006, 104 master's, 32 doctorates awarded. *Degree program information:* Part-time and evening/weekend programs available. Postbaccalaureate distance learning degree programs offered (minimal on-campus study). Offers community health professions (MS); dental hygiene (MS); environmental health (MS); health care administration (MS); health sciences (MPH, MS, MSN, DPT, PhD); health services research (PhD); long-term care administration (MS); nursing (MSN); physical therapy (DPT); public health (MPH); wellness and promotion (MS). *Application deadline:* Applications are processed on a rolling basis. *Application fee:* $40. Electronic applications accepted. *Application Contact:* Dr. Brenda Stevenson Marshall, Assistant Dean for Education, 757-683-6482, Fax: 757-683-4753, E-mail: bmarshal@odu.edu. *Dean,* Dr. Andrew Balas, 757-683-4960, Fax: 757-683-3674, E-mail: abalas@odu.edu.

College of Sciences Students: 146 full-time (74 women), 359 part-time (175 women); includes 57 minority (28 African Americans, 2 American Indian/Alaska Native, 16 Asian Americans or Pacific Islanders, 11 Hispanic Americans), 197 international. Average age 29. 592 applicants, 51% accepted. *Faculty:* 142 full-time (32 women), 3 part-time/adjunct (2 women). Expenses: Contact institution. *Financial support:* In 2006–07, 3 fellowships (averaging $5,000 per year), 158 research assistantships with tuition reimbursements (averaging $18,000 per year), 101 teaching assistantships with tuition reimbursements (averaging $16,000 per year) were awarded; career-related internships or fieldwork, scholarships/grants, and tuition waivers (partial) also available. Support available to part-time students. Financial award application deadline: 2/15; financial award applicants required to submit FAFSA. In 2006, 101 master's, 19 doctorates awarded. *Degree program information:* Part-time and evening/weekend programs available. Offers analytical chemistry (MS); applied experimental psychology (PhD); biochemistry (MS); biology (MS); biomedical sciences (PhD); clinical chemistry (MS); clinical psychology (Psy D); computational and applied mathematics (MS, PhD); computer science (MS, PhD); ecological sciences (PhD); environmental chemistry (MS); human factors psychology (PhD); industrial/organizational psychology (PhD); ocean and earth sciences (MS); oceanography (PhD); organic chemistry (MS); physical chemistry (MS); physics (MS, PhD); psychology (MS, PhD); sciences (MS, PhD, Psy D). *Application fee:* $40. Electronic applications accepted. *Interim Dean,* Dr. Chris Platsucas, 757-683-3274, Fax: 757-683-3034, E-mail: cpatsou@odu.edu.

Darden College of Education Students: 453 full-time (359 women), 961 part-time (720 women); includes 207 minority (173 African Americans, 9 American Indian/Alaska Native, 17 Asian Americans or Pacific Islanders, 8 Hispanic Americans), 17 international. Average age 34. 1,125 applicants, 72% accepted. *Faculty:* 93 full-time (50 women), 65 part-time/adjunct (44 women). Expenses: Contact institution. *Financial support:* In 2006–07, 4 fellowships with full tuition reimbursements (averaging $15,000 per year), 60 research assistantships with full and partial tuition reimbursements (averaging $9,000 per year), 25 teaching assistantships with full and partial tuition reimbursements (averaging $9,000 per year) were awarded; career-related internships or fieldwork, Federal Work-Study, institutionally sponsored loans, scholarships/grants, tuition waivers (partial), and unspecified assistantships also available. Support available to part-time students. Financial award application deadline: 2/15; financial award applicants required to submit CSS PROFILE or FAFSA. In 2006, 606 master's, 7 doctorates, 11 other advanced degrees awarded. *Degree program information:* Part-time and evening/weekend programs available. Postbaccalaureate distance learning degree programs offered (no on-campus study). Offers athletic training (MS Ed); biology (MS Ed); business and industry training (MS); career and technical education (PhD); chemistry (MS Ed); community college leadership (PhD); community college teaching (MS); counseling (MS Ed, PhD, Ed S); curriculum and instruction (MS Ed); early childhood education (MS Ed, PhD); education (MS, MS Ed, PhD, Ed S); educational leadership (MS Ed, PhD, Ed S); educational media (MS Ed); educational training (MS Ed); elementary education (MS Ed); English (MS Ed); exercise and wellness (MS Ed); higher education (MS Ed, PhD, Ed S); human movement science (PhD); human resources training (PhD); instructional design and technology (PhD); instructional technology (MS Ed); library science (MS Ed); literacy leadership (PhD); middle and secondary teaching (MS); middle school education (MS Ed); principal preparation (MS Ed); reading education (MS Ed); recreation and tourism studies (MS Ed); secondary education (MS Ed); special education (MS Ed, PhD); speech-language pathology (MS Ed); sport management (MS Ed); technology education (PhD). *Application deadline:* For fall admission, 6/1 priority date for domestic students; for spring admission, 11/1 priority date for domestic students. Applications are processed on a rolling basis. *Application fee:* $40. Electronic applications accepted. *Dean,* Dr. William H. Graves, 757-683-3938, Fax: 757-683-5083, E-mail: wgraves@odu.edu.

See Close-Up on page 987.

OLIVET COLLEGE, Olivet, MI 49076-9701

General Information Independent-religious, coed, comprehensive institution.

GRADUATE UNITS

Program in Education Offers education (MAT). Electronic applications accepted.

OLIVET NAZARENE UNIVERSITY, Bourbonnais, IL 60914-2271

General Information Independent-religious, coed, comprehensive institution. *Graduate housing:* Room and/or apartments available to single students; on-campus housing not available to married students. Housing application deadline: 8/15.

Olivet Nazarene University (continued)

GRADUATE UNITS

Graduate School *Degree program information:* Part-time and evening/weekend programs available. Offers business administration (MBA); practical ministries (MPM).

Division of Education *Degree program information:* Evening/weekend programs available. Offers curriculum and instruction (MAE); elementary education (MAT); secondary education (MAT).

Division of Religion and Philosophy *Degree program information:* Part-time programs available. Offers biblical literature (MA); religion (MA); theology (MA).

Institute for Church Management *Degree program information:* Part-time programs available. Offers church management (MCM); pastoral counseling (MPC).

Program in Organizational Leadership Offers organizational leadership (MOL).

ORAL ROBERTS UNIVERSITY, Tulsa, OK 74171-0001

General Information Independent-religious, coed, comprehensive institution. *Enrollment:* 3,244 graduate, professional, and undergraduate students; 381 full-time matriculated graduate/professional students (180 women), 393 part-time matriculated graduate/professional students (208 women). *Enrollment by degree level:* 563 master's, 211 doctoral. *Graduate faculty:* 35 full-time (5 women), 13 part-time/adjunct (6 women). *Graduate housing:* Room and/or apartments available on a first-come, first-served basis to single students; on-campus housing not available to married students. *Student services:* Campus employment opportunities, career counseling, disabled student services, exercise/wellness program, free psychological counseling, international student services, low-cost health insurance, teacher training. *Library facilities:* John D. Messick Resources Center plus 1 other. *Online resources:* library catalog, web page, access to other libraries' catalogs. *Collection:* 216,691 titles, 600 serial subscriptions.

Computer facilities: 253 computers available on campus for general student use. A campuswide network can be accessed from student residence rooms and from off campus. Internet access is available. *Web address:* http://www.oru.edu/.

General Application Contact: Graduate Admissions Coordinator, 918-495-6989, Fax: 918-495-7965, E-mail: alsc@oru.edu.

GRADUATE UNITS

School of Business Students: 33 full-time (18 women), 67 part-time (28 women); includes 28 minority (17 African Americans, 3 American Indian/Alaska Native, 6 Asian Americans or Pacific Islanders, 2 Hispanic Americans), 15 international. Average age 29. 69 applicants, 84% accepted, 33 enrolled. *Faculty:* 9 full-time (2 women), 4 part-time/adjunct (2 women). Expenses: Contact institution. *Financial support:* In 2006–07, 9 research assistantships (averaging $3,600 per year) were awarded; scholarships/grants and unspecified assistantships also available. Financial award application deadline: 6/1; financial award applicants required to submit FAFSA. In 2006, 21 degrees awarded. *Degree program information:* Part-time programs available. Postbaccalaureate distance learning degree programs offered (minimal on-campus study). Offers accounting (MBA); finance (MBA); international business (MBA); management (MBA); marketing (MBA); non-profit management (M Man, MBA); organizational dynamics (M Man); sales marketing (M Man). *Application deadline:* For fall admission, 7/1 priority date for domestic students, 5/1 priority date for international students; for spring admission, 12/1 priority date for domestic students, 10/1 priority date for international students. Applications are processed on a rolling basis. *Application fee:* $35. *Application Contact:* 918-495-6989, Fax: 918-495-7965, E-mail: alsc@oru.edu. *Dean,* Dr. Mark Lewandowski, 918-495-7040, Fax: 918-495-7876, E-mail: mlewandowski@oru.edu.

School of Education Students: 331 full-time (217 women); includes 118 minority (96 African Americans, 7 American Indian/Alaska Native, 10 Asian Americans or Pacific Islanders, 5 Hispanic Americans). 125 applicants, 96% accepted, 116 enrolled. *Faculty:* 9 full-time (2 women), 9 part-time/adjunct (4 women). Expenses: Contact institution. *Financial support:* In 2006–07, 4 research assistantships (averaging $5,000 per year) were awarded; scholarships/grants and unspecified assistantships also available. Financial award application deadline: 6/1; financial award applicants required to submit FAFSA. In 2006, 25 master's, 10 doctorates awarded. *Degree program information:* Part-time programs available. Postbaccalaureate distance learning degree programs offered (minimal on-campus study). Offers Christian school administration (MA Ed, Ed D); Christian school administration (K-12) (MA Ed, Ed D); Christian school curriculum development (MA Ed); college and higher education administration (MA Ed, Ed D); public school administration (K-12) (MA Ed, Ed D); public school teaching (MA Ed); teaching English as a second language (MA Ed). *Application deadline:* For fall admission, 7/1 priority date for domestic students, 5/1 priority date for international students; for spring admission, 12/1 priority date for domestic students, 10/1 priority date for international students. Applications are processed on a rolling basis. *Application fee:* $35. *Application Contact:* Kim Schmeisser, Graduate Admissions, 918-495-6058, Fax: 918-495-6222, E-mail: gradeducation@oru.edu. *Dean,* Dr. David Hand, 918-495-7084, Fax: 918-495-6050, E-mail: dhand@oru.edu.

School of Theology and Missions Students: 346 full-time (142 women), 133 part-time (61 women); includes 188 minority (129 African Americans, 32 Asian Americans or Pacific Islanders, 27 Hispanic Americans), 52 international. Average age 36. 170 applicants, 95% accepted, 124 enrolled. *Faculty:* 17 full-time (2 women). Expenses: Contact institution. *Financial support:* In 2006–07, teaching assistantships (averaging $3,600 per year); scholarships/grants and employment assistantships also available. Financial award application deadline: 6/1; financial award applicants required to submit FAFSA. In 2006, 41 M Divs, 51 master's, 21 doctorates awarded. *Degree program information:* Part-time programs available. Postbaccalaureate distance learning degree programs offered (minimal on-campus study). Offers biblical literature (MA); Christian counseling (MA); Christian education (MA); divinity (M Div); missions (MA); practical theology (MA); theological/historical studies (MA); theology (D Min). *Application deadline:* For fall admission, 7/1 priority date for domestic students, 5/1 priority date for international students; for spring admission, 12/1 priority date for domestic students, 10/1 priority date for international students. Applications are processed on a rolling basis. *Application fee:* $35. *Application Contact:* 918-495-6989, Fax: 918-495-7965, E-mail: alsc@oru.edu. *Dean,* Dr. Thomson K. Mathew, 918-495-7016, Fax: 918-495-6259, E-mail: tmathew@oru.edu.

OREGON COLLEGE OF ORIENTAL MEDICINE, Portland, OR 97216

General Information Independent, coed, graduate-only institution. *Enrollment by degree level:* 228 master's, 38 doctoral. *Graduate faculty:* 12 full-time (5 women), 46 part-time/adjunct (26 women). *Graduate housing:* On-campus housing not available. *Student services:* Campus employment opportunities, campus safety program, low-cost health insurance, teacher training. *Library facilities:* Oregon College of Oriental Medicine Library. *Online resources:* library catalog, access to other libraries' catalogs. *Collection:* 3,100 titles, 43 serial subscriptions, 750 audiovisual materials.

Computer facilities: 6 computers available on campus for general student use. A campuswide network can be accessed. Internet access is available. *Web address:* http://www.ocom.edu/.

General Application Contact: Nicola Moll, Admissions Coordinator, 503-253-3443 Ext. 113, Fax: 503-253-2701, E-mail: nmoll@ocom.edu.

GRADUATE UNITS

Graduate Program in Acupuncture and Oriental Medicine Students: 243 full-time (184 women), 23 part-time (20 women); includes 38 minority (5 African Americans, 1 American Indian/Alaska Native, 30 Asian Americans or Pacific Islanders, 2 Hispanic Americans), 2 international. Average age 35. 142 applicants, 70% accepted, 74 enrolled. *Faculty:* 12 full-time (5 women), 47 part-time/adjunct (26 women). Expenses: Contact institution. *Financial support:* In 2006–07, 208 students received support, including 5 fellowships (averaging $14,000 per year), 1 research assistantship (averaging $14,175 per year); Federal Work-Study also available. Support available to part-time students. Financial award applicants required to submit FAFSA. In 2006, 63 master's, 15 doctorates awarded. *Degree program information:* Part-time programs available. Offers acupuncture and Oriental medicine (M Ac OM, MAcOM, DAOM). *Application deadline:* Applications are processed on a rolling basis. *Application fee:* $50. *Application Contact:* Nicola Moll, Admissions Coordinator, 503-253-3443 Ext. 113, Fax: 503-253-2701, E-mail: nmoll@ocom.edu. *President,* Dr. Michael Gaeta, 503-253-3443 Ext. 107, Fax: 503-253-2701.

OREGON HEALTH & SCIENCE UNIVERSITY, Portland, OR 97239-3098

General Information State-related, coed, upper-level institution. *Graduate housing:* Room and/or apartments available to single students; on-campus housing not available to married students. *Research affiliation:* Oregon Regional Primate Research Center.

GRADUATE UNITS

School of Dentistry Offers dental materials (MS); dentistry (DMD, MS, Certificate); endodontics (MS, Certificate); oral molecular biology (MS); oral pathology (Certificate); orthodontics (MS, Certificate); periodontology (MS, Certificate). Electronic applications accepted.

School of Medicine *Degree program information:* Part-time programs available. Offers epidemiology and biostatistics (MPH); integrative biomedical sciences (PhD); medicine (MD, MPH, MS, PhD, Certificate).

Graduate Programs in Medicine *Degree program information:* Part-time programs available. Offers behavioral neuroscience (MS, PhD); biochemistry and molecular biology (PhD); biomedical informatics (MS, PhD, Certificate); cell and developmental biology (PhD); medicine (MS, PhD, Certificate); molecular and medical genetics (PhD); molecular microbiology and immunology (PhD); neuroscience (PhD); pharmacology (PhD); physiology (PhD).

School of Nursing *Degree program information:* Part-time programs available. Offers adult health and illness nursing (MS, Post Master's Certificate); adult nurse practitioner (MS, Post Master's Certificate); community health care systems (MS, Post Master's Certificate); families in health, illness, and transition (PhD); family nurse practitioner (MS, Post Master's Certificate); geriatric nurse practitioner (Post Master's Certificate); geriatric/adult nurse practitioner (MS); gerontological nursing (PhD); mental health nursing (MS, Post Master's Certificate); nurse midwifery (MS, Post Master's Certificate); nursing (MPH, MS, PhD, Post Master's Certificate); pediatric nurse practitioner (MS, Post Master's Certificate); public health nursing (MPH); women's health care nurse practitioner (MS, Post Master's Certificate). Electronic applications accepted.

OREGON STATE UNIVERSITY, Corvallis, OR 97331

General Information State-supported, coed, university. CGS member. *Enrollment:* 19,362 graduate, professional, and undergraduate students; 2,640 full-time matriculated graduate/professional students (1,341 women), 893 part-time matriculated graduate/professional students (479 women). *Enrollment by degree level:* 532 first professional, 1,415 master's, 1,137 doctoral, 449 other advanced degrees. *Graduate faculty:* 1,393 full-time (508 women), 207 part-time/adjunct (104 women). *Graduate housing:* Rooms and/or apartments available on a first-come, first-served basis to single and married students. Housing application deadline: 9/10. *Student services:* Campus employment opportunities, campus safety program, career counseling, child daycare facilities, disabled student services, exercise/wellness program, free psychological counseling, international student services, low-cost health insurance, multicultural affairs office, teacher training, writing training. *Library facilities:* Valley Library. *Online resources:* library catalog, web page, access to other libraries' catalogs. *Collection:* 689,119 titles, 12,254 serial subscriptions. *Research affiliation:* Comer Science and Educational Foundation (Science), George and Betty Moore Foundation (Medical Research, science education), William and Flora Hewett Foundation (Science, engineering), W.M. Keck Foundation (Science, engineering), David and Lucille Packard Foundation (Science, environmental science).

Computer facilities: 2,251 computers available on campus for general student use. A campuswide network can be accessed from student residence rooms and from off campus. Internet access and online class registration are available. *Web address:* http://oregonstate.edu/.

General Application Contact: Dr. Sally K. Francis, Dean of the Graduate School, 541-737-4881, Fax: 541-737-3313, E-mail: franciss@oregonstate.edu.

GRADUATE UNITS

College of Pharmacy Students: 351 full-time (205 women), 8 part-time (5 women); includes 122 minority (4 African Americans, 1 American Indian/Alaska Native, 103 Asian Americans or Pacific Islanders, 14 Hispanic Americans), 15 international. Average age 27. *Faculty:* 35 full-time (16 women). Expenses: Contact institution. *Financial support:* Fellowships, research assistantships, teaching assistantships, career-related internships or fieldwork, Federal Work-Study, and institutionally sponsored loans available. Support available to part-time students. Financial award application deadline: 2/1. In 2006, 80 first professional degrees, 1 master's, 2 doctorates awarded. *Degree program information:* Part-time programs available. Offers pharmacy (Pharm D, MAIS, MS, PhD). *Application deadline:* For fall admission, 3/1 for domestic students. Applications are processed on a rolling basis. *Application fee:* $50. *Application Contact:* 541-737-5784, Fax: 541-737-3999. *Dean,* Dr. Wayne A. Kradjan, 541-737-3424, Fax: 541-737-3424, E-mail: wayne.kradjan@orst.edu.

College of Veterinary Medicine Students: 198 full-time (163 women), 1 part-time; includes 10 minority (1 African American, 2 American Indian/Alaska Native, 5 Asian Americans or Pacific Islanders, 2 Hispanic Americans), 1 international. Average age 26. *Faculty:* 37 full-time (13 women), 6 part-time/adjunct (2 women). Expenses: Contact institution. *Financial support:* Fellowships, research assistantships, Federal Work-Study, institutionally sponsored loans, and scholarships/grants available. Support available to part-time students. Financial award application deadline: 2/1. In 2006, 38 degrees awarded. *Degree program information:* Part-time programs available. Offers comparative veterinary medicine (PhD); microbiology (MS); pathology (MS); toxicology (MS); veterinary medicine (DVM, MS, PhD). DVM admissions open only to residents of Oregon and other states participating in the Western Interstate Commission for Higher Education (WICHE). *Application deadline:* For fall admission, 11/1 for domestic students. *Application fee:* $50. *Application Contact:* Dr. Linda L. Blythe, Associate Dean, 541-737-2098, Fax: 541-737-4245, E-mail: linda.blythe@orst.edu. *Dean,* Dr. Cyril Clarke, 541-737-2098, Fax: 541-737-4245.

Graduate School Students: 2,620 full-time (1,321 women), 913 part-time (499 women); includes 417 minority (49 African Americans, 34 American Indian/Alaska Native, 228 Asian Americans or Pacific Islanders, 106 Hispanic Americans), 604 international. Average age 31. *Faculty:* 766 full-time (313 women), 404 part-time/adjunct (217 women). Expenses: Contact institution. *Financial support:* Fellowships, research assistantships, teaching assistantships, career-related internships or fieldwork, Federal Work-Study, institutionally sponsored loans, and unspecified assistantships available. Support available to part-time students. Financial award application deadline: 2/1. In 2006, 660 master's, 166 doctorates awarded. *Degree program information:* Part-time programs available. Offers environmental sciences (MA, MS, PhD); interdisciplinary studies (MAIS); molecular and cellular biology (MS, PhD); plant physiology (MS, PhD); water resources engineering (MS, PhD). *Application fee:* $50. *Application Contact:* Stephen F. Massott, Assistant Director of Admissions and Orientation, 541-737-4411, Fax: 541-737-2482. *Dean,* Dr. Sally K. Francis, 541-737-4881, Fax: 541-737-3313, E-mail: franciss@oregonstate.edu.

College of Agricultural Sciences Students: 244 full-time (120 women), 31 part-time (16 women); includes 21 minority (2 African Americans, 4 American Indian/Alaska Native, 8 Asian Americans or Pacific Islanders, 7 Hispanic Americans), 76 international. Average age 31. Expenses: Contact institution. *Financial support:* Fellowships, research assistantships, teaching assistantships, career-related internships or fieldwork, Federal Work-Study, and institutionally sponsored loans available. Support available to part-time students. Financial award application deadline: 2/1. In 2006, 60 master's, 34 doctorates awarded. *Degree program information:* Part-time programs available. Offers agricultural and resource economics (M Agr, MAIS, MS, PhD); agricultural education (M Agr, MAIS, MAT, MS); agricultural sciences (M Ag, M Agr, MA, MAIS, MAT, MS, PhD); animal science (M Agr, MAIS, MS, PhD); crop science (M Agr, MAIS, MS, PhD); economics (MS, PhD); fisheries science (M Agr, MAIS, MS, PhD); food science and technology (M Agr, MAIS, MS, PhD); genetics (MA, MAIS, MS, PhD); horticulture (M Ag, MAIS, MS, PhD); poultry science (M Agr, MAIS, MS, PhD); rangeland ecology and management (M Agr, MAIS, MS, PhD); soil science (M Agr, MAIS, MS, PhD); toxicology (MS, PhD); wildlife science (MAIS, MS, PhD). *Applica-*

tion fee: $50. *Application Contact:* Dr. Michael J. Burke, Associate Dean, 541-737-2211, Fax: 541-737-2256, E-mail: mike.burke@orst.edu. *Dean,* Dr. Thayne R. Dutson, 541-737-2331, Fax: 541-737-4574, E-mail: thayne.dutson@orst.edu.

College of Business Students: 53 full-time (21 women), 22 part-time (13 women); includes 5 minority (1 American Indian/Alaska Native, 2 Asian Americans or Pacific Islanders, 2 Hispanic Americans), 24 international. Average age 30. *Faculty:* 37 full-time (7 women), 12 part-time/adjunct (2 women). Expenses: Contact institution. *Financial support:* Fellowships, teaching assistantships, career-related internships or fieldwork, Federal Work-Study, and institutionally sponsored loans available. Financial award application deadline: 2/1. In 2006, 39 degrees awarded. *Degree program information:* Part-time programs available. Offers business (MAIS, MBA, Certificate). *Application deadline:* For fall admission, 3/15 for domestic students. Applications are processed on a rolling basis. *Application fee:* $50. *Application Contact:* Clara Horne, Head Advisor, 541-737-3716, Fax: 541-737-4890, E-mail: horne@bus.orst.edu. *Dean,* Dr. Ilene K. Kleinsorge, 541-737-6024, Fax: 541-737-3033.

College of Education Students: 114 full-time (85 women), 193 part-time (135 women); includes 58 minority (15 African Americans, 6 American Indian/Alaska Native, 15 Asian Americans or Pacific Islanders, 22 Hispanic Americans), 9 international. Average age 38. *Faculty:* 51 full-time (37 women), 24 part-time/adjunct (18 women). Expenses: Contact institution. *Financial support:* Fellowships, research assistantships, teaching assistantships, career-related internships or fieldwork, Federal Work-Study, and institutionally sponsored loans available. Support available to part-time students. Financial award application deadline: 2/1. In 2006, 132 master's, 16 doctorates awarded. *Degree program information:* Part-time programs available. Offers adult education and higher education leadership (Ed M, MAIS); college student service administration (Ed M, MS); counseling (MS, PhD); education (Ed M, MAIS, MAT, MS, Ed D, PhD); elementary education (MAT); family and consumer sciences education (MAT, MS); general education (Ed M, MAIS, MS, Ed D, PhD); language arts education (MAT); music education (MAT). *Application fee:* $50. *Dean,* Dr. Sam Stern, 541-737-6392, Fax: 541-737-2040.

College of Engineering Students: 352 full-time (61 women), 83 part-time (14 women); includes 44 minority (5 African Americans, 33 Asian Americans or Pacific Islanders, 6 Hispanic Americans), 159 international. Average age 28. 816 applicants, 50% accepted, 156 enrolled. *Faculty:* 119 full-time (18 women). Expenses: Contact institution. *Financial support:* In 2006–07, 20 fellowships with full tuition reimbursements (averaging $11,608 per year), 192 research assistantships with full tuition reimbursements (averaging $12,639 per year), 129 teaching assistantships with full tuition reimbursements (averaging $9,965 per year) were awarded; career-related internships or fieldwork, Federal Work-Study, institutionally sponsored loans, and instructorships also available. Support available to part-time students. Financial award application deadline: 2/1. In 2006, 131 master's, 32 doctorates awarded. *Degree program information:* Part-time programs available. Offers bioscience engineering (MS, PhD); chemical engineering (MS, PhD); civil engineering (MS, PhD); construction engineering management (MBE); electrical engineering and computer science (MA, MAIS, MS, PhD); engineering (M Engr, M Oc E, MA, MAIS, MBE, MS, PhD); industrial engineering (MS, PhD); manufacturing engineering (M Engr); materials science (MAIS, MS, PhD); mechanical engineering (MS, PhD); nuclear engineering (MS, PhD); ocean engineering (M Oc E); radiation health physics (MS, PhD). *Application deadline:* Applications are processed on a rolling basis. *Application fee:* $50. *Application Contact:* Chris A. Bell, Associate Dean, 541-737-1598, Fax: 541-737-1805, E-mail: chris.a.bell@oregonstate.edu. *Dean,* Dr. Ronald L. Adams, 541-737-7722, Fax: 541-737-1805, E-mail: ronald.lynn.adams@orst.edu.

College of Forestry Students: 127 full-time (45 women), 15 part-time (5 women); includes 5 minority (1 African American, 1 Asian American or Pacific Islander, 3 Hispanic Americans), 31 international. Average age 30. *Faculty:* 49 full-time (5 women), 13 part-time/adjunct (2 women). Expenses: Contact institution. *Financial support:* Fellowships, research assistantships, teaching assistantships, career-related internships or fieldwork, Federal Work-Study, institutionally sponsored loans, and unspecified assistantships available. Support available to part-time students. Financial award application deadline: 2/1. In 2006, 33 master's, 10 doctorates awarded. *Degree program information:* Part-time programs available. Offers economics (MS, PhD); forest engineering (MAIS, MF, MS, PhD); forest products (MAIS, MF, MS, PhD); forest resources (MAIS, MF, MS, PhD); forest science (MAIS, MF, MS, PhD); forestry (MAIS, MF, MS, PhD); wood science and technology (MF, MS, PhD). *Application deadline:* Applications are processed on a rolling basis. *Application fee:* $50. *Application Contact:* Deborah J. Bird, Head Advisor, 541-737-2052, Fax: 541-737-8508, E-mail: birdd@for.orst.edu. *Dean,* Hal J. Salwasser, 541-737-1585, Fax: 541-737-2906, E-mail: salwassh@for.orst.edu.

College of Health and Human Sciences Students: 187 full-time (141 women), 50 part-time (31 women); includes 34 minority (7 African Americans, 2 American Indian/Alaska Native, 17 Asian Americans or Pacific Islanders, 8 Hispanic Americans), 41 international. Average age 31. *Faculty:* 57 full-time (39 women), 55 part-time/adjunct (39 women). Expenses: Contact institution. *Financial support:* Fellowships, research assistantships, teaching assistantships, career-related internships or fieldwork, Federal Work-Study, and institutionally sponsored loans available. Support available to part-time students. Financial award application deadline: 2/1. In 2006, 59 master's, 14 doctorates awarded. Offers design and human environment (MA, MAIS, MS, PhD); environmental health and occupational safety management (MAIS, MS); exercise and sport science (MS, PhD); gerontology (MAIS); health and human sciences (MA, MAIS, MAT, MPH, MS, PhD); health management and policy (MS); health promotion and health behavior (MAIS, MAT, MS); human development and family studies (MS, PhD); human performance (MAIS, MS, PhD); movement studies in disabilities (MAIS, MS); nutrition and food management (MAIS, MS, PhD); physical education teacher education (MAT); public health (MPH, PhD). *Application deadline:* Applications are processed on a rolling basis. *Application fee:* $50. *Application Contact:* Linda Johnson, Head Adviser, 541-737-3718, Fax: 541-737-4230, E-mail: linda.johnson@orst.edu. *Dean,* Dr. Tammy Bray, 541-737-3220, Fax: 541-737-3220.

College of Liberal Arts Students: 36 full-time (18 women), 5 part-time (4 women); includes 1 minority (Asian American or Pacific Islander), 15 international. Average age 32. *Faculty:* 48 full-time (18 women), 9 part-time/adjunct (4 women). Expenses: Contact institution. *Financial support:* Fellowships, research assistantships, teaching assistantships, career-related internships or fieldwork, Federal Work-Study, and institutionally sponsored loans available. Support available to part-time students. Financial award application deadline:2/1. In 2006, 32 master's, 3 doctorates awarded. *Degree program information:* Part-time programs available. Offers anthropology (MAIS); applied anthropology (MA); economics (MA, MS, PhD); English (MA, MAIS, MFA); history (MA, MS, PhD); liberal arts (MA, MAIS, MAT, MFA, MS, PhD); music education (MAT). *Application deadline:* Applications are processed on a rolling basis. *Application fee:* $50. *Application Contact:* Polly Jeneva, Adviser, 541-737-6193, Fax: 541-737-2434, E-mail: polly.jeneva@orst.edu. *Dean,* Dr. Kay F. Schaffer, 541-737-4582, Fax: 541-737-2434, E-mail: kschaffer@orst.edu.

College of Oceanic and Atmospheric Sciences Students: 71 full-time (33 women), 11 part-time (5 women); includes 5 minority (1 African American, 1 American Indian/Alaska Native, 1 Asian American or Pacific Islander, 2 Hispanic Americans), 12 international. Average age 30. *Faculty:* 60 full-time (9 women), 15 part-time/adjunct (4 women). Expenses: Contact institution. *Financial support:* Fellowships, research assistantships, teaching assistantships, career-related internships or fieldwork, Federal Work-Study, and institutionally sponsored loans available. Support available to part-time students. Financial award application deadline: 2/1. In 2006, 17 master's, 7 doctorates awarded. Offers atmospheric sciences (MA, MS, PhD); geophysics (MA, MS, PhD); marine resource management (MA, MS); oceanography (MA, MS, PhD). *Application deadline:* For fall admission, 2/1 priority date for domestic students. Applications are processed on a rolling basis. *Application fee:* $50. *Application Contact:* Irma Delson, Assistant Director, Student Services, 541-737-5189, Fax: 541-737-2064, E-mail: student_adviser@oce.orst.edu. *Dean,* Dr. Mark R. Abbott, 541-737-3504, Fax: 541-737-2064, E-mail: mark@oce.orst.edu.

College of Science Students: 408 full-time (158 women), 51 part-time (17 women); includes 32 minority (3 African Americans, 2 American Indian/Alaska Native, 17 Asian Americans or Pacific Islanders, 10 Hispanic Americans), 104 international. Average age 30. *Faculty:* 141 full-time (43 women), 40 part-time/adjunct (12 women). Expenses: Contact institution. *Financial support:* Fellowships, research assistantships, teaching assistantships, career-related internships or fieldwork, Federal Work-Study, and institutionally sponsored loans available. Support available to part-time students. Financial award application deadline:2/1. In 2006, 123 master's, 41 doctorates awarded. *Degree program information:* Part-time programs available. Offers advanced mathematics education (MAT); analytical chemistry (MS, PhD); applied statistics (MA, MS, PhD); biochemistry and biophysics (MA, MAIS, MS, PhD); biology education (MAT); biometry (MA, MS, PhD); chemistry (MA, MAIS); chemistry education (MAT); ecology (MA, MAIS, MS, PhD); environmental statistics (MA, MS, PhD); general science (MA, MS, PhD); genetics (MA, MAIS, MS, PhD); geography (MA, MAIS, MS, PhD); geology (MA, MAIS, MS, PhD); inorganic chemistry (MS, PhD); integrated science education (MAT); mathematical statistics (MA, MS, PhD); mathematics (MA, MAIS, MS, PhD); mathematics education (MA, MAT, MS, PhD); microbiology (MA, MAIS, MS, PhD); molecular and cellular biology (MA, MAIS, MS, PhD); mycology (MA, MAIS, MS, PhD); nuclear and radiation chemistry (MS, PhD); operations research (MA, MAIS, MS); organic chemistry (MS, PhD); physical chemistry (MS, PhD); physics (MA, MS, PhD); physics education (MAT); plant pathology (MA, MAIS, MS, PhD); plant physiology (MA, MAIS, MS, PhD); science (MA, MAIS, MAT, MS, PhD); science education (MA, MAT, MS, PhD); statistics (MA, MS, PhD); structural botany (MA, MAIS, MS, PhD); systematics (MA, MAIS, MS, PhD); zoology (MA, MAIS, MS, PhD). *Application deadline:* Applications are processed on a rolling basis. *Application fee:* $50. *Application Contact:* Carolyn Brumley, Graduate Secretary, 541-737-6707, Fax: 541-737-2062, E-mail: carolyn.brumley@orst.edu. *Dean,* Dr. Sherman H. Bloomer, 541-737-4811, Fax: 541-737-1009, E-mail: bloomers@geo.orst.edu.

OREGON STATE UNIVERSITY–CASCADES, Bend, OR 97701

General Information State-supported, coed, comprehensive institution.

GRADUATE UNITS

Program in Counseling Offers community counseling (MS); school counseling (MS).

Program in Education Offers education (MAT).

OTIS COLLEGE OF ART AND DESIGN, Los Angeles, CA 90045-9785

General Information Independent, coed, comprehensive institution. *Enrollment:* 1,125 graduate, professional, and undergraduate students; 38 full-time matriculated graduate/professional students (22 women), 20 part-time matriculated graduate/professional students (14 women). *Enrollment by degree level:* 58 master's. *Graduate faculty:* 3 full-time (1 woman), 14 part-time/adjunct (7 women). *Tuition:* Full-time $28,596. *Required fees:* $600. *Graduate housing:* On-campus housing not available. *Student services:* Campus employment opportunities, campus safety program, career counseling, free psychological counseling, international student services, low-cost health insurance, writing training. *Library facilities:* Milliard Sheets Library. *Online resources:* library catalog, web page, access to other libraries' catalogs. *Collection:* 42,000 titles, 150 serial subscriptions.

Computer facilities: 220 computers available on campus for general student use. A campuswide network can be accessed. Internet access is available. *Web address:* http://www.otis.edu/.

General Application Contact: Yvette Sobky, Assistant Dean of Admissions, 310-665-6819, Fax: 310-665-6821, E-mail: ysobky@otis.edu.

GRADUATE UNITS

Program in Fine Arts Students: 38 full-time (22 women), 14 part-time (9 women). Average age 32. 94 applicants, 31% accepted, 14 enrolled. *Faculty:* 2 full-time (1 woman), 9 part-time/adjunct (5 women). Expenses: Contact institution. *Financial support:* In 2006–07, 20 students received support. Career-related internships or fieldwork, Federal Work-Study, scholarships/grants, and tuition waivers (partial) available. Financial award applicants required to submit FAFSA. In 2006, 12 degrees awarded. Offers new genres (MFA); painting (MFA); photography (MFA); sculpture (MFA). *Application deadline:* For fall admission, 2/15 for domestic and international students. *Application fee:* $50. Electronic applications accepted. *Application Contact:* Yvette Sobky, Assistant Dean of Admissions, 310-665-6819, Fax: 310-665-6821, E-mail: ysobky@otis.edu. *Chair,* Roy Dowell, 310-665-6893, Fax: 310-665-6998, E-mail: gradsfa@fbc.global.net.

Program in Writing Students: 13 full-time (11 women), 11 part-time (8 women); includes 8 minority (4 African Americans, 2 Asian Americans or Pacific Islanders, 2 Hispanic Americans), 1 international. Average age 34. 20 applicants, 75% accepted, 9 enrolled. *Faculty:* 1 full-time (0 women), 5 part-time/adjunct (2 women). Expenses: Contact institution. *Financial support:* Federal Work-Study, scholarships/grants, and tuition waivers (partial) available. Financial award applicants required to submit FAFSA. Offers writing (MFA). *Application deadline:* For fall admission, 2/15 for domestic and international students. *Application fee:* $50. Electronic applications accepted. *Application Contact:* Yvette Sobky, Assistant Dean of Admissions, 310-665-6819, Fax: 310-665-6821, E-mail: ysobky@otis.edu. *Chair,* Paul Vangelisti, 310-665-6891, Fax: 310-665-6890, E-mail: pvangel@otis.edu.

OTTAWA UNIVERSITY, Ottawa, KS 66067-3399

General Information Independent-religious, coed, comprehensive institution. *Enrollment:* 41 full-time matriculated graduate/professional students (30 women), 611 part-time matriculated graduate/professional students (446 women). *Enrollment by degree level:* 603 master's. *Graduate faculty:* 18 full-time (8 women), 50 part-time/adjunct (23 women). *Graduate housing:* On-campus housing not available. *Library facilities:* Myers Library. *Online resources:* access to other libraries' catalogs. *Collection:* 75,401 titles, 808 serial subscriptions, 15 audiovisual materials.

Computer facilities: 71 computers available on campus for general student use. A campuswide network can be accessed from student residence rooms and from off campus. Internet access and online class registration are available. *Web address:* http://www.ottawa.edu/.

General Application Contact: Office of Admissions, 785-242-5200 Ext. 5421, Fax: 785-229-1008, E-mail: admiss@ottawa.edu.

GRADUATE UNITS

Graduate Studies-Arizona Students: 34 full-time (24 women), 505 part-time (378 women); includes 75 minority (29 African Americans, 4 American Indian/Alaska Native, 5 Asian Americans or Pacific Islanders, 37 Hispanic Americans), 6 international. Average age 37. *Faculty:* 12 full-time (6 women), 37 part-time/adjunct (15 women). Expenses: Contact institution. *Financial support:* Career-related internships or fieldwork available. In 2006, 151 degrees awarded. *Degree program information:* Part-time and evening/weekend programs available. Postbaccalaureate distance learning degree programs offered. Offers business administration (MBA); Christian counseling (MA); community college counseling (MA); curriculum and instruction (MA); early childhood (MA); education intervention (MA); education leadership (MA); education technology (MA); expressive arts therapy (MA); finance (MBA); human resources (MA, MBA); leadership (MBA); marketing (MBA); marriage and family therapy (MA); Montessori early childhood education (MA); Montessori elementary education (MA); professional development (MA); school guidance counseling (MA); special education—cross categorical (MA); treatment of trauma, abuse and deprivation (MA). *Application deadline:* For fall admission, 7/1 priority date for domestic students; for winter admission, 11/1 priority date for domestic students; for spring admission, 2/1 priority date for domestic students. Applications are processed on a rolling basis. *Application fee:* $50. Electronic applications accepted. *Dean of Instruction,* Dr. June Wiley, 602-371-1188, Fax: 602-371-0035, E-mail: june.wiley@ottawa.edu.

Graduate Studies-International Students: 3 full-time (2 women), 22 part-time (11 women), (all international). Average age 35. *Faculty:* 1 full-time (0 women), 2 part-time/adjunct (1 woman). Expenses: Contact institution. In 2006, 21 degrees awarded. Postbaccalaureate distance learning degree programs offered (minimal on-campus study). Offers business administration (MBA). *Application deadline:* Applications are processed on a rolling basis. *Application fee:* $50. Electronic applications accepted. *Application Contact:* Misti Thuro,

Ottawa University (continued)

Admissions Coordinator, 785-242-5200, Fax: 785-229-1007, E-mail: misti.thuro@ottawa.edu. *Program Coordinator,* Buddy Jo Tanck, 785-242-5200, E-mail: tanckb@ottawa.edu.

Graduate Studies-Kansas City Students: 4 full-time (all women), 63 part-time (42 women); includes 10 minority (7 African Americans, 2 Asian Americans or Pacific Islanders, 1 Hispanic American). Average age 37. *Faculty:* 4 full-time (1 woman), 8 part-time/adjunct (4 women). Expenses: Contact institution. In 2006, 30 degrees awarded. *Degree program information:* Part-time and evening/weekend programs available. Postbaccalaureate distance learning degree programs offered (minimal on-campus study). Offers business administration (MBA); human resources (MA). *Application deadline:* Applications are processed on a rolling basis. *Application fee:* $65. Electronic applications accepted. *Application Contact:* Alisa Jones, Enrollment Coordinator, 913-451-1431, Fax: 913-451-0806, E-mail: alisa.jones@ottawa.edu. *Director of Graduate Studies,* Dr. W. A. Breytspraak, 913-451-1431, Fax: 913-451-0806, E-mail: breytspraak@ottawa.edu.

Graduate Studies-Wisconsin Average age 39. *Faculty:* 1 (woman) full-time, 5 part-time/adjunct (4 women). Expenses: Contact institution. In 2006, 2 degrees awarded. *Degree program information:* Part-time and evening/weekend programs available. Postbaccalaureate distance learning degree programs offered. Offers business administration (MBA). *Application deadline:* Applications are processed on a rolling basis. *Application fee:* $50. Electronic applications accepted. *Application Contact:* Trisha Frederick, Enrollment Manager, 262-879-0200, Fax: 262-879-0096, E-mail: trisha.frederick@ottawa.edu. *Instructor in Business Administration,* Elaine George, 262-879-0200, Fax: 262-879-0096, E-mail: elaine.george@ottawa.edu.

OTTERBEIN COLLEGE, Westerville, OH 43081

General Information Independent-religious, coed, comprehensive institution. *Enrollment:* 3,176 graduate, professional, and undergraduate students; 90 full-time matriculated graduate/professional students (51 women), 290 part-time matriculated graduate/professional students (240 women). *Enrollment by degree level:* 380 master's. *Graduate faculty:* 30 full-time (23 women), 10 part-time/adjunct (3 women). *Tuition:* Full-time $7,560; part-time $315 per credit. Tuition and fees vary according to program. *Graduate housing:* On-campus housing not available. *Student services:* Campus employment opportunities, career counseling, disabled student services, international student services, low-cost health insurance, multicultural affairs office. *Library facilities:* Courtright Memorial Library. *Online resources:* library catalog, web page. *Collection:* 182,629 titles, 1,012 serial subscriptions.

Computer facilities: 146 computers available on campus for general student use. A campuswide network can be accessed from student residence rooms and from off campus. Internet access is available. *Web address:* http://www.otterbein.edu/.

General Application Contact: Deb Williams, Administrative Assistant, Office of Graduate Programs, 614-823-3210, Fax: 614-823-3208, E-mail: grad@otterbein.edu.

GRADUATE UNITS

Department of Business, Accounting and Economics Students: 53 full-time, 50 part-time; includes 13 minority (7 African Americans, 5 Asian Americans or Pacific Islanders, 1 Hispanic American). Average age 33. 23 applicants, 83% accepted, 14 enrolled. Expenses: Contact institution. *Financial support:* Available to part-time students. Applicants required to submit FAFSA. In 2006, 55 degrees awarded. *Degree program information:* Part-time and evening/weekend programs available. Offers business, accounting and economics (MBA). *Application deadline:* For fall admission, 8/10 priority date for domestic students, 7/10 priority date for international students; for winter admission, 12/7 priority date for domestic students, 11/7 priority date for international students; for spring admission, 2/28 priority date for domestic students, 1/31 priority date for international students. Applications are processed on a rolling basis. *Application fee:* $35. *Application Contact:* Deb Williams, Administrative Assistant, Office of Graduate Programs, 614-823-3210, Fax: 614-823-3208, E-mail: grad@otterbein.edu. *Chair,* Dr. Don Eskew, 614-823-1212, Fax: 614-823-1014, E-mail: deskew@otterbein.edu.

Department of Education Students: 24 full-time, 65 part-time. Average age 34. Expenses: Contact institution. *Financial support:* Unspecified assistantships available. Support available to part-time students. Financial award applicants required to submit FAFSA. In 2006, 27 degrees awarded. Offers education (MAE, MAT). *Application deadline:* Applications are processed on a rolling basis. *Application fee:* $0. *Application Contact:* Deb Williams, Administrative Assistant, Office of Graduate Programs, 614-823-3210, Fax: 614-823-3208, E-mail: grad@otterbein.edu. *Chair,* Dr. Harriet Fayne, 614-823-1788, Fax: 614-823-3036, E-mail: hfayne@otterbein.edu.

Department of Nursing Students: 7 full-time, 118 part-time; includes 5 minority (4 African Americans, 1 Hispanic American). Average age 40. 47 applicants, 94% accepted, 33 enrolled. Expenses: Contact institution. *Financial support:* Traineeships available. Support available to part-time students. Financial award applicants required to submit FAFSA. In 2006, 37 degrees awarded. *Degree program information:* Part-time and evening/weekend programs available. Postbaccalaureate distance learning degree programs offered (minimal on-campus study). Offers adult nurse practitioner (MSN, Certificate); clinical nurse leader (MSN); family nurse practitioner (MSN, Certificate); nurse service administration (MSN). *Application deadline:* For fall admission, 8/10 priority date for domestic students, 7/10 for international students; for winter admission, 12/7 priority date for domestic students, 11/7 for international students; for spring admission, 2/28 priority date for domestic students, 1/31 for international students. Applications are processed on a rolling basis. *Application Contact:* Vicki Miller, Administrative Assistant, Office of Graduate Programs, 614-823-3210, Fax: 614-823-3208, E-mail: grad@otterbein.edu. *Chair,* Dr. Barbara Schaffner, 614-823-1735, Fax: 614-823-3131, E-mail: bschaffner@otterbein.edu.

OUR LADY OF HOLY CROSS COLLEGE, New Orleans, LA 70131-7399

General Information Independent-religious, coed, comprehensive institution. *Graduate housing:* On-campus housing not available.

GRADUATE UNITS

Program in Education and Counseling *Degree program information:* Part-time and evening/weekend programs available. Offers administration and supervision (M Ed); curriculum and instruction (M Ed); marriage and family counseling (MA); school counseling (M Ed, MA).

OUR LADY OF THE LAKE UNIVERSITY OF SAN ANTONIO, San Antonio, TX 78207-4689

General Information Independent-religious, coed, comprehensive institution. *Graduate housing:* Room and/or apartments available on a first-come, first-served basis to single students; on-campus housing not available to married students. Housing application deadline: 7/15.

GRADUATE UNITS

College of Arts and Sciences *Degree program information:* Part-time and evening/weekend programs available. Offers English (MA); English communication arts (MA); language and literature (MA). Electronic applications accepted.

School of Business *Degree program information:* Part-time and evening/weekend programs available. Offers general (MBA); health care management (MBA). Electronic applications accepted.

School of Education and Clinical Studies *Degree program information:* Part-time and evening/weekend programs available. Offers communication and learning disorders (MA); counseling psychology (MS, Psy D); curriculum and instruction (M Ed); human sciences (MA); leadership studies (PhD); learning resources (M Ed); marriage and family therapy (MS); principal (M Ed); school counseling (M Ed); school psychology (MS); sociology (MA); special education (MA). Electronic applications accepted.

Worden School of Social Service *Degree program information:* Part-time programs available. Offers social service (MSW). Electronic applications accepted.

OXFORD GRADUATE SCHOOL, Dayton, TN 37321-6736

General Information Independent-religious, coed, graduate-only institution. *Enrollment by degree level:* 14 master's, 74 doctoral. *Graduate faculty:* 10 full-time (2 women), 18 part-time/adjunct (3 women). *Tuition:* Part-time $202 per credit hour. One-time fee: $415 part-time. Tuition and fees vary according to degree level and program. *Graduate housing:* Rooms and/or apartments guaranteed to single students and available to married students. Typical cost: $3,150 per year ($6,030 including board) for single students; $3,750 per year ($6,630 including board) for married students. *Student services:* Campus employment opportunities, campus safety program, disabled student services, grant writing training, international student services, teacher training, writing training. *Online resources:* library catalog, web page, access to other libraries' catalogs. *Collection:* 117,309 titles, 4,541 serial subscriptions, 2,117 audiovisual materials.

Computer facilities: 15 computers available on campus for general student use. A campuswide network can be accessed from off campus. Internet access, extensive research databases are available. *Web address:* http://www.oxnet.com/.

General Application Contact: Joanne Phillips, Information Contact, 423-775-6596, E-mail: oxnet@oxnetedu.org.

GRADUATE UNITS

Graduate Programs Expenses: Contact institution. Offers family life education (M Litt); organizational leadership in nonprofits (M Litt); religion and society (D Phil).

PACE UNIVERSITY, New York, NY 10038

General Information Independent, coed, university. CGS member. *Enrollment:* 13,463 graduate, professional, and undergraduate students; 677 full-time matriculated graduate/professional students (452 women), 3,832 part-time matriculated graduate/professional students (2,314 women). *Enrollment by degree level:* 4,225 master's, 284 doctoral. *Graduate faculty:* 189 full-time, 139 part-time/adjunct. *Tuition:* Part-time $890 per credit. *Graduate housing:* Room and/or apartments available on a first-come, first-served basis to single students; on-campus housing not available to married students. *Student services:* Campus employment opportunities, career counseling, free psychological counseling, international student services, low-cost health insurance, multicultural affairs office, teacher training, writing training. *Library facilities:* Henry Birnbaum Library plus 3 others. *Online resources:* library catalog, web page, access to other libraries' catalogs. *Collection:* 824,533 titles, 4,151 serial subscriptions, 2,248 audiovisual materials.

Computer facilities: 246 computers available on campus for general student use. A campuswide network can be accessed from student residence rooms and from off campus. Internet access and online class registration are available. *Web address:* http://www.pace.edu/.

General Application Contact: Joanna Broda, Director of Admissions, 212-346-1652, Fax: 212-346-1585, E-mail: gradnyc@pace.edu.

GRADUATE UNITS

Dyson College of Arts and Sciences Students: 261 full-time (209 women), 270 part-time (207 women); includes 130 minority (59 African Americans, 1 American Indian/Alaska Native, 29 Asian Americans or Pacific Islanders, 41 Hispanic Americans), 26 international. Average age 27. 845 applicants, 51% accepted, 151 enrolled. *Faculty:* 27 full-time, 56 part-time/adjunct. Expenses: Contact institution. *Financial support:* Research assistantships, teaching assistantships, career-related internships or fieldwork, Federal Work-Study, and tuition waivers (partial) available. Support available to part-time students. Financial award application deadline: 5/15; financial award applicants required to submit FAFSA. In 2006, 147 master's, 12 doctorates awarded. *Degree program information:* Part-time and evening/weekend programs available. Offers acting (MFA); arts and sciences (MA, MFA, MPA, MS, MS Ed, Psy D); bilingual school psychology (MS Ed); counseling-substance abuse (MS); environmental science (MS); forensic science (MS); government management (MPA); health care administration (MPA); nonprofit management (MPA); psychology (MA); publishing (MS); school psychology (MS Ed); school-clinical child psychology (Psy D). *Application deadline:* Applications are processed on a rolling basis. *Application fee:* $65. Electronic applications accepted. *Application Contact:* Joanna Broda, Director of Admissions, 212-346-1652, Fax: 212-346-1585, E-mail: gradnyc@pace.edu. *Dean,* Dr. Nira Herrmann, 212-346-1517.

Lienhard School of Nursing Students: 20 full-time (19 women), 171 part-time (156 women); includes 96 minority (55 African Americans, 1 American Indian/Alaska Native, 27 Asian Americans or Pacific Islanders, 13 Hispanic Americans), 5 international. Average age 37. 84 applicants, 93% accepted, 43 enrolled. *Faculty:* 2 full-time (both women). Expenses: Contact institution. *Financial support:* Research assistantships, career-related internships or fieldwork, Federal Work-Study, and tuition waivers (partial) available. Support available to part-time students. Financial award applicants required to submit FAFSA. In 2006, 38 master's, 2 other advanced degrees awarded. *Degree program information:* Part-time and evening/weekend programs available. Offers nursing (MS, Advanced Certificate). *Application deadline:* For fall admission, 7/31 priority date for domestic students; for spring admission, 11/30 for domestic students. Applications are processed on a rolling basis. *Application fee:* $65. Electronic applications accepted. *Application Contact:* Joanna Broda, Director of Admissions, 212-346-1652, Fax: 212-346-1585, E-mail: gradnyc@pace.edu. *Dean,* Dr. Harriet Feldman, 914-773-3341.

Lubin School of Business Students: 159 full-time (84 women), 844 part-time (349 women); includes 236 minority (46 African Americans, 134 Asian Americans or Pacific Islanders, 56 Hispanic Americans), 250 international. Average age 30. 995 applicants, 58% accepted, 233 enrolled. *Faculty:* 128 full-time, 62 part-time/adjunct. Expenses: Contact institution. *Financial support:* Research assistantships, career-related internships or fieldwork, Federal Work-Study, and tuition waivers (full and partial) available. Support available to part-time students. Financial award applicants required to submit FAFSA. In 2006, 483 master's, 7 doctorates, 4 other advanced degrees awarded. *Degree program information:* Part-time and evening/weekend programs available. Postbaccalaureate distance learning degree programs offered (minimal on-campus study). Offers banking and finance (MBA); business (MBA, MS, DPS, APC); corporate economic planning (MBA); corporate financial management (MBA); financial economics (MBA); financial management (MBA); information systems (MBA); international business (MBA); international economics (MBA); investment management (MBA, MS); management (MBA); management science (MBA); managerial accounting (MBA); marketing management (MBA); marketing research (MBA); operations management (MBA); professional studies (DPS); public accounting (MBA, MS); taxation (MBA, MS). *Application deadline:* For fall admission, 7/31 priority date for domestic students; for spring admission, 11/30 for domestic students. Applications are processed on a rolling basis. *Application fee:* $65. Electronic applications accepted. *Application Contact:* Joanna Broda, Director of Admissions, 212-346-1652, Fax: 212-346-1585, E-mail: gradnyc@pace.edu. *Dean,* Dr. Arthur Centonze, 212-346-1963.

School of Computer Science and Information Systems Students: 107 full-time (34 women), 396 part-time (118 women); includes 184 minority (62 African Americans, 2 American Indian/Alaska Native, 64 Asian Americans or Pacific Islanders, 56 Hispanic Americans), 78 international. Average age 31. 434 applicants, 69% accepted, 142 enrolled. *Faculty:* 23 full-time, 9 part-time/adjunct. Expenses: Contact institution. *Financial support:* Research assistantships, career-related internships or fieldwork available. Support available to part-time students. Financial award applicants required to submit FAFSA. In 2006, 186 master's, 8 doctorates awarded. *Degree program information:* Part-time and evening/weekend programs available. Offers computer communications and networks (Certificate); computer science (MS); computing studies (DPS); information systems (MS); object-oriented programming (Certificate); telecommunications (MS, Certificate). *Application deadline:* For fall admission, 7/31 priority date for domestic students; for spring admission, 11/30 for domestic students. Applications are processed on a rolling basis. *Application fee:* $65. Electronic applications accepted. *Application Contact:* Joanna Broda, Director of Admissions, 212-346-1652, Fax: 212-346-1585, E-mail: gradnyc@pace.edu. *Dean,* Dr. Susan Merritt, 914-422-4375.

School of Education Students: 130 full-time (106 women), 2,151 part-time (1,484 women); includes 96 minority (50 African Americans, 2 American Indian/Alaska Native, 21 Asian

Americans or Pacific Islanders, 23 Hispanic Americans), 6 international. Average age 27. 229 applicants, 70% accepted, 70 enrolled. *Faculty:* 9 full-time, 12 part-time/adjunct. Expenses: Contact institution. *Financial support:* Research assistantships, career-related internships or fieldwork and Federal Work-Study available. Support available to part-time students. Financial award applicants required to submit FAFSA. In 2006, 550 master's, 23 other advanced degrees awarded. *Degree program information:* Part-time and evening/weekend programs available. Offers administration and supervision (MS Ed); curriculum and instruction (MS); education (MST); school business management (Certificate). *Application deadline:* For fall admission, 7/31 priority date for domestic students; for spring admission, 11/30 for domestic students. Applications are processed on a rolling basis. *Application fee:* $65. Electronic applications accepted. *Application Contact:* Joanna Broda, Director of Admissions, 212-346-1652, Fax: 212-346-1585, E-mail: gradnyc@pace.edu. *Interim Dean,* Dr. Harriet Feldman, 212-346-1512.

School of Law Students: 511 full-time (305 women), 279 part-time (149 women); includes 138 minority (24 African Americans, 1 American Indian/Alaska Native, 73 Asian Americans or Pacific Islanders, 40 Hispanic Americans), 15 international. Average age 26. 2,935 applicants, 31% accepted, 273 enrolled. *Faculty:* 44 full-time, 56 part-time/adjunct. Expenses: Contact institution. *Financial support:* Career-related internships or fieldwork, Federal Work-Study, institutionally sponsored loans, and scholarships/grants available. Support available to part-time students. Financial award application deadline: 2/1; financial award applicants required to submit FAFSA. In 2006, 224 JDs, 20 master's awarded. *Degree program information:* Part-time and evening/weekend programs available. Offers comparative legal studies (LL M); environmental law (LL M, SJD); law (JD). *Application deadline:* For fall admission, 3/1 priority date for domestic students. Applications are processed on a rolling basis. *Application fee:* $65. Electronic applications accepted. *Application Contact:* Cathy Alexander, Director of Law Admissions, 914-422-4210, Fax: 914-989-8714, E-mail: calexander@law.pace.edu. *Dean,* Stephen J. Friedman, 914-422-4407, E-mail: sfriedman@law.pace.edu.

PACIFICA GRADUATE INSTITUTE, Carpinteria, CA 93013

General Information Proprietary, coed, graduate-only institution. *Graduate housing:* Rooms and/or apartments guaranteed to single and married students. Housing application deadline: 8/15. *Research affiliation:* EBSCO—Elton B. Stevens Company (journal management), American Psychological Association (psychology-research), North California consortium of Psychology Libraries (psychology).

GRADUATE UNITS

Graduate Programs Offers clinical psychology (PhD); counseling psychology (MA); depth psychology (MA, PhD); mythological studies (MA, PhD).

PACIFIC COLLEGE OF ORIENTAL MEDICINE, San Diego, CA 92108

General Information Proprietary, coed, graduate-only institution. *Graduate housing:* On-campus housing not available. *Research affiliation:* National Institutes of Health (complementary and alternative medicine).

GRADUATE UNITS

Graduate Program *Degree program information:* Part-time and evening/weekend programs available. Offers Oriental medicine (MSTOM, DAOM).

PACIFIC COLLEGE OF ORIENTAL MEDICINE-CHICAGO, Chicago, IL 60613

General Information Proprietary, coed, graduate-only institution. *Graduate housing:* On-campus housing not available. *Research affiliation:* Children's Memorial Hospital of Chicago (pediatric research).

GRADUATE UNITS

Graduate Program *Degree program information:* Part-time and evening/weekend programs available. Offers oriental medicine (MTOM).

PACIFIC COLLEGE OF ORIENTAL MEDICINE-NEW YORK, New York, NY 10010

General Information Proprietary, coed, graduate-only institution. *Graduate housing:* On-campus housing not available.

GRADUATE UNITS

Graduate Program *Degree program information:* Part-time and evening/weekend programs available. Offers Oriental medicine (MSTOM).

PACIFIC GRADUATE SCHOOL OF PSYCHOLOGY, Palo Alto, CA 94303-4232

General Information Independent, coed, graduate-only institution. *Graduate housing:* On-campus housing not available.

GRADUATE UNITS

Distance Learning Program in Psychology Postbaccalaureate distance learning degree programs offered (no on-campus study). Offers psychology (MS). Electronic applications accepted.

PGSP-Stanford Psy D Consortium Program Offers psychology (Psy D). Electronic applications accepted.

Program in Clinical Psychology Offers clinical psychology (PhD). Electronic applications accepted.

PACIFIC LUTHERAN THEOLOGICAL SEMINARY, Berkeley, CA 94708-1597

General Information Independent-religious, coed, graduate-only institution. *Graduate faculty:* 14 full-time (4 women), 10 part-time/adjunct (1 woman). *Tuition:* Full-time $10,200; part-time $510 per unit. Tuition and fees vary according to course load and program. *Graduate housing:* Rooms and/or apartments available on a first-come, first-served basis to single and married students. Housing application deadline: 8/1. *Student services:* Campus employment opportunities, career counseling, international student services, multicultural affairs office. *Library facilities:* Flora Lamson Hewlett Library. *Online resources:* library catalog, access to other libraries' catalogs. *Collection:* 355,000 titles, 2,400 serial subscriptions.

Computer facilities: 5 computers available on campus for general student use. Internet access is available. *Web address:* http://www.plts.edu/.

General Application Contact: Rev. Greg Schaefer, Director of Admissions, 510-559-2738, Fax: 510-524-2408, E-mail: admissions@plts.edu.

GRADUATE UNITS

Graduate and Professional Programs Students: 161 (80 women); includes 16 minority (4 African Americans, 9 Asian Americans or Pacific Islanders, 3 Hispanic Americans) 3 international. 83 applicants, 69% accepted. *Faculty:* 11 full-time (5 women), 10 part-time/adjunct (2 women). Expenses: Contact institution. *Financial support:* In 2006–07, 104 students received support. Career-related internships or fieldwork, Federal Work-Study, institutionally sponsored loans, and scholarships/grants available. Support available to part-time students. Financial award application deadline: 3/15; financial award applicants required to submit FAFSA. In 2006, 17 M Divs, 1 master's, 5 other advanced degrees awarded. *Degree program information:* Part-time programs available. Offers theology (M Div, MA, MCM, MTS, PhD, Th D, Certificate). *Application deadline:* For fall admission, 8/1 priority date for domestic students; for spring admission, 1/1 priority date for domestic students. Applications are processed on a rolling basis. *Application fee:* $35. *Dean of Faculty,* Michael B. Aune, 510-524-5264, E-mail: maune@plts.edu.

PACIFIC LUTHERAN UNIVERSITY, Tacoma, WA 98447

General Information Independent-religious, coed, comprehensive institution. *Enrollment:* 3,640 graduate, professional, and undergraduate students; 186 full-time matriculated graduate/professional students (123 women), 105 part-time matriculated graduate/professional students (78 women). *Enrollment by degree level:* 291 master's. *Graduate faculty:* 16 full-time (3 women), 15 part-time/adjunct (9 women). *Tuition:* Full-time $17,544. Part-time tuition and fees vary according to program. *Graduate housing:* Rooms and/or apartments available on a first-come, first-served basis to single and married students. Typical cost: $3,150 per year ($7,140 including board) for single students; $3,150 per year ($7,140 including board) for married students. Housing application deadline: 5/1. *Student services:* Campus employment opportunities, campus safety program, career counseling, disabled student services, exercise/wellness program, free psychological counseling, international student services, low-cost health insurance, multicultural affairs office, teacher training, writing training. *Library facilities:* Mortvedt Library. *Online resources:* library catalog, web page. *Collection:* 350,750 titles, 3,433 serial subscriptions, 12,954 audiovisual materials.

Computer facilities: Computer purchase and lease plans are available. 200 computers available on campus for general student use. A campuswide network can be accessed from student residence rooms and from off campus. Internet access and online class registration are available. *Web address:* http://www.plu.edu/.

General Application Contact: Linda DuBay, Senior Office Assistant, 253-535-7151, Fax: 253-536-5136, E-mail: admissions@plu.edu.

GRADUATE UNITS

Division of Graduate Studies Students: 186 full-time (123 women), 105 part-time (78 women); includes 27 minority (8 African Americans, 1 American Indian/Alaska Native, 12 Asian Americans or Pacific Islanders, 6 Hispanic Americans), 17 international. Average age 33. 314 applicants, 63% accepted, 136 enrolled. *Faculty:* 15 full-time (3 women), 16 part-time/adjunct (9 women). Expenses: Contact institution. *Financial support:* In 2006–07, 111 students received support, including 38 fellowships; career-related internships or fieldwork, Federal Work-Study, scholarships/grants, and unspecified assistantships also available. Support available to part-time students. Financial award application deadline: 3/1; financial award applicants required to submit FAFSA. In 2006, 143 degrees awarded. *Degree program information:* Part-time and evening/weekend programs available. *Application deadline:* Applications are processed on a rolling basis. *Application fee:* $40. Electronic applications accepted. *Application Contact:* Linda DuBay, Senior Office Assistant, 253-535-7151, Fax: 253-536-5136, E-mail: admissions@plu.edu. *Provost and Dean of Graduate Studies,* Dr. Patricia O'Connell Killen, 253-535-7126, Fax: 253-535-5103, E-mail: provost@plu.edu.

Division of Humanities Average age 45. 31 applicants, 61% accepted, 16 enrolled. *Faculty:* 1 full-time (0 women), 4 part-time/adjunct (1 woman). Expenses: Contact institution. *Financial support:* In 2006–07, 1 fellowship (averaging $2,000 per year) was awarded; unspecified assistantships also available. In 2006, 2 degrees awarded. *Degree program information:* Part-time programs available. Offers creative writing (MFA). Offered during summer only. *Application fee:* $40. *Application Contact:* Stan Sanvel Rubin, Director of MFA in Creative Writing Program, 253-535-7221, E-mail: mfa@plu.edu. *Dean,* Dr. Douglas E. Oakman, 253-535-7317, Fax: 253-536-7132, E-mail: oakmande@plu.edu.

Division of Social Sciences Students: 35 full-time (27 women), 7 part-time (6 women); includes 5 minority (2 African Americans, 2 Asian Americans or Pacific Islanders, 1 Hispanic American). Average age 28. 63 applicants, 52% accepted, 20 enrolled. *Faculty:* 2 full-time (1 woman), 4 part-time/adjunct (1 woman). Expenses: Contact institution. *Financial support:* In 2006–07, 14 students received support, including 12 fellowships (averaging $23,046 per year); career-related internships or fieldwork, Federal Work-Study, scholarships/grants, and unspecified assistantships also available. Financial award application deadline: 3/1; financial award applicants required to submit FAFSA. In 2006, 17 degrees awarded. Offers marriage and family therapy (MA); social sciences (MA). *Application deadline:* For fall admission, 1/31 priority date for domestic and international students. *Application fee:* $40. Electronic applications accepted. *Application Contact:* Linda DuBay, Senior Office Assistant, 253-535-7151, Fax: 253-536-5136, E-mail: admissions@plu.edu. *Dean,* Dr. Norris Peterson, 253-535-7196.

School of Business Students: 49 full-time (15 women), 24 part-time (11 women); includes 9 minority (3 African Americans, 4 Asian Americans or Pacific Islanders, 2 Hispanic Americans), 15 international. Average age 31. 46 applicants, 100% accepted, 30 enrolled. *Faculty:* 8 full-time (4 women), 2 part-time/adjunct (0 women). Expenses: Contact institution. *Financial support:* In 2006–07, 10 students received support, including 7 fellowships (averaging $20,066 per year); career-related internships or fieldwork, Federal Work-Study, scholarships/grants, and unspecified assistantships also available. Financial award application deadline: 3/1. In 2006, 27 degrees awarded. *Degree program information:* Part-time and evening/weekend programs available. Offers business administration (MBA). *Application deadline:* Applications are processed on a rolling basis. *Application fee:* $40. *Application Contact:* Abby Wigstrom, Director, MBA Program, Fax: 253-535-8723, E-mail: wigstraj@plu.edu. *Dean,* Dr. Andrew Turner, 253-535-7445, Fax: 253-535-8723.

School of Education Students: 32 full-time (19 women), 19 part-time (15 women); includes 7 minority (2 African Americans, 4 Asian Americans or Pacific Islanders, 1 Hispanic American), 1 international. Average age 29. 65 applicants, 100% accepted, 46 enrolled. *Faculty:* 5 full-time (2 women), 3 part-time/adjunct (2 women). Expenses: Contact institution. *Financial support:* In 2006–07, 42 students received support, including 17 fellowships (averaging $47,500 per year); Federal Work-Study, scholarships/grants, and unspecified assistantships also available. Financial award application deadline: 3/1. In 2006, 67 degrees awarded. *Degree program information:* Part-time and evening/weekend programs available. Offers education (MA); educational leadership (MA); teaching (MA). *Application deadline:* Applications are processed on a rolling basis. *Application fee:* $40. *Application Contact:* Linda DuBay, Senior Office Assistant, 253-535-7151, Fax: 253-536-5136, E-mail: admissions@plu.edu. *Dean,* Dr. John Lee, 253-535-7272.

School of Nursing Students: 69 full-time (62 women), 2 part-time (both women); includes 4 minority (1 African American, 2 Asian Americans or Pacific Islanders, 1 Hispanic American), 1 international. Average age 34. 63 applicants, 56% accepted, 24 enrolled. *Faculty:* 4 full-time (3 women), 3 part-time/adjunct (1 woman). Expenses: Contact institution. *Financial support:* In 2006–07, 4 students received support, including 1 fellowship (averaging $2,500 per year); Federal Work-Study, scholarships/grants, and unspecified assistantships also available. Financial award application deadline: 3/1. In 2006, 30 degrees awarded. *Degree program information:* Part-time and evening/weekend programs available. Offers client systems management (MSN); entry level nursing (MSN); family nurse practitioner (MSN); health care systems management (MSN); nursing (MSN). *Application deadline:* For fall admission, 4/1 priority date for domestic students. Applications are processed on a rolling basis. *Application fee:* $40. *Application Contact:* Linda DuBay, Senior Office Assistant, 253-535-7151, Fax: 253-536-5136, E-mail: admissions@plu.edu. *Dean and Graduate Program Director,* Dr. Terry Miller, 253-535-7672, Fax: 253-535-7590, E-mail: millertw@plu.edu.

See Close-Up on page 989.

PACIFIC OAKS COLLEGE, Pasadena, CA 91103

General Information Independent, coed, primarily women, upper-level institution. *Enrollment:* 1,028 graduate, professional, and undergraduate students; 163 full-time matriculated graduate/professional students (141 women), 608 part-time matriculated graduate/professional students (561 women). *Enrollment by degree level:* 771 master's. *Graduate faculty:* 27 full-time (22 women), 98 part-time/adjunct. *Tuition:* Full-time $11,760; part-time $735 per unit. *Required fees:* $30 per semester. *Graduate housing:* Room and/or apartments available to single students; on-campus housing not available to married students. Typical cost: $9,900 (including board). *Student services:* Campus employment opportunities, career counseling, disabled student services, international student services, teacher training, writing training. *Library facilities:* Andrew Norman Library plus 1 other. *Online resources:* library catalog, web page, access to other libraries' catalogs. *Collection:* 36,000 titles, 87 serial subscriptions, 125 audiovisual materials.

Pacific Oaks College (continued)

Computer facilities: 25 computers available on campus for general student use. A campuswide network can be accessed from off campus. Internet access, online class listings are available. *Web address:* http://www.pacificoaks.edu/.

General Application Contact: Amy Peterson, Admissions Coordinator, 626-397-1349, Fax: 626-666-1220, E-mail: admissions@pacificoaks.edu.

GRADUATE UNITS

Graduate School Students: 163 full-time (141 women), 608 part-time (561 women); includes 121 minority (24 African Americans, 4 American Indian/Alaska Native, 14 Asian Americans or Pacific Islanders, 79 Hispanic Americans). Average age 35. 208 applicants, 72% accepted, 109 enrolled. *Faculty:* 27 full-time (22 women), 98 part-time/adjunct. Expenses: Contact institution. *Financial support:* In 2006–07, 385 students received support. Federal Work-Study and scholarships/grants available. Support available to part-time students. Financial award application deadline: 4/15; financial award applicants required to submit FAFSA. In 2006, 147 degrees awarded. *Degree program information:* Part-time and evening/weekend programs available. Postbaccalaureate distance learning degree programs offered (minimal on-campus study). Offers human development (MA); marriage, family and child counseling (MA). *Application deadline:* For fall admission, 6/1 priority date for domestic and international students; for spring admission, 10/1 priority date for domestic and international students. Applications are processed on a rolling basis. *Application fee:* $55. *Application Contact:* Amy Peterson, Admissions Coordinator, 626-397-1349, Fax: 626-666-1220, E-mail: admissions@pacificoaks.edu. *President,* Dr. Carolyn Denham, 626-583-6039.

PACIFIC SCHOOL OF RELIGION, Berkeley, CA 94709-1323

General Information Independent, coed, graduate-only institution. *Graduate housing:* Rooms and/or apartments guaranteed to single and married students. Housing application deadline: 4/1. *Research affiliation:* Center for Women and Religion (women's studies), Center for Ethics and Social Policy (business ethics), Disciples Seminary Foundation (theology), Swedenborgean House of Studies (theology), Bay Area Faith and Health Consortium (public health).

GRADUATE UNITS

Graduate and Professional Programs *Degree program information:* Part-time programs available. Offers religion (M Div, MA, MTS, D Min, PhD, Th D, CAPS, CMS, CSS, CTS). Electronic applications accepted.

PACIFIC STATES UNIVERSITY, Los Angeles, CA 90006

General Information Independent, coed, comprehensive institution. *Enrollment:* 157 full-time matriculated graduate/professional students (70 women). *Graduate faculty:* 4 full-time (0 women), 15 part-time/adjunct (0 women). *Tuition:* Full-time $6,360. *Required fees:* $1,080. Full-time tuition and fees vary according to course load and degree level. *Graduate housing:* Room and/or apartments available on a first-come, first-served basis to single students; on-campus housing not available to married students. *Student services:* Campus employment opportunities, international student services. *Library facilities:* University Library plus 1 other. *Online resources:* library catalog, access to other libraries' catalogs. *Collection:* 15,000 titles, 108 serial subscriptions.

Computer facilities: 25 computers available on campus for general student use. *Web address:* http://www.psuca.edu/.

General Application Contact: Marina Miller, Assistant Director of Admissions, 323-731-2383 Ext. 11, Fax: 323-731-7276, E-mail: admissions@psuca.edu.

GRADUATE UNITS

College of Business Students: 106 full-time (47 women); includes 10 minority (all Asian Americans or Pacific Islanders), 96 international. Average age 32. 36 applicants, 81% accepted, 26 enrolled. *Faculty:* 3 full-time (0 women), 11 part-time/adjunct (0 women). Expenses: Contact institution. *Financial support:* Fellowships, research assistantships, teaching assistantships, scholarships/grants available. Financial award applicants required to submit FAFSA. In 2006, 68 degrees awarded. *Degree program information:* Part-time and evening/weekend programs available. Postbaccalaureate distance learning degree programs offered (no on-campus study). Offers accounting (MBA); business administration (DBA); finance (MBA); international business (MBA); management of information technology (MBA); real estate management (MBA). *Application deadline:* For fall admission, 8/15 priority date for domestic students; for winter admission, 10/15 priority date for domestic students; for spring admission, 1/15 priority date for domestic students. Applications are processed on a rolling basis. *Application fee:* $100. *Application Contact:* Marina Miller, Assistant Director of Admissions, 323-731-2383 Ext. 11, Fax: 323-731-7276, E-mail: admissions@psuca.edu. *Director,* Dr. Kamol Somvichian, 888-200-0383, Fax: 323-731-2383, E-mail: admission@psuca.edu.

College of Computer Science Students: 15 full-time (4 women); includes 2 minority (both Asian Americans or Pacific Islanders), 13 international. Average age 27. 11 applicants, 73% accepted, 6 enrolled. *Faculty:* 1 full-time (0 women), 3 part-time/adjunct (0 women). Expenses: Contact institution. *Financial support:* Scholarships/grants available. Financial award applicants required to submit FAFSA. In 2006, 6 degrees awarded. *Degree program information:* Part-time and evening/weekend programs available. Offers computer science (MSCS); information systems (MSCS). *Application deadline:* For fall admission, 8/15 priority date for domestic students; for winter admission, 10/15 priority date for domestic students; for spring admission, 1/15 priority date for domestic students. Applications are processed on a rolling basis. *Application fee:* $100. *Application Contact:* Namyoung Chah, Registrar, 323-731-2383, Fax: 323-731-7276, E-mail: registrar@psuca.edu. *Director,* Dr. Myung K. Yoo, 888-200-0383, Fax: 323-731-7276, E-mail: admission@psuca.edu.

PACIFIC UNION COLLEGE, Angwin, CA 94508-9707

General Information Independent-religious, coed, comprehensive institution. *Enrollment:* 1,397 graduate, professional, and undergraduate students; 4 full-time matriculated graduate/professional students (all women), 14 part-time matriculated graduate/professional students (10 women). *Enrollment by degree level:* 18 master's. *Graduate faculty:* 4 full-time (2 women). *Tuition:* Full-time $20,130; part-time $584 per quarter hour. *Required fees:* $135. Tuition and fees vary according to course load and student's religious affiliation. *Graduate housing:* Rooms and/or apartments guaranteed to single students and available on a first-come, first-served basis to married students. Typical cost: $3,447 per year ($5,652 including board) for single students. Room and board charges vary according to campus/location and housing facility selected. Housing application deadline: 8/31. *Student services:* Campus employment opportunities, campus safety program, career counseling, child daycare facilities, disabled student services, exercise/wellness program, free psychological counseling, international student services, teacher training, writing training. *Library facilities:* W. E. Nelson Memorial Library. *Online resources:* library catalog, web page, access to other libraries' catalogs. *Collection:* 173,839 titles, 812 serial subscriptions.

Computer facilities: 150 computers available on campus for general student use. A campuswide network can be accessed from student residence rooms and from off campus. Internet access and online class registration are available. *Web address:* http://www.puc.edu/.

General Application Contact: Marsha Crow, Credential Analyst, 707-965-6643, Fax: 707-965-6645, E-mail: mcrow@puc.edu.

GRADUATE UNITS

Department of Education Students: 4 full-time (all women), 14 part-time (10 women); includes 3 minority (all Asian Americans or Pacific Islanders) Average age 29. 5 applicants, 100% accepted. *Faculty:* 4 full-time (2 women). Expenses: Contact institution. *Financial support:* In 2006–07, 2 students received support, including 2 teaching assistantships with full tuition reimbursements available (averaging $2,600 per year); Federal Work-Study, scholarships/grants, and unspecified assistantships also available. Support available to part-time students. Financial award application deadline: 3/1. In 2006, 6 degrees awarded. *Degree program information:* Part-time programs available. Offers teacher leadership (M Ed). *Application deadline:* For fall admission, 7/1 priority date for domestic students. Applications are processed on a rolling basis. *Application fee:* $0. *Application Contact:* Marsha Crow, Credential Analyst, 707-965-6643, Fax: 707-965-6645, E-mail: mcrow@puc.edu. *Chair,* Dr. Jim Roy, 707-965-6644, Fax: 707-965-6645, E-mail: jroy@puc.edu.

PACIFIC UNIVERSITY, Forest Grove, OR 97116-1797

General Information Independent, coed, comprehensive institution. *Enrollment:* 2,790 graduate, professional, and undergraduate students; 1,183 full-time matriculated graduate/professional students (753 women), 190 part-time matriculated graduate/professional students (158 women). *Enrollment by degree level:* 431 first professional, 567 master's, 375 doctoral. *Graduate faculty:* 108 full-time (56 women), 86 part-time/adjunct (47 women). *Graduate housing:* On-campus housing not available. *Student services:* Campus employment opportunities, campus safety program, career counseling, disabled student services, exercise/wellness program, free psychological counseling, international student services, low-cost health insurance. *Library facilities:* Pacific University Library. *Online resources:* library catalog, web page, access to other libraries' catalogs. *Collection:* 206,198 titles, 20,908 serial subscriptions, 8,580 audiovisual materials. *Research affiliation:* Ohio State University/Vistakon Johnson & Johnson (achieve study, adolescent and child vision care), Cooper Vision (contact lens), CIBA Vision (contact lens), BSK (student thesis projects), NEI/PEDIG—JAEB Center of Health Research (amblyopia treatment study), Jacob Lieberman, O.D. (contact lens, vision research, sports vision).

Computer facilities: Computer purchase and lease plans are available. 150 computers available on campus for general student use. A campuswide network can be accessed from student residence rooms and from off campus. Internet access, e-mail, Web space, printing, student and academic information, WebCT, wireless, computer peripherals are available. *Web address:* http://www.pacificu.edu/.

General Application Contact: Jon-Erik Larsen, Director of Graduate and Professional Admissions, 503-352-7221, Fax: 503-352-7290, E-mail: admissions@pacificu.edu.

GRADUATE UNITS

College of Education Students: 222 full-time (151 women), 115 part-time (90 women); includes 30 minority (3 African Americans, 5 American Indian/Alaska Native, 12 Asian Americans or Pacific Islanders, 10 Hispanic Americans). Average age 32. 92 applicants, 83% accepted, 69 enrolled. *Faculty:* 20 full-time (12 women), 40 part-time/adjunct (21 women). Expenses: Contact institution. *Financial support:* In 2006–07, 287 students received support; fellowships, research assistantships, teaching assistantships, career-related internships or fieldwork, institutionally sponsored loans, and scholarships/grants available. Support available to part-time students. Financial award application deadline: 5/1; financial award applicants required to submit FAFSA. In 2006, 257 degrees awarded. *Degree program information:* Part-time and evening/weekend programs available. Offers early childhood education (MAT); education (MAE); elementary education (MAT); high school education (MAT); middle school education (MAT); special education (MAT); visual function in learning (M Ed). *Application deadline:* For fall admission, 6/15 priority date for domestic students; for spring admission, 10/15 for domestic students. Applications are processed on a rolling basis. *Application fee:* $35. Electronic applications accepted. *Application Contact:* Diana Watkins, Assistant Director Graduate and Professional Admissions, 503-352-2958, Fax: 503-352-2907, E-mail: teach@pacificu.edu. *Acting Dean,* Dr. Mark Ankeny, 503-352-2102, E-mail: mankeny@pacificu.edu.

College of Optometry Students: 363 full-time (175 women), 1 (woman) part-time; includes 53 minority (1 African American, 1 American Indian/Alaska Native, 44 Asian Americans or Pacific Islanders, 7 Hispanic Americans), 4 international. Average age 26. 332 applicants, 37% accepted, 90 enrolled. *Faculty:* 28 full-time (9 women), 12 part-time/adjunct (7 women). Expenses: Contact institution. *Financial support:* In 2006–07, 309 students received support, including 1 teaching assistantship (averaging $6,000 per year); fellowships, research assistantships, career-related internships or fieldwork, Federal Work-Study, and scholarships/grants also available. Support available to part-time students. Financial award applicants required to submit FAFSA. In 2006, 80 ODs, 1 master's awarded. Offers optometry (OD, MS). *Application deadline:* For fall admission, 1/15 priority date for domestic students, 1/10 for international students; for spring admission, 4/15 for domestic students. Applications are processed on a rolling basis. *Application fee:* $55. Electronic applications accepted. *Application Contact:* Janelle Holmboe, Assistant Director of Graduate and Professional Admissions, 503-352-2900, Fax: 503-352-2975, E-mail: admissions@pacificu.edu. *Dean,* Dr. James E. Sheedy, 503-352-2884.

School of Occupational Therapy Students: 64 full-time (57 women), 1 (woman) part-time; includes 8 minority (5 Asian Americans or Pacific Islanders, 3 Hispanic Americans). Average age 27. 55 applicants, 58% accepted, 22 enrolled. *Faculty:* 6 full-time (4 women), 4 part-time/adjunct (all women). Expenses: Contact institution. *Financial support:* In 2006–07, 65 students received support; fellowships, research assistantships, teaching assistantships, career-related internships or fieldwork, Federal Work-Study, and scholarships/grants available. Support available to part-time students. Financial award applicants required to submit FAFSA. In 2006, 17 degrees awarded. Offers occupational therapy (MOT). *Application deadline:* For fall admission, 12/1 priority date for domestic students. Applications are processed on a rolling basis. *Application fee:* $55. Electronic applications accepted. *Application Contact:* Jon-Erik Larsen, Director of Graduate and Professional Admissions, 503-352-2900, Fax: 503-352-2975, E-mail: admissions@pacificu.edu. *Director,* Dr. John A. White, 503-352-7355, Fax: 503-352-2980, E-mail: whiteja@pacificu.edu.

School of Pharmacy Students: 68 full-time (32 women); includes 30 minority (4 African Americans, 24 Asian Americans or Pacific Islanders, 2 Hispanic Americans). Average age 27. *Faculty:* 10 full-time (3 women). Expenses: Contact institution. *Financial support:* In 2006–07, 68 students received support; fellowships, research assistantships, teaching assistantships, career-related internships or fieldwork and Federal Work-Study available. Offers pharmacy (Pharm D). *Application Contact:* Kent Steinmetz, Information Contact, 503-352-7225, Fax: 503-352-7290, E-mail: ksteinmetz@pacificu.edu. *Director,* Dr. Robert Rosenow, 503-352-7271.

School of Physical Therapy Students: 116 full-time (82 women), 13 part-time (11 women); includes 12 minority (9 Asian Americans or Pacific Islanders, 3 Hispanic Americans). Average age 28. 278 applicants, 25% accepted, 38 enrolled. *Faculty:* 11 full-time (7 women), 2 part-time/adjunct (0 women). Expenses: Contact institution. *Financial support:* In 2006–07, 108 students received support, including 1 fellowship (averaging $3,000 per year); research assistantships, teaching assistantships, career-related internships or fieldwork, Federal Work-Study, and scholarships/grants also available. Financial award application deadline: 5/1; financial award applicants required to submit FAFSA. In 2006, 41 degrees awarded. Offers entry level (DPT); post-professional (DPT). *Application deadline:* For fall admission, 12/1 for domestic and international students. *Application fee:* $25. Electronic applications accepted. *Application Contact:* Stephanie Krusemark, Assistant Director of Graduate and Professional Admissions, 503-352-2900, Fax: 503-352-2975, E-mail: admissions@pacificcu.edu. *Director,* Dr. Richard Rutt, 503-352-7377, E-mail: ruttra@pacificu.edu.

School of Physician Assistant Studies Students: 82 full-time (53 women), 4 part-time (1 woman); includes 11 minority (4 African Americans, 2 Asian Americans or Pacific Islanders, 5 Hispanic Americans). Average age 31. 542 applicants, 12% accepted, 42 enrolled. *Faculty:* 8 full-time (4 women), 2 part-time/adjunct (0 women). Expenses: Contact institution. *Financial support:* In 2006–07, 80 students received support; fellowships, research assistantships, teaching assistantships, career-related internships or fieldwork and Federal Work-Study available. Financial award applicants required to submit FAFSA. In 2006, 44 degrees awarded. Offers physician assistant studies (MHS, MS). *Application deadline:* For fall admission, 10/20 for domestic and international students. *Application fee:* $55. *Application Contact:* Stephanie Krusemark, Assistant Director of Graduate and Professional Admissions, 503-352-2900, Fax: 503-352-2975, E-mail: admissions@pacificcu.edu. *Director,* Randy Randolph, 503-352-2898, Fax: 503-359-2977, E-mail: pa@pacificu.edu.

School of Professional Psychology Students: 255 full-time (182 women), 69 part-time (54 women); includes 28 minority (2 African Americans, 3 American Indian/Alaska Native, 16 Asian Americans or Pacific Islanders, 7 Hispanic Americans). Average age 29. 336 applicants, 43% accepted, 93 enrolled. *Faculty:* 22 full-time (14 women), 20 part-time/adjunct (10 women). Expenses: Contact institution. *Financial support:* In 2006–07, 58 students received support, including 36 research assistantships (averaging $2,806 per year), 22 teaching assistantships (averaging $1,878 per year); fellowships, career-related internships or fieldwork, Federal Work-Study, scholarships/grants, and unspecified assistantships also available. Support available to part-time students. Financial award applicants required to submit FAFSA. In 2006, 67 master's, 28 doctorates awarded. *Degree program information:* Part-time programs available. Offers clinical psychology (MS, Psy D); counseling psychology (MA). *Application deadline:* For fall admission, 1/10 priority date for domestic students; for winter admission, 3/5 priority date for domestic students. *Application fee:* $40. Electronic applications accepted. *Application Contact:* Janelle Holmboe, Assistant Director of Graduate and Professional Admissions, 503-352-3145, Fax: 503-352-2975, E-mail: admissions@pacificu.edu. *Dean,* Dr. Michel Hersen, 503-352-7330, Fax: 503-352-7320, E-mail: spp@pacificu.edu.

PALM BEACH ATLANTIC UNIVERSITY, West Palm Beach, FL 33416-4708

General Information Independent-religious, coed, comprehensive institution. *Enrollment:* 3,264 graduate, professional, and undergraduate students; 548 full-time matriculated graduate/professional students (385 women), 192 part-time matriculated graduate/professional students (117 women). *Enrollment by degree level:* 319 first professional, 421 master's. *Graduate faculty:* 26 full-time (15 women), 31 part-time/adjunct (12 women). *Tuition:* Full-time $10,665; part-time $395 per credit. *Required fees:* $90 per semester. *Graduate housing:* On-campus housing not available. *Student services:* Campus safety program, career counseling, exercise/wellness program, free psychological counseling, international student services, low-cost health insurance, multicultural affairs office, teacher training. *Library facilities:* Warren Library. *Online resources:* library catalog, web page. *Collection:* 147,514 titles, 332 serial subscriptions, 4,540 audiovisual materials.

Computer facilities: 147 computers available on campus for general student use. A campuswide network can be accessed from student residence rooms and from off campus. Internet access and online class registration are available. *Web address:* http://www.pba.edu/.

General Application Contact: Laura A. Leinweber, Director of Graduate and Evening Admissions, 888-468-6722, Fax: 561-803-2115, E-mail: grad@pba.edu.

GRADUATE UNITS

MacArthur School of Continuing Education Students: 10 full-time (8 women), 21 part-time (10 women); includes 13 minority (10 African Americans, 3 Hispanic Americans), 2 international. Average age 39. 21 applicants, 90% accepted, 16 enrolled. *Faculty:* 5 full-time (3 women), 1 (woman) part-time/adjunct. Expenses: Contact institution. *Financial support:* Tuition waivers (partial) and unspecified assistantships available. Financial award applicants required to submit FAFSA. In 2006, 28 degrees awarded. *Degree program information:* Part-time and evening/weekend programs available. Offers organizational leadership (MS). *Application deadline:* For fall admission, 7/15 priority date for domestic students; for spring admission, 11/15 priority date for domestic students. Applications are processed on a rolling basis. *Application fee:* $35. Electronic applications accepted. *Application Contact:* Laura A. Leinweber, Director of Graduate and Evening Admissions, 888-468-6722, Fax: 561-803-2115, E-mail: grad@pba.edu. *Dean,* Dr. Jim Laub, 561-803-2318, Fax: 561-803-2306, E-mail: jim_laub@pba.edu.

Rinker School of Business Students: 27 full-time (16 women), 86 part-time (42 women); includes 31 minority (15 African Americans, 1 American Indian/Alaska Native, 5 Asian Americans or Pacific Islanders, 10 Hispanic Americans), 11 international. Average age 33. 36 applicants, 94% accepted, 31 enrolled. *Faculty:* 6 full-time (2 women), 5 part-time/adjunct (0 women). Expenses: Contact institution. *Financial support:* Career-related internships or fieldwork and unspecified assistantships available. Support available to part-time students. Financial award applicants required to submit FAFSA. In 2006, 46 degrees awarded. *Degree program information:* Part-time and evening/weekend programs available. Offers business (MBA). *Application deadline:* For fall admission, 7/15 priority date for domestic students; for spring admission, 11/15 priority date for domestic students. Applications are processed on a rolling basis. *Application fee:* $35. Electronic applications accepted. *Application Contact:* Laura A. Leinweber, Director of Graduate and Evening Admissions, 888-468-6722, Fax: 561-803-2115, E-mail: grad@pba.edu. *Interim Dean,* Dr. Edgar Langlois, 561-803-2462, E-mail: edgar_langlois@pba.edu.

School of Education and Behavioral Studies Students: 211 full-time (169 women), 66 part-time (55 women); includes 103 minority (61 African Americans, 4 Asian Americans or Pacific Islanders, 38 Hispanic Americans), 7 international. Average age 36. 98 applicants, 71% accepted, 51 enrolled. *Faculty:* 13 full-time (3 women), 6 part-time/adjunct (5 women). Expenses: Contact institution. *Financial support:* Unspecified assistantships available. Support available to part-time students. Financial award applicants required to submit FAFSA. In 2006, 49 degrees awarded. *Degree program information:* Part-time and evening/weekend programs available. Offers counseling psychology (MSCP); elementary education (M Ed). *Application deadline:* For fall admission, 7/15 priority date for domestic students; for spring admission, 11/15 priority date for domestic students. Applications are processed on a rolling basis. *Application fee:* $35. Electronic applications accepted. *Application Contact:* Laura A. Leinweber, Director of Graduate and Evening Admissions, 888-468-6722, Fax: 561-803-2115, E-mail: grad@pba.edu. *Dean,* Dr. Melise Bunker, 561-803-2350, Fax: 561-803-2186, E-mail: melise_bunker@pba.edu.

School of Pharmacy Students: 300 full-time (192 women), 19 part-time (10 women); includes 123 minority (20 African Americans, 1 American Indian/Alaska Native, 54 Asian Americans or Pacific Islanders, 48 Hispanic Americans), 15 international. Average age 27. 1,201 applicants, 15% accepted, 79 enrolled. *Faculty:* 18 full-time (12 women), 4 part-time/adjunct (2 women). Expenses: Contact institution. *Financial support:* Fellowships, unspecified assistantships available. In 2006, 45 degrees awarded. Offers pharmacy (Pharm D). *Application deadline:* For fall admission, 5/31 priority date for domestic and international students. Applications are processed on a rolling basis. *Application fee:* $50. Electronic applications accepted. *Application Contact:* Laura A. Leinweber, Director of Graduate and Evening Admissions, 888-468-6722, Fax: 561-803-2115, E-mail: grad@pba.edu. *Dean,* Dr. Daniel Brown, 561-803-2702, E-mail: daniel_brown@pba.edu.

PALMER COLLEGE OF CHIROPRACTIC, Davenport, IA 52803-5287

General Information Independent, coed, comprehensive institution. *Enrollment:* 1,505 graduate, professional, and undergraduate students; 1,395 full-time matriculated graduate/professional students (493 women), 15 part-time matriculated graduate/professional students (4 women). *Enrollment by degree level:* 1,398 first professional, 12 master's. *Graduate faculty:* 133 full-time (40 women). *Tuition:* Full-time $21,690; part-time $282 per credit hour. *Required fees:* $60. *Graduate housing:* On-campus housing not available. *Student services:* Campus employment opportunities, campus safety program, career counseling, child daycare facilities, disabled student services, exercise/wellness program, free psychological counseling, international student services, low-cost health insurance. *Library facilities:* D. D. Palmer Health Sciences Library. *Online resources:* library catalog, web page. *Collection:* 55,278 titles, 525 serial subscriptions.

Computer facilities: 75 computers available on campus for general student use. A campuswide network can be accessed from off campus. Internet access is available. *Web address:* http://www.palmer.edu/.

General Application Contact: Karen Eden, Director of Admissions, 563-884-5656, Fax: 563-884-5414, E-mail: pcadmit@palmer.edu.

GRADUATE UNITS

Division of Graduate Studies Students: 8 full-time (3 women), 4 part-time (1 woman). *Faculty:* 133 full-time (40 women). Expenses: Contact institution. *Financial support:* In 2006–07, 5 students received support, including teaching assistantships with full and partial tuition reimbursements available (averaging $6,269 per year); research assistantships, Federal Work-Study, institutionally sponsored loans, tuition waivers (full), and stipends also available. Support available to part-time students. Financial award application deadline: 4/1; financial award applicants required to submit FAFSA. Offers anatomy (MS); clinical research (MS). *Application deadline:* For fall admission, 9/1 for domestic students; for spring admission, 5/28 for domestic students. Applications are processed on a rolling basis. *Application fee:* $50. Electronic applications accepted. *Application Contact:* Dr. Brian McMaster, Assistant Dean, 563-884-5163, Fax: 563-884-5226, E-mail: brian.mcmaster@palmer.edu. *Administrator,* Dr. Jean Murray, 563-884-5672, Fax: 563-884-5505, E-mail: jean.murray@palmer.edu.

Professional Program Students: 1,395 full-time (493 women), 15 part-time (4 women). Average age 25. *Faculty:* 133 full-time (40 women). Expenses: Contact institution. *Financial support:* Federal Work-Study, institutionally sponsored loans, scholarships/grants, and tuition waivers available. Support available to part-time students. Financial award applicants required to submit FAFSA. In 2006, 480 degrees awarded. *Degree program information:* Part-time programs available. Offers chiropractic (DC). *Application deadline:* For fall admission, 10/1 priority date for domestic students; for spring admission, 2/1 priority date for domestic students. Applications are processed on a rolling basis. *Application fee:* $50. *Application Contact:* Karen Eden, Director of Admissions, 563-884-5656, Fax: 563-884-5414, E-mail: pcadmit@palmer.edu. *Vice President for Academic Affairs,* Dr. Dennis Marchiori, 563-884-5466, Fax: 563-884-5624, E-mail: marchiori_d@palmer.edu.

Professional Program–West Campus Students: 249 full-time (94 women), 18 part-time (9 women); includes 81 minority (1 African American, 2 American Indian/Alaska Native, 62 Asian Americans or Pacific Islanders, 16 Hispanic Americans). Average age 28. 73 applicants, 60% accepted, 35 enrolled. *Faculty:* 26 full-time (5 women), 14 part-time/adjunct (4 women). Expenses: Contact institution. *Financial support:* Career-related internships or fieldwork and Federal Work-Study available. Support available to part-time students. Financial award applicants required to submit FAFSA. In 2006, 117 degrees awarded. Offers chiropractic (DC). *Application deadline:* Applications are processed on a rolling basis. *Application fee:* $50. Electronic applications accepted. *Application Contact:* Armando Andrews, Senior Admissions Representative, 408-944-6031, Fax: 408-944-6032, E-mail: armando.andrews@palmer.edu.

PARKER COLLEGE OF CHIROPRACTIC, Dallas, TX 75229-5668

General Information Independent, coed, graduate-only institution. *Enrollment by degree level:* 950 first professional. *Graduate faculty:* 100 full-time. *Graduate housing:* On-campus housing not available. *Student services:* Campus employment opportunities, campus safety program, career counseling, free psychological counseling, international student services, low-cost health insurance. *Library facilities:* Parker College Library plus 1 other. *Online resources:* library catalog. *Collection:* 12,000 titles, 250 serial subscriptions, 8,000 audiovisual materials.

Computer facilities: 30 computers available on campus for general student use. A campuswide network can be accessed from off campus. Internet access is available. *Web address:* http://www.parkercc.edu/.

General Application Contact: Selena Reagan, Assistant Director of Recruitment, 972-438-6932 Ext. 7007, E-mail: sreagan@parkercc.edu.

GRADUATE UNITS

First Professional Degree Program Students: 950 full-time. Average age 26. 300 applicants, 47% accepted. *Faculty:* 100 full-time. Expenses: Contact institution. *Financial support:* Federal Work-Study and institutionally sponsored loans available. Support available to part-time students. In 2006, 360 degrees awarded. *Degree program information:* Part-time programs available. Offers chiropractic (DC). *Application deadline:* For fall admission, 6/1 priority date for domestic students; for spring admission, 10/1 priority date for domestic students. Applications are processed on a rolling basis. *Application fee:* $50. Electronic applications accepted. *Application Contact:* Selena Reagan, Assistant Director of Recruitment, 972-438-6932 Ext. 7007, E-mail: sreagan@parkercc.edu. *President,* Dr. Fabrizio Mancini, 972-438-6932.

PARK UNIVERSITY, Parkville, MO 64152-3795

General Information Independent, coed, comprehensive institution. *Graduate housing:* Room and/or apartments available on a first-come, first-served basis to single students; on-campus housing not available to married students.

GRADUATE UNITS

College of Graduate and Professional Studies *Degree program information:* Part-time and evening/weekend programs available. Postbaccalaureate distance learning degree programs offered (no on-campus study). Offers adult education (M Ed); at-risk students (M Ed); disaster and emergency management (MPA); educational administration (M Ed); entrepreneurship (MBA); general business (MBA); general education (M Ed); government/business relations (MPA); healthcare/services management (MBA, MPA); international business (MBA); K-12 certification (MAT); management information systems (MBA); management of information systems (MPA); middle school certification (MAT); multi-cultural education (M Ed); nonprofit management (MPA); public management (MPA); school law (M Ed); secondary school certification (MAT); special education (M Ed). Electronic applications accepted.

PAYNE THEOLOGICAL SEMINARY, Wilberforce, OH 45384-3474

General Information Independent-religious, coed, primarily women, graduate-only institution. *Graduate housing:* Rooms and/or apartments available on a first-come, first-served basis to single and married students. Housing application deadline: 8/25.

GRADUATE UNITS

Program in Theology *Degree program information:* Part-time and evening/weekend programs available. Offers theology (M Div).

PENN STATE DICKINSON SCHOOL OF LAW, Carlisle, PA 17013-2899

General Information State-related, coed, graduate-only institution. *Enrollment by degree level:* 609 first professional. *Graduate faculty:* 56 full-time (23 women), 39 part-time/adjunct (9 women). *Graduate housing:* Rooms and/or apartments available on a first-come, first-served basis to single students and available to married students. Typical cost: $5,760 per year ($8,960 including board) for single students; $6,705 per year ($8,200 including board) for married students. Room and board charges vary according to board plan and housing facility selected. Housing application deadline: 5/15. *Student services:* Campus employment opportunities, campus safety program, career counseling, disabled student services, international student services, low-cost health insurance, teacher training, writing training. *Library facilities:* Sheely-Lee Law Library. *Online resources:* library catalog, web page, access to other libraries' catalogs. *Collection:* 282,099 titles, 6,829 serial subscriptions, 1,092 audiovisual materials.

Computer facilities: 113 computers available on campus for general student use. A campuswide network can be accessed from student residence rooms and from off campus. Internet access and online class registration are available. *Web address:* http://www.dsl.psu.edu/.

General Application Contact: Barbara W. Guillaume, Director, Law Admissions, 717-240-5207, Fax: 717-241-3503, E-mail: dsladmit@psu.edu.

GRADUATE UNITS

Graduate and Professional Programs Students: 552 full-time (249 women), 68 part-time (36 women); includes 108 minority (59 African Americans, 1 American Indian/Alaska Native, 42 Asian Americans or Pacific Islanders, 6 Hispanic Americans), 24 international. Average age 25. 3,350 applicants, 31% accepted, 237 enrolled. *Faculty:* 56 full-time (23 women), 39 part-time/adjunct (9 women). Expenses: Contact institution. *Financial support:* In 2006–07, 519 students received support; research assistantships, Federal Work-Study, institutionally sponsored loans, and scholarships/grants available. Support available to part-time students. Financial award application deadline: 3/1; financial award applicants required to submit FAFSA. In 2006, 200 JDs, 9 master's awarded. *Degree program information:* Part-time programs available. Offers comparative law (LL M); law (JD). *Application deadline:* For fall admission, 3/1 priority date for domestic students. Applications are processed on a rolling basis. *Application fee:* $60. Electronic applications accepted. *Application Contact:* Barbara W. Guillaume, Director, Law Admissions, 717-240-5207, Fax: 717-241-3503, E-mail: dsladmit@psu.edu. *Dean,* Philip J. McConnaughay, 717-240-5000, Fax: 717-240-5213, E-mail: pjm30@psu.edu.

PENN STATE ERIE, THE BEHREND COLLEGE, Erie, PA 16563-0001

General Information State-related, coed, comprehensive institution. Tuition, state resident: full-time $13,972. Tuition, nonresident: full-time $19,488. Tuition and fees vary according to course load and program. *Graduate housing:* Room and/or apartments available on a first-come, first-served basis to single students; on-campus housing not available to married students. *Student services:* Campus employment opportunities, campus safety program, career counseling, child daycare facilities, disabled student services, exercise/wellness program, free psychological counseling, grant writing training, international student services, low-cost health insurance, multicultural affairs office. *Library facilities:* John M. Lilley Library. *Online resources:* library catalog, web page, access to other libraries' catalogs. *Collection:* 5 million titles, 68,445 serial subscriptions, 163,643 audiovisual materials.

Computer facilities: Computer purchase and lease plans are available. 448 computers available on campus for general student use. A campuswide network can be accessed from student residence rooms and from off campus. Internet access and online class registration are available. *Web address:* http://www.pserie.psu.edu/.

General Application Contact: Ann M. Burbules, Graduate Admissions Counselor, 866-374-3378, Fax: 814-898-6044, E-mail: amb29@psu.edu.

GRADUATE UNITS

Graduate School Students: 57 full-time (24 women), 107 part-time (34 women); includes 10 minority (4 African Americans, 3 Asian Americans or Pacific Islanders, 3 Hispanic Americans), 12 international. Average age 29. 111 applicants, 68% accepted, 61 enrolled. Expenses: Contact institution. *Financial support:* Federal Work-Study available. Financial award application deadline: 2/15; financial award applicants required to submit FAFSA. In 2006, 65 degrees awarded. *Degree program information:* Part-time programs available. *Application deadline:* Applications are processed on a rolling basis. *Application fee:* $45. Electronic applications accepted. *Application Contact:* Ann M. Burbules, Graduate Admissions Counselor, 866-374-3378, Fax: 814-898-6044, E-mail: amb29@psu.edu. *CEO and Dean,* Dr. John D. Burke, 814-898-6160, Fax: 814-898-6461, E-mail: jdb1@psu.edu.

PENN STATE GREAT VALLEY, Malvern, PA 19355-1488

General Information State-related, coed, graduate-only institution. Tuition, state resident: full-time $13,224; part-time $551 per credit. Tuition, nonresident: full-time $26,064; part-time $1,003 per credit. *Required fees:* $69 per semester. *Graduate housing:* On-campus housing not available. *Student services:* Campus employment opportunities, campus safety program, career counseling, disabled student services, grant writing training, international student services, low-cost health insurance, multicultural affairs office. *Library facilities:* Great Valley Library. *Online resources:* library catalog, web page, access to other libraries' catalogs. *Collection:* 37,363 titles, 604 serial subscriptions, 2,515 audiovisual materials.

Computer facilities: 331 computers available on campus for general student use. A campuswide network can be accessed from off campus. Internet access and online class registration are available. *Web address:* http://www.gv.psu.edu/.

General Application Contact: Dr. Kathy Mingioni, Assistant Director of Admissions, 610-648-3315, Fax: 610-725-5296, E-mail: kgm2@psu.edu.

GRADUATE UNITS

Graduate Studies Students: 71 full-time (25 women), 1,248 part-time (523 women); includes 218 minority (77 African Americans, 1 American Indian/Alaska Native, 116 Asian Americans or Pacific Islanders, 24 Hispanic Americans), 28 international. Average age 33. 684 applicants, 85% accepted, 450 enrolled. Expenses: Contact institution. *Financial support:* In 2006–07, 2 research assistantships, 1 teaching assistantship were awarded; fellowships, Federal Work-Study, scholarships/grants, health care benefits, and unspecified assistantships also available. Support available to part-time students. Financial award application deadline: 2/15; financial award applicants required to submit FAFSA. In 2006, 359 degrees awarded. *Degree program information:* Evening/weekend programs available. *Application deadline:* Applications are processed on a rolling basis. *Application fee:* $45. Electronic applications accepted. *Application Contact:* 610-648-3242, Fax: 610-889-1334. *Chancellor,* Dr. Diane M. Disney, 610-648-3301, Fax: 610-889-1334, E-mail: d2d5@psu.edu.

Education Division Expenses: Contact institution. Offers curriculum and instruction (M Ed); instructional systems (M Ed, MS); special education (M Ed, MS). *Application Contact:* Dr. Arlene Mitchell, Academic Division Head, 610-648-3355, E-mail: ahm13@psu.edu. *Academic Division Head,* Dr. Arlene Mitchell, 610-648-3355, E-mail: ahm13@psu.edu.

Engineering Division Expenses: Contact institution. Offers information science (MSIS); software engineering (MSE); systems engineering (M Eng). *Application Contact:* Unit Head, 610-648-3200. *Unit Head,* 610-648-3200.

Management Division Expenses: Contact institution. Offers biotechnology and health industry management (MBA); business administration (MBA); finance (M Fin); leadership development (MLD); management (M Fin, MBA, MLD); new venture and entrepreneurial studies (MBA).

PENN STATE HARRISBURG, Middletown, PA 17057-4898

General Information State-related, coed, comprehensive institution. Tuition, state resident: full-time $13,224; part-time $551 per credit. Tuition, nonresident: full-time $18,652; part-time $777 per credit. *Required fees:* $84 per semester. *Graduate housing:* Room and/or apartments available on a first-come, first-served basis to single students; on-campus housing not available to married students. *Student services:* Campus employment opportunities, campus safety program, career counseling, child daycare facilities, disabled student services, exercise/wellness program, free psychological counseling, grant writing training, international student services, low-cost health insurance, multicultural affairs office, writing training. *Library facilities:* Penn State Harrisburg Library. *Online resources:* library catalog, web page, access to other libraries' catalogs. *Collection:* 5 million titles, 68,445 serial subscriptions, 163,643 audiovisual materials.

Computer facilities: Computer purchase and lease plans are available. 132 computers available on campus for general student use. A campuswide network can be accessed from student residence rooms and from off campus. Internet access and online class registration are available. *Web address:* http://www.hbg.psu.edu/.

General Application Contact: Robert Coffman, Director of Admissions, 717-948-6250, Fax: 717-948-6325, E-mail: ric1@psu.edu.

GRADUATE UNITS

Graduate School Students: 215 full-time (131 women), 1,325 part-time (839 women); includes 129 minority (69 African Americans, 4 American Indian/Alaska Native, 31 Asian Americans or Pacific Islanders, 25 Hispanic Americans), 38 international. Average age 31. 829 applicants, 75% accepted, 412 enrolled. Expenses: Contact institution. *Financial support:* In 2006–07, 1 fellowship, 9 research assistantships, 22 teaching assistantships were awarded; career-related internships or fieldwork, Federal Work-Study, and unspecified assistantships also available. Support available to part-time students. Financial award application deadline: 2/15; financial award applicants required to submit FAFSA. In 2006, 498 master's, 8 doctorates awarded. *Degree program information:* Part-time and evening/weekend programs available. *Application deadline:* Applications are processed on a rolling basis. *Application fee:* $45. Electronic applications accepted. *Application Contact:* Robert Coffman, Director of Admissions, 717-948-6250, Fax: 717-948-6325, E-mail: ric1@psu.edu. *Chancellor,* Dr. Madlyn L. Hanes, 717-948-6000, Fax: 717-948-6100, E-mail: mqh3@psu.edu.

School of Behavioral Sciences and Education Expenses: Contact institution. *Financial support:* Career-related internships or fieldwork available. *Degree program information:* Part-time and evening/weekend programs available. Offers adult education (D Ed); applied behavior analysis (MA); applied clinical psychology (MA); applied psychological research (MA); community psychology and social change (MA); health education (M Ed); teaching and curriculum (M Ed); training and development (M Ed). *Director,* Dr. William D. Milheim, 717-948-6205, Fax: 717-948-6209, E-mail: wdm2@psu.edu.

School of Business Administration Expenses: Contact institution. Offers business administration (MBA); information systems (MS). *Professor,* Dr. Mukund S. Kulkarni, 717-948-6141, E-mail: msk5@psu.edu.

School of Humanities Expenses: Contact institution. *Degree program information:* Evening/weekend programs available. Offers American studies (MA); humanities (MA). *Professor,* Kathryn Robinson, 717-948-6470, E-mail: kdr12@psu.edu.

School of Public Affairs Expenses: Contact institution. Offers criminal justice (MA); health administration (MHA); public administration (MPA); public affairs (PhD). *Professor of Politics,* Dr. Steven A. Peterson, 717-948-6058, E-mail: sap12@psu.edu.

School of Science, Engineering and Technology Expenses: Contact institution. *Degree program information:* Evening/weekend programs available. Offers computer science (MS); electrical engineering (M Eng); engineering science (M Eng); environmental engineering (M Eng); environmental pollution control (M Eng, MEPC, MS). *Director,* Dr. Omid Ansary, 717-948-6541, E-mail: axa8@psu.edu.

See Close-Up on page 991.

PENN STATE HERSHEY MEDICAL CENTER, Hershey, PA 17033-2360

General Information State-related, coed, graduate-only institution. *Graduate housing:* Rooms and/or apartments available on a first-come, first-served basis to single and married students. *Student services:* Campus employment opportunities, campus safety program, career counseling, child daycare facilities, disabled student services, exercise/wellness program, free psychological counseling, grant writing training, international student services, low-cost health insurance, multicultural affairs office. *Library facilities:* George T. Harrell Library plus 1 other. *Online resources:* library catalog, web page, access to other libraries' catalogs. *Collection:* 130,837 titles, 7,000 serial subscriptions.

Computer facilities: A campuswide network can be accessed from student residence rooms and from off campus. Internet access and online class registration are available. *Web address:* http://www.hmc.psu.edu/college/.

General Application Contact: Dr. Ronald E. Domen, Associate Dean of Graduate Medical Education, 717-531-8892, Fax: 717-531-4139, E-mail: grad-hmc@psu.edu.

GRADUATE UNITS

College of Medicine Students: 541 full-time (297 women); includes 131 minority (39 African Americans, 3 American Indian/Alaska Native, 85 Asian Americans or Pacific Islanders, 4 Hispanic Americans), 19 international. Average age 27. 154 applicants, 49% accepted. *Faculty:* 707 full-time (151 women), 65 part-time/adjunct (43 women). Expenses: Contact institution. *Financial support:* In 2006–07, 10 fellowships, 44 research assistantships, 42 teaching assistantships were awarded; scholarships/grants and health care benefits also available. Financial award application deadline: 2/15; financial award applicants required to submit FAFSA. In 2006, 116 degrees awarded. Offers medicine (MD, MS, PhD). *Application deadline:* For fall admission, 11/15 for domestic students. *Application fee:* $54. *Senior Vice President and Dean,* Dr. Harold L. Paz, 717-531-8521, Fax: 717-531-5351.

Graduate School Programs in the Biomedical Sciences 548 applicants, 11% accepted, 47 enrolled. Expenses: Contact institution. *Financial support:* Fellowships with full tuition reimbursements, research assistantships with full tuition reimbursements, teaching assistantships with tuition reimbursements, scholarships/grants, health care benefits, tuition waivers (full), and unspecified assistantships available. Financial award applicants required to submit FAFSA. In 2006, 14 master's, 30 doctorates awarded. Offers anatomy (MS, PhD); biochemistry and molecular biology (MS, PhD); bioengineering (MS, PhD); biomedical sciences (MS, PhD); cell and molecular biology (MS, PhD); genetics (PhD); health evaluation sciences (MS); immunology (MS, PhD); integrative biosciences (MS, PhD); laboratory animal medicine (MS); life sciences (MS, PhD); microbiology (MS); microbiology/virology (PhD); molecular biology (PhD); molecular medicine (MS, PhD); molecular toxicology (MS, PhD); neuroscience (MS, PhD); pharmacology (MS, PhD); physiology (MS, PhD). *Application deadline:* For fall admission, 2/1 priority date for domestic students, 2/1 for international students. Applications are processed on a rolling basis. *Application fee:* $45. Electronic applications accepted. *Application Contact:* Kathleen M. Simon, Administrative Assistant, 717-531-8892, Fax: 717-531-0786, E-mail: grad-hmc@psu.edu. *Associate Dean for Graduate Studies,* Dr. Michael F. Verderame, 717-531-8892, Fax: 717-531-0786, E-mail: grad-hmc@psu.edu.

PENN STATE UNIVERSITY PARK, State College, University Park, PA 16802-1503

General Information State-related, coed, university. CGS member. *Graduate housing:* Rooms and/or apartments available on a first-come, first-served basis to single and married students. *Student services:* Campus employment opportunities, campus safety program, career counseling, child daycare facilities, disabled student services, exercise/wellness program, free psychological counseling, grant writing training, international student services, low-cost health insurance, multicultural affairs office, teacher training, writing training. *Library facilities:* Pattee Library plus 14 others. *Online resources:* library catalog, web page, access to other libraries' catalogs. *Collection:* 5 million titles, 68,445 serial subscriptions, 163,643 audiovisual materials.

Computer facilities: 3,589 computers available on campus for general student use. A campuswide network can be accessed from student residence rooms and from off campus. Internet access and online class registration are available. *Web address:* http://www.psu.edu/.

General Application Contact: Cynthia E. Nicosia, Director, Graduate Enrollment Services, 814-865-1834, Fax: 814-865-4627, E-mail: cey1@psu.edu.

GRADUATE UNITS

Graduate School Expenses: Contact institution. *Financial support:* Fellowships, research assistantships, teaching assistantships, Federal Work-Study, traineeships, health care benefits, tuition waivers (full), and unspecified assistantships available. Support available to part-time students. Financial award application deadline: 2/15; financial award applicants required to submit FAFSA. In 2006, 1,150 master's, 646 doctorates awarded. *Degree program information:* Part-time programs available. Postbaccalaureate distance learning degree programs offered. Offers acoustics (M Eng, MS, PhD); bioengineering (MS, PhD); ecology (MS, PhD); environmental pollution control (MEPC, MS); genetics (MS, PhD); integrative biosciences (MS, PhD); mass communications (PhD); nutrition (MS, PhD); physiology (MS, PhD); plant physiology (MS, PhD); quality and manufacturing management (MMM). *Application deadline:* Applications are processed on a rolling basis. *Application fee:* $45. Electronic applications accepted. *Application Contact:* Cynthia E. Nicosia, Director, Graduate Enrollment Services, 814-865-1795, Fax: 814-865-4627, E-mail: cey1@psu.edu. *Vice President, Research and Dean of the Graduate School,* Dr. Eva J. Pell, 814-863-9580, Fax: 814-863-9659, E-mail: gswww@psu.edu.

College of Agricultural Sciences Students: 318 full-time (168 women), 53 part-time (22 women); includes 27 minority (12 African Americans, 1 American Indian/Alaska Native, 4 Asian Americans or Pacific Islanders, 10 Hispanic Americans), 149 international. Average age 28. 461 applicants, 36% accepted, 103 enrolled. Expenses: Contact institution. *Financial support:* In 2006–07, 13 fellowships, 217 research assistantships, 27 teaching assistantships were awarded. Financial award applicants required to submit FAFSA. In 2006, 75 master's, 27 doctorates awarded. Offers agricultural and biological engineering (MS, PhD); agricultural and extension education (M Ed, MS, D Ed, PhD); agricultural sciences (M Agr, M Ed, MFR, MS, D Ed, PhD); agricultural, environmental and regional economics (M Agr, MS, PhD); agronomy (M Agr, MS, PhD); animal science (M Agr, MS, PhD); entomology (M Agr, MS, PhD); food science (MS, PhD); forest resources (M Agr, MFR, MS, PhD); horticulture (M Agr, MS, PhD); pathobiology (PhD); plant pathology (M Agr, MS, PhD); rural sociology (M Agr, MS, PhD); soil science (M Agr, PhD); wildlife and fisheries sciences (M Agr, MFR, MS, PhD); youth and family education (M Ed). *Application deadline:* Applications are processed on a rolling basis. Electronic applications accepted. *Application Contact:* Cynthia E. Nicosia, Director Graduate Enrollment Services, 814-865-1834, Fax: 814-865-

4627, E-mail: cey1@psu.edu. *Dean,* Dr. Robert D. Steele, 814-865-2541, Fax: 814-865-3103, E-mail: rds17@psu.edu.

College of Arts and Architecture Students: 190 full-time (120 women), 32 part-time (24 women); includes 18 minority (6 African Americans, 1 American Indian/Alaska Native, 3 Asian Americans or Pacific Islanders, 8 Hispanic Americans), 41 international. Average age 29. 315 applicants, 40% accepted, 74 enrolled. Expenses: Contact institution. *Financial support:* In 2006–07, 8 fellowships, 4 research assistantships, 135 teaching assistantships were awarded. Financial award applicants required to submit FAFSA. In 2006, 65 master's, 7 doctorates awarded. Offers architecture (M Arch); art (MFA); art education (M Ed, MS, PhD); art history (MA, PhD); arts and architecture (M Arch, M Ed, M Mus, MA, MFA, MLA, MME, MS, PhD); composition/theory (M Mus); conducting (M Mus); landscape architecture (MLA); music education (MME, PhD); music theory (MA); music theory and history (MA); musicology (MA); performance (M Mus); piano, pedagogy and performance (M Mus); theatre (MFA); voice performance and pedagogy (M Mus). *Application Contact:* Cynthia E. Nicosia, Director Graduate Enrollment Services, 814-865-1834, Fax: 814-865-4627, E-mail: cey1@psu.edu. *Interim Dean,* Dr. Yvonne M. Gaudelius, 814-865-2591, Fax: 814-865-2018, E-mail: ymg100@psu.edu.

College of Communications Students: 70 full-time (44 women), 8 part-time (7 women); includes 12 minority (5 African Americans, 1 American Indian/Alaska Native, 4 Asian Americans or Pacific Islanders, 2 Hispanic Americans), 30 international. Average age 31. 190 applicants, 26% accepted, 18 enrolled. Expenses: Contact institution. *Financial support:* In 2006–07, 5 fellowships, 1 research assistantship, 38 teaching assistantships were awarded. Financial award applicants required to submit FAFSA. In 2006, 8 master's, 7 doctorates awarded. Offers communications (MA, PhD); mass communications (PhD); media studies (MA); telecommunications studies (MA). *Application Contact:* Cynthia E. Nicosia, Director Graduate Enrollment Services, 814-865-1834, Fax: 814-865-4627, E-mail: cey1@psu.edu. *Dean,* Dr. Douglas A. Anderson, 814-863-1484, Fax: 814-863-8044, E-mail: doug-anderson@psu.edu.

College of Earth and Mineral Sciences Students: 290 full-time (106 women), 21 part-time (4 women); includes 25 minority (7 African Americans, 1 American Indian/Alaska Native, 7 Asian Americans or Pacific Islanders, 10 Hispanic Americans), 116 international. Average age 28. 435 applicants, 37% accepted, 78 enrolled. Expenses: Contact institution. *Financial support:* In 2006–07, 16 fellowships, 208 research assistantships, 106 teaching assistantships were awarded. Financial award applicants required to submit FAFSA. In 2006, 73 master's, 52 doctorates awarded. Offers astrobiology (PhD); ceramic science (MS, PhD); earth and mineral sciences (M Ed, M Eng, MGIS, MS, PhD); energy and geo-environmental engineering (MS, PhD); fuel science (MS, PhD); geography (MS, PhD); geosciences (MS, PhD); industrial health and safety (MS); metals science and engineering (MS, PhD); meteorology (MS, PhD); mineral processing (MS, PhD); mining engineering (MS, PhD); petroleum and mining engineering (MS, PhD); polymer science (MS, PhD). *Application Contact:* Cynthia E. Nicosia, Director Graduate Enrollment Services, 814-865-1834, Fax: 814-865-4627, E-mail: cey1@psu.edu. *Dean,* Dr. Rob G. Crane, 814-865-6546, Fax: 814-863-7708, E-mail: rqc3@psu.edu.

College of Education Students: 509 full-time (333 women), 316 part-time (182 women); includes 127 minority (64 African Americans, 8 American Indian/Alaska Native, 28 Asian Americans or Pacific Islanders, 27 Hispanic Americans), 144 international. Average age 35. 746 applicants, 49% accepted, 207 enrolled. Expenses: Contact institution. *Financial support:* In 2006–07, 38 fellowships, 36 research assistantships, 146 teaching assistantships were awarded. Financial award applicants required to submit FAFSA. In 2006, 199 master's, 101 doctorates awarded. Offers adult education (M Ed, D Ed, PhD); bilingual education (M Ed, MS, PhD); college student affairs (M Ed); counseling psychology (PhD); counselor education (M Ed, MS); counselor education, counseling psychology and rehabilitation services (D Ed); early childhood education (M Ed, MS, PhD); education (M Ed, MA, MS, D Ed, PhD); educational leadership (M Ed, MS, D Ed, PhD); educational psychology (MS, PhD); educational theory and policy (MA, PhD); elementary education (M Ed, MS, PhD); higher education (M Ed, D Ed, PhD); instructional systems (M Ed, MS, D Ed, PhD); language arts and reading (M Ed, MS, PhD); school psychology (M Ed, MS, PhD); science education (M Ed, MS, PhD); social studies education (MS, PhD); special education (M Ed, MS, PhD); supervisor and curriculum development (M Ed, MS, PhD); workforce education and development (M Ed, MS, D Ed, PhD). *Application deadline:* Applications are processed on a rolling basis. Electronic applications accepted. *Application Contact:* Cynthia E. Nicosia, Director Graduate Enrollment Services, 814-865-1834, Fax: 814-865-4627, E-mail: cey1@psu.edu. *Dean,* Dr. David H. Monk, 814-865-2526, Fax: 814-865-0555, E-mail: dhm6@psu.edu.

College of Engineering Students: 1,130 full-time (223 women), 120 part-time (17 women); includes 70 minority (16 African Americans, 2 American Indian/Alaska Native, 32 Asian Americans or Pacific Islanders, 20 Hispanic Americans), 774 international. Average age 27. 3,095 applicants, 38% accepted, 384 enrolled. Expenses: Contact institution. *Financial support:* In 2006–07, 37 fellowships, 560 research assistantships, 258 teaching assistantships were awarded. Financial award applicants required to submit FAFSA. In 2006, 251 master's, 134 doctorates awarded. Offers aerospace engineering (M Eng, MS, PhD); architectural engineering (M Eng, MAE, MS, PhD); chemical engineering (MS, PhD); civil engineering (M Eng, MS, PhD); computer science and engineering (M Eng, MS, PhD); electrical engineering (MS, PhD); engineering (M Eng, MAE, MS, PhD); engineering mechanics (M Eng, MS, PhD); engineering science (M Eng, MS, PhD); engineering science and mechanics (M Eng, MS, PhD); environmental engineering (M Eng, MS, PhD); industrial engineering (M Eng, MS, PhD); manufacturing engineering (M Eng); mechanical engineering (M Eng, MS, PhD); nuclear engineering (M Eng, MS, PhD); structural engineering (M Eng, MS, PhD); transportation and highway engineering (M Eng, MS, PhD); water resources engineering (M Eng, MS, PhD). *Application Contact:* Cynthia E. Nicosia, Director Graduate Enrollment Services, 814-865-1834, Fax: 814-865-4627, E-mail: cey1@psu.edu. *Dean,* Dr. David N. Wormley, 814-865-7537, Fax: 814-865-8767, E-mail: dnw2@engr.psu.edu.

College of Health and Human Development Students: 340 full-time (251 women), 53 part-time (41 women); includes 29 minority (16 African Americans, 9 Asian Americans or Pacific Islanders, 4 Hispanic Americans), 99 international. Average age 30. 564 applicants, 32% accepted, 117 enrolled. Expenses: Contact institution. *Financial support:* In 2006–07, 38 fellowships, 67 research assistantships, 153 teaching assistantships were awarded. Financial award applicants required to submit FAFSA. In 2006, 70 master's, 46 doctorates awarded. Offers biobehavioral health (MS, PhD); communication sciences and disorders (MS, PhD); health and human development (M Ed, MHA, MHRIM, MS, PhD); health policy and administration (MHA, MS, PhD); hospitality management (MHRIM, MS, PhD); hotel, restaurant, and institutional management (MHRIM, MS, PhD); human development and family studies (MS, PhD); human nutrition (M Ed); kinesiology (MS, PhD); leisure studies (MS, PhD); nursing (MS, PhD); nutrition (MS, PhD); recreation, park and tourism management (M Ed). *Application deadline:* Applications are processed on a rolling basis. Electronic applications accepted. *Dean,* Dr. Ann Crouter, 814-865-1428, Fax: 814-865-3282, E-mail: ac1@psu.edu.

College of Information Sciences and Technology Students: 75 full-time (23 women), 5 part-time (2 women); includes 10 minority (4 African Americans, 4 Asian Americans or Pacific Islanders, 2 Hispanic Americans), 42 international. Average age 30. 108 applicants, 35% accepted, 19 enrolled. Expenses: Contact institution. *Financial support:* In 2006–07, 28 research assistantships, 35 teaching assistantships were awarded; fellowships also available. Financial award applicants required to submit FAFSA. In 2006, 5 master's, 5 doctorates awarded. Offers information sciences and technology (MS, PhD). *Application deadline:* Applications are processed on a rolling basis. Electronic applications accepted. *Application Contact:* Dr. Henry Foley, Dean, 814-863-3528, Fax: 814-865-5604, E-mail: hcf2@psu.edu. *Dean,* Dr. Henry Foley, 814-863-3528, Fax: 814-865-5604, E-mail: hcf2@psu.edu.

College of the Liberal Arts Students: 730 full-time (426 women), 70 part-time (55 women); includes 82 minority (30 African Americans, 2 American Indian/Alaska Native, 22 Asian Americans or Pacific Islanders, 28 Hispanic Americans), 217 international. Average age 28. 2,378 applicants, 15% accepted, 176 enrolled. Expenses: Contact institution. *Financial support:* In 2006–07, 43 fellowships, 66 research assistantships, 500 teaching assistantships were awarded. Financial award applicants required to submit FAFSA. In 2006, 118 master's, 89 doctorates awarded. Offers anthropology (MA, PhD); applied linguistics (PhD); classical American philosophy (MA, PhD); clinical psychology (MS, PhD); cognitive psychology (MS, PhD); communication arts and sciences (MA, PhD); comparative literature (MA, PhD); contemporary European philosophy (MA, PhD); crime, law, and justice (MA, PhD); developmental psychology (MS, PhD); economics (MA, PhD); English (MA, MFA, PhD); French (MA, PhD); German (MA, PhD); history (MA, PhD); history of philosophy (MA, PhD); industrial relations and human resources (MS); industrial/organizational psychology (MS, PhD); liberal arts (MA, MFA, MS, PhD); political science (MA, PhD); psychobiology (MS, PhD); Russian and comparative literature (MA); social psychology (MS, PhD); sociology (MA, PhD); Spanish (MA, PhD); teaching English as a second language (MA). *Dean,* Dr. Susan Welch, 814-865-7691, Fax: 814-863-2085, E-mail: swelch@psu.edu.

Eberly College of Science Students: 660 full-time (232 women), 31 part-time (14 women); includes 46 minority (6 African Americans, 2 American Indian/Alaska Native, 20 Asian Americans or Pacific Islanders, 18 Hispanic Americans), 325 international. Average age 26. 1,419 applicants, 16% accepted, 129 enrolled. Expenses: Contact institution. *Financial support:* In 2006–07, 14 fellowships, 300 research assistantships, 312 teaching assistantships were awarded. Financial award applicants required to submit FAFSA. In 2006, 54 master's, 108 doctorates awarded. Offers applied statistics (MAS); astronomy and astrophysics (MS, PhD); biochemistry, microbiology, and molecular biology (MS, PhD); biology (MS, PhD); biotechnology (MS); cell and developmental biology (MS, PhD); chemistry (MS, PhD); mathematics (M Ed, MA, D Ed, PhD); molecular evolutionary biology (MS, PhD); physics (M Ed, MS, D Ed, PhD); science (M Ed, MA, MAS, MS, D Ed, PhD); statistics (MA, MAS, MS, PhD). *Dean,* Dr. Daniel J. Larson, 814-865-9591, Fax: 814-863-0491, E-mail: djlarson@psu.edu.

The Mary Jean and Frank P. Smeal College of Business Administration Students: 287 full-time (79 women), 5 part-time (2 women); includes 39 minority (22 African Americans, 11 Asian Americans or Pacific Islanders, 6 Hispanic Americans), 93 international. Average age 31. 841 applicants, 31% accepted, 150 enrolled. Expenses: Contact institution. *Financial support:* In 2006–07, 1 fellowship, 11 research assistantships, 143 teaching assistantships were awarded. Financial award applicants required to submit FAFSA. In 2006, 107 master's, 11 doctorates awarded. Offers accounting (PhD); business administration (MBA); finance (PhD); management and organization (PhD); management science/operations/logistics (PhD); marketing (PhD); real estate (PhD); supply chain and information systems (PhD). *Dean,* Dr. Kenneth B. Thomas, 814-863-0448, Fax: 814-865-7064, E-mail: j2t@psu.edu.

See Close-Up on page 993.

PENNSYLVANIA ACADEMY OF THE FINE ARTS, Philadelphia, PA 19102

General Information Independent, coed, graduate-only institution. *Graduate housing:* On-campus housing not available.

GRADUATE UNITS

Graduate School Offers drawing (MFA, Postbaccalaureate Certificate); painting (MFA, Postbaccalaureate Certificate); printmaking (MFA, Postbaccalaureate Certificate); sculpture (MFA, Postbaccalaureate Certificate). Electronic applications accepted.

PENNSYLVANIA COLLEGE OF OPTOMETRY, Elkins Park, PA 19027-1598

General Information Independent, coed, graduate-only institution. *Graduate housing:* Rooms and/or apartments available to single and married students. *Research affiliation:* Charles River Laboratories (photobiology).

GRADUATE UNITS

Graduate Studies in Vision Impairment and Audiology *Degree program information:* Part-time programs available. Offers audiology (Au D); education of children and youth with visual and multiple impairments (M Ed, Certificate); low vision rehabilitation (MS, Certificate); orientation and mobility therapy (MS, Certificate); rehabilitation teaching (MS, Certificate).

Professional Program Postbaccalaureate distance learning degree programs offered. Offers optometry (OD). Electronic applications accepted.

PEPPERDINE UNIVERSITY, Los Angeles, CA 90045

General Information Independent-religious, coed, upper-level institution. *Enrollment by degree level:* 2,554 master's, 451 doctoral. *Graduate faculty:* 147 full-time (43 women), 155 part-time/adjunct (75 women). *Graduate housing:* On-campus housing not available. *Student services:* Campus employment opportunities, career counseling, disabled student services, exercise/wellness program, international student services, low-cost health insurance, teacher training. *Web address:* http://www.pepperdine.edu/.

General Application Contact: Information Contact, 310-568-5500.

GRADUATE UNITS

Graduate School of Education and Psychology Students: 598 full-time (496 women), 1,035 part-time (733 women); includes 480 minority (169 African Americans, 8 American Indian/Alaska Native, 121 Asian Americans or Pacific Islanders, 182 Hispanic Americans), 50 international. 812 applicants, 77% accepted, 518 enrolled. *Faculty:* 64 full-time (28 women), 108 part-time/adjunct (64 women). Expenses: Contact institution. *Financial support:* Research assistantships, teaching assistantships, career-related internships or fieldwork, Federal Work-Study, institutionally sponsored loans, scholarships/grants, and unspecified assistantships available. Support available to part-time students. Financial award application deadline: 7/1; financial award applicants required to submit FAFSA. In 2006, 621 master's, 70 doctorates awarded. *Degree program information:* Part-time and evening/weekend programs available. Postbaccalaureate distance learning degree programs offered (minimal on-campus study). Offers education and psychology (MA, MS, Ed D, Psy D). *Application deadline:* Applications are processed on a rolling basis. *Application fee:* $45. *Application Contact:* Anne McLintock, Admissions Specialist, 310-258-2848, E-mail: anne.mclintock@pepperdine.edu. *Dean,* Dr. Margaret J. Weber, 310-568-5600, E-mail: margaret.weber@pepperdine.edu.

Division of Education Students: 275 full-time (225 women), 502 part-time (284 women); includes 252 minority (93 African Americans, 3 American Indian/Alaska Native, 62 Asian Americans or Pacific Islanders, 94 Hispanic Americans), 26 international. 394 applicants, 86% accepted, 291 enrolled. *Faculty:* 32 full-time (17 women), 32 part-time/adjunct (22 women). Expenses: Contact institution. *Financial support:* Research assistantships, teaching assistantships, career-related internships or fieldwork, institutionally sponsored loans, and scholarships/grants available. Support available to part-time students. Financial award application deadline: 7/1; financial award applicants required to submit FAFSA. In 2006, 413 master's, 52 doctorates awarded. *Degree program information:* Part-time and evening/weekend programs available. Postbaccalaureate distance learning degree programs offered (minimal on-campus study). Offers education (MS); educational leadership, administration, and policy (Ed D); educational technology (Ed D); organization change (Ed D); organizational leadership (Ed D). *Application deadline:* Applications are processed on a rolling basis. *Application fee:* $45. *Application Contact:* Anne McLintock, Admissions Specialist, 310-258-2848, E-mail: anne.mclintock@pepperdine.edu. *Associate Dean,* Dr. Chester McCall, 310-568-2323, E-mail: chester.mccall@pepperdine.edu.

Division of Psychology Students: 323 full-time (271 women), 533 part-time (449 women); includes 228 minority (76 African Americans, 5 American Indian/Alaska Native, 59 Asian Americans or Pacific Islanders, 88 Hispanic Americans), 24 international. 434 applicants, 66% accepted, 227 enrolled. *Faculty:* 32 full-time (11 women), 76 part-time/adjunct (42 women). Expenses: Contact institution. *Financial support:* Research assistantships, teaching assistantships, career-related internships or fieldwork and scholarships/grants available. Support available to part-time students. Financial award application deadline: 7/1; financial award applicants required to submit FAFSA. In 2006, 244 master's, 22 doctorates awarded. *Degree program information:* Part-time and evening/weekend programs available. Offers clinical psychology (MA); psychology (MA, Psy D). *Application deadline:* For fall admission, 2/1 for domestic students. Applications are processed on a rolling basis. *Application fee:* $55. *Application Contact:* Christine M. Runyan, Program Administrator, 310-568-5605,

Pepperdine University (continued)

E-mail: christine.runyan@pepperdine.edu. *Associate Dean*, Dr. Robert deMayo, 310-568-5747, E-mail: robert.demayo@pepperdine.edu.

The Graziadio School of Business and Management Students: 606 full-time (229 women), 766 part-time (301 women); includes 433 minority (43 African Americans, 6 American Indian/Alaska Native, 250 Asian Americans or Pacific Islanders, 134 Hispanic Americans), 54 international. 764 applicants, 71% accepted, 415 enrolled. *Faculty:* 83 full-time (15 women), 47 part-time/adjunct (11 women). Expenses: Contact institution. *Financial support:* Career-related internships or fieldwork, institutionally sponsored loans, scholarships/grants, and unspecified assistantships available. Support available to part-time students. Financial award applicants required to submit FAFSA. In 2006, 681 degrees awarded. *Degree program information:* Part-time and evening/weekend programs available. Offers business (MBA); executive business administration (MBAA); organizational development (MSOD); technology management (MSTM). *Application deadline:* For fall admission, 6/28 for domestic students. Applications are processed on a rolling basis. *Application fee:* $45. *Application Contact:* Darrell Eriksen, Director of Admission and Student Accounts, 310-568-5525, E-mail: darrell.eriksen@pepperdine.edu. *Dean*, Dr. Linda A. Livingstone, 310-568-5689, Fax: 310-568-5766, E-mail: linda.livingstone@pepperdine.edu.

See Close-Up on page 995.

PEPPERDINE UNIVERSITY, Malibu, CA 90263

General Information Independent-religious, coed, university. CGS member. *Enrollment:* 7,593 graduate, professional, and undergraduate students; 1,080 full-time matriculated graduate/professional students (577 women), 157 part-time matriculated graduate/professional students (80 women). *Enrollment by degree level:* 639 first professional, 598 master's. *Graduate faculty:* 96 full-time (25 women), 41 part-time/adjunct (12 women). *Tuition:* Full-time $32,744; part-time $1,026 per unit. Full-time tuition and fees vary according to program. *Graduate housing:* Rooms and/or apartments available on a first-come, first-served basis to single and married students. *Student services:* Campus employment opportunities, career counseling, exercise/wellness program, international student services, low-cost health insurance, teacher training. *Library facilities:* Payson Library plus 2 others. *Online resources:* library catalog, web page, access to other libraries' catalogs. *Collection:* 1.5 million titles, 103,654 serial subscriptions.

Computer facilities: Computer purchase and lease plans are available. 292 computers available on campus for general student use. A campuswide network can be accessed from student residence rooms. Internet access and online class registration are available. *Web address:* http://www.pepperdine.edu/.

General Application Contact: Paul A. Long, Dean of Admission and Enrollment Management, 310-506-6165, Fax: 310-506-4861, E-mail: admission-seaver@pepperdine.edu.

GRADUATE UNITS

Graduate School of Education and Psychology Students: 86 full-time (76 women); includes 13 minority (5 African Americans, 3 Asian Americans or Pacific Islanders, 5 Hispanic Americans). *Faculty:* 4 full-time (2 women). Expenses: Contact institution. Offers clinical psychology (MA). *Application deadline:* For fall admission, 1/2 for domestic students; for spring admission, 1/1 for domestic students. Applications are processed on a rolling basis. *Application fee:* $55. Electronic applications accepted. *Application Contact:* Fionnbarr Kelly, Director, Recruitment and Admissions, 310-568-5744, E-mail: fionnbarr.kelly@pepperdine.edu. *Dean of Graduate School of Education and Psychology*, Dr. Margaret J. Weber, 310-568-5000, E-mail: margaret.weber@pepperdine.edu.

Malibu Graduate Business Programs Students: 241 full-time (111 women), 3 part-time; includes 34 minority (1 African American, 1 American Indian/Alaska Native, 24 Asian Americans or Pacific Islanders, 8 Hispanic Americans), 94 international. 627 applicants, 62% accepted, 164 enrolled. *Faculty:* 10 full-time (4 women). Expenses: Contact institution. *Financial support:* Career-related internships or fieldwork, institutionally sponsored loans, scholarships/grants, and unspecified assistantships available. Financial award application deadline: 6/1; financial award applicants required to submit FAFSA. In 2006, 86 degrees awarded. Offers business administration (MBA); international business (MIB). *Application deadline:* For fall admission, 5/1 for domestic and international students. Applications are processed on a rolling basis. *Application fee:* $45. Electronic applications accepted. *Application Contact:* Paul E. Pinckley, Executive Director, Recruitment and Student Recruitment, 310-506-4858, Fax: 310-506-4126, E-mail: paul.pinckley@pepperdine.edu. *Director, Full-Time Programs*, Dr. Mark Mallinger, 310-506-6962, Fax: 310-506-4126, E-mail: mark.mallinger@pepperdine.edu.

School of Law Students: 644 full-time (325 women), 53 part-time (27 women); includes 118 minority (27 African Americans, 3 American Indian/Alaska Native, 52 Asian Americans or Pacific Islanders, 36 Hispanic Americans), 12 international. 3,162 applicants, 30% accepted, 233 enrolled. *Faculty:* 40 full-time (11 women), 36 part-time/adjunct (11 women). Expenses: Contact institution. *Financial support:* Fellowships, research assistantships, teaching assistantships, career-related internships or fieldwork, Federal Work-Study, institutionally sponsored loans, and scholarships/grants available. Support available to part-time students. Financial award application deadline: 4/1; financial award applicants required to submit FAFSA. In 2006, 204 JDs, 36 master's awarded. Offers dispute resolution (LL M, MDR); law (JD, LL M, MDR). *Application deadline:* For fall admission, 2/1 for domestic students, 3/1 for international students. Applications are processed on a rolling basis. *Application fee:* $50. Electronic applications accepted. *Application Contact:* Shannon Phillips, Director of Admissions/Records, 310-506-4631, Fax: 310-506-4266, E-mail: shannon.phillips@pepperdine.edu. *Dean*, Kenneth W. Starr, 310-506-4621, Fax: 310-506-4266, E-mail: ken.starr@pepperdine.edu.

School of Public Policy Students: 104 full-time (63 women), 6 part-time (2 women); includes 18 minority (5 African Americans, 1 American Indian/Alaska Native, 9 Asian Americans or Pacific Islanders, 3 Hispanic Americans), 10 international. 149 applicants, 74% accepted, 45 enrolled. *Faculty:* 6 full-time (1 woman), 5 part-time/adjunct (1 woman). Expenses: Contact institution. *Financial support:* Research assistantships, teaching assistantships, institutionally sponsored loans and scholarships/grants available. Financial award application deadline: 5/1; financial award applicants required to submit FAFSA. In 2006, 27 degrees awarded. Offers American politics (MPP); economics (MPP); international relations (MPP); public policy (MPP); state and local policy (MPP). *Application deadline:* For fall admission, 4/15 for domestic students. Applications are processed on a rolling basis. *Application fee:* $50. Electronic applications accepted. *Application Contact:* Melinda E. van Hemert, Director of Recruitment and Career Services, 310-506-7492, Fax: 310-506-7494, E-mail: melinda.vanhemert@pepperdine.edu. *Dean*, Dr. James R. Wilburn, 310-506-7490, Fax: 310-506-7494, E-mail: james.wilburn@pepperdine.edu.

Seaver College Students: 5 full-time (2 women), 95 part-time (51 women); includes 10 minority (3 African Americans, 3 Asian Americans or Pacific Islanders, 4 Hispanic Americans). 121 applicants, 77% accepted, 60 enrolled. *Faculty:* 36 full-time (7 women). Expenses: Contact institution. *Financial support:* Fellowships, research assistantships, teaching assistantships, career-related internships or fieldwork, Federal Work-Study, institutionally sponsored loans, scholarships/grants, and tuition waivers (partial) available. Support available to part-time students. Financial award application deadline: 2/15; financial award applicants required to submit FAFSA. In 2006, 27 degrees awarded. *Degree program information:* Part-time and evening/weekend programs available. Offers American studies (MA); communication (MA); history (MA); ministry (MS); religion (M Div, MA). *Application deadline:* For fall admission, 5/1 for domestic students. Applications are processed on a rolling basis. *Application fee:* $55. *Application Contact:* Paul A. Long, Dean of Admission and Enrollment Management, 310-506-6165, Fax: 310-506-4861, E-mail: admission-seaver@pepperdine.edu. *Dean*, Dr. David W. Baird, 310-506-4280, E-mail: david.baird@pepperdine.edu.

See Close-Up on page 995.

PERU STATE COLLEGE, Peru, NE 68421

General Information State-supported, coed, comprehensive institution. *Graduate housing:* Rooms and/or apartments available to single and married students.

GRADUATE UNITS

Graduate Studies *Degree program information:* Part-time programs available. Offers education (MS Ed).

PFEIFFER UNIVERSITY, Misenheimer, NC 28109-0960

General Information Independent-religious, coed, comprehensive institution. *Enrollment:* 2,116 graduate, professional, and undergraduate students; 179 full-time matriculated graduate/professional students (100 women), 803 part-time matriculated graduate/professional students (563 women). *Enrollment by degree level:* 982 master's. *Graduate faculty:* 24 full-time (9 women), 29 part-time/adjunct (5 women). *Tuition:* Part-time $380 per semester hour. Tuition and fees vary according to campus/location. *Graduate housing:* On-campus housing not available. *Student services:* Campus employment opportunities, campus safety program, career counseling, international student services, teacher training, writing training. *Library facilities:* Gustavus A. Pfeiffer Library. *Online resources:* library catalog, web page, access to other libraries' catalogs. *Collection:* 125,972 titles, 288 serial subscriptions, 3,702 audiovisual materials.

Computer facilities: 90 computers available on campus for general student use. A campuswide network can be accessed from student residence rooms and from off campus. Internet access, e-mail are available. *Web address:* http://www.pfeiffer.edu/.

General Application Contact: Michael Utsman, Assistant Dean, 704-521-9116 Ext. 253, Fax: 704-521-8617, E-mail: mutsman@pfeiffer.edu.

GRADUATE UNITS

Program in Business Administration Students: 108 full-time (46 women), 395 part-time (248 women); includes 202 minority (182 African Americans, 9 Asian Americans or Pacific Islanders, 11 Hispanic Americans), 43 international. Average age 36. *Faculty:* 13 full-time (3 women), 15 part-time/adjunct (2 women). Expenses: Contact institution. *Financial support:* Unspecified assistantships available. Support available to part-time students. Financial award applicants required to submit FAFSA. In 2006, 223 degrees awarded. *Degree program information:* Part-time and evening/weekend programs available. Postbaccalaureate distance learning degree programs offered (minimal on-campus study). Offers business administration (MBA); organizational management (MS). *Application deadline:* For fall admission, 8/21 for domestic students. Applications are processed on a rolling basis. *Application fee:* $75. *Director of the MBA Program*, Dr. Robert K. Spear, 704-521-9116 Ext. 244, Fax: 704-521-8617, E-mail: rks@pfeiffer.edu.

Program in Health Administration Students: 71 full-time (54 women), 299 part-time (238 women); includes 149 minority (138 African Americans, 1 American Indian/Alaska Native, 5 Asian Americans or Pacific Islanders, 5 Hispanic Americans), 3 international. Average age 38. *Faculty:* 5 full-time (1 woman), 10 part-time/adjunct (2 women). Expenses: Contact institution. *Financial support:* Applicants required to submit FAFSA. In 2006, 81 degrees awarded. Offers health administration (MHA). *Director*, Dr. Joel Vickers, 204-521-9116 Ext. 228.

Program in Organizational Change and Leadership Students: 24 full-time (15 women), 155 part-time (114 women); includes 80 minority (78 African Americans, 2 American Indian/Alaska Native), 10 international. Average age 38. *Faculty:* 7 full-time (3 women), 8 part-time/adjunct (2 women). Expenses: Contact institution. *Financial support:* Unspecified assistantships available. Support available to part-time students. Financial award applicants required to submit FAFSA. In 2006, 50 degrees awarded. Offers organizational change and leadership (MS). *Application fee:* $75. *Director*, Dr. Ron Hunady, 704-521-9116 Ext. 224, E-mail: rhunady@pfeiffer.edu.

School of Education Students: 5 full-time (all women), 60 part-time (52 women); includes 22 minority (21 African Americans, 1 Hispanic American), 1 international. Average age 39. *Faculty:* 4 full-time (3 women), 2 part-time/adjunct (1 woman). Expenses: Contact institution. *Financial support:* Unspecified assistantships available. Support available to part-time students. Financial award applicants required to submit FAFSA. In 2006, 29 degrees awarded. Offers elementary education (MS); teaching (MAT). *Application deadline:* Applications are processed on a rolling basis. *Application fee:* $75. *Director of Teacher Education*, Dr. Sandra Loehr, 704-521-9116 Ext. 239.

School of Religion and Christian Education Students: 1 (woman) full-time, 51 part-time (40 women); includes 12 minority (all African Americans), 1 international. Average age 40. *Faculty:* 4 full-time (2 women). Expenses: Contact institution. *Financial support:* Scholarships/grants available. Support available to part-time students. Financial award applicants required to submit FAFSA. In 2006, 12 degrees awarded. *Degree program information:* Part-time and evening/weekend programs available. Offers religion and Christian education (MACE). *Application deadline:* For fall admission, 8/21 priority date for domestic students. Applications are processed on a rolling basis. *Application fee:* $75. *Coordinator*, Kathleen Kilbourne, 704-521-9116 Ext. 236, E-mail: kbourne@pfeiffer.edu.

PHILADELPHIA BIBLICAL UNIVERSITY, Langhorne, PA 19047-2990

General Information Independent-religious, coed, comprehensive institution. *Enrollment:* 1,389 graduate, professional, and undergraduate students; 29 full-time matriculated graduate/professional students (13 women), 302 part-time matriculated graduate/professional students (162 women). *Enrollment by degree level:* 44 first professional, 287 master's. *Graduate faculty:* 18 full-time (7 women), 21 part-time/adjunct (9 women). *Tuition:* Full-time $8,820; part-time $490 per credit. *Graduate housing:* Rooms and/or apartments available on a first-come, first-served basis to single and married students. Typical cost: $7,092 per year ($10,242 including board) for single students; $8,271 per year ($14,571 including board) for married students. *Student services:* Campus employment opportunities, campus safety program, career counseling, disabled student services, exercise/wellness program, international student services, low-cost health insurance, teacher training. *Library facilities:* Masland Learning Resource Center. *Online resources:* library catalog, web page. *Collection:* 109,085 titles, 803 serial subscriptions, 8,452 audiovisual materials.

Computer facilities: Computer purchase and lease plans are available. 85 computers available on campus for general student use. A campuswide network can be accessed from student residence rooms and from off campus. Internet access and online class registration are available. *Web address:* http://www.pbu.edu/.

General Application Contact: Binu Abraham, Assistant Director, Graduate Admissions, 800-572-2472, Fax: 215-702-4248, E-mail: babraham@pbu.edu.

GRADUATE UNITS

School of Biblical Studies Students: 18 full-time (4 women), 77 part-time (17 women); includes 39 minority (32 African Americans, 6 Asian Americans or Pacific Islanders, 1 Hispanic American), 2 international. Average age 40. 50 applicants, 54% accepted, 17 enrolled. *Faculty:* 5 full-time (0 women), 6 part-time/adjunct (0 women). Expenses: Contact institution. *Financial support:* In 2006–07, 43 students received support. Scholarships/grants available. Support available to part-time students. Financial award applicants required to submit FAFSA. In 2006, 3 first professional degrees, 16 master's awarded. *Degree program information:* Part-time and evening/weekend programs available. Offers biblical studies (M Div, MSB). *Application deadline:* Applications are processed on a rolling basis. *Application fee:* $25. Electronic applications accepted. *Application Contact:* Binu Abraham, Assistant Director, Graduate Admissions, 800-572-2472, Fax: 215-702-4248, E-mail: babraham@pbu.edu. *Dean*, Dr. O. Herbert Hirt, 215-702-4354, Fax: 215-702-4359, E-mail: bible@pbu.edu.

School of Business and Leadership Average age 40. 12 applicants, 75% accepted, 6 enrolled. *Faculty:* 1 full-time (0 women), 3 part-time/adjunct (1 woman). Expenses: Contact institution. *Financial support:* In 2006–07, 18 students received support. Scholarships/grants available. Support available to part-time students. Financial award applicants required to submit FAFSA. In 2006, 12 degrees awarded. *Degree program information:* Part-time and evening/weekend programs available. Offers organizational leadership (MSOL). *Application deadline:* Applications are processed on a rolling basis. *Application fee:* $25. Electronic applications accepted. *Application Contact:* Binu Abraham, Assistant Director, Graduate Admissions, 800-572-2472, Fax: 215-702-4248, E-mail: babraham@pbu.edu. *Dean*, Ron Ferner, 215-702-9260, Fax: 215-702-4248.

School of Church and Community Ministries Students: 5 full-time (4 women), 118 part-time (86 women); includes 40 minority (28 African Americans, 7 Asian Americans or Pacific Islanders, 5 Hispanic Americans), 1 international. Average age 37. 87 applicants, 51% accepted, 36 enrolled. *Faculty:* 4 full-time (1 woman), 9 part-time/adjunct (6 women). Expenses:

Contact institution. *Financial support:* In 2006–07, 63 students received support. Scholarships/grants available. Support available to part-time students. Financial award applicants required to submit FAFSA. In 2006, 41 degrees awarded. *Degree program information:* Part-time and evening/weekend programs available. Offers Christian counseling (MSCC). *Application deadline:* Applications are processed on a rolling basis. *Application fee:* $25. Electronic applications accepted. *Application Contact:* Gwen Dorsey, Enrollment Counselor, Graduate Counseling, 800-572-2472, Fax: 215-702-4248, E-mail: gdorsey@pbu.edu. *Dean,* Donald Cheyney, 215-702-4546, E-mail: dcheyney@pbu.edu.

School of Education Students: 6 full-time (5 women), 70 part-time (42 women); includes 12 minority (4 African Americans, 7 Asian Americans or Pacific Islanders, 1 Hispanic American), 3 international. Average age 35. 29 applicants, 55% accepted, 12 enrolled. *Faculty:* 8 full-time (6 women), 3 part-time/adjunct (2 women). Expenses: Contact institution. *Financial support:* In 2006–07, 27 students received support. Scholarships/grants available. Support available to part-time students. Financial award applicants required to submit FAFSA. In 2006, 30 degrees awarded. *Degree program information:* Part-time and evening/weekend programs available. Offers educational leadership and administration (MS El); teacher education (MS Ed). *Application deadline:* Applications are processed on a rolling basis. *Application fee:* $25. Electronic applications accepted. *Application Contact:* Katerina Penkova, Enrollment Counselor, Graduate Education, 800-572-2472, Fax: 215-702-4248, E-mail: kpenkova@pbu.edu. *Dean,* Dr. Martha MacCullough, 215-702-4387, E-mail: teacher.ed@pbu.edu.

PHILADELPHIA COLLEGE OF OSTEOPATHIC MEDICINE, Philadelphia, PA 19131-1694

General Information Independent, coed, graduate-only institution. *Enrollment by degree level:* 1,047 first professional, 357 master's, 208 doctoral, 102 other advanced degrees. *Graduate faculty:* 112 full-time (48 women), 1,035 part-time/adjunct (179 women). *Graduate housing:* On-campus housing not available. *Student services:* Campus employment opportunities, campus safety program, career counseling, disabled student services, exercise/wellness program, free psychological counseling, low-cost health insurance, multicultural affairs office. *Library facilities:* O. J. Snyder Memorial Medical Library. *Online resources:* library catalog, web page, access to other libraries' catalogs. *Collection:* 24,128 titles, 6,100 serial subscriptions, 6,668 audiovisual materials. *Research affiliation:* Lankenau Institute for Medical Research (cell differentiation), Albert Einstein Medical Center (clinical pain studies; chronic inflammation), Neuromuscular Engineering (exercise), Mount Sinai School of Medicine (joint and bone disease), Medical College of Georgia (coronary artery disease).

Computer facilities: 75 computers available on campus for general student use. A campuswide network can be accessed from student residence rooms and from off campus. Internet access is available. *Web address:* http://www.pcom.edu/.

General Application Contact: Carol A. Fox, Associate Vice President for Enrollment Management, 215-871-6700, Fax: 215-871-6719, E-mail: carolf@pcom.edu.

GRADUATE UNITS

Graduate and Professional Programs Students: 1,714 full-time (1,085 women); includes 388 minority (158 African Americans, 3 American Indian/Alaska Native, 184 Asian Americans or Pacific Islanders, 43 Hispanic Americans), 8 international. Average age 28. 3,727 applicants, 17% accepted, 441 enrolled. *Faculty:* 87 full-time (37 women), 927 part-time/adjunct (146 women). Expenses: Contact institution. *Financial support:* In 2006–07, 1,230 students received support; fellowships, research assistantships, career-related internships or fieldwork, Federal Work-Study, institutionally sponsored loans, and scholarships/grants available. Financial award application deadline: 4/15; financial award applicants required to submit FAFSA. In 2006, 235 DOs, 71 master's, 14 doctorates, 1 other advanced degree awarded. Offers biomedical sciences (MS, Certificate); clinical health psychology (MS); clinical psychology (Psy D); forensic medicine (MS); health sciences (MS); organizational leadership and development (MS); osteopathic medicine (DO); school psychology (Psy D). *Application deadline:* Applications are processed on a rolling basis. *Application fee:* $50. *Associate Vice President for Enrollment Management,* Carol A. Fox, 215-871-6700, Fax: 215-871-6719, E-mail: carolf@pcom.edu.

PHILADELPHIA UNIVERSITY, Philadelphia, PA 19144-5497

General Information Independent, coed, comprehensive institution. *Enrollment:* 3,256 graduate, professional, and undergraduate students; 224 full-time matriculated graduate/professional students (164 women), 262 part-time matriculated graduate/professional students (152 women). *Enrollment by degree level:* 413 master's, 2 doctoral, 71 other advanced degrees. *Graduate faculty:* 42 full-time (12 women), 40 part-time/adjunct (12 women). *Graduate housing:* On-campus housing not available. *Student services:* Campus employment opportunities, campus safety program, career counseling, disabled student services, free psychological counseling, international student services, low-cost health insurance. *Library facilities:* Paul J. Gutman Library plus 1 other. *Online resources:* library catalog, web page. *Collection:* 108,141 titles, 991 serial subscriptions, 47,818 audiovisual materials.

Computer facilities: 400 computers available on campus for general student use. A campuswide network can be accessed from student residence rooms and from off campus. Internet access and online class registration are available. *Web address:* http://www.philau.edu/.

General Application Contact: Jack A. Klett, Director of Graduate Admissions, 215-951-2943, Fax: 215-951-2907, E-mail: gradadm@philau.edu.

GRADUATE UNITS

School of Business Administration Students: 47 full-time (27 women), 117 part-time (58 women). 178 applicants, 55% accepted, 46 enrolled. *Faculty:* 12 full-time (2 women), 12 part-time/adjunct (0 women). Expenses: Contact institution. *Financial support:* In 2006–07, research assistantships with full tuition reimbursements (averaging $2,500 per year); career-related internships or fieldwork, Federal Work-Study, scholarships/grants, and unspecified assistantships also available. Support available to part-time students. Financial award applicants required to submit FAFSA. In 2006, 114 degrees awarded. *Degree program information:* Part-time and evening/weekend programs available. Postbaccalaureate distance learning degree programs offered (no on-campus study). Offers business (MBA, MS, PhD); business administration (MBA); finance (MBA); health care management (MBA); international business (MBA); marketing (MBA); taxation (MS). *Application deadline:* Applications are processed on a rolling basis. *Application fee:* $35. Electronic applications accepted. *Application Contact:* Jack A. Klett, Director of Graduate Admissions, 215-951-2943, Fax: 215-951-2907, E-mail: gradadm@philau.edu. *Dean,* Dr. Elmore Alexander, 215-951-2827, Fax: 215-951-2652, E-mail: alexandere@philau.edu.

School of Design and Media Students: 9 full-time (2 women), 68 part-time (28 women); includes 1 American Indian/Alaska Native. 42 applicants, 74% accepted, 25 enrolled. *Faculty:* 6 full-time (0 women), 16 part-time/adjunct (4 women). Expenses: Contact institution. *Financial support:* In 2006–07, research assistantships with full tuition reimbursements (averaging $2,500 per year). *Degree program information:* Part-time and evening/weekend programs available. Offers design and media (MS); digital design (MS); instructional design and technology (MS). *Application fee:* $35. *Application Contact:* Jack A. Klett, Director of Graduate Admissions, 215-951-2943, Fax: 215-951-2907, E-mail: gradadm@philau.edu.

School of Engineering and Textiles Students: 51 full-time (35 women), 12 part-time (10 women); includes 2 Asian Americans or Pacific Islanders, 2 Hispanic Americans. Average age 28. 65 applicants, 46% accepted, 19 enrolled. *Faculty:* 14 full-time (4 women), 4 part-time/adjunct (2 women). Expenses: Contact institution. *Financial support:* In 2006–07, research assistantships with full tuition reimbursements (averaging $2,500 per year); career-related internships or fieldwork, Federal Work-Study, and unspecified assistantships also available. Support available to part-time students. Financial award applicants required to submit FAFSA. In 2006, 17 degrees awarded. *Degree program information:* Part-time programs available. Offers engineering and textiles (MS, PhD); fashion-apparel studies (MS); textile design (MS); textile engineering (MS, PhD). *Application deadline:* Applications are processed on a rolling basis. *Application fee:* $35. Electronic applications accepted. *Application Contact:* Jack A. Klett, Director of Graduate Admissions, 215-951-2943, Fax: 215-951-2907, E-mail: gradadm@philau.edu. *Dean,* Dr. David Brookstein, 215-951-2751, Fax: 215-951-2651, E-mail: brooksteind@philau.edu.

School of Science and Health Students: 114 full-time (100 women), 36 part-time (35 women); includes 1 African American. Average age 38. 589 applicants, 26% accepted, 78 enrolled. *Faculty:* 10 full-time (6 women), 8 part-time/adjunct (6 women). Expenses: Contact institution. *Financial support:* In 2006–07, research assistantships with full tuition reimbursements (averaging $2,500 per year); career-related internships or fieldwork, Federal Work-Study, and unspecified assistantships also available. Support available to part-time students. Financial award applicants required to submit FAFSA. In 2006, 67 degrees awarded. *Degree program information:* Part-time and evening/weekend programs available. Postbaccalaureate distance learning degree programs offered (minimal on-campus study). Offers midwifery (MS); nurse midwifery (Postbaccalaureate Certificate); occupational therapy (MS); physician assistant studies (MS); science and health (MS, Postbaccalaureate Certificate). *Application deadline:* Applications are processed on a rolling basis. *Application fee:* $35. Electronic applications accepted. *Application Contact:* Jack A. Klett, Director of Graduate Admissions, 215-951-2943, Fax: 215-951-2907, E-mail: gradadm@philau.edu. *Dean,* Matt Dane Baker, 215-951-2874, Fax: 215-951-2615, E-mail: bakerm@philau.edu.

PHILLIPS GRADUATE INSTITUTE, Encino, CA 91316-1509

General Information Independent, coed, graduate-only institution. *Graduate housing:* On-campus housing not available.

GRADUATE UNITS

Program in Clinical Family Psychology *Degree program information:* Evening/weekend programs available. Offers clinical family psychology (Psy D).

Program in Marriage and Family Therapy, Organizational Behavior and School Counseling *Degree program information:* Evening/weekend programs available. Offers marital and family therapy (MA); organizational consulting (MA); school counseling (MA).

PHILLIPS THEOLOGICAL SEMINARY, Tulsa, OK 74116

General Information Independent-religious, coed, graduate-only institution. *Graduate housing:* On-campus housing not available.

GRADUATE UNITS

Programs in Theology *Degree program information:* Part-time programs available. Postbaccalaureate distance learning degree programs offered (minimal on-campus study). Offers administration of church agencies (M Div); campus ministry (M Div); church-related social work (M Div); college and seminary teaching (M Div); global mission work (M Div); institutional chaplaincy (M Div); ministerial vocations in Christian education (M Div); ministry (D Min); ministry and culture (MAMC); ministry of music (M Div); parish ministry (D Min); pastoral care and counseling (M Div); pastoral counseling (D Min); pastoral ministry (M Div); practices of ministry (D Min); theological studies (MTS).

PHOENIX SEMINARY, Scottsdale, AZ 85254

General Information Independent-religious, coed, graduate-only institution.

GRADUATE UNITS

Graduate Programs

PIEDMONT BAPTIST COLLEGE AND GRADUATE SCHOOL, Winston-Salem, NC 27101-5197

General Information Independent-religious, coed, comprehensive institution. *Enrollment:* 13 full-time matriculated graduate/professional students (1 woman), 71 part-time matriculated graduate/professional students (6 women). *Enrollment by degree level:* 74 master's, 10 doctoral. *Graduate faculty:* 5 full-time (0 women), 8 part-time/adjunct (1 woman). *Graduate housing:* Rooms and/or apartments available on a first-come, first-served basis to single and married students. Typical cost: $2,000 per year for single students; $2,000 per year ($2,700 including board) for married students. Housing application deadline: 5/1. *Student services:* Campus employment opportunities, campus safety program, career counseling, writing training. *Library facilities:* George Manuel Memorial Library. *Collection:* 50,000 titles, 204 serial subscriptions.

Computer facilities: 26 computers available on campus for general student use. A campuswide network can be accessed. *Web address:* http://www.pbc.edu/.

General Application Contact: Kathy Holritz, Director of Admissions, 336-725-8344 Ext. 2328, Fax: 336-725-5522, E-mail: admissions@pbc.edu.

GRADUATE UNITS

Piedmont Baptist Graduate School Students: 84; includes 3 minority (2 African Americans, 1 Asian American or Pacific Islander). Average age 35. 12 applicants, 100% accepted. *Faculty:* 5 full-time (0 women), 8 part-time/adjunct (1 woman). Expenses: Contact institution. *Financial support:* Career-related internships or fieldwork available. Support available to part-time students. Financial award applicants required to submit CSS PROFILE. In 2006, 18 degrees awarded. *Degree program information:* Part-time programs available. Postbaccalaureate distance learning degree programs offered (no on-campus study). Offers chaplaincy track (MABS); non-language track (MABS); PhD preparation track (MABS); theology (M Min, PhD). *Application deadline:* For fall admission, 8/15 priority date for domestic students; for spring admission, 1/1 for domestic students. Applications are processed on a rolling basis. *Application fee:* $30. Electronic applications accepted. *Application Contact:* Patti Kurar, Admissions Director, 336-725-8344, Fax: 336-725-5522, E-mail: holritz@pbc.edu. *School Director,* Dr. Barkev Trachian, 336-725-8344, Fax: 336-714-2715, E-mail: trachian@pbc.edu.

PIEDMONT COLLEGE, Demorest, GA 30535-0010

General Information Independent-religious, coed, comprehensive institution. *Enrollment:* 2,118 graduate, professional, and undergraduate students; 311 full-time matriculated graduate/professional students (213 women), 858 part-time matriculated graduate/professional students (730 women). *Graduate faculty:* 40 full-time (29 women), 50 part-time/adjunct (23 women). *Tuition:* Part-time $310 per credit hour. *Graduate housing:* On-campus housing not available. *Student services:* Campus employment opportunities, career counseling, disabled student services, exercise/wellness program, free psychological counseling, low-cost health insurance, teacher training, writing training. *Library facilities:* Arrendale Library. *Online resources:* library catalog, web page, access to other libraries' catalogs. *Collection:* 115,400 titles, 365 serial subscriptions, 2,500 audiovisual materials.

Computer facilities: 150 computers available on campus for general student use. A campuswide network can be accessed from student residence rooms and from off campus. Internet access, e-mail are available. *Web address:* http://www.piedmont.edu/.

General Application Contact: Carol E. Kokesh, Director of Graduate Studies, 706-778-8500 Ext. 1181, Fax: 706-776-6635, E-mail: ckokesh@piedmont.edu.

GRADUATE UNITS

School of Business Students: 77 full-time (32 women), 36 part-time (15 women); includes 17 minority (all African Americans) 37 applicants, 89% accepted, 27 enrolled. *Faculty:* 3 full-time (1 woman), 10 part-time/adjunct (4 women). Expenses: Contact institution. *Financial support:* Unspecified assistantships available. Financial award applicants required to submit FAFSA. In 2006, 29 degrees awarded. Offers business (MBA). *Application deadline:* For fall admission, 7/15 for domestic students; for spring admission, 12/1 for domestic students. *Application fee:* $30. *Application Contact:* Carol E. Kokesh, Director of Graduate Studies, 706-778-8500 Ext. 1181, Fax: 706-776-6635, E-mail: ckokesh@piedmont.edu. *Dean,* Dr. William Piper, 706-778-3000 Ext. 1349, Fax: 706-778-0701, E-mail: bpiper@piedmont.edu.

School of Education Students: 210 full-time (158 women), 846 part-time (734 women); includes 95 minority (72 African Americans, 2 American Indian/Alaska Native, 10 Asian Americans or Pacific Islanders, 11 Hispanic Americans), 7 international. 327 applicants, 92% accepted, 235 enrolled. *Faculty:* 20 full-time (17 women), 22 part-time/adjunct (5 women). Expenses: Contact institution. *Financial support:* Career-related internships or fieldwork,

Piedmont College (continued)

Federal Work-Study, institutionally sponsored loans, and unspecified assistantships available. Support available to part-time students. Financial award applicants required to submit FAFSA. In 2006, 422 master's, 203 other advanced degrees awarded. *Degree program information:* Part-time and evening/weekend programs available. Offers early childhood education (MA, MAT); instruction (Ed S); secondary education (MA, MAT). *Application deadline:* For fall admission, 7/15 for domestic students; for spring admission, 12/1 for domestic students. *Application fee:* $30. *Application Contact:* Carol E. Kokesh, Director of Graduate Studies, 706-778-8500 Ext. 1181, Fax: 706-776-6635, E-mail: ckokesh@piedmont.edu. *Dean,* Dr. Jane McFerrin, 706-778-3000 Ext. 1201, Fax: 706-776-9608, E-mail: jmcferrin@piedmont.edu.

PIKEVILLE COLLEGE, Pikeville, KY 41501

General Information Independent-religious, coed, comprehensive institution. *Graduate housing:* Room and/or apartments available on a first-come, first-served basis to married students; on-campus housing not available to single students.

GRADUATE UNITS

School of Osteopathic Medicine Offers osteopathic medicine (DO).

PITTSBURGH THEOLOGICAL SEMINARY, Pittsburgh, PA 15206-2596

General Information Independent-religious, coed, graduate-only institution. *Graduate faculty:* 20 full-time (5 women), 7 part-time/adjunct (2 women). *Tuition:* Part-time $292 per credit. *Required fees:* $46 per term. Full-time tuition and fees vary according to course load. *Graduate housing:* Rooms and/or apartments available on a first-come, first-served basis to single students and married students. Typical cost: $4,440 per year for single students; $4,440 per year for married students. Housing application deadline: 6/1. *Student services:* Campus employment opportunities, career counseling, child daycare facilities, disabled student services, exercise/wellness program, free psychological counseling, international student services, low-cost health insurance, writing training. *Library facilities:* Clifford E. Barbour Library. *Online resources:* library catalog, web page, access to other libraries' catalogs. *Collection:* 279,795 titles, 896 serial subscriptions, 16,131 audiovisual materials.

Computer facilities: 11 computers available on campus for general student use. A campuswide network can be accessed from student residence rooms. Internet access is available. *Web address:* http://www.pts.edu/.

General Application Contact: Sherry Sparks, Director of Admissions, 412-362-5610 Ext. 2115, Fax: 412-363-3260, E-mail: ssparks@pts.edu.

GRADUATE UNITS

Graduate and Professional Programs Students: 297 full-time (104 women), 73 part-time (37 women); includes 59 minority (49 African Americans, 2 American Indian/Alaska Native, 1 Asian American or Pacific Islander, 7 Hispanic Americans), 12 international. Average age 36. 134 applicants, 73% accepted, 81 enrolled. *Faculty:* 20 full-time (5 women), 7 part-time/adjunct (2 women). Expenses: Contact institution. *Financial support:* In 2006–07, 84 students received support. Career-related internships or fieldwork and scholarships/grants available. Financial award application deadline: 4/15; financial award applicants required to submit FAFSA. In 2006, 39 M Divs, 12 master's, 21 doctorates awarded. *Degree program information:* Part-time and evening/weekend programs available. Offers divinity (M Div); ministry (D Min); theology (MA, STM). *Application deadline:* For fall admission, 6/15 priority date for domestic students, 1/1 for international students; for winter admission, 10/15 priority date for domestic students; for spring admission, 1/15 priority date for domestic students. Applications are processed on a rolling basis. *Application fee:* $25. *Application Contact:* Sherry Sparks, Director of Admissions, 412-362-5610 Ext. 2115, Fax: 412-363-3260, E-mail: ssparks@pts.edu. *Interim Dean,* Dr. Byron H. Jackson, 412-362-5610 Ext. 2118, Fax: 412-363-3260, E-mail: bjackson@pts.edu.

PITTSBURG STATE UNIVERSITY, Pittsburg, KS 66762

General Information State-supported, coed, comprehensive institution. CGS member. *Enrollment:* 6,859 graduate, professional, and undergraduate students; 374 full-time matriculated graduate/professional students (213 women), 738 part-time matriculated graduate/professional students (497 women). *Graduate faculty:* 223 full-time (74 women), 129 part-time/adjunct (68 women). Tuition, state resident: full-time $2,144; part-time $181 per credit hour. Tuition, nonresident: full-time $5,273; part-time $442 per credit hour. Tuition and fees vary according to course load and campus/location. *Graduate housing:* Rooms and/or apartments available on a first-come, first-served basis to single students and available to married students. Typical cost: $5,250 (including board) for single students; $4,140 per year for married students. Room and board charges vary according to board plan and housing facility selected. *Student services:* Campus employment opportunities, campus safety program, career counseling, disabled student services, exercise/wellness program, international student services, low-cost health insurance, multicultural affairs office, writing training. *Library facilities:* Leonard H. Axe Library plus 1 other. *Online resources:* library catalog, web page, access to other libraries' catalogs. *Collection:* 705,267 titles, 9,436 serial subscriptions, 3,710 audiovisual materials. *Research affiliation:* Cargill Inc. (Vegetable Oil).

Computer facilities: A campuswide network can be accessed from student residence rooms and from off campus. Internet access and online class registration are available. *Web address:* http://www.pittstate.edu/.

General Application Contact: Jamie Vanderbeck, Assistant Director, 620-235-4223, Fax: 620-235-4219, E-mail: jvanderb@pittstate.edu.

GRADUATE UNITS

Graduate School Students: 374 full-time (213 women), 738 part-time (497 women). *Faculty:* 223 full-time (74 women), 129 part-time/adjunct (68 women). Expenses: Contact institution. *Financial support:* In 2006–07, 134 teaching assistantships (averaging $5,000 per year) were awarded; research assistantships, career-related internships or fieldwork, Federal Work-Study, and unspecified assistantships also available. In 2006, 316 master's awarded. *Degree program information:* Part-time and evening/weekend programs available. Postbaccalaureate distance learning degree programs offered (no on-campus study). *Application deadline:* Applications are processed on a rolling basis. *Application fee:* $35 ($60 for international students). Electronic applications accepted. *Application Contact:* Jamie Vanderbeck, Assistant Director, 620-235-4223, Fax: 620-235-4219, E-mail: jvanderb@pittstate.edu. *Dean of Continuing and Graduate Studies,* Dr. Peggy Snyder, 620-235-4179, Fax: 620-235-4219, E-mail: psnyder@pittstate.edu.

College of Arts and Sciences Students: 155. Expenses: Contact institution. *Financial support:* In 2006–07, teaching assistantships (averaging $5,000 per year); research assistantships, career-related internships or fieldwork, Federal Work-Study, and unspecified assistantships also available. Offers applied communication (MA); applied physics (MS); art education (MA); arts and sciences (MA, MM, MS, MSN); biology (MS); chemistry (MS); communication education (MA); English (MA); history (MA); instrumental music education (MM); mathematics (MS); music history/music literature (MM); nursing (MSN); performance (MM); physics (MS); professional physics (MS); studio art (MA); theatre (MA); theory and composition (MM); vocal music education (MM). *Application fee:* $35 ($60 for international students). *Application Contact:* Jamie Vanderbeck, Assistant Director, 620-235-4223, Fax: 620-235-4219, E-mail: jvanderb@pittstate.edu. *Dean,* Dr. Lynette Olson, 620-235-4684.

College of Education Students: 474. Expenses: Contact institution. *Financial support:* In 2006–07, teaching assistantships (averaging $5,000 per year); career-related internships or fieldwork, Federal Work-Study, and unspecified assistantships also available. Offers behavioral disorders (MS); classroom reading teacher (MS); community college and higher education (Ed S); counseling (MS); counselor education (MS); early childhood education (MS); education (MAT, MS, Ed S); educational leadership (MS); educational technology (MS); elementary education (MS); learning disabilities (MS); mentally retarded (MS); physical education (MS); psychology (MS); reading (MS); reading specialist (MS); school psychology (Ed S); secondary education (MS); special education teaching (MS); teaching (MAT). *Application fee:* $35 ($60 for international students). *Application Contact:* Jamie Vanderbeck, Assistant Director, 620-235-4223, Fax: 620-235-4219, E-mail: jvanderb@pittstate.edu. *Dean,* 620-235-4500.

College of Technology Students: 127. Expenses: Contact institution. *Financial support:* In 2006–07, teaching assistantships (averaging $5,000 per year); career-related internships or fieldwork, Federal Work-Study, and unspecified assistantships also available. Offers engineering technology (MET); human resource development (MS, Ed S); industrial education (Ed S); technical teacher education (MS); technology (MS); technology education (MS). *Application fee:* $35 ($60 for international students). *Application Contact:* Jamie Vanderbeck, Assistant Director, 620-235-4223, Fax: 620-235-4219, E-mail: jvanderb@pittstate.edu. *Dean,* Dr. Bruce Dallman, 620-235-4365.

Kelce College of Business Students: 109. Expenses: Contact institution. *Financial support:* In 2006–07, teaching assistantships (averaging $5,000 per year); research assistantships, career-related internships or fieldwork, Federal Work-Study, and unspecified assistantships also available. Financial award application deadline: 3/1. Offers accounting (MBA); business (MBA); general administration (MBA). *Application fee:* $35 ($60 for international students). *Application Contact:* Jamie Vanderbeck, Assistant Director, 620-235-4223, Fax: 620-235-4219, E-mail: jvanderb@pittstate.edu. *Dean,* 620-235-4590.

PLYMOUTH STATE UNIVERSITY, Plymouth, NH 03264-1595

General Information State-supported, coed, comprehensive institution. *Enrollment:* 5,872 graduate, professional, and undergraduate students; 28 full-time matriculated graduate/professional students (21 women), 1,692 part-time matriculated graduate/professional students (1,225 women). *Enrollment by degree level:* 1,517 master's, 203 other advanced degrees. *Graduate faculty:* 73 full-time (33 women), 95 part-time/adjunct (54 women). Tuition, state resident: part-time $369 per credit. Tuition, nonresident: part-time $407 per credit. Tuition and fees vary according to course level. *Graduate housing:* Rooms and/or apartments available on a first-come, first-served basis to single students and guaranteed to married students. Housing application deadline: 5/1. *Student services:* Campus employment opportunities, campus safety program, career counseling, child daycare facilities, disabled student services, exercise/wellness program, free psychological counseling, grant writing training, teacher training, writing training. *Library facilities:* Lamson Library. *Online resources:* library catalog, web page, access to other libraries' catalogs. *Collection:* 335,230 titles, 2,213 serial subscriptions. *Research affiliation:* Hubbard Brook Experimental Forest (science), NH Department of Environmental Services (science), White Mountain National Forest (science), National Oceanic and Atmospheric Admdu (NOAA) (science).

Computer facilities: Computer purchase and lease plans are available. 500 computers available on campus for general student use. A campuswide network can be accessed from student residence rooms and from off campus. Internet access and online class registration, degree audit, academic history, account status are available. *Web address:* http://www.plymouth.edu/.

General Application Contact: Cheryl B. Baker, Director of Recruitment and Outreach, 603-535-2737, Fax: 603-535-2572, E-mail: cbaker@plymouth.edu.

GRADUATE UNITS

College of Graduate Studies Students: 28 full-time (21 women), 1,692 part-time (1,225 women); includes 46 minority (15 African Americans, 2 American Indian/Alaska Native, 15 Asian Americans or Pacific Islanders, 14 Hispanic Americans). Average age 39. 407 applicants, 99% accepted, 404 enrolled. *Faculty:* 73 full-time (33 women), 95 part-time/adjunct (54 women). Expenses: Contact institution. *Financial support:* In 2006–07, 1 fellowship with partial tuition reimbursement (averaging $10,000 per year), 17 teaching assistantships with full tuition reimbursements (averaging $4,000 per year) were awarded; career-related internships or fieldwork, institutionally sponsored loans, scholarships/grants, tuition waivers (full), and unspecified assistantships also available. Support available to part-time students. Financial award application deadline: 4/15; financial award applicants required to submit FAFSA. In 2006, 308 master's, 32 other advanced degrees awarded. *Degree program information:* Part-time and evening/weekend programs available. Postbaccalaureate distance learning degree programs offered (minimal on-campus study). Offers business (MBA). *Application deadline:* For fall admission, 5/15 for international students; for winter admission, 5/15 for international students; for spring admission, 10/15 for international students. Applications are processed on a rolling basis. *Application fee:* $75. *Application Contact:* Cheryl B. Baker, Director of Recruitment and Outreach, 603-535-2737, Fax: 603-535-2572, E-mail: cbaker@plymouth.edu. *Associate Vice President,* Dr. Dennise M. Maslakowski, 603-535-2286, Fax: 603-535-2572, E-mail: dmmaslakowski@plymouth.edu.

Graduate Studies in Education Students: 20 full-time (18 women), 1,278 part-time (959 women); includes 26 minority (9 African Americans, 11 Asian Americans or Pacific Islanders, 6 Hispanic Americans). Average age 39. 358 applicants, 100% accepted, 357 enrolled. *Faculty:* 52 full-time (29 women), 91 part-time/adjunct (53 women). Expenses: Contact institution. *Financial support:* In 2006–07, fellowships with partial tuition reimbursements (averaging $10,000 per year), teaching assistantships with full tuition reimbursements (averaging $4,000 per year) were awarded; career-related internships or fieldwork, institutionally sponsored loans, scholarships/grants, and unspecified assistantships also available. Support available to part-time students. Financial award application deadline: 4/15; financial award applicants required to submit FAFSA. In 2006, 264 master's, 32 other advanced degrees awarded. *Degree program information:* Part-time and evening/weekend programs available. Postbaccalaureate distance learning degree programs offered (minimal on-campus study). Offers applied meteorology (MS); athletic training (M Ed, MS); counselor education (M Ed); education (CAGS); educational leadership (M Ed); elementary education (M Ed); English education (M Ed); environmental science and policy (MS); health education (M Ed); k-12 education (M Ed); mathematics education (M Ed); reading and writing specialist (M Ed); science (MS); science education (MS); secondary education (M Ed); special education administration (M Ed); special education k-12 (M Ed); teaching (MAT). *Application deadline:* For fall admission, 5/15 for international students; for winter admission, 5/15 for international students; for spring admission, 10/15 for international students. Applications are processed on a rolling basis. *Application fee:* $75. *Application Contact:* Cheryl B. Baker, Director of Recruitment and Outreach, 603-535-2737, Fax: 603-535-2572, E-mail: cbaker@plymouth.edu.

POINT LOMA NAZARENE UNIVERSITY, San Diego, CA 92106-2899

General Information Independent-religious, coed, comprehensive institution. *Enrollment:* 3,437 graduate, professional, and undergraduate students; 528 full-time matriculated graduate/professional students (366 women), 621 part-time matriculated graduate/professional students (424 women). *Enrollment by degree level:* 752 master's, 397 other advanced degrees. *Graduate faculty:* 31 full-time (18 women), 83 part-time/adjunct (50 women). *Graduate housing:* On-campus housing not available. *Student services:* Campus employment opportunities, campus safety program, career counseling, disabled student services, free psychological counseling, international student services, low-cost health insurance, teacher training. *Library facilities:* Ryan Library. *Online resources:* library catalog, web page, access to other libraries' catalogs. *Collection:* 152,377 titles, 25,505 serial subscriptions.

Computer facilities: 196 computers available on campus for general student use. A campuswide network can be accessed from student residence rooms and from off campus. Internet access and online class registration are available. *Web address:* http://www.pointloma.edu/.

General Application Contact: Steve Guthrie, Director of Graduate Admissions, 866-692-4723, E-mail: admissions@pointloma.edu.

GRADUATE UNITS

Graduate Studies Students: 407 full-time (279 women), 168 part-time (102 women); includes 218 minority (26 African Americans, 6 American Indian/Alaska Native, 43 Asian Americans or Pacific Islanders, 143 Hispanic Americans), 2 international. Average age 35. *Faculty:* 31 full-time (18 women), 83 part-time/adjunct (50 women). Expenses: Contact institution. *Financial support:* Career-related internships or fieldwork available. Support available to part-time students. Financial award application deadline: 4/10. In 2006, 290 degrees awarded. *Degree program information:* Part-time and evening/weekend programs available. Postbaccalaureate distance learning degree programs offered (minimal on-campus study). Offers biology (MA, MS); business administration (MBA); education (MA, Ed S); nursing (MSN); religion (M Min, MA). *Application deadline:* For fall admission, 5/15 priority date for domestic students; for spring admission, 11/1 for domestic students. Applications are processed on a rolling basis. *Application fee:* $25. *Vice Provost for Graduate Studies,* Dr. Maggie Bailey, 619-849-2200, Fax: 619-849-7018, E-mail: mbailey@pointloma.edu.

POINT PARK UNIVERSITY, Pittsburgh, PA 15222-1984

General Information Independent, coed, comprehensive institution. *Enrollment:* 3,546 graduate, professional, and undergraduate students; 219 full-time matriculated graduate/professional students (128 women), 255 part-time matriculated graduate/professional students (154 women). *Enrollment by degree level:* 474 master's. *Graduate faculty:* 31 full-time, 60 part-time/adjunct. *Tuition:* Full-time $9,828; part-time $546 per credit. *Required fees:* $360; $20 per credit. *Graduate housing:* Room and/or apartments available on a first-come, first-served basis to single students; on-campus housing not available to married students. Typical cost: $5,500 per year ($9,500 including board). Room and board charges vary according to board plan, campus/location and housing facility selected. Housing application deadline: 7/31. *Student services:* Campus employment opportunities, career counseling, child daycare facilities, disabled student services, free psychological counseling, international student services. *Library facilities:* Point Park University Library. *Online resources:* library catalog, access to other libraries' catalogs. *Collection:* 125,000 titles, 230 serial subscriptions.

Computer facilities: 170 computers available on campus for general student use. A campuswide network can be accessed from student residence rooms and from off campus. Internet access is available. *Web address:* http://www.pointpark.edu/.

General Application Contact: Marty Paonessa, Associate Director, Graduate and Adult Enrollment, 412-392-3915, Fax: 412-392-6164, E-mail: mpaonessa@pointpark.edu.

GRADUATE UNITS

Conservatory of Performing Arts Students: 6 full-time (3 women), 1 part-time. Average age 40. 3 applicants, 67% accepted, 2 enrolled. *Faculty:* 3 full-time, 1 part-time/adjunct. Expenses: Contact institution. *Financial support:* Teaching assistantships with full tuition reimbursements, scholarships/grants available. Financial award application deadline: 5/1; financial award applicants required to submit FAFSA. Offers theatre arts-acting (MFA). *Application deadline:* Applications are processed on a rolling basis. *Application fee:* $30. Electronic applications accepted. *Application Contact:* Debbie P. Bateman, Director, Adult Academic Services, 412-392-3433, Fax: 412-392-6164, E-mail: dbateman@pointpark.edu. *Dean/ Artistic Producing Director,* Ronald Allan-Lindblom, 412-392-3454, Fax: 412-392-2424, E-mail: rlindblom@pointpark.edu.

School of Adult and Professional Studies Students: 33 full-time (23 women), 4 part-time (3 women); includes 16 minority (all African Americans) Average age 32. 48 applicants, 58% accepted, 24 enrolled. *Faculty:* 5 full-time, 3 part-time/adjunct. Expenses: Contact institution. *Financial support:* In 2006–07, 12 students received support. Scholarships/grants and unspecified assistantships available. Financial award application deadline: 5/1; financial award applicants required to submit FAFSA. In 2006, 33 degrees awarded. *Degree program information:* Evening/weekend programs available. Offers criminal justice administration (MS). *Application deadline:* Applications are processed on a rolling basis. Electronic applications accepted. *Application Contact:* Lynn Ribar, Assistant Director of Adult Enrollment, 412-392-3908, Fax: 412-392-6164, E-mail: lribar@pointpark.edu. *Dean,* Judy Bolsinger, 412-392-3830, Fax: 412-392-4781, E-mail: jbolsinger@pointpark.edu.

School of Arts and Sciences Students: 46 full-time (30 women), 99 part-time (60 women); includes 24 minority (20 African Americans, 1 American Indian/Alaska Native, 2 Asian Americans or Pacific Islanders, 1 Hispanic American), 5 international. Average age 30. 164 applicants, 55% accepted, 60 enrolled. *Faculty:* 10 full-time, 35 part-time/adjunct. Expenses: Contact institution. *Financial support:* In 2006–07, 20 students received support. Application deadline: 5/1; In 2006, 46 degrees awarded. *Degree program information:* Part-time and evening/ weekend programs available. Offers arts and sciences (MA, MS); curriculum and instruction (MA); educational administration (MA); engineering management (MS); journalism and mass communication (MA). *Application deadline:* Applications are processed on a rolling basis. *Application fee:* $30. Electronic applications accepted. *Application Contact:* Kathryn B. Ballas, Director, Adult Enrollment, 412-392-3808, Fax: 412-392-6164, E-mail: kballas@pointpark.edu. *Dean,* Dr. Kathleen Rourke, 412-392-3938, E-mail: krourke@pointpark.edu.

School of Business Students: 133 full-time (72 women), 138 part-time (85 women); includes 60 minority (55 African Americans, 1 American Indian/Alaska Native, 2 Asian Americans or Pacific Islanders, 2 Hispanic Americans), 24 international. Average age 31. 269 applicants, 74% accepted, 140 enrolled. *Faculty:* 13 full-time, 21 part-time/adjunct. Expenses: Contact institution. *Financial support:* In 2006–07, 29 students received support, including 3 research assistantships with full tuition reimbursements available (averaging $5,400 per year); career-related internships or fieldwork and scholarships/grants also available. Support available to part-time students. Financial award application deadline: 5/1; financial award applicants required to submit FAFSA. In 2006, 132 degrees awarded. *Degree program information:* Part-time and evening/weekend programs available. Offers business (MBA); organizational leadership (MA). *Application deadline:* Applications are processed on a rolling basis. *Application fee:* $30. Electronic applications accepted. *Application Contact:* Kathryn B. Ballas, Director, Adult Enrollment, 412-392-3808, Fax: 412-392-6164, E-mail: kballas@pointpark.edu. *Interim Dean,* Margaret Gilfillan, 412-392-3942, Fax: 412-765-2570, E-mail: mgilfillan@pointpark.edu.

POLYTECHNIC UNIVERSITY, BROOKLYN CAMPUS, Brooklyn, NY 11201-2990

General Information Independent, coed, university. CGS member. *Enrollment:* 2,919 graduate, professional, and undergraduate students; 806 full-time matriculated graduate/professional students (202 women), 457 part-time matriculated graduate/professional students (111 women). *Enrollment by degree level:* 1,087 master's, 160 doctoral, 16 other advanced degrees. *Graduate faculty:* 138 full-time (24 women), 135 part-time/adjunct (29 women). *Tuition:* Full-time $17,784; part-time $988 per credit. *Graduate housing:* Room and/or apartments available on a first-come, first-served basis to single students; on-campus housing not available to married students. Typical cost: $8,500 (including board). Housing application deadline: 6/30. *Student services:* Campus employment opportunities, campus safety program, career counseling, international student services, low-cost health insurance. *Library facilities:* Bern Dibner Library plus 1 other. *Online resources:* library catalog, web page, access to other libraries' catalogs. *Collection:* 150,000 titles, 1,621 serial subscriptions.

Computer facilities: Computer purchase and lease plans are available. 1,334 computers available on campus for general student use. A campuswide network can be accessed from student residence rooms and from off campus. Internet access is available. *Web address:* http://www.poly.edu/.

General Application Contact: Prof. Sunil Kumar, Associate Provost for Graduate School, 718-260-3482, Fax: 718-260-3624, E-mail: gradinfo@poly.edu.

GRADUATE UNITS

Department of Chemical and Biological Sciences Expenses: Contact institution. Offers biomedical engineering (MS, PhD); biotechnology and entrepreneurship (MS); chemistry (MS); materials chemistry (PhD); polymer science and engineering (MS).

Department of Civil Engineering Students: 44 full-time (10 women), 85 part-time (21 women); includes 33 minority (14 African Americans, 14 Asian Americans or Pacific Islanders, 5 Hispanic Americans), 26 international. Average age 32. 150 applicants, 78% accepted, 45 enrolled. *Faculty:* 8 full-time (1 woman), 7 part-time/adjunct (0 women). Expenses: Contact institution. *Financial support:* In 2006–07, 2 fellowships with partial tuition reimbursements (averaging $16,440 per year), 1 research assistantship (averaging $19,800 per year) were awarded; teaching assistantships, institutionally sponsored loans also available. Support available to part-time students. Financial award applicants required to submit FAFSA. In 2006, 28 master's, 3 doctorates awarded. *Degree program information:* Part-time and evening/ weekend programs available. Offers civil engineering (MS, PhD); construction management (MS); environmental engineering (MS); environmental science (MS); transportation management (MS); transportation planning and engineering (MS, PhD). *Application deadline:* For fall admission, 7/15 priority date for domestic students, 4/1 priority date for international students; for spring admission, 12/15 priority date for domestic students, 10/1 priority date for international students. Applications are processed on a rolling basis. *Application fee:* $55. Electronic applications accepted. *Application Contact:* Anthea Jeffrey, Graduate Admissions, 718-260-3200, Fax: 718-260-3624, E-mail: gradinfo@poly.edu. *Head,* Dr. Roger Roess, 718-260-3018, Fax: 718-260-3433, E-mail: rroess@poly.edu.

Department of Computer and Information Science Students: 121 full-time (26 women), 72 part-time (15 women); includes 26 minority (3 African Americans, 22 Asian Americans or Pacific Islanders, 1 Hispanic American), 111 international. Average age 32. 513 applicants, 78% accepted, 78 enrolled. *Faculty:* 17 full-time (1 woman), 11 part-time/adjunct (0 women). Expenses: Contact institution. *Financial support:* In 2006–07, 38 fellowships with partial tuition reimbursements (averaging $19,596 per year) were awarded; research assistantships, teaching assistantships, institutionally sponsored loans also available. Support available to part-time students. Financial award applicants required to submit FAFSA. In 2006, 64 master's, 6 doctorates awarded. *Degree program information:* Part-time and evening/weekend programs available. Offers computer science (MS, PhD); cyber security (Graduate Certificate); software engineering (Graduate Certificate). *Application deadline:* For fall admission, 7/15 priority date for domestic students, 4/1 priority date for international students; for spring admission, 12/15 priority date for domestic students, 10/1 priority date for international students. Applications are processed on a rolling basis. *Application fee:* $55. Electronic applications accepted. *Application Contact:* Anthea Jeffrey, Graduate Admissions, 718-260-3200, Fax: 718-260-3624, E-mail: gradinfo@poly.edu. *Head,* Dr. Stuart Steele, 718-260-3357, Fax: 718-260-3609, E-mail: ssteele@rama.poly.edu.

Department of Electrical and Computer Engineering Students: 263 full-time (47 women), 114 part-time (13 women); includes 47 minority (6 African Americans, 36 Asian Americans or Pacific Islanders, 5 Hispanic Americans), 247 international. Average age 32. 1,041 applicants, 79% accepted, 166 enrolled. *Faculty:* 17 full-time (3 women), 9 part-time/adjunct (1 woman). Expenses: Contact institution. *Financial support:* In 2006–07, 47 fellowships with partial tuition reimbursements (averaging $19,524 per year) were awarded; research assistantships with partial tuition reimbursements, teaching assistantships, institutionally sponsored loans also available. Support available to part-time students. Financial award applicants required to submit FAFSA. In 2006, 104 master's, 9 doctorates awarded. *Degree program information:* Part-time and evening/weekend programs available. Offers computer engineering (MS, Certificate); electrical engineering (MS, PhD); electrophysics (MS); image processing (Certificate); systems engineering (MS); telecommunication networks (MS); wireless communications (Certificate). *Application deadline:* For fall admission, 7/15 priority date for domestic students, 4/1 priority date for international students; for spring admission, 12/15 priority date for domestic students, 10/1 priority date for international students. Applications are processed on a rolling basis. *Application fee:* $55. Electronic applications accepted. *Application Contact:* Anthea Jeffrey, Graduate Admissions, 718-260-3200, Fax: 718-260-3624, E-mail: gradinfo@poly.edu. *Head,* Dr. Jonathan Chao, 718-860-3478, Fax: 718-260-3302, E-mail: chao@poly.edu.

Department of Finance and Risk Engineering Students: 114 full-time (29 women), 67 part-time (15 women); includes 21 minority (5 African Americans, 16 Asian Americans or Pacific Islanders), 85 international. Average age 32. 216 applicants, 87% accepted, 89 enrolled. Expenses: Contact institution. *Financial support:* Applicants required to submit FAFSA. In 2006, 35 degrees awarded. *Degree program information:* Part-time and evening/weekend programs available. Offers financial engineering (MS, Advanced Certificate); financial technology management (Advanced Certificate); risk management (Advanced Certificate). *Application deadline:* For fall admission, 7/15 priority date for domestic students, 4/1 priority date for international students; for spring admission, 12/15 priority date for domestic students, 10/1 priority date for international students. Applications are processed on a rolling basis. *Application fee:* $55. Electronic applications accepted. *Academic Director,* Frederick Novomestky, 718-260-3436, Fax: 718-260-3874, E-mail: fnovomes@poly.edu.

Department of Humanities and Social Sciences Students: 14 full-time (6 women), 14 part-time (4 women); includes 8 minority (4 African Americans, 3 Asian Americans or Pacific Islanders, 1 Hispanic American), 4 international. Average age 32. 24 applicants, 96% accepted, 16 enrolled. *Faculty:* 4 full-time (0 women), 1 part-time/adjunct (0 women). Expenses: Contact institution. *Financial support:* Fellowships, research assistantships, teaching assistantships, career-related internships or fieldwork and institutionally sponsored loans available. Support available to part-time students. Financial award applicants required to submit FAFSA. In 2006, 11 degrees awarded. *Degree program information:* Part-time and evening/weekend programs available. Offers environment-behavior studies (MS); history of science (MS); integrated digital media (MS, Graduate Certificate); technical communication (Graduate Certificate); technical writing and specialized journalism (MS). *Application deadline:* For fall admission, 7/15 priority date for domestic students, 4/1 priority date for international students; for spring admission, 12/15 priority date for domestic students, 10/1 priority date for international students. Applications are processed on a rolling basis. *Application fee:* $55. Electronic applications accepted. *Application Contact:* Anthea Jeffrey, Graduate Admissions, 718-260-3200, Fax: 718-260-3624, E-mail: gradinfo@poly.edu. *Head,* Dr. Harold Sjursen, 718-260-3597, Fax: 718-260-3289, E-mail: hsjursen@poly.edu.

Department of Management Students: 234 full-time (75 women), 113 part-time (41 women); includes 57 minority (23 African Americans, 30 Asian Americans or Pacific Islanders, 4 Hispanic Americans), 115 international. Average age 32. 398 applicants, 89% accepted, 177 enrolled. *Faculty:* 8 full-time (1 woman), 33 part-time/adjunct (4 women). Expenses: Contact institution. *Financial support:* Fellowships, research assistantships, teaching assistantships available. In 2006, 125 degrees awarded. *Degree program information:* Part-time and evening/weekend programs available. Offers management (MS); management of technology (MS); organizational behavior (MS); technology management (PhD); telecommunications and information management (MS). *Application deadline:* For fall admission, 7/15 priority date for domestic students, 4/1 priority date for international students; for spring admission, 12/15 priority date for domestic students, 10/1 priority date for international students. Applications are processed on a rolling basis. *Application fee:* $55. Electronic applications accepted. *Application Contact:* Anthea Jeffrey, Graduate Admissions, 718-260-3200, Fax: 718-260-3624, E-mail: gradinfo@poly.edu. *Associate Dean,* Dr. Barry Blecherman, 718-260-3760, Fax: 718-260-3874, E-mail: blecherm@poly.edu.

Department of Mathematics Students: 15 full-time (3 women), 9 part-time (3 women); includes 7 minority (2 African Americans, 5 Asian Americans or Pacific Islanders), 5 international. Average age 32. 32 applicants, 84% accepted, 8 enrolled. *Faculty:* 1 full-time (0 women). Expenses: Contact institution. *Financial support:* Fellowships, research assistantships, teaching assistantships, institutionally sponsored loans available. Support available to part-time students. Financial award applicants required to submit FAFSA. In 2006, 1 degree awarded. *Degree program information:* Part-time and evening/weekend programs available. Offers mathematics (MS, PhD). *Application deadline:* For fall admission, 7/15 priority date for domestic students, 4/1 priority date for international students; for spring admission, 12/15 priority date for domestic students, 10/1 priority date for international students. Applications are processed on a rolling basis. *Application fee:* $55. Electronic applications accepted. *Application Contact:* Anthea Jeffrey, Graduate Admissions, 718-260-3200, Fax: 718-260-3624, E-mail: gradinfo@poly.edu. *Head,* Dr. Erwin Lutwak, 718-260-3366, Fax: 718-260-3139, E-mail: lutwak@magnus.poly.edu.

Department of Mechanical and Aerospace Engineering Students: 42 full-time (5 women), 18 part-time (1 woman); includes 7 minority (2 African Americans, 5 Asian Americans or Pacific Islanders), 29 international. Average age 32. 210 applicants, 80% accepted, 36 enrolled. *Faculty:* 3 full-time (0 women), 4 part-time/adjunct (0 women). Expenses: Contact institution. *Financial support:* In 2006–07, 19 fellowships with partial tuition reimbursements (averaging $18,936 per year), 7 research assistantships with partial tuition reimbursements (averaging $18,456 per year) were awarded; teaching assistantships, career-related internships or fieldwork and institutionally sponsored loans also available. Support available to part-time students. Financial award applicants required to submit FAFSA. In 2006, 24 master's, 2 doctorates awarded. *Degree program information:* Part-time and evening/weekend programs available. Offers industrial engineering (MS); manufacturing engineering (MS); materials science (MS); mechanical engineering (MS, PhD). *Application deadline:* For fall admission, 7/15

Polytechnic University, Brooklyn Campus (continued)

priority date for domestic students, 4/1 priority date for international students; for spring admission, 12/15 priority date for domestic students, 10/1 priority date for international students. Applications are processed on a rolling basis. *Application fee:* $55. Electronic applications accepted. *Application Contact:* Anthea Jeffrey, Graduate Admissions, 718-260-3200, Fax: 718-260-3624, E-mail: gradinfo@poly.edu. *Head,* Dr. Said Nourbaksh, 718-260-3566, Fax: 718-260-3532, E-mail: snourbak@poly.edu.

Department of Physics Expenses: Contact institution. *Financial support:* Fellowships, research assistantships, teaching assistantships, institutionally sponsored loans available. Support available to part-time students. Financial award applicants required to submit FAFSA. *Degree program information:* Part-time and evening/weekend programs available. Offers physics (MS, PhD). *Application deadline:* For fall admission, 7/15 priority date for domestic students, 4/1 priority date for international students; for spring admission, 12/15 priority date for domestic students, 10/1 priority date for international students. Applications are processed on a rolling basis. *Application fee:* $55. Electronic applications accepted. *Head,* Dr. Edward Wolf, 718-260-3629, E-mail: ewolf@poly.edu.

Othmer-Jacobs Department of Chemical and Biological Engineering Students: 19 full-time (4 women), 9 part-time (3 women); includes 5 minority (2 African Americans, 3 Asian Americans or Pacific Islanders), 20 international. Average age 32. 66 applicants, 71% accepted, 5 enrolled. *Faculty:* 6 full-time (0 women), 1 part-time/adjunct (0 women). Expenses: Contact institution. *Financial support:* In 2006–07, 29 fellowships with partial tuition reimbursements (averaging $19,560 per year), 1 research assistantship with partial tuition reimbursement (averaging $18,204 per year) were awarded; teaching assistantships, institutionally sponsored loans also available. Support available to part-time students. Financial award applicants required to submit FAFSA. In 2006, 5 master's, 1 doctorate awarded. *Degree program information:* Part-time and evening/weekend programs available. Offers bioinformatics (MS); chemical engineering (MS, PhD). *Application deadline:* For fall admission, 7/15 priority date for domestic students, 4/1 priority date for international students; for spring admission, 12/15 priority date for domestic students, 10/1 priority date for international students. Applications are processed on a rolling basis. *Application fee:* $55. Electronic applications accepted. *Application Contact:* Anthea Jeffrey, Graduate Admissions, 718-260-3200, Fax: 718-260-3624, E-mail: gradinfo@poly.edu. *Head,* Dr. Jovan Mijovic, 718-260-3579, Fax: 718-260-3125.

POLYTECHNIC UNIVERSITY, LONG ISLAND GRADUATE CENTER, Melville, NY 11747

General Information Independent, coed, graduate-only institution. *Enrollment:* 17 full-time matriculated graduate/professional students (2 women), 117 part-time matriculated graduate/professional students (17 women). *Enrollment by degree level:* 107 master's, 2 doctoral, 25 other advanced degrees. *Graduate faculty:* 66 full-time (6 women), 66 part-time/adjunct (5 women). *Tuition:* Full-time $17,184. *Graduate housing:* Room and/or apartments available to single students; on-campus housing not available to married students. *Student services:* Campus employment opportunities, career counseling, international student services. *Library facilities:* Dibner Library. *Online resources:* library catalog, web page, access to other libraries' catalogs. *Collection:* 150,200 titles, 1,621 serial subscriptions, 337 audiovisual materials.

Computer facilities: A campuswide network can be accessed from off campus. Internet access and online class registration are available. *Web address:* http://rama.poly.edu/.

General Application Contact: Prof. Sunil Kumar, Graduate Admissions, 718-260-3482, Fax: 718-260-3624, E-mail: gradinfo@poly.edu.

GRADUATE UNITS

Graduate Programs Students: 17 full-time (2 women), 117 part-time (17 women); includes 28 minority (4 African Americans, 18 Asian Americans or Pacific Islanders, 6 Hispanic Americans), 8 international. Average age 32. 57 applicants, 72% accepted, 34 enrolled. *Faculty:* 66 full-time (6 women), 66 part-time/adjunct (5 women). Expenses: Contact institution. *Financial support:* Institutionally sponsored loans available. Support available to part-time students. Financial award applicants required to submit FAFSA. In 2006, 32 degrees awarded. *Degree program information:* Part-time and evening/weekend programs available. Offers aeronautics and astronautics (MS); bioinstrumentation (Certificate); biomedical engineering (MS, PhD); biomedical materials (Certificate); biotechnology (MS); biotechnology and entrepreneurship (MS); chemical engineering (MS, PhD); chemistry (MS, PhD); civil engineering (MS, PhD); computer engineering (MS); computer science (MS, PhD); distributed information systems engineering (MS); electrical engineering (MS, PhD); electrophysics (MS); environmental engineering (MS); financial engineering (MS, AC); industrial engineering (MS); management (MS); manufacturing engineering (MS); materials chemistry (PhD); mechanical engineering (MS, PhD); software engineering (MS); systems engineering (MS); telecommunication networks (MS); transportation planning and engineering (MS); wireless innovation (M Engr). *Application deadline:* For fall admission, 7/15 priority date for domestic students, 4/1 priority date for international students; for spring admission, 12/15 priority date for domestic students, 10/1 priority date for international students. Applications are processed on a rolling basis. *Application fee:* $55. Electronic applications accepted. *Application Contact:* Prof. Sunil Kumar, Graduate Admissions, 718-260-3482, Fax: 718-260-3624, E-mail: gradinfo@poly.edu. *Director, Long Island Graduate Center,* Dr. Frank Cassara, 516-755-4300, Fax: 516-755-4404, E-mail: cassara@poly.edu.

POLYTECHNIC UNIVERSITY OF PUERTO RICO, Hato Rey, PR 00919

General Information Independent, coed, comprehensive institution. *Graduate housing:* On-campus housing not available. *Research affiliation:* University of Missouri-Columbia (engineering, mathematics and science), University of Puerto Rico-Mayagüez (electrical engineering), Virginia Polytechnic Institute (mechanical/electrical engineering), Navy Research Laboratories (mechanical/electrical engineering), Department of Energy Laboratories (electrical engineering).

GRADUATE UNITS

Graduate School *Degree program information:* Part-time and evening/weekend programs available.

POLYTECHNIC UNIVERSITY OF THE AMERICAS–MIAMI CAMPUS, Miami, FL 33166

General Information Independent, comprehensive institution. *Enrollment:* 29 full-time matriculated graduate/professional students (15 women). *Enrollment by degree level:* 29 master's. *Graduate faculty:* 8 part-time/adjunct (1 woman). *Tuition:* Full-time $7,110; part-time $395 per credit. *Required fees:* $620. One-time fee: $30 full-time. *Student services:* Career counseling. *Library facilities:* Main library plus 1 other. *Online resources:* web page. *Web address:* http://www.pupr.edu/miami/.

General Application Contact: Ernesto Castro, Academic and Enrollment Director, 888-729-7659 Ext. 206, Fax: 305-418-4325, E-mail: ecastro@pupr.edu.

GRADUATE UNITS

Graduate School Students: 29 full-time (15 women); includes 28 minority (2 African Americans, 26 Hispanic Americans). Average age 35. *Faculty:* 8 part-time/adjunct (1 woman). Expenses: Contact institution. *Financial support:* In 2006–07, 13 students received support. Applicants required to submit FAFSA. In 2006, 4 degrees awarded. *Degree program information:* Part-time and evening/weekend programs available. Postbaccalaureate distance learning degree programs offered (no on-campus study). *Application deadline:* Applications are processed on a rolling basis. *Application fee:* $30 ($250 for international students). Electronic applications accepted. *Application Contact:* Ernesto Castro, Academic and Enrollment Director, 305-418-4220 Ext. 206, Fax: 305-418-4325, E-mail: ecastro@pupr.edu. *Campus Director,* Gustavo B. Marin, 305-418-4220 Ext. 205, Fax: 305-418-4325, E-mail: gmarin@pupr.edu.

POLYTECHNIC UNIVERSITY OF THE AMERICAS–ORLANDO CAMPUS, Orlando, FL 32792

General Information Independent, comprehensive institution. *Enrollment by degree level:* 12 master's. *Graduate faculty:* 5 part-time/adjunct (1 woman). *Graduate housing:* On-campus housing not available. *Student services:* Campus employment opportunities, campus safety program, career counseling, teacher training, writing training. *Web address:* http://www.pupr.edu/orlando/.

General Application Contact: Luis Mercado, Admissions Director, 407-677-5661, Fax: 407-677-5082, E-mail: lmercado@pupr.edu.

GRADUATE UNITS

Graduate School Students: 12 full-time (6 women); all minorities (all Hispanic Americans) Average age 30. 5 applicants, 100% accepted, 5 enrolled. *Faculty:* 5 part-time/adjunct (1 woman). Expenses: Contact institution. *Financial support:* Applicants required to submit FAFSA. In 2006, 5 degrees awarded. *Degree program information:* Part-time and evening/weekend programs available. Postbaccalaureate distance learning degree programs offered (no on-campus study). *Application deadline:* For fall admission, 8/6 priority date for domestic students, 7/6 priority date for international students; for winter admission, 11/6 priority date for domestic students, 10/6 priority date for international students; for spring admission, 3/7 priority date for domestic students, 2/7 priority date for international students. Applications are processed on a rolling basis. *Application fee:* $30. Electronic applications accepted. *Application Contact:* Luis Mercado, Admissions Director, 407-677-5661, Fax: 407-677-5082, E-mail: lmercado@pupr.edu. *Campus Director,* Carlos Perez, 407-677-5661 Ext. 301, Fax: 407-677-5082, E-mail: cperez@pupr.edu.

POLYTECHNIC UNIVERSITY, WESTCHESTER GRADUATE CENTER, Hawthorne, NY 10532-1507

General Information Independent, coed, graduate-only institution. *Enrollment by degree level:* 42 master's. *Graduate faculty:* 66 full-time (6 women), 66 part-time/adjunct (5 women). *Tuition:* Full-time $17,184; part-time $988 per credit. *Graduate housing:* Room and/or apartments available to single students; on-campus housing not available to married students. *Student services:* Campus employment opportunities, career counseling, international student services. *Library facilities:* Dibner Library. *Online resources:* library catalog, web page, access to other libraries' catalogs. *Collection:* 160,200 titles, 1,621 serial subscriptions, 337 audiovisual materials.

Computer facilities: 30 computers available on campus for general student use. A campuswide network can be accessed from off campus. Internet access is available. *Web address:* http://west.poly.edu/~www/.

General Application Contact: Prof. Sunil Kumar, Graduate Admissions, 718-260-3482, Fax: 718-260-3624, E-mail: gradinfo@poly.edu.

GRADUATE UNITS

Graduate Programs Students: 13 full-time (5 women), 29 part-time (4 women); includes 6 minority (1 American Indian/Alaska Native, 5 Asian Americans or Pacific Islanders), 6 international. Average age 32. 27 applicants, 89% accepted, 8 enrolled. *Faculty:* 66 full-time (6 women), 66 part-time/adjunct (5 women). Expenses: Contact institution. *Financial support:* Fellowships, research assistantships, teaching assistantships, institutionally sponsored loans available. Support available to part-time students. Financial award applicants required to submit FAFSA. In 2006, 39 degrees awarded. *Degree program information:* Part-time and evening/weekend programs available. Offers chemical engineering (MS); chemistry (MS); computer engineering (MS); computer science (MS, PhD); electrical engineering (MS, PhD); information systems engineering (MS); materials chemistry (PhD); telecommunication networks (MS). *Application deadline:* For fall admission, 7/15 priority date for domestic students, 4/1 priority date for international students; for spring admission, 12/15 priority date for domestic students, 10/1 priority date for international students. Applications are processed on a rolling basis. *Application fee:* $55. Electronic applications accepted. *Application Contact:* Prof. Sunil Kumar, Graduate Admissions, 718-260-3482, Fax: 718-260-3624, E-mail: gradinfo@poly.edu. *Director of Campus Operations,* LaVerne Clark, 914-323-2002, E-mail: lclark@poly.edu.

Department of Management Average age 32. *Faculty:* 8 full-time (1 woman), 33 part-time/adjunct (4 women). Expenses: Contact institution. *Financial support:* Institutionally sponsored loans available. Support available to part-time students. Financial award applicants required to submit FAFSA. In 2006, 2 degrees awarded. *Degree program information:* Part-time and evening/weekend programs available. Offers capital markets (MS); computational finance (MS); financial engineering (MS, AC); financial technology (MS); financial technology management (AC); information management (AC); management (MS); management of technology (MS). *Application deadline:* For fall admission, 7/15 priority date for domestic students, 4/1 priority date for international students; for spring admission, 12/15 priority date for domestic students, 10/1 priority date for international students. Applications are processed on a rolling basis. *Application fee:* $55. Electronic applications accepted. *Application Contact:* Anthea Jeffrey, Graduate Admissions, 718-260-3200, Fax: 718-260-3624, E-mail: gradinfo@poly.edu. *Associate Dean,* Dr. Barry Blecherman, 718-260-3610, Fax: 718-260-3874.

PONCE SCHOOL OF MEDICINE, Ponce, PR 00732-7004

General Information Independent, coed, graduate-only institution. *Graduate housing:* On-campus housing not available.

GRADUATE UNITS

Professional Program Offers medicine (MD). Electronic applications accepted.

Program in Biomedical Sciences Offers biomedical sciences (PhD).

Program in Clinical Psychology Offers clinical psychology (Psy D).

Program in Public Health Offers public health (MPH).

PONTIFICAL CATHOLIC UNIVERSITY OF PUERTO RICO, Ponce, PR 00717-0777

General Information Independent-religious, coed, university. *Graduate housing:* Room and/or apartments available to single students; on-campus housing not available to married students. Housing application deadline: 7/15.

GRADUATE UNITS

College of Arts and Humanities *Degree program information:* Part-time and evening/weekend programs available. Offers arts and humanities (MA); Hispanic studies (MA); history (MA); theology and philosophy (M Div).

College of Business Administration *Degree program information:* Part-time and evening/weekend programs available. Offers accounting (MBA); business administration (PhD); finance (MBA); general business (MBA); human resources (MBA); international business (MBA); management (MBA); management information systems (MBA); marketing (MBA); office administration (MBA).

College of Education *Degree program information:* Part-time and evening/weekend programs available. Offers commercial education (MRE); curriculum instruction (M Ed); education (PhD); education-general (MRE); English as a second language (MRE); religious education (MA Ed); scholar psychology (MRE).

College of Sciences *Degree program information:* Part-time and evening/weekend programs available. Offers chemistry (MS); environmental sciences (MS); medical technology (Certificate); medical-surgical nursing (MS); mental health and psychiatric nursing (MS); sciences (MS, Certificate).

Institute of Graduate Studies in Behavioral Science and Community Affairs *Degree program information:* Part-time and evening/weekend programs available. Offers clinical psychology (MA, MS); clinical social work (MSW); criminology (MA); industrial psychology (MS); psychology (PhD); public administration (MA).

School of Law *Degree program information:* Part-time and evening/weekend programs available. Offers law (JD).

PONTIFICAL COLLEGE JOSEPHINUM, Columbus, OH 43235-1498

General Information Independent-religious, coed, primarily men, comprehensive institution. *Enrollment:* 153 graduate, professional, and undergraduate students; 49 full-time matriculated graduate/professional students, 2 part-time matriculated graduate/professional students. *Enrollment by degree level:* 49 first professional, 2 master's. *Graduate faculty:* 16 full-time (1 woman), 5 part-time/adjunct (1 woman). *Tuition:* Full-time $18,720; part-time $588 per credit hour. *Required fees:* $660. *Graduate housing:* Room and/or apartments guaranteed to single students; on-campus housing not available to married students. Typical cost: $7,280 (including board). Housing application deadline: 8/15. *Student services:* Campus employment opportunities, free psychological counseling, international student services, low-cost health insurance. *Library facilities:* Wehrle Memorial Library. *Online resources:* web page. *Collection:* 137,883 titles, 465 serial subscriptions.

Computer facilities: 10 computers available on campus for general student use. A campuswide network can be accessed from student residence rooms. Internet access is available. *Web address:* http://www.pcj.edu/.

General Application Contact: Dr. Perry Cahall, Director of Admissions, 614-885-5585, Fax: 614-885-2307, E-mail: pcahall@pcj.edu.

GRADUATE UNITS

School of Theology Students: 49 full-time (0 women), 2 part-time; includes 5 minority (2 Asian Americans or Pacific Islanders, 3 Hispanic Americans), 10 international. Average age 28. 16 applicants, 88% accepted, 14 enrolled. *Faculty:* 16 full-time (1 woman), 5 part-time/adjunct (1 woman). Expenses: Contact institution. *Financial support:* Career-related internships or fieldwork and Federal Work-Study available. Financial award application deadline: 8/15; financial award applicants required to submit FAFSA. In 2006, 9 M Divs, 4 master's awarded. *Degree program information:* Part-time programs available. Offers theology (M Div, MA). *Application deadline:* For fall admission, 8/15 for domestic students. Applications are processed on a rolling basis. *Application fee:* $35. *Application Contact:* Dr. Perry Cahall, Director of Admissions, 614-885-5585, Fax: 614-885-2307, E-mail: pcahall@pcj.edu. *Vice Rector,* Rev. Msgr. Nevin Klinger, 614-885-5585, Fax: 614-885-2307.

PORTLAND STATE UNIVERSITY, Portland, OR 97207-0751

General Information State-supported, coed, university. CGS member. *Enrollment:* 24,254 graduate, professional, and undergraduate students; 2,244 full-time matriculated graduate/professional students (1,341 women), 2,319 part-time matriculated graduate/professional students (1,356 women). *Enrollment by degree level:* 3,679 master's, 539 doctoral, 345 other advanced degrees. *Graduate faculty:* 643 full-time (261 women), 414 part-time/adjunct (194 women). Tuition, state resident: full-time $6,426; part-time $238 per credit. Tuition, nonresident: full-time $11,016; part-time $408 per credit. Tuition and fees vary according to course load. *Graduate housing:* Rooms and/or apartments available on a first-come, first-served basis to single and married students. Typical cost: $6,300 per year ($8,940 including board) for single students; $6,300 per year ($8,940 including board) for married students. *Student services:* Campus employment opportunities, campus safety program, career counseling, child daycare facilities, disabled student services, free psychological counseling, international student services, low-cost health insurance, multicultural affairs office, teacher training. *Library facilities:* Branford P. Millar Library plus 1 other. *Online resources:* library catalog, web page, access to other libraries' catalogs. *Collection:* 1.8 million titles, 10,308 serial subscriptions. *Research affiliation:* Tektronix (electrical engineering), Tri-County Metropolitan Transportation District of Oregon, City of Portland (civil engineering, urban planning), Intel Corporation (electronic cooling, engineering), Battelle Pacific Northwest Laboratories (computer science, geographic information systems, mechanical engineering, science education), Bonneville Power Administration (civil and mechanical engineering, geology, urban studies).

Computer facilities: 800 computers available on campus for general student use. A campuswide network can be accessed from student residence rooms and from off campus. Internet access and online class registration are available. *Web address:* http://www.pdx.edu/.

General Application Contact: Information Contact, 503-725-3511, Fax: 503-725-5525, E-mail: admissions@pdx.edu.

GRADUATE UNITS

Graduate Studies Students: 4,563; includes 555 minority (90 African Americans, 48 American Indian/Alaska Native, 216 Asian Americans or Pacific Islanders, 201 Hispanic Americans), 552 international. Average age 33. 3,956 applicants, 75% accepted, 1673 enrolled. *Faculty:* 643 full-time (261 women), 414 part-time/adjunct (194 women). Expenses: Contact institution. *Financial support:* In 2006–07, 178 research assistantships with full tuition reimbursements (averaging $9,557 per year), 168 teaching assistantships with full tuition reimbursements (averaging $9,214 per year) were awarded; fellowships, career-related internships or fieldwork, Federal Work-Study, scholarships/grants, tuition waivers (partial), and unspecified assistantships also available. Support available to part-time students. Financial award application deadline: 3/1; financial award applicants required to submit FAFSA. In 2006, 1,453 master's, 41 doctorates awarded. *Degree program information:* Part-time and evening/weekend programs available. Postbaccalaureate distance learning degree programs offered (minimal on-campus study). Offers computational intelligence (Certificate); computer modeling and simulation (Certificate); systems science (MS); systems science/anthropology (PhD); systems science/business administration (PhD); systems science/civil engineering (PhD); systems science/economics (PhD); systems science/engineering management (PhD); systems science/general (PhD); systems science/mathematical sciences (PhD); systems science/mechanical engineering (PhD); systems science/psychology (PhD); systems science/sociology (PhD). *Application deadline:* For fall admission, 4/1 for domestic students, 3/1 for international students; for winter admission, 9/1 for domestic students, 7/1 for international students; for spring admission, 11/1 for domestic and international students. Applications are processed on a rolling basis. *Application fee:* $50. *Application Contact:* 503-725*3511, Fax: 503-725-5525. *Vice Provost for Sponsored Research/Dean of Graduate Studies,* Dr. William H. Feyerherm, 503-725-3423, Fax: 503-725-3416.

College of Liberal Arts and Sciences Students: 650 full-time (399 women), 486 part-time (293 women); includes 110 minority (17 African Americans, 8 American Indian/Alaska Native, 41 Asian Americans or Pacific Islanders, 44 Hispanic Americans), 107 international. Average age 33. 775 applicants, 68% accepted, 338 enrolled. *Faculty:* 294 full-time (115 women), 133 part-time/adjunct (75 women). Expenses: Contact institution. *Financial support:* In 2006–07, 51 research assistantships with full tuition reimbursements (averaging $9,911 per year), 156 teaching assistantships with full tuition reimbursements (averaging $9,162 per year) were awarded; career-related internships or fieldwork, Federal Work-Study, scholarships/grants, and tuition waivers (partial) also available. Support available to part-time students. Financial award application deadline: 3/1; financial award applicants required to submit FAFSA. In 2006, 276 master's, 8 doctorates awarded. *Degree program information:* Part-time and evening/weekend programs available. Offers anthropology (MA); applied economics (MA, MS); biology (MA, MS, PhD); chemistry (MA, MS, PhD); conflict resolution (MA, MS); economics (PhD); English (MA); environmental management (MEM); environmental sciences and resources (PhD); environmental sciences/biology (PhD); environmental sciences/chemistry (PhD); environmental sciences/civil engineering (PhD); environmental sciences/geography (PhD); environmental sciences/geology (PhD); environmental sciences/physics (PhD); environmental studies (MS); foreign literature and language (MA); French (MA); general arts and letters education (MAT, MST); general economics (MA, MS); general science education (MAT, MST); general social science education (MAT, MST); general speech communication (MA, MS, Certificate); geography (MA, MAT, MS, MST, PhD); geology (MA, MS); German (MA); history (MA); Japanese (MA); liberal arts and sciences (MA, MAT, MEM, MS, MST, MST, PhD, Certificate); mathematical sciences (PhD); mathematics education (PhD); physics (MA, MS, PhD); psychology (MA, MS, PhD); science/environmental science (MST); science/geology (MAT, MST); sociology (MA, MS, PhD); Spanish (MA); speech-language pathology (MA, MS); statistics (MS); teaching English to speakers of other languages (MA). *Application deadline:* Applications are processed on a rolling basis. *Application fee:* $50. *Dean,* Dr. Marvin Kaiser, 503-725-3514, Fax: 503-725-3693, E-mail: marvin@clas.pdx.edu.

College of Urban and Public Affairs Students: 304 full-time (197 women), 352 part-time (212 women); includes 75 minority (18 African Americans, 10 American Indian/Alaska Native, 19 Asian Americans or Pacific Islanders, 28 Hispanic Americans), 37 international. Average age 33. 518 applicants, 73% accepted, 214 enrolled. *Faculty:* 62 full-time (26 women), 49 part-time/adjunct (20 women). Expenses: Contact institution. *Financial support:* In 2006–07, 29 research assistantships with full tuition reimbursements (averaging $8,187 per year), 4 teaching assistantships with full tuition reimbursements (averaging $10,373 per year) were awarded; fellowships, career-related internships or fieldwork, Federal Work-Study, scholarships/grants, tuition waivers (partial), and unspecified assistantships also available. Support available to part-time students. Financial award application deadline: 3/1; financial award applicants required to submit FAFSA. In 2006, 159 master's, 10 doctorates awarded. *Degree program information:* Part-time and evening/weekend programs available. Offers criminology and criminal justice (MS, PhD); gerontology (Certificate); government (MA, MAT, MPA, MS, MST, PhD); health administration (MPA); health administration and policy (MPH); health education (MA, MS); health education and health promotion (MPH); health studies (MPA, MPH); political science (MA, MAT, MS, MST, PhD); public administration (MPA); public administration and policy (PhD); urban and public affairs (MA, MAT, MPA, MPH, MS, MST, MURP, MUS, PhD, Certificate); urban and regional planning (MURP); urban studies (MUS, PhD); urban studies and planning (MURP, MUS, PhD). *Application fee:* $50. *Application Contact:* Rod Johnson, Admissions Officer, 503-725-4044, Fax: 503-725-5199, E-mail: rod@pdx.edu. *Dean,* Dr. Lawrence Wallack, 503-725-4043, Fax: 503-725-5199, E-mail: wallackl@pdx.edu.

Graduate School of Social Work Students: 314 full-time (248 women), 154 part-time (127 women); includes 69 minority (15 African Americans, 9 American Indian/Alaska Native, 15 Asian Americans or Pacific Islanders, 30 Hispanic Americans), 4 international. Average age 35. 474 applicants, 69% accepted, 221 enrolled. *Faculty:* 35 full-time (24 women), 14 part-time/adjunct (6 women). Expenses: Contact institution. *Financial support:* In 2006–07, 8 research assistantships with full tuition reimbursements (averaging $10,022 per year), 2 teaching assistantships with full tuition reimbursements (averaging $13,161 per year) were awarded; career-related internships or fieldwork, Federal Work-Study, scholarships/grants, tuition waivers (partial), and unspecified assistantships also available. Support available to part-time students. Financial award application deadline: 3/1; financial award applicants required to submit FAFSA. In 2006, 141 master's, 2 doctorates awarded. *Degree program information:* Part-time programs available. Offers social work (MSW); social work and social research (PhD). *Application deadline:* For fall admission, 2/1 for domestic and international students. *Application fee:* $50. *Application Contact:* Janet Putnam, Director of Student Affairs, 503-725-4712, Fax: 503-725-5545, E-mail: putnamj@pdx.edu. *Dean,* Dr. Kristine E. Nelson, 503-725-4712, Fax: 503-725-5545, E-mail: nelsonk@pdx.edu.

Maseeh College of Engineering and Computer Science Students: 289 full-time (71 women), 260 part-time (71 women); includes 71 minority (4 African Americans, 3 American Indian/Alaska Native, 48 Asian Americans or Pacific Islanders, 16 Hispanic Americans), 305 international. Average age 29. 593 applicants, 72% accepted, 202 enrolled. *Faculty:* 78 full-time (14 women), 16 part-time/adjunct (2 women). Expenses: Contact institution. *Financial support:* In 2006–07, 28 research assistantships with full tuition reimbursements (averaging $14,559 per year), 3 teaching assistantships with full tuition reimbursements (averaging $9,252 per year) were awarded; career-related internships or fieldwork, Federal Work-Study, scholarships/grants, and unspecified assistantships also available. Support available to part-time students. Financial award application deadline: 3/1; financial award applicants required to submit FAFSA. In 2006, 165 master's, 4 doctorates awarded. *Degree program information:* Part-time and evening/weekend programs available. Offers civil and environmental engineering (M Eng, MS); civil and environmental engineering management (M Eng); civilian and environmental engineering (PhD); computer science (MS, PhD); electrical and computer engineering (M Eng, MS, PhD); engineering and computer science (M Eng, ME, MS, MSE, PhD, Certificate); engineering and technology management (M Eng); engineering management (MS); environmental sciences and resources (PhD); manufacturing engineering (ME); manufacturing management (M Eng); mechanical engineering (M Eng, MS, PhD); software engineering (MSE); systems engineering (M Eng); systems engineering fundamentals (Certificate); systems science (PhD); systems science/engineering management (PhD). *Application deadline:* For fall admission, 6/15 for domestic and international students; for winter admission, 11/1 for domestic and international students; for spring admission, 2/1 for domestic and international students. Applications are processed on a rolling basis. *Application fee:* $50. *Application Contact:* Marcia Fischer, Assistant Dean for Enrollment, 503-725-4289, Fax: 503-725-4298, E-mail: fischerm@cecs.pdx.edu. *Dean,* Dr. Robert D. Dryden, 503-725-4631, Fax: 503-725-4298, E-mail: drydenr@cecspdx.edu.

School of Business Administration Students: 205 full-time (85 women), 233 part-time (91 women); includes 67 minority (8 African Americans, 2 American Indian/Alaska Native, 45 Asian Americans or Pacific Islanders, 12 Hispanic Americans), 54 international. Average age 31. 328 applicants, 84% accepted, 199 enrolled. *Faculty:* 60 full-time (24 women), 44 part-time/adjunct (7 women). Expenses: Contact institution. *Financial support:* Research assistantships with full tuition reimbursements, teaching assistantships with full tuition reimbursements, career-related internships or fieldwork, Federal Work-Study, scholarships/grants, tuition waivers (partial), and unspecified assistantships available. Support available to part-time students. Financial award application deadline: 3/1; financial award applicants required to submit FAFSA. In 2006, 156 degrees awarded. *Degree program information:* Part-time and evening/weekend programs available. Offers business administration (MBA, MIM, MSFA, PhD); financial analysis (MSFA); international management (MIM). *Application deadline:* For fall admission, 4/1 for domestic students, 3/1 for international students. Applications are processed on a rolling basis. *Application fee:* $50. *Application Contact:* Pam Mitchell, Administrator, 503-725-3730, Fax: 503-725-5850, E-mail: pamm@sba.pdx.edu. *Dean,* Dr. Scott Dawson, 503-725-3721, Fax: 503-725-5850, E-mail: scottd@sba.pdx.edu.

School of Education Students: 372 full-time (288 women), 634 part-time (452 women); includes 119 minority (21 African Americans, 16 American Indian/Alaska Native, 28 Asian Americans or Pacific Islanders, 54 Hispanic Americans), 25 international. Average age 36. 846 applicants, 85% accepted, 367 enrolled. *Faculty:* 50 full-time (29 women), 50 part-time/adjunct (29 women). Expenses: Contact institution. *Financial support:* In 2006–07, 21 research assistantships with full tuition reimbursements (averaging $5,742 per year) were awarded; teaching assistantships with full tuition reimbursements, career-related internships or fieldwork, Federal Work-Study, institutionally sponsored loans, scholarships/grants, and unspecified assistantships also available. Support available to part-time students. Financial award application deadline: 3/1; financial award applicants required to submit FAFSA. In 2006, 532 master's, 8 doctorates awarded. *Degree program information:* Part-time and evening/weekend programs available. Offers counselor education (MA, MS); early childhood education (MA, MS); education (M Ed, MA, MS); educational leadership (MA, MS, Ed D); educational leadership: curriculum and instruction (Ed D); educational media/school librarianship (MA, MS); elementary education (M Ed, MAT, MST); postsecondary, adult and continuing education (Ed D); reading (MA, MS); secondary education (M Ed, MAT, MST); special and counselor education (Ed D); special education (MA, MS). *Application deadline:* For fall admission, 4/1 for domestic and international students; for winter admission, 9/1 for domestic and international students; for spring admission, 11/1 for domestic and international students. *Application fee:* $50. *Application Contact:* Tasa Lehman, 503-725-4619, Fax: 503-725-5599, E-mail: lehmant@pdx.edu. *Dean,* Dr. Randy Hitz, 503-725-4697, Fax: 503-725-5399.

School of Fine and Performing Arts Students: 49 full-time (28 women), 15 part-time (5 women); includes 7 minority (2 Asian Americans or Pacific Islanders, 5 Hispanic Americans), 4 international. Average age 30. 92 applicants, 34% accepted, 26 enrolled. *Faculty:* 59 full-time (27 women), 67 part-time/adjunct (28 women). Expenses: Contact institution. *Financial support:* Research assistantships with full tuition reimbursements, teaching assistantships with full tuition reimbursements, career-related internships or fieldwork, Federal Work-Study, scholarships/grants, tuition waivers (partial), and unspecified assistant-

Portland State University (continued)

ships available. Support available to part-time students. Financial award application deadline: 3/1; financial award applicants required to submit FAFSA. In 2006, 23 degrees awarded. *Degree program information:* Part-time programs available. Offers conducting (MMC); drawing (MFA); fine and performing arts (MA, MAT, MFA, MMC, MMP, MS, MST); mixed media (MFA); music education (MAT, MST); painting (MFA); performance (MMP); printmaking (MFA); sculpture (MFA); theater arts (MA, MS). *Application deadline:* For fall admission, 3/1 for domestic and international students. Applications are processed on a rolling basis. *Application fee:* $50. *Dean,* Barbara Sestak, 503-725-3340, Fax: 503-725-3351.

PRATT INSTITUTE, Brooklyn, NY 11205-3899

General Information Independent, coed, comprehensive institution. *Enrollment:* 4,673 graduate, professional, and undergraduate students; 1,281 full-time matriculated graduate/professional students (886 women), 324 part-time matriculated graduate/professional students (234 women). *Enrollment by degree level:* 1,605 master's. *Graduate faculty:* 57 full-time (22 women), 362 part-time/adjunct (164 women). *Tuition:* Full-time $24,240. Tuition and fees vary according to course load and program. *Graduate housing:* Rooms and/or apartments available on a first-come, first-served basis to single and married students. Typical cost: $5,552 per year ($8,752 including board) for single students; $5,552 per year ($88,752 including board) for married students. Room and board charges vary according to board plan, campus/location and housing facility selected. Housing application deadline: 5/1. *Student services:* Campus employment opportunities, campus safety program, career counseling, disabled student services, exercise/wellness program, free psychological counseling, grant writing training, international student services, low-cost health insurance, multicultural affairs office, teacher training, writing training. *Library facilities:* Pratt Institute Library. *Online resources:* library catalog, web page, access to other libraries' catalogs. *Collection:* 172,000 titles, 540 serial subscriptions. *Research affiliation:* Ford Motor Company (transportation), The Procter & Gamble Company (product design), General Motors Corporation (transportation).

Computer facilities: 250 computers available on campus for general student use. A campuswide network can be accessed from student residence rooms and from off campus. Internet access and online class registration are available. *Web address:* http://www.pratt.edu/.

General Application Contact: Young Hah, Director of Graduate Admissions, 718-636-3683, Fax: 718-399-4242, E-mail: yhah@pratt.edu.

GRADUATE UNITS

School of Architecture Students: 217 full-time (112 women), 22 part-time (12 women); includes 54 minority (17 African Americans, 18 Asian Americans or Pacific Islanders, 19 Hispanic Americans), 66 international. Average age 29. 576 applicants, 62% accepted, 101 enrolled. *Faculty:* 13 full-time (5 women), 74 part-time/adjunct (27 women). Expenses: Contact institution. *Financial support:* In 2006–07, 20 fellowships (averaging $2,000 per year) were awarded; research assistantships, career-related internships or fieldwork, Federal Work-Study, institutionally sponsored loans, scholarships/grants, health care benefits, and unspecified assistantships also available. Support available to part-time students. Financial award application deadline: 2/1; financial award applicants required to submit FAFSA. In 2006, 42 master's awarded. *Degree program information:* Part-time and evening/weekend programs available. Offers architecture (M Arch, MS, MS Arch, MSCRP, MSUD, MSUESM); architecture and urban design (MS); city and regional planning (MSCRP); facilities management (MS); historic preservation (MS); urban environmental systems management (MSUESM). *Application deadline:* For fall admission, 2/1 for domestic students; for spring admission, 10/1 for domestic students. Applications are processed on a rolling basis. *Application fee:* $40 ($90 for international students). Electronic applications accepted. *Application Contact:* Young Hah, Director of Graduate Admissions, 718-636-3683, Fax: 718-399-4242, E-mail: yhah@pratt.edu. *Dean,* Thomas Hanrahan, 718-399-4304, Fax: 718-399-4315, E-mail: hanrahan@pratt.edu.

School of Art and Design Students: 943 full-time (681 women), 78 part-time (57 women); includes 210 minority (72 African Americans, 5 American Indian/Alaska Native, 80 Asian Americans or Pacific Islanders, 53 Hispanic Americans), 341 international. Average age 28. 1,480 applicants, 46% accepted, 324 enrolled. *Faculty:* 41 full-time (17 women), 200 part-time/adjunct (99 women). Expenses: Contact institution. *Financial support:* In 2006–07, 15 fellowships (averaging $3,500 per year), 75 research assistantships (averaging $1,500 per year) were awarded; teaching assistantships, career-related internships or fieldwork, Federal Work-Study, institutionally sponsored loans, scholarships/grants, tuition waivers (full), and unspecified assistantships also available. Support available to part-time students. Financial award application deadline: 2/1; financial award applicants required to submit FAFSA. In 2006, 332 degrees awarded. *Degree program information:* Part-time and evening/weekend programs available. Offers art and design (MFA, MID, MPS, MS); art and design education (MS); art history (MS); art therapy and creativity development (MPS); art therapy-special education (MPS); arts and cultural management (MPS); ceramics (MFA); communications design (MS); computer graphics (MFA); dance/movement therapy (MS); design management (MPS); industrial design (MID); interior design (MS); metals (MFA); new forms (MFA); package design (MS); painting (MFA); photography (MFA); printmaking (MFA); sculpture (MFA); theory and criticism (MS). *Application deadline:* For fall admission, 2/1 for domestic students; for spring admission, 10/1 for domestic students. *Application fee:* $40 ($90 for international students). Electronic applications accepted. *Application Contact:* Young Hah, Director of Graduate Admissions, 718-636-3683, Fax: 718-399-4242, E-mail: yhah@pratt.edu. *Chairperson,* Frank Lind, 718-636-3602, E-mail: flind@pratt.edu.

School of Information and Library Science Students: 121 full-time (93 women), 224 part-time (165 women); includes 78 minority (33 African Americans, 1 American Indian/Alaska Native, 21 Asian Americans or Pacific Islanders, 23 Hispanic Americans), 9 international. Average age 33. 254 applicants, 81% accepted, 110 enrolled. *Faculty:* 9 full-time (6 women), 27 part-time/adjunct (15 women). Expenses: Contact institution. *Financial support:* In 2006–07, 10 fellowships (averaging $2,000 per year), 10 research assistantships (averaging $2,500 per year) were awarded; career-related internships or fieldwork, institutionally sponsored loans, scholarships/grants, and unspecified assistantships also available. Support available to part-time students. Financial award application deadline: 2/1; financial award applicants required to submit FAFSA. In 2006, 100 degrees awarded. *Degree program information:* Part-time and evening/weekend programs available. Offers information and library science (MS, Adv C). *Application deadline:* For fall admission, 2/1 for domestic students; for spring admission, 10/1 for domestic students. *Application fee:* $40 ($90 for international students). Electronic applications accepted. *Application Contact:* Young Hah, Director of Graduate Admissions, 718-636-3683, Fax: 718-399-4242, E-mail: yhah@pratt.edu. *Dean,* Tula Giannini, 212-647-7682.

PRESCOTT COLLEGE, Prescott, AZ 86301

General Information Independent, coed, comprehensive institution. *Enrollment:* 1,053 graduate, professional, and undergraduate students; 195 full-time matriculated graduate/professional students (138 women), 100 part-time matriculated graduate/professional students (60 women). *Enrollment by degree level:* 275 master's, 20 doctoral. *Graduate faculty:* 5 full-time (2 women), 172 part-time/adjunct (92 women). *Tuition:* Full-time $12,408; part-time $517 per credit. One-time fee: $130. *Graduate housing:* On-campus housing not available. *Student services:* Campus employment opportunities, career counseling, disabled student services, free psychological counseling, international student services, low-cost health insurance. *Library facilities:* Prescott College Library. *Online resources:* library catalog, web page, access to other libraries' catalogs. *Collection:* 26,169 titles, 248 serial subscriptions.

Computer facilities: 30 computers available on campus for general student use. A campuswide network can be accessed. Internet access is available. *Web address:* http://www.prescott.edu/.

General Application Contact: Kerstin Alicki, Admissions Counselor, 877-350-2100 Ext. 2102, Fax: 928-776-5242, E-mail: admissions@prescott.edu.

GRADUATE UNITS

Graduate Programs Students: 194 full-time (137 women), 100 part-time (60 women); includes 41 minority (10 African Americans, 9 American Indian/Alaska Native, 2 Asian Americans or Pacific Islanders, 20 Hispanic Americans), 2 international. Average age 38. 153 applicants, 70% accepted, 101 enrolled. *Faculty:* 5 full-time (2 women), 172 part-time/adjunct (92 women). Expenses: Contact institution. *Financial support:* Career-related internships or fieldwork and Federal Work-Study available. Financial award applicants required to submit FAFSA. In 2006, 84 degrees awarded. *Degree program information:* Part-time programs available. Postbaccalaureate distance learning degree programs offered (minimal on-campus study). Offers adventure education/wilderness leadership (MA); agroecology (MA); bilingual education (MA); counseling and psychology (MA); ecopsychology (MA); education (MA, PhD); environmental education (MA); environmental studies (MA); humanities (MA); multicultural education (MA); Southwestern regional history (MA); sustainability (MA). *Application deadline:* For fall admission, 5/1 priority date for domestic students; for spring admission, 11/1 priority date for domestic students. Applications are processed on a rolling basis. *Application fee:* $40. Electronic applications accepted. *Application Contact:* Kerstin Alicki, Admissions Counselor, 877-350-2100 Ext. 2102, Fax: 928-776-5242, E-mail: admissions@prescott.edu. *Interim Dean,* Paul Burkhart, 928-350-3210, Fax: 928-776-5151, E-mail: pburkhart@prescott.edu.

PRINCETON THEOLOGICAL SEMINARY, Princeton, NJ 08542-0803

General Information Independent-religious, coed, graduate-only institution. *Graduate housing:* Rooms and/or apartments available on a first-come, first-served basis to single and married students. *Research affiliation:* Center of Theological Inquiry.

GRADUATE UNITS

Graduate and Professional Programs *Degree program information:* Part-time programs available. Offers theology (M Div, MA, Th M, D Min, PhD). Electronic applications accepted.

PRINCETON UNIVERSITY, Princeton, NJ 08544-1019

General Information Independent, coed, university. CGS member. *Graduate housing:* Rooms and/or apartments available to single and married students. Housing application deadline: 4/15. *Research affiliation:* Institute for Advanced Study (physics and mathematics), Brookhaven National Laboratory (experimental physics), Textile Research Institute (polymer research), NOAA-GFD Laboratory (weather prediction).

GRADUATE UNITS

Center for Photonic and Optoelectronic Materials (POEM) Offers photonic and optoelectronic materials (PhD).

Graduate School Offers ancient history (PhD); ancient Near Eastern studies (PhD); anthropology (PhD); applied and computational mathematics (PhD); applied physics (M Eng, MSE, PhD); astrophysical sciences (PhD); atmospheric and oceanic sciences (PhD); biology (PhD); chemical engineering (M Eng, MSE, PhD); chemistry (PhD); Chinese and Japanese art and archaeology (PhD); classical archaeology (PhD); classical art and archaeology (PhD); classical philosophy (PhD); community college history teaching (PhD); comparative literature (PhD); composition (PhD); computational methods (M Eng, MSE); computer science (M Eng, MSE, PhD); demography (PhD, Certificate); demography and public affairs (PhD); dynamics and control systems (M Eng, MSE, PhD); East Asian civilizations (PhD); East Asian studies (PhD); economics (PhD); economics and demography (PhD); electrical engineering (M Eng, MSE, PhD); energy and environmental policy (M Eng, MSE, PhD); energy conversion, propulsion, and combustion (M Eng, MSE, PhD); English (PhD); environmental engineering and water resources (PhD); financial engineering (M Eng); flight science and technology (M Eng, MSE, PhD); fluid mechanics (M Eng, MSE, PhD); French and Italian (PhD); geological and geophysical sciences (PhD); Germanic languages and literatures (PhD); history (PhD); history of science (PhD); history, archaeology and religions of the ancient world (PhD); industrial chemistry (MS); Islamic studies (PhD); mathematical physics (PhD); mathematics (PhD); mechanics, materials, and structures (M Eng, MSE, PhD); molecular biology (PhD); molecular biophysics (PhD); musicology (PhD); Near Eastern studies (MA); neuroscience (PhD); operations research and financial engineering (MSE, PhD); philosophy (PhD); physics (PhD); physics and chemical physics (PhD); plasma physics (PhD); plasma science and technology (MSE, PhD); political philosophy (PhD); politics (PhD); polymer sciences and materials (MSE, PhD); psychology (PhD); religion (PhD); Slavic languages and literatures (PhD); sociology (PhD); sociology and demography (PhD); Spanish and Portuguese languages and cultures (PhD); statistics and operations research (MSE, PhD); transportation systems (MSE, PhD). Electronic applications accepted.

Bendheim Center for Finance Offers finance (M Fin). Electronic applications accepted.

School of Architecture Offers architecture (M Arch, PhD). Electronic applications accepted.

Woodrow Wilson School of Public and International Affairs Offers public and international affairs (MPA, MPA-URP, MPP, PhD). Electronic applications accepted.

THE PROTESTANT EPISCOPAL THEOLOGICAL SEMINARY IN VIRGINIA, Alexandria, VA 22304

General Information Independent-religious, coed, graduate-only institution. *Graduate housing:* Room and/or apartments available on a first-come, first-served basis to single students; on-campus housing not available to married students. Housing application deadline: 5/1.

GRADUATE UNITS

Graduate and Professional Programs *Degree program information:* Part-time programs available. Offers theology (M Div, MACE, MTS, D Min).

PROVIDENCE COLLEGE, Providence, RI 02918

General Information Independent-religious, coed, comprehensive institution. *Enrollment:* 4,835 graduate, professional, and undergraduate students; 111 full-time matriculated graduate/professional students (72 women), 387 part-time matriculated graduate/professional students (246 women). *Enrollment by degree level:* 498 master's. *Graduate faculty:* 33 full-time (9 women), 55 part-time/adjunct (25 women). *Tuition:* Full-time $6,573; part-time $939 per unit. *Graduate housing:* On-campus housing not available. *Student services:* Campus employment opportunities, career counseling, disabled student services, international student services, multicultural affairs office, teacher training. *Library facilities:* Phillips Memorial Library. *Online resources:* library catalog, web page, access to other libraries' catalogs. *Collection:* 567,761 titles, 26,766 serial subscriptions.

Computer facilities: 164 computers available on campus for general student use. A campuswide network can be accessed from student residence rooms and from off campus. Internet access and online class registration are available. *Web address:* http://www.providence.edu/.

General Application Contact: Dr. Thomas Flaherty, Dean of Graduate Studies, 401-865-2247, Fax: 401-865-2057, E-mail: tflaherty@providence.edu.

GRADUATE UNITS

Graduate Studies Students: 111 full-time (72 women), 387 part-time (246 women); includes 16 minority (7 African Americans, 1 Asian American or Pacific Islander, 8 Hispanic Americans), 9 international. Average age 32. 159 applicants, 87% accepted. *Faculty:* 33 full-time (9 women), 55 part-time/adjunct (25 women). Expenses: Contact institution. *Financial support:* In 2006–07, 58 research assistantships with full tuition reimbursements (averaging $8,400 per year) were awarded; career-related internships or fieldwork, Federal Work-Study, institutionally sponsored loans, and unspecified assistantships also available. Support available to part-time students. Financial award application deadline: 8/1; financial award applicants required to submit FAFSA. In 2006, 198 degrees awarded. *Degree program information:* Part-time and evening/weekend programs available. Offers administration (M Ed); biblical studies (MA); business administration (MBA); education literacy (M Ed); elementary administration (M Ed); guidance and counseling (M Ed); history (MA); mathematics (MAT); pastoral ministry (MA); religious education (MA); religious studies (MA); secondary administration (M Ed); special education (M Ed). *Application deadline:* For fall admission, 8/1 priority date for domestic students, 8/1 for international students. Applications are processed on a rolling basis. *Application fee:* $55. *Dean, Graduate Studies,* Dr. Thomas Flaherty, 401-865-2247, E-mail: tflahert@providence.edu.

PROVIDENCE COLLEGE AND THEOLOGICAL SEMINARY, Otterburne, MB R0A 1G0, Canada

General Information Independent-religious, coed, comprehensive institution. *Graduate housing:* Rooms and/or apartments guaranteed to single students and available on a first-come, first-served basis to married students. Housing application deadline: 8/15.

GRADUATE UNITS

Theological Seminary *Degree program information:* Part-time programs available. Offers children's ministry (Certificate); Christian studies (MA, Certificate); counseling (MA); cross-cultural discipleship (Certificate); divinity (M Div); educational studies (MA); global studies (MA); lay counseling (Diploma); ministry (D Min); teaching English to speakers of other languages (Certificate); theological studies (MA); training teacher of English to speakers of other languages (Certificate); youth ministry (Certificate).

PSYCHOLOGICAL STUDIES INSTITUTE, Atlanta, GA 30327

General Information Independent-religious, coed, graduate-only institution.

GRADUATE UNITS

Graduate Programs

PURCHASE COLLEGE, STATE UNIVERSITY OF NEW YORK, Purchase, NY 10577-1400

General Information State-supported, coed, comprehensive institution. *Enrollment:* 3,901 graduate, professional, and undergraduate students; 134 full-time matriculated graduate/professional students (74 women), 13 part-time matriculated graduate/professional students (9 women). *Enrollment by degree level:* 147 master's. *Graduate faculty:* 266. Tuition, state resident: full-time $6,900; part-time $288 per credit. Tuition, nonresident: full-time $10,920; part-time $455 per credit. *Graduate housing:* Room and/or apartments available on a first-come, first-served basis to single students; on-campus housing not available to married students. *Student services:* Campus employment opportunities, campus safety program, career counseling, child daycare facilities, disabled student services, exercise/wellness program, free psychological counseling, international student services, low-cost health insurance. *Library facilities:* Purchase College Library. *Online resources:* library catalog, web page, access to other libraries' catalogs. *Collection:* 281,686 titles, 1,990 serial subscriptions.

Computer facilities: 350 computers available on campus for general student use. A campuswide network can be accessed from student residence rooms and from off campus. Internet access, e-mail are available. *Web address:* http://www.purchase.edu/.

General Application Contact: Sabrina Johnston, Counselor, 914-251-6479, Fax: 914-251-6314, E-mail: admissn@purchase.edu.

GRADUATE UNITS

Conservatory of Dance Offers choreography (MFA); performance and pedagogy (MFA). Electronic applications accepted.

Conservatory of Music Offers composition (MFA); instrumental (MFA); voice (MFA). Electronic applications accepted.

Conservatory of Theatre Arts and Film Offers theatre design (MFA); theatre technology (MFA). Electronic applications accepted.

Division of Humanities Students: 9 full-time (6 women), 5 part-time (4 women), 2 international. Average age 31. 13 applicants, 85% accepted, 6 enrolled. *Faculty:* 3 full-time (all women), 2 part-time/adjunct (1 woman). Expenses: Contact institution. *Financial support:* In 2006–07, 1 student received support, including 1 fellowship (averaging $5,000 per year); Federal Work-Study, scholarships/grants, and tuition waivers (partial) also available. Support available to part-time students. Financial award application deadline: 3/15; financial award applicants required to submit FAFSA. In 2006, 5 degrees awarded. Offers art history (MA). *Application deadline:* For fall admission, 3/15 for domestic students. *Application fee:* $50. *Application Contact:* Sabrina Johnston, Counselor, 914-251-6479, Fax: 914-251-6314, E-mail: admissn@purchase.edu. *Dean, Division of Humanities,* Jonathan Levin, 914-251-6000.

School of Art and Design Offers art and design (MFA). Electronic applications accepted.

PURDUE UNIVERSITY, West Lafayette, IN 47907

General Information State-supported, coed, university. CGS member. *Enrollment:* 39,228 graduate, professional, and undergraduate students; 5,762 full-time matriculated graduate/professional students (2,499 women), 1,939 part-time matriculated graduate/professional students (725 women). *Enrollment by degree level:* 915 first professional, 2,677 master's, 4,082 doctoral, 27 other advanced degrees. *Graduate faculty:* 1,721 full-time (405 women), 305 part-time/adjunct (74 women). *Graduate housing:* Rooms and/or apartments available on a first-come, first-served basis to single and married students. Housing application deadline: 3/1. *Student services:* Campus employment opportunities, campus safety program, career counseling, disabled student services, exercise/wellness program, free psychological counseling, grant writing training, international student services, low-cost health insurance, multicultural affairs office, teacher training, writing training. *Library facilities:* Hicks Undergraduate Library plus 13 others. *Online resources:* library catalog, web page, access to other libraries' catalogs. *Collection:* 2.5 million titles, 20,829 serial subscriptions.

Computer facilities: 2,925 computers available on campus for general student use. A campuswide network can be accessed from student residence rooms and from off campus. Internet access is available. *Web address:* http://www.purdue.edu/.

General Application Contact: Graduate School Admissions, 765-494-2600, Fax: 765-494-0136, E-mail: gradinfo@purdue.edu.

GRADUATE UNITS

College of Engineering Students: 1,528 full-time (310 women), 683 part-time (119 women); includes 168 minority (53 African Americans, 3 American Indian/Alaska Native, 71 Asian Americans or Pacific Islanders, 41 Hispanic Americans), 1,194 international. Average age 25. 4,405 applicants, 30% accepted, 548 enrolled. *Faculty:* 339 full-time (43 women), 27 part-time/adjunct (7 women). Expenses: Contact institution. *Financial support:* Fellowships with full tuition reimbursements, research assistantships with partial tuition reimbursements, teaching assistantships with partial tuition reimbursements, career-related internships or fieldwork, health care benefits, and unspecified assistantships available. Financial award applicants required to submit FAFSA. In 2006, 461 master's, 192 doctorates awarded. *Degree program information:* Part-time programs available. Postbaccalaureate distance learning degree programs offered (no on-campus study). Offers agricultural and biological engineering (MS, MSABE, MSE, PhD); engineering (MS, MSAAE, MSABE, MSBME, MSCE, MSChE, MSE, MSECE, MSIE, MSME, MSMSE, MSNE, PhD, Certificate); engineering education (PhD); engineering professional education (MS, MSE). *Application deadline:* Applications are processed on a rolling basis. *Application fee:* $55. Electronic applications accepted. *Dean,* Dr. Leah H. Jamieson, 765-494-5346.

School of Aeronautics and Astronautics Engineering Students: 148 full-time (22 women), 63 part-time (9 women); includes 15 minority (2 African Americans, 10 Asian Americans or Pacific Islanders, 3 Hispanic Americans), 80 international. 202 applicants, 67% accepted, 80 enrolled. *Faculty:* 27 full-time (3 women), 4 part-time/adjunct (0 women). Expenses: Contact institution. *Financial support:* Fellowships, research assistantships, teaching assistantships, career-related internships or fieldwork and health care benefits available. Support available to part-time students. Financial award applicants required to submit FAFSA. In 2006, 42 master's, 12 doctorates awarded. Offers aeronautics and astronautics engineering (MS, MSAAE, MSE, PhD). *Application deadline:* For fall admission, 1/15 priority date for domestic and international students; for spring admission, 8/15 priority date for domestic and international students. Applications are processed on a rolling basis. *Application fee:* $55. Electronic applications accepted. *Application Contact:* Linda Flack, Administrative Assistant, 765-494-5152, Fax: 765-494-0307, E-mail: flack@ecn.purdue.edu. *Graduate Chair,* Prof. Anastasias Lyrintzis, 765-494-5142, E-mail: aaegrdos@ecn.purdue.edu.

School of Chemical Engineering Students: 103 full-time (27 women), 12 part-time (1 woman); includes 6 minority (3 African Americans, 3 Asian Americans or Pacific Islanders), 72 international. 286 applicants, 14% accepted, 21 enrolled. *Faculty:* 22 full-time (2 women), 1 part-time/adjunct (0 women). Expenses: Contact institution. *Financial support:* Fellowships with partial tuition reimbursements, research assistantships with partial tuition reimbursements, teaching assistantships with partial tuition reimbursements, career-related internships or fieldwork available. Support available to part-time students. Financial award applicants required to submit FAFSA. In 2006, 12 master's, 17 doctorates awarded. Offers chemical engineering (MSChE, PhD). *Application deadline:* For fall admission, 1/15 priority date for domestic students; for spring admission, 11/1 priority date for domestic students. Applications are processed on a rolling basis. *Application fee:* $55. Electronic applications accepted. *Application Contact:* Deborah Bowman, Graduate Administrator, 765-494-4057, Fax: 765-494-0805, E-mail: gordonde@ecn.purdue.edu. *Graduate Chair,* Osman Basaran, 765-494-4057, Fax: 765-494-0805.

School of Civil Engineering Students: 208 full-time (55 women), 38 part-time (7 women); includes 18 minority (4 African Americans, 1 American Indian/Alaska Native, 4 Asian Americans or Pacific Islanders, 9 Hispanic Americans), 130 international. 379 applicants, 55% accepted, 65 enrolled. *Faculty:* 51 full-time (6 women). Expenses: Contact institution. *Financial support:* Fellowships, research assistantships, teaching assistantships available. Support available to part-time students. Financial award application deadline: 6/30; financial award applicants required to submit FAFSA. In 2006, 83 master's, 26 doctorates awarded. *Degree program information:* Part-time programs available. Offers civil engineering (MS, MSCE, MSE, PhD). *Application deadline:* For fall admission, 1/1 for domestic and international students; for spring admission, 9/15 for domestic and international students. Applications are processed on a rolling basis. *Application fee:* $55. Electronic applications accepted. *Application Contact:* Maeve Drummond, Student Contact, 765-494-2156, Fax: 765-494-0395, E-mail: cegrad@purdue.edu. *Associate Head,* Darcy Bullock, 765-494-3204, E-mail: cegrad@purdue.edu.

School of Electrical and Computer Engineering Students: 422 full-time (73 women), 152 part-time (22 women); includes 45 minority (16 African Americans, 19 Asian Americans or Pacific Islanders, 10 Hispanic Americans), 415 international. 1,550 applicants, 30% accepted, 149 enrolled. *Faculty:* 83 full-time (7 women), 9 part-time/adjunct (3 women). Expenses: Contact institution. *Financial support:* Fellowships with partial tuition reimbursements, research assistantships with partial tuition reimbursements, teaching assistantships with partial tuition reimbursements available. Financial award application deadline: 1/5. In 2006, 58 master's, 52 doctorates awarded. *Degree program information:* Part-time programs available. Postbaccalaureate distance learning degree programs offered (no on-campus study). Offers electrical and computer engineering (MS, MSE, MSECE, PhD). MS and PhD degree programs in biomedical engineering offered jointly with School of Mechanical Engineering and School of Chemical Engineering. *Application deadline:* For fall admission, 1/5 priority date for domestic and international students; for winter admission, 9/15 for domestic students; for spring admission, 9/15 for domestic and international students. Applications are processed on a rolling basis. *Application fee:* $55. Electronic applications accepted. *Application Contact:* Karen Jurss, Admissions Representative, 765-494-3392, Fax: 765-494-3393, E-mail: ecegrad@ecn.purdue.edu. *Graduate Coordinator,* Chee-Mun Ong, 765-494-3484, Fax: 765-494-3393, E-mail: ecegrad@purdue.edu.

School of Industrial Engineering Students: 115 full-time (32 women), 40 part-time (6 women); includes 6 minority (1 African American, 3 Asian Americans or Pacific Islanders, 2 Hispanic Americans), 127 international. 366 applicants, 38% accepted, 42 enrolled. *Faculty:* 25 full-time (3 women), 1 (woman) part-time/adjunct. Expenses: Contact institution. *Financial support:* In 2006–07, 6 fellowships with full tuition reimbursements (averaging $20,000 per year), 36 research assistantships with full tuition reimbursements (averaging $14,000 per year), 36 teaching assistantships with full tuition reimbursements (averaging $12,500 per year) were awarded. Support available to part-time students. Financial award application deadline: 3/15; financial award applicants required to submit FAFSA. In 2006, 61 master's, 7 doctorates awarded. *Degree program information:* Part-time programs available. Offers industrial engineering (MS, MSIE, PhD). *Application deadline:* For fall admission, 3/15 for domestic and international students; for spring admission, 9/1 for domestic and international students. Applications are processed on a rolling basis. *Application fee:* $55. Electronic applications accepted. *Application Contact:* Sandra Morgeson, 765-494-5434, E-mail: sandy@purdue.edu. *Associate Head,* Srinivasan Chandrasekar, 765-494-3623, Fax: 765-494-1299, E-mail: engi@ecn.purdue.edu.

School of Materials Engineering Students: 56 full-time (14 women), 7 part-time (4 women); includes 1 minority (African American), 30 international. 192 applicants, 16% accepted, 16 enrolled. *Faculty:* 20 full-time (2 women), 2 part-time/adjunct (0 women). Expenses: Contact institution. *Financial support:* Fellowships, research assistantships with full tuition reimbursements, teaching assistantships available. Support available to part-time students. Financial award applicants required to submit FAFSA. In 2006, 14 master's, 4 doctorates awarded. *Degree program information:* Part-time programs available. Offers materials engineering (MSMSE, PhD). *Application deadline:* For fall admission, 1/1 priority date for domestic students, 1/1 for international students. Applications are processed on a rolling basis. *Application fee:* $55. Electronic applications accepted. *Application Contact:* Vicki Cline, Academic Program Administrator, 765-494-4103, E-mail: msegrad@purdue.edu. *Graduate Coordinator,* David Johnson, 765-494-7009, E-mail: msegrad@purdue.edu.

School of Mechanical Engineering Students: 296 full-time (37 women), 67 part-time (8 women); includes 17 minority (2 African Americans, 1 American Indian/Alaska Native, 12 Asian Americans or Pacific Islanders, 2 Hispanic Americans), 191 international. 401 applicants, 42% accepted, 77 enrolled. *Faculty:* 55 full-time (4 women), 1 part-time/adjunct (0 women). Expenses: Contact institution. *Financial support:* Career-related internships or fieldwork available. Support available to part-time students. Financial award applicants required to submit FAFSA. In 2006, 81 master's, 35 doctorates awarded. Offers mechanical engineering (MS, MSE, MSME, PhD, Certificate). MS and PhD degree programs in biomedical engineering offered jointly with School of Electrical and Computer Engineering and School of Chemical Engineering. *Application deadline:* For fall admission, 3/1 priority date for domestic students, 1/31 priority date for international students; for spring admission, 10/1 for domestic students, 9/15 for international students. Applications are processed on a rolling basis. *Application fee:* $55. Electronic applications accepted. *Application Contact:* Julayne C. Mott, Graduate Administrator, 765-494-5729, Fax: 765-494-0539, E-mail: purdueme@ecn.purdue.edu. *Associate Head,* Arill K. Bajaj, 765-494-5730, Fax: 765-494-0539.

School of Nuclear Engineering Students: 37 full-time (2 women), 8 part-time, 32 international. 43 applicants, 100% accepted, 6 enrolled. *Faculty:* 11 full-time (2 women), 4 part-time/adjunct (1 woman). Expenses: Contact institution. *Financial support:* Fellowships with full tuition reimbursements, research assistantships with full tuition reimbursements, teaching assistantships with full tuition reimbursements available. Support available to part-time students. Financial award application deadline: 5/1; financial award applicants required to submit FAFSA. In 2006, 8 master's, 4 doctorates awarded. *Degree program information:* Part-time programs available. Offers nuclear engineering (MS, MSNE, PhD). *Application deadline:* For fall admission, 12/31 priority date for domestic and international students; for spring admission, 8/15 priority date for domestic and international students. Applications are processed on a rolling basis. *Application fee:* $55. Electronic applications accepted. *Application Contact:* Dr. Erica A Timmerman, Graduate Contact, 765-494-5741, Fax: 765-94-9570, E-mail: grad@ecn.purdue.edu. *Graduate Chair,* Chan Choi, 765-494-5742, Fax: 765-494-9570, E-mail: grad@ecn.purdue.edu.

Weldon School of Biomedical Engineering Students: 69 full-time (22 women); includes 15 minority (5 African Americans, 1 American Indian/Alaska Native, 7 Asian Americans or Pacific Islanders, 2 Hispanic Americans), 19 international. 292 applicants, 15% accepted, 12 enrolled. *Faculty:* 10 full-time (5 women), 4 part-time/adjunct (1 woman). Expenses: Contact institution. *Financial support:* Fellowships, research assistantships, teaching assistantships available. Support available to part-time students. Financial award applicants required to submit FAFSA. In 2006, 8 master's, 2 doctorates awarded. Offers biomedical engineering (MSBME, PhD). Degree programs offered jointly with School of Mechanical Engineering, School of Electrical and Computer Engineering, and School of Chemical Engineering. *Application deadline:* For fall admission, 1/5 priority date for domestic and international students. Applications are processed on a rolling basis. *Application fee:* $55. Electronic applications accepted. *Application Contact:* Jennifer Groh, Graduate

Purdue University (continued)

Administrator, 765-494-2982, Fax: 765-494-1193, E-mail: weldonbmegrad@purdue.edu. *Assistant Head*, Andrew Brightman, 765-494-3537, Fax: 765-494-1193.

College of Pharmacy and Pharmacal Sciences Students: 796 full-time (495 women), 51 part-time (31 women); includes 112 minority (41 African Americans, 52 Asian Americans or Pacific Islanders, 19 Hispanic Americans), 84 international. Average age 24. 1,077 applicants, 33% accepted, 70 enrolled. *Faculty:* 73 full-time (20 women), 65 part-time/adjunct (11 women). Expenses: Contact institution. *Financial support:* Fellowships, research assistantships, teaching assistantships, career-related internships or fieldwork, Federal Work-Study, scholarships/grants, and traineeships available. Support available to part-time students. Financial award applicants required to submit FAFSA. In 2006, 162 Pharm Ds, 20 master's, 20 doctorates awarded. *Degree program information:* Part-time programs available. Offers pharmacy and pharmacal sciences (Pharm D, MS, PhD, Certificate). *Application deadline:* Applications are processed on a rolling basis. *Application fee:* $55. Electronic applications accepted. *Application Contact:* Dr. G. Marc Loudon, Associate Dean for Graduate Programs, 765-494-1362, Fax: 765-494-7880, E-mail: marc.loudon@purdue.edu. *Dean*, Dr. Craig Svensson, 765-494-1368.

Graduate Programs in Pharmacy and Pharmacal Sciences Students: 160 full-time (89 women), 39 part-time (23 women); includes 18 minority (7 African Americans, 4 Asian Americans or Pacific Islanders, 7 Hispanic Americans), 64 international. Average age 28. 322 applicants, 35% accepted, 66 enrolled. *Faculty:* 78 full-time (25 women), 60 part-time/adjunct (7 women). Expenses: Contact institution. *Financial support:* Fellowships, research assistantships, teaching assistantships, career-related internships or fieldwork and traineeships available. Support available to part-time students. Financial award applicants required to submit FAFSA. In 2006, 20 master's, 20 doctorates awarded. *Degree program information:* Part-time programs available. Offers analytical medicinal chemistry (PhD); clinical pharmacy (MS, PhD); computational and biophysical medicinal chemistry (PhD); industrial and physical pharmacy (MS, PhD, Certificate); medicinal and bioorganic chemistry (PhD); medicinal biochemistry and molecular biology (PhD); medicinal chemistry and molecular pharmacology (MS, PhD); molecular pharmacology and toxicology (PhD); natural products and pharmacognosy (PhD); nuclear pharmacy (MS); pharmaceutics (PhD); pharmacy administration (MS, PhD); pharmacy practice (MS, PhD); radiopharmaceutical chemistry and nuclear pharmacy (PhD); regulatory quality compliance (MS, Certificate). *Application deadline:* Applications are processed on a rolling basis. *Application fee:* $55. Electronic applications accepted. *Associate Dean*, Dr. G. Marc Loudon, 765-494-1462, Fax: 765-494-7880, E-mail: marc.loudon@purdue.edu.

Graduate School Students: 4,858 full-time (1,880 women), 1,901 part-time (697 women); includes 591 minority (229 African Americans, 21 American Indian/Alaska Native, 183 Asian Americans or Pacific Islanders, 158 Hispanic Americans), 2,892 international. Average age 29. 11,744 applicants, 34% accepted, 1822 enrolled. *Faculty:* 1,678 full-time (379 women), 300 part-time/adjunct (73 women). Expenses: Contact institution. *Financial support:* Fellowships with tuition reimbursements, research assistantships with tuition reimbursements, teaching assistantships with tuition reimbursements, career-related internships or fieldwork, scholarships/grants, tuition waivers (full and partial), and instructorships available. Support available to part-time students. Financial award applicants required to submit FAFSA. In 2006, 1,420 master's, 566 doctorates, 2 other advanced degrees awarded. *Degree program information:* Part-time and evening/weekend programs available. Postbaccalaureate distance learning degree programs offered (no on-campus study). Offers life sciences (PhD). *Application deadline:* Applications are processed on a rolling basis. *Application fee:* $55. Electronic applications accepted. *Application Contact:* Graduate School Admissions, 765-494-2600, Fax: 765-494-0136, E-mail: gradinfo@purdue.edu. *Interim Dean*, Dr. Cindy H. Nakatsu, 765-494-2604, Fax: 765-494-0136.

Center for Education and Research in Information Assurance and Security (CERIAS) Expenses: Contact institution. Offers information security (MS). *Application Contact:* Graduate School Admissions, 765-494-2600, Fax: 765-494-0136, E-mail: gradinfo@purdue.edu.

College of Agriculture Students: 425 full-time (186 women), 104 part-time (40 women); includes 30 minority (13 African Americans, 7 Asian Americans or Pacific Islanders, 10 Hispanic Americans), 222 international. 591 applicants, 35% accepted, 134 enrolled. *Faculty:* 296 full-time (49 women), 60 part-time/adjunct (13 women). Expenses: Contact institution. *Financial support:* Fellowships with tuition reimbursements, research assistantships with tuition reimbursements, teaching assistantships with tuition reimbursements, career-related internships or fieldwork and tuition waivers (partial) available. Support available to part-time students. Financial award applicants required to submit FAFSA. In 2006, 85 master's, 59 doctorates awarded. *Degree program information:* Part-time programs available. Offers agricultural economics (MS, PhD); agriculture (EMBA, M Agr, MA, MS, MSF, PhD); agronomy (MS, PhD); animal sciences (MS, PhD); aquaculture, fisheries, aquatic science (MSF); aquaculture, fisheries, aquatic sciences (MS, PhD); biochemistry (MS, PhD); botany and plant pathology (MS, PhD); entomology (MS, PhD); food and agricultural business (EMBA); food science (MS, PhD); forest biology (MS, MSF, PhD); horticulture (M Agr, MS, PhD); natural resources and environmental policy (MS, MSF); natural resources environmental policy (PhD); quantitative resource analysis (MS, MSF, PhD); wildlife science (MS, MSF, PhD); wood science and technology (MS, MSF, PhD); youth development and agricultural education (MA, PhD). *Application deadline:* Applications are processed on a rolling basis. *Application fee:* $55. Electronic applications accepted. *Dean*, Dr. Victor L. Lechtenberg, 765-494-8392.

College of Consumer and Family Sciences Students: 129 full-time (98 women), 40 part-time (35 women); includes 16 minority (10 African Americans, 3 Asian Americans or Pacific Islanders, 3 Hispanic Americans), 91 international. Average age 30. 261 applicants, 31% accepted, 40 enrolled. *Faculty:* 54 full-time (24 women), 18 part-time/adjunct (13 women). Expenses: Contact institution. *Financial support:* Fellowships, research assistantships, teaching assistantships, career-related internships or fieldwork available. Support available to part-time students. Financial award applicants required to submit FAFSA. In 2006, 30 master's, 23 doctorates awarded. *Degree program information:* Part-time programs available. Offers consumer and family sciences (MS, PhD); consumer behavior (MS, PhD); developmental studies (MS, PhD); family and consumer economics (MS, PhD); family studies (MS, PhD); hospitality and tourism management (MS, PhD); marriage and family therapy (MS, PhD); nutrition (MS, PhD); retail management (MS, PhD); textile science (MS, PhD). *Application deadline:* Applications are processed on a rolling basis. *Application fee:* $55. Electronic applications accepted. *Dean*, Dr. Dennis A. Savaiano, 765-494-8210.

College of Liberal Arts Students: 792 full-time (499 women), 334 part-time (196 women); includes 107 minority (55 African Americans, 7 American Indian/Alaska Native, 20 Asian Americans or Pacific Islanders, 25 Hispanic Americans), 253 international. Average age 30. 1,801 applicants, 33% accepted, 293 enrolled. *Faculty:* 347 full-time (133 women), 33 part-time/adjunct (12 women). Expenses: Contact institution. *Financial support:* Fellowships, research assistantships, teaching assistantships, career-related internships or fieldwork, scholarships/grants, and tuition waivers (full) available. Support available to part-time students. Financial award applicants required to submit FAFSA. In 2006, 182 master's, 80 doctorates awarded. *Degree program information:* Part-time and evening/weekend programs available. Offers American studies (MA, PhD); anthropology (MS, PhD); art and design (MA); audiology (MS, Au D, PhD); communication (MA, MS, PhD); comparative literature (MA, PhD); creative writing (MFA); exercise, human physiology of movement and sport (PhD); French (MA, MAT, PhD); German (MA, MAT, PhD); health and fitness (MS); health promotion (MS); health promotion and disease prevention (PhD); history (MA, PhD); liberal arts (MA, MAT, MFA, MS, Au D, PhD); linguistics (MS, PhD); literature (MA, PhD); movement and sport science (MS); pedagogy and administration (MS); pedagogy of physical activity and health (PhD); philosophy (MA, PhD); political science (MA, PhD); psychological sciences (PhD); psychology of sport and exercise, and motor behavior (PhD); sociology (MS, PhD); Spanish (MA, MAT, PhD); speech and hearing science (MS, PhD); speech-language pathology (MS, PhD); theatre (MA, MFA). *Application deadline:* Applications are processed on a rolling basis. *Application fee:* $55. Electronic applications accepted. *Dean*, Dr. John J. Contreni, 765-496-2373, Fax: 765-494-3780.

College of Science Students: 861 full-time (296 women), 188 part-time (67 women); includes 87 minority (31 African Americans, 2 American Indian/Alaska Native, 18 Asian Americans or Pacific Islanders, 36 Hispanic Americans), 568 international. Average age 27. 2,265 applicants, 21% accepted, 199 enrolled. *Faculty:* 294 full-time (47 women), 21 part-time/adjunct (3 women). Expenses: Contact institution. *Financial support:* Fellowships with tuition reimbursements, research assistantships with tuition reimbursements, teaching assistantships with tuition reimbursements, career-related internships or fieldwork and tuition waivers (partial) available. Support available to part-time students. Financial award applicants required to submit FAFSA. In 2006, 112 master's, 120 doctorates awarded. *Degree program information:* Part-time programs available. Offers analytical chemistry (MS, PhD); biochemistry (MS, PhD); biophysics (PhD); cell and developmental biology (PhD); chemical education (MS, PhD); computer sciences (MS, PhD); earth and atmospheric sciences (MS, PhD); ecology, evolutionary and population biology (MS, PhD); genetics (MS, PhD); inorganic chemistry (MS, PhD); mathematics (MS, PhD); microbiology (MS, PhD); molecular biology (PhD); neurobiology (MS, PhD); organic chemistry (MS, PhD); physical chemistry (MS, PhD); physics (MS, PhD); plant physiology (PhD); science (MS, PhD, Certificate); statistics (MS, PhD, Certificate). *Application fee:* $55. Electronic applications accepted. *Application Contact:* Dr. Aditya Mathur, Associate Dean for Graduate Studies and International Programs, 765-496-2212, E-mail: apm@purdue.edu. *Dean*, Dr. Jeffrey S Vitter, 765-494-1730.

College of Technology Students: 79 full-time (24 women), 185 part-time (33 women); includes 24 minority (12 African Americans, 1 American Indian/Alaska Native, 6 Asian Americans or Pacific Islanders, 5 Hispanic Americans), 40 international. Average age 29. 173 applicants, 68% accepted, 90 enrolled. *Faculty:* 145 full-time (24 women), 5 part-time/adjunct (0 women). Expenses: Contact institution. *Financial support:* In 2006–07, 37 teaching assistantships were awarded; fellowships also available. Support available to part-time students. Financial award applicants required to submit FAFSA. In 2006, 67 master's awarded. Postbaccalaureate distance learning degree programs offered. Offers industrial technology (MS); technology (MS). *Application deadline:* For fall admission, 4/1 for domestic and international students; for spring admission, 10/1 for domestic students, 9/1 for international students. Applications are processed on a rolling basis. *Application fee:* $55. Electronic applications accepted. *Application Contact:* Debbie L. Hulsey, Graduate Contact, 765-494-6875, E-mail: dhulsey@purdue.edu. *Dean*, Dr. Dennis R Depew, 765-494-2552.

Krannert School of Management Expenses: Contact institution. *Financial support:* Application deadline: 2/15; Offers accounting (PhD); business (EMBA, MBA); business administration (MBA); economics (PhD); executive business administration (EMBA); finance (PhD); human resource management (MS); industrial administration (MSIA); management (EMBA, MBA, MS, MSIA, PhD); management information systems (PhD); marketing (PhD); operations management (PhD); organizational behavior and human resource management (MS, PhD); quantitative methods (PhD); strategic management (PhD). *Application deadline:* Applications are processed on a rolling basis. *Application fee:* $55. Electronic applications accepted. *Dean*, Dr. R. A. Cosier, 765-494-4366.

School of Education Students: 159 full-time (108 women), 238 part-time (147 women); includes 56 minority (32 African Americans, 5 American Indian/Alaska Native, 10 Asian Americans or Pacific Islanders, 9 Hispanic Americans), 71 international. Average age 35. 251 applicants, 65% accepted, 97 enrolled. *Faculty:* 58 full-time (32 women), 3 part-time/adjunct (all women). Expenses: Contact institution. *Financial support:* Fellowships with full tuition reimbursements, research assistantships with full tuition reimbursements, teaching assistantships with full tuition reimbursements, career-related internships or fieldwork and tuition waivers (full) available. Support available to part-time students. Financial award application deadline: 3/1; financial award applicants required to submit FAFSA. In 2006, 103 master's, 40 doctorates, 5 other advanced degrees awarded. *Degree program information:* Part-time and evening/weekend programs available. Offers administration (MS Ed, PhD, Ed S); agricultural and extension education (PhD, Ed S); agriculture and extension education (MS, MS Ed); art education (PhD); consumer and family sciences and extension education (MS Ed, PhD, Ed S); counseling and development (MS Ed, PhD); curriculum studies (MS Ed, PhD, Ed S); education (MS, MS Ed, PhD, Ed S); education of the gifted (MS Ed); educational psychology (MS Ed, PhD); educational technology (MS Ed, PhD, Ed S); elementary education (MS Ed); foreign language education (MS Ed, PhD, Ed S); foundations of education (MS Ed, PhD); higher education administration (MS Ed, PhD); industrial technology (PhD, Ed S); language arts (MS Ed, PhD, Ed S); literacy (MS Ed, PhD, Ed S); mathematics/science education (MS, MS Ed, PhD, Ed S); social studies (MS Ed, PhD); social studies education (Ed S); special education (MS Ed, PhD); vocational/industrial education (MS Ed, PhD, Ed S); vocational/technical education (MS Ed, PhD, Ed S). *Application deadline:* For fall admission, 1/15 for domestic students; for spring admission, 9/15 for domestic students. *Application fee:* $55. Electronic applications accepted. *Application Contact:* Lauren Franks, Graduate Admissions Specialist, 765-494-2345, E-mail: lfranks@purdue.edu. *Head*, Dr. George W Hynd, 765-494-2326, Fax: 765-496-1622.

School of Health Sciences Students: 38 full-time (18 women), 4 part-time (1 woman); includes 4 minority (1 African American, 1 Asian American or Pacific Islander, 2 Hispanic Americans), 12 international. Average age 32. 85 applicants, 46% accepted, 20 enrolled. *Faculty:* 10 full-time (0 women), 20 part-time/adjunct (2 women). Expenses: Contact institution. *Financial support:* In 2006–07, 10 students received support, including 5 fellowships, 2 research assistantships, 3 teaching assistantships; career-related internships or fieldwork and traineeships also available. Support available to part-time students. Financial award applicants required to submit FAFSA. In 2006, 9 master's, 5 doctorates awarded. *Degree program information:* Part-time programs available. Offers health sciences (MS, PhD). *Application deadline:* For fall admission, 5/15 for domestic and international students; for spring admission, 10/15 for domestic and international students. Applications are processed on a rolling basis. *Application fee:* $55. Electronic applications accepted. *Application Contact:* Dr. Wei Zheng, Graduate Chairperson, 765-494-1412, Fax: 765-496-1377, E-mail: wzheng@purdue.edu. *Head*, Dr. George A. Sandison, 765-494-7863, Fax: 765-496-1377, E-mail: sandison@purdue.edu.

School of Veterinary Medicine Students: 339 full-time (248 women), 27 part-time (18 women); includes 19 minority (5 African Americans, 4 Asian Americans or Pacific Islanders, 10 Hispanic Americans), 51 international. Average age 27. *Faculty:* 100 full-time (31 women), 8 part-time/adjunct (4 women). Expenses: Contact institution. *Financial support:* In 2006–07, 6 fellowships, 16 research assistantships, 2 teaching assistantships were awarded; career-related internships or fieldwork, Federal Work-Study, institutionally sponsored loans, scholarships/grants, and tuition waivers (full and partial) also available. Support available to part-time students. Financial award application deadline: 3/1; financial award applicants required to submit FAFSA. In 2006, 58 DVMs, 12 master's, 5 doctorates awarded. *Degree program information:* Part-time and evening/weekend programs available. Offers anatomy (MS, PhD); basic medical sciences (MS, PhD); biochemistry and molecular biology (MS, PhD); comparative epidemiology (MS, PhD); comparative pathobiology (MS, PhD); epidemiology (MS, PhD); immunology (MS, PhD); infectious diseases (MS, PhD); interdisciplinary genetics (PhD); laboratory animal medicine (MS, PhD); microbiology (MS, PhD); molecular virology (MS, PhD); parasitology (MS, PhD); pathobiology (MS, PhD); pharmacology (MS, PhD); physiology (MS, PhD); public health epidemiology (MS, PhD); toxicology (MS, PhD); veterinary anatomic pathology (MS, PhD); veterinary clinical pathology (MS, PhD); veterinary clinical sciences (MS, PhD); veterinary medicine (DVM, MS, PhD); virology (MS, PhD). *Application Contact:* Denise A. Ottinger, Director, Student Services and Admissions, 765-494-7893, Fax: 765-496-2891, E-mail: vetadmissions@purdue.edu. *Dean*, Dr. Willie Reed, 765-494-7608.

PURDUE UNIVERSITY CALUMET, Hammond, IN 46323-2094

General Information State-supported, coed, comprehensive institution. *Graduate housing:* On-campus housing not available.

GRADUATE UNITS

Graduate School *Degree program information:* Part-time and evening/weekend programs available. Electronic applications accepted.

School of Education Offers counseling and personnel services (MS Ed); educational administration (MS Ed); elementary education (MS Ed); instructional development (MS Ed); media sciences (MS Ed); secondary education (MS Ed).

School of Engineering, Mathematics, and Science *Degree program information:* Part-time and evening/weekend programs available. Postbaccalaureate distance learning degree programs offered (minimal on-campus study). Offers biology (MS); biology teaching (MS); biotechnology (MS); engineering (MSE); engineering, mathematics, and science (MAT, MS, MSE); mathematics (MAT, MS). Electronic applications accepted.

School of Liberal Arts and Sciences *Degree program information:* Part-time programs available. Offers communication (MA); English and philosophy (MA); history and political science (MA); liberal arts and sciences (MA, MS); marriage and family therapy (MS).

School of Management *Degree program information:* Part-time and evening/weekend programs available. Offers accountancy (M Acc); business administration (MBA). Electronic applications accepted.

School of Nursing *Degree program information:* Part-time programs available. Postbaccalaureate distance learning degree programs offered (minimal on-campus study). Offers nursing (MS). Electronic applications accepted.

PURDUE UNIVERSITY NORTH CENTRAL, Westville, IN 46391-9542

General Information State-supported, coed, comprehensive institution. *Graduate housing:* On-campus housing not available.

GRADUATE UNITS

Program in Education *Degree program information:* Part-time and evening/weekend programs available. Offers elementary education (MS Ed).

QUEENS COLLEGE OF THE CITY UNIVERSITY OF NEW YORK, Flushing, NY 11367-1597

General Information State and locally supported, coed, comprehensive institution. CGS member. *Enrollment:* 18,107 graduate, professional, and undergraduate students; 379 full-time matriculated graduate/professional students (282 women), 4,066 part-time matriculated graduate/professional students (2,883 women). *Enrollment by degree level:* 3,913 master's, 532 other advanced degrees. *Graduate faculty:* 582 full-time (244 women). *Graduate housing:* On-campus housing not available. *Student services:* Campus employment opportunities, career counseling, child daycare facilities, disabled student services, free psychological counseling, international student services, low-cost health insurance, multicultural affairs office, teacher training, writing training. *Library facilities:* Main library plus 1 other. *Online resources:* library catalog, web page, access to other libraries' catalogs. *Collection:* 1.1 million titles, 2,689 serial subscriptions, 35,721 audiovisual materials. *Research affiliation:* Brookhaven National Laboratory/SUNY Stony Brook (physics), The New York Times.

Computer facilities: 1,000 computers available on campus for general student use. A campuswide network can be accessed from off campus. Internet access is available. *Web address:* http://www.qc.cuny.edu/.

General Application Contact: Mario Caruso, Director of Graduate Admissions, 718-997-5200, Fax: 718-997-5193, E-mail: graduate_admissions@qc.edu.

GRADUATE UNITS

Division of Graduate Studies Students: 379 full-time (282 women), 4,066 part-time (2,883 women); includes 1,422 minority (431 African Americans, 74 American Indian/Alaska Native, 410 Asian Americans or Pacific Islanders, 507 Hispanic Americans). Average age 26. 3,040 applicants, 75% accepted, 1753 enrolled. *Faculty:* 582 full-time (244 women). Expenses: Contact institution. *Financial support:* Career-related internships or fieldwork, Federal Work-Study, institutionally sponsored loans, tuition waivers (partial), unspecified assistantships, and adjunct lectureships available. Support available to part-time students. Financial award application deadline: 4/1; financial award applicants required to submit FAFSA. In 2006, 1,319 master's, 134 other advanced degrees awarded. *Degree program information:* Part-time and evening/weekend programs available. *Application deadline:* For fall admission, 4/1 priority date for domestic students, 3/1 priority date for international students; for winter admission, 11/1 priority date for domestic students, 10/1 priority date for international students; for spring admission, 11/1 priority date for domestic students, 10/1 priority date for international students. Applications are processed on a rolling basis. *Application fee:* $125. *Application Contact:* Mario Caruso, Director of Graduate Admissions, 718-997-5200, Fax: 718-997-5193, E-mail: graduate_admissions@qc.edu. *Acting Dean of Research and Graduate Services,* Dr. Steven Schwarz, 718-997-5190, Fax: 718-997-5493, E-mail: steven_schwarz@qc.edu.

Arts and Humanities Division Students: 65 full-time (45 women), 301 part-time (197 women). Average age 26. 559 applicants, 59% accepted, 227 enrolled. *Faculty:* 136 full-time (61 women). Expenses: Contact institution. *Financial support:* Career-related internships or fieldwork, Federal Work-Study, institutionally sponsored loans, tuition waivers (partial), and adjunct lectureships available. Support available to part-time students. Financial award application deadline: 4/1; financial award applicants required to submit FAFSA. In 2006, 118 degrees awarded. *Degree program information:* Part-time and evening/weekend programs available. Offers applied linguistics (MA); art history (MA); arts and humanities (MA, MFA, MS Ed); creative writing (MA); English language and literature (MA); fine arts (MFA); French (MA); Italian (MA); music (MA); Spanish (MA); speech pathology (MA); teaching English to speakers of other languages (MS Ed). *Application deadline:* Applications are processed on a rolling basis. *Application fee:* $125. *Application Contact:* Mario Caruso, Director of Graduate Admissions, 718-997-5200, Fax: 718-997-5193, E-mail: graduate_admissions@qc.edu. *Dean,* Dr. Tamara Evans, 718-997-5790, E-mail: tamara_evans@qc.edu.

Division of Education Students: 211 full-time (168 women), 2,185 part-time (1,640 women). 1,518 applicants, 73% accepted, 893 enrolled. *Faculty:* 73 full-time (50 women). Expenses: Contact institution. *Financial support:* Career-related internships or fieldwork, Federal Work-Study, institutionally sponsored loans, and tuition waivers (partial) available. Support available to part-time students. Financial award application deadline: 4/1; financial award applicants required to submit FAFSA. In 2006, 671 master's, 124 other advanced degrees awarded. *Degree program information:* Part-time and evening/weekend programs available. Offers art (MS Ed); bilingual education (MS Ed); biology (MS Ed, AC); chemistry (MS Ed, AC); childhood education (MA); counselor education (MS Ed); early childhood education (MA); earth sciences (MS Ed, AC); education (MA, MS Ed, AC); educational leadership (AC); elementary education (MS Ed, AC); English (MS Ed, AC); French (MS Ed, AC); Italian (MS Ed, AC); literacy (MS Ed); mathematics (MS Ed, AC); music (MS Ed, AC); physics (MS Ed, AC); school psychology (MS Ed, AC); social studies (MS Ed, AC); Spanish (MS Ed, AC); special education (MS Ed). *Application deadline:* For fall admission, 4/1 for domestic students; for spring admission, 11/1 for domestic students. Applications are processed on a rolling basis. *Application fee:* $125. *Application Contact:* Mario Caruso, Director of Graduate Admissions, 718-997-5200, Fax: 718-997-5193, E-mail: graduate_admissions@qc.edu. *Dean,* Dr. Penny Hammrich, 718-997-5220.

Mathematics and Natural Sciences Division Students: 48 full-time (26 women), 300 part-time (157 women). Average age 26. 374 applicants, 85% accepted, 221 enrolled. *Faculty:* 149 full-time (46 women). Expenses: Contact institution. *Financial support:* Career-related internships or fieldwork, Federal Work-Study, institutionally sponsored loans, tuition waivers (partial), unspecified assistantships, and adjunct lectureships available. Support available to part-time students. Financial award application deadline: 4/1; financial award applicants required to submit FAFSA. In 2006, 97 degrees awarded. *Degree program information:* Part-time and evening/weekend programs available. Offers biochemistry (MA); biology (MA); chemistry (MA); clinical behavioral applications in mental health settings (MA); computer science (MA); earth and environmental sciences (MA); home economics (MS Ed); mathematics (MA); mathematics and natural sciences (MA, MS Ed, PhD); physical education and exercise sciences (MS Ed); physics (MA, PhD); psychology (MA). *Application deadline:* For fall admission, 4/1 for domestic students; for spring admission, 11/1 for domestic students. Applications are processed on a rolling basis. *Application fee:* $125. *Application Contact:* Mario Caruso, Director of Graduate Admissions, 718-997-5200, Fax: 718-997-5193, E-mail: graduate_admissions@qc.edu. *Dean,* Dr. Thomas Strekas, 718-997-4105, E-mail: thomas_strekas@qc.edu.

Social Science Division Students: 43 full-time (36 women), 704 part-time (494 women). 589 applicants, 91% accepted, 412 enrolled. *Faculty:* 98 full-time (37 women). Expenses: Contact institution. *Financial support:* Career-related internships or fieldwork, Federal Work-Study, institutionally sponsored loans, and tuition waivers (partial) available. Support available to part-time students. Financial award application deadline: 4/1; financial award applicants required to submit FAFSA. In 2006, 332 degrees awarded. *Degree program information:* Part-time and evening/weekend programs available. Offers accounting (MS); history (MA); liberal studies (MALS); library and information studies (MLS, AC); social science (MA, MALS, MASS, MLS, MS, AC); social sciences (MASS); sociology (MA); urban studies (MA). *Application deadline:* For fall admission, 4/1 for domestic students; for spring admission, 11/1 for domestic students. Applications are processed on a rolling basis. *Application fee:* $125. *Application Contact:* Mario Caruso, Director of Graduate Admissions, 718-997-5200, Fax: 718-997-5193, E-mail: graduate_admissions@qc.edu. *Dean,* Dr. Elizabeth Hendrey, 718-997-5210.

See Close-Up on page 997.

QUEEN'S UNIVERSITY AT KINGSTON, Kingston, ON K7L 3N6, Canada

General Information Province-supported, coed, university. *Graduate housing:* Rooms and/or apartments available to single students and available on a first-come, first-served basis to married students. Housing application deadline: 6/15.

GRADUATE UNITS

Faculty of Law *Degree program information:* Part-time programs available. Offers law (LL B, LL M).

Queens School of Business Offers business (M Sc, MBA, PhD); business administration (MBA); business administration for science and technology (MBA).

Queen's Theological College *Degree program information:* Part-time programs available. Offers theology (M Div, MTS).

School of Graduate Studies and Research *Degree program information:* Part-time programs available.

Faculty of Applied Science *Degree program information:* Part-time programs available. Offers applied science (M Sc, M Sc Eng, PhD); chemical engineering (M Sc, M Sc Eng, PhD); civil engineering (M Sc, M Sc Eng, PhD); electrical and computer engineering (M Sc, M Sc Eng, PhD); mechanical engineering (M Sc, M Sc Eng, PhD); mining engineering (M Sc, M Sc Eng, PhD). Electronic applications accepted.

Faculty of Arts and Sciences *Degree program information:* Part-time programs available. Offers arts and sciences (M Sc, M Sc Eng, MA, MTS, PhD); biology (M Sc, PhD); brain behavior and cognitive science (MA, PhD); chemistry (M Sc, PhD); classics, Greek, Latin (MA); clinical psychology (MA, PhD); computing (M Sc, PhD); developmental psychology (MA, PhD); English language and literature (MA, PhD); French studies (MA, PhD); geography (M Sc, MA, PhD); geological sciences and geological engineering (M Sc, M Sc Eng, PhD); German language and literature (MA, PhD); mathematics (M Sc, M Sc Eng, PhD); philosophy (MA, PhD); physics (M Sc, M Sc Eng, PhD); political studies (MA, PhD); religious studies (MA); social personality psychology (MA, PhD); sociology (MA, PhD); Spanish (MA); statistics (M Sc, M Sc Eng, PhD). Electronic applications accepted.

Faculty of Education *Degree program information:* Part-time programs available. Offers education (M Ed, PhD).

Faculty of Health Sciences *Degree program information:* Part-time programs available. Offers anatomy and cell biology (M Sc, PhD); biochemistry (M Sc, PhD); epidemiology (M Sc); health sciences (M Sc, PhD); microbiology and immunology (M Sc, PhD); nursing (M Sc); pathology (M Sc, PhD); pharmacology and toxicology (M Sc, PhD); physiology (M Sc, PhD); rehabilitation therapy (M Sc, PhD). Electronic applications accepted.

School of Industrial Relations *Degree program information:* Part-time programs available. Offers industrial relations (MIR).

School of Physical and Health Education *Degree program information:* Part-time programs available. Offers applied exercise science (PhD); biomechanics/ergonomics (M Sc); exercise physiology rehabilitation (M Sc); social psychology of sport and exercise rehabilitation (MA); sociology of sport (MA). Electronic applications accepted.

School of Policy Studies *Degree program information:* Part-time programs available. Offers policy studies (MPA).

School of Urban and Regional Planning *Degree program information:* Part-time programs available. Offers urban and regional planning (M Pl).

School of Medicine Offers medicine (MD). Electronic applications accepted.

QUEENS UNIVERSITY OF CHARLOTTE, Charlotte, NC 28274-0002

General Information Independent-religious, coed, comprehensive institution. *Enrollment:* 2,118 graduate, professional, and undergraduate students; 150 full-time matriculated graduate/professional students (91 women), 255 part-time matriculated graduate/professional students (173 women). *Enrollment by degree level:* 405 master's. *Graduate faculty:* 24 full-time (9 women), 11 part-time/adjunct (8 women). *Graduate housing:* On-campus housing not available. *Student services:* Campus safety program, international student services, teacher training. *Library facilities:* Everett Library plus 1 other. *Online resources:* library catalog, web page, access to other libraries' catalogs. *Collection:* 126,242 titles, 592 serial subscriptions.

Computer facilities: Computer purchase and lease plans are available. 125 computers available on campus for general student use. A campuswide network can be accessed from student residence rooms and from off campus. Internet access is available. *Web address:* http://www.queens.edu/.

General Application Contact: Robert Mobley, Director of MBA Admissions, 704-337-2224, Fax: 704-337-2594.

GRADUATE UNITS

College of Arts and Sciences Students: 78 full-time (60 women); includes 6 minority (all African Americans) 43 applicants, 65% accepted, 25 enrolled. *Faculty:* 4 full-time (1 woman), 2 part-time/adjunct (1 woman). Expenses: Contact institution. In 2006, 27 degrees awarded. *Degree program information:* Part-time programs available. Postbaccalaureate distance learning degree programs offered (minimal on-campus study). Offers creative writing (MFA). *Application deadline:* Applications are processed on a rolling basis. *Application fee:* $45. Electronic applications accepted. *Application Contact:* Jennifer Matz, Information Contact, 704-337-2404, Fax: 704-337-2503. *Dean,* Dr. Betty J. Powell, 704-337-2463, Fax: 704-337-2325.

Hayworth College Students: 20 full-time (19 women), 128 part-time (115 women); includes 22 minority (15 African Americans, 1 American Indian/Alaska Native, 6 Hispanic Americans), 3 international. Average age 29. 82 applicants, 83% accepted, 47 enrolled. *Faculty:* 9 full-time (6 women), 6 part-time/adjunct (all women). Expenses: Contact institution. *Financial support:* In 2006–07, 30 students received support, including 5 fellowships; institutionally sponsored loans also available. Support available to part-time students. Financial award applicants required to submit FAFSA. In 2006, 64 degrees awarded. *Degree program information:* Part-time and evening/weekend programs available. Offers elementary education (MAT); organizational communications (MA). *Application deadline:* Applications are processed on a rolling basis. *Application fee:* $40. Electronic applications accepted. *Application Contact:* Holly Boyd, Director of Admissions, 704-337-2574, Fax: 704-337-2415. *Dean,* Dr. Darrel L. Miller, 704-337-2574, Fax: 704-337-2415.

Division of Nursing Students: 2 full-time (both women), 17 part-time (13 women); includes 6 minority (all African Americans) Average age 27. 11 applicants, 82% accepted, 9 enrolled. *Faculty:* 2 full-time (both women), 3 part-time/adjunct (all women). Expenses: Contact institution. In 2006, 10 degrees awarded. Offers nursing management (MSN). *Application deadline:* Applications are processed on a rolling basis. *Application fee:* $40. Electronic applications accepted. *Application Contact:* Holly Boyd, Director of Admissions, 704-337-2574, Fax: 704-337-2415. *Chair,* Dr. William K. Cody, 704-337-2542.

Queens University of Charlotte (continued)

McColl Graduate School of Business Students: 52 full-time (12 women), 127 part-time (58 women); includes 25 minority (14 African Americans, 6 Asian Americans or Pacific Islanders, 5 Hispanic Americans), 3 international. Average age 31. 62 applicants, 85% accepted, 37 enrolled. *Faculty:* 11 full-time (2 women), 3 part-time/adjunct (1 woman). Expenses: Contact institution. *Financial support:* In 2006–07, 40 fellowships were awarded; institutionally sponsored loans also available. Support available to part-time students. In 2006, 55 degrees awarded. *Degree program information:* Part-time and evening/weekend programs available. Offers business (EMBA, MBA). *Application deadline:* Applications are processed on a rolling basis. *Application fee:* $50. Electronic applications accepted. *Application Contact:* Robert Mobley, Director of MBA Admissions, 704-337-2224, Fax: 704-337-2594. *Chair,* Terry Broderick, 704-337-2234.

QUINCY UNIVERSITY, Quincy, IL 62301-2699

General Information Independent-religious, coed, comprehensive institution. *Enrollment:* 1,250 graduate, professional, and undergraduate students; 40 full-time matriculated graduate/professional students (24 women), 152 part-time matriculated graduate/professional students (115 women). *Enrollment by degree level:* 192 master's. *Graduate faculty:* 14 full-time (7 women), 12 part-time/adjunct (6 women). *Graduate housing:* On-campus housing not available. *Student services:* Campus safety program, career counseling, exercise/wellness program, free psychological counseling, international student services, teacher training. *Library facilities:* Brenner Library. *Online resources:* library catalog, web page, access to other libraries' catalogs. *Collection:* 204,557 titles, 365 serial subscriptions, 9,293 audiovisual materials.

Computer facilities: 190 computers available on campus for general student use. A campuswide network can be accessed from student residence rooms and from off campus. Internet access and online class registration are available. *Web address:* http://www.quincy.edu/.

General Application Contact: Syndi Peck, Director of Admissions, 217-228-5215, Fax: 217-228-5648, E-mail: admissions@quincy.edu.

GRADUATE UNITS

Division of Business Students: 10 full-time (4 women), 34 part-time (18 women); includes 1 minority (Hispanic American), 2 international. Average age 29. *Faculty:* 6 full-time (3 women). Expenses: Contact institution. *Financial support:* In 2006–07, 26 students received support. Available to part-time students. Applicants required to submit FAFSA. In 2006, 14 degrees awarded. *Degree program information:* Part-time and evening/weekend programs available. Offers business (MBA). *Application deadline:* Applications are processed on a rolling basis. *Application fee:* $25. *Application Contact:* Kevin Brown, Director of Admissions, 217-228-5210, Fax: 217-228-5648, E-mail: admissions@quincy.edu. *Director, MBA Program,* Dr. John Palmer, 217-228-5387, E-mail: palmejo@quincy.edu.

Division of Education Students: 25 full-time (15 women), 61 part-time (47 women); includes 4 minority (1 Asian American or Pacific Islander, 3 Hispanic Americans). Average age 34. *Faculty:* 4 full-time (3 women), 9 part-time/adjunct (5 women). Expenses: Contact institution. *Financial support:* In 2006–07, 45 students received support. Available to part-time students. Applicants required to submit FAFSA. In 2006, 22 degrees awarded. *Degree program information:* Part-time programs available. Offers education (MS Ed). *Application deadline:* Applications are processed on a rolling basis. *Application fee:* $25. *Application Contact:* Syndi Peck, Director of Admissions, 217-228-5215, Fax: 217-228-5648, E-mail: admissions@quincy.edu. *Director,* Dr. Alice Mills, 217-228-5420, E-mail: millsal@quincy.edu.

QUINNIPIAC UNIVERSITY, Hamden, CT 06518-1940

General Information Independent, coed, comprehensive institution. *Enrollment:* 7,341 graduate, professional, and undergraduate students; 531 full-time matriculated graduate/professional students (377 women), 314 part-time matriculated graduate/professional students (189 women). *Enrollment by degree level:* 814 master's, 31 doctoral. *Tuition:* Part-time $675 per credit. *Required fees:* $30 per credit. *Graduate housing:* On-campus housing not available. *Student services:* Campus employment opportunities, campus safety program, career counseling, exercise/wellness program, free psychological counseling, international student services, low-cost health insurance, multicultural affairs office. *Library facilities:* Arnold Bernhard Library plus 1 other. *Online resources:* library catalog, web page, access to other libraries' catalogs. *Collection:* 285,000 titles, 5,500 serial subscriptions.

Computer facilities: Computer purchase and lease plans are available. 600 computers available on campus for general student use. A campuswide network can be accessed from student residence rooms and from off campus. Internet access and online class registration are available. *Web address:* http://www.quinnipiac.edu/.

General Application Contact: Information Contact, 800-462-1944, Fax: 203-582-3443, E-mail: graduate@quinnipiac.edu.

GRADUATE UNITS

Division of Education Students: 147 full-time (116 women); includes 10 minority (2 African Americans, 8 Hispanic Americans), 1 international. Average age 26. 145 applicants, 91% accepted, 110 enrolled. *Faculty:* 7 full-time (5 women), 23 part-time/adjunct (14 women). Expenses: Contact institution. *Financial support:* Career-related internships or fieldwork, tuition waivers (partial), and unspecified assistantships available. Financial award application deadline: 4/15; financial award applicants required to submit FAFSA. In 2006, 101 degrees awarded. *Degree program information:* Part-time programs available. Offers biology (MAT); chemistry (MAT); education (MAT); elementary education (MAT); English (MAT); French (MAT); history/social studies (MAT); mathematics (MAT); physics (MAT); Spanish (MAT). *Application deadline:* For fall admission, 7/30 priority date for domestic students; for spring admission, 12/15 priority date for domestic students. Applications are processed on a rolling basis. *Application fee:* $45. Electronic applications accepted. *Application Contact:* 800-462-1944, Fax: 203-582-3443, E-mail: graduate@quinnipiac.edu. *Dean—Division of Education, College of Liberal Arts,* Dr. Cynthia Dubea, 203-582-8730, Fax: 203-582-8709, E-mail: cynthia.dubea@quinnipiac.edu.

School of Business Students: 76 full-time (31 women), 157 part-time (63 women); includes 25 minority (6 African Americans, 1 American Indian/Alaska Native, 11 Asian Americans or Pacific Islanders, 7 Hispanic Americans), 14 international. Average age 27. 135 applicants, 70% accepted, 65 enrolled. *Faculty:* 26 full-time (6 women), 9 part-time/adjunct (3 women). Expenses: Contact institution. *Financial support:* Career-related internships or fieldwork, tuition waivers (partial), and unspecified assistantships available. Support available to part-time students. Financial award application deadline: 4/15; financial award applicants required to submit FAFSA. In 2006, 107 degrees awarded. *Degree program information:* Part-time and evening/weekend programs available. Offers accounting (MBA); business (MBA, MS); chartered financial analyst (MBA); economics (MBA); finance (MBA); health care management (MBA); healthcare management (MBA); information systems (MS); information systems management (MBA); international business (MBA); management (MBA); marketing (MBA). *Application deadline:* For fall admission, 7/30 priority date for domestic students, 5/30 priority date for international students; for spring admission, 12/15 priority date for domestic students, 10/15 priority date for international students. Applications are processed on a rolling basis. *Application fee:* $45. Electronic applications accepted. *Application Contact:* 800-462-1944, Fax: 203-582-3443, E-mail: graduate@quinnipiac.edu. *Dean,* Dr. Mark Thompson, 203-582-8914, Fax: 203-582-8664, E-mail: mark.thompson@quinnipiac.edu.

School of Communications Students: 36 full-time (18 women), 52 part-time (30 women); includes 13 minority (10 African Americans, 1 Asian American or Pacific Islander, 2 Hispanic Americans), 3 international. Average age 28. 68 applicants, 90% accepted, 45 enrolled. *Faculty:* 7 full-time (2 women), 11 part-time/adjunct (1 woman). Expenses: Contact institution. *Financial support:* In 2006–07, 1 fellowship with full tuition reimbursement was awarded; career-related internships or fieldwork and unspecified assistantships also available. Support available to part-time students. Financial award application deadline: 4/15; financial award applicants required to submit FAFSA. In 2006, 45 degrees awarded. *Degree program information:* Part-time and evening/weekend programs available. Offers communications (MS); interactive communications (MS); journalism (MS). *Application deadline:* For fall admission, 7/30 priority date for domestic students, 5/30 priority date for international students; for spring admission, 12/15 priority date for domestic students, 10/15 priority date for international students. Applications are processed on a rolling basis. *Application fee:* $45. Electronic applications accepted. *Application Contact:* Scott Farber, E-mail: graduate@quinnipiac.edu. *Dean,* Dr. David Donnelly, 203-582-3641, Fax: 203-582-5310, E-mail: david.donnelly@quinnipiac.edu.

School of Health Sciences Students: 272 full-time (212 women), 105 part-time (96 women); includes 54 minority (14 African Americans, 1 American Indian/Alaska Native, 23 Asian Americans or Pacific Islanders, 16 Hispanic Americans), 8 international. Average age 27. 642 applicants, 35% accepted, 186 enrolled. *Faculty:* 49 full-time (33 women), 67 part-time/adjunct (38 women). Expenses: Contact institution. *Financial support:* Career-related internships or fieldwork, traineeships, tuition waivers (partial), and unspecified assistantships available. Support available to part-time students. Financial award application deadline: 4/15; financial award applicants required to submit FAFSA. In 2006, 201 master's, 1 other advanced degree awarded. Offers adult nurse practitioner (MSN, Post Master's Certificate); biomedical sciences (MHS); family nurse practitioner (MSN, Post Master's Certificate); forensic nurse clinical specialist (MSN, Post Master's Certificate); health sciences (MHS, MOT, MS, MSN, DPT, Post Master's Certificate); laboratory management (MHS); microbiology (MHS); molecular and cell biology (MS); occupational therapy (MOT); pathologists' assistant (MHS); physical therapy (DPT); physician assistant (MHS). *Application deadline:* For fall admission, 5/30 priority date for international students; for spring admission, 10/15 priority date for international students. Applications are processed on a rolling basis. *Application fee:* $45. Electronic applications accepted. *Application Contact:* 800-462-1944, Fax: 203-582-3443, E-mail: graduate@quinnipiac.edu. *Dean,* Dr. Edward O'Connor, 203-582-8710, Fax: 203-582-8706.

School of Law Students: 393 full-time (202 women), 153 part-time (79 women); includes 52 minority (10 African Americans, 2 American Indian/Alaska Native, 28 Asian Americans or Pacific Islanders, 12 Hispanic Americans). Average age 28. 2,550 applicants, 24% accepted, 132 enrolled. *Faculty:* 33 full-time (15 women), 36 part-time/adjunct (10 women). Expenses: Contact institution. *Financial support:* In 2006–07, 516 students received support, including 23 fellowships (averaging $1,330 per year), 47 research assistantships (averaging $620 per year); career-related internships or fieldwork, Federal Work-Study, and scholarships/grants also available. Support available to part-time students. Financial award application deadline: 4/15; financial award applicants required to submit FAFSA. In 2006, 205 degrees awarded. *Degree program information:* Part-time and evening/weekend programs available. Offers health law (LL M); law (JD). *Application deadline:* For fall admission, 3/1 priority date for domestic students. Applications are processed on a rolling basis. *Application fee:* $40. Electronic applications accepted. *Application Contact:* Edwin Wilkes, Executive Dean of Law School Admissions, 203-582-3400, Fax: 203-582-3339, E-mail: ladm@quinnipiac.edu. *Dean,* Brad Saxton, 203-582-3200, Fax: 203-582-3209, E-mail: ladm@quinnipiac.edu.

RABBI ISAAC ELCHANAN THEOLOGICAL SEMINARY, New York, NY 10033-2807

General Information Independent-religious, men only, graduate-only institution. *Graduate housing:* Rooms and/or apartments guaranteed to single students and available on a first-come, first-served basis to married students. Housing application deadline: 6/1.

GRADUATE UNITS

Graduate Program Offers theology (Certificate of Advanced Ordination, Certificate of Ordination).

RABBINICAL ACADEMY MESIVTA RABBI CHAIM BERLIN, Brooklyn, NY 11230-4715

General Information Independent-religious, men only, comprehensive institution. *Enrollment:* 90 full-time matriculated graduate/professional students. *Graduate faculty:* 4 full-time. *Graduate housing:* Room and/or apartments available to single students; on-campus housing not available to married students. Housing application deadline: 9/30. *Student services:* Campus employment opportunities, career counseling, international student services.

General Application Contact: Eli Rabinowitz, Associate Director, 718-377-0777, Fax: 718-338-5578, E-mail: eli.rabinowitz@myrcb.org.

GRADUATE UNITS

School of Talmudic Law and Rabbinics Students: 90 full-time (0 women), 26 international. Average age 23. 25 applicants, 80% accepted. *Faculty:* 4 full-time. Expenses: Contact institution. *Financial support:* In 2006–07, 20 research assistantships, 10 teaching assistantships were awarded; fellowships, career-related internships or fieldwork and Federal Work-Study also available. Support available to part-time students. Financial award application deadline: 9/30. In 2006, 30 degrees awarded. Offers Talmudic law and rabbinics (Advanced Talmudic Degree, Second Talmudic Degree). *Application Contact:* Eli Rabinowitz, Associate Director, 718-377-0777, Fax: 718-338-5578, E-mail: eli.rabinowitz@myrcb.org. *President,* Rabbi Aaron Schechter, 718-377-0777.

RABBINICAL COLLEGE BETH SHRAGA, Monsey, NY 10952-3035

General Information Independent-religious, men only, comprehensive institution.

GRADUATE UNITS

Graduate Programs Offers theology).

RABBINICAL COLLEGE BOBOVER YESHIVA B'NEI ZION, Brooklyn, NY 11219

General Information Independent-religious, men only, comprehensive institution. *Graduate housing:* Room and/or apartments available to single students; on-campus housing not available to married students.

GRADUATE UNITS

Graduate Programs Offers theology).

RABBINICAL COLLEGE CH'SAN SOFER, Brooklyn, NY 11204

General Information Independent-religious, men only, comprehensive institution.

GRADUATE UNITS

Graduate Programs Offers theology).

RABBINICAL COLLEGE OF LONG ISLAND, Long Beach, NY 11561-3305

General Information Independent-religious, men only, comprehensive institution.

GRADUATE UNITS

Graduate Programs Offers theology).

RABBINICAL SEMINARY M'KOR CHAIM, Brooklyn, NY 11219

General Information Independent-religious, men only, comprehensive institution.

GRADUATE UNITS

Graduate Programs Offers theology).

RABBINICAL SEMINARY OF AMERICA, Flushing, NY 11367

General Information Independent-religious, men only, comprehensive institution. *Enrollment:* 207 full-time matriculated graduate/professional students. *Graduate faculty:* 7 full-time (0 women), 4 part-time/adjunct (0 women). *Tuition:* Full-time $6,000. *Graduate housing:* Room and/or apartments available to single students; on-campus housing not available to married students. Typical cost: $4,000 (including board). Housing application deadline: 6/15. *Student services:* Career counseling, free psychological counseling, low-cost health insurance. *Library* *facilities:* Rabbinical Seminary of America Otzar HaSeforim Library plus 3 others. *Collection:* 30,000 titles, 50 serial subscriptions.

General Application Contact: Abraham Semnel, Registrar, 718-268-4700 Ext. 122.

GRADUATE UNITS

Graduate Programs Students: 207 full-time. *Faculty:* 7 full-time, 4 part-time/adjunct. Expenses: Contact institution. School offers a master's and first professional degree. *Application Contact:* Abraham Semnel, Registrar, 718-268-4700 Ext. 122.

RADFORD UNIVERSITY, Radford, VA 24142

General Information State-supported, coed, comprehensive institution. CGS member. *Enrollment:* 9,220 graduate, professional, and undergraduate students; 501 full-time matriculated graduate/professional students (389 women), 585 part-time matriculated graduate/professional students (463 women). *Enrollment by degree level:* 915 master's, 171 other advanced degrees. *Graduate faculty:* 111 full-time (54 women), 36 part-time/adjunct (24 women). Tuition, state resident: full-time $4,680; part-time $260 per credit hour. Tuition, nonresident: full-time $8,604; part-time $478 per credit hour. *Graduate housing:* Room and/or apartments guaranteed to single students; on-campus housing not available to married students. Housing application deadline: 5/1. *Student services:* Campus employment opportunities, campus safety program, career counseling, disabled student services, exercise/wellness program, free psychological counseling, international student services, low-cost health insurance, multicultural affairs office, teacher training, writing training. *Library facilities:* McConnell Library plus 1 other. *Online resources:* library catalog, web page, access to other libraries' catalogs. *Collection:* 377,110 titles, 4,801 serial subscriptions, 16,388 audiovisual materials. *Research affiliation:* National Science Foundation (biology, physical science, mathematics), NASA (physical science), Department of Transportation (communications), State Government (communications, physical science, social science, business and management, education), Department of Defense (psychology), U.S. Army (computer science).

Computer facilities: 500 computers available on campus for general student use. A campuswide network can be accessed from student residence rooms and from off campus. Internet access and online class registration, online financial aid status and student accounts payable are available. *Web address:* http://www.radford.edu/.

General Application Contact: Graduate Admissions Office, 540-831-5431, Fax: 540-831-6061, E-mail: gradcollege@radford.edu.

GRADUATE UNITS

Graduate College Students: 501 full-time (389 women), 585 part-time (463 women); includes 116 minority (83 African Americans, 2 American Indian/Alaska Native, 19 Asian Americans or Pacific Islanders, 12 Hispanic Americans). Average age 31. 524 applicants, 76% accepted, 258 enrolled. *Faculty:* 111 full-time (54 women), 36 part-time/adjunct (24 women). Expenses: Contact institution. *Financial support:* In 2006–07, 384 students received support, including 257 research assistantships with partial tuition reimbursements available (averaging $8,000 per year), 22 teaching assistantships with partial tuition reimbursements available (averaging $8,700 per year); career-related internships or fieldwork, Federal Work-Study, institutionally sponsored loans, scholarships/grants, and unspecified assistantships also available. Financial award application deadline: 3/1; financial award applicants required to submit FAFSA. In 2006, 261 master's, 10 other advanced degrees awarded. *Degree program information:* Part-time and evening/weekend programs available. Postbaccalaureate distance learning degree programs offered (minimal on-campus study). *Application deadline:* For fall admission, 3/1 priority date for domestic students, 4/1 for international students; for spring admission, 10/1 for domestic students, 8/1 for international students. Applications are processed on a rolling basis. *Application fee:* $40. Electronic applications accepted. *Application Contact:* Sharon D. Gunter, Graduate Admissions and Coordinator, 540-831-5431, Fax: 540-831-6061, E-mail: gradcollege@radford.edu. *Dean,* Dr. Carole L. Seyfrit, 540-831-5724, Fax: 540-831-6061, E-mail: gradcollege@radford.edu.

College of Arts and Sciences Students: 156 full-time (109 women), 57 part-time (35 women); includes 24 minority (14 African Americans, 1 American Indian/Alaska Native, 4 Asian Americans or Pacific Islanders, 5 Hispanic Americans). Average age 27. 200 applicants, 59% accepted, 69 enrolled. *Faculty:* 38 full-time (17 women). Expenses: Contact institution. *Financial support:* In 2006–07, 140 students received support, including 102 research assistantships with partial tuition reimbursements available (averaging $8,000 per year), 18 teaching assistantships with partial tuition reimbursements available (averaging $8,700 per year); career-related internships or fieldwork, Federal Work-Study, institutionally sponsored loans, scholarships/grants, and unspecified assistantships also available. Financial award application deadline: 3/1; financial award applicants required to submit FAFSA. In 2006, 66 master's, 10 other advanced degrees awarded. *Degree program information:* Part-time and evening/weekend programs available. Postbaccalaureate distance learning degree programs offered (minimal on-campus study). Offers arts and sciences (MA, MS, Psy D, Ed S); clinical psychology (MA, MS); corporate and professional communication (MS); counseling psychology (Psy D); criminal justice (MA, MS); English (MA, MS); experimental psychology (MA); industrial-organizational psychology (MA, MS); school psychology (Ed S). *Application deadline:* For fall admission, 3/1 priority date for domestic students, 4/1 for international students; for spring admission, 10/1 priority date for domestic students, 8/1 for international students. Applications are processed on a rolling basis. *Application fee:* $40. Electronic applications accepted. *Application Contact:* Graduate Admissions Office, 540-831-5431, Fax: 540-831-6061, E-mail: gradcollege@radford.edu. *Acting Dean,* Dr. Judy Niehaus, 540-831-5149, Fax: 540-831-5970.

College of Business and Economics Students: 33 full-time (11 women), 30 part-time (13 women); includes 13 minority (all African Americans) Average age 30. 43 applicants, 91% accepted, 28 enrolled. *Faculty:* 7 full-time (1 woman). Expenses: Contact institution. *Financial support:* In 2006–07, 23 students received support, including 21 research assistantships with partial tuition reimbursements available (averaging $8,000 per year), teaching assistantships with partial tuition reimbursements available (averaging $8,700 per year); career-related internships or fieldwork, Federal Work-Study, institutionally sponsored loans, scholarships/grants, and unspecified assistantships also available. Financial award application deadline: 3/1; financial award applicants required to submit FAFSA. In 2006, 27 degrees awarded. *Degree program information:* Part-time and evening/weekend programs available. Postbaccalaureate distance learning degree programs offered (minimal on-campus study). Offers business administration (MBA); business and economics (MBA). *Application deadline:* For fall admission, 3/1 priority date for domestic students, 4/1 for international students; for spring admission, 10/1 for domestic students, 8/1 for international students. Applications are processed on a rolling basis. *Application fee:* $40. Electronic applications accepted. *Dean,* Dr. William A. Dempsey, 540-831-5187, Fax: 540-831-6103, E-mail: wdempsey@radford.edu.

College of Education and Human Development Students: 172 full-time (135 women), 324 part-time (276 women); includes 40 minority (29 African Americans, 7 Asian Americans or Pacific Islanders, 4 Hispanic Americans). Average age 32. 171 applicants, 95% accepted, 103 enrolled. *Faculty:* 30 full-time (16 women), 17 part-time/adjunct (9 women). Expenses: Contact institution. *Financial support:* In 2006–07, 104 students received support, including 69 research assistantships with partial tuition reimbursements available (averaging $8,000 per year), teaching assistantships with partial tuition reimbursements available (averaging $8,700 per year); career-related internships or fieldwork, Federal Work-Study, institutionally sponsored loans, scholarships/grants, and unspecified assistantships also available. Financial award application deadline: 3/1; financial award applicants required to submit FAFSA. In 2006, 121 degrees awarded. *Degree program information:* Part-time and evening/weekend programs available. Postbaccalaureate distance learning degree programs offered (minimal on-campus study). Offers content area studies (MS); counseling and human development (MS); curriculum and instruction (MS); deaf and hard of hearing (MS); early childhood education (MS); early childhood special education (MS); education (MS); education and human development (MS); educational leadership (MS); educational technology (MS); high incidence disability (MS); library media (MS); reading (MS); severe disability (MS); special education (MS); teaching English as second language (MS). *Application deadline:* For fall admission, 3/1 priority date for domestic students, 4/1 for international students; for spring admission, 10/1 for domestic students, 8/1 for international students. Applications are processed on a rolling basis. *Application fee:* $40. Electronic applications accepted. *Acting Dean,* Dr. Patricia Shoemaker, 540-831-5277, Fax: 540-831-6053, E-mail: pshoemak@radford.edu.

College of Visual and Performing Arts Students: 34 full-time (22 women), 13 part-time (9 women); includes 10 minority (4 African Americans, 5 Asian Americans or Pacific Islanders, 1 Hispanic American). Average age 31. 26 applicants, 65% accepted, 15 enrolled. *Faculty:* 20 full-time (5 women), 6 part-time/adjunct (4 women). Expenses: Contact institution. *Financial support:* In 2006–07, 27 students received support, including 18 research assistantships with partial tuition reimbursements available (averaging $8,000 per year), 5 teaching assistantships with partial tuition reimbursements available (averaging $8,700 per year); career-related internships or fieldwork, Federal Work-Study, institutionally sponsored loans, scholarships/grants, and unspecified assistantships also available. Financial award application deadline: 3/1; financial award applicants required to submit FAFSA. In 2006, 12 degrees awarded. *Degree program information:* Part-time programs available. Offers art (MFA); music (MA); music therapy (MS); visual and performing arts (MA, MFA, MS). *Application deadline:* For fall admission, 3/1 priority date for domestic students, 4/1 for international students; for spring admission, 10/1 for domestic students, 8/1 for international students. Applications are processed on a rolling basis. *Application fee:* $40. Electronic applications accepted. *Dean,* Dr. Joseph P. Scartelli, 540-831-5141, Fax: 540-831-6313, E-mail: jscartel@radford.edu.

Waldron College of Health and Human Services Students: 132 full-time (130 women), 61 part-time (55 women); includes 23 minority (21 African Americans, 1 Asian American or Pacific Islander, 1 Hispanic American). Average age 34. 121 applicants, 83% accepted, 67 enrolled. *Faculty:* 16 full-time (14 women), 13 part-time/adjunct (11 women). Expenses: Contact institution. *Financial support:* In 2006–07, 90 students received support, including 70 research assistantships with partial tuition reimbursements available (averaging $8,000 per year), teaching assistantships with partial tuition reimbursements available (averaging $8,700 per year); career-related internships or fieldwork, Federal Work-Study, institutionally sponsored loans, and scholarships/grants also available. Financial award application deadline: 3/1; financial award applicants required to submit FAFSA. In 2006, 51 degrees awarded. *Degree program information:* Part-time and evening/weekend programs available. Postbaccalaureate distance learning degree programs offered (minimal on-campus study). Offers communication science and disorders (MA, MS); health and human services (MA, MS, MSN, MSW); nursing (MSN); social work (MSW). *Application deadline:* For fall admission, 3/1 priority date for domestic students, 4/1 for international students; for spring admission, 10/1 for domestic students, 8/1 for international students. Applications are processed on a rolling basis. *Application fee:* $40. Electronic applications accepted. *Acting Dean,* Dr. Raymond Linville, 540-831-7600, Fax: 540-831-6314, E-mail: rlinville@radford.edu.

RAMAPO COLLEGE OF NEW JERSEY, Mahwah, NJ 07430-1680

General Information State-supported, coed, comprehensive institution. *Enrollment:* 5,499 graduate, professional, and undergraduate students; 47 matriculated graduate/professional students (31 women). *Enrollment by degree level:* 47 master's. *Graduate faculty:* 16. Tuition, state resident: part-time $450 per credit. Tuition, nonresident: part-time $578 per credit. *Graduate housing:* On-campus housing not available. *Student services:* Career counseling, child daycare facilities, disabled student services, free psychological counseling, international student services. *Library facilities:* George T. Potter Library. *Online resources:* library catalog, web page, access to other libraries' catalogs. *Collection:* 168,408 titles, 453 serial subscriptions, 5,038 audiovisual materials.

Computer facilities: 580 computers available on campus for general student use. A campuswide network can be accessed from student residence rooms and from off campus. Internet access and online class registration, part of the campus is WI FI accessible are available. *Web address:* http://www.ramapo.edu/.

General Application Contact: Dr. Anthony T. Padovano, Director, 201-684-7430, Fax: 201-684-7973, E-mail: apadovan@ramapo.edu.

GRADUATE UNITS

Program in Liberal Studies Students: 47 (31 women); includes 3 minority (2 African Americans, 1 Asian American or Pacific Islander). 13 applicants, 100% accepted, 10 enrolled. *Faculty:* 16 part-time/adjunct (8 women). Expenses: Contact institution. *Financial support:* Tuition waivers (full) available. Financial award applicants required to submit FAFSA. In 2006, 13 degrees awarded. *Degree program information:* Part-time and evening/weekend programs available. Offers liberal studies (MALS). *Application deadline:* For fall admission, 9/1 priority date for domestic and international students; for spring admission, 1/30 priority date for domestic and international students. Applications are processed on a rolling basis. *Application fee:* $55. Electronic applications accepted. *Application Contact:* Melissa C. Kupfer, MALS Secretary, 201-684-7709, Fax: 201-684-7973, E-mail: mkupfer@ramapo.edu. *Director,* Dr. Anthony T. Padovano, 201-684-7430, Fax: 201-684-7973, E-mail: apadovan@ramapo.edu.

RECONSTRUCTIONIST RABBINICAL COLLEGE, Wyncote, PA 19095-1898

General Information Independent-religious, coed, graduate-only institution. *Enrollment by degree level:* 67 first professional, 2 master's. *Graduate faculty:* 10 full-time (5 women), 25 part-time/adjunct (14 women). *Tuition:* Full-time $12,000; part-time $1,500 per course. *Required fees:* $27. One-time fee: $27 part-time. *Graduate housing:* On-campus housing not available. *Student services:* Campus employment opportunities, career counseling, disabled student services, international student services, low-cost health insurance, writing training. *Library facilities:* Mordecai M. Kaplan Library. *Online resources:* library catalog, access to other libraries' catalogs. *Collection:* 49,600 titles, 125 serial subscriptions, 68 audiovisual materials.

Computer facilities: 20 computers available on campus for general student use. A campuswide network can be accessed from off campus. Internet access, class materials are available. *Web address:* http://www.rrc.edu/.

General Application Contact: Rabbi Amber Powers, Dean of Recruitment and Admissions, 215-576-0800 Ext. 145, Fax: 215-576-6143, E-mail: apowers@rrc.edu.

GRADUATE UNITS

Graduate Program Students: 64 full-time (42 women), 5 part-time (3 women). Average age 32. 30 applicants, 47% accepted, 12 enrolled. *Faculty:* 10 full-time (5 women), 25 part-time/adjunct (14 women). Expenses: Contact institution. *Financial support:* In 2006–07, 47 students received support, including 4 fellowships with full tuition reimbursements available (averaging $9,800 per year), 1 research assistantship with partial tuition reimbursement available (averaging $4,900 per year), 5 teaching assistantships (averaging $4,900 per year); career-related internships or fieldwork, institutionally sponsored loans, and scholarships/grants also available. Financial award application deadline: 4/15; financial award applicants required to submit FAFSA. In 2006, 9 degrees awarded. *Degree program information:* Part-time programs available. Offers rabbinical studies (MAHL, MAJS, DHL, Certificate). *Application deadline:* For spring admission, 4/30 priority date for domestic and international students. Applications are processed on a rolling basis. *Application fee:* $50. *Application Contact:* Rabbi Amber Powers, Dean of Recruitment and Admissions, 215-576-0800 Ext. 145, Fax: 215-576-6143, E-mail: apowers@rrc.edu. *President,* Rabbi Dan Ehrenkrantz, 215-576-0800 Ext. 129, Fax: 215-576-6143, E-mail: dehrenkrantz@rrc.edu.

REED COLLEGE, Portland, OR 97202-8199

General Information Independent, coed, comprehensive institution. *Enrollment:* 1,436 graduate, professional, and undergraduate students; 29 part-time matriculated graduate/professional students (20 women). *Enrollment by degree level:* 29 master's. *Graduate faculty:* 16 part-time/adjunct (6 women). *Tuition:* Part-time $3,110 per unit. Part-time tuition and fees vary according to course load. *Graduate housing:* On-campus housing not available. *Student services:* Campus employment opportunities, campus safety program, career counseling, disabled student services, exercise/wellness program, free psychological counseling, low-cost health insurance, multicultural affairs office, writing training. *Library facilities:* Hauser Library.

Reed College (continued)

Online resources: library catalog, web page, access to other libraries' catalogs. *Collection:* 564,598 titles, 23,290 serial subscriptions, 21,538 audiovisual materials.

Computer facilities: Computer purchase and lease plans are available. 360 computers available on campus for general student use. A campuswide network can be accessed from student residence rooms and from off campus. Internet access and online class registration are available. *Web address:* http://www.reed.edu/.

General Application Contact: Barbara A. Amen, Director, Graduate Studies, 503-777-7259, Fax: 503-517-7345, E-mail: bamen@reed.edu.

GRADUATE UNITS

Graduate Program in Liberal Studies Average age 35. 10 applicants, 50% accepted, 5 enrolled. *Faculty:* 16 part-time/adjunct (6 women). Expenses: Contact institution. *Financial support:* In 2006–07, 5 students received support. Scholarships/grants and health care benefits available. Support available to part-time students. Financial award application deadline: 5/1; financial award applicants required to submit CSS PROFILE or FAFSA. In 2006, 11 degrees awarded. *Degree program information:* Part-time and evening/weekend programs available. Offers liberal studies (MALS). *Application deadline:* For fall admission, 7/1 priority date for domestic students; for spring admission, 12/1 priority date for domestic students. Applications are processed on a rolling basis. *Application fee:* $60. *Director, Graduate Studies,* Barbara A. Amen, 503-777-7259, Fax: 503-517-7345, E-mail: bamen@reed.edu.

REFORMED PRESBYTERIAN THEOLOGICAL SEMINARY, Pittsburgh, PA 15208-2594

General Information Independent-religious, coed, primarily men, graduate-only institution. *Enrollment by degree level:* 44 first professional, 22 master's, 2 other advanced degrees. *Graduate faculty:* 5 full-time (0 women), 9 part-time/adjunct (0 women). *Tuition:* Full-time $8,136; part-time $226 per quarter hour. *Graduate housing:* Rooms and/or apartments available on a first-come, first-served basis to single and married students. *Student services:* Campus employment opportunities, career counseling. *Library facilities:* Reformed Presbyterian Theological Seminary. *Online resources:* library catalog. *Collection:* 67,000 titles, 240 serial subscriptions, 1,500 audiovisual materials.

Computer facilities: 10 computers available on campus for general student use. Internet access, wi-fi access (free) are available. *Web address:* http://www.rpts.edu/.

General Application Contact: Matthew T. Filbert, Admissions Director, 412-731-8690, Fax: 412-731-4834, E-mail: mfilbert@rpts.edu.

GRADUATE UNITS

Graduate and Professional Programs Students: 30 full-time (2 women), 48 part-time (14 women); includes 21 minority (all African Americans), 2 international. Average age 32. 33 applicants, 70% accepted, 21 enrolled. *Faculty:* 5 full-time (0 women), 9 part-time/adjunct (0 women). Expenses: Contact institution. *Financial support:* In 2006–07, 52 students received support. Scholarships/grants available. In 2006, 4 M Divs, 5 master's awarded. *Degree program information:* Part-time and evening/weekend programs available. Offers theology (M Div, MTS, D Min). *Application deadline:* Applications are processed on a rolling basis. *Application fee:* $35. Electronic applications accepted. *Application Contact:* Matthew T. Filbert, Admissions Director, 412-731-8690, Fax: 412-731-4834, E-mail: mfilbert@rpts.edu. *President,* Dr. Jerry F. O'Neill, 412-731-8690, Fax: 412-731-4834, E-mail: joneill@rpts.edu.

REFORMED THEOLOGICAL SEMINARY–CHARLOTTE CAMPUS, Charlotte, NC 28226-6318

General Information Independent-religious, coed, primarily men, graduate-only institution. *Graduate faculty:* 9 full-time. *Tuition:* Part-time $325 per semester hour. *Graduate housing:* On-campus housing not available. *Student services:* Campus employment opportunities. *Online resources:* library catalog. *Collection:* 46,000 titles, 375 serial subscriptions, 730 audiovisual materials.

Computer facilities: 6 computers available on campus for general student use. A campuswide network can be accessed. Internet access and online class registration are available. *Web address:* http://www.rts.edu/.

General Application Contact: Stephane Jeanrenaud, Director of Admissions, 800-755-2429, E-mail: admissions.charlotte@rts.edu.

GRADUATE UNITS

Graduate and Professional Programs Students: 362. *Faculty:* 9 full-time. Expenses: Contact institution. *Financial support:* In 2006–07, teaching assistantships (averaging $1,600 per year). Financial award application deadline: 5/1. *Degree program information:* Part-time programs available. Postbaccalaureate distance learning degree programs offered (minimal on-campus study). Offers biblical studies (MA); Christian education/youth ministry (M Div); ministry (D Min); theological studies (MA). *Application deadline:* For fall admission, 5/1 priority date for domestic students; for winter admission, 10/1 priority date for domestic students; for spring admission, 11/1 priority date for domestic students. Applications are processed on a rolling basis. *Application fee:* $25. *Application Contact:* Stephane Jeanrenaud, Director of Admissions, 800-755-2429, E-mail: admissions.charlotte@rts.edu.

REFORMED THEOLOGICAL SEMINARY–JACKSON CAMPUS, Jackson, MS 39209-3099

General Information Independent-religious, coed, primarily men, graduate-only institution. *Graduate housing:* Rooms and/or apartments available on a first-come, first-served basis to single and married students.

GRADUATE UNITS

Graduate and Professional Programs Offers Bible, theology, and missions (Certificate); biblical studies (MA); Christian education (M Div, MA); counseling (M Div); divinity (M Div, Diploma); marriage and family therapy (MA); ministry (D Min); missions (M Div, MA, D Min); New Testament (Th M); Old Testament (Th M); theological studies (MA); theology (Th M).

REFORMED THEOLOGICAL SEMINARY–ORLANDO CAMPUS, Oviedo, FL 32765-7197

General Information Independent-religious, coed, primarily men, graduate-only institution. *Enrollment by degree level:* 196 first professional, 207 master's, 67 doctoral, 2 other advanced degrees. *Graduate faculty:* 15 full-time (0 women), 5 part-time/adjunct (0 women). *Graduate housing:* Room and/or apartments available to married students; on-campus housing not available to single students. *Student services:* Campus employment opportunities, career counseling, free psychological counseling, international student services, low-cost health insurance, writing training. *Library facilities:* Reformed Theological Seminary Library. *Online resources:* library catalog. *Collection:* 70,000 titles, 330 serial subscriptions, 500 audiovisual materials.

Computer facilities: 5 computers available on campus for general student use. A campuswide network can be accessed from off campus. Internet access and online class registration are available. *Web address:* http://www.rts.edu/.

General Application Contact: David S. Kirkendall, Director of Student Relations, 800-752-4382, Fax: 407-366-9425, E-mail: dkirkendall@rts.edu.

GRADUATE UNITS

Graduate Program Students: 472; includes 42 minority (12 African Americans, 20 Asian Americans or Pacific Islanders, 10 Hispanic Americans), 20 international. 549 applicants, 82% accepted, 398 enrolled. *Faculty:* 15 full-time (0 women), 5 part-time/adjunct (0 women). Expenses: Contact institution. In 2006, 40 M Divs, 35 master's, 21 doctorates awarded. *Degree program information:* Part-time programs available. Postbaccalaureate distance learning degree programs offered (minimal on-campus study). Offers biblical studies (MA); Christian thought (MA); counseling (MA); ministry (D Min); reformation studies (Th M); theological studies (MA); theology (M Div). *Application deadline:* For fall admission, 5/21 priority date for domestic students; for winter admission, 10/3 priority date for domestic students; for spring admission, 11/5 priority date for domestic students. Applications are processed on a rolling basis. *Application fee:* $50. *Application Contact:* David S. Kirkendall, Director of Student Relations, 800-752-4382, Fax: 407-366-9425, E-mail: dkirkendall@rts.edu. *President,* Dr. Frank A. James, 407-366-9493, Fax: 407-366-9425, E-mail: fjames@rts.edu.

REFORMED THEOLOGICAL SEMINARY–WASHINGTON D.C., Fairfax, VA 22033

General Information Independent-religious, coed, primarily men, graduate-only institution. *Graduate housing:* On-campus housing not available.

GRADUATE UNITS

Graduate and Professional Programs *Degree program information:* Part-time and evening/weekend programs available. Offers religion (MA). Electronic applications accepted.

REGENT COLLEGE, Vancouver, BC V6T 2E4, Canada

General Information Independent-religious, coed, graduate-only institution. *Enrollment by degree level:* 204 first professional, 308 master's, 111 other advanced degrees. *Graduate faculty:* 21 full-time (4 women), 15 part-time/adjunct (2 women). *Graduate housing:* On-campus housing not available. *Student services:* Campus employment opportunities, campus safety program, career counseling, disabled student services, international student services, low-cost health insurance, writing training. *Library facilities:* Regent-Carey Library. *Online resources:* library catalog, web page, access to other libraries' catalogs. *Collection:* 120,236 titles, 385 serial subscriptions, 9,905 audiovisual materials.

Computer facilities: 6 computers available on campus for general student use. A campuswide network can be accessed from off campus. Internet access is available. *Web address:* http://www.regent-college.edu/.

General Application Contact: Cindy Aalders, Assistant Registrar, 604-224-3245 Ext. 335, Fax: 604-224-3097, E-mail: admissions@regent-college.edu.

GRADUATE UNITS

Program in Theology Students: 309 full-time (89 women), 314 part-time (125 women); includes 161 minority (7 African Americans, 1 American Indian/Alaska Native, 143 Asian Americans or Pacific Islanders, 10 Hispanic Americans). Average age 33. 261 applicants, 88% accepted, 169 enrolled. *Faculty:* 21 full-time (4 women), 15 part-time/adjunct (2 women). Expenses: Contact institution. *Financial support:* In 2006–07, 116 students received support, including 100 teaching assistantships (averaging $2,900 Canadian dollars per year); career-related internships or fieldwork, scholarships/grants, and health care benefits also available. Financial award application deadline: 3/1. In 2006, 34 first professional degrees, 76 master's, 62 other advanced degrees awarded. *Degree program information:* Part-time and evening/weekend programs available. Offers theology (M Div, MCS, Th M, Dip CS). *Application deadline:* For fall admission, 2/1 priority date for domestic students, 1/1 priority date for international students; for winter admission, 7/2 priority date for domestic students, 7/2 for international students; for spring admission, 2/1 priority date for domestic students. *Application fee:* $60 Canadian dollars. *Application Contact:* Cindy Aalders, Assistant Registrar, 604-224-3245 Ext. 335, Fax: 604-224-3097, E-mail: admissions@regent-college.edu. *President,* Dr. Rod J.K. Wilson, 604-224-3245 Ext. 318, Fax: 604-222-2476, E-mail: presidentsoffice@regent-college.edu.

REGENT UNIVERSITY, Virginia Beach, VA 23464-9800

General Information Independent, coed, comprehensive institution. *Enrollment:* 4,266 graduate, professional, and undergraduate students; 1,408 full-time matriculated graduate/professional students (833 women), 1,812 part-time matriculated graduate/professional students (965 women). *Enrollment by degree level:* 895 first professional, 1,316 master's, 826 doctoral, 183 other advanced degrees. *Graduate faculty:* 144 full-time (42 women), 326 part-time/adjunct (138 women). *Graduate housing:* Rooms and/or apartments available on a first-come, first-served basis to single and married students. Typical cost: $6,850 per year for single students; $6,850 per year for married students. Room charges vary according to housing facility selected. Housing application deadline: 8/30. *Student services:* Campus employment opportunities, campus safety program, career counseling, disabled student services, free psychological counseling, international student services, low-cost health insurance, teacher training, writing training. *Library facilities:* Regent University Library plus 1 other. *Online resources:* library catalog, web page, access to other libraries' catalogs. *Collection:* 769,590 titles, 1,335 serial subscriptions, 18,438 audiovisual materials. *Web address:* http://www.regent.edu/.

General Application Contact: Althea Bishard, Registrar and Executive Director of Enrollment and Academic Services, 800-373-5504, Fax: 757-226-4381, E-mail: admissions@regent.edu.

GRADUATE UNITS

Graduate School Students: 1,408 full-time (833 women), 1,812 part-time (965 women); includes 911 minority (721 African Americans, 19 American Indian/Alaska Native, 69 Asian Americans or Pacific Islanders, 102 Hispanic Americans), 125 international. Average age 35. 2,713 applicants, 52% accepted, 831 enrolled. *Faculty:* 144 full-time (42 women), 326 part-time/adjunct (138 women). Expenses: Contact institution. *Financial support:* In 2006–07, 15 fellowships with full and partial tuition reimbursements (averaging $7,591 per year), 16 research assistantships with full and partial tuition reimbursements (averaging $3,125 per year), 11 teaching assistantships with full and partial tuition reimbursements (averaging $11,433 per year) were awarded; career-related internships or fieldwork, scholarships/grants, and tuition waivers (full and partial) also available. Support available to part-time students. Financial award application deadline: 9/1. In 2006, 189 first professional degrees, 480 master's, 129 doctorates awarded. *Degree program information:* Part-time and evening/weekend programs available. Postbaccalaureate distance learning degree programs offered (minimal on-campus study). *Application deadline:* Applications are processed on a rolling basis. *Application fee:* $50. Electronic applications accepted. *Application Contact:* Althea Bishard, Registrar and Executive Director of Enrollment and Academic Services, 800-373-5504, Fax: 757-226-4381, E-mail: admissions@regent.edu. *Vice President for Academic Affairs,* Dr. Randall Pannell, 757-266-4624, Fax: 757-226-4075, E-mail: randpan@regent.edu.

Robertson School of Government Students: 73 full-time (48 women), 78 part-time (40 women); includes 42 minority (28 African Americans, 5 Asian Americans or Pacific Islanders, 9 Hispanic Americans), 3 international. Average age 31. 189 applicants, 51% accepted, 63 enrolled. *Faculty:* 7 full-time (2 women), 7 part-time/adjunct (0 women). Expenses: Contact institution. *Financial support:* In 2006–07, 151 students received support. Scholarships/grants and unspecified assistantships available. Support available to part-time students. Financial award application deadline: 9/1; financial award applicants required to submit FAFSA. In 2006, 31 degrees awarded. *Degree program information:* Part-time programs available. Offers health care policy and administration (MA); international politics (MA); law and public policy (MA); political leadership and management (MA); political management (MA); public administration (MA); public policy (MA); terrorism and homeland defense (MA); world economies and political development (MA). *Application deadline:* For fall admission, 5/1 priority date for domestic students; for spring admission, 11/1 priority date for domestic students. Applications are processed on a rolling basis. *Application fee:* $50. Electronic applications accepted. *Application Contact:* Althea Bishard, Registrar and Executive Director of Enrollment and Academic Services, 800-373-5504, Fax: 757-226-4381, E-mail: admissions@regent.edu. *Dean,* Dr. Charles W. Dunn, 757-226-4322, Fax: 757-226-4643, E-mail: cwdunn@regent.edu.

School of Communication and the Arts Students: 115 full-time (64 women), 162 part-time (98 women); includes 53 minority (41 African Americans, 3 American Indian/Alaska Native, 2 Asian Americans or Pacific Islanders, 7 Hispanic Americans), 9 international. Average age 33. 226 applicants, 50% accepted, 59 enrolled. *Faculty:* 21 full-time (3 women), 27 part-time/adjunct (9 women). Expenses: Contact institution. *Financial support:* In 2006–07, 14 fellowships with full and partial tuition reimbursements (averaging $7,896 per year) were awarded; scholarships/grants, tuition waivers (full and partial), and unspecified assistantships also available. Support available to part-time students. Financial award application deadline: 9/1; financial award applicants required to submit FAFSA. In 2006, 72 master's, 10 doctorates awarded. *Degree program information:* Part-time programs available. Postbaccalaureate distance learning degree programs offered (minimal on-campus study). Offers acting and directing (MFA); cinema arts (MA); communication (MA, PhD); fine arts (MFA); journalism (MA); script and screenwriting (MFA); television arts (MA); theatre arts (MA). *Application deadline:* For fall admission, 3/1 priority date for domestic students; for spring admission, 10/1 priority date for domestic students. Applications are processed on a rolling basis. *Application fee:* $50. Electronic applications accepted. *Application Contact:* Althea Bishard, Registrar and Executive Director of Enrollment and Academic Services, 800-373-5504, Fax: 757-226-4381, E-mail: admissions@regent.edu. *Dean,* Michael Patrick, 757-226-4970, Fax: 757-226-4279, E-mail: michpat@regent.edu.

School of Divinity Students: 219 full-time (87 women), 416 part-time (156 women); includes 256 minority (219 African Americans, 4 American Indian/Alaska Native, 16 Asian Americans or Pacific Islanders, 17 Hispanic Americans), 50 international. Average age 38. 299 applicants, 62% accepted, 117 enrolled. *Faculty:* 20 full-time (5 women), 38 part-time/adjunct (8 women). Expenses: Contact institution. *Financial support:* In 2006–07, 1 fellowship with full and partial tuition reimbursement (averaging $3,328 per year) was awarded; career-related internships or fieldwork, scholarships/grants, tuition waivers (full and partial), and unspecified assistantships also available. Support available to part-time students. Financial award application deadline: 9/1; financial award applicants required to submit FAFSA. In 2006, 47 M Divs, 27 master's, 7 doctorates awarded. *Degree program information:* Part-time programs available. Postbaccalaureate distance learning degree programs offered (minimal on-campus study). Offers biblical studies (MA); leadership and renewal (D Min); missiology (M Div, MA); practical theology (M Div, MA); renewal studies (PhD). *Application deadline:* For fall admission, 5/1 priority date for domestic students. Applications are processed on a rolling basis. *Application fee:* $50. Electronic applications accepted. *Application Contact:* Althea Bishard, Registrar and Executive Director of Enrollment and Academic Services, 800-373-5504, Fax: 757-226-4381, E-mail: admissions@regent.edu. *Dean,* Dr. Michael Palmer, 757-226-4406, Fax: 757-226-4597, E-mail: mpalmer@regent.edu.

School of Education Students: 220 full-time (176 women), 501 part-time (374 women); includes 264 minority (229 African Americans, 9 Asian Americans or Pacific Islanders, 26 Hispanic Americans), 13 international. Average age 38. 472 applicants, 79% accepted, 256 enrolled. *Faculty:* 25 full-time (11 women), 132 part-time/adjunct (90 women). Expenses: Contact institution. *Financial support:* In 2006–07, 721 students received support; fellowships, career-related internships or fieldwork, scholarships/grants, tuition waivers (full and partial), and unspecified assistantships available. Support available to part-time students. Financial award application deadline: 4/1; financial award applicants required to submit FAFSA. In 2006, 185 master's, 5 doctorates awarded. *Degree program information:* Part-time and evening/weekend programs available. Postbaccalaureate distance learning degree programs offered (minimal on-campus study). Offers Christian school program (M Ed); cross-categorical special education (M Ed); education (M Ed, Ed D); educational leadership (M Ed); elementary education (M Ed); individual degree plan (M Ed); master teacher (M Ed); special education leadership (Ed S); TESOL (M Ed). *Application deadline:* For fall admission, 4/1 priority date for domestic students; for spring admission, 10/15 priority date for domestic students. Applications are processed on a rolling basis. *Application fee:* $50. Electronic applications accepted. *Application Contact:* Althea Bishard, Registrar and Executive Director of Enrollment and Academic Services, 800-373-5504, Fax: 757-226-4381, E-mail: admissions@regent.edu. *Dean,* Dr. Alan A. Arroyo, 757-226-4261, Fax: 757-226-4318, E-mail: alanarr@regent.edu.

School of Global Leadership and Entrepreneurship Students: 68 full-time (40 women), 482 part-time (170 women); includes 144 minority (110 African Americans, 6 American Indian/Alaska Native, 9 Asian Americans or Pacific Islanders, 19 Hispanic Americans), 37 international. Average age 40. 395 applicants, 37% accepted, 64 enrolled. *Faculty:* 20 full-time (3 women), 36 part-time/adjunct (6 women). Expenses: Contact institution. *Financial support:* In 2006–07, 321 students received support. Scholarships/grants and tuition waivers (full and partial) available. Support available to part-time students. Financial award application deadline: 9/1. In 2006, 100 master's, 69 doctorates awarded. *Degree program information:* Part-time programs available. Postbaccalaureate distance learning degree programs offered (minimal on-campus study). Offers business administration (MBA); management (MA); organizational leadership (MA, PhD, Certificate); strategic foresight (MA); strategic leadership (DSL). *Application deadline:* For fall admission, 5/1 priority date for domestic students; for spring admission, 10/1 priority date for domestic students. Applications are processed on a rolling basis. *Application fee:* $50. Electronic applications accepted. *Application Contact:* Althea Bishard, Registrar and Executive Director of Enrollment and Academic Services, 800-373-5504, Fax: 757-226-4381, E-mail: admissions@regent.edu. *Dean,* Dr. Bruce Winston, 757-226-4306, Fax: 757-226-4634, E-mail: brucwin@regent.edu.

School of Law Students: 475 full-time (237 women), 8 part-time (5 women); includes 55 minority (26 African Americans, 4 American Indian/Alaska Native, 16 Asian Americans or Pacific Islanders, 9 Hispanic Americans), 3 international. Average age 27. 698 applicants, 44% accepted, 167 enrolled. *Faculty:* 26 full-time (5 women), 59 part-time/adjunct (12 women). Expenses: Contact institution. *Financial support:* Scholarships/grants and tuition waivers (full and partial) available. Support available to part-time students. Financial award application deadline: 2/1. In 2006, 142 degrees awarded. *Degree program information:* Part-time and evening/weekend programs available. Postbaccalaureate distance learning degree programs offered (minimal on-campus study). Offers law (JD). *Application deadline:* For fall admission, 3/1 for domestic students. Applications are processed on a rolling basis. *Application fee:* $50. Electronic applications accepted. *Application Contact:* Althea Bishard, Registrar and Executive Director of Enrollment and Academic Services, 800-373-5504, Fax: 757-226-4381, E-mail: admissions@regent.edu. *Dean,* Jeffrey Brauch, 757-226-4040, Fax: 757-226-4595, E-mail: jeffbra@regent.edu.

School of Psychology and Counseling Students: 238 full-time (181 women), 165 part-time (121 women); includes 97 minority (68 African Americans, 2 American Indian/Alaska Native, 12 Asian Americans or Pacific Islanders, 15 Hispanic Americans), 10 international. Average age 31. 434 applicants, 44% accepted, 105 enrolled. *Faculty:* 25 full-time (13 women), 27 part-time/adjunct (13 women). Expenses: Contact institution. *Financial support:* In 2006–07, 16 research assistantships with full and partial tuition reimbursements (averaging $3,125 per year), 11 teaching assistantships with full and partial tuition reimbursements (averaging $11,433 per year) were awarded; career-related internships or fieldwork, scholarships/grants, tuition waivers (full and partial) also available. Support available to part-time students. Financial award application deadline: 9/1. In 2006, 65 master's, 38 doctorates awarded. *Degree program information:* Part-time programs available. Postbaccalaureate distance learning degree programs offered. Offers clinical psychology (Psy D); counseling (MA); counseling studies (CAGS); counselor education and supervision (PhD). PhD program offered online only. *Application deadline:* For fall admission, 4/1 priority date for domestic students; for spring admission, 11/1 priority date for domestic students. Applications are processed on a rolling basis. *Application fee:* $50. Electronic applications accepted. *Application Contact:* Althea Bishard, Registrar and Executive Director of Enrollment and Academic Services, 800-373-5504, Fax: 757-226-4381, E-mail: admissions@regent.edu. *Dean,* Dr. Rosemarie Hughes, 757-226-4269, Fax: 757-226-4282, E-mail: rosehug@regent.edu.

Announcement: With faith as the foundation of its mission, Regent prepares leaders to have a positive impact on American society and the world. Regent's highly motivated students choose to pursue degrees at the Virginia Beach Campus, at the Washington, DC, Campus in Alexandria, Virginia, or online via the Worldwide Campus. Regent University is accredited by the Commission on Colleges of the Southern Association of Colleges and Schools to award bachelor's, master's, and doctoral degrees. The School of Law is accredited by the ABA, the School of Divinity is accredited by the Association of Theological Schools, and the School of Psychology & Counseling's MA in Counseling (School and Community) is accredited by CACREP and the PsyD is accredited by the American Psychological Association's Committee on Accreditation.

See Close-Up on page 999.

REGIONS UNIVERSITY, Montgomery, AL 36117

General Information Independent-religious, coed, university. *Graduate housing:* On-campus housing not available.

GRADUATE UNITS

Graduate and Professional Programs *Degree program information:* Part-time and evening/weekend programs available. Postbaccalaureate distance learning degree programs offered (no on-campus study). Offers behavioral leadership and management (MA); biblical studies (MA, D Min, PhD); Christian ministry (M Div); family therapy (D Min, PhD); leadership and management (MS); marriage and family therapy (M Div, MA); ministerial leadership (M Div, MS); pastoral counseling (M Div, MS); practical theology (MA); professional counseling (M Div, MA). Electronic applications accepted.

REGIS COLLEGE, Toronto, ON M4Y 2R5, Canada

General Information Independent-religious, coed, graduate-only institution. *Enrollment by degree level:* 66 first professional, 69 master's, 25 doctoral, 55 other advanced degrees. *Graduate faculty:* 14 full-time (3 women), 11 part-time/adjunct (3 women). *Graduate housing:* On-campus housing not available. *Library facilities:* Regis College Library. *Online resources:* library catalog, web page, access to other libraries' catalogs. *Collection:* 101,051 titles, 270 serial subscriptions, 186 audiovisual materials.

Computer facilities: 10 computers available on campus for general student use. A campuswide network can be accessed from off campus. Internet access and online class registration are available. *Web address:* http://www.regiscollege.ca/.

General Application Contact: Elaine Chu, Registrar, 416-922-5474 Ext. 226, Fax: 416-922-2898, E-mail: regis.registrar@utoronto.ca.

GRADUATE UNITS

Graduate and Professional Programs Students: 83 full-time (24 women), 132 part-time (78 women); includes 75 minority (21 African Americans, 1 American Indian/Alaska Native, 46 Asian Americans or Pacific Islanders, 7 Hispanic Americans). Average age 45. 56 applicants, 84% accepted, 37 enrolled. *Faculty:* 14 full-time (3 women), 11 part-time/adjunct (3 women). Expenses: Contact institution. *Financial support:* In 2006–07, 44 students received support. Career-related internships or fieldwork and scholarships/grants available. Support available to part-time students. Financial award application deadline: 3/15. In 2006, 15 M Divs, 16 master's, 2 doctorates, 10 other advanced degrees awarded. Offers ministry (D Min); ministry and spirituality (MAMS); sacred theology (STB, STM, STD, STL); theological study (MTS); theology (M Div, MA, Th M, PhD, Th D). *Application deadline:* For fall admission, 3/15 priority date for domestic and international students; for winter admission, 12/1 for domestic and international students; for spring admission, 3/15 for domestic and international students. Applications are processed on a rolling basis. *Application fee:* $25. *Application Contact:* Elaine Chu, Registrar, 416-922-5474 Ext. 226, Fax: 416-922-2898, E-mail: regis.registrar@utoronto.ca. *Dean,* Dr. Gordon Rixon, 416-922-5474 Ext. 225, Fax: 416-922-2898, E-mail: gordon.rixon@utoronto.ca.

REGIS COLLEGE, Weston, MA 02493

General Information Independent-religious, coed, comprehensive institution. *Enrollment:* 1,314 graduate, professional, and undergraduate students; 166 full-time matriculated graduate/professional students (150 women), 289 part-time matriculated graduate/professional students (267 women). *Enrollment by degree level:* 445 master's, 10 other advanced degrees. *Graduate faculty:* 24 full-time (22 women), 39 part-time/adjunct (33 women). *Tuition:* Full-time $23,680; part-time $665 per credit hour. *Graduate housing:* Room and/or apartments available on a first-come, first-served basis to single students; on-campus housing not available to married students. Typical cost: $5,370 per year ($10,560 including board). *Student services:* Campus employment opportunities, campus safety program, career counseling, exercise/wellness program, low-cost health insurance, multicultural affairs office, teacher training. *Library facilities:* Regis College Library. *Online resources:* library catalog, web page, access to other libraries' catalogs. *Collection:* 139,837 titles, 787 serial subscriptions, 6,204 audiovisual materials. *Research affiliation:* Lahey Clinic Medical Center (nursing), Boston Medical Center (nursing), Caritas Norwood Hospital (nursing).

Computer facilities: 159 computers available on campus for general student use. A campuswide network can be accessed from student residence rooms and from off campus. Internet access and online class registration are available. *Web address:* http://www.regiscollege.edu/.

General Application Contact: Christine Petherick, Administrative Coordinator—Graduate Admission, 866-438-7344, Fax: 781-768-7071, E-mail: christine.petherick@regiscollege.edu.

GRADUATE UNITS

Department of Education Students: 5 full-time (all women), 48 part-time (45 women); includes 4 minority (1 African American, 3 Asian Americans or Pacific Islanders), 1 international. Average age 35. 12 applicants, 100% accepted, 10 enrolled. *Faculty:* 3 full-time (all women), 4 part-time/adjunct (all women). Expenses: Contact institution. *Financial support:* In 2006–07, 7 students received support, including 1 fellowship with full tuition reimbursement available (averaging $11,970 per year); Federal Work-Study also available. Financial award applicants required to submit FAFSA. In 2006, 13 degrees awarded. *Degree program information:* Part-time and evening/weekend programs available. Offers education (MAT). *Application deadline:* Applications are processed on a rolling basis. *Application fee:* $40. Electronic applications accepted. *Program Director,* Dr. Leona McCaughey-Oreszak, 781-768-7421, Fax: 781-768-7159, E-mail: leona.mccaughey-oreszak@regiscollege.edu.

Department of Health Product Regulation and Health Policy Students: 2 full-time (1 woman), 25 part-time (20 women); includes 2 minority (1 African American, 1 Asian American or Pacific Islander). Average age 35. 11 applicants, 100% accepted, 9 enrolled. *Faculty:* 2 part-time/adjunct (1 woman). Expenses: Contact institution. *Financial support:* Career-related internships or fieldwork available. Financial award applicants required to submit FAFSA. In 2006, 6 degrees awarded. *Degree program information:* Part-time and evening/weekend programs available. Offers health product regulation and health policy (MS). *Application fee:* $50. *Director,* Charles Burr, 781-768-7008, E-mail: charles.burr@regiscollege.edu.

Department of Management and Leadership Students: 1 (woman) full-time, 17 part-time (15 women); includes 3 minority (1 Asian American or Pacific Islander, 2 Hispanic Americans). Average age 36. 5 applicants, 100% accepted, 5 enrolled. *Faculty:* 1 full-time (0 women), 1 part-time/adjunct (0 women). Expenses: Contact institution. *Financial support:* Applicants required to submit FAFSA. In 2006, 9 degrees awarded. *Degree program information:* Part-time and evening/weekend programs available. Offers leadership and organizational change (MS). *Application deadline:* Applications are processed on a rolling basis. *Application fee:* $50. *Director,* Dr. Phillip Jutras, 781-768-7436, Fax: 781-768-7159, E-mail: phillip.jutras@regiscollege.edu.

Department of Nursing Students: 157 full-time (142 women), 176 part-time (166 women); includes 49 minority (35 African Americans, 1 American Indian/Alaska Native, 9 Asian Americans or Pacific Islanders, 4 Hispanic Americans). Average age 36. 167 applicants, 83% accepted, 139 enrolled. *Faculty:* 14 full-time (13 women), 18 part-time/adjunct (15 women). Expenses: Contact institution. *Financial support:* In 2006–07, 31 students received support, including 8 research assistantships (averaging $35,000 per year); Federal Work-Study, scholarships/grants, traineeships, and unspecified assistantships also available. Support available to part-time students. Financial award applicants required to submit FAFSA. In 2006, 45 master's, 13 other advanced degrees awarded. *Degree program information:* Part-time and evening/weekend programs available. Offers nurse educator (Certificate); nurse practitioner (Certificate); nursing (MS). *Application deadline:* Applications are processed on a rolling basis. *Application fee:* $50. Electronic applications accepted. *Dean, School of Nursing and Health Professions,* Dr. Antoinette Hays, 781-768-7091, Fax: 781-768-8339, E-mail: antoinette.hays@regiscollege.edu.

Department of Organizational and Professional Communication Students: 1 (woman) full-time, 23 part-time (21 women); includes 4 minority (all African Americans) Average age 30. 6 applicants, 100% accepted, 5 enrolled. *Faculty:* 2 full-time (both women), 1 (woman) part-time/adjunct. Expenses: Contact institution. *Financial support:* Applicants required to

Regis College (continued)
submit FAFSA. In 2006, 6 degrees awarded. *Degree program information:* Part-time and evening/weekend programs available. Offers organizational and professional communication (MS). *Application deadline:* Applications are processed on a rolling basis. *Application fee:* $50. *Director,* Dr. Joan Murray, 781-768-7416, Fax: 781-768-7159, E-mail: joan.murray@regiscollege.edu.

REGIS UNIVERSITY, Denver, CO 80221-1099

General Information Independent-religious, coed, comprehensive institution. *Enrollment:* 16,004 graduate, professional, and undergraduate students; 5,328 matriculated graduate/professional students. *Enrollment by degree level:* 4,785 master's. *Graduate faculty:* 730. *Graduate housing:* On-campus housing not available. *Student services:* Campus employment opportunities, campus safety program, career counseling, disabled student services, exercise/wellness program, grant writing training, international student services, teacher training, writing training. *Library facilities:* Dayton Memorial Library. *Online resources:* library catalog, web page, access to other libraries' catalogs. *Collection:* 350,000 titles, 20,800 serial subscriptions. *Research affiliation:* Learning Anytime Anywhere Partnership (Internet based technology).

Computer facilities: 300 computers available on campus for general student use. A campuswide network can be accessed from student residence rooms and from off campus. Internet access and online class registration are available. *Web address:* http://www.regis.edu/.

General Application Contact: Information Contact, 303-458-4300, Fax: 303-964-5274, E-mail: masters@regis.edu.

GRADUATE UNITS

Regis College Students: 129. Average age 35. 5 applicants, 100% accepted. *Faculty:* 13. Expenses: Contact institution. *Financial support:* Available to part-time students. Application deadline: 3/15; In 2006, 23 degrees awarded. *Degree program information:* Part-time and evening/weekend programs available. Offers education (MA). Offered at Northwest Denver Campus. *Application deadline:* Applications are processed on a rolling basis. *Application fee:* $75. *Application Contact:* Kathleen Nutting, Director, 303-458-4349, Fax: 303-964-5421, E-mail: knutting@regis.edu. *Dean,* Dr. Paul Ewald, 303-458-4040.

Rueckert-Hartman School for Health Professions Students: 453. *Faculty:* 3 full-time (all women), 7 part-time/adjunct (4 women). Expenses: Contact institution. *Financial support:* Career-related internships or fieldwork and Federal Work-Study available. In 2006, 55 degrees awarded. Offers clinical leadership for physician assistants (MS); health services administration (MS); nursing (MSN); physical therapy (DPT, TDPT). *Application deadline:* Applications are processed on a rolling basis. *Application Contact:* Donna Eastman, Assistant to the Dean, 303-458-4174, Fax: 303-964-5533, E-mail: deastman@regis.edu. *Academic Dean,* Dr. Patricia Ladewig, 303-458-4174, E-mail: pladewig@regis.edu.

School for Professional Studies Students: 4,117 (2,124 women). Average age 35. *Faculty:* 478. Expenses: Contact institution. *Financial support:* Career-related internships or fieldwork and Federal Work-Study available. Support available to part-time students. Financial award applicants required to submit FAFSA. In 2006, 1211 degrees awarded. *Degree program information:* Part-time and evening/weekend programs available. Postbaccalaureate distance learning degree programs offered (no on-campus study). Offers accounting (MS); adult learning, training, and development (M Ed); business administration (MBA); community counseling (MAC); computer information technology (MSOL); counseling children and adolescents (Post-Graduate Certificate); curriculum, instruction, and assessment (M Ed); database administration with IBM DB2 (Certificate); database administration with Oracle (Certificate); database development (Certificate); database technologies (MSCIT); early childhood (M Ed); educational technology (Certificate); elementary (M Ed); enterprise Java software development (Certificate); ESL (M Ed); executive information technologies (Certificate); executive information technology (MSCIT); executive international management (Certificate); executive leadership (Certificate); finance (MBA); finance and accounting (MBA); fine arts (M Ed); fine arts administration (Certificate); human resource management (MSOL); information assurance (Certificate); instructional technology (M Ed); international business (MBA); language and communication (MA); leadership (Certificate); marketing (MBA); marriage and family therapy (Post-Graduate Certificate); mediation (Certificate); nonprofit management (MNM); operations management (MBA); organization leadership (MS); organizational leadership (MSOL); professional leadership (M Ed); program management (Certificate); project leadership and management (MSOL, Certificate); project management (Certificate); psychology (MA); reading (M Ed); resource development (Certificate); secondary (M Ed); self-designed (M Ed); social justice, peace, and reconciliation (Certificate); social science (MA); software and information systems (M Sc); software engineering (MSCIT, Certificate); space studies (M Ed); special education (M Ed); storage area networks (Certificate); strategic business (Certificate); strategic human resource (Certificate); systems engineering (MSCIT, Certificate); teacher licensure (M Ed); technical communication (Certificate); technical management (Certificate). *Application deadline:* For fall admission, 8/6 priority date for domestic students; for winter admission, 10/1 priority date for domestic students; for spring admission, 12/14 priority date for domestic students. Applications are processed on a rolling basis. *Application fee:* $75. Electronic applications accepted. *Application Contact:* 800-677-9270, Fax: 303-964-5538, E-mail: masters@regis.edu. *Dean,* Dr. Steven Berkshire, 303-964-5240, Fax: 303-964-5538.

RENSSELAER AT HARTFORD, Hartford, CT 06120-2991

General Information Independent, coed, graduate-only institution. *Graduate housing:* On-campus housing not available.

GRADUATE UNITS

Department of Computer and Information Science *Degree program information:* Part-time and evening/weekend programs available. Offers computer science (MS); information technology (MS). Electronic applications accepted.

Department of Engineering *Degree program information:* Part-time and evening/weekend programs available. Offers computer and systems engineering (ME); electrical engineering (MS); engineering (ME, MS); mechanical engineering (MS). Electronic applications accepted.

Lally School of Management and Technology *Degree program information:* Part-time and evening/weekend programs available. Postbaccalaureate distance learning degree programs offered (no on-campus study). Offers management and technology (MBA, MS). Electronic applications accepted.

RENSSELAER POLYTECHNIC INSTITUTE, Troy, NY 12180-3590

General Information Independent, coed, university. CGS member. *Enrollment:* 7,433 graduate, professional, and undergraduate students; 1,131 full-time matriculated graduate/professional students (344 women), 1,109 part-time matriculated graduate/professional students (326 women). *Enrollment by degree level:* 1,354 master's, 886 doctoral. *Graduate faculty:* 393 full-time (82 women), 78 part-time/adjunct (21 women). *Tuition:* Full-time $32,600; part-time $1,358 per credit. *Required fees:* $1,629. *Graduate housing:* Rooms and/or apartments available on a first-come, first-served basis to single and married students. Typical cost: $9,000 (including board) for single students. Room and board charges vary according to board plan, campus/location and housing facility selected. *Student services:* Campus employment opportunities, campus safety program, career counseling, disabled student services, exercise/wellness program, free psychological counseling, grant writing training, international student services, low-cost health insurance, multicultural affairs office, teacher training, writing training. *Library facilities:* Folsom Library plus 1 other. *Online resources:* library catalog, web page, access to other libraries' catalogs. *Collection:* 309,171 titles, 10,210 serial subscriptions. *Research affiliation:* IBM (broadband technologies, modeling and simulation of complex systems), Lockheed Martin (advanced sensors systems, THz detection technologies), Semiconductor Research Corporation (high density magnetic storage devices), Cleveland Clinic Foundation (tissue engineering and regenerative medicine, imaging, bio-nano materials), New York State Energy Research and Development Authority (fuel cells, polymer membranes, renewable energy sources).

Computer facilities: Computer purchase and lease plans are available. 5,588 computers available on campus for general student use. A campuswide network can be accessed from student residence rooms and from off campus. Internet access and online class registration are available. *Web address:* http://www.rpi.edu/.

General Application Contact: James G. Nondorf, Vice President for Enrollment, 518-276-6216, Fax: 518-276-4072, E-mail: admissions@rpi.edu.

GRADUATE UNITS

Graduate School Students: 1,131 full-time (344 women), 1,109 part-time (326 women); includes 200 minority (52 African Americans, 2 American Indian/Alaska Native, 79 Asian Americans or Pacific Islanders, 67 Hispanic Americans), 1,153 international. Average age 28. 2,535 applicants, 34% accepted, 352 enrolled. *Faculty:* 393 full-time (82 women), 78 part-time/adjunct (21 women). Expenses: Contact institution. *Financial support:* In 2006–07, 867 students received support, including 103 fellowships with full tuition reimbursements available (averaging $21,000 per year), 424 research assistantships with full tuition reimbursements available (averaging $19,330 per year), 335 teaching assistantships with full tuition reimbursements available (averaging $14,500 per year); career-related internships or fieldwork, institutionally sponsored loans, scholarships/grants, health care benefits, tuition waivers (partial), and unspecified assistantships also available. Financial award application deadline: 1/15. In 2006, 739 master's, 146 doctorates awarded. *Degree program information:* Part-time and evening/weekend programs available. Postbaccalaureate distance learning degree programs offered (no on-campus study). *Application deadline:* For fall admission, 1/1 priority date for domestic and international students; for spring admission, 8/15 priority date for domestic and international students. Applications are processed on a rolling basis. *Application fee:* $75. Electronic applications accepted. *Application Contact:* James G. Nondorf, Vice President for Enrollment, 518-276-6216, Fax: 518-276-4072, E-mail: admissions@rpi.edu. *Vice Provost and Dean of Graduate Education, Acting,* Dr. Lester A. Gerhardt, 518-276-6400, Fax: 518-276-8788, E-mail: gerhal@rpi.edu.

Lally School of Management and Technology Students: 121 full-time (62 women), 525 part-time (184 women); includes 137 minority (43 African Americans, 60 Asian Americans or Pacific Islanders, 34 Hispanic Americans), 71 international. Average age 28. 416 applicants, 70% accepted, 240 enrolled. *Faculty:* 50 full-time (9 women), 1 part-time/adjunct (0 women). Expenses: Contact institution. *Financial support:* In 2006–07, 48 students received support; fellowships with partial tuition reimbursements available, research assistantships with partial tuition reimbursements available, teaching assistantships with partial tuition reimbursements available, career-related internships or fieldwork, institutionally sponsored loans, and scholarships/grants available. Financial award application deadline: 3/15; financial award applicants required to submit FAFSA. In 2006, 215 master's, 6 doctorates awarded. *Degree program information:* Part-time and evening/weekend programs available. Postbaccalaureate distance learning degree programs offered (no on-campus study). Offers finance (MBA, MS); financial technology (MS); management (PhD); management and technology (MBA, MS, PhD); management information systems (MBA, MS); new product development and marketing (MBA); new production and operations management (MS); product development and marketing (MS); production and operations management (MBA); technical commercialization (MS); technological entrepreneurship (MBA, MS). *Application deadline:* For fall admission, 3/15 priority date for domestic and international students. Applications are processed on a rolling basis. *Application fee:* $75. Electronic applications accepted. *Application Contact:* Michele M. Martens, Manager of Graduate Programs, 518-276-6586, Fax: 518-276-2665, E-mail: martem@rpi.edu. *Dean,* Dr. David A. Gautschi, 518-276-6586, Fax: 518-276-2665, E-mail: lallymba@rpi.edu.

School of Architecture Students: 53 full-time (19 women), 13 part-time (9 women); includes 7 minority (3 African Americans, 1 Asian American or Pacific Islander, 3 Hispanic Americans), 21 international. Average age 26. 94 applicants, 62% accepted, 28 enrolled. *Faculty:* 16 full-time (4 women), 16 part-time/adjunct (5 women). Expenses: Contact institution. *Financial support:* In 2006–07, 37 students received support, including 6 fellowships with full tuition reimbursements available (averaging $20,000 per year), 15 research assistantships with full tuition reimbursements available (averaging $14,500 per year), 2 teaching assistantships with full tuition reimbursements available (averaging $14,500 per year); career-related internships or fieldwork, institutionally sponsored loans, scholarships/grants, tuition waivers (partial), and unspecified assistantships also available. Financial award application deadline: 1/15. In 2006, 25 master's awarded. *Degree program information:* Part-time programs available. Offers architectural science (MS, PhD); architecture (M Arch); building conservation (MS); lighting (MS). *Application deadline:* For fall admission, 1/15 priority date for domestic and international students. Applications are processed on a rolling basis. *Application fee:* $75. Electronic applications accepted. *Application Contact:* Kathleen G. O'Connor, Senior Program Administrator, Graduate Programs, 518-276-6466, Fax: 518-276-3034, E-mail: oconnk2@rpi.edu. *Chair,* Prof. Ted Krueger, 518-276-2562, Fax: 518-276-3034, E-mail: krueger@rpi.edu.

School of Engineering Students: 530 full-time (130 women), 48 part-time (10 women); includes 53 minority (10 African Americans, 25 Asian Americans or Pacific Islanders, 18 Hispanic Americans), 325 international. Average age 27. 1,460 applicants, 27% accepted, 155 enrolled. *Faculty:* 141 full-time (7 women), 30 part-time/adjunct (5 women). Expenses: Contact institution. *Financial support:* In 2006–07, fellowships with full tuition reimbursements (averaging $19,000 per year), research assistantships with full and partial tuition reimbursements (averaging $15,000 per year), teaching assistantships with full and partial tuition reimbursements (averaging $14,000 per year) were awarded; career-related internships or fieldwork, institutionally sponsored loans, scholarships/grants, tuition waivers (full and partial), and unspecified assistantships also available. Financial award application deadline: 2/1. In 2006, 159 master's, 86 doctorates awarded. *Degree program information:* Part-time and evening/weekend programs available. Postbaccalaureate distance learning degree programs offered (no on-campus study). Offers aerospace engineering (M Eng, MS, PhD); biomedical engineering (MS, PhD); ceramics and glass science (M Eng, MS, PhD); chemical and biological engineering (M Eng, MS, D Eng, PhD); civil engineering (M Eng, MS, D Eng, PhD); composites (M Eng, MS, PhD); computer and systems engineering (M Eng, MS, D Eng, PhD); decision sciences and engineering systems (PhD); electric power engineering (M Eng, MS, D Eng, PhD); electrical engineering (M Eng, MS, D Eng, PhD); electronic materials (M Eng, MS, PhD); engineering (M Eng, MS, D Eng, PhD); engineering physics (MS, PhD); engineering science (M Eng, MS, PhD); environmental engineering (M Eng, MS, D Eng, PhD); geotechnical engineering (M Eng, MS, D Eng, PhD); industrial and management engineering (M Eng, MS, PhD); manufacturing systems engineering (M Eng, MS, PhD); mechanical engineering (M Eng, MS, PhD); mechanics of composite materials and structures (M Eng, MS, D Eng, PhD); metallurgy (M Eng, MS, PhD); nuclear engineering (M Eng, MS, PhD); nuclear engineering and science (PhD); operations research and statistics (M Eng, MS, PhD); polymers (M Eng, MS, PhD); structural engineering (M Eng, MS, D Eng, PhD); transportation engineering (M Eng, MS, D Eng, PhD). *Application deadline:* For fall admission, 1/1 priority date for domestic and international students; for spring admission, 8/15 priority date for domestic and international students. Applications are processed on a rolling basis. *Application fee:* $75. Electronic applications accepted. *Application Contact:* James G. Nondorf, Vice President for Enrollment, 518-276-6216, Fax: 518-276-4072, E-mail: admissions@rpi.edu. *Dean,* Dr. Alan W. Cramb, 518-276-6298, Fax: 518-276-8788, E-mail: cramb@rpi.edu.

School of Humanities and Social Sciences Students: 97 full-time (40 women), 4 part-time (1 woman); includes 10 minority (3 African Americans, 1 American Indian/Alaska Native, 2 Asian Americans or Pacific Islanders, 4 Hispanic Americans), 28 international. Average age 32. 173 applicants, 48% accepted, 32 enrolled. *Faculty:* 63 full-time (20 women), 9 part-time/adjunct (4 women). Expenses: Contact institution. *Financial support:* In 2006–07, fellowships with full tuition reimbursements (averaging $16,000 per year), research assistantships with full and partial tuition reimbursements (averaging $16,000 per year), teaching assistantships with full and partial tuition reimbursements (averaging $16,000 per year) were awarded; career-related internships or fieldwork, institutionally sponsored loans, and tuition waivers (full and partial) also available. Financial award application deadline: 2/1. In 2006, 26 master's, 11 doctorates awarded. *Degree program information:* Part-time and evening/weekend programs available. Postbaccalaureate distance learning degree programs offered (no on-campus study). Offers cognitive science (PhD); communication and rhetoric

(MS, PhD); ecological economics (PhD); ecological economics, values, and policy (MS); economics (MS); electronic arts (MFA); human-computer interaction (MS); humanities and social sciences (MFA, MS, PhD); science and technology studies (MS, PhD); technical communication (MS). *Application deadline:* For fall admission, 1/1 priority date for domestic students, 1/15 priority date for international students; for spring admission, 8/15 priority date for domestic and international students. Applications are processed on a rolling basis. *Application fee:* $75. Electronic applications accepted. *Application Contact:* Karen Long, Acting Dean, Enrollment Management, 518-276-6216, Fax: 518-276-4072, E-mail: admissions@rpi.edu. *Dean,* Dr. John P. Harrington, 518-276-6575, Fax: 518-276-4871, E-mail: harrij2@rpi.edu.

School of Science Students: 307 full-time (103 women), 7 part-time (2 women); includes 24 minority (8 African Americans, 11 Asian Americans or Pacific Islanders, 5 Hispanic Americans), 171 international. Average age 26. 571 applicants, 33% accepted, 72 enrolled. *Faculty:* 115 full-time (16 women). Expenses: Contact institution. *Financial support:* In 2006–07, 24 fellowships with full tuition reimbursements (averaging $20,000 per year), 14 research assistantships with full tuition reimbursements (averaging $14,500 per year), 154 teaching assistantships with full tuition reimbursements (averaging $14,500 per year) were awarded; career-related internships or fieldwork, institutionally sponsored loans, and tuition waivers (full) also available. Financial award application deadline: 2/1. In 2006, 88 master's, 43 doctorates awarded. *Degree program information:* Part-time and evening/weekend programs available. Postbaccalaureate distance learning degree programs offered (no on-campus study). Offers analytical chemistry (MS, PhD); applied mathematics (MS); applied science (MS); biochemistry (MS, PhD); biophysics (MS, PhD); cell biology (MS, PhD); computer science (MS, PhD); developmental biology (MS, PhD); environmental chemistry (MS, PhD); geochemistry (MS, PhD); geology (MS, PhD); geophysics (MS, PhD); information technology (MS); inorganic chemistry (MS, PhD); mathematics (MS, PhD); microbiology (MS, PhD); molecular biology (MS, PhD); multidisciplinary science (MS, PhD); natural sciences (MS); organic chemistry (MS, PhD); petrology (MS, PhD); physical chemistry (MS, PhD); physics (MS, PhD); polymer chemistry (MS, PhD); science (MS, PhD). *Application deadline:* For fall admission, 1/1 priority date for domestic students, 1/15 priority date for international students. Applications are processed on a rolling basis. *Application fee:* $75. Electronic applications accepted. *Application Contact:* James G. Nondorf, Vice President for Enrollment, 518-276-6216, Fax: 518-276-4072, E-mail: admissions@rpi.edu. *Dean,* Dr. Wei Zhao, 518-276-6305, Fax: 518-276-2825, E-mail: zhaow3@rpi.edu.

See Close-Up on page 1001.

RESEARCH COLLEGE OF NURSING, Kansas City, MO 64132

General Information Independent, coed, primarily women, comprehensive institution. *Enrollment:* 406 graduate, professional, and undergraduate students; 64 part-time matriculated graduate/professional students (59 women). *Enrollment by degree level:* 64 master's. *Graduate faculty:* 11 full-time (all women). *Tuition:* Part-time $350 per credit hour. *Graduate housing:* Rooms and/or apartments available on a first-come, first-served basis to single and married students. Typical cost: $5,000 per year for single students; $5,000 per year for married students. *Student services:* Campus safety program, child daycare facilities, disabled student services, low-cost health insurance, writing training. *Library facilities:* Greenlease Library. *Online resources:* library catalog, web page, access to other libraries' catalogs. *Collection:* 150,000 titles, 675 serial subscriptions.

Computer facilities: 125 computers available on campus for general student use. A campuswide network can be accessed from student residence rooms and from off campus. Internet access and online class registration are available. *Web address:* http://www.researchcollege.edu/.

General Application Contact: Leslie Ann Mendenhall, Director of Transfer and Graduate Recruitment, 816-995-2820, Fax: 816-995-2813, E-mail: leslie.mendenhall@researchcollege.edu.

GRADUATE UNITS

Nursing Program Average age 30. *Faculty:* 11 full-time (all women). Expenses: Contact institution. *Financial support:* Applicants required to submit FAFSA. In 2006, 6 degrees awarded. *Degree program information:* Part-time programs available. Postbaccalaureate distance learning degree programs offered (no on-campus study). Offers executive nurse practitioner (MSN); family nurse practitioner (MSN); nursing education (MSN). *Application deadline:* For spring admission, 10/1 priority date for domestic students. Applications are processed on a rolling basis. *Application fee:* $50. *Application Contact:* Leslie Ann Mendenhall, Director of Transfer and Graduate Recruitment, 816-995-2820, Fax: 816-995-2813, E-mail: leslie.mendenhall@researchcollege.edu. *President and Dean,* Dr. Nancy O. De Basio, 816-995-2815, Fax: 816-995-2817, E-mail: nancy.debasio@researchcollege.edu.

RHODE ISLAND COLLEGE, Providence, RI 02908-1991

General Information State-supported, coed, comprehensive institution. *Enrollment:* 8,939 graduate, professional, and undergraduate students; 230 full-time matriculated graduate/professional students (192 women), 410 part-time matriculated graduate/professional students (329 women). *Enrollment by degree level:* 525 master's, 53 doctoral, 62 other advanced degrees. *Graduate faculty:* 135 full-time (62 women), 46 part-time/adjunct (27 women). Tuition, state resident: part-time $244 per credit. Tuition, nonresident: part-time $512 per credit. *Required fees:* $12 per credit. $66 per term. Tuition and fees vary according to degree level, program and reciprocity agreements. *Graduate housing:* On-campus housing not available. *Student services:* Campus employment opportunities, career counseling, child daycare facilities, disabled student services, free psychological counseling, international student services, low-cost health insurance, multicultural affairs office. *Library facilities:* Adams Library. *Online resources:* library catalog, web page, access to other libraries' catalogs. *Collection:* 664,667 titles, 2,251 serial subscriptions.

Computer facilities: Computer purchase and lease plans are available. 350 computers available on campus for general student use. A campuswide network can be accessed from student residence rooms and from off campus. Internet access and online class registration are available. *Web address:* http://www.ric.edu/.

General Application Contact: Dean of Graduate Studies, 401-456-8700.

GRADUATE UNITS

School of Graduate Studies Students: 230 full-time (192 women), 410 part-time (329 women); includes 36 minority (13 African Americans, 1 American Indian/Alaska Native, 7 Asian Americans or Pacific Islanders, 15 Hispanic Americans), 1 international. Average age 35. *Faculty:* 135 full-time (62 women), 46 part-time/adjunct (27 women). Expenses: Contact institution. *Financial support:* In 2006–07, 12 teaching assistantships with full tuition reimbursements (averaging $4,550 per year) were awarded; research assistantships with partial tuition reimbursements, career-related internships or fieldwork, Federal Work-Study, traineeships, health care benefits, tuition waivers (partial), and unspecified assistantships also available. Support available to part-time students. Financial award application deadline: 5/15; financial award applicants required to submit FAFSA. In 2006, 295 master's, 1 doctorate, 12 other advanced degrees awarded. *Degree program information:* Part-time and evening/weekend programs available. Offers nursing (MSN). *Application deadline:* For fall admission, 4/1 priority date for domestic students; for spring admission, 11/1 for domestic students. Applications are processed on a rolling basis. *Application fee:* $50. *Dean,* 401-456-8700.

Faculty of Arts and Sciences Students: 36 full-time (23 women), 55 part-time (33 women); includes 7 minority (3 African Americans, 1 American Indian/Alaska Native, 2 Asian Americans or Pacific Islanders, 1 Hispanic American). Average age 33. *Faculty:* 72 full-time (31 women), 8 part-time/adjunct (4 women). Expenses: Contact institution. *Financial support:* Research assistantships with tuition reimbursements, teaching assistantships with full tuition reimbursements, career-related internships or fieldwork, Federal Work-Study, scholarships/grants, health care benefits, and unspecified assistantships available. Support available to part-time students. Financial award application deadline: 5/15; financial award applicants required to submit FAFSA. In 2006, 34 degrees awarded. *Degree program information:* Part-time and evening/weekend programs available. Offers art (MA); art education (MAT); arts and sciences (MA, MAT, MFA, MM Ed, MPA); biology (MA); creative writing (MA); English (MA); history (MA); mathematics (MA); media studies (MA); music education (MAT, MM Ed); psychology (MA); public administration (MPA); theatre (MFA). *Application deadline:* For fall admission, 4/1 for domestic students; for spring admission, 11/1 for domestic students. Applications are processed on a rolling basis. *Application fee:* $50. *Dean,* Dr. Richard R. Weiner, 401-456-8106, E-mail: rweiner@ric.edu.

Feinstein School of Education and Human Development Students: 91 full-time (80 women), 320 part-time (270 women); includes 17 minority (6 African Americans, 2 American Indian/Alaska Native, 2 Asian Americans or Pacific Islanders, 7 Hispanic Americans). Average age 35. *Faculty:* 43 full-time (20 women), 31 part-time/adjunct (18 women). Expenses: Contact institution. *Financial support:* Teaching assistantships with full tuition reimbursements, career-related internships or fieldwork, Federal Work-Study, scholarships/grants, health care benefits, and unspecified assistantships available. Support available to part-time students. Financial award application deadline: 5/15; financial award applicants required to submit FAFSA. In 2006, 181 master's, 1 doctorate, 12 other advanced degrees awarded. *Degree program information:* Part-time and evening/weekend programs available. Offers bilingual/bicultural education (M Ed); counseling (MA); early childhood education (M Ed); education (PhD); education and human development (M Ed, MA, MAT, PhD, CAGS); educational administration (CAGS); educational leadership (M Ed); elementary education (M Ed, MAT); English (MAT); French (MAT); health education (M Ed); history (MAT); math (MAT); reading (M Ed); school administration (M Ed); school counseling (CAGS); secondary education (M Ed); Spanish (MAT); special education (M Ed, CAGS); teaching English as a second language (M Ed, MAT); technology education (M Ed). *Application deadline:* For fall admission, 3/15 for domestic students; for spring admission, 11/1 for domestic students. Applications are processed on a rolling basis. *Application fee:* $50. *Interim Dean,* Dr. Julie Wollman, 401-456-8110, E-mail: jwollman@ric.edu.

School of Management Students: 2 full-time (both women), 13 part-time (6 women); includes 2 minority (1 African American, 1 Hispanic American), 1 international. Average age 37. *Faculty:* 9 full-time (3 women). Expenses: Contact institution. *Financial support:* Federal Work-Study, scholarships/grants, health care benefits, and unspecified assistantships available. Support available to part-time students. Financial award application deadline: 5/15; financial award applicants required to submit FAFSA. In 2006, 8 degrees awarded. *Degree program information:* Part-time and evening/weekend programs available. Offers accounting (MP Ac); management (MP Ac); personal financial planning (MP Ac). *Application deadline:* For fall admission, 4/1 for domestic students; for spring admission, 11/1 for domestic students. Applications are processed on a rolling basis. *Application fee:* $50. *Dean,* Dr. James Schweikart, 401-456-8009, E-mail: jschweikart@ric.edu.

School of Social Work Students: 101 full-time (87 women), 22 part-time (19 women); includes 13 minority (3 African Americans, 3 Asian Americans or Pacific Islanders, 7 Hispanic Americans). Average age 34. *Faculty:* 10 full-time (8 women), 6 part-time/adjunct (5 women). Expenses: Contact institution. *Financial support:* Career-related internships or fieldwork, Federal Work-Study, scholarships/grants, health care benefits, and unspecified assistantships available. Support available to part-time students. Financial award application deadline: 5/15; financial award applicants required to submit FAFSA. In 2006, 61 degrees awarded. *Degree program information:* Part-time programs available. Offers social work (MSW). *Application deadline:* For fall admission, 2/15 for domestic students. Applications are processed on a rolling basis. *Application fee:* $50. *Dean,* Dr. Carol Bennett-Speight, 401-456-8043.

RHODE ISLAND SCHOOL OF DESIGN, Providence, RI 02903-2784

General Information Independent, coed, comprehensive institution. *Graduate housing:* Room and/or apartments available on a first-come, first-served basis to single students; on-campus housing not available to married students.

GRADUATE UNITS

Graduate Studies Offers art education (MA, MAT); digital media (MFA). Electronic applications accepted.

Division of Architecture and Design Offers architecture (M Arch); architecture and design (M Arch, MFA, MIA, MID, MLA); furniture design (MFA); graphic design (MFA); industrial design (MID); interior architecture (MIA); landscape architecture (MLA).

Division of Fine Arts Offers ceramics (MFA); glass (MFA); jewelry and light metals (MFA); painting (MFA); photography (MFA); printmaking (MFA); sculpture (MFA); textiles (MFA).

RHODES COLLEGE, Memphis, TN 38112-1690

General Information Independent-religious, coed, comprehensive institution. *Graduate housing:* Room and/or apartments available to single students; on-campus housing not available to married students. Housing application deadline: 3/1.

GRADUATE UNITS

Department of Economics/Business Administration *Degree program information:* Part-time programs available. Offers accounting (MS).

RICE UNIVERSITY, Houston, TX 77251-1892

General Information Independent, coed, university. CGS member. *Enrollment:* 5,119 graduate, professional, and undergraduate students; 1,916 full-time matriculated graduate/professional students (672 women), 89 part-time matriculated graduate/professional students (53 women). *Enrollment by degree level:* 800 master's, 1,205 doctoral. *Graduate faculty:* 597 full-time, 387 part-time/adjunct. *Tuition:* Full-time $23,400; part-time $1,300 per hour. *Required fees:* $150; $75 per semester. Tuition and fees vary according to program. *Graduate housing:* Rooms and/or apartments available on a first-come, first-served basis to single and married students. Typical cost: $6,200 per year ($9,590 including board) for single students. Housing application deadline: 7/15. *Student services:* Campus employment opportunities, campus safety program, career counseling, exercise/wellness program, free psychological counseling, international student services, low-cost health insurance, multicultural affairs office, teacher training. *Library facilities:* Fondren Library. *Online resources:* library catalog, web page, access to other libraries' catalogs. *Collection:* 2.5 million titles, 13,486 serial subscriptions, 57,728 audiovisual materials. *Research affiliation:* Fermi National Accelerator Laboratory, Los Alamos National Laboratory, Brookhaven National Laboratory, Arecibo Observatory, Houston Area Research Center.

Computer facilities: 523 computers available on campus for general student use. A campuswide network can be accessed from student residence rooms and from off campus. Internet access and online class registration are available. *Web address:* http://www.rice.edu/.

General Application Contact: Office of Graduate Studies, 713-348-4002, E-mail: graduate@rice.edu.

GRADUATE UNITS

Graduate Programs Students: 1,916 full-time (672 women), 89 part-time (53 women); includes 347 minority (73 African Americans, 5 American Indian/Alaska Native, 150 Asian Americans or Pacific Islanders, 119 Hispanic Americans), 665 international. 4,929 applicants, 22% accepted, 597 enrolled. Expenses: Contact institution. *Financial support:* Fellowships, research assistantships, teaching assistantships, career-related internships or fieldwork, Federal Work-Study, institutionally sponsored loans, scholarships/grants, tuition waivers (full and partial), and unspecified assistantships available. Financial award applicants required to submit CSS PROFILE or FAFSA. In 2006, 485 master's, 147 doctorates awarded. *Degree program information:* Part-time programs available. Offers education (MAT). *Application deadline:* For fall admission, 2/15 for domestic and international students; for spring admission, 12/1 for domestic students. *Application fee:* $35. Electronic applications accepted. *Application Contact:* Susan Massey, Admissions and Enrollment Manager, 713-348-4002, Fax: 713-348-4806, E-mail: graduate@rice.edu. *Vice Provost for Research and Graduate Studies,* Jordan Konisky, 713-348-4002, Fax: 713-348-4806, E-mail: graduate@rice.edu.

George R. Brown School of Engineering Students: 473 full-time (121 women), 16 part-time (4 women); includes 84 minority (12 African Americans, 1 American Indian/Alaska Native, 42 Asian Americans or Pacific Islanders, 29 Hispanic Americans), 234 international. 1,543

Rice University (continued)

applicants, 15% accepted, 112 enrolled. *Faculty:* 122 full-time, 129 part-time/adjunct. Expenses: Contact institution. *Financial support:* In 2006–07, 216 fellowships with full tuition reimbursements (averaging $20,500 per year), 270 research assistantships with full tuition reimbursements (averaging $20,640 per year), 19 teaching assistantships with full tuition reimbursements (averaging $16,200 per year) were awarded; institutionally sponsored loans, scholarships/grants, tuition waivers (full), and unspecified assistantships also available. Financial award applicants required to submit FAFSA. In 2006, 58 master's, 72 doctorates awarded. *Degree program information:* Part-time programs available. Offers bioengineering (MS, PhD); biostatistics (PhD); chemical and biomolecular engineering (MS, PhD); chemical engineering (M Ch E); circuits, controls, and communication systems (MS, PhD); civil engineering (MCE, MS, PhD); computational and applied mathematics (MA, MCAM, PhD); computational finance (PhD); computational science and engineering (MCSE, PhD); computer science (MCS, MS, PhD); computer science and engineering (MS, PhD); computer science in bioinformatics (MCS); electrical engineering (MEE); engineering (M Ch E, M Stat, MA, MBE, MCAM, MCE, MCS, MCSE, MEE, MEE, MES, MME, MMS, MS, PhD); environmental engineering (MEE, MES, MS, PhD); environmental science (MEE, MES, MS, PhD); lasers, microwaves, and solid-state electronics (MS, PhD); materials science (MMS, MS, PhD); mechanical engineering (MME, MS, PhD); statistics (M Stat, MA, PhD). *Application deadline:* For fall admission, 2/1 for domestic and international students; for spring admission, 11/1 priority date for domestic and international students. Applications are processed on a rolling basis. *Application fee:* $35. Electronic applications accepted. *Dean of Engineering,* Dr. Sallie Keller-McNulty, 713-348-4009, Fax: 713-348-5300, E-mail: deng@rice.edu.

Jesse H. Jones Graduate School of Management Students: 459 full-time (125 women); includes 125 minority (28 African Americans, 1 American Indian/Alaska Native, 55 Asian Americans or Pacific Islanders, 41 Hispanic Americans), 91 international. 437 applicants, 48% accepted, 105 enrolled. *Faculty:* 58 full-time (16 women), 46 part-time/adjunct (8 women). Expenses: Contact institution. *Financial support:* Fellowships, career-related internships or fieldwork, Federal Work-Study, institutionally sponsored loans, scholarships/grants, and tuition waivers (full and partial) available. Financial award application deadline: 5/15; financial award applicants required to submit FAFSA. In 2006, 160 degrees awarded. *Degree program information:* Evening/weekend programs available. Offers business administration (EMBA, MBA, PMBA). *Application deadline:* For fall admission, 11/13 priority date for domestic and international students; for winter admission, 1/22 priority date for domestic and international students; for spring admission, 3/26 priority date for domestic and international students. Applications are processed on a rolling basis. *Application fee:* $100. Electronic applications accepted. *Application Contact:* Lisa W. Anderson, Director of Admissions, 713-348-4918, Fax: 713-348-6147, E-mail: ricemba@rice.edu. *Dean,* Dr. William H. Glick, 713-348-4838, Fax: 713-348-5110, E-mail: bill.glick@rice.edu.

School of Architecture Students: 70 full-time (32 women); includes 12 minority (1 African American, 6 Asian Americans or Pacific Islanders, 5 Hispanic Americans), 13 international. Average age 25. 273 applicants, 26% accepted, 27 enrolled. *Faculty:* 14 full-time (2 women), 25 part-time/adjunct (2 women). Expenses: Contact institution. *Financial support:* In 2006–07, 82 fellowships were awarded; Federal Work-Study also available. In 2006, 29 degrees awarded. Offers architecture (M Arch, D Arch); urban design (M Arch UD). *Application deadline:* For fall admission, 2/1 for domestic and international students. *Application fee:* $35. *Application Contact:* Graduate Programs, 713-348-5202, Fax: 713-348-5277, E-mail: arch@rice.edu. *Dean,* Lars Lerup, 713-348-4044, Fax: 713-348-5277, E-mail: arch@rice.edu.

School of Humanities Students: 176 full-time (93 women); includes 24 minority (9 African Americans, 6 Asian Americans or Pacific Islanders, 9 Hispanic Americans), 44 international. Average age 28. 372 applicants, 17% accepted, 33 enrolled. *Faculty:* 88 full-time (34 women), 10 part-time/adjunct (4 women). Expenses: Contact institution. *Financial support:* In 2006–07, 115 students received support, including 105 fellowships (averaging $12,400 per year), 10 teaching assistantships with full tuition reimbursements available (averaging $4,600 per year); Federal Work-Study, institutionally sponsored loans, scholarships/grants, and tuition waivers (full and partial) also available. Financial award applicants required to submit CSS PROFILE or FAFSA. In 2006, 21 master's, 13 doctorates awarded. Offers English (MA, PhD); French studies (MA, PhD); history (MA, PhD); humanities (MA, PhD); linguistics (MA, PhD); philosophy (MA, PhD); religious studies (PhD); Spanish (MA). *Application deadline:* For fall admission, 2/1 for domestic students. *Application fee:* $35. *Dean,* Gary Wihl, 713-348-4810, E-mail: humadmin@rice.edu.

School of Social Sciences Students: 140 full-time (76 women), 1 part-time; includes 19 minority (4 African Americans, 4 Asian Americans or Pacific Islanders, 11 Hispanic Americans), 63 international. 449 applicants, 9% accepted, 34 enrolled. *Faculty:* 63 full-time (14 women), 22 part-time/adjunct (12 women). Expenses: Contact institution. *Financial support:* In 2006–07, 76 fellowships, 10 research assistantships, 46 teaching assistantships were awarded; Federal Work-Study and tuition waivers (full and partial) also available. In 2006, 23 master's, 16 doctorates awarded. Offers anthropology (MA, PhD); cognitive sciences (MA, PhD); economics (MA, PhD); industrial-organizational/social psychology (MA, PhD); political science (MA, PhD); psychology (MA, PhD); social sciences (MA, PhD). *Application deadline:* For fall admission, 2/1 priority date for domestic and international students; for spring admission, 11/1 for domestic and international students. Applications are processed on a rolling basis. *Application fee:* $35. *Dean,* Lyn Ragsdale, 713-348-4824, Fax: 713-348-5161, E-mail: dssc@rice.edu.

Shepherd School of Music Students: 166 full-time (82 women), 5 part-time (2 women); includes 23 minority (2 African Americans, 1 American Indian/Alaska Native, 17 Asian Americans or Pacific Islanders, 3 Hispanic Americans), 36 international. Average age 24. 489 applicants, 17% accepted, 57 enrolled. *Faculty:* 39 full-time (11 women), 19 part-time/adjunct (6 women). Expenses: Contact institution. *Financial support:* In 2006–07, 168 students received support, including fellowships with full and partial tuition reimbursements available (averaging $16,020 per year), teaching assistantships with full tuition reimbursements available (averaging $25,700 per year); scholarships/grants and tuition waivers (full and partial) also available. Financial award application deadline: 1/2. In 2006, 44 master's, 5 doctorates awarded. Offers composition (MM, DMA); conducting (MM); history (MM); performance (MM, DMA); theory (MM). *Application deadline:* For fall admission, 1/2 for domestic and international students; for spring admission, 11/1 for domestic and international students. Applications are processed on a rolling basis. *Application fee:* $35. Electronic applications accepted. *Application Contact:* Suzanne Taylor, Admissions Assistant, 713-348-4854, Fax: 713-348-5317, E-mail: musi@rice.edu. *Dean,* Dr. Robert Yekovich, 713-348-4854, Fax: 713-348-5317, E-mail: musi@rice.edu.

Wiess School of Natural Sciences Students: 364 full-time (124 women), 7 part-time (3 women); includes 40 minority (6 African Americans, 1 American Indian/Alaska Native, 16 Asian Americans or Pacific Islanders, 17 Hispanic Americans), 149 international. 1,140 applicants, 15% accepted, 71 enrolled. *Faculty:* 116 full-time (15 women), 4 part-time/adjunct (0 women). Expenses: Contact institution. *Financial support:* In 2006–07, 150 fellowships (averaging $20,000 per year), 181 research assistantships (averaging $20,000 per year) were awarded; Federal Work-Study and tuition waivers (full and partial) also available. *Degree program information:* Part-time programs available. Offers biochemistry and cell biology (MA, PhD); chemistry (MA, PhD); ecology and evolutionary biology (MA, MS, PhD); environmental analysis and decision making (MS); geophysics (MS); inorganic chemistry (PhD); mathematics (MA, PhD); nanoscale physics (MS); natural sciences (MA, MS, MST, PhD); organic chemistry (PhD); physical chemistry (PhD); physics (MA); physics and astronomy (MS, MST, PhD). *Application deadline:* Applications are processed on a rolling basis. *Application fee:* $35. Electronic applications accepted. *Application Contact:* Rachel S. Miller, Assistant Dean, 713-348-6148, Fax: 713-348-6149, E-mail: gradinfo@rice.edu. *Dean,* Dr. Kathleen S. Matthews, 713-348-3350, Fax: 713-348-6149.

Rice Quantum Institute Students: 50 full-time (11 women); includes 5 minority (3 African Americans, 1 Asian American or Pacific Islander, 1 Hispanic American), 35 international. Average age 24. 60 applicants, 25% accepted, 7 enrolled. *Faculty:* 57 full-time (6 women). Expenses: Contact institution. *Financial support:* Fellowships, research assistantships available. In 2006, 2 master's, 1 doctorate awarded. Offers quantum physics (MS, PhD). *Application deadline:* For fall admission, 2/1 for domestic and international students. *Application fee:* $35. Electronic applications accepted. *Application Contact:* Yvonne Creed, Executive Assistant, 713-348-6356, Fax: 713-348-5401, E-mail: ycreed@rice.edu. *Director,* Dr. Peter Nordlander, 713-348-6356, Fax: 713-348-5401, E-mail: quantum@rice.edu.

THE RICHARD STOCKTON COLLEGE OF NEW JERSEY, Pomona, NJ 08240-0195

General Information State-supported, coed, comprehensive institution. *Enrollment:* 7,212 graduate, professional, and undergraduate students; 127 full-time matriculated graduate/professional students (101 women), 361 part-time matriculated graduate/professional students (257 women). *Enrollment by degree level:* 488 master's. *Graduate faculty:* 85 full-time (53 women), 22 part-time/adjunct (12 women). Tuition, state resident: full-time $9,746. Tuition, nonresident: full-time $14,462. *Required fees:* $2,340. *Graduate housing:* Room and/or apartments available to single students; on-campus housing not available to married students. Typical cost: $5,989 per year ($8,345 including board). Room and board charges vary according to board plan. Housing application deadline: 4/1. *Student services:* Campus employment opportunities, campus safety program, career counseling, child daycare facilities, disabled student services, exercise/wellness program, free psychological counseling, international student services, low-cost health insurance, teacher training, writing training. *Library facilities:* The Richard Stockton College of New Jersey Library. *Online resources:* library catalog, web page. *Collection:* 268,411 titles, 24,364 serial subscriptions, 14,834 audiovisual materials. *Research affiliation:* Wetlands Institute (marine biology), Jewish Foundation (Holocaust studies), Buildner Family Foundation (diversity projects), Association of State Colleges & Universities (civic engagement), Nature Conservancy of NJ (environmental studies), Aviation Research & Technology Park (aviation research).

Computer facilities: 1,375 computers available on campus for general student use. A campuswide network can be accessed from student residence rooms and from off campus. Internet access and online class registration are available. *Web address:* http://www.stockton.edu/.

General Application Contact: John Iacovelli, Dean of Enrollment Management, 866-RSC-2885, Fax: 609-748-5541, E-mail: admissions@stockton.edu.

GRADUATE UNITS

Graduate Programs Students: 127 full-time (101 women), 361 part-time (257 women); includes 68 minority (30 African Americans, 2 American Indian/Alaska Native, 17 Asian Americans or Pacific Islanders, 19 Hispanic Americans). Average age 42. 302 applicants, 57% accepted. *Faculty:* 85 full-time (53 women), 22 part-time/adjunct (12 women). Expenses: Contact institution. *Financial support:* In 2006–07, 82 students received support; research assistantships, career-related internships or fieldwork, Federal Work-Study, and scholarships/grants available. Support available to part-time students. Financial award application deadline: 3/1; financial award applicants required to submit FAFSA. In 2006, 100 degrees awarded. *Degree program information:* Part-time programs available. Offers business studies (MBA); criminal justice (MA); education (MA); Holocaust and genocide studies (MA); instructional technology (MA); nursing (MSN); occupational therapy (MSOT); paralegal (Certificate); physical therapy (MPT, DPT). *Application deadline:* Applications are processed on a rolling basis. *Application fee:* $50. Electronic applications accepted. *Application Contact:* John Iacovelli, Dean of Enrollment Management, 866-RSC-2885, Fax: 609-748-5541, E-mail: admissions@stockton.edu. *Dean of Graduate Studies,* Dr. Deborah M. Figart, 609-652-4298, E-mail: graduatestudies@stockton.edu.

RICHMOND, THE AMERICAN INTERNATIONAL UNIVERSITY IN LONDON, Richmond, Surrey TW10 6JP, United Kingdom

General Information Independent, coed, comprehensive institution. *Graduate housing:* Room and/or apartments available on a first-come, first-served basis to single students; on-campus housing not available to married students. Housing application deadline: 8/1.

GRADUATE UNITS

Program in Art History *Degree program information:* Part-time programs available. Offers art history (MA). Electronic applications accepted.

RIDER UNIVERSITY, Lawrenceville, NJ 08648-3001

General Information Independent, coed, comprehensive institution. *Enrollment:* 5,790 graduate, professional, and undergraduate students; 255 full-time matriculated graduate/professional students (165 women), 749 part-time matriculated graduate/professional students (513 women). *Enrollment by degree level:* 1,004 master's. *Graduate faculty:* 78 full-time (27 women), 78 part-time/adjunct (35 women). *Tuition:* Part-time $525 per credit. *Required fees:* $35 per course. $30 per semester. *Graduate housing:* Room and/or apartments available on a first-come, first-served basis to single students; on-campus housing not available to married students. Typical cost: $6,740 per year ($10,800 including board). Housing application deadline: 7/1. *Student services:* Campus employment opportunities, campus safety program, career counseling, disabled student services, exercise/wellness program, free psychological counseling, international student services, multicultural affairs office. *Library facilities:* Franklin F. Moore Library plus 1 other. *Online resources:* library catalog, web page, access to other libraries' catalogs. *Collection:* 430,197 titles, 30,125 serial subscriptions, 21,471 audiovisual materials.

Computer facilities: Computer purchase and lease plans are available. 403 computers available on campus for general student use. A campuswide network can be accessed from student residence rooms and from off campus. Internet access and online class registration are available. *Web address:* http://www.rider.edu/.

General Application Contact: Jamie L Mitchell, Director of Graduate Admissions, 609-896-5036, Fax: 609-895-5680, E-mail: jmitchell@rider.edu.

GRADUATE UNITS

College of Business Administration Students: 68 full-time (27 women), 270 part-time (124 women); includes 69 minority (19 African Americans, 1 American Indian/Alaska Native, 39 Asian Americans or Pacific Islanders, 10 Hispanic Americans), 18 international. Average age 29. 129 applicants, 71% accepted, 62 enrolled. *Faculty:* 23 full-time (6 women), 12 part-time/adjunct (0 women). Expenses: Contact institution. *Financial support:* In 2006–07, 90 students received support. Career-related internships or fieldwork, Federal Work-Study, institutionally sponsored loans, unspecified assistantships, and institutional work-study available. Support available to part-time students. Financial award applicants required to submit FAFSA. In 2006, 112 degrees awarded. *Degree program information:* Part-time and evening/weekend programs available. Offers accountancy (M Acc); business administration (M Acc, MBA). *Application deadline:* For fall admission, 8/1 priority date for domestic students, 6/1 priority date for international students; for spring admission, 12/1 priority date for domestic students, 11/1 priority date for international students. Applications are processed on a rolling basis. *Application fee:* $50. Electronic applications accepted. *Application Contact:* Jamie L Mitchell, Director of Graduate Admissions, 609-896-5036, Fax: 609-895-5680, E-mail: jmitchell@rider.edu. *MBA Program Director,* Dr. John Farrell, 609-895-5776, Fax: 609-896-5304.

Department of Graduate Education, Leadership and Counseling Students: 90 full-time (75 women), 457 part-time (369 women); includes 73 minority (50 African Americans, 2 American Indian/Alaska Native, 6 Asian Americans or Pacific Islanders, 15 Hispanic Americans), 1 international. Average age 32. 314 applicants, 61% accepted, 138 enrolled. *Faculty:* 24 full-time (12 women), 30 part-time/adjunct (15 women). Expenses: Contact institution. *Financial support:* In 2006–07, 271 students received support. Career-related internships or fieldwork, Federal Work-Study, institutionally sponsored loans, and unspecified assistantships available. Support available to part-time students. Financial award applicants required to submit FAFSA. In 2006, 116 master's, 19 other advanced degrees awarded. *Degree program information:* Part-time and evening/weekend programs available. Offers business education (Certificate); counseling services (MA, Ed S); curriculum, instruction and supervision (MA); director of school counseling services (Certificate); educational administration (MA); elementary education (Certificate); English as a second language (Certificate); English education (Certificate); mathematics education (Certificate); organizational leadership (MA); preschool to grade 3 (Certificate); principal (Certificate); reading specialist (Certificate); reading/language arts (MA, Certificate); school business administrator (Certificate); school counseling services (Certificate);

school psychology (Ed S); science education (Certificate); social studies education (Certificate); special education (MA); supervisor (Certificate); teacher certification (Certificate); teaching (MA); world languages (Certificate). *Application deadline:* For fall admission, 5/1 priority date for domestic students, 6/1 priority date for international students; for spring admission, 11/1 priority date for domestic and international students. Applications are processed on a rolling basis. *Application fee:* $50. Electronic applications accepted. *Application Contact:* Jamie L Mitchell, Director of Graduate Admissions, 609-896-5036, Fax: 609-895-5680, E-mail: jmitchell@rider.edu. *Chair,* Dr. Dennis C. Buss, 609-895-5353, Fax: 609-896-5362, E-mail: dbuss@rider.edu.

RIVIER COLLEGE, Nashua, NH 03060

General Information Independent-religious, coed, comprehensive institution. *Enrollment:* 2,320 graduate, professional, and undergraduate students; 73 full-time matriculated graduate/professional students (40 women), 674 part-time matriculated graduate/professional students (530 women). *Enrollment by degree level:* 747 master's. *Graduate faculty:* 35 full-time (17 women), 71 part-time/adjunct (39 women). *Graduate housing:* On-campus housing not available. *Student services:* Campus safety program, career counseling, disabled student services, free psychological counseling, international student services, low-cost health insurance, multicultural affairs office, teacher training. *Library facilities:* Regina Library plus 1 other. *Online resources:* library catalog, web page, access to other libraries' catalogs. *Collection:* 92,000 titles, 500 serial subscriptions, 4,000 audiovisual materials.

Computer facilities: 93 computers available on campus for general student use. A campuswide network can be accessed from student residence rooms and from off campus. *Web address:* http://www.rivier.edu/.

General Application Contact: Diane Monahan, Director of Graduate Admissions, 603-897-8129, Fax: 603-897-8810, E-mail: gradadm@rivier.edu.

GRADUATE UNITS

School of Graduate Studies Students: 73 full-time (40 women), 674 part-time (530 women); includes 25 minority (5 African Americans, 9 Asian Americans or Pacific Islanders, 11 Hispanic Americans), 17 international. Average age 36. *Faculty:* 35 full-time (17 women), 71 part-time/adjunct (39 women). Expenses: Contact institution. *Financial support:* Available to part-time students. Application deadline: 2/1; In 2006, 178 master's, 18 other advanced degrees awarded. *Degree program information:* Part-time programs available. Offers arts and sciences (EMBA, M Ed, MA, MAT, MBA, MS, CAGS); business administration (MBA); computer information systems (MS); computer science (MS); curriculum and instruction (M Ed); early childhood education (M Ed); educational administration (M Ed); educational studies (M Ed); elementary education (M Ed); elementary education and general special education (M Ed); emotional and behavioral disorders (M Ed); English (MA, MAT); family nurse practitioner (MS); general social education (M Ed); health care administration (MBA); human resources management (MS); leadership and learning (CAGS); learning disabilities (M Ed); learning disabilities and reading (M Ed); mathematics (MAT); mental health counseling (MA); nursing education (MS); organizational leadership (EMBA); reading (M Ed); school counseling (M Ed); social studies education (MAT); Spanish (MAT); writing and literature (MA). *Application deadline:* Applications are processed on a rolling basis. *Application fee:* $25. Electronic applications accepted. *Application Contact:* Diane Monahan, Director of Graduate Admissions, 603-897-8129, Fax: 603-897-8810, E-mail: gradadm@rivier.edu. *Dean,* Dr. Albert DeCiccio, 603-888-1311.

ROBERT MORRIS UNIVERSITY, Moon Township, PA 15108-1189

General Information Independent, coed, university. *Enrollment:* 5,065 graduate, professional, and undergraduate students; 1,121 part-time matriculated graduate/professional students (537 women). *Enrollment by degree level:* 936 master's, 79 doctoral, 106 other advanced degrees. *Graduate faculty:* 65 full-time (23 women), 26 part-time/adjunct (9 women). *Tuition:* Part-time $580 per credit. Part-time tuition and fees vary according to degree level and program. *Graduate housing:* Room and/or apartments available on a first-come, first-served basis to single students; on-campus housing not available to married students. Typical cost: $4,890 per year ($8,410 including board). Room and board charges vary according to board plan and housing facility selected. Housing application deadline: 5/1. *Student services:* Campus employment opportunities, campus safety program, career counseling, disabled student services, international student services. *Library facilities:* Robert Morris University Library plus 1 other. *Online resources:* library catalog, access to other libraries' catalogs. *Collection:* 135,806 titles, 580 serial subscriptions, 2,852 audiovisual materials.

Computer facilities: 300 computers available on campus for general student use. A campuswide network can be accessed from student residence rooms and from off campus. Internet access and online class registration are available. *Web address:* http://www.rmu.edu/.

General Application Contact: Kellie L. Laurenzi, Dean of Enrollment, 412-262-8235, Fax: 412-299-2425, E-mail: laurenzi@rmu.edu.

GRADUATE UNITS

Graduate Studies Average age 33. 718 applicants, 62% accepted, 298 enrolled. *Faculty:* 65 full-time (23 women), 26 part-time/adjunct (9 women). Expenses: Contact institution. *Financial support:* In 2006–07, 125 students received support, including 6 research assistantships with partial tuition reimbursements available; Federal Work-Study, institutionally sponsored loans, and unspecified assistantships also available. Support available to part-time students. Financial award application deadline: 5/1; financial award applicants required to submit FAFSA. In 2006, 352 master's, 6 doctorates awarded. *Degree program information:* Part-time and evening/weekend programs available. *Application deadline:* For fall admission, 7/1 priority date for domestic and international students; for spring admission, 11/1 priority date for domestic and international students. Applications are processed on a rolling basis. *Application fee:* $35. Electronic applications accepted. *Application Contact:* Kellie L. Laurenzi, Dean of Enrollment, 412-262-8235, Fax: 412-299-2425, E-mail: laurenzi@rmu.edu. *Senior Vice President for Academic and Student Affairs,* Dr. William J. Katip, 412-262-8285, Fax: 412-604-2528.

School of Adult and Continuing Education Average age 31. 36 applicants, 67% accepted, 23 enrolled. *Faculty:* 3 full-time (1 woman), 1 part-time/adjunct (0 women). Expenses: Contact institution. *Financial support:* Federal Work-Study, institutionally sponsored loans, and unspecified assistantships available. Financial award application deadline: 5/1. In 2006, 29 degrees awarded. *Degree program information:* Part-time and evening/weekend programs available. Offers adult and continuing education (MS). *Application deadline:* For fall admission, 7/1 priority date for domestic and international students; for spring admission, 11/1 priority date for domestic and international students. Applications are processed on a rolling basis. *Application fee:* $35. Electronic applications accepted. *Application Contact:* Kellie L. Laurenzi, Dean of Enrollment, 412-262-8235, Fax: 412-299-2425, E-mail: laurenzi@rmu.edu. *Dean,* Dr. Kathleen V. Davis, 412-397-6808, Fax: 412-397-5539, E-mail: daviska@rmu.edu.

School of Business Average age 31. 253 applicants, 59% accepted, 103 enrolled. *Faculty:* 27 full-time (12 women), 6 part-time/adjunct (1 woman). Expenses: Contact institution. *Financial support:* Research assistantships with partial tuition reimbursements, Federal Work-Study, institutionally sponsored loans, and unspecified assistantships available. Support available to part-time students. Financial award application deadline: 5/1; financial award applicants required to submit FAFSA. In 2006, 139 degrees awarded. *Degree program information:* Part-time and evening/weekend programs available. Offers accounting (MS); business administration and management (MBA); finance (MS); human resource management (MS); nonprofit management (MS); sport management (MS); taxation (MS). *Application deadline:* For fall admission, 7/1 priority date for domestic and international students; for spring admission, 11/1 priority date for domestic and international students. Applications are processed on a rolling basis. *Application fee:* $35. Electronic applications accepted. *Application Contact:* Kellie L. Laurenzi, Dean of Enrollment, 412-262-8235, Fax: 412-299-2425, E-mail: laurenzi@rmu.edu. *Dean,* Dr. Derya A. Jacobs, 412-262-8451, Fax: 412-262-8494, E-mail: jacobs@rmu.edu.

School of Communications and Information Systems Average age 33. 200 applicants, 59% accepted, 72 enrolled. *Faculty:* 21 full-time (6 women), 6 part-time/adjunct (2 women). Expenses: Contact institution. *Financial support:* Research assistantships with partial tuition reimbursements, institutionally sponsored loans and unspecified assistantships available. Support available to part-time students. Financial award application deadline: 5/1. In 2006, 81 master's, 6 doctorates awarded. *Degree program information:* Part-time and evening/weekend programs available. Offers communications and information systems (MS); competitive intelligence systems (MS); information security and assurance (MS); information systems and communications (D Sc); information systems management (MS); Internet information systems (MS); IT project management (MS). *Application deadline:* For fall admission, 7/1 priority date for domestic and international students; for spring admission, 11/1 priority date for domestic and international students. Applications are processed on a rolling basis. *Application fee:* $35. Electronic applications accepted. *Application Contact:* Kellie L. Laurenzi, Dean of Enrollment, 412-262-8235, Fax: 412-299-2425, E-mail: laurenzi@rmu.edu. *Dean,* Dr. David L. Jamison, 412-604-2591, Fax: 412-262-8483, E-mail: jamison@rmu.edu.

School of Education and Social Sciences Average age 31. 168 applicants, 73% accepted, 80 enrolled. *Faculty:* 12 full-time (4 women), 13 part-time/adjunct (5 women). Expenses: Contact institution. In 2006, 71 master's, 137 other advanced degrees awarded. *Degree program information:* Part-time and evening/weekend programs available. Offers education and social sciences (MS, PhD, Postbaccalaureate Certificate). *Application deadline:* For fall admission, 7/1 priority date for domestic and international students; for spring admission, 11/1 priority date for domestic and international students. Applications are processed on a rolling basis. *Application fee:* $35. Electronic applications accepted. *Application Contact:* Kellie L. Laurenzi, Dean of Enrollment, 412-262-8235, Fax: 412-299-2425, E-mail: laurenzi@rmu.edu. *Dean,* Dr. John E. Graham, 412-262-8228, E-mail: graham@rmu.edu.

School of Engineering, Mathematics and Science Average age 33. 39 applicants, 36% accepted, 7 enrolled. *Faculty:* 3 full-time (0 women), 1 (woman) part-time/adjunct. Expenses: Contact institution. *Financial support:* Federal Work-Study, institutionally sponsored loans, and unspecified assistantships available. Financial award application deadline: 5/1; financial award applicants required to submit FAFSA. In 2006, 22 degrees awarded. *Degree program information:* Part-time and evening/weekend programs available. Offers engineering, mathematics and science (MS, PhD). *Application deadline:* For fall admission, 7/1 priority date for domestic and international students; for spring admission, 11/1 priority date for domestic and international students. Applications are processed on a rolling basis. *Application fee:* $35. Electronic applications accepted. *Application Contact:* Kellie L. Laurenzi, Dean of Enrollment, 412-262-8235, Fax: 412-299-2425, E-mail: laurenzi@rmu.edu. *Dean,* Dr. Winston F. Erevelles, 412-262-8616, Fax: 412-262-8494, E-mail: erevelles@rmu.edu.

School of Nursing Average age 38. 17 applicants, 82% accepted, 10 enrolled. *Faculty:* 2 full-time (both women). Expenses: Contact institution. *Financial support:* Federal Work-Study, institutionally sponsored loans, and unspecified assistantships available. Financial award application deadline: 5/1; financial award applicants required to submit FAFSA. In 2006, 8 degrees awarded. *Degree program information:* Part-time and evening/weekend programs available. Offers nursing (MS). *Application deadline:* For fall admission, 7/1 priority date for domestic and international students; for spring admission, 11/1 priority date for domestic and international students. Applications are processed on a rolling basis. *Application fee:* $35. Electronic applications accepted. *Application Contact:* Kellie L. Laurenzi, Assistant Dean, Enrollment Services, 412-262-8235, Fax: 412-299-2425, E-mail: laurenzi@rmu.edu. *Dean,* Dr. Lynda J. Davidson, 412-269-3859, Fax: 412-262-8494, E-mail: davidsonl@rmu.edu.

See Close-Up on page 1003.

ROBERTS WESLEYAN COLLEGE, Rochester, NY 14624-1997

General Information Independent-religious, coed, comprehensive institution. *Enrollment:* 1,903 graduate, professional, and undergraduate students; 168 full-time matriculated graduate/professional students (116 women), 121 part-time matriculated graduate/professional students (81 women). *Enrollment by degree level:* 222 master's, 67 other advanced degrees. *Graduate faculty:* 11 full-time (2 women), 31 part-time/adjunct (10 women). *Graduate housing:* Room and/or apartments available on a first-come, first-served basis to single students; on-campus housing not available to married students. *Student services:* Career counseling, disabled student services, low-cost health insurance, teacher training, writing training. *Library facilities:* Ora A. Sprague Library. *Online resources:* library catalog, web page, access to other libraries' catalogs. *Collection:* 123,434 titles, 1,057 serial subscriptions, 3,895 audiovisual materials.

Computer facilities: 170 computers available on campus for general student use. A campuswide network can be accessed from student residence rooms and from off campus. Internet access and online class registration are available. *Web address:* http://www.roberts.edu/.

General Application Contact: Office of Admissions, 800-777-4RWC, E-mail: admissions@roberts.edu.

GRADUATE UNITS

Division of Adult Professional Studies Students: 57 full-time (28 women). Average age 34. *Faculty:* 2 full-time (0 women), 9 part-time/adjunct (5 women). Expenses: Contact institution. *Financial support:* In 2006–07, 15 students received support. Applicants required to submit FAFSA. In 2006, 26 degrees awarded. *Degree program information:* Evening/weekend programs available. Offers health administration (MS). *Application deadline:* Applications are processed on a rolling basis. *Application fee:* $35. *Application Contact:* Cheryl Johnson, Program Coordinator, 585-594-6452, E-mail: johnson_cheryl@roberts.edu. *Chair,* Dr. William Walence, 585-594-6210.

Division of Business Students: 57 full-time (28 women). Average age 34. 45 applicants, 89% accepted. *Faculty:* 3 full-time (0 women), 13 part-time/adjunct (3 women). Expenses: Contact institution. *Financial support:* In 2006–07, 15 students received support. Applicants required to submit FAFSA. In 2006, 26 degrees awarded. *Degree program information:* Evening/weekend programs available. Offers nonprofit leadership (Certificate); strategic leadership (MS); strategic marketing (MS). *Application deadline:* Applications are processed on a rolling basis. *Application fee:* $35. *Chair,* Dr. Steven Bovee, 716-594-6571, Fax: 716-594-6316, E-mail: bovees@roberts.edu.

Division of Social Work Students: 75 full-time (66 women), 23 part-time (16 women). Average age 35. 75 applicants, 75% accepted. *Faculty:* 11. Expenses: Contact institution. *Financial support:* In 2006–07, 84 students received support, including 35 fellowships (averaging $1,863 per year); career-related internships or fieldwork, scholarships/grants, and tuition waivers (partial) also available. Financial award applicants required to submit FAFSA. In 2006, 49 degrees awarded. Offers child and family practice (MSW); congregational and community practice (MSW); mental health practice (MSW). *Application deadline:* For fall admission, 4/1 priority date for domestic students. Applications are processed on a rolling basis. *Application fee:* $35. *Application Contact:* Beverly Keim, Graduate Admissions Coordinator, 585-594-6232, E-mail: keimb@roberts.edu. *Chair,* Dr. Harmon Meldrim, 585-594-6487, E-mail: meldrimh@roberts.edu.

Division of Teacher Education Students: 1 (woman) full-time, 66 part-time (47 women). Average age 33. 52 applicants, 63% accepted. *Faculty:* 17 part-time/adjunct (7 women). Expenses: Contact institution. *Financial support:* In 2006–07, 7 students received support. Career-related internships or fieldwork available. Financial award application deadline: 9/1; financial award applicants required to submit FAFSA. In 2006, 20 degrees awarded. *Degree program information:* Part-time and evening/weekend programs available. Offers adolescence education (M Ed); childhood and special education (M Ed); literacy education (M Ed); urban education (M Ed). *Application deadline:* For fall admission, 8/1 priority date for domestic students; for spring admission, 12/1 for domestic students. Applications are processed on a rolling basis. *Application fee:* $35. *Application Contact:* Paula Finch, Graduate Admissions Coordinator, 585-594-6683, E-mail: finch_paula@roberts.edu. *Chair,* Dr. Richard Mace, 585-594-6934.

ROCHESTER INSTITUTE OF TECHNOLOGY, Rochester, NY 14623-5603

General Information Independent, coed, comprehensive institution. CGS member. *Enrollment:* 15,557 graduate, professional, and undergraduate students; 1,279 full-time

Rochester Institute of Technology (continued)

matriculated graduate/professional students (498 women), 976 part-time matriculated graduate/professional students (347 women). *Enrollment by degree level:* 2,158 master's, 88 doctoral. *Tuition:* Full-time $28,491; part-time $800 per credit. *Required fees:* $201. *Graduate housing:* Rooms and/or apartments available on a first-come, first-served basis to single and married students. Typical cost: $7,356 (including board) for single students. Housing application deadline: 4/30. *Student services:* Campus employment opportunities, campus safety program, career counseling, child daycare facilities, disabled student services, free psychological counseling, international student services, low-cost health insurance, multicultural affairs office. *Library facilities:* Wallace Memorial Library. *Online resources:* library catalog, web page, access to other libraries' catalogs. *Collection:* 408,000 titles, 2,800 serial subscriptions.

Computer facilities: 2,500 computers available on campus for general student use. A campuswide network can be accessed from student residence rooms and from off campus. Internet access and online class registration, student account information are available. *Web address:* http://www.rit.edu/.

General Application Contact: Diane Ellison, Director, Graduate Enrollment Services, 585-475-7284, Fax: 585-475-7164, E-mail: dmeges@rit.edu.

GRADUATE UNITS

Graduate Enrollment Services Students: 1,279 full-time (498 women), 976 part-time (347 women); includes 239 minority (93 African Americans, 1 American Indian/Alaska Native, 97 Asian Americans or Pacific Islanders, 48 Hispanic Americans), 648 international. 2,647 applicants, 62% accepted, 784 enrolled. Expenses: Contact institution. *Financial support:* Fellowships, research assistantships, teaching assistantships, career-related internships or fieldwork, Federal Work-Study, institutionally sponsored loans, scholarships/grants, tuition waivers (full and partial), and unspecified assistantships available. Support available to part-time students. In 2006, 839 master's, 11 doctorates, 15 other advanced degrees awarded. *Degree program information:* Part-time and evening/weekend programs available. Postbaccalaureate distance learning degree programs offered. *Application deadline:* For fall admission, 2/15 priority date for domestic students. Applications are processed on a rolling basis. *Application fee:* $50. Electronic applications accepted. *Director, Graduate Enrollment Services,* Diane Ellison, 585-475-7284, Fax: 585-475-7164, E-mail: dmeges@rit.edu.

College of Applied Science and Technology Students: 103 full-time (35 women), 230 part-time (108 women); includes 47 minority (25 African Americans, 1 American Indian/Alaska Native, 12 Asian Americans or Pacific Islanders, 9 Hispanic Americans), 92 international. 255 applicants, 62% accepted, 92 enrolled. Expenses: Contact institution. *Financial support:* Research assistantships, teaching assistantships, scholarships/grants and unspecified assistantships available. In 2006, 111 master's, 5 other advanced degrees awarded. *Degree program information:* Part-time and evening/weekend programs available. Postbaccalaureate distance learning degree programs offered. Offers applied science and technology (MS, AC); cross-disciplinary professional studies (MS); environmental management (MS); health systems administration (MS, AC); health systems-finance (AC); hospitality-tourism management (MS); human resources development (MS, AC); integrated health systems (AC); manufacturing and mechanical systems integration (MS); multidisciplinary studies (MS, AC); packaging science (MS); senior living management (AC); service management (MS); technical information design (AC); telecommunications engineering technology (MS). *Application deadline:* For fall admission, 3/1 priority date for domestic students. Applications are processed on a rolling basis. *Application fee:* $50. Electronic applications accepted. *Interim Dean,* Dr. Carol Richardson, 585-475-2369, E-mail: carite@rit.edu.

College of Engineering Students: 201 full-time (45 women), 204 part-time (47 women); includes 46 minority (15 African Americans, 20 Asian Americans or Pacific Islanders, 11 Hispanic Americans), 143 international. 619 applicants, 60% accepted, 123 enrolled. Expenses: Contact institution. *Financial support:* Fellowships, research assistantships, teaching assistantships, career-related internships or fieldwork, Federal Work-Study, institutionally sponsored loans, and tuition waivers (partial) available. Support available to part-time students. In 2006, 167 master's, 4 doctorates, 7 other advanced degrees awarded. *Degree program information:* Part-time and evening/weekend programs available. Offers applied statistics (MS); computer engineering (MS); electrical engineering (MSEE); engineering (ME, MS, MSEE, PhD, AC); engineering management (ME); industrial engineering (ME, MS); manufacturing engineering (ME, MS); manufacturing leadership (MS); mechanical engineering (ME, MS); microelectronic engineering (MS); microelectronic manufacturing engineering (ME); microsystems engineering (PhD); product development (MS); statistical quality (AC); systems engineering (ME). *Application deadline:* For fall admission, 3/1 priority date for domestic students. Applications are processed on a rolling basis. *Application fee:* $50. *Application Contact:* Dr. Richard Reeve, Associate Dean, 585-475-5382, E-mail: nrreie@rit.edu. *Dean,* Dr. Harvey Palmer, 585-475-2146.

College of Imaging Arts and Sciences Students: 254 full-time (129 women), 70 part-time (40 women); includes 26 minority (8 African Americans, 12 Asian Americans or Pacific Islanders, 6 Hispanic Americans), 96 international. 508 applicants, 49% accepted, 129 enrolled. Expenses: Contact institution. *Financial support:* Fellowships, research assistantships, teaching assistantships, career-related internships or fieldwork, institutionally sponsored loans, tuition waivers (partial), and unspecified assistantships available. In 2006, 105 master's awarded. *Degree program information:* Part-time programs available. Offers art education (MST); ceramics (MFA); computer graphics design (MFA); fine arts (MFA, MST); fine arts studio (MST); glass (MFA); graphic design (MFA); imaging arts (MFA); imaging arts and sciences (MFA, MS, MST); industrial design (MFA); medical illustration (MFA); metal crafts and jewelry (MFA); painting (MFA); print media (MS); printmaking (MFA); woodworking and furniture design (MFA). *Application deadline:* For fall admission, 3/1 priority date for domestic students. Applications are processed on a rolling basis. *Application fee:* $50. *Dean,* Dr. Joan Stone, 585-475-7249, E-mail: jbsntm@rit.edu.

College of Liberal Arts Students: 86 full-time (64 women), 27 part-time (19 women); includes 8 minority (7 African Americans, 1 Asian American or Pacific Islander), 4 international. 115 applicants, 54% accepted, 44 enrolled. Expenses: Contact institution. *Financial support:* Teaching assistantships available. In 2006, 24 degrees awarded. Offers communication and media technologies (MS); liberal arts (MS, AC); psychology (MS); public policy (MS); school psychology (MS, AC). *Application deadline:* For fall admission, 3/1 priority date for domestic students. Applications are processed on a rolling basis. *Application fee:* $50. *Interim Dean,* Dr. Glenn Kist, 585-475-2446, E-mail: gjkgsh@rit.edu.

College of Science Students: 126 full-time (49 women), 60 part-time (17 women); includes 17 minority (2 African Americans, 11 Asian Americans or Pacific Islanders, 4 Hispanic Americans), 64 international. 199 applicants, 57% accepted, 61 enrolled. Expenses: Contact institution. *Financial support:* Research assistantships, teaching assistantships, career-related internships or fieldwork, Federal Work-Study, institutionally sponsored loans, and tuition waivers (full and partial) available. Support available to part-time students. In 2006, 57 master's, 7 doctorates awarded. *Degree program information:* Part-time and evening/weekend programs available. Offers bioinformatics (MS); chemistry (MS); clinical chemistry (MS); color science (MS, PhD); environmental science (MS); imaging science (MS, PhD); industrial and applied mathematics (MS); materials science and engineering (MS); science (MS, PhD). *Application deadline:* For fall admission, 3/1 priority date for domestic students. Applications are processed on a rolling basis. *Application fee:* $50. *Dean,* Dr. Ian Gatley, 585-475-2483, E-mail: ixgpci@rit.edu.

E. Philip Saunders College of Business Students: 246 full-time (91 women), 152 part-time (63 women); includes 38 minority (12 African Americans, 16 Asian Americans or Pacific Islanders, 10 Hispanic Americans), 95 international. 396 applicants, 70% accepted, 148 enrolled. Expenses: Contact institution. *Financial support:* Research assistantships, career-related internships or fieldwork and scholarships/grants available. Support available to part-time students. In 2006, 210 degrees awarded. *Degree program information:* Part-time and evening/weekend programs available. Offers accounting (MBA, MS); business (Exec MBA, MBA, MS); business administration (MBA); executive business administration (Exec MBA); finance (MS); management (MS). *Application deadline:* For fall admission, 3/1 priority date for domestic students. Applications are processed on a rolling basis. *Application fee:* $50. *Dean,* Ashok Rao, 585-475-7042, E-mail: axrbbu@rit.edu.

Golisano College of Computing and Information Sciences Students: 214 full-time (48 women), 228 part-time (48 women); includes 50 minority (17 African Americans, 25 Asian Americans or Pacific Islanders, 8 Hispanic Americans), 152 international. 521 applicants, 72% accepted, 161 enrolled. Expenses: Contact institution. In 2006, 140 master's, 1 other advanced degree awarded. Offers computer science (MS); computing and information sciences (MS, AC); game design and development (MS); information technology (MS); interactive multimedia development (AC); learning and knowledge management systems (MS); networking and systems administration (AC); security and information assurance (MS); software development and management (MS). *Application deadline:* For fall admission, 3/1 priority date for domestic students. Applications are processed on a rolling basis. *Application fee:* $50. Electronic applications accepted. *Dean,* Jorge Diaz-Herrera, 585-475-4786, E-mail: jdiaz@gccis.rit.edu.

National Technical Institute for the Deaf Students: 49 full-time (37 women), 5 part-time (all women); includes 7 minority (all African Americans), 2 international. 34 applicants, 88% accepted, 26 enrolled. Expenses: Contact institution. In 2006, 25 degrees awarded. Offers deaf studies (MS); secondary education (MS). *Application deadline:* For fall admission, 3/1 priority date for domestic students. Applications are processed on a rolling basis. *Application fee:* $50. *Dean,* Dr. Alan Hurwitz, 585-475-6443, E-mail: alan_hurwitz@rit.edu.

See Close-Up on page 1005.

THE ROCKEFELLER UNIVERSITY, New York, NY 10021-6399

General Information Independent, coed, graduate-only institution. CGS member. *Enrollment by degree level:* 199 doctoral. *Graduate faculty:* 111 full-time (26 women), 180 part-time/adjunct (46 women). *Graduate housing:* Rooms and/or apartments guaranteed to single and married students. Housing application deadline: 6/1. *Student services:* Campus safety program, child daycare facilities, exercise/wellness program, free psychological counseling, low-cost health insurance. *Library facilities:* Rita and Frits Markus Library. *Online resources:* library catalog, web page, access to other libraries' catalogs. *Collection:* 47,080 titles, 900 serial subscriptions, 38 audiovisual materials.

Computer facilities: 25 computers available on campus for general student use. A campuswide network can be accessed from student residence rooms and from off campus. Internet access is available. *Web address:* http://www.rockefeller.edu/.

General Application Contact: Dr. Sidney Strickland, Dean of Graduate Studies, 212-327-8086, Fax: 212-327-8505, E-mail: phd@rockefeller.edu.

GRADUATE UNITS

Program in Biomedical Sciences Students: 199 full-time (92 women); includes 37 minority (10 African Americans, 1 American Indian/Alaska Native, 21 Asian Americans or Pacific Islanders, 5 Hispanic Americans), 76 international. Average age 28. 721 applicants, 10% accepted, 22 enrolled. *Faculty:* 111 full-time (26 women), 180 part-time/adjunct (46 women). Expenses: Contact institution. *Financial support:* In 2006–07, 199 fellowships with full tuition reimbursements (averaging $26,750 per year) were awarded; institutionally sponsored loans, scholarships/grants, traineeships, and health care benefits also available. In 2006, 28 doctorates awarded. Offers biomedical sciences (PhD). *Application deadline:* For winter admission, 12/7 for domestic and international students. *Application fee:* $80. Electronic applications accepted. *Application Contact:* Kristen Cullen, Admissions and Records Administrator, 212-327-8088, Fax: 212-327-8505, E-mail: cullenk@rockefeller.edu. *Dean of Graduate Studies,* Dr. Sidney Strickland, 212-327-8086, Fax: 212-327-8505, E-mail: phd@rockefeller.edu.

ROCKFORD COLLEGE, Rockford, IL 61108-2393

General Information Independent, coed, comprehensive institution. *Graduate housing:* Room and/or apartments available to single students; on-campus housing not available to married students.

GRADUATE UNITS

Graduate Studies *Degree program information:* Part-time and evening/weekend programs available. Offers art education (MAT); business administration (MBA); elementary education (MAT); English (MAT); history (MAT); learning disabilities (MAT); political science (MAT); reading (MAT); secondary education (MAT); social sciences (MAT). Electronic applications accepted.

ROCKHURST UNIVERSITY, Kansas City, MO 64110-2561

General Information Independent-religious, coed, comprehensive institution. CGS member. *Enrollment:* 3,066 graduate, professional, and undergraduate students; 347 full-time matriculated graduate/professional students (221 women), 497 part-time matriculated graduate/professional students (259 women). *Enrollment by degree level:* 742 master's, 102 doctoral. *Graduate faculty:* 59 full-time (31 women), 23 part-time/adjunct (9 women). *Tuition:* Full-time $9,810; part-time $6,540 per year. *Required fees:* $400 per term. *Graduate housing:* Room and/or apartments available on a first-come, first-served basis to single students; on-campus housing not available to married students. Typical cost: $3,200 per year ($5,900 including board). Housing application deadline: 6/10. *Student services:* Campus employment opportunities, campus safety program, career counseling, free psychological counseling, international student services, multicultural affairs office, teacher training. *Library facilities:* Greenlease Library. *Online resources:* library catalog, web page, access to other libraries' catalogs. *Collection:* 450,000 titles, 278,790 serial subscriptions, 3,394 audiovisual materials.

Computer facilities: 500 computers available on campus for general student use. A campuswide network can be accessed from student residence rooms and from off campus. Internet access is available. *Web address:* http://www.rockhurst.edu/.

General Application Contact: Director of Graduate Recruitment, 816-501-4100, Fax: 816-501-4241, E-mail: graduate.admission@rockhurst.edu.

GRADUATE UNITS

Helzberg School of Management Students: 112 full-time (33 women), 341 part-time (135 women); includes 58 minority (23 African Americans, 1 American Indian/Alaska Native, 24 Asian Americans or Pacific Islanders, 10 Hispanic Americans), 4 international. Average age 30. 184 applicants, 47% accepted, 74 enrolled. *Faculty:* 29 full-time (6 women), 14 part-time/adjunct (3 women). Expenses: Contact institution. *Financial support:* Career-related internships or fieldwork available. Support available to part-time students. Financial award application deadline: 4/1; financial award applicants required to submit FAFSA. In 2006, 179 degrees awarded. *Degree program information:* Part-time and evening/weekend programs available. Postbaccalaureate distance learning degree programs offered (minimal on-campus study). Offers management (MBA). *Application deadline:* For fall admission, 7/25 priority date for domestic students; for spring admission, 12/15 for domestic students. Applications are processed on a rolling basis. *Application fee:* $0. Electronic applications accepted. *Application Contact:* Ron Filipowicz, Director of Graduate Admission, 816-501-4731, Fax: 816-501-4241, E-mail: ron.filipowicz@rockhurst.edu. *Dean,* Dr. James Daley, 816-501-4201, Fax: 816-501-4650, E-mail: james.daley@rockhurst.edu.

School of Graduate and Professional Studies Students: 235 full-time (188 women), 156 part-time (124 women); includes 29 minority (19 African Americans, 1 American Indian/Alaska Native, 9 Hispanic Americans), 2 international. Average age 28. 377 applicants, 51% accepted, 126 enrolled. *Faculty:* 30 full-time (22 women), 12 part-time/adjunct (9 women). Expenses: Contact institution. *Financial support:* In 2006–07, 10 research assistantships, 20 teaching assistantships were awarded; career-related internships or fieldwork, institutionally sponsored loans, and unspecified assistantships also available. Financial award application deadline: 4/1; financial award applicants required to submit FAFSA. In 2006, 123 degrees awarded. *Degree program information:* Part-time programs available. Offers arts and sciences (M Ed, MOT, MS, DPT); communication sciences and disorders (MS); education (M Ed); occupational therapy (MOT); physical therapy (DPT). *Application deadline:* Applications are processed on a rolling basis. *Application fee:* $25. Electronic applications accepted. *Application Contact:* Michele Huiatt, Director of Graduate Recruitment Admission, 816-501-3490, Fax: 816-501-4241, E-mail: michele.huiatt@rockhurst.edu. *Dean,* Dr. Robin Bowen, 816-501-4767, E-mail: robin.bowen@rockhurst.edu.

ROCKY MOUNTAIN COLLEGE, Billings, MT 59102-1796

General Information Independent-religious, coed, comprehensive institution.

GRADUATE UNITS

Graduate Programs

ROGER WILLIAMS UNIVERSITY, Bristol, RI 02809

General Information Independent, coed, comprehensive institution. *Enrollment:* 5,172 graduate, professional, and undergraduate students; 602 full-time matriculated graduate/professional students (298 women), 221 part-time matriculated graduate/professional students (132 women). *Enrollment by degree level:* 593 first professional, 230 master's. *Graduate faculty:* 30 full-time (13 women), 7 part-time/adjunct (3 women). *Tuition:* Part-time $362 per credit. Tuition and fees vary according to program. *Graduate housing:* Rooms and/or apartments available on a first-come, first-served basis to single students and available to married students. *Student services:* Campus employment opportunities, campus safety program, career counseling, disabled student services, exercise/wellness program, international student services, low-cost health insurance, multicultural affairs office, teacher training, writing training. *Library facilities:* Roger Williams University Library plus 2 others. *Online resources:* library catalog, web page, access to other libraries' catalogs. *Collection:* 216,424 titles, 1,332 serial subscriptions, 2,728 audiovisual materials.

Computer facilities: Computer purchase and lease plans are available. 410 computers available on campus for general student use. A campuswide network can be accessed from student residence rooms and from off campus. Internet access and online class registration, telephone registration are available. *Web address:* http://www.rwu.edu/.

General Application Contact: Suzanne Faubl, Director of Graduate Admissions, 401-254-3809, Fax: 401-254-3557, E-mail: sfaubl@rwu.edu.

GRADUATE UNITS

Feinstein College of Arts and Sciences Students: 20 full-time (12 women), 32 part-time (17 women); includes 4 minority (all Hispanic Americans), 3 international. Average age 39. 40 applicants, 78% accepted, 18 enrolled. *Faculty:* 7 full-time (1 woman), 1 (woman) part-time/adjunct. Expenses: Contact institution. *Financial support:* In 2006–07, 2 students received support. In 2006, 12 degrees awarded. *Degree program information:* Part-time programs available. Offers arts and sciences (MA, MPA); forensic psychology (MA); public administration (MPA). *Application deadline:* Applications are processed on a rolling basis. *Application fee:* $50. Electronic applications accepted. *Interim Dean,* Dr. Robert Cole, 401-254-3149.

Ralph R. Papitto School of Law Students: 533 full-time (262 women), 60 part-time (24 women); includes 69 minority (19 African Americans, 2 American Indian/Alaska Native, 27 Asian Americans or Pacific Islanders, 21 Hispanic Americans), 5 international. Average age 27. 1,677 applicants, 51% accepted, 204 enrolled. *Faculty:* 32 full-time (13 women), 31 part-time/adjunct (11 women). Expenses: Contact institution. *Financial support:* In 2006–07, 245 students received support, including 6 fellowships, 40 research assistantships; career-related internships or fieldwork, Federal Work-Study, scholarships/grants, and tuition waivers (full and partial) also available. Financial award application deadline: 3/15; financial award applicants required to submit FAFSA. In 2006, 177 degrees awarded. Offers law (JD). *Application deadline:* For fall admission, 3/15 priority date for domestic and international students. Applications are processed on a rolling basis. *Application fee:* $60. Electronic applications accepted. *Application Contact:* Michael W. Boylen, Assistant Dean of Admissions, 401-254-4555, Fax: 401-254-4516, E-mail: mboylen@rwu.edu. *Dean,* David A. Logan, 401-254-4500, Fax: 401-254-3525, E-mail: dlogan@rwu.edu.

School of Architecture, Art and Historic Preservation Students: 23 full-time (7 women), 2 part-time (both women); includes 2 minority (1 American Indian/Alaska Native, 1 Asian American or Pacific Islander), 2 international. Average age 24. 14 applicants, 93% accepted, 8 enrolled. *Faculty:* 6 full-time (1 woman), 2 part-time/adjunct (0 women). Expenses: Contact institution. *Financial support:* In 2006–07, 20 students received support; fellowships, career-related internships or fieldwork, scholarships/grants, health care benefits, and unspecified assistantships available. Financial award applicants required to submit FAFSA. In 2006, 11 degrees awarded. Offers architecture (M Arch). Students begin 5-6 year dual degree sequence as undergraduates. *Application deadline:* For fall admission, 3/15 priority date for domestic students. Applications are processed on a rolling basis. *Application fee:* $50. Electronic applications accepted. *Application Contact:* Suzanne Faubl, Director of Graduate Admissions, 401-254-3809, Fax: 401-254-3557, E-mail: sfaubl@rwu.edu. *Dean,* Stephen White, 401-254-3607, E-mail: swhite@rwu.edu.

School of Education Students: 18 full-time (15 women), 84 part-time (78 women); includes 2 minority (1 Asian American or Pacific Islander, 1 Hispanic American). Average age 33. 20 applicants, 90% accepted, 13 enrolled. *Faculty:* 11 full-time (8 women), 3 part-time/adjunct (2 women). Expenses: Contact institution. *Financial support:* In 2006–07, 41 students received support. Career-related internships or fieldwork and health care benefits available. Financial award applicants required to submit FAFSA. In 2006, 44 degrees awarded. *Degree program information:* Part-time and evening/weekend programs available. Offers education (MA, MAT); elementary education (MAT); literacy (MA). *Application deadline:* Applications are processed on a rolling basis. *Application fee:* $50. Electronic applications accepted. *Application Contact:* Suzanne Faubl, Director of Graduate Admissions, 401-254-3809, Fax: 401-254-3557, E-mail: sfaubl@rwu.edu. *Dean,* Dr. Bruce Marlowe, 401-254-3427, E-mail: bmarlowe@rwu.edu.

School of Justice Studies Students: 8 full-time (2 women), 48 part-time (15 women); includes 2 minority (1 African American, 1 Hispanic American). Average age 31. 29 applicants, 93% accepted, 14 enrolled. *Faculty:* 6 full-time (3 women), 1 part-time/adjunct (0 women). Expenses: Contact institution. *Financial support:* In 2006–07, 23 students received support; research assistantships with partial tuition reimbursements available, career-related internships or fieldwork and health care benefits available. Financial award applicants required to submit FAFSA. In 2006, 25 degrees awarded. *Degree program information:* Part-time and evening/weekend programs available. Offers criminal justice (MS). *Application deadline:* For fall admission, 8/1 priority date for domestic students; for spring admission, 12/1 priority date for domestic students. Applications are processed on a rolling basis. *Application fee:* $50. Electronic applications accepted. *Application Contact:* Suzanne Faubl, Director of Graduate Admissions, 401-254-3809, Fax: 401-254-3557, E-mail: sfaubl@rwu.edu. *Dean,* Stephanie Manzi, 401-254-3715, Fax: 401-254-3431, E-mail: smanzi@rwu.edu.

ROLLINS COLLEGE, Winter Park, FL 32789-4499

General Information Independent, coed, comprehensive institution. *Enrollment:* 2,454 graduate, professional, and undergraduate students; 343 full-time matriculated graduate/professional students (176 women), 391 part-time matriculated graduate/professional students (237 women). *Enrollment by degree level:* 734 master's. *Graduate faculty:* 23 full-time (3 women). *Graduate housing:* On-campus housing not available. *Student services:* Campus employment opportunities, campus safety program, career counseling, disabled student services, exercise/wellness program, free psychological counseling, international student services, low-cost health insurance, multicultural affairs office. *Library facilities:* Olin Library. *Online resources:* library catalog, web page, access to other libraries' catalogs. *Collection:* 303,519 titles, 17,874 serial subscriptions, 5,406 audiovisual materials.

Computer facilities: 195 computers available on campus for general student use. A campuswide network can be accessed from student residence rooms and from off campus. Internet access is available. *Web address:* http://www.rollins.edu/.

General Application Contact: Information Contact, 407-646-2000.

GRADUATE UNITS

Crummer Graduate School of Business Students: 261 full-time (105 women), 171 part-time (65 women); includes 83 minority (24 African Americans, 2 American Indian/Alaska Native, 21 Asian Americans or Pacific Islanders, 36 Hispanic Americans), 17 international. Average age 30. *Faculty:* 23 full-time (3 women). Expenses: Contact institution. *Financial support:* Fellowships, research assistantships, career-related internships or fieldwork, Federal Work-Study, scholarships/grants, and tuition waivers (full) available. In 2006, 175 degrees awarded. *Degree program information:* Part-time and evening/weekend programs available. Offers business (MBA). *Application deadline:* For fall admission, 4/1 priority date for domestic students; for spring admission, 12/1 for domestic students. Applications are processed on a rolling basis. *Application fee:* $50. Electronic applications accepted. *Application Contact:* Student Admissions Office, 407-646-2405, Fax: 407-646-1550. *Dean,* Dr. Craig M. McAllaster, 407-646-2249, Fax: 407-646-1550, E-mail: cmcallaster@rollins.edu.

Hamilton Holt School Students: 82 full-time (71 women), 220 part-time (172 women); includes 42 minority (15 African Americans, 5 Asian Americans or Pacific Islanders, 22 Hispanic Americans), 9 international. Average age 31. *Faculty:* 5 full-time (4 women). Expenses: Contact institution. *Financial support:* Teaching assistantships, institutionally sponsored loans and scholarships/grants available. Support available to part-time students. In 2006, 101 degrees awarded. *Degree program information:* Part-time and evening/weekend programs available. Offers elementary education (M Ed, MAT); human resources (MA); liberal studies (MLS); mental health counseling (MA); school counseling (MA); secondary education (MAT). *Application deadline:* Applications are processed on a rolling basis. *Application fee:* $50. Electronic applications accepted. *Application Contact:* Graduate Program Admission, 407-646-2292, Fax: 407-646-1551. *Dean,* Dr. Sharon M. Carrier, 407-646-2292, Fax: 407-646-1551, E-mail: scarrier@rollins.edu.

ROOSEVELT UNIVERSITY, Chicago, IL 60605-1394

General Information Independent, coed, comprehensive institution. *Enrollment:* 7,186 graduate, professional, and undergraduate students; 853 full-time matriculated graduate/professional students (572 women), 2,277 part-time matriculated graduate/professional students (1,597 women). *Enrollment by degree level:* 3,044 master's, 86 doctoral. *Graduate faculty:* 210 full-time (85 women), 424 part-time/adjunct (181 women). *Graduate housing:* Room and/or apartments available on a first-come, first-served basis to single students; on-campus housing not available to married students. Housing application deadline: 7/1. *Student services:* Campus employment opportunities, campus safety program, career counseling, child daycare facilities, disabled student services, exercise/wellness program, free psychological counseling, international student services, low-cost health insurance, teacher training, writing training. *Library facilities:* Murray-Green Library plus 4 others. *Online resources:* library catalog, web page, access to other libraries' catalogs. *Collection:* 186,944 titles, 1,195 serial subscriptions.

Computer facilities: 250 computers available on campus for general student use. A campuswide network can be accessed from student residence rooms and from off campus. Internet access and online class registration are available. *Web address:* http://www.roosevelt.edu/.

General Application Contact: Joanne Canyon-Heller, Coordinator of Graduate Admission, 877-APPLY RU, Fax: 312-281-3356, E-mail: applyru@roosevelt.edu.

GRADUATE UNITS

Graduate Division Students: 853 full-time (572 women), 2,277 part-time (1,597 women); includes 986 minority (699 African Americans, 7 American Indian/Alaska Native, 121 Asian Americans or Pacific Islanders, 159 Hispanic Americans), 170 international. Average age 34. 2,684 applicants, 59% accepted, 1351 enrolled. *Faculty:* 212 full-time (82 women), 437 part-time/adjunct (187 women). Expenses: Contact institution. *Financial support:* In 2006–07, 175 students received support, including 36 research assistantships with full tuition reimbursements available (averaging $5,700 per year); career-related internships or fieldwork, Federal Work-Study, scholarships/grants, tuition waivers (full and partial), and unspecified assistantships also available. Support available to part-time students. Financial award application deadline: 5/1; financial award applicants required to submit FAFSA. In 2006, 948 master's, 10 doctorates awarded. *Degree program information:* Part-time and evening/weekend programs available. *Application deadline:* For fall admission, 6/1 priority date for domestic students; for spring admission, 12/1 for domestic students. Applications are processed on a rolling basis. *Application fee:* $25 ($35 for international students). Electronic applications accepted. *Application Contact:* Joanne Canyon-Heller, Coordinator of Graduate Admission, 877-APPLY RU, Fax: 312-281-3356, E-mail: applyru@roosevelt.edu. *Dean of Graduate Studies,* Dr. Janett Trubatch, 312-341-3616, Fax: 312-341-2013.

Chicago College of Performing Arts Students: 149 full-time (73 women), 22 part-time (11 women); includes 19 minority (9 African Americans, 4 Asian Americans or Pacific Islanders, 6 Hispanic Americans), 45 international. Average age 26. 340 applicants, 43% accepted, 71 enrolled. *Faculty:* 31 full-time (10 women), 33 part-time/adjunct. Expenses: Contact institution. *Financial support:* Research assistantships, career-related internships or fieldwork, Federal Work-Study, scholarships/grants, and tuition waivers (full and partial) available. Support available to part-time students. In 2006, 72 degrees awarded. *Degree program information:* Part-time and evening/weekend programs available. Offers directing and dramaturgy (MFA); music (MM); musical theatre (MFA); performing arts (MA, MFA, MM, Diploma); piano pedagogy (Diploma); theatre (MA, MFA); theatre-directing (MA); theatre-performance (MFA). *Application deadline:* For fall admission, 6/1 priority date for domestic students. Applications are processed on a rolling basis. *Application fee:* $25 ($35 for international students). *Application Contact:* Joanne Canyon-Heller, Coordinator of Graduate Admission, 877-APPLY RU, Fax: 312-281-3356, E-mail: applyru@roosevelt.edu. *Dean,* James Gandre, 312-341-3782, E-mail: jgandre@roosevelt.edu.

College of Arts and Sciences Students: 345 full-time (238 women), 667 part-time (471 women); includes 330 minority (233 African Americans, 40 Asian Americans or Pacific Islanders, 57 Hispanic Americans), 87 international. Average age 31. 1,037 applicants, 58% accepted, 524 enrolled. *Faculty:* 97 full-time (34 women), 224 part-time/adjunct. Expenses: Contact institution. *Financial support:* Research assistantships, teaching assistantships, career-related internships or fieldwork, Federal Work-Study, institutionally sponsored loans, scholarships/grants, and tuition waivers (full and partial) available. Support available to part-time students. Financial award application deadline: 2/15. In 2006, 250 master's, 3 doctorates awarded. *Degree program information:* Part-time and evening/weekend programs available. Offers anthropology (MA); applied economics (MA); arts and sciences (MA, MFA, MPA, MS, MSC, MSIMC, MSJ, MST, Psy D, Certificate); biotechnology and chemical science (MS); clinical professional psychology (MA, Psy D); computer science (MSC); creative writing (MFA); economics (MA); English (MA); history (MA); industrial/organizational psychology (MA); integrated marketing communications (MSIMC); journalism (MSJ); mathematical sciences (MS); mathematics (MS); political science (MA); psychology (Psy D); public administration (MPA); sociology (MA); Spanish (MA); telecommunications (MST); women's and gender studies (MA, Certificate). *Application deadline:* For fall admission, 6/1 priority date for domestic students. Applications are processed on a rolling basis. *Application fee:* $25 ($35 for international students). *Application Contact:* Joanne Canyon-Heller, Coordinator of Graduate Admission, 877-APPLY RU, Fax: 312-281-3356, E-mail: applyru@roosevelt.edu. *Dean,* Lynn Weiner, 312-341-2134, E-mail: lweiner@roosevelt.edu.

College of Education Students: 219 full-time (176 women), 721 part-time (554 women); includes 261 minority (198 African Americans, 2 American Indian/Alaska Native, 21 Asian Americans or Pacific Islanders, 40 Hispanic Americans). Average age 37. 637 applicants, 64% accepted, 352 enrolled. *Faculty:* 35 full-time (26 women), 75 part-time/adjunct. Expenses: Contact institution. *Financial support:* Federal Work-Study available. Support available to part-time students. Financial award application deadline: 2/15. In 2006, 315 master's, 7 doctorates awarded. *Degree program information:* Part-time and evening/weekend programs available. Offers counseling and human services (MA); early childhood education/early childhood professions (MA); education (MA, Ed D); educational leadership and organizational change (MA, Ed D); elementary education (MA); reading teacher education (MA); secondary education (MA); special education (MA); teacher leadership (MA). *Application deadline:* For fall admission, 6/1 priority date for domestic students. Applications are processed on a rolling basis. *Application fee:* $25 ($35 for international students). *Application Contact:* Joanne Canyon-Heller, Coordinator of Graduate Admission, 877-APPLY RU, Fax: 312-281-3356, E-mail: applyru@roosevelt.edu. *Interim Dean,* James Gandre, 312-341-3700, E-mail: jgandre@roosevelt.edu.

Evelyn T. Stone University College Students: 28 full-time (24 women), 172 part-time (142 women); includes 33 minority (23 African Americans, 1 American Indian/Alaska Native, 5 Asian Americans or Pacific Islanders, 4 Hispanic Americans), 7 international. Average age 37. 177 applicants, 59% accepted, 90 enrolled. *Faculty:* 18 full-time (5 women), 50 part-time/adjunct. Expenses: Contact institution. *Financial support:* Federal Work-Study available. Support available to part-time students. Financial award application deadline: 2/15. In

Roosevelt University (continued)

2006, 37 degrees awarded. *Degree program information:* Part-time and evening/weekend programs available. Offers hospitality management (MS); training and development (MA). *Application deadline:* For fall admission, 6/1 priority date for domestic students. Applications are processed on a rolling basis. *Application fee:* $25 ($35 for international students). *Application Contact:* Joanne Canyon-Heller, Coordinator of Graduate Admission, 877-APPLY RU, Fax: 312-281-3356, E-mail: applyru@roosevelt.edu. *Interim Dean,* Douglas G. Knerr, 312-281-3376.

Walter E. Heller College of Business Administration Students: 112 full-time (61 women), 695 part-time (419 women); includes 293 minority (186 African Americans, 4 American Indian/Alaska Native, 51 Asian Americans or Pacific Islanders, 52 Hispanic Americans), 31 international. Average age 33. 493 applicants, 67% accepted, 309 enrolled. *Faculty:* 30 full-time (8 women), 47 part-time/adjunct. Expenses: Contact institution. *Financial support:* Career-related internships or fieldwork, Federal Work-Study, and tuition waivers (partial) available. Support available to part-time students. Financial award application deadline: 2/15. In 2006, 460 degrees awarded. *Degree program information:* Part-time and evening/weekend programs available. Offers accounting (MSA); business administration (MBA, MS, MSA, MSHRM, MSIB, MSIS, Certificate); commercial real estate development (Certificate); human resource management (MSHRM); information systems (MSIS); international business (MSIB); real estate (MBA, MS). *Application deadline:* For fall admission, 6/1 priority date for domestic students. Applications are processed on a rolling basis. *Application fee:* $25 ($35 for international students). *Application Contact:* Joanne Canyon-Heller, Coordinator of Graduate Admission, 877-APPLY RU, Fax: 312-281-3356, E-mail: applyru@roosevelt.edu. *Interim Dean,* Joe Chan, 312-281-3254, Fax: 847-619-4852.

See Close-Up on page 1007.

ROSALIND FRANKLIN UNIVERSITY OF MEDICINE AND SCIENCE, North Chicago, IL 60064-3095

General Information Independent, coed, graduate-only institution. CGS member. *Graduate housing:* Rooms and/or apartments available on a first-come, first-served basis to single students and available to married students. *Research affiliation:* Veterans Administration Hospital (pulmonary medicine), Argonne National Laboratory (medical physics).

GRADUATE UNITS

The Chicago Medical School Students: 750 full-time (325 women); includes 390 minority (34 African Americans, 1 American Indian/Alaska Native, 346 Asian Americans or Pacific Islanders, 9 Hispanic Americans), 16 international. Average age 26. 7,210 applicants, 6% accepted, 184 enrolled. *Faculty:* 376 full-time (101 women), 298 part-time/adjunct (81 women). Expenses: Contact institution. *Financial support:* Federal Work-Study, institutionally sponsored loans, and scholarships/grants available. Financial award application deadline: 5/18; financial award applicants required to submit FAFSA. In 2006, 181 degrees awarded. Offers medicine (MD). *Application deadline:* For fall admission, 11/1 for domestic and international students. Applications are processed on a rolling basis. *Application fee:* $95. *Application Contact:* Maryann DeCaire, Executive Director of Admissions, Records, and Financial Aid, 847-578-3204, Fax: 847-578-3284, E-mail: maryann.decaire@rosalindfranklin.edu. *Dean,* Dr. Arthur J. Ross, 847-578-3300, E-mail: arthur.ross@rosalindfranklin.edu.

College of Health Professions *Degree program information:* Part-time and evening/weekend programs available. Postbaccalaureate distance learning degree programs offered (minimal on-campus study). Offers clinical education (MS); clinical laboratory science (MS); clinical nutrition (MS); health professions (MS, PhD, TDPT); healthcare management (MS); healthcare risk management (MS); medical radiation physics (MS, PhD); pathologist assistant (MS); physical therapy (MS, TDPT); physician assistant (MS); physician assistant studies (MS).

The Dr. William M. Scholl College of Podiatric Medicine Offers podiatric medicine (DPM).

Integrated Bioscience Program Offers integrated bioscience).

School of Graduate and Postdoctoral Studies *Degree program information:* Part-time programs available. Offers anatomy (MS, PhD); applied physiology (MS); biochemistry (MS, PhD); cell biology (MS, PhD); cellular and molecular pharmacology (MS, PhD); clinical psychology (MS, PhD); medical microbiology (MS, PhD); microbiology and immunology (MS, PhD); neuroscience (PhD); pathology (MS, PhD); physiology (MS, PhD).

ROSE-HULMAN INSTITUTE OF TECHNOLOGY, Terre Haute, IN 47803-3999

General Information Independent, coed, primarily men, comprehensive institution. *Enrollment:* 1,963 graduate, professional, and undergraduate students; 42 full-time matriculated graduate/professional students (5 women), 59 part-time matriculated graduate/professional students (20 women). *Enrollment by degree level:* 101 master's. *Graduate faculty:* 88 full-time (16 women), 4 part-time/adjunct (0 women). *Graduate housing:* Room and/or apartments available on a first-come, first-served basis to single students; on-campus housing not available to married students. Housing application deadline: 4/15. *Student services:* Campus employment opportunities, career counseling, exercise/wellness program, free psychological counseling, international student services, low-cost health insurance. *Library facilities:* Logan Library. *Online resources:* library catalog, web page, access to other libraries' catalogs. *Collection:* 80,094 titles, 20,934 serial subscriptions, 429 audiovisual materials.

Computer facilities: Computer purchase and lease plans are available. 45 computers available on campus for general student use. A campuswide network can be accessed from student residence rooms and from off campus. Internet access and online class registration are available. *Web address:* http://www.rose-hulman.edu/.

General Application Contact: Dr. Daniel J. Moore, Associate Dean of the Faculty, 812-877-8110, Fax: 812-877-8061, E-mail: daniel.j.moore@rose-hulman.edu.

GRADUATE UNITS

Faculty of Engineering and Applied Sciences Students: 42 full-time (5 women), 59 part-time (20 women); includes 4 minority (1 African American, 1 Asian American or Pacific Islander, 2 Hispanic Americans), 18 international. Average age 28. 56 applicants, 68% accepted, 32 enrolled. *Faculty:* 88 full-time (16 women), 4 part-time/adjunct (0 women). Expenses: Contact institution. *Financial support:* In 2006–07, 45 students received support; fellowships with full and partial tuition reimbursements available, research assistantships with full and partial tuition reimbursements available, institutionally sponsored loans, scholarships/grants, and tuition waivers (full and partial) available. In 2006, 32 degrees awarded. *Degree program information:* Part-time and evening/weekend programs available. Postbaccalaureate distance learning degree programs offered (minimal on-campus study). Offers biomedical engineering (MS); chemical engineering (MS); civil engineering (MS); electrical engineering (MS); engineering and applied sciences (MS); engineering management (MS); environmental engineering (MS); mechanical engineering (MS); optical engineering (MS). *Application deadline:* For fall admission, 2/1 priority date for domestic students. Applications are processed on a rolling basis. *Application fee:* $0. *Associate Dean of the Faculty,* Dr. Daniel J. Moore, 812-877-8110, Fax: 812-877-8061, E-mail: daniel.j.moore@rose-hulman.edu.

ROSEMONT COLLEGE, Rosemont, PA 19010-1699

General Information Independent-religious, Undergraduate: women only; graduate: coed, comprehensive institution. *Graduate housing:* Room and/or apartments available to single students; on-campus housing not available to married students.

GRADUATE UNITS

Graduate School *Degree program information:* Part-time and evening/weekend programs available. Offers arts/culture/project management (MSM); business administration (MBA); criminal justice (MSM); elementary certification (MA); English (MA); English and publishing (MA); human services (MA); middle level education (M Ed); not for profit (MSM); school counseling (MA); technology in education (M Ed); training and leadership (MSM). Electronic applications accepted.

See Close-Up on page 1009.

ROWAN UNIVERSITY, Glassboro, NJ 08028-1701

General Information State-supported, coed, comprehensive institution. CGS member. *Enrollment:* 9,578 graduate, professional, and undergraduate students; 199 full-time matriculated graduate/professional students (143 women), 582 part-time matriculated graduate/professional students (438 women). *Enrollment by degree level:* 721 master's, 60 doctoral. *Graduate faculty:* 90 full-time (39 women), 24 part-time/adjunct (7 women). Tuition, state resident: full-time $9,882; part-time $549 per credit. Tuition, nonresident: full-time $9,882; part-time $549 per credit. Tuition and fees vary according to degree level. *Graduate housing:* Rooms and/or apartments available on a first-come, first-served basis to single and married students. Housing application deadline: 5/1. *Student services:* Campus employment opportunities, campus safety program, career counseling, child daycare facilities, disabled student services, exercise/wellness program, free psychological counseling, international student services, low-cost health insurance, multicultural affairs office, teacher training, writing training. *Library facilities:* Keith and Shirley Campbell Library plus 2 others. *Online resources:* library catalog, web page, access to other libraries' catalogs. *Collection:* 316,500 titles, 1,858 serial subscriptions, 52,834 audiovisual materials.

Computer facilities: 350 computers available on campus for general student use. A campuswide network can be accessed from student residence rooms and from off campus. Internet access and online class registration are available. *Web address:* http://www.rowan.edu/.

General Application Contact: Dr. Jay Kuder, Dean, Graduate School, 856-256-4050, Fax: 856-256-4436, E-mail: kuder@rowan.edu.

GRADUATE UNITS

Graduate School Students: 199 full-time (143 women), 582 part-time (438 women); includes 103 minority (58 African Americans, 4 American Indian/Alaska Native, 18 Asian Americans or Pacific Islanders, 23 Hispanic Americans). Average age 32. 153 applicants, 58% accepted, 88 enrolled. Expenses: Contact institution. *Financial support:* In 2006–07, 97 students received support. Career-related internships or fieldwork, Federal Work-Study, and unspecified assistantships available. Support available to part-time students. In 2006, 324 master's, 5 doctorates awarded. *Degree program information:* Part-time and evening/weekend programs available. *Application deadline:* Applications are processed on a rolling basis. *Application fee:* $50. Electronic applications accepted. *Application Contact:* Dorie Gilchrist, Director of Graduate Admissions, 856-256-4054, Fax: 856-256-4436, E-mail: gilchrist@rowan.edu. *Dean, Graduate School,* Dr. Jay Kuder, 856-256-4050, Fax: 856-256-4436, E-mail: kuder@rowan.edu.

College of Communication Students: 18 full-time (12 women), 42 part-time (29 women); includes 6 minority (3 African Americans, 1 Asian American or Pacific Islander, 2 Hispanic Americans). Average age 33. 20 applicants, 75% accepted, 15 enrolled. Expenses: Contact institution. *Financial support:* Career-related internships or fieldwork and unspecified assistantships available. Support available to part-time students. In 2006, 23 degrees awarded. *Degree program information:* Part-time and evening/weekend programs available. Offers public relations (MA); writing (MA). *Application deadline:* Applications are processed on a rolling basis. *Application fee:* $50. *Application Contact:* Dr. J. Basso, Adviser, 856-256-4609, E-mail: basso@rowan.edu. *Dean,* Dr. Craig Monroe, 856-256-4340.

College of Education Students: 131 full-time (111 women), 438 part-time (359 women); includes 77 minority (49 African Americans, 3 American Indian/Alaska Native, 11 Asian Americans or Pacific Islanders, 14 Hispanic Americans). Average age 34. 95 applicants, 52% accepted, 49 enrolled. Expenses: Contact institution. *Financial support:* Career-related internships or fieldwork, Federal Work-Study, and unspecified assistantships available. Support available to part-time students. In 2006, 234 master's, 5 doctorates awarded. *Degree program information:* Part-time and evening/weekend programs available. Offers business administration (MA); collaborative teaching (MST); counseling in educational settings (MA); education (M Ed, MA, MST, Ed D, CAGS, Ed S); educational leadership (Ed D); higher education administration (MA); learning disabilities (MA); music education (MA); principal preparation (MA); reading education (MA); school administration (MA, CAGS); school and public librarianship (MA); school psychology (MA, Ed S); special education (MA); standards-based practice (M Ed); supervision and curriculum development (MA); teaching-secondary (MST). *Application deadline:* Applications are processed on a rolling basis. *Application fee:* $50. Electronic applications accepted. *Dean,* Dr. Carol Sharp, 856-256-4750.

College of Engineering Students: 16 full-time (1 woman), 10 part-time; includes 6 minority (1 African American, 1 Asian American or Pacific Islander, 4 Hispanic Americans). Average age 25. 6 applicants, 33% accepted, 2 enrolled. Expenses: Contact institution. *Financial support:* Career-related internships or fieldwork, Federal Work-Study, and unspecified assistantships available. Support available to part-time students. In 2006, 17 degrees awarded. *Degree program information:* Part-time and evening/weekend programs available. Offers engineering (MS). *Application deadline:* Applications are processed on a rolling basis. *Application fee:* $50. Electronic applications accepted. *Application Contact:* Dr. Ralph Dusseau, Program Adviser, 856-256-5332. *Dean,* Dr. Dianne Dorland, 856-256-5301.

College of Fine and Performing Arts Students: 4 full-time (2 women), 4 part-time (1 woman); includes 1 minority (Asian American or Pacific Islander) Average age 31. 4 applicants, 75% accepted, 3 enrolled. Expenses: Contact institution. *Financial support:* Career-related internships or fieldwork, Federal Work-Study, and unspecified assistantships available. Support available to part-time students. In 2006, 6 degrees awarded. *Degree program information:* Part-time and evening/weekend programs available. Offers fine and performing arts (MA, MM); music (MM); theatre (MA). *Application deadline:* Applications are processed on a rolling basis. *Application fee:* $50. Electronic applications accepted. *Dean,* Dr. Donald Gephardt, 856-256-4552.

College of Liberal Arts and Sciences Students: 17 full-time (12 women), 31 part-time (24 women); includes 6 minority (2 African Americans, 1 American Indian/Alaska Native, 1 Asian American or Pacific Islander, 2 Hispanic Americans). Average age 28. 15 applicants, 80% accepted, 12 enrolled. Expenses: Contact institution. *Financial support:* Career-related internships or fieldwork, Federal Work-Study, and unspecified assistantships available. Support available to part-time students. In 2006, 15 degrees awarded. *Degree program information:* Part-time and evening/weekend programs available. Offers liberal arts and sciences (MA, CAGS); mathematics (MA); mental health counseling and applied psychology (MA, CAGS). *Application deadline:* Applications are processed on a rolling basis. *Application fee:* $50. Electronic applications accepted. *Dean,* Dr. Jay Harper, 856-256-4850.

William G. Rohrer College of Business Students: 13 full-time (5 women), 57 part-time (25 women); includes 7 minority (3 African Americans, 3 Asian Americans or Pacific Islanders, 1 Hispanic American). Average age 30. 13 applicants, 54% accepted, 7 enrolled. Expenses: Contact institution. *Financial support:* Federal Work-Study and unspecified assistantships available. Support available to part-time students. In 2006, 24 degrees awarded. *Degree program information:* Part-time and evening/weekend programs available. Offers business (MBA); business administration (MBA). *Application deadline:* Applications are processed on a rolling basis. *Application fee:* $50. Electronic applications accepted. *Application Contact:* Dr. Daniel McFarland, Director, MBA Program, 856-256-5426, E-mail: mcfarland@rowan.edu. *Dean,* Dr. Edward Schoen, 856-256-4025.

ROYAL MILITARY COLLEGE OF CANADA, Kingston, ON K7K 7B4, Canada

General Information Federally supported, coed, comprehensive institution.

GRADUATE UNITS

Division of Graduate Studies and Research *Degree program information:* Part-time programs available. Postbaccalaureate distance learning degree programs offered (minimal on-campus study). Electronic applications accepted.

Continuing Studies Offers arts (MA, MBA, MDS); business administration (MBA); defense management and policy (MA); defense studies (MDS); war studies (MA). Electronic applications accepted.

Engineering Division Offers civil engineering (M Eng, MA Sc, PhD); computer engineering (M Eng, MA Sc, PhD); electrical engineering (M Eng, MA Sc, PhD); engineering (M Eng, M Sc, MA Sc, PhD); environmental engineering (M Eng, MA Sc, PhD); environmental science (M Sc, PhD); materials science (M Sc, PhD); mechanical engineering (M Eng, MA Sc, PhD); nuclear engineering (M Eng, MA Sc, PhD); nuclear science (M Sc, PhD); software engineering (M Eng, MA Sc, PhD). Electronic applications accepted.

Science Division Offers chemical engineering (M Eng, MA Sc, PhD); chemistry (M Sc, PhD); computer science (M Sc); mathematics (M Sc); physics (M Sc); science (M Eng, M Sc, MA Sc, PhD). Electronic applications accepted.

ROYAL ROADS UNIVERSITY, Victoria, BC V9B 5Y2, Canada

General Information Province-supported, coed, upper-level institution. *Graduate housing:* Room and/or apartments available on a first-come, first-served basis to single students; on-campus housing not available to married students.

GRADUATE UNITS

Graduate Studies Postbaccalaureate distance learning degree programs offered (minimal on-campus study). Offers conflict analysis and management (MA); distributed learning (MA); environment and management (M Sc, MA); knowledge management (MA); leadership and training (MA). Electronic applications accepted.

School of Business Postbaccalaureate distance learning degree programs offered (minimal on-campus study). Offers digital technologies management (MBA); executive management (MBA); human resources management (MBA); public relations and communications management (MBA). Electronic applications accepted.

RUSH UNIVERSITY, Chicago, IL 60612-3832

General Information Independent, coed, upper-level institution. CGS member. *Graduate housing:* Rooms and/or apartments available on a first-come, first-served basis to single and married students. Housing application deadline: 6/1.

GRADUATE UNITS

College of Health Sciences *Degree program information:* Part-time and evening/weekend programs available. Offers audiology (Au D); clinical laboratory management (MS); clinical laboratory science (MS); clinical nutrition (MS); health sciences (MA, MS, Au D, DHSc, Graduate Certificate); health systems management (MS, DHSc); healthcare ethics (MA, Graduate Certificate); occupational therapy (MS); speech-language pathology (MS). Electronic applications accepted.

College of Nursing Students: 66 full-time (54 women), 239 part-time (225 women); includes 41 minority (15 African Americans, 9 Asian Americans or Pacific Islanders, 17 Hispanic Americans). Average age 34. 197 applicants, 83% accepted, 153 enrolled. *Faculty:* 42 full-time (40 women), 31 part-time/adjunct (29 women). Expenses: Contact institution. *Financial support:* In 2006–07, 237 students received support, including 6 teaching assistantships with partial tuition reimbursements available (averaging $22,000 per year); fellowships, research assistantships, Federal Work-Study, institutionally sponsored loans, scholarships/grants, and traineeships also available. Support available to part-time students. Financial award application deadline: 4/15; financial award applicants required to submit FAFSA. In 2006, 57 master's, 13 doctorates awarded. *Degree program information:* Part-time programs available. Postbaccalaureate distance learning degree programs offered (minimal on-campus study). Offers acute care nurse practitioner (MSN, Post-Master's Certificate); adult health nursing (DN Sc, DNP); adult nurse practitioner (MSN, Post-Master's Certificate); adult/gerontological nurse practitioner (MSN); anesthesia nurse practitioner (MSN, Post-Master's Certificate); community and mental health nursing (DN Sc, DNP); critical care clinical specialist (MSN); family nurse practitioner (MSN, Post-Master's Certificate); gerontological nurse practitioner (MSN, Post-Master's Certificate); medical surgical clinical specialist (MSN); neonatal nurse practitioner (MSN, Post-Master's Certificate); nursing (MSN, DN Sc, DNP, Post-Master's Certificate); pediatric acute/chronic care nurse practitioner (MSN); pediatric clinical nurse specialist (MSN); pediatric nurse practitioner (MSN, Post-Master's Certificate); psychiatric clinical specialist (MSN); psychiatric nurse practitioner—adult (MSN); psychiatric nurse practitioner—family (MSN); psychiatric-mental health clinical specialist (Post-Master's Certificate); psychiatric-mental health nurse practitioner (Post-Master's Certificate); public health nursing (MSN); women's and children's health nursing (DN Sc, DNP). *Application deadline:* For fall admission, 7/1 for domestic students; for winter admission, 11/1 for domestic students; for spring admission, 1/15 for domestic students. Applications are processed on a rolling basis. *Application fee:* $40. Electronic applications accepted. *Application Contact:* Hicela Castruita Woods, Director, College Admissions Services, 312-942-7100, Fax: 312-942-2219, E-mail: hicela_castruita@rush.edu. *Dean,* Dr. Melanie Dreher, 312-942-7117, Fax: 312-942-3043.

Graduate College *Degree program information:* Part-time programs available. Offers anatomy and cell biology (MS, PhD); biochemistry (PhD); clinical research (MS); immunology (MS, PhD); medical physics (MS, PhD); microbiology (PhD); pharmacology (MS, PhD); physiology (PhD); virology (MS, PhD). Electronic applications accepted.

Division of Neuroscience Offers neuroscience (MS, PhD). Electronic applications accepted.

Rush Medical College Offers medicine (MD).

RUTGERS, THE STATE UNIVERSITY OF NEW JERSEY, CAMDEN, Camden, NJ 08102-1401

General Information State-supported, coed, university. *Enrollment:* 5,165 graduate, professional, and undergraduate students; 744 full-time matriculated graduate/professional students (349 women), 727 part-time matriculated graduate/professional students (318 women). *Enrollment by degree level:* 765 first professional. *Graduate faculty:* 228 full-time (88 women), 173 part-time/adjunct (65 women). *Graduate housing:* Rooms and/or apartments available to single and married students. *Student services:* Campus employment opportunities, campus safety program, career counseling, child daycare facilities, disabled student services, free psychological counseling, low-cost health insurance, multicultural affairs office, teacher training. *Library facilities:* Paul Robeson Library plus 2 others. *Collection:* 714,447 titles, 5,189 serial subscriptions, 326 audiovisual materials.

Computer facilities: 184 computers available on campus for general student use. A campuswide network can be accessed from student residence rooms and from off campus. Internet access, online grade reports are available. *Web address:* http://camden-www.rutgers.edu/.

General Application Contact: Information Contact, 856-225-6149, Fax: 856-225-6498, E-mail: camden@ugadm.rutgers.edu.

GRADUATE UNITS

Graduate School of Arts and Sciences Students: 152 full-time (98 women), 288 part-time (161 women); includes 102 minority (51 African Americans, 28 Asian Americans or Pacific Islanders, 23 Hispanic Americans), 4 international. Average age 27. 378 applicants, 62% accepted, 149 enrolled. *Faculty:* 128 full-time (46 women), 4 part-time/adjunct (1 woman). Expenses: Contact institution. *Financial support:* In 2006–07, 194 students received support, including 27 fellowships with partial tuition reimbursements available, 1 research assistantship with full tuition reimbursement available (averaging $16,988 per year), 16 teaching assistantships with full tuition reimbursements available (averaging $16,988 per year); career-related internships or fieldwork, Federal Work-Study, institutionally sponsored loans, scholarships/grants, and unspecified assistantships also available. Support available to part-time students. Financial award application deadline: 6/15; financial award applicants required to submit FAFSA. In 2006, 105 degrees awarded. *Degree program information:* Part-time and evening/weekend programs available. Offers American and public history (MA); biology (MS); chemistry (MS); childhood studies (MA, PhD); computer science (MS); criminal justice (MA); education policy and leadership (MPA); English (MA); international public service and development (MPA); liberal studies (MA); mathematics (MS); physical therapy (MPT); psychology (MA); public management (MPA). *Application deadline:* For fall admission, 4/15 priority date for domestic and international students; for spring admission, 11/15 priority date for domestic and international students. Applications are processed on a rolling basis. *Application fee:* $50. Electronic applications accepted. *Application Contact:* Kathryn B. Gallagher, Admissions Counselor, 856-225-6105, Fax: 856-225-6498. *Interim Dean,* Dr. Michael Palis, 856-225-6097, Fax: 856-225-6603.

School of Business Students: 40 full-time, 226 part-time; includes 61 minority (16 African Americans, 41 Asian Americans or Pacific Islanders, 4 Hispanic Americans). Average age 28. 186 applicants, 74% accepted, 76 enrolled. *Faculty:* 33 full-time (9 women), 7 part-time/adjunct (2 women). Expenses: Contact institution. *Financial support:* In 2006–07, 5 students received support. Career-related internships or fieldwork and scholarships/grants available. Financial award applicants required to submit FAFSA. In 2006, 94 degrees awarded. *Degree program information:* Part-time and evening/weekend programs available. Offers business (MBA). *Application deadline:* For fall admission, 7/1 priority date for domestic students, 2/1 for international students; for spring admission, 11/1 priority date for domestic students, 9/1 for international students. Applications are processed on a rolling basis. *Application fee:* $50. Electronic applications accepted. *Application Contact:* Barbara Bickart, MBA Director, 856-225-6593, Fax: 856-225-6231, E-mail: bickart@camden.rutgers.edu. *Dean,* Mitchell P. Koza, 856-225-6217, Fax: 856-225-6231, E-mail: mitchell.koza@camden.rutgers.edu.

School of Law *Degree program information:* Part-time and evening/weekend programs available. Offers law (JD). Electronic applications accepted.

RUTGERS, THE STATE UNIVERSITY OF NEW JERSEY, NEWARK, Newark, NJ 07102

General Information State-supported, coed, university. CGS member. *Enrollment:* 10,203 graduate, professional, and undergraduate students; 1,406 full-time matriculated graduate/professional students (632 women), 2,294 part-time matriculated graduate/professional students (1,044 women). *Enrollment by degree level:* 815 first professional. *Graduate faculty:* 403 full-time (151 women), 203 part-time/adjunct (85 women). *Graduate housing:* Room and/or apartments available to single students; on-campus housing not available to married students. Housing application deadline: 5/15. *Student services:* Career counseling, free psychological counseling, low-cost health insurance. *Library facilities:* John Cotton Dana Library plus 4 others. *Collection:* 941,103 titles, 6,408 serial subscriptions, 34,994 audiovisual materials.

Computer facilities: 708 computers available on campus for general student use. A campuswide network can be accessed from student residence rooms and from off campus. Internet access, online grade reports are available. *Web address:* http://www.newark.rutgers.edu/.

General Application Contact: Information Contact, 973-353-5205, Fax: 973-353-1191, E-mail: gradnwk@andromeda.rutgers.edu.

GRADUATE UNITS

Graduate School Students: 447 full-time (221 women), 889 part-time (553 women); includes 549 minority (220 African Americans, 3 American Indian/Alaska Native, 244 Asian Americans or Pacific Islanders, 82 Hispanic Americans). 1,784 applicants, 48% accepted, 403 enrolled. *Faculty:* 395 full-time (116 women), 36 part-time/adjunct (12 women). Expenses: Contact institution. *Financial support:* In 2006–07, 43 fellowships with partial tuition reimbursements (averaging $18,000 per year), 18 research assistantships with partial tuition reimbursements (averaging $18,347 per year), teaching assistantships with partial tuition reimbursements (averaging $16,988 per year) were awarded; career-related internships or fieldwork, Federal Work-Study, tuition waivers (full and partial), and unspecified assistantships also available. Support available to part-time students. In 2006, 217 master's, 43 doctorates awarded. *Degree program information:* Part-time and evening/weekend programs available. Offers accounting (PhD); accounting information systems (PhD); American political system (MA); analytical chemistry (MS, PhD); applied physics (MS, PhD); biochemistry (MS, PhD); biology (MS, PhD); cognitive neuroscience (PhD); cognitive science (PhD); computational biology (MS); computer information systems (PhD); criminal justice (PhD); economics (MA); English (MA); environmental geology (MS); environmental science (MS, PhD); finance (PhD); health care administration (MPA); history (MA, MAT); human resources administration (MPA); information technology (PhD); inorganic chemistry (MS, PhD); integrative neuroscience (PhD); international business (PhD); international relations (MA); jazz history and research (MA); liberal studies (MALS); management science (PhD); marketing (PhD); mathematical sciences (PhD); nursing (MS); organic chemistry (MS, PhD); organization management (PhD); perception (PhD); physical chemistry (MS, PhD); psychobiology (PhD); public administration (PhD); public management (MPA); public policy analysis (MPA); social cognition (PhD); urban systems (PhD); urban systems and issues (MPA). *Application deadline:* Applications are processed on a rolling basis. *Application fee:* $50. Electronic applications accepted. *Application Contact:* Jason Hand, Director of Admissions, 973-353-5205, Fax: 973-353-1440. *Associate Dean,* Dr. Barry R. Komisarwk, 973-353-5834 Ext. 10, Fax: 973-353-1191, E-mail: brk@psychology.rutgers.edu.

Division of Global Affairs *Degree program information:* Part-time and evening/weekend programs available. Offers global affairs (MS, PhD). Electronic applications accepted.

School of Criminal Justice *Degree program information:* Part-time and evening/weekend programs available. Offers criminal justice (MA, PhD). Electronic applications accepted.

Rutgers Business School: Graduate Programs-Newark/New Brunswick *Degree program information:* Part-time and evening/weekend programs available. Offers accounting (PhD); accounting information systems (PhD); business (M Accy, MBA, MQF, PhD, Certificate); business environment (MBA); customized concentration (MBA); finance (PhD); finance and economics (MBA, MQF); global business (MBA); government financial management (Certificate); governmental accounting (M Accy); individualized study (PhD); information technology (PhD); international business (PhD); management and business strategy (MBA); management science (PhD); management science and information systems (MBA); marketing (MBA); organizational management (PhD); professional accounting (MBA); supply chain management (PhD); taxation (M Accy). Electronic applications accepted.

School of Law *Degree program information:* Part-time and evening/weekend programs available. Offers law (JD).

See Close-Up on page 1011.

RUTGERS, THE STATE UNIVERSITY OF NEW JERSEY, NEW BRUNSWICK, New Brunswick, NJ 08901-1281

General Information State-supported, coed, university. CGS member. *Enrollment:* 34,392 graduate, professional, and undergraduate students; 3,894 full-time matriculated graduate/professional students (2,349 women), 3,807 part-time matriculated graduate/professional students (2,540 women). *Enrollment by degree level:* 449 first professional. *Graduate faculty:* 1,527 full-time (488 women), 685 part-time/adjunct (335 women). *Graduate housing:* Rooms and/or apartments available to single and married students. *Student services:* Campus employment opportunities, career counseling, child daycare facilities, free psychological counseling, international student services, low-cost health insurance. *Library facilities:* Archibald S. Alexander Library plus 14 others. *Online resources:* library catalog, web page, access to other libraries' catalogs. *Collection:* 4.7 million titles, 17,182 serial subscriptions, 91,657 audiovisual materials.

Computer facilities: 1,450 computers available on campus for general student use. A campuswide network can be accessed from student residence rooms and from off campus. Internet access, online grade reports are available. *Web address:* http://www.rutgers.edu/.

General Application Contact: Information Contact, 732-932-7711, Fax: 732-932-7407, E-mail: gradadm@rci.rutgers.edu.

GRADUATE UNITS

Edward J. Bloustein School of Planning and Public Policy *Degree program information:* Part-time and evening/weekend programs available. Offers planning and public policy (MCRP, MCRS, MPAP, MPH, MPP, Dr PH, PhD); public health (MPH, Dr PH, PhD); public policy (MPAP, MPP); urban planning and policy development (MCRP, MCRS, PhD). Electronic applications accepted.

Ernest Mario School of Pharmacy Offers pharmacy (Pharm D). Electronic applications accepted.

Rutgers, The State University of New Jersey, New Brunswick (continued)

Graduate School *Degree program information:* Part-time and evening/weekend programs available. Postbaccalaureate distance learning degree programs offered. Offers African diaspora (PhD); air resources (MS, PhD); American political institutions (PhD); analytical chemistry (MS, PhD); anthropology (MA, PhD); applied mathematics (MS, PhD); applied microbiology (MS, PhD); aquatic biology (MS, PhD); aquatic chemistry (MS, PhD); art history (MA, PhD); astronomy (MS, PhD); atmospheric science (MS, PhD); biochemistry (MS, PhD); biological chemistry (PhD); biomedical engineering (MS, PhD); biophysics (PhD); biopsychology and behavioral neuroscience (PhD); bioresource engineering (MS); cell biology (MS, PhD); cellular and molecular pharmacology (PhD); ceramic and materials science and engineering (MS, PhD); chemical and biochemical engineering (MS, PhD); chemistry and physics of aerosol and hydrosol systems (MS, PhD); chemistry education (MST); civil and environmental engineering (MS, PhD); classics (MA, MAT, PhD); clinical microbiology (MS, PhD); clinical psychology (PhD); cognitive psychology (PhD); communication, information and library studies (PhD); communications and solid-state electronics (MS, PhD); comparative literature (MA, PhD); comparative politics (PhD); composition (MA, PhD); computational biology and molecular biophysics (PhD); computational fluid dynamics (MS, PhD); computational molecular biology (PhD); computer engineering (MS, PhD); computer science (MS, PhD); condensed matter physics (MS, PhD); control systems (MS, PhD); design and dynamics (MS, PhD); developmental biology (MS, PhD); digital signal processing (MS, PhD); diplomatic history (PhD); direct intervention in interpersonal situations (PhD); early American history (PhD); early modern European history (PhD); ecology and evolution (MS, PhD); economics (MA, PhD); elementary particle physics (MS, PhD); endocrine control of growth and metabolism (MS, PhD); entomology (MS, PhD); environmental chemistry (MS, PhD); environmental microbiology (MS, PhD); environmental toxicology (MS, PhD); exposure assessment (PhD); fate and effects of pollutants (MS, PhD); fluid mechanics (MS, PhD); food and business economics (MS); food science (M Phil, MS, PhD); French (MA, PhD); French studies (MAT); geography (MA, MS, PhD); geological sciences (MS, PhD); German (PhD); global/comparative history (PhD); heat transfer (MS, PhD); historic preservation (PhD); history (PhD); history of technology, environment and health (PhD); horticulture (MS, PhD); immunology (MS, PhD); industrial and systems engineering (MS, PhD); industrial relations and human resources (PhD); industrial-occupational toxicology (MS, PhD); information technology (MS); inorganic chemistry (MS, PhD); interdisciplinary developmental psychology (PhD); interdisciplinary health psychology (PhD); intermediate energy nuclear physics (MS); international relations (PhD); Italian (MA); Italian history (PhD); Italian literature and literary criticism (MA, PhD); language, literature and civilization (MAT); Latin American history (PhD); linguistics (PhD); literature (MA, PhD); literatures in English (PhD); manufacturing systems (MS); math finance (MS); mathematics (MS, PhD); mechanics (MS, PhD); medicinal chemistry (MS, PhD); medieval history (PhD); microbial biochemistry (MS, PhD); modern American history (PhD); modern British history (PhD); modern European history (PhD); molecular and cell biology (PhD); molecular biology (MS, PhD); molecular biology and biochemistry (MS, PhD); molecular biosciences (PhD); molecular genetics (MS, PhD); museum studies (MA); music history (MA, PhD); neuroscience (PhD); nuclear physics (MS, PhD); nutrition of ruminant and nonruminant animals (MS, PhD); nutritional sciences (MS, PhD); nutritional toxicology (MS, PhD); oceanography (MS, PhD); operations research (PhD); organic chemistry (MS, PhD); pathology (MS, PhD); pharmaceutical science (MS, PhD); pharmaceutical toxicology (MS, PhD); philosophy (PhD); physical chemistry (MS, PhD); physics (MST); physiology and neurobiology (PhD); plant ecology (MS, PhD); plant genetics (PhD); plant physiology (MS, PhD); political and cultural history (PhD); political economy (PhD); political theory (PhD); pollution prevention and control (MS, PhD); production and management (MS); public law (PhD); quality and productivity management (MS); quality and reliability engineering (MS); reproductive endocrinology and neuroendocrinology (MS, PhD); social policy analysis and administration (PhD); social psychology (PhD); social work (PhD); sociology (MA, PhD); solid mechanics (MS, PhD); Spanish (MA, MAT, PhD); Spanish-American literature (MA, PhD); statistics (MS, PhD); structure and plant groups (MS, PhD); surface science (PhD); theoretical physics (MS, PhD); translation (MA); virology (MS, PhD); water and wastewater treatment (MS, PhD); water resources (MS, PhD); women and politics (PhD); women's and gender studies (MA, PhD); women's history (PhD).

Eagleton Institute of Politics *Degree program information:* Part-time programs available. Offers politics (MS).

Graduate School of Applied and Professional Psychology Students: 194 full-time (146 women), 8 part-time (all women); includes 59 minority (26 African Americans, 14 Asian Americans or Pacific Islanders, 19 Hispanic Americans), 6 international. Average age 31. 535 applicants, 8% accepted, 32 enrolled. *Faculty:* 21 full-time (8 women), 16 part-time/adjunct (13 women). Expenses: Contact institution. *Financial support:* In 2006–07, 43 fellowships with partial tuition reimbursements (averaging $10,000 per year), 1 research assistantship with full tuition reimbursement (averaging $16,988 per year), 8 teaching assistantships with full tuition reimbursements (averaging $16,988 per year) were awarded; career-related internships or fieldwork, Federal Work-Study, institutionally sponsored loans, scholarships/grants, traineeships, and unspecified assistantships also available. Support available to part-time students. Financial award application deadline: 3/15; financial award applicants required to submit FAFSA. In 2006, 23 master's, 15 doctorates awarded. Offers applied and professional psychology (Psy M, Psy D); clinical psychology (Psy M, Psy D); organizational psychology (Psy M, Psy D); school psychology (Psy M, Psy D). *Application deadline:* For fall admission, 1/5 for domestic and international students. *Application fee:* $50. Electronic applications accepted. *Application Contact:* Narda Acevedo, Associate Dean, 732-445-2000 Ext. 113, Fax: 732-445-4888, E-mail: nacevedo@rci.rutgers.edu. *Dean,* Dr. Stanley B. Messer, 732-445-2000 Ext. 110, Fax: 732-445-4888, E-mail: smesser@rci.rutgers.edu.

Graduate School of Education Students: 313 full-time (244 women), 462 part-time (333 women); includes 115 minority (39 African Americans, 45 Asian Americans or Pacific Islanders, 31 Hispanic Americans), 42 international. 946 applicants, 51% accepted, 337 enrolled. *Faculty:* 52 full-time (29 women), 54 part-time/adjunct (34 women). Expenses: Contact institution. *Financial support:* In 2006–07, 142 students received support, including 7 fellowships with full and partial tuition reimbursements available, 8 research assistantships with full tuition reimbursements available (averaging $18,347 per year), 9 teaching assistantships with full tuition reimbursements available (averaging $18,347 per year); career-related internships or fieldwork, Federal Work-Study, institutionally sponsored loans, and scholarships/grants also available. Support available to part-time students. Financial award application deadline: 3/15; financial award applicants required to submit FAFSA. In 2006, 304 master's, 24 doctorates awarded. *Degree program information:* Part-time and evening/weekend programs available. Offers adult and continuing education (Ed M); counseling psychology (Ed M); early childhood/elementary education (Ed M, Ed D); education (Ed M, Ed D, PhD); educational administration and supervision (Ed M, Ed D); educational policy (PhD); educational psychology (PhD); educational statistics, measurement and evaluation (Ed M); English as a second language education (Ed M); English education (Ed M); language education (Ed M, Ed D); learning, cognition and development (Ed M); literacy education (Ed M, Ed D, PhD); mathematics education (Ed M, Ed D, PhD); reading education (Ed M); science education (Ed M, Ed D); social and philosophical foundations of education (Ed M, Ed D); social studies education (Ed M, Ed D); special education (Ed M, Ed D). *Application fee:* $60. Electronic applications accepted. *Application Contact:* Dr. Warren Crown, Associate Dean for Academic Affairs, 732-932-7496 Ext. 8102, Fax: 732-932-8206, E-mail: wcrown@rci.rutgers.edu. *Dean,* Dr. Richard DeLisi, 732-932-7496 Ext. 8117, Fax: 732-932-8206, E-mail: delisi@rci.rutgers.edu.

Mason Gross School of the Arts Students: 211 full-time (122 women), 117 part-time (67 women); includes 114 minority (22 African Americans, 78 Asian Americans or Pacific Islanders, 14 Hispanic Americans). Average age 28. 664 applicants, 21% accepted, 89 enrolled. *Faculty:* 67 full-time (26 women), 67 part-time/adjunct (20 women). Expenses: Contact institution. *Financial support:* Fellowships, teaching assistantships, career-related internships or fieldwork, Federal Work-Study, institutionally sponsored loans, and tuition waivers (full and partial) available. Support available to part-time students. In 2006, 73 master's, 20 doctorates awarded. *Degree program information:* Part-time programs available. Offers acting (MFA); arts (MFA, MM, DMA, AD); collaborative piano (MM, DMA); conducting: choral (MM, DMA); conducting: instrumental (MM, DMA); conducting: orchestral (MM, DMA); design (MFA); directing (MFA); drawing (MFA); jazz studies (MM); music (DMA, AD); music education (MM, DMA); music performance (MM); painting (MFA); playwriting (MFA); sculpture (MFA); stage management (MFA). *Application deadline:* Applications are processed on a rolling basis. *Application fee:* $50. *Dean,* George B. Stauffer, 732-932-9360 Ext. 507, Fax: 732-932-8794.

Programs in Engineering Offers engineering (MS, PhD). Degrees offered through the Graduate School.

School of Communication, Information and Library Studies Students: 193 full-time (161 women), 204 part-time (155 women); includes 47 minority (7 African Americans, 1 American Indian/Alaska Native, 25 Asian Americans or Pacific Islanders, 14 Hispanic Americans), 18 international. Average age 32. 311 applicants, 55% accepted, 76 enrolled. *Faculty:* 38 full-time (18 women), 14 part-time/adjunct (7 women). Expenses: Contact institution. *Financial support:* In 2006–07, 7 fellowships with full tuition reimbursements (averaging $18,348 per year) were awarded; research assistantships, teaching assistantships, career-related internships or fieldwork, Federal Work-Study, institutionally sponsored loans, scholarships/grants, and tuition waivers also available. Support available to part-time students. Financial award application deadline: 4/2; financial award applicants required to submit FAFSA. In 2006, 175 degrees awarded. *Degree program information:* Part-time programs available. Postbaccalaureate distance learning degree programs offered (no on-campus study). Offers communication and information studies (MCIS); library and information science (MLS). *Application deadline:* For fall admission, 5/2 priority date for domestic students, 4/2 for international students. Applications are processed on a rolling basis. *Application fee:* $50. Electronic applications accepted. *Application Contact:* Linda J. Costa, Director of Graduate Admissions, 732-932-7711, Fax: 732-932-8231, E-mail: smeds@rci.rutgers.edu. *Dean,* Dr. Gustav W. Friedrich, 732-932-7500, Fax: 732-932-6916, E-mail: gusf@scils.rutgers.edu.

School of Management and Labor Relations *Degree program information:* Part-time and evening/weekend programs available. Offers human resource management (MHRM); labor and employment relations (MLER); management and labor relations (MHRM, MLER). Electronic applications accepted.

School of Social Work *Degree program information:* Part-time programs available. Offers social work (MSW, PhD). PhD offered through the Graduate School. Electronic applications accepted.

RYERSON UNIVERSITY, Toronto, ON M5B 2K3, Canada

General Information Province-supported, coed, comprehensive institution. CGS member.

GRADUATE UNITS

School of Graduate Studies Offers photographic preservation and collections management (MA).

SACRED HEART MAJOR SEMINARY, Detroit, MI 48206-1799

General Information Independent-religious, coed, comprehensive institution. *Graduate housing:* Room and/or apartments guaranteed to single students; on-campus housing not available to married students. Housing application deadline: 8/1.

GRADUATE UNITS

School of Theology *Degree program information:* Part-time and evening/weekend programs available. Offers pastoral studies (MAPS); theology (M Div, MA).

SACRED HEART SCHOOL OF THEOLOGY, Hales Corners, WI 53130-0429

General Information Independent-religious, coed, primarily men, graduate-only institution. *Enrollment by degree level:* 79 first professional, 21 master's, 2 other advanced degrees. *Graduate faculty:* 29 full-time (7 women), 15 part-time/adjunct (7 women). *Tuition:* Full-time $11,650; part-time $390 per credit. Tuition and fees vary according to program. *Graduate housing:* Room and/or apartments guaranteed to single students; on-campus housing not available to married students. Typical cost: $7,750 (including board). *Student services:* Campus employment opportunities, career counseling, disabled student services, exercise/wellness program, free psychological counseling, international student services, multicultural affairs office, writing training. *Library facilities:* Leo Dehon Library. *Online resources:* library catalog, access to other libraries' catalogs. *Collection:* 98,003 titles, 433 serial subscriptions, 17,982 audiovisual materials.

Computer facilities: 4 computers available on campus for general student use. A campuswide network can be accessed from student residence rooms and from off campus. Internet access, Intranet are available. *Web address:* http://www.shst.edu.

General Application Contact: Rev. Thomas L. Knoebel, Director of Admissions, 414-425-8300 Ext. 6984, Fax: 414-529-6999, E-mail: tknoebel@shst.edu.

GRADUATE UNITS

Graduate and Professional Programs Students: 81 full-time (0 women), 21 part-time (11 women); includes 5 minority (2 Asian Americans or Pacific Islanders, 3 Hispanic Americans), 17 international. Average age 44. 26 applicants, 100% accepted, 25 enrolled. *Faculty:* 29 full-time (7 women), 15 part-time/adjunct (7 women). Expenses: Contact institution. *Financial support:* In 2006–07, 8 students received support. Career-related internships or fieldwork and scholarships/grants available. Financial award application deadline: 9/30; financial award applicants required to submit FAFSA. In 2006, 11 M Divs, 3 master's awarded. *Degree program information:* Part-time programs available. Offers theology (M Div, MA). *Application deadline:* For fall admission, 8/25 for domestic students; for spring admission, 12/20 for domestic students. *Application fee:* $50. *Application Contact:* Rev. Thomas L. Knoebel, Director of Admissions, 414-425-8300 Ext. 6984, Fax: 414-529-6999, E-mail: tknoebel@shst.edu. *President-Rector,* Very Rev. Thomas P. Cassidy, SCJ, 414-425-8300 Ext. 6986, Fax: 414-529-6999, E-mail: tcassidy@shst.edu.

SACRED HEART UNIVERSITY, Fairfield, CT 06825-1000

General Information Independent-religious, coed, comprehensive institution. *Enrollment:* 5,756 graduate, professional, and undergraduate students; 548 full-time matriculated graduate/professional students (407 women), 1,005 part-time matriculated graduate/professional students (698 women). *Enrollment by degree level:* 1,460 master's, 93 doctoral. *Graduate faculty:* 62 full-time (35 women), 81 part-time/adjunct (40 women). *Tuition:* Part-time $510 per credit. *Required fees:* $118 per term. Full-time tuition and fees vary according to degree level and program. *Graduate housing:* On-campus housing not available. *Student services:* Campus employment opportunities, campus safety program, career counseling, exercise/wellness program, free psychological counseling, international student services, low-cost health insurance, multicultural affairs office, teacher training. *Library facilities:* Ryan-Matura Library. *Online resources:* library catalog, web page, access to other libraries' catalogs. *Collection:* 134,348 titles, 860 serial subscriptions, 1,797 audiovisual materials.

Computer facilities: Computer purchase and lease plans are available. 330 computers available on campus for general student use. A campuswide network can be accessed from student residence rooms and from off campus. Internet access and online class registration, intranet are available. *Web address:* http://www.sacredheart.edu/.

General Application Contact: Alexis Haakonsen, Dean of Graduate Admissions, 203-365-7619, Fax: 203-365-4732, E-mail: gradstudies@sacredheart.edu.

GRADUATE UNITS

Graduate Studies Students: 548 full-time (407 women), 1,005 part-time (698 women); includes 104 minority (43 African Americans, 6 American Indian/Alaska Native, 23 Asian Americans or Pacific Islanders, 32 Hispanic Americans), 30 international. Average age 33. 599 applicants, 87% accepted, 454 enrolled. *Faculty:* 62 full-time (35 women), 81 part-time/adjunct (40 women). Expenses: Contact institution. *Financial support:* In 2006–07, 220 students received support. Career-related internships or fieldwork, institutionally sponsored loans, traineeships, tuition waivers (partial), and unspecified assistantships available. Support available to part-time students. Financial award applicants required to submit FAFSA. In 2006, 518 master's, 59 other advanced degrees awarded. *Degree program information:*

Part-time and evening/weekend programs available. Postbaccalaureate distance learning degree programs offered (minimal on-campus study). *Application deadline:* Applications are processed on a rolling basis. *Application fee:* $50 ($100 for international students). Electronic applications accepted. *Application Contact:* Alexis Haakonsen, Dean of Graduate Admissions, 203-365-7619, Fax: 203-365-4732, E-mail: haakonsena@sacredheart.edu.

College of Arts and Sciences Students: 18 full-time (7 women), 103 part-time (49 women); includes 13 minority (5 African Americans, 2 American Indian/Alaska Native, 4 Asian Americans or Pacific Islanders, 2 Hispanic Americans), 16 international. Average age 33. 42 applicants, 81% accepted. Expenses: Contact institution. *Financial support:* Career-related internships or fieldwork, institutionally sponsored loans, and unspecified assistantships available. Support available to part-time students. Financial award applicants required to submit FAFSA. In 2006, 30 degrees awarded. *Degree program information:* Part-time and evening/weekend programs available. Offers arts and sciences (MA, MS, CPS); chemistry (MS); computer science (MS, CPS); criminal justice (MA); information technology (MS, CPS); information technology and network security (CPS); interactive multimedia (CPS); religious studies (MA); Web development (CPS). *Application deadline:* Applications are processed on a rolling basis. *Application fee:* $50 ($100 for international students). Electronic applications accepted. *Application Contact:* Alexis Haakonsen, Dean of Graduate Admissions, 203-365-7619, Fax: 203-365-4732, E-mail: haakonsena@sacredheart.edu. *Dean,* Dr. Claire Paolini, 203-396-8020.

College of Education and Health Professions Students: 464 full-time (364 women), 804 part-time (603 women); includes 58 minority (23 African Americans, 4 American Indian/Alaska Native, 10 Asian Americans or Pacific Islanders, 21 Hispanic Americans), 7 international. Average age 33. 499 applicants, 88% accepted, 367 enrolled. Expenses: Contact institution. *Financial support:* Research assistantships, career-related internships or fieldwork, institutionally sponsored loans, traineeships, tuition waivers (partial), and unspecified assistantships available. Support available to part-time students. Financial award applicants required to submit FAFSA. In 2006, 362 master's, 59 other advanced degrees awarded. *Degree program information:* Part-time and evening/weekend programs available. Postbaccalaureate distance learning degree programs offered (minimal on-campus study). Offers administration (CAS); clinical nurse leader (MSN); education and health professions (MAT, MS, MSN, MSOT, DPT, CAS); educational technology (MAT); elementary education (MAT); family nurse practitioner (MSN); geriatric health and wellness (MS); occupational therapy (MSOT); patient care services administration (MSN); physical therapy (DPT); reading (CAS); secondary education (MAT); teaching (CAS). *Application deadline:* Applications are processed on a rolling basis. *Application fee:* $50 ($100 for international students). Electronic applications accepted. *Application Contact:* Alexis Haakonsen, Dean of Graduate Admissions, 203-365-7619, Fax: 203-365-4732, E-mail: haakonsena@sacredheart.edu. *Dean,* Dr. Patricia Walker, 203-396-8024.

The John F. Welch College of Business Students: 26 full-time (10 women), 138 part-time (72 women); includes 30 minority (13 African Americans, 8 Asian Americans or Pacific Islanders, 9 Hispanic Americans), 7 international. Average age 32. 58 applicants, 90% accepted, 47 enrolled. *Faculty:* 35 full-time, 27 part-time/adjunct. Expenses: Contact institution. *Financial support:* Career-related internships or fieldwork, institutionally sponsored loans, and unspecified assistantships available. Support available to part-time students. Financial award applicants required to submit FAFSA. In 2006, 88 degrees awarded. *Degree program information:* Part-time and evening/weekend programs available. Offers business (MBA). *Application deadline:* Applications are processed on a rolling basis. *Application fee:* $50 ($100 for international students). Electronic applications accepted. *Application Contact:* Meredith Woerz, Director of Graduate Admissions, 203-365-2619, Fax: 203-365-4732, E-mail: gradstudies@sacredheart.edu. *Dean,* Dr. Stephen Brown, 203-396-8084.

See Close-Up on page 1013.

SAGE GRADUATE SCHOOL, Troy, NY 12180-4115

General Information Independent, coed, graduate-only institution. *Enrollment by degree level:* 790 master's, 88 doctoral, 24 other advanced degrees. *Graduate faculty:* 44 full-time (38 women), 46 part-time/adjunct (37 women). *Tuition:* Full-time $9,270; part-time $515 per credit hour. *Graduate housing:* Room and/or apartments available on a first-come, first-served basis to single students; on-campus housing not available to married students. Typical cost: $4,430 per year ($8,520 including board). Housing application deadline: 5/1. *Student services:* Career counseling, low-cost health insurance. *Library facilities:* James Wheelock Clark Library plus 1 other. *Online resources:* library catalog, web page. *Collection:* 341,098 titles, 658 serial subscriptions, 32,648 audiovisual materials. *Research affiliation:* Enlarged City School District of Troy (education), Albany Medical College (occupational therapy), Samaritan Hospital (nursing), Ellis Hospital (nursing), Samuel Stratton Veterans Administration Hospital (nursing).

Computer facilities: 319 computers available on campus for general student use. A campuswide network can be accessed from student residence rooms and from off campus. Internet access is available. *Web address:* http://www.sage.edu/.

General Application Contact: Shannon K. Easton, Director of Graduate and Adult Admission, 518-244-2443, Fax: 518-244-6880, E-mail: sgsadm@sage.edu.

GRADUATE UNITS

Graduate School Students: 355 full-time (301 women), 547 part-time (458 women); includes 67 minority (33 African Americans, 4 American Indian/Alaska Native, 11 Asian Americans or Pacific Islanders, 19 Hispanic Americans), 4 international. Average age 30. 575 applicants, 73% accepted, 264 enrolled. *Faculty:* 44 full-time (38 women), 46 part-time/adjunct (37 women). Expenses: Contact institution. *Financial support:* Career-related internships or fieldwork, scholarships/grants, and unspecified assistantships available. Support available to part-time students. Financial award application deadline: 3/1; financial award applicants required to submit FAFSA. In 2006, 295 master's, 37 doctorates, 29 other advanced degrees awarded. *Degree program information:* Part-time and evening/weekend programs available. *Application deadline:* Applications are processed on a rolling basis. *Application fee:* $40. *Application Contact:* Shannon K. Easton, Director of Graduate and Adult Admission, 518-244-2443, Fax: 518-244-6880, E-mail: sgsadm@sage.edu. *Dean,* Dr. John A. Tribble, 518-244-2264, E-mail: tribbj@sage.edu.

Division of Education Students: 171 full-time (147 women), 230 part-time (194 women); includes 19 minority (7 African Americans, 1 American Indian/Alaska Native, 5 Asian Americans or Pacific Islanders, 6 Hispanic Americans). Average age 27. 267 applicants, 68% accepted, 107 enrolled. *Faculty:* 11 full-time (8 women), 20 part-time/adjunct (15 women). Expenses: Contact institution. *Financial support:* Career-related internships or fieldwork, scholarships/grants, and unspecified assistantships available. Support available to part-time students. Financial award application deadline: 3/1; financial award applicants required to submit FAFSA. In 2006, 187 master's, 5 other advanced degrees awarded. *Degree program information:* Part-time and evening/weekend programs available. Offers art education (MAT); biology (MAT); childhood education (MS Ed); childhood education/literacy (MS); childhood special education (MS Ed); English (MAT); guidance and counseling (MS, Post Master's Certificate); literacy (MS Ed); literacy/childhood special education (MS Ed); mathematics (MAT); school health education (MS); social studies (MAT); teaching (MAT). *Application deadline:* Applications are processed on a rolling basis. *Application fee:* $40. *Application Contact:* Shannon K. Easton, Director of Graduate and Adult Admission, 518-244-2443, Fax: 518-244-6880, E-mail: sgsadm@sage.edu. *Dean,* Dr. Connell G. Frazer, 518-244-2326, Fax: 518-244-2334, E-mail: frazec@sage.edu.

Division of Health and Rehabilitation Sciences Students: 82 full-time (69 women), 73 part-time (59 women); includes 6 minority (2 African Americans, 1 Asian American or Pacific Islander, 3 Hispanic Americans), 1 international. Average age 28. 65 applicants, 88% accepted, 44 enrolled. *Faculty:* 18 full-time (17 women), 9 part-time/adjunct (all women). Expenses: Contact institution. *Financial support:* Career-related internships or fieldwork, scholarships/grants, and unspecified assistantships available. Support available to part-time students. Financial award application deadline: 3/1; financial award applicants required to submit FAFSA. In 2006, 8 master's, 37 doctorates, 11 other advanced degrees awarded. Offers applied nutrition (MS); dietetic internship (Certificate); nutrition (MS); occupational therapy (MS); physical therapy (PhD). *Application deadline:* Applications are processed on a rolling basis. *Application fee:* $40. *Application Contact:* Shannon K. Easton, Director of Graduate and Adult Admission, 518-244-2443, Fax: 518-244-6880, E-mail: sgsadm@sage.edu.

Division of Management, Communications and Legal Studies Students: 13 full-time (9 women), 107 part-time (76 women); includes 17 minority (13 African Americans, 4 Hispanic Americans), 2 international. Average age 32. 83 applicants, 73% accepted, 46 enrolled. *Faculty:* 3 full-time (1 woman), 4 part-time/adjunct (2 women). Expenses: Contact institution. *Financial support:* Career-related internships or fieldwork, scholarships/grants, and unspecified assistantships available. Support available to part-time students. Financial award application deadline: 3/1; financial award applicants required to submit FAFSA. In 2006, 31 degrees awarded. *Degree program information:* Part-time and evening/weekend programs available. Offers business strategy (MBA); finance (MBA); gerontology (MS); health education (MS); human resources (MBA); human services administration (MS); management (MS); management, communications and legal studies (MBA, MS); marketing (MBA); organizational management (MS); public management (MS). *Application deadline:* Applications are processed on a rolling basis. *Application fee:* $40. *Application Contact:* Shannon K. Easton, Director of Graduate and Adult Admission, 518-244-2443, Fax: 518-244-6880, E-mail: sgsadm@sage.edu. *Director,* James Murtagh, 518-292-1770, Fax: 518-292-5414, E-mail: murtaj@sage.edu.

Division of Nursing Students: 38 full-time (34 women), 63 part-time (60 women); includes 9 minority (4 African Americans, 1 American Indian/Alaska Native, 3 Asian Americans or Pacific Islanders, 1 Hispanic American). Average age 40. 67 applicants, 79% accepted, 31 enrolled. *Faculty:* 8 full-time (all women), 3 part-time/adjunct (all women). Expenses: Contact institution. *Financial support:* Career-related internships or fieldwork, scholarships/grants, and unspecified assistantships available. Support available to part-time students. Financial award application deadline: 3/1; financial award applicants required to submit FAFSA. In 2006, 39 master's, 11 other advanced degrees awarded. *Degree program information:* Part-time and evening/weekend programs available. Offers adult health (MS); adult nurse practitioner (MS, Post Master's Certificate); community health (MS); family nurse practitioner (MS, Post Master's Certificate); nursing (Post Master's Certificate); nursing-medical surgical (MS); psychiatric mental health (MS); psychiatric mental health nurse practitioner (MS). *Application deadline:* Applications are processed on a rolling basis. *Application fee:* $40. *Application Contact:* Shannon K. Easton, Director of Graduate and Adult Admission, 518-244-2443, Fax: 518-244-6880, E-mail: sgsadm@sage.edu. *Chair,* Dr. Glenda Kelman, 518-244-2001, E-mail: kelmag@sage.edu.

Division of Psychology Students: 51 full-time (42 women), 71 part-time (66 women); includes 16 minority (7 African Americans, 2 American Indian/Alaska Native, 2 Asian Americans or Pacific Islanders, 5 Hispanic Americans), 1 international. Average age 29. 90 applicants, 71% accepted, 29 enrolled. *Faculty:* 4 full-time (all women), 6 part-time/adjunct (5 women). Expenses: Contact institution. *Financial support:* Career-related internships or fieldwork, scholarships/grants, and unspecified assistantships available. Support available to part-time students. Financial award application deadline: 3/1; financial award applicants required to submit FAFSA. In 2006, 30 degrees awarded. *Degree program information:* Part-time and evening/weekend programs available. Offers child care and children's services (MA); community counseling (MA); community health education (MA); community psychology (MA); forensic psychology (Certificate); general psychology (MA). *Application deadline:* Applications are processed on a rolling basis. *Application fee:* $40. *Application Contact:* Shannon K. Easton, Director of Graduate and Adult Admission, 518-244-2443, Fax: 518-244-6880, E-mail: sgsadm@sage.edu. *Chair,* Dr. Jean Poppei, 518-244-2076, Fax: 518-244-4545, E-mail: poppei@sage.edu.

SAGINAW VALLEY STATE UNIVERSITY, University Center, MI 48710

General Information State-supported, coed, comprehensive institution. *Enrollment:* 9,543 graduate, professional, and undergraduate students; 154 full-time matriculated graduate/professional students (107 women), 1,456 part-time matriculated graduate/professional students (1,097 women). *Enrollment by degree level:* 1,519 master's, 91 other advanced degrees. *Graduate faculty:* 81 full-time (47 women), 55 part-time/adjunct (37 women). Tuition, state resident: full-time $7,225; part-time $301 per credit hour. Tuition, nonresident: full-time $13,888; part-time $579 per credit hour. *Required fees:* $330; $14 per credit hour. Tuition and fees vary according to course load. *Graduate housing:* Room and/or apartments available on a first-come, first-served basis to single students; on-campus housing not available to married students. Typical cost: $4,470 per year ($7,020 including board). Housing application deadline: 6/5. *Student services:* Campus employment opportunities, career counseling, disabled student services, free psychological counseling, international student services, multicultural affairs office, writing training. *Library facilities:* Zahnow Library. *Online resources:* library catalog, web page, access to other libraries' catalogs. *Collection:* 641,190 titles, 11,770 serial subscriptions, 6,380 audiovisual materials.

Computer facilities: Computer purchase and lease plans are available. 1,033 computers available on campus for general student use. A campuswide network can be accessed from student residence rooms and from off campus. Internet access and online class registration are available. *Web address:* http://www.svsu.edu/.

General Application Contact: Information Contact, 989-964-4200, Fax: 989-790-0180, E-mail: gradadm@svsu.edu.

GRADUATE UNITS

College of Arts and Behavioral Sciences Students: 28 full-time (14 women), 79 part-time (53 women); includes 25 minority (18 African Americans, 1 Asian American or Pacific Islander, 6 Hispanic Americans), 8 international. Average age 34. 75 applicants, 92% accepted, 45 enrolled. *Faculty:* 9 full-time (3 women), 5 part-time/adjunct (4 women). Expenses: Contact institution. *Financial support:* Federal Work-Study available. Support available to part-time students. Financial award applicants required to submit FAFSA. In 2006, 44 degrees awarded. *Degree program information:* Part-time and evening/weekend programs available. Offers administrative science (MA); arts and behavioral sciences (MA); communication and multimedia (MA). *Application deadline:* Applications are processed on a rolling basis. *Application fee:* $25. Electronic applications accepted. *Dean,* Dr. Mary Hedberg, 989-964-7144, E-mail: hedberg@svsu.edu.

College of Business and Management Students: 22 full-time (7 women), 44 part-time (15 women); includes 4 minority (2 African Americans, 2 Asian Americans or Pacific Islanders), 17 international. Average age 30. 50 applicants, 88% accepted, 19 enrolled. *Faculty:* 10 full-time (3 women), 1 part-time/adjunct (0 women). Expenses: Contact institution. *Financial support:* In 2006–07, 1 research assistantship with full tuition reimbursement (averaging $5,000 per year) was awarded; fellowships with partial tuition reimbursements, Federal Work-Study also available. Support available to part-time students. Financial award application deadline: 4/1; financial award applicants required to submit FAFSA. In 2006, 23 degrees awarded. *Degree program information:* Part-time and evening/weekend programs available. Offers business administration (MBA); business and management (MBA). *Application deadline:* Applications are processed on a rolling basis. *Application fee:* $25. Electronic applications accepted. *Dean,* Dr. Marwan A. Wafa, 989-964-4064, Fax: 989-964-7497, E-mail: cbmdean@svsu.edu.

College of Education Students: 74 full-time (58 women), 1,264 part-time (968 women); includes 48 minority (29 African Americans, 1 American Indian/Alaska Native, 7 Asian Americans or Pacific Islanders, 11 Hispanic Americans), 1 international. Average age 34. 280 applicants, 100% accepted, 211 enrolled. *Faculty:* 40 full-time (29 women), 44 part-time/adjunct (33 women). Expenses: Contact institution. *Financial support:* Federal Work-Study available. Support available to part-time students. Financial award applicants required to submit FAFSA. In 2006, 387 master's, 16 other advanced degrees awarded. *Degree program information:* Part-time and evening/weekend programs available. Offers adapted physical activity (MAT); chief business officers (M Ed); early childhood education (MAT); education (M Ed, MAT, Ed S); education leadership (Ed S); educational administration and supervision (M Ed); elementary (MAT); elementary classroom teaching (MAT); instructional technology (MAT); learning and behavioral disorders (MAT); middle school (MAT); middle school classroom teaching (MAT); principalship (M Ed); reading education (MAT); secondary classroom teaching (MAT); secondary school (MAT); special education (MAT); superintendency (M Ed). *Applica-*

Saginaw Valley State University (continued)

tion deadline: Applications are processed on a rolling basis. *Application fee:* $25. Electronic applications accepted. *Application Contact:* Jeanne Chipman, Certification Officer, 989-964-4083, Fax: 989-964-4385, E-mail: jdc@svsu.edu. *Dean,* Dr. Steve P. Barbus, 989-964-6067, Fax: 989-790-4385, E-mail: barbus@svsu.edu.

College of Science, Engineering, and Technology Students: 1 full-time (0 women), 8 part-time, 3 international. Average age 37. 1 applicant, 100% accepted, 1 enrolled. *Faculty:* 11 full-time (2 women), 5 part-time/adjunct (0 women). Expenses: Contact institution. *Financial support:* In 2006–07, 1 fellowship with partial tuition reimbursement, 1 research assistantship with full tuition reimbursement (averaging $2,500 per year) were awarded; Federal Work-Study also available. Support available to part-time students. Financial award application deadline: 4/1; financial award applicants required to submit FAFSA. In 2006, 8 degrees awarded. *Degree program information:* Part-time and evening/weekend programs available. Offers science, engineering, and technology (MS); technological processes (MS). *Application deadline:* Applications are processed on a rolling basis. *Application fee:* $25. Electronic applications accepted. *Dean,* Dr. Ron Williams, 989-964-4144, Fax: 989-790-2717, E-mail: rrwillia@svsu.edu.

Crystal M. Lange College of Nursing and Health Sciences Students: 29 full-time (28 women), 61 part-time (all women); includes 5 minority (3 African Americans, 1 Asian American or Pacific Islander, 1 Hispanic American). Average age 35. 21 applicants, 95% accepted, 16 enrolled. *Faculty:* 12 full-time (10 women). Expenses: Contact institution. *Financial support:* Fellowships with partial tuition reimbursements, research assistantships with full tuition reimbursements, Federal Work-Study available. Support available to part-time students. Financial award application deadline: 4/1; financial award applicants required to submit FAFSA. In 2006, 4 degrees awarded. *Degree program information:* Part-time and evening/weekend programs available. Offers clinical nurse specialist (MSN); health system nurse specialist (MSN); nurse practitioner (MSN); nursing (MSN); nursing and health sciences (MSN, MSOT); occupational therapy (MSOT). *Application deadline:* Applications are processed on a rolling basis. *Application fee:* $25. Electronic applications accepted. *Dean,* Dr. Janalou Blecke, 989-964-4145, Fax: 989-964-4024, E-mail: blecke@svsu.edu.

ST. AMBROSE UNIVERSITY, Davenport, IA 52803-2898

General Information Independent-religious, coed, comprehensive institution. CGS member. *Enrollment:* 3,780 graduate, professional, and undergraduate students; 310 full-time matriculated graduate/professional students (214 women), 641 part-time matriculated graduate/professional students (379 women). *Enrollment by degree level:* 861 master's, 90 doctoral. *Graduate faculty:* 75 full-time (22 women), 50 part-time/adjunct (22 women). *Graduate housing:* Room and/or apartments available on a first-come, first-served basis to single students; on-campus housing not available to married students. Typical cost: $3,835 per year ($7,525 including board). Room and board charges vary according to board plan and housing facility selected. Housing application deadline: 8/15. *Student services:* Campus employment opportunities, campus safety program, career counseling, child daycare facilities, disabled student services, free psychological counseling, international student services, multicultural affairs office, teacher training, writing training. *Library facilities:* O'Keefe Library plus 1 other. *Online resources:* library catalog, web page, access to other libraries' catalogs. *Collection:* 150,328 titles, 738 serial subscriptions, 3,687 audiovisual materials.

Computer facilities: Computer purchase and lease plans are available. 190 computers available on campus for general student use. A campuswide network can be accessed from student residence rooms and from off campus. Internet access and online class registration, online course syllabi, class listings, grades are available. *Web address:* http://www.sau.edu/.

General Application Contact: Elizabeth Berridge, Director of Graduate Student Recruitment, 563-333-6271, Fax: 563-333-6268, E-mail: berridgeelizabethb@sau.edu.

GRADUATE UNITS

College of Arts and Sciences Students: 80 full-time (61 women), 134 part-time (86 women); includes 25 minority (15 African Americans, 2 Asian Americans or Pacific Islanders, 8 Hispanic Americans), 3 international. Average age 35. 110 applicants, 78% accepted, 73 enrolled. *Faculty:* 19 full-time (4 women), 13 part-time/adjunct (9 women). Expenses: Contact institution. *Financial support:* In 2006–07, 189 students received support, including 9 research assistantships with partial tuition reimbursements available (averaging $3,290 per year); career-related internships or fieldwork, scholarships/grants, and tuition waivers (partial) also available. Support available to part-time students. Financial award application deadline: 8/15; financial award applicants required to submit FAFSA. In 2006, 76 degrees awarded. *Degree program information:* Part-time and evening/weekend programs available. Offers arts and sciences (MCJ, MOL, MPS, MSW); criminal justice (MCJ); juvenile justice education (MCJ); leadership studies (MOL); pastoral studies (MPS); social work (MSW). *Application deadline:* For fall admission, 8/1 priority date for domestic students; for winter admission, 12/15 priority date for domestic students; for spring admission, 1/1 priority date for domestic students. Applications are processed on a rolling basis. *Application fee:* $25. Electronic applications accepted. *Application Contact:* Elizabeth Berridge, Director of Graduate Student Recruitment, 563-333-6271, Fax: 563-333-6268, E-mail: berridgeelizabethb@sau.edu. *Dean,* Dr. Aron R. Aji, 563-333-6053, Fax: 563-333-6052, E-mail: aronajir@sau.edu.

College of Business Students: 107 full-time (50 women), 383 part-time (185 women); includes 50 minority (28 African Americans, 8 Asian Americans or Pacific Islanders, 14 Hispanic Americans), 20 international. Average age 35. 234 applicants, 81% accepted, 125 enrolled. *Faculty:* 35 full-time (6 women), 26 part-time/adjunct (6 women). Expenses: Contact institution. *Financial support:* In 2006–07, 350 students received support, including 10 research assistantships with partial tuition reimbursements available; career-related internships or fieldwork, scholarships/grants, and tuition waivers (partial) also available. Support available to part-time students. Financial award application deadline: 3/15; financial award applicants required to submit FAFSA. In 2006, 134 master's, 5 doctorates awarded. *Degree program information:* Part-time and evening/weekend programs available. Offers accounting (M Ac); business (M Ac, MBA, MSITM, DBA); business administration (DBA); health care (MBA); human resources (MBA); information technology management (MSITM). *Application deadline:* For fall admission, 8/15 priority date for domestic students; for winter admission, 12/15 for domestic students; for spring admission, 1/1 for domestic students. Applications are processed on a rolling basis. *Application fee:* $25. Electronic applications accepted. *Application Contact:* Elizabeth Berridge, Director of Graduate Student Recruitment, 563-333-6271, Fax: 563-333-6268, E-mail: berridgeelizabethb@sau.edu. *Dean,* Dr. Richard M. Dienesch, 563-333-6270, Fax: 563-333-6268.

College of Education and Health Sciences Students: 123 full-time (103 women), 124 part-time (108 women); includes 10 minority (1 Asian American or Pacific Islander, 9 Hispanic Americans). Average age 33. 105 applicants, 91% accepted, 87 enrolled. *Faculty:* 21 full-time (12 women), 11 part-time/adjunct (7 women). Expenses: Contact institution. *Financial support:* In 2006–07, 73 students received support, including 13 research assistantships with partial tuition reimbursements available (averaging $3,662 per year); career-related internships or fieldwork, scholarships/grants, tuition waivers (full and partial), and unspecified assistantships also available. Support available to part-time students. Financial award application deadline: 3/15; financial award applicants required to submit FAFSA. In 2006, 30 master's, 34 doctorates awarded. *Degree program information:* Part-time and evening/weekend programs available. Postbaccalaureate distance learning degree programs offered (no on-campus study). Offers education and health sciences (M Ed, MEA, MOT, MSN, DPT); educational leadership (MEA); occupational therapy (MOT); physical therapy (DPT); special education (M Ed); teaching (M Ed). *Application deadline:* For fall admission, 8/15 priority date for domestic students; for winter admission, 12/15 priority date for domestic students; for spring admission, 1/1 priority date for domestic students. Applications are processed on a rolling basis. *Application fee:* $25. Electronic applications accepted. *Application Contact:* Elizabeth Berridge, Director of Graduate Student Recruitment, 563-333-6271, Fax: 563-333-6268, E-mail: berridgeelizabethb@sau.edu. *Dean,* Dr. Robert Ristow, 563-333-6078, Fax: 563-333-6297, E-mail: rristow@sau.edu.

ST. ANDREW'S COLLEGE, Saskatoon, SK S7N 0W3, Canada

General Information Independent-religious, coed, graduate-only institution.

GRADUATE UNITS

Graduate Programs in Theology Offers theology (M Div, MPC, MTS, STM).

ST. ANDREW'S COLLEGE IN WINNIPEG, Winnipeg, MB R3T 2M7, Canada

General Information Independent-religious, coed, primarily men, graduate-only institution. *Graduate housing:* Rooms and/or apartments available to single and married students. Housing application deadline: 7/31.

GRADUATE UNITS

Graduate Programs Offers theology (M Div).

ST. AUGUSTINE'S SEMINARY OF TORONTO, Scarborough, ON M1M 1M3, Canada

General Information Independent-religious, coed, primarily men, graduate-only institution. *Enrollment by degree level:* 63 first professional, 59 master's, 72 other advanced degrees. *Graduate faculty:* 11 full-time (4 women), 20 part-time/adjunct (4 women). *Tuition:* Full-time $4,352; part-time $435 per course. *Required fees:* $54 per term. Tuition and fees vary according to course load. *Graduate housing:* On-campus housing not available. *Library facilities:* St. Augustine's Seminary Library. *Online resources:* library catalog, access to other libraries' catalogs. *Collection:* 37,387 titles, 194 serial subscriptions, 1,328 audiovisual materials.

Computer facilities: 2 computers available on campus for general student use. A campuswide network can be accessed from student residence rooms and from off campus. Internet access is available. *Web address:* http://www.staugustines.on.ca/.

General Application Contact: Theresa Mary Vicioso, Registrar/Administrative Assistant to the Dean of Studies, 416-261-7207 Ext. 230, Fax: 416-261-2529, E-mail: t.vicioso@utoronto.ca.

GRADUATE UNITS

Graduate and Professional Programs Students: 53 full-time (2 women), 141 part-time (62 women), 16 international. Average age 42. 45 applicants, 91% accepted, 37 enrolled. *Faculty:* 11 full-time (4 women), 20 part-time/adjunct (4 women). Expenses: Contact institution. In 2006, 7 M Divs, 12 master's awarded. *Degree program information:* Part-time and evening/weekend programs available. Postbaccalaureate distance learning degree programs offered (minimal on-campus study). Offers divinity (M Div); lay ministry (Diploma); religious education (MRE); theological studies (MTS, Diploma). *Application deadline:* For fall admission, 7/15 priority date for domestic and international students; for winter admission, 11/15 priority date for domestic and international students; for spring admission, 4/15 priority date for domestic and international students. *Application fee:* $25 Canadian dollars. *Application Contact:* Theresa Mary Vicioso, Registrar/Administrative Assistant to the Dean of Studies, 416-261-7207 Ext. 230, Fax: 416-261-2529, E-mail: t.vicioso@utoronto.ca. *Dean of Studies,* Rev. Michael Mcgourty, 416-261-7207, Fax: 416-261-2529.

SAINT BERNARD'S SCHOOL OF THEOLOGY AND MINISTRY, Rochester, NY 14618

General Information Independent-religious, coed, graduate-only institution. *Enrollment by degree level:* 18 first professional, 110 master's, 12 other advanced degrees. *Graduate faculty:* 7 full-time (4 women), 4 part-time/adjunct (0 women). *Tuition:* Full-time $7,596; part-time $1,266 per course. *Graduate housing:* On-campus housing not available. *Student services:* Writing training. *Library facilities:* Rush Rhees Library at University of Rochester. *Online resources:* library catalog, access to other libraries' catalogs. *Collection:* 64,950 titles, 315 serial subscriptions, 284 audiovisual materials. *Research affiliation:* Colgate Rochester Divinity School.

Computer facilities: 2 computers available on campus for general student use. Internet access, word processing, scanning, image editing, chat utilities are available. *Web address:* http://www.stbernards.edu/.

General Application Contact: Thomas McDade Clay, Director of Admissions and Recruitment, 585-271-3657 Ext. 289, Fax: 585-271-2045, E-mail: tmcdadeclay@stbernards.edu.

GRADUATE UNITS

Graduate and Professional Programs Students: 6 full-time (3 women), 134 part-time (70 women); includes 15 minority (5 African Americans, 1 American Indian/Alaska Native, 4 Asian Americans or Pacific Islanders, 5 Hispanic Americans). Average age 50. 28 applicants, 100% accepted, 28 enrolled. *Faculty:* 7 full-time (4 women), 4 part-time/adjunct (0 women). Expenses: Contact institution. *Financial support:* In 2006–07, 50 students received support. Career-related internships or fieldwork, scholarships/grants, and tuition waivers (partial) available. Support available to part-time students. Financial award application deadline: 4/15; financial award applicants required to submit FAFSA. In 2006, 3 M Divs, 18 master's awarded. *Degree program information:* Part-time and evening/weekend programs available. Offers pastoral studies (MA, Certificate); theological studies (MA); theology (M Div). *Application deadline:* Applications are processed on a rolling basis. *Application fee:* $50. *Application Contact:* Thomas McDade Clay, Director of Admissions and Recruitment, 585-271-3657 Ext. 289, Fax: 585-271-2045, E-mail: tmcdadeclay@stbernards.edu. *President,* Dr. Patricia Schoelles, 585-271-3657 Ext. 276, Fax: 585-271-2045, E-mail: pschoelles@stbernards.edu.

ST. BONAVENTURE UNIVERSITY, St. Bonaventure, NY 14778-2284

General Information Independent-religious, coed, comprehensive institution. CGS member. *Graduate housing:* Room and/or apartments available to single students; on-campus housing not available to married students. Housing application deadline: 3/19.

GRADUATE UNITS

School of Graduate Studies *Degree program information:* Part-time and evening/weekend programs available.

School of Arts and Sciences *Degree program information:* Part-time and evening/weekend programs available. Offers arts and sciences (MA); English (MA).

School of Business *Degree program information:* Part-time and evening/weekend programs available. Offers accounting (Adv C); accounting and finance (MBA); finance (Adv C); management (Adv C); management and marketing (MBA); marketing (Adv C); professional leadership (Adv C).

School of Education *Degree program information:* Part-time and evening/weekend programs available. Offers counseling education (Adv C); counseling education-agency (MS, MS Ed); counseling education-school (MS, MS Ed); education (MS, MS Ed, Adv C); educational leadership (MS Ed, Adv C); literacy (MS Ed).

School of Franciscan Studies *Degree program information:* Part-time programs available. Offers Franciscan studies (MA, Adv C).

ST. CHARLES BORROMEO SEMINARY, OVERBROOK, Wynnewood, PA 19096

General Information Independent-religious, Undergraduate: men only; graduate: coed, comprehensive institution. *Enrollment:* 293 graduate, professional, and undergraduate students; 63 full-time matriculated graduate/professional students, 68 part-time matriculated graduate/professional students (42 women). *Enrollment by degree level:* 50 first professional, 81 master's. *Graduate faculty:* 16 full-time (4 women), 7 part-time/adjunct (0 women). *Tuition:* Full-time $12,968; part-time $372 per credit. *Graduate housing:* Room and/or apartments guaranteed to single students; on-campus housing not available to married students. Typical cost: $7,875 (including board). Housing application deadline: 7/15. *Student services:* Campus employment opportunities, career counseling. *Library facilities:* Ryan Memorial Library. *Online resources:* web page. *Collection:* 113,761 titles, 575 serial subscriptions.

Computer facilities: 60 computers available on campus for general student use. A campuswide network can be accessed. Internet access and online class registration are available. *Web address:* http://www.scs.edu/.

General Application Contact: Msgr. Michael J. Fitzgerald, Vice Rector, 610-785-6271, Fax: 610-617-9267, E-mail: frmfitzg@adphila.org.

GRADUATE UNITS

Graduate and Professional Programs Students: 63 full-time (0 women), 68 part-time (42 women); includes 11 minority (5 African Americans, 5 Asian Americans or Pacific Islanders, 1 Hispanic American), 1 international. Average age 39. 44 applicants, 100% accepted, 41 enrolled. *Faculty:* 16 full-time (4 women), 7 part-time/adjunct (0 women). Expenses: Contact institution. *Financial support:* In 2006–07, 74 students received support. Federal Work-Study and scholarships/grants available. Financial award application deadline: 7/15; financial award applicants required to submit CSS PROFILE. In 2006, 16 M Divs, 28 master's awarded. *Degree program information:* Part-time programs available. Offers religious studies (MA); theology (M Div, MA). *Application deadline:* For fall admission, 7/15 for domestic students, 3/15 priority date for international students. Applications are processed on a rolling basis. *Application fee:* $0. *Application Contact:* Msgr. Michael J. Fitzgerald, Vice Rector, 610-785-6271, Fax: 610-617-9267, E-mail: frmfitzg@adphila.org. *Rector and President,* Msgr. Joseph G. Prior, 610-785-6200, Fax: 610-667-7635, E-mail: igprior@adphila.org.

ST. CLOUD STATE UNIVERSITY, St. Cloud, MN 56301-4498

General Information State-supported, coed, comprehensive institution. CGS member. *Enrollment:* 15,964 graduate, professional, and undergraduate students; 641 full-time matriculated graduate/professional students (375 women), 951 part-time matriculated graduate/professional students (604 women). *Enrollment by degree level:* 1,592 master's. *Graduate faculty:* 540 full-time (194 women), 34 part-time/adjunct (16 women). *Graduate housing:* Room and/or apartments available on a first-come, first-served basis to single students; on-campus housing not available to married students. Housing application deadline: 4/15. *Student services:* Campus employment opportunities, campus safety program, career counseling, child daycare facilities, disabled student services, exercise/wellness program, free psychological counseling, international student services, low-cost health insurance, multicultural affairs office, writing training. *Library facilities:* James W. Miller Learning Resources Center. *Online resources:* library catalog, web page, access to other libraries' catalogs. *Collection:* 897,973 titles, 1,737 serial subscriptions, 24,929 audiovisual materials.

Computer facilities: Computer purchase and lease plans are available. 1,335 computers available on campus for general student use. A campuswide network can be accessed from student residence rooms and from off campus. Internet access and online class registration are available. *Web address:* http://www.stcloudstate.edu/.

General Application Contact: Dr. Dennis Nunes, Dean of Graduate Studies, 320-308-2113, Fax: 320-308-5371, E-mail: dlnunes@stcloudstate.edu.

GRADUATE UNITS

School of Graduate Studies Students: 641 full-time (375 women), 951 part-time (604 women); includes 77 minority (29 African Americans, 9 American Indian/Alaska Native, 22 Asian Americans or Pacific Islanders, 17 Hispanic Americans), 225 international. 742 applicants, 84% accepted. *Faculty:* 540 full-time (194 women), 34 part-time/adjunct (16 women). Expenses: Contact institution. *Financial support:* In 2006–07, 250 research assistantships with partial tuition reimbursements (averaging $9,700 per year) were awarded; career-related internships or fieldwork, Federal Work-Study, scholarships/grants, and unspecified assistantships also available. Financial award application deadline: 3/1. In 2006, 445 degrees awarded. *Degree program information:* Part-time and evening/weekend programs available. Postbaccalaureate distance learning degree programs offered (no on-campus study). *Application deadline:* Applications are processed on a rolling basis. *Application fee:* $35. *Application Contact:* Linda Lou Krueger, Admission Specialist, 320-308-2113, Fax: 320-308-5371, E-mail: ledrueger@stcloudstate.edu. *Dean,* Dr. Dennis Nunes, 320-308-2113, Fax: 320-308-5371, E-mail: dlnunes@stcloudstate.edu.

College of Education Students: 207 full-time (145 women), 350 part-time (271 women); includes 25 minority (11 African Americans, 3 American Indian/Alaska Native, 5 Asian Americans or Pacific Islanders, 6 Hispanic Americans), 26 international. 390 applicants, 60% accepted. *Faculty:* 96 full-time (52 women), 18 part-time/adjunct (14 women). Expenses: Contact institution. *Financial support:* Career-related internships or fieldwork, Federal Work-Study, scholarships/grants, and unspecified assistantships available. Financial award application deadline: 3/1. In 2006, 186 degrees awarded. *Degree program information:* Part-time and evening/weekend programs available. Offers applied behavior analysis (MS); child and family studies (MS); college counseling and student development (MS); community counseling (MS); curriculum and instruction (MS); educable mentally handicapped (MS); education (MS, Spt); educational administration and leadership (MS); educational leadership and community psychology (Spt); emotionally disturbed (MS); exercise science (MS); gifted and talented (MS); higher education administration (MS); information media (MS); learning disabled (MS); marriage and family therapy (MS); physical education (MS); rehabilitation counseling (MS); school counseling (MS); social responsibility (MS); special education (MS); sports management (MS); trainable mentally retarded (MS). *Application deadline:* Applications are processed on a rolling basis. *Application fee:* $35. *Application Contact:* Linda Lou Krueger, School of Graduate Studies, 320-308-2113, Fax: 320-308-5371, E-mail: lekrueger@stcloudstate.edu. *Interim Dean,* Dr. Kate Steffens, 320-308-3023, Fax: 320-308-4237, E-mail: ksteffens@stcloudstate.edu.

College of Fine Arts and Humanities Students: 87 full-time (65 women), 52 part-time (36 women); includes 3 minority (1 Asian American or Pacific Islander, 2 Hispanic Americans), 19 international. 76 applicants, 80% accepted. *Faculty:* 80 full-time (38 women), 2 part-time/adjunct (1 woman). Expenses: Contact institution. *Financial support:* Federal Work-Study, scholarships/grants, and unspecified assistantships available. Financial award application deadline: 3/1. In 2006, 42 degrees awarded. Offers communication sciences and disorders (MS); conducting and literature (MM); English (MA, MS); fine arts and humanities (MA, MM, MS); mass communication (MS); music education (MM); piano pedagogy (MM); teaching English as a second language (MA). *Application fee:* $35. *Application Contact:* Linda Lou Krueger, School of Graduate Studies, 320-308-2113, Fax: 320-308-5371, E-mail: lekrueger@stcloudstate.edu. *Dean,* Dr. Roland Specht-Jarvis, 320-308-3093, Fax: 320-308-4716.

College of Science and Engineering Students: 87 full-time (25 women), 52 part-time (12 women); includes 5 minority (3 Asian Americans or Pacific Islanders, 2 Hispanic Americans), 100 international. 144 applicants, 41% accepted. *Faculty:* 85 full-time (19 women). Expenses: Contact institution. *Financial support:* Federal Work-Study and unspecified assistantships available. Financial award application deadline: 3/1. In 2006, 33 degrees awarded. Offers applied statistics (MS); biological sciences (MA, MS); computer science (MS); electrical engineering and computer engineering (MS); engineering management (MEM); environmental and technological studies (MS); mathematics (MS); mechanical engineering (MS); science and engineering (MA, MEM, MS). *Application fee:* $35. Electronic applications accepted. *Application Contact:* Linda Lou Krueger, School of Graduate Studies, 320-308-2113, Fax: 320-308-5371, E-mail: lekrueger@stcloudstate.edu. *Chairperson,* Dr. David DeGroote, 320-308-2036, Fax: 320-308-4166.

College of Social Sciences Students: 51 full-time (33 women), 34 part-time (21 women); includes 8 minority (3 African Americans, 2 American Indian/Alaska Native, 2 Asian Americans or Pacific Islanders, 1 Hispanic American), 13 international. 51 applicants, 96% accepted. *Faculty:* 81 full-time (32 women), 16 part-time/adjunct (2 women). Expenses: Contact institution. *Financial support:* Federal Work-Study and unspecified assistantships available. Financial award application deadline: 3/1. In 2006, 46 degrees awarded. *Degree program information:* Part-time programs available. Offers applied economics (MS); criminal justice administration (MS); criminal justice counseling (MS); geography (MS); gerontology (MS); history (MA, MS); industrial-organizational psychology (MS); public and nonprofit institutions (MS); public safety executive leadership (MS); social sciences (MA, MS). *Application deadline:* Applications are processed on a rolling basis. *Application fee:* $35. Electronic applications accepted. *Application Contact:* Linda Lou Krueger, School of Graduate Studies, 320-308-2113, Fax: 320-308-5371, E-mail: lekrueger@stcloudstate.edu. *Interim Dean,* Dr. Sharon Cogdill, 320-308-4790, E-mail: scogdill@stcloudstate.edu.

G.R. Herberger College of Business Students: 35 full-time (11 women), 98 part-time (39 women); includes 9 minority (5 African Americans, 1 American Indian/Alaska Native, 3 Asian Americans or Pacific Islanders), 21 international. 67 applicants, 84% accepted. *Faculty:* 62 full-time (17 women), 4 part-time/adjunct (1 woman). Expenses: Contact institution. *Financial support:* Federal Work-Study, scholarships/grants, and unspecified assistantships available. Financial award application deadline: 3/1. In 2006, 87 degrees awarded. *Degree program information:* Part-time and evening/weekend programs available. Offers management and finance (MBA); marketing and general business (MBA). *Application deadline:* For fall admission, 6/1 priority date for domestic students, 4/1 for international students; for spring admission, 10/1 priority date for domestic students, 8/1 for international students. Applications are processed on a rolling basis. *Application fee:* $35. Electronic applications accepted. *Application Contact:* Linda Lou Krueger, School of Graduate Studies, 320-308-2113, Fax: 320-308-5371, E-mail: lekrueger@stcloudstate.edu. *Graduate Director,* Dr. P.N. Subba, 320-308-3212.

ST. EDWARD'S UNIVERSITY, Austin, TX 78704

General Information Independent-religious, coed, comprehensive institution. *Enrollment:* 5,224 graduate, professional, and undergraduate students; 158 full-time matriculated graduate/professional students (115 women), 802 part-time matriculated graduate/professional students (450 women). *Enrollment by degree level:* 960 master's. *Graduate faculty:* 48 full-time (22 women), 52 part-time/adjunct (17 women). *Tuition:* Full-time $11,682; part-time $649 per credit hour. Full-time tuition and fees vary according to course load and program. *Graduate housing:* Room and/or apartments available on a first-come, first-served basis to single students; on-campus housing not available to married students. Typical cost: $6,340 per year ($9,340 including board). Room and board charges vary according to board plan and housing facility selected. *Student services:* Campus employment opportunities, campus safety program, career counseling, disabled student services, exercise/wellness program, free psychological counseling, international student services, low-cost health insurance. *Library facilities:* Scarborough-Phillips Library. *Online resources:* library catalog, web page. *Collection:* 188,256 titles, 464 serial subscriptions, 3,177 audiovisual materials. *Research affiliation:* Samaritan Center (ethics in business).

Computer facilities: 475 computers available on campus for general student use. A campuswide network can be accessed from student residence rooms and from off campus. Internet access and online class registration are available. *Web address:* http://www.stedwards.edu/.

General Application Contact: Bridget Sowinski, Director, Center for Academic Progress, 512-428-1061, Fax: 512-428-1032, E-mail: bridgets@stedwards.edu.

GRADUATE UNITS

New College Students: 89 full-time (75 women), 225 part-time (162 women); includes 71 minority (19 African Americans, 1 American Indian/Alaska Native, 5 Asian Americans or Pacific Islanders, 46 Hispanic Americans), 1 international. Average age 35. 115 applicants, 78% accepted, 74 enrolled. *Faculty:* 5 full-time (4 women), 19 part-time/adjunct (10 women). Expenses: Contact institution. *Financial support:* In 2006–07, 9 students received support. Scholarships/grants available. Financial award applicants required to submit FAFSA. In 2006, 109 degrees awarded. *Degree program information:* Part-time and evening/weekend programs available. Offers counseling (MA); liberal arts (MLA, Certificate). *Application deadline:* For fall admission, 8/1 for domestic students, 7/1 for international students; for spring admission, 12/1 for domestic students, 11/1 for international students. Applications are processed on a rolling basis. *Application fee:* $45 ($50 for international students). Electronic applications accepted. *Application Contact:* Bridget Sowinski, Director, Center for Academic Progress, 512-428-1061, Fax: 512-428-1032, E-mail: bridgets@stedwards.edu. *Dean,* Dr. H. Ramsey Fowler, 512-448-8648, Fax: 512-448-8492, E-mail: ramseyf@stedwards.edu.

School of Education Average age 35. 10 applicants, 70% accepted, 7 enrolled. Expenses: Contact institution. *Financial support:* Scholarships/grants available. *Degree program information:* Part-time and evening/weekend programs available. Offers education (MA). *Application deadline:* For fall admission, 8/1 for domestic students, 7/1 for international students; for spring admission, 12/1 for domestic students, 11/1 for international students. Applications are processed on a rolling basis. *Application fee:* $45 ($50 for international students). Electronic applications accepted. *Application Contact:* Kay L. Arnold, Graduate Admissions Coordinator, 512-233-1636, Fax: 512-428-1032, E-mail: kayla@stedwards.edu. *Dean,* Dr. Karen Jenlink, 512-448-8655, Fax: 512-428-1372, E-mail: karenj@stedwards.edu.

School of Management and Business Students: 69 full-time (40 women), 569 part-time (281 women); includes 179 minority (40 African Americans, 3 American Indian/Alaska Native, 36 Asian Americans or Pacific Islanders, 100 Hispanic Americans), 27 international. Average age 34. 254 applicants, 76% accepted, 160 enrolled. *Faculty:* 21 full-time (9 women), 33 part-time/adjunct (8 women). Expenses: Contact institution. *Financial support:* In 2006–07, 9 students received support. Scholarships/grants available. Financial award applicants required to submit FAFSA. In 2006, 218 degrees awarded. *Degree program information:* Part-time and evening/weekend programs available. Offers accounting (MBA); business management (MBA); computer information systems (MS); conflict resolution (Certificate); digital media management (MBA); entrepreneurship (MBA, Certificate); finance—general (MBA, Certificate); global business (MBA, Certificate); human resource management (MBA, Certificate); human services (MA); management and business (MA, MBA, MS, Certificate); management information systems (MBA, Certificate); marketing (MBA, Certificate); operations management (MBA, Certificate); organizational leadership and ethics (MS); personal financial planner (MBA, Certificate); project management (MS); sports management (MBA, Certificate). *Application deadline:* For fall admission, 8/1 for domestic students, 7/1 for international students; for spring admission, 12/1 for domestic students, 11/1 for international students. Applications are processed on a rolling basis. *Application fee:* $45 ($50 for international students). Electronic applications accepted. *Application Contact:* Bridget Sowinski, Director, Center for Academic Progress, 512-428-1061, Fax: 512-428-1032, E-mail: bridgets@stedwards.edu. *Dean,* Marsha Kelliher, 512-448-8588, Fax: 512-448-8492, E-mail: marshak@stedwards.edu.

SAINT FRANCIS MEDICAL CENTER COLLEGE OF NURSING, Peoria, IL 61603-3783

General Information Independent-religious, coed, primarily women, upper-level institution. *Enrollment:* 347 graduate, professional, and undergraduate students; 3 full-time matriculated graduate/professional students (all women), 74 part-time matriculated graduate/professional students (69 women). *Enrollment by degree level:* 58 master's. *Graduate faculty:* 1 (woman) full-time, 5 part-time/adjunct (all women). *Tuition:* Part-time $440 per semester hour. *Required fees:* $130. *Graduate housing:* Room and/or apartments guaranteed to single students; on-campus housing not available to married students. Typical cost: $1,000 per year. Housing application deadline: 6/1. *Student services:* Campus safety program, exercise/wellness program, free psychological counseling, low-cost health insurance. *Library facilities:* Saint Francis Medical Center College of Nursing Library. *Collection:* 6,215 titles, 125 serial subscriptions.

Computer facilities: 6 computers available on campus for general student use. Internet access is available. *Web address:* http://www.sfmccon.edu/.

General Application Contact: Dr. Janice F. Boundy, Associate Dean Graduate Program, 309-655-2230, Fax: 309-624-8973, E-mail: jan.f.boundy@osfhealthcare.org.

GRADUATE UNITS

Graduate Program Students: 3 full-time (all women), 74 part-time (69 women); includes 5 minority (1 Asian American or Pacific Islander, 4 Hispanic Americans). Average age 28. 23 applicants, 100% accepted, 19 enrolled. *Faculty:* 1 (woman) full-time, 5 part-time/adjunct (all women). Expenses: Contact institution. *Financial support:* In 2006–07, 1 student received support. Application deadline: 6/15; In 2006, 5 degrees awarded. *Degree program information:* Part-time programs available. Postbaccalaureate distance learning degree programs offered (minimal on-campus study). Offers child and family nursing (MSN); medical-surgical nursing (MSN); nurse clinician (Post-Graduate Certificate); nurse educator (Post-Graduate Certificate).

Saint Francis Medical Center College of Nursing (continued)

Application deadline: For fall admission, 6/1 priority date for domestic and international students; for spring admission, 11/15 priority date for domestic and international students. Applications are processed on a rolling basis. *Application fee:* $50. Electronic applications accepted. *Application Contact:* Dr. Janice F. Boundy, Associate Dean Graduate Program, 309-655-2230, Fax: 309-624-8973, E-mail: jan.f.boundy@osfhealthcare.org. *Dean,* Dr. Lois J. Hamilton, 309-655-2201, Fax: 309-624-8973, E-mail: lois.j.hamilton@osfhealthcare.org.

SAINT FRANCIS SEMINARY, St. Francis, WI 53235-3795

General Information Independent-religious, coed, graduate-only institution. *Graduate housing:* Room and/or apartments available to single students; on-campus housing not available to married students. Housing application deadline: 7/15.

GRADUATE UNITS

Graduate and Professional Programs *Degree program information:* Part-time programs available. Offers theology (M Div, MAPS).

SAINT FRANCIS UNIVERSITY, Loretto, PA 15940-0600

General Information Independent-religious, coed, comprehensive institution. *Enrollment:* 2,014 graduate, professional, and undergraduate students; 188 full-time matriculated graduate/professional students (133 women), 291 part-time matriculated graduate/professional students (153 women). *Graduate faculty:* 22 full-time (14 women), 52 part-time/adjunct (12 women). *Tuition:* Part-time $661 per credit. Tuition and fees vary according to program. *Graduate housing:* Rooms and/or apartments available on a first-come, first-served basis to single and married students. Typical cost: $1,920 per year ($3,820 including board) for single students. Room and board charges vary according to board plan and housing facility selected. *Student services:* Campus employment opportunities, campus safety program, career counseling, exercise/wellness program, free psychological counseling, low-cost health insurance, multicultural affairs office, writing training. *Library facilities:* Pasquerella Library. *Online resources:* library catalog, web page, access to other libraries' catalogs. *Collection:* 118,333 titles, 7,202 serial subscriptions.

Computer facilities: Computer purchase and lease plans are available. 60 computers available on campus for general student use. A campuswide network can be accessed from student residence rooms and from off campus. Internet access, billing, schedules and grades are available. *Web address:* http://www.francis.edu/.

General Application Contact: Dr. Peter Raymond Skoner, Associate Vice President for Academic Affairs, 814-472-3085, Fax: 814-472-3365, E-mail: pskoner@francis.edu.

GRADUATE UNITS

Department of Education and Educational Leadership Average age 30. 19 applicants, 100% accepted, 19 enrolled. *Faculty:* 24 part-time/adjunct (8 women). Expenses: Contact institution. *Financial support:* Research assistantships with full and partial tuition reimbursements, teaching assistantships with full and partial tuition reimbursements, career-related internships or fieldwork and unspecified assistantships available. In 2006, 35 degrees awarded. *Degree program information:* Part-time and evening/weekend programs available. Offers education (M Ed); educational leadership (MEDL); reading (M Ed). *Application deadline:* Applications are processed on a rolling basis. *Application fee:* $30. *Director, Graduate Education,* Dr. Janette D. Kelly, 814-472-3058, Fax: 814-472-3864, E-mail: jkelly@francis.edu.

Department of Occupational Therapy Students: 11 full-time (9 women). Average age 22. 11 applicants, 100% accepted, 11 enrolled. *Faculty:* 5 full-time (3 women). Expenses: Contact institution. In 2006, 19 degrees awarded. Offers occupational therapy (MOT). *Chair,* Dr. Donald Walkovich, 814-472-3899, Fax: 814-472-3950, E-mail: dwalkovich@francis.edu.

Department of Physical Therapy Students: 55 full-time (39 women); includes 3 minority (1 African American, 2 Asian Americans or Pacific Islanders). Average age 24. 30 applicants, 63% accepted, 10 enrolled. *Faculty:* 8 full-time (5 women), 1 part-time/adjunct (0 women). Expenses: Contact institution. *Financial support:* In 2006–07, 8 students received support, including 8 teaching assistantships with partial tuition reimbursements available; career-related internships or fieldwork also available. In 2006, 16 degrees awarded. Offers physical therapy (DPT). *Application deadline:* For winter admission, 1/15 for domestic and international students. *Application fee:* $30. Electronic applications accepted. *Interim Department Chair/Associate Professor,* Dr. Patricia I. Fitzgerald, 814-472-3199, Fax: 814-472-3140, E-mail: pfitzgerald@francis.edu.

Department of Physician Assistant Sciences Students: 109 full-time (78 women), 2 part-time (1 woman); includes 9 minority (3 African Americans, 6 Asian Americans or Pacific Islanders). Average age 25. 403 applicants, 16% accepted, 26 enrolled. *Faculty:* 10 full-time (8 women), 3 part-time/adjunct (0 women). Expenses: Contact institution. *Financial support:* Applicants required to submit FAFSA. In 2006, 50 degrees awarded. Offers health science (MHS); medical science (MMS); physician assistant sciences (MPAS). *Application deadline:* For fall admission, 11/1 for domestic and international students. Applications are processed on a rolling basis. *Application fee:* $160. Electronic applications accepted. *Application Contact:* Marie S. Link, Director of Research, 814-472-3138, Fax: 814-472-3137, E-mail: mslpa1@mail.francis.edu. *Chair,* Donna L. Yeisley, 814-472-3130, Fax: 814-472-3137, E-mail: dyeisley@francis.edu.

ST. FRANCIS XAVIER UNIVERSITY, Antigonish, NS B2G 2W5, Canada

General Information Independent-religious, coed, comprehensive institution. *Enrollment:* 95 full-time matriculated graduate/professional students, 138 part-time matriculated graduate/professional students. *Graduate faculty:* 32 full-time (8 women), 22 part-time/adjunct (10 women). *Graduate housing:* Room and/or apartments available on a first-come, first-served basis to single students; on-campus housing not available to married students. Housing application deadline: 7/1. *Student services:* Campus employment opportunities, campus safety program, career counseling, child daycare facilities, disabled student services, exercise/wellness program, free psychological counseling, international student services, low-cost health insurance, writing training. *Library facilities:* Angus L. MacDonald Library plus 1 other. *Online resources:* library catalog, web page, access to other libraries' catalogs. *Collection:* 632,575 titles, 3,282 serial subscriptions, 6,598 audiovisual materials.

Computer facilities: 350 computers available on campus for general student use. A campuswide network can be accessed from student residence rooms and from off campus. Internet access and online class registration are available. *Web address:* http://www.stfx.ca/.

General Application Contact: Chair, Committee on Graduate Studies, 902-867-2341, Fax: 902-867-3243.

GRADUATE UNITS

Graduate Studies Students: 95 full-time, 138 part-time. *Faculty:* 24 full-time (3 women), 18 part-time/adjunct (8 women). Expenses: Contact institution. *Financial support:* Teaching assistantships, scholarships/grants and tuition waivers (partial) available. In 2006, 122 degrees awarded. *Degree program information:* Part-time programs available. Post-baccalaureate distance learning degree programs offered (minimal on-campus study). Offers adult education (M Ad Ed); biology (M Sc); Celtic studies (MA); chemistry (M Sc); computer science (M Sc); curriculum and instruction (M Ed); earth sciences (M Sc); educational administration and leadership (M Ed); physics (M Sc). *Application deadline:* For fall admission, 7/1 priority date for domestic students. Applications are processed on a rolling basis. *Application fee:* $40. *Application Contact:* 902-867-2219, Fax: 902-867-2329, E-mail: admit@stfx.ca. *Chair, Committee on Graduate Studies,* 902-867-2341, Fax: 902-867-3243.

ST. JOHN FISHER COLLEGE, Rochester, NY 14618-3597

General Information Independent-religious, coed, comprehensive institution. *Enrollment:* 3,704 graduate, professional, and undergraduate students; 274 full-time matriculated graduate/professional students (182 women), 637 part-time matriculated graduate/professional students (468 women). *Enrollment by degree level:* 55 first professional, 829 master's, 27 doctoral. *Graduate faculty:* 60 full-time (27 women), 40 part-time/adjunct (25 women). *Tuition:* Part-time $615 per credit. Tuition and fees vary according to program. *Graduate housing:* On-campus housing not available. *Student services:* Campus employment opportunities, campus safety program, career counseling, child daycare facilities, disabled student services, free psychological counseling, international student services, low-cost health insurance, multicultural affairs office, teacher training, writing training. *Library facilities:* Charles J. Lavery Library. *Online resources:* library catalog, web page, access to other libraries' catalogs. *Collection:* 190,903 titles, 8,964 serial subscriptions.

Computer facilities: 260 computers available on campus for general student use. A campuswide network can be accessed from student residence rooms and from off campus. Internet access and online class registration are available. *Web address:* http://www.sjfc.edu/.

General Application Contact: Shannon Cleverley, Director of Graduate Admissions, 585-385-8161, Fax: 585-385-8344, E-mail: scleverley@sjfc.edu.

GRADUATE UNITS

Office of the Provost Students: 274 full-time (182 women), 637 part-time (468 women); includes 101 minority (67 African Americans, 4 American Indian/Alaska Native, 15 Asian Americans or Pacific Islanders, 15 Hispanic Americans). Average age 32. 698 applicants, 63% accepted, 258 enrolled. *Faculty:* 60 full-time (27 women), 40 part-time/adjunct (25 women). Expenses: Contact institution. *Financial support:* Federal Work-Study, scholarships/grants, and traineeships available. Financial award application deadline: 2/15; financial award applicants required to submit FAFSA. In 2006, 314 degrees awarded. *Degree program information:* Part-time and evening/weekend programs available. Offers advanced practice nursing (MS); arts and sciences (MS); clinical nurse specialist (Certificate); family nurse practitioner (Certificate); human resources development (MS); human service administration (MS); international studies (MS); mathematics/science/technology education (MS); mental health counseling (MS); nurse educator (Certificate); nursing (MS, Certificate); pharmacy (Pharm D). *Application deadline:* For fall admission, 7/1 for domestic students; for spring admission, 10/30 for domestic students. Applications are processed on a rolling basis. *Application fee:* $30. *Application Contact:* Shannon Cleverley, Director of Graduate Admissions, 585-385-8161, Fax: 585-385-8344, E-mail: scleverley@sjfc.edu. *Provost and Dean of the College,* Dr. Ronald J. Ambrosetti, 585-385-8116, Fax: 585-385-8203, E-mail: rambrosetti@sjfc.edu.

Ralph C. Wilson Jr. School of Education Students: 137 full-time (104 women), 377 part-time (289 women); includes 66 minority (46 African Americans, 3 American Indian/Alaska Native, 5 Asian Americans or Pacific Islanders, 12 Hispanic Americans). Average age 31. 319 applicants, 85% accepted, 189 enrolled. *Faculty:* 25 full-time (12 women), 30 part-time/adjunct (22 women). Expenses: Contact institution. *Financial support:* In 2006–07, 4 students received support. Federal Work-Study and scholarships/grants available. Financial award application deadline: 2/15; financial award applicants required to submit FAFSA. In 2006, 214 degrees awarded. Offers adolescence English (MS Ed); adolescence French (MS Ed); adolescence social studies (MS Ed); adolescence Spanish (MS Ed); childhood education (MS Ed); education (MS, MS Ed, Ed D, Certificate); educational leadership (MS Ed); executive leadership (Ed D); literacy birth to grade 6 (MS); literacy grades 5 to 12 (MS); special education (MS, Certificate). *Application deadline:* For spring admission, 10/30 for domestic students. Applications are processed on a rolling basis. *Application fee:* $30. *Application Contact:* Shannon Cleverley, Director of Graduate Admissions, 585-385-8161, Fax: 585-385-8344, E-mail: scleverley@sjfc.edu. *Dean,* Dr. Arthur Walton, 585-385-8387, E-mail: awalton@sjfc.edu.

Ronald L. Bittner School of Business Students: 34 full-time (21 women), 54 part-time (20 women); includes 4 African Americans, 3 Asian Americans or Pacific Islanders, 1 Hispanic American. Average age 33. 74 applicants, 61% accepted, 35 enrolled. *Faculty:* 11 full-time (2 women), 1 part-time/adjunct (0 women). Expenses: Contact institution. *Financial support:* Federal Work-Study and scholarships/grants available. Financial award application deadline: 2/15; financial award applicants required to submit FAFSA. In 2006, 41 degrees awarded. *Degree program information:* Part-time and evening/weekend programs available. Offers business (MBA); business administration and management (MBA). *Application deadline:* For fall admission, 7/1 for domestic students; for spring admission, 10/30 for domestic students. Applications are processed on a rolling basis. *Application fee:* $30. *Application Contact:* Dina Natale, MBA Admissions Coordinator, 585-385-8357, Fax: 585-385-8344, E-mail: dnatale@sjfc.edu. *Interim Dean,* Dr. Selim Ilter, 585-385-8079, Fax: 585-385-8094, E-mail: silter@sjfc.edu.

ST. JOHN'S COLLEGE, Annapolis, MD 21404

General Information Independent, coed, comprehensive institution. *Enrollment:* 600 graduate, professional, and undergraduate students; 90 matriculated graduate/professional students (34 women). *Enrollment by degree level:* 90 master's. *Graduate faculty:* 13 full-time (2 women), 5 part-time/adjunct (1 woman). *Tuition:* Full-time $12,762. *Required fees:* $582. *Graduate housing:* On-campus housing not available. *Student services:* Campus safety program, career counseling, disabled student services, exercise/wellness program, free psychological counseling, international student services, low-cost health insurance, writing training. *Library facilities:* Greenfield Library plus 1 other. *Online resources:* library catalog, web page. *Collection:* 124,500 titles, 123 serial subscriptions, 4,200 audiovisual materials.

Computer facilities: 16 computers available on campus for general student use. A campuswide network can be accessed from student residence rooms and from off campus. Internet access is available. *Web address:* http://www.stjohnscollege.edu/.

General Application Contact: Miriam L. Callahan-Hean, Graduate Admissions Administrator, 410-626-2541, Fax: 410-626-2880, E-mail: giadm@sjca.edu.

GRADUATE UNITS

Graduate Institute in Liberal Education Students: 85 full-time (34 women), 5 part-time; includes 7 minority (3 African Americans, 1 Asian American or Pacific Islander, 3 Hispanic Americans). Average age 32. 93 applicants, 65% accepted, 46 enrolled. *Faculty:* 17 full-time (1 woman), 1 (woman) part-time/adjunct. Expenses: Contact institution. *Financial support:* In 2006–07, 81 students received support. Scholarships/grants available. Financial award applicants required to submit FAFSA. In 2006, 50 degrees awarded. *Degree program information:* Evening/weekend programs available. Offers liberal arts (MA). *Application deadline:* For fall admission, 4/1 priority date for domestic and international students; for winter admission, 9/1 priority date for domestic and international students; for spring admission, 3/1 priority date for domestic and international students. Applications are processed on a rolling basis. *Application fee:* $0. Electronic applications accepted. *Application Contact:* Miriam L. Callahan-Hean, Graduate Admissions Administrator, 410-626-2541, Fax: 410-626-2880, E-mail: giadm@sjca.edu. *Director,* Dr. Joan E. Silver, 410-626-2542, Fax: 410-626-2880.

ST. JOHN'S COLLEGE, Santa Fe, NM 87505-4599

General Information Independent, coed, comprehensive institution. *Graduate housing:* Rooms and/or apartments available on a first-come, first-served basis to single and married students. Housing application deadline: 4/1.

GRADUATE UNITS

Graduate Institute in Liberal Education *Degree program information:* Evening/weekend programs available. Offers Eastern classics (MA); liberal arts (MA); liberal education (MA).

ST. JOHN'S SEMINARY, Camarillo, CA 93012-2598

General Information Independent-religious, coed, primarily men, graduate-only institution. *Enrollment by degree level:* 85 first professional, 17 master's. *Graduate faculty:* 24 full-time (5 women), 6 part-time/adjunct (0 women). *Tuition:* Full-time $11,250; part-time $375 per unit. *Graduate housing:* Room and/or apartments guaranteed to single students; on-campus housing not available to married students. Typical cost: $8,750 (including board). *Student services:* Campus employment opportunities, career counseling, free psychological counseling, international student services, low-cost health insurance, writing training. *Library facilities:* Edward Laurence Doheny Memorial Library plus 1 other. *Online resources:* library catalog, web page. *Collection:* 57,443 titles, 247 serial subscriptions, 3,162 audiovisual materials.

Computer facilities: 17 computers available on campus for general student use. A campuswide network can be accessed from student residence rooms and from off campus. Internet access is available. *Web address:* http://www.stjohnsem.edu.

General Application Contact: Dr. Mark F. Fischer, Director of Admissions, 805-482-2755 Ext. 1063, Fax: 805-482-3470, E-mail: fischer@stjohnsem.edu.

GRADUATE UNITS

Graduate and Professional Programs Students: 88 full-time (1 woman), 14 part-time (6 women); includes 54 minority (30 Asian Americans or Pacific Islanders, 24 Hispanic Americans), 15 international. Average age 34. 37 applicants, 84% accepted, 29 enrolled. *Faculty:* 24 full-time (5 women), 6 part-time/adjunct (0 women). Expenses: Contact institution. In 2006, 13 M Divs, 6 master's awarded. *Degree program information:* Part-time programs available. Offers divinity (M Div); pastoral ministry (MAPM); theology (MA). *Application deadline:* For fall admission, 7/15 priority date for domestic students. Applications are processed on a rolling basis. *Application fee:* $0. *Application Contact:* Esmé M. Takahashi, Registrar, 805-482-2755 Ext. 1014, Fax: 805-482-3470, E-mail: registrar-sjs@stjohnsem.edu. *Academic Dean,* Rev. Richard Benson, CM, 805-482-2755, Fax: 805-482-3470, E-mail: rbensoncm@sjs-sc.org.

SAINT JOHN'S SEMINARY, Brighton, MA 02135

General Information Independent-religious, coed, primarily men, graduate-only institution. *Graduate housing:* Room and/or apartments guaranteed to single students; on-campus housing not available to married students. Housing application deadline: 8/1.

GRADUATE UNITS

Graduate Programs Offers theology (M Div, MA Th, MAM).

SAINT JOHN'S UNIVERSITY, Collegeville, MN 56321

General Information Independent-religious, coed, primarily men, comprehensive institution. *Graduate housing:* Rooms and/or apartments available on a first-come, first-served basis to single and married students. *Research affiliation:* Hill Monastic Manuscript Library (monastic studies, liturgy, spirituality), Center for Ecumenical and Cultural Research, Arca Artium (visual and book arts).

GRADUATE UNITS

Saint John's School of Theology and Seminary *Degree program information:* Part-time programs available. Postbaccalaureate distance learning degree programs offered (no on-campus study). Offers divinity (M Div); liturgical music (MA); liturgical studies (MA); pastoral ministry (MA); theology (MA). Electronic applications accepted.

ST. JOHN'S UNIVERSITY, Queens, NY 11439

General Information Independent-religious, coed, university. CGS member. *Enrollment:* 20,069 graduate, professional, and undergraduate students; 1,962 full-time matriculated graduate/professional students (1,231 women), 3,124 part-time matriculated graduate/professional students (2,077 women). *Enrollment by degree level:* 1,415 first professional, 3,067 master's, 538 doctoral, 66 other advanced degrees. *Graduate faculty:* 648 full-time (250 women), 865 part-time/adjunct (346 women). *Tuition:* Full-time $18,480; part-time $770 per credit. *Required fees:* $125 per semester. Tuition and fees vary according to program. *Graduate housing:* On-campus housing not available. *Student services:* Campus employment opportunities, campus safety program, career counseling, disabled student services, exercise/wellness program, free psychological counseling, international student services, low-cost health insurance, writing training. *Library facilities:* St. John's University Library plus 1 other. *Online resources:* library catalog, web page, access to other libraries' catalogs. *Collection:* 1.2 million titles, 27,423 serial subscriptions, 20,556 audiovisual materials. *Research affiliation:* Clinical Directors' Network (social science), American Cancer Society (chemical research), Mt. Sinai School of Medicine (medical science), Brookhaven Medical Center (medical services), Institute for Fraud Protection (fraud prevention research).

Computer facilities: Computer purchase and lease plans are available. 1,025 computers available on campus for general student use. A campuswide network can be accessed from student residence rooms and from off campus. Internet access and online class registration, various software packages are available. *Web address:* http://www.stjohns.edu/.

General Application Contact: Br. Shamus McGrenra, Senior Associate Director, Office of Admission, 718-990-1601, Fax: 718-990-2346, E-mail: gradhelp@stjohns.edu.

GRADUATE UNITS

College of Pharmacy and Allied Health Professions Students: 476 full-time (350 women), 219 part-time (121 women); includes 320 minority (29 African Americans, 270 Asian Americans or Pacific Islanders, 21 Hispanic Americans), 156 international. Average age 25. 418 applicants, 39% accepted, 63 enrolled. *Faculty:* 65 full-time (27 women), 18 part-time/adjunct (6 women). Expenses: Contact institution. *Financial support:* In 2006–07, 133 students received support, including 24 fellowships with full and partial tuition reimbursements available (averaging $8,769 per year), 1 research assistantship with full and partial tuition reimbursement available (averaging $10,920 per year), 59 teaching assistantships with full and partial tuition reimbursements available (averaging $12,052 per year); career-related internships or fieldwork, scholarships/grants, and unspecified assistantships also available. Support available to part-time students. Financial award application deadline: 3/1; financial award applicants required to submit FAFSA. In 2006, 191 Pharm Ds, 33 master's, 3 doctorates awarded. *Degree program information:* Part-time and evening/weekend programs available. Offers pharmaceutical sciences (MS, PhD); pharmacy (Pharm D, MS, PhD); pharmacy administration (MS); pharmacy and allied health professions (Pharm D, MS, PhD); toxicology (MS). *Application deadline:* For fall admission, 4/1 for domestic students, 5/1 priority date for international students; for spring admission, 12/1 for domestic students, 11/1 priority date for international students. Applications are processed on a rolling basis. *Application fee:* $40. Electronic applications accepted. *Application Contact:* Br. Shamus McGrenra, Senior Associate Director, Office of Admission, 718-990-1601, Fax: 718-990-2346, E-mail: gradhelp@stjohns.edu. *Dean,* Dr. Robert Mangione, 718-990-6411, Fax: 718-990-1871, E-mail: mangionr@stjohns.edu.

College of Professional Studies Students: 10 full-time (7 women), 64 part-time (34 women); includes 25 minority (11 African Americans, 1 American Indian/Alaska Native, 3 Asian Americans or Pacific Islanders, 10 Hispanic Americans), 1 international. Average age 29. 39 applicants, 69% accepted, 15 enrolled. *Faculty:* 15 full-time (5 women), 44 part-time/adjunct (10 women). Expenses: Contact institution. *Financial support:* In 2006–07, 73 students received support; research assistantships available. Financial award application deadline: 3/1. In 2006, 50 degrees awarded. Offers criminal justice and legal studies (MPS). *Application deadline:* For fall admission, 5/1 priority date for domestic and international students; for spring admission, 11/1 priority date for domestic and international students. Applications are processed on a rolling basis. *Application fee:* $40. Electronic applications accepted. *Application Contact:* Br. Shamus McGrenra, Senior Associate Director, Office of Admission, 718-990-1601, Fax: 718-990-2346, E-mail: gradhelp@stjohns.edu. *Dean,* Dr. Kathleen Voute MacDonald, 718-990-6435, Fax: 718-990-1882, E-mail: macdonk@stjohns.edu.

The Peter J. Tobin College of Business Students: 239 full-time (125 women), 434 part-time (192 women); includes 162 minority (52 African Americans, 66 Asian Americans or Pacific Islanders, 44 Hispanic Americans), 202 international. Average age 27. 716 applicants, 66% accepted, 225 enrolled. *Faculty:* 98 full-time (20 women), 65 part-time/adjunct (13 women). Expenses: Contact institution. *Financial support:* In 2006–07, 364 students received support, including 47 research assistantships with full and partial tuition reimbursements available (averaging $15,894 per year); scholarships/grants also available. Support available to part-time students. Financial award application deadline: 3/1; financial award applicants required to submit FAFSA. In 2006, 300 degrees awarded. *Degree program information:* Part-time and evening/weekend programs available. Offers accounting (MBA, MS, Adv C); business (MBA, MS, Adv C); computer information systems and decision sciences (MBA, Adv C); finance (MBA, Adv C); international business (MBA, Adv C); management (MBA, Adv C); marketing (MBA, Adv C); taxation (MBA, MS, Adv C). *Application deadline:* For fall admission, 5/1 priority date for domestic and international students; for spring admission, 11/1 priority date for domestic and international students. Applications are processed on a rolling basis. *Application fee:* $40. Electronic applications accepted. *Application Contact:* Nicole T. Bryan, Assistant Dean, 718-990-2599, Fax: 718-990-5242, E-mail: mbaadmissions@stjohns.edu. *Dean,* Dr. Steven Papamarcos, 718-990-6477, Fax: 718-990-5966, E-mail: papamars@stjohns.edu.

School of Risk Management and Actuarial Science Students: 16 full-time (9 women), 33 part-time (18 women); includes 7 minority (2 African Americans, 2 Asian Americans or Pacific Islanders, 3 Hispanic Americans), 32 international. Average age 27. 68 applicants, 71% accepted, 24 enrolled. *Faculty:* 7 full-time (0 women), 5 part-time/adjunct (2 women). Expenses: Contact institution. *Financial support:* Research assistantships available. In 2006, 9 degrees awarded. Offers risk management and actuarial science (MBA, MS). *Application deadline:* For fall admission, 5/1 priority date for domestic and international students; for spring admission, 11/1 priority date for domestic and international students. Applications are processed on a rolling basis. *Application fee:* $40. Electronic applications accepted. *Application Contact:* Nicole T. Bryan, Assistant Dean, 718-990-2599, Fax: 718-990-5242, E-mail: mbaadmissions@stjohns.edu. *Chair,* Dr. Nicos Scordis, 212-277-5193, E-mail: scordisn@stjohns.edu.

St. John's College of Liberal Arts and Sciences Students: 367 full-time (289 women), 693 part-time (471 women); includes 262 minority (90 African Americans, 3 American Indian/Alaska Native, 57 Asian Americans or Pacific Islanders, 112 Hispanic Americans), 94 international. Average age 30. 1,293 applicants, 44% accepted, 290 enrolled. *Faculty:* 254 full-time (97 women), 354 part-time/adjunct (161 women). Expenses: Contact institution. *Financial support:* In 2006–07, 796 students received support, including 123 fellowships with full and partial tuition reimbursements available (averaging $15,266 per year), 76 research assistantships with full and partial tuition reimbursements available (averaging $12,690 per year), 21 teaching assistantships with full and partial tuition reimbursements available (averaging $10,751 per year); career-related internships or fieldwork, scholarships/grants, and unspecified assistantships also available. Support available to part-time students. Financial award application deadline: 3/1; financial award applicants required to submit FAFSA. In 2006, 258 master's, 48 doctorates awarded. *Degree program information:* Part-time and evening/weekend programs available. Offers algebra (MA); analysis (MA); applied mathematics (MA); biological sciences (MS, PhD); chemistry (MS); clinical psychology (PhD); clinical psychology-child (PhD); clinical psychology-general (PhD); computer science (MA); criminology and justice (MA); English (MA, DA); general experimental psychology (MA); geometry-topology (MA); government and politics (MA, Adv C); history (MA); international law and diplomacy (Adv C); languages and literatures (Adv C); liberal arts and sciences (M Div, MA, MLS, MS, Au D, DA, PhD, Psy D, Adv C, Advanced Diploma, Certificate); liberal studies (MA); library and information science (MLS, Adv C); logic and foundations (MA); modern world history (DA); pastoral ministry (Certificate); philosophy (MA); priestly studies (M Div); probability and statistics (MA); school psychology (MS, Psy D); sociology (MA); Spanish (MA); speech, communication sciences and theatre (MA, Advanced Diploma); theology (MA, Certificate). *Application deadline:* For fall admission, 5/1 priority date for domestic and international students; for spring admission, 11/1 priority date for domestic and international students. Applications are processed on a rolling basis. *Application fee:* $40. Electronic applications accepted. *Application Contact:* Br. Shamus McGrenra, Senior Associate Director, Office of Admission, 718-990-1601, Fax: 718-990-2346, E-mail: gradhelp@stjohns.edu. *Dean,* Dr. Jeffrey Fagen, 718-990-6068, Fax: 718-990-6593, E-mail: fagenj@stjohns.edu.

Institute of Asian Studies Students: 4 full-time (3 women), 9 part-time (5 women); includes 2 minority (1 Asian American or Pacific Islander, 1 Hispanic American), 8 international. Average age 34. 17 applicants, 82% accepted, 1 enrolled. *Faculty:* 1 (woman) full-time, 9 part-time/adjunct (7 women). Expenses: Contact institution. *Financial support:* Research assistantships, scholarships/grants available. Support available to part-time students. Financial award application deadline: 3/1; financial award applicants required to submit FAFSA. In 2006, 4 degrees awarded. *Degree program information:* Part-time and evening/weekend programs available. Offers Asian and African cultural studies (Adv C); Asian studies (Adv C); Chinese studies (MA, Adv C); East Asian culture studies (Adv C); East Asian studies (MA). *Application deadline:* For fall admission, 5/1 priority date for domestic and international students; for spring admission, 11/1 priority date for domestic and international students. Applications are processed on a rolling basis. *Application fee:* $40. Electronic applications accepted. *Application Contact:* Br. Shamus McGrenra, Senior Associate Director, Office of Admission, 718-990-1601, Fax: 718-990-2346, E-mail: gradhelp@stjohns.edu. *Chair,* Dr. Bernadette Li, 718-990-1657, E-mail: lib@stjohns.edu.

The School of Education Students: 138 full-time (109 women), 1,512 part-time (1,160 women); includes 396 minority (179 African Americans, 4 American Indian/Alaska Native, 69 Asian Americans or Pacific Islanders, 144 Hispanic Americans), 43 international. Average age 33. 889 applicants, 74% accepted, 410 enrolled. *Faculty:* 42 full-time (24 women), 111 part-time/adjunct (63 women). Expenses: Contact institution. *Financial support:* In 2006–07, 1,576 students received support, including 156 fellowships with full and partial tuition reimbursements available (averaging $12,986 per year), 8 research assistantships with full and partial tuition reimbursements available (averaging $10,049 per year); teaching assistantships with full and partial tuition reimbursements available, career-related internships or fieldwork and scholarships/grants also available. Support available to part-time students. Financial award application deadline: 3/1; financial award applicants required to submit FAFSA. In 2006, 403 master's, 21 doctorates, 37 other advanced degrees awarded. *Degree program information:* Part-time and evening/weekend programs available. Offers bilingual school counseling (MS Ed); bilingual/multicultural education/teaching English to speakers of other languages (MS Ed); education (MS Ed, Ed D, PD); instructional leadership (Ed D, PD); literacy (MS Ed, PD); rehabilitation counseling (MS Ed, PD); school building leadership (MS Ed, PD); school counseling (MS Ed, PD); school district leader (PD); student development practice in higher education (PD); teaching children with disabilities (MS Ed). *Application deadline:* For fall admission, 4/15 for domestic students, 5/1 priority date for international students; for spring admission, 11/1 priority date for international students. Applications are processed on a rolling basis. *Application fee:* $40. Electronic applications accepted. *Application Contact:* Kelly Ronayne, Assistant Dean, 718-990-2303, Fax: 718-990-6069, E-mail: graded@stjohns.edu. *Dean,* Dr. Jerrold Ross, 718-990-1305, Fax: 718-990-6096, E-mail: rossj@stjohns.edu.

Division of Early Childhood, Childhood and Adolescent Education Students: 63 full-time (51 women), 690 part-time (543 women); includes 185 minority (74 African Americans, 1 American Indian/Alaska Native, 51 Asian Americans or Pacific Islanders, 59 Hispanic Americans), 12 international. Average age 29. 466 applicants, 83% accepted, 230 enrolled. *Faculty:* 15 full-time (13 women), 65 part-time/adjunct (35 women). Expenses: Contact institution. *Financial support:* Research assistantships available. In 2006, 232 degrees awarded. Offers adolescent education (MS Ed); childhood education (MS Ed); early childhood education (MS Ed). *Application deadline:* For fall admission, 4/15 for domestic students, 5/1 priority date for international students; for spring admission, 11/1 priority date for international students. Applications are processed on a rolling basis. *Application fee:* $40. Electronic applications accepted. *Application Contact:* Kelly Ronayne, Assistant Dean, 718-990-2303, Fax: 718-990-6069, E-mail: graded@stjohns.edu. *Chair,* Dr. Peter Quinn, 718-990-6775, Fax: 718-990-3803, E-mail: quinnp@stjohns.edu.

School of Law Students: 732 full-time (351 women), 201 part-time (98 women); includes 223 minority (55 African Americans, 2 American Indian/Alaska Native, 94 Asian Americans or Pacific Islanders, 72 Hispanic Americans), 10 international. Average age 27. 3,658 applicants, 35% accepted, 310 enrolled. *Faculty:* 55 full-time (23 women), 43 part-time/adjunct (11 women). Expenses: Contact institution. *Financial support:* In 2006–07, 827 students received support; research assistantships, career-related internships or fieldwork and scholarships/grants available. Support available to part-time students. Financial award application deadline: 3/1; financial award applicants required to submit FAFSA. In 2006, 328 degrees awarded. *Degree program information:* Part-time and evening/weekend programs available. Offers bankruptcy (LL M); law (JD, LL M). *Application deadline:* For fall admission, 4/1 priority date for domestic students, 5/1 priority date for international students; for spring admission, 11/1 priority date for domestic and international students. Applications are processed on a rolling basis. *Application fee:* $50. Electronic applications accepted. *Application Contact:* Robert Harrison, Assistant Dean and Director of Admissions, 718-990-2310, Fax: 718-990-6699, E-mail: lawinfo@stjohns.edu. *Dean,* Mary C. Daly, 718-990-6601, Fax: 718-990-6694, E-mail: dalym@stjohns.edu.

SAINT JOSEPH COLLEGE, West Hartford, CT 06117-2700

General Information Independent-religious, Undergraduate: women only; graduate: coed, comprehensive institution. *Graduate housing:* On-campus housing not available.

GRADUATE UNITS

Graduate Division *Degree program information:* Part-time and evening/weekend programs available. Postbaccalaureate distance learning degree programs offered. Offers biology (MS); biology/chemistry (MS); chemistry (MS); community counseling (MA); early childhood education (MA); education (MA); family health nurse practitioner (MS); family health nursing (MS); management science (MS); marriage and family therapy (MA, Certificate); nursing (Post Master's Certificate); psychiatric/mental health nursing (MS); special education (MA); spirituality (Certificate). Electronic applications accepted.

Institute in Gerontology *Degree program information:* Part-time and evening/weekend programs available. Offers human development/gerontology (Certificate). Electronic applications accepted.

SAINT JOSEPH'S COLLEGE, Rensselaer, IN 47978

General Information Independent-religious, coed, comprehensive institution. *Graduate housing:* Rooms and/or apartments available on a first-come, first-served basis to single students and available to married students. Housing application deadline: 6/20.

GRADUATE UNITS

Rensselaer Program of Church Music and Liturgy *Degree program information:* Part-time programs available. Offers music (MA); pastoral liturgy (Diploma). Offered during summer only.

ST. JOSEPH'S COLLEGE, NEW YORK, Brooklyn, NY 11205-3688

General Information Independent, coed, comprehensive institution.

GRADUATE UNITS

Graduate Programs Offers accounting (MBA); executive business administration (EMBA); infant/toddler early childhood special education (MA); literacy and cognition (MA); management (MS); nursing (MS); severe and multiple disabilities (MA); special education (MA).

SAINT JOSEPH'S COLLEGE OF MAINE, Standish, ME 04084-5263

General Information Independent-religious, coed, comprehensive institution. *Enrollment:* 1,050 graduate, professional, and undergraduate students; 884 matriculated graduate/professional students (678 women). *Enrollment by degree level:* 884 master's. *Graduate faculty:* 5 full-time (4 women), 67 part-time/adjunct (46 women). *Tuition:* Part-time $350 per credit. *Graduate housing:* On-campus housing not available. *Student services:* Campus safety program, career counseling, free psychological counseling, international student services, teacher training. *Library facilities:* Wellehan Library. *Online resources:* library catalog, web page, access to other libraries' catalogs. *Collection:* 113,453 titles, 15,646 serial subscriptions, 1,043 audiovisual materials.

Computer facilities: Computer purchase and lease plans are available. 102 computers available on campus for general student use. A campuswide network can be accessed from student residence rooms. Internet access is available. *Web address:* http://www.sjcme.edu/.

General Application Contact: Admissions Department/Graduate and Professional Studies, 800-752-4723, Fax: 207-892-7480, E-mail: info@sjcme.edu.

GRADUATE UNITS

Department of Nursing Average age 43. 65 applicants, 91% accepted, 54 enrolled. *Faculty:* 2 full-time (both women), 8 part-time/adjunct (all women). Expenses: Contact institution. *Financial support:* Institutionally sponsored loans available. Support available to part-time students. In 2006, 26 degrees awarded. *Degree program information:* Part-time programs available. Postbaccalaureate distance learning degree programs offered (minimal on-campus study). Offers nursing (MS); nursing administration and leadership (Certificate); nursing and health care education (Certificate). MS degree offered only through faculty-directed independent study. *Application deadline:* Applications are processed on a rolling basis. *Application fee:* $50. Electronic applications accepted. *Application Contact:* 800-752-4723, Fax: 207-892-7480, E-mail: info@sjcme.edu. *Chair,* Dr. Margaret Hourigan, 207-893-7970, Fax: 207-892-7423, E-mail: mhourigan@sjcme.edu.

Program in Business Administration Average age 40. 71 applicants, 93% accepted, 61 enrolled. *Faculty:* 15 part-time/adjunct (5 women). Expenses: Contact institution. *Degree program information:* Part-time programs available. Offers quality leadership (MBA). *Application Contact:* 800-752-4723, Fax: 207-892-7480, E-mail: info@sjcme.edu. *Director,* Dr. Gregory Gull, 207-893-7988, Fax: 207-892-7423, E-mail: ggull@sjcme.edu.

Program in Health Services Administration Average age 43. 93 applicants, 94% accepted, 82 enrolled. *Faculty:* 3 full-time (2 women), 15 part-time/adjunct (8 women). Expenses: Contact institution. *Financial support:* Institutionally sponsored loans available. Support available to part-time students. In 2006, 35 degrees awarded. *Degree program information:* Part-time programs available. Postbaccalaureate distance learning degree programs offered (minimal on-campus study). Offers health services administration (MHSA). Degree program is external; available only by correspondence and online. *Application deadline:* Applications are processed on a rolling basis. *Application fee:* $50. Electronic applications accepted. *Application Contact:* 800-752-4723, Fax: 207-892-7480, E-mail: info@sjcme.edu. *Interim Director,* John Pratt, 207-893-7981, Fax: 207-893-7987.

Program in Teacher Education Students: 266 (195 women); includes 13 minority (3 African Americans, 1 American Indian/Alaska Native, 2 Asian Americans or Pacific Islanders, 7 Hispanic Americans). Average age 43. 164 applicants, 97% accepted, 154 enrolled. *Faculty:* 19 part-time/adjunct (15 women). Expenses: Contact institution. *Financial support:* Institutionally sponsored loans available. Support available to part-time students. In 2006, 25 degrees awarded. *Degree program information:* Part-time programs available. Postbaccalaureate distance learning degree programs offered (minimal on-campus study). Offers teacher education (MS). Program available by correspondence. *Application deadline:* Applications are processed on a rolling basis. *Application fee:* $50. Electronic applications accepted. *Application Contact:* 800-752-4723, Fax: 207-892-7480, E-mail: info@sjcme.edu. *Director,* Dr. Richard Willis, 207-893-7992, Fax: 207-892-7987, E-mail: rwillis@sjcme.edu.

ST. JOSEPH'S COLLEGE, SUFFOLK CAMPUS, Patchogue, NY 11772-2399

General Information Independent, coed, comprehensive institution. *Graduate housing:* On-campus housing not available.

GRADUATE UNITS

Executive MBA Program Offers business administration (EMBA).

Program in Accounting Offers accounting (MBA).

Program in Infant/Toddler Early Childhood Special Education *Degree program information:* Part-time and evening/weekend programs available. Offers infant/toddler early childhood special education (MA).

Program in Literacy and Cognition Offers literacy and cognition (MA).

Program in Management Offers health care (AC); health care management (MS); human resource management (AC); human resources management (MS); organizational management (MS).

Program in Nursing Offers nursing (MS).

ST. JOSEPH'S SEMINARY, Yonkers, NY 10704

General Information Independent-religious, coed, graduate-only institution. *Graduate housing:* Room and/or apartments guaranteed to single students; on-campus housing not available to married students.

GRADUATE UNITS

Institute of Religious Studies *Degree program information:* Part-time and evening/weekend programs available. Offers religious studies (MA). Electronic applications accepted.

Professional Program Offers divinity (M Div); theology (MA).

SAINT JOSEPH'S UNIVERSITY, Philadelphia, PA 19131-1395

General Information Independent-religious, coed, comprehensive institution. *Enrollment:* 7,535 graduate, professional, and undergraduate students; 440 full-time matriculated graduate/professional students (223 women), 1,653 part-time matriculated graduate/professional students (982 women). *Graduate faculty:* 95 full-time (40 women), 139 part-time/adjunct (53 women). *Graduate housing:* On-campus housing not available. *Student services:* Campus employment opportunities, campus safety program, career counseling, disabled student services, free psychological counseling, international student services, low-cost health insurance, multicultural affairs office, teacher training, writing training. *Library facilities:* Francis A. Drexel Library plus 1 other. *Online resources:* library catalog, web page, access to other libraries' catalogs. *Collection:* 366,300 titles, 11,700 serial subscriptions, 5,200 audiovisual materials. *Research affiliation:* Sepracor, Inc. (psychology).

Computer facilities: Computer purchase and lease plans are available. 400 computers available on campus for general student use. A campuswide network can be accessed from student residence rooms and from off campus. Internet access and online class registration are available. *Web address:* http://www.sju.edu/.

General Application Contact: Susan P. Kassab, Director of Admissions, 610-660-1306, Fax: 610-660-1314, E-mail: skassab@sju.edu.

GRADUATE UNITS

College of Arts and Sciences Students: 254 full-time (157 women), 979 part-time (667 women); includes 268 minority (225 African Americans, 2 American Indian/Alaska Native, 14 Asian Americans or Pacific Islanders, 27 Hispanic Americans), 72 international. Average age 32. *Faculty:* 56 full-time (31 women), 112 part-time/adjunct (48 women). Expenses: Contact institution. *Financial support:* In 2006–07, 45 students received support, including research assistantships with full and partial tuition reimbursements available (averaging $4,000 per year), teaching assistantships with full and partial tuition reimbursements available (averaging $4,000 per year); scholarships/grants and unspecified assistantships also available. Financial award applicants required to submit FAFSA. In 2006, 517 master's, 5 doctorates awarded. *Degree program information:* Part-time and evening/weekend programs available. Postbaccalaureate distance learning degree programs offered. Offers administration/police executive (MS); arts and sciences (MA, MS, Ed D, Certificate, Post-Master's Certificate); behavior analysis (MS); behavior management and justice (MS); biology (MA, MS); computer science (MS); criminal justice (MS, Post-Master's Certificate); criminology (MS); educational leadership (Ed D); elementary education (MS); federal law (MS); gerontological counseling (MS); gerontological services (Post-Master's Certificate); health administration (MS); health education (MS); human services administration (MS); instructional technology (MS); intelligence and crime (MS); mathematics and computer science (Post-Master's Certificate); nurse anesthesia (MS); probation, parole, and corrections (MS); professional education (MS); psychology (MS); reading (MS); secondary education (MS); special education (MS); training and organizational development (MS, Certificate); writing studies (MA). *Application deadline:* For fall admission, 7/15 priority date for domestic students, 4/15 for international students; for winter admission, 1/15 for international students; for spring admission, 11/15 priority date for domestic students, 10/15 for international students. Applications are processed on a rolling basis. *Application fee:* $35. Electronic applications accepted. *Application Contact:* Sena Owereko-Andah, Assistant Director of Graduate Admissions, 610-660-1108, Fax: 610-660-1224, E-mail: sowereko@sju.edu. *Dean of Graduate and Continuing Studies,* Dr. Robert H. Palestini, 610-660-1289, Fax: 610-660-3230, E-mail: rpalesti@sju.edu.

Public Safety and Environmental Protection Institute Students: 10 full-time (4 women), 72 part-time (13 women); includes 10 minority (all African Americans) Average age 36. Expenses: Contact institution. In 2006, 28 degrees awarded. Offers environmental protection and safety management (MS, Post-Master's Certificate); public safety (MS, Post-Master's Certificate). *Application deadline:* For fall admission, 7/15 for domestic students. *Application fee:* $35. *Director,* Dr. Vincent P. McNally, 610-660-1641, Fax: 610-660-2903, E-mail: vmcnally@sju.edu.

Erivan K. Haub School of Business Students: 186 full-time (66 women), 674 part-time (315 women); includes 117 minority (60 African Americans, 1 American Indian/Alaska Native, 35 Asian Americans or Pacific Islanders, 21 Hispanic Americans), 61 international. Average age 32. *Faculty:* 39 full-time (9 women), 27 part-time/adjunct (5 women). Expenses: Contact institution. *Financial support:* In 2006–07, 29 students received support, including research assistantships with full and partial tuition reimbursements available (averaging $4,000 per year), teaching assistantships with full and partial tuition reimbursements available (averaging $4,000 per year); scholarships/grants and unspecified assistantships also available. Financial award application deadline: 2/1; financial award applicants required to submit FAFSA. In 2006, 326 degrees awarded. *Degree program information:* Part-time and evening/weekend programs available. Postbaccalaureate distance learning degree programs offered (minimal on-campus study). Offers accounting (MBA); business (MBA, MS, Certificate, Post Master's Certificate); certified financial planner (Certificate); decision and system sciences (MBA); e-business (MBA); executive business administration (MBA); executive pharmaceutical marketing (MBA, Post Master's Certificate); finance (MBA, Certificate); financial services (MS); food marketing (MBA, MS); general business (MBA); health and medical services administration (MBA); human resource management (MBA); information systems (MBA); international business (MBA); international marketing (MBA); management (MBA); marketing (MBA). *Application deadline:* For fall admission, 7/15 priority date for domestic students, 4/15 for international students; for winter admission, 1/15 for international students; for spring admission, 11/15 priority date for domestic students, 10/15 for international students. Applications are processed on a rolling basis. *Application fee:* $35. Electronic applications accepted. *Application Contact:* Sena Owereko-Andah, Assistant Director of Graduate Admissions, 610-660-1108, Fax: 610-660-1224, E-mail: sowereko@sju.edu. *Dean,* Dr. Joseph A. DiAngelo, 610-660-1645, Fax: 610-660-1649, E-mail: jodiange@sju.edu.

ST. LAWRENCE UNIVERSITY, Canton, NY 13617-1455

General Information Independent, coed, comprehensive institution. *Graduate housing:* Room and/or apartments available on a first-come, first-served basis to single students; on-campus housing not available to married students. Housing application deadline: 4/1.

GRADUATE UNITS

Department of Education *Degree program information:* Part-time and evening/weekend programs available. Offers counseling and human development (M Ed, CAS); education (Certificate); educational administration (M Ed, CAS); general studies (M Ed).

SAINT LEO UNIVERSITY, Saint Leo, FL 33574-6665

General Information Independent-religious, coed, comprehensive institution. *Enrollment:* 2,774 graduate, professional, and undergraduate students; 483 full-time matriculated graduate/professional students (317 women), 724 part-time matriculated graduate/professional students (453 women). *Enrollment by degree level:* 1,207 master's. *Graduate faculty:* 37 full-time (11 women), 44 part-time/adjunct (18 women). *Graduate housing:* Room and/or apartments available on a first-come, first-served basis to single students; on-campus housing not available to married students. Typical cost: $5,030 per year ($8,686 including board). Room and board charges vary according to board plan and housing facility selected. *Student services:* Campus employment opportunities, career counseling, disabled student services, exercise/wellness program, free psychological counseling, international student services, low-cost health insurance, multicultural affairs office, teacher training, writing training. *Library facilities:* Cannon Memorial Library. *Online resources:* library catalog, web page, access to other libraries' catalogs. *Collection:* 208,110 titles, 890 serial subscriptions, 6,542 audiovisual materials. *Research affiliation:* American Jewish Committee (religion).

Computer facilities: 750 computers available on campus for general student use. A campuswide network can be accessed from student residence rooms and from off campus. Internet access and online class registration are available. *Web address:* http://www.saintleo.edu/.

General Application Contact: Scott Cathcart, Vice President of Enrollment, 800-707-8846, Fax: 352-588-7873, E-mail: grad.admission@saintleo.edu.

GRADUATE UNITS

Graduate Business Studies Students: 298 full-time (187 women), 368 part-time (215 women); includes 195 minority (132 African Americans, 3 American Indian/Alaska Native, 23 Asian Americans or Pacific Islanders, 37 Hispanic Americans), 6 international. Average age 36. 863 applicants, 59% accepted, 282 enrolled. *Faculty:* 17 full-time (5 women), 24 part-time/adjunct (6 women). Expenses: Contact institution. *Financial support:* In 2006–07, 39 students received support. Career-related internships or fieldwork, Federal Work-Study, and scholarships/grants available. Support available to part-time students. Financial award application deadline: 3/1; financial award applicants required to submit FAFSA. In 2006, 156 degrees awarded. *Degree program information:* Part-time and evening/weekend programs available. Postbaccalaureate distance learning degree programs offered (no on-campus study). Offers accounting (MBA); business (MBA); criminal justice (MBA); human resource administration (MBA); information security management (MBA); sport business (MBA). *Application deadline:* For fall admission, 7/1 priority date for domestic students; for spring admission, 11/12 priority date for domestic students. Applications are processed on a rolling basis. *Application fee:* $45. Electronic applications accepted. *Application Contact:* Scott Cathcart, Vice President of Enrollment, 800-707-8846, Fax: 352-588-7873, E-mail: grad.admission@saintleo.edu. *Director*, Dr. Robert Robertson, 352-588-8758, Fax: 352-588-8912, E-mail: mba@saintleo.edu.

Graduate Pastoral Studies Students: 23 full-time (13 women), 43 part-time (16 women); includes 2 minority (1 African American, 1 Hispanic American), 1 international. Average age 51. 69 applicants, 71% accepted, 27 enrolled. *Faculty:* 3 full-time (0 women), 1 (woman) part-time/adjunct. Expenses: Contact institution. *Financial support:* In 2006–07, 66 students received support. Federal Work-Study and scholarships/grants available. Support available to part-time students. *Degree program information:* Part-time and evening/weekend programs available. Offers pastoral studies (MA). *Application deadline:* For fall admission, 7/1 priority date for domestic and international students; for spring admission, 11/1 priority date for domestic and international students. Applications are processed on a rolling basis. *Application fee:* $45. Electronic applications accepted. *Application Contact:* Scott Cathcart, Vice President of Enrollment, 800-707-8846, Fax: 352-588-7873, E-mail: grad.admission@saintleo.edu. *Director*, Dr. Michael Tkacik, 352-588-7297, E-mail: michael.tkacik@saintleo.edu.

Graduate Studies in Criminal Justice Students: 45 full-time (23 women), 124 part-time (62 women); includes 57 minority (44 African Americans, 1 American Indian/Alaska Native, 12 Hispanic Americans), 1 international. Average age 36. 262 applicants, 77% accepted, 96 enrolled. *Faculty:* 6 full-time (1 woman), 8 part-time/adjunct (0 women). Expenses: Contact institution. *Financial support:* In 2006–07, 11 students received support. Federal Work-Study and scholarships/grants available. Support available to part-time students. In 2006, 22 degrees awarded. *Degree program information:* Part-time and evening/weekend programs available. Postbaccalaureate distance learning degree programs offered (no on-campus study). Offers criminal justice (MS); critical incident management (MS). *Application deadline:* For fall admission, 7/1 priority date for domestic and international students; for spring admission, 11/1 priority date for domestic and international students. Applications are processed on a rolling basis. *Application fee:* $45. Electronic applications accepted. *Application Contact:* Scott Cathcart, Vice President of Enrollment, 800-707-8846, Fax: 352-588-7873, E-mail: grad.admission@saintleo.edu. *Director*, Dr. Robert Diemer, 352-588-8974, E-mail: robert.diemer@saintleo.edu.

Graduate Studies in Education Students: 96 full-time (77 women), 169 part-time (143 women); includes 22 minority (16 African Americans, 6 Hispanic Americans), 2 international. Average age 35. 365 applicants, 54% accepted, 116 enrolled. *Faculty:* 8 full-time (5 women), 10 part-time/adjunct (all women). Expenses: Contact institution. *Financial support:* In 2006–07, 242 students received support. Career-related internships or fieldwork, Federal Work-Study, and scholarships/grants available. Support available to part-time students. Financial award application deadline: 3/1; financial award applicants required to submit FAFSA. In 2006, 39 degrees awarded. *Degree program information:* Part-time and evening/weekend programs available. Postbaccalaureate distance learning degree programs offered (minimal on-campus study). Offers education (MAT); educational leadership (M Ed); exceptional student education (M Ed); instructional leadership (M Ed); reading (M Ed). *Application deadline:* For fall admission, 7/1 priority date for domestic students; for spring admission, 11/12 priority date for domestic students. Applications are processed on a rolling basis. *Application fee:* $45. Electronic applications accepted. *Application Contact:* Scott Cathcart, Vice President of Enrollment, 800-707-8846, Fax: 352-588-7873, E-mail: grad.admission@saintleo.edu. *Director*, Dr. John Smith, 352-588-8309, Fax: 352-588-8861, E-mail: med@saintleo.edu.

ST. LOUIS COLLEGE OF PHARMACY, St. Louis, MO 63110-1088

General Information Independent, coed, comprehensive institution. *Enrollment:* 1,126 graduate, professional, and undergraduate students; 1,124 full-time matriculated graduate/professional students (668 women), 2 part-time matriculated graduate/professional students (1 woman). *Enrollment by degree level:* 1,124 first professional. *Graduate faculty:* 64 full-time (37 women), 37 part-time/adjunct (21 women). *Graduate housing:* Rooms and/or apartments available on a first-come, first-served basis to single and married students. Housing application deadline: 5/1. *Student services:* Campus safety program, career counseling, disabled student services, exercise/wellness program, free psychological counseling, low-cost health insurance, multicultural affairs office, writing training. *Library facilities:* O. J. Cloughly Alumni Library. *Online resources:* library catalog, web page, access to other libraries' catalogs. *Collection:* 73,411 titles, 153 serial subscriptions, 50 audiovisual materials.

Computer facilities: Computer purchase and lease plans are available. 75 computers available on campus for general student use. A campuswide network can be accessed from student residence rooms and from off campus. Internet access and online class registration are available. *Web address:* http://www.stlcop.edu/.

General Application Contact: Penny Myers Bryant, Director of Admissions/Registrar, 314-446-8313, Fax: 314-446-8310, E-mail: pbryant@stlcop.edu.

GRADUATE UNITS

Professional Program in Pharmacy Students: 1,124 full-time (668 women); includes 181 minority (24 African Americans, 1 American Indian/Alaska Native, 147 Asian Americans or Pacific Islanders, 9 Hispanic Americans), 6 international. Average age 22. 538 applicants, 83% accepted, 297 enrolled. Expenses: Contact institution. *Financial support:* In 2006–07, 583 students received support. Federal Work-Study and scholarships/grants available. Financial award application deadline: 12/15; financial award applicants required to submit FAFSA. In 2006, 67 Pharm Ds awarded. Offers pharmacy (Pharm D). *Application deadline:* For fall admission, 12/15 for domestic and international students; for spring admission, 2/1 for domestic and international students. *Application fee:* $50. Electronic applications accepted. *Director of Admissions/Registrar*, Penny Myers Bryant, 314-446-8313, Fax: 314-446-8310, E-mail: pbryant@stlcop.edu.

Program in Pharmacy Administration Average age 35. *Faculty:* 1 full-time (0 women), 3 part-time/adjunct (0 women). Expenses: Contact institution. In 2006, 1 degree awarded. *Degree program information:* Part-time and evening/weekend programs available. Postbaccalaureate distance learning degree programs offered (minimal on-campus study). Offers managed care pharmacy (MS, Certificate). *Application deadline:* For fall admission, 8/1 priority date for domestic students; for winter admission, 12/20 priority date for domestic students; for spring admission, 3/15 priority date for domestic students. Applications are processed on a rolling basis. *Application fee:* $50.

SAINT LOUIS UNIVERSITY, St. Louis, MO 63103-2097

General Information Independent-religious, coed, university. CGS member. *Enrollment:* 12,034 graduate, professional, and undergraduate students; 2,937 full-time matriculated graduate/professional students (1,615 women). *Enrollment by degree level:* 1,496 master's, 913 doctoral, 125 other advanced degrees. *Graduate faculty:* 1,051 full-time (382 women), 477 part-time/adjunct (223 women). *Tuition:* Part-time $800 per credit hour. *Required fees:* $105 per semester. *Student services:* Campus employment opportunities, campus safety program, career counseling, disabled student services, exercise/wellness program, free psychological counseling, grant writing training, international student services, low-cost health insurance, multicultural affairs office, teacher training, writing training. *Library facilities:* Pius XII Memorial Library plus 2 others. *Online resources:* library catalog, web page, access to other libraries' catalogs. *Collection:* 1.9 million titles, 14,395 serial subscriptions, 174,702 audiovisual materials. *Research affiliation:* National Center for Atmospheric Research (earth and atmospheric sciences), Argonne National Laboratory (energy/physics/chemistry/mathematics and computer science), Small Business Administration (business, administration and entrepreneurship), Monsanto Chemical Corporation (chemistry), Missouri Botanical Garden (biology/plant science), ATT Foundation (communication).

Computer facilities: Computer purchase and lease plans are available. 1,350 computers available on campus for general student use. A campuswide network can be accessed from student residence rooms and from off campus. Internet access and online class registration are available. *Web address:* http://www.slu.edu.

General Application Contact: Gary Behrman, Associate Dean of the Graduate School, 314-977-3827, E-mail: behrmang@slu.edu.

GRADUATE UNITS

Graduate School Students: 1,002 full-time (646 women), 1,109 part-time (714 women); includes 267 minority (146 African Americans, 10 American Indian/Alaska Native, 60 Asian Americans or Pacific Islanders, 51 Hispanic Americans), 132 international. Average age 36. 2,041 applicants, 57% accepted, 617 enrolled. *Faculty:* 527 full-time (220 women), 347 part-time/adjunct (175 women). Expenses: Contact institution. *Financial support:* In 2006–07, 983 students received support, including 27 fellowships with full tuition reimbursements available, 85 research assistantships with full tuition reimbursements available, 226 teaching assistantships with full tuition reimbursements available; career-related internships or fieldwork, Federal Work-Study, scholarships/grants, traineeships, health care benefits, tuition waivers (full and partial), and unspecified assistantships also available. Support available to part-time students. Financial award application deadline: 6/1; financial award applicants required to submit FAFSA. In 2006, 285 master's, 115 doctorates, 26 other advanced degrees awarded. *Degree program information:* Part-time and evening/weekend programs available. Postbaccalaureate distance learning degree programs offered (minimal on-campus study). Offers biochemistry and molecular biology (PhD); biomedical sciences (PhD); molecular microbiology and immunology (PhD); pathology (PhD); pharmacological and physiological science (PhD). *Application deadline:* For fall admission, 7/1 for domestic and international students; for spring admission, 11/1 for domestic and international students. Applications are processed on a rolling basis. *Application fee:* $40. *Application Contact:* Gary Behrman, Associate Dean of the Graduate School, 314-977-3827, E-mail: behrmang@slu.edu. *Interim Dean*, Dr. Donald G. Brennan, 314-977-2244, Fax: 314-977-3943, E-mail: brennand@slu.edu.

Center for Advanced Dental Education Students: 59 full-time (20 women), 4 part-time (1 woman); includes 12 minority (1 African American, 2 American Indian/Alaska Native, 7 Asian Americans or Pacific Islanders, 2 Hispanic Americans), 8 international. Average age 29. 256 applicants, 8% accepted, 21 enrolled. *Faculty:* 7 full-time (1 woman), 34 part-time/adjunct (4 women). Expenses: Contact institution. *Financial support:* In 2006–07, 33 students received support. Application deadline: 6/1. In 2006, 19 degrees awarded. Offers dentistry (MS). *Application deadline:* For fall admission, 9/15 for domestic and international students. *Application fee:* $40. *Application Contact:* Gary Behrman, Associate Dean of the Graduate School, 314-977-3827, E-mail: behrmang@slu.edu. *Executive Director*, Dr. Rolf Behrents, 314-977-8600, E-mail: behrents@slu.edu.

Center for Health Care Ethics Students: 14 full-time (7 women), 20 part-time (8 women); includes 3 minority (all Hispanic Americans), 2 international. Average age 37. 37 applicants, 89% accepted, 16 enrolled. *Faculty:* 4 full-time (1 woman), 1 (woman) part-time/adjunct. Expenses: Contact institution. *Financial support:* In 2006–07, 11 students received support, including 6 teaching assistantships with full tuition reimbursements available (averaging $11,000 per year); career-related internships or fieldwork, Federal Work-Study, scholarships/grants, traineeships, health care benefits, tuition waivers (full), and unspecified assistantships also available. Support available to part-time students. Financial award application deadline: 6/1; financial award applicants required to submit FAFSA. In 2006, 1 degree awarded. Offers clinical health care ethics (Certificate); health care ethics (PhD). *Application deadline:* For fall admission, 7/1 for domestic and international students. Applications are processed on a rolling basis. *Application fee:* $40. *Application Contact:* Gary Behrman, Associate Dean of the Graduate School, 314-977-3827, E-mail: behrmang@slu.edu. *Executive Director*, Rev. Gerard Magill, PhD, 314-977-6666, Fax: 314-977-5150, E-mail: magill@slu.edu.

College of Arts and Sciences Students: 342 full-time (188 women), 191 part-time (98 women); includes 59 minority (26 African Americans, 2 American Indian/Alaska Native, 10 Asian Americans or Pacific Islanders, 21 Hispanic Americans), 44 international. Average age 31. 633 applicants, 48% accepted, 132 enrolled. *Faculty:* 258 full-time (76 women), 151 part-time/adjunct (83 women). Expenses: Contact institution. *Financial support:* In 2006–07, 410 students received support, including 65 research assistantships with full tuition reimbursements available (averaging $13,092 per year), 144 teaching assistantships with full tuition reimbursements available (averaging $12,021 per year); career-related internships or fieldwork, Federal Work-Study, scholarships/grants, traineeships, health care benefits, tuition waivers (partial), and unspecified assistantships also available. Support available to part-time students. Financial award application deadline: 6/1; financial award applicants required to submit FAFSA. In 2006, 117 master's, 54 doctorates awarded. *Degree program information:* Part-time and evening/weekend programs available. Offers administration of justice (MA); American studies (MA, PhD); arts and sciences (M Pr Met, MA, MA-R, MS, MS-R, PhD); biology (MS, MS-R, PhD); chemistry (MS, MS-R); clinical psychology (MS-R, PhD); communication (MA, MA-R); English (MA, MA-R, PhD); experimental psychology (MS-R, PhD); French (MA); geophysics (PhD); geoscience (MS); historical theology (MA, PhD); history (MA, PhD); industrial-organizational psychology (PhD); mathematics (MA, MA-R, PhD); meteorology (M Pr Met, MS-R, PhD); philosophy (MA, PhD); psychology (PhD); Spanish (MA); theology (MA). *Application deadline:* For fall admission, 7/1 for domestic students, 7/11 for international students; for spring admission, 11/1 for domestic and international students. Applications are processed on a rolling basis. *Application fee:* $40. *Application Contact:* Gary Behrman, Associate Dean of the Graduate School, 314-977-3827, E-mail: behrmang@slu.edu. *Interim Dean*, Dr. Donald G. Brennan, 314-977-2244, Fax: 314-977-3943, E-mail: brennand@slu.edu.

College of Public Service Students: 205 full-time (151 women), 443 part-time (259 women); includes 80 minority (59 African Americans, 2 American Indian/Alaska Native, 11 Asian Americans or Pacific Islanders, 8 Hispanic Americans), 9 international. Average age 35. 417 applicants, 76% accepted, 182 enrolled. *Faculty:* 48 full-time (24 women), 49 part-time/adjunct (29 women). Expenses: Contact institution. *Financial support:* In 2006–07, 215 students received support, including 4 research assistantships with full tuition reimbursements available (averaging $14,700 per year), 31 teaching assistantships with full tuition reimbursements available (averaging $11,300 per year); Federal Work-Study, scholarships/grants, traineeships, health care benefits, tuition waivers, and unspecified assistantships also available. Support available to part-time students. Financial award application deadline: 6/1; financial award applicants required to submit FAFSA. In 2006, 65 master's, 78 doctorates awarded. *Degree program information:* Part-time programs available. Offers Catholic school leadership (MA); communication sciences and disorders (MA, MA-R); counseling and family therapy (PhD); curriculum and instruction (MA, Ed D, PhD); educational administration (MA, Ed D, PhD, Ed S); educational foundations (MA, Ed D, PhD); geographic information systems (Certificate); higher education (MA, Ed D, PhD); human development counseling (MA); marriage and family therapy (Certificate); organizational development (Certificate); public administration (MAPA); public policy analysis (PhD); public service (MA, MA-R, MAPA, MAT, MAUA, MSW, MUPRED, Ed D, PhD, Certificate, Ed S); school counseling (MA, MA-R); social work (MSW); special education (MA); student personnel administration (MA); teaching (MAT); urban affairs (MAUA); urban planning and real estate development (MUPRED). *Application deadline:* For fall admission, 7/11 for domestic and

Saint Louis University (continued)

international students; for spring admission, 11/1 for domestic and international students. Applications are processed on a rolling basis. *Application fee:* $40. *Application Contact:* Gary Behrman, Associate Dean of the Graduate School, 314-977-3827, E-mail: behrmang@slu.edu. *Interim Dean,* Marla Berg-Weger, 314-977-3078, Fax: 314-977-3290, E-mail: bergwm@slu.edu.

Doisy College of Health Sciences Students: 219 full-time (182 women), 30 part-time (27 women); includes 16 minority (4 African Americans, 3 American Indian/Alaska Native, 7 Asian Americans or Pacific Islanders, 2 Hispanic Americans), 2 international. Average age 25. 662 applicants, 12% accepted, 68 enrolled. *Faculty:* 43 full-time (36 women), 15 part-time/adjunct (13 women). Expenses: Contact institution. *Financial support:* In 2006–07, 16 students received support, including 11 research assistantships with full tuition reimbursements available (averaging $12,255 per year), 5 teaching assistantships with full tuition reimbursements available (averaging $12,000 per year); career-related internships or fieldwork, Federal Work-Study, scholarships/grants, traineeships, health care benefits, and unspecified assistantships also available. Support available to part-time students. Financial award application deadline: 6/1; financial award applicants required to submit FAFSA. In 2006, 131 master's, 15 doctorates awarded. *Degree program information:* Part-time programs available. Offers health sciences (MMS, MOT, MS, MSN, MSN-R, MSPT, DPT, PhD, Certificate); nursing (MSN, MSN-R, PhD, Certificate); nutrition and dietetics (MS); occupational science and occupational therapy (MOT); physical therapy (MSPT, DPT); physician assistant (MMS). *Application deadline:* For fall admission, 7/1 for domestic and international students; for spring admission, 11/1 for domestic and international students. Applications are processed on a rolling basis. *Application fee:* $40. *Dean,* Dr. Charlotte Royeen, 314-977-8501, Fax: 314-977-8503, E-mail: royeencb@slu.edu.

John Cook School of Business Students: 84 full-time (29 women), 318 part-time (115 women); includes 40 minority (15 African Americans, 1 American Indian/Alaska Native, 15 Asian Americans or Pacific Islanders, 9 Hispanic Americans), 17 international. Average age 29. 387 applicants, 60% accepted, 169 enrolled. *Faculty:* 60 full-time (16 women), 19 part-time/adjunct (4 women). Expenses: Contact institution. *Financial support:* In 2006–07, 117 students received support, including 5 teaching assistantships with full tuition reimbursements available (averaging $11,000 per year); Federal Work-Study, traineeships, health care benefits, and unspecified assistantships also available. Support available to part-time students. Financial award application deadline: 6/1; financial award applicants required to submit FAFSA. In 2006, 111 degrees awarded. *Degree program information:* Part-time and evening/weekend programs available. Offers accounting (M Acct, MBA); business (EMIB, M Acct, MBA, MSF, PhD); business administration (PhD); executive international business (EMIB); finance (MBA, MSF); international business (MBA). *Application deadline:* For fall admission, 4/15 priority date for domestic and international students. Applications are processed on a rolling basis. *Application fee:* $90. Electronic applications accepted. *Dean,* Dr. Ellen Harshman, 314-977-3833, Fax: 314-977-1416, E-mail: harshman@slu.edu.

Parks College of Engineering, Aviation, and Technology Students: 9 full-time (4 women), 23 part-time (6 women); includes 5 minority (3 African Americans, 1 Asian American or Pacific Islander, 1 Hispanic American), 3 international. Average age 30. 26 applicants, 88% accepted, 13 enrolled. *Faculty:* 23 full-time (4 women), 8 part-time/adjunct (1 woman). Expenses: Contact institution. *Financial support:* In 2006–07, 20 students received support, including 6 teaching assistantships with full tuition reimbursements available (averaging $13,300 per year); health care benefits and tuition waivers (partial) also available. Financial award application deadline: 6/1; financial award applicants required to submit FAFSA. In 2006, 8 degrees awarded. *Degree program information:* Part-time programs available. Postbaccalaureate distance learning degree programs offered (minimal on-campus study). Offers biomedical engineering (MS, MS-R, PhD); engineering, aviation, and technology (MS, MS-R, PhD). *Application deadline:* For fall admission, 7/1 for domestic and international students; for spring admission, 11/1 for domestic and international students. Applications are processed on a rolling basis. *Application fee:* $40. *Application Contact:* Gary Behrman, Associate Dean of the Graduate School, 314-977-3827, E-mail: behrmang@slu.edu. *Interim Dean,* Dr. Neil E Seitz, 314-977-8203, Fax: 314-977-8403, E-mail: seitzne@slu.edu.

School of Medicine Students: 668 full-time (285 women); includes 175 minority (17 African Americans, 1 American Indian/Alaska Native, 144 Asian Americans or Pacific Islanders, 13 Hispanic Americans), 14 international. Average age 25. 5,635 applicants, 11% accepted, 177 enrolled. *Faculty:* 481 full-time (144 women), 103 part-time/adjunct (38 women). Expenses: Contact institution. *Financial support:* Application deadline: 6/1; In 2006, 147 degrees awarded. Offers anatomy (MS-R, PhD); medicine (MD, MS-R, PhD). *Application deadline:* For fall admission, 2/15 for international students; for winter admission, 2/15 for domestic students. Applications are processed on a rolling basis. Electronic applications accepted. *Application Contact:* Dr. James Willmore, Associate Dean of Admissions, 314-577-8205, Fax: 314-577-8214, E-mail: willmore@slu.edu. *Dean,* Dr. Patricia L. Monteleone, 314-977-9801, Fax: 314-977-8253, E-mail: montelpl@slu.edu.

School of Public Health Students: 170 full-time (127 women), 112 part-time (69 women); includes 58 minority (32 African Americans, 21 Asian Americans or Pacific Islanders, 5 Hispanic Americans), 28 international. Average age 31. 313 applicants, 66% accepted, 98 enrolled. *Faculty:* 43 full-time (20 women), 36 part-time/adjunct (7 women). Expenses: Contact institution. *Financial support:* In 2006–07, 106 students received support, including 11 research assistantships with full tuition reimbursements available (averaging $12,255 per year), 5 teaching assistantships with full tuition reimbursements available (averaging $12,000 per year); Federal Work-Study, scholarships/grants, traineeships, health care benefits, and unspecified assistantships also available. Support available to part-time students. Financial award application deadline: 6/1; financial award applicants required to submit FAFSA. In 2006, 94 master's, 8 doctorates awarded. *Degree program information:* Part-time programs available. Offers biosecurity (Certificate); community health (MPH); health administration (MHA); health management and policy (MHA, PhD); public health (PhD); public health studies (PhD). *Application deadline:* For fall admission, 7/1 for domestic and international students; for spring admission, 11/1 for domestic students. Applications are processed on a rolling basis. *Application fee:* $40. *Application Contact:* Gary Behrman, Associate Dean of the Graduate School, 314-977-3827, E-mail: behrmang@slu.edu. *Dean,* Dr. Connie J. Evashwick, 314-977-8144, Fax: 314-977-8150, E-mail: cevashwi@slu.edu.

School of Law Students: 716 full-time (357 women), 234 part-time (108 women); includes 103 minority (48 African Americans, 5 American Indian/Alaska Native, 32 Asian Americans or Pacific Islanders, 18 Hispanic Americans), 12 international. Average age 26. 2,278 applicants, 47% accepted, 346 enrolled. *Faculty:* 43 full-time (18 women), 27 part-time/adjunct (10 women). Expenses: Contact institution. *Financial support:* In 2006–07, 372 students received support. Federal Work-Study, scholarships/grants, traineeships, health care benefits, tuition waivers, and unspecified assistantships available. Support available to part-time students. Financial award application deadline: 6/1; financial award applicants required to submit FAFSA. In 2006, 247 JDs, 6 master's awarded. *Degree program information:* Part-time and evening/weekend programs available. Offers law (JD, LL M). *Application deadline:* For fall admission, 3/1 for domestic and international students. Applications are processed on a rolling basis. *Application fee:* $55. Electronic applications accepted. *Application Contact:* Michael J. Kolnik, Director of Admissions, 314-977-2800, E-mail: kolnikmj@slu.edu. *Dean,* Dr. Jeffrey E. Lewis, 314-977-2766, Fax: 314-977-3333, E-mail: lewisje@slu.edu.

See Close-Up on page 1015.

SAINT LOUIS UNIVERSITY, MADRID, 28003 Madrid, Spain

General Information Independent-religious, coed, comprehensive institution. *Enrollment:* 650 graduate, professional, and undergraduate students; 29 full-time matriculated graduate/professional students (23 women), 34 part-time matriculated graduate/professional students (25 women). *Enrollment by degree level:* 63 master's. *Graduate faculty:* 54 full-time (26 women), 7 part-time/adjunct (3 women). *Graduate tuition:* Tuition charges are reported in euros. *Tuition:* Part-time 360 euros per credit hour. *Graduate housing:* Rooms and/or apartments available on a first-come, first-served basis to single and married students. Typical cost: 4,340 euros per year (6,906 euros including board) for single students. Housing application deadline: 5/30. *Student services:* Campus employment opportunities, career counseling, disabled student services, exercise/wellness program, free psychological counseling, international student services, low-cost health insurance, teacher training, writing training. *Library facilities:* Main library plus 1 other. *Online resources:* library catalog. *Collection:* 8,000 titles, 75 serial subscriptions. *Research affiliation:* Universidad Autónoma de Madrid (Filología Inglesa).

Computer facilities: 72 computers available on campus for general student use. A campuswide network can be accessed from student residence rooms. Internet access and online class registration are available. *Web address:* http://spain.slu.edu/.

General Application Contact: Phyllis Chaney, Director of Admissions, 34-91-554-58-58 Ext. 232, Fax: 34-91-554-62-02, E-mail: chaney@madrid.sluiberica.slu.edu.

GRADUATE UNITS

Graduate Programs Tuition charges are reported in euros. *Degree program information:* Part-time programs available. Offers English (MA); Spanish (MA); Spanish language and literature (MA).

SAINT MARTIN'S UNIVERSITY, Lacey, WA 98503-1297

General Information Independent-religious, coed, comprehensive institution. *Graduate housing:* Room and/or apartments available on a first-come, first-served basis to single students; on-campus housing not available to married students. Housing application deadline: 3/15.

GRADUATE UNITS

Graduate Programs *Degree program information:* Part-time and evening/weekend programs available. Offers administration (M Ed); civil engineering (MCE); counseling psychology (MAC); engineering management (M Eng Mgt); English as a second language (M Ed); guidance and counseling (M Ed); reading (M Ed); special education (M Ed); teaching (MIT); technology in education (M Ed).

Division of Economics and Business Administration *Degree program information:* Part-time and evening/weekend programs available. Offers economics and business administration (MBA).

SAINT MARY-OF-THE-WOODS COLLEGE, Saint Mary-of-the-Woods, IN 47876

General Information Independent-religious, Undergraduate: women only; graduate: coed, comprehensive institution. *Enrollment:* 1,668 graduate, professional, and undergraduate students; 117 part-time matriculated graduate/professional students (98 women). *Enrollment by degree level:* 117 master's. *Graduate faculty:* 8 full-time (4 women), 27 part-time/adjunct (23 women). *Graduate housing:* Rooms and/or apartments guaranteed to single students and available to married students. *Student services:* Campus safety program, career counseling, child daycare facilities, disabled student services, international student services, teacher training, writing training. *Library facilities:* Rooney Library. *Online resources:* library catalog, access to other libraries' catalogs. *Collection:* 155,771 titles, 150 serial subscriptions.

Computer facilities: 65 computers available on campus for general student use. A campuswide network can be accessed from student residence rooms and from off campus. Internet access is available. *Web address:* http://www.smwc.edu/.

General Application Contact: Kathi Kortz, Administrative Assistant, Graduate Studies, 812-535-5206, Fax: 812-535-5177, E-mail: kkortz@smwc.edu.

GRADUATE UNITS

Program in Art Therapy Average age 39. 20 applicants, 50% accepted, 3 enrolled. *Faculty:* 3 full-time (2 women), 6 part-time/adjunct (5 women). Expenses: Contact institution. *Financial support:* Scholarships/grants available. Financial award applicants required to submit FAFSA. In 2006, 1 degree awarded. *Degree program information:* Part-time and evening/weekend programs available. Postbaccalaureate distance learning degree programs offered (minimal on-campus study). Offers art therapy (MA, Post-Master's Certificate). *Application deadline:* For fall admission, 5/20 priority date for domestic students; for winter admission, 12/7 priority date for domestic students. *Application fee:* $35. Electronic applications accepted. *Director,* Kathy Jeanne Gotshall, 812-535-5162, Fax: 812-535-4613, E-mail: kgotshall@smwc.edu.

Program in Earth Literacy Students: 1 (woman) full-time, 31 part-time (29 women). Average age 43. 17 applicants, 100% accepted. *Faculty:* 11 part-time/adjunct (9 women). Expenses: Contact institution. *Financial support:* Career-related internships or fieldwork available. Financial award application deadline: 3/1; financial award applicants required to submit FAFSA. In 2006, 3 degrees awarded. *Degree program information:* Part-time programs available. Postbaccalaureate distance learning degree programs offered (minimal on-campus study). Offers earth literacy (MA). *Application deadline:* Applications are processed on a rolling basis. *Application fee:* $35. Electronic applications accepted. *Director,* Dr. Mary Louise Dolan, CSJ, 812-535-5160, Fax: 812-535-5127, E-mail: mldolan@smwc.edu.

Program in Music Therapy Average age 32. 2 applicants, 100% accepted. *Faculty:* 3 full-time (2 women), 6 part-time/adjunct (5 women). Expenses: Contact institution. *Financial support:* In 2006–07, 2 students received support. In 2006, 2 degrees awarded. *Degree program information:* Part-time programs available. Postbaccalaureate distance learning degree programs offered (minimal on-campus study). Offers music therapy (MA). *Application deadline:* Applications are processed on a rolling basis. *Application fee:* $35. Electronic applications accepted. *Director,* Tracy Gay Richardson, 812-535-5154, Fax: 812-535-4613, E-mail: trichard@smwc.edu.

Program in Pastoral Theology Average age 45. 11 applicants, 100% accepted. *Faculty:* 2 full-time (0 women), 4 part-time/adjunct (all women). Expenses: Contact institution. *Financial support:* In 2006–07, 3 students received support. Scholarships/grants and tuition waivers (partial) available. Financial award applicants required to submit FAFSA. In 2006, 12 degrees awarded. *Degree program information:* Part-time and evening/weekend programs available. Postbaccalaureate distance learning degree programs offered (minimal on-campus study). Offers pastoral theology (MA); youth ministry (Graduate Certificate). *Application deadline:* For fall admission, 8/1 priority date for domestic students; for winter admission, 12/1 priority date for domestic students; for spring admission, 4/1 priority date for domestic students. Applications are processed on a rolling basis. *Application fee:* $35. *Director,* Dr. Virginia Unverzagt, 812-535-5206, Fax: 812-535-5177, E-mail: vunverzagt@smwc.edu.

SAINT MARY'S COLLEGE OF CALIFORNIA, Moraga, CA 94575

General Information Independent-religious, coed, comprehensive institution. *Enrollment:* 3,962 graduate, professional, and undergraduate students; 540 full-time matriculated graduate/professional students (310 women), 587 part-time matriculated graduate/professional students (488 women). *Enrollment by degree level:* 1,065 master's, 62 doctoral. *Graduate faculty:* 111 full-time (61 women), 277 part-time/adjunct (154 women). *Graduate housing:* On-campus housing not available. *Student services:* Campus employment opportunities, campus safety program, career counseling, disabled student services, international student services, low-cost health insurance, multicultural affairs office, teacher training. *Library facilities:* St. Albert Hall. *Online resources:* library catalog, web page, access to other libraries' catalogs. *Collection:* 220,337 titles, 15,000 serial subscriptions, 5,670 audiovisual materials.

Computer facilities: 250 computers available on campus for general student use. A campuswide network can be accessed from student residence rooms and from off campus. Internet access and online class registration are available. *Web address:* http://www.stmarys-ca.edu/.

General Application Contact: Michael Beseda, Vice Provost for Enrollment, 925-631-4277, Fax: 925-376-8339, E-mail: mbeseda@stmarys-ca.edu.

GRADUATE UNITS

Graduate Business Programs Students: 158 full-time (54 women), 83 part-time (36 women); includes 67 minority (9 African Americans, 33 Asian Americans or Pacific Islanders, 25 Hispanic Americans), 1 international. Average age 33. 125 applicants, 86% accepted, 90 enrolled. *Faculty:* 13 full-time (3 women), 14 part-time/adjunct (0 women). Expenses: Contact institution. *Financial support:* Career-related internships or fieldwork available. Support available to part-time students. Financial award application deadline: 3/2; financial award applicants required to submit FAFSA. In 2006, 120 degrees awarded. *Degree program information:* Part-time and evening/weekend programs available. Offers business (MBA); business administration (MBA); executive business administration (MBA). *Application deadline:* Applications are processed on a rolling basis. *Application fee:* $50. *Application Contact:* Bob Peterson, Director of Admissions, 925-631-4505, Fax: 925-376-6521, E-mail: smcmba@stmarys-ca.edu. *Associate Dean, Director,* Guido Krickx, 925-631-4514, Fax: 925-376-6521, E-mail: gakl@stmarys-ca.edu.

School of Education Students: 230 full-time (188 women), 408 part-time (310 women); includes 133 minority (40 African Americans, 4 American Indian/Alaska Native, 32 Asian Americans or Pacific Islanders, 57 Hispanic Americans), 26 international. Average age 29. 409 applicants, 98% accepted. *Faculty:* 28 full-time (22 women), 82 part-time/adjunct (63 women). Expenses: Contact institution. *Financial support:* In 2006–07, 44 students received support. Career-related internships or fieldwork and tuition waivers (partial) available. Support available to part-time students. Financial award application deadline: 2/15; financial award applicants required to submit FAFSA. In 2006, 102 master's, 8 doctorates awarded. *Degree program information:* Part-time and evening/weekend programs available. Offers early childhood education and Montessori teacher training (M Ed, MA); education (M Ed, MA, MAT, PhD); educational leadership (MA, PhD); general counseling (MA); instruction (M Ed); marital and family therapy (MA); reading leadership (MA); school counseling (MA); special education (M Ed, MA); teachers for tomorrow (MAT); teaching leadership (MA). *Application deadline:* Applications are processed on a rolling basis. *Application fee:* $50. *Application Contact:* Jane Joyce, Coordinator Recruitment and Admissions, 925-631-4700, Fax: 925-376-8379, E-mail: soereq@stmarys-ca.edu. *Dean,* Dr. Nancy L. Sorenson, 925-631-4309, Fax: 925-376-8379, E-mail: nsorenso@stmarys-ca.edu.

School of Liberal Arts Students: 91 full-time (39 women), 107 part-time (72 women); includes 56 minority (18 African Americans, 16 Asian Americans or Pacific Islanders, 22 Hispanic Americans), 1 international. Average age 26. *Faculty:* 13 full-time (6 women), 39 part-time/adjunct (18 women). Expenses: Contact institution. *Financial support:* Fellowships, teaching assistantships, career-related internships or fieldwork, institutionally sponsored loans, and tuition waivers (partial) available. Support available to part-time students. Financial award applicants required to submit FAFSA. In 2006, 50 degrees awarded. *Degree program information:* Part-time programs available. Offers creative writing (MFA); kinesiology (MA); leadership (MA); liberal arts (MA, MFA); liberal studies (MA). *Dean,* Stephen Woolpert, 925-631-4609, Fax: 925-631-4490, E-mail: woolpert@stmarys-ca.edu.

SAINT MARY SEMINARY AND GRADUATE SCHOOL OF THEOLOGY, Wickliffe, OH 44092-2527

General Information Independent-religious, coed, primarily men, graduate-only institution. *Graduate housing:* Room and/or apartments available to single students; on-campus housing not available to married students.

GRADUATE UNITS

School of Theology *Degree program information:* Part-time programs available. Offers theology (M Div, MA, D Min).

ST. MARY'S SEMINARY AND UNIVERSITY, Baltimore, MD 21210-1994

General Information Independent-religious, coed, primarily men, graduate-only institution. *Graduate housing:* Room and/or apartments guaranteed to single students; on-campus housing not available to married students. Housing application deadline: 8/15.

GRADUATE UNITS

Ecumenical Institute of Theology *Degree program information:* Part-time and evening/weekend programs available. Offers church ministries (MA); theology (MA Th, Certificate).

School of Theology *Degree program information:* Part-time programs available. Offers theology (M Div, STB, MA Th, STD, STL).

SAINT MARY'S UNIVERSITY, Halifax, NS B3H 3C3, Canada

General Information Province-supported, coed, comprehensive institution. *Graduate housing:* Rooms and/or apartments available on a first-come, first-served basis to single students and available to married students. Housing application deadline: 3/30.

GRADUATE UNITS

Faculty of Arts *Degree program information:* Part-time and evening/weekend programs available. Offers arts (MA); Atlantic Canada studies (MA); criminology (MA); history (MA); international development studies (MA); philosophy (MA); women's studies (MA).

Faculty of Commerce *Degree program information:* Part-time and evening/weekend programs available. Offers business administration (MBA); management (PhD).

Faculty of Science *Degree program information:* Part-time programs available. Offers applied psychology (M Sc); astronomy (M Sc); science (M Sc).

SAINT MARY'S UNIVERSITY OF MINNESOTA, Winona, MN 55987-1399

General Information Independent-religious, coed, comprehensive institution. *Enrollment:* 5,566 graduate, professional, and undergraduate students; 592 full-time matriculated graduate/professional students (379 women), 3,012 part-time matriculated graduate/professional students (2,001 women). *Enrollment by degree level:* 2,981 master's, 219 doctoral, 404 other advanced degrees. *Graduate faculty:* 8 full-time (2 women), 368 part-time/adjunct (169 women). *Student services:* Campus safety program, disabled student services, teacher training, writing training. *Library facilities:* Fitzgerald Library plus 1 other. *Online resources:* library catalog, web page, access to other libraries' catalogs. *Collection:* 222,153 titles, 19,948 serial subscriptions, 8,650 audiovisual materials.

Computer facilities: 374 computers available on campus for general student use. A campuswide network can be accessed from student residence rooms and from off campus. Internet access and online class registration are available. *Web address:* http://www.smumn.edu/.

General Application Contact: Becky Copper, Director of Admissions for Graduate and Professional Programs, 612-728-5207, Fax: 612-728-5121, E-mail: bcopper@smumn.edu.

GRADUATE UNITS

School of Graduate and Professional Programs Students: 592 full-time (379 women), 3,012 part-time (2,001 women); includes 305 minority (159 African Americans, 10 American Indian/Alaska Native, 76 Asian Americans or Pacific Islanders, 60 Hispanic Americans), 89 international. Average age 35. Expenses: Contact institution. Offers arts and cultural management (MA); business administration (MBA); counseling and psychological services (MA); education (MA); educational administration (MA, Certificate, Ed S); educational leadership (Ed D); executive business leadership (Certificate); finance manager (Certificate); geographic information science (MS, Certificate); health and human services administration (MA); human development (MA); human resource management (MA); instruction (MA, Certificate); international business (MA); K-12 reading teacher (Certificate); literacy education (MA); management (MA); marriage and family therapy (MA, Certificate); nurse anesthesia (MS); organizational leadership (MA); philanthropy and development (MA); project management (MS); public safety administration (MA); teaching and learning (M Ed); telecommunications (MS). *Application Contact:* Becky Copper, Director of Admissions for Graduate and Professional Programs, 612-728-5207, Fax: 612-728-5121, E-mail: bcopper@smumn.edu. *Vice President, Graduate and Professional Programs,* James M. Bedtke, 507-457-1458, Fax: 507-457-1752, E-mail: jbedtke@smumn.edu.

Institute in Pastoral Ministries Expenses: Contact institution. Offers pastoral administration (MA); pastoral ministries (MA). *Application Contact:* Jami Spitzer, Information Contact, 507-457-7500, E-mail: jspitzer@smumn.edu. *Director,* Dr. Gregory Sobolewski, 507-457-1767, Fax: 507-457-1752, E-mail: gsobolew@smumn.edu.

ST. MARY'S UNIVERSITY OF SAN ANTONIO, San Antonio, TX 78228-8507

General Information Independent-religious, coed, comprehensive institution. *Enrollment:* 3,904 graduate, professional, and undergraduate students; 964 full-time matriculated graduate/professional students (464 women), 540 part-time matriculated graduate/professional students (287 women). *Enrollment by degree level:* 749 first professional, 698 master's, 57 doctoral. *Graduate faculty:* 44 full-time (14 women), 89 part-time/adjunct (30 women). *Tuition:* Full-time $10,890; part-time $605 per hour. *Required fees:* $500. Tuition and fees vary according to degree level. *Graduate housing:* Room and/or apartments available on a first-come, first-served basis to single students; on-campus housing not available to married students. Typical cost: $3,900 per year ($6,780 including board). Housing application deadline: 5/1. *Student services:* Campus employment opportunities, career counseling, disabled student services, exercise/wellness program, free psychological counseling, international student services, low-cost health insurance. *Library facilities:* Louis J. Blume Library plus 1 other. *Online resources:* library catalog, web page, access to other libraries' catalogs. *Collection:* 481,137 titles, 1,213 serial subscriptions. *Research affiliation:* Southeast Research Consortium (behavioral science, biomedical engineering, social science).

Computer facilities: Computer purchase and lease plans are available. 100 computers available on campus for general student use. A campuswide network can be accessed from student residence rooms and from off campus. Internet access and online class registration, wireless campus; e-mail are available. *Web address:* http://www.stmarytx.edu/.

General Application Contact: Dr. Henry Flores, Dean of the Graduate School, 210-436-3101, Fax: 210-431-2220, E-mail: hflores@stmarytx.edu.

GRADUATE UNITS

Graduate School Students: 230 full-time (152 women), 525 part-time (280 women); includes 297 minority (21 African Americans, 1 American Indian/Alaska Native, 17 Asian Americans or Pacific Islanders, 258 Hispanic Americans), 28 international. Average age 32. *Faculty:* 8 full-time (3 women), 75 part-time/adjunct (25 women). Expenses: Contact institution. *Financial support:* Career-related internships or fieldwork, Federal Work-Study, institutionally sponsored loans, scholarships/grants, health care benefits, tuition waivers (full), unspecified assistantships, and employer tuition benefit available. Financial award application deadline: 3/31; financial award applicants required to submit FAFSA. In 2006, 119 master's, 8 doctorates awarded. *Degree program information:* Part-time and evening/weekend programs available. Postbaccalaureate distance learning degree programs offered (minimal on-campus study). Offers Catholic principalship (Certificate); Catholic school administrators (Certificate); Catholic school leadership (MA, Certificate); Catholic school teachers (Certificate); clinical psychology (MA, MS); communication studies (MA); community counseling (MA); computer information systems (MS); computer science (MS); counseling (Sp C); counseling education and supervision (PhD); educational leadership (MA, Certificate); electrical engineering (MS); electrical/computer engineering (MS); engineering administration (MS); engineering computer applications (MS); engineering management (MS); engineering systems management (MS); English literature and language (MA); industrial engineering (MS); industrial/organizational psychology (MA, MS); inter-American administration (MPA); international relations (MA); marriage and family relations (Certificate); marriage and family therapy (MA, PhD); mental health (MA); mental health and substance abuse counseling (Certificate); operations research (MS); pastoral ministry (MA); political communications and applied science (MA); political science (MA); principalship (mid-management) (Certificate); public administration (MPA); public management (MPA); reading (MA); school psychology (MA); software engineering (MS); substance abuse (MA); theology (MA). *Application deadline:* Applications are processed on a rolling basis. *Application fee:* $30. Electronic applications accepted. *Dean of the Graduate School,* Dr. Henry Flores, 210-436-3101, Fax: 210-431-2220, E-mail: hflores@stmarytx.edu.

Bill Greehey School of Business Students: 20 full-time (9 women), 88 part-time (42 women); includes 45 minority (2 African Americans, 2 Asian Americans or Pacific Islanders, 41 Hispanic Americans), 4 international. Average age 30. *Faculty:* 17 full-time (6 women), 1 part-time/adjunct (0 women). Expenses: Contact institution. *Financial support:* Research assistantships, career-related internships or fieldwork, Federal Work-Study, institutionally sponsored loans, scholarships/grants, health care benefits, and unspecified assistantships available. Financial award application deadline: 3/31. In 2006, 37 degrees awarded. *Degree program information:* Part-time and evening/weekend programs available. Postbaccalaureate distance learning degree programs offered (minimal on-campus study). Offers accounting (M Acc); business administration (MBA); finance (MBA); international business (MBA); management (MBA); taxation (M Acc). *Application deadline:* Applications are processed on a rolling basis. *Application fee:* $30. Electronic applications accepted. *Dean,* Dr. Keith A Russell.

School of Law Students: 734 full-time, 15 part-time; includes 205 minority (15 African Americans, 8 American Indian/Alaska Native, 26 Asian Americans or Pacific Islanders, 156 Hispanic Americans), 6 international. Average age 27. 2,170 applicants, 32% accepted, 295 enrolled. *Faculty:* 36 full-time (11 women), 14 part-time/adjunct (5 women). Expenses: Contact institution. *Financial support:* In 2006–07, 59 research assistantships (averaging $1,000 per year), 35 teaching assistantships (averaging $1,250 per year) were awarded; career-related internships or fieldwork, Federal Work-Study, institutionally sponsored loans, scholarships/grants, and health care benefits also available. Financial award application deadline: 2/15; financial award applicants required to submit FAFSA. In 2006, 242 degrees awarded. Offers law (JD). *Application deadline:* For fall admission, 3/1 for domestic students. *Application fee:* $55. Electronic applications accepted. *Application Contact:* Dr. William Charles Wilson, Assistant Dean and Director of Admissions, 210-436-3523, Fax: 210-431-4202. *Dean,* Robert William Piatt, 210-436-3424, Fax: 210-436-3515.

SAINT MEINRAD SCHOOL OF THEOLOGY, Saint Meinrad, IN 47577

General Information Independent-religious, coed, primarily men, graduate-only institution. *Enrollment by degree level:* 74 first professional, 97 master's. *Graduate faculty:* 23 full-time (3 women), 7 part-time/adjunct (1 woman). *Tuition:* Full-time $15,759; part-time $325 per credit hour. *Required fees:* $350; $25 per course. One-time fee: $250 full-time. *Graduate housing:* Room and/or apartments guaranteed to single students; on-campus housing not available to married students. Typical cost: $8,179 (including board). Housing application deadline: 7/15. *Student services:* Campus employment opportunities, campus safety program, exercise/wellness program, free psychological counseling, low-cost health insurance, writing training. *Library facilities:* Archabbey Library. *Online resources:* library catalog, access to other libraries' catalogs. *Collection:* 172,926 titles, 335 serial subscriptions, 6,389 audiovisual materials.

Computer facilities: 30 computers available on campus for general student use. A campuswide network can be accessed from student residence rooms and from off campus. Internet access is available. *Web address:* http://www.saintmeinrad.edu/.

General Application Contact: Rev. Jonathan Fassero, OSB, Director of Enrollment, 812-357-6762, Fax: 812-357-6462, E-mail: jfassero@saintmeinrad.edu.

GRADUATE UNITS

Professional Program Students: 74 full-time (0 women); includes 17 minority (6 African Americans, 8 Asian Americans or Pacific Islanders, 3 Hispanic Americans), 2 international. Average age 32. 22 applicants, 95% accepted, 21 enrolled. *Faculty:* 23 full-time (3 women), 7 part-time/adjunct (1 woman). Expenses: Contact institution. *Financial support:* In 2006–07, 64 students received support. Career-related internships or fieldwork, Federal Work-Study, institutionally sponsored loans, and scholarships/grants available. Support available to part-time students. Financial award application deadline: 7/31; financial award applicants required to submit FAFSA. In 2006, 12 degrees awarded. Offers theology (M Div). *Application deadline:* For fall admission, 7/31 for domestic and international students; for winter admission, 11/15 for domestic and international students. Applications are processed on a rolling basis. *Application fee:* $0. *Application Contact:* Rev. Jonathan Fassero, OSB, Director of Enrollment, 812-357-6762, Fax: 812-357-6462, E-mail: jfassero@saintmeinrad.edu. *Academic Dean,* Dr. Thomas P. Walters, 812-357-6543, Fax: 812-357-6792, E-mail: twalters@saintmeinrad.edu.

Saint Meinrad School of Theology (continued)

Program in Catholic Thought and Life Students: 5 full-time (2 women), 21 part-time (11 women); includes 1 minority (Asian American or Pacific Islander) Average age 40. 47 applicants, 89% accepted. *Faculty:* 23 full-time (3 women), 7 part-time/adjunct (1 woman). Expenses: Contact institution. *Financial support:* In 2006–07, 8 students received support. Federal Work-Study, institutionally sponsored loans, and scholarships/grants available. Support available to part-time students. Financial award application deadline: 7/31; financial award applicants required to submit FAFSA. In 2006, 7 degrees awarded. *Degree program information:* Part-time and evening/weekend programs available. Offers Catholic thought and life (MA). *Application deadline:* For fall admission, 7/31 for domestic and international students; for winter admission, 11/15 for domestic and international students. Applications are processed on a rolling basis. *Application fee:* $25. *Application Contact:* Kyle Kramer, Director of Lay Degree Programs, 812-357-6678, Fax: 812-357-6792, E-mail: kkramer@saintmeinrad.edu. *Director of Lay Degree Programs,* Kyle Kramer, 812-357-6678, Fax: 812-357-6792, E-mail: kkramer@saintmeinrad.edu.

Program in Theological Studies Students: 3 full-time (2 women), 51 part-time (33 women). 47 applicants, 89% accepted. *Faculty:* 23 full-time (3 women), 7 part-time/adjunct (1 woman). Expenses: Contact institution. *Financial support:* In 2006–07, 26 students received support. Federal Work-Study, institutionally sponsored loans, and scholarships/grants available. Support available to part-time students. Financial award application deadline: 7/31; financial award applicants required to submit FAFSA. In 2006, 9 degrees awarded. *Degree program information:* Part-time and evening/weekend programs available. Offers theological studies (MTS). *Application deadline:* For fall admission, 7/31 for domestic and international students; for winter admission, 11/15 for domestic and international students. Applications are processed on a rolling basis. *Application fee:* $25. *Application Contact:* Kyle Kramer, Director of Lay Degree Programs, 812-357-6678, Fax: 812-357-6792, E-mail: kkramer@saintmeinrad.edu. *Director of Lay Degree Programs,* Kyle Kramer, 812-357-6678, Fax: 812-357-6792, E-mail: kkramer@saintmeinrad.edu.

SAINT MICHAEL'S COLLEGE, Colchester, VT 05439

General Information Independent-religious, coed, comprehensive institution. *Enrollment:* 2,437 graduate, professional, and undergraduate students; 86 full-time matriculated graduate/professional students (60 women), 220 part-time matriculated graduate/professional students (158 women). *Enrollment by degree level:* 299 master's, 7 other advanced degrees. *Graduate faculty:* 25 full-time (11 women), 84 part-time/adjunct (49 women). *Graduate housing:* On-campus housing not available. *Student services:* Campus employment opportunities, campus safety program, career counseling, international student services. *Library facilities:* Durick Library. *Online resources:* library catalog, web page, access to other libraries' catalogs. *Collection:* 241,574 titles, 2,337 serial subscriptions, 7,616 audiovisual materials.

Computer facilities: 233 computers available on campus for general student use. A campuswide network can be accessed from student residence rooms and from off campus. Internet access and online class registration are available. *Web address:* http://www.smcvt.edu/.

General Application Contact: Dee M. Goodrich, Director of Admissions and Marketing, Graduate Programs, 802-654-2251, Fax: 802-654-2906, E-mail: dgoodrich@smcvt.edu.

GRADUATE UNITS

Graduate Programs Students: 85 full-time (59 women), 214 part-time (153 women); includes 7 minority (1 African American, 1 American Indian/Alaska Native, 3 Asian Americans or Pacific Islanders, 2 Hispanic Americans). Average age 35. 116 applicants, 78% accepted, 74 enrolled. *Faculty:* 25 full-time (11 women), 84 part-time/adjunct (49 women). Expenses: Contact institution. *Financial support:* Fellowships, research assistantships, teaching assistantships with full tuition reimbursements, career-related internships or fieldwork, Federal Work-Study, institutionally sponsored loans, scholarships/grants, tuition waivers (partial), and unspecified assistantships available. Financial award applicants required to submit FAFSA. In 2006, 136 degrees awarded. *Degree program information:* Part-time and evening/weekend programs available. Offers administration (M Ed, CAGS); administration and management (MSA, CAMS); arts in education (CAGS); clinical psychology (MA); curriculum and instruction (M Ed, CAGS); information technology (CAGS); reading (M Ed); special education (M Ed, CAGS); teaching English as a second language (MATESL, Certificate); technology (M Ed); theology (MA, CAS, Certificate). *Application deadline:* Applications are processed on a rolling basis. *Application fee:* $35. Electronic applications accepted. *Dean,* Dr. Jeffrey Trumbower, 802-654-2100, Fax: 802-654-2664.

ST. NORBERT COLLEGE, De Pere, WI 54115-2099

General Information Independent-religious, coed, comprehensive institution. *Enrollment:* 2,072 graduate, professional, and undergraduate students; 73 part-time matriculated graduate/professional students (44 women). *Enrollment by degree level:* 73 master's. *Graduate faculty:* 2 full-time (both women), 5 part-time/adjunct (3 women). *Tuition:* Part-time $335 per credit. *Graduate housing:* On-campus housing not available. *Student services:* Campus employment opportunities, campus safety program, career counseling, child daycare facilities, disabled student services, exercise/wellness program, free psychological counseling, international student services, low-cost health insurance, multicultural affairs office, teacher training, writing training. *Library facilities:* Todd Wehr Library. *Online resources:* library catalog, web page, access to other libraries' catalogs. *Collection:* 223,096 titles, 580 serial subscriptions, 6,640 audiovisual materials.

Computer facilities: Computer purchase and lease plans are available. 219 computers available on campus for general student use. A campuswide network can be accessed from student residence rooms and from off campus. Internet access and online class registration are available. *Web address:* http://www.snc.edu/.

General Application Contact: DeEtte L. Radant, Program Coordinator, 920-403-3957, Fax: 920-403-4086, E-mail: deette.radant@snc.edu.

GRADUATE UNITS

Program in Education 30 applicants, 53% accepted, 15 enrolled. *Faculty:* 2 full-time (both women), 1 (woman) part-time/adjunct. Expenses: Contact institution. *Financial support:* Scholarships/grants and tuition waivers (partial) available. Support available to part-time students. *Degree program information:* Part-time and evening/weekend programs available. Offers education (MS). *Application deadline:* Applications are processed on a rolling basis. *Application fee:* $35. Electronic applications accepted. *Application Contact:* Karen L. Cleereman, Office Manager, Fax: 920-403-4078, E-mail: karen.cleereman@snc.edu. *Director/Professor,* Dr. Susan Landt, 920-403-1328, Fax: 920-403-4078, E-mail: susan.landt@snc.edu.

Program in Theological Studies 2 applicants, 100% accepted, 1 enrolled. *Faculty:* 4 part-time/adjunct (2 women). Expenses: Contact institution. *Financial support:* In 2006–07, 8 students received support. Scholarships/grants available. Support available to part-time students. In 2006, 3 degrees awarded. *Degree program information:* Part-time programs available. Offers theological studies (MTS). *Application deadline:* Applications are processed on a rolling basis. *Application fee:* $50. Electronic applications accepted. *Application Contact:* DeEtte L. Radant, Program Coordinator, 920-403-3957, Fax: 920-403-4086, E-mail: deette.radant@snc.edu. *Director,* Dr. Howard Ebert, 920-403-3956, Fax: 920-403-4086, E-mail: howard.ebert@snc.edu.

ST. PATRICK'S SEMINARY & UNIVERSITY, Menlo Park, CA 94025-3596

General Information Independent-religious, coed, primarily men, graduate-only institution. *Enrollment by degree level:* 63 first professional, 14 master's. *Graduate faculty:* 15 full-time (4 women), 12 part-time/adjunct (4 women). *Tuition:* Full-time $11,632; part-time $300 per unit. *Required fees:* $600. One-time fee: $2,800 full-time. *Graduate housing:* Room and/or apartments guaranteed to single students; on-campus housing not available to married students. Typical cost: $9,675 (including board). Housing application deadline: 8/15. *Student services:* Campus employment opportunities, campus safety program, career counseling, disabled student services, free psychological counseling, international student services, writing training. *Library facilities:* McKeon Memorial Library. *Online resources:* library catalog, access to other libraries' catalogs. *Collection:* 120,233 titles, 313 serial subscriptions, 1,432 audiovisual materials.

Computer facilities: 12 computers available on campus for general student use. A campuswide network can be accessed from student residence rooms. Internet access is available. *Web address:* http://www.stpatricksseminary.org/.

General Application Contact: Dr. Dorothy A. Tully, Academic Dean, 650-325-5621 Ext. 109, Fax: 650-322-0997, E-mail: dtully@stpatricksseminary.org.

GRADUATE UNITS

School of Theology Students: 77 full-time (0 women); includes 25 minority (16 Asian Americans or Pacific Islanders, 9 Hispanic Americans), 35 international. Average age 35. 13 applicants, 100% accepted, 13 enrolled. *Faculty:* 15 full-time (4 women), 12 part-time/adjunct (4 women). Expenses: Contact institution. *Financial support:* Tuition waivers (partial) available. Financial award application deadline: 10/1. In 2006, 12 M Divs, 2 master's awarded. *Degree program information:* Part-time programs available. Offers theology (M Div, STB, MA). *Application deadline:* For fall admission, 8/15 priority date for domestic and international students; for spring admission, 1/3 priority date for domestic and international students. Applications are processed on a rolling basis. *Application fee:* $200. *Application Contact:* Rev. Gerald L. Brown, President/Rector, 650-325-5621, Fax: 650-322-0997, E-mail: jbrown07@ix.netcom.com. *Academic Dean,* Dr. Dorothy A. Tully, 650-325-5621 Ext. 109, Fax: 650-322-0997, E-mail: dtully@stpatricksseminary.org.

SAINT PAUL SCHOOL OF THEOLOGY, Kansas City, MO 64127-2440

General Information Independent-religious, coed, graduate-only institution. *Graduate housing:* Rooms and/or apartments available to single and married students. Housing application deadline: 5/31.

GRADUATE UNITS

Graduate and Professional Programs *Degree program information:* Part-time programs available. Offers theology (M Div, MTS, D Min).

SAINT PAUL UNIVERSITY, Ottawa, ON K1S 1C4, Canada

General Information Province-supported, coed, university. *Graduate housing:* Room and/or apartments available to single students; on-campus housing not available to married students.

GRADUATE UNITS

Faculty of Canon Law Students: 55 full-time (6 women), 1 (woman) part-time; includes 27 minority (14 African Americans, 13 Asian Americans or Pacific Islanders). Average age 40. 23 applicants, 87% accepted, 11 enrolled. *Faculty:* 10 full-time (1 woman), 9 part-time/adjunct (2 women). Expenses: Contact institution. *Financial support:* In 2006–07, 3 students received support. Scholarships/grants and bursaries available. In 2006, 13 master's, 3 doctorates, 27 other advanced degrees awarded. *Degree program information:* Part-time programs available. Offers canon law (MCL, JCD, PhD, Graduate Certificate, JCL); canonical practice (Graduate Certificate); ecclesiastical administration (Graduate Certificate). *Application deadline:* For fall admission, 8/15 priority date for domestic students, 5/15 priority date for international students. Applications are processed on a rolling basis. *Application fee:* $60 Canadian dollars. *Application Contact:* Beverly Ruth Kavanaugh, Administrative Assistant, 613-751-4018, Fax: 613-751-4036, E-mail: bkavanaugh@ustpaul.ca. *Dean,* Dr. Roland Jacques, 613-751-4035, Fax: 613-751-4036, E-mail: rjacques@ustpaul.ca.

Faculty of Human Sciences Students: 78 full-time (53 women), 15 part-time (10 women), 5 international. 50 applicants, 70% accepted, 28 enrolled. *Faculty:* 16 full-time. Expenses: Contact institution. *Financial support:* Research assistantships, institutionally sponsored loans available. In 2006, 25 degrees awarded. Offers conflict studies (MA); counseling and spirituality (MA); individual and/or marital/couple counseling (MA Past St); mission and inter-religious studies (MA); pastoral care in health care services (MA Past St). Program offered in French and English. *Application deadline:* For fall admission, 3/31 priority date for domestic and international students; for spring admission, 5/1 priority date for domestic students. *Application fee:* $60. *Application Contact:* Janik Lowe. *Dean,* Dr. Giles Fortias, 613-236-1393, E-mail: dogenfsh@ustpaul.ca.

Faculty of Theology Students: 63 full-time (23 women), 14 part-time (9 women), 20 international. *Faculty:* 26 full-time (6 women), 8 part-time/adjunct (0 women). Expenses: Contact institution. In 2006, 10 master's, 5 doctorates, 9 other advanced degrees awarded. Offers theology (MA Th, MP Th, MRE, D Min, D Th, PhD, L Th). *Application deadline:* For fall admission, 6/15 priority date for domestic students; for winter admission, 10/15 for domestic students. Applications are processed on a rolling basis. *Application fee:* $60. *Application Contact:* Francine Forgues, Associate Registrar, 613-236-1393 Ext. 2237, Fax: 613-782-3014, E-mail: fforgues@ustpaul.ca. *Dean,* Dr. Normand Bonneau, 613-236-1393 Ext. 2277, Fax: 613-751-4016, E-mail: nbonneau@ustpaul.ca.

ST. PETERSBURG THEOLOGICAL SEMINARY, St. Petersburg, FL 33708

General Information Independent-religious, coed, upper-level institution.

GRADUATE UNITS

Graduate Programs

SAINT PETER'S COLLEGE, Jersey City, NJ 07306-5997

General Information Independent-religious, coed, comprehensive institution. *Graduate housing:* On-campus housing not available.

GRADUATE UNITS

Graduate Programs in Education *Degree program information:* Part-time and evening/weekend programs available. Offers administration and supervision (MA); elementary teacher (Certificate); reading specialist (MA); supervisor of instruction (Certificate); teaching (MA, Certificate); urban education (MA).

MBA Programs *Degree program information:* Part-time and evening/weekend programs available. Offers finance (MBA); international business (MBA); management (MBA); management information systems (MBA); marketing (MBA).

Nursing Program *Degree program information:* Part-time and evening/weekend programs available. Offers nursing (MSN).

Program in Accountancy *Degree program information:* Part-time and evening/weekend programs available. Offers accountancy (MS, Certificate).

See Close-Up on page 1017.

ST. PETER'S SEMINARY, London, ON N6A 3Y1, Canada

General Information Independent-religious, coed, primarily men, graduate-only institution.

GRADUATE UNITS

Department of Theology Offers theology (M Div, MTS).

SAINTS CYRIL AND METHODIUS SEMINARY, Orchard Lake, MI 48324

General Information Independent-religious, coed, graduate-only institution. *Graduate housing:* Room and/or apartments guaranteed to single students; on-campus housing not available to married students. Housing application deadline: 7/1.

GRADUATE UNITS

Graduate and Professional Programs *Degree program information:* Part-time programs available. Offers pastoral ministry (MAPM); religious education (MARE); theology (M Div, MA).

ST. STEPHEN'S COLLEGE, Edmonton, AB T6G 2J6, Canada

General Information Independent-religious, coed, graduate-only institution. *Graduate housing:* On-campus housing not available.

GRADUATE UNITS

Programs in Theology *Degree program information:* Part-time and evening/weekend programs available. Postbaccalaureate distance learning degree programs offered (minimal on-campus study). Offers ministry (D Min); pastoral counseling (MA); social transformation ministry (MA); spirituality and liturgy (MA); theological studies (MTS); theology (M Th). Electronic applications accepted.

ST. THOMAS AQUINAS COLLEGE, Sparkill, NY 10976

General Information Independent, coed, comprehensive institution. *Graduate housing:* On-campus housing not available. *Research affiliation:* Lederle Laboratories (science education), Lamont Doherty Laboratories (science education).

GRADUATE UNITS

Division of Business Administration *Degree program information:* Part-time and evening/weekend programs available. Offers business administration (MBA); finance (MBA); management (MBA); marketing (MBA). Electronic applications accepted.

Division of Teacher Education *Degree program information:* Part-time and evening/weekend programs available. Offers adolescence education (MST); childhood and special education (MST); childhood education (MST); reading (MS Ed, PMC); special education (MS Ed, PMC); teaching (MS Ed). Electronic applications accepted.

ST. THOMAS UNIVERSITY, Miami Gardens, FL 33054-6459

General Information Independent-religious, coed, comprehensive institution. *Graduate housing:* Room and/or apartments available on a first-come, first-served basis to single students; on-campus housing not available to married students. Housing application deadline: 7/1.

GRADUATE UNITS

School of Graduate Studies *Degree program information:* Part-time and evening/weekend programs available. Offers accounting (MBA); business administration (M Acc, MBA, Certificate); communication arts (MA); educational administration (MS, Certificate); educational leadership (Ed D); elementary education (MS); general management (MSM, Certificate); guidance and counseling (MS, Post-Master's Certificate); health management (MBA, MSM, Certificate); Hispanic media (MA, Certificate); human resource management (MBA, MSM, Certificate); international business (MBA, MIB, MSM, Certificate); justice administration (MSM, Certificate); management accounting (MSM, Certificate); marriage and family therapy (MS, Post-Master's Certificate); mental health counseling (MS); public management (MSM, Certificate); reading (MS); special education (MS). Electronic applications accepted.

Institute for Pastoral Ministries *Degree program information:* Part-time and evening/weekend programs available. Offers pastoral ministries (MA, Certificate); practical theology (PhD). Electronic applications accepted.

School of Law Postbaccalaureate distance learning degree programs offered (no on-campus study). Offers international human rights (LL M); international taxation (LL M); law (JD). Electronic applications accepted.

ST. TIKHON'S ORTHODOX THEOLOGICAL SEMINARY, South Canaan, PA 18459

General Information Independent-religious, men only, graduate-only institution. *Enrollment by degree level:* 55 first professional. *Graduate faculty:* 8 full-time (1 woman), 6 part-time/adjunct (0 women). *Tuition:* Full-time $2,550; part-time $85 per credit. *Required fees:* $10 per term. One-time fee: $150. *Graduate housing:* Room and/or apartments guaranteed to single students; on-campus housing not available to married students. Typical cost: $600 per year ($1,650 including board). *Student services:* Career counseling. *Library facilities:* Patriarch Tikhon. *Online resources:* library catalog, web page, access to other libraries' catalogs. *Collection:* 47,000 titles, 232 serial subscriptions, 533 audiovisual materials.

Computer facilities: 25 computers available on campus for general student use. Internet access is available. *Web address:* http://www.stots.edu/.

General Application Contact: Fr. Michael Dahulich, Dean and Director of Admissions, 570-937-4411 Ext. 113, Fax: 570-937-3100, E-mail: fr.michael@stots.edu.

GRADUATE UNITS

Divinity Program Students: 48 full-time (0 women), 7 part-time, 5 international. 35 applicants, 80% accepted, 28 enrolled. *Faculty:* 8 full-time (1 woman), 6 part-time/adjunct (0 women). Expenses: Contact institution. *Financial support:* Fellowships with partial tuition reimbursements, career-related internships or fieldwork, institutionally sponsored loans, scholarships/grants, and tuition waivers (partial) available. In 2006, 13 degrees awarded. Offers divinity (M Div). *Application deadline:* For fall admission, 7/30 for domestic students, 6/30 for international students. Applications are processed on a rolling basis. *Application fee:* $15. *Application Contact:* Fr. Michael Dahulich, Dean, Director of Admissions, 570-937-4411, Fax: 570-937-3100, E-mail: fr.michael@stots.edu. *Rector,* Bp. Tikhon Mollard, 570-937-4411, Fax: 570-937-4139, E-mail: bp.tikhon@stots.edu.

SAINT VINCENT COLLEGE, Latrobe, PA 15650-2690

General Information Independent-religious, coed, comprehensive institution. *Graduate housing:* Room and/or apartments available on a first-come, first-served basis to single students; on-campus housing not available to married students.

GRADUATE UNITS

Program in Accounting *Degree program information:* Part-time and evening/weekend programs available. Offers accounting (MS).

Program in Education *Degree program information:* Part-time and evening/weekend programs available. Offers curriculum and instruction (MS); environmental education (MS); library media management (MS); school administration (MS); special education (MS).

SAINT VINCENT DE PAUL REGIONAL SEMINARY, Boynton Beach, FL 33436-4899

General Information Independent-religious, coed, primarily men, graduate-only institution. *Graduate housing:* Room and/or apartments guaranteed to single students; on-campus housing not available to married students.

GRADUATE UNITS

Graduate and Professional Programs *Degree program information:* Part-time programs available. Offers theology (M Div, MA Th).

SAINT VINCENT SEMINARY, Latrobe, PA 15650-2690

General Information Independent-religious, coed, primarily men, graduate-only institution. *Enrollment by degree level:* 52 first professional, 8 master's. *Graduate faculty:* 5 full-time (1 woman), 15 part-time/adjunct (0 women). *Tuition:* Part-time $560 per credit. *Required fees:* $156 per semester. *Graduate housing:* Room and/or apartments guaranteed to single students; on-campus housing not available to married students. Typical cost: $126 (including board). Housing application deadline: 8/1. *Student services:* Campus safety program, disabled student services, exercise/wellness program, international student services, writing training. *Library facilities:* Saint Vincent College Library. *Online resources:* library catalog, web page, access to other libraries' catalogs. *Collection:* 271,481 titles, 683 serial subscriptions, 4,271 audiovisual materials.

Computer facilities: 68 computers available on campus for general student use. A campuswide network can be accessed from student residence rooms and from off campus. Internet access is available. *Web address:* http://www.benedictine.stvincent.edu/seminary/.

General Application Contact: Rev. Cyprian G. Constantine, OSB, Academic Dean, 724-805-2324, Fax: 724-532-5052, E-mail: cyprian.constantine@email.stvincent.edu.

GRADUATE UNITS

School of Theology Students: 55 full-time (0 women), 5 part-time (4 women); includes 4 minority (2 Asian Americans or Pacific Islanders, 2 Hispanic Americans), 11 international. Average age 33. 21 applicants, 95% accepted, 19 enrolled. *Faculty:* 5 full-time (1 woman), 15 part-time/adjunct (0 women). Expenses: Contact institution. *Financial support:* In 2006–07, 60 students received support. Scholarships/grants available. Support available to part-time students. Financial award application deadline: 8/1; financial award applicants required to submit FAFSA. In 2006, 10 M Divs, 7 master's awarded. *Degree program information:* Part-time programs available. Offers theology (M Div, MA). *Application deadline:* For fall admission, 8/1 priority date for domestic students, 8/1 for international students. Applications are processed on a rolling basis. *Application fee:* $33. Electronic applications accepted. *Application Contact:* Rev. Cyprian G. Constantine, OSB, Academic Dean, 724-805-2324, Fax: 724-532-5052, E-mail: cyprian.constantine@email.stvincent.edu. *President/Rector,* Very Rev. Justin Matro, 724-537-4592, Fax: 724-532-5052, E-mail: justin.matro@email.stvincent.edu.

ST. VLADIMIR'S ORTHODOX THEOLOGICAL SEMINARY, Crestwood, NY 10707-1699

General Information Independent-religious, coed, primarily men, graduate-only institution. *Graduate housing:* Rooms and/or apartments available on a first-come, first-served basis to single and married students. Housing application deadline: 5/1.

GRADUATE UNITS

Graduate School of Theology *Degree program information:* Part-time programs available. Offers general theological studies (MA); liturgical music (MA); religious education (MA); theology (M Div, M Th, D Min). MA in general theological studies, M Div offered jointly with St. Nersess Seminary.

SAINT XAVIER UNIVERSITY, Chicago, IL 60655-3105

General Information Independent-religious, coed, comprehensive institution. *Enrollment:* 5,657 graduate, professional, and undergraduate students; 221 full-time matriculated graduate/professional students (147 women), 2,120 part-time matriculated graduate/professional students (1,717 women). *Graduate faculty:* 152. *Graduate housing:* Room and/or apartments available on a first-come, first-served basis to single students; on-campus housing not available to married students. Housing application deadline: 8/15. *Student services:* Campus employment opportunities, career counseling, child daycare facilities, free psychological counseling, international student services, low-cost health insurance, teacher training. *Library facilities:* Byrne Memorial Library. *Online resources:* library catalog, web page, access to other libraries' catalogs. *Collection:* 170,753 titles, 717 serial subscriptions. *Research affiliation:* Alexian Brothers Hospital, Holy Cross Hospital, Little Company of Mary Hospital, Mercy Center for Health Care Services.

Computer facilities: 306 computers available on campus for general student use. A campuswide network can be accessed from student residence rooms and from off campus. Internet access is available. *Web address:* http://www.sxu.edu/.

General Application Contact: Beth Gierach, Vice President of Enrollment Services, 773-298-3050, Fax: 773-298-3076, E-mail: gierach@sxu.edu.

GRADUATE UNITS

Graduate Studies Students: 221 full-time (147 women), 2,120 part-time (1,717 women). Average age 33. *Faculty:* 152. Expenses: Contact institution. *Financial support:* Research assistantships, teaching assistantships, career-related internships or fieldwork available. Support available to part-time students. Financial award applicants required to submit FAFSA. In 2006, 1087 degrees awarded. *Degree program information:* Part-time and evening/weekend programs available. *Application deadline:* Applications are processed on a rolling basis. *Application fee:* $35. Electronic applications accepted. *Application Contact:* Beth Gierach, Managing Director of Admission, 773-298-3053, Fax: 773-298-3076, E-mail: gierach@sxu.edu. *Vice President of Academic Affairs,* 773-298-3194, Fax: 773-298-3002.

Graham School of Management Students: 67 full-time (32 women), 291 part-time (152 women). Average age 35. *Faculty:* 27. Expenses: Contact institution. *Financial support:* Career-related internships or fieldwork available. Support available to part-time students. Financial award applicants required to submit FAFSA. In 2006, 61 degrees awarded. *Degree program information:* Part-time and evening/weekend programs available. Offers e-commerce (MBA); employee health benefits (Certificate); finance (MBA, MS); financial analysis and investments (MBA); financial planning (MBA, Certificate); financial trading and practice (MBA, Certificate); generalist/administration (MBA); health administration (MBA, MS); managed care (Certificate); management (MBA, MS); marketing (MBA); public and non-profit management (MBA); public health (MPH); service management (MBA); training and performance management (MBA). *Application deadline:* For fall admission, 8/15 for domestic students. Applications are processed on a rolling basis. *Application fee:* $35. Electronic applications accepted. *Application Contact:* Beth Gierach, Managing Director of Admission, 773-298-3053, Fax: 773-298-3076, E-mail: gierach@sxu.edu. *Dean,* Dr. John Eber, 773-298-3601, Fax: 773-298-3601, E-mail: eber@sxu.edu.

School of Arts and Sciences Students: 18 full-time (10 women), 101 part-time (72 women). *Faculty:* 19. Expenses: Contact institution. *Financial support:* Research assistantships, teaching assistantships, career-related internships or fieldwork available. Support available to part-time students. Financial award applicants required to submit FAFSA. In 2006, 36 degrees awarded. *Degree program information:* Part-time and evening/weekend programs available. Offers adult counseling (Certificate); applied computer science in Internet information systems (MS); arts and sciences (MA, MS, CAS, Certificate); child/adolescent counseling (Certificate); core counseling (Certificate); counseling psychology (MA); English (CAS); literary studies (MA); mathematics and computer science (MA); speech-language pathology (MS); teaching of writing (MA); writing pedagogy (CAS). *Application deadline:* For fall admission, 8/15 for domestic students. *Application fee:* $35. *Application Contact:* Beth Gierach, Managing Director of Admission, 773-298-3053, Fax: 773-298-3076, E-mail: gierach@sxu.edu. *Dean,* Dr. Lawrence Frank, 773-298-3090, Fax: 773-779-9061, E-mail: lfrank@sxu.edu.

School of Education Students: 45 full-time (35 women), 1,529 part-time (1,309 women). *Faculty:* 92. Expenses: Contact institution. *Financial support:* Career-related internships or fieldwork available. Support available to part-time students. Financial award applicants required to submit FAFSA. In 2006, 474 degrees awarded. *Degree program information:* Part-time and evening/weekend programs available. Offers counseling (MA); counselor education (MA); curriculum and instruction (MA); early childhood education (MA); education (CAS); educational administration (MA); elementary education (MA); field-based education (MA); general educational studies (MA); individualized program (MA); learning disabilities (MA); reading (MA); secondary education (MA). *Application deadline:* For fall admission, 8/15 priority date for domestic students. Applications are processed on a rolling basis. *Application fee:* $35. *Application Contact:* Beth Gierach, Managing Director of Admission, 773-298-3053, Fax: 773-298-3076, E-mail: gierach@sxu.edu. *Dean,* Dr. Beverly Gulley, 773-298-3221, Fax: 773-779-9061, E-mail: gulley@sxu.edu.

School of Nursing Students: 20 full-time (14 women), 120 part-time (113 women). Average age 40. *Faculty:* 11. Expenses: Contact institution. *Financial support:* Available to part-time students. Applicants required to submit FAFSA. In 2006, 36 degrees awarded. *Degree program information:* Part-time and evening/weekend programs available. Offers adult health clinical nurse specialist (MS); family nurse practitioner (MS, PMC); leadership in community health nursing (MS); psychiatric-mental health clinical nurse specialist (MS); psychiatric-mental health clinical specialist (PMC). *Application deadline:* For fall admission, 2/15 for domestic students; for spring admission, 9/15 for domestic students. Applications are processed on a rolling basis. *Application fee:* $35. *Managing Director of Admission,* Beth Gierach, 773-298-3053, Fax: 773-298-3076, E-mail: gierach@sxu.edu.

SALEM COLLEGE, Winston-Salem, NC 27108-0548

General Information Independent-religious, Undergraduate: women only; graduate: coed, comprehensive institution. *Enrollment:* 1,094 graduate, professional, and undergraduate students; 8 full-time matriculated graduate/professional students (all women), 250 part-time matriculated graduate/professional students (238 women). *Enrollment by degree level:* 258 master's. *Graduate faculty:* 8 full-time (6 women), 5 part-time/adjunct (all women). *Graduate housing:* On-campus housing not available. *Student services:* Campus employment opportunities, campus safety program, career counseling, teacher training, writing training. *Library facilities:* Gramley Library plus 1 other. *Online resources:* library catalog, web page, access to other libraries' catalogs. *Collection:* 151,719 titles, 679 serial subscriptions, 14,187 audiovisual materials.

Computer facilities: 54 computers available on campus for general student use. A campuswide network can be accessed from student residence rooms and from off campus. Internet access, e-mail are available. *Web address:* http://www.salem.edu/.

General Application Contact: Dr. Paula Grubbs, Director of Teacher Education, 336-721-2610, Fax: 336-721-2683, E-mail: grubbs@salem.edu.

GRADUATE UNITS

Department of Education Students: 8 full-time (all women), 250 part-time (238 women); includes 19 minority (16 African Americans, 1 Asian American or Pacific Islander, 2 Hispanic Americans). Average age 33. 110 applicants, 65% accepted, 68 enrolled. *Faculty:* 8 full-time (6 women), 5 part-time/adjunct (all women). Expenses: Contact institution. *Financial support:* In 2006–07, 152 students received support. Federal Work-Study and scholarships/grants available. Support available to part-time students. Financial award applicants required to submit FAFSA. In 2006, 34 degrees awarded. *Degree program information:* Part-time and evening/weekend programs available. Offers early education and leadership (MAT); elementary education (MAT); English as a second language (MAT); language and literacy (M Ed); middle school education (MAT); secondary education (MAT); special education (MAT). *Application deadline:* Applications are processed on a rolling basis. *Application fee:* $30. *Director of Teacher Education,* Dr. Paula Grubbs, 336-721-2610, Fax: 336-721-2683, E-mail: grubbs@salem.edu.

SALEM INTERNATIONAL UNIVERSITY, Salem, WV 26426-0500

General Information Independent, coed, comprehensive institution. *Enrollment:* 786 graduate, professional, and undergraduate students; 124 full-time matriculated graduate/professional students (67 women), 242 part-time matriculated graduate/professional students (106 women). *Enrollment by degree level:* 366 master's. *Graduate faculty:* 13 full-time (6 women), 30 part-time/adjunct (12 women). *Tuition:* Part-time $340 per credit hour. One-time fee: $25 part-time. Tuition and fees vary according to program. *Graduate housing:* Rooms and/or apartments available on a first-come, first-served basis to single students and available to married students. Typical cost: $1,990 per year ($5,360 including board) for single students; $1,990 per year ($5,360 including board) for married students. Room and board charges vary according to board plan. *Student services:* Campus employment opportunities, career counseling, disabled student services, international student services, low-cost health insurance. *Library facilities:* Benedum Library. *Online resources:* library catalog, web page. *Collection:* 106,991 titles, 43 serial subscriptions, 1,173 audiovisual materials.

Computer facilities: 50 computers available on campus for general student use. A campuswide network can be accessed from off campus. *Web address:* http://www.salemu.edu/.

General Application Contact: Gina Cossey, Vice President/Recruiting and Admissions, 304-326-1359, Fax: 304-326-1592, E-mail: admissions@salemiu.edu.

GRADUATE UNITS

School of Business Students: 50 full-time (22 women), 88 part-time (31 women); includes 1 minority (African American), 87 international. 9 applicants, 56% accepted, 5 enrolled. *Faculty:* 8 full-time (2 women), 13 part-time/adjunct (4 women). Expenses: Contact institution. *Financial support:* In 2006–07, 1 student received support. Career-related internships or fieldwork, institutionally sponsored loans, and tuition waivers (partial) available. In 2006, 1 degree awarded. *Degree program information:* Part-time programs available. Postbaccalaureate distance learning degree programs offered (no on-campus study). Offers information security (eMBA); international business (MBA). *Application deadline:* For fall admission, 8/15 priority date for domestic and international students; for winter admission, 12/15 priority date for domestic and international students; for spring admission, 4/15 priority date for domestic and international students. Applications are processed on a rolling basis. *Application fee:* $25. Electronic applications accepted. *Application Contact:* Thomas White, Director of Admissions, 304-326-1549, Fax: 304-326-1246, E-mail: admission@salemiu.edu. *Dean,* 304-326-1609, Fax: 304-326-1246.

School of Education Students: 74 full-time (45 women), 154 part-time (75 women); includes 7 minority (2 African Americans, 5 Asian Americans or Pacific Islanders), 28 international. Average age 41. 200 applicants, 75% accepted, 130 enrolled. *Faculty:* 5 full-time (4 women), 17 part-time/adjunct (8 women). Expenses: Contact institution. *Financial support:* Application deadline: 4/15; In 2006, 18 degrees awarded. *Degree program information:* Part-time and evening/weekend programs available. Postbaccalaureate distance learning degree programs offered. Offers curriculum and instruction (M Ed); educational administration (M Ed). *Application deadline:* Applications are processed on a rolling basis. *Application fee:* $25. Electronic applications accepted. *Application Contact:* Thomas White, Director of Admissions, 304-326-1549, Fax: 304-326-1246, E-mail: admission@salemiu.edu. *Dean, School of Education,* 304-326-1253, Fax: 304-326-1246.

SALEM STATE COLLEGE, Salem, MA 01970-5353

General Information State-supported, coed, comprehensive institution. CGS member. *Enrollment:* 10,230 graduate, professional, and undergraduate students; 271 full-time matriculated graduate/professional students (223 women), 1,108 part-time matriculated graduate/professional students (869 women). *Enrollment by degree level:* 1,379 master's. *Graduate faculty:* 320 full-time (160 women), 397 part-time/adjunct (169 women). *Graduate housing:* On-campus housing not available. *Student services:* Campus employment opportunities, campus safety program, career counseling, child daycare facilities, disabled student services, exercise/wellness program, free psychological counseling, international student services, low-cost health insurance, multicultural affairs office, teacher training, writing training. *Library facilities:* Salem State College Library. *Online resources:* library catalog, web page, access to other libraries' catalogs. *Collection:* 277,985 titles, 1,914 serial subscriptions, 3,811 audiovisual materials.

Computer facilities: Computer purchase and lease plans are available. 426 computers available on campus for general student use. A campuswide network can be accessed from student residence rooms and from off campus. Internet access is available. *Web address:* http://www.salemstate.edu/.

General Application Contact: Dr. Marc Glasser, Dean of the Graduate School, 978-542-6323, Fax: 978-542-7215.

GRADUATE UNITS

Graduate School Students: 271 full-time (223 women), 1,108 part-time (869 women); includes 76 minority (26 African Americans, 3 American Indian/Alaska Native, 16 Asian Americans or Pacific Islanders, 31 Hispanic Americans), 36 international. Average age 35. *Faculty:* 392 full-time (232 women), 285 part-time/adjunct (57 women). Expenses: Contact institution. *Financial support:* Fellowships with partial tuition reimbursements, research assistantships with full tuition reimbursements, career-related internships or fieldwork and Federal Work-Study available. Support available to part-time students. In 2006, 468 master's, 42 other advanced degrees awarded. *Degree program information:* Part-time and evening/weekend programs available. Offers advanced practice in rehabilitation (MSN); art (MAT); bilingual education (M Ed); biology (MAT); business administration (MBA); chemistry (MAT); counseling and psychological services (MS); criminal justice (MS); direct entry nursing (MSN); early childhood education (M Ed); educational leadership (CAGS); elementary education (M Ed); English (MA, MAT); English as a second language (MAT); field-based education (M Ed); geo-information science (MS); higher education in student affairs (M Ed); history (MA, MAT); innovative practices (CAGS); library media studies (M Ed); mathematics (MS); middle school education (M Ed, MAT); nursing (MSN); physical education 5-12 (M Ed); physical education K-9 (M Ed); reading (M Ed, CAGS); reading, literacy and language (CAGS); school business officer (M Ed); school counseling (M Ed); secondary education (M Ed); social work (MSW); Spanish (MAT); special education (M Ed, MAT); teaching English as a second language (MAT); technology in education (M Ed). *Application deadline:* Applications are processed on a rolling basis. *Application fee:* $35. *Dean of the Graduate School,* Dr. Marc Glasser, 978-542-6323, Fax: 978-542-7215.

SALISBURY UNIVERSITY, Salisbury, MD 21801-6837

General Information State-supported, coed, comprehensive institution. *Enrollment:* 7,383 graduate, professional, and undergraduate students; 147 full-time matriculated graduate/professional students (100 women), 287 part-time matriculated graduate/professional students (221 women). *Enrollment by degree level:* 434 master's. *Graduate faculty:* 71 full-time (30 women), 14 part-time/adjunct (12 women). Tuition, state resident: part-time $260 per credit hour. Tuition, nonresident: part-time $546 per credit hour. *Required fees:* $52 per credit hour. *Student services:* Campus employment opportunities, campus safety program, career counseling, disabled student services, free psychological counseling, international student services, multicultural affairs office. *Library facilities:* Blackwell Library plus 1 other. *Online resources:* library catalog, web page, access to other libraries' catalogs. *Collection:* 269,550 titles, 1,235 serial subscriptions. *Research affiliation:* NASA (mathematics, physics).

Computer facilities: Computer purchase and lease plans are available. 275 computers available on campus for general student use. A campuswide network can be accessed from student residence rooms and from off campus. Internet access and online class registration, e-mail services/accounts for all students are available. *Web address:* http://www.ssu.edu/.

General Application Contact: Gary E. Grodzicki, Associate Dean of Admissions, 410-543-6161, Fax: 410-546-6016, E-mail: admissions@salisbury.edu.

GRADUATE UNITS

Graduate Division Students: 147 full-time (100 women), 287 part-time (221 women); includes 39 African Americans, 3 Asian Americans or Pacific Islanders, 8 Hispanic Americans, 16 international. Average age 32. 235 applicants, 70% accepted, 150 enrolled. *Faculty:* 71 full-time (30 women), 14 part-time/adjunct (12 women). Expenses: Contact institution. *Financial support:* In 2006–07, 350 students received support; fellowships, research assistantships with full tuition reimbursements available, teaching assistantships with full tuition reimbursements available, career-related internships or fieldwork, institutionally sponsored loans, scholarships/grants, and unspecified assistantships available. Support available to part-time students. Financial award application deadline: 2/1; financial award applicants required to submit FAFSA. In 2006, 209 degrees awarded. *Degree program information:* Part-time and evening/weekend programs available. Offers applied health physiology (MS); art (MAT); biology (MAT); business administration (MBA); business education (MAT); chemistry (MAT); composition, language and rhetoric (MA); early childhood education (M Ed); educational administration (M Ed); elementary education (M Ed); English (M Ed, MAT); French (MAT); geography (MAT); history (MAT); literature (MA); mathematics (MAT); mathematics education (MS); media and technology (MAT); music (MAT); nursing (MS); psychology (MAT); public school administration (MS Ed); reading (M Ed); reading education (MAT); science (MAT); secondary education (MAT); social studies (MAT); social work (MSW); Spanish (MAT); teaching English to speakers of other languages (MA). *Application deadline:* Applications are processed on a rolling basis. *Application fee:* $45. Electronic applications accepted. *Application Contact:* Laura J Thorpe, Director of Admissions, 410-543-6161, Fax: 410-546-6016, E-mail: admissions@salisbury.edu.

SALVE REGINA UNIVERSITY, Newport, RI 02840-4192

General Information Independent-religious, coed, comprehensive institution. *Enrollment:* 2,589 graduate, professional, and undergraduate students; 76 full-time matriculated graduate/professional students (47 women), 333 part-time matriculated graduate/professional students (183 women). *Enrollment by degree level:* 352 master's, 57 doctoral. *Graduate faculty:* 8 full-time (3 women), 32 part-time/adjunct (12 women). *Graduate housing:* On-campus housing not available. *Student services:* Campus employment opportunities, campus safety program, career counseling, disabled student services, free psychological counseling, international student services, multicultural affairs office, writing training. *Library facilities:* McKillop Library. *Online resources:* library catalog, web page, access to other libraries' catalogs. *Collection:* 139,161 titles, 1,221 serial subscriptions.

Computer facilities: 163 computers available on campus for general student use. A campuswide network can be accessed from student residence rooms and from off campus. Internet access is available. *Web address:* http://www.salve.edu/.

General Application Contact: Karen E. Johnson, Graduate Admissions Counselor, 401-341-2153, Fax: 401-341-2973, E-mail: johnsonke@salve.edu.

GRADUATE UNITS

Graduate Studies Students: 77 full-time (51 women), 335 part-time (193 women); includes 5 minority (1 African American, 1 American Indian/Alaska Native, 1 Asian American or Pacific Islander, 2 Hispanic Americans). Average age 39. 266 applicants, 74% accepted, 169 enrolled. *Faculty:* 8 full-time (3 women), 32 part-time/adjunct (12 women). Expenses: Contact institution. *Financial support:* Career-related internships or fieldwork and Federal Work-Study available. Support available to part-time students. Financial award application deadline: 3/1. In 2006, 120 master's, 6 doctorates, 13 other advanced degrees awarded. *Degree program information:* Part-time and evening/weekend programs available. Postbaccalaureate distance learning degree programs offered (minimal on-campus study). Offers business administration (MBA); business studies (Certificate); expressive and creative arts (CAGS); health services administration (MS, Certificate); holistic counseling (MA); homeland security (Certificate); human resources management (Certificate); humanities (MA, PhD); international relations (MA, Certificate); justice and homeland security (MS); law enforcement leadership (MS, MSM); management (Certificate); mental health (CAGS); mental health counseling (CAGS); organizational development (Certificate); rehabilitation counseling (MA). *Application deadline:* For fall admission, 3/15 priority date for domestic and international students; for spring admission, 9/15 priority date for domestic and international students. Applications are processed on a rolling basis. *Application fee:* $50. Electronic applications accepted. *Application Contact:* Karen E. Johnson, Graduate Admissions Counselor, 401-341-2153, Fax: 401-341-2973, E-mail: johnsonke@salve.edu. *Dean,* Dr. Thomas M. Sabbagh, 401-341-2477, Fax: 401-341-2973, E-mail: thomas.sabbagh@salve.edu.

See Close-Up on page 1019.

SAMFORD UNIVERSITY, Birmingham, AL 35229-0002

General Information Independent-religious, coed, university. *Enrollment:* 4,478 graduate, professional, and undergraduate students; 1,295 full-time matriculated graduate/professional students (661 women), 301 part-time matriculated graduate/professional students (192 women). *Enrollment by degree level:* 1,139 first professional, 275 master's, 119 doctoral, 63 other advanced degrees. *Graduate faculty:* 128 full-time (45 women), 27 part-time/adjunct (10 women). *Tuition:* Part-time $500 per credit. One-time fee: $25 part-time. Full-time tuition and fees vary according to program and student level. *Graduate housing:* On-campus housing not available. *Student services:* Campus employment opportunities, campus safety program, career counseling, disabled student services, free psychological counseling, international student services, low-cost health insurance. *Library facilities:* Samford University Library plus 3 others. *Online resources:* library catalog, web page, access to other libraries' catalogs. *Collection:* 439,760 titles, 3,724 serial subscriptions. *Research affiliation:* Alabama Marine Consortium (marine research), Amazon Center for Environmental Education and Research (Amazon environmental research).

Computer facilities: Computer purchase and lease plans are available. 350 computers available on campus for general student use. A campuswide network can be accessed from student residence rooms. Internet access is available. *Web address:* http://www.samford.edu/.

General Application Contact: Dr. Phil Kimrey, Dean of Admissions and Financial Aid, 205-726-2871, Fax: 205-726-2171, E-mail: ppkimrey@samford.edu.

GRADUATE UNITS

Beeson School of Divinity Students: 199 full-time (44 women), 13 part-time (6 women); includes 37 minority (34 African Americans, 1 Asian American or Pacific Islander, 2 Hispanic Americans), 5 international. Average age 32. 99 applicants, 57% accepted, 48 enrolled. *Faculty:* 14 full-time (3 women), 2 part-time/adjunct (1 woman). Expenses: Contact institution. *Financial support:* In 2006–07, 167 students received support. Scholarships/grants and tuition waivers (full and partial) available. Financial award applicants required to submit FAFSA. In 2006, 32 M Divs, 9 master's, 10 doctorates awarded. *Degree program information:* Part-time programs available. Offers divinity (M Div, MTS, D Min). *Application deadline:* For fall admission, 3/1 for domestic students; for spring admission, 10/1 for domestic students. *Application fee:* $50. *Dean,* Dr. Timothy George, 205-726-2632, E-mail: tgeorge@samford.edu.

Cumberland School of Law Students: 492 full-time (210 women), 7 part-time (4 women); includes 60 minority (43 African Americans, 4 American Indian/Alaska Native, 7 Asian Americans or Pacific Islanders, 6 Hispanic Americans). Average age 25. 1,425 applicants, 15% accepted, 199 enrolled. *Faculty:* 26 full-time (6 women), 14 part-time/adjunct (5 women). Expenses: Contact institution. *Financial support:* In 2006–07, 196 students received support. Career-related internships or fieldwork, Federal Work-Study, institutionally sponsored loans, and scholarships/grants available. Financial award application deadline: 3/1; financial award applicants required to submit FAFSA. In 2006, 193 JDs, 3 master's awarded. Offers law (JD, MCL). *Application deadline:* For fall admission, 2/28 priority date for domestic students. Applications are processed on a rolling basis. *Application fee:* $50. *Application Contact:* M. Giselle Gauthier, Director of Admissions, 205-726-2702, Fax: 205-726-2057, E-mail: law.admissions@samford.edu. *Dean,* John L. Carroll, 205-726-2704, Fax: 205-726-4107, E-mail: jlcarrol@samford.edu.

Howard College of Arts and Sciences Students: 2 full-time (1 woman), 13 part-time (6 women). Average age 30. 14 applicants, 100% accepted, 4 enrolled. *Faculty:* 8 full-time (0 women), 1 part-time/adjunct (0 women). Expenses: Contact institution. *Financial support:* In 2006–07, 1 student received support. In 2006, 10 degrees awarded. *Degree program information:* Part-time and evening/weekend programs available. Offers arts and sciences (MSEM). *Application deadline:* For fall admission, 8/30 for domestic students; for spring admission, 1/2 for domestic students. *Application fee:* $25. *Application Contact:* Dr. Ron Hunsinger, Head, 205-726-2944, Fax: 205-726-2479, E-mail: mhunsin@samford.edu. *Dean,* Dr. David W. Chapman, 205-726-2771, Fax: 205-726-2279.

Ida V. Moffett School of Nursing Students: 84 full-time (62 women), 21 part-time (15 women); includes 8 minority (6 African Americans, 2 Asian Americans or Pacific Islanders). Average age 33. 112 applicants, 62% accepted, 38 enrolled. *Faculty:* 8 full-time (all women). Expenses: Contact institution. *Financial support:* In 2006–07, 20 students received support. Career-related internships or fieldwork, Federal Work-Study, and institutionally sponsored loans available. Financial award application deadline: 3/1; financial award applicants required to submit FAFSA. In 2006, 32 degrees awarded. *Degree program information:* Part-time programs available. Offers nursing (MSN, MSNA). *Application deadline:* For spring admission, 1/2 for domestic students. Applications are processed on a rolling basis. *Application fee:* $25. *Application Contact:* Stacy W. Miner, Graduate Admissions and Alumni Administrator, 205-726-2047, Fax: 205-870-4179, E-mail: sewaldre@samford.edu. *Dean,* Dr. Nena F. Sanders, 205-726-2629, E-mail: nfsander@samford.edu.

McWhorter School of Pharmacy Students: 476 full-time (321 women), 13 part-time (8 women); includes 36 minority (17 African Americans, 2 American Indian/Alaska Native, 15 Asian Americans or Pacific Islanders, 2 Hispanic Americans), 5 international. Average age 24. 1,068 applicants, 12% accepted, 88 enrolled. *Faculty:* 38 full-time (17 women). Expenses: Contact institution. *Financial support:* In 2006–07, 103 students received support. Career-related internships or fieldwork, Federal Work-Study, and institutionally sponsored loans available. Financial award application deadline: 5/2; financial award applicants required to submit FAFSA. In 2006, 104 degrees awarded. Postbaccalaureate distance learning degree programs offered (minimal on-campus study). Offers pharmacy (Pharm D). *Application deadline:* For winter admission, 2/1 for domestic students. Applications are processed on a rolling basis. *Application fee:* $50. *Application Contact:* C. Bruce Foster, Assistant Dean for Student/Alumni Affairs, 205-726-2053, Fax: 205-726-2759, E-mail: cbfoster@samford.edu. *Dean,* Dr. Bobby G. Bryant, 205-726-2820, Fax: 205-726-2759, E-mail: bgbryant@samford.edu.

School of Business Students: 20 full-time (13 women), 69 part-time (44 women); includes 15 minority (14 African Americans, 1 Hispanic American), 3 international. Average age 29. 67 applicants, 79% accepted, 18 enrolled. *Faculty:* 11 full-time (1 woman). Expenses: Contact institution. *Financial support:* In 2006–07, 6 students received support. Career-related internships or fieldwork and institutionally sponsored loans available. Support available to part-time students. Financial award applicants required to submit FAFSA. In 2006, 39 degrees awarded. *Degree program information:* Part-time and evening/weekend programs available. Offers business (M Acc, MBA). *Application deadline:* For fall admission, 7/15 priority date for domestic students; for spring admission, 12/15 for domestic students. Applications are processed on a rolling basis. *Application fee:* $25. *Application Contact:* Doug Smith, Director of Graduate Programs, 205-726-2931, Fax: 205-726-2540, E-mail: dusmith@samford.edu. *Dean,* Dr. Beck Taylor, 205-726-2364, Fax: 205-726-2464, E-mail: btaylor@samford.edu.

School of Education Students: 16 full-time (14 women), 160 part-time (124 women); includes 25 minority (all African Americans) Average age 38. 45 applicants, 100% accepted, 17 enrolled. *Faculty:* 12 full-time (7 women), 8 part-time/adjunct (4 women). Expenses: Contact institution. *Financial support:* In 2006–07, 54 students received support; research assistantships, career-related internships or fieldwork, Federal Work-Study, scholarships/grants, and tuition waivers (partial) available. Support available to part-time students. Financial award applicants required to submit FAFSA. In 2006, 15 master's, 20 doctorates, 20 other advanced degrees awarded. *Degree program information:* Part-time programs available. Offers early childhood education (Ed S); early childhood/elementary education (MS Ed); educational administration (Ed S); educational leadership (Ed D); elementary education (Ed S); gifted education (MS Ed). *Application deadline:* Applications are processed on a rolling basis. *Application fee:* $25. *Application Contact:* Dr. Maurice Persall, Director, Graduate Office, 205-726-2019, E-mail: jmpersal@samford.edu. *Dean,* Dr. Jean Ann Box, 205-726-2559, E-mail: jabox@samford.edu.

School of Performing Arts Students: 6 full-time (2 women), 3 part-time (2 women). Average age 24. 1 applicant, 100% accepted, 1 enrolled. *Faculty:* 11 full-time (3 women), 2 part-time/adjunct (0 women). Expenses: Contact institution. *Financial support:* In 2006–07, 7 students received support. Federal Work-Study, scholarships/grants, and tuition waivers (partial) available. Financial award application deadline: 9/1. In 2006, 3 degrees awarded. *Degree program information:* Part-time programs available. Offers church music (MM); music education (MME). *Application deadline:* For fall admission, 9/1 for domestic students; for spring admission, 1/20 for domestic students. *Application fee:* $25. *Application Contact:* Dr. Paul Richardson, Assistant Dean for Graduate Studies, 205-726-2496, Fax: 205-726-2165. *Dean,* Dr. Joseph H. Hopkins, 205-726-2165, E-mail: jhhopkin@samford.edu.

SAM HOUSTON STATE UNIVERSITY, Huntsville, TX 77341

General Information State-supported, coed, university. *Enrollment:* 15,935 graduate, professional, and undergraduate students; 485 full-time matriculated graduate/professional students (297 women), 1,397 part-time matriculated graduate/professional students (999 women). *Enrollment by degree level:* 1,634 master's, 248 doctoral. *Graduate faculty:* 213 full-time (68 women), 1 part-time/adjunct (0 women). Tuition, state resident: full-time $5,904; part-time $164 per semester hour. Tuition, nonresident: full-time $15,804; part-time $439 per semester hour. *Required fees:* $1,374; $462 per semester. *Graduate housing:* Room and/or apartments available on a first-come, first-served basis to single students; on-campus housing not available to married students. Typical cost: $3,177 per year ($5,598 including board). Room and board charges vary according to board plan and housing facility selected. *Student services:* Campus employment opportunities, campus safety program, career counseling, child daycare facilities, disabled student services, exercise/wellness program, free psychological counseling, grant writing training, international student services, multicultural affairs office, writing training. *Library facilities:* Newton Gresham Library. *Online resources:* library catalog, web page, access to other libraries' catalogs. *Collection:* 1.2 million titles, 4,521 serial subscriptions. *Research affiliation:* Texas Department of Corrections, Research Division, Texas Criminal Justice Division.

Computer facilities: 552 computers available on campus for general student use. A campuswide network can be accessed from student residence rooms and from off campus. Internet access and online class registration are available. *Web address:* http://www.shsu.edu/.

General Application Contact: Dr. Mitchell Muehsam, Dean of Graduate Studies and Associate Vice President for Academic Affairs, 936-294-1971, Fax: 936-294-1271, E-mail: graduate@shsu.edu.

GRADUATE UNITS

College of Arts and Sciences Students: 76 full-time (32 women), 69 part-time (44 women); includes 17 minority (4 African Americans, 1 American Indian/Alaska Native, 3 Asian Americans or Pacific Islanders, 9 Hispanic Americans), 37 international. Average age 29. *Faculty:* 59 full-time (12 women), 1 part-time/adjunct (0 women). Expenses: Contact institution. *Financial support:* Research assistantships, teaching assistantships, career-related internships or fieldwork, Federal Work-Study, institutionally sponsored loans, scholarships/grants, and tuition waivers (partial) available. Support available to part-time students. Financial award application deadline: 5/31; financial award applicants required to submit FAFSA. In 2006, 46 degrees awarded. *Degree program information:* Part-time and evening/weekend programs available. Offers agriculture (MS); art (MA, MFA); arts and sciences (M Ed, MA, MFA, MM, MS); biology (MA, MS); chemistry (MS); computing and information science (MS); dance (MFA); industrial education (M Ed, MA); industrial technology (MA); mathematics (MA, MS); statistics (MS); vocational education (M Ed). *Application deadline:* For fall admission, 8/1 for domestic students; for spring admission, 12/1 for domestic students. Applications are processed on a rolling basis. *Application fee:* $20. Electronic applications accepted. *Application Contact:* Anita Shipman, Advisor, 936-294-3962. *Dean,* Dr. Jaimie Hebert, 936-294-1401, Fax: 936-294-1598, E-mail: mth_jlh@shsu.edu.

School of Music Students: 7 full-time (2 women), 1 (woman) part-time; includes 1 minority (Hispanic American), 2 international. Average age 26. *Faculty:* 8 full-time (3 women). Expenses: Contact institution. *Financial support:* Teaching assistantships, Federal Work-Study and scholarships/grants available. Financial award application deadline: 5/31; financial award applicants required to submit FAFSA. In 2006, 9 degrees awarded. *Degree program information:* Part-time programs available. Offers conducting (MM); music (MM); music education (M Ed, MM). *Application deadline:* For fall admission, 8/1 for domestic students; for spring admission, 12/1 for domestic students. Applications are processed on a rolling basis. *Application fee:* $20. *Application Contact:* Scott Plugge, Advisor, 936-294-1393, E-mail: plugge@shsu.edu. *Chair,* Dr. James Bankhead, 936-294-3808, Fax: 936-294-3765, E-mail: bankhead@shsu.edu.

College of Business Administration Students: 95 full-time (40 women), 118 part-time (56 women); includes 37 minority (12 African Americans, 1 American Indian/Alaska Native, 6 Asian Americans or Pacific Islanders, 18 Hispanic Americans), 15 international. Average age 30. *Faculty:* 31 full-time (7 women). Expenses: Contact institution. *Financial support:* Research assistantships, Federal Work-Study, institutionally sponsored loans, and unspecified assistantships available. Financial award application deadline: 5/31; financial award applicants required to submit FAFSA. In 2006, 81 degrees awarded. *Degree program information:* Part-time and evening/weekend programs available. Offers business administration (MBA); finance (MS); general business and finance (MS). *Application deadline:* For fall admission, 8/1 for domestic students; for spring admission, 12/1 for domestic students. Applications are processed on a rolling basis. *Application fee:* $20. *Application Contact:* Dr. Leroy Ashorn, Advisor, 936-294-4040, E-mail: busgrad@shsu.edu. *Dean,* Dr. R. Dean Lewis, 936-294-1254, Fax: 936-294-3612, E-mail: bed_rdl@shsu.edu.

College of Criminal Justice Students: 76 full-time (44 women), 113 part-time (40 women); includes 25 minority (8 African Americans, 1 American Indian/Alaska Native, 1 Asian American or Pacific Islander, 15 Hispanic Americans), 39 international. Average age 32. *Faculty:* 16 full-time (3 women). Expenses: Contact institution. *Financial support:* Fellowships, research assistantships, teaching assistantships, career-related internships or fieldwork, Federal Work-Study, institutionally sponsored loans, and unspecified assistantships available. Support available to part-time students. Financial award application deadline: 5/31; financial award applicants required to submit FAFSA. In 2006, 53 master's, 16 doctorates awarded. Offers criminal justice (MS, PhD); criminal justice and criminology (MA); criminal justice management (MS); forensic science (MS). *Application deadline:* For fall admission, 8/1 for domestic students; for spring admission, 12/1 for domestic students. Applications are processed on a rolling basis. *Application fee:* $20. *Application Contact:* Doris Powell, Advisor, 936-294-3637. *Dean,* Dr. Vincent Webb, 936-294-1632, Fax: 936-294-1653, E-mail: vwebb@shsu.edu.

College of Education and Applied Science Students: 123 full-time (97 women), 963 part-time (783 women); includes 298 minority (96 African Americans, 5 American Indian/Alaska Native, 6 Asian Americans or Pacific Islanders, 191 Hispanic Americans), 12 international. Average age 36. *Faculty:* 33 full-time (21 women). Expenses: Contact institution. *Financial support:* Research assistantships, teaching assistantships, career-related internships or fieldwork, Federal Work-Study, institutionally sponsored loans, and tuition waivers (partial) available. Support available to part-time students. Financial award application deadline: 5/31; financial award applicants required to submit FAFSA. In 2006, 380 master's, 20 doctorates awarded. *Degree program information:* Part-time and evening/weekend programs available. Offers administration (M Ed, MA); counseling (M Ed, MA); counselor education (MA, PhD); early childhood education (M Ed); education and applied science (M Ed, MA, MLS, Ed D, PhD); educational leadership (Ed D); elementary education (M Ed, MA); health and kinesiology (M Ed, MA); instructional leadership (M Ed, MA); library science (MLS); reading (M Ed, MA); secondary education (M Ed, MA); special education (M Ed, MA). *Application deadline:* For fall admission, 8/1 for domestic students; for spring admission, 12/1 for domestic students. *Application fee:* $20. *Application Contact:* Molly Doughtie, Advisor, 936-294-1105, E-mail: edu_mxd@shsu.edu. *Dean,* Dr. Genevieve Brown, 936-294-1101, Fax: 936-294-1102, E-mail: edu_gxb@shsu.edu.

College of Humanities and Social Sciences Students: 115 full-time (84 women), 134 part-time (76 women); includes 30 minority (9 African Americans, 1 American Indian/Alaska Native, 8 Asian Americans or Pacific Islanders, 12 Hispanic Americans), 3 international. Average age 31. *Faculty:* 69 full-time (25 women). Expenses: Contact institution. In 2006, 70 master's, 6 doctorates awarded. Offers clinical psychology (MA, PhD); English (MA); family and consumer sciences (MA); history (MA); humanities and social sciences (MA, MPA, PhD); political science (MA); psychology (MA); public administration (MPA); school psychology (MA); sociology (MA). *Dean,* Dr. John deCastro, 936-294-2200, Fax: 936-294-2207, E-mail: jmd018@shsu.edu.

SAMRA UNIVERSITY OF ORIENTAL MEDICINE, Los Angeles, CA 90034

General Information Independent, coed, graduate-only institution. *Graduate faculty:* 10 full-time (5 women), 60 part-time/adjunct (30 women). *Graduate housing:* On-campus housing not available. *Student services:* Career counseling, exercise/wellness program, international student services, low-cost health insurance. *Library facilities:* Samra University Library plus 1 other. *Collection:* 4,000 titles, 50 serial subscriptions.

Computer facilities: 3 computers available on campus for general student use. Internet access is available. *Web address:* http://www.samra.edu/.

General Application Contact: Taula Jackson, Admissions Director, 310-202-6444 Ext. 104, Fax: 310-202-6007, E-mail: tjackson@samra.edu.

GRADUATE UNITS

Program in Oriental Medicine Students: 322 full-time, 138 part-time. *Faculty:* 10 full-time (5 women), 60 part-time/adjunct (30 women). Expenses: Contact institution. *Financial support:* Available to part-time students. *Degree program information:* Part-time and evening/weekend programs available. Offers Oriental medicine (MS, DAOM). *Application deadline:* Applications are processed on a rolling basis. *Application fee:* $100. *Application Contact:* Taula Jackson, Admissions Director, 310-202-6444 Ext. 104, Fax: 310-202-6007, E-mail: tjackson@samra.

Samra University of Oriental Medicine (continued)

edu. *Provost*, Dr. Katsuyuki P. Sakamoto, 310-202-6444 Ext. 113, Fax: 310-202-6004, E-mail: ksakamoto@samra.edu.

SAMUEL MERRITT COLLEGE, Oakland, CA 94609-3108

General Information Independent, coed, primarily women, upper-level institution. *Graduate housing:* Room and/or apartments available to single students; on-campus housing not available to married students. *Research affiliation:* Summit Medical Center (nursing).

GRADUATE UNITS

Department of Occupational Therapy Offers occupational therapy (MOT).

Department of Physical Therapy Offers physical therapy (MPT, MSPT).

Department of Physician Assistant Studies Offers physician assistant studies (MPA).

School of Nursing *Degree program information:* Part-time and evening/weekend programs available. Offers case management (MSN); family nurse practitioner (MSN, Certificate); nurse anesthetist (MSN, Certificate); nursing (MSN).

SAN DIEGO STATE UNIVERSITY, San Diego, CA 92182

General Information State-supported, coed, university. CGS member. *Enrollment:* 34,305 graduate, professional, and undergraduate students; 3,038 full-time matriculated graduate/professional students (1,983 women), 2,520 part-time matriculated graduate/professional students (1,437 women). *Graduate faculty:* 741 full-time (299 women). *Graduate housing:* Room and/or apartments available on a first-come, first-served basis to single students; on-campus housing not available to married students. Housing application deadline: 5/1. *Student services:* Campus employment opportunities, campus safety program, career counseling, child daycare facilities, disabled student services, free psychological counseling, international student services, low-cost health insurance. *Library facilities:* Malcolm A. Love Library. *Online resources:* library catalog, web page, access to other libraries' catalogs. *Collection:* 1.3 million titles, 8,245 serial subscriptions. *Research affiliation:* Children's Hospital and Research Center (children's health), Qualcomm (wireless and telecommunications), Robert Wood Johnson Foundation (public health), General Atomics Corporation (technical student services), William and Flora Hewlit Foundation (teacher education), American Heart Association (biology).

Computer facilities: 400 computers available on campus for general student use. A campuswide network can be accessed from student residence rooms and from off campus. Internet access and online class registration are available. *Web address:* http://www.sdsu.edu/.

General Application Contact: Information Contact, 619-594-5213, Fax: 619-594-0189, E-mail: gra@mail.sdsu.edu.

GRADUATE UNITS

Graduate and Research Affairs Students: 3,038 full-time (1,983 women), 2,520 part-time (1,437 women); includes 1,412 minority (149 African Americans, 34 American Indian/Alaska Native, 500 Asian Americans or Pacific Islanders, 729 Hispanic Americans), 750 international. 6,714 applicants, 53% accepted, 1020 enrolled. Expenses: Contact institution. *Financial support:* In 2006–07, 1,850 students received support, including 933 teaching assistantships; fellowships, research assistantships, career-related internships or fieldwork, Federal Work-Study, institutionally sponsored loans, scholarships/grants, traineeships, tuition waivers (partial), and unspecified assistantships also available. Support available to part-time students. Financial award applicants required to submit CSS PROFILE or FAFSA. In 2006, 1,637 master's, 49 doctorates awarded. *Degree program information:* Part-time and evening/weekend programs available. Offers interdisciplinary studies (MA, MS). *Application deadline:* For fall admission, 5/1 for domestic and international students; for spring admission, 11/1 for domestic students, 10/1 for international students. *Application fee:* $55. Electronic applications accepted. *Application Contact:* Graduate Admissions, 619-594-0884, E-mail: gra@mail.sdsu.edu. *Graduate Dean*, 619-594-4163.

College of Arts and Letters Students: 356 full-time (206 women), 355 part-time (189 women); includes 189 minority (14 African Americans, 6 American Indian/Alaska Native, 38 Asian Americans or Pacific Islanders, 131 Hispanic Americans), 64 international. Average age 30. 647 applicants, 62% accepted, 158 enrolled. Expenses: Contact institution. *Financial support:* In 2006–07, 256 teaching assistantships were awarded; fellowships, research assistantships, career-related internships or fieldwork, Federal Work-Study, institutionally sponsored loans, scholarships/grants, tuition waivers (partial), and unspecified assistantships also available. Support available to part-time students. Financial award applicants required to submit FAFSA. In 2006, 193 master's, 5 doctorates awarded. *Degree program information:* Part-time and evening/weekend programs available. Offers anthropology (MA); applied linguistics and English as a second language (CAL); arts and letters (MA, MFA, PhD, CAL); Asian studies (MA); computational linguistics (MA); creative writing (MFA); economics (MA); English (MA); English as a second language/applied linguistics (MA); European studies (MA); general linguistics (MA); geography (MA, PhD); history (MA); Latin American studies (MA); liberal arts and sciences (MA); philosophy (MA); political science (MA); rhetoric and writing (MA); sociology (MA); Spanish (MA); women's studies (MA). *Application deadline:* For fall admission, 5/1 for domestic and international students; for spring admission, 11/1 for domestic students, 10/1 for international students. Applications are processed on a rolling basis. *Application fee:* $55. Electronic applications accepted. *Dean*, Paul Wong, 619-594-5456, Fax: 619-594-6281, E-mail: paul.wong@sdsu.edu.

College of Business Administration Students: 324 full-time (155 women), 376 part-time (153 women); includes 110 minority (3 African Americans, 6 American Indian/Alaska Native, 69 Asian Americans or Pacific Islanders, 32 Hispanic Americans), 167 international. Average age 28. 872 applicants, 52% accepted, 148 enrolled. Expenses: Contact institution. *Financial support:* In 2006–07, 65 teaching assistantships were awarded; fellowships, research assistantships, career-related internships or fieldwork and Federal Work-Study also available. Support available to part-time students. In 2006, 301 degrees awarded. *Degree program information:* Part-time and evening/weekend programs available. Offers accountancy (MS); business administration (MBA, MS); entrepreneurship (MS); finance (MS); human resources management (MS); information and decision systems (MS); international business (MS); management science (MS); marketing (MS); production and operations management (MS). *Application deadline:* For fall admission, 4/15 priority date for domestic students; for spring admission, 11/1 for domestic students. Applications are processed on a rolling basis. *Application fee:* $55. Electronic applications accepted. *Application Contact:* Information Contact, E-mail: sdsumba@mail.sdsu.edu. *Dean*, Dr. Gail K. Naughton, 619-594-8872, Fax: 619-594-1573, E-mail: gail.naughton@sdsu.edu.

College of Education Students: 330 full-time (257 women), 374 part-time (304 women); includes 250 minority (39 African Americans, 10 American Indian/Alaska Native, 56 Asian Americans or Pacific Islanders, 145 Hispanic Americans), 20 international. Average age 31. 707 applicants, 53% accepted, 104 enrolled. Expenses: Contact institution. *Financial support:* In 2006–07, 28 teaching assistantships were awarded; fellowships, research assistantships, career-related internships or fieldwork also available. Support available to part-time students. Financial award applicants required to submit FAFSA. In 2006, 395 master's, 10 doctorates awarded. *Degree program information:* Part-time and evening/weekend programs available. Offers counseling and school psychology (MS); education (MA, MS, Ed D, PhD); educational leadership (MA); educational leadership in post-secondary education (MA); educational technology (MA); educational technology and teaching and learning (Ed D); elementary curriculum and instruction (MA); multi-cultural emphasis (PhD); policy studies in language and cross cultural education (MA); reading education (MA); rehabilitation counseling (MS); secondary curriculum and instruction (MA); special education (MA). *Application fee:* $55. Electronic applications accepted. *Dean*, Lionel R. Meno, 619-594-1424, Fax: 619-594-7082, E-mail: lmeno@mail.sdsu.edu.

College of Engineering Students: 149 full-time (39 women), 174 part-time (43 women); includes 63 minority (4 African Americans, 1 American Indian/Alaska Native, 39 Asian Americans or Pacific Islanders, 19 Hispanic Americans), 165 international. Average age 29. 513 applicants, 57% accepted, 105 enrolled. Expenses: Contact institution. *Financial support:* In 2006–07, 26 teaching assistantships were awarded; fellowships, research assistantships, career-related internships or fieldwork and Federal Work-Study also available. Support available to part-time students. Financial award applicants required to submit FAFSA. In 2006, 70 master's, 3 doctorates awarded. *Degree program information:* Part-time and evening/weekend programs available. Offers aerospace engineering (MS); civil engineering (MS); electrical engineering (MS); engineering (MS, PhD); engineering mechanics (MS); engineering sciences and applied mechanics (PhD); flight dynamics (MS); fluid dynamics (MS); manufacture and design (MS); mechanical engineering (MS). *Application deadline:* For fall admission, 5/1 for domestic and international students; for spring admission, 11/1 for domestic students, 10/1 for international students. Applications are processed on a rolling basis. *Application fee:* $55. Electronic applications accepted. *Dean*, David A. Hayhurst, 619-594-6061, Fax: 619-594-6005, E-mail: hayhurst@engineering.sdsu.edu.

College of Health and Human Services Students: 556 full-time (480 women), 256 part-time (194 women); includes 227 minority (33 African Americans, 3 American Indian/Alaska Native, 81 Asian Americans or Pacific Islanders, 110 Hispanic Americans), 47 international. 1,080 applicants, 49% accepted, 189 enrolled. Expenses: Contact institution. *Financial support:* In 2006–07, 71 teaching assistantships were awarded; fellowships, research assistantships, career-related internships or fieldwork, Federal Work-Study, institutionally sponsored loans, and traineeships also available. Support available to part-time students. In 2006, 296 master's, 9 doctorates awarded. *Degree program information:* Part-time and evening/weekend programs available. Offers audiology (Au D); communicative disorders (MA); environmental health (MPH); epidemiology (MPH, PhD); gerontology (MS); global emergency preparedness and response (MS); health and human services (MA, MPH, MS, MSW, Au D, PhD); health behavior (PhD); health promotion (MPH); health services administration (MPH); language and communicative disorders (PhD); nursing (MS); social work (MSW); toxicology (MS). *Application fee:* $55. Electronic applications accepted. *Dean*, Marilyn Newhoff, 619-594-6516, Fax: 619-594-7103, E-mail: mnewhoff@mail.sdsu.edu.

College of Professional Studies and Fine Arts Students: 290 full-time (170 women), 217 part-time (145 women); includes 99 minority (17 African Americans, 32 Asian Americans or Pacific Islanders, 50 Hispanic Americans), 29 international. 721 applicants, 47% accepted, 141 enrolled. Expenses: Contact institution. *Financial support:* Fellowships, teaching assistantships, career-related internships or fieldwork and unspecified assistantships available. Support available to part-time students. In 2006, 180 degrees awarded. *Degree program information:* Part-time programs available. Offers advertising and public relations (MA); art history (MA); child development (MS); city planning (MCP); composition (acoustic and electronic) (MM); conducting (MM); criminal justice administration (MPA); criminal justice and criminology (MS); critical-cultural studies (MA); ethnomusicology (MA); exercise physiology (MA); interaction studies (MA); intercultural and international studies (MA); jazz studies (MM); musicology (MA); new media studies (MA); news and information studies (MA); nutritional science (MS); nutritional sciences (MS); performance (MM); physical education (MS); piano pedagogy (MA); professional studies and fine arts (MA, MCP, MFA, MM, MPA, MS); public administration (MPA); studio arts (MA, MFA); telecommunications and media management (MA); television, film, and new media production (MA); theatre arts (MA, MFA); theory (MA). *Application deadline:* Applications are processed on a rolling basis. *Application fee:* $55. *Application Contact:* John Baxter, Administrative Support Coordinator, 619-594-1343, E-mail: jbaxter@mail.sdsu.edu. *Dean*, Joyce M. Gattas, 619-594-4464, Fax: 619-594-4987, E-mail: gattas@mail.sdsu.edu.

College of Sciences Students: 414 full-time (206 women), 477 part-time (202 women); includes 172 minority (14 African Americans, 2 American Indian/Alaska Native, 98 Asian Americans or Pacific Islanders, 58 Hispanic Americans), 252 international. Average age 30. 1,331 applicants, 39% accepted, 172 enrolled. Expenses: Contact institution. *Financial support:* Fellowships, research assistantships, teaching assistantships, career-related internships or fieldwork, Federal Work-Study, institutionally sponsored loans, and unspecified assistantships available. Support available to part-time students. Financial award applicants required to submit CSS PROFILE or FAFSA. In 2006, 194 master's, 22 doctorates awarded. *Degree program information:* Part-time programs available. Offers applied mathematics (MS); astronomy (MS); biology (MA, MS); biostatistics and biometry (PhD); cell and molecular biology (PhD); chemistry (MA, MS, PhD); clinical psychology (MS, PhD); computational science (MS, PhD); computer science (MS); ecology (MS, PhD); geological sciences (MS); industrial and organizational psychology (MS); mathematics (MA); mathematics and science education (PhD); microbiology (MS); molecular biology (MA, MS); physics (MA, MS); program evaluation (MS); psychology (MA); radiological physics (MS); regulatory affairs (MS); sciences (MA, MS, PhD); statistics (MS). *Application deadline:* For fall admission, 5/1 for domestic students; for spring admission, 11/1 for domestic students, 10/1 for international students. *Application fee:* $55. Electronic applications accepted. *Interim Dean*, 619-594-5142, Fax: 619-594-6381, E-mail: deanasst@sciences.sdsu.edu.

SAN FRANCISCO ART INSTITUTE, San Francisco, CA 94133

General Information Independent, coed, comprehensive institution. *Enrollment:* 652 graduate, professional, and undergraduate students; 171 full-time matriculated graduate/professional students (99 women), 42 part-time matriculated graduate/professional students (33 women). *Enrollment by degree level:* 194 master's, 19 other advanced degrees. *Graduate faculty:* 10 full-time (3 women), 48 part-time/adjunct (24 women). *Tuition:* Full-time $30,210; part-time $1,400 per unit. *Required fees:* $35 per semester. Tuition and fees vary according to course load and program. *Graduate housing:* Room and/or apartments available on a first-come, first-served basis to single students; on-campus housing not available to married students. *Student services:* Campus employment opportunities, campus safety program, career counseling, international student services, low-cost health insurance. *Library facilities:* Anne Bremer Memorial Library. *Online resources:* library catalog, web page. *Collection:* 35,500 titles, 210 serial subscriptions, 1,250 audiovisual materials. *Research affiliation:* Exploratorium (museum of science, art, and human perception).

Computer facilities: 30 computers available on campus for general student use. A campuswide network can be accessed. Internet access is available. *Web address:* http://www.sfai.edu/.

General Application Contact: Director of Admissions, 800-345-7324, Fax: 415-749-4592, E-mail: admissions@sfai.edu.

GRADUATE UNITS

Graduate Program Students: 171 full-time (99 women), 42 part-time (33 women); includes 38 minority (7 African Americans, 1 American Indian/Alaska Native, 12 Asian Americans or Pacific Islanders, 18 Hispanic Americans), 23 international. Average age 31. 415 applicants, 30% accepted, 86 enrolled. *Faculty:* 32 full-time (12 women), 30 part-time/adjunct (19 women). Expenses: Contact institution. *Financial support:* In 2006–07, 11 fellowships with full tuition reimbursements were awarded; teaching assistantships, career-related internships or fieldwork, Federal Work-Study, and scholarships/grants also available. Support available to part-time students. Financial award application deadline: 3/2; financial award applicants required to submit FAFSA. In 2006, 92 master's, 18 other advanced degrees awarded. *Degree program information:* Part-time programs available. Offers design and technology (MFA, Certificate); exhibition and museum studies (MA); film (MFA, Certificate); fine arts (MA, MFA, Certificate); history and theory of contemporary art (MA); new genres (Certificate); painting (MFA, Certificate); performance/video (MFA); photography (MFA, Certificate); printmaking (MFA, Certificate); sculpture (MFA, Certificate); urban studies (MA). *Application deadline:* For fall admission, 1/15 priority date for domestic and international students. *Application fee:* $75 ($85 for international students). Electronic applications accepted. *Application Contact:* Director of Admissions, 800-345-7324, Fax: 415-749-4592, E-mail: admissions@sfai.edu. *Dean of Graduate Programs*, Rene,&e Green, 415-641-1241 Ext. 1000, Fax: 415-641-1260, E-mail: rgreen@sfai.edu.

SAN FRANCISCO CONSERVATORY OF MUSIC, San Francisco, CA 94122-4411

General Information Independent, coed, comprehensive institution. *Graduate housing:* On-campus housing not available.

GRADUATE UNITS

Graduate Division *Degree program information:* Part-time programs available. Offers chamber music (MM); classical guitar (MM); composition (MM); conducting (MM); keyboards (MM); orchestral instruments (MM); voice (MM). Electronic applications accepted.

SAN FRANCISCO STATE UNIVERSITY, San Francisco, CA 94132-1722

General Information State-supported, coed, comprehensive institution. CGS member. *Enrollment:* 29,628 graduate, professional, and undergraduate students; 4,642 matriculated graduate/professional students. *Graduate faculty:* 795 full-time (285 women). *Graduate housing:* Room and/or apartments available on a first-come, first-served basis to single students; on-campus housing not available to married students. *Student services:* Campus employment opportunities, campus safety program, career counseling, child daycare facilities, disabled student services, exercise/wellness program, free psychological counseling, international student services, low-cost health insurance, multicultural affairs office, teacher training. *Library facilities:* J. Paul Leonard Library. *Online resources:* library catalog, web page, access to other libraries' catalogs. *Collection:* 1.2 million titles, 15,644 serial subscriptions, 192,862 audiovisual materials.

Computer facilities: 1,474 computers available on campus for general student use. A campuswide network can be accessed from student residence rooms and from off campus. *Web address:* http://www.sfsu.edu/.

General Application Contact: Brian Gallagher, Director of Admissions, Division of Graduate Studies, 415-338-2234, Fax: 415-338-0942, E-mail: gadmit@sfsu.edu.

GRADUATE UNITS

Division of Graduate Studies Students: 4,642. *Faculty:* 795. Expenses: Contact institution. *Financial support:* Fellowships, research assistantships, teaching assistantships, career-related internships or fieldwork, Federal Work-Study, institutionally sponsored loans, tuition waivers (partial), and unspecified assistantships available. Support available to part-time students. Financial award application deadline: 3/1; financial award applicants required to submit FAFSA. In 2006, 4 degrees awarded. *Degree program information:* Part-time and evening/weekend programs available. *Application fee:* $55. *Application Contact:* Marsha Harris, Assistant to Graduate Dean, 415-338-2232, Fax: 415-338-0942, E-mail: mch7@sfsu.edu. *Dean,* Dr. Ann Hallum, 415-338-2231, Fax: 415-338-0942, E-mail: glider@sfsu.edu.

College of Behavioral and Social Sciences Expenses: Contact institution. *Financial support:* Fellowships, research assistantships, teaching assistantships, career-related internships or fieldwork and Federal Work-Study available. Support available to part-time students. Financial award application deadline: 3/1. *Degree program information:* Part-time and evening/weekend programs available. Offers anthropology (MA); behavioral and social sciences (MA, MPA, MS); economics (MA); geography (MA); history (MA); human sexuality studies (MA); integrated and collaborative services (MPA); international relations (MA); nonprofit administration (MPA); policy analysis (MPA); political science (MA); psychology (MA, MS); public management (MPA); social science (MA); urban administration (MPA). *Application fee:* $55. *Dean,* Joel Kassiola, 415-338-1846, E-mail: kassiola@sfsu.edu.

College of Business Students: 850 (408 women). Average age 30. 839 applicants, 56% accepted, 241 enrolled. *Faculty:* 100. Expenses: Contact institution. *Financial support:* Career-related internships or fieldwork, Federal Work-Study, and unspecified assistantships available. Financial award application deadline: 3/1; financial award applicants required to submit FAFSA. In 2006, 220 degrees awarded. *Degree program information:* Part-time and evening/weekend programs available. Offers business (MBA); business administration (MBA). *Application deadline:* For fall admission, 5/1 for domestic students, 4/1 for international students; for spring admission, 11/1 for domestic students, 10/15 for international students. Applications are processed on a rolling basis. *Application fee:* $55. *Application Contact:* Armaan Moattori, Graduate Admission Coordinator, 415-338-1395, Fax: 415-405-0495, E-mail: amoatt@sfsu.edu. *Dean,* Nancy Mayes, 415-338-2670.

College of Creative Arts Students: 241 (128 women). *Faculty:* 80 full-time (26 women), 50 part-time/adjunct (20 women). Expenses: Contact institution. *Financial support:* Fellowships, research assistantships, teaching assistantships, career-related internships or fieldwork, Federal Work-Study, and unspecified assistantships available. Financial award application deadline: 3/1. *Degree program information:* Part-time and evening/weekend programs available. Offers art (MFA); art history (MA); chamber music (MM); cinema (MFA); cinema studies (MA); classical performance (MM); composition (MA); conducting (MM); creative arts (MA, MFA, MM); drama (MA); industrial arts (MA); music education (MA); music history (MA); radio and television (MA); theatre arts (MFA). *Application fee:* $55. *Interim Dean,* Ron Compesi, 415-338-7618.

College of Education Students: 1,500. *Faculty:* 95 full-time, 121 part-time/adjunct. Expenses: Contact institution. *Financial support:* Fellowships, career-related internships or fieldwork and Federal Work-Study available. Financial award application deadline: 3/1. *Degree program information:* Part-time and evening/weekend programs available. Offers adult education (MA Ed, AC); communicative disorders (MS); early childhood education (MA); education (MA, MA Ed, MS, Ed D, PhD, AC); educational administration (MA, AC); educational technology (MA); elementary education (MA); equity and social justice (AC); equity and social justice in education (MA Ed); language and literacy education (MA); mathematics education (MA); secondary education (MA Ed); special education (MA, Ed D, PhD, AC); special interest (MA Ed); training systems development (AC). *Application deadline:* For fall admission, 11/30 priority date for domestic students. Applications are processed on a rolling basis. *Application fee:* $55. *Application Contact:* Dr. David Hemphill, Associate Dean, 415-338-2684, E-mail: hemphill@sfsu.edu. *Dean,* Dr. Jacob Perea, 415-338-2687, E-mail: pjoost@sfsu.edu.

College of Ethnic Studies *Faculty:* 20. Expenses: Contact institution. *Financial support:* Application deadline: 3/1. In 2006, 4 degrees awarded. *Degree program information:* Part-time programs available. Offers Asian American studies (MA); ethnic studies (MA). *Application deadline:* For fall admission, 3/31 for domestic students. *Application fee:* $55. *Application Contact:* Dr. Jim Okutsu, Associate Dean and Graduate Coordinator, 415-338-1693, E-mail: jokutsu@sfsu.edu. *Dean,* Dr. Kenneth P. Montiero, 415-338-1693.

College of Health and Human Services *Faculty:* 22 full-time (13 women), 10 part-time/adjunct (6 women). Expenses: Contact institution. *Financial support:* Fellowships, research assistantships, teaching assistantships, career-related internships or fieldwork, Federal Work-Study, institutionally sponsored loans, and unspecified assistantships available. Financial award application deadline: 3/1. In 2006, 52 degrees awarded. *Degree program information:* Part-time programs available. Offers case management (MS); counseling (MS); family and consumer sciences (MA); geriatric care management (MA); health and human services (MA, MPH, MS, MSC, MSW, DPT, Dr Sc PT); health education (MPH); health, wellness and aging (MA); kinesiology (MS); long-term care administration (MA); marriage, family, and child counseling (MSC); nursing administration (MS); nursing education (MS); physical therapy (MS, DPT, Dr Sc PT); recreation (MS); rehabilitation counseling (MS); social work (MSW). *Application fee:* $55. *Application Contact:* Dr. Ann Hallum, Dean, 415-338-2231, Fax: 415-338-0942, E-mail: glider@sfsu.edu. *Dean,* Dr. Don Taylor, 415-338-3326.

College of Humanities Students: 651 (442 women). Expenses: Contact institution. *Financial support:* Teaching assistantships, career-related internships or fieldwork and Federal Work-Study available. Financial award application deadline: 3/1. In 2006, 247 degrees awarded. *Degree program information:* Part-time and evening/weekend programs available. Offers Chinese (MA); classics (MA); communication studies (MA); comparative literature (MA); composition (MA, Certificate); creative writing (MA, MFA); French (MA); German (MA); humanities (MA, MFA, Certificate); Italian (MA); Japanese (MA); linguistics (MA); literature (MA); museum studies (MA); philosophy (MA); Spanish (MA); teaching composition (Certificate); teaching critical thinking (Certificate); teaching English to speakers of other languages (MA); teaching post-secondary reading (Certificate); women studies (MA). *Application fee:* $55. *Dean,* Dr. Paul Sherwin, 415-338-1541, Fax: 415-338-7030, E-mail: psherwin@sfsu.edu.

College of Science and Engineering Students: 632 (313 women); includes 199 minority (22 African Americans, 5 American Indian/Alaska Native, 131 Asian Americans or Pacific Islanders, 41 Hispanic Americans) 156 international. *Faculty:* 143 full-time. Expenses: Contact institution. *Financial support:* Fellowships, research assistantships, teaching assistantships, career-related internships or fieldwork, Federal Work-Study, institutionally sponsored loans, scholarships/grants, tuition waivers (partial), and unspecified assistantships available. Financial award application deadline: 3/1. In 2006, 107 degrees awarded. *Degree program information:* Part-time programs available. Offers applied geosciences (MS); biomedical laboratory science (MS); cell and molecular biology (MS); chemistry (MS); computer science (MS); conservation biology (MS); ecology and systematic biology (MS); engineering (MS); marine biology (MS); marine science (MS); mathematics (MA); microbiology (MS); physics (MS); physiology and behavioral biology (MS); science and engineering (MA, MS). *Application deadline:* For fall admission, 11/30 priority date for domestic and international students; for spring admission, 9/30 priority date for domestic students. Applications are processed on a rolling basis. *Application fee:* $55. Electronic applications accepted. *Application Contact:* Dr. Sung C. Hu, Associate Dean, 415-338-1571, Fax: 415-338-6136, E-mail: shu@sfsu.edu. *Dean,* Dr. Sheldon Axler, 415-338-1571, Fax: 415-338-6136, E-mail: axler@sfsu.edu.

SAN FRANCISCO THEOLOGICAL SEMINARY, San Anselmo, CA 94960-2997

General Information Independent-religious, coed, graduate-only institution. *Graduate housing:* Rooms and/or apartments available on a first-come, first-served basis to single and married students. Housing application deadline: 5/1.

GRADUATE UNITS

Graduate and Professional Programs *Degree program information:* Part-time programs available. Offers theology (M Div, MA, MATS, D Min, PhD, Th D).

SAN JOAQUIN COLLEGE OF LAW, Clovis, CA 93612-1312

General Information Independent, coed, graduate-only institution. *Graduate housing:* On-campus housing not available.

GRADUATE UNITS

Law Program *Degree program information:* Part-time and evening/weekend programs available. Offers law (JD).

SAN JOSE STATE UNIVERSITY, San Jose, CA 95192-0001

General Information State-supported, coed, comprehensive institution. CGS member. *Enrollment:* 29,604 graduate, professional, and undergraduate students; 3,555 full-time matriculated graduate/professional students (2,312 women), 3,567 part-time matriculated graduate/professional students (2,229 women). *Enrollment by degree level:* 7,122 master's. *Graduate housing:* Room and/or apartments available on a first-come, first-served basis to single students; on-campus housing not available to married students. Typical cost: $6,647 per year ($10,163 including board). Room and board charges vary according to board plan and housing facility selected. *Student services:* Campus employment opportunities, campus safety program, career counseling, child daycare facilities, disabled student services, free psychological counseling, international student services, low-cost health insurance, multicultural affairs office. *Library facilities:* Dr. Martin Luther King Jr. Library plus 1 other. *Online resources:* library catalog, web page, access to other libraries' catalogs. *Collection:* 1.8 million titles, 35,390 serial subscriptions, 32,270 audiovisual materials. *Research affiliation:* Moss Landing Marine Laboratories.

Computer facilities: A campuswide network can be accessed from student residence rooms and from off campus. Internet access and online class registration are available. *Web address:* http://www.sjsu.edu/.

General Application Contact: Andy Hernandez, Associate Director, Undergraduate and Graduate Admissions, 408-924-2359, Fax: 408-924-2050, E-mail: andy.hernandez@sjsu.edu.

GRADUATE UNITS

Graduate Studies and Research Students: 3,555 full-time (2,312 women), 3,567 part-time (2,229 women); includes 2,183 minority (186 African Americans, 23 American Indian/Alaska Native, 1,275 Asian Americans or Pacific Islanders, 699 Hispanic Americans), 1,413 international. Average age 33. Expenses: Contact institution. *Financial support:* Fellowships, research assistantships, teaching assistantships, career-related internships or fieldwork, Federal Work-Study, institutionally sponsored loans, scholarships/grants, and tuition waivers (partial) available. Support available to part-time students. Financial award applicants required to submit FAFSA. In 2006, 2474 degrees awarded. *Degree program information:* Part-time and evening/weekend programs available. Postbaccalaureate distance learning degree programs offered (minimal on-campus study). Offers human factors and ergonomics (MS); interdisciplinary studies (MA, MS). *Application deadline:* For fall admission, 6/29 for domestic students; for spring admission, 11/30 for domestic students. Applications are processed on a rolling basis. *Application fee:* $55. Electronic applications accepted. *Application Contact:* 408-924-2480, Fax: 408-924-2477. *Associate Vice President,* Dr. Pam Stacks, 408-924-2427, Fax: 408-924-2477.

College of Applied Sciences and Arts Students: 793 full-time (648 women), 919 part-time (743 women); includes 496 minority (63 African Americans, 11 American Indian/Alaska Native, 217 Asian Americans or Pacific Islanders, 205 Hispanic Americans), 56 international. Average age 32. 1,614 applicants, 69% accepted, 569 enrolled. Expenses: Contact institution. *Financial support:* Career-related internships or fieldwork, Federal Work-Study, institutionally sponsored loans, and scholarships/grants available. Support available to part-time students. Financial award applicants required to submit FAFSA. In 2006, 710 degrees awarded. *Degree program information:* Part-time and evening/weekend programs available. Offers applied sciences and arts (MA, MLIS, MPH, MS, MSW, Certificate); applied social gerontology (Certificate); community health education (MPH); gerontology nurse practitioner (MS); justice studies (MS); kinesiology (MA); library and information science (MLIS); mass communication (MS); nursing (Certificate); nursing administration (MS); nursing education (MS); nutritional science (MS); occupational therapy (MS); recreation (MS); social work (MSW, Certificate). *Application deadline:* For fall admission, 6/29 for domestic students; for spring admission, 11/30 for domestic students. Applications are processed on a rolling basis. *Application fee:* $59. Electronic applications accepted. *Interim Dean,* Barbara Conry, 408-924-2900, Fax: 408-924-2901, E-mail: bjconry@casa.sjsu.edu.

College of Education Students: 1,217 full-time (940 women), 667 part-time (519 women); includes 629 minority (58 African Americans, 5 American Indian/Alaska Native, 260 Asian Americans or Pacific Islanders, 306 Hispanic Americans), 35 international. Average age 35. 1,308 applicants, 81% accepted, 773 enrolled. Expenses: Contact institution. *Financial support:* Career-related internships or fieldwork available. Financial award applicants required to submit FAFSA. In 2006, 506 degrees awarded. *Degree program information:* Evening/weekend programs available. Offers child and adolescent development (MA); education (MA, Certificate); education (counseling and student personnel) (MA); educational administration (MA); elementary education (MA, Certificate); higher education administration (MA); instructional technology (MA, Certificate); school business management (Certificate); secondary education (Certificate); special education (MA, Certificate); speech pathology (MA). *Application deadline:* For fall admission, 6/29 for domestic students; for spring admission, 11/30 for domestic students. Applications are processed on a rolling basis. *Application fee:* $59. Electronic applications accepted. *Dean,* Dr. Susan Meyers, 408-924-3600, Fax: 408-924-3713.

College of Engineering Students: 838 full-time (311 women), 1,067 part-time (446 women); includes 554 minority (20 African Americans, 2 American Indian/Alaska Native, 497 Asian Americans or Pacific Islanders, 35 Hispanic Americans), 1,052 international. Average age 30. 1,396 applicants, 72% accepted, 539 enrolled. Expenses: Contact institution. *Financial support:* Teaching assistantships, career-related internships or fieldwork, Federal Work-Study, and institutionally sponsored loans available. Support available to part-time students. Financial award applicants required to submit FAFSA. In 2006, 646 degrees awarded. *Degree program information:* Part-time programs available. Offers aerospace engineering (MS); chemical engineering (MS); civil engineering (MS); computer engineering (MS);

San Jose State University (continued)

electrical engineering (MS); engineering (MS); general engineering (MS); industrial and systems engineering (MS); materials engineering (MS); mechanical engineering (MS); quality assurance (MS); software engineering (MS). *Application deadline:* For fall admission, 6/29 for domestic students; for spring admission, 11/30 for domestic students. Applications are processed on a rolling basis. *Application fee:* $59. Electronic applications accepted. *Dean,* Dr. Belle Wei, 408-924-3800, Fax: 408-924-3818.

College of Humanities and the Arts Students: 196 full-time (125 women), 188 part-time (132 women); includes 88 minority (12 African Americans, 1 American Indian/Alaska Native, 32 Asian Americans or Pacific Islanders, 43 Hispanic Americans), 44 international. Average age 34. 357 applicants, 65% accepted, 143 enrolled. Expenses: Contact institution. *Financial support:* Applicants required to submit FAFSA. In 2006, 135 degrees awarded. Offers art history (MA); computational linguistics (Certificate); creative writing (MFA); digital media arts (MFA); English (MA); French (MA); humanities and the arts (MA, MFA, Certificate); linguistics (MA, Certificate); music (MA); philosophy (MA, Certificate); photography (MFA); pictorial arts (MFA); secondary English education (Certificate); Spanish (MA); spatial arts (MFA); teaching English to speakers of other languages (MA, Certificate); theatre arts (MA). *Application deadline:* For fall admission, 6/29 for domestic students; for spring admission, 11/30 for domestic students. Applications are processed on a rolling basis. *Application fee:* $59. Electronic applications accepted. *Dean,* Karl Toepfer, 408-924-4300, Fax: 408-924-4365.

College of Science Students: 157 full-time (72 women), 258 part-time (129 women); includes 140 minority (6 African Americans, 120 Asian Americans or Pacific Islanders, 14 Hispanic Americans), 104 international. Average age 32. 632 applicants, 62% accepted, 226 enrolled. Expenses: Contact institution. *Financial support:* Teaching assistantships, career-related internships or fieldwork, Federal Work-Study, and institutionally sponsored loans available. Support available to part-time students. Financial award applicants required to submit FAFSA. In 2006, 107 degrees awarded. *Degree program information:* Part-time and evening/weekend programs available. Offers biological sciences (MA, MS); chemistry (MA, MS); computational physics (MS); computer science (MS, Certificate); geology (MS); marine science (MS); mathematics (MA, MS); mathematics education (MA); meteorology (MS); molecular biology and microbiology (MS); organismal biology, conservation and ecology (MS); physics (MS); physiology (MS); science (MA, MS, Certificate). *Application deadline:* For fall admission, 6/29 for domestic students; for spring admission, 11/30 for domestic students. Applications are processed on a rolling basis. *Application fee:* $59. Electronic applications accepted. *Dean,* J. Michael Parrish, 408-924-4800, Fax: 408-924-4815.

College of Social Sciences Students: 274 full-time (171 women), 312 part-time (190 women); includes 181 minority (22 African Americans, 4 American Indian/Alaska Native, 70 Asian Americans or Pacific Islanders, 85 Hispanic Americans), 71 international. Average age 33. 508 applicants, 61% accepted, 214 enrolled. Expenses: Contact institution. *Financial support:* In 2006–07, 29 teaching assistantships were awarded; career-related internships or fieldwork, Federal Work-Study, institutionally sponsored loans, scholarships/grants, and tuition waivers (partial) also available. Support available to part-time students. Financial award applicants required to submit FAFSA. In 2006, 159 degrees awarded. *Degree program information:* Part-time and evening/weekend programs available. Offers applied economics (MA); clinical psychology (MS); communication (MA); criminology (MA); economics (MA); environmental studies (MS); experimental psychology (MA); geography (MA, Certificate); history (MA); history education (MA); industrial/organizational psychology (MS); Mexican-American studies (MA); psychology (MA); public administration (MPA); social sciences (MA, MPA, MS, MUP, Certificate); sociology (MA); urban and regional planning (MUP, Certificate). *Application deadline:* For fall admission, 6/29 for domestic students; for spring admission, 11/30 for domestic students. Applications are processed on a rolling basis. *Application fee:* $59. Electronic applications accepted. *Dean,* Tim Hegstrom, 408-924-5300, Fax: 408-924-5303.

Lucas Graduate School of Business Students: 76 full-time (44 women), 143 part-time (61 women); includes 86 minority (1 African American, 76 Asian Americans or Pacific Islanders, 9 Hispanic Americans), 51 international. Average age 32. 591 applicants, 54% accepted, 96 enrolled. Expenses: Contact institution. *Financial support:* Applicants required to submit FAFSA. In 2006, 206 degrees awarded. *Degree program information:* Part-time and evening/weekend programs available. Postbaccalaureate distance learning degree programs offered (minimal on-campus study). Offers accounting (MS); business (MBA, MS); business administration (MBA); taxation (MS); transportation management (MS). *Application deadline:* For fall admission, 6/29 for domestic students; for spring admission, 11/30 for domestic students. Applications are processed on a rolling basis. *Application fee:* $59. Electronic applications accepted. *Application Contact:* Karen Pieniaszek, Administrative Analyst, 408-924-3423, Fax: 408-924-3426, E-mail: pieniaszek_k@cob.sjsu.edu. *Interim Dean,* Dr. Nancie Fimbel, 408-924-3400, Fax: 408-924-3419, E-mail: fimbel_n@cob.sjsu.edu.

SAN JUAN BAUTISTA SCHOOL OF MEDICINE, Caguas, PR 00726-4968

General Information Independent, coed, graduate-only institution. *Enrollment by degree level:* 199 first professional. *Graduate faculty:* 30 full-time (12 women), 33 part-time/adjunct (9 women). *Graduate housing:* On-campus housing not available. *Student services:* Campus employment opportunities, career counseling, low-cost health insurance. *Library facilities:* San Juan Bautista School of Medicine Library. *Online resources:* library catalog, web page. *Collection:* 7,447 titles, 1,288 serial subscriptions, 8,659 audiovisual materials.

Computer facilities: 50 computers available on campus for general student use. A campuswide network can be accessed from off campus. Internet access is available. *Web address:* http://www.sanjuanbautista.edu/.

General Application Contact: Jaymi Sanchez, Admissions/Financial Aid Officer, 787-743-3038 Ext. 236, Fax: 787-746-3093, E-mail: jsanchez@sanjuanbautista.edu.

GRADUATE UNITS

Professional Program Students: 199 full-time (136 women); all minorities (all Hispanic Americans) 110 applicants, 67% accepted, 48 enrolled. *Faculty:* 30 full-time (12 women), 33 part-time/adjunct (9 women). Expenses: Contact institution. In 2006, 31 degrees awarded. Offers medicine (MD). *Application deadline:* For fall admission, 7/20 priority date for domestic students. Applications are processed on a rolling basis. *Application fee:* $75. *Application Contact:* Jaymi Sanchez, Admissions/Financial Aid Officer, 787-743-3038 Ext. 236, Fax: 787-746-3093, E-mail: jsanchez@sanjuanbautista.edu. *Academic Dean,* Dr. Myrna Borges, 787-743-3038 Ext. 254, E-mail: mborges@sanjuanbautista.edu.

SANTA CLARA UNIVERSITY, Santa Clara, CA 95053

General Information Independent-religious, coed, university. CGS member. *Enrollment:* 7,952 graduate, professional, and undergraduate students; 1,407 full-time matriculated graduate/professional students (703 women), 1,736 part-time matriculated graduate/professional students (681 women). *Enrollment by degree level:* 929 first professional, 1,935 master's, 48 doctoral, 231 other advanced degrees. *Graduate faculty:* 212 full-time (68 women), 124 part-time/adjunct (38 women). *Tuition:* Part-time $627 per unit. Tuition and fees vary according to program. *Graduate housing:* On-campus housing not available. *Student services:* Campus employment opportunities, campus safety program, career counseling, child daycare facilities, exercise/wellness program, free psychological counseling, international student services, multicultural affairs office. *Library facilities:* University Library plus 1 other. *Online resources:* library catalog, web page, access to other libraries' catalogs. *Collection:* 786,360 titles, 4,459 serial subscriptions, 10,493 audiovisual materials.

Computer facilities: Computer purchase and lease plans are available. 800 computers available on campus for general student use. A campuswide network can be accessed from student residence rooms and from off campus. Internet access and online class registration are available. *Web address:* http://www.scu.edu/.

General Application Contact: Ricahrd Toomey, Associate Vice Provost, Enrollment Mangement, 408-554-4966, E-mail: rtoomey@scu.edu.

GRADUATE UNITS

Leavey School of Business Students: 226 full-time (80 women), 869 part-time (254 women); includes 392 minority (11 African Americans, 3 American Indian/Alaska Native, 356 Asian Americans or Pacific Islanders, 22 Hispanic Americans), 231 international. Average age 33. 454 applicants, 73% accepted, 218 enrolled. *Faculty:* 83 full-time (16 women), 16 part-time/adjunct (3 women). Expenses: Contact institution. *Financial support:* Fellowships, research assistantships, career-related internships or fieldwork, Federal Work-Study, institutionally sponsored loans, and scholarships/grants available. Support available to part-time students. Financial award application deadline: 3/1; financial award applicants required to submit FAFSA. In 2006, 309 degrees awarded. *Degree program information:* Part-time and evening/weekend programs available. Offers business (EMBA, MBA, MSIS); business administration (EMBA, MBA); information systems (MSIS). *Application deadline:* For fall admission, 6/1 for domestic students; for winter admission, 9/1 for domestic students; for spring admission, 12/1 for domestic students. Applications are processed on a rolling basis. *Application fee:* $75 ($100 for international students). Electronic applications accepted. *Application Contact:* Elizabeth Ford, Assistant Dean of Admissions, 408-554-2752, Fax: 408-554-4571. *Dean,* Dr. Barry Posner, 408-554-4523.

School of Education, Counseling Psychology, and Pastoral Ministries Students: 172 full-time (148 women), 398 part-time (316 women); includes 131 minority (14 African Americans, 1 American Indian/Alaska Native, 53 Asian Americans or Pacific Islanders, 63 Hispanic Americans), 16 international. Average age 35. 287 applicants, 82% accepted, 171 enrolled. *Faculty:* 31 full-time (12 women), 27 part-time/adjunct (13 women). Expenses: Contact institution. *Financial support:* Fellowships, teaching assistantships, career-related internships or fieldwork, Federal Work-Study, institutionally sponsored loans, and scholarships/grants available. Support available to part-time students. Financial award application deadline: 3/1; financial award applicants required to submit FAFSA. In 2006, 178 master's, 33 other advanced degrees awarded. *Degree program information:* Part-time and evening/weekend programs available. Offers catechetics (MA); counseling (MA); counseling psychology (MA); education (MA); education, counseling psychology, and pastoral ministries (MA, Certificate); educational administration (MA); liturgical music (MA); multiple subject teaching (Certificate); pastoral liturgy (MA); single subject teaching (Certificate); special education (MA, Certificate); spirituality (MA); teacher education (Certificate). *Application deadline:* Applications are processed on a rolling basis. *Application fee:* $50. *Application Contact:* Helen Valine, Director of Admissions and Records, 408-554-7884, Fax: 408-551-4367, E-mail: hvaline@scu.edu. *Interim Dean,* Dr. Terry Shoup, 408-551-7069.

School of Engineering Students: 128 full-time (36 women), 416 part-time (82 women); includes 212 minority (3 African Americans, 1 American Indian/Alaska Native, 172 Asian Americans or Pacific Islanders, 36 Hispanic Americans), 142 international. Average age 31. 384 applicants, 66% accepted, 152 enrolled. *Faculty:* 40 full-time (11 women), 47 part-time/adjunct (7 women). Expenses: Contact institution. *Financial support:* Fellowships, research assistantships, teaching assistantships, career-related internships or fieldwork, Federal Work-Study, institutionally sponsored loans, and scholarships/grants available. Support available to part-time students. Financial award application deadline: 3/1; financial award applicants required to submit FAFSA. In 2006, 225 master's, 5 doctorates awarded. *Degree program information:* Part-time and evening/weekend programs available. Offers analog circuit design (Certificate); applied mathematics (MSAM); ASIC design and test (Certificate); civil engineering (MSCE); computer science and engineering (MSCSE, PhD, Engineer); controls (Certificate); data storage technologies (Certificate); digital signal processing (Certificate); dynamics (Certificate); electrical engineering (MSEE, PhD, Engineer); engineering (MS, MSAM, MSCE, MSCSE, MSE, MSE Mgt, MSEE, MSME, PhD, Certificate, Engineer); engineering management (MSE Mgt); fundamentals of electrical engineering (Certificate); grid computing (Certificate); information assurance (Certificate); materials engineering (Certificate); mechanical design analysis (Certificate); mechanical engineering (MSME, PhD, Engineer); mechatronics systems engineering (Certificate); networking (Certificate); software engineering (MS, Certificate); technology jump-start (Certificate); telecommunications management (Certificate); thermofluids (Certificate). *Application deadline:* For fall admission, 7/18 for domestic students; for spring admission, 2/1 for domestic students. Applications are processed on a rolling basis. *Application fee:* $60. Electronic applications accepted. *Application Contact:* Diana McDonald, Assistant Director for Admissions and Recruiting, 408-554-4313, Fax: 408-554-5474, E-mail: engrgrad@engr.scu.edu. *Dean,* Daniel Pitt, 408-554-4600.

School of Law Students: 881 full-time (439 women), 53 part-time (29 women); includes 362 minority (45 African Americans, 4 American Indian/Alaska Native, 229 Asian Americans or Pacific Islanders, 84 Hispanic Americans), 16 international. Average age 28. 3,782 applicants, 41% accepted, 329 enrolled. *Faculty:* 58 full-time (29 women), 34 part-time/adjunct (15 women). Expenses: Contact institution. *Financial support:* Fellowships, research assistantships, career-related internships or fieldwork, Federal Work-Study, institutionally sponsored loans, and scholarships/grants available. Support available to part-time students. Financial award application deadline: 2/1; financial award applicants required to submit FAFSA. In 2006, 286 JDs, 17 master's awarded. *Degree program information:* Part-time and evening/weekend programs available. Offers high technology law (Certificate); intellectual property law (LL M); international and comparative law (LL M); international law (Certificate); law (JD); public interest and social justice law (Certificate); U.S. law for foreign lawyers (LL M). *Application deadline:* For fall admission, 2/1 for domestic students. *Application fee:* $75. *Application Contact:* Julia Yaffee, Director of Admissions, 408-554-4800, Fax: 408-554-7897. *Dean,* Donald Polden, 408-554-4361.

SARAH LAWRENCE COLLEGE, Bronxville, NY 10708-5999

General Information Independent, coed, comprehensive institution. CGS member. *Enrollment:* 1,709 graduate, professional, and undergraduate students; 219 full-time matriculated graduate/professional students (180 women), 99 part-time matriculated graduate/professional students (92 women). *Enrollment by degree level:* 318 master's. *Graduate faculty:* 134 part-time/adjunct (78 women). *Tuition:* Full-time $23,520. *Required fees:* $404. Tuition and fees vary according to program and student level. *Graduate housing:* On-campus housing not available. *Student services:* Campus employment opportunities, career counseling, disabled student services, exercise/wellness program, free psychological counseling, grant writing training, international student services, low-cost health insurance, multicultural affairs office, teacher training, writing training. *Library facilities:* Esther Rauschenbush Library plus 2 others. *Online resources:* library catalog, web page, access to other libraries' catalogs. *Collection:* 298,611 titles, 917 serial subscriptions, 10,251 audiovisual materials. *Research affiliation:* Columbia University Medical Center, New York University Medical Center, Albert Einstein College of Medicine of Yeshiva University, New York Hospital–Cornell Medical Center, Westchester/New York Medical College.

Computer facilities: 110 computers available on campus for general student use. A campuswide network can be accessed from student residence rooms and from off campus. Internet access is available. *Web address:* http://www.sarahlawrence.edu/.

General Application Contact: Susan Guma, Dean of Graduate Studies, 914-395-2373, E-mail: sguma@mail.slc.edu.

GRADUATE UNITS

Graduate Studies Students: 219 full-time (180 women), 99 part-time (92 women); includes 48 minority (17 African Americans, 5 American Indian/Alaska Native, 17 Asian Americans or Pacific Islanders, 9 Hispanic Americans), 17 international. 706 applicants, 42% accepted, 141 enrolled. *Faculty:* 134 part-time/adjunct (78 women). Expenses: Contact institution. *Financial support:* In 2006–07, 201 students received support, including 188 fellowships (averaging $4,476 per year); career-related internships or fieldwork, Federal Work-Study, scholarships/grants, and unspecified assistantships also available. Support available to part-time students. Financial award application deadline: 3/1; financial award applicants required to submit CSS PROFILE or FAFSA. In 2006, 128 degrees awarded. *Degree program information:* Part-time programs available. Offers art of teaching (MS Ed); child development (MA); creative non-fiction (MFA); dance (MFA); fiction (MFA); health advocacy (MA); human genetics (MS); individualized study (MA); poetry (MFA); theater (MFA); women's history (MA). *Application fee:* $60. *Dean of Graduate Studies,* Susan Guma, 914-395-2373, E-mail: sguma@mail.slc.edu.

See Close-Up on page 1021.

SAVANNAH COLLEGE OF ART AND DESIGN, Savannah, GA 31402-3146

General Information Independent, coed, comprehensive institution. CGS member. *Enrollment:* 8,236 graduate, professional, and undergraduate students; 1,075 full-time matriculated graduate/professional students (559 women), 248 part-time matriculated graduate/professional students (135 women). *Enrollment by degree level:* 1,323 master's. *Graduate faculty:* 137 full-time (59 women), 13 part-time/adjunct (2 women). *Tuition:* Full-time $23,400; part-time $520 per credit. One-time fee: $500. *Graduate housing:* Room and/or apartments available on a first-come, first-served basis to single students; on-campus housing not available to married students. Typical cost: $6,350 per year ($9,700 including board). Room and board charges vary according to board plan and housing facility selected. Housing application deadline: 4/1. *Student services:* Campus employment opportunities, campus safety program, career counseling, disabled student services, exercise/wellness program, free psychological counseling, international student services, multicultural affairs office, teacher training, writing training. *Library facilities:* Jen Library plus 1 other. *Online resources:* library catalog, web page. *Collection:* 170,909 titles, 948 serial subscriptions, 5,710 audiovisual materials.

Computer facilities: Computer purchase and lease plans are available. 2,220 computers available on campus for general student use. A campuswide network can be accessed from student residence rooms and from off campus. Internet access and online class registration are available. *Web address:* http://www.scad.edu/.

General Application Contact: Darrell Tutchton, Director of Graduate and International Enrollment, 912-525-5961, Fax: 912-525-5985, E-mail: admission@scad.edu.

GRADUATE UNITS

Graduate School Students: 1,074 full-time (559 women), 251 part-time (135 women); includes 129 minority (85 African Americans, 4 American Indian/Alaska Native, 11 Asian Americans or Pacific Islanders, 29 Hispanic Americans), 284 international. Average age 25. 1,720 applicants, 52% accepted, 466 enrolled. *Faculty:* 244 full-time (95 women), 19 part-time/adjunct (5 women). Expenses: Contact institution. *Financial support:* Fellowships, career-related internships or fieldwork, Federal Work-Study, and scholarships/grants available. Financial award application deadline: 4/1; financial award applicants required to submit FAFSA. In 2006, 391 degrees awarded. *Degree program information:* Part-time programs available. Offers advertising design (MA, MFA); animation (MA, MFA); architectural history (MA, MFA); architecture (M Arch); art history (MA, MFA); arts administration (MA); broadcast design (MA, MFA); cinema studies (MA); commercial photography (MA); contemporary writing (MFA); digital photography (MA); documentary photography (MA); fashion (MA, MFA); fibers (MA, MFA); film and television (MA, MFA); furniture design (MA, MFA); graphic design (MA, MFA); historic preservation (MA, MFA); illustration (MA, MFA); illustration design (MA); industrial design (MA, MFA); interactive design and game development (MA, MFA); interior design (MA, MFA); metals and jewelry (MA, MFA); painting (MA, MFA); performing arts (MA, MFA); photography (MA, MFA); printmaking (MA, MFA); production design (MA, MFA); sculpture (MA, MFA); sequential art (MA, MFA); sound design (MA, MFA); typeface design (MA); urban design and development (MA); visual effects (MA, MFA). *Application deadline:* For fall admission, 4/1 priority date for domestic and international students. Applications are processed on a rolling basis. *Application fee:* $50. Electronic applications accepted. *Application Contact:* Darrell Tutchton, Director of Graduate and International Enrollment, 912-525-5961, Fax: 912-525-5985, E-mail: admission@scad.edu.

SAVANNAH STATE UNIVERSITY, Savannah, GA 31404

General Information State-supported, coed, comprehensive institution. *Graduate housing:* On-campus housing not available.

GRADUATE UNITS

Program in Marine Science *Degree program information:* Part-time programs available. Offers marine science (MS). Electronic applications accepted.

Program in Public Administration Offers public administration (MPA).

Program in Social Work Offers social work (MSW).

Program in Urban Studies *Degree program information:* Part-time programs available. Offers urban studies (MS).

SAYBROOK GRADUATE SCHOOL AND RESEARCH CENTER, San Francisco, CA 94111-1920

General Information Independent, coed, graduate-only institution. *Enrollment by degree level:* 97 master's, 382 doctoral. *Graduate faculty:* 19 full-time (8 women), 109 part-time/adjunct (38 women). *Graduate housing:* On-campus housing not available. *Library facilities:* Library and Information Services plus 1 other. *Online resources:* library catalog, web page. *Collection:* 20,000 titles, 10,000 serial subscriptions, 20 audiovisual materials. *Research affiliation:* Rollo May Center for Humanistic Studies.

Computer facilities: A campuswide network can be accessed from off campus. Internet access and online class registration are available. *Web address:* http://www.saybrook.edu/.

General Application Contact: Director of Admissions, 800-825-4480, Fax: 415-433-9271, E-mail: admissions@saybrook.edu.

GRADUATE UNITS

Program in Psychology, Human Science and Organizational Systems Students: 479 full-time (333 women); includes 62 minority (30 African Americans, 1 American Indian/Alaska Native, 13 Asian Americans or Pacific Islanders, 18 Hispanic Americans), 18 international. Average age 43. 280 applicants, 52% accepted, 105 enrolled. *Faculty:* 15 full-time (5 women), 83 part-time/adjunct (34 women). Expenses: Contact institution. *Financial support:* In 2006–07, 335 students received support. Scholarships/grants available. Financial award applicants required to submit FAFSA. In 2006, 28 master's, 43 doctorates awarded. Postbaccalaureate distance learning degree programs offered (minimal on-campus study). Offers human science (MA, PhD); organizational systems (MA, PhD); psychology (MA, PhD). *Application deadline:* For fall admission, 6/1 priority date for domestic students; for spring admission, 12/16 priority date for domestic students. *Application fee:* $50. Electronic applications accepted. *Application Contact:* Director of Admissions, 800-825-4480, Fax: 415-433-9271, E-mail: admissions@saybrook.edu. *President,* Lorne Buchman, 800-825-4480, Fax: 415-433-9271.

SCHILLER INTERNATIONAL UNIVERSITY, D-69121 Heidelberg, Germany

General Information Independent, coed, comprehensive institution. *Enrollment:* 175 graduate, professional, and undergraduate students; 25 full-time matriculated graduate/professional students, 7 part-time matriculated graduate/professional students. *Enrollment by degree level:* 32 master's. *Graduate faculty:* 7 full-time (3 women), 14 part-time/adjunct (4 women). *Graduate tuition:* Tuition charges are reported in euros. *Tuition:* Full-time 20,938 euros; part-time 1,651 euros per course. *Graduate housing:* Room and/or apartments available on a first-come, first-served basis to single students; on-campus housing not available to married students. Typical cost: 1,783 euros (including board). *Student services:* Campus employment opportunities, career counseling, international student services, low-cost health insurance. *Library facilities:* SIU Library plus 1 other. *Collection:* 8,000 titles, 94 serial subscriptions.

Computer facilities: 16 computers available on campus for general student use. *Web address:* http://www.schiller.edu/.

General Application Contact: Susan Russeff, Assistant Director of Admissions, 727-736-5082, Fax: 727-734-0359, E-mail: admissions@schiller.edu.

GRADUATE UNITS

MBA Programs, Heidelberg, Germany Students: 28 full-time, 4 part-time. Average age 28. *Faculty:* 7 full-time (3 women), 14 part-time/adjunct (4 women). Expenses: Contact institution. *Financial support:* In 2006–07, 32 students received support. Scholarships/grants, tuition waivers (partial), and unspecified assistantships available. Support available to part-time students. Financial award application deadline: 3/30; financial award applicants required to submit FAFSA. In 2006, 15 degrees awarded. *Degree program information:* Part-time and evening/weekend programs available. Offers international business (MBA, MIM); management of information technology (MBA). *Application deadline:* For fall admission, 8/1 priority date for domestic and international students; for spring admission, 12/1 priority date for domestic and international students. Applications are processed on a rolling basis. *Application fee:* $60. *Application Contact:* Susan Russeff, Assistant Director of Admissions, 727-736-5082, Fax: 727-734-0359, E-mail: admissions@schiller.edu. *Director,* Dr. Nicolle Macho, 49-6221-458135, Fax: 49-6221-402703, E-mail: campus@siu-heidelberg.de.

SCHILLER INTERNATIONAL UNIVERSITY, F-75017 Paris, France

General Information Independent, coed, comprehensive institution. *Enrollment:* 145 graduate, professional, and undergraduate students; 22 full-time matriculated graduate/professional students, 28 part-time matriculated graduate/professional students. *Enrollment by degree level:* 50 master's. *Graduate faculty:* 5 full-time (1 woman), 10 part-time/adjunct (5 women). *Graduate tuition:* Tuition charges are reported in euros. *Tuition:* Full-time 21,812 euros; part-time 1,724 euros per course. Tuition and fees vary according to degree level. *Graduate housing:* On-campus housing not available. *Student services:* Campus employment opportunities, career counseling, international student services, low-cost health insurance. *Library facilities:* Schiller Library plus 1 other. *Online resources:* library catalog, access to other libraries' catalogs. *Collection:* 3,797 titles, 41 serial subscriptions.

Computer facilities: 11 computers available on campus for general student use. *Web address:* http://www.schiller.edu/.

General Application Contact: Susan Russeff, Associate Director of Admissions, 727-736-5082 Ext. 239, Fax: 727-734-0359, E-mail: admissions@schiller.edu.

GRADUATE UNITS

MBA Program Paris, France Students: 50. *Faculty:* 5 full-time (1 woman), 10 part-time/adjunct (5 women). Expenses: Contact institution. *Financial support:* In 2006–07, 14 students received support; teaching assistantships, scholarships/grants, tuition waivers (partial), and unspecified assistantships available. Support available to part-time students. Financial award application deadline: 3/30; financial award applicants required to submit FAFSA. In 2006, 12 degrees awarded. *Degree program information:* Part-time and evening/weekend programs available. Offers international business (MBA). Bilingual French/English MBA available for native French speakers. *Application deadline:* For fall admission, 8/1 priority date for domestic and international students; for spring admission, 12/1 priority date for domestic and international students. Applications are processed on a rolling basis. *Application fee:* $60. *Application Contact:* Kamala Dontamsetti, Associate Director of Admissions, 813-736-5082 Ext. 240, Fax: 813-734-0359, E-mail: admissions@schiller.edu. *Adviser,* Hassan Mansoor, 1-4538-5601, Fax: 1-4538-5430, E-mail: info-schiller@schillerparis.com.

Program in International Relations and Diplomacy Students: 11 full-time, 19 part-time. Average age 25. Expenses: Contact institution. *Financial support:* Teaching assistantships, scholarships/grants and unspecified assistantships available. Support available to part-time students. Financial award application deadline: 3/30; financial award applicants required to submit FAFSA. *Degree program information:* Part-time and evening/weekend programs available. Offers international relations and diplomacy (MA). *Application deadline:* For fall admission, 8/1 priority date for domestic and international students; for spring admission, 12/1 priority date for domestic and international students. Applications are processed on a rolling basis. *Application fee:* $50. *Application Contact:* Kamala Dontamsetti, Associate Director of Admissions, 813-736-5082 Ext. 240, Fax: 813-734-0359, E-mail: admissions@schiller.edu.

SCHILLER INTERNATIONAL UNIVERSITY, 28015 Madrid, Spain

General Information Independent, coed, comprehensive institution. *Enrollment:* 90 graduate, professional, and undergraduate students; 11 full-time matriculated graduate/professional students, 3 part-time matriculated graduate/professional students. *Enrollment by degree level:* 14 master's. *Graduate faculty:* 6 full-time, 4 part-time/adjunct. *Tuition:* Full-time $20,958; part-time $1,652 per course. Tuition and fees vary according to degree level. *Graduate housing:* On-campus housing not available. *Student services:* Campus employment opportunities, career counseling, international student services, low-cost health insurance. *Library facilities:* Schiller Library plus 1 other. *Online resources:* library catalog, access to other libraries' catalogs. *Collection:* 4,216 titles, 58 serial subscriptions.

Computer facilities: 8 computers available on campus for general student use. *Web address:* http://www.schillermadrid.edu/.

General Application Contact: Susan Russeff, Associate Director of Admissions, 727-736-5082, Fax: 727-734-0359, E-mail: admissions@schiller.edu.

GRADUATE UNITS

MBA Program, Madrid, Spain Students: 7 full-time, 3 part-time. Average age 28. *Faculty:* 6 full-time, 4 part-time/adjunct. Expenses: Contact institution. *Financial support:* In 2006–07, 8 students received support. Career-related internships or fieldwork, scholarships/grants, tuition waivers (partial), and unspecified assistantships available. Support available to part-time students. Financial award application deadline: 3/30; financial award applicants required to submit FAFSA. *Degree program information:* Part-time programs available. Offers international business (MBA). *Application deadline:* For fall admission, 8/1 priority date for domestic and international students; for spring admission, 12/1 priority date for domestic and international students. Applications are processed on a rolling basis. *Application fee:* $60. *Application Contact:* Susan Russeff, Associate Director of Admissions, 727-736-5082, Fax: 727-734-0359, E-mail: admissions@schiller.edu. *Adviser,* Lynn Bergunde, 34-91-448-2488, Fax: 34-91-445-2110, E-mail: admissions@schillermadrid.edu.

SCHILLER INTERNATIONAL UNIVERSITY, F-67000 Strasbourg, France

General Information Independent, coed, graduate-only institution. *Enrollment by degree level:* 11 master's. *Graduate faculty:* 3 full-time, 5 part-time/adjunct. *Tuition:* Part-time $1,282 per course. *Graduate housing:* Rooms and/or apartments available to single and married students. Housing application deadline: 8/1. *Student services:* Campus employment opportunities, career counseling, international student services, low-cost health insurance. *Collection:* 30 titles. *Web address:* http://www.schiller.edu/.

General Application Contact: Kamala Dontamsetti, Associate Director of Admissions, 727-736-5082 Ext. 240, Fax: 727-734-0359, E-mail: admissions@schiller.edu.

GRADUATE UNITS

MBA Program, Strasbourg, France Campus Average age 28. *Faculty:* 8. Expenses: Contact institution. *Financial support:* Teaching assistantships, tuition waivers (partial) and unspecified assistantships available. Support available to part-time students. Financial award application deadline: 3/30; financial award applicants required to submit FAFSA. In 2006, 13 degrees awarded. *Degree program information:* Part-time and evening/weekend programs available. Postbaccalaureate distance learning degree programs offered (no on-campus study). Offers international business (MBA). *Application deadline:* For fall admission, 8/1 priority date for domestic and international students; for spring admission, 12/1 priority date for domestic and international students. Applications are processed on a rolling basis. *Application fee:* $60. *Application Contact:* Kamala Dontamsetti, Associate Director of Admissions, 727-736-5082 Ext. 240, Fax: 727-734-0359, E-mail: admissions@schiller.edu. *Director,* Anne Zedler, 33-3884-58464, Fax: 33-3884-58460, E-mail: siustrmba@aol.com.

SCHILLER INTERNATIONAL UNIVERSITY, London SE1 8TX, United Kingdom

General Information Independent, coed, comprehensive institution. *Enrollment:* 383 graduate, professional, and undergraduate students; 46 full-time matriculated graduate/professional students (30 women). *Enrollment by degree level:* 46 master's. *Graduate faculty:* 7 full-time (1 woman), 9 part-time/adjunct (0 women). *Tuition:* Full-time $20,306; part-time $1,601 per course. *Graduate housing:* Room and/or apartments available on a first-come, first-served basis to single students; on-campus housing not available to married students. Typical cost:

Schiller International University (continued)

$3,612 per year ($5,955 including board). Housing application deadline: 8/1. *Student services:* Campus employment opportunities, career counseling, free psychological counseling, international student services, low-cost health insurance, multicultural affairs office. *Library facilities:* SIU Library. *Collection:* 21,603 titles, 143 serial subscriptions.

Computer facilities: 39 computers available on campus for general student use. *Web address:* http://www.schiller.edu/.

General Application Contact: Susan Russeff, Associate Director of Admissions, 727-736-5082, Fax: 727-734-0359, E-mail: admissions@schiller.edu.

GRADUATE UNITS

Graduate Programs, London Students: 46 full-time. Average age 24. 50 applicants, 92% accepted, 46 enrolled. *Faculty:* 6 full-time (1 woman), 9 part-time/adjunct (0 women). Expenses: Contact institution. *Financial support:* In 2006–07, 11 students received support. Scholarships/grants and administrative assistantships available. Support available to part-time students. Financial award application deadline: 3/30; financial award applicants required to submit FAFSA. In 2006, 57 degrees awarded. *Degree program information:* Part-time and evening/weekend programs available. Postbaccalaureate distance learning degree programs offered (no on-campus study). Offers business communication (MA); international business (MBA); international hotel and tourism management (MA, MBA); international management (MIM); international relations and diplomacy (MA); management of information technology (MBA). *Application deadline:* For fall admission, 8/1 priority date for domestic and international students; for spring admission, 12/1 priority date for domestic and international students. Applications are processed on a rolling basis. *Application fee:* $60. *Application Contact:* Susan Russeff, Associate Director of Admissions, 727-736-5082, Fax: 727-734-0359, E-mail: admissions@schiller.edu. *Director,* Dr. Elizabeth Nunn, 44-207-928-1372, Fax: 44-207-620-1226, E-mail: admissions@schillerlondon.ac.uk.

SCHILLER INTERNATIONAL UNIVERSITY, Largo, FL 33770

General Information Independent, coed, comprehensive institution. *Enrollment:* 246 graduate, professional, and undergraduate students; 146 matriculated graduate/professional students. *Enrollment by degree level:* 146 master's. *Graduate faculty:* 5 full-time (0 women), 10 part-time/adjunct (1 woman). *Tuition:* Full-time $17,920; part-time $1,420 per course. *Graduate housing:* Room and/or apartments available on a first-come, first-served basis to single students; on-campus housing not available to married students. Typical cost: $9,525 (including board). Housing application deadline: 8/1. *Student services:* Campus employment opportunities, career counseling, free psychological counseling, international student services, multicultural affairs office. *Library facilities:* SIU Library. *Collection:* 1,918 titles, 34 serial subscriptions.

Computer facilities: 17 computers available on campus for general student use. Internet access is available. *Web address:* http://www.schiller.edu/.

General Application Contact: Susan Russeff, Associate Director of Admissions, 727-736-5082, Fax: 727-734-0359, E-mail: admissions@schiller.edu.

GRADUATE UNITS

MBA Programs, Florida Students: 146. Average age 25. *Faculty:* 5 full-time (0 women), 10 part-time/adjunct (1 woman). Expenses: Contact institution. *Financial support:* Federal Work-Study, scholarships/grants, tuition waivers (partial), and unspecified assistantships available. Support available to part-time students. Financial award application deadline: 3/30; financial award applicants required to submit FAFSA. In 2006, 39 degrees awarded. *Degree program information:* Part-time and evening/weekend programs available. Postbaccalaureate distance learning degree programs offered (no on-campus study). Offers financial planning (MBA); information technology (MBA); international business (MBA); international hotel and tourism management (MBA). *Application deadline:* For fall admission, 8/1 priority date for domestic and international students; for spring admission, 12/1 priority date for domestic and international students. Applications are processed on a rolling basis. *Application fee:* $60. *Application Contact:* Susan Russeff, Associate Director of Admissions, 727-736-5082, Fax: 727-734-0359, E-mail: admissions@schiller.edu. *Head,* Dr. Cathy Eberhart, 727-736-5082, Fax: 727-734-0359.

SCHILLER INTERNATIONAL UNIVERSITY, AMERICAN COLLEGE OF SWITZERLAND, CH-1854 Leysin, Switzerland

General Information Independent, coed, comprehensive institution. *Enrollment:* 83 graduate, professional, and undergraduate students; 8 full-time matriculated graduate/professional students. *Enrollment by degree level:* 8 master's. *Graduate faculty:* 18. *Tuition:* Full-time $22,622; part-time $1,178 per course. *Graduate housing:* Room and/or apartments available to single students; on-campus housing not available to married students. Typical cost: $4,503 (including board). Housing application deadline: 8/15. *Student services:* Campus employment opportunities, career counseling, low-cost health insurance. *Collection:* 48,355 titles, 200 serial subscriptions.

Computer facilities: 17 computers available on campus for general student use. Internet access is available. *Web address:* http://www.american-college.com/.

General Application Contact: Bethani Ann Delong Vehapi, Director of Admissions, 41-244930309, Fax: 41-244930300, E-mail: siuadmissions@bluewin.ch.

GRADUATE UNITS

MBA Program Students: 8 full-time. Average age 23. *Faculty:* 6. Expenses: Contact institution. *Financial support:* In 2006–07, 3 students received support, including teaching assistantships (averaging $6,895 per year); career-related internships or fieldwork, scholarships/grants, tuition waivers (partial), and unspecified assistantships also available. Support available to part-time students. Financial award application deadline: 4/1; financial award applicants required to submit FAFSA. *Degree program information:* Part-time programs available. Postbaccalaureate distance learning degree programs offered (no on-campus study). Offers international business (MBA). *Application deadline:* For fall admission, 8/1 priority date for domestic and international students; for spring admission, 12/1 priority date for domestic and international students. Applications are processed on a rolling basis. *Application fee:* $60. *Application Contact:* Bethani Ann Delong Vehapi, Director of Admissions, 41-244930309, Fax: 41-244930300, E-mail: siuadmissions@bluewin.ch. *Provost,* Nancy Carroll, 41-244930303, Fax: 41-244930300, E-mail: acs_provost@bluewin.ch.

SCHOOL FOR INTERNATIONAL TRAINING, Brattleboro, VT 05302-0676

General Information Independent, coed, graduate-only institution. *Enrollment by degree level:* 620 master's. *Graduate faculty:* 27 full-time (12 women), 19 part-time/adjunct (8 women). *Tuition:* Full-time $27,355; part-time $638 per credit hour. *Required fees:* $1,092. *Graduate housing:* Rooms and/or apartments available on a first-come, first-served basis to single and married students. Typical cost: $2,654 per year ($6,074 including board) for single students. Room and board charges vary according to board plan. *Student services:* Campus employment opportunities, campus safety program, career counseling, disabled student services, exercise/wellness program, free psychological counseling, international student services, low-cost health insurance, multicultural affairs office, teacher training, writing training. *Library facilities:* Donald B. Watt Library. *Online resources:* library catalog, web page. *Collection:* 32,000 titles, 450 serial subscriptions, 2,000 audiovisual materials.

Computer facilities: 55 computers available on campus for general student use. A campuswide network can be accessed from student residence rooms and from off campus. Internet access is available. *Web address:* http://www.sit.edu/.

General Application Contact: Information Contact, 800-336-1616, Fax: 802-258-3500, E-mail: admissions@sit.edu.

GRADUATE UNITS

Graduate Programs Students: 237 full-time (161 women), 383 part-time (276 women); includes 75 minority (33 African Americans, 3 American Indian/Alaska Native, 15 Asian Americans or Pacific Islanders, 24 Hispanic Americans), 129 international. Average age 32. 769 applicants, 75% accepted, 214 enrolled. *Faculty:* 27 full-time (12 women), 19 part-time/adjunct (8 women). Expenses: Contact institution. *Financial support:* In 2006–07, 397 students received support. Career-related internships or fieldwork, Federal Work-Study, institutionally sponsored loans, and scholarships/grants available. Financial award application deadline: 3/1; financial award applicants required to submit FAFSA. In 2006, 145 master's awarded. Postbaccalaureate distance learning degree programs offered (minimal on-campus study). Offers conflict transformation (MA); English for speakers of other languages (MAT); French (MAT); intercultural service, leadership, and management (MA); international education (MA); management (MS); social justice in intercultural relations (MA); Spanish (MAT); sustainable development (MA). *Application deadline:* Applications are processed on a rolling basis. *Application fee:* $50. Electronic applications accepted. *Application Contact:* Information Contact, 800-336-1616, Fax: 802-258-3500, E-mail: admissions@sit.edu. *Provost/Executive Vice President,* Adam Weinberg, 802-258-3357, Fax: 802-258-3110, E-mail: adam.weinberg@sit.edu.

See Close-Up on page 1023.

SCHOOL OF ADVANCED AIR AND SPACE STUDIES, Maxwell AFB, AL 36112-6424

General Information Federally supported, graduate-only institution.

GRADUATE UNITS

Program in Airpower Art and Science Offers airpower art and science (MA). Available to active duty military officers only.

SCHOOL OF THE ART INSTITUTE OF CHICAGO, Chicago, IL 60603-3103

General Information Independent, coed, comprehensive institution. *Graduate housing:* Room and/or apartments available on a first-come, first-served basis to single students; on-campus housing not available to married students. Housing application deadline: 3/21.

GRADUATE UNITS

Graduate Division *Degree program information:* Part-time programs available. Offers art and technology (MFA); art education (MAAE, Certificate); art history, theory, and criticism (MA, Certificate); art therapy (MAAT); arts administration (MAAA); ceramics (MFA); fiber (MFA); filmmaking (MFA); historic preservation (MSHP); interior architecture (MFA); painting and drawing (MFA); performance art (MFA); photography (MFA); printmaking (MFA); sculpture (MFA); video (MFA); visual communication (MFA); writing (MFA).

SCHOOL OF THE MUSEUM OF FINE ARTS, BOSTON, Boston, MA 02115

General Information Independent, coed, comprehensive institution. *Graduate housing:* On-campus housing not available.

GRADUATE UNITS

Graduate Program Offers fine arts (MAT, MFA).

SCHOOL OF VISUAL ARTS, New York, NY 10010-3994

General Information Proprietary, coed, comprehensive institution. *Enrollment:* 3,715 graduate, professional, and undergraduate students; 380 full-time matriculated graduate/professional students (241 women), 27 part-time matriculated graduate/professional students (17 women). *Enrollment by degree level:* 407 master's. *Graduate faculty:* 8 full-time (1 woman), 106 part-time/adjunct (38 women). *Tuition:* Full-time $22,400. Full-time tuition and fees vary according to program. *Graduate housing:* Room and/or apartments available on a first-come, first-served basis to single students; on-campus housing not available to married students. Typical cost: $10,800 per year. Room charges vary according to housing facility selected. *Student services:* Campus employment opportunities, campus safety program, career counseling, disabled student services, free psychological counseling, grant writing training, international student services, low-cost health insurance, writing training. *Library facilities:* School of Visual Arts Library. *Online resources:* library catalog, access to other libraries' catalogs. *Collection:* 71,490 titles, 340 serial subscriptions, 1,000 audiovisual materials.

Computer facilities: Computer purchase and lease plans are available. 600 computers available on campus for general student use. A campuswide network can be accessed from student residence rooms and from off campus. Internet access is available. *Web address:* http://www.schoolofvisualarts.edu/.

General Application Contact: Randal Lynch, Assistant Manager Graduate Admissions, 212-592-2100, Fax: 212-592-2116, E-mail: gradadmissions@sva.edu.

GRADUATE UNITS

Graduate Programs Students: 380 full-time (241 women), 27 part-time (17 women); includes 61 minority (12 African Americans, 27 Asian Americans or Pacific Islanders, 22 Hispanic Americans), 129 international. Average age 28. 1,290 applicants, 36% accepted, 205 enrolled. *Faculty:* 8 full-time (1 woman), 106 part-time/adjunct (38 women). Expenses: Contact institution. *Financial support:* In 2006–07, 176 students received support. Career-related internships or fieldwork, scholarships/grants, and unspecified assistantships available. Financial award application deadline: 2/1; financial award applicants required to submit FAFSA. In 2006, 182 degrees awarded. Offers art criticism and writing (MFA); art education (MAT); art therapy (MPS); computer art (MFA); design (MFA); digital photography (MPS); illustration (MFA); painting (MFA); photography (MFA); printmaking (MFA); sculpture (MFA). *Application deadline:* For fall admission, 2/1 for domestic students. *Application fee:* $70 ($80 for international students). Electronic applications accepted. *President,* David Rhodes, 212-592-2350, Fax: 212-260-7621, E-mail: president@sva.edu.

See Close-Up on page 1025.

SCHREINER UNIVERSITY, Kerrville, TX 78028-5697

General Information Independent-religious, coed, comprehensive institution. *Graduate housing:* Rooms and/or apartments available on a first-come, first-served basis to single and married students. Housing application deadline: 8/1.

GRADUATE UNITS

Program in Education *Degree program information:* Evening/weekend programs available. Offers education (M Ed, MET). Electronic applications accepted.

THE SCRIPPS RESEARCH INSTITUTE, La Jolla, CA 92037

General Information Independent, coed, graduate-only institution. *Enrollment by degree level:* 200 doctoral. *Graduate faculty:* 119 full-time (21 women). *Tuition:* Full-time $5,000. *Graduate housing:* On-campus housing not available. *Student services:* Campus employment opportunities, campus safety program, career counseling, disabled student services, exercise/wellness program, free psychological counseling, grant writing training, international student services, low-cost health insurance, multicultural affairs office, teacher training, writing training. *Library facilities:* Kresge Library. *Online resources:* library catalog, web page, access to other libraries' catalogs. *Collection:* 45,865 titles, 765 serial subscriptions, 255 audiovisual materials.

Computer facilities: 257 computers available on campus for general student use. A campuswide network can be accessed from student residence rooms and from off campus. Internet access is available. *Web address:* http://www.scripps.edu/.

General Application Contact: Marylyn Rinaldi, Administrative Director, 858-784-8469, Fax: 858-784-2802, E-mail: mrinaldi@scripps.edu.

GRADUATE UNITS

Kellogg School of Science and Technology Students: 230 full-time (85 women). Average age 22. 590 applicants, 22% accepted, 45 enrolled. *Faculty:* 119 full-time (21 women). Expenses: Contact institution. *Financial support:* Institutionally sponsored loans and stipends available. In 2006, 27 degrees awarded. Offers biology (PhD); biophysics (PhD);

chemical biology (PhD); chemistry (PhD); science and technology (PhD). *Application deadline:* For fall admission, 1/1 for domestic and international students. *Application fee:* $0. *Application Contact:* Marylyn Rinaldi, Administrative Director, 858-784-8469, Fax: 858-784-2802, E-mail: mrinaldi@scripps.edu. *Dean,* Dr. Jeffery W. Kelly, 858-784-8469, Fax: 858-784-2801, E-mail: gradprgm@scripps.edu.

SEABURY-WESTERN THEOLOGICAL SEMINARY, Evanston, IL 60201-2976

General Information Independent-religious, coed, graduate-only institution. *Graduate housing:* Rooms and/or apartments available to single students and available on a first-come, first-served basis to married students. Housing application deadline: 5/30.

GRADUATE UNITS

School of Theology *Degree program information:* Part-time programs available. Offers Anglican ministries (D Min); congregational development (MTS, D Min); preaching (D Min); theological studies (MTS); theology (M Div, L Th). MTS and D Min (congregational development) offered in summer only.

SEATTLE INSTITUTE OF ORIENTAL MEDICINE, Seattle, WA 98115

General Information Proprietary, coed, primarily women, graduate-only institution. *Enrollment by degree level:* 31 master's. *Graduate faculty:* 2 full-time (0 women), 9 part-time/adjunct (3 women). *Tuition:* Part-time $5,100 per trimester. *Graduate housing:* On-campus housing not available. *Student services:* Low-cost health insurance. *Library facilities:* SIOM Library. *Collection:* 500 titles, 25 serial subscriptions.

Computer facilities: 2 computers available on campus for general student use. Internet access is available. *Web address:* http://www.siom.edu/.

General Application Contact: Paul D. Karsten, President, 206-517-4541, Fax: 206-526-1932, E-mail: pkarsten@siom.edu.

GRADUATE UNITS

Graduate Program Students: 31 full-time (23 women). Average age 37. 38 applicants, 55% accepted, 14 enrolled. *Faculty:* 2 full-time (0 women), 9 part-time/adjunct (3 women). Expenses: Contact institution. In 2006, 12 degrees awarded. Offers Oriental medicine (M Ac OM). *Application deadline:* Applications are processed on a rolling basis. *Application fee:* $50. *Application Contact:* Anna Couch, Registrar, 206-517-4541 Ext. 1, Fax: 206-526-1932, E-mail: acouch@siom.edu. *President,* Paul D. Karsten, 206-517-4541, Fax: 206-526-1932, E-mail: pkarsten@siom.edu.

SEATTLE PACIFIC UNIVERSITY, Seattle, WA 98119-1997

General Information Independent-religious, coed, comprehensive institution. *Enrollment:* 3,830 graduate, professional, and undergraduate students; 217 full-time matriculated graduate/professional students (159 women), 523 part-time matriculated graduate/professional students (366 women). *Enrollment by degree level:* 571 master's, 169 doctoral. *Graduate faculty:* 52 full-time (23 women). *Graduate housing:* Rooms and/or apartments available on a first-come, first-served basis to single and married students. Housing application deadline: 8/1. *Student services:* Campus employment opportunities, campus safety program, career counseling, disabled student services, exercise/wellness program, free psychological counseling, international student services, low-cost health insurance, multicultural affairs office, teacher training, writing training. *Library facilities:* Seattle Pacific University Library. *Online resources:* library catalog, web page, access to other libraries' catalogs. *Collection:* 191,807 titles, 1,230 serial subscriptions, 4,408 audiovisual materials. *Research affiliation:* Fred Hutchinson Cancer Research Center (cancer and tumors), Washington Research Center/Gates Foundation (education effectiveness), Battelle Research Center (business marketing).

Computer facilities: 150 computers available on campus for general student use. A campuswide network can be accessed from student residence rooms and from off campus. Internet access and online class registration are available. *Web address:* http://www.spu.edu/.

General Application Contact: John Glancy, Director, Graduate Admissions/Marketing, 206-281-2325, Fax: 206-281-2877, E-mail: jglancy@spu.edu.

GRADUATE UNITS

Graduate School Students: 217 full-time (159 women), 523 part-time (366 women); includes 91 minority (8 African Americans, 50 American Indian/Alaska Native, 21 Asian Americans or Pacific Islanders, 12 Hispanic Americans), 20 international. Average age 36. 589 applicants, 60% accepted, 275 enrolled. *Faculty:* 52 full-time (23 women). Expenses: Contact institution. *Financial support:* In 2006–07, 366 students received support; research assistantships, teaching assistantships, career-related internships or fieldwork, traineeships, and unspecified assistantships available. Financial award applicants required to submit FAFSA. In 2006, 204 master's, 29 doctorates awarded. *Degree program information:* Part-time and evening/weekend programs available. Postbaccalaureate distance learning degree programs offered (no on-campus study). *Application deadline:* Applications are processed on a rolling basis. *Application fee:* $50. *Application Contact:* John Glancy, Director, Graduate Admissions/Marketing, 206-281-2325, Fax: 206-281-2877, E-mail: jglancy@spu.edu. *Vice President for Academic Affairs,* Dr. Les L. Steele, 206-281-2125, Fax: 206-281-2115, E-mail: lsteele@spu.edu.

College of Arts and Sciences Students: 10 full-time (8 women), 41 part-time (27 women); includes 8 minority (2 African Americans, 5 American Indian/Alaska Native, 1 Asian American or Pacific Islander), 6 international. 54 applicants, 35% accepted, 14 enrolled. *Faculty:* 5 full-time (3 women). Expenses: Contact institution. *Financial support:* Research assistantships, career-related internships or fieldwork and unspecified assistantships available. Financial award applicants required to submit FAFSA. In 2006, 28 degrees awarded. *Degree program information:* Part-time and evening/weekend programs available. Offers arts and sciences (MA); fine arts (MA); teaching English as a second language (MA). *Application deadline:* Applications are processed on a rolling basis. *Dean,* Dr. Bruce Congdon, 206-281-2165.

School of Business and Economics Students: 19 full-time (8 women), 91 part-time (40 women); includes 21 minority (6 African Americans, 1 American Indian/Alaska Native, 12 Asian Americans or Pacific Islanders, 2 Hispanic Americans), 8 international. 57 applicants, 81% accepted, 26 enrolled. *Faculty:* 14 full-time (4 women). Expenses: Contact institution. *Financial support:* In 2006–07, 5 students received support, including 2 research assistantships; career-related internships or fieldwork also available. Financial award applicants required to submit FAFSA. In 2006, 52 degrees awarded. *Degree program information:* Part-time and evening/weekend programs available. Offers business administration (MBA); business and economics (MBA, MS); information systems management (MS). *Application deadline:* For fall admission, 8/1 priority date for domestic students; for winter admission, 11/1 for domestic students; for spring admission, 2/1 for domestic students. Applications are processed on a rolling basis. *Application Contact:* Debbie Wysomierski, Assistant Graduate Director, 206-281-2753, Fax: 206-281-2733, E-mail: mba@spu.edu. *Graduate Director,* Gary Karns, 206-281-2753, Fax: 206-281-2733.

School of Education Students: 65 full-time (50 women), 263 part-time (190 women); includes 25 minority (7 African Americans, 3 American Indian/Alaska Native, 12 Asian Americans or Pacific Islanders, 3 Hispanic Americans), 3 international. 255 applicants, 73% accepted, 151 enrolled. *Faculty:* 16 full-time (5 women). Expenses: Contact institution. *Financial support:* In 2006–07, 5 research assistantships (averaging $4,500 per year) were awarded; career-related internships or fieldwork also available. Financial award applicants required to submit FAFSA. In 2006, 89 master's, 7 doctorates awarded. *Degree program information:* Part-time and evening/weekend programs available. Offers education (M Ed, MAT, Ed D); educational leadership (M Ed, Ed D); reading/language arts education (M Ed); school counseling (M Ed); secondary teaching (MAT). *Application deadline:* Applications are processed on a rolling basis. *Application Contact:* Allan Blomquist, Graduate Programs Manager, 206-281-2378, Fax: 206-281-2756, E-mail: blomqa@spu.edu. *Director of Graduate Programs,* Dr. Rick Eigenbrood, 206-281-2214.

School of Health Sciences 17 applicants, 71% accepted, 8 enrolled. *Faculty:* 2 full-time (both women). Expenses: Contact institution. *Financial support:* In 2006–07, 2 teaching assistantships were awarded; career-related internships or fieldwork and traineeships also available. Financial award applicants required to submit FAFSA. In 2006, 15 degrees awarded. *Degree program information:* Part-time and evening/weekend programs available. Offers health sciences (MSN, Certificate); nurse practitioner (Certificate); nursing leadership (MSN). *Application deadline:* For fall admission, 9/1 priority date for domestic students. Applications are processed on a rolling basis. *Application fee:* $50. *Application Contact:* Dr. Donna J. Allis, Director, 206-281-2649, Fax: 206-281-2767, E-mail: dallis@spu.edu. *Dean,* Dr. Lucille Kelley, 206-281-2608, Fax: 206-281-2767, E-mail: lkelley@spu.edu.

School of Psychology, Family and Community Students: 123 full-time (93 women), 98 part-time (80 women); includes 33 minority (6 African Americans, 2 American Indian/Alaska Native, 19 Asian Americans or Pacific Islanders, 6 Hispanic Americans), 3 international. 206 applicants, 44% accepted, 76 enrolled. *Faculty:* 15 full-time (9 women). Expenses: Contact institution. *Financial support:* Research assistantships, career-related internships or fieldwork and unspecified assistantships available. Financial award applicants required to submit FAFSA. In 2006, 32 master's, 10 doctorates awarded. *Degree program information:* Part-time programs available. Offers clinical psychology (PhD); marriage and family therapy (MS); organizational psychology (MA, PhD); psychology, family and community (MA, MS, PhD). *Application fee:* $50. *Application Contact:* John Glancy, Director, Graduate Admissions/Marketing, 206-281-2325, Fax: 206-281-2877, E-mail: jglancy@spu.edu. *Dean,* Dr. Michèal Roe, 206-281-2987.

SEATTLE UNIVERSITY, Seattle, WA 98122-1090

General Information Independent-religious, coed, comprehensive institution. *Enrollment:* 7,226 graduate, professional, and undergraduate students; 1,415 full-time matriculated graduate/professional students (839 women), 1,547 part-time matriculated graduate/professional students (916 women). *Enrollment by degree level:* 1,185 first professional, 1,712 master's, 65 doctoral. *Graduate faculty:* 167 full-time (94 women), 85 part-time/adjunct (47 women). *Graduate housing:* Room and/or apartments available on a first-come, first-served basis to single students; on-campus housing not available to married students. *Student services:* Campus employment opportunities, campus safety program, career counseling, disabled student services, exercise/wellness program, free psychological counseling, international student services, low-cost health insurance, multicultural affairs office, teacher training, writing training. *Library facilities:* Lemieux Library plus 1 other. *Online resources:* library catalog, web page, access to other libraries' catalogs. *Collection:* 141,478 titles, 2,701 serial subscriptions, 5,649 audiovisual materials. *Research affiliation:* Swedish Medical Centers (nursing).

Computer facilities: 401 computers available on campus for general student use. A campuswide network can be accessed from student residence rooms and from off campus. Internet access and online class registration are available. *Web address:* http://www.seattleu.edu/.

General Application Contact: Janet Shandley, Associate Dean of Graduate Admissions, 206-296-5900, Fax: 206-298-5656, E-mail: grad_admissions@seattleu.edu.

GRADUATE UNITS

Albers School of Business and Economics Students: 159 full-time (69 women), 615 part-time (247 women); includes 147 minority (14 African Americans, 2 American Indian/Alaska Native, 117 Asian Americans or Pacific Islanders, 14 Hispanic Americans), 91 international. Average age 32. 443 applicants, 60% accepted, 205 enrolled. *Faculty:* 51 full-time (16 women), 16 part-time/adjunct (7 women). Expenses: Contact institution. *Financial support:* Career-related internships or fieldwork, Federal Work-Study, and unspecified assistantships available. Support available to part-time students. Financial award applicants required to submit FAFSA. In 2006, 208 master's, 4 other advanced degrees awarded. *Degree program information:* Part-time and evening/weekend programs available. Offers business administration (MBA, MIB, Certificate); business and economics (EMBA, MBA, MIB, MPAC, MSF, Certificate); finance (MSF, Certificate); leadership formation (EMBA, Certificate); professional accounting (MPAC). *Application deadline:* For fall admission, 8/20 priority date for domestic students; for winter admission, 11/20 for domestic students; for spring admission, 2/20 for domestic students. Applications are processed on a rolling basis. *Application fee:* $55. *Application Contact:* Janet Shandley, Associate Dean of Graduate Admissions, 206-296-5900, Fax: 206-298-5656, E-mail: grad_admissions@seattleu.edu. *Dean,* Dr. Joseph Phillips, 206-296-5700, Fax: 206-296-5795.

College of Arts and Sciences Students: 102 full-time (70 women), 218 part-time (139 women); includes 79 minority (26 African Americans, 5 American Indian/Alaska Native, 35 Asian Americans or Pacific Islanders, 13 Hispanic Americans), 6 international. Average age 33. 181 applicants, 57% accepted, 93 enrolled. *Faculty:* 23 full-time (12 women), 24 part-time/adjunct (9 women). Expenses: Contact institution. *Financial support:* Career-related internships or fieldwork and Federal Work-Study available. Support available to part-time students. Financial award applicants required to submit FAFSA. In 2006, 84 degrees awarded. Offers arts and sciences (MA Psych, MACJ, MNPL, MPA, MSAL); criminal justice (MACJ); existential and phenomenological therapeutic psychology (MA Psych); sport and exercise (MSAL). *Application fee:* $55. *Application Contact:* Janet Shandley, Associate Dean of Graduate Admissions, 206-296-5900, Fax: 206-298-5656, E-mail: grad_admissions@seattleu.edu. *Dean,* Dr. Wallace Loh, 206-296-5300, E-mail: lohw@seattleu.edu.

The Center for Nonprofit and Social Enterprise Management Students: 38 full-time (33 women), 40 part-time (29 women); includes 11 minority (2 African Americans, 5 Asian Americans or Pacific Islanders, 4 Hispanic Americans). Average age 37. Expenses: Contact institution. *Financial support:* Career-related internships or fieldwork and Federal Work-Study available. Support available to part-time students. Financial award applicants required to submit FAFSA. In 2006, 14 degrees awarded. Offers nonprofit and social enterprise management (MNPL). *Application deadline:* For fall admission, 3/1 for domestic students. *Application fee:* $55. *Application Contact:* Janet Shandley, Associate Dean of Graduate Admissions, 206-296-5900, Fax: 206-298-5656, E-mail: grad_admissions@seattleu.edu. *Director,* Dr. Michael Bisesi, 206-296-5435, Fax: 206-296-5997, E-mail: bisesim@seattleu.edu.

Institute of Public Service Students: 22 full-time (14 women), 116 part-time (78 women); includes 48 minority (17 African Americans, 4 American Indian/Alaska Native, 21 Asian Americans or Pacific Islanders, 6 Hispanic Americans), 3 international. Average age 33. 35 applicants, 77% accepted, 20 enrolled. *Faculty:* 9 full-time (3 women), 14 part-time/adjunct (5 women). Expenses: Contact institution. *Financial support:* Career-related internships or fieldwork, Federal Work-Study, and unspecified assistantships available. Support available to part-time students. Financial award applicants required to submit FAFSA. In 2006, 25 degrees awarded. Offers public service (MPA). *Application deadline:* For fall admission, 8/20 priority date for domestic students; for winter admission, 11/20 priority date for domestic students; for spring admission, 2/20 priority date for domestic students. *Application fee:* $55. *Application Contact:* Janet Shandley, Associate Dean of Graduate Admissions, 206-296-5900, Fax: 206-298-5656, E-mail: grad_admissions@seattleu.edu. *Director,* Dr. Russell Lidman, 206-296-5440, Fax: 206-296-5997, E-mail: lidmanr@seattleu.edu.

College of Education Students: 166 full-time (132 women), 323 part-time (252 women); includes 80 minority (17 African Americans, 3 American Indian/Alaska Native, 38 Asian Americans or Pacific Islanders, 22 Hispanic Americans), 11 international. Average age 33. 496 applicants, 38% accepted, 136 enrolled. *Faculty:* 29 full-time (16 women), 13 part-time/adjunct (9 women). Expenses: Contact institution. *Financial support:* Career-related internships or fieldwork, Federal Work-Study, and unspecified assistantships available. Support available to part-time students. Financial award applicants required to submit FAFSA. In 2006, 215 master's, 16 doctorates, 29 other advanced degrees awarded. *Degree program information:* Part-time and evening/weekend programs available. Offers adult education and training (M Ed, MA, Certificate); counseling and school psychology (MA, Certificate, Ed S); curriculum and instruction (M Ed, MA, Certificate); education (M Ed, MA, MIT, Ed D, Certificate, Ed S, Post-Master's Certificate); educational administration (M Ed, MA, Certificate, Ed S); educational leadership (Ed D); literacy (M Ed, Post-Master's Certificate); special education (M Ed, MA, Certificate); student development administration (M Ed, MA); teacher education

Seattle University (continued)

(MIT); teaching English to speakers of other languages (M Ed, MA, Certificate). *Application fee:* $55. *Application Contact:* Janet Shandley, Associate Dean of Graduate Admissions, 206-296-5900, Fax: 206-298-5656, E-mail: grad_admissions@seattleu.edu. *Dean,* Dr. Sue Schmitt, 206-296-5760, E-mail: sschmitt@seattleu.edu.

College of Nursing Students: 71 full-time (63 women), 8 part-time (7 women); includes 11 minority (3 African Americans, 1 American Indian/Alaska Native, 7 Asian Americans or Pacific Islanders). Average age 32. 22 applicants, 55% accepted, 12 enrolled. *Faculty:* 42 full-time (40 women), 14 part-time/adjunct (12 women). Expenses: Contact institution. *Financial support:* Fellowships, research assistantships, career-related internships or fieldwork and Federal Work-Study available. Support available to part-time students. Financial award applicants required to submit FAFSA. In 2006, 21 master's awarded. *Degree program information:* Part-time and evening/weekend programs available. Offers advanced practice nursing immersion (MSN); leadership in community nursing (MSN); nursing (MSN); primary care nurse practitioner (MSN). *Application deadline:* For fall admission, 7/1 for domestic students. *Application fee:* $55. *Application Contact:* Janet Shandley, Associate Dean of Graduate Admissions, 206-296-5900, Fax: 206-298-5656, E-mail: grad_admissions@seattleu.edu. *Dean,* Dr. Mary Walker, 206-296-5676.

College of Science and Engineering Students: 8 full-time (3 women), 46 part-time (9 women); includes 12 minority (2 African Americans, 10 Asian Americans or Pacific Islanders), 11 international. Average age 31. 34 applicants, 68% accepted, 16 enrolled. *Faculty:* 10 full-time (4 women), 1 (woman) part-time/adjunct. Expenses: Contact institution. *Financial support:* Career-related internships or fieldwork and Federal Work-Study available. Support available to part-time students. Financial award applicants required to submit FAFSA. In 2006, 17 degrees awarded. *Degree program information:* Part-time and evening/weekend programs available. Offers science and engineering (MSE); software engineering (MSE). *Application deadline:* For fall admission, 7/1 for domestic students. *Application fee:* $55. *Application Contact:* Janet Shandley, Associate Dean of Graduate Admissions, 206-296-5900, Fax: 206-298-5656, E-mail: grad_admissions@seattleu.edu. *Dean,* Dr. Michael Quinn, 206-296-5500, Fax: 206-296-2071.

School of Law Students: 861 full-time (470 women), 229 part-time (107 women); includes 265 minority (47 African Americans, 16 American Indian/Alaska Native, 142 Asian Americans or Pacific Islanders, 60 Hispanic Americans), 9 international. Average age 28. 3,151 applicants, 29% accepted, 352 enrolled. *Faculty:* 67 full-time (33 women), 40 part-time/adjunct (9 women). Expenses: Contact institution. *Financial support:* Career-related internships or fieldwork, Federal Work-Study, institutionally sponsored loans, and scholarships/grants available. Support available to part-time students. Financial award application deadline: 4/1; financial award applicants required to submit FAFSA. In 2006, 343 degrees awarded. *Degree program information:* Part-time programs available. Offers law (JD). *Application deadline:* For fall admission, 4/1 priority date for domestic and international students. Applications are processed on a rolling basis. *Application fee:* $50. Electronic applications accepted. *Application Contact:* Carol T. Cochran, Assistant Dean for Admission, 206-398-4200, Fax: 206-398-4058, E-mail: lawadmis@seattleu.edu. *Dean,* Kellye Y. Testy, 206-398-4309, Fax: 206-398-4310, E-mail: ktesty@seattleu.edu.

School of Theology and Ministry Students: 37 full-time (25 women), 183 part-time (138 women); includes 37 minority (14 African Americans, 2 American Indian/Alaska Native, 10 Asian Americans or Pacific Islanders, 11 Hispanic Americans). Average age 46. 85 applicants, 74% accepted, 55 enrolled. *Faculty:* 12 full-time (6 women), 17 part-time/adjunct (9 women). Expenses: Contact institution. *Financial support:* Career-related internships or fieldwork and Federal Work-Study available. Support available to part-time students. Financial award applicants required to submit FAFSA. In 2006, 11 M Divs, 24 master's, 4 other advanced degrees awarded. *Degree program information:* Part-time and evening/weekend programs available. Offers divinity (M Div); pastoral counseling (MA); pastoral studies (MAPS); theology and ministry (M Div, MA, MAPS, MATS, Certificate); transforming spirituality (MATS, Certificate). *Application deadline:* For fall admission, 7/1 for domestic students. *Application fee:* $55. *Application Contact:* Catherine Kehoe Fallon, Admissions Coordinator, 206-296-5333, Fax: 206-296-5329, E-mail: fallon@seattleu.edu. *Dean,* Dr. Mark Markuly, 206-296-5330, Fax: 206-296-5329.

SEMINARY OF THE IMMACULATE CONCEPTION, Huntington, NY 11743-1696

General Information Independent-religious, coed, graduate-only institution. *Graduate housing:* Room and/or apartments guaranteed to single students; on-campus housing not available to married students. Housing application deadline: 8/30.

GRADUATE UNITS

School of Theology *Degree program information:* Part-time and evening/weekend programs available. Offers pastoral studies (MA); theology (M Div, MA, D Min, Certificate).

SETON HALL UNIVERSITY, South Orange, NJ 07079-2697

General Information Independent-religious, coed, university. CGS member. *Graduate housing:* Room and/or apartments available on a first-come, first-served basis to single students; on-campus housing not available to married students.

GRADUATE UNITS

College of Arts and Sciences *Degree program information:* Part-time and evening/weekend programs available. Postbaccalaureate distance learning degree programs offered (minimal on-campus study). Offers analytical chemistry (MS, PhD); arts administration (MPA); arts and sciences (MA, MHA, MPA, MS, PhD); Asian studies (MA); biochemistry (MS, PhD); biology (MS); Catholic history (MA); chemistry (MS); corporate and public communication (MA); English (MA); European history (MA); experimental psychology (MS); global history (MA); health policy and management (MPA); healthcare administration (MHA); inorganic chemistry (MS, PhD); Jewish-Christian studies (MA); microbiology (MS); molecular bioscience (PhD); museum professions (MA); nonprofit organization management (MPA); organic chemistry (MS, PhD); physical chemistry (MS, PhD); public service: leadership, governance, and policy (MPA); strategic communication and leadership (MA); US history (MA). Electronic applications accepted.

College of Education and Human Services Students: 320 full-time (201 women), 746 part-time (469 women); includes 110 minority (71 African Americans, 2 American Indian/Alaska Native, 10 Asian Americans or Pacific Islanders, 27 Hispanic Americans), 11 international. Average age 35. 365 applicants, 86% accepted, 201 enrolled. *Faculty:* 39 full-time (21 women), 116 part-time/adjunct (32 women). Expenses: Contact institution. *Financial support:* In 2006–07, 13 students received support; fellowships, research assistantships, career-related internships or fieldwork, institutionally sponsored loans, and unspecified assistantships available. Financial award application deadline: 2/1. In 2006, 286 master's, 53 doctorates, 47 other advanced degrees awarded. *Degree program information:* Part-time and evening/weekend programs available. Offers bilingual education (Ed S); Catholic school leadership (MA); Catholic school teaching EPICS (MA); college student personnel administration (MA); counseling psychology (MA, PhD); counselor preparation (MA); education and human services (MA, MS, Ed S, Exec Ed D, PhD, Ed S); education media specialist (MA); higher education administration (PhD); human resource training and development (MA); instructional design (MA); K–12 administration and supervision (Ed D, Exec Ed D, Ed S); K–12 leadership, management and policy (Ed D, Exec Ed D, Ed S); marriage and family therapy (MS, Ed S); professional development (MA); psychological studies (MA); school psychology (Ed S). *Application deadline:* Applications are processed on a rolling basis. *Application fee:* $50. Electronic applications accepted. *Application Contact:* Dr. Manina Urgolo Huckvale, Associate Dean, 973-761-9668, Fax: 973-275-2187, E-mail: huckvama@shu.edu. *Dean,* Dr. Joseph V. De Pierro, 973-761-9025.

College of Nursing *Degree program information:* Part-time programs available. Offers acute care nurse practitioner (MSN); adult nurse practitioner (MSN); advanced practice in acute care nursing (MSN); advanced practice in primary health care (MSN); gerontological nurse practitioner (MSN); health systems administration (MSN); nursing (PhD); nursing case management (MSN); nursing education (MA); pediatric nurse practitioner (MSN); school nurse (MSN); women's health nurse practitioner (MSN). Electronic applications accepted.

Immaculate Conception Seminary School of Theology *Degree program information:* Part-time and evening/weekend programs available. Offers pastoral ministry (M Div, MA); theology (MA, Certificate). Electronic applications accepted.

School of Graduate Medical Education Students: 275 full-time (225 women), 114 part-time (71 women); includes 30 minority (12 African Americans, 1 American Indian/Alaska Native, 5 Asian Americans or Pacific Islanders, 12 Hispanic Americans), 1 international. 368 applicants, 50% accepted, 103 enrolled. *Faculty:* 29 full-time (19 women), 68 part-time/adjunct (30 women). Expenses: Contact institution. *Financial support:* In 2006–07, 12 research assistantships with partial tuition reimbursements (averaging $8,000 per year) were awarded; Federal Work-Study, institutionally sponsored loans, scholarships/grants, and unspecified assistantships also available. In 2006, 72 master's, 18 doctorates awarded. *Degree program information:* Part-time and evening/weekend programs available. Offers athletic training (MS); health sciences (MS, PhD); medical education (MS, DPT, PhD); occupational therapy (MS); physician assistant (MS); professional physical therapy (DPT); speech-language pathology (MS). *Application deadline:* Applications are processed on a rolling basis. *Application fee:* $75. Electronic applications accepted. *Application Contact:* Deborah Ann Verderosa, Director of Admissions, 973-275-2062, Fax: 973-275-2370, E-mail: verderde@shu.edu. *Dean,* Dr. Brian B. Shulman, 973-275-2800, Fax: 973-275-2370, E-mail: gradmeded@shu.edu.

School of Law Students: 729 full-time (313 women), 435 part-time (224 women); includes 219 minority (52 African Americans, 3 American Indian/Alaska Native, 107 Asian Americans or Pacific Islanders, 57 Hispanic Americans). Average age 27. 3,005 applicants, 36% accepted, 359 enrolled. *Faculty:* 61 full-time (24 women), 81 part-time/adjunct (24 women). Expenses: Contact institution. *Financial support:* In 2006–07, 979 students received support, including 26 fellowships (averaging $3,000 per year), 95 research assistantships (averaging $3,731 per year), 2 teaching assistantships (averaging $3,000 per year); career-related internships or fieldwork, Federal Work-Study, institutionally sponsored loans, scholarships/grants, and unspecified assistantships also available. Support available to part-time students. Financial award application deadline: 4/1; financial award applicants required to submit FAFSA. In 2006, 370 JDs, 17 master's awarded. *Degree program information:* Part-time and evening/weekend programs available. Offers law (JD, LL M, MSJ). *Application deadline:* For fall admission, 4/1 for domestic and international students. Applications are processed on a rolling basis. *Application fee:* $65. Electronic applications accepted. *Application Contact:* Gisele Joachim, Assistant Dean for Admissions and Financial Resource Management, 973-642-8747, Fax: 973-642-8876, E-mail: admitme@shu.edu. *Dean and Professor of Law,* Patrick E. Hobbs, 973-642-8750, Fax: 973-642-8031, E-mail: hobbspat@shu.edu.

Stillman School of Business Students: 70 full-time (19 women), 404 part-time (165 women); includes 52 minority (20 African Americans, 19 Asian Americans or Pacific Islanders, 13 Hispanic Americans). Average age 27. 271 applicants, 49% accepted, 77 enrolled. *Faculty:* 57 full-time (13 women), 30 part-time/adjunct (3 women). Expenses: Contact institution. *Financial support:* In 2006–07, 60 students received support, including research assistantships with full and partial tuition reimbursements available (averaging $5,400 per year); career-related internships or fieldwork, Federal Work-Study, scholarships/grants, health care benefits, and unspecified assistantships also available. Support available to part-time students. Financial award application deadline: 6/1; financial award applicants required to submit FAFSA. In 2006, 195 degrees awarded. *Degree program information:* Part-time and evening/weekend programs available. Offers accounting (MBA, MS); business (MBA, MS, Certificate); finance (MBA); financial markets, institutions and instruments (MBA); healthcare management (MBA); information systems (MBA); international business (MBA); management (MBA); marketing (MBA); pharmaceutical management (MBA); professional accounting (MS); sport management (MBA); taxation (MS). *Application deadline:* For fall admission, 6/1 priority date for domestic students, 5/1 for international students; for spring admission, 11/1 priority date for domestic students, 10/1 for international students. Applications are processed on a rolling basis. *Application fee:* $75 ($100 for international students). Electronic applications accepted. *Application Contact:* Catherine Bianchi, Director of Graduate Admissions, 973-761-9220, Fax: 973-761-9208, E-mail: biancha@shu.edu. *Dean,* Dr. Karen E. Boroff, 973-761-9013, Fax: 973-275-2465, E-mail: boroffka@shu.edu.

Whitehead School of Diplomacy and International Relations Average age 26. 325 applicants, 62% accepted. *Faculty:* 14 full-time (3 women), 20 part-time/adjunct (9 women). Expenses: Contact institution. *Financial support:* Career-related internships or fieldwork, Federal Work-Study, scholarships/grants, tuition waivers (full and partial), and unspecified assistantships available. Support available to part-time students. *Degree program information:* Part-time and evening/weekend programs available. Offers diplomacy and international relations (MA). *Application deadline:* For fall admission, 5/1 priority date for domestic and international students; for winter admission, 10/1 priority date for domestic and international students; for spring admission, 2/1 priority date for domestic and international students. Applications are processed on a rolling basis. *Application fee:* $50. Electronic applications accepted. *Application Contact:* Catherine Ruby, Director of Graduate Admissions, 973-275-2142, Fax: 973-275-2519, E-mail: rubycath@shu.edu. *Assistant Dean of Graduate Studies,* Ursula Sanjamino, 973-313-6210, Fax: 973-275-2519, E-mail: sanjamur@shu.edu.

SETON HILL UNIVERSITY, Greensburg, PA 15601

General Information Independent-religious, coed, comprehensive institution. *Enrollment:* 1,895 graduate, professional, and undergraduate students; 125 full-time matriculated graduate/professional students (100 women), 220 part-time matriculated graduate/professional students (168 women). *Enrollment by degree level:* 345 master's. *Graduate faculty:* 24 full-time (15 women), 36 part-time/adjunct (16 women). *Tuition:* Part-time $620 per credit. *Required fees:* $100 per semester. *Graduate housing:* Room and/or apartments guaranteed to single students; on-campus housing not available to married students. Housing application deadline: 8/15. *Student services:* Campus employment opportunities, campus safety program, career counseling, disabled student services, exercise/wellness program, free psychological counseling, international student services, multicultural affairs office, teacher training, writing training. *Library facilities:* Reeves Memorial Library. *Online resources:* library catalog, web page, access to other libraries' catalogs. *Collection:* 123,538 titles, 423 serial subscriptions, 6,684 audiovisual materials.

Computer facilities: 259 computers available on campus for general student use. A campuswide network can be accessed from student residence rooms and from off campus. Internet access and online class registration, e-mail are available. *Web address:* http://www.setonhill.edu/.

General Application Contact: Christine Schaeffer, Director of Graduate and Adult Studies, 724-838-4283, Fax: 724-830-1891, E-mail: schaeffer@setonhill.edu.

GRADUATE UNITS

Program in Art Therapy Students: 20 full-time (19 women), 15 part-time (13 women); includes 1 minority (Hispanic American) Average age 29. 32 applicants, 75% accepted, 15 enrolled. *Faculty:* 1 (woman) full-time, 2 part-time/adjunct (both women). Expenses: Contact institution. *Financial support:* In 2006–07, 32 students received support. Federal Work-Study, scholarships/grants, tuition waivers (partial), and unspecified assistantships available. Support available to part-time students. Financial award application deadline: 8/15; financial award applicants required to submit FAFSA. In 2006, 4 degrees awarded. *Degree program information:* Part-time programs available. Offers art therapy (MA, Certificate). *Application deadline:* For fall admission, 8/15 priority date for domestic students; for spring admission, 12/15 for domestic students. Applications are processed on a rolling basis. *Application fee:* $35. Electronic applications accepted. *Application Contact:* Dane Zimmer, Advisor, 724-838-4209, Fax: 724-830-1891, E-mail: zimmer@setonhill.edu. *Director,* Nina Denninger, 724-830-1047, Fax: 724-830-1294, E-mail: denninger@setonhill.edu.

Program in Business Administration Students: 34 full-time (24 women), 64 part-time (41 women); includes 8 minority (5 African Americans, 2 Asian Americans or Pacific Islanders, 1 Hispanic American), 5 international. Average age 33. 49 applicants, 84% accepted, 34 enrolled. *Faculty:* 4 full-time (2 women), 8 part-time/adjunct (2 women). Expenses: Contact institution. *Financial support:* In 2006–07, 84 students received support. Scholarships/grants, tuition waivers (partial), and unspecified assistantships available. Support available to part-time students. Financial award application deadline: 8/15; financial award applicants required to submit FAFSA. In 2006, 52 master's awarded. *Degree program information:* Part-time and evening/weekend programs available. Offers business administration (MBA). *Application deadline:* For fall admission, 8/15 priority date for domestic students; for spring admission, 12/15 for domestic students. Applications are processed on a rolling basis. *Application fee:* $35. Electronic applications accepted. *Application Contact:* Michelle Kelly, Advisor, 724-830-4634, Fax: 724-830-1891, E-mail: mkelly@setonhill.edu. *Interim Director,* Paul Mahady, 724-830-1012, Fax: 724-830-1294, E-mail: mahady@setonhill.edu.

Program in Elementary Education Students: 15 full-time (13 women), 28 part-time (25 women); includes 1 minority (Asian American or Pacific Islander) Average age 31. 21 applicants, 90% accepted, 14 enrolled. *Faculty:* 7 full-time (5 women), 4 part-time/adjunct (2 women). Expenses: Contact institution. *Financial support:* In 2006–07, 36 students received support. Scholarships/grants, tuition waivers (partial), and unspecified assistantships available. Support available to part-time students. Financial award application deadline: 8/15; financial award applicants required to submit FAFSA. In 2006, 12 master's awarded. *Degree program information:* Part-time and evening/weekend programs available. Offers elementary education (MA, Teaching Certificate). *Application deadline:* For fall admission, 8/15 priority date for domestic students; for spring admission, 12/15 for domestic students. Applications are processed on a rolling basis. *Application fee:* $35. Electronic applications accepted. *Application Contact:* Dane Zimmer, Advisor, 724-838-4209, Fax: 724-830-1891, E-mail: zimmer@setonhill.edu. *Director,* Dr. Michele H. Conway, 724-830-4732, Fax: 724-830-1294, E-mail: conway@setonhill.edu.

Program in Instructional Design Students: 6 full-time (3 women), 7 part-time (all women); includes 2 minority (1 African American, 1 Hispanic American). Average age 36. 12 applicants, 75% accepted, 7 enrolled. *Faculty:* 3 full-time (2 women), 3 part-time/adjunct (2 women). Expenses: Contact institution. *Financial support:* In 2006–07, 7 students received support. Scholarships/grants, tuition waivers (partial), and unspecified assistantships available. Support available to part-time students. Financial award application deadline: 8/15; financial award applicants required to submit FAFSA. In 2006, 3 degrees awarded. *Degree program information:* Part-time and evening/weekend programs available. Offers instructional design (M Ed). *Application deadline:* For fall admission, 8/15 priority date for domestic students; for spring admission, 12/15 for domestic students. Applications are processed on a rolling basis. *Application fee:* $35. Electronic applications accepted. *Application Contact:* Dane Zimmer, Advisor, 724-838-4209, Fax: 724-830-1891, E-mail: zimmer@setonhill.edu. *Director,* Dr. Shirley Campbell, 724-830-1007, Fax: 724-830-1294.

Program in Marriage and Family Therapy Students: 20 full-time (18 women), 11 part-time (9 women); includes 3 minority (all African Americans) Average age 31. 26 applicants, 54% accepted, 9 enrolled. *Faculty:* 3 full-time (2 women), 4 part-time/adjunct (3 women). Expenses: Contact institution. *Financial support:* In 2006–07, 30 students received support. Scholarships/grants, tuition waivers (partial), and unspecified assistantships available. Support available to part-time students. Financial award application deadline: 8/15; financial award applicants required to submit FAFSA. In 2006, 9 degrees awarded. *Degree program information:* Part-time and evening/weekend programs available. Offers marriage and family therapy (MA). *Application deadline:* For fall admission, 8/15 priority date for domestic students; for spring admission, 12/15 for domestic students. Applications are processed on a rolling basis. *Application fee:* $35. Electronic applications accepted. *Application Contact:* Dane Zimmer, Advisor, 724-838-4209, Fax: 724-830-1891, E-mail: zimmer@setonhill.edu. *Director,* Dr. Susan Cooley, 724-838-7816, E-mail: cooley@setonhill.edu.

Program in Physician Assistant Students: 22 full-time (18 women); includes 5 minority (2 African Americans, 2 American Indian/Alaska Native, 1 Asian American or Pacific Islander). Average age 29. 285 applicants, 12% accepted, 22 enrolled. *Faculty:* 5 full-time (3 women), 6 part-time/adjunct (3 women). Expenses: Contact institution. *Financial support:* Application deadline: 8/15; In 2006, 18 degrees awarded. Offers physician assistant (MS). *Application deadline:* For spring admission, 3/1 for domestic and international students. *Application fee:* $110. Electronic applications accepted. *Application Contact:* Christine Schaeffer, Director of Graduate and Adult Studies, 724-838-4283, Fax: 724-830-1891, E-mail: schaeffer@setonhill.edu. *Director,* Cathy Shallenberger, 724-838-2455, Fax: 724-838-7843, E-mail: shallenberger@setonhill.edu.

Program in Special Education Students: 10 full-time (7 women), 28 part-time (26 women). Average age 31. 16 applicants, 88% accepted, 14 enrolled. *Faculty:* 7 full-time (5 women), 4 part-time/adjunct (2 women). Expenses: Contact institution. *Financial support:* In 2006–07, 38 students received support. Scholarships/grants, tuition waivers (partial), and unspecified assistantships available. Support available to part-time students. Financial award application deadline: 8/15; financial award applicants required to submit FAFSA. In 2006, 20 master's awarded. *Degree program information:* Part-time and evening/weekend programs available. Offers special education (MA, Teaching Certificate). *Application deadline:* For fall admission, 8/15 priority date for domestic students; for spring admission, 12/15 for domestic students. Applications are processed on a rolling basis. *Application fee:* $35. Electronic applications accepted. *Application Contact:* Dane Zimmer, Advisor, 724-838-4209, Fax: 724-830-1891, E-mail: zimmer@setonhill.edu. *Director,* Dr. Sondra Lettrich, 724-830-1010, Fax: 724-830-1294, E-mail: lettrich@setonhill.edu.

Program in Writing Popular Fiction Students: 1 (woman) full-time, 63 part-time (46 women); includes 6 minority (2 African Americans, 4 Hispanic Americans), 4 international. Average age 36. 29 applicants, 83% accepted, 20 enrolled. *Faculty:* 3 full-time (1 woman), 16 part-time/adjunct (8 women). Expenses: Contact institution. *Financial support:* In 2006–07, 59 students received support. Scholarships/grants, tuition waivers (partial), and unspecified assistantships available. Support available to part-time students. Financial award application deadline: 8/15; financial award applicants required to submit FAFSA. In 2006, 26 master's awarded. *Degree program information:* Part-time programs available. Postbaccalaureate distance learning degree programs offered (minimal on-campus study). Offers writing popular fiction (MA). *Application deadline:* For fall admission, 6/1 for domestic students; for spring admission, 12/15 for domestic students. Applications are processed on a rolling basis. *Application fee:* $35. Electronic applications accepted. *Application Contact:* Dane Zimmer, Advisor, 724-838-4209, Fax: 724-830-1891, E-mail: zimmer@setonhill.edu. *Director,* Dr. Lee McClain, 724-830-1040, Fax: 724-830-1294, E-mail: mcclain@setonhill.edu.

See Close-Up on page 1027.

SEWANEE: THE UNIVERSITY OF THE SOUTH, Sewanee, TN 37383-1000

General Information Independent-religious, coed, comprehensive institution. *Enrollment:* 1,611 graduate, professional, and undergraduate students; 88 full-time matriculated graduate/professional students (45 women), 2 part-time matriculated graduate/professional students (1 woman). *Enrollment by degree level:* 78 first professional, 5 master's, 7 other advanced degrees. *Graduate faculty:* 13 full-time (3 women), 9 part-time/adjunct (5 women). *Tuition:* Full-time $14,764; part-time $615 per credit hour. *Required fees:* $521. Tuition and fees vary according to course load, degree level and program. *Graduate housing:* Rooms and/or apartments available on a first-come, first-served basis to single and married students. *Student services:* Campus employment opportunities, campus safety program, career counseling, child daycare facilities, free psychological counseling, international student services, multicultural affairs office. *Library facilities:* Jessie Ball duPont Library. *Online resources:* library catalog, web page. *Collection:* 648,459 titles, 3,444 serial subscriptions.

Computer facilities: 92 computers available on campus for general student use. A campuswide network can be accessed from student residence rooms and from off campus. *Web address:* http://www.sewanee.edu/.

General Application Contact: Roslyn Dianne Weaver, Director of Admissions/Registrar, 931-598-1283, Fax: 931-598-1852, E-mail: rweaver@sewanee.edu.

GRADUATE UNITS

School of Theology Students: 88 full-time (45 women), 2 part-time (1 woman); includes 2 minority (both African Americans), 1 international. Average age 43. 56 applicants, 80% accepted, 36 enrolled. *Faculty:* 13 full-time (3 women), 9 part-time/adjunct (5 women). Expenses: Contact institution. *Financial support:* Institutionally sponsored loans and scholarships/grants available. Support available to part-time students. Financial award application deadline: 5/1; financial award applicants required to submit FAFSA. In 2006, 26 M Divs, 2 master's, 7 doctorates awarded. *Degree program information:* Part-time programs available. Offers theology (M Div, MA, STM, D Min). MA open to foreign students. *Application deadline:* For fall admission, 4/1 priority date for domestic students, 4/1 for international students. Applications are processed on a rolling basis. *Application fee:* $25. *Application Contact:* Roslyn Dianne Weaver, Director of Admissions/Registrar, 931-598-1283, Fax: 931-598-1852, E-mail: rweaver@sewanee.edu. *Dean,* Very Rev. William S. Stafford, 931-598-1288, Fax: 931-598-1412, E-mail: wstafford@sewanee.edu.

Sewanee School of Letters Expenses: Contact institution. *Financial support:* Application deadline: 4/1; *Degree program information:* Part-time programs available. Offers American literature and English literature (MA); creative writing (MFA). Programs offered only during the summer. *Application deadline:* For spring admission, 2/1 priority date for domestic and international students. Applications are processed on a rolling basis. *Application fee:* $40. Electronic applications accepted. *Application Contact:* Margaret D Binnicker, Coordinator, Sewanee School of Letters, 931-598-1636, Fax: 931-598-3303, E-mail: mbinnick@sewanee.edu. *Director, Sewanee School of Letters,* Dr. John M Grammer, 931-598-1483, Fax: 931-598-3303, E-mail: jgrammer@sewanee.edu.

SHASTA BIBLE COLLEGE, Redding, CA 96002

General Information Independent-religious, coed, comprehensive institution. *Graduate housing:* Rooms and/or apartments available on a first-come, first-served basis to single and married students.

GRADUATE UNITS

Program in Biblical Counseling *Degree program information:* Part-time programs available. Offers biblical counseling and Christian family life education (MA).

Program in School/Church Administration *Degree program information:* Part-time and evening/weekend programs available. Offers school/church administration (MS).

SHAW UNIVERSITY, Raleigh, NC 27601-2399

General Information Independent-religious, coed, comprehensive institution. *Graduate housing:* Room and/or apartments available on a first-come, first-served basis to single students; on-campus housing not available to married students. *Research affiliation:* Old North State Medical Society (health and spirituality), The University of North Carolina at Chapel Hill (health disparities in the African American community), General Baptist State Convention (domestic violence prevention), Wabash Center (philosophy of religious education).

GRADUATE UNITS

Department of Education *Degree program information:* Part-time and evening/weekend programs available. Offers curriculum and instruction (MS). Electronic applications accepted.

Divinity School *Degree program information:* Part-time and evening/weekend programs available. Offers divinity (M Div, MRE). Electronic applications accepted.

SHENANDOAH UNIVERSITY, Winchester, VA 22601-5195

General Information Independent-religious, coed, comprehensive institution. *Enrollment:* 3,105 graduate, professional, and undergraduate students; 663 full-time matriculated graduate/professional students (458 women), 649 part-time matriculated graduate/professional students (442 women). *Enrollment by degree level:* 407 first professional, 579 master's, 276 doctoral, 50 other advanced degrees. *Graduate faculty:* 116 full-time (56 women), 37 part-time/adjunct (17 women). *Tuition:* Full-time $12,200; part-time $610 per credit. *Required fees:* $150. Full-time tuition and fees vary according to course load and program. *Graduate housing:* Room and/or apartments available on a first-come, first-served basis to single students; on-campus housing not available to married students. Typical cost: $7,650 (including board). Room and board charges vary according to board plan. Housing application deadline: 4/3. *Student services:* Campus employment opportunities, campus safety program, career counseling, child daycare facilities, disabled student services, exercise/wellness program, free psychological counseling, international student services, low-cost health insurance, multicultural affairs office. *Library facilities:* Alson H. Smith Jr. Library plus 1 other. *Online resources:* library catalog, web page, access to other libraries' catalogs. *Collection:* 131,174 titles, 19,479 serial subscriptions, 31,143 audiovisual materials.

Computer facilities: Computer purchase and lease plans are available. 175 computers available on campus for general student use. A campuswide network can be accessed from student residence rooms and from off campus. Internet access and online class registration, online grades and student account information are available. *Web address:* http://www.su.edu/.

General Application Contact: David Anthony, Dean of Admissions, 540-665-4581, Fax: 540-665-4627, E-mail: admit@su.edu.

GRADUATE UNITS

Byrd School of Business Students: 23 full-time (9 women), 10 part-time (3 women); includes 1 minority (Asian American or Pacific Islander), 7 international. Average age 29. 27 applicants, 59% accepted, 12 enrolled. *Faculty:* 11 full-time (2 women), 1 part-time/adjunct (0 women). Expenses: Contact institution. *Financial support:* In 2006–07, 28 students received support, including 4 fellowships with partial tuition reimbursements available (averaging $1,518 per year), 8 teaching assistantships with partial tuition reimbursements available (averaging $4,278 per year); career-related internships or fieldwork, institutionally sponsored loans, and unspecified assistantships also available. Support available to part-time students. Financial award application deadline: 3/15; financial award applicants required to submit FAFSA. In 2006, 23 degrees awarded. *Degree program information:* Part-time and evening/weekend programs available. Offers business administration (MBA); health care management (Certificate); information systems and computer technology (Certificate). *Application deadline:* Applications are processed on a rolling basis. *Application fee:* $30. Electronic applications accepted. *Application Contact:* David Anthony, Dean of Admissions, 540-665-4581, Fax: 540-665-4627, E-mail: admit@su.edu. *Dean,* Dr. Randy Boxx, 540-665-4572, Fax: 540-665-5437, E-mail: rboxx@su.edu.

College of Arts and Sciences Students: 28 full-time (16 women), 283 part-time (208 women); includes 8 minority (3 African Americans, 1 American Indian/Alaska Native, 3 Asian Americans or Pacific Islanders, 1 Hispanic American), 26 international. Average age 40. 182 applicants, 68% accepted, 98 enrolled. *Faculty:* 14 full-time (9 women), 7 part-time/adjunct (4 women). Expenses: Contact institution. *Financial support:* In 2006–07, fellowships with partial tuition reimbursements (averaging $2,581 per year); career-related internships or fieldwork, institutionally sponsored loans, and unspecified assistantships also available. Support available to part-time students. Financial award application deadline: 3/15; financial award applicants required to submit FAFSA. In 2006, 96 master's, 6 doctorates, 22 other advanced degrees awarded. *Degree program information:* Part-time and evening/weekend programs available. Postbaccalaureate distance learning degree programs offered (minimal on-campus study). Offers administrative leadership (D Ed); advanced professional teaching English to speakers of other languages (Certificate); education (MSE); elementary education (Certificate); middle school education (Certificate); professional studies (Certificate); professional teaching English to speakers of other languages (Certificate); public management (Certificate); secondary education (Certificate); women's studies (Certificate). *Application deadline:* For fall admission, 7/15 for domestic students; for spring admission, 10/15 for domestic students. Applications are processed on a rolling basis. *Application fee:* $30. Electronic applications accepted. *Application Contact:* David Anthony, Dean of Admissions, 540-665-4581, Fax: 540-665-4627, E-mail: admit@su.edu. *Dean,* Dr. Calvin Allen, 540-665-4587, Fax: 540-665-4644, E-mail: callen@su.edu.

School of Health Professions Expenses: Contact institution. Offers health professions (MS, MSN, DPT, Certificate). *Application Contact:* Information Contact, 540-665-5500, Fax: 540-665-5519.

Division of Athletic Training Students: 22 full-time (12 women), 1 part-time, 1 international. Average age 25. *Faculty:* 3 full-time (1 woman), 1 part-time/adjunct (0 women). Expenses:

Shenandoah University (continued)

Contact institution. *Financial support:* In 2006–07, 12 students received support. Institutionally sponsored loans available. Support available to part-time students. Financial award application deadline: 3/15; financial award applicants required to submit FAFSA. In 2006, 6 degrees awarded. Offers athletic training (MS). *Application deadline:* Applications are processed on a rolling basis. *Application fee:* $30. Electronic applications accepted. *Application Contact:* David Anthony, Dean of Admissions, 540-665-4581, Fax: 540-665-4627, E-mail: admit@su.edu. *Director,* Dr. Rose A. Schmieg, 540-665-5534, Fax: 540-545-7387, E-mail: rschmieg@su.edu.

Division of Nursing Students: 5 full-time (all women), 19 part-time (18 women). Average age 37. 40 applicants, 78% accepted, 19 enrolled. *Faculty:* 9 full-time (all women), 2 part-time/adjunct (both women). Expenses: Contact institution. *Financial support:* In 2006–07, 21 students received support, including 3 fellowships with partial tuition reimbursements available (averaging $1,500 per year), 2 teaching assistantships with partial tuition reimbursements available (averaging $3,482 per year); institutionally sponsored loans and scholarships/grants also available. Support available to part-time students. Financial award application deadline: 3/15; financial award applicants required to submit FAFSA. In 2006, 11 master's, 4 other advanced degrees awarded. *Degree program information:* Part-time programs available. Offers family nurse practitioner (Certificate); nurse-midwifery (Certificate); nursing (MSN); psychiatric mental health nurse practitioner (Certificate). *Application deadline:* For fall admission, 6/15 priority date for domestic and international students. Applications are processed on a rolling basis. *Application fee:* $30. Electronic applications accepted. *Application Contact:* David Anthony, Dean of Admissions, 540-665-4581, Fax: 540-665-4627, E-mail: admit@su.edu. *Director,* Dr. Sheila Ralph, 540-678-4381, Fax: 540-665-5519, E-mail: ssparks@su.edu.

Division of Occupational Therapy Students: 30 full-time (28 women), 20 part-time (19 women). Average age 26. 25 applicants, 52% accepted, 11 enrolled. *Faculty:* 3 full-time (all women), 2 part-time/adjunct (both women). Expenses: Contact institution. *Financial support:* In 2006–07, 40 students received support. Institutionally sponsored loans, scholarships/grants, and ACT and FED loans available. Support available to part-time students. Financial award application deadline: 3/15; financial award applicants required to submit FAFSA. In 2006, 20 degrees awarded. Offers occupational therapy (MS). *Application deadline:* For fall admission, 7/1 for domestic students. Applications are processed on a rolling basis. *Application fee:* $30. Electronic applications accepted. *Application Contact:* David Anthony, Dean of Admissions, 540-665-4581, Fax: 540-665-4627, E-mail: admit@su.edu. *Director,* Dr. Deborah Maar, 540-665-5542, Fax: 540-665-5564, E-mail: dmaar@su.edu.

Division of Physical Therapy Students: 104 full-time (86 women), 78 part-time (50 women); includes 1 minority (African American), 5 international. Average age 32. 235 applicants, 66% accepted, 95 enrolled. *Faculty:* 7 full-time (4 women), 4 part-time/adjunct (2 women). Expenses: Contact institution. *Financial support:* In 2006–07, 74 students received support. Institutionally sponsored loans and scholarships/grants available. Support available to part-time students. Financial award application deadline: 3/15; financial award applicants required to submit FAFSA. In 2006, 46 degrees awarded. *Degree program information:* Part-time programs available. Postbaccalaureate distance learning degree programs offered. Offers physical therapy and non-traditional physical therapy (DPT). *Application deadline:* For fall admission, 3/31 for domestic students. Applications are processed on a rolling basis. *Application fee:* $30. Electronic applications accepted. *Application Contact:* David Anthony, Dean of Admissions, 540-665-4581, Fax: 540-665-4627, E-mail: admit@su.edu. *Director,* Dr. Rose A. Schmieg, 540-665-5534, Fax: 540-545-7387, E-mail: rschmieg@su.edu.

Division of Physician Assistant Studies Students: 94 full-time (82 women), 2 part-time (both women); includes 1 minority (Asian American or Pacific Islander) Average age 28. 332 applicants, 19% accepted, 37 enrolled. *Faculty:* 5 full-time (2 women). Expenses: Contact institution. *Financial support:* In 2006–07, 68 students received support. Institutionally sponsored loans and scholarships/grants available. Support available to part-time students. Financial award application deadline: 3/15; financial award applicants required to submit FAFSA. In 2006, 23 degrees awarded. Offers physician assistant (MS). *Application deadline:* For fall admission, 2/1 for domestic students. Applications are processed on a rolling basis. *Application fee:* $30. Electronic applications accepted. *Application Contact:* David Anthony, Dean of Admissions, 540-665-4581, Fax: 540-665-4627, E-mail: admit@su.edu. *Director,* Anthony A. Miller, 540-545-7257, Fax: 540-542-6210, E-mail: amiller@su.edu.

School of Pharmacy Students: 299 full-time (180 women), 108 part-time (61 women); includes 13 minority (3 African Americans, 8 Asian Americans or Pacific Islanders, 2 Hispanic Americans), 5 international. Average age 30. 1,285 applicants, 14% accepted, 112 enrolled. *Faculty:* 18 full-time (6 women). Expenses: Contact institution. *Financial support:* In 2006–07, 306 students received support. Institutionally sponsored loans and scholarships/grants available. Support available to part-time students. Financial award application deadline: 3/15; financial award applicants required to submit FAFSA. In 2006, 126 degrees awarded. *Degree program information:* Part-time programs available. Postbaccalaureate distance learning degree programs offered (minimal on-campus study). Offers pharmacy and non-traditional pharmacy (Pharm D). *Application deadline:* For fall admission, 2/1 for domestic and international students. Applications are processed on a rolling basis. *Application fee:* $30. Electronic applications accepted. *Application Contact:* David Anthony, Dean of Admissions, 540-665-4581, Fax: 540-665-4627, E-mail: admit@su.edu. *Dean,* Dr. Alan McKay, 540-665-1280, Fax: 540-665-1283, E-mail: amckay@su.edu.

Shenandoah Conservatory Students: 45 full-time (28 women), 113 part-time (67 women), 20 international. Average age 36. 88 applicants, 48% accepted, 33 enrolled. *Faculty:* 46 full-time (20 women), 20 part-time/adjunct (7 women). Expenses: Contact institution. *Financial support:* In 2006–07, 158 students received support, including fellowships with partial tuition reimbursements available (averaging $2,020 per year), teaching assistantships with partial tuition reimbursements available (averaging $5,727 per year); career-related internships or fieldwork, institutionally sponsored loans, scholarships/grants, and unspecified assistantships also available. Support available to part-time students. Financial award application deadline: 3/15; financial award applicants required to submit FAFSA. In 2006, 37 master's, 10 doctorates, 4 other advanced degrees awarded. *Degree program information:* Part-time and evening/weekend programs available. Offers arts administration (MS); church music (MM, Certificate); composition (MM); conducting (MM); dance (MA, MFA, MS); dance accompanying (MM); music (MS); music education (MME, DMA); music therapy (MMT); pedagogy (MM); performance (MM, DMA, Artist Diploma); piano accompanying (MM). *Application deadline:* Applications are processed on a rolling basis. *Application fee:* $30. Electronic applications accepted. *Application Contact:* David Anthony, Dean of Admissions, 540-665-4581, Fax: 540-665-4627, E-mail: admit@su.edu. *Dean,* Dr. Laurence A. Kaptain, 540-665-4600, Fax: 540-665-5402, E-mail: lkaptain@su.edu.

SHEPHERD UNIVERSITY, Shepherdstown, WV 25443-3210

General Information State-supported, coed, comprehensive institution.

GRADUATE UNITS

Program in Curriculum and Instruction Offers curriculum and instruction (MA).

SHERMAN COLLEGE OF STRAIGHT CHIROPRACTIC, Spartanburg, SC 29304-1452

General Information Independent, coed, graduate-only institution. *Enrollment by degree level:* 311 first professional. *Graduate faculty:* 33 full-time (12 women), 10 part-time/adjunct (8 women). *Graduate housing:* On-campus housing not available. *Student services:* Campus employment opportunities, campus safety program, career counseling, exercise/wellness program, free psychological counseling, international student services, low-cost health insurance. *Library facilities:* Tom and Mae Bahan Library. *Collection:* 13,154 titles, 165 serial subscriptions, 1,462 audiovisual materials. *Research affiliation:* Foundation for Chiropractic Education and Research, American Public Health Service (chiropractic research).

Computer facilities: 80 computers available on campus for general student use. A campuswide network can be accessed from off campus. Internet access is available. *Web address:* http://www.sherman.edu/.

General Application Contact: Lisa A. Hildebrand, Director of Admissions, 864-578-8770 Ext. 222, Fax: 864-599-4860, E-mail: lhildebrand@sherman.edu.

GRADUATE UNITS

Professional Program Students: 311 full-time (141 women). Average age 28. 101 applicants, 60% accepted, 37 enrolled. *Faculty:* 33 full-time (12 women), 10 part-time/adjunct (8 women). Expenses: Contact institution. *Financial support:* Career-related internships or fieldwork, Federal Work-Study, institutionally sponsored loans, and scholarships/grants available. Support available to part-time students. Financial award applicants required to submit FAFSA. In 2006, 102 degrees awarded. Offers chiropractic (DC). *Application deadline:* Applications are processed on a rolling basis. *Application fee:* $35. Electronic applications accepted. *Application Contact:* Susan Newlin, Vice President for Enrollment Management, 864-578-8770 Ext. 223, Fax: 864-599-4860, E-mail: admissions@sherman.edu.

SHIPPENSBURG UNIVERSITY OF PENNSYLVANIA, Shippensburg, PA 17257-2299

General Information State-supported, coed, comprehensive institution. CGS member. *Enrollment:* 7,516 graduate, professional, and undergraduate students; 239 full-time matriculated graduate/professional students (151 women), 712 part-time matriculated graduate/professional students (470 women). *Enrollment by degree level:* 951 master's. *Graduate faculty:* 146 full-time (51 women), 13 part-time/adjunct (6 women). Tuition, state resident: part-time $336 per credit. Tuition, nonresident: part-time $538 per credit. *Graduate housing:* On-campus housing not available. *Student services:* Campus employment opportunities, campus safety program, career counseling, child daycare facilities, disabled student services, exercise/wellness program, free psychological counseling, grant writing training, international student services, low-cost health insurance, multicultural affairs office, teacher training, writing training. *Library facilities:* Ezra Lehman Memorial Library. *Online resources:* library catalog, web page, access to other libraries' catalogs. *Collection:* 450,517 titles, 1,243 serial subscriptions, 78,144 audiovisual materials.

Computer facilities: 800 computers available on campus for general student use. A campuswide network can be accessed from student residence rooms and from off campus. Internet access, personal Web pages are available. *Web address:* http://www.ship.edu/.

General Application Contact: Renee Payne, Associate Dean of Graduate Admissions, 717-477-1231, Fax: 717-477-4016, E-mail: rmpayn@ship.edu.

GRADUATE UNITS

School of Graduate Studies Students: 239 full-time (151 women), 712 part-time (470 women); includes 59 minority (34 African Americans, 1 American Indian/Alaska Native, 15 Asian Americans or Pacific Islanders, 9 Hispanic Americans), 11 international. Average age 30. 675 applicants, 67% accepted, 293 enrolled. *Faculty:* 146 full-time (51 women), 13 part-time/adjunct (6 women). Expenses: Contact institution. *Financial support:* In 2006–07, 151 research assistantships with full tuition reimbursements (averaging $3,125 per year) were awarded; career-related internships or fieldwork, scholarships/grants, and unspecified assistantships also available. Support available to part-time students. Financial award application deadline: 3/1; financial award applicants required to submit FAFSA. In 2006, 290 degrees awarded. *Degree program information:* Part-time and evening/weekend programs available. Postbaccalaureate distance learning degree programs offered (minimal on-campus study). *Application deadline:* For fall admission, 3/1 for international students; for spring admission, 7/1 for international students. Applications are processed on a rolling basis. *Application fee:* $30. Electronic applications accepted. *Application Contact:* Renee Payne, Associate Dean of Graduate Admissions, 717-477-1231, Fax: 717-477-4016, E-mail: rmpayn@ship.edu. *Interim Dean of Graduate Studies/Associate Provost,* Dr. Tracy Schoolcraft, 717-477-1148, Fax: 717-477-4038, E-mail: tascho@ship.edu.

College of Arts and Sciences Students: 114 full-time (57 women), 178 part-time (92 women); includes 23 minority (11 African Americans, 1 American Indian/Alaska Native, 9 Asian Americans or Pacific Islanders, 2 Hispanic Americans), 7 international. Average age 30. 221 applicants, 72% accepted, 84 enrolled. *Faculty:* 80 full-time (22 women), 2 part-time/adjunct (0 women). Expenses: Contact institution. *Financial support:* In 2006–07, 77 research assistantships with full tuition reimbursements (averaging $3,125 per year) were awarded; career-related internships or fieldwork, scholarships/grants, and unspecified assistantships also available. Support available to part-time students. Financial award application deadline: 3/1; financial award applicants required to submit FAFSA. In 2006, 101 degrees awarded. *Degree program information:* Part-time and evening/weekend programs available. Postbaccalaureate distance learning degree programs offered. Offers applied history (MA, Certificate); arts and sciences (MA, MPA, MS, Certificate); biology (MS); communication studies (MS); computer science (MS); geoenvironmental studies (MS); information studies (MS); organizational development and leadership (MS); psychology (MS); public administration (MPA). *Application deadline:* For fall admission, 3/1 for international students; for spring admission, 7/1 for international students. Applications are processed on a rolling basis. *Application fee:* $30. Electronic applications accepted. *Application Contact:* Renee Payne, Associate Dean of Graduate Admissions, 717-477-1231, Fax: 717-477-4016, E-mail: rmpayn@ship.edu. *Dean,* Dr. James Mike, 717-477-1151, Fax: 717-477-4026, E-mail: jhmike@ship.edu.

College of Education and Human Services Students: 112 full-time (89 women), 438 part-time (340 women); includes 28 minority (20 African Americans, 3 Asian Americans or Pacific Islanders, 5 Hispanic Americans), 3 international. Average age 30. 303 applicants, 54% accepted, 122 enrolled. *Faculty:* 45 full-time (22 women), 8 part-time/adjunct (6 women). Expenses: Contact institution. *Financial support:* In 2006–07, 70 research assistantships with full tuition reimbursements (averaging $3,125 per year) were awarded; career-related internships or fieldwork, scholarships/grants, and unspecified assistantships also available. Support available to part-time students. Financial award application deadline: 3/1; financial award applicants required to submit FAFSA. In 2006, 168 degrees awarded. *Degree program information:* Part-time and evening/weekend programs available. Offers Adlerian studies (Certificate); administration of justice (MS); advanced study in counseling (Certificate); counseling (MS); couple and family counseling (Certificate); curriculum and instruction (M Ed); education and human services (M Ed, MS, MSW, Certificate); guidance and counseling (M Ed); reading (M Ed); school administration (M Ed); social work (MSW); special education (M Ed). *Application deadline:* For fall admission, 3/1 for international students; for spring admission, 7/1 for international students. Applications are processed on a rolling basis. *Application fee:* $30. Electronic applications accepted. *Application Contact:* Renee Payne, Associate Dean of Graduate Admissions, 717-477-1231, Fax: 717-477-4016, E-mail: rmpayn@ship.edu. *Dean,* Dr. Robert B. Bartos, 717-477-1373, Fax: 717-477-4012, E-mail: rbbart@ship.edu.

John L. Grove College of Business Students: 13 full-time (5 women), 96 part-time (38 women); includes 8 minority (3 African Americans, 3 Asian Americans or Pacific Islanders, 2 Hispanic Americans), 1 international. Average age 30. 76 applicants, 66% accepted, 34 enrolled. *Faculty:* 21 full-time (7 women), 3 part-time/adjunct (0 women). Expenses: Contact institution. *Financial support:* In 2006–07, 4 research assistantships with full tuition reimbursements (averaging $3,125 per year) were awarded; career-related internships or fieldwork, scholarships/grants, and unspecified assistantships also available. Support available to part-time students. Financial award application deadline: 3/1; financial award applicants required to submit FAFSA. In 2006, 21 degrees awarded. *Degree program information:* Part-time and evening/weekend programs available. Postbaccalaureate distance learning degree programs offered (minimal on-campus study). Offers business administration (MBA). *Application deadline:* For fall admission, 3/1 for international students; for spring admission, 7/1 for international students. Applications are processed on a rolling basis. *Application fee:* $30. Electronic applications accepted. *Application Contact:* Renee Payne, Associate Dean of Graduate Admissions, 717-477-1231, Fax: 717-477-4016, E-mail: rmpayn@ship.edu. *Director,* Dr. Robert Rollins, 717-477-1483, Fax: 717-477-4015, E-mail: rdroll@ship.edu.

See Close-Up on page 1029.

SHORTER COLLEGE, Rome, GA 30165

General Information Independent-religious, coed, comprehensive institution. *Graduate housing:* On-campus housing not available.

GRADUATE UNITS

School of Business *Degree program information:* Evening/weekend programs available. Offers business administration (MBA); leadership (MA).

SH'OR YOSHUV RABBINICAL COLLEGE, Lawrence, NY 11559-1714

General Information Independent-religious, men only, comprehensive institution.

GRADUATE UNITS

Graduate Programs

SIENA HEIGHTS UNIVERSITY, Adrian, MI 49221-1796

General Information Independent-religious, coed, comprehensive institution. *Graduate housing:* Room and/or apartments available on a first-come, first-served basis to single students; on-campus housing not available to married students. Housing application deadline: 4/1.

GRADUATE UNITS

Graduate College *Degree program information:* Part-time and evening/weekend programs available. Offers agency counseling (MA); community counseling (Spt); curriculum and instruction (MA); early childhood education (MA); elementary education (MA); elementary education/reading (MA); human resource development (MA); middle school education (MA); Montessori education (MA); school counseling (MA); secondary education (MA); secondary education/reading (MA).

SIERRA NEVADA COLLEGE, Incline Village, NV 89451

General Information Independent, coed, comprehensive institution. *Enrollment:* 492 graduate, professional, and undergraduate students; 179 full-time matriculated graduate/professional students (136 women), 85 part-time matriculated graduate/professional students (58 women). *Enrollment by degree level:* 264 master's. *Graduate faculty:* 2 full-time (both women), 26 part-time/adjunct (16 women). *Tuition:* Full-time $3,590; part-time $350 per credit. *Graduate housing:* On-campus housing not available. *Student services:* Campus employment opportunities, career counseling, disabled student services, free psychological counseling, low-cost health insurance, teacher training, writing training. *Library facilities:* Primm Library. *Online resources:* library catalog, web page, access to other libraries' catalogs. *Collection:* 35,000 titles, 175 serial subscriptions.

Computer facilities: 50 computers available on campus for general student use. A campuswide network can be accessed from student residence rooms and from off campus. Internet access is available. *Web address:* http://www.sierranevada.edu/.

General Application Contact: Katrina Midgley, Teacher Education Admissions Counselor, 775-831-1314 Ext. 7517, Fax: 775-832-1694, E-mail: kmidgley@sierranevada.edu.

GRADUATE UNITS

Teacher Education Program Students: 179 full-time (136 women), 85 part-time (58 women); includes 21 minority (6 African Americans, 1 American Indian/Alaska Native, 2 Asian Americans or Pacific Islanders, 12 Hispanic Americans). Average age 35. *Faculty:* 2 full-time (both women), 26 part-time/adjunct (16 women). Expenses: Contact institution. *Financial support:* In 2006–07, 230 students received support. Federal Work-Study available. Support available to part-time students. Financial award application deadline: 8/16; financial award applicants required to submit FAFSA. In 2006, 29 degrees awarded. *Degree program information:* Part-time and evening/weekend programs available. Offers elementary education (MAT); secondary education (MAT). *Application deadline:* For fall admission, 8/16 priority date for domestic students; for winter admission, 1/10 priority date for domestic students; for spring admission, 5/25 priority date for domestic students. Applications are processed on a rolling basis. *Application fee:* $50. *Application Contact:* Katrina Midgley, Teacher Education Admissions Counselor, 775-831-1314 Ext. 7517, Fax: 775-832-1694, E-mail: kmidgley@sierranevada.edu. *Statewide Director,* Dr. Francesca Bero, 775-831-1314, Fax: 775-832-1686, E-mail: fbero@sierranevada.edu.

SILICON VALLEY UNIVERSITY, San Jose, CA 95131

General Information Proprietary, coed, comprehensive institution.

GRADUATE UNITS

Graduate Programs

SILVER LAKE COLLEGE, Manitowoc, WI 54220-9319

General Information Independent-religious, coed, comprehensive institution. *Enrollment:* 939 graduate, professional, and undergraduate students; 18 full-time matriculated graduate/professional students (16 women), 293 part-time matriculated graduate/professional students (230 women). *Enrollment by degree level:* 140 master's. *Graduate faculty:* 6 full-time (all women), 54 part-time/adjunct (33 women). *Tuition:* Full-time $6,120; part-time $340 per credit. *Graduate housing:* Room and/or apartments available on a first-come, first-served basis to single students; on-campus housing not available to married students. Typical cost: $4,400 per year. *Student services:* Campus employment opportunities, campus safety program, career counseling, disabled student services, international student services, low-cost health insurance, teacher training, writing training. *Library facilities:* The Erma M. and Theodore M. Zigmunt Library. *Online resources:* library catalog, access to other libraries' catalogs. *Collection:* 61,574 titles, 277 serial subscriptions, 8,631 audiovisual materials.

Computer facilities: 50 computers available on campus for general student use. A campuswide network can be accessed from off campus. Internet access is available. *Web address:* http://www.sl.edu/.

General Application Contact: Jamie Grant, Associate Director- Admissions, 800-236-4752 Ext. 186, Fax: 920-684-7082, E-mail: jgrant@silver.sl.edu.

GRADUATE UNITS

Division of Graduate Studies Students: 58 full-time (39 women), 274 part-time (192 women); includes 15 minority (2 African Americans, 7 American Indian/Alaska Native, 5 Asian Americans or Pacific Islanders, 1 Hispanic American). Average age 35. 70 applicants, 61% accepted, 23 enrolled. *Faculty:* 5 full-time (all women), 81 part-time/adjunct (45 women). Expenses: Contact institution. *Financial support:* Career-related internships or fieldwork, Federal Work-Study, and scholarships/grants available. Support available to part-time students. Financial award applicants required to submit FAFSA. In 2006, 86 degrees awarded. *Degree program information:* Part-time and evening/weekend programs available. Postbaccalaureate distance learning degree programs offered (minimal on-campus study). Offers administrative leadership (MA); management and organizational behavior (MS); music education-Kodaly emphasis (MM); teacher leadership (MA). *Application deadline:* Applications are processed on a rolling basis. *Application fee:* $35. Electronic applications accepted. *Application Contact:* Jamie Grant, Associate Director- Admissions, 800-236-4752 Ext. 186, Fax: 920-684-7082, E-mail: jgrant@silver.sl.edu.

SIMMONS COLLEGE, Boston, MA 02115

General Information Independent, Undergraduate: women only; graduate: coed, university. *Enrollment:* 4,849 graduate, professional, and undergraduate students; 568 full-time matriculated graduate/professional students (498 women), 1,765 part-time matriculated graduate/professional students (1,509 women). *Enrollment by degree level:* 2,062 master's, 235 doctoral, 36 other advanced degrees. *Graduate faculty:* 143 full-time (107 women), 220 part-time/adjunct (155 women). *Graduate housing:* Room and/or apartments available on a first-come, first-served basis to single students; on-campus housing not available to married students. Housing application deadline: 7/15. *Student services:* Campus employment opportunities, campus safety program, career counseling, disabled student services, free psychological counseling, international student services, low-cost health insurance. *Library facilities:* Beatley Library plus 2 others. *Online resources:* library catalog, web page, access to other libraries' catalogs. *Collection:* 243,161 titles, 1,696 serial subscriptions, 6,202 audiovisual materials.

Computer facilities: 420 computers available on campus for general student use. A campuswide network can be accessed from student residence rooms and from off campus. Internet access and online class registration are available. *Web address:* http://www.simmons.edu/.

General Application Contact: Donna M. Dolan, Registrar, 617-521-2111, Fax: 617-521-3144, E-mail: donna.dolan@simmons.edu.

GRADUATE UNITS

Graduate School Students: 151 full-time (135 women), 718 part-time (624 women); includes 87 minority (33 African Americans, 3 American Indian/Alaska Native, 21 Asian Americans or Pacific Islanders, 30 Hispanic Americans), 11 international. Average age 27. *Faculty:* 59 full-time (41 women), 78 part-time/adjunct (51 women). Expenses: Contact institution. *Financial support:* Fellowships, research assistantships, teaching assistantships, career-related internships or fieldwork, Federal Work-Study, institutionally sponsored loans, scholarships/grants, tuition waivers (partial), and unspecified assistantships available. Support available to part-time students. Financial award application deadline: 3/1; financial award applicants required to submit FAFSA. In 2006, 300 master's, 39 other advanced degrees awarded. *Degree program information:* Part-time programs available. *Application deadline:* Applications are processed on a rolling basis. Electronic applications accepted. *Application Contact:* Kristen Haack, Director, Graduate Studies Admission, 617-521-2915, Fax: 617-521-3058, E-mail: gsa@simmons.edu. *Dean,* Dr. Diane Raymond, 617-521-2910, Fax: 617-521-3058, E-mail: gsa@simmons.edu.

College of Arts and Sciences Graduate Studies Expenses: Contact institution. *Financial support:* Research assistantships, teaching assistantships available. Financial award application deadline: 3/1; financial award applicants required to submit FAFSA. Offers applied behavior analysis (PhD); arts and sciences (MA, MAT, MFA, MS, MS Ed, PhD, CAGS, Ed S); assistive technology (MS Ed, Ed S); behavioral education (MS Ed, Ed S); children's literature (MA); communications management (MS); educational leadership (MS Ed, CAGS); elementary education (MAT, CAGS); English (MA); gender/cultural studies (MA); general education (CAGS); general purposes (MS); health professions education (PhD); language and literacy (MS Ed, Ed S); middle school education (MAT, CAGS); moderate disabilities (Ed S); moderate special needs (MS Ed); professional license (CAGS); professional license: elementary (MS Ed); professional license: middle/high (MS Ed); secondary education (MAT, CAGS); severe disabilities (Ed S); severe special needs (MS Ed); Spanish (MA); special education (MS Ed, PhD, Ed S); special education administration (MS Ed, PhD, Ed S); teacher preparation (MAT, MS, MS Ed, CAGS); teaching English as a second language (MAT); urban education (MS Ed, CAGS); writing for children (MFA). *Application deadline:* For fall admission, 8/1 priority date for domestic students; for winter admission, 12/15 priority date for domestic students; for spring admission, 5/1 priority date for domestic students. Applications are processed on a rolling basis. *Application fee:* $35. Electronic applications accepted.

Graduate School of Library and Information Science Students: 26 full-time (20 women), 528 part-time (412 women); includes 41 minority (13 African Americans, 2 American Indian/Alaska Native, 16 Asian Americans or Pacific Islanders, 10 Hispanic Americans), 7 international. Average age 35. 342 applicants, 86% accepted, 159 enrolled. *Faculty:* 17 full-time (11 women), 30 part-time/adjunct (21 women). Expenses: Contact institution. *Financial support:* In 2006–07, 4 research assistantships with full tuition reimbursements were awarded; career-related internships or fieldwork, Federal Work-Study, institutionally sponsored loans, scholarships/grants, and tuition waivers (full and partial) also available. Support available to part-time students. Financial award application deadline: 3/1; financial award applicants required to submit FAFSA. In 2006, 314 master's, 1 doctorate awarded. *Degree program information:* Part-time and evening/weekend programs available. Offers history and archives management); library and information science (PhD); school library teacher (MS, Certificate). MS/DA and MS/MA offered jointly with Department of History. *Application deadline:* For fall admission, 3/1 priority date for domestic students, 3/1 for international students; for spring admission, 7/1 priority date for domestic students. Applications are processed on a rolling basis. *Application fee:* $35. Electronic applications accepted. *Application Contact:* Denise Davis, Assistant Dean for Admission and Recruitment, 617-521-2801, Fax: 617-521-3192, E-mail: denise.davis@simmons.edu. *Dean,* Dr. Michele V. Cloonan, 617-521-2806, Fax: 617-521-3192, E-mail: cloonan@simmons.edu.

School for Health Studies Students: 125 full-time (110 women), 266 part-time (234 women); includes 42 minority (11 African Americans, 1 American Indian/Alaska Native, 21 Asian Americans or Pacific Islanders, 9 Hispanic Americans), 2 international. Average age 27. 427 applicants, 61% accepted, 155 enrolled. *Faculty:* 21 full-time (17 women), 36 part-time/adjunct (33 women). Expenses: Contact institution. *Financial support:* Fellowships, research assistantships, teaching assistantships, scholarships/grants, traineeships, and unspecified assistantships available. Financial award application deadline: 3/1; financial award applicants required to submit FAFSA. In 2006, 46 master's, 124 doctorates, 9 other advanced degrees awarded. *Degree program information:* Part-time and evening/weekend programs available. Postbaccalaureate distance learning degree programs offered (no on-campus study). Offers didactic program in dietetics (Certificate); health care administration (MHA, CAGS); health professions education (PhD); health studies (MHA, MS, DPT, PhD, CAGS, Certificate); nutrition (dietetic internship) (Certificate); nutrition and health promotion (MS); physical therapy (DPT); primary health care nursing (MS, CAGS); sports nutrition (Certificate). *Application deadline:* For fall admission, 6/1 for domestic and international students; for spring admission, 11/1 for domestic students. *Application fee:* $50. Electronic applications accepted. *Application Contact:* Vilma Torres, Administrative Assistant, 617-521-2654, Fax: 617-521-3137, E-mail: shs@simmons.edu. *Dean,* Dr. Gerald P. Koocher, 617-521-2605, Fax: 617-521-3137, E-mail: gerald.koocher@simmons.edu.

School of Social Work Students: 234 full-time (201 women), 136 part-time (122 women); includes 60 minority (32 African Americans, 12 Asian Americans or Pacific Islanders, 16 Hispanic Americans), 7 international. Average age 27. 540 applicants, 85% accepted, 160 enrolled. *Faculty:* 21 full-time (17 women), 68 part-time/adjunct (46 women). Expenses: Contact institution. *Financial support:* Fellowships with full tuition reimbursements, career-related internships or fieldwork, Federal Work-Study, institutionally sponsored loans, and tuition waivers (full) available. Support available to part-time students. Financial award application deadline: 3/1; financial award applicants required to submit FAFSA. In 2006, 141 master's, 4 doctorates awarded. *Degree program information:* Part-time programs available. Offers clinical social work (MSW, PhD). *Application deadline:* For fall admission, 12/15 priority date for domestic students; for winter admission, 2/15 for domestic students. *Application fee:* $45. *Dean,* Dr. Stefan Krug, 617-521-3929, Fax: 617-521-3980, E-mail: stefan.krug@simmons.edu.

Simmons School of Management Students: 32 full-time (all women), 117 part-time (all women); includes 23 minority (14 African Americans, 7 Asian Americans or Pacific Islanders, 2 Hispanic Americans), 2 international. Average age 31. 98 applicants, 82% accepted, 53 enrolled. *Faculty:* 25 full-time (21 women), 8 part-time/adjunct (4 women). Expenses: Contact institution. *Financial support:* Institutionally sponsored loans, scholarships/grants, and unspecified assistantships available. Support available to part-time students. Financial award application deadline: 3/1; financial award applicants required to submit FAFSA. In 2006, 99 master's, 5 other advanced degrees awarded. *Degree program information:* Part-time and evening/weekend programs available. Offers entrepreneurship (Certificate); management (MBA). *Application deadline:* For fall admission, 6/30 priority date for domestic and international students; for spring admission, 12/1 priority date for domestic students, 11/15 priority date for international students. Applications are processed on a rolling basis. *Application fee:* $75. Electronic applications accepted. *Application Contact:* Denise Haile, Director of Admissions, 617-521-3840, Fax: 617-521-3880, E-mail: somadm@simmons.edu. *Dean,* Dr. Deborah Merrill-Sands, 617-521-3827, Fax: 617-521-3881.

SIMON FRASER UNIVERSITY, Burnaby, BC V5A 1S6, Canada

General Information Province-supported, coed, university. *Enrollment:* 24,842 graduate, professional, and undergraduate students; 2,990 full-time matriculated graduate/professional

Simon Fraser University (continued)

students (2,032 women), 276 part-time matriculated graduate/professional students (193 women). *Enrollment by degree level:* 2,060 master's, 834 doctoral, 352 other advanced degrees. *Graduate faculty:* 624 full-time (152 women), 7 part-time/adjunct (2 women). *Graduate housing:* Rooms and/or apartments available on a first-come, first-served basis to single and married students. Housing application deadline: 1/2. *Student services:* Campus employment opportunities, campus safety program, career counseling, child daycare facilities, disabled student services, exercise/wellness program, free psychological counseling, grant writing training, international student services, low-cost health insurance, teacher training, writing training. *Library facilities:* W. A. C. Bennett Library. *Online resources:* library catalog, web page, access to other libraries' catalogs. *Collection:* 20,000 serial subscriptions. *Research affiliation:* Bamfield Marine Research Station.

Computer facilities: 900 computers available on campus for general student use. A campuswide network can be accessed from off campus. Internet access and online class registration are available. *Web address:* http://www.sfu.ca/.

General Application Contact: B. Williamson, Director of Graduate Records, Admission and Registration, 778-782-3042, Fax: 778-782-3080, E-mail: dgs-sfu@sfu.ca.

GRADUATE UNITS

Graduate Studies Students: 1,668. Average age 35. *Faculty:* 624 full-time (152 women), 7 part-time/adjunct (2 women). Expenses: Contact institution. *Financial support:* In 2006–07, 456 fellowships were awarded; research assistantships, teaching assistantships, career-related internships or fieldwork, Federal Work-Study, institutionally sponsored loans, and scholarships/grants also available. Support available to part-time students. In 2006, 438 master's, 72 doctorates awarded. *Degree program information:* Part-time and evening/weekend programs available. Offers population and public health (M Sc). *Application fee:* $55. *Dean,* Dr. Jonathan Driver, 778-782-4255, Fax: 778-782-5666, E-mail: driver@sfu.ca.

Faculty of Applied Sciences Students: 411. *Faculty:* 103 full-time (17 women). Expenses: Contact institution. *Financial support:* In 2006–07, 124 fellowships were awarded; research assistantships, teaching assistantships, career-related internships or fieldwork, Federal Work-Study, and institutionally sponsored loans also available. In 2006, 59 master's, 14 doctorates awarded. Offers applied sciences (M Eng, M Sc, MA, MA Sc, MRM, PhD); communication (MA, PhD); computing science (M Sc, PhD); engineering science (M Eng, MA Sc, PhD); information technology (M Sc, PhD); interactive arts (M Sc, PhD); kinesiology (M Sc, PhD); resource and environmental management (MRM, PhD). *Application fee:* $55.

Faculty of Arts and Social Sciences Students: 740. *Faculty:* 303 full-time (93 women), 4 part-time/adjunct (2 women). Expenses: Contact institution. *Financial support:* In 2006–07, 168 fellowships were awarded; research assistantships, teaching assistantships. In 2006, 103 master's, 29 doctorates awarded. *Degree program information:* Part-time and evening/weekend programs available. Offers anthropology (MA, PhD); archaeology (MA, PhD); arts and social sciences (M Pub, M Sc, MA, MALS, MFA, MPP, MUS, PhD, Graduate Diploma); contemporary arts (MFA); criminology (MA, PhD); economics (MA, PhD); English (MA, PhD); French (MA); geography (M Sc, MA, PhD); gerontology (MA, PhD); history (MA, PhD); Latin American studies (MA); liberal studies (MALS); linguistics (MA, PhD); philosophy (MA, PhD); political science (MA, PhD); psychology (MA, PhD); public policy (MPP); publishing (M Pub); sociology (MA, PhD); urban studies (MUS, Graduate Diploma); women's studies (MA, PhD). *Application fee:* $55. *Dean,* Dr. John T. Pierce, 778-782-4414, Fax: 778-782-3033, E-mail: pierce@sfu.ca.

Faculty of Business Administration Students: 293 full-time (107 women). Average age 28. 286 applicants. *Faculty:* 60 full-time (18 women). Expenses: Contact institution. *Financial support:* In 2006–07, 41 fellowships (averaging $4,400 per year) were awarded; research assistantships with partial tuition reimbursements, teaching assistantships with partial tuition reimbursements, career-related internships or fieldwork and scholarships/grants also available. In 2006, 43 degrees awarded. Postbaccalaureate distance learning degree programs offered. Offers business administration (EMBA, PhD); financial management (MA); general business (MBA); global asset and wealth management (MBA); management of technology/biotechnology (MBA). *Application deadline:* For fall admission, 4/2 for domestic students; for winter admission, 10/1 for domestic students; for spring admission, 2/2 for domestic students. Applications are processed on a rolling basis. *Application fee:* $100. *Application Contact:* Program Assistant, 604-291-3047, Fax: 604-291-3404, E-mail: mba@sfu.ca. *Associate Dean,* Ed Bukszar, 778-782-5195, E-mail: bukszar@sfu.ca.

Faculty of Education Students: 379 full-time (263 women), 153 part-time (118 women). Average age 40. *Faculty:* 41 full-time (19 women). Expenses: Contact institution. *Financial support:* In 2006–07, 16 fellowships were awarded; research assistantships, teaching assistantships. In 2006, 129 master's, 3 doctorates awarded. Offers administrative leadership (M Ed, MA, Ed D); arts education (M Ed, MA, PhD); counseling psychology (M Ed, MA); curriculum theory and implementation (PhD); education (M Ed, M Sc, MA, Ed D, PhD); educational psychology (M Ed, MA, PhD); educational technology and learning design (M Ed, MA, PhD); foundations (M Ed, MA); mathematics education (M Ed, M Sc, PhD); philosophy of education (PhD); teaching English as a second/foreign language (M Ed). *Application fee:* $55. *Application Contact:* Mauvereen Walker, Graduate Secretary, 778-782-4787, E-mail: mauve@sfu.ca. *Director, Graduate Programs,* Dr. Tom O'Shea, 778-782-3984, E-mail: oshea@sfu.ca.

Faculty of Science Students: 342. *Faculty:* 130 full-time (11 women), 2 part-time/adjunct (0 women). Expenses: Contact institution. *Financial support:* In 2006–07, 98 fellowships were awarded; research assistantships, teaching assistantships, career-related internships or fieldwork also available. In 2006, 48 master's, 25 doctorates awarded. *Degree program information:* Part-time programs available. Offers applied and computational mathematics (M Sc, PhD); biological sciences (M Sc, PhD); biophysics (M Sc, PhD); chemical physics (M Sc, PhD); chemistry (PhD); earth sciences (M Sc, PhD); environmental toxicology (MET); mathematics (M Sc, PhD); molecular biology and biochemistry (M Sc, PhD); pest management (MPM); physics (M Sc, PhD); science (M Sc, MET, MPM, PhD); statistics and actuarial science (M Sc, PhD). *Application fee:* $55. *Dean,* Michael Plischke, 778-782-3771, E-mail: scdean@sfu.ca.

SIMPSON UNIVERSITY, Redding, CA 96003-8606

General Information Independent-religious, coed, comprehensive institution. *Graduate housing:* On-campus housing not available.

GRADUATE UNITS

A.W. Tozer Theological Seminary Students: 3 full-time (1 woman), 57 part-time (14 women); includes 10 minority (3 African Americans, 5 Asian Americans or Pacific Islanders, 2 Hispanic Americans), 1 international. Average age 35. 22 applicants, 73% accepted, 16 enrolled. *Faculty:* 37 part-time/adjunct (4 women). Expenses: Contact institution. *Financial support:* In 2006–07, 26 students received support. Scholarships/grants available. Support available to part-time students. Financial award application deadline: 3/20; financial award applicants required to submit FAFSA. In 2006, 8 degrees awarded. *Degree program information:* Part-time programs available. Postbaccalaureate distance learning degree programs offered (minimal on-campus study). Offers Christian leadership (MA); Christian studies (MA); intercultural studies (MA); ministry (M Div). *Application deadline:* For fall admission, 9/4 priority date for domestic students, 9/4 for international students; for spring admission, 1/8 priority date for domestic students, 1/8 for international students. Applications are processed on a rolling basis. *Application fee:* $20. Electronic applications accepted. *Application Contact:* Jeff Williams, Director of Enrollment Development, 530-226-4611, Fax: 530-226-4861, E-mail: jwilliams@simpsonuniversity.edu. *Dean,* Dr. Rolda Redman, 530-226-4144, Fax: 530-326-4871, E-mail: rredman@simpsonuniversity.edu.

School of Education *Degree program information:* Part-time programs available. Offers education (MA); education and preliminary administrative services (MA); education and preliminary teaching (MA); teaching (MA). Electronic applications accepted.

SINTE GLESKA UNIVERSITY, Rosebud, SD 57555

General Information Independent, coed, comprehensive institution. *Graduate housing:* Rooms and/or apartments available on a first-come, first-served basis to single and married students.

GRADUATE UNITS

Graduate Education Program *Degree program information:* Part-time and evening/weekend programs available. Offers elementary education (M Ed).

SIOUX FALLS SEMINARY, Sioux Falls, SD 57105-1599

General Information Independent-religious, coed, graduate-only institution. *Graduate faculty:* 8 full-time (1 woman), 18 part-time/adjunct (6 women). *Graduate housing:* Rooms and/or apartments available to single and married students. Housing application deadline: 7/1. *Student services:* Campus employment opportunities, career counseling, exercise/wellness program, free psychological counseling, international student services, low-cost health insurance. *Library facilities:* Kaiser-Ramaker Library. *Online resources:* library catalog, access to other libraries' catalogs. *Collection:* 72,156 titles, 313 serial subscriptions, 9,321 audiovisual materials.

Computer facilities: Internet access is available. *Web address:* http://sfseminary.edu/.

General Application Contact: Bryce H. Eben, Director of Enrollment Development, 605-336-6588, Fax: 605-335-9090, E-mail: beben@nabs.edu.

GRADUATE UNITS

Graduate and Professional Programs Students: 66 full-time (20 women), 34 part-time (14 women). *Faculty:* 8 full-time (1 woman), 18 part-time/adjunct (6 women). Expenses: Contact institution. *Financial support:* Career-related internships or fieldwork and scholarships/grants available. Support available to part-time students. *Degree program information:* Part-time programs available. Offers Bible and theology (MA); Christian leadership (MA); counseling (MA); marriage and family therapy (MA); ministry (D Min); pastoral ministry (M Div); religious studies (MA); theological studies (Certificate). *Application deadline:* Applications are processed on a rolling basis. *Application fee:* $35. *Application Contact:* Bryce H. Eben, Director of Enrollment Development, 605-336-6588, Fax: 605-335-9090, E-mail: beben@nabs.edu. *Academic Vice President and Dean,* Dr. Ronald D. Sisk, 605-336-6588, Fax: 605-335-9090, E-mail: rsisk@nabs.edu.

SKIDMORE COLLEGE, Saratoga Springs, NY 12866-1632

General Information Independent, coed, comprehensive institution. *Enrollment:* 2,816 graduate, professional, and undergraduate students; 57 part-time matriculated graduate/professional students (45 women). *Enrollment by degree level:* 57 master's. *Graduate faculty:* 78 full-time (38 women), 3 part-time/adjunct (1 woman). *Graduate housing:* On-campus housing not available. *Student services:* Career counseling. *Library facilities:* Scribner Library plus 1 other. *Online resources:* library catalog, web page, access to other libraries' catalogs. *Collection:* 376,682 titles, 959 serial subscriptions, 11,078 audiovisual materials.

Computer facilities: 173 computers available on campus for general student use. A campuswide network can be accessed from student residence rooms and from off campus. Internet access is available. *Web address:* http://www.skidmore.edu/.

General Application Contact: Dr. John Anzalone, Director, 518-580-5480, Fax: 518-580-5486.

GRADUATE UNITS

Liberal Studies Program Average age 42. 29 applicants, 45% accepted, 9 enrolled. *Faculty:* 78 full-time (38 women), 3 part-time/adjunct (1 woman). Expenses: Contact institution. *Financial support:* In 2006–07, 4 students received support. Career-related internships or fieldwork and scholarships/grants available. Support available to part-time students. Financial award applicants required to submit FAFSA. In 2006, 10 degrees awarded. *Degree program information:* Part-time programs available. Postbaccalaureate distance learning degree programs offered (minimal on-campus study). Offers liberal studies (MA). *Application deadline:* For fall admission, 6/1 priority date for domestic and international students; for spring admission, 10/1 priority date for domestic and international students. Applications are processed on a rolling basis. *Application fee:* $60. Electronic applications accepted. *Application Contact:* Information Contact, 518-580-5480, Fax: 518-580-5486, E-mail: mals@skidmore.edu. *Director,* Dr. John Anzalone, 518-580-5480, Fax: 518-580-5486.

SLIPPERY ROCK UNIVERSITY OF PENNSYLVANIA, Slippery Rock, PA 16057-1383

General Information State-supported, coed, comprehensive institution. *Enrollment:* 8,230 graduate, professional, and undergraduate students; 311 full-time matriculated graduate/professional students (201 women), 374 part-time matriculated graduate/professional students (274 women). *Enrollment by degree level:* 497 master's, 128 doctoral, 60 other advanced degrees. *Graduate faculty:* 62 full-time (34 women), 6 part-time/adjunct (4 women). Tuition, state resident: part-time $336 per credit. Tuition, nonresident: part-time $538 per credit. *Required fees:* $84 per credit. $37 per semester. *Graduate housing:* Room and/or apartments available on a first-come, first-served basis to single students; on-campus housing not available to married students. Typical cost: $2,822 per year ($4,998 including board). Room and board charges vary according to board plan and housing facility selected. *Student services:* Campus employment opportunities, campus safety program, career counseling, child daycare facilities, disabled student services, exercise/wellness program, free psychological counseling, international student services, multicultural affairs office, writing training. *Library facilities:* Bailey Library. *Online resources:* library catalog, web page, access to other libraries' catalogs. *Collection:* 503,376 titles, 599 serial subscriptions.

Computer facilities: Computer purchase and lease plans are available. 940 computers available on campus for general student use. A campuswide network can be accessed from student residence rooms and from off campus. Internet access and online class registration are available. *Web address:* http://www.sru.edu/.

General Application Contact: April Longwell, Interim Director of Graduate Studies, 724-738-2051 Ext. 2116, Fax: 724-738-2146, E-mail: graduate.studies@sru.edu.

GRADUATE UNITS

Graduate Studies (Recruitment) Students: 310 full-time (200 women), 315 part-time (233 women); includes 23 minority (17 African Americans, 2 American Indian/Alaska Native, 1 Asian American or Pacific Islander, 3 Hispanic Americans), 7 international. Average age 30. 660 applicants, 67% accepted, 282 enrolled. *Faculty:* 62 full-time (34 women), 6 part-time/adjunct (4 women). Expenses: Contact institution. *Financial support:* In 2006–07, 140 students received support. Career-related internships or fieldwork, Federal Work-Study, institutionally sponsored loans, scholarships/grants, tuition waivers (full), and unspecified assistantships available. Support available to part-time students. Financial award application deadline: 5/1; financial award applicants required to submit FAFSA. In 2006, 216 master's, 48 doctorates awarded. *Degree program information:* Part-time and evening/weekend programs available. Postbaccalaureate distance learning degree programs offered (no on-campus study). *Application deadline:* For fall admission, 7/1 priority date for domestic and international students; for spring admission, 11/1 priority date for domestic and international students. Applications are processed on a rolling basis. *Application fee:* $25. Electronic applications accepted. *Interim Director of Graduate Studies,* April Longwell, 724-738-2051 Ext. 2116, Fax: 724-738-2146, E-mail: graduate.studies@sru.edu.

College of Business, Information, and Social Sciences Expenses: Contact institution. *Financial support:* Career-related internships or fieldwork, Federal Work-Study, scholarships/grants, and unspecified assistantships available. Support available to part-time students. Financial award application deadline: 5/1; financial award applicants required to submit FAFSA. *Degree program information:* Part-time programs available. Offers business, information, and social sciences (MS). *Application deadline:* For fall admission, 7/1 priority date for domestic and international students; for spring admission, 11/1 priority date for domestic and international students. Applications are processed on a rolling basis. *Application fee:* $25. Electronic applications accepted. *Application Contact:* April Longwell, Interim Director of Graduate Studies, 724-738-2051 Ext. 2116, Fax: 724-738-2146, E-mail: graduate.studies@sru.edu. *Dean,* Dr. Bruce Russell, 724-738-2607, Fax: 724-738-4767, E-mail: bruce.russell@sru.edu.

College of Education Expenses: Contact institution. *Financial support:* Career-related internships or fieldwork, Federal Work-Study, scholarships/grants, and unspecified assistantships available. Support available to part-time students. Financial award application deadline: 5/1; financial award applicants required to submit FAFSA. *Degree program information:* Part-time and evening/weekend programs available. Offers community counseling (MA); early childhood education (M Ed); education (M Ed, MA, MS); elementary guidance and counseling (M Ed); master teacher (M Ed); math/science (M Ed); physical education (M Ed); reading (M Ed); secondary education in math/science (M Ed); secondary guidance and counseling (M Ed); sport management (MS); student personnel (MA); supervision (M Ed). *Application deadline:* For fall admission, 7/1 priority date for domestic and international students; for spring admission, 11/1 priority date for domestic and international students. Applications are processed on a rolling basis. *Application fee:* $25. Electronic applications accepted. *Application Contact:* Dr. Duncan M. Sargent, Director of Graduate Studies, 724-738-2051 Ext. 2116, Fax: 724-738-2146, E-mail: graduate.studies@sru.edu. *Interim Director of Graduate Studies,* Dr. Jay Hertzog, 724-738-2685, Fax: 724-738-2146, E-mail: graduate.studies@sru.edu.

College of Health, Environment, and Science Expenses: Contact institution. *Financial support:* Career-related internships or fieldwork, Federal Work-Study, institutionally sponsored loans, scholarships/grants, and unspecified assistantships available. Support available to part-time students. Financial award application deadline: 5/1; financial award applicants required to submit FAFSA. *Degree program information:* Part-time and evening/weekend programs available. Offers environmental education (M Ed); health, environment, and science (M Ed, MS, MSN, DPT); nursing (MSN); physical therapy (DPT); resource management (MS); sustainable systems (MS). *Application deadline:* For fall admission, 7/1 priority date for domestic and international students; for spring admission, 11/1 priority date for domestic and international students. Applications are processed on a rolling basis. *Application fee:* $25. Electronic applications accepted. *Application Contact:* April Longwell, Interim Director of Graduate Studies, 724-738-2051 Ext. 2116, Fax: 724-738-2146, E-mail: graduate.studies@sru.edu. *Dean,* Dr. Susan Hannam, 724-738-4862, Fax: 724-738-2881, E-mail: susan.hannam@sru.edu.

College of Humanities, Fine and Performing Arts Expenses: Contact institution. *Financial support:* Career-related internships or fieldwork, scholarships/grants, and unspecified assistantships available. Support available to part-time students. Financial award application deadline: 5/1; financial award applicants required to submit FAFSA. *Degree program information:* Part-time and evening/weekend programs available. Offers English (MA); history (MA); humanities, fine and performing arts (MA). *Application deadline:* For fall admission, 7/1 priority date for domestic and international students; for spring admission, 11/1 priority date for domestic and international students. Applications are processed on a rolling basis. *Application fee:* $25. Electronic applications accepted. *Application Contact:* April Longwell, Interim Director of Graduate Studies, 724-738-2051 Ext. 2116, Fax: 724-738-2146, E-mail: graduate.studies@sru.edu. *Dean,* Dr. William McKinney, 724-738-4863 Ext. 4866, Fax: 724-738-2188, E-mail: william.mckinney@sru.edu.

See Close-Up on page 1031.

SMITH COLLEGE, Northampton, MA 01063

General Information Independent, Undergraduate: women only; graduate: coed, comprehensive institution. *Enrollment:* 3,092 graduate, professional, and undergraduate students; 47 full-time matriculated graduate/professional students (37 women), 20 part-time matriculated graduate/professional students (18 women). *Enrollment by degree level:* 67 master's. *Graduate faculty:* 285 full-time (153 women), 28 part-time/adjunct (14 women). *Tuition:* Full-time $32,320; part-time $1,010 per credit. Tuition and fees vary according to course load. *Graduate housing:* Room and/or apartments available on a first-come, first-served basis to single students; on-campus housing not available to married students. Typical cost: $5,460 per year. Housing application deadline: 5/1. *Student services:* Campus employment opportunities, campus safety program, career counseling, child daycare facilities, disabled student services, exercise/wellness program, international student services, low-cost health insurance, multicultural affairs office, teacher training, writing training. *Library facilities:* Neilson Library plus 3 others. *Online resources:* library catalog, web page, access to other libraries' catalogs. *Collection:* 1.4 million titles, 8,741 serial subscriptions, 68,550 audiovisual materials.

Computer facilities: Computer purchase and lease plans are available. 585 computers available on campus for general student use. A campuswide network can be accessed from student residence rooms and from off campus. Internet access and online class registration, e-mail are available. *Web address:* http://www.smith.edu/.

General Application Contact: Susan Etheredge, Director, 413-585-3050, Fax: 413-585-3054, E-mail: gradstudy@smith.edu.

GRADUATE UNITS

Graduate Programs Students: 47 full-time (37 women), 20 part-time (18 women); includes 5 minority (1 African American, 3 Asian Americans or Pacific Islanders, 1 Hispanic American), 7 international. Average age 28. 128 applicants, 56% accepted, 58 enrolled. *Faculty:* 285 full-time (153 women), 28 part-time/adjunct (14 women). Expenses: Contact institution. *Financial support:* In 2006–07, 64 students received support, including teaching assistantships with full tuition reimbursements available (averaging $11,150 per year); fellowships, research assistantships, career-related internships or fieldwork, institutionally sponsored loans, and scholarships/grants also available. Support available to part-time students. Financial award application deadline: 1/15; financial award applicants required to submit CSS PROFILE or FAFSA. In 2006, 43 degrees awarded. *Degree program information:* Part-time programs available. Offers biological sciences (MA, MAT); biological sciences education (MAT); chemistry (MAT); chemistry education (MAT); dance (MFA); education of the deaf (MED); elementary education (Ed M); English education (MAT); English language and literature (MAT); exercise and sport studies (MS); French education (MAT); French language and literature (MAT); geology education (MAT); government education (MAT); history (MAT); history education (MAT); mathematics education (MAT); middle school education (Ed M); physics education (MAT); playwriting (MFA); secondary education (MAT); Spanish education (MAT). *Application deadline:* For fall admission, 1/15 for domestic and international students; for spring admission, 12/1 for domestic students. *Application fee:* $60. *Application Contact:* Ruth Morgan, Administrative Assistant, 413-585-3050, Fax: 413-585-3054, E-mail: gradstdy@smith.edu. *Director,* Susan Etheredge, 413-585-3050, Fax: 413-585-3054, E-mail: gradstudy@smith.edu.

School for Social Work Students: 373 full-time (332 women); includes 74 minority (33 African Americans, 4 American Indian/Alaska Native, 11 Asian Americans or Pacific Islanders, 26 Hispanic Americans), 6 international. Average age 32. 346 applicants, 70% accepted, 124 enrolled. *Faculty:* 10 full-time (7 women), 98 part-time/adjunct (75 women). Expenses: Contact institution. *Financial support:* In 2006–07, 218 students received support. Career-related internships or fieldwork, institutionally sponsored loans, and scholarships/grants available. Financial award application deadline: 4/1; financial award applicants required to submit FAFSA. In 2006, 114 master's, 6 doctorates awarded. Offers social work (MSW, PhD). *Application deadline:* For fall admission, 2/21 for domestic students. Applications are processed on a rolling basis. *Application fee:* $60. *Application Contact:* Irene Rodriguez Martin, Director of Enrollment Management and Continuing Education, 413-585-7960, Fax: 413-585-7994, E-mail: imartin@smith.edu. *Dean,* Dr. Carolyn Jacobs, 413-585-7977, E-mail: cjacobs@smith.edu.

SOJOURNER-DOUGLASS COLLEGE, Baltimore, MD 21205-1814

General Information Independent, coed, primarily women, comprehensive institution.

GRADUATE UNITS

Graduate Program

SONOMA STATE UNIVERSITY, Rohnert Park, CA 94928-3609

General Information State-supported, coed, comprehensive institution. *Enrollment:* 7,749 graduate, professional, and undergraduate students; 746 full-time matriculated graduate/professional students (539 women), 416 part-time matriculated graduate/professional students (297 women). *Enrollment by degree level:* 1,162 master's. *Graduate faculty:* 71 full-time (34 women), 16 part-time/adjunct (12 women). Tuition, nonresident: part-time $339 per unit. *Required fees:* $1,464 per term. *Graduate housing:* Room and/or apartments available on a first-come, first-served basis to single students; on-campus housing not available to married students. Housing application deadline: 1/1. *Student services:* Campus employment opportunities, career counseling, child daycare facilities, disabled student services, exercise/wellness program, free psychological counseling, international student services, multicultural affairs office. *Library facilities:* Jean and Charles Schultz Information Center. *Online resources:* library catalog, web page, access to other libraries' catalogs. *Collection:* 636,613 titles, 21,115 serial subscriptions.

Computer facilities: 400 computers available on campus for general student use. A campuswide network can be accessed from student residence rooms and from off campus. Internet access is available. *Web address:* http://www.sonoma.edu/.

General Application Contact: Elaine Sundberg, Associate Vice Provost, Academic Programs/Graduate Studies, 707-664-2215, Fax: 707-664-4060, E-mail: elaine.sundberg@sonoma.edu.

GRADUATE UNITS

Institute of Interdisciplinary Studies/Special Major Students: 4 full-time (3 women), 28 part-time (19 women); includes 2 minority (1 American Indian/Alaska Native, 1 Hispanic American). Average age 37. 13 applicants, 100% accepted, 12 enrolled. *Faculty:* 1 (woman) full-time. Expenses: Contact institution. *Financial support:* Career-related internships or fieldwork, Federal Work-Study, and institutionally sponsored loans available. Support available to part-time students. In 2006, 10 degrees awarded. *Degree program information:* Part-time programs available. Offers special major (MA, MS). *Application deadline:* For fall admission, 1/31 for domestic students; for spring admission, 10/31 for domestic students. *Application fee:* $55. *Coordinator,* Dr. Ellen Carlton, 707-664-3918, E-mail: ellen.carlton@sonoma.edu.

School of Arts and Humanities Students: 8 full-time (all women), 28 part-time (21 women); includes 2 minority (1 Asian American or Pacific Islander, 1 Hispanic American). Average age 36. 14 applicants, 93% accepted, 6 enrolled. *Faculty:* 8 full-time (5 women), 1 part-time/adjunct (0 women). Expenses: Contact institution. *Financial support:* In 2006–07, 9 teaching assistantships with partial tuition reimbursements were awarded; fellowships, career-related internships or fieldwork and Federal Work-Study also available. Support available to part-time students. Financial award application deadline: 3/2. In 2006, 8 degrees awarded. *Degree program information:* Part-time and evening/weekend programs available. Offers American literature (MA); arts and humanities (MA); creative writing (MA); English literature (MA); world literature (MA). *Application deadline:* For fall admission, 11/30 priority date for domestic students. *Application fee:* $55. *Application Contact:* Dr. Tim Wandling, Chair, 707-664-2140, E-mail: tim.wandling@sonoma.edu. *Dean,* Dr. William Babula, 707-664-2146, E-mail: william.babula@sonoma.edu.

School of Business and Economics Students: 4 full-time (1 woman), 37 part-time (13 women); includes 1 minority (African American) Average age 31. 24 applicants, 63% accepted, 7 enrolled. *Faculty:* 5 full-time (1 woman), 1 part-time/adjunct (0 women). Expenses: Contact institution. *Financial support:* Fellowships, career-related internships or fieldwork, Federal Work-Study, and institutionally sponsored loans available. Support available to part-time students. Financial award application deadline: 3/2. In 2006, 21 degrees awarded. *Degree program information:* Part-time and evening/weekend programs available. Offers business administration (MBA); business and economics (MBA). *Application deadline:* For fall admission, 1/31 priority date for domestic students; for spring admission, 8/31 for domestic students. Applications are processed on a rolling basis. *Application fee:* $55. *Dean,* Jim Robertson, 707-664-2377, E-mail: jimrobertson@sonoma.edu.

School of Education Students: 7 full-time (5 women), 148 part-time (108 women); includes 20 minority (1 African American, 2 American Indian/Alaska Native, 5 Asian Americans or Pacific Islanders, 12 Hispanic Americans). Average age 40. 77 applicants, 88% accepted, 51 enrolled. *Faculty:* 20 full-time (6 women), 1 (woman) part-time/adjunct. Expenses: Contact institution. *Financial support:* Fellowships, career-related internships or fieldwork and Federal Work-Study available. Support available to part-time students. Financial award application deadline: 3/2. In 2006, 23 degrees awarded. *Degree program information:* Part-time and evening/weekend programs available. Offers curriculum and secondary education (MA); education (MA); educational leadership (MA); literacy studies and elementary education (MA); special education (MA). *Application fee:* $55. *Dean,* Dr. Mary Gendernalik-Cooper, 707-664-2132, E-mail: gendernm@sonoma.edu.

School of Science and Technology Students: 100 full-time (20 women), 44 part-time (25 women); includes 14 minority (6 African Americans, 1 American Indian/Alaska Native, 1 Asian American or Pacific Islander, 6 Hispanic Americans). Average age 35. 99 applicants, 93% accepted, 55 enrolled. *Faculty:* 28 full-time (16 women), 5 part-time/adjunct (all women). Expenses: Contact institution. *Financial support:* Fellowships, research assistantships, teaching assistantships, career-related internships or fieldwork and Federal Work-Study available. Support available to part-time students. Financial award application deadline: 3/2. In 2006, 30 degrees awarded. *Degree program information:* Part-time programs available. Offers computer and engineering sciences (MSCES); environmental biology (MA); family nurse practitioner (MS); general biology (MA); kinesiology (MA); science and technology (MA, MS, MSCES). *Application deadline:* For fall admission, 11/30 for domestic students. *Application fee:* $55. *Dean,* Dr. Saeid Rahimi, 707-664-2171, E-mail: saeid.rahimi@sonoma.edu.

School of Social Sciences Students: 51 full-time (40 women), 92 part-time (62 women); includes 18 minority (2 African Americans, 2 American Indian/Alaska Native, 2 Asian Americans or Pacific Islanders, 12 Hispanic Americans). Average age 36. 141 applicants, 56% accepted, 59 enrolled. *Faculty:* 12 full-time (6 women), 4 part-time/adjunct (2 women). Expenses: Contact institution. *Financial support:* Career-related internships or fieldwork and Federal Work-Study available. Support available to part-time students. Financial award application deadline: 3/2. In 2006, 42 degrees awarded. *Degree program information:* Part-time and evening/weekend programs available. Offers counseling (MA); cultural resources management (MA); history (MA); marriage, family, and child counseling (MA); public administration (MPA); pupil personnel services (MA); social sciences (MA, MPA). *Application deadline:* For fall admission, 11/30 for domestic students. *Application fee:* $55. *Dean,* Dr. Elaine Leeder, 707-664-2112, E-mail: elaine.leeder@sonoma.edu.

SOUTH BAYLO UNIVERSITY, Anaheim, CA 92801-1701

General Information Independent, coed, graduate-only institution. *Graduate housing:* On-campus housing not available. *Research affiliation:* University of California Irvine College of Medicine (complimentary and alternative medicine), National Nutritional Foods Association (herbs and nutritional supplements), Henan College of Traditional Chinese Medicine, China (herbology and acupuncture), Kaiser Permanente (patient care: acupuncture and oriental medicine), University of Illinois at Chicago (testing of herbal formulations).

GRADUATE UNITS

Program in Oriental Medicine and Acupuncture *Degree program information:* Evening/weekend programs available. Offers Oriental medicine and acupuncture (MS). Electronic applications accepted.

SOUTH CAROLINA STATE UNIVERSITY, Orangeburg, SC 29117-0001

General Information State-supported, coed, comprehensive institution. CGS member. *Enrollment:* 4,384 graduate, professional, and undergraduate students; 226 full-time matriculated graduate/professional students (167 women), 272 part-time matriculated graduate/professional students (201 women). *Enrollment by degree level:* 405 master's, 93 doctoral. *Graduate faculty:* 61 full-time (30 women), 13 part-time/adjunct (5 women). Tuition, state resident: full-time $7,278. Tuition, nonresident: full-time $14,322. *Graduate housing:* Room and/or apartments available to married students; on-campus housing not available to single students. *Student services:* Campus employment opportunities, career counseling, disabled student services, exercise/wellness program, free psychological counseling, international student services, low-cost health insurance, teacher training, writing training. *Library facilities:* Miller F. Whittaker Library. *Online resources:* library catalog, web page, access to other libraries' catalogs. *Collection:* 1.5 million titles.

Computer facilities: 300 computers available on campus for general student use. A campuswide network can be accessed. Internet access is available. *Web address:* http://www.scsu.edu/.

South Carolina State University (continued)

General Application Contact: Dr. Thomas Thompson, Dean of the School of Graduate Studies, 803-516-4734, Fax: 803-536-8812, E-mail: tthompson@scsu.edu.

GRADUATE UNITS

School of Graduate Studies Students: 226 full-time (167 women), 272 part-time (201 women); includes 441 minority (434 African Americans, 2 American Indian/Alaska Native, 4 Asian Americans or Pacific Islanders, 1 Hispanic American), 2 international. Average age 35. 323 applicants, 73% accepted, 163 enrolled. *Faculty:* 61 full-time (30 women), 13 part-time/adjunct (5 women). Expenses: Contact institution. *Financial support:* Fellowships, research assistantships, career-related internships or fieldwork, Federal Work-Study, institutionally sponsored loans, scholarships/grants, and unspecified assistantships available. Financial award application deadline: 6/1. In 2006, 104 master's, 27 doctorates, 28 other advanced degrees awarded. *Degree program information:* Part-time and evening/weekend programs available. Offers agribusiness (MS); agribusiness and entrepreneurship (MBA); civil and mechanical engineering (MA, MS); early childhood and special education (M Ed); early childhood education (MAT); educational leadership (Ed D, Ed S); elementary counselor education (M Ed); elementary education (M Ed, MAT); engineering (MAT); general science (MAT); individual and family development (MS); mathematics (MAT); nutritional sciences (MS); rehabilitation counseling (MA); secondary counselor education (M Ed); secondary education (M Ed); special education (M Ed); speech/language pathology (MA). *Application deadline:* For fall admission, 6/15 for domestic and international students; for spring admission, 11/1 for domestic and international students. *Application fee:* $25. Electronic applications accepted. *Application Contact:* Annette Hazzard-Jones, Program Coordinator II, 803-536-8809, Fax: 803-536-8812, E-mail: zs_ahazzard@scsu.edu. *Dean of the School of Graduate Studies,* Dr. Thomas Thompson, 803-516-4734, Fax: 803-536-8812, E-mail: tthompson@scsu.edu.

SOUTH DAKOTA SCHOOL OF MINES AND TECHNOLOGY, Rapid City, SD 57701-3995

General Information State-supported, coed, university. CGS member. *Graduate housing:* Rooms and/or apartments available on a first-come, first-served basis to single students and available to married students. *Research affiliation:* CEA USA, Inc. (radium/nickel extraction), Black Hills Corporation (wind power), EG & G Idaho, Inc. (ground-probing radar), RE/SPEC, Inc. (preparation of new plant growth regulators), Homestake Mining Company (gold ore exploration and development), Horizons, Inc. (interferometric synthetic aperture radar).

GRADUATE UNITS

Graduate Division *Degree program information:* Part-time programs available. Offers chemical engineering (PhD); chemistry (MS, PhD); chemistry and chemical engineering (MS); civil engineering (MS, PhD); electrical engineering (PhD); electrical engineering and computer engineering (MS); engineering (MS, PhD); geology and geological engineering (MS, PhD); mechanical engineering (PhD); metallurgical engineering (MS, PhD); nanoscience and nanoengineering (PhD); paleontology (MS); physics (MS, PhD); technology management (MS). Electronic applications accepted.

College of Science and Letters Offers atmospheric sciences (MS); atmospheric, environmental, and water resources (PhD); computer science (MS); science and letters (MS, PhD).

See Close-Up on page 1033.

SOUTH DAKOTA STATE UNIVERSITY, Brookings, SD 57007

General Information State-supported, coed, university. CGS member. *Enrollment:* 11,303 graduate, professional, and undergraduate students; 317 full-time matriculated graduate/professional students (155 women), 964 part-time matriculated graduate/professional students (585 women). *Enrollment by degree level:* 1,104 master's, 177 doctoral. *Graduate housing:* Rooms and/or apartments available to single and married students. *Student services:* Campus employment opportunities, campus safety program, career counseling, child daycare facilities, disabled student services, exercise/wellness program, free psychological counseling, grant writing training, international student services, low-cost health insurance, multicultural affairs office, teacher training, writing training. *Library facilities:* H. M. Briggs Library. *Online resources:* library catalog, web page, access to other libraries' catalogs. *Collection:* 1 million titles, 29,255 serial subscriptions, 13,123 audiovisual materials.

Computer facilities: 1,022 computers available on campus for general student use. A campuswide network can be accessed from student residence rooms and from off campus. Internet access and online class registration are available. *Web address:* http://www.sdstate.edu/.

General Application Contact: Traci Johnson, Application Contact, 605-688-4181, Fax: 605-688-6167, E-mail: traci.johnson@sdstate.edu.

GRADUATE UNITS

Graduate School Students: 317 full-time (155 women), 964 part-time (585 women); includes 224 minority (21 African Americans, 22 American Indian/Alaska Native, 166 Asian Americans or Pacific Islanders, 15 Hispanic Americans). 1,016 applicants, 53% accepted. *Faculty:* 285 full-time (56 women). Expenses: Contact institution. *Financial support:* Fellowships with tuition reimbursements, research assistantships with partial tuition reimbursements, teaching assistantships with partial tuition reimbursements, career-related internships or fieldwork, Federal Work-Study, and unspecified assistantships available. In 2006, 262 master's, 20 doctorates awarded. *Degree program information:* Part-time and evening/weekend programs available. Postbaccalaureate distance learning degree programs offered (no on-campus study). *Application deadline:* For fall admission, 4/15 priority date for international students; for spring admission, 8/15 priority date for international students. Applications are processed on a rolling basis. *Application fee:* $35. *Dean,* Dr. Kevin Kephart, 605-688-4181, Fax: 605-688-6167, E-mail: kevin.kephart@sdstate.edu.

College of Agriculture and Biological Sciences Expenses: Contact institution. *Financial support:* Fellowships, research assistantships, teaching assistantships, career-related internships or fieldwork, Federal Work-Study, and unspecified assistantships available. *Degree program information:* Part-time programs available. Offers agriculture and biological sciences (MS, PhD); agronomy (PhD); animal science (MS, PhD); animal sciences (MS, PhD); biological science (MS, PhD); biological sciences (MS, PhD); economics (MS); plant science (MS); rural sociology (MS); sociology (PhD); wildlife and fisheries sciences (MS, PhD). *Application deadline:* Applications are processed on a rolling basis. *Application fee:* $35. *Application Contact:* Gene Arnold, Associate Dean, 605-688-4148. *Dean,* Dr. Fred Cholick, 605-688-4148.

College of Arts and Science Expenses: Contact institution. *Financial support:* Research assistantships, teaching assistantships, career-related internships or fieldwork, Federal Work-Study, and unspecified assistantships available. *Degree program information:* Part-time programs available. Offers arts and science (MA, MS, PhD); chemistry (MS, PhD); communication studies and journalism (MS); English (MA); geography (MS); health, physical education and recreation (MS). *Application deadline:* Applications are processed on a rolling basis. *Application fee:* $35. *Dean,* Dr. Herbert Cheever, 605-688-6619.

College of Education and Counseling Expenses: Contact institution. *Financial support:* Research assistantships, teaching assistantships, Federal Work-Study and unspecified assistantships available. *Degree program information:* Part-time programs available. Offers counseling and human resource development (MS); curriculum and instruction (M Ed); education and counseling (M Ed, MS); educational administration (M Ed). *Application deadline:* Applications are processed on a rolling basis. *Application fee:* $35. *Dean,* Dr. Dee Hopkins, 605-688-4321.

College of Engineering Expenses: Contact institution. *Financial support:* Fellowships, research assistantships, teaching assistantships, career-related internships or fieldwork, Federal Work-Study, and unspecified assistantships available. *Degree program information:* Part-time programs available. Offers biological sciences (MS, PhD); computational science and statistics (PhD); electrical engineering (PhD); engineering (MS); geospatial science and engineering (PhD); industrial management (MS); mathematics (MS). *Application deadline:* Applications are processed on a rolling basis. *Application fee:* $35. *Application Contact:* Dr. Virgil G. Ellerbruch, Assistant Dean, 605-688-4161. *Dean,* Dr. Duane Sander, 605-688-4161.

College of Family and Consumer Sciences Expenses: Contact institution. *Financial support:* Research assistantships, teaching assistantships, Federal Work-Study and unspecified assistantships available. Offers apparel merchandising and interior design (MFCS); family and consumer sciences (MFCS); human development, consumer and family sciences (MFCS); nutrition, food science and hospitality (MFCS). *Application deadline:* Applications are processed on a rolling basis. *Application fee:* $35. *Dean,* Dr. Laurie Stenberg Nichols, 605-688-6181, Fax: 605-688-4439, E-mail: nicholsl@mg.sdstate.edu.

College of Nursing Students: 6 full-time (all women), 168 part-time (162 women); includes 5 minority (1 African American, 2 American Indian/Alaska Native, 1 Asian American or Pacific Islander, 1 Hispanic American). 15 applicants, 93% accepted. *Faculty:* 20 full-time (18 women). Expenses: Contact institution. *Financial support:* In 2006–07, 2 fellowships, 1 research assistantship, 3 teaching assistantships were awarded; career-related internships or fieldwork, Federal Work-Study, scholarships/grants, and unspecified assistantships also available. In 2006, 26 degrees awarded. *Degree program information:* Part-time and evening/weekend programs available. Postbaccalaureate distance learning degree programs offered. Offers nursing (MS, PhD). *Application deadline:* For fall admission, 3/1 priority date for domestic students. *Application fee:* $15. *Application Contact:* LeAnn K. Nelson, Senior Secretary, 605-688-4114, Fax: 605-688-5827, E-mail: leann.nelson@sdstate.edu. *Department Head, Graduate Nursing,* Dr. Sandra J. Bunkers, 605-688-4114, Fax: 605-688-5827.

College of Pharmacy Expenses: Contact institution. *Financial support:* Research assistantships, teaching assistantships, Federal Work-Study available. Financial award application deadline: 3/1; financial award applicants required to submit FAFSA. Offers biological science (MS, PhD); pharmacy (Pharm D, MS, PhD). *Application deadline:* For fall admission, 3/1 for domestic students. Applications are processed on a rolling basis. *Application fee:* $15. *Application Contact:* Dr. Chandradhar Dwivedi, Coordinator of Graduate Studies, 605-688-4247. *Dean,* Dr. Danny Lattin, 605-688-6197, Fax: 605-688-6232.

SOUTHEASTERN BAPTIST THEOLOGICAL SEMINARY, Wake Forest, NC 27588-1889

General Information Independent-religious, coed, comprehensive institution. *Graduate housing:* Rooms and/or apartments available on a first-come, first-served basis to single and married students.

GRADUATE UNITS

Graduate and Professional Programs Offers advanced biblical studies (M Div); Christian education (M Div, MACE); Christian ethics (PhD); Christian ministry (M Div); Christian planting (M Div); church music (MACM); counseling (MACO); evangelism (PhD); language (M Div); ministry (D Min); New Testament (PhD); Old Testament (PhD); philosophy (PhD); theology (Th M, PhD); women's studies (M Div).

SOUTHEASTERN LOUISIANA UNIVERSITY, Hammond, LA 70402

General Information State-supported, coed, comprehensive institution. *Enrollment:* 15,118 graduate, professional, and undergraduate students; 369 full-time matriculated graduate/professional students (241 women), 742 part-time matriculated graduate/professional students (587 women). *Enrollment by degree level:* 1,101 master's, 10 doctoral. *Graduate faculty:* 182 full-time (80 women), 3 part-time/adjunct (1 woman). Tuition, state resident: full-time $2,216; part-time $123 per credit. Tuition, nonresident: full-time $6,212; part-time $345 per credit. *Required fees:* $986; $55 per credit. Part-time tuition and fees vary according to course load. *Graduate housing:* Room and/or apartments available on a first-come, first-served basis to single students; on-campus housing not available to married students. Typical cost: $3,600 per year ($5,750 including board). Room and board charges vary according to board plan and housing facility selected. *Student services:* Campus employment opportunities, campus safety program, career counseling, disabled student services, exercise/wellness program, free psychological counseling, international student services, low-cost health insurance, multicultural affairs office, teacher training, writing training. *Library facilities:* Sims Memorial Library. *Online resources:* library catalog, web page, access to other libraries' catalogs. *Collection:* 623,746 titles, 2,707 serial subscriptions, 9,905 audiovisual materials. *Research affiliation:* MECOM (environmental resources), Lake Ponchartrain Basin Foundation (water quality), Coypu Foundation (environmental resources), Bishop Museum (fish studies), Cox Walker & Associates, Inc. (chemistry).

Computer facilities: 837 computers available on campus for general student use. A campuswide network can be accessed from student residence rooms and from off campus. Internet access and online class registration, campus Webmail, student newspaper, transcripts, bookstore are available. *Web address:* http://www.selu.edu/.

General Application Contact: Sandra Meyers, Graduate Admissions Analyst, 985-549-2066, Fax: 985-549-5632, E-mail: admissions@selu.edu.

GRADUATE UNITS

College of Arts, Humanities and Social Sciences Students: 72 full-time (44 women), 104 part-time (62 women); includes 38 minority (33 African Americans, 3 American Indian/Alaska Native, 2 Hispanic Americans), 8 international. Average age 30. 72 applicants, 96% accepted, 53 enrolled. *Faculty:* 59 full-time (20 women), 1 part-time/adjunct (0 women). Expenses: Contact institution. *Financial support:* In 2006–07, 18 research assistantships with full tuition reimbursements (averaging $5,500 per year) were awarded; career-related internships or fieldwork, Federal Work-Study, institutionally sponsored loans, scholarships/grants, unspecified assistantships, and administrative assistantship also available. Support available to part-time students. Financial award application deadline: 5/1; financial award applicants required to submit FAFSA. In 2006, 51 degrees awarded. *Degree program information:* Part-time programs available. Offers applied sociology (MS); arts, humanities and social sciences (M Mus, MA, MS); English (MA); history (MA); music (M Mus); organizational communication (MA); psychology (MA). *Application deadline:* For fall admission, 7/15 priority date for domestic students, 6/1 priority date for international students; for spring admission, 12/1 priority date for domestic students, 10/1 priority date for international students. Applications are processed on a rolling basis. *Application fee:* $20 ($30 for international students). Electronic applications accepted. *Application Contact:* Sandra Meyers, Graduate Admissions Analyst, 985-549-2066, Fax: 985-549-5632, E-mail: admissions@selu.edu. *Dean,* Dr. Tammy Bourg, 985-549-2101, Fax: 985-549-5014, E-mail: tbourg@selu.edu.

College of Business Students: 111 full-time (51 women), 61 part-time (26 women); includes 19 minority (9 African Americans, 1 American Indian/Alaska Native, 4 Asian Americans or Pacific Islanders, 5 Hispanic Americans), 27 international. Average age 27. 65 applicants, 78% accepted, 38 enrolled. *Faculty:* 25 full-time (4 women). Expenses: Contact institution. *Financial support:* Career-related internships or fieldwork, Federal Work-Study, institutionally sponsored loans, scholarships/grants, unspecified assistantships, and administrative assistantships available. Support available to part-time students. Financial award application deadline: 5/1; financial award applicants required to submit FAFSA. In 2006, 85 degrees awarded. *Degree program information:* Part-time and evening/weekend programs available. Offers business administration (MBA). *Application deadline:* For fall admission, 7/15 priority date for domestic students, 6/1 priority date for international students; for spring admission, 12/1 priority date for domestic students, 10/1 priority date for international students. Applications are processed on a rolling basis. *Application fee:* $20 ($30 for international students). Electronic applications accepted. *Application Contact:* Sandra Meyers, Graduate Admissions Analyst, 985-549-2066, Fax: 985-549-5632, E-mail: admissions@selu.edu. *Dean,* Dr. Randy Settoon, 985-549-2258, Fax: 985-549-5038, E-mail: rsettoon@selu.edu.

College of Education and Human Development Students: 86 full-time (74 women), 447 part-time (392 women); includes 74 minority (60 African Americans, 3 Asian Americans or Pacific Islanders, 11 Hispanic Americans), 4 international. Average age 33. 110 applicants, 99% accepted, 79 enrolled. *Faculty:* 41 full-time (27 women), 1 (woman) part-time/adjunct. Expenses: Contact institution. *Financial support:* In 2006–07, 1 research assistantship with full tuition reimbursement (averaging $5,500 per year) was awarded; career-related internships or fieldwork, Federal Work-Study, institutionally sponsored loans, scholarships/grants, unspecified assistantships, and administrative assistantships also available. Support available to part-time students. Financial award application deadline: 5/1; financial award applicants required to submit FAFSA. In 2006, 184 degrees awarded. *Degree program information:* Part-time programs available. Offers counselor education (M Ed); curriculum and instruction (M Ed); education and human development (M Ed, MAT, Ed D); educational leadership (M Ed, Ed D); elementary education (MAT); secondary education (MAT); special education (M Ed, MAT). *Application deadline:* For fall admission, 7/15 priority date for domestic students, 6/1 priority date for international students; for spring admission, 12/1 priority date for domestic students, 10/1 priority date for international students. Applications are processed on a rolling basis. *Application fee:* $20 ($30 for international students). Electronic applications accepted. *Application Contact:* Sandra Meyers, Graduate Admissions Analyst, 985-549-2066, Fax: 985-549-5632, E-mail: admissions@selu.edu. *Dean,* Dr. Diane Allen, 985-549-2217, Fax: 985-549-2070, E-mail: dallen@selu.edu.

College of Nursing and Health Sciences Students: 71 full-time (60 women), 110 part-time (98 women); includes 21 minority (20 African Americans, 1 Hispanic American), 5 international. Average age 31. 76 applicants, 99% accepted, 56 enrolled. *Faculty:* 26 full-time (19 women). Expenses: Contact institution. *Financial support:* In 2006–07, 8 research assistantships with full tuition reimbursements (averaging $5,500 per year), 3 teaching assistantships with full tuition reimbursements (averaging $5,500 per year) were awarded; career-related internships or fieldwork, Federal Work-Study, institutionally sponsored loans, scholarships/grants, unspecified assistantships, and administrative assistantship also available. Support available to part-time students. Financial award application deadline: 5/1; financial award applicants required to submit FAFSA. In 2006, 53 degrees awarded. *Degree program information:* Part-time programs available. Offers communication sciences and disorders (MS); health and kinesiology (MA); nursing and health sciences (MA, MS, MSN). *Application deadline:* For fall admission, 7/15 priority date for domestic students, 6/1 priority date for international students; for spring admission, 12/1 priority date for domestic students, 10/1 priority date for international students. Applications are processed on a rolling basis. *Application fee:* $20 ($30 for international students). Electronic applications accepted. *Application Contact:* Sandra Meyers, Graduate Admissions Analyst, 985-549-2066, Fax: 985-549-5632, E-mail: admissions@selu.edu. *Dean,* Dr. Donnie Booth, 985-549-5045, Fax: 985-549-5087, E-mail: dbooth@selu.edu.

School of Nursing Students: 13 full-time (10 women), 60 part-time (52 women); includes 6 minority (5 African Americans, 1 Hispanic American), 1 international. Average age 36. 29 applicants, 100% accepted, 24 enrolled. *Faculty:* 11 full-time (all women). Expenses: Contact institution. *Financial support:* Career-related internships or fieldwork, Federal Work-Study, institutionally sponsored loans, scholarships/grants, unspecified assistantships, and administrative assistantship available. Support available to part-time students. Financial award application deadline: 5/1; financial award applicants required to submit FAFSA. In 2006, 6 degrees awarded. *Degree program information:* Part-time programs available. Offers nursing (MSN). *Application deadline:* For fall admission, 7/15 priority date for domestic students, 6/1 priority date for international students; for spring admission, 12/1 priority date for domestic students, 10/1 priority date for international students. Applications are processed on a rolling basis. *Application fee:* $20 ($30 for international students). Electronic applications accepted. *Application Contact:* Sandra Meyers, Graduate Admissions Analyst, 985-549-2066, Fax: 985-549-5632, E-mail: admissions@selu.edu. *Director,* Dr. Barbara Moffett, 985-549-2156, Fax: 985-549-2869, E-mail: bmoffett@selu.edu.

College of Science and Technology Students: 29 full-time (12 women), 20 part-time (9 women); includes 4 minority (2 African Americans, 2 Hispanic Americans), 12 international. Average age 28. 15 applicants, 87% accepted, 11 enrolled. *Faculty:* 31 full-time (10 women), 1 part-time/adjunct (0 women). Expenses: Contact institution. *Financial support:* In 2006–07, 4 fellowships with full tuition reimbursements (averaging $8,000 per year), 12 research assistantships with full tuition reimbursements (averaging $5,500 per year), 6 teaching assistantships with full tuition reimbursements (averaging $5,500 per year) were awarded; career-related internships or fieldwork, Federal Work-Study, institutionally sponsored loans, unspecified assistantships, and administrative assistantships also available. Support available to part-time students. Financial award application deadline: 5/1; financial award applicants required to submit FAFSA. In 2006, 12 degrees awarded. *Degree program information:* Part-time programs available. Offers biology (MS); integrated science and technology (MS); science and technology (MS). *Application deadline:* For fall admission, 7/15 priority date for domestic students, 6/1 priority date for international students; for spring admission, 12/1 priority date for domestic students, 10/1 priority date for international students. Applications are processed on a rolling basis. *Application fee:* $20 ($30 for international students). Electronic applications accepted. *Application Contact:* Sandra Meyers, Graduate Admissions Analyst, 985-549-2066, Fax: 985-549-5632, E-mail: admissions@selu.edu. *Dean,* Dr. Daniel McCarthy, 985-549-2055, Fax: 985-549-3396, E-mail: dmccarthy@selu.edu.

SOUTHEASTERN OKLAHOMA STATE UNIVERSITY, Durant, OK 74701-0609

General Information State-supported, coed, comprehensive institution. *Graduate housing:* Room and/or apartments available on a first-come, first-served basis to single students; on-campus housing not available to married students. Housing application deadline: 8/1. *Research affiliation:* Oklahoma Small Business Development Center (business development), J. J. Keller Foundation (occupational safety research), United States Department of Agriculture (biological sciences), Virginia Polytechnic Institute (physical sciences).

GRADUATE UNITS

Graduate School *Degree program information:* Part-time and evening/weekend programs available. Offers aerospace administration (MS). Electronic applications accepted.

School of Arts and Sciences *Degree program information:* Part-time and evening/weekend programs available. Offers technology (MT). Electronic applications accepted.

School of Behavioral Sciences *Degree program information:* Part-time and evening/weekend programs available. Offers guidance and counseling (MBS). Electronic applications accepted.

School of Business *Degree program information:* Part-time and evening/weekend programs available. Offers business (MBA, MS). Electronic applications accepted.

School of Education *Degree program information:* Part-time and evening/weekend programs available. Offers educational administration (M Ed); educational instruction and leadership (M Ed); educational technology (M Ed); elementary education (M Ed); school counseling (M Ed); secondary education (M Ed). Electronic applications accepted.

SOUTHEASTERN UNIVERSITY, Washington, DC 20024-2788

General Information Independent, coed, comprehensive institution. *Graduate housing:* On-campus housing not available.

GRADUATE UNITS

College of Graduate Studies *Degree program information:* Part-time and evening/weekend programs available. Offers accounting (MBA); business (MBA, MPA, MS, MSMOT); computer science (MBA, MS); financial management (MBA); government program management (MPA, MSMOT); health services administration (MPA); international management (MBA); management (MBA); management information systems (MBA); marketing (MBA); public administration (MPA); taxation (MS).

SOUTHEAST MISSOURI STATE UNIVERSITY, Cape Girardeau, MO 63701-4799

General Information State-supported, coed, comprehensive institution. CGS member. *Enrollment:* 10,477 graduate, professional, and undergraduate students; 231 full-time matriculated graduate/professional students (163 women), 1,269 part-time matriculated graduate/professional students (1,033 women). *Enrollment by degree level:* 1,374 master's, 115 other advanced degrees. *Graduate faculty:* 215 full-time (85 women). *Graduate housing:* Room and/or apartments available on a first-come, first-served basis to single students. Typical cost: $3,493 per year ($5,647 including board). *Student services:* Campus employment opportunities, campus safety program, career counseling, child daycare facilities, disabled student services, exercise/wellness program, free psychological counseling, international student services, low-cost health insurance, multicultural affairs office, teacher training, writing training. *Library facilities:* Kent Library. *Online resources:* library catalog, web page, access to other libraries' catalogs. *Collection:* 429,108 titles, 32,455 serial subscriptions, 14,279 audiovisual materials.

Computer facilities: 1,022 computers available on campus for general student use. A campuswide network can be accessed from student residence rooms and from off campus. Internet access and online class registration are available. *Web address:* http://www.semo.edu/.

General Application Contact: Dr. Fred Janzow, Dean of the School of Graduate Studies, 573-651-2192, Fax: 573-651-2001, E-mail: fjanzow@semo.edu.

GRADUATE UNITS

School of Graduate Studies Students: 231 full-time (163 women), 1,258 part-time (1,025 women); includes 72 minority (43 African Americans, 9 American Indian/Alaska Native, 13 Asian Americans or Pacific Islanders, 7 Hispanic Americans), 35 international. Average age 35. 357 applicants, 88% accepted. *Faculty:* 215 full-time (85 women). Expenses: Contact institution. *Financial support:* In 2006–07, 387 students received support, including 100 research assistantships with full tuition reimbursements available (averaging $7,100 per year), 58 teaching assistantships with full tuition reimbursements available (averaging $7,100 per year); career-related internships or fieldwork, Federal Work-Study, and unspecified assistantships also available. Financial award applicants required to submit FAFSA. In 2006, 189 master's, 16 other advanced degrees awarded. *Degree program information:* Part-time and evening/weekend programs available. Postbaccalaureate distance learning degree programs offered. Offers biology (MNS); chemistry (MNS); communication disorders (MA); community counseling (MA); community wellness and leisure services (MPA); counseling education (Ed S); criminal justice (MS); educational administration (MA, Ed S); educational studies (MA); elementary education (MA); English (MA); exceptional child education (MA); guidance and counseling (MA, Ed S); higher education (MA); history (MA); home economics (MA); human environmental studies (MA); mathematics (MNS); middle level education (MA); music education (MME); nursing (MSN); nutrition and exercise science (MS); political science, philosophy and religion (MPA); school counseling (MA); teaching English to speakers of other languages (MA). *Application deadline:* For fall admission, 8/1 for domestic students, 4/1 for international students; for spring admission, 11/21 for domestic students, 10/1 for international students. Applications are processed on a rolling basis. *Application fee:* $20 ($100 for international students). Electronic applications accepted. *Application Contact:* Marsha L. Arant, Senior Administrative Assistant, 573-651-2192, Fax: 573-651-2001, E-mail: marant@semo.edu. *Dean,* Dr. Fred Janzow, 573-651-2192, Fax: 573-651-2001, E-mail: fjanzow@semo.edu.

Godwin Center for Science and Mathematics Education Students: 1 (woman) full-time, 7 part-time (5 women). Average age 32. 2 applicants, 100% accepted. Expenses: Contact institution. *Financial support:* In 2006–07, 1 student received support. Applicants required to submit FAFSA. In 2006, 3 degrees awarded. *Degree program information:* Part-time programs available. Offers science education (MNS). *Application deadline:* For fall admission, 8/1 for domestic students, 4/1 for international students; for spring admission, 11/21 for domestic students, 10/1 for international students. Applications are processed on a rolling basis. *Application fee:* $20 ($100 for international students). Electronic applications accepted. *Application Contact:* Marsha L. Arant, Senior Administrative Assistant, Office of Graduate Studies, 573-651-2192, Fax: 573-651-2001, E-mail: marant@semo.edu. *Director,* Dr. Sharon Coleman, 573-651-2372, Fax: 573-986-6792, E-mail: godwin@semo.edu.

Harrison College of Business Students: 35 full-time (18 women), 40 part-time (24 women); includes 5 minority (2 African Americans, 3 Asian Americans or Pacific Islanders), 9 international. Average age 27. 35 applicants, 86% accepted. *Faculty:* 33 full-time (10 women). Expenses: Contact institution. *Financial support:* In 2006–07, 54 students received support, including 31 research assistantships with full tuition reimbursements available (averaging $7,100 per year); career-related internships or fieldwork and unspecified assistantships also available. Financial award applicants required to submit FAFSA. In 2006, 23 degrees awarded. *Degree program information:* Part-time and evening/weekend programs available. Postbaccalaureate distance learning degree programs offered (no on-campus study). Offers accounting (MBA); environmental management (MBA); finance (MBA); general management (MBA); health administration (MBA); industrial management (MBA); international business (MBA). *Application deadline:* For fall admission, 8/1 for domestic students, 4/1 for international students; for spring admission, 11/21 for domestic students, 10/1 for international students. Applications are processed on a rolling basis. *Application fee:* $20 ($100 for international students). *Application Contact:* Marsha L. Arant, Senior Administrative Assistant, Office of Graduate Studies, 573-651-2192, Fax: 573-651-2001, E-mail: marant@semo.edu. *Director MBA Program,* Dr. Kenneth Heischmidt, 573-651-2912, Fax: 573-651-5032, E-mail: kheischmidt@semo.edu.

School of Polytechnic Studies Students: 6 full-time (1 woman), 21 part-time (3 women); includes 3 minority (all African Americans), 2 international. Average age 30. 10 applicants, 90% accepted. *Faculty:* 9 full-time (1 woman). Expenses: Contact institution. *Financial support:* In 2006–07, 10 students received support, including 2 research assistantships with full tuition reimbursements available (averaging $7,100 per year), 5 teaching assistantships with full tuition reimbursements available (averaging $7,100 per year); unspecified assistantships also available. Financial award applicants required to submit FAFSA. In 2006, 9 master's awarded. *Degree program information:* Part-time and evening/weekend programs available. Postbaccalaureate distance learning degree programs offered (no on-campus study). Offers industrial management (MS). *Application deadline:* For fall admission, 8/1 for domestic students, 4/1 for international students; for spring admission, 11/21 for domestic students, 10/1 for international students. Applications are processed on a rolling basis. *Application fee:* $20 ($100 for international students). *Application Contact:* Marsha L. Arant, Senior Administrative Assistant, Office of Graduate Studies, 573-651-2192, Fax: 573-651-2001, E-mail: marant@semo.edu. *Dean,* Dr. Randall Shaw, 573-651-5915, Fax: 573-651-2827, E-mail: rshaw@semo.edu.

SOUTHERN ADVENTIST UNIVERSITY, Collegedale, TN 37315-0370

General Information Independent-religious, coed, comprehensive institution. *Enrollment:* 2,593 graduate, professional, and undergraduate students; 43 full-time matriculated graduate/professional students (28 women), 99 part-time matriculated graduate/professional students (65 women). *Enrollment by degree level:* 142 master's. *Graduate faculty:* 8 full-time (4 women), 14 part-time/adjunct (4 women). *Graduate housing:* Rooms and/or apartments available on a first-come, first-served basis to single and married students. Typical cost: $6,000 per year ($9,000 including board) for single students. *Student services:* Campus employment opportunities, campus safety program, career counseling, disabled student services, exercise/wellness program, free psychological counseling, international student services, low-cost health insurance, multicultural affairs office, teacher training, writing training. *Library facilities:* McKee Library. *Online resources:* library catalog, web page. *Collection:* 154,987 titles, 21,123 serial subscriptions, 6,410 audiovisual materials.

Computer facilities: 200 computers available on campus for general student use. A campuswide network can be accessed from student residence rooms and from off campus. Internet access is available. *Web address:* http://www.southern.edu/.

General Application Contact: Dr. Carleton Swafford, Dean of Graduate Studies, 423-236-2694, Fax: 423-236-1694, E-mail: graduatestudies@southern.edu.

GRADUATE UNITS

School of Business and Management Students: 18 full-time (8 women), 66 part-time (37 women); includes 15 minority (6 African Americans, 7 Asian Americans or Pacific Islanders, 2 Hispanic Americans). Average age 35. 32 applicants, 84% accepted, 24 enrolled. *Faculty:* 7 full-time (0 women), 2 part-time/adjunct (1 woman). Expenses: Contact institution. *Financial support:* In 2006–07, 32 students received support. Scholarships/grants available. Financial award application deadline: 9/1; financial award applicants required to submit FAFSA. In

Southern Adventist University (continued)

2006, 11 degrees awarded. *Degree program information:* Part-time and evening/weekend programs available. Postbaccalaureate distance learning degree programs offered (no on-campus study). Offers accounting (MBA); administration (MS); financial services (MFS); health care administration (MBA); human resource management (MBA); management (MBA); marketing (MBA). *Application deadline:* For fall admission, 8/1 priority date for domestic students, 7/1 for international students; for winter admission, 12/1 priority date for domestic students, 11/1 for international students; for spring admission, 4/1 priority date for domestic students, 3/1 for international students. Applications are processed on a rolling basis. *Application fee:* $25. Electronic applications accepted. *Application Contact:* Linda Wilhelm, Admissions Coordinator, 423-236-2751, Fax: 423-236-1527, E-mail: sbm@southern.edu. *Dean,* Dr. Don Van Ornam, 423-236-2750, Fax: 423-236-1527, E-mail: dvanorna@southern.edu.

School of Education and Psychology Students: 36 full-time (29 women), 7 part-time (6 women); includes 8 minority (6 African Americans, 2 Hispanic Americans). Average age 30. 15 applicants, 100% accepted, 15 enrolled. *Faculty:* 11 full-time (5 women), 1 (woman) part-time/adjunct. Expenses: Contact institution. *Financial support:* In 2006–07, 7 students received support, including 4 research assistantships with full tuition reimbursements available (averaging $10,000 per year); career-related internships or fieldwork, scholarships/grants, tuition waivers (partial), and unspecified assistantships also available. Support available to part-time students. Financial award application deadline: 4/1; financial award applicants required to submit FAFSA. In 2006, 25 degrees awarded. *Degree program information:* Part-time and evening/weekend programs available. Offers curriculum and instruction (MS Ed); educational administration and supervision (MS Ed); inclusive education (MS Ed); literacy education (MS Ed); outdoor teacher education (MS Ed); professional counseling (MS); school counseling (MS). *Application deadline:* For fall admission, 5/15 priority date for domestic and international students; for winter admission, 10/15 priority date for domestic and international students; for spring admission, 3/31 priority date for domestic and international students. Applications are processed on a rolling basis. *Application fee:* $25. Electronic applications accepted. *Application Contact:* Mikhaile Spence, Information Contact, 423-236-2496, Fax: 423-236-1765, E-mail: maspence@southern.edu. *Dean,* Dr. Denise Dunzweiler, 423-236-2776, Fax: 423-236-1765, E-mail: denise@southern.edu.

School of Nursing Students: 45 full-time (41 women), 17 part-time (14 women); includes 5 minority (2 African Americans, 2 Asian Americans or Pacific Islanders, 1 Hispanic American). Average age 35. 40 applicants, 95% accepted, 31 enrolled. *Faculty:* 1 (woman) full-time, 5 part-time/adjunct (all women). Expenses: Contact institution. *Financial support:* In 2006–07, 1 teaching assistantship with partial tuition reimbursement (averaging $5,000 per year) was awarded. In 2006, 20 degrees awarded. *Degree program information:* Part-time programs available. Offers adult nurse practitioner (MSN); family nurse practitioner (MSN); nurse educator (MSN). *Application deadline:* For fall admission, 7/1 for domestic and international students; for winter admission, 12/1 for domestic and international students. Applications are processed on a rolling basis. *Application fee:* $25. Electronic applications accepted. *Application Contact:* Diane Proffitt, Enrollment Counselor, 423-236-2941, Fax: 423-236-1940, E-mail: dproffitt@southern.edu. *Dean,* Dr. Barbara James, 423-236-2940, Fax: 423-236-1940, E-mail: bjames@southern.edu.

School of Religion Students: 3 full-time (0 women), 6 part-time (1 woman); includes 3 minority (1 African American, 2 Asian Americans or Pacific Islanders). Average age 36. 9 applicants, 100% accepted, 9 enrolled. *Faculty:* 10 full-time (0 women), 5 part-time/adjunct (0 women). Expenses: Contact institution. *Financial support:* In 2006–07, 4 students received support. Tuition waivers (full) available. Support available to part-time students. Financial award application deadline: 4/1; financial award applicants required to submit FAFSA. In 2006, 6 degrees awarded. *Degree program information:* Part-time programs available. Offers church leadership and management (MA); evangelism (MA); homiletics (MA); religious education (MA); religious studies (MA). Summer program only. *Application deadline:* For spring admission, 4/30 priority date for domestic students, 12/30 for international students. Applications are processed on a rolling basis. *Application fee:* $25. *Application Contact:* Susan L. Brown, Administrative Assistant, 423-236-2977, Fax: 423-236-1977, E-mail: sbrown@southern.edu. *Dean,* Dr. Greg A. King, 423-236-2975, Fax: 423-236-1976, E-mail: gking@southern.edu.

SOUTHERN ARKANSAS UNIVERSITY–MAGNOLIA, Magnolia, AR 71753

General Information State-supported, coed, comprehensive institution. *Graduate housing:* Room and/or apartments available on a first-come, first-served basis to single students. Housing application deadline: 6/1.

GRADUATE UNITS

Graduate Programs *Degree program information:* Part-time and evening/weekend programs available. Offers computer and information sciences (MS); counseling (MS); education (M Ed); kinesiology (MS); library media and information specialist (M Ed); school counseling (M Ed); teaching (MAT).

SOUTHERN BAPTIST THEOLOGICAL SEMINARY, Louisville, KY 40280-0004

General Information Independent-religious, coed, comprehensive institution. *Graduate housing:* Rooms and/or apartments available on a first-come, first-served basis to single and married students.

GRADUATE UNITS

Billy Graham School of Missions, Evangelism, and Church Growth *Degree program information:* Part-time and evening/weekend programs available. Postbaccalaureate distance learning degree programs offered (minimal on-campus study). Offers Christian mission/world religion (PhD); evangelism/church growth (PhD); ministry (D Min); missiology (MA, D Miss); missions, evangelism, and church growth (M Div); theology (Th M).

School of Church Music and Worship Offers church music and worship (M Div, MCM, DMA, DMM).

School of Leadership and Church Ministry *Degree program information:* Part-time programs available. Postbaccalaureate distance learning degree programs offered (minimal on-campus study). Offers leadership and church ministry (M Div, MACE, Ed D, PhD).

School of Theology *Degree program information:* Part-time and evening/weekend programs available. Postbaccalaureate distance learning degree programs offered (minimal on-campus study). Offers theology (M Div, Th M, D Min, PhD).

SOUTHERN CALIFORNIA COLLEGE OF OPTOMETRY, Fullerton, CA 92831-1615

General Information Independent, coed, graduate-only institution. *Graduate housing:* On-campus housing not available. *Research affiliation:* Alcon Laboratories (Ophthalmic Products), Essilor (Spectacle Lenses), Allergan (Ophthalmic products).

GRADUATE UNITS

Professional Program Offers optometry (OD). Electronic applications accepted.

SOUTHERN CALIFORNIA INSTITUTE OF ARCHITECTURE, Los Angeles, CA 90013

General Information Independent, coed, comprehensive institution. *Graduate housing:* On-campus housing not available.

GRADUATE UNITS

Graduate Program in Architecture Offers architecture design (M Arch).

SOUTHERN CALIFORNIA SEMINARY, El Cajon, CA 92019

General Information Independent-religious, comprehensive institution. *Enrollment by degree level:* 38 first professional, 65 master's, 14 doctoral. *Graduate faculty:* 7 full-time (0 women), 19 part-time/adjunct (4 women). *Tuition:* Full-time $8,640; part-time $240 per credit hour. *Graduate housing:* Rooms and/or apartments available on a first-come, first-served basis to single and married students. *Student services:* Campus employment opportunities, career counseling, international student services, teacher training, writing training. *Web address:* http://www.socalsem.edu/.

General Application Contact: Steve Perdue, Director, 619-590-2129, E-mail: sperdue@socalsem.edu.

GRADUATE UNITS

Graduate and Professional Programs Students: 91 full-time (54 women), 40 part-time (10 women); includes 29 minority (13 African Americans, 5 Asian Americans or Pacific Islanders, 11 Hispanic Americans), 5 international. Average age 38. *Faculty:* 7 full-time (0 women), 17 part-time/adjunct (2 women). Expenses: Contact institution. *Financial support:* In 2006–07, 29 students received support. Federal Work-Study, scholarships/grants, and tuition waivers (partial) available. Financial award application deadline: 3/1; financial award applicants required to submit FAFSA. In 2006, 4 first professional degrees, 39 master's awarded. *Degree program information:* Part-time and evening/weekend programs available. Postbaccalaureate distance learning degree programs offered (minimal on-campus study). Offers biblical studies (MA); counseling psychology (MACP); psychology (Psy D); religious studies (MRS); theology (M Div). *Application deadline:* For fall admission, 8/15 for domestic students; for spring admission, 12/11 for domestic students. *Application fee:* $25. Electronic applications accepted. *Application Contact:* Steve Perdue, Director, 619-590-2129, E-mail: sperdue@socalsem.edu. *Academic Officer,* Dr. Paul Boatner, 619-590-2124, E-mail: aletting@socalsem.edu.

SOUTHERN CALIFORNIA UNIVERSITY OF HEALTH SCIENCES, Whittier, CA 90609-1166

General Information Independent, coed, graduate-only institution. *Enrollment by degree level:* 471 first professional, 158 master's. *Graduate faculty:* 45 full-time (12 women), 74 part-time/adjunct (40 women). *Graduate housing:* On-campus housing not available. *Student services:* Campus employment opportunities, campus safety program, career counseling, disabled student services, international student services, low-cost health insurance, multicultural affairs office. *Library facilities:* Learning Resource Center. *Collection:* 27,227 titles, 527 serial subscriptions, 1,077 audiovisual materials.

Computer facilities: 50 computers available on campus for general student use. A campuswide network can be accessed. Internet access and online class registration are available. *Web address:* http://www.scuhs.edu/.

General Application Contact: Len Rosenthal, Executive Director of Marketing and Enrollment, 562-947-8755 Ext. 305, Fax: 562-947-5724, E-mail: lenrosenthal@scuhs.edu.

GRADUATE UNITS

College of Acupuncture and Oriental Medicine Students: 66 full-time (40 women), 92 part-time (41 women); includes 104 minority (5 African Americans, 2 American Indian/Alaska Native, 84 Asian Americans or Pacific Islanders, 13 Hispanic Americans). Average age 28. 97 applicants, 51% accepted, 39 enrolled. *Faculty:* 10 full-time (3 women), 15 part-time/adjunct (8 women). Expenses: Contact institution. *Financial support:* In 2006–07, 104 students received support. Federal Work-Study available. Financial award applicants required to submit FAFSA. In 2006, 33 degrees awarded. *Degree program information:* Part-time and evening/weekend programs available. Offers acupuncture and Oriental medicine (MAOM). *Application deadline:* Applications are processed on a rolling basis. *Application fee:* $50. Electronic applications accepted. *Application Contact:* Len Rosenthal, Executive Director of Marketing and Enrollment, 562-947-8755 Ext. 305, Fax: 562-947-5724, E-mail: lenrosenthal@scuhs.edu. *Dean,* Dr. Wen–Shuo Wu, 562-947-8755 Ext. 7028, E-mail: wen-shuowu@scuhs.edu.

Los Angeles College of Chiropractic Students: 456 full-time (163 women), 15 part-time (5 women); includes 200 minority (9 African Americans, 4 American Indian/Alaska Native, 129 Asian Americans or Pacific Islanders, 58 Hispanic Americans). Average age 28. 244 applicants, 61% accepted, 89 enrolled. *Faculty:* 35 full-time (9 women), 59 part-time/adjunct (32 women). Expenses: Contact institution. *Financial support:* In 2006–07, 469 students received support. Career-related internships or fieldwork, Federal Work-Study, and scholarships/grants available. Financial award applicants required to submit FAFSA. In 2006, 131 degrees awarded. Offers chiropractic (DC). *Application deadline:* Applications are processed on a rolling basis. *Application fee:* $50. Electronic applications accepted. *Application Contact:* Len Rosenthal, Executive Director of Marketing and Enrollment, 562-947-8755 Ext. 305, Fax: 562-947-5724, E-mail: lenrosenthal@scuhs.edu. *Dean,* Dr. Todd Knudsen, 562-947-8755 Ext. 522, Fax: 562-947-5724, E-mail: toddknudsen@scuhs.edu.

SOUTHERN COLLEGE OF OPTOMETRY, Memphis, TN 38104-2222

General Information Independent, coed, graduate-only institution. *Graduate housing:* On-campus housing not available.

GRADUATE UNITS

Professional Program Offers optometry (OD).

SOUTHERN CONNECTICUT STATE UNIVERSITY, New Haven, CT 06515-1355

General Information State-supported, coed, comprehensive institution. CGS member. *Enrollment:* 12,326 graduate, professional, and undergraduate students; 569 full-time matriculated graduate/professional students, 1,490 part-time matriculated graduate/professional students. *Graduate faculty:* 402 full-time (175 women), 337 part-time/adjunct. *Graduate housing:* On-campus housing not available. *Student services:* Campus employment opportunities, campus safety program, career counseling, child daycare facilities, disabled student services, exercise/wellness program, free psychological counseling, grant writing training, international student services, low-cost health insurance, multicultural affairs office, teacher training, writing training. *Library facilities:* Hilton C. Buley Library. *Online resources:* library catalog, web page, access to other libraries' catalogs. *Collection:* 495,660 titles, 3,549 serial subscriptions.

Computer facilities: Computer purchase and lease plans are available. 750 computers available on campus for general student use. A campuswide network can be accessed from student residence rooms and from off campus. Internet access and online class registration are available. *Web address:* http://www.southernct.edu/.

General Application Contact: Lisa Galvin, Assistant Dean, 203-392-5240, Fax: 203-392-5235, E-mail: gradinfo@southernct.edu.

GRADUATE UNITS

School of Graduate Studies Students: 2,059. 1,768 applicants, 56% accepted, 819 enrolled. *Faculty:* 187 full-time, 255 part-time/adjunct. Expenses: Contact institution. *Financial support:* Fellowships, research assistantships, teaching assistantships, career-related internships or fieldwork, Federal Work-Study, and unspecified assistantships available. Support available to part-time students. Financial award application deadline: 4/15; financial award applicants required to submit FAFSA. In 2006, 907 master's, 190 other advanced degrees awarded. *Degree program information:* Part-time and evening/weekend programs available. Postbaccalaureate distance learning degree programs offered (no on-campus study). Offers audiology (MS); health and human services (MFT, MPH, MS, MSN, MSW); marriage and family therapy (MFT); nursing administration (MSN); nursing education (MSN); public health (MPH); recreation and leisure studies (MS); social work (MSW); speech pathology (MS). *Application deadline:* Applications are processed on a rolling basis. *Application fee:* $50. Electronic applications accepted. *Application Contact:* Lisa Galvin, Assistant Dean of Graduate Studies, 203-392-5240, Fax: 203-392-5235, E-mail: galvinl1@southernct.edu. *Dean,* Dr. Sandra C. Holley, 203-392-5240, Fax: 203-392-5235, E-mail: holleys1@southernct.edu.

School of Arts and Sciences Students: 194 full-time, 380 part-time; includes 55 minority (25 African Americans, 1 American Indian/Alaska Native, 9 Asian Americans or Pacific Islanders, 20 Hispanic Americans), 3 international. 343 applicants, 62% accepted, 169 enrolled.

Faculty: 54 full-time, 14 part-time/adjunct. Expenses: Contact institution. *Financial support:* Teaching assistantships, career-related internships or fieldwork available. In 2006, 194 master's, 14 other advanced degrees awarded. Offers art education (MS); arts and sciences (MA, MS, Diploma); biology (MS); biology for nurse anesthetists (MS); chemistry (MS); English (MA, MS); environmental education (MS); French (MA); history (MA, MS); mathematics (MS); multicultural-bilingual education/teaching English to speakers of other languages (MS); political science (MS); psychology (MA); Romance languages (MA); science education (MS, Diploma); sociology (MS); Spanish (MA); urban studies (MS); women's studies (MA). *Application deadline:* Applications are processed on a rolling basis. *Application fee:* $50. Electronic applications accepted. *Dean,* Dr. Donna Jean Fredeen, 203-392-5468, Fax: 203-392-6807, E-mail: fredeend1@southernct.edu.

School of Business Students: 64 full-time (30 women), 109 part-time (46 women); includes 67 minority (34 African Americans, 20 Asian Americans or Pacific Islanders, 13 Hispanic Americans). 107 applicants, 59% accepted, 46 enrolled. *Faculty:* 7 full-time, 2 part-time/adjunct. Expenses: Contact institution. *Financial support:* Application deadline: 4/15; In 2006, 62 degrees awarded. *Degree program information:* Evening/weekend programs available. Offers business (MBA); business administration (MBA). *Application deadline:* For fall admission, 7/1 priority date for domestic students. Applications are processed on a rolling basis. *Application fee:* $50. Electronic applications accepted. *Application Contact:* Dr. Omid Nodoushani, Director, 203-392-7030, Fax: 203-392-5988, E-mail: nodoushanio1@southernct.edu. *Interim Dean,* Dr. Henry Hein, 203-392-5556, Fax: 203-392-6473, E-mail: heinh1@southernct.edu.

School of Communication, Information and Library Science Students: 56 full-time (39 women), 276 part-time (233 women); includes 30 minority (7 African Americans, 19 Asian Americans or Pacific Islanders, 4 Hispanic Americans). 142 applicants, 87% accepted, 106 enrolled. *Faculty:* 18 full-time, 6 part-time/adjunct. Expenses: Contact institution. *Financial support:* Research assistantships available. Financial award application deadline: 4/15; financial award applicants required to submit FAFSA. In 2006, 141 master's, 12 other advanced degrees awarded. *Degree program information:* Part-time and evening/weekend programs available. Postbaccalaureate distance learning degree programs offered (no on-campus study). Offers communication, information and library science (MLS, MS, Diploma); computer science (MS); instructional technology (MS); library science (MLS); library/information studies (Diploma). *Application deadline:* For fall admission, 7/15 priority date for domestic students. Applications are processed on a rolling basis. *Application fee:* $50. Electronic applications accepted. *Dean,* Dr. Edward Harris, 203-392-5701.

School of Education Students: 1,507. 561 applicants, 71% accepted, 326 enrolled. *Faculty:* 52 full-time, 37 part-time/adjunct. Expenses: Contact institution. *Financial support:* Research assistantships, teaching assistantships, career-related internships or fieldwork available. In 2006, 363 master's, 151 other advanced degrees awarded. *Degree program information:* Part-time programs available. Offers classroom teacher specialist (Diploma); community counseling (MS); counseling (Diploma); education (MS, MS Ed, Ed D, Diploma); educational leadership (Ed D, Diploma); elementary education (MS); foundational studies (Diploma); human performance (MS); physical education (MS); reading (MS, Diploma); research, measurement and quantitative analysis (MS); school counseling (MS); school health education (MS); school psychology (MS, Diploma); special education (MS Ed, Diploma); sport psychology (MS). *Application fee:* $50. Electronic applications accepted. *Interim Dean,* Dr. James Granfield, 203-392-5900.

Announcement: The University maintains a high standard of excellence in its programs and seeks to instill in its students a desire for continuing self-education and self-development. Each school of the University has developed its graduate programs in accordance with the highest national standards for the respective fields.

See Close-Up on page 1035.

SOUTHERN EVANGELICAL SEMINARY, Matthews, NC 28105

General Information Independent-religious, coed, primarily men, graduate-only institution. *Enrollment by degree level:* 201 master's, 19 doctoral. *Graduate housing:* On-campus housing not available. *Student services:* Career counseling, international student services, writing training. *Library facilities:* Jamison Library. *Online resources:* library catalog. *Collection:* 46,000 titles, 94 serial subscriptions, 318 audiovisual materials.

Computer facilities: 4 computers available on campus for general student use. A campuswide network can be accessed. Internet access is available. *Web address:* http://www.ses.edu/.

General Application Contact: Dr. Douglas Potter, Admissions Director, 704-847-5600 Ext. 205, Fax: 704-845-1747, E-mail: dpotter@ses.edu.

GRADUATE UNITS

Graduate School of Ministry and Missions 31 applicants, 100% accepted, 20 enrolled. Expenses: Contact institution. *Financial support:* Scholarships/grants available. In 2006, 1 M Div, 5 master's awarded. *Degree program information:* Part-time and evening/weekend programs available. Postbaccalaureate distance learning degree programs offered. Offers Christian education (MA); church ministry (MA, Certificate); divinity (Certificate); Islamic studies (Certificate); theology (M Div). *Application deadline:* For fall admission, 8/15 priority date for domestic students, 8/5 priority date for international students; for winter admission, 12/15 priority date for domestic and international students; for spring admission, 1/15 priority date for domestic and international students. Applications are processed on a rolling basis. *Application fee:* $25. *Dean,* Dr. Barry R. Leventhal, 704-847-5600 Ext. 204, Fax: 704-845-1747, E-mail: dean@ses.edu.

Veritas Graduate School of Apologetics and Counter-Cult Ministry 68 applicants, 100% accepted, 48 enrolled. Expenses: Contact institution. *Financial support:* Scholarships/grants available. In 2006, 16 master's, 2 doctorates awarded. *Degree program information:* Part-time and evening/weekend programs available. Postbaccalaureate distance learning degree programs offered (minimal on-campus study). Offers apologetics (MA, D Min, Certificate); philosophy (MA); religion (MA). *Application deadline:* For fall admission, 8/5 priority date for domestic and international students; for winter admission, 12/15 priority date for domestic and international students; for spring admission, 1/15 priority date for domestic and international students. Applications are processed on a rolling basis. *Application fee:* $25. *Director, Apologetics Program,* Dr. Thomas A. Howe, 704-847-5600 Ext. 209, Fax: 704-845-1747, E-mail: thowe@ses.edu.

SOUTHERN ILLINOIS UNIVERSITY CARBONDALE, Carbondale, IL 62901-4701

General Information State-supported, coed, university. CGS member. *Enrollment:* 21,003 graduate, professional, and undergraduate students; 1,648 full-time matriculated graduate/professional students (851 women), 2,632 part-time matriculated graduate/professional students (1,387 women). *Graduate faculty:* 1,074 full-time (262 women), 112 part-time/adjunct. *Graduate housing:* Rooms and/or apartments available on a first-come, first-served basis to single and married students. *Student services:* Campus employment opportunities, campus safety program, career counseling, child daycare facilities, disabled student services, exercise/wellness program, free psychological counseling, grant writing training, international student services, low-cost health insurance, teacher training. *Library facilities:* Morris Library plus 1 other. *Online resources:* library catalog, web page, access to other libraries' catalogs. *Collection:* 4.2 million titles, 18,271 serial subscriptions, 371,180 audiovisual materials. *Research affiliation:* Argonne National Laboratory, NASA–Ames Research Center.

Computer facilities: Computer purchase and lease plans are available. 1,827 computers available on campus for general student use. A campuswide network can be accessed from student residence rooms and from off campus. Internet access and online class registration are available. *Web address:* http://www.siu.edu/siuc/.

General Application Contact: Associate Dean of the Graduate School, 618-536-7791.

GRADUATE UNITS

Graduate School Students: 1,645 full-time (828 women), 2,354 part-time (1,293 women); includes 483 minority (327 African Americans, 16 American Indian/Alaska Native, 59 Asian Americans or Pacific Islanders, 81 Hispanic Americans), 1,051 international. 3,988 applicants, 39% accepted, 448 enrolled. *Faculty:* 780 full-time (198 women), 14 part-time/adjunct (9 women). Expenses: Contact institution. *Financial support:* In 2006–07, 59 fellowships with full tuition reimbursements, 536 research assistantships with full tuition reimbursements, 980 teaching assistantships with full tuition reimbursements were awarded; career-related internships or fieldwork, Federal Work-Study, institutionally sponsored loans, tuition waivers (full), and dissertation research awards, clinical assistantships also available. Support available to part-time students. In 2006, 837 master's, 148 doctorates awarded. *Degree program information:* Part-time programs available. Offers general law (MLS); health law and policy (MLS); molecular, cellular and systemic physiology (MS); pharmacology (MS, PhD); physiology (MS, PhD). *Application deadline:* Applications are processed on a rolling basis. *Application Contact:* Lu Lyons, Supervisor, Admissions, 618-453-4512, E-mail: llyons@siu.edu. *Dean,* Dr. John Koropchak, 618-536-7791.

College of Agriculture Students: 43 full-time (16 women), 87 part-time (38 women); includes 16 minority (12 African Americans, 2 Asian Americans or Pacific Islanders, 2 Hispanic Americans), 4 international. 78 applicants, 36% accepted, 15 enrolled. *Faculty:* 51 full-time (8 women). Expenses: Contact institution. *Financial support:* In 2006–07, 35 students received support, including 31 research assistantships; fellowships, teaching assistantships, career-related internships or fieldwork, Federal Work-Study, institutionally sponsored loans, and tuition waivers (full) also available. Support available to part-time students. In 2006, 38 degrees awarded. *Degree program information:* Part-time programs available. Offers agribusiness economics (MS); agriculture (MS); animal science (MS); food and nutrition (MS); forestry (MS); horticultural science (MS); plant and soil science (MS). *Application deadline:* Applications are processed on a rolling basis. *Application fee:* $0. *Dean,* Gary L. Minish, 618-453-2469.

College of Business and Administration Students: 125 full-time (58 women), 80 part-time (32 women); includes 15 minority (4 African Americans, 1 American Indian/Alaska Native, 6 Asian Americans or Pacific Islanders, 4 Hispanic Americans), 96 international. Average age 26. 261 applicants, 37% accepted, 25 enrolled. *Faculty:* 42 full-time (4 women). Expenses: Contact institution. *Financial support:* In 2006–07, 123 students received support, including 2 fellowships, 42 research assistantships, 49 teaching assistantships; Federal Work-Study, institutionally sponsored loans, and tuition waivers (full) also available. Support available to part-time students. In 2006, 115 master's, 14 doctorates awarded. *Degree program information:* Part-time programs available. Offers accountancy (M Acc, PhD); business administration (MBA, PhD); business and administration (M Acc, MBA, PhD). *Application deadline:* For fall admission, 6/15 priority date for domestic students. Applications are processed on a rolling basis. *Application fee:* $20. *Application Contact:* Julie Virgo, Administrative Aide, 618-453-3030, Fax: 618-453-7961, E-mail: jvirgo@siu.edu. *Dean,* Dr. Dennis Cradit, 618-453-7960, E-mail: siu50661@siu.edu.

College of Education Students: 441 full-time (318 women), 886 part-time (592 women); includes 210 minority (167 African Americans, 4 American Indian/Alaska Native, 15 Asian Americans or Pacific Islanders, 24 Hispanic Americans), 144 international. Average age 34. 679 applicants, 47% accepted, 77 enrolled. *Faculty:* 175 full-time (74 women), 25 part-time/adjunct (6 women). Expenses: Contact institution. *Financial support:* In 2006–07, 306 students received support, including 8 fellowships, 115 research assistantships, 166 teaching assistantships; career-related internships or fieldwork, Federal Work-Study, institutionally sponsored loans, traineeships, tuition waivers (full), and unspecified assistantships also available. Support available to part-time students. In 2006, 301 master's, 43 doctorates awarded. *Degree program information:* Part-time programs available. Offers behavior analysis and therapy (MS); behavioral analysis and therapy (MS); communication disorders and sciences (MS); community health education (MPH); counselor education (MS Ed, PhD); curriculum and instruction (MS Ed, PhD); education (MPH, MS, MS Ed, MSW, PhD, Rh D); educational administration (MS Ed, PhD); educational psychology (MS Ed, PhD); health education (MS Ed, PhD); higher education (MS Ed); human learning and development (MS Ed); measurement and statistics (PhD); physical education (MS Ed); recreation (MS Ed); rehabilitation (Rh D); rehabilitation administration and services (MS); rehabilitation counseling (MS); social work (MSW); special education (MS Ed); workforce education and development (MS Ed, PhD). *Application fee:* $20. *Interim Dean,* Patricia Elmore, 618-453-2415.

College of Engineering Students: 188 full-time (36 women), 183 part-time (35 women); includes 23 minority (15 African Americans, 7 Asian Americans or Pacific Islanders, 1 Hispanic American), 292 international. 629 applicants, 59% accepted, 88 enrolled. *Faculty:* 55 full-time (3 women), 3 part-time/adjunct (0 women). Expenses: Contact institution. *Financial support:* In 2006–07, 1 fellowship, 58 research assistantships, 95 teaching assistantships were awarded; Federal Work-Study, institutionally sponsored loans, and tuition waivers (full) also available. Support available to part-time students. In 2006, 144 master's, 11 doctorates awarded. Offers civil engineering (MS); electrical and computer engineering (MS, PhD); electrical systems (PhD); engineering (MS, PhD); fossil energy (PhD); manufacturing systems (MS); mechanical engineering and energy processes (MS); mechanics (PhD); mining engineering (MS). *Application deadline:* Applications are processed on a rolling basis. *Application fee:* $20. *Application Contact:* Anna Maria Alms, Student Contact, 618-453-4321, Fax: 618-453-4235, E-mail: amalms@siu.edu. *Dean,* Dr. William Osborne, 618-453-4321, E-mail: osborne@engr.siu.edu.

College of Liberal Arts Students: 472 full-time (243 women), 482 part-time (257 women); includes 113 minority (57 African Americans, 6 American Indian/Alaska Native, 17 Asian Americans or Pacific Islanders, 33 Hispanic Americans), 182 international. 1,054 applicants, 28% accepted, 149 enrolled. *Faculty:* 254 full-time (87 women), 8 part-time/adjunct (3 women). Expenses: Contact institution. *Financial support:* In 2006–07, 608 students received support, including 24 fellowships, 146 research assistantships, 325 teaching assistantships; career-related internships or fieldwork, Federal Work-Study, institutionally sponsored loans, scholarships/grants, and tuition waivers (full) also available. Support available to part-time students. In 2006, 159 master's, 55 doctorates awarded. *Degree program information:* Part-time programs available. Offers administration of justice (MA); anthropology (MA, PhD); applied linguistics (MA); ceramics (MFA); clinical psychology (MA, MS, PhD); composition (MA, PhD); composition and theory (MM); counseling psychology (MA, MS, PhD); creative writing (MFA); drawing (MFA); economics (MA, MS, PhD); experimental psychology (MA, MS, PhD); fiber/weaving (MFA); foreign languages and literatures (MA); geography (MS, PhD); glass (MFA); history (MA, PhD); history and literature (MM); jewelry (MFA); liberal arts (MA, MFA, MM, MPA, MS, PhD); metalsmithing/blacksmithing (MFA); music education (MM); opera/music theater (MM); painting (MFA); performance (MM); philosophy (MA, PhD); piano pedagogy (MM); political science (MA, PhD); printmaking (MFA); public administration (MPA); sculpture (MFA); sociology (MA, PhD); speech communication (MA, MS, PhD); speech/theater (PhD); teaching English to speakers of other languages (MA); theater (MFA). *Application deadline:* Applications are processed on a rolling basis. *Interim Dean,* Dr. Alan Vaux, 618-453-2466.

College of Mass Communication and Media Arts Students: 41 full-time (19 women), 79 part-time (31 women); includes 12 minority (5 African Americans, 2 American Indian/Alaska Native, 1 Asian American or Pacific Islander, 4 Hispanic Americans), 47 international. Average age 28. 91 applicants, 23% accepted, 19 enrolled. *Faculty:* 35 full-time (9 women), 2 part-time/adjunct (0 women). Expenses: Contact institution. *Financial support:* In 2006–07, 75 students received support; fellowships, research assistantships, teaching assistantships, career-related internships or fieldwork, Federal Work-Study, institutionally sponsored loans, and tuition waivers (full) also available. Support available to part-time students. In 2006, 14 master's, 4 doctorates awarded. *Degree program information:* Part-time programs available. Offers journalism (PhD); mass communication and media arts (MA, MFA, PhD); professional media and media management studies (MA); telecommunications (MA). *Application deadline:* Applications are processed on a rolling basis. *Application fee:* $20. *Dean,* Dr. Manjunath Pendakur, 618-453-5794, E-mail: jschool@siu.edu.

College of Science Students: 205 full-time (79 women), 247 part-time (97 women); includes 30 minority (19 African Americans, 2 American Indian/Alaska Native, 4 Asian Americans or Pacific Islanders, 5 Hispanic Americans), 217 international. 702 applicants, 23% accepted, 67 enrolled. *Faculty:* 137 full-time (8 women), 2 part-time/adjunct (0 women). Expenses: Contact institution. *Financial support:* In 2006–07, 11 fellowships, 90 research assistantships, 160 teaching assistantships were awarded; career-related internships or fieldwork, Federal Work-Study, institutionally sponsored loans, scholarships/grants, and tuition waiv-

Southern Illinois University Carbondale (continued)

ers (full) also available. Support available to part-time students. In 2006, 66 master's, 17 doctorates awarded. *Degree program information:* Part-time programs available. Offers biological sciences (MS); chemistry and biochemistry (MS, PhD); computer science (MS, PhD); environmental resources and policy (PhD); geology (MS, PhD); mathematics (MA, MS, PhD); molecular biology, microbiology, and biochemistry (MS, PhD); physics (MS, PhD); plant biology (MS, PhD); science (MA, MS, PhD); statistics (MS); zoology (MS, PhD). *Application deadline:* Applications are processed on a rolling basis. *Application Contact:* William G. Dyer, Associate Dean, 618-536-6666. *Dean,* Dr. Jack Parker, 618-536-6666.

School of Law Students: 380 full-time (143 women), 3 part-time (1 woman); includes 29 minority (9 African Americans, 1 American Indian/Alaska Native, 12 Asian Americans or Pacific Islanders, 7 Hispanic Americans), 2 international. Average age 27. 802 applicants, 50% accepted, 158 enrolled. *Faculty:* 23 full-time (11 women), 12 part-time/adjunct (6 women). Expenses: Contact institution. *Financial support:* In 2006–07, 326 students received support. Career-related internships or fieldwork, Federal Work-Study, institutionally sponsored loans, scholarships/grants, and health care benefits available. Support available to part-time students. Financial award application deadline: 4/1; financial award applicants required to submit FAFSA. In 2006, 107 degrees awarded. *Degree program information:* Part-time programs available. Offers general law (LL M); health law and policy (LL M); law (JD); legal studies (MLS). *Application deadline:* For fall admission, 3/1 for domestic and international students. Applications are processed on a rolling basis. *Application fee:* $50. Electronic applications accepted. *Application Contact:* Michael P. Ruiz, Assistant Dean for Admissions, 618-453-8858, Fax: 618-453-8769, E-mail: lawadmit@siu.edu. *Dean,* Peter C. Alexander, 618-453-8761, Fax: 618-453-8769.

SOUTHERN ILLINOIS UNIVERSITY EDWARDSVILLE, Edwardsville, IL 62026-0001

General Information State-supported, coed, comprehensive institution. CGS member. *Enrollment:* 13,449 graduate, professional, and undergraduate students; 1,033 full-time matriculated graduate/professional students (584 women), 1,257 part-time matriculated graduate/professional students (818 women). *Enrollment by degree level:* 366 first professional, 185 master's, 74 other advanced degrees. *Graduate faculty:* 465 full-time (176 women). *Graduate housing:* Rooms and/or apartments available on a first-come, first-served basis to single and married students. Housing application deadline: 5/1. *Student services:* Campus employment opportunities, campus safety program, career counseling, child daycare facilities, disabled student services, exercise/wellness program, free psychological counseling, grant writing training, international student services, low-cost health insurance, multicultural affairs office, teacher training, writing training. *Library facilities:* Lovejoy Library. *Online resources:* library catalog, web page, access to other libraries' catalogs. *Collection:* 847,631 titles, 24,530 serial subscriptions, 30,078 audiovisual materials.

Computer facilities: Computer purchase and lease plans are available. 600 computers available on campus for general student use. A campuswide network can be accessed from student residence rooms and from off campus. Internet access, online job finder are available. *Web address:* http://www.siue.edu/.

General Application Contact: Dr. Stephen L. Hansen, Dean of Graduate School, 618-650-3010, Fax: 618-650-3523, E-mail: shansen@siue.edu.

GRADUATE UNITS

Graduate Studies and Research Students: 667 full-time (400 women), 1,257 part-time (818 women); includes 165 minority (118 African Americans, 8 American Indian/Alaska Native, 24 Asian Americans or Pacific Islanders, 15 Hispanic Americans), 246 international. Average age 33. 1,745 applicants, 46% accepted. *Faculty:* 433 full-time (172 women). Expenses: Contact institution. *Financial support:* In 2006–07, 19 fellowships with full tuition reimbursements (averaging $7,843 per year), 53 research assistantships with full tuition reimbursements (averaging $7,843 per year), 141 teaching assistantships with full tuition reimbursements (averaging $7,843 per year) were awarded; career-related internships or fieldwork, Federal Work-Study, institutionally sponsored loans, scholarships/grants, traineeships, tuition waivers (full), and unspecified assistantships also available. Support available to part-time students. Financial award application deadline: 3/1; financial award applicants required to submit FAFSA. In 2006, 693 master's, 7 other advanced degrees awarded. *Degree program information:* Part-time programs available. *Application deadline:* For fall admission, 7/20 for domestic students, 6/1 for international students; for spring admission, 12/8 for domestic students, 10/1 for international students. Applications are processed on a rolling basis. *Application fee:* $30. Electronic applications accepted. *Application Contact:* Linda Skelton, Staff Assistant, 618-650-2958, Fax: 618-650-3523, E-mail: lskelto@siue.edu. *Dean of Graduate School,* Dr. Stephen L. Hansen, 618-650-3010, Fax: 618-650-3523, E-mail: shansen@siue.edu.

College of Arts and Sciences Students: 243 full-time (161 women), 345 part-time (228 women); includes 89 minority (68 African Americans, 6 American Indian/Alaska Native, 7 Asian Americans or Pacific Islanders, 8 Hispanic Americans), 52 international. Average age 33. 526 applicants, 52% accepted. *Faculty:* 243 full-time (92 women). Expenses: Contact institution. *Financial support:* In 2006–07, 10 fellowships with full tuition reimbursements, 11 research assistantships with full tuition reimbursements, 105 teaching assistantships with full tuition reimbursements were awarded; career-related internships or fieldwork, Federal Work-Study, institutionally sponsored loans, scholarships/grants, traineeships, and unspecified assistantships also available. Support available to part-time students. Financial award application deadline: 3/1. In 2006, 177 master's, 4 other advanced degrees awarded. *Degree program information:* Part-time programs available. Offers American and English literature (MA, Postbaccalaureate Certificate); art therapy counseling (MA, Postbaccalaureate Certificate); arts and sciences (MA, MFA, MM, MPA, MS, MSW, Postbaccalaureate Certificate); biology (MA, MS); biotechnology management (MS); chemistry (MS); corporate and organizational communication (Postbaccalaureate Certificate); creative writing (MA); environmental science management (MS); environmental sciences (MS); geography (MS); history (MA); mass communications (MS); mathematics (MS); media literacy (Postbaccalaureate Certificate); museum studies (Postbaccalaureate Certificate); music education (MM); music performance (MM); physics (MS); public administration and policy analysis (MPA); social work (MSW); sociology (MA); speech communication (MA); studio art (MFA); teaching English as a second language (MA, Postbaccalaureate Certificate); teaching of writing (MA, Postbaccalaureate Certificate). *Application deadline:* For fall admission, 7/20 for domestic students, 6/1 for international students; for spring admission, 12/14 for domestic students, 10/1 for international students. Applications are processed on a rolling basis. *Application fee:* $30. Electronic applications accepted. *Dean,* Dr. M. Kent Neely, 618-650-5047, E-mail: kneely@siue.edu.

School of Business Students: 83 full-time (35 women), 196 part-time (81 women); includes 17 minority (11 African Americans, 1 American Indian/Alaska Native, 5 Asian Americans or Pacific Islanders), 31 international. Average age 33. 176 applicants, 61% accepted. *Faculty:* 43 full-time (13 women). Expenses: Contact institution. *Financial support:* In 2006–07, 3 fellowships with full tuition reimbursements, 17 research assistantships with full tuition reimbursements were awarded; teaching assistantships with full tuition reimbursements, career-related internships or fieldwork, Federal Work-Study, institutionally sponsored loans, traineeships, and unspecified assistantships also available. Support available to part-time students. Financial award application deadline: 3/1; financial award applicants required to submit FAFSA. In 2006, 140 degrees awarded. *Degree program information:* Part-time programs available. Offers accounting (MSA); business (MA, MBA, MMR, MS, MSA); business administration (MBA); computer management and information systems (MS); economics and finance (MA, MS); management information systems (MBA); marketing research (MMR). *Application deadline:* For fall admission, 7/20 for domestic students, 6/1 for international students; for spring admission, 12/14 for domestic students, 10/1 for international students. *Application fee:* $30. Electronic applications accepted. *Application Contact:* Dr. Timothy Schoenecker, Acting Dean, 618-650-3822, E-mail: tschoen@siue.edu. *Acting Dean,* Dr. Timothy Schoenecker, 618-650-3822, E-mail: tschoen@siue.edu.

School of Education Students: 145 full-time (117 women), 483 part-time (359 women); includes 35 minority (28 African Americans, 2 Asian Americans or Pacific Islanders, 5 Hispanic Americans), 4 international. Average age 33. 381 applicants, 44% accepted. *Faculty:* 74 full-time (39 women). Expenses: Contact institution. *Financial support:* In 2006–07, 2 fellowships with full tuition reimbursements, 5 research assistantships with full tuition reimbursements, 2 teaching assistantships with full tuition reimbursements were awarded; career-related internships or fieldwork, Federal Work-Study, institutionally sponsored loans, traineeships, and unspecified assistantships also available. Support available to part-time students. Financial award application deadline: 3/1; financial award applicants required to submit FAFSA. In 2006, 252 master's, 13 other advanced degrees awarded. *Degree program information:* Part-time programs available. Offers art (MS Ed); biology (MS Ed); chemistry (MS Ed); clinical child and school psychology (MS); clinical-adult psychology (MA); education (MA, MAT, MS, MS Ed, Ed S, Postbaccalaureate Certificate, SD); educational administration (MS Ed, Ed S); elementary education (MS Ed); English (MS Ed); exercise physiology (Postbaccalaureate Certificate); foreign languages (MS Ed); history (MS Ed); industrial-organizational psychology (MA); instructional design and learning technologies (MS Ed); kinesiology (MS Ed); learning, culture and society (MS Ed); literacy education (MS Ed); mathematics (MS Ed); pedagogy administration (Postbaccalaureate Certificate); physics (MS Ed); psychology (MA, MS); reading (MS Ed); school psychology (SD); science (MS Ed); secondary education (MS Ed); special education (MS Ed); speech language pathology (MS); sport and exercise behavior (Postbaccalaureate Certificate); teaching (MAT). *Application deadline:* For fall admission, 7/20 for domestic students, 6/1 for international students; for spring admission, 12/14 for domestic students, 10/1 for international students. *Application fee:* $30. Electronic applications accepted. *Application Contact:* Dr. Lela DeToye, Associate Dean, 618-650-3358, E-mail: ldetoye@siue.edu. *Interim Dean,* Dr. Bill Searcy, 618-650-3350.

School of Engineering Students: 124 full-time (34 women), 97 part-time (25 women); includes 8 minority (3 African Americans, 5 Asian Americans or Pacific Islanders), 159 international. Average age 33. 568 applicants, 40% accepted. *Faculty:* 42 full-time (2 women). Expenses: Contact institution. *Financial support:* In 2006–07, 2 fellowships with full tuition reimbursements, 22 research assistantships with full tuition reimbursements, 31 teaching assistantships with full tuition reimbursements were awarded; career-related internships or fieldwork, Federal Work-Study, institutionally sponsored loans, scholarships/grants, traineeships, and unspecified assistantships also available. Support available to part-time students. Financial award application deadline: 3/1; financial award applicants required to submit FAFSA. In 2006, 76 degrees awarded. *Degree program information:* Part-time programs available. Offers civil engineering (MS); computer science (MS); electrical engineering (MS); engineering (MS); mechanical engineering (MS). *Application deadline:* For fall admission, 7/20 for domestic students, 6/1 for international students; for spring admission, 12/14 for domestic students, 10/1 for international students. *Application fee:* $30. Electronic applications accepted. *Application Contact:* Dr. Jacob Van Roekel, Associate Dean, 618-650-2534, E-mail: jvanroe@siue.edu. *Dean,* Dr. Hasan Sevim, 618-650-2861.

School of Nursing Students: 72 full-time (53 women), 136 part-time (125 women); includes 16 minority (8 African Americans, 1 American Indian/Alaska Native, 5 Asian Americans or Pacific Islanders, 2 Hispanic Americans). Average age 33. 94 applicants, 32% accepted. *Faculty:* 26 full-time (24 women). Expenses: Contact institution. *Financial support:* In 2006–07, 2 fellowships with full tuition reimbursements, 1 research assistantship were awarded; teaching assistantships, career-related internships or fieldwork, Federal Work-Study, institutionally sponsored loans, scholarships/grants, traineeships, and unspecified assistantships also available. Support available to part-time students. Financial award application deadline: 3/1; financial award applicants required to submit FAFSA. In 2006, 35 master's, 3 other advanced degrees awarded. Offers family nurse practitioner (MS, Post-Master's Certificate); health care and nursing administration (MS, Post-Master's Certificate); nurse anesthesia (MS, Post-Master's Certificate); nurse educator (MS, Post-Master's Certificate); nursing (MS, Post-Master's Certificate); public health nursing (MS, Post-Master's Certificate). *Application deadline:* For fall admission, 1/1 for domestic and international students. *Application fee:* $30. Electronic applications accepted. *Application Contact:* Dr. Jacquelyn Clement, Director, 618-650-3923, E-mail: jclemen@siue.edu. *Dean,* Dr. Marcia Maurer, 618-650-3959, E-mail: mamaure@siue.edu.

School of Dental Medicine Students: 205 full-time (93 women); includes 31 minority (12 African Americans, 1 American Indian/Alaska Native, 13 Asian Americans or Pacific Islanders, 5 Hispanic Americans). Average age 25. *Faculty:* 19 full-time (1 woman). Expenses: Contact institution. In 2006, 49 degrees awarded. Offers dental medicine (DMD). *Application deadline:* For fall admission, 2/1 priority date for domestic students. *Application fee:* $20. *Dean,* Dr. Ann Boyle, 618-474-7120, E-mail: aboyle@siue.edu.

School of Pharmacy Students: 161 full-time (91 women); includes 24 minority (8 African Americans, 13 Asian Americans or Pacific Islanders, 3 Hispanic Americans). 463 applicants, 19% accepted. *Faculty:* 13 full-time (3 women). Expenses: Contact institution. Offers pharmacy (Pharm D). *Application deadline:* For fall admission, 12/1 for domestic and international students. *Application fee:* $40. *Head,* Dr. Philip J. Medon.

See Close-Up on page 1037.

SOUTHERN METHODIST UNIVERSITY, Dallas, TX 75275

General Information Independent-religious, coed, university. CGS member. *Enrollment:* 10,941 graduate, professional, and undergraduate students; 2,199 full-time matriculated graduate/professional students (902 women), 2,028 part-time matriculated graduate/professional students (778 women). *Enrollment by degree level:* 1,243 first professional, 2,577 master's, 407 doctoral. *Graduate faculty:* 613 full-time (205 women), 315 part-time/adjunct (111 women). *Graduate housing:* Rooms and/or apartments available on a first-come, first-served basis to single and married students. Housing application deadline: 5/31. *Student services:* Campus employment opportunities, campus safety program, career counseling, child daycare facilities, disabled student services, exercise/wellness program, free psychological counseling, grant writing training, international student services, low-cost health insurance, multicultural affairs office, teacher training. *Library facilities:* Central University Library plus 7 others. *Online resources:* library catalog, web page, access to other libraries' catalogs. *Collection:* 2.8 million titles, 11,701 serial subscriptions, 45,168 audiovisual materials.

Computer facilities: Computer purchase and lease plans are available. 758 computers available on campus for general student use. A campuswide network can be accessed from student residence rooms and from off campus. Internet access and online class registration, online billing/payment processing are available. *Web address:* http://www.smu.edu/.

General Application Contact: Dr. R. Hal Williams, Dean of Research and Graduate Studies, 214-768-4345.

GRADUATE UNITS

Cox School of Business Students: 472 full-time (130 women), 455 part-time (126 women); includes 231 minority (43 African Americans, 4 American Indian/Alaska Native, 112 Asian Americans or Pacific Islanders, 72 Hispanic Americans), 104 international. Average age 30. 318 applicants, 57% accepted, 76 enrolled. *Faculty:* 68 full-time (16 women), 31 part-time/adjunct (8 women). Expenses: Contact institution. *Financial support:* In 2006–07, 165 fellowships (averaging $20,000 per year), 10 research assistantships (averaging $2,800 per year) were awarded; career-related internships or fieldwork, scholarships/grants, and unspecified assistantships also available. Support available to part-time students. Financial award application deadline: 3/1; financial award applicants required to submit FAFSA. In 2006, 391 degrees awarded. *Degree program information:* Part-time and evening/weekend programs available. Offers accounting (MSA); business (Exec MBA, MBA); management (MSM). *Application deadline:* For fall admission, 4/30 priority date for domestic students; for spring admission, 12/30 priority date for domestic students. Applications are processed on a rolling basis. *Application fee:* $75. Electronic applications accepted. *Application Contact:* Path Cudney, Director of MBA Admissions, 214-768-3001, Fax: 214-768-3956, E-mail: pcudney@mail.cox.smu.edu. *Dean,* Dr. Albert W. Niemi, 214-768-3012, Fax: 214-768-3713, E-mail: aniemi@mail.cox.smu.edu.

Dedman College Students: 160 full-time (70 women), 175 part-time (84 women); includes 31 minority (8 African Americans, 13 Asian Americans or Pacific Islanders, 10 Hispanic Americans), 102 international. Average age 35. 555 applicants, 37% accepted, 90 enrolled. *Faculty:* 332

full-time (81 women). Expenses: Contact institution. *Financial support:* In 2006–07, 194 students received support, including research assistantships with full tuition reimbursements available (averaging $16,000 per year), teaching assistantships with full tuition reimbursements available (averaging $16,000 per year); fellowships, career-related internships or fieldwork, Federal Work-Study, institutionally sponsored loans, scholarships/grants, tuition waivers (full and partial), and unspecified assistantships also available. Support available to part-time students. Financial award applicants required to submit FAFSA. In 2006, 71 master's, 3 doctorates awarded. *Degree program information:* Part-time and evening/weekend programs available. Offers anthropology (PhD); applied economics (MA); applied geophysics (MS); biological sciences (MA, MS, PhD); chemistry (MS, PhD); clinical and counseling psychology (MA); clinical psychology (PhD); computational and applied mathematics (MS, PhD); economics (MA, PhD); English (MA, PhD); exploration geophysics (MS); geology (MS, PhD); geophysics (PhD); history (MA, PhD); medical anthropology (MA); medieval studies (MA); physics (MS, PhD); religious studies (MA, PhD); statistical science (MS, PhD). *Application deadline:* For fall admission, 2/1 priority date for domestic and international students; for winter admission, 11/30 priority date for domestic and international students. Applications are processed on a rolling basis. *Application fee:* $75. Electronic applications accepted. *Application Contact:* Barbara Phillips, Assistant Dean, 214-768-4202, Fax: 214-768-4235, E-mail: bphillips@smu.edu. *Interim,* Dr. R. Hal Williams, 214-768-4336.

Dedman School of Law Students: 922 full-time (424 women), 76 part-time (34 women); includes 193 minority (44 African Americans, 8 American Indian/Alaska Native, 75 Asian Americans or Pacific Islanders, 66 Hispanic Americans), 46 international. Average age 27. 2,640 applicants, 23% accepted, 275 enrolled. *Faculty:* 37 full-time (15 women), 27 part-time/adjunct (6 women). Expenses: Contact institution. *Financial support:* Career-related internships or fieldwork, Federal Work-Study, and scholarships/grants available. Financial award application deadline: 2/15; financial award applicants required to submit FAFSA. In 2006, 261 JDs, 45 master's awarded. *Degree program information:* Part-time and evening/weekend programs available. Offers comparative and international law (LL M); law (JD, SJD); law-general (LL M); taxation (LL M). *Application deadline:* For fall admission, 2/15 priority date for domestic students. Applications are processed on a rolling basis. *Application fee:* $75. Electronic applications accepted. *Application Contact:* Virginia Keehan, Assistant Dean for Admissions, 214-768-2550, Fax: 214-768-2549, E-mail: lawadmit@smu.edu. *Dean,* John B. Attanasio, 214-768-8999, Fax: 214-768-2182, E-mail: jba@mail.smu.edu.

Meadows School of the Arts Students: 184 full-time (112 women), 31 part-time (21 women); includes 20 minority (9 African Americans, 2 American Indian/Alaska Native, 2 Asian Americans or Pacific Islanders, 7 Hispanic Americans), 59 international. Average age 27. 219 applicants, 62% accepted, 89 enrolled. *Faculty:* 81 full-time (31 women), 35 part-time/adjunct (13 women). Expenses: Contact institution. *Financial support:* In 2006–07, 136 teaching assistantships (averaging $4,400 per year) were awarded; research assistantships, scholarships/grants and unspecified assistantships also available. Financial award application deadline: 3/1; financial award applicants required to submit FAFSA. In 2006, 67 master's, 12 other advanced degrees awarded. *Degree program information:* Evening/weekend programs available. Offers acting (MFA); art history (MA); arts (MA, MFA, MM, MSM, Certificate); conducting (MM); dance (MFA); design (MFA); joint business); music composition (MM); music education (MM); music history (MM); music theory (MM); performance (MM, Certificate); piano performance and pedagogy (MM); sacred music (MSM); studio art (MFA). *Application fee:* $75. *Application Contact:* Jean Cherry, Director of Graduate Admissions and Records, 214-768-3765, Fax: 214-768-3272, E-mail: jcherry@smu.edu. *Dean,* Jose Antonio Bowen, 214-768-2880.

Division of Cinema—Television Students: 6 full-time (3 women), 4 part-time (2 women); includes 1 minority (African American), 6 international. Average age 30. 9 applicants, 78% accepted, 4 enrolled. *Faculty:* 9 full-time (4 women), 3 part-time/adjunct (0 women). Expenses: Contact institution. *Financial support:* In 2006–07, 7 students received support, including 7 teaching assistantships (averaging $6,500 per year); research assistantships, scholarships/grants, tuition waivers (full), and unspecified assistantships also available. Financial award application deadline: 3/15. In 2006, 5 degrees awarded. *Degree program information:* Part-time and evening/weekend programs available. Offers cinema—television (MA). *Application deadline:* For fall admission, 3/1 priority date for domestic and international students. *Application fee:* $75. *Application Contact:* Jean Cherry, Director of Graduate Admissions and Records, 214-768-3765, Fax: 214-768-3272, E-mail: jcherry@smu.edu. *Chair,* Rick Worland, 214-768-3708, Fax: 214-768-2784, E-mail: rworland@smu.edu.

Perkins School of Theology Students: 233 full-time (104 women), 226 part-time (123 women); includes 113 minority (78 African Americans, 3 American Indian/Alaska Native, 9 Asian Americans or Pacific Islanders, 23 Hispanic Americans), 13 international. Average age 40. 230 applicants, 76% accepted, 97 enrolled. *Faculty:* 30 full-time (11 women), 7 part-time/adjunct (2 women). Expenses: Contact institution. *Financial support:* In 2006–07, 232 students received support, including 3 fellowships (averaging $18,656 per year); career-related internships or fieldwork, Federal Work-Study, scholarships/grants, and minister's family tuition awards also available. Support available to part-time students. Financial award application deadline: 3/1; financial award applicants required to submit FAFSA. In 2006, 48 M Divs, 31 master's, 11 doctorates awarded. *Degree program information:* Part-time programs available. Offers theology (M Div, CMM, MSM, MTS, D Min). *Application deadline:* For fall admission, 5/1 for domestic students, 12/15 for international students; for spring admission, 11/1 for domestic students. Applications are processed on a rolling basis. *Application fee:* $30. *Application Contact:* Jason Pangiarella, Director, Recruitment and Admissions, 214-768-2293, Fax: 214-768-4245, E-mail: theology@smu.edu. *Dean,* Dr. William B. Lawrence, 214-768-2534.

School of Education and Human Development Students: 16 full-time (14 women), 372 part-time (284 women); includes 88 minority (40 African Americans, 4 American Indian/Alaska Native, 8 Asian Americans or Pacific Islanders, 36 Hispanic Americans), 6 international. *Faculty:* 15 full-time (10 women), 48 part-time/adjunct (33 women). Expenses: Contact institution. In 2006, 109 degrees awarded. Offers education and human development (M Ed, MBE, MLS); liberal arts (MLS); literacy and language acquisition (MBE); teacher education (M Ed).

School of Engineering Students: 223 full-time (49 women), 818 part-time (159 women); includes 312 minority (78 African Americans, 10 American Indian/Alaska Native, 138 Asian Americans or Pacific Islanders, 86 Hispanic Americans), 224 international. Average age 31. 672 applicants, 57% accepted, 200 enrolled. *Faculty:* 56 full-time (9 women), 58 part-time/adjunct (2 women). Expenses: Contact institution. *Financial support:* In 2006–07, 72 students received support, including 37 research assistantships with full tuition reimbursements available (averaging $16,800 per year), 35 teaching assistantships with full tuition reimbursements available (averaging $12,600 per year); fellowships, career-related internships or fieldwork, Federal Work-Study, institutionally sponsored loans, scholarships/grants, and tuition waivers (full and partial) also available. Financial award applicants required to submit FAFSA. In 2006, 358 master's, 11 doctorates awarded. *Degree program information:* Part-time and evening/weekend programs available. Postbaccalaureate distance learning degree programs offered (no on-campus study). Offers applied science (MS, PhD); civil engineering (MS, PhD); computer engineering (MS Cp E, PhD); computer science (MS, PhD); electrical engineering (MSEE, PhD); electronic and optical packaging (MS); engineering (MS, MS Cp E, MSEE, MSEM, MSIEM, MSME, DE, PhD); engineering management (MSEM, DE); environmental engineering (MS); environmental science (MS); facilities management (MS); information engineering and management (MSIEM); manufacturing systems management (MS); mechanical engineering (MSME, PhD); operations research (MS, PhD); security engineering (MS); software engineering (MS); systems engineering (MS); telecommunications (MS). *Application deadline:* For fall admission, 7/1 for domestic students, 5/15 for international students; for spring admission, 11/15 for domestic students, 9/1 for international students. Applications are processed on a rolling basis. *Application fee:* $75. *Application Contact:* Marc Valerin, Director of Graduate and Executive Admissions, 214-768-3042, E-mail: valerin@engr.smu.edu. *Dean,* Dr. Geoffrey Orsak, 214-768-3050, Fax: 214-768-3845.

SOUTHERN NAZARENE UNIVERSITY, Bethany, OK 73008

General Information Independent-religious, coed, comprehensive institution. *Enrollment:* 382 full-time matriculated graduate/professional students (214 women), 11 part-time matriculated graduate/professional students (4 women). *Enrollment by degree level:* 393 master's. *Graduate faculty:* 18 full-time (6 women), 36 part-time/adjunct (16 women). *Tuition:* Part-time $507 per credit. *Graduate housing:* Rooms and/or apartments available on a first-come, first-served basis to single and married students. Typical cost: $2,458 per year ($5,378 including board) for single students. Room and board charges vary according to board plan and housing facility selected. Housing application deadline: 8/1. *Student services:* Campus employment opportunities, campus safety program, career counseling, disabled student services, international student services, low-cost health insurance, multicultural affairs office. *Library facilities:* R. T. Williams Learning Resources Center. *Online resources:* library catalog, web page. *Collection:* 95,535 titles, 225 serial subscriptions, 4,257 audiovisual materials.

Computer facilities: 120 computers available on campus for general student use. A campuswide network can be accessed from student residence rooms and from off campus. Internet access is available. *Web address:* http://www.snu.edu/.

General Application Contact: Dr. W. Davis Berryman, Dean of Graduate College, 405-491-6316, Fax: 405-491-6302, E-mail: dberryma@snu.edu.

GRADUATE UNITS

Graduate College Average age 27. Expenses: Contact institution. *Financial support:* Teaching assistantships with full tuition reimbursements, career-related internships or fieldwork and Federal Work-Study available. *Degree program information:* Part-time and evening/weekend programs available. Offers theology (MA). *Application deadline:* For fall admission, 8/1 priority date for domestic students. Applications are processed on a rolling basis. *Application fee:* $25 ($35 for international students). Electronic applications accepted. *Dean of Graduate College,* Dr. W. Davis Berryman, 405-491-6316, Fax: 405-491-6302, E-mail: dberryma@snu.edu.

School of Business Students: 152. Average age 27. Expenses: Contact institution. In 2006, 151 degrees awarded. *Degree program information:* Part-time and evening/weekend programs available. Offers business (MBA, MS Mgt). *Application deadline:* For fall admission, 8/1 priority date for domestic students. Applications are processed on a rolling basis. *Application fee:* $25 ($35 for international students). Electronic applications accepted. *Interim Chair,* Jeff Seyfert, 405-491-6358, E-mail: jseyfert@snu.edu.

School of Education Students: 105. Average age 27. *Faculty:* 10. Expenses: Contact institution. *Financial support:* Teaching assistantships, career-related internships or fieldwork available. In 2006, 23 degrees awarded. *Degree program information:* Part-time and evening/weekend programs available. Offers curriculum and instruction (MA); educational leadership (MA). *Application deadline:* For fall admission, 8/1 priority date for domestic students. Applications are processed on a rolling basis. *Application fee:* $25 ($35 for international students). *Director,* Dr. Rex Tullis, 405-491-6317, E-mail: rtullis@snu.edu.

School of Nursing Students: 30. Expenses: Contact institution. In 2006, 14 degrees awarded. *Degree program information:* Part-time and evening/weekend programs available. Offers nursing education (MS); nursing leadership (MS). *Dean,* Dr. Carol Dorough, 405-491-6365, E-mail: cdorough@snu.edu.

School of Psychology Students: 98. Expenses: Contact institution. In 2006, 49 degrees awarded. Offers counseling psychology (MSCP); marriage and family therapy (MA). *Application deadline:* For fall admission, 8/1 priority date for domestic students. Applications are processed on a rolling basis. *Application fee:* $25 ($35 for international students). *Chair,* Dr. Phil Budd, 405-491-6360.

SOUTHERN NEW ENGLAND SCHOOL OF LAW, North Dartmouth, MA 02747-1252

General Information Independent, coed, graduate-only institution. *Enrollment by degree level:* 266 first professional. *Graduate faculty:* 11 full-time (5 women), 19 part-time/adjunct (5 women). *Tuition:* Full-time $19,486; part-time $685 per credit. *Required fees:* $375. *Graduate housing:* On-campus housing not available. *Student services:* Campus employment opportunities, career counseling, free psychological counseling, low-cost health insurance, writing training. *Library facilities:* Southern New England School of Law Library. *Online resources:* library catalog, web page. *Collection:* 134,284 titles, 1,200 serial subscriptions, 246 audiovisual materials.

Computer facilities: 30 computers available on campus for general student use. A campuswide network can be accessed. Internet access and online class registration, email, listserves, financial aid are available. *Web address:* http://www.snesl.edu/.

General Application Contact: Nancy Fitzsimmons Hebert, Director of Admissions, 508-998-9400 Ext. 113, Fax: 508-998-9561, E-mail: nhebert@snesl.edu.

GRADUATE UNITS

Professional Program Students: 156 full-time (86 women), 110 part-time (69 women); includes 68 minority (41 African Americans, 15 Asian Americans or Pacific Islanders, 12 Hispanic Americans), 7 international. Average age 32. 256 applicants, 82% accepted, 105 enrolled. *Faculty:* 11 full-time (5 women), 19 part-time/adjunct (5 women). Expenses: Contact institution. *Financial support:* In 2006–07, 242 students received support, including 3 research assistantships (averaging $2,400 per year); scholarships/grants, tuition waivers (full and partial), and SNESL summer stipends also available. Support available to part-time students. Financial award application deadline: 6/30; financial award applicants required to submit FAFSA. In 2006, 68 degrees awarded. *Degree program information:* Part-time and evening/weekend programs available. Offers law (JD). *Application deadline:* For fall admission, 6/30 for domestic students. Applications are processed on a rolling basis. *Application fee:* $50. *Application Contact:* Nancy Fitzsimmons Hebert, Director of Admissions, 508-998-9400 Ext. 113, Fax: 508-998-9561, E-mail: nhebert@snesl.edu. *Dean,* Robert V. Ward, 508-998-9600 Ext. 170, Fax: 508-998-9561, E-mail: rward@snesl.edu.

SOUTHERN NEW HAMPSHIRE UNIVERSITY, Manchester, NH 03106-1045

General Information Independent, coed, comprehensive institution. *Enrollment:* 3,490 graduate, professional, and undergraduate students; 467 full-time matriculated graduate/professional students (184 women), 1,104 part-time matriculated graduate/professional students (592 women). *Enrollment by degree level:* 1,571 master's. *Graduate housing:* Room and/or apartments available on a first-come, first-served basis to single students; on-campus housing not available to married students. *Student services:* Campus employment opportunities, campus safety program, career counseling, disabled student services, exercise/wellness program, free psychological counseling, international student services, low-cost health insurance, multicultural affairs office, teacher training, writing training. *Library facilities:* Harry A. B. and Gertrude C. Shapiro Library. *Online resources:* library catalog, web page, access to other libraries' catalogs. *Collection:* 89,338 titles, 47,577 serial subscriptions, 2,752 audiovisual materials.

Computer facilities: Computer purchase and lease plans are available. 557 computers available on campus for general student use. A campuswide network can be accessed from student residence rooms and from off campus. Internet access and online class registration are available. *Web address:* http://www.snhu.edu/.

General Application Contact: Scott Durand, Director of Graduate Enrollment Services, 603-644-3102 Ext. 3338, Fax: 603-644-3144, E-mail: s.durand@snhu.edu.

GRADUATE UNITS

School of Business Students: 427 full-time (184 women), 774 part-time (428 women). Average age 32. *Faculty:* 45 full-time, 75 part-time/adjunct. Expenses: Contact institution. *Financial support:* Career-related internships or fieldwork, Federal Work-Study, institutionally sponsored loans, tuition waivers (partial), and unspecified assistantships available. Support available to part-time students. Financial award applicants required to submit FAFSA. In 2006, 682 master's, 1 doctorate awarded. *Degree program information:* Part-time and evening/weekend programs available. Postbaccalaureate distance learning degree programs offered (no on-campus study). Offers accounting (MS); business administration (MBA, Certificate); finance (MS); hospitality and tourism leadership (Certificate); information technology (MS, Certificate); information technology/international business (Certificate); integrated marketing

Southern New Hampshire University (continued)

communications (Certificate); international business (MS, DBA); marketing (MS); operations and project management (MS); organizational leadership (MS); project management (Certificate); sport management (MS). *Application deadline:* Applications are processed on a rolling basis. *Application fee:* $25. Electronic applications accepted. *Application Contact:* Scott Durand, Director of Graduate Enrollment Services, 603-644-3102 Ext. 3338, Fax: 603-644-3144, E-mail: s.durand@snhu.edu. *Dean,* Dr. Martin Bradley, 603-644-3102, Fax: 603-644-3144, E-mail: m.bradley@snhu.edu.

School of Community Economic Development Students: 130 full-time (78 women), 6 part-time (3 women); includes 91 minority (73 African Americans, 1 Asian American or Pacific Islander, 17 Hispanic Americans), 20 international. Average age 32. 194 applicants, 53% accepted, 92 enrolled. *Faculty:* 6 full-time (2 women), 16 part-time/adjunct (7 women). Expenses: Contact institution. *Financial support:* In 2006–07, 1 research assistantship was awarded; Federal Work-Study also available. Support available to part-time students. Financial award applicants required to submit FAFSA. In 2006, 77 master's, 1 doctorate awarded. *Degree program information:* Part-time and evening/weekend programs available. Offers community economic development (MA, MS, PhD). *Application deadline:* For fall admission, 6/1 for domestic students, 4/1 for international students. Applications are processed on a rolling basis. *Application fee:* $25. Electronic applications accepted. *Application Contact:* Anthony Poore, 603-644-3123, Fax: 603-644-3130, E-mail: p.goolbis@snhu.edu. *Dean,* Dr. Michael Swack, 603-644-3135, Fax: 603-644-3130, E-mail: m.swack@snhc.edu.

School of Education Average age 35. *Faculty:* 6 full-time (3 women), 9 part-time/adjunct (7 women). Expenses: Contact institution. *Financial support:* Institutionally sponsored loans available. Financial award applicants required to submit FAFSA. In 2006, 52 degrees awarded. *Degree program information:* Part-time and evening/weekend programs available. Post-baccalaureate distance learning degree programs offered. Offers business education (MS); child development (M Ed); computer technology education (Certificate); curriculum and instruction (M Ed); education (M Ed, CAS); elementary education (M Ed); general special education (Certificate); school business administrator (Certificate); school counseling (M Ed); school psychology (M Ed); secondary education (M Ed); training and development (Certificate). *Application deadline:* Applications are processed on a rolling basis. *Application fee:* $25. Electronic applications accepted. *Application Contact:* Scott Durand, Director of Graduate Enrollment Services, 603-644-3102 Ext. 3338, Fax: 603-644-3144, E-mail: s.durand@snhu.edu. *Dean,* Dr. Patrick J. Hartwick, 603-668-2211 Ext. 4698, Fax: 603-629-4673, E-mail: p.hartwick@snhu.edu.

School of Liberal Arts Students: 187 full-time, 12 part-time. Average age 35. *Faculty:* 18 full-time. Expenses: Contact institution. *Financial support:* In 2006–07, 4 research assistantships were awarded; career-related internships or fieldwork and scholarships/grants also available. Financial award applicants required to submit FAFSA. In 2006, 35 degrees awarded. *Degree program information:* Part-time and evening/weekend programs available. Offers clinical services for adults psychiatric disabilities (Certificate); clinical services for children and adolescents with psychiatric disabilities (Certificate); clinical services for persons with co-occurring substance abuse and psychiatric disabilities (Certificate); community mental health (MS); fiction writing (MFA); non-fiction writing (MFA); teaching English as a foreign language (MS). *Application deadline:* For fall admission, 7/1 priority date for domestic students; for winter admission, 11/1 priority date for domestic students; for spring admission, 6/1 priority date for domestic students. Applications are processed on a rolling basis. *Application fee:* $40. Electronic applications accepted. *Application Contact:* Scott Durand, Director of Graduate Enrollment Services, 603-644-3102 Ext. 3338, Fax: 603-644-3144, E-mail: s.durand@snhu.edu. *Dean,* Dr. Karen Erickson, 603-668-2211, E-mail: k.erickson@snhu.edu.

SOUTHERN OREGON UNIVERSITY, Ashland, OR 97520

General Information State-supported, coed, comprehensive institution. *Graduate housing:* Rooms and/or apartments available on a first-come, first-served basis to single and married students. *Research affiliation:* U.S. Forest Service (biology, ecology studies), U.S. Fish and Wildlife Service (forensics), Oregon Shakespeare Festival, Crater Lake National Park (scientific studies), Bureau of Land Management (ecological studies), Bear Creek Corporation (environmental studies).

GRADUATE UNITS

Graduate Studies *Degree program information:* Part-time programs available. Electronic applications accepted.

School of Arts and Letters Offers music (MA, MS). Electronic applications accepted.

School of Business Offers business (MA Ed, MIM, MS Ed). Electronic applications accepted.

School of Sciences *Degree program information:* Part-time programs available. Offers environmental education (MA, MS); mathematics/computer science (MA, MS); science (MA, MS).

School of Social Sciences Offers applied psychology (MAP); elementary education (MA Ed, MS Ed); human service-organizational training and development (MA, MS); secondary education (MA Ed, MS Ed); social science (MA, MS); social science, health and physical education (MA, MA Ed, MAP, MAT, MS, MS Ed); teaching (MAT).

SOUTHERN POLYTECHNIC STATE UNIVERSITY, Marietta, GA 30060-2896

General Information State-supported, coed, comprehensive institution. *Enrollment:* 4,206 graduate, professional, and undergraduate students; 163 full-time matriculated graduate/professional students (61 women), 339 part-time matriculated graduate/professional students (115 women). *Enrollment by degree level:* 502 master's. *Graduate faculty:* 46 full-time (15 women), 8 part-time/adjunct (1 woman). Tuition, state resident: part-time $422 per credit hour. Tuition, nonresident: part-time $835 per credit hour. *Graduate housing:* Room and/or apartments available on a first-come, first-served basis to single students. Typical cost: $3,210 per year ($5,610 including board). Housing application deadline: 8/1. *Student services:* Campus employment opportunities, campus safety program, career counseling, disabled student services, exercise/wellness program, free psychological counseling, international student services, low-cost health insurance, multicultural affairs office. *Library facilities:* Lawrence V. Johnson Library. *Online resources:* library catalog, web page, access to other libraries' catalogs. *Collection:* 119,917 titles, 1,124 serial subscriptions, 85 audiovisual materials.

Computer facilities: 1,500 computers available on campus for general student use. A campuswide network can be accessed from student residence rooms and from off campus. Internet access and online class registration are available. *Web address:* http://www.spsu.edu/.

General Application Contact: Virginia A. Head, Director of Admissions, 678-915-4188, Fax: 678-915-7292, E-mail: vhead@spsu.edu.

GRADUATE UNITS

School of Architecture, Civil Engineering Technology and Construction Students: 18 full-time (3 women), 12 part-time (4 women); includes 10 minority (8 African Americans, 2 Asian Americans or Pacific Islanders), 9 international. Average age 34. 30 applicants, 50% accepted, 7 enrolled. *Faculty:* 4 full-time (0 women). Expenses: Contact institution. *Financial support:* In 2006–07, 30 students received support, including 6 research assistantships with tuition reimbursements available (averaging $1,500 per year); career-related internships or fieldwork, scholarships/grants, and unspecified assistantships also available. Support available to part-time students. Financial award application deadline: 5/1; financial award applicants required to submit FAFSA. In 2006, 11 degrees awarded. *Degree program information:* Part-time and evening/weekend programs available. Offers architecture, civil engineering technology and construction (MS); construction (MS). *Application deadline:* For fall admission, 7/1 priority date for domestic students, 5/1 priority date for international students; for spring admission, 11/1 priority date for domestic students, 9/1 priority date for international students. Applications are processed on a rolling basis. *Application fee:* $20. Electronic applications accepted. *Application Contact:* Virginia A. Head, Director of Admissions, 678-915-4188, Fax: 678-915-7292, E-mail: vhead@spsu.edu. *Dean,* Dr. Wilson Barnes, 678-915-5481, Fax: 678-915-3945, E-mail: wbarnes@spsu.edu.

School of Arts and Sciences Students: 2 full-time (1 woman), 35 part-time (24 women); includes 12 minority (all African Americans), 2 international. Average age 41. 30 applicants, 70% accepted, 15 enrolled. *Faculty:* 5 full-time (4 women). Expenses: Contact institution. *Financial support:* In 2006–07, 12 students received support, including 5 research assistantships with tuition reimbursements available (averaging $1,500 per year); career-related internships or fieldwork, scholarships/grants, and unspecified assistantships also available. Support available to part-time students. Financial award application deadline: 5/1; financial award applicants required to submit FAFSA. In 2006, 12 degrees awarded. *Degree program information:* Part-time and evening/weekend programs available. Offers arts and sciences (MS); information design and communication (MS). *Application deadline:* For fall admission, 7/1 priority date for domestic students, 5/1 priority date for international students; for spring admission, 11/1 priority date for domestic students, 9/1 priority date for international students. Applications are processed on a rolling basis. *Application fee:* $20. Electronic applications accepted. *Application Contact:* Virginia A. Head, Director of Admissions, 678-915-4188, Fax: 678-915-7292, E-mail: vhead@spsu.edu. *Dean,* Dr. Alan Gabrielli, 678-915-7464, Fax: 678-915-7292, E-mail: agabriel@spsu.edu.

School of Computing and Software Engineering Students: 79 full-time (37 women), 119 part-time (33 women); includes 52 minority (42 African Americans, 8 Asian Americans or Pacific Islanders, 2 Hispanic Americans), 90 international. 112 applicants, 75% accepted, 57 enrolled. *Faculty:* 21 full-time (5 women), 2 part-time/adjunct (0 women). Expenses: Contact institution. *Financial support:* In 2006–07, 45 students received support, including 43 research assistantships with tuition reimbursements available (averaging $1,500 per year); career-related internships or fieldwork, scholarships/grants, and unspecified assistantships also available. Support available to part-time students. Financial award application deadline: 5/1; financial award applicants required to submit FAFSA. In 2006, 71 degrees awarded. *Degree program information:* Part-time and evening/weekend programs available. Post-baccalaureate distance learning degree programs offered. Offers computer science (MS); computing and software engineering (MS, MS SwE, MSIT); information technology (MSIT); software engineering (MS SwE). *Application deadline:* For fall admission, 7/1 priority date for domestic students, 5/1 priority date for international students; for spring admission, 11/1 priority date for domestic students, 9/1 priority date for international students. Applications are processed on a rolling basis. *Application fee:* $20. Electronic applications accepted. *Application Contact:* Nikki Palamiotis, Director of Graduate Studies, 678-915-4276, Fax: 678-915-7292, E-mail: npalamio@spsu.edu. *Dean,* Dr. Michael G. Murphy, 678-915-5572, Fax: 678-915-5577, E-mail: mmurphy@spsu.edu.

School of Engineering Technology and Management Students: 63 full-time (20 women), 174 part-time (53 women); includes 81 minority (63 African Americans, 13 Asian Americans or Pacific Islanders, 5 Hispanic Americans), 55 international. 168 applicants, 61% accepted, 71 enrolled. *Faculty:* 16 full-time (6 women), 6 part-time/adjunct (1 woman). Expenses: Contact institution. *Financial support:* In 2006–07, 144 students received support, including 22 research assistantships (averaging $1,500 per year); career-related internships or fieldwork, scholarships/grants, and unspecified assistantships also available. Support available to part-time students. Financial award application deadline: 5/1; financial award applicants required to submit FAFSA. In 2006, 63 degrees awarded. *Degree program information:* Part-time and evening/weekend programs available. Postbaccalaureate distance learning degree programs offered. Offers business administration (MBA); engineering technology (MS); engineering technology and management (MBA, MS, MS SEng); quality assurance (MS); systems engineering (MS SEng). *Application deadline:* For fall admission, 7/1 priority date for domestic students, 5/1 priority date for international students; for spring admission, 11/1 priority date for domestic students, 9/1 priority date for international students. Applications are processed on a rolling basis. *Application fee:* $20. Electronic applications accepted. *Application Contact:* Virginia A. Head, Director of Admissions, 678-915-4188, Fax: 678-915-7292, E-mail: vhead@spsu.edu. *Interim Dean,* Dr. David Caudill, 678-915-7234, Fax: 678-915-7134, E-mail: dcaudill@spsu.edu.

SOUTHERN UNIVERSITY AND AGRICULTURAL AND MECHANICAL COLLEGE, Baton Rouge, LA 70813

General Information State-supported, coed, comprehensive institution. CGS member. *Graduate housing:* Room and/or apartments available on a first-come, first-served basis to single students; on-campus housing not available to married students. Housing application deadline: 6/30. *Research affiliation:* NASA (mechanical engineering), Michigan State University (language screening of African-Americans), University of Georgia at Athens (substance abuse prevention), University of Alabama (diabetes), NASA (drinking water remote sensing), Livingston Observatory (gravitational waves/cosmic gravity waves/black waves).

GRADUATE UNITS

Graduate School *Degree program information:* Part-time programs available. Offers criminal justice (MS); public policy analysis (PhD); science/mathematics education (PhD); special education (M Ed, PhD).

College of Agricultural, Family and Consumer Sciences Offers urban forestry (MS).

College of Arts and Humanities Offers arts and humanities (MA); mass communications (MA); social sciences (MA).

College of Business Offers accountancy (MPA); business (MPA).

College of Education Offers administration and supervision (M Ed); counselor education (MA); education (M Ed, MA, MS, PhD); elementary education (M Ed); media (M Ed); mental health counseling (MA); secondary education (M Ed); therapeutic recreation (MS).

College of Engineering Offers engineering (ME).

College of Sciences *Degree program information:* Part-time programs available. Offers analytical chemistry (MS); biochemistry (MS); biology (MS); environmental sciences (MS); information systems (MS); inorganic chemistry (MS); mathematics (MS); micro/minicomputer architecture (MS); operating systems (MS); organic chemistry (MS); physical chemistry (MS); physics (MS); rehabilitation counseling (MS); sciences (MA, MS).

School of Public Policy and Urban Affairs Offers public administration (MPA); public policy (PhD); public policy and urban affairs (MA, MPA, MS, PhD); social sciences (MA).

School of Nursing *Degree program information:* Part-time programs available. Offers educator/administrator (PhD); family health nursing (MSN); family nurse practitioner (Post Master's Certificate); geriatric nurse practitioner/gerontology (PhD).

Southern University Law Center *Degree program information:* Part-time and evening/weekend programs available. Offers law (JD). Electronic applications accepted.

SOUTHERN UNIVERSITY AT NEW ORLEANS, New Orleans, LA 70126-1009

General Information State-supported, coed, comprehensive institution. *Graduate housing:* On-campus housing not available.

GRADUATE UNITS

School of Social Work *Degree program information:* Part-time and evening/weekend programs available. Offers social work (MSW).

SOUTHERN UTAH UNIVERSITY, Cedar City, UT 84720-2498

General Information State-supported, coed, comprehensive institution. *Enrollment:* 7,029 graduate, professional, and undergraduate students; 73 full-time matriculated graduate/professional students (31 women), 355 part-time matriculated graduate/professional students (224 women). *Enrollment by degree level:* 428 master's. *Graduate faculty:* 42 full-time (8 women), 12 part-time/adjunct (4 women). Tuition, state resident: full-time $3,888. Tuition, nonresident: full-time $12,830. *Required fees:* $505. Tuition and fees vary according to program. *Graduate housing:* Room and/or apartments available on a first-come, first-served basis to single students; on-campus housing not available to married students. Typical cost: $1,740 per year ($5,400 including board). Room and board charges vary according to board plan and housing facility selected. *Student services:* Campus employment opportunities, campus safety program, career counseling, disabled student services, exercise/wellness program, free psychological counseling, international student services, low-cost health insurance, multicultural affairs office, teacher training. *Library facilities:* Southern Utah University Library. *Online resources:* library catalog, web page, access to other libraries' catalogs. *Collection:* 180,424 titles, 6,165 serial subscriptions, 13,352 audiovisual materials.

Computer facilities: 300 computers available on campus for general student use. A campuswide network can be accessed from student residence rooms and from off campus. *Web address:* http://www.suu.edu/.

General Application Contact: Abe Harraf, Provost, 435-586-7704, Fax: 435-586-5475.

GRADUATE UNITS

College of Education Students: 18 full-time (9 women), 279 part-time (188 women); includes 9 minority (1 African American, 1 American Indian/Alaska Native, 2 Asian Americans or Pacific Islanders, 5 Hispanic Americans). Average age 39. 120 applicants, 75% accepted. *Faculty:* 7 full-time (3 women), 12 part-time/adjunct (4 women). Expenses: Contact institution. *Financial support:* In 2006–07, 16 teaching assistantships with full and partial tuition reimbursements (averaging $1,215 per year) were awarded; scholarships/grants also available. In 2006, 126 degrees awarded. *Degree program information:* Part-time programs available. Offers education (M Ed). *Application deadline:* Applications are processed on a rolling basis. *Application fee:* $50. *Associate Professor of Teacher Education,* Dr. Prent Klag, 435-586-7803, Fax: 435-865-8485, E-mail: klag@suu.edu.

College of Humanities and Social Sciences Students: 5 full-time (2 women), 31 part-time (16 women); includes 3 minority (1 American Indian/Alaska Native, 1 Asian American or Pacific Islander, 1 Hispanic American). 19 applicants, 95% accepted. *Faculty:* 9 full-time (2 women). Expenses: Contact institution. *Financial support:* In 2006–07, 3 fellowships (averaging $3,000 per year), 6 teaching assistantships (averaging $5,000 per year) were awarded. Offers humanities and social sciences (MPC). *Application fee:* $50. *Dean,* Dean Rodney D. Decker, 435-586-7898, Fax: 435-865-8193, E-mail: decker@suu.edu.

College of Performing and Visual Arts Students: 10 full-time (6 women); includes 1 minority (African American) Average age 26. 20 applicants, 30% accepted. *Faculty:* 1 full-time (0 women). Expenses: Contact institution. *Financial support:* In 2006–07, 10 fellowships with full tuition reimbursements (averaging $7,700 per year) were awarded. In 2006, 10 degrees awarded. Offers arts administration (MFA). *Application deadline:* For fall admission, 3/31 for domestic students. *Application fee:* $50. *Application Contact:* Matt Neves, Director, 435-586-7873, Fax: 435-865-8657, E-mail: neves@suu.edu. *Dean,* Bill Byrnes, 435-865-8554, Fax: 435-865-8580, E-mail: byrnes@suu.edu.

School of Business Students: 30 full-time (7 women), 37 part-time (14 women); includes 2 minority (1 African American, 1 Asian American or Pacific Islander). 112 applicants, 85% accepted. *Faculty:* 13 full-time (2 women). Expenses: Contact institution. *Financial support:* In 2006–07, 10 research assistantships with full tuition reimbursements (averaging $4,916 per year) were awarded; career-related internships or fieldwork, institutionally sponsored loans, tuition waivers (full and partial), and unspecified assistantships also available. In 2006, 32 degrees awarded. *Degree program information:* Part-time programs available. Offers accounting (M Acc); business (M Acc, MBA); business administration (MBA). *Application deadline:* For fall admission, 8/1 priority date for domestic students. Applications are processed on a rolling basis. *Application fee:* $30. *Application Contact:* Paula Alger, Curriculum Coordinator and Adviser, 435-865-8157, Fax: 435-586-5493, E-mail: alger@suu.edu. *Dean,* Dr. Carl Templin, 435-586-7704, Fax: 435-586-5475, E-mail: templin@suu.edu.

SOUTHERN WESLEYAN UNIVERSITY, Central, SC 29630-1020

General Information Independent-religious, coed, comprehensive institution. *Graduate housing:* On-campus housing not available.

GRADUATE UNITS

Program in Business Administration *Degree program information:* Evening/weekend programs available. Offers business administration (MBA).

Program in Christian Ministries *Degree program information:* Evening/weekend programs available. Offers Christian ministries (M Min).

Program in Education *Degree program information:* Evening/weekend programs available. Offers education (M Ed). Program also offered at Greenville, SC site.

Program in Management *Degree program information:* Evening/weekend programs available. Offers management (MSM).

SOUTH TEXAS COLLEGE OF LAW, Houston, TX 77002-7000

General Information Independent, coed, graduate-only institution. *Enrollment by degree level:* 1,237 first professional. *Graduate faculty:* 58 full-time (21 women), 69 part-time/adjunct (18 women). *Tuition:* Full-time $21,840; part-time $14,560 per year. *Required fees:* $600. *Graduate housing:* On-campus housing not available. *Student services:* Campus employment opportunities, campus safety program, career counseling, disabled student services, international student services. *Library facilities:* The Fred Parks Law Library. *Online resources:* library catalog, web page, access to other libraries' catalogs. *Collection:* 239,476 titles, 3,506 serial subscriptions, 733 audiovisual materials.

Computer facilities: 102 computers available on campus for general student use. A campuswide network can be accessed from off campus. Internet access and online class registration, online class schedules, assignments, grades are available. *Web address:* http://www.stcl.edu/.

General Application Contact: Alicia K. Cramer, Assistant Dean of Admissions, 713-646-1810, Fax: 713-646-2906, E-mail: admissions@stcl.edu.

GRADUATE UNITS

Professional Program Students: 913 full-time (412 women), 324 part-time (136 women); includes 279 minority (44 African Americans, 10 American Indian/Alaska Native, 122 Asian Americans or Pacific Islanders, 103 Hispanic Americans), 3 international. Average age 28. 2,185 applicants, 43% accepted, 339 enrolled. *Faculty:* 58 full-time (21 women), 69 part-time/adjunct (18 women). Expenses: Contact institution. *Financial support:* In 2006–07, 1,175 students received support. Federal Work-Study, scholarships/grants, and tuition waivers (full and partial) available. Support available to part-time students. Financial award application deadline: 5/1; financial award applicants required to submit FAFSA. In 2006, 374 degrees awarded. *Degree program information:* Part-time and evening/weekend programs available. Offers law (JD). *Application deadline:* For fall admission, 2/15 for domestic and international students; for spring admission, 10/1 for domestic and international students. *Application fee:* $50. Electronic applications accepted. *Application Contact:* Alicia K. Cramer, Assistant Dean of Admissions, 713-646-1810, Fax: 713-646-2906, E-mail: admissions@stcl.edu. *President and Dean,* James J. Alfini, 713-646-1819, Fax: 713-646-2909, E-mail: jalfini@stcl.edu.

SOUTH UNIVERSITY, Montgomery, AL 36116-1120

General Information Proprietary, coed, comprehensive institution.

GRADUATE UNITS

Program in Counseling Offers counseling (MA).

SOUTH UNIVERSITY, West Palm Beach, FL 33409

General Information Proprietary, coed, comprehensive institution.

GRADUATE UNITS

Program in Counseling Offers counseling (MA).

SOUTH UNIVERSITY, Savannah, GA 31406-4805

General Information Proprietary, coed, comprehensive institution.

GRADUATE UNITS

Graduate Programs

School of Health Professions Offers anesthesiologist assistant (MM Sc); physician assistant studies (MS); professional counseling (MA).

School of Pharmacy Offers pharmacy (Pharm D).

SOUTH UNIVERSITY, Columbia, SC 29203-6400

General Information Proprietary, coed, comprehensive institution.

GRADUATE UNITS

Program in Counseling Offers counseling (MA).

SOUTHWEST ACUPUNCTURE COLLEGE, Santa Fe, NM 87505

General Information Private, coed, primarily women, graduate-only institution. *Enrollment by degree level:* 313 master's. *Graduate faculty:* 19 full-time (7 women), 51 part-time/adjunct (30 women). *Tuition:* Full-time $10,657. *Required fees:* $130. *Graduate housing:* On-campus housing not available. *Student services:* Campus employment opportunities, disabled student services. *Library facilities:* Southwest Acupuncture College Library. *Collection:* 6,785 titles, 152 serial subscriptions, 502 audiovisual materials.

Computer facilities: 11 computers available on campus for general student use. Internet access is available. *Web address:* http://www.acupuncturecollege.edu/.

General Application Contact: Dr. Bing zeng Zou, Academic Dean, 505-888-8898, E-mail: admin@acupuncturecollege.edu.

GRADUATE UNITS

Program in Oriental Medicine, Albuquerque Campus Students: 96 full-time (72 women), 2 part-time (both women); includes 11 minority (2 American Indian/Alaska Native, 4 Asian Americans or Pacific Islanders, 5 Hispanic Americans), 1 international. Average age 36. 38 applicants, 92% accepted, 32 enrolled. *Faculty:* 4 full-time (2 women), 14 part-time/adjunct (7 women). Expenses: Contact institution. *Financial support:* In 2006–07, 39 students received support. Scholarships/grants available. Financial award application deadline: 5/31; financial award applicants required to submit FAFSA. In 2006, 29 degrees awarded. *Degree program information:* Part-time programs available. Offers Oriental medicine (MS). *Application deadline:* For fall admission, 5/15 priority date for domestic students; for winter admission, 12/15 priority date for domestic students. Applications are processed on a rolling basis. *Application fee:* $50. Electronic applications accepted. *Application Contact:* Dr. Bing zeng Zou, Academic Dean, 505-888-8898, E-mail: admin@acupuncturecollege.edu. *Campus Director,* Dr. Li Xu, 505-888-8898, Fax: 505-888-1380, E-mail: drlixu@acupuncturecollege.edu.

Program in Oriental Medicine, Boulder Campus Students: 128 full-time (82 women), 3 part-time (2 women); includes 9 minority (1 African American, 7 Asian Americans or Pacific Islanders, 1 Hispanic American), 1 international. Average age 30. 60 applicants, 90% accepted, 45 enrolled. *Faculty:* 6 full-time (2 women), 23 part-time/adjunct (17 women). Expenses: Contact institution. *Financial support:* Scholarships/grants available. Financial award application deadline: 5/31; financial award applicants required to submit FAFSA. In 2006, 34 degrees awarded. *Degree program information:* Part-time programs available. Offers Oriental medicine (MS). *Application deadline:* For fall admission, 5/15 priority date for domestic students; for winter admission, 12/15 priority date for domestic students. Applications are processed on a rolling basis. *Application fee:* $50. *Application Contact:* Melanie Crane, Academic Dean, 303-581-9955, Fax: 303-581-9944, E-mail: boulder@acupuncturecollege.edu. *Campus Director,* Valerie L. Hobbs, 303-581-9955, Fax: 303-581-9944, E-mail: boulder@acupuncturecollege.edu.

Program in Oriental Medicine, Santa Fe Campus Students: 80 full-time (54 women), 4 part-time (2 women); includes 4 minority (1 African American, 1 American Indian/Alaska Native, 2 Asian Americans or Pacific Islanders), 3 international. Average age 33. 31 applicants, 100% accepted, 28 enrolled. *Faculty:* 9 full-time (3 women), 14 part-time/adjunct (6 women). Expenses: Contact institution. *Financial support:* In 2006–07, 12 students received support. Scholarships/grants available. Financial award application deadline: 5/31; financial award applicants required to submit FAFSA. In 2006, 20 degrees awarded. *Degree program information:* Part-time programs available. Offers Oriental medicine (MS). *Application deadline:* For fall admission, 5/15 priority date for domestic students; for winter admission, 12/15 priority date for domestic students. Applications are processed on a rolling basis. *Application fee:* $50. *Application Contact:* Dr. Dawei Shao, Academic Dean, 505-438-8884, Fax: 505-438-8883, E-mail: admin@acupuncturecollege.edu. *Campus Director,* Terry Lopez, 505-438-8884, Fax: 505-438-8883, E-mail: admin@acupuncturecollege.edu.

SOUTHWEST BAPTIST UNIVERSITY, Bolivar, MO 65613-2597

General Information Independent-religious, coed, comprehensive institution. *Graduate housing:* Room and/or apartments available on a first-come, first-served basis to single students; on-campus housing not available to married students.

GRADUATE UNITS

Graduate Studies *Degree program information:* Part-time and evening/weekend programs available. Offers business administration (MBA); education (MS); educational administration (MS, Ed S); health administration (MBA); physical therapy (DPT).

SOUTHWEST COLLEGE OF NATUROPATHIC MEDICINE AND HEALTH SCIENCES, Tempe, AZ 85282

General Information Independent, coed, graduate-only institution. *Enrollment by degree level:* 335 doctoral. *Graduate faculty:* 21 full-time (7 women), 30 part-time/adjunct (20 women). *Tuition:* Full-time $5,456; part-time $4,331 per quarter. *Graduate housing:* On-campus housing not available. *Student services:* Campus employment opportunities, career counseling, free psychological counseling, low-cost health insurance. *Library facilities:* Southwest College of Neuropathic Medicine Library plus 1 other. *Online resources:* library catalog, web page, access to other libraries' catalogs. *Collection:* 13,000 titles, 100 serial subscriptions, 3,524 audiovisual materials. *Research affiliation:* Gaia Herbs, Inc. (neutraceuticals), Program in Integrative Medicine, College of Medicine, Univ. of Arizona (educational).

Computer facilities: 20 computers available on campus for general student use. A campuswide network can be accessed. Internet access is available. *Web address:* http://www.scnm.edu/.

General Application Contact: Recruitment Specialist, 480-858-9100, Fax: 480-858-9116.

GRADUATE UNITS

Program in Naturopathic Medicine Students: 330 full-time (249 women), 5 part-time (4 women); includes 73 minority (36 African Americans, 4 American Indian/Alaska Native, 18 Asian Americans or Pacific Islanders, 15 Hispanic Americans), 13 international. Average age 31. 239 applicants, 54% accepted, 99 enrolled. *Faculty:* 21 full-time (7 women), 30 part-time/adjunct (20 women). Expenses: Contact institution. *Financial support:* Federal Work-Study and scholarships/grants available. Support available to part-time students. Financial award application deadline: 7/1; financial award applicants required to submit FAFSA. In 2006, 75 degrees awarded. Offers naturopathic medicine (ND). *Application deadline:* For fall admission, 7/1 priority date for domestic students; for spring admission, 2/1 priority date for domestic students. Applications are processed on a rolling basis. *Application fee:* $65 ($90 for international students). *Provost,* Dr. Richard Eberst, 480-858-9100 Ext. 241, Fax: 480-858-9116, E-mail: r.eberst@scnm.edu.

SOUTHWESTERN ADVENTIST UNIVERSITY, Keene, TX 76059

General Information Independent-religious, coed, comprehensive institution. *Graduate housing:* Rooms and/or apartments available on a first-come, first-served basis to single and married students. Housing application deadline: 8/31.

GRADUATE UNITS

Business Department, Graduate Program *Degree program information:* Part-time and evening/weekend programs available. Offers accounting (MBA).

Education Department, Graduate Program *Degree program information:* Part-time and evening/weekend programs available. Offers elementary education (M Ed).

SOUTHWESTERN ASSEMBLIES OF GOD UNIVERSITY, Waxahachie, TX 75165-5735

General Information Independent-religious, coed, comprehensive institution. *Graduate housing:* Room and/or apartments guaranteed to single students.

GRADUATE UNITS

Thomas F. Harrison School of Graduate Studies *Degree program information:* Part-time and evening/weekend programs available. Postbaccalaureate distance learning degree programs offered (minimal on-campus study). Offers Bible and theology (MS); Christian school administration (MS); counseling psychology (MS); curriculum development (MS). Electronic applications accepted.

SOUTHWESTERN BAPTIST THEOLOGICAL SEMINARY, Fort Worth, TX 76122-0000

General Information Independent-religious, coed, primarily men, graduate-only institution. *Graduate housing:* Rooms and/or apartments available on a first-come, first-served basis to single and married students. *Research affiliation:* DAWN Disciple A Whole Nation (evangelical missions), Campus Crusade for Christ/Jesus Film Project (evangelical missions).

GRADUATE UNITS

School of Church Music *Degree program information:* Part-time programs available. Offers church music (MACM, MAWSHP, MM, DMA, PhD, SPCM). Electronic applications accepted.

School of Educational Ministries *Degree program information:* Part-time and evening/weekend programs available. Offers educational ministries (MA Comm, MACC, MACCM, MACE, MACSE, MAMFC, DEM, PhD, SPEM). Electronic applications accepted.

School of Theology *Degree program information:* Part-time and evening/weekend programs available. Offers theology (M Div, MA Islamic, MA Miss, MA Th, Th M, D Min, PhD, SPTH). Electronic applications accepted.

SOUTHWESTERN CHRISTIAN UNIVERSITY, Bethany, OK 73008-0340

General Information Independent-religious, coed, comprehensive institution.

GRADUATE UNITS

Program in Ministry *Degree program information:* Part-time programs available. Offers ministry (M Min). Electronic applications accepted.

SOUTHWESTERN COLLEGE, Winfield, KS 67156-2499

General Information Independent-religious, coed, comprehensive institution. *Graduate housing:* Rooms and/or apartments available on a first-come, first-served basis to single and married students. Housing application deadline: 6/1.

GRADUATE UNITS

Center for Teaching Excellence *Degree program information:* Part-time and evening/weekend programs available. Postbaccalaureate distance learning degree programs offered (minimal on-campus study). Offers special education (M Ed). Electronic applications accepted.

MBA Program

SOUTHWESTERN COLLEGE, Santa Fe, NM 87502-4788

General Information Independent, coed, graduate-only institution. *Enrollment by degree level:* 163 master's. *Graduate faculty:* 37. *Tuition:* Full-time $16,416; part-time $342 per unit. *Graduate housing:* On-campus housing not available. *Student services:* Campus employment opportunities, campus safety program, career counseling. *Library facilities:* Quimby Memorial Library. *Online resources:* library catalog, web page, access to other libraries' catalogs. *Collection:* 21,000 titles, 50 serial subscriptions, 200 audiovisual materials.

Computer facilities: 8 computers available on campus for general student use. A campuswide network can be accessed from off campus. Internet access is available. *Web address:* http://www.swc.edu/.

General Application Contact: Dru Phoenix, Director of Admissions, 505-471-5756 Ext. 26, Fax: 505-471-4071, E-mail: admissions@swc.edu.

GRADUATE UNITS

Program in Art Therapy Students: 52 full-time (50 women), 25 part-time (all women). Average age 36. 52 applicants, 48% accepted, 25 enrolled. *Faculty:* 2 full-time (both women), 8 part-time/adjunct (all women). Expenses: Contact institution. *Financial support:* In 2006–07, 25 students received support. Career-related internships or fieldwork, institutionally sponsored loans, and scholarships/grants available. Support available to part-time students. Financial award application deadline: 6/1; financial award applicants required to submit FAFSA. In 2006, 14 degrees awarded. *Degree program information:* Part-time and evening/weekend programs available. Offers art therapy (MA, Certificate). *Application deadline:* For fall admission, 6/1 priority date for domestic students; for winter admission, 10/15 priority date for domestic students; for spring admission, 1/30 priority date for domestic students. Applications are processed on a rolling basis. *Application fee:* $50. *Application Contact:* Dru Phoenix, Director of Admissions, 505-471-5756 Ext. 26, Fax: 505-471-4071, E-mail: admissions@swc.edu. *Chair,* Debbie Schroder.

Program in Counseling Students: 47 full-time (31 women), 21 part-time (14 women). Average age 37. 34 applicants, 59% accepted, 20 enrolled. *Faculty:* 5 full-time (4 women), 22 part-time/adjunct (15 women). Expenses: Contact institution. *Financial support:* In 2006–07, 46 students received support. Career-related internships or fieldwork, institutionally sponsored loans, and scholarships/grants available. Support available to part-time students. Financial award application deadline: 6/1; financial award applicants required to submit FAFSA. In 2006, 17 degrees awarded. *Degree program information:* Part-time and evening/weekend programs available. Offers counseling (MA). *Application deadline:* For fall admission, 6/1 priority date for domestic students; for winter admission, 10/15 priority date for domestic students; for spring admission, 1/15 priority date for domestic students. Applications are processed on a rolling basis. *Application fee:* $50. *Application Contact:* Dru Phoenix, Director of Admissions, 505-471-5756 Ext. 26, Fax: 505-471-4071, E-mail: admissions@swc.edu. *Chair,* Dr. Carol Parker, 877-471-5756 Ext. 13.

Program in Grief and Loss Counseling Students: 14 full-time (11 women), 6 part-time (5 women). Average age 37. 12 applicants, 83% accepted, 9 enrolled. *Faculty:* 1 (woman) full-time, 2 part-time/adjunct (1 woman). Expenses: Contact institution. In 2006, 11 degrees awarded. Offers grief and loss counseling (MA, Certificate). *Application deadline:* For fall admission, 6/1 priority date for domestic students; for winter admission, 10/15 priority date for domestic students; for spring admission, 1/30 priority date for domestic students. Applications are processed on a rolling basis. *Application fee:* $50. *Application Contact:* Dru Phoenix, Director of Admissions, 505-471-5756 Ext. 26, Fax: 505-471-4071, E-mail: admissions@swc.edu. *Director,* Dr. Janet Schreiber, Fax: 877-471-4071.

Program in Psychodrama and Action Methods Average age 41. 12 applicants, 100% accepted, 12 enrolled. *Faculty:* 2 part-time/adjunct (both women). Expenses: Contact institution. Offers psychodrama and action methods (Certificate). *Application deadline:* Applications are processed on a rolling basis. *Application fee:* $25. *Application Contact:* Dru Phoenix, Director of Admissions, 505-471-5756 Ext. 26, Fax: 505-471-4071, E-mail: admissions@swc.edu. *Director,* Kate Cook, Fax: 877-471-4071.

SOUTHWESTERN LAW SCHOOL, Los Angeles, CA 90010

General Information Independent, coed, graduate-only institution. *Graduate faculty:* 57 full-time (22 women), 24 part-time/adjunct (7 women). *Tuition:* Full-time $31,700; part-time $19,100 per year. *Required fees:* $200. Tuition and fees vary according to class time, course load, program and student level. *Graduate housing:* On-campus housing not available. *Student services:* Campus employment opportunities, campus safety program, career counseling, disabled student services, exercise/wellness program, free psychological counseling, international student services, writing training. *Library facilities:* The Leigh H. Taylor Law Library. *Online resources:* library catalog, web page. *Collection:* 475,147 titles, 4,500 serial subscriptions, 3,506 audiovisual materials.

Computer facilities: 118 computers available on campus for general student use. A campuswide network can be accessed. Internet access and online class registration are available. *Web address:* http://www.swlaw.edu/.

General Application Contact: Lisa Gear, Interim Director of Admissions, 213-738-6717, Fax: 213-383-1688, E-mail: admissions@swlaw.edu.

GRADUATE UNITS

Graduate Program Students: 676 full-time (353 women), 288 part-time (150 women); includes 343 minority (50 African Americans, 7 American Indian/Alaska Native, 175 Asian Americans or Pacific Islanders, 111 Hispanic Americans), 12 international. Average age 27. 3,555 applicants, 31% accepted, 348 enrolled. *Faculty:* 57 full-time (22 women), 24 part-time/adjunct (7 women). Expenses: Contact institution. *Financial support:* Research assistantships, career-related internships or fieldwork, Federal Work-Study, institutionally sponsored loans, scholarships/grants, and tuition waivers (full and partial) available. Support available to part-time students. Financial award application deadline: 6/1; financial award applicants required to submit FAFSA. In 2006, 269 JDs, 7 master's awarded. *Degree program information:* Part-time and evening/weekend programs available. Offers entertainment and media law (LL M); law (JD). *Application deadline:* For fall admission, 4/1 for domestic and international students. Applications are processed on a rolling basis. *Application fee:* $50. Electronic applications accepted. *Application Contact:* Lisa Gear, Interim Director of Admissions, 213-738-6717, Fax: 213-383-1688, E-mail: admissions@swlaw.edu. *Dean,* Bryant Garth, 213-738-6710, Fax: 213-383-1688.

SOUTHWESTERN OKLAHOMA STATE UNIVERSITY, Weatherford, OK 73096-3098

General Information State-supported, coed, comprehensive institution. *Graduate housing:* Rooms and/or apartments available on a first-come, first-served basis to single and married students. Housing application deadline: 8/19. *Research affiliation:* Gulf Coast Research Laboratory.

GRADUATE UNITS

College of Arts and Sciences *Degree program information:* Part-time programs available. Offers art education (M Ed); arts and sciences (M Ed, MM); English (M Ed); mathematics (M Ed); music education (M Ed); natural sciences (M Ed); performance (MM); social sciences (M Ed).

College of Pharmacy Offers pharmacy (Pharm D).

College of Professional and Graduate Studies *Degree program information:* Part-time and evening/weekend programs available. Postbaccalaureate distance learning degree programs offered (minimal on-campus study).

School of Behavioral Sciences and Education *Degree program information:* Part-time and evening/weekend programs available. Postbaccalaureate distance learning degree programs offered (minimal on-campus study). Offers community counseling (M Ed); early childhood education (M Ed); educational administration (M Ed); elementary education (M Ed); health sciences and microbiology (M Ed); kinesiology (M Ed); parks and recreation management (M Ed); school counseling (M Ed); school psychology (MS); school psychometry (M Ed); secondary education (M Ed); special education (M Ed).

School of Business and Technology *Degree program information:* Part-time and evening/weekend programs available. Postbaccalaureate distance learning degree programs offered (minimal on-campus study). Offers business and technology (MBA). MBA distance learning degree program offered to Oklahoma residents only.

SOUTHWEST MINNESOTA STATE UNIVERSITY, Marshall, MN 56258

General Information State-supported, coed, comprehensive institution. *Enrollment:* 6,126 graduate, professional, and undergraduate students; 131 full-time matriculated graduate/professional students (93 women), 305 part-time matriculated graduate/professional students (223 women). *Enrollment by degree level:* 436 master's. *Graduate faculty:* 21 full-time (7 women), 3 part-time/adjunct (2 women). *Tuition, area resident:* Full-time $4,835. Tuition, state resident: full-time $4,835; part-time $269 per credit. Tuition, nonresident: part-time $269 per credit. *Required fees:* $589; $33 per credit. Tuition and fees vary according to course load and reciprocity agreements. *Graduate housing:* Room and/or apartments available to single students; on-campus housing not available to married students. *Student services:* Campus employment opportunities, campus safety program, career counseling, child daycare facilities, disabled student services, exercise/wellness program, free psychological counseling, international student services, low-cost health insurance, multicultural affairs office, teacher training, writing training. *Library facilities:* Southwest State University. *Online resources:* library catalog, web page, access to other libraries' catalogs. *Collection:* 197,057 titles, 768 serial subscriptions, 11,511 audiovisual materials.

Computer facilities: 350 computers available on campus for general student use. A campuswide network can be accessed from student residence rooms and from off campus. Internet access and online class registration are available. *Web address:* http://www.southwest.msus.edu/.

General Application Contact: Rich Shearer, Director of Enrollment Management, 507-537-6286, E-mail: shearerr@southwestmsu.edu.

GRADUATE UNITS

Department of Business Administration Students: 12 full-time (4 women), 60 part-time (28 women); includes 6 minority (3 African Americans, 3 Asian Americans or Pacific Islanders), 10 international. 18 applicants. *Faculty:* 13 full-time (3 women). Expenses: Contact institution. In 2006, 46 degrees awarded. Offers business administration (MBA); management (MS). *Application deadline:* Applications are processed on a rolling basis. *Application fee:* $20. Electronic applications accepted. *Application Contact:* Rich Shearer, Director of Enrollment Management, 507-537-6286, E-mail: shearerr@southwestmsu.edu. *Department Chair,* Dr. Mark Goodenow, 507-537-6260.

Department of Education Students: 119 full-time (89 women), 245 part-time (195 women); includes 5 minority (1 Asian American or Pacific Islander, 4 Hispanic Americans), 1 international. 148 applicants. *Faculty:* 8 full-time (4 women), 3 part-time/adjunct (2 women). Expenses: Contact institution. In 2006, 172 degrees awarded. Offers education (MS); education development and leadership (MS); special education (MS). *Application deadline:* Applications are processed on a rolling basis. *Application fee:* $20. *Application Contact:* Rich Shearer, Director of Enrollment Management, 507-537-6286, E-mail: shearerr@southwestmsu.edu. *Dean,* Donna Burgraff, 507-537-6218, E-mail: burgraff@southwestmsu.edu.

SPALDING UNIVERSITY, Louisville, KY 40203-2188

General Information Independent-religious, coed, comprehensive institution. CGS member. *Graduate housing:* Room and/or apartments available on a first-come, first-served basis to single students; on-campus housing not available to married students.

GRADUATE UNITS

Graduate Studies *Degree program information:* Part-time and evening/weekend programs available.

College of Business and Communication *Degree program information:* Part-time and evening/weekend programs available. Offers business communication (MS). Electronic applications accepted.

College of Education *Degree program information:* Part-time and evening/weekend programs available. Offers education (MA, MAT, Ed D); elementary school education (MAT); general education (MA); high school education (MAT); leadership education (Ed D); middle school education (MAT); school administration (MA); special education (learning and behavioral disorders) (MAT). Electronic applications accepted.

College of Health and Natural Sciences *Degree program information:* Part-time and evening/weekend programs available. Offers adult nurse practitioner (MSN); family nurse practitioner (MSN); health and natural sciences (MS, MSN); leadership in nursing and healthcare (MSN); occupational therapy (advanced-level) (MS); occupational therapy (entry-level) (MS); pediatric nurse practitioner (MSN).

College of Social Sciences and Humanities *Degree program information:* Part-time and evening/weekend programs available. Postbaccalaureate distance learning degree programs offered (minimal on-campus study). Offers clinical psychology (MA, Psy D); social sciences and humanities (MA, MFA, MSW, Psy D); social work (MSW); writing (MFA).

See Close-Up on page 1039.

SPERTUS INSTITUTE OF JEWISH STUDIES, Chicago, IL 60605-1901

General Information Independent, coed, graduate-only institution. *Enrollment by degree level:* 255 master's, 36 doctoral. *Graduate faculty:* 35 part-time/adjunct (12 women). *Graduate housing:* On-campus housing not available. *Student services:* Career counseling, grant writing training, international student services, writing training. *Library facilities:* Asher Library. *Online resources:* library catalog, web page. *Collection:* 115,000 titles, 558 serial subscriptions, 1,000 audiovisual materials.

Computer facilities: 7 computers available on campus for general student use. Internet access is available. *Web address:* http://www.spertus.edu/.

General Application Contact: Nadia Whiteside, Assistant Director of Recruitment and Alumni Affairs, 312-322-1707, Fax: 312-994-5360, E-mail: nwhiteside@spertus.edu.

GRADUATE UNITS

Graduate Programs Average age 39. 80 applicants, 81% accepted. *Faculty:* 35 part-time/adjunct (12 women). Expenses: Contact institution. *Financial support:* Scholarships/grants available. Support available to part-time students. Financial award applicants required to submit FAFSA. In 2006, 10 degrees awarded. *Degree program information:* Part-time and evening/weekend programs available. Postbaccalaureate distance learning degree programs offered (minimal on-campus study). Offers Jewish education (MAJ Ed); Jewish studies (MAJS, MSJE, MSJS, DJS, DSJS); nonprofit management (MSNM). *Application deadline:* Applications are processed on a rolling basis. *Application fee:* $50. *Application Contact:* Dr. Ellen LeVee, Assistant Dean of Jewish Studies, 312-322-1794, Fax: 312-994-5360, E-mail: elevee@spertus.edu. *Dean,* Dr. Dean Phillip Bell, 312-322-1791, Fax: 312-994-5360, E-mail: dbell@spertus.edu.

SPRING ARBOR UNIVERSITY, Spring Arbor, MI 49283-9799

General Information Independent-religious, coed, comprehensive institution. *Enrollment:* 3,714 graduate, professional, and undergraduate students; 759 full-time matriculated graduate/professional students (580 women), 425 part-time matriculated graduate/professional students (310 women). *Enrollment by degree level:* 1,184 master's. *Graduate faculty:* 21 full-time (5 women), 173 part-time/adjunct (76 women). *Tuition:* Full-time $4,200; part-time $350 per credit. *Required fees:* $140; $48 per term. Tuition and fees vary according to course load and program. *Graduate housing:* Rooms and/or apartments available on a first-come, first-served basis to single and married students. Typical cost: $2,850 per year for single students; $2,850 per year for married students. Housing application deadline: 5/1. *Student services:* Campus employment opportunities, campus safety program, career counseling. *Library facilities:* Hugh A. White Library. *Online resources:* library catalog, web page, access to other libraries' catalogs. *Collection:* 111,736 titles, 665 serial subscriptions, 3,775 audiovisual materials.

Computer facilities: 168 computers available on campus for general student use. A campuswide network can be accessed from student residence rooms and from off campus. Internet access and online class registration are available. *Web address:* http://www.arbor.edu/.

General Application Contact: Dale N. Glinz, Graduate Recruiter, Admissions Office, E-mail: dglinz@arbor.edu.

GRADUATE UNITS

School of Adult Studies Students: 575 full-time (443 women), 194 part-time (146 women); includes 161 minority (137 African Americans, 4 American Indian/Alaska Native, 2 Asian Americans or Pacific Islanders, 18 Hispanic Americans), 2 international. Average age 39. *Faculty:* 1 full-time (0 women), 140 part-time/adjunct (59 women). Expenses: Contact institution. *Financial support:* Scholarships/grants available. Support available to part-time students. Financial award applicants required to submit FAFSA. In 2006, 206 degrees awarded. *Degree program information:* Part-time and evening/weekend programs available. Postbaccalaureate distance learning degree programs offered (no on-campus study). Offers counseling (MAC); family studies (MAFS); organizational management (MAOM). *Application deadline:* Applications are processed on a rolling basis. *Application fee:* $30. Electronic applications accepted. *Application Contact:* Dr. Carl Pavey, Director, Graduate Studies, School of Adult Studies, 517-750-1200 Ext. 1653, Fax: 517-750-6602, E-mail: cpavey@arbor.edu. *Dean of Adult Studies,* Natalie Gianetti, 517-750-1200 Ext. 1343, Fax: 517-750-6602, E-mail: gianetti@arbor.edu.

School of Arts and Sciences Students: 50 full-time (32 women), 37 part-time (28 women); includes 12 minority (10 African Americans, 2 Hispanic Americans), 1 international. *Faculty:* 6 full-time (1 woman), 8 part-time/adjunct (3 women). Expenses: Contact institution. *Financial support:* Applicants required to submit FAFSA. *Degree program information:* Part-time programs available. Postbaccalaureate distance learning degree programs offered (no on-campus study). Offers communication (MA); spiritual formation and leadership (MA). *Application fee:* $30. *Application Contact:* Carol Bunnell, Secretary, Department of Communication, 517-750-6483, E-mail: cbunnell@arbor.edu. *Chair of the Department of Communication,* Dr. Wally Metts, 517-750-1200 Ext. 1491, E-mail: wmetts@arbor.edu.

School of Business and Management Students: 40 full-time (21 women), 55 part-time (28 women); includes 10 minority (6 African Americans, 1 Asian American or Pacific Islander, 3 Hispanic Americans), 4 international. Average age 37. 28 applicants, 71% accepted, 18 enrolled. *Faculty:* 9 full-time (3 women), 9 part-time/adjunct (5 women). Expenses: Contact institution. *Financial support:* Career-related internships or fieldwork, scholarships/grants, and tuition waivers (partial) available. Support available to part-time students. Financial award application deadline: 8/25; financial award applicants required to submit FAFSA. In 2006, 41 degrees awarded. *Degree program information:* Part-time and evening/weekend programs available. Offers business and management (MBA). *Application deadline:* Applications are processed on a rolling basis. *Application fee:* $30. *Application Contact:* Michelle Coats, Secretary, School of Business and Management, 517-750-6315, Fax: 517-750-6624, E-mail: mcoats@arbor.edu. *Director, MBA Program,* Dr. Caleb K. Chan, 517-750-6538, Fax: 517-750-6624, E-mail: cchan@arbor.edu.

School of Education Students: 15 full-time (12 women), 218 part-time (180 women); includes 13 minority (11 African Americans, 1 Asian American or Pacific Islander, 1 Hispanic American). *Faculty:* 5 full-time (1 woman), 16 part-time/adjunct (9 women). Expenses: Contact institution. *Financial support:* Applicants required to submit FAFSA. In 2006, 69 degrees awarded. *Degree program information:* Part-time programs available. Offers education (MAE). *Application deadline:* For fall admission, 9/1 priority date for domestic students; for winter admission, 2/1 priority date for domestic students; for spring admission, 2/1 priority date for domestic students. Applications are processed on a rolling basis. *Application fee:* $30. Electronic applications accepted. *Application Contact:* Deb Scott, Graduate Coordinator, 517-750-6677, Fax: 517-750-6629, E-mail: debs@arbor.edu. *Interim Dean of Education,* Carla Koontz, 517-750-6334, Fax: 517-750-6629, E-mail: ckoontz@arbor.edu.

SPRINGFIELD COLLEGE, Springfield, MA 01109-3797

General Information Independent, coed, comprehensive institution. *Enrollment:* 1,170 full-time matriculated graduate/professional students, 323 part-time matriculated graduate/professional students. *Enrollment by degree level:* 1,492 master's, 1 doctoral. *Graduate faculty:* 156 full-time (78 women), 98 part-time/adjunct (46 women). *Tuition:* Full-time $12,222; part-time $679 per credit. *Required fees:* $25; $25 per year. One-time fee: $25 full-time. *Graduate housing:* Rooms and/or apartments available on a first-come, first-served basis to single and married students. Housing application deadline: 5/1. *Student services:* Campus employment opportunities, campus safety program, career counseling, child daycare facilities, disabled student services, exercise/wellness program, free psychological counseling, international student services, low-cost health insurance, multicultural affairs office, teacher training, writing training. *Library facilities:* Babson Library. *Collection:* 125,000 titles, 850 serial subscriptions.

Computer facilities: Computer purchase and lease plans are available. 95 computers available on campus for general student use. A campuswide network can be accessed from student residence rooms and from off campus. Internet access is available. *Web address:* http://www.spfldcol.edu/.

General Application Contact: Donald James Shaw, Director of Graduate Admissions, 413-748-3060, Fax: 413-748-3069, E-mail: donald_shaw_jr@spfldcol.edu.

GRADUATE UNITS

Graduate Programs Students: 1,170 full-time, 323 part-time. Average age 34. 726 applicants, 79% accepted, 357 enrolled. *Faculty:* 156 full-time (78 women), 98 part-time/adjunct (46 women). Expenses: Contact institution. *Financial support:* In 2006–07, 4 fellowships with partial tuition reimbursements, 196 teaching assistantships with partial tuition reimbursements were awarded; career-related internships or fieldwork, Federal Work-Study, institutionally sponsored loans, scholarships/grants, traineeships, and tuition waivers (full and partial) also available. Financial award application deadline: 3/1; financial award applicants required to submit FAFSA. In 2006, 613 master's, 4 doctorates, 4 other advanced degrees awarded. *Degree program information:* Part-time and evening/weekend programs available. Offers adapted physical education (M Ed, MPE, MS); advanced level coaching (M Ed, MPE, MS); alcohol rehabilitation/substance abuse counseling (M Ed, MS, CAS); art therapy (M Ed, MS, CAS); athletic administration (M Ed, MPE, MS); athletic counseling (M Ed, MS, CAS); biomechanics (MS); counseling and secondary education (M Ed, MS); deaf counseling (M Ed, MS, CAS); developmental disabilities (M Ed, MS, CAS); education (M Ed, MS); exercise physiology (MS, DPE); general counseling (M Ed); general counseling and casework (M Ed, MS, CAS); general physical education (DPE, CAS); health care management (MS); health education licensure (MPE, MS); health education licensure program (M Ed); human services (MS); industrial/organizational psychology (MS, CAS); interdisciplinary movement sciences (MS); marriage and family therapy (M Ed, MS, CAS); mental health counseling (M Ed, MS, CAS); occupational therapy (M Ed, MS, CAS); outdoor recreational management (M Ed, MS); physical education licensure (MPE, MS); physical education licensure program (M Ed); physical therapy (MS); physician assistant studies (MS); psychiatric rehabilitation/mental health counseling (M Ed, MS, CAS); recreational management (M Ed, MS); school guidance and counseling (M Ed, MS, CAS); special services (M Ed, MS, CAS); sport management (M Ed, MS); sport performance (M Ed, MPE, MS); sport psychology (MS, DPE); student personnel in higher education (M Ed, MS, CAS); teaching and administration (MS); therapeutic recreational management (M Ed, MS); vocational evaluation and work adjustment (M Ed, MS, CAS). *Application deadline:* For fall admission, 1/15 priority date for domestic and international students; for winter admission, 11/1 priority date for domestic and international students; for spring admission, 11/1 priority date for domestic and international students. Applications are processed on a rolling basis. *Application fee:* $50. Electronic applications accepted. *Application Contact:* Director of Graduate Admissions, 413-748-3225, Fax: 413-748-3694. *Dean,* Dr. Betty L. Mann, 413-748-3125, Fax: 413-748-3764.

School of Social Work Students: 249. Average age 34. 244 applicants, 72% accepted, 110 enrolled. *Faculty:* 11 full-time (5 women), 29 part-time/adjunct (20 women). Expenses: Contact institution. *Financial support:* Fellowships with partial tuition reimbursements, teaching assistantships with partial tuition reimbursements, career-related internships or fieldwork, Federal Work-Study, institutionally sponsored loans, scholarships/grants, and unspecified assistantships available. Financial award application deadline: 3/1. In 2006, 97 degrees awarded. *Degree program information:* Part-time and evening/weekend programs available. Offers advanced generalist (MSW); advanced standing (MSW); practice with children and adolescents (PMC). *Application deadline:* For fall admission, 3/1 priority date for domestic students. Applications are processed on a rolling basis. *Application fee:* $50. Electronic applications accepted. *Application Contact:* Donald James Shaw, Director of Graduate Admissions, 413-748-3060, Fax: 413-748-3069, E-mail: donald_shaw_jr@spfldcol.edu. *Dean,* Dr. Francine Vecchiolla, 413-748-3060, Fax: 413-748-3069, E-mail: francine_vecchiolla@spfldcol.edu.

See Close-Up on page 1041.

SPRING HILL COLLEGE, Mobile, AL 36608-1791

General Information Independent-religious, coed, comprehensive institution. *Enrollment:* 1,446 graduate, professional, and undergraduate students; 23 full-time matriculated graduate/professional students (19 women), 169 part-time matriculated graduate/professional students (107 women). *Enrollment by degree level:* 192 master's. *Graduate faculty:* 16 full-time (7 women), 17 part-time/adjunct (10 women). *Tuition:* Part-time $242 per credit hour. *Graduate housing:* On-campus housing not available. *Student services:* Career counseling, free psychological counseling, international student services, low-cost health insurance, multicultural affairs office, teacher training. *Library facilities:* Marnie and John Burke Memorial Library plus 1 other. *Online resources:* library catalog, web page, access to other libraries' catalogs. *Collection:* 185,868 titles, 2,200 serial subscriptions, 1,201 audiovisual materials.

Computer facilities: 194 computers available on campus for general student use. A campuswide network can be accessed from student residence rooms and from off campus. Internet access is available. *Web address:* http://www.shc.edu/.

General Application Contact: Joyce Genz, Dean of Life Long Learning and Director of Graduate Programs, 251-380-3094, Fax: 251-460-2190, E-mail: grad@shc.edu.

GRADUATE UNITS

Graduate Programs Students: 23 full-time (19 women), 169 part-time (107 women); includes 44 minority (37 African Americans, 2 American Indian/Alaska Native, 1 Asian American or Pacific Islander, 4 Hispanic Americans), 4 international. Average age 40. *Faculty:* 16 full-time (7 women), 17 part-time/adjunct (10 women). Expenses: Contact institution. *Financial support:* In 2006–07, 107 students received support. Career-related internships or fieldwork and scholarships/grants available. Support available to part-time students. Financial award applicants required to submit FAFSA. In 2006, 50 degrees awarded. *Degree program information:* Part-time and evening/weekend programs available. Offers business administration (MBA); clinical nurse leader (MSN); early childhood education (MAT, MS Ed); elementary education (MAT, MS Ed); liberal arts (MLA); secondary education (MAT, MS Ed); theology (MA, MPS, MTS). *Application deadline:* For fall admission, 8/1 priority date for domestic students, 6/1 priority date for international students; for spring admission, 12/1 priority date for domestic students, 11/1 priority date for international students. Applications are processed on a rolling basis. *Application fee:* $25 ($35 for international students). Electronic applications accepted. *Dean of Life Long Learning and Director of Graduate Programs,* Joyce Genz, 251-380-3094, Fax: 251-460-2190, E-mail: grad@shc.edu.

STANFORD UNIVERSITY, Stanford, CA 94305-9991

General Information Independent, coed, university. CGS member. *Graduate housing:* Rooms and/or apartments guaranteed to single and married students. Housing application deadline: 5/5.

GRADUATE UNITS

Graduate School of Business Offers business (MBA, PhD). Electronic applications accepted.

Law School Offers law (JD, JSM, MLS, JSD). Electronic applications accepted.

School of Earth Sciences Offers earth sciences (MS, PhD, Eng); earth systems (MS); geological and environmental sciences (MS, PhD, Eng); geophysics (MS, PhD); petroleum engineering (MS, PhD, Eng). Electronic applications accepted.

School of Education Offers administration and policy analysis (Ed D, PhD); anthropology of education (PhD); art education (MA, PhD); child and adolescent development (PhD); counseling psychology (PhD); dance education (MA); economics of education (PhD); education (MA, Ed D, PhD); educational linguistics (PhD); educational psychology (PhD); English education

Stanford University (continued)

(MA, PhD); evaluation (MA); general curriculum studies (MA, PhD); higher education (PhD); history of education (PhD); interdisciplinary studies (PhD); international comparative education (MA, PhD); international education administration and policy analysis (MA); languages education (MA); learning, design, and technology (MA, PhD); mathematics education (MA, PhD); philosophy of education (PhD); policy analysis (MA); prospective principal's program (MA); science education (MA, PhD); social studies education (MA, PhD); sociology of education (PhD); symbolic systems in education (PhD); teacher education (MA, PhD). Electronic applications accepted.

School of Engineering Offers aeronautics and astronautics (MS, PhD, Eng); biomechanical engineering (MS); chemical engineering (MS, PhD, Eng); civil and environmental engineering (MS, PhD, Eng); computer science (MS, PhD); electrical engineering (MS, PhD, Eng); engineering (MS, PhD, Eng); management science and engineering (MS, PhD); materials science and engineering (MS, PhD, Eng); mechanical engineering (MS, PhD, Eng); product design (MS); scientific computing and computational mathematics (MS, PhD). Electronic applications accepted.

School of Humanities and Sciences Offers anthropological sciences (MA, MS, PhD); applied physics (MS, PhD); art history (PhD); art practice (MFA); biological sciences (MS, PhD); biophysics (PhD); chemistry (PhD); Chinese (MA, PhD); classics (MA, PhD); communication (journalism specialization) (MA); communication theory and research (PhD); comparative literature (PhD); computer-based music theory and acoustics (MA, PhD); cultural and social anthropology (MA, PhD); drama (PhD); economics (PhD); English (MA, PhD); financial mathematics (MS); French (MA, PhD); German studies (MA, PhD); history (MA, PhD); humanities (MA); humanities and sciences (MA, MFA, MS, DMA, PhD); international policy studies (MA); Italian (MA, PhD); Japanese (MA, PhD); linguistics (MA, PhD); mathematics (MS, PhD); modern thought and literature (PhD); music composition (MA, DMA); music history (MA); music, science, and technology (MA); musicology (PhD); philosophy (MA, PhD); physics (PhD); political science (MA, PhD); psychology (PhD); religious studies (MA, PhD); Russian (MA); Slavic languages and literatures (PhD); sociology (PhD); Spanish (MA, PhD); statistics (MS, PhD). Electronic applications accepted.

Center for East Asian Studies Offers East Asian studies (MA). Electronic applications accepted.

Center for Russian and East European Studies Offers Russian and East European studies (MA). Electronic applications accepted.

School of Medicine Offers bioengineering (MS, PhD); medicine (MD, MS, PhD). Electronic applications accepted.

Graduate Programs in Medicine Offers biochemistry (PhD); biomedical informatics (MS, PhD); cancer biology (PhD); developmental biology (PhD); epidemiology (MS, PhD); genetics (PhD); health services research (MS); immunology (PhD); medicine (MS, PhD); microbiology and immunology (PhD); molecular and cellular physiology (PhD); molecular pharmacology (PhD); neurosciences (PhD); structural biology (PhD). Electronic applications accepted.

STARR KING SCHOOL FOR THE MINISTRY, Berkeley, CA 94709-1209

General Information Independent-religious, coed, graduate-only institution. *Graduate housing:* On-campus housing not available.

GRADUATE UNITS

Professional Program Offers theology (M Div).

STATE UNIVERSITY OF NEW YORK AT BINGHAMTON, Binghamton, NY 13902-6000

General Information State-supported, coed, university. CGS member. *Enrollment:* 14,373 graduate, professional, and undergraduate students; 1,589 full-time matriculated graduate/professional students (749 women), 1,157 part-time matriculated graduate/professional students (631 women). *Enrollment by degree level:* 1,590 master's, 1,156 doctoral. *Graduate faculty:* 461 full-time (162 women), 211 part-time/adjunct (92 women). *Graduate housing:* On-campus housing not available. *Student services:* Campus employment opportunities, career counseling, child daycare facilities, disabled student services, exercise/wellness program, free psychological counseling, grant writing training, international student services, low-cost health insurance, teacher training. *Library facilities:* Glenn G. Bartle Library plus 1 other. *Online resources:* library catalog, web page, access to other libraries' catalogs. *Collection:* 2.3 million titles, 41,985 serial subscriptions, 128,055 audiovisual materials. *Research affiliation:* IBM (engineering), Matco Company (engineering), Lockheed Martin Corporation (engineering, management, mathematics), Universal Instruments (engineering).

Computer facilities: Computer purchase and lease plans are available. 7,200 computers available on campus for general student use. A campuswide network can be accessed from student residence rooms and from off campus. Internet access and online class registration are available. *Web address:* http://www.binghamton.edu/.

General Application Contact: Dr. Nancy E. Stamp, Vice Provost and Dean of the Graduate School, 607-777-2070, Fax: 607-777-2501, E-mail: nstamp@binghamton.edu.

GRADUATE UNITS

Graduate School Students: 1,589 full-time (749 women), 1,157 part-time; includes 300 minority (104 African Americans, 3 American Indian/Alaska Native, 113 Asian Americans or Pacific Islanders, 80 Hispanic Americans), 868 international. Average age 32. 3,275 applicants, 58% accepted, 698 enrolled. *Faculty:* 461 full-time (162 women), 211 part-time/adjunct (92 women). Expenses: Contact institution. *Financial support:* In 2006–07, 1,169 students received support, including 138 fellowships with full tuition reimbursements available (averaging $6,332 per year), 188 research assistantships with full tuition reimbursements available (averaging $7,370 per year), 612 teaching assistantships with full tuition reimbursements available (averaging $8,074 per year); career-related internships or fieldwork, Federal Work-Study, institutionally sponsored loans, traineeships, tuition waivers (full and partial), and unspecified assistantships also available. Support available to part-time students. Financial award application deadline: 2/15; financial award applicants required to submit FAFSA. In 2006, 539 master's, 103 doctorates awarded. *Degree program information:* Part-time and evening/weekend programs available. *Application deadline:* For fall admission, 4/5 priority date for domestic students, 1/15 for international students; for spring admission, 11/1 for domestic students, 10/1 for international students. Applications are processed on a rolling basis. *Application fee:* $60. Electronic applications accepted. *Application Contact:* Cheryl Foster, Assistant Dean of the Graduate School, 607-777-2151, Fax: 607-777-2501, E-mail: cfoster@binghamton.edu. *Vice Provost and Dean of the Graduate School,* Dr. Nancy E. Stamp, 607-777-2070, Fax: 607-777-2501, E-mail: nstamp@binghamton.edu.

College of Community and Public Affairs Students: 78 full-time (40 women), 32 part-time (30 women); includes 10 minority (5 African Americans, 2 American Indian/Alaska Native, 1 Asian American or Pacific Islander, 2 Hispanic Americans), 6 international. Average age 33. 51 applicants, 82% accepted, 23 enrolled. *Faculty:* 2 full-time (0 women), 1 part-time/adjunct (0 women). Expenses: Contact institution. *Financial support:* In 2006–07, 10 students received support, including 6 teaching assistantships with full tuition reimbursements available (averaging $5,467 per year); research assistantships, career-related internships or fieldwork, Federal Work-Study, institutionally sponsored loans, and unspecified assistantships also available. Support available to part-time students. Financial award application deadline: 2/15. In 2006, 10 degrees awarded. *Degree program information:* Part-time and evening/weekend programs available. Offers community and public affairs (MASS, MPA, MSW); social science (MASS). *Application deadline:* For fall admission, 4/15 priority date for domestic students, 1/15 priority date for international students; for spring admission, 11/1 for domestic students, 10/1 priority date for international students. Applications are processed on a rolling basis. *Application fee:* $60. Electronic applications accepted. *Dean,* Dr. Patricia Ingraham, 607-777-5572, Fax: 607-777-2406, E-mail: pingraham@binghamton.edu.

Decker School of Nursing Students: 44 full-time (39 women), 36 part-time (35 women); includes 4 minority (3 African Americans, 1 Asian American or Pacific Islander), 6 international. Average age 40. 33 applicants, 97% accepted. *Faculty:* 30 full-time (28 women), 9 part-time/adjunct (8 women). Expenses: Contact institution. *Financial support:* In 2006–07, 43 students received support, including 7 fellowships with partial tuition reimbursements available (averaging $7,743 per year), 3 research assistantships with full tuition reimbursements available (averaging $7,233 per year), 12 teaching assistantships with full tuition reimbursements available (averaging $6,325 per year); career-related internships or fieldwork, Federal Work-Study, institutionally sponsored loans, traineeships, tuition waivers (full and partial), and unspecified assistantships also available. Support available to part-time students. Financial award application deadline: 2/15. In 2006, 24 master's, 4 doctorates, 5 Certificates awarded. *Degree program information:* Part-time and evening/weekend programs available. Offers nursing (MS, PhD, Certificate). *Application deadline:* For fall admission, 4/15 priority date for domestic students, 1/15 priority date for international students; for spring admission, 11/1 for domestic students, 10/1 priority date for international students. Applications are processed on a rolling basis. Electronic applications accepted. *Application Contact:* Theresa Grabo, Director of Graduate Studies, 607-777-6163, Fax: 607-777-4440, E-mail: tgrabo@binghamton.edu. *Dean,* Dr. Joyce Ferrario, 607-777-2311, Fax: 607-777-4440, E-mail: jferrari@binghamton.edu.

School of Arts and Sciences Students: 698 full-time (354 women), 398 part-time (227 women); includes 138 minority (46 African Americans, 4 American Indian/Alaska Native, 38 Asian Americans or Pacific Islanders, 50 Hispanic Americans), 282 international. Average age 32. 1,109 applicants, 47% accepted, 206 enrolled. *Faculty:* 301 full-time (92 women), 141 part-time/adjunct (55 women). Expenses: Contact institution. *Financial support:* In 2006–07, 590 students received support, including 84 fellowships with full tuition reimbursements available (averaging $7,850 per year), 64 research assistantships with full tuition reimbursements available (averaging $9,300 per year), 434 teaching assistantships with full tuition reimbursements available (averaging $8,527 per year); career-related internships or fieldwork, Federal Work-Study, institutionally sponsored loans, tuition waivers (full and partial), and unspecified assistantships also available. Support available to part-time students. Financial award application deadline: 2/15. In 2006, 143 master's, 84 doctorates awarded. *Degree program information:* Part-time and evening/weekend programs available. Offers analytical chemistry (PhD); anthropology (MA, PhD); applied physics (MS); art history (MA, PhD); arts and sciences (MA, MM, MS, PhD, Certificate); behavioral neuroscience (MA, PhD); biological sciences (MA, PhD); chemistry (MA, MS); clinical psychology (MA, PhD); cognitive and behavioral science (MA, PhD); comparative literature (MA, PhD); computer science (MA, PhD); economics (MA, PhD); economics and finance (MA, PhD); English (MA, PhD); French (MA); geography (MA); geological sciences (MA, PhD); history (MA, PhD); inorganic chemistry (PhD); Italian (MA); music (MA, MM); organic chemistry (PhD); philosophy (MA, PhD); physical chemistry (PhD); physics (MA, MS); political science (MA, PhD); probability and statistics (MA, PhD); public policy (MA, PhD); social, legal and legal philosophy (MA, PhD); sociology (MA, PhD); Spanish (MA, Certificate); theater (MA); translation (Certificate); translation research and instruction (Certificate). *Application deadline:* For fall admission, 4/15 priority date for domestic students, 1/15 priority date for international students; for spring admission, 11/1 for domestic students, 10/1 priority date for international students. Applications are processed on a rolling basis. *Application fee:* $60. Electronic applications accepted. *Dean,* Dr. Jean-Pierre Mileur, 607-777-2144, E-mail: jpmileur@binghamton.edu.

School of Education Students: 184 full-time (122 women), 204 part-time (163 women); includes 36 minority (16 African Americans, 1 American Indian/Alaska Native, 6 Asian Americans or Pacific Islanders, 13 Hispanic Americans), 5 international. Average age 32. 239 applicants, 70% accepted. *Faculty:* 23 full-time (14 women), 18 part-time/adjunct (13 women). Expenses: Contact institution. *Financial support:* In 2006–07, 70 students received support, including 14 fellowships with full tuition reimbursements available (averaging $6,866 per year), 6 research assistantships with full tuition reimbursements available (averaging $5,775 per year), 44 teaching assistantships with full tuition reimbursements available (averaging $5,880 per year); career-related internships or fieldwork, Federal Work-Study, institutionally sponsored loans, tuition waivers (full and partial), and unspecified assistantships also available. Support available to part-time students. Financial award application deadline: 2/15. In 2006, 132 master's, 5 doctorates awarded. *Degree program information:* Part-time and evening/weekend programs available. Offers biology education (MAT, MS Ed, MST); early childhood and elementary education (MS Ed); earth science education (MAT, MS Ed, MST); education (MAT, MS Ed, MST, Ed D); educational theory and practice (Ed D); English education (MAT, MS Ed, MST); French education (MAT, MST); mathematical sciences education (MAT, MS Ed, MST); physics (MAT, MS Ed, MST); reading education (MS Ed); social studies (MAT, MS Ed, MST); Spanish education (MAT, MST); special education (MS Ed). *Application deadline:* For fall admission, 4/15 priority date for domestic students, 1/15 priority date for international students; for spring admission, 11/1 for domestic students, 10/1 priority date for international students. Applications are processed on a rolling basis. *Application fee:* $60. Electronic applications accepted. *Interim Dean,* Dr. Susan Strahle, 607-777-7329, E-mail: sstrahle@binghamton.edu.

School of Management Students: 267 full-time (112 women), 31 part-time (11 women); includes 19 minority (3 African Americans, 16 Asian Americans or Pacific Islanders), 143 international. Average age 29. 514 applicants, 52% accepted. *Faculty:* 38 full-time (8 women), 15 part-time/adjunct (2 women). Expenses: Contact institution. *Financial support:* In 2006–07, 44 students received support, including 1 fellowship with full tuition reimbursement available (averaging $8,700 per year), 39 teaching assistantships with full tuition reimbursements available (averaging $7,127 per year); research assistantships, career-related internships or fieldwork, Federal Work-Study, institutionally sponsored loans, tuition waivers (partial), and unspecified assistantships also available. Support available to part-time students. Financial award application deadline: 2/15. In 2006, 114 master's, 2 doctorates awarded. *Degree program information:* Part-time and evening/weekend programs available. Offers accounting (MS, PhD); business administration (MBA, PhD); health care professional executive (MBA); management (MBA, MS, PhD). *Application deadline:* For fall admission, 4/15 priority date for domestic students, 1/15 priority date for international students; for spring admission, 11/1 for domestic students, 10/1 priority date for international students. Applications are processed on a rolling basis. *Application fee:* $60. Electronic applications accepted. *Dean,* Dr. Upinder S. Dhillon, 607-777-2314, E-mail: dhillon@binghamton.edu.

Thomas J. Watson School of Engineering and Applied Science Students: 351 full-time (57 women), 244 part-time (48 women); includes 52 minority (17 African Americans, 31 Asian Americans or Pacific Islanders, 4 Hispanic Americans), 365 international. Average age 28. 1,055 applicants, 41% accepted. *Faculty:* 50 full-time (6 women), 24 part-time/adjunct (6 women). Expenses: Contact institution. *Financial support:* In 2006–07, 7 fellowships with full tuition reimbursements (averaging $6,476 per year), 112 research assistantships with full tuition reimbursements (averaging $6,360 per year), 80 teaching assistantships with full tuition reimbursements (averaging $7,583 per year) were awarded; career-related internships or fieldwork, Federal Work-Study, institutionally sponsored loans, tuition waivers (full and partial), and unspecified assistantships also available. Support available to part-time students. Financial award application deadline: 2/15. In 2006, 104 master's, 7 doctorates awarded. *Degree program information:* Part-time and evening/weekend programs available. Offers computer science (M Eng, MS, PhD); electrical and computer engineering (M Eng, MS, PhD); engineering and applied science (M Eng, MS, MSAT, PhD); materials science and engineering (MS, PhD); mechanical engineering (M Eng, MS, PhD); systems science and industrial engineering (M Eng, MS, MSAT, PhD). *Application deadline:* For fall admission, 4/15 priority date for domestic students, 1/15 priority date for international students; for spring admission, 11/1 for domestic students, 10/1 priority date for international students. Applications are processed on a rolling basis. *Application fee:* $60. Electronic applications accepted. *Dean,* Dr. Seshu Desu, 607-777-2871, E-mail: sdesu@binghamton.edu.

STATE UNIVERSITY OF NEW YORK AT FREDONIA, Fredonia, NY 14063-1136

General Information State-supported, coed, comprehensive institution. *Enrollment:* 5,540 graduate, professional, and undergraduate students; 169 full-time matriculated graduate/professional students (106 women), 171 part-time matriculated graduate/professional students (73 women). *Enrollment by degree level:* 336 master's, 4 other advanced degrees. *Graduate faculty:* 65 full-time (31 women), 9 part-time/adjunct (4 women). Tuition, state resident: full-time $6,900; part-time $288 per credit hour. Tuition, nonresident: full-time $10,920; part-time $455 per credit hour. *Required fees:* $1,132; $47 per credit hour. *Graduate housing:* Room and/or apartments available on a first-come, first-served basis to single students; on-campus housing not available to married students. Typical cost: $4,750 per year ($8,120 including board). Housing application deadline: 7/15. *Student services:* Campus employment opportunities, campus safety program, career counseling, child daycare facilities, free psychological counseling, international student services, low-cost health insurance. *Library facilities:* Reed Library. *Online resources:* library catalog, web page, access to other libraries' catalogs. *Collection:* 396,000 titles, 2,270 serial subscriptions.

Computer facilities: 500 computers available on campus for general student use. A campuswide network can be accessed from student residence rooms and from off campus. *Web address:* http://www.fredonia.edu/.

General Application Contact: Dr. Jacqueline Swansinger, Interim Dean of Graduate Studies, 716-673-3808, Fax: 716-673-3338, E-mail: jacqueline.swansinger@fredonia.edu.

GRADUATE UNITS

Graduate Studies Students: 169 full-time (106 women), 171 part-time (73 women); includes 4 minority (2 American Indian/Alaska Native, 2 Asian Americans or Pacific Islanders). Average age 27. *Faculty:* 65 full-time (31 women), 9 part-time/adjunct (4 women). Expenses: Contact institution. *Financial support:* In 2006–07, 27 teaching assistantships with partial tuition reimbursements (averaging $5,216 per year) were awarded; research assistantships, career-related internships or fieldwork and tuition waivers (full and partial) also available. Support available to part-time students. Financial award application deadline: 3/15. In 2006, 209 master's, 7 other advanced degrees awarded. *Degree program information:* Part-time and evening/weekend programs available. Offers accounting (MS); biology (MS, MS Ed); chemistry (MS); curriculum and instruction science education (MS Ed); English (MA, MS Ed); interdisciplinary studies (MA, MS); mathematical sciences (MS Ed); speech pathology and audiology (MS, MS Ed). *Application deadline:* For fall admission, 8/5 for domestic students; for spring admission, 12/1 for domestic students. Applications are processed on a rolling basis. *Application fee:* $50. Electronic applications accepted. *Dean of Graduate Studies (Interim),* Dr. Jacqueline Swansinger, 716-673-3808, Fax: 716-673-3338, E-mail: jacqueline.swansinger@fredonia.edu.

College of Education Students: 77 full-time (31 women), 131 part-time (46 women); includes 5 minority (2 American Indian/Alaska Native, 3 Hispanic Americans). Average age 28. *Faculty:* 19 full-time (12 women), 4 part-time/adjunct (0 women). Expenses: Contact institution. *Financial support:* In 2006–07, 10 teaching assistantships with partial tuition reimbursements (averaging $6,193 per year) were awarded; research assistantships, career-related internships or fieldwork and tuition waivers (full and partial) also available. Support available to part-time students. Financial award application deadline: 3/15. In 2006, 127 master's, 7 other advanced degrees awarded. *Degree program information:* Part-time and evening/weekend programs available. Offers educational administration (CAS); elementary education (MS Ed); literacy (MS Ed); secondary education (MS Ed); teaching English to speakers of other languages (MS Ed). *Application deadline:* For fall admission, 8/5 for domestic students; for spring admission, 12/1 for domestic students. *Application fee:* $50. *Dean,* Dr. Christine Givner, 716-673-3311, E-mail: christine.givner@fredonia.edu.

School of Music Students: 24 full-time (14 women), 17 part-time (14 women). Average age 27. *Faculty:* 12 full-time (3 women), 2 part-time/adjunct (1 woman). Expenses: Contact institution. *Financial support:* In 2006–07, 3 teaching assistantships with partial tuition reimbursements (averaging $6,620 per year) were awarded; research assistantships, tuition waivers (full and partial) also available. Support available to part-time students. Financial award application deadline: 3/15. In 2006, 26 degrees awarded. *Degree program information:* Part-time and evening/weekend programs available. Offers music (MM); music education (MM). *Application deadline:* For fall admission, 8/5 for domestic students; for spring admission, 12/1 for domestic students. *Application fee:* $50. *Director,* Dr. Karl Boelter, 716-673-3151, E-mail: karl.boelter@fredonia.edu.

STATE UNIVERSITY OF NEW YORK AT NEW PALTZ, New Paltz, NY 12561

General Information State-supported, coed, comprehensive institution. *Enrollment:* 7,699 graduate, professional, and undergraduate students; 525 full-time matriculated graduate/professional students (321 women), 725 part-time matriculated graduate/professional students (503 women). *Enrollment by degree level:* 1,184 master's, 66 other advanced degrees. *Graduate faculty:* 185 full-time (96 women), 218 part-time/adjunct (135 women). Tuition, state resident: full-time $6,900; part-time $288 per credit hour. Tuition, nonresident: full-time $10,920; part-time $455 per credit hour. *Graduate housing:* On-campus housing not available. *Student services:* Campus employment opportunities, campus safety program, career counseling, child daycare facilities, free psychological counseling, low-cost health insurance. *Library facilities:* Sojourner Truth Library. *Online resources:* library catalog, web page. *Collection:* 532,381 titles, 1,515 serial subscriptions, 1,614 audiovisual materials.

Computer facilities: 600 computers available on campus for general student use. A campuswide network can be accessed from student residence rooms and from off campus. Internet access and online class registration, e-mail are available. *Web address:* http://www.newpaltz.edu/.

General Application Contact: Caroline Murphy, Graduate Admissions Advisor, 845-257-3285, Fax: 845-257-3284, E-mail: gradschool@newpaltz.edu.

GRADUATE UNITS

Graduate School Students: 525 full-time (321 women), 725 part-time (503 women); includes 114 minority (26 African Americans, 3 American Indian/Alaska Native, 29 Asian Americans or Pacific Islanders, 56 Hispanic Americans), 178 international. Average age 31. 1,567 applicants. *Faculty:* 185 full-time (96 women), 218 part-time/adjunct (135 women). Expenses: Contact institution. *Financial support:* In 2006–07, 11 fellowships with partial tuition reimbursements, 16 research assistantships with partial tuition reimbursements (averaging $5,000 per year), 43 teaching assistantships with partial tuition reimbursements (averaging $5,000 per year) were awarded; career-related internships or fieldwork, Federal Work-Study, institutionally sponsored loans, tuition waivers (full), and unspecified assistantships also available. Support available to part-time students. Financial award applicants required to submit FAFSA. In 2006, 465 master's, 67 other advanced degrees awarded. *Degree program information:* Part-time and evening/weekend programs available. *Application deadline:* For fall admission, 5/15 priority date for domestic students, 5/15 for international students; for spring admission, 11/15 for domestic and international students. Applications are processed on a rolling basis. *Application fee:* $50. Electronic applications accepted. *Application Contact:* Caroline Murphy, Graduate Admissions Advisor, 845-257-3285, Fax: 845-257-3284, E-mail: gradschool@newpaltz.edu. *Associate Provost for Academic Affairs/Dean of the Graduate School,* Dr. Laurel M. Garrick-Duhaney, 845-257-3285, Fax: 845-257-3284, E-mail: gradschool@newpaltz.edu.

Faculty of Education Students: 210 full-time (168 women), 492 part-time (368 women); includes 66 minority (21 African Americans, 2 American Indian/Alaska Native, 8 Asian Americans or Pacific Islanders, 35 Hispanic Americans), 7 international. Average age 32. 540 applicants. *Faculty:* 33 full-time (24 women), 97 part-time/adjunct (64 women). Expenses: Contact institution. *Financial support:* Career-related internships or fieldwork, Federal Work-Study, and institutionally sponsored loans available. In 2006, 269 master's, 67 other advanced degrees awarded. *Degree program information:* Part-time and evening/weekend programs available. Offers adolescence (7-12) (MS Ed); childhood (1-6) (MS Ed); childhood education (MS Ed); childhood education (1-6) (MST); early childhood education (B-2) (MST); education (MAT, MPS, MS Ed, MST, CAS); educational administration (MS Ed, CAS); English as a second language (MS Ed); humanistic/multicultural education (MPS); literacy education (5-12) (MS Ed); literacy education (B-6) (MS Ed); secondary education (MAT, MS Ed); special education (MS Ed). *Application deadline:* For fall admission, 3/1 priority date for domestic and international students; for spring admission, 10/1 priority date for domestic and international students. *Application fee:* $50. Electronic applications accepted. *Dean,* Dr. Robert Michael, 845-257-2800.

Faculty of Fine and Performing Arts Students: 58 full-time (39 women), 30 part-time (16 women); includes 7 minority (1 Asian American or Pacific Islander, 6 Hispanic Americans), 14 international. Average age 30. 211 applicants. *Faculty:* 30 full-time (22 women), 41 part-time/adjunct (24 women). Expenses: Contact institution. *Financial support:* In 2006–07, 19 students received support, including 3 research assistantships with partial tuition reimbursements available (averaging $5,000 per year), 8 teaching assistantships with partial tuition reimbursements available (averaging $5,000 per year); Federal Work-Study and institutionally sponsored loans also available. In 2006, 40 degrees awarded. *Degree program information:* Part-time and evening/weekend programs available. Offers art studio (MFA); ceramics (MA); fine and performing arts (MA, MFA, MS Ed); interdisciplinary (MA); metal (MA); painting (MA); printmaking (MA); sculpture (MA); visual arts education (MS Ed). *Application deadline:* For fall admission, 2/15 priority date for domestic students, 2/15 for international students. *Application fee:* $50. Electronic applications accepted. *Dean,* Dr. Kurt Daw, 845-257-3860.

Faculty of Liberal Arts and Sciences Students: 79 full-time (66 women), 122 part-time (86 women); includes 13 minority (2 African Americans, 1 American Indian/Alaska Native, 2 Asian Americans or Pacific Islanders, 8 Hispanic Americans), 1 international. Average age 32. *Faculty:* 63 full-time (38 women), 49 part-time/adjunct (30 women). Expenses: Contact institution. *Financial support:* In 2006–07, 33 students received support, including 31 teaching assistantships with partial tuition reimbursements available (averaging $5,000 per year); research assistantships, career-related internships or fieldwork, Federal Work-Study, and institutionally sponsored loans also available. In 2006, 61 degrees awarded. *Degree program information:* Part-time and evening/weekend programs available. Offers biology (MA); clinical nurse specialist adult health (CAS); communication disorders (MS); English (MA); gerontological nursing (MS); liberal arts and sciences (MA, MS, CAS); mental health counseling (MS); psychology (MA). *Application deadline:* For fall admission, 5/15 for domestic and international students; for spring admission, 11/15 for domestic and international students. Applications are processed on a rolling basis. *Application fee:* $50. Electronic applications accepted. *Dean,* Dr. Gerald Benjamin, 845-257-3520.

School of Business Students: 58 full-time (29 women), 48 part-time (24 women); includes 17 minority (3 African Americans, 11 Asian Americans or Pacific Islanders, 3 Hispanic Americans), 31 international. Average age 30. *Faculty:* 25 full-time (6 women), 4 part-time/adjunct (1 woman). Expenses: Contact institution. *Financial support:* In 2006–07, 14 students received support, including 8 research assistantships with partial tuition reimbursements available (averaging $5,000 per year), 1 teaching assistantship with partial tuition reimbursement available (averaging $5,000 per year). In 2006, 51 degrees awarded. *Degree program information:* Part-time and evening/weekend programs available. Offers business administration (MBA); public accountancy (MBA). *Application deadline:* For fall admission, 5/15 priority date for domestic students, 5/15 for international students; for spring admission, 11/15 for domestic and international students. Applications are processed on a rolling basis. *Application fee:* $50. Electronic applications accepted. *Application Contact:* Rania Al-Haddad, Coordinator, 845-257-2968, E-mail: mba@newpaltz.edu. *Dean,* Dr. Hadi Salavitabar, 845-257-3720, E-mail: mba@newpaltz.edu.

School of Science and Engineering Students: 120 full-time (19 women), 33 part-time (9 women); includes 11 minority (7 Asian Americans or Pacific Islanders, 4 Hispanic Americans), 125 international. Average age 22. *Faculty:* 34 full-time (6 women), 27 part-time/adjunct (16 women). Expenses: Contact institution. *Financial support:* In 2006–07, 17 students received support, including 3 teaching assistantships with partial tuition reimbursements available (averaging $5,000 per year); tuition waivers (partial) also available. In 2006, 44 degrees awarded. *Degree program information:* Part-time and evening/weekend programs available. Offers chemistry (MA); computer science (MS); electrical and computer engineering (MS); geological sciences (MA); mathematics (MA); science and engineering (MA, MS). *Application deadline:* For fall admission, 5/15 priority date for domestic students, 5/15 for international students; for spring admission, 11/15 for domestic and international students. Applications are processed on a rolling basis. *Application fee:* $50. Electronic applications accepted. *Dean,* Dr. John Harrington, 845-257-3728.

STATE UNIVERSITY OF NEW YORK AT OSWEGO, Oswego, NY 13126

General Information State-supported, coed, comprehensive institution. *Enrollment:* 8,183 graduate, professional, and undergraduate students; 378 full-time matriculated graduate/professional students (246 women), 481 part-time matriculated graduate/professional students (321 women). *Enrollment by degree level:* 767 master's, 92 other advanced degrees. *Graduate faculty:* 76 full-time, 97 part-time/adjunct. Tuition, state resident: part-time $288 per credit. Tuition, nonresident: part-time $455 per credit. Tuition and fees vary according to program. *Graduate housing:* Room and/or apartments available on a first-come, first-served basis to single students; on-campus housing not available to married students. Typical cost: $5,490 per year ($8,940 including board). Housing application deadline: 4/1. *Student services:* Campus employment opportunities, career counseling, child daycare facilities, disabled student services, exercise/wellness program, free psychological counseling, grant writing training, international student services, low-cost health insurance. *Library facilities:* Penfield Library plus 1 other. *Online resources:* library catalog, web page. *Collection:* 476,709 titles, 2,654 serial subscriptions, 32,359 audiovisual materials. *Research affiliation:* Sun Microsystems, Inc. (research and education), Alcan (research and education), Merck (research and education), Entergy (research and education), Intel (research and education), IBM (research and education).

Computer facilities: Computer purchase and lease plans are available. 600 computers available on campus for general student use. A campuswide network can be accessed from student residence rooms and from off campus. Internet access and online class registration are available. *Web address:* http://www.oswego.edu/.

General Application Contact: Dr. David W. King, Dean of Graduate Studies, 315-312-3152, Fax: 315-312-3577, E-mail: dking@oswego.edu.

GRADUATE UNITS

Graduate Studies Students: 378 full-time (246 women), 481 part-time (321 women); includes 36 minority (17 African Americans, 1 American Indian/Alaska Native, 3 Asian Americans or Pacific Islanders, 15 Hispanic Americans), 22 international. Average age 30. 636 applicants, 86% accepted. *Faculty:* 76 full-time, 97 part-time/adjunct. Expenses: Contact institution. *Financial support:* In 2006–07, 56 students received support, including 10 fellowships with full tuition reimbursements available (averaging $5,100 per year), 1 research assistantship with full tuition reimbursement available (averaging $11,000 per year), 39 teaching assistantships with full and partial tuition reimbursements available (averaging $7,000 per year); career-related internships or fieldwork, Federal Work-Study, institutionally sponsored loans, scholarships/grants, health care benefits, tuition waivers (partial), and unspecified assistantships also available. Support available to part-time students. Financial award application deadline: 4/1; financial award applicants required to submit FAFSA. In 2006, 409 master's, 46 other advanced degrees awarded. *Degree program information:* Part-time programs available. *Application deadline:* For fall admission, 2/1 for domestic students, 4/15 for international students; for spring admission, 10/1 for domestic students, 11/1 for international students. Applications are processed on a rolling basis. *Application fee:* $50. *Dean of Graduate Studies,* Dr. David W. King, 315-312-3152, Fax: 315-312-3577, E-mail: dking@oswego.edu.

College of Arts and Sciences Students: 40 full-time (16 women), 30 part-time (14 women); includes 6 minority (3 African Americans, 3 Hispanic Americans), 2 international. Average age 25. 45 applicants, 87% accepted. *Faculty:* 32 full-time, 13 part-time/adjunct. Expenses: Contact institution. *Financial support:* In 2006–07, 18 students received support, including 1 research assistantship with full tuition reimbursement available, 17 teaching assistantships with full and partial tuition reimbursements available; fellowships, career-related internships or fieldwork, Federal Work-Study, institutionally sponsored loans, scholarships/

State University of New York at Oswego (continued)

grants, health care benefits, tuition waivers (partial), and unspecified assistantships also available. Support available to part-time students. Financial award application deadline: 4/1; financial award applicants required to submit FAFSA. In 2006, 22 degrees awarded. *Degree program information:* Part-time programs available. Offers art (MA); arts and sciences (MA, MS); chemistry (MS); English (MA); history (MA); human computer interaction (MA). *Application deadline:* For fall admission, 4/1 for domestic students; for spring admission, 10/1 for domestic students. Applications are processed on a rolling basis. *Application fee:* $50. *Application Contact:* Dr. David W. King, Dean of Graduate Studies, 315-312-3152, Fax: 315-312-3577, E-mail: dking@oswego.edu. *Interim Dean,* Dr. Rhonda Mandel, 315-312-2285.

School of Business Students: 46 full-time (14 women), 30 part-time (12 women); includes 5 minority (3 African Americans, 2 Asian Americans or Pacific Islanders), 18 international. Average age 32. 87 applicants, 90% accepted. *Faculty:* 6 full-time, 12 part-time/adjunct. Expenses: Contact institution. *Financial support:* In 2006–07, 7 students received support, including 1 fellowship; teaching assistantships with partial tuition reimbursements available, career-related internships or fieldwork, Federal Work-Study, institutionally sponsored loans, scholarships/grants, health care benefits, tuition waivers (partial), and unspecified assistantships also available. Support available to part-time students. Financial award application deadline: 4/1; financial award applicants required to submit FAFSA. In 2006, 30 degrees awarded. *Degree program information:* Part-time and evening/weekend programs available. Offers business (MBA); business administration (MBA). *Application deadline:* For fall admission, 4/15 for domestic students; for spring admission, 11/1 for domestic students. Applications are processed on a rolling basis. *Application fee:* $50. *Application Contact:* Dr. Ding Zhang, Director, 315-312-2911, E-mail: zhang@oswego.edu. *Dean,* Dr. Lanny A. Karns, 315-312-2272.

School of Education Students: 292 full-time (216 women), 421 part-time (295 women); includes 25 minority (11 African Americans, 1 American Indian/Alaska Native, 1 Asian American or Pacific Islander, 12 Hispanic Americans), 2 international. Average age 33. 504 applicants, 85% accepted. *Faculty:* 38 full-time, 72 part-time/adjunct. Expenses: Contact institution. *Financial support:* In 2006–07, 31 students received support, including 9 fellowships, 22 teaching assistantships with full and partial tuition reimbursements available; research assistantships, career-related internships or fieldwork, Federal Work-Study, institutionally sponsored loans, scholarships/grants, health care benefits, and unspecified assistantships also available. Support available to part-time students. Financial award application deadline: 4/1; financial award applicants required to submit FAFSA. In 2006, 356 master's, 46 other advanced degrees awarded. *Degree program information:* Part-time programs available. Offers agriculture (MS Ed); art education (MAT); business and marketing (MS Ed); counseling services (MS, CAS); education (MAT, MS, MS Ed, CAS); educational administration and supervision (CAS); elementary education (MS Ed); family and consumer sciences (MS Ed); health careers (MS Ed); human services/community counseling (MS); literacy education (MS Ed); school building leadership (CAS); school psychology (MS, CAS); secondary education (MS Ed); special education (MS Ed); technical education (MS Ed); technology (MS Ed); trade education (MS Ed). *Application deadline:* For fall admission, 2/1 for domestic students; for spring admission, 10/1 for domestic students. *Application fee:* $50. *Dean,* Dr. Linda Markert, 315-312-2102.

STATE UNIVERSITY OF NEW YORK AT PLATTSBURGH, Plattsburgh, NY 12901-2681

General Information State-supported, coed, comprehensive institution. *Enrollment:* 6,217 graduate, professional, and undergraduate students; 277 full-time matriculated graduate/professional students (204 women), 259 part-time matriculated graduate/professional students (176 women). *Enrollment by degree level:* 440 master's, 96 other advanced degrees. *Graduate faculty:* 54 full-time (31 women), 48 part-time/adjunct (26 women). Tuition, state resident: full-time $6,900; part-time $288 per credit hour. Tuition, nonresident: full-time $10,920; part-time $455 per credit hour. *Graduate housing:* Room and/or apartments available on a first-come, first-served basis to single students; on-campus housing not available to married students. Housing application deadline: 5/1. *Student services:* Campus employment opportunities, campus safety program, career counseling, child daycare facilities, disabled student services, free psychological counseling, international student services, low-cost health insurance, multicultural affairs office, teacher training, writing training. *Library facilities:* Feinberg Library. *Online resources:* library catalog, web page, access to other libraries' catalogs. *Collection:* 1.6 million titles, 4,238 serial subscriptions, 4,626 audiovisual materials. *Research affiliation:* Miner Agricultural Research Institute (environmental science), New York State Sea Grant (environmental science).

Computer facilities: Computer purchase and lease plans are available. 475 computers available on campus for general student use. A campuswide network can be accessed from student residence rooms and from off campus. Internet access and online class registration are available. *Web address:* http://www.plattsburgh.edu/.

General Application Contact: Richard Higgins, Director of Graduate Admissions, 518-564-2040, Fax: 518-564-2045, E-mail: higginrj@splaub.cc.plattsburgh.edu.

GRADUATE UNITS

Division of Education, Health, and Human Services Students: 232 full-time (177 women), 221 part-time (150 women); includes 17 minority (3 African Americans, 1 American Indian/Alaska Native, 5 Asian Americans or Pacific Islanders, 8 Hispanic Americans), 8 international. Average age 30. 235 applicants, 74% accepted, 165 enrolled. *Faculty:* 46 full-time (30 women), 44 part-time/adjunct (24 women). Expenses: Contact institution. *Financial support:* In 2006–07, 139 students received support, including 1 teaching assistantship; research assistantships, career-related internships or fieldwork and Federal Work-Study also available. Support available to part-time students. Financial award application deadline: 4/15; financial award applicants required to submit FAFSA. In 2006, 233 master's, 22 other advanced degrees awarded. *Degree program information:* Part-time programs available. Offers adolescence education (MST); biology 7-12 (MST); birth to grade 2 (MS Ed); birth-grade 6 (MS Ed); chemistry 7-12 (MST); childhood education (grades 1-6) (MST); college/agency counseling (MS); curriculum and instruction (MS Ed); earth science 7-12 (MST); education, health, and human services (MA, MS, MS Ed, MST, CAS); educational leadership (CAS); English 7-12 (MST); French 7-12 (MST); grades 1 to 6 (MS Ed); grades 5-12 (MS Ed); grades 7 to 12 (MS Ed); mathematics 7-12 (MST); physics 7-12 (MST); school counselor (MS Ed, CAS); social studies 7-12 (MST); Spanish 7-12 (MST); speech-language pathology (MA). *Application deadline:* For fall admission, 5/1 priority date for domestic and international students. Applications are processed on a rolling basis. *Application fee:* $50. *Application Contact:* Sharon Derr, Assistant Director, Graduate Admission, 518-564-4723, Fax: 518-564-4722, E-mail: derrsl@plattsburgh.edu. *Dean,* Dr. David Hill, 518-564-3066, E-mail: david.hill@plattsburgh.edu.

Faculty of Arts and Science Students: 23 full-time (17 women), 8 part-time (all women); includes 2 minority (both Hispanic Americans) Average age 27. 24 applicants, 71% accepted, 10 enrolled. *Faculty:* 5 full-time (2 women), 1 (woman) part-time/adjunct. Expenses: Contact institution. *Financial support:* Federal Work-Study available. Support available to part-time students. Financial award application deadline: 4/15; financial award applicants required to submit FAFSA. In 2006, 11 master's, 11 other advanced degrees awarded. *Degree program information:* Part-time and evening/weekend programs available. Offers arts and science (MA, CAS); school psychology (MA, CAS). *Application deadline:* For fall admission, 3/1 priority date for domestic students. Applications are processed on a rolling basis. *Application fee:* $50. *Application Contact:* Sharon Derr, Assistant Director, Graduate Admission, 518-564-4723, Fax: 518-564-4722, E-mail: derrsl@plattsburgh.edu. *Dean,* Dr. Kathleen Lavoie, 518-564-3150.

STATE UNIVERSITY OF NEW YORK COLLEGE AT BROCKPORT, Brockport, NY 14420-2997

General Information State-supported, coed, comprehensive institution. CGS member. *Enrollment:* 8,312 graduate, professional, and undergraduate students; 345 full-time matriculated graduate/professional students (243 women), 870 part-time matriculated graduate/professional students (554 women). *Enrollment by degree level:* 1,067 master's, 148 other advanced degrees. *Graduate faculty:* 141 full-time (66 women), 53 part-time/adjunct (23 women). Tuition, state resident: full-time $6,900; part-time $288 per credit. Tuition, nonresident: full-time $10,920; part-time $455 per credit. *Graduate housing:* Room and/or apartments available on a first-come, first-served basis to single students; on-campus housing not available to married students. Typical cost: $5,090 per year ($7,490 including board). Room and board charges vary according to board plan. Housing application deadline: 6/1. *Student services:* Campus employment opportunities, campus safety program, career counseling, child daycare facilities, disabled student services, exercise/wellness program, free psychological counseling, grant writing training, international student services, low-cost health insurance, multicultural affairs office, teacher training, writing training. *Library facilities:* Drake Memorial Library. *Online resources:* library catalog, web page, access to other libraries' catalogs. *Collection:* 995,618 titles, 26,769 serial subscriptions, 10,303 audiovisual materials.

Computer facilities: 750 computers available on campus for general student use. A campuswide network can be accessed from student residence rooms and from off campus. Internet access and online class registration are available. *Web address:* http://www.brockport.edu/.

General Application Contact: Graduate Admissions Secretary, 585-395-5465, Fax: 585-395-2515.

GRADUATE UNITS

School of Arts and Performance Students: 69 full-time (44 women), 117 part-time (61 women); includes 12 minority (7 African Americans, 1 Asian American or Pacific Islander, 4 Hispanic Americans), 5 international. 95 applicants, 85% accepted, 67 enrolled. Expenses: Contact institution. *Financial support:* In 2006–07, 2 fellowships with tuition reimbursements (averaging $7,500 per year), 1 research assistantship with tuition reimbursement, 13 teaching assistantships with tuition reimbursements (averaging $6,000 per year) were awarded; career-related internships or fieldwork, Federal Work-Study, scholarships/grants, and unspecified assistantships also available. Support available to part-time students. Financial award application deadline: 3/15; financial award applicants required to submit FAFSA. In 2006, 61 degrees awarded. Offers arts and performance (MA, MFA, MS Ed); communication (MA); dance (MA, MFA); physical education and sport (MS Ed); visual studies (MFA). *Application fee:* $50. *Application Contact:* Graduate Admissions Secretary, 585-395-5465, Fax: 585-395-2515, E-mail: gradadmit@brockport.edu. *Dean,* Dr. Francis X. Short, 585-395-2350, E-mail: fshort@brockport.edu.

School of Letters and Sciences Students: 67 full-time (35 women), 123 part-time (67 women); includes 8 minority (1 African American, 1 American Indian/Alaska Native, 5 Asian Americans or Pacific Islanders, 1 Hispanic American), 2 international. 111 applicants, 68% accepted, 66 enrolled. Expenses: Contact institution. *Financial support:* In 2006–07, 2 fellowships with tuition reimbursements (averaging $6,000 per year), 1 research assistantship with tuition reimbursement (averaging $6,000 per year), 16 teaching assistantships with tuition reimbursements (averaging $6,000 per year) were awarded; career-related internships or fieldwork, Federal Work-Study, scholarships/grants, and unspecified assistantships also available. Support available to part-time students. Financial award application deadline: 3/15; financial award applicants required to submit FAFSA. In 2006, 86 degrees awarded. *Degree program information:* Part-time programs available. Offers biological sciences (MS); computational science (MS); English (MA); environmental science and biology (MS); history (MA); letters and sciences (MA, MS); liberal studies (MA); mathematics (MA); psychology (MA). *Application fee:* $50. *Graduate Admission Secretary,* Dr. Stuart Appelle, 585-395-5465, Fax: 585-395-2515, E-mail: gradadmit@brockport.edu.

School of Professions Students: 209 full-time (164 women), 630 part-time (426 women); includes 102 minority (69 African Americans, 3 American Indian/Alaska Native, 6 Asian Americans or Pacific Islanders, 24 Hispanic Americans), 1 international. 405 applicants, 77% accepted, 283 enrolled. Expenses: Contact institution. *Financial support:* In 2006–07, 2 fellowships (averaging $7,500 per year), 4 teaching assistantships with tuition reimbursements (averaging $6,000 per year) were awarded; career-related internships or fieldwork, Federal Work-Study, scholarships/grants, and unspecified assistantships also available. Support available to part-time students. Financial award application deadline: 3/15; financial award applicants required to submit FAFSA. In 2006, 362 master's, 112 other advanced degrees awarded. Offers adolescence education (MS Ed); bilingual education (MS Ed); biology education (MS Ed); chemistry education (MS Ed); childhood curriculum specialist (MS Ed); childhood literacy (MS Ed); college counseling (MS Ed); earth science education (MS Ed); English education (MS Ed); health science (MS Ed); mathematics education (MS Ed); mental health counseling (MS); physics education (MS Ed); public administration (MPA); recreation and leisure studies (MS); school administration and supervision (MS Ed, CAS); school business administration (CAS); school counseling (MS Ed, CAS); school district administration (CAS); social studies education (MS Ed); social work (MSW). *Application fee:* $50. *Dean,* Dr. Christine Murray, 585-395-2510, E-mail: cmurray@brockport.edu.

See Close-Up on page 1043.

STATE UNIVERSITY OF NEW YORK COLLEGE AT CORTLAND, Cortland, NY 13045

General Information State-supported, coed, comprehensive institution. *Graduate housing:* On-campus housing not available.

GRADUATE UNITS

Graduate Studies *Degree program information:* Part-time and evening/weekend programs available.

School of Arts and Sciences *Degree program information:* Part-time and evening/weekend programs available. Offers American civilization and culture (CAS); arts and sciences (MA, MAT, MS Ed, CAS); biology (MAT, MS Ed); chemistry (MAT, MS Ed); earth science (MAT, MS Ed); English (MS Ed); French (MS Ed); history (MA, MS Ed); mathematics (MAT, MS Ed); physics (MAT, MS Ed); second language education (MS Ed); social studies (MS Ed); Spanish (MS Ed).

School of Education *Degree program information:* Part-time and evening/weekend programs available. Offers childhood/early child education (MS Ed, MST); educational leadership (CAS); literacy (MS Ed); teaching students with disabilities (MS Ed).

School of Professional Studies *Degree program information:* Part-time and evening/weekend programs available. Offers exercise science and sport studies (MS); health education (MS Ed, MST); international sport management (MS); physical education (MS Ed); professional studies (MS, MS Ed, MST); recreation and leisure studies (MS, MS Ed); sport management (MS).

STATE UNIVERSITY OF NEW YORK COLLEGE AT GENESEO, Geneseo, NY 14454-1401

General Information State-supported, coed, comprehensive institution. *Enrollment:* 5,530 graduate, professional, and undergraduate students; 78 full-time matriculated graduate/professional students (67 women), 94 part-time matriculated graduate/professional students (70 women). *Enrollment by degree level:* 172 master's. *Graduate faculty:* 25 full-time (11 women), 7 part-time/adjunct (5 women). *Graduate housing:* On-campus housing not available. *Student services:* Campus employment opportunities, campus safety program, career counseling, disabled student services, exercise/wellness program, free psychological counseling, international student services, low-cost health insurance, multicultural affairs office, teacher training. *Library facilities:* Milne Library. *Online resources:* library catalog, web page. *Collection:* 647,100 titles, 25,822 serial subscriptions, 28,134 audiovisual materials. *Research affiliation:* Armor Dynamics, Inc. (physics), Rochester Laboratory for Laser Energetics (nuclear physics), Great Lakes Research Consortium (biology), Rochester National Technical Institute for the Deaf (communicative disorders), Center for Nanomaterials and Nanoelectronics (chemistry), Mt. Hope Family Center (psychology).

Computer facilities: Computer purchase and lease plans are available. 900 computers available on campus for general student use. A campuswide network can be accessed from student residence rooms and from off campus. Internet access and online class registration are available. *Web address:* http://www.geneseo.edu/.

General Application Contact: Dr. Paul Schacht, Interim Dean of the College, 585-245-5546, Fax: 585-245-5005, E-mail: schacht@geneseo.edu.

GRADUATE UNITS

Graduate Studies Students: 60 full-time (57 women), 62 part-time (45 women); includes 4 minority (1 Asian American or Pacific Islander, 3 Hispanic Americans), 1 international. Average age 24. 115 applicants, 65% accepted, 38 enrolled. *Faculty:* 15 full-time (7 women), 3 part-time/adjunct (all women). Expenses: Contact institution. *Financial support:* In 2006–07, 6 students received support; fellowships, research assistantships, teaching assistantships, career-related internships or fieldwork, Federal Work-Study, and institutionally sponsored loans available. Financial award application deadline: 4/1; financial award applicants required to submit FAFSA. *Degree program information:* Part-time and evening/weekend programs available. Offers communicative disorders and sciences (MA). *Application deadline:* For fall admission, 6/1 for domestic students; for spring admission, 10/1 for domestic students. *Application fee:* $35. *Dean of the College,* Dr. Susan Bailey, 585-245-5546, Fax: 585-245-5005, E-mail: baileys@geneseo.edu.

School of Education Students: 31 full-time (26 women), 71 part-time (56 women); includes 3 minority (2 Asian Americans or Pacific Islanders, 1 Hispanic American), 1 international. Average age 24. 50 applicants, 82% accepted, 29 enrolled. *Faculty:* 26 full-time (15 women). Expenses: Contact institution. *Financial support:* In 2006–07, 5 students received support; fellowships, teaching assistantships with tuition reimbursements available, career-related internships or fieldwork, Federal Work-Study, and institutionally sponsored loans available. Financial award application deadline: 4/1; financial award applicants required to submit FAFSA. In 2006, 75 degrees awarded. *Degree program information:* Part-time and evening/weekend programs available. Offers early childhood education (MS Ed); elementary education (MS Ed); reading (MS Ed); secondary education (MS Ed). *Application deadline:* For fall admission, 6/1 priority date for domestic students; for spring admission, 10/1 for domestic students. *Application fee:* $50. *Chairperson,* Dr. Osman Alawiye, 585-245-5560, Fax: 585-245-5220.

STATE UNIVERSITY OF NEW YORK COLLEGE AT OLD WESTBURY, Old Westbury, NY 11568-0210

General Information State-supported, coed, comprehensive institution. *Enrollment:* 3,450 graduate, professional, and undergraduate students; 22 full-time matriculated graduate/professional students (9 women), 17 part-time matriculated graduate/professional students (12 women). *Enrollment by degree level:* 39 master's. *Graduate faculty:* 7 full-time (2 women), 2 part-time/adjunct (0 women). Tuition, state resident: full-time $6,900; part-time $288 per credit. Tuition, nonresident: full-time $10,920; part-time $455 per credit. *Required fees:* $491; $56 per credit. Part-time tuition and fees vary according to course load. *Graduate housing:* Room and/or apartments available to single students; on-campus housing not available to married students. Typical cost: $5,907 per year ($8,667 including board). *Student services:* Campus safety program, career counseling, child daycare facilities, disabled student services. *Library facilities:* SUNY College at Old Westbury Library plus 1 other. *Online resources:* library catalog, web page, access to other libraries' catalogs. *Collection:* 246,811 titles, 3,428 serial subscriptions, 1,986 audiovisual materials.

Computer facilities: 342 computers available on campus for general student use. A campuswide network can be accessed from student residence rooms and from off campus. Internet access and online class registration, grades, financial aid, billing information are available. *Web address:* http://www.oldwestbury.edu/.

General Application Contact: Philip D'Angelo, Graduate Admissions Office, 516-876-3073, E-mail: enroll@oldwestbury.edu.

GRADUATE UNITS

Program in Accounting Students: 22 full-time (9 women), 17 part-time (12 women); includes 7 minority (3 African Americans, 3 Asian Americans or Pacific Islanders, 1 Hispanic American), 2 international. Average age 33. 37 applicants, 35% accepted, 10 enrolled. *Faculty:* 7 full-time (2 women), 2 part-time/adjunct (0 women). Expenses: Contact institution. In 2006, 9 degrees awarded. *Degree program information:* Part-time and evening/weekend programs available. Offers accounting (MS); taxation and finance (MS). *Application deadline:* For fall admission, 6/15 priority date for domestic students; for spring admission, 11/15 priority date for domestic students. Applications are processed on a rolling basis. *Application fee:* $50. Electronic applications accepted. *Application Contact:* Philip D'Angelo, Graduate Admissions Office, 516-876-3073, E-mail: enroll@oldwestbury.edu. *Director of Graduate Business Programs,* Dr. James M. Fornaro, 516-876-2883, E-mail: fornaroj@oldwestbury.edu.

STATE UNIVERSITY OF NEW YORK COLLEGE AT ONEONTA, Oneonta, NY 13820-4015

General Information State-supported, coed, comprehensive institution. *Graduate housing:* Room and/or apartments available on a first-come, first-served basis to single students; on-campus housing not available to married students.

GRADUATE UNITS

Graduate Studies *Degree program information:* Part-time and evening/weekend programs available. Offers biology (MA); earth science (MA); history museum studies (MA).

Division of Education *Degree program information:* Part-time and evening/weekend programs available. Offers adolescence education (MS Ed); childhood education (MS Ed); educational psychology and counseling (MS Ed, CAS); elementary and reading education (MS Ed); family and consumer science education (MS Ed); literacy education (MS Ed); school counselor K-12 (MS Ed, CAS).

STATE UNIVERSITY OF NEW YORK COLLEGE AT POTSDAM, Potsdam, NY 13676

General Information State-supported, coed, comprehensive institution. *Enrollment:* 4,332 graduate, professional, and undergraduate students; 469 full-time matriculated graduate/professional students (351 women), 166 part-time matriculated graduate/professional students (126 women). *Enrollment by degree level:* 635 master's. *Graduate faculty:* 47 full-time (20 women), 21 part-time/adjunct (11 women). *Graduate housing:* Room and/or apartments available on a first-come, first-served basis to single students; on-campus housing not available to married students. *Student services:* Campus employment opportunities, campus safety program, career counseling, child daycare facilities, disabled student services, exercise/wellness program, free psychological counseling, grant writing training, international student services, low-cost health insurance, multicultural affairs office, teacher training, writing training. *Library facilities:* F. W. Crumb Memorial Library plus 1 other. *Online resources:* library catalog, web page, access to other libraries' catalogs. *Collection:* 322,591 titles, 1,035 serial subscriptions, 15,915 audiovisual materials.

Computer facilities: Computer purchase and lease plans are available. 400 computers available on campus for general student use. A campuswide network can be accessed from student residence rooms and from off campus. Internet access and online class registration, online access to grades, financial aid status, and unofficial transcripts are available. *Web address:* http://www.potsdam.edu/.

General Application Contact: Peter Cutler, Graduate Admissions Counselor, 315-267-3154, Fax: 315-267-4802, E-mail: cutlerpj@potsdam.edu.

GRADUATE UNITS

Crane School of Music Students: 16 full-time (10 women), 4 part-time (3 women), 1 international. *Faculty:* 12 full-time (4 women), 1 part-time/adjunct (0 women). Expenses: Contact institution. *Financial support:* Teaching assistantships with full tuition reimbursements, career-related internships or fieldwork, Federal Work-Study, and scholarships/grants available. Support available to part-time students. Financial award applicants required to submit FAFSA. In 2006, 20 degrees awarded. *Degree program information:* Part-time programs available. Offers composition (MM); history and literature (MM); music education (MM); music theory (MM); performance (MM). *Application deadline:* For fall admission, 3/1 for domestic students. Applications are processed on a rolling basis. *Application fee:* $50. *Application Contact:* Peter Cutler, Graduate Admissions Counselor, 315-267-3154, Fax: 315-267-4802, E-mail: cutlerpj@potsdam.edu. *Dean,* Dr. Alan Solomon, 315-267-2415, Fax: 315-267-2413, E-mail: solomon@potsdam.edu.

School of Arts and Sciences Students: 9 full-time (5 women), 5 part-time (4 women). 5 applicants, 100% accepted. *Faculty:* 9 full-time (3 women), 2 part-time/adjunct (1 woman). Expenses: Contact institution. *Financial support:* Teaching assistantships with full tuition reimbursements, Federal Work-Study available. Support available to part-time students. Financial award application deadline: 3/1. In 2006, 4 degrees awarded. *Degree program information:* Part-time and evening/weekend programs available. Offers arts and sciences (MA); English (MA); mathematics (MA). *Application deadline:* Applications are processed on a rolling basis. *Application fee:* $50. *Application Contact:* Peter Cutler, Graduate Admissions Counselor, 315-267-3154, Fax: 315-267-4802, E-mail: cutlerpj@potsdam.edu. *Dean,* Dr. Galen K. Pletcher, 315-267-2231, Fax: 315-267-3140, E-mail: pletchgk@potsdam.edu.

School of Education Students: 444 full-time (336 women), 157 part-time (119 women); includes 2 minority (both American Indian/Alaska Native), 286 international. *Faculty:* 26 full-time (13 women), 18 part-time/adjunct (10 women). Expenses: Contact institution. *Financial support:* Fellowships, teaching assistantships with full tuition reimbursements, career-related internships or fieldwork, Federal Work-Study, scholarships/grants, and tuition waivers (full) available. Support available to part-time students. Financial award application deadline: 3/1. In 2006, 572 degrees awarded. *Degree program information:* Part-time and evening/weekend programs available. Postbaccalaureate distance learning degree programs offered (minimal on-campus study). Offers curriculum and instruction (MS Ed); education (MS Ed, MST); educational technology (MS Ed); elementary education (MS Ed, MST); literacy education (MS Ed); secondary education (MS Ed, MST); special education (MS Ed). *Application deadline:* Applications are processed on a rolling basis. *Application fee:* $50. *Application Contact:* Peter Cutler, Graduate Admissions Counselor, 315-267-3154, Fax: 315-267-4802, E-mail: cutlerpj@potsdam.edu. *Dean of Education and Graduate Studies,* Dr. William Amoriell, 315-267-2515, Fax: 315-267-4802, E-mail: amoriewj@potsdam.edu.

STATE UNIVERSITY OF NEW YORK COLLEGE OF ENVIRONMENTAL SCIENCE AND FORESTRY, Syracuse, NY 13210-2779

General Information State-supported, coed, university. *Enrollment:* 2,069 graduate, professional, and undergraduate students; 281 full-time matriculated graduate/professional students (151 women), 176 part-time matriculated graduate/professional students (77 women). *Enrollment by degree level:* 19 other advanced degrees. *Graduate faculty:* 113 full-time (23 women), 23 part-time/adjunct (6 women). *Graduate housing:* Rooms and/or apartments available to single and married students. Housing application deadline: 5/1. *Student services:* Campus employment opportunities, campus safety program, career counseling, free psychological counseling, international student services, low-cost health insurance. *Library facilities:* F. Franklin Moon Library plus 1 other. *Online resources:* library catalog, web page, access to other libraries' catalogs. *Collection:* 135,341 titles, 2,000 serial subscriptions, 150 audiovisual materials. *Research affiliation:* NYS Department Env. Conservation (NYSDEC), Honeywell International, Department of Commerce, U.S. Department of Agriculture (CREES), NASA.

Computer facilities: 150 computers available on campus for general student use. A campuswide network can be accessed from student residence rooms and from off campus. Internet access and online class registration are available. *Web address:* http://www.esf.edu/.

General Application Contact: Dr. Dudley J. Raynal, Dean, Instruction and Graduate Studies, 315-470-6599, Fax: 315-470-6978, E-mail: esfgrad@esf.edu.

GRADUATE UNITS

Department of Construction Management and Wood Products Engineering Students: 4 full-time (1 woman), 10 part-time (1 woman); includes 1 minority (African American), 3 international. Average age 31. 7 applicants, 57% accepted, 1 enrolled. *Faculty:* 8 full-time (1 woman), 3 part-time/adjunct (1 woman). Expenses: Contact institution. *Financial support:* In 2006–07, 8 students received support, including fellowships with full tuition reimbursements available (averaging $10,500 per year), 4 research assistantships with full tuition reimbursements available (averaging $12,500 per year), 2 teaching assistantships with full tuition reimbursements available (averaging $12,500 per year); career-related internships or fieldwork, Federal Work-Study, institutionally sponsored loans, scholarships/grants, health care benefits, and unspecified assistantships also available. Financial award application deadline: 6/30; financial award applicants required to submit FAFSA. In 2006, 5 master's, 2 doctorates awarded. Offers environmental and resources engineering (MPS, MS, PhD). *Application deadline:* For fall admission, 2/1 priority date for domestic and international students; for spring admission, 11/1 priority date for domestic and international students. Applications are processed on a rolling basis. *Application fee:* $60. *Application Contact:* Dr. Dudley J. Raynal, Dean, Instruction and Graduate Studies, 315-470-6599, Fax: 315-470-6879, E-mail: esfgrad@esf.edu. *Interim Chair,* Dr. Susan E. Anagnost, 315-470-6880, Fax: 315-470-6879, E-mail: seanagno@esf.edu.

Department of Paper and Bioprocess Engineering Students: 17 full-time (5 women), 28 part-time (19 women), 19 international. Average age 31. 16 applicants, 63% accepted, 5 enrolled. *Faculty:* 7 full-time (0 women), 1 part-time/adjunct (0 women). Expenses: Contact institution. *Financial support:* In 2006–07, 3 fellowships with full tuition reimbursements (averaging $10,500 per year), 7 research assistantships with full tuition reimbursements (averaging $12,500 per year), 9 teaching assistantships with full tuition reimbursements (averaging $12,500 per year) were awarded; career-related internships or fieldwork, Federal Work-Study, institutionally sponsored loans, scholarships/grants, health care benefits, and unspecified assistantships also available. Support available to part-time students. Financial award application deadline: 6/30; financial award applicants required to submit FAFSA. In 2006, 2 master's degrees awarded. Offers environmental and resources engineering (MPS, MS, PhD). *Application deadline:* For fall admission, 2/1 priority date for domestic and international students; for spring admission, 11/1 priority date for domestic and international students. Applications are processed on a rolling basis. *Application fee:* $60. *Application Contact:* Dr. Dudley J. Raynal, Dean, Instruction and Graduate Studies, 315-470-6599, Fax: 315-470-6978, E-mail: esfgrad@esf.edu. *Chair,* Dr. Gary M. Scott, 315-470-6524, Fax: 315-470-6945, E-mail: gscott@esf.edu.

Faculty of Chemistry Students: 28 full-time (16 women), 14 part-time (8 women), 14 international. Average age 28. 25 applicants, 88% accepted, 9 enrolled. *Faculty:* 16 full-time (1 woman). Expenses: Contact institution. *Financial support:* In 2006–07, 35 students received support, including fellowships with full tuition reimbursements available (averaging $10,500 per year), 12 research assistantships with full tuition reimbursements available (averaging $17,500 per year), 23 teaching assistantships with full tuition reimbursements available (averaging $17,500 per year); Federal Work-Study, institutionally sponsored loans, scholarships/grants, health care benefits, and unspecified assistantships also available. Financial award application deadline: 6/30; financial award applicants required to submit FAFSA. In 2006, 1 master's, 2 doctorates awarded. Offers biochemistry (MS, PhD); environmental and forest chemistry (MS, PhD); organic chemistry of natural products (MS, PhD); polymer chemistry (MS, PhD). *Application deadline:* For fall admission, 2/1 priority date for domestic and international students; for spring admission, 11/1 priority date for domestic and international students. Applications are processed on a rolling basis. *Application fee:* $60. Electronic applications accepted. *Application Contact:* Dr. Dudley J. Raynal, Dean, Instruction and Graduate Studies, 315-470-6599, Fax: 315-470-6978, E-mail: esfgrad@esf.edu. *Chair,* Dr. Arthur J. Stipanovic, 315-470-6855, Fax: 315-470-6856, E-mail: astipano@esf.edu.

Faculty of Environmental and Forest Biology Students: 89 full-time (55 women), 49 part-time (25 women); includes 2 minority (1 American Indian/Alaska Native, 1 Hispanic American), 12 international. Average age 30. 88 applicants, 52% accepted, 29 enrolled. *Faculty:* 27 full-time (4 women), 3 part-time/adjunct (2 women). Expenses: Contact institution. *Financial support:* In 2006–07, 86 students received support, including 5 fellowships with full and partial tuition reimbursements available (averaging $10,500 per year), 36 research assistantships with full and partial tuition reimbursements available (averaging $12,500 per

State University of New York College of Environmental Science and Forestry (continued)

year), 43 teaching assistantships with full and partial tuition reimbursements available (averaging $12,500 per year); Federal Work-Study, institutionally sponsored loans, scholarships/grants, health care benefits, and unspecified assistantships also available. Financial award application deadline: 6/30. In 2006, 29 master's, 6 doctorates awarded. Offers chemical ecology (MPS, MS, PhD); conservation biology (MPS, MS, PhD); ecology (MPS, MS, PhD); entomology (MPS, MS, PhD); environmental interpretation (MPS, MS, PhD); environmental physiology (MPS, MS, PhD); fish and wildlife biology (MPS, MS, PhD); forest pathology and mycology (MPS, MS, PhD); plant science and biotechnology (MPS, MS, PhD). *Application deadline:* For fall admission, 2/1 priority date for domestic and international students; for spring admission, 11/1 priority date for domestic and international students. Applications are processed on a rolling basis. *Application fee:* $60. *Application Contact:* Dr. Dudley J. Raynal, Dean, Instruction and Graduate Studies, 315-470-6599, Fax: 315-470-6978, E-mail: esfgrad@esf.edu. *Chair,* Dr. Donald J. Leopold, 315-470-6770, Fax: 315-470-6934.

Faculty of Environmental Resources and Forest Engineering Students: 21 full-time (14 women), 18 part-time (5 women); includes 3 minority (1 African American, 2 Asian Americans or Pacific Islanders), 12 international. Average age 31. 31 applicants, 45% accepted, 6 enrolled. *Faculty:* 6 full-time (1 woman), 1 part-time/adjunct (0 women). Expenses: Contact institution. *Financial support:* In 2006–07, 1 fellowship with full and partial tuition reimbursement (averaging $10,500 per year), 13 research assistantships with full and partial tuition reimbursements (averaging $12,500 per year), 10 teaching assistantships with full and partial tuition reimbursements (averaging $12,500 per year) were awarded; Federal Work-Study, institutionally sponsored loans, scholarships/grants, health care benefits, and unspecified assistantships also available. Financial award application deadline: 6/30; financial award applicants required to submit FAFSA. In 2006, 6 degrees awarded. Offers environmental and resources engineering (MPS, MS, PhD). *Application deadline:* For fall admission, 2/1 priority date for domestic and international students; for spring admission, 11/1 priority date for domestic and international students. Applications are processed on a rolling basis. *Application fee:* $60. *Application Contact:* Dr. Dudley J. Raynal, Dean, Instruction and Graduate Studies, 315-470-6599, Fax: 315-470-6978, E-mail: esfgrad@esf.edu. *Chair,* Dr. James M. Hassett, 315-470-6633, Fax: 315-470-6958, E-mail: jhassett@esf.edu.

Faculty of Environmental Studies Students: 38 full-time (23 women), 27 part-time (14 women); includes 2 minority (1 Asian American or Pacific Islander, 1 Hispanic American), 25 international. Average age 33. 63 applicants, 65% accepted, 13 enrolled. *Faculty:* 11 full-time (6 women), 6 part-time/adjunct (2 women). Expenses: Contact institution. *Financial support:* In 2006–07, 5 fellowships with full and partial tuition reimbursements (averaging $10,500 per year), 5 research assistantships with full and partial tuition reimbursements (averaging $12,500 per year), 21 teaching assistantships with full and partial tuition reimbursements (averaging $12,500 per year) were awarded; career-related internships or fieldwork, Federal Work-Study, institutionally sponsored loans, scholarships/grants, health care benefits, and unspecified assistantships also available. Support available to part-time students. Financial award application deadline: 6/30; financial award applicants required to submit FAFSA. In 2006, 15 master's, 3 doctorates awarded. *Degree program information:* Part-time programs available. Offers environmental and community land planning (MPS, MS, PhD); environmental and natural resources policy (PhD); environmental communication and participatory processes (MPS, MS, PhD); environmental policy and democratic processes (MPS, MS, PhD); environmental systems and risk management (MPS, MS, PhD); water and wetland resource studies (MPS, MS, PhD). *Application deadline:* For fall admission, 2/1 priority date for domestic and international students; for spring admission, 11/1 priority date for domestic and international students. Applications are processed on a rolling basis. *Application fee:* $60. *Application Contact:* Dr. Dudley J. Raynal, Dean, Instruction and Graduate Studies, 315-470-6599, Fax: 315-470-6978, E-mail: esfgrad@esf.edu. *Chair,* 315-470-6636, Fax: 315-470-6915.

Faculty of Forest and Natural Resources Management Students: 42 full-time (18 women), 26 part-time (12 women); includes 4 minority (1 American Indian/Alaska Native, 2 Asian Americans or Pacific Islanders, 1 Hispanic American), 19 international. Average age 30. 62 applicants, 68% accepted, 20 enrolled. *Faculty:* 25 full-time (6 women), 1 part-time/adjunct (0 women). Expenses: Contact institution. *Financial support:* In 2006–07, 43 students received support, including 5 fellowships with full and partial tuition reimbursements available (averaging $10,500 per year), 13 research assistantships with full and partial tuition reimbursements available (averaging $12,500 per year), 25 teaching assistantships with full and partial tuition reimbursements available (averaging $12,500 per year); career-related internships or fieldwork, Federal Work-Study, institutionally sponsored loans, scholarships/grants, health care benefits, and unspecified assistantships also available. Financial award application deadline: 6/30; financial award applicants required to submit FAFSA. In 2006, 20 master's, 6 doctorates awarded. Offers environmental and natural resource policy (MS, PhD); environmental and natural resources policy (MPS); forest management and operations (MF); forestry ecosystems science and applications (MPS, MS, PhD); natural resources management (MPS, MS, PhD); quantitative methods and management in forest science (MPS, MS, PhD); recreation and resource management (MPS, MS, PhD); watershed management and forest hydrology (MPS, MS, PhD). *Application deadline:* For fall admission, 2/1 priority date for domestic and international students; for spring admission, 11/1 priority date for domestic and international students. Applications are processed on a rolling basis. *Application fee:* $60. *Application Contact:* Dr. Dudley J. Raynal, Dean, Instruction and Graduate Studies, 315-470-6599, Fax: 315-470-6978, E-mail: esfgrad@esf.edu. *Chair,* Dr. David Newman, 315-470-6536, Fax: 315-470-6535.

Faculty of Landscape Architecture Students: 42 full-time (19 women), 4 part-time (3 women); includes 4 minority (2 Asian Americans or Pacific Islanders, 2 Hispanic Americans), 5 international. Average age 31. 37 applicants, 86% accepted, 17 enrolled. *Faculty:* 13 full-time (4 women), 8 part-time/adjunct (1 woman). Expenses: Contact institution. *Financial support:* In 2006–07, 24 students received support, including 5 fellowships with full and partial tuition reimbursements available (averaging $10,500 per year), 5 research assistantships with full and partial tuition reimbursements available (averaging $12,500 per year), 10 teaching assistantships with full and partial tuition reimbursements available (averaging $10,500 per year); career-related internships or fieldwork and Federal Work-Study also available. Support available to part-time students. Financial award application deadline: 6/30; financial award applicants required to submit FAFSA. In 2006, 1 master's awarded. Offers community design and planning (MLA, MS); cultural landscape studies and conservation (MLA, MS); landscape and urban ecology (MLA, MS). *Application deadline:* For fall admission, 2/1 priority date for domestic and international students; for spring admission, 11/1 priority date for domestic and international students. Applications are processed on a rolling basis. *Application fee:* $60. *Application Contact:* Dr. Dudley J. Raynal, Dean, Instruction and Graduate Studies, 315-470-6599, Fax: 315-470-6978, E-mail: esfgrad@esf.edu. *Chair,* Richard S. Hawks, 315-470-6544, Fax: 315-470-6540, E-mail: rshawks@esf.edu.

STATE UNIVERSITY OF NEW YORK COLLEGE OF OPTOMETRY, New York, NY 10036

General Information State-supported, coed, graduate-only institution. *Enrollment by degree level:* 281 first professional, 21 master's, 4 doctoral. *Graduate faculty:* 45 full-time (10 women), 102 part-time/adjunct (28 women). Tuition, state resident: full-time $13,620. Tuition, nonresident: full-time $26,150. *Required fees:* $370. *Graduate housing:* On-campus housing not available. *Student services:* Campus employment opportunities, campus safety program, career counseling, international student services, low-cost health insurance. *Library facilities:* Harold Kohn Visual Science Library. *Collection:* 3,600 titles, 400 serial subscriptions. *Research affiliation:* Schnurmacher Institute for Vision Research (vision science).

Computer facilities: 32 computers available on campus for general student use. A campuswide network can be accessed from off campus. Internet access is available. *Web address:* http://www.sunyopt.edu/.

General Application Contact: Dr. Edward Johnston, Vice President for Student Affairs and Director of Admissions, 212-938-5500, Fax: 212-938-5504, E-mail: johnston@sunyopt.edu.

GRADUATE UNITS

Graduate Programs Students: 11 full-time (5 women), 14 part-time (9 women). 11 applicants, 36% accepted, 3 enrolled. *Faculty:* 28 full-time (3 women), 1 (woman) part-time/adjunct. Expenses: Contact institution. *Financial support:* In 2006–07, 9 students received support, including 7 teaching assistantships with full tuition reimbursements available (averaging $18,000 per year); fellowships, research assistantships, Federal Work-Study, tuition waivers (full and partial), and unspecified assistantships also available. Financial award application deadline: 3/1. In 2006, 4 master's, 1 doctorate awarded. *Degree program information:* Part-time programs available. Offers vision science (MS, PhD). *Application deadline:* For fall admission, 3/1 priority date for domestic and international students. Applications are processed on a rolling basis. *Application fee:* $75. *Application Contact:* Debra Berger, Assistant to Associate Dean, 212-938-5544, Fax: 212-938-5537, E-mail: berger@sunyopt.edu. *Associate Dean,* Dr. Jerry Feldman, 212-938-5541, Fax: 212-938-5537, E-mail: jfeldman@sunyopt.edu.

Professional Program Students: 281 full-time (196 women); includes 130 minority (9 African Americans, 114 Asian Americans or Pacific Islanders, 7 Hispanic Americans), 19 international. Average age 24. 499 applicants, 28% accepted, 74 enrolled. *Faculty:* 45 full-time (10 women), 102 part-time/adjunct (28 women). Expenses: Contact institution. *Financial support:* In 2006–07, 234 students received support; fellowships, career-related internships or fieldwork, Federal Work-Study, and tuition waivers (full and partial) available. Financial award application deadline: 4/15; financial award applicants required to submit FAFSA. In 2006, 68 degrees awarded. Offers optometry (OD). *Application deadline:* For fall admission, 2/15 priority date for domestic and international students. Applications are processed on a rolling basis. *Application fee:* $75. Electronic applications accepted. *Vice President for Student Affairs and Director of Admissions,* Dr. Edward Johnston, 212-938-5500, Fax: 212-938-5501, E-mail: johnston@sunyopt.edu.

STATE UNIVERSITY OF NEW YORK DOWNSTATE MEDICAL CENTER, Brooklyn, NY 11203-2098

General Information State-supported, coed, upper-level institution. *Enrollment:* 1,609 graduate, professional, and undergraduate students; 932 full-time matriculated graduate/professional students (377 women), 132 part-time matriculated graduate/professional students (all women). *Enrollment by degree level:* 771 first professional, 207 master's, 86 doctoral. *Graduate faculty:* 119 full-time (29 women), 18 part-time/adjunct (8 women). Tuition, state resident: full-time $6,900; part-time $288 per credit. Tuition, nonresident: full-time $10,920; part-time $455 per credit. *Required fees:* $100; $20 per credit. $50 per semester. Tuition and fees vary according to course load. *Graduate housing:* Rooms and/or apartments available on a first-come, first-served basis to single and married students. Typical cost: $6,105 per year for single students; $7,934 per year for married students. Housing application deadline: 5/29. *Student services:* Campus employment opportunities, campus safety program, career counseling, child daycare facilities, exercise/wellness program, free psychological counseling, grant writing training, low-cost health insurance, writing training. *Library facilities:* The Medical Research Library of Brooklyn. *Online resources:* library catalog, web page, access to other libraries' catalogs. *Collection:* 357,209 titles, 2,104 serial subscriptions. *Research affiliation:* Brooklyn Veterans Administration Medical Center, Polytechnic University Brooklyn (Biomedical Engineering).

Computer facilities: 183 computers available on campus for general student use. A campuswide network can be accessed from student residence rooms and from off campus. Internet access is available. *Web address:* http://www.downstate.edu/.

General Application Contact: Denise Sheares, Admissions Officer, 718-270-2738, Fax: 718-270-3378, E-mail: dsheares@downstate.edu.

GRADUATE UNITS

College of Medicine Offers medicine (MD, MPH); urban and immigrant health (MPH).

College of Nursing *Degree program information:* Part-time and evening/weekend programs available. Offers nurse anesthesia (MS); nurse practitioner (MS, Post Master's Certificate); nursing (MS).

School of Graduate Studies Students: 82 full-time (34 women); includes 15 minority (3 African Americans, 12 Asian Americans or Pacific Islanders), 40 international. Average age 30. 92 applicants, 22% accepted, 12 enrolled. *Faculty:* 119 full-time (29 women), 18 part-time/adjunct (8 women). Expenses: Contact institution. *Financial support:* In 2006–07, 70 students received support, including 70 teaching assistantships with tuition reimbursements available (averaging $25,000 per year); fellowships, research assistantships, career-related internships or fieldwork, Federal Work-Study, health care benefits, and tuition waivers (full and partial) also available. In 2006, 1 master's, 10 doctorates awarded. Offers bioimaging and neuroengineering (PhD); biomedical engineering (MS); molecular and cellular biology (PhD); neural and behavioral science (PhD). *Application deadline:* For fall admission, 4/1 for domestic and international students. *Application fee:* $35. *Application Contact:* Denise Sheares, Admissions Officer, 718-270-2738, Fax: 718-270-3378, E-mail: dsheares@downstate.edu. *Dean,* Dr. Susan Schwartz-Giblin, 718-270-1155.

STATE UNIVERSITY OF NEW YORK EMPIRE STATE COLLEGE, Saratoga Springs, NY 12866-4391

General Information State-supported, coed, comprehensive institution. *Graduate housing:* On-campus housing not available.

GRADUATE UNITS

Graduate Studies *Degree program information:* Part-time and evening/weekend programs available. Postbaccalaureate distance learning degree programs offered (minimal on-campus study). Offers business administration (MBA); business and policy studies (MA); labor and policy studies (MA); liberal studies (MA); social policy (MA); teaching (MA). Electronic applications accepted.

STATE UNIVERSITY OF NEW YORK INSTITUTE OF TECHNOLOGY, Utica, NY 13504-3050

General Information State-supported, coed, comprehensive institution. *Enrollment:* 2,587 graduate, professional, and undergraduate students; 123 full-time matriculated graduate/professional students (59 women), 309 part-time matriculated graduate/professional students (145 women). *Enrollment by degree level:* 429 master's, 3 other advanced degrees. *Graduate faculty:* 54 full-time (18 women), 16 part-time/adjunct (8 women). Tuition, state resident: full-time $3,452; part-time $288 per credit hour. Tuition, nonresident: full-time $10,920; part-time $455 per credit hour. *Required fees:* $927; $38 per credit hour. *Graduate housing:* Room and/or apartments available on a first-come, first-served basis to single students; on-campus housing not available to married students. Typical cost: $7,600 (including board). Room and board charges vary according to board plan. *Student services:* Campus employment opportunities, campus safety program, career counseling, disabled student services, exercise/wellness program, free psychological counseling, international student services, low-cost health insurance, multicultural affairs office, writing training. *Library facilities:* Peter J. Cayan Library. *Online resources:* library catalog, web page, access to other libraries' catalogs. *Collection:* 200,730 titles, 372 serial subscriptions, 11,762 audiovisual materials. *Research affiliation:* Wyle Laboratories-Reliability Information Analysis Center (reliability analysis and information).

Computer facilities: 250 computers available on campus for general student use. A campuswide network can be accessed from student residence rooms and from off campus. Internet access and online class registration, various other software applications are available. *Web address:* http://www.sunyit.edu/.

General Application Contact: Marybeth Lyons, Director of Admissions, 315-792-7500, Fax: 315-792-7837, E-mail: smbl@sunyit.edu.

GRADUATE UNITS

School of Arts and Sciences Students: 6 full-time (4 women), 34 part-time (19 women), 2 international. *Faculty:* 9 full-time (5 women), 2 part-time/adjunct (both women). Expenses: Contact institution. *Financial support:* Federal Work-Study, scholarships/grants, and unspecified assistantships available. Financial award applicants required to submit FAFSA. *Degree program information:* Part-time and evening/weekend programs available. Offers applied sociology (MS); information design and technology (MS). *Application deadline:* For fall admission, 6/15 priority date for domestic students. Applications are processed on a rolling basis. *Application fee:* $50. *Application Contact:* Marybeth Lyons, Director of Admissions, 315-792-7500, Fax: 315-792-7837, E-mail: smbl@sunyit.edu. *Dean,* Dr. Thomas McMillan, 315-792-7333, Fax: 315-792-7503, E-mail: thomas.mcmillan@sunyit.edu.

School of Business Students: 62 full-time (27 women), 154 part-time (77 women); includes 25 minority (11 African Americans, 11 Asian Americans or Pacific Islanders, 3 Hispanic Americans), 12 international. *Faculty:* 15 full-time (4 women), 3 part-time/adjunct (0 women). Expenses: Contact institution. *Financial support:* In 2006–07, 1 fellowship (averaging $7,500 per year), 8 research assistantships (averaging $7,500 per year) were awarded; career-related internships or fieldwork, Federal Work-Study, scholarships/grants, health care benefits, and unspecified assistantships also available. Financial award application deadline: 6/1; financial award applicants required to submit FAFSA. *Degree program information:* Part-time and evening/weekend programs available. Postbaccalaureate distance learning degree programs offered (no on-campus study). Offers accountancy (MS); business administration in technology management (MBA); health services administration (MS); technology management (MBA). *Application deadline:* For fall admission, 6/15 priority date for domestic students. Applications are processed on a rolling basis. *Application fee:* $50. *Application Contact:* Marybeth Lyons, Director of Admissions, 315-792-7500, Fax: 315-792-7837, E-mail: smbl@sunyit.edu. *Dean,* Dr. Stephen Havlovic, 315-792-7429, Fax: 315-792-7138.

School of Information Systems and Engineering Technology Students: 34 full-time (8 women), 80 part-time (12 women); includes 4 Asian Americans or Pacific Islanders, 69 international. *Faculty:* 21 full-time (0 women), 6 part-time/adjunct (2 women). Expenses: Contact institution. *Financial support:* In 2006–07, 14 research assistantships (averaging $1,430 per year), 3 teaching assistantships (averaging $7,000 per year) were awarded; Federal Work-Study, scholarships/grants, and unspecified assistantships also available. Financial award applicants required to submit FAFSA. *Degree program information:* Part-time and evening/weekend programs available. Offers advanced technology (MS); computer and information science (MS); telecommunications (MS). *Application deadline:* For fall admission, 6/15 priority date for domestic students. Applications are processed on a rolling basis. *Application fee:* $50. *Application Contact:* Marybeth Lyons, Director of Admissions, 315-792-7500, Fax: 315-792-7837, E-mail: smbl@sunyit.edu. *Interim Dean,* Ray Jesaltis, 315-792-7234, Fax: 315-792-7800, E-mail: ray.jesaltis@sunyit.edu.

School of Nursing and Health Systems Students: 21 full-time (20 women), 38 part-time (36 women), 1 international. *Faculty:* 9 full-time (all women), 5 part-time/adjunct (4 women). Expenses: Contact institution. *Financial support:* Federal Work-Study, scholarships/grants, traineeships, and unspecified assistantships available. Financial award applicants required to submit FAFSA. *Degree program information:* Part-time programs available. Offers adult nurse practitioner (MS, CAS); family nurse practitioner (MS, CAS); gerontological nurse practitioner (MS, CAS); nursing administration (MS, CAS); nursing education (MS, CAS). *Application deadline:* For fall admission, 6/15 priority date for domestic students. Applications are processed on a rolling basis. *Application fee:* $50. *Application Contact:* Marybeth Lyons, Director of Admissions, 315-792-7500, Fax: 315-792-7837, E-mail: smbl@sunyit.edu. *Dean,* Dr. Esther Bankert, 315-792-7295, Fax: 315-792-7555, E-mail: esther.bankert@sunyit.edu.

See Close-Up on page 1045.

STATE UNIVERSITY OF NEW YORK MARITIME COLLEGE, Throggs Neck, NY 10465-4198

General Information State-supported, coed, primarily men, comprehensive institution. *Graduate housing:* Room and/or apartments available to single students; on-campus housing not available to married students. *Research affiliation:* Port Authority of New York and New Jersey (transportation), Transportation Infrastructure Research Consortium, Transportation Research Board (maritime transportation).

GRADUATE UNITS

Program in International Transportation Management *Degree program information:* Part-time and evening/weekend programs available. Offers international transportation management (MS).

STATE UNIVERSITY OF NEW YORK UPSTATE MEDICAL UNIVERSITY, Syracuse, NY 13210-2334

General Information State-supported, coed, upper-level institution. CGS member. *Enrollment:* 1,236 graduate, professional, and undergraduate students; 839 full-time matriculated graduate/professional students (387 women), 57 part-time matriculated graduate/professional students (51 women). *Enrollment by degree level:* 4 master's, 96 doctoral. *Graduate faculty:* 353. Tuition, state resident: full-time $6,900; part-time $288 per credit. Tuition, nonresident: full-time $10,920; part-time $455 per credit. *Required fees:* $496. *Graduate housing:* Rooms and/or apartments available on a first-come, first-served basis to single and married students. Typical cost: $3,931 per year for single students. Housing application deadline: 8/1. *Student services:* Career counseling, child daycare facilities, low-cost health insurance. *Library facilities:* Weiskotten Library. *Online resources:* library catalog, web page, access to other libraries' catalogs. *Collection:* 132,500 titles, 1,800 serial subscriptions.

Computer facilities: 130 computers available on campus for general student use. A campuswide network can be accessed from student residence rooms and from off campus. Internet access is available. *Web address:* http://www.upstate.edu/.

General Application Contact: Dr. Maxwell M. Mozell, Dean of the College of Graduate Studies, 315-464-4538, Fax: 315-464-4544.

GRADUATE UNITS

College of Graduate Studies Students: 125 full-time (65 women), 4 part-time (2 women); includes 16 minority (13 Asian Americans or Pacific Islanders, 3 Hispanic Americans), 41 international. Average age 28. 176 applicants, 35% accepted, 30 enrolled. *Faculty:* 80 full-time (15 women), 15 part-time/adjunct (2 women). Expenses: Contact institution. *Financial support:* In 2006–07, fellowships (averaging $21,514 per year), research assistantships (averaging $21,514 per year) were awarded; Federal Work-Study, institutionally sponsored loans, and scholarships/grants also available. Support available to part-time students. Financial award application deadline: 4/15; financial award applicants required to submit FAFSA. In 2006, 4 master's, 17 doctorates awarded. *Degree program information:* Part-time programs available. Offers anatomy and cell biology (MS, PhD); biochemistry and molecular biology (MS, PhD); microbiology and immunology (MS, PhD); neuroscience (PhD); pharmacology (MS, PhD); physiology (MS, PhD). *Application deadline:* For fall admission, 1/15 priority date for domestic and international students. Applications are processed on a rolling basis. *Application fee:* $40. Electronic applications accepted. *Application Contact:* Therese A. Brown, Information Contact, 315-464-4541, Fax: 315-464-4544, E-mail: browntt@upstate.edu. *Dean,* Dr. Maxwell M. Mozell, 315-464-4538, Fax: 315-464-4544.

College of Medicine Students: 611 full-time (312 women); includes 176 minority (47 African Americans, 5 American Indian/Alaska Native, 119 Asian Americans or Pacific Islanders, 5 Hispanic Americans), 30 international. Average age 25. 3,572 applicants, 12% accepted, 151 enrolled. *Faculty:* 366 full-time (74 women), 182 part-time/adjunct (37 women). Expenses: Contact institution. *Financial support:* In 2006–07, 545 students received support; research assistantships, teaching assistantships, career-related internships or fieldwork, Federal Work-Study, institutionally sponsored loans, scholarships/grants, and tuition waivers (full and partial) available. Support available to part-time students. Financial award application deadline: 3/1; financial award applicants required to submit FAFSA. In 2006, 157 degrees awarded. Offers medicine (MD). *Application deadline:* For fall admission, 12/1 for domestic and international students. Applications are processed on a rolling basis. *Application fee:* $100. Electronic applications accepted. *Application Contact:* Jennifer Welch, Director of Admissions, 315-464-4570, Fax: 315-464-8867, E-mail: welchj@upstate.edu. *Dean,* Dr. Steven J. Scheinman, 315-464-9720, E-mail: scheinms@upstate.edu.

College of Nursing Students: 29 full-time (all women), 62 part-time (56 women); includes 7 minority (4 African Americans, 3 Hispanic Americans). Average age 39. 41 applicants, 95% accepted, 29 enrolled. *Faculty:* 9 full-time (all women), 5 part-time/adjunct (4 women). Expenses: Contact institution. *Financial support:* Federal Work-Study, institutionally sponsored loans, scholarships/grants, and traineeships available. Support available to part-time students. Financial award application deadline: 3/1; financial award applicants required to submit FAFSA. In 2006, 18 master's, 8 other advanced degrees awarded. *Degree program information:* Part-time programs available. Offers nurse practitioner (Post Master's Certificate); nursing (MS). *Application deadline:* For fall admission, 3/15 priority date for domestic and international students. Applications are processed on a rolling basis. *Application fee:* $40. Electronic applications accepted. *Application Contact:* Donna Vavonese, Associate Director of Admissions, 315-464-4570, Fax: 315-464-8867, E-mail: vavonesd@upstate.edu. *Dean,* Dr. Elvira Szigeti, 315-464-4276, Fax: 315-464-5168.

Department of Physical Therapy Students: 67 full-time (49 women), 40 part-time (26 women); includes 5 minority (2 African Americans, 1 Asian American or Pacific Islander, 2 Hispanic Americans), 2 international. Average age 27. 130 applicants, 59% accepted, 60 enrolled. *Faculty:* 9 full-time (5 women), 5 part-time/adjunct (2 women). Expenses: Contact institution. *Financial support:* In 2006–07, 52 students received support. Federal Work-Study and scholarships/grants available. Support available to part-time students. Financial award application deadline: 3/1; financial award applicants required to submit FAFSA. In 2006, 17 degrees awarded. *Degree program information:* Part-time and evening/weekend programs available. Postbaccalaureate distance learning degree programs offered (minimal on-campus study). *Application deadline:* For fall admission, 1/15 for domestic students. Applications are processed on a rolling basis. *Application fee:* $30. *Application Contact:* Donna Vavonese, Associate Director of Admissions, 315-464-4570, Fax: 315-464-8867, E-mail: vavonesd@upstate.edu. *Interim Chair,* Dr. Susan Miller, 315-464-5101, Fax: 315-464-4608.

Program in Medical Technology Students: 9 full-time (6 women), 3 part-time (all women); includes 7 minority (all African Americans), 2 international. 19 applicants, 79% accepted, 7 enrolled. *Faculty:* 5 full-time, 1 part-time/adjunct. Expenses: Contact institution. *Financial support:* Federal Work-Study available. Support available to part-time students. Financial award application deadline: 3/1; financial award applicants required to submit FAFSA. Offers medical technology (MS). *Application deadline:* For fall admission, 4/1 priority date for domestic students. Applications are processed on a rolling basis. *Application fee:* $40. *Application Contact:* Donna Vavonese, Associate Director of Admissions, 315-464-4570, Fax: 315-464-8867, E-mail: vavonesd@upstate.edu. *Department Chair,* Susan S. Graham, 315-464-4608, E-mail: cls@upstate.edu.

STEPHEN F. AUSTIN STATE UNIVERSITY, Nacogdoches, TX 75962

General Information State-supported, coed, comprehensive institution. *Graduate housing:* Rooms and/or apartments available on a first-come, first-served basis to single students and available to married students. Housing application deadline: 6/1. *Research affiliation:* University Health Center at Tyler (biotechnology, environmental science).

GRADUATE UNITS

Graduate School *Degree program information:* Part-time and evening/weekend programs available. Postbaccalaureate distance learning degree programs offered. Electronic applications accepted.

College of Applied Arts and Science *Degree program information:* Part-time programs available. Offers applied arts and science (MA, MIS, MSW); communication (MA); interdisciplinary studies (MIS); mass communication (MA); social work (MSW).

College of Business *Degree program information:* Part-time and evening/weekend programs available. Offers business (MBA); computer science (MS); management and marketing (MBA); professional accountancy (MPAC).

College of Education *Degree program information:* Part-time and evening/weekend programs available. Offers athletic training (MS); counseling (MA); early childhood education (M Ed); education (M Ed, MA, MS, Ed D); educational leadership (Ed D); elementary education (M Ed); human sciences (MS); kinesiology (M Ed); school psychology (MA); secondary education (M Ed); special education (M Ed); speech pathology (MS).

College of Fine Arts *Degree program information:* Part-time programs available. Offers art (MA); design (MFA); drawing (MFA); fine arts (MA, MFA, MM); music (MA, MM); painting (MFA); sculpture (MFA).

College of Forestry and Agriculture Offers agriculture (MS); forestry (MF, MS, PhD); forestry and agriculture (MF, MS, PhD).

College of Liberal Arts *Degree program information:* Part-time and evening/weekend programs available. Offers English (MA); history (MA); liberal arts (MA, MPA); psychology (MA); public administration (MPA).

College of Sciences and Mathematics *Degree program information:* Part-time programs available. Offers biology (MS); biotechnology (MS); chemistry (MS); environmental science (MS); geology (MS, MSNS); mathematics (MS); mathematics education (MS); physics (MS); sciences and mathematics (MS, MSNS); statistics (MS).

STEPHENS COLLEGE, Columbia, MO 65215-0002

General Information Independent, Undergraduate: women only; graduate: coed, comprehensive institution. *Enrollment:* 964 graduate, professional, and undergraduate students; 101 full-time matriculated graduate/professional students (86 women), 18 part-time matriculated graduate/professional students (15 women). *Enrollment by degree level:* 119 master's. *Graduate faculty:* 5 full-time (4 women), 2 part-time/adjunct (both women). *Graduate housing:* On-campus housing not available. *Student services:* Campus safety program, career counseling, exercise/wellness program, international student services, multicultural affairs office. *Library facilities:* Hugh Stephens Library. *Online resources:* library catalog, web page, access to other libraries' catalogs. *Collection:* 125,000 titles, 7,393 serial subscriptions, 850 audiovisual materials.

Computer facilities: 64 computers available on campus for general student use. A campuswide network can be accessed from student residence rooms and from off campus. Internet access is available. *Web address:* http://www.stephens.edu/.

General Application Contact: Dr. Kate Getty, Associate Director, 800-388-7579, E-mail: online@stephens.edu.

GRADUATE UNITS

Division of Graduate and Continuing Studies Students: 101 full-time (86 women), 18 part-time (15 women); includes 1 minority (African American) Average age 40. 45 applicants, 78% accepted, 35 enrolled. *Faculty:* 5 part-time/adjunct. Expenses: Contact institution. In 2006, 8 master's awarded. *Degree program information:* Part-time and evening/weekend programs available. Postbaccalaureate distance learning degree programs offered (minimal on-campus study). Offers business administration (MBA); counseling (M Ed); curriculum and instruction (M Ed); health information administration (Postbaccalaureate Certificate). *Application deadline:* Applications are processed on a rolling basis. *Application fee:* $25. Electronic applications accepted. *Application Contact:* Dr. Kate Getty, Associate Director, 800-388-7579, E-mail: online@stephens.edu. *Director of Graduate and Continuing Studies,* Suzanne Sharp, 573-876-7123, Fax: 573-876-7237, E-mail: ssharp@stephens.edu.

STETSON UNIVERSITY, DeLand, FL 32723

General Information Independent, coed, comprehensive institution. *Enrollment:* 3,762 graduate, professional, and undergraduate students; 999 full-time matriculated graduate/professional students (518 women), 459 part-time matriculated graduate/professional students (270 women). *Enrollment by degree level:* 1,057 first professional, 388 master's, 13 other advanced degrees. *Graduate faculty:* 87 full-time (38 women), 43 part-time/adjunct (20 women). *Graduate housing:* Rooms and/or apartments available to single and married students. *Student services:* Campus employment opportunities, campus safety program, career counseling, free psychological counseling, international student services, multicultural affairs office, teacher training. *Library facilities:* DuPont-Ball Library plus 1 other. *Online resources:* library catalog, web page. *Collection:* 395,069 titles, 20,000 serial subscriptions, 17,260 audiovisual materials.

Stetson University (continued)

Computer facilities: 400 computers available on campus for general student use. A campuswide network can be accessed from student residence rooms and from off campus. Internet access and online class registration are available. *Web address:* http://www.stetson.edu/.

General Application Contact: Office of Graduate Studies, 386-822-7075, Fax: 386-822-7388.

GRADUATE UNITS

College of Arts and Sciences Students: 60 full-time (38 women), 120 part-time (103 women); includes 8 African Americans, 2 Asian Americans or Pacific Islanders, 16 Hispanic Americans, 4 international. Average age 33. Expenses: Contact institution. *Financial support:* Career-related internships or fieldwork, Federal Work-Study, institutionally sponsored loans, scholarships/grants, and tuition waivers (partial) available. Support available to part-time students. In 2006, 91 master's, 5 other advanced degrees awarded. *Degree program information:* Part-time and evening/weekend programs available. Offers arts and sciences (M Ed, MA, MS, Ed S); curriculum and instruction (Ed S); education (M Ed, MS, Ed S); educational leadership (M Ed, Ed S); exceptional student education (M Ed); marriage and family therapy (MS); mental health counseling (MS); reading education (M Ed); school guidance and family consultation (MS). *Application deadline:* For fall admission, 3/1 priority date for domestic students; for spring admission, 11/1 for domestic students. Applications are processed on a rolling basis. *Application fee:* $25. *Application Contact:* Midge McDaniel, Office of Graduate Studies, 386-822-7075, Fax: 386-822-7388, E-mail: mmcdanie@stetson.edu. *Dean,* Dr. Grady Ballenger, 386-822-7515.

Division of Humanities Average age 27. Expenses: Contact institution. In 2006, 1 degree awarded. Offers English (MA); humanities (MA). *Application deadline:* For fall admission, 3/1 priority date for domestic students; for spring admission, 11/1 for domestic students. Applications are processed on a rolling basis. *Application fee:* $25. *Application Contact:* Pat LeClaire, Office of Graduate Studies, 386-822-7075, Fax: 386-822-7388, E-mail: pleclaire@stetson.edu.

College of Law Students: 853 full-time (450 women), 204 part-time (112 women); includes 204 minority (61 African Americans, 6 American Indian/Alaska Native, 27 Asian Americans or Pacific Islanders, 110 Hispanic Americans), 22 international. Average age 27. Expenses: Contact institution. *Financial support:* Research assistantships, teaching assistantships, career-related internships or fieldwork, institutionally sponsored loans, and scholarships/grants available. Financial award application deadline: 4/1; financial award applicants required to submit FAFSA. In 2006, 294 degrees awarded. Offers law (JD, LL M). *Application deadline:* For fall admission, 3/1 priority date for domestic students; for spring admission, 9/1 for domestic students. *Application fee:* $50. *Application Contact:* Pamela Coleman, Assistant Dean and Director of Admissions, 727-562-7802, E-mail: lawadmit@law.stetson.edu. *Dean,* Dr. Darby Dickerson, 727-562-7810.

School of Business Administration Students: 86 full-time (30 women), 135 part-time (55 women); includes 26 minority (8 African Americans, 5 Asian Americans or Pacific Islanders, 13 Hispanic Americans), 16 international. Average age 29. Expenses: Contact institution. *Financial support:* In 2006–07, 3 research assistantships were awarded; Federal Work-Study and institutionally sponsored loans also available. Support available to part-time students. Financial award application deadline: 3/15. In 2006, 127 degrees awarded. *Degree program information:* Part-time and evening/weekend programs available. Offers accounting (M Acc); business administration (M Acc, MBA). *Application deadline:* For fall admission, 7/1 for domestic students. *Application fee:* $25. *Application Contact:* Jeanne Bosco, Administrative Assistant, 386-822-7410, Fax: 386-822-7413, E-mail: jbosco@stetson.edu. *Dean,* Dr. James Scheiner, 386-822-7415.

STEVENS INSTITUTE OF TECHNOLOGY, Hoboken, NJ 07030

General Information Independent, coed, university. *Graduate housing:* Room and/or apartments available on a first-come, first-served basis to single students.

GRADUATE UNITS

Graduate School *Degree program information:* Part-time and evening/weekend programs available. Postbaccalaureate distance learning degree programs offered (no on-campus study). Offers interdisciplinary sciences and engineering (M Eng, MS, PhD). Electronic applications accepted.

Arthur E. Imperatore School of Sciences and Arts *Degree program information:* Part-time and evening/weekend programs available. Offers applied mathematics (MS, PhD); applied optics (Certificate); applied statistics (Certificate); chemical biology (MS, PhD); chemistry (MS, PhD); chemistry and chemical biology (Certificate); cognitive science (Certificate); computer science (MS, PhD); database systems (Certificate); elements of computer science (Certificate); engineering physics (M Eng); information systems (MS); mathematics (MS, PhD); physics (MS, PhD); professional communications (Certificate); quantitative software engineering (MS, Certificate); sciences and arts (M Eng, MS, PhD, Certificate); stochastic systems analysis and optimization (MS, Certificate); surface physics (Certificate); theoretical computer science (Certificate). Electronic applications accepted.

Charles V. Schaefer Jr. School of Engineering *Degree program information:* Part-time and evening/weekend programs available. Postbaccalaureate distance learning degree programs offered. Offers advanced manufacturing (Certificate); agile systems engineering and design (Certificate); air pollution technology (Certificate); armament engineering (M Eng); biomedical engineering (M Eng, Certificate); chemical engineering (M Eng, PhD, Engr); civil engineering (M Eng, PhD, Certificate, Engr); computational fluid mechanics and heat transfer (Certificate); computer and communications security (Certificate); computer and electrical engineering (M Eng); computer architecture and digital system design (M Eng, PhD, Engr); computer engineering (M Eng, PhD, Certificate, Engr); computer systems (M Eng, PhD, Engr); concurrent design management (M Eng); construction accounting/estimating (Certificate); construction engineering (Certificate); construction law/disputes (Certificate); construction management (MS, Certificate); construction/quality management (Certificate); design and production management (Certificate); digital systems and VLSI design (Certificate); electrical engineering (M Eng, MS, PhD, Certificate, Engr); engineering (M Eng, MS, PhD, Certificate, Engr); engineering management (M Eng, PhD, Certificate); environmental compatibility in engineering (Certificate); environmental engineering (M Eng, PhD, Certificate); environmental process (M Eng, PhD, Certificate); geotechnical engineering (Certificate); geotechnical/geoenvironmental engineering (M Eng, PhD, Engr); groundwater and soil pollution control (M Eng, PhD, Certificate); image processing and multimedia (M Eng, PhD, Engr); information networks (Certificate); inland and coastal environmental hydrodynamics (M Eng, PhD, Certificate); integrated product development (M Eng); manufacturing technologies (M Eng); maritime systems (M Eng, MS); materials engineering (M Eng, PhD, Engr); mechanical engineering (M Eng, PhD, Engr); microelectronics and photonics (Certificate); ocean engineering (M Eng, PhD); pharmaceutical manufacturing (M Eng, MS, Certificate); polymer engineering (M Eng, PhD, Engr); power generation (Certificate); product architecture and engineering (M Eng); robotics and control (Certificate); signal processing for communications (M Eng, PhD, Engr); software engineering (M Eng, PhD, Engr); structural analysis and design (Certificate); structural engineering (M Eng, PhD, Engr); systems and supportability engineering (Certificate); systems design and operational effectiveness (M Eng); systems engineering (M Eng, PhD, Certificate); systems engineering and architecting (Certificate); systems reliability and design (M Eng); telecommunications engineering (M Eng, PhD, Engr); telecommunications management (MS, PhD, Certificate); vibration and noise control (Certificate); water quality control (Certificate); water resources engineering (M Eng). Electronic applications accepted.

Wesley J. Howe School of Technology Management *Degree program information:* Part-time and evening/weekend programs available. Postbaccalaureate distance learning degree programs offered. Offers business (MS); computer science (MS); e-commerce (MS, Certificate); engineering management (MBA); entrepreneurial information technology (MS); financial management (MBA); general management (MS); global innovation management (MS); global technology management (MBA); human resource management (MS); information management (MBA, MS, PhD, Certificate); information security (MS); information technology in financial services (MBA); information technology in financial services industry (MS); information technology in the pharmaceutical industry (MBA, MS); information technology outsourcing (MBA); information technology outsourcing management (MS); integrated information architecture (MS); management of wireless networks (MS); online security, technology and business (MS); pharmaceutical technology management (MBA); project management (MBA, MS, Certificate); quantitative software engineering (MS); systems engineering (MS); technical management (MS); technology commercialization (MS); technology management (EMBA, MS, PhD); technology management for experienced professionals (EMTM, MS, MTM, Certificate); telecommunications management (MBA, MS, PhD, Certificate). Electronic applications accepted.

STONEHILL COLLEGE, Easton, MA 02357-5510

General Information Independent-religious, coed, comprehensive institution. *Enrollment:* 2,386 graduate, professional, and undergraduate students; 10 full-time matriculated graduate/professional students (7 women), 5 part-time matriculated graduate/professional students (3 women). *Enrollment by degree level:* 15 master's. *Graduate faculty:* 9 full-time (3 women). *Tuition:* Full-time $27,330; part-time $2,733 per course. *Required fees:* $25 per semester. Part-time tuition and fees vary according to course load. *Graduate housing:* On-campus housing not available. *Student services:* Campus employment opportunities, campus safety program, career counseling, disabled student services, exercise/wellness program, free psychological counseling, international student services, multicultural affairs office. *Library facilities:* Bartley MacPhaidin, C.S.C. Library. *Online resources:* library catalog, web page. *Collection:* 205,400 titles, 2,196 serial subscriptions, 7,123 audiovisual materials.

Computer facilities: 300 computers available on campus for general student use. A campuswide network can be accessed from student residence rooms and from off campus. Internet access and online class registration, online schedules, assignments, grades and student accounts are available. *Web address:* http://www.stonehill.edu/.

General Application Contact: Brian P. Murphy, Dean of Admissions and Enrollment, 508-565-1373, Fax: 508-565-1545, E-mail: admissions@stonehill.edu.

GRADUATE UNITS

Program in Accounting Students: 10 full-time (7 women), 5 part-time (3 women); includes 3 minority (1 African American, 1 Asian American or Pacific Islander, 1 Hispanic American). Average age 28. 13 applicants, 100% accepted, 7 enrolled. *Faculty:* 9 full-time (3 women). Expenses: Contact institution. *Financial support:* Career-related internships or fieldwork, Federal Work-Study, scholarships/grants, and health care benefits available. Support available to part-time students. Financial award application deadline: 3/15; financial award applicants required to submit FAFSA. In 2006, 18 degrees awarded. *Degree program information:* Part-time programs available. Offers accountancy (MSA). *Application deadline:* For fall admission, 3/1 for domestic and international students; for spring admission, 10/1 for domestic and international students. *Application fee:* $50. *Application Contact:* Brian P. Murphy, Dean of Admissions and Enrollment, 508-565-1373, Fax: 508-565-1545, E-mail: admissions@stonehill.edu. *Director,* Richard J. Anderson, 508-565-1224, E-mail: jranderson@stonehill.edu.

STONY BROOK UNIVERSITY, STATE UNIVERSITY OF NEW YORK, Stony Brook, NY 11794

General Information State-supported, coed, university. CGS member. *Enrollment:* 22,522 graduate, professional, and undergraduate students; 4,413 full-time matriculated graduate/professional students (2,296 women), 2,216 part-time matriculated graduate/professional students (1,433 women). *Enrollment by degree level:* 595 first professional, 3,111 master's, 2,420 doctoral, 503 other advanced degrees. *Graduate faculty:* 1,254 full-time (394 women), 445 part-time/adjunct (173 women). Tuition, state resident: full-time $6,900; part-time $288 per credit. Tuition, nonresident: full-time $10,920; part-time $455 per credit. *Graduate housing:* Rooms and/or apartments available to single and married students. *Student services:* Campus employment opportunities, campus safety program, career counseling, child daycare facilities, disabled student services, exercise/wellness program, free psychological counseling, grant writing training, international student services, low-cost health insurance, multicultural affairs office, teacher training, writing training. *Library facilities:* Frank Melville, Jr. Building Library plus 6 others. *Online resources:* library catalog, web page, access to other libraries' catalogs. *Collection:* 1.9 million titles, 29,275 serial subscriptions, 42,764 audiovisual materials. *Research affiliation:* Brookhaven National Laboratory, Cold Spring Harbor Laboratory, Winthrop University Hospital, Nassau University Medical Center, Veterans Affairs Medical Center (Northport, NY).

Computer facilities: 2,600 computers available on campus for general student use. A campuswide network can be accessed from student residence rooms and from off campus. Internet access and online class registration are available. *Web address:* http://www.sunysb.edu/.

General Application Contact: Dr. Kent Marks, Director, Admissions and Records, 631-632-4723, Fax: 631-632-7243, E-mail: kent.marks@sunysb.edu.

GRADUATE UNITS

Graduate School Students: 2,719 full-time (1,197 women), 450 part-time (216 women); includes 404 minority (66 African Americans, 5 American Indian/Alaska Native, 205 Asian Americans or Pacific Islanders, 128 Hispanic Americans), 1,356 international. 6,308 applicants, 32% accepted. *Faculty:* 601 full-time (142 women), 123 part-time/adjunct (38 women). Expenses: Contact institution. *Financial support:* In 2006–07, 113 fellowships, 713 research assistantships, 819 teaching assistantships were awarded; career-related internships or fieldwork, Federal Work-Study, institutionally sponsored loans, scholarships/grants, traineeships, health care benefits, tuition waivers (full), and unspecified assistantships also available. In 2006, 559 master's, 243 doctorates, 45 other advanced degrees awarded. *Degree program information:* Part-time and evening/weekend programs available. *Application deadline:* For fall admission, 1/15 for domestic and international students; for spring admission, 10/1 for domestic and international students. *Application fee:* $60. *Application Contact:* Dr. Kent Marks, Director, Admissions and Records, 631-632-4723, Fax: 631-632-7243, E-mail: kent.marks@sunysb.edu. *Dean,* Dr. Lawrence B. Martin, 631-632-7035, Fax: 631-632-7243.

College of Arts and Sciences Students: 1,815 full-time (918 women), 251 part-time (162 women); includes 249 minority (43 African Americans, 4 American Indian/Alaska Native, 105 Asian Americans or Pacific Islanders, 97 Hispanic Americans), 717 international. 3,655 applicants, 27% accepted. *Faculty:* 421 full-time (112 women), 80 part-time/adjunct (31 women). Expenses: Contact institution. *Financial support:* In 2006–07, 94 fellowships, 479 research assistantships, 674 teaching assistantships were awarded; career-related internships or fieldwork, Federal Work-Study, scholarships/grants, traineeships, health care benefits, and unspecified assistantships also available. In 2006, 284 master's, 172 doctorates, 23 other advanced degrees awarded. *Degree program information:* Part-time and evening/weekend programs available. Offers anthropology (MA, PhD); art history and criticism (MA, PhD); arts and sciences (MA, MAPP, MAT, MFA, MM, MS, DA, DMA, PhD, Certificate); astronomy (MS, PhD); biochemistry and molecular biology (PhD); biochemistry and structural biology (PhD); biological and biomedical sciences (PhD); biological sciences (MA); biopsychology (PhD); cellular and developmental biology (PhD); chemistry (MAT, MS, PhD); clinical psychology (PhD); comparative literature (MA, PhD); composition studies (Certificate); dramaturgy (MFA); earth and space science (MS, PhD); earth and space sciences (MS, PhD); earth science (MAT); ecology and evolution (PhD); economics (MA, PhD); English (MA, MAT, PhD); ethnomusicology (MA, PhD); experimental psychology (PhD); foreign languages (DA); French (MA, MAT, DA); genetics (PhD); German (MA, MAT, DA); Germanic languages and literatures (MA); Hispanic languages and literature (MA, DA, PhD); history (MA, MAT, PhD); immunology and pathology (PhD); Italian (MA, MAT, DA); linguistics (MA, PhD); mathematics (MA, PhD); molecular and cellular biology (MA, PhD); music (MA, PhD); music history, theory and composition (MA, PhD); music performance (MM, DMA); neuroscience (PhD); philosophy (MA, PhD); physics (MA, MAT, MS, PhD); political science (MA, PhD); psychology (MA); public policy (MAPP); Romance languages and literatures (MA); Slavic languages and literatures (MA); social/health psychology (PhD); sociology (MA, PhD); studio art (MFA); teaching English to speakers of other languages (MA, DA); theatre (MA). *Application deadline:* For fall admission, 1/15 for domestic students. *Application fee:* $60. *Dean,* Dr. James V. Staros, 631-632-6999, Fax: 631-632-6900.

College of Business Students: 150 full-time (70 women), 58 part-time (23 women); includes 43 minority (7 African Americans, 24 Asian Americans or Pacific Islanders, 12 Hispanic Americans), 54 international. Average age 29. 144 applicants, 89% accepted. *Faculty:* 18 full-time (1 woman), 20 part-time/adjunct (5 women). Expenses: Contact institution. *Financial support:* In 2006–07, 1 research assistantship, 8 teaching assistantships were awarded. In 2006, 48 master's, 22 other advanced degrees awarded. Offers business (MBA, MS, Certificate); business administration (MBA); finance (Certificate); industrial management (Certificate); management policy (MS); technology management (MS). *Application deadline:* For fall admission, 1/15 for domestic and international students; for spring admission, 10/1 for domestic and international students. *Application fee:* $60. *Application Contact:* Dr. Jeff Casey, Director, Graduate Program, 631-632-7171, E-mail: jcasey@notes.cc.sunysb.edu. *Interim Dean,* William H. Turner, 631-632-7180, E-mail: oss@notes.cc.sunysb.edu.

College of Engineering and Applied Sciences Students: 754 full-time (209 women), 141 part-time (31 women); includes 112 minority (16 African Americans, 1 American Indian/Alaska Native, 76 Asian Americans or Pacific Islanders, 19 Hispanic Americans), 585 international. 2,317 applicants, 39% accepted. *Faculty:* 125 full-time (22 women), 23 part-time/adjunct (2 women). Expenses: Contact institution. *Financial support:* In 2006–07, 19 fellowships, 233 research assistantships, 137 teaching assistantships were awarded; career-related internships or fieldwork also available. In 2006, 227 master's, 71 doctorates awarded. *Degree program information:* Part-time and evening/weekend programs available. Offers applied mathematics and statistics (MS, PhD); biomedical engineering (MS, PhD, Certificate); computer science (MS, PhD); educational technology (MS); electrical and computer engineering (MS, PhD); engineering and applied sciences (MS, PhD, Certificate); global operations management (MS); information systems (Certificate); information systems engineering (MS); materials science and engineering (MS, PhD); mechanical engineering (MS, PhD); medical physics (PhD); optoelectromechanical system engineering (MS); software engineering (Certificate). *Application deadline:* For fall admission, 1/15 for domestic students. *Application fee:* $60. *Dean,* Dr. Yacov Shamash, 631-632-8380, E-mail: yaeou.shamash@storybrook.edu.

Institute for Terrestrial and Planetary Atmospheres Expenses: Contact institution. *Financial support:* Fellowships available. Offers terrestrial and planetary atmospheres (PhD). *Application deadline:* For fall admission, 3/1 for domestic students. *Application fee:* $60. *Director,* Minghua Zhang, 631-632-8318.

Marine Sciences Research Center Students: 109 full-time (59 women), 4 part-time (all women); includes 10 minority (2 African Americans, 2 Asian Americans or Pacific Islanders, 6 Hispanic Americans), 42 international. Average age 28. 71 applicants, 69% accepted. *Faculty:* 37 full-time (7 women). Expenses: Contact institution. *Financial support:* In 2006–07, 26 fellowships, 55 research assistantships, 31 teaching assistantships were awarded; career-related internships or fieldwork and tuition waivers (full) also available. In 2006, 18 master's, 4 doctorates awarded. *Degree program information:* Evening/weekend programs available. Offers marine and atmospheric sciences (MS, PhD). *Application fee:* $60. *Application Contact:* Dr. Glen Lopez, Acting Director, 631-632-8660, Fax: 631-632-8200, E-mail: glopez@notes.cc.sunysb.edu. *Dean and Director,* Dr. David O. Conover, 631-632-8700, Fax: 631-632-8200, E-mail: dconover@notes.cc.sunnysb.edu.

School of Professional Development Students: 322 full-time (202 women), 1,188 part-time (728 women); includes 164 minority (69 African Americans, 2 American Indian/Alaska Native, 29 Asian Americans or Pacific Islanders, 64 Hispanic Americans), 11 international. Average age 28. *Faculty:* 1 full-time (0 women), 118 part-time/adjunct (45 women). Expenses: Contact institution. *Financial support:* In 2006–07, 5 teaching assistantships were awarded; fellowships, research assistantships, career-related internships or fieldwork also available. Support available to part-time students. In 2006, 738 master's, 405 other advanced degrees awarded. *Degree program information:* Part-time and evening/weekend programs available. Postbaccalaureate distance learning degree programs offered. Offers adolescence education: mathematics (Certificate); biology 7-12 (MAT); chemistry-grade 7-12 (MAT); coaching (Certificate); computer integrated engineering (Certificate); cultural studies (Certificate); earth science-grade 7-12 (MAT); educational computing (Advanced Certificate, Certificate); English-grade 7-12 (MAT); environmental and waste management (MS, Advanced Certificate); environmental systems management (Certificate); environmental/occupational health and safety (Certificate); French-grade 7-12 (MAT); German-grade 7-12 (MAT); human resource management (Certificate); industrial management (Certificate); information systems management (Certificate); Italian-grade 7-12 (MAT); liberal studies (MA); liberal studies online (MA); Long Island regional studies (Certificate); operation research (Certificate); physics-grade 7-12 (MAT); Russian-grade 7-12 (MAT); school administration and supervision (Certificate); school district administration (Certificate); social science and the professions (MPS); social studies 7-12 (MAT); waste management (Certificate); women's studies (Certificate). *Application deadline:* Applications are processed on a rolling basis. *Application fee:* $62. *Application Contact:* Sandra Romansky, Director of Admissions and Advisement, 631-632-7050, Fax: 631-632-9046, E-mail: sandra.romansky@sunysb.edu. *Dean,* Dr. Paul J. Edelson, 631-632-7052, Fax: 631-632-9046, E-mail: paul.edelson@sunysb.edu.

Health Sciences Center Students: 812 full-time (601 women), 563 part-time (474 women); includes 356 minority (155 African Americans, 5 American Indian/Alaska Native, 109 Asian Americans or Pacific Islanders, 87 Hispanic Americans), 18 international. 5,625 applicants, 19% accepted. *Faculty:* 108 full-time (69 women), 117 part-time/adjunct (52 women). Expenses: Contact institution. *Financial support:* In 2006–07, 41 fellowships, 74 research assistantships, 19 teaching assistantships were awarded; career-related internships or fieldwork, Federal Work-Study, institutionally sponsored loans, traineeships, and tuition waivers (full) also available. Financial award applicants required to submit FAFSA. In 2006, 158 first professional degrees, 380 master's, 133 doctorates, 64 other advanced degrees awarded. *Degree program information:* Part-time programs available. Offers adult health nurse practitioner (Certificate); adult health/primary care nursing (MS); child health nurse practitioner (Certificate); child health nursing (MS); community health (Advanced Certificate); dental medicine (DDS); endodontics (Certificate); family nurse practitioner (MS, Certificate); gerontological nursing (MS); health care management (Advanced Certificate); health care policy and management (MS); health sciences (DDS, MS, MSW, DPT, PhD, Advanced Certificate, Certificate); mental health nurse practitioner (Certificate); mental health/psychiatric nursing (MS); neonatal nurse practitioner (Certificate); neonatal nursing (MS); nurse-midwifery (MS, Certificate); nursing (MS, Certificate); occupational therapy (MS); oral biology and pathology (PhD); orthodontics (Certificate); perinatal/women's health nurse practitioner (Certificate); perinatal/women's health nursing (MS); periodontics (Certificate); physical therapy (MS, DPT); social welfare (PhD); social work (MSW). *Application fee:* $60. *Interim Executive Dean,* Dr. Craig A. Lehmann, 631-444-2080, Fax: 631-444-6032.

School of Medicine Students: 546 full-time (288 women), 29 part-time (23 women); includes 246 minority (58 African Americans, 2 American Indian/Alaska Native, 159 Asian Americans or Pacific Islanders, 27 Hispanic Americans), 32 international. 3,281 applicants, 10% accepted. *Faculty:* 568 full-time (181 women), 74 part-time/adjunct (32 women). Expenses: Contact institution. *Financial support:* In 2006–07, 33 fellowships, 67 research assistantships, 7 teaching assistantships were awarded; career-related internships or fieldwork, Federal Work-Study, and tuition waivers (full) also available. In 2006, 118 MDs, 6 master's, 24 doctorates awarded. Offers anatomical sciences (PhD); community health (MPH); evaluation sciences (MPH); family violence (MPH); health economics (MPH); medicine (MD, MPH, PhD); molecular and cellular pharmacology (PhD); molecular microbiology (PhD); physiology and biophysics (PhD); population health (MPH); substance abuse (MPH). *Application deadline:* For fall admission, 1/15 for domestic students. *Dean,* Dr. Richard N. Fine, 631-444-2113.

See Close-Up on page 1047.

STRATFORD UNIVERSITY, Falls Church, VA 22043

General Information Proprietary, coed, comprehensive institution. *Enrollment:* 21 full-time matriculated graduate/professional students (9 women), 10 part-time matriculated graduate/professional students (4 women). *Enrollment by degree level:* 31 master's. *Graduate housing:* On-campus housing not available. *Library facilities:* Stratford University Library. *Collection:* 1,800 titles, 75 serial subscriptions, 283 audiovisual materials.

Computer facilities: 7 computers available on campus for general student use. A campuswide network can be accessed. Internet access and online class registration are available. *Web address:* http://www.stratford.edu/.

General Application Contact: Gail Robin, Interim Dean, 703-821-8570, E-mail: grobin@stratford.edu.

GRADUATE UNITS

School of Graduate Studies Students: 21 full-time (9 women), 10 part-time (4 women); includes 5 minority (all African Americans), 19 international. Average age 37. Expenses: Contact institution. *Financial support:* In 2006–07, 9 students received support. Federal Work-Study available. Financial award applicants required to submit FAFSA. In 2006, 9 degrees awarded. *Degree program information:* Part-time and evening/weekend programs available. Postbaccalaureate distance learning degree programs offered (minimal on-campus study). *Application deadline:* Applications are processed on a rolling basis. *Application fee:* $100. Electronic applications accepted. *Interim Dean,* Gail Robin, 703-821-8570, E-mail: grobin@stratford.edu.

STRAYER UNIVERSITY, Washington, DC 20005-2603

General Information Proprietary, coed, comprehensive institution. *Graduate housing:* On-campus housing not available.

GRADUATE UNITS

Graduate Studies *Degree program information:* Part-time and evening/weekend programs available. Postbaccalaureate distance learning degree programs offered (minimal on-campus study). Offers accounting (MS); acquisition (MBA); business administration (MBA); communications technology (MS); educational management (M Ed); finance (MBA); health services administration (MHSA); hospitality and tourism management (MBA); human resource management (MBA); information systems (MS); management (MBA); management information systems (MS); marketing (MBA); professional accounting (MS); public administration (MPA); supply chain management (MBA); technology in education (M Ed). Programs also offered at campus locations in Birmingham, AL; Chamblee, GA; Cobb County, GA; Morrow, GA; White Marsh, MD; Charleston, SC; Columbia, SC; Greensboro, NC; Greenville, SC; Lexington, KY; Louisville, KY; Nashville, TN; North Raleigh, NC; Washington, DC. Electronic applications accepted.

SUFFOLK UNIVERSITY, Boston, MA 02108-2770

General Information Independent, coed, comprehensive institution. *Enrollment:* 8,863 graduate, professional, and undergraduate students; 1,518 full-time matriculated graduate/professional students (804 women), 1,777 part-time matriculated graduate/professional students (1,020 women). *Enrollment by degree level:* 1,644 first professional, 1,444 master's, 66 doctoral, 141 other advanced degrees. *Graduate faculty:* 210 full-time (81 women), 96 part-time/adjunct (30 women). *Graduate housing:* On-campus housing not available. *Student services:* Campus employment opportunities, campus safety program, career counseling, disabled student services, exercise/wellness program, free psychological counseling, grant writing training, international student services, low-cost health insurance, multicultural affairs office, teacher training, writing training. *Library facilities:* Mildred Sawyer Library plus 3 others. *Online resources:* library catalog, web page, access to other libraries' catalogs. *Collection:* 120,389 titles, 24,598 serial subscriptions, 558 audiovisual materials.

Computer facilities: 400 computers available on campus for general student use. A campuswide network can be accessed from student residence rooms and from off campus. Internet access and online class registration are available. *Web address:* http://www.suffolk.edu/.

General Application Contact: Judith Reynolds, Director of Graduate Admissions, 617-573-8302, Fax: 617-523-0116, E-mail: grad.admission@suffolk.edu.

GRADUATE UNITS

College of Arts and Sciences Students: 220 full-time (162 women), 364 part-time (279 women); includes 59 minority (31 African Americans, 3 American Indian/Alaska Native, 16 Asian Americans or Pacific Islanders, 9 Hispanic Americans), 64 international. Average age 29. 853 applicants, 55% accepted, 208 enrolled. *Faculty:* 114 full-time (55 women), 25 part-time/adjunct (7 women). Expenses: Contact institution. *Financial support:* In 2006–07, 248 students received support, including 235 fellowships with full and partial tuition reimbursements available (averaging $8,750 per year); career-related internships or fieldwork, Federal Work-Study, institutionally sponsored loans, scholarships/grants, and unspecified assistantships also available. Support available to part-time students. Financial award application deadline: 4/1; financial award applicants required to submit FAFSA. In 2006, 178 master's, 5 doctorates, 6 CAGSs awarded. *Degree program information:* Part-time and evening/weekend programs available. Offers administration of higher education (M Ed); adult and organizational learning (MS, CAGS); arts and sciences (M Ed, MA, MS, MSCJ, MSEP, MSIE, PhD, CAGS); clinical-developmental psychology (PhD); communication (MA); computer science (MS); counseling and human relations (M Ed, MS, CAGS); criminal justice (MSCJ); economic policy (MSEP); economics (PhD); educational administration (M Ed); foundations of education (M Ed, CAGS); higher education administration (M Ed, CAGS); human resources (MS, CAGS); instructional design (CAGS); international economics (MSIE); leadership (CAGS); mental health counseling (MS); organizational development (CAGS); organizational learning (CAGS); political science (MS); professional development in teaching programs (CAGS); school counseling (M Ed); secondary school teaching (MS). *Application deadline:* For fall admission, 6/15 priority date for domestic students, 6/15 for international students; for spring admission, 11/1 priority date for domestic students, 11/1 for international students. Applications are processed on a rolling basis. *Application fee:* $35. Electronic applications accepted. *Application Contact:* Judith Reynolds, Director of Graduate Admissions, 617-573-8302, Fax: 617-523-0116, E-mail: grad.admission@suffolk.edu. *Dean,* Dr. Kenneth S. Greenberg, 617-573-8527, Fax: 617-573-8513, E-mail: kgreenbe@suffolk.edu.

New England School of Art and Design Students: 51 full-time (49 women), 67 part-time (61 women); includes 8 minority (3 African Americans, 3 Asian Americans or Pacific Islanders, 2 Hispanic Americans), 13 international. Average age 29. 89 applicants, 73% accepted, 30 enrolled. *Faculty:* 18 full-time (9 women), 14 part-time/adjunct (4 women). Expenses: Contact institution. *Financial support:* In 2006–07, 32 fellowships with partial tuition reimbursements (averaging $7,912 per year) were awarded. Financial award application deadline: 4/1. In 2006, 12 degrees awarded. *Degree program information:* Part-time and evening/weekend programs available. Offers graphic design (MA); interior design (MA). *Application deadline:* For fall admission, 6/15 priority date for domestic students, 6/15 for international students; for spring admission, 11/1 priority date for domestic students, 11/1 for international students. Applications are processed on a rolling basis. *Application fee:* $30. Electronic applications accepted. *Application Contact:* Judith Reynolds, Director of Graduate Admissions, 617-573-8302, Fax: 617-523-0116, E-mail: grad.admission@suffolk.edu. *Director,* Dr. William Davis, 617-994-4264, Fax: 617-536-0461, E-mail: wdavis@suffolk.edu.

Law School Students: 1,032 full-time (504 women), 612 part-time (301 women); includes 211 minority (47 African Americans, 8 American Indian/Alaska Native, 105 Asian Americans or Pacific Islanders, 51 Hispanic Americans), 23 international. Average age 26. 3,069 applicants, 49% accepted, 550 enrolled. *Faculty:* 79 full-time (25 women), 124 part-time/adjunct (30 women). Expenses: Contact institution. *Financial support:* In 2006–07, 627 students received support. Career-related internships or fieldwork, Federal Work-Study, institutionally sponsored loans, and scholarships/grants available. Support available to part-time students. Financial award application deadline: 3/1; financial award applicants required to submit FAFSA. In 2006, 498 JDs, 18 master's awarded. *Degree program information:* Part-time and evening/weekend programs available. Offers civil litigation (JD); financial services (JD); global law and technology (LL M); health care/biotechnology law (JD); intellectual property law (JD); international law (JD); U.S. law for international business lawyers (LL M). *Application deadline:* For fall admission, 3/1 priority date for domestic and international students. Applications are processed on a rolling basis. *Application fee:* $60. Electronic applications accepted. *Application Contact:* Ian A. Menchini, Associate Director, Law Admissions, 617-573-8144, Fax: 617-523-1367, E-mail: imenchin@suffolk.edu. *Dean of Admissions,* Gail N. Ellis, 617-573-8144, Fax: 617-523-1367, E-mail: gellis@suffolk.edu.

Suffolk University (continued)

Sawyer Business School Students: 266 full-time (138 women), 801 part-time (440 women); includes 106 minority (42 African Americans, 53 Asian Americans or Pacific Islanders, 11 Hispanic Americans), 157 international. Average age 30. 863 applicants, 76% accepted, 323 enrolled. *Faculty:* 96 full-time (26 women), 71 part-time/adjunct (23 women). Expenses: Contact institution. *Financial support:* In 2006–07, 200 students received support, including 200 fellowships with partial tuition reimbursements available (averaging $9,409 per year); career-related internships or fieldwork, Federal Work-Study, and institutionally sponsored loans also available. Support available to part-time students. Financial award application deadline: 4/1; financial award applicants required to submit FAFSA. In 2006, 471 master's, 3 other advanced degrees awarded. *Degree program information:* Part-time and evening/weekend programs available. Postbaccalaureate distance learning degree programs offered (no on-campus study). Offers accounting (MSA, GDPA); banking and financial services (MS); business (EMBA, GMBA, MBA, MBAH, MHA, MPA, MS, MSA, MSF, MST, APC, CASPA, CPASF, GDPA); business administration (MBA, APC); disability studies (MPA); executive business administration (EMBA); finance (MSF, CPASF); global business administration (GMBA); health administration (MPA); nonprofit management (MPA); public administration (CASPA); public finance and human resources (MPA); state and local government (MPA); taxation (MST). *Application deadline:* For fall admission, 6/15 priority date for domestic students, 6/15 for international students; for spring admission, 11/1 for domestic and international students. Applications are processed on a rolling basis. *Application fee:* $50. Electronic applications accepted. *Application Contact:* Judith Reynolds, Director of Graduate Admissions, 617-573-8302, Fax: 617-523-0116, E-mail: grad.admission@suffolk.edu. *Dean,* Dr. William J. O'Neill, 617-573-2665, Fax: 617-573-8704, E-mail: woneill@suffolk.edu.

SULLIVAN UNIVERSITY, Louisville, KY 40205

General Information Proprietary, coed, comprehensive institution. *Graduate housing:* On-campus housing not available.

GRADUATE UNITS

School of Business Offers business (EMBA, MBA); dispute resolution (MSDR); management of information technology (MSMIT).

SUL ROSS STATE UNIVERSITY, Alpine, TX 79832

General Information State-supported, coed, comprehensive institution. *Graduate housing:* Rooms and/or apartments available to single and married students. *Research affiliation:* Chihuahuan Desert Research Institute (biology, geology), Big Bend National Park (biology, geology).

GRADUATE UNITS

Division of Agricultural and Natural Resource Science *Degree program information:* Part-time programs available. Offers agricultural and natural resource science (M Ag, MS); animal science (M Ag, MS); range and wildlife management (M Ag, MS).

Rio Grande College of Sul Ross State University *Degree program information:* Part-time and evening/weekend programs available. Offers business administration (MBA); teacher education (M Ed).

School of Arts and Sciences *Degree program information:* Part-time and evening/weekend programs available. Offers art education (M Ed); art history (M Ed); arts and sciences (M Ed, MA, MS); biology (MS); English (MA); geology and chemistry (MS); history (MA); political science (MA); psychology (MA); public administration (MA); studio art (M Ed).

School of Professional Studies *Degree program information:* Part-time and evening/weekend programs available. Offers bilingual education (M Ed); counseling (M Ed); criminal justice (MS); educational diagnostics (M Ed); elementary education (M Ed); industrial arts (M Ed); international trade (MBA); management (MBA); physical education (M Ed); professional studies (M Ed, MBA, MS); reading specialist (M Ed); school administration (M Ed); secondary education (M Ed); supervision (M Ed).

SUNBRIDGE COLLEGE, Spring Valley, NY 10977

General Information Independent, graduate-only institution. *Graduate housing:* Room and/or apartments available on a first-come, first-served basis to single students; on-campus housing not available to married students.

GRADUATE UNITS

Programs in Education *Degree program information:* Part-time programs available. Offers Waldorf early childhood education (MS Ed); Waldorf elementary school education (MS Ed).

SWEDISH INSTITUTE, COLLEGE OF HEALTH SCIENCES, New York, NY 10001-6700

General Information Proprietary, coed, comprehensive institution. *Enrollment:* 480 graduate, professional, and undergraduate students; 71 full-time matriculated graduate/professional students (48 women), 40 part-time matriculated graduate/professional students (29 women). *Graduate faculty:* 6 full-time (4 women), 32 part-time/adjunct (16 women). *Tuition:* Full-time $8,700. *Required fees:* $180. One-time fee: $50 full-time. Tuition and fees vary according to class time, course load and student level. *Graduate housing:* On-campus housing not available. *Student services:* Disabled student services. *Library facilities:* The Lillian F. Phillips Library. *Online resources:* library catalog, access to other libraries' catalogs. *Collection:* 2,700 titles, 30 serial subscriptions, 250 audiovisual materials. *Web address:* http://www.swedishinstitute.org/.

General Application Contact: Admissions Advisor, 212-924-5900 Ext. 125, Fax: 212-924-7600, E-mail: admissions@swedishinstitute.edu.

GRADUATE UNITS

Graduate Program Students: 71 full-time (48 women), 40 part-time (29 women); includes 30 minority (3 African Americans, 19 Asian Americans or Pacific Islanders, 8 Hispanic Americans). Average age 36. 36 applicants, 67% accepted, 20 enrolled. *Faculty:* 6 full-time (4 women), 32 part-time/adjunct (16 women). Expenses: Contact institution. *Financial support:* In 2006–07, 3 teaching assistantships with full and partial tuition reimbursements were awarded. In 2006, 19 degrees awarded. *Degree program information:* Part-time and evening/weekend programs available. *Application deadline:* For fall admission, 11/9 priority date for domestic and international students; for winter admission, 7/13 priority date for domestic and international students. *Application fee:* $50.

SWEET BRIAR COLLEGE, Sweet Briar, VA 24595

General Information Independent, women only, comprehensive institution. *Enrollment:* 751 graduate, professional, and undergraduate students; 8 full-time matriculated graduate/professional students (7 women), 2 part-time matriculated graduate/professional students (both women). *Enrollment by degree level:* 10 master's. *Graduate faculty:* 3 full-time (2 women), 4 part-time/adjunct (all women). *Tuition:* Full-time $13,500; part-time $300 per credit. *Required fees:* $300 per credit. Tuition and fees vary according to course load and program. *Student services:* Campus employment opportunities, campus safety program, career counseling, disabled student services, exercise/wellness program, free psychological counseling, international student services, teacher training, writing training. *Library facilities:* Mary Helen Cochran Library plus 3 others. *Online resources:* library catalog, web page, access to other libraries' catalogs. *Collection:* 263,066 titles, 18,676 serial subscriptions, 12,175 audiovisual materials.

Computer facilities: 117 computers available on campus for general student use. A campuswide network can be accessed from student residence rooms and from off campus. Internet access and online class registration are available. *Web address:* http://www.sbc.edu/.

General Application Contact: Jill E. Gavitt, Assistant Director of Admissions, Special Programs Recruitment, 434-381-6240, Fax: 434-381-6152, E-mail: jgavitt@sbc.edu.

GRADUATE UNITS

Department of Education Students: 8 full-time (7 women), 2 part-time (both women); includes 1 minority (Asian American or Pacific Islander) Average age 24. 15 applicants, 73% accepted, 10 enrolled. *Faculty:* 3 full-time (2 women), 4 part-time/adjunct (all women). Expenses: Contact institution. *Financial support:* Available to part-time students. In 2006, 14 degrees awarded. *Degree program information:* Part-time and evening/weekend programs available. Offers education (M Ed, MAT). *Application deadline:* For fall admission, 2/1 for domestic students. *Application fee:* $40. *Application Contact:* Jill E. Gavitt, Assistant Director of Admissions, Special Programs Recruitment, 434-381-6240, Fax: 434-381-6152, E-mail: jgavitt@sbc.edu. *Education Department Chair,* Dr. James L. Alouf, 434-381-6130, E-mail: alouf@sbc.edu.

SYRACUSE UNIVERSITY, Syracuse, NY 13244

General Information Independent, coed, university. CGS member. *Enrollment:* 17,492 graduate, professional, and undergraduate students; 3,229 full-time matriculated graduate/professional students (1,632 women), 1,564 part-time matriculated graduate/professional students (898 women). *Enrollment by degree level:* 3,281 master's, 1,374 doctoral, 138 other advanced degrees. *Tuition:* Full-time $16,920; part-time $940 per credit hour. *Required fees:* $930; $930 per year. *Graduate housing:* Rooms and/or apartments available on a first-come, first-served basis to single and married students. Housing application deadline: 5/1. *Student services:* Campus employment opportunities, campus safety program, career counseling, child daycare facilities, disabled student services, exercise/wellness program, free psychological counseling, grant writing training, international student services, low-cost health insurance, multicultural affairs office, teacher training, writing training. *Library facilities:* E. S. Bird Library plus 7 others. *Online resources:* library catalog, web page, access to other libraries' catalogs. *Collection:* 3.2 million titles, 20,637 serial subscriptions, 430,826 audiovisual materials.

Computer facilities: Computer purchase and lease plans are available. 1,200 computers available on campus for general student use. A campuswide network can be accessed from student residence rooms and from off campus. Internet access and online class registration, online services, networked client and server computing are available. *Web address:* http://www.syracuse.edu/.

General Application Contact: The Graduate Enrollment Management Center, 315-443-4492, Fax: 315-443-3423, E-mail: grad@syr.edu.

GRADUATE UNITS

College of Law *Degree program information:* Part-time programs available. Offers law (JD).

Graduate School Students: 3,229 full-time (1,632 women), 1,564 part-time (898 women); includes 524 minority (239 African Americans, 25 American Indian/Alaska Native, 144 Asian Americans or Pacific Islanders, 116 Hispanic Americans), 1,398 international. 6,439 applicants, 47% accepted. Expenses: Contact institution. *Financial support:* Fellowships with full and partial tuition reimbursements, research assistantships with full and partial tuition reimbursements, teaching assistantships with full and partial tuition reimbursements, career-related internships or fieldwork, Federal Work-Study, institutionally sponsored loans, scholarships/grants, health care benefits, tuition waivers (partial), and unspecified assistantships available. Support available to part-time students. In 2006, 1,532 master's, 150 doctorates, 171 other advanced degrees awarded. *Degree program information:* Part-time and evening/weekend programs available. Postbaccalaureate distance learning degree programs offered. Offers disability studies (CAS). *Application deadline:* Applications are processed on a rolling basis. *Application fee:* $65. Electronic applications accepted. *Application Contact:* Lori Klish, Director of Graduate Admissions, 315-443-4492, E-mail: grad@syr.edu. *Dean,* Dr. Ben Ware, 315-443-4142, E-mail: grad@syr.edu.

College of Arts and Sciences Students: 582 full-time (320 women), 70 part-time (36 women); includes 62 minority (22 African Americans, 4 American Indian/Alaska Native, 19 Asian Americans or Pacific Islanders, 17 Hispanic Americans), 176 international. 1,374 applicants, 29% accepted, 175 enrolled. Expenses: Contact institution. *Financial support:* Fellowships with full and partial tuition reimbursements, research assistantships with full and partial tuition reimbursements, teaching assistantships with full and partial tuition reimbursements, career-related internships or fieldwork, Federal Work-Study, institutionally sponsored loans, scholarships/grants, health care benefits, tuition waivers (full and partial), and unspecified assistantships available. Support available to part-time students. In 2006, 99 master's, 49 doctorates awarded. *Degree program information:* Part-time programs available. Offers applied statistics (MS); art history (MA); arts and sciences (MA, MFA, MS, Au D, PhD); audiology (Au D, PhD); biology (MS, PhD); chemistry (MS, PhD); clinical psychology (PhD); college science teaching (PhD); composition and cultural rhetoric (PhD); creative writing (MFA); English (MA, PhD); experimental psychology (PhD); French language, literature and culture (MA); geology (MA, MS, PhD); linguistic studies (MA); mathematics (MS, PhD); Pan-African studies (MA); philosophy (MA, PhD); physics (MS, PhD); religion (MA, PhD); school psychology (PhD); social psychology (PhD); Spanish language, literature and culture (MA); speech language pathology (MS, PhD); structural biology, biochemistry and biophysics (PhD). *Application deadline:* Applications are processed on a rolling basis. *Application fee:* $65. Electronic applications accepted. *Dean,* Dr. Cathryn Newton, 315-443-2201.

College of Human Services and Health Professions Students: 214 full-time (185 women), 97 part-time (81 women); includes 44 minority (30 African Americans, 3 American Indian/Alaska Native, 5 Asian Americans or Pacific Islanders, 6 Hispanic Americans), 24 international. 308 applicants, 67% accepted, 106 enrolled. *Faculty:* 40 full-time (26 women), 29 part-time/adjunct (21 women). Expenses: Contact institution. *Financial support:* Fellowships with full and partial tuition reimbursements, research assistantships with full and partial tuition reimbursements, teaching assistantships with full and partial tuition reimbursements, career-related internships or fieldwork, Federal Work-Study, institutionally sponsored loans, scholarships/grants, health care benefits, tuition waivers (full and partial), and unspecified assistantships available. Support available to part-time students. Financial award application deadline: 1/15; financial award applicants required to submit FAFSA. In 2006, 102 master's, 7 doctorates awarded. *Degree program information:* Part-time and evening/weekend programs available. Offers child and family studies (MA, MS, PhD); human services and health professions (MA, MS, MSW, PhD); marriage and family therapy (MA, PhD); nutrition science and food management (MA, MS); social work (MSW). *Application deadline:* For spring admission, 11/1 for domestic students. *Application fee:* $65. Electronic applications accepted. *Application Contact:* Felecia Otero, Director, College Relations, 315-443-5555, Fax: 315-443-2562, E-mail: inquire@hshp.syr.edu. *Dean,* Dr. Diane Lyden Murphy, 315-443-5582, Fax: 315-443-2562.

College of Visual and Performing Arts Students: 125 full-time (77 women), 16 part-time (6 women); includes 18 minority (9 African Americans, 1 American Indian/Alaska Native, 5 Asian Americans or Pacific Islanders, 3 Hispanic Americans), 25 international. 274 applicants, 35% accepted, 54 enrolled. *Faculty:* 115 full-time (45 women), 106 part-time/adjunct (58 women). Expenses: Contact institution. *Financial support:* Fellowships with full and partial tuition reimbursements, research assistantships with full and partial tuition reimbursements, teaching assistantships with full and partial tuition reimbursements, Federal Work-Study, institutionally sponsored loans, health care benefits, tuition waivers (full and partial), and unspecified assistantships available. In 2006, 69 degrees awarded. *Degree program information:* Part-time and evening/weekend programs available. Postbaccalaureate distance learning degree programs offered (minimal on-campus study). Offers art (MFA); art photography (MFA); art video (MFA); arts education (MS); ceramics (MFA); communication and rhetorical studies (MA, MS); computer art (MFA); conducting (M Mu); film (MFA); metalsmithing (MFA); museum studies (MA); music composition (M Mus); organ (M Mus); painting (MFA); percussion (M Mus); piano (M Mus); printmaking (MFA); sculpture (MFA); strings (M Mus); transmedia (MFA); visual and performing arts (M Mu, M Mus, MA, MFA, MS); voice (M Mus); wind instruments (M Mus). *Application deadline:* For fall admission, 1/1 priority date for domestic students; for spring admission, 3/1 priority date for domestic students. Applications are processed on a rolling basis. *Application fee:* $65. Electronic applications accepted. *Application Contact:* Harriett Conti, Associate Director, Graduate Student Services, 315-443-3089, E-mail: hmconti@syr.edu. *Dean,* Carole Brzozowski, 315-443-2611.

L. C. Smith College of Engineering and Computer Science Students: 583 full-time (115 women), 169 part-time (22 women); includes 45 minority (15 African Americans, 20 Asian Americans or Pacific Islanders, 10 Hispanic Americans), 538 international. 1,689 applicants, 52% accepted, 280 enrolled. *Faculty:* 60 full-time (6 women), 20 part-time/adjunct (3 women). Expenses: Contact institution. *Financial support:* Fellowships with full and partial tuition reimbursements, research assistantships with full and partial tuition reimbursements, teaching assistantships with full and partial tuition reimbursements, tuition waivers (full and partial) available. In 2006, 205 master's, 24 doctorates awarded. *Degree program information:* Part-time and evening/weekend programs available. Offers bioengineering (ME, MS, PhD); chemical engineering (MS, PhD); civil engineering (MS, PhD); computer and information science and engineering (PhD); computer engineering (MS, CE); computer science (MS); electrical and computer engineering (PhD); electrical engineering (MS, EE); engineering and computer science (ME, MS, PhD, CE, EE); engineering management (MS); environmental engineering (MS); environmental engineering science (MS); mechanical and aerospace engineering (MS, PhD); neuroscience (MS). *Application deadline:* For fall admission, 3/1 for domestic students. Applications are processed on a rolling basis. *Application fee:* $65. Electronic applications accepted. *Application Contact:* Cheryl Anderson, Director of Graduate Recruitment, 315-443-1044, E-mail: topgrads@syr.edu. *Interim Dean,* Dr. Shiu-Kai Chen, 315-443-4341.

Maxwell School of Citizenship and Public Affairs Students: 642 full-time (335 women), 229 part-time (122 women); includes 92 minority (34 African Americans, 6 American Indian/Alaska Native, 25 Asian Americans or Pacific Islanders, 27 Hispanic Americans), 260 international. 1,082 applicants, 47% accepted, 248 enrolled. *Faculty:* 147 full-time (47 women), 27 part-time/adjunct (11 women). Expenses: Contact institution. *Financial support:* Fellowships with full and partial tuition reimbursements, research assistantships with full and partial tuition reimbursements, teaching assistantships with full and partial tuition reimbursements, institutionally sponsored loans, scholarships/grants, health care benefits, and unspecified assistantships available. Support available to part-time students. In 2006, 276 master's, 32 doctorates, 84 other advanced degrees awarded. *Degree program information:* Part-time and evening/weekend programs available. Postbaccalaureate distance learning degree programs offered. Offers anthropology (MA, PhD); citizenship and public affairs (EMPA, MA, MPA, MS Sc, PhD, CAS); economics (MA, PhD); geography (MA, PhD); health services management and policy (CAS); history (MA, PhD); international relations (MA); political science (MA, PhD); public administration (EMPA, MPA, PhD, CAS); social sciences (MS Sc, PhD); sociology (MA, PhD). *Application deadline:* For fall admission, 2/1 priority date for domestic students. Applications are processed on a rolling basis. *Application fee:* $65. Electronic applications accepted. *Dean,* Mitchel Wallerstein, 315-443-2253, Fax: 315-443-3385, E-mail: mwallers@syr.edu.

School of Architecture Students: 85 full-time (39 women), 2 part-time (both women); includes 7 minority (2 African Americans, 3 Asian Americans or Pacific Islanders, 2 Hispanic Americans), 11 international. 139 applicants, 58% accepted, 29 enrolled. *Faculty:* 32 full-time (9 women), 4 part-time/adjunct (0 women). Expenses: Contact institution. *Financial support:* Fellowships with full and partial tuition reimbursements, research assistantships with full and partial tuition reimbursements, teaching assistantships with full and partial tuition reimbursements, Federal Work-Study, institutionally sponsored loans, scholarships/grants, health care benefits, tuition waivers (full and partial), and unspecified assistantships available. In 2006, 24 degrees awarded. Offers architecture (M Arch I, M Arch II). *Application deadline:* For fall admission, 2/1 priority date for domestic students. Applications are processed on a rolling basis. *Application fee:* $65. Electronic applications accepted. *Application Contact:* Mark Linder, Graduate Director, 315-443-1041, Fax: 315-443-5082. *Dean,* Mark Robbins, 315-443-1041, Fax: 315-443-5082.

School of Education Students: 344 full-time (245 women), 321 part-time (233 women); includes 70 minority (37 African Americans, 7 American Indian/Alaska Native, 12 Asian Americans or Pacific Islanders, 14 Hispanic Americans), 62 international. 394 applicants, 71% accepted, 151 enrolled. *Faculty:* 42 full-time (27 women), 33 part-time/adjunct (19 women). Expenses: Contact institution. *Financial support:* Fellowships with full and partial tuition reimbursements, research assistantships with full and partial tuition reimbursements, teaching assistantships with full and partial tuition reimbursements, career-related internships or fieldwork, Federal Work-Study, institutionally sponsored loans, health care benefits, tuition waivers (full and partial), and unspecified assistantships available. Support available to part-time students. In 2006, 178 master's, 23 doctorates, 17 other advanced degrees awarded. Offers art education (MS, CAS); art education/professional certification (MS); art education: preparation (MS); childhood education: (1-6) preparation (MS); community counseling (MS); counselor education (PhD); cultural foundations of education (MS, PhD); early childhood special education (MS); education (M Mus, MS, Ed D, PhD, CAS); educational leadership (MS, Ed D, CAS); English education (PhD); English education: preparation 7-12 (MS); exercise science (MS); higher education (MS, PhD); inclusive special education (grades 1-6) (MS); inclusive special education (grades 7-12) (MS); instructional design, development, and evaluation (MS, PhD, CAS); literacy education (MS); literacy education: birth-grade 6 (MS); literacy education: grades 5-12 (MS); mathematics education (MS, PhD); mathematics education: preparation 7-12 (MS); music education (M Mus, MS); music education/professional certification (M Mus, MS); music education: teacher preparation (MS); reading education (PhD); rehabilitation and community counseling (MS); rehabilitation counseling (MS); school counseling (MS); science education (MS, PhD); science/biology education: preparation 7-12 (MS); science/chemistry education: preparation 7-12 (MS); science/earth science education: preparation 7-12 (MS); science/physics education: preparation 7-12 (MS); social studies education (MS, CAS); social studies education: preparation 7-12 (MS); special education (PhD); teaching and curriculum (MS, PhD). *Application deadline:* For fall admission, 2/1 priority date for domestic students; for spring admission, 10/15 for domestic students. Applications are processed on a rolling basis. *Application fee:* $65. Electronic applications accepted. *Application Contact:* Liza Rochelson, Graduate Admission Recruiter, 315-443-2505, Fax: 315-443-2258, E-mail: gradcrt@gwmail.syr.edu. *Dean,* Dr. Douglas Biklen, 315-443-4751.

School of Information Studies Students: 275 full-time (127 women), 396 part-time (277 women); includes 90 minority (46 African Americans, 4 American Indian/Alaska Native, 23 Asian Americans or Pacific Islanders, 17 Hispanic Americans), 184 international. 498 applicants, 77% accepted, 163 enrolled. *Faculty:* 29 full-time (12 women), 36 part-time/adjunct (8 women). Expenses: Contact institution. *Financial support:* Fellowships with full and partial tuition reimbursements, research assistantships with full and partial tuition reimbursements, teaching assistantships with full and partial tuition reimbursements, career-related internships or fieldwork, Federal Work-Study, institutionally sponsored loans, health care benefits, tuition waivers (partial), and unspecified assistantships available. In 2006, 200 master's, 7 doctorates, 38 other advanced degrees awarded. *Degree program information:* Part-time and evening/weekend programs available. Postbaccalaureate distance learning degree programs offered (minimal on-campus study). Offers digital libraries (CAS); information management (MS); information science and technology (PhD); information security management (CAS); information systems and telecommunications management (CAS); library and information science (MS); school library media (CAS); school media (MS); telecommunications and network management (MS). *Application deadline:* For fall admission, 2/14 for domestic students; for spring admission, 11/1 for domestic students. *Application fee:* $65. Electronic applications accepted. *Application Contact:* Susan Corieri, Director of Enrollment Management, 315-443-6885, E-mail: ist@syr.edu. *Dean,* Dr. Raymond F. von Dran, 315-443-2736, E-mail: vondran@syr.edu.

S. I. Newhouse School of Public Communications Students: 214 full-time (137 women), 79 part-time (58 women); includes 45 minority (20 African Americans, 12 Asian Americans or Pacific Islanders, 13 Hispanic Americans), 43 international. 778 applicants, 62% accepted, 216 enrolled. Expenses: Contact institution. *Financial support:* In 2006–07, fellowships with tuition reimbursements (averaging $11,000 per year), teaching assistantships with tuition reimbursements (averaging $7,500 per year) were awarded; research assistantships with tuition reimbursements, career-related internships or fieldwork, Federal Work-Study, scholarships/grants, and tuition waivers (partial) also available. Support available to part-time students. Financial award application deadline: 2/1; financial award applicants required to submit FAFSA. In 2006, 223 master's, 4 doctorates awarded. Postbaccalaureate distance learning degree programs offered (minimal on-campus study). Offers advertising (MA); arts journalism (MA); broadcast journalism (MS); communications management (MS); documentary film and history (MA); magazine, newspaper and online journalism (MA); mass communications (PhD); media management (MS); media studies (MA); new media (MS); photography (MS); public communications (MA, MS, PhD); public relations (MS). *Application deadline:* For fall admission, 2/1 for domestic students. *Application fee:* $65. Electronic applications accepted. *Application Contact:* Graduate Records Office, 315-443-4039, Fax: 315-443-1834, E-mail: pcgrad@syr.edu. *Dean,* David M. Rubin, 315-443-2302, Fax: 315-443-3946, E-mail: newhouse@syr.edu.

Martin J. Whitman School of Management Students: 115 full-time (36 women), 285 part-time (85 women); includes 84 minority (45 African Americans, 33 Asian Americans or Pacific Islanders, 6 Hispanic Americans), 66 international. 458 applicants, 22% accepted, 39 enrolled. *Faculty:* 71 full-time (16 women), 2 part-time/adjunct (1 woman). Expenses: Contact institution. *Financial support:* In 2006–07, 45 students received support; fellowships with full tuition reimbursements available, research assistantships with partial tuition reimbursements available, teaching assistantships with partial tuition reimbursements available, career-related internships or fieldwork, scholarships/grants, tuition waivers (partial), unspecified assistantships, and paid hourly positions available. Financial award application deadline: 1/30; financial award applicants required to submit FAFSA. In 2006, 146 master's, 8 doctorates awarded. *Degree program information:* Part-time programs available. Postbaccalaureate distance learning degree programs offered (minimal on-campus study). Offers accounting (MBA, PhD); entrepreneurship (MBA); finance (MBA, PhD); management (MBA, MS Acct, MSF, PhD); management information systems (PhD); managerial statistics (PhD); marketing (MBA, PhD); operations management (PhD); organizational behavior (PhD); strategy and human resources (PhD); supply chain management (MBA, PhD). *Application deadline:* For fall admission, 1/30 priority date for domestic and international students. Applications are processed on a rolling basis. *Application fee:* $75. Electronic applications accepted. *Application Contact:* Carol J. Swanberg, Director of Graduate Admissions and Financial Aid, 315-443-9214, Fax: 315-443-9517, E-mail: mbainfo@syr.edu. *Dean,* Dr. Melvin T. Stiten, 315-443-3751.

TABOR COLLEGE, Hillsboro, KS 67063

General Information Independent-religious, coed, comprehensive institution.

GRADUATE UNITS

Graduate Program Offers accounting (MBA). Program offered at the Wichita campus only.

TAI SOPHIA INSTITUTE FOR THE HEALING ARTS, Laurel, MD 20723

General Information Independent, coed, primarily women, graduate-only institution. *Graduate housing:* On-campus housing not available. *Research affiliation:* Maryland State Department of Public Safety and Corrections (acupuncture detox services).

GRADUATE UNITS

Program in Acupuncture Offers acupuncture (MA).

Program in Applied Healing Arts Offers applied healing arts (MA).

Program in Botanical Healing Offers botanical healing (MA).

TALMUDICAL ACADEMY OF NEW JERSEY, Adelphia, NJ 07710

General Information Independent-religious, men only, comprehensive institution.

GRADUATE UNITS

Graduate Program

TALMUDIC COLLEGE OF FLORIDA, Miami Beach, FL 33139

General Information Independent-religious, men only, comprehensive institution. *Enrollment:* 35 graduate, professional, and undergraduate students; 8 full-time matriculated graduate/professional students. *Enrollment by degree level:* 8 master's. *Graduate faculty:* 4 full-time (0 women), 4 part-time/adjunct (0 women). *Tuition:* Full-time $7,500. *Graduate housing:* Rooms and/or apartments available on a first-come, first-served basis to single and married students. Typical cost: $2,500 per year ($5,000 including board) for single students. *Student services:* Campus employment opportunities, career counseling, international student services, teacher training. *Library facilities:* Beis Medrash plus 1 other. *Online resources:* web page. *Collection:* 25,000 titles, 10,000 audiovisual materials.

Computer facilities: A campuswide network can be accessed. Internet access is available. *Web address:* http://www.talmudicu.edu/.

General Application Contact: Rabbi Ira Hill, Administrator, 305-534-7050, Fax: 305-534-8444, E-mail: ryhill@talmudicu.edu.

GRADUATE UNITS

Program in Talmudic Law Students: 8 full-time (0 women); includes 2 minority (both Hispanic Americans), 3 international. Average age 22. 8 applicants, 100% accepted. *Faculty:* 4 full-time (0 women), 4 part-time/adjunct (0 women). Expenses: Contact institution. *Financial support:* In 2006–07, 6 fellowships with partial tuition reimbursements (averaging $16,000 per year) were awarded; research assistantships with partial tuition reimbursements, teaching assistantships with partial tuition reimbursements, Federal Work-Study and scholarships/grants also available. Support available to part-time students. Financial award application deadline: 4/15; financial award applicants required to submit FAFSA. In 2006, 1 degree awarded. Offers Talmudic law (MRE, Master of Talmudic Law, Doctor of Talmudic Law). *Application deadline:* Applications are processed on a rolling basis. *Application fee:* $250. *Application Contact:* Peggy Loewy-Wellisch, Director, 305-534-7550, Fax: 305-534-8444, E-mail: plw@talmudicu.edu. *Administrator,* Rabbi Ira Hill, 305-534-7050, Fax: 305-534-8444, E-mail: ryhill@talmudicu.edu.

TARLETON STATE UNIVERSITY, Stephenville, TX 76402

General Information State-supported, coed, comprehensive institution. *Enrollment:* 9,464 graduate, professional, and undergraduate students; 337 full-time matriculated graduate/professional students (203 women), 1,194 part-time matriculated graduate/professional students (821 women). *Enrollment by degree level:* 1,487 master's, 44 doctoral. *Graduate faculty:* 151 full-time (55 women), 115 part-time/adjunct (39 women). *Graduate housing:* Rooms and/or apartments available on a first-come, first-served basis to single and married students. Housing application deadline: 8/1. *Student services:* Campus employment opportunities, campus safety program, career counseling, child daycare facilities, disabled student services, exercise/wellness program, free psychological counseling, grant writing training, international student services, low-cost health insurance, multicultural affairs office, teacher training, writing training. *Library facilities:* Dick Smith Library plus 1 other. *Online resources:* library catalog, web page, access to other libraries' catalogs. *Collection:* 349,979 titles, 19,844 serial subscriptions, 9,394 audiovisual materials.

Computer facilities: 600 computers available on campus for general student use. A campuswide network can be accessed from student residence rooms and from off campus. Internet access and online class registration are available. *Web address:* http://www.tarleton.edu/.

General Application Contact: Dr. Linda M. Jones, Dean, 254-968-9104, Fax: 254-968-9670, E-mail: ljones@tarleton.edu.

GRADUATE UNITS

College of Graduate Studies Students: 355 full-time (216 women), 1,245 part-time (878 women); includes 329 minority (185 African Americans, 11 American Indian/Alaska Native, 26 Asian Americans or Pacific Islanders, 107 Hispanic Americans), 42 international. Average age 38. 552 applicants, 93% accepted, 404 enrolled. *Faculty:* 152 full-time (45 women), 14 part-time/adjunct (4 women). Expenses: Contact institution. *Financial support:* In 2006–07, 18 research assistantships (averaging $12,000 per year), 34 teaching assistantships with partial tuition reimbursements (averaging $12,000 per year) were awarded; career-related internships or fieldwork, Federal Work-Study, institutionally sponsored loans, scholarships/grants, and tuition waivers (partial) also available. Support available to part-time students. Financial award application deadline: 5/1; financial award applicants required to submit FAFSA.

Tarleton State University (continued)

In 2006, 483 degrees awarded. *Degree program information:* Part-time and evening/weekend programs available. Postbaccalaureate distance learning degree programs offered (minimal on-campus study). *Application deadline:* For fall admission, 8/5 priority date for domestic students; for spring admission, 12/1 for domestic students. Applications are processed on a rolling basis. *Application fee:* $25 ($75 for international students). Electronic applications accepted. *Application Contact:* Information Contact, 254-968-9104, Fax: 254-968-9670, E-mail: gradoffice@tarleton.edu. *Dean,* Dr. Linda M. Jones, 254-968-9104, Fax: 254-968-9670, E-mail: ljones@tarleton.edu.

College of Agriculture and Human Sciences Students: 35 full-time (20 women), 27 part-time (8 women); includes 2 minority (both Hispanic Americans), 2 international. Average age 29. *Faculty:* 19 full-time (1 woman), 1 part-time/adjunct (0 women). Expenses: Contact institution. *Financial support:* In 2006–07, 5 research assistantships (averaging $12,000 per year), 4 teaching assistantships (averaging $12,000 per year) were awarded; career-related internships or fieldwork, Federal Work-Study, and institutionally sponsored loans also available. Support available to part-time students. Financial award application deadline: 5/1; financial award applicants required to submit FAFSA. In 2006, 39 degrees awarded. *Degree program information:* Part-time and evening/weekend programs available. Postbaccalaureate distance learning degree programs offered (minimal on-campus study). Offers agriculture (MS); agriculture and human sciences (MS); agriculture education (MS). *Application deadline:* For fall admission, 8/5 priority date for domestic students; for spring admission, 12/1 for domestic students. Applications are processed on a rolling basis. *Application fee:* $25 ($75 for international students). *Acting Dean,* Dr. Don Cawthon, 254-968-9277.

College of Business Administration Students: 99 full-time (53 women), 290 part-time (164 women); includes 101 minority (62 African Americans, 4 American Indian/Alaska Native, 11 Asian Americans or Pacific Islanders, 24 Hispanic Americans), 31 international. Average age 36. *Faculty:* 31 full-time (5 women), 3 part-time/adjunct (1 woman). Expenses: Contact institution. *Financial support:* In 2006–07, 4 teaching assistantships (averaging $12,000 per year) were awarded; research assistantships, career-related internships or fieldwork, Federal Work-Study, and institutionally sponsored loans also available. Support available to part-time students. Financial award application deadline: 5/1; financial award applicants required to submit FAFSA. In 2006, 117 degrees awarded. *Degree program information:* Part-time and evening/weekend programs available. Postbaccalaureate distance learning degree programs offered (minimal on-campus study). Offers business administration (MBA); human resource management (MS); information systems (MS). *Application deadline:* For fall admission, 8/5 priority date for domestic students; for spring admission, 12/1 for domestic students. Applications are processed on a rolling basis. *Application fee:* $25 ($75 for international students). *Dean,* Dr. Ruby Barker, 254-968-9350.

College of Education Students: 175 full-time (118 women), 833 part-time (646 women); includes 195 minority (112 African Americans, 5 American Indian/Alaska Native, 10 Asian Americans or Pacific Islanders, 68 Hispanic Americans), 2 international. Average age 39. *Faculty:* 61 full-time (34 women), 55 part-time/adjunct (22 women). Expenses: Contact institution. *Financial support:* In 2006–07, 3 research assistantships (averaging $12,000 per year), teaching assistantships with partial tuition reimbursements (averaging $12,000 per year) were awarded; career-related internships or fieldwork, Federal Work-Study, institutionally sponsored loans, and tuition waivers (partial) also available. Support available to part-time students. Financial award application deadline: 5/1; financial award applicants required to submit FAFSA. In 2006, 280 degrees awarded. *Degree program information:* Part-time and evening/weekend programs available. Postbaccalaureate distance learning degree programs offered (minimal on-campus study). Offers counseling (M Ed); counseling and psychology (M Ed); counseling psychology (M Ed); curriculum and instruction (M Ed); education (M Ed, Ed D, Certificate); educational administration (M Ed, Certificate); educational leadership (Ed D); educational psychology (M Ed); physical education (M Ed); secondary education (Certificate); special education (Certificate). *Application deadline:* For fall admission, 8/5 priority date for domestic students; for spring admission, 12/1 for domestic students. Applications are processed on a rolling basis. *Application fee:* $25 ($75 for international students). *Dean,* Dr. Jill Burk, 254-968-9089.

College of Liberal and Fine Arts Students: 31 full-time (16 women), 73 part-time (33 women); includes 22 minority (9 African Americans, 1 American Indian/Alaska Native, 5 Asian Americans or Pacific Islanders, 7 Hispanic Americans), 4 international. Average age 38. *Faculty:* 14 full-time (6 women), 15 part-time/adjunct (6 women). Expenses: Contact institution. *Financial support:* Research assistantships, teaching assistantships available. In 2006, 21 degrees awarded. Offers criminal justice (MCJ); English (MA); history (MA); liberal and fine arts (MA, MCJ, MS); liberal studies (MS); political science (MA). *Application fee:* $25 ($75 for international students). *Dean,* Dr. Dean A. Minix, 254-968-9141.

College of Science and Technology Students: 13 full-time (9 women), 22 part-time (12 women); includes 5 minority (2 African Americans, 3 Hispanic Americans), 2 international. Average age 35. 59 applicants, 90% accepted. *Faculty:* 13 full-time (1 woman), 11 part-time/adjunct (6 women). Expenses: Contact institution. *Financial support:* In 2006–07, 10 research assistantships (averaging $12,000 per year), 17 teaching assistantships (averaging $12,000 per year) were awarded; career-related internships or fieldwork, Federal Work-Study, and tuition waivers (partial) also available. Support available to part-time students. Financial award application deadline: 5/1; financial award applicants required to submit FAFSA. In 2006, 15 degrees awarded. *Degree program information:* Part-time and evening/weekend programs available. Postbaccalaureate distance learning degree programs offered (minimal on-campus study). Offers biology (MS); environmental science (MS); mathematics (MS); science and technology (MS). *Application deadline:* For fall admission, 8/5 priority date for domestic students; for spring admission, 12/1 for domestic students. Applications are processed on a rolling basis. *Application fee:* $25 ($75 for international students). *Dean,* Dr. Rueben Walter, 254-968-9781, Fax: 254-968-9784, E-mail: walter@tarleton.edu.

TAYLOR UNIVERSITY, Upland, IN 46989-1001

General Information Independent-religious, coed, comprehensive institution. *Graduate housing:* On-campus housing not available.

GRADUATE UNITS

Program in Environmental Science Offers environmental science (MES).

TAYLOR UNIVERSITY COLLEGE AND SEMINARY, Edmonton, AB T6J 4T3, Canada

General Information Independent-religious, coed, comprehensive institution. *Enrollment:* 26 full-time matriculated graduate/professional students (4 women), 67 part-time matriculated graduate/professional students (24 women). *Enrollment by degree level:* 72 first professional, 18 master's, 3 other advanced degrees. *Graduate faculty:* 6 full-time (0 women), 5 part-time/adjunct (0 women). *Graduate housing:* Room and/or apartments available on a first-come, first-served basis to single students; on-campus housing not available to married students. Housing application deadline: 8/1. *Student services:* Campus employment opportunities, career counseling, international student services. *Library facilities:* Schalm Library. *Online resources:* library catalog, access to other libraries' catalogs. *Collection:* 50,083 titles, 303 serial subscriptions.

Computer facilities: 16 computers available on campus for general student use. A campuswide network can be accessed. Internet access is available. *Web address:* http://www.taylor-edu.ca/.

General Application Contact: Karen Manzer, Director of Admissions, 780-431-5200, Fax: 780-436-9416, E-mail: karen.manzer@taylor-edu.ca.

GRADUATE UNITS

Graduate and Professional Programs Students: 26 full-time (4 women), 67 part-time (24 women); includes 20 minority (4 African Americans, 15 Asian Americans or Pacific Islanders, 1 Hispanic American). Average age 38. 45 applicants, 56% accepted, 22 enrolled. *Faculty:* 6 full-time (0 women), 5 part-time/adjunct (0 women). Expenses: Contact institution. *Financial support:* In 2006–07, 17 students received support. Career-related internships or fieldwork and scholarships/grants available. Financial award application deadline: 5/1. In 2006, 12 M Divs, 8 master's awarded. *Degree program information:* Part-time programs available. Offers Christian studies (Diploma); intercultural studies (MA, Diploma); theology (M Div, MTS). *Application deadline:* For fall admission, 8/1 priority date for domestic and international students. Applications are processed on a rolling basis. *Application fee:* $35 ($70 for international students). *Application Contact:* Karen Manzer, Director of Admissions, 780-431-5200, Fax: 780-436-9416, E-mail: karen.manzer@taylor-edu.ca. *Academic Vice President,* Dr. Jim Leverette, 780-431-5245, Fax: 780-436-9416, E-mail: jim.leverette@taylor-edu.ca.

TAYLOR UNIVERSITY FORT WAYNE, Fort Wayne, IN 46807-2197

General Information Independent-religious, coed, comprehensive institution. *Research affiliation:* Crane Metamarketing (marketing).

GRADUATE UNITS

Master of Business Administration Program Offers business administration (MBA). Electronic applications accepted.

TEACHERS COLLEGE COLUMBIA UNIVERSITY, New York, NY 10027-6696

General Information Independent, coed, graduate-only institution. *Enrollment by degree level:* 3,061 master's, 1,687 doctoral, 123 other advanced degrees. *Graduate faculty:* 152 full-time (90 women), 260 part-time/adjunct. *Tuition:* Full-time $23,400; part-time $975 per credit. *Required fees:* $320 per term. *Graduate housing:* Rooms and/or apartments available on a first-come, first-served basis to single and married students. Typical cost: $6,200 per year for single students; $13,750 per year for married students. Housing application deadline: 2/1. *Student services:* Campus employment opportunities, campus safety program, career counseling, child daycare facilities, disabled student services, exercise/wellness program, free psychological counseling, grant writing training, international student services, low-cost health insurance, multicultural affairs office, teacher training, writing training. *Library facilities:* Milbank Memorial Library. *Online resources:* library catalog, web page, access to other libraries' catalogs. *Collection:* 417,044 titles, 5,651 audiovisual materials.

Computer facilities: 482 computers available on campus for general student use. A campuswide network can be accessed from student residence rooms and from off campus. Internet access and online class registration are available. *Web address:* http://www.tc.columbia.edu/.

General Application Contact: Thomas Rock, Director of Admissions, 212-678-3083, Fax: 212-678-4171, E-mail: rock@tc.edu.

GRADUATE UNITS

Graduate Faculty of Education Students: 1,582 full-time (1,205 women), 3,290 part-time (2,427 women); includes 1,263 minority (453 African Americans, 8 American Indian/Alaska Native, 517 Asian Americans or Pacific Islanders, 285 Hispanic Americans), 529 international. Average age 32. 5,136 applicants, 58% accepted, 1408 enrolled. *Faculty:* 152 full-time (90 women). Expenses: Contact institution. *Financial support:* Fellowships, research assistantships, teaching assistantships, career-related internships or fieldwork, Federal Work-Study, institutionally sponsored loans, traineeships, tuition waivers (full and partial), and unspecified assistantships available. Support available to part-time students. Financial award application deadline: 2/1. In 2006, 1,518 master's, 210 doctorates awarded. *Degree program information:* Part-time and evening/weekend programs available. Offers administration and supervision in special education (Ed M, MA, Ed D, PhD); adult education (MA, Ed D); anthropology (Ed M, MA, Ed D, PhD); applied educational psychology – school psychology (Ed M, MA, Ed D, PhD); applied linguistics (Ed M, MA, Ed D); art and art education (Ed M, MA, Ed D, Ed DCT); arts administration (MA); behavioral disorders (MA, Ed D, PhD); bilingual and bicultural education (MA); blind and visual impairment (MA, Ed D); childhood/disabilities (Certificate); clinical psychology (MA, PhD); communications (Ed M, MA, Ed D); comparative and international education (Ed M, MA, Ed D, PhD); computing in education (MA); counseling psychology (Ed M, Ed D, PhD); curriculum and teaching (Ed M, MA, Ed D); curriculum and teaching in physical education (Ed M, MA, Ed D); developmental psychology (MA, Ed D, PhD); early childhood education (Ed M, MA, Ed D); early childhood special education (Ed M, MA); economics and education (Ed M, MA, Ed D, PhD); education (Ed M, MA, MS, Ed D, Ed DCT, PhD, Certificate); education leadership (Ed M, MA, Ed D, PhD); education leadership studies (Ed M, MA, Ed D); educational administration (Ed M, MA, Ed D, PhD); educational media/instructional technology (Ed M, MA, Ed D); educational psychology-human cognition and learning (Ed M, MA, Ed D, PhD); elementary/childhood education, preservice (MA); giftedness (MA, Ed D); health education (MA, MS, Ed D); hearing impairment (MA, Ed D); higher education (Ed M, MA, Ed D, PhD); history and education (Ed M, MA, Ed D, PhD); inquiry in education leadership (Ed D); interdisciplinary studies (Ed M, MA, Ed D); international educational development (Ed M, MA, Ed D, PhD); leadership, policy and politics (Ed M, MA, Ed D, PhD); learning disabilities (Ed M, MA, Ed D); literacy specialist (MA); mathematics education (Ed M, MA, MS, Ed D, Ed DCT, PhD); measurement, evaluation, and statistics (MA, MS, Ed D, PhD); mental retardation (MA, Ed D, PhD); motor learning/movement science (Ed M, MA, Ed D); music and music education (Ed M, MA, Ed D, Ed DCT); neuroscience and education (Ed M, Ed D); nurse executive (Ed M, MA, Ed D); nursing, professional role (Ed M, MA, Ed D); nutrition and education (Ed M, MS, Ed D); nutrition education (Ed M, MS, Ed D); nutrition education and public health nutrition (Ed M, MS, Ed D); organizational psychology (MA, Ed D, PhD); philosophy and education (Ed M, MA, Ed D, PhD); physical disabilities (MA, Ed D, PhD); politics and education (Ed M, MA, Ed D, PhD); private school leadership (Ed M, MA, Ed D); public school and school district leadership (Ed M, MA, Ed D); reading specialist (MA); reading/learning disability (Ed M); religion and education (Ed M, MA, Ed D); research in special education (Ed D); science education (Ed M, MA, MS, Ed D, Ed DCT, PhD); social and organizational psychology (MA, Ed D, PhD); social psychology (Ed D, PhD); social studies education (Ed M, MA, Ed D, PhD); sociology and education (Ed M, MA, Ed D, PhD); special education (Ed M, MA, Ed D); speech-language pathology (Ed M, MS, Ed D, PhD); student personnel administration (Ed M, MA, Ed D); teaching English to speakers of other languages (Ed M, MA, Ed D); teaching of English and English education (Ed M, MA, Ed D, PhD); teaching of sign language (MA); teaching of Spanish (Ed M, MA, Ed D, Ed DCT, PhD). *Application fee:* $65. Electronic applications accepted. *Application Contact:* Thomas Rock, Director of Admissions, 212-678-3083, Fax: 212-678-4171, E-mail: rock@tc.edu. *President,* Susan Furhman, 212-678-3050.

See Close-Up on page 1049.

TÉLÉ-UNIVERSITÉ, Québec, QC G1K 9H5, Canada

General Information Province-supported, coed, comprehensive institution. *Graduate housing:* On-campus housing not available.

GRADUATE UNITS

Graduate Programs *Degree program information:* Part-time programs available. Offers computer science (PhD); corporate finance (MS); distance learning (MS).

TELSHE YESHIVA–CHICAGO, Chicago, IL 60625-5598

General Information Independent-religious, men only, comprehensive institution.

GRADUATE UNITS

Graduate Program

TEMPLE BAPTIST SEMINARY, Chattanooga, TN 37404-3530

General Information Independent-religious, coed, primarily men, graduate-only institution. *Graduate housing:* On-campus housing not available.

GRADUATE UNITS

Program in Theology *Degree program information:* Part-time and evening/weekend programs available. Postbaccalaureate distance learning degree programs offered (minimal on-campus study). Offers theology (M Div, MABS, MM, MRE, D Min).

TEMPLE UNIVERSITY, Philadelphia, PA 19122-6096

General Information State-related, coed, university. CGS member. *Enrollment:* 33,865 graduate, professional, and undergraduate students; 4,632 full-time matriculated graduate/professional students (2,471 women), 3,373 part-time matriculated graduate/professional students (1,918 women). *Enrollment by degree level:* 3,093 first professional, 3,043 master's, 1,869 doctoral. *Graduate faculty:* 1,421 full-time (482 women). Tuition, state resident: full-time $12,264; part-time $511 per credit. Tuition, nonresident: full-time $17,904; part-time $746 per credit. *Required fees:* $84 per course. Tuition and fees vary according to program. *Graduate housing:* Rooms and/or apartments available on a first-come, first-served basis to single and married students. Housing application deadline: 5/1. *Student services:* Campus employment opportunities, campus safety program, career counseling, disabled student services, exercise/wellness program, free psychological counseling, grant writing training, international student services, low-cost health insurance, multicultural affairs office, teacher training, writing training. *Library facilities:* Paley Library plus 11 others. *Online resources:* library catalog, web page, access to other libraries' catalogs. *Collection:* 3.3 million titles, 20,980 serial subscriptions.

Computer facilities: 2,000 computers available on campus for general student use. A campuswide network can be accessed from student residence rooms and from off campus. Internet access and online class registration, student account and grade information are available. *Web address:* http://www.temple.edu/.

General Application Contact: Tara Schumacher, Coordinator of Outreach, 215-204-6575, Fax: 215-204-8781, E-mail: tara.schumacher@temple.edu.

GRADUATE UNITS

Ambler College Expenses: Contact institution. *Financial support:* Application deadline: 1/15; Offers community and regional planning (MS). *Application fee:* $50. Electronic applications accepted. *Interim Dean,* Dr. James Hilty, 267-468-8020, E-mail: jhilty@temple.edu.

Graduate School Students: 4,632 full-time (2,471 women), 3,373 part-time (1,918 women); includes 1,558 minority (941 African Americans, 16 American Indian/Alaska Native, 322 Asian Americans or Pacific Islanders, 279 Hispanic Americans), 1,165 international. 7,555 applicants, 41% accepted, 1489 enrolled. *Faculty:* 1,421 full-time (482 women). Expenses: Contact institution. *Financial support:* In 2006–07, fellowships with full tuition reimbursements (averaging $20,000 per year), research assistantships with full and partial tuition reimbursements (averaging $18,660 per year), teaching assistantships with full and partial tuition reimbursements (averaging $18,660 per year) were awarded; career-related internships or fieldwork, Federal Work-Study, institutionally sponsored loans, scholarships/grants, traineeships, health care benefits, tuition waivers (full and partial), and unspecified assistantships also available. Support available to part-time students. Financial award application deadline: 1/15; financial award applicants required to submit FAFSA. In 2006, 1,683 master's, 236 doctorates awarded. *Degree program information:* Part-time and evening/weekend programs available. *Application deadline:* For fall admission, 12/15 for international students; for spring admission, 8/1 for international students. *Application fee:* $50. Electronic applications accepted. *Application Contact:* Tara Schumacher, Coordinator of Outreach, 215-204-6575, Fax: 215-204-8781, E-mail: tara.schumacher@temple.edu. *Dean,* Dr. Aquiles Iglesias, 215-204-6578, Fax: 215-204-8781, E-mail: iglesias@temple.edu.

College of Education Students: 307 full-time (217 women), 930 part-time (630 women); includes 265 minority (185 African Americans, 5 American Indian/Alaska Native, 36 Asian Americans or Pacific Islanders, 39 Hispanic Americans), 48 international. 870 applicants, 49% accepted, 250 enrolled. *Faculty:* 75 full-time (33 women). Expenses: Contact institution. *Financial support:* Fellowships, research assistantships, teaching assistantships, career-related internships or fieldwork and Federal Work-Study available. Financial award application deadline: 1/15; financial award applicants required to submit FAFSA. In 2006, 352 master's, 75 doctorates awarded. *Degree program information:* Part-time and evening/weekend programs available. Offers adult and organizational development (Ed M); applied behavioral analysis (MS Ed); career and technical education (MS Ed); counseling psychology (Ed M, PhD); early childhood education and elementary education (MS Ed); education (Ed M, MS Ed, Ed D, PhD); educational administration (Ed M, Ed D); educational psychology (Ed M, PhD); English education (MS Ed); language arts education (Ed D); math/science education (Ed D); mathematics education (MS Ed); school psychology (Ed M, PhD); science education (MS Ed); second and foreign language education (MS Ed); special education (MS Ed); teaching English as a second language (MS Ed); urban education (Ed M, Ed D). *Application deadline:* For fall admission, 12/15 for international students; for spring admission, 8/1 for international students. Applications are processed on a rolling basis. *Application fee:* $50. Electronic applications accepted. *Application Contact:* Dr. Jan Price Greenough, Associate Dean, 215-204-7962, E-mail: james.earl.davis@temple.edu. *Dean,* Dr. C. Kent McGuire, 215-204-8017, Fax: 215-204-5622, E-mail: kent.mcguire@temple.edu.

College of Engineering Students: 44 full-time (16 women), 55 part-time (9 women); includes 10 minority (4 African Americans, 6 Asian Americans or Pacific Islanders), 64 international. 233 applicants, 47% accepted, 34 enrolled. *Faculty:* 17 full-time (2 women). Expenses: Contact institution. *Financial support:* Fellowships with full tuition reimbursements, research assistantships with full tuition reimbursements, teaching assistantships with full tuition reimbursements, career-related internships or fieldwork, Federal Work-Study, and institutionally sponsored loans available. Financial award application deadline: 1/15. In 2006, 24 master's, 1 doctorate awarded. *Degree program information:* Part-time programs available. Offers civil engineering (MSE); electrical engineering (MSE); engineering (MS, MSE, PhD); mechanical engineering (MSE). *Application deadline:* For fall admission, 7/1 priority date for domestic students, 12/15 for international students; for spring admission, 11/1 priority date for domestic students, 8/1 for international students. Applications are processed on a rolling basis. *Application fee:* $50. Electronic applications accepted. *Dean,* Dr. Keyanoush Sadeghipour, 215-204-5285, Fax: 215-204-6936, E-mail: keya@temple.edu.

College of Liberal Arts Students: 217 full-time (131 women), 540 part-time (263 women); includes 177 minority (117 African Americans, 4 American Indian/Alaska Native, 30 Asian Americans or Pacific Islanders, 26 Hispanic Americans), 62 international. 1,167 applicants, 34% accepted, 184 enrolled. *Faculty:* 193 full-time (74 women). Expenses: Contact institution. *Financial support:* Fellowships, research assistantships, teaching assistantships, career-related internships or fieldwork, Federal Work-Study, institutionally sponsored loans, scholarships/grants, and tuition waivers (full and partial) available. Support available to part-time students. Financial award application deadline: 1/15; financial award applicants required to submit FAFSA. In 2006, 85 master's, 82 doctorates awarded. *Degree program information:* Part-time and evening/weekend programs available. Offers African American studies (MA, PhD); anthropology (PhD); clinical psychology (PhD); cognitive psychology (PhD); creative writing (MA); criminal justice (MA, PhD); developmental psychology (PhD); English (MA, PhD); geography (MA); history (MA, PhD); liberal arts (MA, MLA, PhD); philosophy (MA, PhD); political science (MA, PhD); religion (MA, PhD); social psychology (PhD); sociology (MA, PhD); Spanish (MA, PhD); urban studies (MA). *Application deadline:* For fall admission, 12/15 for international students; for spring admission, 8/1 for international students. *Application fee:* $50. Electronic applications accepted. *Interim Dean,* Dr. Carolyn Adams, 215-204-7743, Fax: 215-204-3731, E-mail: omicron@temple.edu.

College of Science and Technology Students: 83 full-time (25 women), 167 part-time (51 women); includes 28 minority (6 African Americans, 20 Asian Americans or Pacific Islanders, 2 Hispanic Americans), 146 international. 540 applicants, 23% accepted, 52 enrolled. *Faculty:* 85 full-time (12 women). Expenses: Contact institution. *Financial support:* Fellowships, research assistantships, teaching assistantships, career-related internships or fieldwork, Federal Work-Study, institutionally sponsored loans, scholarships/grants, tuition waivers (full and partial), and laboratory assistantships available. Financial award application deadline: 1/15; financial award applicants required to submit FAFSA. In 2006, 49 master's, 14 doctorates awarded. *Degree program information:* Part-time and evening/weekend programs available. Offers applied mathematics (MA); biology (MS, PhD); chemistry (MA, PhD); computer and information sciences (MS, PhD); geology (MS); mathematics (PhD); physics (MA, PhD); pure mathematics (MA); science and technology (MA, MS, PhD). *Application deadline:* For fall admission, 12/15 for international students; for spring admission, 8/1 for international students. *Application fee:* $50. Electronic applications accepted. *Dean,* Dr. Hai-Lung Dai, 215-204-2888, Fax: 215-204-1255, E-mail: hldai@temple.edu.

Esther Boyer College of Music and Dance Students: 120 full-time (87 women), 134 part-time (87 women); includes 35 minority (12 African Americans, 17 Asian Americans or Pacific Islanders, 6 Hispanic Americans), 55 international. 348 applicants, 38% accepted, 76 enrolled. *Faculty:* 43 full-time (16 women). Expenses: Contact institution. *Financial support:* Fellowships with full and partial tuition reimbursements, research assistantships with full and partial tuition reimbursements, teaching assistantships with full and partial tuition reimbursements, career-related internships or fieldwork, Federal Work-Study, and scholarships/grants available. Financial award application deadline: 1/15; financial award applicants required to submit FAFSA. In 2006, 55 master's, 9 doctorates awarded. *Degree program information:* Part-time and evening/weekend programs available. Offers choral activities (MM); composition (MM, DMA); dance (Ed M, MFA, PhD); instrumental studies (MM, DMA); keyboard instruction (MM, DMA); music and dance (Ed M, MFA, MM, MMT, DMA, PhD); music education (MM, PhD); music history (MM); music theory (MM); music therapy (MMT, PhD); voice and opera (MM, DMA). *Application deadline:* For fall admission, 12/15 for international students; for spring admission, 8/1 for international students. Applications are processed on a rolling basis. *Application fee:* $50. Electronic applications accepted. *Dean,* Dr. Robert T. Stroker, 215-204-5527, Fax: 215-204-4957, E-mail: rstroker@temple.edu.

Fox School of Business and Management *Degree program information:* Part-time and evening/weekend programs available. Postbaccalaureate distance learning degree programs offered (minimal on-campus study). Offers accounting (MBA, PhD); accounting and financial management (MS); actuarial science (MS); business administration (EMBA, IMBA, MBA, MS); business and management (EMBA, IMBA, MA, MBA, MS, PhD); e-business (MBA, MS); economics (MA, MBA, PhD); finance (MBA, MS, PhD); general and strategic management (MBA, PhD); healthcare financial management (MS); healthcare management (MBA, PhD); human resource administration (MBA, MS, PhD); international business (IMBA); international business administration (PhD); management information systems (MBA, MS, PhD); management science/operations management (MBA, MS); management science/operations research (PhD); marketing (MBA, MS, PhD); risk management and insurance (MBA); risk, insurance, and health-care management (PhD); statistics (MBA, MS, PhD); tourism (PhD). Electronic applications accepted.

School of Communications and Theater Students: 101 full-time (64 women), 128 part-time (77 women); includes 40 minority (30 African Americans, 1 American Indian/Alaska Native, 3 Asian Americans or Pacific Islanders, 6 Hispanic Americans), 58 international. 435 applicants, 37% accepted, 61 enrolled. *Faculty:* 41 full-time (16 women). Expenses: Contact institution. *Financial support:* Fellowships, research assistantships with partial tuition reimbursements, teaching assistantships with partial tuition reimbursements, career-related internships or fieldwork, Federal Work-Study, institutionally sponsored loans, and tuition waivers (partial) available. Financial award application deadline: 1/15; financial award applicants required to submit FAFSA. In 2006, 49 master's, 6 doctorates awarded. *Degree program information:* Part-time and evening/weekend programs available. Offers acting (MFA); broadcasting, telecommunications and mass media (MA); communication management (MS); communications and theater (MA, MFA, MJ, MS, PhD); design (MFA); directing (MFA); film and media arts (MFA); journalism (MJ); mass media and communication (PhD). *Application deadline:* For fall admission, 12/15 for international students. *Application fee:* $50. Electronic applications accepted. *Dean,* Dr. Concetta M. Stewart, 215-204-8421, Fax: 215-204-4811, E-mail: cstewart@temple.edu.

School of Social Administration Students: 209 full-time (178 women), 290 part-time (224 women); includes 149 minority (123 African Americans, 2 American Indian/Alaska Native, 6 Asian Americans or Pacific Islanders, 18 Hispanic Americans), 5 international. 400 applicants, 71% accepted, 183 enrolled. *Faculty:* 18 full-time (11 women). Expenses: Contact institution. *Financial support:* Fellowships with tuition reimbursements, research assistantships with tuition reimbursements, teaching assistantships with tuition reimbursements, career-related internships or fieldwork, Federal Work-Study, institutionally sponsored loans, scholarships/grants, traineeships, tuition waivers (partial), unspecified assistantships, and field assistantships available. Financial award application deadline: 1/15; financial award applicants required to submit FAFSA. In 2006, 160 degrees awarded. *Degree program information:* Part-time and evening/weekend programs available. Offers social administration (MSW); social work (MSW). *Application deadline:* For fall admission, 2/15 priority date for domestic students, 12/15 for international students; for spring admission, 11/1 priority date for domestic students, 8/1 for international students. Applications are processed on a rolling basis. *Application fee:* $50. Electronic applications accepted. *Interim Dean,* Dr. Linda Mauro, 215-204-8623, Fax: 215-204-9606, E-mail: lmauro@temple.edu.

School of Tourism and Hospitality Management Students: 56 full-time (35 women), 47 part-time (23 women); includes 20 minority (19 African Americans, 1 Asian American or Pacific Islander), 7 international. 153 applicants, 52% accepted, 39 enrolled. *Faculty:* 8 full-time (2 women). Expenses: Contact institution. *Financial support:* Teaching assistantships available. Financial award application deadline: 1/15; financial award applicants required to submit FAFSA. In 2006, 43 degrees awarded. *Degree program information:* Part-time and evening/weekend programs available. Offers sport and recreation administration (Ed M); tourism and hospitality management (Ed M, MTHM). *Application deadline:* For fall admission, 12/15 for international students; for spring admission, 8/1 for international students. *Application fee:* $50. Electronic applications accepted. *Dean,* Dr. M. Moshe Porat, 215-204-1836, Fax: 215-204-8705, E-mail: porat@temple.edu.

Tyler School of Art Students: 88 full-time (62 women), 34 part-time (27 women); includes 5 minority (2 African Americans, 2 Asian Americans or Pacific Islanders, 1 Hispanic American), 9 international. 483 applicants, 21% accepted, 50 enrolled. *Faculty:* 48 full-time (24 women). Expenses: Contact institution. *Financial support:* Fellowships with full tuition reimbursements, research assistantships with full tuition reimbursements, teaching assistantships with full tuition reimbursements, career-related internships or fieldwork, Federal Work-Study, and institutionally sponsored loans available. Support available to part-time students. Financial award application deadline: 1/15; financial award applicants required to submit FAFSA. In 2006, 52 master's, 1 doctorate awarded. *Degree program information:* Part-time and evening/weekend programs available. Offers art (Ed M, MA, MFA, PhD); art and art education (Ed M); art history (MA, PhD); ceramics/glass (MFA); fibers and fabric design (MFA); graphic and interactive design (MFA); metals/jewelry/CAD-CAM (MFA); painting (MFA); photography (MFA); printmaking (MFA); sculpture (MFA). *Application fee:* $50. Electronic applications accepted. *Application Contact:* Carmina Cianciulli, Assistant Dean for Admissions, 215-782-2875, Fax: 215-782-2711, E-mail: tylerart@temple.edu. *Dean,* Keith Morrison, 215-782-2828, Fax: 215-782-2799, E-mail: keitham@temple.edu.

Health Sciences Center Students: 2,399 full-time (1,081 women), 426 part-time (296 women). 3,680 applicants, 11% accepted. *Faculty:* 751. Expenses: Contact institution. *Financial support:* Fellowships, research assistantships, teaching assistantships, career-related internships or fieldwork, Federal Work-Study, institutionally sponsored loans, scholarships/grants, traineeships, and tuition waivers (full and partial) available. Support available to part-time students. Financial award application deadline: 1/15; financial award applicants required to submit FAFSA. In 2006, 451 first professional degrees, 175 master's, 29 doctorates, 26 Certificates awarded. *Degree program information:* Part-time and evening/weekend programs available. Offers health sciences (DMD, DPM, MD, Pharm D, Ed M, MA, MOT, MPH, MS, MSN, DPT, PhD, Certificate). *Application fee:* $50. Electronic applications accepted.

College of Health Professions Students: 254 full-time (207 women), 293 part-time (217 women); includes 123 minority (81 African Americans, 30 Asian Americans or Pacific Islanders, 12 Hispanic Americans). Average age 25. 500 applicants, 60% accepted, 165 enrolled. *Faculty:* 53 full-time (40 women). Expenses: Contact institution. *Financial support:* Fellowships, research assistantships, teaching assistantships with full tuition reimbursements, career-related internships or fieldwork, Federal Work-Study, institutionally sponsored loans, traineeships, and tuition waivers (partial) available. Support available to part-time students. Financial award application deadline: 1/15. In 2006, 113 master's, 105 doctorates awarded. *Degree program information:* Part-time and evening/weekend programs available. Postbaccalaureate distance learning degree programs offered (minimal on-campus study). Offers communication sciences (PhD); community health education

Temple University (continued)

(MPH); environmental health (MS); epidemiology (MS); health professions (Ed M, MA, MOT, MPH, MS, MSN, DPT, PhD); health studies (PhD); kinesiology (Ed M, PhD); linguistics (MA); nursing (MSN); occupational therapy (MOT, MS); physical therapy (DPT, PhD); public health (Ed M, MPH, MS, PhD); school health education (Ed M); speech-language-hearing (MA); therapeutic recreation (Ed M). *Application fee:* $50. *Dean,* Dr. Ronald T. Brown, 215-707-4800, Fax: 215-707-7819, E-mail: rtbrown@temple.edu.

School of Dentistry *Faculty:* 84 full-time (16 women), 91 part-time/adjunct (21 women). Expenses: Contact institution. *Financial support:* Fellowships, career-related internships or fieldwork, institutionally sponsored loans, and scholarships/grants available. Financial award application deadline: 1/15; financial award applicants required to submit FAFSA. *Degree program information:* Part-time programs available. Offers advanced education in general dentistry (Certificate); dentistry (DMD, MS, Certificate); endodontology (Certificate); oral biology (MS); orthodontics (Certificate); periodontology (Certificate). *Application deadline:* For fall admission, 7/1 priority date for domestic students, 12/15 for international students; for spring admission, 11/1 priority date for domestic students, 8/1 for international students. Applications are processed on a rolling basis. *Application fee:* $50. Electronic applications accepted. *Application Contact:* Dr. Lisa P. Deem, Associate Dean for Admissions and Student Affairs, 215-707-2801, Fax: 215-707-5461, E-mail: lisa.deem@temple.edu. *Dean,* Dr. Martin F. Tansy, 215-707-2799, Fax: 215-707-7669, E-mail: mtansy@temple.edu.

School of Medicine Students: 883 full-time (384 women), 80 part-time (39 women); includes 333 minority (111 African Americans, 3 American Indian/Alaska Native, 171 Asian Americans or Pacific Islanders, 48 Hispanic Americans), 53 international. 6,820 applicants, 8% accepted, 221 enrolled. *Faculty:* 495 full-time (135 women), 44 part-time/adjunct (16 women). Expenses: Contact institution. *Financial support:* Fellowships, research assistantships, career-related internships or fieldwork, Federal Work-Study, institutionally sponsored loans, scholarships/grants, and tuition waivers (full and partial) available. Support available to part-time students. Financial award application deadline: 1/15; financial award applicants required to submit FAFSA. In 2006, 163 MDs, 1 master's, 19 doctorates awarded. Offers anatomy and cell biology (MS, PhD); biochemistry (MS, PhD); medicine (MD, MS, PhD); microbiology and immunology (MS, PhD); molecular biology and genetics (PhD); neuroscience (MS, PhD); pathology and laboratory medicine (PhD); pharmacology (PhD); physiology (PhD). *Application fee:* $50. Electronic applications accepted. *Dean,* Dr. John M. Daly, 215-707-7000, Fax: 215-707-8431, E-mail: johndaly@temple.edu.

School of Pharmacy Students: 557 full-time (332 women), 263 part-time (183 women); includes 388 minority (147 African Americans, 4 American Indian/Alaska Native, 223 Asian Americans or Pacific Islanders, 14 Hispanic Americans), 26 international. 901 applicants, 29% accepted, 203 enrolled. *Faculty:* 9 full-time (1 woman). Expenses: Contact institution. *Financial support:* Fellowships with tuition reimbursements, research assistantships with tuition reimbursements, teaching assistantships with tuition reimbursements, career-related internships or fieldwork, Federal Work-Study, and institutionally sponsored loans available. Financial award application deadline: 1/15; financial award applicants required to submit FAFSA. In 2006, 110 first professional degrees, 84 master's, 2 doctorates awarded. *Degree program information:* Part-time and evening/weekend programs available. Post-baccalaureate distance learning degree programs offered (minimal on-campus study). Offers medicinal chemistry (MS, PhD); pharmaceutics (MS, PhD); pharmacodynamics (MS, PhD); pharmacy (Pharm D, MS, PhD); quality assurance/regulatory affairs (MS). *Application fee:* $50. Electronic applications accepted. *Dean,* Dr. Peter H. Doukas, 215-707-4990, Fax: 215-707-5620, E-mail: pdoukas@temple.edu.

School of Podiatric Medicine Offers podiatric medicine (DPM).

James E. Beasley School of Law *Degree program information:* Part-time and evening/weekend programs available. Offers law (JD); taxation (LL M); transnational law (LL M); trial advocacy (LL M). Electronic applications accepted.

Announcement: Located in the fifth-largest U.S. city, Temple University is as diverse academically as it is culturally. With more than 5,000 graduate students (more than 30,000 students total), Temple offers 62 doctoral and 133 master's programs that range from fine arts and sciences to professional degrees. While housed in selective schools, these programs are immersed in the cultural wealth of a comprehensive university.

See Close-Up on page 1051.

TENNESSEE STATE UNIVERSITY, Nashville, TN 37209-1561

General Information State-supported, coed, comprehensive institution. CGS member. *Enrollment:* 9,038 graduate, professional, and undergraduate students; 603 full-time matriculated graduate/professional students (431 women), 1,323 part-time matriculated graduate/professional students (937 women). *Enrollment by degree level:* 1,180 master's, 342 doctoral, 404 other advanced degrees. *Graduate faculty:* 151 full-time (63 women), 20 part-time/adjunct (11 women). *Graduate housing:* Rooms and/or apartments available on a first-come, first-served basis to single and married students. Housing application deadline: 8/1. *Student services:* Campus employment opportunities, campus safety program, career counseling, child daycare facilities, disabled student services, exercise/wellness program, free psychological counseling, international student services, low-cost health insurance, teacher training, writing training. *Library facilities:* Martha M. Brown/Lois H. Daniel Library plus 1 other. *Online resources:* library catalog, web page. *Collection:* 580,650 titles.

Computer facilities: 705 computers available on campus for general student use. A campuswide network can be accessed from student residence rooms and from off campus. Internet access and online class registration are available. *Web address:* http://www.tnstate.edu/.

General Application Contact: Graduate School Contact, 615-963-5901, Fax: 615-963-5963, E-mail: gradschool@tnstate.edu.

GRADUATE UNITS

The School of Graduate Studies and Research Students: 41 full-time (31 women), 253 part-time (186 women); includes 157 minority (150 African Americans, 1 American Indian/Alaska Native, 5 Asian Americans or Pacific Islanders, 1 Hispanic American), 3 international. Average age 34. 921 applicants. *Faculty:* 209 full-time (76 women). Expenses: Contact institution. *Financial support:* In 2006–07, 60 students received support, including 7 fellowships, 19 research assistantships (averaging $5,500 per year), 24 teaching assistantships (averaging $5,500 per year); career-related internships or fieldwork, institutionally sponsored loans, scholarships/grants, traineeships, and unspecified assistantships also available. Support available to part-time students. Financial award applicants required to submit FAFSA. *Application fee:* $25. *Application Contact:* Deborah Chisom, Coordinator of Admissions, 615-963-5962, Fax: 615-963-5963, E-mail: dchiscom@tnstate.edu. *Dean,* Dr. Helen Barrett, 615-963-5139, Fax: 615-963-5963, E-mail: hbarrett@tnstate.edu.

College of Arts and Sciences 83 applicants. Expenses: Contact institution. *Financial support:* Fellowships, research assistantships, teaching assistantships, unspecified assistantships available. Support available to part-time students. *Degree program information:* Part-time and evening/weekend programs available. Offers arts and sciences (MA, MCJ, MS, PhD); biological sciences (MS, PhD); chemistry (MS); criminal justice (MCJ); English (MA); mathematical sciences (MS); music education (MS). *Application deadline:* Applications are processed on a rolling basis. Electronic applications accepted. *Dean,* Dr. William Lawson, 615-963-7519, E-mail: wlawson@tnstate.edu.

College of Business Students: 31 full-time (19 women), 60 part-time (34 women); includes 56 minority (46 African Americans, 9 Asian Americans or Pacific Islanders, 1 Hispanic American), 11 international. Average age 30. 129 applicants, 36% accepted, 37 enrolled. *Faculty:* 13 full-time (3 women), 1 part-time/adjunct (0 women). Expenses: Contact institution. *Financial support:* In 2006–07, 6 research assistantships (averaging $3,198 per year), teaching assistantships (averaging $3,198 per year) were awarded. In 2006, 30 degrees awarded. *Degree program information:* Part-time and evening/weekend programs available. Postbaccalaureate distance learning degree programs offered. Offers business (MBA). *Application fee:* $25. *Application Contact:* Dr. Raovl Russell, Director, 615-963-7170, Fax: 615-963-7139, E-mail: rrussell3@tnstate.edu. *Dean,* Dr. Tilden J. Curry, 615-963-7121, Fax: 615-963-7139, E-mail: tcurry@tnstate.edu.

College of Education Expenses: Contact institution. *Financial support:* Fellowships, research assistantships, teaching assistantships, career-related internships or fieldwork and institutionally sponsored loans available. Support available to part-time students. Financial award application deadline: 5/1; financial award applicants required to submit FAFSA. *Degree program information:* Part-time and evening/weekend programs available. Offers administration and supervision (M Ed, Ed D, Ed S); counseling and guidance (MS); counseling psychology (PhD); curriculum and instruction (M Ed, Ed D); education (M Ed, MA Ed, MS, Ed D, PhD, Ed S); elementary education (M Ed, MA Ed, Ed D); human performance and sports science (MA Ed); psychology (MS, PhD); school psychology (MS, PhD); special education (M Ed, MA Ed, Ed D). *Application deadline:* Applications are processed on a rolling basis. *Application Contact:* Dr. Helen Barrett, Dean, 615-963-5139, Fax: 615-963-5963, E-mail: hbarrett@tnstate.edu. *Dean,* Dr. Leslie Drummonds, 615-963-5451.

College of Engineering, Technology, and Computer Science Students: 36 full-time (13 women), 26 part-time (5 women); includes 35 minority (27 African Americans, 8 Asian Americans or Pacific Islanders), 17 international. Average age 32. 4,615 applicants, 0% accepted, 13 enrolled. *Faculty:* 22 full-time (2 women). Expenses: Contact institution. *Financial support:* In 2006–07, 7 research assistantships, 6 teaching assistantships were awarded. In 2006, 16 degrees awarded. *Degree program information:* Part-time and evening/weekend programs available. Offers computer and information systems engineering (MS); computer information systems engineering (PhD); engineering (ME). *Application fee:* $25. *Application Contact:* Dr. Mohan J. Malkani, Associate Dean, 615-963-5400, Fax: 615-963-5397, E-mail: mmalkani@tnstate.edu. *Dean,* Dr. Decatur B. Rogers, 615-963-5409, Fax: 615-963-5397, E-mail: drogers@tnstate.edu.

College of Health Sciences 120 applicants. Expenses: Contact institution. *Financial support:* Fellowships, research assistantships, teaching assistantships, scholarships/grants available. Financial award application deadline: 3/15. *Degree program information:* Part-time and evening/weekend programs available. Offers health sciences (MPT, MS, DPT); physical therapy (MPT, DPT); speech and hearing science (MS). *Application deadline:* Applications are processed on a rolling basis. Electronic applications accepted. *Application Contact:* Dr. Harold R. Mitchell, Head, Department of Speech Pathology and Audiology, 615-963-7009, Fax: 615-963-7119, E-mail: hmitchell@tnstate.edu. *Dean,* Dr. Kathleen McEnerney, 615-963-5924, Fax: 615-963-5926, E-mail: kmcenerney@tnstate.edu.

Institute of Government Students: 31 full-time (19 women), 104 part-time (65 women); includes 18 minority (16 African Americans, 1 Asian American or Pacific Islander, 1 Hispanic American), 5 international. Average age 36. 114 applicants, 39% accepted, 41 enrolled. *Faculty:* 6 full-time (1 woman), 1 (woman) part-time/adjunct. Expenses: Contact institution. *Financial support:* In 2006–07, 3 research assistantships (averaging $4,185 per year), teaching assistantships (averaging $4,185 per year) were awarded. Support available to part-time students. In 2006, 35 master's, 1 doctorate awarded. *Degree program information:* Part-time and evening/weekend programs available. Offers public administration (MPA, PhD). *Application fee:* $25. *Application Contact:* Dr. Rodney Stonley, Coordinator of Graduate Studies, 615-963-7249, Fax: 615-963-7245, E-mail: rstonleyl@tnstate.edu. *Director,* Dr. Ann-Marie Rizzo, 615-963-7250, Fax: 615-963-7245, E-mail: arizzo@tnstate.edu.

School of Agriculture and Consumer Sciences Students: 6 full-time (3 women), 8 part-time (3 women); includes 10 minority (all African Americans) Average age 31. 9 applicants, 67% accepted, 3 enrolled. *Faculty:* 6 full-time (1 woman). Expenses: Contact institution. *Financial support:* In 2006–07, 2 research assistantships (averaging $6,511 per year), 1 teaching assistantship (averaging $6,511 per year) were awarded. In 2006, 8 degrees awarded. *Degree program information:* Part-time and evening/weekend programs available. Offers agricultural sciences (MS). *Application fee:* $25. *Interim Dean,* Dr. Constantine Fenderson, 615-963-7620, Fax: 615-963-5888, E-mail: cfenderson@tnstate.edu.

School of Nursing Students: 32 full-time (18 women), 71 part-time (69 women); includes 21 minority (29 African Americans, 2 Asian Americans or Pacific Islanders, 1 Hispanic American), 1 international. Average age 37. 78 applicants, 49% accepted, 30 enrolled. *Faculty:* 6 full-time (5 women). Expenses: Contact institution. *Financial support:* In 2006–07, research assistantships (averaging $5,500 per year), 2 teaching assistantships (averaging $5,500 per year) were awarded. In 2006, 7 degrees awarded. Offers family nurse practitioner (MSN); holistic nursing (MSN); nursing administration (MSN); nursing education (MSN); nursing informatics (MSN). *Application deadline:* Applications are processed on a rolling basis. *Interim Dean,* Dr. Bernadeen Fleming, 615-963-7106, Fax: 615-963-5049, E-mail: dfleming@tnstate.edu.

TENNESSEE TECHNOLOGICAL UNIVERSITY, Cookeville, TN 38505

General Information State-supported, coed, university. CGS member. *Enrollment:* 9,733 graduate, professional, and undergraduate students; 655 full-time matriculated graduate/professional students (396 women), 815 part-time matriculated graduate/professional students (535 women). *Graduate faculty:* 341 full-time (62 women). Tuition, state resident: full-time $8,748; part-time $319 per hour. Tuition, nonresident: full-time $23,524; part-time $740 per hour. *Graduate housing:* Rooms and/or apartments available on a first-come, first-served basis to single students and available to married students. Typical cost: $5,166 per year ($9,996 including board) for single students; $6,600 per year ($9,820 including board) for married students. Housing application deadline: 6/1. *Student services:* Campus employment opportunities, campus safety program, career counseling, child daycare facilities, disabled student services, exercise/wellness program, free psychological counseling, international student services, low-cost health insurance, teacher training. *Library facilities:* Angelo and Jennette Volpe Library and Media Center. *Online resources:* library catalog, web page, access to other libraries' catalogs. *Collection:* 640,056 titles, 4,847 serial subscriptions. *Research affiliation:* Center for Excellence in Teacher Evaluation, Appalachian Center for Crafts, Center of Excellence in Water Resources, Center of Excellence in Manufacturing Resources, Center of Excellence in Electric Power.

Computer facilities: 620 computers available on campus for general student use. A campuswide network can be accessed from student residence rooms and from off campus. Internet access and online class registration are available. *Web address:* http://www.tntech.edu/.

General Application Contact: Dr. Francis O. Otuonye, Associate Vice President for Research and Graduate Studies, 931-372-3233, Fax: 931-372-3497, E-mail: fotuonye@tntech.edu.

GRADUATE UNITS

Graduate School Students: 655 full-time (396 women), 815 part-time (535 women); includes 231 minority (87 African Americans, 2 American Indian/Alaska Native, 127 Asian Americans or Pacific Islanders, 15 Hispanic Americans), 2 international. Average age 27. 1,129 applicants, 62% accepted, 474 enrolled. *Faculty:* 341 full-time (62 women). Expenses: Contact institution. *Financial support:* In 2006–07, 50 fellowships (averaging $8,000 per year), 152 research assistantships (averaging $6,973 per year), 103 teaching assistantships (averaging $6,213 per year) were awarded; career-related internships or fieldwork and Federal Work-Study also available. Support available to part-time students. Financial award application deadline: 4/1. In 2006, 533 master's, 13 doctorates, 291 other advanced degrees awarded. *Degree program information:* Part-time and evening/weekend programs available. *Application deadline:* For fall admission, 3/1 priority date for domestic students; for spring admission, 8/1 for domestic students. *Application fee:* $25 ($30 for international students). Electronic applications accepted. *Associate Vice President for Research and Graduate Studies,* Dr. Francis O. Otuonye, 931-372-3233, Fax: 931-372-3497, E-mail: fotuonye@tntech.edu.

College of Arts and Sciences Students: 67 full-time (27 women), 36 part-time (16 women); includes 27 minority (4 African Americans, 20 Asian Americans or Pacific Islanders, 3 Hispanic Americans). Average age 27. 119 applicants, 39% accepted, 24 enrolled. *Faculty:* 78 full-time (15 women). Expenses: Contact institution. *Financial support:* In 2006–07, 30 research assistantships (averaging $7,600 per year), 36 teaching assistantships (averaging $6,630 per year) were awarded; fellowships, career-related internships or fieldwork also available. Support available to part-time students. Financial award application deadline: 4/1. In 2006, 41 degrees awarded. *Degree program information:* Part-time programs available. Offers arts and sciences (MA, MS, PhD); chemistry (MS); computer science (MS); English (MA); environmental biology (MS); environmental sciences (PhD); fish, game, and wildlife management (MS); mathematics (MS). *Application deadline:* For fall admission, 3/1 priority date for domestic students; for spring admission, 8/1 for domestic students. *Application fee:* $25 ($30 for international students). Electronic applications accepted. *Application Contact:* Dr. Francis O. Otuonye, Associate Vice President for Research and Graduate Studies, 931-372-3233, Fax: 931-372-3497, E-mail: fotuonye@tntech.edu. *Dean,* 931-372-3118, Fax: 931-372-6142.

College of Business Administration Students: 42 full-time (21 women), 145 part-time (69 women); includes 19 minority (7 African Americans, 1 American Indian/Alaska Native, 7 Asian Americans or Pacific Islanders, 4 Hispanic Americans). Average age 25. 175 applicants, 59% accepted, 70 enrolled. *Faculty:* 28 full-time (5 women). Expenses: Contact institution. *Financial support:* In 2006–07, 5 fellowships (averaging $10,000 per year), 18 research assistantships (averaging $4,000 per year), teaching assistantships (averaging $4,000 per year) were awarded. Support available to part-time students. Financial award application deadline: 4/1. In 2006, 64 degrees awarded. *Degree program information:* Part-time and evening/weekend programs available. Offers business administration (MBA). *Application deadline:* For fall admission, 3/1 priority date for domestic students; for spring admission, 8/1 for domestic students. *Application fee:* $25 ($30 for international students). *Application Contact:* Dr. Francis O. Otuonye, Associate Vice President for Research and Graduate Studies, 931-372-3233, Fax: 931-372-3497, E-mail: fotuonye@tntech.edu. *Director,* Dr. Bob G. Wood, 931-372-3600, Fax: 931-372-6249.

College of Education Students: 443 full-time (322 women), 551 part-time (412 women); includes 76 minority (62 African Americans, 2 American Indian/Alaska Native, 8 Asian Americans or Pacific Islanders, 4 Hispanic Americans). Average age 27. 449 applicants, 86% accepted, 304 enrolled. *Faculty:* 58 full-time (16 women). Expenses: Contact institution. *Financial support:* In 2006–07, 42 fellowships (averaging $8,000 per year), 33 research assistantships (averaging $4,000 per year), 26 teaching assistantships (averaging $4,000 per year) were awarded; career-related internships or fieldwork also available. Support available to part-time students. Financial award application deadline: 4/1. In 2006, 379 master's, 6 doctorates, 291 other advanced degrees awarded. *Degree program information:* Part-time and evening/weekend programs available. Offers curriculum (MA, Ed S); early childhood education (MA, Ed S); education (MA, PhD, Ed S); educational psychology (MA, Ed S); educational psychology and student personnel (MA, Ed S); elementary education (MA, Ed S); exceptional learning (PhD); exercise science, physical education and wellness (MA); instructional leadership (MA, Ed S); library science (MA); reading (MA, Ed S); secondary education (MA, Ed S); special education (MA, Ed S). *Application deadline:* For fall admission, 3/1 priority date for domestic students; for spring admission, 8/1 for domestic students. *Application fee:* $25 ($30 for international students). Electronic applications accepted. *Application Contact:* Dr. Francis O. Otuonye, Associate Vice President for Research and Graduate Studies, 931-372-3233, Fax: 931-372-3497, E-mail: fotuonye@tntech.edu. *Interim Dean,* Dr. Larry Peach, 931-372-3124, Fax: 931-372-6319, E-mail: lpeach@tntech.edu.

College of Engineering Students: 98 full-time (21 women), 50 part-time (10 women); includes 107 minority (11 African Americans, 92 Asian Americans or Pacific Islanders, 4 Hispanic Americans). Average age 28. 360 applicants, 41% accepted, 37 enrolled. *Faculty:* 76 full-time (2 women). Expenses: Contact institution. *Financial support:* In 2006–07, 3 fellowships (averaging $8,000 per year), 71 research assistantships (averaging $9,293 per year), 41 teaching assistantships (averaging $7,223 per year) were awarded; career-related internships or fieldwork also available. Support available to part-time students. Financial award application deadline: 4/1. In 2006, 51 master's, 7 doctorates awarded. *Degree program information:* Part-time programs available. Offers chemical engineering (MS, PhD); civil engineering (MS, PhD); electrical engineering (MS, PhD); engineering (MS, PhD); mechanical engineering (MS, PhD). *Application deadline:* For fall admission, 3/1 priority date for domestic students; for spring admission, 8/1 for domestic students. *Application fee:* $25 ($30 for international students). *Application Contact:* Dr. Francis O. Otuonye, Associate Vice President for Research and Graduate Studies, 931-372-3233, Fax: 931-372-3497, E-mail: fotuonye@tntech.edu. *Dean,* Dr. Glen Johnson, 931-372-3172, Fax: 931-372-6172.

School of Nursing Students: 4 full-time (all women), 25 part-time (22 women); includes 2 minority (both African Americans) 14 applicants, 64% accepted, 7 enrolled. Expenses: Contact institution. Offers nursing (MSN). *Application fee:* $25 ($30 for international students). *Application Contact:* Dr. Francis Otuonye, Associate Vice President for Research and Graduate Studies, 931-372-3233. *Interim Dean,* Dr. Shelia Green, 931-372-3203, Fax: 931-372-6244, E-mail: sgreen@tntech.edu.

TENNESSEE TEMPLE UNIVERSITY, Chattanooga, TN 37404-3587

General Information Independent-religious, coed, comprehensive institution. *Graduate housing:* Rooms and/or apartments available to single students and available on a first-come, first-served basis to married students. Housing application deadline: 6/1.

GRADUATE UNITS

Graduate Studies Division *Degree program information:* Part-time programs available. Offers curriculum and instruction (MS); educational administration and supervision (MS).

TEXAS A&M HEALTH SCIENCE CENTER, College Station, TX 77840

General Information State-supported, coed, upper-level institution. *Enrollment:* 1,032 matriculated graduate/professional students (541 women). *Enrollment by degree level:* 626 first professional, 178 master's, 93 doctoral, 78 other advanced degrees. *Graduate faculty:* 57 full-time (13 women), 48 part-time/adjunct (17 women). *Graduate housing:* On-campus housing not available. *Student services:* Campus employment opportunities, career counseling, exercise/wellness program, free psychological counseling, low-cost health insurance, multicultural affairs office. *Library facilities:* Baylor Hospital. *Web address:* http://www.tamhsc.edu/.

General Application Contact: Information Contact, 979-458-7200.

GRADUATE UNITS

Baylor College of Dentistry Offers dentistry (DDS, MD, MS, PhD, Certificate).

Graduate Division *Degree program information:* Part-time programs available. Offers biomaterials science (MS); biomedical sciences (MS, PhD); dental hygiene (MS); endodontics (MS, PhD, Certificate); health professions education (MS); oral and maxillofacial pathology (MS, PhD, Certificate); oral and maxillofacial surgery (MD, Certificate); oral biology (MS, PhD); orthodontics (MS, Certificate); pediatric dentistry (MS, Certificate); periodontics (MS, Certificate); prosthodontics (MS, Certificate).

College of Medicine Students: 322 full-time (168 women); includes 129 minority (14 African Americans, 2 American Indian/Alaska Native, 82 Asian Americans or Pacific Islanders, 31 Hispanic Americans), 4 international. Average age 24. 2,909 applicants, 4% accepted, 85 enrolled. *Faculty:* 771 full-time (134 women), 64 part-time/adjunct (12 women). Expenses: Contact institution. *Financial support:* In 2006–07, 2 fellowships, 26 research assistantships were awarded; teaching assistantships, institutionally sponsored loans and scholarships/grants also available. Financial award applicants required to submit FAFSA. Offers medicine (MD, PhD). *Application deadline:* For fall admission, 10/1 for domestic and international students. Applications are processed on a rolling basis. *Application fee:* $45. Electronic applications accepted. *Application Contact:* Filomeno G. Maldonado, Assistant Dean of Admissions, 979-845-7743, Fax: 979-845-5533, E-mail: fgmaldonado@medicine.tamhsc.edu. *Dean,* Dr. Christopher Colenda, 979-845-3431, Fax: 979-847-8663.

Graduate School of Biomedical Sciences Students: 60 full-time (27 women), 24 part-time (14 women); includes 17 minority (2 African Americans, 1 American Indian/Alaska Native, 5 Asian Americans or Pacific Islanders, 9 Hispanic Americans), 23 international. Average age 28. 220 applicants, 12% accepted, 15 enrolled. *Faculty:* 57 full-time (13 women), 48 part-time/adjunct (17 women). Expenses: Contact institution. *Financial support:* In 2006–07, 26 research assistantships (averaging $18,500 per year) were awarded; fellowships, teaching assistantships, institutionally sponsored loans, health care benefits, and unspecified assistantships also available. Financial award applicants required to submit FAFSA. In 2006, 3 degrees awarded. Offers cell and molecular biology (PhD); immunology (PhD); microbial and molecular pathogenesis (PhD); microbiology (PhD); molecular and cellular medicine (PhD); molecular biology (PhD); neuroscience and experimental therapeutics (PhD); systems biology and translational medicine (PhD); virology (PhD). *Application deadline:* For fall admission, 2/1 priority date for domestic students. Applications are processed on a rolling basis. *Application fee:* $50 ($75 for international students). *Head,* Dr. David S. Carlson, 979-458-0807, Fax: 979-845-6509, E-mail: dcarlson@tambcd.tamu.edu.

Institute of Biosciences and Technology Offers medical sciences (PhD). Degree awarded by the Graduate School for Biomedical Sciences.

School of Rural Public Health Students: 43 full-time (27 women), 118 part-time (76 women); includes 63 minority (13 African Americans, 13 Asian Americans or Pacific Islanders, 37 Hispanic Americans), 1 international. Average age 32. 162 applicants, 83% accepted, 118 enrolled. *Faculty:* 16 full-time (7 women), 4 part-time/adjunct (1 woman). Expenses: Contact institution. *Financial support:* In 2006–07, research assistantships (averaging $10,800 per year). In 2006, 10 degrees awarded. *Degree program information:* Part-time programs available. Postbaccalaureate distance learning degree programs offered (no on-campus study). Offers environmental/occupational health (MPH); epidemiology/biostatistics (MPH); health policy/management (MPH); social and behavioral health (MPH). *Application deadline:* For fall admission, 8/27 for domestic students; for spring admission, 1/14 for domestic students. Applications are processed on a rolling basis. *Application fee:* $35 ($75 for international students). Electronic applications accepted. *Application Contact:* Dr. James Robinson, Professor/Special Advisor to the Dean, 409-845-2387, Fax: 409-862-8371, E-mail: jrobinson@medicine.tamu.edu. *Dean,* Dr. Ciro V. Sumaya.

TEXAS A&M INTERNATIONAL UNIVERSITY, Laredo, TX 78041-1900

General Information State-supported, coed, comprehensive institution. *Enrollment:* 4,917 graduate, professional, and undergraduate students; 151 full-time matriculated graduate/professional students, 800 part-time matriculated graduate/professional students. *Enrollment by degree level:* 951 master's. *Graduate faculty:* 70 full-time (20 women), 12 part-time/adjunct (1 woman). Tuition, state resident: full-time $1,580. Tuition, nonresident: full-time $5,432. *Required fees:* $3,808. *Graduate housing:* Rooms and/or apartments available on a first-come, first-served basis to single and married students. Typical cost: $3,200 (including board) for single students. Room and board charges vary according to board plan and housing facility selected. *Student services:* Campus employment opportunities, campus safety program, career counseling, disabled student services, exercise/wellness program, free psychological counseling, international student services, low-cost health insurance, multicultural affairs office, teacher training, writing training. *Library facilities:* Sue and Radcliff Killam Library. *Online resources:* library catalog, web page, access to other libraries' catalogs. *Collection:* 237,705 titles, 5,459 serial subscriptions, 2,959 audiovisual materials.

Computer facilities: 200 computers available on campus for general student use. A campuswide network can be accessed from off campus. *Web address:* http://www.tamiu.edu/.

General Application Contact: Dr. Jeff Brown, Director, office of Graduate Studies, 956-326-2596, Fax: 956-326-3021, E-mail: jbrown@tamiu.edu.

GRADUATE UNITS

Office of Graduate Studies and Research Students: 164 full-time (72 women), 799 part-time (506 women); includes 708 minority (4 African Americans, 1 American Indian/Alaska Native, 3 Asian Americans or Pacific Islanders, 700 Hispanic Americans), 129 international. Average age 31. 789 applicants, 79% accepted, 407 enrolled. *Faculty:* 70 full-time (20 women), 12 part-time/adjunct (1 woman). Expenses: Contact institution. *Financial support:* In 2006–07, 475 students received support, including 40 fellowships with partial tuition reimbursements available; Federal Work-Study, institutionally sponsored loans, and scholarships/grants also available. Support available to part-time students. Financial award application deadline: 11/1; financial award applicants required to submit FAFSA. In 2006, 159 degrees awarded. *Degree program information:* Part-time and evening/weekend programs available. Offers educational administration (MS Ed); generic special education (MS Ed); school counseling (MS). *Application deadline:* For fall admission, 7/1 priority date for domestic students, 6/1 for international students; for spring admission, 11/1 priority date for domestic students, 10/1 for international students. Applications are processed on a rolling basis. *Application fee:* $25. *Application Contact:* Rosie Espinoza-Dickinson, Director of Admissions, 956-326-2200, Fax: 956-326-2199, E-mail: enroll@tamiu.edu. *Director,* Dr. Jeff Brown, 956-326-2596, Fax: 956-326-3021, E-mail: jbrown@tamiu.edu.

College of Arts and Sciences Students: 30 full-time (16 women), 147 part-time (85 women); includes 159 minority (1 American Indian/Alaska Native, 158 Hispanic Americans), 2 international. Average age 32. 130 applicants, 90% accepted, 77 enrolled. *Faculty:* 28 full-time (8 women). Expenses: Contact institution. *Financial support:* In 2006–07, 84 students received support, including 5 research assistantships (averaging $9,100 per year), 5 teaching assistantships (averaging $9,100 per year); fellowships with tuition reimbursements available, Federal Work-Study and institutionally sponsored loans also available. Support available to part-time students. Financial award application deadline: 11/1; financial award applicants required to submit FAFSA. In 2006, 33 degrees awarded. *Degree program information:* Part-time and evening/weekend programs available. Postbaccalaureate distance learning degree programs offered (no on-campus study). Offers arts and sciences (MA, MACP, MAIS, MPA, MS, PhD); biology (MS); counseling psychology (MACP); criminal justice (MS); English (MA); fine and performing arts; Hispanic studies (PhD); history (MA); mathematical and physical science (MA, MAIS); political science (MA); psychology (MS); public administration (MPA); sociology (MA); Spanish (MA). *Application deadline:* For fall admission, 4/30 priority date for domestic students, 4/30 for international students; for spring admission, 11/12 for domestic students, 4/30 for international students. Applications are processed on a rolling basis. *Application fee:* $25. *Application Contact:* Rosie Espinoza-Dickinson, Director of Admissions, 956-326-2200, Fax: 956-326-2199, E-mail: enroll@tamiu.edu. *Dean,* Dr. Nasser Momayezi, 956-326-2460, Fax: 956-326-2459, E-mail: nmomayezi@tamiu.edu.

College of Business Administration Students: 114 full-time (42 women), 155 part-time (53 women); includes 140 minority (1 African American, 2 Asian Americans or Pacific Islanders, 137 Hispanic Americans), 120 international. Average age 28. 272 applicants, 57% accepted, 117 enrolled. *Faculty:* 22 full-time (2 women), 8 part-time/adjunct (0 women). Expenses: Contact institution. *Financial support:* In 2006–07, 105 students received support, including 40 fellowships; Federal Work-Study and institutionally sponsored loans also available. Support available to part-time students. Financial award application deadline: 11/1; financial award applicants required to submit FAFSA. In 2006, 107 degrees awarded. *Degree program information:* Part-time and evening/weekend programs available. Offers accounting (MP Acc); business administration (MBA, MP Acc, MSIS); information systems (MSIS); international banking (MBA); international trade (MBA). *Application deadline:* For fall admission, 7/15 priority date for domestic students; for spring admission, 11/12 for domestic students. Applications are processed on a rolling basis. *Application fee:* $25. *Application Contact:* Imelda Lopez, Graduate Admissions Counselor, 956-326-2485, Fax: 956-326-2459, E-mail: lopez@tamiu.edu. *Dean,* Dr. Jacky So, 956-328-2480.

College of Education Students: 19 full-time (14 women), 472 part-time (352 women); includes 464 minority (3 African Americans, 1 Asian American or Pacific Islander, 460 Hispanic Americans), 7 international. Average age 33. 372 applicants, 90% accepted, 203 enrolled. *Faculty:* 17 full-time (7 women), 3 part-time/adjunct (0 women). Expenses: Contact institution. *Financial support:* In 2006–07, 272 students received support; fellowships, Federal Work-Study and institutionally sponsored loans available. Support available to part-time students. Financial award application deadline: 11/1; financial award applicants required to submit FAFSA. In 2006, 81 degrees awarded. *Degree program information:* Part-time and evening/weekend programs available. Offers bilingual education (PhD); curriculum and instruction (MS, PhD); early childhood education (PhD); education (MS,

Texas A&M International University (continued)

MS Ed, PhD); reading (MS). *Application deadline:* For fall admission, 7/15 priority date for domestic students; for spring admission, 11/12 for domestic students. Applications are processed on a rolling basis. *Application fee:* $25. *Application Contact:* Rosie Espinoza-Dickinson, Director of Admissions, 956-326-2200, Fax: 956-326-2199, E-mail: enroll@tamiu.edu. *Dean,* Dr. Humberto Gonzalez, 956-326-2420, E-mail: hgonzalez@tamiu.edu.

School of Nursing Students: 1 full-time (0 women), 25 part-time (16 women); includes 25 minority (all Hispanic Americans) Average age 53. 12 applicants, 92% accepted, 9 enrolled. *Faculty:* 3 full-time (all women), 1 (woman) part-time/adjunct. Expenses: Contact institution. *Financial support:* In 2006–07, 14 students received support. Offers nursing (MSN). *Application fee:* $25. *Application Contact:* Rosie Espinoza, Director, Office of Admissions, 956-326-2200, Fax: 956-326-2269, E-mail: enroll@tamiu.edu. *Director,* Dr. Susan Walker, 956-326-2574, E-mail: swalker@tamiu.edu.

TEXAS A&M UNIVERSITY, College Station, TX 77843

General Information State-supported, coed, university. CGS member. *Enrollment:* 45,380 graduate, professional, and undergraduate students; 7,085 full-time matriculated graduate/professional students (2,889 women), 1,715 part-time matriculated graduate/professional students (860 women). *Graduate faculty:* 1,205 full-time (249 women), 160 part-time/adjunct (31 women). Tuition, state resident: full-time $4,697. Tuition, nonresident: full-time $11,297. *Required fees:* $2,272. *Graduate housing:* Rooms and/or apartments available on a first-come, first-served basis to single and married students. *Student services:* Campus employment opportunities, campus safety program, career counseling, child daycare facilities, disabled student services, exercise/wellness program, free psychological counseling, grant writing training, international student services, low-cost health insurance, multicultural affairs office, teacher training, writing training. *Library facilities:* Sterling C. Evans Library plus 4 others. *Online resources:* library catalog, web page, access to other libraries' catalogs. *Collection:* 3.6 million titles, 43,949 serial subscriptions, 44,088 audiovisual materials. *Research affiliation:* Joint Oceanographic Institutions, Inc. (geosciences), National Science Foundation (geosciences), US Department of Agriculture (agriculture), Texas Department of Transportation (transportation).

Computer facilities: 1,300 computers available on campus for general student use. A campuswide network can be accessed from student residence rooms and from off campus. Internet access and online class registration are available. *Web address:* http://www.tamu.edu/.

General Application Contact: Graduate Admissions, 979-845-1044, E-mail: admissions@tamu.edu.

GRADUATE UNITS

College of Agriculture and Life Sciences Students: 788 full-time (392 women), 260 part-time (102 women); includes 118 minority (30 African Americans, 5 American Indian/Alaska Native, 14 Asian Americans or Pacific Islanders, 69 Hispanic Americans), 299 international. Average age 29. 628 applicants, 57% accepted, 245 enrolled. *Faculty:* 193 full-time (38 women), 66 part-time/adjunct (10 women). Expenses: Contact institution. *Financial support:* Fellowships, research assistantships, teaching assistantships, career-related internships or fieldwork, Federal Work-Study, institutionally sponsored loans, scholarships/grants, tuition waivers (partial), and unspecified assistantships available. Support available to part-time students. Financial award applicants required to submit FAFSA. In 2006, 167 master's, 73 doctorates awarded. *Degree program information:* Part-time programs available. Post-baccalaureate distance learning degree programs offered (minimal on-campus study). Offers agricultural economics (MAB, MS, PhD); agricultural education (M Ed, MS, Ed D, PhD); agriculture (M Agr); agriculture and life sciences (M Agr, M Ed, M Eng, MAB, MS, DE, Ed D, PhD); agronomy (M Agr, MS, PhD); animal breeding (MS, PhD); animal science (M Agr, MS, PhD); biochemistry (MS, PhD); biological and agricultural engineering (M Agr, M Eng, MS, DE, PhD); biophysics (MS); dairy science (M Agr, MS); entomology (M Agr, MS, PhD); forestry (MS, PhD); genetics (PhD); horticulture (PhD); horticulture and floriculture (M Agr, MS); molecular and environmental plant sciences (MS, PhD); natural resources development (M Agr); nutrition and food science (M Agr, MS, PhD); physiology of reproduction (MS, PhD); plant pathology (MS, PhD); plant protection (M Agr); poultry science (M Agr, MS, PhD); rangeland ecology and management (M Agr, MS, PhD); recreation resources development (M Agr); recreation, park, and tourism sciences (MS, PhD); soil science (MS, PhD); wildlife and fisheries sciences (M Agr, MS, PhD). *Application deadline:* For fall admission, 7/21 priority date for domestic students, 6/1 priority date for international students; for spring admission, 12/1 priority date for domestic students, 10/1 priority date for international students. Applications are processed on a rolling basis. *Application fee:* $50 ($75 for international students). Electronic applications accepted. *Vice Chancellor,* Dr. Elsa Murano, 979-845-4747, Fax: 979-845-9938.

College of Architecture Students: 381 full-time (141 women), 62 part-time (21 women); includes 58 minority (13 African Americans, 2 American Indian/Alaska Native, 17 Asian Americans or Pacific Islanders, 26 Hispanic Americans), 187 international. Average age 29. 375 applicants, 80% accepted, 146 enrolled. *Faculty:* 77 full-time (18 women), 2 part-time/adjunct (0 women). Expenses: Contact institution. *Financial support:* In 2006–07, fellowships with partial tuition reimbursements (averaging $1,000 per year), research assistantships with partial tuition reimbursements (averaging $8,139 per year), teaching assistantships with partial tuition reimbursements (averaging $7,650 per year) were awarded; career-related internships or fieldwork, Federal Work-Study, institutionally sponsored loans, scholarships/grants, and unspecified assistantships also available. Financial award application deadline: 1/15; financial award applicants required to submit FAFSA. In 2006, 115 master's, 23 doctorates awarded. Offers architecture (M Arch, MS Arch, PhD); construction management (MS); land development (MSLD); landscape architecture (MLA); urban and regional science (PhD); urban planning (MUP); visualization science (MS). *Application deadline:* For fall admission, 1/15 priority date for domestic and international students. Applications are processed on a rolling basis. *Application fee:* $50 ($75 for international students). Electronic applications accepted. *Application Contact:* 979-845-6582, Fax: 979-862-7119, E-mail: gradoff@archone.tamu.edu. *Dean,* J. Thomas Regan, 979-845-1221, Fax: 979-845-4491.

College of Education and Human Development Students: 597 full-time (399 women), 643 part-time (472 women); includes 317 minority (123 African Americans, 4 American Indian/Alaska Native, 22 Asian Americans or Pacific Islanders, 168 Hispanic Americans), 127 international. Average age 36. 509 applicants, 66% accepted, 223 enrolled. *Faculty:* 94 full-time (37 women), 11 part-time/adjunct (6 women). Expenses: Contact institution. *Financial support:* In 2006–07, fellowships with partial tuition reimbursements (averaging $12,000 per year), research assistantships with partial tuition reimbursements (averaging $10,000 per year), teaching assistantships with partial tuition reimbursements (averaging $10,000 per year) were awarded; career-related internships or fieldwork, Federal Work-Study, institutionally sponsored loans, scholarships/grants, tuition waivers (partial), and unspecified assistantships also available. Financial award applicants required to submit FAFSA. In 2006, 205 master's, 75 doctorates awarded. *Degree program information:* Part-time and evening/weekend programs available. Postbaccalaureate distance learning degree programs offered (no on-campus study). Offers counseling psychology (PhD); curriculum and instruction (M Ed, MS, PhD); education and human development (M Ed, MS, Ed D, PhD); educational administration and human resource development (M Ed, MS, Ed D, PhD); educational psychology (PhD); educational technology (M Ed); gifted and talented education (M Ed, MS); health education (M Ed, MS, Ed D, PhD); Hispanic bilingual education (M Ed, PhD); human learning and development (MS); intelligence, creativity, and giftedness (PhD); kinesiology (M Ed, MS, Ed D, PhD); learning, development, and instruction (PhD); mathematics education (M Ed, MS, PhD); multicultural/urban/ESL/international education (M Ed, MS, PhD); reading/language arts (M Ed, MS, PhD); research, measurement and statistics (MS); research, measurement, and statistics (PhD); school counseling (M Ed); school psychology (PhD); science education (M Ed, MS, PhD); social studies education (M Ed, MS, PhD); special education (M Ed, PhD). *Application fee:* $50 ($75 for international students). Electronic applications accepted. *Application Contact:* Becky Carr, Assistant Dean, 979-845-5311, Fax: 979-845-6129, E-mail: bcarr@tamu.edu. *Interim Dean,* Doug Palmer, 979-845-5311.

College of Engineering Students: 1,915 full-time (349 women), 291 part-time (47 women); includes 204 minority (55 African Americans, 3 American Indian/Alaska Native, 63 Asian Americans or Pacific Islanders, 83 Hispanic Americans), 1,425 international. 4,401 applicants, 37% accepted, 619 enrolled. *Faculty:* 285 full-time (32 women), 34 part-time/adjunct (2 women). Expenses: Contact institution. *Financial support:* Fellowships, research assistantships, teaching assistantships, career-related internships or fieldwork, institutionally sponsored loans, scholarships/grants, and unspecified assistantships available. Financial award applicants required to submit FAFSA. In 2006, 432 master's, 150 doctorates awarded. *Degree program information:* Part-time programs available. Postbaccalaureate distance learning degree programs offered (minimal on-campus study). Offers aerospace engineering (M Eng, MS, PhD); biomedical engineering (M Eng, MS, D Eng, PhD); chemical engineering (M Eng, MS, PhD); computer engineering (M En, M Eng, MS, PhD); computer science (MCS, MS, PhD); construction engineering and management (M Eng, MS, D Eng, PhD); electrical engineering (MS, PhD); engineering (M En, M Eng, MCS, MID, MS, D Eng, PhD); engineering technology and industrial distribution (MID); environmental engineering (M Eng, MS, D Eng, PhD); geotechnical engineering (M Eng, MS, D Eng, PhD); health physics (MS); industrial and systems engineering (M Eng, MS); industrial engineering (D Eng, PhD); materials engineering (M Eng, MS, D Eng, PhD); mechanical engineering (M Eng, MS, D Eng, PhD); nuclear engineering (M Eng, MS, PhD); ocean engineering (M Eng, MS, D Eng, PhD); petroleum engineering (M Eng, MS, PhD); structural engineering (M Eng, MS, D Eng, PhD); transportation engineering (M Eng, MS, D Eng, PhD); water resources engineering (M Eng, MS, D Eng, PhD). *Application fee:* $50 ($75 for international students). Electronic applications accepted. *Application Contact:* Karen Butler-Purry, Assistant Dean, 979-845-7200, Fax: 979-847-8654, E-mail: eapo@tamu.edu. *Dean,* Dr. G. Kemble Bennett, 979-845-7203, Fax: 979-845-8986.

College of Geosciences Students: 230 full-time (90 women), 43 part-time (19 women); includes 18 minority (3 African Americans, 2 American Indian/Alaska Native, 1 Asian American or Pacific Islander, 12 Hispanic Americans), 109 international. Average age 30. 241 applicants, 55% accepted, 61 enrolled. *Faculty:* 65 full-time (10 women), 14 part-time/adjunct (1 woman). Expenses: Contact institution. *Financial support:* Fellowships with partial tuition reimbursements, research assistantships, teaching assistantships, career-related internships or fieldwork, Federal Work-Study, institutionally sponsored loans, scholarships/grants, tuition waivers (partial), and unspecified assistantships available. Financial award application deadline: 3/1; financial award applicants required to submit FAFSA. In 2006, 51 master's, 15 doctorates awarded. *Degree program information:* Part-time programs available. Offers atmospheric sciences (MS, PhD); geography (MS, PhD); geology (MS, PhD); geophysics (MS, PhD); geosciences (MS, PhD); oceanography (MS, PhD). *Application deadline:* For fall admission, 3/1 priority date for domestic students; for spring admission, 12/1 for domestic students. Applications are processed on a rolling basis. *Application fee:* $50 ($75 for international students). Electronic applications accepted. *Dean,* Dr. Bjorn Kjerfve, 979-845-3651, Fax: 979-845-0056.

College of Liberal Arts Students: 622 full-time (314 women), 164 part-time (86 women); includes 150 minority (33 African Americans, 3 American Indian/Alaska Native, 30 Asian Americans or Pacific Islanders, 84 Hispanic Americans), 181 international. 1,016 applicants, 41% accepted, 196 enrolled. *Faculty:* 190 full-time (54 women), 7 part-time/adjunct (3 women). Expenses: Contact institution. *Financial support:* Fellowships, research assistantships with partial tuition reimbursements, teaching assistantships with partial tuition reimbursements, career-related internships or fieldwork, Federal Work-Study, institutionally sponsored loans, unspecified assistantships, and assistant lecturer positions available. Financial award applicants required to submit FAFSA. In 2006, 92 master's, 71 doctorates awarded. *Degree program information:* Part-time programs available. Offers anthropology (MA, PhD); behavioral and cellular neuroscience (MS, PhD); clinical psychology (MS, PhD); cognitive psychology (MS, PhD); communication (MA, PhD); developmental psychology (MS, PhD); economics (MS, PhD); English (MA, PhD); Hispanic studies (MA, PhD); history (MA, PhD); industrial/organizational psychology (MS, PhD); liberal arts (MA, MS, PhD); philosophy (MA, PhD); political science (MA, PhD); science and technology journalism (MS); social psychology (MS, PhD); sociology (MS, PhD). *Application fee:* $50 ($75 for international students). Electronic applications accepted. *Application Contact:* Dr. Larry J. Oliver, Associate Dean, 979-845-8541, Fax: 979-845-5164, E-mail: l-oliver@tamu.edu. *Dean,* Dr. Charles A. Johnson, 979-845-5141, Fax: 979-845-5164, E-mail: cjohnson@tamu.edu.

College of Science Students: 691 full-time (245 women), 37 part-time (3 women); includes 91 minority (11 African Americans, 4 American Indian/Alaska Native, 34 Asian Americans or Pacific Islanders, 42 Hispanic Americans), 327 international. 842 applicants, 38% accepted, 159 enrolled. *Faculty:* 184 full-time (25 women), 5 part-time/adjunct (0 women). Expenses: Contact institution. *Financial support:* Fellowships, research assistantships, teaching assistantships, career-related internships or fieldwork, institutionally sponsored loans, and scholarships/grants available. Financial award applicants required to submit FAFSA. In 2006, 88 master's, 90 doctorates awarded. *Degree program information:* Part-time programs available. Offers applied physics (PhD); biology (MS, PhD); botany (MS, PhD); chemistry (MS, PhD); mathematics (MS, PhD); microbiology (MS, PhD); molecular and cell biology (PhD); neuroscience (MS, PhD); physics (MS, PhD); science (MS, PhD); statistics (MS, PhD); zoology (MS, PhD). *Application Contact:* James C. Holste, Associate Dean for Graduate Studies, 979-845-7362, Fax: 979-845-6077, E-mail: j-holste@tamu.edu. *Dean,* H. Joseph Newton, 979-845-7361, Fax: 979-845-6077.

College of Veterinary Medicine 187 applicants, 91% accepted, 165 enrolled. *Faculty:* 100 full-time (29 women), 21 part-time/adjunct (9 women). Expenses: Contact institution. *Financial support:* Fellowships, research assistantships, teaching assistantships, career-related internships or fieldwork, Federal Work-Study, institutionally sponsored loans, tuition waivers (partial), and clinical associateships available. Support available to part-time students. Financial award applicants required to submit FAFSA. In 2006, 125 DVMs, 11 master's, 5 doctorates awarded. *Degree program information:* Part-time programs available. Offers veterinary medicine (DVM, MS, PhD). *Dean,* Dr. H. Richard Adams, 979-845-5051, Fax: 979-845-5088.

Graduate Programs in Veterinary Medicine Average age 30. Expenses: Contact institution. *Financial support:* Fellowships, research assistantships, teaching assistantships, career-related internships or fieldwork, Federal Work-Study, institutionally sponsored loans, tuition waivers (partial), and clinical associateships available. Support available to part-time students. Financial award applicants required to submit FAFSA. *Degree program information:* Part-time programs available. Offers epidemiology (MS); food safety/toxicology (MS); genetics (MS, PhD); physiology and pharmacology (MS, PhD); toxicology (MS, PhD); veterinary anatomy (MS, PhD); veterinary integrative biosciences (MS, PhD); veterinary large animal clinical sciences (MS); veterinary medicine and surgery (MS); veterinary microbiology (MS, PhD); veterinary parasitology (MS); veterinary pathobiology (MS, PhD); veterinary pathology (MS, PhD); veterinary physiology and pharmacology (MS, PhD); veterinary public health (MS); veterinary small animal medicine and surgery (MS). *Application fee:* $50 ($75 for international students). *Application Contact:* Kathie Henning, Administrative Assistant, 979-845-5092, Fax: 979-845-5088, E-mail: khenning@cvm.tamu.edu. *Associate Dean, Research and Graduate Studies,* Dr. L. Garry Adams, 979-845-5092, Fax: 979-845-5088, E-mail: gadams@cvm.tamu.edu.

Faculty of Neuroscience *Faculty:* 65. Expenses: Contact institution. *Financial support:* Fellowships, research assistantships, teaching assistantships available. Financial award application deadline: 4/1. Offers neuroscience (MS, PhD). *Application deadline:* For fall admission, 2/1 priority date for domestic students. Applications are processed on a rolling basis. *Application fee:* $50 ($75 for international students).

George Bush School of Government and Public Service Students: 146 full-time (69 women), 53 part-time (12 women); includes 29 minority (6 African Americans, 2 American Indian/Alaska Native, 4 Asian Americans or Pacific Islanders, 17 Hispanic Americans), 12 international. Average age 24. 181 applicants, 56% accepted, 67 enrolled. *Faculty:* 17 full-time (6 women). Expenses: Contact institution. *Financial support:* In 2006–07, fellowships (averaging $11,000 per year), research assistantships (averaging $11,250 per year) were awarded; career-related internships or fieldwork, Federal Work-Study, and institutionally sponsored loans also available. Financial award application deadline: 2/1; financial award applicants required to submit FAFSA. In 2006, 56 degrees awarded. Offers international affairs (MPSA); public service and administration (MPSA). *Application deadline:* For fall admission, 1/24 for domestic and international students. *Application fee:* $50 ($75 for international students). Electronic applications accepted. *Application Contact:* Kathryn Meyer, Recruitment/Placement Officer, 979-458-4767, Fax: 979-845-4155, E-mail: admissions@bushschool.tamu.edu. *Dean,* Richard A. Chilcoat, 979-862-8007, Fax: 979-862-7953, E-mail: bushschool@tamu.edu.

Mays Business School Students: 876 full-time (342 women). Average age 28. 850 applicants, 59% accepted, 202 enrolled. *Faculty:* 178 full-time (40 women), 20 part-time/adjunct (5 women). Expenses: Contact institution. *Financial support:* In 2006–07, 235 students received support; fellowships, research assistantships, teaching assistantships, career-related internships or fieldwork, Federal Work-Study, and institutionally sponsored loans available. Financial award application deadline: 2/1. In 2006, 460 master's, 10 doctorates awarded. Offers accounting (MS, PhD); business (EMBA, MBA, MLERE, MS, PhD); business administration (EMBA, MBA); finance (MS, PhD); human resource management (MS); management (PhD); management information systems (MS, PhD); management science (PhD); marketing (MS, PhD); production and operations management (PhD); real estate (MLERE). *Application deadline:* Applications are processed on a rolling basis. *Application fee:* $50 ($75 for international students). Electronic applications accepted. *Application Contact:* Wendy Flynn, Director, MBA Program, 979-845-4714, Fax: 979-862-2393, E-mail: maysmba@tamu.edu. *Dean,* Dr. Jerry R. Strawser, 979-845-4711.

TEXAS A&M UNIVERSITY AT GALVESTON, Galveston, TX 77553-1675

General Information State-supported, coed, comprehensive institution. *Enrollment:* 1,553 graduate, professional, and undergraduate students; 12 full-time matriculated graduate/professional students (7 women), 21 part-time matriculated graduate/professional students (15 women). *Enrollment by degree level:* 33 master's. *Graduate faculty:* 33 full-time (7 women). Tuition, state resident: full-time $3,523; part-time $196 per hour. Tuition, nonresident: full-time $7,060; part-time $470 per hour. *Graduate housing:* Room and/or apartments available on a first-come, first-served basis to single students; on-campus housing not available to married students. Typical cost: $1,958 per year ($4,870 including board). *Student services:* Campus employment opportunities, career counseling, disabled student services, international student services. *Library facilities:* Jack K. Williams Library. *Online resources:* library catalog, web page, access to other libraries' catalogs. *Collection:* 56,589 titles, 640 serial subscriptions.

Computer facilities: 122 computers available on campus for general student use. A campuswide network can be accessed from student residence rooms and from off campus. Internet access and online class registration, grades, degree plan progress, billing statement are available. *Web address:* http://www.tamug.edu/.

General Application Contact: Dr. Frederick C. Schlemmer, Associate Professor/ Graduate Advisor, 409-740-4518, Fax: 409-740-4429, E-mail: schlemme@tamug.edu.

GRADUATE UNITS

Department of Marine Sciences Students: 12 full-time (7 women), 21 part-time (15 women); includes 5 minority (3 Asian Americans or Pacific Islanders, 2 Hispanic Americans), 2 international. Average age 23. 18 applicants, 83% accepted, 7 enrolled. *Faculty:* 33 full-time (7 women). Expenses: Contact institution. *Financial support:* In 2006–07, 14 students received support, including 1 research assistantship, 2 teaching assistantships; scholarships/grants, health care benefits, and unspecified assistantships also available. Financial award application deadline: 4/1; financial award applicants required to submit FAFSA. In 2006, 12 degrees awarded. Offers marine resources management (MMRM). *Application deadline:* Applications are processed on a rolling basis. *Application fee:* $50 ($75 for international students). Electronic applications accepted. *Application Contact:* Dr. Frederick C. Schlemmer, Associate Professor/ Graduate Advisor, 409-740-4518, Fax: 409-740-4429, E-mail: schlemme@tamug.edu. *Head,* Dr. Ernest Estes, 409-710-4599.

TEXAS A&M UNIVERSITY–COMMERCE, Commerce, TX 75429-3011

General Information State-supported, coed, university. CGS member. *Graduate housing:* Rooms and/or apartments available on a first-come, first-served basis to single and married students. *Research affiliation:* A&M–Commerce Regional Division of Texas Engineering Experiment Station.

GRADUATE UNITS

Graduate School *Degree program information:* Part-time programs available. Electronic applications accepted.

College of Arts and Sciences *Degree program information:* Part-time programs available. Offers agricultural education (M Ed, MS); agricultural sciences (M Ed, MS); art (MA, MS); art history (MA); arts and sciences (M Ed, MA, MFA, MM, MS, MSW, PhD); biological and earth sciences (M Ed, MS); chemistry (M Ed, MS); college teaching of English (PhD); computer science (MS); English (MA, MS); fine arts (MFA); history (MA, MS); mathematics (MA, MS); music (MA, MS); music composition (MA, MM); music education (MA, MM, MS); music literature (MA); music performance (MA, MM); music theory (MA, MM); physics (M Ed, MS); social sciences (M Ed, MS); social work (MSW); sociology (MA, MS); Spanish (MA); studio art (MA); theatre (MA, MS). Electronic applications accepted.

College of Business and Technology *Degree program information:* Part-time programs available. Offers business administration (MBA); business and technology (MA, MBA, MS); economics (MA, MS); industry and technology (MS). Electronic applications accepted.

College of Education and Human Services *Degree program information:* Part-time programs available. Offers counseling (M Ed, MS, Ed D); early childhood education (M Ed, MA, MS); education (M Ed, MA, MS, Ed D, PhD); educational administration (M Ed, MS, Ed D); educational psychology (PhD); elementary education (M Ed, MS); health, kinesiology and sports studies (M Ed, MS, Ed D); higher education (MS); learning technology and information systems (M Ed, MS); psychology (MA, MS); reading (M Ed, MA, MS); secondary education (M Ed, MS); special education (M Ed, MA, MS); supervision of curriculum and instruction: elementary education (Ed D); supervision, curriculum, and instruction (Ed D); training and development (MS). Electronic applications accepted.

TEXAS A&M UNIVERSITY–CORPUS CHRISTI, Corpus Christi, TX 78412-5503

General Information State-supported, coed, comprehensive institution. CGS member. *Graduate housing:* Room and/or apartments available on a first-come, first-served basis to single students; on-campus housing not available to married students. Housing application deadline: 5/1.

GRADUATE UNITS

Graduate Studies and Research *Degree program information:* Part-time and evening/weekend programs available. Postbaccalaureate distance learning degree programs offered (minimal on-campus study). Electronic applications accepted.

College of Business *Degree program information:* Part-time and evening/weekend programs available. Offers accounting (M Acc); health care administration (MBA); international business (MBA). Electronic applications accepted.

College of Education *Degree program information:* Part-time and evening/weekend programs available. Offers counseling (MS, PhD); counselor education (PhD); curriculum and instruction (MS, Ed D); early childhood education (MS); educational administration (MS); educational leadership (Ed D); educational technology (MS); elementary education (MS); kinesiology (MS); occupational training and development (MS); reading (MS); secondary education (MS); special education (MS). Electronic applications accepted.

College of Liberal Arts *Degree program information:* Part-time and evening/weekend programs available. Offers English (MA); history (MA); psychology (MA); public administration (MPA); studio arts (MA, MFA). Electronic applications accepted.

College of Nursing and Health Sciences *Degree program information:* Part-time and evening/weekend programs available. Offers clinical nurse specialist (MSN); family nurse practitioner (MSN); health care administration (MSN); leadership in nursing systems (MSN). Electronic applications accepted.

College of Science and Technology *Degree program information:* Part-time and evening/weekend programs available. Offers applied and computational mathematics (MS); biology (MS); coastal and marine system science (PhD); computer science (MS); curriculum content (MS); environmental science (MS); mariculture (MS); science and technology (MS, PhD). Electronic applications accepted.

TEXAS A&M UNIVERSITY–KINGSVILLE, Kingsville, TX 78363

General Information State-supported, coed, university. *Graduate housing:* Rooms and/or apartments available on a first-come, first-served basis to single and married students. Housing application deadline: 8/1. *Research affiliation:* Gas Research Institute (engineering), U.S. Filters (engineering), Texas A&M University (biology), University of Texas Health Science Center–Houston (biology), University of Texas Health Science Center–San Antonio (biology), Institute of Biosciences and Technology (biology).

GRADUATE UNITS

College of Graduate Studies *Degree program information:* Part-time and evening/weekend programs available. Postbaccalaureate distance learning degree programs offered (minimal on-campus study).

College of Agriculture and Home Economics *Degree program information:* Part-time and evening/weekend programs available. Offers agribusiness (MS); agricultural education (MS); agriculture and home economics (MS, PhD); animal sciences (MS); human sciences (MS); plant and soil sciences (MS, PhD); range and wildlife management (MS); wildlife science (PhD).

College of Arts and Sciences *Degree program information:* Part-time and evening/weekend programs available. Offers applied geology (MS); art (MA, MS); arts and sciences (MA, MM, MS); biology (MS); chemistry (MS); communication (MS); English (MA, MS); gerontology (MS); history and political science (MA, MS); mathematics (MS); music education (MM); psychology (MA, MS); sociology (MA, MS); Spanish (MA).

College of Business Administration *Degree program information:* Part-time and evening/weekend programs available. Offers business administration (MBA, MS).

College of Education *Degree program information:* Part-time and evening/weekend programs available. Offers adult education (M Ed); bilingual education (MA, MS, Ed D); early childhood education (M Ed); education (M Ed, MA, MS, Ed D, PhD); elementary education (MA, MS); English as a second language (M Ed); guidance and counseling (MA, MS); health and kinesiology (MA, MS); higher education administration leadership (PhD); reading (MS); school administration (MA, MS, Ed D); secondary education (MA, MS); special education (M Ed); supervision (MA, MS).

College of Engineering *Degree program information:* Part-time and evening/weekend programs available. Offers chemical engineering (ME, MS); civil engineering (ME, MS); computer science (MS); electrical engineering (ME, MS); engineering (ME, MS, PhD); environmental engineering (ME, MS, PhD); industrial engineering (ME, MS); mechanical engineering (ME, MS); natural gas engineering (ME, MS).

See Close-Up on page 1053.

TEXAS A&M UNIVERSITY–TEXARKANA, Texarkana, TX 75505-5518

General Information State-supported, coed, upper-level institution. *Enrollment:* 1,670 graduate, professional, and undergraduate students; 49 full-time matriculated graduate/professional students (36 women), 465 part-time matriculated graduate/professional students (332 women). *Enrollment by degree level:* 514 master's. Tuition, state resident: part-time $112 per credit hour. Tuition, nonresident: part-time $387 per credit hour. *Required fees:* $8 per credit hour. $8 per term. *Graduate housing:* On-campus housing not available. *Student services:* Campus employment opportunities, career counseling, disabled student services, low-cost health insurance, teacher training, writing training. *Library facilities:* John F. Moss Library plus 1 other. *Online resources:* library catalog, web page. *Collection:* 132,065 titles, 6,561 serial subscriptions, 360 audiovisual materials.

Computer facilities: 133 computers available on campus for general student use. A campuswide network can be accessed from off campus. Internet access and online class registration are available. *Web address:* http://www.tamut.edu/.

General Application Contact: Patricia E. Black, Director of Admissions and Registrar, 903-223-3068, Fax: 903-223-3140, E-mail: pat.black@tamut.edu.

GRADUATE UNITS

Graduate Studies and Research Students: 49 full-time (36 women), 465 part-time (332 women); includes 138 minority (115 African Americans, 4 American Indian/Alaska Native, 1 Asian American or Pacific Islander, 18 Hispanic Americans), 4 international. Average age 32. 136 applicants, 86% accepted. Expenses: Contact institution. *Financial support:* Career-related internships or fieldwork and scholarships/grants available. Financial award application deadline: 3/1; financial award applicants required to submit FAFSA. In 2006, 153 degrees awarded. *Degree program information:* Part-time and evening/weekend programs available. *Application deadline:* For fall admission, 7/15 priority date for domestic students; for spring admission, 12/1 priority date for domestic students. Applications are processed on a rolling basis. *Application fee:* $0 ($25 for international students). Electronic applications accepted. *Application Contact:* Patricia E. Black, Director of Admissions and Registrar, 903-223-3068, Fax: 903-223-3140, E-mail: pat.black@tamut.edu. *Dean,* Dr. David Allard, 903-223-3131, E-mail: david.allard@tamut.edu.

College of Arts and Sciences and Education Students: 285. Average age 32. 41 applicants, 76% accepted. Expenses: Contact institution. *Financial support:* Career-related internships or fieldwork and scholarships/grants available. Financial award applicants required to submit FAFSA. In 2006, 51 degrees awarded. *Degree program information:* Part-time and evening/weekend programs available. Offers adult education (MS); curriculum and instruction (MS); education (MS); educational administration (M Ed); English (MA); history (MS); instructional technology (MS); interdisciplinary studies (MA, MS); special education (M Ed, MS). *Application deadline:* For fall admission, 7/15 priority date for domestic students; for spring admission, 12/1 priority date for domestic students. Applications are processed on a rolling basis. *Application fee:* $0 ($25 for international students). Electronic applications accepted. *Application Contact:* Patricia E. Black, Director of Admissions and Registrar, 903-223-3068, Fax: 903-223-3140, E-mail: pat.black@tamut.edu. *Dean,* Dr. Rosannce Stripling, 903-223-3073, E-mail: rosanne.stripling@tamut.edu.

College of Business Students: 178. Average age 32. 81 applicants, 91% accepted. Expenses: Contact institution. *Financial support:* Career-related internships or fieldwork and scholarships/grants available. Financial award application deadline: 3/1; financial award applicants required to submit FAFSA. In 2006, 87 degrees awarded. *Degree program information:* Part-time and evening/weekend programs available. Offers accounting (MSA); business administration (MBA, MS). *Application deadline:* For fall admission, 7/15 priority date for domestic students; for spring admission, 12/1 priority date for domestic students. Applications are processed on a rolling basis. *Application fee:* $0 ($25 for international students). Electronic applications accepted. *Application Contact:* Patricia E. Black, Director of Admissions and Registrar, 903-223-3068, Fax: 903-223-3140, E-mail: pat.black@tamut.edu. *Dean,* Dr. Edward Bashaw, 903-223-3106, E-mail: edward.bashaw@tamut.edu.

College of Health and Behavioral Sciences Students: 51. 14 applicants, 86% accepted. Expenses: Contact institution. *Financial support:* Career-related internships or fieldwork and scholarships/grants available. In 2006, 5 degrees awarded. *Degree program information:* Part-time and evening/weekend programs available. Offers counseling psychology (MS). *Application deadline:* For fall admission, 7/15 priority date for domestic students; for spring admission, 12/1 priority date for domestic students. Applications are processed on a rolling basis. *Application fee:* $0 ($25 for international students). Electronic applications accepted. *Dean,* Dr. Jo Kahler, 903-223-3175, Fax: 903-223-3107.

TEXAS CHIROPRACTIC COLLEGE, Pasadena, TX 77505-1699

General Information Independent, coed, upper-level institution. *Graduate housing:* On-campus housing not available.

Texas Chiropractic College (continued)

GRADUATE UNITS

Professional Program *Degree program information:* Part-time programs available. Offers chiropractic (DC).

TEXAS CHRISTIAN UNIVERSITY, Fort Worth, TX 76129-0002

General Information Independent-religious, coed, university. CGS member. *Enrollment:* 8,865 graduate, professional, and undergraduate students; 610 full-time matriculated graduate/professional students, 988 part-time matriculated graduate/professional students. *Enrollment by degree level:* 170 first professional, 1,164 master's, 235 doctoral, 29 other advanced degrees. *Tuition:* Part-time $800 per credit hour. *Graduate housing:* Rooms and/or apartments available on a first-come, first-served basis to single and married students. *Student services:* Campus employment opportunities, campus safety program, career counseling, disabled student services, exercise/wellness program, free psychological counseling, international student services, low-cost health insurance, multicultural affairs office, teacher training, writing training. *Library facilities:* Mary Couts Burnett Library. *Online resources:* library catalog, web page, access to other libraries' catalogs. *Collection:* 1.4 million titles, 32,017 serial subscriptions. *Research affiliation:* Laerdal Corporation (engineering), TXU (engineering), Aberdeen Proving Ground (engineering), Botanical Research Institute of Texas, Inc. (biology), Lockheed Martin (engineering), Bell Helicopter (engineering).

Computer facilities: Computer purchase and lease plans are available. A campuswide network can be accessed from student residence rooms and from off campus. Internet access and online class registration are available. *Web address:* http://www.tcu.edu/.

General Application Contact: Admissions, TCU Graduate Studies Office, 817-257-7515, Fax: 817-257-7484, E-mail: frogmail@tcu.edu.

GRADUATE UNITS

AddRan College of Humanities and Social Sciences Expenses: Contact institution. *Financial support:* Unspecified assistantships available. Financial award application deadline: 3/1. *Degree program information:* Part-time and evening/weekend programs available. Offers English (MA, PhD); history (MA, PhD); humanities and social sciences (MA, PhD). *Application deadline:* For fall admission, 3/1 for domestic students; for spring admission, 12/1 for domestic students. Applications are processed on a rolling basis. *Application fee:* $0. *Dean,* Dr. Mary Volcansek, 817-257-7160.

Brite Divinity School Expenses: Contact institution. *Financial support:* Career-related internships or fieldwork and unspecified assistantships available. Financial award application deadline: 3/1. *Degree program information:* Part-time and evening/weekend programs available. Offers Biblical interpretation (PhD); Christian service (MACS); divinity (M Div, D Min); pastoral theology and pastoral counseling (PhD); theological studies (MTS, CTS); theology (Th M). *Application deadline:* For fall admission, 3/1 for domestic students; for spring admission, 12/1 for domestic students. Applications are processed on a rolling basis. *Application fee:* $0. *Application Contact:* Dr. J. Stanley Hagadone, Director of Admissions, 817-921-7804, E-mail: j.hagadone@tcu.edu. *President,* Dr. D. Newell Williams, 817-257-7575.

College of Communication Expenses: Contact institution. *Financial support:* Unspecified assistantships available. Financial award application deadline: 3/1. *Degree program information:* Part-time and evening/weekend programs available. Offers advertising/public relations (MS); communication (MS); communication in human relations (MS); news-editorial (MS). *Application deadline:* For fall admission, 3/1 for domestic students; for spring admission, 12/1 for domestic students. Applications are processed on a rolling basis. *Application fee:* $0. *Application Contact:* Dr. John Burton, Director of Graduate Studies, 817-257-7603, Fax: 817-257-7703, E-mail: j.burton@tcu.edu. *Dean,* Dr. William T. Slater, 817-257-5918, E-mail: w.slater@tcu.edu.

College of Fine Arts Expenses: Contact institution. *Financial support:* Application deadline: 3/1. *Degree program information:* Part-time and evening/weekend programs available. Offers art history (MA); fine arts (M Mus, MA, MFA, MM Ed, Artist Diploma); studio art (MFA). *Application deadline:* For fall admission, 3/1 for domestic students; for spring admission, 12/1 for domestic students. Applications are processed on a rolling basis. *Application fee:* $0. *Dean,* Dr. Scott Sullivan, 817-257-7601.

School of Music Expenses: Contact institution. *Financial support:* Unspecified assistantships available. Financial award application deadline: 3/1. *Degree program information:* Part-time and evening/weekend programs available. Offers conducting (M Mus); music education (MM Ed); musicology (M Mus); organ performance (M Mus); piano (Artist Diploma); piano pedagogy (M Mus); piano performance (M Mus); string performance (M Mus); theory/composition (M Mus); vocal performance (M Mus); voice pedagogy (M Mus); wind and percussion performance (M Mus). *Application deadline:* For fall admission, 3/1 for domestic students; for spring admission, 12/1 for domestic students. Applications are processed on a rolling basis. *Application fee:* $0. *Application Contact:* Dr. Joseph Butler, Associate Dean, College of Fine Arts, E-mail: j.butler@tcu.edu. *Director,* Dr. Richard Gipson, 817-257-7602.

College of Science and Engineering Expenses: Contact institution. *Financial support:* Fellowships, teaching assistantships, unspecified assistantships available. Financial award application deadline: 3/1. *Degree program information:* Part-time and evening/weekend programs available. Offers biology (MA, MS); chemistry (MA, MS, PhD); earth sciences (MS); ecology (MS); environmental sciences (MS); geology (MS); mathematics (MAT); physics (MA, MS, PhD); psychology (MA, MS, PhD); science and engineering (MA, MAT, MS, PhD). *Application deadline:* For fall admission, 3/1 for domestic students; for spring admission, 12/1 for domestic students. Applications are processed on a rolling basis. *Application fee:* $0. *Dean,* Dr. Michael McCracken, 817-257-7727, E-mail: m.mccracken@tcu.edu.

Graduate Studies and Research Expenses: Contact institution. *Financial support:* Application deadline: 3/1. *Degree program information:* Part-time and evening/weekend programs available. Offers liberal arts (MLA). *Application deadline:* For fall admission, 3/1 for domestic students; for spring admission, 12/1 for domestic students. Applications are processed on a rolling basis. *Application fee:* $0. *Application Contact:* Dr. Don Coerver, Director, 817-257-6290, E-mail: d.coerver@tcu.edu. *Director,* Dr. Don Coerver, 817-257-6290, E-mail: d.coerver@tcu.edu.

Harris College of Nursing and Health Sciences Expenses: Contact institution. *Financial support:* Application deadline: 3/1. *Degree program information:* Part-time and evening/weekend programs available. Offers adult nursing (MSN); kinesiology (MS); nursing and health sciences (MS, MSN, MSNA); speech-language pathology (MS). *Application deadline:* For fall admission, 3/1 for domestic students; for spring admission, 12/1 for domestic students. Applications are processed on a rolling basis. *Application fee:* $0. *Dean,* Dr. Paulette Burns, 817-257-7621.

School of Nurse Anesthesia Expenses: Contact institution. Offers nurse anesthesia (MSNA). *Director,* Dr. Kay K. Sanders, 817-257-7887.

M. J. Neeley School of Business Expenses: Contact institution. *Financial support:* Career-related internships or fieldwork, Federal Work-Study, institutionally sponsored loans, and unspecified assistantships available. Support available to part-time students. Financial award application deadline: 5/1; financial award applicants required to submit FAFSA. *Degree program information:* Part-time and evening/weekend programs available. Offers accounting (M Ac); business administration (MBA); international management (MIM). *Application deadline:* For fall admission, 4/30 priority date for domestic students. Applications are processed on a rolling basis. *Application fee:* $50. Electronic applications accepted. *Application Contact:* Peggy Conway, Director, MBA Admissions, 817-257-7531, Fax: 817-257-6431, E-mail: mbainfo@tcu.edu. *Dean,* Dr. Daniel G. Short, 817-257-7527, Fax: 817-257-7227.

School of Education *Faculty:* 21. Expenses: Contact institution. *Financial support:* Career-related internships or fieldwork and unspecified assistantships available. Financial award application deadline: 3/1. *Degree program information:* Part-time and evening/weekend programs available. Offers counseling (M Ed); education (M Ed, PhD, Certificate); educational administration (M Ed); educational foundations (M Ed); educational studies: science education (PhD); elementary education (M Ed, Certificate); school counseling (Certificate); science education (M Ed); special education (M Ed). *Application deadline:* For fall admission, 3/1 for domestic students; for spring admission, 12/1 for domestic students. Applications are processed on a rolling basis. *Application fee:* $50. *Application Contact:* Director of Graduate Studies, 817-257-7664. *Dean,* Dr. Sam Deitz, 817-257-7663, E-mail: s.deitz@tcu.edu.

TEXAS COLLEGE OF TRADITIONAL CHINESE MEDICINE, Austin, TX 78704

General Information Private, coed, graduate-only institution.

GRADUATE UNITS

Program in Acupuncture and Oriental Medicine *Degree program information:* Part-time and evening/weekend programs available. Offers acupuncture and Oriental medicine (MAOM). Electronic applications accepted.

TEXAS SOUTHERN UNIVERSITY, Houston, TX 77004-4584

General Information State-supported, coed, university. CGS member. *Enrollment:* 11,224 graduate, professional, and undergraduate students; 1,434 full-time matriculated graduate/professional students (850 women), 683 part-time matriculated graduate/professional students (455 women). *Enrollment by degree level:* 1,191 first professional, 757 master's, 169 doctoral. *Graduate faculty:* 118 full-time (48 women), 37 part-time/adjunct (11 women). *Graduate housing:* Room and/or apartments available on a first-come, first-served basis to single students; on-campus housing not available to married students. Housing application deadline: 7/15. *Student services:* Campus employment opportunities, campus safety program, career counseling, child daycare facilities, disabled student services, exercise/wellness program, free psychological counseling, international student services, multicultural affairs office. *Library facilities:* Robert J. Terry Library plus 2 others. *Online resources:* library catalog, access to other libraries' catalogs. *Collection:* 264,254 titles, 1,750 serial subscriptions. *Research affiliation:* Texas Space Grant Consortium, Lockheed Missile Company, Inc, American Heart Association (cardiovascular diseases).

Computer facilities: 500 computers available on campus for general student use. A campuswide network can be accessed. Internet access and online class registration, Blackboard Learning and Community Portal System (E-education) are available. *Web address:* http://www.tsu.edu/.

General Application Contact: Dr. Richard Pitre, Dean of the Graduate School, Acting, 713-313-7011 Ext. 7534, Fax: 713-639-1876, E-mail: pitre_rx@tsu.edu.

GRADUATE UNITS

College of Pharmacy and Health Sciences Students: 325 full-time (199 women), 224 part-time (138 women); includes 464 minority (288 African Americans, 134 Asian Americans or Pacific Islanders, 42 Hispanic Americans), 54 international. Average age 29. 127 applicants, 100% accepted, 118 enrolled. *Faculty:* 8 full-time (5 women), 9 part-time/adjunct (4 women). Expenses: Contact institution. *Financial support:* Fellowships, teaching assistantships, career-related internships or fieldwork, scholarships/grants, and tuition waivers (partial) available. Financial award application deadline: 5/1; financial award applicants required to submit FAFSA. In 2006, 90 degrees awarded. Postbaccalaureate distance learning degree programs offered. Offers pharmacy and health sciences (Pharm D, MHCA). *Application deadline:* For fall admission, 3/15 for domestic students. *Application fee:* $50 ($75 for international students). *Application Contact:* LaJoy Kay, Head, 713-313-1880. *Dean,* Dr. Barbara Hayes, 713-313-7164, Fax: 713-313-1091.

Graduate School Students: 459 full-time (308 women), 467 part-time (324 women); includes 835 minority (763 African Americans, 2 American Indian/Alaska Native, 40 Asian Americans or Pacific Islanders, 30 Hispanic Americans), 50 international. Average age 35. 446 applicants, 89% accepted, 278 enrolled. *Faculty:* 118 full-time (48 women), 37 part-time/adjunct (11 women). Expenses: Contact institution. *Financial support:* In 2006–07, 91 students received support, including 4 fellowships with partial tuition reimbursements available (averaging $14,000 per year), 46 research assistantships with partial tuition reimbursements available (averaging $1,305 per year), 24 teaching assistantships with partial tuition reimbursements available (averaging $10,000 per year); career-related internships or fieldwork, Federal Work-Study, institutionally sponsored loans, scholarships/grants, tuition waivers (partial), and unspecified assistantships also available. Financial award application deadline: 5/1. In 2006, 190 master's, 19 doctorates awarded. *Degree program information:* Part-time and evening/weekend programs available. *Application deadline:* For fall admission, 7/15 priority date for domestic students. Applications are processed on a rolling basis. *Application fee:* $75. *Dean of the Graduate School, Acting,* Dr. Richard Pitre, 713-313-7011 Ext. 7534, Fax: 713-639-1876, E-mail: pitre_rx@tsu.edu.

College of Education Students: 149 full-time (118 women), 219 part-time (170 women); includes 337 minority (315 African Americans, 7 Asian Americans or Pacific Islanders, 15 Hispanic Americans), 3 international. Average age 29. 146 applicants, 81% accepted, 97 enrolled. *Faculty:* 26 full-time (13 women), 7 part-time/adjunct (2 women). Expenses: Contact institution. *Financial support:* Fellowships, research assistantships, teaching assistantships, career-related internships or fieldwork, Federal Work-Study, and institutionally sponsored loans available. Financial award application deadline: 5/1. In 2006, 75 master's, 18 doctorates awarded. *Degree program information:* Part-time and evening/weekend programs available. Offers bilingual education (M Ed); counseling (M Ed, Ed D); counseling education (Ed D); curriculum, instruction, and urban education (Ed D); early childhood education (M Ed); education (M Ed, MS, Ed D); educational administration (M Ed, Ed D); elementary education (M Ed); health education (MS); higher education administration (Ed D); mid-management superintending (Ed D); physical education (MS); reading education (M Ed); research education and certification (Ed D); research education and education (Ed D); secondary education (M Ed); special education (M Ed). *Application deadline:* For fall admission, 7/15 priority date for domestic students. Applications are processed on a rolling basis. *Application fee:* $50 ($75 for international students). *Dean,* Dr. Jay Cummings, 713-313-7343.

College of Liberal Arts and Behavioral Sciences Students: 74 full-time (58 women), 65 part-time (50 women); includes 134 minority (126 African Americans, 1 American Indian/Alaska Native, 1 Asian American or Pacific Islander, 6 Hispanic Americans), 3 international. Average age 35. 89 applicants, 90% accepted, 54 enrolled. *Faculty:* 25 full-time (14 women), 6 part-time/adjunct (3 women). Expenses: Contact institution. *Financial support:* Fellowships, research assistantships, teaching assistantships, career-related internships or fieldwork, Federal Work-Study, and institutionally sponsored loans available. Financial award application deadline: 5/1. In 2006, 32 degrees awarded. *Degree program information:* Part-time and evening/weekend programs available. Offers English (MA, MS); history (MA); human services and consumer sciences (MS); liberal arts and behavioral sciences (MA, MS); music (MA); psychology (MA); sociology (MA). *Application deadline:* For fall admission, 7/15 priority date for domestic students. Applications are processed on a rolling basis. *Application fee:* $50 ($75 for international students). *Dean,* Dr. Merline Pitre, 713-313-7210, E-mail: pitre_mx@tsu.edu.

Jesse H. Jones School of Business Students: 57 full-time (33 women), 34 part-time (21 women); includes 82 minority (78 African Americans, 3 Asian Americans or Pacific Islanders, 1 Hispanic American), 9 international. Average age 30. 55 applicants, 82% accepted, 34 enrolled. *Faculty:* 11 full-time (2 women), 5 part-time/adjunct (2 women). Expenses: Contact institution. *Financial support:* In 2006–07, 2 students received support, including 2 research assistantships (averaging $12,000 per year); career-related internships or fieldwork, tuition waivers (partial), and unspecified assistantships also available. Financial award application deadline: 5/1. In 2006, 36 degrees awarded. *Degree program information:* Part-time and evening/weekend programs available. Offers business (MBA); business administration (MBA). *Application deadline:* For fall admission, 7/15 priority date for domestic students; for spring admission, 11/15 for domestic students. Applications are processed on a rolling basis. *Application fee:* $50 ($75 for international students). *Application Contact:* Bobbie J. Richardson, Executive Secretary, 713-313-7309, Fax: 713-313-7705, E-mail: richardson_bj@tsu.edu. *Dean,* Dr. Joseph Boyd, 713-313-7215, Fax: 713-313-7701.

School of Public Affairs Students: 70 full-time (41 women), 54 part-time (29 women); includes 115 minority (109 African Americans, 1 American Indian/Alaska Native, 1 Asian American or Pacific Islander, 4 Hispanic Americans), 8 international. Average age 35. 45 applicants, 89% accepted, 31 enrolled. *Faculty:* 15 full-time (4 women), 5 part-time/

adjunct (0 women). Expenses: Contact institution. *Financial support:* In 2006–07, 6 research assistantships (averaging $12,000 per year) were awarded; fellowships, teaching assistantships, career-related internships or fieldwork, Federal Work-Study, institutionally sponsored loans, and unspecified assistantships also available. Financial award application deadline: 5/1; financial award applicants required to submit FAFSA. In 2006, 11 degrees awarded. *Degree program information:* Part-time programs available. Offers public administration (MPA); public affairs (MCP, MPA); urban planning and environmental policy (MCP). *Application deadline:* For fall admission, 7/15 priority date for domestic students. Applications are processed on a rolling basis. *Application fee:* $50 ($75 for international students). *Application Contact:* Pinkie Cotton, Administrative Assistant, 713-313-7311, E-mail: cotton_pe@tsu.edu. *Interim Dean,* Dr. Theophilus Herrington, 713-313-7447, E-mail: herrington_tx@tsu.edu.

School of Science and Technology Students: 83 full-time (41 women), 59 part-time (29 women); includes 115 minority (86 African Americans, 26 Asian Americans or Pacific Islanders, 3 Hispanic Americans), 20 international. Average age 34. 65 applicants, 85% accepted, 39 enrolled. *Faculty:* 31 full-time (9 women), 4 part-time/adjunct (0 women). Expenses: Contact institution. *Financial support:* In 2006–07, 4 fellowships (averaging $14,000 per year), 12 research assistantships (averaging $9,000 per year), 5 teaching assistantships (averaging $9,000 per year) were awarded; career-related internships or fieldwork, Federal Work-Study, institutionally sponsored loans, scholarships/grants, tuition waivers (partial), and unspecified assistantships also available. Financial award application deadline: 5/1. In 2006, 25 master's, 1 doctorate awarded. *Degree program information:* Part-time and evening/weekend programs available. Offers biology (MS); chemistry (MS); computer science (MS); environmental toxicology (MS, PhD); industrial technology (MS); mathematics (MA, MS); science and technology (MA, MS, PhD); transportation (MS). *Application deadline:* For fall admission, 7/15 priority date for domestic students. Applications are processed on a rolling basis. *Application fee:* $50 ($75 for international students). *Application Contact:* Lulueua Nasser, Administrative Secretary, 713-313-7679, E-mail: nasser_la@tsu.edu. *Interim Dean,* Dr. Victor Obot, 713-313-7830.

Tavis Smiley School of Communication Students: 13 full-time (9 women), 26 part-time (18 women); includes 34 minority (all African Americans), 4 international. Average age 32. 21 applicants, 100% accepted, 12 enrolled. *Faculty:* 2 full-time (1 woman), 1 part-time/adjunct (0 women). Expenses: Contact institution. *Financial support:* In 2006–07, 4 fellowships were awarded; research assistantships, teaching assistantships, career-related internships or fieldwork, Federal Work-Study, and institutionally sponsored loans also available. Financial award application deadline: 5/1. In 2006, 10 degrees awarded. *Degree program information:* Part-time programs available. Offers journalism (MA); speech communications (MA); telecommunications (MA). *Application deadline:* For fall admission, 7/15 priority date for domestic students. Applications are processed on a rolling basis. *Application fee:* $50 ($75 for international students). *Application Contact:* Dr. Louis Browne, Graduate Adviser, 713-313-7024. *Head,* Dr. James Ward, 713-313-7740.

Thurgood Marshall School of Law Students: 663 full-time (351 women), 2 part-time; includes 530 minority (328 African Americans, 6 American Indian/Alaska Native, 47 Asian Americans or Pacific Islanders, 149 Hispanic Americans), 22 international. Average age 28. 308 applicants, 100% accepted, 253 enrolled. *Faculty:* 35 full-time (17 women), 18 part-time/adjunct (7 women). Expenses: Contact institution. *Financial support:* In 2006–07, 75 students received support, including 24 research assistantships (averaging $1,050 per year), 19 teaching assistantships (averaging $1,000 per year); fellowships, career-related internships or fieldwork, Federal Work-Study, institutionally sponsored loans, scholarships/grants, and tuition waivers (partial) also available. Financial award application deadline: 4/1; financial award applicants required to submit FAFSA. In 2006, 195 degrees awarded. Offers law (JD). *Application deadline:* For fall admission, 4/1 priority date for domestic students. Applications are processed on a rolling basis. *Application fee:* $55. Electronic applications accepted. *Application Contact:* Edward Rene, Director of Admissions, 713-313-7115 Ext. 1004, Fax: 713-313-1049, E-mail: erene@tsulaw.edu. *Dean,* McKen V. Carrington, 713-313-1076, Fax: 713-313-1049, E-mail: carrington_mv@tsulaw.edu.

TEXAS STATE UNIVERSITY-SAN MARCOS, San Marcos, TX 78666

General Information State-supported, coed, university. CGS member. *Enrollment:* 27,485 graduate, professional, and undergraduate students; 1,442 full-time matriculated graduate/professional students (905 women), 1,837 part-time matriculated graduate/professional students (1,177 women). *Enrollment by degree level:* 3,101 master's, 178 doctoral. *Graduate faculty:* 360 full-time (143 women), 58 part-time/adjunct (32 women). *Graduate housing:* Rooms and/or apartments available on a first-come, first-served basis to single and married students. Housing application deadline: 7/1. *Student services:* Campus employment opportunities, campus safety program, career counseling, disabled student services, exercise/wellness program, free psychological counseling, international student services, low-cost health insurance, multicultural affairs office, teacher training. *Library facilities:* Alkek Library. *Online resources:* library catalog, web page, access to other libraries' catalogs. *Collection:* 1.4 million titles, 8,330 serial subscriptions, 277,806 audiovisual materials. *Research affiliation:* Texas Engineering Experiment Station, Condhec.

Computer facilities: Computer purchase and lease plans are available. 1,200 computers available on campus for general student use. A campuswide network can be accessed from student residence rooms and from off campus. Internet access and online class registration are available. *Web address:* http://www.txstate.edu/.

General Application Contact: Dr. J. Michael Willoughby, Dean of Graduate School, 512-245-2581, Fax: 512-245-8365, E-mail: gradcollege@txstate.edu.

GRADUATE UNITS

Graduate School Students: 1,442 full-time (905 women), 1,837 part-time (1,177 women); includes 862 minority (163 African Americans, 10 American Indian/Alaska Native, 135 Asian Americans or Pacific Islanders, 554 Hispanic Americans), 136 international. Average age 31. 1,340 applicants, 84% accepted, 1028 enrolled. *Faculty:* 360 full-time (143 women), 58 part-time/adjunct (32 women). Expenses: Contact institution. *Financial support:* In 2006–07, 2,279 students received support, including 168 research assistantships (averaging $6,768 per year), 474 teaching assistantships (averaging $6,971 per year); fellowships, career-related internships or fieldwork, Federal Work-Study, institutionally sponsored loans, scholarships/grants, unspecified assistantships, and laboratory instructorships, stipends also available. Support available to part-time students. Financial award application deadline: 4/1; financial award applicants required to submit FAFSA. In 2006, 1,051 master's, 15 doctorates awarded. *Degree program information:* Part-time and evening/weekend programs available. Postbaccalaureate distance learning degree programs offered (minimal on-campus study). Offers applied sociology (MAIS); biology (MSIS); criminal justice (MSIS); educational administration and psychological services (MAIS); elementary mathematics, science, and technology (MSIS); health, physical education, and recreation (MAIS); interdisciplinary studies in political science (MAIS); international studies (MA); modern languages (MAIS); occupational education (MAIS, MSIS); psychology (MAIS). *Application deadline:* For fall admission, 6/15 for domestic and international students; for spring admission, 10/15 for domestic and international students. Applications are processed on a rolling basis. *Application fee:* $40 ($90 for international students). Electronic applications accepted. *Dean,* Dr. J. Michael Willoughby, 512-245-2581, Fax: 512-245-8365, E-mail: gradcollege@txstate.edu.

College of Applied Arts Students: 52 full-time (41 women), 81 part-time (44 women); includes 46 minority (10 African Americans, 3 Asian Americans or Pacific Islanders, 33 Hispanic Americans), 2 international. Average age 32. 68 applicants, 99% accepted, 39 enrolled. *Faculty:* 12 full-time (8 women), 3 part-time/adjunct (1 woman). Expenses: Contact institution. *Financial support:* In 2006–07, 113 students received support, including 10 research assistantships (averaging $7,446 per year), 21 teaching assistantships (averaging $6,871 per year); career-related internships or fieldwork, Federal Work-Study, and institutionally sponsored loans also available. Support available to part-time students. Financial award application deadline: 4/1; financial award applicants required to submit FAFSA. In 2006, 21 degrees awarded. *Degree program information:* Part-time and evening/weekend programs available. Offers agriculture (M Ed); applied arts (M Ed, MS, MSCJ); criminal justice (MSCJ); family and child studies (MS); management of technical education (M Ed). *Application deadline:* For fall admission, 6/15 priority date for domestic students; for spring admission, 10/15 priority date for domestic students. Applications are processed on a rolling basis. *Application fee:* $40 ($90 for international students). *Application Contact:* Dr. J. Michael Willoughby, Dean of Graduate School, 512-245-2581, Fax: 512-245-8365, E-mail: gradcollege@txstate.edu. *Dean,* Dr. Jaime Chahin, 512-245-3333, Fax: 512-245-3338, E-mail: tc03@txstate.edu.

College of Education Students: 368 full-time (285 women), 768 part-time (607 women); includes 280 minority (55 African Americans, 1 American Indian/Alaska Native, 24 Asian Americans or Pacific Islanders, 200 Hispanic Americans), 24 international. Average age 32. 372 applicants, 84% accepted, 225 enrolled. *Faculty:* 63 full-time (37 women), 33 part-time/adjunct (22 women). Expenses: Contact institution. *Financial support:* In 2006–07, 735 students received support, including 58 research assistantships (averaging $6,801 per year), 45 teaching assistantships (averaging $5,735 per year); fellowships, career-related internships or fieldwork, Federal Work-Study, and institutionally sponsored loans also available. Support available to part-time students. Financial award application deadline: 4/1; financial award applicants required to submit FAFSA. In 2006, 355 master's, 7 doctorates awarded. *Degree program information:* Part-time and evening/weekend programs available. Offers counseling and guidance (M Ed); developmental and adult education (MA, PhD); early childhood education (M Ed, MA); education (M Ed, MA, MSRLS, PhD); educational administration (M Ed, MA); elementary education (M Ed, MA); elementary education-bilingual/bicultural (M Ed, MA); health and physical education (MA); health education (M Ed); physical education (M Ed); professional counseling (MA); reading education (M Ed); recreation and leisure services (MSRLS); school psychology (MA); secondary education (M Ed, MA); special education (M Ed). *Application deadline:* For fall admission, 6/15 priority date for domestic students; for spring admission, 10/15 priority date for domestic students. Applications are processed on a rolling basis. *Application fee:* $40 ($90 for international students). *Application Contact:* Dr. J. Michael Willoughby, Dean of Graduate School, 512-245-2581, Fax: 512-245-8365, E-mail: gradcollege@txstate.edu. *Dean,* Dr. Rosalinda Barrera, 512-245-2150, Fax: 512-245-8345, E-mail: rb43@txstate.edu.

College of Fine Arts and Communication Students: 95 full-time (61 women), 63 part-time (39 women); includes 43 minority (10 African Americans, 1 American Indian/Alaska Native, 4 Asian Americans or Pacific Islanders, 28 Hispanic Americans), 9 international. Average age 29. 77 applicants, 97% accepted, 52 enrolled. *Faculty:* 43 full-time (16 women), 3 part-time/adjunct (1 woman). Expenses: Contact institution. *Financial support:* In 2006–07, 139 students received support, including 4 research assistantships (averaging $4,928 per year), 51 teaching assistantships (averaging $6,135 per year); career-related internships or fieldwork, Federal Work-Study, institutionally sponsored loans, scholarships/grants, and unspecified assistantships also available. Support available to part-time students. Financial award application deadline: 4/1; financial award applicants required to submit FAFSA. In 2006, 63 degrees awarded. *Degree program information:* Part-time and evening/weekend programs available. Offers communication studies (MA); fine arts and communication (MA, MM); journalism and mass communication (MA); music education (MM); music performance (MM); theatre arts (MA). *Application deadline:* For fall admission, 6/15 priority date for domestic students; for spring admission, 10/15 priority date for domestic students. Applications are processed on a rolling basis. *Application fee:* $40 ($90 for international students). *Application Contact:* Dr. J. Michael Willoughby, Dean of Graduate School, 512-245-2581, Fax: 512-245-8365, E-mail: gradcollege@txstate.edu. *Dean,* Dr. T. Richard Cheatham, 512-245-2308, Fax: 512-245-8334, E-mail: tc02@txstate.edu.

College of Health Professions Students: 197 full-time (152 women), 149 part-time (121 women); includes 103 minority (24 African Americans, 1 American Indian/Alaska Native, 13 Asian Americans or Pacific Islanders, 65 Hispanic Americans), 8 international. Average age 30. 174 applicants, 72% accepted, 80 enrolled. *Faculty:* 34 full-time (21 women), 7 part-time/adjunct (4 women). Expenses: Contact institution. *Financial support:* In 2006–07, 286 students received support, including 2 research assistantships (averaging $7,668 per year), 26 teaching assistantships (averaging $3,443 per year); fellowships, career-related internships or fieldwork, Federal Work-Study, institutionally sponsored loans, scholarships/grants, and stipends also available. Support available to part-time students. Financial award application deadline: 4/1; financial award applicants required to submit FAFSA. In 2006, 146 degrees awarded. *Degree program information:* Part-time and evening/weekend programs available. Offers communication disorders (MA, MSCD); health professions (MA, MHA, MS, MSCD, MSPT, MSW); health services and research (MS); health services research (MS); healthcare administration (MHA); healthcare human resources (MS); physical therapy (MSPT); social work (MSW). *Application deadline:* For fall admission, 6/15 for domestic students, 6/1 for international students; for spring admission, 10/15 priority date for domestic students, 10/1 for international students. *Application fee:* $40 ($90 for international students). *Application Contact:* Dr. J. Michael Willoughby, Dean of Graduate School, 512-245-2581, Fax: 512-245-8365, E-mail: gradcollege@txstate.edu. *Dean,* Dr. Ruth Welborn, 512-245-3300, Fax: 512-245-3791, E-mail: mw01@txstate.edu.

College of Liberal Arts Students: 357 full-time (194 women), 425 part-time (220 women); includes 201 minority (39 African Americans, 2 American Indian/Alaska Native, 21 Asian Americans or Pacific Islanders, 139 Hispanic Americans), 15 international. Average age 32. 396 applicants, 80% accepted, 216 enrolled. *Faculty:* 116 full-time (39 women), 9 part-time/adjunct (3 women). Expenses: Contact institution. *Financial support:* In 2006–07, 578 students received support, including 38 research assistantships (averaging $7,754 per year), 166 teaching assistantships (averaging $7,047 per year); fellowships, career-related internships or fieldwork, Federal Work-Study, institutionally sponsored loans, and scholarships/grants also available. Support available to part-time students. Financial award application deadline: 4/1; financial award applicants required to submit FAFSA. In 2006, 187 master's, 8 doctorates awarded. *Degree program information:* Part-time and evening/weekend programs available. Offers anthropology (MA); applied geography (MAG); creative writing (MFA); environmental geography (PhD); environmental geography, geography education, and geography information science (PhD); geographic information science (MAG); geography (MAG, MS); geography education (PhD); health psychology (MA); history (M Ed, MA); information science (PhD); land/area studies (MAG); legal studies (MA); liberal arts (M Ed, MA, MAG, MFA, MPA, MS, PhD); literature (MA); political science (MA); public administration (MPA); resource and environmental studies (MAG); rhetoric and composition (MA); sociology (MA, MS); Spanish (MA); technical communication (MA). *Application deadline:* For fall admission, 6/15 priority date for domestic students; for spring admission, 10/15 priority date for domestic students. Applications are processed on a rolling basis. *Application fee:* $40 ($90 for international students). *Application Contact:* Dr. J. Michael Willoughby, Dean of Graduate School, 512-245-2581, Fax: 512-245-8365, E-mail: gradcollege@txstate.edu. *Dean,* Dr. Ann Marrie Ellis, 512-245-2317, Fax: 512-245-8291, E-mail: ae02@txstate.edu.

College of Science Students: 202 full-time (87 women), 162 part-time (66 women); includes 100 minority (10 African Americans, 1 American Indian/Alaska Native, 39 Asian Americans or Pacific Islanders, 50 Hispanic Americans), 51 international. Average age 31. 149 applicants, 96% accepted, 90 enrolled. *Faculty:* 65 full-time (14 women), 3 part-time/adjunct (1 woman). Expenses: Contact institution. *Financial support:* In 2006–07, 246 students received support, including 30 research assistantships (averaging $8,692 per year), 148 teaching assistantships (averaging $8,253 per year); career-related internships or fieldwork, Federal Work-Study, institutionally sponsored loans, and laboratory instructorships also available. Support available to part-time students. Financial award application deadline: 4/1; financial award applicants required to submit FAFSA. In 2006, 109 degrees awarded. *Degree program information:* Part-time and evening/weekend programs available. Offers aquatic biology (MS); biochemistry (MS); biology (M Ed, MA, MS); chemistry (MA, MS); computer science (MA, MS); industrial mathematics (MS); industrial technology (MST); mathematics (MS); middle school mathematics teaching (M Ed); physics (MS); population and conservation biology (MS); science (M Ed, MA, MS, MST); software engineering (MS); wildlife ecology (MS). *Application deadline:* For fall admission, 6/15 priority date for domestic students, 6/1 priority date for international students; for spring admission, 10/15 priority date for domestic students, 10/1 priority date for international students. Applications are processed on a rolling basis. *Application fee:* $40 ($90 for international students). *Application Contact:* Dr. J. Michael Willoughby, Dean of Graduate School, 512-245-2581, Fax:

Texas State University-San Marcos (continued)

512-245-8365, E-mail: gradcollege@txstate.edu. *Dean,* Dr. Hector E. Flores, 512-245-2119, Fax: 512-245-8095, E-mail: hf12@txstate.edu.

Emmett & Miriam McCoy College of Business Administration Students: 171 full-time (85 women), 189 part-time (80 women); includes 89 minority (15 African Americans, 4 American Indian/Alaska Native, 31 Asian Americans or Pacific Islanders, 39 Hispanic Americans), 27 international. Average age 28. 122 applicants, 84% accepted, 82 enrolled. *Faculty:* 27 full-time (8 women). Expenses: Contact institution. *Financial support:* In 2006–07, 180 students received support, including 5 research assistantships (averaging $4,982 per year), 16 teaching assistantships (averaging $6,324 per year); Federal Work-Study and institutionally sponsored loans also available. Support available to part-time students. Financial award application deadline: 4/1; financial award applicants required to submit FAFSA. In 2006, 148 degrees awarded. *Degree program information:* Part-time programs available. Offers accounting (M Acy); business administration (M Acy, MBA). *Application deadline:* For fall admission, 6/1 for domestic and international students; for spring admission, 10/1 for domestic and international students. Applications are processed on a rolling basis. *Application fee:* $40 ($90 for international students). *Application Contact:* Dr. J. Michael Willoughby, Dean of Graduate School, 512-245-2581, Fax: 512-245-8365, E-mail: gradcollege@txstate.edu. *Dean,* Dr. Denise Smart, 512-245-2311, Fax: 512-245-8375, E-mail: ds37@txstate.edu.

TEXAS TECH UNIVERSITY, Lubbock, TX 79409

General Information State-supported, coed, university. CGS member. *Enrollment:* 27,996 graduate, professional, and undergraduate students; 3,570 full-time matriculated graduate/professional students (1,593 women), 1,575 part-time matriculated graduate/professional students (875 women). *Enrollment by degree level:* 702 first professional, 2,394 master's, 1,482 doctoral, 567 other advanced degrees. *Graduate faculty:* 768 full-time (225 women), 34 part-time/adjunct (5 women). Tuition, state resident: full-time $4,440. Tuition, nonresident: full-time $11,040. *Required fees:* $2,136. *Graduate housing:* Room and/or apartments available on a first-come, first-served basis to single students; on-campus housing not available to married students. Typical cost: $3,883 per year ($7,288 including board). Room and board charges vary according to board plan and housing facility selected. Housing application deadline: 5/1. *Student services:* Campus employment opportunities, campus safety program, career counseling, disabled student services, exercise/wellness program, free psychological counseling, international student services, low-cost health insurance, multicultural affairs office, teacher training, writing training. *Library facilities:* Texas Tech Library plus 3 others. *Online resources:* library catalog, web page, access to other libraries' catalogs. *Collection:* 2.4 million titles, 30,823 serial subscriptions. *Research affiliation:* Lawrence Livermore National Laboratory (atomic force microscopy), Cotton Inc. (improvement of cotton), United Space Alliance (computer systems), Sandia National Lab (chemistry), Meat and Livestock Australia (consumer meat industry), Bayer Crop Science (agriculture genetics).

Computer facilities: Computer purchase and lease plans are available. 3,000 computers available on campus for general student use. A campuswide network can be accessed from student residence rooms and from off campus. Internet access and online class registration, online degree plans, accounts, transcripts, schedules are available. *Web address:* http://www.ttu.edu/.

General Application Contact: Dr. Duane Crawford, Assistant Dean of Graduate Admissions and Recruitment, 806-742-2781, Fax: 806-742-4038, E-mail: gradschool@ttu.edu.

GRADUATE UNITS

Graduate School Students: 2,875 full-time (1,283 women), 1,568 part-time (871 women); includes 634 minority (113 African Americans, 29 American Indian/Alaska Native, 121 Asian Americans or Pacific Islanders, 371 Hispanic Americans), 757 international. Average age 31. 5,179 applicants, 56% accepted, 1354 enrolled. *Faculty:* 757 full-time (221 women), 28 part-time/adjunct (4 women). Expenses: Contact institution. *Financial support:* In 2006–07, 2,494 students received support, including 393 research assistantships with partial tuition reimbursements available (averaging $12,612 per year), 1,016 teaching assistantships with partial tuition reimbursements available (averaging $12,232 per year); career-related internships or fieldwork, Federal Work-Study, institutionally sponsored loans, scholarships/grants, and health care benefits also available. Support available to part-time students. Financial award application deadline: 4/15; financial award applicants required to submit FAFSA. In 2006, 1,052 master's, 220 doctorates awarded. *Degree program information:* Part-time and evening/weekend programs available. Postbaccalaureate distance learning degree programs offered (minimal on-campus study). Offers heritage management (MS); interdisciplinary studies (MA, MS); museum science (MA). *Application deadline:* For fall admission, 3/1 for international students; for spring admission, 11/1 for international students. Applications are processed on a rolling basis. *Application fee:* $50 ($60 for international students). Electronic applications accepted. *Application Contact:* Shannon Samson, Coordinator of Graduate School Recruitment, 806-742-2781 Ext. 239, Fax: 806-742-4038, E-mail: gradschool@ttu.edu. *Dean,* Dr. John Borrelli, 806-742-2781, Fax: 806-742-4038, E-mail: gradschool@ttu.edu.

College of Agricultural Sciences and Natural Resources Students: 178 full-time (76 women), 87 part-time (31 women); includes 22 minority (6 African Americans, 2 American Indian/Alaska Native, 7 Asian Americans or Pacific Islanders, 7 Hispanic Americans), 45 international. Average age 30. 186 applicants, 66% accepted, 73 enrolled. *Faculty:* 65 full-time (9 women), 5 part-time/adjunct (0 women). Expenses: Contact institution. *Financial support:* In 2006–07, 151 students received support, including 107 research assistantships with partial tuition reimbursements available (averaging $11,767 per year), 15 teaching assistantships with partial tuition reimbursements available (averaging $12,383 per year); career-related internships or fieldwork, Federal Work-Study, and institutionally sponsored loans also available. Support available to part-time students. Financial award application deadline: 4/15; financial award applicants required to submit FAFSA. In 2006, 52 master's, 21 doctorates awarded. *Degree program information:* Part-time and evening/weekend programs available. Offers agribusiness (MAB); agricultural and applied economics (MS, PhD); agricultural education (MS, Ed D); agricultural sciences and natural resources (M Agr, MAB, MLA, MS, Ed D, PhD); agronomy (PhD); animal science (MS, PhD); crop science (MS); entomology (MS); fisheries science (MS, PhD); food technology (MS); horticulture (MS); landscape architecture (MLA); range science (MS, PhD); soil science (MS); wildlife science (MS, PhD). *Application deadline:* For fall admission, 3/1 priority date for international students; for spring admission, 11/1 priority date for international students. Applications are processed on a rolling basis. *Application fee:* $50 ($60 for international students). Electronic applications accepted. *Application Contact:* Graduate Adviser, 806-742-2808, Fax: 806-742-2836. *Dean,* Dr. Marvin J. Cepica, 806-742-2808, Fax: 806-742-2836, E-mail: marv.cepica@ttu.edu.

College of Architecture Students: 133 full-time (50 women), 21 part-time (5 women); includes 27 minority (2 African Americans, 2 Asian Americans or Pacific Islanders, 23 Hispanic Americans), 11 international. Average age 26. 90 applicants, 67% accepted, 31 enrolled. *Faculty:* 22 full-time (4 women), 1 part-time/adjunct (0 women). Expenses: Contact institution. *Financial support:* In 2006–07, 92 students received support, including 4 research assistantships with partial tuition reimbursements available (averaging $9,196 per year), 3 teaching assistantships with partial tuition reimbursements available (averaging $15,809 per year); career-related internships or fieldwork, Federal Work-Study, and institutionally sponsored loans also available. Support available to part-time students. Financial award application deadline: 4/15; financial award applicants required to submit FAFSA. In 2006, 61 master's, 4 doctorates awarded. *Degree program information:* Part-time programs available. Offers architecture (M Arch, MS, PhD); community design and development (MS); historical preservation (MS); land-use planning, management, and design (PhD); visualization (MS). *Application deadline:* For fall admission, 3/1 priority date for international students; for spring admission, 11/1 priority date for international students. Applications are processed on a rolling basis. *Application fee:* $50 ($60 for international students). Electronic applications accepted. *Application Contact:* Jess Schwintz, Academic Program Assistant, 806-742-3136 Ext. 272, Fax: 806-742-2855, E-mail: jess.schwintz@ttu.edu. *Dean,* David Andrew Vernooy, 806-742-3136 Ext. 223, Fax: 806-742-2855, E-mail: andrew.vernoy@ttu.edu.

College of Arts and Sciences Students: 878 full-time (380 women), 256 part-time (129 women); includes 173 minority (25 African Americans, 7 American Indian/Alaska Native, 32 Asian Americans or Pacific Islanders, 109 Hispanic Americans), 239 international. Average age 30. 1,225 applicants, 48% accepted, 278 enrolled. *Faculty:* 318 full-time (76 women), 8 part-time/adjunct (2 women). Expenses: Contact institution. *Financial support:* In 2006–07, 69 research assistantships with partial tuition reimbursements (averaging $14,672 per year), 6,383 teaching assistantships with partial tuition reimbursements (averaging $13,211 per year) were awarded; career-related internships or fieldwork, Federal Work-Study, and institutionally sponsored loans also available. Support available to part-time students. Financial award application deadline: 4/15; financial award applicants required to submit FAFSA. In 2006, 263 master's, 92 doctorates awarded. *Degree program information:* Part-time and evening/weekend programs available. Offers anthropology (MA); applied linguistics (MA); applied physics (MS); arts and sciences (MA, MPA, MS, PhD); atmospheric sciences (MS); biological informatics (MS); biology (MS, PhD); biotechnology (MS); chemistry (MS, PhD); classics (MA); clinical psychology (PhD); communication studies (MA); counseling psychology (MA, PhD); economics (MA, PhD); English (MA, PhD); environmental toxicology (MS, PhD); exercise and sport sciences (MS); experimental psychology (MA, PhD); geoscience (MS, PhD); German (MA); history (MA, PhD); mathematics (MA, MS, PhD); microbiology (MS); philosophy (MA); physics (MS, PhD); political science (MA, PhD); psychology (MA, PhD); public administration (MPA); romance language (MA); romance languages—Spanish (MA); Romance languages-French (MA); Romance languages-Spanish (PhD); sociology (MA); sports health (MS); statistics (MS); technical communication (MA); technical communication and rhetoric (PhD); zoology (MS, PhD). *Application deadline:* For fall admission, 3/1 priority date for international students; for spring admission, 11/1 priority date for international students. Applications are processed on a rolling basis. *Application fee:* $50 ($60 for international students). Electronic applications accepted. *Dean,* Dr. Jane L. Winer, 806-742-3831, Fax: 806-742-3893, E-mail: jane.winer@ttu.edu.

College of Education Students: 340 full-time (256 women), 564 part-time (409 women); includes 154 minority (43 African Americans, 1 American Indian/Alaska Native, 9 Asian Americans or Pacific Islanders, 101 Hispanic Americans), 33 international. Average age 35. 825 applicants, 67% accepted, 223 enrolled. *Faculty:* 57 full-time (39 women), 3 part-time/adjunct (0 women). Expenses: Contact institution. *Financial support:* In 2006–07, 575 students received support, including 2 research assistantships with partial tuition reimbursements available (averaging $10,800 per year), 13 teaching assistantships with partial tuition reimbursements available (averaging $10,835 per year); career-related internships or fieldwork, Federal Work-Study, and institutionally sponsored loans also available. Support available to part-time students. Financial award application deadline: 4/15; financial award applicants required to submit FAFSA. In 2006, 171 master's, 23 doctorates awarded. *Degree program information:* Part-time programs available. Offers bilingual education (M Ed); counselor (Certificate); counselor education (M Ed, PhD); curriculum and instruction (M Ed, PhD); education (M Ed, Ed D, PhD, Certificate); education diagnostician (Certificate); educational leadership (M Ed, Ed D); educational psychology (M Ed, PhD); elementary education (M Ed); gifted and talented (Certificate); higher education (M Ed, Ed D, PhD); information processing technologist (Certificate); instructional technology (M Ed, Ed D); language and literacy education (M Ed); principal (Certificate); secondary education (M Ed); special education (M Ed, Ed D); special education counselor (Certificate); superintendent (Certificate); visually handicapped (Certificate). *Application deadline:* For fall admission, 3/1 priority date for international students; for spring admission, 11/1 priority date for international students. Applications are processed on a rolling basis. *Application fee:* $50 ($60 for international students). Electronic applications accepted. *Application Contact:* Patsy Ann Mountz, Administrative Assistant, 806-742-1988 Ext. 434, Fax: 806-742-2179, E-mail: patsy.mountz@ttu.edu. *Dean,* Dr. Sheryl Santos, 806-742-1998 Ext. 450, Fax: 806-742-2179, E-mail: sheryl.santos@ttu.edu.

College of Engineering Students: 399 full-time (77 women), 154 part-time (23 women); includes 52 minority (7 African Americans, 1 American Indian/Alaska Native, 19 Asian Americans or Pacific Islanders, 25 Hispanic Americans), 280 international. Average age 28. 1,176 applicants, 34% accepted, 182 enrolled. *Faculty:* 102 full-time (13 women), 7 part-time/adjunct (1 woman). Expenses: Contact institution. *Financial support:* In 2006–07, 258 students received support, including 145 research assistantships with partial tuition reimbursements available (averaging $12,456 per year), 78 teaching assistantships with partial tuition reimbursements available (averaging $11,262 per year); career-related internships or fieldwork, Federal Work-Study, and institutionally sponsored loans also available. Support available to part-time students. Financial award application deadline: 4/15; financial award applicants required to submit FAFSA. In 2006, 132 master's, 34 doctorates awarded. *Degree program information:* Part-time programs available. Offers chemical engineering (MS Ch E, PhD); civil engineering (MSCE, PhD); computer science (MS, PhD); electrical engineering (MSEE, PhD); engineering (M Engr, MENVEGR, MS, MS Ch E, MSCE, MSEE, MSETM, MSIE, MSME, MSMSE, MSPE, MSSEM, PhD); environmental engineering (MENVEGR); environmental technology and management (MSETM); industrial engineering (MSIE, PhD); manufacturing systems and engineering (MSMSE); mechanical engineering (MSME, PhD); petroleum engineering (MSPE, PhD); software engineering (MS); systems and engineering management (MSSEM). *Application deadline:* For fall admission, 3/1 priority date for international students; for spring admission, 11/1 priority date for international students. Applications are processed on a rolling basis. *Application fee:* $50 ($60 for international students). Electronic applications accepted. *Application Contact:* Dr. Ernst Keisling, Graduate Adviser, 806-742-3451, Fax: 806-742-3493, E-mail: ernst.keisling@ttu.edu. *Dean,* Dr. Pamela A. Eibeck, 806-742-3451, Fax: 806-742-3493.

College of Human Sciences Students: 188 full-time (121 women), 90 part-time (58 women); includes 39 minority (9 African Americans, 3 American Indian/Alaska Native, 9 Asian Americans or Pacific Islanders, 18 Hispanic Americans), 60 international. Average age 31. 231 applicants, 54% accepted, 62 enrolled. *Faculty:* 55 full-time (38 women), 1 part-time/adjunct (0 women). Expenses: Contact institution. *Financial support:* In 2006–07, 186 students received support, including 16 research assistantships with partial tuition reimbursements available (averaging $12,630 per year), 106 teaching assistantships with partial tuition reimbursements available (averaging $12,381 per year); career-related internships or fieldwork, Federal Work-Study, institutionally sponsored loans, and scholarships/grants also available. Support available to part-time students. Financial award application deadline: 4/15; financial award applicants required to submit FAFSA. In 2006, 52 master's, 23 doctorates awarded. *Degree program information:* Part-time and evening/weekend programs available. Postbaccalaureate distance learning degree programs offered (minimal on-campus study). Offers consumer economics and environmental design (PhD); environmental design (MS); environmental design and consumer economics (PhD); family and consumer sciences education (MS, PhD, Certificate); gerontology (MS); hospitality administration (PhD); human development and family studies (MS, PhD); human sciences (MS, PhD, Certificate); marriage and family therapy (MS, PhD); nutritional sciences (MS, PhD); personal financial planning (MS); restaurant, hotel and institutional management (MS); restaurant, hotel, and institutional management (MS, PhD). *Application deadline:* For fall admission, 3/1 priority date for domestic students; for spring admission, 11/1 priority date for domestic students. Applications are processed on a rolling basis. *Application fee:* $50 ($60 for international students). Electronic applications accepted. *Application Contact:* Dr. Steven M. Harris, Associate Dean, 806-742-3031, Fax: 806-742-1849, E-mail: steve.harris@ttu.edu. *Dean,* Dr. Linda C. Hoover, 806-742-3031, Fax: 806-742-1849.

College of Mass Communications Students: 30 full-time (16 women), 10 part-time (5 women); includes 7 minority (1 African American, 1 Asian American or Pacific Islander, 5 Hispanic Americans), 8 international. Average age 28. 58 applicants, 47% accepted, 14 enrolled. *Faculty:* 15 full-time (3 women), 1 (woman) part-time/adjunct. Expenses: Contact institution. *Financial support:* In 2006–07, 28 students received support, including 10 teaching assistantships with partial tuition reimbursements available (averaging $19,332 per year); research assistantships with partial tuition reimbursements available, Federal Work-Study and institutionally sponsored loans also available. Support available to part-time students. Financial award application deadline: 4/15; financial award applicants required to submit FAFSA. In 2006, 11 degrees awarded. *Degree program information:* Part-time programs available. Offers mass communications (MA, PhD). *Application deadline:* For fall admission, 3/1 priority date for international students; for spring admission, 11/1 priority date for international students. Applications are processed on a rolling basis. *Application fee:* $50 ($60 for international students). Electronic applications accepted. *Application Contact:* Dr. Michael Parkinson, Associate Dean Graduate Studies, 806-742-3385 Ext. 254, Fax: 806-742-1085, E-mail: michael.parkinson@ttu.edu. *Dean,* Dr. Jerry C. Hudson, 806-742-3385 Ext. 224, Fax: 806-742-1085, E-mail: jerry.hudson@ttu.edu.

College of Visual and Performing Arts Students: 153 full-time (66 women), 67 part-time (36 women); includes 23 minority (7 African Americans, 3 American Indian/Alaska Native, 3 Asian Americans or Pacific Islanders, 10 Hispanic Americans), 28 international. Average age 37. 154 applicants, 59% accepted, 42 enrolled. *Faculty:* 67 full-time (27 women). Expenses: Contact institution. *Financial support:* In 2006–07, 166 students received support, including 1 research assistantship with partial tuition reimbursement available (averaging $7,350 per year), 127 teaching assistantships with partial tuition reimbursements available (averaging $8,116 per year); career-related internships or fieldwork, Federal Work-Study, and institutionally sponsored loans also available. Support available to part-time students. Financial award application deadline: 4/15. In 2006, 41 master's, 12 doctorates awarded. *Degree program information:* Part-time programs available. Offers art (MFA); art education (MAE); composition (MM, DMA); conducting (DMA); fine arts (PhD); music performance (MM); music theory (MM); musicology (MM); pedagogy (MM); performance (DMA); piano pedagogy (DMA); theatre arts (MA, MFA); visual and performing arts (MA, MAE, MFA, MM, MM Ed, DMA, PhD). *Application deadline:* For fall admission, 3/1 priority date for international students; for spring admission, 11/1 priority date for international students. Applications are processed on a rolling basis. *Application fee:* $50 ($60 for international students). Electronic applications accepted. *Interim Dean,* Dr. Jonathan Marks, 806-742-0700, Fax: 806-742-0695.

Jerry S. Rawls College of Business Administration Students: 240 full-time (89 women), 353 part-time (122 women); includes 87 minority (6 African Americans, 7 American Indian/Alaska Native, 28 Asian Americans or Pacific Islanders, 46 Hispanic Americans), 54 international. Average age 26. 570 applicants, 75% accepted, 342 enrolled. *Faculty:* 66 full-time (8 women), 6 part-time/adjunct (0 women). Expenses: Contact institution. *Financial support:* In 2006–07, 130 students received support, including 63 research assistantships (averaging $8,000 per year), 30 teaching assistantships (averaging $16,930 per year); fellowships, career-related internships or fieldwork, Federal Work-Study, scholarships/grants, health care benefits, and unspecified assistantships also available. Financial award applicants required to submit FAFSA. In 2006, 231 master's, 11 doctorates awarded. *Degree program information:* Part-time and evening/weekend programs available. Offers accounting (PhD); agricultural business (MBA); audit/financial reporting (MSA); business administration (MBA, MBA, MS, MSA, PhD, Certificate); business statistics (MS, PhD); entrepreneurship (MBA); finance (MBA); general business (MBA); health organization management (MBA, MS); international business (MBA); management (PhD); management and leadership skills (MBA); management information systems (MBA, MS, PhD); marketing (MBA, PhD); production and operations management (MS, PhD); statistics (MBA). *Application deadline:* For fall admission, 7/1 priority date for domestic students, 3/1 priority date for international students; for spring admission, 11/1 priority date for domestic students, 9/1 priority date for international students. Applications are processed on a rolling basis. *Application fee:* $50 ($60 for international students). Electronic applications accepted. *Application Contact:* Cynthia D. Barnes, Director, Graduate Services Center, 806-742-3184, Fax: 806-742-3958, E-mail: ba_grad@ttu.edu. *Dean,* Dr. Allen T. McInnes, 806-742-1300, Fax: 806-742-1092, E-mail: allen.mcinnes@ttu.edu.

School of Law Students: 695 full-time (310 women), 7 part-time (4 women); includes 137 minority (28 African Americans, 5 American Indian/Alaska Native, 30 Asian Americans or Pacific Islanders, 74 Hispanic Americans), 2 international. Average age 26. 1,790 applicants, 26% accepted, 225 enrolled. *Faculty:* 11 full-time (4 women), 6 part-time/adjunct (1 woman). Expenses: Contact institution. *Financial support:* In 2006–07, 646 students received support, including 16 teaching assistantships with partial tuition reimbursements available (averaging $6,979 per year); research assistantships with partial tuition reimbursements available, career-related internships or fieldwork, Federal Work-Study, and institutionally sponsored loans also available. Financial award application deadline: 4/15; financial award applicants required to submit FAFSA. In 2006, 200 degrees awarded. Offers law (JD). *Application deadline:* For fall admission, 2/1 priority date for domestic and international students. Applications are processed on a rolling basis. *Application fee:* $50 ($60 for international students). *Application Contact:* Terence Cook, Assistant Dean of Admissions and Recruitment, 806-742-3990, Fax: 806-742-4617, E-mail: terence.cook@ttu.edu. *Dean,* Walter Burl Huffman, 806-742-3990, Fax: 806-742-4014, E-mail: walter.huffman@ttu.edu.

See Close-Up on page 1055.

TEXAS TECH UNIVERSITY HEALTH SCIENCES CENTER, Lubbock, TX 79430

General Information State-supported, coed, graduate-only institution. *Enrollment by degree level:* 17 master's, 80 doctoral. *Graduate faculty:* 94 full-time (21 women), 10 part-time/adjunct (2 women). *Graduate housing:* On-campus housing not available. *Student services:* Campus safety program, international student services. *Library facilities:* Preston Smith Library of the Health Sciences. *Collection:* 259,931 titles, 3,439 serial subscriptions.

Computer facilities: Internet access and online class registration are available. *Web address:* http://www.ttuhsc.edu/.

General Application Contact: Karen Smith, Associate Director of Graduate Programs, 806-743-2556, Fax: 806-743-2656, E-mail: graduate.school@ttuhsc.edu.

GRADUATE UNITS

Graduate School of Biomedical Sciences Students: 79 full-time (32 women), 1 (woman) part-time; includes 9 minority (1 African American, 1 American Indian/Alaska Native, 5 Asian Americans or Pacific Islanders, 2 Hispanic Americans), 34 international. Average age 29. 131 applicants, 12% accepted, 11 enrolled. *Faculty:* 94 full-time (21 women), 10 part-time/adjunct (2 women). Expenses: Contact institution. *Financial support:* In 2006–07, 6 fellowships with partial tuition reimbursements (averaging $20,500 per year), 43 research assistantships with full and partial tuition reimbursements (averaging $20,500 per year) were awarded; institutionally sponsored loans and scholarships/grants also available. Financial award applicants required to submit FAFSA. In 2006, 8 master's, 4 doctorates awarded. Offers biochemistry and molecular genetics (MS, PhD); biomedical sciences (MS, PhD); biotechnology (MS); cell and molecular biology (MS, PhD); medical microbiology (MS, PhD); pharmaceutical sciences (MS, PhD); pharmacology and neuroscience (MS, PhD); physiology (MS, PhD). *Application deadline:* For fall admission, 5/15 priority date for domestic students, 4/15 for international students; for spring admission, 11/15 priority date for domestic students, 10/15 for international students. Applications are processed on a rolling basis. *Application fee:* $45. Electronic applications accepted. *Application Contact:* Pamela Johnson, Director of Graduate Programs, 806-743-2556, Fax: 806-743-2656, E-mail: pamela.johnson@ttuhsc.edu. *Associate Dean,* Dr. Barbara C. Pence, 806-743-2556, Fax: 806-743-2656, E-mail: acagsbs@ttuhsc.edu.

School of Allied Health Sciences Students: 494 full-time (364 women), 132 part-time (82 women); includes 144 minority (35 African Americans, 3 American Indian/Alaska Native, 26 Asian Americans or Pacific Islanders, 80 Hispanic Americans), 3 international. Average age 28. *Faculty:* 53 full-time (21 women), 5 part-time/adjunct (all women). Expenses: Contact institution. *Financial support:* Fellowships, research assistantships, teaching assistantships, career-related internships or fieldwork, institutionally sponsored loans, scholarships/grants, and tuition waivers (full) available. Financial award application deadline: 9/1; financial award applicants required to submit FAFSA. In 2006, 47 master's, 11 doctorates awarded. Offers allied health sciences (MAT, MOT, MPAS, MPT, MRC, MS, Au D, PhD, Sc D); athletic training (MAT); clinical practice management (MS); molecular pathology (MS); occupational therapy (MOT); physical therapy (MPT, Sc D); physician assistant studies (MPAS); rehabilitation counseling (MRC); speech, language and hearing sciences (MS, Au D, PhD). *Application fee:* $35. Electronic applications accepted. *Application Contact:* Jeri Moravcik, Assistant Director of Admissions and Student Affairs, 806-743-3220, Fax: 806-743-2994, E-mail: jeri.moravcik@ttuhsc.edu. *Dean,* Dr. Paul P. Brooke, 806-743-3223, Fax: 806-743-3249, E-mail: paul.brooke@ttuhsc.edu.

School of Medicine Students: 140 full-time (65 women); includes 46 minority (4 African Americans, 1 American Indian/Alaska Native, 30 Asian Americans or Pacific Islanders, 11 Hispanic Americans). Average age 23. 2,856 applicants, 5% accepted, 140 enrolled. *Faculty:* 511 full-time (158 women). Expenses: Contact institution. *Financial support:* Career-related internships or fieldwork, institutionally sponsored loans, and scholarships/grants available. Financial award applicants required to submit FAFSA. In 2006, 118 MDs awarded. Offers medicine (MD). Open only to residents of Texas, eastern New Mexico, and southwestern Oklahoma. *Application deadline:* For winter admission, 10/15 for domestic and international students. Applications are processed on a rolling basis. *Application fee:* $50. Electronic applications accepted. *Application Contact:* Linda Prado, Director of Admissions, 806-743-2297, Fax: 806-743-2725, E-mail: linda.prado@ttuhsc.edu. *Dean,* Dr. Steven L. Berk, 806-743-3003, Fax: 806-743-3021, E-mail: steven.berk@ttuhsc.edu.

School of Nursing Students: 23 full-time (22 women), 161 part-time (137 women); includes 46 minority (8 African Americans, 2 American Indian/Alaska Native, 6 Asian Americans or Pacific Islanders, 30 Hispanic Americans). Average age 37. 97 applicants, 69% accepted, 67 enrolled. *Faculty:* 17 full-time (16 women), 5 part-time/adjunct (all women). Expenses: Contact institution. *Financial support:* In 2006–07, 184 students received support. Institutionally sponsored loans, scholarships/grants, and traineeships available. Support available to part-time students. Financial award application deadline: 12/1; financial award applicants required to submit FAFSA. In 2006, 41 degrees awarded. *Degree program information:* Part-time programs available. Postbaccalaureate distance learning degree programs offered (minimal on-campus study). Offers acute care nurse practitioner (MSN, Certificate); administration (MSN); clinical research management (MSN, Certificate); education (MSN); family nurse practitioner (MSN, Certificate); geriatric nurse practitioner (MSN, Certificate); pediatric nurse practitioner (MSN, Certificate). *Application deadline:* For fall admission, 7/15 priority date for domestic and international students; for spring admission, 11/15 priority date for domestic and international students. Applications are processed on a rolling basis. *Application fee:* $40. *Application Contact:* Lauren K. Sullivan, Recruiter/Transcultural Coordinator, 806-743-2730 Ext. 309, Fax: 806-743-1622, E-mail: lauren.sullivan@ttuhsc.edu. *Associate Dean for Administrative and Student Affairs,* Dr. Barbara A. Johnston, 806-743-3055, Fax: 806-743-1622, E-mail: barbara.johnston@ttuhsc.edu.

TEXAS WESLEYAN UNIVERSITY, Fort Worth, TX 76105-1536

General Information Independent-religious, coed, comprehensive institution. *Enrollment:* 2,930 graduate, professional, and undergraduate students; 648 full-time matriculated graduate/professional students (336 women), 754 part-time matriculated graduate/professional students (429 women). *Enrollment by degree level:* 751 first professional, 651 master's. *Graduate faculty:* 37 full-time (11 women), 40 part-time/adjunct (13 women). *Tuition:* Full-time $4,230; part-time $470 per credit hour. *Required fees:* $53 per credit hour. Tuition and fees vary according to program. *Graduate housing:* Room and/or apartments available on a first-come, first-served basis to single students; on-campus housing not available to married students. Typical cost: $3,850 per year ($6,570 including board). *Student services:* Campus employment opportunities, career counseling, free psychological counseling, international student services, low-cost health insurance, teacher training, writing training. *Library facilities:* Eunice and James L. West Library plus 1 other. *Online resources:* library catalog. *Collection:* 192,044 titles, 632 serial subscriptions.

Computer facilities: 77 computers available on campus for general student use. A campuswide network can be accessed. Internet access is available. *Web address:* http://www.txwesleyan.edu/.

General Application Contact: Holly Kiser, Information Contact, 817-531-4458, Fax: 817-531-4231, E-mail: transfer@txwes.edu.

GRADUATE UNITS

Graduate Programs Students: 204 full-time (128 women), 447 part-time (284 women); includes 159 minority (78 African Americans, 4 American Indian/Alaska Native, 26 Asian Americans or Pacific Islanders, 51 Hispanic Americans). Average age 32. 462 applicants, 57% accepted. *Faculty:* 26 full-time (9 women), 17 part-time/adjunct (6 women). Expenses: Contact institution. *Financial support:* Fellowships with full and partial tuition reimbursements, career-related internships or fieldwork, Federal Work-Study, institutionally sponsored loans, scholarships/grants, and tuition waivers (full and partial) available. Support available to part-time students. Financial award application deadline: 3/15; financial award applicants required to submit FAFSA. In 2006, 154 degrees awarded. *Degree program information:* Part-time and evening/weekend programs available. Postbaccalaureate distance learning degree programs offered (no on-campus study). Offers business administration (MBA); education (M Ed, MAT, MS Ed); geriatrics (MSHA); health administration (MSHA); nurse anesthesia (MHS, MSNA); professional counseling (MA); public health (MSHA); school counseling (MS). *Application deadline:* Applications are processed on a rolling basis. Electronic applications accepted. *Provost,* Dr. Allen Henderson, 817-531-4405.

School of Law Students: 444 full-time (208 women), 307 part-time (145 women); includes 149 minority (40 African Americans, 12 American Indian/Alaska Native, 36 Asian Americans or Pacific Islanders, 61 Hispanic Americans). Average age 29. *Faculty:* 25 full-time (8 women), 28 part-time/adjunct (11 women). Expenses: Contact institution. *Financial support:* Career-related internships or fieldwork, scholarships/grants, and tuition waivers (full and partial) available. Support available to part-time students. Financial award application deadline: 3/15; financial award applicants required to submit FAFSA. In 2006, 151 degrees awarded. *Degree program information:* Part-time and evening/weekend programs available. Offers law (JD). *Application deadline:* For fall admission, 5/1 priority date for domestic students. Applications are processed on a rolling basis. *Application fee:* $50. Electronic applications accepted. *Application Contact:* Lynda Culver, Assistant Dean/Director of Admissions, 817-212-4045, Fax: 817-212-4002, E-mail: law_admissions@law.txwes.edu. *Interim Dean,* Cynthia Fountaine, 817-212-4000, Fax: 817-212-4199.

TEXAS WOMAN'S UNIVERSITY, Denton, TX 76201

General Information State-supported, coed, primarily women, university. CGS member. *Enrollment:* 11,832 graduate, professional, and undergraduate students; 1,812 full-time matriculated graduate/professional students (1,571 women), 2,800 part-time matriculated graduate/professional students (2,529 women). *Enrollment by degree level:* 3,863 master's, 749 doctoral. *Graduate faculty:* 354 full-time (272 women), 418 part-time/adjunct (300 women). *Tuition, area resident:* Part-time $168 per unit. Tuition, state resident: full-time $4,369. Tuition, nonresident: full-time $9,373; part-time $443 per unit. *Required fees:* $20 per unit. $177 per term. *Graduate housing:* Rooms and/or apartments available on a first-come, first-served basis to single and married students. Typical cost: $3,356 per year ($5,576 including board) for single students; $7,062 per year ($9,282 including board) for married students. Room and board charges vary according to board plan and housing facility selected. *Student services:* Campus employment opportunities, campus safety program, career counseling, disabled student services, exercise/wellness program, free psychological counseling, grant writing training, international student services, low-cost health insurance, multicultural affairs office, teacher training, writing training. *Library facilities:* Blagg-Huey Library. *Online resources:* library catalog, web page. *Collection:* 572,500 titles, 2,537 serial subscriptions.

Computer facilities: 700 computers available on campus for general student use. A campuswide network can be accessed from student residence rooms and from off campus. Internet access and online class registration are available. *Web address:* http://www.twu.edu/.

General Application Contact: Samuel Wheeler, Coordinator of Graduate Admissions, 940-898-3188, Fax: 940-898-3081, E-mail: wheelersr@twu.edu.

GRADUATE UNITS

Graduate School Students: 1,812 full-time (1,571 women), 2,800 part-time (2,529 women); includes 1,369 minority (696 African Americans, 34 American Indian/Alaska Native, 232 Asian Americans or Pacific Islanders, 407 Hispanic Americans), 219 international. Average age 35. 3,074 applicants, 59% accepted, 1245 enrolled. Expenses: Contact institution. *Financial support:* In 2006–07, 1,478 students received support, including 1 research assistantship (averaging $10,764 per year), teaching assistantships (averaging $10,764 per year); career-related internships or fieldwork, Federal Work-Study, institutionally sponsored loans,

Texas Woman's University (continued)

scholarships/grants, traineeships, health care benefits, and unspecified assistantships also available. Support available to part-time students. Financial award application deadline: 3/1. In 2006, 1,264 master's, 84 doctorates awarded. *Degree program information:* Part-time and evening/weekend programs available. Postbaccalaureate distance learning degree programs offered. *Application deadline:* For fall admission, 6/30 for domestic students, 4/1 for international students; for spring admission, 12/1 for domestic students, 8/1 for international students. Applications are processed on a rolling basis. *Application fee:* $30 ($50 for international students). Electronic applications accepted. *Application Contact:* Samuel Wheeler, Coordinator of Graduate Admissions, 940-898-3188, Fax: 940-898-3081, E-mail: wheelersr@twu.edu. *Dean of the Graduate School,* Dr. Jennifer L. Martin, 940-898-3415, Fax: 940-898-3412, E-mail: jmartin@twu.edu.

College of Arts and Sciences Students: 615 full-time (505 women), 442 part-time (372 women); includes 379 minority (233 African Americans, 10 American Indian/Alaska Native, 47 Asian Americans or Pacific Islanders, 89 Hispanic Americans), 79 international. Average age 35. Expenses: Contact institution. *Financial support:* In 2006–07, 133 research assistantships (averaging $10,764 per year), 64 teaching assistantships (averaging $10,764 per year) were awarded; career-related internships or fieldwork, Federal Work-Study, institutionally sponsored loans, scholarships/grants, traineeships, health care benefits, and unspecified assistantships also available. Support available to part-time students. Financial award application deadline: 3/1; financial award applicants required to submit FAFSA. In 2006, 314 master's, 16 doctorates awarded. *Degree program information:* Part-time and evening/weekend programs available. Postbaccalaureate distance learning degree programs offered (minimal on-campus study). Offers art (MA, MFA); arts (MA, MFA, PhD); arts and sciences (MA, MBA, MFA, MHSM, MS, PhD, SSP); biology (MS); biology teaching (MS); chemistry (MS); chemistry teaching (MS); counseling psychology (MA, PhD); dance (MA, MFA, PhD); drama (MA); English (MA); government (MA); history (MA); management (MBA, MHSM); mathematics (MA, MS); mathematics teaching (MS); molecular biology (PhD); music (MA); rhetoric (PhD); school psychology (PhD); science teaching (MS); sociology (MA, PhD); women's studies (MA). *Application deadline:* For fall admission, 4/1 for international students; for spring admission, 8/1 for international students. Applications are processed on a rolling basis. *Application fee:* $30 ($50 for international students). Electronic applications accepted. *Application Contact:* Samuel Wheeler, Coordinator of Graduate Admissions, 940-898-3188, Fax: 940-898-3081, E-mail: wheelersr@twu.edu. *Dean,* Dr. Ann Staton, 940-898-3326, Fax: 940-898-3366, E-mail: astaton@mail.twu.edu.

College of Health Sciences Students: 825 full-time (737 women), 524 part-time (448 women); includes 343 minority (115 African Americans, 12 American Indian/Alaska Native, 80 Asian Americans or Pacific Islanders, 136 Hispanic Americans), 85 international. Average age 30. Expenses: Contact institution. *Financial support:* In 2006–07, 76 research assistantships (averaging $10,764 per year), 18 teaching assistantships (averaging $10,764 per year) were awarded; career-related internships or fieldwork, Federal Work-Study, institutionally sponsored loans, scholarships/grants, traineeships, health care benefits, tuition waivers (partial), and unspecified assistantships also available. Support available to part-time students. Financial award application deadline: 3/1; financial award applicants required to submit FAFSA. In 2006, 333 master's, 24 doctorates awarded. *Degree program information:* Part-time and evening/weekend programs available. Postbaccalaureate distance learning degree programs offered. Offers education of the deaf (MS); exercise and sports nutrition (MS); food science (MS); health care administration (MHA); health sciences (MA, MHA, MOT, MS, DPT, Ed D, PhD); health studies (MS, Ed D, PhD); institutional administration (MS); kinesiology (MS, PhD); nutrition (MS, PhD); occupational therapy (MA, MOT, PhD); physical therapy (MS, DPT, PhD); speech-language pathology (MS). *Application deadline:* For fall admission, 4/1 for international students; for spring admission, 8/1 for international students. Applications are processed on a rolling basis. *Application fee:* $30 ($50 for international students). Electronic applications accepted. *Application Contact:* Samuel Wheeler, Coordinator of Graduate Admissions, 940-898-3188, Fax: 940-898-3081, E-mail: wheelersr@twu.edu. *Dean,* Dr. Jimmy Ishee, 940-898-2854, Fax: 940-898-2853, E-mail: jishee@twu.edu.

College of Nursing Students: 41 full-time (38 women), 512 part-time (490 women); includes 211 minority (121 African Americans, 2 American Indian/Alaska Native, 64 Asian Americans or Pacific Islanders, 24 Hispanic Americans), 9 international. Average age 41. Expenses: Contact institution. *Financial support:* In 2006–07, 11 research assistantships (averaging $11,232 per year), 3 teaching assistantships (averaging $11,232 per year) were awarded; career-related internships or fieldwork, Federal Work-Study, institutionally sponsored loans, scholarships/grants, traineeships, health care benefits, and unspecified assistantships also available. Support available to part-time students. Financial award application deadline: 3/1; financial award applicants required to submit FAFSA. In 2006, 129 master's, 16 doctorates awarded. *Degree program information:* Part-time programs available. Postbaccalaureate distance learning degree programs offered. Offers adult health nurse practitioner (MS); health systems management (MS); nursing (MS); nursing education (MS); nursing science (PhD). *Application deadline:* For fall admission, 4/1 for international students; for spring admission, 8/1 for international students. Applications are processed on a rolling basis. *Application fee:* $30 ($50 for international students). Electronic applications accepted. *Application Contact:* Samuel Wheeler, Coordinator of Graduate Admissions, 940-898-3188, Fax: 940-898-3081, E-mail: wheelersr@twu.edu. *Dean,* Dr. Marcia Hern, 940-898-2401, Fax: 940-898-2437, E-mail: mhern@twu.edu.

College of Professional Education Students: 331 full-time (291 women), 1,322 part-time (1,219 women); includes 436 minority (227 African Americans, 10 American Indian/Alaska Native, 41 Asian Americans or Pacific Islanders, 158 Hispanic Americans), 46 international. Average age 37. Expenses: Contact institution. *Financial support:* In 2006–07, 34 research assistantships (averaging $10,764 per year), 14 teaching assistantships (averaging $10,764 per year) were awarded; career-related internships or fieldwork, Federal Work-Study, institutionally sponsored loans, scholarships/grants, traineeships, health care benefits, tuition waivers (partial), and unspecified assistantships also available. Support available to part-time students. Financial award application deadline: 3/1; financial award applicants required to submit FAFSA. In 2006, 488 master's, 28 doctorates awarded. *Degree program information:* Part-time and evening/weekend programs available. Offers child development (MS, PhD); counseling and development (MS); early childhood education (M Ed, MA, MS, Ed D); education administration (M Ed, MA); elementary education (M Ed, MA); family studies (MS, PhD); family therapy (MS, PhD); library science (MA, MLS, PhD); professional education (M Ed, MA, MAT, MLS, MS, Ed D, PhD); reading education (M Ed, MA, MS, Ed D, PhD); special education (M Ed, MA, PhD); teaching (MAT). *Application deadline:* For fall admission, 4/1 for international students; for spring admission, 8/1 for international students. Applications are processed on a rolling basis. *Application fee:* $30 ($50 for international students). Electronic applications accepted. *Application Contact:* Samuel Wheeler, Coordinator of Graduate Admissions, 940-898-3188, Fax: 940-898-3081, E-mail: wheelersr@twu.edu. *Interim Dean,* Dr. Nan L. Restine, 940-898-2202, Fax: 940-898-2611, E-mail: lrestine@mail.twu.edu.

THOMAS COLLEGE, Waterville, ME 04901-5097

General Information Independent, coed, comprehensive institution. *Graduate housing:* On-campus housing not available.

GRADUATE UNITS

Graduate School *Degree program information:* Part-time and evening/weekend programs available. Offers business (MBA); computer technology education (MS); education (MS); human resource management (MBA). Electronic applications accepted.

THOMAS EDISON STATE COLLEGE, Trenton, NJ 08608-1176

General Information State-supported, coed, comprehensive institution. CGS member. *Enrollment:* 13,173 graduate, professional, and undergraduate students; 444 part-time matriculated graduate/professional students (199 women). *Enrollment by degree level:* 444 master's. Tuition, nonresident: part-time $422 per credit. Part-time tuition and fees vary according to program. *Graduate housing:* On-campus housing not available.

Computer facilities: A campuswide network can be accessed from off campus. Internet access and online class registration are available. *Web address:* http://www.tesc.edu/.

General Application Contact: Renee San Giacomo, Director of Admissions, 888-442-8372, Fax: 609-984-8447, E-mail: admissions@tesc.edu.

See Close-Up on page 1057.

THOMAS JEFFERSON SCHOOL OF LAW, San Diego, CA 92110-2905

General Information Independent, coed, graduate-only institution. *Enrollment by degree level:* 770 first professional. *Graduate faculty:* 37 full-time (19 women), 34 part-time/adjunct (11 women). *Tuition:* Full-time $30,100; part-time $9,450 per semester. Tuition and fees vary according to course load. *Graduate housing:* On-campus housing not available. *Student services:* Campus employment opportunities, career counseling, disabled student services, free psychological counseling, international student services, low-cost health insurance. *Library facilities:* Thomas Jefferson School of Law Library. *Online resources:* library catalog, web page, access to other libraries' catalogs. *Collection:* 132,530 titles, 3,376 serial subscriptions, 1,504 audiovisual materials.

Computer facilities: 49 computers available on campus for general student use. A campuswide network can be accessed from student residence rooms and from off campus. Internet access is available. *Web address:* http://www.tjsl.edu/.

General Application Contact: M. Elizabeth Kransberger, Assistant Dean for Admissions, Financial Aid, and Student Counseling Services, 619-297-9700 Ext. 1616, Fax: 619-294-4713, E-mail: bkransberger@tjsl.edu.

GRADUATE UNITS

Professional Program Students: 580 full-time (255 women), 190 part-time (85 women); includes 150 minority (36 African Americans, 4 American Indian/Alaska Native, 56 Asian Americans or Pacific Islanders, 54 Hispanic Americans). Average age 26. 3,285 applicants, 47% accepted, 294 enrolled. *Faculty:* 37 full-time (19 women), 34 part-time/adjunct (11 women). Expenses: Contact institution. *Financial support:* In 2006–07, 346 fellowships with full and partial tuition reimbursements (averaging $11,622 per year) were awarded; career-related internships or fieldwork, Federal Work-Study, scholarships/grants, and tuition waivers also available. Support available to part-time students. Financial award application deadline: 4/30; financial award applicants required to submit FAFSA. In 2006, 279 degrees awarded. *Degree program information:* Part-time and evening/weekend programs available. Offers law (JD). *Application deadline:* For fall admission, 8/20 priority date for domestic students; for spring admission, 1/7 priority date for domestic students. Applications are processed on a rolling basis. *Application fee:* $35. Electronic applications accepted. *Application Contact:* M. Elizabeth Kransberger, Assistant Dean for Admissions, Financial Aid, and Student Counseling Services, 619-297-9700 Ext. 1616, Fax: 619-294-4713, E-mail: bkransberger@tjsl.edu. *Dean and President,* Rudolph C. Hasl, 619-297-9700 Ext. 1404, E-mail: hasl@tjsl.edu.

THOMAS JEFFERSON UNIVERSITY, Philadelphia, PA 19107

General Information Independent, coed, university. CGS member. *Enrollment:* 2,867 graduate, professional, and undergraduate students; 1,226 full-time matriculated graduate/professional students (683 women), 243 part-time matriculated graduate/professional students (195 women). *Enrollment by degree level:* 966 first professional, 336 master's, 141 doctoral, 26 other advanced degrees. *Tuition:* Full-time $15,340; part-time $790 per credit. *Required fees:* $300. *Graduate housing:* Rooms and/or apartments available to single and married students. *Student services:* Campus employment opportunities, campus safety program, career counseling, child daycare facilities, exercise/wellness program, free psychological counseling, international student services, low-cost health insurance, multicultural affairs office. *Library facilities:* Scott Memorial Library plus 1 other. *Online resources:* web page. *Collection:* 170,000 titles, 2,290 serial subscriptions.

Computer facilities: 100 computers available on campus for general student use. A campuswide network can be accessed from off campus. *Web address:* http://www.jefferson.edu/.

General Application Contact: Jessie F. Pervall, Director of Admissions, 215-503-0155, Fax: 215-503-9920, E-mail: jcgs-info@jefferson.edu.

GRADUATE UNITS

Jefferson College of Graduate Studies Students: 138 full-time (79 women), 152 part-time (110 women); includes 76 minority (35 African Americans, 4 American Indian/Alaska Native, 28 Asian Americans or Pacific Islanders, 9 Hispanic Americans), 17 international. Average age 29. 428 applicants, 40% accepted, 89 enrolled. *Faculty:* 165 full-time (37 women), 28 part-time/adjunct (11 women). Expenses: Contact institution. *Financial support:* In 2006–07, 81 students received support, including 138 fellowships with full tuition reimbursements available; research assistantships, Federal Work-Study, institutionally sponsored loans, scholarships/grants, and traineeships also available. Support available to part-time students. Financial award application deadline: 5/1; financial award applicants required to submit FAFSA. In 2006, 57 master's, 19 doctorates awarded. *Degree program information:* Part-time and evening/weekend programs available. Postbaccalaureate distance learning degree programs offered (no on-campus study). Offers biochemistry and molecular biology (PhD); biomedical sciences (MS); cell and developmental biology (MS, PhD); clinical research, public health, and research management (Certificate); genetics (PhD); immunology and microbial pathogenesis (PhD); interdisciplinary biomedical sciences (PhD); microbiology (MS); molecular pharmacology and structural biology (PhD); molecular physiology and biophysics (PhD); neuroscience (PhD); pharmacology (MS); public health (MS); tissue engineering and regenerative medicine (PhD). *Application deadline:* For fall admission, 3/1 priority date for domestic and international students; for winter admission, 6/1 priority date for international students; for spring admission, 9/1 priority date for international students. Applications are processed on a rolling basis. *Application fee:* $50. Electronic applications accepted. *Application Contact:* Jessie F. Pervall, Director of Admissions, 215-503-0155, Fax: 215-503-9920, E-mail: jcgs-info@jefferson.edu. *Dean,* Dr. James H. Keen, 215-503-8982, Fax: 215-503-6690, E-mail: james.keen@jefferson.edu.

Jefferson Medical College Students: 966 full-time (496 women); includes 254 minority (17 African Americans, 4 American Indian/Alaska Native, 199 Asian Americans or Pacific Islanders, 34 Hispanic Americans), 26 international. Average age 26. 7,789 applicants, 6% accepted, 255 enrolled. *Faculty:* 699 full-time (200 women), 25 part-time/adjunct (13 women). Expenses: Contact institution. *Financial support:* In 2006–07, 806 students received support. Federal Work-Study and institutionally sponsored loans available. Financial award application deadline: 3/1; financial award applicants required to submit FAFSA. In 2006, 231 MDs awarded. Offers medicine (MD). *Application deadline:* For fall admission, 11/15 for domestic and international students. Applications are processed on a rolling basis. *Application fee:* $80. Electronic applications accepted. *Application Contact:* Dr. Clara Callahan, Dean for Admissions, 215-955-6983, Fax: 215-923-6939, E-mail: clara.callahan@jefferson.edu. *Senior Vice President and Dean for Academic Affairs,* Dr. Thomas J. Nasca, 215-955-6980, Fax: 215-923-6939.

See Close-Up on page 1059.

THOMAS M. COOLEY LAW SCHOOL, Lansing, MI 48901-3038

General Information Independent, coed, graduate-only institution. *Enrollment by degree level:* 3,606 first professional, 26 other advanced degrees. *Graduate faculty:* 87 full-time (35 women), 154 part-time/adjunct (53 women). *Tuition:* Full-time $24,220. Tuition and fees vary according to course load. *Graduate housing:* Rooms and/or apartments available on a first-come, first-served basis to single and married students. Typical cost: $4,240 per year for single students; $5,480 per year for married students. Room charges vary according to board plan and housing facility selected. *Student services:* Campus employment opportunities, career counseling, disabled student services, multicultural affairs office, writing training. *Library facilities:* Thomas E. Brennan Law School Library plus 5 others. *Online resources:* library catalog, web page. *Collection:* 257,501 titles, 9,478 serial subscriptions, 2,906 audiovisual materials.

Computer facilities: 181 computers available on campus for general student use. A campuswide network can be accessed from off campus. Internet access is available. *Web address:* http://www.cooley.edu/.

General Application Contact: Stephanie Gregg, Dean of Admissions, 517-371-5140, Fax: 517-334-5718, E-mail: greggs@cooley.edu.

GRADUATE UNITS

Professional Program Students: 566 full-time (253 women), 3,066 part-time (1,468 women); includes 810 minority (394 African Americans, 14 American Indian/Alaska Native, 219 Asian Americans or Pacific Islanders, 183 Hispanic Americans), 137 international. Average age 26. 5,718 applicants, 66% accepted, 1691 enrolled. *Faculty:* 87 full-time (35 women), 154 part-time/adjunct (53 women). Expenses: Contact institution. *Financial support:* In 2006–07, 3,304 students received support, including 11 research assistantships with tuition reimbursements available (averaging $5,092 per year), 60 teaching assistantships with tuition reimbursements available; career-related internships or fieldwork, Federal Work-Study, scholarships/grants, and unspecified assistantships also available. Support available to part-time students. Financial award applicants required to submit FAFSA. In 2006, 665 JDs awarded. *Degree program information:* Part-time and evening/weekend programs available. Offers law (JD, LL M). *Application deadline:* For fall admission, 9/1 for domestic students; for winter admission, 1/1 for domestic students; for spring admission, 5/1 for domestic students. Applications are processed on a rolling basis. *Application fee:* $0. Electronic applications accepted. *Application Contact:* Stephanie Gregg, Dean of Admissions, 517-371-5140, Fax: 517-334-5718, E-mail: greggs@cooley.edu.

THOMAS MORE COLLEGE, Crestview Hills, KY 41017-3495

General Information Independent-religious, coed, comprehensive institution. *Enrollment:* 1,400 graduate, professional, and undergraduate students; 75 full-time matriculated graduate/professional students (36 women). *Enrollment by degree level:* 75 master's. *Graduate faculty:* 11 full-time (3 women). *Tuition:* Full-time $10,330. One-time fee: $125 full-time. *Graduate housing:* On-campus housing not available. *Student services:* Career counseling, free psychological counseling, international student services. *Library facilities:* Thomas More Library. *Online resources:* library catalog, web page, access to other libraries' catalogs. *Collection:* 115,345 titles, 498 serial subscriptions, 2,292 audiovisual materials.

Computer facilities: 100 computers available on campus for general student use. A campuswide network can be accessed from student residence rooms and from off campus. Internet access is available. *Web address:* http://www.thomasmore.edu/.

General Application Contact: Nathan Hartman, Director of Lifelong Learning, 859-344-3602, Fax: 859-344-3686, E-mail: nathan.hartman@thomasmore.edu.

GRADUATE UNITS

Program in Business Administration Students: 75 full-time (36 women); includes 4 minority (1 African American, 2 Asian Americans or Pacific Islanders, 1 Hispanic American). Average age 32. 47 applicants, 68% accepted, 28 enrolled. *Faculty:* 11 full-time (3 women). Expenses: Contact institution. *Financial support:* In 2006–07, 60 students received support. Institutionally sponsored loans available. Financial award application deadline: 3/15; financial award applicants required to submit FAFSA. In 2006, 69 degrees awarded. *Degree program information:* Evening/weekend programs available. Offers business administration (MBA). *Application deadline:* Applications are processed on a rolling basis. *Application fee:* $25. Electronic applications accepted. *Director of Lifelong Learning,* Nathan Hartman, 859-344-3602, Fax: 859-344-3686, E-mail: nathan.hartman@thomasmore.edu.

THOMAS UNIVERSITY, Thomasville, GA 31792-7499

General Information Independent, coed, comprehensive institution. *Enrollment:* 684 graduate, professional, and undergraduate students; 48 full-time matriculated graduate/professional students (38 women), 55 part-time matriculated graduate/professional students (45 women). *Enrollment by degree level:* 90 master's, 13 other advanced degrees. *Graduate faculty:* 6 full-time (2 women), 5 part-time/adjunct (2 women). *Tuition:* Part-time $376 per credit. *Required fees:* $130 per semester. *Graduate housing:* Room and/or apartments available on a first-come, first-served basis to single students; on-campus housing not available to married students. Typical cost: $2,500 per year. Housing application deadline: 8/1. *Student services:* Campus employment opportunities, disabled student services. *Library facilities:* Thomas University Library. *Online resources:* library catalog. *Collection:* 41,467 titles, 451 serial subscriptions, 560 audiovisual materials.

Computer facilities: 50 computers available on campus for general student use. A campuswide network can be accessed from student residence rooms and from off campus. *Web address:* http://www.thomasu.edu/.

General Application Contact: Adrienne Diggs, Assistant Director of Admissions, 229-226-1621 Ext. 127, Fax: 229-227-6919, E-mail: adiggs@thomasu.edu.

GRADUATE UNITS

Department of Business Administration Students: 3 full-time (2 women), 7 part-time (6 women); includes 5 minority (all African Americans) Average age 27. *Faculty:* 4 full-time (3 women). Expenses: Contact institution. *Financial support:* Applicants required to submit FAFSA. In 2006, 10 degrees awarded. *Degree program information:* Part-time programs available. Offers business administration (MBA). *Application deadline:* For fall admission, 8/1 priority date for domestic students, 6/1 for international students; for spring admission, 12/1 priority date for domestic students, 10/1 for international students. Applications are processed on a rolling basis. *Application fee:* $50 ($125 for international students). Electronic applications accepted. *Application Contact:* Adrienne Diggs, Assistant Director of Admissions, 229-226-1621 Ext. 127, Fax: 229-227-6919, E-mail: adiggs@thomasu.edu. *Assistant Professor, Chair of Business,* Dr. Jenny Swearingen, 229-226-1621 Ext. 133, Fax: 229-226-1653, E-mail: jswearingen@thomasu.edu.

Department of Human Services Students: 24 full-time (17 women), 30 part-time (23 women); includes 23 minority (all African Americans), 2 international. Average age 33. *Faculty:* 3 full-time (2 women). Expenses: Contact institution. *Financial support:* Applicants required to submit FAFSA. *Degree program information:* Part-time programs available. Offers community counseling (MSCC); rehabilitation counseling (MRC). *Application deadline:* For fall admission, 8/1 priority date for domestic students, 6/1 for international students; for spring admission, 2/1 priority date for domestic students, 10/1 for international students. Applications are processed on a rolling basis. *Application fee:* $50 ($125 for international students). Electronic applications accepted. *Application Contact:* Adrienne Diggs, Assistant Director of Admissions, 229-226-1621 Ext. 127, Fax: 229-227-6919, E-mail: adiggs@thomasu.edu. *Assistant Professor, Chair of Human Services,* Dr. Theresa Reese, 229-226-1621, Fax: 229-226-1653, E-mail: treese@thomasu.edu.

THUNDERBIRD SCHOOL OF GLOBAL MANAGEMENT, Glendale, AZ 85306-6000

General Information Independent, coed, graduate-only institution. *Enrollment by degree level:* 1,106 master's. *Graduate faculty:* 40 full-time (10 women), 3 part-time/adjunct (1 woman). *Tuition:* Full-time $36,630. *Required fees:* $1,220. One-time fee: $625 full-time. Part-time tuition and fees vary according to course load and program. *Graduate housing:* Room and/or apartments available on a first-come, first-served basis to single students; on-campus housing not available to married students. Typical cost: $3,900 (including board). Housing application deadline: 7/15. *Student services:* Campus employment opportunities, campus safety program, career counseling, disabled student services, exercise/wellness program, international student services, low-cost health insurance, multicultural affairs office, writing training. *Library facilities:* The Merle A. Hinrichs International Business Information Centre plus 1 other. *Online resources:* library catalog, web page, access to other libraries' catalogs. *Collection:* 70,000 titles, 1,338 serial subscriptions, 3,616 audiovisual materials. *Research affiliation:* Wiley (publishing).

Computer facilities: 97 computers available on campus for general student use. A campuswide network can be accessed from student residence rooms and from off campus. Internet access and online class registration, My Thunderbird, campus intranet are available. *Web address:* http://www.thunderbird.edu/.

General Application Contact: Judy Johnson, Director of Admissions, 602-978-7210, Fax: 602-439-5432, E-mail: johnsonj@thunderbird.edu.

GRADUATE UNITS

Graduate Programs Students: 534 full-time (167 women), 572 part-time (129 women); includes 91 minority (7 African Americans, 42 Asian Americans or Pacific Islanders, 42 Hispanic Americans), 629 international. *Faculty:* 40 full-time (10 women), 3 part-time/adjunct (1 woman). Expenses: Contact institution. *Financial support:* In 2006–07, 531 students received support. Federal Work-Study and scholarships/grants available. Support available to part-time students. Financial award applicants required to submit FAFSA. In 2006, 661 degrees awarded. *Degree program information:* Part-time and evening/weekend programs available. Postbaccalaureate distance learning degree programs offered (minimal on-campus study). Offers corporate learning (MBA); global affairs and management (MA); global business administration for Latin American managers (GMBA); global business administration on-demand (GMBA); global management (MS). *Application deadline:* Applications are processed on a rolling basis. *Application fee:* $125. Electronic applications accepted. *Application Contact:* Judy Johnson, Director of Admissions, 602-978-7210, Fax: 602-439-5432, E-mail: johnsonj@thunderbird.edu. *Senior Vice President of Academic Programs,* Dr. Robert Widing, 602-978-7872, Fax: 602-547-1356, E-mail: widingr@t-bird.edu.

TIFFIN UNIVERSITY, Tiffin, OH 44883-2161

General Information Independent, coed, comprehensive institution. *Enrollment:* 1,977 graduate, professional, and undergraduate students; 204 full-time matriculated graduate/professional students (143 women), 335 part-time matriculated graduate/professional students (156 women). *Enrollment by degree level:* 539 master's. *Graduate faculty:* 40 full-time (13 women), 40 part-time/adjunct (17 women). *Tuition:* Part-time $700 per credit hour. *Graduate housing:* Room and/or apartments available on a first-come, first-served basis to single students; on-campus housing not available to married students. Typical cost: $3,525 per year ($6,775 including board). Housing application deadline: 8/1. *Student services:* Campus employment opportunities, campus safety program, career counseling, disabled student services, exercise/wellness program, free psychological counseling, international student services, low-cost health insurance, multicultural affairs office. *Library facilities:* Pfeiffer Library. *Online resources:* library catalog, web page, access to other libraries' catalogs. *Collection:* 29,779 titles, 250 serial subscriptions, 536 audiovisual materials.

Computer facilities: 60 computers available on campus for general student use. A campuswide network can be accessed from student residence rooms and from off campus. Internet access and online class registration are available. *Web address:* http://www.tiffin.edu/.

General Application Contact: Kristi Krintzline, Director of Graduate Admissions, 800-968-6446 Ext. 3445, Fax: 419-443-5002, E-mail: krintzlineka@tiffin.edu.

GRADUATE UNITS

Program in Business Administration Students: 89 full-time (54 women), 159 part-time (87 women); includes 31 minority (28 African Americans, 3 Hispanic Americans), 8 international. Average age 31. 182 applicants, 68% accepted, 88 enrolled. *Faculty:* 29 full-time (8 women), 28 part-time/adjunct (9 women). Expenses: Contact institution. *Financial support:* In 2006–07, 94 students received support. Available to part-time students. Application deadline: 7/31; In 2006, 145 degrees awarded. *Degree program information:* Part-time and evening/weekend programs available. Postbaccalaureate distance learning degree programs offered (no on-campus study). Offers general management (MBA); leadership (MBA); safety and security management (MBA); sports management (MBA). *Application deadline:* For fall admission, 9/3 for domestic students, 8/1 for international students; for spring admission, 1/9 for domestic students, 12/1 for international students. Applications are processed on a rolling basis. *Application fee:* $50. Electronic applications accepted. *Application Contact:* Kristi Krintzline, Director of Graduate Admissions, 800-968-6446 Ext. 3445, Fax: 419-443-5002, E-mail: krintzlineka@tiffin.edu. *Dean of the School of Business,* Dr. Shawn P. Daly, 419-448-3404, Fax: 419-443-5002, E-mail: sdaly@tiffin.edu.

Program in Criminal Justice Students: 115 full-time (89 women), 176 part-time (69 women); includes 72 minority (55 African Americans, 3 Asian Americans or Pacific Islanders, 14 Hispanic Americans), 2 international. 319 applicants, 72% accepted, 166 enrolled. *Faculty:* 9 full-time (3 women), 14 part-time/adjunct (5 women). Expenses: Contact institution. *Financial support:* In 2006–07, 64 students received support. Available to part-time students. Application deadline: 7/31; In 2006, 107 degrees awarded. *Degree program information:* Part-time and evening/weekend programs available. Postbaccalaureate distance learning degree programs offered (no on-campus study). Offers crime analysis (MSCJ); criminal behavior (MSCJ); forensic psychology (MSCJ); homeland security administration (MSCJ); justice administration (MSCJ). *Application deadline:* For fall admission, 9/3 for domestic students, 8/1 for international students; for spring admission, 1/9 priority date for domestic students, 12/1 for international students. Applications are processed on a rolling basis. *Application fee:* $50. Electronic applications accepted. *Application Contact:* Kristi Krintzline, Director of Graduate Admissions, 800-968-6446 Ext. 3445, Fax: 419-443-5002, E-mail: krintzlineka@tiffin.edu. *Dean of Criminal Justice and Social Sciences,* Dr. Charles Christensen, 419-448-3268, Fax: 419-443-5002, E-mail: christensenc@tiffin.edu.

TORONTO SCHOOL OF THEOLOGY, Toronto, ON M5S 2C3, Canada

General Information Independent-religious, coed, graduate-only institution. *Graduate housing:* On-campus housing not available.

GRADUATE UNITS

Graduate Programs Offers theology (M Div, M Rel, MA, MAMS, MPS, MRE, MTS, Th M, D Min, PhD, Th D). Federation of seven Toronto-area theological colleges; basic degrees offered through the member colleges co-jointly with the University of Toronto.

TOURO COLLEGE, New York, NY 10010

General Information Independent, coed, comprehensive institution.

GRADUATE UNITS

Barry Z. Levine School of Health Sciences Offers biomedical sciences (MS); health information management (Certificate); occupational therapy (MS); physical therapy (MS).

Jacob D. Fuchsberg Law Center *Degree program information:* Part-time and evening/weekend programs available. Offers law (JD); U.S. law for foreign lawyers (LL M).

School of Jewish Studies *Degree program information:* Part-time programs available. Offers Jewish studies (MA).

TOURO UNIVERSITY COLLEGE OF OSTEOPATHIC MEDICINE, Vallejo, CA 94592

General Information Independent, coed, graduate-only institution. *Enrollment by degree level:* 701 first professional, 142 master's, 107 other advanced degrees. *Graduate faculty:* 61 full-time (26 women), 30 part-time/adjunct (16 women). *Graduate housing:* Room and/or apartments available on a first-come, first-served basis to single students; on-campus housing not available to married students. Typical cost: $600 per year. Housing application deadline: 6/20. *Student services:* Campus safety program, career counseling, exercise/wellness program, free psychological counseling, low-cost health insurance, multicultural affairs office, teacher training. *Library facilities:* Touro University Library plus 1 other. *Online resources:* library catalog, web page, access to other libraries' catalogs. *Collection:* 3,000 serial subscriptions, 100 audiovisual materials.

Computer facilities: 90 computers available on campus for general student use. A campuswide network can be accessed from student residence rooms and from off campus. Internet access is available. *Web address:* http://www.tumi.edu/.

General Application Contact: Dr. Donald Haight, Director of Admissions, 707-638-5226, Fax: 707-638-5250, E-mail: haight@touro.edu.

Touro University College of Osteopathic Medicine (continued)

GRADUATE UNITS

Professional Program Students: 950 full-time (579 women); includes 354 minority (39 African Americans, 5 American Indian/Alaska Native, 258 Asian Americans or Pacific Islanders, 52 Hispanic Americans). Average age 26. 2,113 applicants, 13% accepted, 269 enrolled. *Faculty:* 61 full-time (26 women), 30 part-time/adjunct (16 women). Expenses: Contact institution. *Financial support:* In 2006–07, 3 fellowships (averaging $3,000 per year) were awarded. In 2006, 109 first professional degrees, 43 master's awarded. Offers education (MA); osteopathic medicine (DO); pharmacy (Pharm D); physician assistant studies (MS); public health (MPH). *Application deadline:* For fall admission, 6/1 for domestic students. Applications are processed on a rolling basis. *Application fee:* $100. Electronic applications accepted. *Application Contact:* Steve Davis, Admissions Counselor, 707-638-5527, Fax: 707-638-5270, E-mail: sdavis@touro.edu.

TOURO UNIVERSITY INTERNATIONAL, Cypress, CA 90630

General Information Independent, coed, university. *Enrollment:* 4,519 matriculated graduate/professional students. *Enrollment by degree level:* 3,957 master's, 562 doctoral. *Graduate faculty:* 223. *Tuition:* Part-time $300 per credit hour. Tuition and fees vary according to course level and program. *Library facilities:* Touro Cyber Library. *Online resources:* web page. *Collection:* 30,692 titles, 1,500 serial subscriptions.

Computer facilities: A campuswide network can be accessed from off campus. Internet access and online class registration are available. *Web address:* http://www.tourou.edu/.

General Application Contact: Wei Ren-Finaly, Registrar, 800-375-9878, Fax: 714-827-7407, E-mail: registration@touro.edu.

GRADUATE UNITS

College of Business Administration Expenses: Contact institution. In 2006, 631 master's, 30 doctorates awarded. *Degree program information:* Part-time and evening/weekend programs available. Postbaccalaureate distance learning degree programs offered (no on-campus study). Offers business administration (PhD); conflict and negotiation management (MBA); criminal justice administration (MBA); entrepreneurship (MBA); finance (MBA); general management (MBA); human resource management (MBA); information technology management (MBA); international business (MBA); logistics management (MBA); public management (MBA); strategic leadership (MBA). *Application deadline:* Applications are processed on a rolling basis. *Application fee:* $75. Electronic applications accepted. *Dean,* Dr. Paul Watkins, 714-816-0366 Ext. 2054, Fax: 714-816-0367, E-mail: infocba@tourou.edu.

College of Education Expenses: Contact institution. In 2006, 193 master's, 13 doctorates awarded. *Degree program information:* Part-time and evening/weekend programs available. Postbaccalaureate distance learning degree programs offered (no on-campus study). Offers adult education (MA Ed); aviation education (MA Ed); children's literacy development (MA Ed); e-learning (MA Ed); e-learning leadership (MA Ed, PhD); early childhood education (MA Ed); education (MA Ed, PhD, Certificate); educational leadership (MA Ed); enrollment management (MA Ed); higher education (MA Ed); higher education leadership (PhD); K-12 leadership (PhD); teaching and instruction (MA Ed); technology and learning (MA Ed); training and development (MA Ed). *Application fee:* $75. *Vice President for Academic Affairs,* Dr. Edith Neumann, 714-816-0366 Ext. 2030, Fax: 714-226-9844, E-mail: eneumann@tourou.edu.

College of Health Sciences Expenses: Contact institution. In 2006, 322 master's, 21 doctorates awarded. *Degree program information:* Part-time and evening/weekend programs available. Postbaccalaureate distance learning degree programs offered (no on-campus study). Offers clinical research administration (MS, Certificate); emergency and disaster management (MS, Certificate); environmental health science (Certificate); health care administration (PhD); health care management (MS); health education (MS, Certificate); health informatics (Certificate); health sciences (PhD); international health (MS); international health: educator or researcher option (PhD); international health: practitioner option (PhD); law and expert witness studies (MS, Certificate); public health (MS); quality assurance (Certificate). *Application fee:* $75. *Vice President for Academic Affairs,* Dr. Edith Neumann, 714-816-0366 Ext. 2030, Fax: 714-226-9844, E-mail: eneumann@tourou.edu.

College of Information Systems Expenses: Contact institution. In 2006, 129 degrees awarded. *Degree program information:* Part-time and evening/weekend programs available. Postbaccalaureate distance learning degree programs offered (no on-campus study). Offers business intelligence (Certificate); information technology management (MS). *Dean,* Dr. Paul Watkins, 800-509-3901, Fax: 714-816-0367, E-mail: infocis@tourou.edu.

TOWSON UNIVERSITY, Towson, MD 21252-0001

General Information State-supported, coed, university. CGS member. *Enrollment:* 18,921 graduate, professional, and undergraduate students; 886 full-time matriculated graduate/professional students (663 women), 2,661 part-time matriculated graduate/professional students (1,976 women). *Enrollment by degree level:* 123 doctoral, 105 other advanced degrees. *Graduate faculty:* 484. Tuition, state resident: part-time $275 per unit. Tuition, nonresident: part-time $577 per unit. *Required fees:* $72 per unit. *Graduate housing:* Rooms and/or apartments available on a first-come, first-served basis to single and married students. *Student services:* Campus employment opportunities, campus safety program, career counseling, child daycare facilities, disabled student services, exercise/wellness program, free psychological counseling, international student services, low-cost health insurance, multicultural affairs office, teacher training, writing training. *Library facilities:* Cook Library. *Online resources:* library catalog, web page, access to other libraries' catalogs. *Collection:* 580,036 titles, 4,154 serial subscriptions, 16,761 audiovisual materials.

Computer facilities: A campuswide network can be accessed from student residence rooms and from off campus. Internet access and online class registration are available. *Web address:* http://www.towson.edu/.

General Application Contact: Fran Musotto, Information Contact, 410-704-2501, Fax: 410-704-4675, E-mail: grads@towson.edu.

GRADUATE UNITS

Graduate School Students: 886 full-time (663 women), 2,661 part-time (1,976 women); includes 534 minority (412 African Americans, 4 American Indian/Alaska Native, 76 Asian Americans or Pacific Islanders, 42 Hispanic Americans), 189 international. Average age 31. 2,141 applicants, 70% accepted, 894 enrolled. Expenses: Contact institution. *Financial support:* Fellowships with full and partial tuition reimbursements, research assistantships with full and partial tuition reimbursements, teaching assistantships with full and partial tuition reimbursements, career-related internships or fieldwork, Federal Work-Study, and unspecified assistantships available. Support available to part-time students. Financial award application deadline: 4/1; financial award applicants required to submit FAFSA. In 2006, 964 master's, 10 doctorates, 145 other advanced degrees awarded. *Degree program information:* Part-time and evening/weekend programs available. Postbaccalaureate distance learning degree programs offered. Offers applied and industrial mathematics (MS); applied gerontology (MS, Certificate); applied information technology (MS, D Sc); art education (M Ed); audiology (Au D); biology (MS); clinical psychology (MA); clinician-administrator transition (Certificate); communications management (MS); computer science (MS); counseling psychology (MA, CAS); Dalcroze (Certificate); early childhood education (M Ed, CAS); educational leadership (Certificate); educational leadership (administrator I certification) (CAS); educational technology (MS); elementary education (M Ed); environmental science (MS, Certificate); experimental psychology (MA); family-professional collaboration (Certificate); geography and environmental planning (MA); health science (MS); human resource development (MS); humanities (MA); information security and assurance (Certificate); information systems management (Certificate); instructional design and training (MS); instructional technology (Ed D); integrated homeland security management (MS); Internet application development (Certificate); Kodaly (Certificate); management and leadership development (Certificate); mathematics education (MS); music education (MS); music performance and composition (MM); networking technologies (Certificate); nursing (MS, Certificate); occupational science (Sc D); occupational therapy (MS); Orff (Certificate); organizational change (CAS); physician assistant studies (MS); professional studies (MA); professional writing (MS); reading (M Ed); reading education (CAS); school library media (MS); school psychology (MA, CAS); science education (MS); secondary education (M Ed); security assessment and management (Certificate); social science (MS); software engineering (Certificate); special education certification (M Ed); special education leadership (M Ed); speech-language pathology (MS); strategic public relations and integrated communications (Certificate); studio arts (MFA); teaching (MAT); theatre (MFA); women's studies (MS). *Application deadline:* For fall admission, 4/15 for international students; for spring admission, 10/15 for international students. Applications are processed on a rolling basis. *Application fee:* $50. Electronic applications accepted. *Application Contact:* 410-704-2501, Fax: 410-704-4675, E-mail: grads@towson.edu. *Dean,* Dr. Jin Gong, 410-704-2501, E-mail: jgong@towson.edu.

Joint University of Baltimore/Towson University (UB/Towson) MBA Program Students: 21 full-time (3 women). Expenses: Contact institution. Offers accounting and business advisory services (MS); business administration (MBA). *Application deadline:* Applications are processed on a rolling basis. *Application fee:* $50. Electronic applications accepted. *Application Contact:* Graduate School, 410-837-4777, E-mail: grads@towson.edu. *Graduate Program Director,* Ron Desi, 410-704-3562, E-mail: rdesi@towson.edu.

TRADITIONAL CHINESE MEDICAL COLLEGE OF HAWAII, Kamuela, HI 96743-2288

General Information Proprietary, coed, graduate-only institution.

GRADUATE UNITS

Graduate Programs

TRENT UNIVERSITY, Peterborough, ON K9J 7B8, Canada

General Information Province-supported, coed, university. *Graduate housing:* Room and/or apartments available to single students; on-campus housing not available to married students. Housing application deadline: 7/10. *Research affiliation:* Watershed Science Centre (watershed studies), Ontario Power Generation, Inc. (acid rain deposition), Enbridge Consumers Gas (ozone depletion), Forensics Laboratory (DNA testing).

GRADUATE UNITS

Graduate Studies *Degree program information:* Part-time programs available. Offers anthropology (MA); applications of modeling in the natural and social sciences (MA); biology (M Sc, PhD); Canadian studies and native studies (MA); chemistry (M Sc); computer studies (M Sc); environmental and resource studies (M Sc, PhD); geography (M Sc, PhD); methodologies for the study of Western history and culture (MA); native studies (PhD); physics (M Sc).

TREVECCA NAZARENE UNIVERSITY, Nashville, TN 37210-2877

General Information Independent-religious, coed, comprehensive institution. *Enrollment:* 2,217 graduate, professional, and undergraduate students; 798 full-time matriculated graduate/professional students (565 women), 172 part-time matriculated graduate/professional students (112 women). *Enrollment by degree level:* 876 master's, 94 doctoral. *Graduate faculty:* 48 full-time (28 women), 66 part-time/adjunct (30 women). *Tuition:* Full-time $6,390; part-time $355 per credit. Tuition and fees vary according to degree level and program. *Graduate housing:* Rooms and/or apartments available to single and married students. Housing application deadline: 6/15. *Student services:* Career counseling, free psychological counseling, teacher training. *Library facilities:* Mackey Library. *Online resources:* library catalog, web page, access to other libraries' catalogs. *Collection:* 110,277 titles, 485 serial subscriptions, 3,758 audiovisual materials.

Computer facilities: 200 computers available on campus for general student use. A campuswide network can be accessed from student residence rooms and from off campus. Internet access is available. *Web address:* http://www.trevecca.edu/.

General Application Contact: Dr. Stephen M. Pusey, Provost and Chief Academic Officer, 615-248-1258, Fax: 615-248-1435, E-mail: spusey@trevecca.edu.

GRADUATE UNITS

Graduate Division Students: 798 full-time (565 women), 172 part-time (112 women); includes 192 minority (171 African Americans, 4 American Indian/Alaska Native, 6 Asian Americans or Pacific Islanders, 11 Hispanic Americans), 4 international. Average age 35. *Faculty:* 48 full-time (28 women), 66 part-time/adjunct (30 women). Expenses: Contact institution. *Financial support:* Applicants required to submit FAFSA. In 2006, 385 master's, 24 doctorates awarded. *Degree program information:* Part-time and evening/weekend programs available. *Application deadline:* Applications are processed on a rolling basis. *Application fee:* $25. *Provost and Chief Academic Officer,* Dr. Stephen M. Pusey, 615-248-1258, Fax: 615-248-1435, E-mail: spusey@trevecca.edu.

Division of Natural and Applied Sciences Students: 66 full-time (49 women); includes 1 minority (African American) Average age 26. *Faculty:* 6 full-time (3 women), 6 part-time/adjunct (4 women). Expenses: Contact institution. *Financial support:* Applicants required to submit FAFSA. In 2006, 32 degrees awarded. Offers natural and applied sciences (MS); physician assistant (MS). *Application deadline:* For fall admission, 11/1 for domestic students. *Application fee:* $45. *Application Contact:* Admissions Coordinator, 615-248-1621, Fax: 615-248-1622, E-mail: admissions_pa@trevecca.edu. *Chair,* Dr. Mike Moredock, 615-248-1261, Fax: 615-248-1622, E-mail: mmoredock@trevecca.edu.

Division of Social and Behavioral Sciences Students: 150 full-time (111 women), 57 part-time (47 women); includes 19 African Americans, 1 American Indian/Alaska Native, 1 Hispanic American. Average age 35. *Faculty:* 6 full-time (5 women), 13 part-time/adjunct (7 women). Expenses: Contact institution. *Financial support:* Applicants required to submit FAFSA. In 2006, 61 degrees awarded. *Degree program information:* Part-time and evening/weekend programs available. Offers counseling (MA); counseling psychology (MA); marriage and family therapy (MMFT). *Application deadline:* Applications are processed on a rolling basis. *Application fee:* $25. *Application Contact:* Joyce Houk, Division of Social and Behavior Sciences, 615-248-1417, Fax: 615-248-1366, E-mail: admissions_psy@trevecca.edu. *Chair,* Dr. Peter Wilson, 615-248-1417, Fax: 615-248-1366, E-mail: pwilson@trevecca.edu.

School of Business and Management Students: 83 full-time (44 women), 18 part-time (9 women); includes 24 minority (19 African Americans, 2 Asian Americans or Pacific Islanders, 3 Hispanic Americans). Average age 36. *Faculty:* 10 full-time (2 women), 1 part-time/adjunct (0 women). Expenses: Contact institution. *Financial support:* Applicants required to submit FAFSA. In 2006, 38 degrees awarded. *Degree program information:* Evening/weekend programs available. Offers business administration (MBA); business and management (MBA, MSM); management (MSM). *Application deadline:* Applications are processed on a rolling basis. *Application fee:* $25. *Application Contact:* Marcus Lackey, Admissions Counselor, 615-248-1529, Fax: 615-248-1700, E-mail: management@trevecca.edu. *Dean,* Dr. Jim Hiatt, 615-248-1256, Fax: 615-248-1700, E-mail: jhiatt@trevecca.edu.

School of Education Students: 465 full-time (355 women), 78 part-time (53 women); includes 139 minority (126 African Americans, 3 American Indian/Alaska Native, 3 Asian Americans or Pacific Islanders, 7 Hispanic Americans), 3 international. Average age 36. *Faculty:* 22 full-time (18 women), 42 part-time/adjunct (19 women). Expenses: Contact institution. *Financial support:* Applicants required to submit FAFSA. In 2006, 240 master's, 24 doctorates awarded. *Degree program information:* Part-time and evening/weekend programs available. Offers educational leadership (M Ed); English language learners (PreK-12) (M Ed); instructional effectiveness (M Ed); instructional technology (M Ed); leadership and professional practice (D Ed); library and information science (MLI Sc); reading PreK-12 (M Ed); teaching (MAT); teaching 7-12 (MAT); teaching K-6 (MAT). *Application deadline:* Applications are processed on a rolling basis. *Application fee:* $50. *Application Contact:* Admissions Office, 615-248-1201, Fax: 615-248-1597, E-mail: admissions_ged@trevecca.edu. *Dean,* Dr. Esther Swink, 615-248-1201, Fax: 615-248-1597, E-mail: eswink@trevecca.edu.

School of Religion and Philosophy Students: 34 full-time (6 women), 19 part-time (3 women); includes 7 minority (6 African Americans, 1 Asian American or Pacific Islander), 1 international. Average age 34. *Faculty:* 4 full-time (0 women), 4 part-time/adjunct (0 women). Expenses: Contact institution. *Financial support:* Applicants required to submit FAFSA. In 2006, 14 degrees awarded. *Degree program information:* Part-time programs available. Offers biblical studies (MA); preaching and practical theology (MA); systematic theology/

historical theology (MA). *Application deadline:* Applications are processed on a rolling basis. *Application fee:* $25. *Application Contact:* Sherry Crutchfield, Secretary for the Department of Religion and Philosophy, 615-248-1378, Fax: 615-248-7417, E-mail: admissions_rel@trevecca.edu. *Dean,* Dr. Tim Green, 615-248-1378, Fax: 615-248-7728, E-mail: tgreen@trevecca.edu.

TRINITY BAPTIST COLLEGE, Jacksonville, FL 32221

General Information Independent, coed, comprehensive institution. *Graduate faculty:* 10. *Library facilities:* Travis Hudson Library. *Collection:* 35,070 titles, 191 serial subscriptions.

Computer facilities: 35 computers available on campus for general student use. A campuswide network can be accessed from student residence rooms and from off campus. Internet access and online class registration are available. *Web address:* http://www.tbc.edu/.

General Application Contact: Michael Nichols, Director of Graduate Studies, 904-596-2449, E-mail: graduatestudies@tbc.edu.

GRADUATE UNITS

Graduate Programs *Faculty:* 10. Expenses: Contact institution. Postbaccalaureate distance learning degree programs offered.

TRINITY COLLEGE, Hartford, CT 06106-3100

General Information Independent, coed, comprehensive institution. *Enrollment:* 2,528 graduate, professional, and undergraduate students; 138 part-time matriculated graduate/professional students (62 women). *Enrollment by degree level:* 138 master's. *Graduate faculty:* 8 full-time (3 women), 12 part-time/adjunct (1 woman). *Tuition:* Part-time $1,500 per course. *Required fees:* $50 per term. One-time fee: $25 part-time. *Graduate housing:* On-campus housing not available. *Student services:* Campus safety program, career counseling, disabled student services, exercise/wellness program, free psychological counseling, multicultural affairs office, writing training. *Library facilities:* Trinity College Library plus 1 other. *Online resources:* library catalog, web page, access to other libraries' catalogs. *Collection:* 1 million titles, 1,813 serial subscriptions, 2,349 audiovisual materials.

Computer facilities: 315 computers available on campus for general student use. A campuswide network can be accessed from student residence rooms and from off campus. Internet access and online class registration, e-mail, Web pages are available. *Web address:* http://www.trincoll.edu/.

General Application Contact: Marilyn Murphy, Program Manager for Graduate Studies, 860-297-2151, Fax: 860-297-5362, E-mail: marilyn.murphy@mail.trincoll.edu.

GRADUATE UNITS

Graduate Programs Average age 38. 57 applicants, 88% accepted, 45 enrolled. *Faculty:* 8 full-time (3 women), 12 part-time/adjunct (1 woman). Expenses: Contact institution. *Financial support:* In 2006–07, 20 students received support, including 20 fellowships with partial tuition reimbursements available (averaging $9,000 per year); scholarships/grants and tuition waivers (full) also available. Support available to part-time students. Financial award application deadline: 4/1; financial award applicants required to submit FAFSA. In 2006, 30 degrees awarded. *Degree program information:* Part-time and evening/weekend programs available. Offers American studies (MA); economics (MA); English (MA); history (MA); public policy studies (MA). *Application deadline:* For fall admission, 4/15 for domestic students; for spring admission, 11/15 for domestic students. *Application fee:* $50. Electronic applications accepted. *Application Contact:* Marilyn Murphy, Program Manager for Graduate Studies, 860-297-2151, Fax: 860-297-5362, E-mail: marilyn.murphy@mail.trincoll.edu. *Dean of Graduate Studies,* Dr. Nancy Birch Wagner, 860-297-2527, Fax: 860-297-2529, E-mail: grad-studies@trincoll.edu.

TRINITY EPISCOPAL SCHOOL FOR MINISTRY, Ambridge, PA 15003-2397

General Information Independent-religious, coed, graduate-only institution. *Enrollment by degree level:* 89 first professional, 32 master's, 6 doctoral, 92 other advanced degrees. *Graduate faculty:* 12 full-time (2 women), 4 part-time/adjunct (2 women). *Tuition:* Full-time $8,850; part-time $295 per credit hour. *Required fees:* $60 per semester. Tuition and fees vary according to degree level. *Graduate housing:* On-campus housing not available. *Student services:* Career counseling, free psychological counseling, international student services, low-cost health insurance, writing training. *Library facilities:* Trinity Library. *Online resources:* library catalog, web page. *Collection:* 91,402 titles, 463 serial subscriptions, 5,071 audiovisual materials.

Computer facilities: 8 computers available on campus for general student use. A campuswide network can be accessed from off campus. Internet access and online class registration are available. *Web address:* http://www.tesm.edu/.

General Application Contact: Rev. Tina Lockett, Director of Admissions/Dean of Students, 724-266-3838 Ext. 219, Fax: 724-266-4617, E-mail: tlockett@tesm.edu.

GRADUATE UNITS

Graduate Programs Students: 104 full-time (31 women), 115 part-time (45 women); includes 11 minority (2 African Americans, 2 Asian Americans or Pacific Islanders, 7 Hispanic Americans), 6 international. Average age 38. 23 applicants, 96% accepted, 16 enrolled. *Faculty:* 12 full-time (2 women), 4 part-time/adjunct (2 women). Expenses: Contact institution. *Financial support:* In 2006–07, 56 students received support. Career-related internships or fieldwork and scholarships/grants available. Financial award application deadline: 6/30; financial award applicants required to submit FAFSA. In 2006, 19 M Divs, 2 master's, 6 doctorates, 4 other advanced degrees awarded. *Degree program information:* Part-time programs available. Offers Anglican studies (Diploma); basic Christian studies (Diploma); divinity (M Div); ministry (D Min); mission and evangelism (MAME, Diploma); religion (MAR); youth ministry (Diploma). *Application deadline:* For fall admission, 8/1 priority date for domestic students, 4/1 for international students; for spring admission, 12/1 for domestic students. Applications are processed on a rolling basis. *Application fee:* $25. *Application Contact:* Rev. Tina Lockett, Director of Admissions/Dean of Students, 724-266-3838 Ext. 219, Fax: 724-266-4617, E-mail: tlockett@tesm.edu. *Interim Academic Dean,* Rev. Dr. Grant LeMarquand, 724-266-3838, Fax: 724-266-4617, E-mail: glemarquand@tesm.edu.

TRINITY INTERNATIONAL UNIVERSITY, Deerfield, IL 60015-1284

General Information Independent-religious, coed, university. *Enrollment:* 2,855 graduate, professional, and undergraduate students; 696 full-time matriculated graduate/professional students (215 women), 912 part-time matriculated graduate/professional students (293 women). *Enrollment by degree level:* 557 first professional, 726 master's, 296 doctoral, 29 other advanced degrees. *Graduate faculty:* 47 full-time (7 women), 128 part-time/adjunct (28 women). *Tuition:* Full-time $13,200; part-time $630 per hour. *Required fees:* $43 per semester. *Graduate housing:* Rooms and/or apartments available on a first-come, first-served basis to single and married students. Typical cost: $2,460 per year ($5,440 including board) for single students; $9,000 per year for married students. *Student services:* Campus employment opportunities, campus safety program, career counseling, child daycare facilities, disabled student services, exercise/wellness program, international student services, low-cost health insurance, multicultural affairs office. *Library facilities:* Rolfing Memorial Library. *Online resources:* library catalog, web page, access to other libraries' catalogs. *Collection:* 245,320 titles, 1,176 serial subscriptions.

Computer facilities: 130 computers available on campus for general student use. A campuswide network can be accessed from student residence rooms and from off campus. Internet access and online class registration are available. *Web address:* http://www.tiu.edu/.

General Application Contact: Ron Campbell, Director of Admissions, 800-345-8337, Fax: 847-317-8097, E-mail: rcampbel@tiu.edu.

GRADUATE UNITS

Trinity Evangelical Divinity School Students: 515 full-time (105 women), 716 part-time (180 women); includes 163 minority (32 African Americans, 1 American Indian/Alaska Native, 119 Asian Americans or Pacific Islanders, 11 Hispanic Americans), 135 international. 489 applicants, 88% accepted, 212 enrolled. *Faculty:* 39 full-time (3 women), 68 part-time/adjunct (10 women). Expenses: Contact institution. *Financial support:* In 2006–07, 929 students received support, including 6 fellowships with partial tuition reimbursements available, 12 teaching assistantships with partial tuition reimbursements available; career-related internships or fieldwork, Federal Work-Study, scholarships/grants, and tuition waivers (partial) also available. Financial award application deadline: 4/1; financial award applicants required to submit FAFSA. In 2006, 76 first professional degrees, 136 master's, 47 doctorates, 31 other advanced degrees awarded. *Degree program information:* Part-time programs available. Postbaccalaureate distance learning degree programs offered (minimal on-campus study). Offers Biblical and Near Eastern archaeology and languages (MA); Christian studies (MA, Certificate); Christian thought (MA); church history (MA, Th M); congregational ministry: pastor-teacher (M Div); congregational ministry: team ministry (M Div); counseling ministries (MA); counseling psychology (MA); cross-cultural ministry (M Div); educational studies (PhD); evangelism (MA); general studies (MAR); history of Christianity in America (MA); intercultural studies (MA, PhD); leadership and ministry management (D Min); military chaplaincy (D Min); ministry (MA); mission and evangelism (Th M); missions and evangelism (D Min); New Testament (MA, Th M); Old Testament (Th M); Old Testament and Semitic languages (MA); pastoral care (M Div); pastoral care and counseling (D Min); pastoral counseling and psychology (Th M); pastoral theology (Th M); philosophy of religion (MA); preaching (D Min); research ministry (M Div); systematic theology (Th M); theological studies (PhD); urban ministry (MA, MAR). *Application deadline:* For fall admission, 7/15 priority date for domestic and international students. Applications are processed on a rolling basis. *Application fee:* $25. Electronic applications accepted. *Application Contact:* Ron Campbell, Director of Admissions, 800-345-8337, Fax: 847-317-8097, E-mail: rcampbel@tiu.edu. *Academic Dean,* Dr. Tite Tiénou, 847-317-8086, Fax: 847-317-8014, E-mail: ttienou@teds.edu.

Trinity Graduate School Students: 109 full-time (85 women), 130 part-time (81 women). *Faculty:* 5 full-time (4 women), 39 part-time/adjunct (13 women). Expenses: Contact institution. *Financial support:* Career-related internships or fieldwork, Federal Work-Study, institutionally sponsored loans, and tuition waivers (partial) available. Support available to part-time students. Financial award application deadline: 4/1; financial award applicants required to submit FAFSA. In 2006, 29 degrees awarded. *Degree program information:* Part-time and evening/weekend programs available. Postbaccalaureate distance learning degree programs offered (minimal on-campus study). Offers bioethics (MA); communication and culture (MA); counseling psychology (MA); instructional leadership (M Ed); teaching (MA). *Application deadline:* For fall admission, 7/15 priority date for domestic and international students. Applications are processed on a rolling basis. *Application fee:* $25. Electronic applications accepted. *Application Contact:* Ken Botton, Director of Enrollment Services for University Records and Graduate Admissions, 800-533-0975, Fax: 847-317-8097, E-mail: kbotton@tiu.edu. *Academic Dean,* Dr. James Stamoolis, 847-317-7001, Fax: 847-317-4786.

Trinity Law School Students: 107 full-time (54 women), 65 part-time (32 women). *Faculty:* 3 full-time (0 women), 21 part-time/adjunct (5 women). Expenses: Contact institution. *Financial support:* Scholarships/grants available. Financial award application deadline: 8/15; financial award applicants required to submit FAFSA. In 2006, 37 degrees awarded. *Degree program information:* Part-time and evening/weekend programs available. Offers law (JD). *Application deadline:* For fall admission, 5/1 priority date for domestic and international students; for spring admission, 12/1 priority date for domestic and international students. Applications are processed on a rolling basis. *Application fee:* $30. *Application Contact:* Joseph Wyse, Director of Admissions and Records, 714-796-7141, Fax: 714-796-7190, E-mail: jwyse@tiu.edu. *Academic Dean,* Kevin P. Holsclaw, 714-836-7160, Fax: 714-796-7190, E-mail: kholscla@tiu.edu.

TRINITY INTERNATIONAL UNIVERSITY, SOUTH FLORIDA CAMPUS, Miami, FL 33132-1996

General Information Independent-religious, coed, graduate-only institution. *Graduate housing:* On-campus housing not available.

GRADUATE UNITS

Program in Counseling Psychology Offers counseling psychology (MA).

Program in Religion Offers religion (MA).

TRINITY LUTHERAN SEMINARY, Columbus, OH 43209-2334

General Information Independent-religious, coed, graduate-only institution. *Enrollment by degree level:* 132 first professional, 27 master's. *Graduate faculty:* 20 full-time (9 women), 23 part-time/adjunct (5 women). *Tuition:* Full-time $9,900; part-time $225 per credit. *Required fees:* $60 per quarter. One-time fee: $100 full-time. *Graduate housing:* Rooms and/or apartments available on a first-come, first-served basis to single and married students. Typical cost: $3,080 per year for single students; $3,935 per year for married students. Housing application deadline: 5/15. *Student services:* Campus employment opportunities, international student services, low-cost health insurance, writing training. *Library facilities:* Hamma Library. *Online resources:* library catalog, web page, access to other libraries' catalogs. *Collection:* 137,107 titles, 450 serial subscriptions, 6,349 audiovisual materials.

Computer facilities: 10 computers available on campus for general student use. A campuswide network can be accessed from student residence rooms and from off campus. Internet access is available. *Web address:* http://www.trinitylutheranseminary.edu/.

General Application Contact: Rev. Sheri L. Ayers, Director of Admissions, 614-235-4136 Ext. 4614, Fax: 866-610-8572, E-mail: sayers@trinitylutheranseminary.edu.

GRADUATE UNITS

Graduate and Professional Programs Students: 107 full-time (47 women), 52 part-time (31 women); includes 20 minority (18 African Americans, 1 Asian American or Pacific Islander, 1 Hispanic American), 3 international. Average age 37. 62 applicants, 92% accepted, 44 enrolled. *Faculty:* 20 full-time (9 women), 23 part-time/adjunct (5 women). Expenses: Contact institution. *Financial support:* In 2006–07, 117 students received support. Career-related internships or fieldwork, Federal Work-Study, institutionally sponsored loans, and scholarships/grants available. Support available to part-time students. Financial award application deadline: 5/1; financial award applicants required to submit FAFSA. In 2006, 40 M Divs, 7 master's awarded. *Degree program information:* Part-time programs available. Offers church music (MA); divinity (M Div); lay ministry (MA); sacred theology (STM); theological studies (MTS). *Application deadline:* For fall admission, 7/15 priority date for domestic students. Applications are processed on a rolling basis. *Application fee:* $25. *Application Contact:* Rev. Sheri L. Ayers, Director of Admissions, 614-235-4136 Ext. 4614, Fax: 866-610-8572, E-mail: sayers@trinitylutheranseminary.edu. *Dean,* Dr. Donald L. Huber, 614-235-4136, Fax: 614-236-3129, E-mail: dhuber@trinitylutheranseminary.edu.

TRINITY UNIVERSITY, San Antonio, TX 78212-7200

General Information Independent-religious, coed, comprehensive institution. CGS member. *Enrollment:* 2,693 graduate, professional, and undergraduate students; 119 full-time matriculated graduate/professional students (78 women), 107 part-time matriculated graduate/professional students (66 women). *Enrollment by degree level:* 226 master's. *Graduate faculty:* 15 full-time (7 women), 21 part-time/adjunct (12 women). *Graduate housing:* On-campus housing not available. *Student services:* Campus employment opportunities, campus safety program, career counseling, disabled student services, free psychological counseling, international student services. *Library facilities:* Elizabeth Huth Coates Library. *Online resources:* library catalog, web page, access to other libraries' catalogs. *Collection:* 937,261 titles, 2,118 serial subscriptions, 27,653 audiovisual materials.

Computer facilities: 450 computers available on campus for general student use. A campuswide network can be accessed from student residence rooms and from off campus. Internet access and online class registration are available. *Web address:* http://www.trinity.edu/.

General Application Contact: Dr. Mary E. Stefl, Chair, 210-999-8424, Fax: 210-999-8108, E-mail: mstefl@trinity.edu.

Trinity University (continued)

GRADUATE UNITS

Department of Business Administration Students: 21 full-time (13 women), 2 part-time (1 woman); includes 4 minority (all Hispanic Americans), 1 international. Average age 23. *Faculty:* 4 full-time (2 women). Expenses: Contact institution. *Financial support:* In 2006–07, 12 research assistantships were awarded. Financial award application deadline: 4/1. In 2006, 27 degrees awarded. *Degree program information:* Part-time programs available. Offers accounting (MS). *Application deadline:* For fall admission, 2/1 priority date for domestic students. *Application fee:* $40. *Director of the Accounting Program,* Dr. Petrea K. Sandlin, 210-999-7296, Fax: 210-999-8134, E-mail: psandlin@trinity.edu.

Department of Education Students: 48 full-time (39 women), 43 part-time (33 women); includes 26 minority (3 Asian Americans or Pacific Islanders, 23 Hispanic Americans). Average age 28. *Faculty:* 6 full-time (4 women), 16 part-time/adjunct (11 women). Expenses: Contact institution. *Financial support:* Fellowships, research assistantships, teaching assistantships, career-related internships or fieldwork, Federal Work-Study, institutionally sponsored loans, and scholarships/grants available. Support available to part-time students. Financial award application deadline: 4/1. In 2006, 66 degrees awarded. *Degree program information:* Part-time and evening/weekend programs available. Offers school administration (M Ed); school psychology (MA); teacher education (MAT). *Application deadline:* For fall admission, 5/1 priority date for domestic students. *Application fee:* $30. *Chair,* Dr. Paul Kelleher, 210-999-7501, Fax: 210-999-7592, E-mail: paul.kelleher@trinity.edu.

Department of Health Care Administration Students: 50 full-time (26 women), 50 part-time (20 women); includes 23 minority (8 African Americans, 7 Asian Americans or Pacific Islanders, 8 Hispanic Americans), 2 international. Average age 28. *Faculty:* 5 full-time (1 woman), 5 part-time/adjunct (1 woman). Expenses: Contact institution. *Financial support:* In 2006–07, 9 research assistantships (averaging $9,500 per year) were awarded; career-related internships or fieldwork, institutionally sponsored loans, traineeships, and unspecified assistantships also available. Financial award application deadline: 4/1. In 2006, 27 degrees awarded. *Degree program information:* Part-time programs available. Postbaccalaureate distance learning degree programs offered (minimal on-campus study). Offers health care administration (MS). *Application deadline:* For fall admission, 6/1 priority date for domestic students. Applications are processed on a rolling basis. *Application fee:* $30. *Application Contact:* Sharon Hubenak, Director of Recruiting and Residencies, 210-999-8107, Fax: 210-999-8108, E-mail: shubenak@trinity.edu. *Chair,* Dr. Mary E. Stefl, 210-999-8424, Fax: 210-999-8108, E-mail: mstefl@trinity.edu.

TRINITY (WASHINGTON) UNIVERSITY, Washington, DC 20017-1094

General Information Independent-religious, Undergraduate: women only; graduate: coed, comprehensive institution. *Graduate housing:* Room and/or apartments available on a first-come, first-served basis to single students; on-campus housing not available to married students.

GRADUATE UNITS

School of Education *Degree program information:* Part-time and evening/weekend programs available. Offers democracy, diversity, and social justice (M Ed); early childhood (MAT); educational administration (MSA); elementary education (MAT); English as a second language (M Ed, MAT); literacy and reading education (M Ed); school counseling (MA); secondary education (MAT); special education (MAT).

School of Professional Studies *Degree program information:* Part-time and evening/weekend programs available. Offers business administration (MBA); communication (MA); information security management (MS); organizational management (MSA).

TRINITY WESTERN UNIVERSITY, Langley, BC V2Y 1Y1, Canada

General Information Independent-religious, coed, comprehensive institution. *Graduate housing:* Room and/or apartments available to single students; on-campus housing not available to married students. Housing application deadline: 7/6. *Research affiliation:* Department of National Defense (polymers), Department of Wildlife (weeds).

GRADUATE UNITS

ACTS Seminaries *Degree program information:* Part-time programs available. Offers Christian studies (MA); church ministries (MA); cross cultural ministries (MA); theology (M Div, M Th, MC, MLE, MTS).

Program in Biblical Studies *Degree program information:* Part-time programs available. Offers biblical studies (MA).

Program in Counseling Psychology *Degree program information:* Part-time programs available. Offers counseling psychology (MA).

Program in Leadership Postbaccalaureate distance learning degree programs offered (minimal on-campus study). Offers leadership (MA).

Program in Teaching English as a Second or Other Language (TESOL) Offers teaching English as a second or other language (MA).

TRI STATE COLLEGE OF ACUPUNCTURE, New York, NY 10011

General Information Independent, coed, graduate-only institution. *Graduate housing:* On-campus housing not available.

GRADUATE UNITS

Program in Acupuncture *Degree program information:* Evening/weekend programs available. Offers acupuncture (MS); oriental medicine (MS); traditional Chinese herbology (Certificate).

TRI-STATE UNIVERSITY, Angola, IN 46703-1764

General Information Independent, coed, comprehensive institution. *Graduate housing:* Room and/or apartments available on a first-come, first-served basis to single students; on-campus housing not available to married students. Housing application deadline: 8/1.

GRADUATE UNITS

Department of Engineering Technology *Degree program information:* Part-time and evening/weekend programs available. Offers engineering technology (MS).

TROY UNIVERSITY, Troy, AL 36082

General Information State-supported, coed, comprehensive institution. *Enrollment:* 27,938 graduate, professional, and undergraduate students; 2,748 full-time matriculated graduate/professional students (1,955 women), 5,121 part-time matriculated graduate/professional students (3,294 women). *Enrollment by degree level:* 7,624 master's, 245 other advanced degrees. Tuition, state resident: full-time $4,368; part-time $182 per hour. Tuition, nonresident: full-time $8,736; part-time $364 per hour. *Required fees:* $50 per term. *Graduate housing:* Rooms and/or apartments available to single and married students. Typical cost: $2,350 per year ($4,920 including board) for single students; $3,840 per year ($6,410 including board) for married students. Housing application deadline: 7/31. *Student services:* Campus employment opportunities, campus safety program, career counseling, child daycare facilities, disabled student services, free psychological counseling, international student services, low-cost health insurance, writing training. *Library facilities:* Wallace Library plus 3 others. *Online resources:* library catalog, web page, access to other libraries' catalogs. *Collection:* 504,716 titles, 3,263 serial subscriptions, 19,532 audiovisual materials. *Research affiliation:* Birmingham Audubon Society (Alabama flora and fauna), Systemics Research Fund (protozoan symbionts).

Computer facilities: 557 computers available on campus for general student use. A campuswide network can be accessed from student residence rooms and from off campus. Internet access is available. *Web address:* http://www.troy.edu/.

General Application Contact: Brenda K. Campbell, Director of Graduate Admissions, 334-670-3178, Fax: 334-670-3733, E-mail: bcamp@troy.edu.

GRADUATE UNITS

Graduate School Students: 2,748 full-time (1,955 women), 5,121 part-time (3,294 women); includes 3,999 minority (3,575 African Americans, 38 American Indian/Alaska Native, 152 Asian Americans or Pacific Islanders, 234 Hispanic Americans), 140 international. Average age 33. Expenses: Contact institution. *Financial support:* Fellowships, career-related internships or fieldwork available. Support available to part-time students. Financial award application deadline: 5/1; financial award applicants required to submit FAFSA. In 2006, 3,442 master's, 183 other advanced degrees awarded. *Degree program information:* Part-time and evening/weekend programs available. Offers business administration (EMBA, MBA); human resources management (MS); management (MS, MSM). *Application deadline:* For fall admission, 6/1 for international students; for spring admission, 10/15 for international students. Applications are processed on a rolling basis. *Application fee:* $50. Electronic applications accepted. *Application Contact:* Brenda K. Campbell, Director of Graduate Admissions, 334-670-3178, Fax: 334-670-3733, E-mail: bcamp@troy.edu. *Associate Provost/Dean of Graduate School,* Dr. Dianne Barron, 334-670-3189, Fax: 334-370-3912, E-mail: dlbarron@troy.edu.

College of Arts and Sciences Students: 353 full-time (230 women), 1,295 part-time (824 women); includes 748 minority (594 African Americans, 9 American Indian/Alaska Native, 63 Asian Americans or Pacific Islanders, 82 Hispanic Americans). Average age 33. Expenses: Contact institution. *Financial support:* Available to part-time students. Applicants required to submit FAFSA. In 2006, 519 degrees awarded. *Degree program information:* Part-time and evening/weekend programs available. Offers administration of criminal justice (MS); arts and sciences (MPA, MS); computer and information science (MS); environmental analysis and management (MS); international relations (MS); public administration (MPA). *Application deadline:* For fall admission, 6/1 for international students; for spring admission, 10/15 for international students. Applications are processed on a rolling basis. *Application fee:* $50. Electronic applications accepted. *Application Contact:* Brenda K. Campbell, Director of Graduate Admissions, 334-670-3178, Fax: 334-670-3733, E-mail: bcamp@troy.edu. *Interim Dean,* Dr. Don Jeffrey, 334-670-3399, Fax: 334-670-3673, E-mail: djeffr@troy.edu.

College of Business Students: 1,274 full-time (604 women), 1,592 part-time (818 women); includes 1,615 minority (1,410 African Americans, 13 American Indian/Alaska Native, 97 Asian Americans or Pacific Islanders, 95 Hispanic Americans). Average age 33. Expenses: Contact institution. *Financial support:* In 2006–07, 5 research assistantships were awarded; career-related internships or fieldwork also available. Support available to part-time students. Financial award applicants required to submit FAFSA. In 2006, 1148 degrees awarded. *Degree program information:* Part-time and evening/weekend programs available. Postbaccalaureate distance learning degree programs offered. Offers business administration (EMBA, MBA); human resource management (MS); management (MS, MSM). *Application deadline:* Applications are processed on a rolling basis. *Application fee:* $50. Electronic applications accepted. *Application Contact:* Brenda K. Campbell, Director of Graduate Admissions, 334-670-3178, Fax: 334-670-3733, E-mail: bcamp@troy.edu. *Dean,* Dr. Don Hines, 334-670-3143, Fax: 334-670-3708, E-mail: dhines@troy.edu.

College of Communication and Fine Arts Expenses: Contact institution. In 2006, 6 degrees awarded. Offers communication and fine arts (MS). *Application deadline:* For fall admission, 6/1 for international students; for spring admission, 10/15 for international students. *Application fee:* $50. *Application Contact:* Brenda K. Campbell, Director of Graduate Admissions, 334-670-3178, Fax: 334-670-3733, E-mail: bcamp@troy.edu. *Dean,* Dr. Maryjo Cochran, 334-670-3869, Fax: 334-670-3547, E-mail: macochran@troy.edu.

College of Education Students: 1,042 full-time (852 women), 1,548 part-time (1,189 women); includes 1,332 minority (1,149 African Americans, 116 American Indian/Alaska Native, 16 Asian Americans or Pacific Islanders, 51 Hispanic Americans). Average age 35. Expenses: Contact institution. *Financial support:* Career-related internships or fieldwork available. Support available to part-time students. Financial award applicants required to submit FAFSA. In 2006, 1,735 master's, 183 other advanced degrees awarded. *Degree program information:* Part-time and evening/weekend programs available. Offers adult education (MS); clinical mental health (MS); community counseling (MS, Ed S); counselor education (MS); early childhood education (MS, MSE, Ed S); education (M Ed, ME, MS, MSE, Ed S); educational administration/leadership (MS, Ed S); guidance services (MS); K–6 elementary and collaborative education (MS, MSE, Ed S); postsecondary education (M Ed); rehabilitation counseling (Ed S); school counseling (Ed S); school psychology (MS); secondary education (MS, Ed S); student affairs counseling (MS); teacher education-multiple levels (MS, Ed S). *Application deadline:* For fall admission, 6/1 for international students; for spring admission, 10/15 for international students. Applications are processed on a rolling basis. *Application fee:* $50. Electronic applications accepted. *Application Contact:* Brenda K. Campbell, Director of Graduate Admissions, 334-670-3178, Fax: 334-670-3733, E-mail: bcamp@troy.edu. *Interim Dean,* Dr. Lance Tatum, 334-670-3365, Fax: 334-670-3474, E-mail: ltatum@troy.edu.

College of Health and Human Services Students: 50 full-time (39 women), 109 part-time (79 women); includes 56 minority (55 African Americans, 1 American Indian/Alaska Native). Average age 32. Expenses: Contact institution. *Financial support:* In 2006–07, 4 students received support. Tuition waivers and unspecified assistantships available. Support available to part-time students. Financial award application deadline: 4/5; financial award applicants required to submit FAFSA. In 2006, 34 degrees awarded. *Degree program information:* Part-time and evening/weekend programs available. Offers health and human services (MS, MSN); nursing (MSN); sport and fitness management (MS). *Application deadline:* Applications are processed on a rolling basis. *Application fee:* $50. Electronic applications accepted. *Application Contact:* Brenda K. Campbell, Director of Graduate Admissions, 334-670-3178, Fax: 334-670-3733, E-mail: bcamp@troy.edu. *Interim Dean,* Dr. Edith Smith, 334-670-3712, Fax: 334-670-3743, E-mail: esmith@troy.edu.

TRUMAN STATE UNIVERSITY, Kirksville, MO 63501-4221

General Information State-supported, coed, comprehensive institution. CGS member. *Graduate housing:* Rooms and/or apartments available on a first-come, first-served basis to single and married students. Housing application deadline: 5/1. *Research affiliation:* Gulf Coast Research Laboratory (marine science), Kirksville College of Osteopathic Medicine (biology).

GRADUATE UNITS

Graduate School Electronic applications accepted.

Division of Business and Accountancy Offers accountancy (M Ac); accounting (M Ac). Electronic applications accepted.

Division of Education Offers education (MAE). Electronic applications accepted.

Division of Fine Arts Offers music (MA). Electronic applications accepted.

Division of Human Potential and Performance Offers communication disorders (MA). Electronic applications accepted.

Division of Language and Literature Offers English (MA). Electronic applications accepted.

Division of Science Offers biology (MS). Electronic applications accepted.

See Close-Up on page 1061.

TUFTS UNIVERSITY, Medford, MA 02155

General Information Independent, coed, university. CGS member. *Enrollment:* 9,638 graduate, professional, and undergraduate students; 3,823 full-time matriculated graduate/professional students (2,250 women), 468 part-time matriculated graduate/professional students (242 women). *Enrollment by degree level:* 1,666 first professional, 1,770 master's, 826 doctoral, 29 other advanced degrees. *Graduate faculty:* 789 full-time, 419 part-time/adjunct. *Tuition:* Full-time $33,672. Tuition and fees vary according to degree level and program. *Graduate housing:* Room and/or apartments available on a first-come, first-served basis to single students; on-campus housing not available to married students. Typical cost: $5,814 per year. Room charges vary according to housing facility selected. *Student services:* Campus employment opportunities, campus safety program, career counseling, child daycare facilities, disabled student services, exercise/wellness program, free psychological counseling, international student services, low-cost health insurance, multicultural affairs office, teacher training, writing training. *Library facilities:* Tisch Library plus 1 other. *Online resources:* library catalog, web page, access to other libraries' catalogs. *Collection:* 1.7 million titles, 4,341 serial subscriptions, 40,307 audiovisual materials. *Research affiliation:* Baystate Medical Center (medicine), Lahey Clinic Medical Center (medicine), Tufts-New England medical Center (medicine), Caritas St. Elizabeth's Medical Center (medicine), The Stockholm Environmental Institute (environmental science and policy).

Computer facilities: 254 computers available on campus for general student use. A campuswide network can be accessed from student residence rooms and from off campus. Internet access and online class registration are available. *Web address:* http://www.tufts.edu/.

General Application Contact: Information Contact, 617-628-5000.

GRADUATE UNITS

Cummings School of Veterinary Medicine Students: 345 full-time (297 women); includes 28 minority (2 African Americans, 24 Asian Americans or Pacific Islanders, 2 Hispanic Americans). Average age 27. 736 applicants, 25% accepted, 104 enrolled. *Faculty:* 85 full-time (35 women), 147 part-time/adjunct (59 women). Expenses: Contact institution. *Financial support:* In 2006–07, 68 students received support, including 6 research assistantships with full tuition reimbursements available (averaging $20,774 per year), 2 teaching assistantships (averaging $5,000 per year); career-related internships or fieldwork, Federal Work-Study, institutionally sponsored loans, scholarships/grants, and institutional aid awards also available. Financial award application deadline: 3/10. In 2006, 77 DVMs, 10 master's awarded. Offers animals and public policy (MS); comparative biomedical sciences (PhD); veterinary medicine (DVM, MS, PhD). *Application deadline:* For fall admission, 11/1 for domestic and international students. *Application fee:* $60. Electronic applications accepted. *Application Contact:* Rebecca Russo, Director of Admissions, 508-839-7920, Fax: 508-839-2953, E-mail: rebecca.russo@tufts.edu. *Dean,* Dr. Deborah T. Kochevar, 508-839-5302, Fax: 508-839-2953, E-mail: deborah.kochevar@tufts.edu.

Fletcher School of Law and Diplomacy Students: 527 full-time (268 women), 9 part-time (4 women); includes 61 minority (12 African Americans, 1 American Indian/Alaska Native, 32 Asian Americans or Pacific Islanders, 16 Hispanic Americans), 212 international. Average age 31. 1,605 applicants, 40% accepted, 234 enrolled. *Faculty:* 34 full-time (7 women), 31 part-time/adjunct (8 women). Expenses: Contact institution. *Financial support:* Federal Work-Study, institutionally sponsored loans, scholarships/grants, and tuition waivers (partial) available. Financial award application deadline: 1/15; financial award applicants required to submit FAFSA. In 2006, 203 master's, 10 doctorates awarded. Postbaccalaureate distance learning degree programs offered (minimal on-campus study). Offers law and diplomacy (MA, MAHA, MALD, PhD). *Application deadline:* For fall admission, 1/15 for domestic and international students; for spring admission, 10/15 for domestic and international students. *Application fee:* $65. Electronic applications accepted. *Application Contact:* Laurie A. Hurley, Director of Admissions and Financial Aid, 617-627-2410, Fax: 617-627-3712, E-mail: fletcheradmissions@tufts.edu. *Dean,* Stephen W. Bosworth, 617-627-3050, Fax: 617-627-3712.

The Gerald J. and Dorothy R. Friedman School of Nutrition Science and Policy Students: 183 full-time (155 women), 14 part-time (12 women); includes 20 minority (2 African Americans, 12 Asian Americans or Pacific Islanders, 6 Hispanic Americans), 24 international. Average age 29. 257 applicants, 48% accepted, 63 enrolled. *Faculty:* 12 full-time (8 women), 98 part-time/adjunct (45 women). Expenses: Contact institution. *Financial support:* In 2006–07, 169 students received support, including 3 fellowships with full and partial tuition reimbursements available (averaging $20,000 per year), 36 research assistantships with full and partial tuition reimbursements available (averaging $20,000 per year), teaching assistantships with full and partial tuition reimbursements available (averaging $2,000 per year); career-related internships or fieldwork, Federal Work-Study, institutionally sponsored loans, scholarships/grants, traineeships, health care benefits, and unspecified assistantships also available. Support available to part-time students. Financial award applicants required to submit FAFSA. In 2006, 68 master's, 12 doctorates awarded. *Degree program information:* Part-time programs available. Offers humanitarian assistance (MAHA); nutrition (MS, PhD). *Application deadline:* For fall admission, 1/15 priority date for domestic and international students. Applications are processed on a rolling basis. *Application fee:* $65. Electronic applications accepted. *Application Contact:* Kristina S. Bonanno, Coordinator of Admissions and Recruitment, 617-636-3777, Fax: 617-636-3600, E-mail: nutritionadmissions@tufts.edu. *Director of Student Affairs,* Stacey M. Herman, 617-636-3711, Fax: 617-636-3600, E-mail: stacey.herman@tufts.edu.

Graduate School of Arts and Sciences Students: 1,028 (735 women); includes 139 minority (42 African Americans, 54 Asian Americans or Pacific Islanders, 43 Hispanic Americans) 129 international. Average age 29. 1,891 applicants, 46% accepted, 378 enrolled. *Faculty:* 295 full-time, 188 part-time/adjunct. Expenses: Contact institution. *Financial support:* Fellowships with full and partial tuition reimbursements, research assistantships with full and partial tuition reimbursements, teaching assistantships with full and partial tuition reimbursements, career-related internships or fieldwork, Federal Work-Study, scholarships/grants, tuition waivers (full and partial), and unspecified assistantships available. Support available to part-time students. Financial award applicants required to submit FAFSA. In 2006, 332 master's, 36 doctorates, 12 other advanced degrees awarded. *Degree program information:* Part-time and evening/weekend programs available. Offers analytical chemistry (MS, PhD); applied developmental psychology (PhD); art history (MA); arts and sciences (MA, MAT, MFA, MPP, MS, OTD, PhD, CAGS, Certificate); bioengineering (Certificate); biology (MS, PhD); bioorganic chemistry (MS, PhD); biotechnology (Certificate); biotechnology engineering (Certificate); child development (MA, CAGS); classical archaeology (MA); classics (MA); community development (MA); community environmental studies (Certificate); computer science (Certificate); computer science minor (Certificate); dance (MA, PhD); drama (MA); dramatic literature and criticism (PhD); early childhood education (MAT); economics (MA); education (MA, MAT, MS, PhD); elementary education (MAT); English (MA, PhD); environmental chemistry (MS, PhD); environmental management (Certificate); environmental policy (MA); epidemiology (Certificate); ethnomusicology (MA); French (MA); German (MA); health and human welfare (MA); history (MA, PhD); housing policy (MA); human-computer interaction (Certificate); inorganic chemistry (MS, PhD); international environment/development policy (MA); management of community organizations (Certificate); manufacturing engineering (Certificate); mathematics (MA, MS, PhD); microwave and wireless engineering (Certificate); middle and secondary education (MA, MAT); museum studies (Certificate); music history and literature (MA); music theory and composition (MA); occupational therapy (Certificate); organic chemistry (MS, PhD); philosophy (MA); physical chemistry (MS, PhD); physics (MS, PhD); program evaluation (Certificate); psychology (MS, PhD); public policy (MPP); public policy and citizen participation (MA); school psychology (MA, CAGS); secondary education (MA); studio art (MFA); theater history (PhD). *Application deadline:* For fall admission, 1/15 priority date for domestic students, 12/30 for international students. Applications are processed on a rolling basis. *Application fee:* $70. Electronic applications accepted. *Deam,* Lynne Pepall, 617-327-3395, Fax: 617-627-3016, E-mail: gradschool@ase.tufts.edu.

Sackler School of Graduate Biomedical Sciences Students: 224 full-time (142 women), 1 part-time; includes 34 minority (4 African Americans, 1 American Indian/Alaska Native, 23 Asian Americans or Pacific Islanders, 6 Hispanic Americans), 49 international. Average age 28. 703 applicants, 12% accepted, 32 enrolled. *Faculty:* 172 full-time (50 women). Expenses: Contact institution. *Financial support:* In 2006–07, 225 students received support, including 225 research assistantships with full tuition reimbursements available (averaging $29,000 per year); scholarships/grants, health care benefits, and tuition waivers (full and partial) also available. Financial award application deadline: 1/15. In 2006, 18 master's, 34 doctorates awarded. Offers biochemistry (PhD); biomedical sciences (MS, PhD); cell, molecular and developmental biology (PhD); cellular and molecular physiology (PhD); genetics (PhD); immunology (PhD); integrated studies (PhD); molecular microbiology (PhD); neuroscience (PhD); pharmacology and experimental therapeutics (PhD). *Application deadline:* For fall admission, 1/15 priority date for domestic and international students. Applications are processed on a rolling basis. *Application fee:* $65. Electronic applications accepted. *Application Contact:* 617-636-6767, Fax: 617-636-0375, E-mail: sackler-school@tufts.edu. *Dean,* Naomi Rosenberg, 617-636-6767, Fax: 617-636-0375, E-mail: naomi.rosenberg@tufts.edu.

Division of Clinical Care Research Students: 19 full-time (10 women), 1 part-time; includes 3 minority (all Asian Americans or Pacific Islanders), 3 international. Average age 34. 19 applicants, 47% accepted, 8 enrolled. *Faculty:* 33 full-time (10 women). Expenses: Contact institution. *Financial support:* In 2006–07, 20 fellowships with full tuition reimbursements (averaging $44,000 per year) were awarded. Financial award application deadline: 1/15. In 2006, 13 master's, 1 doctorate awarded. *Degree program information:* Part-time programs available. Offers clinical care research (MS, PhD). *Application deadline:* For fall admission, 1/15 priority date for domestic and international students. Applications are processed on a rolling basis. *Application fee:* $65. Electronic applications accepted. *Application Contact:* 617-636-6767, Fax: 617-636-0375, E-mail: sackler-school@tufts.edu. *Program Director,* Dr. Harry P. Selker, 617-636-5009, Fax: 617-636-8023, E-mail: hselker@lifespan.org.

School of Dental Medicine Offers dental medicine (DMD, MS, Certificate); dentistry (Certificate).

School of Engineering Students: 504 (163 women); includes 50 minority (5 African Americans, 34 Asian Americans or Pacific Islanders, 11 Hispanic Americans) 112 international. 593 applicants, 50% accepted, 150 enrolled. *Faculty:* 67 full-time, 34 part-time/adjunct. Expenses: Contact institution. *Financial support:* Fellowships with full tuition reimbursements, research assistantships with full and partial tuition reimbursements, teaching assistantships with full and partial tuition reimbursements, Federal Work-Study, scholarships/grants, and tuition waivers (partial) available. Support available to part-time students. Financial award application deadline: 1/15; financial award applicants required to submit FAFSA. In 2006, 154 master's, 12 doctorates awarded. *Degree program information:* Part-time programs available. Offers biomedical engineering (ME, MS, PhD); chemical and biological engineering (ME, MS, PhD); civil engineering (ME, MS, PhD); computer science (MS, PhD); electrical engineering (MS, PhD); engineering (ME, MS, MSEM, PhD); environmental engineering (ME, MS, PhD); human factors (MS); mechanical engineering (ME, MS, PhD). *Application deadline:* For fall admission, 1/15 priority date for domestic students, 12/30 for international students; for spring admission, 10/15 for domestic students, 9/15 for international students. Applications are processed on a rolling basis. *Application fee:* $70. Electronic applications accepted. *Dean,* Linda Abriola, 617-627-3237, Fax: 617-627-3819.

The Gordon Institute Students: 106 (26 women); includes 1 minority (Asian American or Pacific Islander) 15 international. 61 applicants, 79% accepted, 40 enrolled. *Faculty:* 7 part-time/adjunct. Expenses: Contact institution. *Financial support:* Fellowships with full tuition reimbursements available. In 2006, 33 degrees awarded. *Degree program information:* Part-time programs available. Offers engineering management (MSEM). *Application deadline:* For fall admission, 3/15 priority date for domestic students. Applications are processed on a rolling basis. *Application fee:* $70. Electronic applications accepted. *Director,* Arthur Winston, 617-627-3111, Fax: 617-627-3180, E-mail: a.winston@tufts.edu.

School of Medicine Expenses: Contact institution. Offers biomedical sciences (MS); health communication (MS); medicine (MD, MPH, MS); pain research, education and policy (MS); public health (MPH). *Dean,* Dr. Michael Rosenblatt, 617-636-6565.

See Close-Up on page 1063.

TULANE UNIVERSITY, New Orleans, LA 70118-5669

General Information Independent, coed, university. CGS member. *Enrollment:* 10,606 graduate, professional, and undergraduate students; 7,110 full-time matriculated graduate/professional students (3,543 women), 1,172 part-time matriculated graduate/professional students (510 women). *Graduate faculty:* 1,428. *Graduate housing:* Rooms and/or apartments available on a first-come, first-served basis to single and married students. Housing application deadline: 3/24. *Student services:* Campus safety program, career counseling, child daycare facilities, disabled student services, exercise/wellness program, free psychological counseling, international student services, low-cost health insurance, multicultural affairs office. *Library facilities:* Howard Tilton Memorial Library plus 8 others. *Online resources:* library catalog, web page. *Collection:* 2.5 million titles, 12,607 serial subscriptions, 1,764 audiovisual materials.

Computer facilities: Computer purchase and lease plans are available. 592 computers available on campus for general student use. A campuswide network can be accessed from student residence rooms and from off campus. Internet access and online class registration, wireless access to the internet are available. *Web address:* http://www.tulane.edu/.

General Application Contact: Dr. Michael Herman, Dean, 504-865-5100, Fax: 504-865-5274, E-mail: graddean@tulane.edu.

GRADUATE UNITS

A. B. Freeman School of Business Students: 337 full-time, 222 part-time; includes 58 minority (30 African Americans, 3 American Indian/Alaska Native, 11 Asian Americans or Pacific Islanders, 14 Hispanic Americans), 177 international. Average age 27. 495 applicants, 72% accepted, 173 enrolled. *Faculty:* 65 full-time (15 women), 64 part-time/adjunct (21 women). Expenses: Contact institution. *Financial support:* In 2006–07, 68 students received support, including 50 fellowships with full and partial tuition reimbursements available; research assistantships, teaching assistantships, career-related internships or fieldwork, Federal Work-Study, tuition waivers (full and partial), and unspecified assistantships also available. Support available to part-time students. Financial award application deadline: 4/15; financial award applicants required to submit FAFSA. In 2006, 325 master's, 16 doctorates awarded. *Degree program information:* Part-time and evening/weekend programs available. Offers business (EMBA, M Acct, M Fin, MBA, PMBA, PhD). *Application deadline:* For fall admission, 5/1 priority date for domestic students; for spring admission, 12/1 priority date for domestic students. *Application fee:* $40 ($50 for international students). Electronic applications accepted. *Application Contact:* Bill D. Sandefer, Director, Graduate Admissions and Financial Aid, 504-865-5410, Fax: 504-865-6770, E-mail: freeman.admissions@tulane.edu. *Dean,* Angelo S. DeNisi, 504-865-5407, Fax: 504-865-5491.

Program in Liberal Arts Students: 16 full-time (9 women), 5 part-time (4 women); includes 5 minority (4 African Americans, 1 Hispanic American). Expenses: Contact institution. *Financial support:* Application deadline: 2/1. In 2006, 5 degrees awarded. *Degree program information:* Part-time programs available. Offers liberal arts (MLA). *Application deadline:* For fall admission, 7/1 for domestic students. *Application fee:* $45. *Director,* Dr. Ronna Burger, 504-861-8640, E-mail: rburger@tulane.edu.

School of Architecture Students: 30 full-time (16 women), 10 part-time (5 women); includes 3 minority (2 African Americans, 1 Hispanic American). 67 applicants, 81% accepted, 14 enrolled. *Faculty:* 21. Expenses: Contact institution. *Financial support:* In 2006–07, 15 students received support, including 1 fellowship; Federal Work-Study and scholarships/grants also available. Support available to part-time students. Financial award application deadline: 2/1; financial award applicants required to submit FAFSA. In 2006, 13 degrees awarded. *Degree program information:* Part-time programs available. Offers architecture (M Arch, MPS). *Application deadline:* For fall admission, 2/15 for domestic and international students. *Application fee:* $35. *Application Contact:* Peggy A. Messina, Director of Academic Affairs, 504-865-5389, Fax: 504-865-8798, E-mail: pmessina@tulane.edu. *Dean,* Reed Kroloff, 504-865-5389, Fax: 504-862-8798, E-mail: rkroloff@tulane.edu.

School of Law Students: 1,023 full-time (513 women), 8 part-time (6 women); includes 182 minority (80 African Americans, 7 American Indian/Alaska Native, 51 Asian Americans or Pacific Islanders, 44 Hispanic Americans), 50 international. Average age 24. 4,100 applicants, 26% accepted, 300 enrolled. *Faculty:* 54 full-time (15 women), 103 part-time/adjunct (18 women). Expenses: Contact institution. *Financial support:* In 2006–07, 625 students received support, including 3 fellowships with full and partial tuition reimbursements available; career-related internships or fieldwork, Federal Work-Study, institutionally sponsored loans, scholarships/grants, and tuition waivers (full and partial) also available. Financial award application deadline: 2/15; financial award applicants required to submit FAFSA. In 2006, 336 JDs, 51 master's, 1 doctorate awarded. Offers admiralty (LL M); American business law (LL M); energy and environment (LL M); international and comparative law (LL M); law (JD, LL M, SJD). *Application deadline:* For fall admission, 3/15 priority date for domestic and international students. Applications are processed on a rolling basis. *Application fee:* $60. Electronic applications accepted. *Application Contact:* Susan Krinsky, Associate Dean, 504-865-5930, Fax: 504-865-6710, E-mail: skrinsky@law.tulane.edu. *Dean,* Lawrence Ponoroff, 504-865-5937, Fax: 504-862-8746, E-mail: lponoroff@law.tulane.edu.

Tulane University (continued)

School of Liberal Arts Students: 1,213 full-time (629 women), 95 part-time (51 women); includes 202 minority (89 African Americans, 6 American Indian/Alaska Native, 39 Asian Americans or Pacific Islanders, 68 Hispanic Americans), 370 international. 1,703 applicants, 37% accepted, 330 enrolled. *Faculty:* 370. Expenses: Contact institution. *Financial support:* Fellowships with full tuition reimbursements, research assistantships with full tuition reimbursements, teaching assistantships with full tuition reimbursements, career-related internships or fieldwork, Federal Work-Study, institutionally sponsored loans, scholarships/grants, traineeships, tuition waivers, and unspecified assistantships available. Financial award application deadline: 2/1; financial award applicants required to submit FAFSA. In 2006, 192 master's, 116 doctorates awarded. *Degree program information:* Part-time programs available. Offers anthropology (MA, PhD); applied mathematics (MS); art (MFA); art history (MA); cell and molecular biology (MS, PhD); chemistry (MS, PhD); classical studies (MA); design and technical production (MFA); ecology and evolutionary biology (MS, PhD); economics (MA, PhD); English (MA, PhD); French (MA, PhD); geology (MS, PhD); history (MA, PhD); liberal arts (MA, MFA, MS, PhD); mathematics (MS, PhD); music (MA, MFA); paleontology (PhD); philosophy (MA, PhD); physics (MS, PhD); political science (MA, PhD); Portuguese (MA); sociology (MA, PhD); Spanish (MA); Spanish and Portuguese (PhD); statistics (MS). *Application deadline:* For fall admission, 2/1 for domestic and international students. *Application fee:* $45. Electronic applications accepted. *Application Contact:* Deborah A. Troescher, Director of Graduate Programs, 504-865-5100, Fax: 504-865-5274, E-mail: deboraht@tulane.edu. *Dean,* George L. Bernstein, 504-865-5225, Fax: 504-865-5224, E-mail: gbernst@tulane.edu.

The Payson Center for International Development and Technology Transfer Students: 58 full-time (36 women), 37 part-time (20 women); includes 15 minority (5 African Americans, 2 American Indian/Alaska Native, 7 Asian Americans or Pacific Islanders, 1 Hispanic American), 35 international. 91 applicants, 81% accepted, 28 enrolled. *Faculty:* 3 full-time. Expenses: Contact institution. *Financial support:* Research assistantships available. In 2006, 13 degrees awarded. *Degree program information:* Part-time programs available. Offers international development (MS, PhD). *Application deadline:* For fall admission, 2/1 for domestic and international students. *Application fee:* $45. Electronic applications accepted. *Academic Director,* Dr. Eamon M. Kelly, 504-865-5240.

Roger Thayer Stone Center for Latin American Studies Students: 45 full-time (29 women), 1 part-time; includes 14 minority (6 African Americans, 1 Asian American or Pacific Islander, 7 Hispanic Americans), 1 international. 71 applicants, 30% accepted, 13 enrolled. *Faculty:* 1 full-time. Expenses: Contact institution. *Financial support:* Fellowships, teaching assistantships, career-related internships or fieldwork, Federal Work-Study, and institutionally sponsored loans available. Financial award application deadline: 2/1. In 2006, 12 master's, 1 doctorate awarded. Offers Latin American studies (MA, PhD). *Application deadline:* For fall admission, 2/1 for domestic and international students. *Application fee:* $45. Electronic applications accepted. *Application Contact:* Dr. James D. Huck, Assistant Director, Graduate Programs, 504-865-5164. *Executive Director,* Dr. Thomas Reese, 504-865-5164.

School of Medicine Students: 631 full-time (276 women); includes 152 minority (43 African Americans, 6 American Indian/Alaska Native, 100 Asian Americans or Pacific Islanders, 3 Hispanic Americans), 8 international. 6,627 applicants, 6% accepted, 155 enrolled. *Faculty:* 490 full-time (143 women), 31 part-time/adjunct. Expenses: Contact institution. *Financial support:* Fellowships, research assistantships, teaching assistantships, career-related internships or fieldwork, Federal Work-Study, institutionally sponsored loans, and scholarships/grants available. Financial award application deadline: 2/1. In 2006, 154 first professional degrees, 36 master's, 1 doctorate awarded. Offers medicine (MD, MBS, MS, PhD). *Application deadline:* For winter admission, 1/15 for domestic and international students. *Application fee:* $95. *Application Contact:* Dr. Joseph Pisano, Associate Dean for Admissions, 504-588-5187, Fax: 504-988-6735, E-mail: medsch@tulane.edu. *Interim Dean,* Dr. L. Lee Hamm, 504-988-5462, Fax: 504-284-2945, E-mail: lhamm@tulane.edu.

Graduate Programs in Biomedical Sciences Students: 211 full-time (114 women), 4 part-time (1 woman); includes 41 minority (18 African Americans, 15 Asian Americans or Pacific Islanders, 8 Hispanic Americans), 46 international. 364 applicants, 46% accepted, 88 enrolled. *Faculty:* 70 full-time (22 women). Expenses: Contact institution. *Financial support:* Fellowships, research assistantships, teaching assistantships, career-related internships or fieldwork, Federal Work-Study, institutionally sponsored loans, scholarships/grants, traineeships, tuition waivers (full), and unspecified assistantships available. Financial award application deadline: 2/1; financial award applicants required to submit FAFSA. In 2006, 35 master's, 18 doctorates awarded. Offers biochemistry (MS, PhD); biomedical sciences (MBS, MS, PhD); human genetics (MBS, PhD); microbiology and immunology (MS, PhD); molecular and cellular biology (PhD); neuroscience (MS, PhD); pharmacology (MS, PhD); physiology (MS, PhD); structural and cellular biology (MS, PhD). *Application deadline:* For fall admission, 2/1 for domestic and international students. *Application fee:* $61. *Dean, Graduate School,* Dr. Michael Herman, 504-865-5100, Fax: 504-865-5274, E-mail: graddean@tulane.edu.

School of Public Health and Tropical Medicine Students: 791 full-time, 412 part-time; includes 135 minority (39 African Americans, 2 American Indian/Alaska Native, 17 Asian Americans or Pacific Islanders, 77 Hispanic Americans), 234 international. 855 applicants, 82% accepted, 380 enrolled. *Faculty:* 118 full-time, 42 part-time/adjunct. Expenses: Contact institution. *Financial support:* Fellowships, research assistantships, teaching assistantships, Federal Work-Study, scholarships/grants, and traineeships available. Support available to part-time students. Financial award application deadline: 4/15; financial award applicants required to submit FAFSA. In 2006, 420 master's, 9 doctorates awarded. *Degree program information:* Part-time and evening/weekend programs available. Postbaccalaureate distance learning degree programs offered (no on-campus study). Offers biostatistics (MS, MSPH, PhD, Sc D); clinical tropical medicine and travelers health (Diploma); environmental health sciences (MPH, MSPH, Dr PH, PhD); epidemiology (MPH, MS, Dr PH, PhD); health education and communication (MPH); health systems management (MHA, MMM, MPH, PhD, Sc D); international health and development (MPH, Dr PH, PhD); maternal and child health (MPH, Dr PH); nutrition (MPH); parasitology (MSPH, PhD); public health and tropical medicine (MPHTM); vector borne infectious diseases (MS, PhD). MS, PhD offered through the Graduate School. *Application deadline:* For fall admission, 4/15 priority date for domestic and international students; for winter admission, 10/15 priority date for domestic and international students. Applications are processed on a rolling basis. *Application fee:* $40. Electronic applications accepted. *Application Contact:* Jeffrey T. Johnson, Associate Dean for Admissions and Student Affairs, 504-588-5387, Fax: 504-584-1667, E-mail: jeff@tulane.edu. *Dean,* Dr. Pierre Beukens, 504-588-5397, Fax: 504-588-5718.

School of Science and Engineering Students: 165 full-time (57 women), 18 part-time (6 women); includes 15 minority (11 African Americans, 1 Asian American or Pacific Islander, 3 Hispanic Americans), 74 international. 219 applicants, 31% accepted, 33 enrolled. *Faculty:* 56 full-time (6 women), 10 part-time/adjunct (1 woman). Expenses: Contact institution. *Financial support:* In 2006–07, 154 students received support, including 18 fellowships with full tuition reimbursements available (averaging $19,500 per year), 41 research assistantships with full tuition reimbursements available (averaging $20,500 per year), 46 teaching assistantships with full tuition reimbursements available (averaging $14,000 per year); career-related internships or fieldwork, Federal Work-Study, institutionally sponsored loans, scholarships/grants, health care benefits, tuition waivers (full and partial), and unspecified assistantships also available. Support available to part-time students. Financial award application deadline: 12/1. In 2006, 36 master's, 19 doctorates awarded. *Degree program information:* Part-time programs available. Offers biomedical engineering (M Eng, MS, PhD); chemical and biomolecular engineering (M Eng, MS, PhD); civil engineering (M Eng, MS, PhD, Sc D); computer science (MS, PhD); electrical engineering (MS, PhD); engineering science (Sc D); environmental engineering (M Eng, Sc D); mechanical engineering (M Eng, MS, PhD, Sc D); psychology (MS, PhD); science and engineering (M Eng, MS, PhD, Sc D). MS and PhD offered through the Graduate School. *Application deadline:* For fall admission, 12/1 priority date for domestic and international students; for spring admission, 5/1 priority date for domestic and international students. Applications are processed on a rolling basis. *Application fee:* $0. Electronic applications accepted. *Application Contact:* Dr. Daniel De Kee, Associate Dean, 504-865-5764, E-mail: engrgrad@tulane.edu. *Dean,* Dr. Nicholas J. Altiero, 504-865-5764, Fax: 504-862-8747, E-mail: engrgrad@tulane.edu.

School of Social Work Students: 29 full-time (22 women), 5 part-time (3 women); includes 12 minority (9 African Americans, 3 Hispanic Americans). Average age 28. 5 applicants, 100% accepted, 4 enrolled. *Faculty:* 18 full-time (13 women), 37 part-time/adjunct (22 women). Expenses: Contact institution. *Financial support:* Fellowships, Federal Work-Study available. Financial award applicants required to submit FAFSA. *Degree program information:* Part-time programs available. Offers social work (MSW). *Application deadline:* For fall admission, 3/31 priority date for domestic students. Applications are processed on a rolling basis. *Application fee:* $25. Electronic applications accepted. *Application Contact:* Dr. Michael J Zakour, Director, 504-865-5314, Fax: 504-862-8727. *Dean,* Dr. Ronald Marks, 504-865-5314, Fax: 504-862-8727, E-mail: rmarks@tulane.edu.

TUSCULUM COLLEGE, Greeneville, TN 37743-9997

General Information Independent-religious, coed, comprehensive institution. *Graduate housing:* On-campus housing not available.

GRADUATE UNITS

Graduate School *Degree program information:* Evening/weekend programs available. Offers adult education (MA Ed); K–12 (MA Ed); organizational management (MAOM).

TUSKEGEE UNIVERSITY, Tuskegee, AL 36088

General Information Independent, coed, comprehensive institution. *Enrollment:* 2,842 graduate, professional, and undergraduate students; 393 full-time matriculated graduate/professional students (270 women), 29 part-time matriculated graduate/professional students (11 women). *Enrollment by degree level:* 236 first professional, 164 master's, 22 doctoral. *Graduate faculty:* 112 full-time (17 women), 11 part-time/adjunct (5 women). *Tuition:* Full-time $13,520; part-time $390 per semester. *Required fees:* $480; $405 per semester. *Graduate housing:* Rooms and/or apartments available to single and married students. Typical cost: $6,460 (including board) for single students. Room and board charges vary according to board plan and housing facility selected. Housing application deadline: 5/1. *Student services:* Campus employment opportunities, campus safety program, career counseling, child daycare facilities, free psychological counseling, international student services, low-cost health insurance. *Library facilities:* Hollis B. Frissell Library plus 3 others. *Online resources:* library catalog. *Collection:* 623,824 titles, 81,157 serial subscriptions.

Computer facilities: 1,000 computers available on campus for general student use. A campuswide network can be accessed from student residence rooms and from off campus. Internet access and online class registration are available. *Web address:* http://www.tuskegee.edu/.

General Application Contact: Dr. Robert L. Laney, Vice President/Director Admissions and Enrollment Management, 334-727-8580, Fax: 334-727-5750, E-mail: planey@tuskegee.edu.

GRADUATE UNITS

Graduate Programs Students: 393 full-time (270 women), 29 part-time (11 women); includes 243 minority (236 African Americans, 3 Asian Americans or Pacific Islanders, 4 Hispanic Americans), 58 international. Average age 28. 370 applicants, 62% accepted, 140 enrolled. *Faculty:* 112 full-time (17 women), 11 part-time/adjunct (5 women). Expenses: Contact institution. *Financial support:* Fellowships, research assistantships, teaching assistantships, career-related internships or fieldwork, Federal Work-Study, institutionally sponsored loans, and scholarships/grants available. Support available to part-time students. Financial award application deadline: 4/15. In 2006, 53 first professional degrees, 41 master's awarded. *Degree program information:* Part-time programs available. *Application deadline:* For fall admission, 7/15 for domestic students. Applications are processed on a rolling basis. *Application fee:* $25 ($35 for international students). *Application Contact:* Dr. Robert L. Laney, Vice President/Director Admissions and Enrollment Management, 334-727-8580, Fax: 334-727-5750, E-mail: planey@tuskegee.edu. *Provost,* Dr. Luther S. Williams, 334-727-8164.

College of Agricultural, Environmental and Natural Sciences Students: 86 full-time (53 women), 14 part-time (6 women); includes 75 minority (74 African Americans, 1 Asian American or Pacific Islander), 19 international. Average age 29. 65 applicants, 65% accepted, 23 enrolled. *Faculty:* 26 full-time (12 women), 1 part-time/adjunct (0 women). Expenses: Contact institution. *Financial support:* Fellowships, research assistantships, teaching assistantships, career-related internships or fieldwork, Federal Work-Study, and institutionally sponsored loans available. Support available to part-time students. Financial award application deadline: 4/15. In 2006, 31 degrees awarded. Offers agricultural and resource economics (MS); agricultural, environmental and natural sciences (MS, PhD); animal and poultry sciences (MS); biology (MS); chemistry (MS); environmental sciences (MS); food and nutritional sciences (MS); integrative biosciences (PhD); plant and soil sciences (MS). *Application deadline:* For fall admission, 7/15 for domestic students. Applications are processed on a rolling basis. *Application fee:* $25 ($35 for international students). *Dean,* Dr. Walter A. Hill, 334-727-8157.

College of Engineering, Architecture and Physical Sciences Students: 48 full-time (16 women), 8 part-time (1 woman); includes 31 minority (30 African Americans, 1 Asian American or Pacific Islander), 21 international. Average age 28. 104 applicants, 59% accepted. *Faculty:* 19 full-time (0 women). Expenses: Contact institution. *Financial support:* Fellowships, research assistantships, teaching assistantships, career-related internships or fieldwork, Federal Work-Study, and institutionally sponsored loans available. Support available to part-time students. Financial award application deadline: 4/15. In 2006, 14 degrees awarded. Offers electrical engineering (MSEE); engineering, architecture and physical sciences (MSEE, MSME, PhD); material science engineering (PhD); mechanical engineering (MSME). *Application deadline:* For fall admission, 7/15 for domestic students. Applications are processed on a rolling basis. *Application fee:* $25 ($35 for international students). *Acting Dean,* Dr. Legand L. Burge, 334-727-8356.

College of Veterinary Medicine, Nursing and Allied Health Average age 27. *Faculty:* 62 full-time (6 women). Expenses: Contact institution. *Financial support:* Fellowships, research assistantships, teaching assistantships, career-related internships or fieldwork, Federal Work-Study, institutionally sponsored loans, and scholarships/grants available. Support available to part-time students. Financial award application deadline: 4/15. In 2006, 53 DVMs, 3 master's awarded. Offers veterinary medicine (DVM, MS); veterinary medicine, nursing and allied health (DVM, MS). *Application deadline:* For fall admission, 7/15 for domestic students. Applications are processed on a rolling basis. *Application fee:* $25 ($35 for international students). *Dean,* Dr. Tsegaye Habtemariam, 334-727-8174, Fax: 334-727-8177.

TYNDALE UNIVERSITY COLLEGE & SEMINARY, Toronto, ON M2M 4B3, Canada

General Information Independent-religious, coed, comprehensive institution. *Graduate housing:* Room and/or apartments available on a first-come, first-served basis to single students; on-campus housing not available to married students.

GRADUATE UNITS

Graduate Programs *Degree program information:* Part-time programs available. Postbaccalaureate distance learning degree programs offered (no on-campus study). Offers Biblical studies (M Div); Christian foundations (MTS); Christian studies (Diploma); counseling (M Div); educational ministry (M Div); missions (M Div, Diploma); pastoral and Chinese ministry (M Div); pastoral ministry (M Div); Pentecostal studies (MTS); spiritual formation (M Div, Diploma); theological studies (M Div); theology (Th M); worship and liturgy (M Div, MTS); youth and family ministry (M Div). Electronic applications accepted.

UNIFICATION THEOLOGICAL SEMINARY, Barrytown, NY 12507

General Information Independent-religious, coed, primarily men, graduate-only institution. *Enrollment by degree level:* 32 first professional, 91 master's. *Graduate faculty:* 6 full-time (1 woman), 11 part-time/adjunct (2 women). *Tuition:* Part-time $385 per credit. *Required fees:* $120 per term. Full-time tuition and fees vary according to course load and program. *Graduate housing:* Rooms and/or apartments guaranteed to single students and available on a first-come, first-served basis to married students. Typical cost: $5,594 (including board) for single students; $5,520 per year ($8,176 including board) for married students. Room and board charges vary according to board plan and housing facility selected. *Student services:* Campus employment opportunities, career counseling, international student services, low-cost health insurance. *Library facilities:* Unification Theological Seminary Library. *Online resources:* library catalog. *Collection:* 55,100 titles, 75 serial subscriptions, 750 audiovisual materials.

Computer facilities: 6 computers available on campus for general student use. A campuswide network can be accessed from student residence rooms. Internet access is available. *Web address:* http://www.uts.edu/.

General Application Contact: Henry Christopher, Director of Admissions, 845-752-3000 Ext. 200, Fax: 845-752-3016, E-mail: hchristopher@uts.edu.

GRADUATE UNITS

Graduate Program, Main Campus Students: 40 full-time (8 women), 17 part-time (6 women). Average age 39. *Faculty:* 6 full-time (1 woman), 4 part-time/adjunct (0 women). Expenses: Contact institution. *Financial support:* Teaching assistantships, career-related internships or fieldwork, institutionally sponsored loans, scholarships/grants, and tuition waivers (partial) available. Financial award applicants required to submit FAFSA. In 2006, 6 first professional degrees, 35 master's awarded. *Degree program information:* Part-time programs available. Offers theology (M Div, MRE, D Min). *Application deadline:* For fall admission, 8/15 priority date for domestic students; for winter admission, 12/15 priority date for domestic students; for spring admission, 3/15 priority date for domestic students. Applications are processed on a rolling basis. *Application fee:* $25. *Application Contact:* Henry Christopher, Director of Admissions, 845-752-3000 Ext. 200, Fax: 845-752-3016, E-mail: admissions@uts.edu. *Academic Dean,* Dr. Andrew Wilson, 845-752-3000 Ext. 228, Fax: 845-752-3014, E-mail: wilson@uts.edu.

Graduate Program, New York Extension Students: 24 full-time (7 women), 42 part-time (20 women). Average age 42. *Faculty:* 2 full-time (0 women), 8 part-time/adjunct (2 women). Expenses: Contact institution. *Financial support:* Career-related internships or fieldwork, institutionally sponsored loans, scholarships/grants, and tuition waivers (partial) available. Financial award applicants required to submit FAFSA. *Degree program information:* Part-time and evening/weekend programs available. Offers theology (M Div, MRE). *Application deadline:* For fall admission, 8/15 priority date for domestic students; for winter admission, 12/15 priority date for domestic students; for spring admission, 3/15 priority date for domestic students. Applications are processed on a rolling basis. *Application fee:* $25. *Application Contact:* Rev. Leander Hardaway, Admissions Officer, 212-563-6647 Ext. 15, Fax: 212-563-6649, E-mail: lwhardaway@aol.com. *Dean of the Extension Center,* Dr. Kathy Winings, 212-563-6647 Ext. 104, Fax: 212-563-6649, E-mail: irffint@aol.com.

UNIFORMED SERVICES UNIVERSITY OF THE HEALTH SCIENCES, Bethesda, MD 20814-4799

General Information Federally supported, coed, graduate-only institution. *Graduate housing:* On-campus housing not available. *Research affiliation:* U.S. Armed Forces Radiobiology Research Institute, National Institutes of Health, National Library of Medicine, Walter Reed Army Institute of Research, Armed Forces Institute of Pathology.

GRADUATE UNITS

Graduate School of Nursing Postbaccalaureate distance learning degree programs offered (no on-campus study). Offers nurse anesthesia (MSN); nurse practitioner (MSN); perioperative clinical nurse specialty (MSN). Available to military officers only. Electronic applications accepted.

School of Medicine Offers medicine (MD, MMH, MPH, MS, MSPH, MTMH, Dr PH, PhD).

Programs in Biomedical Sciences Offers applied human biology (MS); clinical psychology (PhD); comparative pathology (PhD); emerging infectious diseases (PhD); environmental health science (PhD); medical and clinical psychology (PhD); medical history (MMH); medical psychology (PhD); medical zoology (PhD); microbiology and immunology (PhD); molecular and cell biology (PhD); molecular pathobiology (PhD); neuroscience (PhD); pathology (PhD); preventive medicine and biometrics (MPH, MSPH, MTMH, Dr PH, PhD); public health (MPH, MSPH, Dr PH); tropical medicine and hygiene (MTMH); undersea medicine (PhD).

UNION COLLEGE, Barbourville, KY 40906-1499

General Information Independent-religious, coed, comprehensive institution. *Graduate housing:* Rooms and/or apartments available to single and married students.

GRADUATE UNITS

Graduate Programs *Degree program information:* Part-time and evening/weekend programs available. Offers elementary education (MA); elementary principalship (Certificate); health (MA Ed); health and physical education (MA); middle grades (MA); middle grades principalship (Certificate); music education (MA); principalship (MA); reading specialist (MA); secondary education (MA); secondary school principalship (Certificate); special education (MA); supervisor of instruction (Certificate).

UNION COLLEGE, Lincoln, NE 68506-4300

General Information Independent-religious, coed, comprehensive institution.

GRADUATE UNITS

Program in Physician Assistant Studies Offers physician assistant studies (MPAS).

UNION GRADUATE COLLEGE, Schenectady, NY 12308-3107

General Information Independent, coed, graduate-only institution. *Enrollment by degree level:* 569 master's, 32 other advanced degrees. *Graduate faculty:* 14 full-time (4 women), 68 part-time/adjunct (21 women). *Student services:* Campus employment opportunities, career counseling, disabled student services, free psychological counseling, international student services, teacher training. *Library facilities:* Schaeffer Library. *Online resources:* library catalog, web page, access to other libraries' catalogs. *Collection:* 2 million titles, 3,728 serial subscriptions, 9,044 audiovisual materials.

Computer facilities: 50 computers available on campus for general student use. A campuswide network can be accessed from off campus. Internet access is available. *Web address:* http://www.gcuu.edu/.

General Application Contact: Rhonda Sheehan, Director of Graduate Admissions Registrar, 518-388-6238, Fax: 518-388-6686, E-mail: sheehanr@union.edu.

GRADUATE UNITS

Center for Bioethics and Clinical Leadership Students: 68 full-time (39 women), 36 part-time (23 women); includes 37 minority (2 African Americans, 1 American Indian/Alaska Native, 33 Asian Americans or Pacific Islanders, 1 Hispanic American), 2 international. Average age 26. 366 applicants, 24% accepted, 40 enrolled. *Faculty:* 1 full-time (0 women), 10 part-time/adjunct (6 women). Expenses: Contact institution. *Financial support:* Federal Work-Study, scholarships/grants, health care benefits, and tuition waivers (partial) available. Support available to part-time students. Financial award applicants required to submit FAFSA. In 2006, 23 master's awarded. *Degree program information:* Part-time and evening/weekend programs available. Postbaccalaureate distance learning degree programs offered. Offers bioethics (MS); clinical leadership in health management (MS). *Application deadline:* For spring admission, 5/1 for domestic and international students. *Application fee:* $60. *Application Contact:* Rhonda Sheehan, Director of Graduate Admissions Registrar, 518-388-6238, Fax: 518-388-6686, E-mail: sheehanr@union.edu. *Director,* Dr. Robert B. Baker, 518-388-6215, Fax: 518-388-8046, E-mail: bakerr@union.edu.

School of Education Students: 57 full-time (36 women), 21 part-time (14 women); includes 2 African Americans, 2 Hispanic Americans, 2 international. Average age 31. 59 applicants, 83% accepted, 39 enrolled. *Faculty:* 5 full-time (1 woman), 19 part-time/adjunct (10 women). Expenses: Contact institution. *Financial support:* In 2006–07, 12 research assistantships with tuition reimbursements (averaging $3,000 per year) were awarded; Federal Work-Study, scholarships/grants, health care benefits, and tuition waivers (partial) also available. Support available to part-time students. Financial award applicants required to submit FAFSA. In 2006, 56 degrees awarded. Offers biology (MAT, MS); chemistry (MAT); earth science (MAT); English (MAT); French (MAT); general science (MAT); German (MAT); languages (MAT); Latin (MAT); mathematics (MAT); mathematics and technology (MS); physical science (MS); physics (MAT); social studies (MAT); Spanish (MAT). *Application fee:* $60. *Application Contact:* Rhonda Sheehan, Director of Graduate Admissions Registrar, 518-388-6238, Fax: 518-388-6686, E-mail: sheehanr@union.edu. *Dean,* Dr. Patrick Allen, 518-388-6361, Fax: 518-388-6686, E-mail: mat@union.edu.

School of Engineering and Computer Science Students: 13 full-time (1 woman), 86 part-time (13 women); includes 6 Asian Americans or Pacific Islanders, 7 international. Average age 29. 52 applicants, 77% accepted, 38 enrolled. *Faculty:* 30 part-time/adjunct (2 women). Expenses: Contact institution. *Financial support:* Research assistantships, Federal Work-Study, scholarships/grants, health care benefits, and tuition waivers (full and partial) available. Support available to part-time students. Financial award applicants required to submit FAFSA. In 2006, 27 degrees awarded. *Degree program information:* Part-time and evening/weekend programs available. Offers computer science (MS); electrical engineering (MS); engineering and computer science (MS); engineering and management systems (MS); mechanical engineering (MS). *Application deadline:* Applications are processed on a rolling basis. *Application fee:* $60. *Application Contact:* Rhonda Sheehan, Director of Graduate Admissions Registrar, 518-388-6238, Fax: 518-388-6686, E-mail: sheehanr@union.edu. *Dean,* Robert Kozik, 515-388-8068, Fax: 518-388-6789, E-mail: kozikr@union.edu.

School of Management Students: 94 full-time (48 women), 211 part-time (81 women); includes 32 minority (9 African Americans, 17 Asian Americans or Pacific Islanders, 6 Hispanic Americans), 23 international. Average age 27. 116 applicants, 72% accepted, 67 enrolled. Expenses: Contact institution. *Financial support:* Research assistantships, career-related internships or fieldwork, Federal Work-Study, scholarships/grants, health care benefits, and tuition waivers (partial) available. Support available to part-time students. Financial award applicants required to submit FAFSA. In 2006, 58 master's, 2 other advanced degrees awarded. *Degree program information:* Part-time and evening/weekend programs available. Offers business administration (MBA, Certificate); financial management (Certificate); general management (Certificate); health systems administration (MBA, Certificate); healthcare management (Certificate). *Application deadline:* Applications are processed on a rolling basis. *Application fee:* $60. *Application Contact:* Rhonda Sheehan, Director of Graduate Admissions Registrar, 518-388-6238, Fax: 518-388-6686, E-mail: sheehanr@union.edu. *Dean,* Melvin Chudzik, 518-388-6447, Fax: 518-388-6754, E-mail: chudzikm@union.edu.

UNION INSTITUTE & UNIVERSITY, Cincinnati, OH 45206-1925

General Information Independent, coed, university. *Graduate housing:* On-campus housing not available.

GRADUATE UNITS

Program in Education (Florida Campus) Postbaccalaureate distance learning degree programs offered (minimal on-campus study). Offers education (M Ed, Ed S).

Program in Education (Vermont Campus) Offers education (M Ed).

Program in Interdisciplinary Studies (Vermont Campus) *Degree program information:* Evening/weekend programs available. Postbaccalaureate distance learning degree programs offered (no on-campus study). Offers counseling (MA); interdisciplinary studies (MA); psychology (MA). Self-designed studies completed through independent research.

Program in Visual Art (Vermont Campus) Offers visual art (MFA).

Program in Writing (Vermont Campus) Postbaccalaureate distance learning degree programs offered (minimal on-campus study). Offers writing (MFA); writing for children and young adults (MFA).

School of Interdisciplinary Arts and Sciences Offers interdisciplinary studies (PhD). Individually-designed interdisciplinary programs.

School of Professional Psychology Offers clinical psychology (PhD); interdisciplinary studies (PhD).

UNION THEOLOGICAL SEMINARY AND PRESBYTERIAN SCHOOL OF CHRISTIAN EDUCATION, Richmond, VA 23227-4597

General Information Independent-religious, coed, graduate-only institution. *Graduate housing:* Rooms and/or apartments available on a first-come, first-served basis to single and married students.

GRADUATE UNITS

School of Christian Education *Degree program information:* Part-time and evening/weekend programs available. Postbaccalaureate distance learning degree programs offered (minimal on-campus study). Offers Christian education (MA, MATS).

School of Theological Studies Offers theological studies (M Div, Th M, D Min, PhD).

UNION THEOLOGICAL SEMINARY IN THE CITY OF NEW YORK, New York, NY 10027-5710

General Information Independent-religious, coed, graduate-only institution. *Graduate housing:* Rooms and/or apartments available on a first-come, first-served basis to single and married students. Housing application deadline: 5/15.

GRADUATE UNITS

Graduate and Professional Programs *Degree program information:* Part-time programs available. Offers theology (M Div, MA, STM, Ed D, PhD).

UNION UNIVERSITY, Jackson, TN 38305-3697

General Information Independent-religious, coed, comprehensive institution. *Enrollment:* 2,934 graduate, professional, and undergraduate students; 580 full-time matriculated graduate/professional students (379 women), 207 part-time matriculated graduate/professional students (134 women). *Enrollment by degree level:* 657 master's, 130 doctoral. *Graduate faculty:* 69. *Graduate housing:* Rooms and/or apartments available on a first-come, first-served basis to single and married students. *Student services:* Campus employment opportunities, campus safety program, career counseling, exercise/wellness program, free psychological counseling, international student services, teacher training. *Library facilities:* Emma Waters Summar Library plus 1 other. *Online resources:* library catalog, web page, access to other libraries' catalogs. *Collection:* 149,255 titles, 19,919 serial subscriptions, 14,131 audiovisual materials.

Computer facilities: 236 computers available on campus for general student use. A campuswide network can be accessed from student residence rooms and from off campus. Internet access is available. *Web address:* http://www.uu.edu/.

General Application Contact: Robbie Graves, Director of Enrollment Services, 731-661-5008, Fax: 731-661-5017, E-mail: rgraves@uu.edu.

GRADUATE UNITS

Institute for International and Intercultural Studies Students: 47 full-time (36 women); includes 3 minority (1 African American, 1 Asian American or Pacific Islander, 1 Hispanic American), 4 international. 30 applicants, 70% accepted, 21 enrolled. *Faculty:* 5 full-time (2 women), 2 part-time/adjunct (both women). Expenses: Contact institution. In 2006, 23 degrees awarded. *Degree program information:* Part-time and evening/weekend programs available. Offers international and intercultural studies (MAIS). *Application deadline:* For fall admission, 8/15 priority date for domestic and international students. Applications are processed on a rolling basis. *Application fee:* $25 ($50 for international students). Electronic applications accepted. *Application Contact:* Carol Johnson, MAIS Program Coordinator, 731-661-5057, Fax: 731-661-5175, E-mail: cljohnso@uu.edu. *Director,* Dr. Cynthia Powell Jayne, 731-661-5358, Fax: 731-661-5175, E-mail: cjayne@uu.edu.

Union University (continued)

McAfee School of Business Administration *Degree program information:* Evening/weekend programs available. Offers business administration (MBA). Also available at Germantown campus. Electronic applications accepted.

School of Christian Studies Expenses: Contact institution. Offers Christian studies (MCS). *Dean,* Dr. Gregory Thornburg, 731-661-5082, E-mail: gthornbu@uu.edu.

School of Education Students: 254 full-time (207 women), 161 part-time (120 women); includes 197 minority (193 African Americans, 1 American Indian/Alaska Native, 1 Asian American or Pacific Islander, 2 Hispanic Americans). Average age 32. *Faculty:* 19 full-time (11 women), 18 part-time/adjunct (12 women). Expenses: Contact institution. *Financial support:* In 2006–07, 117 students received support. Application deadline: 2/15; In 2006, 184 master's, 22 doctorates, 77 other advanced degrees awarded. *Degree program information:* Part-time and evening/weekend programs available. Offers education (M Ed, MA Ed); education administration generalist (Ed S); educational leadership (Ed D); educational supervision (Ed S); higher education (Ed D). M Ed also available at Germantown campus. *Application deadline:* Applications are processed on a rolling basis. *Application fee:* $25 ($50 for international students). *Application Contact:* Helen F. Fowler, Assistant to the Dean, 731-661-5374, Fax: 731-661-5468, E-mail: hfowler@uu.edu. *Dean,* Dr. Tom R. Rosebrough, 731-661-5523, Fax: 731-661-5468, E-mail: trosebro@uu.edu.

School of Nursing Students: 47 full-time (36 women); includes 12 minority (10 African Americans, 1 American Indian/Alaska Native, 1 Asian American or Pacific Islander). Average age 38. 12 applicants, 100% accepted, 12 enrolled. *Faculty:* 15 full-time (14 women), 3 part-time/adjunct (2 women). Expenses: Contact institution. *Financial support:* Traineeships available. Financial award applicants required to submit FAFSA. In 2006, 9 degrees awarded. Offers nurse anesthetist (PMC); nursing education (MSN, PMC). *Application deadline:* For fall admission, 8/1 priority date for domestic students, 8/1 for international students. *Application fee:* $25. Electronic applications accepted. *Application Contact:* Elsie Cressman, Coordinator of MSN Programs, 731-661-5120, Fax: 731-661-5504, E-mail: ecressman@uu.edu. *Dean,* Dr. Tim Smith, 731-661-5200, Fax: 731-661-5504.

UNITED STATES ARMY COMMAND AND GENERAL STAFF COLLEGE, Fort Leavenworth, KS 66027-1352

General Information Federally supported, coed, primarily men, graduate-only institution. *Graduate housing:* Rooms and/or apartments available to single and married students.

GRADUATE UNITS

Graduate Program Offers military art and science (MMAS). Only career military officers are selected to attend United States Army Command and General Staff College; Graduate Program is voluntary for first-year students, but mandatory for second-year students.

UNITED STATES INTERNATIONAL UNIVERSITY, Nairobi 00800, Kenya

General Information Independent, coed, comprehensive institution. *Graduate housing:* Room and/or apartments available on a first-come, first-served basis to single students; on-campus housing not available to married students. Housing application deadline: 7/31.

GRADUATE UNITS

School of Arts and Sciences *Degree program information:* Part-time and evening/weekend programs available. Offers counseling psychology (MA); international relations (MA).

School of Business Administration *Degree program information:* Part-time and evening/weekend programs available. Offers finance (MBA); information technology management (MBA); integrated studies (MBA); management and organizational development (MS); marketing (MBA); strategic management (MBA).

UNITED STATES SPORTS ACADEMY, Daphne, AL 36526-7055

General Information Independent, coed, upper-level institution. *Enrollment by degree level:* 384 master's, 90 doctoral. *Graduate faculty:* 8 full-time (1 woman), 23 part-time/adjunct (3 women). *Graduate housing:* On-campus housing not available. *Student services:* Campus employment opportunities, campus safety program, career counseling, exercise/wellness program, free psychological counseling, international student services, low-cost health insurance. *Web address:* http://www.ussa.edu/.

General Application Contact: Dr. Albert G. Applin, Dean of Student Services, 251-626-3303 Ext. 147, Fax: 251-626-1035, E-mail: applin@ussa.edu.

GRADUATE UNITS

Graduate Programs Students: 112 full-time (21 women), 362 part-time (104 women); includes 93 minority (56 African Americans, 27 Asian Americans or Pacific Islanders, 10 Hispanic Americans), 15 international. Average age 33. 120 applicants, 94% accepted. *Faculty:* 8 full-time (1 woman), 23 part-time/adjunct (3 women). Expenses: Contact institution. *Financial support:* In 2006–07, 2 research assistantships with full tuition reimbursements (averaging $10,000 per year) were awarded; career-related internships or fieldwork, Federal Work-Study, scholarships/grants, and service assistantships also available. Support available to part-time students. Financial award application deadline: 8/15; financial award applicants required to submit FAFSA. In 2006, 89 master's, 2 doctorates awarded. *Degree program information:* Part-time programs available. Postbaccalaureate distance learning degree programs offered (minimal on-campus study). Offers health and fitness management (MSS); sport coaching (MSS); sport management (MSS, DSM, Ed D); sport studies (MSS); sports medicine (MSS). *Application deadline:* Applications are processed on a rolling basis. *Application fee:* $50 ($125 for international students). Electronic applications accepted. *Application Contact:* Dr. Albert G. Applin, Dean of Student Services, 251-626-3303 Ext. 147, Fax: 251-626-1035, E-mail: applin@ussa.edu. *Dean of Academic Affairs,* Dr. Thomas J. Rosandich, 251-626-3303, Fax: 251-626-1149, E-mail: vicepresident@ussa.edu.

UNITED TALMUDICAL SEMINARY, Brooklyn, NY 11211-7900

General Information Independent-religious, men only, comprehensive institution.

GRADUATE UNITS

Graduate Programs

UNITED THEOLOGICAL SEMINARY, Trotwood, OH 45426

General Information Independent-religious, coed, graduate-only institution. *Enrollment by degree level:* 106 first professional, 28 master's, 161 doctoral. *Graduate faculty:* 12 full-time (4 women), 36 part-time/adjunct (4 women). *Tuition:* Part-time $383 per credit hour. *Required fees:* $30 per semester. Tuition and fees vary according to program. *Graduate housing:* Rooms and/or apartments available on a first-come, first-served basis to single and married students. *Student services:* Campus employment opportunities, international student services, writing training. *Library facilities:* Memorial Library. *Online resources:* library catalog. *Collection:* 145,687 titles, 494 serial subscriptions, 8,239 audiovisual materials.

Computer facilities: 12 computers available on campus for general student use. A campuswide network can be accessed. Internet access is available. *Web address:* http://www.united.edu/.

General Application Contact: Betty J. Stutler, Director of Admissions, 937-529-2201 Ext. 3307, Fax: 937-529-2292, E-mail: utsadmis@united.edu.

GRADUATE UNITS

Graduate and Professional Programs Students: 266 full-time (116 women), 29 part-time (17 women); includes 151 minority (144 African Americans, 1 American Indian/Alaska Native, 3 Asian Americans or Pacific Islanders, 3 Hispanic Americans), 8 international. Average age 41. 130 applicants, 73% accepted, 89 enrolled. *Faculty:* 12 full-time (4 women), 36 part-time/adjunct (4 women). Expenses: Contact institution. *Financial support:* In 2006–07, 87 students received support. Career-related internships or fieldwork, Federal Work-Study, and scholarships/grants available. Financial award application deadline: 4/1; financial award applicants required to submit CSS PROFILE or FAFSA. In 2006, 18 first professional degrees, 6 master's, 54 doctorates awarded. *Degree program information:* Part-time and evening/weekend programs available. Offers theology (M Div, MASM, MATS, D Min). *Application deadline:* For fall admission, 8/1 for domestic students, 1/15 for international students; for spring admission, 2/1 for domestic students. Applications are processed on a rolling basis. *Application fee:* $40. Electronic applications accepted. *Director of Admissions,* Betty J. Stutler, 937-529-2201 Ext. 3307, Fax: 937-529-2292, E-mail: utsadmis@united.edu.

UNITED THEOLOGICAL SEMINARY OF THE TWIN CITIES, New Brighton, MN 55112-2598

General Information Independent-religious, coed, graduate-only institution. *Enrollment by degree level:* 112 first professional, 21 master's, 36 doctoral, 2 other advanced degrees. *Graduate faculty:* 9 full-time (6 women), 21 part-time/adjunct (10 women). *Tuition:* Full-time $6,282; part-time $349 per credit hour. *Required fees:* $85. One-time fee: $180 full-time. *Graduate housing:* Rooms and/or apartments available on a first-come, first-served basis to single and married students. Housing application deadline: 4/1. *Student services:* Campus employment opportunities, free psychological counseling, international student services, multicultural affairs office. *Library facilities:* Spencer Library. *Online resources:* library catalog, web page, access to other libraries' catalogs. *Collection:* 91,276 titles, 249 serial subscriptions, 955 audiovisual materials.

Computer facilities: 6 computers available on campus for general student use. A campuswide network can be accessed from student residence rooms and from off campus. Internet access is available. *Web address:* http://www.unitedseminary.edu/.

General Application Contact: Rev. Glen Herrington-Hall, Director of Admissions, 651-255-6107, Fax: 651-633-4315, E-mail: gherrington-hall@unitedseminary.edu.

GRADUATE UNITS

Graduate and Professional Programs Students: 63 full-time (40 women), 108 part-time (68 women). Average age 48. 51 applicants, 76% accepted, 30 enrolled. *Faculty:* 9 full-time (6 women), 21 part-time/adjunct (10 women). Expenses: Contact institution. *Financial support:* In 2006–07, 103 students received support. Career-related internships or fieldwork, institutionally sponsored loans, and scholarships/grants available. Support available to part-time students. Financial award application deadline: 5/1; financial award applicants required to submit FAFSA. In 2006, 20 M Divs, 12 master's, 2 doctorates, 5 other advanced degrees awarded. *Degree program information:* Part-time programs available. Offers advanced theological studies (Diploma); ministry (D Min); ministry renewal and professional development (Certificate); religion and theology (MA); religious leadership (MARL); theological and religious studies (Certificate); theology (M Div, MA); theology and the arts (MA); women's studies (MA). *Application deadline:* For fall admission, 8/1 priority date for domestic students, 12/1 priority date for international students; for winter admission, 12/1 priority date for domestic students; for spring admission, 1/1 priority date for domestic students. Applications are processed on a rolling basis. *Application fee:* $40. *Application Contact:* Rev. Glen Herrington-Hall, Director of Admissions, 651-255-6107, Fax: 651-633-4315, E-mail: gherrington-hall@unitedseminary.edu. *Dean,* Dr. Richard D. Weis, 651-255-6108, Fax: 651-633-4315, E-mail: rweis@unitedseminary.edu.

UNIVERSIDAD ADVENTISTA DE LAS ANTILLAS, Mayagüez, PR 00681-0118

General Information Independent-religious, coed, comprehensive institution. *Graduate housing:* Rooms and/or apartments available on a first-come, first-served basis to single and married students.

GRADUATE UNITS

Graduate School Electronic applications accepted.

UNIVERSIDAD CENTRAL DEL CARIBE, Bayamón, PR 00960-6032

General Information Independent, coed. *Graduate housing:* On-campus housing not available.

GRADUATE UNITS

Program in Substance Abuse Counseling Offers substance abuse counseling (MHS).

School of Medicine Offers anatomy and cell biology (MA, MS); biochemistry (MS); biomedical sciences (MA); medicine (MD, MA, MS); microbiology and immunology (MA, MS); pharmacology (MS); physiology (MA, MS).

UNIVERSIDAD DE LAS AMERICAS, A.C., 06700 Mexico City, Mexico

General Information Independent, comprehensive institution.

GRADUATE UNITS

Program in Business Administration Offers finance (MBA); marketing research (MBA); production and quality (MBA).

Program in Education Offers education (M Ed).

Program in International Organizations and Institutions Offers international organizations and institutions (MA).

Program in Psychology Offers family therapy (MA).

UNIVERSIDAD DE LAS AMÉRICAS–PUEBLA, 72820 Puebla, Mexico

General Information Independent, coed, comprehensive institution. CGS member. *Graduate housing:* On-campus housing not available. *Research affiliation:* Empacadora San Marcos S.A. de C.U. (food service), Volkswagon de México S.A. de C.U. (mechanical engineering), Institute Mexicano del Tecnologá del agua (electronic engineering), Frugosa S.A. de C.U. (chemical engineering).

GRADUATE UNITS

Division of Graduate Studies *Degree program information:* Part-time and evening/weekend programs available.

School of Business Administration *Degree program information:* Part-time and evening/weekend programs available. Offers business administration (MBA); finance (M Adm).

School of Engineering *Degree program information:* Part-time and evening/weekend programs available. Offers chemical engineering (MS); computer science (MS); construction management (M Adm); electronic engineering (MS); engineering (M Adm, MS, PhD); food sciences (MS); food technology (MS); industrial engineering (MS); manufacturing administration (MS); production management (M Adm).

School of Humanities *Degree program information:* Part-time and evening/weekend programs available. Offers humanities (MA); information design (MA); linguistics (MA); literature (MA).

School of Sciences *Degree program information:* Part-time and evening/weekend programs available. Offers biotechnology (MS); clinical analysis (biomedicine) (MS); sciences (MS).

School of Social Sciences *Degree program information:* Part-time and evening/weekend programs available. Offers American studies (MA); anthropology (MA); archaeology (MA); economics (MA); education (MA); finance (M Adm); psychology (MA); social sciences (M Adm, MA).

UNIVERSIDAD DEL ESTE, Carolina, PR 00983

General Information Independent, coed, comprehensive institution.

GRADUATE UNITS

Graduate School

UNIVERSIDAD DEL TURABO, Gurabo, PR 00778-3030

General Information Independent, coed, comprehensive institution. *Graduate housing:* On-campus housing not available.

GRADUATE UNITS

Graduate Programs *Degree program information:* Part-time and evening/weekend programs available. Offers bilingual education (MA); criminal justice studies (MPA); education administration and supervision (MA); environmental studies (MES); human services administration (MPA); school libraries administration (MA); special education (MA); teaching English as a second language (MA).

School in Business Administration *Degree program information:* Part-time and evening/weekend programs available. Offers accounting (MBA); logistics and materials management (MBA); management (MBA, DBA); management of information systems (DBA); marketing (MBA).

UNIVERSIDAD DE MONTERREY, 66238 San Pedro Garza GarcÝa, NL, Mexico

General Information Independent-religious, coed, comprehensive institution.

GRADUATE UNITS

Graduate Programs

UNIVERSIDAD FLET, Miami, FL 33186

General Information Independent-religious, coed, comprehensive institution.

GRADUATE UNITS

Graduate Program

UNIVERSIDAD METROPOLITANA, San Juan, PR 00928-1150

General Information Independent, coed, comprehensive institution. *Graduate housing:* On-campus housing not available. *Research affiliation:* Berkeley National Laboratories (bioremediation), University Consortium of Atmospheric Research (computer science, atmospheric science), University of Colorado at Boulder (computer science, biology), University of Puerto Rico (physics, chemistry), University of Utah (computational chemistry), Howard University (computational chemistry).

GRADUATE UNITS

Graduate Programs in Education *Degree program information:* Part-time and evening/weekend programs available. Offers curriculum and teaching (MA); educational administration and supervision (MA); environmental education (MA); fitness management (MA); managing leisure services (MA); pre-school centers administration (MA); pre-school education (MA); special education (MA); teaching of physical education (MA). Electronic applications accepted.

School of Business Administration *Degree program information:* Part-time and evening/weekend programs available. Offers accounting (MBA); finance (MBA); human resources management (MBA); international business (MBA); management (MBA); marketing (MBA); public accounting (Certificate). Electronic applications accepted.

School of Environmental Affairs *Degree program information:* Part-time programs available. Offers conservation and management of natural resources (MEM); environmental education (MA); environmental planning (MEM); environmental risk and assessment management (MEM). Electronic applications accepted.

UNIVERSITÉ DE MONCTON, Moncton, NB E1A 3E9, Canada

General Information Province-supported, coed, comprehensive institution. *Graduate housing:* Rooms and/or apartments available on a first-come, first-served basis to single and married students.

GRADUATE UNITS

Faculty of Administration Students: 42 full-time (5 women), 88 part-time (45 women), 34 international. Average age 28. 100 applicants, 45% accepted, 25 enrolled. *Faculty:* 11 full-time (3 women), 2 part-time/adjunct (0 women). Expenses: Contact institution. *Financial support:* In 2006–07, 7 fellowships (averaging $2,500 per year) were awarded; teaching assistantships, institutionally sponsored loans also available. Support available to part-time students. Financial award application deadline: 5/30. In 2006, 36 degrees awarded. *Degree program information:* Part-time and evening/weekend programs available. Postbaccalaureate distance learning degree programs offered (no on-campus study). Offers administration (MBA). *Application deadline:* For fall admission, 6/1 for domestic students, 2/1 for international students; for winter admission, 11/15 for domestic students, 9/1 for international students; for spring admission, 3/31 for domestic students, 1/1 for international students. Applications are processed on a rolling basis. *Application fee:* $39. *Application Contact:* Natalie LeBlanc, Admission Counselor, 506-858-4273, Fax: 506-858-4093, E-mail: natalie.r.leblanc@umoncton.ca. *Director,* Dr. Tania Morris, 506-858-4218, Fax: 506-858-4093, E-mail: tania.morris@umoncton.ca.

Faculty of Arts *Degree program information:* Part-time programs available. Offers arts (M Fr, MA, PhD); French (M Fr, MA, PhD); history (MA). Electronic applications accepted.

Faculty of Education *Degree program information:* Part-time programs available. Offers education (M Ed, MA Ed).

Graduate Studies in Education *Degree program information:* Part-time programs available. Offers educational psychology (M Ed, MA Ed); guidance (M Ed, MA Ed); school administration (M Ed, MA Ed); teaching (M Ed, MA Ed).

Faculty of Law Offers law (LL B, LL M, Diploma). Programs offered exclusively in French.

Faculty of Science *Degree program information:* Part-time programs available. Offers biochemistry (M Sc); biology (M Sc); chemistry (M Sc); information technology (M Sc, Certificate, Diploma); mathematics (M Sc); physics and astronomy (M Sc); science (M Sc, Certificate, Diploma). Electronic applications accepted.

Faculty of Social Sciences *Degree program information:* Part-time and evening/weekend programs available. Offers economics (MA); psychology (MA Ps); public administration (MPA); social sciences (MA, MA Ps, MPA, MSS).

School of Social Work Offers social work (MSS).

School of Engineering Offers civil engineering (M Sc A); electrical engineering (M Sc A); industrial engineering (M Sc A); mechanical engineering (M Sc A).

School of Food Science, Nutrition and Family Studies *Degree program information:* Part-time programs available. Offers foods/nutrition (M Sc). Electronic applications accepted.

UNIVERSITÉ DE MONTRÉAL, Montréal, QC H3C 3J7, Canada

General Information Independent, coed, university. CGS member. *Enrollment:* 55,539 graduate, professional, and undergraduate students; 8,486 full-time matriculated graduate/professional students (5,034 women), 2,238 part-time matriculated graduate/professional students (1,627 women). *Graduate faculty:* 1,576 full-time (475 women), 1,704 part-time/adjunct (613 women). *Graduate housing:* Room and/or apartments available on a first-come, first-served basis to single students; on-campus housing not available to married students. Housing application deadline: 2/1. *Student services:* Campus safety program, career counseling, child daycare facilities, disabled student services, exercise/wellness program, free psychological counseling, international student services, low-cost health insurance. *Library facilities:* Bibliotheque des lettres et sciences humaines plus 18 others. *Online resources:* library catalog, web page. *Collection:* 4 million titles, 18,330 serial subscriptions. *Research affiliation:* Institut Universitaire de gériatric de Montréal (gérontologie clinique et gériatric neurosciences cognitives, soins et services, nutrition et les troubles sensoriels), Institut de Cardiologie de Montréal (cardiologie, médicine et chirurgie cardiovasculaires, prévention et réadaption), Institut de recherches cliniques de Montréal (bioéthique, cancer, chimie bioorganique, génetique, hématologie, immunologie, neurosciences et endocrinologie, systeme cardiovasculaire), Centre de Recherche de L'Hôpital Sacré-Coeur (maladies cardiovasculaires, maladies rénales, maladies respiratoires, neurobiologie psychiatrique et troubles du sommeil et traumatologie), Centre Hospitalier Universitaire Mère-Enfant de l'Hôpital Sainte-Justine (pédiatric, urgentologie pédiatrique et périnatalogie).

Computer facilities: 1,500 computers available on campus for general student use. A campuswide network can be accessed from student residence rooms and from off campus. Internet access and online class registration are available. *Web address:* http://www.umontreal.ca/.

General Application Contact: Louise Béliveau, Dean of Graduate Studies, 514-343-6537, Fax: 514-343-2252, E-mail: louise.beliveau@umontreal.ca.

GRADUATE UNITS

Faculty of Graduate Studies Students: 579 full-time (356 women), 1,160 part-time (947 women). 707 applicants, 33% accepted, 189 enrolled. *Faculty:* 505 full-time (299 women), 195 part-time/adjunct (134 women). Expenses: Contact institution. *Financial support:* Fellowships, research assistantships, teaching assistantships, career-related internships or fieldwork, Federal Work-Study, institutionally sponsored loans, and tuition waivers (full and partial) available. Support available to part-time students. In 2006, 84 master's, 12 doctorates, 65 other advanced degrees awarded. *Degree program information:* Part-time programs available. Offers applied human sciences (PhD); bioethics (MA, DESS); environment and prevention (DESS); ergonomics (DESS); kinesiology (M Sc, DESS); molecular biology (M Sc, PhD); museology (MA); physical activity (M Sc, PhD); physical activity and health promotion (DESS); toxicology and risk analysis (DESS). *Application deadline:* For fall admission, 2/1 priority date for domestic students; for winter admission, 11/1 priority date for domestic students; for spring admission, 2/1 priority date for domestic students. *Application fee:* $30. Electronic applications accepted. *Application Contact:* Jocelyne Rousseau, Admissions Office, 514-343-6426, Fax: 514-343-2252, E-mail: fes-admission@fes.umontreal.ca. *Dean,* Louise Béliveau, 514-343-6537, Fax: 514-343-2252.

Faculty of Arts and Sciences Students: 3,512 full-time (1,944 women), 311 part-time (218 women). 3,532 applicants, 35% accepted, 1068 enrolled. *Faculty:* 698 full-time (191 women), 99 part-time/adjunct (25 women). Expenses: Contact institution. *Financial support:* Fellowships, research assistantships, teaching assistantships, career-related internships or fieldwork, Federal Work-Study, institutionally sponsored loans and tuition waivers (full and partial) available. Support available to part-time students. In 2006, 639 master's, 135 doctorates, 50 other advanced degrees awarded. *Degree program information:* Part-time programs available. Offers anthropology (M Sc, PhD); archival (Certificate); art history (MA, PhD); arts and sciences (M Sc, MA, MBSI, PhD, Certificate, DESS); biological sciences (M Sc, PhD); chemistry (M Sc, PhD); communication (PhD); communication sciences (M Sc); comparative literature (MA); computer systems (M Sc, PhD); criminology (M Sc, PhD); data processing (DESS); demography (M Sc, PhD); economic sciences (M Sc, PhD); English (MA, PhD); film studies (MA); French literature (MA, PhD); geography (M Sc, PhD, DESS); German literature (PhD); German studies (MA); Hispanic literature (PhD); Hispanic studies (MA); history (MA, PhD); industrial relations (M Sc, PhD); information sciences (MBSI, PhD); linguistics and translation (MA, PhD, DESS); literature (PhD); literature and cinema (PhD); management of numerical information (Certificate); mathematics (M Sc, PhD); philosophy (MA, PhD); physics (M Sc, PhD); political science (M Sc, PhD); psychoeducation (M Sc, PhD); psychology (M Sc, PhD); social administration (DESS); social work (M Sc, PhD); sociology (M Sc, PhD); statistics (M Sc, PhD); the phenomenon of narcotics (DESS). *Application deadline:* For fall admission, 2/1 priority date for domestic students; for winter admission, 11/1 priority date for domestic students; for spring admission, 2/1 priority date for domestic students. *Application fee:* $30. Electronic applications accepted. *Dean,* Joseph Hubert, 514-343-6262, Fax: 514-343-2185, E-mail: joseph.hubert@umontreal.ca.

Faculty of Dental Medicine Students: 16 full-time (3 women), 1 (woman) part-time. 49 applicants, 12% accepted, 6 enrolled. *Faculty:* 25 full-time (8 women), 1 (woman) part-time/adjunct. Expenses: Contact institution. In 2006, 5 master's, 8 other advanced degrees awarded. Offers dental medicine (M Sc, Certificate); multidisciplinary residency (Certificate); oral and dental sciences (M Sc); orthodontics (M Sc); pediatric dentistry (M Sc); prosthodontics rehabilitation (M Sc); stomatology residency (Certificate). *Application deadline:* For fall admission, 10/1 for domestic students. *Application fee:* $30. Electronic applications accepted. *Application Contact:* Arlette Kolta, Associate Dean for Research, 514-343-7112, Fax: 514-343-2233. *Dean,* Claude Lamarche, 514-343-6005, Fax: 514-343-2233.

Faculty of Education Students: 2,074 full-time (1,636 women), 955 part-time (701 women). 947 applicants, 64% accepted, 496 enrolled. *Faculty:* 72 full-time (41 women), 29 part-time/adjunct (14 women). Expenses: Contact institution. *Financial support:* Fellowships, research assistantships, teaching assistantships available. In 2006, 64 master's, 23 doctorates, 83 other advanced degrees awarded. *Degree program information:* Part-time and evening/weekend programs available. Offers administration and foundations of education (M Ed, MA, PhD, DESS); didactics (M Ed, MA, PhD, DESS); education (M Ed, MA, PhD, DESS); psychopedagogy and andragogy (M Ed, MA, PhD, DESS). *Application deadline:* For fall admission, 2/1 priority date for domestic students; for winter admission, 11/1 priority date for domestic students; for spring admission, 2/1 priority date for domestic students. *Application fee:* $30. Electronic applications accepted. *Application Contact:* François Bowen, Graduate Chairman and Vice Dean, 514-343-7491, Fax: 514-343-7276, E-mail: francois.bowen@umontreal.ca. *Dean,* Michel D. Laurier, 514-343-6658, Fax: 514-343-7276.

Faculty of Environmental Design and Planning Students: 372 full-time (197 women), 56 part-time (34 women). 440 applicants, 39% accepted, 152 enrolled. *Faculty:* 41 full-time (9 women), 41 part-time/adjunct (12 women). Expenses: Contact institution. In 2006, 94 master's, 3 doctorates, 8 other advanced degrees awarded. Offers environmental design and planning (M Sc A, M Urb, PhD, DESS). *Application deadline:* For fall admission, 2/1 priority date for domestic students; for winter admission, 11/1 priority date for domestic students; for spring admission, 2/1 priority date for domestic students. *Application fee:* $30. Electronic applications accepted. *Dean,* Giovanni de Paoli, 514-343-6001, Fax: 514-343-2183.

Faculty of Law Students: 375 full-time (208 women), 89 part-time (53 women). 698 applicants, 40% accepted, 216 enrolled. *Faculty:* 57 full-time (19 women), 5 part-time/adjunct (2 women). Expenses: Contact institution. *Financial support:* Fellowships, research assistantships, teaching assistantships available. In 2006, 53 master's, 4 doctorates, 78 other advanced degrees awarded. *Degree program information:* Part-time programs available. Offers law (LL B, LL M, LL D, DDN, DESS). *Application deadline:* For fall admission, 2/1 priority date for domestic students; for winter admission, 11/1 priority date for domestic students; for spring admission, 2/1 priority date for domestic students. *Application fee:* $30. Electronic applications accepted. *Application Contact:* Michel Morin, Vice Dean, 514-343-2409, E-mail: michel.morin.3@umontreal.ca. *Dean,* Anne-Marie Boisvert, 514-343-2356, Fax: 514-343-2199, E-mail: anne-marie.boisvert@umontreal.ca.

Faculty of Music Students: 260 full-time (115 women), 1 (woman) part-time. 222 applicants, 43% accepted, 88 enrolled. *Faculty:* 42 full-time (16 women), 38 part-time/adjunct (14 women). Expenses: Contact institution. In 2006, 59 master's, 8 doctorates, 18 other advanced degrees awarded. Offers composition (M Mus, D Mus); musicology and ethnomusicology (MA, PhD); orchestra conducting (M Mus, D Mus); orchestral repertoire (DESS); performance interpretation (DESS); voice and instruments interpretation (M Mus, D Mus). *Application deadline:* For fall admission, 2/1 priority date for domestic students; for winter admission, 11/1 priority date for domestic students; for spring admission, 2/1 priority date for domestic students. *Application fee:* $30. Electronic applications accepted. *Application Contact:* Sylvain Caron, Vice Dean, 514-343-5897, Fax: 514-343-5727, E-mail: sylvain.caron@umontreal.ca. *Dean,* Jacques Boucher, 514-343-6429, Fax: 514-343-5727.

Faculty of Nursing Students: 126 full-time (115 women), 164 part-time (149 women). 218 applicants, 64% accepted, 121 enrolled. *Faculty:* 27 full-time (21 women), 22 part-time/adjunct (20 women). Expenses: Contact institution. *Financial support:* Fellowships, research assistantships, teaching assistantships, career-related internships or fieldwork, Federal Work-Study, and institutionally sponsored loans available. In 2006, 35 master's, 2 doctorates, 8 other advanced degrees awarded. *Degree program information:* Part-time programs available. Offers nursing (M Sc, PhD, DESS). *Application deadline:* For fall admission, 2/1 priority date for domestic students; for winter admission, 11/1 priority date for domestic students; for spring admission, 2/1 priority date for domestic students. Applica-

Université de Montréal (continued)

tions are processed on a rolling basis. *Application fee:* $30. Electronic applications accepted. *Application Contact:* Francine Gratton, Vice Dean of Studies, 514-343-5835, Fax: 514-343-2306, E-mail: francine.gratton@umontreal.ca. *Dean,* Céline Goulet, 514-343-6436, Fax: 514-343-2306.

Faculty of Pharmacy Students: 224 full-time (153 women), 91 part-time (71 women). 236 applicants, 49% accepted, 101 enrolled. *Faculty:* 24 full-time (13 women), 29 part-time/adjunct (16 women). Expenses: Contact institution. *Financial support:* Fellowships, teaching assistantships, career-related internships or fieldwork, Federal Work-Study, and institutionally sponsored loans available. In 2006, 83 master's, 7 doctorates, 50 other advanced degrees awarded. *Degree program information:* Part-time programs available. Offers development of medicine (DESS); master pharmacist (DESS); pharmaceutical cares (DESS); pharmaceutical practice (M Sc); pharmaceutical sciences (M Sc, PhD). *Application deadline:* For fall admission, 2/1 priority date for domestic students; for winter admission, 11/1 priority date for domestic students; for spring admission, 2/1 priority date for domestic students. *Application fee:* $30. Electronic applications accepted. *Application Contact:* Daniel Lamontagne, Vice Dean, 514-343-6467, Fax: 514-343-2102. *Dean,* Pierre Moreau, 514-343-6440, Fax: 514-343-2102.

Faculty of Theology Students: 88 full-time (27 women), 21 part-time (7 women). 46 applicants, 48% accepted, 18 enrolled. *Faculty:* 21 full-time (6 women), 4 part-time/adjunct (1 woman). Expenses: Contact institution. *Financial support:* Research assistantships, teaching assistantships, institutionally sponsored loans and tuition waivers (partial) available. In 2006, 12 master's, 5 doctorates awarded. Offers theology (MA, D Th, PhD, DESS, L Th). *Application deadline:* For fall admission, 2/1 priority date for domestic students; for winter admission, 11/1 priority date for domestic students; for spring admission, 2/1 priority date for domestic students. *Application fee:* $30. Electronic applications accepted. *Application Contact:* Alain Gignac, Vice Dean of Graduate Studies, 514-343-7164, Fax: 514-343-5738. *Dean,* Jean Duhaime, 514-343-7160, Fax: 514-343-5738.

Faculty of Veterinary Medicine Students: 162 full-time (88 women), 35 part-time (16 women). 82 applicants, 48% accepted, 38 enrolled. *Faculty:* 61 full-time (14 women), 55 part-time/adjunct (16 women). Expenses: Contact institution. *Financial support:* Research assistantships, teaching assistantships, career-related internships or fieldwork and scholarships/grants available. In 2006, 30 master's, 7 doctorates, 25 other advanced degrees awarded. Offers veterinary medicine (DVM, M Sc, DES, PhD, Certificate, DESS); veterinary sciences (M Sc, DES, PhD, Certificate, DESS). *Application deadline:* For fall admission, 2/1 priority date for domestic students; for winter admission, 11/1 priority date for domestic students; for spring admission, 2/1 priority date for domestic students. *Application fee:* $30. Electronic applications accepted. *Application Contact:* Diane Blais, Associate Dean, Student Affairs, 450-773-8521, Fax: 450-778-8132. *Dean,* Jean Sirois, 450-773-8521 Ext. 8542, Fax: 450-778-8101, E-mail: jean.sirois@umontreal.ca.

School of Optometry Students: 24 full-time (15 women), 5 part-time (3 women). 26 applicants, 46% accepted, 11 enrolled. *Faculty:* 10 full-time (2 women), 18 part-time/adjunct (8 women). Expenses: Contact institution. *Financial support:* Research assistantships, teaching assistantships, career-related internships or fieldwork available. Support available to part-time students. In 2006, 12 master's, 3 other advanced degrees awarded. *Degree program information:* Part-time programs available. Offers optometry (OD, M Sc, DESS); vision sciences (M Sc). *Application deadline:* For fall admission, 2/1 priority date for domestic students; for winter admission, 11/1 priority date for domestic students; for spring admission, 2/1 priority date for domestic students. *Application fee:* $30. Electronic applications accepted. *Application Contact:* Christian Casanova, Chairperson, 514-343-6325, Fax: 514-343-2382. *Director,* Jacques Gresset, 514-343-6948, Fax: 514-343-2382, E-mail: jacques.gresset@umontreal.ca.

Faculty of Medicine Students: 1,944 full-time (1,259 women), 184 part-time (108 women). 1,162 applicants, 37% accepted, 363 enrolled. *Faculty:* 545 full-time (145 women), 1,342 part-time/adjunct (494 women). Expenses: Contact institution. *Financial support:* Fellowships, research assistantships, teaching assistantships, career-related internships or fieldwork, institutionally sponsored loans, and tuition waivers (full) available. In 2006, 278 master's, 72 doctorates, 157 other advanced degrees awarded. Offers anesthesia (DESS); biochemistry (M Sc, PhD, DEPD); biomedical engineering (M Sc A, PhD, DESS); biomedical sciences (M Sc, PhD); biophysics and molecular physiology (M Sc, PhD); clinical biochemistry (DEPD); communal and public health (M Sc, PhD, DESS); community health (M Sc, DESS); diagnostic radiology (DESS); environmental and occupational health (M Sc, DESS); family medicine (DESS); health administration (M Sc, DESS); health sciences (DESS); medical biochemistry (DESS); medical genetics (DESS); medicine (DESS); microbiology and immunology (M Sc, PhD); microbiology and infectious diseases (DESS); neurological sciences (M Sc, PhD); nuclear medicine (DESS); nutrition (M Sc, PhD); obstetrics and gynecology (DESS); ophthalmology (DESS); pathology and cellular biology (M Sc, PhD); pediatrics (DESS); pharmacology (M Sc, PhD); physiology (M Sc, PhD); psychiatry (DESS); public health (PhD); radiology-oncology (DESS); speech therapy (DESS); speech therapy and audiology (MOA, DESS); speech-language pathology and audiology (MOA); surgery (DESS); virology and immunology (PhD). *Application deadline:* For fall admission, 2/1 priority date for domestic students; for winter admission, 11/1 priority date for domestic students; for spring admission, 2/1 priority date for domestic students. *Application fee:* $30. Electronic applications accepted. *Application Contact:* Dr. Pierre Boyle, Vice Dean of Studies, 514-343-6300, Fax: 514-343-5751, E-mail: pierre.boyle@umontreal.ca. *Dean,* Jean L. Lucien, 514-343-6351, Fax: 514-343-5850.

UNIVERSITÉ DE SHERBROOKE, Sherbrooke, QC J1K 2R1, Canada

General Information Independent, coed, university. *Graduate housing:* Room and/or apartments available to single students; on-campus housing not available to married students. Housing application deadline: 6/1. *Research affiliation:* Société de Microélectronique Industrielle.

GRADUATE UNITS

Faculty of Administration *Degree program information:* Part-time and evening/weekend programs available. Offers accounting (M Sc); administration (EMBA, M Sc, M Tax, MBA, DBA, Diploma); business administration (EMBA, MBA, DBA, Diploma); finance (M Sc); international business (M Sc); management information systems (M Sc); marketing (M Sc); organizational change and intervention (M Sc); taxation (M Tax, Diploma).

Faculty of Education *Degree program information:* Part-time and evening/weekend programs available. Offers education (M Ed, MA, Diploma); elementary education (M Ed, Diploma); postsecondary education training (M Ed, Diploma); school administration (M Ed); sciences of education (MA); special education (M Ed, Diploma).

Faculty of Engineering Students: 408 full-time (78 women), 226 part-time (58 women); includes 60 minority (15 African Americans, 21 Asian Americans or Pacific Islanders, 24 Hispanic Americans), 106 international. 370 applicants, 22% accepted, 46 enrolled. *Faculty:* 82 full-time (5 women). Expenses: Contact institution. In 2006, 64 master's, 20 doctorates awarded. *Degree program information:* Part-time programs available. Offers chemical engineering (M Sc A, PhD); civil engineering (M Sc A, PhD); electrical engineering (M Sc A, PhD); engineering (M Eng, M Env, M Sc A, PhD, Diploma); engineering management (M Eng, Diploma); environment (M Env); mechanical engineering (M Sc A, PhD). *Application deadline:* Applications are processed on a rolling basis. *Application fee:* $70 Canadian dollars. Electronic applications accepted. *Application Contact:* Radhouane Masmoudi, Assistant Dean, Research, 819-821-8000, Fax: 819-821-6994, E-mail: radhouane.masmoudi@usherbrooke.ca. *Dean,* Gérard Lachiver, 819-821-7111, Fax: 819-821-7903, E-mail: gerard.lachiver@usherbrooke.ca.

Faculty of Law *Degree program information:* Part-time and evening/weekend programs available. Offers alternative dispute resolution (LL M, Diploma); biotechnology (LL B); business administration (LL B); business law (Diploma); health law (LL M, Diploma); law (LL B, LL D); legal management (Diploma); notarial law (DDN); transnational law (Diploma). Electronic applications accepted.

Faculty of Letters and Human Sciences *Degree program information:* Part-time programs available. Offers comparative Canadian literature (MA, PhD); economics (MA); French literature (MA, PhD); geography and remote sensing (M Sc, PhD); gerontology (MA); history (MA); letters and human sciences (M Psych, M Sc, MA, MSS, PhD, Diploma); linguistics (MA); lit&erature de création (MA, PhD); philosophy (MA); social service (MSS); theatre (MA).

Institute of Management and Development of Cooperatives Offers management and development of cooperatives (MA, Diploma).

Faculty of Medicine and Health Sciences Students: 879 full-time (624 women), 360 part-time (214 women). 1,909 applicants, 24% accepted, 244 enrolled. Expenses: Contact institution. *Financial support:* Fellowships, research assistantships, tuition waivers (full) available. In 2006, 91 MDs, 98 master's, 34 doctorates awarded. *Degree program information:* Part-time programs available. Offers medicine (MD); medicine and health sciences (MD, M Sc, PhD). Electronic applications accepted. *Dean,* Réjean Hébert, 819-564-5201, E-mail: rejean.hebert@usherbrooke.ca.

Graduate Programs in Medicine Students: 148 full-time (73 women), 180 part-time (107 women). 66 applicants, 39% accepted, 25 enrolled. Expenses: Contact institution. *Financial support:* Fellowships, research assistantships, tuition waivers (full) available. In 2006, 49 master's, 17 doctorates awarded. *Degree program information:* Part-time programs available. Offers biochemistry (M Sc, PhD); cell biology (M Sc, PhD); clinical sciences (M Sc, PhD); immunology (M Sc, PhD); medicine (M Sc, PhD); microbiology (M Sc, PhD); pharmacology (M Sc, PhD); physiology and biophysics (M Sc, PhD); radiobiology (M Sc, PhD). *Application deadline:* For fall admission, 6/30 for domestic students; for winter admission, 10/31 for domestic students; for spring admission, 2/28 for domestic students. *Application fee:* $70. Electronic applications accepted. *Vice Dean for Graduate Studies,* Dr. Claude Asselin, 819-564-5276, E-mail: claude.asselin@usherbrooke.ca.

Faculty of Physical Education *Degree program information:* Part-time programs available. Offers kinanthropology (M Sc); physical activity (Diploma); physical education (M Sc, Diploma).

Faculty of Sciences Offers biology (M Sc, PhD, Diploma); chemistry (M Sc, PhD, Diploma); informatics (M Sc, PhD); mathematics (M Sc, PhD); physics (M Sc, PhD); sciences (M Sc, PhD, Diploma).

Centre de Formation en Technologies de L'information Offers information technologies (M Sc, Diploma). Electronic applications accepted.

Centre Universitaire de Formation en Environnement Postbaccalaureate distance learning degree programs offered (no on-campus study). Offers environment (M Sc, Diploma). Electronic applications accepted.

Faculty of Theology, Ethics and Philosophy *Degree program information:* Part-time and evening/weekend programs available. Postbaccalaureate distance learning degree programs offered. Offers applied ethics (Diploma); human science of religions (MA); intercultural training (Diploma); philosophy (MA, PhD); spiritual anthropology (Diploma); theology (MA, PhD, Diploma).

UNIVERSITÉ DU QUÉBEC À CHICOUTIMI, Chicoutimi, QC G7H 2B1, Canada

General Information Province-supported, coed, university. CGS member. *Graduate housing:* Room and/or apartments available to single students; on-campus housing not available to married students.

GRADUATE UNITS

Graduate Programs *Degree program information:* Part-time programs available. Offers didactics of French-mother tongue (Diploma); earth sciences (M Sc A); education (M Ed, MA, PhD); engineering (M Sc A, PhD); ethics (Diploma); fine arts (MA); genetics (M Sc); linguistics (MA); literary studies (MA); mineral resources (PhD); project management (M Sc); regional studies (MA); renewable resources (M Sc); small and medium-sized organization management (M Sc); theology (pastoral studies) (MA, PhD).

UNIVERSITÉ DU QUÉBEC À MONTRÉAL, Montréal, QC H3C 3P8, Canada

General Information Province-supported, coed, university. CGS member. *Graduate housing:* Room and/or apartments available to single students; on-campus housing not available to married students. *Research affiliation:* Labopharm, Inc. (pharmacology), Hydro-Québec (environmental sciences), Bell (computer sciences), Microcréatif (computer sciences), University Corporation for Atmospheric Resources.

GRADUATE UNITS

Graduate Programs *Degree program information:* Part-time programs available. Offers accounting (M Sc, MPA, Diploma); actuarial sciences (Diploma); art history (PhD); art studies (MA); atmospheric sciences (M Sc); biology (M Sc, PhD); business administration (MBA); business administration (research) (MBA); chemistry (M Sc); communications (MA, PhD); dance (MA); death (Diploma); dramatic arts (MA); economics (M Sc, PhD); education (M Ed, MA, PhD); education of the environmental sciences (Diploma); environmental sciences (M Sc, PhD); ergonomics in occupational health and safety (Diploma); finance (Diploma); fine arts (MA); geographical information systems (Diploma); geography (M Sc); geology-research (M Sc); history (MA, PhD); human movement studies (M Sc); linguistics (MA, PhD); literary studies (MA, PhD); management consultant (Diploma); management information systems (M Sc, M Sc A); mathematics (M Sc, PhD); meteorology (PhD, Diploma); mineral resources (PhD); museology (MA); non-renewable resources (DESS); philosophy (MA, PhD); political science (MA, PhD); project management (MGP, Diploma); psychology (D Ps, PhD); religious sciences (MA, PhD); semiology (PhD); sexology (MA); social and labor law (LL M); social intervention (MA); sociology (MA, PhD); study and practices of the arts (PhD); urban analysis and management (MA); urban studies (PhD).

UNIVERSITÉ DU QUÉBEC À RIMOUSKI, Rimouski, QC G5L 3A1, Canada

General Information Province-supported, coed, comprehensive institution. CGS member. *Graduate faculty:* 176 full-time (52 women), 236 part-time/adjunct (101 women). *Graduate housing:* Room and/or apartments available on a first-come, first-served basis to single students; on-campus housing not available to married students. *Student services:* Campus employment opportunities, career counseling, child daycare facilities, free psychological counseling, international student services, writing training. *Collection:* 263,142 titles, 3,951 serial subscriptions.

Computer facilities: Internet access is available. *Web address:* http://www.uqar.qc.ca/.

General Application Contact: Marc Berube, Office of Admissions, 418-724-1433, Fax: 418-724-1525, E-mail: marc_berube@uqar.ca.

GRADUATE UNITS

Graduate Programs Students: 132 full-time (62 women), 277 part-time (150 women), 72 international. Expenses: Contact institution. *Financial support:* Fellowships, research assistantships, teaching assistantships available. In 2006, 84 master's, 6 doctorates, 8 other advanced degrees awarded. *Degree program information:* Part-time programs available. Offers biology (PhD); business administration (MBA); education (M Ed, MA, PhD, Diploma); engineering (M Sc A); ethics (MA, Diploma); literary studies (MA, PhD); management of marine resources (M Sc, Diploma); management of people in working situation (M Sc, Diploma); nursing studies (M Sc, Diploma); oceanography (M Sc, PhD); project management (M Sc, Diploma); psychosocial studies (MA); regional development (MA, PhD, Diploma); wildlife resources management (M Sc, Diploma). *Application deadline:* For fall admission, 5/1 for domestic students. *Application fee:* $50. *Application Contact:* Marc Berube, Office of Admission, 418-724-1433, Fax: 418-724-1525, E-mail: marc_berube@uqar.ca. *Dean,* Jean-Pierre Ouellet, 418-724-1540, Fax: 418-724-1525.

UNIVERSITÉ DU QUÉBEC À TROIS-RIVIÈRES, Trois-Rivières, QC G9A 5H7, Canada

General Information Province-supported, coed, university. CGS member. *Graduate housing:* Room and/or apartments available to single students; on-campus housing not available to married students. Housing application deadline: 2/1.

GRADUATE UNITS

Graduate Programs *Degree program information:* Part-time programs available. Offers accounting science (DESS); biophysics and cellular biology (M Sc, PhD); business administration (DBA); chemistry (M Sc); education (M Ed, MA, DESS); educational administration (PhD); electrical engineering (M Sc A, PhD); energy sciences (M Sc, PhD); environmental sciences (M Sc, PhD); finance and economic finance (DESS); industrial engineering (M Sc, DESS); labor relations (DESS); leisure, culture and tourism sciences (MA, DESS); literary studies (MA); management of small and medium-sized enterprises and their environment (M Sc); mathematics and computer science (M Sc); nursing sciences (M Sc, DESS); philosophy (MA, PhD); physical education (M Sc); project management (M Sc, MGP, DESS); psychoeducation (M Ed); psychology (MA, PhD); pulp and paper engineering (M Sc A, PhD); Quebec studies (MA, PhD).

UNIVERSITÉ DU QUÉBEC, ÉCOLE DE TECHNOLOGIE SUPÉRIEURE, Montréal, QC H3C 1K3, Canada

General Information Province-supported, coed, primarily men, comprehensive institution. CGS member. *Enrollment:* 487 full-time matriculated graduate/professional students (84 women), 225 part-time matriculated graduate/professional students (42 women). *Enrollment by degree level:* 483 master's, 206 doctoral, 23 other advanced degrees. *Graduate faculty:* 153 full-time, 206 part-time/adjunct. *Graduate housing:* Rooms and/or apartments available on a first-come, first-served basis to single and married students. *Student services:* Campus employment opportunities, free psychological counseling, international student services. *Online resources:* library catalog, web page, access to other libraries' catalogs. *Collection:* 44,195 titles, 630 serial subscriptions. *Web address:* http://www.etsmtl.ca/.

General Application Contact: Francine Gamache, Registrar, 514-396-8885, Fax: 514-396-8831, E-mail: francine.gamache@etsmtl.ca.

GRADUATE UNITS

Graduate Programs Students: 487 full-time (84 women), 225 part-time (42 women). 249 applicants, 75% accepted, 119 enrolled. *Faculty:* 149 full-time, 210 part-time/adjunct. Expenses: Contact institution. *Financial support:* Fellowships, research assistantships, teaching assistantships available. In 2006, 121 master's, 16 doctorates, 12 other advanced degrees awarded. Postbaccalaureate distance learning degree programs offered (minimal on-campus study). Offers engineering (M Eng, PhD, Diploma). *Application deadline:* For fall admission, 5/1 priority date for domestic and international students; for winter admission, 11/1 priority date for domestic students, 8/1 priority date for international students; for spring admission, 3/1 priority date for domestic students, 12/1 priority date for international students. *Application fee:* $40. *Application Contact:* Francine Gamache, Registrar, 514-396-8885, Fax: 514-396-8831, E-mail: francine.gamache@etsmtl.ca. *Head,* Sylvie Doré, E-mail: sylvie.dore@etsmtl.ca.

UNIVERSITÉ DU QUÉBEC, ÉCOLE NATIONALE D'ADMINISTRATION PUBLIQUE, Quebec, QC G1K 9E5, Canada

General Information Province-supported, coed, graduate-only institution. CGS member. *Graduate housing:* On-campus housing not available.

GRADUATE UNITS

Graduate Program in Public Administration *Degree program information:* Part-time programs available. Offers international administration (MAP, Diploma); public administration (MAGU, MAP, PhD, Diploma); urban analysis and management (MAGU).

UNIVERSITÉ DU QUÉBEC EN ABITIBI-TÉMISCAMINGUE, Rouyn-Noranda, QC J9X 5E4, Canada

General Information Province-supported, coed, comprehensive institution. CGS member. *Graduate housing:* Room and/or apartments available on a first-come, first-served basis to single students; on-campus housing not available to married students. Housing application deadline: 3/1.

GRADUATE UNITS

Graduate Programs *Degree program information:* Part-time programs available. Offers business administration (MBA); education (M Ed, MA, PhD); organization management (M Sc); project management (M Sc).

UNIVERSITÉ DU QUÉBEC EN OUTAOUAIS, Gatineau, QC J8X 3X7, Canada

General Information Province-supported, coed, university. CGS member. *Enrollment:* 5,592 graduate, professional, and undergraduate students; 367 full-time matriculated graduate/professional students, 616 part-time matriculated graduate/professional students. *Enrollment by degree level:* 942 master's, 41 doctoral. *Graduate faculty:* 40. *Graduate housing:* Rooms and/or apartments available on a first-come, first-served basis to single students and available to married students. *Student services:* Campus employment opportunities, disabled student services, international student services, low-cost health insurance. *Library facilities:* Brault Library plus 1 other. *Online resources:* library catalog, web page. *Collection:* 230,910 titles, 12,351 serial subscriptions.

Computer facilities: Computer purchase and lease plans are available. 141 computers available on campus for general student use. A campuswide network can be accessed from off campus. Internet access and online class registration are available. *Web address:* http://www.uqo.ca/.

General Application Contact: Registrar's Office, 819-773-1850, Fax: 819-773-1835, E-mail: registraire@ugo.ca.

GRADUATE UNITS

Graduate Programs Students: 1,131, 64 international. *Faculty:* 40. Expenses: Contact institution. *Financial support:* Fellowships, research assistantships, teaching assistantships available. *Degree program information:* Part-time programs available. Offers accounting (DESS); andragogy (DESS); computer network (Diploma); computer science (M Sc); education (M Ed, MA, PhD, Diploma); executive certified management accounting (MBA, Diploma); financial services (MBA, Diploma); industrial relations (M Sc, MA, PhD, Diploma); localisation (Diploma); nursing (M Sc, Diploma); project management (M Sc, MA, Diploma); psychoéducation (M Ed, MA); regional development (MA); social work (MA). *Application deadline:* For fall admission, 6/1 for domestic students, 3/1 for international students; for winter admission, 11/1 for domestic students, 10/1 for international students. *Application fee:* $30 Canadian dollars. *Application Contact:* Registrar's Office, 819-773-1850, Fax: 819-773-1835, E-mail: registraire@ugo.ca. *Dean,* Toussaint Fortin, 819-595-3985, Fax: 819-595-3985, E-mail: toussaint.fortin@uqo.ca.

UNIVERSITÉ DU QUÉBEC, INSTITUT NATIONAL DE LA RECHERCHE SCIENTIFIQUE, Québec, QC G1K 9A9, Canada

General Information Province-supported, coed, graduate-only institution. CGS member. *Enrollment by degree level:* 235 master's, 291 doctoral, 39 other advanced degrees. *Graduate faculty:* 152. *Graduate housing:* On-campus housing not available. *Student services:* Campus employment opportunities, international student services. *Online resources:* library catalog, web page, access to other libraries' catalogs. *Collection:* 47,013 titles, 7,907 serial subscriptions, 250 audiovisual materials.

Computer facilities: A campuswide network can be accessed from student residence rooms and from off campus. Internet access is available. *Web address:* http://www.inrs.ca/.

General Application Contact: Yvonne Boisvert, Registrar, 418-654-3861, Fax: 418-654-3858, E-mail: registrariat@adm.inrs.ca.

GRADUATE UNITS

Graduate Programs Students: 554 full-time (246 women), 29 part-time (6 women), 155 international. Average age 31. *Faculty:* 152. Expenses: Contact institution. *Financial support:* Fellowships, research assistantships, teaching assistantships available. In 2006, 74 master's, 21 doctorates awarded. *Degree program information:* Part-time programs available. *Application deadline:* For fall admission, 3/30 for domestic and international students; for winter admission, 11/1 for domestic and international students. *Application fee:* $30. *Application Contact:* Yvonne Boisvert, Registrar, 418-654-3861, Fax: 418-654-3858, E-mail: registrariat@adm.inrs.ca. *Scientific Director,* Sinh LeQuoc, 418-654-2512, E-mail: sinh_lequoc@adm.inrs.ca.

Research Center—Energy, Materials and Telecommunications Students: 150 full-time (34 women), 13 part-time (1 woman), 64 international. Average age 31. *Faculty:* 39. Expenses: Contact institution. *Financial support:* Fellowships, research assistantships, teaching assistantships available. In 2006, 17 master's, 4 doctorates awarded. *Degree program information:* Part-time programs available. Offers energy and materials science (M Sc, PhD); telecommunications (M Sc, PhD). Programs given in French. *Application deadline:* For fall admission, 3/30 for domestic and international students; for winter admission, 11/1 for domestic and international students. *Application fee:* $30. *Application Contact:* Yvonne Boisvert, Registrar, 418-654-3861, Fax: 418-654-3858, E-mail: registrariat@adm.inrs.ca. *Director,* Jean-Claude Kieffer, 450-929-8100, Fax: 450-8102, E-mail: kieffer@emt.inrs.ca.

Research Center—INRS—Institut Armand-Frappier—Human Health Students: 150 full-time (88 women), 1 part-time, 26 international. Average age 29. *Faculty:* 45. Expenses: Contact institution. *Financial support:* Fellowships, research assistantships, teaching assistantships available. In 2006, 24 master's, 9 doctorates awarded. *Degree program information:* Part-time programs available. Offers applied microbiology (M Sc); biology (PhD); experimental health sciences (M Sc); virology and immunology (M Sc, PhD). Programs given in French. *Application deadline:* For fall admission, 3/30 for domestic and international students; for winter admission, 11/1 for domestic and international students. *Application fee:* $30 Canadian dollars. *Application Contact:* Yvonne Boisvert, Registrar, 418-654-3861, Fax: 418-654-3858, E-mail: registrariat@adm.inrs.ca. *Director,* Pierre Talbot, 450-681-5010 Ext. 4406, E-mail: pierre.talbot@iaf.inrs.ca.

Research Center—Urbanization, Culture and Society Students: 76 full-time (41 women), 8 part-time (3 women), 12 international. Average age 33. *Faculty:* 35. Expenses: Contact institution. *Financial support:* Fellowships, research assistantships, teaching assistantships available. In 2006, 6 master's, 1 doctorate awarded. *Degree program information:* Part-time programs available. Offers demography (MA, PhD); urban studies (MA, PhD). Programs given in French. *Application deadline:* For fall admission, 3/30 for domestic and international students; for winter admission, 11/1 for domestic and international students. *Application fee:* $30. *Application Contact:* Yvonne Boisvert, Registrar, 418-654-3861, Fax: 418-654-3858, E-mail: registrariat@adm.inrs.ca. *Director,* Johanne Charbonneau, 514-499-4001, Fax: 514-499-4065, E-mail: johanne.charbonneau@ucs.inrs.ca.

Research Center—Water, Earth and Environment Students: 178 full-time (83 women), 7 part-time (2 women), 53 international. Average age 30. *Faculty:* 33. Expenses: Contact institution. *Financial support:* Fellowships, research assistantships, teaching assistantships available. In 2006, 27 master's, 7 doctorates awarded. *Degree program information:* Part-time programs available. Offers earth sciences (M Sc, PhD); earth sciences-environmental technologies (M Sc); water sciences (MA, PhD). *Application deadline:* For fall admission, 3/30 for domestic and international students; for winter admission, 11/1 for domestic and international students. *Application fee:* $30. *Application Contact:* Yvonne Boisvert, Registrar, 418-654-3861, Fax: 418-654-3858, E-mail: registrariat@adm.inrs.ca. *Director,* Jean Pierre Villeneuve, 418-654-2575, Fax: 418-654-2615, E-mail: jp_villeneuve@ete.inrs.ca.

UNIVERSITÉ LAVAL, Québec, QC G1K 7P4, Canada

General Information Independent, coed, university. CGS member. *Graduate housing:* Room and/or apartments available on a first-come, first-served basis to single students; on-campus housing not available to married students. *Research affiliation:* Centre Hospitalier Universitaire de Québec (biomedical research), Institut National d'optique (optics and photonics), Centre de Développement de la Geomatique (applied geomatics), Institut Maurice-Lamontagne (oceanography), Forintek Canada (forestry and wood processing), Société des pades de Sciences Naturelles du Québec (biology).

GRADUATE UNITS

Faculty of Administrative Sciences *Degree program information:* Part-time programs available. Postbaccalaureate distance learning degree programs offered (no on-campus study). Offers accounting (MBA); administrative sciences (M Sc, MBA, PhD, Diploma); administrative studies (M Sc, PhD); agri-food management (MBA); electronic business (MBA, Diploma); factory management and logistics (MBA); finance (MBA); financial engineering (M Sc); firm management (MBA); information technology management (MBA); international management (MBA); management (MBA); management accounting (MBA, Diploma); marketing (MBA); modelization and organizational decision (MBA); occupational health and safety management (MBA); organizations management and development (Diploma); pharmacy management (MBA); public accountancy (MBA, Diploma); technological entrepreneurship (Diploma). Electronic applications accepted.

Faculty of Agricultural and Food Sciences *Degree program information:* Part-time programs available. Offers agri-food engineering (M Sc); agricultural and food sciences (M Sc, PhD, Diploma); agricultural economics (M Sc); agricultural microbiology (M Sc, PhD); animal sciences (M Sc, PhD); consumer sciences (Diploma); environmental technology (M Sc); food sciences and technology (M Sc, PhD); integrated rural development (Diploma); nutrition (M Sc, PhD); plant biology (M Sc, PhD); soils and environment science (M Sc, PhD). Electronic applications accepted.

Faculty of Architecture, Planning and Visual Arts Offers architecture, planning and visual arts (M Arch, M Sc, MA, MATDR, PhD); planning and regional development (MATDR, PhD). Electronic applications accepted.

School of Architecture *Degree program information:* Part-time programs available. Offers architecture (M Arch, M Sc). Electronic applications accepted.

School of Visual Arts Offers graphic design and multimedia (MA); visual arts (MA). Electronic applications accepted.

Faculty of Dentistry Offers buccal and maxillofacial surgery (DESS); dentistry (DMD, M Sc, DESS); gerodontology (DESS); multidisciplinary dentistry (DESS); periodontics (DESS). Electronic applications accepted.

Faculty of Education *Degree program information:* Part-time programs available. Offers didactics (MA, PhD); education (MA, PhD, Diploma); educational administration and evaluation (MA, PhD); educational pedagogy (Diploma); educational practice (Diploma); educational psychology (MA, PhD); orientation sciences (MA, PhD); pedagogy management and development (Diploma); school adaptation (Diploma); teaching technology (MA, PhD). Electronic applications accepted.

Faculty of Forestry and Geomatics Offers agroforestry (M Sc); forestry and geomatics (M Sc, M Sc Geogr, PhD); forestry sciences (M Sc, PhD); geographical sciences (M Sc Geogr, PhD); geography (M Sc Geogr, PhD); geomatics sciences (M Sc, PhD); wood sciences (M Sc, PhD). Electronic applications accepted.

Faculty of Law *Degree program information:* Part-time programs available. Offers international and transnational law (Diploma); law (LL M, LL D); law of business (Diploma); notarial law (Diploma). Electronic applications accepted.

Faculty of Letters *Degree program information:* Part-time programs available. Offers ancient civilization (MA, PhD); archaeology (MA, PhD); art history (MA, PhD); English literatures (MA, PhD); ethnology of French-speaking people in North America (MA, PhD); French studies (MA); history (MA, PhD); international journalism (Diploma); letters (MA, PhD, Diploma);

Université Laval (continued)

linguistics (MA, PhD); literary studies (MA, PhD); literature and the screen and stage (MA, PhD); museology (Diploma); public communication (MA); public relations (Diploma); Spanish literature (MA, PhD); terminology and translation (MA, Diploma). Electronic applications accepted.

Faculty of Medicine *Degree program information:* Part-time programs available. Offers accident prevention and occupational health and safety management (Diploma); anatomy and physiology (M Sc, PhD); anatomy–pathology (DESS); anesthesiology (DESS); cardiology (DESS); care of older people (Diploma); cellular and molecular biology (M Sc, PhD); clinical research (DESS); community health (M Sc, PhD, DESS); dermatology (DESS); diagnostic radiology (DESS); emergency medicine (Diploma); epidemiology (M Sc, PhD); experimental medicine (M Sc, PhD); family medicine (DESS); general surgery (DESS); geriatrics (DESS); hematology (DESS); internal medicine (DESS); kinesiology (M Sc, PhD); maternal and fetal medicine (Diploma); medical biochemistry (DESS); medical microbiology and infectious diseases (DESS); medical oncology (DESS); medicine (MD, M Sc, PhD, DESS, Diploma); microbiology-immunology (M Sc, PhD); nephrology (DESS); neurobiology (M Sc, PhD); neurology (DESS); neurosurgery (DESS); obstetrics and gynecology (DESS); ophthalmology (DESS); orthopedic surgery (DESS); oto-rhino-laryngology (DESS); palliative medicine (Diploma); pediatrics (DESS); physiology-endocrinology (M Sc, PhD); plastic surgery (DESS); psychiatry (DESS); pulmonary medicine (DESS); radiology–oncology (DESS); speech therapy (M Sc); thoracic surgery (DESS); urology (DESS). Electronic applications accepted.

Faculty of Music Offers composition (M Mus); instrumental didactics (M Mus); interpretation (M Mus); music (PhD); music education (M Mus); musicology (M Mus). Electronic applications accepted.

Faculty of Nursing Offers nursing (M Sc, Diploma). Electronic applications accepted.

Faculty of Pharmacy *Degree program information:* Part-time programs available. Offers community pharmacy (Diploma); hospital pharmacy (M Sc); pharmacy (M Sc, PhD, Diploma). Electronic applications accepted.

Faculty of Philosophy Offers philosophy (MA, PhD). Electronic applications accepted.

Faculty of Sciences and Engineering *Degree program information:* Part-time programs available. Offers aerospace engineering (M Sc); biochemistry (M Sc, PhD); biology (M Sc, PhD); chemical engineering (M Sc, PhD); chemistry (M Sc, PhD); civil engineering (M Sc, PhD); computer science (M Sc, PhD); earth sciences (M Sc, PhD); electrical engineering (M Sc, PhD); environmental technologies (M Sc); environmental technology (M Sc); geology (M Sc, PhD); industrial engineering (Diploma); mathematics (M Sc, PhD); mechanical engineering (M Sc, PhD); metallurgical engineering (M Sc, PhD); microbiology (M Sc, PhD); mining engineering (M Sc, PhD); oceanography (PhD); physics (M Sc, PhD); sciences and engineering (M Sc, PhD, Diploma); software engineering (Diploma); statistics (M Sc); technological entrepreneurship (Diploma); urban infrastructure engineering (Diploma). Electronic applications accepted.

Faculty of Social Sciences *Degree program information:* Part-time programs available. Offers anthropology (MA, PhD); economics (MA, PhD); feminist studies (Diploma); industrial relations (MA, PhD); political science (MA, PhD); politics analysis (MA); social sciences (M Serv Soc, MA, PhD, Psy D, Diploma); sociology (MA, PhD). Electronic applications accepted.

School of Psychology Offers clinical psychology (PhD); community psychology (PhD); psychology (PhD, Psy D). Electronic applications accepted.

School of Social Work Offers social work (M Serv Soc, PhD). Electronic applications accepted.

Faculty of Theology and Religious Sciences Offers applied ethics (Diploma); human sciences of religion (MA, PhD); practical theology (D Th P); theology (MA, PhD); theology and religious sciences (MA, D Th P, PhD, Diploma). Electronic applications accepted.

Québec Institute for Advanced International Studies Offers advanced international studies (MA); international relations (MA). Electronic applications accepted.

UNIVERSITY AT ALBANY, STATE UNIVERSITY OF NEW YORK, Albany, NY 12222-0001

General Information State-supported, coed, university. CGS member. *Enrollment:* 17,434 graduate, professional, and undergraduate students; 2,336 full-time matriculated graduate/professional students (1,407 women), 2,129 part-time matriculated graduate/professional students (1,308 women). *Enrollment by degree level:* 2,661 master's, 1,651 doctoral, 153 other advanced degrees. *Graduate faculty:* 635 full-time (222 women), 579 part-time/adjunct (275 women). Tuition, state resident: full-time $6,900; part-time $288 per credit. Tuition, nonresident: full-time $10,920; part-time $455 per credit. *Required fees:* $1,139. *Graduate housing:* Rooms and/or apartments available on a first-come, first-served basis to single and married students. Housing application deadline: 9/1. *Student services:* Campus employment opportunities, campus safety program, career counseling, child daycare facilities, disabled student services, free psychological counseling, grant writing training, international student services, low-cost health insurance, multicultural affairs office, teacher training, writing training. *Library facilities:* University Library plus 2 others. *Online resources:* library catalog, web page, access to other libraries' catalogs. *Collection:* 2.2 million titles, 42,829 serial subscriptions, 15,936 audiovisual materials. *Research affiliation:* Woods Hole Oceanographic Institution, Wadsworth Laboratories, New York State Department of Health, IBM–Watson Research Laboratories, General Electric Corporate Research and Development Center, Naval Research Laboratories, Stanford Linear Accelerator Center.

Computer facilities: 500 computers available on campus for general student use. A campuswide network can be accessed from student residence rooms and from off campus. Internet access and online class registration are available. *Web address:* http://www.albany.edu/.

General Application Contact: Michael DeRensis, Director, Graduate Admissions, 518-442-3980, Fax: 518-442-3922, E-mail: graduate@uamail.albany.edu.

GRADUATE UNITS

College of Arts and Sciences Students: 802 full-time (413 women), 506 part-time (254 women); includes 190 minority (79 African Americans, 12 American Indian/Alaska Native, 29 Asian Americans or Pacific Islanders, 70 Hispanic Americans), 270 international. Average age 32. Expenses: Contact institution. *Financial support:* Fellowships, research assistantships, teaching assistantships, career-related internships or fieldwork, Federal Work-Study, institutionally sponsored loans, and unspecified assistantships available. In 2006, 272 master's, 60 doctorates, 30 other advanced degrees awarded. *Degree program information:* Part-time and evening/weekend programs available. Offers African studies (MA); Afro-American studies (MA); anthropology (MA, PhD); art (MA, MFA); arts and sciences (MA, MFA, MRP, MS, DA, PhD, Certificate); atmospheric science (MS, PhD); autism (Certificate); biodiversity, conservation, and policy (MS); biopsychology (PhD); chemistry (MS, PhD); clinical psychology (PhD); communication (MA); demography (Certificate); ecology, evolution, and behavior (MS, PhD); economics (MA, PhD); English (MA, PhD); forensic molecular biology (MS); French (MA, PhD); general/experimental psychology (PhD); geographic information systems and spatial analysis (Certificate); geography (MA, Certificate); geology (MS, PhD); history (MA, PhD); industrial/organizational psychology (PhD); Italian (MA); Latin American, Caribbean, and US Latino studies (MA, Certificate); liberal studies (MA); mathematics (PhD); molecular, cellular, developmental, and neural biology (MS, PhD); philosophy (MA, PhD); physics (MS, PhD); psychology (MA); public history (Certificate); regional planning (MRP); regulatory economics (Certificate); Russian (MA, Certificate); Russian translation (Certificate); secondary teaching (MA); social/personality psychology (PhD); sociology (MA, PhD); sociology and communication (PhD); Spanish (MA, PhD); statistics (MA); theatre (MA); urban policy (Certificate); women's studies (MA, DA). *Application fee:* $75. *Application Contact:* Michael DeRensis, Director, Graduate Admissions, 518-442-3980, Fax: 518-442-3922, E-mail: graduate@uamail.albany.edu. *Director, Graduate Admissions,* Michael DeRensis, 518-442-3980, Fax: 518-442-3922, E-mail: graduate@uamail.albany.edu.

College of Computing and Information Students: 192 full-time (109 women), 134 part-time (84 women); includes 9 African Americans, 9 Asian Americans or Pacific Islanders, 11 Hispanic Americans, 60 international. Average age 33. Expenses: Contact institution. *Financial support:* Fellowships, Federal Work-Study available. Financial award application deadline:4/1. In 2006, 129 master's, 5 doctorates awarded. *Degree program information:* Part-time and evening/weekend programs available. Offers computer science (MS, PhD); information science (MS, PhD); information science and policy (CAS); library science (MLS). *Application deadline:* For fall admission, 3/1 for domestic students. Applications are processed on a rolling basis. *Application fee:* $75. Electronic applications accepted. *Application Contact:* Brian Goodale, Senior Counselor for Graduate and International Admissions, 518-442-3980. *Dean,* Peter Bloniarz, 518-442-5115.

College of Nanoscale Science and Engineering Students: 72 full-time (13 women), 23 part-time (3 women); includes 6 minority (3 African Americans, 3 Asian Americans or Pacific Islanders), 47 international. Average age 28. Expenses: Contact institution. In 2006, 8 master's, 2 doctorates awarded. Offers nanoscale science and engineering (MS, PhD). *Application deadline:* For fall admission, 4/1 for domestic students. *Application fee:* $75. *Dean,* Alain Kaloyeros.

Nelson A. Rockefeller College of Public Affairs and Policy Students: 215 full-time (99 women), 116 part-time (44 women); includes 36 minority (18 African Americans, 7 Asian Americans or Pacific Islanders, 11 Hispanic Americans), 64 international. Average age 31. Expenses: Contact institution. *Financial support:* Fellowships, research assistantships, teaching assistantships, career-related internships or fieldwork, Federal Work-Study, and institutionally sponsored loans available. Financial award application deadline: 2/1. In 2006, 68 master's, 18 doctorates, 4 other advanced degrees awarded. *Degree program information:* Part-time and evening/weekend programs available. Offers administrative behavior (PhD); comparative and development administration (MPA, PhD); human resources (MPA); legislative administration (MPA); nonprofit leadership and management (Certificate); planning and policy analysis (CAS); policy analysis (MPA); political science (MA, PhD); program analysis and evaluation (PhD); public affairs and policy (MA); public finance (MPA, PhD); public management (MPA, PhD); women and public policy (Certificate). *Application deadline:* For fall admission, 2/1 priority date for domestic students, 5/1 for international students. Applications are processed on a rolling basis. *Application fee:* $75. Electronic applications accepted. *Application Contact:* Brian Goodale, Senior Counselor for Graduate and International Admissions, 518-442-3980. *Dean,* Dr. Jeffrey J. Straussman, 518-442-5244.

School of Business Students: 199 full-time (93 women), 189 part-time (74 women); includes 44 minority (11 African Americans, 2 American Indian/Alaska Native, 26 Asian Americans or Pacific Islanders, 5 Hispanic Americans), 53 international. Average age 31. Expenses: Contact institution. *Financial support:* Fellowships, research assistantships, career-related internships or fieldwork and Federal Work-Study available. In 2006, 216 master's awarded. *Degree program information:* Part-time and evening/weekend programs available. Offers accounting (MS); business (MBA, MS); finance (MBA); human resource systems (MBA); information technology management (MBA); marketing (MBA); taxation (MS). *Application deadline:* For fall admission, 3/1 for domestic students, 5/1 for international students. Applications are processed on a rolling basis. *Application fee:* $75. Electronic applications accepted. *Application Contact:* Michael DeRensis, Director, Graduate Admissions, 518-442-3980, Fax: 518-442-3922, E-mail: graduate@uamail.albany.edu. *Dean,* Paul Leonard, 518-442-4910.

School of Criminal Justice Students: 65 full-time (35 women), 57 part-time (38 women); includes 8 African Americans, 4 Asian Americans or Pacific Islanders, 5 Hispanic Americans, 15 international. Average age 32. Expenses: Contact institution. *Financial support:* Fellowships, research assistantships, teaching assistantships, career-related internships or fieldwork, Federal Work-Study, and institutionally sponsored loans available. Financial award application deadline: 4/1. In 2006, 38 master's, 3 doctorates awarded. *Degree program information:* Part-time and evening/weekend programs available. Offers criminal justice (MA, PhD). *Application deadline:* For fall admission, 7/1 for domestic students, 5/1 for international students. Applications are processed on a rolling basis. *Application fee:* $75. Electronic applications accepted. *Dean,* Julie Horney, 518-442-5214.

School of Education Students: 456 full-time (340 women), 669 part-time (520 women); includes 106 minority (45 African Americans, 2 American Indian/Alaska Native, 17 Asian Americans or Pacific Islanders, 42 Hispanic Americans), 63 international. Average age 34. Expenses: Contact institution. *Financial support:* Fellowships, career-related internships or fieldwork and Federal Work-Study available. In 2006, 455 master's, 30 doctorates, 50 other advanced degrees awarded. *Degree program information:* Part-time and evening/weekend programs available. Offers counseling psychology (MS, PhD, CAS); curriculum and instruction (MS, Ed D, CAS); curriculum planning and development (MA); education (MA, MS, Ed D, PhD, Psy D, CAS); educational administration (MS, PhD, CAS); educational communications (MS, CAS); educational psychology (Ed D); educational psychology and statistics (MS); measurements and evaluation (Ed D); reading (MS, Ed D, CAS); rehabilitation counseling (MS); school counselor (CAS); school psychology (Psy D, CAS); special education (MS); statistics and research design (Ed D). *Application fee:* $75. Electronic applications accepted. *Application Contact:* Christine Smith, Assistant to the Dean of Graduate Studies, E-mail: csmith2@albany.edu. *Dean,* Susanne K. Phillips, 518-442-4988.

School of Public Health Students: 227 full-time (156 women), 131 part-time (89 women); includes 33 African Americans, 12 Asian Americans or Pacific Islanders, 14 Hispanic Americans, 89 international. Average age 32. Expenses: Contact institution. *Financial support:* Fellowships, research assistantships available. In 2006, 67 master's, 14 doctorates, 3 other advanced degrees awarded. Offers biochemistry, molecular biology, and genetics (MS, PhD); cell and molecular structure (MS, PhD); environmental and analytical chemistry (MS, PhD); environmental and occupational health (MS, PhD); epidemiology and biostatistics (MS, PhD); health policy, management, and behavior (MS); immunobiology and immunochemistry (MS, PhD); molecular pathogenesis (MS, PhD); neuroscience (MS, PhD); public health (MPH, MS, Dr PH, PhD, Certificate); toxicology (MS, PhD). *Application deadline:* For fall admission, 1/1 for domestic students. Applications are processed on a rolling basis. *Application fee:* $75. Electronic applications accepted. *Application Contact:* Michael DeRensis, Director, Graduate Admissions, 518-442-3980, Fax: 518-442-3922, E-mail: graduate@uamail.albany.edu. *Dean,* Dr. Mary Applegate, 518-485-5500.

School of Social Welfare Students: 253 full-time (220 women), 150 part-time (126 women); includes 77 minority (40 African Americans, 2 American Indian/Alaska Native, 7 Asian Americans or Pacific Islanders, 28 Hispanic Americans), 15 international. Average age 34. Expenses: Contact institution. *Financial support:* Fellowships, career-related internships or fieldwork and Federal Work-Study available. Financial award application deadline: 2/15. In 2006, 133 master's, 8 doctorates awarded. *Degree program information:* Part-time and evening/weekend programs available. Offers social welfare (MSW, PhD). *Application deadline:* For fall admission, 2/15 for domestic and international students. *Application fee:* $75. Electronic applications accepted. *Application Contact:* Brian Goodale, Senior Counselor for Graduate and International Admissions, 518-442-3980. *Dean,* Katharine Briar-Lawson, 518-442-5324.

UNIVERSITY AT BUFFALO, THE STATE UNIVERSITY OF NEW YORK, Buffalo, NY 14260

General Information State-supported, coed, university. CGS member. *Enrollment:* 27,220 graduate, professional, and undergraduate students; 6,969 full-time matriculated graduate/professional students (3,554 women), 2,036 part-time matriculated graduate/professional students (1,154 women). *Enrollment by degree level:* 2,013 first professional, 4,290 master's, 2,508 doctoral, 194 other advanced degrees. *Graduate faculty:* 1,277 full-time (418 women), 1,122 part-time/adjunct (417 women). *Graduate housing:* Rooms and/or apartments available on a first-come, first-served basis to single students and available to married students. Housing application deadline: 5/1. *Student services:* Campus employment opportunities, campus safety program, career counseling, child daycare facilities, disabled student services, exercise/wellness program, free psychological counseling, international student services, low-cost health insurance, multicultural affairs office, teacher training, writing training. *Library facilities:* Lockwood Library plus 7 others. *Online resources:* library catalog, web page, access to other libraries' catalogs. *Collection:* 3.4 million titles, 34,126 serial subscriptions, 188,300 audiovisual materials. *Research affiliation:* Roswell Park Cancer Institute, Calspan–UB Research Center, Veterans Administration Medical Center, Hauptman-Woodward Medical Research Institute, Kaleida Health.

Computer facilities: 2,391 computers available on campus for general student use. A campuswide network can be accessed from student residence rooms and from off campus. Internet access and online class registration are available. *Web address:* http://www.buffalo.edu/.

General Application Contact: Christopher S. Connor, Director of Graduate Student Recruitment Services, 716-645-6968, Fax: 716-645-6998, E-mail: cconnor@buffalo.edu.

GRADUATE UNITS

Graduate School Students: 6,969 full-time (3,554 women), 2,036 part-time (1,154 women); includes 1,045 minority (330 African Americans, 33 American Indian/Alaska Native, 470 Asian Americans or Pacific Islanders, 212 Hispanic Americans), 2,126 international. *Faculty:* 1,277 full-time (418 women), 1,122 part-time/adjunct (417 women). Expenses: Contact institution. *Financial support:* Fellowships with full and partial tuition reimbursements, research assistantships with full and partial tuition reimbursements, teaching assistantships with full and partial tuition reimbursements, career-related internships or fieldwork, Federal Work-Study, institutionally sponsored loans, scholarships/grants, traineeships, tuition waivers (full and partial), unspecified assistantships, and stipends available. Support available to part-time students. Financial award applicants required to submit FAFSA. In 2006, 571 first professional degrees, 1,912 master's, 362 doctorates, 123 other advanced degrees awarded. *Degree program information:* Part-time and evening/weekend programs available. Postbaccalaureate distance learning degree programs offered. Offers cancer pathology and prevention (PhD); cancer research and biomedical sciences (MS, PhD); cellular and molecular biology (PhD); immunology (PhD); molecular and cellular biophysics and biochemistry (PhD); molecular pharmacology and cancer therapeutics (PhD); natural and biomedical sciences (MS). *Application deadline:* Applications are processed on a rolling basis. Electronic applications accepted. *Application Contact:* Christopher S. Connor, Director of Graduate Student Recruitment Services, 716-645-6968, Fax: 716-645-6998, E-mail: cconnor@buffalo.edu. *Associate Provost and Executive Director of the Graduate School,* Dr. Myron A. Thompson, 716-645-6227, Fax: 716-645-6142, E-mail: gradschl@buffalo.edu.

College of Arts and Sciences Students: 1,714 full-time (833 women), 332 part-time (151 women); includes 165 minority (58 African Americans, 11 American Indian/Alaska Native, 42 Asian Americans or Pacific Islanders, 54 Hispanic Americans), 674 international. Average age 29. *Faculty:* 509 full-time (150 women), 257 part-time/adjunct (103 women). Expenses: Contact institution. *Financial support:* Fellowships with full and partial tuition reimbursements, research assistantships with full tuition reimbursements, teaching assistantships with full tuition reimbursements, career-related internships or fieldwork, Federal Work-Study, institutionally sponsored loans, scholarships/grants, tuition waivers (full and partial), and unspecified assistantships available. Support available to part-time students. Financial award applicants required to submit FAFSA. In 2006, 385 master's, 144 doctorates, 31 other advanced degrees awarded. *Degree program information:* Part-time programs available. Offers American studies (MA, PhD); anthropology (MA, PhD); art (MFA); art history (MA, Certificate); arts and sciences (MA, MFA, MM, MS, Au D, PhD, Certificate); audiology (Au D); behavioral neuroscience (PhD); biological sciences (MA, MS, PhD); chemistry (MA, PhD); classics (MA, PhD); clinical psychology (PhD); cognitive psychology (PhD); communication (MA, PhD); communicative disorders and sciences (MA, PhD); comparative literature (MA, PhD); critical museum studies (Certificate); economics (MA, MS, PhD); English (MA, PhD); evolution, ecology and behavior (MS, PhD, Certificate); financial economics (Certificate); fine arts (MFA); French (MA, PhD); general psychology (MA); geographic information science (Certificate); geography (MA, MS, PhD); geology (MA, MS, PhD); health services (Certificate); historical musicology and music theory (PhD); history (MA, PhD); humanities (film studies concentration) (MA); information and Internet economics (Certificate); international economics (Certificate); law and regulation (Certificate); linguistics (MA, PhD); mathematics (MA, PhD); media arts production (MFA); medicinal chemistry (MS, PhD); music composition (MA, PhD); music history (MA); music performance (MM); music theory (MA); new media design (Certificate); philosophy (MA, PhD); physics (MS, PhD); political science (MA, PhD); social-personality psychology (PhD); sociology (MA, PhD); Spanish (MA, PhD); transportation and business geographics (Certificate); urban and regional economics (Certificate). *Application deadline:* Applications are processed on a rolling basis. *Application fee:* $35. Electronic applications accepted. *Application Contact:* Joseph C. Syracuse, Graduate Enrollment Manager, 716-645-2711, Fax: 716-645-3888, E-mail: jcs32@buffalo.edu. *Dean,* Dr. Bruce D. Mc Combe, 716-645-2711, Fax: 716-645-3888, E-mail: cas-dean@buffalo.edu.

Graduate School of Education Students: 835 full-time (620 women), 709 part-time (504 women); includes 145 minority (74 African Americans, 5 American Indian/Alaska Native, 29 Asian Americans or Pacific Islanders, 37 Hispanic Americans), 122 international. 1,248 applicants, 55% accepted, 459 enrolled. *Faculty:* 80 full-time (48 women), 98 part-time/adjunct (68 women). Expenses: Contact institution. *Financial support:* Fellowships with full tuition reimbursements, research assistantships with full tuition reimbursements, teaching assistantships with full tuition reimbursements, career-related internships or fieldwork, Federal Work-Study, institutionally sponsored loans, tuition waivers (full and partial), and unspecified assistantships available. Financial award applicants required to submit FAFSA. In 2006, 527 master's, 55 doctorates, 72 other advanced degrees awarded. *Degree program information:* Part-time programs available. Postbaccalaureate distance learning degree programs offered (minimal on-campus study). Offers adolescence education (Certificate); biology (Ed M); chemistry (Ed M); childhood education (Ed M); counseling/school psychology (PhD); counselor education (PhD); early childhood and childhood education with bilingual extension (Ed M); early childhood education (Ed M); earth science (Ed M); education (Ed M, MA, MLS, MS, Ed D, PhD, Certificate); educational administration (Ed M, Ed D, PhD); educational psychology (MA, PhD); elementary education (Ed D, PhD); English (Ed M); English education (PhD); English for speakers of other languages (Ed M); foreign and second language education (PhD); French (Ed M); general education (Ed M); German (Ed M); higher education (PhD); higher education administration (Ed M); Italian (Ed M); Japanese (Ed M); Latin (Ed M); library and information studies (MLS, Certificate); literary specialist (Ed M); mathematics (Ed M); mathematics education (PhD); mental health counseling (MS); mentoring teachers (Certificate); music education (Ed M, Certificate); physics (Ed M); reading education (PhD); rehabilitation counseling (MS); Russian (Ed M); school administrator and supervisor (Certificate); school business and human resource administration (Certificate); school counseling (Ed M, Certificate); school psychology (MA); science education (PhD); social foundations (PhD); social studies (Ed M); Spanish (Ed M); special education (PhD); specialist in education administration (Certificate); teaching and leading for diversity (Certificate); teaching English to speakers of other languages (Ed M). *Application deadline:* Applications are processed on a rolling basis. *Application fee:* $50. Electronic applications accepted. *Application Contact:* Dr. Radhika Suresh, Director of Graduate Admissions and Student Services, 716-645-2110 Ext. 1209, Fax: 716-645-7937, E-mail: gse-info@buffalo.edu. *Dean,* Dr. Mary H. Gresham, 716-645-6640, Fax: 716-645-2479, E-mail: gse-info@buffalo.edu.

Law School Students: 764 full-time (372 women), 5 part-time (3 women); includes 126 minority (42 African Americans, 4 American Indian/Alaska Native, 48 Asian Americans or Pacific Islanders, 32 Hispanic Americans), 29 international. Average age 25. 1,544 applicants, 36% accepted, 247 enrolled. *Faculty:* 54 full-time (24 women), 51 part-time/adjunct (19 women). Expenses: Contact institution. *Financial support:* In 2006–07, 660 students received support, including 25 fellowships with full and partial tuition reimbursements available (averaging $10,000 per year), 34 research assistantships (averaging $1,135 per year); career-related internships or fieldwork, Federal Work-Study, institutionally sponsored loans, scholarships/grants, tuition waivers (full and partial), and unspecified assistantships also available. Financial award application deadline: 3/1; financial award applicants required to submit FAFSA. In 2006, 248 degrees awarded. Offers criminal law (LL M); general law for international students (LL M); law (JD). *Application deadline:* For fall admission, 3/15 priority date for domestic students. Applications are processed on a rolling basis. *Application fee:* $50. Electronic applications accepted. *Application Contact:* Lillie V. Wiley-Upshaw, Associate Dean and Director of Admissions and Financial Aid, 716-645-2907, Fax: 716-645-6676, E-mail: law-admissions@buffalo.edu. *Dean,* R. Nils Olsen, 716-645-2052, Fax: 716-645-5968, E-mail: law-deans@buffalo.edu.

School of Architecture and Planning Students: 190 full-time (81 women), 17 part-time (11 women); includes 23 minority (9 African Americans, 7 Asian Americans or Pacific Islanders, 7 Hispanic Americans), 38 international. Average age 25. 200 applicants, 75% accepted. *Faculty:* 32 full-time (12 women), 35 part-time/adjunct (9 women). Expenses: Contact institution. *Financial support:* Fellowships with full tuition reimbursements, research assistantships with full tuition reimbursements, teaching assistantships with full and partial tuition reimbursements, career-related internships or fieldwork, Federal Work-Study, institutionally sponsored loans, scholarships/grants, traineeships, tuition waivers (full and partial), and unspecified assistantships available. Support available to part-time students. Financial award applicants required to submit FAFSA. In 2006, 99 degrees awarded. *Degree program information:* Part-time programs available. Offers architecture (M Arch); architecture and planning (M Arch, MUP); planning (MUP). *Application deadline:* Applications are processed on a rolling basis. *Application fee:* $35. Electronic applications accepted. *Application Contact:* Deborah R. Smith, Assistant to the Chair, 716-829-3485 Ext. 105, Fax: 716-829-3256, E-mail: drs5@buffalo.edu. *Dean,* Brian Carter, 716-829-3485 Ext. 121, Fax: 716-829-2297, E-mail: bcarter@buffalo.edu.

School of Dental Medicine Students: 417 full-time (162 women), 7 part-time (2 women); includes 72 minority (1 African American, 63 Asian Americans or Pacific Islanders, 8 Hispanic Americans), 58 international. Average age 24. 1,657 applicants, 12% accepted, 115 enrolled. *Faculty:* 69 full-time (25 women), 109 part-time/adjunct (26 women). Expenses: Contact institution. *Financial support:* Fellowships with full and partial tuition reimbursements, research assistantships with full and partial tuition reimbursements, career-related internships or fieldwork, institutionally sponsored loans, scholarships/grants, and unspecified assistantships available. Financial award applicants required to submit FAFSA. In 2006, 77 DDSs, 14 master's, 1 doctorate awarded. Offers advanced education in general dentistry (Certificate); biomaterials (MS); combined prosthodontics (Certificate); dental medicine (DDS, MS, PhD, Certificate); endodontics (Certificate); general practice residency (Certificate); oral and maxillofacial pathology (Certificate); oral and maxillofacial surgery (Certificate); oral biology (PhD); oral diagnostic sciences (MS); oral sciences (MS); orthodontics (MS, Certificate); pediatric dentistry (Certificate); periodontics (Certificate); temporomandibular disorders and orafacial pain (Certificate). *Application deadline:* For fall admission, 2/1 for domestic and international students. *Application fee:* $50. Electronic applications accepted. *Application Contact:* Dr. Robert Joynt, Director of Admissions, 716-829-2839, Fax: 716-833-3517, E-mail: joynt@buffalo.edu. *Dean,* Dr. Richard N. Buchanan, 716-829-2836, Fax: 716-833-3517, E-mail: rb26@buffalo.edu.

School of Engineering and Applied Sciences Students: 798 full-time (155 women), 152 part-time (29 women); includes 43 minority (16 African Americans, 2 American Indian/Alaska Native, 18 Asian Americans or Pacific Islanders, 7 Hispanic Americans), 671 international. Average age 27. 2,255 applicants, 47% accepted, 224 enrolled. *Faculty:* 138 full-time (17 women), 36 part-time/adjunct (4 women). Expenses: Contact institution. *Financial support:* In 2006–07, 35 fellowships with full tuition reimbursements (averaging $22,000 per year), 157 research assistantships with full and partial tuition reimbursements (averaging $20,700 per year), 183 teaching assistantships with full tuition reimbursements (averaging $19,600 per year) were awarded; career-related internships or fieldwork, Federal Work-Study, institutionally sponsored loans, scholarships/grants, tuition waivers (full and partial), and unspecified assistantships also available. Support available to part-time students. Financial award applicants required to submit FAFSA. In 2006, 300 master's, 58 doctorates awarded. *Degree program information:* Part-time and evening/weekend programs available. Postbaccalaureate distance learning degree programs offered (minimal on-campus study). Offers aerospace engineering (MS, PhD); chemical and biological engineering (M Eng, MS, PhD); civil engineering (M Eng, MS, PhD); computer science and engineering (MS, PhD); electrical engineering (M Eng, MS, PhD); engineering and applied sciences (M Eng, MS, PhD); engineering science (MS); industrial and systems engineering (M Eng, MS, PhD); mechanical engineering (MS, PhD). *Application deadline:* Applications are processed on a rolling basis. *Application fee:* $35. Electronic applications accepted. *Application Contact:* Dr. Rajan Batta, Associate Dean for Graduate Education, 716-645-2771 Ext. 1105, Fax: 716-645-2495, E-mail: batta@eng.buffalo.edu. *Dean,* Dr. Harvey G. Stenger, 716-645-2771 Ext. 1101, Fax: 716-645-2495, E-mail: dean@eng.buffalo.edu.

School of Management Students: 493 full-time (192 women), 212 part-time (55 women); includes 53 minority (11 African Americans, 3 American Indian/Alaska Native, 31 Asian Americans or Pacific Islanders, 8 Hispanic Americans), 283 international. Average age 27. 1,058 applicants, 55% accepted, 369 enrolled. *Faculty:* 65 full-time (18 women), 30 part-time/adjunct (3 women). Expenses: Contact institution. *Financial support:* In 2006–07, 91 students received support, including 17 fellowships with full and partial tuition reimbursements available (averaging $3,917 per year), 38 research assistantships with full and partial tuition reimbursements available (averaging $11,907 per year), 26 teaching assistantships with full and partial tuition reimbursements available (averaging $7,571 per year); career-related internships or fieldwork, Federal Work-Study, institutionally sponsored loans, scholarships/grants, health care benefits, and unspecified assistantships also available. Financial award application deadline: 2/15; financial award applicants required to submit FAFSA. In 2006, 260 master's, 5 doctorates, 3 other advanced degrees awarded. *Degree program information:* Part-time and evening/weekend programs available. Offers accounting (MS); business administration (MBA); finance (MS); information assurance (Certificate); management (PhD); management information systems (MS); supply chains and operations management (MS). *Application deadline:* For fall admission, 6/1 priority date for domestic students, 3/1 priority date for international students. Applications are processed on a rolling basis. *Application fee:* $50. Electronic applications accepted. *Application Contact:* David W. Frasier, Administrative Director of Graduate Programs and Assistant Dean, 716-645-3204, Fax: 716-645-2341, E-mail: davidf@buffalo.edu. *Dean,* John M. Thomas, 716-645-3221, Fax: 716-645-5926, E-mail: jmthomas@buffalo.edu.

School of Medicine and Biomedical Sciences Students: 708 full-time (368 women), 12 part-time (4 women); includes 155 minority (17 African Americans, 5 American Indian/Alaska Native, 124 Asian Americans or Pacific Islanders, 9 Hispanic Americans), 61 international. Average age 25. 3,853 applicants, 13% accepted, 214 enrolled. *Faculty:* 154 full-time (32 women), 351 part-time/adjunct (100 women). Expenses: Contact institution. *Financial support:* In 2006–07, fellowships with full tuition reimbursements (averaging $25,000 per year), research assistantships with full tuition reimbursements (averaging $21,000 per year), teaching assistantships with full tuition reimbursements (averaging $21,000 per year) were awarded; career-related internships or fieldwork, Federal Work-Study, institutionally sponsored loans, scholarships/grants, traineeships, health care benefits, and unspecified assistantships also available. Financial award application deadline: 2/1; financial award applicants required to submit FAFSA. In 2006, 134 MDs, 11 master's, 25 doctorates awarded. Offers anatomical sciences (MA, PhD); biochemical pharmacology (MS); biochemistry (MA, PhD); biomedical sciences (PhD); biophysics (MS, PhD); biotechnology (MS); medicine (MD); medicine and biomedical sciences (MD, MA, MS, PhD); microbiology and immunology (MA, PhD); neuroscience (MS, PhD); pathology (MA, PhD); pharmacology (MA, PhD); physiology (MA, PhD); structural biology (MS, PhD). *Application deadline:* For fall admission, 2/1 priority date for domestic and international students. Applications are processed on a rolling basis. *Application fee:* $50. Electronic applications accepted. *Application Contact:* Amy J. Kuzdale, Staff Associate, 716-829-3398, Fax: 716-829-2437, E-mail: akuzdale@buffalo.edu. *Dean of Medicine,* Dr. Michael E. Cain, 716-829-3955, Fax: 716-829-3395, E-mail: mcain@buffalo.edu.

School of Nursing Students: 131 full-time (108 women), 64 part-time (61 women); includes 29 minority (11 African Americans, 9 Asian Americans or Pacific Islanders, 9 Hispanic Americans), 20 international. Average age 28. 346 applicants, 25% accepted, 51 enrolled. *Faculty:* 38 full-time (34 women), 15 part-time/adjunct (14 women). Expenses: Contact institution. *Financial support:* In 2006–07, 78 students received support, including 13 fellowships with full tuition reimbursements available (averaging $7,220 per year), 10 research assistantships with tuition reimbursements available (averaging $17,881 per year), 23 teaching assistantships with full tuition reimbursements available (averaging $11,245 per year); Federal Work-Study, scholarships/grants, traineeships, health care benefits, and unspecified assistantships also available. Financial award application deadline: 3/15; financial award applicants required to submit FAFSA. In 2006, 49 master's, 3 doctorates, 6 other advanced degrees awarded. *Degree program information:* Part-time programs available. Postbaccalaureate distance learning degree programs offered. Offers acute care nurse practitioner (MS, Certificate); adult health nursing (MS, Certificate); child

University at Buffalo, the State University of New York (continued)

health nursing (MS); family nurse practitioner (Certificate); family nursing (MS); geriatric nurse practitioner (MS, Certificate); maternal and women's health nurse practitioner (Certificate); maternal and women's health nursing (MS); nurse anesthetist (MS); nursing (PhD); nursing education (Certificate); pediatric nurse practitioner (Certificate); psychiatric/mental health nurse practitioner (Certificate); psychiatric/mental health nursing (MS). *Application deadline:* For fall admission, 6/1 priority date for domestic students, 3/1 priority date for international students; for spring admission, 11/1 for domestic students, 9/15 priority date for international students. Applications are processed on a rolling basis. *Application fee:* $50. Electronic applications accepted. *Application Contact:* Dr. Elaine R. Cusker, Assistant Dean, 716-829-2537, Fax: 716-829-2021, E-mail: ecusker@buffalo.edu. *Dean, Interim,* Dr. Jean K. Brown, 716-829-2533, Fax: 716-829-2566, E-mail: jebrown@buffalo.edu.

School of Pharmacy and Pharmaceutical Sciences Students: 385 full-time (233 women), 7 part-time (4 women); includes 74 minority (11 African Americans, 57 Asian Americans or Pacific Islanders, 6 Hispanic Americans), 57 international. Average age 26. 1,553 applicants, 9% accepted, 135 enrolled. *Faculty:* 39 full-time (11 women), 7 part-time/adjunct (3 women). Expenses: Contact institution. *Financial support:* In 2006–07, 27 students received support, including 8 fellowships with full tuition reimbursements available (averaging $22,565 per year), 18 research assistantships with full tuition reimbursements available (averaging $22,565 per year); teaching assistantships, Federal Work-Study, institutionally sponsored loans, scholarships/grants, health care benefits, tuition waivers (full and partial), and unspecified assistantships also available. Financial award application deadline: 2/28; financial award applicants required to submit FAFSA. In 2006, 112 Pharm Ds, 1 master's, 5 doctorates awarded. Postbaccalaureate distance learning degree programs offered (minimal on-campus study). Offers pharmaceutical sciences (MS, PhD); pharmacy (Pharm D); pharmacy and pharmaceutical sciences (Pharm D, MS, PhD). *Application deadline:* For fall admission, 2/1 priority date for domestic and international students. Applications are processed on a rolling basis. Electronic applications accepted. *Application Contact:* Cindy F. Konovitz, Assistant Dean, 716-645-2825, Fax: 716-645-3688, E-mail: pharm-admin@acsu.buffalo.edu. *Dean,* Dr. Wayne K. Anderson, 716-645-2823, Fax: 716-645-3688.

School of Public Health and Health Professions Students: 283 full-time (168 women), 74 part-time (54 women); includes 46 minority (19 African Americans, 1 American Indian/Alaska Native, 21 Asian Americans or Pacific Islanders, 5 Hispanic Americans), 48 international. Average age 30. 614 applicants, 27% accepted, 117 enrolled. *Faculty:* 64 full-time (30 women), 43 part-time/adjunct (26 women). Expenses: Contact institution. *Financial support:* In 2006–07, 15 fellowships with full tuition reimbursements (averaging $2,500 per year), 3 research assistantships with full tuition reimbursements (averaging $15,000 per year), 18 teaching assistantships with full tuition reimbursements (averaging $8,500 per year) were awarded; career-related internships or fieldwork, Federal Work-Study, institutionally sponsored loans, scholarships/grants, tuition waivers (full and partial), and unspecified assistantships also available. Financial award applicants required to submit FAFSA. In 2006, 72 master's, 49 doctorates, 7 other advanced degrees awarded. *Degree program information:* Part-time programs available. Offers assistive and rehabilitation technology (Certificate); biostatistics (MA, PhD); community health (PhD); epidemiology (MS, PhD); exercise science (MS, PhD); nutrition (MS); occupational therapy (MS); physical therapy (DPT); public health (MPH); public health and health professions (MA, MPH, MS, DPT, PhD, Certificate). *Application fee:* $35. Electronic applications accepted. *Application Contact:* Cassandra F. Walker-Whiteside, Senior Advisor, PHHP Student Advisement and Recruitment Services, 716-829-3434 Ext. 410, Fax: 716-829-2034, E-mail: cfwalker@buffalo.edu. *Dean,* Dr. Maurizio Trevisan, 716-829-3434 Ext. 411, Fax: 716-829-2034, E-mail: trevisan@buffalo.edu.

School of Social Work Students: 278 full-time (251 women), 206 part-time (175 women); includes 81 minority (53 African Americans, 2 American Indian/Alaska Native, 4 Asian Americans or Pacific Islanders, 22 Hispanic Americans), 10 international. Average age 32. 425 applicants, 72% accepted, 212 enrolled. *Faculty:* 21 full-time (12 women), 40 part-time/adjunct (28 women). Expenses: Contact institution. *Financial support:* In 2006–07, 67 students received support, including 4 fellowships with full tuition reimbursements available (averaging $7,500 per year), 3 research assistantships with full tuition reimbursements available (averaging $15,000 per year), 6 teaching assistantships with full tuition reimbursements available (averaging $15,000 per year); Federal Work-Study, scholarships/grants, health care benefits, tuition waivers (partial), unspecified assistantships, and instructorships and research grants for PhD students also available. Financial award application deadline: 2/1; financial award applicants required to submit FAFSA. In 2006, 160 master's, 1 doctorate awarded. *Degree program information:* Part-time programs available. Offers social work (MSW, PhD). MSW available in Buffalo, Rochester, Jamestown, and Corning, New York. *Application deadline:* For fall admission, 3/1 priority date for domestic and international students. Applications are processed on a rolling basis. *Application fee:* $50. Electronic applications accepted. *Application Contact:* Maria Soos, Admissions Processor, 716-645-3381, Fax: 716-645-3456, E-mail: sw-info@buffalo.edu. *Dean,* Dr. Nancy J. Smyth, 716-645-3381 Ext. 221, Fax: 716-645-3883, E-mail: njsmyth@buffalo.edu.

See Close-Up on page 1065.

UNIVERSITY COLLEGE OF THE FRASER VALLEY, Abbotsford, BC V2S 7M8, Canada

General Information Province-supported, coed, comprehensive institution.

GRADUATE UNITS

Graduate Studies

UNIVERSITY OF ADVANCING TECHNOLOGY, Tempe, AZ 85283-1042

General Information Proprietary, coed, comprehensive institution. *Graduate housing:* On-campus housing not available.

GRADUATE UNITS

Program in Technology *Degree program information:* Part-time programs available. Offers technology (MS). Electronic applications accepted.

THE UNIVERSITY OF AKRON, Akron, OH 44325

General Information State-supported, coed, university. CGS member. *Enrollment:* 21,882 graduate, professional, and undergraduate students; 2,039 full-time matriculated graduate/professional students (1,110 women), 1,828 part-time matriculated graduate/professional students (1,116 women). *Enrollment by degree level:* 539 first professional, 2,378 master's, 726 doctoral, 224 other advanced degrees. *Graduate faculty:* 524 full-time (176 women), 427 part-time/adjunct (216 women). Tuition, state resident: full-time $6,164; part-time $342 per credit. Tuition, nonresident: full-time $10,575; part-time $588 per credit. *Required fees:* $806; $43 per credit. $12 per term. Tuition and fees vary according to course load, degree level and program. *Graduate housing:* Room and/or apartments available on a first-come, first-served basis to single students; on-campus housing not available to married students. Typical cost: $4,764 per year ($7,640 including board). Room and board charges vary according to board plan and housing facility selected. Housing application deadline: 3/1. *Student services:* Campus employment opportunities, campus safety program, career counseling, child daycare facilities, disabled student services, exercise/wellness program, free psychological counseling, grant writing training, international student services, low-cost health insurance, multicultural affairs office, teacher training, writing training. *Library facilities:* Bierce Library plus 2 others. *Online resources:* library catalog, web page, access to other libraries' catalogs. *Collection:* 1.3 million titles, 13,677 serial subscriptions, 46,248 audiovisual materials.

Computer facilities: Computer purchase and lease plans are available. 2,450 computers available on campus for general student use. A campuswide network can be accessed from student residence rooms and from off campus. Internet access and online class registration, wireless campus, library laptops for student checkout are available. *Web address:* http://www.uakron.edu/.

General Application Contact: Dr. Mark Tausig, Associate Dean, 330-972-6266, Fax: 330-972-6475, E-mail: mtausig@uakron.edu.

GRADUATE UNITS

Graduate School Students: 1,725 full-time (974 women), 1,603 part-time (1,021 women); includes 336 minority (229 African Americans, 11 American Indian/Alaska Native, 49 Asian Americans or Pacific Islanders, 47 Hispanic Americans), 578 international. Average age 32. 2,240 applicants, 55% accepted, 754 enrolled. *Faculty:* 493 full-time (165 women), 403 part-time/adjunct (210 women). Expenses: Contact institution. *Financial support:* In 2006–07, 57 fellowships with full tuition reimbursements, 471 research assistantships with full tuition reimbursements, 584 teaching assistantships with full tuition reimbursements were awarded; career-related internships or fieldwork, Federal Work-Study, institutionally sponsored loans, scholarships/grants, tuition waivers (full and partial), unspecified assistantships, and administrative assistantships also available. Support available to part-time students. In 2006, 830 master's, 118 doctorates awarded. *Degree program information:* Part-time and evening/weekend programs available. *Application deadline:* Applications are processed on a rolling basis. *Application fee:* $30 ($40 for international students). Electronic applications accepted. *Application Contact:* Dr. Mark Tausig, Associate Dean, 330-972-6266, Fax: 330-972-6475, E-mail: mtausig@uakron.edu. *Vice President for Research and Dean of the Graduate School,* Dr. George R. Newkome, 330-972-6458, Fax: 330-972-2413, E-mail: newkome@uakron.edu.

Buchtel College of Arts and Sciences Students: 495 full-time (258 women), 211 part-time (117 women); includes 85 minority (57 African Americans, 2 American Indian/Alaska Native, 10 Asian Americans or Pacific Islanders, 16 Hispanic Americans), 145 international. Average age 30. 635 applicants, 57% accepted, 184 enrolled. *Faculty:* 201 full-time (56 women), 76 part-time/adjunct (26 women). Expenses: Contact institution. *Financial support:* In 2006–07, 2 fellowships with full tuition reimbursements, 72 research assistantships with full tuition reimbursements, 310 teaching assistantships with full tuition reimbursements were awarded; career-related internships or fieldwork, Federal Work-Study, institutionally sponsored loans, scholarships/grants, tuition waivers (full and partial), and unspecified assistantships also available. Support available to part-time students. In 2006, 187 master's, 33 doctorates awarded. *Degree program information:* Part-time and evening/weekend programs available. Offers applied cognitive aging (MA, PhD); applied mathematics (MS); applied politics (MA); arts and sciences (MA, MFA, MPA, MS, PhD); biology (MS); chemistry (MS, PhD); composition (MA); computer science (MS); counseling psychology (MA, PhD); creative writing (MFA); earth science (MS); economics (MA); environmental (MS); geographic information science (MS); geology (MS); geophysics (MS); history (MA, PhD); industrial/gerontological (PhD); industrial/organizational psychology (MA, PhD); integrated bioscience (PhD); literature (MA); mathematics (MS); physics (MS); political science (MA); psychology (MA); public administration (MPA); sociology (MA, PhD); Spanish (MA); statistics (MS); urban planning (MA); urban studies (MA, PhD); urban studies and public affairs (PhD). *Application deadline:* Applications are processed on a rolling basis. *Application fee:* $30 ($40 for international students). Electronic applications accepted. *Dean,* Dr. Ronald Levant, 330-972-7882, E-mail: levant@uakron.edu.

College of Business Administration Students: 179 full-time (75 women), 200 part-time (82 women); includes 17 minority (6 African Americans, 7 Asian Americans or Pacific Islanders, 4 Hispanic Americans), 91 international. Average age 29. 239 applicants, 72% accepted, 109 enrolled. *Faculty:* 45 full-time (8 women), 27 part-time/adjunct (6 women). Expenses: Contact institution. *Financial support:* In 2006–07, 69 research assistantships with full tuition reimbursements, 3 teaching assistantships with full tuition reimbursements were awarded; fellowships with full tuition reimbursements, career-related internships or fieldwork, Federal Work-Study, and tuition waivers (full) also available. In 2006, 119 degrees awarded. *Degree program information:* Part-time and evening/weekend programs available. Offers accountancy (MS); accounting-information systems (MS); business administration (MBA, MS, MSM, MT); electronic business (MBA); entrepreneurship (MBA); finance (MBA); international business (MBA); international business for international executive (MBA); management (MBA); management of technology (MBA); management-health services administration (MSM); management-human resources (MSM); management-information systems (MSM); management-supply chain management (MSM); strategic marketing (MBA); taxation (MT). *Application deadline:* For fall admission, 8/15 for domestic students. Applications are processed on a rolling basis. *Application fee:* $30 ($40 for international students). Electronic applications accepted. *Application Contact:* Dr. James Divoky, Director of Graduate Business Programs, 330-972-7043, Fax: 330-972-6588, E-mail: jdivoky@uakron.edu. *Dean,* Dr. Raj Aggrawal, 330-972-7442, E-mail: cbadean@uakron.edu.

College of Education Students: 342 full-time (245 women), 669 part-time (493 women); includes 120 minority (94 African Americans, 5 American Indian/Alaska Native, 10 Asian Americans or Pacific Islanders, 11 Hispanic Americans), 18 international. Average age 33. 357 applicants, 64% accepted, 175 enrolled. *Faculty:* 53 full-time (34 women), 125 part-time/adjunct (82 women). Expenses: Contact institution. *Financial support:* In 2006–07, 78 research assistantships with full tuition reimbursements, 30 teaching assistantships with full tuition reimbursements were awarded; fellowships with full tuition reimbursements, career-related internships or fieldwork, Federal Work-Study, tuition waivers (full), and unspecified assistantships also available. In 2006, 270 master's, 20 doctorates awarded. *Degree program information:* Part-time programs available. Offers administrative specialist (MA, MS); classroom guidance for teachers (MA, MS); community counseling (MA, MS); counseling psychology (PhD); counselor education and supervision (PhD); education (MA, MS, Ed D, PhD); educational administration (MA, MS, Ed D); elementary education (MA, MS, PhD); elementary education—literacy (MA); elementary education with licensure (MS); exercise physiology/adult fitness (MA, MS); higher education administration (MA, MS); marriage and family therapy (MA, MS); physical education K–12 (MA, MS); principalship (MA, MS); school counseling (MA, MS); school psychology (MS); secondary education (MA, MS, PhD); secondary education with licensure (MS); special education (MA, MS); sports science/coaching (MA, MS); superintendent (MA, MS); technical education (MS); technical education guidance (MS); technical education instructional technology (MS); technical education teaching (MS); technical education training (MS). *Application deadline:* For fall admission, 8/15 for domestic students. Applications are processed on a rolling basis. *Application fee:* $30 ($40 for international students). Electronic applications accepted. *Dean,* Dr. Patricia Nelson, 330-972-7680.

College of Engineering Students: 220 full-time (61 women), 57 part-time (6 women); includes 10 minority (5 African Americans, 3 Asian Americans or Pacific Islanders, 2 Hispanic Americans), 177 international. Average age 28. 451 applicants, 37% accepted, 87 enrolled. *Faculty:* 59 full-time (7 women), 33 part-time/adjunct (1 woman). Expenses: Contact institution. *Financial support:* In 2006–07, 3 fellowships with full tuition reimbursements, 47 research assistantships with full tuition reimbursements, 109 teaching assistantships with full tuition reimbursements were awarded; career-related internships or fieldwork, Federal Work-Study, and tuition waivers (full) also available. In 2006, 59 master's, 22 doctorates awarded. *Degree program information:* Part-time and evening/weekend programs available. Offers biomedical engineering (MS, PhD); chemical and biomolecular engineering (MS, PhD); civil engineering (MS, PhD); electrical and computer engineering (MS, PhD); engineering (MS, PhD); engineering (biomedical engineering specialization) (MS); engineering (management specialization) (MS); engineering (polymer specialization) (MS); engineering-applied mathematics (PhD); mechanical engineering (MS, PhD). *Application deadline:* Applications are processed on a rolling basis. *Application fee:* $30 ($40 for international students). Electronic applications accepted. *Application Contact:* Dr. Subramaniya Hariharan, Associate Dean, Research and Graduate Studies, 330-972-6580, E-mail: hari@uakron.edu. *Dean,* Dr. George Haritos, 330-972-6978, E-mail: haritos@uakron.edu.

College of Fine and Applied Arts Students: 277 full-time (227 women), 83 part-time (53 women); includes 48 minority (30 African Americans, 3 American Indian/Alaska Native, 3 Asian Americans or Pacific Islanders, 12 Hispanic Americans), 24 international. Average age 30. 310 applicants, 65% accepted, 127 enrolled. *Faculty:* 83 full-time (35 women), 109 part-time/adjunct (76 women). Expenses: Contact institution. *Financial support:* In 2006–07, 32 fellowships with full tuition reimbursements, 42 research assistantships with full tuition reimbursements, 11 teaching assistantships with full tuition reimbursements were awarded; career-related internships or fieldwork, Federal Work-Study, institutionally sponsored loans, tuition waivers (partial), and unspecified assistantships also available. Support available to part-time students. In 2006, 127 master's, 10 doctorates awarded. *Degree program information:* Part-time and evening/weekend programs available. Offers arts administration (MA); audiology (Au D); child and family development (MA); child development (MA); child life (MA); clothing, textiles and interiors (MA); communication (MA); composition (MM); family development (MA); fine and applied arts (MA, MM, MS, Au D); music education (MM); music history and literature (MM); music technology (MM); nutrition and dietetics (MS); performance (MM); social work (MS); speech-language pathology (MA); theatre arts (MA); theory (MM). *Application deadline:* Applications are processed on a rolling basis. *Application fee:* $30 ($40 for international students). Electronic applications accepted. *Interim Dean,* Dr. James Lynn, 330-972-7543.

College of Nursing Students: 67 full-time (53 women), 167 part-time (139 women); includes 24 minority (16 African Americans, 8 Asian Americans or Pacific Islanders), 1 international. Average age 36. 67 applicants, 81% accepted, 40 enrolled. *Faculty:* 22 full-time (all women), 17 part-time/adjunct (15 women). Expenses: Contact institution. *Financial support:* In 2006–07, 15 fellowships with full tuition reimbursements, 14 research assistantships with full tuition reimbursements, 12 teaching assistantships with full tuition reimbursements were awarded; career-related internships or fieldwork, Federal Work-Study, and tuition waivers (full) also available. In 2006, 60 master's, 1 doctorate awarded. *Degree program information:* Part-time programs available. Offers nursing (MSN, PhD); public health (MPH). *Application deadline:* For fall admission, 8/15 for domestic students. Applications are processed on a rolling basis. *Application fee:* $30 ($40 for international students). Electronic applications accepted. *Interim Dean,* Dr. Margaret Wineman, 330-972-7551, E-mail: wineman@uakron.edu.

College of Polymer Science and Polymer Engineering Students: 155 full-time (44 women), 28 part-time (9 women); includes 6 minority (2 African Americans, 2 Asian Americans or Pacific Islanders, 2 Hispanic Americans), 130 international. Average age 29. 181 applicants, 23% accepted, 32 enrolled. *Faculty:* 30 full-time (3 women), 16 part-time/adjunct (4 women). Expenses: Contact institution. *Financial support:* In 2006–07, 4 fellowships with full tuition reimbursements, 142 research assistantships with full tuition reimbursements were awarded; teaching assistantships with full tuition reimbursements, scholarships/grants and tuition waivers (full) also available. In 2006, 8 master's, 32 doctorates awarded. *Degree program information:* Part-time and evening/weekend programs available. Offers polymer engineering (MS, PhD); polymer science (MS, PhD). *Application deadline:* Applications are processed on a rolling basis. *Application fee:* $30 ($40 for international students). Electronic applications accepted. *Interim Dean,* Dr. George R. Newkome, 330-972-7500, Fax: 330-972-2413, E-mail: newkome@uakron.edu.

School of Law Students: 314 full-time (136 women), 225 part-time (95 women); includes 71 minority (38 African Americans, 22 Asian Americans or Pacific Islanders, 11 Hispanic Americans), 1 international. Average age 28. 2,230 applicants, 28% accepted, 186 enrolled. *Faculty:* 31 full-time (11 women), 24 part-time/adjunct (6 women). Expenses: Contact institution. *Financial support:* In 2006–07, 197 students received support. Career-related internships or fieldwork, scholarships/grants, and tuition waivers (full and partial) available. Support available to part-time students. Financial award applicants required to submit FAFSA. In 2006, 138 JDs awarded. *Degree program information:* Part-time and evening/weekend programs available. Offers law (JD). *Application deadline:* For fall admission, 3/1 priority date for domestic and international students. Applications are processed on a rolling basis. *Application fee:* $35. Electronic applications accepted. *Application Contact:* Lauri S. File, Assistant Dean of Admission and Financial Aid, 330-972-7331, Fax: 330-258-2343, E-mail: lfile@uakron.edu. *Dean,* Richard L. Aynes, 330-972-7331, Fax: 330-258-2343, E-mail: raynes@uakron.edu.

THE UNIVERSITY OF ALABAMA, Tuscaloosa, AL 35487

General Information State-supported, coed, university. CGS member. *Enrollment:* 23,838 graduate, professional, and undergraduate students; 2,436 full-time matriculated graduate/professional students (1,250 women), 1,686 part-time matriculated graduate/professional students (1,053 women). *Enrollment by degree level:* 586 first professional, 2,319 master's, 1,217 doctoral. *Graduate faculty:* 649 full-time (193 women), 4 part-time/adjunct (2 women). *Graduate housing:* Rooms and/or apartments available on a first-come, first-served basis to single and married students. Housing application deadline: 3/1. *Student services:* Campus employment opportunities, campus safety program, career counseling, child daycare facilities, disabled student services, exercise/wellness program, free psychological counseling, grant writing training, international student services, low-cost health insurance, multicultural affairs office, teacher training, writing training. *Library facilities:* Amelia Gayle Gorgas Library plus 8 others. *Online resources:* library catalog, web page, access to other libraries' catalogs. *Collection:* 2.6 million titles, 34,461 serial subscriptions. *Research affiliation:* DuPont (chemistry), Michael J. Fox Foundation for Parkinson's Research (biological), Information Storage Industry Consortium (magnetic information), IBM Corporation (magnetic information).

Computer facilities: 2,000 computers available on campus for general student use. A campuswide network can be accessed from student residence rooms and from off campus. Internet access and online class registration are available. *Web address:* http://www.ua.edu/.

General Application Contact: Louise F. Labosier, Admissions Officer, 205-348-5921, Fax: 205-348-0400, E-mail: labosier@aalan.ua.edu.

GRADUATE UNITS

Graduate School Students: 1,897 full-time (1,049 women), 1,639 part-time (1,035 women); includes 492 minority (389 African Americans, 19 American Indian/Alaska Native, 37 Asian Americans or Pacific Islanders, 47 Hispanic Americans), 467 international. Average age 31. *Faculty:* 649 full-time (193 women), 4 part-time/adjunct (2 women). Expenses: Contact institution. *Financial support:* In 2006–07, fellowships with full and partial tuition reimbursements (averaging $12,000 per year), research assistantships with full and partial tuition reimbursements (averaging $9,252 per year), teaching assistantships with full and partial tuition reimbursements (averaging $10,000 per year) were awarded; career-related internships or fieldwork, Federal Work-Study, institutionally sponsored loans, scholarships/grants, traineeships, tuition waivers (full and partial), and unspecified assistantships also available. Support available to part-time students. Financial award application deadline: 2/15. *Degree program information:* Part-time and evening/weekend programs available. Postbaccalaureate distance learning degree programs offered. *Application deadline:* For fall admission, 7/1 priority date for domestic students, 3/15 for international students; for spring admission, 11/1 priority date for domestic students, 7/1 for international students. Applications are processed on a rolling basis. *Application fee:* $25. Electronic applications accepted. *Application Contact:* Louise F. Labosier, Admissions Officer, 205-348-5921, Fax: 205-348-0400, E-mail: labosier@aalan.ua.edu. *Dean,* Dr. Ronald W. Rogers, 205-348-8280, Fax: 205-348-0400, E-mail: rrogers@aalan.ua.edu.

Capstone College of Nursing Students: 1 (woman) full-time, 56 part-time (53 women); includes 16 African Americans. Average age 39. 39 applicants, 72% accepted, 23 enrolled. *Faculty:* 15 full-time (14 women). Expenses: Contact institution. *Financial support:* In 2006–07, 4 students received support, including 2 fellowships with full tuition reimbursements available (averaging $14,000 per year); scholarships/grants and traineeships also available. Financial award application deadline: 4/1. In 2006, 16 degrees awarded. *Degree program information:* Part-time and evening/weekend programs available. Offers nursing (MSN). *Application deadline:* For fall admission, 6/1 priority date for domestic students. *Application fee:* $25. *Application Contact:* Dr. Marietta Stanton, Director, Undergraduate Program, 205-348-1020, Fax: 205-348-5559, E-mail: mstanton@bama.ua.edu. *Dean,* Dr. Sara E. Barger, 205-348-1040, Fax: 205-348-5559, E-mail: sbarger@bama.ua.edu.

College of Arts and Sciences Average age 28. *Faculty:* 303 full-time (80 women), 7 part-time/adjunct (3 women). Expenses: Contact institution. *Financial support:* In 2006–07, 555 students received support; fellowships with full tuition reimbursements available, research assistantships with full tuition reimbursements available, teaching assistantships with full and partial tuition reimbursements available, career-related internships or fieldwork, Federal Work-Study, institutionally sponsored loans, scholarships/grants, tuition waivers (full and partial), and unspecified assistantships also available. Support available to part-time students. Financial award applicants required to submit FAFSA. *Degree program information:* Part-time programs available. Postbaccalaureate distance learning degree programs offered. Offers acting (MFA); American studies (MA); anthropology (MA, PhD); applied mathematics (PhD); art history (MA); arts and sciences (MA, MATESOL, MFA, MM, MPA, MS, DMA, PhD); biological sciences (MS, PhD); chemistry (MS, PhD); clinical psychology (PhD); communicative disorders (MS); composition (DMA); composition and rhetoric (PhD); costume design (MFA); creative writing (MFA); criminal justice (MS); directing (MFA); experimental psychology (PhD); French (MA, PhD); French and Spanish (PhD); geography (MS); geological sciences (MS, PhD); German (MA); history (MA, PhD); literature (MA, PhD); mathematics (MA, PhD); musicology (MM); performance (MM, DMA); physics (MS, PhD); political science (MA, PhD); public administration (MPA); pure mathematics (PhD); rhetoric and composition (MA); Romance languages (MA, PhD); scene design/technical production (MFA); Spanish (MA, PhD); stage management (MFA); studio art (MA, MFA); teaching English as a second language (MATESOL); theatre (MFA); theatre management/administration (MFA); theory (DMA); theory and composition (MM); women's studies (MA). *Application fee:* $25. Electronic applications accepted. *Application Contact:* Louise F. Labosier, Admissions Officer, 205-348-5921, Fax: 205-348-0400, E-mail: labosier@aalan.ua.edu. *Dean,* Dr. Robert F. Olin, 205-348-7007, Fax: 205-348-0272, E-mail: olin@as.ua.edu.

College of Communication and Information Sciences Students: 163 full-time (113 women), 162 part-time (131 women); includes 26 minority (20 African Americans, 4 American Indian/Alaska Native, 1 Asian American or Pacific Islander, 1 Hispanic American), 21 international. Average age 31. 256 applicants, 50% accepted, 85 enrolled. *Faculty:* 48 full-time (17 women). Expenses: Contact institution. *Financial support:* In 2006–07, 78 students received support, including 3 fellowships with tuition reimbursements available (averaging $15,000 per year), 34 research assistantships with tuition reimbursements available (averaging $12,300 per year), 38 teaching assistantships with tuition reimbursements available (averaging $12,300 per year); career-related internships or fieldwork, Federal Work-Study, and institutionally sponsored loans also available. Financial award application deadline: 2/15. In 2006, 153 master's, 12 doctorates awarded. Offers advertising and public relations (MA); book arts (MFA); communication and information sciences (MA, MFA, MLIS, PhD); communication studies (MA); journalism (MA); library and information studies (MLIS, PhD); telecommunication and film (MA). *Application deadline:* For fall admission, 2/15 priority date for domestic and international students; for winter admission, 11/1 priority date for international students; for spring admission, 11/1 priority date for domestic students. Applications are processed on a rolling basis. *Application fee:* $25. Electronic applications accepted. *Application Contact:* Diane Shaddix, Information Contact, 205-348-8593, Fax: 205-348-6774, E-mail: dshaddix@bama.ua.edu. *Associate Dean for Graduate Studies,* Dr. Jennings Bryant, 205-348-4787, Fax: 205-348-6774.

College of Education Students: 268 full-time (180 women), 561 part-time (378 women); includes 121 minority (98 African Americans, 9 American Indian/Alaska Native, 4 Asian Americans or Pacific Islanders, 10 Hispanic Americans), 37 international. Average age 34. 465 applicants, 46% accepted, 153 enrolled. *Faculty:* 67 full-time (34 women), 3 part-time/adjunct (1 woman). Expenses: Contact institution. *Financial support:* In 2006–07, 42 research assistantships with full and partial tuition reimbursements were awarded; teaching assistantships with full and partial tuition reimbursements, career-related internships or fieldwork, Federal Work-Study, institutionally sponsored loans, scholarships/grants, and unspecified assistantships also available. Financial award applicants required to submit FAFSA. In 2006, 198 master's, 42 doctorates, 44 other advanced degrees awarded. *Degree program information:* Part-time programs available. Postbaccalaureate distance learning degree programs offered (minimal on-campus study). Offers alternative sport pedagogy (MA); choral music education (MA); collaborative teacher program (M Ed, Ed S); curriculum and instruction (MA, Ed D, PhD, Ed S); early intervention (M Ed, Ed S); education (M Ed, MA, Ed D, PhD, Ed S); educational administration (Ed D, PhD); educational leadership (MA, Ed S); educational studies in psychology, research methodology and counseling (MA, Ed D, PhD, Ed S); exercise science (MA, PhD); gifted education (M Ed, Ed S); higher education administration (MA, Ed D, PhD); human performance (MA); instructional leadership (Ed D, PhD); instrumental music education (MA); multiple abilities program (M Ed); music education (Ed D, PhD, Ed S); special education (Ed D, PhD); sport management (MA); sport pedagogy (MA, PhD). *Application deadline:* For fall admission, 7/1 for domestic and international students; for spring admission, 11/17 for domestic and international students. Applications are processed on a rolling basis. *Application fee:* $25. *Application Contact:* Dr. Kathy S. Wetzel, Assistant Dean for Student Services, 205-348-1154, Fax: 205-348-0080, E-mail: kwetzel@bamaed.ua.edu. *Dean,* Dr. James E. McLean, 205-348-6052.

College of Engineering Students: 179 full-time (37 women), 138 part-time (20 women); includes 19 minority (13 African Americans, 3 Asian Americans or Pacific Islanders, 3 Hispanic Americans), 185 international. Average age 27. 588 applicants, 38% accepted, 69 enrolled. *Faculty:* 96 full-time (10 women), 1 part-time/adjunct (0 women). Expenses: Contact institution. *Financial support:* In 2006–07, 188 students received support, including 11 fellowships with full tuition reimbursements available, 65 research assistantships with full tuition reimbursements available, 81 teaching assistantships with full tuition reimbursements available; career-related internships or fieldwork, Federal Work-Study, and institutionally sponsored loans also available. Financial award application deadline: 2/15. In 2006, 79 master's, 32 doctorates awarded. *Degree program information:* Part-time programs available. Postbaccalaureate distance learning degree programs offered (no on-campus study). Offers aerospace engineering (MAE); chemical and biological engineering (MS Ch E, PhD); civil engineering (MSCE, PhD); computer science (MS, PhD); electrical engineering (MS, PhD); engineering (MAE, MES, MS, MS Ch E, MS Met E, MSCE, MSE, MSIE, PhD); engineering science and mechanics (MES, PhD); environmental engineering (MS); industrial engineering (MSE, MSIE); materials science (PhD); mechanical engineering (MS, PhD); metallurgical and materials engineering (MS Met E, PhD). *Application deadline:* For fall admission, 7/1 for domestic students, 4/15 for international students; for spring admission, 11/15 for domestic students, 9/1 for international students. Applications are processed on a rolling basis. *Application fee:* $25. Electronic applications accepted. *Application Contact:* Ronald Rogers, Assistant Vice President for Academic Affairs and Dean, Graduate School, 205-348-8280, Fax: 205-348-0400, E-mail: rrogers@aalan.ua.edu. *Dean,* Dr. Charles Karr, 205-348-6405, Fax: 205-348-8573.

College of Human Environmental Sciences Average age 31. *Faculty:* 25 full-time (17 women), 2 part-time/adjunct (both women). Expenses: Contact institution. *Financial support:* Fellowships with tuition reimbursements, research assistantships with full tuition reimbursements, teaching assistantships with full tuition reimbursements, career-related internships or fieldwork, Federal Work-Study, institutionally sponsored loans, and scholarships/grants available. *Degree program information:* Part-time and evening/weekend programs available. Postbaccalaureate distance learning degree programs offered (no on-campus study). Offers clothing, textiles, and interior design (MSHES); consumer sciences (MS); health education and promotion (PhD); health studies (MA); human development and family studies (MSHES); human environmental sciences (MA, MS, MSHES, PhD); human nutrition and hospitality management (MSHES). *Application deadline:* For fall admission, 7/6 for domestic students. Applications are processed on a rolling basis. *Application fee:* $25. *Dean,* Dr. Milla D. Boschung, 205-348-6250, Fax: 205-348-1786, E-mail: mboschun@ches.ua.edu.

Manderson Graduate School of Business Average age 26. *Faculty:* 87 full-time (12 women), 3 part-time/adjunct (0 women). Expenses: Contact institution. *Financial support:* Fellowships with full and partial tuition reimbursements, research assistantships with full and partial tuition reimbursements, teaching assistantships with full and partial tuition reimbursements, career-related internships or fieldwork, Federal Work-Study, institutionally sponsored loans, and scholarships/grants available. Support available to part-time students. *Degree program information:* Part-time and evening/weekend programs available. Postbaccalaureate distance learning degree programs offered (no on-campus study). Offers accounting (M Acc, MA, PhD); applied statistics (MS, PhD); business (Exec MBA, M Acc, MA, MBA, MS, MSC, MTA, PhD); economics (MA, PhD); finance (MS, PhD); general commerce and business (MBA); information systems, statistics, and management science—applied statistics (MS, PhD); information systems, statistics, and management science—operations management (MS, PhD); management (MA, MS, PhD); marketing (MS, PhD); operations management (MS, PhD); statistics (MS); tax accounting (MA, MTA). *Application deadline:* Applications are processed on a rolling basis. *Application fee:* $25. Electronic applications accepted.

The University of Alabama (continued)

Application Contact: Pam Vickers, Coordinator of Graduate Recruiting/Admissions, 205-348-9122, Fax: 205-348-4504, E-mail: pvickers@cba.ua.edu. *Dean,* Dr. J. Barry Mason, 205-348-8935, Fax: 205-348-5308, E-mail: jbmason@cba.ua.edu.

School of Social Work Students: 248 full-time (214 women), 50 part-time (39 women); includes 112 minority (103 African Americans, 3 Asian Americans or Pacific Islanders, 6 Hispanic Americans), 11 international. Average age 29. 245 applicants, 54% accepted, 121 enrolled. *Faculty:* 25 full-time (17 women), 13 part-time/adjunct (9 women). Expenses: Contact institution. *Financial support:* In 2006–07, 113 students received support, including 4 fellowships (averaging $3,750 per year), 9 research assistantships with full tuition reimbursements available (averaging $9,394 per year), 3 teaching assistantships with full tuition reimbursements available (averaging $9,396 per year); career-related internships or fieldwork, scholarships/grants, health care benefits, tuition waivers (partial), and unspecified assistantships also available. Financial award application deadline: 2/1. In 2006, 119 master's, 3 doctorates awarded. Postbaccalaureate distance learning degree programs offered (no on-campus study). Offers social work (MSW, PhD). *Application deadline:* For fall admission, 2/1 priority date for domestic students. Applications are processed on a rolling basis. *Application fee:* $30. Electronic applications accepted. *Application Contact:* Dr. Ginny Raymond, Associate Dean, 205-348-3943, Fax: 205-348-9419, E-mail: graymond@sw.ua.edu. *Dean,* Dr. James P. Adams, 205-348-3924, Fax: 205-348-9419, E-mail: jadams@sw.ua.edu.

School of Law Students: 497 full-time (188 women), 2 part-time; includes 53 minority (40 African Americans, 4 American Indian/Alaska Native, 4 Asian Americans or Pacific Islanders, 5 Hispanic Americans), 1 international. Average age 25. 1,071 applicants, 26% accepted, 157 enrolled. *Faculty:* 35 full-time (11 women), 31 part-time/adjunct (5 women). Expenses: Contact institution. *Financial support:* In 2006–07, 383 students received support, including 54 research assistantships; career-related internships or fieldwork, Federal Work-Study, institutionally sponsored loans, and tuition waivers (full and partial) also available. Financial award application deadline: 5/15. In 2006, 176 JDs, 28 master's awarded. Postbaccalaureate distance learning degree programs offered (no on-campus study). Offers law (JD, LL M, LL M in Tax). *Application deadline:* For fall admission, 3/1 for domestic and international students. Applications are processed on a rolling basis. *Application fee:* $35. Electronic applications accepted. *Application Contact:* Marquita Henderson, Admissions Coordinator, 205-348-5440, Fax: 205-348-3917, E-mail: admissions@law.ua.edu. *Dean,* Kenneth C. Randall, 205-348-5117, Fax: 205-348-3917, E-mail: krandall@law.ua.edu.

THE UNIVERSITY OF ALABAMA AT BIRMINGHAM, Birmingham, AL 35294

General Information State-supported, coed, university. CGS member. *Enrollment:* 16,561 graduate, professional, and undergraduate students; 3,243 full-time matriculated graduate/professional students (1,762 women), 1,504 part-time matriculated graduate/professional students (1,003 women). *Enrollment by degree level:* 975 first professional, 2,546 master's, 1,156 doctoral, 70 other advanced degrees. Tuition, state resident: part-time $170 per credit hour. Tuition, nonresident: part-time $425 per credit hour. *Required fees:* $15 per credit hour. $122 per term. Tuition and fees vary according to program. *Graduate housing:* Rooms and/or apartments available to single and married students. *Student services:* Campus employment opportunities, campus safety program, career counseling, child daycare facilities, disabled student services, exercise/wellness program, free psychological counseling, international student services, low-cost health insurance, multicultural affairs office, teacher training. *Library facilities:* Mervyn Sterne Library plus 1 other. *Online resources:* library catalog, web page, access to other libraries' catalogs. *Collection:* 853,445 titles, 3,934 serial subscriptions.

Computer facilities: 400 computers available on campus for general student use. A campuswide network can be accessed from student residence rooms and from off campus. Internet access and online class registration are available. *Web address:* http://main.uab.edu/.

General Application Contact: Julie Bryant, Director of Graduate Admissions, 205-934-8227, Fax: 205-934-8413, E-mail: jbryant@uab.edu.

GRADUATE UNITS

Graduate Programs in Joint Health Sciences Students: 437 full-time (204 women), 11 part-time (7 women); includes 71 minority (35 African Americans, 5 American Indian/Alaska Native, 25 Asian Americans or Pacific Islanders, 6 Hispanic Americans), 156 international. Average age 28. 257 applicants, 30% accepted. Expenses: Contact institution. *Financial support:* Fellowships, career-related internships or fieldwork available. In 2006, 46 degrees awarded. Offers basic medical sciences (MSBMS); biochemistry (PhD); biochemistry and molecular genetics (PhD); biophysical sciences (PhD); cell biology (PhD); cellular and molecular biology (PhD); cellular and molecular physiology (PhD); genetics (PhD); integrative biomedical sciences (PhD); microbiology (PhD); neurobiology (PhD); neuroscience (PhD); pathology (PhD); pharmacology (PhD); pharmacology and toxicology (PhD); physiology and biophysics (MSBMS, PhD); toxicology (PhD). *Application deadline:* Applications are processed on a rolling basis. *Application fee:* $35 ($60 for international students). Electronic applications accepted. *Vice President/Dean, School of Medicine,* Dr. Robert R. Rich, 205-934-1111, Fax: 205-934-0333, E-mail: rrich@uab.edu.

School of Arts and Humanities Students: 28 full-time (18 women), 58 part-time (44 women); includes 14 minority (13 African Americans, 1 Hispanic American). Average age 31. 41 applicants, 83% accepted. Expenses: Contact institution. *Financial support:* In 2006–07, 3 teaching assistantships (averaging $9,500 per year) were awarded; research assistantships, career-related internships or fieldwork, Federal Work-Study, and tuition waivers (partial) also available. Support available to part-time students. In 2006, 26 degrees awarded. Offers art history (MA); arts and humanities (MA); communication studies (MA); English (MA). *Application deadline:* Applications are processed on a rolling basis. *Application fee:* $35 ($60 for international students). Electronic applications accepted. *Dean,* Bert Brouwer, 205-934-2290, E-mail: bbrouwer@uab.edu.

School of Business Students: 149 full-time (65 women), 244 part-time (89 women); includes 68 minority (37 African Americans, 2 American Indian/Alaska Native, 23 Asian Americans or Pacific Islanders, 6 Hispanic Americans), 40 international. Average age 28. 176 applicants, 79% accepted. Expenses: Contact institution. *Financial support:* Fellowships, career-related internships or fieldwork available. In 2006, 166 degrees awarded. Offers business (M Acct, MBA, PhD). *Application deadline:* Applications are processed on a rolling basis. *Application fee:* $35 ($60 for international students). Electronic applications accepted. *Application Contact:* Director, 205-934-8817. *Dean,* Dr. Robert E. Holmes, 205-934-8800, Fax: 205-934-8886, E-mail: holmesr@uab.edu.

School of Dentistry Students: 223 full-time (96 women), 1 (woman) part-time; includes 34 minority (17 African Americans, 3 American Indian/Alaska Native, 9 Asian Americans or Pacific Islanders, 5 Hispanic Americans), 1 international. 726 applicants, 9% accepted. Expenses: Contact institution. *Financial support:* Fellowships, Federal Work-Study available. In 2006, 56 DMDs, 12 master's awarded. Offers dentistry (DMD, MS, MSBMS, PhD); dentistry and oral biology (MS). *Application deadline:* For fall admission, 2/15 for domestic students. *Application fee:* $145. Electronic applications accepted. *Application Contact:* Dr. Steven J. Filler, Director of Dentistry Admissions, 205-934-5424, Fax: 205-975-6519, E-mail: sfiller@uab.edu. *Dean,* Dr. Huw F. Thomas, 205-934-4720, Fax: 205-934-9283.

School of Education Students: 217 full-time (172 women), 535 part-time (426 women); includes 203 minority (189 African Americans, 4 American Indian/Alaska Native, 2 Asian Americans or Pacific Islanders, 8 Hispanic Americans), 15 international. Average age 34. 202 applicants, 83% accepted. Expenses: Contact institution. *Financial support:* Fellowships, career-related internships or fieldwork and Federal Work-Study available. Support available to part-time students. In 2006, 356 master's, 13 doctorates, 59 other advanced degrees awarded. *Degree program information:* Part-time and evening/weekend programs available. Offers agency counseling (MA); arts education (MA Ed); counseling and school psychology (MA, MA Ed); early childhood education (MA Ed, PhD); education (Ed S); educational leadership (MA Ed, Ed D, PhD, Ed S); elementary education (MA Ed); health education (MA Ed); health education/health promotion (PhD); high school education (MA Ed); marriage and family counseling (MA); physical education (MA Ed); rehabilitation counseling (MA); school counseling (MA); school psychology (MA Ed); special education (MA Ed). *Application deadline:* Applications are processed on a rolling basis. *Application fee:* $35 ($60 for international students). Electronic applications accepted. *Dean,* Dr. Michael J. Froning, 205-934-5363, Fax: 205-934-4963.

School of Engineering Students: 135 full-time (37 women), 88 part-time (18 women); includes 29 minority (19 African Americans, 5 Asian Americans or Pacific Islanders, 5 Hispanic Americans), 117 international. Average age 29. 211 applicants, 54% accepted. Expenses: Contact institution. *Financial support:* Fellowships with full tuition reimbursements, research assistantships with full tuition reimbursements, career-related internships or fieldwork, Federal Work-Study, institutionally sponsored loans, and tuition waivers (full and partial) available. Support available to part-time students. In 2006, 78 master's, 19 doctorates awarded. *Degree program information:* Evening/weekend programs available. Offers biomedical engineering (MSBME, PhD); civil engineering (MSCE, PhD); computer engineering (PhD); electrical engineering (MSEE); engineering (MS Mt E, MSBME, MSCE, MSEE, MSME, PhD); environmental health engineering (MSCE); materials engineering (MS Mt E, PhD); materials science (PhD); mechanical engineering (MSME, PhD). *Application deadline:* Applications are processed on a rolling basis. *Application fee:* $35 ($60 for international students). Electronic applications accepted. *Dean,* Dr. Linda C. Lucas, 205-934-8420, Fax: 205-975-4919.

School of Health Professions Students: 632 full-time (439 women), 88 part-time (61 women); includes 107 minority (71 African Americans, 5 American Indian/Alaska Native, 19 Asian Americans or Pacific Islanders, 12 Hispanic Americans), 24 international. Average age 30. 301 applicants, 68% accepted. Expenses: Contact institution. *Financial support:* Fellowships, research assistantships, teaching assistantships, career-related internships or fieldwork, Federal Work-Study, institutionally sponsored loans, scholarships/grants, traineeships, and unspecified assistantships available. Support available to part-time students. In 2006, 150 master's, 17 doctorates awarded. *Degree program information:* Part-time programs available. Offers administration-health services (PhD); clinical laboratory science (MS); clinical nutrition (MS); clinical nutrition and dietetics (MS, Certificate); dietetic internship (Certificate); health administration (MSHA); health informatics (MS); health professions (MNA, MS, MSHA, DPT, Dr Sc PT, PhD, Certificate); low vision rehabilitation (Certificate); nurse anesthesia (MNA); nutrition sciences (PhD); occupational therapy (MS); physical therapy (DPT, Dr Sc PT); physician assistant (MS). *Application fee:* $35 ($60 for international students). Electronic applications accepted. *Dean,* Dr. Harold P. Jones, 205-934-5149, Fax: 205-934-2412, E-mail: jonesh@uab.edu.

School of Medicine Students: 590 full-time (242 women); includes 126 minority (36 African Americans, 3 American Indian/Alaska Native, 81 Asian Americans or Pacific Islanders, 6 Hispanic Americans). Average age 25. 1,914 applicants, 13% accepted. Expenses: Contact institution. *Financial support:* Fellowships, career-related internships or fieldwork available. Financial award application deadline: 5/1; financial award applicants required to submit FAFSA. In 2006, 165 degrees awarded. Offers medicine (MD, MSBMS, PhD). *Application deadline:* For fall admission, 11/1 for domestic students. *Application fee:* $65. Electronic applications accepted. *Application Contact:* Dr. George S. Hand, Assistant Dean for Admissions, 205-934-2333, Fax: 205-934-8724, E-mail: ghand@uab.edu. *Vice President/Dean, School of Medicine,* Dr. Robert R. Rich, 205-934-1111, Fax: 205-934-0333, E-mail: rrich@uab.edu.

School of Natural Sciences and Mathematics Students: 163 full-time (59 women), 33 part-time (13 women); includes 28 minority (20 African Americans, 1 American Indian/Alaska Native, 6 Asian Americans or Pacific Islanders, 1 Hispanic American), 79 international. Average age 29. 173 applicants, 56% accepted. *Faculty:* 72 full-time (7 women), 32 part-time/adjunct (5 women). Expenses: Contact institution. *Financial support:* Fellowships with full tuition reimbursements, research assistantships with full tuition reimbursements, teaching assistantships with full tuition reimbursements, career-related internships or fieldwork, Federal Work-Study, institutionally sponsored loans, scholarships/grants, traineeships, health care benefits, tuition waivers (full and partial), and unspecified assistantships available. Support available to part-time students. Financial award applicants required to submit FAFSA. In 2006, 61 master's, 12 doctorates awarded. Offers applied mathematics (PhD); biology (MS, PhD); chemistry (MS, PhD); computer and information sciences (MS, PhD); mathematics (MS); natural sciences and mathematics (MS, PhD); physics (MS, PhD). *Application deadline:* Applications are processed on a rolling basis. *Application fee:* $35 ($60 for international students). Electronic applications accepted. *Dean,* Dr. Lowell E. Wenger, 205-934-5102.

School of Nursing Students: 75 full-time (71 women), 241 part-time (227 women); includes 56 minority (49 African Americans, 1 American Indian/Alaska Native, 5 Asian Americans or Pacific Islanders, 1 Hispanic American), 7 international. Average age 37. 107 applicants, 94% accepted. Expenses: Contact institution. *Financial support:* In 2006–07, 3 fellowships (averaging $12,833 per year), 1 research assistantship, teaching assistantships (averaging $6,760 per year) were awarded; Federal Work-Study also available. Support available to part-time students. In 2006, 62 master's, 7 doctorates awarded. Offers nursing (MSN, PhD). *Application deadline:* Applications are processed on a rolling basis. *Application fee:* $35 ($60 for international students). Electronic applications accepted. *Application Contact:* Dr. Lynda L. Harrison, Associate for Graduate Studies, 205-934-6787. *Dean,* Dr. Doreen C. Harper, 205-934-5360, E-mail: dcharper@uab.edu.

School of Optometry Students: 184 full-time (113 women), 2 part-time (1 woman); includes 26 minority (10 African Americans, 3 American Indian/Alaska Native, 13 Asian Americans or Pacific Islanders), 9 international. 223 applicants, 26% accepted. Expenses: Contact institution. *Financial support:* In 2006–07, 137 students received support. Federal Work-Study available. Financial award application deadline: 5/1; financial award applicants required to submit FAFSA. In 2006, 40 ODs, 3 doctorates awarded. Offers optometry (OD, MS, PhD); vision science (MS, PhD). *Application deadline:* Applications are processed on a rolling basis. *Application fee:* $40. *Application Contact:* Dr. Gerald Simon, Director, Optometry Student Affairs, 205-935-0739, Fax: 205-934-6758, E-mail: gsimonod@uab.edu. *Dean,* Dr. John F. Amos, 205-934-3036, Fax: 205-975-7052, E-mail: optometrydean@uab.edu.

School of Public Health Students: 288 full-time (165 women), 115 part-time (65 women); includes 91 minority (60 African Americans, 26 Asian Americans or Pacific Islanders, 5 Hispanic Americans), 129 international. Average age 30. 468 applicants, 72% accepted. Expenses: Contact institution. *Financial support:* In 2006–07, 115 students received support; fellowships, career-related internships or fieldwork, Federal Work-Study, scholarships/grants, and unspecified assistantships available. Support available to part-time students. Financial award application deadline: 2/15. In 2006, 130 master's, 15 doctorates awarded. *Degree program information:* Part-time programs available. Offers biomathematics (MS, PhD); biostatistics (MS, PhD); environmental health (PhD); environmental toxicology (PhD); epidemiology (PhD); health care organization and policy (MPH, MSPH); health education promotion (PhD); industrial hygiene (PhD); maternal and child health (MSPH); public health (MPH, MS, MSPH, DPH, PhD). *Application deadline:* Applications are processed on a rolling basis. *Application fee:* $35 ($60 for international students). Electronic applications accepted. *Application Contact:* Nancy O. Pinson, Coordinator of Student Admissions, 205-934-4993, Fax: 205-975-5484. *Dean,* Dr. Max Michael, 205-975-7742, Fax: 205-975-5484, E-mail: maxm@uab.edu.

School of Social and Behavioral Sciences Students: 122 full-time (81 women), 86 part-time (49 women); includes 50 minority (44 African Americans, 1 American Indian/Alaska Native, 3 Asian Americans or Pacific Islanders, 2 Hispanic Americans), 13 international. Average age 30. 176 applicants, 33% accepted. Expenses: Contact institution. *Financial support:* Fellowships, research assistantships, teaching assistantships, career-related internships or fieldwork, Federal Work-Study, and institutionally sponsored loans available. Support available to part-time students. In 2006, 46 master's, 11 doctorates awarded. *Degree program information:* Part-time and evening/weekend programs available. Offers anthropology (MA); behavioral neuroscience (PhD); clinical psychology (PhD); criminal justice (MSCJ); developmental psychology (PhD); forensic science (MSFS); history (MA); medical psychology (PhD); medical sociology (PhD); psychology (MA, PhD); public administration (MPA); social and behavioral sciences (MA, MPA, MSCJ, MSFS, PhD); sociology (MA). *Application deadline:* Applications are processed on a rolling basis. *Application fee:* $35 ($60 for international students).

Electronic applications accepted. *Dean,* Dr. Tennant S. McWilliams, 205-934-5643, Fax: 205-934-5643, E-mail: tsm@uab.edu.

See Close-Up on page 1067.

THE UNIVERSITY OF ALABAMA IN HUNTSVILLE, Huntsville, AL 35899

General Information State-supported, coed, university. CGS member. *Enrollment:* 7,091 graduate, professional, and undergraduate students; 470 full-time matriculated graduate/professional students (209 women), 777 part-time matriculated graduate/professional students (288 women). *Enrollment by degree level:* 967 master's, 252 doctoral, 28 other advanced degrees. *Graduate faculty:* 185 full-time (42 women), 41 part-time/adjunct (12 women). Tuition, state resident: full-time $6,072; part-time $253 per credit hour. Tuition, nonresident: full-time $12,476; part-time $519 per credit hour. *Graduate housing:* Rooms and/or apartments available on a first-come, first-served basis to single and married students. Typical cost: $2,940 per year ($4,690 including board) for single students; $5,520 per year ($7,270 including board) for married students. *Student services:* Campus employment opportunities, campus safety program, career counseling, child daycare facilities, disabled student services, exercise/wellness program, free psychological counseling, international student services, low-cost health insurance, multicultural affairs office, teacher training, writing training. *Library facilities:* University of Alabama in Huntsville Library. *Online resources:* library catalog, web page, access to other libraries' catalogs. *Collection:* 334,684 titles, 926 serial subscriptions. *Research affiliation:* NASA–Marshall Space Flight Center (space science, earth science, information technology, materials science, optical science), Department of Defense/U.S. Army Aviation & Missile Command (missile research, development and engineering and manufacturing technology), Hudson Alpha Institute for Biotechnology (medical, biotechnology, genetic research, molecular biology).

Computer facilities: 1,091 computers available on campus for general student use. A campuswide network can be accessed from student residence rooms and from off campus. Internet access and online class registration are available. *Web address:* http://www.uah.edu/.

General Application Contact: Dr. Debra Moriarity, Dean of Graduate Studies, 256-824-6002, Fax: 256-824-6405, E-mail: deangrad@uah.edu.

GRADUATE UNITS

School of Graduate Studies Students: 470 full-time (209 women), 777 part-time (288 women); includes 137 minority (76 African Americans, 13 American Indian/Alaska Native, 33 Asian Americans or Pacific Islanders, 15 Hispanic Americans), 201 international. Average age 32. 905 applicants, 71% accepted, 368 enrolled. *Faculty:* 185 full-time (42 women), 41 part-time/adjunct (12 women). Expenses: Contact institution. *Financial support:* In 2006–07, 349 students received support, including 63 fellowships with full and partial tuition reimbursements available (averaging $2,063 per year), 125 research assistantships with full and partial tuition reimbursements available (averaging $10,791 per year), 150 teaching assistantships with full and partial tuition reimbursements available (averaging $8,937 per year); career-related internships or fieldwork, Federal Work-Study, institutionally sponsored loans, scholarships/grants, traineeships, and unspecified assistantships also available. Support available to part-time students. Financial award application deadline: 4/1; financial award applicants required to submit FAFSA. In 2006, 343 master's, 31 doctorates, 39 other advanced degrees awarded. *Degree program information:* Part-time and evening/weekend programs available. Postbaccalaureate distance learning degree programs offered (minimal on-campus study). Offers information assurance (Certificate); optical science and engineering (PhD). *Application deadline:* For fall admission, 5/30 priority date for domestic students, 2/28 priority date for international students; for spring admission, 10/10 priority date for domestic students, 9/1 priority date for international students. Applications are processed on a rolling basis. *Application fee:* $40. Electronic applications accepted. *Application Contact:* Kathy Biggs, Manager, 256-824-6199, Fax: 256-824-6405, E-mail: deangrad@uah.edu. *Dean of Graduate Studies,* Dr. Debra Moriarity, 256-824-6002, Fax: 256-824-6405, E-mail: deangrad@uah.edu.

College of Administrative Science Students: 29 full-time (16 women), 131 part-time (54 women); includes 24 minority (12 African Americans, 3 American Indian/Alaska Native, 4 Asian Americans or Pacific Islanders, 5 Hispanic Americans), 11 international. Average age 31. 79 applicants, 82% accepted, 54 enrolled. *Faculty:* 18 full-time (4 women), 9 part-time/adjunct (6 women). Expenses: Contact institution. *Financial support:* In 2006–07, 2 students received support, including 2 fellowships with full and partial tuition reimbursements available (averaging $5,400 per year); research assistantships with full and partial tuition reimbursements available, teaching assistantships with full and partial tuition reimbursements available, career-related internships or fieldwork, Federal Work-Study, institutionally sponsored loans, scholarships/grants, and health care benefits also available. Support available to part-time students. Financial award application deadline: 4/1; financial award applicants required to submit FAFSA. In 2006, 64 master's, 8 other advanced degrees awarded. *Degree program information:* Part-time and evening/weekend programs available. Offers accounting (M Acc, Certificate); administrative science (M Acc, MS, MSM, MSMIS, Certificate); human resource management (Certificate); management (MS, MSM); management information systems (MSMIS, Certificate). *Application deadline:* For fall admission, 8/10 priority date for domestic students, 6/1 priority date for international students; for spring admission, 12/10 priority date for domestic students, 10/1 priority date for international students. Applications are processed on a rolling basis. *Application fee:* $40. *Application Contact:* Dr. Brent Wren, Director of Graduate Programs, 256-824-6681, Fax: 256-824-7571, E-mail: msmprog@email.uah.edu. *Dean,* Dr. C. David Billings, 256-824-6735, Fax: 256-824-6328, E-mail: billind@email.uah.edu.

College of Engineering Students: 167 full-time (38 women), 371 part-time (75 women); includes 61 minority (33 African Americans, 4 American Indian/Alaska Native, 21 Asian Americans or Pacific Islanders, 3 Hispanic Americans), 89 international. Average age 33. 408 applicants, 62% accepted, 117 enrolled. *Faculty:* 60 full-time (9 women), 11 part-time/adjunct (0 women). Expenses: Contact institution. *Financial support:* In 2006–07, 101 students received support, including 1 fellowship with full and partial tuition reimbursement available (averaging $10,800 per year), 46 research assistantships with full and partial tuition reimbursements available (averaging $9,450 per year), 54 teaching assistantships with full and partial tuition reimbursements available (averaging $9,359 per year); career-related internships or fieldwork, Federal Work-Study, institutionally sponsored loans, scholarships/grants, and health care benefits also available. Support available to part-time students. Financial award application deadline: 4/1; financial award applicants required to submit FAFSA. In 2006, 126 master's, 17 doctorates awarded. *Degree program information:* Part-time and evening/weekend programs available. Postbaccalaureate distance learning degree programs offered. Offers aerospace engineering (MSE); biotechnology science and engineering (PhD); chemical engineering (MSE); civil and environmental engineering (MSE, PhD); computer engineering (PhD); electrical and computer engineering (MSE); electrical engineering (PhD); engineering (MSE, MSOR, MSSE, PhD); industrial engineering (MSE, PhD); mechanical engineering (MSE, PhD); operations research (MSOR); optical science and engineering (PhD); software engineering (MSE, MSSE). *Application deadline:* For fall admission, 5/30 priority date for domestic students, 2/28 priority date for international students; for spring admission, 10/10 priority date for domestic students, 7/10 priority date for international students. Applications are processed on a rolling basis. *Application fee:* $40. *Dean,* Dr. Jorge Aunon, 256-824-6474, Fax: 256-824-6843, E-mail: aunon@eng.uah.edu.

College of Liberal Arts Students: 31 full-time (24 women), 71 part-time (45 women); includes 9 minority (8 African Americans, 1 Hispanic American), 2 international. Average age 33. 44 applicants, 98% accepted, 34 enrolled. *Faculty:* 27 full-time (11 women), 2 part-time/adjunct (1 woman). Expenses: Contact institution. *Financial support:* In 2006–07, 20 students received support, including 2 research assistantships with full and partial tuition reimbursements available (averaging $8,460 per year), 8 teaching assistantships with full and partial tuition reimbursements available (averaging $8,370 per year); fellowships with full and partial tuition reimbursements available, career-related internships or fieldwork, Federal Work-Study, institutionally sponsored loans, scholarships/grants, and health care benefits also available. Support available to part-time students. Financial award application deadline: 4/1; financial award applicants required to submit FAFSA. In 2006, 42 master's, 17 other advanced degrees awarded. *Degree program information:* Part-time and evening/weekend programs available. Offers English (MA); history (MA); liberal arts (MA, Certificate); psychology (MA); public affairs (MA); teaching of English to speakers of other languages (Certificate); technical communications (Certificate). *Application deadline:* For fall admission, 5/30 priority date for domestic students, 2/28 priority date for international students; for spring admission, 10/10 priority date for domestic students, 7/10 priority date for international students. Applications are processed on a rolling basis. *Application fee:* $40. *Dean,* Dr. Sue Kirkpatrick, 256-824-6200, Fax: 256-824-6949, E-mail: kirkpas@email.uah.edu.

College of Nursing Students: 54 full-time (53 women), 79 part-time (72 women); includes 22 minority (13 African Americans, 5 American Indian/Alaska Native, 4 Hispanic Americans). Average age 36. 94 applicants, 93% accepted, 70 enrolled. *Faculty:* 11 full-time (10 women), 8 part-time/adjunct (5 women). Expenses: Contact institution. *Financial support:* In 2006–07, 61 students received support, including 54 fellowships with full and partial tuition reimbursements available (averaging $1,937 per year), 7 teaching assistantships with full and partial tuition reimbursements available (averaging $6,540 per year); research assistantships, career-related internships or fieldwork, Federal Work-Study, institutionally sponsored loans, scholarships/grants, traineeships, health care benefits, and unspecified assistantships also available. Support available to part-time students. Financial award application deadline: 4/1; financial award applicants required to submit FAFSA. In 2006, 44 master's, 12 other advanced degrees awarded. *Degree program information:* Part-time and evening/weekend programs available. Postbaccalaureate distance learning degree programs offered. Offers family nurse practitioner (Certificate); nursing (MSN). *Application deadline:* For fall admission, 5/30 priority date for domestic students, 2/28 priority date for international students; for spring admission, 10/10 priority date for domestic students, 7/10 priority date for international students. Applications are processed on a rolling basis. *Application fee:* $40. *Application Contact:* Lavan Wilson, Director of Student Affairs, 256-824-6742, Fax: 256-824-6026, E-mail: wilsonol@email.uah.edu. *Dean,* Dr. Fay Raines, 256-824-6345, Fax: 256-824-6026, E-mail: rainesc@email.uah.edu.

College of Science Students: 189 full-time (78 women), 125 part-time (42 women); includes 21 minority (10 African Americans, 1 American Indian/Alaska Native, 8 Asian Americans or Pacific Islanders, 2 Hispanic Americans), 99 international. Average age 29. 280 applicants, 71% accepted, 93 enrolled. *Faculty:* 69 full-time (8 women), 11 part-time/adjunct (0 women). Expenses: Contact institution. *Financial support:* In 2006–07, 165 students received support, including 6 fellowships with full and partial tuition reimbursements available (averaging $9,000 per year), 77 research assistantships with full and partial tuition reimbursements available (averaging $11,653 per year), 81 teaching assistantships with full and partial tuition reimbursements available (averaging $8,920 per year); career-related internships or fieldwork, Federal Work-Study, institutionally sponsored loans, scholarships/grants, health care benefits, and unspecified assistantships also available. Support available to part-time students. Financial award application deadline: 4/1; financial award applicants required to submit FAFSA. In 2006, 67 master's, 14 doctorates, 2 other advanced degrees awarded. *Degree program information:* Part-time and evening/weekend programs available. Offers applied mathematics (PhD); atmospheric and environmental science (MS, PhD); biological sciences (MS); biotechnology science and engineering (PhD); chemistry (MS); computer science (MS, PhD); materials science (MS, PhD); mathematics (MA, MS); physics (MS, PhD); science (MA, MS, MSSE, PhD, Certificate); software engineering (MSSE, Certificate). *Application deadline:* For fall admission, 5/30 priority date for domestic students, 2/28 priority date for international students; for spring admission, 10/10 priority date for domestic students, 7/10 priority date for international students. Applications are processed on a rolling basis. *Application fee:* $40. *Dean,* Dr. Jack Fix, 256-824-6605, Fax: 256-824-6819, E-mail: fixj@email.uah.edu.

UNIVERSITY OF ALASKA ANCHORAGE, Anchorage, AK 99508-8060

General Information State-supported, coed, comprehensive institution. CGS member. *Enrollment:* 17,023 graduate, professional, and undergraduate students; 242 full-time matriculated graduate/professional students (170 women), 490 part-time matriculated graduate/professional students (327 women). *Enrollment by degree level:* 732 master's. Tuition, state resident: part-time $268 per credit. Tuition, nonresident: part-time $547 per credit. *Required fees:* $124 per semester. Tuition and fees vary according to reciprocity agreements and student level. *Graduate housing:* Room and/or apartments available on a first-come, first-served basis to single students; on-campus housing not available to married students. Typical cost: $2,450 per year. Room charges vary according to board plan and housing facility selected. Housing application deadline: 7/1. *Student services:* Campus employment opportunities, campus safety program, career counseling, child daycare facilities, disabled student services, exercise/wellness program, free psychological counseling, grant writing training, international student services, low-cost health insurance, multicultural affairs office, writing training. *Library facilities:* Consortium Library. *Collection:* 894,080 titles, 3,833 serial subscriptions. *Research affiliation:* Providence Hospital (health care), Municipality of Anchorage (government), BP Alaska (energy).

Computer facilities: 500 computers available on campus for general student use. A campuswide network can be accessed from student residence rooms and from off campus. Internet access is available. *Web address:* http://www.uaa.alaska.edu/.

General Application Contact: Elisa S. Mattison, Coordinator for Graduate Studies, 907-786-1096, Fax: 907-786-1021, E-mail: emattison@uaa.alaska.edu.

GRADUATE UNITS

College of Arts and Sciences Students: 75 full-time (47 women), 65 part-time (43 women); includes 25 minority (5 African Americans, 14 American Indian/Alaska Native, 3 Asian Americans or Pacific Islanders, 3 Hispanic Americans), 2 international. 139 applicants, 32% accepted. Expenses: Contact institution. *Financial support:* Research assistantships with full tuition reimbursements, teaching assistantships with full tuition reimbursements, career-related internships or fieldwork, Federal Work-Study, scholarships/grants, traineeships, tuition waivers, and unspecified assistantships available. Support available to part-time students. Financial award application deadline: 4/1; financial award applicants required to submit FAFSA. In 2006, 33 degrees awarded. *Degree program information:* Part-time programs available. Offers anthropology (MA); arts and sciences (MA, MFA, MS, PhD); biological sciences (MS); clinical psychology (MS); clinical-community psychology with rural-indigenous emphasis (PhD); creative writing and literary arts (MFA); English (MA); interdisciplinary studies (MA, MS). *Application deadline:* For fall admission, 7/1 for domestic and international students; for spring admission, 11/1 for domestic and international students. *Application fee:* $45. *Application Contact:* Deborah Ginsburg, Student Success Coordinator, 907-786-1357, Fax: 907-786-4630, E-mail: andmg@uaa.alaska.edu. *Dean,* Dr. James Liszka, 907-786-1708, Fax: 907-786-4630, E-mail: afjjl@uaa.alaska.edu.

College of Business and Public Policy Students: 29 full-time (20 women), 93 part-time (63 women); includes 25 minority (5 African Americans, 14 American Indian/Alaska Native, 4 Asian Americans or Pacific Islanders, 2 Hispanic Americans), 5 international. 87 applicants, 60% accepted. Expenses: Contact institution. *Financial support:* Research assistantships with full tuition reimbursements, career-related internships or fieldwork, Federal Work-Study, scholarships/grants, health care benefits, and unspecified assistantships available. Support available to part-time students. Financial award application deadline: 4/1; financial award applicants required to submit FAFSA. In 2006, 38 degrees awarded. *Degree program information:* Part-time and evening/weekend programs available. Offers business administration (MBA); business and public policy (MBA, MPA, MS, Certificate); global supply chain management (MS); public administration (MPA); supply chain management (Certificate). *Application deadline:* For fall admission, 7/1 priority date for domestic and international students; for spring admission, 11/1 for domestic and international students. Applications are processed on a rolling basis. *Application fee:* $45. *Application Contact:* Pat Lee, CBPP Graduate Programs Assistant, 907-786-4101, Fax: 907-786-4119, E-mail: pat.lee@uaa.alaska.edu. *Dean,* Gen. Tom Case, 907-786-1753, Fax: 907-786-4119.

College of Education Students: 29 full-time (24 women), 135 part-time (101 women); includes 19 minority (3 African Americans, 7 American Indian/Alaska Native, 5 Asian Americans

University of Alaska Anchorage (continued)

or Pacific Islanders, 4 Hispanic Americans), 8 international. 78 applicants, 40% accepted. Expenses: Contact institution. *Financial support:* Research assistantships, teaching assistantships, career-related internships or fieldwork, Federal Work-Study, scholarships/grants, traineeships, and unspecified assistantships available. Support available to part-time students. Financial award application deadline: 4/1; financial award applicants required to submit FAFSA. In 2006, 72 degrees awarded. *Degree program information:* Part-time programs available. Offers adult education (M Ed); counseling and guidance (M Ed); early childhood special education (M Ed); education (M Ed, MAT, Certificate); educational leadership (M Ed); master teacher (M Ed); principal licensure (Certificate); special education (M Ed, Certificate); superintendent (Certificate); teaching (MAT). *Application deadline:* For fall admission, 3/5 for domestic and international students; for spring admission, 10/15 for domestic and international students. *Application fee:* $45. *Application Contact:* Jane Jordan, Graduate Programs Assistant, 907-786-4401, Fax: 907-786-4445, E-mail: anjmj@uaa.alaska.edu. *Dean,* Dr. Mary Snyder, 907-786-4484.

College of Health and Social Welfare Students: 50 full-time (41 women), 117 part-time (100 women); includes 28 minority (5 African Americans, 11 American Indian/Alaska Native, 6 Asian Americans or Pacific Islanders, 6 Hispanic Americans). 81 applicants, 49% accepted. Expenses: Contact institution. *Financial support:* Career-related internships or fieldwork, Federal Work-Study, and traineeships available. Support available to part-time students. Financial award application deadline: 4/1; financial award applicants required to submit FAFSA. In 2006, 39 degrees awarded. *Degree program information:* Part-time and evening/weekend programs available. Offers health and social welfare (MPH, MS, MSW, Certificate). *Application fee:* $45. *Dean,* Dr. Cheryl Easley, 907-786-4407, Fax: 907-786-4440.

Division of Health Sciences Students: 2 full-time (1 woman), 46 part-time (39 women); includes 10 minority (4 American Indian/Alaska Native, 3 Asian Americans or Pacific Islanders, 3 Hispanic Americans). 23 applicants, 48% accepted. *Faculty:* 2 full-time (both women). Expenses: Contact institution. In 2006, 4 degrees awarded. *Degree program information:* Part-time programs available. Offers public health practice (MPH). *Application deadline:* For fall admission, 3/1 for domestic and international students; for spring admission, 10/1 for domestic and international students. *Application fee:* $45. *Chair,* Dr. Rhonda Johnson, 907-786-6565.

School of Nursing Students: 10 full-time (all women), 38 part-time (34 women); includes 6 minority (3 African Americans, 2 American Indian/Alaska Native, 1 Hispanic American). 15 applicants, 27% accepted. Expenses: Contact institution. *Financial support:* Teaching assistantships, career-related internships or fieldwork, Federal Work-Study, and health care benefits available. Support available to part-time students. Financial award application deadline: 4/1; financial award applicants required to submit FAFSA. In 2006, 12 degrees awarded. *Degree program information:* Part-time and evening/weekend programs available. Offers family nurse practitioner (Certificate); nursing (MS); nursing education (Certificate); psychiatric nurse practitioner (Certificate). *Application deadline:* For fall admission, 3/1 for domestic students; for spring admission, 11/1 for domestic students. *Application fee:* $45. *Application Contact:* Marie Samson, Coordinator of Student Affairs, 907-786-4561. *Director,* Dr. Jean Ballantyne, 907-786-4571, Fax: 907-786-4558.

School of Social Work Students: 38 full-time (30 women), 33 part-time (27 women); includes 12 minority (2 African Americans, 5 American Indian/Alaska Native, 3 Asian Americans or Pacific Islanders, 2 Hispanic Americans). 43 applicants, 58% accepted. Expenses: Contact institution. *Financial support:* Application deadline: 4/1; In 2006, 23 degrees awarded. *Degree program information:* Part-time and evening/weekend programs available. Postbaccalaureate distance learning degree programs offered (no on-campus study). Offers clinical social work practice (Certificate); social work (MSW); social work management (Certificate). *Application deadline:* For fall admission, 1/15 for domestic and international students. *Application fee:* $45. Electronic applications accepted. *Application Contact:* Dr. Randy Magen, MSW Coordinator, 907-786-6901, Fax: 907-786-6912, E-mail: afrhm1@uaa.alaska.edu. *Director,* Dr. Elizabeth Sirles, 907-786-6160, Fax: 907-786-1008.

School of Engineering Students: 10 full-time (6 women), 72 part-time (15 women); includes 13 minority (2 African Americans, 4 American Indian/Alaska Native, 5 Asian Americans or Pacific Islanders, 2 Hispanic Americans), 2 international. 31 applicants, 45% accepted. Expenses: Contact institution. *Financial support:* In 2006–07, 6 research assistantships with full tuition reimbursements were awarded; Federal Work-Study and traineeships also available. Support available to part-time students. Financial award application deadline: 4/1; financial award applicants required to submit FAFSA. In 2006, 18 degrees awarded. *Degree program information:* Part-time and evening/weekend programs available. Offers applied environmental science and technology (M AEST, MS); arctic engineering (MS); civil engineering (MCE, MS); engineering (M AEST, MCE, MS, Certificate); engineering management (MS); port and coastal engineering (Certificate); project management (MS); science management (MS). *Application deadline:* For fall admission, 7/1 priority date for domestic students, 7/1 for international students; for spring admission, 11/1 for domestic and international students. Applications are processed on a rolling basis. *Application fee:* $45. *Application Contact:* Elisa S. Mattison, Coordinator for Graduate Studies, 907-786-1096, Fax: 907-786-1021, E-mail: emattison@uaa.alaska.edu. *Director,* Dr. Robert Lang, 907-786-1859, Fax: 907-786-1079.

UNIVERSITY OF ALASKA FAIRBANKS, Fairbanks, AK 99775-7520

General Information State-supported, coed, university. CGS member. *Enrollment:* 8,341 graduate, professional, and undergraduate students; 600 full-time matriculated graduate/professional students (295 women), 426 part-time matriculated graduate/professional students (251 women). *Enrollment by degree level:* 736 master's, 276 doctoral, 14 other advanced degrees. *Graduate faculty:* 491 full-time (167 women), 13 part-time/adjunct (7 women). *Graduate housing:* Rooms and/or apartments available on a first-come, first-served basis to single and married students. Typical cost: $3,440 per year ($6,030 including board) for single students; $6,930 per year ($9,520 including board) for married students. Housing application deadline: 8/1. *Student services:* Campus employment opportunities, campus safety program, career counseling, child daycare facilities, disabled student services, exercise/wellness program, free psychological counseling, grant writing training, international student services, low-cost health insurance, multicultural affairs office, teacher training, writing training. *Library facilities:* Rasmuson Library plus 1 other. *Online resources:* library catalog, web page, access to other libraries' catalogs. *Collection:* 620,760 titles, 144,583 serial subscriptions, 729,494 audiovisual materials. *Research affiliation:* Alaska Cooperative Fishery and Wildlife Research Unit, Institute of Northern Forestry.

Computer facilities: Computer purchase and lease plans are available. 56 computers available on campus for general student use. A campuswide network can be accessed from student residence rooms and from off campus. Internet access and online class registration, university portal are available. *Web address:* http://www.uaf.edu/.

General Application Contact: Nancy D. Dix, Director of Admissions, 907-474-7500, Fax: 907-474-5379, E-mail: fyapply@uaf.edu.

GRADUATE UNITS

College of Engineering and Mines Students: 81 full-time (18 women), 27 part-time (10 women); includes 4 minority (2 Asian Americans or Pacific Islanders, 2 Hispanic Americans), 69 international. Average age 29. 103 applicants, 39% accepted, 25 enrolled. *Faculty:* 53 full-time (7 women), 1 part-time/adjunct (0 women). Expenses: Contact institution. *Financial support:* In 2006–07, 47 research assistantships with tuition reimbursements (averaging $10,356 per year), 18 teaching assistantships with tuition reimbursements (averaging $10,553 per year) were awarded; fellowships with tuition reimbursements, career-related internships or fieldwork, Federal Work-Study, scholarships/grants, and unspecified assistantships also available. Support available to part-time students. Financial award applicants required to submit FAFSA. In 2006, 23 master's, 2 doctorates awarded. *Degree program information:* Part-time programs available. Offers arctic engineering (MS); civil engineering (MCE, MS); electrical engineering (MEE, MS); engineering (PhD); engineering and mines (MCE, MEE, MS, PhD, EM); engineering and science management (MS); environmental engineering (MS); environmental quality science (MS); geological engineering (MS, EM); mechanical engineering (MS); mineral preparation engineering (MS); mining engineering (MS, EM); petroleum engineering (MS). *Application deadline:* For fall admission, 6/1 for domestic students, 3/1 for international students; for spring admission, 10/15 for domestic students, 9/1 for international students. Applications are processed on a rolling basis. *Application fee:* $50. Electronic applications accepted. *Acting Dean,* Dr. Douglas J. Goering, 907-474-7730, Fax: 907-474-6994, E-mail: fymech@uaf.edu.

College of Liberal Arts Students: 105 full-time (66 women), 100 part-time (66 women); includes 31 minority (5 African Americans, 16 American Indian/Alaska Native, 7 Asian Americans or Pacific Islanders, 3 Hispanic Americans), 15 international. Average age 35. 179 applicants, 53% accepted, 61 enrolled. *Faculty:* 102 full-time (44 women). Expenses: Contact institution. *Financial support:* In 2006–07, 15 research assistantships with tuition reimbursements (averaging $10,965 per year), 77 teaching assistantships with tuition reimbursements (averaging $9,808 per year) were awarded; fellowships with tuition reimbursements, career-related internships or fieldwork, Federal Work-Study, scholarships/grants, and unspecified assistantships also available. Financial award applicants required to submit FAFSA. In 2006, 45 master's, 2 doctorates awarded. *Degree program information:* Part-time programs available. Postbaccalaureate distance learning degree programs offered. Offers Alaskan ethnomusicology (MA); anthropology (MA, PhD); applied linguistics (MA); art (MFA); clinical-community psychology (PhD); creative writing (MFA); criminal justice management and administration (MA); cross cultural studies (MA); English (MA); liberal arts (MA, MFA, PhD); music education (MA); music history (MA); music theory (MA); northern studies (MA); performance (MA); professional communications (MA). *Application deadline:* For fall admission, 6/1 for domestic students, 3/1 for international students; for spring admission, 10/15 for domestic students, 9/1 for international students. Applications are processed on a rolling basis. *Application fee:* $50. Electronic applications accepted. *Dean,* Phyliss Morrow, 907-474-7231, Fax: 907-474-5817, E-mail: fycla@uaf.edu.

College of Natural Sciences and Mathematics Students: 219 full-time (104 women), 78 part-time (38 women); includes 21 minority (2 African Americans, 2 American Indian/Alaska Native, 9 Asian Americans or Pacific Islanders, 8 Hispanic Americans), 49 international. Average age 30. 192 applicants, 45% accepted, 45 enrolled. *Faculty:* 99 full-time (27 women), 4 part-time/adjunct (1 woman). Expenses: Contact institution. *Financial support:* In 2006–07, 95 research assistantships with tuition reimbursements (averaging $12,101 per year), 67 teaching assistantships with tuition reimbursements (averaging $11,900 per year) were awarded; fellowships with tuition reimbursements, career-related internships or fieldwork, Federal Work-Study, scholarships/grants, and unspecified assistantships also available. Financial award applicants required to submit FAFSA. In 2006, 39 master's, 14 doctorates awarded. *Degree program information:* Part-time programs available. Offers atmospheric science (MS, PhD); biochemistry and molecular biology (MS, PhD); biological sciences (MS, PhD); biology (MAT); chemistry (MA, MS); computational physics (MS, PhD); computer science (MS); environmental chemistry (MS, PhD); general physics (MS); geology (MS, PhD); geophysics (MS, PhD); mathematics (MAT, MS, PhD); natural sciences and mathematics (MA, MAT, MS, MSE, PhD); physics (MAT, PhD); software engineering (MSE); space physics (MS, PhD); statistics (MS); wildlife biology (MS, PhD). *Application deadline:* For fall admission, 6/1 for domestic students, 3/1 for international students; for spring admission, 10/15 for domestic students, 9/1 for international students. Applications are processed on a rolling basis. *Application fee:* $50. Electronic applications accepted. *Dean,* Dr. Joan Braddock, 907-474-7608, Fax: 907-474-5101, E-mail: fycnsm@uaf.edu.

College of Rural and Community Development Students: 6 full-time (4 women), 18 part-time (8 women); includes 10 minority (9 American Indian/Alaska Native, 1 Asian American or Pacific Islander), 1 international. Average age 42. 11 applicants, 82% accepted, 6 enrolled. *Faculty:* 31 full-time (15 women), 1 part-time/adjunct (0 women). Expenses: Contact institution. *Financial support:* Fellowships with tuition reimbursements, Federal Work-Study and scholarships/grants available. Financial award applicants required to submit FAFSA. In 2006, 7 degrees awarded. *Degree program information:* Part-time programs available. Offers Alaska native and rural development (MA); rural and community development (MA). *Application deadline:* For fall admission, 7/1 for domestic students, 3/1 for international students; for spring admission, 11/1 for domestic students, 9/1 for international students. Applications are processed on a rolling basis. *Application fee:* $50. Electronic applications accepted. *Vice Chancellor,* Dr. Bernice M. Joseph, 907-474-7143, Fax: 907-474-5824, E-mail: fnbmj@uaf.edu.

Graduate School for Interdisciplinary Studies Students: 30 full-time (18 women), 43 part-time (18 women); includes 15 minority (2 African Americans, 4 American Indian/Alaska Native, 5 Asian Americans or Pacific Islanders, 4 Hispanic Americans), 11 international. Average age 39. 28 applicants, 68% accepted, 16 enrolled. *Faculty:* 3 full-time (0 women), 1 (woman) part-time/adjunct. Expenses: Contact institution. *Financial support:* In 2006–07, 19 research assistantships with tuition reimbursements (averaging $12,584 per year), 6 teaching assistantships with tuition reimbursements (averaging $9,656 per year) were awarded; fellowships with tuition reimbursements, career-related internships or fieldwork, Federal Work-Study, scholarships/grants, and unspecified assistantships also available. Financial award applicants required to submit FAFSA. In 2006, 2 master's, 10 doctorates awarded. *Degree program information:* Part-time programs available. Offers interdisciplinary studies (MA, MS, PhD). *Application deadline:* For fall admission, 6/1 for domestic students, 3/1 for international students; for spring admission, 10/15 for domestic students, 9/1 for international students. Applications are processed on a rolling basis. *Application fee:* $50. Electronic applications accepted. *Application Contact:* Elke G. Richmond, Coordinator of Graduate Student Services, 907-474-7186, Fax: 907-474-7225, E-mail: fygrads@uaf.edu. *Vice Provost,* Dr. Susan M. Henrichs, 907-474-7464, Fax: 907-474-1984, E-mail: fyinds@uaf.edu.

School of Education Students: 56 full-time (40 women), 89 part-time (72 women); includes 31 minority (4 African Americans, 21 American Indian/Alaska Native, 2 Asian Americans or Pacific Islanders, 4 Hispanic Americans), 1 international. Average age 37. 69 applicants, 67% accepted, 42 enrolled. *Faculty:* 18 full-time (10 women), 3 part-time/adjunct (all women). Expenses: Contact institution. *Financial support:* In 2006–07, 2 research assistantships with tuition reimbursements (averaging $6,510 per year), 4 teaching assistantships with tuition reimbursements (averaging $10,441 per year) were awarded; fellowships with tuition reimbursements, career-related internships or fieldwork, Federal Work-Study, and scholarships/grants also available. Financial award applicants required to submit FAFSA. In 2006, 33 degrees awarded. *Degree program information:* Part-time programs available. Postbaccalaureate distance learning degree programs offered. Offers cross cultural education (M Ed); curriculum instruction (M Ed); education (M Ed); guidance and counseling (M Ed); k-12 reading (M Ed); language and literacy (M Ed). *Application deadline:* For fall admission, 3/1 for domestic and international students; for spring admission, 10/1 for domestic students, 9/1 for international students. *Application fee:* $50. Electronic applications accepted. *Dean,* Dr. Eric C. Madsen, 907-474-7341, Fax: 907-474-5451, E-mail: fysoed@uaf.edu.

School of Fisheries and Ocean Sciences Students: 69 full-time (34 women), 48 part-time (24 women); includes 8 minority (3 American Indian/Alaska Native, 2 Asian Americans or Pacific Islanders, 3 Hispanic Americans), 7 international. Average age 32. 86 applicants, 31% accepted, 21 enrolled. *Faculty:* 49 full-time (14 women), 2 part-time/adjunct (1 woman). Expenses: Contact institution. *Financial support:* In 2006–07, 48 research assistantships (averaging $9,837 per year), 12 teaching assistantships with tuition reimbursements (averaging $6,195 per year) were awarded; Federal Work-Study and scholarships/grants also available. Financial award applicants required to submit FAFSA. In 2006, 18 master's, 7 doctorates awarded. *Degree program information:* Part-time programs available. Offers fisheries (MS, PhD); fisheries and ocean sciences (MS, PhD); marine biology (MS, PhD); oceanography (MS, PhD). *Application deadline:* For fall admission, 6/1 for domestic students, 3/1 for international students; for spring admission, 10/15 for domestic students, 9/1 for international students. Applications are processed on a rolling basis. *Application fee:* $50. Electronic applications accepted. *Application Contact:* Katherine Murra, Recruitment and Retention Coordinator, 907-474-7289, Fax: 907-474-7204, E-mail: murra@sfos.uaf.edu. *Dean,* Dr. Denis Wiesenberg, 907-474-7824, Fax: 907-474-7204, E-mail: info@sfos.uaf.edu.

School of Management Students: 23 full-time (6 women), 11 part-time (8 women); includes 3 minority (1 American Indian/Alaska Native, 2 Asian Americans or Pacific Islanders), 7 international. Average age 32. 26 applicants, 62% accepted, 11 enrolled. *Faculty:* 15 full-time (4 women), 2 part-time/adjunct (1 woman). Expenses: Contact institution. *Financial support:*

In 2006–07, 3 research assistantships with tuition reimbursements (averaging $10,403 per year), 10 teaching assistantships with tuition reimbursements (averaging $11,372 per year) were awarded; fellowships with tuition reimbursements, career-related internships or fieldwork, Federal Work-Study, scholarships/grants, and unspecified assistantships also available. Financial award applicants required to submit FAFSA. In 2006, 8 degrees awarded. *Degree program information:* Part-time programs available. Offers capital markets (MBA); general management (MBA); management (MBA, MS); resource economics and applied economics (MS). *Application deadline:* For fall admission, 6/1 priority date for domestic students, 2/15 for international students; for spring admission, 10/15 priority date for domestic students, 9/1 for international students. Applications are processed on a rolling basis. *Application fee:* $50. Electronic applications accepted. *Application Contact:* Dr. Laura Milner, Director, MBA Program, 907-474-5294, Fax: 907-474-5219, E-mail: fflmm@uaf.edu. *Dean,* Dr. Maurice Marr, 907-474-7461, Fax: 907-474-5219, E-mail: dean.som@uaf.edu.

School of Natural Resources and Agricultural Sciences Students: 11 full-time (5 women), 12 part-time (7 women); includes 4 minority (2 American Indian/Alaska Native, 2 Asian Americans or Pacific Islanders). Average age 32. 26 applicants, 42% accepted, 11 enrolled. *Faculty:* 29 full-time (9 women), 1 (woman) part-time/adjunct. Expenses: Contact institution. *Financial support:* In 2006–07, 9 research assistantships with tuition reimbursements (averaging $8,209 per year), 3 teaching assistantships with tuition reimbursements (averaging $6,768 per year) were awarded; fellowships with tuition reimbursements, career-related internships or fieldwork, Federal Work-Study, and scholarships/grants also available. Financial award applicants required to submit FAFSA. In 2006, 5 master's awarded. *Degree program information:* Part-time programs available. Offers natural resources and agricultural sciences (MS); nature resource management (MS). *Application deadline:* For fall admission, 6/1 for domestic students, 3/1 for international students; for spring admission, 10/15 for domestic students, 9/1 for international students. Applications are processed on a rolling basis. *Application fee:* $50. Electronic applications accepted. *Application Contact:* Barbara Pierson, Recruitment Coordinator, 907-474-5276, Fax: 907-474-6567. *Dean,* Dr. Carol E. Lewis, 907-474-7083, Fax: 907-474-6567, E-mail: fysnras@uaf.edu.

UNIVERSITY OF ALASKA SOUTHEAST, Juneau, AK 99801

General Information State-supported, coed, comprehensive institution. *Enrollment:* 2,965 graduate, professional, and undergraduate students; 93 full-time matriculated graduate/professional students (58 women), 174 part-time matriculated graduate/professional students (128 women). *Enrollment by degree level:* 267 master's. *Graduate faculty:* 17 full-time (9 women), 6 part-time/adjunct (5 women). *Graduate housing:* Rooms and/or apartments available on a first-come, first-served basis to single and married students. Typical cost: $4,177 per year ($6,714 including board) for single students; $4,177 per year ($6,714 including board) for married students. Housing application deadline: 5/1. *Student services:* Campus employment opportunities, campus safety program, career counseling, disabled student services, exercise/wellness program, free psychological counseling, grant writing training, international student services, low-cost health insurance, multicultural affairs office, teacher training, writing training. *Library facilities:* Egan Memorial Library plus 1 other. *Online resources:* library catalog, web page, access to other libraries' catalogs. *Collection:* 176,312 titles, 438 serial subscriptions. *Research affiliation:* National Park Service (environmental resources, cultural studies), North Pacific Research Board (marine biology, oceanography), US Department of Education (teaching, early childhood education), Natural Science Foundation (marine biology, undergraduate research), US Department of Agriculture (forest service), Alaska Department of Education (teaching).

Computer facilities: 75 computers available on campus for general student use. A campuswide network can be accessed from student residence rooms and from off campus. Internet access and online class registration are available. *Web address:* http://www.uas.alaska.edu/.

General Application Contact: Susan A. Stuck, Administrative Assistant, 866-465-6424, Fax: 866-465-5159, E-mail: jnsas@uas.alaska.edu.

GRADUATE UNITS

Graduate Programs Students: 93 full-time (58 women), 174 part-time (128 women); includes 37 minority (4 African Americans, 21 American Indian/Alaska Native, 7 Asian Americans or Pacific Islanders, 5 Hispanic Americans), 11 international. Average age 34. *Faculty:* 17 full-time (9 women), 6 part-time/adjunct (5 women). Expenses: Contact institution. *Financial support:* Federal Work-Study, scholarships/grants, and tuition waivers (full and partial) available. Support available to part-time students. Financial award applicants required to submit FAFSA. In 2006, 84 degrees awarded. *Degree program information:* Part-time and evening/weekend programs available. Postbaccalaureate distance learning degree programs offered (minimal on-campus study). Offers business administration (MBA); early childhood education (M Ed, MAT); educational technology (M Ed); elementary education (MAT); public administration (MPA); reading (M Ed); secondary education (MAT). *Application deadline:* For fall admission, 4/1 priority date for domestic and international students; for spring admission, 11/1 priority date for domestic and international students. Applications are processed on a rolling basis. *Application fee:* $50. Electronic applications accepted. *Application Contact:* Susan A. Stuck, Administrative Assistant, 866-465-6424, Fax: 866-465-5159, E-mail: jnsas@uas.alaska.edu. *Provost,* Dr. Roberta Stell, 907-796-6486, Fax: 907-796-6040, E-mail: robbi.stell@uas.alaska.edu.

UNIVERSITY OF ALBERTA, Edmonton, AB T6G 2E1, Canada

General Information Province-supported, coed, university. CGS member. *Enrollment:* 36,562 graduate, professional, and undergraduate students; 4,527 full-time matriculated graduate/professional students (2,205 women), 1,532 part-time matriculated graduate/professional students (886 women). *Enrollment by degree level:* 3,496 master's, 2,452 doctoral, 111 other advanced degrees. *Graduate faculty:* 3,200. *Graduate housing:* Rooms and/or apartments available on a first-come, first-served basis to single and married students. *Student services:* Campus employment opportunities, campus safety program, career counseling, child daycare facilities, disabled student services, exercise/wellness program, free psychological counseling, grant writing training, international student services, multicultural affairs office, teacher training, writing training. *Library facilities:* Cameron Library plus 12 others. *Online resources:* library catalog, web page, access to other libraries' catalogs. *Collection:* 9.7 million titles.

Computer facilities: Computer purchase and lease plans are available. 721 computers available on campus for general student use. A campuswide network can be accessed from student residence rooms and from off campus. Internet access and online class registration, e-mail are available. *Web address:* http://www.ualberta.ca/.

General Application Contact: Information Contact, 780-492-3499, E-mail: grad.mail@ualberta.ca.

GRADUATE UNITS

Faculty of Extension Expenses: Contact institution. Offers communications and technology (MA). *Application Contact:* Susan Petruszczak, Information Contact, 780-492-1538, Fax: 780-492-0627. *Acting Dean,* C. S. McWatters, 780-492-3116.

Faculty of Graduate Studies and Research Students: 4,521 full-time (2,202 women), 1,530 part-time (886 women). Expenses: Contact institution. *Financial support:* In 2006–07, 2,253 fellowships were awarded; research assistantships, teaching assistantships, career-related internships or fieldwork, institutionally sponsored loans, and scholarships/grants also available. Support available to part-time students. In 2006, 1,105 master's, 320 doctorates awarded. *Degree program information:* Part-time and evening/weekend programs available. Offers accounting (PhD); adult education (M Ed, Ed D, PhD); agricultural economics (M Ag, M Sc, PhD); agricultural, food and nutritional science (M Ag, M Eng, M Sc, PhD); agroforestry (M Ag, M Sc, MF); ancient history (PhD); anthropology (MA, PhD); applied linguistics (Germanic, Romance, Slavic) (MA); applied mathematics (M Sc, PhD); applied music (M Mus); astrophysics (M Sc, PhD); biostatistics (M Sc); business administration (Exec MBA); chemical engineering (M Eng, M Sc, PhD); chemistry (M Sc, PhD); Chinese literature (MA); choral conducting (M Mus); classical archaeology (MA, PhD); classical literature (PhD); classics (MA); communications (M Eng, M Sc, PhD); communications and technology (MACT); composition (M Mus); computer engineering (M Eng, M Sc, PhD); computing science (M Sc, PhD); condensed matter (M Sc, PhD); conservation biology (M Sc, PhD); construction engineering and management (M Eng, M Sc, PhD); counseling psychology (M Ed, PhD); criminal justice (MA); demography (MA, PhD); design (MFA); directing (MFA); drama (MA); drawing (MFA); earth and atmospheric sciences (M Sc, MA, PhD); East Asian interdisciplinary studies (MA); economics (MA, PhD); economics and finance (MA); educational administration and leadership (M Ed, Ed D, PhD, Postgraduate Diploma); educational psychology (M Ed, PhD); electromagnetics (M Eng, M Sc, PhD); elementary education (M Ed, Ed D, PhD); engineering management (M Eng); English (MA, PhD); environmental and natural resource economics (PhD); environmental biology and ecology (M Sc, PhD); environmental engineering (M Eng, M Sc, PhD); environmental science (M Sc, PhD); experimental linguistics (M Sc, PhD); family ecology and practice (M Sc, PhD); finance (PhD); First Nations education (M Ed, Ed D, PhD); forest biology and management (M Sc, PhD); forest economics (M Ag, M Sc, PhD); French language, literatures and linguistics (PhD); French language, literatures, and linguistics (MA); geoenvironmental engineering (M Eng, M Sc, PhD); geophysics (M Sc, PhD); geotechnical engineering (M Eng, M Sc, PhD); Germanic languages, literatures and linguistics (PhD); Germanic languages, literatures, and linguistics (MA); history (MA, PhD); history of art, design, and visual culture (MA); human resources/industrial relations (PhD); industrial design (M Des); instructional technology (M Ed); international business (MBA); Italian studies (MA); Japanese literature (MA); land reclamation and remediation (M Sc, PhD); leisure and sport management (MBA); management science (PhD); marketing (PhD); materials engineering (M Eng, M Sc, PhD); mathematical finance (M Sc, PhD); mathematical physics (M Sc, PhD); mathematics (M Sc, PhD); mechanical engineering (M Eng, M Sc, PhD); medical physics (M Sc, PhD); microbiology and biotechnology (M Sc, PhD); mining engineering (M Eng, M Sc, PhD); molecular biology and genetics (M Sc, PhD); music (PhD); nanotechnology and microdevices (M Eng, M Sc, PhD); natural resources and energy (MBA); occupational therapy (M Sc, PhD); organ and choral conductors (D Mus); organizational analysis (PhD); painting (MFA); petroleum engineering (M Eng, M Sc, PhD); pharmacology (M Sc, PhD); philosophy (MA, PhD); physical therapy (M Sc, PhD); physiology and cell biology (M Sc, PhD); piano (D Mus); plant biology (M Sc, PhD); political science (MA, PhD); power/power electronics (M Eng, M Sc, PhD); printmaking (MFA); process control (M Eng, M Sc, PhD); protected areas and wildlands management (M Sc, PhD); psychology (M Sc, MA, PhD); rural sociology (M Ag, M Sc); school counseling (M Ed); school psychology (M Ed, PhD); sculpture (MFA); secondary education (M Ed, Ed D, PhD); Slavic languages and literatures (Russian, Ukrainian) (MA, PhD); Slavic linguistics (Russian, Ukrainian) (MA, PhD); sociology (MA, PhD); soil science (M Ag, M Sc, PhD); Spanish and Latin American studies (MA, PhD); special education (M Ed, PhD); special education-deafness studies (M Ed); speech pathology and audiology (PhD); speech-language pathology (M Sc); statistics (M Sc, PhD, Postgraduate Diploma); structural engineering (M Eng, M Sc, PhD); subatomic physics (M Sc, PhD); systematics and evolution (M Sc, PhD); systems (M Eng, M Sc, PhD); teaching English as a second language (M Ed); technology commercialization (MBA); textiles and clothing (M Sc, MA, PhD); theoretical, cultural and international studies in education (M Ed, Ed D, PhD); Ukrainian folklore (MA, PhD); visual communication design (M Des); water and land resources (M Ag, M Sc, PhD); water resources (M Eng, M Sc, PhD); welding (M Eng); wildlife ecology and management (M Sc, PhD). *Application fee:* $100. *Dean,* Dr. M. T. Dale, 780-492-3499, Fax: 780-492-0692.

Centre for Health Promotion Studies Students: 19 full-time (18 women), 69 part-time (64 women). 100 applicants, 32% accepted, 28 enrolled. *Faculty:* 1 (woman) full-time, 23 part-time/adjunct (18 women). Expenses: Contact institution. *Financial support:* In 2006–07, 10 fellowships with partial tuition reimbursements, 15 research assistantships were awarded; career-related internships or fieldwork and scholarships/grants also available. In 2006, 21 master's, 1 Postgraduate Diploma awarded. *Degree program information:* Part-time programs available. Postbaccalaureate distance learning degree programs offered (minimal on-campus study). Offers health promotion studies (M Sc, Postgraduate Diploma). *Application deadline:* For fall admission, 3/31 for domestic students. *Application fee:* $0. Electronic applications accepted. *Application Contact:* Sue Muhlfeld, Graduate Programs Assistant, 780-492-9347, Fax: 780-492-9579, E-mail: health.promotion@ualberta.ca. *Graduate Coordinator,* Dr. Helen M. Madill, 780-492-8661, Fax: 780-492-9347, E-mail: helen.madill@ualberta.ca.

Facultè Saint Jean Students: 4 full-time (2 women), 64 part-time (50 women). Average age 30. 25 applicants, 92% accepted. *Faculty:* 9 full-time (7 women). Expenses: Contact institution. *Financial support:* In 2006–07, 3 fellowships (averaging $9,000 per year), 1 research assistantship with tuition reimbursement were awarded; teaching assistantships, scholarships/grants also available. In 2006, 9 degrees awarded. *Degree program information:* Part-time and evening/weekend programs available. Postbaccalaureate distance learning degree programs offered (minimal on-campus study). Offers education (M Ed). *Application deadline:* Applications are processed on a rolling basis. *Application fee:* $0. *Application Contact:* Lise Desbiens, Department Office, 403-465-8703, Fax: 403-465-8760, E-mail: medu@ualberta.ca. *Graduate Coordinator,* Dr. M. Cavanagh, 780-465-8770, Fax: 403-465-8760.

Faculty of Nursing Students: 39 full-time (37 women), 154 part-time (149 women). 48 applicants, 88% accepted, 40 enrolled. *Faculty:* 58 full-time (all women), 1 part-time/adjunct (0 women). Expenses: Contact institution. *Financial support:* In 2006–07, 12 fellowships with partial tuition reimbursements (averaging $23,868 per year), 27 research assistantships with partial tuition reimbursements (averaging $6,186 per year), 12 teaching assistantships with partial tuition reimbursements (averaging $2,365 per year) were awarded; institutionally sponsored loans and scholarships/grants also available. In 2006, 13 master's, 6 doctorates awarded. *Degree program information:* Part-time programs available. Offers nursing (MN, PhD). *Application deadline:* For fall admission, 6/1 for domestic and international students; for winter admission, 10/1 for domestic and international students; for spring admission, 2/1 for domestic and international students. Applications are processed on a rolling basis. *Application Contact:* Elaine Carswell, Administrative Assistant, 403-492-4567, Fax: 403-492-2551, E-mail: graduate@nurs.ualberta.ca. *Associate Dean,* Dr. M. Allen, 780-492-4338, Fax: 780-492-2551.

Faculty of Pharmacy and Pharmaceutical Sciences Students: 47. Average age 30. 562 applicants, 2% accepted, 11 enrolled. *Faculty:* 35. Expenses: Contact institution. *Financial support:* In 2006–07, 13 students received support, including 6 teaching assistantships; research assistantships, tuition waivers (partial) also available. In 2006, 3 master's, 5 doctorates awarded. Offers pharmacy and pharmaceutical sciences (M Sc, PhD). *Application deadline:* For fall admission, 6/1 for international students; for winter admission, 9/15 for international students. Applications are processed on a rolling basis. Electronic applications accepted. *Application Contact:* Dr. Edward E. Knaus, Director of Graduate Affairs, 780-492-5993, Fax: 780-492-1217. *Dean,* Dr. Franco M. Pasutto, 780-492-0204, E-mail: fpasutto@pharmacy.ualberta.ca.

Faculty of Physical Education and Recreation Students: 60 full-time (34 women), 55 part-time (28 women), 10 international. 69 applicants, 36% accepted. *Faculty:* 30 full-time (10 women). Expenses: Contact institution. *Financial support:* In 2006–07, 63 students received support, including 28 research assistantships, 35 teaching assistantships; career-related internships or fieldwork and scholarships/grants also available. Support available to part-time students. In 2006, 13 master's, 7 doctorates awarded. *Degree program information:* Part-time programs available. Offers physical education (M Sc); recreation and physical education (MA, PhD). *Application deadline:* For fall admission, 1/1 priority date for domestic students. Applications are processed on a rolling basis. *Application Contact:* Anne Jordan, Department Office, 403-492-3198, Fax: 403-492-2364, E-mail: pergrad@ualberta.ca. *Assistant Dean,* Dr. D. Marshall, 780-492-3198, Fax: 403-492-2364.

Faculty of Rehabilitation Medicine Students: 11 full-time (6 women), 4 part-time (2 women). Average age 32. 10 applicants, 50% accepted, 5 enrolled. *Faculty:* 28 full-time (17 women). Expenses: Contact institution. *Financial support:* In 2006–07, 1 fellowship (averaging $16,000 per year), 7 research assistantships (averaging $2,721 per year), 1 teaching assistantship (averaging $2,535 per year) were awarded; institutionally sponsored loans, scholarships/grants, and traineeships also available. Financial award application deadline: 1/1. In 2006, 2 degrees awarded. Offers rehabilitation medicine (PhD). *Application deadline:* For fall admission, 3/1 for domestic and international students; for winter admission, 7/1 for domestic and international students. Applications are processed on a rolling basis. *Application fee:* $0. Electronic applications accepted. *Application Contact:* Angela Libutti, Administrative Assistant, Graduate Studies, 780-492-1595, Fax: 780-492-1626, E-mail: thesis.info@

University of Alberta (continued)

rehabmed.ualberta.ca. *Associate Dean*, Dr. P. Hagler, 780-492-1595, Fax: 780-492-1626, E-mail: paul.hagler@ualberta.ca.

School of Library and Information Studies Students: 76 full-time (65 women), 22 part-time (20 women). Average age 32. 142 applicants, 32% accepted, 42 enrolled. *Faculty:* 6 full-time (5 women), 12 part-time/adjunct (7 women). Expenses: Contact institution. *Financial support:* In 2006–07, 68 students received support, including 12 research assistantships with partial tuition reimbursements available (averaging $3,536 per year); fellowships, career-related internships or fieldwork and scholarships/grants also available. Support available to part-time students. Financial award application deadline: 7/1. In 2006, 24 degrees awarded. Offers library and information studies (MLIS). *Application deadline:* For fall admission, 7/1 for domestic students, 5/1 for international students. Applications are processed on a rolling basis. Electronic applications accepted. *Application Contact:* Joanne Hilger, Student Services Administrator, 780-492-4578, Fax: 780-492-2430, E-mail: slis@ualberta.ca. *Acting Director*, Anna Altmann, 780-492-4140, Fax: 403-492-2430, E-mail: anna.altmann@ualberta.ca.

Faculty of Law *Degree program information:* Part-time programs available. Offers law (LL B, LL M). Electronic applications accepted.

Faculty of Medicine and Dentistry Students: 516 full-time (252 women), 2 part-time (both women). 1,058 applicants, 125 enrolled. *Faculty:* 375 full-time, 320 part-time/adjunct. Expenses: Contact institution. *Financial support:* Fellowships, research assistantships, teaching assistantships, career-related internships or fieldwork, institutionally sponsored loans, scholarships/grants, tuition waivers (full and partial), and tuition bursaries available. Support available to part-time students. In 2006, 104 degrees awarded. Offers dental hygiene (Diploma); dental sciences (M Sc, PhD); dentistry (DDS, M Sc, PhD); medicine and dentistry (DDS, MD, M Sc, PhD, Diploma); orthodontics (M Sc, PhD). *Application deadline:* For fall admission, 11/1 for domestic students. Applications are processed on a rolling basis. *Application fee:* $60. Electronic applications accepted. *Application Contact:* Marlene Healey, Administrator of Admissions, 780-492-9524, Fax: 780-492-9531, E-mail: marlene.healey@ualberta.ca. *Chair*, Dr. Tom Marrie, 780-407-6234, Fax: 780-407-3132, E-mail: tom.marrie@ualberta.ca.

Graduate Programs in Medicine Students: 396 full-time, 97 part-time. Expenses: Contact institution. *Financial support:* Fellowships, research assistantships, teaching assistantships, career-related internships or fieldwork, institutionally sponsored loans, scholarships/grants, tuition waivers (full and partial), and tuition bursaries available. Support available to part-time students. In 2006, 53 master's, 20 doctorates awarded. *Degree program information:* Part-time programs available. Offers biochemistry (M Sc, PhD); biomedical engineering (M Sc); cell and molecular biology (M Sc, PhD); medical genetics (M Sc, PhD); medical microbiology and immunology (M Sc, PhD); medical sciences (M Sc, PhD); medicine (MD, M Sc, PhD); neuroscience (M Sc, PhD); obstetrics and gynecology (MD); oncology (M Sc, PhD); ophthalmology (M Sc, PhD); pediatrics (M Sc, PhD); physiology (M Sc, PhD); psychiatry (M Sc, PhD); radiology and diagnostic imaging (M Sc); surgery (M Sc, PhD). *Application deadline:* Applications are processed on a rolling basis. *Application fee:* $0. *Application Contact:* Sharon Campbell, Information Contact, 780-407-3131, Fax: 780-407-3134. *Research Administration Officer*, Colleen Iwanicka, 780-492-9720, Fax: 780-492-7303, E-mail: colleen.iwanicka@ualberta.ca.

THE UNIVERSITY OF ARIZONA, Tucson, AZ 85721

General Information State-supported, coed, university. CGS member. *Enrollment:* 36,805 graduate, professional, and undergraduate students; 4,551 full-time matriculated graduate/professional students (2,244 women), 1,759 part-time matriculated graduate/professional students (1,040 women). *Enrollment by degree level:* 3,037 master's, 3,273 doctoral. *Graduate faculty:* 1,392 full-time (362 women), 103 part-time/adjunct (32 women). *Graduate housing:* Rooms and/or apartments available on a first-come, first-served basis to single students and available to married students. Housing application deadline: 5/1. *Student services:* Campus employment opportunities, campus safety program, career counseling, child daycare facilities, disabled student services, exercise/wellness program, free psychological counseling, grant writing training, international student services, low-cost health insurance, multicultural affairs office, teacher training, writing training. *Library facilities:* University of Arizona Main Library plus 5 others. *Online resources:* library catalog, web page, access to other libraries' catalogs. *Collection:* 4.4 million titles, 23,790 serial subscriptions, 51,136 audiovisual materials. *Research affiliation:* Argonne National Laboratory (physics), Kitt Peak National Observatory (astronomy), National Center for Atmospheric Research (atmospheric physics), Smithsonian Astrophysical Observatory (astronomy), Research Corporation (astronomy).

Computer facilities: 1,950 computers available on campus for general student use. A campuswide network can be accessed from student residence rooms and from off campus. Internet access is available. *Web address:* http://www.arizona.edu/.

General Application Contact: Information Contact, 520-621-3132, Fax: 520-621-7112, E-mail: gradadm@grad.arizona.edu.

GRADUATE UNITS

College of Medicine *Degree program information:* Part-time programs available. Offers biochemistry (MS, PhD); cell biology and anatomy (PhD); immunobiology (MS, PhD); medicine (MD, MPH, MS, PhD); public health (MPH). MD program open only to state residents.

College of Optical Sciences Students: 166 full-time (31 women), 65 part-time (10 women); includes 22 minority (3 African Americans, 4 American Indian/Alaska Native, 5 Asian Americans or Pacific Islanders, 10 Hispanic Americans), 68 international. Average age 59. 182 applicants, 31% accepted, 53 enrolled. *Faculty:* 52. Expenses: Contact institution. *Financial support:* Fellowships, research assistantships, teaching assistantships, scholarships/grants available. In 2006, 46 master's, 19 doctorates awarded. *Degree program information:* Part-time programs available. Offers optical sciences (MS, PhD). *Application deadline:* For fall admission, 3/1 for domestic students. Applications are processed on a rolling basis. *Application fee:* $50. *Application Contact:* Dr. Richard L. Shoemaker, Associate Dean, Academic Affairs, 520-621-2825, Fax: 520-621-6778, E-mail: shoemaker@optics.arizona.edu. *Dean*, Dr. James Wyant, 520-621-6997, Fax: 520-621-9613, E-mail: lpalomarez@optics.arizona.edu.

Graduate College Students: 4,635 full-time (2,415 women), 1,746 part-time (736 women); includes 930 minority (94 African Americans, 132 American Indian/Alaska Native, 200 Asian Americans or Pacific Islanders, 504 Hispanic Americans). Average age 32. 7,464 applicants, 46% accepted, 2378 enrolled. *Faculty:* 1,368 full-time (325 women), 75 part-time/adjunct (16 women). Expenses: Contact institution. *Financial support:* Fellowships, research assistantships, teaching assistantships, career-related internships or fieldwork, Federal Work-Study, institutionally sponsored loans, scholarships/grants, and tuition waivers (full and partial) available. Support available to part-time students. In 2006, 1,312 master's, 365 doctorates, 8 other advanced degrees awarded. *Degree program information:* Part-time and evening/weekend programs available. Offers American Indian studies (MA, PhD); anthropology (MA, PhD); applied mathematics (MS, PMS, PhD); arid lands resource sciences (PhD); cancer biology (PhD); communication (MA, PhD); genetics (MS, PhD); geography (MA, PhD); history (MA, PhD); human language technology (MS); insect science (PhD); Latin American studies (MA); library science (MA, PhD); linguistics and anthropology (PhD); mathematical sciences (PMS); Native American linguistics (MA); Near Eastern studies (MA, PhD); neuroscience (PhD); philosophy (MA, PhD); physiological sciences (PhD); political science (MA, PhD); psychology (PhD); second language acquisition and teaching (PhD); social and behavioral sciences (MA, MS, PhD); sociology (MA, PhD); statistics (MS, PhD); theoretical linguistics (PhD); women's studies (MA). *Application fee:* $50. *Application Contact:* General Information, 520-621-3471, Fax: 520-621-7112, E-mail: gradadm@grad.arizona.edu. *Dean*, Dr. Andrew Comrie, 520-621-3512, Fax: 520-621-4101, E-mail: gradadm@grad.arizona.edu.

Arizona Graduate Program in Public Health Offers public health (MPH).

College of Agriculture and Life Sciences Students: 322 full-time (182 women), 118 part-time (65 women); includes 60 minority (7 African Americans, 5 American Indian/Alaska Native, 12 Asian Americans or Pacific Islanders, 36 Hispanic Americans), 125 international. Average age 32. 271 applicants, 47% accepted, 81 enrolled. *Faculty:* 248. Expenses: Contact institution. *Financial support:* Fellowships, research assistantships, teaching assistantships, career-related internships or fieldwork, Federal Work-Study, institutionally sponsored loans, scholarships/grants, and tuition waivers (full and partial) available. In 2006, 64 master's, 38 doctorates awarded. *Degree program information:* Part-time programs available. Offers agricultural and biosystems engineering (MS, PhD); agricultural and resource economics (MS); agricultural education (M Ag Ed, MS); agriculture and life sciences (M Ag Ed, MHE Ed, MS, PhD); animal sciences (MS, PhD); entomology (MS, PhD); family and consumer sciences (MS); family studies and human development (PhD); natural resources (MS, PhD); pathobiology (MS, PhD); plant pathology (MS, PhD); plant sciences (MS, PhD); rangeland ecology and management (MS, PhD); retailing and consumer sciences (MS, PhD); soil, water and environmental science (MS, PhD); watershed resources (MS, PhD); wildlife, fisheries conservation, and management (MS, PhD). *Application deadline:* Applications are processed on a rolling basis. *Application fee:* $50. *Application Contact:* Dr. David E. Cox, Associate Dean, 520-621-3612, Fax: 520-621-8662. *Dean*, Dr. Eugene G. Sander, 520-621-7621, Fax: 520-621-7196.

College of Architecture and Landscape Architecture Students: 65 full-time (37 women), 13 part-time (6 women); includes 2 minority (1 American Indian/Alaska Native, 1 Hispanic American), 14 international. Average age 33. 40 applicants, 48% accepted, 15 enrolled. *Faculty:* 23. Expenses: Contact institution. *Financial support:* In 2006–07, 25 students received support, including 4 fellowships with partial tuition reimbursements available, 3 research assistantships with partial tuition reimbursements available (averaging $4,916 per year), 15 teaching assistantships with partial tuition reimbursements available (averaging $4,916 per year); career-related internships or fieldwork, Federal Work-Study, scholarships/grants, health care benefits, tuition waivers (full), and unspecified assistantships also available. In 2006, 26 degrees awarded. *Degree program information:* Part-time programs available. Offers architecture (M Arch); landscape architecture (ML Arch). *Application deadline:* For fall admission, 3/1 for domestic students, 12/1 for international students; for spring admission, 3/1 priority date for domestic students, 3/1 for international students. Applications are processed on a rolling basis. *Application fee:* $50. *Application Contact:* Susan K.E. Moody, Assistant Dean, 520-621-6751, Fax: 520-621-8700, E-mail: skemoody@u.arizona.edu. *Dean*, Charles Albanese, 520-621-6751, Fax: 520-621-8700, E-mail: cala@u.arizona.edu.

College of Business and Public Administration *Degree program information:* Part-time and evening/weekend programs available. Offers accounting (M Ac); business administration (MBA); business and public administration (M Ac, MA, MBA, MPA, MS, PhD); economics (MA, PhD); finance (MS, PhD); management (MS, PhD); management and organizations (MS, PhD); management information systems (MS); marketing (MS, PhD); public administration (MPA); public administration and policy (PhD).

College of Education Students: 413 full-time (303 women), 410 part-time (292 women); includes 198 minority (29 African Americans, 35 American Indian/Alaska Native, 18 Asian Americans or Pacific Islanders, 116 Hispanic Americans), 67 international. Average age 38. 304 applicants, 56% accepted, 134 enrolled. *Faculty:* 46 full-time (23 women), 14 part-time/adjunct (7 women). Expenses: Contact institution. *Financial support:* In 2006–07, 297 fellowships with tuition reimbursements, 20 research assistantships with tuition reimbursements, 20 teaching assistantships with tuition reimbursements were awarded; career-related internships or fieldwork, Federal Work-Study, institutionally sponsored loans, scholarships/grants, tuition waivers (full and partial), and unspecified assistantships also available. Support available to part-time students. Financial award application deadline:3/1. In 2006, 212 master's, 44 doctorates, 14 other advanced degrees awarded. *Degree program information:* Part-time programs available. Postbaccalaureate distance learning degree programs offered (no on-campus study). Offers bilingual education (M Ed); bilingual/multicultural education (MA); education (M Ed, MA, MS, Ed D, PhD, Ed S); educational leadership (M Ed, Ed D, Ed S); educational psychology (MA, PhD); elementary education (M Ed, Ed D); higher education (MA, PhD); language, reading and culture (MA, Ed D, PhD, Ed S); school counseling and guidance (M Ed); secondary education (M Ed, Ed D); special education, rehabilitation and school psychology (M Ed, MA, MS, Ed D, PhD, Ed S); teaching and teacher education (MA, PhD). *Application deadline:* For fall admission, 2/1 priority date for domestic and international students; for spring admission, 10/1 priority date for domestic students, 9/1 priority date for international students. Applications are processed on a rolling basis. *Application fee:* $50. *Dean*, Dr. Ronald Marx, 520-621-1081, Fax: 520-621-9271.

College of Engineering Students: 446 full-time (113 women), 225 part-time (60 women); includes 74 minority (8 African Americans, 9 American Indian/Alaska Native, 27 Asian Americans or Pacific Islanders, 30 Hispanic Americans), 375 international. Average age 30. 887 applicants, 34% accepted, 121 enrolled. *Faculty:* 143. Expenses: Contact institution. *Financial support:* In 2006–07, 73 fellowships with full tuition reimbursements (averaging $11,250 per year), 240 research assistantships with full tuition reimbursements (averaging $16,670 per year), 90 teaching assistantships with full tuition reimbursements (averaging $15,380 per year) were awarded; institutionally sponsored loans and scholarships/grants also available. In 2006, 132 master's, 63 doctorates awarded. *Degree program information:* Part-time programs available. Postbaccalaureate distance learning degree programs offered (no on-campus study). Offers aerospace engineering (MS, PhD); chemical engineering (MS, PhD); civil engineering (MS, PhD); electrical and computer engineering (M Eng, MS, PhD); engineering (M Eng, ME, MS, PhD); engineering mechanics (MS, PhD); environmental engineering (MS, PhD); geological engineering (MS, PhD); hydrology (MS, PhD); industrial engineering (MS); materials science and engineering (ME, MS, PhD); mechanical engineering (MS, PhD); mine health and safety (Certificate); mine information and production technology (Certificate); mining engineering (M Eng, Certificate); nuclear engineering (MS, PhD); reliability and quality engineering (MS); rock mechanics (Certificate); systems and industrial engineering (PhD); systems engineering (MS); water resources engineering (M Eng). *Application fee:* $50. *Dean*, Dr. Thomas W. Peterson, 520-621-6594, Fax: 520-621-2232, E-mail: twp@engr.arizona.edu.

College of Fine Arts Students: 247 full-time (134 women), 89 part-time (56 women); includes 34 minority (4 African Americans, 3 American Indian/Alaska Native, 10 Asian Americans or Pacific Islanders, 17 Hispanic Americans), 45 international. Average age 31. 445 applicants, 40% accepted, 113 enrolled. *Faculty:* 136. Expenses: Contact institution. *Financial support:* Fellowships, research assistantships, teaching assistantships, career-related internships or fieldwork, Federal Work-Study, institutionally sponsored loans, scholarships/grants, and tuition waivers (full and partial) available. Support available to part-time students. In 2006, 89 master's, 10 doctorates awarded. *Degree program information:* Part-time programs available. Offers art (studio) (MFA); art education (MA); art history (MA, PhD); composition (MM, A Mus D); conducting (MM, A Mus D); fine arts (MA, MFA, MM, A Mus D, PhD); history and theory of art (PhD); media arts (MA); music education (MM, PhD); music theory (MM, PhD); musicology (MM); performance (MM, A Mus D); theatre arts (MA, MFA). *Application fee:* $50. *Dean*, Dr. Maurice Sevigny, 520-621-1778, Fax: 520-621-1307.

College of Humanities *Degree program information:* Part-time programs available. Offers classics (MA); creative writing (MFA); East Asian studies (MA, PhD); English (MA, PhD); English language/linguistics (MA); ESL (MA); French (MA, PhD); German (MA, PhD); humanities (M Ed, MA, MFA, PhD); literature (MA, PhD); rhetoric, composition and teaching of English (PhD); rhetoric, composition, and the teaching of English (MA); Russian (M Ed, MA); Spanish (M Ed, MA, PhD).

College of Nursing Students: 71 full-time (65 women), 81 part-time (72 women); includes 22 minority (2 African Americans, 3 American Indian/Alaska Native, 8 Asian Americans or Pacific Islanders, 9 Hispanic Americans), 15 international. Average age 42. 72 applicants, 63% accepted, 34 enrolled. *Faculty:* 28 full-time (all women), 4 part-time/adjunct (3 women). Expenses: Contact institution. *Financial support:* In 2006–07, 76 students received support, including 22 fellowships (averaging $1,136 per year), 16 research assistantships with partial tuition reimbursements available (averaging $15,000 per year), 2 teaching assistantships with partial tuition reimbursements available (averaging $15,000 per year); career-related internships or fieldwork, institutionally sponsored loans, scholarships/grants, traineeships, and tuition waivers (full) also available. Financial award application deadline: 6/1. In 2006, 21 master's, 11 doctorates awarded. *Degree program information:* Part-time programs available. Postbaccalaureate distance learning degree programs offered (minimal on-campus study). Offers nursing (MS, DNP, PhD). *Application deadline:* For fall admission, 1/15 for domestic students, 12/1 for international students. *Application fee:* $50. Electronic applications accepted. *Application Contact:* Vickie L. Radoye, Assistant Dean,

Student Affairs, 520-626-3808, Fax: 520-626-6424, E-mail: vradoye@nursing.arizona.edu. *Dean,* Dr. Marjorie A. Isenberg, 520-626-6152, Fax: 520-626-6424, E-mail: misenberg@nursing.arizona.edu.

College of Pharmacy Students: 395 full-time (243 women), 16 part-time (9 women); includes 100 minority (3 African Americans, 4 American Indian/Alaska Native, 60 Asian Americans or Pacific Islanders, 33 Hispanic Americans), 31 international. Average age 26. 613 applicants, 36% accepted, 116 enrolled. *Faculty:* 41. Expenses: Contact institution. *Financial support:* Fellowships, research assistantships, teaching assistantships, career-related internships or fieldwork, Federal Work-Study, institutionally sponsored loans, scholarships/grants, and tuition waivers (full and partial) available. Support available to part-time students. In 2006, 67 first professional degrees, 7 master's, 16 doctorates awarded. Offers medical pharmacology (MS, PhD); medicinal and natural products chemistry (MS, PhD); perfusion science (MS); pharmaceutical economics (MS, PhD); pharmaceutics and pharmacokinetics (MS, PhD); pharmacy (Pharm D, MS, PhD). *Application fee:* $50. *Application Contact:* Marty Baker, Coordinator, Recruitment and Admissions, 520-626-4311, E-mail: baker@pharmacy.arizona.edu. *Dean,* Dr. J. Lyle Bootman, 520-626-1657.

College of Science Students: 724 full-time (300 women), 129 part-time (65 women); includes 67 minority (6 African Americans, 8 American Indian/Alaska Native, 31 Asian Americans or Pacific Islanders, 22 Hispanic Americans), 277 international. Average age 29. 984 applicants, 18% accepted, 152 enrolled. *Faculty:* 372. Expenses: Contact institution. *Financial support:* Fellowships, research assistantships, teaching assistantships, career-related internships or fieldwork, Federal Work-Study, institutionally sponsored loans, scholarships/grants, and tuition waivers (full and partial) available. Support available to part-time students. In 2006, 133 master's, 71 doctorates awarded. *Degree program information:* Part-time programs available. Offers applied and industrial physics (MS); applied biosciences (MS); astronomy (MS, PhD); atmospheric sciences (MS, PhD); chemistry (MA, MS, PhD); computer science (MS, PhD); ecology and evolutionary biology (MS, PhD); geosciences (MS, PhD); mathematical sciences (PMS); mathematics (M Ed, MA, MS, PMS, PhD); molecular and cellular biology (MS, PhD); physics (M Ed, MS, PhD); planetary sciences/lunar and planetary laboratory (MS, PhD); science (M Ed, MA, MS, PMS, Au D, PhD); speech and hearing sciences (MS, Au D, PhD). *Application fee:* $50. *Application Contact:* General Information, 520-621-3471, Fax: 520-621-7112. *Dean,* Dr. Joaquin Ruiz.

James E. Rogers College of Law Offers international indigenous peoples' rights and policy (LL M); international trade law (LL M); law (JD). Electronic applications accepted.

UNIVERSITY OF ARKANSAS, Fayetteville, AR 72701-1201

General Information State-supported, coed, university. CGS member. *Enrollment:* 17,926 graduate, professional, and undergraduate students; 3,399 full-time matriculated graduate/professional students (1,684 women). *Graduate faculty:* 655 full-time (169 women), 13 part-time/adjunct (2 women). *Graduate housing:* Rooms and/or apartments available on a first-come, first-served basis to single and married students. *Student services:* Campus employment opportunities, campus safety program, career counseling, disabled student services, exercise/wellness program, free psychological counseling, international student services, low-cost health insurance, multicultural affairs office, teacher training, writing training. *Library facilities:* David W. Mullins Library plus 5 others. *Online resources:* library catalog, web page, access to other libraries' catalogs. *Collection:* 1.8 million titles, 18,173 serial subscriptions. *Research affiliation:* Oak Ridge Associated Universities, Southern Regional Education Board Uncommon Facilities Program, Southeastern Universities Research Association, Southern Regional Education Board, National Minority Graduate Feeder Project, Science Coalition.

Computer facilities: Computer purchase and lease plans are available. 1,252 computers available on campus for general student use. A campuswide network can be accessed from student residence rooms and from off campus. Internet access and online class registration are available. *Web address:* http://www.uark.edu/.

General Application Contact: Lynn Mosesso, Director of Graduate and International Recruitment and Admissions, 479-575-6246, Fax: 479-575-5908, E-mail: gradinfo@uark.edu.

GRADUATE UNITS

Graduate School Students: 1,076 full-time (568 women), 1,912 part-time (893 women); includes 338 minority (201 African Americans, 35 American Indian/Alaska Native, 45 Asian Americans or Pacific Islanders, 57 Hispanic Americans), 596 international. 2,533 applicants, 40% accepted. Expenses: Contact institution. *Financial support:* In 2006–07, 320 fellowships with tuition reimbursements, 546 research assistantships, 453 teaching assistantships with full tuition reimbursements were awarded; career-related internships or fieldwork, Federal Work-Study, institutionally sponsored loans, scholarships/grants, traineeships, and unspecified assistantships also available. Support available to part-time students. Financial award application deadline: 4/1; financial award applicants required to submit FAFSA. In 2006, 897 master's, 127 doctorates awarded. *Degree program information:* Part-time programs available. Postbaccalaureate distance learning degree programs offered (no on-campus study). Offers cell and molecular biology (MS, PhD); environmental dynamics (PhD); microelectronics and photonics (MS, PhD); public policy (PhD); space and planetary science (MS, PhD). *Application deadline:* Applications are processed on a rolling basis. *Application fee:* $40 ($50 for international students). Electronic applications accepted. *Application Contact:* Graduate Admissions, 479-575-6246, Fax: 479-575-5908, E-mail: gradinfo@uark.edu. *Associate Dean,* Dr. Patricia R. Koski, 479-575-4401, Fax: 479-575-5908, E-mail: gradinfo@uark.edu.

College of Education and Health Professions Students: 372 full-time (246 women), 473 part-time (345 women); includes 126 minority (96 African Americans, 13 American Indian/Alaska Native, 5 Asian Americans or Pacific Islanders, 12 Hispanic Americans), 43 international. 461 applicants, 43% accepted. Expenses: Contact institution. *Financial support:* In 2006–07, 39 fellowships with tuition reimbursements, 16 research assistantships, 37 teaching assistantships were awarded; career-related internships or fieldwork and Federal Work-Study also available. Support available to part-time students. Financial award application deadline: 4/1; financial award applicants required to submit FAFSA. In 2006, 296 master's, 35 doctorates awarded. Offers adult education (M Ed, Ed D, Ed S); childhood education (MAT); communication disorders (MS); counseling education (MS, PhD, Ed S); curriculum and instruction (PhD); education and health professions (M Ed, MAT, MS, MSN, Ed D, PhD, Ed S); educational administration (M Ed, Ed D, Ed S); educational foundations (MS, PhD); educational technology (M Ed); elementary education (M Ed, Ed S); health science (MS, PhD); higher education (M Ed, Ed D, Ed S); kinesiology (MS, PhD); middle-level education (MAT); nursing (MSN); physical education (M Ed, MAT); recreation (M Ed, Ed D); rehabilitation (MS, PhD); secondary education (M Ed, MAT, Ed S); special education (M Ed, MAT); vocational education (M Ed, MAT, Ed D, Ed S); workforce development education (M Ed). *Application fee:* $40 ($50 for international students). *Dean,* M. Reed Greenwood, 479-575-3208, Fax: 479-575-3119.

College of Engineering Students: 151 full-time (46 women), 419 part-time (93 women); includes 82 minority (49 African Americans, 7 American Indian/Alaska Native, 14 Asian Americans or Pacific Islanders, 12 Hispanic Americans), 223 international. 784 applicants, 36% accepted. Expenses: Contact institution. *Financial support:* In 2006–07, 27 fellowships with tuition reimbursements, 139 research assistantships, 17 teaching assistantships were awarded; career-related internships or fieldwork and Federal Work-Study also available. Support available to part-time students. Financial award application deadline: 4/1; financial award applicants required to submit FAFSA. In 2006, 146 master's, 16 doctorates awarded. Offers biological and agricultural engineering (MSE, PhD); biological engineering (MSBE); biomedical engineering (MSBME); chemical engineering (MS Ch E, MSE, PhD); civil engineering (MSCE, MSE, PhD); computer engineering (MSCSE, MSE, PhD); computer science (MS, PhD); electrical engineering (MSEE, PhD); engineering (MS, MS Ch E, MS En E, MS Tc E, MSBE, MSBME, MSCE, MSCSE, MSE, MSEE, MSIE, MSME, MSOR, MSTE, PhD); environmental engineering (MS En E, MSE); industrial engineering (MSE, MSIE, PhD); mechanical engineering (MSE, MSME, PhD); operations management (MS); operations research (MSE, MSOR); telecommunications engineering (MS Tc E); transportation engineering (MSE, MSTE). *Application fee:* $40 ($50 for international students). *Dean,* Ashok Saxena, 479-575-4153, Fax: 479-575-4346, E-mail: asaxena@uark.edu.

Dale Bumpers College of Agricultural, Food and Life Sciences Students: 88 full-time (44 women), 199 part-time (93 women); includes 15 minority (10 African Americans, 5 Hispanic Americans), 86 international. 231 applicants, 44% accepted. Expenses: Contact institution. *Financial support:* In 2006–07, 26 fellowships with tuition reimbursements, 138 research assistantships, 2 teaching assistantships were awarded; career-related internships or fieldwork, Federal Work-Study, scholarships/grants, and unspecified assistantships also available. Support available to part-time students. Financial award application deadline: 4/1; financial award applicants required to submit FAFSA. In 2006, 87 master's, 10 doctorates awarded. Offers agricultural and extension education (MS); agricultural economics (MS); agricultural, food and life sciences (MS, PhD); agronomy (MS, PhD); animal science (MS, PhD); entomology (MS, PhD); food science (MS, PhD); horticulture (MS); human environmental sciences (MS); plant pathology (MS); plant science (PhD); poultry science (MS, PhD). *Application fee:* $40 ($50 for international students). *Dean,* Dr. Greg Weidemann, 479-575-2252, Fax: 479-575-6890, E-mail: gweidema@uark.edu.

J. William Fulbright College of Arts and Sciences Students: 339 full-time (173 women), 492 part-time (239 women); includes 60 minority (19 African Americans, 12 American Indian/Alaska Native, 8 Asian Americans or Pacific Islanders, 21 Hispanic Americans), 120 international. 839 applicants, 40% accepted. Expenses: Contact institution. *Financial support:* In 2006–07, 145 fellowships, 105 research assistantships, 349 teaching assistantships with full tuition reimbursements were awarded; career-related internships or fieldwork, Federal Work-Study, institutionally sponsored loans, and traineeships also available. Support available to part-time students. Financial award application deadline: 4/1; financial award applicants required to submit FAFSA. In 2006, 186 master's, 36 doctorates awarded. Offers anthropology (MA); applied physics (MS); art (MFA); arts and sciences (MA, MFA, MM, MPA, MS, MSW, PhD); biology (MA, MS, PhD); chemistry (MS, PhD); communication (MA); comparative literature (MA, PhD); comparative literature and cultural studies (MA, PhD); creative writing (MFA); drama (MA, MFA); English (MA, PhD); French (MA); geography (MA); geology (MS); German (MA); history (MA, PhD); journalism (MA); mathematics (MS, PhD); music (MM); philosophy (MA, PhD); physics (MS, PhD); physics education (MA); political science (MA); psychology (MA, PhD); public administration (MPA); secondary mathematics (MA); social work (MSW); sociology (MA); Spanish (MA); statistics (MS); translation (MFA). *Application fee:* $40 ($50 for international students). *Dean,* Don Bobbitt, 479-575-4801, Fax: 479-575-2642.

Sam M. Walton College of Business Administration Students: 72 full-time (34 women), 154 part-time (43 women); includes 26 minority (7 African Americans, 16 Asian Americans or Pacific Islanders, 3 Hispanic Americans), 38 international. 103 applicants, 60% accepted. Expenses: Contact institution. *Financial support:* In 2006–07, 40 fellowships, 57 research assistantships, 21 teaching assistantships were awarded; career-related internships or fieldwork and Federal Work-Study also available. Support available to part-time students. Financial award application deadline: 4/1; financial award applicants required to submit FAFSA. In 2006, 162 master's, 4 doctorates awarded. Offers accounting (M Acc); business administration (M Acc, MA, MBA, MIS, MTLM, PhD); economics (MA, PhD); information systems (MIS); transportation and logistics management (MTLM). *Application fee:* $40 ($50 for international students). *Application Contact:* Jennifer Williams, Assistant Director of Marketing and Recruiting, 479-575-6123, E-mail: gsb@walton.uark.edu. *Dean,* Dr. Dan Worrell, 479-575-5949.

School of Law Students: 440 full-time (245 women); includes 110 minority (79 African Americans, 8 American Indian/Alaska Native, 14 Asian Americans or Pacific Islanders, 9 Hispanic Americans), 2 international. Expenses: Contact institution. *Financial support:* In 2006–07, 131 students received support, including fellowships with full tuition reimbursements available (averaging $6,000 per year), 10 research assistantships (averaging $2,500 per year), 1 teaching assistantship; career-related internships or fieldwork, Federal Work-Study, and scholarships/grants also available. Support available to part-time students. Financial award application deadline: 4/1; financial award applicants required to submit FAFSA. In 2006, 146 JDs awarded. Offers agricultural law (LL M); law (JD). *Application deadline:* For fall admission, 4/1 for domestic students. Applications are processed on a rolling basis. *Application fee:* $0. *Application Contact:* James K. Miller, Associate Dean for Students, 479-575-3102, E-mail: jkmiller@uark.edu. *Dean,* Cynthia Nance, 479-575-5601, Fax: 479-575-3320, E-mail: cnance@uark.edu.

See Close-Up on page 1069.

UNIVERSITY OF ARKANSAS AT LITTLE ROCK, Little Rock, AR 72204-1099

General Information State-supported, coed, university. CGS member. *Graduate housing:* Room and/or apartments available on a first-come, first-served basis to single students; on-campus housing not available to married students.

GRADUATE UNITS

Graduate School *Degree program information:* Part-time and evening/weekend programs available. Postbaccalaureate distance learning degree programs offered. Electronic applications accepted.

Clinton School of Public Service Offers public service (MPS).

College of Arts, Humanities, and Social Science *Degree program information:* Part-time and evening/weekend programs available. Offers applied gerontology (CG); applied psychology (MAP); art education (MA); art history (MA); arts, humanities, and social science (MA, MALS, MAP, CG); gerontology (MA); philosophy and liberal studies (MALS); professional writing (MA); public history (MA); studio art (MA); technical writing (MA).

College of Business Administration *Degree program information:* Part-time and evening/weekend programs available. Offers business administration (MBA); management information system (MIS).

College of Education *Degree program information:* Part-time and evening/weekend programs available. Offers adult education (M Ed); college student affairs (MA); counseling rehabilitation (MA); counselor education (M Ed); early childhood education (M Ed); early childhood special education (M Ed); education (M Ed, MA, Ed D, Ed S); educational administration (M Ed, Ed D, Ed S); educational administration and supervision (M Ed, Ed D, Ed S); higher education (MA); higher education administration (Ed D); learning systems technology (M Ed); middle childhood education (M Ed); reading (M Ed); rehabilitation of the blind (MA); school counseling (M Ed); secondary education (M Ed); special education (M Ed); teaching deaf and hard of hearing (M Ed); teaching of the mildly disabled student (M Ed); teaching persons with severe disabilities (M Ed); teaching the gifted and talented (M Ed); teaching the visually impaired (M Ed).

College of Information Science and Systems Engineering *Degree program information:* Part-time and evening/weekend programs available. Offers applied science (MS, PhD); bioinformatics (MS, PhD); computer science (MS); information science and systems engineering (MS, PhD).

College of Professional Studies *Degree program information:* Part-time and evening/weekend programs available. Offers clinical social work (MSW); criminal justice (MA); health services administration (MHSA); interpersonal communications (MA); mass communication (MA); organizational communications (MA); professional studies (MA, MHSA, MPA, MSW, CG); public administration (MPA); social program administration (MSW); social work (MSW, CG).

College of Science and Mathematics Offers applied mathematics (MS); biology (MS); chemistry (MA, MS); integrated science and mathematics (MS); science and mathematics (MA, MS).

William H. Bowen School of Law *Degree program information:* Part-time and evening/weekend programs available. Offers law (JD). Electronic applications accepted.

UNIVERSITY OF ARKANSAS AT MONTICELLO, Monticello, AR 71656

General Information State-supported, coed, comprehensive institution. *Enrollment:* 3,179 graduate, professional, and undergraduate students; 25 full-time matriculated graduate/professional students (16 women), 81 part-time matriculated graduate/professional students (57 women). *Enrollment by degree level:* 106 master's. *Graduate faculty:* 48 full-time (14 women), 2 part-time/adjunct (1 woman). Tuition, state resident: full-time $2,646; part-time $135 per hour. Tuition, nonresident: full-time $5,940; part-time $315 per hour. *Required fees:* $594;

University of Arkansas at Monticello (continued)

$30 per hour. Tuition and fees vary according to campus/location. *Graduate housing:* Rooms and/or apartments guaranteed to single students and available on a first-come, first-served basis to married students. Typical cost: $3,550 (including board) for single students; $1,440 per year for married students. Room and board charges vary according to board plan. Housing application deadline: 8/15. *Student services:* Disabled student services, exercise/wellness program, international student services, teacher training, writing training. *Library facilities:* Fred J. Taylor Library and Technology Center. *Collection:* 241,822 titles, 956 serial subscriptions.

Computer facilities: 140 computers available on campus for general student use. *Web address:* http://www.uamont.edu/.

General Application Contact: Mary Whiting, Director, Office of Admissions, 870-460-1026, Fax: 870-460-1926, E-mail: whitingm@uamont.edu.

GRADUATE UNITS

School of Education Students: 21 full-time (14 women), 59 part-time (49 women); includes 10 minority (all African Americans) Average age 36. *Faculty:* 33 full-time (13 women), 1 (woman) part-time/adjunct. Expenses: Contact institution. *Financial support:* In 2006–07, 4 teaching assistantships with full tuition reimbursements were awarded; Federal Work-Study and tuition waivers (partial) also available. Support available to part-time students. In 2006, 59 degrees awarded. *Degree program information:* Part-time and evening/weekend programs available. Postbaccalaureate distance learning degree programs offered (minimal on-campus study). Offers education (M Ed, MAT); educational leadership (M Ed). *Application deadline:* For fall admission, 8/16 priority date for domestic students, 8/1 priority date for international students; for spring admission, 1/3 priority date for domestic students, 12/1 priority date for international students. Applications are processed on a rolling basis. *Application fee:* $0 ($30 for international students). Electronic applications accepted. *Dean,* Dr. Peggy Doss, 870-460-1062, Fax: 870-460-1563, E-mail: dossp@uamont.edu.

School of Forest Resources Students: 4 full-time (2 women), 17 part-time (5 women). Average age 30. *Faculty:* 15 full-time (1 woman). Expenses: Contact institution. *Financial support:* In 2006–07, 21 research assistantships with full tuition reimbursements were awarded. In 2006, 5 degrees awarded. *Degree program information:* Part-time programs available. Offers forest resources (MS). *Application deadline:* For fall admission, 8/16 priority date for domestic students, 8/1 priority date for international students; for spring admission, 1/3 priority date for domestic students, 12/1 priority date for international students. Applications are processed on a rolling basis. *Application fee:* $0 ($30 for international students). Electronic applications accepted. *Dean,* Dr. Richard Kluender, 870-460-1052, Fax: 870-460-1092, E-mail: kluender@uamont.edu.

UNIVERSITY OF ARKANSAS AT PINE BLUFF, Pine Bluff, AR 71601-2799

General Information State-supported, coed, comprehensive institution. *Graduate housing:* Rooms and/or apartments available to single and married students. Housing application deadline: 8/1.

GRADUATE UNITS

Program in Education *Degree program information:* Part-time and evening/weekend programs available. Offers elementary education (M Ed); secondary education (M Ed).

UNIVERSITY OF ARKANSAS FOR MEDICAL SCIENCES, Little Rock, AR 72205-7199

General Information State-supported, coed, upper-level institution. *Enrollment:* 1,766 full-time matriculated graduate/professional students, 562 part-time matriculated graduate/professional students. *Graduate housing:* Rooms and/or apartments available to single and married students. *Student services:* Campus employment opportunities, campus safety program, free psychological counseling, low-cost health insurance. *Library facilities:* Medical Sciences Library. *Online resources:* library catalog, web page. *Collection:* 183,975 titles, 1,567 serial subscriptions. *Research affiliation:* National Center for Toxicological Research, Veterans Administration Hospital, Oak Ridge Associated Universities, Arkansas Children's Hospital.

Computer facilities: A campuswide network can be accessed from student residence rooms and from off campus. Internet access is available. *Web address:* http://www.uams.edu/.

General Application Contact: Dr. Kristen Sterba, Assistant Dean, Office of Graduate Student Recruiting and Retention, 501-526-7396, E-mail: kmsterba@uams.edu.

GRADUATE UNITS

College of Medicine Students: 596 full-time. Expenses: Contact institution. *Financial support:* Fellowships, research assistantships, teaching assistantships, Federal Work-Study and unspecified assistantships available. Support available to part-time students. Offers medicine (MD). *Application Contact:* Tom South, Director of Student Admissions, 501-686-5354, E-mail: southtomg@uams.edu. *Dean,* Dr. Debra Fiser, 501-686-5350.

College of Pharmacy Students: 384 full-time, 8 part-time. Expenses: Contact institution. *Financial support:* Research assistantships available. Support available to part-time students. Offers pharmaceutical evaluation and policy (MS); pharmacy (Pharm D, MS). *Application fee:* $0. *Application Contact:* Dr. Kim Light, Information Contact, 501-686-5557. *Dean,* Dr. Stephanie Gardner, 501-686-5558.

Graduate School Students: 181 full-time, 243 part-time. *Faculty:* 219 full-time (63 women), 52 part-time/adjunct (12 women). Expenses: Contact institution. *Financial support:* Research assistantships, career-related internships or fieldwork, Federal Work-Study, and traineeships available. Support available to part-time students. *Degree program information:* Part-time programs available. Offers clinical nutrition (MS); communicative disorders (MS, PhD); genetic counseling (MS). *Application fee:* $0. *Application Contact:* Dr. Kristen Sterba, Assistant Dean, Office of Graduate Student Recruiting and Retention, 501-526-7396, E-mail: kmsterba@uams.edu. *Dean, Graduate School,* Dr. Robert E. McGehee, 501-686-5454.

College of Nursing Students: 19 full-time, 198 part-time. *Faculty:* 26 full-time (23 women), 8 part-time/adjunct (7 women). Expenses: Contact institution. *Financial support:* Career-related internships or fieldwork and traineeships available. Support available to part-time students. *Degree program information:* Part-time programs available. Offers nursing (MN Sc, PhD). *Application fee:* $0. *Application Contact:* Dr. Elaine Souder, Information Contact, 501-296-1893. *Dean,* Dr. Claudia P. Barone, 501-686-5374.

Graduate Programs in Biomedical Sciences Students: 110 full-time, 13 part-time. Expenses: Contact institution. *Financial support:* Fellowships, research assistantships, teaching assistantships, scholarships/grants and unspecified assistantships available. Support available to part-time students. Offers biochemistry and molecular biology (MS, PhD); biomedical sciences (MS, PhD); microbiology and immunology (MS, PhD); neurobiology and developmental sciences (MS, PhD); occupational and environmental health (MS); pathology (MS); pharmacology (MS, PhD); physiology and biophysics (MS, PhD); toxicology (MS, PhD). *Application fee:* $0. *Application Contact:* Dr. Kristen Sterba, Assistant Dean, Office of Graduate Student Recruiting and Retention, 501-526-7396, E-mail: kmsterba@uams.edu. *Dean, Graduate School,* Dr. Robert E. McGehee, 501-686-5454.

UNIVERSITY OF BALTIMORE, Baltimore, MD 21201-5779

General Information State-supported, coed, upper-level institution. *Enrollment:* 4,948 graduate, professional, and undergraduate students; 1,452 full-time matriculated graduate/professional students (824 women), 1,380 part-time matriculated graduate/professional students (865 women). *Enrollment by degree level:* 1,494 master's, 51 doctoral. *Graduate faculty:* 152 full-time (60 women), 172 part-time/adjunct (49 women). Tuition, state resident: full-time $5,322; part-time $591 per credit. Tuition, nonresident: full-time $7,527; part-time $830 per credit. *Graduate housing:* On-campus housing not available. *Student services:* Campus employment opportunities, career counseling, disabled student services, international student services, low-cost health insurance, multicultural affairs office. *Library facilities:* Langsdale Library plus 1 other. *Online resources:* library catalog, web page, access to other libraries' catalogs. *Collection:* 258,747 titles, 10,738 serial subscriptions.

Computer facilities: 135 computers available on campus for general student use. A campuswide network can be accessed from off campus. Internet access and online class registration are available. *Web address:* http://www.ubalt.edu/.

General Application Contact: Dean Dreibelbis, Assistant Director, Office of Graduate Admissions, 410-837-6565, Fax: 410-837-4793, E-mail: gradadmissions@ubalt.edu.

GRADUATE UNITS

Graduate School Students: 420 full-time (280 women), 1,099 part-time (701 women); includes 521 minority (408 African Americans, 6 American Indian/Alaska Native, 57 Asian Americans or Pacific Islanders, 50 Hispanic Americans), 124 international. Average age 30. 1,946 applicants, 73% accepted, 1051 enrolled. *Faculty:* 146 full-time (55 women), 125 part-time/adjunct (35 women). Expenses: Contact institution. *Financial support:* In 2006–07, 257 students received support, including 73 research assistantships; fellowships, career-related internships or fieldwork, Federal Work-Study, and scholarships/grants also available. Support available to part-time students. Financial award application deadline: 4/1; financial award applicants required to submit FAFSA. In 2006, 443 master's, 6 doctorates awarded. *Degree program information:* Part-time and evening/weekend programs available. Postbaccalaureate distance learning degree programs offered (no on-campus study). *Application deadline:* For fall admission, 8/1 priority date for domestic students, 6/1 for international students; for spring admission, 12/1 for domestic students, 11/1 for international students. Applications are processed on a rolling basis. *Application fee:* $45. Electronic applications accepted. *Application Contact:* Dean Dreibelbis, Assistant Director, Office of Graduate Admissions, 410-837-6565, Fax: 410-837-4793, E-mail: gradadmissions@ubalt.edu. *Provost,* Dr. Wim Wiewel, 410-837-4244, Fax: 410-837-4249.

Merrick School of Business Students: 133 full-time (66 women), 419 part-time (195 women); includes 134 minority (83 African Americans, 2 American Indian/Alaska Native, 35 Asian Americans or Pacific Islanders, 14 Hispanic Americans), 74 international. Average age 31. 543 applicants, 66% accepted, 253 enrolled. *Faculty:* 54 full-time (11 women), 36 part-time/adjunct (6 women). Expenses: Contact institution. *Financial support:* Fellowships, research assistantships, career-related internships or fieldwork and Federal Work-Study available. Support available to part-time students. Financial award application deadline: 4/1; financial award applicants required to submit FAFSA. In 2006, 199 degrees awarded. *Degree program information:* Part-time and evening/weekend programs available. Postbaccalaureate distance learning degree programs offered (no on-campus study). Offers accounting and business advisory services (MS); business (MBA, MS); business/finance (MS); business/management information systems (MS); business/marketing and venturing (MS); taxation (MS). *Application deadline:* For fall admission, 8/1 priority date for domestic students, 6/1 for international students; for spring admission, 12/1 for domestic students, 11/1 for international students. Applications are processed on a rolling basis. *Application fee:* $45. Electronic applications accepted. *Application Contact:* Dean Dreibelbis, Assistant Director, Office of Graduate Admissions, 410-837-6565, Fax: 410-837-4793, E-mail: gradadmissions@ubalt.edu. *Dean,* Dr. Susan Zacur, 410-837-4955.

The Yale Gordon College of Liberal Arts Students: 267 full-time (194 women), 680 part-time (506 women); includes 377 minority (325 African Americans, 4 American Indian/Alaska Native, 22 Asian Americans or Pacific Islanders, 26 Hispanic Americans), 50 international. Average age 33. 540 applicants, 76% accepted, 300 enrolled. *Faculty:* 62 full-time (26 women), 66 part-time/adjunct (26 women). Expenses: Contact institution. *Financial support:* In 2006–07, 35 research assistantships were awarded; fellowships, career-related internships or fieldwork and Federal Work-Study also available. Support available to part-time students. Financial award application deadline: 4/1; financial award applicants required to submit FAFSA. In 2006, 244 master's, 6 doctorates awarded. *Degree program information:* Part-time and evening/weekend programs available. Offers applied psychology (MS); communications design (DCD); creative writing and publishing arts (MFA); criminal justice (MS); health systems management (MS); human services administration (MS); human-computer interaction (MS); integrated design (MFA); interaction design and information technology (MS); legal and ethical studies (MA); liberal arts (MA, MFA, MPA, MS, DCD, DPA); negotiations and conflict management (MS); public administration (MPA, DPA); publications design (MA). *Application deadline:* For fall admission, 8/1 priority date for domestic students, 6/1 for international students; for spring admission, 12/1 for domestic students, 11/1 for international students. Applications are processed on a rolling basis. *Application fee:* $45. Electronic applications accepted. *Application Contact:* Dean Dreibelbis, Assistant Director, Office of Graduate Admissions, 410-837-6565, Fax: 410-837-4793, E-mail: gradadmissions@ubalt.edu. *Dean,* Dr. Larry Thomas, 410-837-5353.

Joint University of Baltimore/Towson University (UB/Towson) MBA Program Students: 103 full-time (48 women), 331 part-time (147 women); includes 113 minority (72 African Americans, 2 American Indian/Alaska Native, 27 Asian Americans or Pacific Islanders, 12 Hispanic Americans), 47 international. Average age 30. 367 applicants, 63% accepted, 151 enrolled. *Faculty:* 44 full-time (12 women), 36 part-time/adjunct (6 women). Expenses: Contact institution. *Financial support:* In 2006–07, 16 research assistantships were awarded; fellowships, career-related internships or fieldwork and Federal Work-Study also available. Support available to part-time students. Financial award application deadline: 4/1; financial award applicants required to submit FAFSA. In 2006, 151 degrees awarded. *Degree program information:* Part-time and evening/weekend programs available. Postbaccalaureate distance learning degree programs offered (no on-campus study). Offers business administration (MBA). *Application deadline:* For fall admission, 8/1 priority date for domestic students, 6/1 for international students; for spring admission, 12/1 for domestic students, 11/1 for international students. Applications are processed on a rolling basis. *Application fee:* $45. *Application Contact:* Dean Dreibelbis, Assistant Director, Office of Graduate Admissions, 410-837-6565, Fax: 410-837-4793, E-mail: gradadmissions@ubalt.edu. *Graduate Advisor,* Ray Frederick, 410-837-4944, E-mail: rfrederick@ubalt.edu.

School of Law Students: 726 full-time, 306 part-time; includes 181 minority (106 African Americans, 5 American Indian/Alaska Native, 50 Asian Americans or Pacific Islanders, 20 Hispanic Americans), 7 international. Average age 27. 2,896 applicants, 41% accepted, 382 enrolled. *Faculty:* 60 full-time (23 women), 92 part-time/adjunct (24 women). Expenses: Contact institution. *Financial support:* In 2006–07, 650 students received support, including 27 teaching assistantships; research assistantships, career-related internships or fieldwork, Federal Work-Study, institutionally sponsored loans, and scholarships/grants also available. Support available to part-time students. Financial award application deadline: 4/1; financial award applicants required to submit FAFSA. In 2006, 276 degrees awarded. *Degree program information:* Part-time and evening/weekend programs available. Offers law (JD); taxation (LL M). *Application deadline:* For fall admission, 3/1 priority date for domestic students. Applications are processed on a rolling basis. *Application fee:* $60. Electronic applications accepted. *Application Contact:* Mark Bell, Assistant Director of Law Admissions, 410-837-4464, Fax: 410-837-4450, E-mail: kbell@ubalt.edu. *Dean,* Phillip J. Closius, 410-837-4458.

UNIVERSITY OF BRIDGEPORT, Bridgeport, CT 06604

General Information Independent, coed, comprehensive institution. CGS member. *Enrollment:* 4,018 graduate, professional, and undergraduate students; 1,263 full-time matriculated graduate/professional students (564 women), 1,061 part-time matriculated graduate/professional students (617 women). *Enrollment by degree level:* 196 first professional, 1,878 master's, 146 doctoral, 104 other advanced degrees. *Graduate faculty:* 102 full-time (31 women), 260 part-time/adjunct (120 women). *Graduate housing:* Room and/or apartments guaranteed to single students; on-campus housing not available to married students. Typical cost: $5,000 per year ($8,200 including board). Housing application deadline: 8/15. *Student services:* Campus employment opportunities, campus safety program, career counseling, disabled student services, exercise/wellness program, free psychological counseling, international student services, low-cost health insurance, multicultural affairs office, teacher training. *Library facilities:* Wahlstrom Library. *Online resources:* library catalog, web page, access to other libraries' catalogs. *Collection:* 272,430 titles, 2,117 serial subscriptions. *Research affiliation:* Burndy Library, Marine Biology Station (Hummingbird Cay, Bahamas), Connecticut Medicine Research Consortia.

Computer facilities: 500 computers available on campus for general student use. A campuswide network can be accessed from student residence rooms and from off campus. Internet access is available. *Web address:* http://www.bridgeport.edu/.

General Application Contact: Audrey Ashton-Savage, Vice President of Enrollment Management, 203-576-4552, Fax: 203-576-4941, E-mail: admit@bridgeport.edu.

GRADUATE UNITS

Acupuncture Institute Students: 15 full-time (12 women), 8 part-time (5 women); includes 6 minority (2 African Americans, 4 Asian Americans or Pacific Islanders), 2 international. Average age 39. 24 applicants, 38% accepted, 8 enrolled. *Faculty:* 2 full-time (1 woman), 5 part-time/adjunct (1 woman). Expenses: Contact institution. In 2006, 9 degrees awarded. Offers acupuncture (MS). *Application deadline:* For fall admission, 3/1 priority date for domestic students; for spring admission, 12/1 priority date for domestic students. Applications are processed on a rolling basis. *Application fee:* $75. Electronic applications accepted. *Director,* Dr. Jennifer Brett, 203-576-4122, Fax: 203-576-4107, E-mail: acup@bridgeport.edu.

College of Chiropractic Students: 193 full-time (74 women), 3 part-time (1 woman); includes 46 minority (17 African Americans, 1 American Indian/Alaska Native, 20 Asian Americans or Pacific Islanders, 8 Hispanic Americans), 9 international. Average age 29. 153 applicants, 46% accepted, 39 enrolled. *Faculty:* 18 full-time (3 women), 16 part-time/adjunct (4 women). Expenses: Contact institution. *Financial support:* In 2006–07, 190 students received support. Federal Work-Study and institutionally sponsored loans available. Support available to part-time students. Financial award application deadline: 6/1; financial award applicants required to submit FAFSA. In 2006, 36 degrees awarded. Offers chiropractic (DC). *Application deadline:* For fall admission, 3/1 priority date for domestic students; for spring admission, 7/1 for domestic students. Applications are processed on a rolling basis. *Application fee:* $75. Electronic applications accepted. *Application Contact:* Michael Grandison, Director of Chiropractic Admissions, 203-576-4348, Fax: 203-576-4941, E-mail: chiro@bridgeport.edu. *Dean,* Dr. Francis A. Zolli, 203-576-4279, E-mail: zolli@bridgeport.edu.

College of Naturopathic Medicine Students: 109 full-time (80 women), 2 part-time (1 woman); includes 34 minority (18 African Americans, 1 American Indian/Alaska Native, 10 Asian Americans or Pacific Islanders, 5 Hispanic Americans), 14 international. Average age 34. 91 applicants, 36% accepted, 24 enrolled. *Faculty:* 6 full-time (3 women), 25 part-time/adjunct (7 women). Expenses: Contact institution. *Financial support:* In 2006–07, 80 students received support. Federal Work-Study, institutionally sponsored loans, and scholarships/grants available. Financial award application deadline: 4/1; financial award applicants required to submit FAFSA. In 2006, 18 degrees awarded. Offers naturopathic medicine (ND). *Application deadline:* For fall admission, 8/1 priority date for domestic students; for spring admission, 12/1 for domestic students. Applications are processed on a rolling basis. *Application fee:* $75. Electronic applications accepted. *Application Contact:* Michael Grandison, Director of Admissions, 203-576-4108, Fax: 203-576-4107, E-mail: natmed@bridgeport.edu. *Dean,* Dr. Guru Sandesh Singh Khalsa, 203-576-4110.

Nutrition Institute Students: 8 full-time (7 women), 190 part-time (136 women); includes 22 minority (10 African Americans, 4 Asian Americans or Pacific Islanders, 8 Hispanic Americans), 28 international. Average age 37. 329 applicants, 57% accepted, 55 enrolled. *Faculty:* 2 full-time (0 women), 16 part-time/adjunct (7 women). Expenses: Contact institution. *Financial support:* In 2006–07, 33 students received support. Available to part-time students. Application deadline: 6/1; In 2006, 71 degrees awarded. *Degree program information:* Part-time and evening/weekend programs available. Postbaccalaureate distance learning degree programs offered (no on-campus study). Offers human nutrition (MS). *Application deadline:* For fall admission, 8/1 priority date for domestic students; for spring admission, 12/1 priority date for domestic students. Applications are processed on a rolling basis. *Application fee:* $25 ($35 for international students). Electronic applications accepted. *Director,* Dr. David M. Brady, 203-576-4667, Fax: 203-576-4591, E-mail: dbrady@bridgeport.edu.

School of Business Students: 227 full-time (100 women), 131 part-time (54 women); includes 46 minority (21 African Americans, 15 Asian Americans or Pacific Islanders, 10 Hispanic Americans), 272 international. Average age 29. 502 applicants, 76% accepted, 141 enrolled. *Faculty:* 11 full-time (2 women), 12 part-time/adjunct (5 women). Expenses: Contact institution. *Financial support:* In 2006–07, 69 students received support; fellowships, research assistantships, teaching assistantships, career-related internships or fieldwork, Federal Work-Study, institutionally sponsored loans, and tuition waivers (partial) available. Support available to part-time students. Financial award application deadline: 6/1; financial award applicants required to submit FAFSA. In 2006, 70 degrees awarded. *Degree program information:* Part-time and evening/weekend programs available. Postbaccalaureate distance learning degree programs offered (minimal on-campus study). Offers business (MBA); business administration (MBA). *Application deadline:* For fall admission, 8/1 priority date for domestic students; for spring admission, 12/1 priority date for domestic students. Applications are processed on a rolling basis. *Application fee:* $25 ($35 for international students). Electronic applications accepted. *Application Contact:* Dr. Ward Thrasher, MBA Director, 203-576-4368, Fax: 203-576-4388, E-mail: mba@bridgeport.edu. *Dean,* Merrill Jay Forgotson, 203-576-4384, Fax: 203-576-4388, E-mail: mjforgotson@bridgeport.edu.

School of Education and Human Resources Students: 332 full-time (241 women), 454 part-time (333 women); includes 121 minority (61 African Americans, 2 American Indian/Alaska Native, 14 Asian Americans or Pacific Islanders, 44 Hispanic Americans), 45 international. Average age 34. 607 applicants, 63% accepted, 223 enrolled. *Faculty:* 20 full-time (8 women), 88 part-time/adjunct (53 women). Expenses: Contact institution. *Financial support:* In 2006–07, 330 students received support; fellowships, research assistantships, teaching assistantships, career-related internships or fieldwork, Federal Work-Study, and institutionally sponsored loans available. Support available to part-time students. Financial award application deadline: 6/1; financial award applicants required to submit FAFSA. In 2006, 297 master's, 4 doctorates, 25 other advanced degrees awarded. *Degree program information:* Part-time and evening/weekend programs available. Offers education and human resources (MS, Ed D, Diploma). *Application deadline:* For fall admission, 8/1 priority date for domestic students; for spring admission, 12/1 priority date for domestic students. Applications are processed on a rolling basis. *Application fee:* $25 ($35 for international students). Electronic applications accepted. *Dean,* Dr. James J. Ritchie, 203-576-4192, Fax: 203-576-4102, E-mail: ritchie@bridgeport.edu.

Division of Education Students: 375 full-time (290 women), 308 part-time (204 women); includes 79 minority (31 African Americans, 1 American Indian/Alaska Native, 13 Asian Americans or Pacific Islanders, 34 Hispanic Americans), 22 international. Average age 33. 523 applicants, 62% accepted, 186 enrolled. *Faculty:* 14 full-time (5 women), 74 part-time/adjunct (44 women). Expenses: Contact institution. *Financial support:* In 2006–07, 303 students received support; fellowships, research assistantships, teaching assistantships, career-related internships or fieldwork, Federal Work-Study, and institutionally sponsored loans available. Support available to part-time students. Financial award application deadline: 6/1; financial award applicants required to submit FAFSA. In 2006, 272 master's, 4 doctorates, 25 other advanced degrees awarded. *Degree program information:* Part-time and evening/weekend programs available. Offers computer specialist (Diploma); early childhood education (MS, Diploma); education (MS); educational management (Ed D, Diploma); elementary education (MS, Diploma); intermediate administrator or supervisor (Diploma); international education (Diploma); leadership (Ed D); reading specialist (MS, Diploma); secondary education (MS, Diploma). *Application deadline:* For fall admission, 8/1 priority date for domestic students; for spring admission, 12/1 priority date for domestic students. Applications are processed on a rolling basis. *Application fee:* $25 ($35 for international students). Electronic applications accepted. *Associate Dean,* Dr. Allen P. Cook, 203-576-4206, Fax: 203-576-4200, E-mail: acook@bridgeport.edu.

Division of Human Resources Students: 27 full-time (21 women), 76 part-time (59 women); includes 42 minority (30 African Americans, 1 American Indian/Alaska Native, 1 Asian American or Pacific Islander, 10 Hispanic Americans), 23 international. Average age 34. 84 applicants, 70% accepted, 37 enrolled. *Faculty:* 6 full-time (3 women), 14 part-time/adjunct (9 women). Expenses: Contact institution. *Financial support:* In 2006–07, 27 students received support; fellowships, research assistantships, teaching assistantships, career-related internships or fieldwork, Federal Work-Study, and institutionally sponsored loans available. Support available to part-time students. Financial award application deadline: 6/1; financial award applicants required to submit FAFSA. In 2006, 25 degrees awarded. *Degree program information:* Part-time and evening/weekend programs available. Offers college student personnel (MS); community counseling (MS); human resource development (MS). *Application deadline:* For fall admission, 8/1 priority date for domestic students; for spring admission, 12/1 priority date for domestic students. Applications are processed on a rolling basis. *Application fee:* $25 ($35 for international students). Electronic applications accepted. *Head,* Dr. Joseph T. Cullen, 203-576-4175.

School of Engineering Students: 378 full-time (49 women), 212 part-time (36 women); includes 7 minority (2 African Americans, 5 Asian Americans or Pacific Islanders), 575 international. Average age 25. 1,757 applicants, 73% accepted, 272 enrolled. *Faculty:* 12 full-time (3 women), 4 part-time/adjunct (1 woman). Expenses: Contact institution. *Financial support:* In 2006–07, 76 students received support; fellowships, research assistantships, teaching assistantships, career-related internships or fieldwork, Federal Work-Study, institutionally sponsored loans, and tuition waivers (partial) available. Support available to part-time students. Financial award application deadline: 6/1; financial award applicants required to submit FAFSA. In 2006, 136 degrees awarded. *Degree program information:* Part-time and evening/weekend programs available. Offers computer engineering (MS); computer science (MS); computer science and engineering (PhD); electrical engineering (MS); engineering (MS, PhD); mechanical engineering (MS); technology management (MS). *Application deadline:* For fall admission, 8/1 priority date for domestic students; for spring admission, 12/1 priority date for domestic students. Applications are processed on a rolling basis. *Application fee:* $25 ($35 for international students). Electronic applications accepted. *Dean,* Dr. Tarek M. Sobh, 203-576-4111, Fax: 203-576-4766, E-mail: sobh@bridgeport.edu.

THE UNIVERSITY OF BRITISH COLUMBIA, Vancouver, BC V6T 1Z1, Canada

General Information Province-supported, coed, university. *Enrollment:* 43,301 graduate, professional, and undergraduate students; 7,002 full-time matriculated graduate/professional students (3,705 women), 874 part-time matriculated graduate/professional students (534 women). *Enrollment by degree level:* 4,900 master's, 2,823 doctoral. *Graduate faculty:* 1,850 full-time (504 women). *Graduate housing:* Rooms and/or apartments available on a first-come, first-served basis to single students and available to married students. Housing application deadline: 3/1. *Student services:* Campus employment opportunities, campus safety program, career counseling, child daycare facilities, disabled student services, exercise/wellness program, free psychological counseling, grant writing training, international student services, low-cost health insurance, multicultural affairs office, teacher training, writing training. *Library facilities:* Walter C. Koerner Library plus 9 others. *Online resources:* library catalog, web page, access to other libraries' catalogs. *Collection:* 5.1 million titles, 51,553 serial subscriptions. *Research affiliation:* Forintek Canada (forest technology), British Columbia Research (chemical and biological science technology), Pacific Biological Station (Nanaimo) (fisheries and oceanography), Pacific Environment Institute, Pulp and Paper Research Institute of Canada (pulp and paper research), National Research Council of Canada Institute of Machinery Research (machinery research).

Computer facilities: 1,500 computers available on campus for general student use. A campuswide network can be accessed from student residence rooms and from off campus. Internet access and online class registration, campus-wide wireless network are available. *Web address:* http://www.ubc.ca/.

General Application Contact: Selene Buendia, Student Academic Services Clerk, 604-822-3907, Fax: 604-822-5802, E-mail: graduate@interchange.ubc.ca.

GRADUATE UNITS

Faculty of Arts Expenses: Contact institution. *Financial support:* Fellowships, research assistantships, teaching assistantships, career-related internships or fieldwork, Federal Work-Study, institutionally sponsored loans, scholarships/grants, tuition waivers (full and partial), and unspecified assistantships available. Support available to part-time students. *Degree program information:* Part-time programs available. Offers ancient culture, religion, and ethnicity (MA); anthropology (MA, PhD); art history (MA, PhD, Diploma); arts (M Mus, M Sc, MA, MAS, MFA, MJ, MLIS, MSW, DMA, PhD, CAS, Diploma); Asian studies (MA, PhD); behavioral neuroscience (MA, PhD); classical and near eastern archaeology (MA); classics (MA, PhD); clinical psychology (MA, PhD); cognitive science (MA, PhD); comparative literature (MA, PhD); creative writing (MFA); creative writing and theatre (MFA); developmental psychology (MA, PhD); economics (MA, PhD); English (MA, PhD); film studies (MA); forensic psychology (MA, PhD); French (MA, PhD); geography (M Sc, MA, PhD); Germanic studies (MA, PhD); health psychology (MA, PhD); Hispanic studies (MA, PhD); history (MA, PhD); linguistics (MA, PhD); philosophy (MA, PhD); political science (MA, PhD); quantitative methods (MA, PhD); religious studies (MA, PhD); social/personality psychology (MA, PhD); sociology (MA, PhD); theatre (MA, MFA, PhD); theatre design (MFA); theatre directing (MFA); visual art (MFA). Electronic applications accepted. *Dean,* Dr. Nancy Gallini, 604-822-3751, Fax: 604-822-6096, E-mail: artsdean@mail.arts.ubc.ca.

The School of Journalism Students: 44 full-time (28 women); includes 13 minority (2 African Americans, 10 Asian Americans or Pacific Islanders, 1 Hispanic American). Average age 24. 199 applicants, 20% accepted, 25 enrolled. *Faculty:* 4 full-time (1 woman), 4 part-time/adjunct (1 woman). Expenses: Contact institution. *Financial support:* In 2006–07, 21 students received support, including 21 fellowships (averaging $12,200 per year); career-related internships or fieldwork also available. Financial award application deadline: 12/1. In 2006, 24 degrees awarded. Offers journalism (MJ). *Application deadline:* For fall admission, 1/1 for domestic and international students. *Application fee:* $90 Canadian dollars ($150 Canadian dollars for international students). Electronic applications accepted. *Application Contact:* Barbara R. Wallin, Acting Department Secretary, 604-822-6688, Fax: 604-822-6707, E-mail: journal@interchange.ubc.ca. *Acting Director,* Prof. Stephen J. Ward, 604-822-6688, Fax: 604-822-6707, E-mail: sjward@interchange.ubc.ca.

School of Library, Archival and Information Studies Students: 232 full-time (183 women), 15 part-time (11 women). Average age 32. 293 applicants, 44% accepted, 88 enrolled. *Faculty:* 13 full-time (10 women), 31 part-time/adjunct (25 women). Expenses: Contact institution. *Financial support:* In 2006–07, 55 students received support, including 2 fellowships (averaging $16,000 per year), 31 research assistantships; teaching assistantships, Federal Work-Study, institutionally sponsored loans, scholarships/grants, tuition waivers (partial), and unspecified assistantships also available. In 2006, 113 degrees awarded. *Degree program information:* Part-time programs available. Offers archival studies (MAS, CAS); archival studies/library and information studies); children's literature (MA); library and information studies (MLIS, CAS); library archival and information studies (PhD). *Application deadline:* For fall admission, 2/1 for domestic and international students; for winter admission, 5/1 for domestic and international students. *Application fee:* $90 Canadian dollars ($150 Canadian dollars for international students). Electronic applications accepted. *Application Contact:* Graduate Admissions Secretary, 604-822-2404, Fax: 604-822-6006, E-mail: slais.admissions@ubc.ca. *Director,* Dr. Edie Rasmussen, 604-822-2404, Fax: 604-822-6006, E-mail: slais@interchange.ubc.ca.

School of Music Students: 115 full-time (49 women); includes 30 minority (23 Asian Americans or Pacific Islanders, 7 Hispanic Americans), 15 international. Average age 24. 234 applicants, 25% accepted, 51 enrolled. *Faculty:* 28 full-time (7 women), 62 part-time/adjunct (22 women). Expenses: Contact institution. *Financial support:* In 2006–07, 72 students received support, including 9 fellowships with tuition reimbursements available (averaging $16,000 Canadian dollars per year), 7 research assistantships (averaging $1,500 Canadian dollars per year), 47 teaching assistantships (averaging $4,000 Canadian dollars per year); institutionally sponsored loans, scholarships/grants, tuition waivers, and doctoral-level tuition waiver also available. Financial award application deadline: 1/30. In 2006, 19 master's, 3 doctorates awarded. *Degree program information:* Part-time programs available. Offers music (M Mus, MA, DMA, PhD). *Application deadline:* For fall admission, 1/30 priority date for domestic and international students. Applications are processed on a rolling basis. *Application fee:* $90 Canadian dollars. Electronic applications accepted. *Application Contact:* Miriam Nechemia, Graduate Admissions Secretary, 604-822-5750, Fax: 604-822-4884, E-mail: miriamn@interchange.ubc.ca. *Director,* Prof. Jesse Read, 604-822-2079, Fax: 604-822-4884, E-mail: jesse.read@ubc.ca.

The University of British Columbia (continued)

School of Social Work and Family Studies Students: 49 full-time (45 women), 27 part-time (22 women). Average age 36. 100 applicants, 57% accepted, 57 enrolled. *Faculty:* 23 full-time (10 women). Expenses: Contact institution. *Financial support:* In 2006–07, 3 fellowships (averaging $2,521 Canadian dollars per year), 26 research assistantships (averaging $5,400 Canadian dollars per year), 15 teaching assistantships (averaging $6,600 Canadian dollars per year) were awarded; career-related internships or fieldwork, Federal Work-Study, institutionally sponsored loans, scholarships/grants, and unspecified assistantships also available. Financial award application deadline: 4/1. In 2006, 48 degrees awarded. *Degree program information:* Part-time programs available. Offers family studies (MA); social work (MSW); social work and family studies (PhD). *Application deadline:* For fall admission, 1/31 for domestic and international students. *Application fee:* $90 Canadian dollars ($150 Canadian dollars for international students). Electronic applications accepted. *Application Contact:* Christine Graham, Program Advisor, 604-822-4119, Fax: 604-822-8656, E-mail: swfs.advisor@ubc.ca. *Director*, Prof. Graham Riches, 604-822-0782, Fax: 604-822-8656, E-mail: griches@interchange.ubc.ca.

Faculty of Dentistry Average age 25. 50 applicants, 18% accepted, 9 enrolled. *Faculty:* 32 full-time (7 women), 3 part-time/adjunct (1 woman). Expenses: Contact institution. *Financial support:* In 2006–07, 3 fellowships with partial tuition reimbursements (averaging $15,000 per year), 2 research assistantships with partial tuition reimbursements (averaging $16,000 per year), 6 teaching assistantships with partial tuition reimbursements (averaging $800 per year) were awarded; career-related internships or fieldwork, Federal Work-Study, scholarships/grants, tuition waivers (full and partial), and unspecified assistantships also available. Financial award application deadline: 12/5. In 2006, 4 degrees awarded. *Degree program information:* Part-time programs available. Offers dental science (M Sc, PhD); dentistry (DMD, M Sc, PhD, Certificate, Diploma); periodontics (Diploma). *Application deadline:* For fall admission, 11/2 for domestic students; for spring admission, 6/8 for international students. Applications are processed on a rolling basis. *Application fee:* $200 Canadian dollars ($400 Canadian dollars for international students). Electronic applications accepted. *Application Contact:* Connie A. Reynolds, Manager, Admissions and Academic Progress, 604-822-1847, Fax: 604-822-8279, E-mail: connier@interchange.ubc.ca. *Dean*, Dr. C. Shuler, 604-822-5773, Fax: 604-822-4532, E-mail: cshuler@interchange.ubc.ca.

Faculty of Graduate Studies Students: 7,876. 9,806 applicants, 38% accepted, 2510 enrolled. *Faculty:* 1,850. Expenses: Contact institution. *Financial support:* Fellowships with full and partial tuition reimbursements, research assistantships with full and partial tuition reimbursements, teaching assistantships with full and partial tuition reimbursements, career-related internships or fieldwork, Federal Work-Study, institutionally sponsored loans, and tuition waivers (full and partial) available. In 2006, 1,466 master's, 305 doctorates awarded. *Degree program information:* Part-time and evening/weekend programs available. Postbaccalaureate distance learning degree programs offered (minimal on-campus study). Offers genetics (M Sc, PhD); resources, environment and sustainability (M Sc, MA, PhD). *Application deadline:* Applications are processed on a rolling basis. *Application fee:* $90 Canadian dollars ($150 Canadian dollars for international students). Electronic applications accepted. *Application Contact:* Leah Billas, Student Academic Services Clerk, 604-822-3907, Fax: 604-822-5802, E-mail: graduate@interchange.ubc.ca. *Dean pro tem*, Dr. Ann Rose, 604-822-2848, Fax: 604-822-5802.

Faculty of Applied Science 1,185 applicants, 51% accepted, 404 enrolled. *Faculty:* 180 full-time (40 women), 68 part-time/adjunct (7 women). Expenses: Contact institution. *Financial support:* In 2006–07, 97 fellowships (averaging $16,000 per year) were awarded; research assistantships, teaching assistantships, career-related internships or fieldwork, Federal Work-Study, institutionally sponsored loans, scholarships/grants, health care benefits, tuition waivers (partial), unspecified assistantships, and full tuition waivers (for all PhD students) also available. Financial award application deadline: 9/30. In 2006, 308 master's, 36 doctorates awarded. *Degree program information:* Part-time programs available. Offers applied science (M Arch, M Eng, M Sc, MA Sc, MASA, MASLA, MLA, MSN, MSS, PhD); architecture (M Arch, MASA); chemical engineering (M Eng, M Sc, MA Sc, PhD); civil engineering (M Eng, MA Sc, PhD); electrical and computer engineering (M Eng, MA Sc, PhD); landscape architecture (MASLA, MLA); materials and metallurgy (M Sc, PhD); mechanical engineering (M Eng, MA Sc, PhD); metals and materials engineering (MA Sc, PhD); mining engineering (M Eng, MA Sc, PhD); nursing (MSN, PhD); software systems (MSS). *Application deadline:* For fall admission, 1/15 for domestic students, 1/1 for international students; for winter admission, 6/1 for domestic and international students. *Application fee:* $90 Canadian dollars ($150 Canadian dollars for international students). Electronic applications accepted. *Application Contact:* Student Inquiries, 604-822-6413, Fax: 604-822-7006. *Dean*, Dr. Michael Isaacson, 604-822-6413, Fax: 604-822-7006.

Faculty of Education Students: 1,332 full-time (943 women), 199 part-time (141 women), 90 international. Average age 38. 1,035 applicants, 55% accepted. *Faculty:* 151 full-time (77 women). Expenses: Contact institution. *Financial support:* Fellowships with full and partial tuition reimbursements, research assistantships with full and partial tuition reimbursements, teaching assistantships with full and partial tuition reimbursements, career-related internships or fieldwork, Federal Work-Study, institutionally sponsored loans, and unspecified assistantships available. In 2006, 366 master's, 49 doctorates awarded. *Degree program information:* Part-time and evening/weekend programs available. Postbaccalaureate distance learning degree programs offered (no on-campus study). Offers adult education (M Ed, MA); adult learning and global change (M Ed); art education (M Ed, MA); counseling psychology (M Ed, MA, PhD); curriculum and instruction (M Ed, MA, PhD); curriculum studies (M Ed, MA, PhD); development, learning and culture (MA, PhD); early childhood education (M Ed, MA); education (M Ed, M Sc, MA, MET, MHK, Ed D, PhD, Diploma); educational administration (M Ed, MA); educational leadership and policy (Ed D); educational studies (M Ed, PhD); guidance studies (Diploma); higher education (M Ed, MA); home economics education (M Ed, MA); human kinetics (M Sc, MA, MHK, PhD); library education (M Ed, MA, PhD); literacy education (M Ed, MA, PhD); math education (M Ed, MA); measurement and evaluation and research methodology (M Ed); measurement, evaluation and research methodology (MA); measurement, evaluation, and research methodology (PhD); modern language education (M Ed, MA, PhD); music education (M Ed, MA); physical education (M Ed, MA); school psychology (M Ed, MA, PhD); science education (M Ed, MA); social studies education (M Ed, MA); society, culture and politics in education (M Ed, MA); special education (M Ed, MA, PhD, Diploma); teaching English as a second language (M Ed, MA, PhD); technical studies education (M Ed, MA). *Application fee:* $90 Canadian dollars ($150 Canadian dollars for international students). Electronic applications accepted. *Application Contact:* Dr. Deborah Butler, Associate Dean, Graduate Programs and Research, 604-822-5513, Fax: 604-822-8971, E-mail: deborah.butler@ubc.ca. *Dean*, Dr. Robert J. Tierney, 604-822-5757, E-mail: dean.educ@ubc.ca.

Faculty of Forestry Students: 241 full-time (81 women), 3 part-time. 150 applicants, 50% accepted, 70 enrolled. *Faculty:* 70 full-time (11 women), 39 part-time/adjunct (6 women). Expenses: Contact institution. *Financial support:* Fellowships, research assistantships, teaching assistantships, scholarships/grants, health care benefits, tuition waivers (full and partial), and unspecified assistantships available. In 2006, 25 master's, 17 doctorates awarded. *Degree program information:* Part-time programs available. Offers forestry (M Sc, MA Sc, MF, PhD). *Application deadline:* For fall admission, 4/1 for domestic students, 3/1 for international students; for winter admission, 8/1 for domestic students, 7/1 for international students; for spring admission, 1/1 for domestic students, 12/1 for international students. Applications are processed on a rolling basis. *Application fee:* $90 Canadian dollars ($150 Canadian dollars for international students). Electronic applications accepted. *Application Contact:* Gayle Kosh, Manager, Graduate Programs, 604-827-4454, Fax: 604-822-8645, E-mail: gayle.kosh@ubc.ca. *Associate Dean, Graduate Studies and Research*, Dr. Cindy E. Prescott, 604-822-4701, Fax: 604-822-8645, E-mail: cindy.prescott@ubc.ca.

Faculty of Land and Food Systems Students: 144 full-time (99 women). Average age 30. 111 applicants, 29% accepted, 24 enrolled. *Faculty:* 54 full-time (14 women), 10 part-time/adjunct (4 women). Expenses: Contact institution. *Financial support:* In 2006–07, 9 fellowships with full and partial tuition reimbursements (averaging $12,300 per year), 50 research assistantships with partial tuition reimbursements (averaging $15,500 per year), 118 teaching assistantships with partial tuition reimbursements (averaging $2,200 per year) were awarded; career-related internships or fieldwork, Federal Work-Study, institutionally sponsored loans, scholarships/grants, and tuition waivers (full and partial) also available. In 2006, 19 master's, 8 doctorates awarded. Offers agricultural economics (M Sc); animal science (M Sc, PhD); food science (M Sc, PhD); human nutrition (M Sc, PhD); land and food systems (M Sc, PhD); plant science (M Sc, PhD); soil science (M Sc, PhD). *Application deadline:* For fall admission, 1/3 for domestic and international students; for winter admission, 6/1 for domestic and international students; for spring admission, 9/1 for domestic and international students. Applications are processed on a rolling basis. *Application fee:* $90 Canadian dollars ($150 Canadian dollars for international students). Electronic applications accepted. *Application Contact:* Lia Maria Dragan, Graduate Programs Assistant, 604-822-8373, Fax: 604-822-4400, E-mail: gradapp@interchange.ubc.ca. *Associate Dean, Graduate Programs*, Dr. Mahesh Upadhyaya, 604-822-6139, Fax: 604-822-4400, E-mail: upadh@interchange.ubc.ca.

Faculty of Law Students: 75 full-time (45 women); includes 24 minority (4 African Americans, 4 American Indian/Alaska Native, 13 Asian Americans or Pacific Islanders, 3 Hispanic Americans), 25 international. Average age 30. 130 applicants, 42% accepted, 33 enrolled. *Faculty:* 44 full-time (11 women), 89 part-time/adjunct. Expenses: Contact institution. *Financial support:* In 2006–07, 10 fellowships (averaging $7,000 per year), 5 research assistantships, 8 teaching assistantships (averaging $9,933 per year) were awarded; Federal Work-Study, scholarships/grants, and unspecified assistantships also available. Financial award application deadline: 9/30. *Degree program information:* Part-time programs available. Offers law (LL M, PhD). *Application deadline:* For fall admission, 2/1 for domestic and international students. Applications are processed on a rolling basis. *Application fee:* $90 ($150 for international students). Electronic applications accepted. *Application Contact:* Joanne Y. Chung, Graduate Administrator, 604-822-6449, Fax: 604-822-4781, E-mail: graduates@law.ubc.ca. *Associate Dean, Graduate Studies and Research*, Prof. Catherine Dauvergne, 604-822-6506, Fax: 604-822-4781.

Faculty of Pharmaceutical Sciences Students: 40 full-time (10 women). Average age 28. 61 applicants, 36% accepted, 19 enrolled. *Faculty:* 30 full-time (9 women), 26 part-time/adjunct (11 women). Expenses: Contact institution. *Financial support:* In 2006–07, fellowships (averaging $16,000 per year), 24 research assistantships (averaging $17,000 per year), 17 teaching assistantships (averaging $10,100 per year) were awarded; career-related internships or fieldwork, institutionally sponsored loans, scholarships/grants, traineeships, health care benefits, tuition waivers (full and partial), and unspecified assistantships also available. In 2006, 8 first professional degrees, 4 master's, 4 doctorates awarded. Offers pharmaceutical sciences (Pharm D, M Sc, PhD). *Application deadline:* For fall admission, 3/15 for domestic students, 2/15 for international students; for spring admission, 4/1 for domestic students. Applications are processed on a rolling basis. *Application fee:* $90 Canadian dollars ($150 Canadian dollars for international students). Electronic applications accepted. *Application Contact:* Dr. Barb Conway, Research Grants Facilitator and Graduate Program Coordinator, 604-822-2390, Fax: 604-822-3035, E-mail: baconway@interchange.ubc.ca. *Dean*, Dr. Robert D. Sindelar, 604-822-2343, Fax: 604-822-3035, E-mail: sindelar@interchange.ubc.ca.

Faculty of Science Expenses: Contact institution. *Financial support:* Fellowships, research assistantships, teaching assistantships, career-related internships or fieldwork, Federal Work-Study, institutionally sponsored loans, and tuition waivers (partial) available. *Degree program information:* Part-time programs available. Offers astronomy (M Sc, PhD); atmospheric science (M Sc, PhD); botany (M Sc, PhD); chemistry (M Sc, PhD); computer science (M Sc, PhD); engineering physics (MA Sc); geological engineering (M Eng, MA Sc, PhD); geological sciences (M Sc, PhD); geophysics (M Sc, MA Sc, PhD); mathematics (M Sc, MA, PhD); microbiology and immunology (M Sc, PhD); oceanography (M Sc, PhD); physics (M Sc, PhD); science (M Eng, M Sc, MA, MA Sc, PhD); statistics (M Sc, PhD); zoology (M Sc, PhD). *Application fee:* $60. Electronic applications accepted. *Dean*, Dr. John Hepburn, 604-822-0220, Fax: 604-822-5558.

Institute of Applied Mathematics Students: 42 full-time (17 women). *Faculty:* 58 full-time (8 women). Expenses: Contact institution. *Financial support:* In 2006–07, 4 fellowships, 21 research assistantships, 21 teaching assistantships were awarded. In 2006, 9 degrees awarded. Offers applied mathematics (M Sc, PhD). *Application fee:* $90 ($128 for international students). *Application Contact:* Marek Labecki, Application Contact, 604-822-4584, Fax: 604-822-0550, E-mail: marek@iam.ubc.ca. *Director*, Michael J. Ward, 604-822-4584, Fax: 604-822-0550, E-mail: ward@math.ubc.ca.

Institute of Asian Research Students: 29 full-time (20 women). Average age 30. 44 applicants, 55% accepted, 14 enrolled. *Faculty:* 9 full-time (1 woman), 3 part-time/adjunct (1 woman). Expenses: Contact institution. *Financial support:* In 2006–07, 5 fellowships with tuition reimbursements (averaging $10,000 Canadian dollars per year), 10 research assistantships (averaging $3,500 Canadian dollars per year) were awarded; career-related internships or fieldwork, institutionally sponsored loans, scholarships/grants, and tuition waivers (partial) also available. In 2006, 14 degrees awarded. *Degree program information:* Part-time programs available. Offers Asian research (MAPPS). *Application deadline:* For fall admission, 3/30 for domestic students, 3/1 for international students. *Application fee:* $90 ($150 for international students). Electronic applications accepted. *Application Contact:* Marietta T. Lao, Administrator, 604-822-2746, Fax: 604-822-5207, E-mail: mlao@interchg.ubc.ca. *Director and Professor of Law*, Pitman B. Potter, 604-822-4686, Fax: 604-822-5207, E-mail: potter@interchg.ubc.ca.

School of Community and Regional Planning Students: 129 full-time (82 women). Average age 26. 250 applicants, 25% accepted, 38 enrolled. *Faculty:* 11 full-time (3 women), 11 part-time/adjunct (1 woman). Expenses: Contact institution. *Financial support:* In 2006–07, 4 fellowships with partial tuition reimbursements (averaging $3,500 per year) were awarded; research assistantships, teaching assistantships, career-related internships or fieldwork, Federal Work-Study, institutionally sponsored loans, scholarships/grants, tuition waivers (full and partial), and research travel bursaries also available. Financial award application deadline: 9/24. In 2006, 26 degrees awarded. Offers community and regional planning (M Sc P, MAP, PhD). *Application deadline:* For fall admission, 12/1 for domestic and international students. *Application fee:* $90 Canadian dollars ($150 Canadian dollars for international students). Electronic applications accepted. *Application Contact:* Patti Toporowski, Secretary, 604-822-5326, Fax: 604-822-3787, E-mail: ptop@interchange.ubc.ca.

School of Occupational and Environmental Hygiene Students: 15 full-time (13 women), 5 part-time (1 woman). Average age 25. 26 applicants, 46% accepted, 7 enrolled. *Faculty:* 4 full-time (1 woman), 22 part-time/adjunct (9 women). Expenses: Contact institution. *Financial support:* In 2006–07, 1 fellowship (averaging $8,000 per year), 4 research assistantships (averaging $16,000 per year), 6 teaching assistantships (averaging $2,300 per year) were awarded; career-related internships or fieldwork and institutionally sponsored loans also available. In 2006, 8 degrees awarded. *Degree program information:* Part-time programs available. Offers occupational and environmental hygiene (M Sc, PhD). *Application deadline:* For fall admission, 1/31 for domestic and international students. *Application fee:* $90 Canadian dollars ($150 Canadian dollars for international students). Electronic applications accepted. *Application Contact:* Dr. Paul Demers, Graduate Advisor, 604-822-0585, Fax: 604-822-9588, E-mail: pdemers@interchange.ubc.ca. *Director*, Dr. Michael Brauer, 604-822-9595, Fax: 604-822-9588, E-mail: brauer@interchange.ubc.ca.

Faculty of Medicine Expenses: Contact institution. *Financial support:* Fellowships, research assistantships, teaching assistantships, career-related internships or fieldwork, Federal Work-Study, and institutionally sponsored loans available. Support available to part-time students. In 2006, 121 degrees awarded. *Degree program information:* Part-time programs available. Offers anatomy and cell biology (M Sc, PhD); anesthesiology, pharmacology and therapeutics (M Sc, PhD); biochemistry and molecular biology (M Sc, PhD); clinical epidemiology (MH Sc); community health (MH Sc); epidemiology/clinical epidemiology (M Sc, PhD); experimental medicine (M Sc, PhD); experimental pathology (M Sc, PhD); health administration (MHA); health services research (M Sc, PhD); medical genetics (M Sc, PhD); medicine (MD, M Sc, MH Sc, MHA, MOT, MPT, MRSc, PhD); occupational and environmental health (M Sc, PhD); occupational health (MH Sc); physiology (M Sc, PhD); reproductive and developmental sciences (M Sc, PhD); surgery (M Sc). Open only to Canadian residents. *Application Contact:*

Dr. J. Carter, Associate Dean of Admissions, 604-822-4482. *Dean,* Dr. Gavin CE Stuart, 604-822-4303.

School of Audiology and Speech Sciences Students: 63 full-time (57 women). Average age 27. 162 applicants, 19% accepted, 30 enrolled. *Faculty:* 9 full-time (6 women), 9 part-time/adjunct (8 women). Expenses: Contact institution. *Financial support:* In 2006–07, 13 students received support, including 3 fellowships with full tuition reimbursements available (averaging $18,000 per year), 4 research assistantships; teaching assistantships, career-related internships or fieldwork, Federal Work-Study, institutionally sponsored loans, scholarships/grants, tuition waivers (full and partial), and unspecified assistantships also available. Financial award application deadline: 1/15. In 2006, 26 degrees awarded. Offers audiology and speech sciences (M Sc, PhD). *Application deadline:* For fall admission, 2/28 for domestic and international students. Applications are processed on a rolling basis. *Application fee:* $90 Canadian dollars ($150 Canadian dollars for international students). Electronic applications accepted. *Application Contact:* Sue Bryant, Graduate Program Assistant, 604-822-5591, Fax: 604-822-6569, E-mail: inquiry@audiospeech.ubc.ca. *Director,* Dr. Valter Ciocca, 604-822-2266, Fax: 604-822-6569, E-mail: director@audiospeech.ubc.ca.

School of Rehabilitation Sciences Students: 186 full-time (155 women). Average age 30. 311 applicants, 27% accepted, 85 enrolled. *Faculty:* 16 full-time (15 women), 7 part-time/adjunct (5 women). Expenses: Contact institution. *Financial support:* In 2006–07, 25 students received support, including 1 fellowship with partial tuition reimbursement available (averaging $16,000 per year), 2 research assistantships, 3 teaching assistantships (averaging $5,000 per year); Federal Work-Study, institutionally sponsored loans, scholarships/grants, and tuition waivers (full and partial) also available. In 2006, 2 master's, 1 doctorate awarded. Offers rehabilitation sciences (M Sc, MOT, MPT, MRSc, PhD). *Application deadline:* For fall admission, 2/1 priority date for domestic and international students; for winter admission, 7/1 priority date for domestic and international students. *Application fee:* $90 Canadian dollars ($150 Canadian dollars for international students). Electronic applications accepted. *Application Contact:* Jacqueline G. Chin, Student Services Program Assistant, 604-822-7050, Fax: 604-822-7624, E-mail: jachin@interchange.ubc.ca. *Interim Director,* Dr. Brenda Loveridge, 604-822-7414, Fax: 604-822-7624.

Sauder School of Business *Degree program information:* Part-time and evening/weekend programs available. Offers accounting (PhD); business (IMBA, M Sc, MBA, MM, PhD); business administration (IMBA, MBA); finance (PhD); international business (PhD); management information systems (PhD); management science (PhD); marketing (PhD); operations research (MM); organizational behavior (PhD); policy analysis and strategy (PhD); transportation and logistics (PhD); urban land economics (PhD). Electronic applications accepted.

UNIVERSITY OF CALGARY, Calgary, AB T2N 1N4, Canada

General Information Province-supported, coed, university. CGS member. *Enrollment:* 4,340 full-time matriculated graduate/professional students (2,118 women), 1,300 part-time matriculated graduate/professional students (714 women). *Enrollment by degree level:* 4,139 master's, 348 doctoral, 153 other advanced degrees. *Graduate faculty:* 425. *Graduate housing:* Rooms and/or apartments available on a first-come, first-served basis to single and married students. Typical cost: $725 per year for married students. Housing application deadline: 3/31. *Student services:* Campus employment opportunities, campus safety program, career counseling, child daycare facilities, disabled student services, exercise/wellness program, free psychological counseling, grant writing training, international student services, low-cost health insurance, multicultural affairs office, teacher training, writing training. *Library facilities:* MacKimmie Library plus 4 others. *Online resources:* library catalog, web page, access to other libraries' catalogs. *Collection:* 2.4 million titles, 20,237 serial subscriptions, 138,759 audiovisual materials. *Research affiliation:* Alta Telecommunications Research Centre, Alberta Sulphur Research, Calgary Society for Students with Learning Difficulties, Canadian Institute of Resources Law, Canadian Music Centre, Canadian Energy Research Institute.

Computer facilities: 800 computers available on campus for general student use. A campuswide network can be accessed from student residence rooms and from off campus. Internet access and online class registration are available. *Web address:* http://www.ucalgary.ca/.

General Application Contact: Warren Veale, Dean of the Faculty of Graduate Studies, 403-220-6356, Fax: 403-289-7635, E-mail: veale@ucalgary.ca.

GRADUATE UNITS

Faculty of Graduate Studies Students: 4,340 full-time (2,118 women), 1,300 part-time (714 women). Average age 33. Expenses: Contact institution. *Financial support:* In 2006–07, fellowships with partial tuition reimbursements (averaging $500 per year), research assistantships with partial tuition reimbursements (averaging $4,100 per year), teaching assistantships with partial tuition reimbursements (averaging $10,886 per year) were awarded; career-related internships or fieldwork, institutionally sponsored loans, scholarships/grants, tuition waivers (full and partial), and unspecified assistantships also available. Financial award application deadline: 2/1. In 2006, 1,227 master's, 182 doctorates, 4 other advanced degrees awarded. *Degree program information:* Part-time and evening/weekend programs available. Postbaccalaureate distance learning degree programs offered (minimal on-campus study). Offers interdisciplinary research (M Sc, MA, PhD); resources and the environment (M Sc, MA, PhD). *Application fee:* $100 ($130 for international students). *Application Contact:* Martha A. Stroud, Executive Officer, 403-220-4932, Fax: 403-282-5262, E-mail: mstroud@ucalgary.ca. *Dean of the Faculty of Graduate Studies,* Warren Veale, 403-220-6356, Fax: 403-289-7635, E-mail: veale@ucalgary.ca.

Centre for Military and Strategic Studies Students: 29 full-time (6 women), 20 part-time (8 women). Average age 28. 32 applicants, 31% accepted, 10 enrolled. Expenses: Contact institution. In 2006, 4 master's, 1 doctorate awarded. *Degree program information:* Part-time programs available. Offers military and strategic studies (MSS, PhD). PhD offered in special cases only. *Application deadline:* For fall admission, 1/15 for domestic and international students. *Application fee:* $100 ($130 for international students). *Application Contact:* Tracy Derksen, Graduate Program Administrator, 403-220-4038, Fax: 403-282-0594, E-mail: tjderkse@ucalgary.ca. *Director,* Dr. David J. Bercuson, 403-220-4038, E-mail: stratnet@ucalgary.ca.

Faculty of Communication and Culture Students: 47 full-time (31 women), 27 part-time (19 women), 7 international. Average age 30. 150 applicants, 11% accepted. *Faculty:* 12 full-time (5 women), 9 part-time/adjunct (4 women). Expenses: Contact institution. *Financial support:* In 2006–07, 22 students received support; research assistantships, teaching assistantships, scholarships/grants and unspecified assistantships available. Financial award application deadline: 2/1. In 2006, 4 degrees awarded. *Degree program information:* Part-time and evening/weekend programs available. Offers communication and culture (MA, MCS, PhD). *Application deadline:* For fall admission, 2/1 for domestic and international students. *Application fee:* $60. Electronic applications accepted. *Associate Dean, Research and Graduate Programs,* Dr. David B. Mitchell, 403-220-6460, Fax: 403-210-8164, E-mail: mitchell@ucalgary.ca.

Faculty of Education Students: 488 full-time (373 women), 541 part-time (376 women). 400 applicants, 50% accepted, 195 enrolled. *Faculty:* 63 full-time, 37 part-time/adjunct. Expenses: Contact institution. *Financial support:* In 2006–07, 20 students received support, including research assistantships (averaging $3,920 per year); fellowships, teaching assistantships, career-related internships or fieldwork, scholarships/grants, and unspecified assistantships also available. In 2006, 50 master's, 10 doctorates awarded. *Degree program information:* Part-time and evening/weekend programs available. Postbaccalaureate distance learning degree programs offered (minimal on-campus study). Offers community rehabilitation and disability studies (M Ed, M Sc, Ed D, PhD, Graduate Certificate, Graduate Diploma); counseling psychology (M Ed, M Sc, PhD); curriculum, teaching and learning (M Ed, M Sc, MA, Ed D, PhD, Graduate Certificate, Graduate Diploma); education (M Ed, M Sc, MA, Ed D, PhD, Graduate Certificate, Graduate Diploma); educational contexts (M Ed, MA, Ed D, PhD, Graduate Certificate, Graduate Diploma); educational leadership (M Ed, MA, Ed D, PhD, Graduate Certificate, Graduate Diploma); educational technology (M Ed, M Sc, MA, Ed D, PhD, Graduate Certificate, Graduate Diploma); gifted education (M Sc, MA, Ed D, PhD, Graduate Certificate, Graduate Diploma); higher education administration (Ed D); human development and learning (M Ed, M Sc, PhD); interpretive studies in education (M Ed, M Sc, MA, Ed D, PhD, Graduate Certificate, Graduate Diploma); school psychology (M Ed, M Sc, PhD); second language teaching (M Ed, Ed D, PhD, Graduate Certificate, Graduate Diploma); special education (M Ed, M Sc, PhD); teaching English as a second language (M Ed, M Sc, MA, Ed D, PhD, Graduate Certificate, Graduate Diploma); workplace and adult learning (M Ed, MA, Ed D, PhD, Graduate Certificate, Graduate Diploma). *Application deadline:* For fall admission, 2/1 for domestic and international students. *Application fee:* $100. Electronic applications accepted. *Application Contact:* Patricia A. Brown, Program Officer, Graduate Division of Educational Research, 403-220-3178, Fax: 403-282-3005, E-mail: brownp@ucalgary.ca. *Dean,* Dr. Annette LaGrange, 403-220-5627, Fax: 403-282-5849, E-mail: avlagran@ucalgary.ca.

Faculty of Environmental Design Offers architecture (M Arch); environmental design (M Env Des, PhD); environmental science (M Env Des); industrial design (M Env Des); planning (M Env Des); urban design (M Env Des).

Faculty of Fine Arts Students: 59 full-time (37 women), 4 part-time (2 women). 74 applicants, 32% accepted. *Faculty:* 41 full-time (13 women), 1 (woman) part-time/adjunct. Expenses: Contact institution. *Financial support:* In 2006–07, 32 students received support; fellowships, research assistantships, teaching assistantships, institutionally sponsored loans, scholarships/grants, and tuition waivers (partial) available. In 2006, 7 master's, 2 doctorates awarded. Offers art (MA, MFA); design and technical theatre (MFA); directing (MFA); fine arts (M Mus, MA, MFA, PhD); music (M Mus, MA, PhD); playwriting (MFA); theatre studies (MFA). *Application deadline:* Applications are processed on a rolling basis. *Application fee:* $100 ($130 for international students). Electronic applications accepted. *Dean,* Dr. A. Calvert, 403-220-5498, Fax: 403-282-6925.

Faculty of Humanities Students: 161 full-time (92 women), 15 part-time (14 women); includes 6 Asian Americans or Pacific Islanders, 9 international. Average age 33. 201 applicants, 35% accepted, 46 enrolled. *Faculty:* 99 full-time (48 women), 20 part-time/adjunct (4 women). Expenses: Contact institution. *Financial support:* In 2006–07, 23 fellowships (averaging $2,850 per year), 55 research assistantships (averaging $3,980 per year), 80 teaching assistantships (averaging $6,599 per year) were awarded; institutionally sponsored loans and scholarships/grants also available. Financial award application deadline: 2/1. In 2006, 27 master's, 6 doctorates awarded. *Degree program information:* Part-time and evening/weekend programs available. Offers English (MA, PhD); French (MA, PhD); German (MA); Greek and Roman studies (MA, PhD); humanities (MA, PhD); performance studies (MA, PhD); philosophy (MA, PhD); religious studies (MA, PhD); Spanish (MA, PhD). *Application deadline:* Applications are processed on a rolling basis. *Application fee:* $100 ($130 for international students). Electronic applications accepted. *Dean,* Dr. Rowland Smith, 403-220-5044, Fax: 403-284-0848.

Faculty of Kinesiology Students: 75 full-time (38 women), 3 part-time (1 woman). Average age 26. 52 applicants, 62% accepted, 25 enrolled. *Faculty:* 59 full-time (13 women), 18 part-time/adjunct (8 women). Expenses: Contact institution. *Financial support:* In 2006–07, 21 students received support, including 3 research assistantships, 18 teaching assistantships; career-related internships or fieldwork and unspecified assistantships also available. Financial award application deadline: 3/31. In 2006, 6 master's, 4 doctorates awarded. Offers biomedical engineering (M Sc, PhD); kinesiology (M Kin, M Sc, PhD). *Application deadline:* For fall admission, 3/31 for domestic students. Applications are processed on a rolling basis. *Application fee:* $100 ($130 for international students). Electronic applications accepted. *Application Contact:* Rosalie Kolstad, Graduate Program Administrator, 403-220-5183, Fax: 403-220-0105, E-mail: knesgrad@ucalgary.ca. *Associate Dean,* Brian R. MacIntosh, 403-220-3421, Fax: 403-220-0105, E-mail: brian@kin.ucalgary.ca.

Faculty of Nursing Students: 86 full-time (81 women), 31 part-time (30 women). Average age 30. 53 applicants, 81% accepted, 33 enrolled. *Faculty:* 46 full-time (44 women), 215 part-time/adjunct (201 women). Expenses: Contact institution. *Financial support:* In 2006–07, 23 students received support, including 8 fellowships (averaging $21,375 per year), 14 teaching assistantships (averaging $6,786 per year); institutionally sponsored loans, scholarships/grants, health care benefits, and unspecified assistantships also available. Support available to part-time students. In 2006, 24 master's, 5 doctorates, 5 other advanced degrees awarded. *Degree program information:* Part-time programs available. Offers nursing (MN, PhD, PMD). *Application deadline:* For fall admission, 2/1 for domestic and international students. *Application fee:* $100 ($130 for international students). Electronic applications accepted. *Application Contact:* Pat Jolly, Graduate Programs Administrator, 403-220-7288, Fax: 403-284-4803, E-mail: pjolly@ucalgary.ca. *Associate Dean, Graduate Programs,* Dr. Carol Ewashen, 403-220-6259, Fax: 403-284-4803.

Faculty of Science Students: 605 full-time (236 women), 47 part-time (13 women). 559 applicants, 35% accepted, 96 enrolled. *Faculty:* 193 full-time (22 women), 37 part-time/adjunct (3 women). Expenses: Contact institution. *Financial support:* Fellowships, research assistantships, teaching assistantships, career-related internships or fieldwork, institutionally sponsored loans, and scholarships/grants available. In 2006, 144 master's, 30 doctorates awarded. *Degree program information:* Part-time programs available. Offers analytical chemistry (M Sc, PhD); applied chemistry (M Sc, PhD); biological sciences (M Sc, PhD); computer science (M Sc, PhD); geology (M Sc, PhD); geophysics (M Sc, PhD); inorganic chemistry (M Sc, PhD); mathematics and statistics (M Sc, PhD); organic chemistry (M Sc, PhD); physical chemistry (M Sc, PhD); physics and astronomy (M Sc, PhD); polymer chemistry (M Sc, PhD); science (M Sc, PhD); software engineering (M Sc); theoretical chemistry (M Sc, PhD). *Application deadline:* Applications are processed on a rolling basis. *Application fee:* $100 ($130 for international students). *Dean,* Sandy J. Murphree, 403-220-6286.

Faculty of Social Sciences Students: 473 full-time (240 women), 78 part-time (27 women). 534 applicants, 35% accepted, 52 enrolled. *Faculty:* 187 full-time (70 women), 24 part-time/adjunct (10 women). Expenses: Contact institution. *Financial support:* Fellowships, research assistantships, teaching assistantships, career-related internships or fieldwork, institutionally sponsored loans, and unspecified assistantships available. In 2006, 102 master's, 25 doctorates awarded. *Degree program information:* Part-time and evening/weekend programs available. Offers anthropology (MA, PhD); archaeology (MA, PhD); clinical psychology (M Sc, PhD); economics (M Ec, MA, PhD); geography (M Sc, MA, MGIS, PhD); history (MA, PhD); linguistics (MA, PhD); political science (MA, PhD); psychology (M Sc, PhD); social sciences (M Ec, M Sc, MA, MGIS, PhD); sociology (MA, PhD). *Application deadline:* Applications are processed on a rolling basis. *Application fee:* $100 ($130 for international students). *Dean,* Stephen J. Randall, 403-220-5400, Fax: 403-282-8606.

Faculty of Social Work Offers social work (MSW, PhD, Postgraduate Diploma). Electronic applications accepted.

Haskayne School of Business Students: 265 full-time (81 women), 140 part-time (52 women). *Faculty:* 52 full-time (15 women), 15 part-time/adjunct (3 women). Expenses: Contact institution. *Financial support:* Fellowships, research assistantships, teaching assistantships available. *Degree program information:* Part-time and evening/weekend programs available. Offers business (EMBA, MBA, PhD); business administration (EMBA, MBA); management (MBA, PhD). *Interim Dean,* Dr. Vern Jones, 403-220-5689, Fax: 403-282-0095, E-mail: vern.jones@haskayne.ucalgary.ca.

Schulich School of Engineering Students: 786 full-time (175 women), 212 part-time (51 women). Average age 25. 1,371 applicants, 24% accepted, 54 enrolled. *Faculty:* 225 full-time (28 women), 62 part-time/adjunct (4 women). Expenses: Contact institution. *Financial support:* In 2006–07, 54 fellowships (averaging $18,000 per year), 93 research assistantships (averaging $5,200 per year), 228 teaching assistantships (averaging $4,630 per year) were awarded; career-related internships or fieldwork, institutionally sponsored loans, scholarships/grants, health care benefits, and unspecified assistantships also available. In 2006, 176 master's, 44 doctorates awarded. *Degree program information:* Part-time and evening/weekend programs available. Offers biomedical engineering (M Eng, M Sc, PhD); chemical and petroleum engineering (M Eng, M Sc, PhD); civil engineering (M Eng, M Sc, MPM, PhD); electrical and computer engineering (M Eng, M Sc, PhD); engineering (M Eng, M Sc, MPM, PhD); geomatics engineering (M Eng, M Sc, PhD); mechanical and manufacturing engineering (M Eng, M Sc, PhD). *Application deadline:* Applications are processed on a rolling basis. *Application fee:* $100 ($130 for international students). *Dean,* Dr. M. Elizabeth Cannon, 403-220-5731, Fax: 403-284-3697, E-mail: cannon@ucalgary.ca.

University of Calgary (continued)

Faculty of Law Students: 241 full-time (138 women). Average age 26. 915 applicants, 9% accepted, 85 enrolled. *Faculty:* 18 full-time (8 women), 23 part-time/adjunct (8 women). Expenses: Contact institution. *Financial support:* In 2006–07, 2 research assistantships (averaging $4,100 per year) were awarded; scholarships/grants and study awards also available. Financial award application deadline: 2/1. In 2006, 69 LL Bs, 2 master's awarded. Offers law (LL B, LL M, Graduate Certificate); natural resources, energy and environmental law (LL M, Graduate Certificate). *Application fee:* $100. *Application Contact:* Karen Argento, Admissions and Student Affairs Officer, 403-220-8154, Fax: 403-210-9662, E-mail: kargento@ucalgary.ca. *Acting Dean,* Alastair Lucas, 403-220-7116, Fax: 403-282-8325, E-mail: lawdean@ucalgary.ca.

Faculty of Medicine Students: 773 full-time (435 women), 8 part-time (3 women), 731 international. Average age 27. 1,944 applicants, 11% accepted. Expenses: Contact institution. *Financial support:* In 2006–07, 81 students received support; fellowships, research assistantships, teaching assistantships, career-related internships or fieldwork, scholarships/grants, and tuition waivers (full and partial) available. Financial award application deadline: 2/1. In 2006, 115 MDs, 75 master's, 40 doctorates awarded. *Degree program information:* Part-time programs available. Offers biochemistry and molecular biology (M Sc, PhD); biomedical technology (MBT); cancer biology (M Sc, PhD); cardiovascular and respiratory sciences (M Sc, PhD); community health sciences (M Sc, MCM, PhD); gastrointestinal sciences (M Sc, PhD); immunology (M Sc, PhD); joint injury and arthritis research (M Sc, PhD); medical education (M Sc, PhD); medical science (M Sc, PhD); medicine (MD, M Sc, MBT, MCM, PhD); microbiology and infectious diseases (M Sc, PhD); mountain medicine and high altitude physiology (M Sc); neuroscience (M Sc, PhD). *Application deadline:* Applications are processed on a rolling basis. *Application fee:* $100 ($130 for international students). Electronic applications accepted. *Associate Dean (Graduate Science Education),* Dr. Frans VanderHoorn, 403-220-6843.

UNIVERSITY OF CALIFORNIA, BERKELEY, Berkeley, CA 94720-1500

General Information State-supported, coed, university. CGS member. *Enrollment:* 33,933 graduate, professional, and undergraduate students; 9,887 matriculated graduate/professional students. *Graduate faculty:* 1,500. *Graduate housing:* Rooms and/or apartments available to single and married students. *Student services:* Campus employment opportunities, campus safety program, career counseling, child daycare facilities, disabled student services, exercise/wellness program, free psychological counseling, grant writing training, international student services, low-cost health insurance, multicultural affairs office. *Library facilities:* Doe Library plus 30 others. *Online resources:* library catalog, web page, access to other libraries' catalogs. *Collection:* 15.2 million titles, 192,030 serial subscriptions, 125,734 audiovisual materials.

Computer facilities: Computer purchase and lease plans are available. 700 computers available on campus for general student use. A campuswide network can be accessed from student residence rooms and from off campus. Internet access and online class registration are available. *Web address:* http://www.berkeley.edu/.

General Application Contact: Information Contact, 510-642-7405.

GRADUATE UNITS

Graduate Division Average age 26. Expenses: Contact institution. *Financial support:* Fellowships, research assistantships, teaching assistantships, career-related internships or fieldwork, Federal Work-Study, institutionally sponsored loans, and tuition waivers (full and partial) available. Support available to part-time students. Financial award applicants required to submit FAFSA. *Degree program information:* Part-time and evening/weekend programs available. Offers ancient history and Mediterranean archaeology (MA, PhD); Asian studies (PhD); bioengineering (PhD); biophysics (PhD); Buddhist studies (PhD); comparative biochemistry (PhD); demography (MA, PhD); East Asian studies (MA); endocrinology (MA, PhD); energy and resources (MA, MS, PhD); ethnic studies (PhD); folklore (MA); French (PhD); international and area studies (MA); Italian (PhD); Jewish studies (PhD); Latin American studies (MA, PhD); neuroscience (PhD); Northeast Asian studies (MA); performance studies (PhD); range management (MS); sociology and demography (PhD); South Asian studies (MA); Southeast Asian studies (MA); Spanish (PhD); vision science (MS, PhD). *Application fee:* $60 ($80 for international students). *Application Contact:* 510-642-7405. *Dean, Graduate Division,* Dr. Mary Ann Mason, 510-642-5473, E-mail: graddean@berkeley.edu.

College of Chemistry *Faculty:* 51 full-time, 3 part-time/adjunct. Expenses: Contact institution. *Financial support:* Fellowships with tuition reimbursements, research assistantships with tuition reimbursements, teaching assistantships with tuition reimbursements, institutionally sponsored loans and unspecified assistantships available. Financial award applicants required to submit FAFSA. Offers chemical engineering (MS, PhD); chemistry (MS, PhD). *Application fee:* $60 ($80 for international students). *Application Contact:* Dr. Judith P. Klinman, Chair, 510-643-0573, Fax: 510-642-9675, E-mail: chemgrad@cchem.berkeley.edu. *Dean, College of Chemistry,* Dr. Charles B. Harris, 510-642-2814, E-mail: harris@socrates.berkeley.edu.

College of Engineering Expenses: Contact institution. *Financial support:* Fellowships, research assistantships, teaching assistantships, career-related internships or fieldwork, Federal Work-Study, institutionally sponsored loans, scholarships/grants, tuition waivers (full and partial), and unspecified assistantships available. Offers applied science and technology (PhD); computer science (MS, PhD); electrical engineering (MS, PhD); engineering (M Eng, MS, D Eng, PhD); engineering and project management (M Eng, MS, D Eng, PhD); engineering science (M Eng, MS, PhD); environmental engineering (M Eng, MS, D Eng, PhD); geoengineering (M Eng, MS, D Eng, PhD); industrial engineering and operations research (M Eng, MS, D Eng, PhD); mechanical engineering (M Eng, MS, D Eng, PhD); nuclear engineering (M Eng, MS, D Eng, PhD); structural engineering, mechanics and materials (M Eng, MS, D Eng, PhD); transportation engineering (M Eng, MS, D Eng, PhD). *Application fee:* $60 ($80 for international students). *Dean, College of Engineering,* Dr. Fiona Doyle, 510-642-5771, E-mail: fmdoyle@berkeley.edu.

College of Environmental Design Students: 383. Expenses: Contact institution. *Financial support:* Fellowships, research assistantships, teaching assistantships, career-related internships or fieldwork, Federal Work-Study, institutionally sponsored loans, and tuition waivers (partial) available. Offers architecture (M Arch); building science (MS, PhD); building structures, construction and materials (MS, PhD); city and regional planning (MCP, PhD); design (MA); design theories, methods, and practices (MS, PhD); environmental design (M Arch, MA, MCP, MLA, MS, MUD, PhD); environmental design in developing countries (MS, PhD); environmental planning (MLA); history of architecture and urbanism (MS, PhD); landscape architecture (MLA); landscape architecture and environmental planning (PhD); landscape design and site planning (MLA); social and cultural processes in architecture and urbanism (MS, PhD); urban and community design (MLA); urban design (MUD). *Application fee:* $60 ($80 for international students). *Dean,* Harrison Fraker, 510-642-0831, E-mail: fraker@berkeley.edu.

College of Letters and Science Expenses: Contact institution. *Financial support:* Fellowships, research assistantships, teaching assistantships, career-related internships or fieldwork, Federal Work-Study, institutionally sponsored loans, tuition waivers (full and partial), and unspecified assistantships available. Financial award applicants required to submit FAFSA. Offers African American studies (PhD); anthropology (PhD); applied mathematics (PhD); art practice (MFA); astrophysics (PhD); Chinese language (PhD); classical archaeology (MA, PhD); classics (MA, PhD); comparative literature (PhD); composition (PhD); Czech (PhD); economics (PhD); English (PhD); ethnomusicology (PhD); French (PhD); geography (PhD); geology (MA, MS, PhD); geophysics (MA, MS, PhD); German (PhD); Greek (MA); Hindi (MA, PhD); Hispanic languages and literature (MA, PhD); history (PhD); history of art (PhD); Indonesian (MA, PhD); integrative biology (PhD); Italian studies (PhD); Japanese language (PhD); Latin (MA); letters and science (MA, MFA, MS, PhD); linguistics (PhD); logic and the methodology of science (PhD); mathematics (MA, PhD); medical anthropology (PhD); molecular and cell biology (PhD); musicology (PhD); Near Eastern religions (PhD); Near Eastern studies (MA, PhD); philosophy (PhD); physics (PhD); Polish (PhD); political science (PhD); psychology (PhD); rhetoric (PhD); Russian (PhD); Sanskrit (MA, PhD); Scandinavian languages and literatures (PhD); Serbo-Croatian (PhD); sociology (PhD); statistics (MA, PhD); Tamil (MA, PhD). *Application fee:* $60 ($80 for international students). Electronic applications accepted. *Chair of Deans,* Dr. Mark Richards, 510-642-5872, E-mail: markr@seismo.berkeley.edu.

College of Natural Resources Expenses: Contact institution. *Financial support:* Fellowships, research assistantships, teaching assistantships, Federal Work-Study, institutionally sponsored loans, tuition waivers (full and partial), and unspecified assistantships available. Financial award applicants required to submit FAFSA. Offers agricultural and environmental chemistry (PhD); agricultural and resource economics (PhD); environmental science, policy, and management (MS, PhD); forestry (MF); microbiology (PhD); molecular and biochemical nutrition (PhD); molecular toxicology (PhD); natural resources (MF, MS, PhD); plant biology (PhD). *Application fee:* $60 ($80 for international students). *Dean, College of Natural Resources,* Paul W. Ludden, 510-642-7171, E-mail: pludden@nature.berkeley.edu.

Graduate School of Journalism *Faculty:* 12 full-time, 12 part-time/adjunct. Expenses: Contact institution. *Financial support:* Fellowships, research assistantships, career-related internships or fieldwork, Federal Work-Study, institutionally sponsored loans, scholarships/grants, tuition waivers (full and partial), and unspecified assistantships available. Financial award applicants required to submit FAFSA. Offers journalism (MJ). *Application deadline:* For fall admission, 12/1 for domestic students. *Application fee:* $60 ($80 for international students). *Application Contact:* Michele Rabin, Director of Admissions, 510-642-3383, Fax: 510-643-9136, E-mail: applysoj@berkeley.edu. *Dean,* Orville Schell, 510-642-3394, E-mail: schell@uclik4.berkeley.edu.

Graduate School of Public Policy Expenses: Contact institution. *Financial support:* Fellowships, research assistantships, teaching assistantships, unspecified assistantships available. Offers public policy (MPP, PhD). *Application deadline:* For fall admission, 12/15 for domestic students. *Application fee:* $60 ($80 for international students). *Application Contact:* Jalilah LaBrie, Graduate Assistant for Admission, 510-642-4670, Fax: 510-643-9657, E-mail: gspp-admissions@berkeley.edu. *Dean,* Michael Nacht, 510-642-4670, E-mail: nacht@socrates.berkeley.edu.

Haas School of Business Students: 653 full-time (214 women), 877 part-time (211 women); includes 520 minority (20 African Americans, 2 American Indian/Alaska Native, 467 Asian Americans or Pacific Islanders, 31 Hispanic Americans), 321 international. *Faculty:* 72 full-time (17 women), 131 part-time/adjunct (22 women). Expenses: Contact institution. *Financial support:* Fellowships, research assistantships, teaching assistantships, career-related internships or fieldwork, Federal Work-Study, institutionally sponsored loans, scholarships/grants, tuition waivers (full), and unspecified assistantships available. Support available to part-time students. Financial award application deadline: 3/2; financial award applicants required to submit FAFSA. In 2006, 541 master's, 17 doctorates awarded. *Degree program information:* Part-time and evening/weekend programs available. Offers accounting (PhD); business (MBA, MFE, PhD); business administration (MBA); business and public policy (PhD); finance (PhD); financial engineering (MFE); marketing (PhD); organizational behavior and industrial relations (PhD); real estate (PhD). *Application Contact:* MBA Admissions Office, 510-642-1405, Fax: 510-643-6659. *Dean,* Tom Campbell, 510-643-2027, Fax: 510-642-9128, E-mail: campbell@haas.berkeley.edu.

School of Education Expenses: Contact institution. *Financial support:* Fellowships, research assistantships, teaching assistantships, career-related internships or fieldwork and unspecified assistantships available. Offers development in mathematics and science (MA); developmental teacher education); education (MA, Ed D, PhD); education and single subject credential: English (MA); education in mathematics, science, and technology (MA, PhD); educational leadership (Ed D); human development and education (MA, PhD); language, literacy, and culture (MA, Ed D, PhD); policy and organizational research (MA, PhD); principal leadership (MA); program evaluation and assessment (Ed D); quantitative methods and evaluation (MA, PhD); school psychology); science and mathematics education); social and cultural studies in education (MA, PhD); special education (PhD). *Application deadline:* For fall admission, 12/1 for domestic students. *Application fee:* $60 ($80 for international students). *Application Contact:* Francisca Cazares, Admissions Assistant, 510-642-0841, Fax: 510-642-4808, E-mail: gse_info@berkeley.edu. *Dean,* Dr. P. David Pearson, 510-643-6644, E-mail: ppearson@socrates.berkeley.edu.

School of Information Management and Systems Expenses: Contact institution. *Financial support:* Fellowships, research assistantships, teaching assistantships, unspecified assistantships available. Offers information management and systems (MIMS, PhD). *Application fee:* $60 ($80 for international students). *Application Contact:* Leticia Sanchez, Student Affairs Officer, 510-642-1464, Fax: 510-642-5814, E-mail: admissions@sims.berkeley.edu. *Dean, School of Information Management and Systems,* AnnaLee Saxenian, 510-642-9980, E-mail: anna@sims.berkeley.edu.

School of Public Health Expenses: Contact institution. *Financial support:* Fellowships, research assistantships, teaching assistantships, career-related internships or fieldwork, Federal Work-Study, institutionally sponsored loans, scholarships/grants, traineeships, tuition waivers (full and partial), and unspecified assistantships available. Financial award applicants required to submit FAFSA. Offers biostatistics (MA, PhD); community health education (MPH); environmental health sciences (MPH, MS, Dr PH, PhD); epidemiology (MPH, MS, PhD); health and medical sciences); health and social behavior (MPH); health policy and management (MPH); health services and policy analysis (PhD); infectious diseases (MPH, PhD); infectious diseases and immunity (PhD); interdisciplinary (MPH); maternal and child health (MPH); public health (MA, MPH, MS, Dr PH, PhD); public health nutrition (MPH). *Application deadline:* For fall admission, 12/1 for domestic students. Applications are processed on a rolling basis. *Application fee:* $60 ($80 for international students). *Application Contact:* Information Contact, 510-643-0881, E-mail: sphinfo@berkeley.edu. *Dean, School of Public Health,* Ralph Catalano, 510-643-3897, E-mail: rayc@berkeley.edu.

School of Social Welfare Expenses: Contact institution. *Financial support:* Fellowships, research assistantships with partial tuition reimbursements, teaching assistantships with partial tuition reimbursements, career-related internships or fieldwork, Federal Work-Study, scholarships/grants, traineeships, health care benefits, and unspecified assistantships available. Financial award applicants required to submit FAFSA. Offers social welfare (MSW, PhD). *Application deadline:* Applications are processed on a rolling basis. *Application fee:* $60 ($80 for international students). *Application Contact:* Rafael Herrera, Director of Admissions, 510-642-9042, Fax: 510-643-6126, E-mail: socwelf@berkeley.edu. *Dean, School of Social Welfare,* Lorraine Midanik, 510-642-5039, E-mail: swdean@berkeley.edu.

School of Law Offers jurisprudence and social policy (PhD); law (JD, LL M, JSD).

School of Optometry 200 applicants, 36% accepted, 61 enrolled. Expenses: Contact institution. *Financial support:* Career-related internships or fieldwork, Federal Work-Study, institutionally sponsored loans, scholarships/grants, and unspecified assistantships available. Financial award application deadline: 3/2; financial award applicants required to submit FAFSA. In 2006, 59 degrees awarded. Offers optometry (OD, Certificate). *Application deadline:* For fall admission, 12/15 for domestic and international students. *Application fee:* $60. Electronic applications accepted. *Application Contact:* Dr. Richard C. Van Sluyters, Associate Dean for Student Affairs/Head Graduate Adviser, 510-642-9537, Fax: 510-643-5109, E-mail: admissions@optometry.berkeley.edu. *Dean,* Dr. Dennis M. Levi, 510-642-3414, Fax: 510-642-7806, E-mail: dlevi@berkeley.edu.

UNIVERSITY OF CALIFORNIA, DAVIS, Davis, CA 95616

General Information State-supported, coed, university. CGS member. *Graduate housing:* Rooms and/or apartments available to single and married students. Housing application deadline: 4/1.

GRADUATE UNITS

College of Engineering *Degree program information:* Part-time programs available. Offers aeronautical engineering (M Engr, MS, D Engr, PhD, Certificate); applied science (MS, PhD); biological systems engineering (M Engr, MS, D Engr, PhD); biomedical engineering (MS, PhD); chemical engineering (MS, PhD); civil and environmental engineering (M Engr, MS, D Engr, PhD, Certificate); computer science (MS, PhD); electrical and computer engineering (MS, PhD); engineering (M Engr, MS, D Engr, PhD, Certificate); materials science and engineering (MS, PhD); mechanical engineering (M Engr, MS, D Engr, PhD, Certificate); transportation, technology and policy (MS, PhD). Electronic applications accepted.

Graduate School of Management Students: 116 full-time (45 women), 314 part-time (79 women); includes 132 minority (6 African Americans, 2 American Indian/Alaska Native, 114 Asian Americans or Pacific Islanders, 10 Hispanic Americans), 29 international. Average age 31. 512 applicants, 47% accepted, 169 enrolled. *Faculty:* 27 full-time (7 women), 19 part-time/adjunct (3 women). Expenses: Contact institution. *Financial support:* In 2006–07, 80 students received support, including 3 research assistantships with partial tuition reimbursements available; teaching assistantships with partial tuition reimbursements available, career-related internships or fieldwork, Federal Work-Study, institutionally sponsored loans, scholarships/grants, health care benefits, tuition waivers (partial), and unspecified assistantships also available. Support available to part-time students. Financial award application deadline: 3/1; financial award applicants required to submit FAFSA. In 2006, 126 degrees awarded. *Degree program information:* Part-time and evening/weekend programs available. Offers business administration (MBA); management (MBA). *Application deadline:* Applications are processed on a rolling basis. *Application fee:* $100. Electronic applications accepted. *Application Contact:* Kathy Gleed, Director, Admissions and Student Services, 530-754-5476, Fax: 530-754-9355, E-mail: krgleed@ucdavis.edu. *Dean,* Nicole W. Biggart, 530-752-7366, Fax: 530-752-2924, E-mail: nwbiggart@ucdavis.edu.

Graduate Studies Offers acting (MFA); agricultural and environmental chemistry (MS, PhD); agricultural and resource economics (MS, PhD); animal behavior (PhD); animal biology (MAM, MS, PhD); anthropology (MA, PhD); applied linguistics (MA, PhD); applied mathematics (MS, PhD); art (MFA); art history (MA); atmospheric sciences (MS, PhD); avian sciences (MS); biochemistry and molecular biology (MS, PhD); biophysics (MS, PhD); biostatistics (MS, PhD); cell and developmental biology (MS, PhD); chemistry (MS, PhD); child development (MS); clinical research (MAS); communication (MA); community development (MS); comparative literature (PhD); comparative pathology (MS, PhD); composition (MA, PhD); conducting (MA, PhD); creative writing (MA); cultural studies (MA, PhD); dramatic art (PhD); ecology (MS, PhD); economics (MA, PhD); education (MA, Ed D); English (MA, PhD); entomology (MS, PhD); epidemiology (MS, PhD); exercise science (MS); food science (MS, PhD); forensic science (MS); French (PhD); genetics (MS, PhD); geography (MA, PhD); geology (MS, PhD); German (MA, PhD); health informatics (MS); history (MA, PhD); horticulture and agronomy (MS); human development (PhD); hydrologic sciences (MS, PhD); immunology (MS, PhD); instructional studies (PhD); integrated pest management (MS); international agricultural development (MS); linguistics (MA); mathematics (MA, MAT, PhD); microbiology (MS, PhD); molecular, cellular and integrative physiology (MS, PhD); musicology (MA, PhD); Native American studies (MA, PhD); neuroscience (PhD); nutrition (MS, PhD); pharmacology/toxicology (MS, PhD); philosophy (MA, PhD); physics (MS, PhD); plant biology (MS, PhD); plant pathology (MS, PhD); political science (MA, PhD); population biology (PhD); psychological studies (PhD); psychology (PhD); sociocultural studies (PhD); sociology (MA, PhD); soils and biogeochemistry (MS, PhD); Spanish (MA, PhD); statistics (MS, PhD); textile arts and costume design (MFA); textiles (MS); viticulture and enology (MS, PhD). Electronic applications accepted.

School of Law Students: 582 full-time (321 women); includes 192 minority (9 African Americans, 2 American Indian/Alaska Native, 133 Asian Americans or Pacific Islanders, 48 Hispanic Americans), 6 international. Average age 24. 3,493 applicants, 28% accepted, 188 enrolled. *Faculty:* 36 full-time (16 women), 16 part-time/adjunct (5 women). Expenses: Contact institution. *Financial support:* In 2006–07, 523 students received support, including 9 research assistantships with partial tuition reimbursements available, 78 teaching assistantships with partial tuition reimbursements available; Federal Work-Study, institutionally sponsored loans, scholarships/grants, health care benefits also available. Financial award application deadline: 3/2; financial award applicants required to submit FAFSA. In 2006, 189 JDs, 10 master's awarded. Offers law (JD, LL M). *Application deadline:* For fall admission, 2/1 for domestic and international students. Applications are processed on a rolling basis. *Application fee:* $75. Electronic applications accepted. *Application Contact:* Sharon Pinkney, Director, Admissions, 530-752-6477, Fax: 530-754-8371, E-mail: lawadmissions@ucdavis.edu. *Dean,* Rex R. Perschbacher, 530-752-0243, Fax: 530-752-7279, E-mail: rrperschbacher@ucdavis.edu.

School of Medicine Students: 402 full-time (220 women). Average age 28. 4,313 applicants, 5% accepted, 90 enrolled. *Faculty:* 582 full-time (175 women), 92 part-time/adjunct (40 women). Expenses: Contact institution. *Financial support:* In 2006–07, 371 students received support, including 15 fellowships with full tuition reimbursements available (averaging $22,036 per year), 11 research assistantships with partial tuition reimbursements available (averaging $19,932 per year), 10 teaching assistantships with partial tuition reimbursements available (averaging $3,469 per year); institutionally sponsored loans and scholarships/grants also available. Financial award application deadline: 3/2; financial award applicants required to submit FAFSA. In 2006, 98 MDs awarded. Offers medicine (MD). *Application deadline:* For fall admission, 11/1 for domestic and international students. Applications are processed on a rolling basis. *Application fee:* $60. Electronic applications accepted. *Application Contact:* Edward D. Dagang, Director of Admissions and Outreach, 916-734-4800, Fax: 916-734-4050, E-mail: ed.dagang@ucdmc.ucdavis.edu. *Dean, School of Medicine; Vice Chancellor, Human Health Services,* Dr. Claire Pomeroy, 916-734-7131, Fax: 916-734-7055, E-mail: claire.pomeroy@ucdmc.ucdavis.edu.

School of Veterinary Medicine Offers preventive veterinary medicine (MPVM); veterinary medicine (DVM, MPVM, Certificate).

UNIVERSITY OF CALIFORNIA, HASTINGS COLLEGE OF THE LAW, San Francisco, CA 94102-4978

General Information State-supported, coed, graduate-only institution. *Graduate housing:* Rooms and/or apartments available on a first-come, first-served basis to single and married students.

GRADUATE UNITS

Graduate Program Offers law (JD, LL M). Electronic applications accepted.

UNIVERSITY OF CALIFORNIA, IRVINE, Irvine, CA 92697

General Information State-supported, coed, university. CGS member. *Enrollment:* 25,229 graduate, professional, and undergraduate students; 4,140 matriculated graduate/professional students. *Graduate faculty:* 1,144. *Graduate housing:* Rooms and/or apartments available on a first-come, first-served basis to single and married students. *Student services:* Campus employment opportunities, campus safety program, career counseling, child daycare facilities, disabled student services, exercise/wellness program, free psychological counseling, grant writing training, international student services, low-cost health insurance, multicultural affairs office, teacher training, writing training.

Computer facilities: 1,732 computers available on campus for general student use. A campuswide network can be accessed from student residence rooms and from off campus. Internet access and online class registration are available. *Web address:* http://www.uci.edu/.

General Application Contact: Ashley Brooks, Office of Graduate Studies, 949-824-4611, Fax: 949-824-9096, E-mail: ogsfront@uci.edu.

GRADUATE UNITS

College of Medicine Students: 472 full-time (228 women); includes 162 minority (5 African Americans, 120 Asian Americans or Pacific Islanders, 37 Hispanic Americans), 6 international. Expenses: Contact institution. *Financial support:* Fellowships, research assistantships with full tuition reimbursements, teaching assistantships, career-related internships or fieldwork, institutionally sponsored loans, traineeships, health care benefits, and unspecified assistantships available. Financial award application deadline: 3/1; financial award applicants required to submit FAFSA. In 2006, 79 MDs, 4 master's, 6 doctorates awarded. Offers biological sciences (MS, PhD); genetic counseling (MS); medicine (MD, MS, PhD); pharmacology and toxicology (MS, PhD); research medical science training). *Application fee:* $60. Electronic applications accepted. *Application Contact:* Gayle Pierce, Director of Admissions, 949-824-5617, Fax: 949-824-2485, E-mail: gjpierce@uci.edu. *Dean,* Dr. Thomas Cesario, 949-824-5926.

Office of Graduate Studies Students: 3,609; includes 835 minority (55 African Americans, 11 American Indian/Alaska Native, 570 Asian Americans or Pacific Islanders, 199 Hispanic Americans), 863 international. Expenses: Contact institution. *Financial support:* Fellowships with full and partial tuition reimbursements, research assistantships with full tuition reimbursements, teaching assistantships with full and partial tuition reimbursements, career-related internships or fieldwork, Federal Work-Study, institutionally sponsored loans, scholarships/grants, traineeships, health care benefits, and unspecified assistantships available. Support available to part-time students. Financial award application deadline: 3/1; financial award applicants required to submit FAFSA. In 2006, 708 master's, 186 doctorates awarded. *Degree program information:* Part-time and evening/weekend programs available. Offers educational administration (Ed D); educational administration and leadership (Ed D); elementary and secondary education (MAT). *Application deadline:* For fall admission, 1/15 for domestic students; for winter admission, 10/15 for domestic students. *Application fee:* $60. Electronic applications accepted. *Application Contact:* Arlene Samano, Office of Graduate Studies, 949-824-4611, Fax: 949-824-9096, E-mail: ogsfront@uci.edu. *Vice Chancellor for Research and Dean of Graduate Studies,* Dr. William H. Parker, 949-824-5796, Fax: 949-824-2095, E-mail: whparker@uci.edu.

Claire Trevor School of the Arts Students: 132 full-time (80 women), 1 part-time; includes 22 minority (5 African Americans, 1 American Indian/Alaska Native, 10 Asian Americans or Pacific Islanders, 6 Hispanic Americans), 12 international. Expenses: Contact institution. *Financial support:* Fellowships, teaching assistantships, institutionally sponsored loans, traineeships, health care benefits, and unspecified assistantships available. Financial award application deadline: 3/1; financial award applicants required to submit FAFSA. In 2006, 47 master's, 1 doctorate awarded. Offers accompanying (MFA); acting (MFA); arts (MFA, PhD); choral conducting (MFA); composition and technology (MFA); dance (MFA); design and stage management (MFA); directing (MFA); drama (MFA); drama and theatre (PhD); guitar/lute performance (MFA); instrumental performance (MFA); jazz instrumental/composition (MFA); piano performance (MFA); studio art (MFA); vocal performance (MFA). *Application deadline:* For fall admission, 1/15 for domestic students; for winter admission, 10/15 for domestic students. Applications are processed on a rolling basis. *Application fee:* $60. Electronic applications accepted. *Application Contact:* Janelle Reinelt, Associate Dean, 949-824-6612, Fax: 949-824-2450, E-mail: jreinelt@uci.edu. *Dean,* Nohema Fernandez, 949-824-8792, Fax: 949-824-2450, E-mail: fernandez@uci.edu.

Donald Bren School of Information and Computer Sciences Students: 255 full-time (60 women), 7 part-time (1 woman); includes 35 minority (1 African American, 1 American Indian/Alaska Native, 29 Asian Americans or Pacific Islanders, 4 Hispanic Americans), 144 international. Expenses: Contact institution. *Financial support:* Fellowships, research assistantships with full tuition reimbursements, teaching assistantships, institutionally sponsored loans, traineeships, health care benefits, and unspecified assistantships available. Financial award application deadline: 3/1; financial award applicants required to submit FAFSA. In 2006, 72 master's, 19 doctorates awarded. Offers information and computer science (MS, PhD); networked systems (MS, PhD). *Application deadline:* For fall admission, 1/15 priority date for domestic students; for winter admission, 10/15 priority date for domestic students. Applications are processed on a rolling basis. *Application fee:* $60. Electronic applications accepted. *Application Contact:* Kris Bolcer, Assistant Director, Graduate Affairs, 949-824-2277, Fax: 949-824-3976, E-mail: kris@ics.uci.edu. *Interim Dean,* Debra J. Richardson, 949-824-7405, Fax: 949-824-3976, E-mail: djr@uci.edu.

The Paul Merage School of Business Students: 784 full-time (258 women), 7 part-time (4 women); includes 176 minority (9 African Americans, 2 American Indian/Alaska Native, 143 Asian Americans or Pacific Islanders, 22 Hispanic Americans), 122 international. Average age 32. Expenses: Contact institution. *Financial support:* Career-related internships or fieldwork, Federal Work-Study, institutionally sponsored loans, scholarships/grants, traineeships, health care benefits, and unspecified assistantships available. Support available to part-time students. Financial award application deadline: 3/1; financial award applicants required to submit FAFSA. In 2006, 363 master's, 2 doctorates awarded. *Degree program information:* Part-time and evening/weekend programs available. Offers business administration (MBA); management (PhD). *Application deadline:* For fall admission, 12/1 priority date for domestic students; for spring admission, 5/1 for domestic students. Applications are processed on a rolling basis. *Application fee:* $75. Electronic applications accepted. *Application Contact:* Wendy Gillett, Admissions Coordinator, 949-824-8318, Fax: 949-824-2944, E-mail: wgillett@uci.edu. *Dean,* Jone Pearce, 949-824-6505, Fax: 949-824-8469, E-mail: jlpearce@uci.edu.

School of Biological Sciences Students: 402 full-time (228 women), 2 part-time (1 woman); includes 130 minority (6 African Americans, 2 American Indian/Alaska Native, 76 Asian Americans or Pacific Islanders, 46 Hispanic Americans), 62 international. Expenses: Contact institution. *Financial support:* Fellowships with full tuition reimbursements, research assistantships with full tuition reimbursements, teaching assistantships with full tuition reimbursements, career-related internships or fieldwork, institutionally sponsored loans, scholarships/grants, traineeships, health care benefits, and unspecified assistantships available. Financial award application deadline: 3/1; financial award applicants required to submit FAFSA. In 2006, 13 master's, 40 doctorates awarded. Offers biological science (MS); biological sciences (MS, PhD); biotechnology (MS). *Application deadline:* For fall admission, 1/15 for domestic students; for winter admission, 10/15 for domestic students. Applications are processed on a rolling basis. *Application fee:* $60. Electronic applications accepted. *Application Contact:* Kimberly McKinney, Administrator, 949-824-8145, Fax: 949-824-1965, E-mail: kamckinn@uci.edu. *Dean,* Dr. Susan V. Bryant, 949-824-5315, E-mail: svbryant@uci.edu.

School of Engineering Students: 588 full-time (147 women), 56 part-time (13 women); includes 150 minority (4 African Americans, 1 American Indian/Alaska Native, 124 Asian Americans or Pacific Islanders, 21 Hispanic Americans), 319 international. Average age 28. Expenses: Contact institution. *Financial support:* In 2006–07, fellowships with tuition reimbursements (averaging $14,656 per year); research assistantships with full tuition reimbursements, teaching assistantships with tuition reimbursements, institutionally sponsored loans, traineeships, health care benefits, and unspecified assistantships also available. Financial award application deadline: 3/1; financial award applicants required to submit FAFSA. In 2006, 179 master's, 70 doctorates awarded. *Degree program information:* Part-time programs available. Offers biomedical engineering (MS, PhD); chemical and biochemical engineering (MS, PhD); civil and environmental engineering (MS, PhD); electrical engineering and computer science (MS, PhD); engineering (MS, PhD); materials science and engineering (MS, PhD); mechanical and aerospace engineering (MS, PhD); networked systems (MS, PhD). *Application deadline:* For fall admission, 1/15 priority date for domestic students. Applications are processed on a rolling basis. *Application fee:* $60 ($80 for international students). Electronic applications accepted. *Application Contact:* Thomas Cahoon, Graduate Counselor, 949-824-3562, Fax: 949-824-3440, E-mail: tcahoon@uci.edu. *Dean,* Dr. Nicolaos G. Alexopoulos, 949-824-6002, Fax: 949-824-7966, E-mail: alfios@uci.edu.

School of Humanities Students: 443 full-time (237 women), 7 part-time (3 women); includes 95 minority (4 African Americans, 2 American Indian/Alaska Native, 39 Asian Americans or Pacific Islanders, 50 Hispanic Americans), 29 international. Expenses: Contact institution. *Financial support:* Fellowships with full and partial tuition reimbursements, research assistantships with full tuition reimbursements, teaching assistantships with full and partial tuition reimbursements, institutionally sponsored loans, traineeships, health care benefits, and unspecified assistantships available. Financial award application deadline: 3/1; financial award applicants required to submit FAFSA. In 2006, 58 master's, 21 doctorates awarded. Offers Chinese (MA, PhD); classics (MA, PhD); comparative literature (MA, PhD); creative writing (MFA); East Asian languages and literatures (MA, PhD); English (MA, PhD); English (summer program) (MA); English and American literature (PhD); French (MA, PhD); German (MA, PhD); history (MA, PhD); humanities (MA, MAT, MFA, PhD); Japanese (MA, PhD); philosophy (MA, PhD); Spanish (MA, MAT, PhD); visual studies (MA, PhD); writing (MFA). *Application deadline:* For fall admission, 1/15 for domestic students; for winter admission, 10/15 for domestic students. Applications are processed on a rolling basis. *Application fee:* $60. Electronic applications accepted. *Application Contact:* Rosemary Humphreys, Graduate Counselor, 949-824-6522, Fax: 949-824-2379, E-mail: rjhumphr@uci.edu. *Dean,* Karen Lawrence, 949-824-5131, Fax: 949-824-2379, E-mail: krlawren@uci.edu.

University of California, Irvine (continued)

School of Physical Sciences Students: 464 full-time (132 women), 2 part-time (1 woman); includes 90 minority (2 African Americans, 62 Asian Americans or Pacific Islanders, 26 Hispanic Americans), 117 international. Expenses: Contact institution. *Financial support:* Fellowships, research assistantships with full tuition reimbursements, teaching assistantships, career-related internships or fieldwork, institutionally sponsored loans, traineeships, health care benefits, and unspecified assistantships available. Financial award application deadline: 3/1; financial award applicants required to submit FAFSA. In 2006, 59 master's, 46 doctorates awarded. Offers chemical and material physics (PhD); chemical and materials physics (MS); chemistry (MS, PhD); earth system science (MS, PhD); mathematics (MS, PhD); physical sciences (MS, PhD); physics (MS, PhD). *Application deadline:* For fall admission, 1/15 priority date for domestic students; for winter admission, 10/15 priority date for domestic students. Applications are processed on a rolling basis. *Application fee:* $60. Electronic applications accepted. *Application Contact:* Robert Doedens, Associate Dean, 949-824-6507, Fax: 949-824-2261, E-mail: rjdoeden@uci.edu. *Dean,* Ronald Stern, 949-824-6022, Fax: 949-824-2261, E-mail: rstern@uci.edu.

School of Social Ecology Students: 276 full-time (171 women), 1 part-time; includes 84 minority (11 African Americans, 2 American Indian/Alaska Native, 48 Asian Americans or Pacific Islanders, 23 Hispanic Americans), 14 international. Average age 31. Expenses: Contact institution. *Financial support:* Fellowships, research assistantships with full tuition reimbursements, teaching assistantships, institutionally sponsored loans, traineeships, health care benefits, and unspecified assistantships available. Financial award application deadline: 3/1; financial award applicants required to submit FAFSA. In 2006, 56 master's, 16 doctorates awarded. Offers criminology, law and society (MAS, PhD); planning, policy and design (PhD); psychology and social behavior (PhD); social ecology (MAS, MS, MURP, PhD); urban and regional planning (MURP). *Application deadline:* For fall admission, 1/15 priority date for domestic students; for winter admission, 10/15 priority date for domestic students. Applications are processed on a rolling basis. *Application fee:* $60. Electronic applications accepted. *Application Contact:* Jill Vidas, Academic Counselor, 949-824-5918, Fax: 949-824-2056, E-mail: jjvidas@uci.edu. *Dean,* C. Ronald Huff, 949-824-6094, Fax: 949-824-1845, E-mail: rhuff@uci.edu.

School of Social Sciences Students: 334 full-time (163 women), 4 part-time (3 women); includes 78 minority (5 African Americans, 47 Asian Americans or Pacific Islanders, 26 Hispanic Americans), 68 international. Expenses: Contact institution. *Financial support:* Fellowships, research assistantships with full tuition reimbursements, teaching assistantships, institutionally sponsored loans, traineeships, health care benefits, and unspecified assistantships available. Financial award application deadline: 3/1; financial award applicants required to submit FAFSA. In 2006, 33 master's, 37 doctorates awarded. Offers anthropology (MA, PhD); demographic and social analysis (MA); economics (MA, PhD); philosophy (PhD); political psychology (PhD); political sciences (PhD); psychology (PhD); public choice (MA, PhD); social networks (PhD); social networks-social science (MA); social science (MA, PhD); social sciences (MA, PhD); sociology and social relations-social science (MA, PhD); transportation economics (MA, PhD); transportation science (MA, PhD). *Application deadline:* For fall admission, 1/15 priority date for domestic students; for winter admission, 10/15 priority date for domestic students. Applications are processed on a rolling basis. *Application fee:* $60. Electronic applications accepted. *Application Contact:* Diane Enriquez, Graduate Counselor, 949-824-5924, Fax: 949-824-3548, E-mail: dmvargas@uci.edu. *Dean,* Barbara Anne Dosher, 949-824-7373, E-mail: bdosher@uci.edu.

UNIVERSITY OF CALIFORNIA, LOS ANGELES, Los Angeles, CA 90095

General Information State-supported, coed, university. CGS member. *Graduate housing:* Rooms and/or apartments available to single and married students. Housing application deadline: 5/15.

GRADUATE UNITS

Graduate Division *Degree program information:* Part-time programs available. Offers East Asian studies (MA). Electronic applications accepted.

College of Letters and Science Offers African studies (MA); Afro-American studies (MA); American Indian studies (MA); anthropology (MA, PhD); applied linguistics (PhD); applied linguistics and teaching English as a second language (MA); archaeology (MA, PhD); art history (MA, PhD); Asian-American studies (MA); astronomy (MAT, MS, PhD); atmospheric sciences (MS, PhD); biochemistry and molecular biology (MS, PhD); biology (MA, PhD); chemistry (MS, PhD); classics (MA, PhD); comparative literature (MA, PhD); East Asian languages and cultures (MA, PhD); economics (MA, PhD); English (MA, PhD); French and Francophone studies (MA, PhD); geochemistry (MS, PhD); geography (MA, PhD); geology (MS, PhD); geophysics and space physics (MS, PhD); German (MA); Germanic languages (MA, PhD); Greek (MA); Hispanic languages and literature (PhD); history (MA, PhD); Indo-European studies (PhD); Islamic studies (MA, PhD); Italian (MA, PhD); Latin (MA); Latin American studies (MA); letters and science (MA, MAT, MS, PhD, Certificate); linguistics (MA, PhD); mathematics (MA, MAT, PhD); molecular and cellular life sciences (PhD); molecular biology (PhD); molecular, cellular and integrative physiology (PhD); musicology (MA, PhD); Near Eastern languages and cultures (MA, PhD); philosophy (MA, PhD); physics (MAT, MS, PhD); physics education (MAT); physiological science (MS, PhD); plant molecular biology (PhD); political science (MA, PhD); Portuguese (MA); psychology (MA, PhD); Romance linguistics and literature (MA, PhD); Scandinavian (MA, PhD); Slavic languages and literatures (MA, PhD); sociology (MA, PhD); Spanish (MA); statistics (MS, PhD); women's studies (MS, PhD). Electronic applications accepted.

Graduate School of Education and Information Studies *Degree program information:* Part-time programs available. Offers archival studies (MLIS); education (M Ed, MA, Ed D, PhD); education and information studies (M Ed, MA, MLIS, Ed D, PhD, Certificate); informatics (MLIS); information studies (PhD); library and information science (Certificate); library studies (MLIS); special education (PhD). Electronic applications accepted.

Henry Samueli School of Engineering and Applied Science Students: 1,295 full-time (263 women); includes 393 minority (9 African Americans, 2 American Indian/Alaska Native, 343 Asian Americans or Pacific Islanders, 39 Hispanic Americans), 516 international. 2,913 applicants, 36% accepted, 404 enrolled. *Faculty:* 152 full-time (14 women). Expenses: Contact institution. *Financial support:* In 2006–07, 594 fellowships, 1,667 research assistantships, 465 teaching assistantships were awarded; career-related internships or fieldwork, Federal Work-Study, institutionally sponsored loans, and tuition waivers (full and partial) also available. Financial award applicants required to submit FAFSA. In 2006, 301 master's, 142 doctorates awarded. Offers aerospace engineering (MS, PhD); biomedical engineering (MS, PhD); ceramics engineering (MS, PhD); chemical and biomolecular engineering (MS, PhD); computer science (MS, PhD); electrical engineering (MS, PhD); engineering and applied science (MS, PhD); engineering optimization/operations research (MS, PhD); environmental engineering (MS, PhD); geotechnical engineering (MS, PhD); hydrology and water resources engineering (MS); manufacturing engineering (MS); mechanical engineering (MS, PhD); metallurgy (MS, PhD); structures (MS, PhD); water resource systems engineering (PhD). *Application fee:* $60 ($80 for international students). Electronic applications accepted. *Application Contact:* Jan Labuda, Student Affairs Officer, 310-825-2514, Fax: 301-825-2473, E-mail: jan@ea.ucla.edu. *Associate Dean, Academic and Student Affairs,* Dr. Stephen E. Jacobsen, 310-825-1704.

School of Nursing Offers nursing (MSN, PhD). Electronic applications accepted.

School of Public Health Offers biostatistics (MS, PhD); environmental health sciences (MS, PhD); environmental science and engineering (D Env); epidemiology (MS, PhD); health services (MS, PhD); molecular toxicology (PhD); public health (MS, PhD); public health for health professionals (MPH). Electronic applications accepted.

School of Public Policy and Social Research Offers public policy (MPP); public policy and social research (MA, MPP, MSW, PhD); social welfare (MSW, PhD); urban planning (MA, PhD). Electronic applications accepted.

School of the Arts and Architecture Offers architecture and urban design (M Arch, MA, PhD); art (MA, MFA); arts and architecture (M Arch, MA, MFA, MM, DMA, PhD); composition (MA, PhD); culture and performance (MA, PhD); dance (MA, MFA); design/media arts (MFA); ethnomusicology (MA, PhD); performance (MM, DMA). Electronic applications accepted.

School of Theater, Film and Television Offers film and television (MA, MFA, PhD); film, television, and digital media (MA, MFA, PhD); theater (MFA, PhD). Electronic applications accepted.

UCLA Anderson School of Management Students: 686 full-time (208 women), 646 part-time (181 women); includes 355 minority (17 African Americans, 302 Asian Americans or Pacific Islanders, 36 Hispanic Americans), 108 international. Average age 28. 3,227 applicants, 32% accepted, 608 enrolled. Expenses: Contact institution. *Financial support:* In 2006–07, 120 fellowships, 23 research assistantships, 25 teaching assistantships were awarded; career-related internships or fieldwork, Federal Work-Study, institutionally sponsored loans, scholarships/grants, and tuition waivers (full and partial) also available. Financial award application deadline: 3/1. In 2006, 607 degrees awarded. *Degree program information:* Part-time programs available. Offers management (MBA, MS, PhD). *Application deadline:* Applications are processed on a rolling basis. *Application fee:* $175. *Application Contact:* Linda Baldwin, Director of Admissions, 310-825-6944, E-mail: mba.admissions@anderson.ucla.edu. *Dean,* Judy D. Olian, 310-825-7982, Fax: 310-206-2073.

School of Dentistry Offers dentistry (DDS, MS, PhD, Certificate); oral biology (MS, PhD).

School of Law Offers law (JD, LL M).

School of Medicine Offers medicine (MD, MA, MS, PhD).

Graduate Programs in Medicine Offers anatomy and cell biology (PhD); biological chemistry (MS, PhD); biomathematics (MS, PhD); biomedical physics (MS, PhD); clinical research (MS); experimental pathology (MS, PhD); human genetics (MS, PhD); medicine (MA, MS, PhD); microbiology, immunology and molecular genetics (MS, PhD); molecular and medical pharmacology (PhD); molecular, cell and developmental biology (MA, PhD); neuroscience (PhD); physiology (MS, PhD).

UNIVERSITY OF CALIFORNIA, RIVERSIDE, Riverside, CA 92521-0102

General Information State-supported, coed, university. CGS member. *Enrollment:* 16,875 graduate, professional, and undergraduate students; 1,944 full-time matriculated graduate/professional students (934 women), 21 part-time matriculated graduate/professional students (8 women). *Enrollment by degree level:* 480 master's, 1,485 doctoral. *Graduate faculty:* 635 full-time (184 women). *Graduate housing:* Rooms and/or apartments available on a first-come, first-served basis to single and married students. Typical cost: $700 per year for single students; $525 per year for married students. Housing application deadline: 6/1. *Student services:* Campus safety program, career counseling, child daycare facilities, disabled student services, exercise/wellness program, free psychological counseling, international student services, low-cost health insurance, multicultural affairs office, teacher training, writing training. *Library facilities:* Tomas Rivera Library plus 6 others. *Online resources:* library catalog, web page, access to other libraries' catalogs. *Collection:* 2.4 million titles, 29,941 serial subscriptions, 27,313 audiovisual materials. *Research affiliation:* Lawrence Livermore National Laboratory (archaeology), J. Paul Getty Museum (art history), U.S. Salinity Laboratory (environmental sciences, biochemistry), Brookhaven National Lab (chemistry, physics), Los Alamos National Laboratory (botany and plant sciences, chemistry, earth sciences, physics), Fermi National Accelerator Laboratory (physics).

Computer facilities: Computer purchase and lease plans are available. 793 computers available on campus for general student use. A campuswide network can be accessed from student residence rooms and from off campus. Internet access and online class registration, online viewing of grades, enrollment data and financial information are available. *Web address:* http://www.ucr.edu/.

General Application Contact: Graduate Admissions, 951-827-3313, Fax: 951-827-2238, E-mail: grdadmis@ucr.edu.

GRADUATE UNITS

Graduate Division Students: 1,944 full-time (934 women), 21 part-time (8 women); includes 417 minority (28 African Americans, 12 American Indian/Alaska Native, 200 Asian Americans or Pacific Islanders, 177 Hispanic Americans), 573 international. Average age 30. *Faculty:* 635 full-time (184 women). Expenses: Contact institution. *Financial support:* In 2006–07, fellowships with full and partial tuition reimbursements (averaging $12,000 per year), research assistantships with full and partial tuition reimbursements (averaging $18,081 per year), teaching assistantships with full and partial tuition reimbursements (averaging $15,610 per year) were awarded; career-related internships or fieldwork, Federal Work-Study, institutionally sponsored loans, scholarships/grants, tuition waivers (full and partial), and readerships also available. Financial award applicants required to submit FAFSA. In 2006, 349 master's, 189 doctorates awarded. *Degree program information:* Part-time and evening/weekend programs available. Offers anthropology (MA, MS, PhD); applied statistics (PhD); archival management (MA); art history (MA); biochemistry and molecular biology (MS, PhD); bioengineering (MS, PhD); biology (MS, PhD); biomedical sciences (PhD); cell, molecular, and developmental biology (MS, PhD); chemical and environmental engineering (MS, PhD); chemistry (MS, PhD); classics (PhD); comparative literature (MA, PhD); computer science (MS, PhD); creative writing (MFA); dance (MFA); dance history and theory (MA, PhD); economics (MA, PhD); electrical engineering (MS, PhD); English (MA, PhD); entomology (MS, PhD); environmental sciences (MS, PhD); environmental toxicology (MS, PhD); evolution, ecology and organismal biology (MS, PhD); genomics and bioinformatics (PhD); geological sciences (MS, PhD); historic preservation (MA); history (MA, PhD); mathematics (MA, MS, PhD); mechanical engineering (MS, PhD); microbiology (MS, PhD); molecular genetics (PhD); museum curatorship (MA); music (MA); neuroscience (PhD); philosophy (MA, PhD); physics and astronomy (MS, PhD); plant biology (MS, PhD); plant biology (plant genetics) (PhD); plant pathology (MS, PhD); political science (MA, PhD); population and evolutionary genetics (PhD); psychology (MA, PhD); sociology (MA, PhD); soil and water sciences (MS, PhD); Spanish (MA, PhD); statistics (MS); visual arts (MFA); writing for the performing arts (MFA). *Application deadline:* For fall admission, 5/1 for domestic students, 2/1 for international students; for winter admission, 2/1 for domestic students, 7/1 for international students; for spring admission, 12/1 for domestic students, 10/1 for international students. Applications are processed on a rolling basis. *Application fee:* $60 ($75 for international students). Electronic applications accepted. *Application Contact:* Graduate Admissions, 951-827-3313, Fax: 951-827-2238, E-mail: grdadmis@ucr.edu. *Dean,* Dr. Dallas Rabenstein, 951-827-3313, Fax: 951-827-2238.

A. Gary Anderson Graduate School of Management Students: 104 full-time (51 women), 11 part-time (5 women); includes 22 minority (18 Asian Americans or Pacific Islanders, 4 Hispanic Americans), 67 international. Average age 26. *Faculty:* 21 full-time (4 women). Expenses: Contact institution. *Financial support:* In 2006–07, teaching assistantships (averaging $15,610 per year); fellowships, research assistantships, career-related internships or fieldwork, Federal Work-Study, institutionally sponsored loans, scholarships/grants, and tuition waivers (full) also available. Financial award application deadline: 2/1; financial award applicants required to submit FAFSA. In 2006, 39 degrees awarded. *Degree program information:* Part-time and evening/weekend programs available. Offers management (MBA). *Application deadline:* For fall admission, 5/1 for domestic students, 2/1 for international students; for winter admission, 9/1 for domestic students, 7/1 for international students; for spring admission, 12/1 for domestic students, 10/1 for international students. Applications are processed on a rolling basis. *Application fee:* $60 ($75 for international students). *Application Contact:* Charlotte Weber, Assistant Dean, 951-827-4551, Fax: 951-827-3970, E-mail: mba@agsmmail.ucr.edu. *Interim Dean,* Dr. Anil Deolalikar, 951-827-1575, Fax: 951-827-5685, E-mail: econgrad@ucr.edu.

Graduate School of Education Students: 229 full-time (168 women), 2 part-time (1 woman); includes 65 minority (9 African Americans, 3 American Indian/Alaska Native, 25 Asian Americans or Pacific Islanders, 28 Hispanic Americans), 7 international. Average age 32. 214 applicants, 61% accepted, 111 enrolled. *Faculty:* 19 full-time (9 women), 36 part-time/adjunct (27 women). Expenses: Contact institution. *Financial support:* In 2006–07, 25 fellowships with full and partial tuition reimbursements, 39 research assistantships with full and partial tuition reimbursements (averaging $10,630 per year), 4 teaching assistantships with full and partial tuition reimbursements (averaging $8,952 per year) were awarded;

career-related internships or fieldwork, Federal Work-Study, institutionally sponsored loans, and tuition waivers (full and partial) also available. Financial award application deadline: 2/15; financial award applicants required to submit FAFSA. In 2006, 84 master's, 6 doctorates awarded. Offers education (M Ed, MA, PhD). *Application deadline:* For fall admission, 5/1 for domestic students, 2/1 for international students; for winter admission, 9/1 for domestic students, 7/1 for international students; for spring admission, 12/1 for domestic students, 10/1 for international students. Applications are processed on a rolling basis. *Application fee:* $60 ($75 for international students). Electronic applications accepted. *Application Contact:* Dr. Judith Sandholtz, Graduate Adviser, 951-827-6362, Fax: 951-827-3942, E-mail: edgrad@ucr.edu. *Dean,* Dr. Steven T. Bossert, 951-827-5802, Fax: 951-827-3942, E-mail: steven.bossert@ucr.edu.

UNIVERSITY OF CALIFORNIA, SAN DIEGO, La Jolla, CA 92093

General Information State-supported, coed, university. CGS member. *Graduate housing:* Rooms and/or apartments available to single and married students. *Research affiliation:* Salk Institute, Veterans Administration Medical Center, Scripps Clinic and Research Foundation, La Jolla Institute.

GRADUATE UNITS

Office of Graduate Studies Students: 3,927 (1,641 women); includes 787 minority (49 African Americans, 12 American Indian/Alaska Native, 506 Asian Americans or Pacific Islanders, 220 Hispanic Americans) 841 international. 11,320 applicants, 24% accepted, 1104 enrolled. *Faculty:* 1,429. Expenses: Contact institution. *Financial support:* Fellowships with full and partial tuition reimbursements, research assistantships with full and partial tuition reimbursements, teaching assistantships with partial tuition reimbursements, career-related internships or fieldwork, institutionally sponsored loans, scholarships/grants, and traineeships available. Support available to part-time students. Financial award applicants required to submit CSS PROFILE or FAFSA. In 2006, 765 master's, 325 doctorates awarded. Offers acting (MFA); aerospace engineering (MS, PhD); anthropology (PhD); applied mathematics (MA); applied mechanics (MS, PhD); applied ocean science (MS, PhD); applied physics (MS, PhD); bilingual education (MA); bioengineering (M Eng, MS, PhD); bioinformatics (PhD); biophysics (MS, PhD); chemical engineering (MS, PhD); chemistry (MS, PhD); clinical psychology (PhD); cognitive science (PhD); cognitive science/anthropology (PhD); cognitive science/communication (PhD); cognitive science/computer science and engineering (PhD); cognitive science/linguistics (PhD); cognitive science/neuroscience (PhD); cognitive science/philosophy (PhD); cognitive science/psychology (PhD); cognitive science/sociology (PhD); communication (MA, PhD); communication theory and systems (MS, PhD); comparative literature (MA, PhD); computer engineering (MS, PhD); computer science (MS, PhD); curriculum design (MA); design (MFA); directing (MFA); drama and theatre (PhD); earth sciences (PhD); economics (PhD); economics and international affairs (PhD); electrical engineering (M Eng); electronic circuits and systems (MS, PhD); engineering physics (MS, PhD); ethnic studies (MA, PhD); French literature (MA); German literature (MA); history (MA, PhD); intelligent systems, robotics and control (MS, PhD); Judaic studies (MA); language and communicative disorders (PhD); Latin American studies (MA); linguistics (PhD); literature (PhD); literatures in English (MA); marine biodiversity and conservation (MAS); marine biology (PhD); materials science and engineering (MS, PhD); mathematics (MA, PhD); mathematics and science education (PhD); mechanical engineering (MS, PhD); music (MA, DMA, PhD); oceanography (PhD); philosophy (PhD); photonics (MS, PhD); physics (MS, PhD); physics/materials physics (MS); playwriting (MFA); political science (PhD); political science and international affairs (PhD); psychology (PhD); public health and epidemiology (PhD); science studies (PhD); signal and image processing (MS, PhD); sociology (PhD); Spanish literature (MA); stage management (MFA); statistics (MS); structural engineering (MS, PhD); teacher education (M Ed); teaching and learning (Ed D); theatre (PhD); visual arts (MFA, PhD). *Application fee:* $60 ($80 for international students). Electronic applications accepted. *Application Contact:* 858-534-1193. *Dean,* Richard Attiyeh, 858-534-3555.

Division of Biological Sciences Offers biochemistry (PhD); biology (MS); cell and developmental biology (PhD); computational neurobiology (PhD); ecology, behavior, and evolution (PhD); genetics and molecular biology (PhD); immunology, virology, and cancer biology (PhD); molecular and cellular biology (PhD); neurobiology (PhD); plant molecular biology (PhD); plant systems biology (PhD); signal transduction (PhD). Offered in association with the Salk Institute. Electronic applications accepted.

Graduate School of International Relations and Pacific Studies Offers economics and international affairs (PhD); Pacific international affairs (MPIA); political science and international affairs (PhD). Electronic applications accepted.

Rady School of Management Offers business administration and management (MBA).

School of Medicine Offers audiology (Au D); bioinformatics (PhD); cancer biology/oncology (PhD); cardiovascular sciences and disease (PhD); clinical research (MAS); leadership in healthcare organizations (MAS); medicine (MD, MAS, Au D, PhD); microbiology (PhD); molecular pathology (PhD); neurological disease (PhD); neurosciences (PhD); stem cell and developmental biology (PhD); structural biology/drug design (PhD).

Graduate Studies in Biomedical Sciences Offers molecular cell biology (PhD); pharmacology (PhD); physiology (PhD); regulatory biology (PhD). Electronic applications accepted.

School of Pharmacy and Pharmaceutical Sciences Offers pharmacy and pharmaceutical sciences (Pharm D).

UNIVERSITY OF CALIFORNIA, SAN FRANCISCO, San Francisco, CA 94143

General Information State-supported, coed, graduate-only institution. CGS member. *Enrollment by degree level:* 1,454 first professional, 516 master's, 917 doctoral, 65 other advanced degrees. *Graduate faculty:* 1,800. *Graduate housing:* Rooms and/or apartments available to single and married students. *Student services:* Campus employment opportunities, campus safety program, child daycare facilities, free psychological counseling, international student services, low-cost health insurance. *Library facilities:* Kalmanovitz Library and Center plus 1 other. *Collection:* 831,922 titles, 6,359 serial subscriptions. *Web address:* http://www.ucsf.edu/.

General Application Contact: Richard Wyllie, Admissions Coordinator, 415-476-2111, Fax: 415-476-9690, E-mail: rick.wyllie@ucsf.edu.

GRADUATE UNITS

Graduate Division Students: 1,461 full-time (981 women), 10 part-time (8 women); includes 431 minority (48 African Americans, 9 American Indian/Alaska Native, 284 Asian Americans or Pacific Islanders, 90 Hispanic Americans), 67 international. 2,349 applicants, 23% accepted. *Faculty:* 400. Expenses: Contact institution. *Financial support:* Fellowships, research assistantships, teaching assistantships, career-related internships or fieldwork, Federal Work-Study, institutionally sponsored loans, and tuition waivers (full and partial) available. Support available to part-time students. Financial award applicants required to submit FAFSA. In 2006, 208 master's, 120 doctorates awarded. *Degree program information:* Part-time programs available. Offers anatomy (PhD); biochemistry and molecular biology (PhD); bioengineering (PhD); cell biology (PhD); developmental biology (PhD); endocrinology (PhD); experimental pathology (PhD); genetics (PhD); history of health sciences (MA, PhD); medical anthropology (PhD); microbiology and immunology (PhD); neuroscience (PhD); oral and craniofacial sciences (MS, PhD); physical therapy (MS, DPT, DPTSc); physiology (PhD). *Application fee:* $60 ($80 for international students). *Dean of Graduate Studies,* Dr. Patricia Calarco, 415-476-2310.

School of Nursing Students: 627 full-time (555 women), 10 part-time (8 women); includes 172 minority (28 African Americans, 5 American Indian/Alaska Native, 93 Asian Americans or Pacific Islanders, 46 Hispanic Americans), 21 international. *Faculty:* 129 full-time (112 women). Expenses: Contact institution. *Financial support:* Fellowships, career-related internships or fieldwork and Federal Work-Study available. Support available to part-time students. Offers nursing (MS, PhD); sociology (PhD). *Application deadline:* For fall admission, 3/1 for domestic students. *Application fee:* $40. *Application Contact:* Jeff Kilmer, Director, Office of Student and Curriculum Services, 415-476-0600, E-mail: jeff.kilmer@nursing.ucsf.edu. *Associate Dean,* Dorrie Fontaine, 415-476-9710, E-mail: dorrie.fontaine@nursing.ucsf.edu.

School of Dentistry Offers dentistry (DDS).

School of Medicine Offers medicine (MD). Electronic applications accepted.

School of Pharmacy Students: 675 full-time (429 women); includes 340 minority (16 African Americans, 4 American Indian/Alaska Native, 287 Asian Americans or Pacific Islanders, 33 Hispanic Americans), 4 international. Average age 26. 1,626 applicants, 11% accepted. *Faculty:* 82 full-time (36 women). Expenses: Contact institution. *Financial support:* In 2006–07, 434 students received support; fellowships, research assistantships, teaching assistantships, career-related internships or fieldwork, Federal Work-Study, institutionally sponsored loans, scholarships/grants, traineeships, and tuition waivers (full) available. Financial award applicants required to submit FAFSA. In 2006, 122 Pharm Ds, 1 master's, 26 doctorates awarded. Offers biological and medical informatics (MS, PhD); biophysics (PhD); chemistry and chemical biology (PhD); pharmaceutical sciences and pharmacogenomics (PhD); pharmacy (Pharm D, MS, PhD). *Application fee:* $60. *Application Contact:* Cynthia Watchmaker, Assistant Dean and Director Student Affairs, 415-476-2732, Fax: 415-476-6805, E-mail: osaca@pharmacy.ucsf.edu. *Dean,* Mary Anne Koda Kimble, 415-476-8010, Fax: 415-476-0688.

UNIVERSITY OF CALIFORNIA, SANTA BARBARA, Santa Barbara, CA 93106

General Information State-supported, coed, university. CGS member. *Enrollment:* 21,062 graduate, professional, and undergraduate students; 2,870 full-time matriculated graduate/professional students (1,265 women). *Graduate faculty:* 684 full-time, 165 part-time/adjunct. *Graduate housing:* Rooms and/or apartments available to single and married students. *Student services:* Campus employment opportunities, campus safety program, career counseling, child daycare facilities, disabled student services, exercise/wellness program, free psychological counseling, grant writing training, international student services, low-cost health insurance, multicultural affairs office, teacher training, writing training. *Library facilities:* Davidson Library. *Online resources:* library catalog, web page, access to other libraries' catalogs. *Collection:* 3.3 million titles, 36,902 serial subscriptions, 125,324 audiovisual materials. *Research affiliation:* National Institute for Theoretical Physics, Center for Black Studies (ethnic studies), Jorge de Sena Center for Portuguese Studies, Center for Quantum Electronic Structures (engineering), David Simonett Center for Spatial Analysis, Center for Theater, Education and Research.

Computer facilities: 3,000 computers available on campus for general student use. A campuswide network can be accessed from off campus. *Web address:* http://www.ucsb.edu/.

General Application Contact: Rebecca Letts, Graduate Admissions Coordinator, 805-893-2278, Fax: 805-893-8259, E-mail: rebecca.letts@graddiv.ucsb.edu.

GRADUATE UNITS

Graduate Division Students: 2,870 full-time (1,265 women); includes 450 minority (38 African Americans, 10 American Indian/Alaska Native, 218 Asian Americans or Pacific Islanders, 184 Hispanic Americans), 512 international. Average age 29. 6,714 applicants, 30% accepted, 750 enrolled. Expenses: Contact institution. *Financial support:* In 2006–07, 1,074 fellowships with full and partial tuition reimbursements (averaging $8,600 per year), 1,116 research assistantships with full and partial tuition reimbursements (averaging $11,400 per year), 1,566 teaching assistantships with full and partial tuition reimbursements (averaging $8,500 per year) were awarded; career-related internships or fieldwork, Federal Work-Study, institutionally sponsored loans, scholarships/grants, traineeships, health care benefits, tuition waivers (full and partial), and unspecified assistantships also available. Support available to part-time students. Financial award applicants required to submit FAFSA. In 2006, 617 master's, 340 doctorates awarded. *Application deadline:* For fall admission, 5/1 for domestic and international students. *Application fee:* $60. Electronic applications accepted. *Application Contact:* Rebecca Letts, Graduate Admissions Coordinator, 805-893-2278, Fax: 805-893-8259, E-mail: rebecca.letts@graddiv.ucsb.edu. *Acting Dean,* Dr. Gale Morrison, 805-893-2013, E-mail: gale.morrison@graddiv.ucsb.edu.

College of Engineering Students: 615 full-time (133 women). Expenses: Contact institution. *Financial support:* Fellowships, research assistantships, teaching assistantships, career-related internships or fieldwork, Federal Work-Study, institutionally sponsored loans, and tuition waivers (full and partial) available. Financial award applicants required to submit FAFSA. Offers chemical engineering (MS, PhD); computer science (MS, PhD); electrical and computer engineering (MS, PhD); engineering (MS, PhD); materials science and engineering (MS, PhD); mechanical engineering (MS, PhD). *Application fee:* $60. Electronic applications accepted. *Application Contact:* 805-893-3207, E-mail: engrdean@engineering.ucsb.edu. *Dean,* Matthew Tirrell, 805-893-3141.

College of Letters and Sciences Expenses: Contact institution. *Financial support:* Fellowships, research assistantships, teaching assistantships, career-related internships or fieldwork, Federal Work-Study, institutionally sponsored loans, and tuition waivers (full and partial) available. Support available to part-time students. Financial award applicants required to submit FAFSA. Offers applied mathematics (MA); applied statistics (MA); archaeology (MA, PhD); art studio (MFA); biochemistry and molecular biology (MS, PhD); biomolecular science and engineering (PhD); biophysics and bioengineering (MS, PhD); biosocial anthropology (PhD); brass (MM); chemistry (MA, MS, PhD); Chicana and Chicano studies (PhD); choral conducting (MM, DMA); classics (MA, PhD); communication (PhD); comparative literature (PhD); composition (MA, PhD); East Asian languages (PhD); East Asian literatures (PhD); ecology, evolution, and marine biology (MA, PhD); economics (MA, PhD); electronic music and sound design (MA, PhD); English literature (PhD); ethnomusicology (MA, PhD); film and media studies); French (MA, PhD); geography (MA, PhD); geological sciences (MS, PhD); geophysics (MS); Germanic languages and literature (MA, PhD); global and international studies (MA); Hispanic languages and literature (PhD); history (PhD); history of art and architecture (PhD); humanities and fine arts (MA, MFA, MM, MS, DMA, PhD); keyboard (MM, DMA); Latin American and Iberian studies (MA); letters and sciences (MA, MFA, MM, MS, DMA, PhD); linguistics (MA, PhD); marine science (MS, PhD); mathematical and empirical finance (PhD); mathematical statistics (MA); mathematics (MA, PhD); mathematics, life, and physical sciences (MA, MS, PhD); molecular, cellular, and developmental biology (MA, PhD); multimedia engineering (MS, PhD); musicology (MA, PhD); philosophy (PhD); physics (MA, PhD); political science (MA, PhD); Portuguese (MA); psychology (PhD); public history (PhD); quantitative methods in the social sciences (PhD); religious studies (MA, PhD); social sciences (MA, PhD); sociocultural anthropology (PhD); sociology (PhD); Spanish (MA); statistics and applied probability (PhD); strings (MM, DMA); theater (MA, PhD); theory (MA, PhD); visual and spatial arts (MA, PhD); voice (MM, DMA); women's studies (PhD); woodwinds (MM). *Application fee:* $60. Electronic applications accepted. *Executive Dean,* David Marshall, 805-893-4327, E-mail: dmarshall@ltsc.ucsb.edu.

Donald Bren School of Environmental Science and Management Students: 164 full-time (100 women); includes 22 minority (1 African American, 1 American Indian/Alaska Native, 17 Asian Americans or Pacific Islanders, 3 Hispanic Americans), 10 international. Average age 25. 270 applicants, 70% accepted, 71 enrolled. *Faculty:* 18 full-time (4 women), 4 part-time/adjunct (0 women). Expenses: Contact institution. *Financial support:* In 2006–07, 91 students received support, including 35 fellowships with full and partial tuition reimbursements available (averaging $8,100 per year), 14 research assistantships with full tuition reimbursements available (averaging $11,140 per year), 18 teaching assistantships with partial tuition reimbursements available (averaging $4,531 per year); career-related internships or fieldwork, Federal Work-Study, institutionally sponsored loans, scholarships/grants, traineeships, health care benefits, and unspecified assistantships also available. Support available to part-time students. Financial award application deadline: 2/1; financial award applicants required to submit FAFSA. In 2006, 64 master's, 5 doctorates awarded. Offers economics and environmental science (PhD); environmental science and management (MESM, PhD). *Application deadline:* For fall admission, 1/10 for domestic and international students. *Application fee:* $60. Electronic applications accepted. *Application Contact:* Chelsea Houdyshell, Graduate Advisor, 805-893-7611, Fax: 805-893-7612, E-mail:

University of California, Santa Barbara (continued)

chelsea@bren.ucsb.edu. *Dean,* Dr. Ernst Von Weizsacker, 805-893-7577, E-mail: ernst@bren.ucsb.edu.

Gevirtz Graduate School of Education Students: 375 full-time (285 women); includes 111 minority (13 African Americans, 2 American Indian/Alaska Native, 33 Asian Americans or Pacific Islanders, 63 Hispanic Americans), 14 international. Average age 29. 777 applicants, 36% accepted, 154 enrolled. *Faculty:* 39 full-time (18 women). Expenses: Contact institution. *Financial support:* In 2006–07, 181 fellowships with full and partial tuition reimbursements (averaging $4,200 per year), 64 research assistantships with full and partial tuition reimbursements (averaging $6,200 per year), 75 teaching assistantships with partial tuition reimbursements (averaging $7,500 per year) were awarded; career-related internships or fieldwork, Federal Work-Study, institutionally sponsored loans, scholarships/grants, traineeships, health care benefits, and unspecified assistantships also available. Support available to part-time students. Financial award application deadline: 12/15; financial award applicants required to submit FAFSA. In 2006, 151 master's, 31 doctorates awarded. Postbaccalaureate distance learning degree programs offered (minimal on-campus study). Offers counseling, clinical and school psychology (PhD); education (M Ed, MA, PhD); educational leadership (Ed D). *Application deadline:* For fall admission, 12/15 for domestic and international students. *Application fee:* $60. Electronic applications accepted. *Application Contact:* Student Affairs Office, 805-893-2137, E-mail: sao@education.ucsb.edu. *Chair,* Dr. Jane Conoley, 805-893-3917, E-mail: jane_conoley@education.ucsb.edu.

UNIVERSITY OF CALIFORNIA, SANTA CRUZ, Santa Cruz, CA 95064

General Information State-supported, coed, university. CGS member. *Graduate housing:* Rooms and/or apartments available to single and married students. *Research affiliation:* Stanford Linear Accelerator Center, Fermi National Accelerator Laboratory, Lawrence Livermore National Laboratory, Scripps Institute of Oceanography (earth sciences), University of Texas Marine Science Institute (earth sciences).

GRADUATE UNITS

Division of Graduate Studies Electronic applications accepted.

Division of Arts Offers arts (MA, MFA, DMA, Certificate); digital arts/new media (MFA); music (MA, DMA); theater arts (Certificate). Electronic applications accepted.

Division of Humanities Offers history (MA, PhD); history of consciousness (PhD); humanities (MA, PhD); linguistics (MA, PhD); literature (MA, PhD); philosophy (MA, PhD). Electronic applications accepted.

Division of Physical and Biological Sciences Offers astronomy and astrophysics (PhD); chemistry and biochemistry (MS, PhD); earth sciences (MS, PhD); ecology and evolutionary biology (MA, PhD); environmental toxicology (MS, PhD); mathematics (MA, PhD); molecular, cellular, and developmental biology (MA, PhD); ocean sciences (MS, PhD); physical and biological sciences (MA, MS, PhD, Certificate); physics (MS, PhD); science communication (Certificate).

Division of Social Sciences Offers anthropology (PhD); applied economics (MS); education (MA, Ed D, PhD); environmental studies (PhD); international economics (PhD); politics (PhD); psychology (PhD); social documentation (MA); social sciences (MA, MS, Ed D, PhD); sociology (PhD).

Jack Baskin School of Engineering Offers bioinformatics (MS, PhD); computer engineering (MS, PhD); computer science (MS, PhD); electrical engineering (MS, PhD); engineering (MS, PhD); network engineering (MS); statistics and stochastic modeling (MS).

UNIVERSITY OF CENTRAL ARKANSAS, Conway, AR 72035-0001

General Information State-supported, coed, comprehensive institution. CGS member. *Enrollment:* 12,330 graduate, professional, and undergraduate students; 585 full-time matriculated graduate/professional students (415 women), 980 part-time matriculated graduate/professional students (782 women). *Enrollment by degree level:* 1,463 master's, 101 doctoral, 1 other advanced degree. *Graduate faculty:* 228 full-time (83 women), 11 part-time/adjunct (5 women). *International tuition:* $6,162 full-time. Tuition, state resident: full-time $4,194; part-time $233 per semester. Tuition, nonresident: full-time $5,963; part-time $429 per semester. *Required fees:* $65; $23 per semester. One-time fee: $65 part-time. *Graduate housing:* Rooms and/or apartments available on a first-come, first-served basis to single and married students. Typical cost: $2,460 per year ($4,320 including board) for single students; $2,460 per year ($4,320 including board) for married students. Room and board charges vary according to board plan, campus/location and housing facility selected. Housing application deadline: 7/1. *Student services:* Campus employment opportunities, campus safety program, career counseling, disabled student services, exercise/wellness program, free psychological counseling, grant writing training, international student services, low-cost health insurance, multicultural affairs office, teacher training, writing training. *Library facilities:* Torreyson Library. *Online resources:* library catalog, web page, access to other libraries' catalogs. *Collection:* 505,000 titles, 2,000 serial subscriptions. *Research affiliation:* 3M Corporation, State Farm Foundation (insurance), Arkansas Game and Fish, Acxiom (math/computers), AETN.

Computer facilities: Computer purchase and lease plans are available. 1,500 computers available on campus for general student use. A campuswide network can be accessed from student residence rooms and from off campus. Internet access and online class registration are available. *Web address:* http://www.uca.edu/.

General Application Contact: Brenda Herring, Admissions Assistant, 501-450-5065, Fax: 501-450-5678, E-mail: bherring@uca.edu.

GRADUATE UNITS

Graduate School Students: 585 full-time (415 women), 980 part-time (782 women); includes 174 minority (134 African Americans, 8 American Indian/Alaska Native, 21 Asian Americans or Pacific Islanders, 11 Hispanic Americans), 46 international. Average age 31. 595 applicants, 97% accepted, 580 enrolled. *Faculty:* 228 full-time (83 women), 11 part-time/adjunct (5 women). Expenses: Contact institution. *Financial support:* In 2006–07, 48 research assistantships with partial tuition reimbursements (averaging $6,000 per year), 34 teaching assistantships with partial tuition reimbursements (averaging $9,000 per year) were awarded; career-related internships or fieldwork, Federal Work-Study, scholarships/grants, traineeships, tuition waivers (partial), and unspecified assistantships also available. Support available to part-time students. Financial award application deadline: 2/15; financial award applicants required to submit FAFSA. In 2006, 314 master's, 29 doctorates awarded. *Degree program information:* Part-time programs available. *Application deadline:* For fall admission, 3/1 priority date for domestic and international students; for spring admission, 10/1 priority date for domestic and international students. Applications are processed on a rolling basis. *Application fee:* $25 ($40 for international students). *Application Contact:* Brenda Herring, Admissions Assistant, 501-450-5065, Fax: 501-450-5678, E-mail: bherring@uca.edu. *Dean,* Dr. Elaine M. McNiece, 501-450-3124, Fax: 501-450-5678, E-mail: elainem@uca.edu.

College of Business Administration Students: 51 full-time (27 women), 45 part-time (21 women); includes 6 minority (2 African Americans, 1 American Indian/Alaska Native, 2 Asian Americans or Pacific Islanders, 1 Hispanic American), 15 international. 55 applicants, 98% accepted, 54 enrolled. *Faculty:* 19 full-time (6 women). Expenses: Contact institution. *Financial support:* In 2006–07, 8 research assistantships with partial tuition reimbursements (averaging $4,000 per year) were awarded; career-related internships or fieldwork, Federal Work-Study, scholarships/grants, and unspecified assistantships also available. Support available to part-time students. Financial award application deadline: 2/15; financial award applicants required to submit FAFSA. In 2006, 56 degrees awarded. *Degree program information:* Part-time and evening/weekend programs available. Offers accounting (M Acc); business administration (M Acc, MBA). *Application deadline:* For fall admission, 3/1 priority date for domestic and international students; for spring admission, 10/1 priority date for domestic and international students. Applications are processed on a rolling basis. *Application fee:* $25 ($40 for international students). *Application Contact:* Brenda Herring, Admissions Assistant, 501-450-5065, Fax: 501-450-5678, E-mail: bherring@uca.edu. *Dean,* Dr. Pat Cantrell, 501-450-5323, E-mail: patc@uca.edu.

College of Education Students: 38 full-time (29 women), 470 part-time (422 women); includes 58 minority (42 African Americans, 1 American Indian/Alaska Native, 11 Asian Americans or Pacific Islanders, 4 Hispanic Americans), 1 international. 195 applicants, 99% accepted, 194 enrolled. *Faculty:* 23 full-time (13 women), 1 (woman) part-time/adjunct. Expenses: Contact institution. *Financial support:* Career-related internships or fieldwork, Federal Work-Study, scholarships/grants, tuition waivers (partial), and unspecified assistantships available. Financial award application deadline: 2/15; financial award applicants required to submit FAFSA. In 2006, 54 degrees awarded. *Degree program information:* Part-time programs available. Offers collaborative instructional specialist (ages 0–8) (MSE); collaborative instructional specialist (grades 4–12) (MSE); early childhood education (MSE); education (MAT, MS, MSE); education media and library science (MS); reading education (MSE); special education (MSE); teaching (MAT); teaching and learning (MSE); training systems (MSE). *Application deadline:* For fall admission, 3/1 priority date for domestic and international students; for spring admission, 10/1 priority date for domestic and international students. Applications are processed on a rolling basis. *Application fee:* $25 ($40 for international students). *Application Contact:* Brenda Herring, Admissions Assistant, 501-450-5065, Fax: 501-450-5678, E-mail: bherring@uca.edu. *Dean,* Dr. Larry Robinson, 501-450-5401, Fax: 501-450-5424, E-mail: lrobinson@uca.edu.

College of Fine Arts and Communication Students: 22 full-time (7 women), 4 part-time; includes 2 minority (both African Americans), 1 international. 16 applicants, 100% accepted, 16 enrolled. *Faculty:* 18 full-time (5 women), 1 part-time/adjunct (0 women). Expenses: Contact institution. *Financial support:* Federal Work-Study, scholarships/grants, tuition waivers (partial), and unspecified assistantships available. Financial award application deadline: 2/15; financial award applicants required to submit FAFSA. In 2006, 5 degrees awarded. *Degree program information:* Part-time programs available. Offers choral conducting (MM); filmmaking (MFA); fine arts and communication (MFA, MM); instrumental conducting (MM); music education (MM); music theory (MM); performance (MM). *Application deadline:* For fall admission, 3/1 priority date for domestic students; for spring admission, 10/1 priority date for domestic students. Applications are processed on a rolling basis. *Application fee:* $25 ($40 for international students). *Application Contact:* Brenda Herring, Admissions Assistant, 501-450-5065, Fax: 501-450-5678, E-mail: bherring@uca.edu. *Dean,* Dr. Rollin Potter, 501-450-3167, Fax: 501-450-3296, E-mail: rpotter@uca.edu.

College of Health and Behavioral Sciences Students: 364 full-time (294 women), 227 part-time (193 women); includes 62 minority (47 African Americans, 5 American Indian/Alaska Native, 7 Asian Americans or Pacific Islanders, 3 Hispanic Americans), 12 international. 212 applicants, 94% accepted, 200 enrolled. *Faculty:* 70 full-time (38 women), 7 part-time/adjunct (4 women). Expenses: Contact institution. *Financial support:* In 2006–07, fellowships with full tuition reimbursements (averaging $6,000 per year), 36 research assistantships with full and partial tuition reimbursements (averaging $6,000 per year), 3 teaching assistantships (averaging $3,000 per year) were awarded; career-related internships or fieldwork, Federal Work-Study, scholarships/grants, traineeships, tuition waivers (partial), and unspecified assistantships also available. Support available to part-time students. Financial award application deadline: 2/15; financial award applicants required to submit FAFSA. In 2006, 128 master's, 29 doctorates awarded. Offers clinical nurse specialist (MSN); community service counseling (MS); counseling psychology (MS); elementary school counseling (MS); family and consumer sciences (MS); health and behavioral sciences (MS, MSN, DPT, PhD); health education (MS); health systems (MS); kinesiology (MS); nurse practitioner (MSN); occupational therapy (MS); physical therapy (DPT, PhD); school counseling (MS); school psychology (MS, PhD); secondary school counseling (MS); speech-language pathology (MS). *Application deadline:* For fall admission, 3/1 priority date for domestic and international students; for spring admission, 10/1 for domestic and international students. Applications are processed on a rolling basis. *Application fee:* $25 ($40 for international students). *Application Contact:* Nanette Fitzhugh, Administrative Assistant, 501-450-5063, Fax: 501-450-5678, E-mail: fitzhugh@uca.edu. *Dean,* Dr. Neil Hattlestad, 501-450-3122, Fax: 501-450-5503, E-mail: neilh@uca.edu.

College of Liberal Arts Students: 26 full-time (16 women), 72 part-time (36 women); includes 6 minority (5 African Americans, 1 Hispanic American). 37 applicants, 100% accepted, 37 enrolled. *Faculty:* 40 full-time (9 women). Expenses: Contact institution. *Financial support:* In 2006–07, 2 teaching assistantships with partial tuition reimbursements (averaging $10,000 per year) were awarded; Federal Work-Study, scholarships/grants, and unspecified assistantships also available. Financial award application deadline: 2/15; financial award applicants required to submit FAFSA. In 2006, 16 degrees awarded. *Degree program information:* Part-time programs available. Offers English (MA); foreign languages (MA); geographic information systems (Certificate); history (MA); liberal arts (MA, Certificate). *Application deadline:* For fall admission, 3/1 priority date for domestic students; for spring admission, 10/1 priority date for domestic students. Applications are processed on a rolling basis. *Application fee:* $25 ($40 for international students). *Application Contact:* Brenda Herring, Admissions Assistant, 501-450-5065, Fax: 501-450-5678, E-mail: bherring@uca.edu. *Dean,* Maurice Lee, 501-450-3167, Fax: 501-450-5185, E-mail: mauricel@uca.edu.

College of Natural Sciences and Math Students: 37 full-time (15 women), 60 part-time (45 women); includes 4 minority (all African Americans), 10 international. 45 applicants, 100% accepted, 45 enrolled. *Faculty:* 51 full-time (10 women). Expenses: Contact institution. *Financial support:* In 2006–07, 4 research assistantships (averaging $8,000 per year) were awarded; career-related internships or fieldwork, Federal Work-Study, and unspecified assistantships also available. Financial award application deadline: 2/15; financial award applicants required to submit FAFSA. In 2006, 22 degrees awarded. *Degree program information:* Part-time programs available. Offers applied computing (MS); biological science (MS); mathematics (MA); natural sciences and math (MA, MS). *Application deadline:* For fall admission, 3/1 priority date for domestic and international students; for spring admission, 10/1 priority date for domestic and international students. Applications are processed on a rolling basis. *Application fee:* $25 ($40 for international students). *Application Contact:* Brenda Herring, Admissions Assistant, 501-450-5065, Fax: 501-450-5678, E-mail: bherring@uca.edu. *Dean,* Dr. Stephen Seidman, 501-450-3199, Fax: 501-450-5084.

Graduate School of Management, Leadership, and Administration Students: 47 full-time (27 women), 102 part-time (65 women); includes 26 minority (22 African Americans, 1 American Indian/Alaska Native, 1 Asian American or Pacific Islander, 2 Hispanic Americans), 20 international. 35 applicants, 100% accepted, 35 enrolled. *Faculty:* 7 full-time (2 women), 2 part-time/adjunct (0 women). Expenses: Contact institution. *Financial support:* Career-related internships or fieldwork, Federal Work-Study, scholarships/grants, tuition waivers, and unspecified assistantships available. Financial award application deadline: 2/15. In 2006, 33 degrees awarded. *Degree program information:* Part-time programs available. Offers college student personnel (MS); community and economic development (MS); educational leadership—district level (Ed S); management, leadership, and administration (MS, Ed S). *Application deadline:* For fall admission, 3/1 priority date for domestic students; for spring admission, 10/1 priority date for domestic students. Applications are processed on a rolling basis. *Application fee:* $25 ($40 for international students). *Application Contact:* Nanette Fitzhugh, Administrative Assistant, 501-450-5063, Fax: 501-450-5678, E-mail: fitzhugh@uca.edu. *Dean,* Dr. Elaine M. McNiece, 501-450-3124, Fax: 501-450-5678, E-mail: elainem@uca.edu.

UNIVERSITY OF CENTRAL FLORIDA, Orlando, FL 32816

General Information State-supported, coed, university. CGS member. *Enrollment:* 46,719 graduate, professional, and undergraduate students; 3,274 full-time matriculated graduate/professional students (1,822 women), 3,097 part-time matriculated graduate/professional students (1,905 women). *Enrollment by degree level:* 4,469 master's, 1,535 doctoral, 367 other advanced degrees. *Graduate faculty:* 1,166 full-time (434 women), 464 part-time/adjunct (255 women). Tuition, state resident: full-time $6,167; part-time $257 per credit hour. Tuition, nonresident: full-time $22,790; part-time $950 per credit hour. *Graduate housing:* Room and/or apartments available on a first-come, first-served basis to single students; on-campus housing not available to married students. Housing application deadline: 3/1. *Student services:* Campus employment opportunities, career counseling, child daycare facilities, disabled student services, exercise/wellness program, free psychological counseling, international student services, low-cost health insurance, multicultural affairs office, writing training. *Library facilities:* University Library. *Online resources:* library catalog, web page, access to other libraries' catalogs. *Collection:* 1.4 million titles, 16,368 serial subscriptions, 42,610 audiovisual materials. *Research affiliation:* Agere Systems, Inc., Lockheed Martin Corporation, Raytheon Company, Image Soft Technologies, American Water Works Association Research Foundation, Raytheon E-Systems, Inc.

Computer facilities: Computer purchase and lease plans are available. 2,420 computers available on campus for general student use. A campuswide network can be accessed from student residence rooms and from off campus. Internet access and online class registration are available. *Web address:* http://www.ucf.edu/.

General Application Contact: Dr. Patricia Bishop, Vice Provost and Dean of Graduate Studies, 407-823-2766, Fax: 407-823-3299, E-mail: graduate@mail.ucf.edu.

GRADUATE UNITS

Burnett College of Biomedical Sciences Students: 77 full-time (40 women), 3 part-time (2 women); includes 8 minority (1 African American, 3 Asian Americans or Pacific Islanders, 4 Hispanic Americans), 30 international. *Faculty:* 17 full-time (3 women), 4 part-time/adjunct (2 women). Expenses: Contact institution. *Financial support:* In 2006–07, 12 fellowships (averaging $2,500 per year), 60 research assistantships (averaging $11,200 per year), 35 teaching assistantships (averaging $6,600 per year) were awarded. In 2006, 10 master's, 3 doctorates awarded. Offers biomedical sciences (MS, PhD); molecular biology and microbiology (MS). *Dean,* Dr. Pappachan E. Kolattukudy, 407-823-1206, Fax: 407-823-0956, E-mail: pk@mail.ucf.edu.

College of Arts and Humanities Students: 250 full-time (132 women), 185 part-time (118 women); includes 91 minority (23 African Americans, 2 American Indian/Alaska Native, 13 Asian Americans or Pacific Islanders, 53 Hispanic Americans), 19 international. *Faculty:* 246 full-time (136 women), 73 part-time/adjunct (42 women). Expenses: Contact institution. *Financial support:* In 2006–07, 77 research assistantships with partial tuition reimbursements (averaging $6,000 per year), 76 teaching assistantships with partial tuition reimbursements (averaging $6,000 per year) were awarded; fellowships with partial tuition reimbursements, career-related internships or fieldwork, Federal Work-Study, institutionally sponsored loans, tuition waivers (partial), and unspecified assistantships also available. Financial award application deadline: 3/1; financial award applicants required to submit FAFSA. In 2006, 75 master's, 19 other advanced degrees awarded. *Degree program information:* Part-time and evening/weekend programs available. Offers arts and humanities (MA, MFA, MS, PhD, Certificate); creative writing (MFA); English (MA, MFA); history (MA); literature (MA); professional writing (Certificate); Spanish (MA); studio art and the computer (MFA); teaching English to speakers of other languages (MA, Certificate); technical writing (MA); texts and technology (PhD); theatre (MA, MFA). *Application fee:* $30. Electronic applications accepted. *Dean, College of Arts an Humanities,* Dr. José Fernandez, 407-823-2373, E-mail: jfernandez@mail.ucf.edu.

School of Film and Digital Media Students: 57 full-time (10 women), 26 part-time (3 women); includes 15 minority (5 African Americans, 1 American Indian/Alaska Native, 3 Asian Americans or Pacific Islanders, 6 Hispanic Americans), 3 international. *Faculty:* 32 full-time (11 women), 5 part-time/adjunct (3 women). Expenses: Contact institution. *Financial support:* In 2006–07, 2 fellowships (averaging $3,800 per year), 2 research assistantships (averaging $4,400 per year), 16 teaching assistantships (averaging $6,600 per year) were awarded. Offers film and digital media (MA, MFA, MS). *Interim Director,* Dr. Terry Frederick, 407-823-6100, E-mail: fred@mail.ucf.edu.

College of Business Administration Students: 458 full-time (216 women), 464 part-time (215 women); includes 183 minority (55 African Americans, 4 American Indian/Alaska Native, 59 Asian Americans or Pacific Islanders, 65 Hispanic Americans), 121 international. *Faculty:* 146 full-time (38 women), 14 part-time/adjunct (4 women). Expenses: Contact institution. *Financial support:* In 2006–07, 40 fellowships with partial tuition reimbursements (averaging $3,000 per year), 117 research assistantships with partial tuition reimbursements (averaging $6,400 per year), 36 teaching assistantships with partial tuition reimbursements (averaging $13,700 per year) were awarded; career-related internships or fieldwork, Federal Work-Study, institutionally sponsored loans, tuition waivers (partial), and unspecified assistantships also available. Financial award application deadline: 3/1; financial award applicants required to submit FAFSA. In 2006, 399 master's, 10 doctorates awarded. *Degree program information:* Part-time and evening/weekend programs available. Offers business administration (MBA, MS, MSA, MSBM, MSM, MST, PhD); economics (MS, PhD); management (MSM); management information systems (MS); sport business management (MSBM). *Application deadline:* For spring admission, 11/1 priority date for domestic students. *Application fee:* $30. Electronic applications accepted. *Application Contact:* Judy Ryder, Director, Graduate Admissions, 407-823-2364, Fax: 407-823-0219, E-mail: judy.ryder@bus.ucf.edu. *Dean,* Dr. Thomas Keon, 407-823-2183, E-mail: thomas.keon@bus.ucf.edu.

Kenneth G. Dixon School of Accounting Students: 77 full-time (50 women), 133 part-time (83 women); includes 34 minority (7 African Americans, 1 American Indian/Alaska Native, 15 Asian Americans or Pacific Islanders, 11 Hispanic Americans), 27 international. Average age 31. *Faculty:* 26 full-time (14 women), 6 part-time/adjunct (2 women). Expenses: Contact institution. *Financial support:* In 2006–07, 2 fellowships with partial tuition reimbursements (averaging $5,000 per year), 20 research assistantships with partial tuition reimbursements (averaging $6,500 per year) were awarded; teaching assistantships with partial tuition reimbursements, career-related internships or fieldwork, Federal Work-Study, institutionally sponsored loans, tuition waivers (partial), and unspecified assistantships also available. Financial award application deadline: 3/1; financial award applicants required to submit FAFSA. In 2006, 79 master's awarded. *Degree program information:* Part-time and evening/weekend programs available. Offers accounting (MSA, MST); taxation (MST). *Application deadline:* For fall admission, 6/15 priority date for domestic students; for spring admission, 11/1 priority date for domestic students. Electronic applications accepted. *Director,* Dr. Robin J. Roberts, 407-823-2876, E-mail: robin.roberts@bus.ucf.edu.

College of Education Students: 556 full-time (437 women), 1,018 part-time (823 women); includes 284 minority (126 African Americans, 7 American Indian/Alaska Native, 31 Asian Americans or Pacific Islanders, 120 Hispanic Americans), 40 international. Average age 35. *Faculty:* 128 full-time (87 women), 95 part-time/adjunct (66 women). Expenses: Contact institution. *Financial support:* In 2006–07, 63 fellowships with partial tuition reimbursements (averaging $2,000 per year), 147 research assistantships with partial tuition reimbursements (averaging $6,400 per year), 10 teaching assistantships with partial tuition reimbursements (averaging $7,000 per year) were awarded; career-related internships or fieldwork, Federal Work-Study, institutionally sponsored loans, tuition waivers (partial), and unspecified assistantships also available. Financial award application deadline: 3/1; financial award applicants required to submit FAFSA. In 2006, 417 master's, 60 doctorates, 144 other advanced degrees awarded. *Degree program information:* Part-time and evening/weekend programs available. Offers art education (M Ed, MA); coaching (Certificate); communication sciences and disorders (PhD); community college education (Certificate); counselor education (M Ed, MA, PhD); curriculum and instruction (PhD); e-learning (MA, Certificate); e-learning professional development (Certificate); early childhood education (M Ed, MA); education (M Ed, MA, Ed D, PhD, Certificate, Ed S); educational leadership (M Ed, MA, Ed D, Ed S); educational media (M Ed); educational studies (M Ed, MA, Ed D, Ed S); educational technology (MA); elementary education (M Ed, MA, PhD); English language arts education (M Ed, MA); exceptional education (M Ed, MA, PhD); foreign language education (Certificate); health and wellness (Certificate); hospitality education (PhD); instructional systems (MA); instructional technology (PhD); instructional technology/media and e-learning (MA); K-8 mathematics and science education (M Ed, Certificate); marriage and family therapy (MA); mathematics education (M Ed, MA, PhD); music education (M Ed, MA); online educational media (Certificate); physical education-exercise physiology (M Ed, MA); pre-kindergarten handicapped endorsement (Certificate); reading education (M Ed, MA, Certificate); school psychology (Ed S); science education (M Ed, MA); social science education (M Ed, MA); sports leadership (Certificate); vocational education (M Ed, MA); world studies education (Certificate); writing education (Certificate). *Application fee:* $30. Electronic applications accepted. *Dean,* Dr. Sandra Robinson, 407-823-5529.

College of Engineering and Computer Science Students: 595 full-time (124 women), 418 part-time (73 women); includes 186 minority (46 African Americans, 2 American Indian/Alaska Native, 51 Asian Americans or Pacific Islanders, 87 Hispanic Americans), 385 international. Average age 30. Expenses: Contact institution. *Financial support:* In 2006–07, 106 fellowships with partial tuition reimbursements (averaging $4,100 per year), 345 research assistantships with partial tuition reimbursements (averaging $11,000 per year), 121 teaching assistantships with partial tuition reimbursements (averaging $9,000 per year) were awarded; career-related internships or fieldwork, Federal Work-Study, institutionally sponsored loans, tuition waivers (partial), and unspecified assistantships also available. Financial award application deadline: 3/1; financial award applicants required to submit FAFSA. In 2006, 265 master's, 55 doctorates, 20 other advanced degrees awarded. *Degree program information:* Part-time and evening/weekend programs available. Offers aerospace engineering (MSAE); applied operations research (Certificate); CAD/CAM technology (Certificate); civil engineering (MS, MSCE, PhD, Certificate); computer-integrated manufacturing (MS); construction engineering (Certificate); design for usability (Certificate); engineering (MS, MS Cp E, MS Env E, MSAE, MSCE, MSEE, MSIE, MSME, MSMSE, PhD, Certificate); engineering management (MS); environmental engineering (MS, MS Env E, PhD, Certificate); HVAC engineering (Certificate); industrial engineering (MSIE); industrial engineering and management systems (PhD); industrial ergonomics and safety (Certificate); launch/spacecraft vehicle processing (Certificate); materials failure analysis (Certificate); materials science and engineering (MSMSE, PhD); mechanical engineering (MSME, PhD, Certificate); operations research (MS); project engineering (Certificate); quality assurance (Certificate); simulation systems (MS); structural engineering (Certificate); surface water modeling (Certificate); systems simulations for engineers (Certificate); training simulation (Certificate); transportation engineering (Certificate); wastewater treatment (Certificate). *Application deadline:* For fall admission, 7/15 for domestic students; for spring admission, 12/1 for domestic students. *Application fee:* $30. Electronic applications accepted. *Dean,* Dr. Neal Gallagher, 407-823-2156, E-mail: nealg@mail.ucf.edu.

School of Electrical Engineering and Computer Science Students: 329 full-time (56 women), 150 part-time (15 women); includes 78 minority (17 African Americans, 32 Asian Americans or Pacific Islanders, 29 Hispanic Americans), 216 international. *Faculty:* 66 full-time (3 women), 4 part-time/adjunct (1 woman). Expenses: Contact institution. *Financial support:* In 2006–07, 58 fellowships with partial tuition reimbursements (averaging $4,300 per year), 153 research assistantships with partial tuition reimbursements (averaging $10,400 per year), 87 teaching assistantships with partial tuition reimbursements (averaging $8,400 per year) were awarded; career-related internships or fieldwork, Federal Work-Study, institutionally sponsored loans, tuition waivers (partial), and unspecified assistantships also available. Financial award application deadline: 3/1; financial award applicants required to submit FAFSA. In 2006, 144 master's, 31 doctorates awarded. *Degree program information:* Part-time and evening/weekend programs available. Offers communications systems (Certificate); computer engineering (MS Cp E, PhD); computer science (MS, PhD); electrical engineering (MSEE, PhD, Certificate); electronic circuits (Certificate). *Application deadline:* For fall admission, 7/15 priority date for domestic students; for spring admission, 12/1 priority date for domestic students. *Application fee:* $30. Electronic applications accepted. *Interim Chair,* Dr. Issa Batarseh, 407-823-0189, Fax: 407-823-5419, E-mail: batarseh@mail.ucf.edu.

College of Health and Public Affairs Students: 666 full-time (551 women), 677 part-time (501 women); includes 312 minority (139 African Americans, 2 American Indian/Alaska Native, 36 Asian Americans or Pacific Islanders, 135 Hispanic Americans), 19 international. *Faculty:* 88 full-time (39 women), 72 part-time/adjunct (33 women). Expenses: Contact institution. *Financial support:* In 2006–07, 57 fellowships with partial tuition reimbursements (averaging $2,500 per year), 111 research assistantships with partial tuition reimbursements (averaging $5,000 per year), 20 teaching assistantships with partial tuition reimbursements (averaging $7,200 per year) were awarded; career-related internships or fieldwork, Federal Work-Study, institutionally sponsored loans, traineeships, tuition waivers (partial), and unspecified assistantships also available. Financial award application deadline: 3/1; financial award applicants required to submit FAFSA. In 2006, 466 master's, 10 doctorates, 10 other advanced degrees awarded. *Degree program information:* Part-time and evening/weekend programs available. Offers child language disorders (Certificate); communication sciences and disorders (MA); corrections leadership (Certificate); crime analysis (Certificate); criminal justice (MS); health and public affairs (MA, MNM, MPA, MS, MSW, DNP, PhD, Certificate, Post-Master's Certificate); health services administration (MS, Certificate); juvenile justice leadership (Certificate); medical speech-language pathology (Certificate); multicultural/multilingual speech-language pathology (Certificate); non-profit management (MNM, Certificate); physical therapy (MS); police leadership (Certificate); public administration (MPA, Certificate); public affairs (PhD); urban and regional planning (Certificate); victim assistance (Certificate). Electronic applications accepted. *Interim Dean,* Dr. Joyce Dorner, 407-823-0521, E-mail: jdorner@mail.cc.ucf.edu.

College of Nursing Students: 84 full-time (75 women), 167 part-time (154 women); includes 41 minority (11 African Americans, 1 American Indian/Alaska Native, 8 Asian Americans or Pacific Islanders, 21 Hispanic Americans), 2 international. Average age 38. *Faculty:* 35 full-time (32 women), 28 part-time/adjunct (25 women). Expenses: Contact institution. *Financial support:* In 2006–07, 35 fellowships with partial tuition reimbursements (averaging $1,550 per year), 9 research assistantships with partial tuition reimbursements (averaging $4,500 per year), 3 teaching assistantships with partial tuition reimbursements (averaging $15,400 per year) were awarded; career-related internships or fieldwork, Federal Work-Study, institutionally sponsored loans, traineeships, and unspecified assistantships also available. Financial award application deadline: 3/1; financial award applicants required to submit FAFSA. In 2006, 30 Post-Master's Certificates awarded. *Degree program information:* Part-time and evening/weekend programs available. Offers adult practitioner (Post-Master's Certificate); family practitioner (Post-Master's Certificate); nursing (DNP, PhD); nursing education (Post-Master's Certificate); pediatric practitioner (Post-Master's Certificate). *Application deadline:* For fall admission, 2/15 for domestic students; for spring admission, 9/15 for domestic students. *Application fee:* $30. Electronic applications accepted. *Dean, College of Nursing,* Dr. Jean D. Leuner, 407-823-5496, Fax: 407-823-5675, E-mail: jleuner@mail.ucf.edu.

School of Social Work Students: 122 full-time (111 women), 100 part-time (85 women); includes 66 minority (33 African Americans, 2 Asian Americans or Pacific Islanders, 31 Hispanic Americans), 1 international. *Faculty:* 17 full-time (11 women), 20 part-time/adjunct (18 women). Expenses: Contact institution. *Financial support:* In 2006–07, 1 fellowship with partial tuition reimbursement (averaging $5,000 per year), 14 research assistantships with partial tuition reimbursements (averaging $5,400 per year) were awarded; teaching assistantships with partial tuition reimbursements, career-related internships or fieldwork, Federal Work-Study, institutionally sponsored loans, and unspecified assistantships also available. Financial award application deadline: 3/1; financial award applicants required to submit FAFSA. In 2006, 103 master's, 18 other advanced degrees awarded. *Degree program information:* Part-time and evening/weekend programs available. Offers addictions (Certificate); aging studies (Certificate); children's services (Certificate); school social work (Certificate); social work (MSW); social work administration (Certificate). *Application deadline:* For fall admission, 3/1 for domestic students. *Application fee:* $30. Electronic applications accepted. *Director,* Dr. John Ronnau, 407-823-2208, Fax: 407-823-5697, E-mail: jronnau@mail.ucf.edu.

College of Optics and Photonics Students: 100 full-time (13 women), 13 part-time (4 women); includes 10 minority (2 African Americans, 5 Asian Americans or Pacific Islanders, 3 Hispanic Americans), 60 international. Average age 28. *Faculty:* 17 full-time (1 woman), 1 part-time/adjunct (0 women). Expenses: Contact institution. *Financial support:* In 2006–07, 20 fellowships with partial tuition reimbursements (averaging $4,600 per year), 83 research assistantships with partial tuition reimbursements (averaging $14,400 per year) were awarded; teaching assistantships with partial tuition reimbursements, career-related internships or fieldwork, Federal Work-Study, institutionally sponsored loans, tuition waivers (partial), and unspecified assistantships also available. Financial award application deadline: 3/1; financial award applicants required to submit FAFSA. In 2006, 12 master's, 16 doctorates awarded. *Degree program information:* Part-time and evening/weekend programs available. Offers optics (MS, PhD). *Application deadline:* For fall admission, 2/1 priority date for domestic students; for spring admission, 12/1 for domestic students. *Application fee:* $30. Electronic applications accepted. *Application Contact:* Dr. David J. Hagan, Coordinator, 407-823-6817,

University of Central Florida (continued)

E-mail: dhagan@creol.ucf.edu. *Dean and Director,* Dr. Eric W. Van Stryland, 407-823-6835, E-mail: cwvs@mail.creol.ucf.edu.

College of Sciences Students: 508 full-time (276 women), 218 part-time (111 women); includes 119 minority (38 African Americans, 3 American Indian/Alaska Native, 20 Asian Americans or Pacific Islanders, 58 Hispanic Americans), 103 international. *Faculty:* 253 full-time (82 women), 73 part-time/adjunct (30 women). Expenses: Contact institution. *Financial support:* In 2006–07, 75 fellowships (averaging $3,000 per year), 185 research assistantships (averaging $10,200 per year), 196 teaching assistantships (averaging $9,400 per year) were awarded. In 2006, 165 master's, 22 doctorates, 29 other advanced degrees awarded. Offers actuarial science (MS); anthropology (MA); applied environmental and human factors psychology (MA); applied experimental and human factors psychology (PhD); applied mathematics (Certificate); applied sociology (MA); biology (MS); chemistry (MS, PhD); clinical psychology (MA, MS, PhD); conservation biology (PhD, Certificate); data mining (MS, Certificate); domestic violence (Certificate); gender studies (Certificate); industrial/organizational psychology (MS, PhD); mathematical science (MS); mathematics (PhD); Mayan studies (Certificate); physics (MS, PhD); political science (MA); sciences (MA, MS, PhD, Certificate); sociology (PhD); statistical computing (MS). *Dean,* Dr. Peter Panousis, 407-823-1911, E-mail: ppanousis@mail.ucf.edu.

Nicholson School of Communication Students: 30 full-time (22 women), 27 part-time (21 women); includes 12 minority (4 African Americans, 2 Asian Americans or Pacific Islanders, 6 Hispanic Americans), 5 international. *Faculty:* 46 full-time (19 women), 28 part-time/adjunct (12 women). Expenses: Contact institution. *Financial support:* In 2006–07, 2 fellowships with partial tuition reimbursements (averaging $5,000 per year), 13 research assistantships with partial tuition reimbursements (averaging $8,000 per year), 5 teaching assistantships with partial tuition reimbursements (averaging $6,000 per year) were awarded; career-related internships or fieldwork, Federal Work-Study, institutionally sponsored loans, tuition waivers (partial), and unspecified assistantships also available. Financial award application deadline: 3/1; financial award applicants required to submit FAFSA. In 2006, 33 degrees awarded. *Degree program information:* Part-time and evening/weekend programs available. Offers communication (MA). *Application deadline:* For fall admission, 7/15 for domestic students; for spring admission, 12/7 for domestic students. *Application fee:* $30. Electronic applications accepted. *Application Contact:* Dr. Burt Pryor, Coordinator, 407-823-2681, Fax: 407-823-6360, E-mail: apryor@pegasus.cc.ucf.edu. *Director,* Dr. Mary Alice Shaver, 407-823-2681, Fax: 407-823-5216, E-mail: mshaver@mail.ucf.edu.

Division of Graduate Studies Students: 77 full-time (35 women), 64 part-time (27 women); includes 21 minority (5 African Americans, 1 American Indian/Alaska Native, 3 Asian Americans or Pacific Islanders, 12 Hispanic Americans), 31 international. Expenses: Contact institution. In 2006, 33 master's, 2 doctorates awarded. Offers interdisciplinary studies (MA, MS); modeling and simulation (MS, PhD). *Vice Provost and Dean,* Dr. Patricia Bishop, 407-823-6432, Fax: 407-823-3299, E-mail: pbishop@mail.ucf.edu.

Rosen College of Hospitality Management Students: 38 full-time (22 women), 38 part-time (31 women); includes 15 minority (5 African Americans, 3 Asian Americans or Pacific Islanders, 7 Hispanic Americans), 10 international. Average age 27. Expenses: Contact institution. *Financial support:* In 2006–07, 1 fellowship with partial tuition reimbursement (averaging $5,000 per year), 19 research assistantships with partial tuition reimbursements (averaging $4,600 per year) were awarded. In 2006, 20 degrees awarded. Offers hospitality and tourism management (MS). *Application deadline:* For fall admission, 2/1 for domestic students. *Application fee:* $30. Electronic applications accepted. *Application Contact:* Dr. Paul Rompf, Coordinator, 407-903-8027, E-mail: prompf@mail.ucf.edu. *Dean,* Dr. Abraham C. Pizam, 407-903-8010, E-mail: apizam@mail.ucf.edu.

UNIVERSITY OF CENTRAL MISSOURI, Warrensburg, MO 64093

General Information State-supported, coed, comprehensive institution. CGS member. *Enrollment:* 10,711 graduate, professional, and undergraduate students; 425 full-time matriculated graduate/professional students (237 women), 1,329 part-time matriculated graduate/professional students (888 women). *Enrollment by degree level:* 1,623 master's, 2 doctoral, 129 other advanced degrees. *Graduate faculty:* 404 full-time (169 women). Tuition, state resident: full-time $5,448; part-time $227 per credit hour. Tuition, nonresident: full-time $10,896; part-time $454 per credit hour. *Required fees:* $336; $14 per credit hour. *Graduate housing:* Rooms and/or apartments available on a first-come, first-served basis to single and married students. Typical cost: $5,412 (including board) for single students. Housing application deadline: 8/1. *Student services:* Campus employment opportunities, campus safety program, career counseling, child daycare facilities, disabled student services, exercise/wellness program, free psychological counseling, international student services, low-cost health insurance, multicultural affairs office, teacher training, writing training. *Library facilities:* James C. Kirkpatrick Library. *Online resources:* library catalog, web page, access to other libraries' catalogs. *Collection:* 2.1 million titles, 1,703 serial subscriptions, 18,434 audiovisual materials.

Computer facilities: 1,220 computers available on campus for general student use. A campuswide network can be accessed from student residence rooms and from off campus. Internet access and online class registration are available. *Web address:* http://www.ucmo.edu/.

General Application Contact: Dr. Novella Perrin, Associate Provost for Research/Dean of the Graduate School, 660-543-4092, Fax: 660-543-8333, E-mail: perrin@cmsu1.cmsu.edu.

GRADUATE UNITS

The Graduate School Students: 425 full-time (237 women), 1,329 part-time (888 women); includes 175 minority (102 African Americans, 7 American Indian/Alaska Native, 36 Asian Americans or Pacific Islanders, 30 Hispanic Americans), 101 international. Average age 34. 541 applicants, 78% accepted, 395 enrolled. *Faculty:* 404 full-time (169 women). Expenses: Contact institution. *Financial support:* In 2006–07, 118 students received support; teaching assistantships with full and partial tuition reimbursements available, career-related internships or fieldwork, Federal Work-Study, scholarships/grants, unspecified assistantships, and administrative assistantships, laboratory assistantships available. Support available to part-time students. Financial award application deadline: 3/1; financial award applicants required to submit FAFSA. In 2006, 448 master's, 20 other advanced degrees awarded. *Degree program information:* Part-time programs available. Offers college student personnel administration (MS); counseling (MS); counselor education (MS); curriculum and instruction (Ed S); education (MS, MSE, Ed D, Ed S); educational leadership (Ed D); educational technology (MSE); elementary education (MSE); human service/guidance counseling (Ed S); human services/ technology and occupational education (Ed S); human services/learning resources (Ed S); K–12 education (MSE); library science and information services (MS, Ed S); literacy education (MSE); school administration (MSE, Ed S); secondary education (MSE); secondary education/business and office education (MSE); special education (MSE, Ed S); special education/human services (Ed S); technology and occupational education (MS). *Application deadline:* For fall admission, 6/1 priority date for domestic students, 5/1 for international students; for spring admission, 10/1 priority date for domestic students, 10/1 for international students. Applications are processed on a rolling basis. *Application fee:* $30 ($50 for international students). Electronic applications accepted. *Assistant Provost for Research/Dean of the Graduate School,* Dr. Novella Perrin, 660-543-4092, Fax: 660-543-8333, E-mail: perrin@cmsu1.cmsu.edu.

College of Arts, Humanities and Social Sciences Students: 60 full-time (38 women), 100 part-time (72 women); includes 15 minority (6 African Americans, 1 American Indian/Alaska Native, 7 Asian Americans or Pacific Islanders, 1 Hispanic American), 15 international. Average age 31. 67 applicants, 87% accepted, 51 enrolled. *Faculty:* 104 full-time (34 women). Expenses: Contact institution. *Financial support:* In 2006–07, 40 students received support; teaching assistantships with full and partial tuition reimbursements available, career-related internships or fieldwork, Federal Work-Study, scholarships/grants, unspecified assistantships, and administrative and laboratory assistantships available. Support available to part-time students. Financial award application deadline: 3/1; financial award applicants required to submit FAFSA. In 2006, 51 degrees awarded. *Degree program information:* Part-time programs available. Offers applied mathematics (MS); arts, humanities and social sciences (MA, MS); biology (MS); communication (MA); English (MA); history (MA); mathematics (MS); music (MA); speech communication (MA); teaching English as a second language (MA); theatre (MA). *Application deadline:* For fall admission, 6/1 priority date for domestic students, 5/1 priority date for international students; for spring admission, 10/1 priority date for domestic students, 10/1 for international students. Applications are processed on a rolling basis. *Application fee:* $30 ($50 for international students). *Interim Dean,* Dr. Steven Boone, 660-543-4750, Fax: 660-543-8271, E-mail: sboone@ucmo.edu.

College of Health and Human Services Students: 108 full-time (74 women), 232 part-time (135 women); includes 36 minority (19 African Americans, 3 American Indian/Alaska Native, 5 Asian Americans or Pacific Islanders, 9 Hispanic Americans), 11 international. Average age 33. 132 applicants, 84% accepted, 82 enrolled. *Faculty:* 101 full-time (48 women). Expenses: Contact institution. *Financial support:* In 2006–07, 36 students received support; teaching assistantships with full and partial tuition reimbursements available, career-related internships or fieldwork, Federal Work-Study, scholarships/grants, unspecified assistantships, and administrative and laboratory assistantships available. Support available to part-time students. Financial award application deadline: 3/1; financial award applicants required to submit FAFSA. In 2006, 87 master's, 1 other advanced degree awarded. *Degree program information:* Part-time programs available. Offers criminal justice (MS); fire science (MS); health and human services (MA, MS, Ed S); human services/public services (Ed S); industrial hygiene (MS); industrial safety management (MS); loss control (MS); occupational safety management (MS); physical education/exercise and sports science (MS); psychology (MS); public safety (MS); rural family nursing (MS); security (MS); social gerontology (MS); sociology (MA); speech pathology and audiology (MS); transportation safety (MS). *Application deadline:* For fall admission, 6/1 priority date for domestic students, 5/1 priority date for international students; for spring admission, 10/1 priority date for domestic students, 10/1 for international students. Applications are processed on a rolling basis. *Application fee:* $30 ($50 for international students). *Interim Dean,* Dr. Rick Sluder, 660-543-4168, Fax: 660-543-4167, E-mail: sluder@ucmo.edu.

College of Science and Technology Students: 65 full-time (19 women), 95 part-time (29 women); includes 22 minority (12 African Americans, 8 Asian Americans or Pacific Islanders, 2 Hispanic Americans), 27 international. Average age 32. 58 applicants, 76% accepted, 41 enrolled. *Faculty:* 80 full-time (26 women). Expenses: Contact institution. *Financial support:* In 2006–07, 15 students received support; teaching assistantships with full and partial tuition reimbursements available, Federal Work-Study, scholarships/grants, unspecified assistantships, and administrative and laboratory assistantships available. Support available to part-time students. Financial award application deadline: 3/1; financial award applicants required to submit FAFSA. In 2006, 68 degrees awarded. *Degree program information:* Part-time programs available. Offers aviation safety (MS); industrial management (MS); science and technology (MS). *Application deadline:* For fall admission, 6/1 priority date for domestic students, 5/1 priority date for international students; for spring admission, 10/1 priority date for domestic students, 10/1 for international students. Applications are processed on a rolling basis. *Application fee:* $30 ($50 for international students). *Dean,* Dr. Alice Greife, 660-543-4450, Fax: 660-543-8031, E-mail: greife@ucmo.edu.

Harmon College of Business Administration Students: 72 full-time (18 women), 26 part-time (7 women); includes 14 minority (4 African Americans, 9 Asian Americans or Pacific Islanders, 1 Hispanic American), 38 international. Average age 27. 53 applicants. *Faculty:* 23 full-time (8 women). Expenses: Contact institution. *Financial support:* In 2006–07, 17 students received support; teaching assistantships with full and partial tuition reimbursements available, career-related internships or fieldwork, Federal Work-Study, scholarships/grants, unspecified assistantships, and administrative and laboratory assistantships available. Support available to part-time students. Financial award application deadline: 3/1; financial award applicants required to submit FAFSA. In 2006, 51 degrees awarded. *Degree program information:* Part-time programs available. Offers accounting (MA); business administration (MBA); information technology (MS). *Application deadline:* For fall admission, 6/1 priority date for domestic students, 5/1 priority date for international students; for spring admission, 10/1 priority date for domestic students, 10/1 for international students. Applications are processed on a rolling basis. *Application fee:* $30 ($50 for international students). *Dean,* Dr. George Wilson, 660-543-4560, Fax: 660-543-8350, E-mail: gwilson@ucmo.edu.

See Close-Up on page 1071.

UNIVERSITY OF CENTRAL OKLAHOMA, Edmond, OK 73034-5209

General Information State-supported, coed, comprehensive institution. CGS member. *Graduate housing:* Rooms and/or apartments available on a first-come, first-served basis to single and married students. Housing application deadline: 7/1. *Research affiliation:* U.S. Department of Agriculture–Agricultural Research Service (grazing lands), National Geographic Society (global positioning system education).

GRADUATE UNITS

College of Graduate Studies and Research *Degree program information:* Part-time and evening/weekend programs available. Electronic applications accepted.

College of Arts, Media, and Design *Degree program information:* Part-time and evening/weekend programs available. Postbaccalaureate distance learning degree programs offered (minimal on-campus study). Offers arts, media, and design (MFA, MM); design and interior design (MFA); music education (MM); performance (MM). Electronic applications accepted.

College of Business Administration *Degree program information:* Part-time programs available. Postbaccalaureate distance learning degree programs offered (minimal on-campus study). Offers business administration (MBA). Electronic applications accepted.

College of Education *Degree program information:* Part-time programs available. Offers adult education (M Ed); community services (M Ed); counseling psychology (MS); early childhood education (M Ed); education (M Ed, MA, MS); educational administration (M Ed); elementary education (M Ed); family and child studies (MS); family and consumer science education (MS); general education (M Ed); gerontology (M Ed); guidance and counseling (M Ed); instructional media (M Ed); interior design (MS); nutrition-food management (MS); professional health occupations (M Ed); psychology (MA); reading (M Ed); secondary education (M Ed); special education (M Ed); speech-language pathology (M Ed). Electronic applications accepted.

College of Liberal Arts *Degree program information:* Part-time programs available. Offers composition skills (MA); contemporary literature (MA); creative writing (MA); criminal justice management and administration (MA); history (MA); international affairs (MA); liberal arts (MA); museum studies (MA); political science (MA); social studies teaching (MA); Southwestern studies (MA); teaching English as a second language (MA); traditional studies (MA); urban affairs (MA). Electronic applications accepted.

College of Mathematics and Science *Degree program information:* Part-time programs available. Offers applied mathematical sciences (MS); biology (MS); chemistry (MS); mathematics and science (MS); physics and engineering (MS). Electronic applications accepted.

UNIVERSITY OF CHARLESTON, Charleston, WV 25304-1099

General Information Independent, coed, comprehensive institution. *Enrollment:* 1,202 graduate, professional, and undergraduate students; 125 full-time matriculated graduate/professional students (60 women), 3 part-time matriculated graduate/professional students (2 women). *Enrollment by degree level:* 49 master's, 79 doctoral. *Graduate faculty:* 1 full-time (0 women). *Graduate housing:* Rooms and/or apartments available to single and married students. Typical cost: $4,200 per year ($7,600 including board) for single students. *Student services:* Campus employment opportunities, campus safety program, career counseling, free psychological counseling, low-cost health insurance. *Library facilities:* Schoenbaum Library. *Online resources:* library catalog, web page, access to other libraries' catalogs. *Collection:* 164,457 titles, 14,192 serial subscriptions, 3,759 audiovisual materials.

Computer facilities: 200 computers available on campus for general student use. A campuswide network can be accessed from student residence rooms and from off campus. Internet access, campus cruiser are available. *Web address:* http://www.ucwv.edu/.

General Application Contact: Brad Parrish, Vice President of Enrollment, 304-357-4750, Fax: 304-357-4715, E-mail: admissions@ucwv.edu.

GRADUATE UNITS

Executive Business Administration Program Students: 33 full-time (10 women). Average age 36. 28 applicants, 96% accepted, 22 enrolled. *Faculty:* 5 full-time (1 woman). Expenses: Contact institution. *Financial support:* In 2006–07, 18 students received support. Available to part-time students. Application deadline: 3/1; In 2006, 11 degrees awarded. *Degree program information:* Part-time and evening/weekend programs available. Offers business administration (EMBA). *Application deadline:* Applications are processed on a rolling basis. *Application fee:* $40. Electronic applications accepted. *Application Contact:* Dr. Robert B. Bliss, Director, 304-357-4865, Fax: 304-357-4872, E-mail: robertbliss@ucwr.edu. *Director,* Dr. Robert B. Bliss, 304-357-4865, Fax: 304-357-4872, E-mail: robertbliss@ucwr.edu.

UNIVERSITY OF CHICAGO, Chicago, IL 60637-1513

General Information Independent, coed, university. CGS member. *Enrollment:* 11,730 graduate, professional, and undergraduate students; 6,844 full-time matriculated graduate/professional students (3,072 women), 2,219 part-time matriculated graduate/professional students (628 women). *Enrollment by degree level:* 1,063 first professional, 4,483 master's, 3,517 doctoral. *Graduate faculty:* 2,261 full-time (656 women), 573 part-time/adjunct (212 women). *Tuition:* Full-time $34,920. *Required fees:* $612. One-time fee: $35 full-time. Full-time tuition and fees vary according to course load, degree level and program. *Graduate housing:* Rooms and/or apartments available on a first-come, first-served basis to single and married students. Typical cost: $10,608 (including board) for single students. *Student services:* Campus employment opportunities, campus safety program, career counseling, disabled student services, exercise/wellness program, free psychological counseling, grant writing training, international student services, low-cost health insurance, multicultural affairs office, teacher training, writing training. *Library facilities:* Joseph Regenstein Library plus 6 others. *Online resources:* library catalog, web page, access to other libraries' catalogs. *Collection:* 7 million titles, 47,000 serial subscriptions. *Research affiliation:* Argonne National Laboratory (energy, materials), Fermilab (high-energy physics), McDonald Observatory (astronomy), Field Museum of Natural History (archaeology, zoology), Smithsonian Tropical Research Institute (biology), National Opinion Research Center (social science).

Computer facilities: 1,000 computers available on campus for general student use. A campuswide network can be accessed from student residence rooms and from off campus. Internet access and online class registration are available. *Web address:* http://www.uchicago.edu/.

General Application Contact: Martha Jackson, Manager, Office of Graduate Affairs, 773-702-7813, Fax: 773-702-1194, E-mail: graduate-affairs-admissions@uchicago.edu.

GRADUATE UNITS

Divinity School *Degree program information:* Part-time programs available. Offers divinity (M Div, AM, AMRS, PhD). Electronic applications accepted.

Division of Social Sciences Students: 1,430. Expenses: Contact institution. *Financial support:* Fellowships, research assistantships, teaching assistantships, Federal Work-Study, institutionally sponsored loans, scholarships/grants, traineeships, health care benefits, and unspecified assistantships available. Financial award application deadline: 12/15; financial award applicants required to submit FAFSA. In 2006, 255 master's, 106 doctorates awarded. Offers anthropology (PhD); comparative human development (PhD); conceptual and historical studies of science (PhD); economics (PhD); history (PhD); international relations (AM); Latin American and Caribbean studies (AM); Middle Eastern studies (AM); political science (PhD); psychology (PhD); social sciences (AM, PhD); social thought (PhD); sociology (PhD). *Application deadline:* For fall admission, 12/10 for domestic and international students. *Application fee:* $55. Electronic applications accepted. *Application Contact:* Office of the Dean of Students, 773-702-8415. *Dean,* Prof. John Mark Hansen, 773-702-8798.

Division of the Biological Sciences Students: 447 full-time (221 women); includes 87 minority (21 African Americans, 1 American Indian/Alaska Native, 45 Asian Americans or Pacific Islanders, 20 Hispanic Americans), 80 international. Average age 27. 1,055 applicants, 16% accepted, 73 enrolled. *Faculty:* 458 full-time (99 women), 18 part-time/adjunct (8 women). Expenses: Contact institution. *Financial support:* In 2006–07, 447 students received support, including fellowships with full tuition reimbursements available (averaging $26,893 per year), research assistantships with full tuition reimbursements available (averaging $26,893 per year); institutionally sponsored loans, scholarships/grants, traineeships, and health care benefits also available. Financial award applicants required to submit FAFSA. In 2006, 21 master's, 56 doctorates awarded. Offers biochemistry and molecular biology (PhD); biological sciences (MD, MS, PhD); biophysics and synthetic biology (PhD); cancer biology (PhD); cell physiology (PhD); cellular and molecular physiology (PhD); cellular differentiation (PhD); computational neuroscience (PhD); developmental biology (PhD); developmental endocrinology (PhD); developmental genetics (PhD); developmental neurobiology (PhD); ecology and evolution (PhD); evolutionary biology (PhD); functional and evolutionary biology (PhD); gene expression (PhD); genetics (PhD); health studies (MS); human genetics (PhD); immunology (PhD); integrative neuroscience (PhD); interdisciplinary scientist training (PhD); microbiology (PhD); molecular genetics and cell biology (PhD); molecular metabolism and nutrition (PhD); neurobiology (PhD); ophthalmology and visual science (PhD); organismal biology and anatomy (PhD); pathology (PhD); pharmacological and physiological sciences (PhD). *Application deadline:* For fall admission, 12/28 priority date for domestic and international students. *Application fee:* $55. Electronic applications accepted. *Application Contact:* Parag M. Shah, Administrator, Graduate Affairs, 773-702-5853, Fax: 773-834-1618, E-mail: pshah@bsd.uchicago.edu. *Dean,* Dr. James Madara, 773-702-9000.

Pritzker School of Medicine Students: 443 full-time (223 women); includes 149 minority (34 African Americans, 1 American Indian/Alaska Native, 90 Asian Americans or Pacific Islanders, 24 Hispanic Americans), 17 international. Average age 24. 7,519 applicants, 4% accepted, 106 enrolled. *Faculty:* 867 full-time. Expenses: Contact institution. *Financial support:* In 2006–07, 361 students received support, including 10 fellowships with full tuition reimbursements available (averaging $20,500 per year), 75 teaching assistantships; career-related internships or fieldwork, Federal Work-Study, institutionally sponsored loans, and scholarships/grants also available. Financial award application deadline: 4/1; financial award applicants required to submit FAFSA. In 2006, 105 degrees awarded. Offers medicine (MD). *Application deadline:* For fall admission, 10/15 for domestic students. Applications are processed on a rolling basis. *Application fee:* $75. Electronic applications accepted. *Application Contact:* Sylvia Robertson, Assistant Dean for Admissions and Financial Aid, 773-702-1937, Fax: 773-834-5412, E-mail: sroberts@bsd.uchicago.edu. *Dean,* Dr. James Madara, 773-702-9000.

Division of the Humanities Students: 1,121 full-time (594 women), 4 part-time (2 women); includes 119 minority (32 African Americans, 1 American Indian/Alaska Native, 59 Asian Americans or Pacific Islanders, 27 Hispanic Americans), 240 international. 1,994 applicants, 42% accepted, 227 enrolled. *Faculty:* 188. Expenses: Contact institution. *Financial support:* Fellowships, teaching assistantships, career-related internships or fieldwork, Federal Work-Study, institutionally sponsored loans, and tuition waivers (full and partial) available. Financial award application deadline: 12/15; financial award applicants required to submit FAFSA. In 2006, 214 master's, 66 doctorates awarded. Offers ancient philosophy (AM, PhD); anthropology and linguistics (PhD); art history (AM, PhD); cinema and media studies (AM, PhD); classical archaeology (AM, PhD); classical languages and literatures (AM, PhD); comparative literature (AM, PhD); East Asian languages and civilizations (AM, PhD); English language and literature (AM, PhD); French (AM, PhD); Germanic languages and literatures (AM, PhD); humanities (AM, MA, MFA, PhD); Italian (AM, PhD); linguistics (AM, PhD); music (AM, PhD); Near Eastern languages and civilizations (AM, PhD); New Testament and early Christian culture (AM, PhD); philosophy (AM, PhD); Slavic languages and literatures (AM, PhD); South Asian languages and civilizations (AM, PhD); Spanish (AM, PhD); visual arts (MFA). *Application deadline:* For fall admission, 12/15 for domestic students. *Application fee:* $55. *Dean of Students,* Thomas B. Thuerer, 773-795-3696, E-mail: thue@uchicago.edu.

Division of the Physical Sciences Students: 544 full-time, 68 part-time. Average age 26. *Faculty:* 173 full-time (7 women), 9 part-time/adjunct (1 woman). Expenses: Contact institution. *Financial support:* Fellowships, research assistantships, teaching assistantships, career-related internships or fieldwork, Federal Work-Study, institutionally sponsored loans, and scholarships/grants available. Support available to part-time students. Financial award applicants required to submit FAFSA. In 2006, 99 master's, 76 doctorates awarded. Offers applied mathematics (SM, PhD); astronomy and astrophysics (MS, PhD); atmospheric sciences (SM, PhD); chemistry (PhD); computer science (SM, PhD); earth sciences (SM, PhD); financial mathematics (MS); mathematics (SM, PhD); paleobiology (PhD); physical sciences (MS, SM, PhD); physics (PhD); planetary and space sciences (SM, PhD); statistics (SM, PhD). *Application fee:* $55. Electronic applications accepted. *Application Contact:* Richard Hefley, Dean of Students, 773-702-8789. *Dean,* Robert Fefferman, 773-702-7950.

Graduate School of Business Students: 1,118 full-time (323 women), 1,924 part-time (398 women). Average age 28. *Faculty:* 127 full-time, 43 part-time/adjunct. Expenses: Contact institution. *Financial support:* In 2006–07, 230 students received support, including 230 fellowships. Financial award applicants required to submit FAFSA. In 2006, 1,260 master's, 16 doctorates awarded. *Degree program information:* Part-time and evening/weekend programs available. Offers business (IMBA, MBA, PhD); business administration (MBA); executive business administration (MBA); international business administration (IMBA). *Application deadline:* For fall admission, 10/18 priority date for domestic and international students; for winter admission, 1/10 for domestic and international students; for spring admission, 3/14 for domestic and international students. *Application fee:* $200. Electronic applications accepted. *Application Contact:* Rosemaria Martinelli, Student Recruitment and Admissions, 773-702-7369, Fax: 773-702-9085, E-mail: admissions@chicagogsb.edu. *Dean,* Edward A. Snyder, 773-702-6680, Fax: 773-702-2225.

The Irving B. Harris Graduate School of Public Policy Studies *Degree program information:* Part-time programs available. Offers environmental science and policy (MS); public policy studies (AM, MPP, PhD). Electronic applications accepted.

The Law School Students: 658 full-time (293 women); includes 179 minority (43 African Americans, 4 American Indian/Alaska Native, 77 Asian Americans or Pacific Islanders, 55 Hispanic Americans), 63 international. Average age 24. 4,818 applicants. *Faculty:* 69 full-time (10 women), 58 part-time/adjunct (11 women). Expenses: Contact institution. *Financial support:* In 2006–07, 307 students received support, including 7 fellowships (averaging $3,000 per year); research assistantships, teaching assistantships, career-related internships or fieldwork, institutionally sponsored loans, and scholarships/grants also available. Financial award application deadline: 3/1; financial award applicants required to submit FAFSA. In 2006, 192 JDs, 51 master's, 1 doctorate awarded. Offers law (JD, LL M, MCL, DCL, JSD). *Application deadline:* For fall admission, 2/1 priority date for domestic students. Applications are processed on a rolling basis. *Application fee:* $75. Electronic applications accepted. *Application Contact:* Ann K. Perry, Dean of Admissions, 773-834-4425, Fax: 773-834-0942, E-mail: admissions@law.uchicago.edu. *Dean,* Saul Levmore, 773-702-9494, Fax: 773-834-4409.

School of Social Service Administration Students: 421 full-time (365 women), 62 part-time (47 women); includes 130 minority (65 African Americans, 2 American Indian/Alaska Native, 28 Asian Americans or Pacific Islanders, 35 Hispanic Americans), 12 international. Average age 28. 594 applicants, 64% accepted, 187 enrolled. *Faculty:* 33 full-time (21 women), 48 part-time/adjunct (32 women). Expenses: Contact institution. *Financial support:* In 2006–07, 415 students received support, including 20 research assistantships with full tuition reimbursements available (averaging $15,000 per year), 20 teaching assistantships with full tuition reimbursements available (averaging $12,000 per year); fellowships, career-related internships or fieldwork, Federal Work-Study, institutionally sponsored loans, scholarships/grants, health care benefits, and unspecified assistantships also available. Support available to part-time students. Financial award application deadline: 4/15; financial award applicants required to submit FAFSA. In 2006, 188 master's, 3 doctorates awarded. *Degree program information:* Part-time and evening/weekend programs available. Offers social service administration (PhD); social work (AM). *Application deadline:* For fall admission, 4/1 priority date for domestic and international students. Applications are processed on a rolling basis. *Application fee:* $60 ($70 for international students). Electronic applications accepted. *Application Contact:* Quenette Walton, Assistant Director of Admissions, 773-834-8104, Fax: 773-834-4751, E-mail: qlwalton@uchicago.edu. *Dean,* Dr. Jeanne Marsh, 773-702-1144, Fax: 773-834-1582, E-mail: j-marsh@uchicago.edu.

UNIVERSITY OF CINCINNATI, Cincinnati, OH 45221

General Information State-supported, coed, university. CGS member. *Graduate housing:* Rooms and/or apartments available on a first-come, first-served basis to single and married students. Housing application deadline: 7/1.

GRADUATE UNITS

College of Law Students: 376 full-time (184 women); includes 66 minority (26 African Americans, 3 American Indian/Alaska Native, 23 Asian Americans or Pacific Islanders, 14 Hispanic Americans). Average age 24. 1,183 applicants, 34% accepted, 113 enrolled. *Faculty:* 32 full-time (16 women), 23 part-time/adjunct (3 women). Expenses: Contact institution. *Financial support:* In 2006–07, 240 students received support, including 240 fellowships (averaging $8,000 per year); research assistantships, career-related internships or fieldwork, Federal Work-Study, scholarships/grants, tuition waivers (full and partial), and unspecified assistantships also available. Financial award application deadline: 4/1; financial award applicants required to submit FAFSA. In 2006, 123 degrees awarded. Offers law (JD). *Application deadline:* For fall admission, 4/1 priority date for domestic students. Applications are processed on a rolling basis. *Application fee:* $35. Electronic applications accepted. *Application Contact:* Al Watson, Assistant Dean and Director of Admissions, 513-556-0077, Fax: 513-556-2391, E-mail: al.watson@uc.edu. *Dean,* Louis D. Bilionois, 513-556-0121, Fax: 513-556-2391, E-mail: louis.bilionis@uc.edu.

Division of Research and Advanced Studies *Degree program information:* Part-time and evening/weekend programs available. Offers neuroscience (PhD). Electronic applications accepted.

College-Conservatory of Music Offers arts administration (MA); choral conducting (MM, DMA); composition (MM, DMA); directing (MFA); keyboard studies (MM, DMA, AD); music (MA, MFA, MM, DMA, PhD, AD); music education (MM); music history (MM); music theory (MM, PhD); musicology (PhD); orchestral conducting (MM, DMA); performance (MM, DMA, AD); theater design and production (MFA); wind conducting (MM, DMA). Electronic applications accepted.

College of Allied Health Sciences *Degree program information:* Part-time programs available. Offers allied health sciences (MA, MS, Au D, DPT, PhD); blood transfusion medicine (MS); cellular therapies (MS); communication sciences and disorders (MA, Au D, PhD); medical genetics (MS); nutritional science (MS); rehabilitation science (DPT).

College of Business Students: 243 full-time (97 women), 432 part-time (153 women); includes 56 minority (30 African Americans, 15 Asian Americans or Pacific Islanders, 11 Hispanic Americans), 177 international. Average age 31. 586 applicants, 67% accepted, 233 enrolled. *Faculty:* 85 full-time (24 women), 23 part-time/adjunct (8 women). Expenses: Contact institution. *Financial support:* In 2006–07, 105 students received support, including 27 research assistantships (averaging $9,800 per year), 20 teaching assistantships (averaging $16,000 per year); scholarships/grants, tuition waivers (full and partial), and unspecified assistantships also available. Financial award application deadline: 2/15; financial award applicants required to submit FAFSA. In 2006, 236 master's, 8 doctorates awarded. *Degree program information:* Part-time and evening/weekend programs available. Offers accounting (MBA); accounting management/organizational behavior (PhD); business (MBA, MS, PhD); construction management (MBA); e-business (MBA); finance (MBA, MS, PhD); general accounting (MS); information systems (MBA, MS); management (MBA, PhD); management of advanced technology and innovation (MBA); marketing (MBA, MS, PhD); operations management (MBA, PhD); quantitative analysis (MBA, MS, PhD); taxation (MS). *Application deadline:* For fall admission, 6/1 priority date for domestic students, 2/15 priority date for international students. Applications are processed on a rolling basis. *Application fee:* $40. Electronic applications accepted. *Application Contact:* Valerie Robinson, Associate Director, MBA Admissions, 513-556-7024, Fax: 513-558-7006, E-mail: valerie.robinson@uc.edu. *Dean,* Dr. Willard McIntosh, 513-556-7001, Fax: 513-556-4891, E-mail: will.mcintosh@uc.edu.

University of Cincinnati (continued)

College of Design, Architecture, Art, and Planning *Degree program information:* Part-time programs available. Offers architecture (M Arch); art education (MA); art history (MA); community planning (MCP); design, architecture, art, and planning (M Arch, M Des, MA, MCP, MFA, PhD); fashion design (M Des); fine arts (MFA); graphic design (M Des); industrial design (M Des); interaction design (M Des); planning (MCP); product development (M Des); regional development planning (PhD). Electronic applications accepted.

College of Education, Criminal Justice, and Human Services *Degree program information:* Part-time programs available. Postbaccalaureate distance learning degree programs offered (no on-campus study). Offers community health (MS); counseling (Ed D); counselor education (CAGS); criminal justice (MS, PhD); curriculum and instruction (M Ed, Ed D); deaf studies (Certificate); early childhood education (M Ed); education, criminal justice, and human services (M Ed, MA, MS, Ed D, PhD, CAGS, Certificate, Ed S); educational leadership (M Ed, Ed S); educational studies (M Ed, Ed D, PhD, Ed S); health education (MS, PhD); health promotion and education (M Ed); human services (M Ed, MA, MS, Ed D, PhD, CAGS, Ed S); mental health (MA); middle childhood education (M Ed); postsecondary literacy instruction (Certificate); reading/literacy (M Ed, Ed D); school counseling (M Ed); school psychology (PhD, Ed S); secondary education (M Ed); special education (M Ed, Ed D); teaching English as a second language (M Ed, Ed D, Certificate); teaching science (MS); urban educational leadership (Ed D). Electronic applications accepted.

College of Engineering *Degree program information:* Part-time and evening/weekend programs available. Offers aerospace engineering and engineering mechanics (MS, PhD); bioinformatics (PhD); biomechanics (PhD); ceramic science and engineering (MS, PhD); chemical engineering (MS, PhD); civil engineering (MS, PhD); computer engineering (MS); computer science (MS); computer science and engineering (PhD); electrical engineering (MS, PhD); engineering (MS, PhD); environmental engineering (MS, PhD); environmental sciences (MS, PhD); health physics (MS); industrial engineering (MS, PhD); materials science and engineering (MS, PhD); materials science and metallurgical engineering (MS, PhD); mechanical engineering (MS, PhD); medical imaging (PhD); metallurgical engineering (MS, PhD); nuclear engineering (MS, PhD); polymer science and engineering (MS, PhD); tissue engineering (PhD).

College of Medicine Students: 888 full-time (370 women), 104 part-time (55 women); includes 218 minority (54 African Americans, 5 American Indian/Alaska Native, 147 Asian Americans or Pacific Islanders, 12 Hispanic Americans), 28 international. 2,626 applicants, 21% accepted, 249 enrolled. *Faculty:* 1,371. Expenses: Contact institution. *Financial support:* In 2006–07, fellowships with full tuition reimbursements (averaging $20,500 per year), research assistantships with full tuition reimbursements (averaging $20,500 per year) were awarded; career-related internships or fieldwork, institutionally sponsored loans, health care benefits, and tuition waivers (partial) also available. Financial award application deadline: 5/1. In 2006, 154 MDs, 19 master's, 41 doctorates awarded. Offers biomedical sciences (MS, PhD); cell and molecular biology (PhD); cell biophysics (PhD); environmental and industrial hygiene (MS, PhD); environmental and occupational medicine (MS); environmental genetics and molecular toxicology (MS, PhD); epidemiology and biostatistics (MS, PhD); immunobiology (MS, PhD); medical physics (MS); medicine (MD, MS, D Sc, PhD); molecular and developmental biology (PhD); molecular genetics, biochemistry and microbiology (MS, PhD); occupational safety and ergonomics (MS, PhD); pathology (PhD); pharmacology (PhD); physiology (PhD); teratology (PhD). *Application deadline:* Applications are processed on a rolling basis. *Application fee:* $40. Electronic applications accepted. *Application Contact:* Laura E. Hildreth, Assistant Dean, Office of Research and Graduate Education, 513-558-6791, Fax: 513-558-2850, E-mail: laura.hildreth@uc.edu. *Dean,* Dr. David Stern, 513-558-1203, Fax: 513-558-1300.

College of Pharmacy *Degree program information:* Part-time programs available. Offers pharmaceutical sciences (MS, PhD); pharmacy (Pharm D, MS, PhD); pharmacy practice (Pharm D).

McMicken College of Arts and Sciences *Degree program information:* Part-time and evening/weekend programs available. Offers analytical chemistry (MS, PhD); anthropology (MA); applied economics (MA); applied mathematics (MS, PhD); arts and sciences (MA, MALER, MAT, MS, PhD, Certificate); biochemistry (MS, PhD); biological sciences (MS, PhD); classics (MA, PhD); clinical psychology (PhD); communication (MA); English (MA, MAT, PhD); experimental psychology (PhD); French (MA); geography (MA, PhD); geology (MS, PhD); German studies (MA, PhD); history (MA, PhD); inorganic chemistry (MS, PhD); interdisciplinary studies (PhD); labor and employment relations (MALER); mathematics education (MAT); organic chemistry (MS, PhD); organizational leadership (MALER); philosophy (MA, PhD); physical chemistry (MS, PhD); physics (MS, PhD); political science (MA, PhD); polymer chemistry (MS, PhD); pure mathematics (MS, PhD); Romance languages and literatures (PhD); sensors (PhD); sociology (MA, PhD); Spanish (MA); statistics (MS, PhD); women's studies (MA, Certificate).

School of Social Work *Degree program information:* Part-time programs available. Offers social work (MSW). Electronic applications accepted.

Graduate School

College of Nursing Students: 159 full-time (125 women), 149 part-time (145 women); includes 40 minority (22 African Americans, 1 American Indian/Alaska Native, 16 Asian Americans or Pacific Islanders, 1 Hispanic American). Average age 34. 385 applicants, 49% accepted, 132 enrolled. *Faculty:* 41 full-time (39 women), 16 part-time/adjunct (15 women). Expenses: Contact institution. *Financial support:* In 2006–07, 164 students received support, including 7 fellowships with full tuition reimbursements available (averaging $13,571 per year), research assistantships with full tuition reimbursements available (averaging $12,000 per year), 8 teaching assistantships with full tuition reimbursements available (averaging $12,000 per year); career-related internships or fieldwork, scholarships/grants, traineeships, tuition waivers (partial), and unspecified assistantships also available. Support available to part-time students. Financial award application deadline: 5/1; financial award applicants required to submit FAFSA. In 2006, 77 master's, 5 doctorates awarded. *Degree program information:* Part-time programs available. Postbaccalaureate distance learning degree programs offered (no on-campus study). Offers clinical nurse specialist (MSN); nurse anesthesia (MSN); nurse midwifery (MSN); nurse practitioner (MSN); nursing (PhD). *Application deadline:* For fall admission, 7/26 priority date for domestic and international students. Applications are processed on a rolling basis. *Application fee:* $40. Electronic applications accepted. *Application Contact:* Loren Carter, Program Coordinator, 513-558-5072, Fax: 513-558-7523, E-mail: loren.carter@uc.edu. *Dean,* Dr. Andrea R. Lindell, 513-558-5330, Fax: 513-558-9030, E-mail: andrea.lindell@uc.edu.

UNIVERSITY OF COLORADO AT BOULDER, Boulder, CO 80309

General Information State-supported, coed, university. CGS member. *Enrollment:* 31,399 graduate, professional, and undergraduate students; 3,675 full-time matriculated graduate/professional students (1,636 women), 1,320 part-time matriculated graduate/professional students (568 women). *Graduate faculty:* 953 full-time (265 women). *Graduate housing:* Rooms and/or apartments available to single and married students. *Student services:* Campus employment opportunities, campus safety program, career counseling, child daycare facilities, free psychological counseling, international student services, low-cost health insurance. *Library facilities:* Norlin Library plus 5 others. *Online resources:* library catalog, web page, access to other libraries' catalogs. *Collection:* 3.6 million titles, 26,152 serial subscriptions, 450,928 audiovisual materials. *Research affiliation:* National Center for Atmospheric Research, National Institute of Standards and Technology, National Oceanic and Atmospheric Administration, U.S. West Advanced Technologies, NASA.

Computer facilities: 1,525 computers available on campus for general student use. A campuswide network can be accessed from student residence rooms and from off campus. Internet access and online class registration, standard and academic software, student government voting are available. *Web address:* http://www.colorado.edu/.

General Application Contact: Philip Distefano, Chancellor, 303-492-8908, E-mail: phil.distefano@colorado.edu.

GRADUATE UNITS

Graduate School Students: 2,999 full-time (1,322 women), 1,206 part-time (548 women); includes 429 minority (45 African Americans, 32 American Indian/Alaska Native, 159 Asian Americans or Pacific Islanders, 193 Hispanic Americans), 641 international. Average age 30. 2,659 applicants, 76% accepted. *Faculty:* 894 full-time (267 women). Expenses: Contact institution. *Financial support:* In 2006–07, 1,113 fellowships with full tuition reimbursements (averaging $6,918 per year), 872 research assistantships with full tuition reimbursements (averaging $15,004 per year), 1,134 teaching assistantships with full tuition reimbursements (averaging $13,181 per year) were awarded; career-related internships or fieldwork, Federal Work-Study, institutionally sponsored loans, scholarships/grants, traineeships, tuition waivers (full and partial), and unspecified assistantships also available. Support available to part-time students. Financial award applicants required to submit FAFSA. In 2006, 891 master's, 305 doctorates awarded. *Degree program information:* Part-time programs available. Postbaccalaureate distance learning degree programs offered. *Application fee:* $50 ($60 for international students). Electronic applications accepted. *Application Contact:* Lisa Hutton, Assistant to the Dean, 303-492-2890, E-mail: lisa.hutton@colorado.edu. *Dean,* Susan Avery, 303-492-2890, Fax: 303-492-5777, E-mail: susan.k.avery@colorado.edu.

College of Arts and Sciences Students: 1,700 full-time (835 women), 501 part-time (251 women); includes 196 minority (16 African Americans, 16 American Indian/Alaska Native, 64 Asian Americans or Pacific Islanders, 100 Hispanic Americans), 273 international. Average age 30. 1,044 applicants, 82% accepted. *Faculty:* 638 full-time (202 women). Expenses: Contact institution. *Financial support:* In 2006–07, 727 fellowships with full tuition reimbursements (averaging $7,078 per year), 513 research assistantships with full tuition reimbursements (averaging $15,456 per year), 960 teaching assistantships with full tuition reimbursements (averaging $12,594 per year) were awarded; career-related internships or fieldwork, Federal Work-Study, institutionally sponsored loans, scholarships/grants, traineeships, tuition waivers (full), and unspecified assistantships also available. Support available to part-time students. In 2006, 334 master's, 194 doctorates awarded. *Degree program information:* Part-time programs available. Offers animal behavior (MA); anthropology (MA, PhD); applied mathematics (MS, PhD); art history (MA); arts and sciences (MA, MFA, MS, Au D, PhD); astrophysics (MS, PhD); atmospheric and oceanic sciences (MS, PhD); audiology (Au D, PhD); biochemistry (PhD); biology (MA, PhD); cellular structure and function (MA, PhD); ceramics (MFA); chemical physics (PhD); chemistry (MS); Chinese (MA, PhD); classics (MA, PhD); clinical research and practice in audiology (PhD); communication (MA, PhD); comparative literature and humanities (MA, PhD); dance (MFA); developmental biology (MA, PhD); drawing (MFA); economics (MA, PhD); environmental biology (MA, PhD); environmental studies (MS, PhD); evolutionary biology (MA, PhD); French (MA, PhD); geography (MA, PhD); geology (MS, PhD); geophysics (PhD); German (MA); Hispanic linguistics (MA); history (MA, PhD); integrative physiology (MS, PhD); international affairs (MA); Japanese (MA, PhD); linguistics (MA, PhD); liquid crystal science and technology (PhD); literature (MA, PhD); mathematical physics (PhD); mathematics (MA, MS, PhD); medical physics (PhD); medieval/early modern Hispanic literatures (PhD); molecular biology (MA, PhD); museum and field studies (MS); neurobiology (MA); optical sciences and engineering (PhD); painting (MFA); philosophy (MA, PhD); photography and media arts (MFA); physics (MS, PhD); planetary science (MS, PhD); political science (MA, PhD); population biology (MA); population genetics (PhD); printmaking (MFA); psychology (MA, PhD); public policy (MA); religious studies (MA); sculpture (MFA); sociology (PhD); Spanish literature (MA, PhD); speech, language and hearing science (MA); speech-language pathology (MA, PhD); speech-language-hearing sciences (PhD); theatre (MA, PhD). *Application fee:* $50 ($60 for international students). Electronic applications accepted. *Application Contact:* Kate Secrest, Assistant to the Dean, 303-492-8799, E-mail: kate.secrest@colorado.edu. *Dean,* Todd T. Gleeson, 303-492-7294, E-mail: gleeson@stripe.colorado.edu.

College of Engineering and Applied Science Students: 837 full-time (198 women), 414 part-time (84 women); includes 138 minority (18 African Americans, 10 American Indian/Alaska Native, 70 Asian Americans or Pacific Islanders, 40 Hispanic Americans), 324 international. Average age 29. 1,146 applicants, 66% accepted. *Faculty:* 160 full-time (24 women). Expenses: Contact institution. *Financial support:* In 2006–07, 170 fellowships with full tuition reimbursements (averaging $10,478 per year), 322 research assistantships with full tuition reimbursements (averaging $14,918 per year), 106 teaching assistantships with full tuition reimbursements (averaging $20,107 per year) were awarded; career-related internships or fieldwork, scholarships/grants, traineeships, and tuition waivers (full) also available. In 2006, 309 master's, 82 doctorates awarded. *Degree program information:* Part-time programs available. Postbaccalaureate distance learning degree programs offered. Offers aerospace engineering sciences (ME, MS, PhD); building systems (MS, PhD); chemical engineering (ME, MS, PhD); computer science (ME, MS, PhD); construction engineering and management (MS, PhD); electrical and computer engineering (ME, MS); electrical engineering (PhD); engineering and applied science (ME, MS, PhD); environmental engineering (MS, PhD); geoenvironmental engineering (MS, PhD); geotechnical engineering (MS, PhD); mechanical engineering (ME, MS, PhD); operations and logistics (ME); quality and process (ME); research and development (ME); structural engineering (MS, PhD); telecommunications (ME, MS); water resources engineering (MS, PhD). *Application fee:* $50 ($60 for international students). Electronic applications accepted. *Dean,* Robert Davis, 303-492-7006, Fax: 303-492-0353, E-mail: robert.davis@colorado.edu.

College of Music Students: 192 full-time (98 women), 52 part-time (23 women); includes 22 minority (2 African Americans, 2 American Indian/Alaska Native, 10 Asian Americans or Pacific Islanders, 8 Hispanic Americans), 32 international. Average age 31. 186 applicants, 82% accepted. *Faculty:* 48 full-time (18 women). Expenses: Contact institution. *Financial support:* In 2006–07, 150 fellowships (averaging $3,030 per year), 11 teaching assistantships (averaging $8,294 per year) were awarded; tuition waivers (full) also available. Financial award application deadline: 3/1. In 2006, 46 master's, 14 doctorates awarded. Offers church music (M Mus); composition (M Mus, D Mus A); conducting (M Mus, D Mus A); music education (M Mus Ed, PhD); music literature (M Mus); musicology (PhD); pedagogy (M Mus, D Mus A); performance (M Mus, D Mus A). *Application deadline:* For fall admission, 3/1 priority date for domestic students, 12/1 for international students. Applications are processed on a rolling basis. *Application fee:* $50 ($60 for international students). Electronic applications accepted. *Application Contact:* Associate Dean for Graduate Studies, 303-492-2207, Fax: 303-492-5619, E-mail: gradmusc@colorado.edu. *Dean,* Daniel P. Sher, 303-492-7505, Fax: 303-492-5619, E-mail: daniel.sher@colorado.edu.

School of Education Students: 165 full-time (123 women), 215 part-time (176 women); includes 57 minority (5 African Americans, 2 American Indian/Alaska Native, 12 Asian Americans or Pacific Islanders, 38 Hispanic Americans), 2 international. Average age 32. 156 applicants, 92% accepted. *Faculty:* 28 full-time (13 women). Expenses: Contact institution. *Financial support:* In 2006–07, 42 fellowships (averaging $5,155 per year), 34 research assistantships (averaging $9,326 per year), 23 teaching assistantships (averaging $9,318 per year) were awarded; career-related internships or fieldwork, Federal Work-Study, scholarships/grants, and tuition waivers (full and partial) also available. Support available to part-time students. Financial award application deadline: 2/1. In 2006, 172 master's, 9 doctorates awarded. *Degree program information:* Part-time programs available. Offers education (MA, PhD); educational and psychological studies (MA, PhD); educational foundations, policy, and practice (MA, PhD); instruction and curriculum (MA, PhD); research and evaluation methodology (PhD); social multicultural and bilingual foundations (MA, PhD). *Application deadline:* For fall admission, 2/1 priority date for domestic students, 12/1 for international students; for spring admission, 9/1 for domestic students, 12/1 for international students. *Application fee:* $50 ($60 for international students). *Application Contact:* Graduate Program Assistant, 303-492-6555, Fax: 303-492-5839, E-mail: edadvise@colorado.edu. *Dean,* Lorrie Shepard, 303-492-6937, Fax: 303-492-7090, E-mail: lorrie.shepard@colorado.edu.

School of Journalism and Mass Communication Students: 91 full-time (58 women), 22 part-time (12 women); includes 12 minority (4 African Americans, 2 Asian Americans or Pacific Islanders, 6 Hispanic Americans), 10 international. Average age 32. 113 applicants, 81% accepted. *Faculty:* 20 full-time (10 women). Expenses: Contact institution. *Financial support:* In 2006–07, 18 fellowships (averaging $4,092 per year), 2 research assistantships with tuition reimbursements (averaging $13,745 per year), 33 teaching assistantships with tuition reimbursements (averaging $12,302 per year) were awarded; institutionally sponsored loans and unspecified assistantships also available. Financial award application deadline: 3/1. In 2006, 21 master's, 6 doctorates awarded. *Degree program information:* Part-time programs available. Offers communication (PhD); mass communication research (MA); media studies (PhD); newsgathering (MA). *Application deadline:* For fall admission, 2/15 for domestic students, 12/1 for international students. Applications are processed on a rolling basis. *Application fee:* $50 ($60 for international students). *Application Contact:* Graduate Program Assistant, 303-492-5008, Fax: 303-492-0969, E-mail: sjmcgrad@colorado.edu. *Dean,* Paul Voakes, 303-492-4364, Fax: 303-492-0969, E-mail: paul.voakes@colorado.edu.

Leeds School of Business Students: 167 full-time (58 women), 113 part-time (20 women); includes 25 minority (16 Asian Americans or Pacific Islanders, 9 Hispanic Americans), 35 international. Average age 30. 135 applicants, 96% accepted. *Faculty:* 48 full-time (11 women). Expenses: Contact institution. *Financial support:* In 2006–07, 7 fellowships (averaging $4,254 per year), 26 research assistantships (averaging $14,883 per year), 20 teaching assistantships (averaging $11,984 per year) were awarded; career-related internships or fieldwork, Federal Work-Study, scholarships/grants, and unspecified assistantships also available. Financial award application deadline: 3/1. In 2006, 121 master's, 8 doctorates awarded. *Degree program information:* Part-time and evening/weekend programs available. Offers accounting (MS, PhD); business (PhD); business administration (MBA, PhD); finance (PhD); management (PhD); marketing (PhD). *Application deadline:* For fall admission, 3/1 priority date for domestic students, 3/1 for international students. Applications are processed on a rolling basis. *Application fee:* $50 ($60 for international students). Electronic applications accepted. *Application Contact:* Information Contact, 303-492-1809, Fax: 303-492-1727, E-mail: busgrad@spot.colorado.edu. *Dean,* Dennis Ahlburg, 303-492-1809, Fax: 303-492-7676, E-mail: dennis.ahlburg@colorado.edu.

School of Law Students: 509 full-time (256 women), 1 part-time; includes 116 minority (19 African Americans, 17 American Indian/Alaska Native, 44 Asian Americans or Pacific Islanders, 36 Hispanic Americans), 5 international. Average age 27. 677 applicants, 100% accepted. *Faculty:* 32 full-time (11 women). Expenses: Contact institution. *Financial support:* In 2006–07, 118 fellowships (averaging $1,613 per year), 11 teaching assistantships (averaging $1,639 per year) were awarded; research assistantships, Federal Work-Study, and institutionally sponsored loans also available. Financial award application deadline: 3/1; financial award applicants required to submit FAFSA. In 2006, 169 JDs awarded. Offers law (JD). *Application deadline:* For fall admission, 2/15 for domestic students. Applications are processed on a rolling basis. *Application fee:* $50 ($60 for international students). *Application Contact:* Graduate Program Assistant, 303-492-7203, Fax: 303-492-2542, E-mail: lawadmin@colorado.edu. *Dean,* Harold H. Bruff, 303-492-8047, Fax: 303-492-1757, E-mail: harold.bruff@colorado.edu.

UNIVERSITY OF COLORADO AT COLORADO SPRINGS, Colorado Springs, CO 80933-7150

General Information State-supported, coed, comprehensive institution. *Enrollment:* 8,583 graduate, professional, and undergraduate students; 865 full-time matriculated graduate/professional students (528 women), 593 part-time matriculated graduate/professional students (330 women). *Enrollment by degree level:* 1,376 master's, 57 doctoral, 25 other advanced degrees. *Graduate faculty:* 157 full-time (56 women), 85 part-time/adjunct (44 women). Tuition, state resident: part-time $303 per credit hour. Tuition, nonresident: part-time $840 per credit hour. Tuition and fees vary according to course load, campus/location and program. *Graduate housing:* Room and/or apartments available on a first-come, first-served basis to single students; on-campus housing not available to married students. Typical cost: $6,738 (including board). Room and board charges vary according to board plan. *Student services:* Campus employment opportunities, campus safety program, career counseling, child daycare facilities, disabled student services, exercise/wellness program, free psychological counseling, international student services, low-cost health insurance, multicultural affairs office, teacher training, writing training. *Library facilities:* University of Colorado at Colorado Springs Kraemer Family Library. *Online resources:* library catalog, web page, access to other libraries' catalogs. *Collection:* 391,638 titles, 2,201 serial subscriptions. *Research affiliation:* Symetrix (ferroelectronics), Colorado Vintage Companies (radon mitigation), Omegatech (genetics).

Computer facilities: 250 computers available on campus for general student use. A campuswide network can be accessed from student residence rooms and from off campus. *Web address:* http://www.uccs.edu/.

General Application Contact: Jackie Francis, Graduate Recruitment Coordinator, 719-262-3072, Fax: 719-262-3045, E-mail: gradschl@uccs.edu.

GRADUATE UNITS

Graduate School Students: 551 full-time (335 women), 387 part-time (211 women); includes 165 minority (45 African Americans, 6 American Indian/Alaska Native, 47 Asian Americans or Pacific Islanders, 67 Hispanic Americans), 24 international. Average age 34. 738 applicants, 88% accepted, 398 enrolled. *Faculty:* 123 full-time (42 women), 42 part-time/adjunct (21 women). Expenses: Contact institution. *Financial support:* Fellowships, research assistantships, teaching assistantships, career-related internships or fieldwork, Federal Work-Study, and institutionally sponsored loans available. Support available to part-time students. Financial award applicants required to submit FAFSA. In 2006, 300 master's, 3 doctorates awarded. *Degree program information:* Part-time and evening/weekend programs available. Postbaccalaureate distance learning degree programs offered (no on-campus study). *Application deadline:* Applications are processed on a rolling basis. *Application fee:* $60 ($75 for international students). *Application Contact:* Information Contact, 719-262-3417, Fax: 719-262-3037, E-mail: gradschl@uccs.edu. *Dean,* Dr. Tom Huber, 719-262-3044, Fax: 719-262-3037, E-mail: thuber@uccs.edu.

Beth-El College of Nursing Students: 84 full-time (77 women), 53 part-time (52 women); includes 22 minority (6 African Americans, 3 American Indian/Alaska Native, 2 Asian Americans or Pacific Islanders, 11 Hispanic Americans). Average age 37. 54 applicants, 85% accepted, 30 enrolled. *Faculty:* 10 full-time (7 women), 14 part-time/adjunct (7 women). Expenses: Contact institution. *Financial support:* Fellowships, career-related internships or fieldwork, Federal Work-Study, and institutionally sponsored loans available. Support available to part-time students. In 2006, 36 degrees awarded. *Degree program information:* Part-time programs available. Postbaccalaureate distance learning degree programs offered (minimal on-campus study). Offers adult health nurse practitioner and clinical specialist (MSN); family practitioner (MSN); gerontology (MSN); neonatal nurse practitioner and clinical specialist (MSN); nursing administration (MSN); women nurse practitioner (MSN). *Application deadline:* For fall admission, 6/1 priority date for domestic students; for spring admission, 11/15 for domestic students. *Application fee:* $60 ($75 for international students). Electronic applications accepted. *Dean,* Dr. Carole Schoffstall, 719-262-4418, Fax: 719-262-4416, E-mail: cschoffs@uccs.edu.

College of Education Students: 331 full-time (246 women), 173 part-time (135 women); includes 85 minority (26 African Americans, 4 American Indian/Alaska Native, 13 Asian Americans or Pacific Islanders, 42 Hispanic Americans). Average age 35. 107 applicants, 93% accepted, 49 enrolled. *Faculty:* 22 full-time (15 women), 29 part-time/adjunct (17 women). Expenses: Contact institution. *Financial support:* Fellowships, career-related internships or fieldwork and Federal Work-Study available. In 2006, 234 degrees awarded. *Degree program information:* Part-time and evening/weekend programs available. Offers counseling and human services (MA); curriculum and instruction (MA); educational administration (MA); educational leadership (MA, PhD); special education (MA). *Application deadline:* For fall admission, 6/15 for domestic students; for spring admission, 10/15 for domestic students. Applications are processed on a rolling basis. *Application fee:* $60 ($75 for international students). *Application Contact:* Connie Wroten, Professional Assistant, 719-262-4102, Fax: 719-262-4110, E-mail: cwroten@uccs.edu. *Dean,* Dr. LaVonne Neal, 719-262-4111, Fax: 719-262-4110, E-mail: lneal@uccs.edu.

College of Engineering and Applied Science Students: 103 full-time (24 women), 137 part-time (27 women); includes 43 minority (7 African Americans, 1 American Indian/Alaska Native, 25 Asian Americans or Pacific Islanders, 10 Hispanic Americans), 22 international. Average age 34. 88 applicants, 91% accepted, 54 enrolled. *Faculty:* 37 full-time (1 woman), 7 part-time/adjunct (2 women). Expenses: Contact institution. *Financial support:* Fellowships, research assistantships, teaching assistantships, career-related internships or fieldwork and Federal Work-Study available. In 2006, 41 master's, 3 doctorates awarded. *Degree program information:* Part-time and evening/weekend programs available. Offers computer science (MS); electrical engineering (MS, PhD); engineering (PhD); engineering and applied science (ME, MS, PhD); engineering management (ME); information operations (ME); manufacturing (ME); mechanical engineering (MS); software engineering (ME); space operations (ME); space systems (MS). *Application deadline:* For fall admission, 5/1 for domestic students; for spring admission, 10/1 for domestic students. Applications are processed on a rolling basis. *Application fee:* $60 ($75 for international students). *Dean,* Dr. Jeremy Haefner, 719-262-3543, Fax: 719-262-3542, E-mail: haefner@cas.uccs.edu.

College of Letters, Arts and Sciences Students: 117 full-time (65 women), 78 part-time (50 women); includes 37 minority (12 African Americans, 1 American Indian/Alaska Native, 9 Asian Americans or Pacific Islanders, 15 Hispanic Americans), 2 international. Average age 32. 290 applicants, 90% accepted, 162 enrolled. *Faculty:* 64 full-time (26 women), 6 part-time/adjunct (2 women). Expenses: Contact institution. *Financial support:* Fellowships, research assistantships, teaching assistantships, career-related internships or fieldwork, Federal Work-Study, and institutionally sponsored loans available. Support available to part-time students. Financial award applicants required to submit FAFSA. In 2006, 45 degrees awarded. *Degree program information:* Part-time and evening/weekend programs available. Offers applied mathematics (MS); communications (MA); geography and environmental studies (MA); geropsychology (PhD); history (MA); letters, arts and sciences (M Sc, MA, MS, PhD); psychology (MA); sciences (M Sc); sociology (MA). *Application deadline:* Applications are processed on a rolling basis. *Dean,* Dr. Tom Christensen, 719-262-4550, Fax: 719-262-3023, E-mail: tchriste@uccs.edu.

Graduate School of Business Administration Students: 158 full-time (70 women), 290 part-time (87 women); includes 48 minority (11 African Americans, 1 American Indian/Alaska Native, 20 Asian Americans or Pacific Islanders, 16 Hispanic Americans), 7 international. Average age 33. 158 applicants, 75% accepted, 51 enrolled. *Faculty:* 15 full-time (4 women), 4 part-time/adjunct (0 women). Expenses: Contact institution. *Financial support:* Career-related internships or fieldwork, Federal Work-Study, and institutionally sponsored loans available. Support available to part-time students. Financial award applicants required to submit FAFSA. In 2006, 119 degrees awarded. *Degree program information:* Part-time and evening/weekend programs available. Offers accounting (MBA); finance (MBA); general health care administration (MBA); information systems (MBA); international business management (MBA); marketing (MBA); service management/technology management (MBA). *Application deadline:* For fall admission, 6/1 for domestic students; for spring admission, 11/1 for domestic students. *Application fee:* $60 ($75 for international students). *Application Contact:* Amy DeLourenco, MBA Program Director, 719-262-3408, Fax: 719-262-3100, E-mail: busadvsr@uccs.edu. *Dean,* Dr. Venkateshwar Reddy, 719-262-3113, Fax: 719-262-3494, E-mail: vreddy@uccs.edu.

Graduate School of Public Affairs Students: 48 full-time (28 women), 41 part-time (25 women); includes 18 minority (5 African Americans, 3 Asian Americans or Pacific Islanders, 10 Hispanic Americans). Average age 35. 32 applicants, 78% accepted, 19 enrolled. *Faculty:* 8 full-time (2 women), 25 part-time/adjunct (15 women). Expenses: Contact institution. *Financial support:* Career-related internships or fieldwork and Federal Work-Study available. Support available to part-time students. In 2006, 22 degrees awarded. *Degree program information:* Part-time and evening/weekend programs available. Offers criminal justice (MCJ); public administration (MPA). *Application deadline:* For fall admission, 6/1 priority date for domestic students; for spring admission, 11/1 for domestic students. Applications are processed on a rolling basis. *Application fee:* $60 ($75 for international students). *Application Contact:* Mary Lou Kartis, Program Assistant, 719-262-4182, Fax: 719-262-4183, E-mail: mkartis@uccs.edu. *Dean,* Dr. Kathleen Beatty, 719-262-4182, Fax: 719-262-4183, E-mail: kbeatty@uccs.edu.

UNIVERSITY OF COLORADO AT DENVER AND HEALTH SCIENCES CENTER, Denver, CO 80217-3364

General Information State-supported, coed, university. CGS member. *Enrollment:* 19,766 graduate, professional, and undergraduate students; 3,611 full-time matriculated graduate/professional students (2,176 women), 2,788 part-time matriculated graduate/professional students (1,651 women). *Enrollment by degree level:* 1,431 first professional, 4,246 master's, 691 doctoral, 31 other advanced degrees. *Graduate faculty:* 2,154 full-time (990 women), 75 part-time/adjunct (34 women). *Graduate housing:* On-campus housing not available. *Student services:* Campus employment opportunities, campus safety program, career counseling, child daycare facilities, disabled student services, exercise/wellness program, free psychological counseling, international student services, low-cost health insurance, teacher training, writing training. *Library facilities:* Auraria Library. *Online resources:* library catalog, web page, access to other libraries' catalogs. *Collection:* 927,468 titles, 88,134 serial subscriptions, 15,366 audiovisual materials. *Research affiliation:* National Jewish Center (immunology, molecular biology), The Children's Hospital (genetic counseling).

Computer facilities: 750 computers available on campus for general student use. A campuswide network can be accessed from student residence rooms and from off campus. Internet access and online class registration are available. *Web address:* http://www.ucdhsc.edu/.

General Application Contact: Graduate School Admissions, 303-556-2400, E-mail: admissions@cudenver.edu.

GRADUATE UNITS

Business School Students: 275 full-time (130 women), 758 part-time (318 women); includes 143 minority (18 African Americans, 7 American Indian/Alaska Native, 67 Asian Americans or Pacific Islanders, 51 Hispanic Americans), 113 international. Average age 27. 535 applicants, 69% accepted, 193 enrolled. *Faculty:* 67 full-time (25 women). Expenses: Contact institution. *Financial support:* Research assistantships, career-related internships or fieldwork, Federal Work-Study, institutionally sponsored loans, scholarships/grants, traineeships, and tuition waivers (partial) available. Support available to part-time students. Financial award application deadline: 4/1; financial award applicants required to submit FAFSA. In 2006, 566 degrees awarded. *Degree program information:* Part-time and evening/weekend programs available. Postbaccalaureate distance learning degree programs offered (minimal on-campus study). Offers accounting (MS); business (Exec MBA, MBA, MS, MSIB, PhD); business administration (Exec MBA, MBA); computer science and information systems (PhD); finance (MS); health administration (MBA); information systems (MS); international business (MSIB); management and organization (MS); marketing (MS); pharmaceutical management (MBA). *Application deadline:* For fall admission, 6/1 for domestic students, 3/15 for international students; for spring admission, 11/1 for domestic students, 10/1 for international students. Applications are processed on a rolling basis. *Application fee:* $50 ($75 for international students). Electronic applications accepted. *Application Contact:* Shelly Townley, Admissions Coordinator, 303-556-5956, Fax: 303-556-5904, E-mail: shelly.townley@cudenver.edu. *Interim Associate Dean,* Cliff Young, 303-556-5803, Fax: 303-556-5914, E-mail: cliff.young@cudenver.edu.

College of Architecture and Planning Students: 394 full-time (157 women), 107 part-time (56 women); includes 52 minority (7 African Americans, 1 American Indian/Alaska Native, 18 Asian Americans or Pacific Islanders, 26 Hispanic Americans), 23 international. Average age 31. 333 applicants, 56% accepted, 150 enrolled. *Faculty:* 52 full-time (17 women). Expenses: Contact institution. *Financial support:* Fellowships with partial tuition reimbursements, research assistantships, teaching assistantships, career-related internships or fieldwork, Federal Work-Study, institutionally sponsored loans, scholarships/grants, and tuition waivers (full and partial) available. Support available to part-time students. Financial award application deadline: 4/1; financial award applicants required to submit FAFSA. In 2006, 175 master's, 5 doctorates awarded. *Degree program information:* Part-time programs available. Offers architecture (M Arch); architecture and planning (M Arch, MLA, MUD, MURP, PhD); design and planning (PhD); landscape architecture (MLA); urban and regional planning (MURP); urban design (MUD). *Application deadline:* For fall admission, 3/15 for domestic students; for spring admission, 10/1 for domestic students. *Application fee:* $50 ($75 for international students). *Application Contact:* Heather Zertuche, Administrative Assistant II, 303-556-3382, Fax: 303-556-3687, E-mail: anpdeansoffice@storm.cudenver.edu. *Dean,* Mark Gelernter, 303-556-5938, Fax: 303-556-3687, E-mail: mark.gelernter@cudenver.edu.

University of Colorado at Denver and Health Sciences Center (continued)

College of Arts and Media Students: 9 full-time (1 woman), 6 part-time; includes 1 minority (African American), 3 international. Average age 29. 18 applicants, 56% accepted, 7 enrolled. *Faculty:* 4 full-time (1 woman). Expenses: Contact institution. *Financial support:* Federal Work-Study, institutionally sponsored loans, and scholarships/grants available. Support available to part-time students. Financial award application deadline: 4/1; financial award applicants required to submit FAFSA. In 2006, 5 degrees awarded. *Degree program information:* Part-time and evening/weekend programs available. Postbaccalaureate distance learning degree programs offered. Offers arts and media (MS); recording arts (MS). *Application deadline:* For fall admission, 2/15 for domestic students; for spring admission, 11/1 for domestic students. Applications are processed on a rolling basis. *Application fee:* $50 ($75 for international students). Electronic applications accepted. *Application Contact:* Dr. Roy Pritts, Program Director, 303-556-2795, Fax: 303-556-2335, E-mail: rpritts@carbon.cudenver.edu. *Dean,* David Dynak, 303-556-6591, Fax: 303-556-2335, E-mail: david.dynak@cudenver.edu.

College of Engineering and Applied Science Students: 54 full-time (20 women), 265 part-time (69 women); includes 62 minority (13 African Americans, 34 Asian Americans or Pacific Islanders, 15 Hispanic Americans), 88 international. Average age 32. 247 applicants, 77% accepted, 81 enrolled. *Faculty:* 40 full-time (5 women). Expenses: Contact institution. *Financial support:* Research assistantships, teaching assistantships, career-related internships or fieldwork and Federal Work-Study available. Financial award application deadline: 4/1; financial award applicants required to submit FAFSA. In 2006, 126 master's, 2 doctorates awarded. *Degree program information:* Part-time and evening/weekend programs available. Offers civil engineering (MS, PhD); computer science and engineering (MS); computer science and information systems (PhD); electrical engineering (M Eng, MS); engineering and applied science (M Eng, MS, PhD); geographic information systems (M Eng); mechanical engineering (M Eng, MS). *Application deadline:* For fall admission, 4/1 for domestic students; for spring admission, 10/1 for domestic students. Applications are processed on a rolling basis. *Application fee:* $50 ($75 for international students). Electronic applications accepted. *Assistant Dean of Student Services,* Paul Rakowski, 303-556-4768, Fax: 303-556-2511, E-mail: gradceo@cudenver.edu.

College of Liberal Arts and Sciences Students: 169 full-time (92 women), 484 part-time (294 women); includes 93 minority (18 African Americans, 5 American Indian/Alaska Native, 22 Asian Americans or Pacific Islanders, 48 Hispanic Americans), 49 international. Average age 33. 410 applicants, 56% accepted, 151 enrolled. *Faculty:* 173 full-time (69 women). Expenses: Contact institution. *Financial support:* Fellowships, research assistantships, teaching assistantships, career-related internships or fieldwork and Federal Work-Study available. Financial award application deadline: 4/1; financial award applicants required to submit FAFSA. In 2006, 181 master's, 11 doctorates awarded. *Degree program information:* Part-time and evening/weekend programs available. Offers anthropology (MA); applied linguistics (MA); applied mathematics (MS, PhD); applied science (MIS); biology (MS); chemistry (MS); communication (MA); computer science (MIS); economics (MA); English studies (MA); environmental sciences (MS); geographic information science (Certificate); health and behavioral sciences (PhD); history (MA); humanities (MH); interactive media (Certificate); liberal arts and sciences (MA, MH, MIS, MS, MSS, PhD, Certificate); literature (MA); mathematics (MIS); political science (MA); psychology (MA); public relations (Certificate); social science (MSS); sociology (MA); Spanish (MA); teaching English to speakers of other languages (Certificate); teaching of writing (MA); technical and professional communication (Certificate); technical communication (MS); usability testing and interface design (Certificate). *Application deadline:* Applications are processed on a rolling basis. *Application fee:* $50 ($75 for international students). Electronic applications accepted. *Application Contact:* Dr. Charles Ferguson, Associate Dean of Student Affairs, 303-556-408, Fax: 303-556-4681, E-mail: charles.ferguson@cudenver.edu. *Dean,* Dr. Jon Harbor, 303-556-2557, Fax: 303-556-4861.

Graduate School Students: 781 full-time (573 women), 78 part-time (61 women); includes 83 minority (12 African Americans, 4 American Indian/Alaska Native, 37 Asian Americans or Pacific Islanders, 30 Hispanic Americans), 69 international. 813 applicants, 78% accepted, 246 enrolled. Expenses: Contact institution. *Financial support:* Fellowships, research assistantships, teaching assistantships, career-related internships or fieldwork, Federal Work-Study, and institutionally sponsored loans available. Support available to part-time students. Financial award application deadline: 3/15; financial award applicants required to submit FAFSA. In 2006, 109 master's, 45 doctorates awarded. *Degree program information:* Part-time programs available. Postbaccalaureate distance learning degree programs offered (minimal on-campus study). Offers analytic health sciences (PhD); analytical health sciences (PhD); bioinformatics (PhD); biostatistics (MS, PhD); clinical science (MS, PhD); epidemiology (PhD); genetic counseling (MS); public health (MSPH). *Application fee:* $50. *Application Contact:* Frances Osterberg, Interim Assistant Dean, 303-315-7928, E-mail: fran.osterberg@uchsc.edu. *Dean,* Dr. John Freed, 303-315-6446, E-mail: john.freed@uchsc.edu.

Graduate School of Public Affairs Students: 69 full-time (28 women), 248 part-time (158 women); includes 45 minority (11 African Americans, 6 Asian Americans or Pacific Islanders, 28 Hispanic Americans), 23 international. Average age 36. 232 applicants, 63% accepted, 82 enrolled. *Faculty:* 21 full-time (8 women). Expenses: Contact institution. *Financial support:* Fellowships with partial tuition reimbursements, research assistantships with partial tuition reimbursements, teaching assistantships with partial tuition reimbursements, career-related internships or fieldwork, Federal Work-Study, institutionally sponsored loans, and scholarships/grants available. Support available to part-time students. Financial award application deadline: 4/1; financial award applicants required to submit FAFSA. In 2006, 149 master's, 5 doctorates awarded. *Degree program information:* Part-time and evening/weekend programs available. Postbaccalaureate distance learning degree programs offered. Offers criminal justice (MCJ); public administration (Exec MPA, MPA); public affairs (Exec MPA, MCJ, MPA, PhD). *Application fee:* $50 ($60 for international students). *Application Contact:* Antoinette Sandoval, Student Service Specialist, 303-556-5972, Fax: 303-556-5971, E-mail: antoinette.sandoval@cudenver.edu. *Dean,* Kathleen Beatty, 303-556-5974, Fax: 303-556-5971, E-mail: kathleen.beatty@cudenver.edu.

Program in Biomedical Sciences Students: 304 full-time (165 women), 18 part-time (11 women); includes 31 minority (4 African Americans, 14 Asian Americans or Pacific Islanders, 13 Hispanic Americans), 44 international. 433 applicants, 84% accepted, 68 enrolled. Expenses: Contact institution. *Financial support:* Fellowships, research assistantships, teaching assistantships, career-related internships or fieldwork, Federal Work-Study, institutionally sponsored loans, and traineeships available. Support available to part-time students. Financial award applicants required to submit FAFSA. In 2006, 30 degrees awarded. Offers biochemistry (PhD); biomedical sciences (PhD); cancer biology (PhD); cell and developmental biology (PhD); human medical genetics (PhD); microbiology (PhD); molecular biology (PhD); neuroscience (PhD); pharmacology (PhD); physiology and biophysics (PhD). *Application fee:* $50. *Application Contact:* Julie Westerdahl, Program Administrator, 303-724-3278, E-mail: julie.westerdahl@uchsc.edu. *Director,* Dr. Steven Anderson, 303-724-3278, E-mail: steven.anderson@uchsc.edu.

School of Dentistry Students: 192 full-time (80 women); includes 26 minority (2 African Americans, 15 Asian Americans or Pacific Islanders, 9 Hispanic Americans), 1 international. Average age 27. 1,322 applicants, 5% accepted, 50 enrolled. *Faculty:* 54 full-time (11 women), 4 part-time/adjunct (0 women). Expenses: Contact institution. *Financial support:* Federal Work-Study and institutionally sponsored loans available. Financial award application deadline: 3/15; financial award applicants required to submit FAFSA. In 2006, 46 degrees awarded. Offers dentistry (DDS). *Application deadline:* For fall admission, 1/1 for domestic students, 3/31 for international students. *Application fee:* $50 ($125 for international students). *Application Contact:* Dr. Randy L. Kluender, Assistant Dean for Admissions and Student Affairs, 303-724-7120. *Interim ean,* Dr. Denise K. Kassebaum, 303-724-7100.

School of Education and Human Development Students: 383 full-time (294 women), 798 part-time (663 women); includes 143 minority (29 African Americans, 10 American Indian/Alaska Native, 30 Asian Americans or Pacific Islanders, 74 Hispanic Americans), 6 international. Average age 34. 389 applicants, 70% accepted, 169 enrolled. *Faculty:* 47 full-time (32 women). Expenses: Contact institution. *Financial support:* Fellowships, research assistantships, teaching assistantships, Federal Work-Study, institutionally sponsored loans, and scholarships/grants available. Support available to part-time students. Financial award application deadline: 4/1; financial award applicants required to submit FAFSA. In 2006, 562 master's, 9 doctorates, 25 other advanced degrees awarded. *Degree program information:* Part-time and evening/weekend programs available. Offers administration leadership and policy studies (MA, Ed S); counseling psychology and counselor education (MA); early childhood education (MA); education and human development (MA, PhD, Ed S); educational leadership and innovation (PhD); educational psychology (MA); professional learning and advancement networks (MA); school psychology (Ed S); special education (MA). *Application deadline:* For fall admission, 4/15 for domestic students; for spring admission, 9/15 for domestic students. Applications are processed on a rolling basis. *Application fee:* $50 ($75 for international students). Electronic applications accepted. *Application Contact:* Lori Sisneros, Student Services Coordinator, 303-556-8854, Fax: 303-556-4479, E-mail: bri.sisneros@cudenver.edu. *Dean,* Lynn K Rhodes, 303-556-2844, Fax: 303-556-4479, E-mail: lynn.rhodes@cudenver.edu.

School of Medicine Students: 778 full-time (445 women), 21 part-time (15 women); includes 129 minority (16 African Americans, 5 American Indian/Alaska Native, 61 Asian Americans or Pacific Islanders, 47 Hispanic Americans), 5 international. Average age 27. 2,994 applicants, 12% accepted, 238 enrolled. *Faculty:* 1,568 full-time (732 women). Expenses: Contact institution. *Financial support:* Fellowships, research assistantships, teaching assistantships, career-related internships or fieldwork, Federal Work-Study, and institutionally sponsored loans available. Support available to part-time students. Financial award application deadline: 3/15; financial award applicants required to submit FAFSA. In 2006, 157 MDs, 24 doctorates awarded. Offers medicine (MD, MPAS, DPT); pediatrics (MPAS); physical therapy (DPT). *Application deadline:* For fall admission, 11/1 for domestic students. *Application fee:* $100. *Application Contact:* Dr. Henry Sondheimer, Associate Dean for Admissions, 303-315-7361, E-mail: somadmin@uchsc.edu. *Dean,* Dr. Richard Krugman, 303-315-7565.

School of Nursing Students: 249 full-time (238 women), 63 part-time (47 women); includes 32 minority (6 African Americans, 4 American Indian/Alaska Native, 12 Asian Americans or Pacific Islanders, 10 Hispanic Americans), 5 international. Average age 35. 262 applicants, 73% accepted, 177 enrolled. Expenses: Contact institution. *Financial support:* Fellowships, research assistantships, teaching assistantships, career-related internships or fieldwork, Federal Work-Study, and institutionally sponsored loans available. Support available to part-time students. Financial award application deadline: 3/15; financial award applicants required to submit FAFSA. In 2006, 69 master's, 6 doctorates awarded. *Degree program information:* Part-time programs available. Offers nursing (MS, PhD, Post Master's Certificate); nursing practice (DNP). *Application deadline:* For fall admission, 5/1 priority date for domestic students; for spring admission, 10/1 for domestic students. *Application fee:* $65. *Dean,* Patricia Moritz, 303-315-1680.

School of Pharmacy Students: 505 full-time (354 women), 8 part-time (5 women); includes 158 minority (33 African Americans, 3 American Indian/Alaska Native, 90 Asian Americans or Pacific Islanders, 32 Hispanic Americans), 4 international. Average age 29. 1,630 applicants, 12% accepted, 131 enrolled. Expenses: Contact institution. *Financial support:* Fellowships, research assistantships, teaching assistantships, career-related internships or fieldwork, Federal Work-Study, and institutionally sponsored loans available. Support available to part-time students. Financial award application deadline: 3/15; financial award applicants required to submit FAFSA. In 2006, 143 degrees awarded. Offers pharmaceutical sciences (PhD); pharmacy (Pharm D, PhD); toxicology (PhD). *Application deadline:* For fall admission, 12/1 for domestic students. *Application fee:* $50. *Application Contact:* Beverly Brunson, Director, 303-315-6100. *Dean,* Ralpha Altiere, 303-315-5055.

UNIVERSITY OF CONNECTICUT, Storrs, CT 06269

General Information State-supported, coed, university. CGS member. *Enrollment:* 23,557 graduate, professional, and undergraduate students; 3,344 full-time matriculated graduate/professional students (1,768 women), 2,244 part-time matriculated graduate/professional students (1,116 women). *Enrollment by degree level:* 3,350 master's, 2,048 doctoral, 190 other advanced degrees. *Graduate faculty:* 1,242 full-time (387 women). *Graduate housing:* Rooms and/or apartments available on a first-come, first-served basis to single and married students. Housing application deadline: 4/1. *Student services:* Campus employment opportunities, campus safety program, career counseling, disabled student services, exercise/wellness program, free psychological counseling, grant writing training, international student services, low-cost health insurance, multicultural affairs office, teacher training, writing training. *Library facilities:* Homer Babbidge Library plus 3 others. *Online resources:* library catalog, web page, access to other libraries' catalogs. *Collection:* 3 million titles, 17,378 serial subscriptions, 61,417 audiovisual materials. *Research affiliation:* Haskins Laboratories, U.S. Navy–Submarine Medical Research Laboratory.

Computer facilities: Computer purchase and lease plans are available. 1,318 computers available on campus for general student use. A campuswide network can be accessed from student residence rooms and from off campus. Internet access and online class registration, e-mail are available. *Web address:* http://www.uconn.edu/.

General Application Contact: Anne K. Lanzit, Associate Director of Graduate Admissions, 860-486-3617, Fax: 860-486-6739, E-mail: anne.lanzit@uconn.edu.

GRADUATE UNITS

Graduate School Students: 3,344 full-time (1,768 women), 2,244 part-time (1,116 women); includes 653 minority (238 African Americans, 16 American Indian/Alaska Native, 206 Asian Americans or Pacific Islanders, 193 Hispanic Americans), 1,172 international. Average age 32. 6,553 applicants, 39% accepted, 2242 enrolled. *Faculty:* 1,242 full-time (387 women). Expenses: Contact institution. *Financial support:* In 2006–07, 1,373 research assistantships with full tuition reimbursements, 850 teaching assistantships with full tuition reimbursements were awarded; fellowships, career-related internships or fieldwork and Federal Work-Study also available. Financial award application deadline: 2/1; financial award applicants required to submit FAFSA. In 2006, 1,387 master's, 298 doctorates, 19 other advanced degrees awarded. *Degree program information:* Part-time and evening/weekend programs available. Postbaccalaureate distance learning degree programs offered (minimal on-campus study). *Application deadline:* For fall admission, 2/1 priority date for domestic and international students; for spring admission, 11/1 for domestic students, 10/1 for international students. Applications are processed on a rolling basis. *Application fee:* $55. Electronic applications accepted. *Application Contact:* Anne K. Lanzit, Associate Director of Graduate Admissions, 860-486-3617, Fax: 860-486-6739, E-mail: anne.lanzit@uconn.edu. *Dean and Vice Provost, Research and Graduate Education,* Janet L. Greger, 860-486-3619, E-mail: jl.greger@uconn.edu.

Center for Continuing Studies Students: 7 full-time (6 women), 121 part-time (52 women); includes 23 minority (13 African Americans, 1 American Indian/Alaska Native, 1 Asian American or Pacific Islander, 8 Hispanic Americans), 3 international. Average age 37. 68 applicants, 63% accepted, 43 enrolled. *Faculty:* 4 full-time (0 women). Expenses: Contact institution. In 2006, 2 master's awarded. Postbaccalaureate distance learning degree programs offered. Offers continuing studies (MPS); homeland security leadership (MPS); humanitarian services administration (MPS); labor relations (MPS); occupational safety and health management (MPS); personnel (MPS). *Application Contact:* Anne K. Lanzit, Associate Director of Graduate Admissions, 860-486-3617, Fax: 860-486-6739, E-mail: anne.lanzit@uconn.edu.

College of Agriculture and Natural Resources Students: 159 full-time (81 women), 41 part-time (23 women); includes 11 minority (4 African Americans, 1 American Indian/Alaska Native, 4 Asian Americans or Pacific Islanders, 2 Hispanic Americans), 78 international. Average age 30. 156 applicants, 43% accepted, 49 enrolled. *Faculty:* 76 full-time (18 women). Expenses: Contact institution. *Financial support:* In 2006–07, 118 research assistantships with full tuition reimbursements, 11 teaching assistantships with full tuition reimbursements were awarded; fellowships, Federal Work-Study, scholarships/grants, health care benefits, and unspecified assistantships also available. Financial award application deadline: 2/1; financial award applicants required to submit FAFSA. In 2006, 33 master's, 29 doctorates awarded. Offers agricultural and resource economics (MS, PhD); agriculture and natural resources (MS, PhD); animal science (MS, PhD); natural resources (MS, PhD); natural resources management and engineering (MS, PhD); nutritional sciences (MS, PhD); pathobiology (MS, PhD); pathobiology and veterinary science (MS, PhD); plant and soil sciences (MS, PhD); plant science (MS, PhD). *Application deadline:* For fall admission, 2/1 priority date for domestic and international students; for spring admission, 11/1 for domestic students, 10/1 for international students. Applications are processed on a rolling basis. *Application fee:* $55. Electronic applications accepted. *Application Contact:* Larissa Hull, Assistant, 860-486-2918, Fax: 860-486-5113, E-mail: larissa.hull@uconn.edu. *Dean*, Kirklyn M. Kerr, 860-486-2917, Fax: 860-486-5113, E-mail: kirklyn.ker@uconn.edu.

College of Liberal Arts and Sciences Students: 1,505 full-time (756 women), 291 part-time (146 women); includes 161 minority (53 African Americans, 6 American Indian/Alaska Native, 45 Asian Americans or Pacific Islanders, 57 Hispanic Americans), 518 international. Average age 29. 3,057 applicants, 31% accepted, 654 enrolled. *Faculty:* 564 full-time (180 women). Expenses: Contact institution. *Financial support:* In 2006–07, 437 research assistantships with full tuition reimbursements, 727 teaching assistantships with full tuition reimbursements were awarded; fellowships, career-related internships or fieldwork, Federal Work-Study, scholarships/grants, health care benefits, and unspecified assistantships also available. Financial award application deadline: 2/1; financial award applicants required to submit FAFSA. In 2006, 294 master's, 139 doctorates, 15 other advanced degrees awarded. Offers actuarial science (MS, PhD); African studies (MA); anthropology (MA, PhD); applied financial mathematics (MS); applied genomics (MS, PSM); audiology (Au D, PhD); behavioral neuroscience (PhD); biobehavioral science (PhD); biochemistry (MS, PhD); biophysics and structural biology (MS, PhD); biopsychology (PhD); biotechnology (MS); botany (MS, PhD); cell and developmental biology (MS, PhD); chemistry (MS, PhD); clinical psychology (MA, PhD); cognition and instruction (PhD); communication processes (MA); communication processes and marketing communication (PhD); communication sciences (MA, Au D, PhD); comparative literature and cultural studies (MA, PhD); comparative physiology (MS, PhD); developmental psychology (MA, PhD); ecological psychology (PhD); ecology (MS, PhD); economics (MA, PhD); English (MA, PhD); entomology (MS, PhD); European studies (MA); experimental psychology (PhD); French (MA, PhD); general psychology (MA, PhD); genetics (MS, PhD); genetics, genomics, and bioinformatics (MS, PhD); geographic information systems (Certificate); geography (MS, PhD); geological sciences (MS, PhD); German (MA, PhD); history (MA, PhD); industrial/organizational psychology (PhD); international studies (MA); Italian (MA, PhD); Italian history and culture (MA); Judaic studies (MA); language and cognition (PhD); Latin American studies (MA); liberal arts and sciences (MA, MPA, MS, PSM, Au D, PhD, Certificate, Graduate Certificate); linguistics (PhD); mathematics (MS, PhD); medieval studies (MA, PhD); microbial systems analysis (MS, PSM); microbiology (MS, PhD); neurobiology (MS, PhD); neuroscience (PhD); nonprofit management (Graduate Certificate); oceanography (MS, PhD); philosophy (MA, PhD); physics (MS, PhD); physiology and neurobiology (MS, PhD); plant cell and molecular biology (MS, PhD); political science (MA, PhD); psychology (MA, PhD); public administration (MPA); public financial management (Graduate Certificate); social psychology (MA, PhD); sociology (MA, PhD); Spanish (MA, PhD); speech-language pathology (MA, PhD); statistics (MS, PhD); survey research (MA); zoology (MS, PhD). *Application deadline:* For fall admission, 2/1 priority date for domestic and international students; for spring admission, 11/1 for domestic students, 10/1 for international students. Applications are processed on a rolling basis. *Application fee:* $55. Electronic applications accepted. *Application Contact:* Ronald Growney, Administrative Specialist, 860-486-2713, Fax: 860-486-0304. *Dean*, Ross D. MacKinnon, 860-486-2713, Fax: 860-486-0304.

Neag School of Education Students: 431 full-time (316 women), 372 part-time (256 women); includes 89 minority (30 African Americans, 5 American Indian/Alaska Native, 18 Asian Americans or Pacific Islanders, 36 Hispanic Americans), 31 international. Average age 32. 917 applicants, 50% accepted, 463 enrolled. *Faculty:* 81 full-time (36 women). Expenses: Contact institution. *Financial support:* In 2006–07, 183 research assistantships with full tuition reimbursements, 9 teaching assistantships with full tuition reimbursements were awarded; fellowships, Federal Work-Study, scholarships/grants, health care benefits, and unspecified assistantships also available. Financial award application deadline: 2/1; financial award applicants required to submit FAFSA. In 2006, 413 master's, 36 doctorates awarded. Offers adult learning (MA, PhD); agriculture education (MA, PhD); bilingual and bicultural education (MA, PhD); cognition and instruction (MA, PhD); counseling psychology (MA, PhD); curriculum and instruction (MA, PhD); education (MA, Ed D, PhD); education policy analysis (PhD); educational administration (Ed D, PhD); educational psychology (MA, PhD); elementary education (MA, PhD); English education (MA, PhD); exercise science (MA, PhD); gifted and talented education (MA, PhD); higher education and student affairs (MA); history and social sciences education (MA, PhD); kinesiology (MA, PhD); learning technology (MA, PhD); mathematics education (MA, PhD); measurement, evaluation, and assessment (MA, PhD); reading education (MA, PhD); school counseling (MA); school psychology (MA, PhD); science education (MA, PhD); secondary education (MA, PhD); special education (MA, PhD); sport management and sociology (MA, PhD); world languages education (MA, PhD). *Application deadline:* For fall admission, 2/1 priority date for domestic and international students; for spring admission, 11/1 for domestic students, 10/1 for international students. Applications are processed on a rolling basis. *Application fee:* $55. Electronic applications accepted. *Application Contact:* Thomas DeFranco, Chairperson, 860-486-3815, Fax: 860-486-0210, E-mail: thomas.defranco@uconn.edu. *Dean*, Richard L. Schwab, 860-486-3813, Fax: 860-486-0210, E-mail: richard.schwab@uconn.edu.

School of Allied Health Students: 39 full-time (25 women), 6 part-time (4 women); includes 4 minority (1 African American, 2 Asian Americans or Pacific Islanders, 1 Hispanic American). Average age 26. 39 applicants, 92% accepted, 36 enrolled. *Faculty:* 17 full-time (7 women). Expenses: Contact institution. *Financial support:* In 2006–07, 11 research assistantships with full tuition reimbursements, 2 teaching assistantships with full tuition reimbursements were awarded; fellowships, Federal Work-Study, scholarships/grants, health care benefits, and unspecified assistantships also available. Financial award application deadline: 2/1; financial award applicants required to submit FAFSA. In 2006, 42 degrees awarded. Offers allied health (MS); physical therapy (MS). *Application deadline:* For fall admission, 2/1 priority date for domestic and international students; for spring admission, 11/1 for domestic students, 10/1 for international students. Applications are processed on a rolling basis. *Application fee:* $55. Electronic applications accepted. *Application Contact:* Thomas Miller, Chairperson, 860-486-2846, Fax: 860-486-5375, E-mail: thomas.miller@uconn.edu. *Dean*, Joseph W. Smey, 860-486-4734, Fax: 860-486-4191.

School of Business Students: 378 full-time (126 women), 852 part-time (322 women); includes 154 minority (43 African Americans, 5 American Indian/Alaska Native, 71 Asian Americans or Pacific Islanders, 35 Hispanic Americans), 171 international. Average age 30. 632 applicants, 72% accepted, 452 enrolled. *Faculty:* 70 full-time (14 women). Expenses: Contact institution. *Financial support:* In 2006–07, 107 research assistantships with full tuition reimbursements, 4 teaching assistantships with full tuition reimbursements were awarded; fellowships, career-related internships or fieldwork, Federal Work-Study, scholarships/grants, health care benefits, and unspecified assistantships also available. Financial award application deadline: 2/1; financial award applicants required to submit FAFSA. In 2006, 413 master's, 9 doctorates awarded. Offers accounting (MS, PhD); business administration (Exec MBA, MBA, PhD); finance (PhD); health care management and insurance studies (MBA); management (PhD); management consulting (MBA); marketing (PhD); marketing intelligence (MBA). *Application deadline:* For fall admission, 2/1 priority date for domestic and international students; for spring admission, 11/1 for domestic students, 10/1 for international students. Applications are processed on a rolling basis. Electronic applications accepted. *Application Contact:* Richard Dino, Admissions Chairperson, 860-486-4483, E-mail: rich.dino@uconn.edu. *Dean*, William Curt Hunter, 860-486-2317, Fax: 860-846-0889, E-mail: william.hunter@uconn.edu.

School of Engineering Students: 384 full-time (86 women), 132 part-time (35 women); includes 38 minority (8 African Americans, 22 Asian Americans or Pacific Islanders, 8 Hispanic Americans), 281 international. Average age 29. 907 applicants, 30% accepted, 164 enrolled. *Faculty:* 178 full-time (19 women). Expenses: Contact institution. *Financial support:* In 2006–07, 261 research assistantships with full tuition reimbursements, 29 teaching assistantships with full tuition reimbursements were awarded; fellowships, career-related internships or fieldwork, Federal Work-Study, scholarships/grants, health care benefits, and unspecified assistantships also available. Financial award application deadline: 2/1; financial award applicants required to submit FAFSA. In 2006, 90 master's, 51 doctorates awarded. Offers artificial intelligence (MS, PhD); biomedical engineering (MS, PhD); chemical engineering (MS, PhD); civil engineering (MS, PhD); computer architecture (MS, PhD); computer science (MS, PhD); electrical engineering (MS, PhD); engineering (M Eng, MS, PhD); environmental engineering (MS, PhD); materials science and engineering (MS, PhD); mechanical engineering (MS, PhD); metallurgy and materials engineering (MS, PhD); operating systems (MS, PhD); polymer science and engineering (MS, PhD); robotics (MS, PhD); software engineering (MS, PhD). *Application deadline:* For fall admission, 2/1 priority date for domestic and international students; for spring admission, 11/1 for domestic students, 10/1 for international students. Applications are processed on a rolling basis. *Application fee:* $55. Electronic applications accepted. *Application Contact:* Ian Greenshields, Associate Dean, 860-486-5003, Fax: 860-486-0318, E-mail: ian@engr.uconn.edu. *Dean*, Amir Faghri, 860-486-2221, Fax: 860-486-0318, E-mail: faghri@engr.uconn.edu.

School of Family Studies Students: 44 full-time (40 women), 9 part-time (6 women); includes 9 minority (3 African Americans, 3 Asian Americans or Pacific Islanders, 3 Hispanic Americans), 9 international. Average age 32. 79 applicants, 30% accepted, 24 enrolled. *Faculty:* 22 full-time (13 women). Expenses: Contact institution. *Financial support:* In 2006–07, 25 research assistantships with full tuition reimbursements, 19 teaching assistantships with full tuition reimbursements were awarded; fellowships, career-related internships or fieldwork, Federal Work-Study, scholarships/grants, health care benefits, and unspecified assistantships also available. Financial award application deadline: 2/1; financial award applicants required to submit FAFSA. In 2006, 16 master's, 10 doctorates awarded. Offers family studies (MA, PhD); human development and family studies (MA, PhD). *Application deadline:* For fall admission, 2/1 priority date for domestic and international students; for spring admission, 11/1 for domestic students, 10/1 for international students. Applications are processed on a rolling basis. *Application fee:* $55. Electronic applications accepted. *Application Contact:* Nancy Sheehan, Associate Dean, 860-486-4721, Fax: 860-486-3452, E-mail: nancy.sheehan@uconn.edu. *Dean*, Charles M. Super, 860-486-4720, Fax: 860-486-3452.

School of Fine Arts Students: 86 full-time (46 women), 34 part-time (21 women); includes 5 minority (1 African American, 2 Asian Americans or Pacific Islanders, 2 Hispanic Americans), 19 international. Average age 29. 153 applicants, 39% accepted, 52 enrolled. *Faculty:* 50 full-time (19 women). Expenses: Contact institution. *Financial support:* In 2006–07, 46 research assistantships, 24 teaching assistantships with full tuition reimbursements were awarded; fellowships, Federal Work-Study, scholarships/grants, health care benefits, and unspecified assistantships also available. Financial award application deadline: 2/1; financial award applicants required to submit FAFSA. In 2006, 25 master's, 1 doctorate, 1 other advanced degree awarded. Offers acting (MFA); art history (MA); conducting (M Mus, DMA); costume design (MFA); dramatic arts (MA, MFA); fine arts (M Mus, MA, MFA, DMA, PhD, Performer's Certificate); historical musicology (MA); lighting design (MFA); music (M Mus, MA, DMA, PhD, Performer's Certificate); music education (M Mus, PhD); music theory (MA); music theory and history (PhD); performance (M Mus, DMA); puppetry (MA, MFA); scenic design (MFA); studio art (MFA). *Application deadline:* For fall admission, 2/1 priority date for domestic and international students; for spring admission, 11/1 for domestic students, 10/1 for international students. Applications are processed on a rolling basis. *Application fee:* $55. Electronic applications accepted. *Application Contact:* Ted Yungclas, Associate Dean, 860-486-1485, E-mail: ted.yungclas@uconn.edu. *Dean*, David G. Woods, 860-486-3016, Fax: 860-486-5845.

School of Nursing Students: 38 full-time (33 women), 70 part-time (65 women); includes 17 minority (3 African Americans, 10 Asian Americans or Pacific Islanders, 4 Hispanic Americans), 1 international. Average age 37. 64 applicants, 100% accepted, 64 enrolled. *Faculty:* 20 full-time (18 women). Expenses: Contact institution. *Financial support:* In 2006–07, 4 research assistantships with full tuition reimbursements, 13 teaching assistantships with full tuition reimbursements were awarded; fellowships, Federal Work-Study, scholarships/grants, health care benefits, and unspecified assistantships also available. Financial award application deadline: 2/1; financial award applicants required to submit FAFSA. In 2006, 25 master's, 7 doctorates, 1 other advanced degree awarded. Offers adult acute care (Post-Master's Certificate); adult primary care (Post-Master's Certificate); community health (Post-Master's Certificate); neonatal acute care (Post-Master's Certificate); nursing (MS, PhD); patient care services and systems administration (Post-Master's Certificate); psychiatric mental health (Post-Master's Certificate). *Application deadline:* For fall admission, 2/1 priority date for domestic and international students; for spring admission, 11/1 for domestic students, 10/1 for international students. Applications are processed on a rolling basis. *Application fee:* $55. Electronic applications accepted. *Application Contact:* Kathleen R. Hiatt, Assistant Dean, 860-486-5261, E-mail: kathleen.hiatt@uconn.edu. *Dean*, Laura Dzurec, 860-486-3716, Fax: 860-486-0001, E-mail: dzurec@uconn.edu.

School of Pharmacy Students: 40 full-time (21 women), 8 part-time (2 women); includes 5 minority (1 African American, 3 Asian Americans or Pacific Islanders, 1 Hispanic American), 26 international. Average age 29. 112 applicants, 13% accepted, 10 enrolled. *Faculty:* 21 full-time (5 women). Expenses: Contact institution. *Financial support:* In 2006–07, 22 research assistantships with full tuition reimbursements, 12 teaching assistantships with full tuition reimbursements were awarded; fellowships, career-related internships or fieldwork, Federal Work-Study, scholarships/grants, traineeships, health care benefits, and unspecified assistantships also available. Financial award application deadline: 2/1; financial award applicants required to submit FAFSA. In 2006, 3 master's, 10 doctorates awarded. Offers medicinal chemistry (MS, PhD); pharmaceutical sciences (MS, PhD); pharmaceutics (MS, PhD); pharmacology (MS, PhD); pharmacology and toxicology (MS, PhD); pharmacy (Pharm D, MS, PhD); toxicology (MS, PhD). *Application deadline:* For fall admission, 2/1 priority date for domestic and international students; for spring admission, 11/1 for domestic students, 10/1 for international students. Applications are processed on a rolling basis. *Application fee:* $55. Electronic applications accepted. *Application Contact:* Kenneth Speranza, Associate Dean, 860-486-2216, Fax: 860-486-4626, E-mail: speranza@uconnvm.uconn.edu. *Dean*, Robert L. McCarthy, 860-486-2129, Fax: 860-486-1553, E-mail: r.mccarthy@uconn.edu.

School of Social Work Students: 316 full-time (261 women), 88 part-time (73 women); includes 129 minority (75 African Americans, 3 American Indian/Alaska Native, 8 Asian Americans or Pacific Islanders, 43 Hispanic Americans), 4 international. Average age 32. 487 applicants, 55% accepted, 236 enrolled. *Faculty:* 32 full-time (23 women). Expenses: Contact institution. *Financial support:* In 2006–07, 9 research assistantships with full tuition reimbursements were awarded; teaching assistantships with full tuition reimbursements, Federal Work-Study, health care benefits, and unspecified assistantships also available. Financial award application deadline: 2/1; financial award applicants required to submit FAFSA. In 2006, 158 degrees awarded. Offers social work (MSW, PhD). *Application deadline:* For fall admission, 2/1 priority date for domestic and international students; for spring admission, 11/1 for domestic students, 10/1 for international students. Applications are processed on a rolling basis. *Application fee:* $55. Electronic applications accepted. *Application Contact:* David Cournoyer, Associate Dean, 860-570-9118. *Dean*, Kay Davidson, 860-570-9118, Fax: 860-570-9139.

University of Connecticut Health Center Students: 189 full-time (109 women), 164 part-time (101 women); includes 52 minority (17 African Americans, 1 American Indian/Alaska Native, 24 Asian Americans or Pacific Islanders, 10 Hispanic Americans), 90 international. Average age 31. 444 applicants, 21% accepted, 92 enrolled. *Faculty:* 218 full-time (55 women). Expenses: Contact institution. *Financial support:* In 2006–07, 150 research assistantships with full tuition reimbursements were awarded; fellowships, teaching assistantships with full tuition reimbursements, Federal Work-Study, scholarships/grants, health care benefits, and unspecified assistantships also available. Financial award application deadline: 2/1; financial award applicants required to submit FAFSA. In 2006, 60 master's, 33 doctorates awarded. Offers biomedical science (PhD); dental science (M Dent Sc); health (M Dent Sc, MPH, PhD); public health (MPH). *Application deadline:* For fall admission, 2/1 priority date for domestic and international students; for spring admission, 11/1 for domestic students, 10/1 for international students. Applications are processed on a rolling basis. *Application fee:* $55. Electronic applications accepted. *Application Contact:* Tricia Avolt, Graduate Coordinator, 860-679-4306, Fax: 860-679-1899, E-mail: robertson@nso2.uchc.edu. *Head*, Dr. Gerald Maxwell, 860-679-3523, Fax: 860-679-8766, E-mail: maxwell@neuron.uchc.edu.

University of Connecticut (continued)

School of Law Students: 480 full-time (230 women), 224 part-time (99 women); includes 117 minority (39 African Americans, 4 American Indian/Alaska Native, 26 Asian Americans or Pacific Islanders, 48 Hispanic Americans), 35 international. Average age 25. 2,017 applicants, 18% accepted, 212 enrolled. *Faculty:* 44 full-time (13 women), 21 part-time/adjunct (5 women). Expenses: Contact institution. *Financial support:* In 2006–07, 364 students received support; research assistantships, teaching assistantships, career-related internships or fieldwork, Federal Work-Study, scholarships/grants, and tuition waivers (full and partial) available. Support available to part-time students. Financial award application deadline: 3/1; financial award applicants required to submit FAFSA. In 2006, 216 JDs awarded. *Degree program information:* Part-time and evening/weekend programs available. Offers law (JD). *Application deadline:* For fall admission, 3/1 for domestic and international students. Applications are processed on a rolling basis. *Application fee:* $30. Electronic applications accepted. *Application Contact:* Karen L. DeMeola, Assistant Dean for Admissions and Student Finance, 860-570-5162, Fax: 860-570-5153, E-mail: karen.demeola@law.uconn.edu. *Associate Dean of Admissions, Career Services, and Student Finance,* Ellen Keane Rutt, 860-570-5100, Fax: 860-570-5153, E-mail: admit@law.uconn.edu.

See Close-Up on page 1073.

UNIVERSITY OF CONNECTICUT HEALTH CENTER, Farmington, CT 06030

General Information State-supported, coed, graduate-only institution. *Graduate housing:* On-campus housing not available.

GRADUATE UNITS

Graduate School *Degree program information:* Part-time and evening/weekend programs available. Offers dental science (MDS); public health (MPH).

Programs in Biomedical Sciences *Degree program information:* Part-time and evening/weekend programs available. Offers biomedical sciences (PhD); cell biology (PhD); cellular and molecular pharmacology (PhD); genetics and developmental biology (PhD); immunology (PhD); molecular biology and biochemistry (PhD); neuroscience (PhD); skeletal, craniofacial and oral biology (PhD). Electronic applications accepted.

School of Dental Medicine Offers dental medicine (DMD, Certificate). Electronic applications accepted.

School of Medicine Offers medicine (MD). Electronic applications accepted.

UNIVERSITY OF DALLAS, Irving, TX 75062-4736

General Information Independent-religious, coed, university. *Enrollment:* 2,941 graduate, professional, and undergraduate students; 388 full-time matriculated graduate/professional students (151 women), 1,365 part-time matriculated graduate/professional students (559 women). *Enrollment by degree level:* 1,560 master's, 67 doctoral, 126 other advanced degrees. *Graduate faculty:* 26 full-time (8 women), 66 part-time/adjunct (12 women). *Graduate housing:* Room and/or apartments available on a first-come, first-served basis to single students; on-campus housing not available to married students. Housing application deadline: 6/1. *Student services:* Campus employment opportunities, campus safety program, career counseling, international student services. *Library facilities:* William A. Blakley Library. *Online resources:* library catalog, web page, access to other libraries' catalogs. *Collection:* 223,350 titles, 691 serial subscriptions.

Computer facilities: Computer purchase and lease plans are available. 125 computers available on campus for general student use. A campuswide network can be accessed from student residence rooms and from off campus. Internet access is available. *Web address:* http://www.udallas.edu/.

General Application Contact: Corey Ellis, Director of Admissions, 972-721-5356, Fax: 972-721-5280, E-mail: graduate@acad.udallas.edu.

GRADUATE UNITS

Braniff Graduate School of Liberal Arts Students: 146 full-time (103 women), 193 part-time (82 women); includes 43 minority (6 African Americans, 3 American Indian/Alaska Native, 12 Asian Americans or Pacific Islanders, 22 Hispanic Americans), 18 international. Average age 35. 180 applicants, 91% accepted, 116 enrolled. *Faculty:* 23 full-time (2 women), 14 part-time/adjunct (1 woman). Expenses: Contact institution. *Financial support:* In 2006–07, 253 students received support. Scholarships/grants available. Financial award application deadline: 2/15; financial award applicants required to submit FAFSA. In 2006, 61 master's, 8 doctorates awarded. *Degree program information:* Part-time programs available. Offers American studies (MAS); art (MA, MFA); English literature (MA, MEL); humanities (M Hum, MA); liberal arts (M Hum, M Pol, M Psych, M Th, MA, MAS, MCSL, MEL, MFA, MPM, MRE, MTS, PhD); philosophy (MA); politics (M Pol, MA); psychology (M Psych, MA); theology (M Th, MA). *Application deadline:* For fall admission, 2/15 priority date for domestic students; for spring admission, 11/15 for domestic students. Applications are processed on a rolling basis. *Application fee:* $50. *Application Contact:* Graduate Coordinator, 972-721-5106, Fax: 972-721-5280, E-mail: graduate@acad.udallas.edu. *Dean,* Dr. David Sweet, 972-721-5288, Fax: 972-721-5280, E-mail: dsweet@udallas.edu.

Institute for Religious and Pastoral Studies Students: 5 full-time (2 women), 88 part-time (53 women); includes 24 minority (3 African Americans, 6 Asian Americans or Pacific Islanders, 15 Hispanic Americans), 1 international. Average age 45. 25 applicants, 100% accepted, 15 enrolled. *Faculty:* 1 full-time (0 women), 9 part-time/adjunct (1 woman). Expenses: Contact institution. *Financial support:* In 2006–07, 81 students received support. Scholarships/grants available. Financial award application deadline: 2/15. In 2006, 11 degrees awarded. *Degree program information:* Part-time and evening/weekend programs available. Postbaccalaureate distance learning degree programs offered (no on-campus study). Offers religious and pastoral studies (MCSL, MPM, MRE, MTS). *Application deadline:* For fall admission, 7/15 for domestic students; for spring admission, 11/15 for domestic students. *Application fee:* $50. *Application Contact:* Program Coordinator, 972-721-5105, Fax: 972-721-4076, E-mail: irps@acad.udallas.edu. *Director,* Dr. Brian Schmisek, 972-721-4068, Fax: 972-721-4076, E-mail: schmisek@acad.udallas.edu.

Institute of Philosophic Studies Students: 53 full-time (16 women), 14 part-time (3 women); includes 4 minority (2 American Indian/Alaska Native, 2 Hispanic Americans), 7 international. Average age 30. 35 applicants, 54% accepted, 15 enrolled. *Faculty:* 12 full-time (1 woman), 4 part-time/adjunct (1 woman). Expenses: Contact institution. *Financial support:* In 2006–07, 53 students received support. Scholarships/grants available. Financial award application deadline: 2/15. In 2006, 8 degrees awarded. Offers literature (PhD); philosophy (PhD); politics (PhD). *Application deadline:* For fall admission, 2/15 priority date for domestic students. *Application fee:* $50. *Application Contact:* Graduate Coordinator, 972-721-5106, Fax: 972-721-5280, E-mail: graduate@udallas.edu.

Graduate School of Management Students: 227 full-time (98 women), 1,160 part-time (446 women); includes 473 minority (209 African Americans, 3 American Indian/Alaska Native, 143 Asian Americans or Pacific Islanders, 118 Hispanic Americans), 224 international. Average age 34. 556 applicants, 86% accepted, 291 enrolled. *Faculty:* 26 full-time (5 women), 85 part-time/adjunct (18 women). Expenses: Contact institution. *Financial support:* In 2006–07, 468 students received support. Scholarships/grants and unspecified assistantships available. Financial award application deadline: 2/15; financial award applicants required to submit FAFSA. In 2006, 476 degrees awarded. *Degree program information:* Part-time and evening/weekend programs available. Postbaccalaureate distance learning degree programs offered (no on-campus study). Offers accounting (MBA, MS); business management (MBA); corporate finance (MBA, MM); engineering management (MBA, MM); entrepreneurship (MBA, MM); financial services (MBA, MM); global business (MBA, MM); health services management (MBA, MM); human resource management (MBA, MM, MS); information assurance (MBA, MM, MS); information technology (MBA, MM, MS); information technology service management (MBA); IT service management (MS); marketing (MM); marketing management (MBA); not-for-profit management (MBA); organization development (MBA); project management (MBA, MM); sports and entertainment management (MBA, MM); strategic leadership (MBA); supply chain management (MBA); supply chain management and market logistics (MM); telecommunications management (MBA, MM). *Application deadline:* Applications are processed on a rolling basis. *Application fee:* $50. Electronic applications accepted. *Application Contact:* Sarah Stivison, Director of Graduate Admissions, 972-721-5198, Fax: 972-721-4009, E-mail: admiss@gsm.udallas.edu. *Dean,* Dr. J. Lee Whittington, 972-721-5230.

UNIVERSITY OF DAYTON, Dayton, OH 45469-1300

General Information Independent-religious, coed, university. CGS member. *Enrollment:* 10,503 graduate, professional, and undergraduate students; 1,235 full-time matriculated graduate/professional students (693 women), 1,172 part-time matriculated graduate/professional students (770 women). *Enrollment by degree level:* 2,235 master's, 172 doctoral. *Graduate faculty:* 494. *Tuition:* Part-time $601 per semester hour. Tuition and fees vary according to degree level and program. *Graduate housing:* Room and/or apartments available on a first-come, first-served basis to single students; on-campus housing not available to married students. Typical cost: $7,300 per year. Room charges vary according to housing facility selected. *Student services:* Campus employment opportunities, campus safety program, career counseling, child daycare facilities, disabled student services, exercise/wellness program, free psychological counseling, international student services, low-cost health insurance, multicultural affairs office, teacher training, writing training. *Library facilities:* Roesch Library plus 2 others. *Online resources:* library catalog, web page, access to other libraries' catalogs. *Collection:* 973,842 titles, 10,481 serial subscriptions, 2,186 audiovisual materials. *Research affiliation:* American Society of Heating Refrigeration and Air Conditioning (civil engineering), Dayton Area Graduate Studies Institute (electrical engineering), Ohio Aerospace Institute (metallurgical and materials engineering), American Chemical Society (environmental science—Earth), Research Corporation (physical sciences—chemistry), Lance Armstrong Foundation (biomedical engineering).

Computer facilities: Computer purchase and lease plans are available. 8,000 computers available on campus for general student use. A campuswide network can be accessed from student residence rooms and from off campus. Internet access and online class registration, apply online, check admission status, confirm enrollment, virtual orientation are available. *Web address:* http://www.udayton.edu/.

General Application Contact: Erika Eavers, Graduate Admission Processor, 937-229-3065, Fax: 937-229-4729, E-mail: erika.eavers@notes.udayton.edu.

GRADUATE UNITS

Graduate School Students: 1,235 full-time (693 women), 1,172 part-time (770 women); includes 248 minority (180 African Americans, 2 American Indian/Alaska Native, 36 Asian Americans or Pacific Islanders, 30 Hispanic Americans), 180 international. 2,576 applicants, 49% accepted, 627 enrolled. *Faculty:* 494. Expenses: Contact institution. *Financial support:* In 2006–07, fellowships (averaging $8,648 per year), research assistantships with full and partial tuition reimbursements (averaging $8,648 per year), teaching assistantships with full tuition reimbursements (averaging $8,648 per year) were awarded. Financial award applicants required to submit FAFSA. In 2006, 817 master's, 16 doctorates awarded. *Degree program information:* Part-time and evening/weekend programs available. Postbaccalaureate distance learning degree programs offered. *Application deadline:* For fall admission, 3/1 priority date for international students. Applications are processed on a rolling basis. *Application fee:* $0. Electronic applications accepted. *Application Contact:* Erika Eavers, Graduate Admissions Processor, 937-229-3065, Fax: 937-229-4729, E-mail: erika.eavers@notes.udayton.edu. *Dean of the Graduate School,* Dr. F. Thomas Eggemeier, 937-229-2390, Fax: 937-229-2400, E-mail: udgradschool@udayton.edu.

College of Arts and Sciences Students: 191 full-time (100 women), 50 part-time (29 women); includes 24 minority (19 African Americans, 1 American Indian/Alaska Native, 1 Asian American or Pacific Islander, 3 Hispanic Americans), 27 international. Average age 26. 604 applicants, 43% accepted, 97 enrolled. *Faculty:* 111 full-time (37 women), 20 part-time/adjunct (6 women). Expenses: Contact institution. *Financial support:* Fellowships with full tuition reimbursements, research assistantships with full tuition reimbursements, teaching assistantships with full tuition reimbursements, career-related internships or fieldwork, Federal Work-Study, institutionally sponsored loans, scholarships/grants, traineeships, health care benefits, tuition waivers (full), and unspecified assistantships available. Support available to part-time students. Financial award application deadline: 3/1; financial award applicants required to submit FAFSA. In 2006, 75 master's, 6 doctorates awarded. *Degree program information:* Part-time and evening/weekend programs available. Offers applied mathematics (MS); arts and sciences (MA, MCS, MPA, MS, PhD); biology (MS, PhD); chemistry (MS); clinical psychology (MA); communication (MA); computer science (MCS); English (MA); financial mathematics (MS); general psychology (MA); mathematics education (MS); pastoral ministry (MA); public administration (MPA); theological studies (MA); theology (PhD). *Application deadline:* For fall admission, 3/1 priority date for domestic and international students. Applications are processed on a rolling basis. *Application fee:* $0. Electronic applications accepted. *Application Contact:* Erika Eavers, Graduate Admission Processor, 937-229-3065, Fax: 937-229-4729, E-mail: erika.eavers@notes.udayton.edu. *Dean,* Dr. Mary Morton, 937-229-2601, Fax: 937-229-2615.

School of Business Administration Students: 115 full-time (43 women), 115 part-time (37 women); includes 25 minority (11 African Americans, 5 Asian Americans or Pacific Islanders, 9 Hispanic Americans), 17 international. Average age 29. 205 applicants, 65% accepted, 77 enrolled. *Faculty:* 80. Expenses: Contact institution. *Financial support:* In 2006–07, 5 fellowships with partial tuition reimbursements, 9 research assistantships with full and partial tuition reimbursements were awarded; career-related internships or fieldwork, institutionally sponsored loans, scholarships/grants, health care benefits, and unspecified assistantships also available. Support available to part-time students. Financial award application deadline: 2/15; financial award applicants required to submit FAFSA. In 2006, 128 degrees awarded. *Degree program information:* Part-time and evening/weekend programs available. Offers business administration (MBA). *Application deadline:* For fall admission, 3/1 priority date for international students. Applications are processed on a rolling basis. *Application fee:* $0. Electronic applications accepted. *Application Contact:* Erika Eavers, Graduate Admission Processor, 937-229-3065, Fax: 937-229-4729, E-mail: erika.eavers@notes.udayton.edu. *Director,* Janice M. Glynn, 937-229-3733, Fax: 937-229-3882, E-mail: mba@udayton.edu.

School of Education and Allied Professions Students: 629 full-time (484 women), 870 part-time (654 women); includes 162 minority (136 African Americans, 4 American Indian/Alaska Native, 6 Asian Americans or Pacific Islanders, 16 Hispanic Americans), 8 international. Average age 33. 619 applicants, 59% accepted, 253 enrolled. *Faculty:* 65 full-time (30 women), 120 part-time/adjunct (59 women). Expenses: Contact institution. *Financial support:* In 2006–07, 29 research assistantships with full tuition reimbursements (averaging $7,620 per year), 13 teaching assistantships with full tuition reimbursements (averaging $8,000 per year) were awarded. Financial award applicants required to submit FAFSA. In 2006, 572 master's, 4 doctorates awarded. *Degree program information:* Part-time and evening/weekend programs available. Postbaccalaureate distance learning degree programs offered (no on-campus study). Offers adolescent/young adult (MS Ed); art education (MS Ed); college student personnel (MS Ed); community counseling (MS Ed); early childhood education (MS Ed); education and allied professions (MS Ed, DPT, PhD, Ed S); educational leadership (MS Ed, PhD, Ed S); exercise sports science (MS Ed); higher education administration (MS Ed); human development services (MS Ed); inclusive early childhood (MS Ed); interdisciplinary education (MS Ed); intervention specialist education, mild/moderate (MS Ed); literacy (MS Ed); middle childhood (MS Ed); multi-age education (MS Ed); music education (MS Ed); physical education (MS Ed); school counseling (MS Ed); school psychology (MS Ed, Ed S); teacher as child/youth development specialist (MS Ed); teacher as leader (MS Ed); technology in education (MS Ed). *Application deadline:* For fall admission, 3/15 priority date for domestic students, 3/1 priority date for international students. Applications are processed on a rolling basis. *Application fee:* $0. Electronic applications accepted. *Application Contact:* Erika Eavers, Graduate Admission Processor, 937-229-3065, Fax: 937-229-4729, E-mail: erika.eavers@notes.udayton.edu. *Dean,* Dr. Thomas J. Lasley, 937-229-3146, Fax: 937-229-3199, E-mail: thomas.lasley@notes.udayton.edu.

School of Engineering Students: 243 full-time (54 women), 118 part-time (23 women); includes 31 minority (13 African Americans, 11 Asian Americans or Pacific Islanders, 7

Hispanic Americans), 88 international. Average age 26. 875 applicants, 38% accepted, 99 enrolled. *Faculty:* 54 full-time (2 women), 52 part-time/adjunct (4 women). Expenses: Contact institution. *Financial support:* In 2006–07, 5 fellowships with full tuition reimbursements (averaging $27,500 per year), 88 research assistantships with full tuition reimbursements (averaging $16,000 per year), 6 teaching assistantships with full tuition reimbursements (averaging $12,000 per year) were awarded; career-related internships or fieldwork, institutionally sponsored loans, health care benefits, tuition waivers (full and partial), and unspecified assistantships also available. In 2006, 112 master's, 11 doctorates awarded. *Degree program information:* Part-time and evening/weekend programs available. Offers aerospace engineering (MSAE, DE, PhD); chemical engineering (MS Ch E); electrical and computer engineering (MSEE, DE, PhD); electro-optics (MSEO, PhD); engineering (MS Ch E, MS Mat E, MSAE, MSCE, MSE, MSEE, MSEM, MSEM, MSEO, MSME, MSMS, DE, PhD); engineering management and systems (MSEM); engineering mechanics (MSEM); environmental engineering (MSCE); management science (MSMS); materials engineering (MS Mat E, DE, PhD); mechanical engineering (MSME, DE, PhD); soil mechanics (MSCE); structural engineering (MSCE); transport engineering (MSCE). *Application deadline:* For fall admission, 8/1 priority date for domestic students, 3/1 priority date for international students. Applications are processed on a rolling basis. *Application fee:* $0. Electronic applications accepted. *Application Contact:* Erika Eavers, Graduate Admission Processor, 937-229-3065, Fax: 937-229-4729, E-mail: erika.eavers@notes.udayton.edu. *Dean,* Dr. Joseph E. Saliba, 937-229-2736, Fax: 937-229-2756, E-mail: jsaliba@engr.udayton.edu.

School of Law Students: 458 full-time (197 women); includes 55 minority (22 African Americans, 4 American Indian/Alaska Native, 12 Asian Americans or Pacific Islanders, 17 Hispanic Americans), 2 international. Average age 25. 2,400 applicants, 39% accepted, 181 enrolled. *Faculty:* 28 full-time, 23 part-time/adjunct. Expenses: Contact institution. *Financial support:* In 2006–07, 245 students received support. Career-related internships or fieldwork, scholarships/grants, and tuition waivers (full and partial) available. Financial award application deadline: 3/1; financial award applicants required to submit FAFSA. In 2006, 164 degrees awarded. Offers law (JD, LL M, MSL). *Application deadline:* For fall admission, 5/1 priority date for domestic students, 3/1 priority date for international students; for spring admission, 2/1 priority date for international students. Applications are processed on a rolling basis. *Application fee:* $0. Electronic applications accepted. *Application Contact:* Janet L. Hein, Assistant Dean, Director of Admissions and Financial Aid, 937-229-3555, Fax: 937-229-4194, E-mail: lawinfo@notes.udayton.edu. *Dean,* Lisa A. Kloppenberg, 937-229-3795, Fax: 937-229-2469.

UNIVERSITY OF DELAWARE, Newark, DE 19716

General Information State-related, coed, university. CGS member. *Graduate housing:* Rooms and/or apartments available to single and married students. Housing application deadline: 3/15. *Research affiliation:* Hagley Museum, Winterthur Museum, Longwood Gardens, Bartol Research Foundation.

GRADUATE UNITS

Alfred Lerner College of Business and Economics *Degree program information:* Part-time and evening/weekend programs available. Offers accounting (MS); business administration (MBA); business and economics (MA, MBA, MS, PhD); economics (MA, MS, PhD); economics for entrepreneurship and educators (MA); information systems and technology management (MS). Electronic applications accepted.

College of Agriculture and Natural Resources *Degree program information:* Part-time programs available. Offers agricultural economics (MS); agriculture and natural resources (MS, PhD); animal sciences (MS, PhD); entomology and applied ecology (MS, PhD); food sciences (MS); operations research (MS, PhD); plant and soil sciences (MS, PhD); public horticulture (MS); statistics (MS). Electronic applications accepted.

College of Arts and Sciences *Degree program information:* Part-time and evening/weekend programs available. Offers acting (MFA); applied mathematics (MS, PhD); art (MA, MFA); art history (MA, PhD); arts and sciences (MA, MALS, MFA, MM, MS, DPT, PhD, Certificate); behavioral neuroscience (PhD); biochemistry (MA, MS, PhD); biomechanics and movement science (MS, PhD); biotechnology (MS); cancer biology (MS, PhD); cell and extracellular matrix biology (MS, PhD); cell and systems physiology (MS, PhD); chemistry (MA, MS, PhD); climatology (PhD); clinical psychology (PhD); cognitive psychology (PhD); communication (MA); composition (MM); computer and information sciences (MS, PhD); criminology (MA, PhD); developmental biology (MS, PhD); early American culture (MA); ecology and evolution (MS, PhD); English and American literature (MA, PhD); foreign languages and literatures (MA); foreign languages pedagogy (MA); geography (MA, MS); geology (MS, PhD); history (MA, PhD); history of technology and industrialization (MA, PhD); liberal studies (MALS); linguistics (MA, PhD); mathematics (MS, PhD); microbiology (MS, PhD); molecular biology and genetics (MS, PhD); museum studies (Certificate); music education (MM); performance (MM); physical therapy (DPT); physics and astronomy (MS, PhD); political science and international relations (MA, PhD); practicing art conservation (MS); social psychology (PhD); sociology (MA, PhD); stage management (MFA); technical production (MFA). Electronic applications accepted.

College of Engineering *Degree program information:* Part-time and evening/weekend programs available. Postbaccalaureate distance learning degree programs offered (minimal on-campus study). Offers chemical engineering (M Ch E, PhD); electrical and computer engineering (MS, MSECE, PhD); engineering (M Ch E, MAS, MCE, MEM, MMSE, MS, MSECE, MSME, PhD); environmental engineering (MAS, MCE, PhD); geotechnical engineering (MAS, MCE, PhD); materials science and engineering (MMSE, PhD); mechanical engineering (MEM, MSME, PhD); ocean engineering (MAS, MCE, PhD); structural engineering (MAS, MCE, PhD); transportation engineering (MAS, MCE, PhD); water resource engineering (MAS, MCE, PhD). Electronic applications accepted.

College of Health Sciences *Degree program information:* Part-time and evening/weekend programs available. Postbaccalaureate distance learning degree programs offered. Offers adult nurse practitioner (MSN, PMC); cardiopulmonary clinical nurse specialist (MSN, PMC); cardiopulmonary clinical nurse specialist/adult nurse practitioner (MSN, PMC); exercise science (MS); family nurse practitioner (MSN, PMC); gerontology clinical nurse specialist (MSN, PMC); gerontology clinical nurse specialist geriatric nurse practitioner (PMC); gerontology clinical nurse specialist/geriatric nurse practitioner (MSN); health promotion (MS); health sciences (MS, MSN, PMC); health services administration (MSN, PMC); human nutrition (MS); nursing of children clinical nurse specialist (MSN, PMC); nursing of children clinical nurse specialist/pediatric nurse practitioner (MSN, PMC); oncology/immune deficiency clinical nurse specialist (MSN, PMC); oncology/immune deficiency clinical nurse specialist/adult nurse practitioner (MSN, PMC); perinatal/women's health clinical nurse specialist (MSN, PMC); perinatal/women's health clinical nurse specialist/women's health nurse practitioner (MSN, PMC); psychiatric nursing clinical nurse specialist (MSN, PMC). Electronic applications accepted.

College of Human Services, Education and Public Policy *Degree program information:* Part-time and evening/weekend programs available. Offers counseling in higher education (M Ed, MA); hospitality information management (MS); human development and family studies (MS, PhD); human services, education and public policy (M Ed, MA, MEEP, MI, MPA, MS, Ed D, PhD). Electronic applications accepted.

Center for Energy and Environmental Policy Offers environmental and energy policy (MEEP, PhD); urban affairs and public policy (MA, PhD). Electronic applications accepted.

School of Education *Degree program information:* Part-time and evening/weekend programs available. Offers curriculum and instruction (M Ed); education (PhD); educational leadership (M Ed, Ed D); exceptional children and youth (M Ed); instruction (MI); school counseling (M Ed); school psychology (MA); teaching English as a second language (TESL) (MA). Electronic applications accepted.

School of Urban Affairs and Public Policy *Degree program information:* Part-time and evening/weekend programs available. Offers community development and nonprofit leadership (MA); energy and environmental policy (MA); governance, planning and management (PhD); historic preservation (MA); public administration (MPA); social and urban policy (PhD); technology, environment and society (PhD); urban affairs and public policy (MA, MPA, PhD). Electronic applications accepted.

College of Marine Studies Offers geology (MS, PhD); marine management (MMM); marine policy (MS); marine studies (MMP, MS, PhD); oceanography (MS, PhD). Electronic applications accepted.

UNIVERSITY OF DENVER, Denver, CO 80208

General Information Independent, coed, university. CGS member. *Enrollment:* 10,374 graduate, professional, and undergraduate students; 3,138 full-time matriculated graduate/professional students (1,827 women), 1,928 part-time matriculated graduate/professional students (1,043 women). *Enrollment by degree level:* 1,132 first professional, 3,284 master's, 515 doctoral, 135 other advanced degrees. *Graduate faculty:* 884. *Tuition:* Full-time $29,628; part-time $823 per credit. *Graduate housing:* Rooms and/or apartments available on a first-come, first-served basis to single and married students. Typical cost: $7,200 per year for single students; $7,200 per year for married students. Room charges vary according to board plan and housing facility selected. *Student services:* Campus employment opportunities, campus safety program, career counseling, disabled student services, exercise/wellness program, free psychological counseling, international student services, low-cost health insurance, multicultural affairs office. *Library facilities:* Penrose Library. *Online resources:* library catalog, web page, access to other libraries' catalogs. *Collection:* 1.2 million titles, 6,283 serial subscriptions. *Research affiliation:* National Center for Atmospheric Research (infrared measurements).

Computer facilities: 150 computers available on campus for general student use. A campuswide network can be accessed from student residence rooms and from off campus. Internet access and online class registration, online grade reports are available. *Web address:* http://www.du.edu/.

General Application Contact: Information Contact, 360-871-2706.

GRADUATE UNITS

College of Education Students: 293 full-time (240 women), 439 part-time (357 women); includes 102 minority (28 African Americans, 7 American Indian/Alaska Native, 14 Asian Americans or Pacific Islanders, 53 Hispanic Americans), 11 international. Average age 34. 574 applicants, 72% accepted. *Faculty:* 28 full-time (18 women). Expenses: Contact institution. *Financial support:* In 2006–07, 51 teaching assistantships with full and partial tuition reimbursements (averaging $6,700 per year) were awarded; career-related internships or fieldwork, Federal Work-Study, institutionally sponsored loans, and scholarships/grants also available. Support available to part-time students. Financial award application deadline: 3/1; financial award applicants required to submit FAFSA. In 2006, 168 master's, 28 doctorates, 67 other advanced degrees awarded. *Degree program information:* Part-time and evening/weekend programs available. Postbaccalaureate distance learning degree programs offered (no on-campus study). Offers counseling psychology (MA, PhD); curriculum and instruction (MA, PhD, Certificate); educational administration and policy studies (Certificate); educational psychology (MA, PhD, Ed S); higher education and adult studies (MA, PhD); library and information science (MLIS); library and information sciences (Certificate); school administration (PhD). *Application deadline:* Applications are processed on a rolling basis. *Application fee:* $50. Electronic applications accepted. *Application Contact:* Linda McCarthy, Contact, 303-871-2509, E-mail: edinfo@du.edu. *Dean,* Dr. Virginia Maloney, 303-871-2509.

College of Law Students: 1,192 full-time (568 women), 136 part-time (74 women); includes 240 minority (61 African Americans, 40 American Indian/Alaska Native, 67 Asian Americans or Pacific Islanders, 72 Hispanic Americans), 24 international. Average age 29. 3,795 applicants, 30% accepted. *Faculty:* 63 full-time (31 women). Expenses: Contact institution. *Financial support:* Career-related internships or fieldwork, Federal Work-Study, institutionally sponsored loans, and tutorships available. Support available to part-time students. Financial award application deadline: 2/15; financial award applicants required to submit FAFSA. In 2006, 366 JDs, 175 master's awarded. *Degree program information:* Part-time and evening/weekend programs available. Offers American and comparative law (LL M); international natural resources law (LL M, MRLS); law (JD, LL M, MRLS, MSLA, MT, Certificate); legal administration (MSLA, Certificate); taxation (LL M, MT). *Application deadline:* For fall admission, 3/1 priority date for domestic students. Applications are processed on a rolling basis. *Application fee:* $60. Electronic applications accepted. *Application Contact:* Forrest Stanford, Director of Admissions, 303-871-6135, Fax: 303-871-6378, E-mail: admissions@law.du.edu. *Dean,* Jose Roberto Juarez, 303-871-6135.

Daniels College of Business Students: 425 full-time (149 women), 479 part-time (146 women); includes 79 minority (12 African Americans, 3 American Indian/Alaska Native, 41 Asian Americans or Pacific Islanders, 23 Hispanic Americans), 173 international. Average age 30. 1,070 applicants, 73% accepted. *Faculty:* 83 full-time (17 women). Expenses: Contact institution. *Financial support:* In 2006–07, 63 teaching assistantships with full and partial tuition reimbursements (averaging $2,027 per year) were awarded; career-related internships or fieldwork, Federal Work-Study, institutionally sponsored loans, and scholarships/grants also available. Support available to part-time students. Financial award application deadline: 2/15; financial award applicants required to submit FAFSA. In 2006, 468 degrees awarded. *Degree program information:* Part-time and evening/weekend programs available. Offers business (IMBA, M Acc, MBA, MS); business administration (MBA); data mining (MS); finance (IMBA, MBA, MS); general business administration (IMBA, MBA, MS); information technology and electronic commerce (IMBA, MBA); international business/management (IMBA, MBA); management (MS); marketing (IMBA, MBA, MS). *Application deadline:* For fall admission, 1/15 priority date for domestic students. Applications are processed on a rolling basis. *Application fee:* $50. Electronic applications accepted. *Application Contact:* Admissions, 303-871-3416, Fax: 303-571-4466, E-mail: daniels@du.edu. *Dean,* Dr. Karen Newman, 303-871-3416.

School of Accountancy Students: 17 full-time (7 women), 27 part-time (15 women); includes 2 minority (1 African American, 1 Asian American or Pacific Islander), 8 international. Average age 28. 66 applicants, 73% accepted. *Faculty:* 12 full-time (4 women). Expenses: Contact institution. *Financial support:* Career-related internships or fieldwork, Federal Work-Study, institutionally sponsored loans, and scholarships/grants available. Support available to part-time students. Financial award application deadline: 2/15; financial award applicants required to submit FAFSA. In 2006, 38 degrees awarded. *Degree program information:* Part-time and evening/weekend programs available. Offers accountancy (M Acc); accounting (IMBA, MBA). *Application deadline:* For fall admission, 1/15 priority date for domestic students. Applications are processed on a rolling basis. *Application fee:* $50. Electronic applications accepted. *Application Contact:* Information Contact, 303-871-3416, Fax: 303-871-4466, E-mail: daniels@du.edu. *Director,* Dr. Ronald Kucic, 303-871-2017.

School of Real Estate and Construction Management Students: 59 full-time (10 women), 84 part-time (17 women); includes 17 minority (5 African Americans, 1 American Indian/Alaska Native, 6 Asian Americans or Pacific Islanders, 5 Hispanic Americans), 14 international. Average age 31. 120 applicants, 88% accepted. *Faculty:* 4 full-time (0 women). Expenses: Contact institution. *Financial support:* In 2006–07, 70 students received support. Career-related internships or fieldwork, Federal Work-Study, institutionally sponsored loans, and scholarships/grants available. Support available to part-time students. Financial award application deadline: 2/15; financial award applicants required to submit FAFSA. In 2006, 52 degrees awarded. *Degree program information:* Part-time programs available. Offers construction management (IMBA, MS); real estate (IMBA, MBA, MS). *Application deadline:* For fall admission, 1/15 priority date for domestic students. Applications are processed on a rolling basis. *Application fee:* $50. Electronic applications accepted. *Application Contact:* Information Contact, 303-871-3416, Fax: 303-871-4466, E-mail: daniels@du.edu. *Director,* Dr. Mark Levine, 303-871-2142.

Faculty of Arts and Humanities/Social Sciences Students: 190 full-time (118 women), 127 part-time (77 women); includes 33 minority (10 African Americans, 3 American Indian/Alaska Native, 6 Asian Americans or Pacific Islanders, 14 Hispanic Americans), 24 international. Average age 28. 799 applicants, 41% accepted. *Faculty:* 199 full-time (98 women). Expenses: Contact institution. *Financial support:* In 2006–07, 13 research assistantships with full and partial tuition reimbursements (averaging $11,350 per year), 135 teaching assistantships with full and partial tuition reimbursements (averaging $8,200 per year) were awarded; career-related internships or fieldwork, Federal Work-Study, institutionally sponsored loans, and scholarships/grants also available. Support available to part-time students. Financial award

University of Denver (continued)

applicants required to submit FAFSA. In 2006, 101 master's, 21 doctorates awarded. *Degree program information:* Part-time programs available. Offers anthropology (MA); arts and humanities/social sciences (MA, MFA, MM, MPP, MS, PhD, Certificate); economics (MA); English (MA, PhD); psychology (MA, PhD); public policy (MPP); religious studies (MA). *Application deadline:* Applications are processed on a rolling basis. *Application fee:* $50. Electronic applications accepted. *Interim Dean,* Dr. George Potts, 303-871-4449.

Lamont School of Music Students: 18 full-time (8 women), 40 part-time (15 women); includes 3 minority (all Hispanic Americans), 8 international. Average age 30. 61 applicants, 67% accepted. *Faculty:* 24 full-time (6 women). Expenses: Contact institution. *Financial support:* In 2006–07, 36 teaching assistantships with full and partial tuition reimbursements (averaging $4,300 per year) were awarded; career-related internships or fieldwork, Federal Work-Study, institutionally sponsored loans, and scholarships/grants also available. Support available to part-time students. Financial award application deadline: 4/15; financial award applicants required to submit FAFSA. In 2006, 13 degrees awarded. *Degree program information:* Part-time programs available. Offers composition (MA); conducting (MA); jazz and commercial music (Certificate); music (MM); music education (MA); music history and literature (MA); Orff-Schulwerk (MA); performance (MA); piano pedagogy (MA); Suzuki pedagogy (MA); Suzuki teaching (Certificate); theory (MA). *Application deadline:* Applications are processed on a rolling basis. *Application fee:* $50. Electronic applications accepted. *Application Contact:* Graduate Adviser, 303-871-6973, E-mail: marhuels@du.edu. *Director,* Joseph Docksey, 303-871-6973.

School of Art and Art History Students: 21 full-time (14 women); includes 2 minority (1 American Indian/Alaska Native, 1 Hispanic American). Average age 26. 44 applicants, 66% accepted. *Faculty:* 14 full-time (8 women). Expenses: Contact institution. *Financial support:* In 2006–07, 9 teaching assistantships with full and partial tuition reimbursements (averaging $6,500 per year) were awarded; career-related internships or fieldwork, Federal Work-Study, institutionally sponsored loans, and scholarships/grants also available. Support available to part-time students. Financial award application deadline: 3/1; financial award applicants required to submit FAFSA. In 2006, 8 degrees awarded. *Degree program information:* Part-time programs available. Offers art history (MA); art history/museum studies (MA); electronic media arts and design (MFA); studio art (MFA). *Application deadline:* Applications are processed on a rolling basis. *Application fee:* $50. Electronic applications accepted. *Application Contact:* Dr. M. Warlick, Graduate Advisor, 303-871-2846, E-mail: saah-interest@du.edu. *Director,* Dr. Annette Stott, 303-871-2846.

School of Communication Students: 59 full-time (37 women), 48 part-time (35 women); includes 12 minority (6 African Americans, 1 American Indian/Alaska Native, 2 Asian Americans or Pacific Islanders, 3 Hispanic Americans), 10 international. Average age 29. 205 applicants, 75% accepted. *Faculty:* 20 full-time (12 women). Expenses: Contact institution. *Financial support:* Career-related internships or fieldwork, Federal Work-Study, institutionally sponsored loans, and scholarships/grants available. Support available to part-time students. In 2006, 39 master's, 6 doctorates awarded. *Degree program information:* Part-time programs available. Offers advertising management (MS); communication (MA, MS, PhD); digital media studies (MA); human communication studies (MA, PhD); international and intercultural communication (MA); mass communications (MA); public relations (MS); video production (MA). *Application deadline:* Applications are processed on a rolling basis. *Application fee:* $50. Electronic applications accepted. *Application Contact:* Information Contact, 303-871-2166, E-mail: mcomadm@du.edu. *Chairperson.*

Faculty of Natural Sciences and Mathematics Students: 17 full-time (11 women), 60 part-time (29 women); includes 5 minority (3 Asian Americans or Pacific Islanders, 2 Hispanic Americans), 13 international. Average age 28. 129 applicants, 60% accepted. *Faculty:* 53 full-time (8 women). Expenses: Contact institution. *Financial support:* In 2006–07, 15 research assistantships with full and partial tuition reimbursements (averaging $12,300 per year), 63 teaching assistantships with full and partial tuition reimbursements (averaging $13,200 per year) were awarded; career-related internships or fieldwork, Federal Work-Study, institutionally sponsored loans, and scholarships/grants also available. Support available to part-time students. Financial award application deadline: 3/1; financial award applicants required to submit FAFSA. In 2006, 26 master's, 5 doctorates awarded. *Degree program information:* Part-time and evening/weekend programs available. Offers applied mathematics (MA, MS); biological sciences (MS, PhD); chemistry (MA, MS, PhD); computer science (MS); geography (MA, MS, PhD); mathematics (PhD); natural sciences and mathematics (MA, MS, PhD); physics and astronomy (MS, PhD). *Application deadline:* Applications are processed on a rolling basis. *Application fee:* $50. Electronic applications accepted. *Application Contact:* Helen Cahill, Assistant to Dean, 303-871-4003. *Dean,* Dr. James Fogleman, 303-871-2693.

Graduate School of International Studies Students: 385 full-time (227 women), 38 part-time (18 women); includes 45 minority (16 African Americans, 14 Asian Americans or Pacific Islanders, 15 Hispanic Americans), 44 international. Average age 27. 723 applicants, 85% accepted. *Faculty:* 22 full-time (5 women). Expenses: Contact institution. *Financial support:* Career-related internships or fieldwork, Federal Work-Study, institutionally sponsored loans, and scholarships/grants available. Support available to part-time students. Financial award application deadline: 2/15; financial award applicants required to submit FAFSA. In 2006, 160 master's, 10 doctorates awarded. *Degree program information:* Part-time and evening/weekend programs available. Offers global studies (MGS); international studies (MA, PhD). *Application deadline:* For fall admission, 1/15 priority date for domestic students. Applications are processed on a rolling basis. *Application fee:* $65. Electronic applications accepted. *Application Contact:* Information Contact, 303-871-3585, E-mail: gsisadm@du.edu. *Dean,* Dr. Tom Farer, 303-871-2544.

Graduate School of Professional Psychology Students: 164 full-time (138 women), 32 part-time (25 women); includes 23 minority (4 African Americans, 2 American Indian/Alaska Native, 12 Asian Americans or Pacific Islanders, 5 Hispanic Americans), 12 international. Average age 26. 486 applicants, 30% accepted. *Faculty:* 8 full-time (5 women). Expenses: Contact institution. *Financial support:* In 2006–07, 34 teaching assistantships with full and partial tuition reimbursements (averaging $2,100 per year) were awarded; career-related internships or fieldwork, Federal Work-Study, institutionally sponsored loans, scholarships/grants, and clinical assistantships also available. Support available to part-time students. Financial award application deadline: 3/1; financial award applicants required to submit FAFSA. In 2006, 62 master's, 29 doctorates awarded. Offers clinical psychology (Psy D); psychology (MA). *Application deadline:* For fall admission, 1/5 for domestic students. *Application fee:* $50. Electronic applications accepted. *Application Contact:* Admissions, 303-871-3873, Fax: 303-871-4220, E-mail: gsppiwfo@du.edu. *Dean,* Dr. Peter Buirski, 303-871-3873.

Graduate School of Social Work Students: 350 full-time (320 women), 30 part-time (24 women); includes 52 minority (11 African Americans, 3 American Indian/Alaska Native, 12 Asian Americans or Pacific Islanders, 26 Hispanic Americans), 6 international. Average age 29. 474 applicants, 89% accepted. *Faculty:* 24 full-time (18 women). Expenses: Contact institution. *Financial support:* In 2006–07, 12 teaching assistantships with full and partial tuition reimbursements (averaging $9,625 per year) were awarded; Federal Work-Study, institutionally sponsored loans, scholarships/grants, and tuition waivers (partial) also available. Support available to part-time students. Financial award application deadline: 2/1; financial award applicants required to submit FAFSA. In 2006, 187 master's, 6 doctorates, 16 other advanced degrees awarded. *Degree program information:* Part-time and evening/weekend programs available. Offers social work (MSW, PhD, Certificate). *Application deadline:* Applications are processed on a rolling basis. *Application fee:* $60. Electronic applications accepted. *Application Contact:* Colin Schneider, Director of Admission and Financial Aid, 303-871-2841, Fax: 303-871-2845, E-mail: gssw-admission@du.edu. *Interim Dean,* Dr. Christian Molidor, 303-871-2841.

Graduate Studies Students: 61 full-time (27 women), 24 part-time (12 women); includes 10 minority (4 African Americans, 2 Asian Americans or Pacific Islanders, 4 Hispanic Americans), 4 international. Average age 35. 63 applicants, 94% accepted. Expenses: Contact institution. *Financial support:* Career-related internships or fieldwork, Federal Work-Study, institutionally sponsored loans, and scholarships/grants available. Support available to part-time students. Financial award applicants required to submit FAFSA. In 2006, 19 degrees awarded. *Degree program information:* Part-time and evening/weekend programs available. Offers joint (PhD). *Application deadline:* Applications are processed on a rolling basis. Electronic applications accepted. *Application Contact:* Karen Fennel, Graduate Studies Executive Assistant, 303-871-2706, Fax: 303-871-4566, E-mail: gfac@du.edu. *Vice Provost,* Dr. James Moran, 303-871-2706.

Conflict Resolution Institute Students: 19 full-time (15 women), 12 part-time (5 women); includes 4 minority (all African Americans) Average age 29. 27 applicants, 89% accepted. *Faculty:* 2 full-time, 13 part-time/adjunct. Expenses: Contact institution. *Financial support:* Career-related internships or fieldwork, Federal Work-Study, scholarships/grants, and tuition waivers (partial) available. Financial award application deadline: 2/15; financial award applicants required to submit FAFSA. In 2006, 9 degrees awarded. *Degree program information:* Part-time programs available. Offers conflict resolution (MA). *Application deadline:* For fall admission, 2/15 priority date for domestic students; for winter admission, 11/1 priority date for domestic students; for spring admission, 1/15 priority date for domestic students. Applications are processed on a rolling basis. *Application fee:* $50. Electronic applications accepted. *Application Contact:* Information Contact, 303-871-6477, E-mail: cri@du.edu. *Director,* Dr. Karen Feste, 303-871-6477, E-mail: kfeste@du.edu.

Intermodal Transportation Institute Students: 35 full-time (10 women); includes 6 minority (2 Asian Americans or Pacific Islanders, 4 Hispanic Americans), 3 international. Average age 40. 19 applicants, 100% accepted. Expenses: Contact institution. *Financial support:* Applicants required to submit FAFSA. In 2006, 10 degrees awarded. Offers intermodal transportation (MS). *Application fee:* $0. *Application Contact:* Cathy Johnson, Administrator, 308-871-4702, E-mail: du-iti@du.edu. *Director,* Dr. Bill Zaranka, 303-871-4146.

School of Engineering and Computer Science Students: 4 full-time (1 woman), 110 part-time (28 women); includes 14 minority (5 African Americans, 2 American Indian/Alaska Native, 5 Asian Americans or Pacific Islanders, 2 Hispanic Americans), 20 international. Average age 30. 166 applicants, 89% accepted. *Faculty:* 25 full-time (4 women). Expenses: Contact institution. *Financial support:* In 2006–07, 14 research assistantships with full and partial tuition reimbursements (averaging $12,400 per year), 18 teaching assistantships with full and partial tuition reimbursements (averaging $13,000 per year) were awarded. Financial award applicants required to submit FAFSA. In 2006, 22 master's, 1 doctorate awarded. Offers computer engineering (MS); computer science (MS, PhD); computer science and engineering (MS); electrical engineering (MS); engineering (PhD); engineering and computer science (MS, PhD); materials science (PhD); mechanical engineering (MS). *Application deadline:* Applications are processed on a rolling basis. *Application fee:* $50. Electronic applications accepted. *Dean,* Dr. Rahmat Shoureshi, 303-871-2621.

University College Students: 57 full-time (28 women), 453 part-time (253 women); includes 84 minority (37 African Americans, 1 American Indian/Alaska Native, 21 Asian Americans or Pacific Islanders, 25 Hispanic Americans), 39 international. Average age 26. 159 applicants, 84% accepted. Expenses: Contact institution. *Financial support:* Applicants required to submit FAFSA. In 2006, 171 master's, 2 other advanced degrees awarded. *Degree program information:* Part-time and evening/weekend programs available. Postbaccalaureate distance learning degree programs offered (no on-campus study). Offers applied communication (MAS, MPS, Certificate); computer information systems (MAS, Certificate); environmental policy and management (MAS, Certificate); geographic information systems (MAS, Certificate); human resource administration (MPS, Certificate); knowledge and information technologies (MAS); liberal studies (MLS, Certificate); modern languages (MLS, Certificate); organizational leadership (MPS, Certificate); security management (Certificate); technology management (MAS, Certificate); telecommunications (MAS, Certificate). *Application deadline:* Applications are processed on a rolling basis. *Application fee:* $75. Electronic applications accepted. *Application Contact:* Information Contact, 303-871-3069. *Dean,* Dr. James Davis, 303-871-2291, Fax: 303-871-4047, E-mail: jdavis@du.edu.

See Close-Up on page 1075.

UNIVERSITY OF DETROIT MERCY, Detroit, MI 48221

General Information Independent-religious, coed, university. *Enrollment:* 1,424 full-time matriculated graduate/professional students (659 women), 964 part-time matriculated graduate/professional students (611 women). *Enrollment by degree level:* 1,045 first professional, 1,234 master's, 61 doctoral, 48 other advanced degrees. *Graduate faculty:* 175. *Tuition:* Full-time $15,750; part-time $875 per credit hour. *Required fees:* $570. *Graduate housing:* Rooms and/or apartments available to single and married students. *Student services:* Campus employment opportunities, campus safety program, career counseling, international student services, low-cost health insurance, teacher training. *Library facilities:* McNichols Campus Library plus 3 others. *Online resources:* library catalog, web page, access to other libraries' catalogs. *Collection:* 9,340 serial subscriptions, 32,053 audiovisual materials.

Computer facilities: 250 computers available on campus for general student use. A campuswide network can be accessed from student residence rooms and from off campus. Internet access is available. *Web address:* http://www.udmercy.edu/.

General Application Contact: Michael Joseph, Vice President, Enrollment Management, 313-993-1245.

GRADUATE UNITS

College of Business Administration Students: 100 full-time (31 women), 180 part-time (82 women); includes 56 minority (49 African Americans, 2 American Indian/Alaska Native, 5 Asian Americans or Pacific Islanders), 105 international. Average age 32. *Faculty:* 23 full-time (4 women). Expenses: Contact institution. *Financial support:* Research assistantships, career-related internships or fieldwork, Federal Work-Study, institutionally sponsored loans, and unspecified assistantships available. Support available to part-time students. Financial award application deadline: 8/1. In 2006, 125 degrees awarded. *Degree program information:* Part-time and evening/weekend programs available. Offers business administration (EMBA, MBA, MS, MSCIS, Certificate); business turnaround management (MS, Certificate); computer information systems (MSCIS); information assurance (MS). *Application deadline:* For fall admission, 8/1 priority date for domestic students. Applications are processed on a rolling basis. *Application fee:* $30 ($50 for international students). *Application Contact:* Dr. Bonnie Naski, Coordinator for Graduate Programs, 313-993-1202, Fax: 313-993-1052, E-mail: gradbusiness@udmercy.edu. *Dean,* Dr. Hossein Nivi, 313-993-1204, Fax: 313-993-1052.

College of Engineering and Science *Degree program information:* Part-time and evening/weekend programs available. Offers automotive engineering (DE); chemical engineering (ME, DE); civil and environmental engineering (ME); computer science (MSCS); electrical engineering (ME, DE); elementary mathematics education (MATM); engineering and science (M Eng Mgt, MATM, ME, MS, MSCS, DE); engineering management (M Eng Mgt); junior high mathematics education (MATM); macromolecular chemistry (MS); manufacturing engineering (DE); mechanical engineering (ME, DE); polymer engineering (ME); secondary mathematics education (MATM); teaching of mathematics (MATM).

College of Health Professions Offers family nurse practitioner (MSN, Certificate); health professions (MS, MSN, Certificate); health services administration (MS); health systems management (MSN); nurse anesthesiology (MS); physician assistant (MS).

College of Liberal Arts and Education *Degree program information:* Part-time and evening/weekend programs available. Offers addiction counseling (MA); addiction studies (Certificate); clinical psychology (MA, PhD); community counseling (MA); counseling (MA); criminal justice (MA); curriculum and instruction (MA); early childhood education (MA); educational administration (MA); emotionally impaired (MA); industrial/organizational psychology (MA); learning disabilities (MA); liberal arts and education (MA, MALS, MS, PhD, Certificate, Spec); liberal studies (MALS); religious studies (MA); school counseling (MA); school psychology (Spec); security administration (MS); special education (MA); teaching and learning (MA).

School of Architecture Offers architecture (M Arch).

School of Dentistry Offers dentistry (DDS, MS, Certificate); endodontics (MS, Certificate); orthodontics (MS, Certificate).

School of Law *Degree program information:* Part-time programs available. Offers law (JD).

UNIVERSITY OF DUBUQUE, Dubuque, IA 52001-5099

General Information Independent-religious, coed, comprehensive institution. *Enrollment:* 20 full-time matriculated graduate/professional students (11 women), 67 part-time matriculated graduate/professional students (33 women). *Enrollment by degree level:* 87 master's. *Graduate faculty:* 9 full-time (1 woman), 5 part-time/adjunct (4 women). *Graduate housing:* Rooms and/or apartments available on a first-come, first-served basis to single students and available to married students. *Student services:* Campus employment opportunities, career counseling, exercise/wellness program, international student services, low-cost health insurance, multicultural affairs office, teacher training. *Library facilities:* Charles C. Myer's Library. *Online resources:* library catalog, web page, access to other libraries' catalogs. *Collection:* 168,579 titles, 484 serial subscriptions, 1,169 audiovisual materials.

Computer facilities: 220 computers available on campus for general student use. A campuswide network can be accessed from student residence rooms and from off campus. Internet access, intranet are available. *Web address:* http://www.dbq.edu/.

General Application Contact: Carol A. Knockle, Graduate Program Coordinator, 563-589-3300, Fax: 563-589-3184, E-mail: cknockle@dbq.edu.

GRADUATE UNITS

Program in Business Administration Students: 18 full-time (10 women), 42 part-time (17 women); includes 13 minority (1 African American, 1 American Indian/Alaska Native, 11 Asian Americans or Pacific Islanders), 1 international. Average age 33. *Faculty:* 5 full-time (1 woman), 4 part-time/adjunct (3 women). Expenses: Contact institution. *Financial support:* In 2006–07, 4 teaching assistantships with full tuition reimbursements were awarded; Federal Work-Study also available. Support available to part-time students. Financial award application deadline: 4/1; financial award applicants required to submit FAFSA. In 2006, 42 degrees awarded. *Degree program information:* Part-time and evening/weekend programs available. Offers business administration (MBA). *Application deadline:* For fall admission, 8/15 priority date for domestic students, 7/15 priority date for international students. Applications are processed on a rolling basis. *Application fee:* $25. Electronic applications accepted. *Application Contact:* Carol A. Knockle, Graduate Program Coordinator, 563-589-3300, Fax: 563-589-3184, E-mail: mba@dbq.edu. *Director of Domestic and International MBA Programs,* Richard Birkenbeuel, 319-589-3417, Fax: 319-589-3184, E-mail: rbirkenb@dbq.edu.

Program in Communication Students: 2 full-time (1 woman), 25 part-time (16 women); includes 2 minority (both African Americans) Average age 35. *Faculty:* 4 full-time (0 women), 1 (woman) part-time/adjunct. Expenses: Contact institution. *Financial support:* Teaching assistantships with full tuition reimbursements, Federal Work-Study available. Support available to part-time students. Financial award application deadline: 4/1. In 2006, 7 degrees awarded. *Degree program information:* Part-time and evening/weekend programs available. Offers communication (MAC). *Application deadline:* For fall admission, 8/15 priority date for domestic students, 7/15 priority date for international students. Applications are processed on a rolling basis. *Application fee:* $25. Electronic applications accepted. *Application Contact:* Carol A. Knockle, Graduate Program Coordinator, 563-589-3300, Fax: 563-589-3184, E-mail: mac@dbq.edu. *Program Director,* Dr. Robert Reid, 563-589-3188, Fax: 563-589-3690, E-mail: rreid@dbq.edu.

Theological Seminary Students: 153 full-time (59 women), 1 (woman) part-time; includes 2 African Americans, 4 Asian Americans or Pacific Islanders, 1 Hispanic American, 4 international. Average age 36. 81 applicants, 72% accepted, 45 enrolled. *Faculty:* 11 full-time (3 women), 16 part-time/adjunct (8 women). Expenses: Contact institution. *Financial support:* In 2006–07, 119 fellowships (averaging $6,940 per year) were awarded; career-related internships or fieldwork, Federal Work-Study, institutionally sponsored loans, scholarships/grants, and tuition waivers (full and partial) also available. Support available to part-time students. Financial award application deadline: 6/1; financial award applicants required to submit FAFSA. In 2006, 22 master's, 7 doctorates awarded. Offers theology (M Div, MAR, D Min). *Application deadline:* For fall admission, 4/15 priority date for domestic students, 12/1 priority date for international students; for spring admission, 11/1 priority date for domestic students. Applications are processed on a rolling basis. *Application fee:* $30. *Application Contact:* Donna F. Warhover, Director of Seminary Admissions, 563-589-3112, Fax: 563-589-3110, E-mail: dwarhove@dbq.edu. *Dean,* Dr. Bradley Longfield, 563-589-3122, Fax: 563-589-3110, E-mail: blongfie@dbq.edu.

UNIVERSITY OF EVANSVILLE, Evansville, IN 47722

General Information Independent-religious, coed, comprehensive institution. *Enrollment:* 2,879 graduate, professional, and undergraduate students; 57 full-time matriculated graduate/professional students (39 women), 9 part-time matriculated graduate/professional students (7 women). *Enrollment by degree level:* 66 master's. *Graduate faculty:* 7 full-time (1 woman), 11 part-time/adjunct (4 women). *Tuition:* Full-time $6,534; part-time $580 per credit hour. Tuition and fees vary according to course load and program. *Graduate housing:* On-campus housing not available. *Student services:* Career counseling, disabled student services, free psychological counseling, international student services, multicultural affairs office. *Library facilities:* Bower Suhrheinrich Library plus 1 other. *Online resources:* library catalog, web page, access to other libraries' catalogs. *Collection:* 289,593 titles, 970 serial subscriptions, 11,534 audiovisual materials. *Research affiliation:* Independent Colleges of Indiana (higher education administration), Associated New American Colleges (higher education administration), Council of Independent Colleges (higher education administration).

Computer facilities: Computer purchase and lease plans are available. 312 computers available on campus for general student use. A campuswide network can be accessed from student residence rooms and from off campus. Internet access and online class registration are available. *Web address:* http://www.evansville.edu/.

General Application Contact: Carla Doty, Interim Director of Continuing Education, 812-488-2981, Fax: 812-488-4079, E-mail: cd39@evansville.edu.

GRADUATE UNITS

Center for Continuing Education Students: 55 full-time (39 women); includes 1 minority (African American), 1 international. Average age 36. 29 applicants, 93% accepted, 20 enrolled. *Faculty:* 6 full-time (1 woman), 6 part-time/adjunct (3 women). Expenses: Contact institution. *Financial support:* In 2006–07, 16 students received support. Available to part-time students. Application deadline: 7/1; In 2006, 24 degrees awarded. *Degree program information:* Part-time and evening/weekend programs available. Offers public service administration (MS). *Application deadline:* For fall admission, 7/15 priority date for domestic students, 7/15 for international students; for spring admission, 11/30 priority date for domestic students, 11/30 for international students. Applications are processed on a rolling basis. *Application fee:* $35 ($50 for international students). *Application Contact:* Carla Doty, Interim Director of Continuing Education, 812-488-2981, Fax: 812-488-4079, E-mail: cd39@evansville.edu. *Interim Director of Continuing Education,* Carla Doty, 812-488-2981, Fax: 812-488-4079, E-mail: cd39@evansville.edu.

College of Education and Health Sciences Students: 1 full-time (0 women), 9 part-time (7 women), 1 international. Average age 42. 2 applicants, 100% accepted, 1 enrolled. *Faculty:* 1 full-time (0 women), 4 part-time/adjunct (1 woman). Expenses: Contact institution. *Financial support:* In 2006–07, 2 students received support. Career-related internships or fieldwork available. Support available to part-time students. Financial award application deadline: 7/1; financial award applicants required to submit FAFSA. In 2006, 11 degrees awarded. *Degree program information:* Part-time and evening/weekend programs available. Offers education and health sciences (MS); health services administration (MS). *Application deadline:* For fall admission, 7/1 priority date for domestic and international students; for spring admission, 10/1 priority date for domestic students. Applications are processed on a rolling basis. *Application fee:* $20 ($50 for international students). *Application Contact:* Dr. William Stroube, Director, Health Services Administration Program, 812-488-2343, Fax: 812-488-2717, E-mail: hsa@evansville.edu. *Director,* Dr. Lynn Penland, 812-488-2981, Fax: 812-488-1146, E-mail: lp22@evansville.edu.

College of Engineering and Computer Science Students: 1 full-time (0 women), 1 international. Average age 22. 10 applicants, 20% accepted, 1 enrolled. *Faculty:* 1 full-time (0 women), 1 part-time/adjunct (0 women). Expenses: Contact institution. *Financial support:* In 2006–07, 1 student received support. Available to part-time students. Application deadline: 7/1; *Degree program information:* Part-time programs available. Offers electrical engineering and computer science (MS); engineering and computer science (MS). *Application deadline:* For fall admission, 5/1 priority date for domestic and international students. Applications are processed on a rolling basis. *Application fee:* $25 ($50 for international students). *Application Contact:* Dr. Dick Blandford, Department Chair, 812-488-2570, Fax: 812-488-2662, E-mail: blandford@evansville.edu. *Dean,* Dr. Philip Gerhart, 812-488-2651, Fax: 812-488-2780, E-mail: pg3@evansville.edu.

THE UNIVERSITY OF FINDLAY, Findlay, OH 45840-3653

General Information Independent-religious, coed, comprehensive institution. CGS member. *Enrollment:* 6,182 graduate, professional, and undergraduate students; 337 full-time matriculated graduate/professional students (208 women), 830 part-time matriculated graduate/professional students (409 women). *Enrollment by degree level:* 1,167 master's. *Graduate faculty:* 43 full-time, 8 part-time/adjunct. *Graduate housing:* Room and/or apartments available on a first-come, first-served basis to single students; on-campus housing not available to married students. Typical cost: $1,953 per year ($3,896 including board). Room and board charges vary according to campus/location and housing facility selected. *Student services:* Campus employment opportunities, campus safety program, career counseling, disabled student services, exercise/wellness program, free psychological counseling, grant writing training, international student services, low-cost health insurance, multicultural affairs office, teacher training. *Library facilities:* Shafer Library. *Online resources:* library catalog, access to other libraries' catalogs. *Collection:* 132,052 titles, 23,128 serial subscriptions. *Research affiliation:* Department of Health and Human Services (terrorism preparedness), Department of Education (technology innovation), Department of Education (bilingual teaching research), Department of Agriculture (wildlife research), Rollin M. Gerstacker Foundation (environmental research), Ohio State University Research Foundation (biology research).

Computer facilities: Computer purchase and lease plans are available. 200 computers available on campus for general student use. A campuswide network can be accessed from student residence rooms and from off campus. Internet access and online class registration are available. *Web address:* http://www.findlay.edu/.

General Application Contact: Heather Riffle, Director, Graduate and Special Programs, 419-434-4640, Fax: 419-434-5517, E-mail: riffle@findlay.edu.

GRADUATE UNITS

Graduate and Professional Studies Students: 337 full-time (208 women), 830 part-time (409 women); includes 42 minority (20 African Americans, 3 American Indian/Alaska Native, 9 Asian Americans or Pacific Islanders, 10 Hispanic Americans), 382 international. Average age 35. 410 applicants, 88% accepted, 345 enrolled. *Faculty:* 43 full-time, 8 part-time/adjunct. Expenses: Contact institution. *Financial support:* In 2006–07, 16 teaching assistantships with full tuition reimbursements (averaging $6,000 per year) were awarded; unspecified assistantships also available. Financial award application deadline: 4/1; financial award applicants required to submit FAFSA. In 2006, 470 degrees awarded. *Degree program information:* Part-time and evening/weekend programs available. Postbaccalaureate distance learning degree programs offered (no on-campus study). Offers administration (MA Ed); early childhood (MA Ed); elementary education (MA Ed); human resource development (MA Ed); leadership (MA Ed); professional studies (MA, MA Ed, MALS, MAT, MBA, MOT, MPT, MSEM); special education (MA Ed); technology (MA Ed); web instruction (MA Ed). *Application deadline:* Applications are processed on a rolling basis. *Application fee:* $25. Electronic applications accepted. *Application Contact:* Heather Riffle, Director, Graduate and Special Programs, 419-434-4640, Fax: 419-434-5517, E-mail: riffle@findlay.edu. *Dean, Graduate and Professional Studies,* Dr. Thomas Dillion, 419-434-4640, Fax: 419-434-5517, E-mail: dillon@findlay.edu.

College of Health Professions Students: 135 full-time (86 women), 10 part-time (8 women); includes 3 minority (1 African American, 1 Asian American or Pacific Islander, 1 Hispanic American), 3 international. Average age 35. 39 applicants, 92% accepted, 36 enrolled. Expenses: Contact institution. In 2006, 71 degrees awarded. Offers athletic training (MAT); health professions (MAT, MOT, MPT); occupational therapy (MOT); physical therapy (MPT). *Application fee:* $25. *Application Contact:* Heather Riffle, Director, Graduate and Special Programs, 419-434-4640, Fax: 419-434-5517, E-mail: riffle@findlay.edu. *Dean, College of Health Professions,* Dr. Lisa Dutton, 419-434-4677, Fax: 419-434-4822, E-mail: dutton@findlay.edu.

College of Liberal Arts Students: 37 full-time (30 women), 31 part-time (23 women); includes 4 minority (1 African American, 2 Asian Americans or Pacific Islanders, 1 Hispanic American), 32 international. Average age 35. 31 applicants, 81% accepted, 24 enrolled. *Faculty:* 11 full-time, 1 part-time/adjunct. Expenses: Contact institution. *Financial support:* In 2006–07, 1 student received support, including 1 teaching assistantship with full tuition reimbursement available (averaging $6,000 per year). Financial award application deadline: 4/1; financial award applicants required to submit FAFSA. In 2006, 19 degrees awarded. *Degree program information:* Part-time and evening/weekend programs available. Offers bilingual and multicultural education (MA); liberal arts (MA, MALS); liberal studies (MALS); teaching English to speakers of other languages (MA). *Application deadline:* Applications are processed on a rolling basis. *Application fee:* $25. Electronic applications accepted. *Application Contact:* Heather Riffle, Director, Graduate and Special Programs, 419-434-4640, Fax: 419-434-5517, E-mail: riffle@findlay.edu. *Dean,* Dr. Dennis Stevens, 419-434-4771, Fax: 419-434-4822, E-mail: stevens@findlay.edu.

College of Science Students: 2 full-time (both women), 109 part-time (42 women); includes 4 minority (2 African Americans, 1 Asian American or Pacific Islander, 1 Hispanic American), 45 international. 41 applicants, 73% accepted, 28 enrolled. *Faculty:* 4 full-time. Expenses: Contact institution. *Financial support:* Unspecified assistantships available. Financial award application deadline: 4/1. In 2006, 24 degrees awarded. *Degree program information:* Part-time and evening/weekend programs available. Offers environmental management (MSEM); science (MSEM). *Application deadline:* Applications are processed on a rolling basis. *Application fee:* $25. Electronic applications accepted. *Application Contact:* Heather Riffle, Director, Graduate and Special Programs, 419-434-4640, Fax: 419-434-5517, E-mail: riffle@findlay.edu.

MBA Program Students: 80 full-time (26 women), 456 part-time (168 women); includes 20 minority (13 African Americans, 1 American Indian/Alaska Native, 4 Asian Americans or Pacific Islanders, 2 Hispanic Americans), 289 international. Average age 35. 208 applicants, 88% accepted, 181 enrolled. *Faculty:* 16 full-time, 1 part-time/adjunct. Expenses: Contact institution. *Financial support:* In 2006–07, 1 student received support, including 1 teaching assistantship with full tuition reimbursement available (averaging $6,000 per year); unspecified assistantships also available. Financial award application deadline: 4/1; financial award applicants required to submit FAFSA. In 2006, 210 degrees awarded. *Degree program information:* Part-time and evening/weekend programs available. Postbaccalaureate distance learning degree programs offered (no on-campus study). Offers financial management (MBA); human resource management (MBA); international management (MBA); management (MBA); marketing (MBA); public management (MBA). *Application deadline:* Applications are processed on a rolling basis. *Application fee:* $25. Electronic applications accepted. *Application Contact:* Heather Riffle, Director, Graduate and Special Programs, 419-434-4640, Fax: 419-434-5517, E-mail: riffle@findlay.edu. *Dean,* Dr. Paul Sears, 419-434-4704, Fax: 419-434-4822.

UNIVERSITY OF FLORIDA, Gainesville, FL 32611

General Information State-supported, coed, university. CGS member. *Enrollment:* 50,822 graduate, professional, and undergraduate students; 13,818 matriculated graduate/professional students. *Graduate faculty:* 3,271 full-time (949 women), 114 part-time/adjunct (44 women). Tuition, state resident: full-time $6,827. Tuition, nonresident: full-time $21,951. *Required fees:* $999. *Graduate housing:* Rooms and/or apartments available on a first-come, first-served basis to single and married students. *Student services:* Campus employment opportunities, campus safety program, career counseling, child daycare facilities, disabled student services, exercise/wellness program, free psychological counseling, grant writing training, international student services, low-cost health insurance, multicultural affairs office, teacher training, writing training. *Library facilities:* George A. Smathers Library plus 8 others. *Online resources:* library catalog, web page, access to other libraries' catalogs. *Collection:*

University of Florida (continued)

5.3 million titles, 25,342 serial subscriptions, 25,953 audiovisual materials. *Research affiliation:* Los Alamos National Laboratory (high magnetic field research), National Center for Automated Information Research (law and business data), Oracle Corporation (database management), IBM (information infrastructure), Association of Universities for Research in Astronomy (Gemini multinational telescope).

Computer facilities: Computer purchase and lease plans are available. 472 computers available on campus for general student use. A campuswide network can be accessed from student residence rooms and from off campus. Internet access and online class registration are available. *Web address:* http://www.ufl.edu/.

General Application Contact: Graduate Admissions, 352-392-3261.

GRADUATE UNITS

College of Dentistry Students: 326 (147 women); includes 101 minority (11 African Americans, 1 American Indian/Alaska Native, 50 Asian Americans or Pacific Islanders, 39 Hispanic Americans). Average age 29. Expenses: Contact institution. *Financial support:* In 2006–07, 320 students received support, including 1 research assistantship (averaging $11,206 per year); Federal Work-Study, institutionally sponsored loans, scholarships/grants, and health care benefits also available. Financial award applicants required to submit FAFSA. In 2006, 78 degrees awarded. Offers dentistry (DMD); endodontics (MS, Certificate); foreign trained dentistry (Certificate); oral biology (PhD); orthodontics (MS, Certificate); periodontology (MS, Certificate); prosthodontics (MS, Certificate). *Application deadline:* For fall admission, 10/15 for domestic students. *Application fee:* $30. *Application Contact:* Dr. Venita Sposetti, Assistant Dean for Admissions and Financial Aid, 352-392-4866, Fax: 352-846-0311, E-mail: sposetti@dental.ufl.edu. *Dean,* Dr. Teresa A. Dolan, 352-392-2911, Fax: 352-392-3070, E-mail: tdolan@dental.ufl.edu.

College of Medicine Average age 28. Expenses: Contact institution. *Financial support:* Fellowships, research assistantships, teaching assistantships, institutionally sponsored loans, scholarships/grants, and traineeships available. Financial award application deadline: 4/1; financial award applicants required to submit FAFSA. In 2006, 115 first professional degrees, 77 master's awarded. Offers biochemistry and molecular biology (MS, PhD); biomedical sciences (PhD); clinical investigation (MS); epidemiology (MS); genetics (PhD); imaging science and technology (MS, PhD); immunology and microbiology (PhD); immunology and molecular pathology (PhD); medicine (MD, MPAS, MPH, MS, PhD); molecular cell biology (PhD); molecular genetics and microbiology (MS, PhD); neuroscience (MS, PhD); pharmacology and therapeutics (PhD); physician assistant (MPAS); physiology and functional genomics (PhD); physiology and pharmacology (PhD); public health (MPH). *Application deadline:* For fall admission, 12/1 for domestic students. *Application fee:* $30. Electronic applications accepted. *Application Contact:* Robyn Sheppard, Admissions Coordinator, 352-392-4569, Fax: 352-392-1307, E-mail: robyn@dean.med.ufl.edu. *Dean,* Dr. C. Craig Tisher, 352-846-2473.

College of Pharmacy Students: 1,892 (1,177 women); includes 581 minority (98 African Americans, 6 American Indian/Alaska Native, 331 Asian Americans or Pacific Islanders, 146 Hispanic Americans) 112 international. *Faculty:* 42 full-time (15 women), 2 part-time/adjunct (1 woman). Expenses: Contact institution. *Financial support:* Fellowships, research assistantships, teaching assistantships, Federal Work-Study, institutionally sponsored loans, tuition waivers (full), and unspecified assistantships available. Support available to part-time students. Financial award applicants required to submit FAFSA. In 2006, 345 degrees awarded. *Degree program information:* Part-time programs available. Postbaccalaureate distance learning degree programs offered (no on-campus study). Offers clinical pharmaceutical sciences (PhD); forensic DNA and serology (MS, Certificate); forensic drug chemistry (MS, Certificate); forensic toxicology (MS, Certificate); medicinal chemistry (Pharm D, MSP, PhD); pharmaceutical sciences (MSP, PhD); pharmaceutics (PhD); pharmacodynamics (MSP, PhD); pharmacology (PhD); pharmacy (Pharm D, MSP, PhD); pharmacy health care administration (MSP, PhD); pharmacy practice (PhD). *Application deadline:* Applications are processed on a rolling basis. *Application fee:* $30. Electronic applications accepted. *Application Contact:* Dr. William J. Millard, Executive Associate Dean, 352-273-6311, Fax: 352-273-6306, E-mail: millard@cop.ufl.edu. *Dean,* Dr. William H. Riffee, 352-273-6309, Fax: 352-273-6306, E-mail: riffee@cop.ufl.edu.

College of Veterinary Medicine Students: 456 (336 women); includes 71 minority (18 African Americans, 2 American Indian/Alaska Native, 11 Asian Americans or Pacific Islanders, 40 Hispanic Americans) 13 international. Average age 27. *Faculty:* 84 full-time (22 women), 7 part-time/adjunct (6 women). Expenses: Contact institution. *Financial support:* In 2006–07, 15 research assistantships (averaging $17,504 per year), 4 teaching assistantships (averaging $15,921 per year) were awarded; fellowships, career-related internships or fieldwork, Federal Work-Study, institutionally sponsored loans, and scholarships/grants also available. Financial award applicants required to submit FAFSA. In 2006, 82 first professional degrees, 32 master's, 3 doctorates awarded. *Degree program information:* Part-time programs available. Offers forensic toxicology (Certificate); veterinary medical sciences (MS, PhD); veterinary medicine (DVM, MS, PhD, Certificate). *Application deadline:* Applications are processed on a rolling basis. *Application Contact:* Dr. Charles H. Courtney, Associate Dean for Research and Graduate Studies, 352-392-4700 Ext. 5100, Fax: 352-392-8351, E-mail: courtneyc@mail.vetmed.ufl.edu. *Interim Dean,* Dr. James P. Thompson, 352-392-4700 Ext. 5000, Fax: 352-392-8351, E-mail: thompsonji@@mail.vetmed.ufl.edu.

Graduate School Students: 9,037. *Faculty:* 3,060. Expenses: Contact institution. *Financial support:* Fellowships, research assistantships, teaching assistantships, career-related internships or fieldwork, Federal Work-Study, institutionally sponsored loans, and unspecified assistantships available. Support available to part-time students. *Degree program information:* Part-time programs available. *Application deadline:* Applications are processed on a rolling basis. *Application fee:* $30. Electronic applications accepted. *Application Contact:* Graduate Admissions, 352-392-1365, E-mail: gradinfo@ufl.edu. *Interim Dean,* Dr. Kenneth J. Gerhardt, 352-392-6622, Fax: 352-392-8729, E-mail: gerhardt@csd.ufl.edu.

College of Agricultural and Life Sciences *Faculty:* 811 full-time (276 women), 13 part-time/adjunct (2 women). Expenses: Contact institution. *Financial support:* In 2006–07, 390 students received support; fellowships with tuition reimbursements available, research assistantships with tuition reimbursements available, teaching assistantships with tuition reimbursements available, career-related internships or fieldwork, Federal Work-Study, institutionally sponsored loans, and unspecified assistantships available. Support available to part-time students. *Degree program information:* Part-time programs available. Offers agricultural and life sciences (M Ag, MAB, MFAS, MFRC, MFYCS, MS, DPM, PhD); agricultural education and communication (M Ag, MS, PhD); agronomy (MS, PhD); anatomy and development (MS, PhD); animal sciences (M Ag, MS, PhD); biochemistry and molecular biology (MS, PhD); breeding and genetics (MS, PhD); ecology (MS, PhD); entomology and nematology (MS, PhD); family, youth, and community sciences (MFYCS, MS); fisheries and aquatic sciences (MFAS, MS, PhD); food and resource economics (MAB, MS, PhD); food science (MS, PhD); forest resources and conservation (MFRC, MS, PhD); microbiology and cell science (MS, PhD); nutritional sciences (MS, PhD); plant biotechnology (MS, PhD); plant breeding and genetics (MS, PhD); plant medicine (DPM); plant molecular and cellular biology (MS, PhD); plant pathology (MS, PhD); plant production and nutrient management (MS, PhD); postharvest biology (MS, PhD); soil and water science (MS, PhD); stress physiology (MS, PhD); sustainable/organic practice (MS, PhD); taxonomy (MS, PhD); tissue culture (MS, PhD); weed science (MS, PhD); wildlife ecology and conservation (MS, PhD). *Application deadline:* Applications are processed on a rolling basis. *Application fee:* $20. Electronic applications accepted. *Application Contact:* Dr. E. Jane Luzar, Associate Dean for Academic Programs, 352-392-2251, Fax: 352-392-8988, E-mail: ejluzar@ufl.edu. *Dean,* R. Kirby Barrick, 352-392-1971.

College of Design, Construction and Planning *Faculty:* 64 full-time (24 women). Expenses: Contact institution. *Financial support:* Fellowships, research assistantships, teaching assistantships, career-related internships or fieldwork, Federal Work-Study, and unspecified assistantships available. Support available to part-time students. In 2006, 5 degrees awarded. *Degree program information:* Part-time programs available. Offers architecture (M Arch, MSAS, PhD); building construction (MBC, MICM, MSBC, PhD); design, construction and planning (M Arch, MAURP, MBC, MICM, MID, MLA, MSAS, MSBC, PhD); interior design (MID, PhD); landscape architecture (MLA, PhD); urban and regional planning (MAURP, PhD). *Application deadline:* Applications are processed on a rolling basis. *Application fee:* $30. Electronic applications accepted. *Dean,* Dr. Christopher Silver, 352-392-4836 Ext. 465, Fax: 352-392-7266, E-mail: silver2@ufl.edu.

College of Education *Faculty:* 91 full-time (57 women). Expenses: Contact institution. *Financial support:* Fellowships with tuition reimbursements, research assistantships with tuition reimbursements, teaching assistantships with tuition reimbursements, career-related internships or fieldwork, Federal Work-Study, and unspecified assistantships available. Support available to part-time students. Financial award application deadline: 1/4; financial award applicants required to submit FAFSA. *Degree program information:* Part-time programs available. Offers bilingual/ESOL education (M Ed, MAE, Ed D, PhD, Ed S); curriculum and instruction (M Ed, MAE, Ed D, PhD, Ed S); early childhood education (Ed D, PhD, Ed S); education (M Ed, MAE, Ed D, PhD, Ed S); educational leadership (M Ed, MAE, Ed D, PhD, Ed S); educational psychology (M Ed, MAE, Ed D, PhD, Ed S); elementary education (M Ed, MAE); English education (M Ed, MAE); higher education administration (Ed D, PhD, Ed S); marriage and family counseling (M Ed, MAE, Ed D, PhD, Ed S); mathematics education (M Ed, MAE); mental health counseling (M Ed, MAE, Ed D, PhD, Ed S); reading education (M Ed, MAE); research and evaluation methodology (M Ed, MAE, Ed D, PhD, Ed S); school counseling and guidance (M Ed, MAE, Ed D, PhD, Ed S); school psychology (M Ed, MAE, Ed D, PhD, Ed S); science education (M Ed, MAE); social foundations (M Ed, MAE, Ed D, PhD); social studies education (M Ed, MAE); special education (M Ed, MAE, Ed D, PhD, Ed S); student personnel in higher education (M Ed, MAE). *Application deadline:* Applications are processed on a rolling basis. *Application fee:* $30. Electronic applications accepted. *Application Contact:* Dr. John H. Kranzler, Associate Dean, 352-392-0728 Ext. 234, Fax: 352-392-6930, E-mail: jkranzler@coe.ufl.edu. *Dean,* Dr. Catherine Emihovich, 352-392-0728 Ext. 226, Fax: 352-392-6930, E-mail: cemihovich@coe.ufl.edu.

College of Engineering *Faculty:* 282 full-time (29 women), 9 part-time/adjunct (2 women). Expenses: Contact institution. *Financial support:* In 2006–07, 1,070 students received support; fellowships with full tuition reimbursements available, research assistantships with full tuition reimbursements available, teaching assistantships with full tuition reimbursements available, career-related internships or fieldwork, Federal Work-Study, institutionally sponsored loans, and unspecified assistantships available. Support available to part-time students. *Degree program information:* Part-time programs available. Offers aerospace engineering (ME, MS, PhD, Engr); agricultural and biological engineering (ME, MS, PhD, Engr); biomedical engineering (ME, MS, PhD, Certificate); chemical engineering (ME, MS, PhD); civil engineering (MCE, MS, PhD, Engr); coastal and oceanographic engineering (ME, MS, PhD, Engr); computer engineering (ME, MS, PhD); computer science (MS); digital arts and sciences (MS); electrical and computer engineering (ME, MS, PhD, Engr); engineering (MCE, ME, MS, PhD, Certificate, Engr); environmental engineering sciences (ME, MS, PhD, Engr); industrial and systems engineering (ME, MS, PhD, Engr); materials science and engineering (ME, MS, PhD, Engr); mechanical engineering (ME, MS, PhD, Engr); nuclear engineering sciences (ME, MS, PhD, Engr). *Application deadline:* For fall admission, 6/1 priority date for domestic students. Applications are processed on a rolling basis. *Application fee:* $30. Electronic applications accepted. *Application Contact:* Dr. Timothy J. Anderson, Associate Dean for Research and Graduate Programs, 352-392-0946, Fax: 352-392-9673, E-mail: tim@ufl.edu. *Dean,* Dr. Pramod P. Khargonekar, 352-392-6000, Fax: 352-392-9673, E-mail: ppk@ufl.edu.

College of Fine Arts *Faculty:* 86 full-time (30 women), 2 part-time/adjunct (1 woman). Expenses: Contact institution. *Financial support:* Fellowships, research assistantships, teaching assistantships, career-related internships or fieldwork, Federal Work-Study, institutionally sponsored loans, and unspecified assistantships available. Support available to part-time students. *Degree program information:* Part-time programs available. Offers art (MFA); art education (MA); art history (MA, PhD); choral conducting (MM, PhD); composition/theory (MM, PhD); digital arts and sciences (MA); ethnomusicology (PhD); fine arts (MA, MFA, MM, PhD); instrumental conducting (MM, PhD); museology (museum studies) (MA); music (MM, PhD); music education (MM, PhD); music history and literature (MM); musicology (PhD); performance (MM); sacred music (MM); theatre (MFA). *Application deadline:* Applications are processed on a rolling basis. *Application fee:* $30. Electronic applications accepted. *Application Contact:* Barbara O. Korner, Interim Dean, 352-392-0207 Ext. 230, Fax: 352-392-3802, E-mail: bkorner@ufl.edu. *Interim Dean,* Lucinda Lavelli, 352-392-0207, Fax: 352-392-3802, E-mail: llavelli@arts.ufl.edu.

College of Health and Human Performance *Faculty:* 45 full-time (12 women), 1 part-time/adjunct (0 women). Expenses: Contact institution. *Financial support:* In 2006–07, 3 research assistantships (averaging $7,864 per year), 44 teaching assistantships (averaging $8,757 per year) were awarded; fellowships, career-related internships or fieldwork, Federal Work-Study, institutionally sponsored loans, and unspecified assistantships also available. Support available to part-time students. In 2006, 9 degrees awarded. *Degree program information:* Part-time programs available. Offers athletic training/sport medicine (MS, PhD); biomechanics (MS, PhD); clinical exercise physiology (MS); exercise physiology (MS, PhD); health and human performance (PhD); health behavior (PhD); health communication (Graduate Certificate); health education and behavior (MS); human performance (MS); motor learning/control (MS, PhD); recreational studies (MS); sport and exercise psychology (MS). *Application deadline:* For fall admission, 6/1 priority date for domestic students. Applications are processed on a rolling basis. *Application fee:* $30. Electronic applications accepted. *Application Contact:* Dr. Bill Chen, Associate Dean, Research and Graduate Programs, 352-392-3187 Ext. 1284, Fax: 352-392-1909, E-mail: wchen@hhp.ufl.edu. *Dean,* Dr. Steve Dorman, 352-392-0578 Ext. 1225, Fax: 352-392-1909, E-mail: dorman@hhp.ufl.edu.

College of Journalism and Communications *Faculty:* 54 full-time (28 women). Expenses: Contact institution. *Financial support:* In 2006–07, 21 research assistantships with full tuition reimbursements (averaging $13,078 per year), 36 teaching assistantships with full tuition reimbursements (averaging $12,077 per year) were awarded; fellowships with full and partial tuition reimbursements, career-related internships or fieldwork, Federal Work-Study, institutionally sponsored loans, and unspecified assistantships also available. Support available to part-time students. Financial award application deadline: 4/15. *Degree program information:* Part-time programs available. Offers advertising (M Adv); journalism (MAMC); mass communication (MAMC, PhD); public relations (MAMC); telecommunication (MAMC). *Application deadline:* For fall admission, 6/1 for domestic students. Applications are processed on a rolling basis. *Application fee:* $30. Electronic applications accepted. *Application Contact:* Dr. Debbie Treise, Associate Dean for Graduate Programs, 352-392-6557, Fax: 352-392-1794, E-mail: dtreise@jou.ufl.edu. *Interim Dean,* Dr. John W. Wright, 352-392-0466.

College of Liberal Arts and Sciences *Faculty:* 651 full-time (178 women), 20 part-time/adjunct (7 women). Expenses: Contact institution. *Financial support:* Fellowships, research assistantships, teaching assistantships, career-related internships or fieldwork, Federal Work-Study, institutionally sponsored loans, and unspecified assistantships available. Support available to part-time students. In 2006, 11 degrees awarded. *Degree program information:* Part-time programs available. Offers African studies (Certificate); anthropology (MA, PhD); astronomy (MS, PhD); behavior analysis (PhD); behavioral neuroscience (MS, PhD); botany (M Ag, MS, MST, PhD); chemistry (MS, MST, PhD); classical studies (MA, PhD); cognitive and sensory processes (PhD); communication sciences and disorders (MA, Au D, PhD); counseling psychology (PhD); creative writing (MFA); criminology and law (MA, PhD); developmental psychology (PhD); English (MA, PhD); French (MA, PhD); gender and development (Graduate Certificate); geography (MA, MS, PhD); geology (MS, MST, PhD); German (MA, PhD); history (MA, PhD); international development policy and administration (MA, Certificate); international relations (MA, MAT); Latin (MA, MAT, ML); Latin American studies (MA, Certificate); liberal arts and sciences (M Ag, M Stat, MA, MAT, MFA, ML, MS, MS Stat, MST, MWS, Au D, PhD, Certificate, Graduate Certificate); linguistics (MA, PhD); mathematics (MA, MAT, MS, MST, PhD); philosophy (MA, PhD); physics (MS, MST, PhD); political campaigning (MA, Certificate); political science (MA, MAT, PhD); public affairs (MA, Certificate); religion (MA, PhD); social psychology (MS, PhD); sociology (MA, PhD); Spanish (MA, PhD); statistics (M Stat, MS Stat, PhD); teaching English as a second language (Certificate); women's studies (MA, MWS, Graduate Certificate); zoology (MS, MST, PhD). *Application deadline:* Applications are processed on a rolling basis. *Application fee:*

$30. Electronic applications accepted. *Application Contact:* Albert Matheny, Associate Dean for Student Affairs, 352-392-1521, Fax: 351-392-3584, E-mail: matheny@polisci.ufl.edu. *Interim Dean,* Joe Glover, 352-392-0780, Fax: 352-392-3584, E-mail: jglover@aa.ufl.edu.

College of Nursing Students: 285 (264 women); includes 39 minority (12 African Americans, 3 American Indian/Alaska Native, 8 Asian Americans or Pacific Islanders, 16 Hispanic Americans). Average age 35. *Faculty:* 28 full-time (26 women). Expenses: Contact institution. *Financial support:* In 2006–07, 2 research assistantships with partial tuition reimbursements (averaging $16,352 per year), 1 teaching assistantship with partial tuition reimbursement (averaging $24,904 per year) were awarded; fellowships with partial tuition reimbursements, career-related internships or fieldwork and Federal Work-Study also available. Support available to part-time students. In 2006, 75 master's, 5 doctorates awarded. *Degree program information:* Part-time programs available. Offers nursing (MSN); nursing sciences (PhD). *Application deadline:* For fall admission, 3/1 priority date for domestic students. Applications are processed on a rolling basis. *Application fee:* $30. Electronic applications accepted. *Application Contact:* Dr. Karin Polifko-Harris, Associate Dean, 352-273-6331, Fax: 352-273-6440, E-mail: kpolifko@nursing.ufl.edu. *Dean,* Dr. Kathleen A. Long, 352-273-6324, Fax: 352-273-6505, E-mail: longka@nursing.ufl.edu.

College of Public Health and Health Professions *Faculty:* 63 full-time (34 women), 9 part-time/adjunct (4 women). Expenses: Contact institution. *Financial support:* Fellowships, research assistantships, teaching assistantships, career-related internships or fieldwork, Federal Work-Study, institutionally sponsored loans, and unspecified assistantships available. Support available to part-time students. In 2006, 8 degrees awarded. *Degree program information:* Part-time programs available. Offers audiology (Au D); biostatistics (MPH); clinical and health psychology (PhD); environmental health (MPH); epidemiology (MPH); health administration (MHA); health services research (PhD); occupational therapy (MHS, MOT); physical therapy (DPT); public health and health professions (MHA, MHS, MOT, MPH, Au D, DPT, PhD); public health management and policy (MPH); public health practice (MPH); rehabilitation counseling (MHS); rehabilitation science (PhD); social and behavioral sciences (MPH). *Application deadline:* Applications are processed on a rolling basis. *Application fee:* $30. Electronic applications accepted. *Application Contact:* Dr. Stephanie Hanson, Associate Dean, 352-273-6377, Fax: 352-273-6199, E-mail: shanson@phhp.ufl.edu. *Dean,* Dr. Robert G. Frank, 352-273-6214, Fax: 352-273-6199, E-mail: rfrank@phhp.ufl.edu.

School of Natural Resources and Environment *Faculty:* 1 full-time (0 women). Expenses: Contact institution. *Financial support:* In 2006–07, 39 research assistantships (averaging $17,109 per year), 10 teaching assistantships (averaging $16,175 per year) were awarded; fellowships also available. Offers interdisciplinary ecology (MS, PhD). *Application deadline:* For fall admission, 2/11 priority date for domestic students. Applications are processed on a rolling basis. *Application fee:* $30. Electronic applications accepted. *Application Contact:* Meisha Wade, Coordinator of Academic Programs, 352-392-9230, Fax: 352-392-9748, E-mail: mwade@ufl.edu. *Senior Associate Dan,* James C. Cato, 352-392-9230, Fax: 352-392-9748, E-mail: jcato@ufl.edu.

Warrington College of Business Administration *Faculty:* 89 full-time (14 women). Expenses: Contact institution. *Financial support:* Fellowships with tuition reimbursements, research assistantships with tuition reimbursements, teaching assistantships with tuition reimbursements, career-related internships or fieldwork, Federal Work-Study, institutionally sponsored loans, and unspecified assistantships available. Support available to part-time students. *Degree program information:* Part-time programs available. Offers accounting (MBA); arts administration (MBA); business administration (MS); business strategy and public policy (MBA); competitive strategy (MBA); decision and information sciences (MBA, MS, PhD); economics (MA, PhD); electronic commerce (MBA); finance (MBA, PhD); financial services (Certificate); general business (MBA); global management (MBA); Graham-Buffett security analysis (MBA); health administration (MBA); human resources management (MBA); insurance (PhD); international business (MAIB); international studies (MBA); Latin American business (MBA); management (MBA, MS, PhD); marketing (MBA); real estate and urban analysis (PhD); sports administration (MBA); supply chain management (MS). *Application deadline:* Applications are processed on a rolling basis. *Application fee:* $30. Electronic applications accepted. *Application Contact:* Dr. W. Andrew McCollough, Senior Associate Dean, 352-392-8436 Ext. 1223, Fax: 352-392-2086, E-mail: andy.mccollough@cba.ufl.edu. *Dean,* Dr. John Kraft, 352-392-2397 Ext. 1217, Fax: 352-392-2086, E-mail: john.kraft@cba.ufl.edu.

Interdisciplinary Concentration in Animal Molecular and Cell Biology Offers animal molecular and cell biology (MS, PhD). Program offered by College of Agricultural and Life Sciences, College of Liberal Arts and Sciences, College of Medicine, and College of Veterinary Medicine.

Levin College of Law Students: 1,364 full-time (636 women); includes 281 minority (82 African Americans, 3 American Indian/Alaska Native, 68 Asian Americans or Pacific Islanders, 128 Hispanic Americans), 51 international. Average age 25. 2,535 applicants, 41% accepted, 447 enrolled. *Faculty:* 61 full-time (31 women), 46 part-time/adjunct (11 women). Expenses: Contact institution. *Financial support:* In 2006–07, 241 students received support, including 4 fellowships (averaging $3,655 per year); Federal Work-Study, institutionally sponsored loans, and scholarships/grants also available. Financial award application deadline: 4/1; financial award applicants required to submit FAFSA. In 2006, 310 first professional degrees awarded. Offers comparative law (LL M); international taxation (LL M); law (JD); taxation (LL M, SJD). *Application deadline:* For fall admission, 1/15 for domestic and international students. Applications are processed on a rolling basis. *Application fee:* $30. Electronic applications accepted. *Application Contact:* J. Michael Patrick, Assistant Dean for Admissions, 352-273-0890, Fax: 352-392-4087, E-mail: patrick@law.ufl.edu. *Dean,* Robert Jerry, 352-273-0600, Fax: 352-392-8727, E-mail: jerryr@law.ufl.edu.

See Close-Up on page 1077.

UNIVERSITY OF GEORGIA, Athens, GA 30602

General Information State-supported, coed, university. CGS member. *Enrollment:* 33,959 graduate, professional, and undergraduate students; 5,982 full-time matriculated graduate/professional students (3,407 women), 2,018 part-time matriculated graduate/professional students (1,260 women). *Enrollment by degree level:* 1,603 first professional, 3,750 master's, 2,594 doctoral, 53 other advanced degrees. *Graduate faculty:* 1,423 full-time (427 women), 13 part-time/adjunct (6 women). *Graduate housing:* Rooms and/or apartments available to single and married students. *Student services:* Career counseling, free psychological counseling. *Library facilities:* Ilah Dunlap Little Memorial Library plus 2 others. *Online resources:* library catalog, web page, access to other libraries' catalogs. *Collection:* 4 million titles, 67,268 serial subscriptions. *Research affiliation:* Organization for Tropical Studies, Russell Research Laboratory, Southeast Water Laboratory, Skidaway Institute of Oceanography.

Computer facilities: Computer purchase and lease plans are available. 2,500 computers available on campus for general student use. A campuswide network can be accessed from student residence rooms and from off campus. Internet access and online class registration, e-mail, Web pages are available. *Web address:* http://www.uga.edu/.

General Application Contact: Krista Haynes, Director of Graduate Admissions, 706-425-1789, Fax: 706-425-3094, E-mail: gradadm@uga.edu.

GRADUATE UNITS

College of Pharmacy Students: 557 full-time (350 women), 52 part-time (38 women); includes 104 minority (42 African Americans, 1 American Indian/Alaska Native, 57 Asian Americans or Pacific Islanders, 4 Hispanic Americans), 37 international. 171 applicants, 16% accepted, 13 enrolled. *Faculty:* 31 full-time (9 women). Expenses: Contact institution. *Financial support:* Fellowships, research assistantships, teaching assistantships, career-related internships or fieldwork, Federal Work-Study, institutionally sponsored loans, tuition waivers, and unspecified assistantships available. Support available to part-time students. Financial award application deadline: 2/15. In 2006, 113 first professional degrees, 2 master's, 4 doctorates awarded. Offers experimental therapeutics (MS, PhD); medicinal chemistry (MS, PhD); pharmaceutical and biomedical regulatory affairs (Certificate); pharmaceutics (MS, PhD); pharmacology (MS, PhD); pharmacy (Pharm D, MS, PhD, Certificate); pharmacy care administration (MS, PhD); toxicology (MS, PhD). *Application deadline:* For fall admission, 7/1 priority date for domestic students; for spring admission, 11/15 for domestic students. *Application fee:* $50. Electronic applications accepted. *Dean,* Dr. Svein Oie, 706-542-1914, Fax: 706-542-5269, E-mail: soie@mail.rx.uga.edu.

College of Public Health Students: 87 full-time (62 women), 19 part-time (15 women); includes 12 African Americans, 4 Asian Americans or Pacific Islanders, 6 Hispanic Americans, 9 international. 121 applicants, 48% accepted, 35 enrolled. *Faculty:* 25 full-time (15 women), 1 (woman) part-time/adjunct. Expenses: Contact institution. In 2006, 19 master's, 6 doctorates awarded. Offers environmental health science (MS, PhD); health promotion and behavior (M Ed, MA, MPH, PhD, Ed S); public health (M Ed, MA, MPH, MS, PhD, Certificate, Ed S). *Application deadline:* For fall admission, 7/1 for domestic students; for spring admission, 11/15 for domestic students. *Application fee:* $50. *Dean,* Dr. Phillip L. Williams, 706-542-0939, Fax: 706-542-6730, E-mail: pwilliam@uga.edu.

Institute of Gerontology Students: 1 (woman) full-time, 5 part-time (all women); includes 1 minority (African American) 1 applicant, 100% accepted, 1 enrolled. *Faculty:* 2 full-time (1 woman). Expenses: Contact institution. Offers gerontology (Certificate). *Director,* Leonard W. Pooh, 706-425-3222, E-mail: lpooh@geron.uga.edu.

College of Veterinary Medicine Students: 494 full-time (361 women), 11 part-time (8 women); includes 35 minority (11 African Americans, 1 American Indian/Alaska Native, 9 Asian Americans or Pacific Islanders, 14 Hispanic Americans), 40 international. 88 applicants, 39% accepted, 24 enrolled. *Faculty:* 71 full-time (25 women). Expenses: Contact institution. *Financial support:* Fellowships, research assistantships, teaching assistantships, Federal Work-Study, scholarships/grants, and unspecified assistantships available. Financial award applicants required to submit FAFSA. In 2006, 88 first professional degrees, 6 master's, 4 doctorates awarded. Offers infectious diseases (MS, PhD); pathology (MS, PhD); pharmacology (MS, PhD); physiology (MS, PhD); physiology and pharmacology (MS, PhD); population health (MAM, MFAM); toxicology (MS, PhD); veterinary anatomy (MS); veterinary anatomy and radiology (MS); veterinary medicine (DVM, MAM, MFAM, MS, PhD). *Application deadline:* For fall admission, 7/1 priority date for domestic students; for spring admission, 11/15 for domestic students. *Application fee:* $50. Electronic applications accepted. *Dean,* Dr. Sheila W. Allen, 706-542-3461, Fax: 706-542-8254, E-mail: sallen@vet.uga.edu.

Graduate School Students: 5,982 full-time (3,407 women), 2,018 part-time (1,260 women); includes 1,075 minority (691 African Americans, 16 American Indian/Alaska Native, 225 Asian Americans or Pacific Islanders, 143 Hispanic Americans), 1,037 international. 7,366 applicants, 42% accepted, 1817 enrolled. *Faculty:* 1,400 full-time (410 women), 6 part-time/adjunct (1 woman). Expenses: Contact institution. *Financial support:* Fellowships, research assistantships, teaching assistantships, career-related internships or fieldwork, Federal Work-Study, institutionally sponsored loans, and unspecified assistantships available. Support available to part-time students. In 2006, 1,463 master's, 382 doctorates, 109 other advanced degrees awarded. *Degree program information:* Part-time programs available. *Application deadline:* For fall admission, 7/1 priority date for domestic students; for spring admission, 11/15 for domestic students. *Application fee:* $50. Electronic applications accepted. *Application Contact:* Krista Haynes, Director of Enrolled Student Services, 706-425-1789, Fax: 706-425-3094, E-mail: gradoff@uga.edu. *Dean,* Dr. Maureen Grasso, 706-542-4788, Fax: 706-583-0278, E-mail: mgrasso@uga.edu.

Biomedical and Health Sciences Institute Students: 6 full-time (5 women), 1 international. 6 applicants, 67% accepted, 3 enrolled. Expenses: Contact institution. Offers neuroscience (PhD). *Director,* Dr. Harry A. Dailey, 706-542-5922, Fax: 706-542-4285, E-mail: hdailey@uga.edu.

College of Agricultural and Environmental Sciences Students: 297 full-time (138 women), 81 part-time (31 women); includes 31 minority (19 African Americans, 8 Asian Americans or Pacific Islanders, 4 Hispanic Americans), 153 international. 262 applicants, 57% accepted, 89 enrolled. *Faculty:* 191 full-time (25 women). Expenses: Contact institution. *Financial support:* Fellowships, research assistantships, teaching assistantships, career-related internships or fieldwork and unspecified assistantships available. In 2006, 69 master's, 30 doctorates awarded. Offers agricultural and environmental sciences (MA Ext, MADS, MAE, MAL, MCCS, MFT, MPPPM, MS, PhD); agricultural economics (MAE, MS, PhD); agricultural engineering (MS); agricultural leadership, education, and communication (MA Ext, MAL); agronomy (MS, PhD); animal and dairy science (PhD); animal and dairy sciences (MADS); animal nutrition (PhD); animal science (MS); biological and agricultural engineering (PhD); biological engineering (MS); crop and soil sciences (MCCS); dairy science (MS); entomology (MS, PhD); environmental economics (MS); food science (MS, PhD); food technology (MFT); horticulture (MS, PhD); plant pathology (MS, PhD); plant protection and pest management (MPPPM); poultry science (MS, PhD). *Application deadline:* For fall admission, 7/1 priority date for domestic students; for spring admission, 11/15 for domestic students. *Application fee:* $50. Electronic applications accepted. *Dean,* Dr. J. Scott Angle, 706-542-3924, Fax: 706-542-0803.

College of Arts and Sciences Students: 1,474 full-time (737 women), 226 part-time (117 women); includes 149 minority (71 African Americans, 3 American Indian/Alaska Native, 39 Asian Americans or Pacific Islanders, 36 Hispanic Americans), 421 international. 2,487 applicants, 31% accepted, 369 enrolled. *Faculty:* 583 full-time (165 women), 1 part-time/adjunct (0 women). Expenses: Contact institution. *Financial support:* Fellowships, research assistantships, teaching assistantships, Federal Work-Study, institutionally sponsored loans, and unspecified assistantships available. In 2006, 217 master's, 156 doctorates awarded. Offers analytical chemistry (MS, PhD); anthropology (MA, PhD); applied mathematical science (MAMS); art (MFA, PhD); art education (MA Ed, Ed D, Ed S); art history (MA); artificial intelligence (MS); arts and sciences (MA, MA Ed, MAMS, MAT, MFA, MM, MS, DMA, Ed D, PhD, Certificate, Ed S); biochemistry and molecular biology (MS, PhD); cellular biology (MS, PhD); classical languages (MA); comparative literature (MA, PhD); computer science (MS, PhD); drama (MFA, PhD); English (MA, MAT, PhD); French (MA, MAT); genetics (MS, PhD); geography (MA, MS, PhD); geology (MS, PhD); German (MA); Greek (MA); history (MA, PhD); inorganic chemistry (MS, PhD); Latin (MA); linguistics (MA, PhD); marine sciences (MS, PhD); mathematics (MA, PhD); microbiology (MS, PhD); music (MA, MM, DMA, PhD); organic chemistry (MS, PhD); philosophy (MA, PhD); physical chemistry (MS, PhD); physics (MS, PhD); plant biology (MS, PhD); psychology (MS, PhD); religion (MA); Romance languages (MA, MAT, PhD); sociology (MA, PhD); Spanish (MA, MAT); speech communication (MA, PhD); statistics (MS, PhD); women's studies (Certificate). *Application deadline:* For fall admission, 7/1 priority date for domestic students; for spring admission, 11/15 for domestic students. *Application fee:* $50. Electronic applications accepted. *Head,* Dr. Garnett Stokes, 706-542-8888, Fax: 706-542-3275, E-mail: gstokes@uga.edu.

College of Education Students: 903 full-time (628 women), 1,175 part-time (840 women); includes 301 minority (235 African Americans, 5 American Indian/Alaska Native, 28 Asian Americans or Pacific Islanders, 33 Hispanic Americans), 153 international. 1,715 applicants, 52% accepted, 549 enrolled. *Faculty:* 170 full-time (84 women). Expenses: Contact institution. *Financial support:* Fellowships, research assistantships, teaching assistantships, unspecified assistantships available. In 2006, 407 master's, 106 doctorates, 109 other advanced degrees awarded. Offers communication sciences and special education (M Ed, MA, Ed D, PhD, Ed S); counseling and human development services (M Ed, MA, Ed D, PhD, Ed S); early childhood education (M Ed, PhD, Ed S); education (M Ed, MA, MAT, MM Ed, Ed D, PhD, Ed S); educational psychology and instructional technology (M Ed, MA, Ed D, PhD, Ed S); elementary and middle school education (M Ed, PhD, Ed S); higher education (Ed D, PhD); kinesiology (M Ed, MA, Ed D, PhD, Ed S); language and literacy education (M Ed, MA, Ed D, PhD, Ed S); lifelong education, administration and policy (M Ed, MA, Ed D, PhD, Ed S); mathematics and science education (M Ed, MA, Ed D, PhD, Ed S); music education (MM Ed, Ed D, Ed S); social foundations of education (PhD); workforce education, leadership and social foundations (M Ed, MA, MAT, Ed D, PhD, Ed S). *Application deadline:* For fall admission, 7/1 priority date for domestic students; for spring admission, 11/15 for domestic students. *Application fee:* $50. Electronic applications accepted. *Dean,* Dr. Louis A. Castenell, 706-542-6446, Fax: 706-542-0360, E-mail: lcastene@coe.uga.edu.

College of Environment and Design Students: 149 full-time (94 women), 29 part-time (16 women); includes 7 minority (2 African Americans, 2 Asian Americans or Pacific Islanders,

University of Georgia (continued)

3 Hispanic Americans), 6 international. 240 applicants, 33% accepted, 46 enrolled. *Faculty:* 42 full-time (10 women). Expenses: Contact institution. In 2006, 48 master's, 10 doctorates awarded. Offers conservation ecology and sustainable development (MS); ecology (MS, PhD); environment and design (MHP, MLA, MS, PhD); environmental design (MHP, MLA); historic preservation (MHP); landscape architecture (MLA). *Application deadline:* For fall admission, 7/1 priority date for domestic students; for spring admission, 11/15 for domestic students. *Application fee:* $50. *Acting Dean,* Prof. Scott S. Weinberg, 706-542-4915, Fax: 706-542-4485, E-mail: weinberg@uga.edu.

College of Family and Consumer Sciences Students: 100 full-time (86 women), 18 part-time (14 women); includes 16 minority (13 African Americans, 1 Asian American or Pacific Islander, 2 Hispanic Americans), 25 international. 149 applicants, 47% accepted, 33 enrolled. *Faculty:* 53 full-time (34 women). Expenses: Contact institution. *Financial support:* Fellowships, research assistantships, teaching assistantships, unspecified assistantships available. In 2006, 16 master's, 13 doctorates awarded. Offers child and family development (MFCS, MS, PhD); family and consumer sciences (MFCS, MS, PhD); foods and nutrition (MFCS, MS, PhD); housing and consumer economics (MS, PhD); textiles, merchandising, and interiors (MS, PhD). *Application deadline:* For fall admission, 7/1 priority date for domestic students; for spring admission, 11/15 for domestic students. *Application fee:* $50. Electronic applications accepted. *Interim Dean,* Dr. Jan M. Hathcote, 706-542-4860, Fax: 706-542-4862, E-mail: jhathcote@fcs.uga.edu.

Grady School of Journalism and Mass Communication Students: 91 full-time (56 women), 16 part-time (10 women); includes 15 minority (14 African Americans, 1 Hispanic American), 23 international. 261 applicants, 34% accepted, 42 enrolled. *Faculty:* 43 full-time (20 women). Expenses: Contact institution. *Financial support:* Research assistantships, teaching assistantships, tuition waivers (full) and unspecified assistantships available. In 2006, 41 master's, 7 doctorates awarded. Offers journalism and mass communication (MA); mass communication (PhD). *Application deadline:* For spring admission, 2/15 for domestic students. *Application fee:* $50. Electronic applications accepted. *Application Contact:* Dr. Jeff Springston, Graduate Coordinator, 706-542-7833, Fax: 706-542-2183, E-mail: jspring@grady.uga.edu. *Dean,* Dr. E. Culpepper Clark, 706-542-1704, Fax: 706-542-2183, E-mail: cully@grady.uga.edu.

School of Forestry and Natural Resources Students: 145 full-time (42 women), 26 part-time (11 women); includes 8 minority (5 African Americans, 1 American Indian/Alaska Native, 2 Hispanic Americans), 23 international. 78 applicants, 69% accepted, 39 enrolled. *Faculty:* 35 full-time (3 women). Expenses: Contact institution. *Financial support:* Fellowships, research assistantships, teaching assistantships, unspecified assistantships available. In 2006, 43 master's, 11 doctorates awarded. Offers forestry and natural resources (MFR, MS, PhD). *Application deadline:* For fall admission, 7/1 priority date for domestic students; for spring admission, 11/15 for domestic students. *Application fee:* $50. Electronic applications accepted. *Application Contact:* Dr. Ronald L. Hendrick, Graduate Coordinator, 706-542-1385, E-mail: rhendrick@uga.edu. *Acting Dean,* Dr. Robert J. Warren, 706-542-6474, Fax: 706-542-8356, E-mail: warren@smokey.forestry.uga.edu.

School of Social Work Students: 290 full-time (251 women), 63 part-time (52 women); includes 104 minority (94 African Americans, 1 American Indian/Alaska Native, 3 Asian Americans or Pacific Islanders, 6 Hispanic Americans), 9 international. Average age 34. 338 applicants, 65% accepted, 138 enrolled. *Faculty:* 20 full-time (11 women). Expenses: Contact institution. *Financial support:* In 2006–07, 39 students received support, including 4 fellowships (averaging $25,000 per year), 35 research assistantships with tuition reimbursements available (averaging $7,500 per year); teaching assistantships with tuition reimbursements available, career-related internships or fieldwork, Federal Work-Study, scholarships/grants, tuition waivers (full and partial), and unspecified assistantships also available. Support available to part-time students. Financial award application deadline: 2/10; financial award applicants required to submit FAFSA. In 2006, 149 master's, 9 doctorates awarded. *Degree program information:* Part-time and evening/weekend programs available. Offers non-profit organizations (MA, Certificate); social work (MA, MSW, PhD, Certificate). *Application deadline:* For fall admission, 7/1 priority date for domestic students, 7/1 for international students; for spring admission, 11/15 for domestic and international students. Applications are processed on a rolling basis. *Application fee:* $50. Electronic applications accepted. *Dean,* Dr. Maurice Daniels, 706-542-5424, Fax: 706-542-3845.

Terry College of Business Students: 540 full-time (182 women), 245 part-time (77 women); includes 126 minority (64 African Americans, 1 American Indian/Alaska Native, 45 Asian Americans or Pacific Islanders, 16 Hispanic Americans), 95 international. 856 applicants, 43% accepted, 298 enrolled. *Faculty:* 79 full-time (18 women). Expenses: Contact institution. *Financial support:* Fellowships, research assistantships, teaching assistantships, unspecified assistantships available. In 2006, 269 master's, 17 doctorates awarded. Offers accounting (M Acc); business (M Acc, MA, MBA, MIT, MMR, PhD); business administration (MA, MBA, PhD); economics (MA, PhD); Internet technology (MIT); marketing (MMR). *Application deadline:* For fall admission, 7/1 priority date for domestic students; for spring admission, 11/15 for domestic students. *Application fee:* $50. Electronic applications accepted. *Application Contact:* Dr. Melvin R. Crask, Interim Associate Dean, 706-542-8068, Fax: 706-542-5351, E-mail: mcrask@terry.uga.edu. *Dean,* Dr. Robert E. Hoyt, 706-542-8100, Fax: 706-542-3835.

School of Law Students: 681 full-time (338 women), 4 part-time (2 women); includes 132 minority (90 African Americans, 2 American Indian/Alaska Native, 25 Asian Americans or Pacific Islanders, 15 Hispanic Americans), 15 international. Expenses: Contact institution. *Financial support:* Fellowships, research assistantships, teaching assistantships, Federal Work-Study, institutionally sponsored loans, tuition waivers (partial), and unspecified assistantships available. Financial award application deadline: 1/31. In 2006, 251 JDs, 9 master's awarded. Offers law (JD, LL M). *Application deadline:* For fall admission, 7/1 priority date for domestic students; for spring admission, 11/15 for domestic students. *Application fee:* $50. Electronic applications accepted. *Application Contact:* Giles Kennedy, Director of Law Admissions, 706-542-7060. *Dean,* Rebecca H. White, 706-542-7140, Fax: 706-542-5556, E-mail: rhwhite@uga.edu.

School of Public and International Affairs Students: 180 full-time (83 women), 72 part-time (40 women); includes 26 minority (19 African Americans, 1 American Indian/Alaska Native, 4 Asian Americans or Pacific Islanders, 2 Hispanic Americans), 36 international. 379 applicants, 34% accepted, 83 enrolled. *Faculty:* 50 full-time (10 women), 1 part-time/adjunct (0 women). Expenses: Contact institution. *Financial support:* Fellowships, research assistantships, teaching assistantships, unspecified assistantships available. In 2006, 71 master's, 6 doctorates awarded. Offers non profit organization (MA); political science (MA, PhD); public administration (MPA, PhD); public and international affairs (MA, MPA, DPA, PhD). *Application deadline:* For fall admission, 7/1 priority date for domestic students; for spring admission, 11/15 for domestic students. *Application fee:* $50. Electronic applications accepted. *Dean,* Dr. Thomas P. Lauth, 706-542-5424, Fax: 706-542-4421, E-mail: tplauth@uga.edu.

UNIVERSITY OF GREAT FALLS, Great Falls, MT 59405

General Information Independent-religious, coed, comprehensive institution. *Enrollment:* 716 graduate, professional, and undergraduate students; 27 full-time matriculated graduate/professional students (22 women), 39 part-time matriculated graduate/professional students (33 women). *Enrollment by degree level:* 66 master's. *Graduate faculty:* 21 full-time (9 women), 19 part-time/adjunct (11 women). *Graduate housing:* Rooms and/or apartments available on a first-come, first-served basis to single and married students. Housing application deadline: 8/1. *Student services:* Campus employment opportunities, campus safety program, career counseling, child daycare facilities, disabled student services, grant writing training, international student services, low-cost health insurance, teacher training. *Library facilities:* University of Great Falls Library. *Online resources:* library catalog, web page. *Collection:* 108,926 titles, 457 serial subscriptions, 1,620 audiovisual materials.

Computer facilities: 110 computers available on campus for general student use. A campuswide network can be accessed from student residence rooms. Internet access and online class registration are available. *Web address:* http://www.ugf.edu/.

General Application Contact: Dr. Richard Fisher, Dean of Graduate Studies, 406-791-5332, Fax: 406-791-5990, E-mail: rfisher02@ugf.edu.

GRADUATE UNITS

Graduate Studies Students: 27 full-time (22 women), 39 part-time (33 women); includes 5 minority (3 American Indian/Alaska Native, 2 Hispanic Americans). Average age 34. 41 applicants, 83% accepted, 24 enrolled. *Faculty:* 21 full-time (9 women), 19 part-time/adjunct (11 women). Expenses: Contact institution. *Financial support:* In 2006–07, 44 students received support. Career-related internships or fieldwork, Federal Work-Study, and institutionally sponsored loans available. Support available to part-time students. Financial award application deadline: 6/1; financial award applicants required to submit FAFSA. In 2006, 33 degrees awarded. *Degree program information:* Part-time and evening/weekend programs available. Postbaccalaureate distance learning degree programs offered (no on-campus study). Offers addictions counseling (MAC, Certificate); counseling psychology (MSC); education (M Ed); effectiveness (MCJ); information systems (MIS); management (MCJ); marriage and family counseling (MSC); organizational management (MS); school psychology (MSC); secondary teaching (MAT). *Application deadline:* For fall admission, 8/15 priority date for domestic students, 6/15 priority date for international students; for spring admission, 12/15 priority date for domestic students, 10/15 priority date for international students. Applications are processed on a rolling basis. *Application fee:* $50. Electronic applications accepted. *Dean of Graduate Studies,* Dr. Richard Fisher, 406-791-5332, Fax: 406-791-5990, E-mail: rfisher02@ugf.edu.

UNIVERSITY OF GUAM, Mangilao, GU 96923

General Information Territory-supported, coed, comprehensive institution. *Graduate housing:* Room and/or apartments available on a first-come, first-served basis to single students; on-campus housing not available to married students. *Research affiliation:* Bernice Pauahi Bishop Museum (science, cultural preservation), Pilar Project, Inc. (salvage of artifacts, archaeology).

GRADUATE UNITS

Graduate School and Research *Degree program information:* Part-time programs available.

College of Arts and Sciences *Degree program information:* Part-time programs available. Offers arts and sciences (MA, MS); ceramics (MA); environmental science (MS); graphics (MA); Micronesian studies (MA); painting (MA); tropical marine biology (MS).

College of Business and Public Administration *Degree program information:* Part-time programs available. Offers business administration (MBA); business and public administration (MBA, MPA); public administration (MPA).

College of Education *Degree program information:* Part-time programs available. Offers administration and supervision (M Ed); counseling (MA); education (M Ed, MA); instructional leadership (MA); language and literacy (M Ed); secondary education (M Ed); special education (M Ed); teaching English to speakers of other languages (M Ed).

UNIVERSITY OF GUELPH, Guelph, ON N1G 2W1, Canada

General Information Province-supported, coed, university. *Enrollment:* 18,616 graduate, professional, and undergraduate students; 1,889 full-time matriculated graduate/professional students (981 women), 185 part-time matriculated graduate/professional students (94 women). *Enrollment by degree level:* 1,343 master's, 720 doctoral, 11 other advanced degrees. *Graduate faculty:* 736. *Graduate housing:* Rooms and/or apartments available to single and married students. Housing application deadline: 6/14. *Student services:* Campus employment opportunities, campus safety program, career counseling, child daycare facilities, disabled student services, exercise/wellness program, free psychological counseling, grant writing training, international student services, low-cost health insurance, multicultural affairs office, teacher training, writing training. *Library facilities:* McLaughlin Library plus 1 other. *Online resources:* library catalog, web page, access to other libraries' catalogs. *Collection:* 2.1 million titles, 7,294 serial subscriptions.

Computer facilities: 1,200 computers available on campus for general student use. A campuswide network can be accessed from student residence rooms and from off campus. Internet access and online class registration are available. *Web address:* http://www.uoguelph.ca/.

General Application Contact: Chris Goody, Graduate Admissions Officer, 519-824-4120 Ext. 56736, Fax: 519-766-0143, E-mail: cgoody@registrar.uoguelph.ca.

GRADUATE UNITS

Graduate Program Services Students: 2,074. *Faculty:* 736. Expenses: Contact institution. *Financial support:* Fellowships with full tuition reimbursements, research assistantships, teaching assistantships with full tuition reimbursements, career-related internships or fieldwork, Federal Work-Study, institutionally sponsored loans, scholarships/grants, tuition waivers (full), unspecified assistantships, and bursaries available. Support available to part-time students. In 2006, 565 master's, 106 doctorates, 7 other advanced degrees awarded. *Degree program information:* Part-time and evening/weekend programs available. Postbaccalaureate distance learning degree programs offered (minimal on-campus study). Offers aquaculture (M Sc); biophysics (M Sc, PhD); food safety and quality assurance (M Sc); rural studies (PhD). *Application deadline:* Applications are processed on a rolling basis. *Application fee:* $75. Electronic applications accepted. *Application Contact:* Chris Goody, Graduate Admissions Officer, 519-824-4120 Ext. 56736, Fax: 519-766-0143, E-mail: cgoody@registrar.uoguelph.ca. *Dean,* Dr. I. Heathcote, 519-824-4120 Ext. 52441, E-mail: iheathco@registrar.uoguelph.ca.

Collaborative International Development Studies Students: 42 full-time (36 women), 2 part-time (1 woman); includes 12 minority (2 African Americans, 7 Asian Americans or Pacific Islanders, 3 Hispanic Americans), 11 international. *Faculty:* 62 full-time (14 women). Expenses: Contact institution. *Financial support:* Fellowships, research assistantships, teaching assistantships available. In 2006, 17 degrees awarded. Offers international development studies (M Eng, M Sc, MA, MBA). MA offered in cooperation with the Departments of Agricultural Economics and Business, Animal and Poultry Science, Economics, Geography, History, Land Resource Science, Philosophy, Political Science, Rural Extension Studies, Rural Planning and Development, and Program in English. *Application fee:* $75. *Application Contact:* Dr. Kerry Preibisch, Graduate Coordinator, E-mail: kpreibis@uoguelph.ca. *Director,* Dr. Sally Anne Humphries, 519-824-4120 Ext. 53542, Fax: 519-837-9561, E-mail: shumphri@uoguelph.ca.

College of Arts *Degree program information:* Part-time programs available. Offers arts (MA, MFA, PhD); drama (MA); English (MA); history (MA, PhD); literary studies/theatre studies (PhD); philosophy (MA, PhD); studio art (MFA).

College of Biological Science *Degree program information:* Part-time programs available. Offers biochemistry (M Sc, PhD); biological science (M Sc, PhD); biophysics (M Sc, PhD); botany (M Sc, PhD); microbiology (M Sc, PhD); molecular biology and genetics (M Sc, PhD); nutritional sciences (M Sc, PhD); zoology (M Sc, PhD).

College of Management and Economics Expenses: Contact institution. Offers agribusiness management (MBA); business administration (MBA); economics (MA, PhD); hospitality and tourism management (MBA); leadership (MA); management and economics (M Sc, MA, MBA, PhD); marketing and consumer studies (M Sc). *Dean,* Dr. Chris J. McKenna, 519-824-4120 Ext. 53141, Fax: 519-763-0526, E-mail: cmckenna@uoguelph.ca.

College of Physical and Engineering Science *Degree program information:* Part-time programs available. Offers applied computer science (M Sc); applied mathematics (PhD); applied statistics (PhD); biochemistry (M Sc, PhD); biological engineering (M Eng, M Sc, PhD); chemistry (M Sc, PhD); computer science (PhD); environmental engineering (M Eng, M Sc, PhD); mathematics and statistics (M Sc); physical and engineering science (M Eng, M Sc, PhD); physics (M Sc, PhD); systems and computer engineering (M Eng, M Sc, PhD); water resources engineering (M Eng, M Sc, PhD).

College of Social and Applied Human Sciences Students: 248 full-time (188 women), 11 part-time (9 women). *Faculty:* 111 full-time (49 women). Expenses: Contact institution. *Financial support:* In 2006–07, 147 teaching assistantships (averaging $9,600 per year) were awarded; fellowships with partial tuition reimbursements, research assistantships, career-related internships or fieldwork, scholarships/grants, tuition waivers (full), and bursaries also available. Support available to part-time students. In 2006, 95 master's, 13 doctorates awarded. *Degree program information:* Part-time programs available. Offers anthropology (MA); applied cognitive science (MA, PhD); applied nutrition (MAN); clinical psychology applied development emphasis (PhD); clinical psychology applied developmental emphasis (MA); crime and criminal justice (MA); crime and criminal justice policy (MA); family relations and human development (M Sc, PhD); geography (M Sc, MA, PhD); industrial/organizational psychology (MA, PhD); neuroscience and applied social psychology (MA, PhD); political science (MA); social and applied human sciences (M Sc, MA, MAN, PhD); sociology (MA). *Application fee:* $75. *Dean,* Alun E. Joseph, 519-824-4120 Ext. 52400, E-mail: csahsdean@uoguelph.ca.

Ontario Agricultural College Students: 514 full-time (273 women), 85 part-time (54 women). *Faculty:* 159. Expenses: Contact institution. *Financial support:* Fellowships, research assistantships, teaching assistantships, scholarships/grants and unspecified assistantships available. Support available to part-time students. In 2006, 162 master's, 45 doctorates, 1 other advanced degree awarded. *Degree program information:* Part-time programs available. Postbaccalaureate distance learning degree programs offered (minimal on-campus study). Offers agricultural economics (M Sc, PhD); agriculture (M Sc, MLA, PhD, Diploma); animal science (M Sc, PhD); atmospheric science (M Sc, PhD); capacity development and extension (M Sc); collaborative international development studies (M Sc, PhD); entomology (M Sc, PhD); environmental and agricultural earth sciences (M Sc, PhD); environmental microbiology and biotechnology (M Sc, PhD); environmental toxicology (M Sc, PhD); food science (M Sc, PhD); international rural planning and development (M Sc); land resources management (M Sc, PhD); landscape architecture (M Sc, MLA); plant agriculture (M Sc, PhD); plant and forest systems (M Sc, PhD); plant pathology (M Sc, PhD); poultry science (M Sc, PhD); resource and environmental economics (PhD); rural planning and development (M Sc); rural planning and development in Canada (M Sc); rural studies (PhD); soil science (M Sc, PhD). *Application fee:* $75. *Dean,* Dr. Mary Buhr, 519-824-4120 Ext. 52285, Fax: 519-766-1423, E-mail: mbuhr@uoguelph.ca.

Ontario Veterinary College Students: 437 (382 women). *Faculty:* 115. Expenses: Contact institution. *Financial support:* Career-related internships or fieldwork and scholarships/grants available. Support available to part-time students. Offers veterinary medicine (DVM, M Sc, DV Sc, PhD, Diploma). *Application deadline:* Applications are processed on a rolling basis. *Application fee:* $75. *Application Contact:* Elizabeth Lowenger, Recruitment Officer, 519-824-4120 Ext. 54430, Fax: 519-837-3230, E-mail: lowenger@uoguelph.ca. *Dean,* Dr. Elizabeth Stone, 519-824-4120 Ext. 54417, Fax: 519-837-3230, E-mail: estone@ovc.uoguelph.ca.

Graduate Programs in Veterinary Sciences Students: 206 (120 women). *Faculty:* 115. Expenses: Contact institution. *Financial support:* In 2006–07, 1 fellowship (averaging $28,000 per year) was awarded; research assistantships, teaching assistantships, career-related internships or fieldwork and scholarships/grants also available. Offers anatomic pathology (DV Sc, Diploma); anesthesiology (M Sc, DV Sc); cardiology (Diploma); clinical pathology (Diploma); clinical studies (Diploma); comparative pathology (M Sc, PhD); emergency/critical care (Diploma); epidemiology (M Sc, DV Sc, PhD); health management (M Sc, DV Sc); immunology (M Sc, PhD); laboratory animal science (DV Sc); medicine (M Sc, DV Sc); morphology (M Sc, DV Sc, PhD); neurology (M Sc, DV Sc); ophthalmology (M Sc, DV Sc); pathology (M Sc, PhD, Diploma); pharmacology (M Sc, DV Sc, PhD); physiology (M Sc, DV Sc, PhD); population medicine (Diploma); surgery (M Sc, DV Sc); theriogenology (M Sc, DV Sc); toxicology (M Sc, DV Sc, PhD); veterinary infectious diseases (M Sc, PhD); veterinary sciences (M Sc, DV Sc, PhD, Diploma); zoo animal/wildlife medicine (DV Sc). *Application deadline:* Applications are processed on a rolling basis. *Application fee:* $75. *Application Contact:* Barb Gaudette, Graduate Coordinator, Dean's Office, 519-824-4120 Ext. 54406, Fax: 519-837-3230, E-mail: bgaudett@ovc.uogelph.ca. *Associate Dean,* Dr. Robert Jacobs, 519-524-4120 Ext. 54796, Fax: 519-837-3230, E-mail: rjacobs@uoguelph.ca.

UNIVERSITY OF HARTFORD, West Hartford, CT 06117-1599

General Information Independent, coed, comprehensive institution. CGS member. *Enrollment:* 7,308 graduate, professional, and undergraduate students; 569 full-time matriculated graduate/professional students (347 women), 1,137 part-time matriculated graduate/professional students (703 women). *Enrollment by degree level:* 1,297 master's, 265 doctoral, 23 other advanced degrees. *Graduate faculty:* 138 full-time (53 women), 97 part-time/adjunct (40 women). *Tuition:* Part-time $515 per credit. *Required fees:* $200 per term. *Graduate housing:* Room and/or apartments available to single students; on-campus housing not available to married students. *Student services:* Campus employment opportunities, career counseling, disabled student services, free psychological counseling, international student services, low-cost health insurance, multicultural affairs office. *Library facilities:* Mortenson Library plus 1 other. *Online resources:* library catalog, web page. *Collection:* 473,115 titles, 2,425 serial subscriptions.

Computer facilities: Computer purchase and lease plans are available. 400 computers available on campus for general student use. A campuswide network can be accessed from student residence rooms and from off campus. Internet access and online class registration, student Web pages are available. *Web address:* http://www.hartford.edu/.

General Application Contact: Reneé Murphy, Assistant Director of Graduate Admissions, 860-768-4373, Fax: 860-768-5160, E-mail: rmurphy@mail.hartford.edu.

GRADUATE UNITS

Barney School of Business Students: 114 full-time (48 women), 426 part-time (166 women); includes 85 minority (31 African Americans, 1 American Indian/Alaska Native, 33 Asian Americans or Pacific Islanders, 20 Hispanic Americans), 45 international. Average age 33. 224 applicants, 73% accepted, 122 enrolled. *Faculty:* 24 full-time (10 women), 14 part-time/adjunct (3 women). Expenses: Contact institution. *Financial support:* In 2006–07, 1 fellowship with full tuition reimbursement (averaging $12,000 per year), 43 research assistantships (averaging $3,400 per year) were awarded; career-related internships or fieldwork and scholarships/grants also available. Financial award application deadline: 5/1. In 2006, 183 degrees awarded. *Degree program information:* Part-time and evening/weekend programs available. Offers business (EMBA, MBA, MSAT, Certificate); business administration (EMBA, MBA); professional accounting (Certificate); taxation (MSAT). *Application deadline:* Applications are processed on a rolling basis. *Application fee:* $40 ($55 for international students). Electronic applications accepted. *Application Contact:* James W. Fairfield-Sonn, Interim Dean, 860-768-4243, Fax: 860-768-4198. *Interim Dean,* James W. Fairfield-Sonn, 860-768-4243, Fax: 860-768-4198.

College of Arts and Sciences Students: 155 full-time (130 women), 144 part-time (119 women); includes 36 minority (15 African Americans, 3 American Indian/Alaska Native, 7 Asian Americans or Pacific Islanders, 11 Hispanic Americans), 22 international. Average age 29. 312 applicants, 53% accepted, 82 enrolled. *Faculty:* 25 full-time (12 women), 16 part-time/adjunct (6 women). Expenses: Contact institution. *Financial support:* In 2006–07, 16 research assistantships (averaging $2,000 per year), 28 teaching assistantships (averaging $2,550 per year) were awarded; fellowships, career-related internships or fieldwork, Federal Work-Study, and tuition waivers (partial) also available. Support available to part-time students. Financial award application deadline: 6/1; financial award applicants required to submit FAFSA. In 2006, 70 master's, 24 doctorates awarded. *Degree program information:* Part-time and evening/weekend programs available. Offers arts and sciences (MA, MS, Psy D); biology (MS); clinical practices (MA, Psy D); communication (MA); general experimental psychology (MA); neuroscience (MS); organizational behavior (MS); psychology (MA); school psychology (MS). *Application deadline:* For fall admission, 7/1 priority date for domestic students; for spring admission, 12/1 for domestic students. Applications are processed on a rolling basis. *Application fee:* $40 ($55 for international students). Electronic applications accepted. *Application Contact:* Reneé Murphy, Assistant Director of Graduate Admissions, 860-768-4371, Fax: 860-768-5160, E-mail: rmurphy@hartford.edu. *Dean,* Dr. Joseph C. Voelker, 860-768-4103, Fax: 860-768-5043, E-mail: voelker@hartford.edu.

College of Education, Nursing, and Health Professions Students: 128 full-time (102 women), 339 part-time (293 women); includes 44 minority (24 African Americans, 1 American Indian/Alaska Native, 3 Asian Americans or Pacific Islanders, 16 Hispanic Americans), 5 international. Average age 38. 130 applicants, 87% accepted, 99 enrolled. *Faculty:* 28 full-time (19 women), 13 part-time/adjunct (10 women). Expenses: Contact institution. *Financial support:* In 2006–07, 3 research assistantships (averaging $4,333 per year) were awarded; teaching assistantships, institutionally sponsored loans and unspecified assistantships also available. Financial award application deadline: 6/1; financial award applicants required to submit FAFSA. In 2006, 112 master's, 21 doctorates, 21 other advanced degrees awarded. *Degree program information:* Part-time and evening/weekend programs available. Offers administration and supervision (CAGS); community/public health nursing (MSN); counseling (M Ed, MS, Sixth Year Certificate); early childhood education (M Ed); education, nursing, and health professions (M Ed, MS, MSN, MSPT, DPT, Ed D, CAGS, Sixth Year Certificate); educational leadership (Ed D, CAGS); educational technology (M Ed); elementary education (M Ed); nursing education (MSN); nursing management (MSN); physical therapy (MSPT, DPT). *Application deadline:* Applications are processed on a rolling basis. *Application fee:* $40 ($55 for international students). Electronic applications accepted. *Application Contact:* Susan Brown, Assistant Dean of Academic Services, 860-768-4692, Fax: 860-768-5043, E-mail: brown@hartford.edu. *Dean,* Dr. Dorothy A. Zeiser, 860-768-4649, Fax: 860-768-5043.

College of Engineering, Technology and Architecture Students: 53 full-time (10 women), 68 part-time (20 women); includes 19 minority (6 African Americans, 1 American Indian/Alaska Native, 4 Asian Americans or Pacific Islanders, 8 Hispanic Americans), 41 international. Average age 29. 120 applicants, 72% accepted, 40 enrolled. *Faculty:* 23 full-time (5 women), 13 part-time/adjunct (3 women). Expenses: Contact institution. *Financial support:* In 2006–07, 22 fellowships (averaging $2,500 per year), 1 research assistantship (averaging $5,000 per year), 2 teaching assistantships (averaging $8,000 per year) were awarded; Federal Work-Study and unspecified assistantships also available. Support available to part-time students. Financial award application deadline: 6/1; financial award applicants required to submit FAFSA. In 2006, 39 degrees awarded. *Degree program information:* Part-time and evening/weekend programs available. Offers architecture (M Arch); engineering (M Eng); engineering, technology and architecture (M Arch, M Eng). *Application deadline:* Applications are processed on a rolling basis. *Application fee:* $40 ($55 for international students). Electronic applications accepted. *Application Contact:* Laurie Granstrand, Manager of Student Services, 860-768-4858, E-mail: granstran@hartford.edu. *Dean,* Louis Manzione, 860-768-4112, Fax: 860-768-5073.

Hartford Art School Students: 9 full-time (4 women), 19 part-time (7 women); includes 2 minority (1 American Indian/Alaska Native, 1 Hispanic American). Average age 44. 40 applicants, 35% accepted, 6 enrolled. *Faculty:* 9 full-time (2 women), 3 part-time/adjunct (0 women). Expenses: Contact institution. *Financial support:* In 2006–07, 9 fellowships with partial tuition reimbursements (averaging $6,000 per year) were awarded; teaching assistantships, Federal Work-Study also available. Support available to part-time students. Financial award application deadline: 6/1; financial award applicants required to submit FAFSA. In 2006, 5 degrees awarded. *Degree program information:* Part-time programs available. Offers art (MFA). *Application deadline:* For fall admission, 3/1 priority date for domestic students. Applications are processed on a rolling basis. *Application fee:* $40 ($55 for international students). Electronic applications accepted. *Application Contact:* Ellen Carey, Director, 860-768-4616, Fax: 860-768-5160, E-mail: ecarey@mail.hartford.edu. *Dean,* Power Boothe.

The Hartt School Students: 108 full-time (53 women), 31 part-time (19 women); includes 11 minority (6 African Americans, 4 Asian Americans or Pacific Islanders, 1 Hispanic American), 31 international. Average age 29. 163 applicants, 55% accepted, 55 enrolled. *Faculty:* 37 full-time (5 women), 33 part-time/adjunct (16 women). Expenses: Contact institution. *Financial support:* Fellowships, teaching assistantships, Federal Work-Study available. Support available to part-time students. Financial award application deadline: 6/1; financial award applicants required to submit FAFSA. In 2006, 49 master's, 9 doctorates, 10 other advanced degrees awarded. *Degree program information:* Part-time programs available. Offers choral conducting (MM Ed); composition (MM, DMA, Artist Diploma, Diploma); conducting (MM, DMA, Artist Diploma, Diploma); early childhood education (MM Ed); instrumental conducting (MM Ed); Kodály (MM Ed); music (CAGS); music education (DMA, PhD); music history (MM); music theory (MM); pedagogy (MM Ed); performance (MM, MM Ed, DMA, Artist Diploma, Diploma); research (MM Ed); technology (MM Ed). *Application deadline:* For fall admission, 4/1 priority date for domestic students. Applications are processed on a rolling basis. *Application fee:* $40 ($55 for international students). Electronic applications accepted. *Application Contact:* Lynne Johnson, Director of Admissions, 860-768-4115, Fax: 860-768-4441, E-mail: johnson@hartford.edu. *Dean,* Dr. Malcolm Morrison, 860-768-4468, E-mail: morrison@mail.hartford.edu.

UNIVERSITY OF HAWAII AT HILO, Hilo, HI 96720-4091

General Information State-supported, coed, comprehensive institution.

GRADUATE UNITS

Program in China-US Relations

UNIVERSITY OF HAWAII AT MANOA, Honolulu, HI 96822

General Information State-supported, coed, university. CGS member. *Graduate housing:* Rooms and/or apartments available to single and married students. Typical cost: $3,742 per year ($5,692 including board) for single students; $7,066 per year ($10,966 including board) for married students. Room and board charges vary according to board plan and housing facility selected. Housing application deadline: 5/1. *Student services:* Campus employment opportunities, campus safety program, career counseling, child daycare facilities, disabled student services, exercise/wellness program, free psychological counseling, international student services, low-cost health insurance, multicultural affairs office, teacher training, writing training. *Library facilities:* Hamilton Library plus 6 others. *Online resources:* library catalog, web page, access to other libraries' catalogs. *Collection:* 3.3 million titles, 28,705 serial subscriptions, 63,942 audiovisual materials. *Research affiliation:* Bernice Pauahi Bishop Museum (anthropology, zoology), Hawaiian Volcano Observatory (geology, geophysics), Honolulu Academy of Arts, East-West Center (communication, geography, economics), U.S. Geological Survey, Hawaii Agriculture Research Center.

Computer facilities: Computer purchase and lease plans are available. 1,400 computers available on campus for general student use. A campuswide network can be accessed from student residence rooms and from off campus. Internet access and online class registration are available. *Web address:* http://www.uhm.hawaii.edu/.

General Application Contact: Joseph Q. Salas, Director of Graduate Admissions, 808-956-8544, Fax: 808-956-4261, E-mail: jaqsalas@hawaii.edu.

GRADUATE UNITS

Graduate Division Students: 3,101 full-time (1,705 women), 1,546 part-time (963 women); includes 1,725 minority (41 African Americans, 18 American Indian/Alaska Native, 1,575 Asian Americans or Pacific Islanders, 91 Hispanic Americans), 1,037 international. 4,108 applicants, 49% accepted, 1210 enrolled. *Faculty:* 1,167 full-time (364 women), 151 part-time/adjunct (28 women). Expenses: Contact institution. *Financial support:* In 2006–07, 757 research assistantships with full tuition reimbursements (averaging $18,369 per year), 534 teaching assistantships with full tuition reimbursements (averaging $14,374 per year) were awarded; fellowships, career-related internships or fieldwork, Federal Work-Study, institutionally sponsored loans, scholarships/grants, and tuition waivers (full and partial) also available. Support available to part-time students. Financial award applicants required to submit FAFSA. In 2006, 1,050 master's, 144 doctorates, 37 other advanced degrees awarded. *Degree program information:* Part-time and evening/weekend programs available. Offers ecology, evolution and conservation biology (MS, PhD); marine biology (MS, PhD). *Application fee:* $50. Electronic applications accepted. *Application Contact:* Graduate Division, 808-956-8594.

College of Education Students: 361 full-time (242 women), 573 part-time (410 women); includes 542 minority (19 African Americans, 3 American Indian/Alaska Native, 497 Asian Americans or Pacific Islanders, 23 Hispanic Americans), 52 international. 594 applicants, 62% accepted, 263 enrolled. *Faculty:* 93 full-time (57 women), 9 part-time/adjunct (4 women). Expenses: Contact institution. *Financial support:* In 2006–07, 34 research assistantships (averaging $16,491 per year), 21 teaching assistantships (averaging $13,610 per year) were awarded; fellowships, career-related internships or fieldwork, Federal Work-Study, institutionally sponsored loans, and tuition waivers (full and partial) also available. Support available to part-time students. In 2006, 233 master's, 19 doctorates, 3 other advanced degrees awarded. *Degree program information:* Part-time and evening/weekend programs available. Offers counseling and guidance (M Ed); curriculum and instruction

University of Hawaii at Manoa (continued)

(PhD); curriculum studies (M Ed); disability studies (Graduate Certificate); early childhood education (M Ed); education (M Ed, M Ed T, MS, PhD, Graduate Certificate); education in teaching (M Ed T); educational administration (PhD); educational foundations (PhD); educational policy studies (PhD); educational psychology (M Ed, PhD); educational technology (M Ed); exceptionalities (PhD); kinesiology (MS); special education (M Ed). *Application fee:* $50. *Application Contact:* Donald Young, Information Contact, 808-956-7703.

College of Engineering Students: 137 full-time (31 women), 40 part-time (13 women); includes 53 minority (1 American Indian/Alaska Native, 51 Asian Americans or Pacific Islanders, 1 Hispanic American), 80 international. 120 applicants, 78% accepted, 55 enrolled. *Faculty:* 46 full-time (3 women). Expenses: Contact institution. *Financial support:* In 2006–07, 81 research assistantships (averaging $17,200 per year), 21 teaching assistantships (averaging $13,996 per year) were awarded; fellowships, career-related internships or fieldwork, Federal Work-Study, and tuition waivers (full and partial) also available. Financial award applicants required to submit FAFSA. In 2006, 29 master's, 10 doctorates awarded. *Degree program information:* Part-time programs available. Offers civil and environmental engineering (MS, PhD); electrical engineering (MS, PhD); engineering (MS, PhD, Graduate Certificate); mechanical engineering (MS, PhD); telecommunications and entrepreneurship (Graduate Certificate). *Application deadline:* Applications are processed on a rolling basis. *Application fee:* $50. *Application Contact:* Peter Crouch, Information Contact, 808-956-7727, Fax: 808-956-2291.

College of Health Sciences and Social Welfare Expenses: Contact institution. *Financial support:* Fellowships with full and partial tuition reimbursements, research assistantships with full and partial tuition reimbursements, teaching assistantships, career-related internships or fieldwork, Federal Work-Study, institutionally sponsored loans, traineeships, and tuition waivers (full) available. Support available to part-time students. *Degree program information:* Part-time programs available. Offers clinical nurse specialist (MS); health sciences and social welfare (MS, MSW, PhD, Graduate Certificate); nurse practitioner (MS); nursing (PhD, Graduate Certificate); nursing administration (MS); social welfare (PhD); social work (MSW). *Application fee:* $50. *Application Contact:* Graduate Division, 808-956-8594.

College of Tropical Agriculture and Human Resources Students: 186 full-time (98 women), 32 part-time (15 women); includes 51 minority (1 African American, 1 American Indian/Alaska Native, 45 Asian Americans or Pacific Islanders, 4 Hispanic Americans), 87 international. 131 applicants, 58% accepted, 48 enrolled. *Faculty:* 120 full-time (21 women), 44 part-time/adjunct (9 women). Expenses: Contact institution. *Financial support:* In 2006–07, 117 research assistantships (averaging $17,071 per year), 30 teaching assistantships (averaging $13,809 per year) were awarded; fellowships, career-related internships or fieldwork, Federal Work-Study, institutionally sponsored loans, tuition waivers (full and partial), and unspecified assistantships also available. In 2006, 41 master's, 13 doctorates awarded. *Degree program information:* Part-time programs available. Offers animal sciences (MS); bioengineering (MS); biosystems engineering (MS); entomology (MS, PhD); food science (MS); human nutrition (MS); molecular biosystems and bioengineering (MS, PhD); natural resources and environmental management (MS, PhD); tropical agriculture and human resources (MS, PhD); tropical plant and soil sciences (MS, PhD); tropical plant pathology (MS, PhD). *Application fee:* $50. *Application Contact:* Dr. Andrew Hashimoto, Dean, 808-956-8234, Fax: 808-956-9105, E-mail: dean@ctahr.hawaii.edu.

Colleges of Arts and Sciences Students: 1,995. *Faculty:* 635. Expenses: Contact institution. *Financial support:* Fellowships, research assistantships, teaching assistantships, career-related internships or fieldwork, Federal Work-Study, institutionally sponsored loans, scholarships/grants, and tuition waivers (full and partial) available. Support available to part-time students. Financial award applicants required to submit CSS PROFILE or FAFSA. *Degree program information:* Part-time and evening/weekend programs available. Offers advanced library and information science (Graduate Certificate); advanced women's studies (Graduate Certificate); American studies (MA, PhD); anthropology (MA, PhD); art (MA); art history (MA); arts and humanities (M Mus, MA, MFA, PhD, Graduate Certificate); arts and sciences (M Mus, MA, MFA, MLI Sc, MPA, MS, MURP, PhD, Graduate Certificate); astronomy (MS, PhD); botany (MS, PhD); chemistry (MS, PhD); Chinese (MA, PhD); classics (MA); clinical psychology (PhD); communication (MA); communication and information science (PhD); community and cultural psychology (PhD); community and culture (MA); community planning and social policy (MURP); computer science (MS, PhD); dance (MA, MFA); economics (MA, PhD); English (MA, PhD); English as a second language (MA, Graduate Certificate); environmental planning and management (MURP); French (MA); geography (MA, PhD); Hawaiian (MA); historic preservation (Graduate Certificate); history (MA, PhD); Japanese (MA, PhD); Korean (MA, PhD); land use and infrastructure planning (MURP); language, linguistics and literature (MA, PhD, Graduate Certificate); library and information science (MLI Sc, PhD, Graduate Certificate); linguistics (MA, PhD); mathematics (MA, PhD); microbiology (MS, PhD); museum studies (Graduate Certificate); music (M Mus, MA, PhD); natural sciences (MA, MLI Sc, MS, PhD, Graduate Certificate); peace (Graduate Certificate); philosophy (MA, PhD); physics (MS, PhD); political science (MA, PhD); population studies (Graduate Certificate); psychology (MA, PhD, Graduate Certificate); public administration (MPA, Graduate Certificate); religion (MA); second language acquisition (PhD); social sciences (MA, MPA, MURP, PhD, Graduate Certificate); sociology (MA, PhD); Spanish (MA); speech (MA); telecommunication and information resource management (Graduate Certificate); theatre (MA, MFA, PhD); urban and regional planning (PhD, Graduate Certificate); urban and regional planning in Asia and Pacific (MURP); visual arts (MFA); zoology (MS, PhD). *Application fee:* $50. *Application Contact:* Graduate Division, 808-956-8594.

School of Architecture Expenses: Contact institution. *Financial support:* Research assistantships, teaching assistantships, tuition waivers (full) available. Offers architecture (D Arch). *Application fee:* $50. *Application Contact:* Joyce Noe, Graduate Field Chairperson, 808-956-3506, Fax: 808-956-7778, E-mail: jmnoe@hawaii.edu.

School of Hawaiian, Asian and Pacific Studies Students: 97 full-time (54 women), 32 part-time (19 women); includes 60 minority (58 Asian Americans or Pacific Islanders, 2 Hispanic Americans), 25 international. 116 applicants, 63% accepted, 37 enrolled. *Faculty:* 128 full-time (44 women), 2 part-time/adjunct (0 women). Expenses: Contact institution. *Financial support:* In 2006–07, 5 research assistantships (averaging $16,440 per year), 15 teaching assistantships (averaging $13,624 per year) were awarded; fellowships, career-related internships or fieldwork, Federal Work-Study, and tuition waivers (full) also available. In 2006, 25 degrees awarded. Offers Asian studies (MA, Graduate Certificate); Hawaiian studies (MA); Hawaiian, Asian and Pacific studies (MA, Graduate Certificate); Pacific Island studies (MA, Graduate Certificate). *Application fee:* $50. *Application Contact:* Ned Shultz, Information Contact, 808-956-8818.

School of Ocean and Earth Science and Technology Students: 174 full-time (74 women), 16 part-time (5 women); includes 26 minority (1 African American, 17 Asian Americans or Pacific Islanders, 8 Hispanic Americans), 71 international. 241 applicants, 24% accepted, 36 enrolled. *Faculty:* 137 full-time (18 women), 30 part-time/adjunct (2 women). Expenses: Contact institution. *Financial support:* In 2006–07, 135 research assistantships (averaging $20,241 per year), teaching assistantships (averaging $18,371 per year) were awarded; fellowships, career-related internships or fieldwork, Federal Work-Study, institutionally sponsored loans, and tuition waivers (full and partial) also available. Financial award applicants required to submit FAFSA. In 2006, 22 master's, 9 doctorates awarded. *Degree program information:* Part-time programs available. Offers high-pressure geophysics and geochemistry (MS, PhD); hydrogeology and engineering geology (MS, PhD); marine geology and geophysics (MS, PhD); meteorology (MS, PhD); ocean and earth science and technology (MS, PhD); ocean and resources engineering (MS, PhD); oceanography (MS, PhD); planetary geosciences and remote sensing (MS, PhD); seismology and solid-earth geophysics (MS, PhD); volcanology, petrology, and geochemistry (MS, PhD). *Application fee:* $50. *Application Contact:* Brian Taylor, Information Contact, 808-956-6182.

School of Travel Industry Management Students: 15 full-time (9 women), 4 part-time (all women); includes 2 minority (both Asian Americans or Pacific Islanders), 3 international. Average age 28. 46 applicants, 43% accepted, 5 enrolled. *Faculty:* 13 full-time (4 women). Expenses: Contact institution. *Financial support:* In 2006–07, 4 fellowships with partial tuition reimbursements were awarded; career-related internships or fieldwork, scholarships/grants, tuition waivers (full and partial), and student assistantships also available. Financial award application deadline: 3/1. In 2006, 14 degrees awarded. *Degree program information:* Part-time programs available. Offers travel industry management (MS). *Application deadline:* For fall admission, 3/1 for domestic and international students; for spring admission, 9/1 for domestic and international students. Applications are processed on a rolling basis. *Application fee:* $50. Electronic applications accepted. *Application Contact:* Harold Richins, Graduate Chair, 808-956-9840, Fax: 808-956-5378.

Shidler College of Business Students: 293 full-time (123 women), 176 part-time (75 women); includes 215 minority (2 African Americans, 1 American Indian/Alaska Native, 208 Asian Americans or Pacific Islanders, 4 Hispanic Americans), 127 international. 349 applicants, 55% accepted, 97 enrolled. Expenses: Contact institution. *Financial support:* In 2006–07, 22 research assistantships (averaging $17,958 per year), 6 teaching assistantships (averaging $14,493 per year) were awarded; career-related internships or fieldwork, Federal Work-Study, and tuition waivers (full) also available. Support available to part-time students. In 2006, 186 master's, 4 doctorates awarded. *Degree program information:* Part-time and evening/weekend programs available. Offers accounting (M Acc); accounting law (M Acc); Asian business studies (MBA); Asian finance (PhD); business administration (MBA); Chinese business studies (MBA); decision sciences (MBA); entrepreneurship (MBA); executive business administration (EMBA); executive education (EMBA); finance (MBA); finance and banking (MBA); global information technology management (PhD); human resources management (MBA, MHRM); information management (MBA); information systems (M Acc); information technology (MBA); international accounting (PhD); international business (MBA); international management (PhD); international marketing (PhD); international organization and strategy (PhD); Japanese business studies (MBA); marketing (MBA); organizational behavior (MBA); organizational management (MBA); real estate (MBA); student-designed track (MBA); taxation (M Acc); Vietnam focused business administration (EMBA). *Application fee:* $50. *Application Contact:* V. Vance Roley, Dean, 808-956-8377.

John A. Burns School of Medicine Students: 110 full-time (74 women), 46 part-time (34 women); includes 73 minority (3 African Americans, 1 American Indian/Alaska Native, 67 Asian Americans or Pacific Islanders, 2 Hispanic Americans), 26 international. 217 applicants, 39% accepted, 48 enrolled. *Faculty:* 46 full-time (20 women), 1 part-time/adjunct (0 women). Expenses: Contact institution. *Financial support:* In 2006–07, 42 research assistantships (averaging $17,907 per year), 6 teaching assistantships (averaging $14,577 per year) were awarded; fellowships, career-related internships or fieldwork, Federal Work-Study, institutionally sponsored loans, and tuition waivers (full and partial) also available. Support available to part-time students. Financial award applicants required to submit FAFSA. In 2006, 45 master's, 5 doctorates, 8 other advanced degrees awarded. *Degree program information:* Part-time programs available. Offers epidemiology (PhD); medicine (MD, MPH, MS, PhD, Graduate Certificate); public health (MPH, MS). *Application fee:* $50. *Application Contact:* Gary K. Ostrander, 808-692-0881.

Center on Aging 1 applicant, 0% accepted. Expenses: Contact institution. In 2006, 8 degrees awarded. Offers gerontology (Graduate Certificate). *Application deadline:* For fall admission, 3/1 for domestic and international students; for spring admission, 9/1 for domestic and international students. *Application fee:* $50. *Application Contact:* Kathryn Braun, Information Contact, 808-956-5768, Fax: 808-956-9582.

Graduate Programs in Biomedical Sciences Students: 2 full-time (both women), 15 part-time (11 women); includes 4 minority (1 African American, 3 Asian Americans or Pacific Islanders). Average age 31. 5 applicants, 40% accepted, 1 enrolled. *Faculty:* 10 full-time (6 women), 1 part-time/adjunct (0 women). Expenses: Contact institution. *Financial support:* Fellowships, research assistantships, teaching assistantships, career-related internships or fieldwork, Federal Work-Study, institutionally sponsored loans, and tuition waivers (full and partial) available. Support available to part-time students. In 2006, 1 degree awarded. *Degree program information:* Part-time programs available. Offers biomedical sciences (MS, PhD); cell and molecular biology (MS, PhD); physiology (MS, PhD); speech pathology and audiology (MS); tropical medicine (MS, PhD). *Application fee:* $50. *Application Contact:* Rosanne Harrigan, Information Contact, 808-692-0904.

William S. Richardson School of Law Expenses: Contact institution. *Financial support:* Fellowships, research assistantships, career-related internships or fieldwork, Federal Work-Study, institutionally sponsored loans, and tuition waivers (full and partial) available. Financial award application deadline: 3/1; financial award applicants required to submit FAFSA. Offers law (JD, Graduate Certificate). *Application Contact:* Laurie A. Tochiki, Assistant Dean, 808-956-7966, Fax: 808-956-3813, E-mail: lawadm@hawaii.edu.

East-West Center Students: 20 full-time (13 women), 2 part-time (both women), 2 international. 3 applicants, 0% accepted. *Faculty:* 11 full-time (6 women). Expenses: Contact institution. *Financial support:* In 2006–07, 2 research assistantships (averaging $17,511 per year), 3 teaching assistantships (averaging $14,212 per year) were awarded. In 2006, 5 degrees awarded. Offers international cultural studies (Graduate Certificate). *Application deadline:* For fall admission, 3/1 for domestic and international students; for spring admission, 9/1 for domestic and international students. *Application fee:* $50. *Application Contact:* Mari Yoshihara, Graduate Chairperson, 808-956-8542, Fax: 808-956-4733, E-mail: myoshiha@hawaii.edu.

UNIVERSITY OF HOUSTON, Houston, TX 77204

General Information State-supported, coed, university. CGS member. *Enrollment:* 34,334 graduate, professional, and undergraduate students; 4,486 full-time matriculated graduate/professional students (2,358 women), 2,448 part-time matriculated graduate/professional students (1,310 women). *Enrollment by degree level:* 1,881 first professional, 3,610 master's, 1,443 doctoral. *Graduate faculty:* 655 full-time (174 women), 331 part-time/adjunct (119 women). Tuition, state resident: full-time $5,429; part-time $226 per credit. Tuition, nonresident: full-time $12,029; part-time $501 per credit. *Required fees:* $2,454. *Graduate housing:* Rooms and/or apartments available on a first-come, first-served basis to single students and available to married students. Typical cost: $4,032 per year ($6,818 including board) for single students. Housing application deadline: 3/1. *Student services:* Campus employment opportunities, campus safety program, career counseling, child daycare facilities, disabled student services, exercise/wellness program, free psychological counseling, international student services, low-cost health insurance, teacher training, writing training. *Library facilities:* M.D. Anderson Library plus 6 others. *Online resources:* library catalog, web page, access to other libraries' catalogs. *Collection:* 2.3 million titles, 21,845 serial subscriptions.

Computer facilities: 825 computers available on campus for general student use. A campuswide network can be accessed from student residence rooms and from off campus. Internet access and online class registration are available. *Web address:* http://www.uh.edu/.

General Application Contact: Jeff Fuller, Executive Associate Director of Admission, 832-842-9047, Fax: 713-743-7542, E-mail: jfuller@uh.edu.

GRADUATE UNITS

Bauer College of Business Students: 461 full-time (195 women), 498 part-time (161 women); includes 317 minority (48 African Americans, 3 American Indian/Alaska Native, 200 Asian Americans or Pacific Islanders, 66 Hispanic Americans), 166 international. Average age 30. 628 applicants, 62% accepted, 294 enrolled. *Faculty:* 52 full-time (12 women), 35 part-time/adjunct (7 women). Expenses: Contact institution. *Financial support:* In 2006–07, 8 fellowships with full tuition reimbursements (averaging $10,150 per year), 97 teaching assistantships with full tuition reimbursements (averaging $7,000 per year) were awarded; research assistantships with full tuition reimbursements, career-related internships or fieldwork, Federal Work-Study, institutionally sponsored loans, scholarships/grants, health care benefits, and unspecified assistantships also available. Support available to part-time students. Financial award application deadline: 3/10; financial award applicants required to submit FAFSA. In 2006, 377 master's, 4 doctorates awarded. *Degree program information:* Part-time and evening/weekend programs available. Offers accountancy (M Acy); accounting (PhD); business (M Acy, MBA, MS, PhD); decision and information sciences (MBA, PhD); finance (MS); management (PhD); marketing and entrepreneurship (PhD). *Application deadline:* For fall admission, 5/1 for domestic students; for spring admission, 10/1 for domestic students. Applications are processed on a rolling basis. *Application fee:* $75 ($150 for international students). *Applica-*

tion Contact: Andrew Wayne Edwards, Office of Student Services, 713-743-4852, Fax: 713-743-4942, E-mail: aedwards@uh.edu. *Dean,* Dr. Arthur Warga, 713-743-4604, Fax: 713-743-4622, E-mail: warga@uh.edu.

College of Architecture Students: 75 full-time (35 women), 5 part-time (3 women); includes 16 minority (2 African Americans, 1 American Indian/Alaska Native, 4 Asian Americans or Pacific Islanders, 9 Hispanic Americans), 15 international. Average age 28. 90 applicants, 68% accepted, 27 enrolled. *Faculty:* 17 full-time (3 women), 15 part-time/adjunct (2 women). Expenses: Contact institution. *Financial support:* In 2006–07, 1 research assistantship with full tuition reimbursement (averaging $9,600 per year), 13 teaching assistantships with full tuition reimbursements (averaging $9,100 per year) were awarded; fellowships with full tuition reimbursements, career-related internships or fieldwork, Federal Work-Study, institutionally sponsored loans, scholarships/grants, health care benefits, and unspecified assistantships also available. Support available to part-time students. Financial award application deadline: 3/10. In 2006, 32 master's awarded. Offers architecture (M Arch, MS). *Application deadline:* For fall admission, 2/1 priority date for domestic students; for spring admission, 10/1 for domestic students. Applications are processed on a rolling basis. *Application fee:* $10 ($75 for international students). *Application Contact:* Thomas M. Colbert, Director of Graduate Studies, 713-743-2380, Fax: 713-743-2358, E-mail: colbert@bayou.uh.edu. *Dean,* Joseph Mashburn, 713-743-2400, Fax: 713-743-2358, E-mail: mashburn@uh.edu.

College of Education Students: 292 full-time (228 women), 648 part-time (490 women); includes 302 minority (124 African Americans, 2 American Indian/Alaska Native, 55 Asian Americans or Pacific Islanders, 121 Hispanic Americans), 27 international. Average age 35. 344 applicants, 57% accepted, 142 enrolled. *Faculty:* 60 full-time (31 women), 39 part-time/adjunct (26 women). Expenses: Contact institution. *Financial support:* In 2006–07, 9 fellowships with full tuition reimbursements (averaging $9,500 per year), 14 research assistantships with full tuition reimbursements (averaging $9,500 per year), 70 teaching assistantships with full tuition reimbursements (averaging $9,500 per year) were awarded; career-related internships or fieldwork, Federal Work-Study, institutionally sponsored loans, scholarships/grants, health care benefits, and unspecified assistantships also available. Support available to part-time students. Financial award application deadline: 3/10; financial award applicants required to submit FAFSA. In 2006, 208 master's, 52 doctorates awarded. *Degree program information:* Part-time and evening/weekend programs available. Offers allied health (M Ed, Ed D); art education (M Ed); bilingual education (M Ed); counseling psychology (M Ed, PhD); curriculum and instruction (Ed D); early childhood education (M Ed); education (M Ed, MS, Ed D, PhD); education of the gifted (M Ed); educational administration (M Ed, Ed D); educational psychology (M Ed); educational psychology and individual differences (PhD); elementary education (M Ed); exercise science (MS); health education (M Ed); higher education (M Ed); historical, social, and cultural foundations of education (M Ed, Ed D); kinesiology (PhD); mathematics education (M Ed); physical education (M Ed, Ed D); reading and language arts education (M Ed); science education (M Ed); second language education (M Ed); secondary education (M Ed); social studies education (M Ed); special education (M Ed, Ed D); teaching (M Ed). *Application fee:* $35 ($75 for international students). *Dean,* Robert K. Wimpelberg, 713-743-5001, Fax: 713-743-5013, E-mail: rwimpelberg@uh.edu.

College of Liberal Arts and Social Sciences Students: 671 full-time (398 women), 362 part-time (225 women); includes 237 minority (72 African Americans, 4 American Indian/Alaska Native, 43 Asian Americans or Pacific Islanders, 118 Hispanic Americans), 127 international. Average age 31. 901 applicants, 43% accepted, 251 enrolled. *Faculty:* 195 full-time (72 women), 61 part-time/adjunct (30 women). Expenses: Contact institution. *Financial support:* In 2006–07, 22 fellowships with full tuition reimbursements (averaging $7,150 per year), 36 research assistantships with full tuition reimbursements (averaging $10,400 per year), 399 teaching assistantships with full tuition reimbursements (averaging $10,400 per year) were awarded; career-related internships or fieldwork, Federal Work-Study, institutionally sponsored loans, scholarships/grants, health care benefits, and unspecified assistantships also available. Support available to part-time students. Financial award application deadline: 3/10; financial award applicants required to submit FAFSA. In 2006, 209 master's, 61 doctorates awarded. *Degree program information:* Part-time and evening/weekend programs available. Postbaccalaureate distance learning degree programs offered. Offers anthropology (MA); applied English linguistics (MA); clinical psychology (PhD); economics (MA, PhD); English and American literature (MA, PhD); French (MA); history (MA, PhD); industrial/organizational psychology (PhD); interior design (MA); liberal arts and social sciences (MA, MFA, MM, DMA, PhD); literature and creative writing (MA, MFA, PhD); painting (MA); philosophy (MA); photography (MA); political science (MA, PhD); psychology (MA); public history (MA); sculpture (MA); social psychology (PhD); sociology (MA); Spanish (MA, PhD); speech language pathology (MA). *Application Contact:* Debra Frazier, Graduate Analyst, 713-743-2991, Fax: 713-743-2990. *Dean,* Dr. John Antel, 713-743-2992, Fax: 713-743-2990, E-mail: antel@uh.edu.

Moores School of Music Students: 88 full-time (40 women), 34 part-time (18 women); includes 18 minority (7 African Americans, 4 Asian Americans or Pacific Islanders, 7 Hispanic Americans), 22 international. Average age 30. 81 applicants, 60% accepted, 34 enrolled. *Faculty:* 27 full-time (7 women), 19 part-time/adjunct (8 women). Expenses: Contact institution. *Financial support:* In 2006–07, 48 teaching assistantships with full tuition reimbursements (averaging $9,800 per year) were awarded; fellowships with full tuition reimbursements, research assistantships with full tuition reimbursements, career-related internships or fieldwork, Federal Work-Study, institutionally sponsored loans, scholarships/grants, health care benefits, and unspecified assistantships also available. Support available to part-time students. Financial award application deadline: 3/10. In 2006, 35 master's, 7 doctorates awarded. *Degree program information:* Part-time programs available. Offers accompanying (MM); applied music (MM); composition (MM, DMA); conducting (DMA); music education (MM, DMA); music literature (MM); music performance and pedagogy (MM); music theory (MM); performance (DMA). *Application deadline:* For fall admission, 7/1 priority date for domestic students. Applications are processed on a rolling basis. *Application fee:* $0 ($75 for international students). *Application Contact:* Howard Pollack, Director of Graduate Studies, 713-743-3314, Fax: 713-743-3166. *Chairperson,* David Ashley White, 713-743-3009, Fax: 713-743-3166, E-mail: daw@orpheus.music.uh.edu.

School of Communication Students: 42 full-time (31 women), 56 part-time (42 women); includes 39 minority (24 African Americans, 1 American Indian/Alaska Native, 4 Asian Americans or Pacific Islanders, 10 Hispanic Americans), 13 international. Average age 29. 62 applicants, 65% accepted, 23 enrolled. *Faculty:* 8 full-time (3 women), 1 part-time/adjunct (0 women). Expenses: Contact institution. *Financial support:* In 2006–07, 3 fellowships with full tuition reimbursements (averaging $9,750 per year), 8 teaching assistantships with full tuition reimbursements (averaging $9,750 per year) were awarded; research assistantships with full tuition reimbursements, career-related internships or fieldwork, Federal Work-Study, institutionally sponsored loans, scholarships/grants, health care benefits, and unspecified assistantships also available. Support available to part-time students. Financial award application deadline: 3/10. In 2006, 13 master's awarded. *Degree program information:* Part-time and evening/weekend programs available. Offers mass communication studies (MA); public relations studies (MA); speech communication (MA). *Application deadline:* For fall admission, 7/3 priority date for domestic students. Applications are processed on a rolling basis. *Application fee:* $25 ($75 for international students). *Application Contact:* Angela Parrish, Graduate Coordinator, 713-743-2873, Fax: 713-743-2876, E-mail: aparrish@bayou.uh.edu. *Chairperson,* Beth Olson, 713-743-2873, Fax: 713-743-2876, E-mail: bolson@uh.edu.

School of Theatre Students: 25 full-time (14 women), 9 part-time (4 women); includes 2 minority (1 African American, 1 Hispanic American), 2 international. Average age 30. 28 applicants, 89% accepted, 21 enrolled. *Faculty:* 10 full-time (2 women), 2 part-time/adjunct (both women). Expenses: Contact institution. *Financial support:* In 2006–07, 11 teaching assistantships with full tuition reimbursements (averaging $9,100 per year) were awarded; fellowships with full tuition reimbursements, research assistantships with full tuition reimbursements, career-related internships or fieldwork, Federal Work-Study, institutionally sponsored loans, scholarships/grants, health care benefits, and unspecified assistantships also available. Support available to part-time students. Financial award application deadline: 3/10. In 2006, 13 master's awarded. *Degree program information:* Part-time programs available. Offers theatre (MA, MFA). *Application fee:* $25. *Chairperson,* Sidney Berger, 713-743-3003, Fax: 713-749-1420, E-mail: sberger@uh.edu.

College of Natural Sciences and Mathematics Students: 587 full-time (193 women), 164 part-time (61 women); includes 70 minority (10 African Americans, 2 American Indian/Alaska Native, 42 Asian Americans or Pacific Islanders, 16 Hispanic Americans), 510 international. Average age 29. 409 applicants, 83% accepted, 164 enrolled. *Faculty:* 132 full-time (14 women), 18 part-time/adjunct (2 women). Expenses: Contact institution. *Financial support:* In 2006–07, 22 fellowships with full tuition reimbursements (averaging $17,000 per year), 280 research assistantships with full tuition reimbursements (averaging $13,000 per year), 234 teaching assistantships with full tuition reimbursements (averaging $13,000 per year) were awarded; career-related internships or fieldwork, Federal Work-Study, institutionally sponsored loans, scholarships/grants, health care benefits, and unspecified assistantships also available. Support available to part-time students. Financial award application deadline: 3/10; financial award applicants required to submit FAFSA. In 2006, 140 master's, 67 doctorates awarded. *Degree program information:* Part-time and evening/weekend programs available. Postbaccalaureate distance learning degree programs offered. Offers biochemistry (MA, MS, PhD); biology (MA, MS, PhD); chemistry (MA, MS, PhD); computer science (MA, MS, PhD); geology (MA, MS, PhD); geophysics (MA, MS, PhD); mathematics (MA, MS, PhD); natural sciences and mathematics (MA, MS, PhD); physics (MA, MS, PhD). *Application deadline:* Applications are processed on a rolling basis. *Application fee:* $0 ($75 for international students). Electronic applications accepted. *Dean,* Dr. John L. Bear, 713-743-2618, Fax: 713-743-8630, E-mail: jbear@uh.edu.

College of Optometry Students: 407 full-time (286 women), 21 part-time (13 women); includes 213 minority (18 African Americans, 2 American Indian/Alaska Native, 158 Asian Americans or Pacific Islanders, 35 Hispanic Americans), 24 international. Average age 26. 101 applicants, 100% accepted, 92 enrolled. *Faculty:* 23 full-time (6 women), 16 part-time/adjunct (11 women). Expenses: Contact institution. *Financial support:* In 2006–07, 13 research assistantships with full tuition reimbursements (averaging $12,950 per year), 14 teaching assistantships with full tuition reimbursements (averaging $12,950 per year) were awarded; fellowships with full tuition reimbursements, career-related internships or fieldwork, Federal Work-Study, institutionally sponsored loans, scholarships/grants, health care benefits, and unspecified assistantships also available. Support available to part-time students. Financial award application deadline: 3/10. In 2006, 89 ODs, 2 master's, 5 doctorates awarded. Offers optometry (OD); physiological optics/vision science (MS Phys Op, PhD). *Application deadline:* Applications are processed on a rolling basis. *Application Contact:* Paul Pease, Director, Student Affairs and Admission, 713-743-2040, Fax: 713-743-2046, E-mail: ppease@uh.edu. *Dean,* Earl Smith, 713-743-1899, Fax: 713-743-0965, E-mail: esmith@uh.edu.

College of Pharmacy Students: 500 full-time (335 women), 31 part-time (23 women); includes 260 minority (25 African Americans, 192 Asian Americans or Pacific Islanders, 43 Hispanic Americans), 55 international. Average age 25. 573 applicants, 27% accepted, 149 enrolled. *Faculty:* 15 full-time (4 women), 17 part-time/adjunct (9 women). Expenses: Contact institution. *Financial support:* In 2006–07, 6 research assistantships with full tuition reimbursements (averaging $14,200 per year), 35 teaching assistantships with full tuition reimbursements (averaging $14,200 per year) were awarded; fellowships with full tuition reimbursements, career-related internships or fieldwork, Federal Work-Study, institutionally sponsored loans, scholarships/grants, health care benefits, and unspecified assistantships also available. Support available to part-time students. Financial award application deadline: 3/10. In 2006, 106 first professional degrees, 6 master's, 4 doctorates awarded. *Degree program information:* Part-time programs available. Offers hospital pharmacy (MSPHR); medical chemistry and pharmacology (MS); pharmaceutics (MS, PhD); pharmacology (MS, PhD); pharmacy (Pharm D); pharmacy administration (MSPHR). *Application deadline:* For spring admission, 3/1 for domestic students. Applications are processed on a rolling basis. *Application fee:* $25 ($75 for international students). *Application Contact:* Shara Zatopek, Assistant Dean for Admissions, 713-743-1262, Fax: 713-743-1259, E-mail: szatopek@uh.edu. *Dean,* Dr. Sunny Ohia, 713-743-1253, Fax: 713-743-1259, E-mail: seohia@uh.edu.

College of Technology Students: 50 full-time (25 women), 58 part-time (27 women); includes 32 minority (9 African Americans, 2 American Indian/Alaska Native, 12 Asian Americans or Pacific Islanders, 9 Hispanic Americans), 31 international. Average age 32. 60 applicants, 80% accepted, 34 enrolled. *Faculty:* 13 full-time (6 women), 7 part-time/adjunct (2 women). Expenses: Contact institution. *Financial support:* In 2006–07, 12 fellowships with full tuition reimbursements (averaging $10,300 per year), 12 teaching assistantships with full tuition reimbursements (averaging $10,300 per year) were awarded; research assistantships with full tuition reimbursements, career-related internships or fieldwork, Federal Work-Study, institutionally sponsored loans, scholarships/grants, health care benefits, and unspecified assistantships also available. Support available to part-time students. Financial award application deadline: 3/10. In 2006, 15 degrees awarded. *Degree program information:* Part-time and evening/weekend programs available. Offers engineering technology (M Tech); human development and consumer science (MS); information and logistics technology (MS); technology (M Tech, MS). *Application deadline:* For fall admission, 7/1 for domestic students; for spring admission, 11/1 for domestic students. *Application fee:* $35 ($110 for international students). *Application Contact:* Holly Rosenthal, Graduate Academic Adviser, 713-743-4098, Fax: 713-743-4032, E-mail: hrosenthal@uh.edu. *Interim Dean,* William Fitzgibbon, 713-743-3465, Fax: 713-743-5699, E-mail: fitz@uh.edu.

Conrad N. Hilton College of Hotel and Restaurant Management Students: 38 full-time (28 women), 22 part-time (15 women); includes 12 minority (2 African Americans, 1 American Indian/Alaska Native, 6 Asian Americans or Pacific Islanders, 3 Hispanic Americans), 29 international. Average age 27. 34 applicants, 71% accepted, 12 enrolled. *Faculty:* 11 full-time (4 women), 9 part-time/adjunct (2 women). Expenses: Contact institution. *Financial support:* In 2006–07, 9 fellowships with full tuition reimbursements (averaging $9,200 per year), 1 research assistantship with full tuition reimbursement (averaging $9,200 per year), 10 teaching assistantships with full tuition reimbursements (averaging $9,200 per year) were awarded; career-related internships or fieldwork, Federal Work-Study, institutionally sponsored loans, scholarships/grants, health care benefits, and unspecified assistantships also available. Support available to part-time students. Financial award application deadline: 3/10. In 2006, 30 degrees awarded. *Degree program information:* Part-time and evening/weekend programs available. Postbaccalaureate distance learning degree programs offered (minimal on-campus study). Offers hotel and restaurant management (MHM, MS). *Application deadline:* For fall admission, 5/1 for domestic students; for spring admission, 10/1 for domestic students. Applications are processed on a rolling basis. *Application fee:* $25 ($75 for international students). Electronic applications accepted. *Application Contact:* Lilian Sutawan-Binns, Program Manager, 713-743-2457, Fax: 713-743-2591, E-mail: lbinns@uh.edu. *Dean,* John Bowen, 713-743-0209, Fax: 713-743-2482, E-mail: jbowen@uh.edu.

Cullen College of Engineering Students: 352 full-time (91 women), 232 part-time (43 women); includes 95 minority (16 African Americans, 47 Asian Americans or Pacific Islanders, 32 Hispanic Americans), 357 international. Average age 29. 688 applicants, 54% accepted, 145 enrolled. *Faculty:* 77 full-time (5 women), 18 part-time/adjunct (1 woman). Expenses: Contact institution. *Financial support:* In 2006–07, 20 fellowships with full tuition reimbursements (averaging $16,300 per year), 151 research assistantships with full tuition reimbursements (averaging $12,250 per year), 83 teaching assistantships with full tuition reimbursements (averaging $12,250 per year) were awarded; career-related internships or fieldwork, Federal Work-Study, institutionally sponsored loans, scholarships/grants, health care benefits, and unspecified assistantships also available. Support available to part-time students. Financial award application deadline: 3/10. In 2006, 167 master's, 42 doctorates awarded. *Degree program information:* Part-time and evening/weekend programs available. Offers aerospace engineering (MS, PhD); biomedical engineering (MS); chemical engineering (M Ch E, MS Ch E, PhD); civil and environmental engineering (MCE, MS Env E, MSCE, PhD); computer and systems engineering (MS, PhD); electrical and computer engineering (MEE, MSEE, PhD); engineering (M Ch E, MCE, MEE, MIE, MME, MS, MS Ch E, MS Env E, MSCE, MSEE, MSIE, MSME, PhD); environmental engineering (MS, PhD); industrial engineering (MIE, MSIE, PhD); materials engineering (MS, PhD); mechanical engineering (MME, MSME); petroleum engineering (MS). *Application deadline:* Applications are processed on a rolling basis. *Application fee:* $25 ($75 for international students). *Application Contact:* Dr. Larry

University of Houston (continued)

Witte, Associate Dean, Graduate Programs, 713-743-4205, Fax: 713-743-4214, E-mail: witte@uh.edu. *Dean,* Dr. Raymond W. Flumerfelt, 713-743-4207, Fax: 713-743-4214, E-mail: rwf@uh.edu.

Graduate School of Social Work Students: 204 full-time (173 women), 160 part-time (142 women); includes 172 minority (90 African Americans, 1 American Indian/Alaska Native, 15 Asian Americans or Pacific Islanders, 66 Hispanic Americans), 9 international. Average age 33. 251 applicants, 53% accepted, 119 enrolled. *Faculty:* 16 full-time (9 women), 15 part-time/adjunct (10 women). Expenses: Contact institution. *Financial support:* In 2006–07, 13 fellowships with full tuition reimbursements (averaging $12,850 per year), 8 research assistantships with full tuition reimbursements (averaging $8,800 per year), 4 teaching assistantships with full tuition reimbursements (averaging $8,800 per year) were awarded; career-related internships or fieldwork, Federal Work-Study, institutionally sponsored loans, scholarships/grants, health care benefits, and unspecified assistantships also available. Support available to part-time students. Financial award application deadline: 3/10; financial award applicants required to submit FAFSA. In 2006, 114 master's, 6 doctorates awarded. *Degree program information:* Part-time programs available. Offers social work (MSW, PhD). *Application deadline:* For fall admission, 3/1 priority date for domestic students. Applications are processed on a rolling basis. *Application fee:* $50 ($125 for international students). *Application Contact:* Colen Skinner, Admissions Office, 713-743-8078, Fax: 713-743-8149, E-mail: cskinner@mail.uh.edu. *Dean,* Dr. Ira C. Colby, 713-743-8085, Fax: 713-743-3267, E-mail: icolby@uh.edu.

Law Center Students: 849 full-time (371 women), 247 part-time (107 women); includes 267 minority (45 African Americans, 11 American Indian/Alaska Native, 115 Asian Americans or Pacific Islanders, 96 Hispanic Americans), 26 international. Average age 28. 991 applicants, 98% accepted, 313 enrolled. *Faculty:* 40 full-time (8 women), 51 part-time/adjunct (14 women). Expenses: Contact institution. *Financial support:* In 2006–07, 691 students received support; fellowships with full tuition reimbursements available, research assistantships with full tuition reimbursements available, teaching assistantships with full tuition reimbursements available, career-related internships or fieldwork, Federal Work-Study, institutionally sponsored loans, scholarships/grants, health care benefits, and unspecified assistantships available. Support available to part-time students. Financial award application deadline: 3/10; financial award applicants required to submit FAFSA. In 2006, 312 JDs, 49 master's awarded. *Degree program information:* Part-time and evening/weekend programs available. Offers law (JD, LL M). *Application deadline:* For fall admission, 2/15 priority date for domestic students. Applications are processed on a rolling basis. *Application fee:* $50 ($75 for international students). Electronic applications accepted. *Application Contact:* Sondra B. Tennessee, Assistant Dean for Admissions, 713-743-2181. *Interim Dean,* Raymond Nimmer, 713-743-2100, Fax: 713-743-2122, E-mail: rnimmer@uh.edu.

UNIVERSITY OF HOUSTON–CLEAR LAKE, Houston, TX 77058-1098

General Information State-supported, coed, upper-level institution. CGS member. *Enrollment:* 1,113 full-time matriculated graduate/professional students (676 women), 2,438 part-time matriculated graduate/professional students (1,559 women). *Enrollment by degree level:* 3,551 master's. *Graduate faculty:* 154 full-time (65 women), 120 part-time/adjunct (56 women). *Graduate housing:* Rooms and/or apartments available on a first-come, first-served basis to single students and available to married students. *Student services:* Campus employment opportunities, campus safety program, career counseling, disabled student services, exercise/wellness program, free psychological counseling, international student services, low-cost health insurance, multicultural affairs office, teacher training, writing training. *Library facilities:* Neumann Library. *Online resources:* library catalog, access to other libraries' catalogs. *Collection:* 650,000 titles, 984 serial subscriptions, 795 audiovisual materials. *Research affiliation:* NASA–Johnson Space Center (computer science, computer engineering), Baylor College of Medicine (life sciences), NABI (biological sciences, life sciences), Smith Kline Beecham Corp. (biological sciences, life sciences), Welch Foundation (chemistry), Tietronix Software Corp. (computer science, computer engineering).

Computer facilities: 383 computers available on campus for general student use. A campuswide network can be accessed from off campus. Internet access and online class registration are available. *Web address:* http://www.uhcl.edu/.

General Application Contact: Janis S. Bigelow, Assistant Director of Admissions, Recruitment and Communications, 281-283-2540, Fax: 281-283-2530, E-mail: bigelow@uhcl.edu.

GRADUATE UNITS

School of Business Students: 385 full-time, 440 part-time; includes 235 minority (64 African Americans, 2 American Indian/Alaska Native, 102 Asian Americans or Pacific Islanders, 67 Hispanic Americans), 197 international. Average age 31. 629 applicants, 53% accepted, 206 enrolled. Expenses: Contact institution. *Financial support:* Fellowships, research assistantships, teaching assistantships, career-related internships or fieldwork, Federal Work-Study, institutionally sponsored loans, and scholarships/grants available. Support available to part-time students. Financial award application deadline: 5/1; financial award applicants required to submit FAFSA. In 2006, 282 degrees awarded. *Degree program information:* Part-time and evening/weekend programs available. Offers accounting (MS); business (MA, MBA, MHA, MS); business administration (MBA); environmental management (MS); finance (MS); healthcare administration (MHA); human resource management (MA); management information systems (MS); professional accounting (MS). *Application deadline:* For fall admission, 8/1 for domestic students, 6/1 for international students; for spring admission, 12/1 for domestic students, 10/1 for international students. Applications are processed on a rolling basis. *Application fee:* $35 ($75 for international students). Electronic applications accepted. *Application Contact:* Janis S. Bigelow, Assistant Director of Admissions, Recruitment and Communications, 281-283-2540, Fax: 281-283-2530, E-mail: bigelow@uhcl.edu. *Dean,* Dr. Wm. Theodore Cummings, 281-283-3102, Fax: 281-283-3951, E-mail: cummings@uhcl.edu.

School of Education Students: 266 full-time (214 women), 1,067 part-time (858 women); includes 504 minority (236 African Americans, 7 American Indian/Alaska Native, 31 Asian Americans or Pacific Islanders, 230 Hispanic Americans), 30 international. Average age 36. *Faculty:* 40 full-time (29 women), 42 part-time/adjunct (23 women). Expenses: Contact institution. *Financial support:* Career-related internships or fieldwork, Federal Work-Study, institutionally sponsored loans, and scholarships/grants available. Support available to part-time students. Financial award application deadline: 5/1; financial award applicants required to submit FAFSA. In 2006, 331 degrees awarded. *Degree program information:* Part-time and evening/weekend programs available. Offers counseling (MS); curriculum and instruction (MS); early childhood education (MS); education (MS, Ed D); educational leadership (Ed D); educational management (MS); instructional technology (MS); multicultural studies (MS); reading (MS); school library and information science (MS). *Application deadline:* For fall admission, 7/1 for domestic students, 6/1 for international students; for spring admission, 10/1 for domestic and international students. Applications are processed on a rolling basis. *Application fee:* $35 ($75 for international students). Electronic applications accepted. *Application Contact:* Janis S. Bigelow, Assistant Director of Admissions, Recruitment and Communications, 281-283-2540, Fax: 281-283-2530, E-mail: bigelow@uhcl.edu. *Dean,* Dr. Dennis Spuck, 281-283-3501, Fax: 281-283-3599, E-mail: spuck@uhcl.edu.

School of Human Sciences and Humanities Students: 339 full-time (245 women), 622 part-time (392 women); includes 320 minority (164 African Americans, 3 American Indian/Alaska Native, 34 Asian Americans or Pacific Islanders, 119 Hispanic Americans), 30 international. Average age 34. *Faculty:* 65 full-time (31 women), 55 part-time/adjunct (34 women). Expenses: Contact institution. *Financial support:* Fellowships, research assistantships, teaching assistantships, career-related internships or fieldwork, Federal Work-Study, institutionally sponsored loans, and scholarships/grants available. Support available to part-time students. Financial award application deadline: 5/1; financial award applicants required to submit FAFSA. In 2006, 224 degrees awarded. *Degree program information:* Part-time and evening/weekend programs available. Offers behavioral sciences (MA); clinical psychology (MA); criminology (MA); cross-cultural studies (MA); family therapy (MA); fitness and human performance (MA); history (MA); human sciences and humanities (MA); humanities (MA); literature (MA); school psychology (MA). *Application deadline:* For fall admission, 7/1 for domestic students, 6/1 for international students; for spring admission, 10/1 for domestic and international students. Applications are processed on a rolling basis. *Application fee:* $35 ($75 for international students). *Application Contact:* Janis S. Bigelow, Assistant Director of Admissions, Recruitment and Communications, 281-283-2540, Fax: 281-283-2530, E-mail: bigelow@uhcl.edu. *Dean,* Dr. Bruce Palmer, 281-283-3301, E-mail: palmer@cl.uh.edu.

School of Science and Computer Engineering Students: 418 (142 women). Average age 32. *Faculty:* 115 full-time (28 women), 65 part-time/adjunct. Expenses: Contact institution. *Financial support:* In 2006–07, 6 fellowships, 14 research assistantships, 95 teaching assistantships were awarded; career-related internships or fieldwork, Federal Work-Study, institutionally sponsored loans, and scholarships/grants also available. Support available to part-time students. Financial award application deadline: 5/1; financial award applicants required to submit FAFSA. In 2006, 146 degrees awarded. *Degree program information:* Part-time and evening/weekend programs available. Offers biological sciences (MS); biotechnology (MS); chemistry (MS); computer engineering (MS); computer information systems (MS); computer science (MS); environmental science (MS); mathematical sciences (MS); physics (MS); science and computer engineering (MS); software engineering (MS); statistics (MS); system engineering (MS). *Application deadline:* For fall admission, 8/1 for domestic students, 6/1 for international students; for spring admission, 12/1 for domestic students, 10/1 for international students. Applications are processed on a rolling basis. *Application fee:* $35 ($75 for international students). *Application Contact:* Dr. Robert Ferebee, Associate Dean, 281-283-3700, Fax: 281-283-3707, E-mail: ferebee@uhcl.edu. *Interim Dean,* Dr. Sadegh Davari, 281-283-3703, Fax: 281-283-3707.

UNIVERSITY OF HOUSTON–DOWNTOWN, Houston, TX 77002-1001

General Information State-supported, coed, comprehensive institution. *Library facilities:* W. I. Dykes Library. *Online resources:* library catalog, web page, access to other libraries' catalogs. *Collection:* 296,000 titles, 1,700 serial subscriptions, 1,900 audiovisual materials.

Computer facilities: 1,200 computers available on campus for general student use. A campuswide network can be accessed from off campus. Internet access and online class registration are available. *Web address:* http://www.uhd.edu/.

General Application Contact: Graduate Admissions, 713-221-8522, Fax: 713-221-8658, E-mail: gradadmissions@uhd.edu.

GRADUATE UNITS

Graduate Programs Expenses: Contact institution. *Financial support:* Scholarships/grants available. Financial award application deadline: 4/1. *Application fee:* $35. *Coordinator of Graduate Admissions,* Yolanda Salinas, 713-221-8522.

UNIVERSITY OF HOUSTON–VICTORIA, Victoria, TX 77901-4450

General Information State-supported, coed, upper-level institution. *Enrollment:* 2,652 graduate, professional, and undergraduate students; 252 full-time matriculated graduate/professional students (153 women), 1,085 part-time matriculated graduate/professional students (692 women). *Enrollment by degree level:* 1,337 master's. *Graduate faculty:* 73 full-time (27 women). Tuition, state resident: full-time $3,168; part-time $176 per semester hour. Tuition, nonresident: full-time $7,218; part-time $401 per semester hour. *Required fees:* $756; $42 per semester hour. Tuition and fees vary according to course load. *Graduate housing:* On-campus housing not available. *Student services:* Campus employment opportunities, campus safety program, career counseling, disabled student services, exercise/wellness program, grant writing training, international student services, low-cost health insurance, teacher training, writing training. *Library facilities:* VC/UHV Library plus 1 other. *Online resources:* library catalog, web page, access to other libraries' catalogs. *Collection:* 50,000 titles, 70,000 serial subscriptions, 12,773 audiovisual materials.

Computer facilities: 150 computers available on campus for general student use. A campuswide network can be accessed from off campus. Internet access and online class registration are available. *Web address:* http://www.uhv.edu/.

General Application Contact: Admissions and Records, 361-570-4114, E-mail: admissions@uhv.edu.

GRADUATE UNITS

School of Arts and Sciences Students: 46 full-time (26 women), 142 part-time (88 women); includes 74 minority (22 African Americans, 1 American Indian/Alaska Native, 16 Asian Americans or Pacific Islanders, 35 Hispanic Americans), 11 international. *Faculty:* 22 full-time (4 women). Expenses: Contact institution. *Financial support:* In 2006–07, research assistantships with partial tuition reimbursements (averaging $2,000 per year), teaching assistantships with partial tuition reimbursements (averaging $2,000 per year) were awarded; career-related internships or fieldwork, Federal Work-Study, scholarships/grants, and unspecified assistantships also available. Support available to part-time students. Financial award application deadline: 4/15. In 2006, 28 master's awarded. *Degree program information:* Part-time and evening/weekend programs available. Postbaccalaureate distance learning degree programs offered (no on-campus study). Offers arts and sciences (MA, MAIS, MS); coputer science (MS); interdisciplinary studies (MAIS); psychology (MA). *Application deadline:* Applications are processed on a rolling basis. *Application fee:* $0. Electronic applications accepted. *Interim Dean,* Dr. Jeffrey Dileo, 361-570-4200, Fax: 361-570-4229, E-mail: dileoj@uhv.edu.

School of Business Administration Students: 144 full-time (75 women), 504 part-time (251 women); includes 356 minority (133 African Americans, 4 American Indian/Alaska Native, 144 Asian Americans or Pacific Islanders, 75 Hispanic Americans), 26 international. Average age 34. *Faculty:* 25 full-time (5 women). Expenses: Contact institution. *Financial support:* In 2006–07, research assistantships with partial tuition reimbursements (averaging $2,000 per year), teaching assistantships with partial tuition reimbursements (averaging $2,000 per year) were awarded; career-related internships or fieldwork, Federal Work-Study, scholarships/grants, and unspecified assistantships also available. Support available to part-time students. Financial award application deadline: 4/15; financial award applicants required to submit FAFSA. In 2006, 158 degrees awarded. *Degree program information:* Part-time and evening/weekend programs available. Postbaccalaureate distance learning degree programs offered (no on-campus study). Offers business administration (MBA). *Application deadline:* For fall admission, 6/1 for international students; for spring admission, 10/1 for international students. Applications are processed on a rolling basis. *Application fee:* $0. Electronic applications accepted. *Application Contact:* Rosie McCusker, Recruitment Coordinator, 832-842-2858, E-mail: mccuskerr@uhv.edu. *Dean,* Charles Bullock, 361-570-4230, Fax: 361-570-4229, E-mail: bullockc@uhv.edu.

School of Education and Human Development Students: 62 full-time (52 women), 439 part-time (353 women); includes 184 minority (112 African Americans, 1 American Indian/Alaska Native, 13 Asian Americans or Pacific Islanders, 58 Hispanic Americans), 2 international. Average age 38. *Faculty:* 22 full-time (15 women). Expenses: Contact institution. *Financial support:* In 2006–07, research assistantships with partial tuition reimbursements (averaging $2,000 per year), teaching assistantships with partial tuition reimbursements (averaging $2,000 per year) were awarded; career-related internships or fieldwork, Federal Work-Study, scholarships/grants, and unspecified assistantships also available. Support available to part-time students. Financial award application deadline: 4/15. In 2006, 125 degrees awarded. *Degree program information:* Part-time and evening/weekend programs available. Postbaccalaureate distance learning degree programs offered (no on-campus study). Offers education (M Ed). *Application deadline:* Applications are processed on a rolling basis. *Application fee:* $0. Electronic applications accepted. *Dean,* Dr. John Stansell, 361-570-4260, Fax: 361-570-4257, E-mail: stansell@uhv.edu.

UNIVERSITY OF IDAHO, Moscow, ID 83844-2282

General Information State-supported, coed, university. CGS member. *Enrollment:* 11,739 graduate, professional, and undergraduate students; 1,246 full-time matriculated graduate/professional students (536 women), 1,099 part-time matriculated graduate/professional students (513 women). *Enrollment by degree level:* 312 first professional, 1,357 master's, 556 doctoral, 120 other advanced degrees. *Graduate faculty:* 407 full-time (96 women), 130 part-time/

adjunct (23 women). Tuition, nonresident: full-time $9,600; part-time $140 per credit. *Required fees:* $4,740; $227 per credit. *Graduate housing:* Rooms and/or apartments available on a first-come, first-served basis to single and married students. Typical cost: $7,236 (including board) for single students. Room and board charges vary according to board plan. *Student services:* Campus employment opportunities, campus safety program, career counseling, child daycare facilities, disabled student services, exercise/wellness program, free psychological counseling, grant writing training, international student services, low-cost health insurance, multicultural affairs office, writing training. *Library facilities:* University of Idaho Library plus 1 other. *Online resources:* library catalog, web page, access to other libraries' catalogs. *Collection:* 1.4 million titles, 14,230 serial subscriptions, 8,717 audiovisual materials. *Research affiliation:* Inland Northwest Research Alliance (INRA), Idaho Nuclear Environmental Engineering Laboratory, Battelle Pacific Northwest Laboratories, Snake River Conservation Research Center, Idaho Research Foundation, Idaho Mining and Materials Resources Research Institute.

Computer facilities: Computer purchase and lease plans are available. 670 computers available on campus for general student use. A campuswide network can be accessed from student residence rooms and from off campus. Internet access and online class registration, student evaluations of teaching are available. *Web address:* http://www.uidaho.edu/.

General Application Contact: Dr. Margrit von Braun, Associate Dean of the College of Graduate Studies, 208-885-6243, Fax: 208-885-6198, E-mail: uigrad@uidaho.edu.

GRADUATE UNITS

College of Graduate Studies Students: 1,198 full-time (485 women), 1,319 part-time (596 women). Expenses: Contact institution. *Financial support:* Fellowships, research assistantships, teaching assistantships, career-related internships or fieldwork, Federal Work-Study, institutionally sponsored loans, scholarships/grants, and tuition waivers (full and partial) available. Support available to part-time students. Financial award application deadline: 2/15. Offers architecture and interior design (M Arch, MS); art (MFA); art and architecture (M Arch, MAT, MFA, MS); art education (MAT); bioinformatics and computational biology (MS, PhD); landscape architecture (MS); neuroscience (MS, PhD). *Application deadline:* For fall admission, 8/1 for domestic students; for spring admission, 12/15 for domestic students. Applications are processed on a rolling basis. *Application fee:* $55 ($60 for international students). *Associate Dean,* Dr. Margrit von Braun, 208-885-6243, Fax: 208-885-6198, E-mail: uigrad@uidaho.edu.

College of Agricultural and Life Sciences Students: 171. Expenses: Contact institution. *Financial support:* Research assistantships, teaching assistantships, career-related internships or fieldwork and Federal Work-Study available. Support available to part-time students. Financial award application deadline: 2/15. In 2006, 37 master's, 18 doctorates awarded. Offers agricultural and life sciences (M Engr, MS, PhD); agricultural economics (MS); agricultural education (MS); animal physiology (PhD); animal science (MS); biological and agricultural engineering (M Engr, MS, PhD); education (PhD); entomology (MS, PhD); family and consumer sciences (MS); food science (MS, PhD); microbiology, molecular biology and biochemistry (MS, PhD); plant science (MS, PhD); soil and land resources (MS, PhD); veterinary science (MS). *Application deadline:* For fall admission, 8/1 for domestic students; for spring admission, 12/15 for domestic students. *Application fee:* $55 ($60 for international students). *Dean,* Dr. John Hammel, 208-885-6681.

College of Business and Economics Students: 15. Expenses: Contact institution. *Financial support:* Research assistantships, teaching assistantships, Federal Work-Study and scholarships/grants available. Support available to part-time students. Financial award application deadline: 2/15. In 2006, 16 degrees awarded. Offers accounting (M Acct); business and economics (M Acct). *Application deadline:* For fall admission, 8/1 for domestic students; for spring admission, 12/15 for domestic students. *Application fee:* $55 ($60 for international students). *Dean,* Dr. John Morris, 208-885-6478.

College of Education Students: 168 full-time (92 women), 490 part-time (310 women). Expenses: Contact institution. *Financial support:* Teaching assistantships, Federal Work-Study available. Support available to part-time students. Financial award application deadline: 2/15. In 2006, 255 master's, 50 doctorates, 62 other advanced degrees awarded. Offers adult and organizational learning (MS, Ed D, PhD, Ed S); counseliing and human services (PhD); counseling and human services (M Ed, MS, Ed D, Ed S); curriculm and intstruction (Ed D); curriculum and instruction (PhD); education (M Ed, MS, Ed D, PhD, Ed S, Ed Sp PTE); educational leadership (M Ed, MS, Ed D, PhD, Ed S); physical education (M Ed, MS, PhD); professional-technical and technology education (M Ed, MS, PhD, Ed Sp PTE); professional-technical and tecnology education (Ed D); recreation (MS); school psychology (Ed S); special education (M Ed, MS, Ed S). *Application deadline:* For fall admission, 8/1 for domestic students; for spring admission, 12/15 for domestic students. *Application fee:* $55 ($60 for international students). *Dean,* Dr. Paul Rowland, 208-885-6773.

College of Engineering Students: 368 (44 women). Expenses: Contact institution. *Financial support:* Fellowships, research assistantships, teaching assistantships, career-related internships or fieldwork and Federal Work-Study available. Support available to part-time students. Financial award application deadline: 2/15. In 2006, 102 master's, 14 doctorates awarded. Offers chemical engineering (M Engr, MS, PhD); civil engineering (M Engr, MS, PhD); computer engineering (M Engr, MS); computer science (MS, PhD); electrical engineering (M Engr, MS, PhD); engineering (M Engr, MS, PhD); environmental engineering (M Engr, MS); geological engineering (MS); materials science and engineering (MS, PhD); mechanical engineering (M Engr, MS, PhD); metallurgical engineering (MS); nuclear engineering (M Engr, MS, PhD); systems engineering (M Engr). *Application deadline:* For fall admission, 8/1 for domestic students; for spring admission, 12/15 for domestic students. *Application fee:* $55 ($60 for international students). *Dean,* Dr. Aicha Elshabini, 208-885-6470.

College of Letters, Arts and Social Sciences Students: 281 (137 women). Expenses: Contact institution. *Financial support:* Fellowships, research assistantships, teaching assistantships, Federal Work-Study available. Support available to part-time students. Financial award application deadline: 2/15. In 2006, 77 master's, 2 doctorates awarded. Offers anthropology (MA); creative writing (MFA); English (MA, MAT); environmental science (MS, PhD); history (MA, MAT, PhD); interdisciplinary studies (MA, MS); letters, arts and social sciences (M Mus, MA, MAT, MFA, MPA, MS, PhD); music (M Mus, MA); political science (MA, PhD); psychology (MS); public administration (MPA); teaching English as a second language (MA); theatre arts (MFA). *Application deadline:* For fall admission, 8/1 for domestic students; for spring admission, 12/15 for domestic students. *Application fee:* $55 ($60 for international students). *Dean,* Dr. Katherine Aiken, 208-885-7885.

College of Natural Resources Students: 174 (80 women). Expenses: Contact institution. *Financial support:* Fellowships, research assistantships, teaching assistantships, Federal Work-Study available. Support available to part-time students. Financial award application deadline: 2/15. In 2006, 45 master's, 13 doctorates awarded. Offers conservation social sciences (MS); fish and wildlife resources (MS); fishery resources (MS); forest products (MS); forest resources (MS); natural resources (MNR, PhD); natural resources management and administration (MNR); rangeland ecology and management (MS); wildlife resources (MS). *Application deadline:* For fall admission, 8/1 for domestic students; for spring admission, 12/15 for domestic students. *Application fee:* $55 ($60 for international students). *Application Contact:* Dr. Ali Moslemi, Graduate Coordinator, 208-885-6126. *Dean,* Steven B. Daley-Laursen, 208-885-6442, Fax: 208-885-6226.

College of Science Students: 192 (69 women). Expenses: Contact institution. In 2006, 45 master's, 12 doctorates awarded. Offers biological sciences (M Nat Sci); chemistry (MAT, MS, PhD); earth science (MAT); geography (MAT, MS, PhD); geology (MS, PhD); hydrology (MS); mathematics (MAT, MS, PhD); physics (MS, PhD); physics education (MAT); science (M Nat Sci, MAT, MS, PhD); statistics (MS). *Application fee:* $55 ($60 for international students). *Dean,* Judith Totman Parrish, 208-885-6195.

College of Law Students: 313 (130 women). Average age 29. Expenses: Contact institution. *Financial support:* Career-related internships or fieldwork, Federal Work-Study, and institutionally sponsored loans available. Financial award application deadline: 2/15. In 2006, 84 degrees awarded. Offers law (JD). *Application deadline:* For fall admission, 2/1 for domestic students. *Application fee:* $55 ($60 for international students). *Dean,* Donald L. Burnett, 208-885-4977.

UNIVERSITY OF ILLINOIS AT CHICAGO, Chicago, IL 60607-7128

General Information State-supported, coed, university. CGS member. *Graduate housing:* Room and/or apartments available on a first-come, first-served basis to single students; on-campus housing not available to married students. Housing application deadline: 3/1. *Research affiliation:* U.S. Department of Energy National Laboratories (physics, environment, computational science), National Surgical Adjuvant Breast and Bowel Project (prevention of breast cancer), Chicago Manufacturing Technology Extension Center (manufacturing research and development, industrial research), Eastern Cooperative Oncology Group (clinical cancer research).

GRADUATE UNITS

College of Dentistry Offers dentistry (DDS, MS); oral sciences (MS). Electronic applications accepted.

College of Medicine *Degree program information:* Part-time programs available. Offers anatomy and cell biology (MS, PhD); biochemistry and molecular biology (MS, PhD); cellular and systems neuroscience and cell biology (PhD); genetics (PhD); health professions education (MHPE); medicine (MD, MHPE, MS, PhD); microbiology and immunology (PhD); molecular genetics (PhD); neuroscience (PhD); pharmacology (PhD); physiology and biophysics (MS, PhD); surgery (MS).

College of Pharmacy Offers forensic science (MS); medicinal chemistry (MS, PhD); pharmaceutics (MS, PhD); pharmacodynamics (MS, PhD); pharmacognosy (MS, PhD); pharmacy (Pharm D, MS, PhD); pharmacy administration (MS, PhD).

Center for Pharmaceutical Biotechnology Offers pharmaceutical biotechnology (MS, PhD).

Graduate College *Degree program information:* Part-time and evening/weekend programs available. Postbaccalaureate distance learning degree programs offered. Offers neuroscience (PhD). Electronic applications accepted.

College of Applied Health Sciences *Degree program information:* Part-time programs available. Offers applied health sciences (MAMS, MS, PhD); biomedical visualization (MAMS); disability and human development (MS); disability studies (PhD); human nutrition and dietetics (MS, PhD); movement sciences (MS); occupational therapy (MS); physical therapy (MS). Electronic applications accepted.

College of Architecture and Art *Degree program information:* Part-time and evening/weekend programs available. Offers architecture (M Arch); architecture and art (M Arch, MA, MFA, PhD); art history (MA, PhD); electronic visualization (MFA); film animation (MFA); graphic design (MFA); industrial design (MFA); photography (MFA); studio arts (MFA). Electronic applications accepted.

College of Education *Degree program information:* Part-time and evening/weekend programs available. Offers curriculum and instruction (PhD); education (M Ed, PhD); educational psychology (PhD); instructional leadership (M Ed); leadership and administration (M Ed); policy and administration (PhD); policy studies in urban education (PhD); special education (M Ed, PhD). Electronic applications accepted.

College of Engineering *Degree program information:* Part-time and evening/weekend programs available. Offers bioengineering (MS, PhD); chemical engineering (MS, PhD); civil and materials engineering (MS, PhD); computer science (MS, PhD); electrical and computer engineering (MS, PhD); engineering (MS, PhD); industrial engineering (MS); industrial engineering and operations research (PhD); mechanical engineering (MS, PhD). Electronic applications accepted.

College of Liberal Arts and Sciences *Degree program information:* Part-time and evening/weekend programs available. Offers anthropology (MA, PhD); applied linguistics (teaching English as a second language) (MA); applied mathematics (MS, DA, PhD); cell and developmental biology (PhD); chemistry (MS, PhD); communication (MA); computer science (MS, DA, PhD); criminal justice (MA); crystallography (MS, PhD); ecology and evolution (MS, DA, PhD); English (MA, PhD); environmental and urban geography (MA); environmental geology (MS, PhD); environmental studies (MA); French (MA); genetics and development (PhD); geochemistry (MS, PhD); geology (MS, PhD); geomorphology (MS, PhD); geophysics (MS, PhD); geotechnical engineering and geosciences (PhD); Germanic studies (MA, PhD); Hispanic studies (MA, PhD); history (MA, MAT, PhD); hydrogeology (MS, PhD); language, literacy, and rhetoric (PhD); liberal arts and sciences (MA, MAT, MS, MST, DA, PhD); linguistics (MA); low-temperature and organic geochemistry (MS, PhD); mass communication (MA); math and information science for the industry (MS); mineralogy (MS, PhD); molecular biology (MS, PhD); neurobiology (MS, PhD); paleoclimatology (MS, PhD); paleontology (MS, PhD); petrology (MS, PhD); philosophy (MA, PhD); physics (MS, PhD); plant biology (MS, DA, PhD); political science (MA, PhD); probability and statistics (MS, DA, PhD); psychology (PhD); pure mathematics (MS, DA, PhD); quaternary geology (MS, PhD); sedimentology (MS, PhD); Slavic languages and literatures (PhD); Slavic studies (MA); sociology (MA, PhD); teaching of mathematics (MST); urban geography (MA); water resources (MS, PhD). Electronic applications accepted.

College of Nursing *Degree program information:* Part-time programs available. Offers maternity nursing/nurse midwifery (MS); nursing (MS, PhD); nursing research (PhD); nursing science (PhD); nursing sciences (medical surgical) (MS); nursing sciences (nursing administration) (MS); nursing sciences (psychiatric nursing) (MS); nursing sciences (public health nursing) (MS); pediatric nursing (MS); perinatal nursing (MS). Electronic applications accepted.

College of Urban Planning and Public Affairs *Degree program information:* Part-time and evening/weekend programs available. Offers public administration (MPA, PhD); public policy analysis (PhD); urban planning and policy (MUPP); urban planning and public affairs (MPA, MUPP, PhD). Electronic applications accepted.

Jane Addams College of Social Work *Degree program information:* Part-time programs available. Offers social work (MSW, PhD). Electronic applications accepted.

Liautaud Graduate School of Business *Degree program information:* Part-time and evening/weekend programs available. Offers accounting (MS); business administration (MA, MBA, MS, PhD); economics (MA, PhD); management information systems (MS, PhD); public policy analysis (PhD). Electronic applications accepted.

School of Public Health *Degree program information:* Part-time programs available. Offers biostatistics (MS, PhD); community health sciences (MPH, MS, Dr PH, PhD); environmental and occupational health sciences (MPH, MS, Dr PH, PhD); epidemiology (MPH, MS, Dr PH, PhD); health policy administration (MPH, MS, Dr PH, PhD). Electronic applications accepted.

UNIVERSITY OF ILLINOIS AT SPRINGFIELD, Springfield, IL 62703-5407

General Information State-supported, coed, comprehensive institution. CGS member. *Enrollment:* 4,761 graduate, professional, and undergraduate students; 508 full-time matriculated graduate/professional students (245 women), 1,246 part-time matriculated graduate/professional students (736 women). *Enrollment by degree level:* 1,734 master's, 20 doctoral. *Graduate faculty:* 180 full-time (71 women), 50 part-time/adjunct (19 women). Tuition, state resident: full-time $4,722; part-time $197 per credit hour. Tuition, nonresident: full-time $12,558; part-time $523 per credit hour. *Required fees:* $1,614; $8 per credit hour. $597 per term. *Graduate housing:* Rooms and/or apartments available on a first-come, first-served basis to single and married students. Housing application deadline: 6/30. *Student services:* Campus employment opportunities, campus safety program, career counseling, child daycare facilities, disabled student services, exercise/wellness program, free psychological counseling, international student services, low-cost health insurance, multicultural affairs office, teacher training, writing training. *Library facilities:* Norris L. Brookens Library. *Online resources:* library catalog, web page, access to other libraries' catalogs. *Collection:* 550,249 titles, 39,357 serial subscriptions, 41,839 audiovisual materials. *Research affiliation:* Interuniversity Consortium for Political and Social Research, Council of Undergraduate Research.

Computer facilities: Computer purchase and lease plans are available. 132 computers available on campus for general student use. A campuswide network can be accessed from student residence rooms and from off campus. Internet access and online class registration are available. *Web address:* http://www.uis.edu/.

University of Illinois at Springfield (continued)

General Application Contact: Dr. Lynn Pardie, Office of Graduate Studies, 800-252-8533, Fax: 217-206-7623, E-mail: pardie.lynn@uis.edu.

GRADUATE UNITS

Graduate Programs Students: 508 full-time (245 women), 1,246 part-time (736 women); includes 183 minority (114 African Americans, 4 American Indian/Alaska Native, 42 Asian Americans or Pacific Islanders, 23 Hispanic Americans), 287 international. Average age 32. 1,689 applicants, 71% accepted, 613 enrolled. *Faculty:* 180 full-time (71 women), 50 part-time/adjunct (19 women). Expenses: Contact institution. *Financial support:* In 2006–07, research assistantships with full tuition reimbursements (averaging $7,425 per year), teaching assistantships with full tuition reimbursements (averaging $7,425 per year) were awarded; career-related internships or fieldwork, Federal Work-Study, scholarships/grants, health care benefits, and unspecified assistantships also available. Support available to part-time students. Financial award application deadline: 11/15; financial award applicants required to submit FAFSA. In 2006, 463 master's, 2 doctorates awarded. *Degree program information:* Part-time and evening/weekend programs available. Postbaccalaureate distance learning degree programs offered (no on-campus study). *Application fee:* $50 ($60 for international students). Electronic applications accepted. *Office of Graduate Studies*, Dr. Lynn Pardie, 800-252-8533, Fax: 217-206-7623, E-mail: pardie.lynn@uis.edu.

College of Business and Management Students: 97 full-time (39 women), 240 part-time (102 women); includes 49 minority (19 African Americans, 2 American Indian/Alaska Native, 22 Asian Americans or Pacific Islanders, 6 Hispanic Americans), 25 international. Average age 33. 241 applicants, 65% accepted, 88 enrolled. *Faculty:* 27 full-time (7 women), 2 part-time/adjunct (1 woman). Expenses: Contact institution. *Financial support:* In 2006–07, research assistantships with full tuition reimbursements (averaging $7,425 per year), teaching assistantships with full tuition reimbursements (averaging $7,425 per year) were awarded; career-related internships or fieldwork, Federal Work-Study, scholarships/grants, health care benefits, and unspecified assistantships also available. Support available to part-time students. Financial award application deadline: 11/15; financial award applicants required to submit FAFSA. In 2006, 109 degrees awarded. *Degree program information:* Part-time and evening/weekend programs available. Postbaccalaureate distance learning degree programs offered (no on-campus study). Offers accountancy (MA); business administration (MBA); business and management (MA, MBA, MS); management information systems (MS). *Application deadline:* Applications are processed on a rolling basis. *Application fee:* $50 ($60 for international students). Electronic applications accepted. *Dean*, Dr. Ronald McNeil, 217-206-6534, Fax: 217-206-7543, E-mail: mcneil.ronald@uis.edu.

College of Education and Human Services Students: 63 full-time (55 women), 500 part-time (368 women); includes 48 minority (38 African Americans, 1 American Indian/Alaska Native, 6 Asian Americans or Pacific Islanders, 3 Hispanic Americans), 3 international. Average age 35. 194 applicants, 58% accepted, 96 enrolled. *Faculty:* 22 full-time (12 women), 29 part-time/adjunct (15 women). Expenses: Contact institution. *Financial support:* In 2006–07, research assistantships with full tuition reimbursements (averaging $7,425 per year), teaching assistantships with full tuition reimbursements (averaging $7,425 per year) were awarded; career-related internships or fieldwork, Federal Work-Study, scholarships/grants, health care benefits, and unspecified assistantships also available. Support available to part-time students. Financial award application deadline: 11/15; financial award applicants required to submit FAFSA. In 2006, 163 degrees awarded. *Degree program information:* Part-time and evening/weekend programs available. Postbaccalaureate distance learning degree programs offered (no on-campus study). Offers alcoholism and substance abuse (MA); child and family services (MA); education and human services (MA); educational leadership (MA); gerontology (MA); human development counseling (MA); social services administration (MA); teacher leadership (MA). *Application fee:* $50 ($60 for international students). Electronic applications accepted. *Dean*, Dr. Larry Stonecipher, 217-206-7815, Fax: 217-206-6775, E-mail: stonecipher.larry@uis.edu.

College of Liberal Arts and Sciences Students: 185 full-time (69 women), 289 part-time (135 women); includes 22 minority (14 African Americans, 1 American Indian/Alaska Native, 6 Asian Americans or Pacific Islanders, 1 Hispanic American), 225 international. Average age 29. 551 applicants, 64% accepted, 127 enrolled. *Faculty:* 47 full-time (19 women), 2 part-time/adjunct (0 women). Expenses: Contact institution. *Financial support:* In 2006–07, research assistantships with full tuition reimbursements (averaging $7,425 per year), teaching assistantships with full tuition reimbursements (averaging $7,425 per year) were awarded; career-related internships or fieldwork, Federal Work-Study, scholarships/grants, health care benefits, tuition waivers (full and partial), and unspecified assistantships also available. Support available to part-time students. Financial award application deadline: 11/15; financial award applicants required to submit FAFSA. In 2006, 85 degrees awarded. *Degree program information:* Part-time and evening/weekend programs available. Postbaccalaureate distance learning degree programs offered (no on-campus study). Offers biology (MS); communication (MA); computer science (MS); English (MA); history (MA); interdisciplinary studies (MA); liberal arts and sciences (MA, MS). *Application fee:* $50 ($60 for international students). Electronic applications accepted. *Dean*, Dr. Margot Duley, 217-206-6512, Fax: 217-206-6217, E-mail: duley.margot@uis.edu.

College of Public Affairs and Administration Students: 163 full-time (82 women), 217 part-time (131 women); includes 64 minority (43 African Americans, 8 Asian Americans or Pacific Islanders, 13 Hispanic Americans), 34 international. Average age 31. 373 applicants, 94% accepted, 128 enrolled. *Faculty:* 30 full-time (12 women), 17 part-time/adjunct (3 women). Expenses: Contact institution. *Financial support:* In 2006–07, research assistantships with full tuition reimbursements (averaging $7,425 per year), teaching assistantships with full tuition reimbursements (averaging $7,425 per year) were awarded; career-related internships or fieldwork, Federal Work-Study, scholarships/grants, health care benefits, and unspecified assistantships also available. Support available to part-time students. Financial award application deadline: 11/15; financial award applicants required to submit FAFSA. In 2006, 106 master's, 2 doctorates awarded. *Degree program information:* Part-time and evening/weekend programs available. Offers environmental science (MS); environmental studies (MA); legal studies (MA); political studies (MA); public administration (MPA, DPA); public affairs and administration (MA, MPA, MPH, MS, DPA); public affairs reporting (MA); public health (MPH). *Application deadline:* Applications are processed on a rolling basis. *Application fee:* $50 ($60 for international students). Electronic applications accepted. *Dean*, Dr. Pinky Sue Wassenberg, 217-206-6523, Fax: 217-206-7807, E-mail: wassenberg.pinky@uis.edu.

UNIVERSITY OF ILLINOIS AT URBANA–CHAMPAIGN, Champaign, IL 61820

General Information State-supported, coed, university. CGS member. *Enrollment:* 42,728 graduate, professional, and undergraduate students; 8,911 full-time matriculated graduate/professional students (3,988 women), 1,896 part-time matriculated graduate/professional students (1,095 women). *Graduate faculty:* 2,083 full-time (599 women), 167 part-time/adjunct (67 women). *Graduate housing:* Rooms and/or apartments available to single and married students. *Student services:* Campus employment opportunities, campus safety program, career counseling, disabled student services, exercise/wellness program, free psychological counseling, international student services, low-cost health insurance, multicultural affairs office, teacher training. *Library facilities:* University Library plus 36 others. *Online resources:* library catalog, web page, access to other libraries' catalogs. *Collection:* 10.4 million titles, 63,413 serial subscriptions, 4,245 audiovisual materials. *Research affiliation:* National Center for Atmospheric Research, Fermi National Accelerator Laboratory, Sandia National Laboratories, Midwest Universities Research Association.

Computer facilities: Computer purchase and lease plans are available. 3,500 computers available on campus for general student use. A campuswide network can be accessed from student residence rooms and from off campus. Internet access and online class registration, wireless available in many buildings are available. *Web address:* http://www.uiuc.edu/.

General Application Contact: William Welburn, Associate Dean, 217-333-6715, Fax: 217-333-8019, E-mail: welburn@uiuc.edu.

GRADUATE UNITS

College of Law Students: 665 full-time (254 women), 6 part-time (1 woman); includes 188 minority (36 African Americans, 3 American Indian/Alaska Native, 100 Asian Americans or Pacific Islanders, 49 Hispanic Americans), 56 international. 958 applicants, 42% accepted, 259 enrolled. *Faculty:* 36 full-time (9 women), 22 part-time/adjunct (11 women). Expenses: Contact institution. *Financial support:* In 2006–07, 1 fellowship, 3 research assistantships, 24 teaching assistantships were awarded; tuition waivers (full and partial) also available. In 2006, 214 JDs, 36 master's, 1 doctorate awarded. Offers law (JD, LL M, MCL, JSD). *Application deadline:* Applications are processed on a rolling basis. *Application fee:* $50 ($60 for international students). Electronic applications accepted. *Application Contact:* Patricia Camp, Admissions Coordinator, 217-244-6415, Fax: 217-244-1478, E-mail: pcamp@law.uiuc.edu. *Dean*, Heidi M. Hurd, 217-333-9857, Fax: 217-244-1478, E-mail: hhurd@law.uiuc.edu.

College of Veterinary Medicine Students: 435 full-time (338 women), 5 part-time (all women); includes 29 minority (3 African Americans, 2 American Indian/Alaska Native, 19 Asian Americans or Pacific Islanders, 5 Hispanic Americans), 15 international. 275 applicants, 73% accepted, 119 enrolled. *Faculty:* 122 full-time (44 women), 15 part-time/adjunct (10 women). Expenses: Contact institution. *Financial support:* In 2006–07, 4 fellowships, 19 research assistantships, 1 teaching assistantship were awarded; career-related internships or fieldwork, Federal Work-Study, and tuition waivers (full and partial) also available. In 2006, 96 first professional degrees, 7 master's, 2 doctorates awarded. *Degree program information:* Part-time programs available. Postbaccalaureate distance learning degree programs offered (minimal on-campus study). Offers pathobiology (MS, PhD); veterinary biosciences (MS, PhD); veterinary clinical medicine (MS, PhD); veterinary medicine (DVM, MS, PhD). *Application fee:* $50 ($60 for international students). Electronic applications accepted. *Dean*, Herbert Whiteley, 217-333-2760, Fax: 217-333-4628, E-mail: hwhitele@uiuc.edu.

Graduate College Students: 8,911 full-time (3,988 women), 1,896 part-time (1,095 women); includes 1,357 minority (426 African Americans, 27 American Indian/Alaska Native, 671 Asian Americans or Pacific Islanders, 233 Hispanic Americans), 3,515 international. 16,785 applicants, 34% accepted, 2707 enrolled. *Faculty:* 2,083 full-time (599 women), 167 part-time/adjunct (67 women). Expenses: Contact institution. *Financial support:* Fellowships, research assistantships, teaching assistantships, career-related internships or fieldwork, Federal Work-Study, institutionally sponsored loans, scholarships/grants, traineeships, and tuition waivers (full and partial) available. Support available to part-time students. Financial award applicants required to submit FAFSA. In 2006, 2,558 master's, 689 doctorates, 10 other advanced degrees awarded. Postbaccalaureate distance learning degree programs offered. Offers medical scholars). *Application deadline:* Applications are processed on a rolling basis. *Application fee:* $50 ($60 for international students). Electronic applications accepted. *Application Contact:* Karen Carney, Associate Dean, 217-333-6715, Fax: 217-333-8019, E-mail: kmcarney@uiuc.edu. *Dean*, Richard P. Wheeler, 217-333-6715, Fax: 217-333-8019, E-mail: rpw@uiuc.edu.

College of Agricultural, Consumer and Environmental Sciences Students: 426 full-time (240 women), 108 part-time (60 women); includes 49 minority (14 African Americans, 22 Asian Americans or Pacific Islanders, 13 Hispanic Americans), 183 international. 464 applicants, 34% accepted, 101 enrolled. *Faculty:* 220 full-time (47 women), 10 part-time/adjunct (2 women). Expenses: Contact institution. *Financial support:* In 2006–07, 71 fellowships, 384 research assistantships, 83 teaching assistantships were awarded; career-related internships or fieldwork and tuition waivers (full and partial) also available. Financial award application deadline: 2/15. In 2006, 103 master's, 47 doctorates awarded. Offers agricultural and biological engineering (MS, PhD); agricultural and consumer economics (MS, PhD); agricultural, consumer and environmental sciences (MS, PhD); animal sciences (MS, PhD); crop sciences (MS, PhD); extension education (MS); food science and human nutrition (MS, PhD); human and community development (MS, PhD); natural resources and environmental science (MS, PhD); nutritional sciences (MS, PhD). *Application deadline:* Applications are processed on a rolling basis. *Application fee:* $50 ($60 for international students). Electronic applications accepted. *Application Contact:* Robert A. Easter, Dean, 217-333-0460, Fax: 217-244-2911, E-mail: reaster@uiuc.edu. *Dean*, Robert A. Easter, 217-333-0460, Fax: 217-244-2911, E-mail: reaster@uiuc.edu.

College of Applied Health Studies Students: 216 full-time (158 women), 22 part-time (13 women); includes 37 minority (22 African Americans, 9 Asian Americans or Pacific Islanders, 6 Hispanic Americans), 42 international. 317 applicants, 33% accepted, 64 enrolled. *Faculty:* 49 full-time (24 women), 1 part-time/adjunct (0 women). Expenses: Contact institution. *Financial support:* In 2006–07, 36 fellowships, 84 research assistantships, 110 teaching assistantships were awarded; career-related internships or fieldwork, Federal Work-Study, institutionally sponsored loans, and tuition waivers (full and partial) also available. Financial award application deadline: 2/15. In 2006, 56 master's, 13 doctorates awarded. Offers applied health studies (MA, MS, MSPH, Au D, PhD); community health (MS, MSPH, PhD); kinesiology (MS, PhD); recreation, sport and tourism (MS, PhD); speech and hearing science (MA, Au D, PhD). *Application deadline:* Applications are processed on a rolling basis. *Application fee:* $50 ($60 for international students). Electronic applications accepted. *Application Contact:* Tanya Gallagher, Dean, 217-333-2131, Fax: 217-333-0404, E-mail: tmgallag@uiuc.edu. *Dean*, Tanya Gallagher, 217-333-2131, Fax: 217-333-0404, E-mail: tmgallag@uiuc.edu.

College of Business Students: 818 full-time (260 women), 39 part-time (8 women); includes 62 minority (7 African Americans, 51 Asian Americans or Pacific Islanders, 4 Hispanic Americans), 372 international. 1,874 applicants, 38% accepted, 325 enrolled. *Faculty:* 87 full-time (21 women), 11 part-time/adjunct (0 women). Expenses: Contact institution. *Financial support:* In 2006–07, 91 fellowships, 102 research assistantships, 127 teaching assistantships were awarded; career-related internships or fieldwork and tuition waivers (full and partial) also available. Financial award application deadline: 2/15. In 2006, 377 master's, 21 doctorates awarded. Offers accountancy (MAS, MS, PhD); business (MAS, MBA, MS, MSTM, PhD); business administration (PhD); finance (MS, PhD); technology management (MSTM). *Application deadline:* Applications are processed on a rolling basis. *Application fee:* $50 ($60 for international students). Electronic applications accepted. *Application Contact:* J.E. Miller, Coordinator of Graduate Programs, 217-244-8002, Fax: 217-244-7969, E-mail: j-miller@uiuc.edu. *Dean*, Avijit Ghosh, 217-333-2747, Fax: 217-244-3118, E-mail: ghosha@uiuc.edu.

College of Communications Students: 99 full-time (56 women), 14 part-time (9 women); includes 20 minority (10 African Americans, 1 American Indian/Alaska Native, 5 Asian Americans or Pacific Islanders, 4 Hispanic Americans), 30 international. 352 applicants, 25% accepted, 41 enrolled. *Faculty:* 35 full-time (12 women). Expenses: Contact institution. *Financial support:* In 2006–07, 18 fellowships, 33 research assistantships, 61 teaching assistantships were awarded; career-related internships or fieldwork, Federal Work-Study, institutionally sponsored loans, and tuition waivers (full and partial) also available. In 2006, 42 master's, 8 doctorates awarded. Offers advertising (MS); communications (PhD); journalism (MS). *Application deadline:* Applications are processed on a rolling basis. *Application fee:* $50 ($60 for international students). Electronic applications accepted. *Application Contact:* Ronald E. Yates, Dean, 217-333-2350, Fax: 217-333-9882, E-mail: ryates@uiuc.edu. *Dean*, Ronald E. Yates, 217-333-2350, Fax: 217-333-9882, E-mail: ryates@uiuc.edu.

College of Education Students: 439 full-time (314 women), 563 part-time (387 women); includes 213 minority (118 African Americans, 6 American Indian/Alaska Native, 52 Asian Americans or Pacific Islanders, 37 Hispanic Americans), 190 international. 676 applicants, 46% accepted, 182 enrolled. *Faculty:* 95 full-time (56 women), 11 part-time/adjunct (6 women). Expenses: Contact institution. *Financial support:* In 2006–07, 99 fellowships, 169 research assistantships, 194 teaching assistantships were awarded; career-related internships or fieldwork, Federal Work-Study, and tuition waivers (full and partial) also available. In 2006, 195 master's, 66 doctorates, 6 other advanced degrees awarded. *Degree program information:* Part-time programs available. Offers curriculum and instruction (Ed M, MA, MS, Ed D, PhD, CAS); education (Ed M, MA, MS, Ed D, PhD, CAS); education, organization and leadership (Ed M, MA, MS, Ed D, PhD, CAS); educational policy studies (Ed M, MA, Ed D, PhD); educational psychology (Ed M, MA, MS, PhD, CAS); human resource education (Ed M, MA, MS, Ed D, PhD, CAS); special education (Ed M, MA, MS, PhD, CAS). *Application deadline:* Applications are processed on a rolling basis. *Application fee:* $50 ($60 for international students). Electronic applications accepted. *Dean*, Mary A. Kalantzis, 217-333-0960, Fax: 217-333-5847, E-mail: marykalantzis@uiuc.edu.

College of Engineering Students: 2,376 full-time (405 women), 288 part-time (27 women); includes 236 minority (24 African Americans, 6 American Indian/Alaska Native, 182 Asian Americans or Pacific Islanders, 24 Hispanic Americans), 1,187 international. 4,782 applicants, 29% accepted, 587 enrolled. *Faculty:* 373 full-time (31 women), 13 part-time/adjunct (2 women). Expenses: Contact institution. *Financial support:* In 2006–07, 338 fellowships, 1,869 research assistantships, 690 teaching assistantships were awarded; Federal Work-Study, institutionally sponsored loans, scholarships/grants, and tuition waivers (full and partial) also available. In 2006, 599 master's, 250 doctorates awarded. Postbaccalaureate distance learning degree programs offered. Offers aerospace engineering (MS, PhD); bioengineering (MS, PhD); civil and environmental engineering (MS, PhD); civil engineering (MS, PhD); computer engineering (MS, PhD); computer science (MCS, MS, PhD); electrical engineering (MS, PhD); engineering (MCS, MS, PhD); health physics (MS, PhD); materials science and engineering (MS, PhD); mechanical engineering (MS, PhD); nuclear engineering (MS, PhD); physics (MS, PhD); systems engineering and engineering design (MS); theoretical and applied mechanics (MS, PhD). *Application deadline:* Applications are processed on a rolling basis. *Application fee:* $50 ($60 for international students). Electronic applications accepted. *Dean,* Dr. Ilesanmi Adesida, 217-333-2150, Fax: 217-244-7705, E-mail: iadesida@uiuc.edu.

College of Fine and Applied Arts Students: 872 full-time (457 women), 100 part-time (64 women); includes 72 minority (22 African Americans, 1 American Indian/Alaska Native, 41 Asian Americans or Pacific Islanders, 8 Hispanic Americans), 252 international. 1,433 applicants, 37% accepted, 297 enrolled. *Faculty:* 190 full-time (58 women), 24 part-time/adjunct (11 women). Expenses: Contact institution. *Financial support:* In 2006–07, 87 fellowships, 103 research assistantships, 308 teaching assistantships were awarded; career-related internships or fieldwork and tuition waivers (full and partial) also available. Financial award application deadline: 2/15. In 2006, 247 master's, 31 doctorates awarded. Offers architecture (M Arch, PhD); art and design (MA, MFA, Ed D, PhD); art education (MA, Ed D); art history (MA, PhD); dance (MFA); fine and applied arts (M Arch, M Mus, MA, MFA, MLA, MME, MS, MUP, DMA, Ed D, PhD); graphics (MFA); industrial design (MFA); landscape architecture (MLA, PhD); music (M Mus, MME, MS, DMA, Ed D, PhD); painting (MFA); photography (MFA); regional planning (PhD); sculpture (MFA); theatre (MA, MFA, PhD); urban and regional planning (MUP). *Application deadline:* Applications are processed on a rolling basis. *Application fee:* $50 ($60 for international students). Electronic applications accepted. *Dean,* Robert F. Graves, 217-333-1660, Fax: 217-244-8381, E-mail: rbgraves@uiuc.edu.

College of Liberal Arts and Sciences Students: 2,180 full-time (965 women), 409 part-time (223 women); includes 259 minority (62 African Americans, 8 American Indian/Alaska Native, 132 Asian Americans or Pacific Islanders, 57 Hispanic Americans), 1,004 international. 4,921 applicants, 25% accepted, 511 enrolled. *Faculty:* 670 full-time (171 women), 30 part-time/adjunct (11 women). Expenses: Contact institution. *Financial support:* In 2006–07, 523 fellowships, 1,001 research assistantships, 1,405 teaching assistantships were awarded; career-related internships or fieldwork, Federal Work-Study, institutionally sponsored loans, traineeships, and tuition waivers (full and partial) also available. In 2006, 360 master's, 258 doctorates awarded. Offers African studies (MA); animal biology (MS, PhD); anthropology (MA, PhD); applied mathematics (MS); astronomy (MS, PhD); atmospheric science (MS, PhD); biochemistry (MS, PhD); biophysics and computational biology (PhD); cell and developmental biology (PhD); chemical and biomolecular engineering (MS, PhD); chemical sciences (MS, PhD); chemistry (MS, PhD); classics (MA, PhD); comparative and world literature (MA, PhD); demography (MA, PhD); earth sciences (MS, PhD); East Asian languages and cultures (MA, PhD); ecology and evolutionary biology (MS, PhD); economics (MS, PhD); English (MA, MFA, PhD); English as an international language (MA); entomology (PhD); French (MA, MAT, PhD); geochemistry (MS, PhD); geography (MA, MS, PhD); geology (MS, PhD); geophysics (MS, PhD); Germanic languages and literatures (MA, MAT, PhD); history (MA, PhD); insect pest management (MS); integrative biology (MS, PhD); Italian (PhD); Latin American and Caribbean studies (MA); liberal arts and sciences (MA, MAT, MFA, MS, PhD, CAS); linguistics (MA, PhD); mathematics (MA, MS, PhD); microbiology (PhD); molecular and cellular biology (MS, PhD); molecular and integrative physiology (MS, PhD); neuroscience (PhD); philosophy (MA, PhD); physiological and molecular plant biology (PhD); plant biology (MS, PhD); political science (MA, PhD); psychology (MA, MS, PhD); Russian (MA, PhD); Russian, East European and Eurasian (MA); second language aquisition and teacher education (CAS); Slavic languages and literatures (MA, PhD); sociology (MA, PhD); Spanish, Italian and Portuguese (MA); speech communication (MA, PhD); statistics (MS, PhD); teaching of mathematics (MS). *Application fee:* $50 ($60 for international students). Electronic applications accepted. *Dean,* Dr. Sarah C. Mangelsdorf, 217-333-1350, Fax: 217-333-9142, E-mail: smangels@uiuc.edu.

Graduate School of Library and Information Science Students: 249 full-time (189 women), 292 part-time (222 women); includes 51 minority (23 African Americans, 24 Asian Americans or Pacific Islanders, 4 Hispanic Americans), 38 international. Average age 31. 571 applicants, 53% accepted, 99 enrolled. *Faculty:* 21 full-time (9 women), 4 part-time/adjunct (3 women). Expenses: Contact institution. *Financial support:* In 2006–07, 33 fellowships, 39 research assistantships, 22 teaching assistantships were awarded; tuition waivers (full and partial) also available. Financial award application deadline: 2/1. In 2006, 197 master's, 4 doctorates, 2 other advanced degrees awarded. Offers biological informatics (MS); digital libraries (CAS); library and information science (MS, PhD, CAS). *Application deadline:* For fall admission, 1/16 priority date for domestic students; for spring admission, 10/16 for domestic students. Applications are processed on a rolling basis. *Application fee:* $50 ($60 for international students). Electronic applications accepted. *Application Contact:* Valerie Youngen, Admissions, 217-333-0734, Fax: 217-244-3302, E-mail: vyoungen@uiuc.edu. *Dean,* John Unsworth, 217-333-3281, Fax: 217-244-3302, E-mail: unsworth@uiuc.edu.

Institute of Labor and Industrial Relations Students: 161 full-time (108 women), 9 part-time (7 women); includes 41 minority (23 African Americans, 1 American Indian/Alaska Native, 12 Asian Americans or Pacific Islanders, 5 Hispanic Americans), 36 international. Average age 25. 198 applicants, 66% accepted, 68 enrolled. *Faculty:* 15 full-time (3 women). Expenses: Contact institution. *Financial support:* In 2006–07, 47 fellowships, 13 research assistantships, 5 teaching assistantships were awarded; career-related internships or fieldwork, Federal Work-Study, scholarships/grants, and tuition waivers (full) also available. Support available to part-time students. Financial award application deadline:2/1. In 2006, 68 master's, 1 doctorate awarded. *Degree program information:* Part-time programs available. Offers human resources (MHRIR, PhD); labor and industrial relations (MHRIR, PhD). *Application deadline:* For fall admission, 2/1 for domestic students; for spring admission, 11/1 for domestic students. *Application fee:* $50 ($60 for international students). Electronic applications accepted. *Application Contact:* Becky Barker, Graduate Admissions, 217-333-2381, Fax: 217-244-9290, E-mail: ebarker@uiuc.edu. *Director,* Dr. Joe Cutcher Gershenfeld, 217-333-1480, Fax: 217-244-9290, E-mail: joelcg@uiuc.edu.

School of Social Work Students: 213 full-time (196 women), 61 part-time (58 women); includes 49 minority (27 African Americans, 8 Asian Americans or Pacific Islanders, 14 Hispanic Americans), 12 international. 270 applicants, 56% accepted, 41 enrolled. *Faculty:* 17 full-time (12 women), 3 part-time/adjunct (2 women). Expenses: Contact institution. *Financial support:* In 2006–07, 11 fellowships, 16 research assistantships, 3 teaching assistantships were awarded; career-related internships or fieldwork and tuition waivers (full and partial) also available. Financial award application deadline: 2/15. In 2006, 143 master's, 2 doctorates awarded. Offers social work (MSW, PhD). *Application deadline:* For fall admission, 3/1 for domestic students; for spring admission, 3/1 for domestic students. Applications are processed on a rolling basis. *Application fee:* $50 ($60 for international students). *Application Contact:* Michele Wintrey, Officer II, 217-333-2261, Fax: 217-244-5220, E-mail: mwinfrey@uiuc.edu. *Dean,* Wynne S. Korr, 217-333-2260, Fax: 217-244-5220, E-mail: wkorr@uiuc.edu.

UNIVERSITY OF INDIANAPOLIS, Indianapolis, IN 46227-3697

General Information Independent-religious, coed, comprehensive institution. *Enrollment:* 4,389 graduate, professional, and undergraduate students; 396 full-time matriculated graduate/professional students (300 women), 630 part-time matriculated graduate/professional students (459 women). *Graduate faculty:* 68 full-time (34 women), 35 part-time/adjunct (20 women). *Graduate housing:* Rooms and/or apartments available on a first-come, first-served basis to single and married students. *Student services:* Campus employment opportunities, campus safety program, career counseling, disabled student services, exercise/wellness program, free psychological counseling, international student services, low-cost health insurance, teacher training, writing training. *Library facilities:* Krannert Memorial Library. *Online resources:* library catalog, web page, access to other libraries' catalogs. *Collection:* 173,363 titles, 1,015 serial subscriptions.

Computer facilities: 218 computers available on campus for general student use. A campuswide network can be accessed from student residence rooms and from off campus. Internet access is available. *Web address:* http://www.uindy.edu/.

General Application Contact: Dr. E. John McIlvried, Associate Provost for Graduate Programs and International Programs, 317-788-3274, Fax: 317-788-3480, E-mail: jmcilvried@uindy.edu.

GRADUATE UNITS

Graduate Programs Students: 396 full-time (300 women), 630 part-time (459 women); includes 62 minority (37 African Americans, 1 American Indian/Alaska Native, 16 Asian Americans or Pacific Islanders, 8 Hispanic Americans), 65 international. Average age 31. *Faculty:* 68 full-time (34 women), 35 part-time/adjunct (20 women). Expenses: Contact institution. *Financial support:* Teaching assistantships, career-related internships or fieldwork, Federal Work-Study, tuition waivers (full and partial), and unspecified assistantships available. Financial award application deadline: 5/1; financial award applicants required to submit FAFSA. In 2006, 243 master's, 60 doctorates awarded. *Degree program information:* Part-time and evening/weekend programs available. *Application deadline:* Applications are processed on a rolling basis. *Associate Provost for Graduate Programs and International Programs,* Dr. E. John McIlvried, 317-788-3274, Fax: 317-788-3480, E-mail: jmcilvried@uindy.edu.

Center for Aging and Community Students: 2 full-time (both women), 15 part-time (12 women); includes 2 minority (1 African American, 1 Hispanic American), 3 international. Average age 36. Expenses: Contact institution. *Financial support:* In 2006–07, 1 research assistantship was awarded; Federal Work-Study and scholarships/grants also available. In 2006, 3 degrees awarded. *Degree program information:* Part-time and evening/weekend programs available. Postbaccalaureate distance learning degree programs offered. Offers gerontology (MS, Certificate). *Application deadline:* Applications are processed on a rolling basis. *Application fee:* $50. *Application Contact:* Tamora Wolske, Academic Program Director, 317-791-5958, Fax: 317-791-5945, E-mail: wolsketl@uindy.edu. *Executive Director,* Dr. Ellen Miller, 317-791-5930, Fax: 317-791-5945, E-mail: emiller@uindy.edu.

College of Arts and Sciences Students: 20 full-time (12 women), 58 part-time (39 women); includes 9 minority (7 African Americans, 1 Asian American or Pacific Islander, 1 Hispanic American), 6 international. Average age 31. *Faculty:* 26 full-time (11 women), 6 part-time/adjunct (3 women). Expenses: Contact institution. *Financial support:* Teaching assistantships, Federal Work-Study available. Financial award application deadline: 5/1; financial award applicants required to submit FAFSA. In 2006, 23 degrees awarded. *Degree program information:* Part-time and evening/weekend programs available. Offers applied sociology (MA); art (MA); arts and sciences (MA, MS); English (MA); history (MA); human biology (MS); international relations (MA). *Application deadline:* Applications are processed on a rolling basis. *Application fee:* $30. *Dean,* Dr. Daniel Briere, 317-788-3277, Fax: 317-788-3480, E-mail: dbriere@uindy.edu.

Krannert School of Physical Therapy Students: 139 full-time (117 women), 107 part-time (73 women); includes 9 minority (5 African Americans, 4 Asian Americans or Pacific Islanders), 39 international. Average age 27. *Faculty:* 11 full-time (4 women), 6 part-time/adjunct (5 women). Expenses: Contact institution. *Financial support:* Teaching assistantships, career-related internships or fieldwork, Federal Work-Study, scholarships/grants, tuition waivers (full and partial), and unspecified assistantships available. Financial award application deadline: 5/1; financial award applicants required to submit FAFSA. In 2006, 36 master's, 52 doctorates awarded. *Degree program information:* Part-time and evening/weekend programs available. Offers physical therapy (MHS, DHS, DPT, TDPT). *Application deadline:* For fall admission, 10/12 for domestic students. *Application fee:* $50. Electronic applications accepted. *Application Contact:* Kelly Wilson, Admissions Counselor, 317-788-4909, Fax: 317-788-3542, E-mail: kwilson@uindy.edu. *Dean of Health Sciences,* Dr. Mary Huer, 317-788-3500, Fax: 317-788-3542, E-mail: huerm@uindy.edu.

School of Business Students: 50 full-time (16 women), 92 part-time (32 women); includes 12 minority (4 African Americans, 7 Asian Americans or Pacific Islanders, 1 Hispanic American), 10 international. Average age 32. *Faculty:* 6 full-time (2 women), 6 part-time/adjunct (1 woman). Expenses: Contact institution. *Financial support:* Federal Work-Study and unspecified assistantships available. Financial award application deadline: 5/1; financial award applicants required to submit FAFSA. In 2006, 57 degrees awarded. *Degree program information:* Part-time and evening/weekend programs available. Offers business (EMBA); business administration (MBA); finance (Graduate Certificate); global supply chains management (Graduate Certificate); marketing (Graduate Certificate); organizational leadership (Graduate Certificate); technology management (Graduate Certificate). *Application deadline:* Applications are processed on a rolling basis. *Application fee:* $50. *Dean,* Dr. Mitch B. Shapiro, 317-788-6096, E-mail: mshapiro@uindy.edu.

School of Education Students: 32 full-time (16 women), 70 part-time (42 women); includes 2 minority (1 African American, 1 Hispanic American). Average age 31. *Faculty:* 4 full-time (2 women), 6 part-time/adjunct (2 women). Expenses: Contact institution. *Financial support:* Federal Work-Study available. Financial award application deadline: 5/1; financial award applicants required to submit FAFSA. In 2006, 51 degrees awarded. *Degree program information:* Part-time and evening/weekend programs available. Offers art education (MAT); biology (MAT); chemistry (MAT); curriculum and instruction (MA); earth sciences (MAT); education (MA, MAT); educational leadership (MA); elementary education (MA); English (MAT); French (MAT); math (MAT); physical education (MAT); physics (MAT); secondary education (MA); social studies (MAT); Spanish (MAT). *Application deadline:* Applications are processed on a rolling basis. *Application fee:* $50. *Dean,* Dr. E. Lynne Weisenbach, 317-788-3446, Fax: 317-788-3300, E-mail: weisenbach@uindy.edu.

School of Nursing Students: 9 full-time (all women), 121 part-time (115 women); includes 17 minority (16 African Americans, 1 Asian American or Pacific Islander). Average age 41. *Faculty:* 7 full-time (all women), 3 part-time/adjunct (all women). Expenses: Contact institution. *Financial support:* Federal Work-Study available. In 2006, 7 degrees awarded. Offers family practice (post-RN) (MSN); gerontological nurse practitioner (MSN); nurse-midwifery (MSN); nursing (MSN); nursing administration (MSN); nursing education (MSN). *Application deadline:* For fall admission, 8/1 for domestic students; for winter admission, 12/15 for domestic students; for spring admission, 4/15 for domestic students. Applications are processed on a rolling basis. *Application fee:* $50. *Application Contact:* T.C. Crum, 317-788-2128, Fax: 317-788-3542, E-mail: tcrum@uindy.edu. *Dean,* Dr. Sharon Isaac, 317-788-3207, E-mail: isaac@uindy.edu.

School of Occupational Therapy Students: 57 full-time (55 women), 112 part-time (102 women); includes 6 minority (1 African American, 3 Asian Americans or Pacific Islanders, 2 Hispanic Americans). Average age 27. *Faculty:* 8 full-time (7 women), 7 part-time/adjunct (5 women). Expenses: Contact institution. *Financial support:* Career-related internships or fieldwork, Federal Work-Study, tuition waivers (full and partial), and unspecified assistantships available. Financial award application deadline: 5/1; financial award applicants required to submit FAFSA. In 2006, 41 degrees awarded. *Degree program information:* Part-time and evening/weekend programs available. Offers occupational therapy (MHS, MOT, DHS). *Application deadline:* For fall admission, 11/1 for domestic students, 2/1 for international students. *Application fee:* $55. *Application Contact:* Jerry Lowery, Admissons Counselor, 317-788-3457, Fax: 317-788-3542, E-mail: loweryj@uindy.edu. *Dean of Health Sciences,* Dr. Mary Huer, 317-788-3500, Fax: 317-788-3542, E-mail: huerm@uindy.edu.

School of Psychological Sciences Students: 87 full-time (73 women), 55 part-time (44 women); includes 5 minority (2 African Americans, 1 American Indian/Alaska Native, 2 Hispanic Americans), 7 international. Average age 28. *Faculty:* 7 full-time (2 women), 1 (woman) part-time/adjunct. Expenses: Contact institution. *Financial support:* Federal Work-Study available. In 2006, 23 master's, 8 doctorates awarded. Offers clinical psychology (Psy D); clinical psychology/mental health counseling (MA). *Application deadline:* For fall

University of Indianapolis (continued)

admission, 2/25 for domestic students. *Application fee:* $50. *Dean,* Dr. E. John McIlvried, 317-788-3247, Fax: 317-788-3480, E-mail: jmcilvried@uindy.edu.

THE UNIVERSITY OF IOWA, Iowa City, IA 52242-1316

General Information State-supported, coed, university. CGS member. *Enrollment:* 28,816 graduate, professional, and undergraduate students; 4,684 full-time matriculated graduate/professional students (2,496 women), 3,892 part-time matriculated graduate/professional students (1,791 women). *Enrollment by degree level:* 3,853 first professional, 1,975 master's, 2,730 doctoral, 18 other advanced degrees. *Graduate faculty:* 1,584 full-time (455 women), 89 part-time/adjunct (23 women). *Graduate housing:* Rooms and/or apartments available on a first-come, first-served basis to single and married students. Typical cost: $4,836 per year ($7,311 including board) for single students. Room and board charges vary according to board plan and housing facility selected. *Student services:* Campus employment opportunities, campus safety program, career counseling, child daycare facilities, disabled student services, exercise/wellness program, free psychological counseling, international student services, low-cost health insurance, multicultural affairs office, teacher training, writing training. *Library facilities:* Main Library plus 12 others. *Online resources:* library catalog, web page, access to other libraries' catalogs. *Collection:* 4 million titles, 44,644 serial subscriptions.

Computer facilities: Computer purchase and lease plans are available. 1,200 computers available on campus for general student use. A campuswide network can be accessed from student residence rooms and from off campus. Internet access and online class registration, online degree process, grades, financial aid summary, bills are available. *Web address:* http://www.uiowa.edu/.

General Application Contact: Betty Wood, Associate Director of Admissions, 319-335-1525, Fax: 319-335-1535, E-mail: admissions@uiowa.edu.

GRADUATE UNITS

College of Dentistry Offers dental public health (MS); dentistry (DDS, MS, PhD, Certificate); endodontics (MS, Certificate); operative dentistry (MS, Certificate); oral and maxillofacial pathology (Certificate); oral and maxillofacial radiology (Certificate); oral and maxillofacial surgery (MS, Certificate); oral pathology, radiology and medicine (MS, Certificate); oral science (MS, PhD); orthodontics (MS, Certificate); pediatric dentistry (Certificate); periodontics (MS, Certificate); preventive and community dentistry (MS); prosthodontics (MS, Certificate); stomatology (MS).

College of Law Students: 655 full-time (311 women); includes 111 minority (28 African Americans, 6 American Indian/Alaska Native, 45 Asian Americans or Pacific Islanders, 32 Hispanic Americans), 8 international. 1,809 applicants, 33% accepted, 210 enrolled. *Faculty:* 43 full-time (14 women), 16 part-time/adjunct (6 women). Expenses: Contact institution. *Financial support:* In 2006–07, 594 students received support, including 25 fellowships with partial tuition reimbursements available, 236 research assistantships with partial tuition reimbursements available (averaging $1,803 per year); career-related internships or fieldwork, Federal Work-Study, institutionally sponsored loans, scholarships/grants, health care benefits, and unspecified assistantships also available. Financial award application deadline: 1/1; financial award applicants required to submit FAFSA. In 2006, 261 JDs, 8 master's awarded. Offers law (JD, LL M). *Application deadline:* For fall admission, 3/1 for domestic and international students. Applications are processed on a rolling basis. *Application fee:* $60 ($85 for international students). Electronic applications accepted. *Application Contact:* Collins Byrd, Associate Dean of Admissions, 319-335-9095, Fax: 319-335-9646, E-mail: law-admissions@uiowa.edu. *Dean,* Carolyn Jones, 319-335-9034, E-mail: carolyn-jones@uiowa.edu.

College of Pharmacy Students: 42 full-time (20 women), 36 part-time (9 women); includes 7 minority (2 African Americans, 1 Asian American or Pacific Islander, 4 Hispanic Americans), 46 international. 158 applicants, 18% accepted, 12 enrolled. *Faculty:* 27 full-time, 314 part-time/adjunct. Expenses: Contact institution. *Financial support:* In 2006–07, 6 fellowships, 50 research assistantships with partial tuition reimbursements, 22 teaching assistantships with partial tuition reimbursements were awarded. Financial award application deadline: 2/1; financial award applicants required to submit FAFSA. In 2006, 3 master's, 9 doctorates awarded. Offers pharmacy (MS, PhD). *Application deadline:* For fall admission, 2/1 priority date for domestic and international students; for spring admission, 8/1 for domestic students, 8/1 priority date for international students. Applications are processed on a rolling basis. *Application fee:* $60 ($85 for international students). Electronic applications accepted. *Dean,* Jordan Cohen, 319-335-8794, Fax: 319-353-5594.

Graduate College Students: 2,581 full-time (1,462 women), 2,142 part-time (1,169 women); includes 437 minority (170 African Americans, 23 American Indian/Alaska Native, 109 Asian Americans or Pacific Islanders, 135 Hispanic Americans), 1,131 international. Average age 30. 6,886 applicants, 29% accepted, 1028 enrolled. *Faculty:* 1,584 full-time (455 women), 89 part-time/adjunct (23 women). Expenses: Contact institution. *Financial support:* In 2006–07, 355 fellowships, 1,409 research assistantships with partial tuition reimbursements, 1,643 teaching assistantships with partial tuition reimbursements were awarded; career-related internships or fieldwork, Federal Work-Study, institutionally sponsored loans, scholarships/grants, and unspecified assistantships also available. Support available to part-time students. Financial award applicants required to submit FAFSA. In 2006, 937 master's, 392 doctorates, 27 other advanced degrees awarded. *Degree program information:* Part-time and evening/weekend programs available. Postbaccalaureate distance learning degree programs offered (minimal on-campus study). Offers applied mathematical and computational sciences (PhD); bioinformatics and computational biology (Certificate); genetics (PhD); health informatics (MS, PhD, Certificate); human toxicology (MS, PhD); immunology (PhD); information science (MS, PhD, Certificate); molecular and cellular biology (PhD); neuroscience (PhD); second language acquisition (PhD); urban and regional planning (MA, MS). *Application fee:* $60 ($85 for international students). Electronic applications accepted. *Application Contact:* Betty Wood, Associate Director of Admissions, 319-335-1525, Fax: 319-335-1535, E-mail: admissions@uiowa.edu. *Dean,* Dr. John C. Keller, 319-335-2144, Fax: 319-335-2806.

College of Education Students: 300 full-time (214 women), 278 part-time (196 women); includes 70 minority (33 African Americans, 3 American Indian/Alaska Native, 15 Asian Americans or Pacific Islanders, 19 Hispanic Americans), 95 international. 335 applicants, 50% accepted, 99 enrolled. *Faculty:* 72 full-time, 15 part-time/adjunct. Expenses: Contact institution. *Financial support:* In 2006–07, 13 fellowships, 147 research assistantships with partial tuition reimbursements, 117 teaching assistantships with partial tuition reimbursements were awarded; career-related internships or fieldwork, Federal Work-Study, institutionally sponsored loans, and unspecified assistantships also available. Financial award applicants required to submit FAFSA. In 2006, 103 master's, 40 doctorates, 5 other advanced degrees awarded. Offers administration and research (PhD); art education (MA, PhD); counseling psychology (PhD); counselor education and supervision (PhD); curriculum and supervision (MA, PhD); curriculum supervision (MA); developmental reading (MA); early childhood and elementary education (MA, PhD); early childhood education and care (MA); education (MA, MAT, PhD, Ed S); educational administration (MA, PhD, Ed S); educational measurement and statistics (MA, PhD); educational psychology (MA, PhD); elementary education (MA, PhD); English education (MA, MAT, PhD); foreign language education (MA, MAT); foreign language/ESL education (PhD); higher education (MA, PhD, Ed S); language, literature and culture (PhD); math education (PhD); mathematics education (MA); music education (MA, PhD); rehabilitation counseling (MA); rehabilitation counselor education (PhD); school counseling (MA); school psychology (PhD, Ed S); secondary education (MA, MAT, PhD); social foundations (MA, PhD); social studies (MA, PhD); special education (MA, PhD); student development (MA, PhD). *Application fee:* $60 ($85 for international students). Electronic applications accepted. *Dean,* Sandra Bowman Damico, 319-335-5380, Fax: 319-335-5386.

College of Engineering Students: 349 full-time (97 women); includes 34 minority (17 African Americans, 6 Asian Americans or Pacific Islanders, 11 Hispanic Americans), 171 international. Average age 28. 493 applicants, 33% accepted, 55 enrolled. *Faculty:* 74 full-time (4 women), 9 part-time/adjunct (3 women). Expenses: Contact institution. *Financial support:* In 2006–07, 34 fellowships with partial tuition reimbursements (averaging $25,000 per year), 234 research assistantships with partial tuition reimbursements (averaging $19,537 per year), 90 teaching assistantships with partial tuition reimbursements (averaging $16,000 per year) were awarded; scholarships/grants, health care benefits, and unspecified assistantships also available. Financial award applicants required to submit FAFSA. In 2006, 73 master's, 36 doctorates awarded. Offers biomedical engineering (MS, PhD); chemical and biochemical engineering (MS, PhD); civil and environmental engineering (MS, PhD); electrical and computer engineering (MS, PhD); engineering (MS, PhD); engineering design and manufacturing (MS, PhD); ergonomics (MS, PhD); information and engineering management (MS, PhD); mechanical engineering (MS, PhD); operations research (MS, PhD); quality engineering (MS, PhD). *Application deadline:* For fall admission, 7/15 for domestic students, 4/15 for international students; for spring admission, 10/1 for domestic and international students. Applications are processed on a rolling basis. *Application fee:* $60 ($85 for international students). Electronic applications accepted. *Dean,* Dr. P. Barry Butler, 319-335-5766, Fax: 319-335-6086, E-mail: patrick-butler@uiowa.edu.

College of Liberal Arts and Sciences Students: 1,361 full-time (754 women), 1,062 part-time (548 women); includes 243 minority (100 African Americans, 15 American Indian/Alaska Native, 51 Asian Americans or Pacific Islanders, 77 Hispanic Americans), 545 international. 4,632 applicants, 26% accepted, 601 enrolled. *Faculty:* 699 full-time, 264 part-time/adjunct. Expenses: Contact institution. *Financial support:* In 2006–07, 226 fellowships, 434 research assistantships with partial tuition reimbursements, 1,231 teaching assistantships with partial tuition reimbursements were awarded; career-related internships or fieldwork, Federal Work-Study, institutionally sponsored loans, and unspecified assistantships also available. Support available to part-time students. Financial award applicants required to submit FAFSA. In 2006, 464 master's, 168 doctorates awarded. *Degree program information:* Part-time programs available. Postbaccalaureate distance learning degree programs offered (minimal on-campus study). Offers African American world studies (MA); American studies (MA, PhD); anthropology (MA, PhD); art (MA, MFA); art history (MA, PhD); Asian languages and literature (MA); astronomy (MS); biology (MS, PhD); cell and developmental biology (MS, PhD); chemistry (MS, PhD); classics (MA, PhD); communication research (MA, PhD); comparative literature (MA, PhD); comparative literature translation (MFA); computer science (MCS, MS, PhD); dance (MFA); English (PhD); evolution (MS, PhD); exercise science (MS, PhD); film and video production (MA, MFA); film studies (MA, PhD); French (MA, PhD); genetics (MS, PhD); geography (MA, PhD); geoscience (MS, PhD); German (MA, PhD); history (MA, PhD); integrative physiology (PhD); leisure and recreational sport management (MA); liberal arts and sciences (MA, MCS, MFA, MS, MSW, Au D, DMA, PhD); linguistics (MA, PhD); linguistics with TESL (MA); literary criticism (PhD); literary history (PhD); literary studies (MA); mass communication (PhD); mathematics (MS, PhD); media communication (MA); music (MA, MFA, DMA, PhD); neural and behavioral sciences (PhD); neurobiology (MS, PhD); nonfiction writing (MFA); philosophy (MA, PhD); physics (MS, PhD); plant biology (MS, PhD); political science (MA, PhD); professional journalism (MA); professional speech pathology and audiology (MA, Au D); psychology (MA, PhD); psychology of sport and physical activity (MA, PhD); religious studies (MA, PhD); rhetorical studies (MA, PhD); rhetorical theory and stylistics (PhD); science education (MS, PhD); social work (MSW, PhD); sociology (MA, PhD); Spanish (MA, PhD); speech and hearing science (PhD); sports studies (MA, PhD); statistics and actuarial science (MS, PhD); theatre arts (MFA); therapeutic recreation (MA); women's studies (PhD); writer's workshop (MFA). *Application fee:* $60 ($85 for international students). Electronic applications accepted. *Dean,* Linda Maxson, 319-335-2610, Fax: 319-335-3755.

College of Nursing Students: 76 full-time (63 women), 128 part-time (121 women); includes 7 minority (2 African Americans, 1 American Indian/Alaska Native, 3 Asian Americans or Pacific Islanders, 1 Hispanic American), 17 international. 78 applicants, 88% accepted, 53 enrolled. *Faculty:* 31 full-time, 103 part-time/adjunct. Expenses: Contact institution. *Financial support:* In 2006–07, 21 fellowships, 29 research assistantships with partial tuition reimbursements, 24 teaching assistantships with partial tuition reimbursements were awarded. Financial award applicants required to submit FAFSA. In 2006, 48 master's, 9 doctorates awarded. Offers nursing (MSN, PhD). *Application fee:* $60 ($85 for international students). Electronic applications accepted. *Interim Dean,* Martha Craft-Rosenberg, 319-335-7009, Fax: 319-335-9990.

College of Public Health Students: 161 full-time (94 women), 100 part-time (62 women); includes 30 minority (6 African Americans, 2 American Indian/Alaska Native, 17 Asian Americans or Pacific Islanders, 5 Hispanic Americans), 64 international. 346 applicants, 37% accepted, 55 enrolled. *Faculty:* 60 full-time, 45 part-time/adjunct. Expenses: Contact institution. *Financial support:* In 2006–07, 3 fellowships, 121 research assistantships with partial tuition reimbursements, 22 teaching assistantships with partial tuition reimbursements were awarded. Financial award applicants required to submit FAFSA. In 2006, 111 master's, 6 doctorates awarded. Offers biostatistics (MS, PhD); clinical investigation (MS); community and behavioral health (MS, PhD); epidemiology (MS, PhD); health management and policy (MHA, PhD); occupational and environmental health (MS, PhD, Certificate); public health (MHA, MPH, MS, PhD, Certificate). *Application deadline:* Applications are processed on a rolling basis. *Application fee:* $60 ($85 for international students). Electronic applications accepted. *Dean,* Dr. James A. Merchant, 319-384-5452, Fax: 319-384-5462, E-mail: james-merchant@uiowa.edu.

School of Library and Information Science Students: 43 full-time (38 women), 23 part-time (19 women); includes 2 minority (1 African American, 1 Hispanic American), 3 international. 88 applicants, 56% accepted, 27 enrolled. *Faculty:* 4 full-time, 9 part-time/adjunct. Expenses: Contact institution. *Financial support:* In 2006–07, 1 fellowship, 11 research assistantships with partial tuition reimbursements, 6 teaching assistantships with partial tuition reimbursements were awarded. Financial award applicants required to submit FAFSA. In 2006, 28 degrees awarded. Offers library and information science (MA). *Application deadline:* For fall admission, 2/1 for domestic and international students. *Application fee:* $60 ($85 for international students). Electronic applications accepted. *Director,* James Elmborg, 319-335-5707.

Henry B. Tippie College of Business *Faculty:* 94 full-time (23 women), 65 part-time/adjunct (21 women). Expenses: Contact institution. *Financial support:* In 2006–07, 219 students received support; fellowships with tuition reimbursements available, research assistantships with tuition reimbursements available, teaching assistantships with tuition reimbursements available, career-related internships or fieldwork, Federal Work-Study, institutionally sponsored loans, scholarships/grants, health care benefits, tuition waivers (full and partial), and unspecified assistantships available. Support available to part-time students. Financial award applicants required to submit FAFSA. *Degree program information:* Part-time and evening/weekend programs available. Offers accountancy (M Ac); business (M Ac, MBA, PhD); business administration (PhD); economics (PhD). *Application deadline:* Applications are processed on a rolling basis. *Application fee:* $60 ($85 for international students). Electronic applications accepted. *Dean,* Prof. William C. (Curt) Hunter, 319-335-0866, Fax: 319-335-0860, E-mail: william-hunter@uiowa.edu.

Henry B. Tippie School of Management Students: 230 full-time (67 women), 712 part-time (234 women); includes 62 minority (6 African Americans, 1 American Indian/Alaska Native, 43 Asian Americans or Pacific Islanders, 12 Hispanic Americans), 127 international. Average age 30. 431 applicants, 61% accepted, 217 enrolled. *Faculty:* 94 full-time (23 women), 65 part-time/adjunct (21 women). Expenses: Contact institution. *Financial support:* In 2006–07, 72 fellowships (averaging $3,892 per year), 55 research assistantships with partial tuition reimbursements (averaging $10,260 per year) were awarded; career-related internships or fieldwork, Federal Work-Study, institutionally sponsored loans, scholarships/grants, health care benefits, and unspecified assistantships also available. Support available to part-time students. Financial award application deadline: 4/15; financial award applicants required to submit FAFSA. In 2006, 363 degrees awarded. *Degree program information:* Part-time and evening/weekend programs available. Offers accounting (MBA); corporate finance (MBA); entrepreneurship (MBA); finance (MBA); individually designed concentration (MBA); investment management (MBA); management information systems (MBA); marketing (MBA); nonprofit management (MBA); operations management (MBA); strategic management and consulting (MBA). *Application deadline:* For fall admission, 7/15 for domestic students, 4/15 for international students; for spring admission, 12/15 priority date for domestic students, 11/1 priority date for international students. Applications are processed on a rolling basis. *Application fee:* $60 ($85 for international students). Electronic applications accepted. *Application Contact:* Jodi Schafer, Director of Student Recruitment and Marketing, 319-335-0864, Fax: 319-335-3604, E-mail: jodi-schafer@uiowa.edu. *Associate*

Dean, MBA Programs, Prof. Gary J. Gaeth, 800-622-4692, Fax: 319-335-3604, E-mail: gary-gaeth@uiowa.edu.

Roy J. and Lucille A. Carver College of Medicine 3,338 applicants, 9% accepted. *Faculty:* 602 full-time (156 women), 523 part-time/adjunct (111 women). Expenses: Contact institution. *Financial support:* Fellowships, research assistantships, teaching assistantships, career-related internships or fieldwork, Federal Work-Study, institutionally sponsored loans, scholarships/grants, and tuition waivers (full and partial) available. Support available to part-time students. Financial award applicants required to submit FAFSA. In 2006, 182 MDs, 99 master's, 56 doctorates awarded. *Degree program information:* Part-time programs available. Offers anatomy and biology (PhD); biochemistry (PhD); biology (PhD); chemistry (PhD); free radical and radiation biology (PhD); genetics (PhD); human toxicology (PhD); immunology (PhD); medicine (MD, MA, MPAS, MS, DPT, PhD); microbiology (PhD); molecular and cellular biology (PhD); molecular physiology and biophysics (PhD); neuroscience (PhD); pharmacology (PhD); speech and hearing (PhD). *Application fee:* $30. Electronic applications accepted. *Dean,* Dr. Jean E. Robillard, 319-335-8064, Fax: 319-335-8318, E-mail: jean-robillard@uiowa.edu.

Graduate Programs in Medicine Expenses: Contact institution. *Financial support:* Fellowships, research assistantships, teaching assistantships, career-related internships or fieldwork, Federal Work-Study, institutionally sponsored loans, and tuition waivers (full and partial) available. Support available to part-time students. Financial award applicants required to submit FAFSA. In 2006, 115 master's, 57 doctorates awarded. *Degree program information:* Part-time programs available. Offers anatomy and cell biology (PhD); biochemistry (MS, PhD); free radical and radiation biology (MS, PhD); general microbiology and microbial physiology (MS, PhD); immunology (MS, PhD); medicine (MA, MPAS, MS, DPT, PhD); microbial genetics (MS, PhD); pathogenic bacteriology (MS, PhD); pathology (MS); pharmacology (MS, PhD); physical therapy (DPT); physician assistant (MPAS); physiology and biophysics (PhD); physiology and biophysiology (MS); rehabilitation science (PhD); translational biomedicine (MS, PhD); virology (MS, PhD). *Application fee:* $30 ($50 for international students). Electronic applications accepted.

UNIVERSITY OF KANSAS, Lawrence, KS 66045

General Information State-supported, coed, university. CGS member. *Enrollment:* 28,924 graduate, professional, and undergraduate students; 4,655 full-time matriculated graduate/professional students (2,549 women), 2,489 part-time matriculated graduate/professional students (1,436 women). *Enrollment by degree level:* 1,431 first professional, 3,637 master's, 2,063 doctoral, 13 other advanced degrees. *Graduate faculty:* 1,953. *Tuition, area resident:* Part-time $227 per credit. Tuition, state resident: part-time $543 per credit. Tuition and fees vary according to course load, campus/location, program and reciprocity agreements. *Graduate housing:* Rooms and/or apartments available on a first-come, first-served basis to single and married students. *Student services:* Campus employment opportunities, campus safety program, career counseling, child daycare facilities, disabled student services, exercise/wellness program, free psychological counseling, grant writing training, international student services, low-cost health insurance, multicultural affairs office, teacher training, writing training. *Library facilities:* Watson Library plus 11 others. *Online resources:* library catalog, web page, access to other libraries' catalogs. *Collection:* 4.9 million titles, 50,992 serial subscriptions, 57,471 audiovisual materials.

Computer facilities: Computer purchase and lease plans are available. 1,500 computers available on campus for general student use. A campuswide network can be accessed from student residence rooms and from off campus. Internet access and online class registration are available. *Web address:* http://www.ku.edu.

General Application Contact: Information Contact, 785-864-6161, Fax: 785-864-4555, E-mail: gradschl@ku.edu.

GRADUATE UNITS

Graduate Studies Students: 3,294 full-time (1,920 women), 2,503 part-time (1,458 women); includes 550 minority (163 African Americans, 73 American Indian/Alaska Native, 173 Asian Americans or Pacific Islanders, 141 Hispanic Americans), 918 international. Average age 31. 4,244 applicants, 53% accepted. *Faculty:* 1,258. Expenses: Contact institution. *Financial support:* Fellowships with full and partial tuition reimbursements, research assistantships with full and partial tuition reimbursements, teaching assistantships with full and partial tuition reimbursements, career-related internships or fieldwork, Federal Work-Study, institutionally sponsored loans, and scholarships/grants available. Support available to part-time students. Financial award applicants required to submit FAFSA. In 2006, 1,498 master's, 239 doctorates, 11 other advanced degrees awarded. *Degree program information:* Part-time and evening/weekend programs available. Postbaccalaureate distance learning degree programs offered. *Application fee:* $55 ($60 for international students). Electronic applications accepted. *Application Contact:* Graduate School, 785-864-6161, Fax: 785-864-4555, E-mail: gradschl@ku.edu. *Associate Vice Provost and Dean of Graduate Studies.*

College of Liberal Arts and Sciences Students: 1,280 full-time (714 women), 610 part-time (319 women); includes 172 minority (36 African Americans, 43 American Indian/Alaska Native, 46 Asian Americans or Pacific Islanders, 47 Hispanic Americans), 375 international. Average age 31. 1,881 applicants, 41% accepted. *Faculty:* 590. Expenses: Contact institution. *Financial support:* Fellowships, research assistantships with partial tuition reimbursements, teaching assistantships with full and partial tuition reimbursements, career-related internships or fieldwork, Federal Work-Study, and institutionally sponsored loans available. Support available to part-time students. Financial award applicants required to submit FAFSA. In 2006, 285 master's, 142 doctorates awarded. *Degree program information:* Part-time and evening/weekend programs available. Offers American studies (MA, PhD); anthropology (MA, PhD); applied behavioral science (MA); applied mathematics (MA, PhD); audiology (PhD); behavioral psychology (PhD); biochemistry and biophysics (MA, PhD); biological sciences (MA, PhD); botany (MA, PhD); Brazilian studies (Certificate); Central American and Mexican studies (Certificate); chemistry (MA, MS, PhD); child language (MA, PhD); Chinese language and literature (MA); classical languages (MA); clinical child psychology (MA, PhD); communication studies (MA, PhD); computational physics and astronomy (MS); creative writing (MFA); developmental and child psychology (PhD); East Asian cultures (MA); ecology and evolutionary biology (MA, PhD); economics (MA, PhD); English (MA, PhD); entomology (MA, PhD); French (MA, PhD); geography (MA, PhD); geology (MS, PhD); German (MA, PhD); gerontology (MA, PhD); history (MA, PhD); history of art (MA, PhD); human development (MA); indigenous nations studies (MA); international studies (MA); Japanese language and literature (MA); Latin American studies (MA); liberal arts and sciences (MA, MFA, MPA, MS, PhD, Certificate); linguistics (MA, PhD); mathematics (MA, PhD); microbiology (MA, PhD); molecular, cellular, and developmental biology (MA, PhD); museum studies (MA); philosophy (MA, PhD); physics (MS, PhD); political science (MA, PhD); psychology (MA, PhD); public administration (MPA, PhD); religious studies (MA); Russian, East European and Eurasian studies (MA); Slavic languages and literatures (MA, PhD); sociology (MA, PhD); Spanish (MA, PhD); speech-language pathology (MA, PhD); systematics and ecology (MA); theatre and film (MA, PhD). *Application fee:* $55 ($60 for international students). Electronic applications accepted. *Dean,* Joseph Steinmetz, 785-864-3661, Fax: 785-864-5331.

Graduate Studies Medical Center Students: 456 full-time (348 women), 390 part-time (318 women); includes 60 minority (33 African Americans, 6 American Indian/Alaska Native, 4 Asian Americans or Pacific Islanders, 17 Hispanic Americans), 44 international. Average age 32. *Faculty:* 292 full-time (141 women), 38 part-time/adjunct (29 women). Expenses: Contact institution. *Financial support:* Fellowships with partial tuition reimbursements, research assistantships with partial tuition reimbursements, teaching assistantships with full and partial tuition reimbursements, career-related internships or fieldwork, Federal Work-Study, institutionally sponsored loans, and traineeships available. Support available to part-time students. In 2006, 160 master's, 32 doctorates awarded. *Degree program information:* Part-time and evening/weekend programs available. Postbaccalaureate distance learning degree programs offered (minimal on-campus study). Offers anatomy and cell biology (MA, PhD); audiology (MA, Au D, PhD); biochemistry and molecular biology (MS, PhD); biomedical sciences (MA, MPH, MS, PhD); health policy and management (MHSA); medicine (MA, MHSA, MOT, MPH, MS, Au D, DPT, PhD, Certificate, PMC); microbiology, molecular genetics and immunology (PhD); molecular and integrative physiology (MS, PhD); pathology and laboratory medicine (MA, PhD); pharmacology (MS, PhD); preventive medicine (MPH, MS); speech-language pathology (MA, PhD); toxicology (MS, PhD). *Application deadline:* For fall admission, 7/1 priority date for domestic and international students; for winter admission, 5/1 for domestic students, 5/1 priority date for international students; for spring admission, 12/1 priority date for domestic and international students. Electronic applications accepted. *Application Contact:* Marcia Jones, Director of Graduate Studies, 913-588-1238, Fax: 913-588-5242, E-mail: mjones@kumc.edu. *Vice Chancellor for Academic Affairs and Dean of Graduate Studies,* Dr. Allen Rawitch, 913-588-1258, Fax: 913-588-5242, E-mail: arawitch@kumc.edu.

School of Allied Health Students: 306 full-time (237 women), 43 part-time (30 women); includes 16 minority (5 African Americans, 8 Asian Americans or Pacific Islanders, 3 Hispanic Americans), 9 international. Average age 27. 107 applicants, 79% accepted. *Faculty:* 82 full-time (43 women), 18 part-time/adjunct (17 women). Expenses: Contact institution. *Financial support:* In 2006–07, 260 students received support, including 1 fellowship, 9 teaching assistantships with full tuition reimbursements available (averaging $20,124 per year); health care benefits and unspecified assistantships also available. Financial award applicants required to submit FAFSA. In 2006, 80 master's, 14 doctorates, 1 other advanced degree awarded. *Degree program information:* Part-time programs available. Postbaccalaureate distance learning degree programs offered (minimal on-campus study). Offers allied health (MA, MOT, MS, Au D, DPT, PhD, Certificate); dietetic internship (Certificate); dietetics and nutrition (MS); nurse anesthesia (MS); occupational therapy (MOT, MS); physical therapy and rehabilitation science (MS, DPT, PhD); therapeutic science (PhD). *Application fee:* $60. Electronic applications accepted. *Application Contact:* Moffett Ferguson, Student Affairs Coordinator, 913-588-5275, E-mail: mfergus1@kumc.edu. *Dean,* Dr. Karen L. Miller, 913-588-5235, Fax: 913-588-5254, E-mail: kmiller@kumc.edu.

School of Nursing Students: 63 full-time (59 women), 200 part-time (190 women); includes 37 minority (16 African Americans, 3 American Indian/Alaska Native, 12 Asian Americans or Pacific Islanders, 6 Hispanic Americans), 4 international. Average age 38. 88 applicants, 82% accepted, 62 enrolled. *Faculty:* 53 full-time (50 women), 3 part-time/adjunct (all women). Expenses: Contact institution. *Financial support:* In 2006–07, 106 students received support, including 7 research assistantships (averaging $19,000 per year), 23 teaching assistantships with full and partial tuition reimbursements available (averaging $19,000 per year); traineeships also available. Financial award application deadline: 7/7. In 2006, 39 master's, 5 doctorates awarded. *Degree program information:* Part-time programs available. Postbaccalaureate distance learning degree programs offered (minimal on-campus study). Offers nurse educator (PMC); nurse midwife (PMC); nursing (MS, PhD); psychiatric/mental health nurse practitioner (PMC). *Application deadline:* For fall admission, 4/1 for domestic students; for winter admission, 7/1 for domestic students; for spring admission, 9/1 for domestic students. *Application fee:* $50. *Application Contact:* Dr. Rita K. Clifford, Associate Dean, Student Affairs, 913-588-1619, Fax: 913-588-1615, E-mail: rcliffor@kumc.edu. *Dean,* Dr. Karen L. Miller, 913-588-1604, Fax: 913-588-1660, E-mail: kmiller@kumc.edu.

School of Architecture and Urban Planning Students: 132 full-time (60 women), 17 part-time (9 women); includes 12 minority (5 African Americans, 1 American Indian/Alaska Native, 2 Asian Americans or Pacific Islanders, 4 Hispanic Americans), 6 international. Average age 26. 100 applicants, 53% accepted. *Faculty:* 31. Expenses: Contact institution. *Financial support:* Fellowships, research assistantships with full and partial tuition reimbursements, teaching assistantships with full and partial tuition reimbursements, career-related internships or fieldwork available. Financial award application deadline: 2/1. In 2006, 39 degrees awarded. *Degree program information:* Part-time programs available. Offers academic track (M Arch); architecture and urban planning (M Arch, MUP); management track (M Arch); professional track (M Arch); urban planning (MUP). *Application deadline:* For fall admission, 3/1 priority date for domestic students, 2/1 priority date for international students; for spring admission, 11/1 priority date for domestic and international students. *Application fee:* $55 ($60 for international students). Electronic applications accepted. *Dean,* John C. Gaunt, 785-864-4281, E-mail: jgaunt@ku.edu.

School of Business Students: 221 full-time (73 women), 210 part-time (60 women); includes 43 minority (8 African Americans, 2 American Indian/Alaska Native, 25 Asian Americans or Pacific Islanders, 8 Hispanic Americans), 58 international. Average age 29. 301 applicants, 57% accepted. *Faculty:* 61. Expenses: Contact institution. *Financial support:* Fellowships, research assistantships with full and partial tuition reimbursements, teaching assistantships with full and partial tuition reimbursements, career-related internships or fieldwork and Federal Work-Study available. Financial award application deadline: 6/1. In 2006, 200 master's, 4 doctorates awarded. *Degree program information:* Part-time and evening/weekend programs available. Offers accounting and information systems (MAIS); business (MAIS, MBA, MS, PhD); business administration (MBA). *Application deadline:* For fall admission, 1/15 priority date for domestic students; for spring admission, 10/1 for domestic students. Applications are processed on a rolling basis. *Application fee:* $65. Electronic applications accepted. *Application Contact:* Student Advising Center, 785-864-4254, Fax: 785-864-5328, E-mail: bschoolgrad@ku.edu. *Head,* William L. Fuerst, 785-864-3795, Fax: 785-864-5328, E-mail: bschoolgrad@ku.edu.

School of Education Students: 493 full-time (378 women), 622 part-time (460 women); includes 100 minority (38 African Americans, 9 American Indian/Alaska Native, 19 Asian Americans or Pacific Islanders, 34 Hispanic Americans), 121 international. Average age 33. 568 applicants, 61% accepted. *Faculty:* 90. Expenses: Contact institution. *Financial support:* Fellowships, research assistantships with partial tuition reimbursements, teaching assistantships with full and partial tuition reimbursements, career-related internships or fieldwork available. Financial award application deadline: 2/1. In 2006, 348 master's, 69 doctorates, 11 other advanced degrees awarded. *Degree program information:* Part-time programs available. Offers counseling psychology (MS, PhD); curriculum and instruction (MA, MS Ed, Ed D, PhD); education (MA, MS, MS Ed, Ed D, PhD, Ed S); education administration (MS Ed, Ed S); educational psychology and research (MS Ed, PhD); foundations (Ed D, PhD); foundations of education (MS Ed); health, sports, and exercise sciences (Ed D, PhD); higher education (Ed D, PhD); higher education administration (MS Ed); physical education (MS Ed, PhD); policy studies (Ed D, PhD); school administration (Ed D, PhD); school psychology (PhD, Ed S); special education (MS Ed, Ed D, PhD). *Application fee:* $55 ($60 for international students). Electronic applications accepted. *Application Contact:* Mary Ann Williams, Graduate Admissions Coordinator, 785-864-4510, Fax: 785-864-3566, E-mail: mwilliam@ku.edu. *Dean,* Dr. Rick Ginsberg, 785-864-4297.

School of Engineering Students: 264 full-time (53 women), 363 part-time (69 women); includes 46 minority (10 African Americans, 2 American Indian/Alaska Native, 25 Asian Americans or Pacific Islanders, 9 Hispanic Americans), 227 international. Average age 29. 551 applicants, 55% accepted. *Faculty:* 108. Expenses: Contact institution. *Financial support:* Fellowships, research assistantships with full and partial tuition reimbursements, teaching assistantships with full and partial tuition reimbursements, career-related internships or fieldwork and Federal Work-Study available. In 2006, 162 master's, 12 doctorates awarded. *Degree program information:* Part-time and evening/weekend programs available. Postbaccalaureate distance learning degree programs offered (no on-campus study). Offers aerospace engineering (ME, MS, DE, PhD); architectural engineering (MS); chemical engineering (MS); chemical/petroleum engineering (PhD); civil engineering (MCE, MS, DE, PhD); computer engineering (MS); computer science (MS, PhD); construction management (MCM); electrical engineering (MS, DE, PhD); engineering (MCE, MCM, ME, MS, DE, PhD); engineering management (MS); environmental engineering (MS, PhD); environmental science (MS, PhD); information technology (MS); mechanical engineering (MS, DE, PhD); petroleum engineering (MS); water resources science (MS). *Application deadline:* Applications are processed on a rolling basis. *Application fee:* $55 ($60 for international students). Electronic applications accepted. *Application Contact:* Glen Marotz, Associate Dean, 785-864-2941, Fax: 785-864-5445, E-mail: gama@ku.edu. *Dean,* Stuart R. Bell, 785-864-3881, E-mail: kuengr@ku.edu.

School of Fine Arts Students: 144 full-time (83 women), 79 part-time (53 women); includes 14 minority (2 African Americans, 1 American Indian/Alaska Native, 4 Asian Americans or Pacific Islanders, 7 Hispanic Americans), 35 international. Average age 30. 234 applicants, 44% accepted. *Faculty:* 104. Expenses: Contact institution. *Financial support:* Fellowships, research assistantships with full and partial tuition reimbursements, teaching assistantships with full and partial tuition reimbursements available. In 2006, 52 master's, 17

University of Kansas (continued)

doctorates awarded. Offers art (MFA); church music (MM, DMA); composition (MM, DMA); conducting (MM, DMA); design (MA, MFA); fine arts (MA, MFA, MM, MME, DMA, PhD); music and dance (MM, MME, DMA, PhD); music education (MME, PhD); music theory (MM, PhD); music therapy (MME); musicology (MM, PhD); opera (MM); performance (MM, DMA); special studies (MA); visual arts education (MA). *Application fee:* $55 ($60 for international students). Electronic applications accepted. *Dean,* Dr. Steven K. Hedden, 785-864-3421, Fax: 785-864-5387, E-mail: finearts@ku.edu.

School of Journalism and Mass Communications Students: 27 full-time (16 women), 50 part-time (37 women); includes 7 minority (3 African Americans, 4 Hispanic Americans), 1 international. Average age 31. 48 applicants, 63% accepted. *Faculty:* 32. Expenses: Contact institution. *Financial support:* Fellowships, research assistantships, teaching assistantships with full and partial tuition reimbursements, career-related internships or fieldwork, scholarships/grants, and unspecified assistantships available. Support available to part-time students. Financial award application deadline: 2/1. In 2006, 25 degrees awarded. *Degree program information:* Part-time programs available. Offers journalism (MS). *Application deadline:* For fall admission, 2/1 for domestic and international students; for spring admission, 11/1 for domestic and international students. *Application fee:* $55 ($60 for international students). Electronic applications accepted. *Application Contact:* Cindy Nesvarba, Graduate Records Coordinator, 785-864-7649, Fax: 785-864-5318, E-mail: cnesvarb@ku.edu. *Dean,* Ann Brill, 785-864-4755, Fax: 785-864-4396.

School of Pharmacy Students: 111 full-time (49 women), 11 part-time (5 women); includes 8 minority (1 American Indian/Alaska Native, 4 Asian Americans or Pacific Islanders, 3 Hispanic Americans), 47 international. Average age 27. 148 applicants, 22% accepted. *Faculty:* 41. Expenses: Contact institution. *Financial support:* Fellowships, research assistantships with full and partial tuition reimbursements, teaching assistantships with full and partial tuition reimbursements, career-related internships or fieldwork and scholarships/grants available. In 2006, 25 master's, 18 doctorates awarded. Offers hospital pharmacy (MS); medicinal chemistry (MS, PhD); neurosciences (MS, PhD); pharmaceutical chemistry (MS, PhD); pharmacology and toxicology (MS, PhD); pharmacy (MS, PhD). *Application fee:* $55 ($60 for international students). Electronic applications accepted. *Dean,* Kenneth L. Audus, 785-864-3591, E-mail: pharmacy@ku.edu.

School of Social Welfare Students: 266 full-time (227 women), 70 part-time (59 women); includes 53 minority (30 African Americans, 8 American Indian/Alaska Native, 6 Asian Americans or Pacific Islanders, 9 Hispanic Americans), 13 international. Average age 33. 237 applicants, 70% accepted. *Faculty:* 26 full-time (17 women). Expenses: Contact institution. *Financial support:* Fellowships, research assistantships with full and partial tuition reimbursements, teaching assistantships with full and partial tuition reimbursements, Federal Work-Study, scholarships/grants, and tuition waivers (partial) available. Support available to part-time students. Financial award applicants required to submit FAFSA. In 2006, 154 master's, 5 doctorates awarded. *Degree program information:* Part-time programs available. Offers social welfare (MSW); social work (PhD). *Application deadline:* For fall admission, 2/15 for domestic and international students; for spring admission, 5/1 priority date for domestic and international students. Applications are processed on a rolling basis. *Application fee:* $55. Electronic applications accepted. *Application Contact:* Becky Hofer, Director of Admissions, 785-864-8956, Fax: 785-864-5277, E-mail: bhofer@ku.edu. *Dean,* Mary Ellen Kondrat, 785-864-4720, Fax: 785-864-5277.

School of Law Students: 482 full-time (190 women); includes 73 minority (9 African Americans, 13 American Indian/Alaska Native, 27 Asian Americans or Pacific Islanders, 24 Hispanic Americans), 18 international. Average age 26. 1,121 applicants, 31% accepted, 160 enrolled. *Faculty:* 39 full-time (16 women), 20 part-time/adjunct (5 women). Expenses: Contact institution. *Financial support:* In 2006–07, 350 students received support, including 38 research assistantships (averaging $1,263 per year), 11 teaching assistantships (averaging $1,700 per year); career-related internships or fieldwork, Federal Work-Study, institutionally sponsored loans, and scholarships/grants also available. Financial award application deadline: 3/1; financial award applicants required to submit FAFSA. In 2006, 173 degrees awarded. Offers law (JD). *Application deadline:* For fall admission, 3/15 for domestic students. Applications are processed on a rolling basis. *Application fee:* $50. Electronic applications accepted. *Application Contact:* Jacqlene Nance, Director of Admissions, 866-220-3654, E-mail: admitlaw@ku.edu. *Dean,* Gail B Agrawal, 785-864-4550, Fax: 785-864-5054.

School of Medicine Students: 780 full-time (363 women), 147 part-time (98 women); includes 190 minority (51 African Americans, 12 American Indian/Alaska Native, 99 Asian Americans or Pacific Islanders, 28 Hispanic Americans), 31 international. Average age 27. *Faculty:* 157 full-time (48 women), 17 part-time/adjunct (9 women). Expenses: Contact institution. In 2006, 171 MDs awarded. Offers medicine (MD). Electronic applications accepted. *Application Contact:* Peggy M. Heinen, Admissions Coordinator, 913-588-5283, Fax: 913-588-5259, E-mail: pheinen@kumc.edu. *Executive Dean,* Dr. Barbara Atkinson, 913-588-5287, Fax: 913-588-5259.

UNIVERSITY OF KENTUCKY, Lexington, KY 40506-0032

General Information State-supported, coed, university. CGS member. *Enrollment:* 26,382 graduate, professional, and undergraduate students; 3,827 full-time matriculated graduate/professional students (2,089 women), 1,444 part-time matriculated graduate/professional students (938 women). *Enrollment by degree level:* 2,951 master's, 2,225 doctoral, 95 other advanced degrees. *Graduate faculty:* 1,881 full-time (510 women), 128 part-time/adjunct (22 women). Tuition, state resident: full-time $7,670; part-time $401 per credit hour. Tuition, nonresident: full-time $16,158; part-time $873 per credit hour. *Graduate housing:* Rooms and/or apartments available to single and married students. *Student services:* Campus employment opportunities, campus safety program, career counseling, child daycare facilities, disabled student services, exercise/wellness program, free psychological counseling, grant writing training, international student services, low-cost health insurance, multicultural affairs office, teacher training, writing training. *Library facilities:* William T. Young Library plus 15 others. *Online resources:* library catalog, web page, access to other libraries' catalogs. *Collection:* 3.1 million titles, 29,633 serial subscriptions, 86,690 audiovisual materials. *Research affiliation:* National Drug Addiction Center (drug abuse and prevention), National Institute of Occupational Health and Safety (environmental health), Oak Ridge National Laboratory (nuclear physics), Continuous Electron Beam Accelerator Facility (high-energy physics), Battelle Pacific Northwest Laboratories (environmental sciences).

Computer facilities: 1,400 computers available on campus for general student use. A campuswide network can be accessed from student residence rooms and from off campus. Internet access and online class registration, various software packages are available. *Web address:* http://www.uky.edu/.

General Application Contact: Dr. Brian Jackson, Senior Associate Dean, 859-257-8176, Fax: 859-323-1928, E-mail: grad.webmaster@email.uky.edu.

GRADUATE UNITS

College of Dentistry Offers dentistry (DMD, MS).

College of Law Offers law (JD). Electronic applications accepted.

College of Medicine Students: 404 full-time (164 women); includes 74 minority (22 African Americans, 49 Asian Americans or Pacific Islanders, 3 Hispanic Americans), 11 international. Average age 23. 1,368 applicants, 14% accepted, 103 enrolled. *Faculty:* 614 full-time (178 women), 283 part-time/adjunct (56 women). Expenses: Contact institution. *Financial support:* Institutionally sponsored loans available. Financial award applicants required to submit FAFSA. In 2006, 90 degrees awarded. Offers medicine (MD). *Application deadline:* For fall admission, 11/1 for domestic students. Applications are processed on a rolling basis. *Application fee:* $50. Electronic applications accepted. *Application Contact:* Kimberly Scott, Assistant Director of Admissions, 859-323-6161, Fax: 859-323-2076, E-mail: kstahlma@email.uky.edu. *Assistant Dean for Admissions,* Dr. Carol L. Elam.

College of Pharmacy Expenses: Contact institution. *Financial support:* Career-related internships or fieldwork, Federal Work-Study, institutionally sponsored loans, scholarships/grants, health care benefits, tuition waivers (full), and unspecified assistantships available. Support available to part-time students. Offers pharmaceutical sciences (MS, PhD); pharmacy (Pharm D, MS, PhD). *Dean,* Dr. Kenneth B. Roberts, 859-323-7601, Fax: 859-257-7297, E-mail: krobe2@pop.uky.edu.

Graduate School Students: 3,832 full-time (2,092 women), 1,451 part-time (941 women); includes 327 minority (220 African Americans, 8 American Indian/Alaska Native, 47 Asian Americans or Pacific Islanders, 52 Hispanic Americans), 1,161 international. Average age 31. 7,303 applicants, 47% accepted, 2054 enrolled. *Faculty:* 1,895 full-time (510 women), 129 part-time/adjunct (23 women). Expenses: Contact institution. *Financial support:* In 2006–07, 353 fellowships with full tuition reimbursements (averaging $3,923 per year), 1,030 research assistantships with full tuition reimbursements (averaging $14,000 per year), 849 teaching assistantships with full tuition reimbursements (averaging $10,600 per year) were awarded; career-related internships or fieldwork, Federal Work-Study, institutionally sponsored loans, scholarships/grants, traineeships, health care benefits, tuition waivers (partial), and unspecified assistantships also available. Support available to part-time students. Financial award application deadline: 3/15. In 2006, 1,297 master's, 293 doctorates, 38 other advanced degrees awarded. *Degree program information:* Part-time and evening/weekend programs available. Offers biomedical engineering (MSBE, PBME, PhD); health administration (MHA); nutritional sciences (MSNS, PhD); public administration (MPA, MPP, PhD). *Application deadline:* For fall admission, 7/17 priority date for domestic students, 2/1 for international students; for spring admission, 12/13 priority date for domestic students, 6/15 for international students. *Application fee:* $40 ($55 for international students). Electronic applications accepted. *Application Contact:* Dr. Brian Jackson, Senior Associate Dean, 859-257-4667, Fax: 859-257-4676, E-mail: brian.jackson@uky.edu. *Dean,* Dr. Jeannine Blackwell, 859-257-1759, Fax: 859-323-1928, E-mail: blackwell@uky.edu.

College of Agriculture Students: 288 full-time (157 women), 59 part-time (29 women); includes 16 minority (13 African Americans, 1 Asian American or Pacific Islander, 2 Hispanic Americans), 109 international. Average age 30. 365 applicants, 52% accepted, 133 enrolled. *Faculty:* 274 full-time (42 women), 26 part-time/adjunct (0 women). Expenses: Contact institution. *Financial support:* In 2006–07, 27 fellowships with full tuition reimbursements (averaging $4,250 per year), 197 research assistantships with full tuition reimbursements (averaging $15,000 per year), 28 teaching assistantships with full tuition reimbursements (averaging $4,800 per year) were awarded; career-related internships or fieldwork, Federal Work-Study, institutionally sponsored loans, scholarships/grants, traineeships, health care benefits, tuition waivers (partial), and unspecified assistantships also available. Support available to part-time students. Financial award application deadline: 3/15. In 2006, 57 master's, 28 doctorates awarded. *Degree program information:* Part-time programs available. Offers agricultural economics (MS, PhD); agriculture (MS, MSFAM, MSFOR, PhD); animal sciences (MS, PhD); biosystems and agricultural engineering (MS, PhD); career, technology and leadership education (MS); crop science (MS, PhD); entomology (MS, PhD); family studies, human development, and resource management (MSFAM, PhD); forestry (MSFOR); hospitality and dietetic administration (MS); plant and soil science (MS); plant pathology (MS, PhD); plant physiology (PhD); soil science (PhD); veterinary science (MS, PhD). *Application deadline:* For fall admission, 7/17 priority date for domestic students, 2/1 priority date for international students; for spring admission, 12/13 priority date for domestic students, 6/15 priority date for international students. *Application fee:* $40 ($55 for international students). Electronic applications accepted. *Application Contact:* Dr. Brian Jackson, Senior Associate Dean, 859-257-4667, Fax: 859-257-4676, E-mail: brian.jackson@uky.edu. *Dean,* Dr. M. Scott Smith, 859-257-4772, Fax: 859-323-2885, E-mail: mssmith@uky.edu.

College of Arts and Sciences Students: 860 full-time (412 women), 131 part-time (57 women); includes 47 minority (26 African Americans, 1 American Indian/Alaska Native, 4 Asian Americans or Pacific Islanders, 16 Hispanic Americans), 229 international. Average age 30. 1,394 applicants, 34% accepted, 241 enrolled. *Faculty:* 405 full-time (108 women), 33 part-time/adjunct (4 women). Expenses: Contact institution. *Financial support:* In 2006–07, 124 fellowships with full tuition reimbursements (averaging $3,000 per year), 153 research assistantships with full tuition reimbursements (averaging $11,074 per year), 449 teaching assistantships with full tuition reimbursements (averaging $11,248 per year) were awarded; career-related internships or fieldwork, Federal Work-Study, institutionally sponsored loans, scholarships/grants, traineeships, health care benefits, tuition waivers (partial), and unspecified assistantships also available. Support available to part-time students. Financial award application deadline: 3/15. In 2006, 140 master's, 84 doctorates awarded. *Degree program information:* Part-time programs available. Offers anthropology (MA, PhD); applied mathematics (MS); arts and sciences (MA, MS, PhD); biology (MS, PhD); chemistry (MS, PhD); classics (MA); clinical psychology (MA); English (MA, PhD); experimental psychology (MA); French (MA); geography (MA, PhD); geology (MS, PhD); German (MA); Hispanic studies (MA, PhD); history (MA, PhD); mathematics (MA, MS, PhD); philosophy (MA, PhD); physics (MS, PhD); political science (MA, PhD); sociology (MA, PhD); statistics (MS, PhD); teaching world languages (MA). *Application deadline:* For fall admission, 7/17 priority date for domestic students, 2/1 priority date for international students; for spring admission, 12/13 priority date for domestic students, 6/15 priority date for international students. Applications are processed on a rolling basis. *Application fee:* $40 ($55 for international students). Electronic applications accepted. *Application Contact:* Dr. Brian Jackson, Senior Associate Dean, 859-257-4667, Fax: 859-257-4676, E-mail: brian.jackson@uky.edu. *Dean,* Dr. Steven Hoch, 859-257-8354, Fax: 859-323-1073, E-mail: steven-hoch@uky.edu.

College of Communications and Information Studies Students: 133 full-time (103 women), 162 part-time (137 women); includes 9 minority (5 African Americans, 1 Asian American or Pacific Islander, 3 Hispanic Americans), 7 international. Average age 33. 254 applicants, 45% accepted, 77 enrolled. *Faculty:* 28 full-time (7 women), 1 part-time/adjunct (0 women). Expenses: Contact institution. *Financial support:* In 2006–07, 6 fellowships (averaging $3,000 per year), 5 research assistantships (averaging $6,200 per year), 29 teaching assistantships (averaging $12,000 per year) were awarded; career-related internships or fieldwork, Federal Work-Study, institutionally sponsored loans, scholarships/grants, traineeships, health care benefits, and unspecified assistantships also available. Support available to part-time students. Financial award application deadline: 3/15; financial award applicants required to submit FAFSA. In 2006, 118 master's, 10 doctorates awarded. *Degree program information:* Part-time programs available. Offers communication (MA, PhD); communications and information studies (MA, MSLS, PhD); library science (MA, MSLS). *Application deadline:* For fall admission, 7/17 priority date for domestic students, 2/1 for international students; for spring admission, 12/13 priority date for domestic students, 6/15 for international students. Applications are processed on a rolling basis. *Application fee:* $40 ($55 for international students). Electronic applications accepted. *Application Contact:* Dr. Brian Jackson, Senior Associate Dean, 859-257-4667, Fax: 859-257-4676, E-mail: brian.jackson@uky.edu. *Dean,* Dr. David Johnson, 859-257-7805, E-mail: joj@uky.edu.

College of Design Students: 17 full-time (6 women); includes 1 minority (Asian American or Pacific Islander), 3 international. Average age 31. 89 applicants, 10% accepted, 8 enrolled. *Faculty:* 11 full-time (1 woman). Expenses: Contact institution. *Financial support:* In 2006–07, 12 students received support, including 2 research assistantships with full tuition reimbursements available (averaging $10,414 per year), 10 teaching assistantships with full tuition reimbursements available (averaging $2,175 per year); fellowships with full tuition reimbursements available, Federal Work-Study, scholarships/grants, traineeships, health care benefits, tuition waivers (partial), and unspecified assistantships also available. Support available to part-time students. Financial award application deadline: 3/15; financial award applicants required to submit FAFSA. In 2006, 4 degrees awarded. Offers architecture (M Arch); design (M Arch, MAIDM, MHP, MSIDM); historic preservation (MHP); interior design, merchandising, and textiles (MAIDM, MSIDM). *Application deadline:* For fall admission, 7/17 priority date for domestic students, 2/1 priority date for international students; for spring admission, 12/13 priority date for domestic students, 6/15 priority date for international students. *Application fee:* $40 ($55 for international students). Electronic applications accepted. *Application Contact:* Dr. Brian Jackson, Senior Associate Dean, 859-257-4667, Fax: 859-257-4676, E-mail: brian.jackson@uky.edu. *Dean,* Dr. David Mohney, 859-257-7619, Fax: 859-323-1990, E-mail: mohney@uky.edu.

College of Education Students: 496 full-time (349 women), 312 part-time (232 women); includes 104 minority (83 African Americans, 2 American Indian/Alaska Native, 13 Asian

Americans or Pacific Islanders, 6 Hispanic Americans), 19 international. Average age 35. 184 applicants, 58% accepted, 78 enrolled. *Faculty:* 77 full-time (44 women), 7 part-time/adjunct (6 women). Expenses: Contact institution. *Financial support:* In 2006–07, 26 fellowships with full tuition reimbursements (averaging $4,500 per year), 57 research assistantships with full tuition reimbursements (averaging $10,810 per year), 64 teaching assistantships with full tuition reimbursements (averaging $8,466 per year) were awarded; career-related internships or fieldwork, Federal Work-Study, institutionally sponsored loans, scholarships/grants, traineeships, health care benefits, tuition waivers (partial), and unspecified assistantships also available. Support available to part-time students. Financial award application deadline: 3/15. In 2006, 199 master's, 29 doctorates, 37 other advanced degrees awarded. *Degree program information:* Part-time and evening/weekend programs available. Offers administration and supervision (Ed S); counseling psychology (MS Ed, PhD, Ed S); curriculum and instruction (MA Ed, Ed D); early childhood special education (MS Ed); education (M Ed, MA Ed, MRC, MS, MS Ed, Ed D, PhD, Ed S); educational and counseling psychology (MS Ed); educational policy studies and evaluation (Ed D); educational psychology (Ed D, PhD, Ed S); exercise science (PhD); higher education (MS Ed, PhD); instruction and administration (Ed D); instruction system design (MS Ed); kinesiology (MS Ed, D); middle school education (MS Ed); rehabilitation counseling (MRC); school administration (M Ed); school psychometrist and school psychology (MA Ed); special education (MS Ed); special education leadership personnel preparation (Ed D). *Application deadline:* For fall admission, 7/17 priority date for domestic students, 2/1 priority date for international students; for spring admission, 12/13 priority date for domestic students, 6/15 priority date for international students. *Application fee:* $40 ($55 for international students). Electronic applications accepted. *Application Contact:* Dr. Brian Jackson, Senior Associate Dean, 859-257-4667, Fax: 859-257-4676, E-mail: brian.jackson@uky.edu. *Dean,* Dr. James Cibulka, 859-257-6076, Fax: 859-323-1046, E-mail: cibulka@uky.edu.

College of Engineering Students: 509 full-time (110 women), 115 part-time (17 women); includes 11 minority (3 African Americans, 6 Asian Americans or Pacific Islanders, 2 Hispanic Americans), 427 international. Average age 28. 1,204 applicants, 47% accepted, 226 enrolled. *Faculty:* 177 full-time (18 women), 13 part-time/adjunct (0 women). Expenses: Contact institution. *Financial support:* In 2006–07, 21 fellowships with full tuition reimbursements (averaging $2,667 per year), 222 research assistantships with full tuition reimbursements (averaging $9,950 per year), 84 teaching assistantships with full tuition reimbursements (averaging $6,750 per year) were awarded; career-related internships or fieldwork, Federal Work-Study, institutionally sponsored loans, scholarships/grants, traineeships, health care benefits, tuition waivers (partial), and unspecified assistantships also available. Support available to part-time students. Financial award application deadline: 3/15. In 2006, 165 master's, 38 doctorates awarded. *Degree program information:* Part-time programs available. Offers chemical engineering (MS, PhD); civil engineering (MCE, MSCE, PhD); computer science (MS, PhD); electrical engineering (MSEE, PhD); engineering (M Eng, MCE, MME, MS, MS Ch E, MS Min, MSCE, MSEE, MSEM, MSMAE, MSME, MSMSE, PhD); manufacturing systems engineering (MSMSE); materials science and engineering (MSMAE, PhD); mechanical engineering (MSME, PhD); mining engineering (MME, MS Min, PhD). *Application deadline:* For fall admission, 7/17 priority date for domestic students, 2/1 priority date for international students; for spring admission, 12/13 priority date for domestic students, 6/15 priority date for international students. *Application fee:* $40 ($55 for international students). Electronic applications accepted. *Application Contact:* Dr. Brian Jackson, Senior Associate Dean, 859-257-4667, Fax: 859-257-4676, E-mail: brian.jackson@uky.edu. *Dean,* Dr. Thomas W. Lester, 859-257-1687, Fax: 859-323-4922, E-mail: lester@engr.uky.edu.

College of Fine Arts Students: 151 full-time (83 women), 41 part-time (23 women); includes 19 minority (11 African Americans, 2 American Indian/Alaska Native, 3 Asian Americans or Pacific Islanders, 3 Hispanic Americans), 14 international. Average age 33. 43 applicants, 47% accepted, 10 enrolled. *Faculty:* 93 full-time (30 women). Expenses: Contact institution. *Financial support:* In 2006–07, 11 fellowships with full tuition reimbursements (averaging $2,721 per year), 14 research assistantships with full tuition reimbursements (averaging $7,603 per year), 60 teaching assistantships with full tuition reimbursements (averaging $10,154 per year) were awarded; Federal Work-Study, institutionally sponsored loans, scholarships/grants, traineeships, health care benefits, tuition waivers (partial), and unspecified assistantships also available. Support available to part-time students. Financial award application deadline: 3/15. In 2006, 33 master's, 7 doctorates awarded. *Degree program information:* Part-time and evening/weekend programs available. Offers art education (MA); art history (MA); art studio (MFA); fine arts (MA, MFA, MM, DMA, PhD); music (PhD); music composition (MM); music education (MM); music performance (MM); music theory (MA); musical arts (DMA); musicology (MA); theatre (MA). *Application deadline:* For fall admission, 7/17 priority date for domestic students, 2/1 priority date for international students; for spring admission, 12/13 priority date for domestic students, 6/15 priority date for international students. *Application fee:* $40 ($55 for international students). Electronic applications accepted. *Application Contact:* Dr. Brian Jackson, Senior Associate Dean, 859-257-4667, Fax: 859-257-4676, E-mail: brian.jackson@uky.edu. *Dean,* Dr. Robert Shay, 859-257-1707, Fax: 859-323-1050, E-mail: robert.shay@uky.edu.

College of Health Sciences Students: 306 full-time (240 women), 26 part-time (24 women); includes 8 minority (4 African Americans, 1 American Indian/Alaska Native, 2 Asian Americans or Pacific Islanders, 1 Hispanic American), 7 international. Average age 28. 149 applicants, 50% accepted, 60 enrolled. *Faculty:* 105 full-time (55 women), 4 part-time/adjunct (2 women). Expenses: Contact institution. *Financial support:* In 2006–07, 9 students received support, including 3 fellowships with full tuition reimbursements available, 5 research assistantships with full tuition reimbursements available (averaging $12,000 per year), 1 teaching assistantship with full tuition reimbursement available (averaging $8,332 per year); career-related internships or fieldwork, Federal Work-Study, institutionally sponsored loans, scholarships/grants, traineeships, health care benefits, tuition waivers (partial), and unspecified assistantships also available. Support available to part-time students. Financial award application deadline: 3/15. In 2006, 143 master's, 3 doctorates awarded. *Degree program information:* Part-time programs available. Offers clinical sciences (MS, DS); communication disorders (MSCD); health physics (MSHP); health sciences (MS, MSCD, MSHP, MSPAS, MSPT, MSRMP, DS, PhD); physical therapy (MSPT); physician assistant studies (MSPAS); radiological medical physics (MSRMP); rehabilitation sciences (PhD). *Application deadline:* For fall admission, 7/17 priority date for domestic students, 2/1 priority date for international students; for spring admission, 12/13 priority date for domestic students, 6/15 priority date for international students. *Application fee:* $40 ($55 for international students). Electronic applications accepted. *Application Contact:* Dr. Brian Jackson, Senior Associate Dean, 859-257-4667, Fax: 859-257-4676, E-mail: brian.jackson@uky.edu. *Dean,* Dr. Lori Gonzalez, 859-323-1100 Ext. 235, Fax: 859-323-1058, E-mail: lsgonz01@pop.uky.edu.

College of Public Health Students: 101 full-time (76 women), 58 part-time (40 women); includes 26 minority (22 African Americans, 1 American Indian/Alaska Native, 2 Asian Americans or Pacific Islanders, 1 Hispanic American), 17 international. Average age 33. 174 applicants, 68% accepted, 60 enrolled. *Faculty:* 44 full-time (16 women), 4 part-time/adjunct (1 woman). Expenses: Contact institution. *Financial support:* In 2006–07, 26 fellowships with full tuition reimbursements (averaging $4,708 per year), 13 research assistantships with full tuition reimbursements (averaging $8,252 per year) were awarded; teaching assistantships with full tuition reimbursements, Federal Work-Study, scholarships/grants, traineeships, health care benefits, tuition waivers (partial), and unspecified assistantships also available. Support available to part-time students. Financial award application deadline: 3/15. In 2006, 30 master's, 9 doctorates awarded. Offers gerontology (PhD); public health (MPH, PhD). *Application deadline:* For fall admission, 7/17 priority date for domestic students, 2/1 priority date for international students; for spring admission, 12/13 priority date for domestic students, 6/15 priority date for international students. *Application fee:* $40 ($55 for international students). Electronic applications accepted. *Application Contact:* Dr. Brian Jackson, Senior Associate Dean, 859-257-4667, Fax: 859-257-4676, E-mail: brian.jackson@uky.edu. *Dean,* Dr. Stephen Wyatt, 859-257-5678, Fax: 859-323-5698, E-mail: steve.wyatt@uky.edu.

College of Social Work Students: 124 full-time (114 women), 171 part-time (148 women); includes 21 minority (16 African Americans, 2 Asian Americans or Pacific Islanders, 3 Hispanic Americans), 3 international. Average age 33. 229 applicants, 72% accepted, 131 enrolled. *Faculty:* 20 full-time (13 women). Expenses: Contact institution. *Financial support:* In 2006–07, 17 students received support, including 7 research assistantships (averaging $1,500 per year), 10 teaching assistantships (averaging $3,000 per year); fellowships, career-related internships or fieldwork, Federal Work-Study, institutionally sponsored loans, scholarships/grants, traineeships, health care benefits, and unspecified assistantships also available. Support available to part-time students. Financial award application deadline: 3/15; financial award applicants required to submit FAFSA. In 2006, 97 master's, 4 doctorates awarded. Offers social work (MSW, PhD). *Application deadline:* For fall admission, 7/17 priority date for domestic students, 2/1 priority date for international students; for spring admission, 12/13 priority date for domestic students, 6/15 priority date for international students. *Application fee:* $40 ($55 for international students). Electronic applications accepted. *Application Contact:* Dr. Brian Jackson, Senior Associate Dean, 859-257-4667, Fax: 859-257-4676, E-mail: brian.jackson@uky.edu. *Dean,* Dr. Kay Hoffman, 859-257-6654, E-mail: khoffma@uky.edu.

Gatton College of Business and Economics Students: 263 full-time (92 women), 137 part-time (53 women); includes 18 minority (10 African Americans, 3 Asian Americans or Pacific Islanders, 5 Hispanic Americans), 152 international. Average age 29. 327 applicants, 34% accepted, 42 enrolled. *Faculty:* 103 full-time (16 women), 3 part-time/adjunct (0 women). Expenses: Contact institution. *Financial support:* In 2006–07, 21 fellowships with full tuition reimbursements (averaging $2,873 per year), 4 research assistantships with full tuition reimbursements (averaging $13,224 per year), 58 teaching assistantships with full tuition reimbursements (averaging $12,450 per year) were awarded; career-related internships or fieldwork, Federal Work-Study, institutionally sponsored loans, scholarships/grants, traineeships, health care benefits, tuition waivers (partial), and unspecified assistantships also available. Support available to part-time students. Financial award application deadline: 3/15; financial award applicants required to submit FAFSA. In 2006, 144 master's, 13 doctorates awarded. *Degree program information:* Part-time and evening/weekend programs available. Offers accounting (MSACC); business administration (MBA, PhD); business and economics (MBA, MS, MSACC, PhD); economics (MS, PhD). *Application deadline:* For fall admission, 7/17 priority date for domestic students, 2/1 priority date for international students; for spring admission, 12/13 priority date for domestic students, 6/15 priority date for international students. *Application fee:* $40 ($50 for international students). Electronic applications accepted. *Application Contact:* Dr. Brian Jackson, Senior Associate Dean, 859-257-4667, Fax: 859-257-4676, E-mail: brian.jackson@uky.edu. *Dean,* Dr. Devanathan Sudharshan, 859-257-8936, Fax: 859-257-8938, E-mail: sudharshan@uky.edu.

Graduate School Programs from the College of Medicine Students: 208 full-time (112 women), 26 part-time (15 women); includes 17 minority (6 African Americans, 5 Asian Americans or Pacific Islanders, 6 Hispanic Americans), 37 international. Average age 29. 430 applicants, 34% accepted, 136 enrolled. *Faculty:* 167 full-time (38 women), 4 part-time/adjunct (1 woman). Expenses: Contact institution. *Financial support:* In 2006–07, 37 fellowships with full tuition reimbursements (averaging $4,846 per year), 207 research assistantships with full tuition reimbursements (averaging $21,000 per year), 10 teaching assistantships with full tuition reimbursements (averaging $21,000 per year) were awarded; Federal Work-Study, scholarships/grants, traineeships, health care benefits, tuition waivers (partial), and unspecified assistantships also available. Support available to part-time students. Financial award application deadline: 3/15; financial award applicants required to submit FAFSA. In 2006, 18 master's, 30 doctorates awarded. Offers anatomy (PhD); biochemistry (PhD); medical science (MS); medicine (MS, PhD); microbiology (PhD); pharmacology (PhD); physiology (MS, PhD); toxicology (MS, PhD). *Application deadline:* For fall admission, 7/17 priority date for domestic students, 2/1 priority date for international students; for spring admission, 12/13 priority date for domestic students, 6/15 priority date for international students. *Application fee:* $40 ($55 for international students). Electronic applications accepted. *Application Contact:* Dr. Brian Jackson, Senior Associate Dean, 859-257-4667, Fax: 859-257-4676, E-mail: brian.jackson@uky.edu. *Dean of College of Medicine,* Dr. Jay Perman, 859-323-6582.

Graduate School Programs in the College of Nursing Students: 72 full-time (66 women), 131 part-time (121 women); includes 6 minority (all African Americans), 8 international. Average age 38. 113 applicants, 59% accepted, 53 enrolled. *Faculty:* 24 full-time (23 women), 3 part-time/adjunct (2 women). Expenses: Contact institution. *Financial support:* In 2006–07, 2 fellowships with full tuition reimbursements (averaging $3,958 per year), 13 research assistantships with full tuition reimbursements (averaging $10,000 per year), 5 teaching assistantships with full tuition reimbursements (averaging $8,160 per year) were awarded; Federal Work-Study, institutionally sponsored loans, scholarships/grants, traineeships, health care benefits, tuition waivers (partial), and unspecified assistantships also available. Support available to part-time students. Financial award application deadline: 3/15; financial award applicants required to submit FAFSA. In 2006, 35 master's, 7 doctorates awarded. Offers nursing (MSN, PhD). *Application deadline:* For fall admission, 7/17 priority date for domestic students, 2/1 priority date for international students; for spring admission, 12/13 priority date for domestic students, 6/15 priority date for international students. *Application fee:* $40 ($55 for international students). Electronic applications accepted. *Application Contact:* Dr. Brian Jackson, Senior Associate Dean, 859-257-4667, Fax: 859-257-4676, E-mail: brian.jackson@uky.edu. *Dean,* Dr. Jane Marie Kirschling, 859-323-1057, Fax: 859-323-1057.

Patterson School of Diplomacy and International Commerce Students: 72 full-time (35 women), 2 part-time (1 woman); includes 1 minority (African American), 16 international. Average age 26. 101 applicants, 51% accepted, 37 enrolled. *Faculty:* 6 full-time (1 woman), 2 part-time/adjunct (0 women). Expenses: Contact institution. *Financial support:* Over half of the incoming students received institutionally-sponsored financial assistance ranging from one-half of tuition up to $20,000 available. Financial award application deadline: 3/15; financial award applicants required to submit FAFSA. In 2006, 32 degrees awarded. Offers diplomacy and international commerce (MA). *Application deadline:* For fall admission, 2/1 for domestic students. *Application fee:* $40 ($55 for international students). Electronic applications accepted. *Application Contact:* Dr. Brian Jackson, Senior Associate Dean, 859-257-4667, Fax: 859-257-4676, E-mail: brian.jackson@uky.edu. *Director of Graduate Studies,* Dr. Evan Hillebrand, 859-257-6928, Fax: 859-257-4676, E-mail: evan.hillebrand@uky.edu.

UNIVERSITY OF LA VERNE, La Verne, CA 91750-4443

General Information Independent, coed, university. *Enrollment:* 3,876 graduate, professional, and undergraduate students; 1,571 full-time matriculated graduate/professional students (987 women), 1,693 part-time matriculated graduate/professional students (1,162 women). *Enrollment by degree level:* 263 first professional, 2,088 master's, 494 doctoral, 419 other advanced degrees. *Graduate faculty:* 70 full-time (34 women), 162 part-time/adjunct (82 women). *Graduate housing:* On-campus housing not available. *Student services:* Campus employment opportunities, campus safety program, career counseling, disabled student services, exercise/wellness program, free psychological counseling, international student services, low-cost health insurance, multicultural affairs office, teacher training, writing training. *Library facilities:* Wilson Library. *Online resources:* library catalog, web page, access to other libraries' catalogs. *Collection:* 195,488 titles, 531,006 serial subscriptions, 1,720 audiovisual materials. *Research affiliation:* Presbyterian Intercommunity Hospital, Riverside Community Hospital, San Antonio Community Hospital, Methodist Hospital of Southern California, Southern California Healthcare Systems, Huntington Memorial Hospital (health services management).

Computer facilities: 150 computers available on campus for general student use. A campuswide network can be accessed from student residence rooms and from off campus. Internet access and online class registration, online grade information are available. *Web address:* http://www.ulv.edu/.

General Application Contact: Jo Nell Baker, Director, Graduate Admissions and Academic Services, 909-593-3511 Ext. 4244, Fax: 909-392-2761, E-mail: gradadmt@ulv.edu.

GRADUATE UNITS

College of Arts and Sciences Students: 88 full-time (75 women), 75 part-time (64 women); includes 93 minority (22 African Americans, 5 Asian Americans or Pacific Islanders, 66

University of La Verne (continued)

Hispanic Americans). Average age 31. *Faculty:* 13 full-time (4 women), 16 part-time/adjunct (10 women). Expenses: Contact institution. *Financial support:* Career-related internships or fieldwork, institutionally sponsored loans, and scholarships/grants available. Financial award application deadline: 3/2; financial award applicants required to submit FAFSA. In 2006, 25 master's, 15 doctorates awarded. *Degree program information:* Part-time programs available. Offers arts and sciences (MS, Psy D); clinical-community psychology (Psy D); counseling (MS); general counseling (MS); higher education counseling (MS); marriage and family therapy (MS). *Application deadline:* Applications are processed on a rolling basis. *Application Contact:* Jo Nell Baker, Director, Graduate Admissions and Academic Services, 909-593-3511 Ext. 4244, Fax: 909-392-2761, E-mail: gradadmt@ulv.edu. *Dean,* Dr. Fred Yaffe, 909-593-3511 Ext. 4198, E-mail: fyaffe@ulv.edu.

College of Business and Public Management Students: 393 full-time (192 women), 273 part-time (163 women); includes 297 minority (86 African Americans, 6 American Indian/Alaska Native, 92 Asian Americans or Pacific Islanders, 113 Hispanic Americans), 171 international. Average age 34. *Faculty:* 29 full-time (13 women), 26 part-time/adjunct (16 women). Expenses: Contact institution. *Financial support:* Career-related internships or fieldwork, institutionally sponsored loans, and scholarships/grants available. Financial award application deadline: 3/2; financial award applicants required to submit FAFSA. In 2006, 208 master's, 13 doctorates awarded. *Degree program information:* Part-time and evening/weekend programs available. Offers accounting (MBA); business (MBIT); business administration (MS); business and public management (MBA, MBA-EP, MBIT, MHA, MPA, MS, DPA, Certificate); counseling (MS); executive management (MBA-EP); finance (MBA, MBA-EP); financial management (MHA); gerontology (Certificate); gerontology administration (MS); health administration (MHA); health services management (MBA, MS); human resources (MHA); information management (MHA); information technology (MBA, MBA-EP); international business (MBA, MBA-EP); leadership (MBA-EP); leadership and management (MHA, MS); managed care (MBA, MHA); management (MBA, MBA-EP); marketing (MBA, MBA-EP); marketing and business development (MHA); nonprofit management (Certificate); organizational leadership (Certificate); public administration (MS). *Application deadline:* Applications are processed on a rolling basis. *Application fee:* $50. *Application Contact:* Dr. Julius Walecki, Marketing Director, 909-593-3511 Ext. 4192, Fax: 909-392-2704, E-mail: cbpm@ulv.edu. *Dean,* Dr. Gordon Badovick, 909-539-3511 Ext. 4216, Fax: 909-392-2704, E-mail: badovick@ulv.edu.

College of Education and Organizational Leadership Students: 383 full-time (293 women), 757 part-time (552 women); includes 451 minority (84 African Americans, 6 American Indian/Alaska Native, 42 Asian Americans or Pacific Islanders, 319 Hispanic Americans), 6 international. Average age 36. *Faculty:* 19 full-time (13 women), 10 part-time/adjunct (9 women). Expenses: Contact institution. *Financial support:* Institutionally sponsored loans, scholarships/grants, and unspecified assistantships available. Financial award application deadline: 3/2; financial award applicants required to submit FAFSA. In 2006, 233 master's, 46 doctorates awarded. *Degree program information:* Part-time programs available. Offers advanced teaching skills (M Ed); child development (MS); child development/child life (MS); child life (MS); education (M Ed); education (special emphasis) (M Ed); education and organizational leadership (M Ed, MS, Ed D, Certificate, Credential); educational management (M Ed, Credential); multiple subject (Credential); organizational leadership (Ed D); preliminary administrative services (Credential); professional administrative services (Credential); pupil personnel services (Credential); reading (M Ed, Certificate, Credential); reading and language arts specialist (Credential); school counseling (MS, Credential); single subject (Credential); teacher education (Credential). *Application deadline:* Applications are processed on a rolling basis. *Application fee:* $50. *Application Contact:* Jo Nell Baker, Director, Graduate Admissions and Academic Services, 909-593-3511 Ext. 4244, Fax: 909-392-2761, E-mail: gradadmt@ulv.edu. *Dean,* Dr. Leonard Pellicer, 909-593-3511 Ext. 4647, E-mail: pellicer@ulv.edu.

College of Law Students: 174 full-time (68 women), 87 part-time (45 women); includes 80 minority (14 African Americans, 1 American Indian/Alaska Native, 30 Asian Americans or Pacific Islanders, 35 Hispanic Americans), 5 international. Average age 27. 641 applicants, 42% accepted, 89 enrolled. *Faculty:* 18 full-time (7 women), 14 part-time/adjunct (2 women). Expenses: Contact institution. *Financial support:* Federal Work-Study and scholarships/grants available. Support available to part-time students. Financial award application deadline: 3/2; financial award applicants required to submit FAFSA. In 2006, 67 degrees awarded. *Degree program information:* Part-time and evening/weekend programs available. Offers law (JD). Also available at San Fernando Valley Campus. *Application deadline:* For fall admission, 7/1 priority date for domestic students; for spring admission, 11/1 priority date for domestic students. Applications are processed on a rolling basis. *Application fee:* $60. Electronic applications accepted. *Application Contact:* Alexis E. Thompson, Assistant Dean of Admissions, 909-460-2001, Fax: 909-460-2082, E-mail: lawadm@ulv.edu. *Dean,* Donald J. Dunn, 909-460-2000, Fax: 909-460-2081, E-mail: lawadm@ulv.edu.

Regional Campus Administration Students: 444 full-time (310 women), 573 part-time (372 women); includes 433 minority (101 African Americans, 14 American Indian/Alaska Native, 66 Asian Americans or Pacific Islanders, 252 Hispanic Americans), 1 international. Average age 37. *Faculty:* 22 full-time (8 women), 100 part-time/adjunct (47 women). Expenses: Contact institution. *Financial support:* Institutionally sponsored loans available. Support available to part-time students. Financial award application deadline: 3/2; financial award applicants required to submit FAFSA. In 2006, 470 degrees awarded. *Degree program information:* Part-time programs available. Offers advanced teaching (M Ed); business (MBA-EP); cross cultural language and academic development (Credential); educational management (M Ed); health administration (MHA); leadership and management (MS); multiple subject (Credential); reading (M Ed); school counseling (MS); single subject (Credential). *Application deadline:* Applications are processed on a rolling basis. *Application fee:* $50. *Dean,* Dr. Stephen E. Lesniak, 909-593-3511 Ext. 5300, E-mail: lesniaks@ulv.edu.

UNIVERSITY OF LETHBRIDGE, Lethbridge, AB T1K 3M4, Canada

General Information Province-supported, coed, university. *Enrollment:* 8,034 graduate, professional, and undergraduate students; 200 full-time matriculated graduate/professional students, 90 part-time matriculated graduate/professional students. *Enrollment by degree level:* 264 master's, 26 doctoral. *Graduate housing:* Rooms and/or apartments available on a first-come, first-served basis to single and married students. Typical cost: $2,800 per year ($4,000 including board) for single students. Room and board charges vary according to board plan and housing facility selected. Housing application deadline: 4/1. *Student services:* Campus employment opportunities, campus safety program, career counseling, disabled student services, exercise/wellness program, free psychological counseling, grant writing training, international student services, low-cost health insurance, multicultural affairs office, teacher training, writing training. *Library facilities:* The University of Lethbridge Library. *Online resources:* library catalog, web page, access to other libraries' catalogs. *Collection:* 560,427 titles, 1,300 serial subscriptions. *Research affiliation:* Pacific Forestry Institution, Monsanto Dow Agro-Sciences.

Computer facilities: Computer purchase and lease plans are available. 600 computers available on campus for general student use. A campuswide network can be accessed from student residence rooms and from off campus. Internet access and online class registration are available. *Web address:* http://www.uleth.ca/.

General Application Contact: Kathy Schrage, Administrative Assistant, School of Graduate Studies, 403-329-2121, Fax: 403-329-2097, E-mail: schrage@uleth.ca.

GRADUATE UNITS

School of Graduate Studies Students: 200 full-time, 90 part-time. Expenses: Contact institution. *Financial support:* Fellowships, research assistantships, teaching assistantships, scholarships/grants, health care benefits, and unspecified assistantships available. In 2006, 105 master's, 3 doctorates awarded. *Degree program information:* Part-time and evening/weekend programs available. Offers accounting (MScM); addictions counseling (M Sc); agricultural biotechnology (M Sc); agricultural studies (M Sc, MA); anthropology (MA); archaeology (MA); art (MA); biochemistry (M Sc); biological sciences (M Sc); biomolecular science (PhD); biosystems and biodiversity (PhD); Canadian studies (MA); chemistry (M Sc); computer science (M Sc); computer science and geographical information science (M Sc); counseling psychology (M Ed); dramatic arts (MA); earth, space, and physical science (PhD); economics (MA); educational leadership (M Ed); English (MA); environmental science (M Sc); evolution and behavior (PhD); exercise science (M Sc); finance (MScM); French (MA); French/German (MA); French/Spanish (MA); general education (M Ed); general management (MScM); geography (M Sc, MA); German (MA); health sciences (M Sc, MA); history (MA); human resource management and labour relations (MScM); individualized multidisciplinary (M Sc, MA); information systems (MScM); international management (MScM); kinesiology (M Sc, MA); management (M Sc, MA); marketing (MScM); mathematics (M Sc); music (MA); Native American studies (MA); neuroscience (M Sc, PhD); new media (MA); nursing (M Sc); philosophy (MA); physics (M Sc); policy and strategy (MScM); political science (MA); psychology (M Sc, MA); religious studies (MA); sociology (MA); theoretical and computational science (PhD); urban and regional studies (MA). *Application fee:* $60 Canadian dollars. *Application Contact:* Kathy Schrage, Administrative Assistant, Office of the Academic Vice President, 403-329-2121, Fax: 403-329-2097, E-mail: inquiries@uleth.ca. *Interim Dean,* Dr. Jo-Anne Fiske, 403-329-2121, Fax: 403-329-2097.

UNIVERSITY OF LOUISIANA AT LAFAYETTE, Lafayette, LA 70504

General Information State-supported, coed, university. CGS member. *Enrollment:* 16,302 graduate, professional, and undergraduate students; 725 full-time matriculated graduate/professional students (342 women), 480 part-time matriculated graduate/professional students (296 women). *Enrollment by degree level:* 906 master's, 299 doctoral. *Graduate faculty:* 322 full-time (100 women), 5 part-time/adjunct (1 woman). Tuition, state resident: full-time $3,247; part-time $93 per credit hour. Tuition, nonresident: full-time $9,427; part-time $350 per credit hour. *Graduate housing:* Rooms and/or apartments available on a first-come, first-served basis to single and married students. Typical cost: $3,996 (including board) for single students. *Student services:* Campus employment opportunities, campus safety program, career counseling, child daycare facilities, disabled student services, free psychological counseling, international student services, low-cost health insurance. *Library facilities:* Edith Garland Dupre Library. *Online resources:* library catalog, web page, access to other libraries' catalogs. *Collection:* 999,913 titles, 2,851 serial subscriptions, 10,807 audiovisual materials. *Research affiliation:* National Wetlands Research Center (biology, wetlands restoration), Louisiana Universities Marine Consortium (marine biology), U.S. Fish and Wildlife Service (ecology), Army Corps of Engineers (wetlands), U.S. Geological Survey, U.S. Department of Agriculture.

Computer facilities: 1,000 computers available on campus for general student use. A campuswide network can be accessed from off campus. Internet access and online class registration are available. *Web address:* http://www.louisiana.edu/.

General Application Contact: Dr. C. E. Palmer, Dean, 337-482-6965, Fax: 337-482-1333, E-mail: palmer@louisiana.edu.

GRADUATE UNITS

Graduate School Students: 725 full-time (342 women), 480 part-time (296 women); includes 110 minority (73 African Americans, 9 American Indian/Alaska Native, 10 Asian Americans or Pacific Islanders, 18 Hispanic Americans), 341 international. Average age 30. 1,259 applicants, 39% accepted, 233 enrolled. *Faculty:* 322 full-time (100 women), 5 part-time/adjunct (1 woman). Expenses: Contact institution. *Financial support:* In 2006–07, 41 fellowships with full tuition reimbursements (averaging $15,371 per year), 176 research assistantships with full tuition reimbursements (averaging $6,582 per year), 136 teaching assistantships with full tuition reimbursements (averaging $9,454 per year) were awarded; career-related internships or fieldwork, Federal Work-Study, institutionally sponsored loans, scholarships/grants, tuition waivers (full), and unspecified assistantships also available. Support available to part-time students. In 2006, 419 master's, 33 doctorates awarded. *Degree program information:* Part-time and evening/weekend programs available. Offers counselor education (MS). *Application deadline:* For fall admission, 5/15 for domestic students. *Application fee:* $25 ($30 for international students). *Dean,* Dr. C. E. Palmer, 337-482-6965, Fax: 337-482-1333, E-mail: palmer@louisiana.edu.

College of Business Administration Students: 68 full-time (28 women), 106 part-time (55 women); includes 18 minority (8 African Americans, 3 American Indian/Alaska Native, 3 Asian Americans or Pacific Islanders, 4 Hispanic Americans), 17 international. Average age 28. 122 applicants, 43% accepted, 38 enrolled. *Faculty:* 34 full-time (11 women). Expenses: Contact institution. *Financial support:* In 2006–07, 15 research assistantships with full tuition reimbursements (averaging $5,500 per year) were awarded; Federal Work-Study, tuition waivers (full), and unspecified assistantships also available. Support available to part-time students. Financial award application deadline: 5/1. In 2006, 63 degrees awarded. *Degree program information:* Part-time programs available. Offers business administration (MBA); health care administration (MBA); health care certification (MBA). *Application deadline:* For fall admission, 5/15 for domestic and international students; for spring admission, 10/1 for domestic and international students. *Application fee:* $25 ($30 for international students). *Application Contact:* Dr. P. Robert Viguerie, Director, MBA, 337-482-6119, Fax: 337-482-5883, E-mail: mbadirector@louisiana.edu. *Acting Dean,* Ellen Cook, 337-482-6491, Fax: 337-482-5883, E-mail: edcook@louisiana.edu.

College of Education Students: 15 full-time (all women), 92 part-time (72 women); includes 20 minority (15 African Americans, 3 American Indian/Alaska Native, 2 Hispanic Americans), 1 international. Average age 36. 44 applicants, 39% accepted, 11 enrolled. *Faculty:* 35 full-time (15 women), 1 part-time/adjunct (0 women). Expenses: Contact institution. *Financial support:* In 2006–07, 14 research assistantships with full tuition reimbursements (averaging $5,500 per year) were awarded; Federal Work-Study and unspecified assistantships also available. Financial award application deadline: 5/1. In 2006, 46 degrees awarded. *Degree program information:* Part-time programs available. Offers administration and supervision (M Ed); curriculum and instruction (M Ed); education (M Ed, Ed D); education of the gifted (M Ed); educational leadership (M Ed, Ed D). *Application deadline:* For fall admission, 5/15 for domestic and international students; for spring admission, 10/1 for domestic and international students. Applications are processed on a rolling basis. *Application fee:* $25 ($30 for international students). Electronic applications accepted. *Application Contact:* Dr. Nathan Roberts, Coordinator, 337-482-6747, Fax: 337-482-5842, E-mail: nmr0713@louisiana.edu. *Dean,* Dr. Gerald B. Carlson, 337-482-6678, Fax: 337-482-5842, E-mail: gcarlson@louisiana.edu.

College of Engineering Students: 242 full-time (55 women), 72 part-time (13 women); includes 15 minority (11 African Americans, 3 Asian Americans or Pacific Islanders, 1 Hispanic American), 239 international. Average age 26. 635 applicants, 34% accepted, 71 enrolled. *Faculty:* 32 full-time (3 women), 1 part-time/adjunct (0 women). Expenses: Contact institution. *Financial support:* In 2006–07, 7 fellowships with full tuition reimbursements (averaging $17,618 per year), 51 research assistantships with full tuition reimbursements (averaging $6,444 per year), 30 teaching assistantships with full tuition reimbursements (averaging $7,474 per year) were awarded; career-related internships or fieldwork, Federal Work-Study, and tuition waivers (full) also available. Support available to part-time students. In 2006, 146 master's, 10 doctorates awarded. *Degree program information:* Part-time and evening/weekend programs available. Offers chemical engineering (MSE); civil engineering (MSE); computer engineering (MS, PhD); computer science (MS, PhD); engineering (MS, MSE, MSET, MSTC, PhD); engineering and technology management (MSET); mechanical engineering (MSE); petroleum engineering (MSE); telecommunications (MSTC). *Application deadline:* For fall admission, 5/15 for domestic and international students; for spring admission, 10/1 for domestic and international students. Applications are processed on a rolling basis. *Application fee:* $25 ($30 for international students). Electronic applications accepted. *Dean,* Dr. Mark Zappi, 337-482-6685, Fax: 337-482-6688, E-mail: zappi@louisiana.edu.

College of Liberal Arts Students: 202 full-time (130 women), 78 part-time (56 women); includes 33 minority (21 African Americans, 2 American Indian/Alaska Native, 2 Asian Americans or Pacific Islanders, 8 Hispanic Americans), 36 international. Average age 31. 237 applicants, 45% accepted, 53 enrolled. *Faculty:* 96 full-time (40 women), 1 part-time/adjunct (0 women). Expenses: Contact institution. *Financial support:* In 2006–07, 15 fellowships with full tuition reimbursements (averaging $14,017 per year), 48 research assistantships with full tuition reimbursements (averaging $6,434 per year), 55 teaching assistantships with full tuition reimbursements (averaging $9,000 per year) were awarded; career-related internships or fieldwork and Federal Work-Study also available. Support available to part-time students. Financial award application deadline: 5/1. In 2006, 71 master's, 15 doctorates awarded. *Degree program information:* Part-time programs available. Offers British and American literature (MA); communicative disorders (MS, PhD); creative writing (PhD); Francophone studies (PhD); French (MA); history (MA); liberal arts (MA, MS, PhD); literature (PhD); mass communications (MS); psychology (MS); rehabilitation counseling (MS); rhetoric (PhD). *Application deadline:* For fall admission, 5/15 for domestic and international students; for spring admission, 10/1 for domestic and international students. Applications are processed on a rolling basis. *Application fee:* $25 ($30 for international students). Electronic applications accepted. *Dean,* Dr. A. David Barry, 337-482-6219, Fax: 337-482-6195, E-mail: dbarry@louisiana.edu.

College of Nursing Students: 13 full-time (10 women), 50 part-time (41 women); includes 9 minority (8 African Americans, 1 American Indian/Alaska Native). Average age 37. 30 applicants, 37% accepted, 10 enrolled. *Faculty:* 11 full-time (all women), 1 (woman) part-time/adjunct. Expenses: Contact institution. *Financial support:* Fellowships with full tuition reimbursements available. In 2006, 17 degrees awarded. Offers nursing (MSN). *Application deadline:* For fall admission, 5/15 for domestic and international students; for spring admission, 10/1 for domestic students. Applications are processed on a rolling basis. *Application fee:* $25 ($30 for international students). Electronic applications accepted. *Application Contact:* Dr. Carolyn P. Delahoussaye, Graduate Coordinator, 337-482-5617, Fax: 337-482-5649, E-mail: cgp6303@louisiana.edu. *Dean,* Dr. Gail Poirrier, 337-482-6808, Fax: 337-482-5649, E-mail: jdc6124@louisiana.edu.

College of Sciences Students: 244 full-time (93 women), 59 part-time (20 women); includes 12 minority (8 African Americans, 2 Asian Americans or Pacific Islanders, 2 Hispanic Americans), 173 international. Average age 28. 346 applicants, 47% accepted, 54 enrolled. *Faculty:* 91 full-time (13 women). Expenses: Contact institution. *Financial support:* In 2006–07, 19 fellowships with full tuition reimbursements (averaging $15,613 per year), 27 research assistantships with full tuition reimbursements (averaging $9,111 per year), 51 teaching assistantships with full tuition reimbursements (averaging $11,110 per year) were awarded; Federal Work-Study, institutionally sponsored loans, and tuition waivers (full) also available. In 2006, 117 master's, 15 doctorates awarded. *Degree program information:* Part-time programs available. Offers biology (MS); cognitive science (PhD); computer science (MS, PhD); environmental and evolutionary biology (PhD); geology (MS); mathematics (MS, PhD); physics (MS); sciences (MS, PhD). *Application deadline:* For fall admission, 5/15 for domestic and international students; for spring admission, 10/1 for domestic and international students. Applications are processed on a rolling basis. *Application fee:* $25 ($30 for international students). Electronic applications accepted. *Dean,* Dr. Bradd D. Clark, 337-482-6986, Fax: 337-482-1247, E-mail: bec1033@louisiana.edu.

College of the Arts Students: 21 full-time (8 women), 7 part-time (2 women); includes 1 minority (Hispanic American), 1 international. Average age 26. 22 applicants, 59% accepted, 13 enrolled. *Faculty:* 22 full-time (6 women), 1 part-time/adjunct (0 women). Expenses: Contact institution. *Financial support:* In 2006–07, 15 research assistantships with full tuition reimbursements (averaging $5,500 per year) were awarded; fellowships, Federal Work-Study and unspecified assistantships also available. Financial award application deadline: 5/1. In 2006, 20 degrees awarded. Offers architecture (M Arch); arts (M Arch, MM); conducting (MM); pedagogy (MM); vocal and instrumental performance (MM). *Application deadline:* For fall admission, 5/15 for domestic and international students; for spring admission, 10/1 for domestic and international students. Applications are processed on a rolling basis. *Application fee:* $25 ($30 for international students). Electronic applications accepted. *Dean,* H. Gordon Brooks, 337-482-6224, Fax: 337-482-5907, E-mail: gbrooks@louisiana.edu.

School of Human Resources Students: 8 full-time (5 women), 8 part-time (7 women); includes 1 minority (Asian American or Pacific Islander), 1 international. Average age 30. *Faculty:* 1 (woman) full-time. Expenses: Contact institution. *Financial support:* In 2006–07, 3 research assistantships with full tuition reimbursements (averaging $5,500 per year) were awarded; fellowships, teaching assistantships, Federal Work-Study also available. Financial award application deadline: 5/1. In 2006, 7 degrees awarded. *Degree program information:* Part-time programs available. Offers human resources (MS). *Application deadline:* For fall admission, 5/15 for domestic and international students; for spring admission, 10/1 for domestic and international students. Applications are processed on a rolling basis. Electronic applications accepted. *Application Contact:* Dr. Janice Weber, Graduate Coordinator, 337-482-6096, Fax: 337-482-5395, E-mail: jweber@louisiana.edu. *Director,* Dr. Rachel Fournet, 337-482-5724, Fax: 337-482-5395, E-mail: rmf0931@louisiana.edu.

UNIVERSITY OF LOUISIANA AT MONROE, Monroe, LA 71209-0001

General Information State-supported, coed, university. *Enrollment:* 8,571 graduate, professional, and undergraduate students; 759 full-time matriculated graduate/professional students (517 women), 351 part-time matriculated graduate/professional students (275 women). *Enrollment by degree level:* 431 first professional, 566 master's, 103 doctoral, 10 other advanced degrees. *Graduate faculty:* 98 full-time (37 women), 9 part-time/adjunct (5 women). Tuition, state resident: part-time $124 per credit hour. Tuition, nonresident: part-time $124 per credit hour. *Graduate housing:* Room and/or apartments available on a first-come, first-served basis to single students; on-campus housing not available to married students. Housing application deadline: 7/28. *Student services:* Campus employment opportunities, career counseling, child daycare facilities, free psychological counseling, international student services. *Library facilities:* University Library. *Online resources:* library catalog, access to other libraries' catalogs. *Collection:* 645,612 titles, 935 audiovisual materials. *Research affiliation:* National Center for Toxicological Research (toxicology), U.S. Army Corps of Engineers (toxicology, environmental science), Xenoport, Inc. (pharmaceutics), Harvard Hughes Medical Institute (biology), Philip Morris, Inc. (medicinal chemistry), Juvenile Diabetes Research Foundation (pharmacology).

Computer facilities: 1,400 computers available on campus for general student use. A campuswide network can be accessed from student residence rooms and from off campus. Internet access and online class registration are available. *Web address:* http://www.ulm.edu/.

General Application Contact: Dr. Virginia Eaton, Executive Director, 318-342-1043, Fax: 318-342-1042, E-mail: logan@ulm.edu.

GRADUATE UNITS

Graduate Studies and Research Students: 759 full-time (517 women), 351 part-time (275 women); includes 263 minority (191 African Americans, 4 American Indian/Alaska Native, 61 Asian Americans or Pacific Islanders, 7 Hispanic Americans), 71 international. Average age 28. *Faculty:* 174 full-time (65 women), 21 part-time/adjunct (15 women). Expenses: Contact institution. *Financial support:* Research assistantships, teaching assistantships, career-related internships or fieldwork, Federal Work-Study, institutionally sponsored loans, unspecified assistantships, and laboratory assistantships available. Support available to part-time students. In 2006, 79 first professional degrees, 262 master's, 18 doctorates awarded. *Degree program information:* Part-time and evening/weekend programs available. Offers pharmaceutical sciences (MS); pharmacy (Pharm D, MS, PhD). *Application deadline:* Applications are processed on a rolling basis. *Application fee:* $20 ($30 for international students). Electronic applications accepted. *Graduate Studies and Research Director,* Dr. Virginia Eaton, 318-342-1036, Fax: 318-342-1042, E-mail: eaton@ulm.edu.

College of Arts and Sciences Students: 103 full-time (67 women), 56 part-time (38 women); includes 41 African Americans, 1 American Indian/Alaska Native, 2 Hispanic Americans, 7 international. Average age 28. *Faculty:* 83 full-time (24 women), 11 part-time/adjunct (9 women). Expenses: Contact institution. *Financial support:* Research assistantships, teaching assistantships, career-related internships or fieldwork, Federal Work-Study, institutionally sponsored loans, unspecified assistantships, and laboratory assistantships available. Support available to part-time students. In 2006, 60 degrees awarded. *Degree program information:* Part-time and evening/weekend programs available. Offers arts and sciences (MA, MM, MS, CGS); biology (MS); communication (MA); criminal justice (MA); English (MA); gerontological studies (CGS); gerontology (MA, CGS); history (MA); music (MM); visual and performing arts (MM). *Application fee:* $20 ($30 for international students). *Application Contact:* Frances Gregory, Assistant Dean, 318-342-1366, Fax: 318-342-1369, E-mail: gregory@ulm.edu. *Dean-Interim,* Dr. Mark Arant, 318-342-1750, Fax: 318-342-1755, E-mail: arant@ulm.edu.

College of Business Administration Students: 27 full-time (19 women), 44 part-time (32 women); includes 12 African Americans, 3 Asian Americans or Pacific Islanders, 8 international. Average age 29. *Faculty:* 14 full-time (4 women). Expenses: Contact institution. *Financial support:* Research assistantships, teaching assistantships, Federal Work-Study available. Financial award application deadline: 7/1. In 2006, 40 degrees awarded. *Degree program information:* Part-time and evening/weekend programs available. Offers business administration (MBA). *Application deadline:* For fall admission, 6/1 for domestic students; for spring admission, 11/1 for domestic students. *Application fee:* $20 ($30 for international students). *Application Contact:* Dr. Donna Luse, Program Chair, 318-342-1106, E-mail: luse@ulm.edu. *Dean,* Dr. Ron Berry, 318-342-1100, E-mail: rberry@ulm.edu.

College of Education and Human Development Students: 126 full-time (103 women), 232 part-time (188 women); includes 111 African Americans, 3 Asian Americans or Pacific Islanders, 2 Hispanic Americans, 8 international. Average age 34. *Faculty:* 43 full-time (21 women), 7 part-time/adjunct (5 women). Expenses: Contact institution. *Financial support:* Research assistantships, teaching assistantships, career-related internships or fieldwork, Federal Work-Study, institutionally sponsored loans, and unspecified assistantships available. Financial award application deadline: 7/1. In 2006, 144 master's, 5 doctorates awarded. *Degree program information:* Part-time and evening/weekend programs available. Offers administration and supervision (M Ed); counseling (M Ed); curriculum and instruction (M Ed, Ed D); education (M Ed, MA, MAT, MS, Ed D, PhD, SSP); educational leadership (Ed D); elementary education (M Ed, MAT); exercise science (MS); marriage and family therapy (MA, PhD); psychology (MS); reading (M Ed); school psychology (SSP); secondary education (M Ed, MAT); special education (M Ed, MAT); substance abuse counseling (MA). *Application fee:* $20 ($30 for international students). *Dean,* Dr. Luke Thomas, 318-342-1305, E-mail: lthomas@ulm.edu.

College of Health Sciences Students: 35 full-time (33 women), 4 part-time (all women); includes 5 African Americans, 1 international. Average age 27. *Faculty:* 8 full-time (all women). Expenses: Contact institution. *Financial support:* Research assistantships, teaching assistantships, Federal Work-Study and unspecified assistantships available. Financial award application deadline: 5/1. In 2006, 18 degrees awarded. Offers communicative disorders (MS); health sciences (MS). *Application deadline:* For fall admission, 5/1 priority date for domestic students. Applications are processed on a rolling basis. *Application fee:* $20 ($30 for international students). *Application Contact:* Dr. Greg Leader, Associate Dean, 318-342-1600. *Dean-Interim,* Dr. Jan Corder, 318-342-1622, Fax: 318-342-1606, E-mail: corder@ulm.edu.

UNIVERSITY OF LOUISVILLE, Louisville, KY 40292-0001

General Information State-supported, coed, university. CGS member. *Enrollment:* 20,804 graduate, professional, and undergraduate students; 3,161 full-time matriculated graduate/professional students (1,668 women), 1,973 part-time matriculated graduate/professional students (1,149 women). *Enrollment by degree level:* 918 first professional, 3,186 master's, 1,030 doctoral. *Graduate faculty:* 1,462 full-time (512 women), 572 part-time/adjunct (252 women). *Graduate housing:* Rooms and/or apartments available to single and married students. *Student services:* Campus employment opportunities, campus safety program, career counseling, child daycare facilities, disabled student services, exercise/wellness program, free psychological counseling, grant writing training, international student services, low-cost health insurance, multicultural affairs office. *Library facilities:* William F. Ekstrom Library plus 5 others. *Online resources:* library catalog, web page. *Collection:* 2.1 million titles, 37,931 serial subscriptions, 32,093 audiovisual materials. *Research affiliation:* Oak Ridge National Laboratory, Argonne National Laboratory.

Computer facilities: Computer purchase and lease plans are available. 265 computers available on campus for general student use. A campuswide network can be accessed from student residence rooms and from off campus. Internet access and online class registration are available. *Web address:* http://www.louisville.edu/.

General Application Contact: Libby Leggett, Information Contact, 502-852-3108, Fax: 502-852-6536, E-mail: gradadm@louisville.edu.

GRADUATE UNITS

Graduate School Students: 2,245 full-time (1,291 women), 1,971 part-time (1,148 women); includes 515 minority (355 African Americans, 8 American Indian/Alaska Native, 104 Asian Americans or Pacific Islanders, 48 Hispanic Americans), 658 international. Average age 33. Expenses: Contact institution. *Financial support:* Fellowships with full tuition reimbursements, research assistantships with full tuition reimbursements, teaching assistantships with full and partial tuition reimbursements, career-related internships or fieldwork, Federal Work-Study, institutionally sponsored loans, scholarships/grants, traineeships, tuition waivers (partial), and unspecified assistantships available. *Degree program information:* Part-time and evening/weekend programs available. *Application deadline:* Applications are processed on a rolling basis. *Application fee:* $50. Electronic applications accepted. *Application Contact:* Libby Leggett, Director, Graduate Admissions, 502-852-3101, Fax: 502-852-6536, E-mail: gradadm@louisville.edu. *Dean,* Dr. Ronald M. Atlas, 502-852-8371, Fax: 502-852-6616, E-mail: r.atlas@louisville.edu.

College of Arts and Sciences Students: 537 full-time (292 women), 368 part-time (212 women); includes 107 minority (69 African Americans, 2 American Indian/Alaska Native, 17 Asian Americans or Pacific Islanders, 19 Hispanic Americans), 123 international. Average age 33. *Faculty:* 366 full-time (151 women), 172 part-time/adjunct (89 women). Expenses: Contact institution. *Financial support:* Fellowships with full tuition reimbursements, research assistantships with full tuition reimbursements, teaching assistantships with full tuition reimbursements, career-related internships or fieldwork, institutionally sponsored loans, scholarships/grants, tuition waivers (partial), and unspecified assistantships available. In 2006, 188 master's, 30 doctorates awarded. *Degree program information:* Part-time and evening/weekend programs available. Offers analytical chemistry (MS, PhD); applied and industrial mathematics (PhD); art history (MA, PhD); arts and sciences (MA, MFA, MPA, MS, MUP, PhD, Certificate); biochemistry (MS, PhD); biology (MS); chemical physics (PhD); clinical psychology (PhD); creative art (MA); English (MA); English literature (MA); English rhetoric and composition (PhD); environmental biology (PhD); experimental psychology (PhD); French (MA); history (MA); humanities (MA, PhD); inorganic chemistry (MS, PhD); justice administration (MS); labor and public management (MPA); mathematics (MA); organic chemistry (MS, PhD); Pan-African studies (MA); performance (MFA); philosophy (MA); physical chemistry (MS, PhD); physics (MS); political science (MA); production (MFA); psychology (MA); public administration (MPA); public policy and administration (MPA); sociology (MA); Spanish (MA); systems science (MA); theatre arts (MA); urban and public affairs (PhD); urban and regional development (MPA); urban planning (MUP); women's and gender studies (MA, Certificate). *Application deadline:* Applications are processed on a rolling basis. *Application fee:* $50. *Dean,* Dr. J. Blaine Hudson, 502-852-2234, Fax: 502-852-6888, E-mail: jbhuds01@louisville.edu.

College of Business Students: 141 full-time (57 women), 248 part-time (99 women); includes 32 minority (10 African Americans, 16 Asian Americans or Pacific Islanders, 6 Hispanic Americans), 86 international. Average age 31. *Faculty:* 73 full-time (14 women), 31 part-time/adjunct (6 women). Expenses: Contact institution. *Financial support:* In 2006–07, 24 research assistantships with full tuition reimbursements were awarded; scholarships/grants, health care benefits, and unspecified assistantships also available. In 2006, 216 degrees awarded. *Degree program information:* Part-time programs available. Offers accountancy (MAC); business (MA, MAC, MBA, PhD); business administration (MBA); entrepreneurship (PhD). *Application deadline:* Applications are processed on a rolling basis. *Application fee:* $50. *Dean,* Dr. Charles Moyer, 502-852-6443, Fax: 502-852-7557.

College of Education and Human Development Students: 514 full-time (354 women), 889 part-time (614 women); includes 173 minority (140 African Americans, 3 American Indian/Alaska Native, 21 Asian Americans or Pacific Islanders, 9 Hispanic Americans), 101

University of Louisville (continued)

international. Average age 34. *Faculty:* 93 full-time (60 women), 97 part-time/adjunct (62 women). Expenses: Contact institution. *Financial support:* In 2006–07, 9 fellowships with full tuition reimbursements (averaging $18,000 per year), 30 research assistantships with full tuition reimbursements, 6 teaching assistantships with full tuition reimbursements were awarded; career-related internships or fieldwork, Federal Work-Study, and scholarships/grants also available. In 2006, 463 master's, 33 doctorates, 11 other advanced degrees awarded. *Degree program information:* Part-time and evening/weekend programs available. Offers art education (MAT); college student personnel services (M Ed); counseling and personnel services (M Ed, PhD); counseling psychology (M Ed, PhD); curriculum and instruction (Ed D); early elementary education (M Ed, MAT); education and human development (M Ed, MA, MAT, MS, Ed D, PhD, Ed S); educational leadership and organizational development (PhD); exercise physiology (MS); expressive therapies (M Ed); foreign language education (MAT); health education (M Ed); higher education (MA, Ed S); human resource education (M Ed); instructional technology (M Ed); interdisciplinary early childhood education (M Ed); mental health counseling (PhD); middle school education (M Ed, MAT); music education (MAT); occupational training and development (M Ed); p-12 educational administration (M Ed, PhD, Ed S); physical education (teacher preparation) (M Ed, MAT); reading education (M Ed); school counseling and guidance (M Ed, PhD); secondary education (M Ed, MAT); special education (M Ed, PhD); sport administration (MS). *Application deadline:* Applications are processed on a rolling basis. *Application fee:* $50. Electronic applications accepted. *Dean,* Dr. Robert Felner, 502-852-6411, Fax: 502-852-0726, E-mail: rifelner@louisville.edu.

Interdisciplinary Studies Average age 45. Expenses: Contact institution. Offers interdisciplinary studies (MA, MS). *Application deadline:* Applications are processed on a rolling basis. *Application fee:* $50.

J.B. Speed School of Engineering Students: 326 full-time (70 women), 210 part-time (41 women); includes 48 minority (16 African Americans, 2 American Indian/Alaska Native, 27 Asian Americans or Pacific Islanders, 3 Hispanic Americans), 243 international. Average age 29. *Faculty:* 95 full-time (16 women), 17 part-time/adjunct (4 women). Expenses: Contact institution. *Financial support:* In 2006–07, 23 fellowships with full tuition reimbursements (averaging $20,000 per year), 78 research assistantships with full tuition reimbursements (averaging $18,313 per year), 47 teaching assistantships with full tuition reimbursements (averaging $17,872 per year) were awarded; Federal Work-Study and scholarships/grants also available. In 2006, 227 master's, 30 doctorates awarded. *Degree program information:* Part-time programs available. Offers chemical engineering (M Eng, MS, PhD); civil and environmental engineering (M Eng, MS, PhD); computer engineering and computer science (M Eng, MS); computer science (MS); computer science and engineering (PhD); electrical and computer engineering (M Eng, MS, PhD); engineering (M Eng, MS, PhD); engineering management (M Eng); industrial engineering (M Eng, MS, PhD); mechanical engineering (M Eng, MS). *Application deadline:* Applications are processed on a rolling basis. *Application fee:* $50. Electronic applications accepted. *Application Contact:* Dr. Mike Day, Associate Dean, 502-852-6100, Fax: 502-852-0392, E-mail: day@louisville.edu. *Dean,* Dr. Mickey R. Wilhelm, 502-852-0802, Fax: 502-852-1577, E-mail: wilhelm@louisville.edu.

Raymond A. Kent School of Social Work Students: 302 full-time (251 women), 96 part-time (83 women); includes 78 minority (71 African Americans, 1 American Indian/Alaska Native, 4 Asian Americans or Pacific Islanders, 2 Hispanic Americans), 10 international. Average age 33. *Faculty:* 25 full-time (16 women), 40 part-time/adjunct (24 women). Expenses: Contact institution. *Financial support:* In 2006–07, 3 fellowships with full tuition reimbursements (averaging $18,000 per year), 11 research assistantships with full tuition reimbursements (averaging $18,000 per year) were awarded; tuition waivers (full) also available. Financial award application deadline: 4/1. In 2006, 141 master's, 7 doctorates awarded. Offers marriage and family therapy (PMC); social work (MSSW, PhD). *Application deadline:* Applications are processed on a rolling basis. *Application fee:* $50. *Dean,* Dr. Terry Singer, 502-852-6402, Fax: 502-852-0422, E-mail: terry.singer@louisville.edu.

School of Music Students: 60 full-time (22 women), 11 part-time (3 women); includes 12 minority (7 African Americans, 3 Asian Americans or Pacific Islanders, 2 Hispanic Americans), 10 international. Average age 27. *Faculty:* 32 full-time (8 women), 38 part-time/adjunct (11 women). Expenses: Contact institution. *Financial support:* In 2006–07, 3 fellowships with full tuition reimbursements (averaging $10,500 per year), 20 teaching assistantships with full tuition reimbursements (averaging $10,500 per year) were awarded; scholarships/grants, health care benefits, tuition waivers (full and partial), and unspecified assistantships also available. In 2006, 31 degrees awarded. *Degree program information:* Part-time programs available. Offers music education (MAT, MME); music history (MM, PhD); music history and literature (MM); music literature (PhD); music performance (MM); music theory and composition (MM); musicology (PhD); performance (MM); theory and composition (MM). *Application deadline:* For fall admission, 3/15 priority date for domestic students. Applications are processed on a rolling basis. *Application fee:* $50. *Application Contact:* Amanda Boyd, Admissions Counselor, 502-852-1623, Fax: 502-852-1874, E-mail: gomusic@louisville.edu. *Dean,* Dr. Christopher Doane, 502-852-6907, Fax: 502-852-1874, E-mail: doane@louisville.edu.

School of Nursing Students: 38 full-time (36 women), 54 part-time (49 women); includes 9 minority (7 African Americans, 1 Asian American or Pacific Islander, 1 Hispanic American). Average age 34. *Faculty:* 30 full-time (28 women), 18 part-time/adjunct (all women). Expenses: Contact institution. *Financial support:* In 2006–07, 10 teaching assistantships were awarded; institutionally sponsored loans, scholarships/grants, and traineeships also available. Financial award application deadline: 4/15; financial award applicants required to submit FAFSA. In 2006, 23 degrees awarded. *Degree program information:* Part-time programs available. Offers nursing (MSN, PhD). *Application deadline:* For fall admission, 5/1 priority date for domestic students; for spring admission, 10/1 priority date for domestic students. Applications are processed on a rolling basis. *Application fee:* $50. *Interim Dean,* Dr. Cynthia A. McCurren, 502-852-8300, Fax: 502-852-5044, E-mail: camccu01@gwise.louisville.edu.

School of Public Health Students: 62 full-time (40 women), 42 part-time (23 women); includes 20 minority (12 African Americans, 6 Asian Americans or Pacific Islanders, 2 Hispanic Americans), 16 international. Average age 35. *Faculty:* 25 full-time (9 women), 4 part-time/adjunct (0 women). Expenses: Contact institution. *Financial support:* In 2006–07, 12 research assistantships with tuition reimbursements (averaging $20,000 per year), 2 teaching assistantships (averaging $20,000 per year) were awarded; fellowships with tuition reimbursements also available. In 2006, 66 master's, 8 doctorates, 3 other advanced degrees awarded. Offers bioinformatics and biostatistics (MS, PhD); clinical investigation (Certificate); clinical investigation sciences (MS, PhD); public health (MPH). *Application fee:* $50. *Application Contact:* Tammi A. Thomas, Assistant Director of Academic/Student Affairs, 502-852-3289, Fax: 502-852-3291, E-mail: tammi.thomas@louisville.edu. *Dean,* Dr. Richard D. Clover, 502-852-3297, Fax: 502-852-3291, E-mail: rdclov01@gwise.louisville.edu.

Louis D. Brandeis School of Law Students: 319 full-time (134 women), 98 part-time (47 women); includes 17 minority (10 African Americans, 2 American Indian/Alaska Native, 1 Asian American or Pacific Islander, 4 Hispanic Americans), 1 international. Average age 24. 1,244 applicants, 32% accepted, 142 enrolled. *Faculty:* 29 full-time (11 women), 6 part-time/adjunct (1 woman). Expenses: Contact institution. *Financial support:* Fellowships, research assistantships, teaching assistantships, career-related internships or fieldwork, Federal Work-Study, scholarships/grants, and tuition waivers (partial) available. Support available to part-time students. Financial award application deadline: 6/1; financial award applicants required to submit FAFSA. In 2006, 104 degrees awarded. *Degree program information:* Part-time and evening/weekend programs available. Offers law (JD). *Application deadline:* For fall admission, 3/1 priority date for domestic students, 3/1 for international students. Applications are processed on a rolling basis. *Application fee:* $50. Electronic applications accepted. *Application Contact:* Jack D Cox, Assistant Dean for Admission and Financial Aid, 502-852-6391, Fax: 502-852-8971, E-mail: lawadmissions@louisville.edu. *Dean,* James Chen, 502-852-6879, E-mail: jim.chen@louisville.edu.

School of Dentistry Students: 337 full-time (136 women), 13 part-time (1 woman); includes 48 minority (23 African Americans, 2 American Indian/Alaska Native, 17 Asian Americans or Pacific Islanders, 6 Hispanic Americans), 4 international. Average age 28. *Faculty:* 67 full-time (18 women), 77 part-time/adjunct (20 women). Expenses: Contact institution. *Financial support:* In 2006–07, 1 fellowship with tuition reimbursement, 10 research assistantships (averaging $3,000 per year) were awarded. In 2006, 77 DMDs, 7 master's awarded. Offers dentistry (DMD, MS); oral biology (MS). *Application fee:* $50. *Application Contact:* Robin Benningfield, Admissions Counselor, 502-852-5081, Fax: 502-852-1210, E-mail: robin.benningfield@louisville.edu. *Acting Dean,* Dr. Wood E. Currens, 502-852-1304, Fax: 502-852-3364, E-mail: wecurr01@louisville.edu.

School of Medicine Students: 844 full-time (410 women), 41 part-time (23 women); includes 133 minority (61 African Americans, 1 American Indian/Alaska Native, 64 Asian Americans or Pacific Islanders, 7 Hispanic Americans), 66 international. Average age 27. *Faculty:* 656 full-time (192 women), 78 part-time/adjunct (18 women). Expenses: Contact institution. *Financial support:* In 2006–07, 30 fellowships with full tuition reimbursements (averaging $20,000 per year) were awarded; career-related internships or fieldwork, institutionally sponsored loans, scholarships/grants, traineeships, tuition waivers (full and partial), and unspecified assistantships also available. In 2006, 139 MDs, 43 master's, 40 doctorates awarded. Offers anatomical sciences and neurobiology (MS, PhD); audiology (Au D); biochemistry and molecular biology (MS, PhD); communicative disorders (MS, Au D); medicine (MD, MS, Au D, PhD); microbiology and immunology (MS, PhD); ophthalmology and visual sciences (PhD); pharmacology and toxicology (MS, PhD); physiology and biophysics (MS, PhD). *Application deadline:* For fall admission, 1/15 for domestic students. Applications are processed on a rolling basis. *Application fee:* $50. *Application Contact:* Director of Admissions, 502-852-5793, Fax: 502-852-6849. *Dean,* Dr. Edward C. Halperin, 502-852-1499, Fax: 502-852-1484, E-mail: edward.halperin@louisville.edu.

See Close-Up on page 1079.

UNIVERSITY OF MAINE, Orono, ME 04469

General Information State-supported, coed, university. CGS member. *Enrollment:* 11,435 graduate, professional, and undergraduate students; 1,110 full-time matriculated graduate/professional students (631 women), 1,160 part-time matriculated graduate/professional students (844 women). *Enrollment by degree level:* 1,212 master's, 440 doctoral, 74 other advanced degrees. *Graduate faculty:* 527 full-time (176 women), 284 part-time/adjunct (158 women). *Graduate housing:* Rooms and/or apartments available on a first-come, first-served basis to single and married students. Housing application deadline: 8/1. *Student services:* Campus employment opportunities, campus safety program, career counseling, child daycare facilities, disabled student services, exercise/wellness program, free psychological counseling, grant writing training, international student services, low-cost health insurance, multicultural affairs office, teacher training, writing training. *Library facilities:* Fogler Library plus 2 others. *Online resources:* library catalog, web page, access to other libraries' catalogs. *Collection:* 1.1 million titles, 13,041 serial subscriptions, 26,647 audiovisual materials. *Research affiliation:* Jackson Laboratory (medical genetics), Bigelow Laboratories for Ocean Sciences (marine science), Mount Desert Island Biological Laboratory (marine molecular biology), Sensor Research Development Corporation (electrical sensors), Maine Medical Center Research Institute (clinical medicine).

Computer facilities: Computer purchase and lease plans are available. 500 computers available on campus for general student use. A campuswide network can be accessed from student residence rooms and from off campus. Internet access and online class registration, online grade and financial aid information, e-mail are available. *Web address:* http://www.umaine.edu/.

General Application Contact: Scott G. Delcourt, Associate Dean of the Graduate School, 207-581-3219, Fax: 207-581-3232, E-mail: graduate@maine.edu.

GRADUATE UNITS

Graduate School Students: 1,073 full-time (599 women), 678 part-time (447 women); includes 60 minority (11 African Americans, 24 American Indian/Alaska Native, 18 Asian Americans or Pacific Islanders, 7 Hispanic Americans), 179 international. Average age 34. 1,244 applicants, 51% accepted, 450 enrolled. *Faculty:* 638. Expenses: Contact institution. *Financial support:* In 2006–07, 30 fellowships with tuition reimbursements (averaging $20,400 per year), 250 research assistantships with tuition reimbursements (averaging $12,000 per year), 250 teaching assistantships with tuition reimbursements (averaging $11,500 per year) were awarded; career-related internships or fieldwork, Federal Work-Study, institutionally sponsored loans, scholarships/grants, tuition waivers (full and partial), and unspecified assistantships also available. Support available to part-time students. Financial award application deadline: 3/1; financial award applicants required to submit FAFSA. In 2006, 574 master's, 50 doctorates, 36 other advanced degrees awarded. *Degree program information:* Part-time and evening/weekend programs available. Offers biomedical sciences (PhD); information systems (MS); interdisciplinary studies (PhD); liberal studies (MA); teaching (MST). *Application deadline:* Applications are processed on a rolling basis. *Application fee:* $50. Electronic applications accepted. *Associate Dean of the Graduate School,* Scott G. Delcourt, 207-581-3219, Fax: 207-581-3232, E-mail: graduate@maine.edu.

Climate Change Institute Students: 12 full-time (5 women), 1 part-time; includes 1 minority (African American), 2 international. Average age 30. 15 applicants, 53% accepted, 4 enrolled. *Faculty:* 9 full-time. Expenses: Contact institution. *Financial support:* In 2006–07, 8 research assistantships with tuition reimbursements (averaging $14,800 per year) were awarded; tuition waivers (full and partial) also available. Financial award application deadline: 3/1. In 2006, 1 degree awarded. *Degree program information:* Part-time programs available. Offers climate change (MS). *Application deadline:* For fall admission, 2/1 priority date for domestic students. Applications are processed on a rolling basis. *Application fee:* $50. Electronic applications accepted. *Application Contact:* Scott G. Delcourt, Associate Dean of the Graduate School, 207-581-3219, Fax: 207-581-3232, E-mail: graduate@maine.edu. *Director,* Dr. Paul Mayewski, 207-581-3019, Fax: 207-581-1203.

College of Business, Public Policy and Health Students: 208 full-time (132 women), 56 part-time (41 women); includes 9 minority (1 African American, 7 American Indian/Alaska Native, 1 Asian American or Pacific Islander), 20 international. Average age 34. 123 applicants, 53% accepted, 60 enrolled. Expenses: Contact institution. *Financial support:* In 2006–07, research assistantships with tuition reimbursements (averaging $9,010 per year), teaching assistantships with tuition reimbursements (averaging $9,010 per year) were awarded; career-related internships or fieldwork, Federal Work-Study, institutionally sponsored loans, scholarships/grants, tuition waivers (full and partial), and unspecified assistantships also available. Support available to part-time students. Financial award application deadline: 3/1. In 2006, 99 master's, 1 doctorate awarded. *Degree program information:* Part-time and evening/weekend programs available. Offers accounting (MS); business administration (MBA); business, public policy and health (MA, MBA, MPA, MS, MSW, PhD, CAS); economics (MA); financial economics (MA); nursing (MS, CAS); public administration (MPA, PhD); social work (MSW). *Application deadline:* Applications are processed on a rolling basis. *Application fee:* $50. Electronic applications accepted. *Application Contact:* Scott G. Delcourt, Associate Dean of the Graduate School, 207-581-3219, Fax: 207-581-3232, E-mail: graduate@maine.edu. *Dean,* Dr. Daniel E. Innis, 207-581-1968, Fax: 207-581-1930.

College of Education and Human Development Students: 232 full-time (177 women), 380 part-time (276 women); includes 16 minority (3 African Americans, 6 American Indian/Alaska Native, 4 Asian Americans or Pacific Islanders, 3 Hispanic Americans), 11 international. Average age 38. 213 applicants, 85% accepted, 154 enrolled. *Faculty:* 34 full-time, 3 part-time/adjunct. Expenses: Contact institution. *Financial support:* In 2006–07, 21 teaching assistantships with tuition reimbursements (averaging $9,010 per year) were awarded; research assistantships with tuition reimbursements, career-related internships or fieldwork, Federal Work-Study, institutionally sponsored loans, and unspecified assistantships also available. Support available to part-time students. Financial award application deadline:3/1. In 2006, 232 master's, 9 doctorates, 36 other advanced degrees awarded. *Degree program information:* Part-time and evening/weekend programs available. Offers counselor education (M Ed, MA, MS, Ed D, CAS); curriculum, assessment, and instruction (M Ed); educational leadership (M Ed, Ed D, CAS); elementary and secondary education (M Ed); elementary education (M Ed, MAT, MS, CAS); higher education (M Ed, MA, MS, Ed D,

CAS); human development (MS); human development and family relations (MS); instructional technology (M Ed); kinesiology and physical education (M Ed, MS); literacy education (M Ed, MA, MS, Ed D, CAS); science education (M Ed, MS, CAS); secondary education (M Ed, MA, MAT, MS, CAS); social studies education (M Ed, MA, MS, CAS); special education (M Ed, CAS). *Application deadline:* For fall admission, 2/1 priority date for domestic students. Applications are processed on a rolling basis. *Application fee:* $50. Electronic applications accepted. *Application Contact:* Scott G. Delcourt, Associate Dean of the Graduate School, 207-581-3219, Fax: 207-581-3232, E-mail: graduate@maine.edu. *Dean,* Dr. Robert A. Cobb, 207-581-2441, Fax: 207-581-2423.

College of Engineering Students: 117 full-time (23 women), 39 part-time (10 women); includes 6 minority (1 American Indian/Alaska Native, 5 Asian Americans or Pacific Islanders), 45 international. Average age 29. 120 applicants, 51% accepted, 38 enrolled. *Faculty:* 55. Expenses: Contact institution. *Financial support:* Fellowships, research assistantships with tuition reimbursements, teaching assistantships with tuition reimbursements, Federal Work-Study, institutionally sponsored loans, scholarships/grants, and tuition waivers (full and partial) available. Financial award application deadline: 3/1. In 2006, 34 master's, 6 doctorates awarded. *Degree program information:* Part-time programs available. Offers biological engineering (MS); chemical engineering (MS, PhD); civil engineering (MS, PhD); computer engineering (MS); electrical engineering (MS, PhD); engineering (MS, PhD); mechanical engineering (MS, PhD); spatial information science and engineering (MS, PhD). *Application deadline:* For fall admission, 2/1 priority date for domestic students. Applications are processed on a rolling basis. *Application fee:* $50. Electronic applications accepted. *Application Contact:* Scott G. Delcourt, Associate Dean of the Graduate School, 207-581-3219, Fax: 207-581-3232, E-mail: graduate@maine.edu. *Interim Dean,* Dr. Dana Humphrey, 207-581-2216, Fax: 207-581-2220.

College of Liberal Arts and Sciences Students: 254 full-time (134 women), 95 part-time (53 women); includes 15 minority (4 African Americans, 5 American Indian/Alaska Native, 4 Asian Americans or Pacific Islanders, 2 Hispanic Americans), 42 international. Average age 31. 405 applicants, 39% accepted, 90 enrolled. Expenses: Contact institution. *Financial support:* Fellowships with tuition reimbursements, research assistantships with tuition reimbursements, teaching assistantships with tuition reimbursements, career-related internships or fieldwork, Federal Work-Study, institutionally sponsored loans, scholarships/grants, and tuition waivers (full and partial) available. Support available to part-time students. Financial award application deadline: 3/1. In 2006, 97 master's, 15 doctorates awarded. *Degree program information:* Part-time and evening/weekend programs available. Offers chemistry (MS, PhD); clinical psychology (PhD); communication (MA); communication sciences and disorders (MA); computer science (MS, PhD); developmental psychology (MA); engineering physics (M Eng); English (MA); experimental psychology (MA, PhD); French (MA, MAT); history (MA, PhD); liberal arts and sciences (M Eng, MA, MAT, MM, MS, PhD); mathematics (MA); music (MM); physics (MS, PhD); social psychology (MA). *Application deadline:* For fall admission, 2/1 priority date for domestic students. Applications are processed on a rolling basis. *Application fee:* $50. Electronic applications accepted. *Application Contact:* Scott G. Delcourt, Associate Dean of the Graduate School, 207-581-3219, Fax: 207-581-3232, E-mail: graduate@maine.edu. *Dean,* Dr. Ann Leffler, 207-581-1954, Fax: 207-581-1947.

College of Natural Sciences, Forestry, and Agriculture Students: 240 full-time (123 women), 92 part-time (55 women); includes 12 minority (3 African Americans, 3 American Indian/Alaska Native, 4 Asian Americans or Pacific Islanders, 2 Hispanic Americans), 58 international. Average age 30. 320 applicants, 33% accepted, 70 enrolled. Expenses: Contact institution. *Financial support:* Fellowships, research assistantships, teaching assistantships, career-related internships or fieldwork, Federal Work-Study, institutionally sponsored loans, scholarships/grants, tuition waivers (full and partial), and unspecified assistantships available. Support available to part-time students. Financial award application deadline: 3/1. In 2006, 102 master's, 19 doctorates awarded. *Degree program information:* Part-time and evening/weekend programs available. Offers animal sciences (MPS, MS); biochemistry (MPS, MS); biochemistry and molecular biology (PhD); biological sciences (PhD); botany and plant pathology (MS); earth sciences (MS, PhD); ecology and environmental science (MS, PhD); ecology and environmental sciences (MS, PhD); entomology (MS); food and nutritional sciences (PhD); food science and human nutrition (MS); forest resources (PhD); forestry (MF, MS); horticulture (MS); marine biology (MS, PhD); marine policy (MS); microbiology (MPS, MS, PhD); natural sciences, forestry, and agriculture (MF, MPS, MS, MWC, PhD); oceanography (MS, PhD); plant science (PhD); plant, soil, and environmental sciences (MS); resource economics and policy (MS); resource utilization (MS); wildlife conservation (MWC); wildlife ecology (MS, PhD); zoology (MS, PhD). *Application deadline:* For fall admission, 2/1 priority date for domestic students. Applications are processed on a rolling basis. *Application fee:* $50. Electronic applications accepted. *Application Contact:* Scott G. Delcourt, Associate Dean of the Graduate School, 207-581-3219, Fax: 207-581-3232, E-mail: graduate@maine.edu. *Dean,* Dr. G. Bruce Wiersma, 207-581-3202, Fax: 207-581-3207.

UNIVERSITY OF MANAGEMENT AND TECHNOLOGY, Arlington, VA 22209

General Information Proprietary, coed, comprehensive institution. *Graduate faculty:* 20 full-time (5 women), 100 part-time/adjunct (25 women). *Graduate housing:* On-campus housing not available. *Student services:* Campus employment opportunities, career counseling, international student services. *Web address:* http://www.umtweb.edu/.

General Application Contact: Scott Wakefield, Admissions, 703-516-2035 Ext. 15, Fax: 703-516-0985, E-mail: admissions@umtweb.edu.

GRADUATE UNITS

Program in Business Administration Expenses: Contact institution. *Degree program information:* Part-time and evening/weekend programs available. Postbaccalaureate distance learning degree programs offered (no on-campus study). Offers acquisition management (DBA); general management (MBA, DBA); project management (MBA, DBA). *Application deadline:* Applications are processed on a rolling basis. *Application fee:* $30. Electronic applications accepted. *Academic Dean,* Dr. J. Davidson Frame, 703-516-0035 Ext. 25.

Program in Computer Science and Information Technology Expenses: Contact institution. *Degree program information:* Part-time and evening/weekend programs available. Postbaccalaureate distance learning degree programs offered (no on-campus study). Offers computer science (MS); information technology (AC); information technology project management (MS, AC); management information systems (MS); multimedia technology (MS); software engineering (MS). *Application deadline:* Applications are processed on a rolling basis. *Application fee:* $30. Electronic applications accepted. *Vice President,* Dr. C. Eric Kirkland, PMP, 703-516-0035, Fax: 703-516-0985, E-mail: eric.kirkland@umtweb.edu.

Program in Management Expenses: Contact institution. *Degree program information:* Part-time and evening/weekend programs available. Postbaccalaureate distance learning degree programs offered (no on-campus study). Offers acquisition management (MS, AC); management (MS); project management (MS, AC); public administration (MPA, MS, AC); public management (MS); telecommunications management (MS). *Application deadline:* Applications are processed on a rolling basis. *Application fee:* $30. Electronic applications accepted. *Academic Dean,* Dr. J. Davidson Frame, 703-516-0035 Ext. 25.

UNIVERSITY OF MANITOBA, Winnipeg, MB R3T 2N2, Canada

General Information Province-supported, coed, university. *Graduate housing:* Rooms and/or apartments available to single and married students. *Research affiliation:* Canada Department of Agriculture Research Station, Freshwater Institute, Atomic Energy of Canada, Manitoba Department of Mines, Resources, and Environmental Management, Northern Scientific Training Program (Northern studies), Taiga Biological Research Trust.

GRADUATE UNITS

Faculty of Dentistry Students: 161 full-time (74 women). Average age 30. 50 applicants, 14% accepted, 7 enrolled. *Faculty:* 30 full-time (8 women), 86 part-time/adjunct (6 women). Expenses: Contact institution. *Financial support:* In 2006–07, 3 fellowships (averaging $15,000 per year), 1 research assistantship were awarded; career-related internships or fieldwork and institutionally sponsored loans also available. Financial award application deadline: 6/30. In 2006, 29 DMDs, 8 master's, 2 doctorates awarded. Offers dental diagnostic and surgical sciences (M Dent); dental materials (M Sc); dentistry (DMD, M Dent, M Sc, PhD); oral and maxillofacial surgery (M Dent); oral biology (M Sc, PhD); oral surgery (M Dent); orthodontics (M Sc); periodontics (M Dent); periodontology (M Dent); preventive dental science (M Sc); restorative dentistry (M Dent, M Sc). *Application deadline:* For fall admission, 9/1 for domestic students. *Application fee:* $50 Canadian dollars ($90 Canadian dollars for international students). *Application Contact:* Dr. J. Elliott Scott, Associate Dean (Research), 204-789-3535, Fax: 204-789-3913, E-mail: jscott@cc.umanitoba.ca. *Dean,* Dr. A. Iacopino, 204-789-3249, Fax: 204-888-4113.

Faculty of Graduate Studies *Degree program information:* Part-time programs available. Offers disability studies (M Sc, MA); foods and nutritional sciences (PhD); interdisciplinary programs (M Sc, MA, PhD); interdisciplinary studies (M Sc, MA, PhD); native studies (M Sc, MA); public administration (MPA).

College Universitaire de Saint Boniface Offers Canadian studies (MA); education (M Ed).

Faculty of Agriculture Offers agribusiness and agricultural economics (M Sc, PhD); agriculture (M Sc, PhD); animal science (M Sc, PhD); entomology (M Sc, PhD); food science (M Sc); horticulture (M Sc, PhD); soil science (M Sc, PhD).

Faculty of Architecture Offers architecture (M Arch, M Land Arch, MCP, MID); city planning (MCP); interior design (MID); landscape architecture (M Land Arch).

Faculty of Arts Offers anthropology (MA, PhD); arts (MA, PhD); classics (MA); clinical psychology (PhD); economics (MA, PhD); English (MA, PhD); French, Spanish and Italian (MA, PhD); German and Slavic studies (MA); history (MA, PhD); Icelandic studies (MA); linguistics (MA, PhD); philosophy (MA); political studies (MA); psychology (MA, PhD); religion (MA, PhD); sociology (MA, PhD).

Faculty of Education Offers adult education (M Ed); education (M Ed, PhD); educational administration (M Ed); general curriculum (M Ed); guidance and counseling (M Ed); inclusive special education (M Ed); language and literacy (M Ed); post-secondary studies (M Ed); special foundations education (M Ed); teaching English as a second language (M Ed).

Faculty of Engineering Offers biosystems engineering (M Eng, M Sc, PhD); civil engineering (M Eng, M Sc, PhD); electrical and computer engineering (M Eng, M Sc, PhD); engineering (M Eng, M Sc, PhD); mechanical and industrial engineering (M Eng, M Sc, PhD).

Faculty of Environment, Earth and Resources Offers environment, earth and resources (M Sc, MA, MNRM, PhD); geography (MA, PhD); geology (M Sc, PhD); geophysics (M Sc, PhD); natural resources and environmental management (PhD); natural resources management (MNRM).

Faculty of Human Ecology Offers clothing and textiles (M Sc); family studies (M Sc); human ecology (M Sc); human nutritional sciences (M Sc).

Faculty of Management Offers business (PhD); business administration (MBA); management (MBA, PhD).

Faculty of Music Offers music (M Mus).

Faculty of Nursing Offers nursing (MN).

Faculty of Pharmacy Offers pharmacy (M Sc, PhD).

Faculty of Physical Education and Recreation Studies Offers physical education and recreation studies (M Sc).

Faculty of Science Offers botany (M Sc, PhD); chemistry (M Sc, PhD); computer science (M Sc, PhD); mathematical, computational and statistical sciences (MMCSS); mathematics (M Sc, PhD); microbiology (M Sc, PhD); physics (M Sc, PhD); science (M Sc, MMCSS, PhD); statistics (M Sc, PhD); zoology (M Sc, PhD).

Faculty of Social Work Offers social work (MSW).

Faculty of Law Offers interdisciplinary studies (MA); law (LL M). Electronic applications accepted.

Faculty of Medicine *Degree program information:* Part-time programs available. Offers medicine (M Sc, PhD). Electronic applications accepted.

Graduate Programs in Medicine *Degree program information:* Part-time programs available. Offers biochemistry and medical genetics (M Sc, PhD); community health sciences (M Sc, PhD); human anatomy and cell science (M Sc, PhD); immunology (M Sc, PhD); medical microbiology (M Sc, PhD); medicine (M Sc, PhD); pathology (M Sc); pediatrics (M Sc); pharmacology and therapeutics (M Sc, PhD); physiology (M Sc, PhD); psychiatry (M Sc); rehabilitation (M Sc); surgery (M Sc).

St. John's College Offers theology (M Div).

Faculty of Theology Offers theology (M Div).

UNIVERSITY OF MARY, Bismarck, ND 58504-9652

General Information Independent-religious, coed, comprehensive institution. *Enrollment:* 2,765 graduate, professional, and undergraduate students; 498 full-time matriculated graduate/professional students (290 women), 161 part-time matriculated graduate/professional students (124 women). *Enrollment by degree level:* 581 master's, 78 doctoral. *Graduate faculty:* 41 full-time (21 women), 34 part-time/adjunct (13 women). *Graduate housing:* Room and/or apartments available on a first-come, first-served basis to single students; on-campus housing not available to married students. Housing application deadline: 7/15. *Student services:* Campus employment opportunities, career counseling, exercise/wellness program, free psychological counseling. *Library facilities:* University of Mary Library. *Online resources:* library catalog, access to other libraries' catalogs. *Collection:* 78,137 titles, 567 serial subscriptions, 7,866 audiovisual materials.

Computer facilities: 233 computers available on campus for general student use. A campuswide network can be accessed from student residence rooms and from off campus. Internet access and online class registration are available. *Web address:* http://www.umary.edu/.

General Application Contact: Dr. Kathy Perrin, Director of Graduate Studies, 701-355-8119, Fax: 701-255-7687, E-mail: kperrin@umary.edu.

GRADUATE UNITS

Department of Occupational Therapy Expenses: Contact institution. *Financial support:* In 2006–07, 2 teaching assistantships with full tuition reimbursements (averaging $2,500 per year) were awarded; career-related internships or fieldwork, Federal Work-Study, institutionally sponsored loans, scholarships/grants, and unspecified assistantships also available. Support available to part-time students. Financial award applicants required to submit FAFSA. In 2006, 10 degrees awarded. Postbaccalaureate distance learning degree programs offered (minimal on-campus study). Offers occupational therapy (MS). *Application deadline:* For spring admission, 1/15 priority date for domestic and international students. Applications are processed on a rolling basis. Electronic applications accepted. *Application Contact:* Geri Toineeta, Program Secretary, 701-355-8216. *Program Director,* Janeene Sibla, 701-255-7500, Fax: 701-255-7687.

Department of Physical Therapy Students: 78 full-time (56 women). 40 applicants, 75% accepted, 29 enrolled. Expenses: Contact institution. *Financial support:* In 2006–07, teaching assistantships with partial tuition reimbursements (averaging $2,500 per year); career-related internships or fieldwork also available. Financial award applicants required to submit FAFSA. Offers physical therapy (DPT). Applications must be requested in writing. *Application deadline:* For fall admission, 1/1 priority date for domestic students; for spring admission, 3/1 priority date for domestic students. Applications are processed on a rolling basis. *Application fee:* $0. Electronic applications accepted. *Program Director,* Joellen Marie Roller, 701-355-8053, Fax: 701-255-7687, E-mail: rollerj@umary.edu.

Division of Nursing Students: 28 full-time (27 women), 22 part-time (all women); includes 2 minority (1 African American, 1 Hispanic American), 1 international. Average age 32. 32 applicants, 66% accepted, 19 enrolled. *Faculty:* 2 full-time (both women), 8 part-time/adjunct (5 women). Expenses: Contact institution. *Financial support:* In 2006–07, 14 fellowships with partial tuition reimbursements, 3 teaching assistantships with partial tuition reimbursements were awarded; institutionally sponsored loans also available. Support avail-

University of Mary (continued)

able to part-time students. Financial award application deadline: 7/1. In 2006, 26 degrees awarded. *Degree program information:* Part-time and evening/weekend programs available. Postbaccalaureate distance learning degree programs offered (minimal on-campus study). Offers family nurse practitioner (MSN); nurse management (MSN); nursing educator (MSN). *Application deadline:* For fall admission, 4/15 priority date for domestic students. Applications are processed on a rolling basis. *Application fee:* $40. Electronic applications accepted. *Application Contact:* Traci L. Schell, Secretary, 701-355-8016, Fax: 701-255-7687, E-mail: tschell@umary.edu. *Director*, Glenda Reemts, 701-255-7500 Ext. 8041, Fax: 701-255-7687.

Program in Business Administration Students: 291 full-time (140 women), 33 part-time (20 women); includes 54 minority (15 African Americans, 30 American Indian/Alaska Native, 6 Asian Americans or Pacific Islanders, 3 Hispanic Americans), 17 international. Average age 34. 177 applicants, 100% accepted, 167 enrolled. *Faculty:* 200 full-time (64 women). Expenses: Contact institution. *Financial support:* Career-related internships or fieldwork available. Support available to part-time students. Financial award applicants required to submit FAFSA. In 2006, 193 degrees awarded. *Degree program information:* Part-time and evening/weekend programs available. Offers business administration (MBA). *Application deadline:* Applications are processed on a rolling basis. *Application fee:* $40. *Application Contact:* Wayne G. Maruska, Graduate Program Advisor, 701-355-8134, Fax: 701-255-7687, E-mail: wmaruska@umary.edu. *Director of the School of Accelerated and Distance Education*, Brenda Kaspari, 701-255-7500.

Program in Education Students: 2 full-time (1 woman), 34 part-time (25 women), 2 international. Average age 35. *Faculty:* 8 full-time (4 women), 12 part-time/adjunct (7 women). Expenses: Contact institution. *Financial support:* In 2006–07, 1 teaching assistantship with full tuition reimbursement was awarded; career-related internships or fieldwork also available. Support available to part-time students. Financial award application deadline: 8/1; financial award applicants required to submit FAFSA. In 2006, 17 degrees awarded. *Degree program information:* Part-time programs available. Offers college teaching (MS Ed); curriculum and instruction (MS Ed); early childhood education (MS Ed); early childhood special education (MS Ed); elementary education administration (MS Ed); reading (MS Ed); secondary education administration (MS Ed); special education (MS Ed). *Application deadline:* Applications are processed on a rolling basis. *Application fee:* $40. *Application Contact:* Leona Friedig, Administrative Secretary, 701-355-8058, E-mail: lfriedig@umary.edu. *Director*, Dr. Rebecca Yunker Salveson, 701-355-8186, E-mail: rysalves@umary.edu.

Program in Management Students: 108 full-time (63 women), 38 part-time (23 women); includes 31 minority (2 African Americans, 24 American Indian/Alaska Native, 5 Hispanic Americans), 3 international. 99 applicants, 100% accepted, 92 enrolled. *Faculty:* 207 part-time/adjunct (72 women). Expenses: Contact institution. *Financial support:* Career-related internships or fieldwork available. Support available to part-time students. Financial award application deadline: 8/1; financial award applicants required to submit FAFSA. In 2006, 146 degrees awarded. *Degree program information:* Part-time and evening/weekend programs available. Postbaccalaureate distance learning degree programs offered (no on-campus study). Offers management (M Mgmt). *Application deadline:* Applications are processed on a rolling basis. *Application fee:* $40. *Application Contact:* Wayne G. Maruska, Graduate Program Advisor, 701-355-8134, Fax: 701-255-7687, E-mail: wmaruska@umary.edu. *Director of the School of Accelerated and Distance Education*, Brenda Kaspari, 701-255-7500.

UNIVERSITY OF MARY HARDIN-BAYLOR, Belton, TX 76513

General Information Independent-religious, coed, comprehensive institution. *Enrollment:* 2,738 graduate, professional, and undergraduate students; 52 full-time matriculated graduate/professional students (31 women), 86 part-time matriculated graduate/professional students (58 women). *Enrollment by degree level:* 138 master's. *Graduate faculty:* 25 full-time (11 women), 6 part-time/adjunct (2 women). *Tuition:* Full-time $8,910; part-time $495 per hour. *Required fees:* $906; $47 per hour. $30 per term. Tuition and fees vary according to course load. *Graduate housing:* Room and/or apartments available on a first-come, first-served basis to single students; on-campus housing not available to married students. Typical cost: $5,728 (including board). *Student services:* Career counseling, disabled student services, exercise/wellness program, free psychological counseling, international student services, multicultural affairs office, teacher training. *Library facilities:* Townsend Memorial Library. *Online resources:* library catalog, web page, access to other libraries' catalogs. *Collection:* 172,855 titles, 990 serial subscriptions, 8,133 audiovisual materials.

Computer facilities: Computer purchase and lease plans are available. 262 computers available on campus for general student use. A campuswide network can be accessed from student residence rooms. Internet access is available. *Web address:* http://www.umhb.edu/.

General Application Contact: Robbin Steen, Director of Admissions and Recruiting, 254-295-4520, Fax: 254-295-5049, E-mail: rsteen@umhb.edu.

GRADUATE UNITS

College of Business Students: 5 full-time (2 women), 28 part-time (14 women); includes 6 minority (1 African American, 1 Asian American or Pacific Islander, 4 Hispanic Americans). Average age 24. *Faculty:* 10 full-time (3 women), 3 part-time/adjunct (1 woman). Expenses: Contact institution. *Financial support:* Federal Work-Study and scholarships (for some active duty military personnel only) available. Support available to part-time students. Financial award application deadline: 6/1; financial award applicants required to submit FAFSA. In 2006, 11 degrees awarded. *Degree program information:* Part-time and evening/weekend programs available. Offers accounting (MBA); business (MBA, MS); information systems (MS); management (MBA); sport management (MBA). *Application deadline:* For fall admission, 6/1 priority date for domestic students; for spring admission, 11/1 for domestic students. Applications are processed on a rolling basis. *Application fee:* $35 ($135 for international students). Electronic applications accepted.

College of Education Students: 8 full-time (3 women), 36 part-time (26 women); includes 8 minority (3 African Americans, 5 Hispanic Americans). Average age 24. *Faculty:* 10 full-time (5 women), 1 part-time/adjunct (0 women). Expenses: Contact institution. *Financial support:* Federal Work-Study, scholarships/grants, and scholarships (for some active duty military personnel only) available. Support available to part-time students. Financial award application deadline: 6/1; financial award applicants required to submit FAFSA. In 2006, 18 degrees awarded. *Degree program information:* Part-time and evening/weekend programs available. Offers educational administration (M Ed, Ed D); educational psychology (M Ed); exercise and sport science (M Ed); general studies (M Ed); reading education (M Ed). *Application deadline:* For fall admission, 6/1 priority date for domestic students; for spring admission, 11/1 for domestic students. Applications are processed on a rolling basis. *Application fee:* $35 ($135 for international students). Electronic applications accepted. *Application Contact:* Dr. Shirley Dahl, Director, Graduate Programs in Education, 254-295-4185, Fax: 254-295-4480, E-mail: sdahl@umhb.edu. *Dean*, Dr. Marlene Zipperlen, 254-295-4572, Fax: 254-295-4480, E-mail: mzipperlen@umhb.edu.

College of Sciences and Humanities Students: 30 full-time (18 women), 29 part-time (21 women); includes 14 minority (6 African Americans, 2 Asian Americans or Pacific Islanders, 6 Hispanic Americans), 1 international. Average age 24. *Faculty:* 5 full-time (3 women), 2 part-time/adjunct (1 woman). Expenses: Contact institution. *Financial support:* Research assistantships with full tuition reimbursements, Federal Work-Study and scholarships (for some active duty military personnel only) available. Support available to part-time students. Financial award applicants required to submit FAFSA. In 2006, 12 degrees awarded. *Degree program information:* Part-time and evening/weekend programs available. Offers community counseling (MA); marriage and family Christian counseling (MA); psychology and counseling (MA); school counseling and psychology (MA); sciences and humanities (MA). *Application deadline:* For fall admission, 6/1 priority date for domestic students; for spring admission, 11/1 for domestic students. Applications are processed on a rolling basis. *Application fee:* $35 ($135 for international students). Electronic applications accepted. *Application Contact:* Dr. Raylene B. Statz, Director, Programs in Psychology and Counseling, 254-295-4548, E-mail: rstatz@umhb.edu.

UNIVERSITY OF MARYLAND, BALTIMORE, Baltimore, MD 21201

General Information State-supported, coed, graduate-only institution. CGS member. *Graduate housing:* Rooms and/or apartments available on a first-come, first-served basis to single and married students. Housing application deadline: 2/18.

GRADUATE UNITS

Graduate School *Degree program information:* Part-time and evening/weekend programs available. Offers biomedical sciences—dental (MS, PhD); dental hygiene (MS); epidemiology (MS); gerontology (PhD); marine-estuarine-environmental sciences (MS, PhD); medical and research technology (MS); oral biology (MS); oral pathology (MS, PhD); pharmaceutical health service research (MS, PhD); pharmaceutical sciences (PhD); pharmacy administration (PhD); social work (MSW, PhD). Electronic applications accepted.

School of Nursing *Degree program information:* Part-time programs available. Offers community health nursing (MS); direct nursing (PhD); gerontological nursing (MS); indirect nursing (PhD); maternal-child nursing (MS); medical-surgical nursing (MS); nurse-midwifery education (MS); nursing (MS, PhD); nursing administration (MS); nursing education (MS); nursing health policy (MS); primary care nursing (MS); psychiatric nursing (MS). Electronic applications accepted.

Professional and Advanced Education Programs in Dentistry Students: 551 full-time (280 women); includes 161 minority (32 African Americans, 1 American Indian/Alaska Native, 111 Asian Americans or Pacific Islanders, 17 Hispanic Americans), 35 international. Average age 25. 2,375 applicants, 130 enrolled. *Faculty:* 123 full-time (48 women), 95 part-time/adjunct (22 women). Expenses: Contact institution. *Financial support:* In 2006–07, research assistantships (averaging $23,000 per year); career-related internships or fieldwork, Federal Work-Study, institutionally sponsored loans, scholarships/grants, and unspecified assistantships also available. Financial award application deadline: 3/1; financial award applicants required to submit FAFSA. In 2006, 103 DDSs, 11 other advanced degrees awarded. Offers advanced general dentistry (Certificate); dentistry (DDS); endodontics (Certificate); oral and experimental pathology (Certificate); oral biology (MS); oral-maxillofacial surgery (Certificate); orthodontics (Certificate); pediatric dentistry (Certificate); periodontics (Certificate); prosthodontics (Certificate). *Application deadline:* For fall admission, 1/15 for domestic students. *Application fee:* $65. *Application Contact:* Dr. Patricia Meehan, Assistant Dean for Admissions and Recruitment, 410-706-7472, Fax: 410-706-0945, E-mail: pmeehan@umaryland.edu. *Dean*, Dr. Christian S. Stohler, 410-706-7461, Fax: 410-706-0406, E-mail: cstohler@dental.umaryland.edu.

Professional Program in Pharmacy Students: 478 full-time (300 women), 3 part-time (1 woman); includes 209 minority (62 African Americans, 1 American Indian/Alaska Native, 133 Asian Americans or Pacific Islanders, 13 Hispanic Americans), 20 international. Average age 24. 1,400 applicants, 11% accepted, 120 enrolled. *Faculty:* 66 full-time (15 women), 585 part-time/adjunct (158 women). Expenses: Contact institution. *Financial support:* In 2006–07, 435 students received support. Career-related internships or fieldwork, Federal Work-Study, institutionally sponsored loans, and scholarships/grants available. Support available to part-time students. Financial award application deadline: 3/1; financial award applicants required to submit FAFSA. In 2006, 122 degrees awarded. Offers pharmacy (Pharm D). *Application deadline:* For fall admission, 12/1 for domestic and international students. *Application fee:* $35. Electronic applications accepted. *Application Contact:* Admissions Office, 410-706-7653, Fax: 410-706-2158, E-mail: pharmdhelp@umaryland.edu. *Associate Dean for Student Affairs*, Dr. Jill Morgan, 410-706-4332, Fax: 410-706-2158, E-mail: jmorgan@rx.umaryland.edu.

School of Law Students: 673 full-time (402 women), 153 part-time (79 women); includes 262 minority (123 African Americans, 4 American Indian/Alaska Native, 81 Asian Americans or Pacific Islanders, 54 Hispanic Americans), 10 international. Average age 26. 4,331 applicants, 16% accepted, 263 enrolled. *Faculty:* 57 full-time (29 women), 64 part-time/adjunct (19 women). Expenses: Contact institution. *Financial support:* In 2006–07, 639 students received support. Federal Work-Study, institutionally sponsored loans, and scholarships/grants available. Support available to part-time students. Financial award application deadline: 3/1; financial award applicants required to submit FAFSA. In 2006, 253 degrees awarded. *Degree program information:* Part-time and evening/weekend programs available. Offers law (JD). *Application deadline:* For fall admission, 3/1 priority date for domestic and international students. Applications are processed on a rolling basis. *Application fee:* $65. Electronic applications accepted. *Application Contact:* Connie Beals, Executive Director of Admissions, 410-706-3492, Fax: 410-706-1793, E-mail: admissions@law.umaryland.edu. *Dean and Marjorie Cook Professor of Law*, Karen H. Rothenberg, 410-706-7214, Fax: 410-706-4045.

School of Medicine *Degree program information:* Part-time and evening/weekend programs available. Offers biochemistry (PhD); biochemistry and molecular biology (PhD); biostatistics (MS); clinical research (MS); epidemiology (MS, PhD); gerontology (PhD); human genetics (MS, PhD); human genetics and genomic medicine (PhD); medical pathology (PhD); medicine (MD, MS, DPT, DS, PhD); molecular and cell biology (MS); molecular and cellular cancer biology (PhD); molecular cell biology and physiology (PhD); molecular epidemiology (PhD); molecular medicine (PhD); molecular microbiology and immunology (PhD); molecular toxicology and pharmacology (PhD); neuroscience (PhD); pathology (MS); pharmacology (MS); physical rehabilitation science (PhD); physical therapy (DPT, DS); physical therapy and rehabilitation science (DPT, DS, PhD); physiology (MS); toxicology (MS, PhD).

UNIVERSITY OF MARYLAND, BALTIMORE COUNTY, Baltimore, MD 21250

General Information State-supported, coed, university. CGS member. *Enrollment:* 11,798 graduate, professional, and undergraduate students; 881 full-time matriculated graduate/professional students (469 women), 1,363 part-time matriculated graduate/professional students (709 women). *Enrollment by degree level:* 1,151 master's, 750 doctoral, 343 other advanced degrees. *Graduate faculty:* 325 full-time, 15 part-time/adjunct. Tuition, state resident: part-time $412 per credit hour. Tuition, nonresident: part-time $681 per credit hour. *Required fees:* $91 per credit hour. One-time fee: $75 part-time. *Graduate housing:* Room and/or apartments available on a first-come, first-served basis to single students; on-campus housing not available to married students. Housing application deadline: 6/1. *Student services:* Campus employment opportunities, campus safety program, career counseling, child daycare facilities, disabled student services, exercise/wellness program, free psychological counseling, grant writing training, international student services, low-cost health insurance, multicultural affairs office, teacher training, writing training. *Library facilities:* Albin O. Kuhn Library and Gallery plus 1 other. *Online resources:* library catalog, web page, access to other libraries' catalogs. *Collection:* 1.3 million titles, 4,170 serial subscriptions, 7,500 audiovisual materials. *Research affiliation:* Fujitsu Laboratories of America (information technology and communications), Pfizer Incorporated (pharmaceuticals), BouMatic (dairy industry), IBM (computers and information technology), Halliburton Energy Services (provider of products and services to oil and gas industries), Sciences Applications International Corp. (information systems and technology).

Computer facilities: Computer purchase and lease plans are available. 762 computers available on campus for general student use. A campuswide network can be accessed from student residence rooms and from off campus. Internet access and online class registration, student account and grade information are available. *Web address:* http://www.umbc.edu/.

General Application Contact: Kathryn Nee, Coordinator of Domestic Admissions, 410-455-2944, E-mail: nee@umbc.edu.

GRADUATE UNITS

Graduate School Students: 881 full-time (469 women), 1,363 part-time (709 women); includes 458 minority (258 African Americans, 8 American Indian/Alaska Native, 143 Asian Americans or Pacific Islanders, 49 Hispanic Americans), 429 international. Average age 32. 1,699 applicants, 44% accepted, 466 enrolled. *Faculty:* 333 full-time, 16 part-time/adjunct. Expenses: Contact institution. *Financial support:* In 2006–07, 345 students received support, including 79 fellowships with tuition reimbursements available (averaging $11,324 per year), 65 research assistantships with tuition reimbursements available (averaging $11,324 per year), 201 teaching assistantships with tuition reimbursements available (averaging $1,324 per year); career-related internships or fieldwork, Federal Work-Study, scholarships/grants, traineeships, health care benefits, and unspecified assistantships also available. Support available to part-time students. Financial award applicants required to submit FAFSA. In 2006, 329 master's, 89 doctorates awarded. *Degree program information:* Part-time and evening/weekend programs available. Postbaccalaureate distance learning degree programs offered (no on-campus study). Offers aging policy for the elderly (PhD); epidemiology of aging (PhD); marine-estuarine-environmental sciences (MS, PhD); social, cultural, and behavioral sciences (PhD). *Application deadline:* For fall admission, 1/1 for international students; for spring admission, 5/1 for international students. Applications are processed on a rolling basis. *Application fee:* $50. Electronic applications accepted. *Application Contact:* Kathryn Nee, Coordinator of Domestic Admissions, 410-455-2944, E-mail: nee@umbc.edu. *Dean and Vice President for Research,* Dr. Scott A. Bass, 410-455-2199.

College of Arts, Humanities and Social Sciences Students: 271 full-time (214 women), 781 part-time (566 women); includes 192 minority (120 African Americans, 3 American Indian/Alaska Native, 40 Asian Americans or Pacific Islanders, 29 Hispanic Americans), 77 international. Average age 31. *Faculty:* 283 full-time, 26 part-time/adjunct. Expenses: Contact institution. *Financial support:* Fellowships, research assistantships, teaching assistantships, career-related internships or fieldwork, scholarships/grants, health care benefits, and unspecified assistantships available. Financial award applicants required to submit FAFSA. In 2006, 170 master's, 35 doctorates awarded. Offers administration, planning, and policy (MS); American contemporary music (Postbaccalaureate Certificate); applied behavioral analysis (MA); applied developmental psychology (PhD); applied sociology (MA, Postbaccalaureate Certificate); arts, humanities and social science (MA, MAT, MFA, MPP, MS, PhD, Postbaccalaureate Certificate); computer/web-based instruction (Postbaccalaureate Certificate); distance education (Postbaccalaureate Certificate); early childhood education (MAT); economic policy analysis (MA); education (MA, MS); elementary education (MAT); emergency health services (MS); ESOL/bilingual education (Postbaccalaureate Certificate); ESOL/bilingual training systems (MA); French (MA); gender and women's studies (Postbaccalaureate Certificate); German (MA); historical studies (MA); human services psychology (MA, PhD); human services psychology/clinical (PhD); imaging and digital arts (MFA); instructional systems development (MA, Postbaccalaureate Certificate); intercultural communication (MA); language, literacy, and culture (PhD); non-profit sector (Postbaccalaureate Certificate); preventive medicine and epidemiology (MS); psychology (MS); public policy (MPP, PhD); Russian (MA); secondary education (MA, MAT); Spanish (MA); teaching (MA). *Application deadline:* For fall admission, 1/1 for international students; for spring admission, 5/1 for international students. Applications are processed on a rolling basis. *Application fee:* $50. Electronic applications accepted. *Dean,* Dr. John Jeffries, 410-455-2312, Fax: 410-455-1045, E-mail: jeffries@umbc.edu.

College of Engineering and Information Technology Students: 264 full-time (81 women), 508 part-time (142 women); includes 166 minority (78 African Americans, 82 Asian Americans or Pacific Islanders, 6 Hispanic Americans), 233 international. Average age 29. 680 applicants, 44% accepted, 171 enrolled. *Faculty:* 87 full-time (20 women), 24 part-time/adjunct (5 women). Expenses: Contact institution. *Financial support:* In 2006–07, 220 students received support, including 21 fellowships with full tuition reimbursements available (averaging $21,000 per year), 122 research assistantships with full tuition reimbursements available (averaging $16,000 per year), 68 teaching assistantships with full tuition reimbursements available (averaging $15,000 per year); career-related internships or fieldwork, traineeships, health care benefits, tuition waivers (partial), and unspecified assistantships also available. Support available to part-time students. Financial award application deadline: 3/1; financial award applicants required to submit FAFSA. In 2006, 132 master's, 26 doctorates awarded. *Degree program information:* Part-time and evening/weekend programs available. Offers biochemical and regulatory engineering (Postbaccalaureate Certificate); biochemical regulatory engineering (Postbaccalaureate Certificate); chemical and biochemical engineering (MS, PhD); chemical engineering (MS, PhD); civil and environmental engineering (MS, PhD); computer engineering (MS, PhD); computer science (MS, PhD); electrical engineering (MS, PhD); engineering and information technology (MS, PhD, Postbaccalaureate Certificate); engineering management (MS); human-centered computing (MS, PhD); information systems (MS, PhD); mechanical engineering (MS, PhD); mechatronics (Postbaccalaureate Certificate); systems engineering (Postbaccalaureate Certificate). *Application deadline:* For fall admission, 7/1 for domestic and international students; for spring admission, 12/1 for domestic and international students. Applications are processed on a rolling basis. *Application fee:* $50. Electronic applications accepted. *Dean,* Dr. Warren DeVries, 410-455-3270, Fax: 410-455-3559, E-mail: wdevries@umbc.edu.

College of Natural and Mathematical Sciences Students: 177 full-time (65 women), 53 part-time (26 women); includes 57 minority (21 African Americans, 32 Asian Americans or Pacific Islanders, 4 Hispanic Americans), 50 international. Average age 27. 282 applicants, 38% accepted, 54 enrolled. *Faculty:* 84 full-time (17 women), 29 part-time/adjunct (2 women). Expenses: Contact institution. *Financial support:* In 2006–07, 16 fellowships with full tuition reimbursements, 45 research assistantships with full tuition reimbursements, 83 teaching assistantships with full tuition reimbursements were awarded. In 2006, 29 master's, 33 doctorates awarded. *Degree program information:* Part-time programs available. Offers applied mathematics (MS, PhD); applied molecular biology (MS); applied physics (MS, PhD); astrophysics (PhD); atmospheric physics (MS, PhD); biochemistry (MS, PhD); biological sciences (MS, PhD); chemistry (MS, PhD); molecular and cell biology (PhD); natural and mathematical sciences (MS, PhD); neurosciences and cognitive sciences (PhD); optics (MS, PhD); quantum optics (PhD); solid state physics (MS, PhD); statistics (MS, PhD). *Application deadline:* Applications are processed on a rolling basis. Electronic applications accepted. *Dean of Natural and Mathematical Sciences,* Dr. Geoffrey P. Summers, 410-455-5827, Fax: 410-455-5831, E-mail: gsummers@umbc.edu.

See Close-Up on page 1081.

UNIVERSITY OF MARYLAND, COLLEGE PARK, College Park, MD 20742

General Information State-supported, coed, university. CGS member. *Enrollment:* 35,300 graduate, professional, and undergraduate students; 6,695 full-time matriculated graduate/professional students (3,247 women), 3,195 part-time matriculated graduate/professional students (1,589 women). *Enrollment by degree level:* 115 first professional, 4,577 master's, 4,632 doctoral, 566 other advanced degrees. *Graduate faculty:* 2,896 full-time (1,012 women), 856 part-time/adjunct (395 women). *Graduate housing:* Rooms and/or apartments available on a first-come, first-served basis to single and married students. *Student services:* Campus employment opportunities, campus safety program, career counseling, child daycare facilities, disabled student services, exercise/wellness program, free psychological counseling, international student services, low-cost health insurance, multicultural affairs office. *Library facilities:* McKeldin Library plus 6 others. *Online resources:* library catalog, web page, access to other libraries' catalogs. *Collection:* 3 million titles, 34,091 serial subscriptions, 244,911 audiovisual materials. *Research affiliation:* Federal-National Rotorcraft Technology Center (aerodynamics), BAE Systems (advanced sensors), Semiconductor Research, Inc. (semiconductors), Fujitsu (computer science), Feaurhaufer USA (computer science).

Computer facilities: Computer purchase and lease plans are available. 773 computers available on campus for general student use. A campuswide network can be accessed from student residence rooms and from off campus. Internet access and online class registration, student account information, financial aid summary are available. *Web address:* http://www.maryland.edu/.

General Application Contact: Dean of Graduate School, 301-405-4190, Fax: 301-314-9305.

GRADUATE UNITS

Graduate Studies Students: 6,695 full-time, 3,195 part-time; includes 1,769 minority (725 African Americans, 28 American Indian/Alaska Native, 683 Asian Americans or Pacific Islanders, 333 Hispanic Americans), 2,448 international. Average age 30. 14,956 applicants, 30% accepted, 2294 enrolled. *Faculty:* 2,896 full-time (1,012 women), 856 part-time/adjunct (395 women). Expenses: Contact institution. *Financial support:* In 2006–07, 5,755 students received support, including 1,107 fellowships with full tuition reimbursements available (averaging $7,083 per year), 1,307 research assistantships with tuition reimbursements available (averaging $18,271 per year), 2,596 teaching assistantships with tuition reimbursements available (averaging $14,274 per year); career-related internships or fieldwork, Federal Work-Study, institutionally sponsored loans, and scholarships/grants also available. Support available to part-time students. Financial award applicants required to submit FAFSA. In 2006, 29 first professional degrees, 2,001 master's, 602 doctorates, 12 other advanced degrees awarded. *Degree program information:* Part-time and evening/weekend programs available. Postbaccalaureate distance learning degree programs offered (no on-campus study). Offers neurosciences and cognitive sciences (PhD). *Application deadline:* For fall admission, 2/1 for domestic and international students; for spring admission, 6/1 for domestic and international students. Applications are processed on a rolling basis. *Application fee:* $60. Electronic applications accepted. *Application Contact:* Dean of Graduate School, 301-405-0358, Fax: 301-314-9305. *Dean of the Graduate School,* Dr. Charles Caramello, 301-405-0358, Fax: 301-314-9305, E-mail: ccaramel@umd.edu.

A. James Clark School of Engineering Students: 1,082 full-time (243 women), 537 part-time (125 women); includes 251 minority (73 African Americans, 5 American Indian/Alaska Native, 126 Asian Americans or Pacific Islanders, 47 Hispanic Americans), 743 international. 2,927 applicants, 24% accepted, 384 enrolled. *Faculty:* 438 full-time (55 women), 95 part-time/adjunct (14 women). Expenses: Contact institution. *Financial support:* In 2006–07, 144 fellowships (averaging $4,992 per year), 536 research assistantships (averaging $19,143 per year), 250 teaching assistantships (averaging $16,604 per year) were awarded; career-related internships or fieldwork, Federal Work-Study, institutionally sponsored loans, and scholarships/grants also available. Support available to part-time students. Financial award applicants required to submit FAFSA. In 2006, 346 master's, 122 doctorates awarded. *Degree program information:* Part-time and evening/weekend programs available. Postbaccalaureate distance learning degree programs offered. Offers aerospace engineering (M Eng); bioengineering (MS, PhD); chemical engineering (M Eng, MS, PhD); civil and environmental engineering (M Eng, MS, PhD); civil engineering (M Eng); electrical and computer engineering (M Eng, MS, PhD); electrical engineering (M Eng, MS, PhD); electronic packaging and reliability (MS, PhD); engineering (Certificate); engineering and public policy (MS); fire protection engineering (M Eng); manufacturing and design (MS, PhD); materials science and engineering (M Eng, MS, PhD); mechanical engineering (M Eng); mechanics and materials (MS, PhD); nuclear engineering (ME, MS, PhD); reliability engineering (M Eng, MS, PhD); systems engineering (M Eng); telecommunications (MS); thermal and fluid sciences (MS, PhD). *Application deadline:* For fall admission, 2/1 for domestic and international students; for spring admission, 6/1 for domestic and international students. Applications are processed on a rolling basis. *Application fee:* $60. Electronic applications accepted. *Application Contact:* Dr. Charles Caramello, Dean of the Graduate School, 301-405-0358, Fax: 301-314-9305, E-mail: ccaramel@umd.edu. *Dean,* Dr. Nariman Farvardin, 301-405-3868, Fax: 301-314-5908, E-mail: farvar@eng.umd.edu.

College of Agriculture and Natural Resources Students: 310 full-time (197 women), 35 part-time (25 women); includes 27 minority (8 African Americans, 2 American Indian/Alaska Native, 13 Asian Americans or Pacific Islanders, 4 Hispanic Americans), 100 international. 297 applicants, 41% accepted, 92 enrolled. *Faculty:* 318 full-time (127 women), 42 part-time/adjunct (26 women). Expenses: Contact institution. *Financial support:* In 2006–07, 28 fellowships with full tuition reimbursements (averaging $7,469 per year), 103 research assistantships with tuition reimbursements (averaging $15,911 per year), 48 teaching assistantships with tuition reimbursements (averaging $14,670 per year) were awarded; career-related internships or fieldwork, Federal Work-Study, and scholarships/grants also available. Support available to part-time students. Financial award applicants required to submit FAFSA. In 2006, 29 first professional degrees, 25 master's, 16 doctorates awarded. *Degree program information:* Part-time and evening/weekend programs available. Offers agriculture and natural resources (DVM, MS, PhD); agriculture economics (MS, PhD); agronomy (MS, PhD); animal sciences (MS, PhD); food science (MS, PhD); horticulture (PhD); natural resource sciences (MS, PhD); nutrition (MS, PhD); resource economics (MS, PhD); veterinary medical sciences (MS, PhD); veterinary medicine (DVM, MS, PhD). *Application deadline:* For fall admission, 5/1 for domestic students, 2/1 for international students; for spring admission, 10/1 for domestic students, 6/1 for international students. Applications are processed on a rolling basis. *Application fee:* $60. Electronic applications accepted. *Application Contact:* Dean of Graduate School, 301-405-0358, Fax: 301-314-9305. *Dean,* Dr. Cheng-i Wei, 301-405-2072, Fax: 301-314-9146, E-mail: wei@umd.edu.

College of Arts and Humanities Students: 940 full-time (603 women), 237 part-time (137 women); includes 184 minority (85 African Americans, 1 American Indian/Alaska Native, 58 Asian Americans or Pacific Islanders, 40 Hispanic Americans), 216 international. 2,242 applicants, 26% accepted, 280 enrolled. *Faculty:* 419 full-time (202 women), 216 part-time/adjunct (116 women). Expenses: Contact institution. *Financial support:* In 2006–07, 143 fellowships with full tuition reimbursements (averaging $7,239 per year), 38 research assistantships with tuition reimbursements (averaging $15,779 per year), 534 teaching assistantships with tuition reimbursements (averaging $14,602 per year) were awarded; career-related internships or fieldwork, Federal Work-Study, and scholarships/grants also available. Support available to part-time students. Financial award applicants required to submit FAFSA. In 2006, 145 master's, 104 doctorates awarded. *Degree program information:* Part-time and evening/weekend programs available. Offers American studies (MA, PhD); art (MFA); art history (MA, PhD); arts and humanities (M Ed, MA, MFA, MM, DMA, Ed D, PhD); classics (MA); communication (MA, PhD); comparative literature (MA, PhD); creative writing (MA, MFA, PhD); dance (MFA); English language and literature (MA, PhD); ethnomusicology (MA); French (MA); French language and literature (MA); German (MA); Germanic language and literature (MA, PhD); history (MA, PhD); Japanese (MA); Jewish studies (MA); languages, literature, and cultures (MA, PhD); linguistics (MA, PhD); modern French studies (PhD); music (M Ed, MA, MM, DMA, Ed D, PhD); philosophy (MA, PhD); Russian (MA); second language instruction (PhD); second language learning (PhD); second language measurement and assessment (PhD); second language use (PhD); Spanish (MA); Spanish and Portuguese (MA, PhD); theatre (MA, MFA, PhD); women's studies (MA, PhD). *Application deadline:* For fall admission, 5/1 for domestic students, 2/1 for international students; for spring admission, 10/1 for domestic students, 6/1 for international students. Applications are processed on a rolling basis. *Application fee:* $60. Electronic applications accepted. *Application Contact:* Dean of Graduate School, 301-405-0358, Fax: 301-314-9305. *Dean,* Dr. James F. Harris, 301-405-0949, Fax: 301-314-9148, E-mail: jfharris@umd.edu.

College of Behavioral and Social Sciences Students: 696 full-time (408 women), 166 part-time (105 women); includes 134 minority (56 African Americans, 3 American Indian/Alaska Native, 41 Asian Americans or Pacific Islanders, 34 Hispanic Americans), 220 international. 2,215 applicants, 24% accepted, 222 enrolled. *Faculty:* 398 full-time (173 women), 115 part-time/adjunct (51 women). Expenses: Contact institution. *Financial support:* In 2006–07, 124 fellowships with full tuition reimbursements (averaging $9,677 per year), 89 research assistantships with tuition reimbursements (averaging $14,614 per year), 366 teaching assistantships with tuition reimbursements (averaging $14,396 per year) were awarded; career-related internships or fieldwork, Federal Work-Study, and scholarships/grants also available. Support available to part-time students. Financial award applicants required to submit FAFSA. In 2006, 142 master's, 94 doctorates awarded. *Degree program information:* Part-time and evening/weekend programs available. Offers American politics (PhD); applied anthropology (MAA); audiology (MA, PhD); behavioral and social sciences (MA, MAA, MS, Au D, PhD); clinical psychology (PhD); comparative politics (PhD); criminology and criminal justice (MA, PhD); developmental psychology (PhD); economics (MA, PhD); experimental psychology (PhD); geography (MA, PhD); hearing and speech sciences (Au D); industrial psychology (MA, MS, PhD); international relations (PhD); language pathology (MA, PhD); neuroscience (PhD); political economy (PhD); political theory (PhD); social psychology (PhD); sociology (MA, PhD); speech (MA, PhD); survey methodology (MS, PhD). *Application deadline:* For fall admission, 5/1 for domestic students, 2/1 for international students; for spring admission, 10/1 for domestic students, 6/1 for international students. Applications are processed on a rolling basis. *Application fee:* $60.

University of Maryland, College Park (continued)

Electronic applications accepted. *Application Contact:* Dean of Graduate School, 301-405-4190, Fax: 301-314-9305. *Dean,* Dr. Edward Montgomery, 301-405-1691, Fax: 301-314-9086, E-mail: montgome@umd.edu.

College of Chemical and Life Sciences Students: 535 full-time (284 women), 163 part-time (99 women); includes 70 minority (21 African Americans, 6 American Indian/Alaska Native, 24 Asian Americans or Pacific Islanders, 19 Hispanic Americans), 190 international. 1,170 applicants, 21% accepted, 151 enrolled. *Faculty:* 265 full-time (101 women), 26 part-time/adjunct (13 women). Expenses: Contact institution. *Financial support:* In 2006–07, 66 fellowships with full tuition reimbursements (averaging $6,484 per year), 95 research assistantships with tuition reimbursements (averaging $17,492 per year), 269 teaching assistantships with tuition reimbursements (averaging $16,769 per year) were awarded; career-related internships or fieldwork, Federal Work-Study, and scholarships/grants also available. Support available to part-time students. Financial award applicants required to submit FAFSA. In 2006, 82 master's, 55 doctorates awarded. *Degree program information:* Part-time and evening/weekend programs available. Offers analytical chemistry (MS, PhD); behavior, ecology, and systematics (PhD); behavior, ecology, evolution, and systematics (MS); biochemistry (MS, PhD); biology (MS, PhD); cell biology and molecular genetics (MS, PhD); chemical and life sciences (MLS, MS, PhD); chemistry (MS, PhD); entomology (MS, PhD); inorganic chemistry (MS, PhD); life sciences (MLS); marine-estuarine-environmental sciences (MS, PhD); molecular and cellular biology (PhD); organic chemistry (MS, PhD); physical chemistry (MS, PhD); plant biology (MS, PhD); sustainable development and conservation biology (MS). *Application deadline:* For fall admission, 5/1 for domestic students, 2/1 for international students; for spring admission, 10/1 for domestic students, 6/1 for international students. Applications are processed on a rolling basis. *Application fee:* $60. Electronic applications accepted. *Application Contact:* Dean of Graduate School, 301-405-0358, Fax: 301-314-9305. *Dean,* Dr. Norma M. Allewell, 301-405-2071, Fax: 301-314-9949, E-mail: allewell@umd.edu.

College of Computer, Mathematical and Physical Sciences Students: 747 full-time (172 women), 97 part-time (28 women); includes 76 minority (27 African Americans, 1 American Indian/Alaska Native, 37 Asian Americans or Pacific Islanders, 11 Hispanic Americans), 357 international. 2,197 applicants, 18% accepted, 148 enrolled. *Faculty:* 588 full-time (97 women), 85 part-time/adjunct (22 women). Expenses: Contact institution. *Financial support:* In 2006–07, 131 fellowships with full tuition reimbursements (averaging $6,805 per year), 350 research assistantships with tuition reimbursements (averaging $17,710 per year), 306 teaching assistantships with tuition reimbursements (averaging $16,525 per year) were awarded; career-related internships or fieldwork, Federal Work-Study, and scholarships/grants also available. Support available to part-time students. Financial award applicants required to submit FAFSA. In 2006, 94 master's, 109 doctorates awarded. *Degree program information:* Part-time and evening/weekend programs available. Postbaccalaureate distance learning degree programs offered. Offers applied mathematics (MS, PhD); astronomy (MS, PhD); atmospheric and oceanic science (MS, PhD); chemical physics (MS, PhD); computer science (MS, PhD); computer, mathematical and physical sciences (MA, MS, PhD); geology (MS, PhD); mathematical statistics (MA, PhD); mathematics (MA, PhD); physics (MS, PhD). *Application deadline:* For fall admission, 12/1 for domestic students, 2/1 for international students; for spring admission, 10/1 for domestic students, 6/1 for international students. Applications are processed on a rolling basis. *Application fee:* $60. Electronic applications accepted. *Application Contact:* Dean of Graduate School, 301-405-0358, Fax: 301-314-9305. *Dean,* Dr. Stephen Halperin, 301-405-2316, Fax: 301-405-9377, E-mail: shalper@umd.edu.

College of Education Students: 732 full-time (567 women), 449 part-time (353 women); includes 336 minority (189 African Americans, 4 American Indian/Alaska Native, 75 Asian Americans or Pacific Islanders, 68 Hispanic Americans), 111 international. 1,141 applicants, 41% accepted, 278 enrolled. *Faculty:* 180 full-time (125 women), 79 part-time/adjunct (70 women). Expenses: Contact institution. *Financial support:* In 2006–07, 151 fellowships with full tuition reimbursements (averaging $5,149 per year), 58 research assistantships with tuition reimbursements (averaging $15,131 per year), 293 teaching assistantships with tuition reimbursements (averaging $14,649 per year) were awarded; career-related internships or fieldwork, Federal Work-Study, and scholarships/grants also available. Support available to part-time students. Financial award applicants required to submit FAFSA. In 2006, 294 master's, 62 doctorates, 12 other advanced degrees awarded. *Degree program information:* Part-time and evening/weekend programs available. Postbaccalaureate distance learning degree programs offered. Offers college student personnel (M Ed, MA); college student personnel administration (PhD); community counseling (CAGS); community/career counseling (M Ed, MA); counseling and personnel services (M Ed, MA, PhD); counseling psychology (PhD); counselor education (PhD); curriculum and educational communications (M Ed, MA, Ed D, PhD); early childhood/elementary education (M Ed, MA, Ed D, PhD); education (M Ed, MA, Ed D, PhD, CAGS); human development (M Ed, MA, Ed D, PhD); measurement (MA, PhD); program evaluation (MA, PhD); reading (M Ed, MA, PhD, CAGS); rehabilitation counseling (M Ed, MA); school counseling (M Ed, MA); school psychology (M Ed, MA, PhD); secondary education (M Ed, MA, Ed D, PhD, CAGS); social foundations of education (M Ed, MA, Ed D, PhD, CAGS); special education (M Ed, MA, PhD, CAGS); statistics (MA, PhD); teaching English to speakers of other languages (M Ed). *Application deadline:* For fall admission, 5/1 for domestic students, 2/1 for international students; for spring admission, 10/1 for domestic students, 6/1 for international students. Applications are processed on a rolling basis. *Application fee:* $60. Electronic applications accepted. *Application Contact:* Dean of Graduate School, 301-405-4190, Fax: 301-314-9305. *Dean,* Dr. Dennis M. Kivlighan, 301-405-2334, Fax: 301-314-9890, E-mail: dennisk@umd.edu.

College of Health and Human Performance Students: 158 full-time (116 women), 43 part-time (36 women); includes 43 minority (26 African Americans, 10 Asian Americans or Pacific Islanders, 7 Hispanic Americans), 37 international. 259 applicants, 32% accepted, 57 enrolled. *Faculty:* 90 full-time (46 women), 21 part-time/adjunct (19 women). Expenses: Contact institution. *Financial support:* In 2006–07, 30 fellowships with full tuition reimbursements (averaging $9,673 per year), 21 research assistantships with tuition reimbursements (averaging $14,596 per year), 72 teaching assistantships with tuition reimbursements (averaging $14,275 per year) were awarded; career-related internships or fieldwork, Federal Work-Study, and scholarships/grants also available. Support available to part-time students. Financial award applicants required to submit FAFSA. In 2006, 32 master's, 9 doctorates awarded. *Degree program information:* Part-time and evening/weekend programs available. Offers community health education (MPH); family studies (PhD); health and human performance (MA, MPH, MS, PhD); kinesiology (MA, PhD); marriage and family therapy (MS); public/community health (PhD). *Application deadline:* For fall admission, 5/1 for domestic students, 2/1 for international students; for spring admission, 10/1 for domestic students, 6/1 for international students. Applications are processed on a rolling basis. *Application fee:* $60. Electronic applications accepted. *Application Contact:* Dean of Graduate School, 301-405-0358, Fax: 301-314-9305. *Dean,* Dr. Robert Gold, 301-405-2437, Fax: 301-314-9167, E-mail: rsgold@umd.edu.

College of Information Studies Students: 205 full-time (151 women), 222 part-time (171 women); includes 52 minority (29 African Americans, 1 American Indian/Alaska Native, 13 Asian Americans or Pacific Islanders, 9 Hispanic Americans), 37 international. 417 applicants, 62% accepted, 128 enrolled. *Faculty:* 18 full-time (9 women), 24 part-time/adjunct (13 women). Expenses: Contact institution. *Financial support:* In 2006–07, 1 fellowship with full tuition reimbursement (averaging $14,140 per year), 6 research assistantships (averaging $17,780 per year), 60 teaching assistantships with tuition reimbursements (averaging $13,992 per year) were awarded; career-related internships or fieldwork, Federal Work-Study, scholarships/grants, and tuition waivers (full and partial) also available. Support available to part-time students. Financial award application deadline: 2/1; financial award applicants required to submit FAFSA. In 2006, 147 degrees awarded. *Degree program information:* Part-time and evening/weekend programs available. Offers information studies (MIM, MLS, PhD). *Application deadline:* For fall admission, 2/1 for domestic and international students; for spring admission, 10/1 for domestic students, 6/1 for international students. Applications are processed on a rolling basis. *Application fee:* $60. Electronic applications accepted. *Application Contact:* Dean of Graduate School, 301-405-0358, Fax: 301-314-9305. *Dean,* Dr. Jennifer Preece, 301-405-2036, Fax: 301-314-9145, E-mail: preece@umd.edu.

Phillip Merrill College of Journalism Students: 73 full-time (41 women), 11 part-time (4 women); includes 14 minority (8 African Americans, 5 Asian Americans or Pacific Islanders, 1 Hispanic American), 11 international. 234 applicants, 34% accepted, 29 enrolled. *Faculty:* 27 full-time (14 women), 40 part-time/adjunct (10 women). Expenses: Contact institution. *Financial support:* In 2006–07, 20 fellowships with full tuition reimbursements (averaging $11,628 per year), 2 research assistantships with tuition reimbursements (averaging $15,751 per year), 16 teaching assistantships with tuition reimbursements (averaging $15,137 per year) were awarded; career-related internships or fieldwork, Federal Work-Study, and scholarships/grants also available. Support available to part-time students. Financial award applicants required to submit FAFSA. In 2006, 28 master's, 2 doctorates awarded. *Degree program information:* Part-time and evening/weekend programs available. Offers broadcast journalism (MA); journalism (MA); journalism and media studies (PhD); online news (MA); public affairs reporting (MA). *Application deadline:* For fall admission, 3/1 for domestic students, 2/1 for international students; for spring admission, 10/1 for domestic students, 6/1 for international students. Applications are processed on a rolling basis. *Application fee:* $60. Electronic applications accepted. *Application Contact:* Dean of Graduate School, 301-405-0358, Fax: 301-314-9305. *Dean,* Thomas Kunkel, 301-405-2383, Fax: 301-314-1978, E-mail: tkunkel@umd.edu.

Robert H. Smith School of Business Students: 862 full-time (289 women), 635 part-time (170 women); includes 392 minority (104 African Americans, 3 American Indian/Alaska Native, 231 Asian Americans or Pacific Islanders, 54 Hispanic Americans), 307 international. 2,123 applicants, 38% accepted, 551 enrolled. *Faculty:* 120 full-time (28 women), 41 part-time/adjunct (10 women). Expenses: Contact institution. *Financial support:* In 2006–07, 91 fellowships with full tuition reimbursements (averaging $11,699 per year), 191 teaching assistantships with tuition reimbursements (averaging $13,998 per year) were awarded; research assistantships with tuition reimbursements, Federal Work-Study and scholarships/grants also available. Support available to part-time students. Financial award applicants required to submit FAFSA. In 2006, 546 master's, 20 doctorates awarded. *Degree program information:* Part-time and evening/weekend programs available. Postbaccalaureate distance learning degree programs offered. Offers business (EMBA, MBA, MS, PhD); business administration (EMBA, MBA); business and management (MS, PhD). *Application deadline:* For fall admission, 5/1 for domestic students, 2/1 for international students; for spring admission, 10/1 for domestic students, 6/1 for international students. Applications are processed on a rolling basis. *Application fee:* $60. Electronic applications accepted. *Application Contact:* Dean of Graduate School, 301-405-0358, Fax: 301-314-9305. *Dean,* Dr. Howard Frank, 301-405-2308, Fax: 301-314-9120, E-mail: hfrank@umd.edu.

School of Architecture, Planning and Preservation Students: 126 full-time (69 women), 37 part-time (25 women); includes 30 minority (12 African Americans, 1 American Indian/Alaska Native, 10 Asian Americans or Pacific Islanders, 7 Hispanic Americans), 26 international. 381 applicants, 43% accepted, 67 enrolled. *Faculty:* 27 full-time (6 women), 11 part-time/adjunct (3 women). Expenses: Contact institution. *Financial support:* In 2006–07, 29 fellowships with full tuition reimbursements (averaging $5,773 per year), 7 research assistantships with tuition reimbursements (averaging $18,818 per year), 91 teaching assistantships with tuition reimbursements (averaging $13,625 per year) were awarded; career-related internships or fieldwork, Federal Work-Study, and scholarships/grants also available. Support available to part-time students. Financial award applicants required to submit FAFSA. In 2006, 62 master's, 1 doctorate awarded. *Degree program information:* Part-time and evening/weekend programs available. Offers architecture (M Arch); architecture, planning and preservation (M Arch, MCP, MHP, PhD, Certificate); historic preservation (MHP, Certificate); urban and regional planning/design (PhD); urban studies and planning (MCP). *Application deadline:* For fall admission, 1/1 for domestic students, 2/1 for international students; for spring admission, 10/15 for domestic students, 6/1 for international students. Applications are processed on a rolling basis. *Application fee:* $60. Electronic applications accepted. *Application Contact:* Dean of Graduate School, 301-405-4190, Fax: 301-314-9305. *Dean,* Garth Rockcastle, 301-405-6283, Fax: 301-314-9583, E-mail: gcr@umd.edu.

School of Public Policy Students: 177 full-time (85 women), 57 part-time (25 women); includes 35 minority (13 African Americans, 1 American Indian/Alaska Native, 11 Asian Americans or Pacific Islanders, 10 Hispanic Americans), 54 international. 463 applicants, 51% accepted, 74 enrolled. *Faculty:* 35 full-time (11 women), 29 part-time/adjunct (8 women). Expenses: Contact institution. *Financial support:* In 2006–07, 64 fellowships with full tuition reimbursements (averaging $6,787 per year), 87 teaching assistantships with tuition reimbursements (averaging $12,991 per year) were awarded; research assistantships with tuition reimbursements, Federal Work-Study and scholarships/grants also available. Support available to part-time students. Financial award applicants required to submit FAFSA. In 2006, 40 master's, 3 doctorates awarded. *Degree program information:* Part-time and evening/weekend programs available. Postbaccalaureate distance learning degree programs offered. Offers policy studies (PhD); public management (MPM); public policy (MPM, MPP, PhD); public policy/law). *Application deadline:* For fall admission, 12/15 for domestic students, 2/1 for international students; for spring admission, 10/1 for domestic students, 6/1 for international students. Applications are processed on a rolling basis. *Application fee:* $60. Electronic applications accepted. *Application Contact:* Dean of Graduate School, 301-405-0358, Fax: 301-314-9305. *Dean,* Dr. Steve Fetter, 301-405-6355, E-mail: sfetter@umd.edu.

National Institutes of Health Sponsored Programs Offers audiology (PhD); language pathology (PhD); neuroscience (PhD); speech (PhD).

UNIVERSITY OF MARYLAND EASTERN SHORE, Princess Anne, MD 21853-1299

General Information State-supported, coed, university. CGS member. *Enrollment:* 190 full-time matriculated graduate/professional students (105 women), 217 part-time matriculated graduate/professional students (131 women). *Enrollment by degree level:* 194 master's, 183 doctoral. *Graduate faculty:* 65 full-time (24 women), 51 part-time/adjunct (15 women). *Graduate housing:* On-campus housing not available. *Student services:* Campus employment opportunities, campus safety program, career counseling, child daycare facilities, disabled student services, exercise/wellness program, free psychological counseling, grant writing training, international student services, teacher training, writing training. *Library facilities:* Frederick Douglass Library. *Online resources:* library catalog, web page, access to other libraries' catalogs. *Collection:* 150,000 titles, 1,260 serial subscriptions.

Computer facilities: Computer purchase and lease plans are available. 120 computers available on campus for general student use. A campuswide network can be accessed. *Web address:* http://www.umes.edu/.

General Application Contact: Dr. C. Dennis Ignasias, Associate Vice President for Academic Affairs, 410-651-6507, Fax: 410-651-7571, E-mail: cdignasias@umes.edu.

GRADUATE UNITS

Graduate Programs Students: 190 full-time (105 women), 217 part-time (131 women); includes 200 minority (187 African Americans, 1 American Indian/Alaska Native, 7 Asian Americans or Pacific Islanders, 5 Hispanic Americans), 63 international. Average age 30. 307 applicants, 56% accepted, 115 enrolled. *Faculty:* 65 full-time (24 women), 51 part-time/adjunct (15 women). Expenses: Contact institution. *Financial support:* In 2006–07, 101 students received support, including 38 research assistantships with full and partial tuition reimbursements available, 53 teaching assistantships with full and partial tuition reimbursements available; career-related internships or fieldwork, scholarships/grants, traineeships, and unspecified assistantships also available. Support available to part-time students. Financial award application deadline: 3/1; financial award applicants required to submit FAFSA. In 2006, 109 master's, 29 doctorates awarded. *Degree program information:* Part-time and evening/weekend programs available. Offers applied computer science (MS); career and technology education (M Ed); criminology and criminal justice (MS); education leadership (Ed D); food and agricultural sciences (MS); food science and technology (PhD); guidance and counseling (M Ed); marine-estuarine-environmental sciences (MS, PhD); organizational leadership (PhD); physical therapy (DPT); rehabilitation counseling (MS); special education (M Ed); teaching (MAT); toxicology (MS, PhD). *Application deadline:* For fall admission, 2/1 priority date for domestic and international students; for winter admission, 10/1 for domestic and international students; for spring admission, 8/1 priority date for domestic students, 6/1 priority date for international students. Applications are processed on a rolling basis. *Application fee:* $30. Electronic applications accepted. *Associate Vice President for Academic Affairs,* Dr. C. Dennis Ignasias, 410-651-6507, Fax: 410-651-7571, E-mail: cdignasias@umes.edu.

See Close-Up on page 1083.

UNIVERSITY OF MARYLAND UNIVERSITY COLLEGE, Adelphi, MD 20783

General Information State-supported, coed, comprehensive institution. CGS member. *Enrollment:* 33,096 graduate, professional, and undergraduate students; 267 full-time matriculated graduate/professional students (150 women), 9,253 part-time matriculated graduate/professional students (4,960 women). *Enrollment by degree level:* 8,927 master's, 137 doctoral, 456 other advanced degrees. *Graduate faculty:* 103 full-time (41 women), 312 part-time/adjunct (88 women). *Graduate housing:* On-campus housing not available. *Student services:* Campus employment opportunities, career counseling, disabled student services, international student services, writing training. *Library facilities:* Information and Library Services plus 1 other. *Online resources:* library catalog, web page, access to other libraries' catalogs. *Collection:* 192,154 serial subscriptions, 25 audiovisual materials.

Computer facilities: 375 computers available on campus for general student use. A campuswide network can be accessed from off campus. *Web address:* http://www.umuc.edu/.

General Application Contact: Coordinator, Graduate Admissions, 301-985-7155, Fax: 301-985-7175, E-mail: gradinfo@umuc.edu.

GRADUATE UNITS

Graduate School of Management and Technology Students: 267 full-time (150 women), 9,253 part-time (4,960 women); includes 4,310 minority (3,135 African Americans, 35 American Indian/Alaska Native, 736 Asian Americans or Pacific Islanders, 404 Hispanic Americans), 191 international. Average age 36. 4,171 applicants, 100% accepted, 2352 enrolled. *Faculty:* 103 full-time (41 women), 312 part-time/adjunct (88 women). Expenses: Contact institution. *Financial support:* Federal Work-Study and scholarships/grants available. Support available to part-time students. Financial award application deadline: 6/1; financial award applicants required to submit FAFSA. In 2006, 1,766 master's, 6 doctorates, 272 other advanced degrees awarded. *Degree program information:* Part-time and evening/weekend programs available. Postbaccalaureate distance learning degree programs offered (no on-campus study). Offers accounting and financial management (MS, Certificate); accounting and information technology (MS, Certificate); biotechnology studies (MS, Certificate); business administration (Exec MBA, MBA); distance education (MDE, Certificate); education (M Ed); environmental management (MS, Certificate); financial management and information systems (MS, Certificate); health administration informatics (MS, Certificate); health care administration (MS, Certificate); information technology (Exec MS, MS, Certificate); international management (MIM, Certificate); management (MS, DM, Certificate); management and technology (Exec MBA, Exec MS, M Ed, MBA, MDE, MIM, MS, DM, Certificate); technology management (Exec MS, MS, Certificate). Offered evenings and weekends only. *Application deadline:* Applications are processed on a rolling basis. *Application fee:* $50. Electronic applications accepted. *Application Contact:* Coordinator, Graduate Admissions, 301-985-7155, Fax: 301-985-7175, E-mail: gradinfo@nova.umuc.edu. *Acting Associate Vice President and Dean of Graduate Studies,* Dr. Christina A. Hannah, 301-985-7040, Fax: 301-985-4611, E-mail: channah@polaris.umuc.edu.

UNIVERSITY OF MARY WASHINGTON, Fredericksburg, VA 22401-5358

General Information State-supported, coed, comprehensive institution. *Enrollment:* 4,862 graduate, professional, and undergraduate students; 121 full-time matriculated graduate/professional students (92 women), 507 part-time matriculated graduate/professional students (367 women). *Graduate faculty:* 25 full-time (17 women), 20 part-time/adjunct (10 women). *Tuition, area resident:* Part-time $275 per credit hour. Tuition, state resident: part-time $626 per credit. *Required fees:* $25 per term. One-time fee: $45 part-time. *Graduate housing:* On-campus housing not available. *Student services:* Campus employment opportunities, career counseling, disabled student services, free psychological counseling, international student services, multicultural affairs office, teacher training, writing training. *Library facilities:* Simpson Library. *Online resources:* library catalog, web page, access to other libraries' catalogs. *Collection:* 355,478 titles, 2,419 serial subscriptions.

Computer facilities: 244 computers available on campus for general student use. A campuswide network can be accessed from student residence rooms and from off campus. Internet access and online class registration are available. *Web address:* http://www.umw.edu/.

General Application Contact: Matthew E. Mejia, Assistant Dean for Graduate and Professional Studies and Dean of the Faculty, 540-286-8017, Fax: 540-286-8085, E-mail: mmejia@umw.edu.

GRADUATE UNITS

College of Graduate and Professional Studies Students: 121 full-time (92 women), 507 part-time (367 women); includes 95 minority (59 African Americans, 1 American Indian/Alaska Native, 10 Asian Americans or Pacific Islanders, 25 Hispanic Americans), 4 international. Average age 35. *Faculty:* 25 full-time (17 women), 20 part-time/adjunct (10 women). Expenses: Contact institution. *Financial support:* In 2006–07, 46 students received support. Scholarships/grants available. Support available to part-time students. Financial award application deadline: 3/15; financial award applicants required to submit FAFSA. In 2006, 14 degrees awarded. *Degree program information:* Part-time and evening/weekend programs available. Offers business administration (MBA); education (M Ed); management information systems (MSMIS). *Application deadline:* For fall admission, 6/1 priority date for domestic students, 6/1 for international students; for spring admission, 10/1 for domestic and international students. *Application fee:* $45. *Application Contact:* Matthew E. Mejia, Assistant Dean for Graduate and Professional Studies and Dean of the Faculty, 540-286-8017, Fax: 540-286-8085, E-mail: mmejia@umw.edu. *Vice President for Graduate and Professional Studies and Dean of the Faculty,* Dr. Meta R. Braymer, 540-286-8000, Fax: 540-286-8005, E-mail: mbraymer@umw.edu.

UNIVERSITY OF MASSACHUSETTS AMHERST, Amherst, MA 01003

General Information State-supported, coed, university. CGS member. *Enrollment:* 25,593 graduate, professional, and undergraduate students; 2,946 full-time matriculated graduate/professional students (1,500 women), 2,125 part-time matriculated graduate/professional students (1,073 women). *Enrollment by degree level:* 2,708 master's, 2,294 doctoral, 69 other advanced degrees. *Graduate faculty:* 1,200 full-time (379 women). Tuition, state resident: full-time $2,640; part-time $110 per credit. Tuition, nonresident: full-time $9,936; part-time $414 per credit. *Required fees:* $8,969; $3,129 per term. One-time fee: $257 full-time. Tuition and fees vary according to class time, course load, campus/location and reciprocity agreements. *Graduate housing:* Rooms and/or apartments available on a first-come, first-served basis to single and married students. Typical cost: $3,700 per year ($6,804 including board) for single students; $6,720 per year ($9,824 including board) for married students. Housing application deadline: 7/15. *Student services:* Campus employment opportunities, campus safety program, career counseling, child daycare facilities, disabled student services, free psychological counseling, grant writing training, international student services, low-cost health insurance. *Library facilities:* W. E. B. Du Bois Library plus 1 other. *Online resources:* library catalog, web page, access to other libraries' catalogs. *Collection:* 3.2 million titles, 40,749 serial subscriptions, 24,180 audiovisual materials.

Computer facilities: 450 computers available on campus for general student use. A campuswide network can be accessed from student residence rooms and from off campus. Internet access and online class registration, online course and grade information are available. *Web address:* http://www.umass.edu/.

General Application Contact: Jean Ames, Supervisor of Admissions, 413-545-0721, Fax: 413-577-0010, E-mail: gradapp@grad.umass.edu.

GRADUATE UNITS

Graduate School Students: 2,946 full-time (1,500 women), 2,125 part-time (1,073 women); includes 582 minority (194 African Americans, 17 American Indian/Alaska Native, 182 Asian Americans or Pacific Islanders, 189 Hispanic Americans), 1,210 international. Average age 32. 7,982 applicants, 32% accepted, 1211 enrolled. *Faculty:* 1,288 full-time (401 women). Expenses: Contact institution. *Financial support:* In 2006–07, 188 fellowships with full tuition reimbursements (averaging $6,116 per year), 1,659 research assistantships with full tuition reimbursements (averaging $11,062 per year), 1,376 teaching assistantships with full tuition reimbursements (averaging $8,149 per year) were awarded; career-related internships or fieldwork, Federal Work-Study, institutionally sponsored loans, scholarships/grants, traineeships, tuition waivers (full), and unspecified assistantships also available. Support available to part-time students. In 2006, 1,146 master's, 267 doctorates awarded. *Degree program information:* Part-time and evening/weekend programs available. Postbaccalaureate distance learning degree programs offered. Offers interdisciplinary studies (MS, PhD); marine science and technology (MS); neuroscience and behavior (MS, PhD); organismic and evolutionary biology (MS, PhD); plant biology (MS, PhD). *Application deadline:* Applications are processed on a rolling basis. *Application fee:* $40 ($65 for international students). Electronic applications accepted. *Application Contact:* Patricia M. Stowell, Graduate Registrar, 413-545-0721, Fax: 413-577-0010, E-mail: pstowell@resgs.umass.edu. *Dean,* Dr. John Mullin, 413-545-5271, Fax: 413-545-3754.

College of Engineering Students: 331 full-time (68 women), 78 part-time (24 women); includes 24 minority (3 African Americans, 14 Asian Americans or Pacific Islanders, 7 Hispanic Americans), 253 international. Average age 28. 1,127 applicants, 28% accepted, 117 enrolled. *Faculty:* 122 full-time (14 women). Expenses: Contact institution. *Financial support:* In 2006–07, 10 fellowships with full tuition reimbursements (averaging $32,157 per year), 323 research assistantships with full tuition reimbursements (averaging $13,094 per year), 61 teaching assistantships with full tuition reimbursements (averaging $2,931 per year) were awarded; career-related internships or fieldwork, Federal Work-Study, scholarships/grants, traineeships, and unspecified assistantships also available. Support available to part-time students. Financial award application deadline: 2/1. In 2006, 80 master's, 21 doctorates awarded. *Degree program information:* Part-time and evening/weekend programs available. Offers chemical engineering (MS, PhD); civil engineering (MS, PhD); electrical and computer engineering (MS, PhD); engineering (MS, PhD); engineering management (MS); environmental engineering (MS); industrial engineering and operations research (MS, PhD); manufacturing engineering (MS); mechanical engineering (MS, PhD). *Application deadline:* Applications are processed on a rolling basis. *Application fee:* $40 ($65 for international students). *Dean,* Dr. Michael Malone, 413-545-6388, Fax: 413-545-6388.

College of Humanities and Fine Arts Students: 467 full-time (260 women), 226 part-time (125 women); includes 91 minority (37 African Americans, 4 American Indian/Alaska Native, 15 Asian Americans or Pacific Islanders, 35 Hispanic Americans), 126 international. Average age 30. 1,608 applicants, 28% accepted, 206 enrolled. *Faculty:* 294 full-time (115 women). Expenses: Contact institution. *Financial support:* In 2006–07, 49 fellowships with full tuition reimbursements (averaging $30,921 per year), 39 research assistantships with full tuition reimbursements (averaging $6,491 per year), 393 teaching assistantships with full tuition reimbursements (averaging $8,554 per year) were awarded; career-related internships or fieldwork, Federal Work-Study, scholarships/grants, traineeships, and unspecified assistantships also available. Support available to part-time students. In 2006, 134 master's, 31 doctorates awarded. *Degree program information:* Part-time programs available. Postbaccalaureate distance learning degree programs offered. Offers Afro-American studies (MA, PhD); ancient history (MA); architecture (M Arch, MS); architecture and design (M Arch); art (MA, MFA); art history (MA); British Empire history (MA); Chinese (MA); comparative literature (MA, PhD); creative writing (MFA); English and American literature (MA, PhD); European (medieval and modern) history (MA, PhD); French and Francophone studies (MA, MAT, PhD); Germanic languages and literatures (MA, PhD); Hispanic literatures and linguistics (MA, PhD); humanities and fine arts (M Arch, MA, MAT, MFA, MM, MS, PhD); interior design (MS); Islamic history (MA); Italian studies (MAT); Japanese (MA); Latin American history (MA, PhD); Latin and classical humanities (MAT); linguistics (MA, PhD); modern global history (MA); music (MM, PhD); philosophy (MA, PhD); public history (MA); science and technology history (MA); teaching Spanish (MAT); theater (MFA); U.S. history (MA, PhD). *Application deadline:* Applications are processed on a rolling basis. *Application fee:* $40 ($65 for international students). Electronic applications accepted. *Dean,* Dr. Joel Martin, 413-545-4169, Fax: 413-545-4171.

College of Natural Resources and the Environment Students: 234 full-time (122 women), 77 part-time (37 women); includes 22 minority (5 African Americans, 1 American Indian/Alaska Native, 9 Asian Americans or Pacific Islanders, 7 Hispanic Americans), 84 international. Average age 29. 424 applicants, 47% accepted, 89 enrolled. *Faculty:* 177 full-time (40 women). Expenses: Contact institution. *Financial support:* In 2006–07, 6 fellowships with full tuition reimbursements (averaging $7,400 per year), 240 research assistantships with full tuition reimbursements (averaging $8,911 per year), 108 teaching assistantships with full tuition reimbursements (averaging $7,246 per year) were awarded; career-related internships or fieldwork, Federal Work-Study, scholarships/grants, traineeships, and unspecified assistantships also available. Support available to part-time students. Financial award application deadline: 2/1. In 2006, 76 master's, 18 doctorates awarded. *Degree program information:* Part-time programs available. Offers entomology (MS, PhD); food science (MS, PhD); forest resources (MS, PhD); landscape architecture (MLA); mammalian and avian biology (MS, PhD); microbiology (MS, PhD); natural resources and the environment (MLA, MRP, MS, PhD); plant science (PhD); regional planning (MRP, PhD); resource economics (MS, PhD); soil science (MS, PhD); wildlife and fisheries conservation (MS, PhD). *Application deadline:* For fall admission, 2/1 priority date for domestic and international students; for spring admission, 10/1 for domestic and international students. Applications are processed on a rolling basis. *Application fee:* $40 ($65 for international students). Electronic applications accepted. *Director,* Dr. Cleve Willis, 413-545-2766, Fax: 413-545-5853, E-mail: willis@resecon.umass.edu.

College of Natural Sciences and Mathematics Students: 598 full-time (213 women), 105 part-time (27 women); includes 42 minority (8 African Americans, 18 Asian Americans or Pacific Islanders, 16 Hispanic Americans), 336 international. Average age 28. 1,835 applicants, 20% accepted, 149 enrolled. *Faculty:* 266 full-time (43 women). Expenses: Contact institution. *Financial support:* In 2006–07, 30 fellowships with full tuition reimbursements (averaging $8,286 per year), 556 research assistantships with full tuition reimbursements (averaging $14,039 per year), 295 teaching assistantships with full tuition reimbursements (averaging $9,581 per year) were awarded; career-related internships or fieldwork, Federal Work-Study, scholarships/grants, traineeships, and unspecified assistantships also available. Support available to part-time students. In 2006, 120 master's, 70 doctorates awarded. *Degree program information:* Part-time programs available. Postbaccalaureate distance learning degree programs offered. Offers applied mathematics (MS); astronomy (MS, PhD); biochemistry (MS, PhD); biological chemistry (PhD); cell and developmental biology (PhD); chemistry (MS, PhD); computer science (MS, PhD); geography (MS); geosciences (MS, PhD); mathematics and statistics (MS, PhD); natural sciences and mathematics (MS, PhD); physics (MS, PhD); polymer science and engineering (MS, PhD). *Application deadline:* Applications are processed on a rolling basis. *Application fee:* $40 ($65 for international students). Electronic applications accepted. *Dean,* Dr. George M. Langford, 413-545-1785, Fax: 413-545-4171.

College of Social and Behavioral Sciences Students: 357 full-time (215 women), 216 part-time (117 women); includes 82 minority (26 African Americans, 4 American Indian/Alaska Native, 19 Asian Americans or Pacific Islanders, 33 Hispanic Americans), 123 international. Average age 33. 1,237 applicants, 19% accepted, 110 enrolled. *Faculty:* 183

University of Massachusetts Amherst (continued)

full-time (71 women). Expenses: Contact institution. *Financial support:* In 2006–07, 24 fellowships with full tuition reimbursements (averaging $6,729 per year), 161 research assistantships with full tuition reimbursements (averaging $7,751 per year), 269 teaching assistantships with full tuition reimbursements (averaging $9,250 per year) were awarded; career-related internships or fieldwork, Federal Work-Study, scholarships/grants, traineeships, and unspecified assistantships also available. Support available to part-time students. In 2006, 80 master's, 49 doctorates awarded. *Degree program information:* Part-time programs available. Offers anthropology (MA, PhD); clinical psychology (MS, PhD); communication (MA, PhD); economics (MA, PhD); labor studies (MS); political science (MA, PhD); public policy and administration (MPA); social and behavioral sciences (MA, MPA, MS, PhD); sociology (MA, PhD). *Application deadline:* Applications are processed on a rolling basis. *Application fee:* $40 ($65 for international students). Electronic applications accepted. *Dean,* Dr. Janet Rifkin, 413-545-4173, Fax: 413-545-4171, E-mail: jrifkin@legal.umass.edu.

Isenberg School of Management Students: 209 full-time (106 women), 647 part-time (195 women); includes 95 minority (13 African Americans, 3 American Indian/Alaska Native, 53 Asian Americans or Pacific Islanders, 26 Hispanic Americans), 103 international. Average age 29. 746 applicants, 52% accepted, 304 enrolled. *Faculty:* 78 full-time (20 women). Expenses: Contact institution. *Financial support:* In 2006–07, 9 fellowships with full tuition reimbursements (averaging $7,590 per year), 132 research assistantships with full tuition reimbursements (averaging $8,969 per year), 58 teaching assistantships with full tuition reimbursements (averaging $7,547 per year) were awarded; career-related internships or fieldwork, Federal Work-Study, scholarships/grants, traineeships, and unspecified assistantships also available. Support available to part-time students. Financial award application deadline: 2/1. In 2006, 252 master's, 13 doctorates awarded. *Degree program information:* Part-time and evening/weekend programs available. Offers accounting (MS); business administration (PMBA); hospitality and tourism management (MS); management (MBA, MS, PMBA, PhD); sport management (MS, PhD). *Application deadline:* For fall admission, 2/1 priority date for domestic and international students. Applications are processed on a rolling basis. *Application fee:* $40 ($65 for international students). *Application Contact:* David A. Butterfield, Director, 413-545-5580, Fax: 413-545-3858, E-mail: dabutter@mgmt.umass.edu. *Dean,* Dr. Soren Bisgaard, 415-545-5581.

School of Education Students: 443 full-time (307 women), 452 part-time (324 women); includes 152 minority (72 African Americans, 4 American Indian/Alaska Native, 31 Asian Americans or Pacific Islanders, 45 Hispanic Americans), 82 international. Average age 34. 612 applicants. *Faculty:* 78 full-time (40 women). Expenses: Contact institution. *Financial support:* In 2006–07, 9 fellowships with full tuition reimbursements (averaging $2,523 per year), 112 research assistantships with full tuition reimbursements (averaging $7,847 per year), 91 teaching assistantships with full tuition reimbursements (averaging $5,106 per year) were awarded; career-related internships or fieldwork, Federal Work-Study, scholarships/grants, traineeships, and unspecified assistantships also available. Support available to part-time students. Financial award application deadline: 1/15. In 2006, 260 master's, 34 doctorates awarded. *Degree program information:* Part-time programs available. Offers cultural diversity and curriculum reform (M Ed, Ed D, CAGS); early childhood education and development (M Ed, Ed D, CAGS); education (M Ed, Ed D, PhD, CAGS); educational administration (M Ed, Ed D, CAGS); elementary teacher education (M Ed, Ed D, CAGS); higher education (M Ed, Ed D, CAGS); international education (M Ed, Ed D, CAGS); mathematics, science, and instructional technology (M Ed, Ed D, CAGS); physical education teacher education (M Ed, Ed D, CAGS); reading and writing (M Ed, Ed D, CAGS); research and evaluation methods (M Ed, Ed D, CAGS); school psychology (PhD); school psychology and school counseling (M Ed, Ed D, CAGS); secondary teacher education (M Ed, Ed D, CAGS); social justice education (M Ed, Ed D, CAGS); special education (M Ed, Ed D, CAGS). *Application deadline:* For fall admission, 1/15 for domestic and international students. Applications are processed on a rolling basis. *Application fee:* $40 ($65 for international students). Electronic applications accepted. *Dean,* Dr. Christine McCormick, 413-545-0233, Fax: 413-545-4240.

School of Nursing Students: 25 full-time (24 women), 59 part-time (58 women); includes 12 minority (6 African Americans, 1 Asian American or Pacific Islander, 5 Hispanic Americans), 3 international. Average age 43. 59 applicants, 85% accepted, 39 enrolled. *Faculty:* 23 full-time (all women). Expenses: Contact institution. *Financial support:* In 2006–07, 27 fellowships with full tuition reimbursements (averaging $404 per year), 3 research assistantships with full tuition reimbursements (averaging $1,877 per year), 29 teaching assistantships with full tuition reimbursements (averaging $8,587 per year) were awarded; career-related internships or fieldwork, Federal Work-Study, scholarships/grants, traineeships, tuition waivers (full), and unspecified assistantships also available. Support available to part-time students. Financial award application deadline: 2/1. In 2006, 10 master's, 1 doctorate awarded. *Degree program information:* Part-time programs available. Offers nursing (MS, PhD). *Application deadline:* For fall admission, 2/1 priority date for domestic and international students; for spring admission, 10/1 for domestic and international students. Applications are processed on a rolling basis. *Application fee:* $40 ($65 for international students). Electronic applications accepted. *Application Contact:* Information Contact, 413-545-5096, Fax: 413-577-2550. *Dean,* Dr. Eileen T. Breslin, 413-545-6883, Fax: 413-545-0086, E-mail: breslin@nursing.umass.edu.

School of Public Health and Health Sciences Students: 185 full-time (127 women), 241 part-time (152 women); includes 48 minority (22 African Americans, 17 Asian Americans or Pacific Islanders, 9 Hispanic Americans), 81 international. Average age 30. 531 applicants, 53% accepted, 77 enrolled. *Faculty:* 66 full-time (35 women). Expenses: Contact institution. *Financial support:* In 2006–07, 6 fellowships with full tuition reimbursements (averaging $8,706 per year), 77 research assistantships with full tuition reimbursements (averaging $6,137 per year), 72 teaching assistantships with full tuition reimbursements (averaging $5,886 per year) were awarded; career-related internships or fieldwork, Federal Work-Study, scholarships/grants, traineeships, tuition waivers (full), and unspecified assistantships also available. Support available to part-time students. Financial award application deadline: 2/1. In 2006, 131 master's, 5 doctorates awarded. *Degree program information:* Part-time programs available. Offers communication disorders (MA, PhD); kinesiology (MS, PhD); nutrition (MPH, MS); public health (PhD); public health and health sciences (MA, MPH, MS, PhD). *Application deadline:* For fall admission, 2/1 priority date for domestic and international students; for spring admission, 10/1 for domestic and international students. Applications are processed on a rolling basis. *Application fee:* $40 ($65 for international students). Electronic applications accepted. *Dean,* Dr. John Cunningham, 413-545-5096, Fax: 413-545-0086, E-mail: jcunningham@provost.umass.edu.

UNIVERSITY OF MASSACHUSETTS BOSTON, Boston, MA 02125-3393

General Information State-supported, coed, university. CGS member. *Enrollment:* 12,362 graduate, professional, and undergraduate students; 913 full-time matriculated graduate/professional students (634 women), 2,203 part-time matriculated graduate/professional students (1,511 women). *Enrollment by degree level:* 2,080 master's, 353 doctoral, 683 other advanced degrees. *Graduate faculty:* 448 full-time (172 women). Tuition, state resident: full-time $2,590; part-time $301 per credit. Tuition, nonresident: full-time $9,758; part-time $427 per credit. One-time fee: $495 full-time. *Graduate housing:* On-campus housing not available. *Student services:* Campus employment opportunities, campus safety program, career counseling, child daycare facilities, disabled student services, exercise/wellness program, free psychological counseling, international student services, low-cost health insurance, multicultural affairs office, teacher training, writing training. *Library facilities:* Joseph P. Healey Library. *Online resources:* library catalog, web page, access to other libraries' catalogs. *Collection:* 584,015 titles, 25,575 serial subscriptions. *Research affiliation:* John F. Kennedy Presidential Library (twentieth century history and politics).

Computer facilities: Computer purchase and lease plans are available. 260 computers available on campus for general student use. A campuswide network can be accessed from off campus. Internet access and online class registration are available. *Web address:* http://www.umb.edu/.

General Application Contact: Peggy Roldan, Graduate Admissions Coordinator, 617-287-6400, Fax: 617-287-6236, E-mail: bos.gadm@dpc.umassp.edu.

GRADUATE UNITS

Office of Graduate Studies Students: 913 full-time (634 women), 2,203 part-time (1,511 women); includes 489 minority (222 African Americans, 6 American Indian/Alaska Native, 145 Asian Americans or Pacific Islanders, 116 Hispanic Americans), 215 international. Average age 34. 2,184 applicants, 50% accepted, 572 enrolled. *Faculty:* 448 full-time (172 women). Expenses: Contact institution. *Financial support:* In 2006–07, 135 research assistantships with full tuition reimbursements (averaging $13,000 per year), 170 teaching assistantships with full tuition reimbursements (averaging $13,000 per year) were awarded; career-related internships or fieldwork, Federal Work-Study, tuition waivers (full), and unspecified assistantships also available. Support available to part-time students. Financial award application deadline: 3/1; financial award applicants required to submit FAFSA. In 2006, 641 master's, 21 doctorates, 92 other advanced degrees awarded. *Degree program information:* Part-time and evening/weekend programs available. Postbaccalaureate distance learning degree programs offered. *Application deadline:* For fall admission, 3/1 priority date for domestic students; for spring admission, 11/1 priority date for domestic students. Applications are processed on a rolling basis. *Application fee:* $25 ($40 for international students). *Application Contact:* Peggy Roldan, Graduate Admissions Coordinator, 617-287-6400, Fax: 617-287-6236, E-mail: bos.gadm@dpc.umassp.edu. *Associate Provost,* Dr. Kristy Alster, 617-287-5700, Fax: 617-287-5699, E-mail: kristine.alster@umb.edu.

College of Liberal Arts Students: 138 full-time (91 women), 292 part-time (186 women); includes 66 minority (23 African Americans, 16 Asian Americans or Pacific Islanders, 27 Hispanic Americans), 25 international. Average age 32. 618 applicants, 38% accepted, 131 enrolled. Expenses: Contact institution. *Financial support:* In 2006–07, 31 research assistantships with full tuition reimbursements (averaging $13,000 per year), 52 teaching assistantships with full tuition reimbursements (averaging $13,000 per year) were awarded; career-related internships or fieldwork, Federal Work-Study, and unspecified assistantships also available. Support available to part-time students. Financial award application deadline: 3/1; financial award applicants required to submit FAFSA. In 2006, 133 master's, 4 doctorates awarded. *Degree program information:* Part-time and evening/weekend programs available. Offers American studies (MA); applied sociology (MA); archival methods (MA); bilingual education (MA); clinical psychology (PhD); English (MA); English as a second language (MA); foreign language pedagogy (MA); historical archaeology (MA); history (MA); liberal arts (MA, PhD). *Application deadline:* For fall admission, 3/1 priority date for domestic students; for spring admission, 1/1 priority date for domestic students. *Application fee:* $25 ($40 for international students). *Application Contact:* Peggy Roldan, Graduate Admissions Coordinator, 617-287-6400, Fax: 617-287-6236, E-mail: bos.gadm@dpc.umassp.edu. *Dean, College of Liberal Arts,* Dr. Donna Kuizenga, 617-287-6500, E-mail: donna.kuizenga@umb.edu.

College of Management Students: 110 full-time (54 women), 259 part-time (120 women); includes 64 minority (19 African Americans, 35 Asian Americans or Pacific Islanders, 10 Hispanic Americans), 62 international. Average age 30. 297 applicants, 38% accepted, 45 enrolled. Expenses: Contact institution. *Financial support:* In 2006–07, 13 research assistantships with full tuition reimbursements (averaging $13,000 per year), teaching assistantships with full tuition reimbursements (averaging $13,000 per year) were awarded; career-related internships or fieldwork, Federal Work-Study, and unspecified assistantships also available. Support available to part-time students. Financial award application deadline: 3/1; financial award applicants required to submit FAFSA. In 2006, 69 degrees awarded. *Degree program information:* Part-time and evening/weekend programs available. Offers business administration (MBA); management (MBA). *Application deadline:* For fall admission, 3/1 priority date for domestic students; for spring admission, 11/1 for domestic students. *Application fee:* $25 ($40 for international students). *Application Contact:* Peggy Roldan, Graduate Admissions Coordinator, 617-287-6400, Fax: 617-287-6236, E-mail: bos.gadm@dpc.umassp.edu. *Dean,* Dr. Philip Quaglieri, 617-287-7700, E-mail: philip.quaglieri@umb.edu.

College of Nursing and Health Sciences Students: 52 full-time (47 women), 104 part-time (100 women); includes 26 minority (16 African Americans, 10 Asian Americans or Pacific Islanders), 2 international. Average age 38. 113 applicants, 72% accepted, 73 enrolled. Expenses: Contact institution. *Financial support:* In 2006–07, 3 research assistantships with full tuition reimbursements (averaging $13,000 per year), 13 teaching assistantships with full tuition reimbursements (averaging $13,000 per year) were awarded; career-related internships or fieldwork, Federal Work-Study, and unspecified assistantships also available. Support available to part-time students. Financial award application deadline: 3/1; financial award applicants required to submit FAFSA. In 2006, 24 master's, 4 doctorates awarded. *Degree program information:* Part-time and evening/weekend programs available. Offers nursing (MS, PhD). *Application deadline:* For fall admission, 3/1 priority date for domestic students; for spring admission, 11/1 for domestic students. *Application fee:* $25. *Application Contact:* Peggy Roldan, Graduate Admissions Coordinator, 617-287-6400, Fax: 617-287-6236, E-mail: bos.gadm@dpc.umassp.edu. *Dean,* Dr. Greer Glazer, 617-287-7500.

College of Public and Community Service Students: 34 full-time (25 women), 52 part-time (36 women); includes 22 minority (14 African Americans, 4 Asian Americans or Pacific Islanders, 4 Hispanic Americans), 1 international. Average age 40. 76 applicants, 55% accepted. Expenses: Contact institution. *Financial support:* In 2006–07, 23 research assistantships with full tuition reimbursements (averaging $13,000 per year), 4 teaching assistantships with full tuition reimbursements (averaging $13,000 per year) were awarded; career-related internships or fieldwork, Federal Work-Study, and unspecified assistantships also available. Support available to part-time students. Financial award application deadline: 3/1; financial award applicants required to submit FAFSA. In 2006, 18 master's, 15 other advanced degrees awarded. *Degree program information:* Part-time and evening/weekend programs available. Offers dispute resolution (MA, Certificate); human services (MS); public and community service (MA, MS, Certificate). *Application deadline:* For fall admission, 3/1 priority date for domestic students. Applications are processed on a rolling basis. *Application fee:* $25 ($40 for international students). *Application Contact:* Peggy Roldan, Graduate Admissions Coordinator, 617-287-6400, Fax: 617-287-6236, E-mail: bos.gadm@dpc.umassp.edu. *Dean,* Adenrele Awotona, 617-287-7231, Fax: 617-287-5699.

College of Science and Mathematics Students: 115 full-time (59 women), 93 part-time (43 women); includes 40 minority (8 African Americans, 2 American Indian/Alaska Native, 25 Asian Americans or Pacific Islanders, 5 Hispanic Americans), 118 international. Average age 31. 386 applicants, 39% accepted, 53 enrolled. Expenses: Contact institution. *Financial support:* In 2006–07, 16 research assistantships with full tuition reimbursements (averaging $13,000 per year), 73 teaching assistantships with full tuition reimbursements (averaging $13,000 per year) were awarded; career-related internships or fieldwork, Federal Work-Study, institutionally sponsored loans, and unspecified assistantships also available. Support available to part-time students. Financial award application deadline: 3/1; financial award applicants required to submit FAFSA. In 2006, 133 master's, 4 doctorates awarded. *Degree program information:* Part-time and evening/weekend programs available. Offers applied physics (MS); biology (MS); biotechnology and biomedical science (MS); chemistry (MS); computer science (MS, PhD); environmental biology (PhD); environmental sciences (MS); environmental, earth and ocean sciences (PhD); molecular, cellular and organismal biology (PhD); science and mathematics (MS, PhD). *Application deadline:* For fall admission, 3/1 priority date for domestic students; for spring admission, 11/1 priority date for domestic students. Applications are processed on a rolling basis. *Application fee:* $25 ($40 for international students). *Application Contact:* Peggy Roldan, Graduate Admissions Coordinator, 617-287-6400, Fax: 617-287-6236, E-mail: bos.gadm@dpc.umassp.edu. *Interim Dean,* Dr. William Hagar, 617-287-5777.

Division of Continuing Education Average age 51. 29 applicants, 76% accepted, 0 enrolled. Expenses: Contact institution. *Financial support:* Career-related internships or fieldwork and Federal Work-Study available. Support available to part-time students. Financial award application deadline: 3/1; financial award applicants required to submit FAFSA. In 2006, 14 degrees awarded. *Degree program information:* Part-time and evening/weekend programs available. Offers continuing education (Certificate); women in politics and government (Certificate). *Application deadline:* For fall admission, 3/1 priority date for domestic students. *Application* *fee:* $25 ($40 for international students). *Application Contact:* Peggy Roldan, Graduate Admissions Coordinator, 617-287-6400, Fax: 617-287-6236, E-mail: bos.gadm@dpc.umassp.edu. *Head,* Dr. Dirk Messelaar, 617-287-7925.

Graduate College of Education Students: 272 full-time (209 women), 629 part-time (475 women); includes 129 minority (68 African Americans, 2 American Indian/Alaska Native, 24 Asian Americans or Pacific Islanders, 35 Hispanic Americans), 17 international. Average age 34. 622 applicants, 60% accepted. Expenses: Contact institution. *Financial support:* In 2006–07, 85 research assistantships with full tuition reimbursements (averaging $3,500 per year), 2 teaching assistantships with full tuition reimbursements (averaging $4,000 per year) were awarded; career-related internships or fieldwork, Federal Work-Study, and unspecified assistantships also available. Support available to part-time students. Financial award application deadline: 3/1; financial award applicants required to submit FAFSA. In 2006, 237 master's, 9 doctorates, 41 other advanced degrees awarded. *Degree program information:* Part-time and evening/weekend programs available. Offers critical and creative thinking (MA, Certificate); education (M Ed, Ed D); educational administration (M Ed, CAGS); elementary and secondary education/certification (M Ed); family therapy (M Ed, CAGS); forensic counseling (M Ed, CAGS); higher education administration (Ed D); instructional design (M Ed); mental health counseling (M Ed, CAGS); rehabilitation counseling (M Ed, CAGS); school guidance counseling (M Ed, CAGS); school psychology (M Ed, CAGS); special education (M Ed); teacher certification (M Ed); urban school leadership (Ed D). *Application deadline:* For fall admission, 3/1 for domestic students. *Application fee:* $25 ($40 for international students). *Application Contact:* Peggy Roldan, Graduate Admissions Coordinator, 617-287-6400, Fax: 617-287-6236, E-mail: bos.gadm@dpc.umassp.edu. *Interim Dean,* Dr. Peter Langer, 617-287-7600.

John W. McCormack Graduate School of Policy Studies Students: 26 full-time (19 women), 104 part-time (68 women); includes 21 minority (14 African Americans, 5 Asian Americans or Pacific Islanders, 2 Hispanic Americans), 12 international. 115 applicants, 63% accepted, 31 enrolled. Expenses: Contact institution. *Financial support:* Research assistantships with full tuition reimbursements, teaching assistantships with full tuition reimbursements, career-related internships or fieldwork, Federal Work-Study, and unspecified assistantships available. Support available to part-time students. Financial award application deadline: 3/1; financial award applicants required to submit FAFSA. In 2006, 20 master's, 7 doctorates, 14 other advanced degrees awarded. *Degree program information:* Part-time and evening/weekend programs available. Offers gerontology (MA, MS, PhD, Certificate); gerontology research (MA); management in aging services (MA); public affairs (MS); public policy (PhD); women in politics and government (Certificate). Certificate program in women in politics and government offered jointly with Division of Continuing Education. *Application Contact:* Peggy Roldan, Graduate Admissions Coordinator, 617-287-6400, Fax: 617-287-6236, E-mail: bos.gadm@dpc.umassp.edu. *Dean,* Dr. Stephen Crosby, 617-287-5550, E-mail: stephen.crosby@umb.edu.

See Close-Up on page 1085.

UNIVERSITY OF MASSACHUSETTS DARTMOUTH, North Dartmouth, MA 02747-2300

General Information State-supported, coed, university. *Enrollment:* 8,756 graduate, professional, and undergraduate students; 342 full-time matriculated graduate/professional students (147 women), 572 part-time matriculated graduate/professional students (330 women). *Enrollment by degree level:* 781 master's, 48 doctoral, 85 other advanced degrees. *Graduate faculty:* 271 full-time (98 women), 134 part-time/adjunct (76 women). Tuition, state resident: full-time $2,071; part-time $86 per credit. Tuition, nonresident: full-time $8,099; part-time $337 per credit. *Graduate housing:* Room and/or apartments available on a first-come, first-served basis to single students; on-campus housing not available to married students. Typical cost: $5,400 per year ($8,162 including board). Room and board charges vary according to board plan and housing facility selected. Housing application deadline: 3/16. *Student services:* Campus employment opportunities, campus safety program, career counseling, child daycare facilities, disabled student services, exercise/wellness program, free psychological counseling, grant writing training, international student services, low-cost health insurance, multicultural affairs office, teacher training, writing training. *Library facilities:* University of Massachusetts Dartmouth Library. *Online resources:* library catalog, web page, access to other libraries' catalogs. *Collection:* 468,266 titles, 2,800 serial subscriptions, 8,179 audiovisual materials. *Research affiliation:* National Textile Center (materials), US Army (materials), Woods Hole Oceanographic Institution (marine sciences), Cape Cod Cranberry Growers Association (agriculture), Massachusetts Institute of Technology (materials), National Aeronautics and Space Administration (NASA) (SMAST).

Computer facilities: Computer purchase and lease plans are available. 368 computers available on campus for general student use. A campuswide network can be accessed from student residence rooms and from off campus. Internet access and online class registration are available. *Web address:* http://www.umassd.edu/.

General Application Contact: Carol Novo, Graduate Admissions Officer, 508-999-8604, Fax: 508-999-8183, E-mail: graduate@umassd.edu.

GRADUATE UNITS

Graduate School Students: 342 full-time (147 women), 572 part-time (330 women); includes 51 minority (13 African Americans, 1 American Indian/Alaska Native, 23 Asian Americans or Pacific Islanders, 14 Hispanic Americans), 286 international. Average age 31. 1,007 applicants, 76% accepted, 347 enrolled. *Faculty:* 271 full-time (98 women), 134 part-time/adjunct (76 women). Expenses: Contact institution. *Financial support:* In 2006–07, 131 research assistantships with full tuition reimbursements (averaging $11,306 per year), 164 teaching assistantships with full tuition reimbursements (averaging $8,082 per year) were awarded; career-related internships or fieldwork, Federal Work-Study, scholarships/grants, and unspecified assistantships also available. Support available to part-time students. Financial award application deadline: 3/1; financial award applicants required to submit FAFSA. In 2006, 224 master's, 4 doctorates, 25 other advanced degrees awarded. *Degree program information:* Part-time programs available. Offers biomedical engineering/biotechnology (PhD). *Application deadline:* Applications are processed on a rolling basis. *Application fee:* $40 ($60 for international students). Electronic applications accepted. *Application Contact:* Carol Novo, Graduate Admissions Officer, 508-999-8604, Fax: 508-999-8183, E-mail: graduate@umassd.edu. *Associate Vice Chancellor for Academic Affairs/Graduate Studies,* Dr. Richard J. Panofsky, 508-999-8029, Fax: 508-999-8375, E-mail: rpanofsky@umassd.edu.

Charlton College of Business Students: 66 full-time (20 women), 111 part-time (54 women); includes 16 minority (5 African Americans, 6 Asian Americans or Pacific Islanders, 5 Hispanic Americans), 46 international. Average age 31. 167 applicants, 83% accepted, 83 enrolled. *Faculty:* 41 full-time (11 women), 22 part-time/adjunct (8 women). Expenses: Contact institution. *Financial support:* In 2006–07, 2 research assistantships with full tuition reimbursements (averaging $11,985 per year), 6 teaching assistantships with full tuition reimbursements (averaging $7,200 per year) were awarded; Federal Work-Study and unspecified assistantships also available. Support available to part-time students. Financial award application deadline: 3/1; financial award applicants required to submit FAFSA. In 2006, 73 master's, 20 other advanced degrees awarded. *Degree program information:* Part-time programs available. Offers accounting (Postbaccalaureate Certificate); business (MBA, PMC, Postbaccalaureate Certificate); business administration (MBA); e-commerce (PMC); finance (PMC); general management (PMC); leadership (PMC); management (Postbaccalaureate Certificate); marketing (PMC); supply chain management (PMC). *Application deadline:* For fall admission, 6/1 for domestic students, 4/1 for international students; for spring admission, 10/1 for domestic students, 8/1 for international students. *Application fee:* $40 ($60 for international students). Electronic applications accepted. *Application Contact:* Carol Novo, Graduate Admissions Officer, 508-999-8604, Fax: 508-999-8183, E-mail: graduate@umassd.edu. *Dean,* Dr. Eileen Peacock, 508-999-8432, Fax: 508-999-8779, E-mail: epeacock@umassd.edu.

College of Arts and Sciences Students: 54 full-time (38 women), 200 part-time (146 women); includes 19 minority (6 African Americans, 8 Asian Americans or Pacific Islanders, 5 Hispanic Americans), 20 international. Average age 32. 202 applicants, 68% accepted, 93 enrolled. *Faculty:* 82 full-time (31 women), 67 part-time/adjunct (38 women). Expenses: Contact institution. *Financial support:* In 2006–07, 7 research assistantships with full tuition reimbursements (averaging $13,882 per year), 53 teaching assistantships with full tuition reimbursements (averaging $10,205 per year) were awarded; career-related internships or fieldwork, Federal Work-Study, and unspecified assistantships also available. Support available to part-time students. Financial award application deadline: 3/1; financial award applicants required to submit FAFSA. In 2006, 54 master's, 2 other advanced degrees awarded. *Degree program information:* Part-time programs available. Offers arts and sciences (MA, MAT, MPP, MS, PhD, Certificate, Postbaccalaureate Certificate); biology (MS); chemistry (MS); clinical psychology (MA); general psychology (MA); marine biology (MS); policy studies (MPP); Portuguese (MA); professional writing (MA, Postbaccalaureate Certificate); teaching (MAT, Certificate); WSO-Afro-Brazilian studies (PhD). *Application fee:* $40 ($60 for international students). *Application Contact:* Carol Novo, Graduate Admissions Officer, 508-999-8604, Fax: 508-999-8183, E-mail: graduate@umassd.edu. *Dean,* Dr. William Hogan, 508-999-8200, Fax: 508-999-8183, E-mail: whogan@umassd.edu.

College of Engineering Students: 140 full-time (37 women), 125 part-time (24 women); includes 2 minority (both Asian Americans or Pacific Islanders), 193 international. Average age 26. 449 applicants, 81% accepted, 100 enrolled. *Faculty:* 69 full-time (9 women), 7 part-time/adjunct (1 woman). Expenses: Contact institution. *Financial support:* In 2006–07, 82 research assistantships with full tuition reimbursements (averaging $9,716 per year), 65 teaching assistantships with full tuition reimbursements (averaging $8,891 per year) were awarded; Federal Work-Study and unspecified assistantships also available. Support available to part-time students. Financial award application deadline: 3/1; financial award applicants required to submit FAFSA. In 2006, 58 master's, 4 doctorates, 1 other advanced degree awarded. *Degree program information:* Part-time programs available. Offers acoustics (Certificate); civil engineering (MS); communications (Certificate); computer engineering (MS); computer science (MS, Certificate); computer systems engineering (Certificate); digital signal processing (Certificate); electrical engineering (MS, PhD); electrical engineering systems (Certificate); engineering (MS, PhD, Certificate); mechanical engineering (MS); physics (MS); textile chemistry (MS); textile technology (MS). *Application deadline:* For fall admission, 4/20 for domestic students, 2/20 for international students; for spring admission, 11/15 for domestic students, 9/15 for international students. Applications are processed on a rolling basis. *Application fee:* $40 ($60 for international students). Electronic applications accepted. *Application Contact:* Carol Novo, Graduate Admissions Officer, 508-999-8604, Fax: 508-999-8183, E-mail: graduate@umassd.edu. *Interim Dean,* Antonio Costa, 508-999-8539, Fax: 508-999-9137, E-mail: acosta@umassd.edu.

College of Nursing Students: 10 full-time (all women), 66 part-time (63 women); includes 4 minority (2 African Americans, 1 American Indian/Alaska Native, 1 Hispanic American). Average age 41. 33 applicants, 94% accepted, 26 enrolled. *Faculty:* 31 full-time (all women), 21 part-time/adjunct (all women). Expenses: Contact institution. *Financial support:* In 2006–07, 10 teaching assistantships with full tuition reimbursements (averaging $4,725 per year) were awarded; research assistantships with full tuition reimbursements, Federal Work-Study, scholarships/grants, and unspecified assistantships also available. Support available to part-time students. Financial award application deadline: 3/1; financial award applicants required to submit FAFSA. In 2006, 20 master's, 2 other advanced degrees awarded. *Degree program information:* Part-time programs available. Offers community nursing (MS, PhD, Certificate, PMC); nursing (MS, PhD, Certificate, PMC). *Application deadline:* For fall admission, 4/20 for domestic students, 2/20 for international students; for spring admission, 11/15 for domestic students, 9/15 for international students. *Application fee:* $40 ($60 for international students). Electronic applications accepted. *Application Contact:* Carol Novo, Graduate Admissions Officer, 508-999-8604, Fax: 508-999-8183, E-mail: graduate@umassd.edu. *Dean,* Dr. James Fain, 508-999-8586, Fax: 508-999-9127, E-mail: jfain@umassd.edu.

College of Visual and Performing Arts Students: 52 full-time (32 women), 46 part-time (37 women); includes 8 minority (6 Asian Americans or Pacific Islanders, 2 Hispanic Americans), 6 international. Average age 32. 107 applicants, 56% accepted, 28 enrolled. *Faculty:* 37 full-time (15 women), 16 part-time/adjunct (8 women). Expenses: Contact institution. *Financial support:* In 2006–07, 35 teaching assistantships with full tuition reimbursements (averaging $3,514 per year) were awarded; research assistantships with full tuition reimbursements, Federal Work-Study and unspecified assistantships also available. Support available to part-time students. Financial award application deadline: 3/1; financial award applicants required to submit FAFSA. In 2006, 17 degrees awarded. *Degree program information:* Part-time programs available. Offers art education (MAE); artisanry (MFA, Certificate); fine arts (MFA); visual and performing arts (MAE, MFA, Certificate); visual design (MFA). *Application deadline:* Applications are processed on a rolling basis. *Application fee:* $40 ($60 for international students). Electronic applications accepted. *Application Contact:* Carol Novo, Graduate Admissions Officer, 508-999-8604, Fax: 508-999-8183, E-mail: graduate@umassd.edu. *Interim Dean,* Michael Taylor, 508-999-8564, Fax: 508-999-9126, E-mail: mtaylor@umassd.edu.

School of Marine Science and Technology Students: 14 full-time (8 women), 18 part-time (5 women); includes 2 minority (1 Asian American or Pacific Islander, 1 Hispanic American), 11 international. Average age 28. 35 applicants, 80% accepted, 14 enrolled. *Faculty:* 11 full-time (1 woman), 1 part-time/adjunct (0 women). Expenses: Contact institution. *Financial support:* In 2006–07, 26 research assistantships (averaging $16,220 per year), 1 teaching assistantship (averaging $14,800 per year) were awarded; unspecified assistantships also available. Financial award application deadline: 3/1; financial award applicants required to submit FAFSA. In 2006, 2 degrees awarded. Offers marine science and technology (MS, PhD). *Application deadline:* For fall admission, 4/20 priority date for domestic students, 2/20 for international students. Applications are processed on a rolling basis. *Application fee:* $40 ($60 for international students). Electronic applications accepted. *Application Contact:* Carol Novo, Graduate Admissions Officer, 508-999-8604, Fax: 508-999-8183, E-mail: graduate@umassd.edu. *Director,* Dr. Avijit Gangopadhyay, 508-910-6330, Fax: 508-999-8183, E-mail: avijit@umassd.edu.

UNIVERSITY OF MASSACHUSETTS LOWELL, Lowell, MA 01854-2881

General Information State-supported, coed, university. CGS member. *Graduate housing:* Rooms and/or apartments available on a first-come, first-served basis to single students and available to married students. Housing application deadline: 4/1.

GRADUATE UNITS

Graduate School *Degree program information:* Part-time and evening/weekend programs available. Electronic applications accepted.

College of Arts and Sciences *Degree program information:* Part-time and evening/weekend programs available. Offers applied mathematics (MS); applied mechanics (PhD); applied physics (MS, PhD); arts and sciences (MA, MM, MMS, MS, MS Eng, PhD, Sc D); biochemistry (PhD); biological sciences (MS); biotechnology (MS); chemistry (MS, PhD); community and social psychology (MA); computational mathematics (PhD); computer science (MS, PhD, Sc D); criminal justice (MA); energy engineering (PhD); environmental studies (PhD); mathematics (MS); music education (MM); music theory (MM); performance (MM); physics (MS, PhD); polymer sciences (MS, PhD); radiological sciences and protection (MS, PhD); regional economic and social development (MS); sound recording technology (MMS).

College of Health Professions *Degree program information:* Part-time programs available. Offers administration of nursing services (PhD); adult psychiatric nursing (MS); advanced practice (MS); clinical laboratory studies (MS); family and community health nursing (MS); gerontological nursing (MS); health professions (MS, PhD); health promotion (PhD); health services administration (MS); occupational health nursing (MS); physical therapy (MS).

College of Management *Degree program information:* Part-time and evening/weekend programs available. Offers business administration (MBA); management (MBA, MMS); manufacturing management (MMS).

Graduate School of Education *Degree program information:* Part-time and evening/weekend programs available. Postbaccalaureate distance learning degree programs offered (no on-campus study). Offers administration, planning, and policy (CAGS); curriculum and instruction (M Ed, CAGS); educational administration (M Ed); language arts and literacy

University of Massachusetts Lowell (continued)

(Ed D); leadership in schooling (Ed D); math and science education (Ed D); reading and language (M Ed, CAGS). Electronic applications accepted.

James B. Francis College of Engineering *Degree program information:* Part-time and evening/weekend programs available. Offers chemical engineering (MS Eng); chemistry (PhD); civil engineering (MS Eng); cleaner production and pollution prevention (MS, Sc D); computer engineering (MS Eng); electrical engineering (MS Eng, D Eng); energy engineering (MS Eng); engineering (MS, MS Eng, D Eng, PhD, Sc D, Certificate); environmental risk assessment (Certificate); environmental studies (MS Eng); identification and control of ergonomic hazards (Certificate); industrial hygiene (MS, Sc D); job stress and healthy job redesign (Certificate); manufacturing (Certificate); mechanical engineering (MS Eng, D Eng); occupational epidemiology (MS, Sc D); occupational ergonomics (MS, Sc D); plastics engineering (MS Eng, D Eng); radiological health physics and general work environment protection (Certificate); work environmental policy (MS, Sc D).

See Close-Up on page 1087.

UNIVERSITY OF MASSACHUSETTS WORCESTER, Worcester, MA 01655-0115

General Information State-supported, coed, graduate-only institution. CGS member. *Enrollment by degree level:* 423 first professional, 199 master's, 354 doctoral, 1 other advanced degree. *Graduate faculty:* 939 full-time (300 women), 119 part-time/adjunct (92 women). Tuition, state resident: full-time $2,640. Tuition, nonresident: full-time $9,856. *Required fees:* $3,942. *Graduate housing:* On-campus housing not available. *Student services:* Career counseling, child daycare facilities, free psychological counseling, international student services, low-cost health insurance. *Library facilities:* Lamar Soutter Library. *Online resources:* library catalog, web page. *Collection:* 236,449 titles, 4,518 serial subscriptions, 1,877 audiovisual materials. *Research affiliation:* Worcester Polytechnic Institute (biomedical engineering).

Computer facilities: 112 computers available on campus for general student use. A campuswide network can be accessed from off campus. Internet access is available. *Web address:* http://www.umass.edu/.

General Application Contact: Karen Lawton, Director of Admissions, 508-856-2303, E-mail: karen.lawton@umassmed.edu.

GRADUATE UNITS

Graduate School of Biomedical Sciences Students: 354 full-time (199 women); includes 30 minority (2 African Americans, 25 Asian Americans or Pacific Islanders, 3 Hispanic Americans), 151 international. Average age 32. 475 applicants, 32% accepted, 52 enrolled. *Faculty:* 289 full-time (66 women). Expenses: Contact institution. *Financial support:* In 2006–07, 139 fellowships with full tuition reimbursements (averaging $25,740 per year), 151 research assistantships with full tuition reimbursements (averaging $25,740 per year) were awarded; institutionally sponsored loans, tuition waivers (full), and unspecified assistantships also available. In 2006, 21 doctorates awarded. Offers biochemistry and molecular pharmacology (PhD); biomedical engineering and medical physics (PhD); biomedical sciences (PhD); cancer biology (PhD); cell biology (PhD); clinical and population health research (PhD); medical sciences (PhD); molecular genetics and microbiology (PhD); neuroscience (PhD); physiology (PhD). *Application deadline:* For fall admission, 12/15 for domestic and international students. Applications are processed on a rolling basis. *Application fee:* $25 ($50 for international students). Electronic applications accepted. *Application Contact:* Michael Cole, Director of Admissions and Recruitment, 508-856-4779, Fax: 508-856-3659, E-mail: michael.cole@umassmed.edu. *Dean,* Dr. Anthony Carruthers, 508-856-4135.

Graduate School of Nursing Students: 46 full-time (43 women), 6 part-time (2 women); includes 5 minority (2 African Americans, 2 Asian Americans or Pacific Islanders, 1 Hispanic American). Average age 38. 42 applicants, 71% accepted. *Faculty:* 39. Expenses: Contact institution. *Financial support:* In 2006–07, 4 students received support. Scholarships/grants and traineeships available. Support available to part-time students. Financial award application deadline: 3/22; financial award applicants required to submit FAFSA. In 2006, 26 master's, 2 doctorates, 6 other advanced degrees awarded. *Degree program information:* Part-time programs available. Offers adult acute/critical care nurse practitioner (MS, Certificate); adult ambulatory/community care nurse practitioner (MS, Certificate); gerontological nurse practitioner (Certificate); nurse educator (MS, Certificate); nursing (PhD). *Application deadline:* For fall admission, 3/15 for domestic students. Applications are processed on a rolling basis. *Application fee:* $40 ($60 for international students). *Application Contact:* Larry Shattuck, Director of Recruitment and Retention, 508-856-5801, Fax: 508-856-6552. *Associate Dean,* Dr. Janet Hale, 508-856-5661, Fax: 508-856-6552.

Medical School Students: 423 full-time (233 women); includes 87 minority (16 African Americans, 4 American Indian/Alaska Native, 60 Asian Americans or Pacific Islanders, 7 Hispanic Americans). Average age 30. 763 applicants, 21% accepted, 103 enrolled. *Faculty:* 939 full-time (300 women), 119 part-time/adjunct (92 women). Expenses: Contact institution. *Financial support:* In 2006–07, 381 students received support. Federal Work-Study, institutionally sponsored loans, scholarships/grants, and tuition waivers (partial) available. Financial award applicants required to submit CSS PROFILE or FAFSA. In 2006, 93 degrees awarded. Offers medicine (MD). *Application deadline:* For fall admission, 12/15 for domestic students. *Application fee:* $75. *Application Contact:* Dr. Jane Cronin, Director of Admissions, 508-856-2303, Fax: 508-856-3629. *Dean,* Dr. Aaron Lazare, 508-856-0011.

UNIVERSITY OF MEDICINE AND DENTISTRY OF NEW JERSEY, Newark, NJ 07107-1709

General Information State-supported, coed, graduate-only institution. CGS member. *Enrollment:* 3,548 full-time matriculated graduate/professional students (2,002 women), 1,078 part-time matriculated graduate/professional students (818 women). *Enrollment by degree level:* 2,101 first professional, 1,316 master's, 1,100 doctoral, 109 other advanced degrees. *Graduate faculty:* 2,109. *Graduate housing:* Rooms and/or apartments available on a first-come, first-served basis to single and married students. Typical cost: $11,700 per year for single students; $21,600 per year for married students. *Student services:* Campus employment opportunities, campus safety program, career counseling, child daycare facilities, exercise/wellness program, free psychological counseling, international student services, low-cost health insurance. *Library facilities:* George F. Smith Library of the Health Sciences. *Online resources:* library catalog, web page, access to other libraries' catalogs. *Collection:* 262,359 titles, 11,224 serial subscriptions, 4,525 audiovisual materials. *Research affiliation:* Coriell Institute for Medical Research (cancer and human development), Kessler Institute for Rehabilitation (physical rehabilitation), Public Health Research Institute (public health), Robert Wood Johnson University Hospital (adult care hospitalization).

Computer facilities: 367 computers available on campus for general student use. A campuswide network can be accessed from student residence rooms and from off campus. Internet access and online class registration, distance learning, continuing education are available. *Web address:* http://www.umdnj.edu/.

General Application Contact: University Registrar, 973-972-5338.

GRADUATE UNITS

Graduate School of Biomedical Sciences Students: 877 full-time (462 women), 121 part-time (82 women); includes 313 minority (76 African Americans, 1 American Indian/Alaska Native, 164 Asian Americans or Pacific Islanders, 72 Hispanic Americans), 317 international. Average age 28. Expenses: Contact institution. *Financial support:* Fellowships, research assistantships, teaching assistantships, career-related internships or fieldwork, Federal Work-Study, institutionally sponsored loans, traineeships, and tuition waivers (full and partial) available. Financial award application deadline: 5/1. In 2006, 54 master's, 24 doctorates awarded. Offers biochemistry and molecular biology (MS, PhD); biomedical engineering (MS, PhD); biomedical sciences (MBS, MS); biomedical sciences (interdisciplinary) (PhD); cell and molecular biology (MS, PhD); cell biology and molecular medicine (PhD); cellular and molecular pharmacology (MS, PhD); environmental sciences/exposure assessment (PhD); experimental pathology (PhD); integrative neuroscience (PhD); microbiology and molecular genetics (PhD); molecular biosciences (PhD); molecular genetics, microbiology and immunology (MS, PhD); neuroscience (MS, PhD); pharmacological sciences (Certificate); pharmacology and physiology (PhD); physiology and integrative biology (MS, PhD). *Application deadline:* Applications are processed on a rolling basis. *Application fee:* $40. Electronic applications accepted. *Interim Dean,* Dr. Kathleen W. Scotto, 973-972-5333, Fax: 973-972-7148, E-mail: scottoka@umdnj.edu.

New Jersey Dental School Students: 404 full-time (224 women), 1 part-time; includes 141 minority (16 African Americans, 1 American Indian/Alaska Native, 106 Asian Americans or Pacific Islanders, 18 Hispanic Americans), 14 international. Average age 26. 1,391 applicants, 14% accepted, 96 enrolled. *Faculty:* 90 full-time (26 women), 118 part-time/adjunct (20 women). Expenses: Contact institution. *Financial support:* Fellowships, research assistantships, teaching assistantships, Federal Work-Study and institutionally sponsored loans available. Financial award application deadline: 5/1. In 2006, 80 DMDs, 4 master's, 17 other advanced degrees awarded. Offers advanced education in general dentistry (Certificate); dental science (MDS); dentistry (DMD, MS); endodontics (Certificate); oral biology (PhD); oral medicine (Certificate); orthodontics (Certificate); pediatric dentistry (Certificate); periodontics (Certificate); prosthodontics (Certificate). *Application deadline:* Applications are processed on a rolling basis. *Application fee:* $75. Electronic applications accepted. *Application Contact:* Dr. Jeffrey Linfante, Director of Admissions and Student Recruitment, 973-972-5362, Fax: 973-972-0309, E-mail: linfante@umdnj.edu. *Dean,* Dr. Cecile A. Feldman, 973-972-4633, Fax: 973-972-3689, E-mail: feldman@umdnj.edu.

New Jersey Medical School Students: 708 full-time (341 women); includes 420 minority (90 African Americans, 2 American Indian/Alaska Native, 225 Asian Americans or Pacific Islanders, 103 Hispanic Americans). Average age 25. 4,233 applicants, 10% accepted, 170 enrolled. *Faculty:* 700 full-time (239 women), 89 part-time/adjunct (24 women). Expenses: Contact institution. *Financial support:* Fellowships, research assistantships, teaching assistantships, Federal Work-Study and institutionally sponsored loans available. Financial award application deadline: 5/1. In 2006, 157 degrees awarded. Offers medicine (MD). *Application deadline:* For fall admission, 8/1 for domestic students. Applications are processed on a rolling basis. *Application fee:* $75. Electronic applications accepted. *Application Contact:* Dr. George F. Heinrich, Assistant Dean, 973-972-4631, Fax: 973-972-7986, E-mail: heinrich@umdnj.edu. *Interim Dean,* Dr. Robert L. Johnson, 973-972-4538, Fax: 973-972-7104, E-mail: rjohnson@umdnj.edu.

Robert Wood Johnson Medical School Students: 659 full-time (349 women); includes 340 minority (75 African Americans, 234 Asian Americans or Pacific Islanders, 31 Hispanic Americans). Average age 25. 2,158 applicants, 16% accepted, 156 enrolled. *Faculty:* 891 full-time (316 women), 144 part-time/adjunct (84 women). Expenses: Contact institution. *Financial support:* Fellowships, research assistantships, teaching assistantships, career-related internships or fieldwork, Federal Work-Study, institutionally sponsored loans, and tuition waivers (partial) available. Support available to part-time students. Financial award application deadline: 5/1; financial award applicants required to submit FAFSA. In 2006, 146 degrees awarded. *Degree program information:* Part-time and evening/weekend programs available. Offers medicine (MD). *Application deadline:* For fall admission, 8/1 for domestic students. Applications are processed on a rolling basis. *Application fee:* $75. Electronic applications accepted. *Application Contact:* Dr. David Seiden, Associate Dean for Student Affairs, 732-235-4576, Fax: 732-235-5078, E-mail: seiden@umdnj.edu. *Interim Dean,* Dr. Peter Amenta, 732-235-6300, Fax: 732-235-6315, E-mail: amenta@umdnj.edu.

School of Health Related Professions Students: 326 full-time (252 women), 396 part-time (282 women); includes 217 minority (78 African Americans, 89 Asian Americans or Pacific Islanders, 50 Hispanic Americans), 32 international. Average age 33. 798 applicants, 46% accepted, 276 enrolled. Expenses: Contact institution. *Financial support:* Fellowships, research assistantships, teaching assistantships, Federal Work-Study and institutionally sponsored loans available. Financial award application deadline: 5/1. In 2006, 96 master's, 66 doctorates, 14 Certificates awarded. *Degree program information:* Part-time programs available. Offers biomedical informatics (MS, PhD); cardiopulmonary sciences (PhD); clinical laboratory sciences (PhD); clinical nutrition (MS, DCN); dietetic internship (Certificate); health care informatics (Certificate); health related professions (MPT, MS, DCN, DPT, PhD, Certificate); health sciences (MS, PhD); health systems (MS); interdisciplinary studies (PhD); nurse midwifery (Certificate); nutrition (PhD); physical therapy (MPT); physical therapy (entry level) (DPT); physical therapy (post-professional level) (DPT); physical therapy/movement science (PhD); physician assistant (MS); professional counseling (Certificate); psychiatric rehabilitation (MS, PhD); radiologist assistant (MS); rehabilitation counseling (MS); vocational rehabilitation (MS). *Application deadline:* Applications are processed on a rolling basis. *Application fee:* $50. Electronic applications accepted. *Application Contact:* Brian Lewis, Assistant Dean, 973-972-5454, Fax: 973-972-7463, E-mail: shrpadm@umdnj.edu. *Dean,* Dr. David M. Gibson, 973-972-4276, E-mail: gibson@umdnj.edu.

School of Nursing Students: 93 full-time (82 women), 307 part-time (274 women); includes 195 minority (92 African Americans, 1 American Indian/Alaska Native, 69 Asian Americans or Pacific Islanders, 33 Hispanic Americans), 1 international. Average age 39. 472 applicants, 63% accepted, 203 enrolled. Expenses: Contact institution. *Financial support:* Teaching assistantships, institutionally sponsored loans and scholarships/grants available. Support available to part-time students. Financial award application deadline: 5/1. In 2006, 57 master's, 6 other advanced degrees awarded. *Degree program information:* Part-time programs available. Offers adult health (MSN); adult occupational health (MSN); advanced practice nursing (MSN, Post Master's Certificate); family nurse practitioner (MSN); nurse anesthesia (MSN); nursing (MSN); nursing education (MSN, Post Master's Certificate); nursing informatics (MSN); urban health (PhD); women's health practitioner (MSN). *Application deadline:* Applications are processed on a rolling basis. *Application fee:* $50. Electronic applications accepted. *Interim Dean,* Dr. Susan Salmond, 973-972-9239, Fax: 973-972-3225, E-mail: salmonsu@umdnj.edu.

School of Osteopathic Medicine Students: 397 full-time (236 women); includes 205 minority (83 African Americans, 1 American Indian/Alaska Native, 91 Asian Americans or Pacific Islanders, 30 Hispanic Americans), 1 international. Average age 26. 2,779 applicants, 6% accepted, 103 enrolled. *Faculty:* 164 full-time (62 women), 31 part-time/adjunct (19 women). Expenses: Contact institution. *Financial support:* Fellowships, research assistantships, teaching assistantships, career-related internships or fieldwork, Federal Work-Study, and institutionally sponsored loans available. Financial award application deadline: 5/1. In 2006, 88 degrees awarded. Offers osteopathic medicine (DO). *Application deadline:* For fall admission, 2/1 for domestic students. Applications are processed on a rolling basis. *Application fee:* $75. Electronic applications accepted. *Interim Dean,* Dr. Thomas A. Cavalieri, 856-566-6996, Fax: 856-566-6865, E-mail: cavalita@umdnj.edu.

UMDNJ–School of Public Health (UMDNJ, Rutgers, NJIT) Newark Campus Expenses: Contact institution. Offers public health (MPH, Dr PH, PhD, Certificate). *Application deadline:* For fall admission, 4/1 for domestic students; for spring admission, 10/1 for domestic students. *Application fee:* $95. Electronic applications accepted. *Application Contact:* Yvette J. Holding-Ford, Information Contact, 973-972-7212, Fax: 973-972-8032, E-mail: holdinys@umdnj.edu. Rhonda Barnes, 973-972-7212, Fax: 973-972-8032, E-mail: barnesb@umdnj.edu.

UMDNJ–School of Public Health (UMDNJ, Rutgers, NJIT) Piscataway/New Brunswick Campus Expenses: Contact institution. Offers biostatistics (MS); epidemiology (Certificate); general public health (Certificate); public health (MPH, Dr PH, PhD). *Application deadline:* For fall admission, 4/1 for domestic students; for spring admission, 10/1 for domestic students. *Application fee:* $95. Electronic applications accepted. *Application Contact:* Dr. Mark G. Robson, Assistant Dean, 732-235-4646, Fax: 732-235-5476, E-mail: robson@eohsi.rutgers.edu. Janet Zamorski, 732-235-4646, Fax: 732-235-5476, E-mail: zamorsja@umdnj.edu.

UMDNJ–School of Public Health (UMDNJ, Rutgers, NJIT) Stratford/Camden Campus Expenses: Contact institution. Offers general public health (Certificate); public health (MPH). *Application deadline:* For fall admission, 4/1 for domestic students; for spring admission, 10/1 for domestic students. *Application fee:* $95. Electronic applications accepted. *Application Contact:* 732-235-4317, Fax: 856-566-2882. Vanessa Jago, 856-566-2790, Fax: 856-566-2882, E-mail: jagovi@umdnj.edu.

UNIVERSITY OF MEMPHIS, Memphis, TN 38152

General Information State-supported, coed, university. CGS member. *Enrollment:* 20,562 graduate, professional, and undergraduate students; 2,076 full-time matriculated graduate/

professional students (1,125 women), 2,559 part-time matriculated graduate/professional students (1,712 women). *Graduate faculty:* 516 full-time (156 women), 63 part-time/adjunct (28 women). *Graduate housing:* Rooms and/or apartments available on a first-come, first-served basis to single students and available to married students. *Student services:* Campus employment opportunities, campus safety program, career counseling, child daycare facilities, disabled student services, exercise/wellness program, free psychological counseling, grant writing training, international student services, low-cost health insurance, multicultural affairs office, teacher training, writing training. *Library facilities:* University of Memphis Libraries: McWherter Libraries plus 6 others. *Online resources:* library catalog, web page, access to other libraries' catalogs. *Collection:* 1.3 million titles, 9,393 serial subscriptions, 27,391 audiovisual materials. *Research affiliation:* Gulf Coast Research Laboratory, St. Jude Children's Research Hospital, Oak Ridge National Laboratory, Federal Express.

Computer facilities: 2,000 computers available on campus for general student use. A campuswide network can be accessed from off campus. Internet access and online class registration are available. *Web address:* http://www.memphis.edu/.

General Application Contact: Information Contact, 901-678-2531, Fax: 901-678-3003, E-mail: gradsch@memphis.edu.

GRADUATE UNITS

Cecil C. Humphreys School of Law Students: 379 full-time (160 women), 29 part-time (20 women); includes 74 minority (63 African Americans, 2 American Indian/Alaska Native, 6 Asian Americans or Pacific Islanders, 3 Hispanic Americans). Average age 25. 1,113 applicants, 26% accepted, 144 enrolled. *Faculty:* 20 full-time (8 women), 24 part-time/adjunct (11 women). Expenses: Contact institution. *Financial support:* In 2006–07, 326 students received support, including 22 research assistantships with full and partial tuition reimbursements available (averaging $3,136 per year), 2 teaching assistantships (averaging $3,000 per year); fellowships, career-related internships or fieldwork, scholarships/grants, tuition waivers (full), and unspecified assistantships also available. Financial award application deadline: 4/1; financial award applicants required to submit FAFSA. In 2006, 125 JDs awarded. *Degree program information:* Part-time programs available. Offers law (JD). *Application deadline:* For fall admission, 3/1 priority date for domestic and international students. Applications are processed on a rolling basis. *Application fee:* $25 ($40 for international students). Electronic applications accepted. *Application Contact:* Dr. Sue Ann McClellan, Assistant Dean for Law Admissions, 901-678-5403, Fax: 901-678-5210, E-mail: smcclell@memphis.edu. *Dean,* James R. Smoot, 901-678-2421, Fax: 901-678-5210, E-mail: jrsmoot@memphis.edu.

Graduate School Students: 1,718 full-time (961 women), 2,574 part-time (1,749 women); includes 1,307 minority (1,186 African Americans, 4 American Indian/Alaska Native, 76 Asian Americans or Pacific Islanders, 41 Hispanic Americans), 531 international. Average age 32. *Faculty:* 516 full-time (156 women), 63 part-time/adjunct (28 women). Expenses: Contact institution. *Financial support:* In 2006–07, 794 students received support, including 10 fellowships with full tuition reimbursements available (averaging $11,000 per year), 130 research assistantships with full tuition reimbursements available (averaging $4,770 per year), 213 teaching assistantships with full tuition reimbursements available (averaging $7,160 per year); career-related internships or fieldwork, Federal Work-Study, institutionally sponsored loans, scholarships/grants, and unspecified assistantships also available. Support available to part-time students. Financial award applicants required to submit CSS PROFILE. *Degree program information:* Part-time and evening/weekend programs available. Postbaccalaureate distance learning degree programs offered. Offers accounting (MBA, MS, PhD); accounting systems (MS); automatic control systems (MS); biomedical engineering (MS, PhD); biomedical systems (MS); business and economics (MA, MBA, MS, PhD); civil engineering (PhD); communications and propagation systems (MS); computer engineering technology (MS); design and mechanical engineering (MS); economics (MBA, PhD); electrical engineering (PhD); electronics engineering technology (MS); energy systems (MS); engineering (MS, PhD); engineering computer systems (MS); environmental engineering (MS); executive business administration (MBA); finance (PhD); finance, insurance, and real estate (MBA, MS); foundation engineering (MS); industrial engineering (MS); international business administration (MBA); management (MBA, MS, PhD); management information systems (MBA, MS, PhD); management science (MBA); manufacturing engineering technology (MS); marketing (MBA, MS); marketing and supply chain management (PhD); mechanical engineering (PhD); mechanical systems (MS); power systems (MS); real estate development (MS); structural engineering (MS); taxation (MS); transportation engineering (MS); water resources engineering (MS). *Application deadline:* Applications are processed on a rolling basis. *Application fee:* $25 ($50 for international students). Electronic applications accepted. *Assistant Vice Provost for Graduate Studies,* Dr. Karen D. Weddle-West, 901-678-2531, Fax: 901-678-2250, E-mail: gradsch@memphis.edu.

College of Arts and Sciences *Degree program information:* Part-time and evening/weekend programs available. Offers anthropology (MA); applied mathematics (MS); applied statistics (PhD); arts and sciences (MA, MCRP, MFA, MHA, MPA, MS, PhD); bioinformatics (MS); biology (MS, PhD); chemistry (MS, PhD); city and regional planning (MCRP); clinical psychology (PhD); computer science (PhD); computer sciences (MS); creative writing (MFA); criminology and criminal justice (MA); earth sciences (MA, MS, PhD); English (MA); experimental psychology (PhD); French (MA); general psychology (MS); health administration (MHA); history (MA, PhD); mathematics (MS, PhD); nonprofit administration (MPA); philosophy (MA, PhD); physics (MS); political science (MA); public management and policy (MPA); school psychology (MA, PhD); sociology (MA); Spanish (MA); statistics (MS, PhD); urban affairs and public policy (MA, MCRP, MHA, MPA); urban management and planning (MPA); writing and language studies (PhD).

College of Communication and Fine Arts *Degree program information:* Part-time programs available. Postbaccalaureate distance learning degree programs offered (no on-campus study). Offers applied music (M Mu, DMA); art history (MA); ceramics (MFA); communication (MA); communication and fine arts (M Mu, MA, MFA, DMA, PhD); communication arts (PhD); composition (M Mu, DMA); conducting (M Mu, DMA); Egyptian art and archaeology (MA); film and video production (MA); general art history (MA); general journalism (MA); graphic design (MFA); historical musicology (PhD); interior design (MFA); jazz and studio performance (M Mu); journalism administration (MA); music education (M Mu, DMA); musicology (M Mu); painting (MFA); printmaking/photography (MFA); sculpture (MFA); theatre (MFA).

College of Education *Degree program information:* Part-time and evening/weekend programs available. Offers adult education (Ed D); clinical nutrition (MS); community education (Ed D); counseling (MS, Ed D); counseling psychology (PhD); early childhood education (MAT, MS, Ed D); education (MAT, MS, Ed D, PhD); educational leadership (Ed D); educational psychology and research (MS, PhD); elementary education (MAT); exercise and sport science (MS); health promotion (MS); higher education (Ed D); instruction and curriculum (MS, Ed D); instruction design and technology (MS, Ed D); leadership (MS); middle grades education (MAT); physical education teacher education (MS); policy studies (Ed D); reading (MS, Ed D); school administration and supervision (MS); secondary education (MAT); special education (MAT, MS, Ed D); sport and leisure commerce (MS); student personnel (MS).

Fogelman College of Business and Economics Average age 30. 535 applicants, 65% accepted. *Faculty:* 118 full-time (20 women), 3 part-time/adjunct (0 women). Expenses: Contact institution. *Financial support:* In 2006–07, 191 students received support; research assistantships with tuition reimbursements available, teaching assistantships with tuition reimbursements available, career-related internships or fieldwork, scholarships/grants, and unspecified assistantships also available. Financial award application deadline: 3/1. In 2006, 232 master's, 12 doctorates awarded. *Degree program information:* Part-time programs available. Offers accounting (MBA, MS, PhD); accounting systems (MS); business and economics (MA, MBA, MS, PhD); economics (MBA, PhD); executive business administration (MBA); finance (PhD); finance, insurance, and real estate (MBA, MS); international business administration (MBA); management (MBA, MS, PhD); management information systems (MBA, MS, PhD); management science (MBA); marketing (MBA, MS); marketing and supply chain management (PhD); real estate development (MS); taxation (MS). *Application deadline:* For fall admission, 8/1 for domestic students; for spring admission, 12/1 for domestic students. *Application fee:* $25 ($50 for international students). *Application Contact:* Dr. Carol V. Danehower, Associate Dean for Programs, 901-678-5402, Fax: 901-678-3579, E-mail: fcbegp@memphis.edu. *Dean,* Rajiv Grover, 901-678-3633, E-mail: rgrover@memphis.edu.

Herff College of Engineering Average age 31. *Faculty:* 55 full-time (4 women), 57 part-time/adjunct (11 women). Expenses: Contact institution. *Financial support:* In 2006–07, 1 fellowship with full tuition reimbursement, 75 research assistantships with full tuition reimbursements, 12 teaching assistantships with full tuition reimbursements were awarded; career-related internships or fieldwork, tuition waivers (full and partial), and unspecified assistantships also available. In 2006, 87 master's, 4 doctorates awarded. *Degree program information:* Part-time programs available. Offers automatic control systems (MS); biomedical engineering (MS, PhD); biomedical systems (MS); civil engineering (PhD); communications and propagation systems (MS); computer engineering technology (MS); design and mechanical engineering (MS); electrical engineering (PhD); electronics engineering technology (MS); energy systems (MS); engineering (MS, PhD); engineering computer systems (MS); environmental engineering (MS); foundation engineering (MS); industrial engineering (MS); manufacturing engineering technology (MS); mechanical engineering (PhD); mechanical systems (MS); power systems (MS); structural engineering (MS); transportation engineering (MS); water resources engineering (MS). *Application deadline:* For fall admission, 8/1 for domestic students; for spring admission, 12/1 for domestic students. *Application fee:* $25 ($50 for international students). Electronic applications accepted. *Application Contact:* Dr. Steven M. Slack, Associate Dean, 901-678-2171, Fax: 901-678-4180, E-mail: sslack@memphis.edu. *Dean,* Dr. Richard C. Warder, 901-678-4306, Fax: 901-678-4180, E-mail: rcwarder@memphis.edu.

School of Audiology and Speech-Language Pathology Students: 50 full-time (43 women), 6 part-time (all women); includes 5 minority (4 African Americans, 1 Hispanic American), 3 international. Average age 27. *Faculty:* 28 full-time (17 women), 2 part-time/adjunct (both women). Expenses: Contact institution. *Financial support:* Research assistantships available. In 2006, 17 master's, 2 doctorates awarded. *Degree program information:* Part-time programs available. Offers audiology and speech-language pathology (MA, Au D, PhD). *Application deadline:* For fall admission, 2/1 for domestic students. *Application fee:* $25 ($50 for international students). *Application Contact:* Dr. David J. Wark, Coordinator of Graduate Studies, 901-678-5800. *Dean,* Dr. Maurice Mendel, 901-678-5800.

University College 20 applicants, 85% accepted, 17 enrolled. *Faculty:* 8 full-time (4 women), 9 part-time/adjunct (3 women). Expenses: Contact institution. *Financial support:* In 2006–07, 5 research assistantships with full tuition reimbursements (averaging $6,000 per year) were awarded; unspecified assistantships also available. Financial award application deadline: 4/1; financial award applicants required to submit FAFSA. In 2006, 20 degrees awarded. *Degree program information:* Part-time and evening/weekend programs available. Offers consumer science and education (MS); family and consumer science (MS); liberal studies (MALS). *Application deadline:* For fall admission, 7/1 for domestic students, 5/1 for international students; for spring admission, 11/1 for domestic students, 9/15 for international students. Applications are processed on a rolling basis. *Application fee:* $55 ($60 for international students). Electronic applications accepted. *Application Contact:* Dr. David Arant, Coordinator of Graduate Studies, 901-678-4596, Fax: 901-678-4913, E-mail: darant@memphis.edu. *Dean,* Dr. Dan Lattimore, 901-678-2991.

See Close-Up on page 1089.

UNIVERSITY OF MIAMI, Coral Gables, FL 33124

General Information Independent, coed, university. CGS member. *Enrollment:* 15,670 graduate, professional, and undergraduate students; 4,485 full-time matriculated graduate/professional students (2,089 women), 550 part-time matriculated graduate/professional students (355 women). *Enrollment by degree level:* 1,974 first professional, 1,940 master's, 1,097 doctoral, 24 other advanced degrees. *Graduate faculty:* 1,192 full-time (314 women), 9 part-time/adjunct (4 women). *Graduate housing:* Room and/or apartments available to single students; on-campus housing not available to married students. *Student services:* Campus employment opportunities, campus safety program, career counseling, child daycare facilities, disabled student services, exercise/wellness program, free psychological counseling, grant writing training, international student services, low-cost health insurance, multicultural affairs office, writing training. *Library facilities:* Otto G. Richter Library plus 7 others. *Online resources:* library catalog, web page, access to other libraries' catalogs. *Collection:* 3 million titles, 45,953 serial subscriptions, 66,094 audiovisual materials. *Research affiliation:* National Center for Atmospheric Research, Organization for Tropical Studies.

Computer facilities: Computer purchase and lease plans are available. 1,800 computers available on campus for general student use. A campuswide network can be accessed from student residence rooms and from off campus. Internet access and online class registration, online student account and grade information are available. *Web address:* http://www.miami.edu/.

General Application Contact: 305-284-4154.

GRADUATE UNITS

Graduate School Students: 2,570 full-time (1,222 women), 491 part-time (331 women); includes 798 minority (152 African Americans, 1 American Indian/Alaska Native, 93 Asian Americans or Pacific Islanders, 552 Hispanic Americans), 632 international. Average age 30. 3,212 applicants, 48% accepted, 778 enrolled. *Faculty:* 797 full-time (215 women), 3 part-time/adjunct (2 women). Expenses: Contact institution. *Financial support:* Fellowships with tuition reimbursements, research assistantships with tuition reimbursements, teaching assistantships with tuition reimbursements, career-related internships or fieldwork, Federal Work-Study, institutionally sponsored loans, scholarships/grants, traineeships, tuition waivers (full and partial), and unspecified assistantships available. Support available to part-time students. Financial award applicants required to submit FAFSA. In 2006, 1,081 master's, 195 doctorates awarded. *Degree program information:* Part-time and evening/weekend programs available. Postbaccalaureate distance learning degree programs offered. *Application fee:* $50. Electronic applications accepted. *Dean,* Dr. Terri A. Scandura, 305-284-4154, Fax: 305-284-5441, E-mail: graduateschool@miami.edu.

College of Arts and Sciences Students: 478 full-time (271 women), 108 part-time (64 women); includes 142 minority (29 African Americans, 17 Asian Americans or Pacific Islanders, 96 Hispanic Americans). Average age 31. 792 applicants, 29% accepted, 139 enrolled. *Faculty:* 246 full-time (82 women). Expenses: Contact institution. *Financial support:* In 2006–07, 33 fellowships with tuition reimbursements (averaging $20,000 per year), 119 research assistantships with tuition reimbursements (averaging $14,846 per year), 244 teaching assistantships with tuition reimbursements (averaging $15,362 per year) were awarded; traineeships and unspecified assistantships also available. Financial award applicants required to submit FAFSA. In 2006, 114 master's, 56 doctorates awarded. *Degree program information:* Part-time and evening/weekend programs available. Offers adult clinical (PhD); applied developmental psychology (PhD); art history (MA); arts and sciences (MA, MAIA, MALS, MFA, MS, DA, PhD); behavioral neuroscience (PhD); biology (MS, PhD); ceramics/glass (MFA); chemistry (MS); child clinical (PhD); computer science (MS); creative writing (MFA); English (MA, PhD); French (PhD); genetics and evolution (MS, PhD); geography (MA); graphic design/multimedia (MFA); health clinical (PhD); history (MA, PhD); inorganic chemistry (PhD); international administration (MAIA); international studies (MA, PhD); liberal studies (MALS); mathematics (MA, MS, DA, PhD); organic chemistry (PhD); painting (MFA); philosophy (MA, PhD); photography/digital imaging (MFA); physical chemistry (PhD); physics (MS, PhD); printmaking (MFA); psychology (MS); sculpture (MFA); sociology (MA, PhD); Spanish (PhD). *Application deadline:* Applications are processed on a rolling basis. *Application fee:* $50. Electronic applications accepted. *Application Contact:* Dr. Charles Mallery, Associate Dean, 305-284-3188, Fax: 305-284-4686, E-mail: gradadmin@mail.as.miami.edu. *Dean,* Dr. Michael R. Halleran, 305-284-4117, Fax: 305-284-4686, E-mail: gradadmin@mail.as.miami.edu.

College of Engineering Students: 203 full-time (45 women), 32 part-time (9 women); includes 63 minority (11 African Americans, 12 Asian Americans or Pacific Islanders, 40 Hispanic Americans), 102 international. Average age 30. 198 applicants, 61% accepted, 44 enrolled. *Faculty:* 56 full-time (0 women). Expenses: Contact institution. *Financial support:* In 2006–07, 3 fellowships with full tuition reimbursements (averaging $19,200 per year), 60 research assistantships with full tuition reimbursements (averaging $19,200 per year), 50 teaching

University of Miami (continued)

assistantships with full tuition reimbursements (averaging $19,200 per year) were awarded; career-related internships or fieldwork, institutionally sponsored loans, tuition waivers (partial), and unspecified assistantships also available. Support available to part-time students. Financial award application deadline: 12/1; financial award applicants required to submit FAFSA. In 2006, 59 master's, 13 doctorates awarded. *Degree program information:* Part-time and evening/weekend programs available. Offers architectural engineering (MSAE); biomedical engineering (MSBE, PhD); civil engineering (MSCE, DA, PhD); electrical and computer engineering (MSECE, PhD); engineering (MS, MSAE, MSBE, MSCE, MSECE, MSEVH, MSIE, MSME, MSOES, DA, PhD); environmental health and safety (MS, MSEVH, MSOES); ergonomics (PhD); industrial engineering (MSIE, PhD); management of technology (MS); mechanical and aerospace engineering (MSME, PhD); occupational ergonomics and safety (MSOES). *Application deadline:* For fall admission, 12/1 priority date for domestic and international students; for spring admission, 11/1 priority date for domestic and international students. Applications are processed on a rolling basis. *Application fee:* $50. Electronic applications accepted. *Application Contact:* Sharon D. Manjarres, Staff Associate, 305-284-2942, Fax: 305-284-2885, E-mail: s.manjarres@miami.edu. *Dean,* Dr. M. Lewis Temares, 305-284-2404, Fax: 305-284-4792, E-mail: mtemares@miami.edu.

Frost School of Music Students: 217 full-time (90 women), 10 part-time (5 women); includes 18 minority (8 African Americans, 3 Asian Americans or Pacific Islanders, 7 Hispanic Americans), 72 international. Average age 28. 324 applicants, 54% accepted, 104 enrolled. *Faculty:* 75 full-time (11 women), 46 part-time/adjunct (16 women). Expenses: Contact institution. *Financial support:* In 2006–07, 2 fellowships with full tuition reimbursements (averaging $18,000 per year), 72 teaching assistantships with full tuition reimbursements (averaging $7,850 per year) were awarded; career-related internships or fieldwork, Federal Work-Study, and tuition waivers (full and partial) also available. Financial award application deadline: 2/1. In 2006, 42 master's, 22 doctorates, 6 other advanced degrees awarded. Offers accompanying and chamber music (MM, DMA); choral conducting (MM, DMA); composition (MM, DMA); electronic music (MM); instrumental conducting (MM, DMA); instrumental performance (MM, DMA, AD); jazz composition (DMA); jazz pedagogy (MM); jazz performance (MM, DMA); keyboard performance and pedagogy (MM, DMA); media writing and production (MM); multiple woodwinds (MM, DMA); music (MM, MS, DMA, PhD, AD, Spec M); music business and entertainment industries (MM); music education (MM, PhD, Spec M); music engineering (MS); music theory (MM); music therapy (MM); musicology (MM); piano performance (MM, DMA, AD); studio jazz writing (MM); vocal pedagogy (DMA); vocal performance (MM, DMA, AD). *Application deadline:* For fall admission, 2/1 priority date for domestic and international students; for spring admission, 11/1 priority date for domestic and international students. Applications are processed on a rolling basis. *Application fee:* $65. Electronic applications accepted. *Application Contact:* Dr. Edward Paul Asmus, Associate Dean for Graduate Studies, 305-284-2241, Fax: 305-284-6475, E-mail: ed.asmus@miami.edu. *Dean,* Shelton Berg, 305-284-2241, Fax: 305-284-6475.

Miller School of Medicine Students: 1,026 (519 women); includes 355 minority (52 African Americans, 4 American Indian/Alaska Native, 161 Asian Americans or Pacific Islanders, 138 Hispanic Americans) 92 international. Expenses: Contact institution. *Financial support:* In 2006–07, 480 students received support; fellowships with partial tuition reimbursements available, research assistantships with partial tuition reimbursements available, teaching assistantships, Federal Work-Study, institutionally sponsored loans, scholarships/grants, and health care benefits available. Financial award applicants required to submit FAFSA. In 2006, 131 degrees awarded. Offers biochemistry and molecular biology (PhD); cancer biology (PhD); epidemiology (PhD); medicine (MD, MPH, MSPH, DPT, PhD); microbiology and immunology (PhD); molecular and cellular pharmacology (PhD); molecular cell and developmental biology (PhD); neuroscience (PhD); physical therapy (DPT, PhD); physiology and biophysics (PhD); public health (MPH, MSPH). *Application deadline:* Applications are processed on a rolling basis. Electronic applications accepted. *Application Contact:* Dr. John L. Bixby, Associate Dean, 305-243-1094, Fax: 305-243-3593, E-mail: biomedgrad@miami.edu. *Vice President for Medical Affairs/Dean,* Dr. Paschal Goldschmidt, 305-243-6545.

Rosenstiel School of Marine and Atmospheric Science Students: 183 full-time (85 women), 13 part-time (3 women); includes 17 minority (4 African Americans, 3 Asian Americans or Pacific Islanders, 10 Hispanic Americans), 57 international. Average age 30. 213 applicants, 34% accepted, 37 enrolled. *Faculty:* 100 full-time (17 women), 95 part-time/adjunct (22 women). Expenses: Contact institution. *Financial support:* In 2006–07, 153 students received support, including 30 fellowships with full tuition reimbursements available (averaging $23,000 per year), 104 research assistantships with full tuition reimbursements available (averaging $23,000 per year), 13 teaching assistantships with full tuition reimbursements available (averaging $23,000 per year); career-related internships or fieldwork, Federal Work-Study, institutionally sponsored loans, scholarships/grants, and unspecified assistantships also available. Financial award application deadline: 3/1; financial award applicants required to submit FAFSA. In 2006, 22 master's, 14 doctorates awarded. *Degree program information:* Part-time programs available. Offers applied marine physics (MS, PhD); marine affairs and policy (MA, MS); marine and atmospheric chemistry (MS, PhD); marine and atmospheric science (MA, MS, PhD); marine biology and fisheries (MA, MS, PhD); marine geology and geophysics (MS, PhD); meteorology (PhD); physical oceanography (MS, PhD). *Application deadline:* For fall admission, 1/1 priority date for domestic and international students. Applications are processed on a rolling basis. *Application fee:* $50. Electronic applications accepted. *Application Contact:* Dr. Larry Peterson, Associate Dean, 305-421-4155, Fax: 305-421-4771, E-mail: gso@rsmas.miami.edu. *Dean,* Dr. Otis Brown, 305-421-4000, Fax: 305-421-4711, E-mail: obrown@rsmas.miami.edu.

School of Architecture Students: 62 full-time (34 women); includes 14 minority (3 African Americans, 1 American Indian/Alaska Native, 2 Asian Americans or Pacific Islanders, 8 Hispanic Americans), 8 international. Average age 26. 78 applicants, 73% accepted, 21 enrolled. *Faculty:* 30 full-time (4 women), 22 part-time/adjunct (5 women). Expenses: Contact institution. *Financial support:* Research assistantships, teaching assistantships, career-related internships or fieldwork, Federal Work-Study, institutionally sponsored loans, scholarships/grants, tuition waivers (partial), and unspecified assistantships available. Support available to part-time students. Financial award application deadline: 2/1; financial award applicants required to submit FAFSA. In 2006, 25 degrees awarded. Offers architecture (M Arch); suburb and town design (M Arch). *Application deadline:* For fall admission, 3/1 priority date for domestic students. Applications are processed on a rolling basis. *Application fee:* $50. *Application Contact:* Jude Alexander, Coordinator, 305-284-3060, Fax: 305-284-6879, E-mail: jude@miami.edu.

School of Business Administration Students: 794 full-time (302 women), 51 part-time (18 women); includes 223 minority (28 African Americans, 1 American Indian/Alaska Native, 33 Asian Americans or Pacific Islanders, 161 Hispanic Americans), 135 international. Average age 31. 531 applicants, 72% accepted, 170 enrolled. *Faculty:* 105 full-time (25 women). Expenses: Contact institution. *Financial support:* In 2006–07, 496 students received support; fellowships, research assistantships, career-related internships or fieldwork, Federal Work-Study, institutionally sponsored loans, scholarships/grants, and unspecified assistantships available. Support available to part-time students. Financial award application deadline: 3/1; financial award applicants required to submit FAFSA. In 2006, 460 master's, 5 doctorates awarded. *Degree program information:* Part-time and evening/weekend programs available. Offers accounting (MBA); business administration (MA, MBA, MP Acc, MPA, MS, MS Tax, MSPM, PhD); computer information systems (MBA); economic development (MA, PhD); environmental economics (PhD); executive and professional (MBA); finance (MBA); human resource economics (MA, PhD); international business (MBA); international economics (MA, PhD); macroeconomics (PhD); management (MBA); management science (MBA, MS); marketing (MBA); political science (MPA); professional accounting (MP Acc); professional management (MSPM); taxation (MS Tax). *Application deadline:* For fall admission, 7/31 priority date for domestic students, 6/30 priority date for international students; for spring admission, 12/31 priority date for domestic students, 10/31 priority date for international students. Applications are processed on a rolling basis. *Application fee:* $50. Electronic applications accepted. *Application Contact:* David S. Green, Director of Graduate Business Recruiting and Admissions, 305-284-4607, Fax: 305-284-1878, E-mail: mba@miami.edu. *Vice Dean,* Dr. Harold W. Berkman, 305-284-2510, Fax: 305-284-5905.

School of Communication Students: 107 full-time (57 women), 24 part-time (15 women); includes 38 minority (10 African Americans, 3 Asian Americans or Pacific Islanders, 25 Hispanic Americans), 15 international. Average age 27. 330 applicants, 44% accepted, 64 enrolled. *Faculty:* 39 full-time (12 women). Expenses: Contact institution. *Financial support:* In 2006–07, 8 teaching assistantships with full tuition reimbursements were awarded; fellowships with full tuition reimbursements, Federal Work-Study, institutionally sponsored loans, scholarships/grants, tuition waivers (partial), and unspecified assistantships also available. Financial award application deadline: 3/1; financial award applicants required to submit FAFSA. In 2006, 54 degrees awarded. *Degree program information:* Part-time programs available. Offers communication (PhD); communication studies (MA); film studies (MA, PhD); motion pictures (MFA); print journalism (MA); public relations (MA); Spanish language journalism (MA); television broadcast journalism (MA). *Application deadline:* For fall admission, 12/15 priority date for domestic and international students. Applications are processed on a rolling basis. *Application fee:* $50. Electronic applications accepted. *Application Contact:* Dr. Leonardo C. Ferreira, Director of Graduate Studies, 305-284-3180, Fax: 305-284-8701, E-mail: lferreira@miami.edu. *Dean,* Dr. Sam L. Grogg, 305-284-3420, Fax: 305-284-2454, E-mail: sgrogg@miami.edu.

School of Education Students: 167 full-time (125 women), 212 part-time (181 women); includes 162 minority (44 African Americans, 3 Asian Americans or Pacific Islanders, 115 Hispanic Americans), 40 international. Average age 31. 331 applicants, 62% accepted, 106 enrolled. *Faculty:* 47 full-time (26 women), 43 part-time/adjunct (21 women). Expenses: Contact institution. *Financial support:* In 2006–07, 3 fellowships with full tuition reimbursements (averaging $20,000 per year), 17 research assistantships with full and partial tuition reimbursements (averaging $18,000 per year), 12 teaching assistantships with full and partial tuition reimbursements (averaging $18,000 per year) were awarded; career-related internships or fieldwork, Federal Work-Study, institutionally sponsored loans, tuition waivers (full and partial), and unspecified assistantships also available. Support available to part-time students. Financial award application deadline: 3/1; financial award applicants required to submit FAFSA. In 2006, 188 master's, 9 doctorates awarded. *Degree program information:* Part-time and evening/weekend programs available. Offers advanced professional studies (MS Ed, Ed S); bilingual and bicultural counseling (Certificate); counseling (MS Ed, Certificate); counseling psychology (PhD); education (MS Ed, PhD, Certificate, Ed S); elementary education/TESOL (MS Ed); exceptional student education (PhD); exceptional student education, pre–K disabilities and ESOL (Ed S); exceptional student education, pre-K disabilities and ESOL (MS Ed); exceptional student education, reading and ESOL (MS Ed, Ed S); exercise physiology (MS Ed, PhD); higher education administration (MS Ed, Certificate); higher education administration/enrollment management (Certificate); marriage and family therapy (MS Ed); mathematics and science education (PhD); mathematics and science resource teaching (MS Ed, Ed S); mental health counseling (MS Ed); reading (MS Ed, PhD, Ed S); research, measurement, and evaluation (MS Ed, PhD); sport administration (MS Ed); sports medicine (MS Ed); teaching and learning (PhD); teaching English to speakers of other languages (PhD). *Application deadline:* Applications are processed on a rolling basis. *Application fee:* $50. Electronic applications accepted. *Application Contact:* SOE Directory, 305-284-3711, Fax: 305-284-3003, E-mail: soe@miami.edu. *Dean,* Dr. Isaac Prilleltensky, 305-284-3505, Fax: 305-284-3003, E-mail: isaacp@miami.edu.

School of Law Students: 1,163 full-time (518 women), 45 part-time (8 women); includes 280 minority (84 African Americans, 3 American Indian/Alaska Native, 51 Asian Americans or Pacific Islanders, 142 Hispanic Americans), 51 international. Average age 24. 4,923 applicants, 48% accepted, 420 enrolled. *Faculty:* 55 full-time (17 women), 42 part-time/adjunct (15 women). Expenses: Contact institution. *Financial support:* In 2006–07, 991 students received support, including 77 fellowships (averaging $2,200 per year), 80 research assistantships (averaging $1,800 per year); career-related internships or fieldwork, Federal Work-Study, institutionally sponsored loans, scholarships/grants, and unspecified assistantships also available. Financial award application deadline: 3/1; financial award applicants required to submit FAFSA. In 2006, 331 JDs awarded. Offers comparative law (LL M); estate planning (LL M); inter-American law (LL M); international law (LL M); law (JD); ocean and coastal law (LL M); real property development (LL M); taxation (LL M). *Application deadline:* For fall admission, 2/5 priority date for domestic and international students. Applications are processed on a rolling basis. *Application fee:* $60. Electronic applications accepted. *Application Contact:* Therese Lambert, Director of Student Recruiting, 305-284-6746, Fax: 305-284-3084, E-mail: tlambert@law.miami.edu. *Assistant Dean of Admissions,* Michael Goodnight, 305-284-2527, Fax: 305-284-3084, E-mail: mgoodnig@law.miami.edu.

School of Nursing and Health Studies Students: 33 full-time (24 women), 27 part-time (24 women); includes 28 minority (7 African Americans, 5 Asian Americans or Pacific Islanders, 16 Hispanic Americans), 2 international. Average age 34. 108 applicants, 48% accepted, 30 enrolled. *Faculty:* 10 full-time (8 women), 1 (woman) part-time/adjunct. Expenses: Contact institution. *Financial support:* In 2006–07, 12 students received support, including 3 research assistantships with tuition reimbursements available (averaging $9,000 per year), 5 teaching assistantships with tuition reimbursements available (averaging $9,000 per year); fellowships, Federal Work-Study, institutionally sponsored loans, scholarships/grants, and unspecified assistantships also available. Support available to part-time students. Financial award application deadline: 3/1; financial award applicants required to submit FAFSA. In 2006, 15 master's, 1 doctorate awarded. *Degree program information:* Part-time programs available. Offers acute care (MSN); community health (MSN); nursing (PhD); primary care (MSN). *Application deadline:* For fall admission, 4/30 priority date for domestic students; for spring admission, 11/1 priority date for domestic students. Applications are processed on a rolling basis. *Application fee:* $50. Electronic applications accepted. *Application Contact:* Anne Stabb, Graduate Advisor, 305-284-2533, Fax: 305-284-4827, E-mail: astabb@miami.edu. *Dean,* Dr. Nilda Peragallo, 305-284-2107, Fax: 305-667-3787, E-mail: nperagallo@miami.edu.

See Close-Up on page 1091.

UNIVERSITY OF MICHIGAN, Ann Arbor, MI 48109

General Information State-supported, coed, university. CGS member. *Graduate housing:* Rooms and/or apartments available on a first-come, first-served basis to single and married students. Housing application deadline: 4/21. *Research affiliation:* Freer Art Gallery, McGraw-Hill Observatory.

GRADUATE UNITS

A. Alfred Taubman College of Architecture and Urban Planning *Degree program information:* Part-time programs available. Offers architecture (M Arch, M Sc, PhD); architecture and urban planning (M Arch, M Sc, MUD, MUP, PhD, Certificate); real estate development (Certificate); urban and regional planning (MUP, PhD, Certificate); urban design (MUD); urban planning (MUP). Electronic applications accepted.

College of Pharmacy Offers medicinal chemistry (PhD); pharmaceutical sciences (PhD); pharmacy (Pharm D, PhD); social and administrative sciences (PhD).

Horace H. Rackham School of Graduate Studies Offers biophysics (PhD); chemical biology (PhD); education and psychology (PhD); English and education (PhD); modern Middle Eastern and North African studies (AM); neuroscience (PhD); survey methodology (MS, PhD, Certificate). Electronic applications accepted.

College of Engineering *Degree program information:* Part-time programs available. Post-baccalaureate distance learning degree programs offered (no on-campus study). Offers aerospace engineering (M Eng, MS, MSE, PhD); applied physics (PhD); atmospheric (MS); atmospheric and space sciences (PhD); automotive engineering (M Eng); biomedical engineering (MS, MSE, PhD); chemical engineering (MSE, PhD, Ch E); civil engineering (MSE, PhD, CE); computer science and engineering (MS, MSE, PhD); concurrent marine design (M Eng); construction engineering and management (M Eng, MSE); electrical engineering (MS, MSE, PhD); electrical engineering systems (MS, MSE, PhD); engineering (M Eng, MS, MSE, D Eng, PhD, CE, Certificate, Ch E, Mar Eng, Nav Arch, Nuc E); environmental engineering (MSE, PhD); financial engineering (MS); geoscience and remote sensing (PhD); global automotive and manufacturing engineering (M Eng); industrial and operations engineering (MS, MSE, PhD); integrated microsystems (M Eng); macromolecular science and engineering (MS, MSE, PhD); manufacturing (M Eng, D Eng); materials science and engineering (MS, PhD); mechanical engineering (MSE, PhD); naval architecture and marine engineering (MS, MSE, PhD, Mar Eng, Nav Arch); nuclear engineering (Nuc E); nuclear engineering and radiological sciences (MSE, PhD); nuclear science (MS, PhD); pharmaceutical engineering (M Eng); space and planetary sciences (PhD); space engineering (M Eng); space sciences (MS); structural engineering (M Eng). Electronic applications accepted.

College of Literature, Science, and the Arts *Degree program information:* Part-time programs available. Offers American culture (AM, PhD); analytical chemistry (PhD); ancient Israel/Hebrew Bible (AM, PhD); anthropology (PhD); anthropology and history (PhD); applied and interdisciplinary mathematics (AM, MS, PhD); applied economics (AM); applied statistics (AM); Arabic (AM, PhD); Armenian (AM, PhD); Asian languages and cultures (MA, PhD); astronomy (MS, PhD); biopsychology (PhD); Chinese studies (AM); classical art and archaeology (PhD); classical studies (PhD); clinical psychology (PhD); cognition and perception (PhD); communication studies (PhD); comparative literature (PhD); creative writing (MFA); developmental psychology (PhD); early Christian studies (AM, PhD); ecology and evolutionary biology (MS, PhD); economics (AM, PhD); Egyptology (AM, PhD); English and education (PhD); English and women's studies (PhD); English language and literature (PhD); film and video studies (Certificate); French (PhD); general linguistics (PhD); geology (MS, PhD); German (AM, PhD); Greek (AM); Greek and Roman history (PhD, Certificate); Hebrew (AM, PhD); history (PhD); history and women's studies (PhD); history of art (PhD); inorganic chemistry (PhD); Islamic studies (AM, PhD); Japanese studies (AM); Latin (AM); linguistics and Germanic languages and literatures (PhD); literature, science, and the arts (AM, MA, MAT, MFA, MS, PhD, Certificate); material chemistry (PhD); mathematics (AM, MS, PhD); Mesopotamian and ancient Near Eastern studies (AM, PhD); mineralogy (MS, PhD); molecular, cellular, and developmental biology (MS, PhD); oceanography: marine geology and geochemistry (MS, PhD); organic chemistry (PhD); organizational psychology (PhD); Persian (AM, PhD); personality psychology (PhD); philosophy (AM, PhD); physical chemistry (PhD); physics (MS, PhD); political science (AM, PhD); psychology and women's studies (PhD); public policy and economics (PhD); public policy and sociology (PhD); Romance linguistics (PhD); Russian (AM, PhD); Russian and East European studies (AM, Certificate); screen arts and cultures (PhD, Certificate); social psychology (PhD); social work and economics (PhD); social work and political science (PhD); social work and sociology (PhD); sociology (PhD); South Asian studies (AM, Certificate); Southeast Asian studies (AM); Spanish (PhD); statistics (AM, PhD); teaching Latin (MAT); teaching of Arabic as a foreign Language (AM); Turkish (AM, PhD); women's studies (Certificate); women's studies and sociology (PhD).

Division of Kinesiology Offers kinesiology (MS, PhD); sport management (AM). Electronic applications accepted.

Gerald R. Ford School of Public Policy Offers public policy (MPA, MPP, PhD).

School of Art and Design Offers art and design (MFA). Electronic applications accepted.

School of Education Students: 325 full-time (245 women), 67 part-time (56 women); includes 88 minority (42 African Americans, 2 American Indian/Alaska Native, 26 Asian Americans or Pacific Islanders, 18 Hispanic Americans), 37 international. 674 applicants, 41% accepted, 175 enrolled. *Faculty:* 51 full-time (27 women). Expenses: Contact institution. *Financial support:* In 2006–07, 215 fellowships (averaging $5,852 per year), 109 research assistantships with full tuition reimbursements (averaging $14,695 per year), 32 teaching assistantships with full tuition reimbursements (averaging $14,756 per year) were awarded; career-related internships or fieldwork, Federal Work-Study, institutionally sponsored loans, scholarships/grants, health care benefits, tuition waivers, and unspecified assistantships also available. Support available to part-time students. Financial award applicants required to submit FAFSA. In 2006, 134 master's, 43 doctorates awarded. Offers academic affairs and student development (PhD); curriculum development (MA); early childhood education (MA, PhD); education (AM); educational administration and policy (MA, PhD); educational foundation, administration, policy, and research methods (MA); educational foundations and policy (MA, PhD); elementary education (MA, PhD); English education (MA); English language learning in school settings (MA); higher education (AM); individually designed concentration (PhD); learning technologies (MA, PhD); literacy, language, and culture (MA, PhD); mathematics education (MA, PhD); organizational behavior and management (PhD); public policy (PhD); research methods (MA); research, evaluation, and assessment (PhD); science education (MA, PhD); secondary education (MA, PhD); social studies education (MA); special education (PhD); teaching and teacher education (PhD). *Application deadline:* For fall admission, 12/1 priority date for domestic students, 12/1 for international students. *Application fee:* $60 ($75 for international students). Electronic applications accepted. *Application Contact:* Roberta Perry, Office of Student Services, 734-764-7563, Fax: 734-763-1495, E-mail: ed.grad.admit@umich.edu. *Dean,* Deborah Loewenberg Ball, 734-764-9470, Fax: 734-763-1229, E-mail: dball@umich.edu.

School of Information *Degree program information:* Part-time programs available. Offers archives and records management (MS); human-computer interaction (MS); information (MS, PhD); information economics, management and policy (MS); library and information services (MS). Electronic applications accepted.

The School of Music, Theatre, and Dance Offers composition (MA, MM, A Mus D); composition and theory (PhD); conducting (MM, A Mus D); design (MFA); media arts (MA); modern dance performance and choreography (MFA); music education (MM, PhD, Spec M); music, theatre, and dance (MA, MFA, MM, A Mus D, PhD, Spec M); musicology (MA, PhD); performance (MM, A Mus D, Spec M); theatre (PhD); theory (MA, PhD). Electronic applications accepted.

School of Nursing *Degree program information:* Part-time programs available. Postbaccalaureate distance learning degree programs offered (minimal on-campus study). Offers adult acute care nurse practitioner (MS); adult primary care/adult nurse practitioner (MS); community care/home care (MS); community health nursing (MS); family nurse practitioner (MS); gerontology nurse practitioner (MS); gerontology nursing (MS); infant, child, adolescent health nurse practitioner (MS); medical-surgical clinical nurse specialist (MS); nurse midwifery (MS); nursing (MS, PhD, Post Master's Certificate); nursing business and health systems (MS); occupational health nursing (MS); parent-child nursing (MS); psychiatric mental health nurse practitioner (MS); psychiatric mental health nursing (MS); women's health (Post Master's Certificate). Electronic applications accepted.

Law School Offers comparative law (MCL); law (JD, LL M, SJD).

Medical School *Degree program information:* Part-time programs available. Offers bioinformatics (MS, PhD); biological chemistry (PhD); biomedical sciences (MS, PhD); cell and developmental biology (MS, PhD); cellular and molecular biology (PhD); human genetics (MS, PhD); immunology (PhD); medicine (MD, MS, PhD); microbiology and immunology (PhD); pathology (PhD); pharmacology (PhD); physiology (PhD). Electronic applications accepted.

Ross School of Business at the University of Michigan *Degree program information:* Part-time and evening/weekend programs available. Offers business (M Acc, MBA); business administration (PhD). Electronic applications accepted.

School of Dentistry *Degree program information:* Part-time programs available. Offers dentistry (DDS, MS, PhD, Certificate). Electronic applications accepted.

School of Natural Resources and Environment Students: 239 (131 women); includes 35 minority (9 African Americans, 1 American Indian/Alaska Native, 19 Asian Americans or Pacific Islanders, 6 Hispanic Americans) 34 international. Average age 31. 365 applicants, 69% accepted. *Faculty:* 39 full-time, 23 part-time/adjunct. Expenses: Contact institution. *Financial support:* Fellowships with tuition reimbursements, research assistantships with tuition reimbursements, teaching assistantships with tuition reimbursements, career-related internships or fieldwork, Federal Work-Study, institutionally sponsored loans, scholarships/grants, health care benefits, and unspecified assistantships available. Support available to part-time students. Financial award application deadline: 1/5; financial award applicants required to submit FAFSA. In 2006, 76 master's, 10 doctorates awarded. Offers aquatic sciences: research and management (MS); behavior, education and communication (MS); conservation biology (MS); environmental informatics (MS); environmental justice (MS); environmental policy and planning (MS); industrial ecology (Certificate); landscape architecture (MLA, PhD); natural resources and environment (MS, PhD); spatial analysis (Certificate); sustainable systems (MS); terrestrial ecosystems (MS). *Application deadline:* For fall admission, 1/5 priority date for domestic and international students. Applications are processed on a rolling basis. *Application fee:* $60 ($75 for international students). Electronic applications accepted. *Application Contact:* 734-764-6453, Fax: 734-936-2195, E-mail: snre.gradteam@umich.edu. *Dean,* Dr. Rosina Bierbaum, 734-764-2550, Fax: 734-763-8965, E-mail: rbierbau@umich.edu.

School of Public Health *Degree program information:* Part-time and evening/weekend programs available. Offers biostatistics (MPH, MS, PhD); clinical research design and statistical analysis (MS); dental public health (MPH); environmental health (MPH, MS, Dr PH, PhD); epidemiological science (PhD); epidemiology (MPH, Dr PH); health behavior and health education (MPH, PhD); health management and policy (MHSA, MPH); health services organization and policy (PhD); hospital and molecular epidemiology (MPH); human nutrition (MPH, MS); industrial hygiene (MS, PhD); international health (MPH); occupational and environmental epidemiology (MPH); occupational health (MPH, MS, PhD); public health (MHSA, MPH, MS, Dr PH, PhD); toxicology (MPH, MS, PhD). MS and PhD offered through the Horace H. Rackham School of Graduate Studies. Electronic applications accepted.

School of Social Work Offers social work (MSW, PhD); social work and social science (PhD). PhD offered through the Horace H. Rackham School of Graduate Studies. Electronic applications accepted.

UNIVERSITY OF MICHIGAN–DEARBORN, Dearborn, MI 48128-1491

General Information State-supported, coed, comprehensive institution. *Graduate housing:* On-campus housing not available.

GRADUATE UNITS

College of Arts, Sciences, and Letters *Degree program information:* Part-time and evening/weekend programs available. Offers applied and computational mathematics (MS); arts, sciences, and letters (MA, MPP, MS); environmental science (MS); health psychology (MS); liberal studies (MA); public policy (MPP). Electronic applications accepted.

College of Engineering and Computer Science *Degree program information:* Part-time and evening/weekend programs available. Offers automotive systems engineering (MSE); computer and information science (MS); computer engineering (MSE); electrical engineering (MSE); engineering (MS, MSE); engineering management (MS); industrial and systems engineering (MSE); information systems and technology (MS); manufacturing systems engineering (MSE, D Eng); mechanical engineering (MSE); software engineering (MS). Electronic applications accepted.

School of Education *Degree program information:* Part-time and evening/weekend programs available. Offers education (M Ed, MA, MPA, Certificate); educational administration (Certificate); emotional impairments endorsement (M Ed); inclusion specialist (M Ed); learning disabilities endorsement (M Ed); nonprofit leadership (Certificate); public administration (MPA); teaching (MA). Electronic applications accepted.

School of Management *Degree program information:* Part-time and evening/weekend programs available. Postbaccalaureate distance learning degree programs offered (no on-campus study). Offers accounting (MS); finance (MS); management (MBA).

See Close-Up on page 1093.

UNIVERSITY OF MICHIGAN–FLINT, Flint, MI 48502-1950

General Information State-supported, coed, comprehensive institution. *Enrollment:* 6,527 graduate, professional, and undergraduate students; 207 full-time matriculated graduate/professional students (150 women), 720 part-time matriculated graduate/professional students (467 women). *Enrollment by degree level:* 860 master's, 67 doctoral. *Graduate faculty:* 69 full-time (35 women), 27 part-time/adjunct (14 women). Tuition, state resident: full-time $6,790; part-time $377 per credit. Tuition, nonresident: full-time $10,186; part-time $566 per credit. *Required fees:* $258 per term. Full-time tuition and fees vary according to degree level and program. Part-time tuition and fees vary according to course load and degree level. *Graduate housing:* On-campus housing not available. *Student services:* Campus employment opportunities, campus safety program, career counseling, child daycare facilities, disabled student services, exercise/wellness program, free psychological counseling, low-cost health insurance, teacher training, writing training. *Library facilities:* Frances Willson Thompson Library. *Online resources:* library catalog, web page, access to other libraries' catalogs. *Collection:* 259,260 titles, 911 serial subscriptions.

Computer facilities: 213 computers available on campus for general student use. A campuswide network can be accessed from off campus. Internet access and online class registration are available. *Web address:* http://www.umflint.edu/.

General Application Contact: Bradley T. Maki, Director of Graduate Admissions, 810-762-3171, Fax: 810-766-6789, E-mail: bmaki@umflint.edu.

GRADUATE UNITS

College of Arts and Sciences Students: 16 full-time (8 women), 64 part-time (26 women); includes 5 minority (3 African Americans, 2 Asian Americans or Pacific Islanders), 2 international. Average age 34. 65 applicants, 78% accepted, 41 enrolled. *Faculty:* 15 full-time (4 women), 1 (woman) part-time/adjunct. Expenses: Contact institution. *Financial support:* Fellowships, Federal Work-Study and scholarships/grants available. Support available to part-time students. Financial award applicants required to submit FAFSA. In 2006, 6 degrees awarded. *Degree program information:* Part-time programs available. Offers arts and sciences (MA, MS); biology (MS); computer science (MS); English (MA); information systems (MS); social sciences (MA). *Application deadline:* For fall admission, 8/1 priority date for domestic students, 3/1 priority date for international students; for winter admission, 11/15 priority date for domestic students, 7/1 priority date for international students; for spring admission, 3/15 priority date for domestic students, 11/1 priority date for international students. Applications are processed on a rolling basis. *Application fee:* $55. Electronic applications accepted. *Application Contact:* Bradley T. Maki, Director of Graduate Admissions, 810-762-3171, Fax: 810-766-6789, E-mail: bmaki@umflint.edu. *Dean,* Dr. D. J. Trela, 810-762-3234, Fax: 810-762-3006, E-mail: djtrela@umflint.edu.

Graduate Programs Students: 31 full-time (18 women), 169 part-time (109 women); includes 47 minority (39 African Americans, 1 American Indian/Alaska Native, 4 Asian Americans or Pacific Islanders, 3 Hispanic Americans), 1 international. Average age 36. 90 applicants, 79% accepted, 57 enrolled. *Faculty:* 10 full-time (2 women), 3 part-time/adjunct (0 women). Expenses: Contact institution. *Financial support:* In 2006–07, 5 fellowships were awarded; career-related internships or fieldwork, Federal Work-Study, and scholarships/grants also available. Support available to part-time students. Financial award application deadline: 5/1; financial award applicants required to submit FAFSA. In 2006, 34 degrees awarded. *Degree program information:* Part-time and evening/weekend programs available. Postbaccalaureate distance learning degree programs offered (minimal on-campus study). Offers American culture (MLS); public administration (MPA). *Application deadline:* For fall admission, 8/1 for domestic students, 3/1 for international students; for winter admission, 11/15 for domestic students, 7/1 for international students; for spring admission, 3/15 for domestic students, 11/1 for international students. *Application fee:* $55. Electronic applications accepted. *Application Contact:* Bradley T. Maki, Director of Graduate Admissions, 810-762-3171, Fax: 810-766-6789, E-mail: bmaki@umflint.edu. *Associate Provost,* Dr. Vahid Lotfi, 810-762-3171, Fax: 810-766-6789, E-mail: vahid@umflint.edu.

School of Education and Human Services Students: 42 full-time (36 women), 200 part-time (173 women); includes 20 minority (16 African Americans, 2 American Indian/Alaska Native, 2 Hispanic Americans), 2 international. Average age 35. 109 applicants, 80% accepted, 65 enrolled. *Faculty:* 19 full-time (15 women), 9 part-time/adjunct (6 women). Expenses: Contact institution. *Financial support:* In 2006–07, 101 students received support. Federal Work-Study and scholarships/grants available. Support available to part-time students. Financial award applicants required to submit FAFSA. In 2006, 54 degrees awarded. *Degree program information:* Part-time programs available. Offers early childhood education (MA, MA Ed); education (MA Ed); elementary education with teacher certification (MA); elementary educa-

University of Michigan–Flint (continued)

tion with teaching certificate (MA Ed); literacy (K-12) (MA, MA Ed); special education (MA, MA Ed); technology in education (MA); urban and multicultural education (MA, MA Ed). *Application deadline:* For fall admission, 8/1 priority date for domestic students, 3/1 priority date for international students; for winter admission, 11/15 priority date for domestic students, 7/15 priority date for international students; for spring admission, 3/15 priority date for domestic students, 11/15 priority date for international students. Applications are processed on a rolling basis. *Application fee:* $55. *Application Contact:* Beulah Alexander, Executive Secretary, 810-766-6879, Fax: 810-766-6891, E-mail: beulaha@umflint.edu. *Dean,* Dr. Susanne Chandler, 810-766-6878, Fax: 810-766-6891, E-mail: chandes@umflint.edu.

School of Health Professions and Studies Students: 106 full-time (82 women), 90 part-time (78 women); includes 38 minority (23 African Americans, 11 Asian Americans or Pacific Islanders, 4 Hispanic Americans), 2 international. Average age 31. 208 applicants, 54% accepted, 72 enrolled. *Faculty:* 22 full-time (17 women), 10 part-time/adjunct (5 women). Expenses: Contact institution. *Financial support:* Fellowships, career-related internships or fieldwork, Federal Work-Study, scholarships/grants, and traineeships available. Support available to part-time students. In 2006, 54 degrees awarded. *Degree program information:* Part-time programs available. Offers anesthesia (MSA); health education (MS); health professions and studies (MS, MSA, MSN, DPT); nursing (MSN); physical therapy (DPT). *Application deadline:* For fall admission, 8/1 priority date for domestic students, 3/1 priority date for international students; for winter admission, 11/15 priority date for domestic students, 7/1 priority date for international students; for spring admission, 3/15 priority date for domestic students, 11/1 priority date for international students. Applications are processed on a rolling basis. *Application fee:* $55. Electronic applications accepted. *Application Contact:* Sandra Johnson, Executive Secretary, 810-237-6503, Fax: 810-237-6532, E-mail: setherly@umflint.edu. *Dean,* Dr. Augustine O. Agho, 810-237-6503, Fax: 810-237-6532, E-mail: aagho@umflint.edu.

School of Management Students: 12 full-time (6 women), 174 part-time (64 women); includes 21 minority (12 African Americans, 1 American Indian/Alaska Native, 7 Asian Americans or Pacific Islanders, 1 Hispanic American), 15 international. Average age 32. 92 applicants, 77% accepted, 62 enrolled. *Faculty:* 12 full-time (2 women), 2 part-time/adjunct (0 women). Expenses: Contact institution. *Financial support:* Federal Work-Study and scholarships/grants available. Support available to part-time students. Financial award applicants required to submit FAFSA. In 2006, 77 degrees awarded. *Degree program information:* Part-time programs available. Postbaccalaureate distance learning degree programs offered (minimal on-campus study). Offers management (MBA). *Application deadline:* For fall admission, 8/1 priority date for domestic and international students; for winter admission, 12/1 priority date for domestic and international students; for spring admission, 2/15 priority date for domestic and international students. Applications are processed on a rolling basis. *Application fee:* $55. Electronic applications accepted. *Application Contact:* D. Nicol Taylor, MBA Program Coordinator, 810-237-6591, Fax: 810-237-6685, E-mail: dntaylor@umflint.edu. *Dean,* Dr. Douglas Moon, 810-762-3160, Fax: 810-762-3287.

UNIVERSITY OF MINNESOTA, DULUTH, Duluth, MN 55812-2496

General Information State-supported, coed, comprehensive institution. *Enrollment:* 11,090 graduate, professional, and undergraduate students; 443 full-time matriculated graduate/professional students (257 women), 153 part-time matriculated graduate/professional students (76 women). *Graduate faculty:* 284 full-time (71 women), 68 part-time/adjunct (23 women). *Graduate housing:* Room and/or apartments available to single students; on-campus housing not available to married students. Housing application deadline: 3/1. *Student services:* Campus employment opportunities, career counseling, child daycare facilities, disabled student services, exercise/wellness program, free psychological counseling, grant writing training, international student services, low-cost health insurance, multicultural affairs office, teacher training. *Library facilities:* University of Minnesota Duluth Library. *Online resources:* library catalog, web page, access to other libraries' catalogs. *Collection:* 608,579 titles, 52,595 serial subscriptions, 21,204 audiovisual materials. *Research affiliation:* Environmental Protection Agency Environmental Research Laboratory (aquatic biology), Minnesota Geological Survey, Northeastern Minnesota National Historical Center (local history), U.S. Forest Service, Northcentral Forest Experiment Station.

Computer facilities: 680 computers available on campus for general student use. A campuswide network can be accessed from student residence rooms and from off campus. Internet access and online class registration are available. *Web address:* http://www.d.umn.edu/.

General Application Contact: M.J. Leone, Executive Administrative Specialist, 218-726-7523, Fax: 218-726-6970, E-mail: grad@d.umn.edu.

GRADUATE UNITS

Graduate School Students: 324 full-time (179 women), 123 part-time (53 women). Average age 32. 369 applicants, 67% accepted, 160 enrolled. *Faculty:* 284 full-time (71 women), 68 part-time/adjunct (23 women). Expenses: Contact institution. *Financial support:* In 2006–07, 65 fellowships with full tuition reimbursements, 26 research assistantships with full tuition reimbursements, 93 teaching assistantships with full tuition reimbursements were awarded; career-related internships or fieldwork, Federal Work-Study, institutionally sponsored loans, scholarships/grants, traineeships, tuition waivers (full and partial), and unspecified assistantships also available. Support available to part-time students. Financial award applicants required to submit FAFSA. In 2006, 75 degrees awarded. *Degree program information:* Part-time and evening/weekend programs available. Postbaccalaureate distance learning degree programs offered (minimal on-campus study). Offers toxicology (MS, PhD). *Application deadline:* For fall admission, 7/15 for domestic students. Applications are processed on a rolling basis. *Application fee:* $55 ($75 for international students). *Application Contact:* M.J. Leone, Executive Administrative Specialist, 218-726-7523, Fax: 218-726-6970, E-mail: grad@d.umn.edu. *Associate Dean,* Larry Knopp, 218-726-6246, Fax: 218-726-6970, E-mail: lknupp@d.umn.edu.

College of Education and Human Service Professions Students: 117 full-time (99 women), 3 part-time (all women); includes 16 minority (1 African American, 13 American Indian/Alaska Native, 2 Asian Americans or Pacific Islanders). Average age 30. 150 applicants, 65% accepted, 68 enrolled. *Faculty:* 14 full-time (9 women), 10 part-time/adjunct (7 women). Expenses: Contact institution. *Financial support:* In 2006–07, 9 fellowships with full and partial tuition reimbursements (averaging $4,111 per year), 5 teaching assistantships with full tuition reimbursements (averaging $11,582 per year) were awarded; career-related internships or fieldwork, Federal Work-Study, institutionally sponsored loans, scholarships/grants, traineeships, and tuition waivers (full and partial) also available. Support available to part-time students. Financial award application deadline: 3/14. In 2006, 49 degrees awarded. *Degree program information:* Part-time and evening/weekend programs available. Postbaccalaureate distance learning degree programs offered (minimal on-campus study). Offers communication sciences and disorders (MA); education (Ed D); education and human service professions (MA, MSW, Ed D); social work (MSW). *Application deadline:* For fall admission, 1/13 priority date for domestic and international students. *Application fee:* $55 ($75 for international students). *Application Contact:* Prof. Jackie Millslagle, Associate Dean, 218-726-7191, Fax: 218-726-7073, E-mail: jmillsla@d.umn.edu. *Dean,* Dr. Paul N. Deputy, 218-726-6537, Fax: 218-726-7073, E-mail: pdeputy@d.umn.edu.

College of Liberal Arts Students: 27 full-time (20 women), 19 part-time (12 women); includes 1 minority (Asian American or Pacific Islander) Average age 36. 33 applicants, 79% accepted, 21 enrolled. *Faculty:* 34 full-time (11 women), 29 part-time/adjunct (12 women). Expenses: Contact institution. *Financial support:* In 2006–07, 12 students received support, including 2 fellowships with full and partial tuition reimbursements available (averaging $4,087 per year), 9 teaching assistantships with full tuition reimbursements available (averaging $8,950 per year); career-related internships or fieldwork, Federal Work-Study, institutionally sponsored loans, and tuition waivers (full and partial) also available. Support available to part-time students. Financial award application deadline: 4/15; financial award applicants required to submit FAFSA. In 2006, 16 degrees awarded. *Degree program information:* Part-time programs available. Offers criminology (MA); English (MA); liberal arts (MA, MLS); liberal studies (MLS). *Application deadline:* For fall admission, 7/15 for domestic students; for spring admission, 11/15 for domestic students. Applications are processed on a rolling basis. *Application fee:* $55 ($75 for international students). *Dean,* Dr. Linda Krug, 218-726-8981, Fax: 218-726-6386.

College of Science and Engineering Students: 162 full-time (52 women), 34 part-time (10 women); includes 6 minority (4 Asian Americans or Pacific Islanders, 2 Hispanic Americans), 56 international. Average age 26. 206 applicants, 58% accepted, 78 enrolled. *Faculty:* 147 full-time (24 women), 14 part-time/adjunct (2 women). Expenses: Contact institution. *Financial support:* In 2006–07, 18 fellowships with full tuition reimbursements (averaging $5,369 per year), 26 research assistantships with full tuition reimbursements (averaging $13,974 per year), 91 teaching assistantships with full tuition reimbursements (averaging $11,970 per year) were awarded; career-related internships or fieldwork, Federal Work-Study, institutionally sponsored loans, scholarships/grants, traineeships, tuition waivers (full and partial), and unspecified assistantships also available. Support available to part-time students. In 2006, 61 master's, 2 doctorates awarded. *Degree program information:* Part-time and evening/weekend programs available. Postbaccalaureate distance learning degree programs offered (minimal on-campus study). Offers applied and computational mathematics (MS); chemistry and biochemistry (MS); computer science (MS); electrical and computer engineering (MSECE); engineering management (MSEM); environmental health and safety (MEHS); geological sciences (MS, PhD); integrated biosciences (MS); physics (MS); science and engineering (MEHS, MS, MSECE, MSEM, PhD). *Application deadline:* For fall admission, 7/15 for domestic students. Applications are processed on a rolling basis. *Application fee:* $55 ($75 for international students). *Dean,* Dr. James Riehl, 218-726-6397, E-mail: jpriehl@d.umn.edu.

Labovitz School of Business and Economics Average age 34. 19 applicants, 89% accepted, 16 enrolled. *Faculty:* 36 full-time (7 women). Expenses: Contact institution. *Financial support:* In 2006–07, 6 students received support, including 6 research assistantships with full and partial tuition reimbursements available (averaging $12,000 per year); institutionally sponsored loans also available. Financial award application deadline: 5/1; financial award applicants required to submit FAFSA. In 2006, 15 degrees awarded. *Degree program information:* Part-time and evening/weekend programs available. Offers business administration (MBA); business and economics (MBA). *Application deadline:* For fall admission, 7/15 for domestic and international students; for spring admission, 11/1 for domestic and international students. Applications are processed on a rolling basis. *Application fee:* $55 ($75 for international students). *Dean,* Kjell Knudsen, 218-726-7288.

School of Fine Arts Students: 12 full-time (7 women), 4 part-time (3 women). Average age 35. 12 applicants, 58% accepted, 6 enrolled. *Faculty:* 34 full-time (18 women), 2 part-time/adjunct (1 woman). Expenses: Contact institution. *Financial support:* In 2006–07, 13 students received support, including 8 fellowships with full tuition reimbursements available (averaging $1,200 per year), research assistantships (averaging $10,000 per year), teaching assistantships with full tuition reimbursements available (averaging $6,000 per year); career-related internships or fieldwork, Federal Work-Study, institutionally sponsored loans, and scholarships/grants also available. In 2006, 6 degrees awarded. *Degree program information:* Part-time programs available. Offers fine arts (MFA, MM); graphic design (MFA); music education (MM); performance (MM). *Application deadline:* For fall admission, 7/15 for domestic students; for spring admission, 11/15 for domestic students. Applications are processed on a rolling basis. *Application fee:* $55 ($75 for international students). *Dean,* Dr. Jack Bowman, 218-726-7261, Fax: 218-726-6969, E-mail: sfa@d.umn.edu.

Medical School Students: 117 full-time (58 women); includes 8 minority (4 American Indian/Alaska Native, 4 Asian Americans or Pacific Islanders). Average age 24. 478 applicants, 17% accepted, 54 enrolled. *Faculty:* 25 full-time (7 women). Expenses: Contact institution. *Financial support:* In 2006–07, 93 students received support, including 8 research assistantships with full tuition reimbursements available (averaging $18,000 per year), 1 teaching assistantship with full tuition reimbursement available (averaging $18,000 per year); fellowships with full tuition reimbursements available, career-related internships or fieldwork, Federal Work-Study, institutionally sponsored loans, and scholarships/grants also available. Support available to part-time students. Financial award application deadline: 4/1; financial award applicants required to submit FAFSA. *Degree program information:* Part-time programs available. Offers biochemistry, molecular biology and biophysics (MS, PhD); medicine (MD, MS, PhD); microbiology, immunology and molecular pathobiology (MS, PhD); pharmacology (MS, PhD); physiology (MS, PhD). *Application deadline:* For fall admission, 11/15 for domestic students. Applications are processed on a rolling basis. *Application fee:* $75. *Application Contact:* Dr. Lillian A. Repesh, Associate Dean for Admissions and Student Affairs, 218-726-8511, Fax: 218-726-7057, E-mail: lrepesh@d.umn.edu. *Dean,* Dr. Richard J. Ziegler, 218-726-7572.

UNIVERSITY OF MINNESOTA, TWIN CITIES CAMPUS, Minneapolis, MN 55455-0213

General Information State-supported, coed, university. CGS member. *Enrollment:* 50,402 graduate, professional, and undergraduate students; 10,904 matriculated graduate/professional students (5,675 women). *Enrollment by degree level:* 5,039 master's, 5,729 doctoral, 136 other advanced degrees. *Graduate faculty:* 2,405. Tuition, state resident: full-time $9,302; part-time $775 per credit. Tuition, nonresident: full-time $16,400; part-time $1,367 per credit. Full-time tuition and fees vary according to class time, course load, program, reciprocity agreements and student level. *Graduate housing:* Rooms and/or apartments available on a first-come, first-served basis to single and married students. Housing application deadline:5/1. *Student services:* Campus employment opportunities, campus safety program, career counseling, child daycare facilities, disabled student services, exercise/wellness program, free psychological counseling, grant writing training, international student services, low-cost health insurance, multicultural affairs office, teacher training, writing training. *Library facilities:* Wilson Library plus 17 others. *Online resources:* library catalog, web page, access to other libraries' catalogs. *Collection:* 5.7 million titles, 45,000 serial subscriptions, 1.2 million audiovisual materials.

Computer facilities: Computer purchase and lease plans are available. A campuswide network can be accessed from student residence rooms and from off campus. Internet access and online class registration, e-mail are available. *Web address:* http://www.umn.edu/tc/.

General Application Contact: Information Contact, 612-625-3014, Fax: 612-625-6002, E-mail: gsquest@umn.edu.

GRADUATE UNITS

Carlson School of Management Students: 2,517 (767 women). Average age 29. *Faculty:* 126 full-time (28 women), 120 part-time/adjunct. Expenses: Contact institution. *Financial support:* In 2006–07, 247 fellowships with full and partial tuition reimbursements, 85 research assistantships with full tuition reimbursements, 84 teaching assistantships with full and partial tuition reimbursements were awarded; career-related internships or fieldwork, Federal Work-Study, institutionally sponsored loans, scholarships/grants, health care benefits, tuition waivers (full and partial), and unspecified assistantships also available. Support available to part-time students. Financial award application deadline: 4/1; financial award applicants required to submit FAFSA. In 2006, 581 master's, 20 doctorates awarded. *Degree program information:* Part-time and evening/weekend programs available. Offers accountancy (M Acc); accounting (MBA, PhD); business administration (MBA, PhD); business taxation (MBT); entrepreneurship (MBA); finance (MBA, PhD); healthcare management (MBA); human resources and industrial relations (MA, PhD); information and decision sciences (MBA, PhD); international business (MBA); management (EMBA, M Acc, MA, MBA, MBT, MS, MSMOT, PhD); marketing and logistics management (MBA, PhD); operations and management science (MBA, PhD); strategic management and organization (MBA, PhD); supply chain management (MBA). Electronic applications accepted. *Dean,* Dr. Allison Davis-Blake, 612-624-7876, Fax: 612-624-6374, E-mail: adavis-blake@csom.umn.edu.

College of Pharmacy *Degree program information:* Part-time programs available. Offers medicinal chemistry (MS, PhD); pharmaceutics (MS, PhD); pharmacy (Pharm D, MS, PhD); social and administrative pharmacy (MS, PhD).

College of Veterinary Medicine Students: 455 full-time (356 women); includes 24 minority (1 African American, 2 American Indian/Alaska Native, 15 Asian Americans or Pacific Islanders, 6 Hispanic Americans), 47 international. 973 applicants, 15% accepted, 105 enrolled.

Faculty: 137 full-time (54 women). Expenses: Contact institution. *Financial support:* In 2006–07, 2 fellowships with full tuition reimbursements (averaging $21,000 per year), 48 research assistantships with full tuition reimbursements (averaging $20,772 per year), 15 teaching assistantships with full tuition reimbursements (averaging $26,500 per year) were awarded; career-related internships or fieldwork, Federal Work-Study, traineeships, health care benefits, and unspecified assistantships also available. Support available to part-time students. Financial award applicants required to submit FAFSA. In 2006, 82 DVMs, 8 master's, 10 doctorates awarded. *Degree program information:* Part-time programs available. Offers comparative and molecular bioscience (MS, PhD); veterinary medicine (MS, PhD). *Application deadline:* For fall admission, 10/1 for domestic and international students. Electronic applications accepted. *Dean,* Dr. Jeffrey Klausner, 612-624-6244, Fax: 612-624-8753.

Graduate School Students: 10,907 (5,695 women) 2,612 international. 12,463 applicants, 35% accepted, 2260 enrolled. *Faculty:* 2,405. Expenses: Contact institution. *Financial support:* In 2006–07, 60 fellowships with full tuition reimbursements (averaging $21,500 per year) were awarded; research assistantships with full and partial tuition reimbursements, teaching assistantships with full and partial tuition reimbursements, career-related internships or fieldwork, Federal Work-Study, institutionally sponsored loans, scholarships/grants, traineeships, health care benefits, tuition waivers (full and partial), and unspecified assistantships also available. Support available to part-time students. Financial award application deadline: 4/1; financial award applicants required to submit FAFSA. In 2006, 1,903 master's, 750 doctorates awarded. *Degree program information:* Part-time and evening/weekend programs available. Postbaccalaureate distance learning degree programs offered (minimal on-campus study). Offers biophysical sciences and medical physics (MS, PhD); cellular and integrative physiology (MS, PhD); genetic counseling (MS); health informatics (MHI, MS, PhD); history of science, technology and medicine (MA, PhD); microbial engineering (MS); microbiology, immunology and cancer biology (PhD); molecular, cellular, developmental biology and genetics (PhD); natural resource sciences and management (MS, PhD); neuroscience (MS, PhD); scientific computation (MS, PhD). *Application deadline:* For fall admission, 6/15 for domestic and international students; for spring admission, 10/15 for domestic and international students. Applications are processed on a rolling basis. *Application fee:* $55 ($75 for international students). Electronic applications accepted. *Application Contact:* 612-625-3014, Fax: 612-625-6002, E-mail: gsquest@umn.edu. *Vice Provost and Dean,* Dr. Gail Dubrow, 612-625-2809, Fax: 612-625-6820.

College of Biological Sciences Expenses: Contact institution. *Financial support:* Fellowships with full tuition reimbursements, research assistantships with full tuition reimbursements, teaching assistantships with full tuition reimbursements, career-related internships or fieldwork, Federal Work-Study, institutionally sponsored loans, scholarships/grants, traineeships, and tuition waivers (full and partial) available. Financial award applicants required to submit FAFSA. *Degree program information:* Part-time programs available. Offers biochemistry, molecular biology and biophysics (PhD); biological science (MBS); biological sciences (MBS, MS, PhD); ecology, evolution, and behavior (MS, PhD); plant biological sciences (MS, PhD). *Application fee:* $50 ($55 for international students). Electronic applications accepted. *Dean,* Dr. Robert Elde, 612-624-2244, Fax: 612-624-2785.

College of Design Students: 293 full-time (142 women), 45 part-time (25 women); includes 29 minority (2 African Americans, 25 Asian Americans or Pacific Islanders, 2 Hispanic Americans), 27 international. Average age 27. 350 applicants, 33% accepted, 93 enrolled. *Faculty:* 19 full-time (6 women), 47 part-time/adjunct (10 women). Expenses: Contact institution. *Financial support:* In 2006–07, 104 students received support, including 28 fellowships (averaging $1,600 per year), 18 research assistantships with partial tuition reimbursements available (averaging $4,824 per year), 58 teaching assistantships with partial tuition reimbursements available (averaging $4,824 per year); career-related internships or fieldwork, Federal Work-Study, institutionally sponsored loans, tuition waivers (full and partial), and thesis awards also available. Financial award application deadline: 1/15. In 2006, 83 master's, 7 doctorates awarded. Offers apparel (MA, MS, PhD); architecture (M Arch); design (M Arch, MA, MFA, MLA, MS, PhD, Postbaccalaureate Certificate); design communication (MA, MS, PhD); housing studies (MA, MS, PhD, Postbaccalaureate Certificate); interactive design (MFA); interior design (MA, MS, PhD); landscape architecture (MLA, MS); sustainable design (MS). *Application deadline:* For fall admission, 1/15 for domestic and international students. *Application fee:* $50 ($55 for international students). Electronic applications accepted. *Application Contact:* Terrence Rafferty, Director of Graduate Admissions and Recruitment, 612-624-8817, E-mail: raffe013@umn.edu. *Dean,* Thomas Fisher, 612-626-1000, Fax: 612-625-7525, E-mail: fishe033@tc.umn.edu.

College of Education and Human Development Students: 1,687 full-time (1,240 women), 1,194 part-time (810 women); includes 315 minority (120 African Americans, 35 American Indian/Alaska Native, 104 Asian Americans or Pacific Islanders, 56 Hispanic Americans), 256 international. Average age 28. 2,019 applicants, 63% accepted, 977 enrolled. *Faculty:* 156 full-time (69 women). Expenses: Contact institution. *Financial support:* In 2006–07, 59 fellowships, 278 research assistantships with full tuition reimbursements (averaging $24,775 per year), 238 teaching assistantships with full tuition reimbursements (averaging $24,775 per year) were awarded; scholarships/grants and tuition waivers (partial) also available. Financial award applicants required to submit FAFSA. In 2006, 1,147 master's, 185 doctorates, 94 other advanced degrees awarded. *Degree program information:* Part-time programs available. Offers adapted physical education (MA, PhD); adult education (M Ed, MA, Ed D, PhD, Certificate); agricultural, food and environmental education (M Ed, MA, Ed D, PhD); art education (M Ed, MA, PhD); biomechanics (MA); biomechanics and neural control (PhD); business and industry education (M Ed, MA, Ed D, PhD); business education (M Ed); child psychology (MA, PhD); children's literature (M Ed, MA, PhD); Chinese (M Ed); coaching (Certificate); comparative and international development education (MA, PhD); counseling and student personnel psychology (MA, PhD, Ed S); curriculum and instruction (MA, PhD); developmental adapted physical education (M Ed); disability policy and services (Certificate); early childhood education (M Ed, MA, PhD); earth science (M Ed); education and human development (M Ed, MA, MSW, Ed D, PhD, Certificate, Ed S); educational administration (MA, Ed D, PhD); educational psychology (PhD); elementary education (M Ed, MA, PhD); elementary special education (M Ed); English (M Ed); English as a second language (M Ed); English education (MA, PhD); environmental education (M Ed); evaluation studies (MA, PhD); exercise physiology (MA, PhD); family education (M Ed, MA, Ed D, PhD); French (M Ed); German (M Ed); Hebrew (M Ed); higher education (MA, PhD); human factors/ergonomics (MA, PhD); human resource development (M Ed, MA, Ed D, PhD, Certificate); instructional systems and technology (M Ed, MA, PhD); international/comparative sport (MA, PhD); Japanese (M Ed); kinesiology (M Ed, MA, PhD); language arts (MA, PhD); language immersion education (Certificate); leisure services/management (MA, PhD); life sciences (M Ed); literacy education (MA); marketing education (M Ed); marriage and family therapy (MA, PhD); mathematics (M Ed); mathematics education (MA, PhD); middle school science (M Ed); motor development (MA, PhD); motor learning/control (MA, PhD); outdoor education/recreation (MA, PhD); physical education (M Ed); postsecondary administration (Ed D); program evaluation (Certificate); psychological foundations of education (MA, PhD, Ed S); reading education (MA, PhD); recreation, park, and leisure studies (M Ed, MA, PhD); school psychology (MA, PhD, Ed S); school-to-work (Certificate); science (M Ed); science education (MA, PhD); second languages and cultures (M Ed); second languages and cultures education (MA, PhD); social studies (M Ed); social studies education (MA, PhD); social work (MSW, PhD); Spanish (M Ed); special education (M Ed, MA, PhD, Ed S); sport and exercise science (M Ed); sport management (M Ed, MA, PhD); sport psychology (MA, PhD); sport sociology (MA, PhD); staff development (Certificate); talent development and gifted education (Certificate); teacher leadership (M Ed); teaching (M Ed); technical education (Certificate); technology education (M Ed, MA); technology enhanced learning (Certificate); therapeutic recreation (MA, PhD); work and human resource education (M Ed, MA, Ed D, PhD); writing education (M Ed, MA, PhD); youth development leadership (M Ed). *Application fee:* $55. *Application Contact:* Dr. Mary Bents, Associate Dean, 612-625-6501, Fax: 612-626-1580, E-mail: mbents@tc.umn.edu. *Dean,* Dr. Darlyne Bailey, 612-626-9252, Fax: 612-626-1580, E-mail: dbailey@umn.edu.

College of Food, Agricultural and Natural Resource Sciences Students: 442 full-time (243 women), 326 part-time (172 women); includes 46 minority (11 African Americans, 4 American Indian/Alaska Native, 17 Asian Americans or Pacific Islanders, 14 Hispanic Americans), 174 international. Average age 30. 587 applicants, 24% accepted, 119 enrolled. Expenses: Contact institution. *Financial support:* Fellowships, research assistantships, teaching assistantships, career-related internships or fieldwork, Federal Work-Study, institutionally sponsored loans, and tuition waivers (full) available. Support available to part-time students. Financial award application deadline: 1/1; financial award applicants required to submit CSS PROFILE. In 2006, 86 master's, 72 doctorates awarded. *Degree program information:* Part-time and evening/weekend programs available. Offers animal science (MS, PhD); applied economics (MS, PhD); applied plant sciences (MS, PhD); biosystems and agricultural engineering (MBAE, MSBAE, PhD); conservation biology (MS, PhD); entomology (MS, PhD); food science (MS, PhD); food, agricultural and natural resource sciences (MBAE, MS, MSBAE, PhD); natural resources science and management (MS, PhD); natural resources, science and management (MS, PhD); nutrition (MS, PhD); plant pathology (MS, PhD); soil science (MS, PhD); water resources science (MS, PhD). *Application deadline:* For fall admission, 1/1 priority date for domestic and international students; for spring admission, 10/15 for domestic and international students. Applications are processed on a rolling basis. *Application fee:* $50 ($55 for international students). Electronic applications accepted. *Application Contact:* Lisa Wiley, Student Support Services Assistant, 612-624-2748, Fax: 612-625-8737, E-mail: lwiley@umn.edu. *Dean,* Dr. Allen S. Levine, 612-624-4772.

College of Liberal Arts Expenses: Contact institution. *Financial support:* Fellowships, research assistantships, teaching assistantships, career-related internships or fieldwork, Federal Work-Study, institutionally sponsored loans, and tuition waivers (full and partial) available. Support available to part-time students. Financial award applicants required to submit CSS PROFILE or FAFSA. *Degree program information:* Part-time and evening/weekend programs available. Offers American studies (MA, PhD); ancient and medieval art and archaeology (MA, PhD); anthropology (MA, PhD); art (MFA); art history (MA, PhD); Asian literatures, cultures, and media (PhD); audiology (Au D); biological psychopathology (PhD); classics (MA, PhD); clinical psychology (PhD); cognitive and biological psychology (PhD); communication studies (MA, PhD); comparative literature (PhD); comparative studies in discourse and society (PhD); counseling psychology (PhD); design technology (MFA); economics (PhD); English (MA, MFA, PhD); English as a second language (MA); feminist studies (PhD); French (MA, PhD); geographic information science (MGIS); geography (MA, PhD); Germanic studies: German and Scandinavian studies track (PhD); Germanic studies: German track (MA, PhD); Germanic studies: Germanic medieval studies track (MA, PhD); Germanic studies: Scandinavian studies track (MA); Germanic studies: teaching track (MA); Greek (MA, PhD); health journalism (professional program) (MA); Hispanic and Luso-Brazilian literatures and linguistics (PhD); Hispanic linguistics (MA); Hispanic literature (MA); history (MA, PhD); industrial/organizational psychology (PhD); Latin (MA, PhD); liberal arts (MA, MFA, MGIS, MM, MS, Au D, DMA, PhD); linguistics (MA, PhD); Lusophone literature (MA); mass communication (MA, PhD); music (MA, MM, DMA, PhD); personality, individual differences, and behavior genetics (PhD); philosophy (MA, PhD); political science (MA, PhD); quantitative/psychometric methods (PhD); religions in antiquity (MA); school psychology (PhD); social psychology (PhD); sociology (MA, PhD); speech-language pathology (MA); speech-language-hearing sciences (PhD); statistics (MS, PhD); strategic communication (professional program) (MA); theater arts and dance (MA); theatre arts and dance (PhD). Electronic applications accepted. *Dean,* Steven J. Rosenstone, 612-624-2535, Fax: 612-624-6839, E-mail: sjr@umn.edu.

Hubert H. Humphrey Institute of Public Affairs *Degree program information:* Part-time and evening/weekend programs available. Offers advanced policy analysis methods (MPP); economic and community development (MPP); environmental planning (MURP); foreign policy (MPP); housing and community development (MURP); land use and urban design (MURP); public affairs (MPA, MPP, MS, MURP); public and nonprofit leadership and management (MPP); regional, economic and workforce development (MURP); science technology and environmental policy (MPP); science, technology, and environmental policy (MS); social policy (MPP); transportation planning (MURP); women and public policy (MPP). Electronic applications accepted.

School of Nursing Students: 167 full-time (152 women), 183 part-time (166 women); includes 28 minority (9 African Americans, 3 American Indian/Alaska Native, 8 Asian Americans or Pacific Islanders, 8 Hispanic Americans). Average age 37. 220 applicants, 76% accepted. *Faculty:* 58 full-time (56 women), 22 part-time/adjunct (20 women). Expenses: Contact institution. *Financial support:* Fellowships, research assistantships, teaching assistantships, career-related internships or fieldwork and traineeships available. Financial award applicants required to submit FAFSA. In 2006, 87 master's, 7 doctorates awarded. *Degree program information:* Part-time programs available. Postbaccalaureate distance learning degree programs offered (minimal on-campus study). Offers adolescent nursing (MS); adult health clinical nurse specialist (MS); advanced clinical specialist in gerontology (MS); children with special health care needs (MS); family nurse practitioner (MS); gerontological nurse practitioner (MS); nurse anesthetist (MS); nurse midwifery (MS); nursing (MN, MS, DNP, PhD); nursing and health care systems administration (MS); pediatric clinical nurse specialist (MS); pediatric nurse practitioner (MS); psychiatric mental health clinical nurse specialist (MS); public health nursing (MS); women's health nurse practitioner (MS). *Application fee:* $55 ($75 for international students). *Application Contact:* Information Contact, 612-624-4454, Fax: 612-624-3174, E-mail: nurseoss@umn.edu. *Dean,* Dr. Connie Delaney, 612-624-5959, Fax: 612-626-2359.

Institute of Technology Students: 1,690 (359 women); includes 94 minority (13 African Americans, 1 American Indian/Alaska Native, 65 Asian Americans or Pacific Islanders, 15 Hispanic Americans) 720 international. Average age 30. 3,024 applicants, 34% accepted. *Faculty:* 412. Expenses: Contact institution. *Financial support:* Fellowships, research assistantships, teaching assistantships, career-related internships or fieldwork, Federal Work-Study, institutionally sponsored loans, and tuition waivers (full and partial) available. Support available to part-time students. Financial award applicants required to submit FAFSA. In 2006, 295 master's, 217 doctorates awarded. *Degree program information:* Part-time and evening/weekend programs available. Postbaccalaureate distance learning degree programs offered (minimal on-campus study). Offers aerospace engineering (M Aero E); aerospace engineering and mechanics (MS, PhD); biomedical engineering (MS, PhD); chemical engineering (M Ch E, MS Ch E, PhD); chemistry (MS, PhD); civil engineering (MCE, MS, PhD); computer and information sciences (MCIS, MS, PhD); computer engineering (M Comp E, MS); electrical engineering (MEE, MSEE, PhD); geological engineering (M Geo E, MS, PhD); geology (MS, PhD); geophysics (MS, PhD); history of science and technology (MA, PhD); industrial engineering (MSIE, PhD); materials science and engineering (M Mat SE, MS Mat SE, PhD); mechanical engineering (MSME, PhD); technology (M Aero E, M Ch E, M Comp E, M Geo E, M Mat SE, MA, MCE, MCIS, MCS, MEE, MS, MS Ch E, MS Mat SE, MS, MSEE, MSIE, MSME, MSMOT, PhD). *Application fee:* $40 ($50 for international students). Electronic applications accepted. *Application Contact:* Admissions Office, 612-625-3014, E-mail: gsadmit@tc.umn.edu. *Dean,* H. Ted Davis, 612-624-2006, Fax: 612-624-2841, E-mail: davis@itdean.umn.edu.

Center for the Development of Technological Leadership Students: 67 (8 women). 60 applicants, 63% accepted, 31 enrolled. *Faculty:* 24 part-time/adjunct (2 women). Expenses: Contact institution. *Financial support:* In 2006–07, 8 fellowships with tuition reimbursements (averaging $2,500 per year) were awarded; institutionally sponsored loans also available. Support available to part-time students. Financial award application deadline: 7/15; financial award applicants required to submit FAFSA. In 2006, 39 degrees awarded. *Degree program information:* Evening/weekend programs available. Offers infrastructure systems engineering (MS); management of technology (MSMOT). *Application deadline:* For fall admission, 6/1 priority date for domestic students. Applications are processed on a rolling basis. *Application fee:* $50 ($55 for international students). Electronic applications accepted. *Application Contact:* Ann Bechtell, Admission Associate, 612-624-5747, Fax: 612-624-7510, E-mail: mot-cdtl@umn.edu. *Director,* Dr. Massond Amin, 612-624-5747, Fax: 612-624-7510.

School of Mathematics Students: 102 full-time (26 women), 4 part-time (2 women); includes 1 minority (African American), 56 international. Average age 28. 198 applicants, 22% accepted. *Faculty:* 73 full-time (1 woman), 13 part-time/adjunct (2 women). Expenses: Contact institution. *Financial support:* In 2006–07, 85 students received support, including 5 research assistantships, 78 teaching assistantships; fellowships, career-related intern-

University of Minnesota, Twin Cities Campus (continued)

ships or fieldwork and institutionally sponsored loans also available. Financial award application deadline: 2/15. In 2006, 13 master's, 15 doctorates awarded. *Degree program information:* Part-time programs available. Offers mathematics (MS, PhD). *Application deadline:* For fall admission, 7/15 for domestic students. Applications are processed on a rolling basis. *Application fee:* $40 ($50 for international students). *Application Contact:* Donald Kahn, Director of Graduate Studies, 612-625-1306, E-mail: gradprog@math.umn.edu. *Head,* Naresh Jain, 612-625-5591, E-mail: dept@math.umn.edu.

School of Physics and Astronomy Students: 136 full-time (27 women), 1 part-time; includes 12 minority (6 African Americans, 3 Asian Americans or Pacific Islanders, 3 Hispanic Americans). Expenses: Contact institution. *Financial support:* Fellowships, research assistantships, teaching assistantships, Federal Work-Study and institutionally sponsored loans available. In 2006, 10 master's, 9 doctorates awarded. *Degree program information:* Part-time programs available. Offers astronomy (MS, PhD); astrophysics (MS, PhD); physics (MS, PhD). *Application deadline:* For fall admission, 7/15 for domestic students. Applications are processed on a rolling basis. *Application fee:* $40 ($50 for international students). *Application Contact:* Director of Graduate Studies, 612-624-6366. *Head,* Allen M. Goldman, 612-624-6062, Fax: 612-624-4578.

Law School Offers law (JD, LL M). Electronic applications accepted.

Medical School Students: 813 full-time (383 women); includes 132 minority (12 African Americans, 18 American Indian/Alaska Native, 86 Asian Americans or Pacific Islanders, 16 Hispanic Americans), 8 international. *Faculty:* 1,323 full-time. Expenses: Contact institution. *Financial support:* Fellowships, research assistantships, teaching assistantships, career-related internships or fieldwork, Federal Work-Study, institutionally sponsored loans, and tuition waivers (full and partial) available. *Degree program information:* Part-time and evening/weekend programs available. Offers medicine (MD, MA, MS, DPT, PhD); pharmacology (MS, PhD). *Application Contact:* Information Contact, 612-625-7977.

Graduate Programs in Medicine Expenses: Contact institution. *Financial support:* Fellowships, research assistantships, teaching assistantships, career-related internships or fieldwork, Federal Work-Study, institutionally sponsored loans, and tuition waivers (full and partial) available. *Degree program information:* Part-time and evening/weekend programs available. Offers biochemistry, molecular biology and biophysics (PhD); experimental surgery (MS); medicine (MA, MS, DPT, PhD); physical therapy (DPT); surgery (MS, PhD). *Application Contact:* Information Contact, 612-625-7977.

School of Dentistry Offers dentistry (DDS, MS, PhD, Certificate); endodontics (MS, Certificate); oral biology (MS, PhD); oral health services for older adults (geriatrics) (MS, Certificate); orthodontics (MS); pediatric dentistry (MS); periodontology (MS); prosthodontics (MS); temporomandibular joint disorders (MS).

School of Public Health *Degree program information:* Part-time programs available. Postbaccalaureate distance learning degree programs offered (minimal on-campus study). Offers biostatistics (MPH, MS, PhD); clinical research (MS); community health education (MPH); core concepts (Certificate); environmental and occupational epidemiology (MPH, MS, PhD); environmental chemistry (MS, PhD); environmental health policy (MPH, MS, PhD); environmental infectious diseases (MPH, MS, PhD); environmental toxicology (MPH, MS, PhD); epidemiology (MPH, PhD); food safety and biosecurity (Certificate); general environmental health (MPH, MS); health services research, policy, and administration (MS, PhD); healthcare management (MHA); industrial hygiene (MPH, MS, PhD); maternal and child health (MPH); occupational health and safety (Certificate); occupational health nursing (MPH, MS, PhD); occupational medicine (MPH); preparedness, response and recovery (Certificate); public health (MHA, MPH, MS, PhD, Certificate); public health administration and policy (MPH); public health nutrition (MPH); public health practice (MPH). Electronic applications accepted.

UNIVERSITY OF MISSISSIPPI, Oxford, University, MS 38677

General Information State-supported, coed, university. CGS member. *Enrollment:* 15,220 graduate, professional, and undergraduate students; 1,766 full-time matriculated graduate/professional students (900 women), 646 part-time matriculated graduate/professional students (433 women). *Enrollment by degree level:* 664 first professional, 1,068 master's, 618 doctoral, 62 other advanced degrees. *Graduate faculty:* 565 full-time (205 women), 116 part-time/adjunct (61 women). Tuition, state resident: full-time $4,602; part-time $256 per credit hour. Tuition, nonresident: full-time $10,566; part-time $587 per credit hour. *Graduate housing:* Rooms and/or apartments available to single and married students. Typical cost: $5,892 (including board) for single students. *Student services:* Campus employment opportunities, campus safety program, career counseling, free psychological counseling, international student services, low-cost health insurance, teacher training. *Library facilities:* J. D. Williams Library plus 3 others. *Online resources:* library catalog, web page, access to other libraries' catalogs. *Collection:* 1.3 million titles, 11,523 serial subscriptions. *Research affiliation:* Cumberland Emerging Technologies (pharmaceutics), Research Corporation (advancement of science), Combustion Research and Flow Technology, Inc. (fluid dynamics), Greenstone Industries (engineering), ElSohly Laboratories (national products research).

Computer facilities: Computer purchase and lease plans are available. 3,500 computers available on campus for general student use. A campuswide network can be accessed from student residence rooms and from off campus. Internet access and online class registration, application for admission, registration for orientation are available. *Web address:* http://www.olemiss.edu/.

General Application Contact: Dr. Christy M. Wyandt, Associate Dean of Graduate School, 662-915-7474, Fax: 662-915-7577, E-mail: cwyandt@olemiss.edu.

GRADUATE UNITS

Graduate School Students: 1,261 full-time (672 women), 645 part-time (432 women); includes 348 minority (290 African Americans, 5 American Indian/Alaska Native, 36 Asian Americans or Pacific Islanders, 17 Hispanic Americans), 294 international. 2,061 applicants, 43% accepted, 556 enrolled. *Faculty:* 539 full-time (196 women), 106 part-time/adjunct (58 women). Expenses: Contact institution. *Financial support:* Fellowships, research assistantships, teaching assistantships, career-related internships or fieldwork, Federal Work-Study, institutionally sponsored loans, scholarships/grants, tuition waivers (full), and unspecified assistantships available. Financial award application deadline: 3/1; financial award applicants required to submit FAFSA. In 2006, 275 first professional degrees, 506 master's, 97 doctorates, 33 other advanced degrees awarded. *Degree program information:* Part-time programs available. *Application deadline:* For fall admission, 4/1 for domestic students; for spring admission, 10/1 for domestic students. Applications are processed on a rolling basis. *Application fee:* $25. Electronic applications accepted. *Application Contact:* Dr. Christy M. Wyandt, Associate Dean, 662-915-7474, Fax: 662-915-7577, E-mail: cwyandt@olemiss.edu. *Dean,* Dr. Maurice Eftink, 662-915-7474, E-mail: eftink@olemiss.edu.

College of Liberal Arts Students: 432 full-time (216 women), 93 part-time (49 women); includes 84 minority (70 African Americans, 4 American Indian/Alaska Native, 3 Asian Americans or Pacific Islanders, 7 Hispanic Americans), 68 international. 639 applicants, 45% accepted, 171 enrolled. *Faculty:* 324 full-time (118 women), 59 part-time/adjunct (35 women). Expenses: Contact institution. *Financial support:* Fellowships, research assistantships, teaching assistantships, career-related internships or fieldwork, Federal Work-Study, institutionally sponsored loans, scholarships/grants, and unspecified assistantships available. Financial award application deadline: 3/1; financial award applicants required to submit FAFSA. In 2006, 87 master's, 42 doctorates awarded. *Degree program information:* Part-time programs available. Offers anthropology (MA); art education (MA); art history (MA); biology (MS, PhD); chemistry (MS, DA, PhD); classics (MA); clinical psychology (PhD); economics (MA, PhD); English (MA, PhD); experimental psychology (PhD); fine arts (MFA); French (MA); German (MA); history (MA, PhD); journalism (MA); liberal arts (MA, MFA, MM, MS, MSS, DA, PhD); mathematics (MA, MS, PhD); music (MM, DA); philosophy (MA); physics (MA, MS, PhD); political science (MA, PhD); psychology (MA); sociology (MA, MSS); Southern studies (MA); Spanish (MA); theatre arts (MFA). *Application deadline:* For fall admission, 4/1 for domestic students; for spring admission, 10/1 for domestic students. Applications are processed on a rolling basis. *Application fee:* $25. Electronic applications accepted. *Dean,* Dr. Glenn Hopkins, 662-915-7177, Fax: 662-915-5792, E-mail: ghopkins@olemiss.edu.

School of Accountancy Students: 76 full-time (34 women), 25 part-time (13 women); includes 9 minority (7 African Americans, 1 American Indian/Alaska Native, 1 Asian American or Pacific Islander), 6 international. 116 applicants, 78% accepted, 72 enrolled. *Faculty:* 11 full-time (4 women), 1 part-time/adjunct (0 women). Expenses: Contact institution. *Financial support:* Scholarships/grants available. Financial award application deadline: 3/1; financial award applicants required to submit FAFSA. In 2006, 62 master's, 3 doctorates awarded. Offers accountancy (M Acc, PhD); taxation accounting (M Tax). *Application deadline:* For fall admission, 4/1 for domestic students; for spring admission, 10/1 for domestic students. Applications are processed on a rolling basis. *Application fee:* $25. *Interim Dean,* Dr. Mark Wilder, 662-915-7468, Fax: 662-915-7483, E-mail: acwilder@olemiss.edu.

School of Applied Sciences Students: 66 full-time (54 women), 11 part-time (8 women); includes 17 minority (14 African Americans, 1 Asian American or Pacific Islander, 2 Hispanic Americans), 3 international. 127 applicants, 42% accepted, 35 enrolled. *Faculty:* 20 full-time (8 women), 9 part-time/adjunct (7 women). Expenses: Contact institution. *Financial support:* Scholarships/grants available. Financial award application deadline: 3/1; financial award applicants required to submit FAFSA. In 2006, 23 master's, 4 doctorates awarded. Offers applied sciences (MA, MS, PhD); communicative disorders (MS); exercise science (MA, MS); exercise science and leisure management (PhD); leisure management (MA); park and recreation management (MA); wellness (MS). *Application deadline:* For fall admission, 4/1 for domestic students; for spring admission, 10/1 for domestic students. Applications are processed on a rolling basis. *Application fee:* $25. Electronic applications accepted. *Dean,* Dr. Linda Chitwood, 662-915-7900, Fax: 662-915-5717, E-mail: lchitwoo@olemiss.edu.

School of Business Administration Students: 62 full-time (19 women), 26 part-time (7 women); includes 2 Asian Americans or Pacific Islanders, 17 international. 203 applicants, 39% accepted, 55 enrolled. *Faculty:* 44 full-time (13 women), 18 part-time/adjunct (5 women). Expenses: Contact institution. *Financial support:* Fellowships, career-related internships or fieldwork, scholarships/grants, tuition waivers (full), and unspecified assistantships available. Financial award application deadline: 3/1; financial award applicants required to submit FAFSA. In 2006, 36 master's, 11 doctorates awarded. Offers business administration (MBA, PhD); systems management (MS). *Application deadline:* For fall admission, 2/1 for domestic students; for spring admission, 10/1 for domestic students. Applications are processed on a rolling basis. *Application fee:* $25. Electronic applications accepted. *Dean,* Dr. Brian Reithel, 662-915-5820, Fax: 662-915-5821, E-mail: breithel@bus.olemiss.edu.

School of Education Students: 666 (509 women); includes 199 minority (182 African Americans, 12 Asian Americans or Pacific Islanders, 5 Hispanic Americans) 17 international. 702 applicants, 56% accepted, 306 enrolled. *Faculty:* 44 full-time (33 women), 10 part-time/adjunct (7 women). Expenses: Contact institution. *Financial support:* Scholarships/grants available. Financial award application deadline: 3/1; financial award applicants required to submit FAFSA. In 2006, 238 master's, 17 doctorates, 33 other advanced degrees awarded. Offers counselor education (M Ed, PhD, Specialist); curriculum and instruction (M Ed, Ed D, Ed S); education (PhD); educational leadership (PhD); educational leadership and counselor education (M Ed, MA, Ed D, Ed S); higher education/student personnel (MA); secondary education (MA). *Application deadline:* For fall admission, 4/1 for domestic students; for spring admission, 10/1 for domestic students. Applications are processed on a rolling basis. *Application fee:* $25. Electronic applications accepted. *Dean,* Dr. Tom Burnham, 662-915-7063, Fax: 662-915-7249, E-mail: tburnham@olemiss.edu.

School of Engineering Students: 140 full-time (32 women), 56 part-time (15 women); includes 15 minority (10 African Americans, 4 Asian Americans or Pacific Islanders, 1 Hispanic American), 122 international. 295 applicants, 49% accepted, 50 enrolled. *Faculty:* 48 full-time (6 women), 4 part-time/adjunct (1 woman). Expenses: Contact institution. *Financial support:* Scholarships/grants available. Financial award application deadline: 3/1; financial award applicants required to submit FAFSA. In 2006, 55 master's, 9 doctorates awarded. Offers computational engineering science (MS, PhD); engineering science (MS, PhD). *Application deadline:* For fall admission, 4/1 for domestic students; for spring admission, 10/1 for domestic students. Applications are processed on a rolling basis. *Application fee:* $25. Electronic applications accepted. *Dean,* Dr. Kai-Fong Lee, 662-915-7407, Fax: 662-915-1287; E-mail: engineer@olemiss.edu.

School of Pharmacy Students: 245 full-time (145 women), 8 part-time (3 women); includes 22 minority (7 African Americans, 13 Asian Americans or Pacific Islanders, 2 Hispanic Americans), 61 international. 239 applicants, 15% accepted, 21 enrolled. *Faculty:* 48 full-time (14 women), 5 part-time/adjunct (2 women). Expenses: Contact institution. *Financial support:* Scholarships/grants available. Financial award application deadline: 3/1; financial award applicants required to submit FAFSA. In 2006, 67 first professional degrees, 5 master's, 11 doctorates awarded. Offers medicinal chemistry (MS, PhD); pharmaceutics (MS, PhD); pharmacognosy (MS, PhD); pharmacology (MS, PhD); pharmacy (Pharm D, MS, PhD); pharmacy administration (MS, PhD). *Application deadline:* For fall admission, 4/1 for domestic students. Applications are processed on a rolling basis. *Application fee:* $25. *Dean,* Dr. Barbara G. Wells, 662-915-7265, Fax: 662-915-5704, E-mail: pharmacy@olemiss.edu.

School of Law Students: 505 full-time (228 women), 1 (woman) part-time; includes 62 minority (50 African Americans, 2 American Indian/Alaska Native, 7 Asian Americans or Pacific Islanders, 3 Hispanic Americans), 2 international. Average age 24. 1,069 applicants, 42% accepted, 160 enrolled. *Faculty:* 26 full-time (9 women), 10 part-time/adjunct (3 women). Expenses: Contact institution. *Financial support:* Fellowships, research assistantships, teaching assistantships, career-related internships or fieldwork, Federal Work-Study, institutionally sponsored loans, and scholarships/grants available. Support available to part-time students. Financial award application deadline: 3/1; financial award applicants required to submit FAFSA. In 2006, 208 degrees awarded. Offers law (JD). *Application deadline:* For fall admission, 4/1 for domestic students. *Application fee:* $40. *Application Contact:* Barbara Vinson, Coordinator of Admissions, 662-915-7361, E-mail: bvinson@olemiss.edu. *Dean,* Dr. Samuel Davis, 662-915-7361, Fax: 662-915-5313, E-mail: smdavis@olemiss.edu.

UNIVERSITY OF MISSISSIPPI MEDICAL CENTER, Jackson, MS 39216-4505

General Information State-supported, coed, upper-level institution. *Enrollment:* 2,092 graduate, professional, and undergraduate students; 1,384 full-time matriculated graduate/professional students (673 women), 137 part-time matriculated graduate/professional students (106 women). *Enrollment by degree level:* 531 first professional, 231 master's, 273 doctoral, 486 other advanced degrees. *Graduate faculty:* 564 full-time (210 women), 116 part-time/adjunct (45 women). Tuition, state resident: full-time $4,523. Tuition, nonresident: full-time $10,566. *Graduate housing:* Rooms and/or apartments available on a first-come, first-served basis to single and married students. *Student services:* Campus employment opportunities, campus safety program, career counseling, disabled student services, exercise/wellness program, free psychological counseling, international student services, low-cost health insurance, multicultural affairs office. *Library facilities:* Rowland Medical Library. *Online resources:* library catalog, web page, access to other libraries' catalogs. *Collection:* 310,016 titles, 2,732 serial subscriptions. *Research affiliation:* Gulf Coast Research Laboratory (microbiology), Oak Ridge National Laboratory (physiology, biomedical engineering), Catfish Genetics Research Unit (immunology), NASA–Stennis Space Center (imaging technology).

Computer facilities: Computer purchase and lease plans are available. 90 computers available on campus for general student use. A campuswide network can be accessed from off campus. Internet access is available. *Web address:* http://umc.edu/.

General Application Contact: Barbara Westerfield, Director, Student Records and Registrar, 601-984-1080, Fax: 601-984-1079, E-mail: bwesterfield@registrar.umsmed.edu.

GRADUATE UNITS

School of Dentistry Students: 124 full-time (55 women); includes 25 minority (18 African Americans, 4 Asian Americans or Pacific Islanders, 3 Hispanic Americans). Average age 25. 97 applicants, 32% accepted, 30 enrolled. *Faculty:* 28 full-time (6 women), 36 part-time/adjunct (7 women). Expenses: Contact institution. *Financial support:* Institutionally sponsored loans and scholarships/grants available. Financial award application deadline: 4/1; financial award applicants required to submit FAFSA. In 2006, 28 degrees awarded. Offers craniofacial and dental research (MS, PhD); dentistry (DMD, MS, PhD). *Application deadline:* For fall admission, 12/1 for domestic students. Applications are processed on a rolling basis. *Application fee:* $10. *Application Contact:* Barbara Westerfield, Director, Student Records and Registrar, 601-984-1080, Fax: 601-984-1079, E-mail: bwesterfield@registrar.umsmed.edu. *Dean,* Dr. James Hupp, 601-984-6000, Fax: 601-984-6014, E-mail: dentistry@sod.umsmed.edu.

School of Graduate Studies in the Health Sciences Students: 184 full-time (129 women), 106 part-time (83 women); includes 21 minority (3 African Americans, 15 Asian Americans or Pacific Islanders, 3 Hispanic Americans). Average age 28. 172 applicants, 54% accepted, 68 enrolled. *Faculty:* 101 full-time (28 women), 6 part-time/adjunct (3 women). Expenses: Contact institution. *Financial support:* In 2006–07, 71 students received support, including 71 research assistantships (averaging $16,234 per year). Financial award application deadline: 3/15; financial award applicants required to submit FAFSA. In 2006, 31 master's, 15 doctorates awarded. Offers anatomy (MS, PhD); biochemistry (MS, PhD); clinical health sciences (MS, PhD); health sciences (MS, MSN, PhD); maternal-fetal medicine (MS); microbiology (MS, PhD); nursing (MSN, PhD); pathology (MS, PhD); pharmacology (MS, PhD); physiology and biophysics (MS, PhD); preventive medicine (MS, PhD); toxicology (MS, PhD). *Application deadline:* Applications are processed on a rolling basis. *Application fee:* $10. *Application Contact:* Barbara Westerfield, Director, Student Records and Registrar, 601-984-1080, Fax: 601-984-1079, E-mail: bwesterfield@registrar.umsmed.edu. *Dean,* Dr. Joey Granger, 601-984-1600, Fax: 601-984-1637, E-mail: jgranger@pharmacology.umsmed.edu.

School of Health Related Professions Students: 180 full-time (146 women), 29 part-time (21 women); includes 64 minority (59 African Americans, 5 Asian Americans or Pacific Islanders). 67 applicants, 57% accepted, 36 enrolled. *Faculty:* 26 full-time (21 women). Expenses: Contact institution. *Financial support:* Institutionally sponsored loans and scholarships/grants available. Support available to part-time students. Financial award application deadline: 4/1; financial award applicants required to submit FAFSA. In 2006, 25 degrees awarded. *Degree program information:* Part-time programs available. Offers health related professions (MOT, MPT); occupational therapy (MOT); physical therapy (MPT). *Application deadline:* Applications are processed on a rolling basis. *Application fee:* $10. *Dean,* Dr. Ben L. Mitchell, 601-984-6300, Fax: 601-984-6344, E-mail: bmitchell@shrp.umsmed.edu.

School of Medicine Students: 407 full-time (176 women); includes 81 minority (32 African Americans, 1 American Indian/Alaska Native, 41 Asian Americans or Pacific Islanders, 7 Hispanic Americans). Average age 24. *Faculty:* 409 full-time (155 women), 74 part-time/adjunct (35 women). Expenses: Contact institution. *Financial support:* In 2006–07, 374 students received support. Institutionally sponsored loans and scholarships/grants available. Financial award application deadline: 4/1. In 2006, 103 degrees awarded. Offers medicine (MD). *Application deadline:* For fall admission, 9/15 for domestic students; for winter admission, 12/1 for domestic students. Applications are processed on a rolling basis. *Application fee:* $10. *Application Contact:* Dr. Steven T. Case, Associate Dean for Medical School Admissions, 601-984-5010, Fax: 601-984-5008, E-mail: admitmd@som.umsmed.edu. *Dean,* Dr. Daniel W. Jones, 601-984-1010.

UNIVERSITY OF MISSOURI–COLUMBIA, Columbia, MO 65211

General Information State-supported, coed, university. CGS member. *Enrollment:* 28,253 graduate, professional, and undergraduate students; 3,885 full-time matriculated graduate/professional students (2,134 women), 2,817 part-time matriculated graduate/professional students (1,749 women). *Enrollment by degree level:* 1,102 first professional, 1,427 master's, 2,101 doctoral, 72 other advanced degrees. *Graduate faculty:* 1,678 full-time (520 women), 70 part-time/adjunct (32 women). *Graduate housing:* Rooms and/or apartments available on a first-come, first-served basis to single and married students. Housing application deadline: 10/1. *Student services:* Campus employment opportunities, campus safety program, career counseling, child daycare facilities, disabled student services, exercise/wellness program, free psychological counseling, grant writing training, international student services, low-cost health insurance, multicultural affairs office, teacher training, writing training. *Library facilities:* Ellis Library plus 11 others. *Online resources:* library catalog, web page, access to other libraries' catalogs. *Collection:* 3.2 million titles, 36,244 serial subscriptions, 4,870 audiovisual materials.

Computer facilities: Computer purchase and lease plans are available. 1,615 computers available on campus for general student use. A campuswide network can be accessed from student residence rooms and from off campus. Internet access and online class registration, telephone registration are available. *Web address:* http://www.missouri.edu/.

General Application Contact: Norma J. Jackson, Coordinator of Graduate Student Affairs, 573-882-3292, E-mail: jacksonnj@missouri.edu.

GRADUATE UNITS

College of Veterinary Medicine Students: 321 full-time (217 women), 38 part-time (21 women); includes 24 minority (8 African Americans, 1 American Indian/Alaska Native, 6 Asian Americans or Pacific Islanders, 9 Hispanic Americans), 24 international. *Faculty:* 109 full-time (32 women), 3 part-time/adjunct (2 women). Expenses: Contact institution. *Financial support:* Fellowships, research assistantships, teaching assistantships, career-related internships or fieldwork, institutionally sponsored loans, and tuition waivers (full and partial) available. Support available to part-time students. In 2006, 64 first professional degrees, 9 master's, 9 doctorates awarded. Offers laboratory animal medicine (MS); pathobiology (MS, PhD); veterinary biomedical sciences (MS); veterinary clinical sciences (MS); veterinary medicine (DVM); veterinary medicine and surgery (MS); veterinary pathobiology (MS, PhD). *Application Contact:* Dr. Ronald Terjung, Associate Dean for Research and Postdoctoral Studies, 573-882-2635, E-mail: terjungr@missouri.edu. *Dean,* Dr. Joe Kornegay, 573-882-3768, Fax: 573-884-5044, E-mail: kornegayj@missouri.edu.

Graduate School Students: 4,605 full-time (2,478 women), 2,094 part-time (1,403 women); includes 548 minority (243 African Americans, 38 American Indian/Alaska Native, 157 Asian Americans or Pacific Islanders, 110 Hispanic Americans), 1,095 international. *Faculty:* 1,678 full-time (520 women), 70 part-time/adjunct (32 women). Expenses: Contact institution. *Financial support:* Fellowships with full and partial tuition reimbursements, research assistantships with full and partial tuition reimbursements, teaching assistantships with full and partial tuition reimbursements, career-related internships or fieldwork, institutionally sponsored loans, scholarships/grants, traineeships, and tuition waivers (full and partial) available. Support available to part-time students. In 2006, 1,335 master's, 277 doctorates, 84 other advanced degrees awarded. *Degree program information:* Part-time and evening/weekend programs available. Offers dispute resolution (LL M); genetics (PhD); health administration (MHA); health informatics (MHA); health services management (MHA). *Application deadline:* Applications are processed on a rolling basis. *Application fee:* $45 ($60 for international students). *Vice-Provost for Advanced Studies and Dean of the Graduate School,* Dr. Pamela Benoit, 573-884-4178, E-mail: benoitp@missouri.edu.

College of Agriculture, Food and Natural Resources Students: 286 full-time (126 women), 117 part-time (47 women); includes 18 minority (11 African Americans, 2 American Indian/Alaska Native, 4 Asian Americans or Pacific Islanders, 1 Hispanic American), 141 international. *Faculty:* 199 full-time (35 women), 3 part-time/adjunct (1 woman). Expenses: Contact institution. *Financial support:* Fellowships, research assistantships, teaching assistantships, institutionally sponsored loans available. In 2006, 48 master's, 29 doctorates awarded. *Degree program information:* Part-time programs available. Offers agricultural economics (MS, PhD); agricultural education (MS, PhD); agriculture, food and natural resources (MS, PhD); animal sciences (MS, PhD); entomology (MS, PhD); food science (MS, PhD); foods and food systems management (MS); horticulture (MS, PhD); human nutrition (MS); nutrition (MS, PhD); plant pathology and microbiology (MS, PhD); plant sciences (MS, PhD); rural sociology (MS, PhD). *Application deadline:* Applications are processed on a rolling basis. *Application fee:* $45 ($60 for international students). *Dean,* Dr. Thomas T. Payne, 573-882-3846, E-mail: paynet@missouri.edu.

College of Arts and Sciences Students: 948 full-time (438 women), 166 part-time (76 women); includes 75 minority (28 African Americans, 6 American Indian/Alaska Native, 22 Asian Americans or Pacific Islanders, 19 Hispanic Americans), 307 international. *Faculty:* 500 full-time (165 women), 8 part-time/adjunct (4 women). Expenses: Contact institution. *Financial support:* Fellowships, research assistantships, teaching assistantships, career-related internships or fieldwork, institutionally sponsored loans, and tuition waivers (full and partial) available. In 2006, 146 master's, 96 doctorates awarded. *Degree program information:* Part-time programs available. Offers analytical chemistry (MS, PhD); anthropology (MA, PhD); applied mathematics (MS); art (MFA); art history and archaeology (MA, PhD); arts and sciences (MA, MFA, MM, MS, MST, PhD); classical studies (MA, PhD); communication (MA, PhD); economics (MA, PhD); English (MA, PhD); evolutionary biology and ecology (MA, PhD); French (MA, PhD); genetic, cellular and developmental biology (MA, PhD); geography (MA); geological sciences (MS, PhD); German (MA); history (MA, PhD); inorganic chemistry (MS, PhD); literature (MA); mathematics (MA, MST, PhD); music (MA, MM); neurobiology and behavior (MA, PhD); organic chemistry (MS, PhD); philosophy (MA, PhD); physical chemistry (MS, PhD); physics and astronomy (MS, PhD); political science (MA, PhD); psychological sciences (MA, MS, PhD); religious studies (MA); sociology (MA, PhD); Spanish (MA, PhD); statistics (MA, PhD); teaching (MA); theatre (MA, PhD). *Application deadline:* Applications are processed on a rolling basis. *Application fee:* $45 ($60 for international students). *Dean,* Dr. Richard Schwartz, 573-882-4422.

College of Business Students: 325 full-time (139 women), 13 part-time (6 women); includes 15 minority (2 African Americans, 10 Asian Americans or Pacific Islanders, 3 Hispanic Americans), 83 international. *Faculty:* 62 full-time (15 women). Expenses: Contact institution. *Financial support:* Fellowships, research assistantships, teaching assistantships, institutionally sponsored loans available. In 2006, 186 master's, 13 doctorates awarded. *Degree program information:* Part-time programs available. Offers accountancy (M Acc, PhD); business (M Acc, MBA, PhD). *Application deadline:* Applications are processed on a rolling basis. *Application fee:* $45 ($60 for international students). *Dean,* Dr. Bruce Walker, 573-882-6688.

College of Education Students: 728 full-time (520 women), 743 part-time (570 women); includes 118 minority (58 African Americans, 12 American Indian/Alaska Native, 24 Asian Americans or Pacific Islanders, 24 Hispanic Americans), 100 international. *Faculty:* 96 full-time (47 women), 1 (woman) part-time/adjunct. Expenses: Contact institution. *Financial support:* Fellowships, research assistantships, teaching assistantships, institutionally sponsored loans and scholarships/grants available. In 2006, 456 master's, 68 doctorates, 25 other advanced degrees awarded. *Degree program information:* Part-time and evening/weekend programs available. Offers administration and supervision of special education (PhD); agricultural education (M Ed, PhD, Ed S); art education (M Ed, PhD, Ed S); behavior disorders (M Ed, PhD); business and office education (M Ed, PhD, Ed S); counseling psychology (M Ed, MA, PhD, Ed S); curriculum development of exceptional students (M Ed, PhD); early childhood education (M Ed, PhD, Ed S); early childhood special education (M Ed, PhD); education (M Ed, MA, Ed D, PhD, Ed S); education administration (M Ed, MA, Ed D, PhD, Ed S); educational psychology (M Ed, MA, PhD, Ed S); educational technology (M Ed, Ed S); elementary education (M Ed, PhD, Ed S); English education (M Ed, PhD, Ed S); foreign language education (M Ed, PhD, Ed S); general special education (M Ed, MA, PhD); health education and promotion (M Ed, PhD); higher and adult education (M Ed, MA, Ed D, PhD, Ed S); information science and learning technology (PhD); learning and instruction (M Ed); learning disabilities (M Ed, PhD); library science (MA); marketing education (M Ed, PhD, Ed S); mathematics education (M Ed, PhD, Ed S); mental retardation (M Ed, PhD); music education (M Ed, PhD, Ed S); reading education (M Ed, PhD, Ed S); school psychology (M Ed, MA, PhD, Ed S); science education (M Ed, PhD, Ed S); social studies education (M Ed, PhD, Ed S); vocational education (M Ed, PhD, Ed S). *Application deadline:* Applications are processed on a rolling basis. *Application fee:* $45 ($60 for international students). *Dean,* Dr. Carolyn D. Herrington, 573-882-8311.

College of Engineering Students: 255 full-time (54 women), 144 part-time (25 women); includes 23 minority (8 African Americans, 1 American Indian/Alaska Native, 8 Asian Americans or Pacific Islanders, 6 Hispanic Americans), 261 international. *Faculty:* 101 full-time (7 women). Expenses: Contact institution. *Financial support:* Fellowships, research assistantships, teaching assistantships, institutionally sponsored loans available. In 2006, 62 master's, 33 doctorates awarded. *Degree program information:* Part-time programs available. Offers agricultural engineering (MS); biological engineering (MS, PhD); chemical engineering (MS, PhD); civil engineering (MS, PhD); computer science (MS, PhD); electrical and computer engineering (MS, PhD); engineering (MS, PhD); environmental engineering (MS, PhD); geotechnical engineering (MS, PhD); industrial and manufacturing systems engineering (MS, PhD); mechanical and aerospace engineering (MS, PhD); nuclear power engineering (MS, PhD); structural engineering (MS, PhD); transportation and highway engineering (MS); water resources (MS, PhD). *Application deadline:* Applications are processed on a rolling basis. *Application fee:* $45 ($60 for international students). *Dean,* Dr. James Thompson, 573-882-4378, E-mail: thompsonje@missouri.edu.

College of Human Environmental Science Students: 88 full-time (65 women), 40 part-time (27 women); includes 16 minority (9 African Americans, 4 Asian Americans or Pacific Islanders, 3 Hispanic Americans), 28 international. *Faculty:* 49 full-time (32 women), 1 (woman) part-time/adjunct. Expenses: Contact institution. *Financial support:* Fellowships, research assistantships, teaching assistantships, institutionally sponsored loans available. In 2006, 14 master's, 6 doctorates awarded. *Degree program information:* Part-time programs available. Offers design with digital media (MA, MS); environmental design (MS); exercise physiology (MA, PhD); human development and family studies (MA, MS, PhD); human environmental science (MA, MS, PhD); nutritional sciences (MS, PhD); personal financial planning (MS); textile and apparel management (MA, MS). *Application deadline:* Applications are processed on a rolling basis. *Application fee:* $45 ($60 for international students). *Dean,* Dr. Stephen R. Jorgensen, 573-882-6227, E-mail: jorgens@missouri.edu.

Harry S Truman School of Public Affairs Students: 59 full-time (34 women), 37 part-time (22 women); includes 7 minority (4 African Americans, 2 Asian Americans or Pacific Islanders, 1 Hispanic American), 21 international. *Faculty:* 13 full-time (3 women). Expenses: Contact institution. *Financial support:* Fellowships, research assistantships, teaching assistantships, institutionally sponsored loans available. In 2006, 48 master's awarded. Offers public affairs (MPA). *Application deadline:* For fall admission, 2/15 priority date for domestic students. Applications are processed on a rolling basis. *Application fee:* $45 ($60 for international students). *Director of Graduate Studies,* Guy B. Adams, 573-882-5443, E-mail: adamsgb@missouri.edu.

School of Journalism Students: 193 full-time (127 women), 90 part-time (62 women); includes 37 minority (14 African Americans, 4 American Indian/Alaska Native, 6 Asian Americans or Pacific Islanders, 13 Hispanic Americans), 70 international. *Faculty:* 64 full-time (29 women). Expenses: Contact institution. *Financial support:* Fellowships, research assistantships, teaching assistantships, career-related internships or fieldwork and institutionally sponsored loans available. In 2006, 75 master's, 7 doctorates awarded. *Degree program information:* Part-time programs available. Offers journalism (MA, PhD). *Application deadline:* For fall admission, 2/1 priority date for domestic students; for winter admission, 9/1 priority date for domestic students. Applications are processed on a rolling basis. *Application fee:* $45 ($60 for international students). *Associate Dean,* Dr. Esther Thorson, 573-882-9590, E-mail: thorsone@missouri.edu.

School of Natural Resources Students: 67 full-time (21 women), 40 part-time (16 women); includes 7 minority (5 African Americans, 1 Asian American or Pacific Islander, 1 Hispanic American), 20 international. *Faculty:* 33 full-time (2 women), 1 part-time/adjunct (0 women). Expenses: Contact institution. *Financial support:* Fellowships, research assistantships, teaching assistantships, institutionally sponsored loans and scholarships/grants available. In 2006, 29 master's, 8 doctorates awarded. *Degree program information:* Part-time programs available. Offers atmospheric science (MS, PhD); fisheries and wildlife (MS, PhD); forestry (MS, PhD); natural resources (MS, PhD); parks, recreation and tourism (MS); soil science (MS, PhD). *Application deadline:* Applications are processed on a rolling basis. *Application fee:* $45 ($60 for international students). *Director,* Dr. Harold Gene Garrett, 573-882-6646, E-mail: garretth@missouri.edu.

School of Social Work Students: 153 full-time (138 women), 33 part-time (28 women); includes 16 minority (12 African Americans, 2 Asian Americans or Pacific Islanders, 2 Hispanic Americans), 8 international. *Faculty:* 17 full-time (12 women). Expenses: Contact institution. *Financial support:* Fellowships, research assistantships, teaching assistant-

University of Missouri–Columbia (continued)

ships, institutionally sponsored loans available. In 2006, 108 degrees awarded. *Degree program information:* Part-time programs available. Offers social work (MSW). *Application deadline:* For fall admission, 1/15 priority date for domestic students. Applications are processed on a rolling basis. *Application fee:* $45 ($60 for international students). *Director of Graduate Studies,* Dr. Colleen Galambos, 573-882-3701, E-mail: galambos@missouri.edu.

Sinclair School of Nursing Students: 59 full-time (52 women), 149 part-time (144 women); includes 16 minority (8 African Americans, 5 American Indian/Alaska Native, 2 Asian Americans or Pacific Islanders, 1 Hispanic American), 4 international. *Faculty:* 23 full-time (21 women). Expenses: Contact institution. *Financial support:* Fellowships, research assistantships, teaching assistantships, career-related internships or fieldwork, institutionally sponsored loans, traineeships, and tuition waivers (full) available. In 2006, 28 master's, 4 doctorates awarded. *Degree program information:* Part-time programs available. Offers nursing (MS, PhD). *Application deadline:* For fall admission, 2/1 priority date for domestic students. Applications are processed on a rolling basis. *Application fee:* $45 ($60 for international students). *Director of Graduate Studies,* Dr. Roxanne W. McDaniel, 573-882-0257, E-mail: mcdanielr@missouri.edu.

School of Health Professions Students: 97 full-time (85 women), 6 part-time (5 women); includes 6 minority (3 African Americans, 2 Asian Americans or Pacific Islanders, 1 Hispanic American), 2 international. *Faculty:* 36 full-time (23 women), 3 part-time/adjunct (all women). Expenses: Contact institution. *Financial support:* Fellowships, research assistantships, teaching assistantships, institutionally sponsored loans available. In 2006, 63 degrees awarded. Offers communication science and disorders (MHS); diagnostic medical ultrasound (MHS); health professions (MHS, MOT, MPT); occupational therapy (MOT); physical therapy (MPT). *Application deadline:* For fall admission, 3/1 priority date for domestic students. Applications are processed on a rolling basis. *Application fee:* $45 ($60 for international students). *Dean,* Dr. Richard E. Oliver, 573-884-6705, E-mail: oliverr@health.missouri.edu.

School of Law Students: 455 full-time (176 women), 12 part-time (6 women); includes 54 minority (23 African Americans, 5 American Indian/Alaska Native, 16 Asian Americans or Pacific Islanders, 10 Hispanic Americans), 11 international. Average age 25. *Faculty:* 32 full-time (10 women). Expenses: Contact institution. *Financial support:* Fellowships, Federal Work-Study and institutionally sponsored loans available. Financial award application deadline: 3/1; financial award applicants required to submit FAFSA. In 2006, 143 JDs, 11 master's awarded. Offers law (JD, LL M). *Application deadline:* For fall admission, 3/1 priority date for domestic students. Applications are processed on a rolling basis. *Dean,* Dr. R. Lawrence Dessem, 573-882-3246, E-mail: dessemrl@law.missouri.edu.

School of Medicine Students: 472 full-time (232 women), 5 part-time (3 women); includes 78 minority (27 African Americans, 2 American Indian/Alaska Native, 46 Asian Americans or Pacific Islanders, 3 Hispanic Americans), 33 international. *Faculty:* 375 full-time (96 women), 51 part-time/adjunct (20 women). Expenses: Contact institution. *Financial support:* Fellowships, research assistantships, teaching assistantships, career-related internships or fieldwork, institutionally sponsored loans, and scholarships/grants available. Support available to part-time students. Financial award applicants required to submit FAFSA. In 2006, 89 MDs, 7 master's, 11 doctorates awarded. *Degree program information:* Part-time programs available. Offers medicine (MD, MPH, MS, PhD). *Application deadline:* Applications are processed on a rolling basis. *Dean,* Dr. William M. Crist, 573-884-8733, E-mail: cristwm@missouri.edu.

Graduate Programs in Medicine Students: 101 full-time (50 women), 5 part-time (3 women); includes 12 minority (9 African Americans, 2 Asian Americans or Pacific Islanders, 1 Hispanic American), 32 international. *Faculty:* 72 full-time (19 women), 5 part-time/adjunct (2 women). Expenses: Contact institution. *Financial support:* Fellowships, research assistantships, teaching assistantships, career-related internships or fieldwork and institutionally sponsored loans available. In 2006, 7 master's, 11 doctorates awarded. *Degree program information:* Part-time programs available. Offers biochemistry (MS, PhD); medicine (MPH, MS, PhD); molecular microbiology and immunology (MS, PhD); pharmacology (MS, PhD); physiology (MS, PhD); public health (MPH). *Application deadline:* Applications are processed on a rolling basis. *Application fee:* $45 ($60 for international students). *Application Contact:* Dr. William Altemeier, Associate Dean for Students, 573-882-3490, E-mail: altemeirw@missouri.edu.

UNIVERSITY OF MISSOURI–KANSAS CITY, Kansas City, MO 64110-2499

General Information State-supported, coed, university. CGS member. *Enrollment:* 14,213 graduate, professional, and undergraduate students; 2,616 full-time matriculated graduate/professional students (1,395 women), 1,979 part-time matriculated graduate/professional students (1,185 women). *Enrollment by degree level:* 1,502 first professional, 2,477 master's, 522 doctoral, 94 other advanced degrees. *Graduate faculty:* 662 full-time (276 women), 439 part-time/adjunct (227 women). Tuition, state resident: full-time $4,975; part-time $276 per credit. Tuition, nonresident: full-time $12,847; part-time $713 per credit. *Required fees:* $595; $595 per year. *Graduate housing:* Room and/or apartments available on a first-come, first-served basis to single students; on-campus housing not available to married students. Typical cost: $6,823 (including board). Room and board charges vary according to board plan and housing facility selected. *Student services:* Campus employment opportunities, campus safety program, career counseling, child daycare facilities, disabled student services, exercise/wellness program, free psychological counseling, international student services, multicultural affairs office, writing training. *Library facilities:* Miller-Nichols Library plus 3 others. *Online resources:* library catalog, web page, access to other libraries' catalogs. *Collection:* 1.3 million titles, 25,022 serial subscriptions, 421,713 audiovisual materials. *Research affiliation:* Midwest Research Institute (health sciences), Veterans Administration Hospital (health sciences), Truman Medical Center (health sciences), Children's Mercy Hospital (health sciences), St. Luke's Hospital (health sciences).

Computer facilities: Computer purchase and lease plans are available. 671 computers available on campus for general student use. A campuswide network can be accessed from student residence rooms and from off campus. Internet access and online class registration are available. *Web address:* http://www.umkc.edu/.

General Application Contact: Jennifer DeHaemeas, Director of Admissions, 816-235-1111, Fax: 816-235-5544, E-mail: admit@umkc.edu.

GRADUATE UNITS

College of Arts and Sciences Students: 303 full-time (200 women), 312 part-time (211 women); includes 122 minority (90 African Americans, 1 American Indian/Alaska Native, 12 Asian Americans or Pacific Islanders, 19 Hispanic Americans), 26 international. Average age 33. 616 applicants, 71% accepted, 313 enrolled. *Faculty:* 208 full-time (84 women), 201 part-time/adjunct (113 women). Expenses: Contact institution. *Financial support:* In 2006–07, 2 fellowships with partial tuition reimbursements (averaging $33,000 per year), 25 research assistantships with full and partial tuition reimbursements (averaging $14,657 per year), 190 teaching assistantships with full and partial tuition reimbursements (averaging $12,938 per year) were awarded; career-related internships or fieldwork, Federal Work-Study, institutionally sponsored loans, scholarships/grants, and tuition waivers (full and partial) also available. Support available to part-time students. Financial award applicants required to submit FAFSA. In 2006, 189 master's, 4 doctorates awarded. *Degree program information:* Part-time and evening/weekend programs available. Offers acting (MFA); analytical chemistry (MS, PhD); art history (MA, PhD); arts and sciences (MA, MFA, MS, MSW, PhD); criminal justice and criminology (MS); design technology (MFA); economics (MA, PhD); English (MA, PhD); environmental and urban geosciences (MS); geosciences (PhD); history (MA, PhD); inorganic chemistry (MS, PhD); mathematics and statistics (MA, MS, PhD); organic chemistry (MS, PhD); physical chemistry (MS, PhD); physics (MS, PhD); political science (MA, PhD); polymer chemistry (MS, PhD); psychology (MA, PhD); Romance languages and literatures (MA); sociology (MA, PhD); studio art (MA); theatre (MA). *Application deadline:* Applications are processed on a rolling basis. *Application fee:* $35 ($50 for international students). Electronic applications accepted. *Dean,* Dr. Karen Vorst, 816-235-1307, Fax: 816-235-1308.

School of Social Work Students: 118 full-time (103 women), 41 part-time (33 women); includes 46 minority (36 African Americans, 1 American Indian/Alaska Native, 3 Asian Americans or Pacific Islanders, 6 Hispanic Americans), 3 international. Average age 34. 118 applicants, 87% accepted, 83 enrolled. *Faculty:* 7 full-time (all women), 16 part-time/adjunct (12 women). Expenses: Contact institution. *Financial support:* In 2006–07, 37 students received support, including 4 research assistantships with partial tuition reimbursements available (averaging $11,280 per year); career-related internships or fieldwork and institutionally sponsored loans also available. In 2006, 66 degrees awarded. *Degree program information:* Part-time and evening/weekend programs available. Offers social work (MSW). *Application deadline:* For fall admission, 4/1 priority date for domestic students, 7/31 priority date for international students; for winter admission, 12/15 priority date for international students; for spring admission, 9/1 priority date for domestic students. Applications are processed on a rolling basis. *Application fee:* $35 ($50 for international students). *Chair,* Dr. Walter Boulden, 816-235-6308, E-mail: bouldenw@umkc.edu.

Conservatory of Music Students: 138 full-time (78 women), 100 part-time (50 women); includes 14 minority (3 African Americans, 3 American Indian/Alaska Native, 6 Asian Americans or Pacific Islanders, 2 Hispanic Americans), 54 international. Average age 29. 228 applicants, 56% accepted, 74 enrolled. *Faculty:* 52 full-time (21 women), 35 part-time/adjunct (17 women). Expenses: Contact institution. *Financial support:* In 2006–07, 135 students received support, including 95 teaching assistantships with partial tuition reimbursements available (averaging $8,526 per year); fellowships with partial tuition reimbursements available, career-related internships or fieldwork, Federal Work-Study, institutionally sponsored loans, scholarships/grants, tuition waivers (partial), and unspecified assistantships also available. Support available to part-time students. In 2006, 36 master's, 9 doctorates awarded. *Degree program information:* Part-time programs available. Offers composition (MM, DMA); conducting (MM, DMA); music (MA); music education (MME, PhD); music history and literature (MM); music theory (MM); performance (MM, DMA). *Application deadline:* For fall admission, 3/1 priority date for domestic students, 2/1 for international students; for winter admission, 1/5 priority date for domestic students, 11/1 for international students; for spring admission, 4/15 for domestic students. *Application fee:* $35 ($50 for international students). *Application Contact:* James Elswick, Associate Director, 816-235-2932, Fax: 816-235-5264, E-mail: cadmissions@umkc.edu. *Dean,* Dr. Randall G. Pembrook, 816-235-2731, Fax: 816-235-5265, E-mail: pembrookr@umkc.edu.

Henry W. Bloch School of Business and Public Administration Students: 201 full-time (104 women), 395 part-time (177 women); includes 80 minority (41 African Americans, 5 American Indian/Alaska Native, 21 Asian Americans or Pacific Islanders, 13 Hispanic Americans), 41 international. Average age 30. 464 applicants, 63% accepted, 226 enrolled. *Faculty:* 42 full-time (11 women), 16 part-time/adjunct (7 women). Expenses: Contact institution. *Financial support:* In 2006–07, 407 students received support, including 26 research assistantships with partial tuition reimbursements available (averaging $10,483 per year), 3 teaching assistantships with partial tuition reimbursements available (averaging $11,080 per year); fellowships, career-related internships or fieldwork, Federal Work-Study, institutionally sponsored loans, scholarships/grants, tuition waivers (full and partial), and unspecified assistantships also available. Support available to part-time students. Financial award application deadline: 3/1; financial award applicants required to submit FAFSA. In 2006, 186 degrees awarded. *Degree program information:* Part-time and evening/weekend programs available. Offers accounting (MS); business administration (MBA); public affairs (MPA, PhD). *Application deadline:* For fall admission, 5/1 priority date for domestic students, 4/1 priority date for international students; for winter admission, 10/1 priority date for domestic students, 9/1 priority date for international students. Applications are processed on a rolling basis. *Application fee:* $35 ($50 for international students). Electronic applications accepted. *Application Contact:* 816-235-1111, E-mail: admit@umkc.edu. *Dean,* Dr. O. Homer Erekson, 816-235-2204, Fax: 816-235-2206, E-mail: ereksonh@umkc.edu.

School of Biological Sciences Students: 18 full-time (10 women), 27 part-time (17 women); includes 4 minority (2 African Americans, 1 American Indian/Alaska Native, 1 Asian American or Pacific Islander), 2 international. Average age 33. 35 applicants, 71% accepted, 15 enrolled. *Faculty:* 37 full-time (7 women), 4 part-time/adjunct (2 women). Expenses: Contact institution. *Financial support:* In 2006–07, 42 research assistantships with full tuition reimbursements (averaging $24,638 per year), 7 teaching assistantships with full tuition reimbursements (averaging $21,999 per year) were awarded; Federal Work-Study, institutionally sponsored loans, scholarships/grants, tuition waivers (full and partial), and unspecified assistantships also available. Support available to part-time students. In 2006, 16 degrees awarded. *Degree program information:* Part-time and evening/weekend programs available. Offers biology (MA); cell biology and biophysics (PhD); cellular and molecular biology (MS); molecular biology and biochemistry (PhD). *Application deadline:* Applications are processed on a rolling basis. *Application fee:* $35 ($50 for international students). *Application Contact:* Laura Batenic, Information Contact, 816-235-2352, Fax: 816-235-5158, E-mail: batenicl@umkc.edu. *Dean,* Dr. Lawrence A. Dreyfus, 816-235-5246, Fax: 816-235-5158, E-mail: dreyfusl@umkc.edu.

School of Computing and Engineering Students: 169 full-time (34 women), 98 part-time (23 women); includes 11 minority (6 African Americans, 4 Asian Americans or Pacific Islanders, 1 Hispanic American), 210 international. Average age 26. 229 applicants, 71% accepted, 70 enrolled. *Faculty:* 35 full-time (5 women), 17 part-time/adjunct (0 women). Expenses: Contact institution. *Financial support:* In 2006–07, 12 research assistantships with partial tuition reimbursements (averaging $13,190 per year), 25 teaching assistantships with partial tuition reimbursements (averaging $10,777 per year) were awarded; fellowships, career-related internships or fieldwork, Federal Work-Study, scholarships/grants, tuition waivers (partial), and unspecified assistantships also available. Support available to part-time students. Financial award application deadline: 3/1; financial award applicants required to submit FAFSA. In 2006, 76 degrees awarded. *Degree program information:* Part-time programs available. Offers civil engineering (MS); computer and electrical engineering (PhD); computer science (MS); computer science and informatics (PhD); computing (PhD); electrical engineering (MS); engineering (PhD); mechanical engineering (MS); telecommunications (PhD). PhD offered through the School of Graduate Studies. *Application deadline:* For fall admission, 4/1 priority date for domestic students, 4/1 for international students; for spring admission, 10/1 for domestic and international students. Applications are processed on a rolling basis. *Application fee:* $35 ($50 for international students). *Application Contact:* Pamela Bernard, Manager, Student Recruitment and Enrollment Services, 816-235-1512, Fax: 816-235-5159, E-mail: bernardp@umkc.edu. *Dean,* Dr. Khosrow Sohraby, 816-235-2399, Fax: 816-235-5159, E-mail: sohrabyk@umkc.edu.

School of Dentistry Students: 424 full-time (155 women), 34 part-time (27 women); includes 60 minority (10 African Americans, 2 American Indian/Alaska Native, 38 Asian Americans or Pacific Islanders, 10 Hispanic Americans), 12 international. Average age 27. 687 applicants, 17% accepted, 110 enrolled. *Faculty:* 102 full-time (36 women), 77 part-time/adjunct (22 women). Expenses: Contact institution. *Financial support:* In 2006–07, 8 fellowships (averaging $42,540 per year), 28 research assistantships (averaging $21,670 per year) were awarded; career-related internships or fieldwork, Federal Work-Study, institutionally sponsored loans, and tuition waivers (full and partial) also available. Support available to part-time students. Financial award applicants required to submit FAFSA. In 2006, 92 DDSs, 25 other advanced degrees awarded. Offers advanced education in dentistry (Graduate Dental Certificate); dental hygiene education (MS); dental specialties (Graduate Dental Certificate); dentistry (DDS); diagnostic sciences (Graduate Dental Certificate); oral and maxillofacial surgery (Graduate Dental Certificate); oral biology (MS, PhD); orthodontics and dentofacial orthopedics (Graduate Dental Certificate); pediatric dentistry (Graduate Dental Certificate); periodontics (Graduate Dental Certificate); prosthodontics (Graduate Dental Certificate). *Application fee:* $35 ($50 for international students). *Application Contact:* 816-235-2080. *Dean,* Dr. Michael Reed, 816-235-2010, E-mail: reedm@umkc.edu.

School of Education Students: 182 full-time (151 women), 470 part-time (344 women); includes 148 minority (117 African Americans, 5 American Indian/Alaska Native, 8 Asian Americans or Pacific Islanders, 18 Hispanic Americans), 9 international. Average age 34. 560 applicants, 79% accepted, 253 enrolled. *Faculty:* 59 full-time (46 women), 39 part-time/adjunct (29 women). Expenses: Contact institution. *Financial support:* In 2006–07, 361 students received support, including 13 research assistantships with partial tuition reimbursements available (averaging $10,560 per year); fellowships with full tuition reimbursements available, teaching assistantships, career-related internships or fieldwork, Federal Work-Study, institutionally sponsored loans, and tuition waivers (full and partial) also available. Support available to part-time students. Financial award application deadline: 3/1. In 2006, 196 master's, 4 doctorates, 41 other advanced degrees awarded. *Degree program information:* Part-time and evening/weekend programs available. Offers administration (Ed D); counseling and guidance (MA, Ed S); counseling psychology (PhD); curriculum and instruction (MA, Ed S); education (PhD); educational administration (Ed S); reading education (MA, Ed S); special education (MA). *Application deadline:* For fall admission, 4/1 priority date for domestic students, 4/1 for international students; for winter admission, 10/1 priority date for domestic students, 10/1 for international students; for spring admission, 10/1 priority date for domestic students, 10/1 for international students. Applications are processed on a rolling basis. *Application fee:* $35 ($50 for international students). *Application Contact:* Dr. Lori Reesor, Assistant Dean, 816-235-1473, Fax: 816-235-5270, E-mail: reesorl@umkc.edu. *Dean,* Dr. Linda Edwards, 816-235-2236, Fax: 816-235-5270, E-mail: edwardsli@umkc.edu.

School of Graduate Studies Students: 68 full-time (34 women), 264 part-time (112 women); includes 29 minority (17 African Americans, 2 American Indian/Alaska Native, 5 Asian Americans or Pacific Islanders, 5 Hispanic Americans), 127 international. Average age 36. 240 applicants, 27% accepted, 47 enrolled. Expenses: Contact institution. *Financial support:* In 2006–07, 78 fellowships with partial tuition reimbursements, 87 research assistantships with partial tuition reimbursements (averaging $7,151 per year), 209 teaching assistantships with partial tuition reimbursements (averaging $12,147 per year) were awarded; career-related internships or fieldwork, Federal Work-Study, tuition waivers (partial), and unspecified assistantships also available. Support available to part-time students. Financial award application deadline: 2/28. In 2006, 43 degrees awarded. Offers interdisciplinary studies (PhD). Students select two or more subjects. *Application deadline:* For fall admission, 1/15 priority date for domestic students; for spring admission, 9/1 priority date for domestic students. Applications are processed on a rolling basis. *Application fee:* $35 ($50 for international students). Electronic applications accepted. *Application Contact:* Qunicy Bennett, Administrative Assistant, 816-235-1559, Fax: 816-235-1310, E-mail: bennettq@umkc.edu. *Dean,* Dr. Ronald MacQuarrie, 816-235-1301, Fax: 816-235-1310, E-mail: macquarrier@umkc.edu.

School of Law Students: 496 full-time (214 women), 41 part-time (20 women); includes 45 minority (15 African Americans, 3 American Indian/Alaska Native, 17 Asian Americans or Pacific Islanders, 10 Hispanic Americans), 6 international. Average age 27. 1,327 applicants, 40% accepted, 216 enrolled. *Faculty:* 34 full-time (13 women). Expenses: Contact institution. *Financial support:* In 2006–07, 162 students received support, including 1 research assistantship (averaging $54,667 per year), 38 teaching assistantships with partial tuition reimbursements available (averaging $2,587 per year); fellowships with partial tuition reimbursements available, career-related internships or fieldwork, Federal Work-Study, institutionally sponsored loans, scholarships/grants, and tuition waivers (full and partial) also available. Support available to part-time students. In 2006, 156 JDs, 22 master's awarded. *Degree program information:* Part-time programs available. Offers law (JD, LL M). *Application deadline:* For fall admission, 4/1 priority date for domestic students. Applications are processed on a rolling basis. *Application fee:* $50. Electronic applications accepted. *Application Contact:* Debbie Brooks, Director of Admissions, 816-325-1644, Fax: 816-235-5276, E-mail: brooksdv@umkc.edu. *Dean,* Ellen Y. Suni, 816-235-1677, Fax: 816-235-5276, E-mail: sunie@umkc.edu.

School of Medicine Students: 363 full-time (220 women); includes 157 minority (15 African Americans, 3 American Indian/Alaska Native, 130 Asian Americans or Pacific Islanders, 9 Hispanic Americans). Average age 22. 586 applicants, 23% accepted, 102 enrolled. *Faculty:* 26 full-time (9 women), 6 part-time/adjunct (2 women). Expenses: Contact institution. *Financial support:* In 2006–07, 323 students received support, including 3 fellowships (averaging $31,364 per year), 13 research assistantships (averaging $12,740 per year); career-related internships or fieldwork, Federal Work-Study, institutionally sponsored loans, scholarships/grants, and tuition waivers (partial) also available. Financial award application deadline: 3/15; financial award applicants required to submit FAFSA. In 2006, 90 degrees awarded. Offers medicine (MD). *Application deadline:* For fall admission, 12/1 for domestic students. *Application fee:* $50. *Application Contact:* MaryAnne Morgenegg, Selection Administrative Assistant, 816-235-1870, Fax: 816-235-6579, E-mail: morgeneggm@umkc.edu. *Dean,* Dr. Betty Drees, 816-235-1808, E-mail: dreesb@umkc.edu.

School of Nursing Students: 36 full-time (all women), 213 part-time (202 women); includes 23 minority (6 African Americans, 2 American Indian/Alaska Native, 6 Asian Americans or Pacific Islanders, 9 Hispanic Americans). Average age 36. 121 applicants, 72% accepted, 71 enrolled. *Faculty:* 31 full-time (26 women), 32 part-time/adjunct (31 women). Expenses: Contact institution. *Financial support:* In 2006–07, 30 students received support, including 6 research assistantships (averaging $3,450 per year), 7 teaching assistantships with partial tuition reimbursements available (averaging $12,650 per year); fellowships, career-related internships or fieldwork, Federal Work-Study, institutionally sponsored loans, and tuition waivers (full and partial) also available. Support available to part-time students. Financial award application deadline: 6/30; financial award applicants required to submit FAFSA. In 2006, 69 master's, 1 doctorate awarded. *Degree program information:* Part-time programs available. Postbaccalaureate distance learning degree programs offered (minimal on-campus study). Offers adult clinical nurse specialist (MSN); family nurse practitioner (MSN); neonatal nurse practitioner (MSN); nurse educator (MSN); nurse executive (MSN); nursing (PhD); pediatric nurse practitioner (MSN). *Application deadline:* For fall admission, 2/1 priority date for domestic students; for spring admission, 9/15 priority date for domestic students. *Application fee:* $25. *Application Contact:* Leah Wilder, Coordinator for Admissions and Recruitment, 816-235-5768, Fax: 816-235-1701, E-mail: wilderl@umkc.edu. *Dean,* Dr. Lora Lacey-Haun, 816-235-1700, Fax: 816-235-1701, E-mail: lacey-haunc@umkc.edu.

School of Pharmacy Students: 238 full-time (159 women), 5 part-time (2 women); includes 30 minority (10 African Americans, 1 American Indian/Alaska Native, 17 Asian Americans or Pacific Islanders, 2 Hispanic Americans), 7 international. Average age 26. 567 applicants, 39% accepted, 213 enrolled. *Faculty:* 34 full-time (17 women), 11 part-time/adjunct (4 women). Expenses: Contact institution. *Financial support:* In 2006–07, 2 fellowships (averaging $28,200 per year), 17 research assistantships with full and partial tuition reimbursements (averaging $13,800 per year), 10 teaching assistantships with full tuition reimbursements (averaging $12,819 per year) were awarded; career-related internships or fieldwork, Federal Work-Study, institutionally sponsored loans, tuition waivers (full and partial), and unspecified assistantships also available. Financial award application deadline: 3/1; financial award applicants required to submit FAFSA. In 2006, 77 first professional degrees, 3 master's awarded. Postbaccalaureate distance learning degree programs offered (minimal on-campus study). Offers pharmaceutical sciences (MS, PhD); pharmacy (Pharm D). *Application deadline:* For fall admission, 3/1 for domestic students; for spring admission, 10/1 for domestic students. Applications are processed on a rolling basis. *Application fee:* $35 ($50 for international students). Electronic applications accepted. *Application Contact:* Shelly M. Janasz, Director, Student Services, 816-235-2400, Fax: 816-235-5190, E-mail: janaszs@umkc.edu. *Dean,* Dr. Robert W. Piepho, 816-235-1609, Fax: 816-235-5190, E-mail: piephor@umkc.edu.

UNIVERSITY OF MISSOURI–ROLLA, Rolla, MO 65409-0910

General Information State-supported, coed, university. *Enrollment:* 5,858 graduate, professional, and undergraduate students; 847 full-time matriculated graduate/professional students (186 women), 373 part-time matriculated graduate/professional students (74 women). *Enrollment by degree level:* 843 master's, 377 doctoral. *Graduate faculty:* 238 full-time (13 women), 4 part-time/adjunct (0 women). *Graduate housing:* Rooms and/or apartments available on a first-come, first-served basis to single and married students. *Student services:* Campus employment opportunities, campus safety program, career counseling, exercise/wellness program, free psychological counseling, international student services, low-cost health insurance, multicultural affairs office. *Library facilities:* Curtis Laws Wilson Library. *Online resources:* library catalog, web page. *Collection:* 255,768 titles, 1,495 serial subscriptions, 6,353 audiovisual materials.

Computer facilities: 800 computers available on campus for general student use. A campuswide network can be accessed from student residence rooms and from off campus. Internet access and online class registration are available. *Web address:* http://www.umr.edu/.

General Application Contact: Debbie Schwertz, Admissions Coordinator, 573-341-6013, Fax: 573-341-6271, E-mail: schwartz@umr.edu.

GRADUATE UNITS

Graduate School Students: 847 full-time (186 women), 373 part-time (74 women); includes 92 minority (42 African Americans, 3 American Indian/Alaska Native, 30 Asian Americans or Pacific Islanders, 17 Hispanic Americans), 500 international. Average age 30. 2,659 applicants, 56% accepted, 348 enrolled. *Faculty:* 238 full-time (13 women), 4 part-time/adjunct (0 women). Expenses: Contact institution. *Financial support:* In 2006–07, 68 fellowships with full and partial tuition reimbursements, 390 research assistantships with full and partial tuition reimbursements, 194 teaching assistantships with full and partial tuition reimbursements were awarded; career-related internships or fieldwork, Federal Work-Study, institutionally sponsored loans, traineeships, and tuition waivers (partial) also available. Support available to part-time students. In 2006, 502 master's, 61 doctorates awarded. *Degree program information:* Part-time and evening/weekend programs available. Offers applied and environmental biology (MS); applied mathematics (MS); chemistry (MS, PhD); computer science (MS, PhD); information science and technology (MS); mathematics (MST, PhD); mathematics education (MST); physics (MS, PhD); statistics (PhD). *Application deadline:* Applications are processed on a rolling basis. *Application fee:* $50. Electronic applications accepted. *Application Contact:* Debbie Schwertz, Admissions Coordinator, 573-341-6013, Fax: 573-341-6271, E-mail: schwartz@umr.edu. *Provost and Executive Vice Chancellor,* Dr. Warren K. Wray, 573-341-4138, Fax: 573-341-6306.

School of Engineering Students: 897; includes 67 minority (32 African Americans, 2 American Indian/Alaska Native, 23 Asian Americans or Pacific Islanders, 10 Hispanic Americans), 306 international. Average age 30. 1,783 applicants, 53% accepted, 189 enrolled. *Faculty:* 112 full-time (5 women), 2 part-time/adjunct (0 women). Expenses: Contact institution. *Financial support:* In 2006–07, 85 fellowships with full and partial tuition reimbursements, 267 research assistantships with full and partial tuition reimbursements, 109 teaching assistantships with full and partial tuition reimbursements were awarded; career-related internships or fieldwork, Federal Work-Study, institutionally sponsored loans, traineeships, and tuition waivers (partial) also available. Support available to part-time students. In 2006, 381 master's, 31 doctorates awarded. *Degree program information:* Part-time and evening/weekend programs available. Offers aerospace engineering (MS, PhD); ceramic engineering (MS, DE, PhD); chemical engineering (MS, DE, PhD); civil engineering (MS, DE, PhD); computer engineering (MS, DE, PhD); construction engineering (MS, DE, PhD); electrical engineering (MS, DE, PhD); engineering (M Eng, MS, DE, PhD); engineering management (MS, DE, PhD); environmental engineering (MS); fluid mechanics (MS, DE, PhD); geochemistry (MS, PhD); geological engineering (MS, DE, PhD); geology (MS, PhD); geology and geophysics (MS, PhD); geophysics (MS, PhD); geotechnical engineering (MS, DE, PhD); groundwater and environmental geology (MS, PhD); hydrology and hydraulic engineering (MS, DE, PhD); manufacturing engineering (M Eng, MS); mechanical engineering (MS, DE, PhD); metallurgical engineering (MS, PhD); mining engineering (MS, DE, PhD); nuclear engineering (MS, DE, PhD); petroleum engineering (MS, DE, PhD); systems engineering (MS, PhD). *Application deadline:* Applications are processed on a rolling basis. *Application fee:* $50. Electronic applications accepted. *Dean,* Dr. O. Robert Mitchell, 573-341-4151, Fax: 573-341-4979, E-mail: mit@umr.edu.

UNIVERSITY OF MISSOURI–ST. LOUIS, St. Louis, MO 63121

General Information State-supported, coed, university. CGS member. *Enrollment:* 15,540 graduate, professional, and undergraduate students; 694 full-time matriculated graduate/professional students (407 women), 2,093 part-time matriculated graduate/professional students (1,366 women). *Enrollment by degree level:* 2,205 master's, 516 doctoral, 66 other advanced degrees. *Graduate faculty:* 347 full-time (139 women), 50 part-time/adjunct (15 women). Tuition, state resident: part-time $332 per credit hour. Tuition, nonresident: part-time $770 per credit hour. *Graduate housing:* Rooms and/or apartments available on a first-come, first-served basis to single and married students. Housing application deadline: 7/1. *Student services:* Campus employment opportunities, campus safety program, career counseling, child daycare facilities, disabled student services, exercise/wellness program, free psychological counseling, grant writing training, international student services, low-cost health insurance, multicultural affairs office. *Library facilities:* Thomas Jefferson Library plus 2 others. *Online resources:* library catalog, web page, access to other libraries' catalogs. *Collection:* 1.2 million titles, 3,174 serial subscriptions, 3,902 audiovisual materials. *Research affiliation:* Donald Danforth Plant Science Center (biology), Missouri Botanical Garden (biology), St. Louis Zoo (biology).

Computer facilities: Computer purchase and lease plans are available. 1,000 computers available on campus for general student use. A campuswide network can be accessed from student residence rooms and from off campus. Internet access and online class registration are available. *Web address:* http://www.umsl.edu/.

General Application Contact: Graduate Admissions, 314-516-5458, Fax: 314-516-6996, E-mail: gradadm@umsl.edu.

GRADUATE UNITS

College of Arts and Sciences Students: 336 full-time (179 women), 351 part-time (170 women); includes 69 minority (38 African Americans, 2 American Indian/Alaska Native, 22 Asian Americans or Pacific Islanders, 7 Hispanic Americans), 129 international. Average age 31. *Faculty:* 179 full-time (60 women), 32 part-time/adjunct (6 women). Expenses: Contact institution. *Financial support:* In 2006–07, 1 fellowship with full and partial tuition reimbursement (averaging $30,000 per year), 83 research assistantships with full and partial tuition reimbursements (averaging $11,256 per year), 132 teaching assistantships with full and partial tuition reimbursements (averaging $10,202 per year) were awarded; career-related internships or fieldwork, Federal Work-Study, health care benefits, and unspecified assistantships also available. Support available to part-time students. In 2006, 191 master's, 31 doctorates awarded. *Degree program information:* Part-time and evening/weekend programs available. Offers advanced social perspective (MA); American literature (MA); American politics (MA); applied mathematics (MA, PhD); applied physics (MS); arts and sciences (MA, MFA, MS, MSW, PhD, Certificate, Graduate Certificate); astrophysics (MS); behavioral neuroscience (PhD); biology (MS, PhD); biotechnology (Certificate); chemistry (MS, PhD); clinical psychology respecialization (Certificate); community conflict intervention (MA); community psychology (PhD); comparative politics (MA); computer science (MS, PhD); creative writing (MFA); criminology and criminal justice (MA, PhD); English (MA); English literature (MA); general economics (MA); general psychology (MA); industrial/organizational psychology (PhD); international politics (MA); linguistics (MA); managerial economics (Certificate); mathematics (PhD); museum studies (MA, Certificate); philosophy (MA); physics (PhD); political process and behavior (MA); political science (PhD); program design and evaluation research (MA); public administration and public policy (MA); social policy planning and administration (MA); teaching of writing (Graduate Certificate); tropical biology and conservation (Certificate); urban and regional politics (MA). *Application deadline:* Applications are processed on a rolling basis. *Application fee:* $35 ($40 for international students). Electronic applications accepted. *Application Contact:* Graduate Admissions, 314-516-5458, Fax: 314-516-6996, E-mail: gradadm@umsl.edu. *Dean,* Dr. Mark Burkholder, 314-516-5501.

School of Social Work Students: 53 full-time (50 women), 38 part-time (36 women); includes 13 minority (11 African Americans, 1 Asian American or Pacific Islander, 1 Hispanic American), 1 international. Average age 31. *Faculty:* 9 full-time (8 women). Expenses: Contact institution. *Financial support:* In 2006–07, 10 teaching assistantships with full tuition reimbursements (averaging $10,125 per year) were awarded; research assistantships. In 2006, 34 degrees awarded. Offers social work (MSW). *Application deadline:* For fall admission, 2/15 for domestic students. *Application fee:* $35 ($40 for international students). *Application Contact:* 314-516-5458, Fax: 314-516-6996, E-mail: gradadm@umsl.edu. *Director,* Dr. Lois Pierce, 314-516-6364, Fax: 314-516-5816, E-mail: socialwork@umsl.edu.

College of Business Administration Students: 182 full-time (81 women), 332 part-time (140 women); includes 54 minority (18 African Americans, 1 American Indian/Alaska Native, 32 Asian Americans or Pacific Islanders, 3 Hispanic Americans), 116 international. Average age 34. *Faculty:* 41 full-time (12 women), 6 part-time/adjunct (3 women). Expenses: Contact institution. *Financial support:* In 2006–07, 17 research assistantships with full and

University of Missouri–St. Louis (continued)

partial tuition reimbursements (averaging $9,857 per year), 7 teaching assistantships with full and partial tuition reimbursements (averaging $8,643 per year) were awarded; career-related internships or fieldwork, Federal Work-Study, and institutionally sponsored loans also available. Support available to part-time students. Financial award application deadline: 4/1; financial award applicants required to submit FAFSA. In 2006, 171 master's, 1 doctorate awarded. *Degree program information:* Part-time and evening/weekend programs available. Offers accounting (MBA); business administration (Certificate); finance (MBA); human resource management (Certificate); information systems (MSMIS, PhD); logistics and supply chain management (MBA, PhD, Certificate); management (MBA); marketing (MBA); marketing management (Certificate); operations (MBA); quantitative management science (MBA); telecommunications management (Certificate). *Application deadline:* For fall admission, 7/1 priority date for domestic students; for spring admission, 11/1 priority date for domestic students. Applications are processed on a rolling basis. *Application fee:* $35 ($40 for international students). Electronic applications accepted. *Application Contact:* 314-516-5458, Fax: 314-516-6996, E-mail: gradadm@umsl.edu. *Assistant Director,* Karl Kottemann, 314-516-5885, Fax: 314-516-6420, E-mail: mba@umsl.edu.

College of Education Students: 178 full-time (123 women), 927 part-time (685 women); includes 271 minority (233 African Americans, 2 American Indian/Alaska Native, 11 Asian Americans or Pacific Islanders, 25 Hispanic Americans), 15 international. Average age 37. *Faculty:* 52 full-time (26 women), 9 part-time/adjunct (5 women). Expenses: Contact institution. *Financial support:* In 2006–07, 24 research assistantships with full tuition reimbursements (averaging $11,161 per year), 9 teaching assistantships with full tuition reimbursements (averaging $14,200 per year) were awarded. Support available to part-time students. In 2006, 247 master's, 16 doctorates, 40 other advanced degrees awarded. *Degree program information:* Part-time and evening/weekend programs available. Offers education (M Ed, Ed D, PhD, Certificate, Ed S). *Application deadline:* Applications are processed on a rolling basis. *Application fee:* $35 ($40 for international students). Electronic applications accepted. *Application Contact:* 314-516-5458, Fax: 314-516-6996, E-mail: gradadm@umsl.edu. *Director of Graduate Studies,* Dr. Kathleen Haywood, 314-516-5483, Fax: 314-516-5227, E-mail: kathleen_haywood@umsl.edu.

Division of Counseling Students: 58 full-time (49 women), 177 part-time (141 women); includes 50 minority (39 African Americans, 4 Asian Americans or Pacific Islanders, 7 Hispanic Americans), 5 international. Average age 32. *Faculty:* 7 full-time (3 women). Expenses: Contact institution. *Financial support:* In 2006–07, 2 research assistantships with full and partial tuition reimbursements (averaging $18,000 per year) were awarded. In 2006, 47 master's awarded. Offers community counseling (M Ed); elementary school counseling (M Ed); secondary school counseling (M Ed). *Application deadline:* Applications are processed on a rolling basis. *Application fee:* $35 ($40 for international students). Electronic applications accepted. *Application Contact:* 314-516-5458, Fax: 314-516-6996, E-mail: gradadm@umsl.edu. *Chair,* Dr. Mark Pope, 314-516-5782.

Division of Educational Leadership and Policy Studies Students: 37 full-time (27 women), 325 part-time (214 women); includes 130 minority (118 African Americans, 1 American Indian/Alaska Native, 4 Asian Americans or Pacific Islanders, 7 Hispanic Americans), 4 international. Average age 39. *Faculty:* 15 full-time (8 women), 2 part-time/adjunct (0 women). Expenses: Contact institution. *Financial support:* In 2006–07, 6 research assistantships (averaging $8,235 per year) were awarded. In 2006, 64 master's, 12 doctorates, 32 other advanced degrees awarded. Offers adult and higher education (M Ed, Ed D); educational administration (M Ed, Ed D, Ed S); educational leadership and policy studies (PhD); institutional research (Certificate). *Application deadline:* Applications are processed on a rolling basis. *Application fee:* $35 ($40 for international students). Electronic applications accepted. *Application Contact:* 314-516-5458, Fax: 314-516-6996, E-mail: gradadm@umsl.edu. *Chair,* Dr. E. Paulette Savage, 514-516-5944.

Division of Educational Psychology, Research, and Evaluation Students: 15 full-time (13 women), 21 part-time (18 women); includes 1 minority (African American), 2 international. Average age 33. *Faculty:* 10 full-time (2 women), 2 part-time/adjunct (1 woman). Expenses: Contact institution. *Financial support:* In 2006–07, 1 research assistantship (averaging $25,500 per year) was awarded; teaching assistantships. In 2006, 5 degrees awarded. Offers education (Ed D); educational psychology (PhD); school psychology (Certificate, Ed S). *Application deadline:* For fall admission, 2/15 for domestic students; for spring admission, 9/15 for domestic students. *Application fee:* $35 ($40 for international students). Electronic applications accepted. *Application Contact:* 314-516-5458, Fax: 314-516-6996, E-mail: gradadm@umsl.edu. *Chairperson,* Dr. Matthew Keefer, 314-516-5783, Fax: 314-516-5784, E-mail: keefer@umsl.edu.

Division of Teaching and Learning Students: 118 full-time (84 women), 353 part-time (311 women); includes 90 minority (75 African Americans, 1 American Indian/Alaska Native, 3 Asian Americans or Pacific Islanders, 11 Hispanic Americans), 4 international. Average age 36. *Faculty:* 20 full-time (13 women), 5 part-time/adjunct (4 women). Expenses: Contact institution. *Financial support:* In 2006–07, 9 teaching assistantships (averaging $14,250 per year) were awarded; research assistantships. In 2006, 136 master's, 3 doctorates awarded. Offers elementary education (M Ed); secondary education (M Ed); special education (M Ed); teaching-learning processes (Ed D, PhD). *Application deadline:* For fall admission, 7/15 for domestic students; for spring admission, 12/15 for domestic students. *Application Contact:* 314-516-5458, Fax: 314-516-6996, E-mail: gadadm@umsl.edu. *Chair,* Dr. Gayle Wilkinson, 314-516-5791.

College of Fine Arts and Communication Students: 11 full-time (8 women), 49 part-time (34 women); includes 6 minority (5 African Americans, 1 Hispanic American), 4 international. Average age 29. *Faculty:* 16 full-time (7 women). Expenses: Contact institution. *Financial support:* In 2006–07, 4 teaching assistantships (averaging $12,000 per year) were awarded. In 2006, 21 master's awarded. Offers communication (MA); fine arts and communication (MA, MME); music education (MME). *Application deadline:* For fall admission, 7/15 for domestic students; for winter admission, 12/15 for domestic students. *Application fee:* $35 ($40 for international students). *Application Contact:* 314-516-5458, Fax: 314-516-6996, E-mail: gradadm@umsl.edu. *Dean,* Dr. John Hylton, 314-516-5911, Fax: 314-516-5910.

College of Nursing Students: 22 full-time (19 women), 154 part-time (152 women); includes 23 minority (17 African Americans, 3 Asian Americans or Pacific Islanders, 3 Hispanic Americans), 1 international. Average age 36. *Faculty:* 11 full-time (all women), 2 part-time/adjunct (both women). Expenses: Contact institution. *Financial support:* In 2006–07, 2 research assistantships with full and partial tuition reimbursements (averaging $11,520 per year) were awarded; teaching assistantships with full and partial tuition reimbursements. In 2006, 39 master's, 6 doctorates awarded. Offers nurse practitioner (Certificate); nursing (MSN, PhD). *Application deadline:* For fall admission, 4/1 for domestic students; for winter admission, 10/30 for domestic students; for spring admission, 7/1 for domestic students. Applications are processed on a rolling basis. *Application fee:* $35 ($40 for international students). Electronic applications accepted. *Application Contact:* 314-516-5458, Fax: 314-516-6996, E-mail: gradadm@umsl.edu. *Dean,* Dean Juliann Sebastian, 314-516-6066.

College of Optometry Students: 178 full-time (103 women), 2 part-time (1 woman); includes 19 minority (7 African Americans, 2 American Indian/Alaska Native, 7 Asian Americans or Pacific Islanders, 3 Hispanic Americans), 9 international. Average age 23. 364 applicants, 25% accepted, 45 enrolled. *Faculty:* 23 full-time (6 women), 14 part-time/adjunct (4 women). Expenses: Contact institution. *Financial support:* In 2006–07, 165 students received support, including 4 research assistantships with full and partial tuition reimbursements available (averaging $500 per year), 5 teaching assistantships with full and partial tuition reimbursements available (averaging $16,100 per year); fellowships with full tuition reimbursements available, Federal Work-Study, institutionally sponsored loans, scholarships/grants, tuition waivers (partial), and unspecified assistantships also available. Financial award applicants required to submit FAFSA. In 2006, 44 ODs, 1 doctorate awarded. Offers optometry (OD, MS, PhD); vision science (MS, PhD). *Application deadline:* For fall admission, 2/15 for domestic and international students. Applications are processed on a rolling basis. *Application fee:* $50. Electronic applications accepted. *Application Contact:* Dr. Edward S. Bennett, Director, Student Services, 314-516-6263, Fax: 314-516-6708, E-mail: optstuff@umsl.edu. *Dean,* Dr. Larry J. Davis, 314-516-5606, Fax: 314-516-6708, E-mail: optometry@umsl.edu.

Graduate School Students: 26 full-time (17 women), 77 part-time (47 women); includes 26 minority (21 African Americans, 1 American Indian/Alaska Native, 3 Asian Americans or Pacific Islanders, 1 Hispanic American), 5 international. Average age 39. *Faculty:* 347 full-time (139 women), 48 part-time/adjunct (13 women). Expenses: Contact institution. *Financial support:* In 2006–07, 23 fellowships with full tuition reimbursements (averaging $23,222 per year), 7 research assistantships with full tuition reimbursements (averaging $11,529 per year) were awarded; teaching assistantships with full tuition reimbursements, career-related internships or fieldwork, Federal Work-Study, and institutionally sponsored loans also available. Support available to part-time students. Financial award applicants required to submit FAFSA. In 2006, 26 degrees awarded. *Degree program information:* Part-time and evening/weekend programs available. Offers gerontology (MS, Certificate); health policy (MPPA); local government management (MPPA); long term care administration (Certificate); managing human resources and organization (MPPA); nonprofit organization management (MPPA); nonprofit organization management and leadership (Certificate); policy research and analysis (MPPA); public sector human resources management (MPPA). *Application deadline:* For fall admission, 7/15 priority date for domestic students; for spring admission, 12/15 priority date for domestic students. Applications are processed on a rolling basis. *Application fee:* $35 ($40 for international students). Electronic applications accepted. *Application Contact:* Graduate Admissions, 314-516-5458, Fax: 314-516-6996, E-mail: gradadm@umsl.edu. *Dean,* Dr. Judith Walker de Félix, 314-516-5898, Fax: 314-516-7017, E-mail: graduate@umsl.edu.

See Close-Up on page 1095.

UNIVERSITY OF MOBILE, Mobile, AL 36613

General Information Independent-religious, coed, comprehensive institution. *Enrollment:* 1,639 graduate, professional, and undergraduate students; 62 full-time matriculated graduate/professional students (54 women), 132 part-time matriculated graduate/professional students (105 women). *Enrollment by degree level:* 194 master's. *Graduate faculty:* 28 full-time (15 women), 36 part-time/adjunct (17 women). *Tuition:* Part-time $340 per hour. *Required fees:* $121 per term. Tuition and fees vary according to course load. *Graduate housing:* Room and/or apartments available on a first-come, first-served basis to single students; on-campus housing not available to married students. Housing application deadline: 8/15. *Student services:* Campus employment opportunities, career counseling, free psychological counseling, international student services, low-cost health insurance. *Library facilities:* J. L. Bedsole Library. *Online resources:* library catalog, web page. *Collection:* 81,852 titles, 401 serial subscriptions, 1,680 audiovisual materials.

Computer facilities: 110 computers available on campus for general student use. A campuswide network can be accessed from off campus. Internet access is available. *Web address:* http://www.umobile.edu/.

General Application Contact: Dr. Kaye F. Brown, Associate Vice President for Academic Affairs, 251-442-2289, Fax: 251-442-2523, E-mail: kayeb@mail.umobile.edu.

GRADUATE UNITS

Graduate Programs Students: 62 full-time (54 women), 132 part-time (105 women); includes 86 minority (85 African Americans, 1 American Indian/Alaska Native), 2 international. Average age 36. *Faculty:* 28 full-time (15 women), 36 part-time/adjunct (17 women). Expenses: Contact institution. *Financial support:* Career-related internships or fieldwork and Federal Work-Study available. Support available to part-time students. Financial award application deadline: 8/1. In 2006, 67 degrees awarded. *Degree program information:* Part-time and evening/weekend programs available. Offers biblical/theological studies (MA); business administration (MBA); education (MA); marriage and family counseling (MA); nursing (MSN); religious studies (MA). *Application deadline:* For fall admission, 8/3 priority date for domestic students. Applications are processed on a rolling basis. *Application fee:* $40 ($50 for international students). *Dean,* Dr. Kaye F. Brown, 251-442-2289, Fax: 251-442-2523, E-mail: kayebrown@free.umobile.edu.

THE UNIVERSITY OF MONTANA, Missoula, MT 59812-0002

General Information State-supported, coed, university. CGS member. *Graduate housing:* Rooms and/or apartments available on a first-come, first-served basis to single and married students. *Research affiliation:* Arthur Carhart National Wilderness Training Center (environmental), Nature Center at Ft. Missoula Museum (environmental), World Trade Center (business), Rocky Mountain National Laboratories (medical), Community Hospital Medical Center (medical), Aldo Leopold Wilderness Institute (forestry).

GRADUATE UNITS

Graduate School *Degree program information:* Part-time programs available. Offers individual interdisciplinary programs (IIP) (PhD); interdisciplinary studies (MIS).

College of Arts and Sciences *Degree program information:* Part-time programs available. Offers anthropology (MA); applied geoscience (PhD); arts and sciences (MA, MFA, MPA, MS, PhD, Ed S); biochemistry (MS); biochemistry and microbiology (MS, PhD); chemistry (MS, PhD); clinical psychology (PhD); communication studies (MA); computer science (MS); creative writing (MFA); criminology (MA); cultural heritage (MA); cultural heritage studies (PhD); ecology of infectious disease (PhD); economics (MA); environmental studies (MS); experimental psychology (PhD); fiction (MFA); forensic anthropology (MA); French (MA); geography (MA); geology (MS, PhD); German (MA); historical anthropology (PhD); history (MA, PhD); integrative microbiology and biochemistry (PhD); linguistics (MA); literature (MA); mathematics (MA, PhD); mathematics education (MA); microbial ecology (MS, PhD); microbiology (MS); non-fiction (MFA); organismal biology and ecology (MS, PhD); philosophy (MA); poetry (MFA); political science (MA); public administration (MPA); rural and environmental change (MA); school psychology (MA, PhD, Ed S); sociology (MA); Spanish (MA); teaching (MA).

College of Forestry and Conservation Offers ecosystem management (MEM, MS); fish and wildlife biology (PhD); forestry (MS, PhD); recreation management (MS); resource conservation (MS); wildlife biology (MS).

School of Business Administration *Degree program information:* Part-time and evening/weekend programs available. Postbaccalaureate distance learning degree programs offered (minimal on-campus study). Offers accounting (M Acct); business administration (M Acct, MBA).

School of Education *Degree program information:* Part-time programs available. Offers counselor education (MA, Ed D, Ed S); counselor education and supervision (Ed D); curriculum and instruction (M Ed, Ed D); education (M Ed, MA, MS, Ed D, Ed S); educational leadership (M Ed, Ed D, Ed S); exercise science (MS); health and human performance (MS); health promotion (MS); mental health counseling (MA); school counseling (MA).

School of Fine Arts Offers fine arts (MA, MFA); music (MM).

School of Journalism Offers journalism (MA).

School of Pharmacy and Allied Health Sciences Offers pharmaceutical sciences (MS); pharmacology (PhD); pharmacy and allied health sciences (MS, DPT, PhD); toxicology (MS, PhD). Electronic applications accepted.

Programs in Public Health Offers public health (MPH, CPH).

School of Law Offers law (JD).

School of Physical Therapy and Rehabilitation Science Offers physical therapy (DPT). Electronic applications accepted.

UNIVERSITY OF MONTEVALLO, Montevallo, AL 35115

General Information State-supported, coed, comprehensive institution. *Graduate housing:* Room and/or apartments guaranteed to single students; on-campus housing not available to married students.

GRADUATE UNITS

College of Arts and Sciences *Degree program information:* Part-time and evening/weekend programs available. Offers arts and sciences (MA, MS); English (MA); speech pathology and audiology (MS).

College of Education *Degree program information:* Part-time and evening/weekend programs available. Offers early childhood education (M Ed); education (M Ed, Ed S);

educational administration (M Ed, Ed S); elementary education (M Ed); guidance and counseling (M Ed); secondary education (M Ed); teacher leader (Ed S).

College of Fine Arts *Degree program information:* Part-time programs available. Offers fine arts (MM); music (MM).

UNIVERSITY OF NEBRASKA AT KEARNEY, Kearney, NE 68849-0001

General Information State-supported, coed, comprehensive institution. CGS member. *Enrollment:* 6,468 graduate, professional, and undergraduate students; 141 full-time matriculated graduate/professional students (99 women), 657 part-time matriculated graduate/professional students (422 women). *Enrollment by degree level:* 724 master's, 74 other advanced degrees. *Graduate faculty:* 109 full-time (52 women). Tuition, state resident: part-time $161 per hour. Tuition, nonresident: part-time $332 per hour. *Required fees:* $57 per hour. *Graduate housing:* Rooms and/or apartments available on a first-come, first-served basis to single and married students. Typical cost: $1,469 per year for single students. Room charges vary according to board plan and housing facility selected. *Student services:* Campus employment opportunities, campus safety program, career counseling, child daycare facilities, disabled student services, exercise/wellness program, free psychological counseling, grant writing training, international student services, low-cost health insurance, multicultural affairs office, teacher training, writing training. *Library facilities:* Calvin T. Ryan Library. *Online resources:* library catalog, web page, access to other libraries' catalogs. *Collection:* 320,915 titles, 1,657 serial subscriptions.

Computer facilities: 277 computers available on campus for general student use. A campuswide network can be accessed from student residence rooms and from off campus. Internet access and online class registration, online grade reports are available. *Web address:* http://www.unk.edu/.

General Application Contact: Dr. Kenya Taylor, Graduate Dean, 308-856-8843, Fax: 308-865-8837, E-mail: taylorks@unk.edu.

GRADUATE UNITS

College of Graduate Study Students: 141 full-time (99 women), 657 part-time (422 women); includes 25 minority (8 African Americans, 1 American Indian/Alaska Native, 6 Asian Americans or Pacific Islanders, 10 Hispanic Americans), 26 international. 255 applicants, 69% accepted. *Faculty:* 109 full-time (52 women). Expenses: Contact institution. *Financial support:* In 2006–07, 37 research assistantships with full tuition reimbursements (averaging $8,200 per year), 24 teaching assistantships with full tuition reimbursements (averaging $8,200 per year) were awarded; career-related internships or fieldwork, scholarships/grants, and unspecified assistantships also available. Support available to part-time students. Financial award application deadline: 3/1; financial award applicants required to submit FAFSA. In 2006, 210 master's, 18 other advanced degrees awarded. *Degree program information:* Part-time and evening/weekend programs available. *Application fee:* $45. *Application Contact:* Linda Johnson, Director, Graduate Admissions and Programs, 308-865-8841, Fax: 308-865-8837, E-mail: johnsonli@unk.edu. *Graduate Dean,* Dr. Kenya Taylor, 308-856-8843, Fax: 308-865-8837, E-mail: taylorks@unk.edu.

College of Business and Technology Students: 17 full-time (10 women), 21 part-time (9 women), 5 international. 12 applicants, 75% accepted. *Faculty:* 19 full-time (9 women). Expenses: Contact institution. *Financial support:* In 2006–07, 9 research assistantships with full tuition reimbursements (averaging $8,200 per year) were awarded; career-related internships or fieldwork, scholarships/grants, and unspecified assistantships also available. Support available to part-time students. Financial award application deadline: 3/1; financial award applicants required to submit FAFSA. In 2006, 13 degrees awarded. *Degree program information:* Part-time and evening/weekend programs available. Offers business administration (MBA); business and technology (MBA). *Application deadline:* For fall admission, 5/1 for domestic and international students; for spring admission, 8/15 for domestic students, 8/1 for international students. *Application fee:* $45. Electronic applications accepted. *Dean,* Dr. Bruce A. Forster, 308-865-8342, E-mail: forsterba@unk.edu.

College of Education Students: 98 full-time (74 women), 471 part-time (311 women); includes 12 minority (2 African Americans, 1 Asian American or Pacific Islander, 9 Hispanic Americans), 16 international. 255 applicants, 69% accepted. *Faculty:* 27 full-time (15 women). Expenses: Contact institution. *Financial support:* In 2006–07, 22 research assistantships with full tuition reimbursements (averaging $8,200 per year), 11 teaching assistantships with full tuition reimbursements (averaging $8,200 per year) were awarded; career-related internships or fieldwork, scholarships/grants, and unspecified assistantships also available. Support available to part-time students. Financial award application deadline: 3/1; financial award applicants required to submit FAFSA. In 2006, 210 master's, 18 other advanced degrees awarded. *Degree program information:* Part-time and evening/weekend programs available. Offers adapted physical education (MA Ed); counseling (MS Ed, Ed S); curriculum and instruction (MS Ed); education (MA Ed, MS Ed, Ed S); educational administration (MA Ed, Ed S); exercise science (MA Ed); instructional technology (MS Ed); master teacher (MA Ed); reading education (MA Ed); school psychology (Ed S); special education (MA Ed); speech pathology (MS Ed); supervisor (MA Ed). *Application deadline:* Applications are processed on a rolling basis. *Application fee:* $45. Electronic applications accepted. *Dean,* Dr. Ed Scantling, 308-865-8502, E-mail: scantlinge@unk.edu.

College of Fine Arts and Humanities Students: 4 full-time (3 women), 10 part-time (8 women), 1 international. 6 applicants, 50% accepted. *Faculty:* 38 full-time (18 women). Expenses: Contact institution. *Financial support:* In 2006–07, 1 research assistantship (averaging $8,200 per year), 5 teaching assistantships with full tuition reimbursements (averaging $8,200 per year) were awarded; career-related internships or fieldwork, scholarships/grants, and unspecified assistantships also available. Support available to part-time students. Financial award application deadline: 3/1; financial award applicants required to submit FAFSA. In 2006, 9 degrees awarded. *Degree program information:* Part-time and evening/weekend programs available. Offers art education (MA Ed); creative writing (MA); fine arts and humanities (MA, MA Ed); French (MA Ed); German (MA Ed); literature (MA); music education (MA Ed); Spanish (MA Ed). *Application deadline:* For fall admission, 5/1 for domestic and international students; for spring admission, 8/15 for domestic and international students. *Application fee:* $45. Electronic applications accepted. *Dean,* Dr. William Jurma.

College of Natural and Social Sciences Students: 22 full-time (12 women), 155 part-time (94 women); includes 13 minority (6 African Americans, 1 American Indian/Alaska Native, 5 Asian Americans or Pacific Islanders, 1 Hispanic American), 4 international. 64 applicants, 78% accepted. *Faculty:* 23 full-time (10 women). Expenses: Contact institution. *Financial support:* In 2006–07, 5 research assistantships with full tuition reimbursements (averaging $8,200 per year), 8 teaching assistantships with full tuition reimbursements (averaging $8,200 per year) were awarded; career-related internships or fieldwork, scholarships/grants, and unspecified assistantships also available. Support available to part-time students. Financial award application deadline: 3/1; financial award applicants required to submit FAFSA. In 2006, 26 degrees awarded. *Degree program information:* Part-time and evening/weekend programs available. Offers biology (MS); history (MA); natural and social sciences (MA, MS, MS Ed); science education (MS Ed). *Application deadline:* For fall admission, 5/1 for domestic and international students; for spring admission, 8/15 for domestic and international students. *Application fee:* $45. Electronic applications accepted. *Dean,* Dr. Francis Harrold, 308-865-8518.

UNIVERSITY OF NEBRASKA AT OMAHA, Omaha, NE 68182

General Information State-supported, coed, university. CGS member. *Enrollment:* 13,906 graduate, professional, and undergraduate students; 565 full-time matriculated graduate/professional students (344 women), 1,716 part-time matriculated graduate/professional students (1,047 women). *Graduate faculty:* 338 full-time (114 women). *Graduate housing:* Room and/or apartments available on a first-come, first-served basis to single students; on-campus housing not available to married students. *Student services:* Campus employment opportunities, campus safety program, career counseling, child daycare facilities, disabled student services, exercise/wellness program, free psychological counseling, grant writing training, international student services, low-cost health insurance, multicultural affairs office, teacher training, writing training. *Library facilities:* Criss Library. *Online resources:* library catalog, web page, access to other libraries' catalogs. *Collection:* 700,000 titles, 37,000 serial subscriptions.

Computer facilities: 2,000 computers available on campus for general student use. A campuswide network can be accessed from student residence rooms and from off campus. Internet access and online class registration are available. *Web address:* http://www.unomaha.edu/.

General Application Contact: Penny Harmoney, Director, Graduate Studies, 402-554-2341, Fax: 402-554-3143, E-mail: graduate@unomaha.edu.

GRADUATE UNITS

Graduate Studies and Research Students: 624 full-time (357 women), 1,663 part-time (1,035 women); includes 184 minority (86 African Americans, 3 American Indian/Alaska Native, 52 Asian Americans or Pacific Islanders, 43 Hispanic Americans), 178 international. Average age 31. 1,351 applicants, 60% accepted, 514 enrolled. *Faculty:* 367 full-time (153 women). Expenses: Contact institution. *Financial support:* In 2006–07, 1,249 students received support; fellowships, research assistantships with tuition reimbursements available, teaching assistantships with tuition reimbursements available, career-related internships or fieldwork, Federal Work-Study, institutionally sponsored loans, tuition waivers (partial), and unspecified assistantships available. Support available to part-time students. Financial award application deadline: 3/1; financial award applicants required to submit FAFSA. In 2006, 655 master's, 13 doctorates, 35 other advanced degrees awarded. *Degree program information:* Part-time programs available. Postbaccalaureate distance learning degree programs offered (no on-campus study). Offers public health (MPH); writing (MFA). *Application deadline:* Applications are processed on a rolling basis. *Application fee:* $45. Electronic applications accepted. *Application Contact:* Penny Harmoney, Director, Graduate Studies, 402-554-2341, Fax: 402-554-3143, E-mail: graduate@unomaha.edu. *Dean for Graduate Studies,* Dr. Thomas Bragg, 402-554-2341.

College of Arts and Sciences Students: 99 full-time (51 women), 212 part-time (114 women); includes 22 minority (12 African Americans, 3 Asian Americans or Pacific Islanders, 7 Hispanic Americans), 16 international. Average age 30. 241 applicants, 61% accepted, 95 enrolled. *Faculty:* 138 full-time (58 women). Expenses: Contact institution. *Financial support:* In 2006–07, 212 students received support; fellowships, research assistantships with tuition reimbursements available, teaching assistantships with tuition reimbursements available, career-related internships or fieldwork, Federal Work-Study, institutionally sponsored loans, scholarships/grants, tuition waivers (partial), and unspecified assistantships available. Support available to part-time students. Financial award application deadline: 3/1; financial award applicants required to submit FAFSA. In 2006, 71 master's, 23 other advanced degrees awarded. *Degree program information:* Part-time and evening/weekend programs available. Offers advanced writing (Certificate); arts and sciences (MA, MAT, MS, PhD, Certificate, Ed S); biology (MS); developmental psychology (PhD); English (MA); geographic information science (Certificate); geography (MA); history (MA); industrial/organizational psychology (MS, PhD); language teaching (MA); mathematics (MA, MAT, MS); political science (MS); psychobiology (PhD); psychology (MA); school psychology (MS, Ed S); teaching English to speakers of other languages (Certificate); technical communication (Certificate). *Application deadline:* For fall admission, 3/1 priority date for domestic students; for spring admission, 10/1 priority date for domestic students. Applications are processed on a rolling basis. *Application fee:* $45. Electronic applications accepted. *Dean,* Dr. Shelton Hendricks, 402-554-2338.

College of Business Administration Students: 101 full-time (32 women), 246 part-time (96 women); includes 18 minority (4 African Americans, 9 Asian Americans or Pacific Islanders, 5 Hispanic Americans), 58 international. Average age 30. 216 applicants, 54% accepted, 83 enrolled. *Faculty:* 46 full-time (11 women). Expenses: Contact institution. *Financial support:* In 2006–07, 140 students received support; fellowships, research assistantships with tuition reimbursements available, career-related internships or fieldwork, Federal Work-Study, institutionally sponsored loans, scholarships/grants, tuition waivers (partial), and unspecified assistantships available. Support available to part-time students. Financial award application deadline: 3/1; financial award applicants required to submit FAFSA. In 2006, 118 degrees awarded. *Degree program information:* Part-time and evening/weekend programs available. Offers accounting (M Acc); business administration (EMBA, M Acc, MA, MBA, MS); economics (MA, MS). *Application deadline:* For fall admission, 7/1 priority date for domestic students; for spring admission, 12/1 priority date for domestic students. Applications are processed on a rolling basis. *Application fee:* $45. Electronic applications accepted. *Application Contact:* Lex Kaczmarek, Director, 402-554-2303. *Associate,* Dr. Louis Pol, 402-554-2303.

College of Communication, Fine Arts and Media Students: 21 full-time (14 women), 74 part-time (56 women); includes 10 minority (5 African Americans, 4 Asian Americans or Pacific Islanders, 1 Hispanic American), 5 international. Average age 33. 47 applicants, 64% accepted, 19 enrolled. *Faculty:* 51 full-time (26 women). Expenses: Contact institution. *Financial support:* In 2006–07, 55 students received support; fellowships, research assistantships with tuition reimbursements available, career-related internships or fieldwork, Federal Work-Study, institutionally sponsored loans, traineeships, tuition waivers (full), and unspecified assistantships available. Support available to part-time students. Financial award application deadline: 3/1; financial award applicants required to submit FAFSA. In 2006, 25 degrees awarded. *Degree program information:* Part-time and evening/weekend programs available. Offers communication (MA); communication, fine arts and media (MA, MM); music (MM); theatre (MA). *Application deadline:* For fall admission, 7/1 priority date for domestic students; for spring admission, 12/1 priority date for domestic students. Applications are processed on a rolling basis. *Application fee:* $45. Electronic applications accepted. *Dean,* Dr. Gail Baker, 402-554-2231.

College of Education Students: 148 full-time (109 women), 656 part-time (509 women); includes 54 minority (31 African Americans, 10 Asian Americans or Pacific Islanders, 13 Hispanic Americans), 9 international. Average age 32. 317 applicants, 66% accepted, 124 enrolled. *Faculty:* 56 full-time (28 women). Expenses: Contact institution. *Financial support:* In 2006–07, 385 students received support; fellowships, research assistantships with tuition reimbursements available, teaching assistantships with tuition reimbursements available, career-related internships or fieldwork, Federal Work-Study, institutionally sponsored loans, scholarships/grants, tuition waivers (full), and unspecified assistantships available. Support available to part-time students. Financial award application deadline: 3/1; financial award applicants required to submit FAFSA. In 2006, 273 master's, 6 doctorates, 5 other advanced degrees awarded. *Degree program information:* Part-time and evening/weekend programs available. Offers community counseling (MA, MS); counseling gerontology (MA, MS); education (MA, MS, Ed D, Certificate, Ed S); educational administration and supervision (MS, Ed D, Ed S); elementary education (MA, MS); health, physical education, and recreation (MA, MS); instruction in urban schools (Certificate); instructional technology (Certificate); reading education (MS); school counseling-elementary (MA, MS); school counseling-secondary (MA, MS); secondary education (MA, MS); special education (MS); speech-language pathology (MA, MS); student affairs practice in higher education (MA, MS). *Application deadline:* For fall admission, 3/1 priority date for domestic students; for spring admission, 10/1 priority date for domestic students. Applications are processed on a rolling basis. *Application fee:* $45. *Chairperson,* Dr. John Langan, 402-554-2212.

College of Information Science and Technology Students: 70 full-time (10 women), 147 part-time (42 women); includes 22 minority (5 African Americans, 16 Asian Americans or Pacific Islanders, 1 Hispanic American), 70 international. Average age 31. 167 applicants, 49% accepted, 42 enrolled. *Faculty:* 28 full-time (8 women). Expenses: Contact institution. *Financial support:* In 2006–07, 117 students received support; fellowships, research assistantships with tuition reimbursements available, teaching assistantships with tuition reimbursements available, career-related internships or fieldwork, Federal Work-Study, institutionally sponsored loans, scholarships/grants, tuition waivers (full), and unspecified assistantships available. Financial award application deadline: 3/1; financial award applicants required to submit FAFSA. In 2006, 52 master's, 2 doctorates awarded. *Degree program information:* Part-time and evening/weekend programs available. Offers computer science (MA, MS); information science and technology (MA, MS, PhD); information technology (PhD); management information systems (MS). *Application deadline:* For fall admission, 7/1 priority date

University of Nebraska at Omaha (continued)

for domestic students; for spring admission, 12/1 priority date for domestic students. Applications are processed on a rolling basis. *Application fee:* $45. Electronic applications accepted. *Dean,* Dr. Hesham Ali, 402-554-2276.

College of Public Affairs and Community Service Students: 156 full-time (121 women), 311 part-time (205 women); includes 51 minority (26 African Americans, 2 American Indian/Alaska Native, 9 Asian Americans or Pacific Islanders, 14 Hispanic Americans), 19 international. Average age 31. 329 applicants, 62% accepted, 137 enrolled. *Faculty:* 48 full-time (22 women). Expenses: Contact institution. *Financial support:* In 2006–07, 308 students received support, including 28 research assistantships with tuition reimbursements available; fellowships, teaching assistantships with tuition reimbursements available, career-related internships or fieldwork, Federal Work-Study, institutionally sponsored loans, scholarships/grants, tuition waivers (partial), and unspecified assistantships also available. Support available to part-time students. Financial award application deadline: 3/1; financial award applicants required to submit FAFSA. In 2006, 113 master's, 5 doctorates, 2 other advanced degrees awarded. *Degree program information:* Part-time and evening/weekend programs available. Postbaccalaureate distance learning degree programs offered (no on-campus study). Offers criminal justice (MA, MS, PhD); gerontology (Certificate); public administration (MPA, PhD); public affairs and community service (MA, MPA, MS, MSW, PhD, Certificate); social gerontology (MA); social work (MSW); urban studies (MS). *Application deadline:* Applications are processed on a rolling basis. *Application fee:* $45. Electronic applications accepted. *Chairperson,* Dr. Burton J. Reed, 402-554-2276.

UNIVERSITY OF NEBRASKA–LINCOLN, Lincoln, NE 68588

General Information State-supported, coed, university. CGS member. *Graduate housing:* Rooms and/or apartments available on a first-come, first-served basis to single students and available to married students. Housing application deadline: 7/1. *Research affiliation:* U.S. Meat Animal Research Center.

GRADUATE UNITS

College of Law Offers law (JD, MLS); legal studies (MLS). Electronic applications accepted.

Graduate College *Degree program information:* Part-time and evening/weekend programs available. Postbaccalaureate distance learning degree programs offered. Offers museum studies (MA, MS); survey research and methodology (MS); toxicology (MS, PhD). Electronic applications accepted.

College of Agricultural Sciences and Natural Resources Offers agricultural economics (MS, PhD); agricultural leadership, education and communication (MS); agricultural sciences and natural resources (M Ag, MA, MS, PhD); agriculture (M Ag); agronomy (MS, PhD); animal science (MS, PhD); biochemistry (MS, PhD); biometry (MS); entomology (MS, PhD); food science and technology (MS, PhD); horticulture (MS, PhD); mechanized systems management (MS); natural resources (MS, PhD); nutrition (MS, PhD); veterinary and biomedical sciences (MS, PhD). Electronic applications accepted.

College of Architecture Offers architecture (M Arch, MS); community and regional planning (MCRP). Electronic applications accepted.

College of Arts and Sciences Offers analytical chemistry (PhD); anthropology (MA); arts and sciences (M Sc T, MA, MAT, MS, PhD); astronomy (MS, PhD); biological sciences (MA, MS, PhD); chemistry (MS); classics and religious studies (MA); communication studies and theatre arts (PhD); communications studies (MA); computer engineering (PhD); computer science (MS, PhD); English (MA, PhD); French (MA, PhD); geography (MA, PhD); geosciences (MS, PhD); German (MA, PhD); history (MA, PhD); inorganic chemistry (PhD); mathematics and statistics (M Sc T, MA, MAT, MS, PhD); organic chemistry (PhD); philosophy (MA, PhD); physical chemistry (PhD); physics (MS, PhD); political science (MA, PhD); psychology (MA, PhD); sociology (MA, PhD); Spanish (MA, PhD). Electronic applications accepted.

College of Business Administration *Degree program information:* Part-time and evening/weekend programs available. Offers accountancy (PhD); actuarial science (MS); business (MA, MBA, PhD); business administration (MA, MBA, MPA, MS, PhD); economics (MA, PhD); finance (MA, PhD); management (MA, PhD); marketing (MA, PhD). Electronic applications accepted.

College of Education and Human Sciences Offers family and consumer sciences (MS); human resources and family sciences (PhD); nutritional science and dietetics (MS); textiles, clothing and design (MA, MS). Electronic applications accepted.

College of Education and Human Services Offers administration, curriculum and instruction (Ed D, PhD); community and human resources (Ed D, PhD); curriculum and instruction (M Ed, MA, MST, Ed S); education (M Ed, MA, MPE, MS, MST, Ed D, PhD, Certificate, Ed S); educational administration (M Ed, MA, Ed D, Certificate); educational psychology (MA, Ed S); health, physical education, and recreation (M Ed, MPE); psychological and cultural studies (Ed D, PhD); special education (M Ed, MA); special education and communication disorders (Ed S); speech-language pathology and audiology (MS). Electronic applications accepted.

College of Engineering and Technology Offers agricultural and biological systems engineering (MS, PhD); architectural engineering (MAE); chemical engineering (MS); civil engineering (MS); electrical engineering (MS); engineering (M Eng, PhD); engineering and technology (M Eng, MAE, MEE, MS, PhD); engineering mechanics (MS); environmental engineering (MS); industrial and management systems engineering (MS); manufacturing systems engineering (MS); mechanical engineering (MS); mechanized systems management (MS). Electronic applications accepted.

College of Fine and Performing Arts Offers art and art history (MFA); fine and performing arts (MFA, MM, DMA); music (MM, DMA); theatre arts (MFA). Electronic applications accepted.

College of Journalism and Mass Communications Postbaccalaureate distance learning degree programs offered (no on-campus study). Offers journalism and mass communications (MA). Electronic applications accepted.

UNIVERSITY OF NEBRASKA MEDICAL CENTER, Omaha, NE 68198

General Information State-supported, coed, upper-level institution. CGS member. *Enrollment:* 2,995 graduate, professional, and undergraduate students; 1,449 full-time matriculated graduate/professional students (843 women), 352 part-time matriculated graduate/professional students (306 women). *Enrollment by degree level:* 922 first professional, 499 master's, 338 doctoral, 40 other advanced degrees. *Graduate faculty:* 816 full-time (308 women), 190 part-time/adjunct (98 women). *Graduate housing:* On-campus housing not available. *Student services:* Campus employment opportunities, campus safety program, child daycare facilities, disabled student services, exercise/wellness program, free psychological counseling, international student services, low-cost health insurance, multicultural affairs office. *Library facilities:* McGoogan Medical Library. *Online resources:* library catalog, web page, access to other libraries' catalogs. *Collection:* 241,551 titles, 4,280 serial subscriptions. *Research affiliation:* UNeMed Corporation (biotechnology).

Computer facilities: 65 computers available on campus for general student use. A campuswide network can be accessed from student residence rooms and from off campus. Internet access, various software packages are available. *Web address:* http://www.unmc.edu/.

General Application Contact: Tymaree Tonjes, Student Records Technician, 402-559-6468, Fax: 402-559-6796, E-mail: ttonjes@unmc.edu.

GRADUATE UNITS

College of Dentistry Students: 181 full-time (82 women), 1 part-time; includes 16 minority (3 African Americans, 1 American Indian/Alaska Native, 6 Asian Americans or Pacific Islanders, 6 Hispanic Americans), 1 international. 881 applicants, 6% accepted, 45 enrolled. *Faculty:* 57 full-time (9 women), 30 part-time/adjunct (6 women). Expenses: Contact institution. *Financial support:* Federal Work-Study, scholarships/grants, and stipends available. Support available to part-time students. Financial award application deadline: 3/10; financial award applicants required to submit FAFSA. In 2006, 43 degrees awarded. Offers dentistry (DDS, Certificate). *Application deadline:* For fall admission, 12/1 priority date for domestic students; for spring admission, 2/1 for domestic students. *Application fee:* $50. *Application Contact:* Glenda Canfield, Admissions Secretary, 402-472-1363, Fax: 402-472-5290, E-mail: gmcanfie@unmc.edu. *Dean,* Dr. John W. Reinhardt, 402-472-1344.

College of Medicine Students: 476 full-time (207 women); includes 35 minority (13 African Americans, 4 American Indian/Alaska Native, 17 Asian Americans or Pacific Islanders, 1 Hispanic American). Average age 22. 1,268 applicants, 13% accepted, 123 enrolled. *Faculty:* 554 full-time, 107 part-time/adjunct. Expenses: Contact institution. *Financial support:* Career-related internships or fieldwork, Federal Work-Study, institutionally sponsored loans, and tuition waivers (full) available. Support available to part-time students. Financial award application deadline: 2/1; financial award applicants required to submit FAFSA. In 2006, 119 degrees awarded. Offers medicine (MD, Certificate). *Application deadline:* For fall admission, 11/1 for domestic students. Applications are processed on a rolling basis. *Application fee:* $45. Electronic applications accepted. *Application Contact:* Gigi R. Rogers, Administrative Coordinator, 402-559-2259, Fax: 402-559-6840, E-mail: grrogers@unmc.edu. *Dean,* Dr. John L. Gollan, 402-559-4146, Fax: 402-559-4148.

College of Pharmacy Students: 256 full-time (191 women), 2 part-time (1 woman); includes 24 minority (6 African Americans, 1 American Indian/Alaska Native, 12 Asian Americans or Pacific Islanders, 5 Hispanic Americans). Average age 23. 256 applicants, 26% accepted, 66 enrolled. *Faculty:* 28 full-time (4 women), 4 part-time/adjunct (2 women). Expenses: Contact institution. *Financial support:* Career-related internships or fieldwork, Federal Work-Study, institutionally sponsored loans, and scholarships/grants available. Support available to part-time students. Financial award application deadline: 4/1; financial award applicants required to submit FAFSA. In 2006, 65 degrees awarded. Offers pharmacy (Pharm D). *Application deadline:* For fall admission, 1/1 for domestic students. *Application fee:* $45. Electronic applications accepted. *Application Contact:* Dr. Charles H. Krobot, Associate Dean for Academic Affairs, 402-559-4333, Fax: 402-559-5060, E-mail: ckrobot@unmc.edu. *Dean,* Dr. Clarence T. Ueda, 402-559-4333, Fax: 402-559-5060, E-mail: cueda@unmc.edu.

Graduate Studies Students: 260 full-time (159 women), 288 part-time (260 women); includes 38 minority (16 African Americans, 2 American Indian/Alaska Native, 11 Asian Americans or Pacific Islanders, 9 Hispanic Americans), 107 international. 404 applicants, 48% accepted, 157 enrolled. *Faculty:* 360 full-time (100 women), 66 part-time/adjunct (18 women). Expenses: Contact institution. *Financial support:* In 2006–07, 8 fellowships with tuition reimbursements (averaging $21,000 per year), 26 research assistantships with tuition reimbursements (averaging $21,000 per year), teaching assistantships with tuition reimbursements (averaging $16,500 per year) were awarded; career-related internships or fieldwork, institutionally sponsored loans, scholarships/grants, traineeships, tuition waivers (full), and unspecified assistantships also available. Support available to part-time students. In 2006, 78 master's, 20 doctorates awarded. *Degree program information:* Part-time programs available. Postbaccalaureate distance learning degree programs offered. Offers biochemistry and molecular biology (MS, PhD); cancer research (MS, PhD); genetics, cell biology and anatomy (MS, PhD); medical sciences (MS, PhD); neuroscience (MS, PhD); nursing (MSN, PhD); pathology and microbiology (MS, PhD); pharmaceutical sciences (MS, PhD); pharmacology (MS, PhD); physiology (MS, PhD); public health (MPH); toxicology (MS, PhD). *Application deadline:* For fall admission, 6/1 for domestic students, 4/1 for international students; for spring admission, 10/1 for domestic students, 8/1 for international students. Applications are processed on a rolling basis. *Application fee:* $45. Electronic applications accepted. *Application Contact:* Dan Teet, Graduate Studies Associate, 402-559-6531, Fax: 402-559-7845, E-mail: unmcgraduatestudies@unmc.edu. *Executive Associate Dean for Graduate Studies,* Dr. David A. Crouse, 402-559-6531, Fax: 402-559-7845, E-mail: dcrouse@unmc.edu.

School of Allied Health Professions Expenses: Contact institution. Offers allied health professions (MPAS, MPS, DPT, Certificate); cytotechnology (Certificate); dietetic internship (Certificate); perfusion science (MPS); physical therapy education (DPT); physician assistant education (MPAS). *Associate Dean,* Kyle P. Meyer, 402-559-6680, E-mail: kpmeyer@unmc.edu.

UNIVERSITY OF NEVADA, LAS VEGAS, Las Vegas, NV 89154-9900

General Information State-supported, coed, university. CGS member. *Enrollment:* 27,933 graduate, professional, and undergraduate students; 1,836 full-time matriculated graduate/professional students (1,084 women), 1,972 part-time matriculated graduate/professional students (1,226 women). *Enrollment by degree level:* 2,948 master's, 773 doctoral, 87 other advanced degrees. *Graduate faculty:* 776 full-time (238 women), 296 part-time/adjunct (115 women). *Graduate housing:* Room and/or apartments available on a first-come, first-served basis to single students; on-campus housing not available to married students. Typical cost: $8,624 (including board). Housing application deadline: 7/1. *Student services:* Campus employment opportunities, campus safety program, career counseling, child daycare facilities, disabled student services, free psychological counseling, grant writing training, international student services, low-cost health insurance, multicultural affairs office, teacher training, writing training. *Library facilities:* Lied Library. *Online resources:* library catalog, web page, access to other libraries' catalogs. *Collection:* 1.3 million titles, 18,568 serial subscriptions, 14,235 audiovisual materials. *Research affiliation:* National Center for Energy Management Building Technologies, National Renewable Energy Laboratory, Lawrence Berkley National Lab, Pacific Northwest National Lab, Lawrence Livermore National Lab, National Security Technologies.

Computer facilities: 1,900 computers available on campus for general student use. A campuswide network can be accessed from student residence rooms and from off campus. Internet access and online class registration are available. *Web address:* http://www.unlv.edu/.

General Application Contact: Karen Maldonado, Administrative Assistant I, 702-895-3320, Fax: 702-895-4180, E-mail: karen.maldanado@unlv.edu.

GRADUATE UNITS

Graduate College Students: 1,836 full-time (1,084 women), 1,972 part-time (1,226 women); includes 702 minority (221 African Americans, 29 American Indian/Alaska Native, 241 Asian Americans or Pacific Islanders, 211 Hispanic Americans), 306 international. Average age 26. 2,938 applicants, 53% accepted, 1167 enrolled. *Faculty:* 776 full-time (238 women), 296 part-time/adjunct (115 women). Expenses: Contact institution. *Financial support:* In 2006–07, 683 students received support, including 6 fellowships with full tuition reimbursements available (averaging $14,600 per year), 185 research assistantships with full and partial tuition reimbursements available (averaging $10,600 per year), 415 teaching assistantships with partial tuition reimbursements available (averaging $10,500 per year); career-related internships or fieldwork, Federal Work-Study, institutionally sponsored loans, scholarships/grants, health care benefits, and unspecified assistantships also available. Support available to part-time students. Financial award application deadline: 3/1. In 2006, 1,055 master's, 63 doctorates, 34 other advanced degrees awarded. *Degree program information:* Part-time and evening/weekend programs available. *Application deadline:* For fall admission, 6/15 for domestic students, 5/1 for international students; for spring admission, 11/15 for domestic students, 10/1 for international students. *Application fee:* $60 ($75 for international students). Electronic applications accepted. *Application Contact:* Graduate College Admissions Evaluator, 702-895-3320, Fax: 702-895-4180, E-mail: gradcollege@unlv.edu. *Interim Vice President of Research and Graduate Dean,* Dr. Ronald Smith, 702-895-4070, Fax: 702-895-4180.

College of Business Students: 214 full-time (86 women), 147 part-time (64 women); includes 71 minority (11 African Americans, 1 American Indian/Alaska Native, 43 Asian Americans or Pacific Islanders, 16 Hispanic Americans), 45 international. 376 applicants, 46% accepted, 129 enrolled. *Faculty:* 80 full-time (10 women), 6 part-time/adjunct (0 women). Expenses: Contact institution. *Financial support:* In 2006–07, 27 research assistantships with partial tuition reimbursements (averaging $10,000 per year), 2 teaching assistantships with partial tuition reimbursements (averaging $10,000 per year) were awarded; career-related internships or fieldwork, Federal Work-Study, institutionally sponsored loans, scholarships/grants, health care benefits, and unspecified assistantships also available. Support available to part-time students. Financial award application deadline: 3/1. In 2006, 106 degrees awarded.

Degree program information: Part-time and evening/weekend programs available. Offers accounting (MS); business (MA, MBA, MS); business administration (MBA); economics (MA); management information systems (MS). *Application deadline:* For fall admission, 5/1 for international students; for spring admission, 10/1 for international students. *Application fee:* $60 ($75 for international students). Electronic applications accepted. *Application Contact:* Graduate College Admissions Evaluator, 702-895-3320, Fax: 702-895-4180, E-mail: gradcollege@unlv.edu. *Dean,* Dr. Richard Flaherty, 702-895-3362.

College of Education Students: 549 full-time (398 women), 888 part-time (642 women); includes 266 minority (97 African Americans, 8 American Indian/Alaska Native, 70 Asian Americans or Pacific Islanders, 91 Hispanic Americans), 31 international. 766 applicants, 67% accepted, 445 enrolled. *Faculty:* 104 full-time (53 women), 66 part-time/adjunct (42 women). Expenses: Contact institution. *Financial support:* In 2006–07, 78 research assistantships with partial tuition reimbursements (averaging $10,400 per year), 25 teaching assistantships with partial tuition reimbursements (averaging $11,800 per year) were awarded; career-related internships or fieldwork, Federal Work-Study, institutionally sponsored loans, scholarships/grants, health care benefits, and unspecified assistantships also available. Support available to part-time students. Financial award application deadline: 3/1. In 2006, 492 master's, 30 doctorates, 17 other advanced degrees awarded. *Degree program information:* Part-time and evening/weekend programs available. Offers assistive technology (Ed S); curriculum and instruction (Ed D, PhD, Ed S); education (M Ed, MS, Ed D, PhD, Ed S); education psychology (MS); educational administration (M Ed, Ed D, PhD, Ed S); educational leadership (MS); educational psychology (PhD); elementary education (M Ed, MS); emotional disturbance (Ed D); English education (M Ed, MS); general special education (Ed D); gifted and talented education (Ed D); learning and technology (PhD); learning disabilities (Ed D); library science (M Ed, MS); literacy education (M Ed, MS); mathematics education (M Ed, MS); mental retardation (Ed D); multicultural education (M Ed, MS); reading specialist (M Ed, MS); school counseling (M Ed); school counselor education (PhD); school psychology (PhD, Ed S); secondary education (M Ed, MS); special education (M Ed, MS, PhD, Ed S); sports education leadership (M Ed, MS, PhD); teacher leadership (M Ed, MS); teaching English as a second language (M Ed, MS); technology integration and leadership (M Ed, MS). *Application fee:* $60 ($75 for international students). Electronic applications accepted. *Application Contact:* Graduate College Admissions Evaluator, 702-895-3320, E-mail: gradcollege@unlv.edu. *Interim Dean,* Dr. Jane McCarthy, 702-895-9974.

College of Fine Arts Students: 145 full-time (70 women), 49 part-time (20 women); includes 27 minority (9 African Americans, 2 American Indian/Alaska Native, 7 Asian Americans or Pacific Islanders, 9 Hispanic Americans), 11 international. 226 applicants, 38% accepted, 61 enrolled. *Faculty:* 79 full-time (19 women), 33 part-time/adjunct (8 women). Expenses: Contact institution. *Financial support:* In 2006–07, 11 research assistantships with partial tuition reimbursements (averaging $10,000 per year), 55 teaching assistantships with partial tuition reimbursements (averaging $10,250 per year) were awarded; career-related internships or fieldwork, Federal Work-Study, institutionally sponsored loans, scholarships/grants, health care benefits, and unspecified assistantships also available. Support available to part-time students. Financial award application deadline: 3/1. In 2006, 52 degrees awarded. *Degree program information:* Part-time programs available. Offers applied music (performance) (MM); architecture (M Arch); art (MFA); composition/theory (MM); design/technology (MFA); directing (MFA); fine arts (M Arch, MA, MFA, MM, DMA); music education (MM); performance (MFA); performance studies (DMA); playwriting (MFA); screenwriting (MFA); stage management (MFA); theatre (MA); theatre arts (MFA). *Application fee:* $60 ($75 for international students). Electronic applications accepted. *Dean,* Dr. Jeffrey Koep, 702-895-4210.

College of Liberal Arts Students: 181 full-time (107 women), 191 part-time (110 women); includes 49 minority (14 African Americans, 2 American Indian/Alaska Native, 11 Asian Americans or Pacific Islanders, 22 Hispanic Americans), 5 international. 325 applicants, 35% accepted, 76 enrolled. *Faculty:* 148 full-time (55 women), 32 part-time/adjunct (12 women). Expenses: Contact institution. *Financial support:* In 2006–07, 63 research assistantships with full and partial tuition reimbursements (averaging $11,000 per year), 104 teaching assistantships with partial tuition reimbursements (averaging $11,800 per year) were awarded; career-related internships or fieldwork, Federal Work-Study, institutionally sponsored loans, scholarships/grants, health care benefits, and unspecified assistantships also available. Support available to part-time students. Financial award application deadline: 3/1. In 2006, 49 master's, 15 doctorates awarded. *Degree program information:* Part-time programs available. Offers anthropology (MA, PhD); clinical psychology (PhD); creative writing (MFA); English (PhD); ethics and policy studies (MA); experimental psychology (PhD); general psychology (MA); history (MA, PhD); language/composition theory study (MA); liberal arts (MA, MFA, PhD, Certificate); literature study (MA); political science (MA); sociology (MA, PhD); Spanish language, culture and technology (MA); women's studies (Certificate). *Application fee:* $60 ($75 for international students). Electronic applications accepted. *Application Contact:* Graduate College Admissions Evaluator, 702-895-3320, Fax: 702-895-4180, E-mail: gradcollege@unlv.edu. *Dean,* Dr. Edward Shoben, 702-895-3401.

College of Science Students: 145 full-time (61 women), 100 part-time (45 women); includes 29 minority (5 African Americans, 1 American Indian/Alaska Native, 11 Asian Americans or Pacific Islanders, 12 Hispanic Americans), 42 international. 185 applicants, 39% accepted, 49 enrolled. *Faculty:* 124 full-time (23 women), 62 part-time/adjunct (11 women). Expenses: Contact institution. *Financial support:* In 2006–07, 28 research assistantships with partial tuition reimbursements (averaging $10,900 per year), 89 teaching assistantships with partial tuition reimbursements (averaging $10,700 per year) were awarded; career-related internships or fieldwork, Federal Work-Study, institutionally sponsored loans, scholarships/grants, health care benefits, and unspecified assistantships also available. Support available to part-time students. Financial award application deadline: 3/1. In 2006, 35 master's, 5 doctorates awarded. *Degree program information:* Part-time programs available. Offers applied mathematics (MS, PhD); applied statistics (MS); biochemistry (MS); chemistry (MS); computational mathematics (PhD); environmental science/chemistry (PhD); geoscience (MS, PhD); life sciences (MS, PhD); physics (MS, PhD); pure mathematics (MS, PhD); radiochemistry (PhD); science (MAS, MS, PhD); statistics (PhD); teaching mathematics (MS); water resources management (MS). *Application fee:* $60 ($75 for international students). Electronic applications accepted. *Application Contact:* Graduate College Admissions Evaluator, 702-895-3320, Fax: 702-895-4180, E-mail: gradcollege@unlv.edu. *Dean,* Dr. Ronald Yasbin, 702-895-3567.

Division of Health Sciences Students: 211 full-time (140 women), 161 part-time (128 women); includes 78 minority (20 African Americans, 1 American Indian/Alaska Native, 40 Asian Americans or Pacific Islanders, 17 Hispanic Americans), 56 international. 315 applicants, 66% accepted, 159 enrolled. *Faculty:* 58 full-time (30 women), 34 part-time/adjunct (20 women). Expenses: Contact institution. *Financial support:* In 2006–07, 35 research assistantships with partial tuition reimbursements (averaging $10,400 per year), 5 teaching assistantships with partial tuition reimbursements (averaging $10,400 per year) were awarded; career-related internships or fieldwork, Federal Work-Study, institutionally sponsored loans, scholarships/grants, health care benefits, and unspecified assistantships also available. Support available to part-time students. Financial award application deadline: 3/1. In 2006, 54 degrees awarded. *Degree program information:* Part-time programs available. Offers exercise physiology (MS); family nurse practitioner (MS, Post-Master's Certificate); health physics (MS); health promotion (M Ed); health sciences (M Ed, MPH, MS, DPT, PhD, Post-Master's Certificate); kinesiology (MS); nursing (PhD); nursing education (MS, Post-Master's Certificate); pediatric nurse practitioner (MS); physical therapy (MS, DPT); public health (MPH). *Application fee:* $60 ($75 for international students). Electronic applications accepted. *Application Contact:* Graduate College Admissions Evaluator, 702-895-3320, Fax: 702-895-4180, E-mail: gradcollege@unlv.edu. *Interim Director,* Dr. Harvey Wallmann, 702-895-3693.

Greenspun College of Urban Affairs Students: 204 full-time (158 women), 250 part-time (161 women); includes 122 minority (55 African Americans, 3 American Indian/Alaska Native, 24 Asian Americans or Pacific Islanders, 40 Hispanic Americans), 6 international. 344 applicants, 56% accepted, 133 enrolled. *Faculty:* 70 full-time (28 women), 24 part-time/adjunct (14 women). Expenses: Contact institution. *Financial support:* In 2006–07, 14 research assistantships (averaging $10,000 per year), 31 teaching assistantships with partial tuition reimbursements (averaging $10,000 per year) were awarded; career-related internships or fieldwork, Federal Work-Study, institutionally sponsored loans, scholarships/grants, health care benefits, and unspecified assistantships also available. Support available to part-time students. Financial award application deadline: 3/1. In 2006, 117 master's, 1 doctorate, 17 other advanced degrees awarded. *Degree program information:* Part-time and evening/weekend programs available. Offers communication studies (MA); community agency counseling (MS); criminal justice (MA); crisis and emergency management (MS); environmental science (MS, PhD); journalism and media studies (MA); marriage and family counseling (MS); marriage and family therapy (Certificate); public administration (MPA); public affairs (PhD); public management (Certificate); rehabilitation counseling (MS); social work (MSW); urban affairs (MA, MPA, MS, MSW, PhD, Certificate). *Application fee:* $60 ($75 for international students). Electronic applications accepted. *Application Contact:* Graduate College Admissions Evaluator, 702-895-3320, Fax: 702-895-4180, E-mail: gradcollege@unlv.edu. *Dean,* Dr. Martha Watson, 702-895-3291.

Howard R. Hughes College of Engineering Students: 136 full-time (37 women), 124 part-time (24 women); includes 36 minority (4 African Americans, 24 Asian Americans or Pacific Islanders, 8 Hispanic Americans), 98 international. 252 applicants, 55% accepted, 76 enrolled. *Faculty:* 70 full-time (7 women), 28 part-time/adjunct (4 women). Expenses: Contact institution. *Financial support:* In 2006–07, 26 research assistantships with full and partial tuition reimbursements (averaging $8,500 per year), 30 teaching assistantships with partial tuition reimbursements (averaging $9,350 per year) were awarded; fellowships, career-related internships or fieldwork, Federal Work-Study, institutionally sponsored loans, scholarships/grants, health care benefits, tuition waivers (full), and unspecified assistantships also available. Support available to part-time students. Financial award application deadline: 3/1. In 2006, 81 master's, 5 doctorates awarded. *Degree program information:* Part-time programs available. Offers civil engineering (MSE, PhD); computer science (MS, PhD); construction (MSE); construction management (MS); electrical and computer engineering (MSE, PhD); engineering (MS, MSE, PhD); informatics (MS, PhD); mechanical engineering (MSE, PhD); transportation (MS, MSE). *Application fee:* $60 ($75 for international students). Electronic applications accepted. *Application Contact:* Graduate College Admissions Evaluator, 702-895-3320, Fax: 702-895-4180, E-mail: gradcollege@unlv.edu. *Dean,* Dr. Eric Sandgren, 702-895-3699.

William F. Harrah College of Hotel Administration Students: 48 full-time (25 women), 60 part-time (30 women); includes 18 minority (4 African Americans, 8 American Indian/Alaska Native, 4 Asian Americans or Pacific Islanders, 2 Hispanic Americans), 19 international. 149 applicants, 33% accepted, 39 enrolled. *Faculty:* 43 full-time (13 women), 11 part-time/adjunct (4 women). Expenses: Contact institution. *Financial support:* In 2006–07, 20 research assistantships with partial tuition reimbursements (averaging $11,200 per year), 2 teaching assistantships with partial tuition reimbursements (averaging $11,000 per year) were awarded; career-related internships or fieldwork, Federal Work-Study, institutionally sponsored loans, scholarships/grants, health care benefits, and unspecified assistantships also available. Support available to part-time students. Financial award application deadline: 3/1. In 2006, 61 master's, 7 doctorates awarded. *Degree program information:* Part-time programs available. Offers hospitality administration (MHA, PhD); hotel administration (MS); leisure studies (MS). *Application deadline:* For fall admission, 6/15 for domestic students, 5/1 for international students; for spring admission, 11/15 for domestic students, 10/1 for international students. *Application fee:* $60 ($75 for international students). Electronic applications accepted. *Application Contact:* Graduate College Admissions Evaluator, 702-895-3320, Fax: 702-895-4180, E-mail: gradcollege@unlv.edu. *Dean,* Dr. Stuart Mann, 702-895-3308.

William S. Boyd School of Law Students: 338 full-time (168 women), 133 part-time (60 women); includes 127 minority (22 African Americans, 6 American Indian/Alaska Native, 57 Asian Americans or Pacific Islanders, 42 Hispanic Americans). 2,206 applicants, 16% accepted, 156 enrolled. *Faculty:* 42 full-time (21 women), 23 part-time/adjunct (5 women). Expenses: Contact institution. *Financial support:* In 2006–07, 343 students received support. Career-related internships or fieldwork and scholarships/grants available. Support available to part-time students. Financial award application deadline: 2/1; financial award applicants required to submit FAFSA. In 2006, 124 degrees awarded. *Degree program information:* Part-time and evening/weekend programs available. Offers law (JD). *Application deadline:* For fall admission, 3/15 priority date for domestic and international students. Applications are processed on a rolling basis. *Application fee:* $50. Electronic applications accepted. *Application Contact:* Gerald Sequiera, Director of Admissions, E-mail: gerald.sequeira@unlv.edu. *Dean,* Richard J. Morgan, 702-895-3671, Fax: 702-895-1095, E-mail: morgan@ccmail.nevada.edu.

See Close-Up on page 1097.

UNIVERSITY OF NEVADA, RENO, Reno, NV 89557

General Information State-supported, coed, university. CGS member. *Enrollment:* 16,663 graduate, professional, and undergraduate students; 980 full-time matriculated graduate/professional students (575 women), 1,475 part-time matriculated graduate/professional students (815 women). *Enrollment by degree level:* 57 first professional, 1,616 master's, 765 doctoral, 17 other advanced degrees. *Graduate faculty:* 999. *Graduate housing:* Rooms and/or apartments available on a first-come, first-served basis to single and married students. *Student services:* Campus employment opportunities, campus safety program, career counseling, child daycare facilities, disabled student services, exercise/wellness program, free psychological counseling, grant writing training, international student services, low-cost health insurance, multicultural affairs office, teacher training, writing training. *Library facilities:* Getchell Library plus 6 others. *Online resources:* library catalog, web page, access to other libraries' catalogs. *Collection:* 1.2 million titles, 19,058 serial subscriptions, 49,433 audiovisual materials. *Research affiliation:* Desert Research Institute (natural resource sciences), Division of Atmospheric Sciences (atmospheric sciences), Division of Earth and Ecosystem Sciences (earth sciences), Division of Hydrologic Sciences (hydrologic sciences), Center for Watersheds and Environmental Sustainability (watershed management).

Computer facilities: Computer purchase and lease plans are available. 298 computers available on campus for general student use. A campuswide network can be accessed from student residence rooms and from off campus. Internet access and online class registration are available. *Web address:* http://www.unr.edu/.

General Application Contact: John C. Green, Application Contact, 775-784-6869, Fax: 775-784-6064, E-mail: gradschool@unr.edu.

GRADUATE UNITS

Graduate School Students: 1,020 full-time (565 women), 1,312 part-time (758 women). Average age 33. 1,096 applicants, 82% accepted, 551 enrolled. *Faculty:* 999. Expenses: Contact institution. *Financial support:* In 2006–07, 423 research assistantships with tuition reimbursements (averaging $14,000 per year), 485 teaching assistantships with tuition reimbursements (averaging $14,000 per year) were awarded; fellowships with tuition reimbursements, career-related internships or fieldwork, Federal Work-Study, institutionally sponsored loans, health care benefits, tuition waivers (full and partial), and unspecified assistantships also available. Support available to part-time students. Financial award application deadline: 3/1. In 2006, 471 master's, 87 doctorates, 5 other advanced degrees awarded. *Degree program information:* Part-time and evening/weekend programs available. Offers biomedical engineering (MS, PhD); environmental sciences and health (MS, PhD); judicial studies (MJS). *Application deadline:* Applications are processed on a rolling basis. *Application fee:* $60 ($95 for international students). Electronic applications accepted. *Application Contact:* John C. Green, Application Contact, 775-784-6869, Fax: 775-784-6064, E-mail: gradschool@unr.edu. *Associate Dean of the Graduate School,* Dr. Marsha Read, 775-784-6869, Fax: 775-784-6064, E-mail: read@unr.nevada.edu.

College of Agriculture, Biotechnology and Natural Resources Students: 25 full-time (18 women), 46 part-time (20 women); includes 6 minority (1 African American, 2 Asian Americans or Pacific Islanders, 3 Hispanic Americans), 13 international. Average age 29. 28 applicants, 71% accepted, 14 enrolled. *Faculty:* 35. Expenses: Contact institution. *Financial support:* In 2006–07, 4 teaching assistantships were awarded; research assistantships, Federal Work-Study and institutionally sponsored loans also available. Financial

University of Nevada, Reno (continued)

award application deadline: 3/1. In 2006, 16 master's, 4 doctorates awarded. Offers agriculture, biotechnology and natural resources (MS, PhD); animal science (MS); biochemistry (MS, PhD); natural resources and environmental sciences (MS); nutrition (MS); resource economics (MS, PhD). *Application deadline:* For fall admission, 3/1 priority date for domestic students. Applications are processed on a rolling basis. *Application fee:* $60 ($95 for international students). *Dean,* Dr. David Thawley, 775-784-1660.

College of Business Administration Students: 81 full-time (40 women), 192 part-time (83 women); includes 41 minority (2 American Indian/Alaska Native, 29 Asian Americans or Pacific Islanders, 10 Hispanic Americans), 23 international. Average age 32. 108 applicants, 81% accepted, 61 enrolled. *Faculty:* 47. Expenses: Contact institution. *Financial support:* In 2006–07, 7 research assistantships with tuition reimbursements, 1 teaching assistantship with tuition reimbursement were awarded; Federal Work-Study, institutionally sponsored loans, tuition waivers (full), and unspecified assistantships also available. Financial award application deadline: 3/1. In 2006, 71 degrees awarded. *Degree program information:* Part-time and evening/weekend programs available. Offers accounting and information systems (M Acc); business administration (M Acc, MA, MBA, MS); economics (MA, MS); finance (MS). *Application deadline:* For fall admission, 2/1 priority date for domestic students; for spring admission, 11/1 for domestic students. Applications are processed on a rolling basis. *Application fee:* $60 ($95 for international students). *Application Contact:* Dr. Brent Bowman, Application Contact, 775-784-4912, E-mail: bowman@unr.edu. *Interim Dean,* Dr. Dana Edberg, 775-784-4912.

College of Education Students: 276 full-time (204 women), 434 part-time (337 women); includes 73 minority (9 African Americans, 9 American Indian/Alaska Native, 21 Asian Americans or Pacific Islanders, 34 Hispanic Americans), 31 international. Average age 36. 285 applicants, 84% accepted, 227 enrolled. *Faculty:* 57. Expenses: Contact institution. *Financial support:* In 2006–07, 27 research assistantships with tuition reimbursements, 9 teaching assistantships with tuition reimbursements were awarded; Federal Work-Study, institutionally sponsored loans, and unspecified assistantships also available. Financial award application deadline: 3/1. In 2006, 117 master's, 19 doctorates, 5 other advanced degrees awarded. Offers counseling and educational psychology (M Ed, MA, MS, Ed D, PhD, Ed S); curriculum, teaching and learning (Ed D, PhD); education (M Ed, MA, MS, Ed D, PhD, Ed S); educational leadership (M Ed, MA, MS, Ed D, PhD, Ed S); educational specialties (MA, MS, PhD, Ed S); elementary education (M Ed, MA, Ed S); literacy studies (M Ed, MA, Ed D, PhD); secondary education (M Ed, MA, MS, Ed S); special education (M Ed); special education and disability studies (PhD); teaching English as a second language (MA). *Application fee:* $60 ($95 for international students). *Dean,* Dr. William E. Sparkman, 775-784-4345.

College of Engineering Students: 94 full-time (14 women), 154 part-time (28 women); includes 31 minority (3 African Americans, 22 Asian Americans or Pacific Islanders, 6 Hispanic Americans), 112 international. Average age 29. 212 applicants, 70% accepted, 63 enrolled. *Faculty:* 48. Expenses: Contact institution. *Financial support:* In 2006–07, 50 research assistantships, 32 teaching assistantships were awarded; fellowships, Federal Work-Study, institutionally sponsored loans, and tuition waivers (full) also available. Financial award application deadline: 3/1. In 2006, 54 master's, 13 doctorates awarded. Offers chemical engineering (MS, PhD); civil engineering (MS, PhD); computer engineering (MS); computer science (MS); computer science and engineering (PhD); electrical engineering (MS, PhD); engineering (MS, PhD, Met E); mechanical engineering (MS, PhD); metallurgical engineering (MS, PhD, Met E). *Application deadline:* For fall admission, 3/1 priority date for domestic students. Applications are processed on a rolling basis. *Application fee:* $60 ($95 for international students). *Dean,* Dr. Theodore Batchman, 775-784-6925, E-mail: batch_t@unr.edu.

College of Health and Human Sciences Students: 77 full-time (61 women), 62 part-time (56 women); includes 6 Asian Americans or Pacific Islanders, 3 Hispanic Americans, 4 international. Average age 37. 135 applicants, 60% accepted, 43 enrolled. *Faculty:* 54. Expenses: Contact institution. *Financial support:* In 2006–07, 25 research assistantships with tuition reimbursements, 2 teaching assistantships with tuition reimbursements were awarded; Federal Work-Study, institutionally sponsored loans, tuition waivers (full), and unspecified assistantships also available. Financial award application deadline: 3/1. In 2006, 56 degrees awarded. *Degree program information:* Part-time and evening/weekend programs available. Offers criminal justice (MA); health and human sciences (MA, MPH, MS, MSN, MSW); human development and family studies (MS); nursing (MSN); public health (MPH); social work (MSW). *Application fee:* $60 ($95 for international students). Electronic applications accepted. *Acting Dean,* Dr. Charles Bullock, 702-784-6977.

College of Liberal Arts Students: 197 full-time (124 women), 275 part-time (168 women); includes 59 minority (6 African Americans, 2 American Indian/Alaska Native, 17 Asian Americans or Pacific Islanders, 34 Hispanic Americans), 27 international. Average age 33. 237 applicants, 76% accepted, 105 enrolled. *Faculty:* 243. Expenses: Contact institution. *Financial support:* In 2006–07, 112 research assistantships, 182 teaching assistantships were awarded; fellowships, Federal Work-Study, institutionally sponsored loans, tuition waivers (full), and unspecified assistantships also available. Financial award application deadline: 3/1. In 2006, 71 master's, 17 doctorates awarded. *Degree program information:* Part-time and evening/weekend programs available. Offers anthropology (MA, PhD); Basque studies (PhD); English (MA, MATE, PhD); fine arts (MFA); French (MA); German (MA); history (MA, PhD); liberal arts (MA, MATE, MFA, MM, MPA, MS, PhD); music (MA, MM); philosophy (MA); political science (MA, PhD); psychology (MA, PhD); public administration (MPA); public administration and policy (MPA); social psychology (PhD); sociology (MA); Spanish (MA); speech communications (MA). *Application fee:* $60 ($95 for international students). *Dean,* Dr. Heather Hardy, 775-784-6155.

College of Science Students: 148 full-time (60 women), 239 part-time (84 women); includes 26 minority (4 African Americans, 1 American Indian/Alaska Native, 11 Asian Americans or Pacific Islanders, 10 Hispanic Americans), 98 international. Average age 31. 135 applicants, 87% accepted, 82 enrolled. Expenses: Contact institution. In 2006, 56 master's, 19 doctorates awarded. Offers atmospheric sciences (MS, PhD); biology (MS); biotechnology (MS); chemical physics (PhD); chemistry (MS, PhD); earth sciences and engineering (MS, PhD, EM, Geol E); ecology, evolution, and conservation biology (PhD); geochemistry (MS, PhD); geography (MS, PhD); geological engineering (MS, Geol E); geology (MS, PhD); geophysics (MS, PhD); hydrogeology (MS, PhD); hydrology (MS, PhD); land use planning (MS); mathematics (MS); mining engineering (MS, EM); physics (MS, PhD); science (MATM, MS, PhD, EM, Geol E); teaching mathematics (MATM). *Application fee:* $60 ($95 for international students). *Acting Dean,* Dr. Jeff Thompson, 775-784-4591, Fax: 775-784-4592.

Donald W. Reynolds School of Journalism Students: 13 full-time (7 women), 5 part-time (3 women); includes 1 minority (American Indian/Alaska Native), 3 international. Average age 32. 19 applicants, 68% accepted, 12 enrolled. *Faculty:* 4. Expenses: Contact institution. *Financial support:* In 2006–07, 6 research assistantships were awarded; teaching assistantships, Federal Work-Study and institutionally sponsored loans also available. Financial award application deadline: 3/1. In 2006, 4 degrees awarded. Offers journalism (MA). *Application deadline:* For fall admission, 4/15 priority date for domestic students; for spring admission, 12/1 for domestic students. Applications are processed on a rolling basis. *Application fee:* $60 ($95 for international students). *Graduate Program Director,* Dr. Donica Mensing, 775-784-4187.

School of Medicine Expenses: Contact institution. *Financial support:* Fellowships, research assistantships, teaching assistantships, Federal Work-Study and institutionally sponsored loans available. Support available to part-time students. Financial award application deadline: 3/1. Offers medicine (MD, MS, PhD). *Application deadline:* Applications are processed on a rolling basis. *Dean,* Dr. David Lupan, 775-784-4125.

Graduate Programs in Medicine Students: 59 full-time (42 women), 37 part-time (19 women); includes 13 minority (1 African American, 7 Asian Americans or Pacific Islanders, 5 Hispanic Americans), 25 international. Average age 28. 52 applicants, 79% accepted, 31 enrolled. *Faculty:* 5. Expenses: Contact institution. *Financial support:* Fellowships, research assistantships, teaching assistantships, Federal Work-Study available. Support available to part-time students. Financial award application deadline: 3/1. In 2006, 20 master's, 11 doctorates awarded. Offers cell and molecular biology (MS, PhD); cellular and molecular pharmacology and physiology (MS, PhD); medicine (MS, PhD); speech pathology (PhD); speech pathology and audiology (MS). *Application deadline:* For fall admission, 3/1 for domestic students. Applications are processed on a rolling basis. *Application fee:* $60 ($95 for international students).

UNIVERSITY OF NEW BRUNSWICK FREDERICTON, Fredericton, NB E3B 5A3, Canada

General Information Province-supported, coed, university. *Enrollment:* 9,090 graduate, professional, and undergraduate students; 1,009 full-time matriculated graduate/professional students (451 women), 456 part-time matriculated graduate/professional students (301 women). *Graduate housing:* Rooms and/or apartments available to single students and available on a first-come, first-served basis to married students. Typical cost: $5,835 per year ($8,180 including board) for single students. Room and board charges vary according to board plan and housing facility selected. *Student services:* Campus employment opportunities, campus safety program, career counseling, child daycare facilities, disabled student services, exercise/wellness program, free psychological counseling, international student services, low-cost health insurance, teacher training, writing training. *Library facilities:* Harriet Irving Library plus 3 others. *Online resources:* library catalog, web page, access to other libraries' catalogs. *Collection:* 1.1 million titles, 4,817 serial subscriptions. *Research affiliation:* National Research Council Institute for Information Technology (informaton technology), Pulp and Paper Research Institute of Canada (pulp and paper), Atlantic Hydrogen Inc. (hydrogen), Atlantic Associate for Research in the Mathematical Sciences (mathematical sciences), Huntsman Marine Science Centre (marine sciences), Petroleum Research Atlantic Canada (petroleum).

Computer facilities: 1,100 computers available on campus for general student use. A campuswide network can be accessed from student residence rooms and from off campus. Internet access and online class registration are available. *Web address:* http://www.unb.ca/.

General Application Contact: Dr. Gwen Davies, Dean of Graduate Studies, 506-458-7150, Fax: 506-453-4817, E-mail: daviesg@unb.ca.

GRADUATE UNITS

Faculty of Law Students: 245 full-time (126 women). Average age 24. 831 applicants, 24% accepted, 89 enrolled. *Faculty:* 20 full-time (6 women), 12 part-time/adjunct (6 women). Expenses: Contact institution. *Financial support:* Scholarships/grants available. In 2006, 64 degrees awarded. Offers law (LL B). *Application deadline:* For fall admission, 3/1 for domestic students. Applications are processed on a rolling basis. *Application fee:* $50. Electronic applications accepted. *Application Contact:* Robin Dickson, Director of Admissions, 506-453-4693, Fax: 506-458-7722, E-mail: rjd@unb.ca. *Dean,* Philip Bryden, 506-453-4627, Fax: 506-453-4604, E-mail: bryden@unb.ca.

School of Graduate Studies Students: 1,009 full-time (451 women), 456 part-time (301 women). *Faculty:* 582 full-time. Expenses: Contact institution. *Financial support:* In 2006–07, 36 fellowships (averaging $3,884 per year), 628 research assistantships, 380 teaching assistantships were awarded; career-related internships or fieldwork, institutionally sponsored loans, scholarships/grants, health care benefits, and unspecified assistantships also available. Support available to part-time students. In 2006, 342 master's, 57 doctorates awarded. *Degree program information:* Part-time programs available. Offers advance nurse practitioner (MN); applied health services (MA); interdisciplinary studies (MA, PhD); nursing (MN); people, property and alternative dispute resolution (M Phil); philosophy politics and economics (M Phil); sustainable development (M Phil). *Application deadline:* 1/31 for domestic and international students. Applications are processed on a rolling basis. *Application fee:* $50 Canadian dollars. *Dean of Graduate Studies,* Dr. Gwen Davies, 506-458-7150, Fax: 506-453-4817, E-mail: daviesg@unb.ca.

Faculty of Arts Students: 211 full-time (125 women), 37 part-time (21 women). *Faculty:* 129 full-time. Expenses: Contact institution. *Financial support:* In 2006–07, 13 fellowships (averaging $6,565 per year), 79 research assistantships, 69 teaching assistantships were awarded. In 2006, 42 master's, 17 doctorates awarded. *Degree program information:* Part-time programs available. Offers anthropology (MA); arts (MA, PhD); classics (MA); economics (MA); English (MA, PhD); history (MA, PhD); political science (MA); psychology (PhD); sociology (MA, PhD). *Application deadline:* For fall admission, 1/31 priority date for domestic students; for winter admission, 1/31 priority date for domestic students; for spring admission, 1/31 priority date for domestic students. Applications are processed on a rolling basis. *Application fee:* $50 Canadian dollars. *Dean,* Dr. James Murray, 506-458-7485, Fax: 506-453-5102, E-mail: jsm@unb.ca.

Faculty of Business Administration Students: 57 full-time (30 women), 46 part-time (21 women). *Faculty:* 34 full-time (9 women). Expenses: Contact institution. *Financial support:* In 2006–07, 19 teaching assistantships were awarded. In 2006, 29 degrees awarded. *Degree program information:* Part-time programs available. Offers administration (MBA). *Application deadline:* For fall admission, 3/1 priority date for domestic students. Applications are processed on a rolling basis. *Application fee:* $50 Canadian dollars. *Application Contact:* Karen Hansen, Graduate Secretary, 506-453-4766, Fax: 506-453-3561, E-mail: karen@unb.ca. *Dean,* Daniel Coleman, 506-543-4869, Fax: 506-453-3561, E-mail: dan@unb.ca.

Faculty of Computer Science Students: 77 full-time (19 women), 20 part-time (6 women). *Faculty:* 28 full-time (7 women). Expenses: Contact institution. *Financial support:* In 2006–07, 67 research assistantships, 27 teaching assistantships were awarded; fellowships also available. In 2006, 29 master's, 1 doctorate awarded. *Degree program information:* Part-time programs available. Offers computer science (M Sc CS, PhD). *Application deadline:* For fall admission, 3/1 priority date for domestic students. Applications are processed on a rolling basis. *Application fee:* $50 Canadian dollars. Electronic applications accepted. *Application Contact:* Melanie Lawson, Acting Secretary, 506-458-7285, Fax: 506-453-3566, E-mail: melanie@unb.ca. *Director of Graduate Studies,* Dr. Patricia Evans, 506-458-7276, Fax: 506-453-3566, E-mail: pevans@unb.ca.

Faculty of Education Students: 80 full-time (66 women), 190 part-time (161 women). *Faculty:* 42 full-time (22 women). Expenses: Contact institution. *Financial support:* In 2006–07, 3 fellowships (averaging $4,500 per year), 27 research assistantships, 9 teaching assistantships were awarded; career-related internships or fieldwork also available. In 2006, 101 master's, 4 doctorates awarded. *Degree program information:* Part-time programs available. Offers education (M Ed, PhD). *Application deadline:* 1/31 priority date for domestic and international students. Applications are processed on a rolling basis. *Application fee:* $50 Canadian dollars. *Application Contact:* Carolyn King, Graduate Secretary, 506-458-7147, Fax: 506-453-3569, E-mail: kingc@unb.ca. *Dean,* Sharon Rich, 506-453-5018, Fax: 506-453-3569, E-mail: srich@unb.ca.

Faculty of Engineering Students: 225 full-time (47 women), 49 part-time (9 women). *Faculty:* 105 full-time. Expenses: Contact institution. *Financial support:* In 2006–07, 2 fellowships (averaging $2,750 per year), 184 research assistantships, 117 teaching assistantships were awarded; career-related internships or fieldwork also available. In 2006, 67 master's, 16 doctorates awarded. *Degree program information:* Part-time programs available. Offers academic proficiency in hydrographic surveying (Certificate); applied mechanics (M Eng, M Sc E, PhD); chemical engineering (M Eng, M Sc E, PhD); construction engineering and management (M Eng, M Sc E, PhD); electrical and computer engineering (M Eng, M Sc E, PhD); engineering (M Eng, M Sc E, PhD, Certificate, Diploma); environmental engineering (M Eng, M Sc E, PhD); field proficiency in hydrographic surveying (Certificate); geotechnical engineering (M Eng, M Sc E, PhD); groundwater/hydrology (M Eng, M Sc E, PhD); land information management (Diploma); mapping, charting and geodesy (Diploma); materials (M Eng, M Sc E, PhD); mechanical engineering (M Eng, M Sc E, PhD); pavements (M Eng, M Sc E, PhD); structures (M Eng, M Sc E, PhD); surveying engineering (M Eng, M Sc E, PhD); transportation (M Eng, M Sc E, PhD). *Application deadline:* For fall admission, 3/1 priority date for domestic students. Applications are processed on a rolling basis. *Application fee:* $50 Canadian dollars. *Dean,* Dr. David Coleman, 506-453-4570, Fax: 506-453-4569, E-mail: dcoleman@unb.ca.

Faculty of Forestry and Environmental Management Students: 87 full-time (34 women), 22 part-time (8 women). *Faculty:* 34 full-time (4 women). Expenses: Contact institution. *Financial support:* In 2006–07, 55 research assistantships, 17 teaching assistantships were awarded; fellowships also available. In 2006, 13 master's, 5 doctorates awarded. *Degree program information:* Part-time programs available. Offers ecological foundations of forest management (PhD); forest engineering (M Sc FE, MFE); forest products marketing (MBA); forest resources (M Sc F, MF, PhD). *Application deadline:* For fall admission, 3/1 priority date for domestic students. Applications are processed on a rolling basis. *Application fee:* $50 Canadian dollars. *Application Contact:* Faith Sharpe, Graduate Secretary, 506-458-7520, Fax: 506-453-3538, E-mail: fsharpe@unb.ca. *Director of Graduate Studies,* Dr. John Kershaw, 506-453-4933, Fax: 506-453-3538, E-mail: kershaw@unb.ca.

Faculty of Kinesiology Students: 45 full-time (20 women), 8 part-time (6 women). *Faculty:* 16 full-time (6 women). Expenses: Contact institution. *Financial support:* In 2006–07, 24 research assistantships, 23 teaching assistantships were awarded; fellowships with tuition reimbursements, career-related internships or fieldwork and scholarships/grants also available. In 2006, 8 degrees awarded. *Degree program information:* Part-time programs available. Offers exercise and sport science (M Sc); sport and recreation administration (MA). *Application deadline:* For fall admission, 3/1 priority date for domestic students. Applications are processed on a rolling basis. *Application fee:* $50 Canadian dollars. Electronic applications accepted. *Application Contact:* Linda O'Brien, Graduate Secretary, 506-453-4576, Fax: 506-453-3511, E-mail: lobrien@unb.ca. *Acting Director of Graduate Studies,* Dr. Chris Stevenson, 506-453-5063, Fax: 506-453-3511, E-mail: cls@unb.ca.

Faculty of Science Students: 179 full-time (76 women), 15 part-time (9 women). *Faculty:* 148 full-time. Expenses: Contact institution. *Financial support:* In 2006–07, 18 fellowships (averaging $2,000 per year), 178 research assistantships, 91 teaching assistantships were awarded. In 2006, 27 master's, 13 doctorates awarded. *Degree program information:* Part-time programs available. Offers biology (M Sc, PhD); chemistry (M Sc, PhD); geology (M Sc, PhD); mathematics and statistics (M Sc, PhD); physics (M Sc, PhD); science (M Sc, PhD). *Application deadline:* For fall admission, 3/1 priority date for domestic students. Applications are processed on a rolling basis. *Application fee:* $50 Canadian dollars. *Dean,* Dr. Allan Sharp, 506-453-4841, Fax: 506-453-3570, E-mail: sharp@unb.ca.

UNIVERSITY OF NEW BRUNSWICK SAINT JOHN, Saint John, NB E2L 4L5, Canada

General Information Province-supported, coed, comprehensive institution. *Graduate housing:* Rooms and/or apartments available on a first-come, first-served basis to single and married students. Housing application deadline: 3/31.

GRADUATE UNITS

Faculty of Arts Offers psychology (MA). Electronic applications accepted.

Faculty of Business *Degree program information:* Part-time programs available. Offers administration (MBA); electronic commerce (MBA); international business (MBA); natural resource management (MBA).

Faculty of Science, Applied Science and Engineering *Degree program information:* Part-time programs available. Offers biology (M Sc, PhD).

UNIVERSITY OF NEW ENGLAND, Biddeford, ME 04005-9526

General Information Independent, coed, comprehensive institution. *Enrollment:* 3,379 graduate, professional, and undergraduate students; 870 full-time matriculated graduate/professional students (543 women), 558 part-time matriculated graduate/professional students (422 women). *Enrollment by degree level:* 500 first professional, 891 master's, 37 other advanced degrees. *Graduate faculty:* 125 full-time (66 women), 119 part-time/adjunct (59 women). *Graduate housing:* On-campus housing not available. *Student services:* Campus employment opportunities, campus safety program, career counseling, disabled student services, exercise/wellness program, free psychological counseling, low-cost health insurance, multicultural affairs office. *Library facilities:* Ketchum Library plus 1 other. *Online resources:* library catalog, web page, access to other libraries' catalogs. *Collection:* 144,632 titles, 27,285 serial subscriptions, 10,690 audiovisual materials.

Computer facilities: 150 computers available on campus for general student use. A campuswide network can be accessed from student residence rooms and from off campus. Internet access and online class registration are available. *Web address:* http://www.une.edu/.

General Application Contact: Peggy Warden, Assistant Dean of Graduate Admissions, 207-221-4225, Fax: 207-221-4898, E-mail: admissions@une.edu.

GRADUATE UNITS

College of Arts and Sciences Students: 19 full-time (11 women), 463 part-time (343 women); includes 12 minority (3 African Americans, 1 American Indian/Alaska Native, 4 Asian Americans or Pacific Islanders, 4 Hispanic Americans), 3 international. Average age 37. 167 applicants, 100% accepted, 127 enrolled. *Faculty:* 27 full-time (13 women), 31 part-time/adjunct (17 women). Expenses: Contact institution. *Financial support:* Available to part-time students. Application deadline: 5/1; In 2006, 242 master's, 11 other advanced degrees awarded. *Degree program information:* Part-time programs available. Postbaccalaureate distance learning degree programs offered (minimal on-campus study). Offers applied biosciences (MS); arts and sciences (MS, MS Ed, CAGS); educational leadership (CAGS); general studies (MS Ed); literacy (MS Ed); marine science (MS); teaching methodologies (MS Ed). *Application deadline:* Applications are processed on a rolling basis. *Application fee:* $40. *Application Contact:* Robert Pecchia, Associate Dean of Admissions, 207-283-0171 Ext. 2297, Fax: 207-602-5900, E-mail: admissions@une.edu. *Interim Dean,* Paul Burlin, 207-283-0171 Ext. 2371, E-mail: pburlin@une.edu.

College of Health Professions Students: 348 full-time (262 women), 63 part-time (55 women); includes 23 minority (6 African Americans, 2 American Indian/Alaska Native, 7 Asian Americans or Pacific Islanders, 8 Hispanic Americans), 6 international. Average age 32. 796 applicants, 35% accepted, 188 enrolled. *Faculty:* 40 full-time (24 women), 42 part-time/adjunct (20 women). Expenses: Contact institution. *Financial support:* Career-related internships or fieldwork and Federal Work-Study available. Support available to part-time students. Financial award application deadline: 5/1; financial award applicants required to submit FAFSA. In 2006, 157 master's, 1 other advanced degree awarded. *Degree program information:* Part-time programs available. Postbaccalaureate distance learning degree programs offered (minimal on-campus study). Offers health professions (MS, MSW, DPT, Certificate); nurse anesthesia (MS); occupational therapy (MS); physical therapy (DPT); physician assistant (MS); post professional occupational therapy (MS); post professional physical therapy (DPT). *Application deadline:* Applications are processed on a rolling basis. *Application fee:* $40. *Application Contact:* Peggy Warden, Assistant Dean of Graduate Admissions, 207-221-4225, Fax: 207-221-4898, E-mail: admissions@une.edu. *Dean,* Dr. David Ward, 207-283-0171 Ext. 4520, E-mail: dward1@une.edu.

School of Social Work Students: 116 full-time (103 women), 41 part-time (34 women); includes 4 minority (1 African American, 2 American Indian/Alaska Native, 1 Asian American or Pacific Islander), 4 international. Average age 32. 110 applicants, 86% accepted, 55 enrolled. *Faculty:* 14 full-time (8 women), 5 part-time/adjunct (4 women). Expenses: Contact institution. *Financial support:* In 2006–07, 40 students received support. Scholarships/grants and tuition waivers (partial) available. Financial award application deadline: 5/1; financial award applicants required to submit FAFSA. In 2006, 55 master's, 1 other advanced degree awarded. *Degree program information:* Part-time programs available. Offers addictions counseling (Certificate); gerontology (Certificate); social work (MSW). *Application deadline:* For fall admission, 1/15 priority date for domestic students; for spring admission, 3/31 priority date for domestic students, 3/31 for international students. Applications are processed on a rolling basis. *Application fee:* $40. Electronic applications accepted. *Application Contact:* Peggy Warden, Assistant Dean of Graduate Admissions, 207-221-4225, Fax: 207-221-4898, E-mail: admissions@une.edu. *Director,* Martha Wilson, 207-283-0171 Ext. 4513, E-mail: mwilson@une.edu.

College of Osteopathic Medicine Students: 503 full-time (270 women), 32 part-time (24 women); includes 41 minority (8 African Americans, 2 American Indian/Alaska Native, 23 Asian Americans or Pacific Islanders, 8 Hispanic Americans), 2 international. Average age 28. 201 applicants, 100% accepted, 143 enrolled. *Faculty:* 58 full-time (29 women), 40 part-time/adjunct (16 women). Expenses: Contact institution. *Financial support:* In 2006–07, 4 fellowships with full tuition reimbursements (averaging $5,000 per year) were awarded; Federal Work-Study, institutionally sponsored loans, and scholarships/grants also available. Support available to part-time students. Financial award application deadline: 5/1; financial award applicants required to submit FAFSA. In 2006, 117 DOs, 1 other advanced degree awarded. Offers osteopathic medicine (DO, MPH, Certificate); public health (MPH, Certificate). *Application deadline:* For fall admission, 3/1 for domestic students. *Application fee:* $55. *Application Contact:* Lisa Lane, Assistant Director, Graduate Medical Programs, 207-283-0171 Ext. 2297, Fax: 207-602-5900, E-mail: llacroixlane@une.edu. *Dean,* Dr. Boyd Buser, 207-283-0171 Ext. 2340, Fax: 207-878-2434.

UNIVERSITY OF NEW HAMPSHIRE, Durham, NH 03824

General Information State-supported, coed, university. CGS member. *Enrollment:* 14,848 graduate, professional, and undergraduate students; 1,254 full-time matriculated graduate/professional students (773 women), 1,180 part-time matriculated graduate/professional students (682 women). *Enrollment by degree level:* 1,922 master's, 488 doctoral, 24 other advanced degrees. *Graduate faculty:* 605 full-time. Tuition, state resident: full-time $8,540; part-time $474 per credit hour. Tuition, nonresident: full-time $20,990; part-time $862 per credit hour. *Required fees:* $1,343; $356 per term. Tuition and fees vary according to course load, program and reciprocity agreements. *Graduate housing:* Rooms and/or apartments available on a first-come, first-served basis to single and married students. Housing application deadline: 7/15. *Student services:* Campus employment opportunities, campus safety program, career counseling, child daycare facilities, disabled student services, exercise/wellness program, free psychological counseling, international student services, low-cost health insurance, multicultural affairs office. *Library facilities:* Dimond Library plus 4 others. *Online resources:* library catalog, web page, access to other libraries' catalogs. *Collection:* 1.8 million titles, 36,313 serial subscriptions, 39,508 audiovisual materials.

Computer facilities: 389 computers available on campus for general student use. A campuswide network can be accessed from student residence rooms and from off campus. Internet access and online class registration are available. *Web address:* http://www.unh.edu/.

General Application Contact: Graduate Admissions Office, 603-862-3000, Fax: 603-862-0275, E-mail: grad.school@unh.edu.

GRADUATE UNITS

Graduate School Students: 1,254 full-time (773 women), 1,180 part-time (682 women); includes 105 minority (25 African Americans, 6 American Indian/Alaska Native, 48 Asian Americans or Pacific Islanders, 26 Hispanic Americans), 228 international. Average age 28. 1,769 applicants, 71% accepted, 695 enrolled. *Faculty:* 605 full-time. Expenses: Contact institution. *Financial support:* In 2006–07, 69 fellowships, 206 research assistantships, 377 teaching assistantships were awarded; career-related internships or fieldwork, Federal Work-Study, scholarships/grants, and tuition waivers (full and partial) also available. Support available to part-time students. Financial award application deadline: 2/15; financial award applicants required to submit FAFSA. In 2006, 877 master's, 55 doctorates, 4 other advanced degrees awarded. *Degree program information:* Part-time and evening/weekend programs available. Offers college teaching (MST); earth and environmental science (PhD); environmental education (MA); natural resources and environmental studies (PhD). *Application deadline:* For fall admission, 4/1 priority date for domestic and international students; for winter admission, 12/1 priority date for domestic students; for spring admission, 4/1 for domestic students. Applications are processed on a rolling basis. *Application fee:* $60. Electronic applications accepted. *Application Contact:* 603-862-3000, Fax: 603-862-0275, E-mail: grad.school@unh.edu. *Dean,* Dr. Harry J. Richards, 603-862-3005, Fax: 603-862-0275, E-mail: harry.richards@unh.edu.

College of Engineering and Physical Sciences Students: 210 full-time (65 women), 213 part-time (64 women); includes 21 minority (3 African Americans, 14 Asian Americans or Pacific Islanders, 4 Hispanic Americans), 142 international. Average age 30. 384 applicants, 74% accepted, 126 enrolled. *Faculty:* 178 full-time. Expenses: Contact institution. *Financial support:* In 2006–07, 12 fellowships, 122 research assistantships, 128 teaching assistantships were awarded; career-related internships or fieldwork, Federal Work-Study, scholarships/grants, and tuition waivers (full and partial) also available. Support available to part-time students. Financial award application deadline: 2/15; financial award applicants required to submit FAFSA. In 2006, 69 master's, 16 doctorates awarded. *Degree program information:* Part-time and evening/weekend programs available. Offers applied mathematics (MS); chemical engineering (MS, PhD); chemistry (MS, MST, PhD); chemistry education (PhD); civil engineering (MS, PhD); computer science (MS, PhD); earth sciences (MS); electrical engineering (MS, PhD); engineering and physical sciences (MS, MST, PhD); hydrology (MS); materials science (MS, PhD); mathematics (MS, MST, PhD); mathematics education (PhD); mechanical engineering (MS, PhD); ocean engineering (MS, PhD); ocean mapping (MS); physics (MS, PhD); statistics (MS); systems design (PhD). *Application deadline:* For fall admission, 4/1 priority date for domestic students, 4/1 for international students; for winter admission, 12/1 priority date for domestic students. Applications are processed on a rolling basis. *Application fee:* $60. Electronic applications accepted. *Dean,* Dr. Arthur Greenberg, 603-862-1781.

College of Liberal Arts Students: 390 full-time (285 women), 507 part-time (333 women); includes 41 minority (9 African Americans, 6 American Indian/Alaska Native, 10 Asian Americans or Pacific Islanders, 16 Hispanic Americans), 15 international. Average age 34. 628 applicants, 62% accepted, 211 enrolled. *Faculty:* 188 full-time. Expenses: Contact institution. *Financial support:* In 2006–07, 32 fellowships, 7 research assistantships, 133 teaching assistantships were awarded; career-related internships or fieldwork, Federal Work-Study, scholarships/grants, and tuition waivers (full and partial) also available. Support available to part-time students. Financial award application deadline: 2/15. In 2006, 372 master's, 12 doctorates, 4 other advanced degrees awarded. *Degree program information:* Part-time programs available. Offers counseling (M Ed, MA); early childhood education (M Ed); education (PhD); educational administration (M Ed, CAGS); elementary education (M Ed, MAT); English (PhD); English education (MST); history (MA, PhD); justice studies (MA); language and linguistics (MA); liberal arts (M Ed, MA, MALS, MAT, MFA, MPA, MST, PhD, CAGS); liberal studies (MALS); literature (MA); museum studies (MA); music education (MA); music history (MA); painting (MFA); political science (MA); psychology (PhD); public administration (MPA); reading (M Ed); secondary education (M Ed, MAT); sociology (MA, PhD); Spanish (MA); special education (M Ed); special needs (M Ed); teacher leadership (M Ed); writing (MA). *Application deadline:* For fall admission, 4/1 for domestic students; for winter admission, 12/1 for domestic students; for spring admission, 4/1 for domestic students. Applications are processed on a rolling basis. *Application fee:* $60. Electronic applications accepted. *Dean,* Dr. Marilyn Hoskin, 603-862-2062.

College of Life Sciences and Agriculture Students: 100 full-time (62 women), 107 part-time (66 women); includes 7 minority (1 African American, 5 Asian Americans or Pacific Islanders, 1 Hispanic American), 17 international. Average age 34. 137 applicants, 55% accepted, 47 enrolled. *Faculty:* 141 full-time. Expenses: Contact institution. *Financial support:* In 2006–07, 1 fellowship, 49 research assistantships, 72 teaching assistantships were awarded; career-related internships or fieldwork, Federal Work-Study, scholarships/grants, and tuition waivers (full and partial) also available. Support available to part-time students. Financial award application deadline: 2/15. In 2006, 42 master's, 11 doctorates awarded. *Degree program information:* Part-time programs available. Offers animal and nutritional sciences (PhD); animal science (MS); biochemistry (MS, PhD); environmental conservation (MS); forestry (MS); genetics (MS, PhD); life sciences and agriculture (MS, PhD); microbiology (MS, PhD); nutritional sciences (MS); plant biology (MS, PhD); resource administration (MS); resource economics (MS); soil science (MS); water resources management (MS); wildlife (MS); zoology (MS, PhD). *Application deadline:* For fall admission, 4/1 for domestic and international students. Applications are processed on a rolling basis. *Application fee:* $60. Electronic applications accepted. *Dean,* 603-862-1450.

School of Health and Human Services Students: 295 full-time (262 women), 198 part-time (167 women); includes 12 minority (7 African Americans, 3 Asian Americans or Pacific Islanders, 2 Hispanic Americans), 5 international. Average age 31. 355 applicants, 79% accepted, 162 enrolled. *Faculty:* 66 full-time. Expenses: Contact institution. *Financial support:* In 2006–07, 10 fellowships, 1 research assistantship, 29 teaching assistantships were

University of New Hampshire (continued)

awarded; career-related internships or fieldwork, Federal Work-Study, scholarships/grants, and tuition waivers (full and partial) also available. Support available to part-time students. Financial award application deadline: 2/15. In 2006, 217 degrees awarded. *Degree program information:* Part-time and evening/weekend programs available. Offers early childhood intervention (MS); family studies (MS); health and human services (MPH, MS, MSW); kinesiology (MS); language and literature disabilities (MS); marriage and family therapy (MS); nursing (MS); occupational therapy (MS); public health: ecology (MPH); public health: nursing (MPH); public health: policy and management (MPH); recreation administration (MS); social work (MSW); therapeutic recreation (MS). *Application deadline:* For fall admission, 4/1 priority date for domestic students, 4/1 for international students; for winter admission, 12/1 priority date for domestic students. Applications are processed on a rolling basis. *Application fee:* $60. Electronic applications accepted. *Dean,* Dr. James McCarthy, 603-862-1178.

Whittemore School of Business and Economics Students: 199 full-time (70 women), 133 part-time (42 women); includes 20 minority (4 African Americans, 15 Asian Americans or Pacific Islanders, 1 Hispanic American), 36 international. Average age 34. 232 applicants, 84% accepted, 140 enrolled. *Faculty:* 43 full-time. Expenses: Contact institution. *Financial support:* In 2006–07, 8 fellowships, 4 research assistantships, 11 teaching assistantships were awarded; career-related internships or fieldwork, Federal Work-Study, scholarships/grants, and tuition waivers (full and partial) also available. Support available to part-time students. Financial award application deadline: 2/15. In 2006, 110 master's, 3 doctorates awarded. *Degree program information:* Part-time and evening/weekend programs available. Offers accounting (MS); business administration (MBA); business and economics (MA, MBA, MS, PhD); economics (MA, PhD); executive business administration (MBA); health management (MBA); management of technology (MS). *Application deadline:* For fall admission, 4/1 for domestic and international students; for winter admission, 12/1 for domestic students. Applications are processed on a rolling basis. *Application fee:* $60. Electronic applications accepted. *Dean,* Dr. Steve Bolander, 603-862-1981.

See Close-Up on page 1099.

UNIVERSITY OF NEW HAMPSHIRE AT MANCHESTER, Manchester, NH 03101-1113

General Information State-supported, coed, comprehensive institution.

GRADUATE UNITS

Center for Graduate and Professional Studies

UNIVERSITY OF NEW HAVEN, West Haven, CT 06516-1916

General Information Independent, coed, comprehensive institution. CGS member. *Graduate housing:* On-campus housing not available.

GRADUATE UNITS

Graduate School *Degree program information:* Part-time and evening/weekend programs available.

College of Arts and Sciences *Degree program information:* Part-time and evening/weekend programs available. Offers arts and sciences (MA, MS, Certificate); cellular and molecular biology (MS); community psychology (MA, Certificate); education (MS); environmental sciences (MS); executive tourism and hospitality (MS); hotel, restaurant, tourism and dietetics administration (MS); human nutrition (MS); industrial and organizational psychology (MA, Certificate); tourism and hospitality management (MS).

Henry C. Lee College of Criminal Justice and Forensic Sciences *Degree program information:* Part-time and evening/weekend programs available. Offers advanced investigation (MS); correctional counseling (MS); criminal justice and forensic sciences (MS); criminal justice management (MS); criminalistics (MS); fire science (MS); forensic science (MS); industrial hygiene (MS); occupational safety and health management (MS); security management (MS).

School of Business *Degree program information:* Part-time and evening/weekend programs available. Offers accounting (MBA); business (EMBA, MBA, MPA, MS); business administration (EMBA, MBA); business policy and strategy (MBA); corporate taxation (MS); finance (MBA); finance and financial services (MS); financial accounting (MS); health care administration (MS); health care management (MBA, MPA); human resources management (MBA); industrial relations (MS); international business (MBA); managerial accounting (MS); marketing (MBA); personnel and labor relations (MPA); public relations (MBA); public taxation (MS); sports management (MBA); taxation (MS); technology management (MBA).

Tagliatela College of Engineering *Degree program information:* Part-time and evening/weekend programs available. Offers applications software (MS); civil engineering design (Certificate); electrical engineering (MSEE); engineering (EMS, MS, MSEE, MSIE, MSME, Certificate); engineering management (EMS); environmental engineering (MS); industrial engineering (MSIE); logistics (Certificate); management information systems (MS); mechanical engineering (MSME); operations research (MS); systems software (MS).

See Close-Up on page 1101.

UNIVERSITY OF NEW MEXICO, Albuquerque, NM 87131-2039

General Information State-supported, coed, university. CGS member. *Enrollment:* 26,172 graduate, professional, and undergraduate students; 3,085 full-time matriculated graduate/professional students (1,699 women), 2,757 part-time matriculated graduate/professional students (1,603 women). *Enrollment by degree level:* 1,009 first professional, 3,797 master's, 1,033 doctoral, 3 other advanced degrees. *Graduate faculty:* 1,509 full-time (666 women), 682 part-time/adjunct (359 women). *Graduate housing:* Rooms and/or apartments available on a first-come, first-served basis to single and married students. *Student services:* Campus employment opportunities, campus safety program, career counseling, child daycare facilities, disabled student services, exercise/wellness program, free psychological counseling, international student services, low-cost health insurance, teacher training. *Library facilities:* The University of New Mexico General Library plus 7 others. *Online resources:* library catalog, web page, access to other libraries' catalogs. *Collection:* 2.7 million titles, 592,243 serial subscriptions. *Research affiliation:* Sandia National Laboratories, Los Alamos National Laboratory, Lovelace Respiratory Research Institute, Phillips Laboratory.

Computer facilities: Computer purchase and lease plans are available. 446 computers available on campus for general student use. A campuswide network can be accessed from student residence rooms and from off campus. Internet access and online class registration are available. *Web address:* http://www.unm.edu/.

General Application Contact: Edwina Chavez-Salazar, Enrollment Management Specialist, 505-277-2711, Fax: 505-277-7405, E-mail: edwinac@unm.edu.

GRADUATE UNITS

Graduate School Students: 1,925 full-time (1,049 women), 2,439 part-time (1,463 women); includes 1,157 minority (81 African Americans, 194 American Indian/Alaska Native, 108 Asian Americans or Pacific Islanders, 774 Hispanic Americans), 554 international. Average age 35. 3,226 applicants, 40% accepted, 891 enrolled. *Faculty:* 831 full-time (359 women), 453 part-time/adjunct (252 women). Expenses: Contact institution. *Financial support:* In 2006–07, 1,593 students received support, including 174 fellowships (averaging $15,503 per year), 700 research assistantships (averaging $11,083 per year), 657 teaching assistantships (averaging $8,391 per year); career-related internships or fieldwork, Federal Work-Study, institutionally sponsored loans, scholarships/grants, health care benefits, tuition waivers (full and partial), unspecified assistantships, and project assistantships, residencies also available. Support available to part-time students. Financial award application deadline: 3/1; financial award applicants required to submit FAFSA. In 2006, 821 master's, 178 doctorates awarded. *Degree program information:* Part-time and evening/weekend programs available. Post-baccalaureate distance learning degree programs offered. Offers water resources (MWR). *Application deadline:* For fall admission, 3/1 priority date for domestic and international students; for spring admission, 8/1 priority date for domestic and international students. *Application fee:* $50. Electronic applications accepted. *Application Contact:* Edwina Chavez-Salazar, Enrollment Management Specialist, 505-277-2711, Fax: 505-277-7405, E-mail: edwinac@unm.edu. *Dean,* Dr. Teresita E. Aguilar, 505-277-2711, Fax: 505-277-7405.

College of Arts and Sciences Students: 797 full-time (431 women), 638 part-time (349 women); includes 296 minority (16 African Americans, 29 American Indian/Alaska Native, 32 Asian Americans or Pacific Islanders, 219 Hispanic Americans), 246 international. Average age 33. 1,473 applicants, 34% accepted, 315 enrolled. *Faculty:* 412 full-time (160 women), 169 part-time/adjunct (88 women). Expenses: Contact institution. *Financial support:* In 2006–07, 521 students received support, including fellowships (averaging $10,712 per year), research assistantships (averaging $10,264 per year), teaching assistantships (averaging $9,263 per year); scholarships/grants, health care benefits, tuition waivers (full and partial), and unspecified assistantships also available. Financial award application deadline: 3/1; financial award applicants required to submit FAFSA. In 2006, 211 master's, 90 doctorates awarded. *Degree program information:* Part-time and evening/weekend programs available. Offers American studies (MA, PhD); anthropology (MA, MS, PhD); arts and sciences (MA, MFA, MS, PhD); biology (MS, PhD); biomedical physics (MS, PhD); chemistry (MS, PhD); clinical psychology (MS, PhD); communication (MA, PhD); comparative literature and cultural studies (MA); earth and planetary sciences (MS, PhD); economics (MA, PhD); English (MA, MFA, MS, PhD); French (MA); French studies (PhD); geography (MS); German studies (MA); history (MA, PhD); Latin American studies (MA, PhD); linguistics (MA, PhD); mathematics (MS, PhD); optical science and engineering (MS); optical sciences and engineering (PhD); philosophy (MA, PhD); physics (MS, PhD); political science (MA, PhD); Portuguese (MA); psychology (MS, PhD); sociology (MA, PhD); Spanish (MA); Spanish and Portuguese (PhD); speech and hearing sciences (MS); statistics (MS, PhD). *Application fee:* $50. Electronic applications accepted. *Application Contact:* Vicki Hall, Academic Administrator III, 505-277-6131, Fax: 505-277-0351, E-mail: vhall@unm.edu. *Dean,* Dr. Vera Norwood, 505-277-3046, Fax: 505-277-0351, E-mail: vnorwood@unm.edu.

College of Education Students: 368 full-time (237 women), 891 part-time (647 women); includes 422 minority (42 African Americans, 90 American Indian/Alaska Native, 28 Asian Americans or Pacific Islanders, 262 Hispanic Americans), 54 international. Average age 39. 619 applicants, 49% accepted, 234 enrolled. *Faculty:* 107 full-time (73 women), 89 part-time/adjunct (71 women). Expenses: Contact institution. *Financial support:* In 2006–07, 475 students received support, including 79 fellowships with partial tuition reimbursements available (averaging $19,768 per year), 10 research assistantships with partial tuition reimbursements available (averaging $7,069 per year), 85 teaching assistantships with full tuition reimbursements available (averaging $7,964 per year); scholarships/grants and unspecified assistantships also available. Financial award application deadline: 3/1; financial award applicants required to submit FAFSA. In 2006, 342 master's, 38 doctorates, 16 other advanced degrees awarded. Offers art education (MA); counselor education (MA, PhD); education (MA, MS, Ed D, PhD, EDSPC); educational leadership (MA, Ed D, EDSPC); educational linguistics (Ed D, PhD); educational psychology (MA, PhD); elementary education (MA, EDSPC); family studies (MA, PhD); health education (MS); language, literacy and sociocultural studies (MA, Ed D, PhD); multicultural teacher and childhood education (Ed D, PhD, EDSPC); nutrition (MS); organizational learning and instructional technologies (MA, PhD, EDSPC); physical education (MS, Ed D, PhD, EDSPC); secondary education (MA, EDSPC); special education (MA, Ed D, PhD, EDSPC); teacher education (MA, EDSPC). *Application deadline:* For fall admission, 3/1 for domestic students; for spring admission, 8/1 for domestic students. *Application fee:* $50. Electronic applications accepted. *Application Contact:* Ed O'Brien, Receptionist, 505-277-3190, Fax: 505-277-8427, E-mail: edob@unm.edu. *Dean,* Dr. Viola E. Florez, 505-277-7267, Fax: 505-277-8427, E-mail: vflorez@unm.edu.

College of Fine Arts Students: 80 full-time (49 women), 114 part-time (65 women); includes 45 minority (1 African American, 7 American Indian/Alaska Native, 9 Asian Americans or Pacific Islanders, 28 Hispanic Americans), 17 international. Average age 32. 301 applicants, 34% accepted, 70 enrolled. *Faculty:* 66 full-time (31 women), 91 part-time/adjunct (59 women). Expenses: Contact institution. *Financial support:* In 2006–07, 99 students received support, including 7 research assistantships (averaging $7,377 per year), 84 teaching assistantships (averaging $6,123 per year); fellowships, health care benefits and unspecified assistantships also available. Financial award application deadline: 3/1; financial award applicants required to submit FAFSA. In 2006, 27 master's, 14 doctorates awarded. *Degree program information:* Part-time programs available. Offers art history (MA, PhD); dramatic writing (MFA); fine arts (M Mu, MA, MFA, PhD); music (M Mu); studio arts (MFA); theater and dance (MA). *Application fee:* $50. *Dean,* Dr. James S. Moy, 505-277-2111, Fax: 505-277-0708.

College of Nursing Students: 66 full-time (63 women), 147 part-time (136 women); includes 53 minority (5 African Americans, 8 American Indian/Alaska Native, 2 Asian Americans or Pacific Islanders, 38 Hispanic Americans), 2 international. Average age 42. 119 applicants, 57% accepted, 55 enrolled. *Faculty:* 44 full-time (39 women), 9 part-time/adjunct (all women). Expenses: Contact institution. *Financial support:* In 2006–07, 64 students received support, including 1 research assistantship (averaging $3,000 per year), 9 teaching assistantships with partial tuition reimbursements available (averaging $5,800 per year); scholarships/grants, traineeships, and tuition waivers (full) also available. Financial award application deadline: 3/1; financial award applicants required to submit FAFSA. In 2006, 39 master's awarded. *Degree program information:* Part-time programs available. Post-baccalaureate distance learning degree programs offered. Offers nursing (MSN, PhD). *Application fee:* $50. Electronic applications accepted. *Application Contact:* Elizabeth Rowe, Student Program Advisor, 505-272-4223, Fax: 505-272-3970, E-mail: erowe@unm.edu. *Senior Associate Dean of Academic Affairs,* Dr. Robin Meize-Grochowski, 505-272-8327, Fax: 505-272-3970, E-mail: rmeize@salud.unm.edu.

College of Pharmacy Students: 339 full-time (221 women), 29 part-time (20 women); includes 177 minority (8 African Americans, 19 American Indian/Alaska Native, 36 Asian Americans or Pacific Islanders, 114 Hispanic Americans), 3 international. Average age 31. 22 applicants, 0% accepted. *Faculty:* 36 full-time (17 women), 5 part-time/adjunct (3 women). Expenses: Contact institution. *Financial support:* In 2006–07, 281 students received support, including 6 research assistantships (averaging $21,500 per year); residencies also available. Financial award application deadline: 3/1; financial award applicants required to submit FAFSA. In 2006, 78 first professional degrees, 3 master's, 1 doctorate awarded. *Degree program information:* Part-time programs available. Offers pharmaceutical sciences (MS, PhD); pharmacy (Pharm D, MS, PhD). *Application deadline:* For fall admission, 2/1 for domestic students. Electronic applications accepted. *Application Contact:* Vanessa G. Harris, Supervisor, Academic Advisement, 505-272-0912, Fax: 505-272-8324, E-mail: vgharris@salud.unm.edu. *Dean,* Dr. John Pieper, 505-272-3241, E-mail: jpieper@salud.unm.edu.

School of Architecture and Planning Students: 147 full-time (74 women), 58 part-time (34 women); includes 57 minority (4 African Americans, 15 American Indian/Alaska Native, 3 Asian Americans or Pacific Islanders, 35 Hispanic Americans), 10 international. Average age 34. 169 applicants, 64% accepted, 65 enrolled. *Faculty:* 20 full-time (6 women), 29 part-time/adjunct (11 women). Expenses: Contact institution. *Financial support:* In 2006–07, 102 students received support, including 1 fellowship (averaging $2,700 per year), 15 research assistantships (averaging $5,917 per year), 2 teaching assistantships (averaging $2,088 per year); health care benefits also available. Financial award application deadline: 3/1; financial award applicants required to submit FAFSA. In 2006, 50 master's awarded. *Degree program information:* Part-time programs available. Offers architecture (M Arch); architecture and planning (M Arch, MCRP, MLA); community and regional planning (MCRP); landscape architecture (MLA). *Application fee:* $50. *Application Contact:* Lois A. Kennedy, Senior Academic Adviser, 505-277-4847, Fax: 505-277-0076, E-mail: loisk@unm.edu. *Dean,* Dr. Roger L. Schluntz, 505-277-2879, Fax: 505-277-0076, E-mail: schluntz@unm.edu.

School of Engineering Students: 254 full-time (49 women), 339 part-time (70 women); includes 109 minority (5 African Americans, 5 American Indian/Alaska Native, 23 Asian Americans or Pacific Islanders, 76 Hispanic Americans), 192 international. Average age 31. 444 applicants, 35% accepted, 114 enrolled. *Faculty:* 94 full-time (10 women), 45 part-time/adjunct (5 women). Expenses: Contact institution. *Financial support:* In 2006–07, 9 fellowships (averaging $7,667 per year), 325 research assistantships (averaging $14,484 per year), 40 teaching assistantships (averaging $12,394 per year) were awarded. Financial award application deadline: 3/1; financial award applicants required to submit FAFSA. In 2006, 113 master's, 35 doctorates awarded. Offers chemical engineering (MS, PhD); civil engineering (MS); computer science (MS, PhD); construction management (MCM); electrical engineering (MS); engineering (PhD); manufacturing engineering (MEME); mechanical engineering (MS); nuclear engineering (MS, PhD); optical sciences (PhD). *Application deadline:* Applications are processed on a rolling basis. *Application fee:* $50. Electronic applications accepted. *Dean,* Dr. Joseph L. Cecchi, 505-277-5522, Fax: 505-277-1422, E-mail: cecchi@unm.edu.

School of Public Administration Students: 38 full-time (21 women), 102 part-time (70 women); includes 74 minority (4 African Americans, 22 American Indian/Alaska Native, 1 Asian American or Pacific Islander, 47 Hispanic Americans), 4 international. Average age 37. 57 applicants, 74% accepted, 29 enrolled. *Faculty:* 5 full-time (2 women), 1 part-time/adjunct (0 women). Expenses: Contact institution. *Financial support:* In 2006–07, 45 students received support; fellowships, institutionally sponsored loans and scholarships/grants available. Financial award application deadline: 3/31; financial award applicants required to submit FAFSA. In 2006, 28 degrees awarded. *Degree program information:* Part-time and evening/weekend programs available. Postbaccalaureate distance learning degree programs offered (no on-campus study). Offers public administration (MPA). *Application deadline:* For fall admission, 6/1 for domestic students; for spring admission, 11/1 for domestic students. *Application fee:* $50. Electronic applications accepted. *Application Contact:* Linda Barril, Department Administrator, 505-277-1092, Fax: 505-277-2529, E-mail: spagrad@mgt.unm.edu. *Interim Director,* Dr. F. Lee Brown, 505-277-1092, Fax: 505-277-2529, E-mail: flbrown@unm.edu.

Robert O. Anderson Graduate School of Management *Degree program information:* Part-time and evening/weekend programs available. Offers accounting (M Acc, MBA); financial management (MBA); financial, international and technology management (MBA); human resources management (MBA); international management (MBA); international management in Latin America (MBA); management information systems (MBA); management of technology (MBA); marketing management (MBA); marketing, information and decision sciences (MBA); operations management (MBA); organizational studies (MBA); policy and planning (MBA); tax accounting (MBA).

School of Law Students: 343 full-time; includes 155 minority (12 African Americans, 40 American Indian/Alaska Native, 9 Asian Americans or Pacific Islanders, 94 Hispanic Americans). 1,405 applicants, 18% accepted, 115 enrolled. *Faculty:* 34 full-time (18 women), 27 part-time/adjunct (12 women). Expenses: Contact institution. *Financial support:* Career-related internships or fieldwork, Federal Work-Study, and scholarships/grants available. Financial award application deadline: 3/1; financial award applicants required to submit FAFSA. In 2006, 119 degrees awarded. Offers law (JD). *Application deadline:* For fall admission, 2/15 priority date for domestic students, 2/15 for international students. Applications are processed on a rolling basis. *Application fee:* $50. Electronic applications accepted. *Application Contact:* Susan L. Mitchell, Assistant Dean for Admissions and Financial Aid, 505-277-0959, Fax: 505-277-9958, E-mail: mitchell@law.unm.edu. *Dean,* Suellyn Scarnecchia, 505-277-4700, Fax: 505-277-1597, E-mail: scarnecchia@law.unm.edu.

School of Medicine Offers biochemistry and molecular biology (MS, PhD); cell biology and physiology (MS, PhD); dental hygiene (MS); medicine (MD, MOT, MPH, MPT, MS, PhD); molecular genetics and microbiology (MS, PhD); neuroscience (MS, PhD); occupational therapy (MOT); pathology (MS, PhD); physical therapy (MPT); public health (MPH); toxicology (MS, PhD). Electronic applications accepted.

See Close-Up on page 1103.

UNIVERSITY OF NEW ORLEANS, New Orleans, LA 70148

General Information State-supported, coed, university. CGS member. *Enrollment:* 11,747 graduate, professional, and undergraduate students; 2,591 matriculated graduate/professional students (1,566 women). *Graduate faculty:* 679. Tuition, state resident: full-time $3,292. Tuition, nonresident: full-time $10,336. *Required fees:* $158. *Graduate housing:* Rooms and/or apartments available on a first-come, first-served basis to single students and available to married students. *Student services:* Campus employment opportunities, campus safety program, career counseling, child daycare facilities, disabled student services, exercise/wellness program, free psychological counseling, grant writing training, international student services, low-cost health insurance, multicultural affairs office, writing training. *Library facilities:* Earl K. Long Library. *Online resources:* library catalog, web page, access to other libraries' catalogs. *Collection:* 896,000 titles, 4,950 serial subscriptions, 22,775 audiovisual materials. *Research affiliation:* Lockheed-Martin Corporation (materials), Applied Research Lab-Penn State University (engineering), Paratek Microwave, Inc. (Nanotechnology), TJ Watson Research Center-IBM (chemistry), Northrop Grumman Corp. (engineering), John C. Stennis Space Center (acoustics, computer science).

Computer facilities: 1,084 computers available on campus for general student use. A campuswide network can be accessed from student residence rooms and from off campus. Internet access is available. *Web address:* http://www.uno.edu/.

General Application Contact: Amanda M. Athey, Coordinator of Program Reviews and Electronic Theses and Dissertations, 504-280-1155, Fax: 504-280-6298, E-mail: gradschool@uno.edu.

GRADUATE UNITS

Graduate School Students: 2,508; includes 634 minority (420 African Americans, 9 American Indian/Alaska Native, 77 Asian Americans or Pacific Islanders, 128 Hispanic Americans), 288 international. Average age 33. Expenses: Contact institution. *Financial support:* In 2006–07, 1,350 students received support; fellowships, research assistantships, teaching assistantships, career-related internships or fieldwork, Federal Work-Study, institutionally sponsored loans, scholarships/grants, tuition waivers (full and partial), and unspecified assistantships available. Financial award application deadline: 3/15; financial award applicants required to submit FAFSA. In 2006, 751 master's, 51 doctorates awarded. *Degree program information:* Part-time and evening/weekend programs available. Postbaccalaureate distance learning degree programs offered (minimal on-campus study). *Application deadline:* For fall admission, 7/1 priority date for domestic students, 6/1 for international students; for spring admission, 11/15 priority date for domestic students, 10/1 for international students. Applications are processed on a rolling basis. *Application fee:* $40. Electronic applications accepted. *Dean,* Dr. Robert Cashner, 504-280-6237, Fax: 504-280-6298, E-mail: rcashner@uno.edu.

College of Business Administration Students: 715 (369 women). Average age 31. Expenses: Contact institution. *Financial support:* Fellowships, research assistantships, teaching assistantships, Federal Work-Study available. Financial award application deadline: 3/15; financial award applicants required to submit FAFSA. In 2006, 106 master's, 1 doctorate awarded. *Degree program information:* Part-time and evening/weekend programs available. Offers accounting (MS); business administration (MBA, MS, PhD); economics and finance (MS); financial economics (PhD); health care management (MS); hospitality and tourism management (MS); taxation (MS). *Application deadline:* For fall admission, 7/1 priority date for domestic students, 6/1 for international students; for spring admission, 11/15 priority date for domestic students, 10/1 for international students. Applications are processed on a rolling basis. *Application fee:* $40. Electronic applications accepted. *Application Contact:* Dr. Paul Hensel, Associate Dean, 504-280-6954, Fax: 504-280-6693, E-mail: phensel@uno.edu. *Dean,* 504-280-6954, Fax: 504-280-6958.

College of Education and Human Development Students: 738 (592 women). Average age 39. Expenses: Contact institution. *Financial support:* Fellowships, research assistantships, teaching assistantships, career-related internships or fieldwork, institutionally sponsored loans, scholarships/grants, and tuition waivers (partial) available. Financial award application deadline: 3/15; financial award applicants required to submit FAFSA. In 2006, 163 master's, 18 doctorates awarded. *Degree program information:* Evening/weekend programs available. Offers counselor education (M Ed, PhD, GCE); curriculum and instruction (M Ed, PhD, GCE); education and human development (M Ed, PhD, GCE); educational leadership (M Ed, PhD, GCE); special education (M Ed, PhD, GCE). *Application deadline:* For fall admission, 7/1 priority date for domestic students, 6/1 for international students; for spring admission, 11/15 priority date for domestic students, 10/1 for international students. Applications are processed on a rolling basis. *Application fee:* $40. Electronic applications accepted. *Application Contact:* Dr. William Sharpton, Associate Dean, 504-280-6253, Fax: 504-280-6065. *Dean,* Dr. James Meza, 504-280-6028, Fax: 504-280-6065, E-mail: jmeza@uno.edu.

College of Engineering Students: 172 (38 women). Average age 32. Expenses: Contact institution. *Financial support:* Fellowships, research assistantships, teaching assistantships, institutionally sponsored loans available. Financial award application deadline: 3/15; financial award applicants required to submit FAFSA. In 2006, 41 master's, 6 doctorates awarded. *Degree program information:* Part-time and evening/weekend programs available. Offers engineering (MS, PhD, Certificate); engineering and applied sciences (PhD); engineering management (MS, Certificate); mechanical engineering (MS). *Application deadline:* For fall admission, 7/1 priority date for domestic students, 6/1 for international students; for spring admission, 10/1 for international students. Applications are processed on a rolling basis. *Application fee:* $40. Electronic applications accepted. *Application Contact:* Dr. Paul Chirlian, Associate Director, 504-280-5504, Fax: 504-280-7413, E-mail: pchirlia@uno.edu. *Dean,* Dr. Russell Trahan, 504-280-6825, Fax: 504-286-7413, E-mail: rtrahan@uno.edu.

College of Liberal Arts Students: 605 (356 women). Average age 32. Expenses: Contact institution. *Financial support:* Fellowships, research assistantships, teaching assistantships, career-related internships or fieldwork, Federal Work-Study, institutionally sponsored loans, and tuition waivers (full and partial) available. Financial award application deadline: 5/15; financial award applicants required to submit FAFSA. In 2006, 118 master's, 4 doctorates awarded. *Degree program information:* Part-time and evening/weekend programs available. Offers arts administration (MA); English (MA); English teaching (MAET); film production (MFA); fine arts (MFA); foreign languages (MA); geography (MA); history (MA); history teaching (MAHT); liberal arts (MA, MAET, MAHT, MFA, MM, MPA, MS, MURP, PhD); music (MM); political science (MA, PhD); public administration (MPA); sociology (MA); theatre directing (MFA); theatre performance (MFA); urban and regional planning (MURP); urban planning and regional studies (MS, MURP, PhD); urban studies (MS, PhD). *Application deadline:* For fall admission, 7/1 priority date for domestic students, 6/1 for international students; for spring admission, 11/15 priority date for domestic students, 10/1 for international students. Applications are processed on a rolling basis. *Application fee:* $40. Electronic applications accepted. *Application Contact:* Dr. Kevin Graves, Professor and Associate Dean, 504-280-6268, Fax: 504-280-6468, E-mail: kgraves@uno.edu. *Dean,* Dr. Susan Krantz, 504-280-6267, Fax: 504-280-6468, E-mail: susan.krantz@uno.edu.

College of Sciences Students: 255 (121 women). Average age 30. Expenses: Contact institution. *Financial support:* Fellowships, research assistantships, teaching assistantships, career-related internships or fieldwork, Federal Work-Study, institutionally sponsored loans, and unspecified assistantships available. Financial award application deadline: 3/15; financial award applicants required to submit FAFSA. *Degree program information:* Part-time and evening/weekend programs available. Offers biological sciences (MS, PhD); chemistry (MS, PhD); computer science (MS); earth and environmental sciences (MS); mathematics (MS); physics (MS, PhD); psychology (MS, PhD); science teaching (MAST); sciences (MAST, MS, PhD). *Application deadline:* For fall admission, 7/1 priority date for domestic students, 6/1 for international students; for spring admission, 11/15 priority date for domestic students, 10/1 for international students. Applications are processed on a rolling basis. *Application fee:* $40. Electronic applications accepted. *Application Contact:* Dr. Steve Stevenson, Associate Dean, 504-280-6783, Fax: 504-280-7483, E-mail: mmsteven@uno.edu. *Dean,* Dr. Joe King, 504-280-6563, Fax: 504-280-7483, E-mail: jmking@uno.edu.

UNIVERSITY OF NORTH ALABAMA, Florence, AL 35632-0001

General Information State-supported, coed, comprehensive institution. *Enrollment:* 6,810 graduate, professional, and undergraduate students; 349 full-time matriculated graduate/professional students (182 women), 721 part-time matriculated graduate/professional students (440 women). *Enrollment by degree level:* 1,044 master's, 26 other advanced degrees. *Graduate faculty:* 7 full-time (3 women), 69 part-time/adjunct (26 women). Tuition, state resident: full-time $4,080. Tuition, nonresident: full-time $8,160. *Required fees:* $764. *Graduate housing:* Rooms and/or apartments available on a first-come, first-served basis to single and married students. *Student services:* Campus employment opportunities, career counseling, child daycare facilities, exercise/wellness program, grant writing training, international student services, multicultural affairs office. *Library facilities:* Collier Library. *Online resources:* library catalog, web page, access to other libraries' catalogs. *Collection:* 380,361 titles, 3,760 serial subscriptions, 11,869 audiovisual materials.

Computer facilities: 750 computers available on campus for general student use. A campuswide network can be accessed from student residence rooms and from off campus. Internet access and online class registration are available. *Web address:* http://www.una.edu/.

General Application Contact: Kim Mauldin, Director of Admissions, 256-765-4608, Fax: 256-765-4960, E-mail: komauldin@una.edu.

GRADUATE UNITS

College of Arts and Sciences Students: 35 full-time (26 women), 19 part-time (12 women); includes 8 minority (7 African Americans, 1 American Indian/Alaska Native), 1 international. Average age 32. *Faculty:* 9 part-time/adjunct (3 women). Expenses: Contact institution. In 2006, 29 degrees awarded. *Degree program information:* Part-time and evening/weekend programs available. Offers arts and sciences (MAEN, MSCJ); criminal justice (MSCJ); English (MAEN). *Application deadline:* For fall admission, 7/1 priority date for domestic students; for spring admission, 12/1 for domestic students. Applications are processed on a rolling basis. *Application fee:* $25. *Application Contact:* Dr. Sue Wilson, Dean of Enrollment Management, 256-765-4316, Fax: 256-765-4349, E-mail: sjwilson@una.edu. *Dean,* Dr. Vagn Hansen, 256-765-4288, Fax: 256-765-4778, E-mail: vhansen@una.edu.

College of Business Students: 214 full-time (87 women), 410 part-time (195 women); includes 183 minority (49 African Americans, 5 American Indian/Alaska Native, 125 Asian Americans or Pacific Islanders, 4 Hispanic Americans), 92 international. Average age 31. *Faculty:* 1 full-time (0 women), 18 part-time/adjunct (3 women). Expenses: Contact institution. *Financial support:* Federal Work-Study available. Support available to part-time students. Financial award application deadline: 4/1. In 2006, 190 degrees awarded. *Degree program information:* Part-time and evening/weekend programs available. Offers business (MBA). *Application deadline:* For fall admission, 7/1 priority date for domestic students; for spring admission, 12/1 for domestic students. Applications are processed on a rolling basis. *Application fee:* $25. Electronic applications accepted. *Application Contact:* Dr. Sue Wilson, Dean of Enrollment Management, 256-765-4316, Fax: 256-765-4349, E-mail: sjwilson@una.edu. *Dean,* Dr. Kerry Gatlin, 256-765-4261, Fax: 256-765-4170, E-mail: kpgatlin@una.edu.

College of Education Students: 100 full-time (69 women), 264 part-time (208 women); includes 34 minority (23 African Americans, 6 American Indian/Alaska Native, 3 Asian Americans or Pacific Islanders, 2 Hispanic Americans), 7 international. Average age 33. *Faculty:* 6 full-time (3 women), 37 part-time/adjunct (19 women). Expenses: Contact institution. *Financial support:* Federal Work-Study available. Support available to part-time students. Financial award application deadline: 4/1. In 2006, 125 master's, 9 other advanced degrees awarded. *Degree program information:* Part-time and evening/weekend programs available. Offers counseling (MA, MA Ed); education (MA, MA Ed, Ed S); education leadership (Ed S); elementary education (MA Ed, Ed S); learning disabilities (MA Ed); mentally retarded (MA Ed); mild learning handicapped (MA Ed); non-school-based counseling (MA); non-school-based teaching (MA); principalship (MA Ed); principalship, superintendency, and supervision of instruction (MA Ed); secondary education (MA Ed); special education (MA Ed); superintendency (MA Ed); supervision of instruction (MA Ed). *Application deadline:* For fall admission, 7/1 priority date for domestic students; for spring admission, 12/1 for domestic students. Applications are processed on a rolling basis. *Application fee:* $25. Electronic applications accepted. *Application Contact:* Dr. Sue Wilson, Dean of Enrollment Management, 256-765-4316, Fax: 256-765-4349, E-mail: sjwilson@una.edu. *Dean,* Dr. Donna Jacobs, 256-765-4252, Fax: 256-765-4664, E-mail: dpjacobs@una.edu.

College of Nursing *Faculty:* 1 (woman) part-time/adjunct. Expenses: Contact institution. Offers nursing (MSN). *Application Contact:* Dr. Sue Wilson, Dean of Enrollment Man-

University of North Alabama (continued)

agement, 256-765-4316, Fax: 256-765-4349, E-mail: sjwilson@una.edu. *Dean*, Dr. Birdie Bailey, 256-765-4984, E-mail: bibailey@una.edu.

THE UNIVERSITY OF NORTH CAROLINA AT ASHEVILLE, Asheville, NC 28804-3299

General Information State-supported, coed, comprehensive institution. *Enrollment:* 3,635 graduate, professional, and undergraduate students; 1 (woman) full-time matriculated graduate/professional student, 19 part-time matriculated graduate/professional students (15 women). *Enrollment by degree level:* 20 master's. *Graduate faculty:* 9 full-time (6 women). Tuition, state resident: full-time $2,530. Tuition, nonresident: full-time $12,469. *Required fees:* $1,709. *Graduate housing:* On-campus housing not available. *Student services:* Campus employment opportunities, career counseling, disabled student services, exercise/wellness program, free psychological counseling, international student services, low-cost health insurance, multicultural affairs office, writing training. *Library facilities:* D. Hidden Ramsey Library. *Online resources:* library catalog, web page, access to other libraries' catalogs. *Collection:* 264,248 titles, 6,405 serial subscriptions, 12,319 audiovisual materials.

Computer facilities: Computer purchase and lease plans are available. 376 computers available on campus for general student use. A campuswide network can be accessed from student residence rooms and from off campus. Internet access and online class registration, online grade reports are available. *Web address:* http://www.unca.edu/.

General Application Contact: Dr. Melissa Burchard, Director, 828-232-2990, Fax: 828-232-2990, E-mail: mburchard@unca.edu.

GRADUATE UNITS

Graduate Studies Students: 1 (woman) full-time, 19 part-time (15 women); includes 1 minority (African American) Average age 42. 6 applicants, 33% accepted, 0 enrolled. *Faculty:* 9 full-time (6 women). Expenses: Contact institution. *Financial support:* Federal Work-Study and institutionally sponsored loans available. Support available to part-time students. Financial award application deadline: 5/1; financial award applicants required to submit FAFSA. In 2006, 6 degrees awarded. *Degree program information:* Part-time and evening/weekend programs available. *Application deadline:* For fall admission, 4/15 for domestic students; for spring admission, 11/15 for domestic students. Applications are processed on a rolling basis. *Application fee:* $50. *Director*, Dr. Melissa Burchard, 828-251-6620, Fax: 828-232-2990, E-mail: mburchard@unca.edu.

THE UNIVERSITY OF NORTH CAROLINA AT CHAPEL HILL, Chapel Hill, NC 27599

General Information State-supported, coed, university. CGS member. *Graduate housing:* Rooms and/or apartments available on a first-come, first-served basis to single and married students. *Research affiliation:* Centers for Disease Control, Research Triangle Institute, Triangle Universities Nuclear Laboratory.

GRADUATE UNITS

Graduate School Postbaccalaureate distance learning degree programs offered (minimal on-campus study). Offers materials science (MS, PhD); public policy (PhD); Russian and east European studies (MA). Electronic applications accepted.

College of Arts and Sciences *Degree program information:* Part-time programs available. Offers acting (MFA); anthropology (MA, PhD); art history (MA, PhD); arts and sciences (MA, MFA, MPA, MRP, MS, MSRA, PhD, Certificate); athletic training (MA); biological psychology (PhD); botany (MA, MS, PhD); cell biology, development, and physiology (MA, MS, PhD); cell motility and cytoskeleton (PhD); chemistry (MA, MS, PhD); city and regional planning (MRP); classical archaeology (MA, PhD); classics (MA, PhD); clinical psychology (PhD); cognitive psychology (PhD); communication studies (MA, PhD); comparative literature (MA, PhD); computer science (MS, PhD); costume production (MFA); developmental psychology (PhD); ecology (MA, MS, PhD); ecology and behavior (MA, MS, PhD); economics (MS, PhD); English (MA, PhD); exercise physiology (MA); folklore (MA); French (MA, PhD); genetics and molecular biology (MA, MS, PhD); geography (MA, PhD); geological sciences (MS, PhD); history (MA, PhD); Italian (MA, PhD); Latin American studies (Certificate); linguistics (MA, PhD); literature and linguistics (MA, PhD); marine sciences (MS, PhD); mathematics (MA, MS, PhD); morphology, systematics, and evolution (MA, MS, PhD); music (MA, PhD); operations research (MS, PhD); philosophy (MA, PhD); physics (MS, PhD); planning (PhD); Polish literature (PhD); political science (MA, PhD); Portuguese (MA, PhD); public administration (MPA); public policy analysis (PhD); quantitative psychology (PhD); recreation and leisure studies (MSRA); religious studies (MA, PhD); Romance languages (MA, PhD); Romance philology (MA, PhD); Russian literature (MA, PhD); Serbo-Croatian literature (PhD); Slavic linguistics (MA, PhD); social psychology (PhD); sociology (MA, PhD); Spanish (MA, PhD); sport administration (MA); statistics (MS, PhD); studio art (MFA); technical production (MFA); trans-Atlantic studies (MA). Electronic applications accepted.

School of Education *Faculty:* 59 full-time (32 women), 34 part-time/adjunct (17 women). Expenses: Contact institution. *Financial support:* In 2006–07, 105 students received support, including 13 fellowships with full and partial tuition reimbursements available, 61 research assistantships with full and partial tuition reimbursements available, 26 teaching assistantships with full tuition reimbursements available; Federal Work-Study, traineeships, and unspecified assistantships also available. Support available to part-time students. Financial award application deadline: 3/1; financial award applicants required to submit FAFSA. In 2006, 118 master's, 30 doctorates awarded. *Degree program information:* Part-time programs available. Offers culture, curriculum and change (PhD); culture, curriculum, and change (MA); curriculum and instruction (Ed D); early childhood, families, and literacy studies (MA, PhD); education (M Ed, MA, MAT, MSA, Ed D, PhD); education for experienced teachers (M Ed); education for experienced teachers, early childhood intervention and family studies (birth-K) (M Ed); educational leadership (Ed D); educational psychology measurements, and evaluation (PhD); educational psychology, measurement, and evaluation (MA); English (Grades 9-12) (MAT); French (Grades K-12) (MAT); German (Grades K-12) (MAT); Japanese (Grades K-12) (MAT); Latin (Grades 9-12) (MAT); mathematics (Grades 9-12) (MAT); music (Grades K-12) (MAT); school administration (MSA); school counseling (M Ed); school psychology (M Ed, MA, PhD); science (Grades 9-12) (MAT); social studies/social science (Grades 9-12) (MAT); Spanish (Grades K-12) (MAT). *Application deadline:* For fall admission, 1/1 priority date for domestic and international students. Applications are processed on a rolling basis. *Application fee:* $60. Electronic applications accepted. *Application Contact:* Janet Carroll, Registrar, 919-962-8690, Fax: 919-962-1533, E-mail: jscarrol@email.unc.edu. *Interim Dean*, Dr. Jill Fitzgerald, 919-966-7000, Fax: 919-962-1533.

School of Information and Library Science Students: 289 full-time (186 women), 34 part-time (20 women); includes 30 minority (19 African Americans, 3 American Indian/Alaska Native, 5 Asian Americans or Pacific Islanders, 3 Hispanic Americans), 19 international. Average age 28. 326 applicants, 62% accepted, 120 enrolled. *Faculty:* 22 full-time (13 women), 46 part-time/adjunct (23 women). Expenses: Contact institution. *Financial support:* In 2006–07, 71 fellowships with full tuition reimbursements (averaging $2,445 per year), 138 research assistantships with full tuition reimbursements (averaging $11,836 per year), 4 teaching assistantships with full tuition reimbursements (averaging $11,000 per year) were awarded; career-related internships or fieldwork, Federal Work-Study, institutionally sponsored loans, health care benefits, and unspecified assistantships also available. Financial award application deadline: 1/1. In 2006, 105 master's, 4 doctorates awarded. *Degree program information:* Part-time programs available. Offers information and library science (MSIS, MSLS, PhD, CAS). *Application deadline:* For fall admission, 1/1 priority date for domestic and international students; for spring admission, 10/15 for domestic and international students. Applications are processed on a rolling basis. *Application fee:* $70. Electronic applications accepted. *Application Contact:* Lara Bailey, Student Services Manager, 919-962-8366, Fax: 919-962-8071, E-mail: info@ils.unc.edu. *Dean*, Dr. Jose-Marie Griffiths, 919-962-8366, Fax: 919-962-8071, E-mail: info@ils.unc.edu.

School of Journalism and Mass Communication Students: 80 full-time (44 women), 2 part-time (both women); includes 18 minority (3 African Americans, 11 Asian Americans or Pacific Islanders, 4 Hispanic Americans). 202 applicants, 28% accepted, 32 enrolled. *Faculty:* 38 full-time (15 women), 2 part-time/adjunct (0 women). Expenses: Contact institution. *Financial support:* In 2006–07, 14 research assistantships with full tuition reimbursements (averaging $13,000 per year), 14 teaching assistantships with full tuition reimbursements (averaging $13,000 per year) were awarded; institutionally sponsored loans and health care benefits also available. Financial award application deadline: 3/1; financial award applicants required to submit FAFSA. In 2006, 25 master's, 12 doctorates awarded. *Degree program information:* Part-time programs available. Offers mass communication (MA, PhD). *Application deadline:* For fall admission, 1/1 for domestic and international students. *Application fee:* $70. Electronic applications accepted. *Application Contact:* Dr. Ruth Walden, Associate Dean for Graduate Studies, 919-962-3372, Fax: 919-962-0620, E-mail: jomcgrad@unc.edu. *Dean*, Dr. Jean Folkerts, 919-962-1204, Fax: 919-962-0620.

School of Public Health Students: 1,204 full-time (839 women); includes 246 minority (120 African Americans, 9 American Indian/Alaska Native, 88 Asian Americans or Pacific Islanders, 29 Hispanic Americans), 142 international. Average age 27. 1,792 applicants, 43% accepted, 489 enrolled. *Faculty:* 212 full-time (99 women), 328 part-time/adjunct. Expenses: Contact institution. *Financial support:* In 2006–07, 148 fellowships with full and partial tuition reimbursements (averaging $20,000 per year), 298 research assistantships with partial tuition reimbursements (averaging $12,023 per year), 79 teaching assistantships with partial tuition reimbursements (averaging $8,375 per year) were awarded; career-related internships or fieldwork, Federal Work-Study, institutionally sponsored loans, scholarships/grants, traineeships, and unspecified assistantships also available. Support available to part-time students. Financial award application deadline: 1/1; financial award applicants required to submit FAFSA. In 2006, 372 master's, 72 doctorates awarded. *Degree program information:* Part-time programs available. Postbaccalaureate distance learning degree programs offered (minimal on-campus study). Offers air, radiation and industrial hygiene (MPH, MS, MSEE, MSPH, PhD); aquatic and atmospheric sciences (MPH, MS, MSPH, PhD); biostatistics (MPH, MS, Dr PH, PhD); environmental engineering (MPH, MS, MSEE, MSPH, PhD); environmental health sciences (MPH, MS, MSPH, PhD); environmental management and policy (MPH, MS, MSPH, PhD); epidemiology (MPH, MSPH, PhD); health behavior and health education (MPH, PhD); health care and prevention (MPH); health policy and administration (MHA, MPH, MSPH, Dr PH, PhD); leadership (MPH); maternal and child health (MPH, MSPH, Dr PH, PhD); nutrition (MPH, Dr PH, PhD); nutritional biochemistry (MS); occupational health nursing (MPH); professional practice program (MPH); public health (MHA, MPH, MS, MSEE, MSPH, Dr PH, PhD); public health nursing (MS). *Application deadline:* For fall admission, 1/1 priority date for domestic and international students. Applications are processed on a rolling basis. *Application fee:* $70. Electronic applications accepted. *Application Contact:* Sherry Rhodes, Director of Student Services, 919-966-2499, Fax: 919-966-6352, E-mail: srhodes@email.unc.edu. *Dean*, Dr. Barbara K. Rimer, 919-966-3245, Fax: 919-966-7678.

School of Social Work *Degree program information:* Part-time programs available. Offers social work (MSW, PhD). Electronic applications accepted.

Kenan-Flagler Business School *Degree program information:* Evening/weekend programs available. Postbaccalaureate distance learning degree programs offered (minimal on-campus study). Offers accounting (PhD); business (MAC, MBA, PhD); business administration (MBA, PhD); finance (PhD); marketing (PhD); operations management (PhD); organizational behavior (PhD); strategy (PhD). Electronic applications accepted.

National Institutes of Health Sponsored Programs Offers cell motility and cytoskeleton (PhD).

School of Dentistry Average age 26. Expenses: Contact institution. *Financial support:* Fellowships, research assistantships, teaching assistantships, Federal Work-Study, institutionally sponsored loans, and scholarships/grants available. Financial award application deadline: 3/1; financial award applicants required to submit FAFSA. Offers dentistry (MS); oral biology (PhD). Electronic applications accepted. *Application Contact:* Dr. Albert David Guckes, Assistant Dean for Predoctoral Education, 919-966-4451, Fax: 919-966-5795, E-mail: ad_guckes@dentistry.unc.edu. *Dean*, Dr. John N. Williams, 919-966-2731, Fax: 919-966-4049, E-mail: john_williams@dentistry.unc.edu.

School of Law Offers law (JD). Electronic applications accepted.

School of Medicine Offers allied health sciences (MPT, MS, Au D, DPT, PhD); audiology (Au D); biochemistry and biophysics (MS, PhD); biomedical engineering (MS, PhD); cell and developmental biology (PhD); cell and molecular physiology (PhD); experimental pathology (PhD); genetics and molecular biology (PhD); human movement science (MS, PhD); immunology (MS, PhD); medicine (MD, MPT, MS, Au D, DPT, PhD); microbiology (MS, PhD); microbiology and immunology (MS, PhD); neurobiology (PhD); occupational science (MS, PhD); pathology and laboratory medicine (PhD); pharmacology (PhD); physical therapy (MPT, MS, DPT); rehabilitation counseling and psychology (MS); speech and hearing sciences (MS, Au D, PhD); toxicology (MS, PhD). Electronic applications accepted.

School of Nursing *Degree program information:* Part-time programs available. Offers nursing (MSN, PhD).

School of Pharmacy Students: 78 full-time (41 women), 2 part-time (1 woman); includes 15 minority (8 African Americans, 6 Asian Americans or Pacific Islanders, 1 Hispanic American), 35 international. Average age 28. 132 applicants, 30% accepted, 25 enrolled. *Faculty:* 39 full-time (10 women), 24 part-time/adjunct (5 women). Expenses: Contact institution. *Financial support:* In 2006–07, 15 fellowships with full tuition reimbursements (averaging $21,000 per year), 25 research assistantships with full tuition reimbursements (averaging $21,000 per year), 35 teaching assistantships with full tuition reimbursements (averaging $21,000 per year) were awarded; career-related internships or fieldwork, Federal Work-Study, institutionally sponsored loans, scholarships/grants, traineeships, health care benefits, and unspecified assistantships also available. Financial award application deadline: 4/1. In 2006, 16 degrees awarded. *Degree program information:* Part-time programs available. Postbaccalaureate distance learning degree programs offered (minimal on-campus study). Offers pharmacy (MS, PhD). *Application deadline:* For fall admission, 4/1 for domestic and international students; for spring admission, 10/15 for domestic and international students. Applications are processed on a rolling basis. *Application fee:* $65. Electronic applications accepted. *Application Contact:* Amber M. Allen, Graduate Services Manager, 919-843-9759, Fax: 919-966-3525, E-mail: amber_allen@unc.edu. *Dean*, Dr. Robert A. Blouin, 919-966-1122, Fax: 919-966-6919, E-mail: bob_blouin@unc.edu.

THE UNIVERSITY OF NORTH CAROLINA AT CHARLOTTE, Charlotte, NC 28223-0001

General Information State-supported, coed, university. CGS member. *Enrollment:* 21,519 graduate, professional, and undergraduate students; 1,191 full-time matriculated graduate/professional students (667 women), 1,980 part-time matriculated graduate/professional students (1,213 women). *Enrollment by degree level:* 2,636 master's, 535 doctoral. *Graduate faculty:* 594 full-time (226 women), 63 part-time/adjunct (33 women). Tuition, state resident: full-time $2,719; part-time $170 per credit. Tuition, nonresident: full-time $12,926; part-time $808 per credit. *Required fees:* $1,555. *Graduate housing:* Room and/or apartments available on a first-come, first-served basis to single students; on-campus housing not available to married students. Typical cost: $4,045 per year ($6,799 including board). Room and board charges vary according to board plan and housing facility selected. Housing application deadline: 5/1. *Student services:* Campus employment opportunities, campus safety program, career counseling, disabled student services, free psychological counseling, grant writing training, international student services, low-cost health insurance, multicultural affairs office, writing training. *Library facilities:* J. Murrey Atkins Library. *Online resources:* library catalog, web page, access to other libraries' catalogs. *Collection:* 969,680 titles, 32,486 serial subscriptions, 164,103 audiovisual materials.

Computer facilities: Computer purchase and lease plans are available. 1,400 computers available on campus for general student use. A campuswide network can be accessed from student residence rooms and from off campus. Internet access and online class registration are available. *Web address:* http://www.uncc.edu/.

General Application Contact: Dr. Thomas L. Reynolds, Dean and Associate Provost, 704-687-3372, Fax: 687-547-3279, E-mail: gradadm@email.uncc.edu.

GRADUATE UNITS

Graduate School Students: 1,191 full-time (667 women), 1,980 part-time (1,213 women); includes 411 minority (272 African Americans, 9 American Indian/Alaska Native, 72 Asian Americans or Pacific Islanders, 58 Hispanic Americans), 557 international. Average age 31. 2,720 applicants, 63% accepted, 1011 enrolled. *Faculty:* 594 full-time (226 women), 63 part-time/adjunct (33 women). Expenses: Contact institution. *Financial support:* In 2006–07, 2,000 students received support, including 6 fellowships (averaging $20,834 per year), 453 research assistantships (averaging $7,580 per year), 707 teaching assistantships (averaging $7,624 per year); career-related internships or fieldwork, Federal Work-Study, institutionally sponsored loans, scholarships/grants, traineeships, and unspecified assistantships also available. Support available to part-time students. Financial award application deadline: 4/1; financial award applicants required to submit FAFSA. In 2006, 851 master's, 43 doctorates awarded. *Degree program information:* Part-time and evening/weekend programs available. Postbaccalaureate distance learning degree programs offered (no on-campus study). *Application deadline:* For fall admission, 7/15 for domestic students, 5/1 for international students; for spring admission, 11/15 for domestic students, 10/1 for international students. Applications are processed on a rolling basis. *Application fee:* $55. Electronic applications accepted. *Application Contact:* Kathy B. Giddings, Director of Graduate Admissions, 704-687-3366, Fax: 704-687-3279, E-mail: gradadm@email.uncc.edu. *Dean and Associate Provost,* Dr. Thomas L. Reynolds, 704-687-3372, Fax: 687-547-3279, E-mail: gradadm@email.uncc.edu.

Belk College of Business Administration Students: 144 full-time (62 women), 380 part-time (104 women); includes 59 minority (28 African Americans, 3 American Indian/Alaska Native, 23 Asian Americans or Pacific Islanders, 5 Hispanic Americans), 117 international. Average age 30. 446 applicants, 68% accepted, 142 enrolled. *Faculty:* 68 full-time (17 women), 3 part-time/adjunct (0 women). Expenses: Contact institution. *Financial support:* In 2006–07, 1 fellowship (averaging $10,000 per year), 1 research assistantship (averaging $6,300 per year), 56 teaching assistantships (averaging $6,022 per year) were awarded; career-related internships or fieldwork, Federal Work-Study, institutionally sponsored loans, scholarships/grants, and unspecified assistantships also available. Support available to part-time students. Financial award application deadline: 4/1; financial award applicants required to submit FAFSA. In 2006, 146 degrees awarded. *Degree program information:* Part-time and evening/weekend programs available. Offers accounting (M Acc); business administration (M Acc, MBA, MS, PhD); economics (MS); mathematical finance (MS); sports marketing management (MS). *Application deadline:* For fall admission, 7/15 for domestic students, 5/1 for international students; for spring admission, 11/15 for domestic students, 10/1 for international students. Applications are processed on a rolling basis. *Application fee:* $55. Electronic applications accepted. *Application Contact:* Kathy B. Giddings, Director of Graduate Admissions, 704-687-3366, Fax: 704-687-3279, E-mail: gradadm@email.uncc.edu. *Dean,* Dr. Claude C. Lilly, 704-687-2165, Fax: 704-687-4014, E-mail: cclilly@email.uncc.edu.

College of Architecture Students: 49 full-time (28 women), 2 part-time (1 woman); includes 2 minority (1 African American, 1 Asian American or Pacific Islander), 2 international. Average age 27. 87 applicants, 48% accepted, 22 enrolled. *Faculty:* 20 full-time (4 women), 1 part-time/adjunct (0 women). Expenses: Contact institution. *Financial support:* In 2006–07, 2 research assistantships (averaging $2,050 per year), 7 teaching assistantships (averaging $6,018 per year) were awarded; fellowships, career-related internships or fieldwork, Federal Work-Study, institutionally sponsored loans, scholarships/grants, and unspecified assistantships also available. Support available to part-time students. Financial award application deadline: 4/1; financial award applicants required to submit FAFSA. In 2006, 10 degrees awarded. Offers architecture (M Arch). *Application deadline:* For fall admission, 2/15 for domestic students, 1/31 for international students. *Application fee:* $55. Electronic applications accepted. *Application Contact:* Kathy B. Giddings, Director of Graduate Admissions, 704-687-3366, Fax: 704-687-3279, E-mail: gradadm@email.uncc.edu. *Dean,* Kenneth A. Lambla, 704-687-4841, Fax: 704-687-3353, E-mail: kalambla@email.uncc.edu.

College of Arts and Sciences Students: 251 full-time (145 women), 449 part-time (272 women); includes 75 minority (38 African Americans, 1 American Indian/Alaska Native, 14 Asian Americans or Pacific Islanders, 22 Hispanic Americans), 96 international. Average age 30. 646 applicants, 45% accepted, 187 enrolled. *Faculty:* 263 full-time (98 women), 11 part-time/adjunct (6 women). Expenses: Contact institution. *Financial support:* In 2006–07, 5 fellowships (averaging $20,000 per year), 131 research assistantships (averaging $8,757 per year), 257 teaching assistantships (averaging $11,215 per year) were awarded; career-related internships or fieldwork, Federal Work-Study, institutionally sponsored loans, scholarships/grants, and unspecified assistantships also available. Support available to part-time students. Financial award application deadline: 4/1; financial award applicants required to submit FAFSA. In 2006, 168 master's, 10 doctorates awarded. *Degree program information:* Part-time and evening/weekend programs available. Offers applied mathematics (MS, PhD); applied physics (MS); arts and sciences (MA, MPA, MS, PhD); biology (MA, MS, PhD); chemistry (MS); communication studies (MA); community/clinical psychology (MA); criminal justice (MS); earth sciences (MS); English (MA); English education (MA); geography (MA); geography and urban and regional analysis (PhD); gerontology (MA); health psychology (PhD); history (MA); industrial/organizational psychology (MA); liberal studies (MA); mathematics (MS); mathematics education (MA); optical science and engineering (MS, PhD); organizational science (PhD); public administration (MPA); public policy (PhD); religious studies (MA); sociology (MA); Spanish (MA). *Application deadline:* For fall admission, 7/15 for domestic students, 5/1 for international students; for spring admission, 11/15 for domestic students, 10/1 for international students. Applications are processed on a rolling basis. *Application fee:* $55. Electronic applications accepted. *Application Contact:* Kathy B. Giddings, Director of Graduate Admissions, 704-687-3366, Fax: 704-687-3279, E-mail: gradadm@email.uncc.edu. *Dean,* Dr. Nancy A Gutierrez, 704-687-4303, Fax: 704-687-3228, E-mail: ngutierr@email.uncc.edu.

College of Computing and Informatics Students: 144 full-time (38 women), 101 part-time (30 women); includes 26 minority (13 African Americans, 1 American Indian/Alaska Native, 10 Asian Americans or Pacific Islanders, 2 Hispanic Americans), 128 international. Average age 29. 301 applicants, 78% accepted, 81 enrolled. *Faculty:* 37 full-time (9 women), 3 part-time/adjunct (0 women). Expenses: Contact institution. *Financial support:* In 2006–07, 1 fellowship (averaging $25,000 per year), 36 research assistantships (averaging $12,456 per year), 58 teaching assistantships (averaging $12,765 per year) were awarded; career-related internships or fieldwork, Federal Work-Study, institutionally sponsored loans, scholarships/grants, and unspecified assistantships also available. Support available to part-time students. Financial award application deadline: 4/1; financial award applicants required to submit FAFSA. In 2006, 84 master's, 5 doctorates awarded. *Degree program information:* Part-time and evening/weekend programs available. Offers computer science (MS); computing and informatics (MS, PhD); information technology (MS, PhD). *Application deadline:* For fall admission, 7/1 for domestic students, 5/1 for international students; for spring admission, 11/1 for domestic students, 10/1 for international students. Applications are processed on a rolling basis. *Application fee:* $55. Electronic applications accepted. *Application Contact:* Kathy B. Giddings, Director of Graduate Admissions, 704-687-3366, Fax: 704-687-3279, E-mail: gradadm@email.uncc.edu. *Dean,* Dr. Mirsad Hadzikadic, 704-687-3119, Fax: 704-687-6979, E-mail: mirsad@email.uncc.edu.

College of Education Students: 214 full-time (181 women), 751 part-time (634 women); includes 173 minority (144 African Americans, 3 American Indian/Alaska Native, 10 Asian Americans or Pacific Islanders, 16 Hispanic Americans), 10 international. Average age 34. 494 applicants, 69% accepted, 272 enrolled. *Faculty:* 100 full-time (59 women), 26 part-time/adjunct (18 women). Expenses: Contact institution. *Financial support:* In 2006–07, 23 research assistantships (averaging $10,862 per year), 33 teaching assistantships (averaging $8,255 per year) were awarded; fellowships, career-related internships or fieldwork, Federal Work-Study, institutionally sponsored loans, scholarships/grants, and unspecified assistantships also available. Support available to part-time students. Financial award application deadline: 4/1; financial award applicants required to submit FAFSA. In 2006, 233 master's, 17 doctorates awarded. *Degree program information:* Part-time and evening/weekend programs available. Postbaccalaureate distance learning degree programs offered (no on-campus study). Offers art education (K-12) (MAT); counseling (MA, PhD); curriculum and supervision (M Ed); dance education (K-12) (MAT); education (M Ed, MA, MAT, MSA, Ed D, PhD, CAS); educational administration (CAS); educational leadership (Ed D); elementary education (M Ed); elementary education (K-6) (MAT); English as a second language (K-12) (MAT); foreign language education (K-12) (MAT); general teacher education (MAT); instructional systems technology (M Ed); middle grades and secondary education (M Ed); middle grades education (6-9) (MAT); music education (K-12) (MAT); reading education (M Ed); school administration (MSA); secondary education (9-12) (MAT); special education (M Ed, PhD); special education (K-12) (MAT); teaching English as a second language (M Ed); theatre education (K-12) (MAT); urban education (PhD); urban literacy (PhD); urban math (PhD). *Application deadline:* For fall admission, 7/1 for domestic students, 5/1 for international students; for spring admission, 11/1 for domestic students, 10/1 for international students. Applications are processed on a rolling basis. *Application fee:* $55. Electronic applications accepted. *Application Contact:* Kathy B. Giddings, Director of Graduate Admissions, 704-687-3366, Fax: 704-687-3279, E-mail: gradadm@email.uncc.edu. *Dean,* Dr. Mary Lynne Calhoun, 704-687-8722, Fax: 704-687-4705, E-mail: mlcalhou@email.uncc.edu.

College of Health and Human Services Students: 213 full-time (175 women), 162 part-time (144 women); includes 59 minority (41 African Americans, 10 Asian Americans or Pacific Islanders, 8 Hispanic Americans), 18 international. Average age 32. 329 applicants, 71% accepted, 145 enrolled. *Faculty:* 39 full-time (27 women), 16 part-time/adjunct (10 women). Expenses: Contact institution. *Financial support:* In 2006–07, 18 research assistantships (averaging $5,893 per year), 7 teaching assistantships (averaging $8,210 per year) were awarded; fellowships, career-related internships or fieldwork, Federal Work-Study, institutionally sponsored loans, scholarships/grants, traineeships, and unspecified assistantships also available. Support available to part-time students. Financial award application deadline: 4/1; financial award applicants required to submit FAFSA. In 2006, 113 degrees awarded. *Degree program information:* Part-time and evening/weekend programs available. Postbaccalaureate distance learning degree programs offered (no on-campus study). Offers clinical exercise physiology (MS); family nurse practitioner (MSN); health and human services (MHA, MS, MSN, MSPH, MSW, PhD); health behavior and administration (MHA); health services research (PhD); nursing (MSN); nursing adult health (MSN); nursing-anesthesia (MSN); nursing-community health (MSN); public health (MSPH); social work (MSW). *Application deadline:* For fall admission, 7/1 for domestic students, 5/1 for international students; for spring admission, 11/1 for domestic students, 10/1 for international students. Applications are processed on a rolling basis. *Application fee:* $55. Electronic applications accepted. *Application Contact:* Kathy B. Giddings, Director of Graduate Admissions, 704-687-3366, Fax: 704-687-3279, E-mail: gradadm@email.uncc.edu. *Dean,* Dr. Karen Schmaling, 704-687-4651, Fax: 704-687-3180.

The William States Lee College of Engineering Students: 176 full-time (38 women), 135 part-time (28 women); includes 17 minority (7 African Americans, 1 American Indian/Alaska Native, 4 Asian Americans or Pacific Islanders, 5 Hispanic Americans), 186 international. Average age 27. 417 applicants, 67% accepted, 98 enrolled. *Faculty:* 64 full-time (10 women), 2 part-time/adjunct (0 women). Expenses: Contact institution. *Financial support:* In 2006–07, 31 research assistantships (averaging $8,372 per year), 86 teaching assistantships (averaging $7,369 per year) were awarded; fellowships, career-related internships or fieldwork, Federal Work-Study, institutionally sponsored loans, scholarships/grants, and unspecified assistantships also available. Support available to part-time students. Financial award application deadline: 4/1; financial award applicants required to submit FAFSA. In 2006, 97 master's, 11 doctorates awarded. *Degree program information:* Part-time and evening/weekend programs available. Offers civil engineering (MSCE); electrical engineering (MSEE, PhD); engineering (MS, MSCE, MSE, MSEE, MSME, PhD); engineering management (MS); infrastructure and environmental systems (PhD); infrastructure and environmental systems design (PhD); infrastructure and environmental systems management (PhD); infrastructure and environmental systems science (PhD); mechanical engineering (MSME, PhD). *Application deadline:* For fall admission, 7/1 for domestic students, 5/1 for international students; for spring admission, 11/1 for domestic students, 10/1 for international students. Applications are processed on a rolling basis. *Application fee:* $55. Electronic applications accepted. *Application Contact:* Kathy B. Giddings, Director of Graduate Admissions, 704-687-3366, Fax: 704-687-3279, E-mail: gradadm@email.uncc.edu. *Dean,* Dr. Robert E. Johnson, 704-687-2301, Fax: 704-687-2352, E-mail: robejohn@email.uncc.edu.

THE UNIVERSITY OF NORTH CAROLINA AT GREENSBORO, Greensboro, NC 27412-5001

General Information State-supported, coed, university. CGS member. *Enrollment:* 16,728 graduate, professional, and undergraduate students; 2,270 full-time matriculated graduate/professional students (1,565 women), 1,537 part-time matriculated graduate/professional students (1,107 women). *Enrollment by degree level:* 73 first professional, 2,614 master's, 612 doctoral, 508 other advanced degrees. *Graduate faculty:* 614 full-time (270 women), 163 part-time/adjunct (96 women). Tuition, state resident: full-time $2,692. Tuition, nonresident: full-time $13,742. *Graduate housing:* Room and/or apartments available to single students; on-campus housing not available to married students. Housing application deadline: 5/15. *Student services:* Campus employment opportunities, campus safety program, career counseling, child daycare facilities, disabled student services, exercise/wellness program, free psychological counseling, grant writing training, international student services, low-cost health insurance, multicultural affairs office, writing training. *Library facilities:* Jackson Library plus 1 other. *Online resources:* library catalog, web page. *Collection:* 740,000 titles, 4,000 serial subscriptions. *Research affiliation:* Moses Cone Memorial Hospital, North Carolina Zoological Park, North Carolina Baptist Hospital.

Computer facilities: Computer purchase and lease plans are available. 500 computers available on campus for general student use. A campuswide network can be accessed from student residence rooms and from off campus. Internet access and online class registration are available. *Web address:* http://www.uncg.edu/.

General Application Contact: Michelle Harkleroad, Director of Graduate Admissions, 336-334-4884, Fax: 336-334-4424, E-mail: mbharkle@uncg.edu.

GRADUATE UNITS

Graduate School Students: 2,270 full-time (1,565 women), 1,537 part-time (1,107 women); includes 782 minority (516 African Americans, 16 American Indian/Alaska Native, 182 Asian Americans or Pacific Islanders, 68 Hispanic Americans). 3,179 applicants, 33% accepted. *Faculty:* 614 full-time (270 women), 163 part-time/adjunct (96 women). Expenses: Contact institution. *Financial support:* In 2006–07, 838 students received support; fellowships, research assistantships, teaching assistantships, career-related internships or fieldwork, Federal Work-Study, institutionally sponsored loans, traineeships, and unspecified assistantships available. Support available to part-time students. Financial award application deadline: 3/1; financial award applicants required to submit FAFSA. *Degree program information:* Part-time and evening/weekend programs available. Postbaccalaureate distance learning degree programs offered (minimal on-campus study). Offers conflict resolution (MA, Certificate); genetic counseling (MS); gerontology (MS, Certificate); liberal studies (MALS). *Application fee:* $45. Electronic applications accepted. *Application Contact:* Michelle Harkleroad, Director of Graduate Admissions, 336-334-4884, Fax: 336-334-4424, E-mail: mbharkle@uncg.edu. *Dean,* Dr. James Peterson, 336-334-5596, Fax: 336-334-4424, E-mail: jcpeters@office.uncg.edu.

Bryan School of Business and Economics Students: 343 full-time (139 women), 123 part-time (53 women); includes 124 minority (40 African Americans, 1 American Indian/Alaska Native, 71 Asian Americans or Pacific Islanders, 12 Hispanic Americans). 376 applicants, 35% accepted. *Faculty:* 57 full-time (8 women), 18 part-time/adjunct (6 women). Expenses: Contact institution. *Financial support:* Fellowships with full tuition reimbursements, research assistantships with full tuition reimbursements, teaching assistantships, career-related internships or fieldwork, Federal Work-Study, scholarships/grants, trainee-

The University of North Carolina at Greensboro (continued)

ships, and unspecified assistantships available. Support available to part-time students. *Degree program information:* Part-time programs available. Offers accounting (MS); accounting systems (MS); applied economics (MA); business administration (MBA, PMC, Post-baccalaureate Certificate); business and economics (MA, MBA, MS, PhD, Certificate, PMC, Postbaccalaureate Certificate); economics (PhD); financial accounting and reporting (MS); financial analysis (PMC); financial economics (MA); information systems (PhD); information technology (Certificate); information technology and management (MS); supply chain management (Certificate); tax concentration (MS). *Application deadline:* For fall admission, 7/1 priority date for domestic students; for spring admission, 11/1 for domestic students. Applications are processed on a rolling basis. *Application fee:* $45. Electronic applications accepted. *Application Contact:* Michelle Harkleroad, Director of Graduate Admissions, 336-334-4884, Fax: 336-334-4424, E-mail: mbharkle@uncg.edu. *Dean,* James K. Weeks, 336-334-5338, Fax: 336-334-4044, E-mail: jim_weeks@uncg.edu.

College of Arts and Sciences Students: 491 full-time (289 women), 158 part-time (95 women); includes 113 minority (70 African Americans, 4 American Indian/Alaska Native, 28 Asian Americans or Pacific Islanders, 11 Hispanic Americans). 970 applicants, 24% accepted. *Faculty:* 277 full-time (102 women), 24 part-time/adjunct (11 women). Expenses: Contact institution. *Financial support:* In 2006–07, 16 fellowships with full tuition reimbursements, 135 research assistantships with full tuition reimbursements, 127 teaching assistantships with full tuition reimbursements were awarded; unspecified assistantships also available. In 2006, 140 master's, 13 doctorates awarded. *Degree program information:* Part-time programs available. Offers acting (MFA); advanced Spanish language and Hispanic cultural studies (Certificate); American literature (PhD); applied geography (MA); arts and sciences (M Ed, MA, MFA, MPA, MS, PhD, Certificate); biochemistry (MS); biology (MS); chemistry (MS); clinical psychology (MA, PhD); cognitive psychology (MA, PhD); communication studies (MA); computer science (MS); creative writing (MFA); criminology (MA); design (MFA); developmental psychology (MA, PhD); directing (MFA); English (M Ed, MA, PhD, Certificate); English literature (PhD); French (MA); geographic information science (Certificate); geography (PhD); historic preservation (Certificate); history (MA); Latin (M Ed); mathematics (M Ed, MA); museum studies (Certificate); nonprofit management (Certificate); public affairs (MPA); rhetoric and composition (PhD); social psychology (MA, PhD); sociology (MA); Spanish (MA, Certificate); studio arts (MFA); theater education (M Ed); theater for youth (MFA); U.S. history (PhD); urban and economic development (Certificate); women's and gender studies (MA, Certificate). *Application fee:* $45. Electronic applications accepted. *Application Contact:* Michelle Harkleroad, Director of Graduate Admissions, 336-334-4884, Fax: 336-334-4424, E-mail: mbharkle@uncg.edu. *Dean,* Timothy Johnston, 336-334-5241, Fax: 336-334-4260, E-mail: johnston@uncg.edu.

School of Education Students: 492 full-time (396 women), 551 part-time (453 women); includes 200 minority (163 African Americans, 4 American Indian/Alaska Native, 21 Asian Americans or Pacific Islanders, 12 Hispanic Americans). 780 applicants, 33% accepted. *Faculty:* 73 full-time (44 women), 33 part-time/adjunct (17 women). Expenses: Contact institution. *Financial support:* Fellowships with full tuition reimbursements, research assistantships with full tuition reimbursements, teaching assistantships with full tuition reimbursements, career-related internships or fieldwork, institutionally sponsored loans, and unspecified assistantships available. *Degree program information:* Part-time and evening/weekend programs available. Offers advanced school counseling (PMC); college teaching and adult learning (Certificate); counseling and counselor education (PhD); counseling and educational development (MS); couple and family counseling (PMC); cross-categorical special education (M Ed); curriculum and instruction (M Ed); curriculum and teaching (PhD); education (M Ed, MLIS, MS, MSA, Ed D, PhD, Certificate, Ed S, PMC); educational leadership (Ed D, Ed S); educational research, measurement and evaluation (PhD); English as a second language (Certificate); higher education (M Ed, PhD); interdisciplinary studies in special education (M Ed); leadership early care and education (Certificate); library and information studies (MLIS); school administration (MSA); school counseling (PMC); special education (M Ed, PhD); supervision (M Ed); teacher education and development (PhD). *Application fee:* $45. Electronic applications accepted. *Application Contact:* Michelle Harkleroad, Director of Graduate Admissions, 336-334-4884, Fax: 336-334-4424, E-mail: mbharkle@uncg.edu. *Dean,* Dr. Dale Schunk, 336-334-3403, Fax: 336-334-4120, E-mail: dhschunk@uncg.edu.

School of Health and Human Performance Students: 243 full-time (180 women), 50 part-time (30 women); includes 66 minority (40 African Americans, 19 Asian Americans or Pacific Islanders, 7 Hispanic Americans). 399 applicants, 33% accepted. *Faculty:* 63 full-time (34 women), 32 part-time/adjunct (22 women). Expenses: Contact institution. *Financial support:* Fellowships with full tuition reimbursements, research assistantships with full tuition reimbursements, teaching assistantships with full tuition reimbursements, unspecified assistantships available. Offers community health education (MPH, Dr PH); dance (MA, MFA); exercise and sports science (M Ed, MS, Ed D, PhD); health and human performance (M Ed, MA, MFA, MPH, MS, Dr PH, Ed D, PhD); parks and recreation management (MS); speech language pathology (PhD); speech pathology and audiology (MA). *Application deadline:* For fall admission, 2/15 priority date for domestic students. *Application fee:* $45. Electronic applications accepted. *Application Contact:* Michelle Harkleroad, Director of Graduate Admissions, 336-334-4884, Fax: 336-334-4424, E-mail: mbharkle@uncg.edu. *Dean,* David Perrin, 336-334-5744, Fax: 336-334-3238, E-mail: dhperrin@uncg.edu.

School of Human Environmental Sciences Students: 221 full-time (199 women), 13 part-time (10 women); includes 78 minority (57 African Americans, 1 American Indian/Alaska Native, 14 Asian Americans or Pacific Islanders, 6 Hispanic Americans). 152 applicants, 39% accepted. *Faculty:* 59 full-time (40 women), 11 part-time/adjunct (8 women). Expenses: Contact institution. *Financial support:* Fellowships with full tuition reimbursements, research assistantships with full tuition reimbursements, teaching assistantships with full tuition reimbursements, unspecified assistantships available. Offers consumer, apparel, and retail studies (MS, PhD); historic preservation (Certificate); human development and family studies (M Ed, MS, PhD); human environmental sciences (M Ed, MS, MSW, PhD, Certificate); interior architecture (MS); museum studies (Certificate); nutrition (MS, PhD); social work (MSW). *Application fee:* $45. Electronic applications accepted. *Application Contact:* Michelle Harkleroad, Director of Graduate Admissions, 336-334-4884, Fax: 336-334-4424, E-mail: mbharkle@uncg.edu. *Dean,* Laura S. Sims, 336-334-5980, Fax: 336-334-5089, E-mail: lssims@uncg.edu.

School of Music Students: 138 full-time (79 women), 56 part-time (34 women); includes 26 minority (13 African Americans, 1 American Indian/Alaska Native, 10 Asian Americans or Pacific Islanders, 2 Hispanic Americans). 213 applicants, 41% accepted. *Faculty:* 56 full-time (14 women), 11 part-time/adjunct (5 women). Expenses: Contact institution. *Financial support:* Fellowships with full tuition reimbursements, research assistantships with full tuition reimbursements, teaching assistantships with full tuition reimbursements, unspecified assistantships available. Offers composition (MM); education (MM); music education (PhD); performance (MM, DMA). *Application deadline:* For fall admission, 3/1 for domestic students. *Application fee:* $45. Electronic applications accepted. *Application Contact:* Michelle Harkleroad, Director of Graduate Admissions, 336-334-4884, Fax: 336-334-4424, E-mail: mbharkle@uncg.edu. *Dean,* Dr. John J. Deal, 336-334-5789, Fax: 336-334-5497, E-mail: jjdeal@uncg.edu.

School of Nursing Students: 231 full-time (197 women), 98 part-time (83 women); includes 56 minority (41 African Americans, 3 American Indian/Alaska Native, 9 Asian Americans or Pacific Islanders, 3 Hispanic Americans). 206 applicants, 59% accepted. *Faculty:* 24 full-time (23 women), 27 part-time/adjunct (22 women). Expenses: Contact institution. *Financial support:* Research assistantships with full tuition reimbursements, career-related internships or fieldwork, Federal Work-Study, scholarships/grants, and traineeships available. Support available to part-time students. Offers adult clinical nurse specialist (MSN, PMC); adult/gerontological nurse practitioner (MSN, PMC); nurse anesthesia (MSN, PMC); nursing (PhD); nursing administration (MSN); nursing education (MSN). *Application fee:* $45. Electronic applications accepted. *Application Contact:* Michelle Harkleroad, Director of Graduate Admissions, 336-334-4884, Fax: 336-334-4424, E-mail: mbharkle@uncg.edu. *Dean,* Dr. Lynne Pearcey, 336-334-5177, Fax: 336-334-3628, E-mail: l_pearce@uncg.edu.

See Close-Up on page 1105.

THE UNIVERSITY OF NORTH CAROLINA AT PEMBROKE, Pembroke, NC 28372-1510

General Information State-supported, coed, comprehensive institution. CGS member. *Enrollment:* 5,827 graduate, professional, and undergraduate students; 82 full-time matriculated graduate/professional students (49 women), 587 part-time matriculated graduate/professional students (400 women). *Enrollment by degree level:* 669 master's. *Graduate faculty:* 27 full-time (9 women), 2 part-time/adjunct (1 woman). Tuition, state resident: full-time $3,516; part-time $1,091 per semester. Tuition, nonresident: full-time $12,924; part-time $4,619 per semester. Tuition and fees vary according to class time, course load, degree level and campus/location. *Graduate housing:* Room and/or apartments available on a first-come, first-served basis to single students; on-campus housing not available to married students. Typical cost: $3,800 per year ($6,170 including board). Housing application deadline: 4/15. *Student services:* Career counseling, disabled student services, exercise/wellness program, free psychological counseling, international student services, low-cost health insurance, multicultural affairs office. *Library facilities:* Sampson-Livermore Library. *Online resources:* library catalog, web page, access to other libraries' catalogs. *Collection:* 342,723 titles, 113,823 serial subscriptions, 3,577 audiovisual materials.

Computer facilities: 650 computers available on campus for general student use. A campuswide network can be accessed from student residence rooms and from off campus. Internet access and online class registration are available. *Web address:* http://www.uncp.edu/.

General Application Contact: Dr. Kathleen C. Hilton, Dean of Graduate Studies, 910-521-6271, Fax: 910-521-6751, E-mail: grad@uncp.edu.

GRADUATE UNITS

Graduate Studies Students: 82 full-time (49 women), 587 part-time (400 women); includes 232 minority (122 African Americans, 100 American Indian/Alaska Native, 6 Asian Americans or Pacific Islanders, 4 Hispanic Americans), 11 international. Average age 34. 669 applicants, 100% accepted, 669 enrolled. *Faculty:* 27 full-time (9 women), 2 part-time/adjunct (1 woman). Expenses: Contact institution. *Financial support:* In 2006–07, 29 research assistantships with full tuition reimbursements (averaging $6,000 per year) were awarded; career-related internships or fieldwork and unspecified assistantships also available. Support available to part-time students. Financial award application deadline: 4/15; financial award applicants required to submit FAFSA. In 2006, 125 degrees awarded. *Degree program information:* Part-time and evening/weekend programs available. Offers art education (MA, MAT); English education (MA, MAT); mathematics education (MA, MAT); music education (MA, MAT); physical education (MA, MAT); public administration (MPA); school counseling (MA); science education (MA); service agency counseling (MA); social studies education (MA, MAT). *Application deadline:* For fall admission, 7/15 priority date for domestic and international students; for spring admission, 12/1 priority date for domestic and international students. Applications are processed on a rolling basis. *Application fee:* $40. *Dean of Graduate Studies,* Dr. Kathleen C. Hilton, 910-521-6271, Fax: 910-521-6751, E-mail: grad@uncp.edu.

School of Business Students: 13 full-time (7 women), 23 part-time (4 women); includes 6 minority (2 African Americans, 2 American Indian/Alaska Native, 2 Asian Americans or Pacific Islanders). Average age 34. 36 applicants, 100% accepted, 36 enrolled. *Faculty:* 6 full-time (0 women). Expenses: Contact institution. *Financial support:* In 2006–07, 1 research assistantship with full tuition reimbursement (averaging $6,000 per year) was awarded; unspecified assistantships also available. Support available to part-time students. Financial award application deadline: 4/15; financial award applicants required to submit FAFSA. In 2006, 5 degrees awarded. *Degree program information:* Part-time and evening/weekend programs available. Offers business (MBA); business administration (MBA). *Application deadline:* For fall admission, 7/15 priority date for domestic and international students; for spring admission, 12/1 priority date for domestic and international students. Applications are processed on a rolling basis. *Application fee:* $40. *Application Contact:* Dr. Kathleen C. Hilton, Dean of Graduate Studies, 910-521-6271, Fax: 910-521-6751, E-mail: grad@uncp.edu. *Dean,* Dr. Eric Dent, 910-521-6214, Fax: 910-521-6564, E-mail: eric.dent@uncp.edu.

School of Education Students: 3 full-time (all women), 169 part-time (138 women); includes 42 minority (20 African Americans, 22 American Indian/Alaska Native). Average age 35. 172 applicants, 100% accepted, 172 enrolled. *Faculty:* 8 full-time (2 women), 1 part-time/adjunct (0 women). Expenses: Contact institution. *Financial support:* In 2006–07, research assistantships with full tuition reimbursements (averaging $6,000 per year); career-related internships or fieldwork and unspecified assistantships also available. Support available to part-time students. Financial award application deadline: 4/15. In 2006, 45 degrees awarded. *Degree program information:* Part-time and evening/weekend programs available. Offers elementary education (MA Ed); middle grades education (MA Ed, MAT); reading education (MA Ed); school administration (MSA). *Application deadline:* For fall admission, 7/15 priority date for domestic and international students; for spring admission, 12/1 priority date for domestic and international students. Applications are processed on a rolling basis. *Application fee:* $40. *Application Contact:* Dr. Kathleen C. Hilton, Dean of Graduate Studies, 910-521-6271, Fax: 910-521-6751, E-mail: grad@uncp.edu. *Dean,* Dr. Zoe Locklear, 910-775-4041, Fax: 910-521-6165, E-mail: zoe.locklear@uncp.edu.

THE UNIVERSITY OF NORTH CAROLINA WILMINGTON, Wilmington, NC 28403-3297

General Information State-supported, coed, comprehensive institution. CGS member. *Enrollment:* 11,793 graduate, professional, and undergraduate students; 384 full-time matriculated graduate/professional students (238 women), 582 part-time matriculated graduate/professional students (371 women). *Enrollment by degree level:* 956 master's, 10 doctoral. *Graduate faculty:* 325 full-time (101 women), 35 part-time/adjunct (15 women). *Graduate housing:* Room and/or apartments available on a first-come, first-served basis to single students; on-campus housing not available to married students. Typical cost: $6,722 (including board). Housing application deadline: 3/31. *Student services:* Campus employment opportunities, campus safety program, career counseling, disabled student services, exercise/wellness program, free psychological counseling, international student services, low-cost health insurance. *Library facilities:* William M. Randall Library. *Online resources:* library catalog, web page, access to other libraries' catalogs. *Collection:* 553,391 titles, 22,218 serial subscriptions.

Computer facilities: Computer purchase and lease plans are available. 778 computers available on campus for general student use. A campuswide network can be accessed from student residence rooms and from off campus. Internet access and online class registration are available. *Web address:* http://www.uncw.edu/.

General Application Contact: Dr. Robert D. Roer, Dean, Graduate School, 910-962-4117, Fax: 910-962-3787, E-mail: roer@uncw.edu.

GRADUATE UNITS

College of Arts and Sciences Students: 249 full-time (153 women), 378 part-time (229 women); includes 64 minority (33 African Americans, 3 American Indian/Alaska Native, 9 Asian Americans or Pacific Islanders, 19 Hispanic Americans), 14 international. Average age 31. 708 applicants, 39% accepted, 201 enrolled. *Faculty:* 239 full-time (65 women), 29 part-time/adjunct (11 women). Expenses: Contact institution. *Financial support:* In 2006–07, 110 teaching assistantships were awarded; career-related internships or fieldwork and Federal Work-Study also available. Support available to part-time students. Financial award application deadline: 3/15. In 2006, 162 degrees awarded. *Degree program information:* Part-time programs available. Offers arts and sciences (MA, MALS, MFA, MPA, MS, MSW, PhD, Graduate Certificate); biology (MS); chemistry (MS); computer science and information systems (MS); creative writing (MFA); criminology (MA); English (MA); geology (MS); Hispanic studies (Graduate Certificate); history (MA); liberal studies (MALS); marine biology (MS, PhD); marine science (MS); mathematical sciences (MA, MS); psychology (MA); public administration (MPA); public sociology (MA); social work (MSW). *Application deadline:* Applications are processed on a rolling basis. *Application fee:* $45. *Application Contact:* Dr. Robert D. Roer, Dean, Graduate School, 910-962-4117, Fax: 910-962-3787, E-mail: roer@uncw.edu. *Dean,* Dr. David Cordle, 910-962-3111.

School of Business Students: 55 full-time (25 women), 78 part-time (34 women); includes 13 minority (5 African Americans, 1 American Indian/Alaska Native, 2 Asian Americans or Pacific Islanders, 5 Hispanic Americans). Average age 29. 145 applicants, 70% accepted, 95 enrolled. *Faculty:* 43 full-time (9 women), 2 part-time/adjunct (1 woman). Expenses: Contact institution. *Financial support:* In 2006–07, 25 teaching assistantships were awarded; career-related internships or fieldwork, Federal Work-Study, and unspecified assistantships also available. Support available to part-time students. Financial award application deadline: 3/15. In 2006, 104 degrees awarded. *Degree program information:* Part-time and evening/weekend programs available. Offers accountancy (MSA); business (MBA, MSA); business administration (MBA). *Application deadline:* Applications are processed on a rolling basis. *Application fee:* $45. *Application Contact:* Dr. Robert D. Roer, Dean, Graduate School, 910-962-4117, Fax: 910-962-3787, E-mail: roer@uncw.edu. *Dean,* Dr. Lawrence Clark, 910-962-7672, E-mail: clarkl@uncw.edu.

School of Education Students: 69 full-time (51 women), 117 part-time (100 women); includes 14 minority (9 African Americans, 2 American Indian/Alaska Native, 3 Hispanic Americans), 1 international. Average age 37. 110 applicants, 69% accepted, 59 enrolled. *Faculty:* 34 full-time (18 women), 3 part-time/adjunct (2 women). Expenses: Contact institution. *Financial support:* In 2006–07, 12 teaching assistantships were awarded; career-related internships or fieldwork, Federal Work-Study, and unspecified assistantships also available. Support available to part-time students. Financial award application deadline: 3/15. In 2006, 84 degrees awarded. *Degree program information:* Part-time and evening/weekend programs available. Offers curriculum, instruction and supervision (M Ed); education (M Ed, MAT, MS, MSA); educational leadership (MSA); elementary education (M Ed); instructional technology (MS); language and literacy education (M Ed); middle grades education (M Ed); secondary education (M Ed); special education (M Ed); teaching (MAT). *Application deadline:* For fall admission, 6/1 for domestic students. Applications are processed on a rolling basis. *Application fee:* $45. *Application Contact:* Dr. Robert D. Roer, Dean, Graduate School, 910-962-4117, Fax: 910-962-3787, E-mail: roer@uncw.edu. *Dean,* Dr. Cathy L. Barlow, 910-962-3354, E-mail: barlowc@uncwil.edu.

School of Nursing Students: 11 full-time (9 women), 9 part-time (8 women); includes 1 minority (American Indian/Alaska Native). Average age 34. 25 applicants, 88% accepted, 16 enrolled. *Faculty:* 9 full-time (all women), 1 (woman) part-time/adjunct. Expenses: Contact institution. *Financial support:* In 2006–07, 2 teaching assistantships were awarded. Financial award application deadline: 3/15. In 2006, 9 degrees awarded. Offers nursing (MSN). *Application deadline:* For fall admission, 3/1 for domestic students. Applications are processed on a rolling basis. *Application fee:* $45. Electronic applications accepted. *Application Contact:* Dr. Robert D. Roer, Dean, Graduate School, 910-962-4117, Fax: 910-962-3787, E-mail: roer@uncw.edu. *Dean,* Dr. Virginia W. Adams, 910-962-7410, E-mail: adamsv@uncw.edu.

UNIVERSITY OF NORTH DAKOTA, Grand Forks, ND 58202

General Information State-supported, coed, university. CGS member. *Enrollment:* 12,834 graduate, professional, and undergraduate students; 846 full-time matriculated graduate/professional students (512 women), 1,289 part-time matriculated graduate/professional students (777 women). *Graduate faculty:* 492 full-time (161 women), 69 part-time/adjunct (12 women). Tuition, state resident: full-time $5,650; part-time $214 per credit. Tuition, nonresident: full-time $14,248; part-time $572 per credit. *Required fees:* $1,008; $42 per credit. Tuition and fees vary according to reciprocity agreements. *Graduate housing:* Rooms and/or apartments available on a first-come, first-served basis to single and married students. Typical cost: $2,663 per year ($5,896 including board) for single students; $3,537 per year ($5,130 including board) for married students. Room and board charges vary according to board plan, campus/location and housing facility selected. *Student services:* Campus employment opportunities, campus safety program, career counseling, child daycare facilities, disabled student services, exercise/wellness program, free psychological counseling, grant writing training, international student services, low-cost health insurance, multicultural affairs office, writing training. *Library facilities:* Chester Fritz Library plus 2 others. *Online resources:* library catalog, web page, access to other libraries' catalogs. *Collection:* 1.5 million titles, 16,153 serial subscriptions, 2,928 audiovisual materials. *Research affiliation:* North Dakota Geological Survey, U.S. Department of Agriculture–Human Nutrition Laboratory, Neuropsychiatric Research Institute (neurosciences), Environmental Energy Research Center.

Computer facilities: Computer purchase and lease plans are available. 1,100 computers available on campus for general student use. A campuswide network can be accessed from student residence rooms and from off campus. Internet access and online class registration are available. *Web address:* http://www.und.nodak.edu/.

General Application Contact: Linda M. Baeza, Admissions Officer, 701-777-2945, Fax: 701-777-3619, E-mail: gradschool@mail.und.nodak.edu.

GRADUATE UNITS

Graduate School Students: 846 full-time (512 women), 1,289 part-time (777 women); includes 206 minority (20 African Americans, 138 American Indian/Alaska Native, 20 Asian Americans or Pacific Islanders, 28 Hispanic Americans), 313 international. Average age 34. 1,158 applicants, 57% accepted, 477 enrolled. *Faculty:* 492 full-time (161 women), 69 part-time/adjunct (12 women). Expenses: Contact institution. *Financial support:* In 2006–07, 477 students received support, including 146 research assistantships with full tuition reimbursements available (averaging $13,000 per year), 194 teaching assistantships with full tuition reimbursements available (averaging $13,000 per year); fellowships, career-related internships or fieldwork, Federal Work-Study, institutionally sponsored loans, scholarships/grants, traineeships, health care benefits, tuition waivers (full and partial), and unspecified assistantships also available. Support available to part-time students. Financial award application deadline: 3/15; financial award applicants required to submit FAFSA. In 2006, 430 master's, 109 doctorates, 2 other advanced degrees awarded. *Degree program information:* Part-time and evening/weekend programs available. Postbaccalaureate distance learning degree programs offered (minimal on-campus study). Offers earth system science and policy (MEM, MS, PhD). *Application deadline:* For fall admission, 8/1 for domestic students, 3/15 priority date for international students; for spring admission, 12/15 for domestic students, 10/15 priority date for international students. Applications are processed on a rolling basis. *Application fee:* $35. Electronic applications accepted. *Application Contact:* Linda M. Baeza, Admissions Officer, 701-777-2945, Fax: 701-777-3619, E-mail: gradschool@mail.und.nodak.edu. *Dean,* Dr. Joseph N. Benoit, 701-777-2786, Fax: 701-777-3619, E-mail: joseph.benoit@und.edu.

College of Arts and Sciences Students: 222 full-time (138 women), 222 part-time (121 women); includes 44 minority (7 African Americans, 31 American Indian/Alaska Native, 2 Asian Americans or Pacific Islanders, 4 Hispanic Americans), 93 international. 345 applicants, 41% accepted, 105 enrolled. *Faculty:* 163 full-time (56 women). Expenses: Contact institution. *Financial support:* In 2006–07, 53 research assistantships with full tuition reimbursements (averaging $8,763 per year), 143 teaching assistantships with full tuition reimbursements (averaging $9,300 per year) were awarded; fellowships, career-related internships or fieldwork, Federal Work-Study, institutionally sponsored loans, scholarships/grants, health care benefits, tuition waivers (full and partial), and unspecified assistantships also available. Support available to part-time students. Financial award application deadline: 3/15; financial award applicants required to submit FAFSA. In 2006, 32 master's, 14 doctorates awarded. *Degree program information:* Part-time programs available. Postbaccalaureate distance learning degree programs offered. Offers arts and sciences (M Ed, M Mus, MA, MFA, MS, DA, DMEd, PhD); botany (MS, PhD); chemistry (MS, PhD); clinical psychology (PhD); communication (MA, PhD); communication sciences and disorders (PhD); counseling psychology (PhD); criminal justice (PhD); ecology (MS, PhD); English (MA, PhD); entomology (MS, PhD); environmental biology (MS, PhD); experimental psychology (PhD); fisheries/wildlife (MS, PhD); forensic psychology (MA, MS); genetics (MS, PhD); geography (MA, MS); history (MA, DA, PhD); linguistics (MA); mathematics (M Ed, MS); music (M Mus); music education (M Mus, DMEd); physics (MS, PhD); psychology (MA); sociology (MA); speech-language pathology (MS); theatre arts (MA); visual arts (MFA); zoology (MS, PhD). *Application deadline:* For fall admission, 8/1 for domestic and international students; for spring admission, 12/15 for domestic and international students. *Application fee:* $35. Electronic applications accepted. *Application Contact:* Linda M. Baeza, Admissions Officer, 701-777-2945, Fax: 701-777-3619, E-mail: gradschool@mail.und.nodak.edu. *Dean,* Dr. Martha Potvin, 701-777-2749, Fax: 701-777-4397, E-mail: martha.potvin@und.nodak.edu.

College of Business and Public Administration Students: 60 full-time (27 women), 108 part-time (43 women); includes 14 minority (3 African Americans, 7 American Indian/Alaska Native, 1 Asian American or Pacific Islander, 3 Hispanic Americans), 28 international. 74 applicants, 57% accepted, 40 enrolled. *Faculty:* 57 full-time (15 women). Expenses: Contact institution. *Financial support:* In 2006–07, 38 students received support, including 17 research assistantships with full tuition reimbursements available (averaging $5,625 per year), 14 teaching assistantships with full tuition reimbursements available (averaging $6,728 per year); fellowships, Federal Work-Study, institutionally sponsored loans, scholarships/grants, tuition waivers (full and partial), and unspecified assistantships also available. Support available to part-time students. Financial award application deadline: 3/15; financial award applicants required to submit FAFSA. In 2006, 14 degrees awarded. *Degree program information:* Part-time and evening/weekend programs available. Postbaccalaureate distance learning degree programs offered. Offers applied economics (MSAE); business administration (MBA); business and public administration (MBA, MPA, MS, MSAE); career and technical education (MS); public administration (MPA); technology education (MS). *Application deadline:* For fall admission, 2/15 priority date for domestic and international students; for spring admission, 10/15 priority date for domestic and international students. Applications are processed on a rolling basis. *Application fee:* $35. Electronic applications accepted. *Application Contact:* Brenda Halle, Admissions Specialist, 701-777-2947, Fax: 701-777-3619, E-mail: gradschool@und.edu. *Dean,* Dr. Dennis J. Elbert, 701-777-2135, Fax: 701-777-5099, E-mail: dennis.elbert@mail.und.nodak.edu.

College of Education and Human Development Students: 213 full-time (159 women), 488 part-time (364 women); includes 76 American Indian/Alaska Native, 4 Asian Americans or Pacific Islanders, 11 Hispanic Americans, 25 international. 254 applicants, 70% accepted, 123 enrolled. *Faculty:* 61 full-time (35 women), 7 part-time/adjunct (4 women). Expenses: Contact institution. *Financial support:* In 2006–07, 108 students received support, including 33 research assistantships with full tuition reimbursements available (averaging $7,232 per year), 60 teaching assistantships with full tuition reimbursements available (averaging $8,026 per year); fellowships, career-related internships or fieldwork, Federal Work-Study, institutionally sponsored loans, scholarships/grants, tuition waivers (full and partial), and unspecified assistantships also available. Support available to part-time students. Financial award application deadline: 3/15; financial award applicants required to submit FAFSA. In 2006, 60 master's, 24 doctorates awarded. *Degree program information:* Part-time and evening/weekend programs available. Postbaccalaureate distance learning degree programs offered (minimal on-campus study). Offers counseling (MA); early childhood education (MS); education and human development (M Ed, MA, MS, MSW, Ed D, PhD, Specialist); education/general studies (MS); educational leadership (M Ed, MS, Ed D, PhD, Specialist); elementary education (Ed D, PhD); instructional design and technology (M Ed, MS); kinesiology (MS); measurement and statistics (Ed D, PhD); reading education (M Ed, MS); secondary education (Ed D, PhD); social work (MSW); special education (Ed D, PhD). *Application deadline:* Applications are processed on a rolling basis. *Application fee:* $35. Electronic applications accepted. *Dean,* Dr. Dan R. Rice, 701-777-4255, Fax: 701-777-4393, E-mail: dan.rice@mail.und.nodak.edu.

College of Nursing Students: 61 full-time (45 women), 51 part-time (45 women); includes 8 American Indian/Alaska Native, 25 international. 92 applicants, 46% accepted, 39 enrolled. *Faculty:* 18 full-time (all women). Expenses: Contact institution. *Financial support:* In 2006–07, 4 research assistantships (averaging $10,498 per year), 7 teaching assistantships with full tuition reimbursements (averaging $10,669 per year) were awarded; fellowships, Federal Work-Study, institutionally sponsored loans, scholarships/grants, traineeships, and tuition waivers (full and partial) also available. Support available to part-time students. Financial award application deadline: 3/15; financial award applicants required to submit FAFSA. *Degree program information:* Part-time programs available. Postbaccalaureate distance learning degree programs offered (minimal on-campus study). Offers nursing (MS, PhD). *Application deadline:* For fall admission, 12/1 for domestic and international students. *Application fee:* $35. Electronic applications accepted. *Application Contact:* Brenda Halle, Admissions Specialist, 701-777-2947, Fax: 701-777-3619, E-mail: brendahalle@mail.und.edu. *Dean,* Dr. Chandice Covington, 701-777-4555, Fax: 701-777-4096, E-mail: chandicecovington@mail.und.edu.

John D. Odegard School of Aerospace Sciences Students: 42 full-time (9 women), 133 part-time (35 women); includes 2 African Americans, 3 American Indian/Alaska Native, 43 international. 99 applicants, 33% accepted, 32 enrolled. *Faculty:* 36 full-time (2 women). Expenses: Contact institution. *Financial support:* In 2006–07, 39 students received support, including 30 research assistantships with full tuition reimbursements available (averaging $8,146 per year), 9 teaching assistantships with full tuition reimbursements available (averaging $8,460 per year); fellowships, career-related internships or fieldwork, Federal Work-Study, institutionally sponsored loans, scholarships/grants, tuition waivers (full and partial), and unspecified assistantships also available. Support available to part-time students. Financial award application deadline: 3/15; financial award applicants required to submit FAFSA. In 2006, 38 degrees awarded. *Degree program information:* Part-time programs available. Postbaccalaureate distance learning degree programs offered (minimal on-campus study). Offers aerospace sciences (MS); atmospheric sciences (MS); aviation (MS); computer science (MS); space studies (MS). *Application deadline:* For fall admission, 2/15 priority date for domestic and international students; for spring admission, 10/15 priority date for domestic and international students. Applications are processed on a rolling basis. *Application fee:* $35. Electronic applications accepted. *Dean,* Bruce A. Smith, 701-777-2791, Fax: 701-777-3016, E-mail: bsmith@aero.und.nodak.edu.

School of Engineering and Mines Students: 58 full-time (5 women), 45 part-time (10 women); includes 1 minority (American Indian/Alaska Native), 51 international. 124 applicants, 51% accepted, 24 enrolled. *Faculty:* 44 full-time (0 women), 4 part-time/adjunct (0 women). Expenses: Contact institution. *Financial support:* In 2006–07, 46 research assistantships with full tuition reimbursements (averaging $7,685 per year), 23 teaching assistantships with full tuition reimbursements (averaging $7,059 per year) were awarded; fellowships, career-related internships or fieldwork, Federal Work-Study, institutionally sponsored loans, scholarships/grants, tuition waivers (full and partial), and unspecified assistantships also available. Support available to part-time students. Financial award application deadline: 3/15; financial award applicants required to submit FAFSA. In 2006, 8 master's, 2 doctorates awarded. *Degree program information:* Part-time programs available. Offers chemical engineering (M Engr, MS); civil engineering (M Engr); electrical engineering (M Engr, MS); engineering (PhD); engineering and mines (M Engr, MA, MS, PhD); environmental engineering (M Engr, MS); geological engineering (MS); geology (MA, MS, PhD); mechanical engineering (M Engr, MS); sanitary engineering (M Engr). *Application deadline:* For fall admission, 2/15 priority date for domestic and international students; for spring admission, 10/15 priority date for domestic and international students. Applications are processed on a rolling basis. *Application fee:* $35. Electronic applications accepted. *Dean,* Dr. John L. Watson, 701-777-3411, Fax: 701-777-4838, E-mail: john.watson@mail.und.nodak.edu.

School of Law Students: 238 full-time (110 women); includes 20 minority (1 African American, 5 American Indian/Alaska Native, 9 Asian Americans or Pacific Islanders, 5 Hispanic Americans), 7 international. Average age 27. 650 applicants, 13% accepted, 76 enrolled. *Faculty:* 15 full-time (8 women). Expenses: Contact institution. *Financial support:* In 2006–07, 4 teaching assistantships with full tuition reimbursements were awarded; career-related internships or fieldwork, Federal Work-Study, scholarships/grants, and tuition waivers (full and partial) also available. Financial award application deadline: 4/15; financial award applicants required to submit FAFSA. In 2006, 60 degrees awarded. Offers law (JD). *Application deadline:* For fall admission, 4/1 priority date for domestic students. Applications are processed on a rolling basis. *Application fee:* $35. *Application Contact:* Ben Hoffman, Admissions and Records Officer, 701-777-2260, Fax: 701-777-2217, E-mail: benjam.n.hoffman@thor.law.und.nodak.edu. *Dean,* Paul LeBel, 701-777-2104.

School of Medicine Students: 430 full-time (250 women), 199 part-time (131 women); includes 26 American Indian/Alaska Native, 17 Asian Americans or Pacific Islanders, 8 Hispanic Americans, 37 international. 182 applicants, 74% accepted, 132 enrolled. *Faculty:* 165 full-time (28 women), 91 part-time/adjunct. Expenses: Contact institution. *Financial support:*

University of North Dakota (continued)

In 2006–07, 39 research assistantships, 13 teaching assistantships were awarded; fellowships, Federal Work-Study, institutionally sponsored loans, and tuition waivers (full and partial) also available. Support available to part-time students. Financial award applicants required to submit FAFSA. In 2006, 57 MDs, 7 master's, 3 doctorates awarded. Postbaccalaureate distance learning degree programs offered (minimal on-campus study). Offers anatomy (MS, PhD); biochemistry (MS, PhD); clinical laboratory science (MS); medicine (MD, MOT, MPAS, MPT, MS, DPT, PhD); microbiology and immunology (MS, PhD); occupational therapy (MOT); pharmacology (MS, PhD); physical therapy (MPT, DPT); physician assistant (MPAS); physiology (MS, PhD). *Application Contact:* Judy L. DeMers, Associate Dean, Student Affairs and Admissions, 701-777-4221, Fax: 701-777-4942. *Dean,* Dr. H. David Wilson, 701-777-2514, Fax: 701-777-3527, E-mail: hdwilson@medicine.nodak.edu.

UNIVERSITY OF NORTHERN BRITISH COLUMBIA, Prince George, BC V2N 4Z9, Canada

General Information Province-supported, coed, university. *Graduate housing:* Room and/or apartments available on a first-come, first-served basis to single students; on-campus housing not available to married students. Housing application deadline: 2/15. *Research affiliation:* Houston Forest Products (forestry—wood debris management), TRC Cedar Ltd. (forestry—cyanolicen growth rate study), Remote Law Online Systems Corp. (computer science), Canadian Natural Oils Ltd. (chemistry—oil fractionation), Stella Jones Inc. (forestry—douglas fir cores), Insurance Corporation of BC (moose involved in highway traffic accidents).

GRADUATE UNITS

Office of Graduate Studies *Degree program information:* Part-time and evening/weekend programs available. Postbaccalaureate distance learning degree programs offered (no on-campus study).

UNIVERSITY OF NORTHERN COLORADO, Greeley, CO 80639

General Information State-supported, coed, university. CGS member. *Enrollment:* 12,981 graduate, professional, and undergraduate students; 977 full-time matriculated graduate/professional students (680 women), 521 part-time matriculated graduate/professional students (376 women). *Enrollment by degree level:* 927 master's, 377 doctoral, 32 other advanced degrees. *Graduate faculty:* 240 full-time (112 women). Tuition, state resident: full-time $5,118; part-time $213 per credit hour. Tuition, nonresident: full-time $14,832; part-time $618 per credit hour. *Required fees:* $674; $34 per credit hour. *Graduate housing:* Rooms and/or apartments available to single students and available on a first-come, first-served basis to married students. Typical cost: $3,260 per year ($6,832 including board) for single students. Housing application deadline: 5/30. *Student services:* Campus employment opportunities, campus safety program, career counseling, disabled student services, exercise/wellness program, free psychological counseling, international student services, low-cost health insurance, multicultural affairs office, teacher training. *Library facilities:* James A. Michener Library plus 2 others. *Online resources:* library catalog, web page, access to other libraries' catalogs. *Collection:* 1 million titles, 3,417 serial subscriptions.

Computer facilities: Computer purchase and lease plans are available. 1,100 computers available on campus for general student use. A campuswide network can be accessed from student residence rooms and from off campus. Internet access and online class registration are available. *Web address:* http://www.unco.edu/.

General Application Contact: Linda Sisson, Graduate Student Admission Coordinator, 970-351-1807, Fax: 970-351-2371, E-mail: linda.sisson@unco.edu.

GRADUATE UNITS

Graduate School Students: 977 full-time (680 women), 521 part-time (376 women); includes 129 minority (23 African Americans, 11 American Indian/Alaska Native, 25 Asian Americans or Pacific Islanders, 70 Hispanic Americans), 60 international. Average age 34. 874 applicants, 75% accepted, 297 enrolled. *Faculty:* 240 full-time (112 women). Expenses: Contact institution. *Financial support:* In 2006–07, 998 students received support, including 105 fellowships (averaging $1,636 per year), 165 research assistantships (averaging $10,165 per year), 143 teaching assistantships (averaging $10,313 per year); career-related internships or fieldwork, Federal Work-Study, institutionally sponsored loans, scholarships/grants, traineeships, tuition waivers (partial), and unspecified assistantships also available. Support available to part-time students. Financial award application deadline: 3/1; financial award applicants required to submit FAFSA. In 2006, 620 master's, 59 doctorates, 34 other advanced degrees awarded. *Degree program information:* Part-time and evening/weekend programs available. Postbaccalaureate distance learning degree programs offered (minimal on-campus study). Offers interdisciplinary studies (MA). *Application deadline:* Applications are processed on a rolling basis. *Application fee:* $50 ($60 for international students). Electronic applications accepted. *Application Contact:* Linda Sisson, Graduate Student Admission Coordinator, 970-351-1807, Fax: 970-351-2371, E-mail: linda.sisson@unco.edu. *Assistant Vice President, Research and Extended Studies/Dean of Graduate School,* Dr. Robbyn Wacker, 970-351-2817, Fax: 970-351-2371.

College of Education and Behavioral Sciences Students: 453 full-time (331 women), 272 part-time (200 women); includes 64 minority (11 African Americans, 5 American Indian/Alaska Native, 13 Asian Americans or Pacific Islanders, 35 Hispanic Americans), 24 international. Average age 35. 311 applicants, 79% accepted, 115 enrolled. *Faculty:* 65 full-time (35 women). Expenses: Contact institution. *Financial support:* In 2006–07, 554 students received support, including 49 fellowships (averaging $1,789 per year), 76 research assistantships (averaging $11,856 per year), 42 teaching assistantships (averaging $10,310 per year); unspecified assistantships also available. Financial award application deadline: 3/1; financial award applicants required to submit FAFSA. In 2006, 387 master's, 27 doctorates, 34 other advanced degrees awarded. *Degree program information:* Part-time programs available. Postbaccalaureate distance learning degree programs offered. Offers applied psychology and counselor education (PhD, Psy D, Ed S); applied statistics and research methods (MS, PhD); counseling psychology (Psy D); counselor education and supervision (PhD); early childhood education (MA); education and behavioral sciences (MA, MAT, MS, Ed D, PhD, Psy D, Ed S); educational leadership (MA, Ed D, Ed S); educational media (MA); educational psychology (MA, PhD); educational research, leadership and technology (MA, MS, Ed D, PhD, Ed S); educational studies (Ed D); educational technology (MA, PhD); elementary education (MAT); interdisciplinary studies (MA); psychological sciences (MA, PhD); reading (MA); school psychology (PhD, Ed S); special education (MA, Ed D); teacher education (MA, MAT, Ed D). *Application deadline:* Applications are processed on a rolling basis. *Application fee:* $50 ($60 for international students). *Dean,* Dr. Eugene P. Sheehan, 970-351-2817, Fax: 970-351-2312, E-mail: coeinfo@unco.edu.

College of Humanities and Social Sciences Students: 60 full-time (36 women), 19 part-time (13 women); includes 11 minority (5 African Americans, 6 Hispanic Americans), 2 international. Average age 31. 48 applicants, 77% accepted, 23 enrolled. *Faculty:* 50 full-time (20 women). Expenses: Contact institution. *Financial support:* In 2006–07, 60 students received support, including 7 fellowships (averaging $714 per year), 10 research assistantships (averaging $5,503 per year), 28 teaching assistantships (averaging $10,120 per year); unspecified assistantships also available. Financial award application deadline: 3/1; financial award applicants required to submit FAFSA. In 2006, 41 degrees awarded. *Degree program information:* Part-time programs available. Offers clinical sociology (MA); communication (MA); English (MA); history (MA); humanities and social sciences (MA); modern languages and cultural studies (MA); social sciences (MA); Spanish/teaching (MA). *Application deadline:* Applications are processed on a rolling basis. *Application fee:* $50 ($60 for international students). Electronic applications accepted. *Dean,* Dr. David Caldwell, 970-351-2707, Fax: 970-351-1571.

College of Natural and Health Sciences Students: 320 full-time (228 women), 108 part-time (73 women); includes 34 minority (3 African Americans, 4 American Indian/Alaska Native, 8 Asian Americans or Pacific Islanders, 19 Hispanic Americans), 20 international. Average age 33. 385 applicants, 66% accepted, 107 enrolled. *Faculty:* 74 full-time (41 women). Expenses: Contact institution. *Financial support:* In 2006–07, 302 students received support, including 41 fellowships (averaging $1,500 per year), 54 research assistantships (averaging $10,539 per year), 51 teaching assistantships (averaging $11,791 per year); unspecified assistantships also available. Financial award application deadline: 3/1; financial award applicants required to submit FAFSA. In 2006, 165 master's, 24 doctorates awarded. Offers audiology (Au D); biological education (PhD); biological sciences (MS); chemistry education (PhD); chemistry, earth sciences and physics (MA, MS, PhD); chemistry: education (MS); chemistry: research (MS); clinical nurse specialist in chronic illness (MS); earth sciences (MA); exercise science (MS, PhD); family nurse practitioner (MS); gerontology (MA); human rehabilitation (PhD); human sciences (MA, MPH, MS, Au D, PhD); mathematical teaching (MA); mathematics education (PhD); mathematics: liberal arts (MA); middle level mathematics (MA); natural and health sciences (MA, MPH, MS, Au D, PhD); natural sciences (MA); nursing education (MS, PhD); public health education (MPH); rehabilitation counseling (MA); speech language pathology (MA); sport administration (MS, PhD); sport pedagogy (MS, PhD). *Application deadline:* Applications are processed on a rolling basis. *Application fee:* $50 ($60 for international students). Electronic applications accepted. *Dean,* Dr. Denise A. Battles, 970-351-2877, Fax: 970-351-2176.

College of Performing and Visual Arts Students: 87 full-time (44 women), 21 part-time (8 women); includes 5 minority (1 African American, 1 American Indian/Alaska Native, 2 Asian Americans or Pacific Islanders, 1 Hispanic American), 9 international. Average age 31. 66 applicants, 92% accepted, 34 enrolled. *Faculty:* 35 full-time (13 women). Expenses: Contact institution. *Financial support:* In 2006–07, 74 students received support, including 6 fellowships (averaging $2,513 per year), 25 research assistantships (averaging $6,082 per year), 21 teaching assistantships (averaging $6,852 per year); unspecified assistantships also available. Financial award application deadline: 3/1; financial award applicants required to submit FAFSA. In 2006, 27 master's, 8 doctorates awarded. *Degree program information:* Part-time programs available. Offers collaborative keyboard (MM); conducting (MM); instrumental performance (MM); jazz studies (MM); music conducting (DA); music education (MM, DA); music history and literature (MM, DA); music performance (DA); music theory and composition (MM, DA); performing and visual arts (MA, MM, MME, DA); visual arts (MA); vocal performance (MM). *Application deadline:* Applications are processed on a rolling basis. *Application fee:* $50 ($60 for international students). Electronic applications accepted. *Dean,* Dr. Andrew J. Svedlow, 970-351-2515, Fax: 970-351-2699.

See Close-Up on page 1107.

UNIVERSITY OF NORTHERN IOWA, Cedar Falls, IA 50614

General Information State-supported, coed, comprehensive institution. CGS member. *Enrollment:* 12,327 graduate, professional, and undergraduate students; 624 full-time matriculated graduate/professional students (396 women), 615 part-time matriculated graduate/professional students (426 women). *Enrollment by degree level:* 1,124 master's, 96 doctoral, 19 other advanced degrees. Tuition, state resident: full-time $5,936. Tuition, nonresident: full-time $14,074. *Graduate housing:* Rooms and/or apartments available on a first-come, first-served basis to single students and available to married students. Typical cost: $5,740 (including board) for single students. *Student services:* Campus employment opportunities, campus safety program, career counseling, child daycare facilities, disabled student services, exercise/wellness program, free psychological counseling, grant writing training, international student services, low-cost health insurance, multicultural affairs office. *Library facilities:* Rod Library. *Online resources:* library catalog, web page, access to other libraries' catalogs. *Collection:* 1.2 million titles, 6,839 serial subscriptions, 28,408 audiovisual materials.

Computer facilities: Computer purchase and lease plans are available. 1,900 computers available on campus for general student use. A campuswide network can be accessed from student residence rooms and from off campus. Internet access and online class registration, course registration, student account and grade information, degree audit, program of study are available. *Web address:* http://www.uni.edu/.

General Application Contact: Laurie S. Russell, Record Analyst, 319-273-2623, Fax: 319-273-6792, E-mail: laurie.russell@uni.edu.

GRADUATE UNITS

Graduate College Students: 624 full-time (396 women), 615 part-time (426 women); includes 103 minority (74 African Americans, 4 American Indian/Alaska Native, 12 Asian Americans or Pacific Islanders, 13 Hispanic Americans), 174 international. Average age 32. 855 applicants, 66% accepted, 368 enrolled. Expenses: Contact institution. *Financial support:* Fellowships, research assistantships, teaching assistantships, career-related internships or fieldwork, Federal Work-Study, institutionally sponsored loans, scholarships/grants, tuition waivers (full and partial), and unspecified assistantships available. Support available to part-time students. Financial award application deadline: 2/1. In 2006, 430 master's, 18 doctorates, 7 other advanced degrees awarded. *Degree program information:* Part-time and evening/weekend programs available. Offers philanthropy/nonprofit development (MA); public policy (MPP); women's and gender studies (MA). *Application deadline:* Applications are processed on a rolling basis. *Application fee:* $30 ($50 for international students). Electronic applications accepted. *Application Contact:* Laurie S. Russell, Record Analyst, 319-273-2623, Fax: 319-273-6792, E-mail: laurie.russell@uni.edu. *Dean,* Dr. Susan Koch, 319-273-2748, Fax: 319-273-2243, E-mail: susan.koch@uni.edu.

College of Business Administration Students: 56 full-time (26 women), 39 part-time (14 women); includes 1 minority (Asian American or Pacific Islander), 47 international. 55 applicants, 73% accepted, 28 enrolled. Expenses: Contact institution. *Financial support:* Career-related internships or fieldwork, Federal Work-Study, scholarships/grants, and tuition waivers (full and partial) available. Support available to part-time students. Financial award application deadline: 2/1. In 2006, 81 degrees awarded. *Degree program information:* Part-time and evening/weekend programs available. Offers accounting (M Acc); business administration (M Acc, MBA). *Application deadline:* For fall admission, 8/1 priority date for domestic students. Applications are processed on a rolling basis. *Application fee:* $30 ($50 for international students). *Dean,* Dr. Farzad Moussavi, 319-273-6240, Fax: 319-273-2922, E-mail: farzad.moussavi@uni.edu.

College of Education Students: 211 full-time (140 women), 403 part-time (291 women); includes 56 minority (42 African Americans, 2 American Indian/Alaska Native, 4 Asian Americans or Pacific Islanders, 8 Hispanic Americans), 40 international. 327 applicants, 70% accepted, 175 enrolled. Expenses: Contact institution. *Financial support:* Career-related internships or fieldwork, Federal Work-Study, institutionally sponsored loans, scholarships/grants, and tuition waivers (full and partial) available. Support available to part-time students. Financial award application deadline: 2/1. In 2006, 156 master's, 15 doctorates, 7 other advanced degrees awarded. *Degree program information:* Part-time and evening/weekend programs available. Offers communication and training technology (MA); community health education (Ed D); counseling (MA, MAE, Ed D); curriculum and instruction (MAE, Ed D); early childhood education (MAE); education (MA, MAE, Ed D, Ed S); educational administration (Ed D); educational leadership (MAE, Ed D); educational media (MA); educational psychology (MAE); educational technology (MA); elementary education (MAE); elementary principal (MAE); elementary reading and language arts (MAE); health education (MA, Ed D); leisure services (MA, Ed D); middle school/junior high education (MAE); physical education (MA); postsecondary education (MAE); program administration (MA); reading (MAE); reading education (MAE); rehabilitation studies (Ed D); school counseling (MAE); school library media studies (MA); school psychology (Ed S); scientific basis of physical education (MA); secondary principal (MAE); secondary reading (MAE); special education (MAE, Ed D); student affairs (MAE); teaching/coaching (MA); youth/human services administration (MA). *Application deadline:* For fall admission, 8/1 priority date for domestic students. Applications are processed on a rolling basis. *Application fee:* $30 ($50 for international students). Electronic applications accepted. *Dean,* Dr. Jeffrey Cornett, 319-273-2717, Fax: 319-273-2607, E-mail: jeffrey.cornett@uni.edu.

College of Humanities and Fine Arts Students: 172 full-time (129 women), 70 part-time (60 women); includes 19 minority (15 African Americans, 3 Asian Americans or Pacific Islanders, 1 Hispanic American), 52 international. 203 applicants, 66% accepted, 64 enrolled. *Faculty:* 125 full-time (52 women), 2 part-time/adjunct (1 woman). Expenses: Contact institution. *Financial support:* Career-related internships or fieldwork, Federal Work-Study, scholarships/grants, and tuition waivers (full and partial) available. Support available to part-time students. Financial award application deadline: 2/1. In 2006, 106 degrees awarded. *Degree program information:* Part-time and evening/weekend programs available. Offers art (MA); art education (MA); audiology (MA); communication studies (MA); composition (MM); conducting (MM); English (MA); French (MA); German (MA); humanities and fine arts (MA, MM); jazz pedagogy (MM); music (MA, MM); music education (MA, MM); music history (MM); performance (MM); piano performance and pedagogy (MM); Spanish (MA); speech pathology (MA); teaching English to speakers of other languages (MA); teaching English to speakers of other languages/French (MA); teaching English to speakers of other languages/German (MA); teaching English to speakers of other languages/Spanish (MA); two languages (MA). *Application deadline:* For fall admission, 8/1 priority date for domestic students. Applications are processed on a rolling basis. *Application fee:* $30 ($50 for international students). Electronic applications accepted. *Interim Dean,* Dr. Reinhold Bubser, 319-273-2725, Fax: 319-273-2731, E-mail: reinhold.bubser@uni.edu.

College of Natural Sciences Students: 47 full-time (11 women), 60 part-time (35 women); includes 8 minority (7 African Americans, 1 Hispanic American), 19 international. 71 applicants, 68% accepted, 31 enrolled. Expenses: Contact institution. *Financial support:* Teaching assistantships, career-related internships or fieldwork, Federal Work-Study, scholarships/grants, and tuition waivers (full and partial) available. Support available to part-time students. Financial award application deadline: 2/1. In 2006, 34 master's, 3 doctorates awarded. *Degree program information:* Part-time and evening/weekend programs available. Offers biology (MA, MS, PSM); chemistry (MA, MS, PSM); computer science (MA, MS); environmental health (MS); environmental science (MS); environmental technology (MS); industrial technology (MA, PSM, DIT); mathematics (MA); mathematics for middle grades (MA); natural sciences (MA, MS, PSM, DIT, SP); physics (MA, PSM); science education (MA, SP). *Application deadline:* For fall admission, 8/1 priority date for domestic students. Applications are processed on a rolling basis. *Application fee:* $30 ($50 for international students). Electronic applications accepted. *Interim Dean,* Dr. Joel Haack, 319-273-2585, Fax: 319-273-2893, E-mail: joel.haack@uni.edu.

College of Social and Behavioral Sciences Students: 106 full-time (71 women), 20 part-time (10 women); includes 13 minority (6 African Americans, 2 American Indian/Alaska Native, 3 Asian Americans or Pacific Islanders, 2 Hispanic Americans), 9 international. 160 applicants, 51% accepted, 41 enrolled. Expenses: Contact institution. *Financial support:* Career-related internships or fieldwork, Federal Work-Study, scholarships/grants, and tuition waivers (full and partial) available. Support available to part-time students. Financial award application deadline: 2/1. In 2006, 54 degrees awarded. *Degree program information:* Part-time and evening/weekend programs available. Offers criminology (MA); geography (MA); history (MA); psychology (MA); social and behavioral sciences (MA, MSW); social work (MSW); sociology (MA). *Application deadline:* For fall admission, 8/1 priority date for domestic students. Applications are processed on a rolling basis. *Application fee:* $30 ($50 for international students). Electronic applications accepted. *Dean,* Dr. Julia E. Wallace, 319-273-2221, Fax: 319-273-2222, E-mail: julia.wallace@uni.edu.

UNIVERSITY OF NORTHERN VIRGINIA, Manassas, VA 20109

General Information Proprietary, coed, comprehensive institution. *Graduate housing:* Room and/or apartments available on a first-come, first-served basis to single students; on-campus housing not available to married students.

GRADUATE UNITS

Graduate Programs *Degree program information:* Part-time and evening/weekend programs available. Postbaccalaureate distance learning degree programs offered (no on-campus study). Offers accountancy (MS); accounting (MBA); business administration (DBA); computer science (MS); counseling education (M Ed); early childhood education (M Ed); educational communication and instructional technology (M Ed); educational leadership (M Ed); finance (MBA); information systems technology (MS); management (MBA); marketing (MBA); project management (MBA); public administration (MPA); teaching English to speakers of other languages (M Ed). Electronic applications accepted.

UNIVERSITY OF NORTH FLORIDA, Jacksonville, FL 32224-2645

General Information State-supported, coed, comprehensive institution. *Enrollment:* 15,954 graduate, professional, and undergraduate students; 603 full-time matriculated graduate/professional students (422 women), 1,009 part-time matriculated graduate/professional students (615 women). *Enrollment by degree level:* 1,501 master's, 111 doctoral. *Graduate faculty:* 309 full-time (118 women). Tuition, state resident: full-time $4,948; part-time $206 per semester hour. Tuition, nonresident: full-time $19,140; part-time $408 per semester hour. *Graduate housing:* Rooms and/or apartments available on a first-come, first-served basis to single and married students. Typical cost: $3,866 per year ($6,268 including board) for single students; $3,866 per year ($6,268 including board) for married students. Housing application deadline: 7/1. *Student services:* Campus employment opportunities, campus safety program, career counseling, child daycare facilities, disabled student services, exercise/wellness program, free psychological counseling, international student services, low-cost health insurance, multicultural affairs office, teacher training, writing training. *Library facilities:* Thomas G. Carpenter Library. *Online resources:* library catalog, web page, access to other libraries' catalogs. *Collection:* 798,321 titles, 3,101 serial subscriptions, 26,885 audiovisual materials.

Computer facilities: 750 computers available on campus for general student use. A campuswide network can be accessed from student residence rooms and from off campus. Internet access and online class registration, applications software are available. *Web address:* http://www.unf.edu/.

General Application Contact: Michelle Mouton, Graduate Coordinator, The Graduate School, 904-620-1360, Fax: 904-620-1362, E-mail: mmouton@unf.edu.

GRADUATE UNITS

Coggin College of Business Students: 146 full-time (74 women), 361 part-time (164 women); includes 74 minority (30 African Americans, 32 Asian Americans or Pacific Islanders, 12 Hispanic Americans), 34 international. Average age 30. 315 applicants, 52% accepted, 124 enrolled. *Faculty:* 55 full-time (11 women). Expenses: Contact institution. *Financial support:* In 2006–07, 124 students received support, including 1 teaching assistantship (averaging $3,356 per year); fellowships, research assistantships, career-related internships or fieldwork, Federal Work-Study, scholarships/grants, and tuition waivers (partial) also available. Support available to part-time students. Financial award application deadline: 4/1; financial award applicants required to submit FAFSA. In 2006, 209 degrees awarded. *Degree program information:* Part-time and evening/weekend programs available. Offers accounting (M Acct); business (M Acct, MBA); business administration (MBA). *Application deadline:* For fall admission, 7/1 priority date for domestic students, 5/1 for international students; for spring admission, 11/1 priority date for domestic students, 10/1 for international students. Applications are processed on a rolling basis. *Application fee:* $30. Electronic applications accepted. *Application Contact:* Denise Guerra, Graduate Adviser, 904-620-1453, Fax: 904-620-2832, E-mail: dguerra@unf.edu. *Dean,* Dr. John P McAllister, 904-620-2590, Fax: 904-620-3861, E-mail: jmcallis@unf.edu.

College of Arts and Sciences Students: 145 full-time (104 women), 162 part-time (100 women); includes 47 minority (23 African Americans, 3 American Indian/Alaska Native, 5 Asian Americans or Pacific Islanders, 16 Hispanic Americans), 8 international. Average age 31. 271 applicants, 48% accepted, 86 enrolled. *Faculty:* 125 full-time (36 women). Expenses: Contact institution. *Financial support:* In 2006–07, 148 students received support, including 50 teaching assistantships (averaging $5,627 per year); research assistantships, career-related internships or fieldwork, Federal Work-Study, scholarships/grants, and tuition waivers (partial) also available. Support available to part-time students. Financial award application deadline: 4/1; financial award applicants required to submit FAFSA. In 2006, 67 degrees awarded. *Degree program information:* Part-time and evening/weekend programs available. Offers applied ethics (Graduate Certificate); applied sociology (MS); arts and sciences (MA, MAC, MPA, MS, MSCJ, Graduate Certificate); biology (MA, MS); counseling psychology (MAC); criminal justice (MSCJ); English (MA); European history (MA); general psychology (MA); mathematical sciences (MS); practical philosophy and applied ethics (MA); public administration (MPA); statistics (MS); US history (MA). *Application deadline:* For fall admission, 7/1 priority date for domestic students, 5/1 for international students; for spring admission, 11/1 priority date for domestic students, 10/1 for international students. Applications are processed on a rolling basis. *Application fee:* $30. Electronic applications accepted. *Application Contact:* Michelle Mouton, Graduate Coordinator, 904-620-1360, Fax: 904-620-1362, E-mail: mmouton@unf.edu. *Acting Dean,* Dr. Dale L. Clifford, 904-620-2560, Fax: 904-620-2929, E-mail: clifford@unf.edu.

College of Computing, Engineering, and Construction Students: 13 full-time (2 women), 43 part-time (13 women); includes 13 minority (3 African Americans, 10 Asian Americans or Pacific Islanders), 13 international. Average age 31. 30 applicants, 53% accepted, 7 enrolled. *Faculty:* 21 full-time (4 women). Expenses: Contact institution. *Financial support:* In 2006–07, 12 students received support, including 6 teaching assistantships (averaging $7,324 per year); research assistantships, Federal Work-Study and tuition waivers (partial) also available. Support available to part-time students. Financial award application deadline: 4/1; financial award applicants required to submit FAFSA. In 2006, 12 degrees awarded. *Degree program information:* Part-time programs available. Offers computer and information sciences (MS). *Application deadline:* For fall admission, 7/1 priority date for domestic students, 5/1 for international students; for spring admission, 11/1 priority date for domestic students, 10/1 for international students. Applications are processed on a rolling basis. *Application fee:* $30. Electronic applications accepted. *Application Contact:* Dr. Charles Winton, Director of Graduate Studies, 904-320-2985, Fax: 904-620-2988, E-mail: cwinton@unf.edu. *Dean,* Dr. Neal Coulter, 904-620-1350, E-mail: ncoulter@unf.edu.

College of Education and Human Services Students: 132 full-time (114 women), 357 part-time (270 women); includes 121 minority (92 African Americans, 2 American Indian/Alaska Native, 7 Asian Americans or Pacific Islanders, 20 Hispanic Americans), 7 international. Average age 36. 245 applicants, 49% accepted, 97 enrolled. *Faculty:* 57 full-time (32 women). Expenses: Contact institution. *Financial support:* In 2006–07, 170 students received support, including 3 teaching assistantships (averaging $3,004 per year); research assistantships, career-related internships or fieldwork, Federal Work-Study, scholarships/grants, and tuition waivers (partial) also available. Support available to part-time students. Financial award application deadline: 4/1; financial award applicants required to submit FAFSA. In 2006, 174 master's, 13 doctorates awarded. *Degree program information:* Part-time and evening/weekend programs available. Offers counselor education (M Ed); deaf education (M Ed); disability services (M Ed); education and human services (M Ed, Ed D); educational leadership (M Ed, Ed D); exceptional student education (M Ed); instructional leadership (M Ed); mental health counseling (M Ed); school counseling (M Ed). *Application deadline:* For fall admission, 7/1 priority date for domestic students, 5/1 for international students; for spring admission, 11/1 priority date for domestic students, 10/1 for international students. Applications are processed on a rolling basis. *Application fee:* $30. Electronic applications accepted. *Application Contact:* Dr. John Kemppainen, Director, Office of Student Services, 904-620-2530, Fax: 904-620-1135, E-mail: jkemppai@unf.edu. *Dean,* Dr. Larry Daniel, 904-620-2520, E-mail: ldaniel@unf.edu.

Division of Curriculum and Instruction Students: 24 full-time (18 women), 90 part-time (80 women); includes 18 minority (11 African Americans, 1 American Indian/Alaska Native, 1 Asian American or Pacific Islander, 5 Hispanic Americans), 3 international. Average age 34. 74 applicants, 55% accepted, 27 enrolled. *Faculty:* 31 full-time (17 women). Expenses: Contact institution. *Financial support:* In 2006–07, 31 students received support, including 1 teaching assistantship (averaging $4,000 per year); career-related internships or fieldwork, Federal Work-Study, and tuition waivers (partial) also available. Support available to part-time students. Financial award application deadline: 4/1; financial award applicants required to submit FAFSA. In 2006, 51 degrees awarded. *Degree program information:* Part-time and evening/weekend programs available. Offers elementary education (M Ed); secondary education (M Ed). *Application deadline:* For fall admission, 7/1 priority date for domestic students, 5/1 for international students; for spring admission, 11/1 priority date for domestic students, 10/1 for international students. Applications are processed on a rolling basis. *Application fee:* $30. Electronic applications accepted. *Application Contact:* Dr. John Kemppainen, Director, Office of Student Services, 904-620-2530, Fax: 904-620-1135, E-mail: jkemppai@unf.edu. *Chair,* Dr. Sandra Gupton, 904-620-2610, E-mail: sgupton@unf.edu.

College of Health Students: 167 full-time (128 women), 86 part-time (68 women); includes 52 minority (25 African Americans, 1 American Indian/Alaska Native, 13 Asian Americans or Pacific Islanders, 13 Hispanic Americans), 12 international. Average age 32. 392 applicants, 41% accepted, 102 enrolled. *Faculty:* 38 full-time (28 women). Expenses: Contact institution. *Financial support:* In 2006–07, 136 students received support, including 14 teaching assistantships (averaging $2,570 per year); research assistantships, career-related internships or fieldwork, Federal Work-Study, scholarships/grants, and tuition waivers (partial) also available. Support available to part-time students. Financial award application deadline: 4/1; financial award applicants required to submit FAFSA. In 2006, 84 degrees awarded. *Degree program information:* Part-time and evening/weekend programs available. Offers community health (MPH); geriatric management (MSH); health (MHA, MPH, MPT, MS, MSH, MSN, Certificate); health administration (MHA); health behavior research and evaluation (Certificate); nutrition (MSH); physical therapy (MPT); rehabilitation counseling (MS). *Application deadline:* For fall admission, 7/1 priority date for domestic students, 5/1 for international students; for spring admission, 11/1 priority date for domestic students, 10/1 for international students. Applications are processed on a rolling basis. *Application fee:* $30. Electronic applications accepted. *Application Contact:* Rachel Broderick, Director of Advising, 904-620-2817, Fax: 904-620-1770, E-mail: rbroderi@unf.edu. *Dean,* Dr. Pamela Chally, 904-620-2810, E-mail: pchally@unf.edu.

School of Nursing Students: 36 full-time (28 women), 29 part-time (25 women); includes 11 minority (3 African Americans, 1 American Indian/Alaska Native, 3 Asian Americans or Pacific Islanders, 4 Hispanic Americans), 2 international. Average age 35. 104 applicants, 45% accepted, 39 enrolled. *Faculty:* 12 full-time (11 women). Expenses: Contact institution. *Financial support:* In 2006–07, 33 students received support; research assistantships available. Financial award application deadline: 4/1; financial award applicants required to submit FAFSA. In 2006, 11 degrees awarded. Offers advanced practice nursing (MSN); primary care nurse practitioner (Certificate). *Application deadline:* For fall admission, 5/1 for domestic and international students. Applications are processed on a rolling basis. *Application fee:* $30. Electronic applications accepted. *Director,* Dr. Lilia Loriz, 904-620-2684, E-mail: lloriz@unf.edu.

UNIVERSITY OF NORTH TEXAS, Denton, TX 76203

General Information State-supported, coed, university. CGS member. *Enrollment:* 33,443 graduate, professional, and undergraduate students; 2,519 full-time matriculated graduate/professional students (1,424 women), 4,326 part-time matriculated graduate/professional students (2,836 women). *Enrollment by degree level:* 3,865 master's, 1,581 doctoral, 1,399 other advanced degrees. *Graduate faculty:* 924 full-time (335 women). Tuition, state resident: full-time $3,573; part-time $198 per credit. Tuition, nonresident: full-time $8,577; part-time $476 per credit. *Required fees:* $1,258; $126 per credit. One-time fee: $150 full-time. Tuition and fees vary according to course load. *Graduate housing:* Rooms and/or apartments available on a first-come, first-served basis to single and married students. Typical cost: $3,278 per year ($5,293 including board) for single students. Room and board charges vary according to board plan, campus/location and housing facility selected. *Student services:* Campus employment opportunities, campus safety program, career counseling, child daycare facilities, disabled student services, exercise/wellness program, free psychological counseling, international student services, low-cost health insurance, multicultural affairs office, teacher training. *Library facilities:* Willis Library plus 4 others. *Online resources:* library catalog, web page, access to other libraries' catalogs. *Collection:* 2.1 million titles, 30,391 serial subscriptions, 141,822 audiovisual materials. *Research affiliation:* Texas Utilities (physical science), Sematech (physical science), Semiconductor Research Corporation (materials science), Delta and Pine Land Company (natural science), Cotton Incorporated (natural science), Texas Instruments, Inc. (physics and material science).

Computer facilities: 2,006 computers available on campus for general student use. A campuswide network can be accessed from student residence rooms and from off campus. *Web address:* http://www.unt.edu/.

General Application Contact: Dr. Sandra L. Terrell, Dean, 940-565-2383, Fax: 940-565-2141, E-mail: terrell@unt.edu.

University of North Texas (continued)

GRADUATE UNITS

Robert B. Toulouse School of Graduate Studies Students: 2,519 full-time (1,424 women), 4,326 part-time (2,836 women); includes 1,351 minority (530 African Americans, 56 American Indian/Alaska Native, 236 Asian Americans or Pacific Islanders, 529 Hispanic Americans), 820 international. Average age 32. 5,156 applicants, 56% accepted, 1525 enrolled. *Faculty:* 941 full-time (338 women). Expenses: Contact institution. *Financial support:* Fellowships, research assistantships, teaching assistantships, career-related internships or fieldwork, Federal Work-Study, institutionally sponsored loans, scholarships/grants, tuition waivers (full and partial), unspecified assistantships, and library assistantships available. Support available to part-time students. Financial award applicants required to submit FAFSA. In 2006, 1,494 master's, 183 doctorates awarded. *Degree program information:* Part-time and evening/weekend programs available. Postbaccalaureate distance learning degree programs offered. *Application deadline:* For fall admission, 7/13 for domestic students; for spring admission, 11/15 for domestic students. Applications are processed on a rolling basis. *Application fee:* $50 ($75 for international students). Electronic applications accepted. *Application Contact:* Dr. Lawrence J. Schneider, Interim Associate Dean, 940-565-2383, Fax: 940-565-2141. *Dean,* Dr. Sandra L. Terrell, 940-565-2383, Fax: 940-565-2141, E-mail: terrell@unt.edu.

College of Arts and Sciences Students: 763 full-time (424 women), 547 part-time (286 women); includes 198 minority (58 African Americans, 10 American Indian/Alaska Native, 42 Asian Americans or Pacific Islanders, 88 Hispanic Americans), 173 international. Average age 29. 1,391 applicants, 43% accepted, 331 enrolled. *Faculty:* 380 full-time (131 women). Expenses: Contact institution. *Financial support:* Fellowships, research assistantships, teaching assistantships, career-related internships or fieldwork, Federal Work-Study, institutionally sponsored loans, tuition waivers (partial), and unspecified assistantships available. Support available to part-time students. In 2006, 200 master's, 55 doctorates awarded. *Degree program information:* Part-time and evening/weekend programs available. Offers applied geography (MS); arts and sciences (MA, MFA, MJ, MS, Au D, PhD); audiology (Au D); biochemistry (MS, PhD); biology (MA, MS, PhD); chemistry (MS, PhD); clinical psychology (PhD); communication studies (MA, MS); counseling psychology (MA, MS, PhD); drama (MA, MS); economic research (MS); economics (MA); English (MA, PhD); environmental science (MS, PhD); experimental psychology (MA, MS, PhD); French (MA); health psychology and behavioral medicine (PhD); history (MA, MS, PhD); industrial psychology (MA, MS); journalism (MA, MJ); labor and industrial relations (MS); mathematics (MA, MS, PhD); molecular biology (MA, MS, PhD); philosophy (MA, PhD); physics (MA, MS, PhD); political science (MA, MS, PhD); psychology (MA, MS); radio, television and film (MA, MFA, MS); school psychology (MA, MS); Spanish (MA); speech-language pathology (MA, MS). *Application fee:* $50 ($75 for international students). *Dean,* Dr. Warren Burggren, 940-565-2497, Fax: 940-565-4517, E-mail: burggren@unt.edu.

College of Business Administration Students: 224 full-time (103 women), 337 part-time (139 women); includes 121 minority (52 African Americans, 3 American Indian/Alaska Native, 32 Asian Americans or Pacific Islanders, 34 Hispanic Americans), 109 international. Average age 28. 562 applicants, 81% accepted, 104 enrolled. *Faculty:* 108 full-time (24 women). Expenses: Contact institution. *Financial support:* Fellowships, research assistantships, teaching assistantships, career-related internships or fieldwork, Federal Work-Study, and institutionally sponsored loans available. In 2006, 181 master's, 9 doctorates awarded. *Degree program information:* Part-time and evening/weekend programs available. Offers accounting (MS, PhD); administrative management (MBA); banking (MBA, PhD); business administration (EMBA, MBA, MS, PhD); decision technologies (MS); finance (MBA, PhD); finance, insurance, real estate, and law (MS); information systems (PhD); information technology (MS); insurance (MBA); management (EMBA, MBA); management science (PhD); marketing and logistics (MBA, PhD); organization theory and policy (PhD); personnel and industrial relations (MBA, PhD); production/operations management (MBA, PhD); real estate (MBA). *Application deadline:* For fall admission, 7/15 for domestic students. Applications are processed on a rolling basis. *Application fee:* $50 ($75 for international students). *Application Contact:* Denise Galubenski, Graduate Advisor, 940-565-3027, Fax: 940-369-8978, E-mail: galubens@cobaf.unt.edu. *Dean,* Dr. Kathleen Cooper, 940-565-3037, Fax: 940-565-4930, E-mail: cooperk@unt.edu.

College of Education Students: 358 full-time (271 women), 1,208 part-time (893 women); includes 347 minority (184 African Americans, 16 American Indian/Alaska Native, 32 Asian Americans or Pacific Islanders, 115 Hispanic Americans), 65 international. Average age 34. 615 applicants, 62% accepted, 233 enrolled. *Faculty:* 124 full-time (68 women). Expenses: Contact institution. *Financial support:* Fellowships, research assistantships, teaching assistantships, career-related internships or fieldwork, Federal Work-Study, institutionally sponsored loans, and tuition waivers (partial) available. Support available to part-time students. Financial award application deadline: 4/1. In 2006, 448 master's, 61 doctorates awarded. *Degree program information:* Part-time and evening/weekend programs available. Offers applied technology, training and development (M Ed, MS, Ed D, PhD); community health (MS); computer education and cognitive systems (MS, PhD); counseling (M Ed, MS, PhD); counseling and student services (M Ed, MS, PhD); counselor education (MS); curriculum and instruction (Ed D, PhD); development and family studies (MS); development, family studies, and early childhood education (MS, Ed D); early childhood education (MS, Ed D); education (M Ed, MS, Ed D, PhD, Certificate); educational administration (M Ed, Ed D, PhD); educational research (PhD); health promotion (MS); higher education (M Ed, MS, Ed D, PhD); kinesiology (MS); reading (M Ed, MS, Ed D, PhD); recreation and leisure studies (MS, Certificate); school health (MS); secondary education (M Ed, MS); special education (M Ed, MS, PhD). *Application deadline:* For fall admission, 7/15 for domestic students; for spring admission, 11/15 for domestic students. *Application fee:* $50 ($75 for international students). *Dean,* Dr. Jean Keller, 940-565-2233, Fax: 940-565-4415, E-mail: jkeller@unt.edu.

College of Engineering Students: 165 full-time (47 women), 68 part-time (21 women); includes 18 minority (4 African Americans, 1 American Indian/Alaska Native, 11 Asian Americans or Pacific Islanders, 2 Hispanic Americans), 161 international. Average age 26. 297 applicants, 78% accepted, 66 enrolled. *Faculty:* 61 full-time (7 women). Expenses: Contact institution. In 2006, 59 master's, 7 doctorates awarded. Offers computer science (MS, PhD); electrical engineering (MS); engineering (MS, PhD); engineering technology (MS); materials science (MS, PhD). *Dean,* Dr. Oscar Garcia, 940-565-4300, Fax: 940-369-8570, E-mail: ogarcia@unt.edu.

College of Music Students: 351 full-time (156 women), 185 part-time (67 women); includes 72 minority (10 African Americans, 3 American Indian/Alaska Native, 24 Asian Americans or Pacific Islanders, 35 Hispanic Americans), 147 international. Average age 29. 416 applicants, 66% accepted, 141 enrolled. *Faculty:* 103 full-time (26 women). Expenses: Contact institution. *Financial support:* Fellowships, research assistantships, teaching assistantships, career-related internships or fieldwork, Federal Work-Study, institutionally sponsored loans, and scholarships/grants available. Financial award application deadline: 4/1. In 2006, 83 master's, 30 doctorates awarded. Offers composition (MM, DMA, PhD); jazz studies (MM); music (MA); music education (MM, MME, PhD); music theory (MM, PhD); musicology (MM, PhD); performance (MM, DMA). *Application deadline:* For fall admission, 7/15 for domestic students. *Application fee:* $50 ($75 for international students). *Application Contact:* Dr. Graham Phipps, Graduate Adviser, 940-565-4566, Fax: 940-565-2002, E-mail: phipps@music.unt.edu. *Dean,* Dr. James C. Scott, 940-565-3704, Fax: 940-565-2002.

College of Public Affairs and Community Service Students: 219 full-time (137 women), 342 part-time (215 women); includes 141 minority (77 African Americans, 6 American Indian/Alaska Native, 12 Asian Americans or Pacific Islanders, 46 Hispanic Americans), 47 international. Average age 33. 391 applicants, 58% accepted, 166 enrolled. *Faculty:* 81 full-time (34 women). Expenses: Contact institution. *Financial support:* Fellowships, research assistantships, teaching assistantships, career-related internships or fieldwork, Federal Work-Study, institutionally sponsored loans, scholarships/grants, and tuition waivers (full and partial) available. Support available to part-time students. Financial award applicants required to submit FAFSA. In 2006, 107 master's, 7 doctorates awarded. *Degree program information:* Part-time and evening/weekend programs available. Offers aging (Certificate); applied anthropology (MA); applied economics (MS); applied gerontology (PhD); behavior analysis (MS); criminal justice (MS); general studies in aging (MA, MS); long term care, senior housing, and aging services (MA, MS); public administration (MPA); public affairs and community service (MA, MPA, MS, PhD, Certificate); rehabilitation counseling (MS); rehabilitation studies (MS); sociology (MA, MS, PhD); vocational evaluation (MS); work adjustment services (MS). *Application deadline:* For fall admission, 7/15 for domestic students. Applications are processed on a rolling basis. *Application fee:* $50 ($75 for international students). *Dean,* Dr. David W. Hartman, 940-565-2239, Fax: 940-565-4663, E-mail: hartmand@unt.edu.

Interdisciplinary Studies Students: 1 (woman) full-time, 9 part-time (7 women); includes 5 minority (4 African Americans, 1 Hispanic American). Average age 44. 2 applicants, 100% accepted, 1 enrolled. Expenses: Contact institution. *Financial support:* Career-related internships or fieldwork, Federal Work-Study, and institutionally sponsored loans available. Financial award application deadline: 4/1. In 2006, 2 degrees awarded. *Degree program information:* Part-time programs available. Offers interdisciplinary studies (MA, MS). *Application deadline:* For fall admission, 7/17 for domestic students. *Application fee:* $50 ($75 for international students). *Head,* Donna Hughes, 940-565-2383, Fax: 940-565-2141, E-mail: hughesd@unt.edu.

School of Library and Information Sciences Students: 123 full-time (86 women), 755 part-time (626 women); includes 159 minority (39 African Americans, 6 American Indian/Alaska Native, 21 Asian Americans or Pacific Islanders, 93 Hispanic Americans), 45 international. Average age 36. 355 applicants, 72% accepted, 138 enrolled. *Faculty:* 15 full-time (8 women). Expenses: Contact institution. *Financial support:* Fellowships, research assistantships, teaching assistantships, career-related internships or fieldwork, Federal Work-Study, institutionally sponsored loans, and library assistantships available. Financial award application deadline: 4/1. In 2006, 362 master's, 11 doctorates awarded. *Degree program information:* Part-time and evening/weekend programs available. Offers information science (MS, PhD); library science (MS). *Application deadline:* For fall admission, 7/15 for domestic students; for spring admission, 11/30 for domestic students. Applications are processed on a rolling basis. *Application fee:* $50 ($75 for international students). *Application Contact:* Dr. Brian O'Connor, Graduate Adviser, 940-565-2347, Fax: 940-565-3101, E-mail: boconnor@lis.admin.unt.edu. *Dean,* Dr. Herman Totten, 940-565-2058, E-mail: totten@lis.admin.unt.edu.

School of Merchandising and Hospitality Management Students: 24 full-time (19 women), 10 part-time (7 women); includes 16 minority (8 African Americans, 1 American Indian/Alaska Native, 4 Asian Americans or Pacific Islanders, 3 Hispanic Americans), 9 international. Average age 26. 43 applicants, 47% accepted, 12 enrolled. *Faculty:* 19 full-time (14 women). Expenses: Contact institution. *Financial support:* Fellowships, research assistantships, teaching assistantships, career-related internships or fieldwork, Federal Work-Study, and institutionally sponsored loans available. Financial award application deadline: 4/1. In 2006, 6 degrees awarded. *Degree program information:* Part-time programs available. Offers hotel/restaurant management (MS); merchandising and fabric analytics (MS). *Application deadline:* For fall admission, 7/15 for domestic students. *Application fee:* $50 ($75 for international students). *Application Contact:* Lynne Hale, Graduate Adviser, 940-565-3518, Fax: 940-565-4348, E-mail: lhale@unt.edu. *Dean,* Dr. Judith C. Forney, 940-565-2436, Fax: 940-565-4348, E-mail: forney@smhm.cmm.unt.edu.

School of Visual Arts Students: 83 full-time (63 women), 72 part-time (53 women); includes 23 minority (4 African Americans, 1 American Indian/Alaska Native, 5 Asian Americans or Pacific Islanders, 13 Hispanic Americans), 14 international. Average age 31. 133 applicants, 56% accepted, 37 enrolled. *Faculty:* 50 full-time (26 women). Expenses: Contact institution. *Financial support:* Fellowships, teaching assistantships, career-related internships or fieldwork, Federal Work-Study, and institutionally sponsored loans available. Support available to part-time students. Financial award application deadline: 4/1. In 2006, 46 master's, 3 doctorates awarded. *Degree program information:* Part-time programs available. Offers art (PhD); art education (MA, MFA, PhD); art history (MA, MFA); ceramics (MFA); communication design (MFA); fashion design (MFA); fibers (MFA); interior design (MFA); metalsmithing and jewelry (MFA); painting and drawing (MFA); photography (MFA); printmaking (MFA); sculpture (MFA). *Application deadline:* For fall admission, 7/15 priority date for domestic students; for spring admission, 10/1 for domestic students. Applications are processed on a rolling basis. *Application fee:* $50 ($75 for international students). *Dean,* Dr. Robert Milnes, 940-565-4003, Fax: 940-565-4717, E-mail: milnes@unt.edu.

See Close-Up on page 1109.

UNIVERSITY OF NORTH TEXAS HEALTH SCIENCE CENTER AT FORT WORTH, Fort Worth, TX 76107-2699

General Information State-supported, coed, graduate-only institution. CGS member. *Graduate housing:* On-campus housing not available. *Research affiliation:* Botanical Research Institutions of Texas, Genelink (familial DNA depository), Ethnobotanical Product Investigation Consortium (natural plant products), My-tech, Inc. (cardiovascular research), Myogen, Inc. (cardiac research), Novopharm, Inc. (gene control).

GRADUATE UNITS

Graduate School of Biomedical Sciences Offers anatomy and cell biology (MS, PhD); biochemistry and molecular biology (MS, PhD); biomedical sciences (MS, PhD); biotechnology (MS); forensic genetics (MS); integrative physiology (MS, PhD); medical science (MS); microbiology and immunology (MS, PhD); pharmacology (MS, PhD); science education (MS).

School of Public Health *Degree program information:* Part-time and evening/weekend programs available. Offers biostatistics (MPH); community health (MPH); disease control and prevention (Dr PH); environmental health (MPH); epidemiology (MPH); health behavior (MPH); health policy and management (MPH, Dr PH). Electronic applications accepted.

Texas College of Osteopathic Medicine Offers osteopathic medicine (DO); physician assistant studies (MPAS). Electronic applications accepted.

UNIVERSITY OF NOTRE DAME, Notre Dame, IN 46556

General Information Independent-religious, coed, university. CGS member. *Graduate housing:* Rooms and/or apartments available on a first-come, first-served basis to single and married students. Housing application deadline: 5/1. *Student services:* Campus employment opportunities, campus safety program, career counseling, child daycare facilities, disabled student services, exercise/wellness program, free psychological counseling, grant writing training, international student services, low-cost health insurance, multicultural affairs office, teacher training, writing training. *Library facilities:* University Libraries of Notre Dame plus 9 others. *Online resources:* library catalog, web page, access to other libraries' catalogs. *Collection:* 2.9 million titles, 10,553 serial subscriptions, 21,095 audiovisual materials. *Research affiliation:* Argonne National Laboratory, Fermi National Accelerator Laboratory, Brookhaven National Laboratory, Space Telescope Science Institute.

Computer facilities: Computer purchase and lease plans are available. 400 computers available on campus for general student use. A campuswide network can be accessed from student residence rooms and from off campus. Internet access and online class registration are available. *Web address:* http://www.nd.edu/.

General Application Contact: Dr. Cecilia Lucero, Director of Graduate Admissions, 574-631-7706, Fax: 574-631-4183, E-mail: gradad@nd.edu.

GRADUATE UNITS

Graduate School Expenses: Contact institution. *Financial support:* In 2006–07, fellowships with full tuition reimbursements (averaging $22,000 per year), research assistantships with full tuition reimbursements (averaging $15,000 per year), teaching assistantships with full tuition reimbursements (averaging $15,000 per year) were awarded; career-related internships or fieldwork, Federal Work-Study, institutionally sponsored loans, scholarships/grants, traineeships, tuition waivers (full and partial), and unspecified assistantships also available. Support available to part-time students. *Degree program information:* Part-time programs available. *Application deadline:* Applications are processed on a rolling basis. *Application fee:* $50. Electronic applications accepted. *Application Contact:* Dr. Cecilia Lucero, Director of Graduate Admissions, 574-631-7706, Fax: 574-631-4183, E-mail: gradad@nd.edu. *Vice President for Gradu-*

ate Studies and Research and Dean of the Graduate School, Dr. Donald Pope-Davis, 574-631-6291, Fax: 574-631-4183, E-mail: gradsch@nd.edu.

College of Arts and Letters Expenses: Contact institution. *Financial support:* Fellowships with full tuition reimbursements, research assistantships with full tuition reimbursements, teaching assistantships with full tuition reimbursements, career-related internships or fieldwork, scholarships/grants, and tuition waivers (full and partial) available. Support available to part-time students. *Degree program information:* Part-time programs available. Offers art history (MA); arts and letters (M Div, M Ed, MA, MFA, MMS, MSM, MTS, PhD); cognitive psychology (PhD); counseling psychology (PhD); creative writing (MFA); design (MFA); developmental psychology (PhD); early Christian studies (MA); economics and econometrics (MA, PhD); educational initiatives (M Ed); English (MA, PhD); French and Francophone studies (MA); history (MA, PhD); history and philosophy of science (MA, PhD); humanities (M Div, MA, MFA, MMS, MSM, MTS, PhD); Iberian and Latin American studies (MA); international peace studies (MA); Italian studies (MA); literature (PhD); medieval studies (MMS, PhD); philosophy (PhD); political science (PhD); quantitative psychology (PhD); Romance literatures (MA); social science (M Ed, MA, PhD); sociology (PhD); studio art (MFA); theology (M Div, MA, MSM, MTS, PhD). *Application deadline:* Applications are processed on a rolling basis. *Application fee:* $50. *Application Contact:* Dr. Cecilia Lucero, Director of Graduate Admissions, 574-631-7706, Fax: 574-631-4183, E-mail: gradad@nd.edu. *Dean*, Dr. Mark W. Roche, 574-631-7085.

College of Engineering Expenses: Contact institution. *Financial support:* Fellowships with full tuition reimbursements, research assistantships with full tuition reimbursements, teaching assistantships with full tuition reimbursements, scholarships/grants, tuition waivers (full), and unspecified assistantships available. Financial award application deadline: 2/1. *Degree program information:* Part-time programs available. Offers aerospace and mechanical engineering (M Eng, PhD); aerospace engineering (MS Aero E); bioengineering (MS Bio E); chemical and biomolecular engineering (MS Ch E, PhD); civil engineering (MSCE); civil engineering and geological sciences (PhD); computer science and engineering (MSCSE, PhD); electrical engineering (MSEE, PhD); engineering (M Eng, MEME, MS, MS Aero E, MS Bio E, MS Ch E, MS Env E, MSCE, MSCSE, MSEE, MSME, PhD); environmental engineering (MS Env E); geological sciences (MS); mechanical engineering (MEME, MSME). *Application deadline:* For fall admission, 2/1 priority date for domestic students. Applications are processed on a rolling basis. *Application fee:* $50. Electronic applications accepted. *Application Contact:* Dr. Cecilia Lucero, Director of Graduate Admissions, 574-631-7706, Fax: 574-631-4183, E-mail: gradad@nd.edu. *Dean*, Dr. James Merz, 574-631-5534, Fax: 574-631-8007.

College of Science Expenses: Contact institution. *Financial support:* Fellowships with full tuition reimbursements, research assistantships with full tuition reimbursements, teaching assistantships with full tuition reimbursements, traineeships and tuition waivers (full) available. Financial award application deadline: 2/1. Offers algebra (PhD); algebraic geometry (PhD); applied mathematics (MSAM); aquatic ecology, evolution and environmental biology (MS, PhD); biochemistry (MS, PhD); cellular and molecular biology (MS, PhD); complex analysis (PhD); differential geometry (PhD); genetics (MS, PhD); inorganic chemistry (MS, PhD); logic (PhD); organic chemistry (MS, PhD); partial differential equations (PhD); physical chemistry (MS, PhD); physics (PhD); physiology (MS, PhD); science (MS, MSAM, PhD); topology (PhD); vector biology and parasitology (MS, PhD). *Application deadline:* For fall admission, 2/1 priority date for domestic students. Applications are processed on a rolling basis. *Application fee:* $50. Electronic applications accepted. *Application Contact:* Dr. Cecilia Lucero, Director of Graduate Admissions, 574-631-7706, Fax: 574-631-4183, E-mail: gradad@nd.edu. *Dean*, Dr. Joseph P. Marino, 574-631-6456, E-mail: jmarino@nd.edu.

School of Architecture Students: 34 full-time (13 women); includes 5 minority (1 African American, 2 Asian Americans or Pacific Islanders, 2 Hispanic Americans), 2 international. 82 applicants, 29% accepted, 19 enrolled. *Faculty:* 20 full-time (2 women), 1 part-time/adjunct (0 women). Expenses: Contact institution. *Financial support:* In 2006–07, 16 students received support, including 14 fellowships with full tuition reimbursements available (averaging $12,000 per year); research assistantships, teaching assistantships, institutionally sponsored loans and tuition waivers (full) also available. Financial award application deadline: 2/1. In 2006, 8 degrees awarded. Offers architectural design and urbanism (M ADU, M Arch); architecture (M Arch). *Application deadline:* For fall admission, 2/1 priority date for domestic and international students. Applications are processed on a rolling basis. *Application fee:* $50. Electronic applications accepted. *Application Contact:* Dr. Cecilia Lucero, Director of Graduate Admissions, 574-631-7706, Fax: 574-631-4183, E-mail: gradad@nd.edu. *Director of Graduate Studies*, Prof. Philip Bess, 574-631-3096, Fax: 574-631-8486.

Law School Students: 570 full-time (210 women), 1 (woman) part-time; includes 128 minority (28 African Americans, 9 American Indian/Alaska Native, 42 Asian Americans or Pacific Islanders, 49 Hispanic Americans), 6 international. 3,502 applicants, 24% accepted, 199 enrolled. *Faculty:* 47 full-time (14 women), 41 part-time/adjunct (18 women). Expenses: Contact institution. *Financial support:* In 2006–07, 376 fellowships (averaging $13,446 per year), 29 research assistantships (averaging $3,000 per year), 7 teaching assistantships were awarded; career-related internships or fieldwork, Federal Work-Study, institutionally sponsored loans, scholarships/grants, and university dormitory rector assistants also available. Financial award application deadline: 3/1; financial award applicants required to submit FAFSA. In 2006, 173 JDs, 20 master's, 2 doctorates awarded. Offers human rights (LL M, JSD); international and comparative law (LL M); law (JD). *Application deadline:* For fall admission, 11/1 priority date for domestic students; for winter admission, 3/1 for domestic students. Applications are processed on a rolling basis. *Application fee:* $55. Electronic applications accepted. *Application Contact:* Marie E. Bensman, Director of Admissions and Financial Aid, 574-631-6626, Fax: 574-631-5474, E-mail: lawadmit@nd.edu. *Dean*, Patricia A. O'Hara, 574-631-6789, Fax: 574-631-8400, E-mail: o'hara.3@nd.edu.

Mendoza College of Business Students: 677 full-time (163 women), 35 part-time (21 women); includes 87 minority (17 African Americans, 3 American Indian/Alaska Native, 32 Asian Americans or Pacific Islanders, 35 Hispanic Americans), 105 international. Average age 29. 1,225 applicants, 49% accepted, 394 enrolled. *Faculty:* 99 full-time (33 women), 39 part-time/adjunct (6 women). Expenses: Contact institution. *Financial support:* In 2006–07, 443 students received support, including 322 fellowships with full and partial tuition reimbursements available (averaging $10,683 per year), 99 teaching assistantships (averaging $3,000 per year); career-related internships or fieldwork, Federal Work-Study, institutionally sponsored loans, scholarships/grants, tuition waivers (full and partial), and unspecified assistantships also available. Financial award applicants required to submit FAFSA. In 2006, 391 degrees awarded. *Degree program information:* Part-time and evening/weekend programs available. Postbaccalaureate distance learning degree programs offered (minimal on-campus study). Offers accountancy (MS); administration (MNA); business (MBA, MNA, MS); business administration (MBA); executive business administration (MBA). *Application deadline:* Applications are processed on a rolling basis. Electronic applications accepted. *Dean*, Dr. Carolyn Y. Woo, 574-631-7236, Fax: 574-631-4825, E-mail: woo.5@nd.edu.

UNIVERSITY OF OKLAHOMA, Norman, OK 73019-0390

General Information State-supported, coed, university. CGS member. *Enrollment:* 26,002 graduate, professional, and undergraduate students; 3,219 full-time matriculated graduate/professional students (1,644 women), 3,142 part-time matriculated graduate/professional students (1,648 women). *Enrollment by degree level:* 504 first professional, 4,320 master's, 1,501 doctoral, 36 other advanced degrees. *Graduate faculty:* 1,130 full-time (341 women), 256 part-time/adjunct (115 women). Tuition, state resident: full-time $3,180; part-time $133 per credit hour. Tuition, nonresident: full-time $11,347; part-time $473 per credit hour. *Required fees:* $1,729; $62 per credit hour. $117 per semester. Tuition and fees vary according to course load and program. *Graduate housing:* Rooms and/or apartments available on a first-come, first-served basis to single and married students. Typical cost: $5,474 per year ($8,584 including board) for single students; $5,474 per year ($8,584 including board) for married students. *Student services:* Campus employment opportunities, campus safety program, career counseling, child daycare facilities, disabled student services, exercise/wellness program, free psychological counseling, grant writing training, international student services, low-cost health insurance, writing training. *Library facilities:* Bizzell Memorial Library plus 8 others. *Online resources:* library catalog, web page, access to other libraries' catalogs. *Collection:* 4.6 million titles, 58,399 serial subscriptions, 6,703 audiovisual materials. *Research affiliation:* Oklahoma Climatological Survey, National Severe Storms Laboratory, Oklahoma Geological Survey, Federal Aviation Administration Aeronautical Center.

Computer facilities: Computer purchase and lease plans are available. 2,356 computers available on campus for general student use. A campuswide network can be accessed from student residence rooms and from off campus. Internet access and online class registration are available. *Web address:* http://www.ou.edu/.

General Application Contact: Patricia Lynch, Director of Admissions, 405-325-2251, Fax: 405-325-7124, E-mail: plynch@ou.edu.

GRADUATE UNITS

College of Law Students: 501 full-time (224 women); includes 122 minority (28 African Americans, 52 American Indian/Alaska Native, 22 Asian Americans or Pacific Islanders, 20 Hispanic Americans). Average age 23. 1,055 applicants, 32% accepted, 164 enrolled. *Faculty:* 37 full-time (15 women), 17 part-time/adjunct (6 women). Expenses: Contact institution. *Financial support:* In 2006–07, 414 students received support. Career-related internships or fieldwork, Federal Work-Study, institutionally sponsored loans, scholarships/grants, and tuition waivers (full and partial) available. Support available to part-time students. Financial award application deadline: 3/1; financial award applicants required to submit FAFSA. In 2006, 169 degrees awarded. Offers law (JD). *Application deadline:* For fall admission, 3/15 for domestic students. Applications are processed on a rolling basis. *Application fee:* $50. Electronic applications accepted. *Application Contact:* Kathie Madden, Admissions Coordinator, 405-325-4728, Fax: 405-325-0502, E-mail: kmadden@ou.edu. *Dean*, Dr. Andrew M. Coats, 405-325-4699, Fax: 405-325-7712, E-mail: acoats@ou.edu.

Graduate College Students: 3,258 full-time (1,664 women), 3,356 part-time (1,760 women); includes 1,319 minority (555 African Americans, 303 American Indian/Alaska Native, 212 Asian Americans or Pacific Islanders, 249 Hispanic Americans), 811 international. Average age 30. 2,501 applicants, 75% accepted, 1360 enrolled. *Faculty:* 1,130 full-time (341 women), 256 part-time/adjunct (115 women). Expenses: Contact institution. *Financial support:* In 2006–07, 123 fellowships with full tuition reimbursements (averaging $3,958 per year), 713 research assistantships with full and partial tuition reimbursements (averaging $11,056 per year), 881 teaching assistantships with full and partial tuition reimbursements (averaging $11,770 per year) were awarded; career-related internships or fieldwork, Federal Work-Study, institutionally sponsored loans, scholarships/grants, traineeships, health care benefits, tuition waivers (full and partial), and unspecified assistantships also available. Support available to part-time students. Financial award applicants required to submit FAFSA. In 2006, 1,511 master's, 159 doctorates awarded. Postbaccalaureate distance learning degree programs offered (no on-campus study). Offers interdisciplinary studies (MA, MS, PhD). *Application deadline:* For fall admission, 6/1 for domestic students, 4/1 for international students; for spring admission, 11/1 for domestic students, 9/1 for international students. Applications are processed on a rolling basis. *Application fee:* $40 ($90 for international students). Electronic applications accepted. *Application Contact:* Miranda Sowell, Coordinator of Graduate Admissions, 405-325-3811, Fax: 405-325-5346, E-mail: mgsowell@ou.edu. *Dean*, Lee Williams, 405-325-3811, Fax: 405-325-5346, E-mail: lwilliams@ou.edu.

College of Architecture Students: 64 full-time (32 women), 30 part-time (6 women); includes 12 minority (2 African Americans, 7 American Indian/Alaska Native, 3 Hispanic Americans), 23 international. 57 applicants, 88% accepted, 30 enrolled. *Faculty:* 33 full-time (7 women), 6 part-time/adjunct (2 women). Expenses: Contact institution. *Financial support:* In 2006–07, 45 students received support, including 16 research assistantships with partial tuition reimbursements available (averaging $9,380 per year), 6 teaching assistantships with partial tuition reimbursements available (averaging $9,450 per year); career-related internships or fieldwork, Federal Work-Study, institutionally sponsored loans, scholarships/grants, health care benefits, tuition waivers (full and partial), and unspecified assistantships also available. Support available to part-time students. Financial award applicants required to submit FAFSA. In 2006, 27 degrees awarded. *Degree program information:* Part-time programs available. Offers architecture (M Arch, MLA, MRCP, MS); construction science (MS); landscape architecture (MLA); regional and city planning (MRCP). *Application deadline:* For fall admission, 6/1 for domestic students, 4/1 for international students; for spring admission, 11/1 for domestic students, 9/1 for international students. Applications are processed on a rolling basis. *Application fee:* $40 ($90 for international students). *Application Contact:* Terry Patterson, Professor/Graduate Liaison, 405-325-3869, Fax: 405-325-7558, E-mail: tpatterson@ou.edu. *Dean*, Bob G. Fillpot, 405-325-2444, Fax: 405-325-7558, E-mail: bfillpot@au.edu.

College of Arts and Sciences Students: 1,336 full-time (762 women), 1,622 part-time (941 women); includes 712 minority (344 African Americans, 123 American Indian/Alaska Native, 112 Asian Americans or Pacific Islanders, 133 Hispanic Americans), 260 international. 1,133 applicants, 78% accepted, 607 enrolled. *Faculty:* 512 full-time (177 women), 131 part-time/adjunct (66 women). Expenses: Contact institution. *Financial support:* In 2006–07, 1,014 students received support, including 66 fellowships with full tuition reimbursements available (averaging $4,204 per year), 184 research assistantships with full and partial tuition reimbursements available (averaging $12,392 per year), 560 teaching assistantships with full and partial tuition reimbursements available (averaging $13,272 per year); career-related internships or fieldwork, Federal Work-Study, institutionally sponsored loans, scholarships/grants, traineeships, health care benefits, tuition waivers (full and partial), and unspecified assistantships also available. Support available to part-time students. Financial award applicants required to submit FAFSA. In 2006, 852 master's, 62 doctorates awarded. Offers anthropology (MA, PhD); arts and sciences (M Nat Sci, MA, MHR, MLIS, MPA, MS, MSW, PhD, Certificate); astrophysics (MS, PhD); botany (MS, PhD); chemistry and biochemistry (MS, PhD); communication (MA, PhD); economics (MA, PhD); English (MA, PhD); French (MA, PhD); German (MA); health and exercise science (MS, PhD); history (MA, PhD); history of science (MA, PhD); human relations (MHR); international studies (MA); knowledge management (MS); library and information studies (MLIS); mathematics (MA, MS, PhD); microbiology (MS, PhD); Native American studies (MA); organizational dynamics (MS); philosophy (MA, PhD); physics (MS, PhD); political science (MA, PhD); psychology (MS, PhD); public administration (MPA); school library media specialist (Certificate); social work (MSW); sociology (MA, PhD); Spanish (MA, PhD); zoology (M Nat Sci, MS, PhD). *Application deadline:* For fall admission, 4/1 for domestic and international students; for spring admission, 11/1 for domestic students, 9/1 for international students. Applications are processed on a rolling basis. *Application fee:* $40 ($90 for international students).

College of Atmospheric and Geographic Sciences Students: 106 full-time (34 women), 36 part-time (13 women); includes 10 minority (4 African Americans, 3 American Indian/Alaska Native, 1 Asian American or Pacific Islander, 2 Hispanic Americans), 29 international. 82 applicants, 49% accepted, 18 enrolled. *Faculty:* 61 full-time (6 women), 12 part-time/adjunct (2 women). Expenses: Contact institution. *Financial support:* In 2006–07, 17 fellowships with full tuition reimbursements (averaging $5,000 per year), 71 research assistantships with partial tuition reimbursements (averaging $15,278 per year), 34 teaching assistantships with partial tuition reimbursements (averaging $14,267 per year) were awarded; career-related internships or fieldwork, scholarships/grants, health care benefits, tuition waivers (partial), and unspecified assistantships also available. Financial award application deadline: 2/1; financial award applicants required to submit FAFSA. In 2006, 21 master's, 4 doctorates awarded. *Degree program information:* Part-time programs available. Offers atmospheric and geographic sciences (M Pr Met, MA, MS, MS Metr, PhD); geography (MA, PhD); meteorology (M Pr Met, MS Metr, PhD). *Application deadline:* For fall admission, 2/1 priority date for domestic students, 4/1 for international students; for spring admission, 11/1 for domestic students, 9/1 for international students. Applications are processed on a rolling basis. *Application fee:* $40 ($90 for international students). *Dean*, Dr. John T. Snow, 405-325-3101, Fax: 405-325-3148, E-mail: jsnow@ou.edu.

College of Earth and Energy Students: 97 full-time (32 women), 47 part-time (9 women); includes 6 minority (2 African Americans, 2 Asian Americans or Pacific Islanders, 2 Hispanic Americans), 101 international. 83 applicants, 55% accepted, 29 enrolled. *Faculty:* 44 full-time (2 women), 6 part-time/adjunct (1 woman). Expenses: Contact institution. *Financial support:* In 2006–07, 1 fellowship (averaging $1,500 per year), 62 research assistantships (averaging $11,916 per year), 34 teaching assistantships (averaging $13,043 per year)

University of Oklahoma (continued)

were awarded; career-related internships or fieldwork, scholarships/grants, tuition waivers (partial), and unspecified assistantships also available. Financial award applicants required to submit FAFSA. In 2006, 48 master's, 5 doctorates awarded. Offers earth and energy (MS, PhD); geological engineering (MS, PhD); geology (MS, PhD); geophysics (MS); natural gas engineering (MS); petroleum engineering (MS, PhD). *Application deadline:* For fall admission, 2/1 priority date for domestic students, 4/1 for international students; for spring admission, 9/1 for domestic and international students. Applications are processed on a rolling basis. *Application fee:* $40 ($90 for international students). *Application Contact:* Linda Goeringer, Academic Counselor, 405-325-3821, Fax: 405-325-3180, E-mail: lgoeringer@ou.edu. *Dean*, Larry R Grillot, 405-325-3821, Fax: 405-325-3180, E-mail: lrgrillot@ou.edu.

College of Education Students: 314 full-time (234 women), 408 part-time (287 women); includes 161 minority (73 African Americans, 60 American Indian/Alaska Native, 10 Asian Americans or Pacific Islanders, 18 Hispanic Americans), 33 international. 230 applicants, 75% accepted, 130 enrolled. *Faculty:* 89 full-time (47 women), 44 part-time/adjunct (27 women). Expenses: Contact institution. *Financial support:* In 2006–07, 329 students received support, including 13 fellowships with full tuition reimbursements available (averaging $3,564 per year), 78 research assistantships with partial tuition reimbursements available (averaging $11,254 per year), 21 teaching assistantships with partial tuition reimbursements available (averaging $10,428 per year); career-related internships or fieldwork, Federal Work-Study, institutionally sponsored loans, scholarships/grants, tuition waivers (full and partial), and unspecified assistantships also available. Support available to part-time students. Financial award applicants required to submit FAFSA. In 2006, 127 master's, 36 doctorates awarded. *Degree program information:* Evening/weekend programs available. Postbaccalaureate distance learning degree programs offered (no on-campus study). Offers adult and higher education (M Ed, PhD); community counseling (M Ed); counseling psychology (PhD); education (Certificate); educational administration, curriculum and supervision (M Ed, Ed D, PhD); educational studies (M Ed, PhD); historical, philosophical, and social foundations of education (M Ed, PhD); instructional leadership and academic curriculum (M Ed, PhD); instructional psychology (M Ed, PhD); school counseling (M Ed); special education (M Ed, PhD). *Application deadline:* For fall admission, 6/1 for domestic students, 4/1 for international students; for spring admission, 11/1 for domestic students, 9/1 for international students. Applications are processed on a rolling basis. *Application fee:* $40 ($90 for international students). *Dean*, Dr. Joan Karen Smith, 405-325-1081, Fax: 405-325-2620, E-mail: jksmith@ou.edu.

College of Engineering Students: 322 full-time (77 women), 134 part-time (21 women); includes 37 minority (6 African Americans, 7 American Indian/Alaska Native, 12 Asian Americans or Pacific Islanders, 12 Hispanic Americans), 241 international. 287 applicants, 71% accepted, 82 enrolled. *Faculty:* 127 full-time (15 women), 12 part-time/adjunct (1 woman). Expenses: Contact institution. *Financial support:* In 2006–07, 7 fellowships with full tuition reimbursements (averaging $4,928 per year), 168 research assistantships with partial tuition reimbursements (averaging $12,619 per year), 80 teaching assistantships with partial tuition reimbursements (averaging $11,928 per year) were awarded; career-related internships or fieldwork, Federal Work-Study, institutionally sponsored loans, scholarships/grants, traineeships, tuition waivers (full and partial), and unspecified assistantships also available. Support available to part-time students. Financial award applicants required to submit FAFSA. In 2006, 131 master's, 24 doctorates awarded. Offers aerospace engineering (MS, PhD); air (M Env Sc); bioengineering (MS, PhD); chemical engineering (MS, PhD); civil engineering (MS, PhD); computer science (MS, PhD); electrical and computer engineering (MS, PhD); engineering (M Env Sc, MS, D Engr, PhD); engineering physics (MS, PhD); environmental engineering (MS); environmental science (M Env Sc, PhD); geotechnical engineering (MS); groundwater management (M Env Sc); hazardous solid waste (M Env Sc); industrial engineering (MS, PhD); mechanical engineering (MS, PhD); occupational safety and health (M Env Sc); process design (M Env Sc); structures (MS); telecommunication systems (MS); water quality resources (M Env Sc). *Application deadline:* For fall admission, 6/1 for domestic students, 4/1 for international students; for spring admission, 11/1 for domestic students, 9/1 for international students. Applications are processed on a rolling basis. *Application fee:* $40 ($90 for international students). *Dean*, Dr. Thomas Landers, 405-325-2621, Fax: 405-325-7508, E-mail: landers@ou.edu.

College of Fine Arts Students: 136 full-time (80 women), 69 part-time (38 women); includes 15 minority (1 African American, 9 American Indian/Alaska Native, 3 Asian Americans or Pacific Islanders, 2 Hispanic Americans), 27 international. 105 applicants, 64% accepted, 41 enrolled. *Faculty:* 105 full-time (40 women), 3 part-time/adjunct (0 women). Expenses: Contact institution. *Financial support:* In 2006–07, 8 fellowships (averaging $6,000 per year), 29 research assistantships with partial tuition reimbursements (averaging $9,647 per year), 93 teaching assistantships with partial tuition reimbursements (averaging $9,739 per year) were awarded; scholarships/grants, health care benefits, tuition waivers (partial), and unspecified assistantships also available. Financial award application deadline: 4/7; financial award applicants required to submit FAFSA. In 2006, 52 master's, 15 doctorates awarded. *Degree program information:* Part-time programs available. Offers acting (MFA); art (MA, MFA); art history (MA, MFA); ceramics (MFA); choral conducting (M Mus); conducting (M Mus Ed, DMA); dance (MFA); design (MFA); directing (MFA); drama (MA); film and video (MFA); fine arts (M Mus, M Mus Ed, MA, MFA, DMA, PhD); general (M Mus Ed); instrumental (M Mus Ed); instrumental conducting (M Mus); music composition (M Mus, DMA); music education (M Mus Ed, PhD); music theory (M Mus); musicology (M Mus); organ (M Mus, DMA); painting (MFA); photography (MFA); piano (M Mus, DMA); printmaking (MFA); visual communications (MFA); voice (M Mus, DMA); wind/percussion/string (M Mus, DMA). *Application deadline:* For fall admission, 6/1 for domestic students, 4/1 for international students; for spring admission, 11/1 for domestic students, 9/1 for international students. Applications are processed on a rolling basis. *Application fee:* $40 ($90 for international students). *Dean*, Eugene J. Enrico, 405-325-7370, Fax: 405-325-1667, E-mail: ejenrico@ou.edu.

College of Liberal Studies Students: 13 full-time (10 women), 210 part-time (120 women); includes 45 minority (25 African Americans, 8 American Indian/Alaska Native, 4 Asian Americans or Pacific Islanders, 8 Hispanic Americans). 103 applicants, 95% accepted, 40 enrolled. *Faculty:* 15 full-time (6 women), 23 part-time/adjunct (8 women). Expenses: Contact institution. *Financial support:* In 2006–07, 83 students received support; research assistantships with full tuition reimbursements available, career-related internships or fieldwork, scholarships/grants, and tuition waivers (partial) available. Support available to part-time students. Financial award applicants required to submit FAFSA. In 2006, 37 degrees awarded. *Degree program information:* Part-time programs available. Postbaccalaureate distance learning degree programs offered (no on-campus study). Offers administrative leadership (MLS); integrated studies (MLS); interprofessional human and health services (MLS); museum studies (MLS). *Application deadline:* For fall admission, 7/15 priority date for domestic students, 4/1 for international students; for spring admission, 12/1 for domestic students, 9/1 for international students. Applications are processed on a rolling basis. *Application fee:* $40 ($90 for international students). *Application Contact:* Dr. Julie Raadschelders, MA Program Coordinator, 405-325-1061, Fax: 405-325-9632, E-mail: jraadschelders@ou.edu. *Dean*, Dr. James Pappas, 405-325-1061, Fax: 405-325-7132, E-mail: jpappas@ou.edu.

Gaylord College of Journalism and Mass Communication Students: 45 full-time (30 women), 60 part-time (37 women); includes 11 minority (2 African Americans, 4 American Indian/Alaska Native, 1 Asian American or Pacific Islander, 4 Hispanic Americans), 12 international. 30 applicants, 93% accepted, 24 enrolled. *Faculty:* 31 full-time (8 women). Expenses: Contact institution. *Financial support:* In 2006–07, 32 students received support, including 1 research assistantship (averaging $10,000 per year), 23 teaching assistantships (averaging $9,985 per year); Federal Work-Study, scholarships/grants, health care benefits, tuition waivers (full and partial), and unspecified assistantships also available. Support available to part-time students. Financial award application deadline: 2/1; financial award applicants required to submit FAFSA. In 2006, 15 degrees awarded. *Degree program information:* Part-time programs available. Offers advertising and public relations (MA); information gathering and distribution (MA); journalism and mass communication (MA); mass communication management and policy (MA); professional writing (MA, MPW); telecommunication and new technology (MA). *Application deadline:* For fall admission, 7/1 for domestic students, 4/1 for international students; for spring admission, 11/1 for domestic students, 9/1 for international students. *Application fee:* $40 ($90 for international students). *Application Contact:* David Craig, Director of Graduate Studies, 405-325-5206, Fax: 405-325-7565, E-mail: dcraig@ou.edu. *Dean*, Joe Foote, 405-325-2721, Fax: 405-325-7565, E-mail: jfoote@ou.edu.

Michael F. Price College of Business Students: 192 full-time (76 women), 143 part-time (37 women); includes 40 minority (4 African Americans, 14 American Indian/Alaska Native, 15 Asian Americans or Pacific Islanders, 7 Hispanic Americans), 58 international. 182 applicants, 55% accepted, 79 enrolled. *Faculty:* 61 full-time (15 women), 9 part-time/adjunct (4 women). Expenses: Contact institution. *Financial support:* In 2006–07, 13 fellowships with full tuition reimbursements (averaging $1,196 per year), 50 research assistantships with partial tuition reimbursements (averaging $11,023 per year), 22 teaching assistantships with partial tuition reimbursements (averaging $13,683 per year) were awarded; career-related internships or fieldwork, Federal Work-Study, scholarships/grants, tuition waivers (full and partial), and unspecified assistantships also available. Support available to part-time students. Financial award applicants required to submit FAFSA. In 2006, 108 master's, 5 doctorates awarded. Offers accounting (M Acc); business administration (MBA, PhD); management (MS); management information systems (MS). *Application deadline:* For fall admission, 4/1 for domestic and international students; for spring admission, 11/1 for domestic students, 9/1 for international students. Applications are processed on a rolling basis. *Application fee:* $40 ($90 for international students). *Application Contact:* Gina Amundson, Director of Graduate Programs, 405-325-4107, Fax: 405-325-7753, E-mail: gamundson@ou.edu. *Dean*, Dr. Kenneth Evans, 405-325-0100, Fax: 405-325-3421, E-mail: evansk@ou.edu.

See Close-Up on page 1111.

UNIVERSITY OF OKLAHOMA HEALTH SCIENCES CENTER, Oklahoma City, OK 73190

General Information State-supported, coed, upper-level institution. CGS member. *Graduate housing:* Rooms and/or apartments available on a first-come, first-served basis to single and married students. *Research affiliation:* Dean A. McGee Eye Institute (ophthalmology), Oklahoma Medical Research Foundation, University of Oklahoma Medical Center, Veterans Administration Medical Center (clinical and applied medicine), Oklahoma Children's Memorial Hospital (pediatrics).

GRADUATE UNITS

College of Dentistry Students: 251 full-time (74 women); includes 47 minority (2 African Americans, 24 American Indian/Alaska Native, 17 Asian Americans or Pacific Islanders, 4 Hispanic Americans), 9 international. Average age 28. 813 applicants, 8% accepted, 64 enrolled. *Faculty:* 43 full-time (9 women), 86 part-time/adjunct (15 women). Expenses: Contact institution. *Financial support:* In 2006–07, 225 students received support, including 14 teaching assistantships (averaging $6,000 per year); institutionally sponsored loans and tuition waivers (partial) also available. Financial award applicants required to submit FAFSA. In 2006, 60 DDSs, 6 master's awarded. Offers dentistry (DDS, MS); orthodontics (MS); periodontics (MS). *Application deadline:* Applications are processed on a rolling basis. *Application fee:* $65 ($90 for international students). *Dean*, Dr. Stephen K. Young, 405-271-5444, Fax: 405-271-3423, E-mail: stephen-young@ouhsc.edu.

College of Medicine *Degree program information:* Part-time programs available. Offers biochemistry (MS, PhD); biochemistry and molecular biology (MS, PhD); biological psychology (MS, PhD); cell biology (MS, PhD); genetic counseling (MS); immunology (MS, PhD); medical radiation physics (MS, PhD); medical sciences (MS); medicine (MD, MHS, MS, PhD); microbiology (MS, PhD); microbiology and immunology (MS, PhD); molecular biology (MS, PhD); neuroscience (MS, PhD); pathology (PhD); physician associate (MHS); physiology (MS, PhD); psychiatry and behavioral sciences (MS, PhD); radiological sciences (MS, PhD). Electronic applications accepted.

College of Pharmacy Offers pharmacy (Pharm D, MS, PhD).

Graduate College *Degree program information:* Part-time and evening/weekend programs available.

College of Allied Health *Degree program information:* Part-time programs available. Offers allied health (MOT, MPT, MS, Au D, PhD, Certificate); allied health sciences (PhD); audiology (MS, Au D, PhD); communication sciences and disorders (Certificate); education of the deaf (MS); nutritional sciences (MS); occupational therapy (MOT); physical therapy (MPT); rehabilitation sciences (MS); speech-language pathology (MS, PhD).

College of Nursing *Degree program information:* Part-time programs available. Offers nursing (MS).

College of Public Health *Degree program information:* Part-time programs available. Offers biostatistics (MPH, MS, Dr PH, PhD); epidemiology (MPH, MS, Dr PH, PhD); general public health (MPH, Dr PH); health administration and policy (MHA, MPH, MS, Dr PH, PhD); health promotion sciences (MPH, MS, Dr PH, PhD); occupational and environmental health (MPH, MS, Dr PH, PhD); preparedness and terrorism (MPH); public health (MHA, MPH, MS, Dr PH, PhD).

UNIVERSITY OF OREGON, Eugene, OR 97403

General Information State-supported, coed, university. CGS member. *Enrollment:* 20,348 graduate, professional, and undergraduate students; 3,349 full-time matriculated graduate/professional students (1,782 women), 536 part-time matriculated graduate/professional students (285 women). *Enrollment by degree level:* 573 first professional, 1,733 master's, 1,098 doctoral. *Graduate faculty:* 715 full-time (273 women), 188 part-time/adjunct (106 women). *Graduate housing:* Rooms and/or apartments available to single and married students. *Student services:* Campus employment opportunities, campus safety program, career counseling, child daycare facilities, disabled student services, exercise/wellness program, free psychological counseling, grant writing training, international student services, low-cost health insurance, multicultural affairs office, teacher training, writing training. *Library facilities:* Knight Library plus 6 others. *Online resources:* library catalog, web page, access to other libraries' catalogs. *Collection:* 2.7 million titles, 18,826 serial subscriptions, 443,827 audiovisual materials. *Research affiliation:* Oregon Research Institute, Decision Research, Battelle Pacific Northwest Laboratories, National Renewable Energy Laboratory, Stanford Linear Accelerator Center, Naval Research Laboratories.

Computer facilities: 1,600 computers available on campus for general student use. A campuswide network can be accessed from student residence rooms and from off campus. Internet access and online class registration are available. *Web address:* http://www.uoregon.edu/.

General Application Contact: Information Contact, 541-346-5129, E-mail: gradsch@oregon.uoregon.edu.

GRADUATE UNITS

Graduate School Students: 3,349 full-time (1,782 women), 536 part-time (285 women); includes 387 minority (53 African Americans, 47 American Indian/Alaska Native, 159 Asian Americans or Pacific Islanders, 128 Hispanic Americans), 433 international. Average age 30. 3,225 applicants, 32% accepted. *Faculty:* 715 full-time (273 women), 188 part-time/adjunct (106 women). Expenses: Contact institution. *Financial support:* In 2006–07, 1,194 teaching assistantships were awarded; fellowships, research assistantships, career-related internships or fieldwork, Federal Work-Study, institutionally sponsored loans, and tuition waivers (full) also available. Support available to part-time students. Financial award applicants required to submit FAFSA. In 2006, 795 master's, 169 doctorates awarded. *Degree program information:* Part-time and evening/weekend programs available. Offers applied information management (MS). *Application fee:* $50. *Associate Dean*, Marian Friestad, 541-346-2834.

Charles H. Lundquist College of Business Students: 168 full-time (66 women), 44 part-time (17 women); includes 19 minority (2 African Americans, 12 Asian Americans or Pacific Islanders, 5 Hispanic Americans), 37 international. 260 applicants, 49% accepted. *Faculty:* 44 full-time (4 women), 5 part-time/adjunct (3 women). Expenses: Contact institution. *Financial support:* In 2006–07, 63 teaching assistantships were awarded; fellowships, research assistantships, career-related internships or fieldwork, Federal Work-Study, and institutionally sponsored loans also available. Support available to part-time students. In 2006, 128 master's, 6 doctorates awarded. *Degree program information:* Part-time and evening/weekend programs available. Offers accounting (M Actg, PhD); business (M Actg, MA, MBA, MS, PhD); decision sciences (MA, MS); finance (PhD); management (PhD); management: general business (MBA); marketing (PhD). *Application fee:* $50. *Application Contact:* Perri McGee, Admissions Contact, 541-346-1462, E-mail: pcrone@uoregon.edu. *Dean,* James C. Bean, 541-346-3300.

College of Arts and Sciences Students: 1,076 full-time (483 women), 91 part-time (39 women); includes 81 minority (17 African Americans, 8 American Indian/Alaska Native, 36 Asian Americans or Pacific Islanders, 20 Hispanic Americans), 239 international. 1,785 applicants, 22% accepted. *Faculty:* 418 full-time (140 women), 78 part-time/adjunct (36 women). Expenses: Contact institution. *Financial support:* In 2006–07, 787 teaching assistantships were awarded; fellowships, research assistantships, career-related internships or fieldwork, Federal Work-Study, and institutionally sponsored loans also available. Support available to part-time students. Financial award applicants required to submit FAFSA. In 2006, 246 master's, 113 doctorates awarded. *Degree program information:* Part-time and evening/weekend programs available. Offers anthropology (MA, MS, PhD); arts and sciences (MA, MFA, MS, PhD); Asian studies (MA); biochemistry (MA, MS, PhD); chemistry (MA, MS, PhD); Chinese (MA, PhD); classical civilization (MA); classics (MA); clinical psychology (PhD); cognitive psychology (MA, MS, PhD); comparative literature (MA, PhD); computer and information science (MA, MS, PhD); creative writing (MFA); developmental psychology (MA, MS, PhD); ecology and evolution (MA, MS, PhD); economics (MA, MS, PhD); English (MA, PhD); environmental science, studies, and policy (PhD); environmental studies (MA, MS); French (MA); geography (MA, MS, PhD); geological sciences (MA, MS, PhD); Germanic languages and literatures (MA, PhD); Greek (MA); history (MA, PhD); human physiology (MS, PhD); independent study: folklore (MA, MS); international studies (MA); Italian (MA); Japanese (MA, PhD); Latin (MA); linguistics (MA, PhD); marine biology (MA, MS, PhD); mathematics (MA, MS, PhD); molecular, cellular and genetic biology (PhD); neuroscience and development (PhD); philosophy (MA, PhD); physics (MA, MS, PhD); physiological psychology (MA, MS, PhD); political science (MA, MS, PhD); psychology (MA, MS, PhD); Romance languages (MA, PhD); Russian and East European Studies (MA); social/personality psychology (MA, MS, PhD); sociology (MA, MS, PhD); Spanish (MA); theater arts (MA, MFA, MS, PhD). *Application fee:* $50. *Dean,* Wendy Larson, 541-346-3902.

College of Education Students: 465 full-time (350 women), 211 part-time (132 women); includes 84 minority (9 African Americans, 16 American Indian/Alaska Native, 22 Asian Americans or Pacific Islanders, 37 Hispanic Americans), 72 international. 390 applicants, 32% accepted. *Faculty:* 107 full-time (70 women), 76 part-time/adjunct (55 women). Expenses: Contact institution. *Financial support:* In 2006–07, 86 teaching assistantships were awarded; fellowships, research assistantships, career-related internships or fieldwork, Federal Work-Study, institutionally sponsored loans, and tuition waivers (full) also available. In 2006, 225 master's, 25 doctorates awarded. *Degree program information:* Part-time programs available. Offers education (M Ed, MA, MS, D Ed, PhD). *Application fee:* $50. *Application Contact:* Ron Tuomi, Admissions Contact, 541-346-3528, Fax: 541-346-5818, E-mail: rtuomi@uoregon.edu. *Dean,* Michael Bullis, 541-346-1396.

School of Architecture and Allied Arts Students: 419 full-time (240 women), 53 part-time (37 women); includes 37 minority (1 African American, 4 American Indian/Alaska Native, 14 Asian Americans or Pacific Islanders, 18 Hispanic Americans), 35 international. 515 applicants, 46% accepted. *Faculty:* 69 full-time (31 women), 19 part-time/adjunct (8 women). Expenses: Contact institution. *Financial support:* In 2006–07, 119 teaching assistantships were awarded; fellowships, research assistantships, career-related internships or fieldwork, Federal Work-Study, and institutionally sponsored loans also available. Support available to part-time students. In 2006, 152 master's, 1 doctorate awarded. *Degree program information:* Part-time and evening/weekend programs available. Offers architecture (M Arch); architecture and allied arts (M Arch, MA, MCRP, MFA, MI Arch, MLA, MPA, MS, PhD); art (MFA); art history (MA, PhD); arts management (MA, MS); community and regional planning (MCRP); historic preservation (MS); interior architecture (MI Arch); landscape architecture (MLA); public policy and management (MA, MPA, MS). *Application fee:* $50. *Dean,* Frances Bronet, 541-346-3631.

School of Journalism and Communication Students: 69 full-time (43 women), 9 part-time (4 women); includes 8 minority (1 American Indian/Alaska Native, 3 Asian Americans or Pacific Islanders, 4 Hispanic Americans), 9 international. 66 applicants, 47% accepted. *Faculty:* 16 full-time (7 women), 1 (woman) part-time/adjunct. Expenses: Contact institution. *Financial support:* In 2006–07, 37 teaching assistantships were awarded; career-related internships or fieldwork, Federal Work-Study, institutionally sponsored loans, and scholarships/grants also available. Financial award application deadline: 3/31. In 2006, 13 master's, 5 doctorates awarded. *Degree program information:* Part-time programs available. Offers journalism and communication (MA, MS, PhD). *Application fee:* $50. *Application Contact:* Petra Hagen, Graduate Secretary, 541-346-2136, E-mail: phagen@uoregon.edu. *Dean,* Timothy W. Gleason, 541-346-3739.

School of Music Students: 121 full-time (66 women), 35 part-time (20 women); includes 10 minority (1 American Indian/Alaska Native, 9 Asian Americans or Pacific Islanders), 19 international. 166 applicants, 49% accepted. *Faculty:* 34 full-time (11 women), 5 part-time/adjunct (2 women). Expenses: Contact institution. *Financial support:* In 2006–07, 75 teaching assistantships were awarded; career-related internships or fieldwork, Federal Work-Study, institutionally sponsored loans, and scholarships/grants also available. In 2006, 18 master's, 6 doctorates awarded. *Degree program information:* Part-time programs available. Offers composition (M Mus, DMA, PhD); conducting (M Mus); dance (MA, MS); jazz studies (M Mus); music (MA); music education (M Mus, DMA, PhD); music history (PhD); music theory (PhD); performance (M Mus, DMA); piano pedagogy (M Mus). *Application fee:* $50. *Application Contact:* Anne Merydith, Admissions Contact, 541-346-5664, E-mail: gradmus@uoregon.edu. *Dean,* C. Brad Foley, 541-346-5664.

School of Law Students: 558 full-time (243 women), 36 part-time (15 women); includes 99 minority (19 African Americans, 10 American Indian/Alaska Native, 40 Asian Americans or Pacific Islanders, 30 Hispanic Americans), 8 international. 1,174 applicants, 53% accepted. *Faculty:* 27 full-time (10 women), 4 part-time/adjunct (1 woman). Expenses: Contact institution. *Financial support:* In 2006–07, 27 teaching assistantships were awarded; career-related internships or fieldwork, Federal Work-Study, institutionally sponsored loans, and tuition waivers (partial) also available. Financial award application deadline: 2/1; financial award applicants required to submit FAFSA. In 2006, 149 degrees awarded. Offers law (JD, MA, MS). *Application deadline:* For fall admission, 2/15 priority date for domestic students. *Application fee:* $50. *Application Contact:* Jee Muntz, Information Contact, Office of Admissions, 541-346-1810, Fax: 541-346-1564. *Interim Dean,* Margaret Paris, 541-346-3852, Fax: 541-346-1564.

UNIVERSITY OF OTTAWA, Ottawa, ON K1N 6N5, Canada

General Information Province-supported, coed, university. CGS member. *Graduate housing:* Rooms and/or apartments available on a first-come, first-served basis to single and married students. *Research affiliation:* Bell Canada (telecommunications, data security), Virox Technologies (disinfectants), Shipley (advanced materials), EnPharma Pharmaceuticals (medical drug development), Communications and Information Technology Ontario (CITO) (telecommunications), Oncology, Inc. (cancer, neuromuscular diseases, genetics).

GRADUATE UNITS

Faculty of Graduate and Postdoctoral Studies *Degree program information:* Part-time and evening/weekend programs available. Offers biomedical engineering (MA Sc); e-business technologies (M Sc, MEBT); globalization and international development (MA); population health (PhD); systems science (M Sc, M Sys Sc, Certificate). Electronic applications accepted.

Faculty of Arts *Degree program information:* Part-time and evening/weekend programs available. Offers arts (M Geog, M Mus, M Sc, MA, PhD, Certificate); classical studies (MA); communication (MA); directing for theatre (MA); economics (PhD); English (PhD); geography (PhD); history (PhD); interpreting (MA); lettres Françaises (PhD); linguistics (PhD); music (M Mus, MA); orchestral studies (Certificate); philosophy (PhD); piano pedagogy research (Certificate); political science (PhD); psychology (PhD); religious studies (PhD); Spanish (MA, PhD); Spanish translation (MA); translation (MA); translation studies (PhD). Electronic applications accepted.

Faculty of Education Postbaccalaureate distance learning degree programs offered (minimal on-campus study). Offers education (M Ed, MA Ed, PhD, Certificate). Electronic applications accepted.

Faculty of Engineering Offers chemical engineering (M Eng, MA Sc, PhD); civil engineering (M Eng, MA Sc, PhD); computer science (MCS, PhD); electrical and computer engineering (M Eng, MA Sc, PhD); engineering (M Eng, MA Sc, MCS, PhD, Certificate); engineering management (M Eng); information technology (Certificate); mechanical and aerospace engineering (M Eng, MA Sc, PhD); project management (Certificate). Electronic applications accepted.

Faculty of Health Sciences *Degree program information:* Part-time and evening/weekend programs available. Offers audiology (M Sc); health sciences (M Sc, MA, PhD, Certificate); human kinetics (MA); nurse practitioner (Certificate); nursing (M Sc, PhD); nursing/primary health care (M Sc); orthophony (M Sc). Electronic applications accepted.

Faculty of Law *Degree program information:* Part-time and evening/weekend programs available. Offers law (LL M, LL D). Electronic applications accepted.

Faculty of Medicine Offers biochemistry (M Sc, PhD); cellular and molecular medicine (M Sc, PhD); epidemiology (M Sc); medicine (MD, M Sc, PhD); microbiology and immunology (M Sc, PhD). Electronic applications accepted.

Faculty of Science *Degree program information:* Part-time and evening/weekend programs available. Offers biology (M Sc, PhD); chemistry (M Sc, PhD); earth sciences (M Sc, PhD); mathematics and statistics (M Sc, PhD); physics (M Sc, PhD); science (M Sc, PhD). Electronic applications accepted.

Faculty of Social Sciences *Degree program information:* Part-time and evening/weekend programs available. Offers criminology (MA, MCA); economics (MA, PhD); education (MA); English (MA); history (MA); human kinetics (MA); law (LL M); lettres Françaises (MA); nursing (M Sc); pastoral studies (MA); political science (MA); political studies (MA, PhD); psychology (PhD); religious studies (MA); social sciences (LL M, M Sc, MA, MCA, MSS, PhD); social work (MSS); sociology (MA); sociology and anthropology (MA). Electronic applications accepted.

School of Management *Degree program information:* Part-time and evening/weekend programs available. Offers business administration (MBA); executive business administration (EMBA); health administration (MHA); management (EMBA, MBA, MHA). Electronic applications accepted.

UNIVERSITY OF PENNSYLVANIA, Philadelphia, PA 19104

General Information Independent, coed, university. CGS member. *Enrollment:* 18,809 graduate, professional, and undergraduate students; 9,296 full-time matriculated graduate/professional students (4,603 women), 2,204 part-time matriculated graduate/professional students (1,302 women). *Enrollment by degree level:* 2,368 first professional, 5,540 master's, 3,360 doctoral, 232 other advanced degrees. *Graduate faculty:* 2,471 full-time (689 women), 1,871 part-time/adjunct (517 women). *Graduate housing:* Rooms and/or apartments available to single and married students. Housing application deadline: 4/1. *Student services:* Campus employment opportunities, campus safety program, career counseling, disabled student services, exercise/wellness program, free psychological counseling, international student services, low-cost health insurance, multicultural affairs office, writing training. *Library facilities:* University of Pennsylvania Libraries plus 15 others. *Online resources:* library catalog, web page, access to other libraries' catalogs. *Collection:* 5.9 million titles, 47,787 serial subscriptions. *Research affiliation:* Regional Nanotechnology Center, BioAdvance, Wistar Institute of Anatomy and Biology, Children's Hospital of Philadelphia.

Computer facilities: 975 computers available on campus for general student use. A campuswide network can be accessed from student residence rooms and from off campus. Internet access and online class registration, billing information, financial aid application, status, academic records, student services are available. *Web address:* http://www.upenn.edu/.

General Application Contact: Karen Lawrence, Assistant Vice Provost for Graduate Education, 215-898-1842, Fax: 215-898-6567, E-mail: graded@pobox.upenn.edu.

GRADUATE UNITS

Annenberg School for Communication Students: 88 full-time (54 women), 3 part-time (2 women); includes 10 minority (8 African Americans, 2 Hispanic Americans), 25 international. 392 applicants, 7% accepted, 16 enrolled. *Faculty:* 16 full-time (3 women), 10 part-time/adjunct (2 women). Expenses: Contact institution. *Financial support:* Fellowships, research assistantships, teaching assistantships, career-related internships or fieldwork and Federal Work-Study available. Financial award application deadline: 1/2. In 2006, 7 doctorates awarded. Offers communication (PhD). *Application deadline:* For fall admission, 1/2 for domestic students. *Application fee:* $70. Electronic applications accepted. *Application Contact:* Beverly Henry, Graduate Studies Coordinator, 215-573-1091, Fax: 215-898-2024, E-mail: bhenry@asc.upenn.edu. *Graduate Dean,* Joseph Turow, 215-898-7041.

Graduate School of Education Students: 510 full-time (409 women), 511 part-time (351 women); includes 146 minority (77 African Americans, 3 American Indian/Alaska Native, 49 Asian Americans or Pacific Islanders, 17 Hispanic Americans), 145 international. 1,487 applicants, 59% accepted, 499 enrolled. *Faculty:* 36 full-time (20 women), 108 part-time/adjunct (65 women). Expenses: Contact institution. *Financial support:* Fellowships, research assistantships, teaching assistantships, career-related internships or fieldwork, Federal Work-Study, institutionally sponsored loans, scholarships/grants, tuition waivers (partial), and unspecified assistantships available. Support available to part-time students. Financial award applicants required to submit FAFSA. In 2006, 297 master's, 86 doctorates awarded. *Degree program information:* Part-time programs available. Offers applied psychology and human development (MS Ed, Ed D, PhD); counseling psychology (MS Ed); early childhood education (MS Ed); education (MS Ed, Ed D, PhD); education, culture and society (MS Ed, PhD); educational linguistics (PhD); educational policy and leadership (MS Ed, Ed D, PhD); elementary education (MS Ed); foundations and practices in education (MS Ed, Ed D, PhD); human development (MS Ed, PhD); human sexuality education (MS Ed, Ed D, PhD); intercultural communication (MS Ed, Ed D, PhD); policy, management and evaluation (MS Ed, Ed D, PhD); reading, writing, and literacy (MS Ed, Ed D, PhD); school, community, and clinical child psychology (PhD); secondary education (MS Ed); teaching English to speakers of other languages (MS Ed); teaching English to speakers of other languages and intercultural communication (MS Ed, PhD). *Application deadline:* For fall admission, 12/15 priority date for domestic students. Applications are processed on a rolling basis. *Application fee:* $70. Electronic applications accepted. *Application Contact:* Alyssa D'Alconzo, Associate Director, Admissions, 215-898-6415, Fax: 215-746-6884, E-mail: admissions@gse.upenn.edu. *Graduate Dean,* Dr. Andrew Porter, 215-898-7014.

Law School Students: 762 full-time (355 women); includes 231 minority (61 African Americans, 5 American Indian/Alaska Native, 110 Asian Americans or Pacific Islanders, 55 Hispanic Americans), 35 international. Average age 24. 5,649 applicants, 16% accepted, 249 enrolled. *Faculty:* 53 full-time (13 women), 41 part-time/adjunct (11 women). Expenses: Contact institution. *Financial support:* In 2006–07, 644 students received support, including 2 research assistantships with tuition reimbursements available (averaging $16,500 per year), 21 teaching assistantships (averaging $1,750 per year); fellowships, career-related internships or fieldwork, Federal Work-Study, institutionally sponsored loans, and scholarships/grants also available. Financial award application deadline: 3/1; financial award applicants required to submit FAFSA. In 2006, 274 JDs, 93 master's, 2 doctorates awarded. Offers law (JD, LL CM, LL M, SJD). *Application deadline:* For fall admission, 2/15 for domestic students. Applications are processed on a rolling basis. *Application fee:* $75. Electronic applications accepted. *Application Contact:* Renee Post, Associate Dean of Admissions and Financial Aid, 215-898-7400, Fax: 215-898-9606, E-mail: admissions@law.upenn.edu. *Dean,* Michael A. Fitts, 215-898-7400, Fax: 215-573-2025.

School of Arts and Sciences Students: 1,591 full-time (772 women), 731 part-time (427 women); includes 205 minority (88 African Americans, 7 American Indian/Alaska Native, 69

University of Pennsylvania (continued)

Asian Americans or Pacific Islanders, 41 Hispanic Americans), 571 international. 5,531 applicants, 19% accepted, 589 enrolled. *Faculty:* 511 full-time (151 women), 712 part-time/adjunct (154 women). Expenses: Contact institution. *Financial support:* Fellowships, research assistantships, teaching assistantships, career-related internships or fieldwork, Federal Work-Study, institutionally sponsored loans, scholarships/grants, traineeships, and lectureships available. Support available to part-time students. Financial award applicants required to submit FAFSA. In 2006, 466 master's, 207 doctorates awarded. *Degree program information:* Part-time and evening/weekend programs available. Offers American civilization (AM, PhD); ancient history (AM, PhD); anthropology (AM, MS, PhD); art and archaeology of the Mediterranean world (AM, PhD); arts and sciences (AM, M Bioethics, MA, MBA, MES, MGA, MLA, MS, PhD); bioethics (M Bioethics); biology (PhD); chemistry (MS, PhD); classical studies (AM, PhD); comparative literature (AM, PhD); criminology (MA, MS, PhD); demography (AM, PhD); East Asian languages and civilization (AM, PhD); economics (AM, PhD); English (AM, PhD); folklore and folklife (AM, PhD); French (AM, PhD); geology (MS, PhD); Germanic languages (AM, PhD); history (AM, PhD); history and sociology of science (AM, PhD); history of art (AM, PhD); international studies (AM); Italian (AM, PhD); linguistics (AM, PhD); literary theory (AM, PhD); mathematics (AM, PhD); medical physics (MS); music (AM, PhD); near eastern languages and civilization (AM, PhD); organizational dynamics (MS); philosophy (AM, PhD); physics (PhD); political science (AM, PhD); psychology (PhD); religious studies (PhD); sociology (AM, PhD); South Asian regional studies (AM, PhD); Spanish (AM, PhD). *Application deadline:* For fall admission, 12/15 priority date for domestic students. Applications are processed on a rolling basis. *Application fee:* $70. Electronic applications accepted. *Application Contact:* Patricia Rea, Coordinator for Admissions, 215-573-5816, Fax: 215-573-8068, E-mail: gdasadmis@sas.upenn.edu. *Associate Dean,* Jack Nagel, 215-898-7156, Fax: 215-573-8068, E-mail: gdasdmis@sas.upenn.edu.

College of General Studies Students: 78 full-time (47 women), 307 part-time (193 women); includes 42 minority (18 African Americans, 15 Asian Americans or Pacific Islanders, 9 Hispanic Americans), 24 international. 264 applicants, 67% accepted, 108 enrolled. *Faculty:* 9 part-time/adjunct (4 women). Expenses: Contact institution. In 2006, 113 master's awarded. Offers environmental studies (MES); individualized study (MLA). *Application deadline:* For fall admission, 12/1 priority date for domestic students. *Application fee:* $70. Electronic applications accepted. *Application Contact:* Patricia Rea, Coordinator for Admissions, 215-573-5816, Fax: 215-573-8068, E-mail: gdasadmis@sas.upenn.edu.

Fels Institute of Government Students: 51 full-time (29 women), 73 part-time (42 women); includes 31 minority (16 African Americans, 6 Asian Americans or Pacific Islanders, 9 Hispanic Americans), 18 international. 219 applicants, 42% accepted, 51 enrolled. *Faculty:* 21 part-time/adjunct (3 women). Expenses: Contact institution. *Financial support:* Fellowships, career-related internships or fieldwork, Federal Work-Study, institutionally sponsored loans, and scholarships/grants available. Support available to part-time students. Financial award application deadline: 12/15; financial award applicants required to submit FAFSA. In 2006, 55 master's awarded. *Degree program information:* Part-time and evening/weekend programs available. Offers government (MGA). *Application deadline:* For fall admission, 12/15 priority date for domestic students. Applications are processed on a rolling basis. *Application fee:* $70. *Application Contact:* Patricia Rea, Coordinator for Admissions, 215-573-5816, Fax: 215-573-8068, E-mail: gdasadmis@sas.upenn.edu. *Director,* Donald F. Kettl, 215-746-4600.

Joseph H. Lauder Institute of Management and International Studies Students: 118 full-time (27 women). Average age 27. 200 applicants, 36% accepted. Expenses: Contact institution. *Financial support:* Fellowships with tuition reimbursements, career-related internships or fieldwork and scholarships/grants available. In 2006, 57 degrees awarded. Offers international studies (MA); management and international studies (MBA). Applications made concurrently and separately to Lauder Institute and Wharton MBA program. *Application deadline:* For fall admission, 10/12 for domestic students; for winter admission, 1/4 for domestic students. Electronic applications accepted. *Application Contact:* Marcy R. Bevan, Directorof Admissions, 215-898-1215, Fax: 215-898-2067, E-mail: lauderinfo@wharton.upenn.edu. *Director,* Dr. Richard J. Herring, 215-898-1215.

School of Dental Medicine Students: 516 full-time (294 women); includes 248 minority (33 African Americans, 1 American Indian/Alaska Native, 194 Asian Americans or Pacific Islanders, 20 Hispanic Americans). Average age 24. 2,205 applicants, 13% accepted, 117 enrolled. *Faculty:* 68 full-time (21 women), 376 part-time/adjunct (70 women). Expenses: Contact institution. *Financial support:* In 2006–07, 223 students received support. Federal Work-Study and scholarships/grants available. Financial award application deadline: 6/30; financial award applicants required to submit FAFSA. In 2006, 128 DMDs awarded. Offers dental medicine (DMD). *Application deadline:* For fall admission, 1/1 for domestic students. Applications are processed on a rolling basis. *Application fee:* $50. *Application Contact:* Corky Cacas, Director of Admissions, 215-898-8943, Fax: 215-898-5243, E-mail: dental-admissions@pobox.upenn.edu. *Dean,* Dr. Marjorie Jeffcoat, 215-898-8941, Fax: 215-573-4075.

School of Design Students: 688 full-time (413 women), 62 part-time (38 women); includes 143 minority (47 African Americans, 9 American Indian/Alaska Native, 55 Asian Americans or Pacific Islanders, 32 Hispanic Americans), 136 international. 1,426 applicants, 42% accepted, 224 enrolled. *Faculty:* 50 full-time (13 women), 127 part-time/adjunct (37 women). Expenses: Contact institution. *Financial support:* Fellowships, research assistantships, teaching assistantships, career-related internships or fieldwork, Federal Work-Study, institutionally sponsored loans, scholarships/grants, and tuition waivers (full and partial) available. Support available to part-time students. Financial award application deadline: 1/2; financial award applicants required to submit FAFSA. In 2006, 214 master's, 31 doctorates, 12 other advanced degrees awarded. *Degree program information:* Part-time programs available. Offers architecture (M Arch, PhD); city and regional planning (MCP, PhD, Certificate); conservation and heritage management (Certificate); design (M Arch, MCP, MFA, MLA, MS, PhD, Certificate); fine arts (MFA); historic conservation (Certificate); historic preservation (MS); landscape architecture and regional planning (MLA); landscape studies (Certificate); real estate design and development (PhD, Certificate); urban design (PhD, Certificate). *Application deadline:* For fall admission, 1/2 priority date for domestic students. *Application fee:* $70. *Application Contact:* Joan Weston, Director of Admissions, 215-898-6520, Fax: 215-573-3927, E-mail: admissions@design.upenn.edu. *Graduate Dean,* David Leatherbarrow, 215-898-5728, Fax: 215-573-2192, E-mail: admissions@design.upenn.edu.

School of Engineering and Applied Science Students: 679 full-time (199 women), 256 part-time (74 women); includes 122 minority (17 African Americans, 1 American Indian/Alaska Native, 90 Asian Americans or Pacific Islanders, 14 Hispanic Americans), 484 international. 2,537 applicants, 32% accepted, 323 enrolled. *Faculty:* 147 full-time (12 women), 159 part-time/adjunct (12 women). Expenses: Contact institution. *Financial support:* Fellowships, research assistantships, teaching assistantships, Federal Work-Study, institutionally sponsored loans, and scholarships/grants available. In 2006, 319 master's, 48 doctorates awarded. *Degree program information:* Part-time and evening/weekend programs available. Offers applied mechanics (MSE, PhD); bioengineering (MSE, PhD); biotechnology (MS); chemical engineering (MSE, PhD); computer and information science (MCIT, MSE, PhD); computer graphics and game technology (MSE); electrical and systems engineering (MSE, PhD); engineering and applied science (EMBA, MCIT, MS, MSE, PhD, AC); materials science and engineering (MSE, PhD); mechanical engineering (MSE, PhD); technology management (EMBA); telecommunications and networking (MSE). *Application deadline:* For fall admission, 6/1 priority date for domestic students, 5/1 priority date for international students; for spring admission, 11/1 priority date for domestic students, 10/1 priority date for international students. Applications are processed on a rolling basis. *Application fee:* $70. Electronic applications accepted. *Application Contact:* Ellen Eckert, Associate Director for Admissions, 215-898-4813, Fax: 215-573-2018, E-mail: engadmis@seas.upenn.edu. *Dean,* Eduardo D. Glandt, 215-898-7244, Fax: 215-573-5577, E-mail: apo@seas.upenn.edu.

School of Medicine Students: 2,133 full-time (1,078 women), 52 part-time (28 women); includes 557 minority (111 African Americans, 12 American Indian/Alaska Native, 311 Asian Americans or Pacific Islanders, 123 Hispanic Americans), 255 international. Average age 24. *Faculty:* 2,093 full-time (668 women), 968 part-time/adjunct (357 women). Expenses: Contact institution. *Financial support:* Fellowships, research assistantships, teaching assistantships, career-related internships or fieldwork, Federal Work-Study, institutionally sponsored loans, scholarships/grants, and unspecified assistantships available. Financial award application deadline: 1/2; financial award applicants required to submit FAFSA. In 2006, 148 MDs, 28 master's, 86 doctorates awarded. *Degree program information:* Part-time programs available. Offers medicine (MD, MS, MSCE, PhD). *Application deadline:* Applications are processed on a rolling basis. Electronic applications accepted. *Application Contact:* Gaye Sheffler, Director, Admissions, 215-898-8001, Fax: 215-898-0833, E-mail: sheffler@mail.med.upenn.edu. *Dean,* Dr. Arthur M. Rubenstein, 215-898-6796, Fax: 215-573-2030, E-mail: amrdean@mail.med.upenn.edu.

Biomedical Graduate Studies Students: 665 full-time (337 women); includes 128 minority (24 African Americans, 3 American Indian/Alaska Native, 67 Asian Americans or Pacific Islanders, 34 Hispanic Americans), 124 international. 1,125 applicants, 22% accepted, 103 enrolled. *Faculty:* 602. Expenses: Contact institution. *Financial support:* Fellowships, research assistantships, scholarships/grants, traineeships, and unspecified assistantships available. In 2006, 17 master's, 97 doctorates awarded. *Degree program information:* Part-time programs available. Offers biochemistry and molecular biophysics (PhD); biomedical studies (MS, PhD); biostatistics (MS, PhD); cell biology and physiology (PhD); cell growth and cancer (PhD); developmental biology (PhD); gene therapy and vaccines (PhD); genetics and gene regulation (PhD); genomics and computational biology (PhD); immunology (PhD); microbiology, virology, and parasitology (PhD); neuroscience (PhD); pharmacology (PhD). *Application deadline:* For fall admission, 12/15 priority date for domestic students, 12/1 priority date for international students. Applications are processed on a rolling basis. *Application fee:* $70. Electronic applications accepted. *Application Contact:* Sarah Gormley, Admissions Coordinator, 215-898-1030, Fax: 215-898-2671, E-mail: gormley@mail.med.upenn.edu. *Director,* Dr. Susan R. Ross, 215-898-1030.

Center for Clinical Epidemiology and Biostatistics Students: 70 full-time (40 women), 42 part-time (22 women); includes 31 minority (6 African Americans, 22 Asian Americans or Pacific Islanders, 3 Hispanic Americans). Average age 30. 56 applicants, 88% accepted, 41 enrolled. *Faculty:* 64 full-time (27 women), 117 part-time/adjunct (39 women). Expenses: Contact institution. *Financial support:* In 2006–07, 65 students received support, including 60 fellowships with full and partial tuition reimbursements available (averaging $40,000 per year); career-related internships or fieldwork, scholarships/grants, health care benefits, unspecified assistantships, and faculty/staff benefits for partial tuition coverage also available. Financial award application deadline: 1/15. In 2006, 27 degrees awarded. *Degree program information:* Part-time programs available. Offers clinical epidemiology (MSCE); epidemiology (PhD). PhD offered through the School of Arts and Sciences. *Application deadline:* For fall admission, 1/15 priority date for domestic and international students. Applications are processed on a rolling basis. *Application Contact:* Shanta C. Layton, Associate Director for Graduate Training in Epidemiology, 215-573-2382, Fax: 215-573-5315, E-mail: shanta2@mail.med.upenn.edu. *Director,* Dr. Harold I. Feldman, 215-573-2382, Fax: 215-573-2265, E-mail: hfeldman@mail.med.upenn.edu.

School of Nursing Students: 191 full-time (168 women), 225 part-time (213 women); includes 64 minority (30 African Americans, 2 American Indian/Alaska Native, 25 Asian Americans or Pacific Islanders, 7 Hispanic Americans), 12 international. 317 applicants, 61% accepted, 152 enrolled. *Faculty:* 45 full-time (42 women), 109 part-time/adjunct (89 women). Expenses: Contact institution. *Financial support:* Fellowships, research assistantships, teaching assistantships, career-related internships or fieldwork, Federal Work-Study, and institutionally sponsored loans available. Support available to part-time students. Financial award application deadline: 12/15; financial award applicants required to submit FAFSA. In 2006, 151 master's, 11 doctorates, 1 other advanced degree awarded. *Degree program information:* Part-time programs available. Postbaccalaureate distance learning degree programs offered. Offers acute care nurse practitioner (MSN); administration/consulting (MSN); adult and special populations (MSN); adult health nurse practitioner (MSN); adult oncology nurse practitioner (MSN); child and family (MSN); family health nurse practitioner (MSN, Certificate); geropsychiatrics (MSN); health leadership (MSN); neonatal nurse practitioner (MSN); nurse anesthetist (MSN); nurse midwifery (MSN); nursing (MSN, PhD, Certificate); nursing and health care administration (MSN, PhD); pediatric acute/chronic care nurse practitioner (MSN); pediatric critical care nurse practitioner (MSN); pediatric nurse practitioner (MSN); pediatric oncology nurse practitioner (MSN); perinatal advanced practice nurse specialist (MSN); primary care (MSN); women's healthcare nurse practitioner (MSN). *Application deadline:* For fall admission, 2/15 priority date for domestic students. Applications are processed on a rolling basis. *Application fee:* $70. *Application Contact:* Nursing Admissions, 215-898-4271, Fax: 215-573-8439, E-mail: admissions@nursing.upenn.edu. *Graduate Dean,* Anne Keane, 215-898-8281, Fax: 215-573-8439, E-mail: admissions@nursing.upenn.edu.

School of Social Policy and Practice Students: 211 full-time (185 women), 86 part-time (72 women); includes 83 minority (49 African Americans, 3 American Indian/Alaska Native, 15 Asian Americans or Pacific Islanders, 16 Hispanic Americans), 7 international. Average age 25. 373 applicants, 76% accepted, 149 enrolled. *Faculty:* 19 full-time (10 women), 42 part-time/adjunct (27 women). Expenses: Contact institution. *Financial support:* In 2006–07, 230 students received support; fellowships, career-related internships or fieldwork, Federal Work-Study, institutionally sponsored loans, scholarships/grants, tuition waivers (partial), and unspecified assistantships available. Support available to part-time students. Financial award application deadline: 4/15; financial award applicants required to submit FAFSA. In 2006, 136 master's, 3 doctorates awarded. Offers social policy and practice (MSW, PhD); social welfare (PhD); social work (MSW). *Application deadline:* For fall admission, 3/31 for domestic and international students. Applications are processed on a rolling basis. *Application fee:* $65. Electronic applications accepted. *Application Contact:* Mary C. Mazzola, Director of Admissions and Recruitment, 215-898-5550, Fax: 215-573-2099, E-mail: mmazzola@sp2.upenn.edu. *Dean,* Richard Gelles, 215-898-5541, Fax: 215-573-2099, E-mail: gelles@sp2.upenn.edu.

School of Veterinary Medicine Students: 438 full-time (346 women); includes 38 minority (8 African Americans, 2 American Indian/Alaska Native, 22 Asian Americans or Pacific Islanders, 6 Hispanic Americans). Average age 24. 1,478 applicants, 11% accepted, 112 enrolled. *Faculty:* 185 full-time (80 women). Expenses: Contact institution. *Financial support:* Career-related internships or fieldwork, Federal Work-Study, and institutionally sponsored loans available. Offers veterinary medicine (VMD). *Application deadline:* For fall admission, 10/1 for domestic students. *Application fee:* $0. *Application Contact:* Malcolm Keiter, Assistant Dean for Admissions, 215-898-5434, Fax: 215-573-8819, E-mail: admissions@vet.upenn.edu. *Dean,* Dr. Joan C. Hendricks, 215-898-8841, Fax: 215-573-8837, E-mail: vetdean@vet.upenn.edu.

Wharton School *Degree program information:* Evening/weekend programs available. Offers accounting (PhD); business (MBA, PhD); business and public policy (PhD); finance (PhD); health care systems (PhD); insurance and risk management (PhD); management (PhD); marketing (PhD); operations and information management (MBA, PhD); operations and information management operations research (PhD); real estate (PhD); statistics (PhD). Electronic applications accepted.

Wharton Executive MBA Division *Degree program information:* Evening/weekend programs available. Offers executive business administration (MBA).

Wharton MBA Division Offers business administration (MBA). Electronic applications accepted.

See Close-Up on page 1113.

UNIVERSITY OF PHOENIX–ATLANTA CAMPUS, Sandy Springs, GA 30350-4153

General Information Proprietary, coed, comprehensive institution. *Enrollment:* 2,518 graduate, professional, and undergraduate students; 691 full-time matriculated graduate/professional students (427 women). *Enrollment by degree level:* 691 master's. *Graduate faculty:* 45 full-time (23 women), 271 part-time/adjunct (66 women). *Tuition:* Full-time $10,560. *Required fees:* $760. *Graduate housing:* On-campus housing not available. *Student services:* Campus safety program, disabled student services, writing training. *Library facilities:* University Library. *Online resources:* library catalog, web page. *Collection:* 1,759 titles, 692 serial subscriptions.

Computer facilities: A campuswide network can be accessed from off campus. *Web address:* http://www.phoenix.edu/.

General Application Contact: Campus Information Center, 678-731-0555, Fax: 678-731-9666.

GRADUATE UNITS

The Artemis School Students: 52 full-time (38 women); includes 28 minority (26 African Americans, 2 Asian Americans or Pacific Islanders). Average age 35. *Faculty:* 9 full-time (5 women), 64 part-time/adjunct (26 women). Expenses: Contact institution. *Financial support:* Institutionally sponsored loans and scholarships/grants available. Financial award applicants required to submit FAFSA. In 2006, 26 degrees awarded. *Degree program information:* Evening/weekend programs available. *Application deadline:* Applications are processed on a rolling basis. *Application fee:* $45. Electronic applications accepted. *Provost*, Dr. Adam Honea, 480-557-1659, E-mail: adam.honea@phoenix.edu.

College of Health and Human Services Students: 52 full-time (38 women); includes 28 minority (26 African Americans, 2 Asian Americans or Pacific Islanders). *Faculty:* 9 full-time (5 women), 56 part-time/adjunct (24 women). Expenses: Contact institution. *Financial support:* Institutionally sponsored loans and scholarships/grants available. Financial award applicants required to submit FAFSA. In 2006, 26 degrees awarded. *Degree program information:* Evening/weekend programs available. Offers health care management (MBA). *Application deadline:* Applications are processed on a rolling basis. *Application fee:* $45. Electronic applications accepted. *Dean/Executive Director*, Dr. Gil Linne, 480-557-1221, E-mail: gil.linne@phoenix.edu.

John Sperling School of Business Students: 639 full-time (389 women); includes 344 minority (321 African Americans, 1 American Indian/Alaska Native, 13 Asian Americans or Pacific Islanders, 9 Hispanic Americans), 26 international. Average age 36. *Faculty:* 36 full-time (18 women), 203 part-time/adjunct (40 women). Expenses: Contact institution. *Financial support:* Institutionally sponsored loans and scholarships/grants available. Financial award applicants required to submit FAFSA. In 2006, 178 degrees awarded. *Degree program information:* Evening/weekend programs available. Offers business (MBA, MIS, MM). *Application deadline:* Applications are processed on a rolling basis. *Application fee:* $45. Electronic applications accepted. *Application Contact:* Campus College Chair, 678-731-0555, Fax: 678-731-9666. *Provost*, Dr. Adam Honea, 480-557-1659, E-mail: adam.honea@phoenix.edu.

College of Graduate Business and Management Students: 605 full-time (375 women); includes 323 minority (303 African Americans, 1 American Indian/Alaska Native, 10 Asian Americans or Pacific Islanders, 9 Hispanic Americans), 22 international. Average age 36. *Faculty:* 25 full-time (15 women), 151 part-time/adjunct (31 women). Expenses: Contact institution. *Financial support:* Institutionally sponsored loans and scholarships/grants available. Financial award applicants required to submit FAFSA. In 2006, 156 degrees awarded. *Degree program information:* Evening/weekend programs available. Offers business administration (MBA); global management (MBA); human resources management (MBA); management (MM). *Application deadline:* Applications are processed on a rolling basis. *Application Contact:* Chair, 678-731-0555, Fax: 678-731-9666. *Associate Vice President and Dean/Executive Director*, Dr. Brian Lindquist, 480-557-1221, E-mail: brian.lindquist@phoenix.edu.

College of Information Systems and Technology Students: 34 full-time (14 women); includes 21 minority (18 African Americans, 3 Asian Americans or Pacific Islanders), 4 international. Average age 37. *Faculty:* 11 full-time (3 women), 52 part-time/adjunct (9 women). Expenses: Contact institution. *Financial support:* Institutionally sponsored loans and scholarships/grants available. Financial award applicants required to submit FAFSA. In 2006, 22 degrees awarded. *Degree program information:* Evening/weekend programs available. Offers information systems (MIS); technology management (MBA). *Application deadline:* Applications are processed on a rolling basis. *Application fee:* $45. Electronic applications accepted. *Application Contact:* Chair, 678-731-0555, Fax: 678-731-9666.

UNIVERSITY OF PHOENIX–BAY AREA CAMPUS, Pleasanton, CA 94588-3677

General Information Proprietary, coed, comprehensive institution. *Enrollment:* 3,139 graduate, professional, and undergraduate students; 903 full-time matriculated graduate/professional students (506 women). *Enrollment by degree level:* 903 master's. *Graduate faculty:* 79 full-time (15 women), 844 part-time/adjunct (278 women). *Tuition:* Full-time $12,648. *Required fees:* $760. *Graduate housing:* On-campus housing not available. *Student services:* Campus safety program, disabled student services, writing training. *Library facilities:* University Library. *Online resources:* library catalog, web page. *Collection:* 1,759 titles, 692 serial subscriptions.

Computer facilities: A campuswide network can be accessed from off campus. *Web address:* http://www.phoenix.edu/.

General Application Contact: Campus Information Center, 408-435-8500, Fax: 408-435-8250.

GRADUATE UNITS

The Artemis School Students: 285 full-time (207 women); includes 72 minority (21 African Americans, 2 American Indian/Alaska Native, 31 Asian Americans or Pacific Islanders, 18 Hispanic Americans), 28 international. Average age 37. *Faculty:* 30 full-time (11 women), 284 part-time/adjunct (137 women). Expenses: Contact institution. *Financial support:* Institutionally sponsored loans and scholarships/grants available. Financial award applicants required to submit FAFSA. In 2006, 128 degrees awarded. *Degree program information:* Evening/weekend programs available. *Application deadline:* Applications are processed on a rolling basis. *Application fee:* $45. Electronic applications accepted. *Provost*, Dr. Adam Honea, 480-447-1659, E-mail: adam.honea@phoenix.edu.

College of Education Students: 227 full-time (156 women); includes 50 minority (15 African Americans, 2 American Indian/Alaska Native, 19 Asian Americans or Pacific Islanders, 14 Hispanic Americans), 22 international. Average age 36. *Faculty:* 11 full-time (3 women), 100 part-time/adjunct (52 women). Expenses: Contact institution. *Financial support:* Institutionally sponsored loans and scholarships/grants available. Financial award applicants required to submit FAFSA. In 2006, 115 degrees awarded. *Degree program information:* Evening/weekend programs available. Offers curriculum instruction (MA Ed); curriculum instruction—adult education (MA Ed). *Application deadline:* Applications are processed on a rolling basis. *Application fee:* $45. Electronic applications accepted. *Application Contact:* Chair, 408-435-8500, Fax: 408-435-8250. *Dean/Executive Director*, Dr. Marla LaRue, 480-557-1218, E-mail: marla.larue@phoenix.edu.

College of Health and Human Services Students: 58 full-time (51 women); includes 22 minority (6 African Americans, 12 Asian Americans or Pacific Islanders, 4 Hispanic Americans), 6 international. Average age 42. *Faculty:* 19 full-time (8 women), 184 part-time/adjunct (85 women). Expenses: Contact institution. *Financial support:* Institutionally sponsored loans and scholarships/grants available. Financial award applicants required to submit FAFSA. In 2006, 13 degrees awarded. *Degree program information:* Evening/weekend programs available. Offers administration of justice and security (MS); family nurse practitioner (MSN); health care management (MBA); marriage, family and child therapy (MSC). *Application deadline:* Applications are processed on a rolling basis. *Application fee:* $45. Electronic applications accepted. *Application Contact:* Chair, 877-416-4100. *Dean/Executive Director*, Dr. Gil Linne, 480-557-1751, E-mail: gil.linne@phoenix.edu.

John Sperling School of Business Students: 617 full-time (298 women); includes 211 minority (44 African Americans, 2 American Indian/Alaska Native, 128 Asian Americans or Pacific Islanders, 37 Hispanic Americans), 114 international. Average age 38. *Faculty:* 49 full-time (4 women), 556 part-time/adjunct (141 women). Expenses: Contact institution. *Financial support:* Institutionally sponsored loans and scholarships/grants available. Financial award applicants required to submit FAFSA. In 2006, 295 degrees awarded. *Degree program information:* Evening/weekend programs available. Offers business (MBA). *Application deadline:* Applications are processed on a rolling basis. *Application fee:* $45. Electronic applications accepted. *Provost*, Dr. Adam Honea, 408-557-1659, E-mail: adam.honea@phoenix.edu.

College of Graduate Business and Management Students: 523 full-time (279 women); includes 185 minority (40 African Americans, 2 American Indian/Alaska Native, 110 Asian Americans or Pacific Islanders, 33 Hispanic Americans), 84 international. Average age 37. *Faculty:* 30 full-time (3 women), 390 part-time/adjunct (106 women). Expenses: Contact institution. *Financial support:* Institutionally sponsored loans and scholarships/grants available. Financial award applicants required to submit FAFSA. In 2006, 205 degrees awarded. *Degree program information:* Evening/weekend programs available. Offers accounting (MBA); business administration (MBA); global management (MBA); human resource management (MBA); marketing (MBA); public administration (MBA). *Application deadline:* Applications are processed on a rolling basis. *Application fee:* $45. Electronic applications accepted. *Application Contact:* Chair, 408-435-8500, Fax: 408-435-8250. *Associate Vice President and Dean/Executive Director*, Dr. Brian Lindquist, 408-557-1221, E-mail: brian.lindquist@phoenix.edu.

College of Information Systems and Technology Students: 94 full-time (19 women); includes 26 minority (4 African Americans, 18 Asian Americans or Pacific Islanders, 4 Hispanic Americans), 30 international. Average age 38. *Faculty:* 19 full-time (1 woman), 166 part-time/adjunct (35 women). Expenses: Contact institution. *Financial support:* Institutionally sponsored loans and scholarships/grants available. Financial award applicants required to submit FAFSA. In 2006, 90 degrees awarded. *Degree program information:* Evening/weekend programs available. Offers e-business (MBA); technology management (MBA). *Application deadline:* Applications are processed on a rolling basis. *Application fee:* $45. Electronic applications accepted. *Application Contact:* Chair, 408-435-8500, Fax: 408-435-8250. *Dean/Executive Director*, Dr. Adam Honea, 480-557-1659, E-mail: adam.honea@phoenix.edu.

UNIVERSITY OF PHOENIX–BOSTON CAMPUS, Braintree, MA 02184-4949

General Information Proprietary, coed, comprehensive institution. *Enrollment:* 634 graduate, professional, and undergraduate students; 164 full-time matriculated graduate/professional students (85 women). *Enrollment by degree level:* 164 master's. *Graduate faculty:* 5 full-time (0 women), 226 part-time/adjunct (44 women). *Tuition:* Full-time $13,848. *Required fees:* $760. *Graduate housing:* On-campus housing not available. *Student services:* Campus safety program, disabled student services, writing training. *Library facilities:* University Library. *Online resources:* library catalog, web page. *Collection:* 1,759 titles, 692 serial subscriptions.

Computer facilities: A campuswide network can be accessed from off campus. Internet access is available. *Web address:* http://www.phoenix.edu/.

General Application Contact: Campus Information Center, 781-843-0844, Fax: 781-843-8646.

GRADUATE UNITS

John Sperling School of Business Students: 164 full-time (85 women); includes 34 minority (23 African Americans, 9 Asian Americans or Pacific Islanders, 2 Hispanic Americans), 16 international. Average age 36. *Faculty:* 4 full-time (0 women), 218 part-time/adjunct (41 women). Expenses: Contact institution. *Financial support:* Institutionally sponsored loans and scholarships/grants available. Financial award applicants required to submit FAFSA. In 2006, 65 degrees awarded. *Degree program information:* Evening/weekend programs available. Offers business (MBA). *Application deadline:* Applications are processed on a rolling basis. *Application fee:* $45. Electronic applications accepted. *Application Contact:* College Chair, 781-843-0844. *Provost*, Dr. Adam Honea, 480-557-1659, Fax: 480-929-7164, E-mail: adam.honea@phoenix.edu.

College of Graduate Business and Management Students: 136 full-time (76 women). Average age 36. *Faculty:* 34 full-time (30 women), 126 part-time/adjunct (0 women). Expenses: Contact institution. *Financial support:* Institutionally sponsored loans and scholarships/grants available. Financial award applicants required to submit FAFSA. In 2006, 55 degrees awarded. *Degree program information:* Evening/weekend programs available. Offers administration (MBA); global management (MBA). *Application deadline:* Applications are processed on a rolling basis. *Application fee:* $45. *Application Contact:* Chair, 781-843-0844, Fax: 781-843-8646. *Associate Vice President and Dean/Executive Director*, Dr. Brian Lindquist, 480-557-1221, E-mail: brian.lindquist@phoenix.edu.

College of Information Systems and Technology Students: 28 full-time (9 women); includes 4 minority (2 African Americans, 2 Asian Americans or Pacific Islanders), 3 international. Average age 40. *Faculty:* 62 part-time/adjunct (11 women). Expenses: Contact institution. *Financial support:* Institutionally sponsored loans and scholarships/grants available. In 2006, 10 degrees awarded. *Degree program information:* Evening/weekend programs available. Offers technology management (MBA). *Application deadline:* Applications are processed on a rolling basis. *Application fee:* $45. Electronic applications accepted. *Application Contact:* Campus College Chair, 781-843-0844. *Dean and Executive Director*, Dr. Adam Honea, 480-557-1659, Fax: 480-929-7164, E-mail: adam.honea@phoenix.edu.

UNIVERSITY OF PHOENIX–CENTRAL FLORIDA CAMPUS, Maitland, FL 32751-7057

General Information Proprietary, coed, comprehensive institution. *Enrollment:* 2,072 graduate, professional, and undergraduate students; 510 full-time matriculated graduate/professional students (329 women). *Enrollment by degree level:* 510 master's. *Graduate faculty:* 110 full-time (38 women), 264 part-time/adjunct (74 women). *Tuition:* Full-time $9,450. *Required fees:* $760. *Graduate housing:* On-campus housing not available. *Student services:* Campus safety program, disabled student services, writing training. *Library facilities:* University Library. *Online resources:* library catalog, web page. *Collection:* 1,759 titles, 692 serial subscriptions.

Computer facilities: A campuswide network can be accessed from off campus. Internet access is available. *Web address:* http://www.phoenix.edu/.

General Application Contact: Campus Information Center, 407-667-0555, Fax: 407-667-0560.

GRADUATE UNITS

The Artemis School Students: 69 full-time (64 women); includes 20 minority (11 African Americans, 2 Asian Americans or Pacific Islanders, 7 Hispanic Americans), 8 international. Average age 42. *Faculty:* 34 full-time (26 women), 62 part-time/adjunct (33 women). Expenses: Contact institution. *Financial support:* Institutionally sponsored loans and scholarships/grants available. Financial award applicants required to submit FAFSA. In 2006, 50 degrees awarded. *Degree program information:* Evening/weekend programs available. *Application deadline:* Applications are processed on a rolling basis. *Application fee:* $45. Electronic applications accepted. *Provost/Dean/Vice President of Research and Development*, Dr. Adam Honea, 480-557-1659, E-mail: adam.honea@phoenix.edu.

College of Education Students: 20 full-time (18 women); includes 5 minority (3 African Americans, 2 Hispanic Americans), 1 international. Average age 38. *Faculty:* 10 full-time (9 women), 16 part-time/adjunct (6 women). Expenses: Contact institution. *Financial support:* Institutionally sponsored loans and scholarships/grants available. Financial award applicants required to submit FAFSA. In 2006, 7 degrees awarded. *Degree program information:* Evening/weekend programs available. Offers administration and supervision (MA Ed); curriculum and instruction (MA Ed); elementary teacher education (MA Ed); secondary teacher education (MA Ed). *Application deadline:* Applications are processed on a rolling basis. *Application fee:* $45. Electronic applications accepted. *Application Contact:* Chair, 407-667-0555, Fax: 407-667-0560. *Dean/Executive Director*, Dr. Marla LaRue, 480-557-1218.

College of Health and Human Services Students: 49 full-time (46 women); includes 15 minority (8 African Americans, 2 Asian Americans or Pacific Islanders, 5 Hispanic Americans), 7 international. Average age 44. *Faculty:* 24 full-time (17 women), 46 part-time/adjunct (27 women). Expenses: Contact institution. *Financial support:* Institutionally sponsored loans and scholarships/grants available. Financial award applicants required to submit FAFSA. In 2006, 43 degrees awarded. *Degree program information:* Evening/weekend programs available. Offers health administration (MHA); health and human services (MSN); health care management (MBA). *Application deadline:* Applications are processed on a rolling basis. *Application fee:* $45. Electronic applications accepted. *Application Contact:* Chair, 407-667-0525, Fax: 407-667-0560. *Dean/Executive Director*, Dr. Gil Linne, 480-557-1751, E-mail: gil.linne@phoenix.edu.

John Sperling School of Business Students: 441 full-time (265 women); includes 176 minority (102 African Americans, 4 American Indian/Alaska Native, 17 Asian Americans or Pacific Islanders, 53 Hispanic Americans), 38 international. Average age 36. *Faculty:* 75 full-time (12 women), 198 part-time/adjunct (41 women). Expenses: Contact institution. *Financial*

University of Phoenix–Central Florida Campus (continued)

support: Institutionally sponsored loans and scholarships/grants available. Financial award applicants required to submit FAFSA. In 2006, 173 degrees awarded. *Degree program information:* Evening/weekend programs available. Offers business (MBA, MIS, MM). *Application deadline:* Applications are processed on a rolling basis. *Application fee:* $45. Electronic applications accepted. *Provost/Dean/Vice President of Research and Development*, Dr. Adam Honea, 480-557-1659, E-mail: adam.honea@phoenix.edu.

College of Graduate Business and Management Students: 440 full-time (265 women); includes 175 minority (102 African Americans, 4 American Indian/Alaska Native, 16 Asian Americans or Pacific Islanders, 53 Hispanic Americans), 38 international. Average age 36. *Faculty:* 50 full-time (11 women), 136 part-time/adjunct (32 women). Expenses: Contact institution. *Financial support:* Institutionally sponsored loans and scholarships/grants available. Financial award applicants required to submit FAFSA. In 2006, 149 degrees awarded. *Degree program information:* Evening/weekend programs available. Offers accounting (MBA); business administration (MBA); business and management (MM); global management (MBA); management (MM); marketing (MBA). *Application deadline:* Applications are processed on a rolling basis. *Application fee:* $45. Electronic applications accepted. *Application Contact:* Chair, 407-667-0555, Fax: 407-667-0560. *Associate Vice President and Dean/Executive Director*, Dr. Brian Lindquist, 480-557-1221, E-mail: brian.lindquist@phoenix.edu.

College of Information Systems and Technology Students: 1 full-time (0 women); minority (Asian American or Pacific Islander) Average age 39. *Faculty:* 25 full-time (1 woman), 62 part-time/adjunct (9 women). Expenses: Contact institution. *Financial support:* Institutionally sponsored loans and scholarships/grants available. Financial award applicants required to submit FAFSA. In 2006, 24 degrees awarded. *Degree program information:* Evening/weekend programs available. Offers management (MIS); technology management (MBA). *Application deadline:* Applications are processed on a rolling basis. *Application fee:* $45. Electronic applications accepted. *Application Contact:* Chair, 407-667-0555, Fax: 407-667-0560.

UNIVERSITY OF PHOENIX–CENTRAL MASSACHUSETTS CAMPUS, Westborough, MA 01581-3906

General Information Proprietary, coed, comprehensive institution. *Enrollment:* 267 graduate, professional, and undergraduate students; 75 full-time matriculated graduate/professional students (31 women). *Enrollment by degree level:* 75 master's. *Graduate faculty:* 22 full-time (8 women), 135 part-time/adjunct (25 women). *Tuition:* Full-time $13,848. *Required fees:* $760. *Graduate housing:* On-campus housing not available. *Student services:* Campus safety program, disabled student services, writing training. *Library facilities:* University Library. *Online resources:* library catalog, web page. *Collection:* 1,759 titles, 692 serial subscriptions.

Computer facilities: A campuswide network can be accessed from off campus. Internet access is available. *Web address:* http://www.phoenix.edu/.

General Application Contact: Campus Information Center, 508-614-4100.

GRADUATE UNITS

The Artemis School Expenses: Contact institution. *Financial support:* Institutionally sponsored loans and scholarships/grants available. Financial award applicants required to submit FAFSA. *Degree program information:* Evening/weekend programs available. *Application deadline:* Applications are processed on a rolling basis. *Application fee:* $45. Electronic applications accepted. *Provost*, Dr. Adam Honea, 480-551-1659, E-mail: adam.honea@phoenix.edu.

College of Education Average age 24. Expenses: Contact institution. *Financial support:* Institutionally sponsored loans and scholarships/grants available. Financial award applicants required to submit FAFSA. *Degree program information:* Evening/weekend programs available. Offers education (MA Ed). *Application deadline:* Applications are processed on a rolling basis. *Application fee:* $45. Electronic applications accepted. *Dean/Executive Director*, Dr. Marla LaRue, 480-557-1218, E-mail: marla.larue@phoenix.edu.

John Sperling School of Business Students: 75 full-time (31 women); includes 16 minority (6 African Americans, 6 Asian Americans or Pacific Islanders, 4 Hispanic Americans), 2 international. Average age 39. *Faculty:* 18 full-time (8 women), 133 part-time/adjunct (25 women). Expenses: Contact institution. *Financial support:* Institutionally sponsored loans and scholarships/grants available. Financial award applicants required to submit FAFSA. In 2006, 27 degrees awarded. *Degree program information:* Evening/weekend programs available. Offers business (MBA). *Application deadline:* Applications are processed on a rolling basis. *Application fee:* $45. Electronic applications accepted. *Application Contact:* Campus College Chair, 508-614-4100. *Provost*, Dr. Adam Honea, 480-551-1659, E-mail: adam.honea@phoenix.edu.

College of Graduate Business and Management Students: 58 full-time (27 women); includes 9 minority (5 African Americans, 4 Hispanic Americans), 1 international. Average age 39. *Faculty:* 11 full-time (5 women), 84 part-time/adjunct (14 women). Expenses: Contact institution. *Financial support:* Institutionally sponsored loans available. Financial award applicants required to submit FAFSA. In 2006, 18 degrees awarded. *Degree program information:* Evening/weekend programs available. Offers business administration (MBA); global management (MBA). *Application deadline:* Applications are processed on a rolling basis. *Application fee:* $45. Electronic applications accepted. *Application Contact:* Campus College Chair, 508-614-4100. *Associate Vice President and Dean/Executive Director*, Dr. Brian Lindquist, 480-557-1221, E-mail: brian.lindquist@phoenix.edu.

College of Information Systems and Technology Students: 17 full-time (4 women); includes 7 minority (1 African American, 6 Asian Americans or Pacific Islanders), 1 international. Average age 37. *Faculty:* 7 full-time (3 women), 49 part-time/adjunct (11 women). Expenses: Contact institution. *Financial support:* Institutionally sponsored loans and scholarships/grants available. Financial award applicants required to submit FAFSA. In 2006, 9 degrees awarded. *Degree program information:* Evening/weekend programs available. Offers technology management (MBA). *Application deadline:* Applications are processed on a rolling basis. *Application fee:* $45. Electronic applications accepted. *Application Contact:* Campus College Chair, 508-614-4100.

UNIVERSITY OF PHOENIX–CENTRAL VALLEY CAMPUS, Fresno, CA 93720

General Information Proprietary, coed, comprehensive institution.

GRADUATE UNITS

College of Education Offers curriculum and instruction (MA Ed); elementary teacher education (MA Ed); secondary teacher education (MA Ed).

College of Graduate Business and Management Offers accounting (MBA); business administration (MBA); global management (MBA); human resources management (MBA); management (MM); marketing (MBA); public administration (MBA).

College of Health and Human Services Offers health care management (MBA); nursing (MSN).

College of Information Systems and Technology Offers technology management (MBA).

College of Social and Behavioral Science Offers marriage, family and child therapy (MSC).

UNIVERSITY OF PHOENIX–CHARLOTTE CAMPUS, Charlotte, NC 28273-3409

General Information Proprietary, coed, comprehensive institution. *Enrollment:* 1,604 graduate, professional, and undergraduate students; 529 full-time matriculated graduate/professional students (342 women). *Enrollment by degree level:* 529 master's. *Graduate faculty:* 24 full-time (5 women), 179 part-time/adjunct (50 women). *Tuition:* Full-time $10,320. *Required fees:* $760. *Graduate housing:* On-campus housing not available. *Student services:* Campus safety program, disabled student services, writing training. *Library facilities:* University Library. *Online resources:* library catalog, web page. *Collection:* 1,759 titles, 692 serial subscriptions.

Computer facilities: A campuswide network can be accessed from off campus. Internet access is available. *Web address:* http://www.phoenix.edu/.

General Application Contact: Campus Information Center, 704-504-5409, Fax: 704-504-5360.

GRADUATE UNITS

The Artemis School Students: 68 full-time (57 women); includes 35 minority (34 African Americans, 1 Asian American or Pacific Islander), 4 international. Average age 38. *Faculty:* 1 full-time (0 women), 14 part-time/adjunct (9 women). Expenses: Contact institution. *Financial support:* Institutionally sponsored loans and scholarships/grants available. Financial award applicants required to submit FAFSA. In 2006, 12 degrees awarded. *Degree program information:* Evening/weekend programs available. *Application deadline:* Applications are processed on a rolling basis. *Application fee:* $45. Electronic applications accepted. *Provost*, Dr. Adam Honea, 480-557-1659, E-mail: adam.honea@phoenix.edu.

College of Health and Human Services Students: 68 full-time (57 women); includes 35 minority (34 African Americans, 1 Asian American or Pacific Islander), 4 international. *Faculty:* 1 full-time (0 women), 12 part-time/adjunct (7 women). Expenses: Contact institution. *Financial support:* Institutionally sponsored loans and scholarships/grants available. Financial award applicants required to submit FAFSA. In 2006, 12 degrees awarded. *Degree program information:* Evening/weekend programs available. Offers health care management (MBA). *Application deadline:* Applications are processed on a rolling basis. *Application fee:* $45. Electronic applications accepted. *Application Contact:* College Chair, 704-504-5409. *Dean/Executive Director*, Dr. Gil Linne, 480-557-1757, E-mail: gil.linne@phoenix.edu.

John Sperling School of Business Students: 461 full-time (285 women); includes 235 minority (224 African Americans, 6 Asian Americans or Pacific Islanders, 5 Hispanic Americans), 22 international. Average age 36. *Faculty:* 22 full-time (4 women), 162 part-time/adjunct (40 women). Expenses: Contact institution. *Financial support:* Institutionally sponsored loans and scholarships/grants available. Financial award applicants required to submit FAFSA. In 2006, 89 degrees awarded. *Degree program information:* Evening/weekend programs available. Offers business (MBA, MIS, MISM). *Application deadline:* Applications are processed on a rolling basis. *Application fee:* $45. Electronic applications accepted. *Provost*, Dr. Adam Honea, 480-557-1659, E-mail: adam.honea@phoenix.edu.

College of Graduate Business and Management Students: 423 full-time (272 women); includes 221 minority (211 African Americans, 6 Asian Americans or Pacific Islanders, 4 Hispanic Americans), 21 international. Average age 36. *Faculty:* 18 full-time (2 women), 111 part-time/adjunct (33 women). Expenses: Contact institution. *Financial support:* Institutionally sponsored loans and scholarships/grants available. Financial award applicants required to submit FAFSA. In 2006, 78 degrees awarded. *Degree program information:* Evening/weekend programs available. Offers accounting (MBA); administration (MBA); global management (MBA). *Application deadline:* Applications are processed on a rolling basis. *Application fee:* $45. Electronic applications accepted. *Application Contact:* College Chair, 704-504-5409, Fax: 704-504-5360. *Associate Vice President and Dean/Executive Director*, Dr. Brian Lindquist, 480-557-1221, E-mail: brian.lindquist@phoenix.edu.

College of Information Systems and Technology Students: 38 full-time (13 women); includes 14 minority (13 African Americans, 1 Hispanic American), 1 international. Average age 39. *Faculty:* 4 full-time (2 women), 51 part-time/adjunct (7 women). Expenses: Contact institution. *Financial support:* Institutionally sponsored loans and scholarships/grants available. Financial award applicants required to submit FAFSA. In 2006, 11 degrees awarded. *Degree program information:* Evening/weekend programs available. Offers information systems (MIS); information systems management (MISM); technology management (MBA). *Application deadline:* Applications are processed on a rolling basis. *Application fee:* $45. Electronic applications accepted. *Application Contact:* College Chair, 704-504-5409, Fax: 704-504-5360.

UNIVERSITY OF PHOENIX–CHICAGO CAMPUS, Schaumburg, IL 60173-4399

General Information Proprietary, coed, comprehensive institution. *Enrollment:* 1,590 graduate, professional, and undergraduate students; 269 full-time matriculated graduate/professional students (160 women). *Enrollment by degree level:* 269 master's. *Graduate faculty:* 46 full-time (18 women), 155 part-time/adjunct (40 women). *Tuition:* Full-time $12,120. *Required fees:* $760. *Graduate housing:* On-campus housing not available. *Student services:* Campus safety program, disabled student services, writing training. *Library facilities:* University Library. *Online resources:* library catalog, web page. *Collection:* 1,756 titles, 692 serial subscriptions.

Computer facilities: A campuswide network can be accessed from off campus. Internet access is available. *Web address:* http://www.phoenix.edu/.

General Application Contact: Campus Information Center, 847-413-1922, Fax: 847-413-8706.

GRADUATE UNITS

John Sperling School of Business Students: 269 full-time (160 women); includes 105 minority (70 African Americans, 1 American Indian/Alaska Native, 20 Asian Americans or Pacific Islanders, 14 Hispanic Americans), 21 international. Average age 37. *Faculty:* 43 full-time (15 women), 147 part-time/adjunct (36 women). Expenses: Contact institution. *Financial support:* Institutionally sponsored loans and scholarships/grants available. Financial award applicants required to submit FAFSA. In 2006, 110 degrees awarded. *Degree program information:* Evening/weekend programs available. Offers business (MBA, MIS, MM). *Application deadline:* Applications are processed on a rolling basis. *Application fee:* $45. *Provost*, Adam Honea, 480-557-1659, E-mail: adam.honea@phoenix.edu.

College of Graduate Business and Management Students: 259 full-time (156 women); includes 99 minority (69 African Americans, 1 American Indian/Alaska Native, 17 Asian Americans or Pacific Islanders, 12 Hispanic Americans), 21 international. Average age 37. *Faculty:* 39 full-time (12 women), 109 part-time/adjunct (28 women). Expenses: Contact institution. *Financial support:* Institutionally sponsored loans and scholarships/grants available. Financial award applicants required to submit FAFSA. In 2006, 91 degrees awarded. *Degree program information:* Evening/weekend programs available. Offers administration (MBA); global management (MBA); information systems (MIS); management (MM). *Application deadline:* Applications are processed on a rolling basis. *Application fee:* $45. Electronic applications accepted. *Application Contact:* Campus College Chair—Graduate Business, 847-413-1922, Fax: 847-413-8706. *Associate Vice President and Dean/Executive Director*, Dr. Brian Lindquist, 480-557-1221, E-mail: brian.lindquist@phoenix.edu.

College of Information Systems and Technology Students: 10 full-time (4 women); includes 6 minority (1 African American, 3 Asian Americans or Pacific Islanders, 2 Hispanic Americans). Average age 37. *Faculty:* 4 full-time (3 women), 38 part-time/adjunct (8 women). Expenses: Contact institution. *Financial support:* Institutionally sponsored loans and scholarships/grants available. Financial award applicants required to submit FAFSA. In 2006, 19 degrees awarded. *Degree program information:* Evening/weekend programs available. Offers e-business (MBA); information systems (MIS); management (MM); technology management (MBA). *Application deadline:* Applications are processed on a rolling basis. *Application fee:* $45. Electronic applications accepted. *Application Contact:* Campus College Chair—Technology, 847-413-1922, Fax: 847-413-8706.

UNIVERSITY OF PHOENIX–CINCINNATI CAMPUS, West Chester, OH 45069-4875

General Information Proprietary, coed, comprehensive institution. *Enrollment:* 646 graduate, professional, and undergraduate students; 183 full-time matriculated graduate/professional students (134 women). *Enrollment by degree level:* 183 master's. *Graduate faculty:* 32 full-time (7 women), 72 part-time/adjunct (21 women). *Tuition:* Full-time $11,832. *Required fees:* $760. *Graduate housing:* On-campus housing not available. *Student services:* Campus safety program, disabled student services, writing training. *Library facilities:* University Library. *Online resources:* library catalog, web page. *Collection:* 1,759 titles, 692 serial subscriptions.

Computer facilities: A campuswide network can be accessed from off campus. Internet access is available. *Web address:* http://www.phoenix.edu/.

General Application Contact: Campus Information Center, 513-772-9600, Fax: 513-772-3645.

GRADUATE UNITS

The Artemis School Expenses: Contact institution. *Financial support:* Institutionally sponsored loans and scholarships/grants available. Financial award applicants required to submit FAFSA. *Degree program information:* Evening/weekend programs available. *Application deadline:* Applications are processed on a rolling basis. *Application fee:* $45. Electronic applications accepted. *Provost*, Dr. Adam Honea, 480-557-1659, E-mail: adam.honea@phoenix.edu.

College of Health and Human Services Expenses: Contact institution. *Financial support:* Institutionally sponsored loans and scholarships/grants available. Financial award applicants required to submit FAFSA. *Degree program information:* Evening/weekend programs available. Offers health care management (MBA). *Application deadline:* Applications are processed on a rolling basis. *Application fee:* $45. Electronic applications accepted. *Application Contact:* College Chair, 573-772-9600. *Dean/Executive Director*, Dr. Gil Linne, 480-557-1221, E-mail: gil.linne@phoenix.edu.

John Sperling School of Business Students: 183 full-time (134 women); includes 54 minority (49 African Americans, 3 Asian Americans or Pacific Islanders, 2 Hispanic Americans), 6 international. Average age 38. *Faculty:* 30 full-time (7 women), 71 part-time/adjunct (20 women). Expenses: Contact institution. *Financial support:* Institutionally sponsored loans and scholarships/grants available. Financial award applicants required to submit FAFSA. In 2006, 85 degrees awarded. *Degree program information:* Evening/weekend programs available. Offers business (MBA). *Application deadline:* Applications are processed on a rolling basis. *Application fee:* $45. Electronic applications accepted. *Application Contact:* College Chair, 513-775-9600. *Provost*, Dr. Adam Honea, 480-557-1659, E-mail: adam.honea@phoenix.edu.

College of Graduate Business and Management Students: 183 full-time (134 women); includes 54 minority (49 African Americans, 3 Asian Americans or Pacific Islanders, 2 Hispanic Americans), 6 international. Average age 38. *Faculty:* 26 full-time (7 women), 53 part-time/adjunct (15 women). Expenses: Contact institution. *Financial support:* Institutionally sponsored loans and scholarships/grants available. Financial award applicants required to submit FAFSA. In 2006, 85 degrees awarded. *Degree program information:* Evening/weekend programs available. Offers business and management (MBA). *Application deadline:* Applications are processed on a rolling basis. *Application fee:* $45. Electronic applications accepted. *Application Contact:* College Chair, 573-772-9600. *Associate Vice President and Dean/Executive Director*, Dr. Brian Lindquist, 480-557-1221.

College of Information Systems and Technology Expenses: Contact institution. *Financial support:* Institutionally sponsored loans and scholarships/grants available. Financial award applicants required to submit FAFSA. *Degree program information:* Evening/weekend programs available. Offers electronic business (MBA); technology management (MBA). *Application deadline:* Applications are processed on a rolling basis. *Application fee:* $45. Electronic applications accepted. *Application Contact:* College Chair, 513-772-9600. *Dean/Executive Director*, Dr. Adam Honea, 480-557-1659, E-mail: adam.honea@phoenix.edu.

UNIVERSITY OF PHOENIX–CLEVELAND CAMPUS, Independence, OH 44131-2194

General Information Proprietary, coed, comprehensive institution. *Enrollment:* 865 graduate, professional, and undergraduate students; 202 full-time matriculated graduate/professional students (130 women). *Enrollment by degree level:* 202 master's. *Graduate faculty:* 20 full-time (1 woman), 115 part-time/adjunct (42 women). *Tuition:* Full-time $11,608. *Required fees:* $760. *Graduate housing:* On-campus housing not available. *Student services:* Campus safety program, disabled student services, writing training. *Library facilities:* University Library. *Online resources:* library catalog, web page. *Collection:* 1,759 titles, 692 serial subscriptions.

Computer facilities: A campuswide network can be accessed from off campus. Internet access is available. *Web address:* http://www.phoenix.edu/.

General Application Contact: Campus Information Center, 216-447-8807, Fax: 216-447-9144.

GRADUATE UNITS

The Artemis School Students: 23 full-time (all women); includes 9 minority (all African Americans), 3 international. Average age 47. *Faculty:* 3 full-time (0 women), 24 part-time/adjunct (18 women). Expenses: Contact institution. *Financial support:* Institutionally sponsored loans and scholarships/grants available. Financial award applicants required to submit FAFSA. In 2006, 13 degrees awarded. *Degree program information:* Evening/weekend programs available. *Application deadline:* Applications are processed on a rolling basis. *Application fee:* $45. Electronic applications accepted. *Application Contact:* Campus College Chair, 216-447-8807. *Provost*, Dr. Adam Honea, 480-557-1659, E-mail: adam.honea@phoenix.edu.

College of Health and Human Services Students: 23 full-time (all women); includes 9 minority (all African Americans), 3 international. Average age 47. *Faculty:* 3 full-time (0 women), 24 part-time/adjunct (18 women). Expenses: Contact institution. *Financial support:* Institutionally sponsored loans and scholarships/grants available. Financial award applicants required to submit FAFSA. In 2006, 3 degrees awarded. *Degree program information:* Evening/weekend programs available. Offers administration of justice and security (MS); health care management (MBA); nursing (MSN); psychology (MS). *Application deadline:* Applications are processed on a rolling basis. *Application fee:* $45. Electronic applications accepted. *Application Contact:* Campus College Chair, 216-447-8807. *Dean/Executive Director*, Dr. Gil Linne, 480-557-1751, E-mail: gil.linne@phoenix.edu.

John Sperling School of Business Students: 179 full-time (107 women); includes 73 minority (67 African Americans, 1 American Indian/Alaska Native, 5 Hispanic Americans), 9 international. Average age 37. *Faculty:* 17 full-time (1 woman), 91 part-time/adjunct (24 women). Expenses: Contact institution. *Financial support:* Institutionally sponsored loans and scholarships/grants available. Financial award applicants required to submit FAFSA. In 2006, 25 degrees awarded. *Degree program information:* Evening/weekend programs available. Offers business (MBA, MIS, MM). *Application deadline:* Applications are processed on a rolling basis. *Application fee:* $45. Electronic applications accepted. *Application Contact:* Campus College Chair, 216-447-8807. *Provost*, Dr. Adam Honea, 480-557-1659, E-mail: adam.honea@phoenix.edu.

College of Graduate Business and Management Students: 178 full-time (107 women); includes 115 minority (66 African Americans, 1 American Indian/Alaska Native, 5 Asian Americans or Pacific Islanders, 43 Hispanic Americans), 9 international. Average age 37. *Faculty:* 10 full-time (1 woman), 68 part-time/adjunct (16 women). Expenses: Contact institution. *Financial support:* Institutionally sponsored loans and scholarships/grants available. Financial award applicants required to submit FAFSA. In 2006, 25 degrees awarded. *Degree program information:* Evening/weekend programs available. Offers accounting (MBA); business administration (MBA); global management (MBA); human resources management (MM); management (MM); marketing (MBA); public administration (MBA, MM). *Application deadline:* Applications are processed on a rolling basis. *Application fee:* $45. Electronic applications accepted. *Application Contact:* Chair, 216-447-8807, Fax: 216-447-9144. *Associate Vice President and Dean/Executive Director*, Dr. Brian Lindquist, 480-557-1221, E-mail: brian.linquist@phoenix.edu.

College of Information Systems and Technology Students: 1 (woman) full-time; minority (African American) Average age 32. *Faculty:* 7 full-time (0 women), 23 part-time/adjunct (8 women). Expenses: Contact institution. *Financial support:* Institutionally sponsored loans and scholarships/grants available. Financial award applicants required to submit FAFSA. *Degree program information:* Evening/weekend programs available. Offers information management (MIS); technology management (MBA). *Application deadline:* Applications are processed on a rolling basis. *Application fee:* $45. Electronic applications accepted. *Application Contact:* 216-447-8807, Fax: 216-447-9144. *Provost/Dean, Vice President Academic Research and Development*, Dr. Adam Honea, 480-557-1659, E-mail: adam.honea@phoenix.edu.

UNIVERSITY OF PHOENIX–COLUMBUS GEORGIA CAMPUS, Columbus, GA 31904-6321

General Information Proprietary, coed, comprehensive institution. *Enrollment:* 819 graduate, professional, and undergraduate students; 67 full-time matriculated graduate/professional students (42 women). *Enrollment by degree level:* 67 master's. *Graduate faculty:* 28 full-time (5 women), 90 part-time/adjunct (31 women). *Tuition:* Full-time $10,200. *Required fees:* $760. *Graduate housing:* On-campus housing not available. *Student services:* Campus safety program, disabled student services, writing training. *Library facilities:* University Library. *Online resources:* library catalog, web page. *Collection:* 1,756 titles, 692 serial subscriptions.

Computer facilities: A campuswide network can be accessed from off campus. Internet access is available. *Web address:* http://www.phoenix.edu/.

General Application Contact: Campus Information Center, 706-320-1262.

GRADUATE UNITS

The Artemis School Students: 7 full-time (5 women); includes 3 minority (2 African Americans, 1 Hispanic American). Average age 38. *Faculty:* 11 full-time (4 women), 25 part-time/adjunct (12 women). Expenses: Contact institution. *Financial support:* Institutionally sponsored loans and scholarships/grants available. Financial award applicants required to submit FAFSA. In 2006, 10 degrees awarded. *Degree program information:* Evening/weekend programs available. *Application deadline:* Applications are processed on a rolling basis. *Application fee:* $45. Electronic applications accepted. *Application Contact:* Dr. Adam Honea, Provost, 480-557-1659, E-mail: adam.honea@phoenix.edu. *Provost*, Dr. Adam Honea, 480-557-1659, E-mail: adam.honea@phoenix.edu.

College of Health and Human Services Students: 7 full-time (5 women); includes 3 minority (2 African Americans, 1 Hispanic American). Average age 38. *Faculty:* 11 full-time (4 women), 25 part-time/adjunct (12 women). Expenses: Contact institution. *Financial support:* Institutionally sponsored loans and scholarships/grants available. Financial award applicants required to submit FAFSA. In 2006, 10 master's awarded. Offers health care management (MBA). *Application deadline:* Applications are processed on a rolling basis. *Application fee:* $45. Electronic applications accepted. *Dean/Executive Director*, Dr. Gil Linne, 480-557-1751, E-mail: gil.linne@phoenix.edu.

John Sperling School of Business Students: 60 full-time (37 women); includes 32 minority (27 African Americans, 1 Asian American or Pacific Islander, 4 Hispanic Americans). Average age 38. *Faculty:* 17 full-time (1 woman), 65 part-time/adjunct (19 women). Expenses: Contact institution. *Financial support:* Institutionally sponsored loans and scholarships/grants available. Financial award applicants required to submit FAFSA. In 2006, 17 degrees awarded. *Degree program information:* Evening/weekend programs available. Offers business (MBA). *Application deadline:* Applications are processed on a rolling basis. *Application fee:* $45. Electronic applications accepted. *Provost*, Dr. Adam Honea, 480-557-1659, E-mail: adam.honea@phoenix.edu.

College of Graduate Business and Management Students: 52 full-time (35 women); includes 27 minority (22 African Americans, 1 Asian American or Pacific Islander, 4 Hispanic Americans). Average age 37. *Faculty:* 11 full-time (1 woman), 53 part-time/adjunct (15 women). Expenses: Contact institution. *Financial support:* Institutionally sponsored loans and scholarships/grants available. Financial award applicants required to submit FAFSA. In 2006, 10 degrees awarded. *Degree program information:* Evening/weekend programs available. Offers accounting (MBA); administration (MBA); global management (MBA); human resource management (MBA); marketing (MBA); public administration (MBA). *Application deadline:* Applications are processed on a rolling basis. *Application fee:* $45. Electronic applications accepted. *Application Contact:* College Chair, 706-320-1262. *Associate Vice President/Dean/Executive Director*, Dr. Brian Lindquist, 480-557-1221, E-mail: brian.lindquist@phoenix.edu.

College of Information Systems and Technology Students: 8 full-time (2 women); includes 5 minority (all African Americans) Average age 44. *Faculty:* 6 full-time (0 women), 12 part-time/adjunct (4 women). Expenses: Contact institution. *Financial support:* Institutionally sponsored loans and scholarships/grants available. Financial award applicants required to submit FAFSA. In 2006, 10 degrees awarded. *Degree program information:* Evening/weekend programs available. Offers e-business (MBA); technology management (MBA). *Application deadline:* Applications are processed on a rolling basis. *Application fee:* $45. Electronic applications accepted. *Application Contact:* College Chair, 706-320-1262. *Dean/Executive Director*, Dr. Adam Honea, 480-557-1659, E-mail: adam.honea@phoenix.edu.

UNIVERSITY OF PHOENIX–COLUMBUS OHIO CAMPUS, Columbus, OH 43240-4032

General Information Proprietary, coed, comprehensive institution. *Enrollment:* 471 graduate, professional, and undergraduate students; 145 full-time matriculated graduate/professional students (88 women). *Enrollment by degree level:* 145 master's. *Graduate faculty:* 14 full-time (6 women), 31 part-time/adjunct (3 women). *Tuition:* Full-time $11,832. *Required fees:* $760. *Graduate housing:* On-campus housing not available. *Student services:* Campus safety program, disabled student services, writing training. *Online resources:* library catalog, web page. *Collection:* 1,756 titles, 692 serial subscriptions.

Computer facilities: A campuswide network can be accessed from off campus. *Web address:* http://www.phoenix.edu/.

General Application Contact: Campus Information Center, 614-433-0095.

GRADUATE UNITS

The Artemis School Expenses: Contact institution. *Financial support:* Institutionally sponsored loans and scholarships/grants available. Financial award applicants required to submit FAFSA. *Degree program information:* Evening/weekend programs available. *Application deadline:* Applications are processed on a rolling basis. *Application fee:* $45. Electronic applications accepted. *Provost*, Dr. Adam Honea, 480-557-1659, E-mail: adam.honea@phoenix.edu.

College of Health and Human Services Expenses: Contact institution. *Financial support:* Institutionally sponsored loans and scholarships/grants available. Financial award applicants required to submit FAFSA. *Degree program information:* Evening/weekend programs available. Offers health care management (MBA). *Application deadline:* Applications are processed on a rolling basis. *Application fee:* $45. Electronic applications accepted. *Application Contact:* College Chair, 614-433-0095. *Dean/Executive Director*, Dr. Gil Linne, 480-557-1221, E-mail: gil.linne@phoenix.edu.

John Sperling School of Business Students: 145 full-time (88 women); includes 40 minority (36 African Americans, 3 Asian Americans or Pacific Islanders, 1 Hispanic American), 6 international. Average age 37. *Faculty:* 13 full-time (5 women), 28 part-time/adjunct (3 women). Expenses: Contact institution. *Financial support:* Institutionally sponsored loans and scholarships/grants available. Financial award applicants required to submit FAFSA. In 2006, 40 degrees awarded. *Degree program information:* Evening/weekend programs available. Offers business (MBA). *Application deadline:* Applications are processed on a rolling basis. *Application fee:* $45. Electronic applications accepted. *Application Contact:* Campus College Chair, 614-433-0095. *Provost*, Dr. Adam Honea, 480-557-1659, E-mail: adam.honea@phoenix.edu.

College of Graduate Business and Management Students: 145 full-time (88 women); includes 40 minority (36 African Americans, 3 Asian Americans or Pacific Islanders, 1 Hispanic American), 6 international. Average age 37. *Faculty:* 12 full-time (5 women), 27 part-time/adjunct (3 women). Expenses: Contact institution. *Financial support:* Institutionally sponsored loans and scholarships/grants available. Financial award applicants required to submit FAFSA. In 2006, 40 degrees awarded. *Degree program information:* Evening/weekend programs available. Offers administration (MBA); marketing (MBA). *Application deadline:* Applications are processed on a rolling basis. *Application fee:* $45. Electronic applications accepted. *Associate Vice President and Dean/Executive Director*, Dr. Brian Lindquist, 480-557-1221, E-mail: brian.lindquist@phoenix.edu.

UNIVERSITY OF PHOENIX–DALLAS CAMPUS, Dallas, TX 75251-2009

General Information Proprietary, coed, comprehensive institution. *Enrollment:* 2,539 graduate, professional, and undergraduate students; 564 full-time matriculated graduate/professional students (345 women). *Enrollment by degree level:* 564 master's. *Graduate faculty:* 39 full-time (6 women), 170 part-time/adjunct (40 women). *Tuition:* Full-time $11,832. *Required fees:* $760. *Graduate housing:* On-campus housing not available. *Student services:* Campus safety program, disabled student services, writing training. *Online resources:* library catalog, web page. *Collection:* 1,759 titles, 692 serial subscriptions.

Computer facilities: A campuswide network can be accessed from off campus. Internet access is available. *Web address:* http://www.phoenix.edu/.

General Application Contact: Campus Information Center, 972-385-1055, Fax: 972-385-1700.

GRADUATE UNITS

The Artemis School Students: 32 full-time (22 women); includes 13 minority (11 African Americans, 2 Hispanic Americans), 3 international. Average age 37. *Faculty:* 2 full-time (1 woman), 7 part-time/adjunct (1 woman). Expenses: Contact institution. *Financial support:* Institutionally sponsored loans and scholarships/grants available. In 2006, 11 degrees awarded. *Degree program information:* Evening/weekend programs available. *Application deadline:* Applications are processed on a rolling basis. *Application fee:* $45. Electronic applications accepted. *Application Contact:* Chair, 972-385-1055, Fax: 972-385-1700. *Provost,* Dr. Adam Honea, 480-557-1659, E-mail: adam.honea@phoenix.edu.

College of Health and Human Services Students: 32 full-time (22 women); includes 14 minority (11 African Americans, 3 Hispanic Americans), 3 international. Average age 37. *Faculty:* 6 part-time/adjunct (1 woman). Expenses: Contact institution. *Financial support:* Institutionally sponsored loans and scholarships/grants available. In 2006, 11 degrees awarded. Offers health care management (MBA). *Application deadline:* Applications are processed on a rolling basis. *Application fee:* $45. Electronic applications accepted. *Application Contact:* Chair, 972-385-1055, Fax: 972-385-1700. *Dean/Executive Director,* Dr. Gil Linne, 480-557-1221, E-mail: gil.linne@phoenix.edu.

John Sperling School of Business Students: 532 full-time (323 women); includes 220 minority (168 African Americans, 7 American Indian/Alaska Native, 12 Asian Americans or Pacific Islanders, 33 Hispanic Americans), 70 international. Average age 37. *Faculty:* 37 full-time (5 women), 162 part-time/adjunct (38 women). Expenses: Contact institution. *Financial support:* Institutionally sponsored loans and scholarships/grants available. Financial award applicants required to submit FAFSA. In 2006, 131 degrees awarded. *Degree program information:* Evening/weekend programs available. Offers business (MBA, MM). *Application deadline:* Applications are processed on a rolling basis. *Application fee:* $45. *Application Contact:* Campus College Chair, 972-385-1055, Fax: 972-385-1700. *Provost,* Dr. Adam Honea, 480-557-1659, E-mail: adam.honea@phoenix.edu.

College of Graduate Business and Management Students: 517 full-time (320 women); includes 217 minority (166 African Americans, 7 American Indian/Alaska Native, 11 Asian Americans or Pacific Islanders, 33 Hispanic Americans), 68 international. Average age 37. *Faculty:* 27 full-time (5 women), 130 part-time/adjunct (34 women). Expenses: Contact institution. *Financial support:* Institutionally sponsored loans and scholarships/grants available. Financial award applicants required to submit FAFSA. In 2006, 127 degrees awarded. *Degree program information:* Evening/weekend programs available. Offers accounting (MBA); administration (MBA); human resources management (MBA, MM); management (MM); marketing (MBA); public administration (MBA, MM). *Application deadline:* Applications are processed on a rolling basis. *Application fee:* $45. Electronic applications accepted. *Application Contact:* Chair, 972-385-1055, Fax: 972-385-1700. *Associate Vice President and Dean/Executive Director,* Dr. Brian Lindquist, 480-557-1221, E-mail: brian.lindquist@phoenix.edu.

College of Information Systems and Technology Students: 15 full-time (3 women); includes 3 minority (2 African Americans, 1 Asian American or Pacific Islander), 2 international. Average age 46. *Faculty:* 10 full-time (0 women), 32 part-time/adjunct (4 women). Expenses: Contact institution. *Financial support:* Institutionally sponsored loans and scholarships/grants available. In 2006, 4 degrees awarded. *Degree program information:* Evening/weekend programs available. Offers e-business (MBA); technology management (MBA). *Application deadline:* Applications are processed on a rolling basis. *Application fee:* $45. Electronic applications accepted. *Application Contact:* Campus College Chair, 972-385-1055, Fax: 972-385-1700. *Dean,* Dr. Adam Honea, 480-557-1659, E-mail: adam.honea@phoenix.edu.

UNIVERSITY OF PHOENIX–DENVER CAMPUS, Lone Tree, CO 80124-5453

General Information Proprietary, coed, comprehensive institution. *Enrollment:* 2,948 graduate, professional, and undergraduate students; 564 full-time matriculated graduate/professional students (345 women). *Enrollment by degree level:* 564 master's. *Graduate faculty:* 125 full-time (52 women), 639 part-time/adjunct (227 women). *Tuition:* Full-time $10,032. *Required fees:* $760. *Graduate housing:* On-campus housing not available. *Student services:* Campus safety program, disabled student services, writing training. *Library facilities:* University Library. *Online resources:* library catalog, web page. *Collection:* 1,759 titles, 692 serial subscriptions.

Computer facilities: A campuswide network can be accessed from off campus. *Web address:* http://www.phoenix.edu/.

General Application Contact: Campus Information Center, 303-694-9093, Fax: 303-662-0911.

GRADUATE UNITS

The Artemis School Students: 935 full-time (668 women); includes 98 minority (37 African Americans, 5 American Indian/Alaska Native, 11 Asian Americans or Pacific Islanders, 45 Hispanic Americans), 87 international. Average age 35. *Faculty:* 36 full-time (21 women), 267 part-time/adjunct (146 women). Expenses: Contact institution. *Financial support:* Institutionally sponsored loans and scholarships/grants available. Financial award applicants required to submit FAFSA. In 2006, 469 master's awarded. *Degree program information:* Evening/weekend programs available. *Application deadline:* Applications are processed on a rolling basis. *Application fee:* $45. Electronic applications accepted. *Application Contact:* College Chair, 303-694-9093. *Provost,* Dr. Adam Honea, 480-557-1659, E-mail: adam.honea@phoenix.edu.

College of Education Students: 738 full-time (513 women); includes 72 minority (27 African Americans, 4 American Indian/Alaska Native, 9 Asian Americans or Pacific Islanders, 32 Hispanic Americans), 66 international. Average age 37. *Faculty:* 19 full-time (14 women), 141 part-time/adjunct (84 women). Expenses: Contact institution. *Financial support:* Institutionally sponsored loans and scholarships/grants available. Financial award applicants required to submit FAFSA. In 2006, 435 master's awarded. *Degree program information:* Evening/weekend programs available. Offers administration and supervision (MAEd); curriculum instruction (MAEd); elementary teacher education (MAEd); school counseling (MSC); secondary teacher education (MAEd). *Application deadline:* Applications are processed on a rolling basis. *Application fee:* $45. Electronic applications accepted. *Application Contact:* Chair, 303-694-9093, Fax: 303-662-0911. *Dean/Executive Director,* Dr. Marla LaRue, 480-557-1218, E-mail: marla.larue@phoenix.edu.

College of Health and Human Services Students: 147 full-time (114 women); includes 18 minority (9 African Americans, 1 American Indian/Alaska Native, 1 Asian American or Pacific Islander, 7 Hispanic Americans), 16 international. Average age 39. *Faculty:* 17 full-time (7 women), 126 part-time/adjunct (62 women). Expenses: Contact institution. *Financial support:* Institutionally sponsored loans and scholarships/grants available. Financial award applicants required to submit FAFSA. In 2006, 34 master's awarded. *Degree program information:* Evening/weekend programs available. Offers community counseling (MSC); health care management (MBA); marriage, family and child therapy (MSC); nursing (MSN). *Application deadline:* Applications are processed on a rolling basis. *Application fee:* $45. Electronic applications accepted. *Application Contact:* Chair, 303-694-9093, Fax: 303-662-0911. *Dean/Executive Director,* Dr. Gil Linne, 480-557-1751, E-mail: gil.linne@phoenix.edu.

John Sperling School of Business Students: 296 full-time (141 women); includes 60 minority (25 African Americans, 1 American Indian/Alaska Native, 9 Asian Americans or Pacific Islanders, 25 Hispanic Americans), 20 international. Average age 37. *Faculty:* 89 full-time (31 women), 372 part-time/adjunct (81 women). Expenses: Contact institution. *Financial support:* Institutionally sponsored loans and scholarships/grants available. Financial award applicants required to submit FAFSA. In 2006, 104 master's awarded. *Degree program information:* Evening/weekend programs available. Offers business (MBA, MIS, MM). *Application deadline:* Applications are processed on a rolling basis. *Application fee:* $45. Electronic applications accepted. *Provost,* Dr. Adam Honea, 480-557-1659, E-mail: adam.honea@phoenix.edu.

College of Graduate Business and Management Students: 289 full-time (139 women); includes 59 minority (25 African Americans, 1 American Indian/Alaska Native, 9 Asian Americans or Pacific Islanders, 24 Hispanic Americans), 20 international. Average age 37. *Faculty:* 63 full-time (22 women), 254 part-time/adjunct (56 women). Expenses: Contact institution. *Financial support:* Institutionally sponsored loans and scholarships/grants available. Financial award applicants required to submit FAFSA. In 2006, 93 degrees awarded. *Degree program information:* Evening/weekend programs available. Offers accounting (MBA); business administration (MBA); e-business (MBA); global management (MBA); human resources management (MBA, MM); management (MM); marketing (MBA); public administration (MBA, MM). *Application deadline:* Applications are processed on a rolling basis. *Application fee:* $45. Electronic applications accepted. *Application Contact:* Chair, 303-694-9093, Fax: 303-662-0911. *Associate Vice President and Dean/Executive Director,* Dr. Brian Lindquist, 480-557-1221, E-mail: brian.lindquist@phoenix.edu.

College of Information Systems and Technology Students: 7 full-time (2 women); includes 1 minority (Hispanic American) Average age 38. *Faculty:* 26 full-time (9 women), 108 part-time/adjunct (25 women). Expenses: Contact institution. *Financial support:* Institutionally sponsored loans and scholarships/grants available. Financial award applicants required to submit FAFSA. In 2006, 11 master's awarded. *Degree program information:* Evening/weekend programs available. Offers e-business (MBA); management (MIS); technology management (MBA). *Application deadline:* Applications are processed on a rolling basis. *Application fee:* $45. Electronic applications accepted. *Application Contact:* Chair, 303-694-9093, Fax: 303-662-0911. *Dean/Executive Director,* Dr. Adam Honea, 480-557-1659, E-mail: adam.honea@phoenix.edu.

UNIVERSITY OF PHOENIX–EASTERN WASHINGTON CAMPUS, Spokane Valley, WA 99212-2531

General Information Proprietary, coed, comprehensive institution. *Enrollment:* 294 graduate, professional, and undergraduate students; 39 full-time matriculated graduate/professional students (20 women). *Enrollment by degree level:* 39 master's. *Graduate faculty:* 20 full-time (1 woman), 121 part-time/adjunct (28 women). *Tuition:* Full-time $9,120. *Required fees:* $760. *Graduate housing:* On-campus housing not available. *Student services:* Campus safety program, disabled student services, writing training. *Library facilities:* University Library. *Online resources:* library catalog, web page. *Collection:* 1,759 titles, 692 serial subscriptions.

Computer facilities: A campuswide network can be accessed from off campus. Internet access is available. *Web address:* http://www.phoenix.edu/.

General Application Contact: Campus Information Center, 509-327-2443.

GRADUATE UNITS

The Artemis School Students: 1 (woman) full-time. Average age 27. *Faculty:* 4 full-time (1 woman), 22 part-time/adjunct (7 women). Expenses: Contact institution. *Financial support:* Institutionally sponsored loans and scholarships/grants available. Financial award applicants required to submit FAFSA. *Degree program information:* Evening/weekend programs available. *Application deadline:* Applications are processed on a rolling basis. *Application fee:* $45. Electronic applications accepted. *Application Contact:* Ginger Pauley, Institutional Reporting Manager, 480-557-1142, Fax: 480-557-1551, E-mail: giner.pauley@phoenix.edu. *Provost,* Dr. Adam Honea, 480-557-1659, E-mail: adam.honea@phoenix.edu.

College of Health and Human Services Students: 1 full-time (0 women). Average age 27. *Faculty:* 4 full-time (1 woman), 19 part-time/adjunct (5 women). Expenses: Contact institution. *Financial support:* Institutionally sponsored loans and scholarships/grants available. Financial award applicants required to submit FAFSA. *Degree program information:* Evening/weekend programs available. Offers health care management (MBA). *Application deadline:* Applications are processed on a rolling basis. *Application fee:* $45. Electronic applications accepted. *Dean/Executive Director,* Dr. Gil Linne, 480-557-1251, E-mail: gil.linne@phoenix.edu.

John Sperling School of Business Students: 38 full-time (19 women); includes 1 minority (African American), 10 international. Average age 34. *Faculty:* 16 full-time (0 women), 98 part-time/adjunct (21 women). Expenses: Contact institution. *Financial support:* Institutionally sponsored loans and scholarships/grants available. Financial award applicants required to submit FAFSA. In 2006, 11 degrees awarded. *Degree program information:* Evening/weekend programs available. Offers business (MBA). *Application deadline:* Applications are processed on a rolling basis. *Application fee:* $45. Electronic applications accepted. *Application Contact:* Campus College Chair, 509-327-2443. *Provost,* Dr. Adam Honea, 480-557-1659, E-mail: adam.honea@phoenix.edu.

College of Graduate Business and Management Students: 38 full-time (19 women); includes 1 minority (American Indian/Alaska Native), 10 international. Average age 34. *Faculty:* 14 full-time (0 women), 62 part-time/adjunct (15 women). Expenses: Contact institution. *Financial support:* Institutionally sponsored loans and scholarships/grants available. Financial award applicants required to submit FAFSA. In 2006, 11 degrees awarded. *Degree program information:* Evening/weekend programs available. Offers business and management (MBA). *Application deadline:* Applications are processed on a rolling basis. *Application fee:* $45. Electronic applications accepted. *Associate Vice President and Dean/Executive Director,* Dr. Brian Lindquist, 480-557-1221, E-mail: brian.lindquist@phoenix.edu.

UNIVERSITY OF PHOENIX–FORT LAUDERDALE CAMPUS, Fort Lauderdale, FL 33309

General Information Proprietary, coed, comprehensive institution. *Enrollment:* 3,121 graduate, professional, and undergraduate students; 778 full-time matriculated graduate/professional students (568 women). *Enrollment by degree level:* 778 master's. *Graduate faculty:* 77 full-time (32 women), 256 part-time/adjunct (72 women). *Tuition:* Full-time $9,450. *Required fees:* $760. *Graduate housing:* On-campus housing not available. *Student services:* Campus safety program, disabled student services, writing training. *Library facilities:* University Library. *Online resources:* library catalog, web page. *Collection:* 1,759 titles, 692 serial subscriptions.

Computer facilities: A campuswide network can be accessed from off campus. Internet access is available. *Web address:* http://www.phoenix.edu/.

General Application Contact: Campus Information Center, 954-832-5503, Fax: 954-382-5304.

GRADUATE UNITS

The Artemis School Students: 329 full-time (287 women); includes 133 minority (112 African Americans, 3 Asian Americans or Pacific Islanders, 18 Hispanic Americans), 38 international. Average age 41. *Faculty:* 32 full-time (15 women), 83 part-time/adjunct (35 women). Expenses: Contact institution. *Financial support:* Institutionally sponsored loans and scholarships/grants available. Financial award applicants required to submit FAFSA. In 2006, 77 degrees awarded. *Degree program information:* Evening/weekend programs available. *Application deadline:* Applications are processed on a rolling basis. *Application fee:* $45. Electronic applications accepted. *Provost,* Dr. Adam Honea, 480-557-1659, E-mail: adam.honea@phoenix.edu.

College of Education Students: 132 full-time (114 women); includes 60 minority (52 African Americans, 1 Asian American or Pacific Islander, 7 Hispanic Americans), 5 international. Average age 39. *Faculty:* 10 full-time (5 women), 17 part-time/adjunct (7 women). Expenses: Contact institution. *Financial support:* Institutionally sponsored loans and scholarships/grants available. Financial award applicants required to submit FAFSA. In 2006, 25 degrees awarded. *Degree program information:* Evening/weekend programs available. Offers administration and supervision (MA Ed); computer education (MA Ed); curriculum and instruction (MA Ed); elementary teacher education (MA Ed); secondary teacher education (MA Ed). *Application deadline:* Applications are processed on a rolling basis. *Application fee:* $45. Electronic applications accepted. *Application Contact:* Chair, 954-382-5303, Fax: 954-382-5304. *Dean/Executive Director,* Dr. Marla LaRue, 480-557-1218.

College of Health and Human Services Students: 197 full-time (173 women); includes 73 minority (60 African Americans, 2 Asian Americans or Pacific Islanders, 11 Hispanic Americans), 33 international. Average age 43. *Faculty:* 22 full-time (10 women), 56 part-time/adjunct (28 women). Expenses: Contact institution. *Financial support:* Institutionally sponsored loans and scholarships/grants available. Financial award applicants required to submit FAFSA. In 2006, 52 degrees awarded. *Degree program information:* Evening/weekend programs available. Offers health administration (MHA); health care education (MSN); health care management (MBA); nursing (MSN). *Application deadline:* Applications are processed on a rolling basis. *Application fee:* $45. Electronic applications accepted. *Application Contact:* 954-382-5303, Fax: 954-382-5303. *Dean/Executive Director,* Dr. Gil Linne, 480-557-1751, E-mail: gil.linne@phoenix.edu.

John Sperling School of Business Students: 449 full-time (281 women); includes 204 minority (118 African Americans, 3 American Indian/Alaska Native, 8 Asian Americans or Pacific Islanders, 75 Hispanic Americans), 66 international. Average age 39. *Faculty:* 42 full-time (16 women), 170 part-time/adjunct (37 women). Expenses: Contact institution. *Financial support:* Institutionally sponsored loans and scholarships/grants available. Financial award applicants required to submit FAFSA. In 2006, 122 degrees awarded. *Degree program information:* Evening/weekend programs available. Offers business (MBA, MIS, MM). *Application deadline:* Applications are processed on a rolling basis. *Application fee:* $45. Electronic applications accepted. *Provost,* Dr. Adam Honea, 480-557-1659, E-mail: adam.honea@phoenix.edu.

College of Graduate Business and Management Students: 433 full-time (273 women); includes 196 minority (113 African Americans, 3 American Indian/Alaska Native, 8 Asian Americans or Pacific Islanders, 72 Hispanic Americans), 64 international. Average age 38. *Faculty:* 31 full-time (13 women), 117 part-time/adjunct (33 women). Expenses: Contact institution. *Financial support:* Institutionally sponsored loans and scholarships/grants available. Financial award applicants required to submit FAFSA. In 2006, 112 degrees awarded. *Degree program information:* Evening/weekend programs available. Offers accounting (MBA); business administration (MBA); global management (MBA); human resource management (MBA); human resources management (MM); management (MM); marketing (MBA); public administration (MBA). *Application deadline:* Applications are processed on a rolling basis. *Application fee:* $45. Electronic applications accepted. *Application Contact:* Chair, 954-382-5303, Fax: 954-382-5304. *Associate Vice President and Dean/Executive Director,* Dr. Brian Linquist, 480-557-1221, E-mail: brian.linquist@phoenix.edu.

College of Information Systems and Technology Students: 16 full-time (8 women); includes 9 minority (5 African Americans, 4 Hispanic Americans), 2 international. Average age 40. *Faculty:* 11 full-time (3 women), 53 part-time/adjunct (4 women). Expenses: Contact institution. *Financial support:* Institutionally sponsored loans and scholarships/grants available. Financial award applicants required to submit FAFSA. In 2006, 10 degrees awarded. *Degree program information:* Evening/weekend programs available. Offers management (MIS); technology management (MBA). *Application deadline:* Applications are processed on a rolling basis. *Application fee:* $45. Electronic applications accepted. *Application Contact:* Chair, 954-382-5303, Fax: 954-382-5304.

UNIVERSITY OF PHOENIX–HAWAII CAMPUS, Honolulu, HI 96813-4317

General Information Proprietary, coed, comprehensive institution. *Enrollment:* 1,730 graduate, professional, and undergraduate students; 396 full-time matriculated graduate/professional students (254 women). *Enrollment by degree level:* 396 master's. *Graduate faculty:* 54 full-time (24 women), 295 part-time/adjunct (111 women). *Tuition:* Full-time $11,520. *Required fees:* $760. *Graduate housing:* On-campus housing not available. *Student services:* Campus safety program, disabled student services, writing training. *Library facilities:* University Library. *Online resources:* library catalog, web page. *Collection:* 1,759 titles, 692 serial subscriptions.

Computer facilities: A campuswide network can be accessed from off campus. Internet access is available. *Web address:* http://www.phoenix.edu/.

General Application Contact: Campus Information Center, 808-536-2686, Fax: 808-536-3848.

GRADUATE UNITS

The Artemis School Students: 308 full-time (212 women); includes 81 minority (3 African Americans, 1 American Indian/Alaska Native, 68 Asian Americans or Pacific Islanders, 9 Hispanic Americans), 115 international. Average age 36. *Faculty:* 30 full-time (19 women), 142 part-time/adjunct (80 women). Expenses: Contact institution. *Financial support:* Institutionally sponsored loans and scholarships/grants available. Financial award applicants required to submit FAFSA. In 2006, 164 degrees awarded. *Degree program information:* Evening/weekend programs available. *Application deadline:* Applications are processed on a rolling basis. *Application fee:* $45. Electronic applications accepted. *Provost,* Dr. Adam Honea, 408-557-1659, E-mail: adam.honea@phoenix.edu.

College of Education Students: 261 full-time (176 women); includes 61 minority (1 African American, 1 American Indian/Alaska Native, 53 Asian Americans or Pacific Islanders, 6 Hispanic Americans), 106 international. Average age 36. *Faculty:* 10 full-time (7 women), 58 part-time/adjunct (34 women). Expenses: Contact institution. *Financial support:* Institutionally sponsored loans and scholarships/grants available. Financial award applicants required to submit FAFSA. In 2006, 151 degrees awarded. *Degree program information:* Evening/weekend programs available. Offers administration and supervision (MA Ed); curriculum and instruction (MA Ed); elementary education (MA Ed); secondary education (MA Ed); teacher education for elementary licensure (MA Ed). *Application deadline:* Applications are processed on a rolling basis. *Application fee:* $45. Electronic applications accepted. *Application Contact:* Chair, 580-536-2686, Fax: 808-536-3848. *Dean/Executive Director,* Dr. Marla LaRue, 480-557-1309, E-mail: marla.larue@phoenix.edu.

College of Health and Human Services Students: 47 full-time (36 women); includes 20 minority (2 African Americans, 15 Asian Americans or Pacific Islanders, 3 Hispanic Americans), 9 international. Average age 41. *Faculty:* 20 full-time (12 women), 84 part-time/adjunct (46 women). Expenses: Contact institution. *Financial support:* Institutionally sponsored loans and scholarships/grants available. Financial award applicants required to submit FAFSA. In 2006, 13 degrees awarded. *Degree program information:* Evening/weekend programs available. Offers administration of justice and security (MS); community counseling (MSC); family nurse practitioner (MSN); health administration (MHA); health care management (MBA); marriage, family and child therapy (MSC); nursing (MSN); psychology (MS). *Application deadline:* Applications are processed on a rolling basis. *Application fee:* $45. Electronic applications accepted. *Application Contact:* Chair, 808-536-2686, Fax: 808-536-3848. *Dean/Executive Director,* Dr. Gil Linne, 480-557-1751, E-mail: gil.linne@phoenix.edu.

John Sperling School of Business Students: 88 full-time (42 women); includes 23 minority (5 African Americans, 16 Asian Americans or Pacific Islanders, 2 Hispanic Americans), 36 international. Average age 37. *Faculty:* 24 full-time (5 women), 149 part-time/adjunct (30 women). Expenses: Contact institution. *Financial support:* Institutionally sponsored loans and scholarships/grants available. Financial award applicants required to submit FAFSA. In 2006, 31 degrees awarded. *Degree program information:* Evening/weekend programs available. Offers business (MBA, MIS, MM). *Application deadline:* Applications are processed on a rolling basis. *Application fee:* $45. Electronic applications accepted. *Provost,* Dr. Adam Honea, 480-557-1659, E-mail: adam.honea@phoenix.edu.

College of Graduate Business and Management Students: 72 full-time (39 women); includes 18 minority (3 African Americans, 13 Asian Americans or Pacific Islanders, 2 Hispanic Americans), 30 international. Average age 37. *Faculty:* 17 full-time (4 women), 92 part-time/adjunct (23 women). Expenses: Contact institution. *Financial support:* Institutionally sponsored loans and scholarships/grants available. Financial award applicants required to submit FAFSA. In 2006, 20 master's awarded. *Degree program information:* Evening/weekend programs available. Offers accounting (MBA); business administration (MBA); global management (MBA); human resources management (MBA, MM); management (MM); marketing (MBA); public administration (MBA, MM). *Application deadline:* Applications are processed on a rolling basis. *Application fee:* $45. Electronic applications accepted. *Application Contact:* Chair, 808-536-2686, Fax: 808-536-3848. *Associate Vice President and Dean/Executive Director,* Dr. Brian Lindquist, 480-557-1221, E-mail: brian.lindquist@phoenix.edu.

College of Information Systems and Technology Students: 16 full-time (3 women); includes 5 minority (2 African Americans, 3 Asian Americans or Pacific Islanders), 6 international. Average age 37. *Faculty:* 7 full-time (1 woman), 57 part-time/adjunct (7 women). Expenses: Contact institution. *Financial support:* Institutionally sponsored loans and scholarships/grants available. Financial award applicants required to submit FAFSA. In 2006, 11 degrees awarded. *Degree program information:* Evening/weekend programs available. Offers management (MIS); technology management (MBA). *Application deadline:* Applications are processed on a rolling basis. *Application fee:* $45. Electronic applications accepted. *Application Contact:* Chair, 808-536-2686, Fax: 808-536-3848. *Dean/Executive Director,* Dr. Adam Honea, 480-557-1659, E-mail: adam.honea@phoenix.edu.

UNIVERSITY OF PHOENIX–HOUSTON CAMPUS, Houston, TX 77079-2004

General Information Proprietary, coed, comprehensive institution. *Enrollment:* 4,532 graduate, professional, and undergraduate students; 827 full-time matriculated graduate/professional students (523 women). *Enrollment by degree level:* 827 master's. *Graduate faculty:* 33 full-time (10 women), 228 part-time/adjunct (61 women). *Tuition:* Full-time $11,832. *Required fees:* $760. *Graduate housing:* On-campus housing not available. *Student services:* Campus safety program, disabled student services, writing training. *Library facilities:* University Library. *Online resources:* library catalog, web page. *Collection:* 1,759 titles, 692 serial subscriptions.

Computer facilities: A campuswide network can be accessed from off campus. Internet access is available. *Web address:* http://www.phoenix.edu/.

General Application Contact: Campus Information Center, 713-465-9966, Fax: 713-465-2686.

GRADUATE UNITS

The Artemis School Students: 110 full-time (87 women); includes 60 minority (42 African Americans, 6 Asian Americans or Pacific Islanders, 12 Hispanic Americans), 5 international. Average age 37. *Faculty:* 2 full-time (1 woman), 23 part-time/adjunct (10 women). Expenses: Contact institution. *Financial support:* Institutionally sponsored loans and scholarships/grants available. In 2006, 22 degrees awarded. *Degree program information:* Evening/weekend programs available. *Application deadline:* Applications are processed on a rolling basis. *Application fee:* $45. Electronic applications accepted. *Application Contact:* Campus College Chair, 713-465-9966, Fax: 713-465-2686. *Provost,* Dr. Adam Honea, 480-557-1659, E-mail: adam.honea@phoenix.edu.

College of Health and Human Services Students: 110 full-time (87 women); includes 60 minority (42 African Americans, 6 Asian Americans or Pacific Islanders, 12 Hispanic Americans), 5 international. Average age 37. *Faculty:* 2 full-time (1 woman), 13 part-time/adjunct (0 women). Expenses: Contact institution. *Financial support:* Institutionally sponsored loans and scholarships/grants available. In 2006, 22 degrees awarded. Offers health care management (MBA). *Application deadline:* Applications are processed on a rolling basis. *Application fee:* $45. Electronic applications accepted. *Application Contact:* Campus College Chair, 913-465-9966, Fax: 713-465-2628. *Dean/Executive Director,* Dr. Gil Linne, 480-557-1751, E-mail: gil.linne@phoenix.edu.

John Sperling School of Business Students: 717 full-time (436 women); includes 377 minority (293 African Americans, 1 American Indian/Alaska Native, 38 Asian Americans or Pacific Islanders, 45 Hispanic Americans), 50 international. Average age 38. *Faculty:* 30 full-time (9 women), 201 part-time/adjunct (49 women). Expenses: Contact institution. *Financial support:* Institutionally sponsored loans available. Financial award applicants required to submit FAFSA. In 2006, 269 degrees awarded. *Degree program information:* Evening/weekend programs available. Offers business (MBA). *Application deadline:* Applications are processed on a rolling basis. *Application fee:* $45. Electronic applications accepted. *Provost,* Dr. Adam Honea, 480-557-1659, E-mail: adam.honea@phoenix.edu.

College of Graduate Business and Management Students: 666 full-time (417 women); includes 350 minority (274 African Americans, 1 American Indian/Alaska Native, 34 Asian Americans or Pacific Islanders, 41 Hispanic Americans), 45 international. Average age 37. *Faculty:* 28 full-time (9 women), 149 part-time/adjunct (43 women). Expenses: Contact institution. *Financial support:* Institutionally sponsored loans available. Financial award applicants required to submit FAFSA. In 2006, 244 degrees awarded. *Degree program information:* Evening/weekend programs available. Offers business administration (MBA); global management (MBA); human resources management (MBA); public administration (MBA). *Application deadline:* Applications are processed on a rolling basis. *Application fee:* $45. Electronic applications accepted. *Application Contact:* 713-465-9966, Fax: 713-465-2686. *Associate Vice President and Dean/Executive Director,* Dr. Brian Lindquist, 480-557-1221, E-mail: brian.lindquist@phoenix.edu.

College of Information Systems and Technology Students: 51 full-time (19 women); includes 27 minority (19 African Americans, 4 Asian Americans or Pacific Islanders, 4 Hispanic Americans), 5 international. Average age 41. *Faculty:* 2 full-time (0 women), 52 part-time/adjunct (6 women). Expenses: Contact institution. *Financial support:* Institutionally sponsored loans available. *Degree program information:* Evening/weekend programs available. Offers e-business (MBA); technology management (MBA). *Application deadline:* Applications are processed on a rolling basis. *Application fee:* $45. Electronic applications accepted. *Application Contact:* Campus College Chair, 713-465-9966, Fax: 713-465-2686. *Dean,* Dr. Adam Honea, 480-557-1659, E-mail: adam.honea@phoenix.edu.

UNIVERSITY OF PHOENIX–IDAHO CAMPUS, Meridian, ID 83642-3014

General Information Proprietary, coed, comprehensive institution. *Enrollment:* 659 graduate, professional, and undergraduate students; 125 full-time matriculated graduate/professional students (42 women). *Enrollment by degree level:* 125 master's. *Graduate faculty:* 15 full-time (1 woman), 93 part-time/adjunct (22 women). *Tuition:* Full-time $9,104. *Graduate housing:* On-campus housing not available. *Student services:* Disabled student services, writing training. *Library facilities:* University Library. *Online resources:* library catalog, web page. *Collection:* 1,759 titles, 692 serial subscriptions.

Computer facilities: A campuswide network can be accessed from off campus. Internet access is available. *Web address:* http://www.phoenix.edu/.

General Application Contact: Campus Information Center, 208-888-1505, Fax: 208-888-4775.

GRADUATE UNITS

The Artemis School Students: 20 full-time (8 women); includes 1 Asian American or Pacific Islander. Average age 39. *Faculty:* 4 full-time (1 woman), 29 part-time/adjunct (7 women). Expenses: Contact institution. *Financial support:* Institutionally sponsored loans and scholarships/grants available. In 2006, 1 degree awarded. *Degree program information:* Evening/weekend programs available. *Application deadline:* Applications are processed on a rolling basis. *Application fee:* $45. Electronic applications accepted. *Application Contact:* College Chair, 208-888-1505, Fax: 208-888-4775. *Provost,* Dr. Adam Honea, 480-557-1659, E-mail: adam.honea@phoenix.edu.

College of Education Students: 20 full-time (8 women); includes 1 Asian American or Pacific Islander. Average age 39. *Faculty:* 7 part-time/adjunct (3 women). Expenses: Contact

University of Phoenix–Idaho Campus (continued)

institution. *Financial support:* Institutionally sponsored loans and scholarships/grants available. In 2006, 1 degree awarded. *Degree program information:* Evening/weekend programs available. Offers education (MA Ed). *Application deadline:* Applications are processed on a rolling basis. *Application fee:* $45. Electronic applications accepted. *Application Contact:* College Chair, 208-888-1505, Fax: 208-888-4775. *Dean/Executive Director,* Dr. Marla LaRue, 480-557-1218, E-mail: marla.larue@phoenix.edu.

College of Health and Human Services *Faculty:* 4 full-time (1 woman), 22 part-time/adjunct (4 women). Expenses: Contact institution. *Financial support:* Institutionally sponsored loans and scholarships/grants available. *Degree program information:* Evening/weekend programs available. Offers health administration (MHA); health care management (MBA); psychology (MS). *Application deadline:* Applications are processed on a rolling basis. *Application fee:* $45. Electronic applications accepted. *Application Contact:* College Chair, 208-888-1505, Fax: 208-888-4775. *Dean/Executive Director,* Dr. Gil Linne, 480-557-1751, E-mail: gil.linne@phoenix.edu.

John Sperling School of Business Students: 105 full-time (34 women); includes 6 minority (1 African American, 2 Asian Americans or Pacific Islanders, 3 Hispanic Americans), 12 international. Average age 35. *Faculty:* 11 full-time (0 women), 64 part-time/adjunct (15 women). Expenses: Contact institution. *Financial support:* Institutionally sponsored loans and scholarships/grants available. Financial award applicants required to submit FAFSA. In 2006, 23 degrees awarded. *Degree program information:* Evening/weekend programs available. Offers business (MBA, MIS, MM). *Application deadline:* Applications are processed on a rolling basis. *Application fee:* $45. Electronic applications accepted. *Application Contact:* Chair, 208-888-1505, Fax: 208-888-4775. *Provost,* Dr. Adam Honea, 480-557-1659, E-mail: adam.honea@phoenix.edu.

College of Graduate Business and Management Students: 104 full-time (34 women); includes 6 minority (1 African American, 2 Asian Americans or Pacific Islanders, 3 Hispanic Americans), 11 international. Average age 35. *Faculty:* 7 full-time (0 women), 52 part-time/adjunct (12 women). Expenses: Contact institution. *Financial support:* Institutionally sponsored loans and scholarships/grants available. Financial award applicants required to submit FAFSA. In 2006, 22 degrees awarded. *Degree program information:* Evening/weekend programs available. Offers accounting (MBA); administration (MBA); management (MM). *Application deadline:* Applications are processed on a rolling basis. *Application fee:* $45. Electronic applications accepted. *Application Contact:* Chair, 208-888-1505, Fax: 208-888-4775. *Dean,* Dr. Brian Lindquist, 480-557-1221, E-mail: brian.lindquist@phoenix.edu.

College of Information Systems and Technology Students: 1 full-time (0 women), 1 international. Average age 52. *Faculty:* 4 full-time (0 women), 12 part-time/adjunct (3 women). Expenses: Contact institution. *Financial support:* Institutionally sponsored loans and scholarships/grants available. In 2006, 1 degree awarded. *Degree program information:* Evening/weekend programs available. Offers information systems (MIS); technology management (MBA). *Application deadline:* Applications are processed on a rolling basis. *Application fee:* $45. Electronic applications accepted. *Application Contact:* College Chair, 208-888-1505, Fax: 208-888-4775.

UNIVERSITY OF PHOENIX–INDIANAPOLIS CAMPUS, Indianapolis, IN 46250-932

General Information Proprietary, coed, comprehensive institution. *Enrollment:* 602 graduate, professional, and undergraduate students; 104 full-time matriculated graduate/professional students (53 women). *Enrollment by degree level:* 104 master's. *Graduate faculty:* 17 full-time (9 women), 130 part-time/adjunct (34 women). *Tuition:* Full-time $10,320. *Required fees:* $760. *Graduate housing:* On-campus housing not available. *Student services:* Campus safety program, disabled student services, writing training. *Library facilities:* University Library. *Online resources:* library catalog, web page. *Collection:* 1,756 titles, 692 serial subscriptions.

Computer facilities: A campuswide network can be accessed from off campus. Internet access is available. *Web address:* http://www.phoenix.edu/.

General Application Contact: Campus Information Center, 317-585-8610.

GRADUATE UNITS

John Sperling School of Business Students: 103 full-time (52 women); includes 28 minority (24 African Americans, 3 Asian Americans or Pacific Islanders, 1 Hispanic American), 11 international. Average age 38. *Faculty:* 16 full-time (9 women), 118 part-time/adjunct (28 women). Expenses: Contact institution. *Financial support:* Institutionally sponsored loans and scholarships/grants available. Financial award applicants required to submit FAFSA. In 2006, 36 degrees awarded. *Degree program information:* Evening/weekend programs available. Offers business (MBA, MIS, MM). *Application deadline:* Applications are processed on a rolling basis. *Application fee:* $45. Electronic applications accepted. *Provost,* Dr. Adam Honea, 480-557-1659, E-mail: adam.honea@phoenix.edu.

College of Graduate Business and Management Students: 102 full-time (52 women); includes 28 minority (24 African Americans, 3 Asian Americans or Pacific Islanders, 1 Hispanic American), 10 international. Average age 36. *Faculty:* 13 full-time (6 women), 77 part-time/adjunct (22 women). Expenses: Contact institution. *Financial support:* Institutionally sponsored loans and scholarships/grants available. Financial award applicants required to submit FAFSA. In 2006, 35 degrees awarded. *Degree program information:* Evening/weekend programs available. Offers business and management (MBA); management (MM). *Application deadline:* Applications are processed on a rolling basis. *Application fee:* $45. Electronic applications accepted. *Application Contact:* Chair, 317-585-8616. *Provost,* Dr. Brian Lindquist, 480-557-1221, E-mail: brian.lindquist@phoenix.edu.

College of Information Systems and Technology Students: 1 full-time (0 women), 1 international. Average age 39. *Faculty:* 3 full-time (0 women), 41 part-time/adjunct (6 women). Expenses: Contact institution. *Financial support:* Institutionally sponsored loans and scholarships/grants available. Financial award applicants required to submit FAFSA. In 2006, 1 degree awarded. *Degree program information:* Evening/weekend programs available. Offers information systems (MIS); technology management (MBA). *Application deadline:* Applications are processed on a rolling basis. *Application fee:* $45. Electronic applications accepted. *Application Contact:* Chair, 317-585-8610. *Dean/Executive Director,* Dr. Adam Honea, 480-557-1659, E-mail: adam.honea@phoenix.edu.

UNIVERSITY OF PHOENIX–KANSAS CITY CAMPUS, Kansas City, MO 64131-4517

General Information Proprietary, coed, comprehensive institution. *Enrollment:* 1,201 graduate, professional, and undergraduate students; 272 full-time matriculated graduate/professional students (126 women). *Enrollment by degree level:* 272 master's. *Graduate faculty:* 37 full-time (4 women), 120 part-time/adjunct (28 women). *Tuition:* Full-time $11,064. *Required fees:* $760. *Graduate housing:* On-campus housing not available. *Student services:* Campus safety program, disabled student services, writing training. *Library facilities:* University Library. *Online resources:* library catalog, web page. *Collection:* 1,759 titles, 692 serial subscriptions.

Computer facilities: A campuswide network can be accessed from off campus. Internet access is available. *Web address:* http://www.phoenix.edu/.

General Application Contact: Campus Information Center, 816-943-9600, Fax: 816-943-6675.

GRADUATE UNITS

The Artemis School Students: 16 full-time (15 women); includes 1 minority (African American), 5 international. Average age 44. *Faculty:* 4 full-time (0 women), 16 part-time/adjunct (7 women). Expenses: Contact institution. *Financial support:* Institutionally sponsored loans and scholarships/grants available. Financial award applicants required to submit FAFSA. In 2006, 1 degree awarded. *Degree program information:* Evening/weekend programs available. Offers education (MA Ed). *Application deadline:* Applications are processed on a rolling basis. *Application fee:* $45. Electronic applications accepted. *Provost,* Dr. Adam Honea, 470-557-1659, E-mail: adam.honea@phoenix.edu.

College of Health and Human Services Students: 16 full-time (15 women); includes 1 minority (African American), 5 international. Average age 44. *Faculty:* 4 full-time (0 women), 16 part-time/adjunct (7 women). Expenses: Contact institution. *Financial support:* Institutionally sponsored loans and scholarships/grants available. In 2006, 2 degrees awarded. *Degree program information:* Evening/weekend programs available. Offers administration of justice and security (MS); community counseling (MSC); health administration (MHA); health care management (MBA); nursing (MSN). *Application fee:* $45. *Application Contact:* Chair, 816-943-9600, Fax: 816-943-6675. *Dean/Executive Director,* Dr. Gil Linne, 480-557-1751, E-mail: gil.linne@phoenix.edu.

John Sperling School of Business Students: 256 full-time (111 women); includes 60 minority (38 African Americans, 1 American Indian/Alaska Native, 13 Asian Americans or Pacific Islanders, 8 Hispanic Americans), 35 international. Average age 44. *Faculty:* 31 full-time (4 women), 102 part-time/adjunct (20 women). Expenses: Contact institution. *Financial support:* Institutionally sponsored loans and scholarships/grants available. Financial award applicants required to submit FAFSA. In 2006, 83 degrees awarded. *Degree program information:* Evening/weekend programs available. Offers business (MBA, MIS, MM). *Application deadline:* Applications are processed on a rolling basis. *Application fee:* $45. Electronic applications accepted. *Application Contact:* Chair, 816-943-9600, Fax: 816-943-6675. *Provost,* Dr. Adam Honea, 480-557-1659, E-mail: adam.honea@phoenix.edu.

College of Graduate Business and Management Students: 226 full-time (105 women); includes 44 minority (36 African Americans, 1 American Indian/Alaska Native, 7 Hispanic Americans), 32 international. Average age 34. *Faculty:* 22 full-time (3 women), 143 part-time/adjunct (34 women). Expenses: Contact institution. *Financial support:* Institutionally sponsored loans and scholarships/grants available. Financial award applicants required to submit FAFSA. In 2006, 78 degrees awarded. *Degree program information:* Evening/weekend programs available. Offers business administration (MBA); management (MM). *Application deadline:* Applications are processed on a rolling basis. *Application fee:* $45. Electronic applications accepted. *Application Contact:* Chair, 816-943-9600, Fax: 816-943-6675. *Associate Vice President/Dean/Executive Director,* Dr. Brian Lindquist, 480-557-1142.

College of Information Systems and Technology Students: 30 full-time (6 women); includes 5 minority (2 African Americans, 2 Asian Americans or Pacific Islanders, 1 Hispanic American), 3 international. Average age 38. *Faculty:* 9 full-time (1 woman), 34 part-time/adjunct (2 women). Expenses: Contact institution. *Financial support:* Institutionally sponsored loans and scholarships/grants available. Financial award applicants required to submit FAFSA. In 2006, 5 degrees awarded. *Degree program information:* Evening/weekend programs available. Offers management (MIS); technology management (MBA). *Application deadline:* Applications are processed on a rolling basis. *Application fee:* $45. Electronic applications accepted. *Application Contact:* Campus College Chair, 816-943-9600, Fax: 816-943-6675. *Dean,* Dr. Adam Honea, 480-557-1659, E-mail: adam.honea@phoenix.edu.

UNIVERSITY OF PHOENIX–LAS VEGAS CAMPUS, Las Vegas, NV 89128

General Information Proprietary, coed, comprehensive institution. *Enrollment:* 3,484 graduate, professional, and undergraduate students; 1,106 full-time matriculated graduate/professional students (757 women). *Enrollment by degree level:* 1,106 master's. *Graduate faculty:* 56 full-time (17 women), 335 part-time/adjunct (114 women). *Tuition:* Full-time $9,576. *Required fees:* $760. *Graduate housing:* On-campus housing not available. *Student services:* Campus safety program, disabled student services, writing training. *Library facilities:* University Library. *Online resources:* library catalog, web page. *Collection:* 1,759 titles, 692 serial subscriptions.

Computer facilities: A campuswide network can be accessed from off campus. Internet access is available. *Web address:* http://www.phoenix.edu/.

General Application Contact: Campus Information Center, 702-638-7249, Fax: 702-638-8035.

GRADUATE UNITS

The Artemis School Students: 625 full-time (490 women); includes 139 minority (77 African Americans, 4 American Indian/Alaska Native, 18 Asian Americans or Pacific Islanders, 40 Hispanic Americans), 12 international. Average age 36. *Faculty:* 17 full-time (9 women), 127 part-time/adjunct (74 women). Expenses: Contact institution. *Financial support:* Institutionally sponsored loans and scholarships/grants available. Financial award applicants required to submit FAFSA. In 2006, 228 degrees awarded. *Degree program information:* Evening/weekend programs available. *Application deadline:* Applications are processed on a rolling basis. *Application fee:* $45. Electronic applications accepted. *Provost,* Dr. Adam Honea, 480-557-1659, E-mail: adam.honea@phoenix.edu.

College of Education Students: 494 full-time (388 women); includes 105 minority (51 African Americans, 2 American Indian/Alaska Native, 18 Asian Americans or Pacific Islanders, 34 Hispanic Americans), 9 international. Average age 35. *Faculty:* 9 full-time (8 women), 45 part-time/adjunct (27 women). Expenses: Contact institution. *Financial support:* Institutionally sponsored loans and scholarships/grants available. Financial award applicants required to submit FAFSA. In 2006, 227 degrees awarded. *Degree program information:* Evening/weekend programs available. Offers administration and supervision (MA Ed); curriculum and instruction (MA Ed); school counseling (MSC); teacher education-elementary licensure (MA Ed). *Application deadline:* Applications are processed on a rolling basis. *Application fee:* $45. Electronic applications accepted. *Application Contact:* Chair, 702-638-7249, Fax: 702-638-8085. *Dean/Executive Director,* Dr. Marla LaRue, 480-557-1218, E-mail: marla.larue@phoenix.edu.

College of Health and Human Services Students: 71 full-time (55 women); includes 18 minority (14 African Americans, 1 American Indian/Alaska Native, 3 Hispanic Americans), 2 international. Average age 39. *Faculty:* 8 full-time (4 women), 72 part-time/adjunct (37 women). Expenses: Contact institution. *Financial support:* Institutionally sponsored loans and scholarships/grants available. Financial award applicants required to submit FAFSA. In 2006, 1 degree awarded. Offers marriage, family, and child therapy (MSC); mental health counseling (MSC). *Application deadline:* Applications are processed on a rolling basis. *Application fee:* $45. Electronic applications accepted. *Application Contact:* Chair, 702-638-7249, Fax: 702-638-8085. *Dean/Executive Director,* Dr. Gil Linne, 480-557-1751, E-mail: gil.linne@phoenix.edu.

John Sperling School of Business Students: 481 full-time (267 women); includes 150 minority (93 African Americans, 5 American Indian/Alaska Native, 17 Asian Americans or Pacific Islanders, 35 Hispanic Americans), 19 international. Average age 37. *Faculty:* 39 full-time (8 women), 208 part-time/adjunct (40 women). Expenses: Contact institution. *Financial support:* Institutionally sponsored loans and scholarships/grants available. Financial award applicants required to submit FAFSA. In 2006, 168 degrees awarded. *Degree program information:* Evening/weekend programs available. Offers business (MBA, MIS, MM). *Application deadline:* Applications are processed on a rolling basis. *Application fee:* $45. Electronic applications accepted. *Provost,* Dr. Adam Honea, 508-557-1659, E-mail: adam.honea@phoenix.edu.

College of Graduate Business and Management Students: 467 full-time (261 women); includes 152 minority (97 African Americans, 5 American Indian/Alaska Native, 17 Asian Americans or Pacific Islanders, 33 Hispanic Americans), 19 international. Average age 37. *Faculty:* 28 full-time (6 women), 144 part-time/adjunct (30 women). Expenses: Contact institution. *Financial support:* Institutionally sponsored loans and scholarships/grants available. Financial award applicants required to submit FAFSA. In 2006, 155 degrees awarded. *Degree program information:* Evening/weekend programs available. Offers business administration (MBA); management (MM). *Application deadline:* Applications are processed on a rolling basis. *Application fee:* $45. Electronic applications accepted. *Application Contact:* Chair, 702-638-7249, Fax: 702-638-8035. *Associate Vice President and Dean/Executive Director,* Dr. Brian Lindquist, 480-557-1221, E-mail: brian.lindquist@phoenix.edu.

College of Information Systems and Technology Students: 14 full-time (6 women); includes 4 minority (2 African Americans, 2 Hispanic Americans). Average age 37. *Faculty:* 11 full-time (2 women), 64 part-time/adjunct (10 women). Expenses: Contact institution. *Financial support:* Institutionally sponsored loans and scholarships/grants available. Financial award applicants required to submit FAFSA. In 2006, 13 degrees awarded. *Degree program information:* Evening/weekend programs available. Offers information systems (MIS); technology management (MBA). *Application deadline:* Applications are processed on a rolling basis. *Application fee:* $45. Electronic applications accepted. *Application Contact:* Chair, 702-638-7249, Fax: 702-638-8035. *Dean/Executive Director,* Dr. Adam Honea, 480-557-1659, E-mail: adam.honea@phoenix.edu.

UNIVERSITY OF PHOENIX–LITTLE ROCK CAMPUS, Little Rock, AR 72211-3500

General Information Proprietary, coed, comprehensive institution. *Enrollment:* 498 graduate, professional, and undergraduate students; 170 full-time matriculated graduate/professional students (113 women). *Enrollment by degree level:* 170 master's. *Graduate faculty:* 8 full-time (5 women), 138 part-time/adjunct (42 women). *Tuition:* Full-time $9,576. *Required fees:* $760. *Graduate housing:* On-campus housing not available. *Student services:* Campus safety program, disabled student services, writing training. *Library facilities:* University Library. *Online resources:* library catalog, web page. *Collection:* 1,759 titles, 692 serial subscriptions.

Computer facilities: Computer purchase and lease plans are available. A campuswide network can be accessed from off campus. Internet access is available. *Web address:* http://www.phoenix.edu/.

General Application Contact: Campus Information Center, 501-225-9337.

GRADUATE UNITS

John Sperling School of Business Students: 170 full-time (113 women); includes 89 minority (88 African Americans, 1 Asian American or Pacific Islander). Average age 35. *Faculty:* 8 full-time (5 women), 122 part-time/adjunct (34 women). Expenses: Contact institution. *Financial support:* Institutionally sponsored loans and scholarships/grants available. Financial award applicants required to submit FAFSA. In 2006, 32 degrees awarded. *Degree program information:* Evening/weekend programs available. Offers business (MBA, MM). *Application deadline:* Applications are processed on a rolling basis. *Application fee:* $45. Electronic applications accepted. *Application Contact:* Chair, 501-225-9337. *Provost,* Dr. Adam Honea, 480-557-1659, E-mail: adam.honea@phoenix.edu.

College of Graduate Business and Management Students: 170 full-time (113 women); includes 89 minority (88 African Americans, 1 Asian American or Pacific Islander). Average age 33. *Faculty:* 6 full-time (3 women), 85 part-time/adjunct (23 women). Expenses: Contact institution. *Financial support:* Institutionally sponsored loans and scholarships/grants available. Financial award applicants required to submit FAFSA. In 2006, 32 degrees awarded. *Degree program information:* Evening/weekend programs available. Offers business and management (MBA, MM). *Application deadline:* Applications are processed on a rolling basis. *Application fee:* $45. Electronic applications accepted. *Application Contact:* Campus College Chair, 501-225-9337. *Associate Vice President/Dean/Executive Director,* Dr. Brian Lindquist, 480-557-1221, E-mail: brian.lindquist@phoenix.edu.

UNIVERSITY OF PHOENIX–LOUISIANA CAMPUS, Metairie, LA 70001-2082

General Information Proprietary, coed, comprehensive institution. *Enrollment:* 481 full-time matriculated graduate/professional students (367 women). *Enrollment by degree level:* 481 master's. *Graduate faculty:* 25 full-time (12 women), 240 part-time/adjunct (99 women). *Tuition:* Full-time $11,832. *Required fees:* $760. *Graduate housing:* On-campus housing not available. *Student services:* Campus safety program. *Library facilities:* University Library. *Online resources:* library catalog, web page. *Collection:* 444 titles, 666 serial subscriptions.

Computer facilities: A campuswide network can be accessed from off campus. Internet access is available. *Web address:* http://www.phoenix.edu/.

General Application Contact: Campus Information Center, 504-461-8852, Fax: 504-464-6373.

GRADUATE UNITS

The Artemis School Students: 29 full-time (23 women); includes 14 minority (13 African Americans, 1 Asian American or Pacific Islander), 2 international. Average age 34. *Faculty:* 2 full-time (both women), 61 part-time/adjunct (39 women). Expenses: Contact institution. *Financial support:* Institutionally sponsored loans and scholarships/grants available. Financial award applicants required to submit FAFSA. In 2006, 17 degrees awarded. *Degree program information:* Evening/weekend programs available. Offers early childhood education (MA Ed). *Application deadline:* Applications are processed on a rolling basis. *Application fee:* $45. Electronic applications accepted. *Application Contact:* Campus College Chair, 504-461-8852, Fax: 504-464-0373. *Provost,* Dr. Adam Honea, 480-557-1659, E-mail: adam.honea@phoenix.edu.

College of Health and Human Services Students: 29 full-time (23 women); includes 14 minority (13 African Americans, 1 Asian American or Pacific Islander), 2 international. Average age 34. *Faculty:* 2 full-time (both women), 52 part-time/adjunct (32 women). Expenses: Contact institution. *Financial support:* Institutionally sponsored loans and scholarships/grants available. Financial award applicants required to submit FAFSA. In 2006, 17 degrees awarded. *Degree program information:* Evening/weekend programs available. Offers administration of justice and security (MS); health care management (MBA); nursing (MSN); psychology (MS). *Application deadline:* Applications are processed on a rolling basis. *Application fee:* $45. Electronic applications accepted. *Application Contact:* Chair, 504-461-8852, Fax: 504-464-6373. *Dean/Executive Director,* Dr. Gil Linne, 480-557-1751, E-mail: gil.linne@phoenix.edu.

John Sperling School of Business Students: 482 full-time (344 women); includes 239 minority (231 African Americans, 6 Asian Americans or Pacific Islanders, 2 Hispanic Americans), 42 international. Average age 35. *Faculty:* 23 full-time (10 women), 179 part-time/adjunct (60 women). Expenses: Contact institution. *Financial support:* Institutionally sponsored loans and scholarships/grants available. Financial award applicants required to submit FAFSA. In 2006, 132 degrees awarded. *Degree program information:* Evening/weekend programs available. Offers business (MBA, MIS, MM). *Application deadline:* Applications are processed on a rolling basis. *Application fee:* $45. Electronic applications accepted. *Application Contact:* Campus College Chair, 504-461-8852, Fax: 504-464-6373. *Provost,* Dr. Adam Honea, 480-557-1659, E-mail: adam.honea@phoenix.edu.

College of Graduate Business and Management Students: 445 full-time (325 women); includes 225 minority (218 African Americans, 6 Asian Americans or Pacific Islanders, 1 Hispanic American), 38 international. Average age 35. *Faculty:* 14 full-time (6 women), 123 part-time/adjunct (40 women). Expenses: Contact institution. *Financial support:* Institutionally sponsored loans and scholarships/grants available. Financial award applicants required to submit FAFSA. In 2006, 126 degrees awarded. *Degree program information:* Evening/weekend programs available. Offers business administration (MBA); human resource management (MBA, MM); public administration (MBA). *Application deadline:* Applications are processed on a rolling basis. *Application fee:* $45. Electronic applications accepted. *Application Contact:* Chair, 504-461-8852, Fax: 504-464-6373. *Associate Vice President and Dean/Executive Director,* Dr. Brian Lindquist, 480-557-1221, E-mail: brian.linguist@phoenix.edu.

College of Information Systems and Technology Students: 37 full-time (19 women); includes 14 minority (13 African Americans, 1 Asian American or Pacific Islander), 4 international. Average age 33. *Faculty:* 9 full-time (4 women), 56 part-time/adjunct (20 women). Expenses: Contact institution. *Financial support:* Institutionally sponsored loans and scholarships/grants available. In 2006, 6 degrees awarded. *Degree program information:* Evening/weekend programs available. Offers information systems/management (MIS); technology management (MBA). *Application deadline:* Applications are processed on a rolling basis. *Application fee:* $45. Electronic applications accepted. *Application Contact:* Campus College Chair, 504-461-8852, Fax: 504-464-6373. *Dean,* Dr. Adam Honea, 480-557-1659, E-mail: adam.honea@phoenix.edu.

UNIVERSITY OF PHOENIX–MARYLAND CAMPUS, Columbia, MD 21045-5424

General Information Proprietary, coed, comprehensive institution. *Enrollment:* 1,823 graduate, professional, and undergraduate students; 389 full-time matriculated graduate/professional students (241 women). *Enrollment by degree level:* 389 master's. *Graduate faculty:* 34 full-time (11 women), 203 part-time/adjunct (50 women). *Tuition:* Full-time $13,200. *Required fees:* $760. *Graduate housing:* On-campus housing not available. *Student services:* Campus safety program, disabled student services, writing training. *Library facilities:* University Library. *Online resources:* library catalog, web page. *Collection:* 1,759 titles, 692 serial subscriptions.

Computer facilities: A campuswide network can be accessed from off campus. Internet access is available. *Web address:* http://www.phoenix.edu/.

General Application Contact: Campus Information Center, 410-872-9001, Fax: 410-536-5727.

GRADUATE UNITS

College of Health and Human Services Students: 1 (woman) full-time; minority (African American) Average age 27. *Faculty:* 8 part-time/adjunct (7 women). Expenses: Contact institution. *Financial support:* Institutionally sponsored loans and scholarships/grants available. Financial award applicants required to submit FAFSA. *Degree program information:* Evening/weekend programs available. Offers administration of justice and security (MS); nursing (MSN); nursing education (MSN); psychology (MS). *Application deadline:* Applications are processed on a rolling basis. *Application fee:* $45. Electronic applications accepted. *Application Contact:* Campus Chair, 410-872-9001. *Dean/Executive Director,* Dr. Gil Linne, 480-557-1751, E-mail: gil.line@phoenix.com.

John Sperling School of Business Students: 388 full-time (240 women); includes 159 minority (139 African Americans, 2 American Indian/Alaska Native, 9 Asian Americans or Pacific Islanders, 9 Hispanic Americans), 45 international. Average age 37. *Faculty:* 33 full-time (11 women), 190 part-time/adjunct (42 women). Expenses: Contact institution. *Financial support:* Institutionally sponsored loans and scholarships/grants available. Financial award applicants required to submit FAFSA. In 2006, 151 degrees awarded. *Degree program information:* Evening/weekend programs available. Offers business (MBA, MIS, MM). *Application deadline:* Applications are processed on a rolling basis. *Application fee:* $45. Electronic applications accepted. *Provost,* Dr. Adam Honea, 480-557-1659, E-mail: adam.honea@phoenix.edu.

College of Graduate Business and Management Students: 357 full-time (223 women); includes 148 minority (128 African Americans, 2 American Indian/Alaska Native, 9 Asian Americans or Pacific Islanders, 9 Hispanic Americans), 38 international. Average age 37. *Faculty:* 22 full-time (6 women), 136 part-time/adjunct (35 women). Expenses: Contact institution. *Financial support:* Institutionally sponsored loans and scholarships/grants available. Financial award applicants required to submit FAFSA. In 2006, 111 master's awarded. *Degree program information:* Evening/weekend programs available. Offers business administration (MBA); e-business (MBA); global management (MBA); human resources management (MBA, MM); marketing (MBA); public administration (MBA, MM). *Application deadline:* Applications are processed on a rolling basis. *Application fee:* $45. Electronic applications accepted. *Application Contact:* Chair, 410-872-9001, Fax: 410-536-5727. *Associate Vice President and Dean/Executive Director,* Dr. Brian Lindquist, 480-557-1221, E-mail: brian.lindquist@phoenix.edu.

College of Information Systems and Technology Students: 31 full-time (17 women); includes 11 minority (all African Americans), 7 international. Average age 39. *Faculty:* 11 full-time (5 women), 54 part-time/adjunct (7 women). Expenses: Contact institution. *Financial support:* Institutionally sponsored loans and scholarships/grants available. Financial award applicants required to submit FAFSA. In 2006, 40 degrees awarded. *Degree program information:* Evening/weekend programs available. Offers information systems (MIS); technology management (MBA). *Application deadline:* Applications are processed on a rolling basis. *Application fee:* $45. Electronic applications accepted. *Application Contact:* Chair, 410-872-9001, Fax: 410-536-5727. *Dean/Executive Director,* Dr. Adam Honea, 480-537-1659, E-mail: adam.honea@phoenix.edu.

UNIVERSITY OF PHOENIX–METRO DETROIT CAMPUS, Troy, MI 48098-2623

General Information Proprietary, coed, comprehensive institution. *Enrollment:* 3,918 graduate, professional, and undergraduate students; 969 full-time matriculated graduate/professional students (679 women). *Enrollment by degree level:* 969 master's. *Graduate faculty:* 75 full-time (26 women), 438 part-time/adjunct (153 women). *Tuition:* Full-time $12,168. *Required fees:* $760. *Graduate housing:* On-campus housing not available. *Student services:* Campus safety program, disabled student services, writing training. *Library facilities:* University Library. *Online resources:* library catalog, web page. *Collection:* 1,759 titles, 692 serial subscriptions.

Computer facilities: A campuswide network can be accessed from off campus. Internet access is available. *Web address:* http://www.phoenix.edu/.

General Application Contact: Campus Information Center, 800-834-2438, Fax: 248-267-0147.

GRADUATE UNITS

The Artemis School Students: 313 full-time (265 women); includes 154 minority (149 African Americans, 1 American Indian/Alaska Native, 3 Asian Americans or Pacific Islanders, 1 Hispanic American), 6 international. Average age 40. *Faculty:* 21 full-time (11 women), 110 part-time/adjunct (71 women). Expenses: Contact institution. *Financial support:* Institutionally sponsored loans and scholarships/grants available. Financial award applicants required to submit FAFSA. In 2006, 81 master's awarded. *Degree program information:* Evening/weekend programs available. *Application deadline:* Applications are processed on a rolling basis. *Application fee:* $45. Electronic applications accepted. *Application Contact:* Campus College Chair, 800-834-2438, Fax: 208-267-0147. *Provost,* Dr. Adam Honea, 480-557-1659, E-mail: adam.honea@phoenix.edu.

College of Education Students: 102 full-time (75 women); includes 59 minority (57 African Americans, 1 American Indian/Alaska Native, 1 Asian American or Pacific Islander), 1 international. Average age 40. *Faculty:* 8 full-time (3 women), 27 part-time/adjunct (21 women). Expenses: Contact institution. *Financial support:* Institutionally sponsored loans and scholarships/grants available. Financial award applicants required to submit FAFSA. In 2006, 30 master's awarded. *Degree program information:* Evening/weekend programs available. Offers administration and supervision (MA Ed); adult education and distance learning (MA Ed); curriculum and development (MA Ed); special education (MA Ed); teacher education elementary (MA Ed). *Application deadline:* Applications are processed on a rolling basis. *Application fee:* $45. Electronic applications accepted. *Application Contact:* Chair, 800-834-2438, Fax: 248-267-0147. *Dean/Executive Director,* Dr. Marla LaRue, 480-557-1218.

College of Health and Human Services Students: 211 full-time (190 women); includes 95 minority (92 African Americans, 2 Asian Americans or Pacific Islanders, 1 Hispanic American), 5 international. Average age 40. *Faculty:* 13 full-time (8 women), 83 part-time/adjunct (50 women). Expenses: Contact institution. *Financial support:* Institutionally sponsored loans and scholarships/grants available. Financial award applicants required to submit FAFSA. In 2006, 57 master's awarded. *Degree program information:* Evening/weekend programs available. Offers health care management (MBA); nursing (MSN). *Application deadline:* Applications are processed on a rolling basis. *Application fee:* $45. Electronic applications accepted. *Application Contact:* Chair, 800-834-2438, Fax: 248-267-0147. *Dean/Executive Director,* Dr. Gil Linne, 480-557-1751, E-mail: gil.linne@phoenix.edu.

John Sperling School of Business Students: 656 full-time (414 women); includes 286 minority (271 African Americans, 3 American Indian/Alaska Native, 9 Asian Americans or Pacific Islanders, 3 Hispanic Americans), 26 international. Average age 39. *Faculty:* 52 full-time (14 women), 321 part-time/adjunct (79 women). Expenses: Contact institution. *Financial support:* Institutionally sponsored loans and scholarships/grants available. Financial award applicants required to submit FAFSA. In 2006, 248 master's awarded. *Degree program information:* Evening/weekend programs available. Offers business (MBA, MIS). *Application deadline:* Applications are processed on a rolling basis. *Application fee:* $45. Electronic applications accepted. *Application Contact:* Campus College Chair, 800-834-2438, Fax: 248-267-0147. *Provost,* Dr. Adam Honea, 480-557-1659, E-mail: adam.honea@phoenix.edu.

College of Graduate Business and Management Students: 607 full-time (394 women); includes 267 minority (254 African Americans, 3 American Indian/Alaska Native, 7 Asian

University of Phoenix–Metro Detroit Campus (continued)

Americans or Pacific Islanders, 3 Hispanic Americans), 19 international. Average age 39. *Faculty:* 32 full-time (9 women), 223 part-time/adjunct (61 women). Expenses: Contact institution. *Financial support:* Institutionally sponsored loans and scholarships/grants available. Financial award applicants required to submit FAFSA. In 2006, 216 master's awarded. *Degree program information:* Evening/weekend programs available. Offers business administration (MBA); global management (MBA). *Application deadline:* Applications are processed on a rolling basis. *Application fee:* $45. Electronic applications accepted. *Application Contact:* Chair, 800-834-2438, Fax: 248-267-0147. *Associate Vice President and Dean/Executive Director,* Dr. Brian Lindquist, 480-557-1221, E-mail: brian.lindquist@phoenix.edu.

College of Information Systems and Technology Students: 49 full-time (20 women); includes 19 minority (17 African Americans, 2 Asian Americans or Pacific Islanders), 7 international. Average age 38. *Faculty:* 20 full-time (5 women), 98 part-time/adjunct (18 women). Expenses: Contact institution. *Financial support:* Institutionally sponsored loans and scholarships/grants available. Financial award applicants required to submit FAFSA. In 2006, 32 degrees awarded. *Degree program information:* Evening/weekend programs available. Offers management (MIS); technology management (MBA). *Application deadline:* Applications are processed on a rolling basis. *Application fee:* $45. Electronic applications accepted. *Application Contact:* Chair, 800-834-2438, Fax: 248-267-0147. *Dean/Executive Director,* Dr. Adam Honea, 480-557-1659, E-mail: adam.honea@phoenix.edu.

UNIVERSITY OF PHOENIX–NASHVILLE CAMPUS, Nashville, TN 37214-5048

General Information Proprietary, coed, comprehensive institution. *Enrollment:* 1,290 graduate, professional, and undergraduate students; 332 full-time matriculated graduate/professional students (198 women). *Enrollment by degree level:* 332 master's. *Graduate faculty:* 50 full-time (5 women), 109 part-time/adjunct (34 women). *Tuition:* Full-time $10,104. *Required fees:* $760. *Graduate housing:* On-campus housing not available. *Student services:* Campus safety program, disabled student services, writing training. *Library facilities:* University Library. *Online resources:* library catalog, web page. *Collection:* 1,759 titles, 692 serial subscriptions.

Computer facilities: A campuswide network can be accessed from off campus. Internet access is available. *Web address:* http://www.phoenix.edu/.

General Application Contact: Campus Information Center, 615-872-3390.

GRADUATE UNITS

The Artemis School Students: 52 full-time (37 women); includes 21 minority (19 African Americans, 1 American Indian/Alaska Native, 1 Asian American or Pacific Islander), 1 international. Average age 38. *Faculty:* 5 full-time (2 women), 19 part-time/adjunct (8 women). Expenses: Contact institution. *Financial support:* Institutionally sponsored loans and scholarships/grants available. Financial award applicants required to submit FAFSA. In 2006, 37 degrees awarded. *Degree program information:* Evening/weekend programs available. Offers administration and supervision (MA Ed); curriculum and instruction (MA Ed); elementary teacher education (MA Ed); secondary teacher education (MA Ed). *Application deadline:* Applications are processed on a rolling basis. *Application fee:* $45. Electronic applications accepted. *Provost,* Dr. Adam Honea, 480-557-1659, E-mail: adam.honea@phoenix.edu.

College of Health and Human Services Students: 52 full-time (37 women); includes 21 minority (19 African Americans, 1 American Indian/Alaska Native, 1 Asian American or Pacific Islander), 1 international. Average age 38. *Faculty:* 3 full-time (0 women), 18 part-time/adjunct (7 women). Expenses: Contact institution. *Financial support:* Institutionally sponsored loans and scholarships/grants available. Financial award applicants required to submit FAFSA. In 2006, 37 degrees awarded. *Degree program information:* Evening/weekend programs available. Offers health administration (MHA); health care management (MBA). *Application deadline:* Applications are processed on a rolling basis. *Application fee:* $45. Electronic applications accepted. *Application Contact:* Chair, 615-872-0188. *Dean/Executive Director,* Dr. Gil Linne, 480-559-1751, E-mail: gil.linne@phoenix.edu.

John Sperling School of Business Students: 280 full-time (161 women); includes 109 minority (103 African Americans, 1 American Indian/Alaska Native, 1 Asian American or Pacific Islander, 4 Hispanic Americans), 8 international. Average age 36. *Faculty:* 44 full-time (2 women), 89 part-time/adjunct (25 women). Expenses: Contact institution. *Financial support:* Institutionally sponsored loans and scholarships/grants available. Financial award applicants required to submit FAFSA. In 2006, 71 degrees awarded. *Degree program information:* Evening/weekend programs available. Offers business (MBA, MM). *Application deadline:* Applications are processed on a rolling basis. *Application fee:* $45. Electronic applications accepted. *Provost,* Dr. Adam Honea, 480-557-1659, E-mail: adam.honea@phoenix.edu.

College of Graduate Business and Management Students: 246 full-time (145 women); includes 95 minority (90 African Americans, 1 American Indian/Alaska Native, 1 Asian American or Pacific Islander, 3 Hispanic Americans), 7 international. Average age 36. *Faculty:* 29 full-time (2 women), 66 part-time/adjunct (20 women). Expenses: Contact institution. *Financial support:* Institutionally sponsored loans and scholarships/grants available. Financial award applicants required to submit FAFSA. In 2006, 61 degrees awarded. *Degree program information:* Evening/weekend programs available. Offers business administration (MBA); human resource management (MBA); management (MM). *Application deadline:* Applications are processed on a rolling basis. *Application fee:* $45. Electronic applications accepted. *Application Contact:* Chair, 615-872-0188. *Associate Vice President and Dean/Executive Director,* Dr. Brian Lindquist, 480-557-1221.

College of Information Systems and Technology Students: 34 full-time (16 women); includes 14 minority (13 African Americans, 1 Hispanic American), 1 international. Average age 34. *Faculty:* 15 full-time (0 women), 23 part-time/adjunct (5 women). Expenses: Contact institution. *Financial support:* Institutionally sponsored loans and scholarships/grants available. Financial award applicants required to submit FAFSA. In 2006, 10 degrees awarded. *Degree program information:* Evening/weekend programs available. Offers technology management (MBA). *Application deadline:* Applications are processed on a rolling basis. *Application fee:* $45. Electronic applications accepted. *Application Contact:* Chair, 615-872-0188. *Dean/Executive Director,* Dr. Adam Honea, 480-557-1659, E-mail: adam.honea@phoenix.edu.

UNIVERSITY OF PHOENIX–NEW MEXICO CAMPUS, Albuquerque, NM 87109-4645

General Information Proprietary, coed, comprehensive institution. *Enrollment:* 4,586 graduate, professional, and undergraduate students; 1,047 full-time matriculated graduate/professional students (669 women). *Enrollment by degree level:* 1,047 master's. *Graduate faculty:* 60 full-time (28 women), 621 part-time/adjunct (208 women). *Tuition:* Full-time $9,005. *Required fees:* $760. *Graduate housing:* On-campus housing not available. *Student services:* Campus safety program, disabled student services, writing training. *Library facilities:* University Library. *Online resources:* library catalog, web page. *Collection:* 1,759 titles, 692 serial subscriptions.

Computer facilities: A campuswide network can be accessed from off campus. Internet access is available. *Web address:* http://www.phoenix.edu/.

General Application Contact: Campus Information Center, 505-821-4800, Fax: 505-821-5551.

GRADUATE UNITS

The Artemis School Students: 520 full-time (388 women); includes 230 minority (16 African Americans, 5 American Indian/Alaska Native, 8 Asian Americans or Pacific Islanders, 201 Hispanic Americans), 36 international. Average age 39. *Faculty:* 28 full-time (20 women), 197 part-time/adjunct (115 women). Expenses: Contact institution. *Financial support:* Institutionally sponsored loans and scholarships/grants available. Financial award applicants required to submit FAFSA. In 2006, 171 degrees awarded. *Degree program information:* Evening/weekend programs available. *Application deadline:* Applications are processed on a rolling basis. *Application fee:* $45. Electronic applications accepted. *Provost,* Dr. Adam Honea, 480-557-1659, E-mail: adam.honea@phoenix.edu.

College of Education Students: 234 full-time (181 women); includes 116 minority (5 African Americans, 1 Asian American or Pacific Islander, 110 Hispanic Americans), 10 international. Average age 39. *Faculty:* 9 full-time (5 women), 62 part-time/adjunct (40 women). Expenses: Contact institution. *Financial support:* Institutionally sponsored loans and scholarships/grants available. Financial award applicants required to submit FAFSA. In 2006, 131 degrees awarded. *Degree program information:* Evening/weekend programs available. Offers administration (MAEd); curriculum and instruction (MAEd); teacher education (MAEd). *Application deadline:* Applications are processed on a rolling basis. *Application fee:* $45. Electronic applications accepted. *Application Contact:* Chair, 505-821-4800, Fax: 505-821-5551. *Dean/Executive Director,* Dr. Marla LaRue, 480-557-1218, E-mail: marla.larue@phoenix.edu.

College of Health and Human Services Students: 217 full-time (156 women); includes 93 minority (9 African Americans, 4 American Indian/Alaska Native, 4 Asian Americans or Pacific Islanders, 76 Hispanic Americans), 17 international. Average age 39. *Faculty:* 19 full-time (12 women), 135 part-time/adjunct (75 women). Expenses: Contact institution. *Financial support:* Institutionally sponsored loans and scholarships/grants available. Financial award applicants required to submit FAFSA. In 2006, 40 degrees awarded. *Degree program information:* Evening/weekend programs available. Offers health care management (MBA); marriage and family therapy (MSC). *Application deadline:* Applications are processed on a rolling basis. *Application fee:* $45. Electronic applications accepted. *Application Contact:* Campus College Chair-Nursing, 505-821-4800, Fax: 505-821-5551. *Dean/Executive Director,* Dr. Gil Linne, 480-557-1751, E-mail: gil.linne@phoenix.edu.

John Sperling School of Business Students: 527 full-time (281 women); includes 244 minority (12 African Americans, 9 American Indian/Alaska Native, 8 Asian Americans or Pacific Islanders, 215 Hispanic Americans), 21 international. Average age 37. *Faculty:* 32 full-time (8 women), 420 part-time/adjunct (91 women). Expenses: Contact institution. *Financial support:* Institutionally sponsored loans and scholarships/grants available. Financial award applicants required to submit FAFSA. In 2006, 165 degrees awarded. *Degree program information:* Evening/weekend programs available. Offers business (MBA). *Application deadline:* Applications are processed on a rolling basis. *Application fee:* $45. Electronic applications accepted. *Provost,* Dr. Adam Honea, 480-557-1659, E-mail: adam.honea@phoenix.edu.

College of Graduate Business and Management Students: 507 full-time (273 women); includes 235 minority (12 African Americans, 9 American Indian/Alaska Native, 7 Asian Americans or Pacific Islanders, 207 Hispanic Americans), 21 international. Average age 37. *Faculty:* 25 full-time (6 women), 305 part-time/adjunct (77 women). Expenses: Contact institution. *Financial support:* Institutionally sponsored loans and scholarships/grants available. Financial award applicants required to submit FAFSA. In 2006, 129 degrees awarded. *Degree program information:* Evening/weekend programs available. Offers business administration (MBA); global management (MBA); human resource management (MBA). *Application deadline:* Applications are processed on a rolling basis. *Application fee:* $45. Electronic applications accepted. *Application Contact:* Graduate Business Chair, 505-821-4800, Fax: 505-821-5551. *Associate Vice President and Dean/Executive Director,* Dr. Brian Lindquist, 480-557-1221, E-mail: brian.lindquist@phoenix.edu.

College of Information Systems and Technology Students: 20 full-time (8 women); includes 9 minority (1 Asian American or Pacific Islander, 8 Hispanic Americans). Average age 37. *Faculty:* 7 full-time (2 women), 115 part-time/adjunct (14 women). Expenses: Contact institution. *Financial support:* Institutionally sponsored loans and scholarships/grants available. Financial award applicants required to submit FAFSA. In 2006, 36 degrees awarded. *Degree program information:* Evening/weekend programs available. Offers e-business (MBA); technology management (MBA). *Application deadline:* Applications are processed on a rolling basis. *Application fee:* $45. Electronic applications accepted. *Application Contact:* Chair, 505-821-4800, Fax: 505-821-5551. *Dean/Executive Director,* Dr. Adam Honea, 480-557-1659, E-mail: adam.honea@phoenix.edu.

UNIVERSITY OF PHOENIX–NORTHERN VIRGINIA CAMPUS, Reston, VA 20190

General Information Proprietary, coed, comprehensive institution.

GRADUATE UNITS

College of Education Offers administration and supervision (MA Ed).

College of Graduate Business and Management Offers accounting (MBA); business administration (MBA); e-business (MBA); global management (MBA); human resources management (MBA, MM); management (MM); marketing (MBA); public administration (MBA).

College of Health and Human Services Offers health administration (MHA); health care management (MBA); nursing (MSN).

College of Information Systems and Technology Offers information systems and technology (MIS); management (MIS); technology management (MBA).

College of Social and Behavioral Science Offers administration of justice and security (MS).

UNIVERSITY OF PHOENIX–NORTH FLORIDA CAMPUS, Jacksonville, FL 32216-0959

General Information Proprietary, coed, comprehensive institution. *Enrollment:* 2,211 graduate, professional, and undergraduate students; 579 full-time matriculated graduate/professional students (370 women). *Enrollment by degree level:* 579 master's. *Graduate faculty:* 84 full-time (35 women), 228 part-time/adjunct (79 women). *Graduate housing:* On-campus housing not available. *Student services:* Campus safety program, disabled student services, writing training. *Library facilities:* University Library. *Online resources:* library catalog, web page. *Collection:* 1,759 titles, 692 serial subscriptions.

Computer facilities: A campuswide network can be accessed from off campus. Internet access is available. *Web address:* http://www.phoenix.edu/.

General Application Contact: Campus Information Center, 904-636-6645, Fax: 904-636-0998.

GRADUATE UNITS

The Artemis School Students: 167 full-time (130 women); includes 74 minority (63 African Americans, 5 Asian Americans or Pacific Islanders, 6 Hispanic Americans), 8 international. Average age 39. *Faculty:* 22 full-time (15 women), 68 part-time/adjunct (46 women). Expenses: Contact institution. *Financial support:* Institutionally sponsored loans and scholarships/grants available. Financial award applicants required to submit FAFSA. In 2006, 37 master's awarded. *Degree program information:* Evening/weekend programs available. *Application deadline:* Applications are processed on a rolling basis. *Application fee:* $45. Electronic applications accepted. *Provost,* Dr. Adam Honea, 480-557-1659, E-mail: adam.honea@phoenix.edu.

College of Education Students: 98 full-time (78 women); includes 41 minority (37 African Americans, 4 Hispanic Americans), 1 international. Average age 37. *Faculty:* 9 full-time (5 women), 10 part-time/adjunct (4 women). Expenses: Contact institution. *Financial support:* Institutionally sponsored loans and scholarships/grants available. Financial award applicants required to submit FAFSA. In 2006, 22 master's awarded. *Degree program information:* Evening/weekend programs available. Offers administration (MA Ed); curriculum and instruction (MA Ed); curriculum and instruction—computer education (MA Ed); elementary teacher education (MA Ed); secondary teacher education (MA Ed). *Application deadline:* Applications are processed on a rolling basis. *Application fee:* $45. Electronic applications accepted. *Application Contact:* Chair, 904-636-6645, Fax: 904-636-0998. *Dean,* Dr. Marla LaRue, 480-557-1218, E-mail: marla.larue@phoenix.edu.

College of Health and Human Services Students: 69 full-time (52 women); includes 33 minority (26 African Americans, 5 Asian Americans or Pacific Islanders, 2 Hispanic Americans), 7 international. Average age 41. *Faculty:* 13 full-time (10 women), 58 part-time/adjunct (42 women). Expenses: Contact institution. *Financial support:* Institutionally sponsored loans and scholarships/grants available. Financial award applicants required to submit FAFSA.

In 2006, 15 master's awarded. *Degree program information:* Evening/weekend programs available. Offers health administration (MHA); health care education (MSN); health care management (MBA); nursing (MSN). *Application deadline:* Applications are processed on a rolling basis. *Application fee:* $45. Electronic applications accepted. *Application Contact:* Chair, 904-636-6645, Fax: 904-636-0998. *Dean,* Dr. Gil Linne, 480-557-1751, E-mail: gil.linne@phoenix.edu.

John Sperling School of Business Students: 412 full-time (240 women); includes 139 minority (120 African Americans, 1 American Indian/Alaska Native, 13 Asian Americans or Pacific Islanders, 5 Hispanic Americans), 23 international. Average age 38. *Faculty:* 60 full-time (20 women), 155 part-time/adjunct (31 women). Expenses: Contact institution. *Financial support:* Institutionally sponsored loans and scholarships/grants available. In 2006, 138 master's awarded. *Degree program information:* Evening/weekend programs available. Offers business (MBA, MIS, MM). *Application deadline:* Applications are processed on a rolling basis. *Application fee:* $45. Electronic applications accepted. *Provost,* Dr. Adam Honea, 480-557-1659, E-mail: adam.honea@phoenix.edu.

College of Graduate Business and Management Students: 392 full-time (237 women); includes 135 minority (117 African Americans, 1 American Indian/Alaska Native, 12 Asian Americans or Pacific Islanders, 5 Hispanic Americans), 20 international. Average age 31. *Faculty:* 40 full-time (15 women), 105 part-time/adjunct (25 women). Expenses: Contact institution. *Financial support:* Institutionally sponsored loans available. Financial award applicants required to submit FAFSA. In 2006, 134 degrees awarded. *Degree program information:* Evening/weekend programs available. Offers accounting (MBA); business administration (MBA); global management (MBA); human resources management (MBA, MM); management (MM); marketing (MBA); public administration (MBA). *Application deadline:* Applications are processed on a rolling basis. *Application fee:* $45. Electronic applications accepted. *Application Contact:* Chair, 904-636-6645, Fax: 904-636-0998. *Associate Vice President and Dean/Executive Director,* Dr. Brian Lindquist, 480-557-1221, E-mail: brian.lindquist@phoenix.edu.

College of Information Systems and Technology Students: 20 full-time (3 women); includes 4 minority (3 African Americans, 1 Asian American or Pacific Islander), 3 international. Average age 36. *Faculty:* 20 full-time (5 women), 50 part-time/adjunct (6 women). Expenses: Contact institution. *Financial support:* Institutionally sponsored loans and scholarships/grants available. Financial award applicants required to submit FAFSA. In 2006, 4 master's awarded. *Degree program information:* Evening/weekend programs available. Offers information systems (MIS); management (MIS). *Application deadline:* Applications are processed on a rolling basis. *Application fee:* $45. Electronic applications accepted. *Application Contact:* Chair, 904-636-6645, Fax: 904-636-0998. *Dean,* Dr. Adam Honea, 480-557-1659, E-mail: adam.honea@phoenix.edu.

UNIVERSITY OF PHOENIX–OKLAHOMA CITY CAMPUS, Oklahoma City, OK 73116-8244

General Information Proprietary, coed, comprehensive institution. *Enrollment:* 1,080 graduate, professional, and undergraduate students; 159 full-time matriculated graduate/professional students (98 women). *Enrollment by degree level:* 159 master's. *Graduate faculty:* 23 full-time (7 women), 238 part-time/adjunct (61 women). *Tuition:* Full-time $10,608. *Required fees:* $760. *Graduate housing:* On-campus housing not available. *Student services:* Campus safety program, disabled student services, writing training. *Library facilities:* University Library. *Online resources:* library catalog, web page. *Collection:* 1,759 titles, 692 serial subscriptions.

Computer facilities: A campuswide network can be accessed from off campus. Internet access is available. *Web address:* http://www.phoenix.edu/.

General Application Contact: Campus Information Center, 405-842-8007, Fax: 405-841-3386.

GRADUATE UNITS

John Sperling School of Business Students: 152 full-time (92 women); includes 46 minority (32 African Americans, 3 American Indian/Alaska Native, 4 Asian Americans or Pacific Islanders, 7 Hispanic Americans), 12 international. Average age 37. *Faculty:* 14 full-time (0 women), 184 part-time/adjunct (39 women). Expenses: Contact institution. *Financial support:* Institutionally sponsored loans and scholarships/grants available. Financial award applicants required to submit FAFSA. In 2006, 57 degrees awarded. *Degree program information:* Evening/weekend programs available. Offers business (MBA). *Application deadline:* Applications are processed on a rolling basis. *Application fee:* $45. Electronic applications accepted. *Provost/Dean,* Dr. Adam Honea, 480-557-1659, E-mail: adam.honea@phoenix.edu.

College of Graduate Business and Management Students: 150 full-time (92 women); includes 45 minority (32 African Americans, 3 American Indian/Alaska Native, 4 Asian Americans or Pacific Islanders, 6 Hispanic Americans), 12 international. Average age 37. *Faculty:* 10 full-time (0 women), 135 part-time/adjunct (33 women). Expenses: Contact institution. *Financial support:* Institutionally sponsored loans and scholarships/grants available. Financial award applicants required to submit FAFSA. In 2006, 41 degrees awarded. *Degree program information:* Evening/weekend programs available. Offers business administration (MBA); business and management (MM); human resource management (MBA). *Application deadline:* Applications are processed on a rolling basis. *Application fee:* $45. Electronic applications accepted. *Application Contact:* Chair, 405-842-8007, Fax: 405-841-3386. *Associate Vice President and Dean/Executive Director,* Dr. Brian Lindquist, 480-557-1221, E-mail: brian.lindquist@phoenix.edu.

College of Information Systems and Technology Students: 2 full-time (0 women); both minorities (both American Indian/Alaska Native). Average age 39. *Faculty:* 4 full-time (0 women), 49 part-time/adjunct (6 women). Expenses: Contact institution. *Financial support:* Institutionally sponsored loans and scholarships/grants available. Financial award applicants required to submit FAFSA. In 2006, 10 degrees awarded. *Degree program information:* Evening/weekend programs available. Offers e-business (MBA); technology management (MBA). *Application deadline:* Applications are processed on a rolling basis. *Application fee:* $45. Electronic applications accepted. *Application Contact:* Chair, 405-842-8007, Fax: 405-841-3386. *Provost/Dean,* Dr. Adam Honea, 480-557-1659, E-mail: adam.honea@phoenix.edu.

UNIVERSITY OF PHOENIX ONLINE CAMPUS, Phoenix, AZ 85034-7209

General Information Proprietary, coed, comprehensive institution. *Enrollment:* 160,150 graduate, professional, and undergraduate students; 46,920 full-time matriculated graduate/professional students (31,156 women). *Enrollment by degree level:* 42,362 master's, 4,544 doctoral. *Graduate faculty:* 61 full-time (37 women), 10,799 part-time/adjunct (4,201 women). *Tuition:* Full-time $12,664. *Required fees:* $760. *Graduate housing:* On-campus housing not available. *Student services:* Disabled student services, writing training. *Library facilities:* University Library. *Online resources:* library catalog, web page. *Collection:* 1,759 titles, 692 serial subscriptions.

Computer facilities: A campuswide network can be accessed from off campus. *Web address:* http://www.uopxonline.com/.

GRADUATE UNITS

The Artemis School Students: 20,133 full-time (16,312 women); includes 4,888 minority (3,511 African Americans, 130 American Indian/Alaska Native, 473 Asian Americans or Pacific Islanders, 774 Hispanic Americans), 1,755 international. Average age 38. *Faculty:* 22 full-time (14 women), 3,209 part-time/adjunct (1,998 women). Expenses: Contact institution. *Financial support:* Institutionally sponsored loans and scholarships/grants available. Financial award applicants required to submit FAFSA. *Degree program information:* Evening/weekend programs available. *Application deadline:* Applications are processed on a rolling basis. *Application fee:* $45. Electronic applications accepted. *Application Contact:* Program Chair, 602-387-7000. *Provost,* Dr. Adam Honea, 480-557-1659, E-mail: adam.honea@phoenix.edu.

College of Education Students: 11,937 full-time (9,375 women); includes 2,972 minority (2,210 African Americans, 74 American Indian/Alaska Native, 205 Asian Americans or Pacific Islanders, 483 Hispanic Americans), 906 international. Average age 36. *Faculty:* 12 full-time (5 women), 8,196 part-time/adjunct (6,937 women). Expenses: Contact institution. *Financial support:* Institutionally sponsored loans and scholarships/grants available. Financial award applicants required to submit FAFSA. *Degree program information:* Evening/weekend programs available. Postbaccalaureate distance learning degree programs offered (no on-campus study). Offers administration and supervision (MAEd); adult education and training (MAEd); curriculum and instruction-adult education (MAEd); curriculum and instruction-English and language arts education (MAEd); curriculum and instruction-mathematics education (MAEd); curriculum education (MAEd); curriculum instruction (MAEd); early childhood (MAEd); English as a second language (MAEd); teacher education elementary (MAEd); teacher education secondary (MAEd). *Application deadline:* Applications are processed on a rolling basis. *Application fee:* $45. Electronic applications accepted. *Application Contact:* Dr. Marla LaRue, Dean/Executive Director, 480-557-1218, E-mail: marla.larue@phoenix.edu. *Dean/Executive Director,* Dr. Marla LaRue, 480-557-1218, E-mail: marla.larue@phoenix.edu.

College of Health and Human Services Students: 8,196 full-time (6,937 women); includes 1,916 minority (1,301 African Americans, 56 American Indian/Alaska Native, 268 Asian Americans or Pacific Islanders, 291 Hispanic Americans), 849 international. Average age 40. *Faculty:* 10 full-time (9 women), 1,743 part-time/adjunct (1,042 women). Expenses: Contact institution. *Financial support:* Institutionally sponsored loans and scholarships/grants available. Financial award applicants required to submit FAFSA. In 2006, 6,951 master's awarded. *Degree program information:* Evening/weekend programs available. Offers administration of justice and security (MS); health care administration (MHA); health care management (MBA, MSN); nurse practitioner (MSN); nursing (MSN); nursing education (MSN); psychology (MS). *Application deadline:* Applications are processed on a rolling basis. *Application fee:* $45. Electronic applications accepted. *Application Contact:* Dr. Gil Linne, Dean/Executive Director, 480-552-1751, E-mail: gil.linne@phoenix.edu. *Dean/Executive Director,* Dr. Gil Linne, 480-552-1751, E-mail: gil.linne@phoenix.edu.

John Sperling School of Business Students: 23,972 full-time (13,078 women); includes 5,950 minority (3,811 African Americans, 132 American Indian/Alaska Native, 873 Asian Americans or Pacific Islanders, 1,134 Hispanic Americans), 2,386 international. Average age 36. *Faculty:* 32 full-time (18 women), 7,178 part-time/adjunct (2,032 women). Expenses: Contact institution. *Financial support:* Institutionally sponsored loans and scholarships/grants available. Financial award applicants required to submit FAFSA. *Degree program information:* Evening/weekend programs available. Offers business (MBA, MIS, MM). *Application deadline:* Applications are processed on a rolling basis. *Application fee:* $45. Electronic applications accepted. *Provost,* Dr. Adam Honea, 480-557-1659, E-mail: adam.honea@phoenix.edu.

College of Graduate Business and Management Students: 17,914 full-time (10,655 women); includes 4,983 minority (3,259 African Americans, 113 American Indian/Alaska Native, 651 Asian Americans or Pacific Islanders, 960 Hispanic Americans), 1,805 international. Average age 36. *Faculty:* 25 full-time (15 women), 4,861 part-time/adjunct (1,504 women). Expenses: Contact institution. *Financial support:* Institutionally sponsored loans and scholarships/grants available. Financial award applicants required to submit FAFSA. In 2006, 1,740 master's awarded. *Degree program information:* Evening/weekend programs available. Offers accounting (MBA); administration (MBA); global management (MBA); human resources management (MBA); management (MM); marketing (MBA); public administration (MBA, MM). *Application deadline:* Applications are processed on a rolling basis. *Application fee:* $45. Electronic applications accepted. *Application Contact:* Brian Lindquist, Dean/Executive Director and Associate Vice President, 480-557-1221, E-mail: brian.lindquist@phoenix.edu. *Dean/Executive Director and Associate Vice President,* Brian Lindquist, 480-557-1221, E-mail: brian.lindquist@phoenix.edu.

College of Information Systems and Technology Students: 4,315 full-time (1,423 women); includes 967 minority (552 African Americans, 19 American Indian/Alaska Native, 222 Asian Americans or Pacific Islanders, 174 Hispanic Americans), 581 international. Average age 38. *Faculty:* 7 full-time (3 women), 2,317 part-time/adjunct (528 women). Expenses: Contact institution. *Financial support:* Institutionally sponsored loans and scholarships/grants available. Financial award applicants required to submit FAFSA. In 2006, 7359 degrees awarded. *Degree program information:* Evening/weekend programs available. Offers e-business (MBA); management (MIS); technology management (MBA). *Application deadline:* Applications are processed on a rolling basis. *Application fee:* $45. Electronic applications accepted. *Application Contact:* Dr. Adam Honea, Dean/Executive Director, 480-557-1659, E-mail: adam.honea@phoenix.edu. *Dean/Executive Director,* Dr. Adam Honea, 480-557-1659, E-mail: adam.honea@phoenix.edu.

School of Advanced Studies Students: 4,544 full-time (2,756 women); includes 1,550 minority (1,136 African Americans, 32 American Indian/Alaska Native, 152 Asian Americans or Pacific Islanders, 230 Hispanic Americans), 378 international. Average age 44. *Faculty:* 36 full-time (13 women), 551 part-time/adjunct (224 women). Expenses: Contact institution. *Financial support:* Institutionally sponsored loans and scholarships/grants available. Financial award applicants required to submit FAFSA. In 2006, 210 degrees awarded. *Degree program information:* Evening/weekend programs available. Offers business administration (DBA); education (Ed D); health administration (DHA); organizational management (DM). *Application deadline:* Applications are processed on a rolling basis. *Application fee:* $45. Electronic applications accepted. *Application Contact:* Information Contact, 800-697-8223. *Dean/Executive Director,* Dr. Dawn Iwamoto, 480-557-3228, E-mail: dawn.iwamoto@phoenix.edu.

UNIVERSITY OF PHOENIX–OREGON CAMPUS, Tigard, OR 97223

General Information Proprietary, coed, comprehensive institution. *Enrollment:* 1,836 graduate, professional, and undergraduate students; 355 full-time matriculated graduate/professional students (170 women). *Enrollment by degree level:* 355 master's. *Graduate faculty:* 50 full-time (10 women), 250 part-time/adjunct (75 women). *Tuition:* Full-time $10,200. *Required fees:* $760. *Graduate housing:* On-campus housing not available. *Student services:* Campus safety program, disabled student services, writing training. *Library facilities:* University Library. *Online resources:* library catalog, web page. *Collection:* 1,759 titles, 692 serial subscriptions.

Computer facilities: A campuswide network can be accessed from off campus. Internet access is available. *Web address:* http://www.phoenix.edu/.

General Application Contact: Campus Information Center, 503-403-2900, Fax: 503-670-0614.

GRADUATE UNITS

The Artemis School Students: 92 full-time (60 women); includes 7 minority (4 African Americans, 1 American Indian/Alaska Native, 2 Hispanic Americans), 16 international. Average age 36. *Faculty:* 12 full-time (6 women), 86 part-time/adjunct (39 women). Expenses: Contact institution. *Financial support:* Institutionally sponsored loans and scholarships/grants available. Financial award applicants required to submit FAFSA. In 2006, 12 degrees awarded. *Degree program information:* Evening/weekend programs available. *Application deadline:* Applications are processed on a rolling basis. *Application fee:* $45. Electronic applications accepted. *Provost,* Dr. Adam Honea, 460-557-1659, E-mail: adam.honea@phoenix.edu.

College of Education Students: 90 full-time (59 women); includes 7 minority (4 African Americans, 1 American Indian/Alaska Native, 2 Hispanic Americans), 14 international. Average age 36. *Faculty:* 3 full-time (2 women), 33 part-time/adjunct (14 women). Expenses: Contact institution. *Financial support:* Institutionally sponsored loans and scholarships/grants available. Financial award applicants required to submit FAFSA. In 2006, 12 degrees awarded. *Degree program information:* Evening/weekend programs available. Offers early childhood and elementary education (MA Ed); secondary education (MA Ed). *Application deadline:* Applications are processed on a rolling basis. *Application fee:* $45. Electronic applications accepted. *Application Contact:* Chair, 503-403-2500, Fax: 503-670-0614. *Dean/Executive Director,* Dr. Marla LaRue, 480-557-1218, E-mail: marla.larue@phoenix.edu.

College of Health and Human Services Students: 2 full-time (1 woman), (both international). Average age 36. *Faculty:* 9 full-time (4 women), 53 part-time/adjunct (25 women). Expenses: Contact institution. *Financial support:* Institutionally sponsored loans and scholarships/grants available. *Degree program information:* Evening/weekend programs available. Offers

University of Phoenix–Oregon Campus (continued)

administration of justice and security (MS); health administration (MHA); health care management (MBA); nursing (MSN); psychology (MS). *Application deadline:* Applications are processed on a rolling basis. *Application fee:* $45. Electronic applications accepted. *Application Contact:* College Chair, 503-403-1250. *Dean/Executive Director,* Dr. Gil Linne, 480-557-1221, E-mail: gil.linne@phoenix.edu.

The John Sperling School of Business Students: 263 full-time (110 women); includes 35 minority (7 African Americans, 4 American Indian/Alaska Native, 16 Asian Americans or Pacific Islanders, 8 Hispanic Americans), 25 international. Average age 39. *Faculty:* 38 full-time (4 women), 164 part-time/adjunct (36 women). Expenses: Contact institution. *Financial support:* Institutionally sponsored loans and scholarships/grants available. Financial award applicants required to submit FAFSA. In 2006, 107 degrees awarded. *Degree program information:* Evening/weekend programs available. Offers business (MBA, MIS, MM). *Application deadline:* Applications are processed on a rolling basis. *Application fee:* $45. Electronic applications accepted. *Application Contact:* Chair, 503-403-2900, Fax: 503-670-0614. *Provost,* Dr. Adam Honea, 480-557-1659, E-mail: adam.honea@phoenix.edu.

College of Graduate Business and Management Students: 241 full-time (103 women); includes 31 minority (7 African Americans, 4 American Indian/Alaska Native, 14 Asian Americans or Pacific Islanders, 6 Hispanic Americans), 21 international. Average age 39. *Faculty:* 28 full-time (4 women), 104 part-time/adjunct (24 women). Expenses: Contact institution. *Financial support:* Institutionally sponsored loans and scholarships/grants available. Financial award applicants required to submit FAFSA. In 2006, 66 degrees awarded. *Degree program information:* Evening/weekend programs available. Offers accounting (MBA); business administration (MBA); global management (MBA); human resource management (MM); human resources management (MBA); management (MM). *Application deadline:* Applications are processed on a rolling basis. *Application fee:* $45. Electronic applications accepted. *Application Contact:* Chair, 503-403-2900, Fax: 503-670-0614. *Associate Vice President and Dean/Executive Director,* Dr. Brian Lindquist, 480-557-1221, E-mail: brian.lindquist@phoenix.edu.

College of Information Systems and Technology Students: 22 full-time (7 women); includes 2 minority (both Hispanic Americans), 4 international. Average age 41. *Faculty:* 10 full-time (0 women), 60 part-time/adjunct (12 women). Expenses: Contact institution. *Financial support:* Institutionally sponsored loans and scholarships/grants available. Financial award applicants required to submit FAFSA. In 2006, 41 degrees awarded. *Degree program information:* Evening/weekend programs available. Offers information systems (MIS); technology management (MBA). *Application deadline:* Applications are processed on a rolling basis. *Application fee:* $45. Electronic applications accepted. *Application Contact:* Chair, 503-403-2900, Fax: 503-670-0614. *Provost/Dean,* Dr. Adam Honea, 480-557-1689, E-mail: adam.honea@phoenix.edu.

UNIVERSITY OF PHOENIX–PHILADELPHIA CAMPUS, Wayne, PA 19087-2121

General Information Proprietary, coed, comprehensive institution. *Enrollment:* 1,611 graduate, professional, and undergraduate students; 340 full-time matriculated graduate/professional students (199 women). *Enrollment by degree level:* 340 master's. *Graduate faculty:* 32 full-time (4 women), 133 part-time/adjunct (26 women). *Tuition:* Full-time $13,560. *Required fees:* $760. *Graduate housing:* On-campus housing not available. *Student services:* Campus safety program, disabled student services, writing training. *Library facilities:* University Library. *Online resources:* library catalog, web page. *Collection:* 1,759 titles, 692 serial subscriptions.

Computer facilities: A campuswide network can be accessed from off campus. Internet access is available. *Web address:* http://www.phoenix.edu/.

General Application Contact: Campus Information Center, 610-989-0880, Fax: 610-989-0881.

GRADUATE UNITS

The Artemis School Students: 37 full-time (30 women); includes 20 minority (16 African Americans, 1 American Indian/Alaska Native, 2 Asian Americans or Pacific Islanders, 1 Hispanic American), 5 international. Average age 37. *Faculty:* 2 full-time (0 women), 13 part-time/adjunct (5 women). Expenses: Contact institution. *Financial support:* Institutionally sponsored loans and scholarships/grants available. In 2006, 8 degrees awarded. *Degree program information:* Evening/weekend programs available. *Application deadline:* Applications are processed on a rolling basis. *Application fee:* $45. Electronic applications accepted. *Provost,* Dr. Adam Honea, 480-557-1659, Fax: 480-929-7164, E-mail: adam.honea@phoenix.edu.

College of Health and Human Services Students: 37 full-time (30 women); includes 20 minority (16 African Americans, 1 American Indian/Alaska Native, 2 Asian Americans or Pacific Islanders, 1 Hispanic American), 5 international. Average age 36. *Faculty:* 2 full-time (0 women), 12 part-time/adjunct (4 women). Expenses: Contact institution. *Financial support:* Institutionally sponsored loans and scholarships/grants available. In 2006, 8 degrees awarded. *Degree program information:* Evening/weekend programs available. Offers health care management (MBA). *Application deadline:* Applications are processed on a rolling basis. *Application fee:* $45. Electronic applications accepted. *Dean/Executive Director,* Dr. Gil Linne, 480-557-1751, E-mail: gin.linne@phoenix.edu.

The John Sperling School of Business Students: 303 full-time (169 women); includes 110 minority (96 African Americans, 3 American Indian/Alaska Native, 7 Asian Americans or Pacific Islanders, 4 Hispanic Americans), 20 international. Average age 36. *Faculty:* 30 full-time (4 women), 119 part-time/adjunct (21 women). Expenses: Contact institution. *Financial support:* Institutionally sponsored loans and scholarships/grants available. Financial award applicants required to submit FAFSA. In 2006, 118 degrees awarded. *Degree program information:* Evening/weekend programs available. Offers business (MBA, MIS, MM). *Application deadline:* Applications are processed on a rolling basis. *Application fee:* $45. Electronic applications accepted. *Application Contact:* Campus College Chair, 610-984-0880, Fax: 610-989-0881. *Provost,* Dr. Adam Honea, 480-557-1659, Fax: 480-929-7164, E-mail: adam.honea@phoenix.edu.

College of Graduate Business and Management Students: 271 full-time (160 women); includes 96 minority (86 African Americans, 3 American Indian/Alaska Native, 5 Asian Americans or Pacific Islanders, 2 Hispanic Americans), 18 international. Average age 36. *Faculty:* 21 full-time (4 women), 85 part-time/adjunct (19 women). Expenses: Contact institution. *Financial support:* Institutionally sponsored loans and scholarships/grants available. Financial award applicants required to submit FAFSA. In 2006, 102 degrees awarded. *Degree program information:* Evening/weekend programs available. Offers business administration (MBA); global management (MBA); management (MM). *Application deadline:* Applications are processed on a rolling basis. *Application fee:* $45. Electronic applications accepted. *Application Contact:* Campus College Chair, 610-984-0880, Fax: 610-989-0881. *Associate Vice President and Dean/Executive Director,* Dr. Brian Lindquist, 480-557-1221, E-mail: brian.lindquist@phoenix.edu.

College of Information Systems and Technology Students: 32 full-time (9 women); includes 14 minority (10 African Americans, 2 Asian Americans or Pacific Islanders, 2 Hispanic Americans), 2 international. Average age 39. *Faculty:* 9 full-time (0 women), 34 part-time/adjunct (2 women). Expenses: Contact institution. *Financial support:* Institutionally sponsored loans and scholarships/grants available. Financial award applicants required to submit FAFSA. In 2006, 16 degrees awarded. *Degree program information:* Evening/weekend programs available. Offers information systems (MIS); technology management (MBA). *Application deadline:* Applications are processed on a rolling basis. *Application fee:* $45. Electronic applications accepted. *Application Contact:* Campus College Chair, 610-984-0880, Fax: 610-989-0881. *Provost/Dean, Vice President Academic Research and Development,* Dr. Adam Honea, 480-557-1659, Fax: 480-929-7164, E-mail: adam.honea@phoenix.edu.

UNIVERSITY OF PHOENIX–PHOENIX CAMPUS, Phoenix, AZ 85040-1958

General Information Proprietary, coed, comprehensive institution. CGS member. *Enrollment:* 8,497 graduate, professional, and undergraduate students; 2,734 full-time matriculated graduate/professional students (1,710 women). *Enrollment by degree level:* 2,734 master's. *Graduate faculty:* 178 full-time (61 women), 2,189 part-time/adjunct (868 women). *Graduate housing:* On-campus housing not available. *Student services:* Campus safety program, disabled student services, writing training. *Library facilities:* University Library. *Online resources:* library catalog, web page. *Collection:* 1,759 titles, 692 serial subscriptions.

Computer facilities: Computer purchase and lease plans are available. A campuswide network can be accessed from off campus. Internet access is available. *Web address:* http://www.phoenix.edu/.

General Application Contact: Campus Information Center, 480-804-7600, Fax: 480-537-2320.

GRADUATE UNITS

The Artemis School Students: 1,379 full-time (1,062 women); includes 218 minority (63 African Americans, 11 American Indian/Alaska Native, 40 Asian Americans or Pacific Islanders, 104 Hispanic Americans), 29 international. Average age 36. *Faculty:* 84 full-time (43 women), 932 part-time/adjunct (563 women). Expenses: Contact institution. *Financial support:* Institutionally sponsored loans and scholarships/grants available. Financial award applicants required to submit FAFSA. In 2006, 666 degrees awarded. *Degree program information:* Evening/weekend programs available. *Application deadline:* Applications are processed on a rolling basis. *Application fee:* $45. Electronic applications accepted. *Provost,* Dr. Adam Honea, 480-557-1659, E-mail: adam.honea@phoenix.edu.

College of Education Students: 850 full-time (614 women); includes 135 minority (45 African Americans, 7 American Indian/Alaska Native, 20 Asian Americans or Pacific Islanders, 63 Hispanic Americans), 15 international. Average age 35. *Faculty:* 39 full-time (23 women), 422 part-time/adjunct (255 women). Expenses: Contact institution. *Financial support:* Institutionally sponsored loans and scholarships/grants available. Financial award applicants required to submit FAFSA. In 2006, 500 degrees awarded. *Degree program information:* Evening/weekend programs available. Offers administration and supervision (MA Ed); curriculum and instruction (MA Ed); elementary licensure (MA Ed); secondary licensure (MA Ed). *Application deadline:* Applications are processed on a rolling basis. *Application fee:* $45. Electronic applications accepted. *Application Contact:* College Chair, 480-804-7400, Fax: 480-557-2320. *Dean/Executive Director,* Dr. Marla LaRue, 480-557-1218, E-mail: marla.larue@phoenix.edu.

College of Health and Human Services Students: 493 full-time (420 women); includes 79 minority (17 African Americans, 4 American Indian/Alaska Native, 20 Asian Americans or Pacific Islanders, 38 Hispanic Americans), 12 international. Average age 38. *Faculty:* 45 full-time (20 women), 510 part-time/adjunct (308 women). Expenses: Contact institution. *Financial support:* Institutionally sponsored loans and scholarships/grants available. Financial award applicants required to submit FAFSA. In 2006, 166 degrees awarded. *Degree program information:* Evening/weekend programs available. Offers community counseling (MSC); family nurse practitioner (MSN); health care management (MBA); nurse practitioner (Certificate); nursing (MSN); nursing health care education (Certificate). *Application deadline:* Applications are processed on a rolling basis. *Application fee:* $45. Electronic applications accepted. *Application Contact:* Chair, 480-804-7400, Fax: 480-557-2320. *Dean/Executive Director,* Dr. Gil Linne, 480-557-1751, E-mail: gil.linne@phoenix.edu.

The John Sperling School of Business Students: 1,321 full-time (624 women); includes 271 minority (77 African Americans, 13 American Indian/Alaska Native, 55 Asian Americans or Pacific Islanders, 126 Hispanic Americans), 89 international. Average age 35. *Faculty:* 87 full-time (17 women), 1,226 part-time/adjunct (291 women). Expenses: Contact institution. *Financial support:* Institutionally sponsored loans and scholarships/grants available. Financial award applicants required to submit FAFSA. In 2006, 561 degrees awarded. *Degree program information:* Evening/weekend programs available. Offers business (MBA, MIS, MM). *Application deadline:* Applications are processed on a rolling basis. *Application fee:* $45. Electronic applications accepted. *Provost,* Dr. Adam Honea, 480-557-1659, E-mail: adam.honea@phoenix.edu.

College of Graduate Business and Management Students: 1,291 full-time (615 women); includes 265 minority (73 African Americans, 12 American Indian/Alaska Native, 55 Asian Americans or Pacific Islanders, 125 Hispanic Americans), 86 international. Average age 35. *Faculty:* 63 full-time (14 women), 833 part-time/adjunct (228 women). Expenses: Contact institution. *Financial support:* Institutionally sponsored loans and scholarships/grants available. Financial award applicants required to submit FAFSA. In 2006, 496 degrees awarded. *Degree program information:* Evening/weekend programs available. Offers business administration (MBA); management (MM). *Application deadline:* Applications are processed on a rolling basis. *Application fee:* $45. Electronic applications accepted. *Application Contact:* Campus College Chair, 480-804-7400, Fax: 480-557-2320. *Dean/Executive Director,* Dr. Brian Lindquist, 480-557-1221, E-mail: brian.lindquist@phoenix.edu.

College of Information Systems and Technology Students: 30 full-time (9 women); includes 6 minority (4 African Americans, 1 American Indian/Alaska Native, 1 Hispanic American), 3 international. Average age 40. *Faculty:* 24 full-time (3 women), 393 part-time/adjunct (63 women). Expenses: Contact institution. *Financial support:* Institutionally sponsored loans and scholarships/grants available. Financial award applicants required to submit FAFSA. In 2006, 65 degrees awarded. *Degree program information:* Evening/weekend programs available. Offers management (MIS). *Application deadline:* Applications are processed on a rolling basis. *Application fee:* $45. Electronic applications accepted. *Application Contact:* Campus College Chair, 480-804-7400, Fax: 480-557-2320. *Provost,* Dr. Adam Honea, 480-557-1659, E-mail: adam.honea@phoenix.edu.

UNIVERSITY OF PHOENIX–PITTSBURGH CAMPUS, Pittsburgh, PA 15276

General Information Proprietary, coed, comprehensive institution. *Enrollment:* 408 graduate, professional, and undergraduate students; 107 full-time matriculated graduate/professional students (54 women). *Enrollment by degree level:* 107 master's. *Graduate faculty:* 32 full-time (9 women), 85 part-time/adjunct (18 women). *Tuition:* Full-time $13,560. *Required fees:* $760. *Graduate housing:* On-campus housing not available. *Student services:* Campus safety program, disabled student services, writing training. *Library facilities:* University Library. *Online resources:* library catalog, web page. *Collection:* 1,759 titles, 692 serial subscriptions.

Computer facilities: A campuswide network can be accessed from off campus. Internet access is available. *Web address:* http://www.phoenix.edu/.

General Application Contact: Campus Information Center, 412-747-9000, Fax: 412-747-0676.

GRADUATE UNITS

The Artemis School Students: 11 full-time (8 women); includes 3 minority (all African Americans) Average age 36. *Faculty:* 2 full-time (0 women), 13 part-time/adjunct (4 women). Expenses: Contact institution. *Financial support:* Institutionally sponsored loans and scholarships/grants available. Financial award applicants required to submit FAFSA. In 2006, 1 degree awarded. *Degree program information:* Evening/weekend programs available. *Application deadline:* Applications are processed on a rolling basis. *Application fee:* $45. Electronic applications accepted. *Provost,* Dr. Adam Honea, 460-557-1659, E-mail: adam.honea@phoenix.edu.

College of Health and Human Services Students: 11 full-time (8 women); includes 3 minority (all African Americans) Average age 36. *Faculty:* 2 full-time (0 women), 10 part-time/adjunct (1 woman). Expenses: Contact institution. *Financial support:* Institutionally sponsored loans and scholarships/grants available. In 2006, 1 degree awarded. *Degree program information:* Evening/weekend programs available. Offers administration of justice and security (MS); health administration (MHA); health care management (MBA); nursing (MSN); nursing education (MSN); psychology (MS). *Application deadline:* Applications are processed on a rolling basis. *Application fee:* $45. Electronic applications accepted. *Dean/Executive Director,* Dr. Gil Linne, 480-557-1751, E-mail: gil.linne@phoenix.edu.

John Sperling School of Business Students: 96 full-time (46 women); includes 19 minority (15 African Americans, 3 Asian Americans or Pacific Islanders, 1 Hispanic American), 4 international. Average age 37. *Faculty:* 30 full-time (9 women), 70 part-time/adjunct (13 women). Expenses: Contact institution. *Financial support:* Institutionally sponsored loans and scholarships/grants available. Financial award applicants required to submit FAFSA. In 2006, 43 degrees awarded. *Degree program information:* Evening/weekend programs available. Offers business (MBA, MIS, MM). *Application deadline:* Applications are processed on a rolling basis. *Application fee:* $45. Electronic applications accepted. *Application Contact:* Campus College Chair, 412-747-9000, Fax: 412-747-0676. *Provost,* Dr. Adam Honea, 480-557-1659, E-mail: adam.honea@phoenix.edu.

College of Graduate Business and Management Students: 84 full-time (43 women); includes 16 minority (13 African Americans, 2 Asian Americans or Pacific Islanders, 1 Hispanic American), 4 international. Average age 37. *Faculty:* 19 full-time (6 women), 49 part-time/adjunct (13 women). Expenses: Contact institution. *Financial support:* Institutionally sponsored loans and scholarships/grants available. Financial award applicants required to submit FAFSA. In 2006, 35 degrees awarded. *Degree program information:* Evening/weekend programs available. Offers accounting (MBA); business administration (MBA); global management (MBA); human resource management (MBA); human resources management (MM); management (MM); marketing (MBA); public administration (MBA, MM). *Application deadline:* Applications are processed on a rolling basis. *Application fee:* $45. Electronic applications accepted. *Application Contact:* College Chair, 412-747-9000, Fax: 412-747-0676. *Associate Vice President and Dean/Executive Director,* Dr. Brian Lindquist, 480-551-1221, E-mail: brian.lindquist@phoenix.edu.

College of Information Systems and Technology Students: 12 full-time (3 women); includes 3 minority (2 African Americans, 1 Asian American or Pacific Islander). Average age 36. *Faculty:* 11 full-time (3 women), 21 part-time/adjunct (0 women). Expenses: Contact institution. *Financial support:* Institutionally sponsored loans and scholarships/grants available. Financial award applicants required to submit FAFSA. In 2006, 8 degrees awarded. *Degree program information:* Evening/weekend programs available. Offers e-business (MBA); information systems (MIS); technology management (MBA). *Application deadline:* Applications are processed on a rolling basis. *Application fee:* $45. Electronic applications accepted. *Application Contact:* Campus College Chair, 412-747-9000, Fax: 412-747-0676. *Provost/Dean, Vice President Research and Development,* Dr. Adam Honea, 480-557-1659, E-mail: adam.honea@phoenix.edu.

UNIVERSITY OF PHOENIX–PUERTO RICO CAMPUS, Guaynabo, PR 00968

General Information Proprietary, coed, comprehensive institution. *Enrollment:* 2,853 graduate, professional, and undergraduate students; 1,774 full-time matriculated graduate/professional students (1,089 women). *Enrollment by degree level:* 1,774 master's. *Graduate faculty:* 35 full-time (20 women), 134 part-time/adjunct (61 women). *Tuition:* Full-time $5,816. *Required fees:* $760. *Graduate housing:* On-campus housing not available. *Student services:* Campus safety program, disabled student services, writing training. *Library facilities:* University Library plus 1 other. *Online resources:* library catalog, web page. *Collection:* 1,756 titles, 692 serial subscriptions.

Computer facilities: A campuswide network can be accessed from off campus. Internet access is available. *Web address:* http://www.phoenix.edu/.

General Application Contact: Campus Information Center, 787-731-5400, Fax: 787-731-1510.

GRADUATE UNITS

The Artemis School Students: 380 full-time (305 women); includes 188 minority (1 African American, 1 American Indian/Alaska Native, 186 Hispanic Americans), 8 international. Average age 36. *Faculty:* 12 full-time (11 women), 48 part-time/adjunct (35 women). Expenses: Contact institution. *Financial support:* Institutionally sponsored loans and scholarships/grants available. Financial award applicants required to submit FAFSA. In 2006, 120 degrees awarded. *Degree program information:* Evening/weekend programs available. *Application deadline:* Applications are processed on a rolling basis. *Application fee:* $45. Electronic applications accepted. *Provost,* Dr. Adam Honea, 480-557-1659, E-mail: adam.honea@phoenix.edu.

College of Education Students: 186 full-time (156 women); includes 91 minority (1 African American, 1 American Indian/Alaska Native, 89 Hispanic Americans), 4 international. Average age 37. *Faculty:* 8 full-time (all women), 28 part-time/adjunct (21 women). Expenses: Contact institution. *Financial support:* Institutionally sponsored loans and scholarships/grants available. Financial award applicants required to submit FAFSA. In 2006, 39 degrees awarded. *Degree program information:* Evening/weekend programs available. Offers administration and supervision (MA Ed); early childhood education (MA Ed); school counselor (MSC). *Application deadline:* Applications are processed on a rolling basis. *Application fee:* $45. Electronic applications accepted. *Application Contact:* Chair, 787-731-5400, Fax: 787-731-1510. *Dean/Executive Director,* Dr. Marla LaRue, 480-557-1218, E-mail: marla.larue@phoenix.edu.

College of Health and Human Services Students: 160 full-time (122 women); includes 84 minority (all Hispanic Americans), 4 international. Average age 35. *Faculty:* 4 full-time (3 women), 20 part-time/adjunct (14 women). Expenses: Contact institution. *Financial support:* Institutionally sponsored loans and scholarships/grants available. Financial award applicants required to submit FAFSA. In 2006, 67 degrees awarded. *Degree program information:* Evening/weekend programs available. Offers marriage, family and child therapy (MSC); mental health counseling (MSC). *Application deadline:* Applications are processed on a rolling basis. *Application fee:* $45. Electronic applications accepted. *Application Contact:* Chair, 787-731-5400, Fax: 787-731-1510. *Dean/Executive Director,* Dr. Gil Linne, 480-557-1074, E-mail: gil.linne@phoenix.edu.

John Sperling School of Business Students: 1,394 full-time (784 women); includes 795 minority (2 African Americans, 5 American Indian/Alaska Native, 4 Asian Americans or Pacific Islanders, 784 Hispanic Americans), 36 international. Average age 34. *Faculty:* 23 full-time (9 women), 86 part-time/adjunct (26 women). Expenses: Contact institution. *Financial support:* Institutionally sponsored loans and scholarships/grants available. Financial award applicants required to submit FAFSA. In 2006, 385 degrees awarded. *Degree program information:* Evening/weekend programs available. Offers business (MBA). *Application deadline:* Applications are processed on a rolling basis. *Application fee:* $45. Electronic applications accepted. *Application Contact:* Chair, 787-931-5400, Fax: 787-931-1510. *Provost,* Dr. Adam Honea, 480-557-1659, E-mail: adam.honea@phoenix.edu.

College of Graduate Business and Management Students: 1,122 full-time (671 women); includes 636 minority (2 African Americans, 3 American Indian/Alaska Native, 3 Asian Americans or Pacific Islanders, 628 Hispanic Americans), 31 international. Average age 34. *Faculty:* 19 full-time (8 women), 73 part-time/adjunct (25 women). Expenses: Contact institution. *Financial support:* Institutionally sponsored loans and scholarships/grants available. Financial award applicants required to submit FAFSA. In 2006, 281 degrees awarded. *Degree program information:* Evening/weekend programs available. Offers accounting (MBA); business administration (MBA); global management (MBA); human resource management (MBA); marketing (MBA). *Application deadline:* Applications are processed on a rolling basis. *Application fee:* $45. Electronic applications accepted. *Application Contact:* Chair, 787-931-5400, Fax: 787-931-1510. *Associate Vice President and Dean/Executive Director,* Dr. Brian Lindquist, 480-557-1221, E-mail: brian.lindquist@phoenix.edu.

College of Information Systems and Technology Students: 272 full-time (113 women); includes 159 minority (2 American Indian/Alaska Native, 1 Asian American or Pacific Islander, 156 Hispanic Americans), 5 international. Average age 34. *Faculty:* 4 full-time (1 woman), 13 part-time/adjunct (1 woman). Expenses: Contact institution. *Financial support:* Institutionally sponsored loans and scholarships/grants available. In 2006, 104 degrees awarded. *Degree program information:* Evening/weekend programs available. Offers technology management (MBA). *Application deadline:* Applications are processed on a rolling basis. *Application fee:* $45. Electronic applications accepted. *Application Contact:* Campus College Chair, 787-931-5400, Fax: 787-931-1510. *Provost/Dean, Vice President Research and Development,* Dr. Adam Honea, 480-557-1659, E-mail: adam.honea@phoenix.edu.

UNIVERSITY OF PHOENIX–RALEIGH CAMPUS, Raleigh, NC 27606

General Information Proprietary, coed, comprehensive institution.

GRADUATE UNITS

College of Graduate Business and Management Offers accounting (MBA); business administration (MBA); e-business (MBA); global management (MBA).

College of Health and Human Services Offers health care management (MBA).

College of Information Systems and Technology Offers information systems and technology (MIS); management (MIS); technology management (MBA).

UNIVERSITY OF PHOENIX–RICHMOND CAMPUS, Richmond, VA 23230

General Information Proprietary, coed, comprehensive institution. *Enrollment:* 351 graduate, professional, and undergraduate students; 123 full-time matriculated graduate/professional students (88 women). *Enrollment by degree level:* 123 master's. *Graduate faculty:* 9 full-time (7 women), 88 part-time/adjunct (13 women). *Graduate housing:* On-campus housing not available. *Student services:* Campus safety program, disabled student services, writing training. *Library facilities:* University Library. *Online resources:* library catalog, web page. *Collection:* 1,759 titles, 692 serial subscriptions.

Computer facilities: A campuswide network can be accessed from off campus. Internet access is available. *Web address:* http://www.phoenix.edu/.

General Application Contact: Campus Information Center, 804-288-3390.

GRADUATE UNITS

College of Health and Human Services Students: 2 full-time (1 woman); includes 1 minority (African American) Average age 38. *Faculty:* 4 part-time/adjunct (1 woman). Expenses: Contact institution. *Financial support:* Institutionally sponsored loans and scholarships/grants available. Financial award applicants required to submit FAFSA. *Degree program information:* Evening/weekend programs available. Offers administration of justice and security (MS); health administration (MHA); health care management (MBA); nursing (MSN); psychology (MS). *Application deadline:* Applications are processed on a rolling basis. *Application fee:* $45. Electronic applications accepted. *Application Contact:* Chair, 804-288-3390. *Dean/Executive Director,* Dr. Gil Linne, 480-557-1751, E-mail: gil.linne@phoenix.edu.

College of Graduate Business and Management Students: 103 full-time (73 women); includes 42 minority (38 African Americans, 1 American Indian/Alaska Native, 2 Asian Americans or Pacific Islanders, 1 Hispanic American), 10 international. Average age 36. *Faculty:* 6 full-time (4 women), 60 part-time/adjunct (7 women). Expenses: Contact institution. *Financial support:* Institutionally sponsored loans and scholarships/grants available. Financial award applicants required to submit FAFSA. In 2006, 1 degree awarded. *Degree program information:* Evening/weekend programs available. Offers accounting (MBA); business administration (MBA); global management (MBA); human resources management (MBA, MM); management (MM); marketing (MBA); public administration (MBA, MM). *Application deadline:* Applications are processed on a rolling basis. *Application fee:* $45. Electronic applications accepted. *Application Contact:* Chair, 804-288-3390. *Associate Vice President/Dean,* Dr. Brian Lindquist, 480-557-1221, E-mail: brian.lindquist@phoenix.edu.

College of Information Systems and Technology Students: 6 full-time (3 women); includes 2 minority (both African Americans) Average age 42. *Faculty:* 3 full-time (all women), 20 part-time/adjunct (2 women). Expenses: Contact institution. *Financial support:* Institutionally sponsored loans and scholarships/grants available. Financial award applicants required to submit FAFSA. *Degree program information:* Evening/weekend programs available. Offers information systems (MIS); technology management (MBA). *Application deadline:* Applications are processed on a rolling basis. *Application fee:* $45. Electronic applications accepted. *Application Contact:* Chair, 804-288-3390. *Provost,* Dr. Adam Honea, 480-557-1659, E-mail: adam.honea@phoenix.edu.

UNIVERSITY OF PHOENIX–SACRAMENTO VALLEY CAMPUS, Sacramento, CA 95833-3632

General Information Proprietary, coed, comprehensive institution. *Enrollment:* 4,585 graduate, professional, and undergraduate students; 1,103 full-time matriculated graduate/professional students (728 women). *Enrollment by degree level:* 1,103 master's. *Graduate faculty:* 96 full-time (55 women), 801 part-time/adjunct (271 women). *Tuition:* Full-time $12,024. *Required fees:* $760. *Graduate housing:* On-campus housing not available. *Student services:* Campus safety program, disabled student services, writing training. *Library facilities:* University Library. *Online resources:* library catalog, web page. *Collection:* 1,759 titles, 692 serial subscriptions.

Computer facilities: A campuswide network can be accessed from off campus. Internet access is available. *Web address:* http://www.phoenix.edu/.

General Application Contact: Campus Information Center, 916-923-2107, Fax: 916-923-3914.

GRADUATE UNITS

The Artemis School Students: 689 full-time (529 women); includes 159 minority (77 African Americans, 5 American Indian/Alaska Native, 32 Asian Americans or Pacific Islanders, 45 Hispanic Americans), 50 international. Average age 39. *Faculty:* 45 full-time (32 women), 465 part-time/adjunct (162 women). Expenses: Contact institution. *Financial support:* Institutionally sponsored loans and scholarships/grants available. Financial award applicants required to submit FAFSA. In 2006, 162 degrees awarded. *Degree program information:* Evening/weekend programs available. *Application deadline:* Applications are processed on a rolling basis. *Application fee:* $45. Electronic applications accepted. *Provost,* Dr. Adam Honea, 480-557-1659, E-mail: adam.honea@phoenix.edu.

College of Education Students: 234 full-time (161 women); includes 51 minority (20 African Americans, 2 American Indian/Alaska Native, 9 Asian Americans or Pacific Islanders, 20 Hispanic Americans), 15 international. Average age 36. *Faculty:* 9 full-time (5 women), 95 part-time/adjunct (41 women). Expenses: Contact institution. *Financial support:* Institutionally sponsored loans and scholarships/grants available. Financial award applicants required to submit FAFSA. In 2006, 80 degrees awarded. *Degree program information:* Evening/weekend programs available. Offers adult education (MA Ed); curriculum instruction (MA Ed); elementary education (MA Ed); secondary education (MA Ed); teacher education (Certificate). *Application deadline:* Applications are processed on a rolling basis. *Application fee:* $45. Electronic applications accepted. *Application Contact:* Campus College Chair, 916-923-2107, Fax: 916-923-3914. *Dean,* Dr. Marla LaRue, 480-557-1218, E-mail: marla.larue@phoenix.edu.

College of Health and Human Services Students: 330 full-time (266 women); includes 73 minority (38 African Americans, 2 American Indian/Alaska Native, 16 Asian Americans or Pacific Islanders, 17 Hispanic Americans), 29 international. Average age 40. *Faculty:* 36 full-time (27 women), 270 part-time/adjunct (121 women). Expenses: Contact institution. *Financial support:* Institutionally sponsored loans and scholarships/grants available. Financial award applicants required to submit FAFSA. In 2006, 82 degrees awarded. *Degree program information:* Evening/weekend programs available. Offers administration of justice and security (MS); family nurse practitioner (MSN); health care management (MBA); marriage, family and child counseling (MSC); nursing (MSN); nursing education (MSN). *Application deadline:* Applications are processed on a rolling basis. *Application fee:* $45. Electronic applications accepted. *Application Contact:* College Chair, 916-923-2107, Fax: 916-923-3914. *Dean/Executive Director,* Dr. Gil Linne, 480-557-1757, E-mail: gil.linne@phoenix.edu.

John Sperling School of Business Students: 414 full-time (199 women); includes 128 minority (66 African Americans, 2 American Indian/Alaska Native, 35 Asian Americans or Pacific Islanders, 25 Hispanic Americans), 36 international. Average age 37. *Faculty:* 51 full-time (23 women), 435 part-time/adjunct (108 women). Expenses: Contact institution. *Financial support:* Institutionally sponsored loans and scholarships/grants available. Financial award applicants required to submit FAFSA. In 2006, 160 degrees awarded. *Degree program information:* Evening/weekend programs available. Offers business (MBA, MIS). *Application deadline:* Applications are processed on a rolling basis. *Application fee:* $45. Electronic

University of Phoenix–Sacramento Valley Campus (continued)

applications accepted. *Provost*, Dr. Adam Honea, 480-557-1659, E-mail: adam.honea@phoenix.edu.

College of Graduate Business and Management Students: 395 full-time (197 women); includes 120 minority (62 African Americans, 2 American Indian/Alaska Native, 32 Asian Americans or Pacific Islanders, 24 Hispanic Americans), 34 international. Average age 37. *Faculty:* 36 full-time (19 women), 291 part-time/adjunct (83 women). Expenses: Contact institution. *Financial support:* Institutionally sponsored loans and scholarships/grants available. Financial award applicants required to submit FAFSA. In 2006, 138 master's awarded. *Degree program information:* Evening/weekend programs available. Offers accounting (MBA); business administration (MBA); global management (MBA); human resources management (MBA); marketing (MBA); public administration (MBA). *Application deadline:* Applications are processed on a rolling basis. *Application fee:* $45. Electronic applications accepted. *Application Contact:* Campus College Chair, 916-923-2107, Fax: 916-923-3914. *Associate Vice President and Dean/Executive Director*, Dr. Brian Lindquist, 480-557-1221, E-mail: brian.lindquist@phoenix.edu.

College of Information Systems and Technology Students: 19 full-time (2 women); includes 8 minority (4 African Americans, 3 Asian Americans or Pacific Islanders, 1 Hispanic American), 2 international. Average age 41. *Faculty:* 15 full-time (4 women), 144 part-time/adjunct (25 women). Expenses: Contact institution. *Financial support:* Institutionally sponsored loans and scholarships/grants available. Financial award applicants required to submit FAFSA. In 2006, 22 degrees awarded. *Degree program information:* Evening/weekend programs available. Offers management (MIS); technology management (MBA). *Application deadline:* Applications are processed on a rolling basis. *Application fee:* $45. Electronic applications accepted. *Application Contact:* Campus College Chair, 916-923-2107, Fax: 916-923-3914. *Provost/Dean, Vice President Academic Research and Development*, Dr. Adam Honea, 480-557-1659, E-mail: adam.honea@phoenix.edu.

UNIVERSITY OF PHOENIX–ST. LOUIS CAMPUS, St. Louis, MO 63043-4828

General Information Proprietary, coed, comprehensive institution. *Enrollment:* 964 graduate, professional, and undergraduate students; 130 full-time matriculated graduate/professional students (88 women). *Enrollment by degree level:* 130 master's. *Graduate faculty:* 21 full-time (10 women), 114 part-time/adjunct (26 women). *Tuition:* Full-time $11,832. *Required fees:* $762. *Graduate housing:* On-campus housing not available. *Student services:* Campus safety program, disabled student services, writing training. *Library facilities:* University Library. *Online resources:* library catalog, web page. *Collection:* 1,759 titles, 692 serial subscriptions.

Computer facilities: A campuswide network can be accessed from off campus. Internet access is available. *Web address:* http://www.phoenix.edu/.

General Application Contact: Campus Information Center, 314-298-9755, Fax: 314-291-2901.

GRADUATE UNITS

The Artemis School *Faculty:* 11 part-time/adjunct (1 woman). Expenses: Contact institution. *Financial support:* Institutionally sponsored loans and scholarships/grants available. Financial award applicants required to submit FAFSA. *Degree program information:* Evening/weekend programs available. *Application deadline:* Applications are processed on a rolling basis. *Application fee:* $45. Electronic applications accepted. *Provost*, Dr. Adam Honea, 480-557-1659, E-mail: adam.honea@phoenix.edu.

College of Health and Human Services Students: 1 full-time (0 women). *Faculty:* 10 part-time/adjunct (1 woman). Expenses: Contact institution. *Financial support:* Institutionally sponsored loans and scholarships/grants available. *Degree program information:* Evening/weekend programs available. Offers health care management (MBA). *Application deadline:* Applications are processed on a rolling basis. *Application fee:* $45. Electronic applications accepted. *Application Contact:* College Chair, 314-298-9755. *Dean/Executive Director*, Dr. Gil Linne, 480-557-1751, E-mail: gin.linne@phoenix.edu.

John Sperling School of Business Students: 129 full-time (88 women); includes 34 minority (26 African Americans, 1 American Indian/Alaska Native, 5 Asian Americans or Pacific Islanders, 2 Hispanic Americans), 4 international. Average age 36. *Faculty:* 21 full-time (10 women), 101 part-time/adjunct (25 women). Expenses: Contact institution. *Financial support:* Institutionally sponsored loans and scholarships/grants available. Financial award applicants required to submit FAFSA. In 2006, 51 degrees awarded. *Degree program information:* Evening/weekend programs available. Offers business (MBA). *Application deadline:* Applications are processed on a rolling basis. *Application fee:* $45. Electronic applications accepted. *Provost*, Dr. Adam Honea, 480-557-1659, E-mail: adam.honea@phoenix.edu.

College of Graduate Business and Management Students: 129 full-time (88 women); includes 34 minority (26 African Americans, 1 American Indian/Alaska Native, 5 Asian Americans or Pacific Islanders, 2 Hispanic Americans), 4 international. Average age 36. *Faculty:* 14 full-time (8 women), 64 part-time/adjunct (14 women). Expenses: Contact institution. *Financial support:* Institutionally sponsored loans available. Financial award applicants required to submit FAFSA. In 2006, 57 master's awarded. *Degree program information:* Evening/weekend programs available. Offers business administration (MBA). *Application deadline:* Applications are processed on a rolling basis. *Application fee:* $45. Electronic applications accepted. *Application Contact:* Campus College Chair—Graduate Business, 314-298-9755, Fax: 314-291-2901. *Associate Vice President and Dean/Executive Director*, Dr. Brian Lindquist, 480-557-1221, E-mail: brain.lindquist@phoenix.edu.

College of Information Systems and Technology *Faculty:* 7 full-time (2 women), 37 part-time/adjunct (11 women). Expenses: Contact institution. *Financial support:* Institutionally sponsored loans available. Financial award applicants required to submit FAFSA. *Degree program information:* Evening/weekend programs available. Offers technology management (MBA). *Application deadline:* Applications are processed on a rolling basis. *Application fee:* $45. Electronic applications accepted. *Application Contact:* College Chair, 314-298-9755, Fax: 314-291-2901. *Dean/Executive Director*, Dr. Adam Honea, 480-557-1659, E-mail: adam.honea@phoenix.edu.

UNIVERSITY OF PHOENIX–SAN DIEGO CAMPUS, San Diego, CA 92123

General Information Proprietary, coed, comprehensive institution. *Enrollment:* 3,781 graduate, professional, and undergraduate students; 999 full-time matriculated graduate/professional students (625 women). *Enrollment by degree level:* 999 master's. *Graduate faculty:* 90 full-time (27 women), 585 part-time/adjunct (158 women). *Tuition:* Full-time $11,419. *Required fees:* $760. *Graduate housing:* On-campus housing not available. *Student services:* Campus safety program, disabled student services, writing training. *Library facilities:* University Library. *Online resources:* library catalog, web page. *Collection:* 1,759 titles, 692 serial subscriptions.

Computer facilities: A campuswide network can be accessed from off campus. Internet access is available. *Web address:* http://www.phoenix.edu/.

General Application Contact: Campus Information Center, 888-UOP-INFO, Fax: 858-509-4399.

GRADUATE UNITS

The Artemis School Students: 536 full-time (408 women); includes 137 minority (34 African Americans, 1 American Indian/Alaska Native, 33 Asian Americans or Pacific Islanders, 69 Hispanic Americans), 28 international. Average age 38. *Faculty:* 38 full-time (23 women), 229 part-time/adjunct (102 women). Expenses: Contact institution. *Financial support:* Institutionally sponsored loans and scholarships/grants available. Financial award applicants required to submit FAFSA. In 2006, 143 degrees awarded. *Degree program information:* Evening/weekend programs available. *Application deadline:* Applications are processed on a rolling basis. *Application fee:* $45. Electronic applications accepted. *Provost*, Dr. Adam Honea, 480-557-1659, E-mail: adam.honea@phoenix.edu.

College of Education Students: 165 full-time (110 women); includes 42 minority (9 African Americans, 8 Asian Americans or Pacific Islanders, 25 Hispanic Americans), 12 international. Average age 34. *Faculty:* 6 full-time (3 women), 69 part-time/adjunct (36 women). Expenses: Contact institution. *Financial support:* Institutionally sponsored loans and scholarships/grants available. Financial award applicants required to submit FAFSA. In 2006, 81 degrees awarded. *Degree program information:* Evening/weekend programs available. Offers curriculum and instruction (MA Ed); elementary education (MA Ed); secondary education (MA Ed). *Application deadline:* Applications are processed on a rolling basis. *Application fee:* $45. Electronic applications accepted. *Application Contact:* Campus College Chair, 888-UOP-INFO, Fax: 858-509-4399. *Dean/Executive Director*, Dr. Marla LaRue, 480-557-1218, E-mail: marla.larue@phoenix.edu.

College of Health and Human Services Students: 281 full-time (225 women); includes 75 minority (20 African Americans, 1 American Indian/Alaska Native, 21 Asian Americans or Pacific Islanders, 33 Hispanic Americans), 15 international. Average age 37. *Faculty:* 32 full-time (20 women), 160 part-time/adjunct (66 women). Expenses: Contact institution. *Financial support:* Institutionally sponsored loans and scholarships/grants available. Financial award applicants required to submit FAFSA. In 2006, 81 degrees awarded. *Degree program information:* Evening/weekend programs available. Offers administration of justice and security (MS); marriage, family and child counseling (MSC); marriage, family and child therapy (MSC); nursing (MSN). *Application deadline:* Applications are processed on a rolling basis. *Application fee:* $45. Electronic applications accepted. *Application Contact:* Campus College Chair, 888-UOP-INFO, Fax: 858-509-4399. *Dean/Executive Director*, Dr. Gil Linne, 480-557-1751, E-mail: gil.linne@phoenix.edu.

John Sperling School of Business Students: 460 full-time (215 women); includes 142 minority (33 African Americans, 2 American Indian/Alaska Native, 48 Asian Americans or Pacific Islanders, 59 Hispanic Americans), 25 international. Average age 35. *Faculty:* 52 full-time (4 women), 350 part-time/adjunct (52 women). Expenses: Contact institution. *Financial support:* Institutionally sponsored loans and scholarships/grants available. Financial award applicants required to submit FAFSA. In 2006, 166 degrees awarded. *Degree program information:* Evening/weekend programs available. Offers business (MBA, MIS, MM). *Application deadline:* Applications are processed on a rolling basis. *Application fee:* $45. Electronic applications accepted. *Provost*, Dr. Adam Honea, 480-557-1659, E-mail: adam.honea@phoenix.edu.

College of Graduate Business and Management Students: 437 full-time (211 women); includes 139 minority (32 African Americans, 2 American Indian/Alaska Native, 48 Asian Americans or Pacific Islanders, 57 Hispanic Americans), 24 international. Average age 36. *Faculty:* 39 full-time (4 women), 217 part-time/adjunct (39 women). Expenses: Contact institution. *Financial support:* Institutionally sponsored loans and scholarships/grants available. Financial award applicants required to submit FAFSA. In 2006, 127 degrees awarded. *Degree program information:* Evening/weekend programs available. Offers business administration (MBA); global management (MBA); management (MM). *Application deadline:* Applications are processed on a rolling basis. *Application fee:* $45. Electronic applications accepted. *Application Contact:* Campus Information Center, 888-UOP-INFO, Fax: 858-509-4399. *Associate Vice President and Dean/Executive Director*, Dr. Brian Lindquist, 480-557-1221, E-mail: brian.lindquist@phoenix.edu.

College of Information Systems and Technology Students: 23 full-time (4 women); includes 3 minority (1 African American, 2 Hispanic Americans), 1 international. Average age 40. *Faculty:* 13 full-time (0 women), 133 part-time/adjunct (13 women). Expenses: Contact institution. *Financial support:* Institutionally sponsored loans and scholarships/grants available. Financial award applicants required to submit FAFSA. In 2006, 39 degrees awarded. *Degree program information:* Evening/weekend programs available. Offers management (MIS); technology management (MBA). *Application deadline:* Applications are processed on a rolling basis. *Application fee:* $45. Electronic applications accepted. *Application Contact:* Campus College Chair, 888-UOP-INFO, Fax: 858-509-4399. *Provost/Dean, Vice President Academic Research and Development*, Dr. Adam Honea, 480-557-1659, E-mail: adam.honea@phoenix.edu.

UNIVERSITY OF PHOENIX–SOUTHERN ARIZONA CAMPUS, Tucson, AZ 85712-2732

General Information Proprietary, coed, comprehensive institution. *Enrollment:* 2,839 graduate, professional, and undergraduate students; 742 full-time matriculated graduate/professional students (434 women). *Enrollment by degree level:* 742 master's. *Graduate faculty:* 91 full-time (51 women), 644 part-time/adjunct (243 women). *Tuition:* Full-time $8,669. *Required fees:* $760. *Graduate housing:* On-campus housing not available. *Student services:* Campus safety program, disabled student services, writing training. *Library facilities:* University Library. *Online resources:* library catalog, web page. *Collection:* 1,759 titles, 692 serial subscriptions.

Computer facilities: A campuswide network can be accessed from off campus. Internet access is available. *Web address:* http://www.phoenix.edu/.

General Application Contact: Campus Information Center, 520-881-6512, Fax: 520-795-6177.

GRADUATE UNITS

The Artemis School Students: 267 full-time (213 women); includes 54 minority (18 African Americans, 1 American Indian/Alaska Native, 4 Asian Americans or Pacific Islanders, 31 Hispanic Americans), 18 international. Average age 39. *Faculty:* 48 full-time (33 women), 313 part-time/adjunct (187 women). Expenses: Contact institution. *Financial support:* Institutionally sponsored loans and scholarships/grants available. Financial award applicants required to submit FAFSA. In 2006, 147 degrees awarded. *Degree program information:* Evening/weekend programs available. *Application deadline:* Applications are processed on a rolling basis. *Application fee:* $45. Electronic applications accepted. *Provost*, Dr. Adam Honea, 480-557-1659, E-mail: adam.honea@phoenix.edu.

College of Education Students: 75 full-time (55 women); includes 16 minority (2 African Americans, 1 American Indian/Alaska Native, 1 Asian American or Pacific Islander, 12 Hispanic Americans), 2 international. Average age 38. *Faculty:* 101. Expenses: Contact institution. *Financial support:* Institutionally sponsored loans and scholarships/grants available. Financial award applicants required to submit FAFSA. In 2006, 113 degrees awarded. *Degree program information:* Evening/weekend programs available. Offers curriculum instruction (MA Ed); educational counseling (MA Ed); elementary licensure (MA Ed); school counseling (MSC); secondary licensure (MA Ed); special education (Certificate). *Application deadline:* Applications are processed on a rolling basis. *Application fee:* $45. Electronic applications accepted. *Application Contact:* Campus College Chair, 520-881-6512, Fax: 520-795-6177. *Dean/Executive Director*, Dr. Marla LaRue, 480-557-1218, E-mail: marla.larue@phoenix.edu.

College of Health and Human Services Students: 192 full-time (158 women); includes 38 minority (16 African Americans, 3 Asian Americans or Pacific Islanders, 19 Hispanic Americans), 16 international. *Faculty:* 24 full-time (17 women), 212 part-time/adjunct (127 women). Expenses: Contact institution. *Financial support:* Institutionally sponsored loans and scholarships/grants available. Financial award applicants required to submit FAFSA. In 2006, 34 degrees awarded. *Degree program information:* Evening/weekend programs available. Offers administration of justice and security (MS); family nurse practitioner (Certificate); health administration (MHA); marriage, family and child therapy (MSC); nursing (MSN). *Application deadline:* Applications are processed on a rolling basis. *Application fee:* $45. Electronic applications accepted. *Application Contact:* Campus College Chair, 520-881-6512, Fax: 520-795-6177. *Dean/Executive Director*, Dr. Gil Linne, 480-557-1757, E-mail: gil.linne@phoenix.edu.

John Sperling School of Business Students: 475 full-time (221 women); includes 123 minority (29 African Americans, 8 American Indian/Alaska Native, 11 Asian Americans or Pacific Islanders, 75 Hispanic Americans), 31 international. Average age 38. *Faculty:* 42 full-time (17 women), 356 part-time/adjunct (56 women). Expenses: Contact institution. *Financial support:* Institutionally sponsored loans and scholarships/grants available. Financial award applicants required to submit FAFSA. In 2006, 209 degrees awarded. *Degree program information:* Evening/weekend programs available. Offers business (MBA, MIS, MM). *Application deadline:* Applications are processed on a rolling basis. *Application fee:* $45. Electronic applications accepted. *Provost*, Dr. Adam Honea, 480-557-1659, E-mail: adam.honea@phoenix.edu.

College of Graduate Business and Management Students: 412 full-time (205 women); includes 107 minority (23 African Americans, 7 American Indian/Alaska Native, 10 Asian Americans or Pacific Islanders, 67 Hispanic Americans), 24 international. Average age 36. *Faculty:* 29 full-time (13 women), 207 part-time/adjunct (40 women). Expenses: Contact institution. *Financial support:* Institutionally sponsored loans and scholarships/grants available. Financial award applicants required to submit FAFSA. In 2006, 141 degrees awarded. *Degree program information:* Evening/weekend programs available. Offers accounting (MBA); business administration (MBA); global management (MBA); management (MM). *Application deadline:* Applications are processed on a rolling basis. *Application fee:* $45. Electronic applications accepted. *Application Contact:* Campus College Chair, 520-881-6512, Fax: 520-795-6177. *Associate Vice President and Dean/Executive Director,* Dr. Brian Lindquist, 480-557-1221, E-mail: brian.lindquist@phoenix.edu.

College of Information Systems and Technology Students: 63 full-time (16 women); includes 16 minority (6 African Americans, 1 American Indian/Alaska Native, 1 Asian American or Pacific Islander, 8 Hispanic Americans), 7 international. Average age 37. *Faculty:* 13 full-time (4 women), 120 part-time/adjunct (16 women). Expenses: Contact institution. *Financial support:* Institutionally sponsored loans and scholarships/grants available. Financial award applicants required to submit FAFSA. In 2006, 68 degrees awarded. *Degree program information:* Evening/weekend programs available. Offers information systems (MIS); technology management (MBA). *Application deadline:* Applications are processed on a rolling basis. *Application fee:* $45. Electronic applications accepted. *Application Contact:* Campus College Chair-Technology, 520-881-6512, Fax: 520-795-6177. *Provost/Dean, Vice President Academic Research and Development,* Dr. Adam Honea, 480-557-1659, E-mail: adam.honea@phoenix.edu.

UNIVERSITY OF PHOENIX–SOUTHERN CALIFORNIA CAMPUS, Costa Mesa, CA 92626

General Information Proprietary, coed, comprehensive institution. *Enrollment:* 14,760 graduate, professional, and undergraduate students; 3,593 full-time matriculated graduate/professional students (2,460 women). *Enrollment by degree level:* 3,593 master's. *Graduate faculty:* 147 full-time (63 women), 1,450 part-time/adjunct (535 women). *Tuition:* Full-time $13,512. *Required fees:* $760. *Graduate housing:* On-campus housing not available. *Student services:* Campus safety program, disabled student services, writing training. *Library facilities:* University Library. *Online resources:* library catalog, web page. *Collection:* 1,759 titles, 692 serial subscriptions.

Computer facilities: A campuswide network can be accessed from off campus. Internet access is available. *Web address:* http://www.phoenix.edu/.

General Application Contact: Campus Information Center, 714-378-1878, Fax: 714-378-5875.

GRADUATE UNITS

The Artemis School Students: 1,989 full-time (1,566 women); includes 743 minority (278 African Americans, 10 American Indian/Alaska Native, 125 Asian Americans or Pacific Islanders, 330 Hispanic Americans), 142 international. Average age 36. *Faculty:* 75 full-time (41 women), 651 part-time/adjunct (348 women). Expenses: Contact institution. *Financial support:* Institutionally sponsored loans and scholarships/grants available. Financial award applicants required to submit FAFSA. In 2006, 472 degrees awarded. *Degree program information:* Evening/weekend programs available. *Application deadline:* Applications are processed on a rolling basis. *Application fee:* $45. Electronic applications accepted. *Provost,* Dr. Adam Honea, 480-557-1659, E-mail: adam.honea@phoenix.edu.

College of Education Students: 1,152 full-time (858 women); includes 420 minority (135 African Americans, 7 American Indian/Alaska Native, 59 Asian Americans or Pacific Islanders, 219 Hispanic Americans), 78 international. Average age 34. *Faculty:* 22 full-time (9 women), 195 part-time/adjunct (108 women). Expenses: Contact institution. *Financial support:* Institutionally sponsored loans and scholarships/grants available. Financial award applicants required to submit FAFSA. In 2006, 359 degrees awarded. *Degree program information:* Evening/weekend programs available. Offers curriculum and instruction (MA Ed); elementary education (MA Ed); secondary education (MA Ed). *Application deadline:* Applications are processed on a rolling basis. *Application fee:* $45. Electronic applications accepted. *Application Contact:* Campus College Chair, 714-378-1878, Fax: 714-378-5875. *Dean/Executive Director,* Dr. Marla LaRue, 480-557-1218, E-mail: marla.larue@phoenix.edu.

College of Health and Human Services Students: 623 full-time (524 women); includes 237 minority (98 African Americans, 2 American Indian/Alaska Native, 62 Asian Americans or Pacific Islanders, 75 Hispanic Americans), 59 international. Average age 40. *Faculty:* 53 full-time (32 women), 456 part-time/adjunct (240 women). Expenses: Contact institution. *Financial support:* Institutionally sponsored loans and scholarships/grants available. Financial award applicants required to submit FAFSA. In 2006, 113 degrees awarded. *Degree program information:* Evening/weekend programs available. Offers family nurse practitioner (MSN, Certificate); health care education (MSN); health care management (MBA); marriage, family and child therapy (MSC); nursing (MSN). *Application deadline:* Applications are processed on a rolling basis. *Application fee:* $45. Electronic applications accepted. *Application Contact:* Campus College Chair, 714-398-1878, Fax: 714-378-5856. *Dean/Executive Director,* Dr. Gil Linne, 480-557-1751, E-mail: gil.linne@phoenix.edu.

John Sperling School of Business Students: 1,578 full-time (872 women); includes 583 minority (242 African Americans, 7 American Indian/Alaska Native, 129 Asian Americans or Pacific Islanders, 205 Hispanic Americans), 128 international. Average age 38. *Faculty:* 71 full-time (22 women), 791 part-time/adjunct (183 women). Expenses: Contact institution. *Financial support:* Institutionally sponsored loans and scholarships/grants available. Financial award applicants required to submit FAFSA. In 2006, 461 degrees awarded. *Degree program information:* Evening/weekend programs available. Offers business (MBA, MM). *Application deadline:* Applications are processed on a rolling basis. *Application fee:* $45. Electronic applications accepted. *Provost,* Dr. Adam Honea, 480-557-1659, E-mail: adam.honea@phoenix.edu.

College of Graduate Business and Management Students: 1,491 full-time (852 women); includes 558 minority (233 African Americans, 7 American Indian/Alaska Native, 124 Asian Americans or Pacific Islanders, 194 Hispanic Americans), 116 international. Average age 38. *Faculty:* 47 full-time (13 women), 513 part-time/adjunct (138 women). Expenses: Contact institution. *Financial support:* Institutionally sponsored loans and scholarships/grants available. Financial award applicants required to submit FAFSA. In 2006, 401 degrees awarded. *Degree program information:* Evening/weekend programs available. Offers accounting (MBA); business administration (MBA); business and management (MM); human resource management (MBA); marketing (MBA). *Application deadline:* Applications are processed on a rolling basis. *Application fee:* $45. Electronic applications accepted. *Application Contact:* Campus College Chair, 714-378-1878, Fax: 714-378-5875. *Associate Vice President and Dean/Executive Director,* Dr. Brian Lindquist, 480-557-1221, E-mail: brian.lindquist@phoenix.edu.

College of Information Systems and Technology Students: 87 full-time (20 women); includes 25 minority (9 African Americans, 5 Asian Americans or Pacific Islanders, 11 Hispanic Americans), 12 international. Average age 39. *Faculty:* 24 full-time (9 women), 278 part-time/adjunct (45 women). Expenses: Contact institution. *Financial support:* Institutionally sponsored loans and scholarships/grants available. Financial award applicants required to submit FAFSA. In 2006, 60 degrees awarded. *Degree program information:* Evening/weekend programs available. Offers technology management (MBA). *Application deadline:* Applications are processed on a rolling basis. *Application fee:* $45. Electronic applications accepted. *Application Contact:* Campus College Chair, 714-378-1878. *Provost/Dean, Vice President Academic Research and Development,* Dr. Adam Honea, 480-557-1659, E-mail: adam.honea@phoenix.edu.

UNIVERSITY OF PHOENIX–SOUTHERN COLORADO CAMPUS, Colorado Springs, CO 80919-2335

General Information Proprietary, coed, comprehensive institution. *Enrollment:* 1,090 graduate, professional, and undergraduate students; 471 full-time matriculated graduate/professional students (306 women). *Enrollment by degree level:* 471 master's. *Graduate faculty:* 13 full-time (5 women), 489 part-time/adjunct (161 women). *Tuition:* Full-time $10,291. *Required fees:* $760. *Graduate housing:* On-campus housing not available. *Student services:* Campus safety program, disabled student services, writing training. *Library facilities:* University Library. *Online resources:* library catalog, web page. *Collection:* 1,759 titles, 692 serial subscriptions.

Computer facilities: A campuswide network can be accessed from off campus. Internet access is available. *Web address:* http://www.phoenix.edu/.

General Application Contact: Campus Information Center, 719-599-5282, Fax: 719-599-7973.

GRADUATE UNITS

The Artemis School Students: 328 full-time (234 women); includes 36 minority (11 African Americans, 4 American Indian/Alaska Native, 4 Asian Americans or Pacific Islanders, 17 Hispanic Americans), 31 international. Average age 37. *Faculty:* 9 full-time (5 women), 190 part-time/adjunct (90 women). Expenses: Contact institution. *Financial support:* Institutionally sponsored loans and scholarships/grants available. Financial award applicants required to submit FAFSA. In 2006, 142 degrees awarded. *Degree program information:* Evening/weekend programs available. *Application deadline:* Applications are processed on a rolling basis. *Application fee:* $45. Electronic applications accepted. *Provost,* Dr. Adam Honea, 480-557-1659, E-mail: adam.honea@phoenix.edu.

College of Education Students: 220 full-time (162 women); includes 22 minority (7 African Americans, 1 American Indian/Alaska Native, 4 Asian Americans or Pacific Islanders, 10 Hispanic Americans), 15 international. Average age 37. *Faculty:* 7 full-time (3 women), 90 part-time/adjunct (53 women). Expenses: Contact institution. *Financial support:* Institutionally sponsored loans and scholarships/grants available. Financial award applicants required to submit FAFSA. In 2006, 122 degrees awarded. *Degree program information:* Evening/weekend programs available. Offers administration and supervision (MA Ed); curriculum and instruction (MA Ed); elementary licensure (MA Ed); principal licensure certification (Certificate); school counseling (MSC); secondary licensure (MA Ed). *Application deadline:* Applications are processed on a rolling basis. *Application fee:* $45. Electronic applications accepted. *Application Contact:* Chair, 719-599-5282, Fax: 719-599-7973. *Dean/Executive Director,* Dr. Marla LaRue, 480-557-1218, E-mail: marla.larue@phoenix.edu.

College of Health and Human Services Students: 76 full-time (52 women); includes 10 minority (3 African Americans, 2 American Indian/Alaska Native, 5 Hispanic Americans). Average age 38. *Faculty:* 2 full-time (both women), 100 part-time/adjunct (37 women). Expenses: Contact institution. *Financial support:* Institutionally sponsored loans and scholarships/grants available. Financial award applicants required to submit FAFSA. In 2006, 20 degrees awarded. *Degree program information:* Evening/weekend programs available. Offers community counseling (MSC); health care management (MBA); marriage, family and child therapy (MSC); nursing (MSN). *Application deadline:* Applications are processed on a rolling basis. *Application fee:* $45. Electronic applications accepted. *Application Contact:* Chair, 719-599-5282, Fax: 719-599-7973. *Dean/Executive Director,* Dr. Gil Linne, 480-557-1751, E-mail: gil.linne@phoenix.edu.

John Sperling School of Business Students: 108 full-time (53 women); includes 21 minority (8 African Americans, 1 American Indian/Alaska Native, 5 Asian Americans or Pacific Islanders, 7 Hispanic Americans), 4 international. Average age 38. *Faculty:* 4 full-time (0 women), 298 part-time/adjunct (71 women). Expenses: Contact institution. *Financial support:* Institutionally sponsored loans and scholarships/grants available. Financial award applicants required to submit FAFSA. In 2006, 53 degrees awarded. *Degree program information:* Evening/weekend programs available. Offers business (MBA). *Application deadline:* Applications are processed on a rolling basis. *Application fee:* $45. Electronic applications accepted. *Provost and Senior Vice President of Academic Affairs,* Dr. William Pepicello, 480-557-1925, E-mail: bill.pepicello@phoenix.edu.

College of Graduate Business and Management Students: 107 full-time (53 women); includes 21 minority (8 African Americans, 1 American Indian/Alaska Native, 5 Asian Americans or Pacific Islanders, 7 Hispanic Americans), 4 international. Average age 38. *Faculty:* 209 part-time/adjunct (51 women). Expenses: Contact institution. *Financial support:* Institutionally sponsored loans and scholarships/grants available. Financial award applicants required to submit FAFSA. In 2006, 47 master's awarded. *Degree program information:* Evening/weekend programs available. Offers business administration (MBA). *Application deadline:* Applications are processed on a rolling basis. *Application fee:* $45. Electronic applications accepted. *Application Contact:* Chair, 719-599-5282, Fax: 719-599-7973. *Associate Vice President and Dean/Executive Director,* Dr. Brian Lindquist, 480-557-1221, E-mail: brian.lindquist@phoenix.edu.

College of Information Systems and Technology Students: 1 full-time (0 women). Average age 25. *Faculty:* 4 full-time (0 women), 89 part-time/adjunct (20 women). Expenses: Contact institution. *Financial support:* Institutionally sponsored loans and scholarships/grants available. Financial award applicants required to submit FAFSA. In 2006, 6 degrees awarded. *Degree program information:* Evening/weekend programs available. Offers technology management (MBA). *Application deadline:* Applications are processed on a rolling basis. *Application fee:* $45. Electronic applications accepted. *Application Contact:* Chair, 719-599-5282, Fax: 719-599-7973. *Provost/Dean, Vice President Academic Research and Development,* Dr. Adam Honea, 480-557-1659, E-mail: adam.honea@phoenix.edu.

UNIVERSITY OF PHOENIX–SPRINGFIELD CAMPUS, Springfield, MO 65804-7211

General Information Proprietary, coed, comprehensive institution.

GRADUATE UNITS

College of Education Offers administration and supervision (MA Ed); curriculum and instruction (MA Ed); curriculum and instruction/adult education (MA Ed); curriculum and instruction/computer education (MA Ed); curriculum and instruction/English as a second language (MA Ed); English and language arts education (MA Ed); mathematics education (MA Ed).

College of Graduate Business and Management Offers accounting (MBA); business and management (MBA); global management (MBA); human resources management (MBA, MM); management (MM); marketing (MBA); public administration (MBA, MM).

College of Health and Human Services Offers administration/health care management (MSN); health administration (MHA); health care management (MBA); nursing (MSN).

College of Information Systems and Technology Offers information systems and technology (MIS); technology management (MBA).

College of Social and Behavioral Science Offers administration of justice and security (MS).

UNIVERSITY OF PHOENIX–TULSA CAMPUS, Tulsa, OK 74146-3801

General Information Proprietary, coed, comprehensive institution. *Enrollment:* 1,169 graduate, professional, and undergraduate students; 150 full-time matriculated graduate/professional students (77 women). *Enrollment by degree level:* 150 master's. *Graduate faculty:* 27 full-time (7 women), 276 part-time/adjunct (87 women). *Tuition:* Full-time $10,608. *Required fees:* $760. *Graduate housing:* On-campus housing not available. *Student services:* Campus safety program, disabled student services, writing training. *Library facilities:* University Library. *Online resources:* library catalog, web page. *Collection:* 1,759 titles, 692 serial subscriptions.

Computer facilities: A campuswide network can be accessed from off campus. Internet access is available. *Web address:* http://www.phoenix.edu/.

General Application Contact: Campus Information Center, 918-622-4877, Fax: 618-622-4981.

GRADUATE UNITS

John Sperling School of Business Students: 146 full-time (73 women); includes 31 minority (21 African Americans, 3 American Indian/Alaska Native, 2 Asian Americans or Pacific Islanders, 5 Hispanic Americans), 17 international. Average age 38. *Faculty:* 24 full-time (7 women), 213 part-time/adjunct (57 women). Expenses: Contact institution. *Financial support:* Institutionally sponsored loans and scholarships/grants available. Financial award applicants required to submit FAFSA. In 2006, 60 degrees awarded. *Degree program information:*

University of Phoenix–Tulsa Campus (continued)

Evening/weekend programs available. Offers business (MBA, MM). *Application deadline:* Applications are processed on a rolling basis. *Application fee:* $45. *Application Contact:* Chair, 918-622-4877, Fax: 918-622-4981. *Provost,* Dr. Adam Honea, 480-557-1659, E-mail: adam.honea@phoenix.edu.

College of Graduate Business and Management Students: 142 full-time (71 women); includes 30 minority (20 African Americans, 3 American Indian/Alaska Native, 2 Asian Americans or Pacific Islanders, 5 Hispanic Americans), 17 international. Average age 38. *Faculty:* 16 full-time (7 women), 160 part-time/adjunct (50 women). Expenses: Contact institution. *Financial support:* Institutionally sponsored loans and scholarships/grants available. Financial award applicants required to submit FAFSA. In 2006, 50 degrees awarded. *Degree program information:* Evening/weekend programs available. Offers business administration (MBA); business and management (MM). *Application deadline:* Applications are processed on a rolling basis. *Application fee:* $45. *Application Contact:* Campus College Chair, 918-622-4877, Fax: 918-622-4981. *Associate Vice President and Dean/Executive Director,* Dr. Brian Lindquist, 480-557-1221, E-mail: brian.lindquist@phoenix.edu.

UNIVERSITY OF PHOENIX–UTAH CAMPUS, Salt Lake City, UT 84123-4617

General Information Proprietary, coed, comprehensive institution. *Enrollment:* 3,986 graduate, professional, and undergraduate students; 1,427 full-time matriculated graduate/professional students (671 women). *Enrollment by degree level:* 1,427 master's. *Graduate faculty:* 124 full-time (24 women), 404 part-time/adjunct (103 women). *Tuition:* Full-time $9,104. *Required fees:* $760. *Graduate housing:* On-campus housing not available. *Student services:* Campus safety program, disabled student services, writing training. *Library facilities:* University Library. *Online resources:* library catalog, web page. *Collection:* 1,759 titles, 692 serial subscriptions.

Computer facilities: A campuswide network can be accessed from off campus. Internet access is available. *Web address:* http://www.phoenix.edu/.

General Application Contact: Campus Information Center, 801-263-1444, Fax: 801-269-9766.

GRADUATE UNITS

The Artemis School Students: 776 full-time (510 women); includes 40 minority (4 African Americans, 2 American Indian/Alaska Native, 16 Asian Americans or Pacific Islanders, 18 Hispanic Americans), 13 international. Average age 37. *Faculty:* 39 full-time (16 women), 127 part-time/adjunct (98 women). Expenses: Contact institution. *Financial support:* Institutionally sponsored loans and scholarships/grants available. Financial award applicants required to submit FAFSA. In 2006, 292 degrees awarded. *Degree program information:* Evening/weekend programs available. *Application deadline:* Applications are processed on a rolling basis. *Application fee:* $45. Electronic applications accepted. *Provost,* Dr. Adam Honea, 480-577-1659, E-mail: adam.honea@phoenix.edu.

College of Education Students: 395 full-time (246 women); includes 20 minority (2 African Americans, 1 American Indian/Alaska Native, 8 Asian Americans or Pacific Islanders, 9 Hispanic Americans), 4 international. Average age 37. *Faculty:* 14 full-time (8 women), 78 part-time/adjunct (39 women). Expenses: Contact institution. *Financial support:* Institutionally sponsored loans and scholarships/grants available. Financial award applicants required to submit FAFSA. In 2006, 233 degrees awarded. *Degree program information:* Evening/weekend programs available. Offers administration and supervision (MA Ed); curriculum and instruction (MA Ed); elementary education (MA Ed); school counseling (MSC); secondary education (MA Ed). *Application deadline:* Applications are processed on a rolling basis. *Application fee:* $45. Electronic applications accepted. *Application Contact:* Chair, 801-263-1444, Fax: 801-269-9766. *Dean/Executive Director,* Dr. Marla LaRue, 480-557-1218, E-mail: marla.larue@phoenix.edu.

College of Health and Human Services Students: 381 full-time (264 women); includes 20 minority (2 African Americans, 1 American Indian/Alaska Native, 8 Asian Americans or Pacific Islanders, 9 Hispanic Americans), 9 international. Average age 38. *Faculty:* 25 full-time (8 women), 105 part-time/adjunct (46 women). Expenses: Contact institution. *Financial support:* Institutionally sponsored loans and scholarships/grants available. Financial award applicants required to submit FAFSA. In 2006, 59 degrees awarded. *Degree program information:* Evening/weekend programs available. Offers business administration healthcare (MSN); mental health counseling (MSC); nursing (MSN). *Application deadline:* Applications are processed on a rolling basis. *Application fee:* $45. Electronic applications accepted. *Application Contact:* Chair, 801-263-1444, Fax: 801-269-9766. *Dean/Executive Director,* Dr. Gil Linne, 480-557-1751, E-mail: gil.linne@phoenix.edu.

John Sperling School of Business Students: 651 full-time (161 women); includes 82 minority (4 African Americans, 3 American Indian/Alaska Native, 14 Asian Americans or Pacific Islanders, 61 Hispanic Americans), 21 international. Average age 37. *Faculty:* 85 full-time (8 women), 219 part-time/adjunct (18 women). Expenses: Contact institution. *Financial support:* Institutionally sponsored loans and scholarships/grants available. Financial award applicants required to submit FAFSA. In 2006, 266 degrees awarded. *Degree program information:* Evening/weekend programs available. Offers business (MBA, MIS). *Application deadline:* Applications are processed on a rolling basis. *Application fee:* $45. Electronic applications accepted. *Application Contact:* College Chair, 801-263-1444, Fax: 801-269-9766. *Provost and Senior Vice Presidnet of Academic Affairs,* Dr. William Pepicello, 480-559-1925, E-mail: will.pepicello@phoenix.edu.

College of Graduate Business and Management Students: 618 full-time (158 women); includes 32 minority (4 African Americans, 3 American Indian/Alaska Native, 14 Asian Americans or Pacific Islanders, 11 Hispanic Americans), 21 international. Average age 36. *Faculty:* 58 full-time (7 women), 155 part-time/adjunct (14 women). Expenses: Contact institution. *Financial support:* Institutionally sponsored loans and scholarships/grants available. Financial award applicants required to submit FAFSA. In 2006, 251 degrees awarded. *Degree program information:* Evening/weekend programs available. Offers business administration (MBA). *Application deadline:* Applications are processed on a rolling basis. *Application fee:* $45. Electronic applications accepted. *Application Contact:* Chair, 801-263-1444, Fax: 801-269-9766. *Associate Vice President and Dean/Executive Director,* Dr. Brian Lindquist, 480-557-1221, E-mail: brian.lindquist@phoenix.edu.

College of Information Systems and Technology Students: 33 full-time (3 women); includes 1 minority (Asian American or Pacific Islander) Average age 32. *Faculty:* 27 full-time (1 woman), 64 part-time/adjunct (4 women). Expenses: Contact institution. *Financial support:* Institutionally sponsored loans and scholarships/grants available. Financial award applicants required to submit FAFSA. In 2006, 15 degrees awarded. *Degree program information:* Evening/weekend programs available. Offers information systems and technology (MIS). *Application deadline:* Applications are processed on a rolling basis. *Application fee:* $45. Electronic applications accepted. *Application Contact:* Chair, 801-263-1444, Fax: 801-269-9766. *Provost/Dean, Vice President Academic Research and Development,* Dr. Adam Honea, 480-557-1659, E-mail: adam.honea@phoenix.edu.

UNIVERSITY OF PHOENIX–VANCOUVER CAMPUS, Burnaby, BC V5C 6G9, Canada

General Information Proprietary, coed, comprehensive institution. *Enrollment:* 263 full-time matriculated graduate/professional students (129 women). *Enrollment by degree level:* 263 master's. *Graduate faculty:* 71. *Tuition:* Full-time $12,840. *Required fees:* $760. *Graduate housing:* On-campus housing not available. *Student services:* Campus safety program, disabled student services, writing training. *Library facilities:* University Library. *Online resources:* library catalog, web page. *Collection:* 444 titles, 666 serial subscriptions.

Computer facilities: A campuswide network can be accessed from off campus. Internet access is available. *Web address:* http://www.phoenix.edu/.

General Application Contact: Campus Information Center, 604-205-6999.

GRADUATE UNITS

The Artemis School Students: 131 full-time (79 women); includes 6 minority (all Asian Americans or Pacific Islanders) Average age 40. *Faculty:* 25. Expenses: Contact institution. *Financial support:* Institutionally sponsored loans and scholarships/grants available. In 2006, 55 degrees awarded. *Degree program information:* Evening/weekend programs available. *Application deadline:* Applications are processed on a rolling basis. *Application fee:* $45. Electronic applications accepted. *Provost,* Dr. Adam Honea, 480-557-1659, E-mail: adam.honea@phoenix.edu.

College of Education Students: 131 full-time (79 women); includes 6 minority (all Asian Americans or Pacific Islanders) Average age 40. *Faculty:* 25. Expenses: Contact institution. *Financial support:* Institutionally sponsored loans and scholarships/grants available. In 2006, 49 degrees awarded. *Degree program information:* Evening/weekend programs available. Offers administration and supervision (MA Ed); curriculum and instruction (MA Ed). *Application deadline:* Applications are processed on a rolling basis. *Application fee:* $45. Electronic applications accepted. *Application Contact:* Chair, 404-205-6999. *Dean/Executive Director,* Dr. Marla LaRue, 480-557-1218, E-mail: marla.larue@phoenix.edu.

College of Health and Human Services Students: 2 full-time (0 women). Average age 36. Expenses: Contact institution. *Financial support:* Institutionally sponsored loans available. *Degree program information:* Evening/weekend programs available. Offers health care management (MBA). *Application deadline:* Applications are processed on a rolling basis. *Application fee:* $45. Electronic applications accepted. *Dean/Executive Director,* Dr. Gil Linne, 480-557-1751, E-mail: gil.linne@phoenix.edu.

John Sperling School of Business Students: 116 full-time (41 women); includes 50 minority (2 African Americans, 1 American Indian/Alaska Native, 45 Asian Americans or Pacific Islanders, 2 Hispanic Americans). Average age 36. *Faculty:* 46. Expenses: Contact institution. *Financial support:* Institutionally sponsored loans and scholarships/grants available. In 2006, 42 degrees awarded. *Degree program information:* Evening/weekend programs available. Offers business (MBA). *Application deadline:* Applications are processed on a rolling basis. *Application fee:* $45. Electronic applications accepted. *Provost,* Dr. Adam Honea, 480-557-1659, E-mail: adam.honea@phoenix.edu.

College of Graduate Business and Management Students: 101 full-time (38 women); includes 45 minority (2 African Americans, 1 American Indian/Alaska Native, 40 Asian Americans or Pacific Islanders, 2 Hispanic Americans). Average age 36. *Faculty:* 39. Expenses: Contact institution. *Financial support:* Institutionally sponsored loans and scholarships/grants available. In 2006, 38 degrees awarded. *Degree program information:* Evening/weekend programs available. Offers business administration (MBA). *Application deadline:* Applications are processed on a rolling basis. *Application fee:* $45. Electronic applications accepted. *Application Contact:* Chair, 604-205-6999. *Associate Vice President and Dean/Executive Director,* Dr. Brian Lindquist, 480-557-1221, E-mail: brian.lindquist@phoenix.edu.

College of Information Systems and Technology Students: 15 full-time (3 women); includes 5 minority (all Asian Americans or Pacific Islanders) Average age 35. *Faculty:* 7. Expenses: Contact institution. *Financial support:* Institutionally sponsored loans and scholarships/grants available. In 2006, 4 degrees awarded. *Degree program information:* Evening/weekend programs available. Offers technology management (MBA). *Application deadline:* Applications are processed on a rolling basis. *Application fee:* $45. Electronic applications accepted. *Application Contact:* Campus College Chair, 604-205-6999. *Dean,* Dr. Adam Honea, 480-557-1659, E-mail: adam.honea@phoenix.edu.

UNIVERSITY OF PHOENIX–WASHINGTON CAMPUS, Seattle, WA 98188-7500

General Information Proprietary, coed, comprehensive institution. *Enrollment:* 1,758 graduate, professional, and undergraduate students; 323 full-time matriculated graduate/professional students (153 women). *Enrollment by degree level:* 323 master's. *Graduate faculty:* 48 full-time (17 women), 225 part-time/adjunct (64 women). *Tuition:* Full-time $10,200. *Required fees:* $760. *Graduate housing:* On-campus housing not available. *Student services:* Campus safety program, disabled student services, writing training. *Library facilities:* University Library. *Online resources:* library catalog, web page. *Collection:* 1,759 titles, 692 serial subscriptions.

Computer facilities: A campuswide network can be accessed from off campus. Internet access is available. *Web address:* http://www.phoenix.edu/.

General Application Contact: Campus Information Center, 206-268-5800, Fax: 206-241-8848.

GRADUATE UNITS

The Artemis School Students: 20 full-time (16 women); includes 8 minority (4 African Americans, 3 Asian Americans or Pacific Islanders, 1 Hispanic American), 1 international. Average age 37. *Faculty:* 9 full-time (3 women), 47 part-time/adjunct (23 women). Expenses: Contact institution. *Financial support:* Institutionally sponsored loans and scholarships/grants available. *Degree program information:* Evening/weekend programs available. *Application deadline:* Applications are processed on a rolling basis. *Application fee:* $45. Electronic applications accepted. *Provost,* Dr. Adam Honea, 480-557-1659, E-mail: adam.honea@phoenix.edu.

College of Health and Human Services Students: 20 full-time (16 women); includes 8 minority (4 African Americans, 3 Asian Americans or Pacific Islanders, 1 Hispanic American), 1 international. Average age 37. *Faculty:* 1 full-time (0 women), 35 part-time/adjunct (17 women). Expenses: Contact institution. *Financial support:* Institutionally sponsored loans and scholarships/grants available. *Degree program information:* Evening/weekend programs available. Offers health care management (MBA). *Application deadline:* Applications are processed on a rolling basis. *Application fee:* $45. Electronic applications accepted. *Application Contact:* College Chair, 206-268-5800, Fax: 206-241-8848. *Dean/Executive Director,* Dr. Gil Linne, 480-557-1221, E-mail: gil.linne@phoenix.edu.

John Sperling School of Business Students: 303 full-time (137 women); includes 66 minority (17 African Americans, 1 American Indian/Alaska Native, 29 Asian Americans or Pacific Islanders, 19 Hispanic Americans), 12 international. Average age 38. *Faculty:* 37 full-time (13 women), 177 part-time/adjunct (41 women). Expenses: Contact institution. *Financial support:* Institutionally sponsored loans and scholarships/grants available. Financial award applicants required to submit FAFSA. In 2006, 109 degrees awarded. *Degree program information:* Evening/weekend programs available. Offers business (MBA). *Application deadline:* Applications are processed on a rolling basis. *Application fee:* $45. Electronic applications accepted. *Provost,* Dr. Adam Honea, 480-557-1659, E-mail: adam.honea@phoenix.edu.

College of Graduate Business and Management Students: 262 full-time (125 women); includes 57 minority (15 African Americans, 1 American Indian/Alaska Native, 27 Asian Americans or Pacific Islanders, 14 Hispanic Americans), 7 international. Average age 37. *Faculty:* 30 full-time (11 women), 117 part-time/adjunct (27 women). Expenses: Contact institution. *Financial support:* Institutionally sponsored loans and scholarships/grants available. Financial award applicants required to submit FAFSA. In 2006, 109 degrees awarded. *Degree program information:* Evening/weekend programs available. Offers business administration (MBA). *Application deadline:* Applications are processed on a rolling basis. *Application fee:* $45. Electronic applications accepted. *Application Contact:* Chair, 206-268-5800, Fax: 206-241-8848. *Associate Vice President and Dean/Executive Director,* Dr. Brian Lindquist, 480-557-1221, E-mail: brian.lindquist@phoenix.edu.

UNIVERSITY OF PHOENIX–WEST FLORIDA CAMPUS, Temple Terrace, FL 33637

General Information Proprietary, coed, comprehensive institution. *Enrollment:* 2,659 graduate, professional, and undergraduate students; 675 full-time matriculated graduate/professional students (422 women). *Enrollment by degree level:* 674 master's. *Graduate faculty:* 84 full-time (42 women), 316 part-time/adjunct (85 women). *Tuition:* Full-time $9,450. *Required fees:* $760. *Graduate housing:* On-campus housing not available. *Student services:* Campus safety program, disabled student services, writing training. *Library facilities:* University Library. *Online resources:* library catalog, web page. *Collection:* 1,759 titles, 692 serial subscriptions.

Computer facilities: A campuswide network can be accessed from off campus. Internet access is available. *Web address:* http://www.phoenix.edu/.

General Application Contact: Campus Information Center, 813-626-7911, Fax: 813-977-1449.

GRADUATE UNITS

The Artemis School Students: 154 full-time (140 women); includes 34 minority (21 African Americans, 2 Asian Americans or Pacific Islanders, 11 Hispanic Americans), 13 international. Average age 43. *Faculty:* 29 full-time (20 women), 71 part-time/adjunct (38 women). Expenses: Contact institution. *Financial support:* Institutionally sponsored loans and scholarships/grants available. Financial award applicants required to submit FAFSA. In 2006, 26 degrees awarded. *Degree program information:* Evening/weekend programs available. *Application deadline:* Applications are processed on a rolling basis. *Application fee:* $45. Electronic applications accepted. *Provost,* Dr. Adam Honea, 480-557-1659, E-mail: adam.honea@phoenix.edu.

College of Education Students: 67 full-time (61 women); includes 24 minority (20 African Americans, 1 American Indian/Alaska Native, 3 Hispanic Americans), 3 international. Average age 40. *Faculty:* 10 full-time (8 women), 15 part-time/adjunct (7 women). Expenses: Contact institution. *Financial support:* Institutionally sponsored loans and scholarships/grants available. Financial award applicants required to submit FAFSA. In 2006, 8 degrees awarded. *Degree program information:* Evening/weekend programs available. Offers administration and supervision (MA Ed); curriculum and instruction (MA Ed); curriculum and technology (MA Ed); elementary teacher education (MA Ed); secondary teacher education (MA Ed). *Application fee:* $45. *Application Contact:* Chair, 813-626-7911, Fax: 813-977-1449. *Dean,* Dr. Marla LaRue, 480-557-1218, E-mail: marla.larue@phoenix.edu.

College of Health and Human Services Students: 87 full-time (79 women); includes 21 minority (12 African Americans, 1 Asian American or Pacific Islander, 8 Hispanic Americans), 10 international. Average age 45. *Faculty:* 19 full-time (12 women), 56 part-time/adjunct (31 women). Expenses: Contact institution. *Financial support:* Institutionally sponsored loans and scholarships/grants available. Financial award applicants required to submit FAFSA. In 2006, 18 degrees awarded. *Degree program information:* Evening/weekend programs available. Postbaccalaureate distance learning degree programs offered. Offers health administration (MHA); health care education (MSN); health care management (MHA). *Application deadline:* Applications are processed on a rolling basis. *Application fee:* $45. Electronic applications accepted. *Application Contact:* Chair, 813-626-7911, Fax: 813-977-1449. *Dean,* Dr. Gil Linne, 480-557-1751, E-mail: gil.linne@phoenix.edu.

The John Sperling School of Business Students: 521 full-time (282 women); includes 168 minority (105 African Americans, 5 American Indian/Alaska Native, 12 Asian Americans or Pacific Islanders, 46 Hispanic Americans), 52 international. Average age 37. *Faculty:* 55 full-time (22 women), 244 part-time/adjunct (47 women). Expenses: Contact institution. *Financial support:* Institutionally sponsored loans and scholarships/grants available. Financial award applicants required to submit FAFSA. In 2006, 198 degrees awarded. *Degree program information:* Evening/weekend programs available. Offers business (MBA, MIS, MM). *Application deadline:* Applications are processed on a rolling basis. *Application fee:* $45. Electronic applications accepted. *Provost,* Dr. Adam Honea, 480-557-1659, E-mail: adam.honea@phoenix.edu.

College of Graduate Business and Management Students: 475 full-time (272 women); includes 150 minority (98 African Americans, 4 American Indian/Alaska Native, 9 Asian Americans or Pacific Islanders, 39 Hispanic Americans), 43 international. Average age 36. *Faculty:* 39 full-time (19 women), 145 part-time/adjunct (45 women). Expenses: Contact institution. *Financial support:* Institutionally sponsored loans and scholarships/grants available. Financial award applicants required to submit FAFSA. In 2006, 165 degrees awarded. *Degree program information:* Evening/weekend programs available. Offers business administration (MBA); global management (MBA); human resource management (MBA); human resources management (MM); management (MM); marketing (MBA); public administration (MBA). *Application deadline:* Applications are processed on a rolling basis. *Application fee:* $45. Electronic applications accepted. *Application Contact:* Chair, 813-626-7911, Fax: 813-977-1449. *Associate Vice President and Dean/Executive Director,* Dr. Brian Lindquist, 480-557-1221, E-mail: brian.lindquist@phoenix.edu.

College of Information Systems and Technology Students: 46 full-time (10 women); includes 18 minority (7 African Americans, 1 American Indian/Alaska Native, 3 Asian Americans or Pacific Islanders, 7 Hispanic Americans), 9 international. Average age 39. *Faculty:* 16 full-time (3 women), 79 part-time/adjunct (2 women). Expenses: Contact institution. *Financial support:* Institutionally sponsored loans and scholarships/grants available. Financial award applicants required to submit FAFSA. In 2006, 33 degrees awarded. *Degree program information:* Evening/weekend programs available. Offers information systems and technology (MIS); technology management (MBA). *Application deadline:* Applications are processed on a rolling basis. *Application fee:* $45. Electronic applications accepted. *Application Contact:* Chair, 813-626-7911, Fax: 813-977-1449.

UNIVERSITY OF PHOENIX–WEST MICHIGAN CAMPUS, Walker, MI 49544

General Information Proprietary, coed, comprehensive institution. *Enrollment:* 1,004 graduate, professional, and undergraduate students; 170 full-time matriculated graduate/professional students (97 women). *Enrollment by degree level:* 170 master's. *Graduate faculty:* 48 full-time (4 women), 187 part-time/adjunct (88 women). *Tuition:* Full-time $12,043. *Required fees:* $760. *Graduate housing:* On-campus housing not available. *Student services:* Campus safety program, disabled student services, writing training. *Library facilities:* University Library. *Online resources:* library catalog, web page. *Collection:* 1,759 titles, 692 serial subscriptions.

Computer facilities: A campuswide network can be accessed from off campus. Internet access is available. *Web address:* http://www.phoenix.edu/.

General Application Contact: Campus Information Center, 888-345-9699, Fax: 616-784-5300.

GRADUATE UNITS

The Artemis School Students: 40 full-time (35 women); includes 8 minority (6 African Americans, 2 Hispanic Americans), 3 international. Average age 39. *Faculty:* 14 full-time (4 women), 64 part-time/adjunct (37 women). Expenses: Contact institution. *Financial support:* Institutionally sponsored loans and scholarships/grants available. Financial award applicants required to submit FAFSA. In 2006, 12 master's awarded. *Degree program information:* Evening/weekend programs available. *Application deadline:* Applications are processed on a rolling basis. *Application fee:* $45. Electronic applications accepted. *Provost,* Dr. Adam Honea, 480-557-1659, E-mail: adam.honea@phoenix.edu.

College of Education *Faculty:* 5 full-time (1 woman), 15 part-time/adjunct (9 women). Expenses: Contact institution. *Financial support:* Institutionally sponsored loans and scholarships/grants available. Financial award applicants required to submit FAFSA. In 2006, 5 master's awarded. *Degree program information:* Evening/weekend programs available. Offers administration and supervision (MA Ed); curriculum and instruction (MA Ed). *Application deadline:* Applications are processed on a rolling basis. *Application fee:* $45. Electronic applications accepted. *Application Contact:* Chair, 888-345-9699, Fax: 616-784-5300. *Dean/Executive Director,* Dr. Marla LaRue, 480-557-1218, E-mail: marla.larue@phoenix.edu.

College of Health and Human Services Students: 40 full-time (35 women); includes 8 minority (6 African Americans, 2 Hispanic Americans), 3 international. Average age 39. *Faculty:* 9 full-time (3 women), 49 part-time/adjunct (28 women). Expenses: Contact institution. *Financial support:* Institutionally sponsored loans and scholarships/grants available. Financial award applicants required to submit FAFSA. In 2006, 7 master's awarded. *Degree program information:* Evening/weekend programs available. Offers health care management (MBA); nursing (MSN). *Application deadline:* Applications are processed on a rolling basis. *Application fee:* $45. Electronic applications accepted. *Application Contact:* Chair, 888-345-9699, Fax: 616-784-5300. *Dean/Executive Director,* Dr. Gil Linne, 480-557-1751, E-mail: gil.linne@phoenix.edu.

The John Sperling School of Business Students: 130 full-time (62 women); includes 19 minority (16 African Americans, 2 Asian Americans or Pacific Islanders, 1 Hispanic American), 4 international. Average age 37. *Faculty:* 34 full-time (0 women), 121 part-time/adjunct (49 women). Expenses: Contact institution. *Financial support:* Institutionally sponsored loans and scholarships/grants available. Financial award applicants required to submit FAFSA. In 2006, 61 degrees awarded. *Degree program information:* Evening/weekend programs available. Offers business (MBA). *Application deadline:* Applications are processed on a rolling basis. *Application fee:* $45. Electronic applications accepted. *Application Contact:* Chair, 888-345-9699, Fax: 616-784-5300. *Provost,* Dr. Adam Honea, 480-557-1659, E-mail: adam.honea@phoenix.edu.

College of Graduate Business and Management Students: 124 full-time (62 women); includes 16 minority (15 African Americans, 1 Hispanic American), 4 international. Average age 37. *Faculty:* 26 full-time (0 women), 95 part-time/adjunct (42 women). Expenses: Contact institution. *Financial support:* Institutionally sponsored loans and scholarships/grants available. Financial award applicants required to submit FAFSA. In 2006, 50 degrees awarded. *Degree program information:* Evening/weekend programs available. Offers accounting (MBA); business administration (MBA); global management (MBA); human resource management (MBA). *Application deadline:* Applications are processed on a rolling basis. *Application fee:* $45. Electronic applications accepted. *Application Contact:* Chair, 888-345-9699, Fax: 616-784-5300. *Associate Vice President and Dean/Executive Director,* Dr. Brian Lindquist, 480-557-1221, E-mail: brian.lindquist@phoenix.edu.

College of Information Systems and Technology Students: 6 full-time (0 women); includes 1 minority (African American) Average age 33. *Faculty:* 8 full-time (0 women), 26 part-time/adjunct (7 women). Expenses: Contact institution. *Financial support:* Institutionally sponsored loans available. Financial award applicants required to submit FAFSA. In 2006, 11 master's awarded. *Degree program information:* Evening/weekend programs available. Offers e-business (MBA); technology management (MBA). *Application deadline:* Applications are processed on a rolling basis. *Application fee:* $45. Electronic applications accepted. *Application Contact:* Chair, 888-345-9699, Fax: 616-784-5300. *Dean/Executive Director,* Dr. Adam Honea, 408-557-1659, E-mail: adam.honea@phoenix.edu.

UNIVERSITY OF PHOENIX–WICHITA CAMPUS, Wichita, KS 67226-4011

General Information Proprietary, coed, comprehensive institution. *Enrollment:* 406 graduate, professional, and undergraduate students; 64 full-time matriculated graduate/professional students (41 women). *Enrollment by degree level:* 64 master's. *Graduate faculty:* 15 full-time (3 women), 84 part-time/adjunct (22 women). *Tuition:* Full-time $10,560. *Required fees:* $760. *Graduate housing:* On-campus housing not available. *Student services:* Campus safety program, disabled student services, writing training. *Library facilities:* University Library. *Online resources:* library catalog, web page. *Collection:* 1,759 titles, 692 serial subscriptions.

Computer facilities: A campuswide network can be accessed from off campus. Internet access is available. *Web address:* http://www.phoenix.edu/.

General Application Contact: Campus Information Center, 316-630-8121.

GRADUATE UNITS

John Sperling School of Business Students: 73 full-time (40 women); includes 11 minority (4 African Americans, 1 American Indian/Alaska Native, 5 Asian Americans or Pacific Islanders, 1 Hispanic American), 13 international. Average age 38. *Faculty:* 12 full-time (1 woman), 65 part-time/adjunct (14 women). Expenses: Contact institution. *Financial support:* Institutionally sponsored loans and scholarships/grants available. Financial award applicants required to submit FAFSA. In 2006, 2 degrees awarded. *Degree program information:* Evening/weekend programs available. Offers business and management (MBA). *Application deadline:* Applications are processed on a rolling basis. *Application fee:* $45. Electronic applications accepted. *Application Contact:* Campus College Chair, 316-630-8121. *Provost,* Dr. Adam T. Honea, 480-557-1659, E-mail: adam.honea@phoenix.edu.

College of Graduate Business and Management Students: 59 full-time (38 women); includes 11 minority (4 African Americans, 1 American Indian/Alaska Native, 5 Asian Americans or Pacific Islanders, 1 Hispanic American), 12 international. Average age 37. *Faculty:* 8 full-time (1 woman), 55 part-time/adjunct (12 women). Expenses: Contact institution. *Financial support:* Institutionally sponsored loans and scholarships/grants available. Financial award applicants required to submit FAFSA. In 2006, 15 degrees awarded. *Degree program information:* Evening/weekend programs available. Offers business and management (MBA). *Application deadline:* Applications are processed on a rolling basis. *Application fee:* $45. Electronic applications accepted. *Application Contact:* Campus College Chair, 316-630-8121. *Associate Vice President and Dean/Executive Director,* Dr. Brian Lindquist, 480-557-1221, E-mail: brian.lindquist@phoenix.edu.

UNIVERSITY OF PHOENIX–WISCONSIN CAMPUS, Brookfield, WI 53045-6608

General Information Proprietary, coed, comprehensive institution. *Enrollment:* 1,132 graduate, professional, and undergraduate students; 249 full-time matriculated graduate/professional students (138 women). *Enrollment by degree level:* 249 master's. *Graduate faculty:* 19 full-time (12 women), 190 part-time/adjunct (68 women). *Tuition:* Full-time $10,944. *Required fees:* $760. *Graduate housing:* On-campus housing not available. *Student services:* Campus safety program, disabled student services, writing training. *Library facilities:* University Library. *Online resources:* library catalog, web page. *Collection:* 1,959 titles, 692 serial subscriptions.

Computer facilities: A campuswide network can be accessed from off campus. Internet access is available. *Web address:* http://www.phoenix.edu/.

General Application Contact: Campus Information Center, 262-785-0608.

GRADUATE UNITS

The Artemis School Students: 2 full-time (1 woman). Average age 48. *Faculty:* 11 part-time/adjunct (8 women). Expenses: Contact institution. *Financial support:* Institutionally sponsored loans and scholarships/grants available. Financial award applicants required to submit FAFSA. *Degree program information:* Evening/weekend programs available. *Application deadline:* Applications are processed on a rolling basis. *Application fee:* $45. Electronic applications accepted. *Provost,* Dr. Adam Honea, 480-557-1659, E-mail: adam.honea@phoenix.edu.

College of Health and Human Services Students: 2 full-time (1 woman). Average age 48. *Faculty:* 8 part-time/adjunct (6 women). Expenses: Contact institution. *Financial support:* Institutionally sponsored loans and scholarships/grants available. Financial award applicants required to submit FAFSA. *Degree program information:* Evening/weekend programs available. Offers health and human services). *Application deadline:* Applications are processed on a rolling basis. *Application fee:* $45. Electronic applications accepted. *Dean/Executive Director,* Dr. Gil Linne, 480-557-1751, E-mail: gin.linne@phoenix.edu.

John Sperling School of Business Students: 247 full-time (137 women); includes 51 minority (37 African Americans, 5 American Indian/Alaska Native, 5 Asian Americans or Pacific Islanders, 4 Hispanic Americans), 9 international. Average age 35. *Faculty:* 19 full-time (12 women), 177 part-time/adjunct (59 women). Expenses: Contact institution. *Financial support:* Institutionally sponsored loans and scholarships/grants available. Financial award applicants required to submit FAFSA. In 2006, 64 degrees awarded. *Degree program information:* Evening/weekend programs available. Offers business (MBA, MIS). *Application deadline:* Applications are processed on a rolling basis. *Application fee:* $45. Electronic applications accepted. *Provost,* Dr. Adam Honea, 480-557-1659, E-mail: adam.honea@phoenix.edu.

College of Graduate Business and Management Students: 245 full-time (137 women); includes 51 minority (37 African Americans, 5 American Indian/Alaska Native, 5 Asian Americans or Pacific Islanders, 4 Hispanic Americans), 9 international. Average age 35. *Faculty:* 15 full-time (10 women), 135 part-time/adjunct (48 women). Expenses: Contact institution. *Financial support:* Institutionally sponsored loans and scholarships/grants available. Financial award applicants required to submit FAFSA. In 2006, 64 degrees awarded. *Degree program information:* Evening/weekend programs available. Offers administration (MBA). *Application deadline:* Applications are processed on a rolling basis. *Application*

University of Phoenix–Wisconsin Campus (continued)

fee: $45. Electronic applications accepted. *Application Contact:* Chair, 262-785-0608, Fax: 262-785-0977. *Associate Vice President/Dean,* Dr. Brian Lindquist, 480-557-1221, E-mail: brian.lindquist@phoenix.edu.

College of Information Systems and Technology Students: 2 full-time (0 women). Average age 46. *Faculty:* 4 full-time (2 women), 42 part-time/adjunct (11 women). Expenses: Contact institution. *Financial support:* Institutionally sponsored loans available. Financial award applicants required to submit FAFSA. In 2006, 11 degrees awarded. *Degree program information:* Evening/weekend programs available. Offers information systems (MIS); technology management (MBA). *Application deadline:* Applications are processed on a rolling basis. *Application fee:* $45. Electronic applications accepted. *Application Contact:* Chair, 262-785-0608, Fax: 262-785-0977. *Provost,* Dr. Adam Honea, 480-557-1659, E-mail: adam.honea@phoenix.edu.

UNIVERSITY OF PITTSBURGH, Pittsburgh, PA 15260

General Information State-related, coed, university. CGS member. *Enrollment:* 26,860 graduate, professional, and undergraduate students; 6,701 full-time matriculated graduate/professional students (3,572 women), 2,913 part-time matriculated graduate/professional students (1,822 women). *Enrollment by degree level:* 1,860 first professional, 7,754 master's. *Graduate faculty:* 3,655 full-time (1,345 women). *Graduate housing:* Room and/or apartments available to married students. *Student services:* Campus employment opportunities, campus safety program, career counseling, disabled student services, exercise/wellness program, free psychological counseling, international student services, low-cost health insurance. *Library facilities:* Hillman Library plus 25 others. *Online resources:* library catalog, web page, access to other libraries' catalogs. *Collection:* 4.6 million titles, 3,767 serial subscriptions. *Research affiliation:* Pittsburgh Life Sciences Greenhouse, Innovation Works (formerly Ben Franklin Technology Center of Western Pennsylvania), Technology Collaboration (formerly Pittsburgh Digital Greenhouse).

Computer facilities: Computer purchase and lease plans are available. 600 computers available on campus for general student use. A campuswide network can be accessed from student residence rooms and from off campus. Internet access, online class listings are available. *Web address:* http://www.pitt.edu/.

General Application Contact: Information Contact, 412-624-4141, E-mail: graduate@pitt.edu.

GRADUATE UNITS

Center for Neuroscience Students: 80 full-time (40 women); includes 15 minority (4 African Americans, 1 American Indian/Alaska Native, 5 Asian Americans or Pacific Islanders, 5 Hispanic Americans), 16 international. Average age 25. 152 applicants, 23% accepted, 17 enrolled. *Faculty:* 86 full-time (18 women). Expenses: Contact institution. *Financial support:* In 2006–07, 38 fellowships with full tuition reimbursements (averaging $21,500 per year), 40 research assistantships with full tuition reimbursements (averaging $21,500 per year), 3 teaching assistantships with full tuition reimbursements (averaging $21,500 per year) were awarded. Financial award application deadline: 1/2. In 2006, 11 doctorates awarded. Offers neurobiology (PhD); neuroscience (PhD). *Application deadline:* For fall admission, 1/2 priority date for domestic and international students. *Application fee:* $50. Electronic applications accepted. *Application Contact:* Joan M. Blaney, Administrator, 412-624-5043, Fax: 412-624-9198, E-mail: jblaney@pitt.edu. *Co-Director, Graduate Program,* Dr. Alan Sved, 412-624-6996, Fax: 412-624-9188.

Graduate School of Public and International Affairs Students: 315 full-time, 92 part-time; includes 52 minority (28 African Americans, 16 Asian Americans or Pacific Islanders, 8 Hispanic Americans), 60 international. Average age 25. 499 applicants, 76% accepted, 170 enrolled. *Faculty:* 35 full-time (11 women), 16 part-time/adjunct (9 women). Expenses: Contact institution. *Financial support:* In 2006–07, 119 students received support, including 119 fellowships (averaging $10,921 per year); career-related internships or fieldwork, scholarships/grants, and unspecified assistantships also available. Financial award application deadline: 2/1. In 2006, 189 master's, 5 doctorates awarded. *Degree program information:* Part-time and evening/weekend programs available. Offers development planning (MPPM); development policy (PhD); foreign and security policy (PhD); international development (MPPM); international political economy (MPPM, PhD); international security studies (MPPM); management of non profit organizations (MPPM); metropolitan management and regional development (MPPM); policy analysis and evaluation (MPPM); public administration (PhD); public and international affairs (MID, MPA, MPIA, MPPM, PhD, Certificate); public policy (PhD). *Application deadline:* For fall admission, 2/1 for domestic students, 3/1 for international students; for spring admission, 10/1 for domestic students, 8/1 for international students. *Application fee:* $50. Electronic applications accepted. *Application Contact:* Jessica Hatherill, Associate Director of Student Services, 412-648-7648, Fax: 412-648-7641, E-mail: hatherill@gspia.pitt.edu. *Interim Dean,* Dr. David Miller, 412-648-1665, Fax: 412-648-2605, E-mail: dymiller@gspia.pitt.edu.

Division of International Development Students: 61 full-time (47 women), 4 part-time (1 woman); includes 14 minority (7 African Americans, 6 Asian Americans or Pacific Islanders, 1 Hispanic American), 13 international. Average age 27. 100 applicants, 77% accepted, 35 enrolled. *Faculty:* 35 full-time (11 women), 16 part-time/adjunct (9 women). Expenses: Contact institution. *Financial support:* In 2006–07, 25 students received support, including 25 fellowships (averaging $8,063 per year); scholarships/grants and unspecified assistantships also available. Financial award application deadline: 2/1. In 2006, 39 degrees awarded. *Degree program information:* Part-time programs available. Offers development planning and environmental sustainability (MID); international development (MID); nongovernmental organizations and civil society (MID). *Application deadline:* For fall admission, 2/1 for domestic and international students; for spring admission, 10/1 for domestic students, 8/1 for international students. *Application fee:* $50. Electronic applications accepted. *Application Contact:* Maureen O'Malley, Admissions Counselor, 412-648-7640, Fax: 412-648-7641, E-mail: pronobis@birch.gspia.pitt.edu. *Director, International Affairs and International Development Divisions,* Dr. Martin Staniland, 412-648-7656, Fax: 412-648-2605, E-mail: mstan@pitt.edu.

Division of Public and Urban Affairs Students: 65 full-time (39 women), 17 part-time (13 women); includes 3 minority (1 African American, 1 Asian American or Pacific Islander, 1 Hispanic American), 6 international. Average age 27. 96 applicants, 81% accepted, 35 enrolled. *Faculty:* 35 full-time (11 women), 16 part-time/adjunct (9 women). Expenses: Contact institution. *Financial support:* In 2006–07, 27 students received support, including 27 fellowships (averaging $10,027 per year). Financial award application deadline: 2/1. In 2006, 34 degrees awarded. *Degree program information:* Part-time and evening/weekend programs available. Offers policy research and analysis (MPA); public and nonprofit management (MPA); public and urban affairs (MPA); urban and regional affairs (MPA). *Application deadline:* For fall admission, 2/1 for domestic and international students; for spring admission, 10/1 for domestic students, 8/1 for international students. *Application fee:* $50. *Application Contact:* Maureen O'Malley, Admissions Counselor, 412-648-7640, Fax: 412-648-7641, E-mail: pronobis@birch.gspia.pitt.edu. *Director, Public and Urban Affairs Division,* Dr. Louise Comfort, 412-648-7606, Fax: 412-648-2605, E-mail: comfort@gspia.pitt.edu.

International Affairs Division Students: 140 full-time (56 women), 13 part-time (8 women); includes 11 minority (5 African Americans, 3 Asian Americans or Pacific Islanders, 3 Hispanic Americans), 21 international. Average age 23. 196 applicants, 86% accepted, 67 enrolled. *Faculty:* 35 full-time (11 women), 16 part-time/adjunct (9 women). Expenses: Contact institution. *Financial support:* In 2006–07, 50 students received support, including 50 fellowships (averaging $7,103 per year); career-related internships or fieldwork, scholarships/grants, and unspecified assistantships also available. Financial award application deadline: 2/1. In 2006, 79 degrees awarded. *Degree program information:* Part-time and evening/weekend programs available. Offers global political economy (MPIA); human security (MPIA); security and intelligence studies (MPIA). *Application deadline:* For fall admission, 2/1 for domestic and international students; for spring admission, 10/1 for domestic students, 8/1 for international students. *Application fee:* $50. Electronic applications accepted. *Application Contact:* Jessica Hatherill, Associate Director of Student Services, 412-648-7648, Fax: 412-648-7641, E-mail: hatherill@gspia.pitt.edu. *Director, International Affairs and International Development Divisions,* Dr. Martin Staniland, 412-648-7656, Fax: 412-648-2605, E-mail: mstan@pitt.edu.

Graduate School of Public Health Students: 349 full-time (243 women), 179 part-time (121 women); includes 93 minority (47 African Americans, 1 American Indian/Alaska Native, 35 Asian Americans or Pacific Islanders, 10 Hispanic Americans), 138 international. Average age 31. 885 applicants, 60% accepted, 185 enrolled. *Faculty:* 162 full-time (71 women), 110 part-time/adjunct (36 women). Expenses: Contact institution. *Financial support:* In 2006–07, 4 fellowships with full tuition reimbursements, 149 research assistantships with full tuition reimbursements (averaging $20,575 per year), 13 teaching assistantships with full tuition reimbursements (averaging $13,996 per year) were awarded; career-related internships or fieldwork, scholarships/grants, traineeships, health care benefits, tuition waivers (partial), and unspecified assistantships also available. Support available to part-time students. Financial award applicants required to submit FAFSA. In 2006, 97 master's, 25 doctorates, 6 other advanced degrees awarded. *Degree program information:* Part-time programs available. Offers behavioral and community health sciences (MPH, Dr PH); biostatistics (MPH, MS, Dr PH, PhD); environmental and occupational health (MPH); epidemiology (MPH, MS, Dr PH, PhD); genetic counseling (MS); health policy and management (MHA, MPH); human genetics (MS, PhD); infectious diseases and microbiology (MPH, MS, Dr PH, PhD); lesbian, gay, bisexual and transgender health and wellness (Certificate); minority health and health disparities (Certificate); molecular toxicology (MS, PhD); occupational medicine (MPH); program evaluation (Certificate); public health (MHA, MPH, MS, Dr PH, PhD, Certificate); public health and aging (Certificate); public health genetics (MPH, Certificate); public health preparedness (Certificate); risk assessment (Certificate). *Application deadline:* For fall admission, 4/1 for international students; for winter admission, 9/1 for international students; for spring admission, 2/1 for international students. Applications are processed on a rolling basis. *Application fee:* $50 ($60 for international students). Electronic applications accepted. *Application Contact:* 412-624-5200, Fax: 412-624-3755, E-mail: stuaff@pitt.edu. *Dean,* Dr. Donald S. Burke, 412-624-3001, Fax: 412-624-3309, E-mail: donburke@pitt.edu.

Joint CMU-Pitt PhD Program in Computational Biology Students: 8 full-time (2 women), 6 international. Average age 27. 94 applicants, 32% accepted. *Faculty:* 67 full-time (13 women). Expenses: Contact institution. *Financial support:* In 2006–07, 8 students received support, including 6 fellowships with full tuition reimbursements available (averaging $24,000 per year). Offers computational biology (PhD). *Application deadline:* For fall admission, 1/15 priority date for domestic and international students. *Application fee:* $50. Electronic applications accepted. *Application Contact:* Dr. Judy Wieber, Research and Education Administrator, Department of Computational Biology, 412-648-8646, Fax: 412-648-3163, E-mail: jwieber@ccbb.pitt.edu. *Chair,* Dr. Ivet Bahar, 412-648-3332.

Joseph M. Katz Graduate School of Business Students: 257 full-time (83 women), 451 part-time (154 women); includes 57 minority (14 African Americans, 1 American Indian/Alaska Native, 35 Asian Americans or Pacific Islanders, 7 Hispanic Americans), 159 international. Average age 29. 1,016 applicants, 50% accepted, 338 enrolled. *Faculty:* 70 full-time (13 women), 27 part-time/adjunct (10 women). Expenses: Contact institution. *Financial support:* Fellowships with tuition reimbursements, research assistantships with tuition reimbursements, teaching assistantships with tuition reimbursements, Federal Work-Study, institutionally sponsored loans, scholarships/grants, tuition waivers (full and partial), and unspecified assistantships available. Financial award application deadline: 3/15; financial award applicants required to submit FAFSA. In 2006, 291 master's, 16 doctorates awarded. *Degree program information:* Part-time and evening/weekend programs available. Offers business (EMBA, MBA, MS, PhD); business administration (EMBA, MBA, MS, PhD); international business (MBA); international business administration (MBA); management of information systems (MS). *Application deadline:* For fall admission, 3/1 for domestic and international students. Applications are processed on a rolling basis. *Application fee:* $50. Electronic applications accepted. *Application Contact:* Kelly R. Wilson, Director, Office of Enrollment Management, 412-648-1700, Fax: 412-648-1659, E-mail: mba@katz.pitt.edu. *Dean,* Dr. Lawrence F Feick, 412-648-1561, Fax: 412-648-1552, E-mail: feick@katz.pitt.edu.

School of Arts and Sciences Students: 1,742 full-time (841 women), 119 part-time (71 women); includes 241 minority (44 African Americans, 2 American Indian/Alaska Native, 123 Asian Americans or Pacific Islanders, 72 Hispanic Americans), 476 international. 4,094 applicants, 24% accepted, 355 enrolled. *Faculty:* 722 full-time (242 women), 111 part-time/adjunct (38 women). Expenses: Contact institution. *Financial support:* In 2006–07, 320 fellowships with full tuition reimbursements, 522 research assistantships with full tuition reimbursements, 683 teaching assistantships with full and partial tuition reimbursements were awarded; career-related internships or fieldwork, Federal Work-Study, institutionally sponsored loans, scholarships/grants, traineeships, health care benefits, tuition waivers (full and partial), and unspecified assistantships also available. Support available to part-time students. Financial award applicants required to submit FAFSA. In 2006, 165 master's, 162 doctorates, 17 other advanced degrees awarded. *Degree program information:* Part-time programs available. Offers anthropology (MA, PhD); applied linguistics (PhD); applied mathematics (MA, MS); applied statistics (MA, MS); arts and sciences (MA, MFA, MS, PM Sc, PMS, PhD, Certificate, Doctoral Certificate, Master's Certificate); chemistry (MS, PhD); classics (MA, PhD); communication (MA, PhD); composition and theory (MA, PhD); computer science (MS, PhD); cultural and critical studies (PhD); East Asian studies (MA); ecology and evolution (PhD); English (MA); ethnomusicology (MA, PhD); financial mathematics (PMS); French (MA, PhD); geographical information systems (PM Sc); geology and planetary science (MS, PhD); Germanic languages and literatures (MA, PhD); Hispanic languages and literatures (MA, PhD); Hispanic linguistics (MA, PhD); historical musicology (MA, PhD); history (MA, PhD); history and philosophy of science (MA, PhD); history of art and architecture (MA, PhD); intelligent systems (MS, PhD); Italian (MA); linguistics (MA); mathematics (MA, MS, PhD); molecular, cellular, and developmental biology (PhD); performance pedagogy (MFA); philosophy (MA, PhD); physics (MS, PhD); political science (MA, PhD); psychology (MS, PhD); religion (PhD); religious studies (MA); Slavic languages and literatures (MA, PhD); sociolinguistics (PhD); sociology (MA, PhD); statistics (MA, MS, PhD); TESOL (Certificate); theatre and performance studies (MA, PhD); women's studies (Doctoral Certificate, Master's Certificate); writing (MFA). *Application deadline:* Applications are processed on a rolling basis. *Application fee:* $50. Electronic applications accepted. *Application Contact:* Jennifer L. Sternick, Administrative Secretary, 412-624-6094, Fax: 412-624-6855, E-mail: sternick@pitt.edu. *Associate Dean, Graduate Studies and Research,* Dr. Nicole Constable, 412-624-6094, Fax: 412-624-6855, E-mail: constable@fcas.pitt.edu.

Center for Bioethics and Health Law Students: 12 full-time (6 women), 6 part-time (2 women). 16 applicants, 56% accepted, 5 enrolled. *Faculty:* 4 full-time (1 woman), 3 part-time/adjunct (1 woman). Expenses: Contact institution. *Financial support:* Tuition waivers (partial) available. *Degree program information:* Part-time programs available. Offers bioethics (MA). *Application deadline:* For fall admission, 2/1 priority date for domestic students, 6/30 for international students. Applications are processed on a rolling basis. *Application fee:* $50. Electronic applications accepted. *Application Contact:* Karen E. Ferris, Administrative Assistant, 412-647-5785, Fax: 412-647-5877, E-mail: bioethic@pitt.edu. *Director of Graduate Education,* Dr. Lisa S. Parker, 412-647-5780, Fax: 412-647-5877, E-mail: lisap@pitt.edu.

Department of Economics Students: 50 full-time (20 women); includes 30 minority (2 African Americans, 23 Asian Americans or Pacific Islanders, 5 Hispanic Americans). Average age 24. 285 applicants, 11% accepted, 8 enrolled. *Faculty:* 23 full-time (3 women), 1 (woman) part-time/adjunct. Expenses: Contact institution. *Financial support:* In 2006–07, 41 students received support, including 10 fellowships with full tuition reimbursements available (averaging $16,450 per year), 3 research assistantships with full tuition reimbursements available (averaging $14,560 per year), 27 teaching assistantships with full tuition reimbursements available (averaging $13,995 per year); institutionally sponsored loans, scholarships/grants, traineeships, health care benefits, tuition waivers (full), and unspecified assistantships also available. Financial award application deadline: 2/1. In 2006, 5 degrees awarded. *Degree program information:* Part-time programs available. Offers economics (PhD). *Application deadline:* For fall admission, 2/1 for domestic and international students. Applications are processed on a rolling basis. *Application fee:* $50. Electronic applications accepted. *Application Contact:* Amy M. Linn, Graduate Administrator, 412-

648-1399, Fax: 412-648-1793, E-mail: amlinn@pitt.edu. *Department Chair,* Dr. David N. De Jong, 412-648-2242, Fax: 41-648-7038, E-mail: dejong@pitt.edu.

School of Dental Medicine Students: 322 full-time (125 women); includes 91 minority (5 African Americans, 3 American Indian/Alaska Native, 59 Asian Americans or Pacific Islanders, 24 Hispanic Americans), 11 international. Average age 26. 1,880 applicants, 14% accepted, 78 enrolled. *Faculty:* 86 full-time (31 women), 81 part-time/adjunct (17 women). Expenses: Contact institution. *Financial support:* In 2006–07, 300 students received support. Federal Work-Study, institutionally sponsored loans, scholarships/grants, and unspecified assistantships available. Financial award application deadline: 4/30; financial award applicants required to submit FAFSA. In 2006, 65 DMDs, 23 other advanced degrees awarded. Offers advanced education in general dentistry (Certificate); craniofacial and maxillofacial surgery (Certificate); dental medicine (DMD, MDS, Certificate); endodontics (MDS, Certificate); oral and maxillofacial surgery (Certificate); orthodontics (MDS, Certificate); pediatric dentistry (MDS, Certificate); periodontics (MDS, Certificate); prosthodontics (MDS, Certificate). *Application deadline:* For fall admission, 12/1 for domestic and international students; for spring admission, 3/30 for domestic and international students. Applications are processed on a rolling basis. *Application fee:* $35 ($50 for international students). Electronic applications accepted. *Application Contact:* Rosemary Mangold, Recruitment/Financial Aid Officer, 412-648-8437, Fax: 412-648-9571, E-mail: mangold@pitt.edu. *Dean,* Dr. Thomas W. Braun, 412-648-8900, Fax: 412-648-8219, E-mail: twb3@pitt.edu.

School of Education Students: 552 full-time (396 women), 665 part-time (499 women); includes 100 minority (70 African Americans, 1 American Indian/Alaska Native, 17 Asian Americans or Pacific Islanders, 12 Hispanic Americans), 77 international. 744 applicants, 78% accepted, 404 enrolled. *Faculty:* 98 full-time (55 women), 115 part-time/adjunct (74 women). Expenses: Contact institution. *Financial support:* In 2006–07, 36 fellowships (averaging $6,464 per year), 40 research assistantships with full and partial tuition reimbursements (averaging $16,555 per year), 102 teaching assistantships with full and partial tuition reimbursements (averaging $14,301 per year) were awarded; career-related internships or fieldwork, Federal Work-Study, traineeships, tuition waivers (partial), and unspecified assistantships also available. Support available to part-time students. Financial award applicants required to submit FAFSA. In 2006, 331 master's, 54 doctorates awarded. *Degree program information:* Part-time and evening/weekend programs available. Postbaccalaureate distance learning degree programs offered (minimal on-campus study). Offers applied developmental psychology (MS, PhD); cognitive studies (PhD); deaf and hard of hearing (M Ed); developmental movement (MS); early childhood education (M Ed); early education of disabled students (M Ed); education (M Ed, MA, MAT, MS, Ed D, PhD); education of students with mental and physical disabilities (M Ed); education of the visually impaired (M Ed); elementary education (M Ed, MAT); English/communications education (M Ed, MAT, Ed D, PhD); exercise physiology (MS, PhD); foreign languages education (M Ed, MAT, Ed D, PhD); general special education (M Ed); higher education (M Ed, Ed D); higher education management (M Ed, Ed D); international development education (MA, PhD); international developmental education (M Ed); mathematics education (M Ed, MAT, Ed D); reading education (M Ed, Ed D, PhD); research methodology (M Ed, MA, PhD); school leadership (M Ed, Ed D); science education (M Ed, MAT, MS, Ed D); secondary education (M Ed, MAT, MS, Ed D, PhD); social and comparative analysis in education (M Ed, MA, PhD); social studies education (M Ed, MAT, Ed D, PhD); social, philosophical, and historical foundations of education (M Ed, MA, PhD); special education (M Ed, Ed D, PhD). *Application deadline:* For fall admission, 2/1 priority date for domestic students; for spring admission, 11/15 priority date for domestic students. Applications are processed on a rolling basis. *Application fee:* $50. Electronic applications accepted. *Application Contact:* Joan M. Cutone, Director, School of Education Student Service Center, 412-648-2230, Fax: 412-648-1899, E-mail: soeinfo@pitt.edu. *Dean,* Dr. Alan Lesgold, 412-648-1773, Fax: 412-648-1825, E-mail: al@pitt.edu.

School of Engineering Students: 390 full-time (120 women), 152 part-time (22 women); includes 37 minority (17 African Americans, 2 American Indian/Alaska Native, 9 Asian Americans or Pacific Islanders, 9 Hispanic Americans), 182 international. 1,273 applicants, 34% accepted, 148 enrolled. *Faculty:* 131 full-time (15 women), 46 part-time/adjunct (0 women). Expenses: Contact institution. *Financial support:* In 2006–07, 372 students received support, including 17 fellowships with full tuition reimbursements available (averaging $20,772 per year), 266 research assistantships with full tuition reimbursements available (averaging $22,000 per year), 81 teaching assistantships with full tuition reimbursements available (averaging $21,000 per year); scholarships/grants, traineeships, and tuition waivers (full and partial) also available. Financial award application deadline: 4/15. In 2006, 116 master's, 49 doctorates awarded. *Degree program information:* Part-time programs available. Offers bioengineering (MSBENG, PhD); chemical engineering (MS Ch E, PhD); civil and environmental engineering (MSCEE, PhD); electrical engineering (MSEE, PhD); engineering (MS Ch E, MSBENG, MSCEE, MSEE, MSIE, MSME, MSPE, PhD); industrial engineering (MSIE, PhD); mechanical engineering and materials science (MSME, PhD); petroleum engineering (MSPE). *Application deadline:* For fall admission, 3/1 priority date for domestic students; for spring admission, 7/1 priority date for domestic students. Applications are processed on a rolling basis. *Application fee:* $50. Electronic applications accepted. *Application Contact:* 412-624-9800, Fax: 412-624-9808, E-mail: admin@engrng.pitt.edu. *Dean,* Dr. Gerald D. Holder, 412-624-9811, Fax: 412-624-0412, E-mail: holder@engrng.pitt.edu.

School of Health and Rehabilitation Sciences Students: 462 full-time (362 women), 93 part-time (64 women); includes 48 minority (21 African Americans, 1 American Indian/Alaska Native, 25 Asian Americans or Pacific Islanders, 1 Hispanic American), 51 international. Average age 30. 555 applicants, 66% accepted, 195 enrolled. *Faculty:* 56 full-time (34 women), 4 part-time/adjunct (2 women). Expenses: Contact institution. *Financial support:* In 2006–07, 1 fellowship with full tuition reimbursement (averaging $15,398 per year), 35 research assistantships with full and partial tuition reimbursements (averaging $20,461 per year), 1 teaching assistantship with full tuition reimbursement (averaging $14,560 per year) were awarded; career-related internships or fieldwork, Federal Work-Study, institutionally sponsored loans, scholarships/grants, traineeships, and unspecified assistantships also available. Support available to part-time students. Financial award applicants required to submit FAFSA. In 2006, 84 master's, 50 doctorates awarded. *Degree program information:* Part-time programs available. Offers assistive rehabilitation technology (Certificate); communication science and disorders (MA, MS, Au D, CScD, PhD); dietetics (MS); disability studies (Certificate); health and rehabilitation sciences (MS); occupational therapy (MOT); physical therapy (DPT); rehabilitation science (PhD); wellness and human performance (MS). *Application deadline:* Applications are processed on a rolling basis. *Application fee:* $50. Electronic applications accepted. *Application Contact:* Shameem Gangjee, Director of Admissions, 412-383-6558, Fax: 412-383-6535, E-mail: admissions@shrs.pitt.edu. *Dean,* Dr. Clifford E. Brubaker, 412-383-6560, Fax: 412-383-6535, E-mail: cliffb@pitt.edu.

School of Information Sciences Students: 324 full-time (150 women), 361 part-time (253 women); includes 77 minority (43 African Americans, 1 American Indian/Alaska Native, 19 Asian Americans or Pacific Islanders, 14 Hispanic Americans), 113 international. 518 applicants, 88% accepted, 170 enrolled. *Faculty:* 26 full-time (5 women), 13 part-time/adjunct (10 women). Expenses: Contact institution. *Financial support:* In 2006–07, 125 fellowships with partial tuition reimbursements (averaging $3,385 per year), 47 research assistantships with full and partial tuition reimbursements (averaging $8,002 per year), 142 teaching assistantships with full and partial tuition reimbursements (averaging $5,519 per year) were awarded; career-related internships or fieldwork, scholarships/grants, traineeships, health care benefits, tuition waivers (full and partial), and unspecified assistantships also available. Support available to part-time students. Financial award application deadline: 1/15; financial award applicants required to submit FAFSA. In 2006, 246 master's, 10 doctorates, 4 other advanced degrees awarded. *Degree program information:* Part-time and evening/weekend programs available. Postbaccalaureate distance learning degree programs offered (minimal on-campus study). Offers information science (MSIS, Certificate); information science telecommunications (PhD); information sciences (MLIS, MSIS, MST, PhD, Certificate); library and information science (MLIS, PhD, Certificate); telecommunications and networking (MST, Certificate). *Application deadline:* For fall admission, 6/1 priority date for domestic students, 4/1 priority date for international students; for winter admission, 10/1 priority date for domestic students; for spring admission, 2/1 priority date for domestic students, 10/1 priority date for international students. Applications are processed on a rolling basis. *Application fee:* $50. Electronic applications accepted. *Application Contact:* Ninette Kay, Admissions Coordinator, 412-624-5146, Fax: 412-624-5231, E-mail: nkay@mail.sis.pitt.edu. *Dean,* Dr. Ronald L. Larsen, 412-624-5139, Fax: 412-624-5231, E-mail: rlarsen@mail.sis.pitt.edu.

School of Law Students: 731 full-time (306 women), 18 part-time (12 women); includes 97 minority (45 African Americans, 1 American Indian/Alaska Native, 40 Asian Americans or Pacific Islanders, 11 Hispanic Americans). 2,456 applicants, 33% accepted, 273 enrolled. *Faculty:* 46 full-time (16 women), 85 part-time/adjunct (23 women). Expenses: Contact institution. *Financial support:* In 2006–07, 387 students received support, including 13 fellowships (averaging $1,200 per year), 36 research assistantships (averaging $5,440 per year); teaching assistantships, career-related internships or fieldwork, Federal Work-Study, scholarships/grants, and unspecified assistantships also available. Financial award application deadline: 3/1; financial award applicants required to submit FAFSA. In 2006, 268 JDs, 11 master's awarded. Offers business law (MSL); civil litigation (Certificate); constitutional law (MSL); criminal justice (MSL); disabilities law (MSL); dispute resolution (MSL); education law (MSL); elder and estate planning law (MSL); employment and labor law (MSL); environment and real estate law (MSL); environmental law, science and policy (Certificate); family law (MSL); general law and jurisprudence (MSL); health law (MSL); intellectual property and technology (MSL); intellectual property and technology law (Certificate); international and comparative law (LL M, MSL); international law (Certificate); law (JD, LL M, MA, MSL, Certificate); personal injury and civil litigation (MSL); regulatory law (MSL); self-designed (MSL). *Application deadline:* For fall admission, 3/1 for domestic students. Applications are processed on a rolling basis. *Application fee:* $55. Electronic applications accepted. *Application Contact:* Charmaine McCall, Assistant Dean of Admissions and Financial Aid, 412-648-1413, Fax: 412-648-1318, E-mail: mccall@law.pitt.edu. *Dean,* Mary Crossley, 412-648-1401, Fax: 412-648-2647, E-mail: crossley@law.pitt.edu.

School of Medicine Students: 909. *Faculty:* 1,896. Expenses: Contact institution. *Financial support:* Fellowships with full tuition reimbursements, research assistantships with full tuition reimbursements, teaching assistantships with tuition reimbursements, Federal Work-Study, institutionally sponsored loans, scholarships/grants, traineeships, health care benefits, and unspecified assistantships available. Financial award applicants required to submit FAFSA. *Degree program information:* Part-time programs available. Postbaccalaureate distance learning degree programs offered (minimal on-campus study). Offers biochemistry and molecular genetics (MS, PhD); biomedical informatics (MS, PhD, Certificate); cell biology and molecular physiology (MS, PhD); cellular and molecular pathology (MS, PhD); clinical research (MS, Certificate); immunology (MS, PhD); integrative molecular biology (PhD); interdisciplinary biomedical sciences (PhD); medical education (MS, Certificate); medical research (Certificate); medicine (MD, MS, PhD, Certificate); molecular biophysics and structural biology (PhD); molecular pharmacology (PhD); molecular virology and microbiology (MS, PhD); neurobiology (MS, PhD). *Application deadline:* Applications are processed on a rolling basis. *Application fee:* $40. Electronic applications accepted. *Application Contact:* Graduate Studies Administrator, 412-648-8957, Fax: 412-648-1077, E-mail: gradstudies@medschool.pitt.edu. *Dean,* Dr. Arthur S. Levine, 412-648-8975, Fax: 412-648-1236, E-mail: alevine@hs.pitt.edu.

School of Nursing Students: 168 full-time (127 women), 175 part-time (161 women); includes 26 minority (13 African Americans, 10 Asian Americans or Pacific Islanders, 3 Hispanic Americans). Average age 38. 197 applicants, 38% accepted, 70 enrolled. *Faculty:* 53 full-time (47 women), 4 part-time/adjunct (all women). Expenses: Contact institution. *Financial support:* In 2006–07, 26 students received support, including 21 research assistantships with full and partial tuition reimbursements available (averaging $17,145 per year), 3 teaching assistantships with full and partial tuition reimbursements available (averaging $20,993 per year); institutionally sponsored loans, scholarships/grants, traineeships, health care benefits, and unspecified assistantships also available. Support available to part-time students. Financial award application deadline: 7/1; financial award applicants required to submit FAFSA. In 2006, 99 master's, 3 doctorates awarded. *Degree program information:* Part-time programs available. Offers acute care nurse practitioner (MSN); adult nurse practitioner (MSN); anesthesia nursing (MSN); family nurse practitioner (MSN); medical/surgical clinical nurse specialist (MSN); nursing (MSN, DNP, PhD); nursing administration (MSN); nursing education (MSN); nursing informatics (MSN); nursing practice (DNP); nursing research (MSN); pediatric nurse practitioner (MSN); psychiatric and mental health clinical nurse specialist (MSN); psychiatric primary care nurse practitioner (MSN). *Application deadline:* Applications are processed on a rolling basis. *Application fee:* $50. Electronic applications accepted. *Application Contact:* Laurie Lapsley, Administrator of Graduate Student Services, 412-624-9670, Fax: 412-624-2409, E-mail: lapsleyl@pitt.edu. *Dean,* Dr. Jacqueline Dunbar-Jacob, 412-624-7838, Fax: 412-624-2401, E-mail: dunbar@pitt.edu.

School of Pharmacy Students: 430 full-time (277 women), 1 part-time; includes 34 minority (13 African Americans, 19 Asian Americans or Pacific Islanders, 2 Hispanic Americans), 16 international. Average age 24. 1,042 applicants, 14% accepted, 115 enrolled. *Faculty:* 89 full-time (40 women), 117 part-time/adjunct (57 women). Expenses: Contact institution. *Financial support:* In 2006–07, 171 students received support, including 2 fellowships (averaging $31,798 per year), 19 teaching assistantships with full tuition reimbursements available (averaging $13,995 per year); career-related internships or fieldwork, Federal Work-Study, institutionally sponsored loans, scholarships/grants, and health care benefits also available. Financial award application deadline: 9/1. In 2006, 93 first professional degrees, 1 doctorate awarded. Offers pharmaceutical sciences (MS, PhD); pharmacy (Pharm D). *Application fee:* $50. *Application Contact:* Marcia L. Borrelli, Director of Student Services, 412-383-9000, Fax: 412-383-9995, E-mail: borrelli@pitt.edu. *Dean,* Dr. Patricia Dowley Kroboth, 412-624-2400, Fax: 412-648-1086.

School of Social Work Students: 308 full-time (256 women), 316 part-time (255 women); includes 105 minority (91 African Americans, 9 Asian Americans or Pacific Islanders, 5 Hispanic Americans), 3 international. Average age 28. 394 applicants, 80% accepted, 242 enrolled. *Faculty:* 19 full-time (10 women), 38 part-time/adjunct (27 women). Expenses: Contact institution. *Financial support:* In 2006–07, 81 students received support, including 3 research assistantships with full tuition reimbursements available (averaging $12,535 per year), 2 teaching assistantships with full tuition reimbursements available (averaging $13,996 per year); fellowships, career-related internships or fieldwork, institutionally sponsored loans, scholarships/grants, traineeships, tuition waivers (full), and unspecified assistantships also available. Financial award application deadline: 3/31; financial award applicants required to submit FAFSA. In 2006, 234 master's, 4 doctorates awarded. *Degree program information:* Part-time programs available. Postbaccalaureate distance learning degree programs offered (no on-campus study). Offers gerontology (Certificate); social work (MSW, PhD, Certificate). *Application deadline:* For fall admission, 5/1 for domestic and international students. Applications are processed on a rolling basis. *Application fee:* $40. Electronic applications accepted. *Application Contact:* Phillip Mack, Director of Admissions, 412-624-6346, Fax: 412-624-6323, E-mail: psm8@pitt.edu. *Dean,* Dr. Larry E. Davis, 412-624-6304, Fax: 412-624-6323, E-mail: ledavis@pitt.edu.

University Center for International Studies Expenses: Contact institution. Offers African studies (Certificate); Asian studies (Certificate); European Union studies (Certificate); global studies (Certificate); Latin American studies (Certificate); Russian and East European studies (Certificate); West European studies (Certificate).

Center for Latin American Studies Students: 141 full-time (80 women), 22 part-time (12 women); includes 22 minority (6 African Americans, 2 Asian Americans or Pacific Islanders, 14 Hispanic Americans), 69 international. *Faculty:* 110 full-time (38 women), 17 part-time/adjunct (7 women). Expenses: Contact institution. *Financial support:* In 2006–07, 30 students received support, including 21 fellowships with full and partial tuition reimbursements available; career-related internships or fieldwork, scholarships/grants, tuition waivers (full and partial), and unspecified assistantships also available. Support available to part-time students. Financial award application deadline: 2/28. In 2006, 20 degrees awarded. *Degree program information:* Part-time and evening/weekend programs available. Offers Latin American studies (Certificate). Students must be enrolled in a separate degree granting program. *Application deadline:* Applications are processed on a rolling basis. *Application fee:* $0. Electronic applications accepted. *Application Contact:* Shirley A. Kregar, Associate Director for Academic Affairs, 412-648-7396, Fax: 412-648-2199, E-mail: kregar@

University of Pittsburgh (continued)

pitt.edu. *Director,* Dr. Kathleen Musante DeWalt, 412-648-7391, Fax: 412-648-2199, E-mail: kmdewalt@pitt.edu.

UNIVERSITY OF PORTLAND, Portland, OR 97203-5798

General Information Independent-religious, coed, comprehensive institution. *Enrollment:* 3,478 graduate, professional, and undergraduate students; 158 full-time matriculated graduate/professional students (91 women), 315 part-time matriculated graduate/professional students (205 women). *Enrollment by degree level:* 473 master's. *Graduate faculty:* 84 full-time (26 women), 11 part-time/adjunct (5 women). *Tuition:* Part-time $728 per semester hour. *Required fees:* $5 per semester hour. Tuition and fees vary according to program. *Graduate housing:* Room and/or apartments available to single students; on-campus housing not available to married students. Housing application deadline: 7/1. *Student services:* Campus employment opportunities, campus safety program, career counseling, disabled student services, exercise/wellness program, free psychological counseling, international student services, low-cost health insurance, multicultural affairs office, teacher training, writing training. *Library facilities:* Wilson M. Clark Library plus 1 other. *Online resources:* library catalog, web page, access to other libraries' catalogs. *Collection:* 350,000 titles, 1,400 serial subscriptions, 11,044 audiovisual materials. *Research affiliation:* Oregon Graduate Institute of Science and Technology (applied engineering, applied physics), Kaiser Center Health Resources, Portland Area Nursing Consortium.

Computer facilities: 575 computers available on campus for general student use. A campuswide network can be accessed from student residence rooms and from off campus. Internet access and online class registration are available. *Web address:* http://www.up.edu/.

General Application Contact: Dr. Patricia L. Chadwick, Assistant to the Provost and Dean of the Graduate School, 503-943-7107, Fax: 503-943-7178, E-mail: chadwick@up.edu.

GRADUATE UNITS

Graduate School Students: 158 full-time (91 women), 315 part-time (205 women). Average age 35. *Faculty:* 84 full-time (26 women), 11 part-time/adjunct (5 women). Expenses: Contact institution. *Financial support:* Career-related internships or fieldwork and Federal Work-Study available. Support available to part-time students. Financial award application deadline: 3/1; financial award applicants required to submit FAFSA. In 2006, 186 degrees awarded. *Degree program information:* Part-time and evening/weekend programs available. Postbaccalaureate distance learning degree programs offered (minimal on-campus study). *Application deadline:* For fall admission, 7/15 priority date for domestic and international students; for spring admission, 12/15 priority date for domestic and international students. Applications are processed on a rolling basis. *Application fee:* $50. *Application Contact:* Chris James Olinger, Administrative Assistant, 503-943-7107, Fax: 503-943-7178, E-mail: olingerc@up.edu. *Assistant to the Provost and Dean of the Graduate School,* Dr. Thomas G. Greene, 503-943-7107, Fax: 503-943-7315, E-mail: greene@up.edu.

College of Arts and Sciences Students: 11 full-time, 26 part-time. *Faculty:* 14 full-time (3 women), 1 part-time/adjunct (0 women). Expenses: Contact institution. *Financial support:* Teaching assistantships, career-related internships or fieldwork, Federal Work-Study, scholarships/grants, and tuition waivers (partial) available. Support available to part-time students. Financial award application deadline: 3/1; financial award applicants required to submit FAFSA. *Degree program information:* Part-time and evening/weekend programs available. Offers arts and sciences (MA, MFA, MS); communication (MA); drama (MFA); management communication (MS); music (MA); pastoral ministry (MA). *Application deadline:* For fall admission, 8/1 priority date for domestic students; for spring admission, 12/1 for domestic students. Applications are processed on a rolling basis. *Application fee:* $50. *Dean,* Dr. Marlene Moore, 503-943-7221, E-mail: moorem@up.edu.

Dr. Robert B. Pamplin, Jr. School of Business Students: 68 full-time, 77 part-time. *Faculty:* 24 full-time (5 women). Expenses: Contact institution. *Financial support:* Federal Work-Study, scholarships/grants, and tuition waivers (partial) available. Support available to part-time students. Financial award application deadline: 3/1; financial award applicants required to submit FAFSA. *Degree program information:* Part-time and evening/weekend programs available. Offers business (MBA). *Application deadline:* For fall admission, 8/1 priority date for domestic students; for spring admission, 12/1 for domestic students. Applications are processed on a rolling basis. *Application fee:* $50. *Application Contact:* Melissa McCarthy, Academic Specialist, 503-943-7225, E-mail: mccarthy@up.edu. *Dean,* Dr. Robin Anderson, 503-943-7224, E-mail: anderson@up.edu.

School of Education Students: 51 full-time, 192 part-time. *Faculty:* 19 full-time (8 women), 10 part-time/adjunct (5 women). Expenses: Contact institution. *Financial support:* Federal Work-Study and scholarships/grants available. Support available to part-time students. Financial award application deadline: 3/1; financial award applicants required to submit FAFSA. *Degree program information:* Part-time and evening/weekend programs available. Offers early childhood education (M Ed, MA, MAT); education (M Ed, MA, MAT); secondary education (M Ed, MA, MAT); special education (M Ed). M Ed also available through the Graduate Outreach Program for teachers residing in the Oregon and Washington State areas. *Application deadline:* For fall admission, 8/1 priority date for domestic students; for spring admission, 12/1 for domestic students. Applications are processed on a rolling basis. *Application fee:* $50. *Application Contact:* Dr. Thomas G. Greene, Associate Dean, 503-943-7135, Fax: 503-943-7315, E-mail: greene@up.edu. *Dean,* Dr. Maria Ciriello, OP, 503-943-7135, Fax: 503-943-8042, E-mail: ciriello@up.edu.

School of Engineering Students: 1 full-time (0 women). 9 applicants, 100% accepted. *Faculty:* 16 full-time (0 women). Expenses: Contact institution. *Financial support:* Teaching assistantships, career-related internships or fieldwork, Federal Work-Study, and scholarships/grants available. Support available to part-time students. Financial award application deadline: 3/1; financial award applicants required to submit FAFSA. *Degree program information:* Part-time and evening/weekend programs available. Offers engineering (ME). *Application deadline:* For fall admission, 8/1 priority date for domestic students; for spring admission, 12/1 for domestic students. Applications are processed on a rolling basis. *Application fee:* $50. *Application Contact:* Dr. Khalid Khan, Director, 503-943-7276, E-mail: khan@up.edu. *Dean,* Dr. Zia Yamayee, 503-943-7314.

School of Nursing Students: 28 full-time, 17 part-time. *Faculty:* 11 full-time (10 women). Expenses: Contact institution. *Financial support:* Fellowships, research assistantships, Federal Work-Study and scholarships/grants available. Support available to part-time students. Financial award application deadline: 3/1; financial award applicants required to submit FAFSA. *Degree program information:* Part-time and evening/weekend programs available. Postbaccalaureate distance learning degree programs offered (minimal on-campus study). Offers nursing (MS). *Application deadline:* Applications are processed on a rolling basis. *Application fee:* $50. *Application Contact:* Dr. Joanne Warner, Associate Dean, 503-943-7211, E-mail: warner@up.edu. *Dean,* Dr. Terry Misener, 503-943-7211, Fax: 503-943-7399, E-mail: misener@up.edu.

UNIVERSITY OF PRINCE EDWARD ISLAND, Charlottetown, PE C1A 4P3, Canada

General Information Province-supported, coed, comprehensive institution. *Enrollment:* 4,075 graduate, professional, and undergraduate students; 335 full-time matriculated graduate/professional students (256 women), 129 part-time matriculated graduate/professional students (101 women). *Enrollment by degree level:* 237 first professional, 198 master's, 29 doctoral. *Graduate faculty:* 76 full-time (25 women), 49 part-time/adjunct (8 women). *Graduate housing:* Room and/or apartments available on a first-come, first-served basis to single students; on-campus housing not available to married students. *Student services:* Campus employment opportunities, campus safety program, career counseling, child daycare facilities, disabled student services, exercise/wellness program, free psychological counseling, international student services, low-cost health insurance, writing training. *Library facilities:* Robertson Library. *Online resources:* library catalog, web page, access to other libraries' catalogs. *Collection:* 359,403 titles, 17,232 serial subscriptions, 1,252 audiovisual materials. *Research affiliation:* Agriculture Canada Research Station, Diagnostic Chemicals, Ltd., Canadian Food Inspection Agency, AquaHealth, NRC Institute for Nutrisciences and Health, PEI Food Technology Centre.

Computer facilities: Computer purchase and lease plans are available. 120 computers available on campus for general student use. A campuswide network can be accessed from student residence rooms and from off campus. Internet access and online class registration are available. *Web address:* http://www.upei.ca/.

General Application Contact: Jack MacDougall, Registrar's Office, 902-566-0781, Fax: 902-566-0795, E-mail: registrar@upei.ca.

GRADUATE UNITS

Atlantic Veterinary College Students: 292 full-time (225 women), 5 part-time (all women). 227 applicants, 36% accepted, 79 enrolled. *Faculty:* 76 full-time (25 women), 49 part-time/adjunct (8 women). Expenses: Contact institution. *Financial support:* Fellowships, research assistantships, career-related internships or fieldwork available. In 2006, 59 first professional degrees, 5 master's, 7 doctorates awarded. *Degree program information:* Part-time programs available. Offers anatomy (M Sc, PhD); bacteriology (M Sc, PhD); clinical pharmacology (M Sc, PhD); clinical sciences (M Sc, PhD); epidemiology (M Sc, PhD); fish health (M Sc, PhD); food animal nutrition (M Sc, PhD); immunology (M Sc, PhD); microanatomy (M Sc, PhD); parasitology (M Sc, PhD); pathology (M Sc, PhD); pharmacology (M Sc, PhD); physiology (M Sc, PhD); toxicology (M Sc, PhD); veterinary medicine (DVM, M Sc, M Vet Sc, PhD); veterinary science (M Vet Sc); virology (M Sc, PhD). *Application deadline:* Applications are processed on a rolling basis. *Application Contact:* Jack MacDougall, Registrar's Office, 902-566-0781, Fax: 902-566-0795, E-mail: registrar@upei.ca. *Dean,* Dr. Tim Ogilvie, 902-566-0800, E-mail: ogilvie@upei.ca.

Faculty of Arts Students: 14 full-time (10 women), 11 part-time (9 women). 8 applicants, 75% accepted, 5 enrolled. Expenses: Contact institution. In 2006, 2 degrees awarded. *Degree program information:* Part-time programs available. Offers island studies (MA). *Application deadline:* For fall admission, 2/1 priority date for domestic and international students. Applications are processed on a rolling basis. *Application fee:* $75 ($100 for international students). *Application Contact:* Wimal Rankadwa, Administrative Assistant, 902-566-0487. *Dean,* Dr. Richard Kurial, 902-566-0307, Fax: 902-566-0304.

Faculty of Education Students: 9 full-time (8 women), 110 part-time (85 women). 106 applicants, 55% accepted, 56 enrolled. Expenses: Contact institution. In 2006, 72 degrees awarded. *Degree program information:* Part-time programs available. Offers leadership and learning (M Ed). *Application deadline:* For fall admission, 1/15 for domestic and international students. *Application fee:* $75 ($100 for international students). *Application Contact:* Dr. Gerald Hopkirk, Graduate Studies Coordinator, 902-566-0622, Fax: 902-566-0416, E-mail: ghopkirk@upei.ca. *Dean,* Dr. Graham Pike, 902-566-0731, Fax: 902-566-0416.

Faculty of Science Students: 20 full-time (13 women), 3 part-time (2 women). 13 applicants, 54% accepted, 7 enrolled. *Faculty:* 15 full-time (4 women), 1 part-time/adjunct (0 women). Expenses: Contact institution. In 2006, 5 degrees awarded. Offers biology (M Sc); chemistry (M Sc). *Application deadline:* For fall admission, 12/15 priority date for domestic and international students. Applications are processed on a rolling basis. *Application fee:* $75 ($100 for international students). *Application Contact:* Jack MacDougall, Registrar's Office, 902-566-0781, Fax: 902-566-0795, E-mail: registrar@upei.ca. *Dean,* Dr. Christian Lacroix, 902-566-0320, Fax: 902-628-4303.

UNIVERSITY OF PUERTO RICO, MAYAGÜEZ CAMPUS, Mayagüez, PR 00681-9000

General Information Commonwealth-supported, coed, university. *Enrollment:* 12,380 graduate, professional, and undergraduate students; 400 full-time matriculated graduate/professional students (178 women), 612 part-time matriculated graduate/professional students (330 women). *Enrollment by degree level:* 853 master's, 157 doctoral. *Graduate faculty:* 568 full-time (190 women). Tuition, nonresident: full-time $4,655. *Required fees:* $210. One-time fee: $77 full-time. Part-time tuition and fees vary according to course load and reciprocity agreements. *Graduate housing:* On-campus housing not available. *Student services:* Career counseling, child daycare facilities, free psychological counseling, international student services, low-cost health insurance, teacher training. *Library facilities:* General Library plus 1 other. *Online resources:* library catalog, access to other libraries' catalogs. *Collection:* 921,392 titles, 590,716 serial subscriptions. *Research affiliation:* Tropical Agriculture Research Station, Corporation for the Development and Administration of Marine Resources of Puerto Rico.

Computer facilities: 1,066 computers available on campus for general student use. A campuswide network can be accessed from off campus. Internet access and online class registration are available. *Web address:* http://www.uprm.edu.

General Application Contact: Dra. Doris Ramírez, Director of Graduate Studies, 787-265-3809, Fax: 787-265-5489, E-mail: dramirez@uprm.edu.

GRADUATE UNITS

Graduate Studies Students: 400 full-time (178 women), 612 part-time (330 women); includes 708 minority (all Hispanic Americans), 304 international. 466 applicants, 70% accepted, 204 enrolled. *Faculty:* 568 full-time (190 women). Expenses: Contact institution. *Financial support:* In 2006–07, 42 fellowships with tuition reimbursements (averaging $12,000 per year), 243 research assistantships with tuition reimbursements (averaging $15,000 per year), 620 teaching assistantships with tuition reimbursements (averaging $8,500 per year) were awarded; career-related internships or fieldwork, Federal Work-Study, and institutionally sponsored loans also available. In 2006, 134 master's, 8 doctorates awarded. *Degree program information:* Part-time and evening/weekend programs available. *Application deadline:* For fall admission, 2/15 for domestic and international students; for spring admission, 9/15 for domestic and international students. Applications are processed on a rolling basis. *Application fee:* $100. *Application Contact:* Carmen Figueroa, Student Affairs Official, 787-265-3809, Fax: 787-265-5489, E-mail: cfigueroa@uprm.edu. *Director of Graduate Studies,* Dra. Doris Ramírez, 787-265-3809, Fax: 787-265-5489, E-mail: dramirez@uprm.edu.

College of Agricultural Sciences Students: 74 full-time (39 women), 100 part-time (53 women); includes 109 minority (all Hispanic Americans), 50 international. 68 applicants, 76% accepted, 41 enrolled. *Faculty:* 62 full-time (23 women). Expenses: Contact institution. *Financial support:* In 2006–07, 89 students received support, including 21 fellowships with tuition reimbursements available (averaging $12,000 per year), 18 research assistantships with tuition reimbursements available (averaging $15,000 per year), 47 teaching assistantships with tuition reimbursements available (averaging $8,500 per year); career-related internships or fieldwork, Federal Work-Study, and institutionally sponsored loans also available. In 2006, 35 degrees awarded. *Degree program information:* Part-time programs available. Offers agricultural economics (MS); agricultural education (MS); agricultural extension (MS); agricultural sciences (MS); agronomy (MS); animal industry (MS); crop protection (MS); food science and technology (MS); horticulture (MS); soils (MS). *Application deadline:* For fall admission, 2/15 for domestic and international students; for spring admission, 9/15 for domestic and international students. Applications are processed on a rolling basis. *Application fee:* $25. *Dean,* Dr. John Fernández-VanCleve, 787-832-4040 Ext. 2181, E-mail: john@uprm.edu.

College of Arts and Sciences Students: 139 full-time (79 women), 268 part-time (171 women). 151 applicants, 72% accepted, 64 enrolled. *Faculty:* 279 full-time (106 women). Expenses: Contact institution. *Financial support:* In 2006–07, 275 students received support, including 14 fellowships (averaging $12,000 per year), 74 research assistantships with tuition reimbursements available (averaging $15,000 per year), 136 teaching assistantships with tuition reimbursements available (averaging $8,500 per year); Federal Work-Study and institutionally sponsored loans also available. In 2006, 79 degrees awarded. *Degree program information:* Part-time programs available. Offers applied chemistry (PhD); applied mathematics (MS); arts and sciences (MA, MS, PhD); biology (MS); chemistry (MS); computational sciences (MS); English education (MA); geology (MS); Hispanic studies (MA); marine sciences (MS, PhD); physics (MS); pure mathematics (MS); statistics (MS). *Application deadline:* For fall admission, 2/15 for domestic and international students; for spring admission, 9/15 for domestic and international students. Applications are processed on a rolling basis. *Application fee:* $25. *Application Contact:* Nancy Damiani, Secretary, 787-832-4040 Ext. 2517, Fax: 787-265-1225, E-mail: ndamiani@uprm.edu. *Dean,* Dr. Moisés Orengo-Avilés, 787-832-4040 Ext. 2517, Fax: 787-265-1225, E-mail: morengo@uprm.edu.

College of Business Administration Students: 32 full-time (15 women), 52 part-time (37 women); includes 73 minority (all Hispanic Americans), 11 international. 47 applicants, 70% accepted, 24 enrolled. *Faculty:* 52 full-time (30 women). Expenses: Contact institution. *Financial support:* In 2006–07, 10 students received support, including fellowships (averaging $12,000 per year), 7 research assistantships (averaging $15,000 per year), 3 teaching assistantships (averaging $8,500 per year); Federal Work-Study and institutionally sponsored loans also available. In 2006, 13 degrees awarded. *Degree program information:* Part-time and evening/weekend programs available. Offers business administration (MBA); finance (MBA); human resources (MBA); industrial management (MBA). *Application deadline:* For fall admission, 2/15 for domestic and international students; for spring admission, 9/15 for domestic and international students. Applications are processed on a rolling basis. *Application fee:* $25. *Application Contact:* Dr. Yolanda Ruiz, Director, 787-265-3887, Fax: 787-832-5320, E-mail: yruiz@caribe.net. *Dean,* Prof. Eva Quinñones, 787-265-3800, Fax: 787-832-5320, E-mail: quinones-e@rigel.uprm.edu.

College of Engineering Students: 155 full-time (45 women), 192 part-time (69 women); includes 232 minority (all Hispanic Americans), 115 international. 200 applicants, 66% accepted, 75 enrolled. *Faculty:* 175 full-time (31 women). Expenses: Contact institution. *Financial support:* In 2006–07, 242 students received support, including 12 fellowships (averaging $12,000 per year), 70 research assistantships (averaging $15,000 per year), 86 teaching assistantships (averaging $8,500 per year); Federal Work-Study and institutionally sponsored loans also available. In 2006, 7 master's, 8 doctorates awarded. *Degree program information:* Part-time programs available. Offers chemical engineering (ME, MS, PhD); civil engineering (ME, MS, PhD); computer engineering (ME, MS); computing information science and engineering (PhD); electrical engineering (ME, MS); engineering (ME, MS, PhD); industrial engineering (ME); management systems (MS); mechanical engineering (ME, MS). *Application deadline:* For fall admission, 2/15 for domestic and international students; for spring admission, 9/15 for domestic and international students. Applications are processed on a rolling basis. *Application fee:* $25. *Application Contact:* Nancy Vega, Secretary, 787-833-1121, Fax: 787-833-1190, E-mail: nvega@uprm.edu. *Dean,* Dr. Ramón Vásquez, 787-265-3822, Fax: 787-833-1190, E-mail: reve@ece.uprm.edu.

UNIVERSITY OF PUERTO RICO, MEDICAL SCIENCES CAMPUS, San Juan, PR 00936-5067

General Information Commonwealth-supported, coed, primarily women, upper-level institution. *Graduate housing:* On-campus housing not available.

GRADUATE UNITS

College of Health Related Professions *Degree program information:* Part-time and evening/weekend programs available. Offers audiology (MS); clinical laboratory science (MS); cytotechnology (Certificate); dietetics (Certificate); health information management (MS); health related professions (MS, Certificate); medical technology (Certificate); physical therapy (MS); speech-language pathology (MS).

Graduate School of Public Health Students: 562 (397 women) 7 international. 484 applicants, 67% accepted. *Faculty:* 62 full-time (37 women). Expenses: Contact institution. *Financial support:* In 2006–07, 56 research assistantships, 8 teaching assistantships were awarded; career-related internships or fieldwork, Federal Work-Study, and institutionally sponsored loans also available. Financial award application deadline: 4/30. In 2006, 154 master's awarded. *Degree program information:* Part-time programs available. Offers biostatistics (MPH); demography (MS); developmental disabilities-early intervention (Certificate); environmental health (MS, Dr PH); epidemiology (MPH, MS); evaluation research of health systems (MS); gerontology (MPH, Certificate); health education (MPHE); health science nutrition (MS); health services administration (MHSA); industrial hygiene (MS); mother and child health (MPH); nurse midwifery (MPH, Certificate); public health (MPH); school health promotion (Certificate). *Application deadline:* For fall admission, 3/15 for domestic students. *Application fee:* $20. *Application Contact:* Prof. Mayra E. Santiago-Vargas, Counselor, 787-756-5244, Fax: 787-759-6719, E-mail: msantiago@rcm.upr.edu. *Dean,* Dr. José F. Cordero, 787-7645975, Fax: 787-759-6719, E-mail: jcordero@rcm.upr.edu.

School of Dentistry Students: 208 full-time (121 women); includes 204 minority (all Hispanic Americans) Average age 25. 132 applicants, 14% accepted, 19 enrolled. *Faculty:* 91 full-time (36 women), 53 part-time/adjunct (18 women). Expenses: Contact institution. *Financial support:* In 2006–07, 41 students received support, including research assistantships (averaging $5,000 per year), teaching assistantships (averaging $5,000 per year); Federal Work-Study, institutionally sponsored loans, scholarships/grants, traineeships, and stipends also available. Financial award application deadline: 3/30. In 2006, 2 master's, 19 other advanced degrees awarded. Offers dentistry (Certificate); general dentistry (Certificate); oral and maxillofacial surgery (MSD, Certificate); orthodontics (MSD, Certificate); pediatric dentistry (MSD, Certificate); prosthodontics (MSD, Certificate). *Application deadline:* For fall admission, 10/15 for domestic students, 10/13 for international students. Applications are processed on a rolling basis. *Application fee:* $0. *Application Contact:* Dr. Aileen Marie Torres, Assistant Dean of Student Affairs, 787-758-2525 Ext. 1113, Fax: 787-751-0990, E-mail: citorres@rcm.upr.edu. *Dean,* Dr. Yilda M. Rivera, 787-758-2525 Ext. 1105, Fax: 787-296-3246, E-mail: yrivera@rcm.upr.edu.

School of Medicine Expenses: Contact institution. *Financial support:* Fellowships, research assistantships, teaching assistantships, career-related internships or fieldwork, Federal Work-Study, institutionally sponsored loans, and tuition waivers (full and partial) available. Support available to part-time students. Offers medicine (MD, MS, PhD). *Application fee:* $15. *Application Contact:* Dr. Gladys González Navarrete, Assistant Dean for Student Affairs, 787-758-2525 Ext. 1810, Fax: 787-764-5740. *Dean,* Dr. Walter R. Frontera, 787-758-2525 Ext. 1801.

Division of Graduate Studies Students: 94 full-time (68 women); includes 92 minority (all Hispanic Americans), 2 international. Average age 23. 49 applicants, 73% accepted, 31 enrolled. *Faculty:* 54 full-time (22 women), 7 part-time/adjunct (2 women). Expenses: Contact institution. *Financial support:* Fellowships, research assistantships, teaching assistantships, career-related internships or fieldwork, Federal Work-Study, institutionally sponsored loans, and tuition waivers (full and partial) available. Support available to part-time students. Financial award application deadline: 4/30. In 2006, 4 master's, 6 doctorates awarded. Offers anatomy and neurobiology (MS, PhD); biochemistry (MS, PhD); biomedical sciences (MS, PhD); medical zoology (MS, PhD); microbiology and medical zoology (MS, PhD); pharmacology and toxicology (MS, PhD); physiology (MS, PhD). *Application deadline:* For fall admission, 9/15 for domestic and international students; for spring admission, 2/15 for domestic and international students. *Application fee:* $20. Electronic applications accepted. *Application Contact:* Lisa E. Santor, Administrative Assistant Graduate Program, 787-758-2525 Ext. 1814, Fax: 787-767-8693, E-mail: lsantos@rcm.upr.edu. *Associate Dean for Biomedical Sciences and Director Graduate Studies,* Dr. Walter I. Silva, 787-758-2525 Ext. 1878, Fax: 787-767-8693, E-mail: wsilva@rcm.upr.edu.

School of Nursing Students: 115 full-time (all women), 13 part-time (9 women); includes 123 minority (all Hispanic Americans), 3 international. 70 applicants, 71% accepted. *Faculty:* 12 full-time (11 women), 3 part-time/adjunct (2 women). Expenses: Contact institution. *Financial support:* In 2006–07, research assistantships with full tuition reimbursements (averaging $28,175 per year), teaching assistantships with full tuition reimbursements (averaging $48,965 per year) were awarded; Federal Work-Study, traineeships, tuition waivers (full), and unspecified assistantships also available. Financial award application deadline: 6/30. In 2006, 40 degrees awarded. *Degree program information:* Part-time and evening/weekend programs available. Offers anesthesia (MSN); clinical specialist (MSN); family nurse practitioner (MSN); nurse administrator (MSN); nursing education (MSN). *Application deadline:* For spring admission, 4/30 priority date for domestic and international students. Applications are processed on a rolling basis. *Application fee:* $33. Electronic applications accepted. *Application Contact:* Dr. Angelica Y. Matos, Director Graduate Department, 787-758-2525, Fax: 787-281-0721. *Dean,* Dr. Suane E. Sánchez, 787-758-2525 Ext. 2100, Fax: 787-281-0721, E-mail: sesanchez@rcm.upr.edu.

School of Pharmacy Students: 234 full-time (178 women), 11 part-time (8 women); all minorities (1 Asian American or Pacific Islander, 244 Hispanic Americans). 130 applicants, 45% accepted, 56 enrolled. *Faculty:* 31 full-time, 22 part-time/adjunct. Expenses: Contact institution. *Financial support:* In 2006–07, 9 research assistantships with full tuition reimbursements (averaging $6,930 per year) were awarded; fellowships with partial tuition reimbursements, teaching assistantships with full tuition reimbursements, career-related internships or fieldwork, Federal Work-Study, institutionally sponsored loans, scholarships/grants, tuition waivers (full), and unspecified assistantships also available. In 2006, 35 first professional degrees, 7 master's awarded. *Degree program information:* Part-time and evening/weekend programs available. Offers industrial pharmacy (MS); pharmaceutical sciences (MS); pharmacy (Pharm D). *Application deadline:* For fall admission, 2/9 for domestic and international students. *Application fee:* $15. *Application Contact:* Miriam Vélez, Assistant Dean of Student Affairs, 787-758-2525 Ext. 5407, Fax: 787-751-5680, E-mail: mivelez@rcm.upr.edu. *Dean,* Dr. Lesbia Hernández, 787-758-2525 Ext. 5427, Fax: 787-751-5680, E-mail: lhernandez@rcm.upr.edu.

UNIVERSITY OF PUERTO RICO, RÍO PIEDRAS, San Juan, PR 00931-3300

General Information Commonwealth-supported, coed, university. CGS member. *Enrollment:* 20,528 graduate, professional, and undergraduate students; 2,467 full-time matriculated graduate/professional students (1,660 women), 1,329 part-time matriculated graduate/professional students (916 women). *Enrollment by degree level:* 714 first professional, 2,215 master's, 832 doctoral, 35 other advanced degrees. Tuition, commonwealth resident: part-time $100 per credit. Tuition, nonresident: part-time $291 per credit. *Required fees:* $72 per semester. *Graduate housing:* Room and/or apartments available to single students; on-campus housing not available to married students. Typical cost: $550 per year ($4,970 including board). Housing application deadline: 6/15. *Student services:* Campus employment opportunities, campus safety program, career counseling, child daycare facilities, free psychological counseling, low-cost health insurance. *Library facilities:* Jose M. Lazaro Library plus 10 others. *Online resources:* library catalog, access to other libraries' catalogs. *Collection:* 1.8 million titles, 5,599 serial subscriptions, 5,599 audiovisual materials.

Computer facilities: 170 computers available on campus for general student use. A campuswide network can be accessed from student residence rooms. Internet access is available. *Web address:* http://www.uprrp.edu/.

General Application Contact: Cruz B. Valentin-Arbelo, Admission Office Director, 787-764-0000 Ext. 5653.

GRADUATE UNITS

College of Business Administration Students: 125 full-time (81 women), 199 part-time (135 women); all minorities (all Hispanic Americans) Expenses: Contact institution. *Financial support:* Fellowships, research assistantships, teaching assistantships, Federal Work-Study, institutionally sponsored loans, and tuition waivers (partial) available. Financial award application deadline: 5/31. In 2006, 50 master's, 3 doctorates awarded. *Degree program information:* Part-time programs available. Offers business administration (MBA, PhD). *Application deadline:* For fall admission, 2/1 for domestic and international students. *Application fee:* $17. *Application Contact:* Information Contact, 787-764-0000 Ext. 4142, Fax: 787-763-6944. *Coordinator of Master Programs,* Dr. Emilio Pontojas, 787-764-0000, Fax: 787-763-6944.

College of Education Students: 229 full-time (187 women), 290 part-time (224 women); all minorities (all Hispanic Americans) Expenses: Contact institution. *Financial support:* Fellowships, research assistantships, teaching assistantships, career-related internships or fieldwork, Federal Work-Study, institutionally sponsored loans, and tuition waivers (partial) available. Financial award application deadline: 5/31. In 2006, 43 master's, 24 doctorates awarded. *Degree program information:* Part-time programs available. Offers biology education (M Ed); chemistry education (M Ed); child education (M Ed); curriculum and teaching (Ed D); education (M Ed, MS, Ed D); educational research and evaluation (M Ed); English education (M Ed); exercise sciences (MS); family ecology and nutrition (M Ed); guidance and counseling (M Ed, Ed D); history education (M Ed); mathematics education (M Ed); physics education (M Ed); school administration and supervision (M Ed, Ed D); secondary education (M Ed); Spanish education (M Ed); special education (M Ed); teaching English as a second language (M Ed). *Application deadline:* For fall admission, 2/1 for domestic and international students. *Application fee:* $17. *Dean,* Dr. Angeles Molina Ilurrondo, 787-764-0000 Ext. 4344, Fax: 787-763-4130.

College of Humanities Students: 306 full-time (214 women), 229 part-time (149 women); includes 532 minority (1 African American, 531 Hispanic Americans). Average age 27. Expenses: Contact institution. *Financial support:* Fellowships, research assistantships, teaching assistantships, Federal Work-Study, institutionally sponsored loans, and tuition waivers (partial) available. Financial award application deadline: 5/31. In 2006, 32 master's, 15 doctorates awarded. *Degree program information:* Part-time programs available. Offers comparative literature (MA); English (MA, PhD); Hispanic studies (MA, PhD); history (MA, PhD); humanities (MA, PhD, Certificate); linguistics (MA); philosophy (MA); translation (MA, Certificate). *Application deadline:* For fall admission, 2/1 for domestic and international students. *Application fee:* $17. *Application Contact:* Information Contact, 787-764-0000 Ext. 3600, Fax: 787-763-5879. *Dean,* Dr. Josè L. Romos Escobor, 787-764-0001 Ext. 3525, Fax: 787-763-5879.

College of Natural Sciences Students: 245 full-time (143 women), 89 part-time (47 women); includes 321 minority (16 Asian Americans or Pacific Islanders, 305 Hispanic Americans). Expenses: Contact institution. *Financial support:* Fellowships, research assistantships, teaching assistantships, Federal Work-Study, institutionally sponsored loans, and tuition waivers (partial) available. Financial award application deadline: 5/31. In 2006, 20 master's, 21 doctorates awarded. *Degree program information:* Part-time programs available. Offers biology (MS, PhD); chemical physics (PhD); chemistry (MS, PhD); mathematics (MS, PhD); natural sciences (MS, PhD); physics (MS). *Application deadline:* For fall admission, 2/1 for domestic and international students. *Application fee:* $17. *Dean,* Dr. Brad Weiner, 787-764-5101.

College of Social Sciences Students: 648 full-time (504 women), 266 part-time (196 women); includes 910 minority (all Hispanic Americans) Average age 24. Expenses: Contact institution. *Financial support:* Fellowships, research assistantships, teaching assistantships, career-related internships or fieldwork, Federal Work-Study, institutionally sponsored loans, and tuition waivers (partial) available. Financial award application deadline: 5/31. In 2006, 141 master's, 27 doctorates awarded. *Degree program information:* Part-time programs available. Offers economics (MA); psychology (MA, PhD); social sciences (MA, MPA, MRC, MSW, PhD); sociology (MA). *Application deadline:* For fall admission, 2/1 for domestic and international students. *Application fee:* $17. *Acting Dean,* Dr. Carlos Severino-Valdés, 787-767-0000 Ext. 4152, Fax: 787-763-5599.

Graduate School of Rehabilitation Counseling Students: 96 full-time (82 women), 6 part-time (4 women); includes 100 minority (all Hispanic Americans) Expenses: Contact institution. *Financial support:* Fellowships, research assistantships, teaching assistantships, career-related internships or fieldwork, Federal Work-Study, institutionally sponsored loans, and tuition waivers (partial) available. Financial award application deadline: 5/31. In 2006, 34 degrees awarded. *Degree program information:* Part-time programs available. Offers rehabilitation counseling (MRC). *Application deadline:* For fall admission, 2/1 for domestic and international students. *Application fee:* $17. *Application Contact:* Information Contact, 787-764-0000 Ext. 2177, Fax: 787-764-0000 Ext. 1212. *Director,* Dr. Marilyn Mendoza-Lugo, 787-764-0000 Ext. 2167, Fax: 787-764-0000.

Graduate School of Social Work Students: 138 full-time (118 women), 48 part-time (34 women); includes 185 minority (all Hispanic Americans) Average age 25. Expenses: Contact institution. *Financial support:* Fellowships, research assistantships, teaching assistantships, career-related internships or fieldwork, Federal Work-Study, institutionally sponsored loans, and tuition waivers (partial) available. Financial award application deadline: 5/31. In 2006, 50 degrees awarded. *Degree program information:* Part-time programs available. Offers social work (MSW, PhD). *Application deadline:* For fall admission, 2/1 for domestic and international students. *Application fee:* $17. *Application Contact:* Information Contact, 787-764-0000 Ext. 5831, Fax: 787-763-3725. *Director,* Dr. Norma Rodriguez, 787-764-0000 Ext. 4268, Fax: 787-763-3725.

School of Public Administration Students: 188 full-time (136 women), 120 part-time (93 women); all minorities (all Hispanic Americans) Average age 24. Expenses: Contact institution.

University of Puerto Rico, Río Piedras (continued)

Financial support: Fellowships, research assistantships, teaching assistantships, Federal Work-Study, institutionally sponsored loans, and tuition waivers (partial) available. Financial award application deadline: 5/31. In 2006, 37 degrees awarded. *Degree program information:* Part-time programs available. Offers public administration (MPA). *Application deadline:* For fall admission, 2/1 for domestic and international students. *Application fee:* $17. *Director*, Dr. Palmira González, 787-764-0000 Ext. 2097, Fax: 787-763-7510.

Graduate School of Information Sciences and Technologies Students: 38 full-time (27 women), 97 part-time (68 women); includes 134 minority (all Hispanic Americans) Expenses: Contact institution. *Financial support:* Fellowships, research assistantships, teaching assistantships, Federal Work-Study, institutionally sponsored loans, and tuition waivers (partial) available. Financial award application deadline: 5/31. In 2006, 18 master's, 28 other advanced degrees awarded. *Degree program information:* Part-time programs available. Offers librarianship (Post-Graduate Certificate); librarianship and information services (MLS). *Application deadline:* For fall admission, 2/1 for domestic and international students. *Application fee:* $17. *Application Contact:* Information Contact, 787-764-0000 Ext. 5827, Fax: 787-764-2311. *Director*, Dr. Nitza M. Hernández, 787-764-0000 Ext. 5207, Fax: 787-764-2311.

Graduate School of Planning Students: 81 full-time (38 women), 63 part-time (31 women); all minorities (all Hispanic Americans) Average age 24. Expenses: Contact institution. *Financial support:* Fellowships, research assistantships, teaching assistantships, Federal Work-Study, institutionally sponsored loans, and tuition waivers (partial) available. Financial award application deadline: 5/31. In 2006, 17 degrees awarded. *Degree program information:* Part-time programs available. Offers planning (MP). *Application deadline:* For fall admission, 2/1 for domestic students. *Application fee:* $17. *Application Contact:* Information Contact, 787-764-0000 Ext. 3182, Fax: 787-763-5375. *Director*, Dr. Elías R. Gutierrez, 787-764-0000 Ext. 5010, Fax: 787-763-5375, E-mail: nvega@rrpac.upr.clu.edu.

School of Architecture Students: 70 full-time (28 women), 11 part-time (4 women); all minorities (all Hispanic Americans) Average age 24. 18 applicants, 100% accepted, 18 enrolled. Expenses: Contact institution. *Financial support:* Fellowships, research assistantships, teaching assistantships, Federal Work-Study, institutionally sponsored loans, and tuition waivers (partial) available. Financial award application deadline: 5/31. In 2006, 18 degrees awarded. *Degree program information:* Part-time programs available. Offers architecture (M Arch). *Application deadline:* For fall admission, 2/1 for domestic and international students. *Application fee:* $45. *Application Contact:* Dr. Humberto Covollin, Graduate Program Coordinator, 787-764-000 Ext. 3449, Fax: 787-763-5377. *Dean*, Dr. Fernando Abruña, 809-763-2101 Ext. 2102.

School of Communication Students: 46 full-time (34 women), 21 part-time (16 women); all minorities (all Hispanic Americans) Average age 24. Expenses: Contact institution. *Financial support:* Fellowships, research assistantships, teaching assistantships, Federal Work-Study, institutionally sponsored loans, and tuition waivers (partial) available. Financial award application deadline: 5/31. In 2006, 10 degrees awarded. *Degree program information:* Part-time programs available. Offers communication (MA). *Application deadline:* For fall admission, 2/1 for domestic students. *Application fee:* $17. *Application Contact:* Information Contact, 787-764-0000 Ext. 5043, Fax: 787-763-5390. *Director*, Dr. Eliseo Colón, 787-764-0000 Ext. 5042, Fax: 787-763-5390.

School of Law Students: 678 full-time (403 women), 41 part-time (27 women); includes 718 minority (all Hispanic Americans) Average age 22. Expenses: Contact institution. *Financial support:* Fellowships, research assistantships, teaching assistantships, career-related internships or fieldwork, Federal Work-Study, institutionally sponsored loans, and tuition waivers (partial) available. Financial award application deadline: 5/31. In 2006, 170 degrees awarded. *Degree program information:* Part-time and evening/weekend programs available. Offers law (JD, LL M). *Application deadline:* For fall admission, 2/1 for domestic students. *Application fee:* $17. *Application Contact:* Information Contact, 787-764-2675 Ext. 3843, Fax: 787-764-2675. *Dean*, Dr. Efrén Rivera-Ramos, 787-999-9527, Fax: 787-764-2765.

UNIVERSITY OF PUGET SOUND, Tacoma, WA 98416

General Information Independent, coed, comprehensive institution. *Enrollment:* 2,819 graduate, professional, and undergraduate students; 198 full-time matriculated graduate/professional students (155 women), 57 part-time matriculated graduate/professional students (48 women). *Enrollment by degree level:* 154 master's, 101 doctoral. *Graduate faculty:* 23 full-time (16 women), 30 part-time/adjunct (25 women). *Tuition:* Full-time $26,390. Tuition and fees vary according to course load. *Graduate housing:* Room and/or apartments available on a first-come, first-served basis to single students; on-campus housing not available to married students. Typical cost: $4,190 per year ($7,670 including board). Room and board charges vary according to board plan and housing facility selected. Housing application deadline: 5/1. *Student services:* Campus employment opportunities, campus safety program, career counseling, disabled student services, exercise/wellness program, free psychological counseling, international student services, low-cost health insurance, multicultural affairs office, teacher training, writing training. *Library facilities:* Collins Memorial Library. *Online resources:* library catalog, web page, access to other libraries' catalogs. *Collection:* 364,662 titles, 20,008 serial subscriptions, 16,868 audiovisual materials.

Computer facilities: 314 computers available on campus for general student use. A campuswide network can be accessed from student residence rooms and from off campus. Internet access, financial aid, admission, student employment, library are available. *Web address:* http://www.ups.edu/.

General Application Contact: Dr. George H. Mills, Vice President for Enrollment, 253-879-3211, Fax: 253-879-3993, E-mail: admission@ups.edu.

GRADUATE UNITS

Graduate Studies Students: 198 full-time (155 women), 57 part-time (48 women); includes 48 minority (11 African Americans, 6 American Indian/Alaska Native, 29 Asian Americans or Pacific Islanders, 2 Hispanic Americans), 4 international. Average age 27. 397 applicants, 65% accepted, 117 enrolled. *Faculty:* 23 full-time (16 women), 30 part-time/adjunct (25 women). Expenses: Contact institution. *Financial support:* In 2006–07, 80 students received support, including 49 fellowships (averaging $7,553 per year), 1 teaching assistantship with tuition reimbursement available (averaging $12,250 per year); career-related internships or fieldwork, scholarships/grants, and tuition waivers (full) also available. Support available to part-time students. Financial award application deadline: 3/31; financial award applicants required to submit FAFSA. In 2006, 83 master's, 48 doctorates awarded. *Application deadline:* For fall admission, 1/15 for domestic and international students. Applications are processed on a rolling basis. *Application fee:* $65. Electronic applications accepted. *Application Contact:* Dr. George H. Mills, Vice President for Enrollment, 253-879-3211, Fax: 253-879-3993, E-mail: admission@ups.edu. *Associate Dean*, Dr. John M. Finney, 253-879-3207.

School of Education Students: 55 full-time (37 women), 28 part-time (22 women); includes 14 minority (7 African Americans, 2 American Indian/Alaska Native, 5 Asian Americans or Pacific Islanders), 2 international. Average age 27. 121 applicants, 82% accepted, 59 enrolled. *Faculty:* 12 full-time (8 women), 3 part-time/adjunct (all women). Expenses: Contact institution. *Financial support:* In 2006–07, 24 students received support, including 16 fellowships (averaging $7,575 per year), 1 teaching assistantship with tuition reimbursement available (averaging $12,250 per year); career-related internships or fieldwork, scholarships/grants, and tuition waivers (full) also available. Support available to part-time students. Financial award application deadline: 3/31; financial award applicants required to submit FAFSA. In 2006, 60 degrees awarded. Offers agency counseling (M Ed); counselor education (M Ed); education (M Ed, MAT); elementary education (MAT); middle school education (MAT); pastoral counseling (M Ed); secondary education (MAT). *Application deadline:* For fall admission, 3/1 priority date for domestic and international students. Applications are processed on a rolling basis. *Application fee:* $65. Electronic applications accepted. *Application Contact:* Dr. George H. Mills, Vice President for Enrollment, 253-879-3211, Fax: 253-879-3993, E-mail: admission@ups.edu. *Dean*, Dr. Christine Kline, 253-879-3377.

School of Occupational Therapy and Physical Therapy Students: 143 full-time (118 women), 29 part-time (26 women); includes 34 minority (4 African Americans, 4 American Indian/Alaska Native, 24 Asian Americans or Pacific Islanders, 2 Hispanic Americans), 2 international. Average age 27. 222 applicants, 56% accepted, 53 enrolled. *Faculty:* 11 full-time (8 women), 27 part-time/adjunct (22 women). Expenses: Contact institution. *Financial support:* In 2006–07, 56 students received support, including 33 fellowships (averaging $7,543 per year); career-related internships or fieldwork and scholarships/grants also available. Support available to part-time students. Financial award application deadline: 3/31; financial award applicants required to submit FAFSA. In 2006, 23 master's, 48 doctorates awarded. Offers occupational therapy (MOT, MSOT); occupational therapy and physical therapy (MOT, MSOT, DPT); physical therapy (DPT). *Application deadline:* For fall admission, 1/15 priority date for domestic and international students. Applications are processed on a rolling basis. *Application fee:* $65. Electronic applications accepted. *Application Contact:* Dr. George H. Mills, Vice President for Enrollment, 253-879-3211, Fax: 253-879-3993, E-mail: admission@ups.edu. *Head*, 253-879-3281.

UNIVERSITY OF REDLANDS, Redlands, CA 92373-0999

General Information Independent, coed, comprehensive institution. *Enrollment:* 2,407 graduate, professional, and undergraduate students; 1,243 full-time matriculated graduate/professional students (727 women), 11 part-time matriculated graduate/professional students (6 women). *Enrollment by degree level:* 909 master's, 19 doctoral, 326 other advanced degrees. *Graduate faculty:* 60 full-time, 217 part-time/adjunct. *Tuition:* Part-time $584 per credit. *Required fees:* $20 per course. Full-time tuition and fees vary according to program. *Graduate housing:* Rooms and/or apartments available on a first-come, first-served basis to single students and available to married students. Housing application deadline: 8/19. *Student services:* Campus employment opportunities, career counseling, free psychological counseling, international student services, low-cost health insurance. *Library facilities:* Armacost Library. *Online resources:* library catalog, web page. *Collection:* 268,387 titles, 11,800 serial subscriptions, 7,134 audiovisual materials. *Research affiliation:* Environmental Systems Research Institute (geographic information systems).

Computer facilities: 655 computers available on campus for general student use. A campuswide network can be accessed from student residence rooms and from off campus. Internet access is available. *Web address:* http://www.redlands.edu/.

GRADUATE UNITS

College of Arts and Sciences Students: 87 full-time (59 women), 7 part-time (3 women); includes 11 minority (4 Asian Americans or Pacific Islanders, 7 Hispanic Americans), 7 international. Average age 27. Expenses: Contact institution. *Financial support:* Application deadline: 3/2; In 2006, 36 degrees awarded. Offers arts and sciences (MM, MS); communicative disorders (MS); geographic information systems (MS). *Application deadline:* Applications are processed on a rolling basis. *Application fee:* $40. Electronic applications accepted. *Acting Dean*, Dr. Barbara Morris, 909-793-2121 Ext. 4080, Fax: 909-335-4076.

School of Music Students: 13 full-time (6 women), 5 part-time (1 woman); includes 2 Hispanic Americans. Average age 25. *Faculty:* 13 full-time, 16 part-time/adjunct. Expenses: Contact institution. *Financial support:* In 2006–07, 5 students received support. Health care benefits and unspecified assistantships available. Financial award application deadline: 3/2; financial award applicants required to submit FAFSA. In 2006, 2 degrees awarded. *Degree program information:* Part-time programs available. Offers music (MM). *Application deadline:* For fall admission, 8/9 for domestic students. Applications are processed on a rolling basis. *Application fee:* $40. *Director*, Dr. Andrew Glendening, 909-793-2121, Fax: 909-793-2029, E-mail: andrew_glendening@redlands.edu.

School of Business Students: 576 full-time (257 women); includes 247 minority (60 African Americans, 8 American Indian/Alaska Native, 54 Asian Americans or Pacific Islanders, 125 Hispanic Americans), 22 international. Average age 36. *Faculty:* 22 full-time, 138 part-time/adjunct. Expenses: Contact institution. *Financial support:* Applicants required to submit FAFSA. In 2006, 275 degrees awarded. *Degree program information:* Evening/weekend programs available. Offers business (MBA); information technology (MS); management (MA). *Application deadline:* For fall admission, 9/1 priority date for domestic students; for spring admission, 2/1 priority date for domestic students. Applications are processed on a rolling basis. *Application fee:* $0. *Application Contact:* Kimmi Grulke, Campus Director, 885-999-9844, Fax: 909-335-5325, E-mail: schoolofbusiness@redlands.edu. *Interim Dean*, Dr. Stuart Noble-Goodman, 909-793-2121, Fax: 909-335-3400.

School of Education Students: 580 full-time (411 women), 4 part-time (3 women); includes 200 minority (45 African Americans, 7 American Indian/Alaska Native, 11 Asian Americans or Pacific Islanders, 137 Hispanic Americans), 7 international. Average age 32. *Faculty:* 15 full-time, 47 part-time/adjunct. Expenses: Contact institution. *Financial support:* Research assistantships with partial tuition reimbursements, health care benefits available. Financial award application deadline: 3/2; financial award applicants required to submit FAFSA. In 2006, 79 master's, 209 other advanced degrees awarded. *Degree program information:* Part-time and evening/weekend programs available. Offers education (MA, Ed D, Certificate). *Application deadline:* For fall admission, 8/6 for domestic students; for winter admission, 1/21 for domestic students. Applications are processed on a rolling basis. *Application fee:* $0. *Application Contact:* Information Contact, 909-748-8064, E-mail: education@redlands.edu. *Dean*, Dr. Hank Robin, 909-748-8064.

UNIVERSITY OF REGINA, Regina, SK S4S 0A2, Canada

General Information Province-supported, coed, university. *Enrollment:* 12,056 graduate, professional, and undergraduate students; 613 full-time matriculated graduate/professional students (305 women), 589 part-time matriculated graduate/professional students (341 women). *Enrollment by degree level:* 1,005 master's, 197 doctoral. *Graduate faculty:* 345 full-time (103 women), 60 part-time/adjunct (14 women). *Graduate housing:* Room and/or apartments available on a first-come, first-served basis to single students; on-campus housing not available to married students. Typical cost: $1,628 Canadian dollars per year ($3,628 Canadian dollars including board). Room and board charges vary according to board plan and campus/location. *Student services:* Campus employment opportunities, campus safety program, career counseling, child daycare facilities, disabled student services, exercise/wellness program, free psychological counseling, international student services, low-cost health insurance, multicultural affairs office, teacher training, writing training. *Library facilities:* Dr. John Archer Library plus 3 others. *Online resources:* library catalog, web page, access to other libraries' catalogs. *Collection:* 1 million titles, 14,055 serial subscriptions, 12,358 audiovisual materials. *Research affiliation:* Institute for Robotics and Intelligent Systems (knowledge-based systems, artificial intelligence), TR Labs (telecommunications), Jefferson Laboratory/Southeastern Universities Research Association, Inc. (electromagnetic physics), Communities of Tomorrow (community sustainability), Petroleum Technology Research Center (greenhouse gas remediation), AUTO 21-The Automobile of the 21st Century (development of automobile and impact on society/environment).

Computer facilities: 300 computers available on campus for general student use. A campuswide network can be accessed from student residence rooms and from off campus. Internet access and online class registration are available. *Web address:* http://www.uregina.ca/.

General Application Contact: Dr. Dongyan Blachford, Associate Dean, 306-585-5186, Fax: 306-337-2444, E-mail: grad.studies@uregina.ca.

GRADUATE UNITS

Faculty of Graduate Studies and Research Students: 613 full-time (305 women), 589 part-time (341 women). 902 applicants, 66% accepted. *Faculty:* 345 full-time (103 women), 60 part-time/adjunct (14 women). Expenses: Contact institution. *Financial support:* In 2006–07, 149 fellowships (averaging $14,886 per year), 35 research assistantships (averaging $12,750 per year), 106 teaching assistantships (averaging $13,501 per year) were awarded; career-related internships or fieldwork, institutionally sponsored loans, and scholarships/grants also available. Financial award application deadline: 6/15. In 2006, 241 master's, 21 doctorates awarded. *Degree program information:* Part-time and evening/weekend programs available. *Application deadline:* For fall admission, 3/15 priority date for domestic students; for winter admission, 7/15 priority date for domestic students; for spring admission, 9/15 priority date for domestic students. Applications are processed on a rolling basis. *Application fee:* $60 ($100 for international students). Electronic applications accepted. *Application Contact:* Dr. Dongyan Blachford, Associate Dean, 306-585-5186, Fax: 306-337-2444, E-mail: dongyan.

blachford@uregina.ca. *Dean,* Dr. Rod Kelln, 306-585-5185, Fax: 306-337-2444, E-mail: rod.kelln@uregina.ca.

Faculty of Arts Students: 132 full-time (92 women), 91 part-time (59 women). 168 applicants, 57% accepted. *Faculty:* 161 full-time (56 women), 11 part-time/adjunct (4 women). Expenses: Contact institution. *Financial support:* In 2006–07, 50 fellowships (averaging $14,886 per year), 19 research assistantships (averaging $12,750 per year), 27 teaching assistantships (averaging $13,501 per year) were awarded; career-related internships or fieldwork and scholarships/grants also available. Financial award application deadline: 6/15. In 2006, 39 master's, 3 doctorates awarded. *Degree program information:* Part-time programs available. Offers anthropology (MA); arts (M Sc, MA, PhD); Canadian plains studies (MA, PhD); clinical psychology (MA, PhD); English (MA, PhD); experimental and applied psychology (MA, PhD); French (MA); geography (M Sc, MA, PhD); gerontology (M Sc, MA); history (MA, PhD); human justice (MA); indigenous studies (MA); justice studies (MA); linguistics (MA); philosophy (MA); police studies (MA); political science (MA, PhD); religious studies (MA, PhD); social and political thought (MA); social studies (MA, PhD); sociology (MA, PhD). *Application deadline:* Applications are processed on a rolling basis. *Application fee:* $60 ($100 for international students). *Dean,* Dr. Thomas Chase, 306-585-4895, Fax: 306-585-5368, E-mail: thomas.chase@uregina.ca.

Faculty of Education Students: 78 full-time (55 women), 241 part-time (168 women). 124 applicants, 81% accepted. *Faculty:* 45 full-time (21 women), 6 part-time/adjunct (5 women). Expenses: Contact institution. *Financial support:* In 2006–07, 23 students received support, including 11 fellowships (averaging $14,886 per year), 3 research assistantships (averaging $12,750 per year), 7 teaching assistantships (averaging $13,501 per year); career-related internships or fieldwork and scholarships/grants also available. Financial award application deadline: 6/15. In 2006, 72 master's, 4 doctorates awarded. *Degree program information:* Part-time programs available. Offers adult education (M Ad Ed); curriculum and instruction (M Ed); education (M Ad Ed, M Ed, MHRD, PhD); educational administration (M Ed); educational psychology (M Ed); human resources development (MHRD). *Application deadline:* For fall admission, 2/15 for domestic students; for winter admission, 2/15 for domestic students; for spring admission, 2/15 for domestic students. *Application fee:* $60 ($100 for international students). *Application Contact:* Vicki Minhinnick, Graduate Program Coordinator, 306-585-4506, Fax: 306-585-5387, E-mail: edgrad@uregina.ca. *Associate Dean, Graduate Program and Research,* Dr. Warren Wessel, 306-585-4816, Fax: 306-585-5387, E-mail: warren.wessel@uregina.ca.

Faculty of Engineering Students: 171 full-time (54 women), 54 part-time (12 women). 159 applicants, 63% accepted. *Faculty:* 36 full-time (7 women), 35 part-time/adjunct (10 women). Expenses: Contact institution. *Financial support:* In 2006–07, 40 fellowships (averaging $14,886 per year), 11 research assistantships (averaging $12,750 per year), 28 teaching assistantships (averaging $13,501 per year) were awarded; career-related internships or fieldwork and scholarships/grants also available. Financial award application deadline: 6/15. In 2006, 48 master's, 9 doctorates awarded. Offers advanced manufacturing and processing (MA Sc); electronic systems engineering (M Eng, MA Sc, PhD); engineering (M Eng, MA Sc, PhD); environmental systems engineering (M Eng, MA Sc, PhD); industrial systems engineering (M Eng, MA Sc, PhD); petroleum systems engineering (M Eng, MA Sc, PhD); process systems engineering (M Eng, MA Sc). *Application deadline:* Applications are processed on a rolling basis. *Application fee:* $60 ($100 for international students). *Acting Dean,* Dr. Paitoon Tontiwachwuthikul, 306-585-4160, Fax: 306-585-4855, E-mail: paitoon.tontiwachwuthikul@uregina.ca.

Faculty of Fine Arts Students: 26 full-time (16 women), 10 part-time (6 women). 19 applicants, 53% accepted. *Faculty:* 23 full-time (13 women). Expenses: Contact institution. *Financial support:* In 2006–07, 13 students received support, including 3 fellowships (averaging $14,886 per year), research assistantships (averaging $12,750 per year), 1 teaching assistantship (averaging $13,501 per year); scholarships/grants also available. Financial award application deadline: 6/15. In 2006, 3 degrees awarded. *Degree program information:* Part-time programs available. Offers fine arts (M Mus, MA, MFA, PhD); music (M Mus); music theory (MA); musicology (MA, PhD); visual arts (MA, MFA). *Application deadline:* For fall admission, 3/15 for domestic students. *Application fee:* $60 ($100 for international students). *Application Contact:* Randal Rogers, Graduate Program Coordinator, 306-585-4746, Fax: 306-585-5544, E-mail: randal.rogers@uregina.ca. *Dean,* Dr. Sheila Petty, 306-585-4188, Fax: 306-585-5544, E-mail: sheila.petty@uregina.ca.

Faculty of Kinesiology and Health Studies Students: 19 full-time (11 women), 11 part-time (6 women). 10 applicants, 100% accepted. *Faculty:* 14 full-time (3 women), 3 part-time/adjunct (0 women). Expenses: Contact institution. *Financial support:* In 2006–07, 3 fellowships (averaging $14,886 per year), 1 research assistantship (averaging $12,750 per year), 3 teaching assistantships (averaging $13,501 per year) were awarded; scholarships/grants also available. In 2006, 3 degrees awarded. Offers kinesiology and health studies (PhD); physical activity studies (M Sc). *Application deadline:* Applications are processed on a rolling basis. *Application fee:* $60 ($100 for international students). *Application Contact:* Dr. Kim Dorsch, Program Coordinator, 306-585-4742, E-mail: kim.dorsch@uregina.ca. *Dean,* Dr. Craig Chamberlin, 306-585-4876, Fax: 306-585-4854, E-mail: craig.chamberlin@uregina.ca.

Faculty of Science Students: 125 full-time (49 women), 48 part-time (18 women). 171 applicants, 47% accepted. *Faculty:* 79 full-time (13 women), 24 part-time/adjunct (1 woman). Expenses: Contact institution. *Financial support:* In 2006–07, 35 fellowships (averaging $14,886 per year), 9 research assistantships (averaging $12,750 per year), 28 teaching assistantships (averaging $13,501 per year) were awarded; career-related internships or fieldwork and scholarships/grants also available. Financial award application deadline: 6/15. In 2006, 23 master's, 5 doctorates awarded. *Degree program information:* Part-time programs available. Offers analytical chemistry (M Sc, PhD); biochemistry (M Sc, PhD); biology (M Sc, PhD); computer science (M Sc, PhD); geology (M Sc, PhD); inorganic chemistry (M Sc, PhD); mathematics (M Sc, MA, PhD); organic chemistry (M Sc, PhD); physical chemistry (M Sc, PhD); physics (M Sc, PhD); science (M Sc, MA, PhD); statistics (M Sc, MA). *Application deadline:* Applications are processed on a rolling basis. *Application fee:* $60 ($100 for international students). *Dean,* Dr. Katherine Bergman, 306-585-4143, Fax: 306-585-4894.

Faculty of Social Work Students: 29 full-time (24 women), 34 part-time (27 women). 32 applicants, 63% accepted. *Faculty:* 16 full-time (8 women), 7 part-time/adjunct (4 women). Expenses: Contact institution. *Financial support:* In 2006–07, 7 fellowships (averaging $14,886 per year), 1 research assistantship (averaging $12,750 per year), 5 teaching assistantships (averaging $13,501 per year) were awarded; career-related internships or fieldwork and scholarships/grants also available. Financial award application deadline: 6/15. In 2006, 18 degrees awarded. *Degree program information:* Part-time programs available. Offers social work (MASW, MSW, PhD). *Application deadline:* For fall admission, 2/15 for domestic students. *Application fee:* $60 ($100 for international students). *Application Contact:* Dr. David Broad, Graduate Coordinator, 306-585-4588, Fax: 306-585-4872, E-mail: david.broad@uregina.ca. *Dean,* Dr. David Schantz, 306-585-4037, E-mail: david.schantz@uregina.ca.

Johnson-Shoyama Graduate School of Public Policy Students: 47 full-time (26 women), 60 part-time (33 women). 115 applicants, 80% accepted. *Faculty:* 5 full-time (2 women). Expenses: Contact institution. *Financial support:* In 2006–07, 5 fellowships (averaging $14,886 per year), 1 research assistantship (averaging $12,750 per year), 4 teaching assistantships (averaging $13,501 per year) were awarded. Financial award application deadline: 6/15. In 2006, 16 degrees awarded. *Degree program information:* Part-time and evening/weekend programs available. Offers economic analysis for public policy (Master's Certificate); non-profit management (Master's Certificate); public management (MPA, Master's Certificate); public policy (MPA, PhD, Master's Certificate). *Application deadline:* Applications are processed on a rolling basis. *Application fee:* $60 ($100 for international students). Electronic applications accepted. *Application Contact:* Devon Anderson, 306-585-5462, E-mail: devon.anderson@uregina.ca. *Associate Dean,* Dr. Ken Rasmussen, 306-585-5463, E-mail: ken.rasmussen@uregina.ca.

Kenneth Levene Graduate School of Business Students: 66 full-time (27 women), 45 part-time (21 women). 104 applicants, 88% accepted. *Faculty:* 24 full-time (5 women), 3 part-time/adjunct (0 women). Expenses: Contact institution. *Financial support:* In 2006–07, 4 fellowships (averaging $14,886 per year), 1 research assistantship (averaging $12,750 per year), 3 teaching assistantships (averaging $13,501 per year) were awarded; scholarships/grants also available. Financial award application deadline: 6/15. In 2006, 17 degrees awarded. *Degree program information:* Part-time and evening/weekend programs available. Offers business (MBA, MHRM, Master's Certificate); business fundamentals (Master's Certificate); general management (Master's Certificate); human resources management (MHRM, Master's Certificate); international business (Master's Certificate). *Application deadline:* Applications are processed on a rolling basis. *Application fee:* $60 ($100 for international students). Electronic applications accepted. *Application Contact:* Heidi Eger, 306-585-4735, E-mail: heidi.eger@uregina.ca. *Director,* Dr. Anne Lavack, 306-585-4716, Fax: 306-585-4805, E-mail: anne.lavack@uregina.ca.

UNIVERSITY OF RHODE ISLAND, Kingston, RI 02881

General Information State-supported, coed, university. CGS member. *Enrollment:* 15,062 graduate, professional, and undergraduate students; 1,564 full-time matriculated graduate/professional students (958 women), 1,623 part-time matriculated graduate/professional students (1,067 women). *Enrollment by degree level:* 556 first professional. *Graduate faculty:* 674 full-time, 32 part-time/adjunct. Tuition, state resident: full-time $6,032; part-time $335 per credit. Tuition, nonresident: full-time $17,288; part-time $960 per credit. *Required fees:* $65 per credit. $30 per semester. One-time fee: $80 part-time. *Graduate housing:* Rooms and/or apartments available on a first-come, first-served basis to single and married students. *Student services:* Campus employment opportunities, campus safety program, career counseling, disabled student services, free psychological counseling, international student services, low-cost health insurance, multicultural affairs office. *Library facilities:* University Library plus 1 other. *Online resources:* library catalog, web page. *Collection:* 1.2 million titles, 7,926 serial subscriptions, 11,671 audiovisual materials.

Computer facilities: 552 computers available on campus for general student use. A campuswide network can be accessed from off campus. *Web address:* http://www.uri.edu.

General Application Contact: Harold D. Bibb, Associate Dean of the Graduate School, 401-874-2262, Fax: 401-874-5491.

GRADUATE UNITS

Graduate School *Faculty:* 659 full-time (213 women), 10 part-time/adjunct (7 women). Expenses: Contact institution. *Financial support:* In 2006–07, 29 fellowships, 342 research assistantships, 385 teaching assistantships were awarded; career-related internships or fieldwork, Federal Work-Study, institutionally sponsored loans, and tuition waivers (full and partial) also available. Support available to part-time students. In 2006, 73 first professional degrees, 491 master's, 95 doctorates awarded. *Degree program information:* Part-time and evening/weekend programs available. *Application deadline:* For fall admission, 4/15 priority date for domestic students. Applications are processed on a rolling basis. *Application fee:* $35. *Interim Vice Provost for Graduate Studies, Research and Outreach,* Karen Markin, 401-874-2223.

College of Arts and Sciences Expenses: Contact institution. *Financial support:* Fellowships, research assistantships, teaching assistantships available. Offers applied mathematics (PhD); arts and sciences (MA, MLIS, MM, MPA, MS, PhD, Certificate, Graduate Certificate); behavioral science (PhD); chemistry (MS, PhD); clinical psychology (PhD); computer science (MS, PhD); digital forensics (Graduate Certificate); English (MA, PhD); history (MA); library and information studies (MLIS); mathematics (MS, PhD); music (MM); physics (MS, PhD); political science (MA); public policy and administration (MA, MPA, Certificate); school psychology (MS, PhD); Spanish (MA); statistics (MS). *Application deadline:* Applications are processed on a rolling basis. *Application fee:* $35. *Dean,* Winifed Brownell, 401-874-4101.

College of Business Administration Expenses: Contact institution. *Financial support:* Unspecified assistantships available. In 2006, 86 master's, 1 doctorate awarded. Offers accounting (MS); business administration (PhD); finance (MBA, PhD); international business (MBA); international sports management (MBA); management (MBA, PhD); management science (MBA); management sciences and information systems (PhD); marketing (MBA, PhD). *Application deadline:* For fall admission, 4/15 priority date for domestic students. Applications are processed on a rolling basis. *Application fee:* $35. *Application Contact:* Dr. Laura Beauvais, Director of Graduate Programs, 401-874-4341. *Dean,* Mark Higgins, 401-874-2337.

College of Continuing Education Expenses: Contact institution. Offers clinical laboratory sciences (MS); communication studies (MA). *Application deadline:* For fall admission, 4/15 priority date for domestic students. Applications are processed on a rolling basis. *Application fee:* $35. *Vice Provost for Urban Programs,* John McCray, 401-277-5080.

College of Engineering Expenses: Contact institution. *Financial support:* Research assistantships, teaching assistantships, tuition waivers (full) available. *Degree program information:* Part-time programs available. Offers chemical engineering (MS, PhD); design/systems (MS, PhD); electrical engineering (MS, PhD); engineering (MS, MSCE, PhD); environmental engineering (MSCE); fluid mechanics (MS, PhD); industrial and manufacturing engineering (PhD); manufacturing systems engineering (MS); ocean engineering (MS, PhD); solid mechanics (MS, PhD); structural engineering (MS, PhD); thermal sciences (MS, PhD); transportation engineering (MS, PhD). *Application deadline:* For fall admission, 4/15 priority date for domestic students. Applications are processed on a rolling basis. *Application fee:* $35. *Application Contact:* Dr. David M. Shao, Associate Dean, 401-874-2186. *Dean,* Bahram Nassersharif, 401-874-2186.

College of Human Science and Services Expenses: Contact institution. *Financial support:* Career-related internships or fieldwork available. *Degree program information:* Evening/weekend programs available. Offers adult education (MA); audiology (Au D); college student personnel (MS); elementary education (MA); exercise science (MS); human development and family studies (MS); human science and services (MA, MM, MS, Au D, DPT); marriage and family therapy (MS); music education (MM); physical education (MS); physical therapy (DPT); psychosocial aspects of physical activity and sport (MS); reading education (MA); secondary education (MA); speech-language pathology (MS); teaching and administration (MS); textiles, fashion merchandising and design (MS). *Application deadline:* For fall admission, 4/15 priority date for domestic students; for spring admission, 11/15 for domestic students. Applications are processed on a rolling basis. *Application fee:* $35. *Dean,* W. Lynn McKinney, 401-874-2244.

College of Nursing Expenses: Contact institution. In 2006, 34 master's, 5 doctorates awarded. Offers administration (MS); clinical specialist in gerontology (MS); clinical specialist in psychiatric/mental health (MS); family nurse practitioner (MS); nurse midwifery (MS); nursing (PhD); nursing education (MS). *Application deadline:* For fall admission, 4/15 for domestic students. *Application fee:* $35. *Dean,* Dayle Joseph, 401-874-2766.

College of Pharmacy Expenses: Contact institution. In 2006, 64 first professional degrees, 7 master's, 2 doctorates awarded. Offers biomedical and pharmaceutical sciences (MS, PhD); medicinal chemistry and pharmacognosy (MS, PhD); pharmaceutical sciences (MS, PhD); pharmaceutics and pharmacokinetics (MS, PhD); pharmacology and toxicology (MS, PhD); pharmacy (Pharm D); pharmacy practice (MS, PhD). *Application deadline:* For fall admission, 4/15 for domestic students. *Application fee:* $35. *Dean,* Donald Letendre, 401-874-2761.

College of the Environment and Life Sciences Expenses: Contact institution. *Financial support:* Fellowships, research assistantships, tuition waivers (full and partial) available. *Degree program information:* Part-time programs available. Offers animal health and disease (MS); animal science (MS); aquaculture (MS); aquatic pathology (MS); biochemistry (MS, PhD); biological sciences (MS, PhD); entomology (MS, PhD); environment and life sciences (MA, MMA, MS, PhD); environmental and natural resource economics (MS, PhD); environmental sciences (PhD); fisheries (MS); food science (MS, PhD); geosciences (MS); marine affairs (MA, MMA, PhD); microbiology (MS, PhD); molecular genetics (MS, PhD); nutrition (MS, PhD); plant sciences (MS, PhD). *Application deadline:* For fall admission, 4/15 priority date for domestic students. Applications are processed on a rolling basis. *Application fee:* $35. *Dean,* Jeffrey Seemann, 401-874-2957.

Graduate School of Oceanography Expenses: Contact institution. In 2006, 4 master's, 10 doctorates awarded. Offers oceanography (MO, MS, PhD). *Application deadline:* For fall

University of Rhode Island (continued)

admission, 4/15 priority date for domestic students. Applications are processed on a rolling basis. *Application fee:* $35. *Dean,* David Farmer, 401-874-6222.

Labor Research Center Average age 32. Expenses: Contact institution. *Financial support:* Fellowships, research assistantships, teaching assistantships, career-related internships or fieldwork, Federal Work-Study, institutionally sponsored loans, and tuition waivers (full and partial) available. Support available to part-time students. In 2006, 4 degrees awarded. *Degree program information:* Part-time and evening/weekend programs available. Offers human resources (MS); labor relations (MS). *Application deadline:* For fall admission, 4/15 priority date for domestic students; for spring admission, 11/15 for domestic students. Applications are processed on a rolling basis. *Application fee:* $35. *Director,* Dr. Richard Scholl, 401-874-4347.

UNIVERSITY OF RICHMOND, Richmond, University of Richmond, VA 23173

General Information Independent, coed, comprehensive institution. *Graduate housing:* On-campus housing not available.

GRADUATE UNITS

Graduate School of Arts and Sciences *Degree program information:* Part-time and evening/weekend programs available. Offers arts and sciences (MA, MLA, MS); biology (MS); English (MA); history (MA); liberal arts (MLA); psychology (MA).

Robins School of Business Average age 29. 78 applicants, 77% accepted, 43 enrolled. *Faculty:* 48 full-time (10 women), 13 part-time/adjunct (4 women). Expenses: Contact institution. *Financial support:* In 2006–07, 59 students received support, including 8 research assistantships with tuition reimbursements available; unspecified assistantships also available. Support available to part-time students. Financial award applicants required to submit FAFSA. In 2006, 38 degrees awarded. *Degree program information:* Part-time and evening/weekend programs available. Offers business (MBA). *Application deadline:* For fall admission, 5/1 for domestic and international students. Applications are processed on a rolling basis. *Application fee:* $50. *Application Contact:* Dr. Richard S. Coughlan, Associate Dean for Graduate and Executive Programs, 804-289-8553, Fax: 804-287-1228, E-mail: rcoughla@richmond.edu. *Dean,* Dr. Jorge Haddock, 804-289-8550, Fax: 804-287-6544, E-mail: jhaddock@richmond.edu.

School of Law Offers law (JD). Electronic applications accepted.

See Close-Up on page 1115.

UNIVERSITY OF RIO GRANDE, Rio Grande, OH 45674

General Information Independent, coed, comprehensive institution. *Graduate housing:* On-campus housing not available.

GRADUATE UNITS

Graduate School *Degree program information:* Part-time and evening/weekend programs available. Offers classroom teaching (M Ed).

UNIVERSITY OF ROCHESTER, Rochester, NY 14627-0250

General Information Independent, coed, university. CGS member. *Graduate housing:* Rooms and/or apartments available on a first-come, first-served basis to single and married students. Housing application deadline: 5/15. *Research affiliation:* Brookhaven National Laboratory, Fermi National Accelerator Laboratory, Argonne National Laboratory, Lawrence Livermore National Laboratory, Los Alamos National Laboratory, Numerous corporations (Biomedical).

GRADUATE UNITS

The College, Arts and Sciences *Degree program information:* Part-time programs available. Offers arts and sciences (MA, MS, PhD); biology (MS, PhD); brain and cognitive sciences (MS, PhD); chemistry (MS, PhD); clinical psychology (PhD); computer science (MS, PhD); developmental psychology (PhD); economics (MA, PhD); English (MA, PhD); geological sciences (MS, PhD); history (MA, PhD); mathematics (MA, MS, PhD); philosophy (MA, PhD); physics (MA, MS, PhD); physics and astronomy (PhD); political science (MA, PhD); psychology (MA); social-personality psychology (PhD); visual and cultural studies (MA, PhD). Electronic applications accepted.

The College, School of Engineering and Applied Sciences *Degree program information:* Part-time programs available. Offers biomedical engineering (MS, PhD); chemical engineering (MS, PhD); electrical and computer engineering (MS, PhD); engineering and applied sciences (MS, PhD); materials science (MS, PhD); mechanical engineering (MS, PhD).

Institute of Optics Offers optics (MS, PhD).

Eastman School of Music *Degree program information:* Part-time programs available. Offers composition (MA, MM, DMA, PhD); conducting (MM, DMA); education (MA, PhD); jazz studies/contemporary media (MM); music education (MM, DMA); musicology (MA, PhD); pedagogy of music theory (MA); performance and literature (MM, DMA); piano accompanying and chamber music (MM, DMA); theory (MA, PhD).

Margaret Warner Graduate School of Education and Human Development *Degree program information:* Part-time and evening/weekend programs available. Offers education and human development (MAT, MS, Ed D, PhD).

School of Medicine and Dentistry *Degree program information:* Part-time programs available. Offers medicine (MD); medicine and dentistry (MD, MA, MPH, MS, PhD, Certificate). Electronic applications accepted.

Graduate Programs in Medicine and Dentistry *Degree program information:* Part-time programs available. Offers biochemistry (MS, PhD); biomedical genetics (MS, PhD); biophysics (MS, PhD); epidemiology (MS, PhD); health services research and policy (PhD); marriage and family therapy (MS); medical statistics (MS); medicine and dentistry (MA, MPH, MS, PhD); microbiology (MS, PhD); neurobiology and anatomy (MS, PhD); neuroscience (MS, PhD); oral biology (MS); pathology (MS, PhD); pharmacology (MS, PhD); physiology (MS, PhD); public health (MPH); statistics (MA, PhD); toxicology (MS, PhD). Electronic applications accepted.

School of Nursing Students: 44 full-time (37 women), 145 part-time (127 women); includes 29 minority (16 African Americans, 1 American Indian/Alaska Native, 7 Asian Americans or Pacific Islanders, 5 Hispanic Americans), 2 international. Average age 38. 33 applicants, 73% accepted, 23 enrolled. *Faculty:* 29 full-time (26 women), 19 part-time/adjunct (17 women). Expenses: Contact institution. *Financial support:* In 2006–07, 13 fellowships with full and partial tuition reimbursements (averaging $13,900 per year), 4 research assistantships (averaging $10,000 per year), 3 teaching assistantships with full and partial tuition reimbursements (averaging $2,800 per year) were awarded; scholarships/grants, traineeships, tuition waivers (partial), and unspecified assistantships also available. Support available to part-time students. Financial award application deadline: 6/30. In 2006, 50 master's, 1 doctorate awarded. *Degree program information:* Part-time programs available. Offers nursing (MS, PhD, Certificate). *Application deadline:* For fall admission, 11/1 priority date for domestic and international students. *Application fee:* $25. *Application Contact:* Elaine Andolina, Director of Admissions, 585-275-2375, Fax: 585-756-8299, E-mail: elaine_andolina@urmc.rochester.edu. *Dean,* Dr. Patricia Chiverton, 585-275-5451, Fax: 585-273-1268, E-mail: patricia_chiverton@urmc.rochester.edu.

William E. Simon Graduate School of Business Administration *Degree program information:* Part-time and evening/weekend programs available. Offers business administration (MBA, MS, PhD).

UNIVERSITY OF ST. AUGUSTINE FOR HEALTH SCIENCES, St. Augustine, FL 32086

General Information Proprietary, coed, graduate-only institution. *Graduate housing:* On-campus housing not available.

GRADUATE UNITS

Graduate Programs *Degree program information:* Part-time programs available. Postbaccalaureate distance learning degree programs offered (minimal on-campus study).

Division of Advanced Studies *Degree program information:* Part-time programs available. Postbaccalaureate distance learning degree programs offered (minimal on-campus study). Offers advanced studies (MH Sc, DH Sc, TDPT).

Division of Entry-Level Physical Therapy Offers entry-level physical therapy (DPT).

Division of Occupational Therapy Offers occupational therapy (MOT, OTD).

Division of Physical Therapy Offers physical therapy (DPT, Certificate).

UNIVERSITY OF ST. FRANCIS, Joliet, IL 60435-6169

General Information Independent-religious, coed, comprehensive institution. *Enrollment:* 2,060 graduate, professional, and undergraduate students; 249 full-time matriculated graduate/professional students (186 women), 1,182 part-time matriculated graduate/professional students (969 women). *Enrollment by degree level:* 1,431 master's. *Graduate faculty:* 33 full-time (22 women), 74 part-time/adjunct (36 women). *Tuition:* Part-time $445 per credit hour. Part-time tuition and fees vary according to campus/location and program. *Graduate housing:* Room and/or apartments available on a first-come, first-served basis to single students; on-campus housing not available to married students. Housing application deadline: 6/30. *Student services:* Campus employment opportunities, campus safety program, career counseling, disabled student services, exercise/wellness program, free psychological counseling, low-cost health insurance, teacher training, writing training. *Library facilities:* University of St. Francis Library. *Online resources:* library catalog, web page, access to other libraries' catalogs. *Collection:* 111,546 titles, 24,985 serial subscriptions, 3,214 audiovisual materials.

Computer facilities: 250 computers available on campus for general student use. A campuswide network can be accessed from student residence rooms and from off campus. Internet access and online class registration are available. *Web address:* http://www.stfrancis.edu/.

General Application Contact: Sandra Sloka, Director of Admissions for Graduate and Degree Completion Programs, 800-735-7500, Fax: 815-740-5032, E-mail: ssloka@stfrancis.edu.

GRADUATE UNITS

College of Business Students: 29 full-time (19 women), 115 part-time (71 women); includes 22 minority (15 African Americans, 2 Asian Americans or Pacific Islanders, 5 Hispanic Americans). Average age 38. 89 applicants, 76% accepted, 47 enrolled. *Faculty:* 4 full-time (0 women), 12 part-time/adjunct (4 women). Expenses: Contact institution. *Financial support:* In 2006–07, 65 students received support. Tuition waivers (partial) available. Support available to part-time students. Financial award applicants required to submit FAFSA. In 2006, 64 degrees awarded. *Degree program information:* Part-time and evening/weekend programs available. Postbaccalaureate distance learning degree programs offered (no on-campus study). Offers business (MBA); management (MS). *Application deadline:* Applications are processed on a rolling basis. *Application fee:* $30. Electronic applications accepted. *Application Contact:* Sandra Sloka, Director of Admissions for Graduate and Degree Completion Programs, 800-735-7500, Fax: 815-740-5032, E-mail: ssloka@stfrancis.edu. *Dean,* Dr. Michael LaRocco, 815-740-3452, Fax: 815-774-2920, E-mail: mlarocco@stfrancis.edu.

College of Education Students: 52 full-time (38 women), 381 part-time (293 women); includes 38 minority (21 African Americans, 1 American Indian/Alaska Native, 4 Asian Americans or Pacific Islanders, 12 Hispanic Americans). Average age 33. 194 applicants, 80% accepted, 117 enrolled. *Faculty:* 11 full-time (10 women), 25 part-time/adjunct (12 women). Expenses: Contact institution. *Financial support:* In 2006–07, 272 students received support. Scholarships/grants, tuition waivers (partial), and unspecified assistantships available. Support available to part-time students. Financial award applicants required to submit FAFSA. In 2006, 165 degrees awarded. *Degree program information:* Part-time and evening/weekend programs available. Offers curriculum and instruction (MS); educational leadership (MS); elementary education certification (M Ed); secondary education certification (M Ed); special education (M Ed); teaching and learning (MS). *Application deadline:* Applications are processed on a rolling basis. *Application fee:* $30. Electronic applications accepted. *Application Contact:* Sandra Sloka, Director of Admissions for Graduate and Degree Completion Programs, 800-735-7500, Fax: 815-740-5032, E-mail: ssloka@stfrancis.edu. *Dean,* Dr. John Gambro, 815-740-3456, Fax: 815-740-2264, E-mail: jgambro@stfrancis.edu.

College of Nursing and Allied Health Students: 61 full-time (42 women), 62 part-time (60 women); includes 30 minority (8 African Americans, 1 American Indian/Alaska Native, 8 Asian Americans or Pacific Islanders, 13 Hispanic Americans). Average age 37. 52 applicants, 71% accepted, 22 enrolled. *Faculty:* 10 full-time (8 women), 1 (woman) part-time/adjunct. Expenses: Contact institution. *Financial support:* In 2006–07, 45 students received support. Scholarships/grants, traineeships, tuition waivers (partial), and unspecified assistantships available. Support available to part-time students. Financial award applicants required to submit FAFSA. In 2006, 30 degrees awarded. *Degree program information:* Part-time and evening/weekend programs available. Offers nursing (MSN); physician assistant studies (MS). *Application deadline:* Applications are processed on a rolling basis. *Application fee:* $30. Electronic applications accepted. *Application Contact:* Sandra Sloka, Director of Admissions for Graduate and Degree Completion Programs, 800-735-7500, Fax: 815-740-5032, E-mail: ssloka@stfrancis.edu. *Dean,* Dr. Maria Connolly, 815-740-3463, Fax: 815-740-4243, E-mail: mconnolly@stfrancis.edu.

College of Professional Studies Students: 95 full-time (78 women), 623 part-time (545 women); includes 98 minority (67 African Americans, 2 American Indian/Alaska Native, 13 Asian Americans or Pacific Islanders, 16 Hispanic Americans), 1 international. Average age 44. 215 applicants, 83% accepted, 136 enrolled. *Faculty:* 4 full-time (1 woman), 36 part-time/adjunct (19 women). Expenses: Contact institution. *Financial support:* In 2006–07, 163 students received support. Tuition waivers (partial) available. Support available to part-time students. Financial award applicants required to submit FAFSA. In 2006, 272 degrees awarded. *Degree program information:* Part-time and evening/weekend programs available. Postbaccalaureate distance learning degree programs offered (no on-campus study). Offers health services administration (MS); training and development (MS). *Application deadline:* Applications are processed on a rolling basis. *Application fee:* $30. Electronic applications accepted. *Application Contact:* Sandra Sloka, Director of Admissions for Graduate and Degree Completion Programs, 800-735-7500, Fax: 815-740-5032, E-mail: ssloka@stfrancis.edu. *Dean,* Dr. Michael LaRocco, 815-740-3452, Fax: 815-774-2920, E-mail: mlarocco@stfrancis.edu.

UNIVERSITY OF SAINT FRANCIS, Fort Wayne, IN 46808-3994

General Information Independent-religious, coed, comprehensive institution. *Enrollment:* 2,039 graduate, professional, and undergraduate students; 94 full-time matriculated graduate/professional students (75 women), 161 part-time matriculated graduate/professional students (120 women). *Enrollment by degree level:* 255 master's. *Graduate faculty:* 36 full-time (24 women), 17 part-time/adjunct (10 women). *Graduate housing:* Room and/or apartments available on a first-come, first-served basis to single students; on-campus housing not available to married students. *Student services:* Campus employment opportunities, career counseling, disabled student services, free psychological counseling, international student services, low-cost health insurance. *Library facilities:* Lee and Jim Vann Library. *Online resources:* library catalog, web page, access to other libraries' catalogs. *Collection:* 50,186 titles, 549 serial subscriptions.

Computer facilities: Computer purchase and lease plans are available. 217 computers available on campus for general student use. A campuswide network can be accessed from student residence rooms. Internet access and online class registration are available. *Web address:* http://www.sf.edu/.

General Application Contact: James Lashdollar, Admissions Counselor, 260-434-3279, E-mail: jcashdollar@sf.edu.

GRADUATE UNITS

Graduate School Students: 94 full-time (75 women), 161 part-time (120 women); includes 15 minority (8 African Americans, 3 Asian Americans or Pacific Islanders, 4 Hispanic Americans).

Average age 35. *Faculty:* 36 full-time (24 women), 17 part-time/adjunct (10 women). Expenses: Contact institution. *Financial support:* Federal Work-Study, scholarships/grants, and unspecified assistantships available. Support available to part-time students. Financial award applicants required to submit FAFSA. In 2006, 56 degrees awarded. *Degree program information:* Part-time and evening/weekend programs available. Offers business administration (MBA, MS); fine art (MA); general psychology (MS); mental health counseling (MS); nursing (MSN); pastoral counseling (MS); physician assistant studies (MS); school counseling (MS Ed); special education (MS Ed). *Application deadline:* For fall admission, 7/1 priority date for domestic students; for spring admission, 11/1 priority date for domestic students. Applications are processed on a rolling basis. *Application fee:* $20. *Application Contact:* James Lashdollar, Admissions Counselor, 260-434-3279, E-mail: jcashdollar@sf.edu. *Chair,* Dr. Rolf Daniel, 260-399-7700 Ext. 8403, Fax: 260-399-8170, E-mail: jpekrul@sf.edu.

UNIVERSITY OF SAINT MARY, Leavenworth, KS 66048-5082

General Information Independent-religious, coed, comprehensive institution. *Graduate housing:* On-campus housing not available.

GRADUATE UNITS

Graduate Programs *Degree program information:* Part-time and evening/weekend programs available. Postbaccalaureate distance learning degree programs offered (no on-campus study). Offers business administration (MBA); curriculum and instruction (MAT); education (MA, MAT); management (MS); psychology (MA); special education (MA); teaching (MA). Electronic applications accepted.

UNIVERSITY OF SAINT MARY OF THE LAKE–MUNDELEIN SEMINARY, Mundelein, IL 60060

General Information Independent-religious, men only, graduate-only institution. *Enrollment by degree level:* 187 first professional, 5 master's, 5 doctoral, 54 other advanced degrees. *Graduate faculty:* 39 full-time (3 women), 9 part-time/adjunct (2 women). *Tuition:* Full-time $11,520; part-time $430 per credit hour. *Required fees:* $394. *Graduate housing:* Room and/or apartments guaranteed to single students; on-campus housing not available to married students. Typical cost: $6,889 (including board). Housing application deadline: 8/1. *Student services:* Campus employment opportunities, campus safety program, free psychological counseling, international student services, low-cost health insurance, multicultural affairs office. *Library facilities:* Feehan Memorial Library. *Online resources:* library catalog. *Collection:* 200,000 titles, 432 serial subscriptions, 629 audiovisual materials.

Computer facilities: 20 computers available on campus for general student use. A campuswide network can be accessed from student residence rooms. Internet access is available. *Web address:* http://www.usml.edu/.

General Application Contact: Very Rev. Dennis J. Lyle, Rector-President, 847-566-6401, Fax: 847-566-7330.

GRADUATE UNITS

School of Theology Students: 250 full-time (4 women); includes 5 minority (all Hispanic Americans), 95 international. Average age 30. 85 applicants, 86% accepted, 73 enrolled. Expenses: Contact institution. *Financial support:* Career-related internships or fieldwork available. In 2006, 27 M Divs, 1 doctorate, 2 other advanced degrees awarded. Offers theology (M Div, STB, D Min, Certificate, STL). *Application deadline:* Applications are processed on a rolling basis. *Application fee:* $0. Electronic applications accepted. *Academic Dean,* Rev. Raymond J. Webb.

UNIVERSITY OF ST. MICHAEL'S COLLEGE, Toronto, ON M5S 1J4, Canada

General Information Independent-religious, coed, graduate-only institution. *Enrollment by degree level:* 56 first professional, 32 master's, 59 doctoral, 88 other advanced degrees. *Graduate faculty:* 10 full-time (3 women), 17 part-time/adjunct (6 women). *Tuition:* Full-time $5,495. Tuition and fees vary according to course load and program. *Graduate housing:* Room and/or apartments available on a first-come, first-served basis to single students; on-campus housing not available to married students. Typical cost: $8,672 (including board). Room and board charges vary according to board plan. Housing application deadline: 8/15. *Student services:* Campus employment opportunities, campus safety program, career counseling, disabled student services, international student services, low-cost health insurance. *Library facilities:* John Kelly Library plus 1 other. *Online resources:* library catalog, web page. *Collection:* 434,743 titles, 427 serial subscriptions, 2,708 audiovisual materials.

Computer facilities: 96 computers available on campus for general student use. A campuswide network can be accessed from student residence rooms and from off campus. Internet access and online class registration are available. *Web address:* http://www.utoronto.ca/stmikes/theology/.

General Application Contact: Mohra Taylor, Student Services Officer, 416-926-7140, Fax: 416-926-7294, E-mail: usmctheology.registrar@utoronto.ca.

GRADUATE UNITS

Faculty of Theology Students: 106 full-time (41 women), 129 part-time (75 women); includes 10 African Americans, 18 Asian Americans or Pacific Islanders, 23 international. Average age 40. 89 applicants, 76% accepted, 66 enrolled. *Faculty:* 10 full-time (3 women), 17 part-time/adjunct (6 women). Expenses: Contact institution. *Financial support:* In 2006–07, 45 students received support, including fellowships with partial tuition reimbursements available (averaging $2,500 per year), research assistantships with partial tuition reimbursements available (averaging $2,500 per year), 11 teaching assistantships with partial tuition reimbursements available (averaging $2,400 per year); scholarships/grants, tuition waivers (partial), and bursaries also available. Financial award application deadline: 2/1. In 2006, 4 first professional degrees, 12 master's, 8 doctorates, 13 other advanced degrees awarded. *Degree program information:* Part-time programs available. Offers Catholic leadership (MA); eastern Christian studies (Certificate, Diploma); religious education (Diploma); theological studies (Diploma); theology (M Div, MA, MRE, MTS, D Min, PhD, Th D); theology and ecology (Certificate); theology and Jewish studies (MA). *Application deadline:* For fall admission, 1/15 for domestic and international students. Applications are processed on a rolling basis. *Application fee:* $25 Canadian dollars. Electronic applications accepted. *Application Contact:* Student Services Officer, 416-926-7140, Fax: 416-926-7294, E-mail: usmetheology.registrar@utoronto.ca. *Dean,* Dr. Anne Anderson, CSJ, 416-926-7265, Fax: 416-926-7294, E-mail: anne.anderson@utoronto.ca.

UNIVERSITY OF ST. THOMAS, St. Paul, MN 55105-1096

General Information Independent-religious, coed, university. *Enrollment:* 10,712 graduate, professional, and undergraduate students; 1,016 full-time matriculated graduate/professional students (563 women), 3,675 part-time matriculated graduate/professional students (1,887 women). *Graduate faculty:* 178 full-time (74 women), 307 part-time/adjunct (103 women). *Graduate housing:* On-campus housing not available. *Student services:* Campus employment opportunities, campus safety program, career counseling, child daycare facilities, disabled student services, exercise/wellness program, free psychological counseling, international student services, low-cost health insurance, multicultural affairs office. *Library facilities:* O'Shaughnessy-Frey Library plus 3 others. *Online resources:* library catalog, web page, access to other libraries' catalogs. *Collection:* 510,355 titles, 2,743 serial subscriptions, 7,824 audiovisual materials.

Computer facilities: 1,549 computers available on campus for general student use. A campuswide network can be accessed from student residence rooms and from off campus. Internet access and online class registration are available. *Web address:* http://www.stthomas.edu/.

General Application Contact: Dr. Angeline Barretta-Herman, Associate Vice President for Academic Affairs, 651-962-6033, Fax: 651-962-6702, E-mail: a9barrettahe@stthomas.edu.

GRADUATE UNITS

Graduate Studies Students: 1,016 full-time (563 women), 3,675 part-time (1,887 women); includes 450 minority (135 African Americans, 24 American Indian/Alaska Native, 210 Asian Americans or Pacific Islanders, 81 Hispanic Americans), 233 international. Average age 33. *Faculty:* 178 full-time (74 women), 307 part-time/adjunct (103 women). Expenses: Contact institution. *Financial support:* Fellowships, research assistantships, teaching assistantships, career-related internships or fieldwork, institutionally sponsored loans, and scholarships/grants available. Support available to part-time students. In 2006, 127 first professional degrees, 1,222 master's, 34 doctorates, 122 other advanced degrees awarded. *Degree program information:* Part-time and evening/weekend programs available. Postbaccalaureate distance learning degree programs offered (no on-campus study). Offers computer security (Certificate); information systems (MSDD, Certificate); software design and development (Certificate); software engineering (MS); software systems (MSS). *Application Contact:* Dr. Angeline Barretta-Herman, Associate Vice President for Academic Affairs, 651-962-6033, Fax: 651-962-6702, E-mail: a9barrettahe@stthomas.edu. *Executive Vice President for Academic Affairs,* Dr. Thomas R. Rochon, 651-962-6720, Fax: 651-962-6702, E-mail: trrochon@stthomas.edu.

College of Arts and Sciences Students: 16 full-time (10 women), 115 part-time (74 women); includes 5 minority (3 American Indian/Alaska Native, 1 Asian American or Pacific Islander, 1 Hispanic American), 2 international. Average age 31. 68 applicants, 88% accepted, 31 enrolled. *Faculty:* 35 full-time (19 women), 45 part-time/adjunct (24 women). Expenses: Contact institution. *Financial support:* In 2006–07, 79 students received support, including 5 fellowships (averaging $4,000 per year); research assistantships, teaching assistantships, career-related internships or fieldwork, institutionally sponsored loans, and scholarships/grants also available. Support available to part-time students. Financial award application deadline: 4/1; financial award applicants required to submit FAFSA. In 2006, 41 degrees awarded. *Degree program information:* Part-time and evening/weekend programs available. Offers art history (MA); arts and sciences (MA); Catholic studies (MA); English (MA); music education (MA). *Application deadline:* For fall admission, 4/1 for domestic students, 5/1 priority date for international students; for spring admission, 11/1 for domestic students, 10/1 priority date for international students. *Application fee:* $50. *Dean,* Dr. Marisa Kelly, 651-962-6000, Fax: 651-962-6004, E-mail: mjkelly1@stthomas.edu.

Graduate School of Professional Psychology Students: 48 full-time (34 women), 137 part-time (103 women); includes 8 minority (3 African Americans, 3 Asian Americans or Pacific Islanders, 2 Hispanic Americans), 6 international. Average age 34. *Faculty:* 8 full-time (4 women), 9 part-time/adjunct (2 women). Expenses: Contact institution. *Financial support:* In 2006–07, 5 fellowships (averaging $3,000 per year), 7 research assistantships (averaging $2,500 per year) were awarded; institutionally sponsored loans and scholarships/grants also available. Support available to part-time students. Financial award application deadline: 8/1; financial award applicants required to submit FAFSA. In 2006, 36 master's, 10 doctorates, 5 other advanced degrees awarded. *Degree program information:* Part-time and evening/weekend programs available. Offers counseling psychology (MA, Psy D); family psychology (Certificate). *Application deadline:* For winter admission, 2/1 for domestic students; for spring admission, 4/1 for domestic students, 3/1 for international students. *Application fee:* $50. *Dean,* Dr. David Welch, 651-962-4650, Fax: 651-962-4651, E-mail: idwelch@stthomas.edu.

Opus College of Business Students: 155 full-time (59 women), 1,682 part-time (754 women); includes 104 minority (19 African Americans, 7 American Indian/Alaska Native, 62 Asian Americans or Pacific Islanders, 16 Hispanic Americans), 67 international. Average age 33. 378 applicants, 62% accepted, 176 enrolled. *Faculty:* 79 full-time (19 women), 168 part-time/adjunct (47 women). Expenses: Contact institution. *Financial support:* In 2006–07, 391 students received support; fellowships, research assistantships, career-related internships or fieldwork, institutionally sponsored loans, and scholarships/grants available. Support available to part-time students. Financial award applicants required to submit FAFSA. In 2006, 664 degrees awarded. *Degree program information:* Part-time and evening/weekend programs available. Postbaccalaureate distance learning degree programs offered. Offers accountancy (MS); business (MBA, MBC, MS); business administration (MBA); business communication (MBC); health care business administration (MBA); real estate (MS). *Application deadline:* For fall admission, 4/1 priority date for domestic students, 3/1 for international students; for spring admission, 12/1 priority date for domestic students, 11/1 for international students. Applications are processed on a rolling basis. *Application fee:* $60 ($90 for international students). *Application Contact:* Anne M. Engler, Director of Admissions, 651-962-8802, Fax: 951-962-8810, E-mail: amengler@stthomas.edu. *Dean,* Dr. Chistopher P. Puto, 651-962-4201, Fax: 651-962-4260, E-mail: cobdean@stthomas.edu.

Saint Paul Seminary School of Divinity Students: 69 full-time (4 women), 18 part-time (5 women); includes 7 minority (4 Asian Americans or Pacific Islanders, 3 Hispanic Americans), 7 international. Average age 37. 32 applicants, 100% accepted, 30 enrolled. *Faculty:* 13 full-time (5 women), 5 part-time/adjunct (2 women). Expenses: Contact institution. *Financial support:* In 2006–07, 52 students received support; fellowships, research assistantships, institutionally sponsored loans and scholarships/grants available. Support available to part-time students. Financial award application deadline: 4/1; financial award applicants required to submit FAFSA. In 2006, 9 first professional degrees, 23 master's awarded. *Degree program information:* Part-time and evening/weekend programs available. Offers divinity (M Div, MA, MARE); religious education (MARE); theology (MA). *Application deadline:* For fall admission, 6/1 priority date for domestic students. Applications are processed on a rolling basis. *Application fee:* $40. Electronic applications accepted. *Application Contact:* Rev. Peter A. Laird, Vice Rector and Admissions Chair, 651-962-5070, Fax: 651-962-5790, E-mail: palaird@stthomas.edu. *Rector,* Rev. Msgr. Aloysius R. Callaghan, 651-962-5052, Fax: 651-962-5790, E-mail: arcallaghan@stthomas.edu.

School of Education Students: 81 full-time (66 women), 990 part-time (678 women); includes 92 minority (46 African Americans, 9 American Indian/Alaska Native, 20 Asian Americans or Pacific Islanders, 17 Hispanic Americans), 13 international. Average age 35. 514 applicants, 93% accepted, 442 enrolled. *Faculty:* 32 full-time (20 women), 68 part-time/adjunct (44 women). Expenses: Contact institution. *Financial support:* In 2006–07, 514 students received support; fellowships, research assistantships, career-related internships or fieldwork, institutionally sponsored loans, and scholarships/grants available. Support available to part-time students. Financial award applicants required to submit FAFSA. In 2006, 277 master's, 23 doctorates, 87 other advanced degrees awarded. *Degree program information:* Part-time and evening/weekend programs available. Offers athletics and activities administration (MA); autism spectrum disorders (Certificate); community education administration (MA); critical pedagogy (Ed D); curriculum and instruction (MA, Ed S); director of special education (Ed S); education (MA, MAT, Ed D, Certificate, Ed S); educational leadership (Ed S); educational leadership and administration (MA); gifted, creative, and talented education (MA, Certificate); leadership (Ed D); leadership in student affairs (MA, Certificate); learning technology (MA, Certificate); organization learning and development (MA, Ed D, Certificate); Orton-Gillingham reading (Certificate); police leadership (MA); public policy and leadership (MA, Certificate); reading (MA); special education (MA); teacher education (MAT). *Application deadline:* For fall admission, 6/1 priority date for domestic students; for spring admission, 11/1 priority date for domestic students. Applications are processed on a rolling basis. *Application fee:* $50. *Application Contact:* Myrna L. Engebretson, Admissions Counselor, 651-962-4430, Fax: 651-962-4169, E-mail: mlengebretso@stthomas.edu. *Dean,* Dr. Miriam Q. Williams, 651-962-4435, Fax: 651-962-4169, E-mail: mqwilliams@stthomas.edu.

School of Engineering Students: 2 full-time (0 women), 210 part-time (58 women); includes 22 minority (3 African Americans, 14 Asian Americans or Pacific Islanders, 5 Hispanic Americans), 23 international. Average age 33. 190 applicants, 94% accepted, 162 enrolled. *Faculty:* 1 full-time (0 women), 40 part-time/adjunct (0 women). Expenses: Contact institution. *Financial support:* In 2006–07, 17 students received support, including 2 research assistantships (averaging $2,443 per year); fellowships, institutionally sponsored loans and scholarships/grants also available. Support available to part-time students. Financial award application deadline: 4/1; financial award applicants required to submit FAFSA. In 2006, 41 master's, 47 Certificates awarded. Offers engineering and technology management (Certificate); manufacturing systems (MS); manufacturing systems engineering (MMSE); systems engineering (MS); technology management (MS). *Application deadline:* For fall admission, 8/1 priority date for domestic students; for spring admission, 1/1 priority date for domestic students. Applications are processed on a rolling basis. *Application fee:* $30.

University of St. Thomas (continued)

Electronic applications accepted. *Application Contact:* Joyce A. Taylor, Student Services Coordinator, 651-962-5756, Fax: 651-962-6419, E-mail: technology@stthomas.edu. *Dean,* Ron Bennett, 651-962-5756, Fax: 651-962-6419, E-mail: rjbennett@stthomas.edu.

School of Law Students: 443 full-time (214 women); includes 64 minority (19 African Americans, 4 American Indian/Alaska Native, 24 Asian Americans or Pacific Islanders, 17 Hispanic Americans). Average age 27. 1,135 applicants, 46% accepted, 155 enrolled. *Faculty:* 29 full-time (12 women), 40 part-time/adjunct (15 women). Expenses: Contact institution. *Financial support:* In 2006–07, 317 students received support. Scholarships/grants available. Financial award application deadline: 7/1; financial award applicants required to submit FAFSA. In 2006, 119 degrees awarded. Offers law (JD). *Application deadline:* For fall admission, 7/1 priority date for domestic and international students. Applications are processed on a rolling basis. *Application fee:* $50. Electronic applications accepted. *Application Contact:* Cari Haaland, Director of Admissions, 651-962-4895, Fax: 651-962-4876, E-mail: lawschool@stthomas.edu. *Dean,* Thomas M. Mengler, 651-962-4880, Fax: 651-962-4881, E-mail: tmmengler@stthomas.edu.

School of Social Work Students: 174 full-time (161 women), 126 part-time (108 women); includes 34 minority (14 African Americans, 1 American Indian/Alaska Native, 8 Asian Americans or Pacific Islanders, 11 Hispanic Americans), 5 international. Average age 31. 198 applicants, 85% accepted, 111 enrolled. *Faculty:* 12 full-time (8 women), 17 part-time/adjunct (14 women). Expenses: Contact institution. *Financial support:* In 2006–07, 178 students received support, including 19 research assistantships (averaging $1,000 per year); fellowships, career-related internships or fieldwork, institutionally sponsored loans, and scholarships/grants also available. Support available to part-time students. Financial award application deadline: 7/1. In 2006, 97 degrees awarded. *Degree program information:* Part-time and evening/weekend programs available. Postbaccalaureate distance learning degree programs offered (minimal on-campus study). Offers social work (MSW). *Application deadline:* For fall admission, 1/10 for domestic students. *Application fee:* $25. Electronic applications accepted. *Application Contact:* Lisa Dalsin, Program Manager, 651-962-5810, Fax: 651-962-5819, E-mail: msw@stthomas.edu. *Dean and Professor,* Dr. Barbara W. Shank, 651-962-5801, Fax: 651-962-5819, E-mail: bwshank@stthomas.edu.

UNIVERSITY OF ST. THOMAS, Houston, TX 77006-4696

General Information Independent-religious, coed, comprehensive institution. CGS member. *Enrollment:* 3,607 graduate, professional, and undergraduate students; 314 full-time matriculated graduate/professional students (136 women), 913 part-time matriculated graduate/professional students (578 women). *Enrollment by degree level:* 89 first professional, 1,126 master's, 12 doctoral. *Graduate faculty:* 50 full-time (19 women), 29 part-time/adjunct (11 women). *Tuition:* Full-time $11,880; part-time $660 per credit. *Required fees:* $52; $21 per semester. *Graduate housing:* Room and/or apartments available on a first-come, first-served basis to single students; on-campus housing not available to married students. *Student services:* Campus employment opportunities, campus safety program, career counseling, disabled student services, free psychological counseling, international student services. *Library facilities:* Doherty Library plus 1 other. *Online resources:* library catalog, web page, access to other libraries' catalogs. *Collection:* 223,898 titles, 19,351 serial subscriptions, 1,474 audiovisual materials.

Computer facilities: 156 computers available on campus for general student use. A campuswide network can be accessed from student residence rooms and from off campus. Internet access is available. *Web address:* http://www.stthom.edu/.

General Application Contact: David Melton, Assistant Vice President of University Admissions, 713-525-3833, Fax: 713-525-6933, E-mail: admissions@stthom.edu.

GRADUATE UNITS

Cameron School of Business Students: 194 full-time (101 women), 359 part-time (172 women); includes 224 minority (64 African Americans, 4 American Indian/Alaska Native, 46 Asian Americans or Pacific Islanders, 110 Hispanic Americans), 103 international. Average age 31. 154 applicants, 97% accepted, 119 enrolled. *Faculty:* 22 full-time (9 women), 17 part-time/adjunct (5 women). Expenses: Contact institution. *Financial support:* In 2006–07, 280 students received support. Federal Work-Study, scholarships/grants, and unspecified assistantships available. Support available to part-time students. Financial award application deadline: 3/1; financial award applicants required to submit FAFSA. In 2006, 237 degrees awarded. *Degree program information:* Part-time and evening/weekend programs available. Offers business (MBA, MIB, MSA, MSIS). *Application deadline:* For fall admission, 6/30 for domestic and international students; for spring admission, 10/31 for domestic and international students. Applications are processed on a rolling basis. *Application fee:* $35. *Application Contact:* Sandra Flanagan, Enrollment Coordinator, 713-525-2115, Fax: 713-525-2110, E-mail: flanags@stthom.edu. *Dean,* Dr. Bahman Mirshab, 713-525-2100, Fax: 713-525-2110, E-mail: mirshab@stthom.edu.

Center for Thomistic Studies Students: 5 full-time (1 woman), 16 part-time (1 woman); includes 2 Asian Americans or Pacific Islanders, 2 Hispanic Americans, 1 international. Average age 34. 7 applicants, 100% accepted, 2 enrolled. *Faculty:* 5 full-time (1 woman). Expenses: Contact institution. *Financial support:* In 2006–07, 11 students received support. Federal Work-Study, scholarships/grants, and unspecified assistantships available. Support available to part-time students. Financial award application deadline: 3/1; financial award applicants required to submit FAFSA. *Degree program information:* Part-time programs available. Offers philosophy (MA, PhD). *Application deadline:* For fall admission, 2/1 priority date for domestic students. Applications are processed on a rolling basis. *Application fee:* $0. *Director,* Dr. Mary Catherine Sommers, 713-525-3591, Fax: 713-942-3464, E-mail: sommers@stthom.edu.

Program in Liberal Arts Students: 42 full-time (28 women), 100 part-time (76 women); includes 62 minority (24 African Americans, 1 American Indian/Alaska Native, 2 Asian Americans or Pacific Islanders, 35 Hispanic Americans), 2 international. Average age 36. 34 applicants, 100% accepted, 21 enrolled. Expenses: Contact institution. *Financial support:* In 2006–07, 61 students received support. Federal Work-Study and scholarships/grants available. Support available to part-time students. Financial award application deadline: 3/1; financial award applicants required to submit FAFSA. In 2006, 37 degrees awarded. *Degree program information:* Part-time and evening/weekend programs available. Offers liberal arts (MLA). *Application deadline:* Applications are processed on a rolling basis. *Application fee:* $35. *Dean,* Dr. Ravi Srinivas, 713-525-6924, Fax: 713-525-3804, E-mail: srinivas@stthom.edu.

School of Education Students: 3 full-time (all women), 280 part-time (222 women); includes 100 minority (37 African Americans, 2 American Indian/Alaska Native, 7 Asian Americans or Pacific Islanders, 54 Hispanic Americans), 10 international. Average age 36. 101 applicants, 100% accepted, 80 enrolled. *Faculty:* 13 full-time (7 women), 9 part-time/adjunct (6 women). Expenses: Contact institution. *Financial support:* In 2006–07, 36 students received support. Federal Work-Study and scholarships/grants available. Support available to part-time students. Financial award application deadline: 3/1; financial award applicants required to submit FAFSA. In 2006, 69 degrees awarded. *Degree program information:* Part-time and evening/weekend programs available. Offers education (M Ed). *Application deadline:* Applications are processed on a rolling basis. *Application fee:* $35. *Application Contact:* Paula C. Hollis, Administrative Assistant, 713-525-3541, Fax: 713-525-3871, E-mail: hollisp@stthom.edu. *Dean,* Dr. Ruth M. Strudler, 713-525-3540, Fax: 713-525-3871, E-mail: strudler@stthom.edu.

School of Theology Students: 70 full-time (3 women), 98 part-time (47 women); includes 43 minority (7 African Americans, 16 Asian Americans or Pacific Islanders, 20 Hispanic Americans), 18 international. Average age 41. 15 applicants, 100% accepted, 10 enrolled. *Faculty:* 11 full-time (2 women), 3 part-time/adjunct (0 women). Expenses: Contact institution. *Financial support:* In 2006–07, 17 students received support. Federal Work-Study and scholarships/grants available. Support available to part-time students. Financial award application deadline: 3/1; financial award applicants required to submit FAFSA. In 2006, 13 M Divs, 32 master's awarded. *Degree program information:* Part-time programs available. Offers theology (M Div, MAPS, MAT). *Application deadline:* Applications are processed on a rolling basis. *Application fee:* $35. *Dean,* Dr. Sandra C. Magie, 713-686-4345 Ext. 242, Fax: 713-683-8673, E-mail: smagie@stthom.edu.

UNIVERSITY OF SAN DIEGO, San Diego, CA 92110-2492

General Information Independent-religious, coed, university. CGS member. *Enrollment:* 7,483 graduate, professional, and undergraduate students; 1,358 full-time matriculated graduate/professional students (738 women), 1,112 part-time matriculated graduate/professional students (656 women). *Enrollment by degree level:* 1,035 first professional, 1,164 master's, 167 doctoral, 104 other advanced degrees. *Graduate faculty:* 149 full-time (68 women), 143 part-time/adjunct (79 women). *Graduate housing:* Room and/or apartments available on a first-come, first-served basis to single students; on-campus housing not available to married students. Typical cost: $10,960 (including board). Housing application deadline: 5/1. *Student services:* Campus employment opportunities, career counseling, child daycare facilities, disabled student services, free psychological counseling, international student services, low-cost health insurance, multicultural affairs office, teacher training. *Library facilities:* Helen K. and James S. Copley Library plus 1 other. *Online resources:* library catalog, access to other libraries' catalogs. *Collection:* 714,082 titles, 10,451 serial subscriptions. *Research affiliation:* Old Globe Theater (dramatic arts), Hubbs Seaworld Research Institute (marine science, ocean studies), Community College Leadership Development Initiative (education).

Computer facilities: 260 computers available on campus for general student use. A campuswide network can be accessed from student residence rooms and from off campus. Internet access and online class registration are available. *Web address:* http://www.sandiego.edu/.

General Application Contact: Stephen Pultz, Director of Admissions, 619-260-4524, Fax: 619-260-4158, E-mail: grads@sandiego.edu.

GRADUATE UNITS

College of Arts and Sciences Students: 61 full-time (36 women), 56 part-time (34 women); includes 19 minority (2 African Americans, 4 Asian Americans or Pacific Islanders, 13 Hispanic Americans), 5 international. Average age 30. 422 applicants, 23% accepted, 52 enrolled. *Faculty:* 18 full-time (8 women), 7 part-time/adjunct (2 women). Expenses: Contact institution. *Financial support:* In 2006–07, 24 fellowships were awarded; career-related internships or fieldwork, Federal Work-Study, institutionally sponsored loans, scholarships/grants, tuition waivers (partial), and unspecified assistantships also available. Support available to part-time students. Financial award application deadline: 5/1; financial award applicants required to submit FAFSA. In 2006, 57 degrees awarded. *Degree program information:* Part-time and evening/weekend programs available. Offers arts and sciences (MA, MFA, MS, CAS); dramatic arts (MFA); history (MA); international relations (MA); marine science (MS); pastoral care and counseling (MA, CAS); peace and justice studies (MA). *Application deadline:* For fall admission, 5/1 priority date for domestic and international students; for spring admission, 11/1 priority date for domestic and international students. Applications are processed on a rolling basis. *Application fee:* $45. Electronic applications accepted. *Application Contact:* Stephen Pultz, Director of Admissions, 619-260-4524, Fax: 619-260-4158, E-mail: grads@sandiego.edu. *Dean,* Dr. Nicholas Healy, 619-260-4545.

Hahn School of Nursing and Health Sciences Students: 103 full-time (85 women), 138 part-time (131 women); includes 58 minority (7 African Americans, 3 American Indian/Alaska Native, 26 Asian Americans or Pacific Islanders, 22 Hispanic Americans), 4 international. Average age 37. 261 applicants, 54% accepted, 87 enrolled. *Faculty:* 13 full-time (12 women), 33 part-time/adjunct (all women). Expenses: Contact institution. *Financial support:* Scholarships/grants and traineeships available. Support available to part-time students. Financial award application deadline: 4/1; financial award applicants required to submit FAFSA. In 2006, 35 master's, 19 doctorates awarded. *Degree program information:* Part-time and evening/weekend programs available. Offers accelerated nursing (for RNs only) (MSN); adult clinical nurse specialist (MSN, Post Master's Certificate); adult nurse practitioner (MSN, Post Master's Certificate); clinical nursing (MSN); entry-level nursing (for non-RNs) (MSN); executive nurse leader (MSN); family nurse practitioner (MSN, Post Master's Certificate); nursing science (PhD); pediatric nurse practitioner (MSN, Post Master's Certificate). *Application deadline:* Applications are processed on a rolling basis. *Application fee:* $45. Electronic applications accepted. *Application Contact:* Stephen Pultz, Director of Admissions, 619-260-4524, Fax: 619-260-4158, E-mail: grads@sandiego.edu. *Dean,* Dr. Sally Hardin, 619-260-4550, Fax: 619-260-6814.

School of Business Administration Students: 187 full-time (76 women), 265 part-time (89 women); includes 55 minority (5 African Americans, 1 American Indian/Alaska Native, 32 Asian Americans or Pacific Islanders, 17 Hispanic Americans), 45 international. Average age 32. 517 applicants, 66% accepted, 187 enrolled. *Faculty:* 35 full-time (10 women), 18 part-time/adjunct (4 women). Expenses: Contact institution. *Financial support:* Career-related internships or fieldwork, Federal Work-Study, institutionally sponsored loans, scholarships/grants, tuition waivers (partial), and unspecified assistantships available. Support available to part-time students. Financial award application deadline: 5/1; financial award applicants required to submit FAFSA. In 2006, 256 degrees awarded. *Degree program information:* Part-time and evening/weekend programs available. Offers accounting and financial management (MS); business administration (MBA); executive leadership (MSEL); global leadership (MSGL); international business administration (IMBA); real estate (MSRE); supply chain management (MS, Certificate); taxation (MS). *Application deadline:* For fall admission, 5/1 priority date for domestic students; for spring admission, 11/15 priority date for domestic students. Applications are processed on a rolling basis. *Application fee:* $45. Electronic applications accepted. *Application Contact:* Stephen Pultz, Director of Admissions, 619-260-4524, Fax: 619-260-4158, E-mail: grads@sandiego.edu. *Interim Dean,* Dr. Andy Allen, 619-260-4886, E-mail: sbadean@sandiego.edu.

School of Law Students: 796 full-time (363 women), 333 part-time (151 women); includes 324 minority (34 African Americans, 11 American Indian/Alaska Native, 165 Asian Americans or Pacific Islanders, 114 Hispanic Americans), 21 international. Average age 27. 4,818 applicants, 31% accepted, 342 enrolled. *Faculty:* 53 full-time (20 women), 44 part-time/adjunct (9 women). Expenses: Contact institution. *Financial support:* In 2006–07, 60 research assistantships were awarded; career-related internships or fieldwork, Federal Work-Study, institutionally sponsored loans, and scholarships/grants also available. Support available to part-time students. Financial award application deadline: 3/1; financial award applicants required to submit FAFSA. In 2006, 313 JDs, 59 master's awarded. *Degree program information:* Part-time and evening/weekend programs available. Offers business and corporate law (LL M); comparative law (LL M); general studies (LL M); international law (LL M); law (JD); taxation (LL M, Diploma). *Application deadline:* For fall admission, 2/1 priority date for domestic students. Applications are processed on a rolling basis. *Application fee:* $50. Electronic applications accepted. *Application Contact:* Carl J. Eging, Director of Admissions and Financial Aid, 619-260-4528, Fax: 619-260-2218, E-mail: eging@sandiego.edu. *Dean,* Kevin Cole, 619-260-2330, Fax: 619-260-2218.

School of Leadership and Education Sciences Students: 195 full-time (160 women), 252 part-time (193 women); includes 116 minority (15 African Americans, 4 American Indian/Alaska Native, 20 Asian Americans or Pacific Islanders, 77 Hispanic Americans), 8 international. Average age 31. 451 applicants, 65% accepted, 183 enrolled. *Faculty:* 31 full-time (19 women), 42 part-time/adjunct (31 women). Expenses: Contact institution. *Financial support:* In 2006–07, 50 fellowships were awarded; career-related internships or fieldwork, Federal Work-Study, institutionally sponsored loans, tuition waivers (partial), unspecified assistantships, and stipends also available. Support available to part-time students. Financial award application deadline: 5/1; financial award applicants required to submit FAFSA. In 2006, 196 master's, 11 doctorates awarded. *Degree program information:* Part-time and evening/weekend programs available. Postbaccalaureate distance learning degree programs offered. Offers counseling (MA); educational leadership (M Ed); leadership and education sciences (M Ed, MA, MAT, Ed D, PhD, Certificate); leadership studies (MA, PhD); learning and teaching (M Ed); marital and family therapy (MA); nonprofit leadership and management (Certificate); teaching (MAT); teaching and learning (Ed D). *Application deadline:* For fall admission, 4/1 for domestic students. *Application fee:* $45. *Application Contact:* Stephen Pultz, Director of Admissions, 619-260-4524, Fax: 619-260-4158, E-mail: grads@sandiego.edu. *Dean,* Dr. Paula A. Cordeiro, 619-260-4540, Fax: 619-260-6835, E-mail: cordeiro@sandiego.edu.

See Close-Up on page 1117.

UNIVERSITY OF SAN FRANCISCO, San Francisco, CA 94117-1080

General Information Independent-religious, coed, university. *Enrollment:* 8,549 graduate, professional, and undergraduate students; 2,510 full-time matriculated graduate/professional students (1,467 women), 613 part-time matriculated graduate/professional students (373 women). *Enrollment by degree level:* 702 first professional, 2,151 master's, 270 doctoral. *Graduate faculty:* 139 full-time (50 women), 341 part-time/adjunct (154 women). *Tuition:* Full-time $17,370; part-time $965 per unit. Tuition and fees vary according to degree level, campus/location and program. *Graduate housing:* Room and/or apartments available on a first-come, first-served basis to single students; on-campus housing not available to married students. Typical cost: $6,790 per year ($10,140 including board). Room and board charges vary according to board plan, campus/location and housing facility selected. *Student services:* Campus employment opportunities, career counseling, disabled student services, free psychological counseling, international student services, low-cost health insurance, multicultural affairs office, teacher training. *Library facilities:* Gleeson Library plus 2 others. *Online resources:* library catalog, web page, access to other libraries' catalogs. *Collection:* 1.1 million titles, 5,560 serial subscriptions. *Research affiliation:* NASA–Ames Research Center.

Computer facilities: 350 computers available on campus for general student use. A campuswide network can be accessed from student residence rooms and from off campus. Internet access and online class registration are available. *Web address:* http://www.usfca.edu/.

General Application Contact: Information Contact, 415-422-4723, Fax: 415-422-2217.

GRADUATE UNITS

College of Arts and Sciences Students: 570 full-time (265 women), 81 part-time (39 women); includes 141 minority (28 African Americans, 2 American Indian/Alaska Native, 79 Asian Americans or Pacific Islanders, 32 Hispanic Americans), 171 international. Average age 29. 1,123 applicants, 67% accepted, 303 enrolled. *Faculty:* 52 full-time (15 women), 93 part-time/adjunct (31 women). Expenses: Contact institution. *Financial support:* In 2006–07, 387 students received support; fellowships, research assistantships, teaching assistantships, career-related internships or fieldwork, Federal Work-Study, institutionally sponsored loans, and tuition waivers (partial) available. Support available to part-time students. Financial award application deadline: 3/2; financial award applicants required to submit FAFSA. In 2006, 235 degrees awarded. *Degree program information:* Part-time and evening/weekend programs available. Offers arts and sciences (MA, MFA, MS); Asia Pacific studies (MA); biology (MS); chemistry (MS); computer science (MS); economics (MA); environmental management (MS); financial economics (MS); international and development economics (MA); Internet engineering (MS); sport management (MA); theology (MA); writing (MA, MFA). *Application deadline:* Applications are processed on a rolling basis. *Application fee:* $55 ($65 for international students). *Dean,* Dr. Jennifer Turpin, 415-422-6373.

College of Professional Studies Students: 412 full-time (255 women); includes 148 minority (40 African Americans, 1 American Indian/Alaska Native, 66 Asian Americans or Pacific Islanders, 41 Hispanic Americans), 21 international. Average age 36. 211 applicants, 90% accepted, 115 enrolled. *Faculty:* 9 full-time (4 women), 70 part-time/adjunct (30 women). Expenses: Contact institution. *Financial support:* In 2006–07, 249 students received support. Available to part-time students. Application deadline: 3/2; In 2006, 128 degrees awarded. *Degree program information:* Part-time and evening/weekend programs available. Offers health services administration (MPA); information systems (MS); nonprofit administration (MNA); organization development (MS); professional studies (MNA, MPA, MS); project management (MS); public administration (MPA). *Application fee:* $55 ($65 for international students). *Application Contact:* 415-422-6000. *Dean,* Dr. Larry Brewster, 415-422-6254.

Masagung Graduate School of Management Students: 233 full-time (85 women), 71 part-time (33 women); includes 62 minority (4 African Americans, 1 American Indian/Alaska Native, 43 Asian Americans or Pacific Islanders, 14 Hispanic Americans), 102 international. Average age 30. 398 applicants, 72% accepted, 125 enrolled. *Faculty:* 32 full-time (5 women), 21 part-time/adjunct (7 women). Expenses: Contact institution. *Financial support:* In 2006–07, 123 students received support; fellowships, research assistantships, teaching assistantships, career-related internships or fieldwork, Federal Work-Study, and institutionally sponsored loans available. Support available to part-time students. Financial award application deadline: 3/2; financial award applicants required to submit FAFSA. In 2006, 185 degrees awarded. *Degree program information:* Part-time and evening/weekend programs available. Offers business economics (MBA); e-business (MBA); entrepreneurship (MBA); finance and banking (MBA); international business (MBA); management (MBA); marketing (MBA); professional business administration (MBA); telecommunications management and policy (MBA). *Application deadline:* For fall admission, 7/1 priority date for domestic students; for spring admission, 11/30 for domestic students. Applications are processed on a rolling basis. *Application Contact:* Carol Langlois, Director, MBA Program, 415-422-6314, Fax: 415-422-2502, E-mail: mbausf@usfca.edu. *Dean,* Dr. Michael Duffy, 415-422-6771, Fax: 415-422-2502.

School of Education Students: 595 full-time (459 women), 308 part-time (221 women); includes 319 minority (76 African Americans, 6 American Indian/Alaska Native, 108 Asian Americans or Pacific Islanders, 129 Hispanic Americans), 52 international. Average age 35. 761 applicants, 83% accepted, 299 enrolled. *Faculty:* 25 full-time (16 women), 68 part-time/adjunct (44 women). Expenses: Contact institution. *Financial support:* In 2006–07, 561 students received support; fellowships, research assistantships, teaching assistantships available. Financial award application deadline: 3/2; financial award applicants required to submit FAFSA. In 2006, 287 master's, 46 doctorates awarded. *Degree program information:* Part-time and evening/weekend programs available. Offers Catholic school leadership (MA, Ed D); Catholic school teaching (MA); counseling (MA); counseling psychology (Ed D); digital media and learning (MA); education (MA, Ed D); international and multicultural education (MA, Ed D); learning and instruction (MA, Ed D); multicultural literature for children and young adults (MA); organization and leadership (MA, Ed D); private school administration (Ed D); teaching English as a second language (MA). *Application fee:* $55 ($65 for international students). *Application Contact:* Jan Weiss, Associate Director of Graduate Outreach, 415-422-5467, E-mail: weissj@usfca.edu. *Dean,* Dr. Walter Gmelch, 415-422-6525.

School of Law Students: 567 full-time (292 women), 141 part-time (69 women); includes 216 minority (34 African Americans, 3 American Indian/Alaska Native, 119 Asian Americans or Pacific Islanders, 60 Hispanic Americans), 7 international. Average age 27. 3,512 applicants, 33% accepted, 246 enrolled. *Faculty:* 16 full-time (6 women), 78 part-time/adjunct (32 women). Expenses: Contact institution. *Financial support:* In 2006–07, 629 students received support. Career-related internships or fieldwork, Federal Work-Study, and institutionally sponsored loans available. Support available to part-time students. Financial award application deadline: 3/2; financial award applicants required to submit FAFSA. In 2006, 242 JDs, 6 master's awarded. *Degree program information:* Part-time and evening/weekend programs available. Offers intellectual property and technology law (LL M); international transactions and comparative law (LL M); law (JD, LL M). *Application deadline:* For fall admission, 4/1 for domestic students. Applications are processed on a rolling basis. *Application Contact:* Alan P. Guerrero, Director of Admissions, 415-422-6586, E-mail: lawadmissions@usfca.edu. *Dean,* Jeffrey Brand, 415-422-6304.

School of Nursing Students: 126 full-time (106 women), 11 part-time (10 women); includes 46 minority (3 African Americans, 36 Asian Americans or Pacific Islanders, 7 Hispanic Americans), 5 international. Average age 31. 219 applicants, 65% accepted, 47 enrolled. *Faculty:* 6 full-time (5 women), 10 part-time/adjunct (9 women). Expenses: Contact institution. *Financial support:* In 2006–07, 114 students received support. Institutionally sponsored loans available. Financial award application deadline: 3/2. In 2006, 53 degrees awarded. *Degree program information:* Part-time programs available. Offers advanced practice nursing-nurse practitioner and clinical nurse specialist (MSN); nursing administration (MSN). *Application deadline:* Applications are processed on a rolling basis. *Application fee:* $40. *Dean,* Dr. Judith Karshmer, 415-422-6681, Fax: 415-422-6877, E-mail: nursing@usfca.edu.

UNIVERSITY OF SASKATCHEWAN, Saskatoon, SK S7N 5A2, Canada

General Information Province-supported, coed, university. *Graduate housing:* Rooms and/or apartments available on a first-come, first-served basis to single and married students. *Research affiliation:* Canada Agriculture, Saskatchewan Research Council, University Hospital, Innovation Place.

GRADUATE UNITS

College of Dentistry Students: 111 full-time (40 women). Average age 25. 347 applicants, 8% accepted, 28 enrolled. *Faculty:* 23 full-time (5 women), 61 part-time/adjunct (14 women). Expenses: Contact institution. *Financial support:* In 2006–07, 15 students received support. Career-related internships or fieldwork and scholarships/grants available. In 2006, 28 degrees awarded. Offers dentistry (DMD). *Application deadline:* For fall admission, 1/15 for domestic and international students. *Application fee:* $125 Canadian dollars. Electronic applications accepted. *Application Contact:* Jacquie Fraser, Director of Academic and Student Affairs, 306-966-5119, Fax: 306-966-5126, E-mail: jacquie.fraser@usask.ca. *Acting Dean,* Dr. Gerry Stephen Uswak, 306-966-5122, Fax: 306-966-5126, E-mail: gerry.uswak@usask.ca.

College of Graduate Studies and Research *Degree program information:* Part-time programs available.

College of Agriculture *Degree program information:* Part-time programs available. Offers agricultural economics (M Ag, M Sc, MA, PhD); agriculture (M Ag, M Sc, MA, PhD); animal and poultry science (M Ag, M Sc, PhD); applied microbiology and food science (M Ag, M Sc, PhD); plant sciences (M Ag, M Sc, PhD); soil science (M Ag, M Sc, PhD).

College of Arts and Sciences *Degree program information:* Part-time programs available. Offers archaeology (MA, PhD); art and art history (MFA); arts and sciences (M Math, M Sc, MA, MFA, PhD, Diploma); biology (M Sc, PhD, Diploma); chemistry (M Sc, PhD); computer science (M Sc, PhD); drama (MA); economics (MA); English (MA, PhD); geography (M Sc, MA, PhD); geological sciences (M Sc, PhD, Diploma); history (MA, PhD); languages and linguistics (MA); mathematics and statistics (M Math, MA, PhD); music (MA); native studies (MA, PhD); philosophy (MA); physics ad engineering physics (M Sc, PhD); political studies (MA); psychology (MA, PhD); religious studies and anthropology (MA); sociology (MA, PhD); women's and gender studies (MA, PhD).

College of Commerce *Degree program information:* Part-time programs available. Offers accounting (M Sc, MP Acc); agribusiness management (MBA); biotechnology management (MBA); commerce (M Sc, MBA, MP Acc); finance (M Sc); health services management (MBA); indigenous management (MBA); industrial relations and organizational behavior (M Sc); international business management (MBA); marketing (M Sc).

College of Education *Degree program information:* Part-time programs available. Offers curriculum studies (M Ed, PhD, Diploma); education (M Ed, MC Ed, PhD, Diploma); educational administration (M Ed, PhD, Diploma); educational foundations (M Ed, MC Ed, PhD, Diploma); educational psychology and special education (M Ed, PhD, Diploma).

College of Engineering Offers agricultural and bioresource engineering (M Eng, M Sc, PhD); biomedical engineering (M Eng, M Sc, PhD); chemical engineering (M Eng, M Sc, PhD); civil and geological engineering (M Eng, M Sc, PhD); electrical engineering (M Eng, M Sc, PhD); engineering (M Eng, M Sc, PhD, Diploma); environmental engineering (M Eng, M Sc, PhD, Diploma); mechanical engineering (M Sc, PhD).

College of Kinesiology Offers kinesiology (M Sc, PhD, Diploma).

College of Law *Degree program information:* Part-time programs available. Offers law (LL B, LL M).

College of Nursing *Degree program information:* Part-time programs available. Offers nursing (MN).

College of Pharmacy and Nutrition Offers pharmacy and nutrition (M Sc, PhD).

Toxicology Centre Offers toxicology (M Sc, PhD, Diploma).

College of Medicine Students: 331 full-time, 16 part-time. *Faculty:* 131. Expenses: Contact institution. *Financial support:* In 2006–07, 80 students received support, including 3 fellowships; research assistantships, teaching assistantships, scholarships/grants also available. Financial award application deadline: 1/31. In 2006, 55 first professional degrees, 16 master's, 9 doctorates awarded. Offers anatomy and cell biology (M Sc, PhD); biochemistry (M Sc, PhD); community health and epidemiology (M Sc, PhD); medicine (MD, M Sc, PhD); microbiology and immunology (M Sc, PhD); obstetrics, gynecology and reproductive services (M Sc, PhD); pathology (M Sc, PhD); pharmacology (M Sc, PhD); physiology (M Sc, PhD); psychiatry (M Sc, PhD); surgery (M Sc). *Application deadline:* For fall admission, 7/1 priority date for domestic students. Applications are processed on a rolling basis. *Application fee:* $50. *Dean,* Dr. W. Albritton, 306-966-6149, Fax: 306-966-6164, E-mail: william.albritton@usask.ca.

Western College of Veterinary Medicine Students: 122 full-time (68 women); includes 10 minority (all African Americans) *Faculty:* 65 full-time (22 women). Expenses: Contact institution. *Financial support:* Fellowships, teaching assistantships available. Financial award application deadline: 1/31. In 2006, 19 master's, 7 doctorates awarded. Offers herd medicine and theriogenology (M Sc, M Vet Sc, PhD); large animal clinical sciences (M Sc, M Vet Sc, PhD); small animal clinical sciences (M Sc, M Vet Sc, PhD); veterinary anatomy (M Sc); veterinary anesthesiology, radiology and surgery (M Vet Sc); veterinary biomedical sciences (M Sc, M Vet Sc, PhD); veterinary internal medicine (M Vet Sc); veterinary medicine (M Sc, PhD); veterinary microbiology (M Sc, M Vet Sc, PhD); veterinary pathology (M Sc, M Vet Sc, PhD); veterinary physiological sciences (M Sc, PhD). *Application deadline:* For fall admission, 7/1 priority date for domestic students. *Application fee:* $50. *Application Contact:* Dr. Norman C. Rawlings, Associate Dean, Research, 306-966-7068, Fax: 306-966-8747, E-mail: norman.rawlings@usask.ca. *Dean,* Dr. C. S. Rhodes, 306-966-7447, Fax: 306-966-8747.

Announcement: The University of Saskatchewan offers high-quality graduate education at the master's (MA, MFA, M Math, M PAcc, MN, M Ag, M Sc, M Ed, MC Ed, M Eng, LL M, MBA, and M Vet Sc) and PhD levels in most disciplines. Actual programs of study and areas of research depend on special interests of faculty members and the facilities available. Strong programs are available in basic sciences, applied sciences, the health sciences, veterinary medicine, the humanities, native studies, and the social sciences. Interdisciplinary offerings are available. Innovation Place, an internationally known research park, houses 95 tenants in the agricultural environmental sciences and resources sector. Inquiries are invited.

THE UNIVERSITY OF SCRANTON, Scranton, PA 18510

General Information Independent-religious, coed, comprehensive institution. CGS member. *Enrollment:* 5,353 graduate, professional, and undergraduate students; 327 full-time matriculated graduate/professional students (219 women), 985 part-time matriculated graduate/professional students (664 women). *Enrollment by degree level:* 1,248 master's, 64 doctoral. *Graduate faculty:* 135 full-time (57 women), 68 part-time/adjunct (29 women). *Tuition:* Part-time $684 per credit. *Required fees:* $25 per term. *Graduate housing:* Room and/or apartments available to single students; on-campus housing not available to married students. *Student services:* Campus employment opportunities, career counseling, free psychological counseling, international student services, multicultural affairs office. *Library facilities:* Harry and Jeanette Weinberg Memorial Library plus 1 other. *Online resources:* library catalog, web page, access to other libraries' catalogs. *Collection:* 481,542 titles, 1,579 serial subscriptions. *Research affiliation:* Universidad Iberoamericana (counseling and human services), Lackawanna River Corridor Association (environment), Allied Services (rehabilitation), National Health Management Center (health care management), Community Medical Center (health services), Wyoming Valley Health Care System (nursing).

Computer facilities: 903 computers available on campus for general student use. A campuswide network can be accessed from student residence rooms and from off campus. Internet access and online class registration are available. *Web address:* http://www.scranton.edu/.

General Application Contact: James L. Goonan, Director of Admissions, 570-941-6304, Fax: 570-941-5995, E-mail: goonanj1@scranton.edu.

GRADUATE UNITS

Graduate School Students: 327 full-time (219 women), 985 part-time (664 women); includes 109 minority (56 African Americans, 5 American Indian/Alaska Native, 16 Asian Americans or Pacific Islanders, 32 Hispanic Americans), 48 international. Average age 32. 704 applicants,

The University of Scranton (continued)

92% accepted. *Faculty:* 135 full-time (57 women), 68 part-time/adjunct (29 women). Expenses: Contact institution. *Financial support:* In 2006–07, 86 students received support, including 86 teaching assistantships with full and partial tuition reimbursements available (averaging $6,960 per year); fellowships, career-related internships or fieldwork, Federal Work-Study, and unspecified assistantships also available. Support available to part-time students. Financial award application deadline: 3/1. In 2006, 283 master's, 21 doctorates awarded. *Degree program information:* Part-time and evening/weekend programs available. Postbaccalaureate distance learning degree programs offered (no on-campus study). Offers accounting (MBA); adult health nursing (MSN); biochemistry (MA, MS); chemistry (MA, MS); clinical chemistry (MA, MS); community counseling (MS); curriculum and instruction (MA, MS); early childhood education (MA, MS); educational administration (MS); elementary education (MS); English as a second language (MS); enterprise management technology (MBA); family nurse practitioner (MSN, PMC); finance (MBA); general business administration (MBA); health administration (MHA); history (MA); human resources (MS); human resources administration (MS); human resources development (MS); international business (MBA); management information systems (MBA); marketing (MBA); nurse anesthesia (MSN, PMC); occupational therapy (MS); operations management (MBA); organizational leadership (MS); physical therapy (MPT, DPT); professional counseling (CAGS); reading education (MS); rehabilitation counseling (MS); school counseling (MS); secondary education (MS); software engineering (MS); special education (MS); theology (MA). *Application deadline:* Applications are processed on a rolling basis. *Application fee:* $50. *Application Contact:* James L. Goonan, Director of Admissions, 570-941-6304, Fax: 570-941-5995, E-mail: goonanj1@scranton.edu. *Dean,* Dr. Duncan Perry, 570-941-7600, Fax: 570-941-5995, E-mail: perryd2@scranton.edu.

UNIVERSITY OF SIOUX FALLS, Sioux Falls, SD 57105-1699

General Information Independent-religious, coed, comprehensive institution. *Enrollment:* 1,675 graduate, professional, and undergraduate students; 405 part-time matriculated graduate/professional students (245 women). *Enrollment by degree level:* 374 master's, 31 other advanced degrees. *Graduate faculty:* 20 full-time (11 women), 20 part-time/adjunct (9 women). *Tuition:* Part-time $300 per semester hour. *Required fees:* $15 per term. Part-time tuition and fees vary according to program. *Graduate housing:* Rooms and/or apartments available on a first-come, first-served basis to single and married students. *Student services:* Campus employment opportunities, campus safety program, career counseling, disabled student services, exercise/wellness program, low-cost health insurance, writing training. *Library facilities:* Norman B. Mears Library. *Online resources:* library catalog, web page, access to other libraries' catalogs. *Collection:* 85,713 titles, 378 serial subscriptions.

Computer facilities: 150 computers available on campus for general student use. A campuswide network can be accessed from student residence rooms and from off campus. Internet access is available. *Web address:* http://www.usiouxfalls.edu/.

General Application Contact: Student Contact, 605-331-5000.

GRADUATE UNITS

Program in Business Administration *Faculty:* 8 full-time (3 women), 7 part-time/adjunct (2 women). Expenses: Contact institution. *Financial support:* In 2006–07, 47 students received support. Institutionally sponsored loans and scholarships/grants available. Financial award applicants required to submit FAFSA. In 2006, 15 degrees awarded. *Degree program information:* Part-time and evening/weekend programs available. Offers business administration (MBA). *Application fee:* $25. *Director,* Rebecca T. Murdock, 605-575-2068, E-mail: mba@usiouxfalls.edu.

Program in Education 9 applicants, 100% accepted, 7 enrolled. *Faculty:* 12 full-time (8 women), 13 part-time/adjunct (7 women). Expenses: Contact institution. *Financial support:* In 2006–07, 58 students received support. Scholarships/grants available. Support available to part-time students. In 2006, 46 master's, 26 other advanced degrees awarded. *Degree program information:* Part-time and evening/weekend programs available. Postbaccalaureate distance learning degree programs offered (minimal on-campus study). Offers leadership (M Ed); reading (M Ed); superintendent (Ed S); teaching (M Ed); technology (M Ed). Summer admission only. *Application deadline:* Applications are processed on a rolling basis. *Application fee:* $25. *Director of Graduate Education,* Dawn Olson, 605-575-2063, Fax: 605-575-2079, E-mail: dawn.olson@usiouxfalls.edu.

UNIVERSITY OF SOUTH ALABAMA, Mobile, AL 36688-0002

General Information State-supported, coed, university. CGS member. *Enrollment:* 13,090 graduate, professional, and undergraduate students; 2,270 full-time matriculated graduate/professional students (1,583 women), 742 part-time matriculated graduate/professional students (560 women). *Enrollment by degree level:* 276 first professional, 2,376 master's, 288 doctoral, 72 other advanced degrees. *Graduate faculty:* 492 full-time (150 women), 41 part-time/adjunct (20 women). *Graduate housing:* Rooms and/or apartments available to single and married students. Housing application deadline: 6/1. *Student services:* Campus employment opportunities, campus safety program, career counseling, disabled student services, free psychological counseling, international student services, low-cost health insurance, multicultural affairs office, writing training. *Library facilities:* University Library plus 1 other. *Online resources:* library catalog, web page, access to other libraries' catalogs. *Collection:* 1.1 million titles, 7,344 serial subscriptions. *Research affiliation:* Dauphin Island Marine Laboratory, Alabama Universities/Tennessee Valley Authority Research Consortia (chemical engineering), Naval Aerospace Medical Research Laboratory, Marine Environmental Sciences Consortium.

Computer facilities: 500 computers available on campus for general student use. A campuswide network can be accessed from student residence rooms and from off campus. Internet access and online class registration are available. *Web address:* http://www.usouthal.edu/.

General Application Contact: Dr. B. Keith Harrison, Interim Dean of the Graduate School, 251-460-6310.

GRADUATE UNITS

College of Medicine Students: 313 full-time (164 women); includes 59 minority (30 African Americans, 2 American Indian/Alaska Native, 25 Asian Americans or Pacific Islanders, 2 Hispanic Americans), 7 international. Average age 33. *Faculty:* 194 full-time (48 women), 33 part-time/adjunct (12 women). Expenses: Contact institution. *Financial support:* Fellowships, research assistantships, institutionally sponsored loans available. In 2006, 60 MDs, 8 doctorates awarded. Offers biochemistry and molecular biology (PhD); cell biology and neuroscience (PhD); medicine (MD, PhD); microbiology and immunology (PhD); pharmacology (PhD); physiology (PhD). *Application fee:* $25. *Interim Dean,* Dr. Samuel J Strada, 251-460-7189.

Graduate School Students: 1,957 full-time (1,419 women), 742 part-time (560 women); includes 472 minority (388 African Americans, 25 American Indian/Alaska Native, 38 Asian Americans or Pacific Islanders, 21 Hispanic Americans), 350 international. 1,903 applicants, 66% accepted, 515 enrolled. *Faculty:* 298 full-time (102 women), 8 part-time/adjunct (all women). Expenses: Contact institution. *Financial support:* Fellowships, research assistantships, teaching assistantships, career-related internships or fieldwork, institutionally sponsored loans, and traineeships available. Support available to part-time students. Financial award application deadline: 4/1. In 2006, 695 master's, 7 doctorates, 12 other advanced degrees awarded. *Degree program information:* Part-time and evening/weekend programs available. Offers environmental toxicology (MS); pharmacy (Pharm D). *Application deadline:* For fall admission, 9/1 priority date for domestic students. Applications are processed on a rolling basis. *Application fee:* $25. *Interim Dean of the Graduate School,* Dr. B. Keith Harrison, 251-460-6310.

College of Allied Health Professions Students: 278 full-time (234 women), 30 part-time (21 women); includes 20 minority (13 African Americans, 2 American Indian/Alaska Native, 3 Asian Americans or Pacific Islanders, 2 Hispanic Americans), 5 international. 28 applicants, 82% accepted, 18 enrolled. *Faculty:* 27 full-time (14 women). Expenses: Contact institution. *Financial support:* Fellowships, research assistantships, career-related internships or fieldwork available. Support available to part-time students. Financial award application deadline: 4/1. In 2006, 54 master's, 4 doctorates awarded. Offers allied health professions (MHS, MS, Au D, DPT, PhD); audiology (Au D); communication sciences and disorders (PhD); occupational therapy (MS); physical therapy (DPT, PhD); physician assistant studies (MHS); speech and hearing sciences (MS). *Application deadline:* For fall admission, 9/1 priority date for domestic students. Applications are processed on a rolling basis. *Application fee:* $25. *Dean,* Dr. Richard Talbot, 251-380-2785.

College of Arts and Sciences Students: 178 full-time (106 women), 76 part-time (49 women); includes 30 minority (25 African Americans, 2 American Indian/Alaska Native, 1 Asian American or Pacific Islander, 2 Hispanic Americans), 19 international. 169 applicants, 58% accepted, 67 enrolled. *Faculty:* 132 full-time (33 women). Expenses: Contact institution. *Financial support:* Fellowships, research assistantships, teaching assistantships, career-related internships or fieldwork available. Support available to part-time students. Financial award application deadline: 4/1. In 2006, 58 master's, 1 doctorate awarded. *Degree program information:* Part-time and evening/weekend programs available. Offers arts and sciences (MA, MPA, MS, PhD, Certificate); biological sciences (MS); communication (MA); English (MA); gerontology (Certificate); history (MA); marine sciences (MS, PhD); mathematics (MS); psychology (MS); public administration (MPA); sociology (MA). *Application deadline:* For fall admission, 9/1 priority date for domestic students. Applications are processed on a rolling basis. *Application fee:* $25. *Application Contact:* Dr. S. L. Varghese, Associate Dean, 251-460-6280. *Dean,* Dr. G. David Johnson, 251-460-6280.

College of Education Students: 444 full-time (375 women), 436 part-time (361 women); includes 233 minority (210 African Americans, 13 American Indian/Alaska Native, 7 Asian Americans or Pacific Islanders, 3 Hispanic Americans), 16 international. 426 applicants, 81% accepted, 171 enrolled. *Faculty:* 50 full-time (21 women). Expenses: Contact institution. *Financial support:* In 2006–07, 23 research assistantships, 10 teaching assistantships were awarded; career-related internships or fieldwork also available. Support available to part-time students. Financial award application deadline: 4/1. In 2006, 245 master's, 2 doctorates, 12 other advanced degrees awarded. *Degree program information:* Part-time programs available. Offers community counseling (MS); early childhood education (M Ed); education (M Ed, MS, PhD, Ed S); educational administration (Ed S); educational leadership (M Ed); educational media (M Ed, MS); elementary education (M Ed); exercise science (MS); health education (M Ed); instructional design and development (MS, PhD); physical education (M Ed); reading education (M Ed); rehabilitation counseling (MS); school counseling (M Ed); school psychometry (M Ed); science education (M Ed); secondary education (M Ed); special education (M Ed, Ed S); therapeutic recreation (MS). *Application deadline:* For fall admission, 9/1 priority date for domestic students. Applications are processed on a rolling basis. *Application fee:* $25. *Dean,* Dr. Richard L Hayes, 251-380-2738.

College of Engineering Students: 213 full-time (45 women), 31 part-time (3 women); includes 12 minority (5 African Americans, 7 Asian Americans or Pacific Islanders), 209 international. 694 applicants, 59% accepted, 46 enrolled. *Faculty:* 26 full-time (1 woman). Expenses: Contact institution. *Financial support:* Research assistantships, career-related internships or fieldwork and institutionally sponsored loans available. Support available to part-time students. Financial award application deadline: 4/1. In 2006, 77 degrees awarded. *Degree program information:* Part-time programs available. Offers chemical engineering (MS Ch E); electrical engineering (MSEE); engineering (MS Ch E, MSEE, MSME); mechanical engineering (MSME). *Application deadline:* For fall admission, 9/1 priority date for domestic students. Applications are processed on a rolling basis. *Application fee:* $25. *Application Contact:* Dr. B. Keith Harrison, Director of Graduate Studies, 251-460-6160. *Dean,* Dr. John W. Steadman, 251-460-6140.

College of Nursing Students: 661 full-time (602 women), 127 part-time (108 women); includes 160 minority (123 African Americans, 6 American Indian/Alaska Native, 19 Asian Americans or Pacific Islanders, 12 Hispanic Americans), 1 international. *Faculty:* 25 full-time (23 women), 8 part-time/adjunct (all women). Expenses: Contact institution. In 2006, 166 degrees awarded. Offers adult health nursing (MSN); community/mental health nursing (MSN); maternal/child nursing (MSN); nursing (DSN). *Dean,* Dr. Debra C. Davis, 251-434-3414.

Mitchell College of Business Students: 88 full-time (33 women), 30 part-time (15 women); includes 12 minority (7 African Americans, 2 American Indian/Alaska Native, 1 Asian American or Pacific Islander, 2 Hispanic Americans), 22 international. 140 applicants, 67% accepted, 65 enrolled. *Faculty:* 23 full-time (7 women). Expenses: Contact institution. *Financial support:* Research assistantships available. Support available to part-time students. Financial award application deadline: 4/1. In 2006, 43 degrees awarded. *Degree program information:* Part-time and evening/weekend programs available. Offers accounting (M Acct); business (M Acct, MBA); general management (MBA). *Application deadline:* For fall admission, 9/1 priority date for domestic students. Applications are processed on a rolling basis. *Application fee:* $25. *Dean,* Dr. Carl Moore, 251-460-6419.

School of Computer and Information Sciences Students: 89 full-time (23 women), 12 part-time (3 women); includes 5 minority (all African Americans), 73 international. 231 applicants, 45% accepted, 26 enrolled. *Faculty:* 12 full-time (1 woman). Expenses: Contact institution. *Financial support:* Research assistantships, career-related internships or fieldwork and institutionally sponsored loans available. Support available to part-time students. Financial award application deadline: 4/1. In 2006, 51 degrees awarded. *Degree program information:* Part-time and evening/weekend programs available. Offers computer science (MS); information systems (MS). *Application deadline:* For fall admission, 9/1 priority date for domestic students. Applications are processed on a rolling basis. *Application fee:* $25. *Dean,* Dr. David Feinstein, 251-460-6390.

See Close-Up on page 1119.

UNIVERSITY OF SOUTH CAROLINA, Columbia, SC 29208

General Information State-supported, coed, university. CGS member. *Graduate housing:* Rooms and/or apartments available to single and married students. *Research affiliation:* E. I. du Pont de Nemours and Company (engineering, chemical engineering), Westinghouse/Savannah River Corporation (environmental restoration, hazardous waste remediation), Motorola Corporation–Energy Production Division (electrochemical engineering), Glaxo-Wellcome, Inc. (pharmaceuticals), NCR Corporation (electrical and computer engineering).

GRADUATE UNITS

College of Pharmacy *Degree program information:* Part-time programs available. Offers pharmaceutical sciences (MS, PhD); pharmacy (Pharm D, MS, PhD). Electronic applications accepted.

The Graduate School *Degree program information:* Part-time and evening/weekend programs available. Postbaccalaureate distance learning degree programs offered. Offers biology (MS, PhD); biology education (IMA, MAT); ecology, evolution and organismal biology (MS, PhD); gerontology (Certificate); mathematics (MA, MS, PhD); mathematics education (M Math, MAT); molecular, cellular, and developmental biology (MS, PhD). Electronic applications accepted.

Arnold School of Public Health *Degree program information:* Part-time programs available. Postbaccalaureate distance learning degree programs offered (minimal on-campus study). Offers alcohol and drug studies (Certificate); biostatistics (MPH, MSPH, Dr PH, PhD); communication sciences and disorders (MCD, MSP, PhD); environmental health science (MS); environmental quality (MPH, MSPH, PhD); epidemiology (MPH, MSPH, Dr PH, PhD); exercise science (MS, DPT, PhD); general public health (MPH); hazardous materials management (MPH, MSPH, PhD); health education administration (Ed D); health promotion and education (MAT, MPH, MS, MSPH, Dr PH, PhD); health services policy and management (MHA, MPH, Dr PH, PhD); industrial hygiene (MPH, MSPH, PhD); physical activity and public health (MPH); public health (MAT, MCD, MHA, MPH, MS, MSP, MSPH, DPT, Dr PH, Ed D, PhD, Certificate); school health education (Certificate). Electronic applications accepted.

College of Arts and Sciences *Degree program information:* Part-time and evening/weekend programs available. Offers anthropology (MA, PhD); applied statistics (CAS); archives (MA); art education (IMA, MA, MAT); art history (MA); art studio (MA); arts and sciences (IMA, MA, MAT, MFA, MIS, MMA, MPA, MS, PMS, PSM, PhD, CAS, Certificate); chemistry and biochemistry (IMA, MAT, MS, PhD); clinical/community psychology (MA, PhD); comparative literature (MA, PhD); creative writing (MFA); criminology and criminal justice (MA); English (MA, PhD); English education (MAT); environmental geoscience (PMS); experimental psychology (MA, PhD); foreign languages (MAT); French (MA); general psychology (MA); geography (MA, MS, PhD); geography education (IMA); geological sciences (MS, PhD); German (MA); historic preservation (MA); history (MA, PhD); history education (IMA, MAT); industrial statistics (MIS); international studies (MA, PhD); linguistics (MA, PhD); marine science (MS, PhD); media arts (MMA); museum (MA); museum management (Certificate); philosophy (MA, PhD); physics and astronomy (IMA, MAT, MS, PSM, PhD); political science (MA, PhD); public administration (MPA); public history (MA, Certificate); religious studies (MA); school psychology (PhD); sociology (MA, PhD); Spanish (MA); statistics (MS, PhD); studio art (MFA); teaching English to speakers of other languages (Certificate); theater (IMA, MA, MAT, MFA); women's studies (Certificate). Electronic applications accepted.

College of Education *Degree program information:* Part-time and evening/weekend programs available. Postbaccalaureate distance learning degree programs offered (minimal on-campus study). Offers art education (IMA, MAT); business education (IMA, MAT); community and adult education (M Ed); counseling education (PhD, Ed S); curriculum and instruction (Ed D); early childhood education (M Ed, MAT, PhD); education (IMA, M Ed, MA, MAT, MS, MT, Ed D, PhD, Certificate, Ed S); educational administration (M Ed, MA, PhD, Ed S); educational psychology, research (M Ed, PhD); educational technology (M Ed); elementary education (M Ed, MAT, PhD); English (MAT); foreign language (MAT); foundations in education (PhD); health education (MAT); health education administration (Ed D); higher education and student affairs (M Ed); higher education leadership (Certificate); language and literacy (M Ed, PhD); mathematics (MAT); physical education (IMA, MAT, MS, PhD); science (IMA, MAT); secondary education (IMA, M Ed, MA, MAT, MT, PhD); social studies (IMA, MAT); special education (M Ed, MAT, PhD); teaching (Ed S); theatre and speech (IMA, MAT). Electronic applications accepted.

College of Engineering and Information Technology *Degree program information:* Part-time and evening/weekend programs available. Postbaccalaureate distance learning degree programs offered (minimal on-campus study). Offers chemical engineering (ME, MS, PhD); civil engineering (ME, MS, PhD); computer science and engineering (ME, MS, PhD); electrical engineering (ME, MS, PhD); engineering and information technology (ME, MS, PhD); mechanical engineering (ME, MS, PhD); software engineering (MS). Electronic applications accepted.

College of Hospitality, Retail, and Sport Management *Degree program information:* Part-time programs available. Postbaccalaureate distance learning degree programs offered (minimal on-campus study). Offers hospitality, retail, and sport management (MHRTM, MS); hotel, restaurant and tourism management (MHRTM); live sport and entertainment events (MS); public assembly facilities management (MS); retailing (MS). Electronic applications accepted.

College of Mass Communications and Information Studies Offers journalism and mass communications (MA, MMC, PhD); library and information science (MLIS, Certificate, Specialist); mass communication and information studies (MA, MLIS, MMC, PhD, Certificate, Specialist).

College of Nursing *Degree program information:* Part-time programs available. Offers acute care clinical specialist (MSN); acute care nurse practitioner (MSN, Certificate); adult nurse practitioner (MSN); advanced practice clinical nursing (MSN, Certificate); advanced practice nursing in primary care (MSN, Certificate); advanced practice nursing in psychiatric mental health (MSN, Certificate); clinical nursing (MSN); community mental health and psychiatric health nursing (MSN); community/public health clinical nurse specialist (MSN); family nurse practitioner (MSN); health nursing (MSN); nursing administration (MSN); nursing practice (DNP); nursing science (PhD); pediatric nurse practitioner (MSN); psychiatric/mental health nurse practitioner (MSN); psychiatric/mental health specialist (MSN); women's health nurse practitioner (MSN). Electronic applications accepted.

College of Social Work Offers social work (MSW, PhD). Electronic applications accepted.

The Darla Moore School of Business *Degree program information:* Part-time and evening/weekend programs available. Postbaccalaureate distance learning degree programs offered (minimal on-campus study). Offers accountancy (M Acc); business administration (PMBA, PhD); business measurement and assurance (M Acc); economics (MA, PhD); human resources (MHR); international business administration (IMBA). Electronic applications accepted.

School of Music *Degree program information:* Part-time programs available. Offers composition (MM, DMA); conducting (MM, DMA); jazz studies (MM); music education (MM Ed, PhD); music history (MM); music performance (Certificate); music theory (MM); opera theater (MM); performance (MM, DMA); piano pedagogy (MM, DMA). Electronic applications accepted.

School of the Environment *Degree program information:* Part-time programs available. Postbaccalaureate distance learning degree programs offered (no on-campus study). Offers earth and environmental resources management (MEERM); environment (MEERM). Electronic applications accepted.

School of Law Offers law (JD).

School of Medicine Offers biomedical science (MBS, PhD); genetic counseling (MS); medicine (MD, MBS, MNA, MRC, MS, PhD, Certificate); nurse anesthesia (MNA); psychiatric rehabilitation (Certificate); rehabilitation counseling (MRC, Certificate). Electronic applications accepted.

See Close-Up on page 1121.

UNIVERSITY OF SOUTH CAROLINA AIKEN, Aiken, SC 29801-6309

General Information State-supported, coed, comprehensive institution. *Enrollment:* 3,380 graduate, professional, and undergraduate students; 18 full-time matriculated graduate/professional students (16 women), 121 part-time matriculated graduate/professional students (104 women). *Enrollment by degree level:* 139 master's. *Graduate faculty:* 13 full-time (8 women), 4 part-time/adjunct (2 women). Tuition, state resident: full-time $8,288; part-time $411 per hour. Tuition, nonresident: full-time $17,916; part-time $874 per hour. *Required fees:* $230; $8 per hour. $15 per hour. *Graduate housing:* Room and/or apartments available on a first-come, first-served basis to single students; on-campus housing not available to married students. *Student services:* Campus employment opportunities, campus safety program, career counseling, child daycare facilities, disabled student services, exercise/wellness program, free psychological counseling, international student services, multicultural affairs office. *Library facilities:* Gregg-Graniteville Library. *Online resources:* library catalog, web page, access to other libraries' catalogs. *Collection:* 156,750 titles, 700 serial subscriptions.

Computer facilities: 450 computers available on campus for general student use. A campuswide network can be accessed from student residence rooms and from off campus. Internet access and online class registration, student e-mail are available. *Web address:* http://www.usca.edu/.

General Application Contact: Karen Morris, Graduate Studies Coordinator, 803-641-3489, E-mail: karenm@usca.edu.

GRADUATE UNITS

Program in Applied Clinical Psychology Students: 17 full-time (15 women), 11 part-time (9 women). *Faculty:* 7 full-time (5 women). Expenses: Contact institution. In 2006, 12 degrees awarded. *Degree program information:* Part-time and evening/weekend programs available. Offers clinical psychology (MS). *Application deadline:* Applications are processed on a rolling basis. *Application fee:* $40. Electronic applications accepted. *Application Contact:* Karen Morris, Graduate Studies Coordinator, 803-641-3489, E-mail: karenm@usca.edu. *Chair,* Dr. Edward Callen, 803-641-3446, Fax: 803-641-3726, E-mail: edc@usca.edu.

School of Education Students: 1 (woman) full-time, 110 part-time (95 women); includes 17 minority (16 African Americans, 1 Asian American or Pacific Islander). *Faculty:* 6 full-time (3 women), 4 part-time/adjunct (2 women). Expenses: Contact institution. *Financial support:* Federal Work-Study and unspecified assistantships available. Support available to part-time students. Financial award application deadline: 3/15; financial award applicants required to submit FAFSA. In 2006, 10 degrees awarded. *Degree program information:* Part-time and evening/weekend programs available. Offers education (M Ed); educational technology (M Ed); elementary education (M Ed). *Application deadline:* Applications are processed on a rolling basis. *Application fee:* $40. Electronic applications accepted. *Head,* Dr. Jeff Priest, 803-648-6851, Fax: 803-641-3698, E-mail: jeffp@usca.edu.

UNIVERSITY OF SOUTH CAROLINA UPSTATE, Spartanburg, SC 29303-4999

General Information State-supported, coed, comprehensive institution. *Enrollment:* 4,610 graduate, professional, and undergraduate students; 5 full-time matriculated graduate/professional students (4 women), 29 part-time matriculated graduate/professional students (26 women). *Enrollment by degree level:* 34 master's. *Graduate faculty:* 9 full-time (7 women), 3 part-time/adjunct (all women). Tuition, state resident: full-time $6,890; part-time $342 per semester hour. Tuition, nonresident: full-time $14,920; part-time $727 per semester hour. *Graduate housing:* Room and/or apartments available to single students; on-campus housing not available to married students. *Student services:* Campus employment opportunities, campus safety program, career counseling, child daycare facilities, disabled student services, free psychological counseling, grant writing training, international student services, low-cost health insurance, multicultural affairs office, teacher training. *Library facilities:* University of South Carolina Upstate Library. *Online resources:* library catalog, web page, access to other libraries' catalogs. *Collection:* 188,572 titles, 31,460 serial subscriptions, 6,198 audiovisual materials.

Computer facilities: Computer purchase and lease plans are available. 320 computers available on campus for general student use. A campuswide network can be accessed from student residence rooms. Internet access and online class registration are available. *Web address:* http://www.uscupstate.edu/.

General Application Contact: Dr. Rebecca L. Stevens, Director of Graduate Programs, 864-503-5521, Fax: 864-503-5574, E-mail: rstevens@uscupstate.edu.

GRADUATE UNITS

Graduate Programs Students: 5 full-time (4 women), 29 part-time (26 women); includes 3 minority (all African Americans) Average age 34. 15 applicants, 100% accepted, 9 enrolled. *Faculty:* 9 full-time (7 women). Expenses: Contact institution. *Financial support:* Institutionally sponsored loans and institutional work-study available. Financial award application deadline: 7/15; financial award applicants required to submit FAFSA. In 2006, 9 degrees awarded. *Degree program information:* Part-time and evening/weekend programs available. Offers early childhood education (M Ed); elementary education (M Ed); special education: visual impairment (M Ed). *Application deadline:* Applications are processed on a rolling basis. *Application fee:* $40. *Application Contact:* Donette Stewart, Associate Vice Chancellor for Enrollment Services, 864-503-5280, E-mail: dstewart@uscupstate.edu. *Director,* Dr. Rebecca L. Stevens, 864-503-5521, Fax: 864-503-5574, E-mail: ystevens@uscupstate.edu.

THE UNIVERSITY OF SOUTH DAKOTA, Vermillion, SD 57069-2390

General Information State-supported, coed, university. *Enrollment:* 8,746 graduate, professional, and undergraduate students; 2,233 matriculated graduate/professional students. *Enrollment by degree level:* 456 first professional, 931 master's, 449 doctoral, 397 other advanced degrees. *Graduate faculty:* 422 full-time, 41 part-time/adjunct. Tuition, state resident: part-time $120 per credit hour. Tuition, nonresident: part-time $355 per credit hour. *Required fees:* $90 per credit hour. *Graduate housing:* Rooms and/or apartments available to single students and available on a first-come, first-served basis to married students. *Student services:* Campus employment opportunities, career counseling, child daycare facilities, disabled student services, free psychological counseling, international student services, low-cost health insurance, multicultural affairs office. *Library facilities:* I. D. Weeks Library plus 2 others. *Online resources:* library catalog, access to other libraries' catalogs. *Collection:* 645,672 titles, 2,647 serial subscriptions.

Computer facilities: 834 computers available on campus for general student use. A campuswide network can be accessed from student residence rooms and from off campus. Internet access and online class registration are available. *Web address:* http://www.usd.edu/.

General Application Contact: Jane M Olson, Registration Officer, 605-677-6287, Fax: 605-677-5202, E-mail: jane.olson@usd.edu.

GRADUATE UNITS

Graduate School Students: 1,186 full-time, 1,092 part-time. *Faculty:* 308 full-time (100 women), 27 part-time/adjunct (14 women). Expenses: Contact institution. *Financial support:* In 2006–07, 239 research assistantships with partial tuition reimbursements (averaging $4,812 per year), 178 teaching assistantships with partial tuition reimbursements (averaging $4,812 per year) were awarded; career-related internships or fieldwork, Federal Work-Study, scholarships/grants, unspecified assistantships, and clinical assistantships also available. Support available to part-time students. *Degree program information:* Part-time and evening/weekend programs available. Postbaccalaureate distance learning degree programs offered (no on-campus study). Offers administrative studies (MS); interdisciplinary studies (MA). *Application fee:* $35. Electronic applications accepted. *Application Contact:* Anthony Shaheen, Graduate Recruiter, 605-677-5435, Fax: 605-677-5202, E-mail: anthony.shaheen@usd.edu. *Dean,* Dr. Karen L Olmstead, 605-677-6287, Fax: 605-677-5202, E-mail: kolmstea@usd.edu.

College of Arts and Sciences Students: 224 full-time (134 women), 97 part-time (48 women); includes 14 minority (6 African Americans, 5 American Indian/Alaska Native, 2 Asian Americans or Pacific Islanders, 1 Hispanic American), 30 international. *Faculty:* 115 full-time (32 women), 3 part-time/adjunct (1 woman). Expenses: Contact institution. *Financial support:* In 2006–07, research assistantships with partial tuition reimbursements (averaging $8,000 per year), teaching assistantships with partial tuition reimbursements (averaging $8,000 per year) were awarded; career-related internships or fieldwork, Federal Work-Study, scholarships/grants, unspecified assistantships, and clinical assistantships also available. Support available to part-time students. Financial award applicants required to submit FAFSA. In 2006, 168 master's, 11 doctorates awarded. *Degree program information:* Part-time programs available. Postbaccalaureate distance learning degree programs offered. Offers arts and sciences (MA, MNS, MPA, MS, Au D, PhD); audiology (Au D); biology (MA, MNS, MS, PhD); chemistry (MA, MNS); clinical psychology (MA, PhD); communication studies (MA); communications disorders (MA); computational sciences and statistics (PhD); computer science (MA); English (MA, PhD); history (MA); human factors (MA, PhD); mathematics (MA, MNS); political science (MA); public administration (MPA); speech-language pathology (MA). *Application deadline:* Applications are processed on a rolling basis. *Application fee:* $35. Electronic applications accepted. *Application Contact:* Graduate Recruiter, 605-677-5435. *Dean,* Dr. Matthew Moen, 605-677-5221, E-mail: matthew.moen@usd.edu.

College of Fine Arts Students: 36 full-time (20 women), 9 part-time (7 women); includes 2 minority (both Hispanic Americans) *Faculty:* 33 full-time (11 women), 2 part-time/adjunct (0 women). Expenses: Contact institution. *Financial support:* In 2006–07, research assistantships with partial tuition reimbursements (averaging $4,626 per year), teaching assistantships with partial tuition reimbursements (averaging $4,626 per year) were awarded; Federal Work-Study and unspecified assistantships also available. Financial award applicants required to submit FAFSA. In 2006, 22 degrees awarded. Offers art (MFA); fine arts (MA, MFA, MM); music (MM); theatre (MA, MFA). *Application deadline:* Applications are processed on a rolling basis. *Application fee:* $35. Electronic applications accepted. *Dean,* Daniel Guyette, 605-677-5481, Fax: 605-677-5988, E-mail: daniel.guyette@usd.edu.

School of Business Students: 71 full-time (36 women), 106 part-time (53 women); includes 3 minority (1 American Indian/Alaska Native, 1 Asian American or Pacific Islander, 1 Hispanic American), 18 international. *Faculty:* 31 full-time (6 women), 4 part-time/adjunct (3 women). Expenses: Contact institution. *Financial support:* In 2006–07, research assistantships with partial tuition reimbursements (averaging $9,626 per year), teaching assistantships with partial tuition reimbursements (averaging $4,626 per year) were awarded; career-related internships or fieldwork, Federal Work-Study, and unspecified assistantships

The University of South Dakota (continued)

also available. Support available to part-time students. Financial award applicants required to submit FAFSA. In 2006, 94 degrees awarded. *Degree program information:* Part-time and evening/weekend programs available. Postbaccalaureate distance learning degree programs offered (no on-campus study). Offers business (MBA, MP Acc); business administration (MBA); professional accountancy (MP Acc). *Application deadline:* For fall admission, 6/1 priority date for domestic students, 5/1 priority date for international students; for spring admission, 10/1 priority date for domestic students, 9/1 priority date for international students. Applications are processed on a rolling basis. *Application fee:* $35. Electronic applications accepted. *Application Contact:* Dr. Angeline Lavin, MBA and Executive Education Dean, 605-677-5232, Fax: 605-677-5058, E-mail: mba@usd.edu. *Dean,* Dean Michael Keller, 605-677-5455.

School of Education Students: 182 full-time (119 women), 379 part-time (241 women); includes 23 minority (5 African Americans, 11 American Indian/Alaska Native, 3 Asian Americans or Pacific Islanders, 4 Hispanic Americans), 11 international. *Faculty:* 42 full-time (23 women), 1 (woman) part-time/adjunct. Expenses: Contact institution. *Financial support:* In 2006–07, research assistantships with partial tuition reimbursements (averaging $4,626 per year), teaching assistantships with partial tuition reimbursements (averaging $4,626 per year) were awarded; career-related internships or fieldwork, Federal Work-Study, and unspecified assistantships also available. Support available to part-time students. Financial award applicants required to submit FAFSA. In 2006, 120 master's, 41 doctorates, 24 other advanced degrees awarded. *Degree program information:* Part-time and evening/weekend programs available. Postbaccalaureate distance learning degree programs offered (no on-campus study). Offers counseling and psychology in education (MA, PhD, Ed S); curriculum and instruction (Ed D, Ed S); education (MA, MS, Ed D, PhD, Ed S); educational administration (MA, Ed D, Ed S); elementary education (MA); health, physical education and recreation (MA); secondary education (MA); special education (MA); technology for education and training (MS, Ed S). *Application deadline:* Applications are processed on a rolling basis. *Application fee:* $35. Electronic applications accepted. *Application Contact:* Kathy Peckham, Senior Secretary, 605-677-5051, E-mail: kathy.peckham@usd.edu. *Campus Dean,* Dr. Jeri Engelking, 605-677-5437, Fax: 605-677-5438, E-mail: jengelki@usd.edu.

School of Law Students: 231 full-time (96 women), 4 part-time (3 women); includes 10 minority (1 African American, 4 American Indian/Alaska Native, 1 Asian American or Pacific Islander, 4 Hispanic Americans). Average age 27. 448 applicants, 37% accepted, 72 enrolled. *Faculty:* 16 full-time (4 women), 3 part-time/adjunct (0 women). Expenses: Contact institution. *Financial support:* In 2006–07, 212 students received support, including 15 research assistantships with partial tuition reimbursements available (averaging $4,812 per year); career-related internships or fieldwork, Federal Work-Study, scholarships/grants, and unspecified assistantships also available. Financial award application deadline: 4/1; financial award applicants required to submit FAFSA. In 2006, 90 degrees awarded. *Degree program information:* Part-time programs available. Offers law (JD). *Application deadline:* For fall admission, 3/1 priority date for domestic students. Applications are processed on a rolling basis. *Application fee:* $35. Electronic applications accepted. *Application Contact:* Jean Henriques, Admissions Officer/Registrar, 605-677-5443, Fax: 605-677-5417, E-mail: law.school@usd.edu. *Dean,* Barry R. Vickrey, 605-677-5443.

School of Medicine and Health Sciences Students: 407 full-time (239 women), 3 part-time (all women); includes 15 minority (1 African American, 7 American Indian/Alaska Native, 7 Asian Americans or Pacific Islanders), 25 international. Average age 25. 1,120 applicants, 16% accepted, 132 enrolled. *Faculty:* 329 full-time, 733 part-time/adjunct. Expenses: Contact institution. *Financial support:* In 2006–07, 197 students received support, including 23 fellowships with partial tuition reimbursements available (averaging $20,772 per year), 3 research assistantships with partial tuition reimbursements available (averaging $20,772 per year); teaching assistantships with partial tuition reimbursements available, career-related internships or fieldwork, institutionally sponsored loans, scholarships/grants, traineeships, tuition waivers (partial), and unspecified assistantships also available. Financial award application deadline: 5/1; financial award applicants required to submit FAFSA. In 2006, 52 MDs, 46 master's, 4 doctorates awarded. *Degree program information:* Part-time programs available. Offers cardiovascular research (MS, PhD); cellular and molecular biology (MS, PhD); medicine (MD); medicine and health science (MD, MS, DPT, PhD); molecular microbiology and immunology (MS, PhD); neuroscience (MS, PhD); occupational therapy (MS); physical therapy (MS, DPT); physician assistant studies (MS); physiology and pharmacology (MS, PhD). *Application deadline:* For fall admission, 4/15 for international students. Applications are processed on a rolling basis. *Application fee:* $35. *Application Contact:* Dr. Paul C. Bunger, Dean, Medical Student Affairs, 605-677-5233, Fax: 605-677-5109, E-mail: pbunger@usd.edu. *Dean,* Dr. Rodney R. Parry, 605-357-1300, Fax: 605-375-1311, E-mail: rparry@usd.edu.

See Close-Up on page 1123.

UNIVERSITY OF SOUTHERN CALIFORNIA, Los Angeles, CA 90089

General Information Independent, coed, university. CGS member. *Enrollment:* 33,389 graduate, professional, and undergraduate students; 13,205 full-time matriculated graduate/professional students (6,620 women), 3,454 part-time matriculated graduate/professional students (1,184 women). *Enrollment by degree level:* 2,710 first professional, 8,723 master's, 4,255 doctoral, 196 other advanced degrees. *Graduate faculty:* 1,917 full-time (568 women), 1,024 part-time/adjunct (383 women). *Tuition:* Full-time $33,314; part-time $1,121 per credit. *Required fees:* $522. Full-time tuition and fees vary according to program. *Graduate housing:* Rooms and/or apartments available on a first-come, first-served basis to single and married students. *Student services:* Campus employment opportunities, campus safety program, career counseling, child daycare facilities, disabled student services, exercise/wellness program, free psychological counseling, grant writing training, international student services, low-cost health insurance, multicultural affairs office, teacher training, writing training. *Library facilities:* Doheny Memorial Library plus 19 others. *Online resources:* library catalog, web page, access to other libraries' catalogs. *Collection:* 4 million titles, 60,718 serial subscriptions, 59,824 audiovisual materials. *Research affiliation:* Norris Cancer Hospital (medicine), Doheny Eye Institute (medicine), Children's Hospital Los Angeles (medicine), Rancho Los Amigos Medical Center (medicine), City of Hope Cancer Center (medicine).

Computer facilities: Computer purchase and lease plans are available. 2,500 computers available on campus for general student use. A campuswide network can be accessed from student residence rooms and from off campus. Internet access and online class registration, online degree progress, grades, financial aid summary are available. *Web address:* http://www.usc.edu/.

General Application Contact: Susan Ikerd, Director of Graduate Admission, 213-740-1111, Fax: 213-740-8826, E-mail: gradadm@usc.edu.

GRADUATE UNITS

Graduate School Students: 13,080 full-time (6,553 women), 2,846 part-time (982 women); includes 5,286 minority (668 African Americans, 59 American Indian/Alaska Native, 3,254 Asian Americans or Pacific Islanders, 1,305 Hispanic Americans), 4,070 international. Expenses: Contact institution. *Financial support:* In 2006–07, research assistantships with full tuition reimbursements (averaging $18,500 per year), teaching assistantships with full tuition reimbursements (averaging $18,500 per year) were awarded; fellowships with full tuition reimbursements, career-related internships or fieldwork, Federal Work-Study, institutionally sponsored loans, and scholarships/grants also available. Support available to part-time students. Financial award applicants required to submit FAFSA. In 2006, 559 first professional degrees, 3,849 master's, 699 doctorates, 107 other advanced degrees awarded. *Degree program information:* Part-time programs available. Offers biokinesiology (MS, PhD); occupational science (PhD); occupational therapy (MA, OTD); physical therapy (MS, DPT). *Application deadline:* For fall admission, 12/1 for domestic students. *Application fee:* $85. *Application Contact:* Dr. L. Katherine Harrington, Associate Dean and Executive Director of Admissions, 213-740-1879, Fax: 213-740-7577. *Viec Provost,* Dr. Jean Morrison, 213-740-9033, E-mail: gradsch@usc.edu.

Annenberg School for Communication Students: 414 full-time, 86 part-time; includes 133 minority (28 African Americans, 2 American Indian/Alaska Native, 59 Asian Americans or Pacific Islanders, 44 Hispanic Americans), 100 international. Average age 30. 1,066 applicants, 40% accepted, 206 enrolled. *Faculty:* 64 full-time (23 women), 56 part-time/adjunct (17 women). Expenses: Contact institution. *Financial support:* In 2006–07, 8 fellowships with full tuition reimbursements (averaging $24,079 per year), 11 research assistantships with full tuition reimbursements (averaging $22,968 per year), 73 teaching assistantships with full tuition reimbursements (averaging $21,430 per year) were awarded; career-related internships or fieldwork, Federal Work-Study, institutionally sponsored loans, scholarships/grants, health care benefits, tuition waivers (partial), and unspecified assistantships also available. Support available to part-time students. Financial award application deadline: 1/15; financial award applicants required to submit FAFSA. In 2006, 318 master's, 7 doctorates awarded. *Degree program information:* Part-time and evening/weekend programs available. Offers broadcast journalism (MA); communication (MA, PhD); communication management (MCM); global communication); online journalism (MA); print journalism (MA); public diplomacy (MPD); specialized journalism (MA); strategic public relations (MA). *Application deadline:* For fall admission, 12/15 priority date for domestic and international students; for spring admission, 12/1 priority date for domestic students, 12/1 for international students. Applications are processed on a rolling basis. *Application fee:* $85. Electronic applications accepted. *Application Contact:* Allyson Hill. *Dean,* Ernest Wilson, 213-740-6180, Fax: 213-740-3772.

College of Letters, Arts and Sciences Students: 1,444 full-time (734 women), 113 part-time (52 women); includes 287 minority (46 African Americans, 8 American Indian/Alaska Native, 132 Asian Americans or Pacific Islanders, 101 Hispanic Americans), 545 international. Expenses: Contact institution. *Financial support:* In 2006–07, research assistantships with full tuition reimbursements (averaging $18,500 per year), teaching assistantships with full tuition reimbursements (averaging $18,500 per year) were awarded; fellowships with full tuition reimbursements, career-related internships or fieldwork, Federal Work-Study, institutionally sponsored loans, and scholarships/grants also available. Support available to part-time students. Financial award application deadline: 2/15; financial award applicants required to submit FAFSA. In 2006, 126 master's, 111 doctorates, 9 other advanced degrees awarded. *Degree program information:* Part-time programs available. Offers American studies and ethnicity (PhD); anthropology (MA); applied mathematics (MA, MS, PhD); art history (MA, PhD, Certificate); biological anthropology (PhD); chemical physics (PhD); chemistry (MA, MS, PhD); classics (MA, PhD); clinical psychology (PhD); comparative literature (MA, PhD); computational linguistics (MS); earth sciences (MS, PhD); East Asian area studies (MA); East Asian languages and cultures (MA, PhD); economic development programming (MA); economics (MA, PhD); English (MA, PhD); French (MA, PhD); geography (MA, MS, PhD); Hispanic linguistics (PhD); history (MA, PhD); international relations (MA, PhD); letters, arts and sciences (MA, MPW, MS, PhD, Certificate); linguistics (MA, PhD); marine environmental biology (PhD); mathematics (MA, PhD); molecular and computational biology (PhD); neuroscience (PhD); philosophy (MA, PhD); physics (MA, MS, PhD); political economy (MA); political science (MA, PhD); professional writing (MPW); psychology (MA, PhD); Slavic languages and literatures (MA, PhD); social anthropology (PhD); social ethics (MA, PhD); sociology (MA, PhD); statistics (MS); visual anthropology (Certificate). *Application deadline:* For fall admission, 12/1 for domestic students. *Application fee:* $85. *Dean,* Dr. Peter Starr, 213-740-2531, E-mail: college@usc.edu.

Davis School of Gerontology Students: 40 full-time (32 women), 19 part-time (15 women); includes 16 minority (1 African American, 13 Asian Americans or Pacific Islanders, 2 Hispanic Americans), 6 international. Expenses: Contact institution. *Financial support:* In 2006–07, research assistantships with full tuition reimbursements (averaging $18,500 per year), teaching assistantships with full tuition reimbursements (averaging $18,500 per year) were awarded; fellowships with partial tuition reimbursements, career-related internships or fieldwork, Federal Work-Study, institutionally sponsored loans, and scholarships/grants also available. Financial award application deadline: 2/15; financial award applicants required to submit FAFSA. In 2006, 13 master's, 1 doctorate awarded. *Degree program information:* Part-time programs available. Postbaccalaureate distance learning degree programs offered. Offers gerontology (MS, PhD, Certificate). *Application deadline:* For fall admission, 12/1 priority date for domestic students. Applications are processed on a rolling basis. *Application fee:* $85. *Dean,* Dr. Gerald Davison, 213-740-1354.

Gould School of Law Students: 609 full-time (290 women); includes 225 minority (53 African Americans, 1 American Indian/Alaska Native, 104 Asian Americans or Pacific Islanders, 67 Hispanic Americans), 12 international. Expenses: Contact institution. *Financial support:* Fellowships, research assistantships, teaching assistantships, Federal Work-Study, institutionally sponsored loans, and scholarships/grants available. Support available to part-time students. Financial award application deadline: 2/15; financial award applicants required to submit FAFSA. In 2006, 206 JDs, 64 master's awarded. Offers law (JD, LL M). *Application deadline:* Applications are processed on a rolling basis. *Dean,* Edward McCaffy, 213-740-6473, E-mail: dean@law.usc.edu.

Marshall School of Business Students: 1,385 full-time (432 women), 432 part-time (132 women); includes 708 minority (33 African Americans, 3 American Indian/Alaska Native, 579 Asian Americans or Pacific Islanders, 93 Hispanic Americans), 297 international. Expenses: Contact institution. *Financial support:* In 2006–07, research assistantships (averaging $18,500 per year), teaching assistantships (averaging $18,500 per year) were awarded; fellowships, Federal Work-Study, institutionally sponsored loans, and scholarships/grants also available. Support available to part-time students. Financial award application deadline: 2/15; financial award applicants required to submit FAFSA. In 2006, 698 master's, 8 doctorates awarded. Offers accounting (M Acc); business (M Acc, MBA, MBT, MS, PhD); business administration (MBA, MS, PhD); business taxation (MBT); finance and business economics (MBA); information and operations management (MS); international business (MBA). *Application deadline:* For fall admission, 12/1 priority date for domestic students. *Application fee:* $85. *Dean,* James Ellis, 213-740-6422, E-mail: dean@marshall.usc.edu.

Roski School of Fine Arts Students: 46 full-time (36 women); includes 11 minority (2 African Americans, 2 Asian Americans or Pacific Islanders, 7 Hispanic Americans), 3 international. Expenses: Contact institution. *Financial support:* Fellowships, research assistantships, teaching assistantships with full tuition reimbursements, career-related internships or fieldwork, Federal Work-Study, institutionally sponsored loans, and scholarships/grants available. Financial award application deadline: 2/1; financial award applicants required to submit FAFSA. In 2006, 11 degrees awarded. Offers fine arts (MFA, MPAS); public art studies (MPAS). *Application deadline:* For fall admission, 12/1 priority date for domestic students. *Application fee:* $85. *Application Contact:* Penelope Jones, Director of Admissions, 213-740-9153, Fax: 213-740-8938, E-mail: penelope@usc.edu. *Dean,* Ruth Weisberg, 213-740-2787, Fax: 213-740-8938, E-mail: finearts@usc.edu.

Rossier School of Education Students: 990 full-time (707 women), 97 part-time (69 women); includes 458 minority (120 African Americans, 10 American Indian/Alaska Native, 166 Asian Americans or Pacific Islanders, 162 Hispanic Americans), 90 international. Expenses: Contact institution. *Financial support:* Fellowships, research assistantships, teaching assistantships, Federal Work-Study, institutionally sponsored loans, and scholarships/grants available. Support available to part-time students. Financial award application deadline: 2/15; financial award applicants required to submit FAFSA. In 2006, 134 master's, 110 doctorates awarded. Offers education (MS, Ed D, PhD). *Application fee:* $65 ($75 for international students). *Dean,* Dr. Karen Symms Gallagher, 213-740-5756.

School of Architecture Students: 70 full-time (38 women), 11 part-time (6 women); includes 19 minority (3 African Americans, 8 Asian Americans or Pacific Islanders, 8 Hispanic Americans), 19 international. Expenses: Contact institution. *Financial support:* Fellowships, research assistantships, teaching assistantships, Federal Work-Study, institutionally sponsored loans, and scholarships/grants available. Support available to part-time students. Financial award application deadline: 2/15; financial award applicants required to submit FAFSA. In 2006, 22 master's, 5 other advanced degrees awarded. Offers architecture (M Arch, MBS, ML Arch, AC); building science (MBS); historic preservation (AC); landscape architecture (ML Arch). *Application deadline:* For fall admission, 12/1 priority date for domestic students. *Application fee:* $85. *Application Contact:* Gymeka Williams, Director of Graduate Admissions, 213-740-2723. *Dean,* Qingyun Ma, 213-740-2083, E-mail: archdean@usc.edu.

School of Cinematic Arts Students: 606 full-time (246 women), 31 part-time (8 women); includes 143 minority (40 African Americans, 3 American Indian/Alaska Native, 40 Asian Americans or Pacific Islanders, 60 Hispanic Americans), 80 international. Average age 28. Expenses: Contact institution. *Financial support:* In 2006–07, research assistantships (averaging $18,500 per year), teaching assistantships (averaging $18,500 per year) were awarded; fellowships, Federal Work-Study, institutionally sponsored loans, and scholarships/grants also available. Support available to part-time students. Financial award application deadline: 2/15; financial award applicants required to submit FAFSA. In 2006, 126 master's, 3 doctorates awarded. Offers cinematic arts (MA, MFA, PhD); critical studies (MA, PhD); film and video production (MFA); film, video, and computer animation (MFA); interactive media (MFA); producing (MFA); screen and television writing (MFA). *Application deadline:* For fall admission, 12/1 priority date for domestic students. *Application fee:* $85. *Dean,* Dr. Elizabeth Daley, 213-740-2804.

School of Dentistry Students: 1,322 full-time, 32 part-time; includes 529 minority (29 African Americans, 6 American Indian/Alaska Native, 415 Asian Americans or Pacific Islanders, 79 Hispanic Americans), 108 international. Expenses: Contact institution. *Financial support:* In 2006–07, research assistantships (averaging $18,500 per year), teaching assistantships (averaging $18,500 per year) were awarded; fellowships, Federal Work-Study, institutionally sponsored loans, and scholarships/grants also available. Support available to part-time students. Financial award application deadline: 2/15; financial award applicants required to submit FAFSA. In 2006, 142 DDSs, 92 master's, 102 doctorates, 2 other advanced degrees awarded. Offers craniofacial biology (MS, PhD); dentistry (DDS, MA, MS, DPT, OTD, PhD, Certificate). *Application deadline:* For fall admission, 6/1 for domestic students; for spring admission, 10/15 for domestic students. *Application fee:* $85. *Dean,* Dr. Harold Slavkin, 213-740-2811, E-mail: dentweb@usc.edu.

School of Pharmacy Students: 807 full-time (583 women), 46 part-time (30 women); includes 566 minority (19 African Americans, 1 American Indian/Alaska Native, 508 Asian Americans or Pacific Islanders, 38 Hispanic Americans), 50 international. Expenses: Contact institution. *Financial support:* In 2006–07, research assistantships (averaging $18,500 per year), teaching assistantships (averaging $18,500 per year) were awarded; fellowships, Federal Work-Study, institutionally sponsored loans, and scholarships/grants also available. Support available to part-time students. Financial award application deadline: 2/15; financial award applicants required to submit FAFSA. In 2006, 185 Pharm Ds, 22 master's, 4 doctorates awarded. Offers molecular pharmacology and toxicology (MS, PhD); pharmaceutical economics and policy (MS, PhD); pharmaceutical sciences (MS, PhD); pharmacy (Pharm D, MS, PhD); regulatory sciences (MS). *Application deadline:* For fall admission, 1/12 priority date for domestic students. *Application fee:* $85. *Dean,* Dr. Pete Vanderveen, 323-442-1369, E-mail: pharmadm@usc.edu.

School of Policy, Planning and Development Students: 593 full-time (334 women), 144 part-time (72 women); includes 270 minority (50 African Americans, 3 American Indian/Alaska Native, 124 Asian Americans or Pacific Islanders, 93 Hispanic Americans), 157 international. Expenses: Contact institution. *Financial support:* In 2006–07, research assistantships (averaging $18,500 per year), teaching assistantships (averaging $18,500 per year) were awarded; fellowships, Federal Work-Study, institutionally sponsored loans, and scholarships/grants also available. Support available to part-time students. Financial award application deadline: 2/15; financial award applicants required to submit FAFSA. In 2006, 256 master's, 9 doctorates, 23 other advanced degrees awarded. Offers health administration (MHA); planning (M Pl); planning and development studies (MPDS, DPDS); policy, planning and development (M Pl, MHA, MPA, MPDS, MPP, MRED, DPA, DPDS, PhD, Certificate); public administration (MPA, DPA, PhD, Certificate); public policy (MPP); real estate development (MRED); urban and regional planning (PhD). *Application deadline:* For fall admission, 12/1 priority date for domestic students. *Application fee:* $85. *Dean,* Dr. Jack Knott, 213-740-6842, E-mail: sppd@usc.edu.

School of Social Work Students: 562 full-time (491 women), 111 part-time (101 women); includes 410 minority (91 African Americans, 5 American Indian/Alaska Native, 80 Asian Americans or Pacific Islanders, 234 Hispanic Americans), 28 international. Expenses: Contact institution. *Financial support:* In 2006–07, research assistantships (averaging $18,500 per year), teaching assistantships (averaging $18,500 per year) were awarded; fellowships, Federal Work-Study, institutionally sponsored loans, and scholarships/grants also available. Support available to part-time students. Financial award application deadline: 2/15; financial award applicants required to submit FAFSA. In 2006, 237 master's, 1 doctorate awarded. Offers social work (MSW, PhD). *Application deadline:* For fall admission, 12/1 priority date for domestic students. *Application fee:* $85. *Dean,* Dr. Marilyn L. Flynn, 213-740-8311, E-mail: sswadm@usc.edu.

School of Theatre Students: 20 full-time (8 women); includes 14 minority (7 African Americans, 2 Asian Americans or Pacific Islanders, 5 Hispanic Americans), 1 international. Expenses: Contact institution. *Financial support:* In 2006–07, 15 students received support; fellowships, research assistantships, teaching assistantships with full and partial tuition reimbursements available, Federal Work-Study, institutionally sponsored loans, and scholarships/grants available. Financial award applicants required to submit FAFSA. In 2006, 2 degrees awarded. *Degree program information:* Part-time programs available. Offers acting (MFA); design (MFA); playwriting (MFA). *Application deadline:* For fall admission, 12/1 priority date for domestic students. Applications are processed on a rolling basis. *Application fee:* $85. *Application Contact:* Madeline Puzo, Dean, 213-821-2744, E-mail: thtrinfo@usc.edu. *Dean,* Madeline Puzo, 213-821-2744, E-mail: thtrinfo@usc.edu.

Thornton School of Music Students: 387 full-time (219 women), 59 part-time (30 women); includes 105 minority (19 African Americans, 2 American Indian/Alaska Native, 66 Asian Americans or Pacific Islanders, 18 Hispanic Americans), 116 international. Expenses: Contact institution. *Financial support:* In 2006–07, research assistantships (averaging $18,500 per year), teaching assistantships (averaging $18,500 per year) were awarded; fellowships, Federal Work-Study, institutionally sponsored loans, and scholarships/grants also available. Support available to part-time students. Financial award application deadline: 2/15; financial award applicants required to submit FAFSA. In 2006, 68 master's, 21 doctorates, 32 other advanced degrees awarded. Offers choral and church music (MM, DMA); composition (MA, MM, DMA, PhD); early music performance (MA); jazz studies (MM, DMA); keyboard collaborative arts (MM, DMA, Graduate Certificate); music (MA, MM, MM Ed, DMA, PhD, Graduate Certificate); music education (MM, MM Ed, DMA); music history and literature (MA); organ studies (MM, DMA, Graduate Certificate); strings (MM, DMA, Graduate Certificate); studio/jazz guitar (MM, DMA, Graduate Certificate); vocal arts and opera (MM, DMA, Graduate Certificate); winds and percussion (MM, DMA, Graduate Certificate). *Application deadline:* For fall admission, 12/1 priority date for domestic students. *Application fee:* $85. *Dean,* Dr. Robert A. Cutietta, 213-740-5389, E-mail: uscmusic@usc.edu.

Viterbi School of Engineering Students: 2,220 full-time (452 women), 1,599 part-time (345 women); includes 727 minority (60 African Americans, 7 American Indian/Alaska Native, 549 Asian Americans or Pacific Islanders, 111 Hispanic Americans), 2,151 international. Expenses: Contact institution. *Financial support:* In 2006–07, research assistantships (averaging $18,500 per year), teaching assistantships (averaging $18,500 per year) were awarded; fellowships, Federal Work-Study, institutionally sponsored loans, and scholarships/grants also available. Support available to part-time students. Financial award application deadline: 2/15; financial award applicants required to submit FAFSA. In 2006, 779 master's, 102 doctorates, 42 other advanced degrees awarded. *Degree program information:* Part-time programs available. Offers aerospace engineering (MSAE, PhD, Engr); applied mechanics (MS); astronautical engineering (MS, PhD, Engr, Graduate Certificate); astronautics (MSAE); astronautics and space technology (MS, PhD, Engr, Graduate Certificate); biomedical engineering (MS, PhD); chemical engineering (MS, PhD, Engr); civil engineering (MS, PhD, Engr); coastal and ocean engineering (MS); computer engineering (MS, PhD); computer networks (MS); computer science (MS, PhD); computer-aided engineering (ME, Certificate); construction engineering and management (MS); construction management (MCM); dynamics and control (MSME); earthquake engineering (MS); electrical engineering (MS, PhD, Engr); engineering (MCM, ME, MS, MSAE, MSEE, MSME, PhD, Certificate, Engr, Graduate Certificate); engineering management (MS); environmental engineering (MS, MSEE, PhD); environmental quality management (ME); geotechnical engineering (MS); industrial and systems engineering (MS, PhD, Engr); manufacturing engineering (MS); materials engineering (MS); materials science (MS, PhD, Engr); materials science and engineering (MS, PhD, Engr); mechanical engineering (MSME, PhD, Engr); medical device and diagnostic engineering (MS); medical imaging and imaging informatics (MS); multimedia and creative technologies (MS); neuroengineering (MS); operations research (MS); petroleum engineering (MS, PhD, Engr); robotics and automation (MS); software engineering (MS); structural design (ME); structural engineering (MS); structural mechanics (MS); systems architecture and engineering (MS); transportation engineering (MS); VLSI design (MS); water resources engineering (MS). *Application deadline:* For fall admission, 12/1 priority date for domestic students. *Application fee:* $85. *Dean,* Dr. Yannis Yortsos, 213-740-7832.

Keck School of Medicine Students: 1,265 full-time (739 women), 8 part-time (6 women); includes 526 minority (52 African Americans, 3 American Indian/Alaska Native, 332 Asian Americans or Pacific Islanders, 139 Hispanic Americans), 166 international. Average age 25. 7,461 applicants, 10% accepted, 337 enrolled. *Faculty:* 1,208 full-time (380 women), 54 part-time/adjunct (23 women). Expenses: Contact institution. *Financial support:* In 2006–07, 829 students received support, including 38 fellowships with full tuition reimbursements available, 186 research assistantships with full tuition reimbursements available, 40 teaching assistantships with full tuition reimbursements available; career-related internships or fieldwork, Federal Work-Study, institutionally sponsored loans, scholarships/grants, traineeships, and tuition waivers (full and partial) also available. Support available to part-time students. Financial award application deadline: 2/1. In 2006, 320 MDs, 80 master's, 36 doctorates awarded. Offers medicine (MD, MPAP, MPH, MS, PhD). Electronic applications accepted. *Application Contact:* Oralia Gonzales, Administrative Services Manager, 323-442-1607, Fax: 323-442-1610, E-mail: oraliago@usc.edu. *Dean,* Dr. Brian E. Henderson, 323-442-1900.

Graduate Programs in Medicine Students: 593 full-time (405 women), 8 part-time (6 women); includes 243 minority (28 African Americans, 1 American Indian/Alaska Native, 144 Asian Americans or Pacific Islanders, 70 Hispanic Americans), 155 international. Average age 26. 1,153 applicants, 31% accepted, 175 enrolled. *Faculty:* 249 full-time (84 women), 15 part-time/adjunct (6 women). Expenses: Contact institution. *Financial support:* In 2006–07, 279 students received support, including 19 fellowships with full tuition reimbursements available, 186 research assistantships with full tuition reimbursements available, 40 teaching assistantships with full tuition reimbursements available; career-related internships or fieldwork, Federal Work-Study, institutionally sponsored loans, scholarships/grants, traineeships, and tuition waivers (full and partial) also available. Support available to part-time students. Financial award application deadline: 2/1. In 2006, 80 master's, 36 doctorates awarded. Offers applied biostatistics/epidemiology (MS); biochemistry and molecular biology (MS, PhD); biometry/epidemiology (MPH); biostatistics (MS, PhD); cell and neurobiology (MS, PhD); epidemiology (PhD); experimental and molecular pathology (MS); genetic epidemiology and statistical genetics (PhD); health behavior research (PhD); health communication (MPH); health promotion (MPH); medicine (MPAP, MPH, MS, PhD); molecular epidemiology (MS, PhD); molecular microbiology and immunology (MS, PhD); pathobiology (PhD); physiology and biophysics (MS, PhD); preventive nutrition (MPH); primary care physician assistant (MPAP); public health (MPH). Electronic applications accepted. *Application Contact:* Oralia Gonzales, Administrative Services Manager, 323-442-1607, Fax: 323-442-1610, E-mail: oraliago@hsc.usc.edu. *Associate Dean for Research,* Dr. Francis S. Markland, 323-442-1607, Fax: 323-442-1610.

UNIVERSITY OF SOUTHERN INDIANA, Evansville, IN 47712-3590

General Information State-supported, coed, comprehensive institution. CGS member. *Enrollment:* 10,021 graduate, professional, and undergraduate students; 103 full-time matriculated graduate/professional students (83 women), 521 part-time matriculated graduate/professional students (380 women). *Enrollment by degree level:* 624 master's. *Graduate faculty:* 73 full-time (36 women), 7 part-time/adjunct (4 women). Tuition, state resident: full-time $3,888; part-time $216 per credit hour. Tuition, nonresident: full-time $7,688; part-time $426 per credit hour. *Required fees:* $220; $23 per term. Tuition and fees vary according to course load and reciprocity agreements. *Graduate housing:* Rooms and/or apartments available on a first-come, first-served basis to single and married students. Typical cost: $3,234 per year ($5,972 including board) for single students; $3,234 per year ($5,972 including board) for married students. Housing application deadline: 3/1. *Student services:* Campus employment opportunities, campus safety program, career counseling, child daycare facilities, disabled student services, exercise/wellness program, free psychological counseling, international student services, low-cost health insurance, multicultural affairs office. *Library facilities:* David L. Rice Library plus 1 other. *Online resources:* library catalog, web page, access to other libraries' catalogs. *Collection:* 328,734 titles, 15,153 serial subscriptions, 5,587 audiovisual materials.

Computer facilities: 778 computers available on campus for general student use. A campuswide network can be accessed from student residence rooms and from off campus. Internet access and online class registration are available. *Web address:* http://www.usi.edu/.

General Application Contact: Dr. Peggy F. Harrel, Director, Graduate Studies, 812-465-7015, Fax: 812-464-1956, E-mail: pharrel@usi.edu.

GRADUATE UNITS

Graduate Studies Students: 103 full-time (83 women), 521 part-time (380 women); includes 20 minority (8 African Americans, 2 American Indian/Alaska Native, 5 Asian Americans or Pacific Islanders, 5 Hispanic Americans), 10 international. Average age 35. 221 applicants, 96% accepted, 149 enrolled. *Faculty:* 73 full-time (36 women), 7 part-time/adjunct (4 women). Expenses: Contact institution. *Financial support:* In 2006–07, 250 students received support. Federal Work-Study, scholarships/grants, tuition waivers (full and partial), and unspecified assistantships available. Financial award application deadline: 3/1; financial award applicants required to submit FAFSA. In 2006, 224 degrees awarded. *Degree program information:* Part-time and evening/weekend programs available. *Application deadline:* Applications are processed on a rolling basis. *Application fee:* $25. Electronic applications accepted. *Director,* Dr. Peggy F. Harrel, 812-465-7015, Fax: 812-464-1956, E-mail: pharrel@usi.edu.

College of Business Students: 4 full-time (0 women), 89 part-time (35 women); includes 3 minority (all Hispanic Americans), 2 international. Average age 31. 26 applicants, 85% accepted, 16 enrolled. *Faculty:* 11 full-time (3 women). Expenses: Contact institution. *Financial support:* In 2006–07, 22 students received support. Federal Work-Study, scholarships/grants, tuition waivers (full and partial), and unspecified assistantships available. Financial award application deadline: 3/1; financial award applicants required to submit FAFSA. In 2006, 28 degrees awarded. *Degree program information:* Part-time and evening/weekend programs available. Offers accountancy (MSA); business (MBA, MSA); business administration (MBA). *Application deadline:* For fall admission, 8/15 for domestic students, 3/1 priority date for international students. Applications are processed on a rolling basis. *Application fee:* $25. *Application Contact:* Information Contact, 812-464-1803. *Dean,* Dr. Mohammed F. Khayum, 812-465-1926, E-mail: mkhayum@usi.edu.

College of Education and Human Services Students: 62 full-time (52 women), 91 part-time (67 women); includes 7 minority (3 African Americans, 2 Asian Americans or Pacific Islanders, 2 Hispanic Americans), 4 international. Average age 34. 104 applicants, 97% accepted, 65 enrolled. *Faculty:* 24 full-time (12 women), 5 part-time/adjunct (2 women). Expenses: Contact institution. *Financial support:* In 2006–07, 84 students received support. Federal Work-Study, scholarships/grants, tuition waivers (full and partial), and unspecified assistantships available. Financial award application deadline: 3/1; financial award applicants required to submit FAFSA. In 2006, 96 degrees awarded. *Degree program information:* Part-time and evening/weekend programs available. Offers education and human services (MS, MSW); elementary education (MS); secondary education (MS); social work (MSW). *Application deadline:* Applications are processed on a rolling basis. *Application fee:* $25. *Application Contact:* Dr. Michael L. Slavkin, Director, 812-465-1858, E-mail: mslavkin@usi.edu. *Acting Dean,* Dr. Jane Davis-Brezette, 812-464-1821, E-mail: brezette@usi.edu.

College of Liberal Arts Students: 8 full-time (6 women), 58 part-time (37 women); includes 2 minority (both African Americans), 2 international. Average age 34. 23 applicants, 100% accepted, 20 enrolled. *Faculty:* 21 full-time (8 women), 1 (woman) part-time/adjunct.

University of Southern Indiana (continued)

Expenses: Contact institution. *Financial support:* In 2006–07, 44 students received support. Federal Work-Study, scholarships/grants, tuition waivers (full and partial), and unspecified assistantships available. Financial award application deadline: 3/1; financial award applicants required to submit FAFSA. In 2006, 10 master's awarded. *Degree program information:* Part-time and evening/weekend programs available. Offers liberal arts (MA, MPA); liberal studies (MA); public administration (MPA). *Application deadline:* For fall admission, 8/15 priority date for domestic students, 3/1 priority date for international students. Applications are processed on a rolling basis. *Application fee:* $25. *Application Contact:* Dr. Thomas M. Rivers, Director, 812-464-1753, E-mail: trivers@usi.edu. *Dean,* Dr. David L. Glassman, 812-464-1855.

College of Nursing and Health Professions Students: 28 full-time (24 women), 213 part-time (190 women); includes 6 minority (3 African Americans, 1 American Indian/Alaska Native, 2 Asian Americans or Pacific Islanders), 1 international. Average age 38. 62 applicants, 95% accepted, 42 enrolled. *Faculty:* 15 full-time (13 women), 1 (woman) part-time/adjunct. Expenses: Contact institution. *Financial support:* In 2006–07, 99 students received support. Federal Work-Study, scholarships/grants, tuition waivers (full and partial), and unspecified assistantships available. Financial award application deadline: 3/1; financial award applicants required to submit FAFSA. In 2006, 87 degrees awarded. *Degree program information:* Part-time programs available. Postbaccalaureate distance learning degree programs offered (minimal on-campus study). Offers health administration (MHA); nursing (MSN); nursing and health professions (MHA, MSN, MSOT); occupational therapy (MSOT). *Application deadline:* Applications are processed on a rolling basis. *Application fee:* $25. *Dean,* Dr. Nadine Coudret, 812-465-1151, E-mail: ncoudret@usi.edu.

College of Science and Engineering Average age 34. 6 applicants, 100% accepted, 6 enrolled. *Faculty:* 7 full-time (3 women). Expenses: Contact institution. *Financial support:* In 2006–07, 1 student received support. Federal Work-Study, scholarships/grants, tuition waivers (full and partial), and unspecified assistantships available. Financial award application deadline: 3/1; financial award applicants required to submit FAFSA. In 2006, 3 degrees awarded. *Degree program information:* Part-time and evening/weekend programs available. Offers industrial management (MS); science and engineering (MS). *Application deadline:* For fall admission, 8/15 priority date for domestic students, 3/1 priority date for international students. Applications are processed on a rolling basis. *Application fee:* $25. *Dean,* Dr. Scott A. Gordon, 812-465-7137, E-mail: sgordon@usi.edu.

UNIVERSITY OF SOUTHERN MAINE, Portland, ME 04104-9300

General Information State-supported, coed, comprehensive institution. CGS member. *Enrollment:* 10,478 graduate, professional, and undergraduate students; 511 full-time matriculated graduate/professional students (388 women), 1,798 part-time matriculated graduate/professional students (1,195 women). *Enrollment by degree level:* 2,283 master's, 26 doctoral. *Graduate faculty:* 166. Tuition, state resident: full-time $4,860; part-time $270 per credit hour. Tuition, nonresident: full-time $13,572; part-time $754 per credit hour. *Required fees:* $222 per semester. Tuition and fees vary according to course load. *Graduate housing:* Rooms and/or apartments available on a first-come, first-served basis to single and married students. *Student services:* Campus employment opportunities, campus safety program, career counseling, child daycare facilities, disabled student services, exercise/wellness program, free psychological counseling, international student services, low-cost health insurance, multicultural affairs office, teacher training. *Library facilities:* University of Southern Maine Library plus 4 others. *Online resources:* library catalog, web page, access to other libraries' catalogs. *Collection:* 545,246 titles, 2,585 serial subscriptions, 2,705 audiovisual materials.

Computer facilities: Computer purchase and lease plans are available. 485 computers available on campus for general student use. A campuswide network can be accessed from student residence rooms and from off campus. Internet access and online class registration are available. *Web address:* http://www.usm.maine.edu/.

General Application Contact: Mary Sloan, Director of Graduate Admissions, 207-780-4386, Fax: 207-780-4969, E-mail: gradstudies@usm.maine.edu.

GRADUATE UNITS

College of Arts and Sciences Students: 153 full-time (110 women), 217 part-time (143 women). Average age 37. 208 applicants, 67% accepted, 94 enrolled. *Faculty:* 43 full-time (19 women), 26 part-time/adjunct (19 women). Expenses: Contact institution. *Financial support:* In 2006–07, 15 research assistantships with partial tuition reimbursements (averaging $4,500 per year) were awarded; career-related internships or fieldwork, Federal Work-Study, scholarships/grants, tuition waivers (partial), and unspecified assistantships also available. Support available to part-time students. In 2006, 387 degrees awarded. *Degree program information:* Part-time and evening/weekend programs available. Postbaccalaureate distance learning degree programs offered (minimal on-campus study). Offers American and New England studies (MA); arts and sciences (MA, MFA, MM, MS, MSW); biology (MS); creative writing (MFA); music (MM); social work (MSW); statistics (MS). *Application deadline:* For fall admission, 3/15 priority date for domestic and international students; for spring admission, 10/1 priority date for domestic and international students. *Application fee:* $50. Electronic applications accepted. *Application Contact:* Mary Sloan, Director of Graduate Admissions, 207-780-4386, Fax: 207-780-4969, E-mail: gradstudies@usm.maine.edu. *Dean,* Devinder Malhotra, 207-780-4221, E-mail: malhorta@usm.maine.edu.

College of Education and Human Development Students: 195 full-time (151 women), 435 part-time (324 women); includes 9 minority (4 American Indian/Alaska Native, 2 Asian Americans or Pacific Islanders, 3 Hispanic Americans), 1 international. 430 applicants, 62% accepted, 195 enrolled. *Faculty:* 39 full-time (21 women), 33 part-time/adjunct (17 women). Expenses: Contact institution. *Financial support:* In 2006–07, 81 students received support, including 20 research assistantships (averaging $4,500 per year), 2 teaching assistantships with tuition reimbursements available (averaging $5,000 per year); career-related internships or fieldwork, Federal Work-Study, institutionally sponsored loans, scholarships/grants, and unspecified assistantships also available. Support available to part-time students. Financial award application deadline: 3/1; financial award applicants required to submit FAFSA. In 2006, 211 master's, 27 other advanced degrees awarded. *Degree program information:* Part-time and evening/weekend programs available. Postbaccalaureate distance learning degree programs offered (minimal on-campus study). Offers adult education (MS); adult learning (CAS); applied behavior analysis (Certificate); applied literacy (MS Ed); assistant principal (Certificate); athletic administration (Certificate); counseling (MS, CAS); education and human development (MS, MS Ed, Psy D, CAS, Certificate); educational leadership (MS Ed, CAS); English as a second language (MS Ed, CAS); industrial/technology education (MS Ed); literacy education (MS Ed, CAS, Certificate); mental health rehabilitation technician/community (Certificate); middle-level education (Certificate); school psychology (MS, Psy D); special education (MS); teaching and learning (MS Ed). *Application deadline:* For fall admission, 2/1 for domestic students; for spring admission, 9/15 for domestic students. *Application fee:* $50. Electronic applications accepted. *Application Contact:* Robin Audesse, Associate Director of Graduate Admissions, 207-780-5306, Fax: 207-780-5193, E-mail: raudesse@usm.maine.edu. *Dean,* Betty Lou Whitford, 207-780-5371, Fax: 207-780-5315.

College of Nursing and Health Professions Students: 55 full-time (53 women), 52 part-time (50 women); includes 6 minority (all Asian Americans or Pacific Islanders) Average age 36. 88 applicants, 93% accepted, 57 enrolled. *Faculty:* 13 full-time (all women), 5 part-time/adjunct (4 women). Expenses: Contact institution. *Financial support:* In 2006–07, 14 students received support, including 5 research assistantships with tuition reimbursements available (averaging $3,375 per year), 7 teaching assistantships with tuition reimbursements available (averaging $3,375 per year); career-related internships or fieldwork, Federal Work-Study, scholarships/grants, traineeships, tuition waivers (full and partial), and unspecified assistantships also available. Support available to part-time students. Financial award application deadline: 2/15; financial award applicants required to submit FAFSA. In 2006, 25 degrees awarded. *Degree program information:* Part-time programs available. Offers adult health nursing (PMC); clinical nurse leader (MS); clinical nurse specialist psychiatric-mental health nursing (MS); family nursing (PMC); medical/surgical nursing (MS); nurse practitioner adult health nursing (MS); nurse practitioner family nursing (MS); nurse practitioner psychiatric/mental health nursing (MS); psychiatric-mental health nursing (PMC). *Application deadline:* Applications are processed on a rolling basis. *Application fee:* $50. Electronic applications accepted. *Application Contact:* Mary Sloan, Director of Graduate Admissions, 207-780-4386, Fax: 207-780-4969, E-mail: gradstudies@usm.maine.edu. *Director of Nursing Program,* Susan Sepples, 207-780-4505, Fax: 207-228-8177, E-mail: sepples@usm.maine.edu.

Edmund S. Muskie School of Public Service *Degree program information:* Part-time and evening/weekend programs available. Postbaccalaureate distance learning degree programs offered (minimal on-campus study). Offers child and family policy (Certificate); community planning and development (MCPD, Certificate); health policy and management (MS, Certificate); non-profit management (Certificate); public policy (PhD); public policy and management (MPPM); public service (MCPD, MPPM, MS, PhD, Certificate). Electronic applications accepted.

Program in Occupational Therapy *Degree program information:* Part-time programs available. Offers occupational therapy (MOT). Electronic applications accepted.

School of Applied Science, Engineering, and Technology Students: 30 full-time (10 women), 19 part-time (3 women). Average age 28. 32 applicants, 41% accepted. *Faculty:* 10 full-time (0 women), 31 part-time/adjunct (7 women). Expenses: Contact institution. *Financial support:* In 2006–07, 12 fellowships (averaging $27,500 per year), 13 research assistantships with full and partial tuition reimbursements (averaging $2,000 per year), 3 teaching assistantships (averaging $4,250 per year) were awarded; career-related internships or fieldwork and Federal Work-Study also available. Support available to part-time students. Financial award application deadline: 4/1; financial award applicants required to submit FAFSA. In 2006, 11 degrees awarded. *Degree program information:* Part-time and evening/weekend programs available. Offers applied medical sciences (MS); applied science, engineering, and technology (MS); computer science (MS); manufacturing systems (MS). *Application deadline:* For fall admission, 4/1 priority date for domestic students; for spring admission, 10/1 priority date for domestic students. *Application fee:* $50. Electronic applications accepted. *Application Contact:* Mary Sloan, Director of Graduate Admissions, 207-780-4386, Fax: 207-780-4969, E-mail: gradstudies@usm.maine.edu. *Dean,* Dr. John R. Wright, 207-780-5585, Fax: 207-780-5129, E-mail: jwright@usm.maine.edu.

School of Business Students: 43 full-time (26 women), 117 part-time (45 women); includes 8 minority (1 American Indian/Alaska Native, 7 Asian Americans or Pacific Islanders), 2 international. Average age 32. 77 applicants, 82% accepted, 54 enrolled. *Faculty:* 20 full-time (4 women). Expenses: Contact institution. *Financial support:* In 2006–07, 108 students received support, including 3 research assistantships with partial tuition reimbursements available (averaging $9,000 per year), 3 teaching assistantships with partial tuition reimbursements available (averaging $9,000 per year); career-related internships or fieldwork, Federal Work-Study, scholarships/grants, tuition waivers (full and partial), and unspecified assistantships also available. Support available to part-time students. Financial award application deadline: 2/15; financial award applicants required to submit FAFSA. In 2006, 32 degrees awarded. *Degree program information:* Part-time and evening/weekend programs available. Offers accounting (MSA); business administration (MBA). *Application deadline:* For fall admission, 8/1 priority date for domestic students, 5/1 priority date for international students; for spring admission, 12/1 priority date for domestic students, 9/1 priority date for international students. Applications are processed on a rolling basis. *Application fee:* $50. Electronic applications accepted. *Application Contact:* Alice B. Cash, Graduate Programs Director, 207-780-4184, Fax: 207-780-4662, E-mail: acash@usm.maine.edu. *Dean,* James B. Shaffer, 207-780-4020, Fax: 207-780-4662, E-mail: jshaffer@usm.maine.edu.

University of Maine School of Law Students: 258 full-time (137 women), 3 part-time (2 women); includes 11 minority (3 African Americans, 7 Asian Americans or Pacific Islanders, 1 Hispanic American). Average age 28. 760 applicants, 43% accepted, 101 enrolled. *Faculty:* 18 full-time (11 women), 13 part-time/adjunct (1 woman). Expenses: Contact institution. *Financial support:* In 2006–07, 242 students received support. Career-related internships or fieldwork, Federal Work-Study, scholarships/grants, and tuition waivers (full and partial) available. Support available to part-time students. Financial award application deadline: 2/1; financial award applicants required to submit FAFSA. In 2006, 82 degrees awarded. *Degree program information:* Part-time programs available. Offers law (JD). *Application deadline:* For fall admission, 3/1 for domestic and international students. Applications are processed on a rolling basis. *Application fee:* $50. Electronic applications accepted. *Application Contact:* David Pallozzi, Assistant Dean for Admissions, 207-780-4341, Fax: 207-780-4239, E-mail: mainelaw@usm.maine.edu. *Dean,* Peter R. Pitegoff, 207-780-4344, Fax: 207-780-4239.

UNIVERSITY OF SOUTHERN MISSISSIPPI, Hattiesburg, MS 39406-0001

General Information State-supported, coed, university. CGS member. *Enrollment:* 14,777 graduate, professional, and undergraduate students; 1,358 full-time matriculated graduate/professional students (801 women), 1,297 part-time matriculated graduate/professional students (872 women). *Enrollment by degree level:* 1,622 master's, 748 doctoral, 82 other advanced degrees. *Graduate faculty:* 465 full-time (154 women), 1 part-time/adjunct (0 women). *Graduate housing:* Rooms and/or apartments available on a first-come, first-served basis to single students and available to married students. *Student services:* Campus employment opportunities, career counseling, child daycare facilities, disabled student services, exercise/wellness program, free psychological counseling, grant writing training, international student services, low-cost health insurance, teacher training. *Library facilities:* Cook Memorial Library plus 4 others. *Online resources:* library catalog, web page. *Collection:* 1.5 million titles, 37,095 serial subscriptions, 37,400 audiovisual materials. *Research affiliation:* Geological Sciences, Coastal Sciences (physics), Oak Ridge Associated Universities (US Dept of Energy BSC, CHE.).

Computer facilities: 600 computers available on campus for general student use. Internet access is available. *Web address:* http://www.usm.edu/.

General Application Contact: Dr. Susan Siltanen, University Director, 601-266-4369, Fax: 601-266-5138, E-mail: susan.siltanen@usm.edu.

GRADUATE UNITS

Graduate School Students: 1,358 full-time (801 women), 1,297 part-time (872 women); includes 466 minority (391 African Americans, 9 American Indian/Alaska Native, 19 Asian Americans or Pacific Islanders, 47 Hispanic Americans), 211 international. Average age 37. 1,924 applicants, 50% accepted, 636 enrolled. *Faculty:* 508 full-time (149 women). Expenses: Contact institution. *Financial support:* In 2006–07, 13 fellowships with full and partial tuition reimbursements (averaging $15,000 per year), 365 research assistantships with full and partial tuition reimbursements (averaging $9,227 per year), 469 teaching assistantships with full and partial tuition reimbursements (averaging $9,227 per year) were awarded; career-related internships or fieldwork, Federal Work-Study, institutionally sponsored loans, scholarships/grants, traineeships, and unspecified assistantships also available. Support available to part-time students. Financial award application deadline: 3/15. In 2006, 659 master's, 109 doctorates, 45 other advanced degrees awarded. *Degree program information:* Part-time and evening/weekend programs available. *Application deadline:* For fall admission, 2/1 priority date for domestic and international students. Applications are processed on a rolling basis. *Application fee:* $25 ($30 for international students). Electronic applications accepted. *Application Contact:* Mary Lowry, Manager of Graduate Admissions, 601-266-5139, Fax: 601-266-5138. *University Director,* Dr. Susan Siltanen, 601-266-4369, Fax: 601-266-5138, E-mail: susan.siltanen@usm.edu.

College of Arts and Letters Students: 289 full-time (145 women), 221 part-time (129 women); includes 63 minority (39 African Americans, 4 American Indian/Alaska Native, 4 Asian Americans or Pacific Islanders, 16 Hispanic Americans), 34 international. Average age 32. 290 applicants, 68% accepted, 115 enrolled. *Faculty:* 147 full-time (51 women). Expenses: Contact institution. *Financial support:* In 2006–07, 1 fellowship with full tuition reimbursement (averaging $12,000 per year), 10 research assistantships with full tuition reimbursements (averaging $7,180 per year), 214 teaching assistantships with full tuition reimbursements (averaging $7,180 per year) were awarded; career-related internships or fieldwork, Federal Work-Study, institutionally sponsored loans, scholarships/grants, tuition waivers, and unspecified assistantships also available. Financial award application deadline: 3/15. In 2006, 109 master's, 26 doctorates awarded. *Degree program information:* Part-time and evening/weekend programs available. Postbaccalaureate distance learning degree programs offered. Offers anthropology (MA); art education (MAE); arts and letters (MA,

MAE, MATL, MFA, MM, MME, MS, DMA, PhD); conducting (MM); English (MA, PhD); French (MATL); history (MA, MS, PhD); history and literature (MM); international development (PhD); mass communication (MA, MS, PhD); music education (MME, PhD); performance (MM); performance and pedagogy (DMA); philosophy (MA); political science (MA, MS); public relations (MS); Spanish (MATL); speech communication (MA, MS, PhD); teaching English to speakers of other languages (TESOL) (MATL); theatre (MFA); theory and composition (MM); woodwind performance (MM). *Application deadline:* For fall admission, 5/1 for domestic students, 3/1 for international students. Applications are processed on a rolling basis. *Application fee:* $25 ($30 for international students). Electronic applications accepted. *Application Contact:* Dr. Shonna Breland, Manager of Graduate Admissions, 601-266-4369, Fax: 601-266-5138, E-mail: graduatestudies@usm.edu. *Interim Dean,* Dr. Denise Von Hermann, 601-266-4315, Fax: 601-266-6541, E-mail: denise.vonhermann@usm.edu.

College of Business Students: 52 full-time (19 women), 52 part-time (25 women); includes 18 minority (14 African Americans, 1 Asian American or Pacific Islander, 3 Hispanic Americans), 2 international. Average age 33. 117 applicants, 44% accepted, 40 enrolled. *Faculty:* 53 full-time (10 women). Expenses: Contact institution. *Financial support:* In 2006–07, 19 research assistantships with full tuition reimbursements (averaging $5,400 per year) were awarded; Federal Work-Study and institutionally sponsored loans also available. Support available to part-time students. Financial award application deadline: 3/15. In 2006, 95 degrees awarded. *Degree program information:* Part-time and evening/weekend programs available. Offers accountancy (MPA); business (MBA, MPA); business administration (MBA). *Application deadline:* For fall admission, 7/15 priority date for domestic students, 3/1 for international students; for spring admission, 11/15 priority date for domestic students, 11/5 for international students. Applications are processed on a rolling basis. *Application fee:* $25 ($30 for international students). Electronic applications accepted. *Application Contact:* Dr. Francis Daniel, Graduate Coordinator, 601-266-4664, Fax: 601-266-5814. *Dean,* Dr. Harold Doty, 601-266-4659, Fax: 601-266-5814.

College of Education and Psychology Students: 287 full-time (234 women), 516 part-time (389 women); includes 163 minority (146 African Americans, 2 American Indian/Alaska Native, 6 Asian Americans or Pacific Islanders, 9 Hispanic Americans), 16 international. Average age 35. 533 applicants, 41% accepted, 183 enrolled. *Faculty:* 89 full-time (40 women). Expenses: Contact institution. *Financial support:* In 2006–07, 87 research assistantships with full tuition reimbursements (averaging $7,502 per year), 72 teaching assistantships with full tuition reimbursements (averaging $7,502 per year) were awarded; career-related internships or fieldwork, Federal Work-Study, and institutionally sponsored loans also available. Financial award application deadline: 3/15. In 2006, 232 master's, 48 doctorates, 45 other advanced degrees awarded. *Degree program information:* Part-time programs available. Offers adult education (M Ed, Ed D, PhD, Ed S); alternative secondary teacher education (MAT); business technology education (MS); child and family studies (MS); clinical psychology (MA, PhD); counseling psychology (PhD); early childhood education (M Ed, Ed S); early intervention (MS); education and psychology (M Ed, MA, MAT, MLIS, MS, Ed D, PhD, Ed S, SLS); education of the gifted (M Ed, Ed D, PhD, Ed S); educational administration (M Ed, Ed D, PhD, Ed S); elementary education (M Ed, Ed D, PhD, Ed S); experimental psychology (MA, PhD); higher education (PhD); instructional technology (MS); library and information science (MLIS, SLS); marriage and family therapy (MS); psychology (MS); reading (M Ed, MS, Ed S); school psychology (MA, PhD); secondary education (M Ed, MS, Ed D, PhD, Ed S); special education (M Ed, Ed D, PhD, Ed S); technical occupational education (MS). *Application deadline:* For fall admission, 3/1 for domestic and international students; for spring admission, 11/1 for domestic and international students. Applications are processed on a rolling basis. *Application fee:* $25 ($30 for international students). Electronic applications accepted. *Interim Chair,* Dr. Wanda Maulding, 601-266-4568, Fax: 601-266-4175.

College of Health Students: 332 full-time (240 women), 189 part-time (151 women); includes 137 minority (128 African Americans, 1 American Indian/Alaska Native, 3 Asian Americans or Pacific Islanders, 5 Hispanic Americans), 26 international. Average age 32. 435 applicants, 65% accepted, 176 enrolled. *Faculty:* 70 full-time (35 women). Expenses: Contact institution. *Financial support:* In 2006–07, 42 research assistantships with full tuition reimbursements (averaging $8,335 per year), 25 teaching assistantships with full tuition reimbursements (averaging $8,335 per year) were awarded; fellowships with full tuition reimbursements, career-related internships or fieldwork, Federal Work-Study, institutionally sponsored loans, scholarships/grants, and tuition waivers (partial) also available. Financial award application deadline: 3/15. In 2006, 166 master's, 14 doctorates awarded. *Degree program information:* Part-time and evening/weekend programs available. Offers adult health nursing (MSN); community health nursing (MSN); epidemiology and biostatistics (MPH); ethics (PhD); family nurse practitioner (MSN); health (MA, MPH, MS, MSN, MSW, Au D, Ed D, PhD); health education (MPH); health policy/administration (MPH); human performance (MS, Ed D, PhD); interscholastic athletic administration (MS); leadership (PhD); medical technology (MS); nursing service administration (MSN); nutrition and food systems (MS, PhD); occupational/environmental health (MPH); policy analysis (PhD); psychiatric nursing (MSN); public health nutrition (MPH); recreation and leisure management (MS); social work (MSW); speech and hearing sciences (MA, MS, Au D); sport administration (MS); sport and coaching education (MS); sport management (MS); sports and high performance materials (MS). *Application deadline:* For fall admission, 3/1 for domestic and international students. Applications are processed on a rolling basis. *Application fee:* $25 ($30 for international students). Electronic applications accepted. *Dean,* Dr. Peter Fos, 601-266-4866.

College of Science and Technology Students: 371 full-time (149 women), 145 part-time (62 women); includes 45 minority (33 African Americans, 1 American Indian/Alaska Native, 3 Asian Americans or Pacific Islanders, 8 Hispanic Americans), 129 international. Average age 30. 433 applicants, 50% accepted, 122 enrolled. *Faculty:* 133 full-time (20 women). Expenses: Contact institution. *Financial support:* In 2006–07, 207 research assistantships with full tuition reimbursements (averaging $12,467 per year), 158 teaching assistantships with full tuition reimbursements (averaging $12,467 per year) were awarded; fellowships with full tuition reimbursements, career-related internships or fieldwork, Federal Work-Study, institutionally sponsored loans, and tuition waivers (full) also available. Support available to part-time students. Financial award application deadline: 3/15. In 2006, 58 master's, 21 doctorates awarded. *Degree program information:* Part-time and evening/weekend programs available. Offers administration of justice (PhD); analytical chemistry (MS, PhD); architecture and construction visualization (MS); biochemistry (MS, PhD); coastal sciences (MS, PhD); computational science (MS, PhD); computational science: mathematics (PhD); computer science (MS, PhD); construction management and technology (MS); corrections (MA, MS); economic development (MS); engineering technology (MS); environmental biology (MS, PhD); geography (MS, PhD); geology (MS); human capital development (PhD); hydrographic science (MS); inorganic chemistry (MS, PhD); juvenile justice (MA, MS); law enforcement (MA, MS); logistics management and technology (MS); marine biology (MS, PhD); marine science (MS, PhD); mathematics (MS); microbiology (MS, PhD); molecular biology (MS, PhD); organic chemistry (MS, PhD); physical chemistry (MS, PhD); physics (MS); polymer science (MS); polymer science and engineering (PhD); science and mathematics education (MS, PhD); science and technology (MA, MS, PhD); workforce training and development (MS). *Application deadline:* For fall admission, 3/1 priority date for domestic students, 3/1 for international students. Applications are processed on a rolling basis. *Application fee:* $25 ($30 for international students). *Dean,* Dr. Rex Gandy, 601-266-4883, Fax: 601-266-5829.

UNIVERSITY OF SOUTHERN NEVADA, Henderson, NV 89014

General Information Private, coed, graduate-only institution. *Enrollment by degree level:* 460 first professional. *Tuition:* Full-time $34,500. *Required fees:* $2,700. *Graduate housing:* On-campus housing not available. *Library facilities:* Main library plus 1 other. *Online resources:* web page.

Computer facilities: A campuswide network can be accessed from off campus. Internet access is available. *Web address:* http://www.usn.edu/.

General Application Contact: Dr. Michael DeYoung, Assistant Dean for Admissions, 702-990-4433 Ext. 2006, Fax: 702-990-4435, E-mail: mdeyoung@usn.edu.

GRADUATE UNITS

Program in Pharmacy Students: 460 full-time (273 women); includes 230 minority (19 African Americans, 2 American Indian/Alaska Native, 190 Asian Americans or Pacific Islanders, 19 Hispanic Americans). Average age 26. 1,500 applicants, 194 enrolled. Expenses: Contact institution. In 2006, 109 degrees awarded. Offers pharmacy (Pharm D). *Application deadline:* For fall admission, 1/11 for international students; for winter admission, 1/11 for domestic students. Applications are processed on a rolling basis. *Application fee:* $125.

UNIVERSITY OF SOUTH FLORIDA, Tampa, FL 33620-9951

General Information State-supported, coed, university. CGS member. *Graduate housing:* Rooms and/or apartments available on a first-come, first-served basis to single students and available to married students. Housing application deadline: 7/1. *Student services:* Campus employment opportunities, campus safety program, career counseling, child daycare facilities, disabled student services, exercise/wellness program, free psychological counseling, international student services, low-cost health insurance, multicultural affairs office. *Library facilities:* Tampa Campus Library plus 2 others. *Online resources:* library catalog, web page, access to other libraries' catalogs. *Collection:* 2.1 million titles, 20,440 serial subscriptions. *Research affiliation:* H. L. Moffitt Cancer Center, Shriners Hospitals, Tampa General Hospital, Harris Corporation (electronics), All Children's Hospital, Veterans Administration Medical Center.

Computer facilities: 593 computers available on campus for general student use. A campuswide network can be accessed from student residence rooms and from off campus. Internet access and online class registration are available. *Web address:* http://www.usf.edu.

General Application Contact: Dr. Kelli MacCormack-Brown, Dean, Graduate School, 813-974-2846, Fax: 813-974-5762, E-mail: kbrown@grad.usf.edu.

GRADUATE UNITS

Center for Entrepreneurship *Faculty:* 11 full-time (3 women). Expenses: Contact institution. *Financial support:* Applicants required to submit FAFSA. *Degree program information:* Part-time and evening/weekend programs available. Offers entrepreneurship (MS, Graduate Certificate). *Application deadline:* For fall admission, 3/15 for domestic students, 7/2 for international students; for spring admission, 10/15 for domestic students. *Application fee:* $30. *Director,* Dr. Michael W. Fountain, 813-974-7900, Fax: 813-974-7663, E-mail: fountain@coba.usf.edu.

College of Medicine Students: 195 full-time (121 women), 27 part-time (17 women); includes 79 minority (27 African Americans, 21 Asian Americans or Pacific Islanders, 31 Hispanic Americans), 23 international. Average age 27. 121 applicants, 100% accepted, 121 enrolled. *Faculty:* 185 full-time (63 women), 5 part-time/adjunct (3 women). Expenses: Contact institution. In 2006, 61 master's, 104 doctorates awarded. *Degree program information:* Part-time programs available. Offers anatomy (PhD); biochemistry and molecular biology (MS, PhD); medical microbiology and immunology (PhD); medicine (MD, MS, PhD); pathology (PhD); pharmacology and therapeutics (PhD); physiology and biophysics (PhD). *Application fee:* $30. Electronic applications accepted. *Application Contact:* Dr. Joseph J. Krzanowski, Associate Dean for Research and Graduate Affairs, 813-974-4181, Fax: 813-974-4317, E-mail: jkrzanow@com1.med.usf.edu. *Interim Dean,* Dr. Robert S. Belsole, 813-974-2196, Fax: 813-974-3886, E-mail: rbelsole@hsc.usf.edu.

School of Physical Therapy Students: 53 full-time (40 women), 1 (woman) part-time; includes 15 minority (5 African Americans, 2 Asian Americans or Pacific Islanders, 8 Hispanic Americans). 33 applicants, 100% accepted, 33 enrolled. *Faculty:* 1 (woman) full-time. Expenses: Contact institution. *Financial support:* Applicants required to submit FAFSA. In 2006, 1 degree awarded. Offers physical therapy (MS). *Application deadline:* For fall admission, 9/1 for domestic students, 2/1 for international students. *Application fee:* $30. *Application Contact:* Robin Hudson, Administration Service Coordinator, 813-974-8870, Fax: 813-974-8915, E-mail: dpt@hsc.usf.edu. *Associate Dean/Director,* Dr. William S. Quillen, 813-974-8870, Fax: 813-974-8915, E-mail: dpt@hsc.usf.edu.

Graduate School Students: 3,948 full-time, 4,169 part-time; includes 1,732 minority (659 African Americans, 31 American Indian/Alaska Native, 350 Asian Americans or Pacific Islanders, 692 Hispanic Americans), 758 international. 6,043 applicants, 61% accepted, 2316 enrolled. Expenses: Contact institution. *Financial support:* Applicants required to submit FAFSA. *Degree program information:* Part-time and evening/weekend programs available. Postbaccalaureate distance learning degree programs offered. Offers applied behavior analysis (MA); cancer biology (PhD). *Application deadline:* For fall admission, 3/1 priority date for domestic students, 1/2 priority date for international students; for spring admission, 10/1 priority date for domestic students, 7/1 priority date for international students. Applications are processed on a rolling basis. *Application fee:* $30. Electronic applications accepted. *Application Contact:* Fransisco Vera, Director of Admission, 813-974-8800, Fax: 813-974-7343, E-mail: fvera@grad.usf.edu. *Associate Provost for Research and Graduate Dean,* Delcie Durham, 813-974-2846, Fax: 813-974-5762, E-mail: ddurham@grad.usf.edu.

College of Arts and Sciences Students: 1,294 full-time (842 women), 1,173 part-time (851 women); includes 451 minority (165 African Americans, 6 American Indian/Alaska Native, 63 Asian Americans or Pacific Islanders, 217 Hispanic Americans), 205 international. Average age 24. 2,084 applicants, 51% accepted, 639 enrolled. *Faculty:* 476 full-time (203 women), 103 part-time/adjunct (63 women). Expenses: Contact institution. *Financial support:* Career-related internships or fieldwork, Federal Work-Study, institutionally sponsored loans, scholarships/grants, tuition waivers (full and partial), and unspecified assistantships available. Support available to part-time students. Financial award applicants required to submit FAFSA. In 2006, 554 master's, 81 doctorates awarded. *Degree program information:* Part-time and evening/weekend programs available. Postbaccalaureate distance learning degree programs offered (minimal on-campus study). Offers Africana studies (MLA); aging studies (PhD); American studies (MA); analytical chemistry (MS, PhD); applied anthropology (MA, PhD); applied physics (PhD); arts and sciences (MA, MLA, MPA, MS, MSW, PhD, Graduate Certificate); biochemistry (MS, PhD); biology (PhD); botany (MS); clinical psychology (PhD); communication (MA, PhD); communication sciences and disorders (PhD); criminal justice administration (MA); criminology (MA, PhD); Cuban studies (Graduate Certificate); ecology (PhD); English (MA, PhD); environmental science and policy (MS); experimental psychology (PhD); French (MA); geography (MA); geology (MS, PhD); gerontology (MA); history (MA); industrial/organizational psychology (PhD); inorganic chemistry (MS, PhD); Latin American and Caribbean studies (Graduate Certificate); Latin American, Caribbean and Latino studies (MA); liberal arts (MLA); library and information sciences (MA); linguistics (MA); mass communications (MA); mathematics (MA, PhD, Graduate Certificate); microbiology (MS); organic chemistry (MS, PhD); philosophy (MA, PhD); physical chemistry (MS, PhD); physics (MS); physiology (PhD); political science (MA); polymer chemistry (PhD); psychology (MA); public administration (MPA); rehabilitation and mental health counseling (MA); religious studies (MA); social work (MSW); sociology (MA); Spanish (MA); statistics (MA, Graduate Certificate); women's studies (MA); zoology (MS). *Application deadline:* For fall admission, 6/1 priority date for domestic students, 5/1 priority date for international students; for spring admission, 10/15 priority date for domestic students, 8/1 priority date for international students. *Application fee:* $30. *Application Contact:* Wanda MacLean, Administrative Assistant, 813-974-6922, Fax: 813-974-4075, E-mail: maclean@chuma1.cas.usf.edu. *Interim Dean,* Dr. Kathleen Heide, 813-974-2503, Fax: 813-974-5911, E-mail: kheide@cas.usf.edu.

College of Business Administration Students: 319 full-time (122 women), 447 part-time (173 women); includes 147 minority (30 African Americans, 3 American Indian/Alaska Native, 52 Asian Americans or Pacific Islanders, 62 Hispanic Americans), 112 international. Average age 25. 678 applicants, 63% accepted, 286 enrolled. *Faculty:* 84 full-time (23 women), 30 part-time/adjunct (18 women). Expenses: Contact institution. *Financial support:* Career-related internships or fieldwork, scholarships/grants, health care benefits, and unspecified assistantships available. Financial award applicants required to submit FAFSA. In 2006, 311 master's, 6 doctorates awarded. *Degree program information:* Part-time and evening/weekend programs available. Offers accounting (M Acc); business administration (Exec MBA, M Acc, MA, MBA, MS, MSM, PhD); economics (MA, PhD); finance (MS); management information systems (MS). *Application deadline:* For fall admission, 6/1 for domestic students, 1/2 for international students; for spring admission, 11/1 for domestic

University of South Florida (continued)

students, 7/1 for international students. *Application fee:* $30. *Application Contact:* MBA Program Staff, 813-974-3335, Fax: 813-974-4518, E-mail: mba@coba.usf.edu. *Director, MBA Programs,* Dr. Steve Baumgarten, 813-974-3335, Fax: 813-974-4518, E-mail: sbaumgar@coba.usf.edu.

College of Education Students: 636 full-time (484 women), 1,342 part-time (1,034 women); includes 413 minority (191 African Americans, 7 American Indian/Alaska Native, 37 Asian Americans or Pacific Islanders, 178 Hispanic Americans), 63 international. Average age 30. 1,147 applicants, 68% accepted, 563 enrolled. *Faculty:* 162 full-time (91 women), 69 part-time/adjunct (39 women). Expenses: Contact institution. *Financial support:* Career-related internships or fieldwork, Federal Work-Study, institutionally sponsored loans, and scholarships/grants available. Support available to part-time students. Financial award applicants required to submit FAFSA. In 2006, 538 master's, 54 doctorates awarded. *Degree program information:* Part-time and evening/weekend programs available. Offers adult education (MA, Ed D, PhD, Ed S); career and technical education (MA); college student affairs (M Ed); counselor education (MA, PhD); early childhood education (M Ed, MAT, PhD); education (M Ed, MA, MAT, Ed D, PhD, Ed S); education of the mentally handicapped (MA); educational leadership (M Ed, Ed D, Ed S); educational measurement and research (M Ed, PhD, Ed S); elementary education (MA, Ed D, PhD, Ed S); English education (M Ed, MA, PhD); foreign language education (M Ed, MA); gifted education (online) (MA); higher education/community college teaching (MA, PhD, Ed S); industrial-technical education (MA); instructional technology (M Ed); interdisciplinary education (PhD, Ed S); learning disabilities (MA); mathematics education (M Ed, MA, PhD, Ed S); middle school education (M Ed); physical education (MA); reading education (M Ed, MA, PhD, Ed S); school psychology (PhD, Ed S); science education (M Ed, MA, MAT, PhD); second language acquisition/instructional technology (PhD); secondary education (PhD); social science education (M Ed, MA); varying exceptionalities (MA, MAT); vocational education (Ed D, PhD, Ed S). *Application deadline:* For fall admission, 6/1 for domestic students; for spring admission, 10/15 for domestic students. *Application fee:* $30. Electronic applications accepted. *Application Contact:* Diane Briscoe, 813-974-3406, Fax: 813-974-3391, E-mail: briscoe@tempest.coedu.usf.edu. *Dean,* Colleen S. Kennedy, 813-974-3400, Fax: 813-974-3826.

College of Engineering Students: 421 full-time (120 women), 308 part-time (66 women); includes 153 minority (48 African Americans, 1 American Indian/Alaska Native, 42 Asian Americans or Pacific Islanders, 62 Hispanic Americans), 302 international. Average age 25. 572 applicants, 73% accepted, 189 enrolled. *Faculty:* 110 full-time (13 women), 9 part-time/adjunct (0 women). Expenses: Contact institution. *Financial support:* Career-related internships or fieldwork, Federal Work-Study, scholarships/grants, health care benefits, and unspecified assistantships available. Financial award application deadline: 3/1; financial award applicants required to submit FAFSA. In 2006, 188 master's, 21 doctorates awarded. *Degree program information:* Part-time and evening/weekend programs available. Offers biomedical engineering (MSBE, PhD); chemical engineering (MCHE, ME, MSCH, PhD); civil and environmental engineering (MEVE, MSES, MSEV); civil engineering (MCE, MSCE, PhD); computer science (MSCP, MSCS); computer science and engineering (ME, MSES, PhD); electrical engineering (ME, MSEE, MSES, PhD); engineering (ME); engineering management (MIE, MSIE); engineering science (PhD); industrial engineering (MIE, MSES, MSIE, PhD); mechanical engineering (ME, MME, MSME, PhD). *Application deadline:* For fall admission, 6/1 for domestic students, 1/2 priority date for international students; for spring admission, 10/15 for domestic students, 7/1 priority date for international students. Applications are processed on a rolling basis. *Application fee:* $30. Electronic applications accepted. *Application Contact:* Marsha L. Brett, Administrative Assistant, 813-974-3782, Fax: 813-974-5094, E-mail: brett@eng.usf.edu. *Associate Dean for Academics and Student Affairs,* Dr. Rafael Perez, 813-974-3782, Fax: 813-974-5094, E-mail: perez@eng.usf.edu.

College of Marine Science Students: 77 full-time (49 women), 46 part-time (31 women); includes 21 minority (9 African Americans, 1 Asian American or Pacific Islander, 11 Hispanic Americans), 13 international. Average age 31. 75 applicants, 36% accepted, 17 enrolled. *Faculty:* 30 full-time (6 women). Expenses: Contact institution. In 2006, 15 master's, 5 doctorates awarded. *Degree program information:* Part-time and evening/weekend programs available. Offers marine science (MS, PhD). *Application deadline:* For fall admission, 3/1 for domestic students; for spring admission, 10/1 for domestic students. Applications are processed on a rolling basis. *Application fee:* $30. *Application Contact:* Dr. Edward VanVleet, Coordinator, 727-553-1165, Fax: 727-553-1189, E-mail: advisor@marine.usf.edu. *Dean,* Dr. Peter R. Betzer, 727-553-1130, Fax: 727-553-1189, E-mail: pbetzer@marine.usf.edu.

College of Nursing Students: 122 full-time (110 women), 206 part-time (186 women); includes 58 minority (30 African Americans, 1 American Indian/Alaska Native, 9 Asian Americans or Pacific Islanders, 18 Hispanic Americans), 1 international. Average age 33. 13 applicants, 100% accepted, 13 enrolled. *Faculty:* 41 full-time (36 women), 10 part-time/adjunct (8 women). Expenses: Contact institution. *Financial support:* Federal Work-Study, institutionally sponsored loans, scholarships/grants, traineeships, tuition waivers (partial), and unspecified assistantships available. Financial award application deadline: 2/1; financial award applicants required to submit FAFSA. In 2006, 58 master's, 3 doctorates awarded. *Degree program information:* Part-time programs available. Offers nursing (MS, PhD). *Application deadline:* For fall admission, 6/1 for domestic students, 6/15 for international students; for spring admission, 10/15 for domestic and international students. Applications are processed on a rolling basis. *Application fee:* $30. *Application Contact:* Carl H. Storck, Director of Student Affairs, 813-974-7513, Fax: 813-974-3118, E-mail: cstorck@hsc.usf.edu. *Dean,* Dr. Patricia A. Burns, 813-974-7813, Fax: 813-974-5418, E-mail: pburns@hsc.usf.edu.

College of Public Health Students: 292 full-time (196 women), 312 part-time (204 women); includes 161 minority (68 African Americans, 2 American Indian/Alaska Native, 39 Asian Americans or Pacific Islanders, 52 Hispanic Americans), 92 international. Average age 33. 319 applicants, 68% accepted, 105 enrolled. *Faculty:* 63 full-time (31 women), 22 part-time/adjunct (7 women). Expenses: Contact institution. *Financial support:* In 2006–07, 16 fellowships with full tuition reimbursements (averaging $10,006 per year), 88 research assistantships with full and partial tuition reimbursements (averaging $4,532 per year), 83 teaching assistantships (averaging $3,140 per year) were awarded; career-related internships or fieldwork, Federal Work-Study, institutionally sponsored loans, scholarships/grants, traineeships, and unspecified assistantships also available. Support available to part-time students. Financial award applicants required to submit FAFSA. In 2006, 132 master's, 17 doctorates awarded. *Degree program information:* Part-time and evening/weekend programs available. Postbaccalaureate distance learning degree programs offered (minimal on-campus study). Offers community and family health (MPH, MSPH, PhD); environmental and occupational health (MPH, MSPH, PhD); epidemiology and biostatistics (MPH, MSPH, PhD); global health (MPH, MSPH, PhD); health policy and management (MHA, MPH, MSPH, PhD); public health (MHA, MPH, MSPH, PhD); public health practice (MPH). *Application deadline:* For fall admission, 6/1 for domestic students, 1/2 for international students; for spring admission, 10/15 for domestic students, 7/1 for international students. Applications are processed on a rolling basis. *Application fee:* $30. Electronic applications accepted. *Application Contact:* Michelle Robinson, Academic Advisor, 813-974-6665, Fax: 813-974-8121, E-mail: mrobinso@health.usf.edu. *Dean,* Dr. Donna J. Petersen, 813-974-3623, Fax: 813-974-7390.

College of Visual and Performing Arts Expenses: Contact institution. *Financial support:* Fellowships with partial tuition reimbursements, research assistantships with partial tuition reimbursements, teaching assistantships with partial tuition reimbursements, scholarships/grants and unspecified assistantships available. Financial award applicants required to submit FAFSA. In 2006, 6 degrees awarded. *Degree program information:* Part-time and evening/weekend programs available. Offers art history (MA); chamber music (MM); composition (MM); conducting (MM); electro-acoustic music (MM); jazz studies (MM); performance (MM); piano pedagogy (MM); studio art (MFA); theory (MM); visual and performing arts (MA, MFA, MM). *Application deadline:* For fall admission, 2/15 for domestic students. *Application fee:* $30. *Application Contact:* Barton Lee, Associate Dean, 813-974-9126, Fax: 813-974-2091, E-mail: blee@arts.usf.edu. *Dean,* Ron Jones, 813-974-2301.

School of Architecture and Community Design Students: 77 full-time (22 women), 42 part-time (20 women); includes 27 minority (8 African Americans, 1 Asian American or Pacific Islander, 18 Hispanic Americans), 7 international. Average age 30. 68 applicants, 44% accepted, 16 enrolled. *Faculty:* 9 full-time (1 woman), 9 part-time/adjunct (3 women). Expenses: Contact institution. *Financial support:* Career-related internships or fieldwork, scholarships/grants, and unspecified assistantships available. In 2006, 48 degrees awarded. Offers architecture and community design (M Arch). *Application deadline:* For fall admission, 3/1 priority date for domestic students; for spring admission, 10/5 priority date for domestic students. Applications are processed on a rolling basis. *Application fee:* $30. Electronic applications accepted. *Application Contact:* Carol Trent, Admissions/Registrar Office, 813-974-4031, Fax: 813-974-2557, E-mail: trent@arch.usf.edu. *Director,* Stephen Schreiber, 813-974-4031, Fax: 813-974-2557, E-mail: schreiber@arch.usf.edu.

See Close-Up on page 1125.

THE UNIVERSITY OF TAMPA, Tampa, FL 33606-1490

General Information Independent, coed, comprehensive institution. *Enrollment:* 5,381 graduate, professional, and undergraduate students; 151 full-time matriculated graduate/professional students (60 women), 485 part-time matriculated graduate/professional students (245 women). *Enrollment by degree level:* 636 master's. *Graduate faculty:* 57 full-time (23 women), 22 part-time/adjunct (11 women). *Tuition:* Part-time $426 per credit hour. *Required fees:* $35 per year. *Graduate housing:* Room and/or apartments available on a first-come, first-served basis to single students; on-campus housing not available to married students. Typical cost: $8,710 per year ($6,936 including board). Housing application deadline: 5/15. *Student services:* Campus employment opportunities, campus safety program, career counseling, exercise/wellness program, free psychological counseling, international student services, writing training. *Library facilities:* Macdonald Keloe Library. *Online resources:* library catalog, web page. *Collection:* 288,857 titles, 24,122 serial subscriptions, 7,103 audiovisual materials. *Research affiliation:* Tampa General Hospital (nursing), Human Resources Institute.

Computer facilities: Computer purchase and lease plans are available. 493 computers available on campus for general student use. A campuswide network can be accessed from student residence rooms and from off campus. Internet access and online class registration are available. *Web address:* http://www.utampa.edu/.

General Application Contact: Barbara P. Strickler, Vice President for Enrollment, 888-646-2738, Fax: 813-258-7398, E-mail: admissions@ut.edu.

GRADUATE UNITS

John H. Sykes College of Business Students: 143 full-time (52 women), 381 part-time (158 women); includes 78 minority (18 African Americans, 3 American Indian/Alaska Native, 19 Asian Americans or Pacific Islanders, 38 Hispanic Americans), 89 international. Average age 31. 486 applicants, 59% accepted, 231 enrolled. *Faculty:* 39 full-time (9 women), 1 part-time/adjunct (0 women). Expenses: Contact institution. *Financial support:* In 2006–07, 57 students received support, including 57 research assistantships with tuition reimbursements available (averaging $3,000 per year); career-related internships or fieldwork and unspecified assistantships also available. Support available to part-time students. Financial award applicants required to submit FAFSA. In 2006, 127 degrees awarded. *Degree program information:* Part-time and evening/weekend programs available. Offers accounting (MBA, MS); economics (MBA); entrepreneurship (MBA); finance (MBA, MS); information systems management (MBA); innovation management (MS); international business (MBA); management (MBA); marketing (MBA, MS). *Application deadline:* For fall admission, 2/15 priority date for domestic students, 6/15 for international students; for spring admission, 12/15 for domestic students, 11/15 for international students. Applications are processed on a rolling basis. *Application fee:* $40. Electronic applications accepted. *Application Contact:* Fernais Nolasco, Director of Graduate Studies, 813-253-6211, Fax: 813-259-5403, E-mail: fnolasco@ut.edu. *Dean Graduate Studies,* Dr. William L. Rhey, 813-253-6211, Fax: 813-259-5403, E-mail: wrhey@ut.edu.

Nursing Program Students: 3 full-time (all women), 67 part-time (63 women); includes 2 minority (both African Americans), 1 international. Average age 40. 46 applicants, 61% accepted, 18 enrolled. *Faculty:* 5 full-time (all women), 10 part-time/adjunct (9 women). Expenses: Contact institution. *Financial support:* In 2006–07, 2 students received support, including 2 research assistantships with tuition reimbursements available (averaging $1,500 per year); career-related internships or fieldwork and unspecified assistantships also available. Support available to part-time students. Financial award applicants required to submit FAFSA. In 2006, 29 degrees awarded. *Degree program information:* Part-time and evening/weekend programs available. Offers adult nurse practitioner (MSN); family nurse practitioner (MSN); nursing administration (MSN); nursing education (MSN). *Application deadline:* For fall admission, 8/20 priority date for domestic students. Applications are processed on a rolling basis. *Application fee:* $40. Electronic applications accepted. *Application Contact:* Barbara P. Strickler, Vice President for Enrollment, 888-646-2738, Fax: 813-258-7398, E-mail: admissions@ut.edu. *Director,* Dr. Nancy Ross, 813-253-6223, Fax: 813-258-7214, E-mail: nross@ut.edu.

Program in Teaching 66 applicants, 71% accepted, 40 enrolled. Expenses: Contact institution. Offers education (MAT); math education (MAT); reading (M Ed); science education (MAT). *Application fee:* $40. *Associate Professor of Education,* Dr. Martine Harrison, 813-253-3333 Ext. 3373, E-mail: mharrison@ut.edu.

THE UNIVERSITY OF TENNESSEE, Knoxville, TN 37996

General Information State-supported, coed, university. CGS member. *Enrollment:* 28,901 graduate, professional, and undergraduate students; 3,946 full-time matriculated graduate/professional students (2,223 women), 2,095 part-time matriculated graduate/professional students (1,120 women). *Enrollment by degree level:* 718 first professional, 3,215 master's, 1,666 doctoral, 442 other advanced degrees. *Graduate faculty:* 1,381 full-time (478 women), 31 part-time/adjunct (17 women). Tuition, state resident: full-time $5,574. Tuition, nonresident: full-time $16,840. *Required fees:* $792. *Graduate housing:* Rooms and/or apartments available on a first-come, first-served basis to single and married students. Typical cost: $8,996 (including board) for single students; $436 per year for married students. Housing application deadline: 2/1. *Student services:* Campus employment opportunities, campus safety program, career counseling, disabled student services, exercise/wellness program, free psychological counseling, grant writing training, international student services, low-cost health insurance, multicultural affairs office, teacher training, writing training. *Library facilities:* John C. Hodges Library plus 6 others. *Online resources:* library catalog, web page, access to other libraries' catalogs. *Collection:* 24.4 million titles, 17,628 serial subscriptions. *Research affiliation:* Oak Ridge National Laboratory–Biology Division (engineering, science), Lockheed Martin Corporation (engineering), Exxon Corporation (materials science), Atlantic Richfield Company (chemistry), Control Data Corporation (engineering).

Computer facilities: Computer purchase and lease plans are available. 1,500 computers available on campus for general student use. A campuswide network can be accessed from student residence rooms and from off campus. Internet access and online class registration are available. *Web address:* http://www.tennessee.edu/.

General Application Contact: Michael Ickowitz, Associate Director Graduate and International Admissions, 865-974-3251, Fax: 865-974-6541, E-mail: graduateadmissions@utk.edu.

GRADUATE UNITS

College of Law Students: 449 full-time (226 women); includes 71 minority (61 African Americans, 2 American Indian/Alaska Native, 3 Asian Americans or Pacific Islanders, 5 Hispanic Americans). Average age 24. 1,390 applicants, 28% accepted, 151 enrolled. *Faculty:* 51 full-time (24 women), 66 part-time/adjunct (23 women). Expenses: Contact institution. *Financial support:* In 2006–07, 397 students received support, including 7 research assistantships with full tuition reimbursements available (averaging $4,400 per year); career-related internships or fieldwork, Federal Work-Study, institutionally sponsored loans, scholarships/grants, and unspecified assistantships also available. Support available to part-time students. Financial award application deadline: 3/1; financial award applicants required to submit FAFSA. In 2006, 136 degrees awarded. Offers law (JD). *Application deadline:* For fall admission, 3/1 priority date for domestic and international students. Applications are processed on a rolling basis. *Application fee:* $15. Electronic applications accepted. *Application Contact:* Janet S.

Hatcher, Admissions and Financial Aid Advisor, 865-974-4131, Fax: 865-974-1572, E-mail: hatcher@utk.edu. *Director of Admissions, Financial Aid and Career Services,* Dr. Karen R. Britton, 865-974-4131, Fax: 865-974-1572, E-mail: lawadmit@utk.edu.

Graduate School Students: 3,946 full-time (2,223 women), 2,095 part-time (1,120 women); includes 562 minority (384 African Americans, 19 American Indian/Alaska Native, 97 Asian Americans or Pacific Islanders, 62 Hispanic Americans), 810 international. Expenses: Contact institution. *Financial support:* In 2006–07, 967 research assistantships with full tuition reimbursements, 912 teaching assistantships with full tuition reimbursements were awarded; fellowships with full tuition reimbursements, career-related internships or fieldwork, Federal Work-Study, institutionally sponsored loans, and unspecified assistantships also available. Financial award application deadline: 2/1; financial award applicants required to submit FAFSA. In 2006, 212 first professional degrees, 1,579 master's, 236 doctorates awarded. *Degree program information:* Part-time and evening/weekend programs available. Postbaccalaureate distance learning degree programs offered (minimal on-campus study). Offers aviation systems (MS); comparative and experimental medicine (MS, PhD). *Application deadline:* Applications are processed on a rolling basis. Electronic applications accepted. *Application Contact:* Michael Ickowitz, Associate Director Graduate and International Admissions, 865-974-3251, Fax: 865-974-6541, E-mail: graduateadmissions@utk.edu. *Vice Provost and Dean, Graduate School,* Dr. Carolyn R. Hodges, 865-974-3694, Fax: 865-974-6541, E-mail: chodges@utk.edu.

College of Agricultural Sciences and Natural Resources Students: 116 full-time (52 women), 109 part-time (45 women); includes 10 minority (6 African Americans, 1 American Indian/Alaska Native, 2 Asian Americans or Pacific Islanders, 1 Hispanic American), 47 international. 186 applicants, 50% accepted. *Faculty:* 115 full-time (12 women). Expenses: Contact institution. *Financial support:* In 2006–07, 2 fellowships with full tuition reimbursements, 124 research assistantships with full tuition reimbursements, 23 teaching assistantships with full tuition reimbursements were awarded; career-related internships or fieldwork, Federal Work-Study, institutionally sponsored loans, and unspecified assistantships also available. Financial award application deadline: 2/1; financial award applicants required to submit FAFSA. In 2006, 53 master's, 10 doctorates awarded. *Degree program information:* Part-time programs available. Postbaccalaureate distance learning degree programs offered (minimal on-campus study). Offers agricultural education (MS); agricultural extension education (MS); agricultural sciences and natural resources (MS, PhD); animal anatomy (PhD); biosystems engineering (MS, PhD); biosystems engineering technology (MS); breeding (MS, PhD); entomology (MS, PhD); floriculture (MS); food science and technology (MS, PhD); forestry (MS); integrated pest management and bioactive natural products (PhD); landscape design (MS); management (MS, PhD); nutrition (MS, PhD); physiology (MS, PhD); plant pathology (MS, PhD); public horticulture (MS); turfgrass (MS); wildlife and fisheries science (MS); woody ornamentals (MS). *Application deadline:* For fall admission, 2/1 priority date for domestic students. Applications are processed on a rolling basis. *Application fee:* $35. Electronic applications accepted. *Dean,* Dr. Caula Beyl, 865-974-7303.

College of Architecture and Design Students: 26 full-time (11 women), 2 part-time (1 woman); includes 2 minority (1 African American, 1 Asian American or Pacific Islander). 96 applicants, 36% accepted. *Faculty:* 29 full-time (9 women), 7 part-time/adjunct (1 woman). Expenses: Contact institution. *Financial support:* In 2006–07, 10 teaching assistantships with tuition reimbursements were awarded; fellowships, research assistantships, Federal Work-Study, scholarships/grants, unspecified assistantships, and research/design internships also available. Financial award application deadline: 2/1; financial award applicants required to submit FAFSA. In 2006, 8 degrees awarded. Offers architecture (professional) (M Arch); architecture (research) (M Arch); landscape architecture (MLA); landscape architecture (research) (MA, MS). *Application deadline:* For fall admission, 2/1 priority date for domestic students. Applications are processed on a rolling basis. *Application fee:* $35. Electronic applications accepted. *Application Contact:* Marian Moffett, Interim Associate Dean, 865-974-3273, E-mail: mmoffett@utk.edu. *Interim Dean,* Dr. John McRae, 865-974-5265, Fax: 865-974-0656.

College of Arts and Sciences Students: 984 full-time (497 women), 426 part-time (184 women); includes 90 minority (40 African Americans, 4 American Indian/Alaska Native, 26 Asian Americans or Pacific Islanders, 20 Hispanic Americans), 253 international. *Faculty:* 629 full-time (224 women). Expenses: Contact institution. *Financial support:* In 2006–07, 133 fellowships, 232 research assistantships, 575 teaching assistantships were awarded; career-related internships or fieldwork, Federal Work-Study, institutionally sponsored loans, and unspecified assistantships also available. Financial award application deadline: 2/1; financial award applicants required to submit FAFSA. In 2006, 248 master's, 105 doctorates awarded. *Degree program information:* Part-time and evening/weekend programs available. Offers accompanying (MM); American history (PhD); analytical chemistry (MS, PhD); applied linguistics (PhD); applied mathematics (MS); archaeology (MA, PhD); arts and sciences (M Math, MA, MFA, MM, MPA, MS, PhD); audiology (MA, PhD); behavior (MS, PhD); biochemistry, cellular and molecular biology (MS, PhD); biological anthropology (MA, PhD); ceramics (MFA); chemical physics (PhD); choral conducting (MM); clinical psychology (PhD); composition (MM); computer science (MS, PhD); costume design (MFA); criminology (MA, PhD); cultural anthropology (MA, PhD); drawing (MFA); ecology (MS, PhD); energy, environment, and resource policy (MA, PhD); English (MA, PhD); environmental chemistry (MS, PhD); European history (PhD); evolutionary biology (MS, PhD); experimental psychology (MA, PhD); French (MA, PhD); genome science and technology (MS, PhD); geography (MS, PhD); geology (MS, PhD); German (MA, PhD); graphic design (MFA); hearing science (PhD); history (MA); inorganic chemistry (MS, PhD); instrumental conducting (MM); inter-area studies (MFA); Italian (PhD); jazz (MM); lighting design (MFA); mathematical ecology (PhD); mathematics (M Math, MS, PhD); media arts (MFA); medical ethics (MA, PhD); microbiology (MS, PhD); modern foreign languages (PhD); music education (MM); music theory (MM); musicology (MM); organic chemistry (MS, PhD); painting (MFA); performance (MFA, MM); philosophy (MA, PhD); physical chemistry (MS, PhD); physics (MS, PhD); piano pedagogy and literature (MM); plant physiology and genetics (MS, PhD); political economy (MA, PhD); political science (MA, PhD); polymer chemistry (MS, PhD); Portuguese (PhD); printmaking (MFA); psychology (MA); public administration (MPA); religious studies (MA); Russian (PhD); scene design (MFA); sculpture (MFA); Spanish (MA, PhD); speech and hearing science (PhD); speech and language pathology (PhD); speech and language science (PhD); speech pathology (MA); theatre technology (MFA); theoretical chemistry (PhD); watercolor (MFA); zoo-archaeology (MA, PhD). *Application deadline:* For fall admission, 2/1 for domestic students. *Application fee:* $35. Electronic applications accepted. *Dean,* Dr. Bruce Bursten, 865-974-5331.

College of Business Administration Students: 477 full-time (174 women), 57 part-time (29 women); includes 55 minority (31 African Americans, 4 American Indian/Alaska Native, 11 Asian Americans or Pacific Islanders, 9 Hispanic Americans), 91 international. *Faculty:* 102 full-time (26 women). Expenses: Contact institution. *Financial support:* In 2006–07, 9 fellowships, 6 research assistantships, 91 teaching assistantships were awarded; career-related internships or fieldwork, Federal Work-Study, institutionally sponsored loans, and unspecified assistantships also available. Financial award application deadline: 2/1; financial award applicants required to submit FAFSA. In 2006, 251 master's, 11 doctorates awarded. *Degree program information:* Part-time programs available. Postbaccalaureate distance learning degree programs offered (minimal on-campus study). Offers accounting (M Acc, PhD); business administration (M Acc, MA, MBA, MS, PhD); economics (MA, PhD); finance (MBA, PhD); industrial and organizational psychology (PhD); industrial statistics (MS); logistics and transportation (MBA, PhD); management (PhD); management science (MS, PhD); marketing (MBA, PhD); operations management (MBA); professional business administration (MBA); statistics (MS, PhD); systems (M Acc); taxation (M Acc); teacher licensure (MS); training and development (MS). *Application deadline:* For fall admission, 2/1 for domestic students. Applications are processed on a rolling basis. *Application fee:* $35. Electronic applications accepted. *Application Contact:* Dr. Sarah Gardial, Assistant Dean, 865-974-5033, Fax: 865-974-3826, E-mail: sgardial@utk.edu. *Dean,* Dr. Jan Williams, 865-974-5061.

College of Communication and Information Students: 118 full-time (85 women), 192 part-time (136 women); includes 24 minority (16 African Americans, 2 American Indian/Alaska Native, 5 Asian Americans or Pacific Islanders, 1 Hispanic American), 19 international. 153 applicants, 39% accepted. *Faculty:* 63 full-time (35 women). Expenses: Contact institution. *Financial support:* In 2006–07, 1 fellowship, 1 research assistantship, 19 teaching assistantships were awarded; career-related internships or fieldwork, Federal Work-Study, institutionally sponsored loans, and unspecified assistantships also available. Financial award application deadline: 2/1; financial award applicants required to submit FAFSA. In 2006, 86 master's, 5 doctorates awarded. *Degree program information:* Part-time and evening/weekend programs available. Postbaccalaureate distance learning degree programs offered (no on-campus study). Offers advertising (MS, PhD); broadcasting (MS, PhD); communications (MS, PhD); information sciences (MS, PhD); journalism (MS, PhD); public relations (MS, PhD); speech communication (MS, PhD). *Application deadline:* For fall admission, 2/1 priority date for domestic students. Applications are processed on a rolling basis. *Application fee:* $35. Electronic applications accepted. *Application Contact:* Dr. Edward Caudill, Head, 865-974-6651, Fax: 865-974-3896, E-mail: ccaudill@utk.edu. *Dean,* Dr. Michael Wirth, 865-974-3031, Fax: 865-974-3896.

College of Education, Health and Human Sciences Students: 641 full-time (476 women), 397 part-time (270 women); includes 83 minority (59 African Americans, 3 American Indian/Alaska Native, 12 Asian Americans or Pacific Islanders, 9 Hispanic Americans), 69 international. 701 applicants, 52% accepted. *Faculty:* 140 full-time (81 women). Expenses: Contact institution. *Financial support:* In 2006–07, 6 fellowships, 3 research assistantships, 46 teaching assistantships were awarded; career-related internships or fieldwork, Federal Work-Study, institutionally sponsored loans, and unspecified assistantships also available. Financial award application deadline: 2/1; financial award applicants required to submit FAFSA. In 2006, 499 master's, 52 doctorates awarded. *Degree program information:* Part-time and evening/weekend programs available. Postbaccalaureate distance learning degree programs offered (no on-campus study). Offers adult education (MS); applied educational psychology (MS); art education (MS); biomechanics/sports medicine (MS, PhD); child and family studies (MS, PhD); collaborative learning (Ed D); college student personnel (MS); community health (PhD); community health education (MPH); consumer services management (MS); counseling education (PhD); cultural studies in education (PhD); curriculum (MS, Ed S); curriculum, educational research and evaluation (Ed D, PhD); early childhood education (MS, PhD); early childhood special education (MS); education of deaf and hard of hearing (MS); education, health and human sciences (MPH, MS, Ed D, PhD, Ed S); educational administration and policy studies (Ed D, PhD); educational administration and supervision (MS, Ed S); educational psychology (Ed D, PhD); elementary education (MS, Ed S); elementary teaching (MS); English education (MS, Ed S); exercise physiology (MS, PhD); exercise science (MS, PhD); foreign language/ESL education (MS, Ed S); gerontology (MPH); health planning/administration (MPH); health promotion and health education (MS); hospitality management (MS); hotel, restaurant, and tourism management (MS); instructional technology (MS, Ed D, PhD, Ed S); literacy, language and ESL education (PhD); literacy, language education, and ESL education (Ed D); mathematics education (MS, Ed S); mental health counseling (MS); modified and comprehensive special education (MS); nutrition (MS); nutrition science (PhD); reading education (MS, Ed S); recreation and leisure studies (MS); rehabilitation counseling (MS); retail and consumer sciences (MS); retailing and consumer sciences (PhD); safety (MS); school counseling (MS, Ed S); school psychology (PhD, Ed S); science education (MS, Ed S); secondary teaching (MS); social foundations (MS); social science education (MS, Ed S); socio-cultural foundations of sports and education (PhD); special education (Ed S); sport management (MS); sport studies (MS, PhD); teacher education (Ed D, PhD); textile science (MS, PhD); therapeutic recreation (MS); tourism (MS). *Application deadline:* For fall admission, 2/1 priority date for domestic students. Applications are processed on a rolling basis. *Application fee:* $35. Electronic applications accepted. *Application Contact:* Dr. Tom George, Associate Dean, 865-974-0907, Fax: 865-974-8718, E-mail: tgeorge1@utk.edu. *Dean,* Dr. Robert Rider, 865-974-2201.

College of Engineering Students: 394 full-time (94 women), 396 part-time (64 women); includes 48 minority (22 African Americans, 2 American Indian/Alaska Native, 17 Asian Americans or Pacific Islanders, 7 Hispanic Americans), 288 international. 877 applicants, 58% accepted, 186 enrolled. *Faculty:* 114 full-time (6 women), 55 part-time/adjunct (2 women). Expenses: Contact institution. *Financial support:* Career-related internships or fieldwork, Federal Work-Study, institutionally sponsored loans, health care benefits, and unspecified assistantships available. Financial award application deadline: 2/1; financial award applicants required to submit FAFSA. In 2006, 171 master's, 37 doctorates awarded. *Degree program information:* Part-time and evening/weekend programs available. Postbaccalaureate distance learning degree programs offered. Offers aerospace engineering (MS, PhD); applied artificial intelligence (MS); biomedical engineering (MS, PhD); chemical engineering (MS, PhD); civil engineering (MS, PhD); composite materials (MS, PhD); computational mechanics (MS, PhD); computer engineering (MS, PhD); electrical engineering (MS, PhD); engineering (MS, PhD); engineering management (MS); engineering science (MS, PhD); environmental engineering (MS); fluid mechanics (MS, PhD); human factors engineering (MS); industrial engineering (MS, PhD); information engineering (MS); manufacturing systems engineering (MS); materials science and engineering (MS, PhD); mechanical engineering (MS, PhD); optical engineering (MS, PhD); polymer engineering (MS, PhD); radiological engineering (MS, PhD); solid mechanics (MS, PhD). *Application deadline:* For fall admission, 2/1 priority date for domestic and international students; for spring admission, 6/15 priority date for international students. Applications are processed on a rolling basis. *Application fee:* $35. Electronic applications accepted. *Application Contact:* Dr. Masood Parang, Associate Dean of Student Affairs, 865-974-2454, Fax: 865-974-9871, E-mail: mparang@utk.edu. *Dean,* Dr. Way Kuo, 865-974-5321, Fax: 865-974-8890, E-mail: way@utk.edu.

College of Nursing Students: 115 full-time (96 women), 62 part-time (55 women). *Faculty:* 41 full-time (38 women). Expenses: Contact institution. *Financial support:* In 2006–07, 3 fellowships, 1 research assistantship were awarded; teaching assistantships, Federal Work-Study, institutionally sponsored loans, and unspecified assistantships also available. Financial award application deadline: 2/1; financial award applicants required to submit FAFSA. In 2006, 57 master's, 5 doctorates awarded. *Degree program information:* Part-time programs available. Offers nursing (MSN, PhD). *Application deadline:* For fall admission, 2/1 priority date for domestic students. Applications are processed on a rolling basis. *Application fee:* $35. Electronic applications accepted. *Application Contact:* Dr. Martha Alligood, Graduate Representative, 865-974-7606, E-mail: stuservices@cn.gw.utk.edu. *Dean,* Dr. Joan L. Creasia, 865-974-4151, Fax: 865-974-3569, E-mail: jcreasia@utk.edu.

College of Social Work Students: 306 full-time (270 women), 141 part-time (121 women); includes 128 minority (118 African Americans, 4 Asian Americans or Pacific Islanders, 6 Hispanic Americans), 6 international. *Faculty:* 29 full-time (14 women). Expenses: Contact institution. *Financial support:* In 2006–07, 8 fellowships, 9 research assistantships were awarded; teaching assistantships, career-related internships or fieldwork, Federal Work-Study, institutionally sponsored loans, and unspecified assistantships also available. Financial award application deadline: 2/1; financial award applicants required to submit FAFSA. In 2006, 195 master's, 5 doctorates awarded. *Degree program information:* Part-time programs available. Offers clinical social work practice (MSSW); social welfare management and community practice (MSSW); social work (PhD). *Application deadline:* For fall admission, 2/1 priority date for domestic students. Applications are processed on a rolling basis. *Application fee:* $35. Electronic applications accepted. *Dean,* Dr. Karen Sowers, 865-974-3175, Fax: 865-974-4803, E-mail: kmsowers@utk.edu.

College of Veterinary Medicine Students: 274 full-time (215 women), 2 part-time (both women); includes 11 minority (4 African Americans, 3 Asian Americans or Pacific Islanders, 4 Hispanic Americans). *Faculty:* 92 full-time (35 women). Expenses: Contact institution. *Financial support:* In 2006–07, 1 fellowship, 10 research assistantships, 5 teaching assistantships were awarded; career-related internships or fieldwork, institutionally sponsored loans, and unspecified assistantships also available. Financial award application deadline: 2/1; financial award applicants required to submit FAFSA. In 2006, 65 degrees awarded. Offers veterinary medicine (DVM). *Application deadline:* For fall admission, 11/1 for domestic students. *Application fee:* $25. *Application Contact:* Dr. James Brace, Associate Dean, 865-974-7263, E-mail: jbrace@utk.edu. *Dean,* Dr. Michael J. Blackwell, 865-974-7263, Fax: 865-974-4773.

THE UNIVERSITY OF TENNESSEE AT CHATTANOOGA, Chattanooga, TN 37403-2598

General Information State-supported, coed, comprehensive institution. CGS member. *Enrollment:* 8,923 graduate, professional, and undergraduate students; 534 full-time matriculated graduate/professional students (352 women), 778 part-time matriculated graduate/professional students (452 women). *Enrollment by degree level:* 1,156 master's, 118 doctoral, 38 other advanced degrees. *Graduate faculty:* 145 full-time (59 women), 22 part-time/adjunct (7 women). Tuition, state resident: full-time $5,434; part-time $339 per hour. Tuition, nonresident: full-time $14,830; part-time $861 per hour. *Required fees:* $940; $178 per hour. *Graduate housing:* Room and/or apartments available on a first-come, first-served basis to single students. Typical cost: $4,884 per year ($7,384 including board). Housing application deadline: 8/1. *Student services:* Campus employment opportunities, campus safety program, career counseling, child daycare facilities, disabled student services, exercise/wellness program, free psychological counseling, international student services, teacher training, writing training. *Library facilities:* Lupton Library. *Online resources:* library catalog, web page, access to other libraries' catalogs. *Collection:* 491,179 titles, 1,847 serial subscriptions. *Research affiliation:* Gulf Coast Research Laboratory, Tennessee Valley Authority, Highland Biological Field Station (NC).

Computer facilities: 300 computers available on campus for general student use. A campuswide network can be accessed from student residence rooms and from off campus. Internet access and online class registration are available. *Web address:* http://www.utc.edu/.

General Application Contact: Dr. Deborah E. Arfken, Dean of Graduate Studies, 423-425-4666, Fax: 423-425-5223, E-mail: deborah-arfken@utc.edu.

GRADUATE UNITS

Graduate School Students: 534 full-time (352 women), 778 part-time (452 women); includes 178 minority (126 African Americans, 5 American Indian/Alaska Native, 30 Asian Americans or Pacific Islanders, 17 Hispanic Americans), 33 international. Average age 31. 583 applicants, 72% accepted, 222 enrolled. *Faculty:* 145 full-time (59 women), 22 part-time/adjunct (7 women). Expenses: Contact institution. *Financial support:* Fellowships, research assistantships, career-related internships or fieldwork, Federal Work-Study, institutionally sponsored loans, scholarships/grants, and unspecified assistantships available. Support available to part-time students. Financial award application deadline: 4/1; financial award applicants required to submit FAFSA. In 2006, 345 master's, 27 doctorates, 23 other advanced degrees awarded. *Degree program information:* Part-time and evening/weekend programs available. *Application deadline:* For fall admission, 8/1 priority date for domestic students; for spring admission, 12/1 priority date for domestic students. Applications are processed on a rolling basis. *Application fee:* $30. Electronic applications accepted. *Dean of Graduate Studies*, Dr. Deborah E. Arfken, 423-425-4666, Fax: 423-425-5223, E-mail: deborah-arfken@utc.edu.

College of Arts and Sciences Students: 115 full-time (80 women), 115 part-time (68 women); includes 39 minority (34 African Americans, 2 Asian Americans or Pacific Islanders, 3 Hispanic Americans), 1 international. Average age 28. 149 applicants, 85% accepted, 64 enrolled. *Faculty:* 54 full-time (11 women), 10 part-time/adjunct (2 women). Expenses: Contact institution. *Financial support:* Fellowships, research assistantships, Federal Work-Study and institutionally sponsored loans available. Financial award application deadline: 4/1; financial award applicants required to submit FAFSA. In 2006, 63 degrees awarded. *Degree program information:* Part-time and evening/weekend programs available. Offers arts and sciences (MA, MM, MPA, MS, MSCJ); criminal justice (MSCJ); English (MA); environmental sciences (MS); industrial/organizational psychology (MS); music (MM); public administration (MPA); research psychology (MS). *Application deadline:* For fall admission, 8/1 priority date for domestic students; for spring admission, 12/1 priority date for domestic students. Applications are processed on a rolling basis. *Application fee:* $30. *Application Contact:* Dr. Deborah E. Arfken, Dean of Graduate Studies, 423-425-4666, Fax: 423-425-5223, E-mail: deborah-arfken@utc.edu. *Acting Dean*, Dr. Charles Nelson, 423-425-4635, Fax: 423-425-4279, E-mail: charles-nelson@utc.edu.

College of Business Administration Students: 80 full-time (38 women), 213 part-time (82 women); includes 37 minority (24 African Americans, 8 Asian Americans or Pacific Islanders, 5 Hispanic Americans), 4 international. Average age 32. 115 applicants, 85% accepted, 60 enrolled. *Faculty:* 19 full-time (6 women), 2 part-time/adjunct (1 woman). Expenses: Contact institution. *Financial support:* Fellowships, research assistantships, Federal Work-Study and institutionally sponsored loans available. Support available to part-time students. Financial award application deadline: 4/1; financial award applicants required to submit FAFSA. In 2006, 91 degrees awarded. *Degree program information:* Part-time and evening/weekend programs available. Offers accountancy (M Acc); business administration (M Acc, MBA); general business administration (MBA). *Application deadline:* For fall admission, 8/1 priority date for domestic students; for spring admission, 12/1 priority date for domestic students. Applications are processed on a rolling basis. *Application fee:* $30. *Application Contact:* Dr. Deborah E. Arfken, Dean of Graduate Studies, 423-425-4666, Fax: 423-425-5223, E-mail: deborah-arfken@utc.edu. *Dean*, Dr. Richard P. Casavant, 423-425-4313, Fax: 423-425-5255, E-mail: richard-casavant@utc.edu.

College of Engineering and Computer Science Students: 34 full-time (4 women), 86 part-time (18 women); includes 25 minority (13 African Americans, 10 Asian Americans or Pacific Islanders, 2 Hispanic Americans), 22 international. Average age 31. 78 applicants, 59% accepted, 26 enrolled. *Faculty:* 19 full-time (3 women), 2 part-time/adjunct (0 women). Expenses: Contact institution. *Financial support:* Fellowships, research assistantships, Federal Work-Study and institutionally sponsored loans available. Support available to part-time students. Financial award application deadline: 4/1; financial award applicants required to submit FAFSA. In 2006, 8 master's, 1 doctorate, 2 other advanced degrees awarded. *Degree program information:* Part-time and evening/weekend programs available. Offers computational engineering (PhD); computer science (MS, Graduate Certificate); engineering (MS); engineering and computer science (MS, PhD, Graduate Certificate); engineering management (MS, Graduate Certificate). *Application deadline:* For fall admission, 8/1 priority date for domestic students; for spring admission, 12/1 priority date for domestic students. Applications are processed on a rolling basis. *Application fee:* $30. *Application Contact:* Dr. Deborah E. Arfken, Dean of Graduate Studies, 423-425-4666, Fax: 423-425-5223, E-mail: deborah-arfken@utc.edu. *Dean*, Dr. Ron Bailey, 423-425-2256, Fax: 423-425-5229, E-mail: ronald-bailey@utc.edu.

College of Health, Education and Professional Studies Students: 306 full-time (229 women), 374 part-time (294 women); includes 78 minority (55 African Americans, 4 American Indian/Alaska Native, 12 Asian Americans or Pacific Islanders, 7 Hispanic Americans), 2 international. Average age 33. 241 applicants, 63% accepted, 72 enrolled. *Faculty:* 51 full-time (36 women), 8 part-time/adjunct (4 women). Expenses: Contact institution. *Financial support:* Fellowships, research assistantships, Federal Work-Study and institutionally sponsored loans available. Support available to part-time students. Financial award application deadline: 4/1; financial award applicants required to submit FAFSA. In 2006, 183 master's, 26 doctorates, 27 other advanced degrees awarded. *Degree program information:* Part-time and evening/weekend programs available. Offers administration (MSN); adult health (MSN); counseling (M Ed); education (MSN); educational leadership (Ed D); educational specialist (Ed S); educational technology (Ed S); elementary education (M Ed); family nurse practitioner (MSN); health and human performance (MS); health, education and professional studies (M Ed, MS, MSN, DPT, Ed D, Ed S); nurse anesthesia (MSN); physical therapy (DPT); school leadership (M Ed); school psychology (Ed S); secondary education (M Ed); special education (M Ed). *Application deadline:* For fall admission, 8/1 priority date for domestic students; for spring admission, 12/1 priority date for domestic students. Applications are processed on a rolling basis. *Application fee:* $30. *Application Contact:* Dr. Deborah E. Arfken, Dean of Graduate Studies, 423-425-4666, Fax: 423-425-5223, E-mail: deborah-arfken@utc.edu. *Dean*, Dr. Mary Tanner, 423-425-4249, Fax: 423-425-4044, E-mail: mary-tanner@utc.edu.

Announcement: UTC offers 3 doctorates (computational engineering, learning and leadership, and physical therapy); one education specialist program; 18 master's programs; and certificate programs in accounting, business, computer science, counseling, criminal justice, education, engineering, engineering management, English, environmental science, health and human performance, music, nursing, psychology, and public administration. Concentrations are available: school leadership, MBA, executive MBA, industrial/organizational psychology, nurse anesthesia, family nurse practitioner studies, research psychology, community counseling, school counseling, school psychology, special education, elementary and secondary education, and teacher licensure. Emphasis on small classes/seminars. Graduate assistantships in every program. Excellent computer facilities. Scenic campus within walking distance of Chattanooga's business/tourist district. Easy driving to mountains, lakes, historic parks, major southern cities. www.utc.edu/GraduateSchool.

THE UNIVERSITY OF TENNESSEE AT MARTIN, Martin, TN 38238-1000

General Information State-supported, coed, comprehensive institution. *Enrollment:* 6,893 graduate, professional, and undergraduate students; 501 matriculated graduate/professional students (347 women). *Enrollment by degree level:* 501 master's. *Graduate faculty:* 151. Tuition, state resident: part-time $303 per credit hour. Tuition, nonresident: part-time $829 per credit hour. *Graduate housing:* Rooms and/or apartments guaranteed to single students and available to married students. Typical cost: $4,550 per year for married students. Room charges vary according to housing facility selected. Housing application deadline: 3/1. *Student services:* Campus employment opportunities, campus safety program, career counseling, child daycare facilities, disabled student services, exercise/wellness program, free psychological counseling, international student services, low-cost health insurance, multicultural affairs office, writing training. *Library facilities:* Paul Meek Library. *Online resources:* library catalog, web page, access to other libraries' catalogs. *Collection:* 488,807 titles, 2,016 serial subscriptions, 12,554 audiovisual materials. *Research affiliation:* University of Tennessee Research Foundation (science and technology), National Writing Project (humanities), Department of Education (academic extensions).

Computer facilities: 836 computers available on campus for general student use. A campuswide network can be accessed from student residence rooms and from off campus. Internet access and online class registration, online fee payments, grades, degree progress, financial aid data, housing applications, transcripts are available. *Web address:* http://www.utm.edu/.

General Application Contact: Linda S. Arant, Student Services Specialist, 731-881-7012, Fax: 731-881-7499, E-mail: larant@utm.edu.

GRADUATE UNITS

Graduate Programs Students: 501 (347 women); includes 63 African Americans. 213 applicants, 65% accepted, 97 enrolled. *Faculty:* 151. Expenses: Contact institution. *Financial support:* In 2006–07, 55 students received support, including 1 research assistantship with full tuition reimbursement available (averaging $4,219 per year), 6 teaching assistantships with full tuition reimbursements available (averaging $5,665 per year); career-related internships or fieldwork, scholarships/grants, tuition waivers (partial), and unspecified assistantships also available. Support available to part-time students. Financial award application deadline: 3/1. In 2006, 177 degrees awarded. *Degree program information:* Part-time programs available. Postbaccalaureate distance learning degree programs offered (no on-campus study). *Application deadline:* For fall admission, 8/1 priority date for domestic students, 8/1 for international students; for spring admission, 1/1 priority date for domestic students, 1/1 for international students. Applications are processed on a rolling basis. *Application fee:* $30 ($50 for international students). Electronic applications accepted. *Application Contact:* Linda S. Arant, Student Services Specialist, 731-881-7012, Fax: 731-881-7499, E-mail: larant@utm.edu. *Assistant Vice Chancellor and Dean of Graduate Studies*, Dr. Victoria S. Seng, 731-881-7012, Fax: 731-881-7499, E-mail: vseng@utm.edu.

College of Agriculture and Applied Sciences Students: 43 (34 women); includes 2 African Americans. 33 applicants, 73% accepted, 15 enrolled. *Faculty:* 23. Expenses: Contact institution. *Financial support:* In 2006–07, 5 students received support. Scholarships/grants, tuition waivers (partial), and unspecified assistantships available. Support available to part-time students. Financial award application deadline: 3/1. In 2006, 10 degrees awarded. *Degree program information:* Part-time programs available. Offers agricultural operations management (MSAOM); agriculture and applied sciences (MSAOM, MSFCS); dietetics (MSFCS); general family and consumer sciences (MSFCS). *Application deadline:* For fall admission, 8/1 priority date for domestic students, 8/1 for international students; for spring admission, 1/1 for domestic and international students. Applications are processed on a rolling basis. *Application fee:* $30 ($50 for international students). Electronic applications accepted. *Application Contact:* Linda S. Arant, Student Services Specialist, 731-881-7012, Fax: 731-881-7499, E-mail: larant@utm.edu. *Dean*, Dr. James Byford, 731-881-7250, E-mail: jbyford@utm.edu.

College of Business and Public Affairs Students: 120 (54 women); includes 8 African Americans. 60 applicants, 72% accepted, 35 enrolled. *Faculty:* 30. Expenses: Contact institution. *Financial support:* In 2006–07, 10 students received support, including 1 research assistantship with full tuition reimbursement available (averaging $4,219 per year), 1 teaching assistantship with full tuition reimbursement available (averaging $5,740 per year); career-related internships or fieldwork, tuition waivers (partial), and unspecified assistantships also available. Support available to part-time students. Financial award application deadline: 3/1. In 2006, 66 degrees awarded. *Degree program information:* Part-time programs available. Postbaccalaureate distance learning degree programs offered (no on-campus study). Offers accountancy (M Ac); business (MBA); business and public affairs (M Ac, MBA). *Application deadline:* For fall admission, 8/1 priority date for domestic students, 8/1 for international students; for spring admission, 1/1 priority date for domestic students, 8/1 for international students. Applications are processed on a rolling basis. *Application fee:* $30 ($50 for international students). Electronic applications accepted. *Application Contact:* Dr. Kevin Hammond, Coordinator, 731-881-7236, Fax: 731-881-7241, E-mail: bagrad@utm.edu. *Dean*, Dr. Ernest Moser, 731-881-7227, Fax: 731-881-7241, E-mail: emoser@utm.edu.

College of Education and Behavioral Sciences Students: 338 (259 women); includes 56 African Americans. 120 applicants, 60% accepted, 47 enrolled. *Faculty:* 48. Expenses: Contact institution. *Financial support:* In 2006–07, 30 students received support, including 6 teaching assistantships with full tuition reimbursements available (averaging $5,665 per year); career-related internships or fieldwork, scholarships/grants, tuition waivers (partial), and unspecified assistantships also available. Support available to part-time students. Financial award application deadline: 3/1. In 2006, 101 degrees awarded. *Degree program information:* Part-time programs available. Postbaccalaureate distance learning degree programs offered (minimal on-campus study). Offers advanced elementary (MS Ed); advanced secondary (MS Ed); education and behavioral sciences (MS Ed); educational administration and supervision (MS Ed); initial licensure comprehensive (MS Ed); initial licensure elementary (MS Ed); initial licensure secondary (MS Ed); mental health (MS Ed); school counseling (MS Ed). *Application deadline:* For fall admission, 8/1 priority date for domestic students, 8/1 for international students; for spring admission, 1/1 priority date for domestic students, 1/1 for international students. Applications are processed on a rolling basis. *Application fee:* $30 ($50 for international students). Electronic applications accepted. *Application Contact:* Dr. Suzanne Maniss, Coordinator, 731-881-7163, Fax: 731-881-7975, E-mail: smaniss@utm.edu. *Dean*, Dr. Mary Lee Hall, 731-881-7127, Fax: 731-881-7975, E-mail: mlhall@utm.edu.

THE UNIVERSITY OF TENNESSEE HEALTH SCIENCE CENTER, Memphis, TN 38163-0002

General Information State-supported, coed, upper-level institution. CGS member. *Enrollment by degree level:* 1,513 first professional, 150 master's, 312 doctoral. *Graduate faculty:* 745 full-time, 169 part-time/adjunct. Tuition, state resident: full-time $8,267. Tuition, nonresident: full-time $20,747. *Required fees:* $60. One-time fee: $55 full-time. *Graduate housing:* Room and/or apartments available on a first-come, first-served basis to single students; on-campus housing not available to married students. Typical cost: $3,600 per year. Housing application deadline: 2/28. *Student services:* Campus employment opportunities, campus safety program, career counseling, child daycare facilities, disabled student services, free psychological counseling, low-cost health insurance. *Library facilities:* Health Science Library plus 2 others.

Collection: 165,200 titles, 1,784 serial subscriptions. *Research affiliation:* Saint Jude's Children's Research Hospital, Veterans Administration Medical Center, LePasses Rehabilitation Center, LeBonheur Children's Medical Center.

Computer facilities: 100 computers available on campus for general student use. A campuswide network can be accessed from student residence rooms and from off campus. Internet access is available. *Web address:* http://www.utmem.edu/.

General Application Contact: Eunice Taylor, Interim Director, Enrollment Services, 901-448-5560, Fax: 901-448-7772, E-mail: etaylor@utmem.edu.

GRADUATE UNITS

College of Allied Health Sciences Students: 197 full-time (141 women), 5 part-time (4 women); includes 43 minority (29 African Americans, 1 American Indian/Alaska Native, 13 Asian Americans or Pacific Islanders). Average age 26. 225 applicants, 57% accepted, 120 enrolled. *Faculty:* 23 full-time (18 women), 23 part-time/adjunct (17 women). Expenses: Contact institution. *Financial support:* In 2006–07, 2 teaching assistantships were awarded; Federal Work-Study, institutionally sponsored loans, and scholarships/grants also available. Support available to part-time students. Financial award application deadline: 2/15; financial award applicants required to submit FAFSA. In 2006, 2 master's, 2 doctorates awarded. *Degree program information:* Part-time and evening/weekend programs available. Postbaccalaureate distance learning degree programs offered (minimal on-campus study). Offers allied health sciences (MCP, MDH, MHIIM, MOT, MSCLS, MSPT, DPT, ScDPT, TDPT). *Application deadline:* For fall admission, 1/30 priority date for domestic students; for winter admission, 10/1 priority date for domestic students. *Application fee:* $50. Electronic applications accepted. *Application Contact:* Eunice Taylor, Interim Director, Enrollment Services, 901-448-5560, Fax: 901-448-7772, E-mail: etaylor@utmem.edu. *Interim Dean,* Dr. William R. Frey, 901-528-5581, Fax: 901-528-7545, E-mail: wfrey@utmem.edu.

College of Dentistry Students: 357 full-time (149 women); includes 80 minority (42 African Americans, 32 Asian Americans or Pacific Islanders, 6 Hispanic Americans). Average age 23. 255 applicants, 37% accepted, 95 enrolled. *Faculty:* 57 full-time (8 women), 66 part-time/adjunct (6 women). Expenses: Contact institution. *Financial support:* In 2006–07, 278 students received support. Federal Work-Study and minority scholarships available. Support available to part-time students. Financial award application deadline: 2/15; financial award applicants required to submit FAFSA. In 2006, 72 DDSs, 6 master's awarded. Offers dentistry (DDS); oral and maxillofacial surgery (Certificate); orthodontics (MS); pediatric dentistry (MS, Certificate); periodontics (MS); prosthodontics (Certificate). *Application deadline:* For fall admission, 12/31 for domestic and international students. Applications are processed on a rolling basis. *Application fee:* $50. Electronic applications accepted. *Application Contact:* Dr. Wisdom F. Coleman, Admissions, Associate Dean, 901-448-4200, Fax: 901-448-1625, E-mail: wcoleman@utmem.edu. *Dean,* Dr. Russell O. Gilpatrick, 901-448-6202, Fax: 901-448-1625, E-mail: rgilpatrick@utmem.edu.

College of Graduate Health Sciences Students: 259 full-time (134 women), 29 part-time (16 women); includes 96 minority (29 African Americans, 59 Asian Americans or Pacific Islanders, 8 Hispanic Americans), 51 international. Average age 25. 673 applicants, 10% accepted, 67 enrolled. *Faculty:* 318 full-time (92 women), 59 part-time/adjunct (16 women). Expenses: Contact institution. *Financial support:* In 2006–07, 2 fellowships, 85 research assistantships, 40 teaching assistantships were awarded; career-related internships or fieldwork, Federal Work-Study, institutionally sponsored loans, and tuition waivers (full and partial) also available. Support available to part-time students. Financial award application deadline: 2/25; financial award applicants required to submit FAFSA. In 2006, 16 master's, 29 doctorates awarded. *Degree program information:* Part-time programs available. Offers anatomy and neurobiology (PhD); health sciences (MS, PhD); integrated program in biomedical sciences (MS, PhD); nursing (PhD); pharmaceutical sciences (MS, PhD). *Application deadline:* For fall admission, 5/15 priority date for domestic students. *Application fee:* $0. Electronic applications accepted. *Application Contact:* Eunice Taylor, Interim Director, Enrollment Services, 901-448-5560, Fax: 901-448-7772, E-mail: etaylor@utmem.edu. *Dean,* Dr. Richard Peppler, 901-448-5506.

College of Medicine Students: 611 full-time (245 women); includes 151 minority (64 African Americans, 4 American Indian/Alaska Native, 76 Asian Americans or Pacific Islanders, 7 Hispanic Americans). Average age 25. 1,355 applicants, 11% accepted. *Faculty:* 1,041 full-time (208 women), 990 part-time/adjunct (198 women). Expenses: Contact institution. *Financial support:* In 2006–07, 519 students received support. Career-related internships or fieldwork, Federal Work-Study, and institutionally sponsored loans available. Support available to part-time students. Financial award application deadline: 2/28. In 2006, 144 degrees awarded. Offers biomedical engineering (MS, PhD); medicine (MD, MS, PhD). *Application deadline:* For fall admission, 11/15 for domestic students. Applications are processed on a rolling basis. *Application fee:* $50. Electronic applications accepted. *Application Contact:* Eunice Taylor, Interim Director, Enrollment Services, 901-448-5560, Fax: 901-448-7772, E-mail: etaylor@utmem.edu. *Dean,* Dr. Steve J. Schwab, 901-448-5529, Fax: 901-448-7683, E-mail: jschwab@utmem.edu.

College of Nursing Students: 240 full-time (197 women), 1 (woman) part-time; includes 53 minority (47 African Americans, 1 Asian American or Pacific Islander, 5 Hispanic Americans). Average age 29. 225 applicants, 43% accepted, 79 enrolled. *Faculty:* 19 full-time (17 women), 8 part-time/adjunct (5 women). Expenses: Contact institution. *Financial support:* In 2006–07, 44 students received support; fellowships with partial tuition reimbursements available, teaching assistantships, Federal Work-Study, institutionally sponsored loans, scholarships/grants, and traineeships available. Support available to part-time students. Financial award application deadline: 2/28; financial award applicants required to submit FAFSA. In 2006, 31 master's, 5 doctorates awarded. Postbaccalaureate distance learning degree programs offered (minimal on-campus study). Offers nursing (MSN, DNP, PhD). *Application deadline:* For fall admission, 2/1 for domestic students; for winter admission, 9/1 for domestic students. *Application fee:* $50. Electronic applications accepted. *Application Contact:* Eunice Taylor, Interim Director, Enrollment Services, 901-448-5560, Fax: 901-448-7772, E-mail: etaylor@utmem.edu. *Dean,* Dr. Donna Hathaway, 901-448-6135, Fax: 901-448-4121, E-mail: dhathaway@utmem.edu.

College of Pharmacy Students: 699 full-time (449 women); includes 182 minority (101 African Americans, 4 American Indian/Alaska Native, 65 Asian Americans or Pacific Islanders, 12 Hispanic Americans). Average age 24. 850 applicants, 25% accepted, 215 enrolled. Expenses: Contact institution. *Financial support:* In 2006–07, 215 students received support; fellowships, research assistantships, teaching assistantships, career-related internships or fieldwork, Federal Work-Study, institutionally sponsored loans, and tuition waivers (full) available. Support available to part-time students. Financial award application deadline: 2/15. In 2006, 121 first professional degrees awarded. Offers pharmacy (Pharm D, MS, PhD). *Application deadline:* For fall admission, 2/1 for domestic students. Applications are processed on a rolling basis. *Application fee:* $50. Electronic applications accepted. *Application Contact:* Paula Webber, Enrollment Services Admissions Coordinator, 901-448-5560, E-mail: pwebber@utmem.edu. *Dean,* Dr. Dick R. Gourley, 901-528-6036, Fax: 901-528-7053, E-mail: rgourley@utmem.edu.

THE UNIVERSITY OF TENNESSEE–OAK RIDGE NATIONAL LABORATORY GRADUATE SCHOOL OF GENOME SCIENCE AND TECHNOLOGY, Oak Ridge, TN 37830-8026

General Information State-supported, coed, graduate-only institution. *Graduate housing:* Rooms and/or apartments available on a first-come, first-served basis to single and married students. *Research affiliation:* Oak Ridge National Laboratory.

GRADUATE UNITS

Graduate Program Offers life sciences (MS, PhD). Electronic applications accepted.

THE UNIVERSITY OF TENNESSEE SPACE INSTITUTE, Tullahoma, TN 37388-9700

General Information State-supported, coed, primarily men, graduate-only institution. *Graduate faculty:* 26 full-time (0 women), 10 part-time/adjunct (0 women). Tuition, state resident: full-time $5,574; part-time $310 per semester hour. Tuition, nonresident: full-time $16,840; part-time $920 per semester hour. *Graduate housing:* Room and/or apartments available on a first-come, first-served basis to single students; on-campus housing not available to married students. Typical cost: $3,360 per year. *Student services:* Campus employment opportunities, career counseling, free psychological counseling, international student services, low-cost health insurance, writing training. *Library facilities:* UTSI Library. *Collection:* 24,674 titles, 158 serial subscriptions, 80 audiovisual materials. *Research affiliation:* U.S. Air Force–Arnold Engineering Development Center, Technical University (Aachen, Germany).

Computer facilities: 25 computers available on campus for general student use. A campuswide network can be accessed from student residence rooms and from off campus. Internet access is available. *Web address:* http://www.utsi.edu/.

General Application Contact: Callie Taylor, Coordinator II, 931-393-7432, Fax: 931-393-7346, E-mail: ctaylor@utsi.edu.

GRADUATE UNITS

Graduate Programs Students: 52 full-time (11 women), 126 part-time (17 women); includes 5 minority (1 African American, 3 Asian Americans or Pacific Islanders, 1 Hispanic American), 14 international. *Faculty:* 26 full-time (0 women), 10 part-time/adjunct (0 women). Expenses: Contact institution. *Financial support:* In 2006–07, 9 fellowships with full and partial tuition reimbursements, 35 research assistantships with full tuition reimbursements (averaging $18,234 per year) were awarded; career-related internships or fieldwork, Federal Work-Study, tuition waivers (full and partial), and unspecified assistantships also available. Financial award applicants required to submit FAFSA. In 2006, 33 master's, 2 doctorates awarded. *Degree program information:* Part-time programs available. Postbaccalaureate distance learning degree programs offered. Offers aerospace engineering (MS, PhD); applied mathematics (MS); aviation systems (MS); electrical engineering and computer science (MS, PhD); engineering and applied science (MS, PhD); engineering management (MS, PhD); engineering sciences (MS, PhD); material science and engineering (MS); mechanical engineering (MS, PhD); mechanics (MS, PhD); physics (MS, PhD). *Application deadline:* For fall admission, 2/1 for international students; for spring admission, 6/15 for international students. Applications are processed on a rolling basis. *Application fee:* $35. Electronic applications accepted. *Application Contact:* Callie Taylor, Coordinator II, 931-393-7432, Fax: 931-393-7346, E-mail: ctaylor@utsi.edu. *Dean for Academic Affairs,* Dr. Bruce Bomar, 931-394-7456, Fax: 931-394-7211, E-mail: bbomar@utsi.edu.

THE UNIVERSITY OF TEXAS AT ARLINGTON, Arlington, TX 76019

General Information State-supported, coed, university. CGS member. *Enrollment:* 24,825 graduate, professional, and undergraduate students; 2,364 full-time matriculated graduate/professional students (1,093 women), 3,230 part-time matriculated graduate/professional students (1,884 women). *Enrollment by degree level:* 4,719 master's, 875 doctoral. *Graduate faculty:* 336 full-time (90 women), 66 part-time/adjunct (25 women). *International tuition:* $10,608 full-time. Tuition, state resident: full-time $5,528. Tuition, nonresident: full-time $10,478. *Graduate housing:* Rooms and/or apartments available on a first-come, first-served basis to single and married students. Typical cost: $3,046 per year ($5,533 including board) for single students; $3,046 per year ($5,533 including board) for married students. *Student services:* Campus employment opportunities, campus safety program, career counseling, child daycare facilities, disabled student services, exercise/wellness program, free psychological counseling, international student services, multicultural affairs office, teacher training, writing training. *Library facilities:* Central Library plus 2 others. *Online resources:* library catalog, web page, access to other libraries' catalogs. *Collection:* 1.2 million titles, 40,965 serial subscriptions, 9,200 audiovisual materials.

Computer facilities: 1,000 computers available on campus for general student use. A campuswide network can be accessed from student residence rooms and from off campus. Internet access and online class registration are available. *Web address:* http://www.uta.edu/.

General Application Contact: Dr. Phil Cohen, Dean of Graduate Studies, 817-272-3186, Fax: 817-272-2625, E-mail: graduate.school@uta.edu.

GRADUATE UNITS

Graduate School Students: 2,555 full-time (1,174 women), 3,205 part-time (1,864 women); includes 1,260 minority (526 African Americans, 24 American Indian/Alaska Native, 335 Asian Americans or Pacific Islanders, 375 Hispanic Americans), 1,639 international. Average age 36. 3,568 applicants, 81% accepted, 1427 enrolled. *Faculty:* 336 full-time (90 women), 66 part-time/adjunct (25 women). Expenses: Contact institution. *Financial support:* Fellowships, research assistantships, teaching assistantships, career-related internships or fieldwork, Federal Work-Study, institutionally sponsored loans, scholarships/grants, traineeships, and tuition waivers (partial) available. Financial award application deadline: 6/1; financial award applicants required to submit FAFSA. In 2006, 1,883 master's, 83 doctorates awarded. *Degree program information:* Part-time and evening/weekend programs available. Postbaccalaureate distance learning degree programs offered (no on-campus study). Offers interdisciplinary studies (MA, MS). *Application deadline:* For fall admission, 6/16 for domestic students. Applications are processed on a rolling basis. *Application fee:* $35 ($50 for international students). *Dean of Graduate Studies,* Dr. Phil Cohen, 817-272-3186, Fax: 817-272-2625, E-mail: graduate.school@uta.edu.

College of Business Administration Students: 368 full-time (162 women), 715 part-time (321 women); includes 281 minority (81 African Americans, 5 American Indian/Alaska Native, 127 Asian Americans or Pacific Islanders, 68 Hispanic Americans), 220 international. Average age 31. 785 applicants, 82% accepted, 339 enrolled. *Faculty:* 65 full-time (14 women), 8 part-time/adjunct (1 woman). Expenses: Contact institution. *Financial support:* In 2006–07, 100 students received support, including 5 fellowships (averaging $1,000 per year), 14 research assistantships (averaging $6,432 per year), 80 teaching assistantships (averaging $10,000 per year); career-related internships or fieldwork, Federal Work-Study, institutionally sponsored loans, and scholarships/grants also available. Financial award application deadline: 6/1; financial award applicants required to submit FAFSA. In 2006, 546 master's, 11 doctorates awarded. *Degree program information:* Part-time and evening/weekend programs available. Postbaccalaureate distance learning degree programs offered (no on-campus study). Offers accounting (MP Acc, MS, PhD); business administration (PhD); business statistics (PhD); economics (MA); finance (MBA); health care administration (MS); human resources (MSHRM); information systems (MBA, MS, PhD); management (MBA); management sciences (MBA); marketing (MBA, PhD); marketing research (MS); quantitative finance (MS); real estate (MBA, MS); taxation (MS). *Application deadline:* For fall admission, 6/15 for domestic students, 4/1 for international students; for spring admission, 10/15 for domestic students, 9/1 for international students. Applications are processed on a rolling basis. *Application fee:* $35 ($50 for international students). *Application Contact:* Alisa Johnson, Director, 817-272-3004, Fax: 817-272-5799, E-mail: question@uta.edu. *Dean,* Dr. Daniel Himarios, 817-272-2881, Fax: 817-272-2073, E-mail: himarios@uta.edu.

College of Education Students: 171 full-time (107 women), 579 part-time (474 women); includes 278 minority (130 African Americans, 6 American Indian/Alaska Native, 20 Asian Americans or Pacific Islanders, 122 Hispanic Americans), 40 international. Average age 36. 579 applicants, 88% accepted, 368 enrolled. *Faculty:* 19 full-time (11 women), 3 part-time/adjunct (2 women). Expenses: Contact institution. *Financial support:* In 2006–07, 11 fellowships (averaging $1,000 per year), teaching assistantships with tuition reimbursements (averaging $9,000 per year) were awarded; career-related internships or fieldwork, Federal Work-Study, scholarships/grants, and unspecified assistantships also available. Financial award application deadline: 6/1; financial award applicants required to submit FAFSA. In 2006, 101 degrees awarded. *Degree program information:* Part-time and evening/weekend programs available. Postbaccalaureate distance learning degree programs offered (minimal on-campus study). Offers curriculum and instruction (M Ed); educational leadership and policy studies (M Ed); physiology of exercise (MS); teaching (M Ed T). *Application deadline:* For fall admission, 6/16 priority date for domestic students, 4/9 priority date for international students; for winter admission, 10/22 priority date for domestic students, 9/10 priority date for international students; for spring admission, 3/25 priority date for domestic and international students. Applications are processed on a rolling basis. *Application fee:* $35 ($50 for international students). Electronic applications accepted. *Application Contact:* Brendan

The University of Texas at Arlington (continued)

Hardy, Graduate Advisor, 817-272-2956, Fax: 817-272-7624, E-mail: coedadvising@uta.edu. *Dean,* Dr. Jeanne M. Gerlach, 817-272-2591, Fax: 817-272-2530, E-mail: soeadvising@uta.edu.

College of Engineering Students: 828 full-time (183 women), 566 part-time (117 women); includes 279 minority (30 African Americans, 214 Asian Americans or Pacific Islanders, 35 Hispanic Americans), 864 international. Average age 28. 1,788 applicants, 71% accepted, 359 enrolled. *Faculty:* 96 full-time (7 women), 6 part-time/adjunct (2 women). Expenses: Contact institution. *Financial support:* Fellowships, research assistantships, teaching assistantships, career-related internships or fieldwork, Federal Work-Study, institutionally sponsored loans, scholarships/grants, and tuition waivers (partial) available. Financial award application deadline: 6/1; financial award applicants required to submit FAFSA. In 2006, 409 master's, 32 doctorates awarded. *Degree program information:* Part-time programs available. Offers aerospace engineering (M Engr, MS, PhD); biomedical engineering (MS, PhD); civil and environmental engineering (M Engr, MS, PhD); computer science and engineering (M Engr, M Sw En, MCS, MS, PhD); electrical engineering (M Engr, MS, PhD); engineering (M Engr, M Sw En, MCS, MS, PhD); engineering management (MS); industrial and manufacturing systems engineering (M Engr, PhD); logistics (MS); materials science and engineering (M Engr, MS, PhD); mechanical engineering (M Engr, MS, PhD); systems engineering (MS). *Application deadline:* For fall admission, 6/16 for domestic students. Applications are processed on a rolling basis. *Application fee:* $35 ($50 for international students). *Application Contact:* Dr. Lynn L. Peterson, Associate Dean for Academic Affairs, 817-272-2571, Fax: 817-272-2548, E-mail: peterson@uta.edu. *Dean,* Dr. Bill D. Carroll, 817-272-2571, Fax: 817-272-5110, E-mail: carroll@uta.edu.

College of Liberal Arts Students: 143 full-time (92 women), 429 part-time (246 women); includes 90 minority (31 African Americans, 3 American Indian/Alaska Native, 22 Asian Americans or Pacific Islanders, 34 Hispanic Americans), 83 international. Average age 35. 276 applicants, 87% accepted, 157 enrolled. *Faculty:* 39 full-time (11 women), 6 part-time/adjunct (2 women). Expenses: Contact institution. *Financial support:* Fellowships, research assistantships, teaching assistantships, career-related internships or fieldwork, Federal Work-Study, institutionally sponsored loans, and scholarships/grants available. Financial award application deadline: 3/1; financial award applicants required to submit FAFSA. In 2006, 62 master's, 2 doctorates awarded. Offers anthropology (MA); communication (MA); criminology and criminal justice (MA); English (MA); French (MA); history (MA); humanities (MA); liberal arts (MA, MM, PhD); linguistics (MA, PhD); literature (PhD); music (MM); political science (MA); rhetoric (PhD); sociology (MA); Spanish (MA); teaching English to speakers of other languages (MA); transatlantic history (PhD). *Application deadline:* For fall admission, 6/16 for domestic students. Applications are processed on a rolling basis. *Application fee:* $35 ($50 for international students). *Application Contact:* Dr. Kimberly Van Noort, Associate Dean, 817-272-3291, E-mail: vannoort@uta.edu. *Dean,* Dr. Beth S. Wright, 817-272-3291, Fax: 817-272-3255, E-mail: bwright@uta.edu.

College of Science Students: 265 full-time (118 women), 125 part-time (77 women); includes 60 minority (15 African Americans, 2 American Indian/Alaska Native, 20 Asian Americans or Pacific Islanders, 23 Hispanic Americans), 148 international. Average age 32. 250 applicants, 68% accepted, 97 enrolled. *Faculty:* 44 full-time (6 women), 5 part-time/adjunct (2 women). Expenses: Contact institution. *Financial support:* In 2006–07, 27 fellowships (averaging $1,000 per year), 61 research assistantships (averaging $14,000 per year), 102 teaching assistantships (averaging $15,500 per year) were awarded; career-related internships or fieldwork, Federal Work-Study, institutionally sponsored loans, scholarships/grants, tuition waivers (partial), and unspecified assistantships also available. Financial award application deadline: 6/1; financial award applicants required to submit FAFSA. In 2006, 44 master's, 12 doctorates awarded. *Degree program information:* Part-time and evening/weekend programs available. Offers applied chemistry (PhD); biology (MS); chemistry (MS); environmental and earth sciences (MS, PhD); environmental science (MS, PhD); experimental psychology (PhD); geology (MS); interdisciplinary science (MA); math: geoscience (PhD); mathematical sciences (PhD); mathematics (MS); physics (MS); physics and applied physics (PhD); psychology (MS); quantitative biology (PhD); science (MA, MS, PhD). *Application deadline:* For fall admission, 6/16 for domestic students. Applications are processed on a rolling basis. *Application fee:* $35 ($50 for international students). *Application Contact:* Dr. Robert F. McMahon, Director, 817-272-3492, Fax: 817-272-3511, E-mail: r.mcmahon@uta.edu. *Interim Dean,* Dr. Paul Paulus, 817-272-3491, Fax: 817-272-3511, E-mail: paulus@uta.edu.

School of Architecture Students: 121 full-time (47 women), 36 part-time (19 women); includes 30 minority (4 African Americans, 4 Asian Americans or Pacific Islanders, 22 Hispanic Americans), 17 international. Average age 30. 90 applicants, 70% accepted, 43 enrolled. *Faculty:* 18 full-time (2 women), 6 part-time/adjunct (0 women). Expenses: Contact institution. *Financial support:* In 2006–07, 5 fellowships with partial tuition reimbursements (averaging $1,000 per year), 2 research assistantships with partial tuition reimbursements (averaging $5,700 per year), 8 teaching assistantships with partial tuition reimbursements (averaging $5,700 per year) were awarded; career-related internships or fieldwork, Federal Work-Study, scholarships/grants, health care benefits, tuition waivers (partial), and unspecified assistantships also available. Support available to part-time students. Financial award application deadline: 6/1; financial award applicants required to submit FAFSA. In 2006, 48 degrees awarded. *Degree program information:* Part-time and evening/weekend programs available. Offers architecture (M Arch, MLA); landscape architecture (MLA). *Application deadline:* For fall admission, 6/16 for domestic students. Applications are processed on a rolling basis. *Application fee:* $35 ($50 for international students). Electronic applications accepted. *Application Contact:* David Jones, Associate Dean, 817-272-2801, Fax: 817-272-5098, E-mail: djonesarch@uta.edu. *Director,* Donald Gatzke, 817-272-2801, Fax: 817-272-5098, E-mail: gatzke@uta.edu.

School of Nursing Students: 52 full-time (50 women), 334 part-time (310 women); includes 86 minority (37 African Americans, 6 American Indian/Alaska Native, 24 Asian Americans or Pacific Islanders, 19 Hispanic Americans), 18 international. Average age 37. 178 applicants, 96% accepted, 117 enrolled. *Faculty:* 22 full-time (21 women), 11 part-time/adjunct (10 women). Expenses: Contact institution. *Financial support:* In 2006–07, 37 students received support, including 24 fellowships with partial tuition reimbursements available (averaging $3,000 per year), 6 research assistantships (averaging $7,992 per year), 7 teaching assistantships (averaging $10,080 per year); career-related internships or fieldwork and traineeships also available. Financial award application deadline: 6/1; financial award applicants required to submit FAFSA. In 2006, 30 degrees awarded. *Degree program information:* Part-time and evening/weekend programs available. Offers administration/supervision of nursing (MSN); nurse practitioner (MSN); nursing science (PhD); teaching of nursing (MSN). *Application deadline:* For fall admission, 6/16 for domestic students. Applications are processed on a rolling basis. *Application fee:* $35 ($50 for international students). *Application Contact:* Dr. Susan Grove, Graduate Adviser, 817-272-2776, Fax: 817-272-5006, E-mail: grove@uta.edu. *Dean,* Dr. Elizabeth C. Poster, 817-272-2776, Fax: 817-272-5006, E-mail: poster@uta.edu.

School of Social Work Students: 341 full-time (301 women), 257 part-time (222 women); includes 212 minority (127 African Americans, 7 American Indian/Alaska Native, 17 Asian Americans or Pacific Islanders, 61 Hispanic Americans), 34 international. Average age 32. 253 applicants, 93% accepted, 185 enrolled. *Faculty:* 26 full-time (12 women), 10 part-time/adjunct (8 women). Expenses: Contact institution. *Financial support:* In 2006–07, 355 students received support, including 14 fellowships (averaging $1,000 per year), 10 teaching assistantships (averaging $8,000 per year); research assistantships, career-related internships or fieldwork, Federal Work-Study, institutionally sponsored loans, scholarships/grants, and unspecified assistantships also available. Financial award application deadline: 6/1; financial award applicants required to submit FAFSA. In 2006, 136 master's, 5 doctorates awarded. *Degree program information:* Part-time and evening/weekend programs available. Postbaccalaureate distance learning degree programs offered (minimal on-campus study). Offers social work (MSSW, PhD). *Application deadline:* For fall admission, 3/15 for domestic students. *Application fee:* $35 ($50 for international students). *Application Contact:* Darlene Santee, Director of admissions, 817-272-3613, Fax: 817-272-5229. *Dean,* Dr. Santos H. Hernandez, 817-272-3181, Fax: 817-272-5229, E-mail: herns@uta.edu.

School of Urban and Public Affairs Students: 75 full-time (33 women), 189 part-time (98 women); includes 77 minority (39 African Americans, 1 American Indian/Alaska Native, 7 Asian Americans or Pacific Islanders, 30 Hispanic Americans), 33 international. Average age 34. 144 applicants, 92% accepted, 74 enrolled. *Faculty:* 11 full-time (4 women), 5 part-time/adjunct (0 women). Expenses: Contact institution. *Financial support:* In 2006–07, 10 fellowships (averaging $1,500 per year), 5 research assistantships (averaging $4,000 per year) were awarded; teaching assistantships, career-related internships or fieldwork and Federal Work-Study also available. Financial award application deadline: 6/1; financial award applicants required to submit FAFSA. In 2006, 42 master's, 1 doctorate awarded. *Degree program information:* Part-time and evening/weekend programs available. Offers city and regional planning (MCRP); public administration (MPA); urban and public affairs (MA, MCRP, MPA, PhD). *Application deadline:* For fall admission, 6/16 for domestic students. *Application fee:* $35 ($50 for international students). *Application Contact:* Linda Slaughter, Administrative Clerk, 817-272-3071, Fax: 817-272-5008, E-mail: slaughter@uta.edu. *Dean,* Dr. Richard Cole, 817-272-3071, Fax: 817-272-3255, E-mail: cole@uta.edu.

THE UNIVERSITY OF TEXAS AT AUSTIN, Austin, TX 78712-1111

General Information State-supported, coed, university. CGS member. *Graduate housing:* Rooms and/or apartments available to single students and available on a first-come, first-served basis to married students.

GRADUATE UNITS

College of Pharmacy Offers pharmacy (Pharm D, MS Phr, PhD). Electronic applications accepted.

Graduate School *Degree program information:* Part-time and evening/weekend programs available. Offers computational and applied mathematics (MA, PhD); Russian, East European and Eurasian studies (MA); science and technology commercialization (MS); writing (MFA). Electronic applications accepted.

Cockrell School of Engineering *Degree program information:* Part-time and evening/weekend programs available. Offers aerospace engineering (MSE, PhD); architectural engineering (MSE); biomedical engineering (MSE, PhD); chemical engineering (MSE, PhD); civil engineering (MSE, PhD); electrical and computer engineering (MSE, PhD); energy and mineral resources (MA, MS); engineering (MA, MS, MSE, PhD); engineering mechanics (MSE, PhD); environmental and water resources engineering (MSE); manufacturing systems engineering (MSE); materials science and engineering (MSE, PhD); mechanical engineering (MSE, PhD); operations research and industrial engineering (MSE, PhD); petroleum and geosystems engineering (MSE, PhD). Electronic applications accepted.

College of Communication *Degree program information:* Part-time programs available. Offers advertising (MA, PhD); communication (MA, MFA, PhD); communication sciences and disorders (MA, PhD); communication studies (MA, PhD); film/video production (MFA); journalism (MA, PhD); radio-television-film (MA, PhD). Electronic applications accepted.

College of Education *Degree program information:* Part-time programs available. Offers academic educational psychology (M Ed, MA); counseling education (M Ed); counseling psychology (PhD); curriculum and instruction (M Ed, MA, Ed D, PhD); education (M Ed, MA, MHRDL, Ed D, PhD); educational administration (M Ed, Ed D, PhD); foreign language education (MA, PhD); health education (M Ed, MA, Ed D, PhD); human development and education (PhD); kinesiology (M Ed, MA, Ed D, PhD); learning cognition and instruction (PhD); mathematics education (M Ed, MA, PhD); quantitative methods (PhD); school psychology (PhD); science education (M Ed, MA, PhD); special education (M Ed, MA, Ed D, PhD). Electronic applications accepted.

College of Fine Arts *Degree program information:* Part-time programs available. Offers art education (MA); art history (MA, PhD); dance (MFA); design (MFA); fine arts (M Music, MA, MFA, DMA, PhD); music (M Music, DMA, PhD); studio art (MFA); theatre (MA, MFA, PhD). Electronic applications accepted.

College of Liberal Arts *Degree program information:* Part-time programs available. Offers American studies (MA, PhD); Arabic studies (MA, PhD); archaeology (MA, PhD); Asian cultures and languages (MA, PhD); Asian studies (MA, PhD); classics (MA, PhD); comparative literature (MA, PhD); economics (MA, MS Econ, PhD); English (MA, PhD); folklore and public culture (MA, PhD); French (MA, PhD); geography (MA, PhD); Germanic studies (MA, PhD); government (MA, PhD); Hebrew studies (MA, PhD); Hispanic literature (MA, PhD); history (MA, PhD); Ibero-Romance philology and linguistics (MA, PhD); Latin American studies (MA, PhD); liberal arts (MA, MS Econ, PhD); linguistic anthropology (MA, PhD); linguistics (MA, PhD); Luso-Brazilian literature (MA, PhD); Middle Eastern studies (MA, PhD); Persian studies (MA, PhD); philosophy (MA, PhD); physical anthropology (MA, PhD); psychology (PhD); Romance linguistics (MA, PhD); Slavic languages and literatures (MA, PhD); social anthropology (MA, PhD); sociology (MA, PhD). Electronic applications accepted.

College of Natural Sciences *Degree program information:* Part-time programs available. Offers analytical chemistry (MA, PhD); astronomy (MA, PhD); biochemistry (MA, PhD); biological sciences (MA, PhD); cell and molecular biology (PhD); cellular and molecular biology (PhD); child development and family relations (MA, PhD); computer sciences (MA, MSCS, PhD); ecology, evolution and behavior (PhD); genetics and developmental biology (PhD); geological sciences (MA, MS, PhD); inorganic chemistry (MA, PhD); marine science (MS, PhD); mathematics (MA, PhD); microbiology (MA, PhD); microbiology and immunology (PhD); natural sciences (MA, MS, MS Stat, MSCS, PhD); nutrition (MA); nutritional sciences (MA, PhD); organic chemistry (MA, PhD); physical chemistry (MA, PhD); physics (MA, MS, PhD); plant biology (MA, PhD); statistics (MS Stat). Electronic applications accepted.

Graduate School of Library and Information Science *Degree program information:* Part-time programs available. Offers library and information science (MLIS, PhD). Electronic applications accepted.

The Institute for Neuroscience Offers neuroscience (MA, PhD). Electronic applications accepted.

Lyndon B. Johnson School of Public Affairs *Degree program information:* Part-time programs available. Offers public affairs (MP Aff); public policy (PhD). Electronic applications accepted.

McCombs School of Business Offers accounting (MPA, PhD); business (MBA); business administration (MBA, MHRDL, MPA, PhD); finance (PhD); human resource development leadership (MHRDL); management (PhD); management sciences and information systems (PhD); marketing administration (PhD). Electronic applications accepted.

School of Architecture Offers architecture (M Arch, MLA, MS Arch St, MSCRP, PhD); community and regional planning (MSCRP, PhD). Electronic applications accepted.

School of Nursing *Degree program information:* Part-time programs available. Offers nursing (MSN, PhD). Electronic applications accepted.

School of Social Work *Degree program information:* Part-time programs available. Offers social work (MSSW, PhD).

School of Law Students: 1,365 full-time (556 women); includes 416 minority (77 African Americans, 8 American Indian/Alaska Native, 73 Asian Americans or Pacific Islanders, 258 Hispanic Americans). Average age 24. 4,999 applicants, 22% accepted, 433 enrolled. *Faculty:* 124 full-time (39 women), 41 part-time/adjunct (16 women). Expenses: Contact institution. *Financial support:* In 2006–07, 1,167 students received support, including 100 research assistantships, 32 teaching assistantships (averaging $3,900 per year); career-related internships or fieldwork, scholarships/grants, and tuition waivers (full) also available. Financial award application deadline: 3/31; financial award applicants required to submit FAFSA. In 2006, 542 JDs, 24 master's awarded. Offers law (JD, LL M). *Application deadline:* For fall admission, 2/1 for domestic students. *Application fee:* $70. Electronic applications accepted. *Application Contact:* 512-232-1200, Fax: 512-471-2765, E-mail: admissions@law.texas.edu. *Interim Dean,* Lawrence Sager, 512-232-1120, Fax: 512-471-6987, E-mail: lsager@law.utexas.edu.

THE UNIVERSITY OF TEXAS AT BROWNSVILLE, Brownsville, TX 78520-4991

General Information State-supported, coed, upper-level institution. CGS member. *Graduate housing:* Room and/or apartments available to single students; on-campus housing not available to married students.

GRADUATE UNITS

Graduate Studies *Degree program information:* Part-time and evening/weekend programs available. Postbaccalaureate distance learning degree programs offered (no on-campus study).

College of Liberal Arts *Degree program information:* Part-time and evening/weekend programs available. Offers behavioral sciences (MAIS); English (MA); government (MAIS); history (MAIS); interdisciplinary studies (MAIS); liberal arts (MA, MAIS, MPPM); public policy and management (MPPM); Spanish (MA).

College of Science, Mathematics and Technology *Degree program information:* Part-time and evening/weekend programs available. Offers biological sciences (MS, MSIS); mathematics (MS); physics (MS).

School of Business *Degree program information:* Part-time and evening/weekend programs available. Postbaccalaureate distance learning degree programs offered (minimal on-campus study). Offers business (MBA).

School of Education *Degree program information:* Part-time and evening/weekend programs available. Postbaccalaureate distance learning degree programs offered (minimal on-campus study). Offers bilingual education (M Ed); counseling and guidance (M Ed); curriculum and instruction (M Ed); early childhood education (M Ed); educational administration (M Ed); educational technology (M Ed); English as a second language (M Ed); reading specialist (M Ed); special education/educational diagnostician (M Ed).

School of Health Sciences Offers health sciences (MSN).

THE UNIVERSITY OF TEXAS AT DALLAS, Richardson, TX 75083-0688

General Information State-supported, coed, university. CGS member. *Enrollment:* 14,523 graduate, professional, and undergraduate students; 2,169 full-time matriculated graduate/professional students (954 women), 2,268 part-time matriculated graduate/professional students (990 women). *Enrollment by degree level:* 3,517 master's, 920 doctoral. *Graduate faculty:* 369 full-time (79 women), 25 part-time/adjunct (5 women). *Graduate housing:* Rooms and/or apartments available on a first-come, first-served basis to single and married students. Typical cost: $6,540 (including board) for single students; $6,540 (including board) for married students. *Student services:* Campus employment opportunities, campus safety program, career counseling, child daycare facilities, disabled student services, exercise/wellness program, free psychological counseling, grant writing training, international student services, low-cost health insurance, multicultural affairs office, teacher training, writing training. *Library facilities:* Eugene McDermott Library plus 1 other. *Online resources:* library catalog, web page, access to other libraries' catalogs. *Collection:* 1.5 million titles, 197,047 serial subscriptions, 6,117 audiovisual materials.

Computer facilities: 630 computers available on campus for general student use. A campuswide network can be accessed from student residence rooms and from off campus. Internet access and online class registration, wireless network are available. *Web address:* http://www.utdallas.edu/.

General Application Contact: Dr. Austin Cunningham, Dean for Graduate Studies, 972-883-2234.

GRADUATE UNITS

Erik Jonsson School of Engineering and Computer Science Students: 636 full-time (146 women), 336 part-time (80 women); includes 120 minority (10 African Americans, 97 Asian Americans or Pacific Islanders, 13 Hispanic Americans), 670 international. Average age 27. 1,560 applicants, 53% accepted, 382 enrolled. *Faculty:* 89 full-time (8 women), 3 part-time/adjunct (0 women). Expenses: Contact institution. *Financial support:* In 2006–07, 220 research assistantships with full tuition reimbursements (averaging $17,819 per year), 90 teaching assistantships with full tuition reimbursements (averaging $17,417 per year) were awarded; fellowships with full tuition reimbursements, career-related internships or fieldwork, Federal Work-Study, institutionally sponsored loans, and scholarships/grants also available. Support available to part-time students. Financial award application deadline: 4/30; financial award applicants required to submit FAFSA. In 2006, 291 master's, 44 doctorates awarded. *Degree program information:* Part-time and evening/weekend programs available. Offers computer engineering (MS, PhD); computer science (MS, PhD); electrical engineering (MSEE, PhD); engineering and computer science (MS, MSEE, MSTE, PhD); materials science engineering (MS, PhD); microelectronics (MSEE, PhD); software engineering (MS, PhD); telecommunications (MSEE, MSTE, PhD). *Application deadline:* For fall admission, 7/15 for domestic students; for spring admission, 11/15 for domestic students. Applications are processed on a rolling basis. *Application fee:* $50 ($100 for international students). Electronic applications accepted. *Application Contact:* Lin Maute, Administrative Assistant, 972-883-6851, Fax: 972-883-2813, E-mail: gradecs@utdallas.edu. *Dean,* Dr. Robert Helms, 972-883-2974, Fax: 972-883-2813, E-mail: ecsdean@utdallas.edu.

School of Arts and Humanities Students: 189 full-time (103 women), 208 part-time (125 women); includes 93 minority (31 African Americans, 4 American Indian/Alaska Native, 27 Asian Americans or Pacific Islanders, 31 Hispanic Americans), 33 international. Average age 37. 181 applicants, 75% accepted, 91 enrolled. *Faculty:* 48 full-time (16 women), 4 part-time/adjunct (1 woman). Expenses: Contact institution. *Financial support:* In 2006–07, 2 research assistantships with tuition reimbursements (averaging $14,851 per year), 77 teaching assistantships with tuition reimbursements (averaging $9,585 per year) were awarded; fellowships, Federal Work-Study, institutionally sponsored loans, and scholarships/grants also available. Support available to part-time students. Financial award application deadline: 4/30; financial award applicants required to submit FAFSA. In 2006, 63 master's, 7 doctorates awarded. *Degree program information:* Part-time and evening/weekend programs available. Offers arts and technology (MFA); humanities (MA, MAT, PhD). *Application deadline:* For fall admission, 7/15 for domestic students; for spring admission, 11/15 for domestic students. Applications are processed on a rolling basis. *Application fee:* $50 ($100 for international students). Electronic applications accepted. *Application Contact:* Dr. W. Jackson Rushing, Associate Dean of Graduate Studies, 972-883-2226, Fax: 972-883-2989, E-mail: jackson.rushing@utdallas.edu. *Dean,* Dr. Dennis M. Kratz, 972-883-2984, Fax: 972-883-2989, E-mail: dkratz@utdallas.edu.

School of Behavioral and Brain Sciences Students: 306 full-time (266 women), 72 part-time (57 women); includes 62 minority (10 African Americans, 28 Asian Americans or Pacific Islanders, 24 Hispanic Americans), 45 international. Average age 28. 441 applicants, 47% accepted, 147 enrolled. *Faculty:* 37 full-time (18 women), 2 part-time/adjunct (0 women). Expenses: Contact institution. *Financial support:* In 2006–07, 21 research assistantships with tuition reimbursements (averaging $12,048 per year), 47 teaching assistantships with tuition reimbursements (averaging $10,018 per year) were awarded; fellowships, career-related internships or fieldwork, Federal Work-Study, institutionally sponsored loans, and scholarships/grants also available. Support available to part-time students. Financial award application deadline: 4/30; financial award applicants required to submit FAFSA. In 2006, 135 master's, 16 doctorates awarded. *Degree program information:* Part-time and evening/weekend programs available. Offers audiology (Au D); behavioral and brain sciences (MS, Au D, PhD); cognition and neuroscience (MS, PhD); communication disorders (MS); communication sciences (PhD); early childhood disorders (MS); psychological sciences (MS, PhD). *Application deadline:* For fall admission, 7/15 for domestic students; for spring admission, 11/15 for domestic students. Applications are processed on a rolling basis. *Application fee:* $50 ($100 for international students). Electronic applications accepted. *Application Contact:* Dr. Robert D. Stillman, Head, 972-883-3106, Fax: 972-883-3022, E-mail: stillman@utdallas.edu. *Dean,* Dr. Bert Moore, 972-883-2355, Fax: 972-883-2491, E-mail: bmoore@utdallas.edu.

School of Economic, Political and Policy Sciences Students: 182 full-time (79 women), 219 part-time (117 women); includes 106 minority (50 African Americans, 2 American Indian/Alaska Native, 24 Asian Americans or Pacific Islanders, 30 Hispanic Americans), 91 international. Average age 35. 336 applicants, 76% accepted, 165 enrolled. *Faculty:* 53 full-time (15 women), 1 (woman) part-time/adjunct. Expenses: Contact institution. *Financial support:* In 2006–07, 22 research assistantships with tuition reimbursements (averaging $11,085 per year), 80 teaching assistantships with tuition reimbursements (averaging $10,907 per year) were awarded; fellowships, career-related internships or fieldwork, Federal Work-Study, institutionally sponsored loans, and scholarships/grants also available. Support available to part-time students. Financial award application deadline: 4/30; financial award applicants required to submit FAFSA. In 2006, 67 master's, 9 doctorates awarded. *Degree program information:* Part-time and evening/weekend programs available. Offers applied economics (MS); economic, political and policy sciences (MPA, MPP, MS, PhD); economics (PhD); geospatial information sciences (MS, PhD); international political economy (MS); political science (PhD); public affairs (MPA, PhD); public policy (MPP); public policy and political economy (PhD); sociology (MS). *Application deadline:* For fall admission, 7/15 for domestic students; for spring admission, 11/15 for domestic students. Applications are processed on a rolling basis. *Application fee:* $50 ($100 for international students). Electronic applications accepted. *Application Contact:* Dr. Euel Elliot, Director of Graduate Studies, 972-883-2066, Fax: 972-883-2735, E-mail: eelliott@utdallas.edu. *Dean,* Dr. Brian Berry, 972-883-4932, Fax: 972-883-2735, E-mail: brian.berry@utdallas.edu.

School of General Studies Students: 17 full-time (15 women), 40 part-time (28 women); includes 25 minority (15 African Americans, 1 American Indian/Alaska Native, 3 Asian Americans or Pacific Islanders, 6 Hispanic Americans), 3 international. Average age 38. 59 applicants, 75% accepted, 26 enrolled. *Faculty:* 4 full-time (2 women), 1 (woman) part-time/adjunct. Expenses: Contact institution. *Financial support:* Fellowships, research assistantships, teaching assistantships with tuition reimbursements, career-related internships or fieldwork, Federal Work-Study, institutionally sponsored loans, and scholarships/grants available. Support available to part-time students. Financial award application deadline: 4/30; financial award applicants required to submit FAFSA. In 2006, 12 degrees awarded. *Degree program information:* Part-time and evening/weekend programs available. Offers interdisciplinary studies (MA). *Application deadline:* For fall admission, 7/15 for domestic students; for spring admission, 11/15 for domestic students. Applications are processed on a rolling basis. *Application fee:* $50 ($100 for international students). Electronic applications accepted. *Application Contact:* Janet Carden, Administrative Assistant, 972-883-2350, Fax: 972-883-2440, E-mail: gs-grad-info@utdallas.edu. *Dean,* Dr. George Fair, 972-883-2350, Fax: 972-883-2440, E-mail: gwfair@utdallas.edu.

School of Management Students: 615 full-time (246 women), 1,240 part-time (500 women); includes 523 minority (94 African Americans, 1 American Indian/Alaska Native, 312 Asian Americans or Pacific Islanders, 116 Hispanic Americans), 544 international. Average age 31. 1,724 applicants, 73% accepted, 746 enrolled. *Faculty:* 70 full-time (12 women), 6 part-time/adjunct (2 women). Expenses: Contact institution. *Financial support:* In 2006–07, 12 research assistantships with tuition reimbursements (averaging $9,916 per year), 11 teaching assistantships with tuition reimbursements (averaging $13,359 per year) were awarded; fellowships, career-related internships or fieldwork, Federal Work-Study, institutionally sponsored loans, and scholarships/grants also available. Support available to part-time students. Financial award application deadline: 4/30; financial award applicants required to submit FAFSA. In 2006, 716 master's, 23 doctorates awarded. *Degree program information:* Part-time and evening/weekend programs available. Postbaccalaureate distance learning degree programs offered. Offers accounting and information management (MS); business administration (EMBA, MBA); information technology and management (MS); international management studies (MA, PhD); management (EMBA, MA, MBA, MS, PhD); management and administrative science (MS); management science (PhD); medical management (MS). *Application deadline:* For fall admission, 7/15 for domestic students; for spring admission, 11/15 for domestic students. Applications are processed on a rolling basis. *Application fee:* $50 ($100 for international students). Electronic applications accepted. *Application Contact:* David B. Ritchey, Director of Advising, 972-883-2701, Fax: 972-883-6425, E-mail: davidr@utdallas.edu. *Dean,* Dr. Hasan Pirkul, 972-883-2705, Fax: 972-883-2799, E-mail: hpirkul@utdallas.edu.

School of Natural Sciences and Mathematics Students: 224 full-time (99 women), 153 part-time (83 women); includes 82 minority (15 African Americans, 1 American Indian/Alaska Native, 43 Asian Americans or Pacific Islanders, 23 Hispanic Americans), 154 international. Average age 32. 565 applicants, 64% accepted, 198 enrolled. *Faculty:* 68 full-time (8 women), 8 part-time/adjunct (0 women). Expenses: Contact institution. *Financial support:* In 2006–07, 58 research assistantships with tuition reimbursements (averaging $13,117 per year), 91 teaching assistantships with tuition reimbursements (averaging $10,981 per year) were awarded; fellowships, career-related internships or fieldwork, Federal Work-Study, institutionally sponsored loans, scholarships/grants, and unspecified assistantships also available. Support available to part-time students. Financial award application deadline: 4/30. In 2006, 85 master's, 25 doctorates awarded. *Degree program information:* Part-time and evening/weekend programs available. Offers applied mathematics (MS, PhD); applied physics (MS); bioinformatics and computational biology (MS); biotechnology (MS); chemistry (MS, PhD); engineering mathematics (MS); geosciences (MS, PhD); mathematical science (MS); mathematics education (MAT); molecular and cell biology (MS, PhD); natural sciences and mathematics (MAT, MS, PhD); physics (PhD); science education (MAT); statistics (MS, PhD). *Application deadline:* For fall admission, 7/15 for domestic students; for spring admission, 11/15 for domestic students. Applications are processed on a rolling basis. *Application fee:* $50 ($100 for international students). Electronic applications accepted. *Dean,* Dr. Myrm B. Salamon, 972-883-2416, Fax: 972-883-6371, E-mail: salamon@utdallas.edu.

THE UNIVERSITY OF TEXAS AT EL PASO, El Paso, TX 79968-0001

General Information State-supported, coed, university. CGS member. *Graduate housing:* Room and/or apartments available on a first-come, first-served basis to single students; on-campus housing not available to married students. Housing application deadline: 5/1.

GRADUATE UNITS

Graduate School *Degree program information:* Part-time and evening/weekend programs available. Postbaccalaureate distance learning degree programs offered. Offers environmental science and engineering (PhD); materials science and engineering (PhD). Electronic applications accepted.

College of Business Administration *Degree program information:* Part-time and evening/weekend programs available. Postbaccalaureate distance learning degree programs offered. Offers accounting (MACY); business administration (MACY, MBA, MS); economics and finance (MS). Electronic applications accepted.

College of Education *Degree program information:* Part-time and evening/weekend programs available. Offers education (M Ed, MA, Ed D); educational administration (M Ed, MA, Ed D); educational curriculum and instruction (M Ed, MA). Electronic applications accepted.

College of Engineering *Degree program information:* Part-time and evening/weekend programs available. Offers civil engineering (MS, PhD); computer engineering (MS, PhD); computer science (MS); electrical engineering (MS); engineering (MEENE, MIT, MS, MSENE, PhD); environmental engineering (MEENE, MSENE); industrial engineering (MS); information technology (MIT); mechanical engineering (MS); metallurgical engineering (MS). Electronic applications accepted.

College of Health Sciences *Degree program information:* Part-time and evening/weekend programs available. Postbaccalaureate distance learning degree programs offered. Offers allied health (MPT, MS); community health (MSN); community health/family nurse practitioner (MSN); health and physical education (MS); health sciences (MPT, MS, MSN); kinesiology and sports studies (MS); nurse midwifery (MSN); nursing administration (MSN); nursing-clinical (MSN); physical therapy (MPT); post master's nursing (MSN); speech language pathology (MS); women's health care (MSN). Electronic applications accepted.

College of Liberal Arts *Degree program information:* Part-time and evening/weekend programs available. Offers art (MA); border history (MA); clinical psychology (MA); communication (MA); creative writing in English (MFA); creative writing in Spanish (MFA); English and American literature (MA); experimental psychology (MA); history (MA, PhD);

The University of Texas at El Paso (continued)
liberal arts (MA, MAIS, MAT, MFA, MM, MPA, PhD); linguistics (MA); music education (MM); music performance (MM); political science (MA, MPA); professional writing and rhetoric (MA); psychology (PhD); sociology (MA); Spanish (MA); teaching English (MAT); theatre arts (MA). Electronic applications accepted.

College of Science *Degree program information:* Part-time and evening/weekend programs available. Offers bioinformatics (MS); biological science (MS, PhD); chemistry (MS); environmental science and engineering (PhD); geological sciences (MS, PhD); geophysics (MS); interdisciplinary studies (MSIS); mathematical sciences (MAT); mathematics (MS); physics (MS); science (MAT, MS, MSIS, PhD); statistics (MS). Electronic applications accepted.

THE UNIVERSITY OF TEXAS AT SAN ANTONIO, San Antonio, TX 78249-0617

General Information State-supported, coed, university. CGS member. *Enrollment:* 28,380 graduate, professional, and undergraduate students; 1,283 full-time matriculated graduate/professional students (667 women), 2,565 part-time matriculated graduate/professional students (1,578 women). *Enrollment by degree level:* 3,424 master's, 424 doctoral. *Graduate faculty:* 435 full-time (161 women), 66 part-time/adjunct (16 women). Tuition, state resident: full-time $1,730; part-time $192 per credit hour. Tuition, nonresident: full-time $6,680; part-time $742 per credit hour. *Required fees:* $733; $308,359 per credit hour. *Graduate housing:* Rooms and/or apartments available on a first-come, first-served basis to single and married students. Typical cost: $4,950 per year ($6,630 including board) for single students; $7,560 per year ($9,240 including board) for married students. Room and board charges vary according to board plan and housing facility selected. *Student services:* Campus employment opportunities, campus safety program, career counseling, child daycare facilities, disabled student services, exercise/wellness program, free psychological counseling, grant writing training, international student services, low-cost health insurance, multicultural affairs office, writing training. *Library facilities:* UTSA Library plus 1 other. *Online resources:* library catalog, web page. *Collection:* 730,678 titles, 24,042 serial subscriptions, 47,499 audiovisual materials. *Research affiliation:* Southwest Research Center (engineering).

Computer facilities: 800 computers available on campus for general student use. A campuswide network can be accessed from student residence rooms. Internet access and online class registration are available. *Web address:* http://www.utsa.edu/.

General Application Contact: Dr. Dorothy A. Flannagan, Dean of the Graduate School, 210-458-4330, Fax: 210-458-4332, E-mail: dorothy.flannagan@utsa.edu.

GRADUATE UNITS

College of Business Students: 305 full-time (116 women), 470 part-time (187 women); includes 284 minority (23 African Americans, 60 Asian Americans or Pacific Islanders, 201 Hispanic Americans), 109 international. Average age 31. 536 applicants, 68% accepted, 342 enrolled. *Faculty:* 66 full-time (16 women), 19 part-time/adjunct (4 women). Expenses: Contact institution. *Financial support:* In 2006–07, 36 research assistantships (averaging $23,004 per year), 76 teaching assistantships (averaging $17,659 per year) were awarded; career-related internships or fieldwork, Federal Work-Study, scholarships/grants, and unspecified assistantships also available. Support available to part-time students. Financial award application deadline: 3/31. In 2006, 265 master's, 11 doctorates awarded. *Degree program information:* Part-time and evening/weekend programs available. Offers accounting (MS, PhD); applied statistics (PhD); business (MA, MBA, MS, MSIT, MSMOT, MT, PhD); business economics (MBA); business finance (MBA); economics (MA); finance (MS, PhD); information systems (MBA, PhD); information technology (MSIT); international business (MBA); management (PhD); management accounting (MBA); management science (MBA); management technology (MSMOT); marketing management (MBA); statistics (MS); taxation (MBA, MT). *Application deadline:* For fall admission, 7/1 for domestic students, 4/1 for international students; for spring admission, 11/1 for domestic students, 9/1 for international students. Applications are processed on a rolling basis. *Application fee:* $45 ($80 for international students). Electronic applications accepted. *Application Contact:* Dr. Dorothy A. Flannagan, Dean of the Graduate School, 210-458-4330, Fax: 210-458-4332, E-mail: dorothy.flannagan@utsa.edu. *Dean,* Dr. Lynda Y. de la Viña, 210-458-4317, Fax: 210-458-4308, E-mail: lynda.delavina@utsa.edu.

College of Education and Human Development Students: 297 full-time (224 women), 1,169 part-time (927 women); includes 802 minority (93 African Americans, 6 American Indian/Alaska Native, 22 Asian Americans or Pacific Islanders, 681 Hispanic Americans), 20 international. Average age 34. 560 applicants, 88% accepted, 478 enrolled. *Faculty:* 73 full-time (51 women), 33 part-time/adjunct (10 women). Expenses: Contact institution. *Financial support:* In 2006–07, 3 fellowships (averaging $38,007 per year), 32 research assistantships (averaging $25,064 per year), 14 teaching assistantships (averaging $17,086 per year) were awarded; career-related internships or fieldwork, Federal Work-Study, scholarships/grants, and unspecified assistantships also available. In 2006, 356 master's, 12 doctorates awarded. *Degree program information:* Part-time and evening/weekend programs available. Offers bicultural studies (MA); bicultural-bilingual studies (MA); counseling (MA); counselor education (PhD); culture, literacy, and language (PhD); curriculum and instruction (MA); early childhood and elementary education (MA); education and human development (MA, Ed D, PhD); education-adult and higher education (MA); educational leadership (Ed D); educational leadership and policy studies (MA); educational psychology/special education (MA); instructional technology (MA); reading and literacy (MA); teaching English as a second language (MA). *Application deadline:* For fall admission, 7/1 for domestic students, 4/1 for international students; for spring admission, 11/1 for domestic students, 9/1 for international students. Applications are processed on a rolling basis. *Application fee:* $45 ($80 for international students). Electronic applications accepted. *Dean,* Dr. Betty M. Merchant, 210-458-4370, Fax: 210-458-4487, E-mail: bmerchant@utsa.edu.

College of Engineering Students: 103 full-time (25 women), 122 part-time (29 women); includes 70 minority (12 African Americans, 21 Asian Americans or Pacific Islanders, 37 Hispanic Americans), 95 international. Average age 28. 244 applicants, 86% accepted, 197 enrolled. *Faculty:* 35 full-time (3 women), 5 part-time/adjunct (0 women). Expenses: Contact institution. *Financial support:* In 2006–07, 2 fellowships (averaging $38,822 per year), 26 research assistantships (averaging $28,524 per year), 33 teaching assistantships (averaging $20,793 per year) were awarded; career-related internships or fieldwork, institutionally sponsored loans, and scholarships/grants also available. Financial award application deadline: 3/31. In 2006, 37 master's, 3 doctorates awarded. *Degree program information:* Part-time and evening/weekend programs available. Offers biomedical engineering (PhD); civil engineering (MSCE); electrical engineering (MSEE, PhD); engineering (MSCE, MSEE, MSME, PhD); mechanical engineering (MSME). *Application deadline:* For fall admission, 7/1 for domestic students, 4/1 for international students; for spring admission, 11/1 for domestic students, 9/1 for international students. Applications are processed on a rolling basis. *Application fee:* $45 ($80 for international students). Electronic applications accepted. *Dean,* Dr. C. Mauli Agarwal, 210-458-5526, Fax: 210-458-5556, E-mail: mauli.agarwal@utsa.edu.

College of Liberal and Fine Arts Students: 161 full-time (91 women), 328 part-time (198 women); includes 233 minority (17 African Americans, 2 American Indian/Alaska Native, 10 Asian Americans or Pacific Islanders, 204 Hispanic Americans), 11 international. Average age 33. 306 applicants, 72% accepted, 211 enrolled. *Faculty:* 109 full-time (50 women), 6 part-time/adjunct (2 women). Expenses: Contact institution. *Financial support:* In 2006–07, 36 research assistantships (averaging $22,377 per year), 40 teaching assistantships (averaging $16,458 per year) were awarded; career-related internships or fieldwork, Federal Work-Study, institutionally sponsored loans, scholarships/grants, tuition waivers (partial), and unspecified assistantships also available. Support available to part-time students. In 2006, 91 degrees awarded. *Degree program information:* Part-time and evening/weekend programs available. Offers anthropology (MA, PhD); art history (MA); communication (MA); English (MA, PhD); Hispanic culture (MA); history (MA); liberal and fine arts (MA, MFA, MM, MS, PhD); music (MM); political science (MA); psychology (MS); sociology (MS); Spanish (MA); studio art (MFA). *Application deadline:* For fall admission, 7/1 for domestic students, 4/1 for international students; for spring admission, 11/1 for domestic students, 9/1 for international students. Applications are processed on a rolling basis. *Application fee:* $45 ($80 for international students). Electronic applications accepted. *Dean,* Dr. Daniel J. Gelo, 210-458-4359, Fax: 210-458-4347, E-mail: daniel.gelo@utsa.edu.

College of Public Policy Students: 77 full-time (53 women), 192 part-time (116 women); includes 163 minority (27 African Americans, 1 American Indian/Alaska Native, 4 Asian Americans or Pacific Islanders, 131 Hispanic Americans), 4 international. Average age 33. 127 applicants, 88% accepted, 95 enrolled. *Faculty:* 32 full-time (15 women). Expenses: Contact institution. *Financial support:* In 2006–07, 18 research assistantships (averaging $22,844 per year), 1 teaching assistantship (averaging $24,336 per year) were awarded; career-related internships or fieldwork, Federal Work-Study, scholarships/grants, and unspecified assistantships also available. In 2006, 38 degrees awarded. *Degree program information:* Part-time and evening/weekend programs available. Offers applied demography (PhD); justice policy (MS); public administration (MPA); public policy (MPA, MS, MSW, PhD); social work (MSW). *Application deadline:* For fall admission, 7/1 for domestic students, 4/1 for international students; for spring admission, 11/1 for domestic students, 9/1 for international students. Applications are processed on a rolling basis. *Application fee:* $40 ($80 for international students). Electronic applications accepted. *Vice Provost, Downtown,* Dr. Jesse T. Zapata, 210-458-2700, Fax: 210-458-2424, E-mail: jzapata@utsa.edu.

College of Sciences Students: 292 full-time (139 women), 263 part-time (110 women); includes 169 minority (21 African Americans, 34 Asian Americans or Pacific Islanders, 114 Hispanic Americans), 142 international. Average age 31. 415 applicants, 70% accepted, 280 enrolled. *Faculty:* 109 full-time (23 women), 1 part-time/adjunct (0 women). Expenses: Contact institution. *Financial support:* In 2006–07, 1 fellowship (averaging $40,310 per year), 42 research assistantships (averaging $35,584 per year), 88 teaching assistantships (averaging $24,577 per year) were awarded; career-related internships or fieldwork, Federal Work-Study, institutionally sponsored loans, scholarships/grants, and unspecified assistantships also available. Support available to part-time students. In 2006, 97 master's, 9 doctorates awarded. *Degree program information:* Part-time and evening/weekend programs available. Offers biology (MS, PhD); biotechnology (MS); chemistry (MS, PhD); computer science (MS, PhD); environmental science and engineering (PhD); environmental sciences (MS); geology (MS); mathematics education (MS); physics (MS, PhD); sciences (MS, PhD). *Application deadline:* For fall admission, 7/1 for domestic students, 4/1 for international students; for spring admission, 11/1 for domestic students, 9/1 for international students. Applications are processed on a rolling basis. *Application fee:* $45 ($80 for international students). Electronic applications accepted. *Dean,* Dr. George Perry, 210-458-4450, Fax: 210-458-4445, E-mail: george.perry@utsa.edu.

THE UNIVERSITY OF TEXAS AT TYLER, Tyler, TX 75799-0001

General Information State-supported, coed, comprehensive institution. *Enrollment:* 5,926 graduate, professional, and undergraduate students; 667 matriculated graduate/professional students. *Enrollment by degree level:* 667 master's. Tuition, state resident: part-time $50 per credit hour. Tuition, nonresident: part-time $328 per credit hour. *Required fees:* $107 per credit hour. $426 per term. *Graduate housing:* Rooms and/or apartments available to single and married students. *Student services:* Campus employment opportunities, campus safety program, career counseling, disabled student services, exercise/wellness program, free psychological counseling, grant writing training, teacher training, writing training. *Library facilities:* Robert Muntz Library. *Online resources:* library catalog, web page. *Collection:* 486,895 titles, 525 serial subscriptions, 5,522 audiovisual materials.

Computer facilities: 177 computers available on campus for general student use. A campuswide network can be accessed from student residence rooms and from off campus. Internet access and online class registration are available. *Web address:* http://www.uttyler.edu/.

General Application Contact: Bonnie Purser, Office of Graduate Studies, 903-566-7142, Fax: 903-566-7068, E-mail: bpurser@uttyler.edu.

GRADUATE UNITS

College of Arts and Sciences 70 applicants, 96% accepted, 28 enrolled. Expenses: Contact institution. *Financial support:* In 2006–07, 8 students received support; teaching assistantships, Federal Work-Study available. Support available to part-time students. Financial award application deadline: 7/1; financial award applicants required to submit FAFSA. In 2006, 34 degrees awarded. *Degree program information:* Part-time and evening/weekend programs available. Postbaccalaureate distance learning degree programs offered. Offers art (MA, MAIS, MFA); arts and sciences (MA, MAIS, MAT, MFA, MPA, MS, MSIS); biology (MS); criminal justice (MS); English (MA); history (MA, MAT); interdisciplinary studies (MAIS, MSIS); mathematics (MS, MSIS); music (MAIS); political science (MA, MAT); public administration (MPA); sociology (MAT, MS). *Application deadline:* Applications are processed on a rolling basis. *Application fee:* $0. Electronic applications accepted. *Application Contact:* Bonnie Purser, Office of Graduate Studies, 903-566-7142, Fax: 903-566-7068, E-mail: bpurser@uttyler.edu. *Interim Dean,* Dr. Alisa White, 903-566-7397, Fax: 903-566-7377, E-mail: awhite@uttyler.edu.

College of Education and Psychology 87 applicants, 90% accepted, 65 enrolled. Expenses: Contact institution. *Financial support:* In 2006–07, 30 students received support; teaching assistantships, career-related internships or fieldwork, Federal Work-Study, institutionally sponsored loans, and scholarships/grants available. Support available to part-time students. Financial award application deadline: 4/1; financial award applicants required to submit FAFSA. In 2006, 78 degrees awarded. *Degree program information:* Part-time and evening/weekend programs available. Offers clinical psychology (MS); counseling psychology (MA); curriculum and instruction (M Ed); early childhood education (M Ed, MA); education and psychology (M Ed, MA, MAT, MS, MSIS); educational leadership (M Ed); interdisciplinary studies (MSIS); reading (M Ed, MA); school counseling (MA); secondary teaching (MAT); special education (M Ed, MA). *Application fee:* $0 ($50 for international students). *Application Contact:* Bonnie Purser, Office of Graduate Studies, 903-566-7142, Fax: 903-566-7068, E-mail: bpurser@uttyler.edu. *Dean,* Dr. William Geiger, 903-566-7081, Fax: 903-565-5648, E-mail: wgeiger@mail.uttyl.edu.

College of Engineering and Computer Science 32 applicants, 66% accepted, 21 enrolled. Expenses: Contact institution. *Financial support:* In 2006–07, 5 research assistantships with tuition reimbursements (averaging $2,333 per year), 1 teaching assistantship (averaging $2,333 per year) were awarded. Financial award application deadline: 7/1; financial award applicants required to submit FAFSA. In 2006, 7 degrees awarded. *Degree program information:* Part-time programs available. Offers computer science (MS); engineering (M Engr); engineering and computer science (M Engr, MS, MSIS); interdisciplinary studies (MSIS). *Application deadline:* Applications are processed on a rolling basis. *Application fee:* $0. Electronic applications accepted. *Application Contact:* Bonnie Purser, Office of Graduate Studies, 903-566-7142, Fax: 903-566-7068, E-mail: bpurser@uttyler.edu. *Dean,* Dr. Jim Nelson, 903-566-7267, Fax: 903-566-7148, E-mail: jnelson@uttyler.edu.

College of Nursing and Health Sciences 67 applicants, 88% accepted, 43 enrolled. Expenses: Contact institution. In 2006, 35 degrees awarded. *Degree program information:* Part-time and evening/weekend programs available. Postbaccalaureate distance learning degree programs offered. Offers clinical exercise physiology (MS); health and kinesiology (M Ed); kinesiology (MS); nurse practitioner (MSN); nursing administration (MSN); nursing and health sciences (M Ed, MS, MSN); nursing education (MSN). *Application deadline:* Applications are processed on a rolling basis. *Application fee:* $0. Electronic applications accepted. *Application Contact:* Bonnie Purser, Office of Graduate Studies, 903-566-7142, Fax: 903-566-7068, E-mail: bpurser@uttyler.edu. *Dean,* Dr. Linda Klotz, 903-566-7075, Fax: 903-565-5533, E-mail: lklotz@mail.uttyl.edu.

College of Business and Technology *Degree program information:* Part-time and evening/weekend programs available. Postbaccalaureate distance learning degree programs offered (no on-campus study). Offers business administration (MBA); general management (MBA); health care track (MBA); human resource development (MS); human resource development and technology (MS); industrial distribution (MS); industrial safety (MS); industrial technology (MS); instructional technology (MS); technology systems (MS). Electronic applications accepted.

THE UNIVERSITY OF TEXAS HEALTH SCIENCE CENTER AT HOUSTON, Houston, TX 77225-0036

General Information State-supported, coed, upper-level institution. *Graduate housing:* On-campus housing not available.

GRADUATE UNITS

Graduate School of Biomedical Sciences Students: 545 full-time (306 women); includes 117 minority (25 African Americans, 1 American Indian/Alaska Native, 42 Asian Americans or Pacific Islanders, 49 Hispanic Americans), 194 international. Average age 28. 524 applicants, 41% accepted, 129 enrolled. *Faculty:* 581 full-time (147 women). Expenses: Contact institution. *Financial support:* Fellowships with full tuition reimbursements, research assistantships with full tuition reimbursements, teaching assistantships, institutionally sponsored loans, scholarships/grants, and health care benefits available. Financial award application deadline: 1/15. In 2006, 44 master's, 66 doctorates awarded. Offers biochemistry and molecular biology (MS, PhD); biomathematics and biostatistics (MS, PhD); biomedical sciences (MS, PhD); cancer biology (MS, PhD); cell and regulatory biology (MS, PhD); genes and development (MS, PhD); genetic counseling (MS); human and molecular genetics (MS, PhD); immunology (MS, PhD); medical physics (MS, PhD); microbiology and molecular genetics (MS, PhD); molecular carcinogenesis (MS, PhD); molecular pathology (MS, PhD); neuroscience (MS, PhD); toxicology (MS, PhD); virology and gene therapy (MS, PhD). *Application deadline:* For fall admission, 1/15 priority date for domestic students, 12/15 for international students; for spring admission, 11/1 priority date for domestic students. Applications are processed on a rolling basis. *Application fee:* $10. Electronic applications accepted. *Application Contact:* Dr. Victoria P. Knutson, Assistant Dean of Admissions, 713-500-9860, Fax: 713-500-9877, E-mail: victoria.p.knutson@uth.tmc.edu. *Dean,* Dr. George M. Stancel, 713-500-9880, Fax: 713-500-9877, E-mail: george.m.stancel@uth.tmc.edu.

Medical School Students: 868 full-time (398 women); includes 237 minority (26 African Americans, 4 American Indian/Alaska Native, 101 Asian Americans or Pacific Islanders, 106 Hispanic Americans), 1 international. Average age 23. 3,446 applicants, 8% accepted, 226 enrolled. *Faculty:* 776 full-time (276 women), 94 part-time/adjunct (42 women). Expenses: Contact institution. *Financial support:* In 2006–07, 859 students received support. Scholarships/grants and health care benefits available. Financial award application deadline: 3/1; financial award applicants required to submit FAFSA. In 2006, 208 degrees awarded. Offers medicine (MD). *Application deadline:* For fall admission, 10/1 for domestic and international students. Applications are processed on a rolling basis. *Application fee:* $55 ($100 for international students). Electronic applications accepted. *Application Contact:* Dr. Judianne Kellaway, Assistant Dean of Admissions, 713-500-5116, E-mail: judianne.kellaway@uth.tmc.edu. *Interim Dean,* Dr. Jerry S. Wolinsky, 713-500-5012, E-mail: jerry.s.wolinsky@uth.tmc.edu.

School of Health Information Sciences *Degree program information:* Part-time programs available. Postbaccalaureate distance learning degree programs offered (no on-campus study). Offers health informatics (MS, PhD). Electronic applications accepted.

School of Nursing Students: 225 full-time (125 women), 188 part-time (169 women); includes 113 minority (47 African Americans, 2 American Indian/Alaska Native, 34 Asian Americans or Pacific Islanders, 30 Hispanic Americans), 11 international. Average age 41. 308 applicants, 38% accepted, 94 enrolled. *Faculty:* 76 full-time (69 women), 25 part-time/adjunct (23 women). Expenses: Contact institution. *Financial support:* In 2006–07, 101 students received support; research assistantships with tuition reimbursements available, teaching assistantships with tuition reimbursements available, institutionally sponsored loans, scholarships/grants, traineeships, and tuition waivers (full) available. Support available to part-time students. In 2006, 124 master's, 9 doctorates awarded. *Degree program information:* Part-time programs available. Offers nursing (MSN, DNP, DSN). *Application deadline:* For fall admission, 5/1 priority date for domestic students. Applications are processed on a rolling basis. *Application fee:* $30. Electronic applications accepted. *Application Contact:* Laurie G. Rutherford, Student Affairs, 713-500-2101, Fax: 713-500-2107, E-mail: laurie.g.rutherford@uth.tmc.edu. *Dean,* Dr. Patricia Starck, 713-500-2100, Fax: 713-500-2107.

School of Public Health Students: 347 full-time (219 women), 436 part-time (329 women); includes 287 minority (78 African Americans, 6 American Indian/Alaska Native, 91 Asian Americans or Pacific Islanders, 112 Hispanic Americans), 179 international. Average age 34. 713 applicants, 65% accepted, 261 enrolled. *Faculty:* 139 full-time (64 women), 12 part-time/adjunct (4 women). Expenses: Contact institution. *Financial support:* In 2006–07, 25 fellowships (averaging $31,994 per year), 105 research assistantships (averaging $17,054 per year), 76 teaching assistantships (averaging $17,434 per year) were awarded; career-related internships or fieldwork, institutionally sponsored loans, scholarships/grants, traineeships, health care benefits, and unspecified assistantships also available. Support available to part-time students. Financial award application deadline: 5/5; financial award applicants required to submit FAFSA. In 2006, 175 master's, 32 doctorates awarded. *Degree program information:* Part-time programs available. Offers public health (MPH, MS, Dr PH, PhD, Certificate). *Application deadline:* For fall admission, 2/1 for domestic and international students; for spring admission, 8/1 for domestic and international students. Applications are processed on a rolling basis. *Application fee:* $30. Electronic applications accepted. *Application Contact:* Marius P. Reyes, Pre-Enrollment Services Coordinator, 713-500-9035, Fax: 713-500-9068, E-mail: marius.p.reyes@uth.tmc.edu. *Dean,* Dr. Guy S. Parcel, 713-500-9050, Fax: 713-500-9068, E-mail: guy.s.parcel@uth.tmc.edu.

The University of Texas Dental Branch at Houston Students: 282 full-time (136 women); includes 120 minority (12 African Americans, 1 American Indian/Alaska Native, 107 Hispanic Americans). Average age 26. 1,193 applicants, 14% accepted, 84 enrolled. *Faculty:* 88 full-time (29 women), 72 part-time/adjunct (21 women). Expenses: Contact institution. *Financial support:* In 2006–07, 23 students received support. Institutionally sponsored loans and scholarships/grants available. Financial award applicants required to submit FAFSA. In 2006, 62 degrees awarded. Offers dentistry (DDS, MS). *Application deadline:* For fall admission, 10/15 for domestic students. Applications are processed on a rolling basis. *Application fee:* $80. Electronic applications accepted. *Application Contact:* Dr. H. Philip Pierpont, Associate Dean for Student and Alumni Affairs, 713-500-4151, Fax: 713-500-4425, E-mail: dbstudentaffairs@uthouston.edu. *Dean,* Dr. Catherine M. Flaitz, 713-500-4021, Fax: 713-500-4089.

THE UNIVERSITY OF TEXAS HEALTH SCIENCE CENTER AT SAN ANTONIO, San Antonio, TX 78229-3900

General Information State-supported, coed, upper-level institution. CGS member. *Enrollment:* 1,811 full-time matriculated graduate/professional students (1,021 women), 330 part-time matriculated graduate/professional students (259 women). *Enrollment by degree level:* 1,208 first professional, 599 master's, 286 doctoral, 48 other advanced degrees. *Graduate faculty:* 273 full-time (112 women), 62 part-time/adjunct (10 women). Tuition, state resident: part-time $50 per credit hour. Tuition, nonresident: part-time $325 per credit hour. *Required fees:* $7.5 per credit hour. $155 per term. *Graduate housing:* On-campus housing not available. *Student services:* Campus safety program, exercise/wellness program, free psychological counseling, international student services, low-cost health insurance. *Library facilities:* Dolph Briso Library. *Collection:* 192,576 titles, 2,501 serial subscriptions. *Research affiliation:* Veterans Administration Hospital, Southwest Foundation for Biomedical Research, Southwest Research Institute, University Hospital.

Computer facilities: 1,000 computers available on campus for general student use. A campuswide network can be accessed from off campus. Internet access is available. *Web address:* http://www.uthscsa.edu/.

General Application Contact: Debra Goode, Registrar, 210-567-2621, Fax: 210-567-2685, E-mail: goode@uthscsa.edu.

GRADUATE UNITS

Dental School Students: 353 full-time (159 women); includes 112 minority (8 African Americans, 1 American Indian/Alaska Native, 40 Asian Americans or Pacific Islanders, 63 Hispanic Americans). Average age 26. 1,025 applicants, 9% accepted, 94 enrolled. *Faculty:* 110 full-time (28 women), 85 part-time/adjunct (18 women). Expenses: Contact institution. *Financial support:* In 2006–07, 311 students received support; teaching assistantships, institutionally sponsored loans and scholarships/grants available. Financial award application deadline: 3/1; financial award applicants required to submit FAFSA. In 2006, 81 first professional degrees, 10 master's awarded. Offers dentistry (DDS, MS, Certificate). *Application deadline:* For fall admission, 10/1 for domestic students. *Application fee:* $75. Electronic applications accepted. *Application Contact:* Sofia Almeda, Office of Admissions and Student Services, 210-567-2659, Fax: 210-567-2685, E-mail: almedas@uthscsa.edu. *Associate Dean for Student Affairs,* Dr. D. Denee Thomas, 210-567-3752, Fax: 210-567-4776, E-mail: thomasd@uthscsa.edu.

Graduate School of Biomedical Sciences Students: 287 full-time (151 women), 227 part-time (190 women); includes 185 minority (28 African Americans, 1 American Indian/Alaska Native, 54 Asian Americans or Pacific Islanders, 102 Hispanic Americans), 87 international. Average age 31. 931 applicants, 19% accepted, 174 enrolled. *Faculty:* 273 full-time (112 women), 62 part-time/adjunct (10 women). Expenses: Contact institution. *Financial support:* Fellowships, research assistantships, teaching assistantships, career-related internships or fieldwork, Federal Work-Study, institutionally sponsored loans, and tuition waivers (full) available. Support available to part-time students. Financial award applicants required to submit FAFSA. In 2006, 74 master's, 38 doctorates awarded. *Degree program information:* Part-time and evening/weekend programs available. Offers biochemistry (MS, PhD); biomedical sciences (MS, MSN, PhD); cellular and structural biology (MS, PhD); microbiology and immunology (PhD); molecular medicine (MS, PhD); pharmacology (PhD); physiology (MS, PhD); radiological sciences (MS, PhD). *Application deadline:* For fall admission, 4/1 for domestic and international students; for spring admission, 9/1 for domestic and international students. Applications are processed on a rolling basis. *Application fee:* $10. Electronic applications accepted. *Application Contact:* Janice M. Stong, Information Contact, 210-567-3711, Fax: 210-567-3719, E-mail: stong@uthscsa.edu. *Dean,* Dr. Merle S. Olson, 210-567-3709, Fax: 210-567-3719, E-mail: olsonm@uthscsa.edu.

School of Nursing Students: 40 full-time (32 women), 197 part-time (171 women); includes 91 minority (21 African Americans, 10 Asian Americans or Pacific Islanders, 60 Hispanic Americans). Average age 40. 116 applicants, 53% accepted, 45 enrolled. *Faculty:* 36 full-time (all women), 2 part-time/adjunct (0 women). Expenses: Contact institution. *Financial support:* In 2006–07, 37 students received support; research assistantships, teaching assistantships, institutionally sponsored loans and scholarships/grants available. Financial award application deadline: 4/1. In 2006, 58 master's, 2 doctorates awarded. *Degree program information:* Part-time programs available. Offers nursing (MSN, PhD). *Application deadline:* For fall admission, 2/1 for domestic students; for spring admission, 9/1 for domestic students. *Application fee:* $45. *Application Contact:* Dr. Beverly Robinson, Associate Dean for Graduate Nursing Program and Director of Doctoral Studies, 210-567-5815, Fax: 210-567-3813, E-mail: robinsonb@uthscsa.edu. *Dean,* Dr. Robin Froman, 210-567-5800, E-mail: froman@uthscsa.edu.

Medical School Offers medicine (MD).

School of Allied Health Sciences Offers clinical laboratory sciences (MS); dental hygiene (MS); occupational therapy (MOT); physical therapy (MPT); physician assistant studies (MS).

THE UNIVERSITY OF TEXAS MEDICAL BRANCH, Galveston, TX 77555

General Information State-supported, coed, upper-level institution. CGS member. *Enrollment:* 2,255 graduate, professional, and undergraduate students; 1,525 full-time matriculated graduate/professional students (867 women), 261 part-time matriculated graduate/professional students (218 women). *Enrollment by degree level:* 861 first professional, 574 master's, 309 doctoral. *Graduate faculty:* 321 full-time (85 women). *Graduate housing:* Rooms and/or apartments available on a first-come, first-served basis to single and married students. *Student services:* Campus employment opportunities, campus safety program, career counseling, child daycare facilities, disabled student services, exercise/wellness program, free psychological counseling, international student services, low-cost health insurance, multicultural affairs office. *Library facilities:* Moody Medical Library. *Online resources:* library catalog, web page, access to other libraries' catalogs. *Research affiliation:* Shriners Hospitals (burns and wound healing).

Computer facilities: 200 computers available on campus for general student use. A campuswide network can be accessed from student residence rooms and from off campus. Internet access and online class registration are available. *Web address:* http://www.utmb.edu/.

General Application Contact: Vicki Brewer, University Registrar/Director of Enroll Services, 409-772-9803, Fax: 409-772-5056, E-mail: vbrewer@utmb.edu.

GRADUATE UNITS

Graduate School of Biomedical Sciences Students: 382; includes 69 minority (21 African Americans, 1 American Indian/Alaska Native, 21 Asian Americans or Pacific Islanders, 26 Hispanic Americans), 84 international. Average age 33. *Faculty:* 332 full-time (89 women). Expenses: Contact institution. *Financial support:* In 2006–07, research assistantships with full tuition reimbursements (averaging $25,000 per year); career-related internships or fieldwork, Federal Work-Study, institutionally sponsored loans, scholarships/grants, traineeships, health care benefits, and unspecified assistantships also available. Support available to part-time students. Financial award applicants required to submit FAFSA. In 2006, 18 master's, 36 doctorates awarded. Offers biochemistry (PhD); bioinformatics (PhD); biomedical sciences (MA, MMS, MPH, MS, PhD); biophysics (PhD); cell biology (PhD); cellular physiology and molecular biophysics (MS, PhD); computational biology (PhD); emerging and tropical infectious diseases (PhD); experimental pathology (PhD); medical humanities (MA, PhD); medical science (MMS); microbiology and immunology (MS, PhD); neuroscience (PhD); nursing (PhD); pharmacology (MS); pharmacology/toxicology (PhD); preventive medicine and community health (MPH, MS, PhD); public health (MPH); structural biology (PhD); toxicology (PhD). *Application deadline:* Applications are processed on a rolling basis. *Application fee:* $30 ($75 for international students). Electronic applications accepted. *Application Contact:* Dr. Dorian H. Coppenhaver, Associate Dean for Student Affairs, 409-772-2665, Fax: 409-747-0772, E-mail: dcoppenh@utmb.edu. *Dean,* Dr. Cary W. Cooper, 409-772-2665, Fax: 409-747-0772, E-mail: ccooper@utmb.edu.

Center for Biodefense and Emerging Infectious Diseases Expenses: Contact institution. *Financial support:* Tuition waivers and unspecified assistantships available. Offers biodefense training (PhD). *Executive Director,* Dr. Clarence J. Peters, 409-772-0090, Fax: 409-747-0762, E-mail: cjpeters@utmb.edu.

School of Allied Health Sciences Students: 311 full-time (243 women), 8 part-time (7 women); includes 90 minority (37 African Americans, 1 American Indian/Alaska Native, 22 Asian Americans or Pacific Islanders, 30 Hispanic Americans), 4 international. Average age 26. 846 applicants, 22% accepted, 172 enrolled. *Faculty:* 27 full-time (18 women). Expenses: Contact institution. *Financial support:* Career-related internships or fieldwork, Federal Work-Study, institutionally sponsored loans, and scholarships/grants available. Financial award applicants required to submit FAFSA. In 2006, 86 degrees awarded. Offers allied health sciences (MOT, MPAS, MPT); occupational therapy (MOT); physical therapy (MPT); physician assistant studies (MPAS). *Application deadline:* For fall admission, 11/1 for domestic students. Applications are processed on a rolling basis. *Application fee:* $30. Electronic applications accepted. *Application Contact:* Raymond Lewis, Associate Dean for Admissions and Student Affairs, 409-772-3030, Fax: 409-747-1624, E-mail: ralewis@utmb.edu. *Interim Dean,* Dr. Elizabeth J. Protas, 409-772-3001, Fax: 409-772-1613, E-mail: ejprotas@utmb.edu.

School of Medicine Students: 861 full-time (429 women); includes 372 minority (79 African Americans, 5 American Indian/Alaska Native, 154 Asian Americans or Pacific Islanders, 134 Hispanic Americans), 4 international. Average age 25. Expenses: Contact institution. *Financial support:* Federal Work-Study, institutionally sponsored loans, scholarships/grants, and tuition waivers (full and partial) available. Financial award applicants required to submit FAFSA. In 2006, 183 degrees awarded. Offers medicine (MD). *Application deadline:* For fall admission, 11/1 for domestic students. *Application fee:* $55 ($100 for international students). *Application Contact:* Dr. Lauree Thomas, Associate Dean for Admissions and Student Affairs, 409-772-

The University of Texas Medical Branch (continued)

1442, Fax: 409-772-5148, E-mail: lauthoma@utmb.edu. *Dean,* Dr. Garland D. Anderson, 409-772-4793, Fax: 409-772-9598, E-mail: ganderso@utmb.edu.

School of Nursing Students: 58 full-time (49 women), 190 part-time (172 women); includes 68 minority (26 African Americans, 1 American Indian/Alaska Native, 18 Asian Americans or Pacific Islanders, 23 Hispanic Americans). Average age 44. *Faculty:* 18 full-time (all women), 9 part-time/adjunct (8 women). Expenses: Contact institution. *Financial support:* Research assistantships, teaching assistantships, Federal Work-Study, institutionally sponsored loans, scholarships/grants, and traineeships available. Support available to part-time students. Financial award applicants required to submit FAFSA. In 2006, 50 degrees awarded. *Degree program information:* Part-time programs available. Postbaccalaureate distance learning degree programs offered (minimal on-campus study). Offers nursing (MSN). *Application deadline:* For fall admission, 1/15 for domestic students. Applications are processed on a rolling basis. *Application fee:* $30. Electronic applications accepted. *Application Contact:* Dr. Vince J. Loffeedo, Associate Dean for Student Affairs/Admissions, 409-772-1983, E-mail: vjloffre@utmb.edu. *Dean,* Dr. Pamela G. Watson, 409-772-1510, Fax: 409-772-5118, E-mail: pgwatson@utmb.edu.

THE UNIVERSITY OF TEXAS OF THE PERMIAN BASIN, Odessa, TX 79762-0001

General Information State-supported, coed, comprehensive institution. *Graduate housing:* Rooms and/or apartments available on a first-come, first-served basis to single and married students. Housing application deadline: 6/15.

GRADUATE UNITS

Office of Graduate Studies *Degree program information:* Part-time and evening/weekend programs available.

College of Arts and Sciences *Degree program information:* Part-time and evening/weekend programs available. Offers applied behavioral analysis (MA); arts and sciences (MA, MS); biology (MS); clinical psychology (MA); criminal justice administration (MS); English (MA); geology (MS); history (MA); kinesiology (MS); psychology (MA).

School of Business *Degree program information:* Part-time and evening/weekend programs available. Offers accountancy (MPA); business (MBA, MPA); management (MBA).

School of Education Offers bilingual/English as a second language education (MA); counseling (MA); early childhood education (MA); education (MA); educational leadership (MA); professional education (MA); reading (MA); special education (MA).

THE UNIVERSITY OF TEXAS–PAN AMERICAN, Edinburg, TX 78541-2999

General Information State-supported, coed, comprehensive institution. CGS member. *Enrollment:* 17,337 graduate, professional, and undergraduate students; 608 full-time matriculated graduate/professional students (369 women), 1,653 part-time matriculated graduate/professional students (1,094 women). *Enrollment by degree level:* 2,158 master's, 103 doctoral. *Graduate faculty:* 232 full-time (78 women), 16 part-time/adjunct (9 women). Tuition, state resident: full-time $2,577; part-time $143 per credit hour. Tuition, nonresident: full-time $7,527; part-time $418 per credit hour. *Required fees:* $561. *Graduate housing:* Room and/or apartments available on a first-come, first-served basis to single students; on-campus housing not available to married students. Typical cost: $2,800 per year ($5,612 including board). *Student services:* Campus employment opportunities, campus safety program, career counseling, child daycare facilities, disabled student services, exercise/wellness program, free psychological counseling, grant writing training, international student services, low-cost health insurance, teacher training. *Library facilities:* University Library. *Online resources:* library catalog, web page, access to other libraries' catalogs. *Collection:* 598,008 titles, 35,004 serial subscriptions. *Research affiliation:* Lockheed Martin (manufacturing engineering), Texas Instruments (curriculum and instruction), Pfizer (health disparities), Howard Hughes Medical Institute (Medical Science), Boeing (Engineering), Robert Wood Johnson (Health Science).

Computer facilities: 500 computers available on campus for general student use. A campuswide network can be accessed from off campus. Internet access and online class registration are available. *Web address:* http://www.utpa.edu/.

General Application Contact: Edel de la Garza, Administrative Clerk, 956-381-3661 Ext. 2207, Fax: 956-381-2863, E-mail: delagarzaa@panam.edu.

GRADUATE UNITS

College of Arts and Humanities *Degree program information:* Part-time and evening/weekend programs available. Offers art (MFA); arts and humanities (M Mus, MA, MAIS, MFA, MSIS); communication (MA); English (MA, MAIS); English as a second language (MA); ethnomusicology (M Mus); history (MA, MAIS); interdisciplinary studies (MAIS); music education (M Mus); performance (M Mus); Spanish (MA); theatre (MA).

College of Business Administration *Degree program information:* Part-time and evening/weekend programs available. Offers business administration (MBA, MS, PhD); computer information systems (MS, PhD).

College of Education *Degree program information:* Part-time and evening/weekend programs available. Offers bilingual education (M Ed); counseling (M Ed); early childhood education (M Ed); education (M Ed, MA, MS, Ed D); educational diagnostician (M Ed); educational leadership (M Ed, Ed D); elementary education (M Ed); gifted education (M Ed); kinesiology (MS); reading (M Ed); school psychology (MA); secondary education (M Ed); special education (M Ed).

College of Health Sciences and Human Services Students: 139 full-time (113 women), 126 part-time (108 women); includes 243 minority (3 African Americans, 240 Hispanic Americans). Average age 29. 207 applicants, 59% accepted, 110 enrolled. *Faculty:* 39 full-time (27 women), 2 part-time/adjunct (1 woman). Expenses: Contact institution. *Financial support:* In 2006–07, 25 students received support, including 3 research assistantships (averaging $13,000 per year), 5 teaching assistantships (averaging $12,740 per year); fellowships with full tuition reimbursements available, career-related internships or fieldwork, Federal Work-Study, institutionally sponsored loans, and scholarships/grants also available. Support available to part-time students. Financial award applicants required to submit FAFSA. In 2006, 127 degrees awarded. *Degree program information:* Part-time and evening/weekend programs available. Offers adult health nursing (MSN); communication sciences and disorders (MS); family nurse practitioner (MSN); health sciences and human services (MS, MSN, MSSW); occupational therapy (MS); pediatric nurse practitioner (MSN); rehabilitation counseling (MS); social work (MSSW). *Interim Dean,* Dr. Bruce Reed, 956-381-2292, Fax: 956-384-5054, E-mail: bjreed@panam.edu.

College of Science and Engineering *Degree program information:* Part-time and evening/weekend programs available. Offers biology (MS); computer science (MS); mathematics (MS); science and engineering (MS).

College of Social and Behavioral Sciences Students: 157. Expenses: Contact institution. *Financial support:* Fellowships, research assistantships, teaching assistantships, career-related internships or fieldwork, Federal Work-Study, institutionally sponsored loans, scholarships/grants, and tuition waivers (full and partial) available. Support available to part-time students. Financial award applicants required to submit CSS PROFILE or FAFSA. *Degree program information:* Part-time and evening/weekend programs available. Postbaccalaureate distance learning degree programs offered (minimal on-campus study). Offers criminal justice (MS); psychology (MA); public administration (MPA); social and behavioral sciences (MA, MPA, MS); sociology (MS). *Application fee:* $0. *Dean,* Dr. Van A Reidhead, 956-381-3551, Fax: 956-381-2180, E-mail: reidheadv@panam.edu.

THE UNIVERSITY OF TEXAS SOUTHWESTERN MEDICAL CENTER AT DALLAS, Dallas, TX 75390

General Information State-supported, coed, upper-level institution. *Enrollment:* 2,434 graduate, professional, and undergraduate students; 708 full-time matriculated graduate/professional students (418 women), 537 part-time matriculated graduate/professional students (195 women). *Enrollment by degree level:* 254 master's, 509 doctoral, 482 other advanced degrees. *Graduate faculty:* 341 full-time (78 women), 81 part-time/adjunct (18 women). Tuition, state resident: part-time $120 per semester hour. Tuition, nonresident: part-time $395 per semester hour. *Required fees:* $42 per semester hour. Tuition and fees vary according to program. *Graduate housing:* Rooms and/or apartments available on a first-come, first-served basis to single and married students. Typical cost: $775 per year for single students. *Student services:* Campus employment opportunities, campus safety program, disabled student services, exercise/wellness program, free psychological counseling, grant writing training, international student services, low-cost health insurance, multicultural affairs office, writing training. *Library facilities:* University of Texas Southwestern Library plus 1 other. *Online resources:* library catalog, web page, access to other libraries' catalogs. *Collection:* 257,782 titles, 2,865 serial subscriptions.

Computer facilities: 150 computers available on campus for general student use. A campuswide network can be accessed from off campus. Internet access is available. *Web address:* http://www.utsouthwestern.edu/.

General Application Contact: Dr. Nancy E. Street, Associate Dean, 214-648-6708, Fax: 214-648-2102, E-mail: nancy.street@utsouthwestern.edu.

GRADUATE UNITS

Southwestern Allied Health Sciences School Students: 186 full-time (151 women), 1 part-time; includes 42 minority (6 African Americans, 1 American Indian/Alaska Native, 17 Asian Americans or Pacific Islanders, 18 Hispanic Americans), 2 international. 754 applicants, 12% accepted, 72 enrolled. Expenses: Contact institution. *Financial support:* Application deadline: 3/1. In 2006, 64 degrees awarded. Offers allied health sciences (MPAS, MPT); physical therapy (MPT); physician assistant studies (MPAS). *Dean,* Dr. Raul Caetano, 214-648-1500.

Southwestern Graduate School of Biomedical Sciences Students: 522 full-time (267 women), 568 part-time (206 women); includes 184 minority (19 African Americans, 3 American Indian/Alaska Native, 112 Asian Americans or Pacific Islanders, 50 Hispanic Americans), 504 international. Average age 31. 1,861 applicants, 38% accepted, 619 enrolled. *Faculty:* 345 full-time (80 women), 89 part-time/adjunct (18 women). Expenses: Contact institution. *Financial support:* Fellowships, research assistantships, teaching assistantships, career-related internships or fieldwork, Federal Work-Study, institutionally sponsored loans, scholarships/grants, traineeships, and tuition waivers (full and partial) available. Financial award application deadline: 3/1; financial award applicants required to submit FAFSA. In 2006, 28 master's, 67 doctorates awarded. Offers biological chemistry (PhD); biomedical sciences (MA, MCS, MS, PhD); cell regulation (PhD); genetics and development (PhD); immunology (PhD); integrative biology (PhD); medical scientist training (PhD); molecular biophysics (PhD); molecular microbiology (PhD); neuroscience (PhD). *Application deadline:* For fall admission, 12/15 priority date for domestic students. Applications are processed on a rolling basis. *Application fee:* $0. Electronic applications accepted. *Application Contact:* 214-648-5617, Fax: 214-648-3289, E-mail: admissions@utsouthwestern.edu. *Dean,* Dr. Melanie H. Cobb, 214-645-6122, Fax: 214-648-2102, E-mail: melanie.cobb@utsouthwestern.edu.

Division of Applied Science Students: 46 full-time (24 women), 32 part-time (11 women); includes 14 minority (2 African Americans, 5 Asian Americans or Pacific Islanders, 7 Hispanic Americans), 43 international. 173 applicants, 8% accepted, 12 enrolled. Expenses: Contact institution. In 2006, 8 degrees awarded. Offers biomedical communications (MA); biomedical engineering (MS, PhD). *Application fee:* $0. *Application Contact:* 214-648-5617, Fax: 214-648-3289, E-mail: admissions@utsouthwestern.edu.

Division of Clinical Science Students: 75 full-time (53 women), 48 part-time (22 women); includes 35 minority (5 African Americans, 2 American Indian/Alaska Native, 12 Asian Americans or Pacific Islanders, 16 Hispanic Americans), 5 international. 223 applicants, 30% accepted, 65 enrolled. Expenses: Contact institution. *Financial support:* Applicants required to submit FAFSA. In 2006, 15 master's, 10 doctorates awarded. Offers clinical psychology (PhD); clinical science (MCS); radiological sciences (MS, PhD); rehabilitation counseling psychology (MS). *Application Contact:* 214-648-5617, Fax: 214-648-3289, E-mail: admissions@utsouthwestern.edu.

Southwestern Medical School Offers medicine (MD). Electronic applications accepted.

THE UNIVERSITY OF THE ARTS, Philadelphia, PA 19102-4944

General Information Independent, coed, comprehensive institution. *Graduate housing:* Room and/or apartments available to single students; on-campus housing not available to married students. Housing application deadline: 6/1. *Research affiliation:* The Franklin Institute (general science education), Philadelphia Museum of Art (arts and culture), School District of Philadelphia (education), Ben Franklin Technology Partners (high tech department and creative/cultural production in Philadelphia).

GRADUATE UNITS

College of Art and Design *Degree program information:* Part-time programs available. Offers art and design (MA, MAT, MFA, MID); art education (MA); book arts/printmaking (MFA); ceramics (MFA); industrial design (MID); museum communication (MA); museum education (MA); museum exhibition planning and design (MFA); painting (MFA); sculpture (MFA); visual arts (MAT). Electronic applications accepted.

College of Performing Arts *Degree program information:* Part-time programs available. Offers performing arts (MAT, MM).

School of Music *Degree program information:* Part-time programs available. Offers jazz studies (MM); music education (MAT). Electronic applications accepted.

UNIVERSITY OF THE CUMBERLANDS, Williamsburg, KY 40769-1372

General Information Independent-religious, coed, comprehensive institution. *Graduate housing:* Room and/or apartments available to single students; on-campus housing not available to married students.

GRADUATE UNITS

Graduate Programs in Education *Degree program information:* Part-time and evening/weekend programs available. Offers early childhood education (MA Ed); elementary (P-5) (MA Ed, MAT); elementary education (MA Ed, MAT); elementary/secondary principalship (MA Ed, Certificate); elementary/secondary teaching (MA Ed, MAT, Certificate); middle school (5-9) (MA Ed, MAT); middle school education (MA Ed, MAT); reading and writing specialist (MA Ed); secondary general education (MA Ed, MAT); special education (MA Ed, MAT).

UNIVERSITY OF THE DISTRICT OF COLUMBIA, Washington, DC 20008-1175

General Information District-supported, coed, comprehensive institution. CGS member. *Enrollment:* 5,534 graduate, professional, and undergraduate students; 70 full-time matriculated graduate/professional students (43 women), 92 part-time matriculated graduate/professional students (61 women). *Enrollment by degree level:* 162 master's. *Graduate faculty:* 30. *Graduate housing:* On-campus housing not available. *Student services:* Campus employment opportunities, campus safety program, career counseling, child daycare facilities, disabled student services, free psychological counseling, international student services, low-cost health insurance, multicultural affairs office. *Library facilities:* Learning Resources Division Library plus 1 other. *Online resources:* library catalog, web page, access to other libraries' catalogs. *Collection:* 544,412 titles, 594 serial subscriptions.

Computer facilities: 1,500 computers available on campus for general student use. A campuswide network can be accessed. *Web address:* http://www.udc.edu/.

General Application Contact: LaVerne Hill Flannigan, Processor, Graduate Applications, 202-274-5008.

GRADUATE UNITS

College of Arts and Sciences Students: 70 full-time (43 women), 92 part-time (61 women); includes 129 minority (115 African Americans, 6 Asian Americans or Pacific Islanders, 8 Hispanic Americans). Average age 35. 178 applicants. Expenses: Contact institution. *Financial* *support:* Fellowships, research assistantships, teaching assistantships, career-related internships or fieldwork and Federal Work-Study available. In 2006, 31 degrees awarded. *Degree program information:* Part-time and evening/weekend programs available. Offers arts and sciences (MA, MS, MST); clinical psychology (MS); counseling (MS); early childhood education (MA); English composition and rhetoric (MA); mathematics (MST); special education (MA); speech and language pathology (MS). *Application deadline:* For fall admission, 6/15 priority date for domestic students; for spring admission, 11/1 for domestic students. Applications are processed on a rolling basis. *Application fee:* $20. *Application Contact:* LaVerne Hill Flannigan, Director of Admission, 202-274-6069. *Dean,* Dr. Rachel Petty, 202-274-5194.

David A. Clarke School of Law Offers law (JD). Electronic applications accepted.

School of Business and Public Administration Students: 22 full-time (12 women), 35 part-time (16 women); includes 49 minority (45 African Americans, 3 Asian Americans or Pacific Islanders, 1 Hispanic American). Average age 29. 71 applicants, 55% accepted. Expenses: Contact institution. *Financial support:* Career-related internships or fieldwork and Federal Work-Study available. In 2006, 14 degrees awarded. *Degree program information:* Part-time and evening/weekend programs available. Offers business administration (MBA); business and public administration (MBA, MPA); public administration (MPA). *Application deadline:* For fall admission, 6/15 priority date for domestic students; for spring admission, 11/1 for domestic students. Applications are processed on a rolling basis. *Application fee:* $20. *Application Contact:* LaVerne Hill Flannigan, Director of Admission, 202-274-6069. *Dean,* Dr. Melanie Anderson, 202-282-7000.

UNIVERSITY OF THE INCARNATE WORD, San Antonio, TX 78209-6397

General Information Independent-religious, coed, comprehensive institution. *Enrollment:* 5,619 graduate, professional, and undergraduate students; 137 full-time matriculated graduate/professional students (97 women), 816 part-time matriculated graduate/professional students (529 women). *Enrollment by degree level:* 79 first professional, 716 master's, 158 doctoral. *Graduate faculty:* 67 full-time (37 women), 42 part-time/adjunct (19 women). *Tuition:* Part-time $570 per credit hour. *Required fees:* $54 per credit hour. One-time fee: $195 part-time. Tuition and fees vary according to degree level. *Graduate housing:* Room and/or apartments available to single students; on-campus housing not available to married students. *Student services:* Campus employment opportunities, career counseling, exercise/wellness program, free psychological counseling, international student services, low-cost health insurance. *Library facilities:* J.E. and L.E. Mabee Library plus 1 other. *Online resources:* library catalog, web page. *Collection:* 335,298 titles, 23,551 serial subscriptions, 14,469 audiovisual materials.

Computer facilities: Computer purchase and lease plans are available. 200 computers available on campus for general student use. A campuswide network can be accessed from student residence rooms and from off campus. Internet access and online class registration are available. *Web address:* http://www.uiw.edu/.

General Application Contact: Andrea Cyterski-Acosta, Dean of Enrollment, 210-829-6005, Fax: 210-829-3921, E-mail: cyterski@uiwtx.edu.

GRADUATE UNITS

Felk School of Pharmacy Students: 79 full-time (58 women); includes 44 minority (6 African Americans, 9 Asian Americans or Pacific Islanders, 29 Hispanic Americans), 1 international. *Faculty:* 10. Expenses: Contact institution. Offers pharmacy (Pharm D). *Founding Dean,* Dr. Arcelia Johnson-Fannin, 210-805-3011, Fax: 210-805-3013, E-mail: johnsonf@uiwtx.edu.

School of Graduate Studies and Research Students: 137 full-time (97 women), 816 part-time (529 women); includes 487 minority (82 African Americans, 6 American Indian/Alaska Native, 21 Asian Americans or Pacific Islanders, 378 Hispanic Americans), 116 international. Average age 35. *Faculty:* 67 full-time (37 women), 42 part-time/adjunct (19 women). Expenses: Contact institution. *Financial support:* Federal Work-Study and scholarships/grants available. In 2006, 285 master's, 23 doctorates awarded. *Degree program information:* Part-time and evening/weekend programs available. *Application deadline:* For spring admission, 12/31 for domestic students. Applications are processed on a rolling basis. *Application fee:* $20. *Application Contact:* Andrea Cyterski-Acosta, Dean of Enrollment, 210-829-6005, Fax: 210-829-3921, E-mail: cyterski@uiwtx.edu. *Dean,* Dr. Kevin Vichcales, 210-829-2759, Fax: 210-805-3559, E-mail: vichcale@uiwtx.edu.

College of Humanities, Arts, and Social Sciences Students: 1 full-time (0 women), 17 part-time (12 women); includes 4 African Americans, 7 Hispanic Americans, 1 international. Average age 42. *Faculty:* 5 full-time (2 women), 1 part-time/adjunct (0 women). Expenses: Contact institution. *Financial support:* Federal Work-Study, scholarships/grants, and tuition waivers (partial) available. In 2006, 9 degrees awarded. *Degree program information:* Part-time and evening/weekend programs available. Offers English (MA); humanities, arts, and social sciences (MA); multidisciplinary studies (MA); religious studies (MA). *Application deadline:* For spring admission, 12/31 for domestic students. Applications are processed on a rolling basis. *Application fee:* $20. *Application Contact:* Andrea Cyterski-Acosta, Dean of Enrollment, 210-829-6005, Fax: 210-829-3921, E-mail: cyterski@uiwtx.edu. *Dean,* Dr. Donna Aronson, 210-829-6022, Fax: 210-829-3880, E-mail: aronson@uiwtx.edu.

Dreeben School of Education Students: 26 full-time (17 women), 269 part-time (181 women); includes 127 minority (28 African Americans, 1 American Indian/Alaska Native, 3 Asian Americans or Pacific Islanders, 95 Hispanic Americans), 56 international. Average age 37. *Faculty:* 19 full-time (9 women), 14 part-time/adjunct (9 women). Expenses: Contact institution. *Financial support:* Federal Work-Study and scholarships/grants available. In 2006, 30 master's, 23 doctorates awarded. *Degree program information:* Evening/weekend programs available. Offers adult education (M Ed, MA); diversity education (M Ed, MA); early childhood education (M Ed, MA); education (M Ed, MA, MAT, PhD); elementary teaching (MAT); general education (M Ed, MA); instructional technology (M Ed, MA); international education and entrepreneurship (PhD); kinesiology (M Ed, MA); mathematics education (PhD); organizational leadership (PhD); organizational learning (M Ed, MA); reading (M Ed, MA); secondary teaching (MAT); special education (M Ed, MA). *Application deadline:* For fall admission, 8/15 priority date for domestic students; for spring admission, 12/31 for domestic students. Applications are processed on a rolling basis. *Application fee:* $20. *Application Contact:* Andrea Cyterski-Acosta, Dean of Enrollment, 210-829-6005, Fax: 210-829-3921, E-mail: cyterski@uiwtx.edu. *Dean,* Dr. Denise Staudt, 210-283-5028, Fax: 210-829-3144, E-mail: staudt@uiwtx.edu.

H-E-B School of Business and Administration Students: 20 full-time (13 women), 380 part-time (222 women); includes 223 minority (30 African Americans, 4 American Indian/Alaska Native, 4 Asian Americans or Pacific Islanders, 185 Hispanic Americans), 53 international. Average age 32. *Faculty:* 15 full-time (7 women), 21 part-time/adjunct (6 women). Expenses: Contact institution. *Financial support:* Federal Work-Study, scholarships/grants, and tuition waivers (partial) available. In 2006, 177 degrees awarded. *Degree program information:* Part-time and evening/weekend programs available. Offers adult education (MAA); applied administration (MAA); business and administration (MAA, MBA, Certificate); communication arts (MAA); English (MAA); instructional technology (MAA); international business (MBA, Certificate); multidisciplinary sciences (MAA); nutrition (MAA); organizational development (MAA, Certificate); project management (Certificate); sports management (MAA, MBA); urban administration (MAA). *Application deadline:* For fall admission, 8/15 priority date for domestic students; for spring admission, 12/31 for domestic students. Applications are processed on a rolling basis. *Application fee:* $20. *Application Contact:* Andrea Cyterski-Acosta, Dean of Enrollment, 210-829-6005, Fax: 210-829-3921, E-mail: cyterski@uiwtx.edu. *Dean,* Dr. Robert Ryan, 210-829-3924, Fax: 210-829-3169, E-mail: ryan@uiwtx.edu.

School of Interactive Media and Design Students: 1 full-time (0 women), 33 part-time (19 women); includes 20 minority (3 African Americans, 17 Hispanic Americans), 2 international. Average age 31. *Faculty:* 2 full-time (1 woman), 2 part-time/adjunct (0 women). Expenses: Contact institution. *Financial support:* Federal Work-Study and scholarships/grants available. In 2006, 15 degrees awarded. Offers communication arts (MA); interactive media and design (MA). *Application fee:* $20. *Application Contact:* Andrea Cyterski-Acosta, Dean of Enrollment, 210-829-6005, Fax: 210-829-3921, E-mail: cyterski@uiwtx.edu. *Dean,* Dr. Cheryl Anderson, 210-829-3923, Fax: 210-829-3196, E-mail: cheryla@uiwtx.edu.

School of Mathematics, Sciences, and Engineering Students: 4 full-time (all women), 63 part-time (55 women); includes 30 minority (4 African Americans, 2 Asian Americans or Pacific Islanders, 24 Hispanic Americans). Average age 32. *Faculty:* 9 full-time (6 women), 3 part-time/adjunct (all women). Expenses: Contact institution. *Financial support:* Research assistantships, teaching assistantships, Federal Work-Study and scholarships/grants available. In 2006, 33 degrees awarded. *Degree program information:* Part-time and evening/weekend programs available. Offers biology (MA, MS); mathematics (MS); mathematics, sciences, and engineering (MA, MS); multidisciplinary sciences (MA); nutrition (MS); teaching (MA). *Application deadline:* For fall admission, 8/15 priority date for domestic students; for spring admission, 12/31 for domestic students. Applications are processed on a rolling basis. *Application fee:* $20. *Application Contact:* Andrea Cyterski-Acosta, Dean of Enrollment, 210-829-6005, Fax: 210-829-3921, E-mail: cyterski@uiwtx.edu. *Dean,* Dr. Glen Edward James, 210-829-2717, Fax: 210-829-3153, E-mail: gjames@uiwtx.edu.

School of Nursing and Health Professions Students: 5 full-time (4 women), 53 part-time (40 women); includes 32 minority (7 African Americans, 1 American Indian/Alaska Native, 3 Asian Americans or Pacific Islanders, 21 Hispanic Americans), 1 international. Average age 38. *Faculty:* 9 full-time (6 women), 1 (woman) part-time/adjunct. Expenses: Contact institution. *Financial support:* Research assistantships, teaching assistantships, Federal Work-Study and scholarships/grants available. In 2006, 21 degrees awarded. *Degree program information:* Part-time and evening/weekend programs available. Offers kinesiology (MS); nursing (MSN); nursing and health professions (MS, MSN); sports management (MS). *Application deadline:* For fall admission, 8/15 priority date for domestic students; for spring admission, 12/31 for domestic students. Applications are processed on a rolling basis. *Application fee:* $20. *Application Contact:* Andrea Cyterski-Acosta, Dean of Enrollment, 210-829-6005, Fax: 210-829-3921, E-mail: cyterski@uiwtx.edu. *Dean,* Dr. Kathleen Light, 210-829-3982, Fax: 210-829-3174.

UNIVERSITY OF THE PACIFIC, Stockton, CA 95211-0197

General Information Independent, coed, university. CGS member. *Enrollment:* 6,251 graduate, professional, and undergraduate students; 2,028 full-time matriculated graduate/professional students (1,045 women), 689 part-time matriculated graduate/professional students (376 women). *Enrollment by degree level:* 2,133 first professional, 314 master's, 225 doctoral, 43 other advanced degrees. *Graduate faculty:* 266 full-time (101 women), 255 part-time/adjunct (104 women). *Tuition:* Full-time $26,920. *Required fees:* $430. Tuition and fees vary according to course load. *Graduate housing:* Rooms and/or apartments available on a first-come, first-served basis to single and married students. Typical cost: $5,350 per year ($8,700 including board) for single students; $4,350 per year ($8,700 including board) for married students. Housing application deadline: 7/1. *Student services:* Campus employment opportunities, campus safety program, career counseling, disabled student services, free psychological counseling, international student services, low-cost health insurance, multicultural affairs office, teacher training. *Library facilities:* Holt Memorial Library plus 1 other. *Online resources:* library catalog, web page, access to other libraries' catalogs. *Collection:* 373,759 titles, 1,826 serial subscriptions, 10,755 audiovisual materials. *Research affiliation:* Lawrence Hall of Science.

Computer facilities: Computer purchase and lease plans are available. 350 computers available on campus for general student use. A campuswide network can be accessed from student residence rooms and from off campus. Internet access and online class registration are available. *Web address:* http://www.pacific.edu/.

General Application Contact: Connie Henderson, Graduate Recruit/Admissions Director, 209-946-2261, Fax: 209-946-2858.

GRADUATE UNITS

Arthur A. Dugoni School of Dentistry Expenses: Contact institution. *Financial support:* In 2006–07, 374 students received support. Institutionally sponsored loans, scholarships/grants, and stipends available. Support available to part-time students. Financial award application deadline: 3/2; financial award applicants required to submit FAFSA. Offers advanced education in general dentistry (Certificate); dentistry (MSD); international dental studies (DDS); oral and maxillofacial surgery (Certificate). *Application deadline:* For fall admission, 9/15 priority date for international students. Applications are processed on a rolling basis. Electronic applications accepted. *Application Contact:* Dr. Craig S. Yarborough, Associate Dean for Institutional Advancement and Student Services, 415-929-6491. *Dean,* Dr. Arthur A. Dugoni, 415-929-6424.

College of the Pacific Students: 8 full-time (6 women), 43 part-time (28 women); includes 13 minority (6 Asian Americans or Pacific Islanders, 7 Hispanic Americans), 1 international. Average age 26. 75 applicants, 37% accepted, 20 enrolled. *Faculty:* 38 full-time (13 women), 4 part-time/adjunct (2 women). Expenses: Contact institution. *Financial support:* Teaching assistantships, institutionally sponsored loans available. Support available to part-time students. Financial award application deadline: 3/1; financial award applicants required to submit FAFSA. In 2006, 29 degrees awarded. Offers biological sciences (MS); communication (MA); psychology (MA); sport sciences (MA). *Application fee:* $75. *Application Contact:* Information Contact, 209-946-2261. *Dean,* Dr. Robert Cox, 209-946-2023.

Conservatory of Music Students: 4 full-time (all women), 8 part-time (5 women); includes 3 minority (1 Asian American or Pacific Islander, 2 Hispanic Americans). Average age 28. 9 applicants, 78% accepted, 4 enrolled. *Faculty:* 3 full-time (all women), 4 part-time/adjunct (2 women). Expenses: Contact institution. *Financial support:* Teaching assistantships, institutionally sponsored loans available. Support available to part-time students. Financial award application deadline: 3/1; financial award applicants required to submit FAFSA. In 2006, 2 degrees awarded. Offers music (MA, MM); music education (MM); music therapy (MA). *Application deadline:* For fall admission, 3/1 priority date for domestic students; for spring admission, 10/1 priority date for domestic students. Applications are processed on a rolling basis. *Application fee:* $75. *Application Contact:* Dr. Therese West, Chairperson, 209-946-3194. *Dean,* Dr. Steven Anderson, 209-946-2417.

Eberhardt School of Business Students: 35 full-time (19 women), 11 part-time (4 women); includes 12 minority (1 African American, 8 Asian Americans or Pacific Islanders, 3 Hispanic Americans), 5 international. Average age 27. 85 applicants, 53% accepted, 20 enrolled. *Faculty:* 25 full-time (8 women), 1 part-time/adjunct (0 women). Expenses: Contact institution. *Financial support:* Fellowships, research assistantships, Federal Work-Study and institutionally sponsored loans available. Support available to part-time students. Financial award application deadline: 3/1; financial award applicants required to submit FAFSA. In 2006, 23 degrees awarded. *Degree program information:* Part-time programs available. Offers business (MBA). *Application deadline:* For fall admission, 7/31 priority date for domestic students; for spring admission, 11/30 for domestic students. Applications are processed on a rolling basis. *Application fee:* $75. *Application Contact:* Dr. Chris Lozano, MBA Recruiting Director, 209-946-2597, Fax: 209-946-2586, E-mail: clozano@pacific.edu. *Dean,* Dr. Charles Williams, 209-946-2466, Fax: 209-946-2586.

McGeorge School of Law Students: 686 full-time, 321 part-time. Average age 24. 3,621 applicants, 31% accepted. *Faculty:* 39 full-time (12 women), 31 part-time/adjunct (7 women). Expenses: Contact institution. *Financial support:* In 2006–07, 528 students received support, including 9 fellowships, 20 research assistantships (averaging $6,485 per year); career-related internships or fieldwork, Federal Work-Study, institutionally sponsored loans, and scholarships/grants also available. Support available to part-time students. Financial award applicants required to submit FAFSA. In 2006, 261 JDs, 19 master's awarded. *Degree program information:* Part-time and evening/weekend programs available. Offers government and public policy (LL M); international law (LL M); international waters resources law (LL M); law (JD); transnational business practice (LL M). *Application deadline:* For fall admission, 5/1 priority date for domestic students. Applications are processed on a rolling basis. *Application fee:* $50. Electronic applications accepted. *Application Contact:* 916-739-7105, Fax: 916-739-7134, E-mail: admissionsmcgeorge@uop.edu. *Dean,* Elizabeth Rindskopf Parker, 916-739-7151, E-mail: elizabeth@uop.edu.

School of Education Students: 67 full-time (50 women), 105 part-time (66 women); includes 58 minority (11 African Americans, 1 American Indian/Alaska Native, 20 Asian Americans or Pacific Islanders, 26 Hispanic Americans), 5 international. Average age 33. 116 applicants, 62% accepted, 51 enrolled. *Faculty:* 20 full-time (12 women), 9 part-time/adjunct (4 women).

University of the Pacific (continued)

Expenses: Contact institution. *Financial support:* In 2006–07, 13 teaching assistantships were awarded; institutionally sponsored loans also available. Support available to part-time students. Financial award application deadline: 3/1; financial award applicants required to submit FAFSA. In 2006, 57 master's, 9 doctorates awarded. Offers curriculum and instruction (M Ed, MA, Ed D); education (M Ed); educational administration (MA, Ed D); educational psychology (MA, Ed D); school psychology (Ed S); special education (MA). *Application deadline:* For fall admission, 3/1 priority date for domestic students; for spring admission, 10/15 for domestic students. Applications are processed on a rolling basis. *Application fee:* $75. *Dean,* Dr. Lynn Beck, 209-946-2683, E-mail: lbeck@pacific.edu.

School of International Studies *Faculty:* 6 full-time (3 women), 3 part-time/adjunct (0 women). Expenses: Contact institution. *Financial support:* Application deadline: 3/1; In 2006, 2 degrees awarded. Offers intercultural relations (MA); international studies (MA). *Application fee:* $75. *Dean,* Dr. Margee Ensign, 209-946-2650, E-mail: mensign@pacific.edu.

School of Pharmacy and Health Sciences Students: 737 full-time (468 women), 66 part-time (35 women); includes 450 minority (8 African Americans, 4 American Indian/Alaska Native, 402 Asian Americans or Pacific Islanders, 36 Hispanic Americans), 30 international. Average age 27. 309 applicants, 38% accepted, 66 enrolled. *Faculty:* 59 full-time (26 women), 18 part-time/adjunct (14 women). Expenses: Contact institution. *Financial support:* In 2006–07, 33 teaching assistantships were awarded; career-related internships or fieldwork, Federal Work-Study, and institutionally sponsored loans also available. Support available to part-time students. Financial award application deadline: 3/1; financial award applicants required to submit FAFSA. In 2006, 191 first professional degrees, 27 master's, 34 doctorates awarded. Offers pharmaceutical sciences (MS, PhD); pharmacy (Pharm D, MS, DPT, PhD); physical therapy (MS, DPT); speech-language pathology (MS). *Application fee:* $75. *Application Contact:* Cyndi Porter, Outreach Officer, 209-946-3957, Fax: 209-946-2410, E-mail: cporter@pacific.edu. *Dean,* Dr. Philip Oppenheimer, 209-946-2561, Fax: 209-946-2410.

UNIVERSITY OF THE SACRED HEART, San Juan, PR 00914-0383

General Information Independent-religious, coed, comprehensive institution. *Graduate housing:* Room and/or apartments available on a first-come, first-served basis to single students; on-campus housing not available to married students. Housing application deadline: 5/31.

GRADUATE UNITS

Graduate Programs *Degree program information:* Part-time and evening/weekend programs available. Offers advertising (MA); contemporary culture and means (MA); early childhood education (M Ed); human resource management (MBA); human rights and anti-discriminatory processes (MASJ); instruction systems and education technology (M Ed); journalism and mass communication (MA); literary creation (MA); management information systems (MBA); marketing (MBA); mediation and transformation of conflicts (MASJ); medical technology (Certificate); natural science (Certificate); non-profit organization (MS); occupational health (MS); public relations (MA); security and occupational health (MS); taxation (MBA).

UNIVERSITY OF THE SCIENCES IN PHILADELPHIA, Philadelphia, PA 19104-4495

General Information Independent, coed, university. *Enrollment:* 2,857 graduate, professional, and undergraduate students; 96 full-time matriculated graduate/professional students (56 women), 203 part-time matriculated graduate/professional students (123 women). *Enrollment by degree level:* 14 first professional, 192 master's, 90 doctoral, 3 other advanced degrees. *Graduate faculty:* 68 full-time (19 women), 64 part-time/adjunct (34 women). *Tuition:* Part-time $1,058 per credit. Tuition and fees vary according to program. *Graduate housing:* On-campus housing not available. *Student services:* Campus employment opportunities, campus safety program, career counseling, disabled student services, free psychological counseling, international student services, low-cost health insurance, writing training. *Library facilities:* Joseph W. England Library plus 1 other. *Online resources:* library catalog, web page, access to other libraries' catalogs. *Collection:* 87,125 titles, 9,817 serial subscriptions. *Research affiliation:* Wyeth Pharmaceuticals (cell biology), Merck and Company (cell biology), Johnson and Johnson (cell biology), Encapsulation Systems (analytical chemistry), Pfizer (computational chemistry), Schering-Plough (computational chemistry).

Computer facilities: 120 computers available on campus for general student use. A campuswide network can be accessed from student residence rooms and from off campus. Internet access is available. *Web address:* http://www.usip.edu/.

General Application Contact: Dr. Rodney J. Wigent, Dean, College of Graduate Studies, 215-596-8886, Fax: 215-895-1185, E-mail: graduate@usip.edu.

GRADUATE UNITS

College of Graduate Studies Students: 96 full-time (56 women), 203 part-time (123 women); includes 33 minority (13 African Americans, 19 Asian Americans or Pacific Islanders, 1 Hispanic American), 48 international. Average age 31. *Faculty:* 68 full-time (19 women), 64 part-time/adjunct (34 women). Expenses: Contact institution. *Financial support:* In 2006–07, 87 students received support, including 12 fellowships with full tuition reimbursements available, 1 research assistantship with full tuition reimbursement available, 43 teaching assistantships with full and partial tuition reimbursements available (averaging $21,040 per year); institutionally sponsored loans, scholarships/grants, traineeships, tuition waivers (full and partial), and unspecified assistantships also available. Support available to part-time students. Financial award application deadline: 5/1. In 2006, 13 first professional degrees, 70 master's, 4 doctorates awarded. *Degree program information:* Part-time and evening/weekend programs available. Offers biochemistry (MS, PhD); bioinformatics (MS); biomedical writing (MS); cell biology and biotechnology (MS); chemistry (MS, PhD); health policy (MS, PhD); health psychology (MS); medical marketing writing (Certificate); medicinal chemistry (MS, PhD); pharmaceutical business (MBA); pharmaceutics (MS, PhD); pharmacognosy (MS, PhD); pharmacology (MS, PhD); pharmacy administration (MS); physical therapy (DPT); public health (MPH); regulatory affairs writing (Certificate); toxicology (MS, PhD). *Application deadline:* For fall admission, 5/1 for international students; for winter admission, 10/1 for international students; for spring admission, 3/1 for international students. Applications are processed on a rolling basis. *Application fee:* $50. Electronic applications accepted. *Application Contact:* Joyce D'Angelo, Administrative Assistant, 215-596-8937, E-mail: j.dangel@usip.edu. *Dean,* Dr. Rodney J. Wigent, 215-596-8886, Fax: 215-895-1185, E-mail: graduate@usip.edu.

Philadelphia College of Pharmacy Offers pharmacy (Pharm D); pharmacy practice (Pharm D).

UNIVERSITY OF THE VIRGIN ISLANDS, Saint Thomas, VI 00802-9990

General Information Territory-supported, coed, comprehensive institution. *Enrollment:* 2,487 graduate, professional, and undergraduate students; 30 full-time matriculated graduate/professional students (20 women), 185 part-time matriculated graduate/professional students (158 women). *Enrollment by degree level:* 215 master's. *Graduate faculty:* 19 full-time (6 women), 8 part-time/adjunct (4 women). *Tuition, area resident:* Full-time $4,950; part-time $275 per credit. Tuition, nonresident: full-time $9,900; part-time $550 per credit. *Required fees:* $130 per term. Tuition and fees vary according to course load and degree level. *Graduate housing:* On-campus housing not available. *Student services:* Career counseling. *Library facilities:* Ralph M. Paiewonsky Library. *Online resources:* library catalog, web page. *Collection:* 106,361 titles, 113,623 serial subscriptions, 3,000 audiovisual materials.

Computer facilities: 100 computers available on campus for general student use. A campuswide network can be accessed from off campus. Internet access and online class registration are available. *Web address:* http://www.uvi.edu/.

General Application Contact: Carolyn Cook-Roberts, Director of Admissions, 340-693-1224, Fax: 340-693-1155, E-mail: ccook@uvi.edu.

GRADUATE UNITS

Graduate Programs Students: 29 full-time (19 women), 153 part-time (133 women); includes 141 minority (132 African Americans, 1 American Indian/Alaska Native, 3 Asian Americans or Pacific Islanders, 5 Hispanic Americans), 24 international. Average age 35. 117 applicants, 67% accepted, 61 enrolled. *Faculty:* 19 full-time (6 women), 8 part-time/adjunct (4 women). Expenses: Contact institution. *Financial support:* Career-related internships or fieldwork and scholarships/grants available. Financial award application deadline: 4/15. In 2006, 65 degrees awarded. *Degree program information:* Part-time and evening/weekend programs available. Offers mathematics for secondary teachers (MA); science and mathematics (MA). *Application deadline:* For fall admission, 4/30 for domestic and international students; for spring admission, 10/30 for domestic and international students. Applications are processed on a rolling basis. *Application fee:* $25. *Application Contact:* Carolyn Cook-Roberts, Director of Admissions, 340-693-1224, Fax: 340-693-1155, E-mail: ccook@uvi.edu.

Division of Business Administration Students: 3 full-time (2 women), 21 part-time (17 women); includes 22 minority (21 African Americans, 1 American Indian/Alaska Native), 1 international. Average age 34. 22 applicants, 73% accepted, 16 enrolled. *Faculty:* 6 full-time (0 women). Expenses: Contact institution. *Financial support:* Application deadline: 4/15. In 2006, 14 degrees awarded. *Degree program information:* Part-time and evening/weekend programs available. Offers business administration (MBA). *Application deadline:* For fall admission, 4/30 for domestic and international students; for spring admission, 10/30 for domestic and international students. *Application fee:* $25. *Application Contact:* Carolyn Cook-Roberts, Director of Admissions, 340-693-1224, Fax: 340-693-1155, E-mail: ccook@uvi.edu. *Chairperson,* Dr. Paul G. Simmonds, 340-692-4151, Fax: 340-692-4009, E-mail: psimmon@uvi.edu.

Division of Education Students: 22 full-time (14 women), 118 part-time (105 women); includes 105 minority (97 African Americans, 3 Asian Americans or Pacific Islanders, 5 Hispanic Americans), 21 international. Average age 36. 76 applicants, 66% accepted, 37 enrolled. *Faculty:* 9 full-time (5 women), 6 part-time/adjunct (4 women). Expenses: Contact institution. *Financial support:* Scholarships/grants available. Financial award application deadline: 4/15. In 2006, 29 degrees awarded. *Degree program information:* Part-time and evening/weekend programs available. Offers education (MAE). *Application deadline:* For fall admission, 4/30 for domestic and international students; for spring admission, 11/30 for domestic and international students. *Application fee:* $25. *Application Contact:* Carolyn Cook-Roberts, Director of Admissions, 340-693-1224, Fax: 340-693-1155, E-mail: ccook@uvi.edu. *Chairperson,* Dr. Cynthia L. Jackson, 340-692-4117, Fax: 340-692-4009, E-mail: cjackso2@uvi.edu.

Division of Humanities and Social Sciences Students: 4 full-time (3 women), 6 part-time (4 women); includes 8 minority (all African Americans), 1 international. Average age 38. 12 applicants, 67% accepted, 4 enrolled. *Faculty:* 1 full-time (0 women), 2 part-time/adjunct (0 women). Expenses: Contact institution. *Financial support:* Career-related internships or fieldwork and scholarships/grants available. Financial award application deadline: 4/15. In 2006, 7 degrees awarded. *Degree program information:* Part-time and evening/weekend programs available. Offers humanities and social sciences (MPA). *Application deadline:* For fall admission, 4/30 for domestic and international students; for spring admission, 10/30 for domestic and international students. *Application fee:* $25. *Application Contact:* Carolyn Cook-Roberts, Director of Admissions, 340-693-1224, Fax: 340-693-1155, E-mail: ccook@uvi.edu. *Chairperson,* Dr. Malik Sekou, 340-693-1261, Fax: 340-693-1265, E-mail: msekou@uvi.edu.

UNIVERSITY OF THE WEST, Rosemead, CA 91770

General Information Independent, coed, comprehensive institution. *Graduate housing:* Room and/or apartments guaranteed to single students; on-campus housing not available to married students.

GRADUATE UNITS

Department of Business Administration *Degree program information:* Part-time and evening/weekend programs available. Offers business administration (EMBA); finance (MBA); information technology and management (MBA); international business (MBA); nonprofit organization management (MBA).

Department of Religious Studies *Degree program information:* Part-time and evening/weekend programs available. Offers Buddhist studies (MA, DBS); comparative religions (MA); religious studies (PhD).

THE UNIVERSITY OF TOLEDO, Toledo, OH 43606-3390

General Information State-supported, coed, university. CGS member. *Enrollment:* 19,374 graduate, professional, and undergraduate students; 1,705 full-time matriculated graduate/professional students (928 women), 1,370 part-time matriculated graduate/professional students (870 women). *Enrollment by degree level:* 295 first professional, 2,141 master's, 555 doctoral, 84 other advanced degrees. *Graduate faculty:* 358. *Graduate housing:* Room and/or apartments available to single students; on-campus housing not available to married students. *Student services:* Campus employment opportunities, campus safety program, career counseling, child daycare facilities, disabled student services, exercise/wellness program, free psychological counseling, grant writing training, international student services, low-cost health insurance, multicultural affairs office, teacher training, writing training. *Library facilities:* Carlson Library plus 7 others. *Online resources:* library catalog, web page, access to other libraries' catalogs. *Collection:* 1.8 million titles, 6,500 serial subscriptions. *Research affiliation:* NASA–Glen Research Center at Lewis Field (aerospace engineering), Merck and Company (pharmaceutical research), Midwest Astronomical Data Reduction and Analysis Facility (astronomy), Edison Industrial Systems Center (systems integration, quality control, mathematical modeling), Ohio Aerospace Institute (aerospace research), National Renewable Energy Laboratory (thin films, photovoltaics).

Computer facilities: 2,800 computers available on campus for general student use. A campuswide network can be accessed from student residence rooms and from off campus. Internet access and online class registration, online transcripts, student account and grade information are available. *Web address:* http://www.utoledo.edu/.

General Application Contact: Jamilah Jones, Recruitment Coordinator, 419-530-8582, Fax: 419-530-4724, E-mail: jamilah.jones10@utoledo.edu.

GRADUATE UNITS

College of Graduate Studies Students: 1,705 full-time (928 women), 1,370 part-time (870 women); includes 313 minority (213 African Americans, 5 American Indian/Alaska Native, 47 Asian Americans or Pacific Islanders, 48 Hispanic Americans), 591 international. Average age 30. *Faculty:* 491. Expenses: Contact institution. *Financial support:* In 2006–07, 4 fellowships with tuition reimbursements, 278 research assistantships with tuition reimbursements (averaging $6,481 per year), 550 teaching assistantships with tuition reimbursements (averaging $9,719 per year) were awarded; career-related internships or fieldwork, Federal Work-Study, institutionally sponsored loans, scholarships/grants, tuition waivers (full and partial), unspecified assistantships, and administrative assistantships also available. Support available to part-time students. Financial award applicants required to submit FAFSA. In 2006, 577 master's, 30 doctorates, 22 other advanced degrees awarded. *Degree program information:* Part-time and evening/weekend programs available. Postbaccalaureate distance learning degree programs offered. *Application deadline:* Applications are processed on a rolling basis. *Application fee:* $45. Electronic applications accepted. *Application Contact:* Graduate School Office, 419-530-4723, Fax: 419-530-4724, E-mail: gradsch@utnet.utoledo.edu. *Assistant Dean, Research and Graduate Studies,* Dr. Martin A. Abraham, 419-530-4968, Fax: 419-530-4724, E-mail: martin.abraham@utoledo.edu.

College of Arts and Sciences Students: 406 full-time (181 women), 155 part-time (85 women); includes 47 minority (35 African Americans, 1 American Indian/Alaska Native, 6 Asian Americans or Pacific Islanders, 5 Hispanic Americans), 163 international. Average age 29. 572 applicants, 49% accepted, 183 enrolled. *Faculty:* 163 full-time (26 women), 55 part-time/adjunct (18 women). Expenses: Contact institution. *Financial support:* In 2006–07, 111 research assistantships with full tuition reimbursements (averaging $13,643 per year), 283 teaching assistantships with full tuition reimbursements (averaging $10,700 per year) were awarded; fellowships, career-related internships or fieldwork, Federal Work-

Study, institutionally sponsored loans, scholarships/grants, tuition waivers (full), and administrative assistantships also available. Support available to part-time students. In 2006, 130 master's, 30 doctorates, 6 other advanced degrees awarded. *Degree program information:* Part-time and evening/weekend programs available. Offers analytical chemistry (MS, PhD); applied mathematics (MS, PhD); arts and sciences (MA, MLS, MMP, MPA, MS, PhD, Certificate); behavioral (PhD); biological chemistry (MS, PhD); biology (MS, PhD); biology (ecology track) (MS, PhD); clinical psychology (PhD); communication studies (Certificate); economics (MA); English as a second language (MA); experimental psychology (MA); French (MA); geographic information systems and applied geographics (Certificate); geography (MA); geology (MS); German (MA); health care policy (MPA); health care policy and administration (Certificate); history (MA, PhD); inorganic chemistry (MS, PhD); liberal studies (MLS); literature (MA); mathematics (MA, PhD); municipal administration (MPA); organic chemistry (MS, PhD); performance (MMP); philosophy (MA); physical chemistry (MS, PhD); physics (MS, PhD); planning (MA); political science (MA); public administration (MPA); sociology (MA); Spanish (MA); spatially integrated social sciences (PhD); statistics (MS, PhD); teaching of writing (Certificate). *Application fee:* $45. Electronic applications accepted. *Interim Dean,* Sue Rowlands, 419-530-7842.

College of Business Administration Students: 192 full-time (75 women), 175 part-time (55 women); includes 21 minority (14 African Americans, 2 Asian Americans or Pacific Islanders, 5 Hispanic Americans), 90 international. Average age 29. 260 applicants, 65% accepted, 105 enrolled. *Faculty:* 28 full-time (3 women), 18 part-time/adjunct (1 woman). Expenses: Contact institution. *Financial support:* In 2006–07, 59 research assistantships with tuition reimbursements (averaging $7,500 per year), 1 teaching assistantship with tuition reimbursement (averaging $5,500 per year) were awarded; fellowships, career-related internships or fieldwork, Federal Work-Study, institutionally sponsored loans, scholarships/grants, tuition waivers (full), and administrative assistantships also available. Support available to part-time students. Financial award application deadline: 4/1; financial award applicants required to submit FAFSA. In 2006, 150 master's, 7 doctorates awarded. *Degree program information:* Part-time and evening/weekend programs available. Offers accounting (MBA, MS Acct, MSA); business administration (EMBA, MBA, MS Acct, MSA, DME); business administration-general (MBA); finance and business economics (MBA); human resource management (MBA); information systems (MBA); international business (MBA); management (MBA); manufacturing management (MBA, DME); marketing (MBA); operations management (MBA). *Application deadline:* For fall admission, 8/1 priority date for domestic students. Applications are processed on a rolling basis. *Application fee:* $45. Electronic applications accepted. *Dean,* Dr. Thomas G. Gutteridge, 419-530-4060, Fax: 419-530-7260, E-mail: mba@uoft01.utoledo.edu.

College of Education Students: 244 full-time (176 women), 485 part-time (365 women); includes 115 minority (85 African Americans, 3 American Indian/Alaska Native, 5 Asian Americans or Pacific Islanders, 22 Hispanic Americans), 24 international. Average age 35. 240 applicants, 84% accepted, 148 enrolled. *Faculty:* 38 full-time (18 women), 21 part-time/adjunct (11 women). Expenses: Contact institution. *Financial support:* In 2006–07, 6 research assistantships with full tuition reimbursements (averaging $11,000 per year), 14 teaching assistantships with full tuition reimbursements (averaging $11,000 per year) were awarded; fellowships, career-related internships or fieldwork, Federal Work-Study, institutionally sponsored loans, scholarships/grants, tuition waivers (full), and administrative assistantships also available. Support available to part-time students. Financial award application deadline: 4/1; financial award applicants required to submit FAFSA. In 2006, 182 master's, 13 doctorates, 1 other advanced degree awarded. *Degree program information:* Part-time and evening/weekend programs available. Offers art education (ME); career and technical education (Ed S); career and technical training (ME); curriculum and instruction (ME, DE, PhD, Ed S); early childhood education (ME, Ed S); education (MAE, ME, MES, MME, DE, PhD, Ed S); education and administration supervision (ME); education and biology (MES); education and chemistry (MES); education and economics (MAE); education and English (MAE); education and French (MAE); education and geology (MES); education and German (MAE); education and history (MAE); education and mathematics (MAE, MES); education and physics (MES); education and political science (MAE); education and sociology (MAE); education and Spanish (MAE); educational administration and supervision (DE, Ed S); educational media (DE, PhD, Ed S); educational psychology (ME, DE, PhD); educational research and measurement (ME, PhD); educational sociology (DE, PhD); educational technology (ME); educational theory and social foundations (ME); elementary (PhD, Ed S); English as a second language (MAE); foundations of education (DE, PhD); gifted and talented (Ed S); health education (ME); higher education (ME, PhD); history of education (DE, PhD); middle childhood education (ME); music education (MME); philosophy of education (DE, PhD); physical education (ME); secondary education (ME, DE, PhD, Ed S); special education (ME, DE, PhD, Ed S). *Application deadline:* Applications are processed on a rolling basis. *Application fee:* $45. Electronic applications accepted. *Dean,* Dr. Thomas J. Switzer, 419-530-2026, Fax: 419-530-7719, E-mail: thomas.switzer@utoledo.edu.

College of Engineering Students: 209 full-time (45 women), 92 part-time (14 women); includes 9 minority (3 African Americans, 3 Asian Americans or Pacific Islanders, 3 Hispanic Americans), 199 international. Average age 28. 330 applicants, 66% accepted, 80 enrolled. *Faculty:* 68 full-time (10 women). Expenses: Contact institution. *Financial support:* In 2006–07, 1 fellowship with full tuition reimbursement (averaging $15,300 per year), 61 research assistantships with full tuition reimbursements (averaging $13,816 per year), 96 teaching assistantships with full tuition reimbursements (averaging $13,649 per year) were awarded; Federal Work-Study, scholarships/grants, tuition waivers (full and partial), and unspecified assistantships also available. Support available to part-time students. Financial award application deadline: 4/1. In 2006, 61 master's, 16 doctorates awarded. *Degree program information:* Part-time and evening/weekend programs available. Postbaccalaureate distance learning degree programs offered (minimal on-campus study). Offers bioengineering (MS, PhD); chemical engineering (MS); civil engineering (MS); computer science (MS); electrical engineering (MS); engineering (MS, PhD); engineering sciences (PhD); general engineering (MS); industrial engineering (MS); mechanical engineering (MS). *Application deadline:* For fall admission, 5/31 priority date for domestic students. Applications are processed on a rolling basis. *Application fee:* $45. Electronic applications accepted. *Application Contact:* Dr. Mohamed Samir Hefzy, Associate Dean, Graduate Studies and Research Administration, 419-530-7391, Fax: 419-530-7392, E-mail: mhefzy@eng.utoledo.edu. *Dean,* Dr. Nagi Naganathan, 419-530-8000, Fax: 419-530-8006, E-mail: nagi.naganathan@utoledo.edu.

College of Health Science and Human Service Average age 30. Expenses: Contact institution. *Financial support:* Research assistantships, teaching assistantships available. Offers community counseling (MA); counselor education (MA, PhD, Ed S); counselor education and school psychology (MA, PhD, Ed S); counselor education and supervision (PhD); criminal justice (MA, Certificate); exercise science (MSX, PhD); gerontology (Certificate); guidance/counselor education (PhD); health education (PhD); health science and human service (MA, MOT, MPH, MS, MSBS, MSX, OTD, PhD, Certificate, Ed S); human donation science (MS); juvenile justice (Certificate); kinesiology (MSX, PhD); occupational health (MS); occupational therapy (MOT, OTD); physical therapy (MS, DPT); physician assistant studies (MSBS); public health (MPH); public health and rehabilitative services (MA, MPH); recreation and leisure (MA); school counseling (MA); school psychology (MA, Ed S); severe behavioral spectrum (Certificate); social work (MS); speech-language pathology (MA). *Application deadline:* Applications are processed on a rolling basis. *Dean,* Dr. Jerome M. Sulivan, 419-530-4180.

College of Medicine Students: 151 full-time (58 women), 42 part-time (13 women); includes 28 minority (5 African Americans, 1 American Indian/Alaska Native, 21 Asian Americans or Pacific Islanders, 1 Hispanic American), 70 international. Average age 25. 213 applicants, 48% accepted, 71 enrolled. Expenses: Contact institution. *Financial support:* Career-related internships or fieldwork, Federal Work-Study, institutionally sponsored loans, scholarships/grants, and tuition waivers (full) available. Financial award application deadline: 6/1; financial award applicants required to submit FAFSA. Offers bioinformatics (MS); bioinformatics and proteomics/genomics (MSBS, Certificate); cancer biology (MS, PhD); cardiovascular and metabolic diseases (MS, PhD); cellular and molecular neurobiology (MS, PhD); infection, immunity and transplantation (MS); infection, immunology and transplantation (PhD); medical physics (MS); medical sciences (MS); medicine (MS, MSBS, PhD, Certificate); molecular and cellular biology (MS, PhD); molecular basis of disease (PhD); neurosciences and neurological disorders (MS, PhD); oral biology (MS); orthopedic science (MS); pathology (Certificate); radiology (MS); surgery (MS); urology (MS). *Application deadline:* For fall admission, 5/21 for domestic students. Applications are processed on a rolling basis. *Application fee:* $45. *Application Contact:* Sandy Velliquette, Information Contact, 419-383-4229. *Dean,* Dr. Almira F. Gohara, 419-383-4356.

College of Nursing Students: 64 full-time (58 women), 151 part-time (144 women); includes 13 minority (10 African Americans, 1 Asian American or Pacific Islander, 2 Hispanic Americans), 4 international. Average age 38. 129 applicants, 75% accepted, 87 enrolled. *Faculty:* 29 full-time. Expenses: Contact institution. *Financial support:* Federal Work-Study, institutionally sponsored loans, and scholarships/grants available. In 2006, 36 master's, 4 other advanced degrees awarded. *Degree program information:* Part-time programs available. Offers advanced practice nursing (MSN). *Application deadline:* For fall admission, 5/1 for domestic students; for spring admission, 9/1 for domestic students. *Application fee:* $45. *Application Contact:* Dr. Janet Robinson, Associate Dean, 419-383-5820, E-mail: jrobinson@mco.edu. *Dean,* Dr. Jeri Millstead, 419-383-5858, Fax: 419-383-6140, E-mail: mcogradschool@mco.edu.

College of Pharmacy Students: 41 full-time (16 women); includes 2 minority (1 African American, 1 Asian American or Pacific Islander), 18 international. Average age 26. 126 applicants, 11% accepted, 11 enrolled. *Faculty:* 36 full-time (17 women), 10 part-time/adjunct (4 women). Expenses: Contact institution. *Financial support:* Research assistantships with full tuition reimbursements, teaching assistantships with full tuition reimbursements, unspecified assistantships available. In 2006, 11 master's, 1 doctorate awarded. Offers administrative pharmacy (MSPS); industrial pharmacy (MSPS); medicinal and biological chemistry (MS, PhD); pharmaceutical science (MSPS); pharmacology (MSPS); pharmacy (MS, MSPS, PhD). *Application deadline:* For fall admission, 2/1 priority date for domestic students, 1/1 for international students. *Application fee:* $45. Electronic applications accepted. *Application Contact:* Karen F. Papadakis, Graduate Coordinator for Pharmaceutical Sciences, 419-530-1910, Fax: 419-530-1909, E-mail: kpapada@utnet.utoledo.edu. *Vice Dean Graduate Studies and Research,* Dr. Wayne P. Hoss, 419-530-1997, Fax: 419-530-1907, E-mail: whoss@utnet.utoledo.edu.

College of Law Students: 345 full-time (140 women), 186 part-time (74 women); includes 41 minority (16 African Americans, 2 American Indian/Alaska Native, 10 Asian Americans or Pacific Islanders, 13 Hispanic Americans). Average age 27. 1,216 applicants, 28% accepted, 190 enrolled. *Faculty:* 31 full-time (13 women), 14 part-time/adjunct (5 women). Expenses: Contact institution. *Financial support:* In 2006–07, 455 students received support, including 15 research assistantships (averaging $689 per year), 47 teaching assistantships; career-related internships or fieldwork, Federal Work-Study, and scholarships/grants also available. Support available to part-time students. Financial award application deadline: 8/1; financial award applicants required to submit FAFSA. In 2006, 140 degrees awarded. *Degree program information:* Part-time and evening/weekend programs available. Offers law (JD, MLW). *Application deadline:* For fall admission, 7/31 priority date for domestic students, 7/31 for international students. Applications are processed on a rolling basis. *Application fee:* $45. Electronic applications accepted. *Application Contact:* Carol E. Frendt, Assistant Dean of Law Admissions, 419-530-4131, Fax: 419-530-4345, E-mail: law.admissions@utoledo.edu. *Dean,* Douglas E. Ray, 419-530-2379, Fax: 419-530-4526, E-mail: douglas.ray@utoledo.edu.

See Close-Up on page 1127.

UNIVERSITY OF TORONTO, Toronto, ON M5S 1A1, Canada

General Information Province-supported, coed, university. CGS member. *Graduate housing:* Rooms and/or apartments available on a first-come, first-served basis to single students and available to married students. *Research affiliation:* Center for Addiction and Mental Health, Hospital for Sick Children, Pontifical Institute of Medieval Studies, Royal Ontario Museum, Canadian Institute for Theoretical Astrophysics, Fields Institute for Research in Mathematical Sciences.

GRADUATE UNITS

Faculty of Dentistry Offers dental anesthesia (M Sc); dental public health (M Sc); dentistry (DDS, M Sc, PhD); endodontics (M Sc); oral and maxillofacial surgery and anesthesia (M Sc); oral pathology (M Sc); oral radiology (M Sc); orthodontics (M Sc); pediatric dentistry (M Sc); periodontology (M Sc); prosthodontics (M Sc).

Faculty of Law *Degree program information:* Part-time programs available. Offers law (JD, LL M, MSL, SJD).

Faculty of Medicine Offers medicine (MD, M Sc, M Sc BMC, M Sc OT, M Sc PT, MH Sc, PhD).

School of Graduate Studies *Degree program information:* Part-time and evening/weekend programs available.

Humanities Division *Degree program information:* Part-time programs available. Offers classics (MA, PhD); comparative literature (MA, PhD); composition (Mus M, Mus Doc); drama (MA, PhD); East Asian studies (MA, PhD); English (MA, PhD); French language and literature (MA, PhD); Germanic languages and literatures (MA, PhD); history (MA, PhD); history and philosophy of science and technology (MA, PhD); history of art (MA, PhD); humanities (MA, MM St, Mus M, Mus Doc, PhD); Italian studies (MA, PhD); linguistics (MA, PhD); medieval studies (MA, PhD); museum studies (MM St); music education (Mus M, PhD); musicology/theory (MA, PhD); Near and Middle Eastern civilizations (MA, PhD); philosophy (MA, PhD); religion (MA, PhD); Slavic languages and literatures (MA, PhD); South Asian studies (MA, PhD); Spanish and Portuguese (MA, PhD).

Life Sciences Division *Degree program information:* Part-time programs available. Offers biochemistry (M Sc, PhD); biomedical communications (M Sc BMC); botany (M Sc, PhD); forestry (M Sc F, MFC, PhD); genetic counseling (M Sc); immunology (M Sc, PhD); laboratory medicine and pathobiology (M Sc, PhD); life sciences (M Sc, M Sc BMC, M Sc F, MA, MFC, MH Sc, MN, PhD, Certificate, Diploma); medical biophysics (M Sc, PhD); medical science (M Sc, PhD); molecular and medical genetics (M Sc, PhD); nursing science (MN, PhD, Certificate, Diploma); nutritional sciences (M Sc, PhD); pharmaceutical sciences (M Sc, PhD); pharmacology (M Sc, PhD); physical education and health (M Sc, PhD); physiology (M Sc, PhD); psychology (MA, PhD); public health services (M Sc, MH Sc, PhD, Diploma); rehabilitation science (M Sc); speech-language pathology (M Sc, MH Sc, PhD); zoology (M Sc, PhD).

Physical Sciences Division *Degree program information:* Part-time programs available. Offers aerospace science and engineering (M Eng, MA Sc, PhD); applied science and engineering (M Eng, M Eng Tel, MA Sc, MH Sc, PhD); astronomy (M Sc, PhD); biomedical engineering (MA Sc, PhD); chemical engineering and applied chemistry (M Eng, MA Sc, PhD); chemistry (M Sc, PhD); civil engineering (M Eng, MA Sc, PhD); clinical engineering (MH Sc); computer science (M Sc, PhD); electrical and computer engineering (M Eng, M Eng Tel, MA Sc, PhD); geology (M Sc, MA Sc, PhD); materials science and engineering (M Eng, MA Sc, PhD); mathematics (M Sc, MMF, PhD); mechanical and industrial engineering (M Eng, MA Sc, PhD); physical sciences (M Eng, M Eng Tel, M Sc, MA Sc, MH Sc, MMF, PhD); physics (M Sc, PhD); statistics (M Sc, PhD).

Social Sciences Division *Degree program information:* Part-time and evening/weekend programs available. Offers anthropology (M Sc, MA, PhD); architecture, landscape and design (M Arch, MLA, MUD); criminology (MA, PhD); economics (MA, PhD); education (M Ed, MA, MT, Ed D, PhD); geography (M Sc, MA, PhD); industrial relations (MIR, PhD); information studies (MI St, PhD, Diploma); management (EMBA, MBA, MMPA, PhD); planning (M Sc Pl); political science (MA, PhD); Russian and East European studies (MA); social sciences (EMBA, M Arch, M Ed, M Sc, M Sc Pl, MA, MBA, MI St, MIR, MIS, MLA, MMPA, MSW, MT, MUD, Ed D, PhD, Diploma); social work (MSW, PhD); sociology (MA, PhD).

UNIVERSITY OF TRINITY COLLEGE, Toronto, ON M5S 1H8, Canada

General Information Independent-religious, coed, graduate-only institution. *Enrollment by degree level:* 38 first professional, 26 master's, 27 doctoral, 26 other advanced degrees.

University of Trinity College (continued)

Graduate faculty: 4 full-time (1 woman), 30 part-time/adjunct (6 women). *Graduate housing:* Room and/or apartments available on a first-come, first-served basis to single students; on-campus housing not available to married students. Typical cost: $9,975 (including board). Housing application deadline: 7/15. *Student services:* Campus employment opportunities, campus safety program, career counseling, child daycare facilities, disabled student services, free psychological counseling, international student services, low-cost health insurance. *Library facilities:* The John W. Graham Library. *Online resources:* library catalog, web page, access to other libraries' catalogs. *Collection:* 193,956 titles, 409 serial subscriptions, 2,050 audiovisual materials.

Computer facilities: 43 computers available on campus for general student use. A campuswide network can be accessed from student residence rooms and from off campus. Internet access and online class registration, Microsoft Office Suite are available. *Web address:* http://www.trinity.utoronto.ca/.

General Application Contact: Rachel Richards, Administrative Assistant to the Dean, Faculty of Divinity, 416-978-2133, Fax: 416-978-4949, E-mail: divinity@trinity.utoronto.ca.

GRADUATE UNITS

Faculty of Divinity Students: 64 full-time (25 women), 53 part-time (31 women). Average age 45. 29 applicants, 100% accepted, 20 enrolled. *Faculty:* 4 full-time (1 woman), 30 part-time/adjunct (6 women). Expenses: Contact institution. *Financial support:* In 2006–07, 61 students received support, including 4 fellowships (averaging $4,000 per year); teaching assistantships, career-related internships or fieldwork, institutionally sponsored loans, and bursaries also available. Support available to part-time students. Financial award application deadline: 5/15. In 2006, 15 first professional degrees, 4 master's, 2 doctorates, 2 other advanced degrees awarded. *Degree program information:* Part-time programs available. Offers ministry (Diploma); ministry for church musicians (Diploma); theology (M Div, MTS, Th M, D Min, PhD, Th D, Diploma, L Th). *Application deadline:* For fall admission, 3/31 priority date for domestic and international students; for winter admission, 12/31 for domestic and international students; for spring admission, 4/30 priority date for domestic and international students. Applications are processed on a rolling basis. *Application fee:* $0. *Application Contact:* Rachel Richards, Administrative Assistant to the Dean, 416-978-2133, Fax: 416-978-4949, E-mail: divinity@trinity.utoronto.ca. *Dean,* Dr. David Neelands, 416-978-7750, Fax: 416-978-4949, E-mail: divdean@trinity.utoronto.ca.

UNIVERSITY OF TULSA, Tulsa, OK 74104-3189

General Information Independent-religious, coed, university. CGS member. *Enrollment:* 4,125 graduate, professional, and undergraduate students; 972 full-time matriculated graduate/professional students (362 women), 316 part-time matriculated graduate/professional students (158 women). *Enrollment by degree level:* 503 master's, 148 doctoral, 618 other advanced degrees. *Graduate faculty:* 215 full-time (63 women), 7 part-time/adjunct (4 women). *Tuition:* Full-time $13,338; part-time $741 per credit hour. *Graduate housing:* Rooms and/or apartments available on a first-come, first-served basis to single and married students. Typical cost: $4,090 per year ($7,404 including board) for single students; $4,090 per year ($9,404 including board) for married students. Housing application deadline: 2/9. *Student services:* Campus employment opportunities, campus safety program, career counseling, child daycare facilities, disabled student services, exercise/wellness program, free psychological counseling, international student services, low-cost health insurance, multicultural affairs office, teacher training, writing training. *Library facilities:* McFarlin Library plus 1 other. *Online resources:* library catalog, web page, access to other libraries' catalogs. *Collection:* 1.2 million titles, 26,228 serial subscriptions, 18,905 audiovisual materials. *Research affiliation:* Chevron Texaco (petroleum engineering), NEXT (Network of Excellence in Training) (petrophysics).

Computer facilities: Computer purchase and lease plans are available. 900 computers available on campus for general student use. A campuswide network can be accessed from student residence rooms and from off campus. Internet access and online class registration are available. *Web address:* http://www.utulsa.edu/.

General Application Contact: Dr. Janet A. Haggerty, Associate Vice President of Research and Dean of the Graduate School, 918-631-2336, Fax: 918-631-2156, E-mail: grad@utulsa.edu.

GRADUATE UNITS

College of Law Students: 464 full-time (153 women), 81 part-time (35 women); includes 57 minority (17 African Americans, 24 American Indian/Alaska Native, 6 Asian Americans or Pacific Islanders, 10 Hispanic Americans), 5 international. Average age 28. 1,436 applicants, 41% accepted, 183 enrolled. *Faculty:* 37 full-time (19 women), 31 part-time/adjunct (9 women). Expenses: Contact institution. *Financial support:* In 2006–07, 181 students received support, including fellowships (averaging $25,000 per year); Federal Work-Study and scholarships/grants also available. Support available to part-time students. Financial award applicants required to submit FAFSA. In 2006, 199 JDs, 8 other advanced degrees awarded. *Degree program information:* Part-time programs available. Offers alternative methods of dispute resolution (Certificate); American Indian and indigenous law (LL M); American law for foreign lawyers (LL M); comparative and international law (Certificate); entrepreneurial law (Certificate); health law (Certificate); law (JD); lawyering skills (Certificate); Native American law (Certificate); public policy and regulation (Certificate); resources, energy, and environmental law (Certificate). *Application deadline:* For fall admission, 2/1 priority date for domestic and international students. Applications are processed on a rolling basis. *Application fee:* $30. Electronic applications accepted. *Application Contact:* Martha T. Cordell, Assistant Dean of Admissions and Financial Aid, 918-631-2406, Fax: 918-631-3630, E-mail: martha-cordell@utulsa.edu. *Dean,* Robert Butkin, 918-631-2400, Fax: 918-631-3126, E-mail: robert-butkin@utulsa.edu.

Graduate School Students: 391 full-time (162 women), 274 part-time (113 women); includes 50 minority (12 African Americans, 24 American Indian/Alaska Native, 3 Asian Americans or Pacific Islanders, 11 Hispanic Americans), 192 international. Average age 30. 864 applicants, 49% accepted, 200 enrolled. *Faculty:* 178 full-time (47 women), 7 part-time/adjunct (4 women). Expenses: Contact institution. *Financial support:* In 2006–07, 302 students received support, including 8 fellowships with full and partial tuition reimbursements available (averaging $12,273 per year), 107 research assistantships with full and partial tuition reimbursements available (averaging $11,613 per year), 184 teaching assistantships with full and partial tuition reimbursements available (averaging $10,500 per year); career-related internships or fieldwork, Federal Work-Study, institutionally sponsored loans, scholarships/grants, traineeships, tuition waivers (partial), and unspecified assistantships also available. Support available to part-time students. Financial award application deadline: 2/1; financial award applicants required to submit FAFSA. In 2006, 203 master's, 42 doctorates awarded. *Degree program information:* Part-time and evening/weekend programs available. *Application deadline:* Applications are processed on a rolling basis. *Application fee:* $40. Electronic applications accepted. *Application Contact:* 918-631-2336, Fax: 918-631-2156, E-mail: grad@utulsa.edu. *Associate Vice President of Research and Dean of the Graduate School,* Dr. Janet A. Haggerty, 918-631-2336, Fax: 918-631-2156, E-mail: grad@utulsa.edu.

College of Arts and Sciences Students: 138 full-time (86 women), 70 part-time (41 women); includes 16 minority (5 African Americans, 9 American Indian/Alaska Native, 1 Asian American or Pacific Islander, 1 Hispanic American), 13 international. Average age 30. 249 applicants, 48% accepted, 51 enrolled. *Faculty:* 67 full-time (27 women), 6 part-time/adjunct (4 women). Expenses: Contact institution. *Financial support:* In 2006–07, 6 fellowships with full and partial tuition reimbursements (averaging $12,222 per year), 16 research assistantships with full and partial tuition reimbursements (averaging $10,226 per year), 89 teaching assistantships with full and partial tuition reimbursements (averaging $10,482 per year) were awarded; career-related internships or fieldwork, Federal Work-Study, scholarships/grants, traineeships, tuition waivers (full and partial), and unspecified assistantships also available. Support available to part-time students. Financial award application deadline: 2/1; financial award applicants required to submit FAFSA. In 2006, 34 master's, 19 doctorates awarded. *Degree program information:* Part-time and evening/weekend programs available. Offers anthropology (MA); art (MA, MFA, MTA); arts and sciences (MA, MFA, MS, MSMSE, MTA, PhD); clinical psychology (MA, PhD); education (MA); English language and literature (MA, MTA, PhD); history (MA, MTA); industrial/organizational psychology (MA, PhD); mathematics and science education (MSMSE); speech-language pathology (MS); teaching arts (MTA). *Application deadline:* Applications are processed on a rolling basis. *Application fee:* $40. Electronic applications accepted. *Application Contact:* Graduate School, 918-631-2336, Fax: 918-631-2156, E-mail: grad@utulsa.edu. *Dean,* Dr. Dale Thomas Benediktson, 918-631-2222, Fax: 918-631-3721, E-mail: dale-benediktson@utulsa.edu.

College of Business Administration Students: 80 full-time (32 women), 123 part-time (46 women); includes 23 minority (5 African Americans, 11 American Indian/Alaska Native, 2 Asian Americans or Pacific Islanders, 5 Hispanic Americans), 31 international. Average age 31. 118 applicants, 62% accepted, 60 enrolled. *Faculty:* 35 full-time (10 women), 1 part-time/adjunct (0 women). Expenses: Contact institution. *Financial support:* In 2006–07, 52 students received support, including 3 research assistantships with full and partial tuition reimbursements available (averaging $5,710 per year), 47 teaching assistantships with full and partial tuition reimbursements available (averaging $10,125 per year); fellowships with full and partial tuition reimbursements available, career-related internships or fieldwork, Federal Work-Study, institutionally sponsored loans, scholarships/grants, tuition waivers (full and partial), and unspecified assistantships also available. Support available to part-time students. Financial award application deadline: 2/1; financial award applicants required to submit FAFSA. In 2006, 87 degrees awarded. *Degree program information:* Part-time and evening/weekend programs available. Postbaccalaureate distance learning degree programs offered (minimal on-campus study). Offers business administration (M Tax, MBA, METM, MS); chemical engineering (METM); computer science (METM); corporate finance (MS); electrical engineering (METM); geological science (METM); investments and portfolio management (MS); mathematics (METM); mechanical engineering (METM); petroleum engineering (METM); risk management (MS); taxation (M Tax). *Application deadline:* Applications are processed on a rolling basis. *Application fee:* $40. Electronic applications accepted. *Application Contact:* Information Contact, E-mail: graduate-business@utulsa.edu. *Dean,* Dr. W. Gale Sullenburger, 918-631-2213, E-mail: gale-sullenberger@utulsa.edu.

College of Engineering and Natural Sciences Students: 173 full-time (44 women), 82 part-time (26 women); includes 11 minority (2 African Americans, 4 American Indian/Alaska Native, 5 Hispanic Americans), 149 international. Average age 29. 432 applicants, 47% accepted, 79 enrolled. *Faculty:* 76 full-time (10 women). Expenses: Contact institution. *Financial support:* In 2006–07, 154 students received support, including 2 fellowships with full and partial tuition reimbursements available (averaging $12,325 per year), 88 research assistantships with full and partial tuition reimbursements available (averaging $13,001 per year), 48 teaching assistantships with full and partial tuition reimbursements available (averaging $10,740 per year); career-related internships or fieldwork, Federal Work-Study, scholarships/grants, tuition waivers (full and partial), and unspecified assistantships also available. Support available to part-time students. Financial award application deadline: 2/1; financial award applicants required to submit FAFSA. In 2006, 82 master's, 20 doctorates awarded. *Degree program information:* Part-time programs available. Offers biological sciences (MS, MTA, PhD); chemical engineering (ME, MSE, PhD); chemistry (MS); computer science (MS, PhD); electrical engineering (ME, MSE); engineering and natural sciences (ME, METM, MS, MSE, MTA, PhD); geosciences (MS, PhD); mathematical sciences (MS, MTA); mechanical engineering (ME, MSE, PhD); petroleum engineering (ME, MSE, PhD). *Application deadline:* Applications are processed on a rolling basis. *Application fee:* $40. Electronic applications accepted. *Application Contact:* Graduate School, 918-631-2336, Fax: 918-631-2156, E-mail: grad@utulsa.edu. *Dean,* Dr. Steve J. Bellovich, 918-631-2288, E-mail: steven-bellovich@utulsa.edu.

See Close-Up on page 1129.

UNIVERSITY OF UTAH, Salt Lake City, UT 84112-1107

General Information State-supported, coed, university. CGS member. *Enrollment:* 28,619 graduate, professional, and undergraduate students; 4,844 full-time matriculated graduate/professional students (2,105 women), 1,620 part-time matriculated graduate/professional students (813 women). *Enrollment by degree level:* 971 first professional, 3,358 master's, 2,131 doctoral, 4 other advanced degrees. *Graduate faculty:* 862 full-time (296 women), 185 part-time/adjunct (79 women). Tuition, state resident: full-time $3,208. Tuition, nonresident: full-time $11,326. *Required fees:* $608. Tuition and fees vary according to class time and program. *Graduate housing:* Rooms and/or apartments available on a first-come, first-served basis to single and married students. Typical cost: $2,792 per year ($5,604 including board) for single students; $3,600 per year for married students. Room and board charges vary according to board plan and housing facility selected. Housing application deadline: 4/1. *Student services:* Campus employment opportunities, campus safety program, career counseling, child daycare facilities, disabled student services, exercise/wellness program, free psychological counseling, international student services, low-cost health insurance, multicultural affairs office, writing training. *Library facilities:* Marriott Library plus 3 others. *Online resources:* library catalog, web page, access to other libraries' catalogs. *Collection:* 6.2 million titles, 33,517 serial subscriptions, 74,731 audiovisual materials. *Research affiliation:* Hunter Cancer Institute (cancer treatment and research), Myriad Genetics (pharmaceutical research/manufacturing), Evans and Sutherland (technology development), ARUP, John A. Moran Eye Center (vision treatment and research institute).

Computer facilities: 8,000 computers available on campus for general student use. A campuswide network can be accessed from student residence rooms and from off campus. Internet access and online class registration, online classes are available. *Web address:* http://www.utah.edu/.

General Application Contact: Office of Admissions, 801-581-7281, Fax: 801-585-3034, E-mail: admissionweb_grad@saff.utah.edu.

GRADUATE UNITS

College of Pharmacy *Degree program information:* Part-time programs available. Offers medicinal chemistry (MS, PhD); pharmaceutics and pharmaceutical chemistry (MS, PhD); pharmacology and toxicology (MS, PhD); pharmacy (Pharm D, MS, PhD); pharmacy practice (MS).

The Graduate School Students: 3,691 full-time (1,623 women), 1,470 part-time (737 women); includes 418 minority (32 African Americans, 37 American Indian/Alaska Native, 184 Asian Americans or Pacific Islanders, 165 Hispanic Americans), 830 international. Average age 31. 6,148 applicants, 46% accepted, 1902 enrolled. *Faculty:* 1,013 full-time (342 women), 108 part-time/adjunct (40 women). Expenses: Contact institution. *Financial support:* In 2006–07, 1,870 students received support, including 300 fellowships with full and partial tuition reimbursements available (averaging $12,500 per year), 750 research assistantships with full and partial tuition reimbursements available (averaging $12,500 per year), 760 teaching assistantships with full and partial tuition reimbursements available (averaging $12,500 per year); career-related internships or fieldwork, Federal Work-Study, institutionally sponsored loans, scholarships/grants, traineeships, and health care benefits also available. Support available to part-time students. Financial award application deadline: 2/15; financial award applicants required to submit FAFSA. In 2006, 1,378 master's, 251 doctorates awarded. *Degree program information:* Part-time and evening/weekend programs available. Offers biological chemistry (PhD); biostatistics (MST); biotechnology (PSM); computational engineering and science (MS); computational science (PSM); econometrics (MST); economics (MST); environmental engineering (MS, PhD); environmental science (PSM); mathematics (MST); sciences instrumental (PSM); sociology (MST); statistics (M Stat, MST). *Application deadline:* For fall admission, 4/1 priority date for domestic students, 4/1 for international students; for winter admission, 4/1 for international students; for spring admission, 11/1 priority date for domestic students, 11/1 for international students. Applications are processed on a rolling basis. *Application fee:* $45 ($65 for international students). Electronic applications accepted. *Dean,* Dr. David S. Chapman, 801-581-7642, Fax: 801-585-6749, E-mail: dchapman@admin.utah.edu.

College of Architecture and Planning Students: 88 full-time (22 women), 11 part-time (3 women); includes 2 minority (1 American Indian/Alaska Native, 1 Hispanic American), 2 international. Average age 30. 84 applicants, 65% accepted, 40 enrolled. *Faculty:* 16 full-time (5 women), 9 part-time/adjunct (2 women). Expenses: Contact institution. *Financial support:* In 2006–07, 29 fellowships with full tuition reimbursements, 3 research assistantships with full tuition reimbursements, 29 teaching assistantships with partial tuition reimbursements were awarded; career-related internships or fieldwork, Federal Work-Study, and scholarships/grants also available. Financial award application deadline: 2/1; financial award applicants required to submit FAFSA. In 2006, 44 degrees awarded. *Degree program information:* Part-time programs available. Offers architectural studies (M Arch, MS); urban planning (MUP). *Application deadline:* For fall admission, 4/1 for domestic and international students; for spring admission, 11/1 for domestic and international students. Applications are processed on a rolling basis. *Application fee:* $45 ($65 for international students). Electronic applications accepted. *Application Contact:* Colleen Nielson, Admissions Advisor, 801-581-8254, Fax: 801-581-8217, E-mail: cnielson@arch.utah.edu. *Dean,* Brenda Scheer, 801-581-8254, Fax: 801-581-8217, E-mail: scheer@arch.utah.edu.

College of Education Students: 274 full-time (199 women), 336 part-time (237 women); includes 80 minority (12 African Americans, 18 American Indian/Alaska Native, 14 Asian Americans or Pacific Islanders, 36 Hispanic Americans), 12 international. Average age 35. 594 applicants, 61% accepted, 262 enrolled. *Faculty:* 65 full-time (35 women), 13 part-time/adjunct (6 women). Expenses: Contact institution. *Financial support:* Fellowships with full tuition reimbursements, research assistantships with full tuition reimbursements, teaching assistantships with full and partial tuition reimbursements, career-related internships or fieldwork, Federal Work-Study, institutionally sponsored loans, scholarships/grants, tuition waivers (full and partial), and unspecified assistantships available. Support available to part-time students. Financial award application deadline: 2/1; financial award applicants required to submit FAFSA. In 2006, 215 master's, 34 doctorates awarded. *Degree program information:* Part-time and evening/weekend programs available. Offers counseling psychology (PhD); education (M Ed, M Phil, M Stat, MA, MAT, MS, Ed D, PhD); education, culture, and society (M Ed, MA, MS, PhD); educational leadership and policy (M Ed, M Phil, Ed D, PhD); educational psychology (MA); elementary education (MAT); professional counseling (MS); professional psychology (M Ed); school counseling (M Ed, MS); secondary education (MAT); special education (M Ed, M Phil, MS, PhD); statistics (M Stat); teaching and learning (M Ed, M Phil, MA, MS, PhD). *Application deadline:* For fall admission, 4/1 for domestic and international students; for spring admission, 11/1 for domestic and international students. Applications are processed on a rolling basis. *Application fee:* $45 ($65 for international students). Electronic applications accepted. *Application Contact:* Kristin Anderson, Executive Secretary, 801-581-8221, Fax: 801-581-5223, E-mail: kristin.anderson@ed.utah.edu. *Dean,* David J. Sperry, 801-581-8221, Fax: 801-581-5223, E-mail: david.sperry@ed.utah.edu.

College of Engineering Students: 525 full-time (91 women), 246 part-time (45 women); includes 58 minority (4 African Americans, 1 American Indian/Alaska Native, 40 Asian Americans or Pacific Islanders, 13 Hispanic Americans), 284 international. Average age 29. 1,456 applicants, 35% accepted, 207 enrolled. *Faculty:* 144 full-time (17 women), 31 part-time/adjunct (3 women). Expenses: Contact institution. *Financial support:* Fellowships, research assistantships, teaching assistantships, career-related internships or fieldwork, Federal Work-Study, institutionally sponsored loans, and traineeships available. Support available to part-time students. Financial award application deadline: 2/1; financial award applicants required to submit FAFSA. In 2006, 163 master's, 51 doctorates awarded. *Degree program information:* Part-time programs available. Offers bioengineering (ME, MS, PhD); chemical engineering (ME, MS, PhD); civil engineering (MS, PhD); computer science (M Phil, MS, PhD); computing (MS, PhD); electrical engineering (M Phil, ME, MS, PhD, EE); engineering (M Phil, ME, MS, PhD, EE); environmental engineering (ME, MS, PhD); materials science and engineering (ME, MS, PhD); mechanical engineering (ME, MS, PhD); nuclear engineering (ME, MS, PhD). *Application deadline:* For fall admission, 4/1 for domestic and international students; for spring admission, 11/1 for domestic and international students. Applications are processed on a rolling basis. *Application fee:* $45 ($65 for international students). *Application Contact:* Dianne Leonard, Coordinator, Administrative Program, 801-585-7769, Fax: 801-581-8692, E-mail: dleonard@coe.utah.edu. *Dean,* Dr. Richard B. Brown, 801-581-6912, Fax: 801-581-8692, E-mail: brown@coe.utah.edu.

College of Fine Arts Students: 103 full-time (63 women), 46 part-time (31 women); includes 11 minority (1 American Indian/Alaska Native, 4 Asian Americans or Pacific Islanders, 6 Hispanic Americans), 8 international. Average age 31. 205 applicants, 50% accepted, 74 enrolled. *Faculty:* 82 full-time (35 women), 16 part-time/adjunct (5 women). Expenses: Contact institution. *Financial support:* Fellowships with full tuition reimbursements, research assistantships, teaching assistantships with full and partial tuition reimbursements, career-related internships or fieldwork, Federal Work-Study, institutionally sponsored loans, and scholarships/grants available. Financial award application deadline: 2/1; financial award applicants required to submit FAFSA. In 2006, 45 degrees awarded. *Degree program information:* Part-time programs available. Offers art history (MA); ballet (MFA); ceramics (MFA); community-based art education (MFA); drawing (MFA); film studies (MFA); fine arts (M Mus, MA, MFA, PhD); graphic design (MFA); illustration (MFA); modern dance (MA, MFA); music (M Mus, MA, PhD); painting (MFA); photography/digital imaging (MFA); printmaking (MFA); sculpture/intermedia (MFA). *Application deadline:* For fall admission, 4/1 for domestic and international students; for spring admission, 11/1 for domestic and international students. *Application fee:* $45 ($65 for international students). *Application Contact:* Steve Roens, Associate Dean, 801-581-8420, E-mail: steve.roens@music.utah.edu. *Chair,* Raymond Tymas Jones, 801-581-6764, Fax: 801-581-3066.

College of Health Students: 366 full-time (225 women), 100 part-time (58 women); includes 16 minority (1 African American, 8 Asian Americans or Pacific Islanders, 7 Hispanic Americans), 20 international. Average age 30. 402 applicants, 60% accepted, 151 enrolled. *Faculty:* 65 full-time (32 women), 47 part-time/adjunct (30 women). Expenses: Contact institution. *Financial support:* Fellowships, research assistantships with tuition reimbursements, teaching assistantships, career-related internships or fieldwork, Federal Work-Study, institutionally sponsored loans, scholarships/grants, health care benefits, and unspecified assistantships available. Financial award application deadline: 2/1; financial award applicants required to submit FAFSA. In 2006, 98 master's, 52 doctorates awarded. *Degree program information:* Part-time and evening/weekend programs available. Offers audiology (Au D); exercise and sport science (MS, PhD); health (M Phil, MA, MOT, MS, Au D, DPT, Ed D, PhD, PPDPT); health promotion and education (M Phil, MS, Ed D, PhD); nutrition (MS); occupational therapy (MOT); parks, recreation, and tourism (M Phil, MS, Ed D, PhD); physical therapy (DPT, PPDPT); speech-language pathology (MA, MS, PhD). *Application deadline:* For fall admission, 1/15 for domestic students, 4/1 for international students; for spring admission, 1/15 for domestic students, 11/1 for international students. Applications are processed on a rolling basis. *Application fee:* $45 ($65 for international students). *Application Contact:* Glenn Richardson, Graduate Director, 801-581-8114, E-mail: glenn.richardson@health.utah.edu. *Dean,* Dr. James E. Graves, 801-581-8537, Fax: 801-581-5580, E-mail: james.graves@health.utah.edu.

College of Humanities Students: 243 full-time (131 women), 129 part-time (63 women); includes 28 minority (1 African American, 12 Asian Americans or Pacific Islanders, 15 Hispanic Americans), 35 international. Average age 34. 458 applicants, 36% accepted, 100 enrolled. *Faculty:* 166 full-time (72 women), 2 part-time/adjunct (0 women). Expenses: Contact institution. *Financial support:* In 2006–07, 1 fellowship with full tuition reimbursement (averaging $5,000 per year), 3 research assistantships with full tuition reimbursements (averaging $13,500 per year), 1 teaching assistantship with full tuition reimbursement (averaging $13,500 per year) were awarded; career-related internships or fieldwork, Federal Work-Study, and institutionally sponsored loans also available. Financial award application deadline: 2/1; financial award applicants required to submit FAFSA. In 2006, 67 master's, 26 doctorates awarded. *Degree program information:* Part-time programs available. Offers American studies (MA, PhD); anthropology (MA); applied linguistics (MA, PhD); Arabic (MA, PhD); Arabic and linguistics (MA, PhD); British American literature (MA, PhD); communication (M Phil, MA, MS, PhD); comparative literature (MA, PhD); creative writing (MFA); English (PhD); French (MA, MALP); German (MA, MALP, PhD); Hebrew (MA); history (MA, PhD); humanities (M Phil, MA, MALP, MAT, MFA, MS, PhD); language pedagogy (MALP); linguistics (MA); literature and creative writing (PhD); Persian (MA, PhD); philosophy (MA, MS, PhD); political science (MA, PhD); rhetoric and composition (PhD); Spanish (MA, MALP, PhD); Turkish (MA). *Application deadline:* For fall admission, 4/1 for domestic and international students; for spring admission, 11/1 for domestic and international students. Applications are processed on a rolling basis. *Application fee:* $45 ($65 for international students). *Application Contact:* Mark Bergstrom, Associate Dean, 801-581-6214, Fax: 801-585-5190, E-mail: mark.bergstrom@hum.utah.edu. *Dean and Associate Vice President of Interdisciplinary Studies,* Robert D. Newman, 801-581-6214, Fax: 801-585-5190, E-mail: robert.newman@hum.utah.edu.

College of Mines and Earth Sciences Students: 121 full-time (30 women), 37 part-time (10 women); includes 3 minority (all Asian Americans or Pacific Islanders), 66 international. Average age 30. 169 applicants, 64% accepted, 68 enrolled. *Faculty:* 45 full-time (5 women), 4 part-time/adjunct (0 women). Expenses: Contact institution. *Financial support:* In 2006–07, 8 fellowships (averaging $15,000 per year) were awarded; research assistantships, teaching assistantships, career-related internships or fieldwork and institutionally sponsored loans also available. Support available to part-time students. Financial award application deadline: 2/15; financial award applicants required to submit FAFSA. In 2006, 29 master's, 10 doctorates awarded. *Degree program information:* Part-time programs available. Offers environmental engineering (ME, MS, PhD); geological engineering (ME, MS, PhD); geology (MS, PhD); geophysics (MS, PhD); metallurgical engineering (ME, MS, PhD); meteorology (MS, PhD); mines and earth sciences (ME, MS, PhD); mining engineering (ME, MS, PhD). *Application deadline:* For fall admission, 4/1 for domestic and international students; for spring admission, 11/1 for domestic and international students. *Application fee:* $45 ($65 for international students). Electronic applications accepted. *Application Contact:* Sharon Christenson, Executive Assistant to the Dean, 801-581-8767, Fax: 801-581-5560, E-mail: sharon@mines.utah.edu. *Dean,* Dr. Francis H. Brown, 801-581-8767, Fax: 801-581-5560, E-mail: fbrown@mines.utah.edu.

College of Nursing Students: 102 full-time (92 women), 123 part-time (106 women); includes 16 minority (1 African American, 7 Asian Americans or Pacific Islanders, 8 Hispanic Americans), 3 international. Average age 37. 124 applicants, 62% accepted, 60 enrolled. *Faculty:* 51 full-time (46 women), 15 part-time/adjunct (13 women). Expenses: Contact institution. *Financial support:* Fellowships, research assistantships, teaching assistantships, scholarships/grants available. Financial award application deadline: 2/1; financial award applicants required to submit FAFSA. In 2006, 81 master's, 3 doctorates awarded. *Degree program information:* Part-time programs available. Offers aging (MS, Certificate); nursing (MS, PhD, Certificate). *Application deadline:* For fall admission, 4/1 for domestic and international students; for spring admission, 11/1 for domestic and international students. Applications are processed on a rolling basis. *Application fee:* $45 ($65 for international students). *Application Contact:* Joyce Rathbun, Graduate Adviser, 801-581-8798, Fax: 801-581-4642, E-mail: jrathbun@nursac.nurs.utah.edu. *Dean,* Maureen Keefe, 801-581-8262, Fax: 801-581-4642, E-mail: maureen.keefe@nurs.utah.edu.

College of Science Students: 364 full-time (131 women), 87 part-time (32 women); includes 25 minority (1 African American, 13 Asian Americans or Pacific Islanders, 11 Hispanic Americans), 179 international. Average age 28. 772 applicants, 29% accepted, 101 enrolled. *Faculty:* 143 full-time (15 women), 22 part-time/adjunct (2 women). Expenses: Contact institution. *Financial support:* Fellowships with full tuition reimbursements, research assistantships with full and partial tuition reimbursements, teaching assistantships with full and partial tuition reimbursements, career-related internships or fieldwork, scholarships/grants, and traineeships available. Financial award application deadline: 2/15; financial award applicants required to submit FAFSA. In 2006, 51 master's, 33 doctorates awarded. *Degree program information:* Part-time programs available. Offers biology (MS); chemical physics (PhD); chemistry (M Phil, MA, MS, PhD); ecology and evolutionary biology (MS, PhD); genetics (MS, PhD); mathematics (M Phil, M Stat, MA, MS, PhD); microbiology (PhD); molecular biology (PhD); physics (MA, MS, PhD); plant biology (PhD); science (M Phil, M Stat, MA, MS, PhD); science teacher education (MS). *Application deadline:* For fall admission, 4/1 for domestic and international students; for spring admission, 11/1 for domestic and international students. Applications are processed on a rolling basis. *Application fee:* $45 ($65 for international students). *Application Contact:* Information Contact, 801-581-6958, E-mail: office@science.utah.edu. *Dean,* Peter J. Stang, 801-581-6958, Fax: 801-585-3169, E-mail: stang@chemistry.utah.edu.

College of Social and Behavioral Science Students: 275 full-time (131 women), 197 part-time (91 women); includes 44 minority (4 African Americans, 2 American Indian/Alaska Native, 16 Asian Americans or Pacific Islanders, 22 Hispanic Americans), 84 international. Average age 32. 691 applicants, 47% accepted, 199 enrolled. *Faculty:* 140 full-time (44 women), 13 part-time/adjunct (4 women). Expenses: Contact institution. *Financial support:* Fellowships, research assistantships, teaching assistantships, career-related internships or fieldwork, Federal Work-Study, and institutionally sponsored loans available. Support available to part-time students. Financial award application deadline: 2/1; financial award applicants required to submit FAFSA. In 2006, 94 master's, 16 doctorates awarded. *Degree program information:* Part-time programs available. Offers anthropology (MA, MS, PhD); economics (M Phil, M Stat, MA, MS, PhD); family and consumer studies (MS); geography (MA, MS, PhD); political science (MA, MS, PhD); psychology (M Stat, MA, MS, PhD); public administration (MPA, Certificate); social and behavioral science (M Phil, M Stat, MA, MPA, MS, PhD, Certificate); sociology (M Stat, MA, MS, PhD). *Application deadline:* For fall admission, 4/1 for domestic and international students; for spring admission, 11/1 for domestic and international students. Applications are processed on a rolling basis. *Application fee:* $45 ($65 for international students). *Application Contact:* Stephen E. Reynolds, Associate Dean, 801-581-8620, E-mail: stephen.reynolds@csbs.utah.edu. *Director,* J. Steven Ott, 801-581-6781, Fax: 801-581-6957, E-mail: jsott@cppa.utah.edu.

College of Social Work Students: 307 full-time (213 women), 36 part-time (25 women); includes 34 minority (4 African Americans, 9 American Indian/Alaska Native, 8 Asian Americans or Pacific Islanders, 13 Hispanic Americans), 14 international. Average age 33. 334 applicants, 50% accepted, 126 enrolled. *Faculty:* 33 full-time (19 women), 8 part-time/adjunct (3 women). Expenses: Contact institution. *Financial support:* In 2006–07, 66 fellowships with full and partial tuition reimbursements (averaging $3,026 per year), 38 research assistantships with full and partial tuition reimbursements (averaging $6,300 per year), 7 teaching assistantships with full and partial tuition reimbursements (averaging $5,956 per year) were awarded; Federal Work-Study and institutionally sponsored loans also available. Support available to part-time students. Financial award application deadline: 3/15; financial award applicants required to submit FAFSA. In 2006, 165 master's, 7 doctorates awarded. *Degree program information:* Part-time programs available. Offers social work (MSW, PhD). *Application deadline:* For fall admission, 4/1 for domestic and international students; for spring admission, 11/1 for domestic and international students. Applications are processed on a rolling basis. *Application fee:* $45 ($65 for international students). *Application Contact:* Mary Jane Taylor, Associate Dean, 801-581-8828, Fax: 801-585-3219, E-mail: maryjane.taylor@socwk.utah.edu. *Dean,* Jannah H. Mather, 801-581-6194, Fax: 801-585-3219, E-mail: jannah.mather@socwk.utah.edu.

David Eccles School of Business Students: 610 full-time (137 women), 74 part-time (22 women); includes 66 minority (2 African Americans, 4 American Indian/Alaska Native, 36 Asian Americans or Pacific Islanders, 24 Hispanic Americans), 51 international. Average age 31. 867 applicants, 63% accepted, 418 enrolled. *Faculty:* 63 full-time (18 women), 7 part-time/adjunct (1 woman). Expenses: Contact institution. *Financial support:* In 2006–07, 1 fellowship (averaging $12,000 per year), 41 research assistantships (averaging $750 per year), 39 teaching assistantships with partial tuition reimbursements (averaging $7,635 per year) were awarded; career-related internships or fieldwork, health care benefits, and unspecified assistantships also available. Financial award application deadline: 2/1; financial award applicants required to submit FAFSA. In 2006, 296 master's, 9 doctorates awarded. *Degree program information:* Part-time and evening/weekend programs available. Offers accounting and information systems (M Pr A, PhD); business (M Pr A, M Stat, MBA, MS, PhD); business administration (M Stat, MBA, PhD); finance (MS, PhD); management (MBA, PhD). *Application deadline:* For fall admission, 4/1 for domestic and international students; for spring admission, 11/1 for domestic and international students. *Application fee:* $45 ($65 for international students). Electronic applications accepted. *Application Contact:* Lori Frandsden, Academic Coordinator, 801-581-8625, Fax: 801-587-3380, E-mail: lori.frandsen@business.utah.edu. *Dean,* Dr. Jack Brittain, 801-587-3860, Fax: 801-587-3380, E-mail: jack.brittain@business.utah.edu.

School of Medicine Average age 26. Expenses: Contact institution. *Financial support:* In 2006–07, 4 teaching assistantships were awarded; fellowships with full tuition reimbursements, research assistantships with full tuition reimbursements, career-related internships or

University of Utah (continued)

fieldwork, Federal Work-Study, institutionally sponsored loans, scholarships/grants, and traineeships also available. Support available to part-time students. Offers biochemistry (MS, PhD); biostatistics (M Stat); experimental pathology (PhD); human genetics (MS, PhD); laboratory medicine and biomedical science (MS); medical informatics (MS, PhD); medicine (MD, M Phil, M Stat, MPAS, MPH, MS, MSPH, PhD); neurobiology and anatomy (PhD); neuroscience (PhD); oncological sciences (M Phil, MS, PhD); physician assistant (MPAS); physiology (PhD); public health (MPH, MSPH, PhD). *Executive Dean and Senior Vice President for Health Sciences,* Dr. A. Lorris Betz, 801-581-7480, Fax: 801-585-3109, E-mail: lorris.betz@hsc.utah.edu.

S.J. Quinney College of Law Students: 391 full-time (148 women); includes 40 minority (2 African Americans, 2 American Indian/Alaska Native, 21 Asian Americans or Pacific Islanders, 15 Hispanic Americans), 1 international. Average age 28. 1,130 applicants, 32% accepted, 122 enrolled. *Faculty:* 39 full-time (13 women), 28 part-time/adjunct (6 women). Expenses: Contact institution. *Financial support:* In 2006–07, 167 students received support, including 45 fellowships with full and partial tuition reimbursements available (averaging $1,332 per year), 2 research assistantships with partial tuition reimbursements available (averaging $5,000 per year); career-related internships or fieldwork, Federal Work-Study, institutionally sponsored loans, and scholarships/grants also available. Financial award application deadline: 3/15; financial award applicants required to submit FAFSA. In 2006, 129 JDs, 2 master's awarded. Offers law (JD, LL M). *Application deadline:* For fall admission, 2/1 for domestic and international students. Applications are processed on a rolling basis. *Application fee:* $60. *Application Contact:* Reyes Aguilar, Associate Dean for Admission and Financial Aid, 801-581-7479, Fax: 801-581-6897, E-mail: aguilarr@law.utah.edu. *Dean,* Hiram E. Chodosh, 801-581-6833, Fax: 801-581-6897.

UNIVERSITY OF VERMONT, Burlington, VT 05405

General Information State-supported, coed, university. CGS member. *Enrollment:* 11,870 graduate, professional, and undergraduate students; 1,772 matriculated graduate/professional students (1,068 women). *Enrollment by degree level:* 422 first professional, 913 master's, 437 doctoral. *Graduate faculty:* 702 full-time, 604 part-time/adjunct. Tuition, state resident: part-time $434 per credit. Tuition, nonresident: part-time $1,096 per credit. *Graduate housing:* Rooms and/or apartments available to single and married students. *Student services:* Career counseling, free psychological counseling, low-cost health insurance. *Library facilities:* Bailey-Howe Library plus 3 others. *Online resources:* library catalog, web page. *Collection:* 2.4 million titles, 20,216 serial subscriptions. *Research affiliation:* Miner Institute (animal sciences).

Computer facilities: Computer purchase and lease plans are available. 685 computers available on campus for general student use. A campuswide network can be accessed from student residence rooms and from off campus. Internet access and online class registration, e-mail, Web pages, on-line course support are available. *Web address:* http://www.uvm.edu/.

General Application Contact: Patricia Stokowski, Assistant Dean, 802-656-3160, Fax: 802-656-0519, E-mail: graduate.admissions@uvm.edu.

GRADUATE UNITS

College of Medicine Students: 500 (299 women); includes 74 minority (1 African American, 1 American Indian/Alaska Native, 65 Asian Americans or Pacific Islanders, 7 Hispanic Americans) 33 international. 5,569 applicants, 4% accepted, 117 enrolled. *Faculty:* 284 full-time (59 women), 608 part-time/adjunct. Expenses: Contact institution. *Financial support:* Fellowships, research assistantships, teaching assistantships, Federal Work-Study available. In 2006, 97 MDs, 1 master's, 8 doctorates awarded. Offers anatomy and neurobiology (PhD); biochemistry (MS, PhD); medicine (MD, MS, PhD); microbiology and molecular genetics (MS, PhD); molecular physiology and biophysics (MS, PhD); neuroscience (PhD); pathology (MS); pharmacology (MS, PhD). *Application deadline:* Applications are processed on a rolling basis. *Dean,* Dr. John Evans, 802-656-2156.

Graduate College Students: 1,350 (814 women); includes 63 minority (18 African Americans, 6 American Indian/Alaska Native, 26 Asian Americans or Pacific Islanders, 13 Hispanic Americans) 167 international. 1,990 applicants, 44% accepted, 445 enrolled. *Faculty:* 361. Expenses: Contact institution. *Financial support:* Fellowships, research assistantships, teaching assistantships, career-related internships or fieldwork, Federal Work-Study, traineeships, tuition waivers (full and partial), and analytical assistantships available. Support available to part-time students. In 2006, 357 master's, 60 doctorates awarded. *Degree program information:* Part-time programs available. Offers cell and molecular biology (MS, PhD). *Application deadline:* For fall admission, 4/1 priority date for domestic and international students; for spring admission, 11/15 priority date for domestic and international students. Applications are processed on a rolling basis. *Application fee:* $40. Electronic applications accepted. *Application Contact:* Patricia Stokowski, Assistant Dean, 802-656-3160, Fax: 802-656-0519, E-mail: graduate.admissions@uvm.edu. *Vice President for Research and Dean of the Graduate College,* Dr. Frances E. Carr, 802-656-3160, Fax: 802-656-0519, E-mail: gradcoll@uvm.edu.

College of Agriculture and Life Sciences Students: 128 (81 women); includes 4 minority (1 African American, 1 Asian American or Pacific Islander, 2 Hispanic Americans) 16 international. 178 applicants, 47% accepted, 40 enrolled. Expenses: Contact institution. *Financial support:* Fellowships, research assistantships, teaching assistantships, career-related internships or fieldwork, Federal Work-Study, and tuition waivers (full and partial) available. Financial award application deadline: 3/1. In 2006, 46 master's, 4 doctorates awarded. *Degree program information:* Part-time programs available. Offers agriculture and life sciences (MPA, MS, PhD); animal sciences (MS, PhD); animal, nutrition and food sciences (PhD); botany (MS, PhD); community development and applied economics (MPA, MS); field naturalist (MS); microbiology and molecular genetics (MS, PhD); nutritional sciences (MS); plant and soil science (MS, PhD); public administration (MPA). *Application fee:* $40. *Dean,* Dr. R. K. Johnson, 802-656-2980.

College of Arts and Sciences Students: 273 (165 women); includes 11 minority (3 African Americans, 2 American Indian/Alaska Native, 3 Asian Americans or Pacific Islanders, 3 Hispanic Americans) 42 international. 562 applicants, 32% accepted, 83 enrolled. Expenses: Contact institution. *Financial support:* Fellowships, research assistantships, teaching assistantships, career-related internships or fieldwork and Federal Work-Study available. In 2006, 46 master's, 19 doctorates awarded. *Degree program information:* Part-time programs available. Offers arts and sciences (MA, MAT, MS, MST, PhD); biology (MS, PhD); biology education (MST); chemistry (MS, PhD); clinical psychology (PhD); communication sciences (MS); English (MA); French (MA); geology (MS); German (MA); Greek (MA); Greek and Latin (MAT); historic preservation (MS); history (MA); Latin (MA); physics (MS); psychology (PhD). *Application fee:* $40. *Dean,* Dr. Eleanor Miller, 802-656-3166.

College of Education and Social Services Students: 435 (324 women); includes 25 minority (9 African Americans, 4 American Indian/Alaska Native, 8 Asian Americans or Pacific Islanders, 4 Hispanic Americans) 7 international. 479 applicants, 59% accepted, 175 enrolled. Expenses: Contact institution. *Financial support:* Fellowships, research assistantships, teaching assistantships, career-related internships or fieldwork and Federal Work-Study available. In 2006, 161 master's, 12 doctorates awarded. *Degree program information:* Part-time programs available. Offers counseling (MS); curriculum and instruction (M Ed); education and social services (M Ed, MS, MSW, Ed D); educational leadership (M Ed); educational leadership and policy studies (Ed D); educational studies (M Ed); higher education and student affairs administration (M Ed); interdisciplinary studies (M Ed); reading and language arts (M Ed); social work (MSW); special education (M Ed). *Application fee:* $40. *Dean,* Dr. Fayneese Miller, 802-656-3424.

College of Engineering and Mathematics Students: 145 (42 women); includes 4 minority (1 African American, 3 Asian Americans or Pacific Islanders) 48 international. 257 applicants, 51% accepted, 29 enrolled. Expenses: Contact institution. *Financial support:* Fellowships, research assistantships, teaching assistantships, Federal Work-Study available. Financial award application deadline: 3/1. In 2006, 40 master's, 4 doctorates awarded. *Degree program information:* Part-time programs available. Offers biomedical engineering (MS); biostatistics (MS); civil and environmental engineering (MS, PhD); computer science (MS, PhD); electrical engineering (MS, PhD); engineering and mathematics (MS, MST, PhD); materials science (MS, PhD); mathematics (MS, MST, PhD); mathematics education (MST); mechanical engineering (MS, PhD); statistics (MS). *Application deadline:* For fall admission, 4/1 priority date for domestic students. Applications are processed on a rolling basis. *Application fee:* $40. *Dean,* Dr. Domenico Grasso, 802-656-3390.

College of Nursing and Health Sciences Students: 81 (62 women); includes 5 minority (1 African American, 3 Asian Americans or Pacific Islanders, 1 Hispanic American) 1 international. 146 applicants, 52% accepted, 36 enrolled. Expenses: Contact institution. *Financial support:* Fellowships, research assistantships, teaching assistantships, Federal Work-Study available. Financial award application deadline: 3/1. In 2006, 20 degrees awarded. *Degree program information:* Part-time programs available. Offers nursing (MS); nursing and health sciences (MS, DPT); physical therapy (DPT). *Application deadline:* For fall admission, 4/1 priority date for domestic students. Applications are processed on a rolling basis. *Application fee:* $40. *Dean,* Dr. Betty Rambur, 802-656-3860.

The Rubenstein School of Environment and Natural Resources Students: 111 (53 women); includes 5 minority (3 African Americans, 2 Asian Americans or Pacific Islanders) 12 international. 117 applicants, 38% accepted, 34 enrolled. Expenses: Contact institution. *Financial support:* Fellowships, research assistantships, teaching assistantships, Federal Work-Study available. Financial award application deadline: 3/1. In 2006, 27 master's, 5 doctorates awarded. *Degree program information:* Part-time programs available. Offers environment and natural resources (MS, PhD); natural resources (MS, PhD). *Application deadline:* For fall admission, 3/1 priority date for domestic students. Applications are processed on a rolling basis. *Application fee:* $40. *Application Contact:* Dr. Deane Wang, Coordinator, 802-656-2620. *Dean,* Dr. D. DeHayes, 802-656-4280.

School of Business Administration Students: 56 (24 women); includes 4 minority (all Asian Americans or Pacific Islanders) 6 international. 42 applicants, 71% accepted, 21 enrolled. *Faculty:* 25. Expenses: Contact institution. *Financial support:* Fellowships, teaching assistantships, Federal Work-Study available. Financial award application deadline: 3/1. In 2006, 15 degrees awarded. *Degree program information:* Part-time programs available. Offers business administration (MBA). *Application deadline:* For fall admission, 4/1 priority date for domestic students. Applications are processed on a rolling basis. *Application fee:* $40. *Application Contact:* Dr. W. Averyt, Coordinator, 802-656-3177. *Dean,* Dr. R. DeWitt, 802-656-3177.

UNIVERSITY OF VICTORIA, Victoria, BC V8W 2Y2, Canada

General Information Province-supported, coed, university. *Graduate housing:* Rooms and/or apartments available on a first-come, first-served basis to single and married students. Housing application deadline: 2/1. *Research affiliation:* Dominion Astrophysical Observatory, Bamfield Marine Research Station (marine biology), Tri-University Meson Facility, Canada/France/Hawaii Telescope Observatory, Forest Research Centre (groundwater), Institute of Ocean Sciences (geography, oceanography).

GRADUATE UNITS

Faculty of Graduate Studies *Degree program information:* Part-time programs available. Postbaccalaureate distance learning degree programs offered (no on-campus study). Electronic applications accepted.

Faculty of Business *Degree program information:* Part-time programs available. Offers business (MBA). Electronic applications accepted.

Faculty of Education Offers art (M Ed, MA, PhD); coaching studies (co-operative education) (M Ed); counseling (M Ed, MA); curriculum studies (M Ed, MA, PhD); early childhood (M Ed, MA, PhD); education (M Ed, M Sc, MA, PhD); educational psychology (M Ed, MA, PhD); kinesiology (M Sc, MA); language and literacy (M Ed, MA, PhD); leadership studies (M Ed, MA); leisure service administration (MA); mathematics (M Ed, MA, PhD); music (M Ed, MA); music education (PhD); physical education (MA); science (M Ed, MA, PhD); social studies (M Ed, MA); social, cultural and foundational studies (PhD); technology and environmental education (PhD).

Faculty of Engineering Offers computer science (M Sc, MA, PhD); electrical and computer engineering (M Eng, MA Sc, PhD); engineering (M Eng, M Sc, MA, MA Sc, PhD); mechanical engineering (M Eng, MA Sc, PhD).

Faculty of Fine Arts Offers composition (M Mus); design/production (MFA); digital multi-media (MFA); directing (MFA); drawing (MFA); fine arts (M Mus, MA, MFA, PhD); history in art (MA, PhD); musicology (MA, PhD); musicology with performance (MA); painting (MFA); performance (M Mus); photography (MFA); sculpture (MFA); theatre history (MA).

Faculty of Human and Social Development Offers advanced nursing practice; (leadership option) (MN); advanced nursing practice; (nurse practitioner option) (MN); child and youth care (MA, PhD); dispute resolution (MA); health information science (M Sc); human and social development (MA); indigenous governance (MA); policy and practice (MN); public administration (MPA, PhD); social work (MSW).

Faculty of Humanities Offers applied linguistics (MA); English (MA, PhD); Germanic and Russian studies (MA); Greek and Roman studies (MA); Hispanic and Italian studies (MA); Hispanic studies (MA); history (MA, PhD); humanities (MA, PhD); literature (MA); Pacific and Asian studies (MA); philosophy (MA); teaching emphasis (MA); theoretical linguistics (MA, PhD).

Faculty of Science Offers astronomy and astrophysics (M Sc, PhD); biochemistry (M Sc, PhD); biology (M Sc, PhD); chemistry (M Sc, PhD); condensed matter physics (M Sc, PhD); earth and ocean sciences (M Sc, PhD); experimental particle physics (M Sc, PhD); mathematics and statistics (M Sc, MA, PhD); medical physics (M Sc, PhD); microbiology (M Sc, PhD); ocean physics (PhD); ocean physics and geophysics (M Sc); science (M Sc, MA, PhD); theoretical physics (M Sc, PhD). Electronic applications accepted.

Faculty of Social Sciences Offers anthropology (MA); clinical psychology (neuropsychology) (M Sc, PhD); cognitive psychology (M Sc); economics (MA, PhD); geography (M Sc, MA, PhD); life span development (PhD); political science (MA, PhD); social sciences (M Sc, MA, PhD); sociology (MA, PhD).

Faculty of Law Students: 393 full-time (217 women), 10 part-time (6 women). Average age 26. 1,038 applicants, 27% accepted, 108 enrolled. *Faculty:* 33 full-time (14 women), 33 part-time/adjunct (6 women). Expenses: Contact institution. *Financial support:* In 2006–07, 250 students received support, including 11 fellowships (averaging $8,000 Canadian dollars per year), 20 research assistantships (averaging $8,000 Canadian dollars per year); career-related internships or fieldwork, Federal Work-Study, institutionally sponsored loans, scholarships/grants, health care benefits, unspecified assistantships, and course prizes, merit-based awards also available. Support available to part-time students. Financial award application deadline: 6/1. In 2006, 122 LL Bs, 10 master's awarded. *Degree program information:* Part-time programs available. Offers law (LL B, LL M, PhD). *Application deadline:* For fall admission, 2/1 for domestic and international students. Applications are processed on a rolling basis. *Application fee:* $75 Canadian dollars. Electronic applications accepted. *Application Contact:* Neela Paige, Admissions Assistant, 250-721-8151, Fax: 250-721-6390, E-mail: lawadmss@uvic.ca. *Dean,* Andrew J. Petter, 250-721-8147, Fax: 250-472-7299, E-mail: dean@law.uvic.ca.

UNIVERSITY OF VIRGINIA, Charlottesville, VA 22903

General Information State-supported, coed, university. CGS member. *Enrollment:* 24,068 graduate, professional, and undergraduate students; 5,924 full-time matriculated graduate/professional students (2,637 women), 331 part-time matriculated graduate/professional students (206 women). *Enrollment by degree level:* 1,691 first professional, 2,250 master's, 2,313 doctoral, 1 other advanced degree. *Graduate faculty:* 2,102 full-time (638 women), 202 part-time/adjunct (93 women). *Graduate housing:* Rooms and/or apartments available on a first-come, first-served basis to single and married students. Housing application deadline:6/1. *Student services:* Campus employment opportunities, campus safety program, career counseling, child daycare facilities, disabled student services, exercise/wellness program, free psychological counseling, grant writing training, international student services, low-cost health insurance, multicultural affairs office, teacher training, writing training. *Library facilities:* Alderman Library plus 14 others. *Online resources:* library catalog, web page, access to other libraries' catalogs. *Collection:* 5.4 million titles, 71,832 serial subscriptions, 99,127 audiovisual materials. *Research affiliation:* National Radio Astronomy Observatory, Federal Executive Institute, The Judge Advocate General's School, U.S. Army.

Computer facilities: Computer purchase and lease plans are available. 1,645 computers available on campus for general student use. A campuswide network can be accessed from student residence rooms and from off campus. Internet access and online class registration, online course management tool are available. *Web address:* http://www.virginia.edu/.
General Application Contact: Dean of Appropriate School, 434-924-0311.

GRADUATE UNITS

College and Graduate School of Arts and Sciences Students: 1,535 full-time (749 women), 87 part-time (65 women); includes 96 minority (38 African Americans, 3 American Indian/Alaska Native, 33 Asian Americans or Pacific Islanders, 22 Hispanic Americans), 305 international. Average age 28. 3,817 applicants, 25% accepted, 387 enrolled. *Faculty:* 597 full-time (174 women), 37 part-time/adjunct (17 women). Expenses: Contact institution. *Financial support:* Fellowships with partial tuition reimbursements, research assistantships, teaching assistantships with tuition reimbursements, career-related internships or fieldwork, Federal Work-Study, institutionally sponsored loans, traineeships, tuition waivers (full and partial), and unspecified assistantships available. Financial award applicants required to submit FAFSA. In 2006, 340 master's, 164 doctorates awarded. *Degree program information:* Part-time programs available. Offers anthropology (MA, PhD); arts and sciences (MA, MFA, MS, PhD); astronomy (MS, PhD); biology (MA, MS, PhD); chemistry (MA, MS, PhD); classical art and archaeology (MA, PhD); classics (MA, PhD); creative writing (MFA); drama (MFA); East Asian studies (MA); economics (MA, PhD); English (MA, PhD); environmental sciences (MA, MS, PhD); foreign affairs (MA, PhD); French (MA, PhD); German (MA, PhD); government (MA, PhD); history (MA, PhD); history of art and architecture (MA, PhD); immunology (PhD); Italian (MA); linguistics (MA); mathematics (MA, MS, PhD); music (MA, PhD); philosophy (MA, PhD); physics (MA, MS, PhD); physics education (MA); psychology (MA, PhD); religious studies (MA, PhD); Slavic languages and literatures (MA, PhD); sociology (MA, PhD); Spanish (MA, PhD); statistics (MS, PhD). *Application deadline:* Applications are processed on a rolling basis. *Application fee:* $60. Electronic applications accepted. *Dean,* Edward L. Ayers, 434-924-7184, Fax: 434-924-6737, E-mail: grad-a-s@virginia.edu.

Center for Biomedical Ethics Students: 1 (woman) full-time. Average age 25. 6 applicants, 0% accepted. Expenses: Contact institution. *Financial support:* Applicants required to submit FAFSA. In 2006, 2 degrees awarded. Offers bioethics (MA). *Application fee:* $60. Electronic applications accepted. *Application Contact:* Peter C. Brunjes, Associate Dean for Graduate Programs and Research, 434-924-7184, Fax: 434-924-6737, E-mail: grad-a-s@virginia.edu. *Director, Center for Biomedical Ethics,* Jonathan Moreno, 434-924-5974, E-mail: jdm8n@virginia.edu.

Curry School of Education Students: 729 full-time (540 women), 156 part-time (102 women); includes 88 minority (48 African Americans, 1 American Indian/Alaska Native, 27 Asian Americans or Pacific Islanders, 12 Hispanic Americans), 34 international. Average age 30. 914 applicants, 52% accepted, 233 enrolled. *Faculty:* 100 full-time (56 women), 7 part-time/adjunct (6 women). Expenses: Contact institution. *Financial support:* Fellowships, Federal Work-Study available. Financial award applicants required to submit FAFSA. In 2006, 551 master's, 86 doctorates, 48 other advanced degrees awarded. Offers administration and supervision (M Ed, Ed D, Ed S); clinical and school psychology (Ed D, PhD); communication disorders (M Ed); counselor education (M Ed, Ed D, Ed S); curriculum and instruction (M Ed, Ed D, Ed S); education (M Ed, MT, Ed D, PhD, Ed S); educational policy and evaluation (M Ed, Ed D); educational psychology (M Ed, Ed D, Ed S); health and physical education (M Ed, Ed D); higher education (Ed D, Ed S); kinesiology (M Ed, Ed D); special education (M Ed, Ed D, Ed S). *Application deadline:* Applications are processed on a rolling basis. *Application fee:* $60. Electronic applications accepted. *Application Contact:* Linda Berry, Student Enrollment Coordinator, 434-924-0738, E-mail: curry-admissions@virginia.edu. *Dean,* David W. Breneman, 434-924-3332, Fax: 434-924-0888, E-mail: dbreneman@virginia.edu.

Darden Graduate School of Business Administration Students: 693 full-time (147 women), 1 part-time; includes 92 minority (25 African Americans, 1 American Indian/Alaska Native, 47 Asian Americans or Pacific Islanders, 19 Hispanic Americans), 165 international. Average age 29. 1,780 applicants, 32% accepted, 329 enrolled. *Faculty:* 62 full-time (13 women), 2 part-time/adjunct (1 woman). Expenses: Contact institution. *Financial support:* Fellowships, research assistantships, career-related internships or fieldwork available. Financial award applicants required to submit FAFSA. In 2006, 300 master's, 3 doctorates awarded. Offers business administration (MBA, PhD). *Application deadline:* Applications are processed on a rolling basis. *Application fee:* $140. Electronic applications accepted. *Application Contact:* Dawna Clarke, Director of Admissions, 434-924-4809, E-mail: darden@virginia.edu. *Dean,* Robert F. Bruner, 434-924-7481, E-mail: brunerr@virginia.edu.

McIntire School of Commerce Students: 125 full-time (42 women), 55 part-time (24 women); includes 8 minority (3 African Americans, 2 Asian Americans or Pacific Islanders, 3 Hispanic Americans), 25 international. Average age 27. *Faculty:* 58 full-time (14 women), 4 part-time/adjunct (3 women). Expenses: Contact institution. *Financial support:* Fellowships, research assistantships, teaching assistantships, career-related internships or fieldwork and Federal Work-Study available. Financial award application deadline: 3/15; financial award applicants required to submit FAFSA. In 2006, 172 degrees awarded. Offers accounting (MS); management of information technology (MS). *Application deadline:* For fall admission, 2/15 for domestic students, 1/15 priority date for international students. Applications are processed on a rolling basis. *Application fee:* $60. Electronic applications accepted. *Application Contact:* Cyndy Huddleston, Assistant Dean, Graduate Marketing and Admissions, 434-924-3110, E-mail: mcintiregrad@virginia.edu. *Dean,* Carl P. Zeithaml, 434-924-3110.

School of Architecture Students: 172 full-time (98 women), 2 part-time (both women); includes 14 minority (2 African Americans, 9 Asian Americans or Pacific Islanders, 3 Hispanic Americans), 11 international. Average age 27. 504 applicants, 47% accepted, 96 enrolled. *Faculty:* 39 full-time (14 women), 18 part-time/adjunct (6 women). Expenses: Contact institution. *Financial support:* Fellowships, career-related internships or fieldwork, Federal Work-Study, and institutionally sponsored loans available. Financial award applicants required to submit FAFSA. In 2006, 71 master's, 2 doctorates awarded. Offers architectural history (M Arch H, PhD); architecture (M Arch); landscape architecture (M Land Arch); urban and environmental planning (MUEP). *Application fee:* $60. Electronic applications accepted. *Application Contact:* Tracy Brookman, Admissions Officer, 434-924-6442, E-mail: arch-admissions@virginia.edu. *Dean,* Karen Van Lengen, 434-924-3715.

School of Engineering and Applied Science Students: 628 full-time (156 women), 12 part-time (2 women); includes 58 minority (10 African Americans, 1 American Indian/Alaska Native, 42 Asian Americans or Pacific Islanders, 5 Hispanic Americans), 260 international. Average age 26. 1,566 applicants, 22% accepted, 148 enrolled. *Faculty:* 171 full-time (25 women), 4 part-time/adjunct (1 woman). Expenses: Contact institution. *Financial support:* Fellowships with full tuition reimbursements, research assistantships with full tuition reimbursements, teaching assistantships with full tuition reimbursements, career-related internships or fieldwork available. Financial award application deadline: 1/15; financial award applicants required to submit FAFSA. In 2006, 184 master's, 65 doctorates awarded. *Degree program information:* Part-time programs available. Postbaccalaureate distance learning degree programs offered (no on-campus study). Offers applied mechanics (MAM, MS); biomedical engineering (ME, MS, PhD); chemical engineering (ME, MS, PhD); civil engineering (ME, MS, PhD); computer engineering (ME, MS, PhD); computer science (MCS, MS, PhD); electrical engineering (ME, MS, PhD); engineering and applied science (MAM, MCS, ME, MEP, MMSE, MS, PhD); engineering physics (MEP, MS, PhD); materials science (MMSE, MS, PhD); mechanical and aerospace engineering (ME, MS, PhD); systems and information engineering (ME, MS, PhD). *Application deadline:* For fall admission, 8/1 for domestic students, 4/1 for international students; for winter admission, 12/1 for domestic students; for spring admission, 5/1 for domestic students. Applications are processed on a rolling basis. *Application fee:* $60. Electronic applications accepted. *Application Contact:* Kathryn C. Thornton, Assistant Dean for Graduate Programs, 434-924-3897, Fax: 434-982-2214, E-mail: seas-grad-admission@cs.virginia.edu. *Dean,* James H. Aylor, 434-924-3593, Fax: 434-924-8818.

School of Law Students: 1,174 full-time (461 women), 1 part-time; includes 199 minority (98 African Americans, 8 American Indian/Alaska Native, 72 Asian Americans or Pacific Islanders, 21 Hispanic Americans), 41 international. Average age 25. 5,286 applicants, 27% accepted, 441 enrolled. *Faculty:* 73 full-time (17 women), 2 part-time/adjunct (1 woman). Expenses: Contact institution. *Financial support:* Fellowships, Federal Work-Study available. Financial award application deadline: 1/15; financial award applicants required to submit FAFSA. In 2006, 369 JDs, 30 master's, 1 doctorate awarded. Offers law (JD, LL M, SJD). *Application deadline:* For fall admission, 1/16 priority date for domestic students. Applications are processed on a rolling basis. *Application fee:* $70. *Application Contact:* Susan Palmer, Associate Dean of Admissions, 434-924-7351, Fax: 434-982-2128, E-mail: lawadmit@virginia.edu. *Dean,* John C. Jeffries, 434-924-7354.

School of Medicine Students: 838 full-time (416 women), 12 part-time (6 women); includes 195 minority (53 African Americans, 1 American Indian/Alaska Native, 124 Asian Americans or Pacific Islanders, 17 Hispanic Americans), 62 international. Average age 26. 78 applicants. *Faculty:* 896 full-time (255 women), 118 part-time/adjunct (51 women). Expenses: Contact institution. *Financial support:* Institutionally sponsored loans and scholarships/grants available. Financial award applicants required to submit FAFSA. In 2006, 136 MDs, 30 master's, 29 doctorates awarded. Offers biochemistry (PhD); biological and physical sciences (MS); biophysics (PhD); cell biology (PhD); clinical investigation and patient-oriented research (MS); health evaluation sciences (MS); informatics in medicine (MS); medicine (MD, MPH, MS, PhD); microbiology (PhD); neuroscience (PhD); pharmacology (PhD); physiology (PhD); public health (MPH); surgery (MS). *Application Contact:* Beth A. Bailey, Director, Admissions Office, 434-924-5571, Fax: 434-982-2586, E-mail: bab7g@virginia.edu. *Vice President and Dean,* Arthur Garson, Jr., 434-924-5118.

School of Nursing Students: 30 full-time (28 women), 5 part-time (all women); includes 5 minority (2 African Americans, 2 Asian Americans or Pacific Islanders, 1 Hispanic American). Average age 41. 23 applicants, 57% accepted, 10 enrolled. Expenses: Contact institution. *Financial support:* Fellowships, research assistantships, teaching assistantships, Federal Work-Study and scholarships/grants available. Financial award application deadline: 3/1; financial award applicants required to submit FAFSA. In 2006, 8 degrees awarded. Offers nursing (MSN, PhD). *Application deadline:* For fall admission, 2/1 for domestic students. Applications are processed on a rolling basis. *Application fee:* $60. Electronic applications accepted. *Application Contact:* Clay Hysell, Assistant Dean for Graduate Student Services, 434-924-0141, E-mail: nur-osa@virginia.edu. *Dean,* B. Jeanette Lancaster, 434-924-0141.

UNIVERSITY OF WASHINGTON, Seattle, WA 98195

General Information State-supported, coed, university. CGS member. *Graduate housing:* Rooms and/or apartments available on a first-come, first-served basis to single and married students. Housing application deadline: 5/1. *Research affiliation:* Fred Hutchinson Cancer Research Center, Children's Hospital and Regional Medical Center (pediatric research).

GRADUATE UNITS

Graduate School *Degree program information:* Part-time and evening/weekend programs available. Postbaccalaureate distance learning degree programs offered (minimal on-campus study). Offers biology for teachers (MS); education (M Ed, Professional Certificate); global trade, transportation, and logistics (Certificate); K-8 education (Certificate); museology (MA); Near and Middle Eastern studies (PhD); preservation planning and design (Certificate); principalship (Certificate); quantitative ecology and resource management (MS, PhD); school administration (Certificate); urban design (Certificate). Electronic applications accepted.

Business School *Degree program information:* Part-time and evening/weekend programs available. Offers auditing and assurance (MP Acc); business (PhD); evening part-time (MBA); executive (MBA); full time (MBA); global (MBA); global executive (MBA); taxation (MP Acc); technology management (MBA). Electronic applications accepted.

College of Architecture and Urban Planning *Degree program information:* Part-time and evening/weekend programs available. Offers architecture (M Arch); architecture and urban planning (M Arch, MLA, MS, MSCM, MUP, PhD, Certificate); computer design (Certificate); construction management (MS, MSCM); historic preservation (Certificate); landscape architecture (MLA); lighting (Certificate); urban design (Certificate); urban design and planning (PhD); urban planning (MUP). Electronic applications accepted.

College of Arts and Sciences *Degree program information:* Part-time and evening/weekend programs available. Offers acting (MFA); anthropology (MA, PhD); applied mathematics (MS, PhD); art (MFA); art and design (MFA); art history (MA, PhD); arts and sciences (M Mus, MA, MAIS, MAT, MC, MFA, MM, MS, DMA, PhD); astronomy (MS, PhD); atmospheric sciences (MS, PhD); botany (MS, PhD); Central Asian studies (MAIS); chemistry (MS, PhD); China studies (MAIS); Chinese language and literature (MA, PhD); classics (MA, PhD); classics and philosophy (PhD); communication (MA, MC, PhD); comparative literature (MA, PhD); comparative religion (MAIS); costume design (MFA); dance (MFA); directing (MFA); East European studies (MAIS); economics (MA, PhD); English (MA, MAT, MFA, PhD); English as a second language (MAT); French (MA, PhD); French and Italian studies (MA, PhD); geography (MA, PhD); geology (MS, PhD); geophysics (MS, PhD); German language and literature (MA); German literature and culture (PhD); Hispanic literary and cultural studies (MA); history (PhD); international studies (MAIS); Italian (MA); Japan studies (MAIS); Japanese language and literature (MA, PhD); Korea studies (MAIS); lighting design (MFA); linguistics (MA, PhD); mathematics (MA, MS, PhD); Middle Eastern studies (MAIS); music (M Mus, MA, MM, DMA, PhD); music education (MA, PhD); Near Eastern languages and civilization (MA); philosophy (MA, PhD); physics (MS, PhD); political science (MA, PhD); psychology (PhD); Romance linguistics (MA, PhD); Russian literature (MA, PhD); Russian studies (MAIS); Russian, East European and Central Asian studies (MAIS); Scandinavian studies (MA, PhD); scene design (MFA); Slavic linguistics (MA, PhD); sociology (MA, PhD); South Asian language and literature (MA, PhD); South Asian studies (MAIS); Spanish and Portuguese (MA); speech and hearing sciences (MS, PhD); statistics (MS, PhD); theory and criticism (PhD); women studies (MA, PhD); zoology (PhD). Electronic applications accepted.

College of Education *Degree program information:* Part-time and evening/weekend programs available. Offers curriculum and instruction (M Ed, Ed D, PhD); early childhood education (M Ed, Ed D, PhD); educational leadership and policy studies (M Ed, Ed D, PhD); educational psychology (M Ed, PhD); elementary special education (M Ed, Ed D, PhD); emotional and behavioral disabilities (M Ed); general special education (M Ed, Ed D, PhD); human development and cognition (M Ed, PhD); measurement and research (M Ed, PhD); school counseling (M Ed, PhD); school psychology (M Ed, PhD); severe disabilities (M Ed, Ed D, PhD); special education (M Ed, Ed D, PhD); teacher education (MIT). Electronic applications accepted.

College of Engineering Students: 1,157 full-time (307 women), 283 part-time (48 women); includes 223 minority (22 African Americans, 9 American Indian/Alaska Native, 161 Asian Americans or Pacific Islanders, 31 Hispanic Americans), 408 international. Average age 28. 2,686 applicants, 34% accepted, 399 enrolled. *Faculty:* 194 full-time (32 women), 1 (woman) part-time/adjunct. Expenses: Contact institution. *Financial support:* In 2006–07, 136 fellowships with full tuition reimbursements (averaging $19,854 per year), 538 research assistantships with full tuition reimbursements (averaging $16,306 per year), 199 teaching assistantships with full tuition reimbursements (averaging $14,799 per year) were awarded; career-related internships or fieldwork, Federal Work-Study, institutionally sponsored loans, scholarships/grants, traineeships, health care benefits, tuition waivers (full), unspecified assistantships, and stipend supplements also available. Financial award application deadline: 2/28; financial award applicants required to submit FAFSA. In 2006, 308 master's, 107 doctorates awarded. *Degree program information:* Part-time and evening/weekend programs available. Postbaccalaureate distance learning degree programs offered (minimal on-campus study). Offers aeronautics and astronautics (MAE, MSAA, PhD); bioengineering (MME, MS, PhD); chemical engineering (MS Ch E, MSE, PhD); computer science (MS, PhD); construction engineering (MSCE); electrical engineering (MSEE, PhD); engineering (MAE, MME, MS, MS Ch E, MSAA, MSCE, MSE, MSEE, MSIE, MSME, MSMSE, PhD); environmental engineering (MS, MSCE, MSE, PhD); hydrology, water resources, and environmental fluid mechanics (MS, MSCE, MSE, PhD); industrial engineering (MSE, MSIE, PhD); materials science and engineering (MSE, MSMSE, PhD); materials science and engineering nanotechnology (PhD); mechanical engineering (MSE, MSME, PhD); structural and geotechnical engineering and mechanics (MS, MSCE, MSE, PhD); technical communication (MS, PhD); transportation and construction engineering (MS, MSE, PhD); transportation engineering (MSCE). *Application deadline:* For fall admission, 1/2 for domestic students, 11/1 priority date for international students. *Application fee:* $45. Electronic

University of Washington (continued)

applications accepted. *Application Contact:* Dr. Eve Riskin, Associate Dean, Academic Affairs, 206-543-8590, Fax: 206-616-8554, E-mail: riskin@u.washington.edu. *Dean*, Dr. Matthew O'Donnell, 206-543-0340, Fax: 206-543-0666, E-mail: odonnel@engr.washington.edu.

College of Forest Resources Offers forest economics (MS, PhD); forest ecosystem analysis (MS, PhD); forest engineering/forest hydrology (MS, PhD); forest products marketing (MS, PhD); forest soils (MS, PhD); paper science and engineering (MS, PhD); quantitative resource management (MS, PhD); silviculture (MFR); silviculture and forest protection (MS, PhD); social sciences (MS, PhD); urban horticulture (MFR, MS, PhD); wildlife science (MS, PhD). Electronic applications accepted.

College of Ocean and Fishery Sciences Offers aquatic and fishery sciences (MS, PhD); biological oceanography (MS, PhD); chemical oceanography (MS, PhD); marine affairs (MMA); marine geology and geophysics (MS, PhD); ocean and fishery sciences (MMA, MS, PhD); physical oceanography (MS, PhD). Electronic applications accepted.

Daniel J. Evans School of Public Affairs Students: 251 full-time, 150 part-time; includes 80 minority (15 African Americans, 2 American Indian/Alaska Native, 41 Asian Americans or Pacific Islanders, 22 Hispanic Americans), 39 international. Average age 30. 419 applicants, 67% accepted, 138 enrolled. *Faculty:* 34 full-time (12 women), 10 part-time/adjunct (4 women). Expenses: Contact institution. *Financial support:* Fellowships with full tuition reimbursements, research assistantships with full tuition reimbursements, career-related internships or fieldwork, Federal Work-Study, institutionally sponsored loans, and tuition waivers (full and partial) available. Support available to part-time students. Financial award applicants required to submit FAFSA. In 2006, 157 degrees awarded. *Degree program information:* Part-time and evening/weekend programs available. Offers public affairs (MPA, PhD). *Application deadline:* For fall admission, 1/15 priority date for domestic and international students. *Application fee:* $45. Electronic applications accepted. *Application Contact:* Jason P. Smith, Director of Student Services and Admissions, 206-616-1613, Fax: 206-543-1096, E-mail: evansdss@u.washington.edu. *Dean*, Dr. Sandra Archibald, 206-616-1648, Fax: 206-685-9044, E-mail: sarch@u.washington.edu.

The Information School Students: 201 full-time (138 women), 291 part-time (218 women); includes 67 minority (9 African Americans, 6 American Indian/Alaska Native, 36 Asian Americans or Pacific Islanders, 16 Hispanic Americans), 33 international. Average age 33. 585 applicants, 52% accepted, 193 enrolled. *Faculty:* 32 full-time (13 women), 15 part-time/adjunct (8 women). Expenses: Contact institution. *Financial support:* In 2006–07, 38 fellowships with tuition reimbursements (averaging $3,000 per year), 51 research assistantships with tuition reimbursements (averaging $12,308 per year) were awarded; teaching assistantships with tuition reimbursements, career-related internships or fieldwork, Federal Work-Study, institutionally sponsored loans, scholarships/grants, health care benefits, tuition waivers (full and partial), and unspecified assistantships also available. Support available to part-time students. Financial award application deadline: 2/28; financial award applicants required to submit FAFSA. In 2006, 138 master's, 2 doctorates awarded. *Degree program information:* Part-time and evening/weekend programs available. Postbaccalaureate distance learning degree programs offered (minimal on-campus study). Offers information management (MSIM); information science (PhD); library and information science (MLIS). *Application deadline:* For fall admission, 1/15 for domestic students, 11/1 for international students. *Application fee:* $45. Electronic applications accepted. *Application Contact:* Office and Student and Academic Services (OSAS), 206-543-1794, Fax: 206-616-3152, E-mail: info@ischool.washington.edu. *Professor and Dean*, Harry Bruce, 206-685-9937, Fax: 206-616-3152, E-mail: harryb@u.washington.edu.

School of Nursing *Degree program information:* Part-time programs available. Offers nursing (MN, MS, PhD).

School of Public Health and Community Medicine *Degree program information:* Part-time and evening/weekend programs available. Postbaccalaureate distance learning degree programs offered (minimal on-campus study). Offers biostatistics (MPH, MS, PhD); environmental and occupational health (MPH); environmental and occupational hygiene (PhD); environmental health (MS); epidemiology (MPH, MS, PhD); genetic epidemiology (MS); health services (MS, PhD); health services administration (MHA); health services administration and planning (EMHA); industrial hygiene and safety (MS); international health (MPH); maternal/child health (MPH); nutritional sciences (MPH, MS, PhD); occupational medicine (MPH); pathobiology (MS, PhD); public health (MPH); public health and community medicine (EMHA, MHA, MPH, MS, PhD); public health genetics (MPH, MS, PhD); safety and ergonomics (MS); statistical genetics (PhD); toxicology (MS, PhD).

School of Social Work *Degree program information:* Evening/weekend programs available. Postbaccalaureate distance learning degree programs offered (minimal on-campus study). Offers social work (MSW, PhD).

School of Social Work, Tacoma Campus *Degree program information:* Part-time and evening/weekend programs available. Offers social work (MSW). Electronic applications accepted.

School of Dentistry Offers dentistry (DDS, MS, MSD, PhD).

School of Law Offers Asian law (LL M, PhD); intellectual property law and policy (LL M); law (JD); law of sustainable international development (LL M); taxation (LL M).

School of Medicine *Degree program information:* Part-time programs available. Offers genome sciences (PhD); medicine (MD, MOT, MS, MSE, DPT, PhD). Electronic applications accepted.

Graduate Programs in Medicine Students: 509 full-time (221 women), 20 part-time (15 women). 3,031 applicants, 8% accepted. *Faculty:* 676 full-time (107 women), 146 part-time/adjunct (24 women). Expenses: Contact institution. *Financial support:* Fellowships with full tuition reimbursements, research assistantships with full tuition reimbursements, teaching assistantships with full tuition reimbursements, career-related internships or fieldwork, Federal Work-Study, institutionally sponsored loans, scholarships/grants, traineeships, tuition waivers (full and partial), and stipends available. Support available to part-time students. Financial award applicants required to submit FAFSA. In 2006, 15 master's, 48 doctorates awarded. *Degree program information:* Part-time programs available. Offers biochemistry (PhD); biological structure (PhD); biomedical and health informatics (MS, PhD); immunology (PhD); laboratory medicine (MS); medicine (MOT, MS, MSE, DPT, PhD); microbiology (PhD); molecular and cellular biology (PhD); molecular basis of disease (PhD); neurobiology (PhD); neuroscience (PhD); occupational therapy (MOT); pathology (MS); pharmacology (MS, PhD); physical therapy (DPT); physiology and biophysics (PhD); rehabilitation science (PhD); veterinary science (MS). *Application fee:* $35. Electronic applications accepted. *Application Contact:* Patricia T. Fero, Admissions Officer, 206-543-7212, E-mail: askuwsom@u.washington.edu.

School of Pharmacy *Degree program information:* Part-time and evening/weekend programs available. Postbaccalaureate distance learning degree programs offered. Offers medicinal chemistry (PhD); pharmaceutics (MS, PhD); pharmacy (Pharm D, MS, PhD).

UNIVERSITY OF WASHINGTON, BOTHELL, Bothell, WA 98011-8246

General Information State-supported, coed, upper-level institution. *Enrollment:* 1,683 graduate, professional, and undergraduate students; 119 full-time matriculated graduate/professional students (55 women), 116 part-time matriculated graduate/professional students (96 women). *Enrollment by degree level:* 235 master's. *Graduate faculty:* 30 full-time (17 women), 3 part-time/adjunct (2 women). *Graduate housing:* On-campus housing not available. *Student services:* Campus employment opportunities, campus safety program, career counseling, disabled student services, exercise/wellness program, low-cost health insurance, writing training. *Library facilities:* UW Bothell Library plus 1 other. *Online resources:* library catalog, web page, access to other libraries' catalogs. *Collection:* 73,749 titles, 720 serial subscriptions, 6,100 audiovisual materials. *Web address:* http://www.uwb.edu.

General Application Contact: Hung Dang, Registrar/Assistant Director of Student Affairs, 425-352-5305, E-mail: hdang@uwb.edu.

GRADUATE UNITS

Program in Policy Studies Students: 40 full-time (29 women), 6 part-time (3 women); includes 7 minority (1 African American, 1 American Indian/Alaska Native, 5 Asian Americans or Pacific Islanders). Average age 33. 38 applicants, 84% accepted, 29 enrolled. *Faculty:* 8 full-time (4 women). Expenses: Contact institution. *Financial support:* In 2006–07, 9 students received support, including 5 fellowships (averaging $15,000 per year), 1 research assistantship (averaging $2,000 per year); Federal Work-Study, tuition waivers (full), and unspecified assistantships also available. Financial award applicants required to submit FAFSA. In 2006, 15 degrees awarded. *Degree program information:* Evening/weekend programs available. Offers policy studies (MA). *Application deadline:* For fall admission, 3/1 priority date for domestic students. Applications are processed on a rolling basis. *Application fee:* $45. Electronic applications accepted. *Application Contact:* Andrew Brusletten, Program Manager, 425-352-5427, Fax: 425-352-3462, E-mail: abrusletten@uwb.edu. *Director, Interdisciplinary Studies Program*, Prof. Jolynn Edwards, 425-352-5350, E-mail: jedwards@uwb.edu.

UNIVERSITY OF WASHINGTON, TACOMA, Tacoma, WA 98402-3100

General Information State-supported, coed, upper-level institution.

UNIVERSITY OF WATERLOO, Waterloo, ON N2L 3G1, Canada

General Information Province-supported, coed, university. *Enrollment:* 26,966 graduate, professional, and undergraduate students; 2,546 full-time matriculated graduate/professional students (993 women), 578 part-time matriculated graduate/professional students (223 women). *Enrollment by degree level:* 1,804 master's, 1,316 doctoral. *Graduate faculty:* 1,539. *Graduate housing:* Rooms and/or apartments available on a first-come, first-served basis to single and married students. *Student services:* Campus employment opportunities, campus safety program, career counseling, child daycare facilities, disabled student services, exercise/wellness program, free psychological counseling, international student services, low-cost health insurance, teacher training, writing training. *Library facilities:* Dana Porter Library plus 7 others. *Online resources:* library catalog, web page, access to other libraries' catalogs. *Collection:* 3.8 million titles, 15,000 serial subscriptions, 1,200 audiovisual materials. *Research affiliation:* Waterloo Maple Inc. (symbolic computation research), Bell Canada (bell university labs), GM Canada (basic research), IBM (basic research), Com Dev International (telecommunications), Nortel (telecommunications).

Computer facilities: Computer purchase and lease plans are available. 6,000 computers available on campus for general student use. A campuswide network can be accessed from student residence rooms and from off campus. Internet access and online class registration, e-mail; wireless are available. *Web address:* http://www.uwaterloo.ca/.

General Application Contact: Tracey Sinclair, Recruitment Manager, 519-888-4567 Ext. 36030, Fax: 519-746-3051, E-mail: sinclair@uwaterloo.ca.

GRADUATE UNITS

Graduate Studies Students: 2,546 full-time (993 women), 578 part-time (223 women). 5,132 applicants, 23% accepted, 740 enrolled. *Faculty:* 865 full-time (171 women), 674 part-time/adjunct (127 women). Expenses: Contact institution. *Financial support:* Fellowships with partial tuition reimbursements, research assistantships with partial tuition reimbursements, teaching assistantships with partial tuition reimbursements, career-related internships or fieldwork, Federal Work-Study, institutionally sponsored loans, scholarships/grants, and tuition waivers (partial) available. Support available to part-time students. In 2006, 779 master's, 196 doctorates awarded. *Degree program information:* Part-time and evening/weekend programs available. Postbaccalaureate distance learning degree programs offered (no on-campus study). *Application deadline:* Applications are processed on a rolling basis. *Application fee:* $75 Canadian dollars. Electronic applications accepted. *Application Contact:* Tracey Sinclair, Recruitment Manager, 519-888-4567 Ext. 36030, Fax: 519-746-3051, E-mail: sinclair@uwaterloo.ca. *Dean*, Dr. Ranjana P. Bird, 519-888-4567 Ext. 3439, Fax: 519-746-3051.

Centre for Business, Entrepreneurship and Technology Students: 33 full-time (11 women). 57 applicants, 63% accepted, 23 enrolled. *Faculty:* 15 full-time. Expenses: Contact institution. In 2006, 31 degrees awarded. Offers business, entrepreneurship and technology (MBET). *Application deadline:* Applications are processed on a rolling basis. *Application fee:* $75. Electronic applications accepted. *Application Contact:* Emily Stafford, Administrative Liaison and Support, 519-888-4567 Ext. 31167, Fax: 519-888-7562, E-mail: estaffor@uwaterloo.ca. *Director*, Dr. Howard Armitage, 519-888-4567 Ext. 35776, Fax: 519-888-7562, E-mail: howard@uwaterloo.ca.

Faculty of Applied Health Sciences Students: 146 full-time (107 women), 48 part-time (33 women). 134 applicants, 48% accepted, 51 enrolled. *Faculty:* 59 full-time (23 women), 59 part-time/adjunct (18 women). Expenses: Contact institution. *Financial support:* Research assistantships, teaching assistantships, career-related internships or fieldwork, Federal Work-Study, institutionally sponsored loans, and scholarships/grants available. In 2006, 32 master's, 7 doctorates awarded. *Degree program information:* Part-time programs available. Offers applied health sciences (M Sc, MA, MPH, PhD); health studies and gerontology (M Sc, MPH, PhD); kinesiology (M Sc, PhD); recreation and leisure studies (MA, PhD). *Application deadline:* For fall admission, 2/1 for domestic and international students. *Application fee:* $75 Canadian dollars. Electronic applications accepted. *Application Contact:* Tracy Taves, Graduate Studies Coordinator, 519-888-4567 Ext. 36149, Fax: 519-746-6776, E-mail: tltaves@uwaterloo.ca. *Associate Dean*, Dr. Richard Hughson, 519-888-4567 Ext. 32516, Fax: 519-746-6776, E-mail: hughson@uwaterloo.ca.

Faculty of Arts Students: 740. 1,091 applicants, 31% accepted, 183 enrolled. *Faculty:* 183 full-time (49 women), 114 part-time/adjunct (52 women). Expenses: Contact institution. *Financial support:* Fellowships, research assistantships, teaching assistantships, career-related internships or fieldwork and scholarships/grants available. In 2006, 219 master's, 27 doctorates awarded. *Degree program information:* Part-time and evening/weekend programs available. Offers accounting (M Acc, PhD); anthropology (MA); arts (M Acc, M Tax, MA, MA Sc, MFA, PhD); economics (MA, PhD); English language and literature (PhD); finance (M Acc); French (MA, PhD); German (MA, PhD); global governance (MA, PhD); history (MA, PhD); literary studies (MA); philosophy (MA, PhD); psychology (MA, MA Sc, PhD); public issues (MA); rhetoric and communication design (MA); Russian (MA); sociology (MA, PhD); studio art (MFA); taxation (M Tax). *Application deadline:* Applications are processed on a rolling basis. *Application fee:* $75 Canadian dollars. Electronic applications accepted. *Application Contact:* Dr. Sandra Burt, Associate Dean of the Arts, Graduate Studies and Research, 519-888-4567 Ext. 33133, Fax: 519-725-1749, E-mail: sburt@watarts.uwaterloo.ca. *Dean*, Dr. K. Coates, 519-888-4567 Ext. 32217, Fax: 519-746-4147, E-mail: kcoates@uwaterloo.ca.

Faculty of Engineering Students: 956 full-time (238 women), 268 part-time (60 women). 1,834 applicants, 17% accepted, 227 enrolled. *Faculty:* 230 full-time. Expenses: Contact institution. *Financial support:* Fellowships, research assistantships, teaching assistantships, career-related internships or fieldwork, Federal Work-Study, and institutionally sponsored loans available. In 2006, 310 master's, 62 doctorates awarded. *Degree program information:* Part-time and evening/weekend programs available. Postbaccalaureate distance learning degree programs offered (no on-campus study). Offers applied operations research (MA Sc, MMS, PhD); architecture (M Arch); chemical engineering (M Eng, MA Sc, PhD); civil and environmental engineering (M Eng, MA Sc, PhD); electrical and computer engineering (M Eng, MA Sc, PhD); electrical and computer engineering (software engineering) (MA Sc); engineering (M Arch, M Eng, MA Sc, MBET, MMS, PhD); information systems (MA Sc, MMS, PhD); management of technology (MA Sc, MMS, PhD); mechanical engineering (M Eng, MA Sc, PhD); mechanical engineering design and manufacturing (M Eng); systems design engineering (M Eng, MA Sc, PhD). *Application deadline:* Applications are processed on a rolling basis. *Application fee:* $75 Canadian dollars. Electronic applications accepted. *Application Contact:* Dr. Peter Douglas, Associate Dean of Graduate Studies, 519-888-4567 Ext. 32913, Fax: 519-888-4365, E-mail: pdouglas@engmail.uwaterloo.ca. *Dean*, Dr. Adel Sedra, 519-888-4567 Ext. 33347, Fax: 519-746-1457, E-mail: asedra@ece.uwaterloo.ca.

Faculty of Environmental Studies *Degree program information:* Part-time programs available. Offers environment and resource studies (MES); environmental studies (MA, MAES,

MES, PhD); geography (MA, MES, PhD); local economic development/tourism policy and planning (MAES); planning (MA, MAES, MES, PhD). Electronic applications accepted.

Faculty of Mathematics Students: 478 full-time (126 women), 42 part-time (12 women). 1,026 applicants, 26% accepted. *Faculty:* 209 full-time (37 women), 60 part-time/adjunct (8 women). Expenses: Contact institution. *Financial support:* Research assistantships, teaching assistantships, career-related internships or fieldwork and scholarships/grants available. In 2006, 85 master's, 19 doctorates awarded. Offers actuarial science (M Math, PhD); applied mathematics (M Math, PhD); biostatistics (PhD); combinatorics and optimization (M Math, PhD); computer science (M Math, PhD); computer science (software engineering) (M Math); computer science (statistics-computing) (M Math); mathematics (M Math, PhD); pure mathematics (M Math, PhD); statistics (M Math, PhD); statistics-biostatistics (M Math); statistics-computing (M Math); statistics-finance (M Math). *Application deadline:* For fall admission, 2/1 for domestic and international students. *Application fee:* $75 Canadian dollars. Electronic applications accepted. *Application Contact:* Dr. Kirsten Morris, Associate Dean of Graduate Studies, 519-888-4567 Ext. 33294, E-mail: kmorris@math.uwaterloo.ca. *Dean,* Dr. Tom Coleman, 519-888-4567, Fax: 519-746-0274.

Faculty of Science Students: 372 full-time (164 women), 46 part-time (22 women). 339 applicants, 27% accepted, 68 enrolled. *Faculty:* 178 full-time (40 women), 181 part-time/adjunct (24 women). Expenses: Contact institution. *Financial support:* Fellowships, research assistantships, teaching assistantships, career-related internships or fieldwork and institutionally sponsored loans available. In 2006, 63 master's, 15 doctorates awarded. *Degree program information:* Part-time programs available. Offers biology (M Sc, PhD); chemistry (M Sc, PhD); earth sciences (M Sc, PhD); physics (M Sc, PhD); science (M Sc, PhD); vision science (M Sc, PhD). *Application deadline:* Applications are processed on a rolling basis. Electronic applications accepted. *Application Contact:* A. Kolic, Administrative Assistant, 519-888-4567 Ext. 33525, Fax: 519-746-2543, E-mail: akolic@scimail.uwaterloo.ca. *Associate Dean,* Dr. R. I. Hall, 519-888-4567 Ext. 32450, Fax: 519-746-2543, E-mail: rihall@uwaterloo.ca.

THE UNIVERSITY OF WEST ALABAMA, Livingston, AL 35470

General Information State-supported, coed, comprehensive institution. *Enrollment:* 3,633 graduate, professional, and undergraduate students; 758 full-time matriculated graduate/professional students (636 women), 1,002 part-time matriculated graduate/professional students (855 women). *Enrollment by degree level:* 1,760 master's. *Graduate faculty:* 24 full-time (6 women), 7 part-time/adjunct (2 women). *Graduate housing:* Rooms and/or apartments available on a first-come, first-served basis to single students and available to married students. Typical cost: $3,370 (including board) for single students; $2,820 per year for married students. *Student services:* Campus employment opportunities, career counseling, disabled student services, free psychological counseling, international student services. *Library facilities:* Julia Tutwiler Library. *Online resources:* library catalog, web page, access to other libraries' catalogs. *Collection:* 161,991 titles, 30,000 serial subscriptions, 3,072 audiovisual materials.

Computer facilities: 400 computers available on campus for general student use. A campuswide network can be accessed from student residence rooms and from off campus. Internet access is available. *Web address:* http://www.uwa.edu/.

General Application Contact: Dr. Tom DeVaney, Dean of Graduate Studies, 205-652-3647 Ext. 421, Fax: 205-652-3551, E-mail: twd@uwa.edu.

GRADUATE UNITS

School of Graduate Studies Students: 758 full-time (636 women), 1,002 part-time (855 women); includes 790 minority (756 African Americans, 8 American Indian/Alaska Native, 12 Asian Americans or Pacific Islanders, 14 Hispanic Americans), 2 international. *Faculty:* 33 full-time (10 women), 42 part-time/adjunct (33 women). Expenses: Contact institution. *Financial support:* In 2006–07, 25 students received support. Career-related internships or fieldwork, Federal Work-Study, scholarships/grants, and unspecified assistantships available. Support available to part-time students. Financial award applicants required to submit CSS PROFILE. In 2006, 344 degrees awarded. *Degree program information:* Part-time and evening/weekend programs available. *Application deadline:* For fall admission, 9/10 priority date for domestic students; for spring admission, 3/24 for domestic students. Applications are processed on a rolling basis. *Application fee:* $20 ($50 for international students). *Dean of Graduate Studies,* Dr. Tom DeVaney, 205-652-3647 Ext. 421, Fax: 205-652-3551, E-mail: twd@uwa.edu.

College of Education Students: 709 full-time (601 women), 888 part-time (772 women); includes 707 minority (673 African Americans, 8 American Indian/Alaska Native, 12 Asian Americans or Pacific Islanders, 14 Hispanic Americans), 2 international. *Faculty:* 17 full-time (9 women), 42 part-time/adjunct (33 women). Expenses: Contact institution. *Financial support:* In 2006–07, 13 students received support. Career-related internships or fieldwork, Federal Work-Study, scholarships/grants, and unspecified assistantships available. Support available to part-time students. Financial award applicants required to submit FAFSA. In 2006, 344 degrees awarded. *Degree program information:* Part-time and evening/weekend programs available. Offers continuing education (MSCE); early childhood education (M Ed); education (M Ed, MAT, MSCE); elementary education (M Ed); guidance and counseling (M Ed, MSCE); library media (M Ed); physical education (M Ed, MAT); school administration (M Ed); secondary education (MAT); special education (M Ed). *Application deadline:* For fall admission, 9/10 priority date for domestic students; for spring admission, 3/24 for domestic students. Applications are processed on a rolling basis. *Application fee:* $20 ($50 for international students). *Dean, College of Education,* Dr. Martha Hocutt, 205-652-3421, Fax: 205-652-3706, E-mail: mhocutt@uwa.edu.

College of Liberal Arts Students: 40 full-time (28 women), 79 part-time (60 women); includes 55 minority (all African Americans) *Faculty:* 11 full-time (1 woman). Expenses: Contact institution. *Financial support:* Career-related internships or fieldwork, Federal Work-Study, scholarships/grants, and unspecified assistantships available. Support available to part-time students. Offers history (MAT); language arts (MAT); liberal arts (MAT); social science (MAT). *Application fee:* $20 ($50 for international students). *Dean, College of Liberal Arts,* Dr. Michael Cook, 800-621-8044 Ext. 3457.

College of Natural Sciences and Mathematics Students: 9 full-time (7 women), 35 part-time (23 women); includes 28 minority (all African Americans) *Faculty:* 5 full-time (0 women). Expenses: Contact institution. *Financial support:* Career-related internships or fieldwork, Federal Work-Study, scholarships/grants, and unspecified assistantships available. Support available to part-time students. Offers biological sciences (MAT); mathematics (MAT); natural sciences and mathematics (MAT). *Application fee:* $20 ($50 for international students). *Dean,* Dr. Judy Massey, 800-621-3412.

THE UNIVERSITY OF WESTERN ONTARIO, London, ON N6A 5B8, Canada

General Information Province-supported, coed, university. *Enrollment:* 33,706 graduate, professional, and undergraduate students; 3,349 full-time matriculated graduate/professional students (1,434 women), 368 part-time matriculated graduate/professional students (227 women). *Graduate faculty:* 1,500. *Graduate housing:* Rooms and/or apartments available on a first-come, first-served basis to single and married students. *Student services:* Campus employment opportunities, campus safety program, career counseling, child daycare facilities, disabled student services, exercise/wellness program, free psychological counseling, grant writing training, international student services, low-cost health insurance, multicultural affairs office, teacher training, writing training. *Library facilities:* The University of Western Ontario Libraries plus 7 others. *Online resources:* library catalog, web page, access to other libraries' catalogs. *Collection:* 3.4 million titles, 38,517 serial subscriptions.

Computer facilities: 351 computers available on campus for general student use. A campuswide network can be accessed from student residence rooms and from off campus. Internet access and online class registration are available. *Web address:* http://www.uwo.ca/.

General Application Contact: Clare Ann Tattersall, Coordinator, Graduate Student Recruitment and Retention, 519-661-2111 Ext. 81130, Fax: 519-661-3730, E-mail: ctatter3@uwo.ca.

GRADUATE UNITS

Faculty of Graduate Studies Students: 3,717. *Faculty:* 1,087. Expenses: Contact institution. *Financial support:* Fellowships, research assistantships, teaching assistantships, career-related internships or fieldwork, Federal Work-Study, institutionally sponsored loans, scholarships/grants, traineeships, health care benefits, tuition waivers (full and partial), and unspecified assistantships available. Financial award application deadline: 4/1. In 2006, 113 degrees awarded. *Degree program information:* Part-time and evening/weekend programs available. Postbaccalaureate distance learning degree programs offered. *Application deadline:* For fall admission, 8/15 for domestic and international students; for spring admission, 4/15 for domestic and international students. Applications are processed on a rolling basis. Electronic applications accepted. *Application Contact:* Applications Coordinator, 519-661-2102, E-mail: grduwo@uwo.ca. *Acting Dean and Provost,* Dr. Fred J. Longstaffe, 519-661-2111 Ext. 84607, Fax: 519-661-3730, E-mail: flonga@uwo.ca.

Biosciences Division Expenses: Contact institution. *Financial support:* Fellowships, research assistantships, teaching assistantships, career-related internships or fieldwork, institutionally sponsored loans, scholarships/grants, and traineeships available. Financial award application deadline: 4/1. *Degree program information:* Part-time programs available. Postbaccalaureate distance learning degree programs offered. Offers audiology (M Cl Sc, M Sc); biochemistry (M Sc, PhD); biology (M Sc, PhD); biosciences (M Cl Sc, M Sc, MA, MPT, PhD); clinical neurological sciences (M Sc, PhD); epidemiology and biostatistics (M Sc, PhD); family medicine (M Cl Sc); kinesiology (M Sc, MA, PhD); medical biophysics (M Sc, PhD); microbiology and immunology (M Sc, PhD); occupational therapy (M Sc); pathology (M Sc, PhD); physical therapy (M Sc, MPT); physiology (M Sc, PhD); plant and environmental sciences (M Sc); plant sciences (M Sc, PhD); plant sciences and environmental sciences (PhD); plant sciences and molecular biology (M Sc, PhD); psychology (MA, PhD); speech-language pathology (M Cl Sc, M Sc); zoology (M Sc, PhD). *Application Contact:* Dr. Tony Percival-Smith, Information Contact, 519-661-3014, Fax: 519-661-3936. *Head,* Dr. B. Fenton, 519-661-2111 Ext. 86464.

Center for the Study of Theory and Criticism Students: 25 full-time (13 women). 37 applicants, 41% accepted. *Faculty:* 21. Expenses: Contact institution. *Financial support:* In 2006–07, 18 teaching assistantships with full tuition reimbursements (averaging $8,264 Canadian dollars per year) were awarded; research assistantships with tuition reimbursements, scholarships/grants also available. Financial award application deadline: 4/1. In 2006, 8 degrees awarded. Offers theory and criticism (MA, PhD). *Application deadline:* For fall admission, 1/15 for domestic and international students. *Application fee:* $30 Canadian dollars. *Chair,* Prof. Veronica Schild, 519-661-2111 Ext. 85169, E-mail: theory@uwo.ca.

Faculty of Arts and Humanities Students: 298. *Faculty:* 143. Expenses: Contact institution. *Financial support:* Fellowships, research assistantships, teaching assistantships, career-related internships or fieldwork, institutionally sponsored loans, and tuition waivers (full) available. Financial award application deadline: 4/1. In 2006, 15 master's, 53 doctorates awarded. *Degree program information:* Part-time programs available. Offers arts and humanities (M Mus, MA, PhD); Canadian literature (MA); classical studies (MA); comparative literature (MA, PhD); English (PhD); English literature (MA); French (MA, PhD); music (M Mus, MA, PhD); philosophy (MA, PhD); Spanish (MA). *Dean,* Dr. Kathleen Okruhlik, 519-661-2111 Ext. 83004, E-mail: okruhlik@uwo.ca.

Faculty of Information and Media Studies Students: 229 full-time (168 women), 69 part-time (47 women). *Faculty:* 40 full-time, 15 part-time/adjunct. Expenses: Contact institution. Offers journalism (MA); library and information science (MLIS, PhD); media studies (MA, PhD). *Application Contact:* Shelley Long, Graduate Student Services Secretary, 519-661-4017, Fax: 519-661-3506, E-mail: slong@uwo.ca. *Dean,* Dr. Catherine L. Ross, 519-661-3542, Fax: 519-661-3506.

Health Sciences Division Expenses: Contact institution. Offers health sciences (M Sc N, PhD); nursing (M Sc N, PhD). *Dean,* Dr. Jim Weese, 519-661-2111 Ext. 84239, Fax: 519-850-2347, E-mail: jweese1@uwo.ca.

Physical Sciences Division Expenses: Contact institution. *Financial support:* Fellowships, research assistantships, teaching assistantships, career-related internships or fieldwork, institutionally sponsored loans, and scholarships/grants available. Financial award application deadline: 4/1. *Degree program information:* Part-time programs available. Offers applied mathematics (M Sc, PhD); astronomy (M Sc, PhD); chemistry (M Sc, PhD); computer science (M Sc, PhD); engineering (M Eng, ME Sc, PhD); geology (M Sc, PhD); geology and environmental science (M Sc, PhD); geophysics (M Sc, PhD); geophysics and environmental science (M Sc, PhD); mathematics (M Sc, PhD); physical sciences (M Eng, M Sc, MA, ME Sc, PhD); physics (M Sc, PhD); statistical and actuarial sciences (M Sc, PhD); theoretical physics (PhD). Electronic applications accepted. *Application Contact:* Applications Coordinator, 519-661-2102, E-mail: grduwo@uwo.ca.

Social Sciences Division Expenses: Contact institution. *Financial support:* Fellowships, research assistantships, teaching assistantships, career-related internships or fieldwork, Federal Work-Study, institutionally sponsored loans, scholarships/grants, and tuition waivers (partial) available. Financial award application deadline: 4/1. *Degree program information:* Part-time and evening/weekend programs available. Offers anthropology (MA, PhD); counseling (M Ed); curriculum studies (M Ed); economics (MA, PhD); education (M Ed); educational policy studies (M Ed); educational psychology/special education (M Ed); geography (M Sc, MA, PhD); history (MA, PhD); political science (MA, MPA, PhD); social sciences (M Ed, M Sc, M Sc N, MA, MBA, MLIS, MPA, PhD, Diploma); sociology (MA, PhD). *Application Contact:* Dr. Julie McMullin, Associate Dean, 519-661-2111 Ext. 82053, E-mail: mcmullin@uwo.ca. *Dean,* Dr. Brian Timney, 519-661-2053 Ext. 82053, Fax: 519-661-3868, E-mail: socscidean@uwo.ca.

Faculty of Law Expenses: Contact institution. Offers law (LL B, LL M, Diploma). *Application deadline:* For fall admission, 11/1 for domestic students. Applications are processed on a rolling basis. *Application fee:* $50. *Application Contact:* D. Sandler, Director, Graduate Program, 519-661-3356, E-mail: dsandler@uwo.ca. *Acting Dean,* Dr. Craig Brown, 519-661-2111 Ext. 88442, E-mail: cbrown3@uwo.ca.

Richard Ivey School of Business *Degree program information:* Part-time and evening/weekend programs available. Offers biotechnology stream (MBA); business (EMBA, PhD); certified management accountant (MBA); China business stream (MBA); entrepreneurship (MBA); finance stream (MBA). Electronic applications accepted.

Schulich School of Medicine and Dentistry Expenses: Contact institution. *Financial support:* Fellowships, teaching assistantships, career-related internships or fieldwork, Federal Work-Study, and institutionally sponsored loans available. Offers medicine (MD); medicine and dentistry (DDS, MD, M Cl D, M Cl Sc, M Sc, MA, PhD). *Dean,* Dr. Carol P. Herbert, 519-661-3459 Ext. 3459, E-mail: carol.herbert@schulich.uwo.ca.

School of Dentistry Expenses: Contact institution. *Financial support:* Fellowships, career-related internships or fieldwork, Federal Work-Study, and institutionally sponsored loans available. Offers dentistry (DDS, M Cl D); orthodontics (M Cl D). *Application Contact:* Dr. Thomas W. Mara, Admissions, 519-661-2111 Ext. 86087, Fax: 519-661-2075, E-mail: dental.admissions@schulich.uwo.ca. *Director,* Dr. H. S. Sandhu, 519-661-2111 Ext. 86141, Fax: 519-661-3875, E-mail: harinder.sandhu@schulich.uwo.ca.

UNIVERSITY OF WEST FLORIDA, Pensacola, FL 32514-5750

General Information State-supported, coed, comprehensive institution. CGS member. *Enrollment:* 9,819 graduate, professional, and undergraduate students; 365 full-time matriculated graduate/professional students (240 women), 907 part-time matriculated graduate/professional students (576 women). *Enrollment by degree level:* 1,009 master's, 205 doctoral, 58 other advanced degrees. *Graduate faculty:* 165 full-time (60 women), 56 part-time/adjunct (29 women). Tuition, state resident: full-time $5,871; part-time $245 per credit hour. Tuition, nonresident: full-time $21,241; part-time $885 per credit hour. *Graduate housing:* Room and/or apartments available on a first-come, first-served basis to single students; on-campus housing not available to married students. Typical cost: $6,600 (including board). Room and board charges vary according to housing facility selected. *Student services:* Campus employment opportunities, campus safety program, career counseling, child daycare facilities, disabled student services, exercise/wellness program, free psychological counseling, international student services, low-cost health insurance, multicultural affairs office, teacher training. *Library facilities:* John C. Pace Library plus 2 others. *Online resources:* library catalog, web page, access to other libraries' catalogs. *Collection:* 792,733 titles, 5,122

University of West Florida (continued)

serial subscriptions, 10,061 audiovisual materials. *Research affiliation:* University of Southern Mississippi Consortium on Coastal Estaurine Research (Microbial Biofilms and Coastal Estaurine Research), Computer Science Corporation (CSC) Inc. (Environmentall Assessment (Project Title: Pre-Reefing Environmental Assessment for the ex-Oriskany)), Workforce ESCAROSA Inc. (Alternative Teacher Certification (Project Name: Hometown Teachers Teach)), Software Engineering Research Consortium (Motorola, Northrup Grumman) (Software Engineering (Multiple Projects)), TIP Strategies Inc. (Economic Development (Project Title: TIP Advanced Planning Project)).

Computer facilities: 900 computers available on campus for general student use. A campuswide network can be accessed from student residence rooms and from off campus. Internet access and online class registration are available. *Web address:* http://uwf.edu/.

General Application Contact: Dr. Richard A. Barth, Director of Admissions, 850-474-2230, Fax: 850-474-2082, E-mail: admissions@uwf.edu.

GRADUATE UNITS

College of Arts and Sciences: Arts Students: 89 full-time (58 women), 140 part-time (75 women); includes 33 minority (10 African Americans, 6 American Indian/Alaska Native, 7 Asian Americans or Pacific Islanders, 10 Hispanic Americans), 5 international. Average age 32. 182 applicants, 60% accepted, 84 enrolled. *Faculty:* 49 full-time (18 women), 15 part-time/adjunct (10 women). Expenses: Contact institution. *Financial support:* In 2006–07, 124 students received support, including 10 fellowships with partial tuition reimbursements available (averaging $2,250 per year), 36 research assistantships with partial tuition reimbursements available (averaging $1,723 per year), 16 teaching assistantships with partial tuition reimbursements available (averaging $2,450 per year); career-related internships or fieldwork, Federal Work-Study, institutionally sponsored loans, scholarships/grants, tuition waivers (full and partial), and unspecified assistantships also available. Support available to part-time students. Financial award application deadline: 4/15; financial award applicants required to submit FAFSA. In 2006, 55 degrees awarded. *Degree program information:* Part-time and evening/weekend programs available. Offers anthropology (MA); applied politics (MA); arts and sciences: arts (MA); communication arts (MA); creative writing (MA); historical archaeology (MA); history (MA); interdisciplinary humanities (MA); literature (MA); political science (MA); psychology (MA). *Application deadline:* For fall admission, 6/1 for domestic students, 5/15 for international students; for spring admission, 11/1 for domestic students, 10/1 for international students. Applications are processed on a rolling basis. *Application fee:* $30. *Dean,* Dr. Jane Halonen, 850-474-2688.

College of Arts and Sciences: Sciences Students: 29 full-time (14 women), 85 part-time (43 women); includes 11 minority (4 African Americans, 1 American Indian/Alaska Native, 4 Asian Americans or Pacific Islanders, 2 Hispanic Americans), 8 international. Average age 31. 56 applicants, 70% accepted, 30 enrolled. *Faculty:* 50 full-time (16 women), 6 part-time/adjunct (0 women). Expenses: Contact institution. *Financial support:* In 2006–07, 57 students received support, including 15 research assistantships with partial tuition reimbursements available (averaging $4,700 per year), 24 teaching assistantships with partial tuition reimbursements available (averaging $6,000 per year); career-related internships or fieldwork, Federal Work-Study, institutionally sponsored loans, scholarships/grants, and tuition waivers (full and partial) also available. Support available to part-time students. Financial award application deadline: 4/15; financial award applicants required to submit FAFSA. In 2006, 25 degrees awarded. *Degree program information:* Part-time and evening/weekend programs available. Offers arts and sciences: sciences (MA, MPH, MS, MST); biological chemistry (MS); biology (MS, MST); biology education (MST); coastal zone studies (MS); computer science (MS); environmental biology (MS); environmental science (MS); general biology (MS); health communication (MA); mathematics and statistics (MS); public health (MPH); software engineering (MS). *Application deadline:* For fall admission, 6/1 for domestic students, 5/15 for international students; for spring admission, 11/1 for domestic students, 10/1 for international students. Applications are processed on a rolling basis. *Application fee:* $30. *Dean,* Dr. Jane Halonen, 850-474-2688.

College of Business Students: 38 full-time (19 women), 128 part-time (60 women); includes 25 minority (7 African Americans, 9 Asian Americans or Pacific Islanders, 9 Hispanic Americans), 17 international. Average age 31. 98 applicants, 64% accepted, 55 enrolled. *Faculty:* 30 full-time (7 women), 12 part-time/adjunct (7 women). Expenses: Contact institution. *Financial support:* In 2006–07, 70 fellowships (averaging $500 per year), 28 research assistantships with partial tuition reimbursements (averaging $7,000 per year) were awarded; career-related internships or fieldwork, scholarships/grants, and unspecified assistantships also available. Support available to part-time students. Financial award application deadline: 4/15; financial award applicants required to submit FAFSA. In 2006, 98 degrees awarded. *Degree program information:* Part-time and evening/weekend programs available. Offers accounting (MA); business (MA, MBA); business administration (MBA). *Application deadline:* For fall admission, 6/30 for domestic students, 5/15 for international students; for spring admission, 11/1 for domestic students, 10/1 for international students. Applications are processed on a rolling basis. *Application fee:* $30. *Dean,* Dr. F. Edward Ranelli, 850-474-2348.

College of Professional Studies Students: 209 full-time (149 women), 554 part-time (398 women); includes 168 minority (118 African Americans, 11 American Indian/Alaska Native, 22 Asian Americans or Pacific Islanders, 17 Hispanic Americans), 15 international. Average age 38. 350 applicants, 72% accepted, 194 enrolled. *Faculty:* 36 full-time (19 women), 23 part-time/adjunct (12 women). Expenses: Contact institution. *Financial support:* In 2006–07, 80 students received support, including 44 fellowships (averaging $408 per year), 8 research assistantships (averaging $8,000 per year), 8 teaching assistantships (averaging $8,000 per year); career-related internships or fieldwork, Federal Work-Study, institutionally sponsored loans, scholarships/grants, tuition waivers (full and partial), and unspecified assistantships also available. Support available to part-time students. Financial award application deadline: 4/15; financial award applicants required to submit FAFSA. In 2006, 209 master's, 21 doctorates, 23 other advanced degrees awarded. *Degree program information:* Part-time and evening/weekend programs available. Offers career and technical studies (M Ed); clinical teaching (MA); criminal justice (MSA); curriculum and instruction (M Ed); elementary education (M Ed); guidance and counseling (M Ed); habilitative science (MA); middle and secondary level education (M Ed); primary education (M Ed); professional studies (M Ed, MA, MS, MSA, Ed D, Ed S); reading education (M Ed); teacher education (M Ed, MA). *Application deadline:* For fall admission, 6/1 for domestic students, 5/15 for international students; for spring admission, 11/1 for domestic students, 10/1 for international students. Applications are processed on a rolling basis. *Application fee:* $30. *Dean,* Dr. Donald Chu, 850-474-2769, Fax: 850-474-3205.

Division of Graduate Education Students: 54 full-time (33 women), 303 part-time (200 women); includes 86 minority (64 African Americans, 5 American Indian/Alaska Native, 14 Asian Americans or Pacific Islanders, 3 Hispanic Americans), 5 international. Average age 39. 128 applicants, 63% accepted, 68 enrolled. Expenses: Contact institution. *Financial support:* Fellowships, teaching assistantships, career-related internships or fieldwork, scholarships/grants, and unspecified assistantships available. Support available to part-time students. Financial award application deadline: 4/15; financial award applicants required to submit FAFSA. In 2006, 48 master's, 21 doctorates, 23 other advanced degrees awarded. *Degree program information:* Part-time and evening/weekend programs available. Offers curriculum and instruction (Ed D, Ed S); educational leadership (M Ed, Ed S); instructional technology (M Ed). *Application deadline:* For fall admission, 6/1 for domestic students, 5/15 for international students; for spring admission, 11/1 for domestic students, 10/1 for international students. Applications are processed on a rolling basis. *Application fee:* $30. *Chairperson,* Dr. Thomas J. Kramer, 850-474-2768.

Division of Health, Leisure, and Exercise Science Students: 39 full-time (29 women), 28 part-time (22 women); includes 7 minority (5 African Americans, 1 American Indian/Alaska Native, 1 Hispanic American), 2 international. Average age 28. 33 applicants, 88% accepted, 21 enrolled. Expenses: Contact institution. *Financial support:* In 2006–07, 3 teaching assistantships with partial tuition reimbursements (averaging $10,000 per year) were awarded; fellowships, Federal Work-Study, scholarships/grants, tuition waivers (full and partial), and unspecified assistantships also available. Financial award application deadline: 4/15; financial award applicants required to submit FAFSA. In 2006, 21 degrees awarded. *Degree program information:* Part-time and evening/weekend programs available. Offers exercise science (MS); health education (MS); health, leisure, and exercise science (MS); physical education (MS). *Application deadline:* For fall admission, 6/1 for domestic students, 5/15 for international students; for spring admission, 11/1 for domestic students, 10/1 for international students. Applications are processed on a rolling basis. *Application fee:* $30. *Chairperson,* Dr. Stuart W. Ryan, 850-474-2592.

UNIVERSITY OF WEST GEORGIA, Carrollton, GA 30118

General Information State-supported, coed, comprehensive institution. CGS member. *Enrollment:* 10,163 graduate, professional, and undergraduate students; 360 full-time matriculated graduate/professional students (261 women), 1,328 part-time matriculated graduate/professional students (1,049 women). *Enrollment by degree level:* 220 first professional, 886 master's, 62 doctoral. *Graduate faculty:* 230 full-time (104 women), 20 part-time/adjunct (11 women). Tuition, state resident: full-time $2,286; part-time $127 per credit. Tuition, nonresident: full-time $9,144; part-time $508 per credit. *Required fees:* $494; $27 per credit. $121 per semester. *Graduate housing:* Room and/or apartments available on a first-come, first-served basis to single students. Typical cost: $2,458 per year ($5,162 including board). Room and board charges vary according to board plan and housing facility selected. Housing application deadline: 6/1. *Student services:* Campus employment opportunities, campus safety program, career counseling, child daycare facilities, disabled student services, exercise/wellness program, free psychological counseling, international student services, low-cost health insurance, multicultural affairs office, teacher training, writing training. *Library facilities:* Irvine Sullivan Ingram Library. *Online resources:* library catalog, web page, access to other libraries' catalogs. *Collection:* 563,677 titles, 14,884 serial subscriptions, 11,048 audiovisual materials.

Computer facilities: 745 computers available on campus for general student use. A campuswide network can be accessed from student residence rooms and from off campus. Internet access and online class registration are available. *Web address:* http://www.westga.edu/.

General Application Contact: Dr. Charles W. Clark, Chair, 678-839-6508, E-mail: cclark@westga.edu.

GRADUATE UNITS

Graduate School Students: 360 full-time (261 women), 1,328 part-time (1,049 women); includes 444 minority (416 African Americans, 1 American Indian/Alaska Native, 11 Asian Americans or Pacific Islanders, 16 Hispanic Americans), 19 international. Average age 29. *Faculty:* 230 full-time (104 women), 20 part-time/adjunct (11 women). Expenses: Contact institution. *Financial support:* In 2006–07, 120 research assistantships with partial tuition reimbursements (averaging $5,000 per year) were awarded; career-related internships or fieldwork, tuition waivers (partial), and unspecified assistantships also available. Support available to part-time students. Financial award applicants required to submit FAFSA. In 2006, 491 master's, 2 doctorates, 123 other advanced degrees awarded. *Degree program information:* Part-time and evening/weekend programs available. Postbaccalaureate distance learning degree programs offered (no on-campus study). *Application deadline:* For fall admission, 8/1 priority date for domestic students; for spring admission, 12/18 for domestic students. *Application fee:* $20. Electronic applications accepted. *Application Contact:* Cheryl Lynn Thomas Hill, Director of Graduate Admissions, 678-839-6419, Fax: 678-839-5949, E-mail: gradsch@westga.edu. *Chair,* Dr. Charles W. Clark, 678-839-6508, E-mail: cclark@westga.edu.

College of Arts and Sciences Students: 109 full-time (55 women), 102 part-time (67 women); includes 35 minority (29 African Americans, 4 Asian Americans or Pacific Islanders, 2 Hispanic Americans), 7 international. Average age 28. *Faculty:* 137 full-time (54 women), 7 part-time/adjunct (4 women). Expenses: Contact institution. *Financial support:* In 2006–07, 40 research assistantships with full tuition reimbursements (averaging $6,000 per year) were awarded; career-related internships or fieldwork and unspecified assistantships also available. Support available to part-time students. Financial award applicants required to submit FAFSA. In 2006, 76 degrees awarded. *Degree program information:* Part-time programs available. Offers applied computer science (MS); arts and sciences (M Mus, MA, MPA, MS, MSN, Psy D); biology (MS); consciousness and society (Psy D); English (MA); gerontology (MA); history (MA); music education (M Mus); nursing (MSN); performance (M Mus); psychology (MA); public administration (MPA); rural and small town planning (MS); sociology (MA). *Application deadline:* For fall admission, 8/1 priority date for domestic students; for spring admission, 12/18 for domestic students. *Application fee:* $20. Electronic applications accepted. *Application Contact:* Dr. Charles W. Clark, Chair, 678-839-6508, E-mail: cclark@westga.edu. *Dean,* Dr. David White, 678-839-6405, Fax: 678-839-4898, E-mail: dwhite@westga.edu.

College of Education Students: 226 full-time (192 women), 1,166 part-time (948 women); includes 329 minority (309 African Americans, 1 American Indian/Alaska Native, 6 Asian Americans or Pacific Islanders, 13 Hispanic Americans), 1 international. Average age 29. *Faculty:* 74 full-time (46 women), 12 part-time/adjunct (7 women). Expenses: Contact institution. *Financial support:* In 2006–07, 46 research assistantships with partial tuition reimbursements (averaging $6,000 per year) were awarded; career-related internships or fieldwork and unspecified assistantships also available. Support available to part-time students. Financial award applicants required to submit FAFSA. In 2006, 372 master's, 2 doctorates, 123 other advanced degrees awarded. *Degree program information:* Part-time and evening/weekend programs available. Offers administration and supervision (M Ed, Ed S); art education (M Ed); business education (M Ed, Ed S); counseling and guidance (M Ed, Ed S); curriculum and instruction (Ed S); early childhood education (M Ed, Ed S); education (M Ed, Ed D, Ed S); education-French (M Ed); education-Spanish (M Ed); leadership (Ed S); learning disabled (Ed S); media (M Ed, Ed S); middle grades education (M Ed, Ed S); physical education (M Ed, Ed S); reading education (M Ed); school improvement (Ed D); secondary education—English (M Ed, Ed S); secondary education—mathematics (M Ed, Ed S); secondary education—science (M Ed, Ed S); secondary education—social studies (M Ed, Ed S); special education-behavior disorders (M Ed); special education-emotionally handicapped (M Ed); special education-general (Ed S); special education-interrelated (M Ed); speech-language pathology (M Ed). *Application deadline:* For fall admission, 8/1 for domestic students; for spring admission, 12/18 for domestic students. Applications are processed on a rolling basis. *Application fee:* $20. *Application Contact:* Dr. Charles W. Clark, Chair, 678-839-6508, E-mail: cclark@westga.edu. *Dean,* Dr. Kent Layton, 678-839-6570, Fax: 678-839-6098, E-mail: klayton@westga.edu.

Richards College of Business Students: 18 full-time (9 women), 31 part-time (12 women); includes 3 minority (2 African Americans, 1 Asian American or Pacific Islander), 11 international. Average age 21. *Faculty:* 19 full-time (4 women), 1 part-time/adjunct (0 women). Expenses: Contact institution. *Financial support:* In 2006–07, 10 students received support; research assistantships with full tuition reimbursements available, career-related internships or fieldwork, tuition waivers (partial), and unspecified assistantships available. Financial award application deadline: 7/1; financial award applicants required to submit FAFSA. In 2006, 33 degrees awarded. *Degree program information:* Part-time and evening/weekend programs available. Offers accounting and finance (MP Acc); business (MBA, MP Acc); business administration (MBA). *Application deadline:* For fall admission, 8/1 priority date for domestic students; for spring admission, 12/1 for domestic students. *Application fee:* $20. Electronic applications accepted. *Application Contact:* Dr. Charles W. Clark, Chair, 678-839-6508, E-mail: cclark@westga.edu. *Dean,* Dr. Faye S. McIntyre, 678-839-6467, E-mail: fmcintyr@westga.edu.

UNIVERSITY OF WINDSOR, Windsor, ON N9B 3P4, Canada

General Information Province-supported, coed, university. *Graduate housing:* Rooms and/or apartments available on a first-come, first-served basis to single and married students. Housing application deadline: 6/7. *Research affiliation:* DaimlerChrysler Automotive Research and Development Centre.

GRADUATE UNITS

Faculty of Graduate Studies and Research *Degree program information:* Part-time and evening/weekend programs available. Electronic applications accepted.

Faculty of Arts and Social Sciences *Degree program information:* Part-time programs available. Offers adult clinical (MA, PhD); applied social psychology (MA, PhD); arts and social sciences (MA, MFA, MSW, PhD); child clinical (MA, PhD); clinical neuropsychology (MA, PhD); communication and social justice (MA); English: creative writing and language and literature (MA); English: language and literature (MA); history (MA); philosophy (MA); political science (MA); social work (MSW); sociology (MA); sociology-social justice (PhD); visual arts (MFA). Electronic applications accepted.

Faculty of Education *Degree program information:* Part-time and evening/weekend programs available. Offers education (M Ed); educational studies (PhD). Electronic applications accepted.

Faculty of Engineering *Degree program information:* Part-time programs available. Offers civil engineering (M Eng, MA Sc, PhD); electrical engineering (M Eng, MA Sc, PhD); engineering (M Eng, MA Sc, PhD); engineering materials (M Eng, MA Sc, PhD); environmental engineering (M Eng, MA Sc, PhD); industrial engineering (M Eng, MA Sc); manufacturing systems engineering (PhD); mechanical engineering (M Eng, MA Sc, PhD). Electronic applications accepted.

Faculty of Human Kinetics *Degree program information:* Part-time programs available. Offers human kinetics (MHK). Electronic applications accepted.

Faculty of Nursing Offers nursing (M Sc, MN). Electronic applications accepted.

Faculty of Science *Degree program information:* Part-time programs available. Offers biological sciences (M Sc, PhD); chemistry and biochemistry (M Sc, PhD); computer science (M Sc, PhD); earth sciences (M Sc, PhD); economics (MA); mathematics (M Sc); physics (M Sc, PhD); science (M Sc, MA, PhD); statistics (M Sc, PhD). Electronic applications accepted.

GLIER-Great Lakes Institute for Environmental Research Offers environmental science (M Sc, PhD). Electronic applications accepted.

Odette School of Business *Degree program information:* Evening/weekend programs available. Offers business (MBA, MM). Electronic applications accepted.

THE UNIVERSITY OF WINNIPEG, Winnipeg, MB R3B 2E9, Canada

General Information Province-supported, coed, comprehensive institution. *Graduate housing:* On-campus housing not available.

GRADUATE UNITS

Faculty of Theology *Degree program information:* Part-time programs available. Offers marriage and family therapy (MMFT, Certificate); sacred theology (STM); theology (M Div).

Graduate Studies *Degree program information:* Part-time and evening/weekend programs available. Offers history (MA); public administration (MPA); religious studies (MA).

UNIVERSITY OF WISCONSIN–EAU CLAIRE, Eau Claire, WI 54702-4004

General Information State-supported, coed, comprehensive institution. CGS member. *Enrollment:* 10,505 graduate, professional, and undergraduate students; 111 full-time matriculated graduate/professional students (88 women), 312 part-time matriculated graduate/professional students (192 women). *Enrollment by degree level:* 423 master's. *Graduate faculty:* 345 full-time (128 women), 11 part-time/adjunct (6 women). Tuition, state resident: full-time $6,533; part-time $363 per credit. Tuition, nonresident: full-time $17,143; part-time $952 per credit. Tuition and fees vary according to program and reciprocity agreements. *Graduate housing:* Room and/or apartments available to single students; on-campus housing not available to married students. Typical cost: $2,640 per year ($4,936 including board). Housing application deadline: 4/1. *Student services:* Campus employment opportunities, campus safety program, career counseling, child daycare facilities, disabled student services, exercise/wellness program, free psychological counseling, grant writing training, international student services, low-cost health insurance, multicultural affairs office, teacher training, writing training. *Library facilities:* William D. McIntyre Library plus 1 other. *Online resources:* library catalog, web page, access to other libraries' catalogs. *Collection:* 764,275 titles, 2,448 serial subscriptions. *Research affiliation:* Beckman Coulter, Inc. (biology), American Chemical Society Petroleum Research Fund (chemistry, geology), Ayers and Associates (anthropology/archaeology), Chevron Phillips Chemical Company (chemistry), Camille and Henry Dreyfus Foundation, Inc. (chemistry), Research Corporation (chemistry, geology).

Computer facilities: 1,150 computers available on campus for general student use. A campuswide network can be accessed from student residence rooms and from off campus. Internet access and online class registration are available. *Web address:* http://www.uwec.edu/.

General Application Contact: Kristina Anderson, Director of Admissions, 715-836-5415, Fax: 715-836-2409, E-mail: admissions@uwec.edu.

GRADUATE UNITS

College of Arts and Sciences Students: 33 full-time (22 women), 38 part-time (23 women); includes 6 minority (5 American Indian/Alaska Native, 1 Hispanic American). Average age 28. 82 applicants, 51% accepted, 34 enrolled. *Faculty:* 245 full-time (80 women), 5 part-time/adjunct (2 women). Expenses: Contact institution. *Financial support:* In 2006–07, 49 students received support, including teaching assistantships (averaging $5,500 per year); fellowships, career-related internships or fieldwork and Federal Work-Study also available. Financial award application deadline: 4/15; financial award applicants required to submit FAFSA. In 2006, 33 degrees awarded. Offers arts and sciences (MA, MS, MSE, Ed S); biology (MS); English (MA); history (MA); school psychology (MSE, Ed S). *Application deadline:* Applications are processed on a rolling basis. *Application fee:* $45. *Dean,* Dr. Donald Christian, 715-836-2542, Fax: 715-836-3292, E-mail: christdp@uwec.edu.

College of Business Students: 7 full-time (2 women), 170 part-time (77 women); includes 18 minority (4 African Americans, 3 American Indian/Alaska Native, 7 Asian Americans or Pacific Islanders, 4 Hispanic Americans), 6 international. Average age 31. 108 applicants, 66% accepted, 71 enrolled. *Faculty:* 32 full-time (8 women), 2 part-time/adjunct (0 women). Expenses: Contact institution. *Financial support:* In 2006–07, 23 students received support, including 3 fellowships, 3 teaching assistantships (averaging $3,800 per year); Federal Work-Study also available. Support available to part-time students. Financial award applicants required to submit FAFSA. In 2006, 26 degrees awarded. *Degree program information:* Part-time programs available. Offers business (MBA); business administration (MBA). *Application deadline:* For fall admission, 7/1 for domestic students; for spring admission, 12/1 for domestic students. Applications are processed on a rolling basis. *Application fee:* $45. *Dean,* Dr. V. Thomas Dock, 715-836-5509, Fax: 715-836-4014, E-mail: dockv@uwec.edu.

College of Education and Human Sciences Students: 46 full-time (41 women), 56 part-time (47 women); includes 3 minority (1 American Indian/Alaska Native, 1 Asian American or Pacific Islander, 1 Hispanic American), 3 international. Average age 30. 161 applicants, 38% accepted, 31 enrolled. *Faculty:* 38 full-time (20 women). Expenses: Contact institution. *Financial support:* In 2006–07, 54 students received support, including 6 teaching assistantships (averaging $5,800 per year); career-related internships or fieldwork and Federal Work-Study also available. Financial award application deadline: 3/1; financial award applicants required to submit FAFSA. In 2006, 48 degrees awarded. Offers biology (MAT, MST); communication sciences and disorders (MS); education and human sciences (MAT, MEPD, MS, MSE, MST); education and professional development (MEPD); elementary education (MST); English (MAT, MST); history (MAT, MST); mathematics (MAT, MST); reading (MST); special education (MSE). *Application deadline:* For fall admission, 7/1 for domestic students; for spring admission, 12/1 for domestic students. Applications are processed on a rolling basis. *Application fee:* $45. *Dean,* Dr. Katherine Rhoades, 715-836-3671, Fax: 715-836-3245, E-mail: rhoadeka@uwec.edu.

College of Nursing and Health Sciences Students: 25 full-time (23 women), 48 part-time (45 women); includes 2 minority (both African Americans), 1 international. Average age 35. 41 applicants, 85% accepted, 10 enrolled. *Faculty:* 19 full-time (17 women), 3 part-time/adjunct (all women). Expenses: Contact institution. *Financial support:* In 2006–07, 35 students received support, including 3 teaching assistantships (averaging $3,400 per year); Federal Work-Study also available. Support available to part-time students. Financial award application deadline: 3/1; financial award applicants required to submit FAFSA. In 2006, 18 degrees awarded. *Degree program information:* Part-time programs available. Offers environmental and public health (MS); nursing (MSN); nursing and health sciences (MS, MSN). *Application deadline:* For fall admission, 2/1 priority date for domestic students. Applications are processed on a rolling basis. *Application fee:* $45. *Dean,* Dr. Elaine Wendt, 715-836-5287, Fax: 715-836-5925, E-mail: wendtle@uwec.edu.

Announcement: Programs are offered in the Colleges of Arts and Sciences, Business, Education, and Nursing. Master's programs include elementary education, English, history, business (MBA), nursing (MSN), communication disorders, special education, library science and media education, reading, and school psychology. School psychology is also offered at the educational specialist level.

UNIVERSITY OF WISCONSIN–GREEN BAY, Green Bay, WI 54311-7001

General Information State-supported, coed, comprehensive institution. *Enrollment:* 5,803 graduate, professional, and undergraduate students; 37 full-time matriculated graduate/professional students (22 women), 71 part-time matriculated graduate/professional students (51 women). *Enrollment by degree level:* 108 master's. *Graduate faculty:* 32 full-time (10 women), 14 part-time/adjunct (8 women). Tuition, state resident: full-time $5,910; part-time $246 per credit. Tuition, nonresident: full-time $16,520; part-time $688 per credit. *Required fees:* $1,148; $48 per credit. *Graduate housing:* Room and/or apartments available on a first-come, first-served basis to single students; on-campus housing not available to married students. Typical cost: $3,200 per year. Housing application deadline: 5/1. *Student services:* Campus employment opportunities, campus safety program, career counseling, disabled student services, free psychological counseling, international student services, low-cost health insurance, multicultural affairs office. *Library facilities:* Cofrin Library. *Online resources:* library catalog, web page, access to other libraries' catalogs. *Collection:* 333,482 titles, 5,512 serial subscriptions. *Research affiliation:* Abbott Laboratories (anaerobic digestion systems), Research Corporation (examination of the function structure, gene of Fetuin), Kimberly Clark (sludge recovery), Robert E. Lee & Associates (endangered species survey for Brown County landfill site selection), R. W. Beck (Brown County waste-to-energy study).

Computer facilities: 550 computers available on campus for general student use. A campuswide network can be accessed from student residence rooms and from off campus. Internet access and online class registration, student online degree progress are available. *Web address:* http://www.uwgb.edu/.

General Application Contact: Pam Harvey-Jacobs, Director of Admissions, 920-465-2111, Fax: 920-465-5754, E-mail: uwgb@uwgb.edu.

GRADUATE UNITS

Graduate Studies Students: 37 full-time (22 women), 71 part-time (51 women); includes 10 minority (1 African American, 6 American Indian/Alaska Native, 1 Asian American or Pacific Islander, 2 Hispanic Americans), 2 international. Average age 33. 87 applicants, 75% accepted, 35 enrolled. *Faculty:* 32 full-time (10 women), 14 part-time/adjunct (8 women). Expenses: Contact institution. *Financial support:* In 2006–07, 7 research assistantships, 11 teaching assistantships were awarded; career-related internships or fieldwork, Federal Work-Study, and institutionally sponsored loans also available. Financial award application deadline: 7/15; financial award applicants required to submit FAFSA. In 2006, 52 degrees awarded. *Degree program information:* Part-time and evening/weekend programs available. Offers applied leadership for teaching and learning (MS Ed); environmental science and policy (MS); management (MS); social work (MSW). *Application deadline:* For fall admission, 8/1 for domestic students; for spring admission, 11/1 for domestic students. Applications are processed on a rolling basis. *Application fee:* $45. Electronic applications accepted. *Application Contact:* Pam Harvey-Jacobs, Director of Admissions, 920-465-2111, Fax: 920-465-5754, E-mail: uwgb@uwgb.edu. *Dean of Professional Studies and Outreach,* Fritz Erickson, 920-465-2123, Fax: 920-465-2728, E-mail: ericksof@uwgb.edu.

UNIVERSITY OF WISCONSIN–LA CROSSE, La Crosse, WI 54601-3742

General Information State-supported, coed, comprehensive institution. CGS member. *Enrollment:* 9,818 graduate, professional, and undergraduate students; 411 full-time matriculated graduate/professional students (267 women), 1,164 part-time matriculated graduate/professional students (798 women). *Enrollment by degree level:* 1,164 master's, 45 doctoral. *Graduate faculty:* 121 full-time (44 women), 84 part-time/adjunct (55 women). *Graduate housing:* Room and/or apartments available on a first-come, first-served basis to single students; on-campus housing not available to married students. Housing application deadline: 5/1. *Student services:* Campus employment opportunities, campus safety program, career counseling, child daycare facilities, disabled student services, exercise/wellness program, free psychological counseling, grant writing training, international student services, low-cost health insurance, multicultural affairs office, teacher training, writing training. *Library facilities:* Murphy Library. *Online resources:* library catalog, web page, access to other libraries' catalogs. *Collection:* 687,207 titles, 1,181 serial subscriptions.

Computer facilities: 600 computers available on campus for general student use. A campuswide network can be accessed from student residence rooms and from off campus. Internet access and online class registration are available. *Web address:* http://www.uwlax.edu.

General Application Contact: Kathryn Kiefer, Associate Director of Admissions, 608-785-8939, E-mail: admissions@uwlax.edu.

GRADUATE UNITS

Office of University Graduate Studies Students: 411 full-time (267 women), 1,164 part-time (798 women); includes 54 minority (13 African Americans, 8 American Indian/Alaska Native, 25 Asian Americans or Pacific Islanders, 8 Hispanic Americans), 62 international. Average age 29. 1,191 applicants, 68% accepted, 401 enrolled. *Faculty:* 121 full-time (44 women), 84 part-time/adjunct (55 women). Expenses: Contact institution. *Financial support:* In 2006–07, 184 students received support, including 19 fellowships (averaging $6,000 per year), 26 research assistantships with partial tuition reimbursements available (averaging $6,000 per year); career-related internships or fieldwork, Federal Work-Study, institutionally sponsored loans, scholarships/grants, traineeships, health care benefits, tuition waivers (full and partial), unspecified assistantships, and grant-funded positions, external contracts, contract-funded assistantships also available. Support available to part-time students. Financial award application deadline: 3/15; financial award applicants required to submit FAFSA. In 2006, 498 degrees awarded. *Degree program information:* Part-time and evening/weekend programs available. Postbaccalaureate distance learning degree programs offered (minimal on-campus study). *Application deadline:* For fall admission, 6/15 for international students. *Application fee:* $45. Electronic applications accepted. *Application Contact:* Kathryn Kiefer, Associate Director of Admissions, 608-785-8939, E-mail: admissions@uwlax.edu. *Director,* Dr. Vijendra Agarwal, 608-785-8124, Fax: 608-785-8179, E-mail: agarwal.vije@uwlax.edu.

College of Business Administration Students: 12 full-time (3 women), 32 part-time (13 women); includes 2 minority (1 Asian American or Pacific Islander, 1 Hispanic American), 8 international. Average age 31. 30 applicants, 77% accepted, 14 enrolled. *Faculty:* 26 full-time (5 women), 2 part-time/adjunct (1 woman). Expenses: Contact institution. *Financial support:* In 2006–07, 6 research assistantships with partial tuition reimbursements (averaging $5,914 per year) were awarded; Federal Work-Study, health care benefits, tuition waivers (partial), and unspecified assistantships also available. Support available to part-time students. Financial award application deadline: 3/15; financial award applicants required to submit FAFSA. In 2006, 17 degrees awarded. *Degree program information:* Part-time and evening/weekend programs available. Offers business administration (MBA). *Application deadline:* For fall admission, 5/1 priority date for domestic students; for spring admission, 10/1 priority date for domestic students. Applications are processed on a rolling basis. *Application fee:* $45. *Application Contact:* Amelia Dittman, Assistant to the Dean, 608-785-8092, Fax: 608-785-6700, E-mail: dittman.amel@uwlax.edu. *Dean,* Dr. Bruce May, 608-785-8095, Fax: 608-785-6700, E-mail: may.bruce@uwlax.edu.

University of Wisconsin–La Crosse (continued)

College of Liberal Studies Students: 77 full-time (57 women), 749 part-time (547 women); includes 26 minority (6 African Americans, 1 American Indian/Alaska Native, 14 Asian Americans or Pacific Islanders, 5 Hispanic Americans), 1 international. Average age 30. 320 applicants, 86% accepted, 218 enrolled. *Faculty:* 27 full-time (12 women), 64 part-time/adjunct (44 women). Expenses: Contact institution. *Financial support:* Research assistantships with partial tuition reimbursements, career-related internships or fieldwork, Federal Work-Study, institutionally sponsored loans, scholarships/grants, health care benefits, and unspecified assistantships available. Support available to part-time students. In 2006, 275 degrees awarded. Offers college student development and administration (MS Ed); elementary education (MEPD); emotional disturbance (MS Ed); K–12 (MEPD); learning disabilities (MS Ed); liberal studies (MEPD, MS Ed, Ed S); professional development (MEPD); reading (MS Ed); school psychology (MS Ed, Ed S); secondary education (MEPD); special education (MS Ed). *Application deadline:* For fall admission, 2/15 for domestic students. *Application fee:* $45. Electronic applications accepted. *Application Contact:* Kathryn Kiefer, Associate Director of Admissions, 608-785-8939, E-mail: admissions@uwlax.edu. *Dean,* Dr. John Mason, 608-785-8113, Fax: 608-785-8119, E-mail: mason.john@uwlax.edu.

College of Science and Health Students: 303 full-time (198 women), 206 part-time (97 women); includes 23 minority (6 African Americans, 7 American Indian/Alaska Native, 8 Asian Americans or Pacific Islanders, 2 Hispanic Americans), 34 international. Average age 27. 593 applicants, 45% accepted, 169 enrolled. *Faculty:* 68 full-time (27 women), 18 part-time/adjunct (10 women). Expenses: Contact institution. *Financial support:* Research assistantships with partial tuition reimbursements, career-related internships or fieldwork, Federal Work-Study, scholarships/grants, traineeships, health care benefits, tuition waivers (partial), unspecified assistantships, and grant-funded positions, contract-funded assistantships available. Support available to part-time students. Financial award application deadline: 3/15; financial award applicants required to submit FAFSA. In 2006, 202 degrees awarded. *Degree program information:* Part-time programs available. Offers aquatic sciences (MS); athletic training (MS); biology (MS); cellular and molecular biology (MS); clinical exercise physiology (MS); clinical microbiology (MS); community health education (MPH, MS); human performance (MS); microbiology (MS); nurse anesthesia (MS); occupational therapy (MS); physical education teaching (MS); physical therapy (MSPT, DPT); physician assistant studies (MS); physiology (MS); recreation (MS); school health education (MS); science and health (MPH, MS, MSE, MSPT, DPT); software engineering (MSE); special/adapted physical education (MS); sport administration (MS). Electronic applications accepted. *Application Contact:* Kathryn Kiefer, Associate Director of Admissions, 608-785-8939, E-mail: admissions@uwlax.edu. *Dean,* Dr. Karen Palmer-McLean, 608-785-8218, Fax: 608-785-8221, E-mail: mclean.kare@uwlax.edu.

See Close-Up on page 1131.

UNIVERSITY OF WISCONSIN–MADISON, Madison, WI 53706-1380

General Information State-supported, coed, university. CGS member. *Graduate housing:* Rooms and/or apartments available on a first-come, first-served basis to single and married students. *Research affiliation:* U.S. Department of Agriculture–Dairy Forage Research Center, Institute on Tropical Studies, University Research Association, U.S. Department of Agriculture–Forest Products Laboratory.

GRADUATE UNITS

Development Studies Program Students: 15 full-time (7 women), 1 (woman) part-time. Average age 32. 16 applicants, 63% accepted, 0 enrolled. *Faculty:* 48 full-time (13 women), 2 part-time/adjunct (1 woman). Expenses: Contact institution. *Financial support:* In 2006–07, 5 fellowships with full tuition reimbursements (averaging $7,500 per year), 1 teaching assistantship with full tuition reimbursement (averaging $14,600 per year) were awarded; research assistantships. Financial award application deadline: 12/20. In 2006, 2 degrees awarded. Offers development studies (PhD). *Application deadline:* For fall admission, 3/31 priority date for domestic and international students; for spring admission, 9/30 priority date for domestic and international students. Applications are processed on a rolling basis. *Application fee:* $45. Electronic applications accepted. *Application Contact:* Christine Elholm, Student Services, 608-262-3412, Fax: 608-262-6022, E-mail: caelholm@wisc.edu. *Chairman,* Ian Coxhead, 608-262-3412, Fax: 608-262-6022, E-mail: coxhead@wisc.edu.

Graduate School *Degree program information:* Part-time and evening/weekend programs available. Postbaccalaureate distance learning degree programs offered (minimal on-campus study). Offers biophysics (PhD); cellular and molecular biology (PhD); engineering (PDD); neuroscience (MS, PhD); professional practice (ME); technical Japanese (ME). Electronic applications accepted.

College of Agricultural and Life Sciences *Degree program information:* Part-time programs available. Offers agricultural and applied economics (MA, MS, PhD); agricultural and life sciences (MA, MS, PhD); agricultural journalism (MS); agroecology (MS); agronomy (MS, PhD); animal sciences (MS, PhD); bacteriology (MS); biochemistry (MS, PhD); biological systems engineering (MS, PhD); biometry (MS); dairy science (MS, PhD); entomology (MS, PhD); family and consumer journalism (MS); food science (MS, PhD); forest science (MS, PhD); forestry (PhD); genetics (PhD); horticulture (MS, PhD); landscape architecture (MA, MS); mass communication (PhD); medical genetics (MS); molecular and environmental toxicology (MS, PhD); natural resources (MA, MS, PhD); nutritional sciences (MS, PhD); plant breeding and plant genetics (MS, PhD); plant pathology (MS, PhD); recreation resources management (MS); soil science (MS, PhD); wildlife ecology (MS, PhD). Electronic applications accepted.

College of Engineering Students: 977 full-time (187 women), 43 part-time (9 women); includes 73 minority (11 African Americans, 2 American Indian/Alaska Native, 33 Asian Americans or Pacific Islanders, 27 Hispanic Americans), 245 international. 2,365 applicants, 24% accepted, 218 enrolled. *Faculty:* 196 full-time (28 women), 17 part-time/adjunct (0 women). Expenses: Contact institution. *Financial support:* Fellowships with full and partial tuition reimbursements, research assistantships with full tuition reimbursements, teaching assistantships with full tuition reimbursements, career-related internships or fieldwork, Federal Work-Study, institutionally sponsored loans, scholarships/grants, and unspecified assistantships available. Support available to part-time students. In 2006, 315 master's, 92 doctorates awarded. *Degree program information:* Part-time programs available. Postbaccalaureate distance learning degree programs offered (minimal on-campus study). Offers biomedical engineering (MS, PhD); chemical engineering (MS, PhD); civil and environmental engineering (MS, PhD); electrical engineering (MS, PhD); energy systems (ME); engineering (ME, MS, PhD, PDD); engineering mechanics (MS, PhD); environmental chemistry and technology (MS, PhD); geological engineering (MS, PhD); industrial and systems engineering (MS, PhD); limnology and marine science (MS, PhD); manufacturing systems engineering (MS); materials engineering (MS, PhD); materials science (MS, PhD); mechanical engineering (MS, PhD); nuclear engineering and engineering physics (MS, PhD); polymers (ME). *Application deadline:* Applications are processed on a rolling basis. *Application fee:* $45. Electronic applications accepted. *Application Contact:* 608-262-2433, Fax: 608-262-5134, E-mail: gradadmiss@mail.bascom.wisc.edu. *Dean,* Paul S. Peercy, 608-262-3482, Fax: 608-262-6400, E-mail: peercy@engr.wisc.edu.

College of Letters and Science *Degree program information:* Part-time and evening/weekend programs available. Postbaccalaureate distance learning degree programs offered (minimal on-campus study). Offers African languages and literature (MA, PhD); Afro-American studies (MA); anthropology (MA, MS, PhD); applied English linguistics (MA); art history (MA, PhD); astronomy (PhD); atmospheric and oceanic sciences (MS, PhD); biology of brain and behavior (PhD); botany (MS, PhD); cartography and geographic information systems (MS); chemistry (MS, PhD); Chinese (MA, PhD); choral (MM, DMA); classics (MA, PhD); clinical psychology (PhD); cognitive neurosciences (PhD); communication arts (MA, PhD); communicative disorders (MS, PhD); comparative literature (MA, PhD); composition (MM, DMA); composition studies (PhD); computer sciences (MS, PhD); curriculum and instruction (PhD); developmental psychology (PhD); economics (PhD); English language and linguistics (PhD); ethnomusicology (MM, PhD); family and consumer journalism (PhD); French (MA, PhD); French studies (MFS, Certificate); geographic information systems (Certificate); geography (MS, PhD); geology (MS, PhD); geophysics (MS, PhD); German (MA, PhD); Greek (MA); Hebrew and Semitic studies (MA, PhD); history (MA, PhD); history of science (MA, PhD); industrial relations (MA, MS, PhD); instrumental (MM, DMA); international public affairs (MPIA); Italian (MA, PhD); Japanese (MA, PhD); journalism and mass communication (MA); languages and cultures of Asia (MA, PhD); Latin (MA); Latin American, Caribbean and Iberian studies (MA); letters and science (MA, MFA, MFS, MM, MPA, MPIA, MS, MSSW, DMA, PhD, Certificate); library and information studies (MA, PhD, Certificate); linguistics (MA, PhD); literature (MA, PhD); mass communication (PhD); mathematics (MA, PhD); music (MA, MM, DMA, PhD); music education (MM); musicology (MA, MM, PhD); perception (PhD); performance (MM, DMA); philosophy (MA, PhD); physics (MA, MS, PhD); political science (MA, PhD); Portuguese (MA, PhD); psychology (PhD); public affairs (MPA, MPIA); rural sociology (MS); Scandinavian studies (MA, PhD); Slavic languages and literature (MA, PhD); social and personality psychology (PhD); social welfare (PhD); social work (MSSW); sociology (MS, PhD); Southeast Asian studies (MA); Spanish (MA, PhD); statistics (MS, PhD); theatre and drama (MA, MFA, PhD); theory (MA, MM, PhD); urban and regional planning (MS, PhD); zoology (MA, MS, PhD). Electronic applications accepted.

Gaylord Nelson Institute for Environmental Studies Students: 109 full-time, 46 part-time; includes 12 minority (2 African Americans, 2 American Indian/Alaska Native, 5 Asian Americans or Pacific Islanders, 3 Hispanic Americans), 9 international. Average age 31. 199 applicants, 54% accepted, 40 enrolled. *Faculty:* 3 full-time (2 women), 149 part-time/adjunct (29 women). Expenses: Contact institution. *Financial support:* In 2006–07, 95 students received support, including 13 fellowships with full tuition reimbursements available (averaging $14,400 per year), 26 research assistantships with full tuition reimbursements available (averaging $14,250 per year), 29 teaching assistantships with full tuition reimbursements available (averaging $11,260 per year); career-related internships or fieldwork, Federal Work-Study, scholarships/grants, traineeships, health care benefits, unspecified assistantships, and project assistantships also available. Financial award application deadline: 1/2. In 2006, 44 master's, 5 doctorates awarded. *Degree program information:* Part-time programs available. Offers conservation biology and sustainable development (MS); environmental monitoring (MS, PhD); environmental studies (MS, PhD); land resources (MS, PhD); water resources management (MS). *Application deadline:* For fall admission, 2/1 for domestic and international students; for spring admission, 10/15 for domestic and international students. *Application fee:* $45. Electronic applications accepted. *Application Contact:* James E. Miller, Associate Student Services Coordinator, 608-263-4373, Fax: 608-262-2273, E-mail: jemiller@wisc.edu. *Chair,* Peter J. Nowak, 608-265-3581, Fax: 608-262-2273, E-mail: pnowak@wisc.edu.

School of Business Students: 317 full-time (116 women), 125 part-time (36 women); includes 36 minority (15 African Americans, 1 American Indian/Alaska Native, 11 Asian Americans or Pacific Islanders, 9 Hispanic Americans), 139 international. Average age 29. 1,009 applicants, 27% accepted, 191 enrolled. *Faculty:* 122. Expenses: Contact institution. *Financial support:* In 2006–07, 316 students received support, including 21 fellowships with partial tuition reimbursements available (averaging $16,544 per year), 110 research assistantships with full tuition reimbursements available (averaging $8,345 per year), 92 teaching assistantships with full tuition reimbursements available (averaging $11,898 per year); career-related internships or fieldwork, Federal Work-Study, institutionally sponsored loans, scholarships/grants, health care benefits, and unspecified assistantships also available. Support available to part-time students. In 2006, 164 master's, 15 doctorates awarded. *Degree program information:* Part-time and evening/weekend programs available. Offers accounting and information systems (PhD); actuarial science (MS); applied corporate finance (MBA); applied security analysis (MBA); arts administration (MBA); brand and product management (MBA); business (MBA, MS, PhD); business administration (MBA); business statistics (PhD); entrepreneurial management (MBA); finance, investment, and banking (PhD); information systems (MBA); international business (PhD); management and human resources (PhD); marketing (PhD); marketing research (MBA); operations and technology management (MBA); quantitative financial management (MS); real estate (MBA); real estate and urban land economics (PhD); risk management and insurance (MBA); strategic human resource management (MBA); strategic management in the life and engineering sciences (MBA); supply chain management (MBA). *Application deadline:* Applications are processed on a rolling basis. *Application fee:* $45. Electronic applications accepted. *Application Contact:* Betsy Kacizak, Director of Admissions and Financial Aid, 608-262-4000, Fax: 608-265-4192, E-mail: uwmadmba@bus.wisc.edu. *Dean,* Dr. Michael M. Knetter, 608-262-1758, E-mail: dean@bus.wisc.edu.

School of Education Students: 648 full-time (434 women), 375 part-time (246 women). *Faculty:* 156 full-time (71 women). Expenses: Contact institution. *Financial support:* In 2006–07, 54 fellowships with full tuition reimbursements, 19 research assistantships with full tuition reimbursements, 166 teaching assistantships with full tuition reimbursements were awarded; traineeships and project assistantships also available. In 2006, 203 master's, 86 doctorates awarded. Offers administration (Certificate); art (MA, MFA); art education (MA); counseling (MS); counseling psychology (PhD); curriculum and instruction (MS, PhD); education (MA, MFA, MS, PhD, Certificate); education and mathematics (MA); educational policy (MS, PhD); educational policy studies (MA, PhD); educational psychology (MS, PhD); French education (MA); German education (MA); kinesiology (MS, PhD); music education (MS); occupational therapy (MS, PhD); rehabilitation psychology (MA, MS, PhD); science education (MS); Spanish education (MA); special education (MA, MS, PhD); therapeutic science (MS). *Application fee:* $45. *Dean,* Dr. Julie K. Underwood, 608-262-1763.

School of Human Ecology Students: 62 full-time (52 women), 19 part-time (18 women). Average age 33. 84 applicants, 37% accepted, 22 enrolled. *Faculty:* 46 full-time (28 women), 5 part-time/adjunct (2 women). Expenses: Contact institution. *Financial support:* In 2006–07, 6 students received support; fellowships with full tuition reimbursements available, research assistantships with tuition reimbursements available, teaching assistantships with full tuition reimbursements available, institutionally sponsored loans, scholarships/grants, health care benefits, and unspecified assistantships available. In 2006, 8 master's, 5 doctorates awarded. Offers consumer behavior and family economics (MS, PhD); design studies (MFA, MS, PhD); human development and family studies (MS, PhD). *Application deadline:* For fall admission, 1/10 for domestic and international students. *Application fee:* $45. Electronic applications accepted. *Application Contact:* Colleen D. Foley, Student Academic Affairs, 608-262-1138, E-mail: cdfoley@wisc.edu. *Dean,* Robin A. Douthitt, 608-262-4847.

Law School Students: 802 full-time (368 women), 37 part-time (27 women); includes 205 minority (68 African Americans, 17 American Indian/Alaska Native, 55 Asian Americans or Pacific Islanders, 65 Hispanic Americans), 18 international. Average age 26. 3,037 applicants, 25% accepted, 283 enrolled. *Faculty:* 61 full-time (23 women), 52 part-time/adjunct (26 women). Expenses: Contact institution. *Financial support:* In 2006–07, 700 students received support, including 63 fellowships with partial tuition reimbursements available (averaging $13,214 per year), 8 research assistantships with full tuition reimbursements available (averaging $10,725 per year), 3 teaching assistantships with full tuition reimbursements available (averaging $10,725 per year); career-related internships or fieldwork, Federal Work-Study, institutionally sponsored loans, tuition waivers (partial), and unspecified assistantships also available. Support available to part-time students. Financial award application deadline: 3/1; financial award applicants required to submit FAFSA. In 2006, 272 JDs, 7 master's, 6 doctorates awarded. *Degree program information:* Part-time programs available. Offers law (JD, LL M, MLI, SJD); legal institutions (MLI). *Application deadline:* For fall admission, 2/1 for domestic and international students. Applications are processed on a rolling basis. *Application fee:* $45. Electronic applications accepted. *Application Contact:* Michael A. Hall, Department of Admissions, 608-262-5914, Fax: 608-263-3190, E-mail: admissions@law.wisc.edu. *Dean,* Kenneth B. Davis, 608-262-0618, Fax: 608-262-5485.

School of Medicine and Public Health Expenses: Contact institution. *Financial support:* Fellowships with full tuition reimbursements, research assistantships with full tuition reimbursements, teaching assistantships with full tuition reimbursements, scholarships/grants, traineeships, and tuition waivers (full) available. *Degree program information:* Part-time programs available. Postbaccalaureate distance learning degree programs offered (minimal on-campus study).

Offers biomolecular chemistry (MS, PhD); cancer biology (PhD); endocrinology-reproductive physiology (MS, PhD); genetics and medical genetics (MS, PhD); health physics (MS); medical physics (MS, PhD); medicine (MD, MPH, MS, PhD); medicine and public health (MD, MPH, MS, PhD); microbiology (PhD); molecular and cellular pharmacology (PhD); pathology and laboratory medicine (PhD); physiology (PhD); population health (MPH, MS, PhD). Electronic applications accepted. *Dean,* Dr. Robert N. Golden, 608-263-4910, Fax: 608-265-3286, E-mail: rngolden@wisc.edu.

School of Nursing Students: 58 full-time (all women), 145 part-time (136 women); includes 8 minority (1 African American, 1 American Indian/Alaska Native, 3 Asian Americans or Pacific Islanders, 3 Hispanic Americans). Average age 37. 79 applicants, 73% accepted, 43 enrolled. *Faculty:* 23 full-time (all women). Expenses: Contact institution. *Financial support:* In 2006–07, 88 students received support, including 10 fellowships with tuition reimbursements available (averaging $20,000 per year), 10 research assistantships with tuition reimbursements available (averaging $19,000 per year), 7 teaching assistantships with tuition reimbursements available (averaging $13,000 per year); career-related internships or fieldwork, Federal Work-Study, institutionally sponsored loans, scholarships/grants, traineeships, health care benefits, and unspecified assistantships also available. Support available to part-time students. Financial award application deadline: 6/1. In 2006, 44 master's, 3 doctorates awarded. *Degree program information:* Part-time programs available. Postbaccalaureate distance learning degree programs offered (no on-campus study). Offers nursing (MS, PhD). *Application deadline:* For fall admission, 3/1 priority date for domestic students; for spring admission, 10/1 priority date for domestic students. *Application fee:* $45. Electronic applications accepted. *Application Contact:* Marcia L. Voss, Master's Program Coordinator, 608-263-5258, Fax: 608-263-5332, E-mail: mlvoss@wisc.edu. *Dean,* Dr. Katharyn A. May, 608-263-5155, Fax: 608-263-5323, E-mail: kamay@wisc.edu.

School of Pharmacy Offers pharmaceutical sciences (MS, PhD); pharmacy (Pharm D, MS, PhD); social and administrative sciences in pharmacy (MS, PhD). Electronic applications accepted.

School of Veterinary Medicine Offers anatomy (MS, PhD); biochemistry (MS, PhD); cellular and molecular biology (MS, PhD); comparative biosciences (MS, PhD); environmental toxicology (MS, PhD); neurosciences (MS, PhD); pharmacology (MS, PhD); physiology (MS, PhD); veterinary medicine (DVM, MS, PhD).

UNIVERSITY OF WISCONSIN–MILWAUKEE, Milwaukee, WI 53201-0413

General Information State-supported, coed, university. CGS member. *Enrollment:* 28,309 graduate, professional, and undergraduate students; 2,102 full-time matriculated graduate/professional students (1,250 women), 2,137 part-time matriculated graduate/professional students (1,330 women). *Enrollment by degree level:* 3,235 master's, 1,004 doctoral. *Graduate faculty:* 787 full-time (285 women). Tuition, state resident: part-time $510 per credit. Tuition, nonresident: part-time $1,408 per credit. Tuition and fees vary according to program. *Graduate housing:* Room and/or apartments available on a first-come, first-served basis to single students; on-campus housing not available to married students. Housing application deadline: 4/7. *Student services:* Campus employment opportunities, campus safety program, career counseling, child daycare facilities, disabled student services, free psychological counseling, international student services, low-cost health insurance, multicultural affairs office. *Library facilities:* Golda Meir Library. *Online resources:* library catalog, web page, access to other libraries' catalogs. *Collection:* 1.4 million titles, 8,240 serial subscriptions. *Research affiliation:* Johnson Controls (environment), Wisconsin Electric Power Company (recycling), Electric Power Research Institute (composites), John Deere (surfaces), Astra Arcus USA (medicinal chemistry), Anteon Corporation (optics).

Computer facilities: 310 computers available on campus for general student use. A campuswide network can be accessed from off campus. *Web address:* http://www.uwm.edu/.

General Application Contact: General Information Contact, 414-229-4982, Fax: 414-229-6967, E-mail: gradschool@uwm.edu.

GRADUATE UNITS

Graduate School Students: 2,102 full-time (1,250 women), 2,139 part-time (1,332 women); includes 488 minority (214 African Americans, 36 American Indian/Alaska Native, 120 Asian Americans or Pacific Islanders, 118 Hispanic Americans), 544 international. Average age 32. 3,897 applicants, 52% accepted, 1149 enrolled. *Faculty:* 787 full-time (285 women). Expenses: Contact institution. *Financial support:* In 2006–07, 38 fellowships with partial tuition reimbursements (averaging $15,000 per year), 29 research assistantships with partial tuition reimbursements (averaging $17,200 per year), 714 teaching assistantships with full tuition reimbursements (averaging $18,100 per year) were awarded; career-related internships or fieldwork, Federal Work-Study, tuition waivers (partial), and unspecified assistantships also available. Support available to part-time students. Financial award application deadline: 4/15; financial award applicants required to submit FAFSA. In 2006, 1,173 master's, 97 doctorates awarded. *Degree program information:* Part-time and evening/weekend programs available. Offers multidisciplinary studies (PhD). *Application deadline:* For fall admission, 1/1 priority date for domestic students; for spring admission, 9/1 for domestic students. Applications are processed on a rolling basis. *Application fee:* $45 ($75 for international students). *Application Contact:* General Information Contact, 414-229-4982, Fax: 414-229-6967, E-mail: gradschool@uwm.edu. *Dean of Graduate School/Vice Chancellor for Research,* Dr. Abbas Ourmazd, 414-229-5483, Fax: 414-229-2348, E-mail: ourmazd@uwm.edu.

College of Engineering and Applied Science Students: 112 full-time (29 women), 157 part-time (34 women); includes 23 minority (3 African Americans, 1 American Indian/Alaska Native, 14 Asian Americans or Pacific Islanders, 5 Hispanic Americans), 133 international. 274 applicants, 50% accepted, 53 enrolled. *Faculty:* 60 full-time (5 women). Expenses: Contact institution. *Financial support:* In 2006–07, 4 fellowships, 12 research assistantships, 68 teaching assistantships were awarded; career-related internships or fieldwork, Federal Work-Study, and unspecified assistantships also available. Support available to part-time students. Financial award application deadline: 4/15. In 2006, 54 master's, 10 doctorates awarded. *Degree program information:* Part-time programs available. Offers computer science (MS, PhD); engineering (MS, PhD, Certificate); engineering and applied science (MS, PhD, Certificate); medical informatics (PhD). *Application deadline:* For fall admission, 1/1 priority date for domestic students; for spring admission, 9/1 for domestic students. Applications are processed on a rolling basis. *Application fee:* $45 ($75 for international students). *Interim Dean,* Dr. Al Ghorbanpoor, 414-229-4126.

College of Health Sciences Students: 83 full-time (68 women), 35 part-time (24 women); includes 9 minority (5 African Americans, 3 Asian Americans or Pacific Islanders, 1 Hispanic American), 9 international. Average age 27. 176 applicants, 44% accepted, 28 enrolled. *Faculty:* 42 full-time (24 women). Expenses: Contact institution. *Financial support:* In 2006–07, 6 fellowships, 1 research assistantship, 15 teaching assistantships were awarded; career-related internships or fieldwork, Federal Work-Study, and unspecified assistantships also available. Support available to part-time students. Financial award application deadline: 4/15. In 2006, 59 degrees awarded. *Degree program information:* Part-time programs available. Offers clinical laboratory science (MS); communication sciences and disorders (MS); health sciences (MS, PhD); healthcare informatics (MS); kinesiology (MS); occupational therapy (MS). *Application deadline:* For fall admission, 1/1 priority date for domestic students; for spring admission, 9/1 for domestic students. Applications are processed on a rolling basis. *Application fee:* $45 ($75 for international students). *Dean,* Randall Lambrecht, 414-229-4712, E-mail: rsl@uwm.edu.

College of Letters and Sciences Students: 720 full-time (360 women), 541 part-time (311 women); includes 114 minority (43 African Americans, 13 American Indian/Alaska Native, 18 Asian Americans or Pacific Islanders, 40 Hispanic Americans), 250 international. Average age 32. 1,499 applicants, 44% accepted, 394 enrolled. *Faculty:* 378 full-time (108 women). Expenses: Contact institution. *Financial support:* In 2006–07, 10 fellowships, 16 research assistantships, 539 teaching assistantships were awarded; career-related internships or fieldwork, Federal Work-Study, and unspecified assistantships also available. Support available to part-time students. Financial award application deadline: 4/15. In 2006, 243 master's, 43 doctorates awarded. *Degree program information:* Part-time programs available. Offers anthropology (MS, PhD, Certificate); art history (MA); art museum studies (Certificate); biological sciences (MS, PhD); chemistry (MS, PhD); classics and Hebrew studies (MAFLL); clinical psychology (MS, PhD); communication (MA, Certificate); comparative literature (MAFLL); economics (MA, PhD); English (MA, PhD, Certificate); French and Italian (MAFLL); geography (MA, MS, PhD); geological sciences (MS, PhD); German (MAFLL); history (MA, PhD); human resources and labor relations (MHRLR, Certificate); journalism and mass communication (MA); letters and sciences (MA, MAFLL, MHRLR, MLS, MPA, MS, PhD, Certificate); liberal studies (MLS); mathematics (MS, PhD); philosophy (MA); physics (MS, PhD); political science (MA, PhD); psychology (MS, PhD); public administration (MPA); Slavic studies (MAFLL); sociology (MA); Spanish (MAFLL); urban studies (MS, PhD). *Application deadline:* For fall admission, 1/1 priority date for domestic students; for spring admission, 9/1 for domestic students. Applications are processed on a rolling basis. *Application fee:* $45 ($75 for international students). *Dean,* G. Richard Meadows, 414-229-5895, E-mail: meadows@uwm.edu.

College of Nursing Students: 121 full-time (109 women), 122 part-time (117 women); includes 29 minority (16 African Americans, 1 American Indian/Alaska Native, 6 Asian Americans or Pacific Islanders, 6 Hispanic Americans), 6 international. Average age 39. 110 applicants, 45% accepted, 39 enrolled. *Faculty:* 36 full-time (35 women). Expenses: Contact institution. *Financial support:* In 2006–07, 11 teaching assistantships were awarded; fellowships, research assistantships, career-related internships or fieldwork, Federal Work-Study, and unspecified assistantships also available. Support available to part-time students. Financial award application deadline: 4/15. In 2006, 37 master's, 7 doctorates awarded. *Degree program information:* Part-time programs available. Offers nursing (MS, PhD, Certificate). *Application deadline:* For fall admission, 1/1 priority date for domestic students; for spring admission, 9/1 for domestic students. Applications are processed on a rolling basis. *Application fee:* $45 ($75 for international students). *Application Contact:* Ellen K. Murphy, Representative, 414-229-5468. *Representative,* Karen Morin, 414-229-5474, Fax: 414-229-6474.

Peck School of the Arts Students: 78 full-time (38 women), 33 part-time (17 women); includes 14 minority (2 African Americans, 3 American Indian/Alaska Native, 4 Asian Americans or Pacific Islanders, 5 Hispanic Americans), 8 international. Average age 32. 149 applicants, 35% accepted, 40 enrolled. *Faculty:* 73 full-time (34 women). Expenses: Contact institution. *Financial support:* In 2006–07, 10 fellowships, 19 teaching assistantships were awarded; research assistantships, career-related internships or fieldwork, Federal Work-Study, and unspecified assistantships also available. Support available to part-time students. Financial award application deadline: 4/15. In 2006, 46 degrees awarded. *Degree program information:* Part-time programs available. Offers art (MA, MFA); art education (MA, MFA, MS); arts (MA, MFA, MM, MS, Certificate); dance (MFA); film (MFA); music (MM, Certificate); theatre (MFA). *Application deadline:* For fall admission, 1/1 priority date for domestic students; for spring admission, 9/1 for domestic students. Applications are processed on a rolling basis. *Application fee:* $45 ($75 for international students). *Dean,* William Robert Bucker, 414-229-4762, E-mail: rbucker@uwm.edu.

School of Architecture and Urban Planning Students: 133 full-time (53 women), 21 part-time (6 women); includes 21 minority (4 African Americans, 2 American Indian/Alaska Native, 8 Asian Americans or Pacific Islanders, 7 Hispanic Americans), 15 international. Average age 28. 141 applicants, 69% accepted, 37 enrolled. *Faculty:* 31 full-time (7 women). Expenses: Contact institution. *Financial support:* In 2006–07, 19 teaching assistantships were awarded; fellowships, research assistantships, career-related internships or fieldwork, Federal Work-Study, and unspecified assistantships also available. Support available to part-time students. Financial award application deadline: 4/15. In 2006, 50 master's, 2 doctorates awarded. *Degree program information:* Part-time programs available. Offers architecture (M Arch, PhD, Certificate); architecture and urban planning (M Arch, MUP, PhD, Certificate); urban planning (MUP, Certificate). *Application deadline:* For fall admission, 1/1 priority date for domestic students; for spring admission, 9/1 for domestic students. Applications are processed on a rolling basis. *Application fee:* $45 ($75 for international students). *Dean,* Robert Greenstreet, 414-229-4016, E-mail: bobg@uwm.edu.

School of Education Students: 303 full-time (237 women), 366 part-time (270 women); includes 145 minority (90 African Americans, 10 American Indian/Alaska Native, 19 Asian Americans or Pacific Islanders, 26 Hispanic Americans), 14 international. Average age 35. 467 applicants, 44% accepted, 102 enrolled. *Faculty:* 80 full-time (48 women). Expenses: Contact institution. *Financial support:* In 2006–07, 6 teaching assistantships were awarded; fellowships, research assistantships, career-related internships or fieldwork, Federal Work-Study, and unspecified assistantships also available. Support available to part-time students. Financial award application deadline: 4/15. In 2006, 154 master's, 24 doctorates awarded. *Degree program information:* Part-time programs available. Offers administrative leadership (Certificate); administrative leadership and supervision in education (MS); cultural foundations of education (MS); curriculum planning and instruction improvement (MS); early childhood education (MS); education (MS, PhD, Certificate, Ed S); educational psychology (MS, Ed S); elementary education (MS); exceptional education (MS); junior high/middle school education (MS); reading education (MS); school psychology (Ed S); secondary education (MS); teaching in an urban setting (MS); urban education (PhD). *Application deadline:* For fall admission, 1/1 priority date for domestic students; for spring admission, 9/1 for domestic students. Applications are processed on a rolling basis. *Application fee:* $45 ($75 for international students). *Dean,* Alfonzo Thurman, 414-229-4181, E-mail: athurman@uwm.edu.

School of Information Studies Students: 99 full-time (75 women), 391 part-time (312 women); includes 32 minority (11 African Americans, 12 Asian Americans or Pacific Islanders, 9 Hispanic Americans), 20 international. Average age 36. 239 applicants, 82% accepted, 121 enrolled. *Faculty:* 14 full-time (5 women). Expenses: Contact institution. *Financial support:* In 2006–07, 3 fellowships were awarded; research assistantships, teaching assistantships, career-related internships or fieldwork, Federal Work-Study, and unspecified assistantships also available. Support available to part-time students. Financial award application deadline: 4/15. In 2006, 120 degrees awarded. *Degree program information:* Part-time programs available. Offers information studies (MLIS, CAS). *Application deadline:* For fall admission, 1/1 priority date for domestic students; for spring admission, 9/1 for domestic students. Applications are processed on a rolling basis. *Application fee:* $45 ($75 for international students). *Dean,* Johannes Britz, 414-229-4709, Fax: 414-229-4848.

School of Social Welfare Students: 199 full-time (182 women), 106 part-time (93 women); includes 44 minority (24 African Americans, 2 American Indian/Alaska Native, 7 Asian Americans or Pacific Islanders, 11 Hispanic Americans), 3 international. Average age 31. 334 applicants, 59% accepted, 120 enrolled. *Faculty:* 22 full-time (9 women). Expenses: Contact institution. *Financial support:* In 2006–07, 2 teaching assistantships were awarded; fellowships, research assistantships, career-related internships or fieldwork, Federal Work-Study, and unspecified assistantships also available. Support available to part-time students. Financial award application deadline: 4/15. In 2006, 119 degrees awarded. *Degree program information:* Part-time programs available. Offers criminal justice (MS); social welfare (MS, MSW, Certificate); social work (MSW, Certificate). *Application deadline:* For fall admission, 1/1 priority date for domestic students; for spring admission, 9/1 for domestic students. Applications are processed on a rolling basis. *Application fee:* $45 ($75 for international students). *Dean,* Stan Stojkovic, 414-229-4400.

Sheldon B. Lubar School of Business Students: 247 full-time (96 women), 366 part-time (147 women); includes 57 minority (16 African Americans, 4 American Indian/Alaska Native, 29 Asian Americans or Pacific Islanders, 8 Hispanic Americans), 86 international. Average age 32. 457 applicants, 46% accepted, 172 enrolled. *Faculty:* 64 full-time (17 women). Expenses: Contact institution. *Financial support:* In 2006–07, 5 fellowships, 35 teaching assistantships were awarded; research assistantships, career-related internships or fieldwork, Federal Work-Study, and unspecified assistantships also available. Support available to part-time students. Financial award application deadline: 4/15. In 2006, 291 master's, 11 doctorates awarded. *Degree program information:* Part-time and evening/weekend programs available. Offers business (MBA, MS, PhD, Certificate). *Application deadline:* For fall admission, 1/1 priority date for domestic students; for spring admission, 9/1 for domestic students. Applications are processed on a rolling basis. *Application fee:* $45 ($75 for international students). *Application Contact:* Velagapudi K. Prasad, Associate Dean, 414-229-4235. *Representative,* Sarah Sandin, 414-229-5403, Fax: 414-229-2372, E-mail: ssandin@uwm.edu.

UNIVERSITY OF WISCONSIN–OSHKOSH, Oshkosh, WI 54901

General Information State-supported, coed, comprehensive institution. *Graduate housing:* Room and/or apartments available on a first-come, first-served basis to single students; on-campus housing not available to married students.

GRADUATE UNITS

The School of Graduate Studies *Degree program information:* Part-time and evening/weekend programs available. Offers social work (MSW). Electronic applications accepted.

College of Business Administration *Degree program information:* Part-time programs available. Offers business administration (MBA, MS); information systems (MS). Electronic applications accepted.

College of Education and Human Services *Degree program information:* Part-time and evening/weekend programs available. Offers counseling (MSE); cross-categorical (MSE); curriculum and instruction (MSE); early childhood: exceptional education needs (MSE); education and human services (MS, MSE); educational leadership (MS); non-licensure (MSE); reading education (MSE). Electronic applications accepted.

College of Letters and Science *Degree program information:* Part-time and evening/weekend programs available. Offers biology (MS); English (MA); experimental psychology (MS); general agency (MPA); health care (MPA); industrial/organizational psychology (MS); letters and science (MA, MPA, MS, MSW); mathematics education (MS). Electronic applications accepted.

College of Nursing *Degree program information:* Part-time programs available. Offers adult health and illness (MSN); family nurse practitioner (MSN). Electronic applications accepted.

UNIVERSITY OF WISCONSIN–PARKSIDE, Kenosha, WI 53141-2000

General Information State-supported, coed, comprehensive institution. *Graduate housing:* Room and/or apartments available on a first-come, first-served basis to single students; on-campus housing not available to married students.

GRADUATE UNITS

College of Arts and Sciences Students: 9 full-time (2 women), 4 part-time (1 woman); includes 3 minority (1 Asian American or Pacific Islander, 2 Hispanic Americans). Average age 32. 7 applicants, 71% accepted, 5 enrolled. *Faculty:* 9 full-time (2 women). Expenses: Contact institution. *Financial support:* Research assistantships, career-related internships or fieldwork, Federal Work-Study, and unspecified assistantships available. In 2006, 3 degrees awarded. *Degree program information:* Part-time programs available. Offers applied molecular biology (MAMB); arts and sciences (MAMB). *Application deadline:* For fall admission, 7/1 priority date for domestic students. Applications are processed on a rolling basis. *Application fee:* $45. Electronic applications accepted. *Application Contact:* Dr. David Higgs, Chair of Molecular Biology Programs, 262-595-2786, Fax: 262-595-2056, E-mail: david.higgs@uwp.edu. *Dean,* Dr. Donald Cress, 262-595-2188, Fax: 262-595-2056, E-mail: donald.cress@uwp.edu.

School of Business and Technology Students: 15 full-time (5 women), 82 part-time (34 women); includes 23 minority (8 African Americans, 11 Asian Americans or Pacific Islanders, 4 Hispanic Americans). Average age 30. 28 applicants, 96% accepted, 24 enrolled. *Faculty:* 24 full-time (7 women). Expenses: Contact institution. *Financial support:* Available to part-time students. Application deadline: 7/1. In 2006, 23 degrees awarded. *Degree program information:* Part-time and evening/weekend programs available. Offers business administration (MBA); business and technology (MBA, MSCIS); computer and information systems (MSCIS). *Application deadline:* For fall admission, 8/1 for domestic students, 6/1 for international students; for spring admission, 12/15 for domestic students, 10/1 for international students. Applications are processed on a rolling basis. *Application fee:* $45. Electronic applications accepted. *Application Contact:* Bradley Piazza, Assistant Dean, 262-595-2046, Fax: 262-595-2680, E-mail: piazza@uwp.edu. *Dean,* Dr. Fred Ebeid, 262-595-2243, Fax: 262-595-2680, E-mail: ebeid@uwp.edu.

UNIVERSITY OF WISCONSIN–PLATTEVILLE, Platteville, WI 53818-3099

General Information State-supported, coed, comprehensive institution. *Enrollment:* 6,732 graduate, professional, and undergraduate students; 110 full-time matriculated graduate/professional students (85 women), 401 part-time matriculated graduate/professional students (194 women). *Enrollment by degree level:* 511 master's. *Graduate faculty:* 5 full-time (2 women), 90 part-time/adjunct (16 women). Tuition, state resident: part-time $365 per credit. Tuition, nonresident: part-time $955 per credit. *Graduate housing:* On-campus housing not available. *Student services:* Campus employment opportunities, campus safety program, career counseling, child daycare facilities, disabled student services, exercise/wellness program, free psychological counseling, grant writing training, international student services, low-cost health insurance, multicultural affairs office, teacher training, writing training. *Library facilities:* Karrmann Library. *Online resources:* library catalog, web page, access to other libraries' catalogs. *Collection:* 362,247 titles, 2,116 serial subscriptions.

Computer facilities: 1,000 computers available on campus for general student use. A campuswide network can be accessed from student residence rooms and from off campus. Internet access and online class registration are available. *Web address:* http://www.uwplatt.edu/.

General Application Contact: Kristal Prohaska, Admissions and Enrollment Management, 608-342-1125, Fax: 608-342-1122, E-mail: admit@uwplatt.edu.

GRADUATE UNITS

School of Graduate Studies Students: 110 full-time (85 women), 401 part-time (194 women); includes 52 minority (38 African Americans, 6 Asian Americans or Pacific Islanders, 8 Hispanic Americans), 44 international. 190 applicants, 59% accepted. *Faculty:* 5 full-time (2 women), 90 part-time/adjunct (16 women). Expenses: Contact institution. *Financial support:* Research assistantships with partial tuition reimbursements, career-related internships or fieldwork, Federal Work-Study, institutionally sponsored loans, scholarships/grants, and unspecified assistantships available. Support available to part-time students. In 2006, 160 degrees awarded. *Degree program information:* Part-time and evening/weekend programs available. Postbaccalaureate distance learning degree programs offered (no on-campus study). *Application deadline:* For fall admission, 7/1 priority date for domestic students; for spring admission, 11/1 for domestic students. Applications are processed on a rolling basis. *Application fee:* $45. Electronic applications accepted. *Application Contact:* Kristal Prohaska, Admissions and Enrollment Management, 608-342-1125, Fax: 608-342-1122, E-mail: admit@uwplatt.edu. *Dean,* Dr. David P. Van Buren, 608-342-1262, Fax: 608-342-1270, E-mail: vanburen@uwplatt.edu.

College of Engineering, Mathematics and Science Students: 3 full-time (0 women), 1 international. 2 applicants, 50% accepted. Expenses: Contact institution. *Financial support:* Research assistantships with partial tuition reimbursements available. *Degree program information:* Part-time programs available. Offers computer science (MS); engineering, mathematics and science (MS). *Application deadline:* For fall admission, 7/1 priority date for domestic students; for spring admission, 11/1 for domestic students. *Application fee:* $45. *Application Contact:* Kristal Prohaska, Admissions and Enrollment Management, 608-342-1125, Fax: 608-342-1122, E-mail: admit@uwplatt.edu. *Dean,* Dr. Rich Shultz, 608-342-1561, Fax: 608-342-1566, E-mail: masoom@uwplatt.edu.

College of Liberal Arts and Education Students: 93 full-time (76 women), 126 part-time (90 women); includes 34 minority (28 African Americans, 1 Asian American or Pacific Islander, 5 Hispanic Americans), 39 international. 81 applicants, 56% accepted. *Faculty:* 4 full-time (1 woman), 54 part-time/adjunct (14 women). Expenses: Contact institution. *Financial support:* Research assistantships with partial tuition reimbursements, career-related internships or fieldwork, Federal Work-Study, institutionally sponsored loans, scholarships/grants, and unspecified assistantships available. Support available to part-time students. In 2006, 82 degrees awarded. *Degree program information:* Part-time programs available. Offers adult education (MSE); counselor education (MSE); elementary education (MSE); liberal arts and education (MSE); middle school education (MSE); secondary education (MSE); vocational and technical education (MSE). *Application deadline:* For fall admission, 7/1 priority date for domestic students; for spring admission, 11/1 for domestic students. Applications are processed on a rolling basis. *Application fee:* $45. Electronic applications accepted. *Application Contact:* Kristal Prohaska, Admissions and Enrollment Management, 608-342-1125, Fax: 608-342-1122, E-mail: admit@uwplatt.edu. *Dean,* Dr. Mittie Nimocks, 608-342-1151, Fax: 608-342-1409, E-mail: nimocksm@uwplatt.edu.

Distance Learning Center Students: 14 full-time (9 women), 275 part-time (104 women); includes 18 minority (10 African Americans, 5 Asian Americans or Pacific Islanders, 3 Hispanic Americans), 4 international. 107 applicants, 62% accepted. *Faculty:* 15 part-time/adjunct. Expenses: Contact institution. *Financial support:* Scholarships/grants available. Support available to part-time students. In 2006, 78 degrees awarded. *Degree program information:* Part-time and evening/weekend programs available. Postbaccalaureate distance learning degree programs offered (no on-campus study). Offers criminal justice (MS); engineering (MS); project management (MS). *Application deadline:* For fall admission, 7/1 priority date for domestic students; for spring admission, 11/1 priority date for domestic students. Applications are processed on a rolling basis. *Application fee:* $45. Electronic applications accepted. *Application Contact:* Chris Jentz, Information Contact, 800-362-5460, Fax: 608-342-1071, E-mail: disted@uwplatt.edu. *Executive Director,* Dawn Drake, 800-362-5460, Fax: 608-342-1071, E-mail: disted@uwplatt.edu.

UNIVERSITY OF WISCONSIN–RIVER FALLS, River Falls, WI 54022-5001

General Information State-supported, coed, comprehensive institution. CGS member. *Graduate housing:* Room and/or apartments available on a first-come, first-served basis to single students; on-campus housing not available to married students.

GRADUATE UNITS

Outreach and Graduate Studies *Degree program information:* Part-time programs available. Offers management (MM). Electronic applications accepted.

College of Agriculture, Food, and Environmental Sciences *Degree program information:* Part-time programs available. Offers agricultural education (MS); agriculture, food, and environmental sciences (MS). Electronic applications accepted.

College of Arts and Science *Degree program information:* Part-time programs available. Offers arts and science (MSE); mathematics education (MSE); science education (MSE); social science education (MSE). Electronic applications accepted.

College of Education and Professional Studies *Degree program information:* Part-time programs available. Offers communicative disorders (MS); counseling (MSE); education (MS, MSE, Ed S); elementary education (MSE); reading (MSE); school psychology (MSE, Ed S); secondary education-communicative disorders (MSE).

UNIVERSITY OF WISCONSIN–STEVENS POINT, Stevens Point, WI 54481-3897

General Information State-supported, coed, comprehensive institution. *Enrollment:* 8,842 graduate, professional, and undergraduate students; 115 full-time matriculated graduate/professional students (86 women), 148 part-time matriculated graduate/professional students (109 women). *Enrollment by degree level:* 256 master's, 7 doctoral. *Graduate faculty:* 262 full-time (84 women), 24 part-time/adjunct (10 women). Tuition, state resident: full-time $5,910; part-time $328 per credit. Tuition, nonresident: full-time $16,520; part-time $918 per credit. *Required fees:* $756; $73 per credit. *Graduate housing:* Room and/or apartments available on a first-come, first-served basis to single students; on-campus housing not available to married students. Typical cost: $2,726 per year ($4,542 including board). *Student services:* Campus employment opportunities, campus safety program, career counseling, child daycare facilities, disabled student services, exercise/wellness program, free psychological counseling, grant writing training, international student services, multicultural affairs office, teacher training, writing training. *Library facilities:* Learning Resources Center. *Online resources:* library catalog, web page, access to other libraries' catalogs. *Collection:* 1.1 million titles, 18,428 serial subscriptions, 8,850 audiovisual materials.

Computer facilities: 880 computers available on campus for general student use. A campuswide network can be accessed from student residence rooms and from off campus. Internet access and online class registration are available. *Web address:* http://www.uwsp.edu/.

General Application Contact: Catherine Glennon, Director of Admissions, 715-346-2441, E-mail: admiss@uwsp.edu.

GRADUATE UNITS

College of Fine Arts and Communication Students: 5 full-time (4 women), 19 part-time (14 women); includes 1 minority (African American) *Faculty:* 33 full-time (12 women), 3 part-time/adjunct (0 women). Expenses: Contact institution. *Financial support:* Teaching assistantships, career-related internships or fieldwork, Federal Work-Study, institutionally sponsored loans, and unspecified assistantships available. Support available to part-time students. Financial award application deadline: 5/1; financial award applicants required to submit FAFSA. In 2006, 9 degrees awarded. *Degree program information:* Part-time programs available. Offers fine arts and communication (MA, MM Ed); interpersonal communication (MA); mass communication (MA); music (MM Ed); organizational communication (MA); public relations (MA). *Application deadline:* For fall admission, 5/1 priority date for domestic students. Applications are processed on a rolling basis. *Application fee:* $45. *Dean,* Jeff Morin, 715-346-4920, Fax: 715-346-2718, E-mail: jmorin@uwse.edu.

College of Letters and Science Students: 3 full-time (1 woman), 14 part-time (8 women). *Faculty:* 58 full-time (19 women), 1 part-time/adjunct (0 women). Expenses: Contact institution. *Financial support:* Research assistantships, teaching assistantships, Federal Work-Study and unspecified assistantships available. Support available to part-time students. Financial award application deadline: 5/1; financial award applicants required to submit FAFSA. In 2006, 3 degrees awarded. Offers biology (MST); business and economics (MBA); English (MST); history (MST); letters and science (MBA, MST). *Application deadline:* For fall admission, 5/1 priority date for domestic students. Applications are processed on a rolling basis. *Application fee:* $45. *Dean,* Lance Grahn, 715-346-4224, E-mail: lgrahn@uwsp.edu.

College of Natural Resources Students: 44 full-time (24 women), 31 part-time (15 women); includes 3 minority (1 American Indian/Alaska Native, 1 Asian American or Pacific Islander, 1 Hispanic American), 5 international. *Faculty:* 25 full-time (4 women), 5 part-time/adjunct (2 women). Expenses: Contact institution. *Financial support:* Research assistantships, teaching assistantships, career-related internships or fieldwork, Federal Work-Study, and unspecified assistantships available. Support available to part-time students. Financial award application deadline: 5/1; financial award applicants required to submit FAFSA. In 2006, 19 degrees awarded. *Degree program information:* Part-time programs available. Offers natural resources (MS). *Application deadline:* For fall admission, 3/15 priority date for domestic students; for spring admission, 11/15 for domestic students. Applications are processed on a rolling basis. *Application fee:* $45. *Dean,* Dr. Christine Thomas, 715-346-4617, Fax: 715-346-3624.

College of Professional Studies Students: 62 full-time (56 women), 83 part-time (71 women); includes 7 minority (1 African American, 1 American Indian/Alaska Native, 4 Asian Americans or Pacific Islanders, 1 Hispanic American), 1 international. *Faculty:* 34 full-time (24 women), 1 (woman) part-time/adjunct. Expenses: Contact institution. *Financial support:* Research assistantships, teaching assistantships, career-related internships or fieldwork, Federal Work-Study, and unspecified assistantships available. Support available to part-time students. Financial award application deadline: 5/1; financial award applicants required to submit FAFSA. In 2006, 120 degrees awarded. *Degree program information:* Part-time programs available. *Application deadline:* For fall admission, 5/1 priority date for domestic students. Applications are processed on a rolling basis. *Application fee:* $45. *Dean,* Joan North, 715-346-3169.

School of Communicative Disorders Students: 50 full-time (all women), 4 part-time (all women); includes 3 minority (1 African American, 1 American Indian/Alaska Native, 1 Asian American or Pacific Islander), 1 international. *Faculty:* 11 full-time (8 women). Expenses: Contact institution. *Financial support:* Research assistantships, teaching assistantships,

Federal Work-Study and unspecified assistantships available. Financial award application deadline: 5/1; financial award applicants required to submit FAFSA. In 2006, 29 degrees awarded. Offers communicative disorders (MS, Au D). *Application deadline:* For fall admission, 1/10 for domestic students. *Application fee:* $45. *Application Contact:* Leslie Plonsker, Information Contact, 715-346-2328, Fax: 715-346-2157, E-mail: lplonske@uwsp.edu. *Head,* Dr. Gary Cumley, 715-346-4699, Fax: 715-346-2157, E-mail: gcumley@uwsp.edu.

School of Education Students: 6 full-time (2 women), 66 part-time (54 women); includes 3 minority (2 Asian Americans or Pacific Islanders, 1 Hispanic American). Average age 26. *Faculty:* 13 full-time (11 women). Expenses: Contact institution. *Financial support:* In 2006–07, 4 research assistantships with partial tuition reimbursements (averaging $9,807 per year) were awarded; teaching assistantships, Federal Work-Study, tuition waivers (partial), and unspecified assistantships also available. Support available to part-time students. Financial award application deadline: 5/1; financial award applicants required to submit FAFSA. In 2006, 76 degrees awarded. *Degree program information:* Part-time programs available. Offers education—general/reading (MSE); education—general/special (MSE); educational administration (MSE); elementary education (MSE); guidance and counseling (MSE). *Application deadline:* For fall admission, 5/1 priority date for domestic students. Applications are processed on a rolling basis. *Application fee:* $45. *Application Contact:* Dr. Patricia Caro, Director, 715-346-4403, Fax: 715-346-4846, E-mail: pcaro@uwsp.edu. *Associate Dean,* Dr. JoAnne Katzmarek, 715-346-4430, Fax: 715-346-4846, E-mail: jkatzmar@uwsp.edu.

School of Health Promotion and Human Development Students: 6 full-time (4 women), 13 part-time (all women); includes 1 minority (Asian American or Pacific Islander) *Faculty:* 10 full-time (5 women), 1 (woman) part-time/adjunct. Expenses: Contact institution. *Financial support:* Research assistantships, teaching assistantships, career-related internships or fieldwork, Federal Work-Study, and unspecified assistantships available. Support available to part-time students. Financial award application deadline: 5/1; financial award applicants required to submit FAFSA. In 2006, 15 degrees awarded. *Degree program information:* Part-time programs available. Offers human and community resources (MS); nutritional sciences (MS). *Application deadline:* For fall admission, 5/1 priority date for domestic students. Applications are processed on a rolling basis. *Application fee:* $45. *Application Contact:* Jasia Steinmetz, Information Contact, 715-346-2830, Fax: 715-346-2720, E-mail: jsteinme@uwsp.edu. *Head,* Marty Loy, 715-346-2830, Fax: 715-346-2720.

UNIVERSITY OF WISCONSIN–STOUT, Menomonie, WI 54751

General Information State-supported, coed, comprehensive institution. *Enrollment:* 8,327 graduate, professional, and undergraduate students; 294 full-time matriculated graduate/professional students (218 women), 337 part-time matriculated graduate/professional students (234 women). *Enrollment by degree level:* 595 master's, 36 other advanced degrees. *Graduate faculty:* 196 full-time (81 women). Tuition, state resident: part-time $317 per credit. Tuition, nonresident: part-time $543 per credit. Tuition and fees vary according to reciprocity agreements. *Graduate housing:* Room and/or apartments available on a first-come, first-served basis to single students; on-campus housing not available to married students. Typical cost: $4,328 (including board). Room and board charges vary according to board plan, campus/location and housing facility selected. *Student services:* Campus employment opportunities, career counseling, child daycare facilities, disabled student services, exercise/wellness program, free psychological counseling, grant writing training, international student services, low-cost health insurance, multicultural affairs office, teacher training. *Library facilities:* Library Learning Center. *Online resources:* library catalog, web page, access to other libraries' catalogs. *Collection:* 229,986 titles, 1,784 serial subscriptions, 16,142 audiovisual materials.

Computer facilities: Computer purchase and lease plans are available. 590 computers available on campus for general student use. A campuswide network can be accessed from student residence rooms and from off campus. Internet access and online class registration, all undergraduates receive a laptop computer. are available. *Web address:* http://www.uwstout.edu/.

General Application Contact: Anne E. Johnson, Graduate Student Evaluator, 715-232-1322, Fax: 715-232-2413, E-mail: johnsona@uwstout.edu.

GRADUATE UNITS

Graduate School Students: 294 full-time (218 women), 337 part-time (234 women); includes 41 minority (13 African Americans, 9 American Indian/Alaska Native, 7 Asian Americans or Pacific Islanders, 12 Hispanic Americans), 40 international. Average age 32. 482 applicants, 60% accepted, 165 enrolled. *Faculty:* 196 full-time (81 women). Expenses: Contact institution. *Financial support:* In 2006–07, 83 research assistantships (averaging $4,632 per year), 33 teaching assistantships (averaging $5,115 per year) were awarded; Federal Work-Study, scholarships/grants, health care benefits, tuition waivers (full and partial), and unspecified assistantships also available. Support available to part-time students. Financial award application deadline: 4/1; financial award applicants required to submit FAFSA. In 2006, 210 master's, 12 other advanced degrees awarded. *Degree program information:* Part-time programs available. Postbaccalaureate distance learning degree programs offered (no on-campus study). *Application fee:* $45. Electronic applications accepted. *Application Contact:* Anne E. Johnson, Graduate Student Evaluator, 715-232-1322, Fax: 715-232-2413, E-mail: johnsona@uwstout.edu. *Associate Vice Chancellor,* Dr. Janice Coker, 715-232-2421, E-mail: cokerj@uwstout.edu.

College of Human Development Students: 151 full-time (122 women), 78 part-time (72 women); includes 12 minority (3 African Americans, 3 American Indian/Alaska Native, 3 Asian Americans or Pacific Islanders, 3 Hispanic Americans), 15 international. Average age 31. 206 applicants, 51% accepted, 66 enrolled. *Faculty:* 61 full-time (26 women). Expenses: Contact institution. *Financial support:* In 2006–07, 27 research assistantships with partial tuition reimbursements (averaging $3,436 per year), 24 teaching assistantships with partial tuition reimbursements (averaging $4,210 per year) were awarded; Federal Work-Study, scholarships/grants, health care benefits, tuition waivers (full and partial), and unspecified assistantships also available. Support available to part-time students. Financial award application deadline: 4/1; financial award applicants required to submit FAFSA. In 2006, 89 degrees awarded. *Degree program information:* Part-time programs available. Postbaccalaureate distance learning degree programs offered (no on-campus study). Offers applied psychology (MS); family studies and human development (MS); food and nutritional sciences (MS); human development (MS); marriage and family therapy (MS); mental health counseling (MS); vocational rehabilitation (MS). *Application fee:* $45. Electronic applications accepted. *Application Contact:* Anne E. Johnson, Graduate Student Evaluator, 715-232-1322, Fax: 715-232-2413, E-mail: johnsona@uwstout.edu. *Dean,* Dr. John Wesolek, 715-232-2687, E-mail: wesolekj@uwstout.edu.

College of Technology, Engineering, and Management Students: 51 full-time (21 women), 91 part-time (44 women); includes 7 minority (2 African Americans, 3 American Indian/Alaska Native, 2 Hispanic Americans), 16 international. Average age 34. 99 applicants, 78% accepted, 47 enrolled. *Faculty:* 51 full-time (13 women). Expenses: Contact institution. *Financial support:* In 2006–07, 19 research assistantships with partial tuition reimbursements (averaging $4,019 per year), 2 teaching assistantships (averaging $2,899 per year) were awarded; Federal Work-Study, scholarships/grants, health care benefits, tuition waivers (full and partial), and unspecified assistantships also available. Support available to part-time students. Financial award application deadline: 4/1; financial award applicants required to submit FAFSA. In 2006, 54 degrees awarded. *Degree program information:* Part-time programs available. Offers information and communication technologies (MS); manufacturing engineering (MS); risk control (MS); technology management (MS); technology, engineering, and management (MS); training and development (MS). *Application deadline:* Applications are processed on a rolling basis. *Application fee:* $45. Electronic applications accepted. *Application Contact:* Anne E. Johnson, Graduate Student Evaluator, 715-232-1322, Fax: 715-232-2413, E-mail: johnsona@uwstout.edu. *Dean,* Dr. Bob Meyer, 715-232-1325, Fax: 715-232-1274, E-mail: meyerb@uwstout.edu.

School of Education Students: 83 full-time (69 women), 160 part-time (114 women); includes 19 minority (6 African Americans, 2 American Indian/Alaska Native, 4 Asian Americans or Pacific Islanders, 7 Hispanic Americans), 2 international. Average age 32. 177 applicants, 59% accepted, 52 enrolled. *Faculty:* 30 full-time (20 women). Expenses: Contact institution. *Financial support:* In 2006–07, 15 research assistantships with partial tuition reimbursements (averaging $5,855 per year), 5 teaching assistantships with partial tuition reimbursements (averaging $9,786 per year) were awarded; Federal Work-Study, scholarships/grants, health care benefits, tuition waivers (partial), and unspecified assistantships also available. Support available to part-time students. In 2006, 67 master's, 12 other advanced degrees awarded. *Degree program information:* Part-time programs available. Postbaccalaureate distance learning degree programs offered (no on-campus study). Offers career and technical education (MS, Ed S); education (MS, MS Ed, Ed S); guidance and counseling (MS); industrial/technology education (MS); school psychology (MS Ed, Ed S). *Application fee:* $45. Electronic applications accepted. *Application Contact:* Anne E. Johnson, Graduate Student Evaluator, 715-232-1322, Fax: 715-232-2413, E-mail: johnsona@uwstout.edu. *Interim Dean,* Dr. Mary Hopkins-Best, 715-232-1168, E-mail: hopkinsbestm@uwstout.edu.

UNIVERSITY OF WISCONSIN–SUPERIOR, Superior, WI 54880-4500

General Information State-supported, coed, comprehensive institution. CGS member. *Graduate housing:* Rooms and/or apartments available on a first-come, first-served basis to single students and available to married students. Housing application deadline: 7/1. *Research affiliation:* Great Lakes Indian Fish and Wildlife Commission, Wisconsin Department of Natural Resources (biology), Environmental Protection Agency (biology), The Mexican National Institute for Ecology (biology), The Mexican Marine National Park Service (biology), Coastal Zone Management Institute and Authority of Belize (biology), Fisheries Department, Government of Belize (biology).

GRADUATE UNITS

Graduate Division *Degree program information:* Part-time and evening/weekend programs available. Postbaccalaureate distance learning degree programs offered (minimal on-campus study). Offers art education (MA); art history (MA); art therapy (MA); community counseling (MSE); educational administration (MSE, Ed S); elementary school counseling (MSE); emotional/behavior disabilities (MSE); human relations (MSE); instruction (MSE); learning disabilities (MSE); mass communication (MA); secondary school counseling (MSE); special education (MSE); speech communication (MA); studio arts (MA); teaching reading (MSE); theater (MA).

UNIVERSITY OF WISCONSIN–WHITEWATER, Whitewater, WI 53190-1790

General Information State-supported, coed, comprehensive institution. *Enrollment:* 10,502 graduate, professional, and undergraduate students; 276 full-time matriculated graduate/professional students (164 women), 745 part-time matriculated graduate/professional students (447 women). *Enrollment by degree level:* 1,021 master's. *Graduate faculty:* 332. Tuition, state resident: full-time $3,311. Tuition, nonresident: full-time $8,616. *Required fees:* $368 per credit. *Graduate housing:* Rooms and/or apartments available on a first-come, first-served basis to single students and available to married students. Housing application deadline: 9/1. *Student services:* Campus employment opportunities, campus safety program, career counseling, child daycare facilities, disabled student services, exercise/wellness program, free psychological counseling, grant writing training, international student services, low-cost health insurance, multicultural affairs office. *Library facilities:* Andersen Library. *Online resources:* library catalog, web page, access to other libraries' catalogs. *Collection:* 701,086 titles, 4,589 serial subscriptions, 19,427 audiovisual materials. *Research affiliation:* WEBCO (lightning radioactive transfer), Generac Power Systems (manufacturing), American Ag-Tec International (International Marketing), American Family Insurance (Insurance), R.A Smith and Associates (Civil Engineering), Sho-Deen (property management and development).

Computer facilities: 1,300 computers available on campus for general student use. A campuswide network can be accessed from student residence rooms and from off campus. Internet access and online class registration are available. *Web address:* http://www.uww.edu/.

General Application Contact: Sally A. Lange, School of Graduate Studies, 262-472-1006, Fax: 262-472-5027, E-mail: gradschl@uww.edu.

GRADUATE UNITS

School of Graduate Studies Students: 276 full-time (164 women), 745 part-time (447 women); includes 142 minority (40 African Americans, 2 American Indian/Alaska Native, 63 Asian Americans or Pacific Islanders, 37 Hispanic Americans). Average age 27. 620 applicants, 82% accepted, 198 enrolled. *Faculty:* 332. Expenses: Contact institution. *Financial support:* In 2006–07, 50 students received support, including 38 research assistantships (averaging $9,875 per year); career-related internships or fieldwork, Federal Work-Study, unspecified assistantships, and out of state fee waiver also available. Support available to part-time students. Financial award application deadline: 3/15; financial award applicants required to submit FAFSA. In 2006, 413 degrees awarded. *Degree program information:* Part-time and evening/weekend programs available. Postbaccalaureate distance learning degree programs offered (no on-campus study). *Application deadline:* For fall admission, 7/15 priority date for domestic students; for spring admission, 12/1 priority date for domestic students. Applications are processed on a rolling basis. *Application fee:* $45. Electronic applications accepted. *Application Contact:* Sally A. Lange, School of Graduate Studies, 262-472-1006, Fax: 262-472-5027, E-mail: gradschl@uww.edu. *Dean, School of Graduate Studies,* Dr. John Stone, 262-472-1006, Fax: 262-472-5210, E-mail: gradschl@uww.edu.

College of Arts and Communications Students: 5 full-time (3 women), 17 part-time (7 women); includes 4 minority (1 African American, 2 Asian Americans or Pacific Islanders, 1 Hispanic American). Average age 26. 13 applicants, 85% accepted, 6 enrolled. *Faculty:* 35. Expenses: Contact institution. *Financial support:* Research assistantships, Federal Work-Study, unspecified assistantships, and out-of-state fee waivers available. Support available to part-time students. Financial award application deadline: 3/15; financial award applicants required to submit FAFSA. In 2006, 20 degrees awarded. *Degree program information:* Part-time and evening/weekend programs available. Postbaccalaureate distance learning degree programs offered (no on-campus study). Offers arts and communications (MS); corporate communication (MS); mass communication (MS). *Application deadline:* For fall admission, 7/15 priority date for domestic students, 7/15 for international students; for spring admission, 12/1 priority date for domestic students, 12/1 for international students. Applications are processed on a rolling basis. *Application fee:* $45. Electronic applications accepted. *Application Contact:* Sally A. Lange, School of Graduate Studies, 262-472-1006, Fax: 262-472-5027, E-mail: gradschl@uww.edu. *Dean,* Dr. John Heyer, 262-472-1221, Fax: 262-472-1436, E-mail: heyerj@uww.edu.

College of Business and Economics Students: 150 full-time (66 women), 424 part-time (191 women); includes 96 minority (24 African Americans, 57 Asian Americans or Pacific Islanders, 15 Hispanic Americans). Average age 29. 257 applicants, 65% accepted, 123 enrolled. *Faculty:* 57. Expenses: Contact institution. *Financial support:* In 2006–07, 15 research assistantships (averaging $7,380 per year) were awarded; career-related internships or fieldwork, Federal Work-Study, unspecified assistantships, and out of state fee waiver also available. Support available to part-time students. Financial award application deadline: 3/15; financial award applicants required to submit FAFSA. In 2006, 236 degrees awarded. *Degree program information:* Part-time and evening/weekend programs available. Postbaccalaureate distance learning degree programs offered (no on-campus study). Offers accounting (MPA); business and economics (MBA, MPA, MS, MS Ed); finance (MBA); general business education (MS); human resource management (MBA); information technology management (MBA); international business (MBA); management (MBA); marketing (MBA); operations and supply chain management (MBA); post-secondary business education (MS); school business management (MS Ed); secondary business education (MS); technology and training (MBA). *Application deadline:* For fall admission, 7/15 priority date for domestic students, 7/15 for international students; for spring admission, 12/1 priority date for domestic students, 12/1 for international students. Applications are processed on a rolling basis. *Application fee:* $45. Electronic applications accepted. *Application Contact:* Dr. Donald Zahn, Associate Dean, 262-472-1945, Fax: 262-472-4863, E-mail:

University of Wisconsin–Whitewater (continued)

zahnd@uww.edu. *Dean,* Dr. Christine Clements, 262-472-1343, Fax: 262-472-4863, E-mail: clementc@uww.edu.

College of Education Students: 99 full-time (77 women), 288 part-time (237 women); includes 38 minority (12 African Americans, 2 American Indian/Alaska Native, 3 Asian Americans or Pacific Islanders, 21 Hispanic Americans). Average age 30. 180 applicants, 42% accepted, 42 enrolled. Expenses: Contact institution. *Financial support:* In 2006–07, 1 research assistantship (averaging $9,875 per year) was awarded; career-related internships or fieldwork, Federal Work-Study, unspecified assistantships, and out of state fee waiver also available. Support available to part-time students. Financial award application deadline: 3/15; financial award applicants required to submit FAFSA. In 2006, 142 degrees awarded. *Degree program information:* Part-time and evening/weekend programs available. Postbaccalaureate distance learning degree programs offered (no on-campus study). Offers communicative disorders (MS); community counseling (MS Ed); curriculum and instruction (MS); education (MS, MS Ed); higher education (MS Ed); reading (MS Ed); safety (MS); school counseling (MS Ed); special education (MS Ed). *Application deadline:* For fall admission, 7/15 priority date for domestic students; for spring admission, 12/1 priority date for domestic students. Applications are processed on a rolling basis. *Application fee:* $45. Electronic applications accepted. *Application Contact:* Sally A. Lange, School of Graduate Studies, 262-472-1006, Fax: 262-472-5027, E-mail: gradschl@uww.edu. *Dean,* Dr. Jeffrey Barnett, 262-472-1101, Fax: 262-472-5716, E-mail: barnettj@uww.edu.

College of Letters and Sciences Students: 29 full-time (22 women), 11 part-time (8 women); includes 4 minority (2 African Americans, 1 American Indian/Alaska Native, 1 Asian American or Pacific Islander). Average age 26. 77 applicants, 25% accepted, 19 enrolled. Expenses: Contact institution. *Financial support:* In 2006–07, research assistantships with partial tuition reimbursements (averaging $9,359 per year); Federal Work-Study, unspecified assistantships, and out of state fee waiver also available. Support available to part-time students. Financial award application deadline: 3/15; financial award applicants required to submit FAFSA. In 2006, 10 master's awarded. *Degree program information:* Part-time and evening/weekend programs available. Offers letters and sciences (MS Ed, Ed S); school psychology (MS Ed, Ed S). *Application deadline:* Applications are processed on a rolling basis. *Application fee:* $45. Electronic applications accepted. *Application Contact:* Sally A. Lange, School of Graduate Studies, 262-472-1006, Fax: 262-472-5027, E-mail: gradschl@uww.edu. *Interim Dean,* Dr. Mary Pinkerton, 262-472-1711, Fax: 262-472-5238, E-mail: pinkertm@uww.edu.

UNIVERSITY OF WYOMING, Laramie, WY 82070

General Information State-supported, coed, university. CGS member. *Enrollment:* 13,203 graduate, professional, and undergraduate students; 1,060 full-time matriculated graduate/professional students (500 women), 917 part-time matriculated graduate/professional students (542 women). *Graduate faculty:* 578 full-time (152 women), 108 part-time/adjunct (48 women). *Graduate housing:* Rooms and/or apartments available on a first-come, first-served basis to single and married students. *Student services:* Campus employment opportunities, campus safety program, career counseling, child daycare facilities, disabled student services, free psychological counseling, international student services, low-cost health insurance, multicultural affairs office, teacher training. *Library facilities:* William Robertson Coe Library plus 8 others. *Online resources:* library catalog, web page, access to other libraries' catalogs. *Collection:* 2.4 million titles, 11,668 serial subscriptions, 9,961 audiovisual materials.

Computer facilities: Computer purchase and lease plans are available. 950 computers available on campus for general student use. A campuswide network can be accessed from student residence rooms and from off campus. Internet access and online class registration are available. *Web address:* http://www.uwyo.edu/.

General Application Contact: Michell Anderson, Credentials Analyst/Advising Assistant, 307-766-2287, Fax: 307-766-2374, E-mail: manders2@uwyo.edu.

GRADUATE UNITS

College of Law Students: 233 full-time (107 women), 3 part-time (1 woman); includes 16 minority (1 African American, 2 American Indian/Alaska Native, 6 Asian Americans or Pacific Islanders, 7 Hispanic Americans), 5 international. Average age 29. 780 applicants, 24% accepted, 82 enrolled. *Faculty:* 16 full-time (8 women), 14 part-time/adjunct (8 women). Expenses: Contact institution. *Financial support:* In 2006–07, 161 students received support, including 18 research assistantships (averaging $1,610 per year), 7 teaching assistantships with full and partial tuition reimbursements available (averaging $2,337 per year); fellowships, career-related internships or fieldwork, Federal Work-Study, institutionally sponsored loans, and scholarships/grants also available. Financial award application deadline: 5/1; financial award applicants required to submit FAFSA. In 2006, 69 degrees awarded. Offers law (JD). *Application deadline:* For fall admission, 3/15 for domestic students. Applications are processed on a rolling basis. *Application fee:* $35. *Application Contact:* Sheryl Sullivan, Assistant Dean, 307-766-6416, E-mail: lawadmis@wyo.edu. *Dean,* Jerry Parkinson, 307-766-6416, E-mail: jparkins@wyo.edu.

Graduate School Students: 1,263 full-time (646 women), 930 part-time (528 women); includes 98 minority (14 African Americans, 19 American Indian/Alaska Native, 21 Asian Americans or Pacific Islanders, 44 Hispanic Americans), 241 international. Average age 31. 1,466 applicants, 47% accepted. *Faculty:* 562 full-time (144 women), 94 part-time/adjunct (40 women). Expenses: Contact institution. *Financial support:* In 2006–07, research assistantships with full tuition reimbursements (averaging $10,062 per year), teaching assistantships with full tuition reimbursements (averaging $10,062 per year) were awarded; fellowships, career-related internships or fieldwork, Federal Work-Study, institutionally sponsored loans, scholarships/grants, traineeships, tuition waivers (full and partial), and unspecified assistantships also available. Support available to part-time students. Financial award applicants required to submit FAFSA. In 2006, 113 first professional degrees, 408 master's, 77 doctorates awarded. *Degree program information:* Part-time and evening/weekend programs available. Postbaccalaureate distance learning degree programs offered. *Application deadline:* Applications are processed on a rolling basis. *Application fee:* $50. Electronic applications accepted. *Application Contact:* Michell Anderson, Credentials Analyst/Advising Assistant, 307-766-2287, Fax: 307-766-2374, E-mail: manders2@uwyo.edu. *Dean,* Dr. Don A. Roth, 307-766-2287, Fax: 307-766-2374, E-mail: rothdon@wyo.edu.

College of Agriculture Students: 83 full-time (42 women), 44 part-time (23 women); includes 4 minority (1 Asian American or Pacific Islander, 3 Hispanic Americans), 27 international. Average age 30. 101 applicants, 40% accepted. *Faculty:* 102 full-time (13 women), 10 part-time/adjunct (2 women). Expenses: Contact institution. *Financial support:* In 2006–07, 3 fellowships, 15 research assistantships, 32 teaching assistantships were awarded; career-related internships or fieldwork, Federal Work-Study, institutionally sponsored loans, scholarships/grants, tuition waivers (partial), and unspecified assistantships also available. Financial award application deadline: 3/1. In 2006, 31 master's, 11 doctorates awarded. *Degree program information:* Part-time programs available. Offers agroecology (MS); agricultural and applied economics (MS); agriculture (MS, PhD); agronomy (MS, PhD); animal sciences (MS, PhD); entomology (MS, PhD); entomology/water resources (MS, PhD); family and consumer sciences (MS); food science and human nutrition (MS); molecular biology (MS, PhD); pathobiology (MS); rangeland ecology and watershed management (MS, PhD); rangeland ecology and watershed management/water resources (MS, PhD); reproductive biology (MS, PhD); soil science (MS); soil science/water resources (PhD). *Application deadline:* Applications are processed on a rolling basis. *Application fee:* $50. Electronic applications accepted. *Dean,* Dr. Frank D. Galey, 307-766-4133, E-mail: fgaley@uwyo.edu.

College of Arts and Sciences Students: 361 full-time (167 women), 222 part-time (108 women); includes 26 minority (5 African Americans, 5 American Indian/Alaska Native, 3 Asian Americans or Pacific Islanders, 13 Hispanic Americans), 71 international. Average age 30. 449 applicants, 47% accepted. *Faculty:* 229 full-time (55 women), 47 part-time/adjunct (17 women). Expenses: Contact institution. *Financial support:* Fellowships, research assistantships with full and partial tuition reimbursements, teaching assistantships with full and partial tuition reimbursements, career-related internships or fieldwork, Federal Work-Study, institutionally sponsored loans, scholarships/grants, traineeships, tuition waivers (full and partial), and unspecified assistantships available. Financial award application deadline: 3/1. In 2006, 123 master's, 29 doctorates awarded. *Degree program information:* Part-time programs available. Offers American studies (MA); anthropology (MA, PhD); arts and sciences (MA, MAT, MFA, MM, MP, MPA, MS, MST, PhD); botany (MS, PhD); botany/water resources (MS); chemistry (MS, PhD); communication (MA); community and regional planning and natural resources (MP); creative writing (MFA); English (MA); French (MA); geography (MA, MP, MST); geography/water resources (MA); geology (MS, PhD); geophysics (MS, PhD); German (MA); history (MA, MAT); international peace corps (MA); international studies (MA); mathematics (MA, MAT, MS, MST, PhD); mathematics/computer science (PhD); music education (MA); performance (MM); philosophy (MA); political science (MA); psychology (MA, MS, PhD); public administration (MPA); rural planning and natural resources (MP); sociology (MA); Spanish (MA); statistics (MS, PhD); zoology and physiology (MS, PhD). *Application deadline:* Applications are processed on a rolling basis. *Application fee:* $40. Electronic applications accepted. *Application Contact:* Audrey C. Shalinsky, Associate Dean, 307-766-4106, Fax: 307-766-2697, E-mail: asdean@uwyo.edu. *Dean,* B. Oliver Walter, 307-766-4106, Fax: 307-766-2697, E-mail: asdean@uwyo.edu.

College of Business Students: 75 full-time (28 women), 75 part-time (26 women); includes 5 minority (2 African Americans, 1 American Indian/Alaska Native, 1 Asian American or Pacific Islander, 1 Hispanic American), 32 international. Average age 30. 178 applicants, 48% accepted. *Faculty:* 38 full-time (7 women), 5 part-time/adjunct (1 woman). Expenses: Contact institution. *Financial support:* In 2006–07, 31 research assistantships (averaging $5,192 per year), 10 teaching assistantships were awarded; fellowships, career-related internships or fieldwork, Federal Work-Study, institutionally sponsored loans, and tuition waivers (partial) also available. Financial award application deadline: 3/1; financial award applicants required to submit FAFSA. In 2006, 63 master's, 2 doctorates awarded. *Degree program information:* Part-time and evening/weekend programs available. Postbaccalaureate distance learning degree programs offered (minimal on-campus study). Offers accounting (MS); business (MBA, MS, PhD); business administration (MBA); economics (MS, PhD); economics and finance (MS); finance (MS). *Application deadline:* For fall admission, 2/1 for domestic and international students. Applications are processed on a rolling basis. *Application fee:* $50. *Application Contact:* Lori Lewis, Office Associate, 307-766-2449, Fax: 307-766-4028, E-mail: mba@uwyo.edu. *Dean,* Dr. Brent A. Hathaway, 307-766-4194.

College of Education Students: 95 full-time (72 women), 351 part-time (222 women); includes 31 minority (5 African Americans, 9 American Indian/Alaska Native, 4 Asian Americans or Pacific Islanders, 13 Hispanic Americans), 6 international. Average age 41. 263 applicants, 55% accepted. *Faculty:* 43 full-time (25 women). Expenses: Contact institution. *Financial support:* In 2006–07, 18 teaching assistantships with full tuition reimbursements (averaging $10,384 per year) were awarded; fellowships, research assistantships, career-related internships or fieldwork, Federal Work-Study, scholarships/grants, and unspecified assistantships also available. Financial award application deadline: 1/31. In 2006, 88 master's, 19 doctorates, 4 other advanced degrees awarded. Postbaccalaureate distance learning degree programs offered. Offers adult and post secondary education (Ed S); adult and postsecondary education (MA, Ed D, PhD); counselor education (MS, PhD); curriculum and instruction (MA, Ed D, PhD); distance education (Ed D, PhD); education (MA, MS, MST, Ed D, PhD, Ed S); educational leadership (MA, Ed D, PhD, Ed S); instructional technology (MS, Ed D, PhD); science and mathematics teaching (MS, MST); special education (MA, Ed S). *Application deadline:* Applications are processed on a rolling basis. *Application fee:* $50. Electronic applications accepted. *Application Contact:* Michael Day, Associate Dean, 307-766-3145, Fax: 307-766-6668, E-mail: mikeday@uwyo.edu. *Dean,* Dr. Patricia McClurg, 307-766-3145, Fax: 307-766-6668, E-mail: patmc@uwyo.edu.

College of Engineering Students: 126 full-time (34 women), 67 part-time (10 women); includes 3 minority (2 Asian Americans or Pacific Islanders, 1 Hispanic American), 84 international. Average age 28. 225 applicants, 45% accepted. *Faculty:* 76 full-time (5 women), 9 part-time/adjunct (1 woman). Expenses: Contact institution. *Financial support:* Fellowships, research assistantships, teaching assistantships, career-related internships or fieldwork, Federal Work-Study, and institutionally sponsored loans available. Support available to part-time students. In 2006, 38 master's, 16 doctorates awarded. *Degree program information:* Part-time programs available. Offers atmospheric science (MS, PhD); chemical engineering (MS, PhD); civil engineering (MS, PhD); computer science (MS, PhD); electrical engineering (MS, PhD); engineering (MS, PhD); environmental engineering (MS); mechanical engineering (MS, PhD); petroleum engineering (MS, PhD). *Application deadline:* Applications are processed on a rolling basis. *Application fee:* $50. Electronic applications accepted. *Dean,* Dr. Ovid A. Plumb, 307-766-4257, Fax: 307-766-4444, E-mail: gplumb@uwyo.edu.

College of Health Sciences Students: 290 full-time (196 women), 168 part-time (138 women); includes 19 minority (1 African American, 1 American Indian/Alaska Native, 4 Asian Americans or Pacific Islanders, 13 Hispanic Americans), 10 international. Average age 31. 550 applicants, 28% accepted. *Faculty:* 63 full-time (38 women), 8 part-time/adjunct (4 women). Expenses: Contact institution. *Financial support:* In 2006–07, teaching assistantships with tuition reimbursements (averaging $10,062 per year); fellowships, research assistantships, career-related internships or fieldwork, Federal Work-Study, institutionally sponsored loans, scholarships/grants, traineeships, tuition waivers (full), and unspecified assistantships also available. Support available to part-time students. Financial award application deadline: 3/1. In 2006, 44 first professional degrees, 64 master's awarded. *Degree program information:* Part-time programs available. Postbaccalaureate distance learning degree programs offered (minimal on-campus study). Offers audiology (PhD); health sciences (Pharm D, MS, MSW, PhD); kinesiology and health (MS); neuroscience (PhD); nursing (MS); pharmacy (Pharm D); social work (MSW); speech-language pathology (MS). *Application fee:* $50. Electronic applications accepted. *Application Contact:* Lisa Shipley, Manager Student Advising, 307-766-6706, E-mail: lshipley@uwyo.edu. *Dean,* Dr. Robert O. Kelley, 307-766-6556, Fax: 307-766-6608, E-mail: rokelley@uwyo.edu.

UPPER IOWA UNIVERSITY, Fayette, IA 52142-1857

General Information Independent, coed, comprehensive institution. *Graduate housing:* On-campus housing not available.

GRADUATE UNITS

Online Master's Programs *Degree program information:* Part-time and evening/weekend programs available. Postbaccalaureate distance learning degree programs offered (no on-campus study). Offers accounting (MBA); corporate financial management (MBA); global business (MBA); health and human services (MPA); homeland security (MPA); human resources management (MBA); justice administration (MPA); organizational development (MBA); public personnel management (MPA); quality management (MBA). MBA also available at Madison, Wisconsin campus. Electronic applications accepted.

URBANA UNIVERSITY, Urbana, OH 43078-2091

General Information Independent, coed, comprehensive institution. *Graduate housing:* On-campus housing not available.

GRADUATE UNITS

Division of Business Administration *Degree program information:* Part-time and evening/weekend programs available. Offers business administration (MBA).

Division of Education and Allied Professions *Degree program information:* Part-time and evening/weekend programs available. Offers classroom education (M Ed).

URSULINE COLLEGE, Pepper Pike, OH 44124-4398

General Information Independent-religious, Undergraduate: women only; graduate: coed, comprehensive institution. *Enrollment:* 1,639 graduate, professional, and undergraduate students; 66 full-time matriculated graduate/professional students (59 women), 393 part-time matriculated graduate/professional students (346 women). *Enrollment by degree level:* 459 master's. *Graduate faculty:* 15 full-time (13 women), 27 part-time/adjunct (17 women).

Tuition: Full-time $12,078; part-time $671 per credit hour. *Required fees:* $60 per semester. *Graduate housing:* Room and/or apartments available on a first-come, first-served basis to single students; on-campus housing not available to married students. Typical cost: $6,366 (including board). Housing application deadline: 8/20. *Student services:* Career counseling, disabled student services, exercise/wellness program, free psychological counseling, multicultural affairs office, teacher training. *Library facilities:* Ralph M. Besse Library. *Online resources:* library catalog, web page, access to other libraries' catalogs. *Collection:* 129,621 titles, 14,198 serial subscriptions, 8,719 audiovisual materials.

Computer facilities: 72 computers available on campus for general student use. A campuswide network can be accessed from student residence rooms. Internet access is available. *Web address:* http://www.ursuline.edu/.

General Application Contact: Dean of Graduate Studies, 440-646-8119, Fax: 440-684-6088, E-mail: gradsch@ursuline.edu.

GRADUATE UNITS

School of Graduate Studies Students: 66 full-time (59 women), 393 part-time (346 women); includes 68 minority (58 African Americans, 4 Asian Americans or Pacific Islanders, 6 Hispanic Americans), 1 international. Average age 37. 172 applicants, 100% accepted, 172 enrolled. *Faculty:* 15 full-time (13 women), 27 part-time/adjunct (17 women). Expenses: Contact institution. *Financial support:* In 2006–07, 253 students received support. Federal Work-Study available. Financial award application deadline: 3/1; financial award applicants required to submit FAFSA. In 2006, 110 degrees awarded. *Degree program information:* Part-time programs available. Offers art therapy counseling (MA); education (MA); educational administration (MA); historic preservation (MA); liberal studies (MALS); management (MM); ministry (MA); nursing (MSN). *Application deadline:* For fall admission, 8/1 priority date for domestic students. Applications are processed on a rolling basis. *Application fee:* $25. Electronic applications accepted. *Application Contact:* Jo Mann, Secretary, 440-646-8119, Fax: 440-684-6088, E-mail: gradsch@ursuline.edu. *Dean of Graduate Studies,* 440-646-8119, Fax: 440-684-6088, E-mail: gradsch@ursuline.edu.

UTAH STATE UNIVERSITY, Logan, UT 84322

General Information State-supported, coed, university. CGS member. *Enrollment:* 14,444 graduate, professional, and undergraduate students; 2,030 full-time matriculated graduate/professional students (800 women), 576 part-time matriculated graduate/professional students (276 women). *Enrollment by degree level:* 2,044 master's, 562 doctoral. *Graduate faculty:* 712 full-time (178 women), 163 part-time/adjunct (45 women). *Graduate housing:* Rooms and/or apartments available on a first-come, first-served basis to single and married students. *Student services:* Campus employment opportunities, campus safety program, career counseling, child daycare facilities, disabled student services, exercise/wellness program, free psychological counseling, international student services, low-cost health insurance, multicultural affairs office, teacher training, writing training. *Library facilities:* Merrill Library plus 4 others. *Online resources:* library catalog, web page, access to other libraries' catalogs. *Collection:* 1.5 million titles, 12,369 serial subscriptions, 16,504 audiovisual materials. *Research affiliation:* Boeing Aerospace and Engineering (science and engineering), Duke Energy Corporation (engineering), Kennecott Copper Corporation (natural resources), Kraft, Inc. (agriculture), National Endowment for Financial Education (education).

Computer facilities: Computer purchase and lease plans are available. 875 computers available on campus for general student use. A campuswide network can be accessed from student residence rooms and from off campus. Internet access and online class registration are available. *Web address:* http://www.usu.edu/.

General Application Contact: Peter J. Morris, Admissions Officer, School of Graduate Studies, 435-797-1190, Fax: 435-797-1192, E-mail: gradsch@cc.usu.edu.

GRADUATE UNITS

School of Graduate Studies Students: 1,745 full-time (708 women), 575 part-time (277 women); includes 61 minority (11 African Americans, 8 American Indian/Alaska Native, 14 Asian Americans or Pacific Islanders, 28 Hispanic Americans), 492 international. 2,566 applicants, 49% accepted, 659 enrolled. *Faculty:* 712 full-time (178 women), 163 part-time/adjunct (45 women). Expenses: Contact institution. *Financial support:* In 2006–07, 432 research assistantships with partial tuition reimbursements (averaging $11,000 per year), 195 teaching assistantships with partial tuition reimbursements (averaging $9,500 per year) were awarded; fellowships with partial tuition reimbursements, career-related internships or fieldwork, Federal Work-Study, institutionally sponsored loans, scholarships/grants, tuition waivers (full and partial), unspecified assistantships, and production assistantships, stipends also available. Support available to part-time students. In 2006, 809 master's, 87 doctorates, 2 other advanced degrees awarded. *Degree program information:* Part-time and evening/weekend programs available. Postbaccalaureate distance learning degree programs offered (minimal on-campus study). *Application deadline:* For fall admission, 6/15 for domestic students; for spring admission, 10/15 for domestic students. Applications are processed on a rolling basis. *Application fee:* $50 ($60 for international students). *Application Contact:* Peter J. Morris, Admissions Officer, 435-797-1190, Fax: 435-797-1192, E-mail: pete.morris@grad.usu.edu. *Interim Dean,* Dr. Laurens H. Smith, 435-797-1189, Fax: 435-797-1192, E-mail: lhsmith@cc.usu.edu.

College of Agriculture Students: 78 full-time (33 women), 24 part-time (11 women); includes 3 minority (1 African American, 2 Hispanic Americans), 19 international. Average age 27. 66 applicants, 52% accepted, 20 enrolled. *Faculty:* 92 full-time (19 women), 19 part-time/adjunct (0 women). Expenses: Contact institution. *Financial support:* In 2006–07, fellowships with full and partial tuition reimbursements (averaging $15,000 per year), research assistantships with full and partial tuition reimbursements (averaging $13,000 per year), teaching assistantships with full and partial tuition reimbursements (averaging $8,000 per year) were awarded; career-related internships or fieldwork, Federal Work-Study, institutionally sponsored loans, scholarships/grants, tuition waivers (full and partial), and unspecified assistantships also available. Support available to part-time students. In 2006, 51 master's, 7 doctorates awarded. *Degree program information:* Part-time programs available. Postbaccalaureate distance learning degree programs offered (minimal on-campus study). Offers agricultural systems technology (MS); agriculture (MDA, MFMS, MS, PhD); animal science (MS, PhD); biometeorology (MS, PhD); bioveterinary science (MS, PhD); dairy science (MS); dietetic administration (MDA); ecology (MS, PhD); family and consumer sciences education (MS); food microbiology and safety (MFMS); nutrition and food sciences (MS, PhD); nutrition science (MS, PhD); plant science (MS, PhD); soil science (MS, PhD); toxicology (MS, PhD). *Application deadline:* For fall admission, 6/15 for domestic students; for spring admission, 10/15 for domestic students. Applications are processed on a rolling basis. *Application fee:* $50 ($60 for international students). *Dean,* Noelle E. Cockett, 435-797-2215.

College of Business Students: 290 full-time (83 women), 29 part-time (10 women); includes 7 minority (2 American Indian/Alaska Native, 1 Asian American or Pacific Islander, 4 Hispanic Americans), 49 international. Average age 30. 394 applicants, 50% accepted, 86 enrolled. *Faculty:* 105 full-time (14 women), 1 part-time/adjunct (0 women). Expenses: Contact institution. *Financial support:* In 2006–07, 12 fellowships with partial tuition reimbursements (averaging $5,833 per year), 30 research assistantships with partial tuition reimbursements (averaging $5,750 per year), 24 teaching assistantships with partial tuition reimbursements (averaging $4,500 per year) were awarded; career-related internships or fieldwork, Federal Work-Study, institutionally sponsored loans, tuition waivers (full and partial), and unspecified assistantships also available. In 2006, 161 degrees awarded. *Degree program information:* Part-time and evening/weekend programs available. Postbaccalaureate distance learning degree programs offered (no on-campus study). Offers accountancy (M Acc); applied economics (MS); business (M Acc, MA, MBA, MS, Ed D, PhD); business administration (MBA); business education (MS); business information systems (MS); business information systems and education (Ed D); economics (MA, MS, PhD); education (PhD); human resource management (MS). *Application deadline:* For fall admission, 6/15 for domestic students; for spring admission, 10/15 for domestic students. Applications are processed on a rolling basis. *Application fee:* $50 ($60 for international students). *Dean,* Caryn C. Beck-Dudley, 435-797-2376.

College of Education and Human Services Students: 648 full-time (377 women), 264 part-time (180 women); includes 33 minority (9 African Americans, 4 American Indian/Alaska Native, 6 Asian Americans or Pacific Islanders, 14 Hispanic Americans), 100 international. Average age 32. 662 applicants, 51% accepted, 253 enrolled. *Faculty:* 101 full-time (57 women), 20 part-time/adjunct (11 women). Expenses: Contact institution. *Financial support:* In 2006–07, 7 fellowships with partial tuition reimbursements (averaging $8,163 per year), 58 research assistantships with partial tuition reimbursements (averaging $6,647 per year), 54 teaching assistantships with partial tuition reimbursements (averaging $7,050 per year) were awarded; career-related internships or fieldwork, Federal Work-Study, institutionally sponsored loans, tuition waivers (full and partial), unspecified assistantships, and stipends also available. Support available to part-time students. In 2006, 261 master's, 32 doctorates awarded. *Degree program information:* Part-time and evening/weekend programs available. Postbaccalaureate distance learning degree programs offered (no on-campus study). Offers audiology (Au D, Ed S); business information systems (Ed D, PhD); clinical/counseling/school psychology (PhD); communication disorders and deaf education (M Ed); communicative disorders and deaf education (MA, MS); curriculum and instruction (Ed D, PhD); disability disciplines (PhD); education and human services (M Ed, MA, MFHD, MRC, MS, Au D, Ed D, PhD, Ed S); elementary education (M Ed, MA, MS); family and human development (MFHD); family, consumer, and human development (MS, PhD); health, physical education and recreation (M Ed, MS); instructional technology (M Ed, MS, PhD, Ed S); rehabilitation counselor education (MRC); research and evaluation (PhD); research and evaluation methodology (PhD); school counseling (MS); school psychology (MS); secondary education (M Ed, MA, MS); special education (M Ed, MS, Ed S). *Application deadline:* For fall admission, 6/15 for domestic students; for spring admission, 10/15 for domestic students. Applications are processed on a rolling basis. *Application fee:* $50 ($60 for international students). *Application Contact:* Shannon Johnson, Staff Assistant, 435-797-1470, Fax: 435-797-3939, E-mail: shannon.johnson@usu.edu. *Dean,* Dr. Carol Strong, 435-797-1470, Fax: 435-797-3939.

College of Engineering Students: 229 full-time (24 women), 66 part-time (10 women); includes 2 minority (1 Asian American or Pacific Islander, 1 Hispanic American), 135 international. Average age 28. 622 applicants, 46% accepted, 73 enrolled. *Faculty:* 73 full-time (5 women), 6 part-time/adjunct (2 women). Expenses: Contact institution. *Financial support:* In 2006–07, 281 students received support, including 12 fellowships with partial tuition reimbursements available (averaging $8,200 per year), 130 research assistantships with partial tuition reimbursements available (averaging $9,333 per year), 25 teaching assistantships with partial tuition reimbursements available (averaging $9,000 per year); career-related internships or fieldwork, Federal Work-Study, institutionally sponsored loans, and tuition waivers (partial) also available. Support available to part-time students. In 2006, 133 master's, 14 doctorates awarded. *Degree program information:* Part-time and evening/weekend programs available. Offers aerospace engineering (MS, PhD); biological and agricultural engineering (MS, PhD); civil and environmental engineering (ME, MS, PhD, CE); electrical engineering (ME, MS, PhD); engineering (ME, MS, PhD, CE); industrial technology (MS); irrigation engineering (MS, PhD); mechanical engineering (ME, MS, PhD). *Application deadline:* For fall admission, 6/15 for domestic students; for spring admission, 10/15 for domestic students. Applications are processed on a rolling basis. *Application fee:* $50 ($60 for international students). Electronic applications accepted. *Application Contact:* Wynn R. Walker, Associate Dean, 435-797-2788, Fax: 435-797-2769, E-mail: wynnwalk@cc.usu.edu. *Dean,* H. Scott Hinton, 435-797-2775, E-mail: office@engineering.usu.edu.

College of Humanities, Arts and Social Sciences Students: 185 full-time (88 women), 56 part-time (29 women); includes 8 minority (2 American Indian/Alaska Native, 3 Asian Americans or Pacific Islanders, 3 Hispanic Americans), 44 international. Average age 28. 290 applicants, 61% accepted, 126 enrolled. *Faculty:* 143 full-time (54 women), 32 part-time/adjunct (12 women). Expenses: Contact institution. *Financial support:* In 2006–07, fellowships with partial tuition reimbursements (averaging $11,500 per year), research assistantships with partial tuition reimbursements (averaging $7,000 per year), teaching assistantships with partial tuition reimbursements (averaging $6,000 per year) were awarded; career-related internships or fieldwork, Federal Work-Study, institutionally sponsored loans, scholarships/grants, tuition waivers (partial), and production assistantships also available. In 2006, 85 master's, 1 doctorate awarded. *Degree program information:* Part-time and evening/weekend programs available. Postbaccalaureate distance learning degree programs offered (minimal on-campus study). Offers advanced technical practice (MFA); American studies (MA, MS); art (MA, MFA); bioregional planning (MS); design (MFA); English (MA, MS); folklore (MA, MS); history (MA, MS); humanities, arts and social sciences (MA, MFA, MLA, MS, MSLT, MSS, PhD); interior design (MS); journalism and communication (MA, MS); landscape architecture (MLA); political science (MA, MS); second language teaching (MSLT); sociology (MA, MS, MSS, PhD); theatre arts (MA, MFA); western American literature and culture (MA, MS). *Application deadline:* For fall admission, 6/15 for domestic students; for spring admission, 10/15 for domestic students. *Application fee:* $50 ($60 for international students). *Dean,* Dr. Gary H. Kiger, 435-797-1195, Fax: 435-797-1092, E-mail: gary.kiger@usu.edu.

College of Natural Resources Students: 120 full-time (46 women), 60 part-time (21 women); includes 1 minority (Asian American or Pacific Islander), 23 international. Average age 31. 114 applicants, 39% accepted, 39 enrolled. *Faculty:* 52 full-time (10 women), 28 part-time/adjunct (7 women). Expenses: Contact institution. *Financial support:* In 2006–07, fellowships with partial tuition reimbursements (averaging $12,500 per year), research assistantships with partial tuition reimbursements (averaging $10,500 per year), teaching assistantships with partial tuition reimbursements (averaging $1,200 per year) were awarded; career-related internships or fieldwork, Federal Work-Study, institutionally sponsored loans, and tuition waivers (full and partial) also available. Support available to part-time students. In 2006, 47 master's, 11 doctorates awarded. *Degree program information:* Part-time programs available. Offers bioregional planning (MS); ecology (MS, PhD); fisheries biology (MS, PhD); forestry (MS, PhD); geography (MA, MS); human dimensions of ecosystem science and management (MS, PhD); natural resources (MA, MNR, MS, PhD); range science (MS, PhD); recreation resource management (MS, PhD); watershed science (MS, PhD); wildlife biology (MS, PhD). *Application deadline:* For fall admission, 6/15 for domestic students; for spring admission, 10/15 for domestic students. Applications are processed on a rolling basis. *Application fee:* $50 ($60 for international students). *Dean,* Dr. Nat Frazer, 435-797-2452, E-mail: nat.frazer@usu.edu.

College of Science Students: 195 full-time (57 women), 76 part-time (16 women); includes 7 minority (1 African American, 2 Asian Americans or Pacific Islanders, 4 Hispanic Americans), 122 international. Average age 27. 441 applicants, 44% accepted, 62 enrolled. *Faculty:* 130 full-time (17 women), 20 part-time/adjunct (3 women). Expenses: Contact institution. *Financial support:* In 2006–07, fellowships with partial tuition reimbursements (averaging $14,000 per year), research assistantships with partial tuition reimbursements (averaging $13,000 per year), teaching assistantships with partial tuition reimbursements (averaging $12,500 per year) were awarded; career-related internships or fieldwork, Federal Work-Study, institutionally sponsored loans, scholarships/grants, and tuition waivers (partial) also available. Support available to part-time students. In 2006, 72 master's, 22 doctorates awarded. *Degree program information:* Part-time and evening/weekend programs available. Offers biochemistry (MS, PhD); biology (MS, PhD); chemistry (MS, PhD); computer science (MCS, MS, PhD); ecology (MS, PhD); geology (MS); industrial mathematics (MS); mathematical sciences (PhD); mathematics (M Math, MS); physics (MS, PhD); science (M Math, MCS, MS, PhD); statistics (MS). *Application deadline:* For fall admission, 6/15 for domestic students; for spring admission, 10/15 for domestic students. Applications are processed on a rolling basis. *Application fee:* $50 ($60 for international students). *Dean,* Don Fiesinger, 435-797-2480, E-mail: fataq@cc.usu.edu.

UTICA COLLEGE, Utica, NY 13502-4892

General Information Independent, coed, comprehensive institution. *Enrollment:* 2,952 graduate, professional, and undergraduate students; 117 full-time matriculated graduate/professional students (87 women), 376 part-time matriculated graduate/professional students (240 women). *Enrollment by degree level:* 92 first professional, 399 master's, 2 other advanced degrees. *Graduate faculty:* 65 full-time (28 women). *Tuition:* Full-time $20,480; part-time $550 per

Utica College (continued)

credit hour. *Required fees:* $310; $50 per term. Tuition and fees vary according to course load, degree level and program. *Graduate housing:* Room and/or apartments available on a first-come, first-served basis to single students; on-campus housing not available to married students. Typical cost: $4,990 per year ($9,510 including board). Room and board charges vary according to board plan. Housing application deadline: 3/1. *Student services:* Campus employment opportunities, campus safety program, career counseling, disabled student services. *Library facilities:* Frank E. Gannett Memorial Library. *Online resources:* library catalog, web page. *Collection:* 184,918 titles, 1,249 serial subscriptions, 9,737 audiovisual materials.

Computer facilities: 140 computers available on campus for general student use. A campuswide network can be accessed from student residence rooms. Internet access is available. *Web address:* http://www.utica.edu/.

General Application Contact: John D. Rowe, Director of Graduate Admissions, 315-792-3824, Fax: 315-792-3003, E-mail: jrowe@utica.edu.

GRADUATE UNITS

Department of Physical Therapy Students: 43 full-time (32 women), 66 part-time (46 women); includes 6 minority (2 African Americans, 1 American Indian/Alaska Native, 2 Asian Americans or Pacific Islanders, 1 Hispanic American), 1 international. 45 applicants, 89% accepted, 34 enrolled. *Faculty:* 8 full-time (4 women). Expenses: Contact institution. *Financial support:* In 2006–07, 42 students received support. Career-related internships or fieldwork, scholarships/grants, tuition waivers (partial), and unspecified assistantships available. Support available to part-time students. Financial award application deadline: 3/15. In 2006, 27 degrees awarded. Offers physical therapy (DPT, TDPT). *Application deadline:* Applications are processed on a rolling basis. *Application fee:* $50. Electronic applications accepted. *Application Contact:* John D. Rowe, Director of Graduate Admissions, 315-792-3824, Fax: 315-792-3003, E-mail: jrowe@utica.edu. *Director of Physical Therapy,* Dr. Dale Scalise-Smith, 315-792-3376, E-mail: dscalise-smith@utica.edu.

Program in Economic Crime Management Students: 76 full-time (39 women); includes 10 minority (5 African Americans, 5 Hispanic Americans), 1 international. 12 applicants, 75% accepted, 9 enrolled. *Faculty:* 4 full-time (0 women). Expenses: Contact institution. *Financial support:* In 2006–07, 53 students received support. Career-related internships or fieldwork, scholarships/grants, tuition waivers (partial), and unspecified assistantships available. Support available to part-time students. Financial award applicants required to submit FAFSA. In 2006, 13 degrees awarded. *Degree program information:* Part-time programs available. Postbaccalaureate distance learning degree programs offered (minimal on-campus study). Offers economic crime management (MS). *Application deadline:* Applications are processed on a rolling basis. *Application fee:* $50. Electronic applications accepted. *Application Contact:* John D. Rowe, Director of Graduate Admissions, 315-792-3824, Fax: 315-792-3003, E-mail: jrowe@utica.edu. *Director of Economic Crime Graduate Programs,* Dr. R. Bruce McBride, 315-792-3808, E-mail: rmcbride@utica.edu.

VALDOSTA STATE UNIVERSITY, Valdosta, GA 31698

General Information State-supported, coed, university. CGS member. *Graduate housing:* Rooms and/or apartments available on a first-come, first-served basis to single and married students. Housing application deadline: 7/1.

GRADUATE UNITS

Graduate School *Degree program information:* Part-time and evening/weekend programs available. Postbaccalaureate distance learning degree programs offered (minimal on-campus study). Offers library and information science (MLIS). Electronic applications accepted.

College of Arts and Sciences *Degree program information:* Part-time and evening/weekend programs available. Postbaccalaureate distance learning degree programs offered. Offers arts and sciences (MA, MPA, MS); criminal justice (MS); English (MA); history (MA); marriage and family therapy (MS); public administration (MPA); sociology (MS). Electronic applications accepted.

College of Education *Degree program information:* Part-time and evening/weekend programs available. Offers adult and career education (M Ed, Ed D); business education (M Ed); clinical/counseling psychology (MS); communication disorders (M Ed); curriculum and instruction (Ed D); early childhood education (M Ed, Ed S); education (M Ed, MS, Ed D, Ed S); educational leadership (M Ed, Ed D, Ed S); health and physical education (M Ed); industrial/organizational psychology (MS); instructional technology (M Ed, Ed S); middle grades education (M Ed, Ed S); reading education (M Ed); school counseling (M Ed, Ed S); school psychology (Ed S); secondary education (M Ed, Ed S); special education (M Ed, Ed S). Electronic applications accepted.

College of Nursing *Degree program information:* Part-time programs available. Offers nursing (MSN). Electronic applications accepted.

College of the Fine Arts *Degree program information:* Part-time programs available. Offers arts (MME, MMP); music education (MME); performance (MMP). Electronic applications accepted.

Division of Social Work *Degree program information:* Part-time and evening/weekend programs available. Offers social work (MSW).

Langdale College of Business Administration *Degree program information:* Part-time programs available. Offers business administration (MBA). Electronic applications accepted.

VALPARAISO UNIVERSITY, Valparaiso, IN 46383

General Information Independent-religious, coed, comprehensive institution. *Enrollment:* 3,868 graduate, professional, and undergraduate students; 684 full-time matriculated graduate/professional students (331 women), 197 part-time matriculated graduate/professional students (126 women). *Enrollment by degree level:* 516 first professional, 333 master's, 32 other advanced degrees. *Graduate faculty:* 31 full-time (13 women), 124 part-time/adjunct (55 women). *Tuition:* Part-time $390 per credit hour. *Required fees:* $60 per term. Tuition and fees vary according to program. *Graduate housing:* On-campus housing not available. *Student services:* Campus employment opportunities, campus safety program, career counseling, disabled student services, exercise/wellness program, free psychological counseling, international student services, low-cost health insurance, multicultural affairs office, teacher training, writing training. *Library facilities:* Christopher Center for Library and Information Resources plus 1 other. *Online resources:* library catalog, web page. *Collection:* 471,645 titles, 41,649 serial subscriptions, 5,770 audiovisual materials.

Computer facilities: 634 computers available on campus for general student use. A campuswide network can be accessed from student residence rooms and from off campus. Internet access and online class registration, Web academic information (grades, program evaluation) are available. *Web address:* http://www.valpo.edu/.

General Application Contact: Dr. David L. Rowland, Dean, Graduate Studies and Continuing Education, 219-464-5313, Fax: 219-464-5381, E-mail: david.rowland@valpo.edu.

GRADUATE UNITS

Graduate Division Students: 213 full-time (121 women), 145 part-time (102 women); includes 31 minority (20 African Americans, 1 American Indian/Alaska Native, 2 Asian Americans or Pacific Islanders, 8 Hispanic Americans), 23 international. Average age 29. *Faculty:* 97 part-time/adjunct (44 women). Expenses: Contact institution. *Financial support:* Career-related internships or fieldwork, scholarships/grants, traineeships, and unspecified assistantships available. Support available to part-time students. Financial award applicants required to submit FAFSA. In 2006, 152 master's, 12 other advanced degrees awarded. *Degree program information:* Part-time and evening/weekend programs available. Offers Chinese studies (MA); clinical mental health counseling (MA); community counseling (MA); counseling (Certificate); English (MALS, Post-Master's Certificate); ethics and values (MALS, Post-Master's Certificate); gerontology (MALS, Post-Master's Certificate); history (MALS, Post-Master's Certificate); human behavior and society (MALS, Post-Master's Certificate); initial licensure (M Ed); international commerce and policy (MS); liberal studies (MALS, Post-Master's Certificate); sports administration (MS); teaching and learning (M Ed); theology (MALS, Post-Master's Certificate); theology and ministry (MALS, Post-Master's Certificate). *Application deadline:* Applications are processed on a rolling basis. *Application fee:* $30 ($50 for international students). Electronic applications accepted. *Application Contact:* Jamie Haney, Coordinator of Recruitment Activities, 219-464-5313, Fax: 219-464-5381, E-mail: jamie.haney@valpo.edu. *Dean, Graduate Studies and Continuing Education,* Dr. David L. Rowland, 219-464-5313, Fax: 219-464-5381, E-mail: david.rowland@valpo.edu.

College of Business Administration Students: 32 full-time (13 women), 34 part-time (14 women); includes 4 minority (3 African Americans, 1 Hispanic American), 1 international. Average age 26. *Faculty:* 13 part-time/adjunct (4 women). Expenses: Contact institution. *Financial support:* Available to part-time students. Applicants required to submit FAFSA. In 2006, 25 degrees awarded. *Degree program information:* Part-time and evening/weekend programs available. Offers business administration (MBA); engineering management (MEM); management (Certificate). *Application deadline:* Applications are processed on a rolling basis. *Application fee:* $30 ($50 for international students). Electronic applications accepted. *Application Contact:* Erin Brown, Assistant MBA Director, 219-465-7952, Fax: 219-464-5789, E-mail: erin.brown@valpo.edu. *Director,* Dr. Dean Schroeder, 219-464-5177, Fax: 219-464-5789, E-mail: dean.schroeder@valpo.edu.

College of Nursing Students: 18 full-time (16 women), 25 part-time (24 women); includes 3 minority (2 African Americans, 1 Hispanic American). Average age 40. *Faculty:* 5 part-time/adjunct (all women). Expenses: Contact institution. *Financial support:* Scholarships/grants available. Support available to part-time students. Financial award applicants required to submit FAFSA. In 2006, 16 master's, 7 other advanced degrees awarded. *Degree program information:* Part-time and evening/weekend programs available. Offers management (Certificate); nursing (MSN, Post-Master's Certificate). *Application deadline:* Applications are processed on a rolling basis. *Application fee:* $30 ($50 for international students). Electronic applications accepted. *Dean,* Dr. Janet Brown, 219-464-5289, Fax: 219-464-5425, E-mail: janet.brown@valpo.edu.

School of Law Students: 466 full-time (208 women), 54 part-time (24 women); includes 60 minority (24 African Americans, 1 American Indian/Alaska Native, 11 Asian Americans or Pacific Islanders, 24 Hispanic Americans), 12 international. Average age 24. 2,736 applicants, 30% accepted, 200 enrolled. *Faculty:* 36 full-time (16 women), 25 part-time/adjunct (11 women). Expenses: Contact institution. *Financial support:* In 2006–07, 470 students received support, including 23 research assistantships (averaging $500 per year), 10 teaching assistantships (averaging $2,000 per year); career-related internships or fieldwork, Federal Work-Study, institutionally sponsored loans, scholarships/grants, and tuition waivers (partial) also available. Support available to part-time students. Financial award application deadline: 3/1; financial award applicants required to submit FAFSA. In 2006, 160 JDs, 5 master's awarded. *Degree program information:* Part-time programs available. Offers law (JD, LL M). *Application deadline:* For fall admission, 4/15 priority date for domestic students. Applications are processed on a rolling basis. *Application fee:* $50. Electronic applications accepted. *Application Contact:* Tony O. Credit, Executive Director of Admissions, 219-465-7829, Fax: 219-465-7808, E-mail: tony.credit@valpo.edu. *Dean,* Jay Conison, 219-465-7834, Fax: 219-465-7872, E-mail: jay.conison@valpo.edu.

VANCOUVER SCHOOL OF THEOLOGY, Vancouver, BC V6T 1L4, Canada

General Information Independent-religious, coed, graduate-only institution. *Graduate housing:* Rooms and/or apartments guaranteed to single students and available to married students. Housing application deadline: 4/7.

GRADUATE UNITS

Graduate and Professional Programs Offers theology (M Div, MPS, MTS, Th M, D Min, Dip CS). Electronic applications accepted.

VANDERBILT UNIVERSITY, Nashville, TN 37240-1001

General Information Independent, coed, university. CGS member. *Enrollment:* 11,607 graduate, professional, and undergraduate students; 4,565 full-time matriculated graduate/professional students (2,360 women), 623 part-time matriculated graduate/professional students (407 women). *Enrollment by degree level:* 3,089 first professional, 271 master's, 1,828 doctoral. *Tuition:* Full-time $24,462. *Required fees:* $2,515. One-time fee: $30 full-time. Full-time tuition and fees vary according to course load, degree level and program. *Graduate housing:* On-campus housing not available. *Student services:* Campus employment opportunities, campus safety program, career counseling, child daycare facilities, disabled student services, exercise/wellness program, free psychological counseling, grant writing training, international student services, low-cost health insurance, multicultural affairs office, teacher training, writing training. *Library facilities:* Jean and Alexander Heard Library plus 7 others. *Collection:* 1.8 million titles, 26,885 serial subscriptions, 153,450 audiovisual materials. *Research affiliation:* General Motors Corporation (embedded systems and software infrastructure), Boeing Aerospace Corporation (software systems: fact integration), Raytheon Corporation (distributed real-time embedded infrastructure for command control), Osaka Gas Company (Japan) (intelligent process control system), Honda Motor Corporation (nanoparticles).

Computer facilities: 400 computers available on campus for general student use. A campuswide network can be accessed from student residence rooms and from off campus. Productivity and educational software available. *Web address:* http://www.vanderbilt.edu/.

General Application Contact: Walter B. Bieschke, Program Coordinator for Admissions, 615-343-6321, Fax: 615-343-6687, E-mail: vandygrad@vanderbilt.edu.

GRADUATE UNITS

Divinity School Students: 121 full-time (69 women), 33 part-time (18 women); includes 25 minority (all African Americans), 3 international. Average age 32. 188 applicants, 81% accepted, 81 enrolled. *Faculty:* 30 full-time (11 women), 9 part-time/adjunct (3 women). Expenses: Contact institution. *Financial support:* In 2006–07, 140 students received support. Career-related internships or fieldwork, Federal Work-Study, institutionally sponsored loans, and tuition waivers (full and partial) available. Support available to part-time students. Financial award application deadline: 5/1; financial award applicants required to submit CSS PROFILE or FAFSA. In 2006, 41 M Divs, 25 master's awarded. *Degree program information:* Part-time programs available. Offers divinity (M Div, MTS). *Application deadline:* For fall admission, 5/1 for domestic students, 4/1 for international students; for spring admission, 11/1 for domestic and international students. Applications are processed on a rolling basis. *Application fee:* $50. *Application Contact:* Robert Taylor Phillips, Director of Admissions, 615-343-3963, Fax: 615-322-6091, E-mail: robert.t.phillips@vanderbilt.edu. *Dean,* Dr. James Hudnut-Beumler, 615-322-2776, Fax: 615-343-9957, E-mail: james.hudnut-beumler@vanderbilt.edu.

Graduate School Students: 1,967 full-time (952 women), 132 part-time (62 women); includes 202 minority (109 African Americans, 13 American Indian/Alaska Native, 44 Asian Americans or Pacific Islanders, 36 Hispanic Americans), 566 international. Average age 30. 5,369 applicants, 16% accepted, 473 enrolled. *Faculty:* 951. Expenses: Contact institution. *Financial support:* Fellowships with full and partial tuition reimbursements, research assistantships with full tuition reimbursements, teaching assistantships with full tuition reimbursements, career-related internships or fieldwork, Federal Work-Study, institutionally sponsored loans, scholarships/grants, traineeships, health care benefits, tuition waivers (full and partial), and unspecified assistantships available. Support available to part-time students. In 2006, 234 master's, 232 doctorates awarded. *Degree program information:* Part-time programs available. Offers analytical chemistry (MAT, MS, PhD); anthropology (MA, PhD); astronomy (MS); biochemistry (MS, PhD); biological sciences (MS, PhD); biomedical informatics (MS, PhD); cancer biology (MS, PhD); cell and developmental biology (MS, PhD); cellular and molecular pathology (PhD); classics (MA); community research and action (MS, PhD); creative writing (MFA); earth and environmental sciences (MS); economic development (MA); economics (MA, MAT, PhD); English (MA, MAT, PhD); French (MA, MAT, PhD); German (MA, MAT, PhD); history (MA, MAT, PhD); inorganic chemistry (MAT, MS, PhD); Latin (MAT); Latin American studies (MA); leadership and policy studies (PhD); learning, teaching and diversity (MS, PhD); liberal arts and science (MLAS); mathematics (MA, MAT, MS, PhD); microbiology and immunology (MS, PhD); molecular physiology and biophysics (MS, PhD); neuroscience (PhD); nursing science (PhD); organic chemistry (MAT, MS, PhD); pharmacology (PhD); philosophy (MA, PhD); physical chemistry (MAT, MS, PhD); physics (MA, MAT, MS, PhD); political science (MA, MAT, PhD); Portuguese (MA); psychological sciences (MA, PhD); religion (MA, PhD); sociology (MA, PhD); Spanish (MA, MAT, PhD); Spanish and Portuguese

(PhD); special education (MS, PhD); theoretical chemistry (MAT, MS, PhD). *Application deadline:* For fall admission, 1/15 for domestic and international students. *Application fee:* $0. Electronic applications accepted. *Application Contact:* Walter B. Bieschke, Program Coordinator for Admissions, 615-343-6321, Fax: 615-343-6687, E-mail: vandygrad@vanderbilt.edu. *Associate Provost for Research and Graduate Education,* Dennis G. Hall, 615-322-2809, Fax: 615-343-9936, E-mail: dennis.g.hall@vanderbilt.edu.

Law School Students: 653 full-time (299 women); includes 116 minority (51 African Americans, 5 American Indian/Alaska Native, 41 Asian Americans or Pacific Islanders, 19 Hispanic Americans), 35 international. Average age 25. 3,640 applicants, 25% accepted, 190 enrolled. *Faculty:* 50 full-time (15 women), 70 part-time/adjunct (26 women). Expenses: Contact institution. *Financial support:* In 2006–07, 90 students received support. Career-related internships or fieldwork, Federal Work-Study, institutionally sponsored loans, and scholarships/grants available. Financial award application deadline: 2/15; financial award applicants required to submit FAFSA. In 2006, 203 JDs, 10 master's awarded. Offers law (JD, LL M); law and economics (PhD). *Application deadline:* For fall admission, 3/15 for domestic students. Applications are processed on a rolling basis. *Application fee:* $50. Electronic applications accepted. *Application Contact:* G. Todd Morton, Assistant Dean for Admissions, 615-322-6452, Fax: 615-322-1531. *Dean,* Edward L Rubin, 615-322-2615.

Owen Graduate School of Management Students: 479 full-time (116 women); includes 51 minority (20 African Americans, 2 American Indian/Alaska Native, 25 Asian Americans or Pacific Islanders, 4 Hispanic Americans), 120 international. Average age 28. 1,214 applicants, 38% accepted, 231 enrolled. *Faculty:* 46 full-time (8 women), 25 part-time/adjunct (4 women). Expenses: Contact institution. *Financial support:* In 2006–07, 210 students received support. Scholarships/grants and tuition waivers (full and partial) available. Financial award application deadline: 5/1; financial award applicants required to submit FAFSA. In 2006, 214 master's, 3 doctorates awarded. *Degree program information:* Evening/weekend programs available. Offers business administration (MBA); executive business administration (MBA); finance (PhD); management (MBA, MSF, PhD); marketing (PhD); operations management (PhD); organization studies (PhD). Students in the 5-year MBA program enter as undergraduate freshman. *Application deadline:* For fall admission, 11/15 priority date for domestic students; for winter admission, 3/15 priority date for domestic students; for spring admission, 5/15 for domestic students. Applications are processed on a rolling basis. *Application fee:* $100. Electronic applications accepted. *Application Contact:* Assistant Dean of Admissions and Career Management Services, 615-322-6469, Fax: 615-343-1175, E-mail: admissions@owen.vanderbilt.edu. *Dean,* Dr. James W. Bradford, 615-322-2316, Fax: 615-343-7110.

Peabody College Students: 347 full-time (284 women), 134 part-time (80 women); includes 64 minority (52 African Americans, 7 Asian Americans or Pacific Islanders, 5 Hispanic Americans), 21 international. Average age 29. 502 applicants, 62% accepted, 139 enrolled. *Faculty:* 114 full-time (55 women), 62 part-time/adjunct (38 women). Expenses: Contact institution. *Financial support:* In 2006–07, 303 students received support, including 115 fellowships with full and partial tuition reimbursements available, 153 research assistantships with full and partial tuition reimbursements available, 35 teaching assistantships with full and partial tuition reimbursements available; career-related internships or fieldwork, Federal Work-Study, institutionally sponsored loans, scholarships/grants, traineeships, tuition waivers (partial), and unspecified assistantships also available. Support available to part-time students. Financial award application deadline: 2/1; financial award applicants required to submit FAFSA. In 2006, 181 master's, 16 doctorates awarded. *Degree program information:* Part-time programs available. Offers child studies (M Ed); community development action (M Ed); curriculum and instructional leadership (M Ed); early childhood education (M Ed); early childhood leadership (Ed D); education (M Ed, MPP, Ed D); education policy (MPP); educational leadership and policy (Ed D); elementary education (M Ed); English education (M Ed); English language learners (M Ed); higher education (M Ed); higher education, leadership and policy (Ed D); human development counseling (M Ed); human resource development (M Ed); international education policy and management (M Ed); mathematics education (M Ed); organizational leadership (M Ed); reading education (M Ed); school administration (M Ed); science education (M Ed); secondary education (M Ed); special education (M Ed). *Application deadline:* For fall admission, 12/31 priority date for domestic and international students; for spring admission, 11/1 priority date for domestic and international students. Applications are processed on a rolling basis. *Application fee:* $0. Electronic applications accepted. *Application Contact:* Kimberly Brazil-Tanner, Recruitment Coordinator, 615-332-8410, Fax: 615-322-8401, E-mail: kim.brazil@vanderbilt.edu. *Dean,* Dr. Camilla P. Benbow, 615-322-8407, Fax: 615-322-8501, E-mail: camilla.benbow@vanderbilt.edu.

School of Engineering Students: 365 full-time (101 women), 18 part-time (2 women); includes 33 minority (10 African Americans, 2 American Indian/Alaska Native, 17 Asian Americans or Pacific Islanders, 4 Hispanic Americans), 174 international. Average age 27. 1,206 applicants, 15% accepted, 106 enrolled. *Faculty:* 124 full-time (22 women), 17 part-time/adjunct (2 women). Expenses: Contact institution. *Financial support:* Fellowships with full tuition reimbursements, research assistantships with full tuition reimbursements, teaching assistantships with full tuition reimbursements, career-related internships or fieldwork, Federal Work-Study, institutionally sponsored loans, scholarships/grants, traineeships, health care benefits, and tuition waivers (full and partial) available. Support available to part-time students. Financial award application deadline: 1/15; financial award applicants required to submit CSS PROFILE or FAFSA. In 2006, 40 doctorates awarded. *Degree program information:* Part-time programs available. Offers biomedical engineering (M Eng, MS, PhD); chemical engineering (M Eng, MS, PhD); civil engineering (M Eng, MS, PhD); computer science (M Eng, MS, PhD); electrical engineering (M Eng, MS, PhD); engineering (M Eng, MS, PhD); environmental engineering (M Eng, MS, PhD); environmental management (MS, PhD); materials science (M Eng, MS, PhD); mechanical engineering (M Eng, MS, PhD). MS and PhD offered through the Graduate School. *Application deadline:* For fall admission, 1/15 for domestic and international students; for spring admission, 11/1 for domestic and international students. *Application fee:* $0. Electronic applications accepted. *Application Contact:* Dr. George E. Cook, Associate Dean for Research and Graduate Studies, 615-322-2762, Fax: 615-343-8006, E-mail: george.e.cook@vanderbilt.edu. *Dean,* Dr. Kenneth F. Galloway, 615-322-0720, Fax: 615-343-8006, E-mail: kenneth.f.galloway@vanderbilt.edu.

School of Medicine Students: 895 full-time. Average age 22. 3,699 applicants, 7% accepted, 104 enrolled. *Faculty:* 1,346 full-time, 934 part-time/adjunct. Expenses: Contact institution. *Financial support:* In 2006–07, 333 students received support. Institutionally sponsored loans and scholarships/grants available. Financial award application deadline: 3/1; financial award applicants required to submit FAFSA. In 2006, 25 master's, 2 doctorates awarded. Offers audiology (Au D, PhD); biomedical and biological sciences (PhD); chemical and physical biology (PhD); clinical investigation (MS); education of the deaf (MED); hearing and speech sciences (MS); medical physics (MS); medicine (MED, MPH, MS, Au D, PhD); public health (MPH); speech-language-pathology (MS). *Application deadline:* For fall admission, 10/15 for domestic students. Applications are processed on a rolling basis. *Application fee:* $50. Electronic applications accepted. *Application Contact:* Dr. John A. Zic, Associate Dean for Admissions, 615-322-2145, Fax: 615-343-8397. *Dean,* Dr. Steven G. Gabbe, 615-322-5191, E-mail: steven.gabbe@vanderbilt.edu.

School of Nursing Students: 371 full-time (325 women), 206 part-time (180 women); includes 59 minority (38 African Americans, 2 American Indian/Alaska Native, 7 Asian Americans or Pacific Islanders, 12 Hispanic Americans). Average age 27. 611 applicants, 55% accepted, 308 enrolled. *Faculty:* 95 full-time (83 women), 432 part-time/adjunct (314 women). Expenses: Contact institution. *Financial support:* In 2006–07, 404 students received support, including 5 research assistantships (averaging $8,000 per year); Federal Work-Study, institutionally sponsored loans, and unspecified assistantships also available. Support available to part-time students. Financial award application deadline: 3/15; financial award applicants required to submit CSS PROFILE or FAFSA. In 2006, 256 master's, 2 doctorates awarded. *Degree program information:* Part-time and evening/weekend programs available. Postbaccalaureate distance learning degree programs offered (minimal on-campus study). Offers adult acute care nurse practitioner (MSN); adult health nurse practitioner/forensic (MSN); adult nurse practitioner/cardiovascular disease management and prevention (MSN); adult nurse practitioner/palliative care (MSN); clinical management (clinical nurse leader/specialist) (MSN); family nurse practitioner (MSN); gerontology nurse practitioner (MSN); health systems management (MSN); neonatal nurse practitioner (MSN); nurse midwifery (MSN); nursing informatics (MSN); nursing science (PhD); pediatric acute care nurse practitioner (MSN); pediatric primary care nurse practitioner (MSN); psychiatric-mental health nurse practitioner (MSN); women's health nurse practitioner (MSN). *Application deadline:* For fall admission, 12/1 priority date for domestic and international students. Applications are processed on a rolling basis. *Application fee:* $50. *Application Contact:* Cheryl Feldner, Assistant Director of Admissions, 615-322-3800, Fax: 615-343-0333, E-mail: cheryl.feldner@vanderbilt.edu. *Dean,* Dr. Colleen Conway-Welch, 615-343-8776, Fax: 615-343-7711, E-mail: colleen.conway-welch@vanderbilt.edu.

VANDERCOOK COLLEGE OF MUSIC, Chicago, IL 60616-3731

General Information Independent, coed, comprehensive institution. *Graduate housing:* Rooms and/or apartments available on a first-come, first-served basis to single and married students. Housing application deadline: 6/1.

GRADUATE UNITS

Program in Music Education *Degree program information:* Part-time programs available. Offers music education (MM Ed). Offered during summer only.

VANGUARD UNIVERSITY OF SOUTHERN CALIFORNIA, Costa Mesa, CA 92626-9601

General Information Independent-religious, coed, comprehensive institution. *Enrollment:* 2,146 graduate, professional, and undergraduate students; 120 full-time matriculated graduate/professional students (77 women), 172 part-time matriculated graduate/professional students (89 women). *Enrollment by degree level:* 292 master's. *Graduate faculty:* 16 full-time (7 women), 22 part-time/adjunct (13 women). *Graduate housing:* On-campus housing not available. *Student services:* Campus employment opportunities, career counseling, free psychological counseling, international student services, low-cost health insurance, teacher training. *Library facilities:* O. Cope Budge Library. *Online resources:* library catalog, web page, access to other libraries' catalogs. *Collection:* 157,500 titles, 2,000 serial subscriptions, 6,900 audiovisual materials.

Computer facilities: 150 computers available on campus for general student use. A campuswide network can be accessed from student residence rooms and from off campus. Internet access and online class registration, online registration for select programs are available. *Web address:* http://www.vanguard.edu/.

General Application Contact: Drake Levasheff, Director of Graduate Admissions, 714-966-5499, Fax: 714-966-5471, E-mail: dlevasheff@vanguard.edu.

GRADUATE UNITS

School of Business and Management Students: 17 full-time (6 women), 2 part-time (1 woman); includes 9 minority (2 African Americans, 4 Asian Americans or Pacific Islanders, 3 Hispanic Americans), 1 international. Average age 35. 17 applicants, 53% accepted, 8 enrolled. *Faculty:* 2 full-time (0 women), 4 part-time/adjunct (1 woman). Expenses: Contact institution. *Financial support:* Applicants required to submit FAFSA. In 2006, 12 degrees awarded. *Degree program information:* Part-time and evening/weekend programs available. Offers business and management (MBA). *Application deadline:* For fall admission, 4/1 priority date for domestic and international students; for spring admission, 10/1 priority date for domestic and international students. Applications are processed on a rolling basis. *Application fee:* $45. Electronic applications accepted. *Application Contact:* Jill Zeiger, Graduate Coordinator, 714-556-3610 Ext. 3704, Fax: 714-662-5228, E-mail: jzeiger@vanguard.edu. *Dean,* Dr. David Alford, 714-556-3610 Ext. 3701, Fax: 714-662-5228, E-mail: dalford@vanguard.edu.

School of Education Students: 46 full-time (32 women), 57 part-time (47 women); includes 22 minority (2 American Indian/Alaska Native, 8 Asian Americans or Pacific Islanders, 12 Hispanic Americans), 1 international. Average age 31. 77 applicants, 73% accepted, 42 enrolled. *Faculty:* 4 full-time (3 women), 9 part-time/adjunct (all women). Expenses: Contact institution. *Financial support:* In 2006–07, 103 students received support, including 3 teaching assistantships (averaging $417 per year); scholarships/grants and unspecified assistantships also available. Financial award application deadline: 3/2; financial award applicants required to submit FAFSA. In 2006, 20 degrees awarded. *Degree program information:* Evening/weekend programs available. Offers education (MA). *Application deadline:* For fall admission, 4/1 priority date for domestic and international students; for spring admission, 10/1 priority date for domestic and international students. Applications are processed on a rolling basis. *Application fee:* $45. Electronic applications accepted. *Application Contact:* Michelle Romo, Graduate Education Coordinator, 714-556-3610 Ext. 3302, Fax: 714-966-5495, E-mail: mromo@vanguard.edu. *Dean,* Dr. Jerry Ternes, 714-556-3610 Ext. 3303, Fax: 714-966-5495, E-mail: jternes@vanguard.edu.

School of Psychology Students: 43 full-time (34 women), 23 part-time (16 women); includes 17 minority (1 African American, 1 American Indian/Alaska Native, 2 Asian Americans or Pacific Islanders, 13 Hispanic Americans). Average age 30. 55 applicants, 56% accepted, 24 enrolled. *Faculty:* 3 full-time (all women), 6 part-time/adjunct (3 women). Expenses: Contact institution. *Financial support:* In 2006–07, 62 students received support, including 16 teaching assistantships (averaging $2,469 per year); scholarships/grants and unspecified assistantships also available. Financial award application deadline: 3/2; financial award applicants required to submit FAFSA. In 2006, 26 degrees awarded. *Degree program information:* Part-time and evening/weekend programs available. Offers clinical psychology (MS). *Application deadline:* For fall admission, 4/1 priority date for domestic and international students. Applications are processed on a rolling basis. *Application fee:* $45. Electronic applications accepted. *Application Contact:* Asha Begnell, Graduate Psychology Coordinator, 714-556-3610 Ext. 3550, Fax: 714-662-5226, E-mail: gradpsych@vanguard.edu. *Dean,* Dr. Jerre White, 714-556-3610 Ext. 3550, Fax: 714-662-5226, E-mail: jwhite@vanguard.edu.

School of Religion Students: 14 full-time (5 women), 90 part-time (25 women); includes 34 minority (3 African Americans, 2 American Indian/Alaska Native, 4 Asian Americans or Pacific Islanders, 25 Hispanic Americans), 5 international. Average age 38. 27 applicants, 89% accepted, 19 enrolled. *Faculty:* 7 full-time (1 woman), 3 part-time/adjunct (0 women). Expenses: Contact institution. *Financial support:* In 2006–07, 28 students received support, including 6 teaching assistantships (averaging $1,800 per year); scholarships/grants, tuition waivers (partial), and unspecified assistantships also available. Financial award application deadline: 3/2. In 2006, 22 degrees awarded. *Degree program information:* Part-time and evening/weekend programs available. Offers leadership studies (MA); religion (MA); theological studies (MTS). *Application deadline:* For fall admission, 4/1 priority date for domestic and international students; for spring admission, 10/1 priority date for domestic and international students. Applications are processed on a rolling basis. *Application fee:* $45. Electronic applications accepted. *Application Contact:* John Sim, Graduate Religion Coordinator, 714-556-3610 Ext. 3285, Fax: 714-957-9317, E-mail: jsim@vanguard.edu. *Dean,* April Westbrook, 714-556-3610 Ext. 3236, Fax: 714-957-9317, E-mail: awestbrook@vanguard.edu.

VASSAR COLLEGE, Poughkeepsie, NY 12604

General Information Independent, coed, comprehensive institution. *Enrollment:* 2,424 graduate, professional, and undergraduate students; 1 (woman) part-time matriculated graduate/professional student. *Tuition:* Full-time $35,520. *Graduate housing:* Room and/or apartments available to single students; on-campus housing not available to married students. Typical cost: $4,310 per year ($8,130 including board). *Student services:* Campus employment opportunities, campus safety program, career counseling, child daycare facilities, disabled student services, exercise/wellness program, free psychological counseling, international student services, low-cost health insurance, multicultural affairs office. *Library facilities:* Vassar College Libraries plus 1 other. *Online resources:* library catalog, web page, access to other libraries' catalogs. *Collection:* 886,097 titles, 5,302 serial subscriptions, 20,448 audiovisual materials. *Research affiliation:* Alfred P. Sloan Foundation (humanities, social sciences), Ford Program.

Computer facilities: Computer purchase and lease plans are available. 300 computers available on campus for general student use. A campuswide network can be accessed from student residence rooms and from off campus. Internet access and online class registration, ethernet are available. *Web address:* http://www.vassar.edu/.

Vassar College (continued)

General Application Contact: Alexander M. Thompson, Dean of Studies, 914-437-5257, E-mail: thompson@vassar.edu.

GRADUATE UNITS

Graduate Programs 1 applicant. Expenses: Contact institution. *Financial support:* Career-related internships or fieldwork available. *Degree program information:* Part-time programs available. Offers chemistry (MA, MS). Applicants accepted only if enrolled in undergraduate programs at Vassar College. *Application fee:* $60. *Dean of Studies,* Alexander M. Thompson, 914-437-5257, E-mail: thompson@vassar.edu.

VERMONT LAW SCHOOL, South Royalton, VT 05068-0096

General Information Independent, coed, graduate-only institution. *Enrollment by degree level:* 552 first professional. *Graduate faculty:* 48 full-time (23 women), 28 part-time/adjunct (12 women). *Graduate housing:* On-campus housing not available. *Student services:* Campus employment opportunities, campus safety program, career counseling, child daycare facilities, exercise/wellness program, free psychological counseling, low-cost health insurance, multicultural affairs office, writing training. *Library facilities:* Cornell Library. *Online resources:* library catalog, access to other libraries' catalogs. *Collection:* 245,105 titles, 1,837 serial subscriptions, 3,905 audiovisual materials.

Computer facilities: 54 computers available on campus for general student use. A campuswide network can be accessed from off campus. Internet access is available. *Web address:* http://www.vermontlaw.edu/.

General Application Contact: Kathy Hartman, Associate Dean for Enrollment Management, 802-831-1239, Fax: 802-763-7071, E-mail: admiss@vermontlaw.edu.

GRADUATE UNITS

Law School Students: 552 full-time (288 women); includes 79 minority (39 African Americans, 8 American Indian/Alaska Native, 15 Asian Americans or Pacific Islanders, 17 Hispanic Americans), 4 international. Average age 26. 1,119 applicants, 56% accepted, 202 enrolled. *Faculty:* 48 full-time (23 women), 28 part-time/adjunct (12 women). Expenses: Contact institution. *Financial support:* In 2006–07, 422 students received support, including 2 fellowships with full tuition reimbursements available (averaging $5,000 per year); career-related internships or fieldwork, Federal Work-Study, institutionally sponsored loans, scholarships/grants, and tuition waivers (partial) also available. Support available to part-time students. Financial award application deadline: 2/15; financial award applicants required to submit FAFSA. In 2006, 144 JDs, 82 master's awarded. *Degree program information:* Part-time programs available. Offers law (JD, LL M, MSEL). *Application deadline:* For fall admission, 3/15 priority date for domestic students. Applications are processed on a rolling basis. *Application fee:* $60. Electronic applications accepted. *Application Contact:* Kathy Hartman, Associate Dean for Enrollment Management, 802-831-1239, Fax: 802-763-7071, E-mail: admiss@vermontlaw.edu. *President and Dean,* Geoffrey B. Shields, 802-831-1237, Fax: 802-763-2663, E-mail: hmccarthy@vermontlaw.edu.

Environmental Law Center Students: 43 full-time (28 women), 5 part-time (4 women); includes 3 minority (2 Asian Americans or Pacific Islanders, 1 Hispanic American), 1 international. Average age 30. 74 applicants, 78% accepted, 30 enrolled. *Faculty:* 12 full-time (6 women), 8 part-time/adjunct (4 women). Expenses: Contact institution. *Financial support:* In 2006–07, 2 fellowships with full tuition reimbursements (averaging $5,000 per year) were awarded; career-related internships or fieldwork, Federal Work-Study, institutionally sponsored loans, scholarships/grants, and tuition waivers (partial) also available. Support available to part-time students. Financial award application deadline: 2/15; financial award applicants required to submit FAFSA. In 2006, 82 degrees awarded. *Degree program information:* Part-time programs available. Offers environmental law (LL M, MSEL). *Application deadline:* For fall admission, 3/15 priority date for domestic students. Applications are processed on a rolling basis. *Application fee:* $60. *Application Contact:* Anne Mansfield, Associate Director, 802-831-1338, Fax: 802-763-2940, E-mail: admiss@vermontlaw.edu. *Associate Dean,* Karin Sheldon, 802-831-1342, Fax: 802-763-2490, E-mail: admiss@vermontlaw.edu.

VICTORIA UNIVERSITY, Toronto, ON M5S 1K7, Canada

General Information Independent-religious, coed, graduate-only institution. *Enrollment by degree level:* 77 first professional, 35 master's, 48 doctoral, 13 other advanced degrees. *Graduate faculty:* 11 full-time (5 women), 7 part-time/adjunct (2 women). *Graduate tuition:* Tuition and fees charges are reported in Canadian dollars. *Tuition:* Part-time $435 Canadian dollars per course. *Required fees:* $159 Canadian dollars per course. Tuition and fees vary according to course load and program. *Graduate housing:* Rooms and/or apartments guaranteed to single students and available on a first-come, first-served basis to married students. Typical cost: $6,384 Canadian dollars per year ($8,424 Canadian dollars including board) for single students; $7,000 Canadian dollars per year for married students. Room and board charges vary according to board plan. Housing application deadline: 7/1. *Student services:* Campus employment opportunities, campus safety program, career counseling, disabled student services, free psychological counseling, international student services, writing training. *Library facilities:* Emmanuel Library plus 2 others. *Online resources:* library catalog, web page, access to other libraries' catalogs. *Collection:* 10 million titles, 65,000 serial subscriptions, 224,000 audiovisual materials.

Computer facilities: 110 computers available on campus for general student use. A campuswide network can be accessed from student residence rooms and from off campus. Internet access and online class registration are available. *Web address:* http://www.vicu.utoronto.ca/.

General Application Contact: Dr. Paul Scott Wilson, Director for Advanced Degree Studies, 416-585-4545, Fax: 416-585-4516, E-mail: paul.wilson@utoronto.ca.

GRADUATE UNITS

Emmanuel College Students: 94 full-time (39 women), 79 part-time (52 women); includes 21 minority (6 African Americans, 1 American Indian/Alaska Native, 9 Asian Americans or Pacific Islanders, 5 Hispanic Americans), 16 international. Average age 42. 59 applicants, 86% accepted, 38 enrolled. *Faculty:* 11 full-time (5 women), 7 part-time/adjunct (2 women). Expenses: Contact institution. *Financial support:* In 2006–07, 70 students received support, including 2 fellowships (averaging $11,000 per year), 13 teaching assistantships (averaging $11,000 per year); research assistantships, career-related internships or fieldwork, scholarships/grants, and bursaries, tutorships also available. Support available to part-time students. Financial award application deadline: 5/30. In 2006, 12 M Divs, 9 master's, 3 doctorates, 6 other advanced degrees awarded. *Degree program information:* Part-time programs available. Offers theology (M Div, MA, MPS, MRE, MTS, Th M, D Min, PhD, Th D, Certificate, Diploma, L Th). *Application deadline:* For fall admission, 6/30 for domestic students, 1/15 for international students; for winter admission, 11/30 for domestic students; for spring admission, 3/30 for domestic students. *Application fee:* $0. *Application Contact:* Wanda Chin, Registrar, 416-585-4538, Fax: 416-585-4516, E-mail: wanda.chin@utoronto.ca. *Principal,* Dr. S. Peter Wyatt, 416-585-4540, Fax: 416-585-4516, E-mail: peter.wyatt@utoronto.ca.

VILLA JULIE COLLEGE, Stevenson, MD 21153

General Information Independent, coed, comprehensive institution. *Enrollment:* 3,123 graduate, professional, and undergraduate students; 78 part-time matriculated graduate/professional students (33 women). *Enrollment by degree level:* 78 master's. *Graduate faculty:* 5 full-time (0 women), 6 part-time/adjunct (1 woman). *Tuition:* Full-time $16,020; part-time $450 per credit. *Required fees:* $1,000. *Graduate housing:* On-campus housing not available. *Student services:* Career counseling, international student services. *Library facilities:* Villa Julie College Library. *Online resources:* library catalog, web page, access to other libraries' catalogs. *Collection:* 81,802 titles, 1,058 serial subscriptions, 2,727 audiovisual materials.

Computer facilities: 300 computers available on campus for general student use. A campuswide network can be accessed from student residence rooms and from off campus. Internet access is available. *Web address:* http://www.vjc.edu/.

General Application Contact: Allison Jones, Assistant Director, Graduate Admissions, 410-486-7001, Fax: 443-352-4440, E-mail: adm-alli@mail.vjc.edu.

GRADUATE UNITS

Graduate and Professional Studies Programs Average age 35. *Faculty:* 5 full-time (0 women), 6 part-time/adjunct (1 woman). Expenses: Contact institution. In 2006, 20 degrees awarded. *Degree program information:* Part-time and evening/weekend programs available. Offers advanced information technologies (MS); business and technology management (MS); forensic accounting (MS); forensic legal professional (MS); forensic science (MS); information technology (MS); interdisciplinary track (MS); investigations (MS). *Application deadline:* For fall admission, 8/1 for domestic students; for spring admission, 12/31 for domestic students. Applications are processed on a rolling basis. *Application fee:* $25. *Application Contact:* Jessica Kozera, Director of Transfer, Graduate and Adult Admissions, 443-352-4403, E-mail: adm-jess@mail.vjc.edu. *Assistant Director, Graduate Admissions,* Allison Jones, 410-486-7001, Fax: 443-352-4440, E-mail: adm-alli@mail.vjc.edu.

VILLANOVA UNIVERSITY, Villanova, PA 19085-1699

General Information Independent-religious, coed, comprehensive institution. CGS member. *Enrollment:* 10,456 graduate, professional, and undergraduate students; 1,412 full-time matriculated graduate/professional students (687 women), 1,650 part-time matriculated graduate/professional students (756 women). *Enrollment by degree level:* 729 first professional, 2,173 master's, 71 doctoral, 89 other advanced degrees. *Graduate faculty:* 250. *Tuition:* Part-time $565 per credit. *Graduate housing:* On-campus housing not available. *Student services:* Career counseling, disabled student services, free psychological counseling, international student services, low-cost health insurance, multicultural affairs office. *Library facilities:* Falvey Library plus 2 others. *Online resources:* library catalog, web page, access to other libraries' catalogs. *Collection:* 712,000 titles, 12,000 serial subscriptions, 8,000 audiovisual materials.

Computer facilities: Computer purchase and lease plans are available. 3,711 computers available on campus for general student use. A campuswide network can be accessed from student residence rooms and from off campus. Internet access and online class registration are available. *Web address:* http://www.villanova.edu/.

General Application Contact: Dr. Gerald Long, Dean, Graduate School of Liberal Arts and Sciences, 610-519-7090, Fax: 610-519-7096.

GRADUATE UNITS

College of Engineering Students: 99 full-time (17 women), 267 part-time (69 women); includes 19 minority (5 African Americans, 11 Asian Americans or Pacific Islanders, 3 Hispanic Americans), 76 international. Average age 26. 181 applicants, 66% accepted, 88 enrolled. *Faculty:* 46 full-time (6 women), 10 part-time/adjunct (0 women). Expenses: Contact institution. *Financial support:* In 2006–07, 45 research assistantships with full tuition reimbursements (averaging $12,165 per year) were awarded; Federal Work-Study, scholarships/grants, tuition waivers (full and partial), and unspecified assistantships also available. Support available to part-time students. In 2006, 82 degrees awarded. *Degree program information:* Part-time and evening/weekend programs available. Postbaccalaureate distance learning degree programs offered (minimal on-campus study). Offers chemical engineering (MSChE); civil engineering (MSCE); communications systems (Certificate); composite engineering (Certificate); computer architecture (Certificate); computer engineering (MSCE, Certificate); electrical engineering (MSEE, Certificate); electrical power systems (Certificate); electro-mechanical systems (Certificate); engineering (MSCE, MSChE, MSEE, MSME, MSTE, MSWREE, PhD, Certificate); high frequency systems (Certificate); intelligent systems (Certificate); machinery dynamics (Certificate); manufacturing (Certificate); mechanical engineering (MSME); thermofluid systems (Certificate); transportation engineering (MSTE); water resources and environmental engineering (MSWREE); wireless and digital communications (Certificate). *Application deadline:* For fall admission, 8/1 priority date for domestic students, 4/1 priority date for international students; for spring admission, 12/1 for domestic students, 10/1 for international students. Applications are processed on a rolling basis. *Application fee:* $50. Electronic applications accepted. *Application Contact:* Engineering Graduate Admissions Office, 610-519-5840, Fax: 610-519-4941, E-mail: engineering.grad@villanova.edu. *Dean,* Dr. Gary A. Gabriele, 610-519-4940, Fax: 610-519-5859, E-mail: gary.gabriele@villanova.edu.

College of Nursing Students: 41 full-time (27 women), 164 part-time (128 women); includes 17 minority (8 African Americans, 1 American Indian/Alaska Native, 8 Asian Americans or Pacific Islanders), 6 international. Average age 31. 137 applicants, 50% accepted, 48 enrolled. *Faculty:* 14 full-time (all women), 2 part-time/adjunct (both women). Expenses: Contact institution. *Financial support:* In 2006–07, 50 students received support, including 4 teaching assistantships with full tuition reimbursements available (averaging $12,165 per year); institutionally sponsored loans, scholarships/grants, traineeships, and tuition waivers (full) also available. Financial award application deadline: 3/1; financial award applicants required to submit FAFSA. In 2006, 47 degrees awarded. *Degree program information:* Part-time programs available. Postbaccalaureate distance learning degree programs offered (minimal on-campus study). Offers adult nurse practitioner (MSN, Post Master's Certificate); clinical case management (MSN, Post Master's Certificate); geriatric nurse practitioner (MSN, Post Master's Certificate); health care administration (MSN); nurse anesthetist (MSN, Post Master's Certificate); nursing (PhD); nursing education (MSN, Post Master's Certificate); pediatric nurse practitioner (MSN, Post Master's Certificate). *Application deadline:* For fall admission, 7/1 priority date for domestic students, 7/1 for international students; for spring admission, 12/1 priority date for domestic students, 12/1 for international students. Applications are processed on a rolling basis. *Application fee:* $50. *Assistant Dean and Director, Graduate Program,* Dr. Marguerite K. Schlag, 610-519-4907, Fax: 610-519-7650, E-mail: marguerite.schlag@villanova.edu.

Graduate School of Liberal Arts and Sciences Students: 409 full-time (230 women), 565 part-time (335 women); includes 81 minority (26 African Americans, 2 American Indian/Alaska Native, 32 Asian Americans or Pacific Islanders, 21 Hispanic Americans), 108 international. Average age 28. 940 applicants. *Faculty:* 122 full-time (46 women), 39 part-time/adjunct (13 women). Expenses: Contact institution. *Financial support:* Research assistantships, teaching assistantships, career-related internships or fieldwork, Federal Work-Study, scholarships/grants, and unspecified assistantships available. Support available to part-time students. Financial award applicants required to submit FAFSA. In 2006, 390 master's, 6 doctorates awarded. *Degree program information:* Part-time and evening/weekend programs available. Offers applied statistics (MS); biology (MA, MS); chemistry (MS); classics (MA); communication (MA); community counseling (MS); computing sciences (MS); counseling and human relations (MS); criminal justice administration (MS); educational leadership (MA); elementary school counseling (MS); elementary teacher education (MA); English (MA); Hispanic studies (MA); history (MA); human resource development (MS); liberal arts and sciences (MA, MPA, MS, PhD); liberal studies (MA); mathematical sciences (MA); philosophy (PhD); political science (MA); psychology (MS); public administration (MPA); secondary school counseling (MS); secondary teacher education (MA); theatre (MA); theology (MA). *Application deadline:* For fall admission, 8/1 for domestic and international students; for spring admission, 12/1 for domestic and international students. Applications are processed on a rolling basis. *Application fee:* $50. Electronic applications accepted. *Dean,* Dr. Gerald Long, 610-519-7090, Fax: 610-519-7096.

School of Law Students: 741 full-time (355 women), 66 part-time (25 women); includes 132 minority (40 African Americans, 4 American Indian/Alaska Native, 58 Asian Americans or Pacific Islanders, 30 Hispanic Americans), 8 international. Average age 25. 2,894 applicants, 37% accepted, 269 enrolled. *Faculty:* 47 full-time (22 women), 124 part-time/adjunct (33 women). Expenses: Contact institution. *Financial support:* In 2006–07, 273 students received support, including 91 research assistantships, 13 teaching assistantships; career-related internships or fieldwork, Federal Work-Study, institutionally sponsored loans, and scholarships/grants also available. Support available to part-time students. Financial award application deadline: 3/15; financial award applicants required to submit FAFSA. In 2006, 259 JDs, 32 master's awarded. Offers law (JD, LL M); tax (LL M). *Application deadline:* For fall admission, 3/1 for domestic and international students. Applications are processed on a rolling basis. *Application fee:* $75. Electronic applications accepted. *Application Contact:* Noe Bernal, Assistant Dean for Admissions, 610-519-7010, Fax: 610-519-6291, E-mail: admissions@law.villanova.edu. *Dean,* Mark A. Sargent, 610-519-7007, Fax: 610-519-6472.

Villanova School of Business Students: 695 (201 women); includes 70 minority (15 African Americans, 2 American Indian/Alaska Native, 45 Asian Americans or Pacific Islanders, 8 Hispanic Americans). Average age 32. *Faculty:* 95 full-time, 61 part-time/adjunct. Expenses: Contact institution. *Financial support:* In 2006–07, 19 research assistantships with tuition reimbursements (averaging $12,165 per year) were awarded. Support available to part-time students. Financial award application deadline: 3/31. *Degree program information:* Part-time and evening/weekend programs available. Offers accountancy (M Ac); business (EMBA, M Ac, MBA, MS, MTM); business administration (MBA); executive business administration (EMBA); finance (MS); technology management (MTM). *Application deadline:* Applications are processed on a rolling basis. *Application fee:* $50. Electronic applications accepted. *Application Contact:* Simone L. Pollard, Director of Graduate Business, 610-519-4336, Fax: 610-519-6273, E-mail: simone.pollard@villanova.edu. *Dean,* James M. Danko, 610-519-4331, Fax: 610-519-7864, E-mail: james.danko@villanova.edu.

See Close-Up on page 1133.

VIRGINIA COLLEGE AT BIRMINGHAM, Birmingham, AL 35209

General Information Proprietary, coed, comprehensive institution. *Graduate faculty:* 200. *Student services:* Campus employment opportunities, campus safety program, career counseling, teacher training, writing training. *Library facilities:* Elma Bell Library plus 2 others. *Online resources:* library catalog. *Collection:* 3,900 titles, 120 serial subscriptions, 40 audiovisual materials.

Computer facilities: 80 computers available on campus for general student use. A campuswide network can be accessed. *Web address:* http://www.vc.edu/.

General Application Contact: Joe Rogalski, Director of Admissions, 205-802-1200, E-mail: admissions@vc.edu.

GRADUATE UNITS

Program in Business Administration Expenses: Contact institution. *Financial support:* Career-related internships or fieldwork, Federal Work-Study, institutionally sponsored loans, and scholarships/grants available. Support available to part-time students. *Degree program information:* Part-time and evening/weekend programs available. Postbaccalaureate distance learning degree programs offered (no on-campus study). Offers business administration (MBA). *Application Contact:* Joe Rogalski, Vice President of Admissions, 205-802-1200, E-mail: admissions@vc.edu. *Unit Head,* Mike Largent, 877-812-8428, E-mail: admissions@vc.edu.

Virginia College Online Expenses: Contact institution. *Degree program information:* Part-time and evening/weekend programs available. Postbaccalaureate distance learning degree programs offered (no on-campus study). Offers business administration (MBA); criminal justice (MCJ); cybersecurity (MC). *Application Contact:* Darrel Hanbury, Director of Admissions, 888-827-7770, E-mail: vcoadm@vc.edu. *President, Virginia College Online,* Stan Banks, 888-827-7770, E-mail: vcadm@vc.edu.

VIRGINIA COMMONWEALTH UNIVERSITY, Richmond, VA 23284-9005

General Information State-supported, coed, university. CGS member. *Enrollment:* 30,381 graduate, professional, and undergraduate students; 2,792 full-time matriculated graduate/professional students (1,819 women), 2,247 part-time matriculated graduate/professional students (1,471 women). *Enrollment by degree level:* 4,004 master's, 1,035 doctoral. *Graduate faculty:* 1,012 full-time. *Graduate housing:* Room and/or apartments available on a first-come, first-served basis to single students; on-campus housing not available to married students. Typical cost: $4,171 per year ($5,666 including board). Room and board charges vary according to board plan and housing facility selected. *Student services:* Campus employment opportunities, campus safety program, career counseling, child daycare facilities, disabled student services, exercise/wellness program, free psychological counseling, grant writing training, international student services, low-cost health insurance, multicultural affairs office, teacher training, writing training. *Library facilities:* Virginia Commonwealth University Libraries plus 6 others. *Online resources:* library catalog, web page, access to other libraries' catalogs. *Collection:* 1.9 million titles, 18,000 serial subscriptions. *Research affiliation:* Center for Innovative Technology (biotechnology), Virginia Biotechnology Research Park.

Computer facilities: 400 computers available on campus for general student use. A campuswide network can be accessed from student residence rooms and from off campus. Internet access and online class registration are available. *Web address:* http://www.vcu.edu/.

General Application Contact: Dr. Mark J. Schaefermeyer, Director of Admissions and Recruitment, 804-828-4696, Fax: 804-828-6949, E-mail: mjschaeferme@vcu.edu.

GRADUATE UNITS

Center for the Study of Biological Complexity Offers bioinformatics (MB, MS).

Graduate School Students: 4,299 full-time (2,602 women), 4,585 part-time (3,133 women); includes 1,745 minority (1,022 African Americans, 29 American Indian/Alaska Native, 563 Asian Americans or Pacific Islanders, 131 Hispanic Americans). 4,868 applicants, 58% accepted, 2039 enrolled. *Faculty:* 1,012. Expenses: Contact institution. *Financial support:* Fellowships, research assistantships, teaching assistantships, career-related internships or fieldwork, Federal Work-Study, institutionally sponsored loans, scholarships/grants, and tuition waivers (full and partial) available. Support available to part-time students. Financial award applicants required to submit FAFSA. In 2006, 388 first professional degrees, 1,623 master's, 128 doctorates, 271 other advanced degrees awarded. *Degree program information:* Part-time and evening/weekend programs available. Offers integrative life sciences (PhD); interdisciplinary studies (MIS). *Application fee:* $50. Electronic applications accepted. *Application Contact:* Dr. Sherry T. Sandkam, Associate Dean, 804-828-6916, Fax: 804-827-4546, E-mail: ssandkam@vcu.edu. *Dean, Graduate School,* Dr. F. Douglas Boudinot, 804-828-2233, Fax: 804-827-0724, E-mail: fdboudinot@vcu.edu.

College of Humanities and Sciences Students: 700 full-time (414 women), 444 part-time (262 women); includes 235 minority (160 African Americans, 9 American Indian/Alaska Native, 42 Asian Americans or Pacific Islanders, 24 Hispanic Americans), 96 international. 1,510 applicants, 42% accepted, 435 enrolled. Expenses: Contact institution. *Financial support:* Fellowships, research assistantships, teaching assistantships, career-related internships or fieldwork, Federal Work-Study, institutionally sponsored loans, scholarships/grants, and tuition waivers (full and partial) available. Support available to part-time students. In 2006, 235 master's, 29 doctorates, 14 other advanced degrees awarded. *Degree program information:* Part-time and evening/weekend programs available. Offers account management (MS); account planning (MS); analytical chemistry (MS, PhD); applied mathematics (MS); applied physics (MS); applied social research (CASR); art direction (MS); biology (MS); chemical physics (PhD); clinical psychology (PhD); community revitalization planning (MURP); copywriting (MS); counseling psychology (PhD); creative brand management (MS); creative media planning (MS); creative writing (MFA); criminal justice (MS, CCJA); environmental communication (MIS); environmental health (MIS); environmental planning (MURP); environmental policy (MIS); environmental sciences (MIS); forensic science (MS); gender violence intervention (Certificate); general psychology (PhD); geographic information systems (Certificate); historic preservation planning (Certificate); history (MA); homeland security and emergency preparedness (MA, Graduate Certificate); humanities and sciences (MA, MFA, MIS, MPA, MS, MURP, PhD, CASR, CCJA, CPM, CURP, Certificate); inorganic chemistry (MS, PhD); international development planning (MURP); literature (MA); mass communications (MS, PhD); mathematics (MS); media, art, and text (PhD); medical physics (MS, PhD); metropolitan planning (MURP); nonprofit management (Graduate Certificate); operations research (MS); organic chemistry (MS, PhD); physical chemistry (MS, PhD); physics (MS); planning information systems (Certificate); planning management (MURP); political science and public administration (MPA); public management (CPM); public policy and administration (PhD); scholastic journalism (MS); sociology (MS); statistical sciences and operations research (MS, Certificate); strategic public relations (MS); urban planning (MURP); urban revitalization (CURP); writing and rhetoric (MA). *Application fee:* $50. *Dean,* Dr. Robert D. Holsworth, 804-828-1674.

School of Allied Health Professions Students: 157 full-time (59 women), 370 part-time (320 women); includes 108 minority (75 African Americans, 2 American Indian/Alaska Native, 24 Asian Americans or Pacific Islanders, 7 Hispanic Americans), 7 international. 416 applicants, 56% accepted, 168 enrolled. *Faculty:* 61 full-time (30 women). Expenses: Contact institution. *Financial support:* Fellowships, research assistantships, teaching assistantships, career-related internships or fieldwork and tuition waivers (full and partial) available. In 2006, 108 master's, 60 doctorates, 23 other advanced degrees awarded. *Degree program information:* Part-time programs available. Offers advanced physical therapy (MS); aging studies (CAS); allied health professions (MHA, MS, MSHA, MSNA, MSOT, PhD, CAS, CPC); anatomy and neurobiology (PhD); clinical laboratory sciences (PhD); entry-level physical therapy (MS); gerontology (MS, PhD); health administration (MHA, MSHA, PhD); health related sciences (PhD); health services organization and research (PhD); nurse anesthesia (PhD); occupational therapy (PhD); patient counseling (MS, CPC); physical therapy (PhD); physiology (PhD); radiation sciences (PhD); rehabilitation counseling (MS, CPC); rehabilitation leadership (PhD). *Application fee:* $50. *Application Contact:* Monica L. White, Director of Student Services, 804-828-3273, Fax: 804-828-8656, E-mail: mlwhite1@vcu.edu. *Dean,* Dr. Cecil B. Drain, 804-828-7247, Fax: 804-828-8656, E-mail: cbdrain@vcu.edu.

School of Business 424 applicants, 61% accepted, 171 enrolled. Expenses: Contact institution. *Financial support:* Fellowships, research assistantships, teaching assistantships, Federal Work-Study, institutionally sponsored loans, and tuition waivers (full and partial) available. Support available to part-time students. Financial award application deadline: 3/15. In 2006, 168 master's, 7 doctorates, 5 other advanced degrees awarded. *Degree program information:* Part-time and evening/weekend programs available. Offers accountancy (M Acc, MBA, MS, PhD); accounting (M Acc, MBA, MS, PhD); business administration (MBA, PhD); decision sciences (MBA, MS); economics (MA, MBA, MS); finance, insurance, and real estate (MS); information systems (MS, PhD); management (Certificate); marketing and business law (Certificate); real estate and urban land development (MS, Certificate); tax (MS); taxation (M Tax). *Application deadline:* Applications are processed on a rolling basis. *Application fee:* $50. *Application Contact:* Tracy Green, Graduate Program Director, 804-828-1741, Fax: 804-828-7174, E-mail: tsgreen@vcu.edu. *Dean,* Dr. Michael L. Sesnowitz, 804-827-0072, Fax: 804-828-1600, E-mail: msesnowi@vcu.edu.

School of Education Students: 324 full-time (252 women), 660 part-time (487 women); includes 195 minority (176 African Americans, 8 American Indian/Alaska Native, 5 Asian Americans or Pacific Islanders, 6 Hispanic Americans), 36 international. 551 applicants, 74% accepted, 326 enrolled. Expenses: Contact institution. *Financial support:* Fellowships, research assistantships, teaching assistantships, career-related internships or fieldwork, Federal Work-Study, institutionally sponsored loans, and tuition waivers (full and partial) available. Support available to part-time students. Financial award application deadline:3/1. In 2006, 276 master's, 13 doctorates, 39 other advanced degrees awarded. *Degree program information:* Part-time programs available. Offers adult literacy (M Ed); adults with disabilities (M Ed); athletic training (MS); counselor education (M Ed); curriculum and instruction (M Ed); early childhood (M Ed); early education (MT); education (M Ed, MS, MT, PhD, Certificate); educational leadership (PhD); emotionally disturbed (M Ed, MT); exercise science (MS); human resource development (M Ed); instructional leadership (PhD); learning disabilities (M Ed); mentally retarded (M Ed, MT); middle education (MT); reading (M Ed); recreation, parks and sports leadership (MS); rehabilitation and movement science (PhD); research and evaluation (PhD); secondary education (MT, Certificate); severely/profoundly handicapped (M Ed); special education (MT); teacher education (MS); urban services leadership (PhD). *Application fee:* $50. *Application Contact:* Dr. Michael D. Davis, Director, Graduate Studies, 804-828-6530, Fax: 804-827-0676, E-mail: mddavis@vcu.edu. *Chair,* Dr. Beverly Warren, 804-828-3382, Fax: 804-828-1946, E-mail: bjwarren@vcu.edu.

School of Engineering Students: 108 full-time (30 women), 71 part-time (22 women); includes 37 minority (14 African Americans, 19 Asian Americans or Pacific Islanders, 4 Hispanic Americans), 66 international. 191 applicants, 62% accepted, 51 enrolled. *Faculty:* 50 full-time (8 women). Expenses: Contact institution. In 2006, 26 master's, 3 doctorates awarded. Offers biomedical engineering (MS, PhD); chemical and life science engineering (MS, PhD); computer science (MS, PhD, Certificate); electrical engineering (MS, PhD); engineering (PhD); mechanical engineering (MS, PhD). *Application deadline:* For fall admission, 2/15 for domestic students; for spring admission, 11/15 for domestic students. *Application fee:* $50. *Application Contact:* Dr. L. Thomas Overby, Associate Dean for Graduate Affairs, 804-828-3925, E-mail: ltoverby@vcu.edu. *Dean,* Dr. Russell Jamison, 804-828-0190, Fax: 804-828-9866, E-mail: rjamison@vcu.edu.

School of Nursing Students: 131 full-time (125 women), 137 part-time (129 women); includes 33 minority (19 African Americans, 11 Asian Americans or Pacific Islanders, 3 Hispanic Americans), 12 international. 110 applicants, 82% accepted, 66 enrolled. *Faculty:* 23 full-time (21 women). Expenses: Contact institution. *Financial support:* Fellowships, research assistantships, teaching assistantships, career-related internships or fieldwork and institutionally sponsored loans available. In 2006, 57 master's, 1 doctorate, 3 other advanced degrees awarded. *Degree program information:* Part-time and evening/weekend programs available. Offers adult health nursing (MS); child health nursing (MS); family health nursing (MS); health system (PhD); immunocompetence (PhD); nurse practitioner (MS, Certificate); nursing administration (MS); psychiatric-mental health nursing (MS); risk and resilience (PhD); women's health nursing (MS). *Application deadline:* For fall admission, 2/1 priority date for domestic students. *Application fee:* $50. *Application Contact:* Susan Lipp, Admissions Counselor, 804-828-5171, Fax: 804-828-7743, E-mail: slipp@vcu.edu. *Dean,* Dr. Nancy F. Langston, 804-828-5174, Fax: 804-828-7743, E-mail: nflangst@vcu.edu.

School of Social Work Students: 309 full-time (275 women), 220 part-time (184 women); includes 139 minority (110 African Americans, 1 American Indian/Alaska Native, 15 Asian Americans or Pacific Islanders, 13 Hispanic Americans), 14 international. 464 applicants, 84% accepted. *Faculty:* 33 full-time (20 women). Expenses: Contact institution. *Financial support:* Fellowships, research assistantships, teaching assistantships, career-related internships or fieldwork, Federal Work-Study, institutionally sponsored loans, and tuition waivers (full and partial) available. Support available to part-time students. In 2006, 171 master's, 6 doctorates awarded. Offers social work (MSW, PhD). *Application fee:* $50. *Application Contact:* Joseph M. Mason, Associate Dean, 804-828-0703, Fax: 804-828-0716, E-mail: jamasonl@vcu.edu. *Dean,* Dr. Frank R. Baskind, 804-828-1030, Fax: 804-828-0716, E-mail: fbaskind@saturn.vcu.edu.

School of the Arts Students: 170 full-time (107 women), 125 part-time (93 women); includes 16 minority (6 African Americans, 1 American Indian/Alaska Native, 2 Asian Americans or Pacific Islanders, 7 Hispanic Americans), 17 international. 642 applicants, 22% accepted, 82 enrolled. *Faculty:* 91 full-time (22 women). Expenses: Contact institution. *Financial support:* Fellowships, teaching assistantships, career-related internships or fieldwork, Federal Work-Study, institutionally sponsored loans, and tuition waivers (full and partial) available. Support available to part-time students. In 2006, 103 master's, 4 doctorates awarded. *Degree program information:* Part-time programs available. Offers acting (MFA); architectural history (MA); art education (MAE); art history (MA, PhD); arts (MA, MAE, MFA, MM, PhD); ceramics (MFA); costume design (MFA); design/visual communications (MFA); directing (MFA); education (MM); fibers (MFA); furniture design (MFA); glassworking (MFA); historical studies (MA); interior environment (MFA); jewelry/metalworking (MFA); kinetic imaging (MFA); museum studies (MA); painting (MFA); pedagogy (MFA); photography and film (MFA); printmaking (MFA); scene design/technical theater (MFA); sculpture (MFA). *Application fee:* $50. *Dean,* Dr. Richard E. Toscan, 804-828-2787, Fax: 804-828-6469, E-mail: rtoscan@vcu.edu.

Medical College of Virginia-Professional Programs Students: 1,079 full-time (590 women), 101 part-time (41 women); includes 222 minority (90 African Americans, 3 American Indian/Alaska Native, 104 Asian Americans or Pacific Islanders, 25 Hispanic Americans), 74 international. 1,131 applicants, 59% accepted, 398 enrolled. Expenses: Contact institution. *Financial support:* Fellowships, research assistantships, teaching assistantships, career-related internships or fieldwork, Federal Work-Study, institutionally sponsored loans, and tuition waivers (full and partial) available. In 2006, 241 MDs, 67 master's, 29 doctorates awarded. *Degree program information:* Part-time programs available. Offers medicine

Virginia Commonwealth University (continued)

(DDS, MD, Pharm D, MPH, MS, PhD). *Application deadline:* Applications are processed on a rolling basis. *Application fee:* $50. Electronic applications accepted. *Vice President for Health Sciences,* Dr. Sheldin M. Retchin, 804-828-9771, Fax: 804-828-8002, E-mail: retchin@mcvh-vcu.edu.

School of Dentistry Students: 397 full-time (134 women); includes 78 minority (14 African Americans, 1 American Indian/Alaska Native, 55 Asian Americans or Pacific Islanders, 8 Hispanic Americans), 19 international. 122 applicants, 98% accepted, 109 enrolled. *Faculty:* 46 full-time (7 women). Expenses: Contact institution. *Financial support:* Fellowships available. In 2006, 85 DDSs awarded. Offers dentistry (DDS). *Application deadline:* For fall admission, 1/1 for domestic students. Electronic applications accepted. *Application Contact:* Dr. Carolyn L. Booker, Assistant Dean of Student Affairs and Admissions, 804-828-9953, Fax: 804-828-5288, E-mail: clbooker@vcu.edu. *Dean,* Dr. Ronald J. Hunt, 804-828-9184, Fax: 804-828-6072, E-mail: rjhunt@vcu.edu.

School of Medicine *Faculty:* 211 full-time (56 women). Expenses: Contact institution. *Financial support:* Fellowships, research assistantships, teaching assistantships, career-related internships or fieldwork, Federal Work-Study, institutionally sponsored loans, and tuition waivers (full and partial) available. Offers anatomy (MS, PhD); anatomy and physical therapy (PhD); biochemistry (MS, PhD); biostatistics (MS, PhD); epidemiology and community health (PhD); genetic counseling (MS); human genetics (PhD); medicine (MD, MPH, MS, PhD); microbiology and genetics (MS); microbiology and immunology (MS, PhD); molecular biology and genetics (MS, PhD); neuroscience (MS, PhD); pathology (MS, PhD); pharmacology (PhD); pharmacology and toxicology (MS); physiology (MS, PhD); public health (MPH). *Application deadline:* For fall admission, 11/15 for domestic students. Applications are processed on a rolling basis. Electronic applications accepted. *Application Contact:* Dr. Cynthia M. Heldberg, Associate Dean, Admissions, 804-828-9629, Fax: 804-828-1246, E-mail: cmheldbe@vcu.edu. *Dean,* Dr. Jerome F. Strauss, 804-828-9788.

School of Pharmacy Students: 513 full-time (336 women), 56 part-time (27 women); includes 152 minority (42 African Americans, 1 American Indian/Alaska Native, 102 Asian Americans or Pacific Islanders, 7 Hispanic Americans), 43 international. 1,902 applicants, 7% accepted, 129 enrolled. *Faculty:* 18 full-time (5 women). Expenses: Contact institution. *Financial support:* Fellowships, research assistantships, teaching assistantships, institutionally sponsored loans available. Financial award application deadline: 3/1. In 2006, 105 first professional degrees, 4 master's, 10 doctorates awarded. *Degree program information:* Part-time programs available. Offers pharmaceutics (Pharm D, MS, PhD); pharmacy (Pharm D, MS, PhD). *Application deadline:* For fall admission, 6/1 for domestic students. Applications are processed on a rolling basis. *Application fee:* $30. *Application Contact:* Dr. Howard T. Karnes, Associate Dean, 804-828-3819, Fax: 804-828-7436, E-mail: htkarnes@vcu.edu. *Dean,* Dr. Victor A. Yanchick, 804-828-3006, Fax: 804-827-0002, E-mail: vayanchi@vcu.edu.

See Close-Up on page 1135.

VIRGINIA POLYTECHNIC INSTITUTE AND STATE UNIVERSITY, Blacksburg, VA 24061

General Information State-supported, coed, university. CGS member. *Enrollment:* 28,470 graduate, professional, and undergraduate students; 4,199 full-time matriculated graduate/professional students (1,818 women), 2,274 part-time matriculated graduate/professional students (1,037 women). *Enrollment by degree level:* 362 first professional, 3,662 master's, 2,449 doctoral. *Graduate faculty:* 1,581 full-time (440 women), 18 part-time/adjunct (11 women). *International tuition:* $11,296 full-time. Tuition, state resident: full-time $7,017; part-time $390 per credit hour. Tuition, nonresident: full-time $12,414; part-time $690 per credit hour. *Required fees:* $1,523; $256 per term. *Graduate housing:* Room and/or apartments available on a first-come, first-served basis to single students; on-campus housing not available to married students. Typical cost: $3,962 per year ($1,088 including board). Housing application deadline: 5/16. *Student services:* Campus employment opportunities, career counseling, disabled student services, free psychological counseling, international student services, low-cost health insurance, multicultural affairs office. *Library facilities:* Newman Library plus 4 others. *Online resources:* library catalog, web page. *Collection:* 2.3 million titles, 33,874 serial subscriptions, 26,253 audiovisual materials. *Research affiliation:* VCOM-Virginia College of Osteopathic Medicine (biomedical engineering and sciences), Carillion Biomedical (biomedical engineering and sciences).

Computer facilities: Computer purchase and lease plans are available. 8,000 computers available on campus for general student use. A campuswide network can be accessed from student residence rooms and from off campus. Internet access and online class registration are available. *Web address:* http://www.vt.edu/.

General Application Contact: Graduate School Receptionist, 540-231-9563.

GRADUATE UNITS

Graduate School Students: 4,199 full-time (1,818 women), 2,274 part-time (1,037 women); includes 783 minority (368 African Americans, 24 American Indian/Alaska Native, 265 Asian Americans or Pacific Islanders, 126 Hispanic Americans), 1,542 international. Average age 31. 6,878 applicants, 41% accepted, 1821 enrolled. *Faculty:* 1,581 full-time (440 women), 18 part-time/adjunct (11 women). Expenses: Contact institution. *Financial support:* In 2006–07, 231 fellowships with full tuition reimbursements (averaging $6,685 per year), 1,174 research assistantships with full tuition reimbursements (averaging $15,495 per year), 1,065 teaching assistantships with full tuition reimbursements (averaging $13,381 per year) were awarded; career-related internships or fieldwork, Federal Work-Study, scholarships/grants, and unspecified assistantships also available. In 2006, 1,456 master's, 366 doctorates, 96 other advanced degrees awarded. *Application deadline:* For fall admission, 5/15 for international students; for spring admission, 10/15 for international students. Applications are processed on a rolling basis. *Application fee:* $45. Electronic applications accepted. *Application Contact:* Jacqueline Nottingham, Director of Graduate Admissions and Academic Progress, 540-231-3092, Fax: 540-231-3750, E-mail: ntnghm@vt.edu. *Vice Provost for Graduate Studies and Dean of the Graduate School,* Dr. Karen P. DePauw, 540-231-7581, Fax: 540-231-1670, E-mail: kpdepauw@vt.edu.

College of Agriculture and Life Sciences Students: 281 full-time (157 women), 49 part-time (27 women); includes 26 minority (9 African Americans, 3 American Indian/Alaska Native, 9 Asian Americans or Pacific Islanders, 5 Hispanic Americans), 88 international. Average age 29. 265 applicants, 46% accepted, 86 enrolled. *Faculty:* 231 full-time (47 women), 1 (woman) part-time/adjunct. Expenses: Contact institution. *Financial support:* In 2006–07, 19 fellowships with full tuition reimbursements (averaging $14,977 per year), 128 research assistantships with full tuition reimbursements (averaging $13,823 per year), 71 teaching assistantships with full tuition reimbursements (averaging $13,552 per year) were awarded; career-related internships or fieldwork, Federal Work-Study, scholarships/grants, and unspecified assistantships also available. Financial award application deadline: 4/1. In 2006, 68 master's, 24 doctorates awarded. Offers agribusiness (MS); agricultural economics (MS); agriculture and life sciences (MS, PhD); animal science (MS, PhD); applied economics (MS); crop and soil environmental sciences (MS, PhD); developmental and international economics (PhD); econometrics (PhD); entomology (MS, PhD); food science and technology (MS, PhD); horticulture (MS, PhD); human nutrition, foods and exercise (MS, PhD); life sciences (MS, PhD); macro and micro economics (PhD); markets and industrial organizations (PhD); plant pathology (MS, PhD); plant physiology and weed science (MS, PhD); plant protection (MS); poultry science (MS, PhD); public and regional/urban economics (PhD); resource and environmental economics (PhD). *Application deadline:* For fall admission, 5/15 for international students; for spring admission, 10/15 for international students. Applications are processed on a rolling basis. *Application fee:* $45. Electronic applications accepted. *Application Contact:* Sheila Norman, Department Contact, 540-231-4152, Fax: 540-231-4163, E-mail: snorman@vt.edu. *Dean,* Dr. Sharron Quisenberry, 540-231-6503, Fax: 540-231-4163, E-mail: sharronq@vt.edu.

College of Architecture and Urban Studies Students: 361 full-time (164 women), 236 part-time (112 women); includes 69 minority (35 African Americans, 2 American Indian/Alaska Native, 16 Asian Americans or Pacific Islanders, 16 Hispanic Americans), 91 international. Average age 31. 456 applicants, 64% accepted, 165 enrolled. *Faculty:* 114 full-time (38 women). Expenses: Contact institution. *Financial support:* In 2006–07, 12 research assistantships with full tuition reimbursements (averaging $12,667 per year), 21 teaching assistantships with full tuition reimbursements (averaging $11,543 per year) were awarded; career-related internships or fieldwork, Federal Work-Study, scholarships/grants, tuition waivers (full and partial), and unspecified assistantships also available. Financial award application deadline: 4/1. In 2006, 136 master's, 17 doctorates awarded. Offers architecture and design (M Arch, MS); architecture and urban studies (M Arch, MLA, MPA, MPIA, MS, MURP, PhD, CAGS); building construction (MS); environmental design and planning (PhD); landscape architecture (MLA); public administration and policy (MPA, PhD, CAGS); public and international affairs (MPIA); urban and regional planning (MURP). *Application deadline:* For fall admission, 5/15 for international students; for spring admission, 10/15 for international students. Applications are processed on a rolling basis. *Application fee:* $45. Electronic applications accepted. *Application Contact:* Liz Roberson, Student Contact, 540-231-6416, Fax: 540-231-6332, E-mail: eroberso@vt.edu. *Dean,* Dr. A.J. Davis, 540-231-6416, Fax: 540-231-4487, E-mail: davisa@vt.edu.

College of Engineering Students: 1,310 full-time (260 women), 440 part-time (83 women); includes 168 minority (42 African Americans, 6 American Indian/Alaska Native, 89 Asian Americans or Pacific Islanders, 31 Hispanic Americans), 749 international. Average age 28. 3,172 applicants, 28% accepted, 510 enrolled. Expenses: Contact institution. *Financial support:* In 2006–07, 83 fellowships with full tuition reimbursements (averaging $6,906 per year), 450 research assistantships with full tuition reimbursements (averaging $17,256 per year), 217 teaching assistantships with full tuition reimbursements (averaging $14,767 per year) were awarded; career-related internships or fieldwork, Federal Work-Study, scholarships/grants, and unspecified assistantships also available. Financial award application deadline: 1/15. In 2006, 436 master's, 147 doctorates awarded. Offers aerospace engineering (M Eng, MS, PhD); biological systems engineering (M Eng, MS, PhD); chemical engineering (M Eng, MS, PhD); civil engineering (M Eng, MS, PhD); computer engineering (M Eng, MS, PhD); computer science (MS, PhD); electrical engineering (M Eng, MS, PhD); engineering (M Eng, MEA, MIS, MS, PhD); engineering administration (MEA); engineering mechanics (MS, PhD); environmental engineering (M Eng, MS); environmental sciences and engineering (MS); industrial engineering (M Eng, MS, PhD); information systems (MIS); materials science and engineering (M Eng, MS, PhD); mechanical engineering (M Eng, MS, PhD); mining and minerals engineering (M Eng, MS, PhD); ocean engineering (MS); operations research (M Eng, MS, PhD); systems engineering (M Eng, MS). *Application deadline:* For fall admission, 5/15 for international students; for spring admission, 10/15 for international students. Applications are processed on a rolling basis. *Application fee:* $45. Electronic applications accepted. *Application Contact:* Linda Perkins, 540-231-9752, Fax: 540-231-3362, E-mail: lperkins@vt.edu. *Head,* Dr. Richard C. Benson, 540-231-6641, E-mail: deaneng@vt.edu.

College of Liberal Arts and Human Sciences Students: 695 full-time (468 women), 907 part-time (605 women); includes 268 minority (211 African Americans, 4 American Indian/Alaska Native, 32 Asian Americans or Pacific Islanders, 21 Hispanic Americans), 86 international. Average age 35. 1,051 applicants, 63% accepted, 474 enrolled. *Faculty:* 394 full-time (184 women), 9 part-time/adjunct (6 women). Expenses: Contact institution. *Financial support:* In 2006–07, 32 research assistantships with full tuition reimbursements (averaging $190 per year), 150 teaching assistantships with full tuition reimbursements (averaging $9,911 per year) were awarded; career-related internships or fieldwork, Federal Work-Study, scholarships/grants, and unspecified assistantships also available. In 2006, 383 master's, 82 doctorates, 39 other advanced degrees awarded. *Degree program information:* Part-time programs available. Offers administration and supervision of special education (Ed D, PhD, Ed S); adult and continuing education (MA Ed, Ed D, PhD); adult development and aging (MS, PhD); adult learning and human resource development (MS, PhD); apparel business and economics (MS, PhD); apparel product design and analysis (MS, PhD); apparel quality analysis (MS, PhD); arts administration (MFA); career and technical education (MS Ed, Ed D, PhD, Ed S); child development (MS, PhD); communication (MA); consumer studies (MS, PhD); costume design (MFA); counselor education (MA Ed, Ed D, PhD, Ed S); creative writing (MFA); curriculum and instruction (MA Ed, Ed D, PhD, Ed S); education (ITMA, MA Ed, MS Ed, Ed D, PhD, Ed S); educational counseling (MA Ed, Ed D, PhD, Ed S); educational leadership (MA Ed, Ed D, PhD); educational research and evaluation (PhD); English (MA); family financial management (MS, PhD); family studies (MS, PhD); health and physical education (MS Ed); history (MA); household equipment (MS, PhD); housing (MS, PhD); instructional technology (ITMA); interior design (MS, PhD); liberal arts and human sciences (ITMA, MA, MA Ed, MFA, MS, MS Ed, Ed D, PhD, Ed S); lighting design (MFA); marriage and family therapy (MS, PhD); philosophy (MA); political science (MA); property management (MFA); resource management (MS, PhD); rhetoric and writing (PhD); scenic design (MFA); science and technology studies (MS, PhD); sociology (MS, PhD); stage management (MFA); technical theatre (MFA). *Application deadline:* For fall admission, 5/15 for international students; for spring admission, 10/15 for international students. Applications are processed on a rolling basis. *Application fee:* $45. Electronic applications accepted. *Application Contact:* Emily Oliver, Student Contact, 540-231-6779, Fax: 540-231-7157, E-mail: emilyo@vt.edu.

College of Natural Resources Students: 134 full-time (52 women), 78 part-time (42 women); includes 13 minority (1 African American, 2 American Indian/Alaska Native, 6 Asian Americans or Pacific Islanders, 4 Hispanic Americans), 32 international. Average age 31. 137 applicants, 55% accepted, 60 enrolled. *Faculty:* 62 full-time (13 women). Expenses: Contact institution. *Financial support:* In 2006–07, 1 fellowship with full tuition reimbursement (averaging $458 per year), 64 research assistantships with full tuition reimbursements (averaging $15,084 per year), 26 teaching assistantships with full tuition reimbursements (averaging $10,802 per year) were awarded; career-related internships or fieldwork, Federal Work-Study, scholarships/grants, health care benefits, and unspecified assistantships also available. In 2006, 39 master's, 5 doctorates awarded. Offers fisheries and wildlife sciences (MS, PhD); forest biology (MF, MS, PhD); forest biometry (MF, MS, PhD); forest management/economics (MF, MS, PhD); forest products marketing (MF, MS, PhD); geography (MS, PhD); industrial forestry operations (MF, MS, PhD); natural resources (MF, MNR, MS, PhD); outdoor recreation (MF, MS, PhD); wood science and engineering (MF, MS, PhD). *Application deadline:* For fall admission, 5/15 for international students; for spring admission, 10/15 for international students. Applications are processed on a rolling basis. *Application fee:* $45. Electronic applications accepted. *Application Contact:* Peggy Quarterman, 540-231-3479, Fax: 540-231-7664, E-mail: pquarter@vt.edu. *Dean,* Dr. J. Michael Kelly, 540-231-5481, Fax: 540-231-7664, E-mail: jmkelly@vt.edu.

College of Science Students: 492 full-time (197 women), 46 part-time (19 women); includes 42 minority (16 African Americans, 1 American Indian/Alaska Native, 13 Asian Americans or Pacific Islanders, 12 Hispanic Americans), 200 international. Average age 28. 864 applicants, 29% accepted, 144 enrolled. Expenses: Contact institution. *Financial support:* In 2006–07, 14 fellowships with full tuition reimbursements (averaging $10,336 per year), 111 research assistantships with full tuition reimbursements (averaging $16,689 per year), 268 teaching assistantships with full tuition reimbursements (averaging $13,902 per year) were awarded; career-related internships or fieldwork, Federal Work-Study, scholarships/grants, and unspecified assistantships also available. In 2006, 73 master's, 67 doctorates awarded. Offers applied mathematics (MS, PhD); applied physics (MS, PhD); bio-behavioral sciences (PhD); botany (MS, PhD); chemistry (MS, PhD); clinical psychology (PhD); developmental psychology (PhD); ecology and evolutionary biology (MS, PhD); economics (MA, PhD); genetics and developmental biology (MS, PhD); geological sciences (MS, PhD); geophysics (MS, PhD); industrial/organizational psychology (PhD); mathematical physics (MS, PhD); microbiology (MS, PhD); physics (MS, PhD); psychology (MS); pure mathematics (MS, PhD); science (MA, MS, PhD); statistics (MS, PhD); zoology (MS, PhD). *Application deadline:* For fall admission, 5/15 for international students; for spring admission, 10/15 for international students. Applications are processed on a rolling basis. *Application fee:* $45. Electronic applications accepted. *Application Contact:* Diane Stearns, Student Contact, 540-231-7515, Fax: 540-231-3380, E-mail: dstearns@vt.edu. *Dean,* Dr. Lay Nam Chang, 540-231-5422, Fax: 540-231-3380, E-mail: laynam@vt.edu.

Intercollege Students: 197 full-time (73 women), 292 part-time (72 women); includes 92 minority (28 African Americans, 1 American Indian/Alaska Native, 47 Asian Americans or Pacific Islanders, 16 Hispanic Americans), 127 international. Average age 32. 412 applicants,

54% accepted, 180 enrolled. Expenses: Contact institution. *Financial support:* In 2006–07, 4 fellowships with full tuition reimbursements (averaging $2,625 per year), 43 research assistantships with full tuition reimbursements (averaging $16,635 per year) were awarded; career-related internships or fieldwork, Federal Work-Study, scholarships/grants, and unspecified assistantships also available. In 2006, 129 master's, 9 doctorates awarded. Offers biomedical engineering (MS, PhD); biomedical engineering and sciences (MS, PhD); genetics, bioinformatics and computational biology (PhD); information technology (MIT); interdisciplinary studies (MIT, MS, PhD); macromolecular science and engineering (MS, PhD). *Application deadline:* For fall admission, 5/15 for domestic students; for spring admission, 10/15 for domestic students. *Application fee:* $45. *Application Contact:* Jacqueline Nottingham, Director of Graduate Admissions and Academic Progress, 540-231-3092, Fax: 540-231-3750, E-mail: ntnghm@vt.edu.

Pamplin College of Business Students: 318 full-time (125 women), 192 part-time (54 women); includes 71 minority (18 African Americans, 3 American Indian/Alaska Native, 40 Asian Americans or Pacific Islanders, 10 Hispanic Americans), 134 international. Average age 30. 479 applicants, 57% accepted, 181 enrolled. Expenses: Contact institution. *Financial support:* In 2006–07, 1 research assistantship with full tuition reimbursement (averaging $2,285 per year), 45 teaching assistantships with full tuition reimbursements (averaging $12,379 per year) were awarded; career-related internships or fieldwork, Federal Work-Study, scholarships/grants, and unspecified assistantships also available. Financial award application deadline: 3/1. In 2006, 182 master's, 13 doctorates awarded. Offers accounting and information systems (MACIS, PhD); business (MACIS, MBA, MS, PhD); business administration (PhD); business administration/finance (MS, PhD); business administration/management (MS, PhD); business administration/marketing (MS, PhD); business information technology (MS, PhD); hospitality and tourism management (MS, PhD). *Application deadline:* For fall admission, 5/15 for international students; for spring admission, 10/15 for international students. Applications are processed on a rolling basis. *Application fee:* $45. Electronic applications accepted. *Application Contact:* Denise Jones, Information Contact, 540-231-9647, Fax: 540-231-4487, E-mail: cdjones@vt.edu. *Dean,* Dr. Richard E. Sorensen, 540-231-6152, Fax: 540-231-4487, E-mail: sorensen@vt.edu.

Virginia-Maryland Regional College of Veterinary Medicine Students: 399 full-time (304 women), 34 part-time (21 women); includes 24 minority (6 African Americans, 2 American Indian/Alaska Native, 8 Asian Americans or Pacific Islanders, 8 Hispanic Americans), 31 international. Average age 27. 36 applicants, 44% accepted, 16 enrolled. *Faculty:* 87 full-time (23 women). Expenses: Contact institution. *Financial support:* In 2006–07, 1 fellowship with full tuition reimbursement (averaging $14,013 per year), 11 research assistantships with full tuition reimbursements (averaging $14,487 per year), 22 teaching assistantships with full tuition reimbursements (averaging $18,835 per year) were awarded; career-related internships or fieldwork, Federal Work-Study, scholarships/grants, and unspecified assistantships also available. In 2006, 87 DVMs, 18 master's, 4 doctorates awarded. Offers biomedical and veterinary sciences (MS, PhD); veterinary medicine (DVM, MS, PhD). *Application deadline:* For fall admission, 5/15 for international students; for spring admission, 10/15 for international students. *Application fee:* $45. *Application Contact:* Joyce Morgan, 540-231-7910, Fax: 540-231-7367, E-mail: cvmjom@vt.edu. *Dean,* Dr. Gerhardt G Schurig, 540-231-7666, Fax: 540-231-7367.

VIRGINIA STATE UNIVERSITY, Petersburg, VA 23806-0001

General Information State-supported, coed, comprehensive institution. *Graduate housing:* Room and/or apartments available on a first-come, first-served basis to single students; on-campus housing not available to married students. Housing application deadline: 5/1. *Research affiliation:* Swiss Institute Nuclear Research Laboratory (physics), NASA–Langley Research Center (physics), Brookhaven National Laboratory (physics), Los Alamos National Laboratory–Continuous Electron Beam Accelerator Facility (physics).

GRADUATE UNITS

School of Graduate Studies, Research, and Outreach *Degree program information:* Part-time and evening/weekend programs available. Offers interdisciplinary studies (MIS).

School of Engineering, Science and Technology Offers biology (MS); engineering, science and technology (M Ed, MS); mathematics (MS); mathematics education (M Ed); physics (MS); psychology (MS).

School of Liberal Arts and Education *Degree program information:* Part-time and evening/weekend programs available. Offers economics (MA); education (M Ed, MS); educational administration and supervision (M Ed, MS); English (MA); guidance (M Ed, MS); history (MA); liberal arts and education (M Ed, MA, MS, CAGS); vocational technical education (M Ed, MS, CAGS).

VIRGINIA UNION UNIVERSITY, Richmond, VA 23220-1170

General Information Independent-religious, coed, comprehensive institution. *Graduate housing:* Room and/or apartments available on a first-come, first-served basis to single students; on-campus housing not available to married students.

GRADUATE UNITS

School of Theology *Degree program information:* Part-time and evening/weekend programs available. Offers theology (M Div, D Min).

VIRGINIA UNIVERSITY OF LYNCHBURG, Lynchburg, VA 24501-6417

General Information Independent-religious, coed, comprehensive institution.

GRADUATE UNITS

Graduate Programs

VITERBO UNIVERSITY, La Crosse, WI 54601-4797

General Information Independent-religious, coed, comprehensive institution. *Graduate housing:* Rooms and/or apartments available to single and married students. Housing application deadline: 4/2.

GRADUATE UNITS

Graduate Program in Education *Degree program information:* Part-time and evening/weekend programs available. Offers education (MA). Courses held on weekends and during summer.

Graduate Program in Nursing Students: 53 full-time (52 women), 17 part-time (all women); includes 1 minority (Asian American or Pacific Islander) Average age 37. *Faculty:* 5 full-time, 5 part-time/adjunct. Expenses: Contact institution. *Financial support:* In 2006–07, 8 students received support. Institutionally sponsored loans, scholarships/grants, and traineeships available. Financial award application deadline: 6/1; financial award applicants required to submit FAFSA. In 2006, 15 degrees awarded. *Degree program information:* Part-time programs available. Postbaccalaureate distance learning degree programs offered (minimal on-campus study). Offers nursing (MSN). *Application deadline:* For spring admission, 2/1 priority date for domestic students. Applications are processed on a rolling basis. *Application fee:* $25. *Application Contact:* 608-796-3671. *Director,* Dr. Bonnie Nesbitt, 608-796-3688, Fax: 608-796-3668, E-mail: bjnesbitt@viterbo.edu.

WAGNER COLLEGE, Staten Island, NY 10301-4495

General Information Independent, coed, comprehensive institution. *Enrollment:* 2,280 graduate, professional, and undergraduate students; 210 full-time matriculated graduate/professional students (124 women), 129 part-time matriculated graduate/professional students (99 women). *Enrollment by degree level:* 339 master's. *Graduate faculty:* 24 full-time (13 women), 37 part-time/adjunct (23 women). *Tuition:* Full-time $15,120; part-time $840 per credit. *Graduate housing:* Room and/or apartments available on a first-come, first-served basis to single students; on-campus housing not available to married students. Typical cost: $8,400 (including board). *Student services:* Campus employment opportunities, career counseling, disabled student services, free psychological counseling, international student services. *Library facilities:* August Horrmann Library. *Online resources:* web page. *Collection:* 310,000 titles, 1,000 serial subscriptions, 1,616 audiovisual materials. *Research affiliation:* Staten Island University Hospital.

Computer facilities: 150 computers available on campus for general student use. A campuswide network can be accessed from student residence rooms and from off campus. Internet access is available. *Web address:* http://www.wagner.edu/.

General Application Contact: Susan Rosenberg, Office of Graduate Studies, 718-390-3106, Fax: 718-390-3456, E-mail: graduate@wagner.edu.

GRADUATE UNITS

Division of Graduate Studies Students: 210 full-time (124 women), 129 part-time (99 women); includes 61 minority (23 African Americans, 1 American Indian/Alaska Native, 19 Asian Americans or Pacific Islanders, 18 Hispanic Americans), 3 international. Average age 29. 168 applicants, 91% accepted, 114 enrolled. *Faculty:* 24 full-time (13 women), 37 part-time/adjunct (23 women). Expenses: Contact institution. *Financial support:* Fellowships, career-related internships or fieldwork, Federal Work-Study, tuition waivers (partial), and unspecified assistantships available. Financial award applicants required to submit FAFSA. In 2006, 158 degrees awarded. *Degree program information:* Part-time and evening/weekend programs available. Offers accelerated MBA (MBA); accounting (MS); adolescent education (MS Ed); advanced physician assistant studies (MS); childhood education (MS Ed); early childhood education (birth-grade 2) (MS Ed); educational leadership (Certificate); family nurse practitioner (Certificate); finance (MBA); health care administration (MBA); international business (MBA); literacy (B-6) (MS Ed); management (Exec MBA, MBA); marketing (MBA); microbiology (MS); middle level education (5-9) (MS Ed); nursing (MS); school building leader (Certificate); school district leader (Certificate). *Application deadline:* For fall admission, 8/1 for domestic students, 6/30 priority date for international students; for spring admission, 12/10 for domestic students, 11/15 priority date for international students. Applications are processed on a rolling basis. *Application fee:* $50 ($85 for international students). *Application Contact:* Susan Rosenberg, Office of Graduate Studies, 718-390-3106, Fax: 718-390-3456, E-mail: graduate@wagner.edu. *Coordinator of Graduate Studies,* Dr. Jeffrey Kraus, 718-390-3254, Fax: 718-390-3456, E-mail: jkraus@wagner.edu.

WAKE FOREST UNIVERSITY, Winston-Salem, NC 27109

General Information Independent, coed, university. CGS member. *Enrollment:* 6,739 graduate, professional, and undergraduate students; 2,418 matriculated graduate/professional students. *Graduate faculty:* 1,900. *Graduate housing:* On-campus housing not available. *Student services:* Career counseling, disabled student services, free psychological counseling, grant writing training, international student services, low-cost health insurance, multicultural affairs office, teacher training, writing training. *Library facilities:* Z. Smith Reynolds Library plus 3 others. *Online resources:* library catalog, web page, access to other libraries' catalogs. *Collection:* 923,123 titles, 16,448 serial subscriptions.

Computer facilities: Computer purchase and lease plans are available. 150 computers available on campus for general student use. A campuswide network can be accessed from student residence rooms and from off campus. Internet access and online class registration, laptop computer for all students, financial information online, GPA, drop-add, transcript requests are available. *Web address:* http://www.wfu.edu/.

General Application Contact: Carol DiGiantommaso, Admissions Coordinator, 336-758-5301, Fax: 336-758-4230, E-mail: gradschl@wfu.edu.

GRADUATE UNITS

Babcock Graduate School of Management Students: 521 full-time (145 women); includes 80 minority (38 African Americans, 31 Asian Americans or Pacific Islanders, 11 Hispanic Americans), 56 international. Average age 31. *Faculty:* 36 full-time (5 women), 6 part-time/adjunct (1 woman). Expenses: Contact institution. *Financial support:* In 2006–07, 147 students received support. Scholarships/grants available. Financial award applicants required to submit FAFSA. In 2006, 288 degrees awarded. *Degree program information:* Evening/weekend programs available. Offers business administration (MA, MBA); management (MA, MBA). *Application deadline:* Applications are processed on a rolling basis. *Application fee:* $75. Electronic applications accepted. *Application Contact:* Stacy Owen, Director, Fulltime Admissions, 336-758-5422, Fax: 336-758-5830, E-mail: admissions@mba.wfu.edu. *Dean,* Ajay Patel, 336-758-5418, Fax: 336-758-5830, E-mail: judy.sowers@mba.wfu.edu.

Graduate School Students: 361 full-time (200 women), 55 part-time (37 women); includes 39 minority (28 African Americans, 8 Asian Americans or Pacific Islanders, 3 Hispanic Americans), 46 international. Average age 25. 783 applicants, 32% accepted, 187 enrolled. *Faculty:* 171 full-time (48 women), 14 part-time/adjunct (3 women). Expenses: Contact institution. *Financial support:* In 2006–07, 330 students received support, including 35 fellowships with full tuition reimbursements available (averaging $7,124 per year), 38 research assistantships with full tuition reimbursements available (averaging $16,071 per year), 144 teaching assistantships with full tuition reimbursements available (averaging $12,008 per year); scholarships/grants, tuition waivers (full and partial), and unspecified assistantships also available. Support available to part-time students. Financial award application deadline: 1/15; financial award applicants required to submit FAFSA. In 2006, 185 master's, 10 doctorates awarded. *Degree program information:* Part-time programs available. Offers accountancy (MSA); analytical chemistry (MS, PhD); biology (MS, PhD); computer science (MS); counseling (MA); English (MA); health and exercise science (MS); inorganic chemistry (MS, PhD); liberal studies (MALS); mathematics (MA); organic chemistry (MS, PhD); pastoral counseling (MA); physical chemistry (MS, PhD); physics (MS, PhD); psychology (MA); religion (MA); secondary education (MA Ed); speech communication (MA). *Application deadline:* For fall admission, 1/15 for domestic and international students. *Application fee:* $45 ($55 for international students). Electronic applications accepted. *Application Contact:* Carol DiGiantommaso, Admissions Coordinator, 336-758-5301, Fax: 336-758-4230, E-mail: gradschl@wfu.edu. *Interim Dean,* Dr. Cecilia H. Solano, 336-758-531, Fax: 336-758-4230, E-mail: solano@wfu.edu.

School of Law Students: 471 full-time (221 women), 20 part-time (13 women); includes 51 minority (27 African Americans, 18 Asian Americans or Pacific Islanders, 6 Hispanic Americans), 5 international. Average age 25. 2,142 applicants, 30% accepted. *Faculty:* 45 full-time, 26 part-time/adjunct. Expenses: Contact institution. *Financial support:* In 2006–07, 183 students received support. Career-related internships or fieldwork, Federal Work-Study, institutionally sponsored loans, and scholarships/grants available. Financial award application deadline: 4/30; financial award applicants required to submit FAFSA. In 2006, 171 degrees awarded. Offers law (JD, LL M). LL M for foreign law graduates in American law. *Application deadline:* For fall admission, 3/1 for domestic students. Applications are processed on a rolling basis. *Application fee:* $60. Electronic applications accepted. *Application Contact:* Melanie E. Nutt, Director of Admissions and Financial Aid, 336-758-5437, Fax: 336-758-3930, E-mail: admissions@law.wfu.edu. *Dean,* Robert K. Walsh, 336-758-5435, Fax: 336-758-4632.

School of Medicine Offers medicine (MD, MS, PhD). Electronic applications accepted.

Graduate Programs in Medicine Offers biochemistry (PhD); cancer biology (PhD); clinical epidemiology and health services research (MS); comparative medicine (MS); medicine (MS, PhD); microbiology and immunology (PhD); molecular and cellular pathobiology (MS, PhD); molecular genetics and genomics (PhD); molecular medicine (MS, PhD); neurobiology and anatomy (PhD); neuroscience (PhD); pharmacology (PhD); physiology (PhD). Electronic applications accepted.

Virginia Tech-Wake Forest University School of Biomedical Engineering and Sciences Offers biomedical engineering and sciences (MS, PhD). Electronic applications accepted.

See Close-Up on page 1137.

WALDEN UNIVERSITY, Minneapolis, MN 55401

General Information Proprietary, coed, upper-level institution. CGS member. *Enrollment:* 27,633 graduate, professional, and undergraduate students; 19,263 full-time matriculated graduate/professional students (15,151 women), 6,787 part-time matriculated graduate/professional students (4,920 women). *Enrollment by degree level:* 17,618 master's, 8,412 doctoral, 20 other advanced degrees. *Graduate faculty:* 1,079. *Graduate housing:* On-campus housing not available. *Student services:* Career counseling, disabled student services, writing training. *Web address:* http://www.waldenu.edu/.

Walden University (continued)

General Application Contact: Seth Saunders, Director of Student Enrollment, 866-4-WALDEN, Fax: 410-843-8780, E-mail: request@walden.edu.

GRADUATE UNITS

Graduate Programs Students: 19,263 full-time (15,151 women), 6,787 part-time (4,920 women); includes 5,361 minority (3,996 African Americans, 128 American Indian/Alaska Native, 360 Asian Americans or Pacific Islanders, 877 Hispanic Americans), 128 international. Average age 37. 7,658 applicants, 86% accepted, 5751 enrolled. *Faculty:* 1,079. Expenses: Contact institution. *Financial support:* In 2006–07, 11 fellowships with partial tuition reimbursements were awarded; tuition waivers (partial) also available. Support available to part-time students. Financial award applicants required to submit FAFSA. In 2006, 5,395 master's, 172 doctorates awarded. *Degree program information:* Part-time and evening/weekend programs available. Postbaccalaureate distance learning degree programs offered (minimal on-campus study). *Application deadline:* For fall admission, 8/15 priority date for domestic and international students; for winter admission, 11/15 priority date for domestic and international students; for spring admission, 12/15 priority date for domestic and international students. Applications are processed on a rolling basis. *Application fee:* $50. Electronic applications accepted. *Application Contact:* Seth Saunders, Director of Student Enrollment, 866-4-WALDEN, Fax: 410-843-8780, E-mail: request@walden.edu. *President,* Dr. Paula Peinovich, 612-338-7224, Fax: 612-338-5092, E-mail: paulap@waldenu.edu.

NTU College of Engineering and Applied Science Students: 69 full-time (13 women), 336 part-time (50 women); includes 71 minority (29 African Americans, 2 American Indian/Alaska Native, 24 Asian Americans or Pacific Islanders, 16 Hispanic Americans), 14 international. Average age 33. 220 applicants, 58% accepted, 82 enrolled. *Faculty:* 44. Expenses: Contact institution. In 2006, 13 degrees awarded. *Degree program information:* Part-time and evening/weekend programs available. Postbaccalaureate distance learning degree programs offered (minimal on-campus study). Offers computer engineering (MS); computer science (MS); electrical engineering (MS); engineering (MS); engineering management (MBA, Certificate); high-tech business administration (MBA); software engineering (MS); systems engineering (MS). *Application deadline:* For fall admission, 8/15 priority date for domestic and international students; for winter admission, 11/15 priority date for domestic and international students; for spring admission, 12/15 priority date for domestic and international students. Applications are processed on a rolling basis. *Application fee:* $50. Electronic applications accepted. *Chair,* Dr. Ahmed Naumaan, 800-925-3368.

College of Education Students: 11,618 full-time (9,630 women), 2,152 part-time (1,745 women); includes 2,524 minority (1,744 African Americans, 61 American Indian/Alaska Native, 154 Asian Americans or Pacific Islanders, 565 Hispanic Americans), 29 international. Average age 35. 3,674 applicants, 95% accepted, 3230 enrolled. *Faculty:* 513. Expenses: Contact institution. *Financial support:* In 2006–07, 6 fellowships with partial tuition reimbursements were awarded; scholarships/grants and tuition waivers (partial) also available. Support available to part-time students. Financial award application deadline: 6/1; financial award applicants required to submit FAFSA. In 2006, 4,682 master's, 38 doctorates awarded. *Degree program information:* Part-time and evening/weekend programs available. Postbaccalaureate distance learning degree programs offered (minimal on-campus study). Offers administrator leadership for teaching and learning (Ed D); adult education leadership (PhD); community college leadership (PhD); curriculum, instruction, and assessment (MS); early childhood education (PhD); education (MS); educational leadership (MS); educational technology (PhD); elementary reading and literacy (MS); elementary reading and mathematics (MS); higher education (PhD); integrating technology in the classroom (MS); Kû12 educational leadership (PhD); literacy and learning in the content areas (MS); mathematics (grades 6û8) (MS); mathematics (grades Kû5) (MS); middle level education (MS); science (grades Kû8) (MS); special education (PhD); teacher leadership (Ed D). *Application deadline:* For fall admission, 8/15 priority date for domestic and international students; for winter admission, 11/15 priority date for domestic and international students; for spring admission, 12/15 priority date for domestic and international students. Applications are processed on a rolling basis. *Application fee:* $50. Electronic applications accepted. *Application Contact:* Office of Admissions, 866-4-WALDEN, Fax: 410-843-8780, E-mail: request@waldenu.edu. *Dean,* Dr. Manual Barrera, 800-925-3368, Fax: 612-338-5092.

School of Health Sciences Students: 2,383 full-time (2,074 women), 1,082 part-time (876 women); includes 840 minority (662 African Americans, 18 American Indian/Alaska Native, 83 Asian Americans or Pacific Islanders, 77 Hispanic Americans), 24 international. Average age 42. 1,164 applicants, 85% accepted, 813 enrolled. *Faculty:* 100. Expenses: Contact institution. *Financial support:* Fellowships with partial tuition reimbursements, tuition waivers (partial) available. Support available to part-time students. Financial award applicants required to submit FAFSA. In 2006, 212 master's, 30 doctorates awarded. *Degree program information:* Part-time and evening/weekend programs available. Postbaccalaureate distance learning degree programs offered (minimal on-campus study). Offers health services (PhD); human services (PhD); nursing (MS); public health (MPH, PhD). *Application deadline:* For fall admission, 8/15 priority date for domestic and international students; for winter admission, 11/15 priority date for domestic and international students; for spring admission, 12/15 priority date for domestic and international students. Applications are processed on a rolling basis. *Application fee:* $50. Electronic applications accepted. *Application Contact:* 866-4-WALDEN, Fax: 410-843-8780, E-mail: request@waldenu.edu. *Dean,* Dr. Gary J. Burkholder, 800-925-3368, Fax: 612-338-5092.

School of Management Students: 2,212 full-time (1,216 women), 752 part-time (390 women); includes 756 minority (626 African Americans, 11 American Indian/Alaska Native, 49 Asian Americans or Pacific Islanders, 70 Hispanic Americans), 22 international. Average age 40. 967 applicants, 83% accepted, 600 enrolled. *Faculty:* 264. Expenses: Contact institution. *Financial support:* In 2006–07, 1 fellowship with partial tuition reimbursement (averaging $750 per year) was awarded; scholarships/grants and tuition waivers (partial) also available. Support available to part-time students. Financial award application deadline: 6/1; financial award applicants required to submit FAFSA. In 2006, 267 master's, 55 doctorates awarded. *Degree program information:* Part-time and evening/weekend programs available. Postbaccalaureate distance learning degree programs offered (minimal on-campus study). Offers applied management and decision sciences (PhD); business administration (MBA); human resource management (MBA); marketing (MBA); technology (MBA). *Application deadline:* For fall admission, 8/15 priority date for domestic and international students; for winter admission, 11/15 priority date for domestic and international students; for spring admission, 12/15 priority date for domestic and international students. Applications are processed on a rolling basis. *Application fee:* $50. Electronic applications accepted. *Application Contact:* 866-4-WALDEN, Fax: 410-843-8780, E-mail: request@waldenu.edu. *Chair,* Dr. Kathleen Simmons, 800-925-3368, Fax: 612-338-5092.

School of Psychology Students: 2,125 full-time (1,700 women), 2,084 part-time (1,614 women); includes 829 minority (637 African Americans, 30 American Indian/Alaska Native, 43 Asian Americans or Pacific Islanders, 119 Hispanic Americans), 36 international. Average age 37. 1,308 applicants, 73% accepted, 814 enrolled. *Faculty:* 194. Expenses: Contact institution. *Financial support:* In 2006–07, 1 fellowship with partial tuition reimbursement was awarded; tuition waivers (partial) also available. Support available to part-time students. Financial award applicants required to submit FAFSA. In 2006, 167 master's, 45 doctorates awarded. *Degree program information:* Part-time and evening/weekend programs available. Postbaccalaureate distance learning degree programs offered (minimal on-campus study). Offers mental health counseling (MS); psychology (MS, PhD). *Application deadline:* For fall admission, 8/15 priority date for domestic and international students; for winter admission, 11/15 priority date for domestic and international students; for spring admission, 12/15 priority date for domestic and international students. Applications are processed on a rolling basis. *Application fee:* $50. Electronic applications accepted. *Application Contact:* 866-4-WALDEN, Fax: 410-843-8780, E-mail: request@waldenu.edu. *Interim Dean,* Dr. Nina Nabors, 800-925-3368.

School of Public Policy and Administration Students: 726 full-time (426 women), 355 part-time (225 women); includes 303 minority (260 African Americans, 5 American Indian/Alaska Native, 11 Asian Americans or Pacific Islanders, 27 Hispanic Americans), 3 international. Average age 39. 325 applicants, 74% accepted, 212 enrolled. *Faculty:* 43. Expenses: Contact institution. *Financial support:* In 2006–07, 1 fellowship with partial tuition reimbursement was awarded; scholarships/grants also available. Financial award application deadline: 6/1; financial award applicants required to submit FAFSA. In 2006, 54 master's, 4 doctorates awarded. *Degree program information:* Part-time and evening/weekend programs available. Postbaccalaureate distance learning degree programs offered (minimal on-campus study). Offers public policy and administration (MPA, PhD). *Application deadline:* For fall admission, 8/15 priority date for domestic and international students; for winter admission, 11/15 priority date for domestic and international students; for spring admission, 12/15 priority date for domestic and international students. Applications are processed on a rolling basis. *Application fee:* $50. Electronic applications accepted. *Application Contact:* 866-4-WALDEN, Fax: 410-843-8780, E-mail: request@waldenu.edu. *Dean,* Dr. Marion Angelica, 800-925-3368, Fax: 612-338-5092.

See Close-Up on page 1139.

WALLA WALLA COLLEGE, College Place, WA 99324-1198

General Information Independent-religious, coed, comprehensive institution. *Enrollment:* 1,876 graduate, professional, and undergraduate students; 203 full-time matriculated graduate/professional students (156 women), 38 part-time matriculated graduate/professional students (23 women). *Enrollment by degree level:* 241 master's. *Graduate faculty:* 29 full-time (16 women), 22 part-time/adjunct (15 women). *Tuition:* Full-time $20,124; part-time $516 per quarter hour. *Graduate housing:* Rooms and/or apartments available on a first-come, first-served basis to single and married students. Typical cost: $9,000 per year ($11,700 including board) for single students. *Student services:* Campus employment opportunities, career counseling, disabled student services, free psychological counseling, international student services, low-cost health insurance, multicultural affairs office. *Library facilities:* Peterson Memorial Library plus 3 others. *Online resources:* library catalog, web page, access to other libraries' catalogs. *Collection:* 178,450 titles, 1,105 serial subscriptions.

Computer facilities: 118 computers available on campus for general student use. A campuswide network can be accessed from student residence rooms and from off campus. Internet access and online class registration are available. *Web address:* http://www.wwc.edu/.

General Application Contact: Dr. Joe G. Galusha, Dean of Graduate Studies, 509-527-2421, Fax: 509-527-2237, E-mail: galujo@wwc.edu.

GRADUATE UNITS

Graduate School Students: 203 full-time (156 women), 38 part-time (23 women); includes 48 minority (3 African Americans, 26 American Indian/Alaska Native, 6 Asian Americans or Pacific Islanders, 13 Hispanic Americans), 4 international. Average age 37. 221 applicants, 79% accepted, 123 enrolled. *Faculty:* 29 full-time (16 women), 22 part-time/adjunct (15 women). Expenses: Contact institution. *Financial support:* In 2006–07, 216 students received support, including 10 teaching assistantships (averaging $10,147 per year); research assistantships, career-related internships or fieldwork, Federal Work-Study, scholarships/grants, tuition waivers (partial), and unspecified assistantships also available. Support available to part-time students. Financial award application deadline: 4/1; financial award applicants required to submit FAFSA. In 2006, 150 master's awarded. *Degree program information:* Part-time and evening/weekend programs available. Offers biology (MS). *Application deadline:* Applications are processed on a rolling basis. *Application fee:* $50. Electronic applications accepted. *Application Contact:* Donna J. Fisher, Administrative Assistant to Graduate Dean, 509-527-2421, Fax: 509-527-2237, E-mail: fishdo@wwc.edu. *Dean,* Dr. Joe G. Galusha, 509-527-2421, Fax: 509-527-2237, E-mail: galujo@wwc.edu.

School of Education and Psychology Students: 18 full-time (9 women), 4 part-time (3 women); includes 1 minority (Asian American or Pacific Islander), 1 international. Average age 30. 46 applicants, 61% accepted, 13 enrolled. *Faculty:* 7 full-time (3 women), 6 part-time/adjunct (4 women). Expenses: Contact institution. *Financial support:* In 2006–07, 16 students received support; research assistantships, teaching assistantships, Federal Work-Study and tuition waivers (partial) available. Support available to part-time students. Financial award application deadline: 4/1; financial award applicants required to submit FAFSA. In 2006, 16 master's awarded. *Degree program information:* Part-time programs available. Offers counseling psychology (MA); curriculum and instruction (M Ed, MA, MAT); educational leadership (M Ed, MA, MAT); literacy instruction (M Ed, MA, MAT); students at risk (M Ed, MA, MAT); teaching (MAT). *Application deadline:* For fall admission, 4/1 priority date for domestic students. Applications are processed on a rolling basis. *Application fee:* $50. Electronic applications accepted. *Application Contact:* Dr. Joe G. Galusha, Dean of Graduate Studies, 509-527-2421, Fax: 509-527-2237, E-mail: galujo@wwc.edu. *Dean,* Dr. Julian Melgosa, 509-527-2272, Fax: 509-527-2248, E-mail: melgju@wwc.edu.

School of Social Work Students: 183 full-time (145 women), 26 part-time (16 women); includes 46 minority (3 African Americans, 26 American Indian/Alaska Native, 4 Asian Americans or Pacific Islanders, 13 Hispanic Americans), 2 international. Average age 38. 167 applicants, 84% accepted, 105 enrolled. *Faculty:* 17 full-time (12 women), 15 part-time/adjunct (11 women). Expenses: Contact institution. *Financial support:* In 2006–07, 184 students received support. Career-related internships or fieldwork, Federal Work-Study, and scholarships/grants available. Support available to part-time students. Financial award application deadline: 4/1; financial award applicants required to submit FAFSA. In 2006, 130 master's awarded. *Degree program information:* Part-time programs available. Offers social work (MSW). *Application deadline:* For fall admission, 7/15 priority date for domestic students. Applications are processed on a rolling basis. *Application fee:* $50. Electronic applications accepted. *Application Contact:* Dr. Joe G. Galusha, Dean of Graduate Studies, 509-527-2421, Fax: 509-527-2237, E-mail: galujo@wwc.edu. *Dean,* Dr. Pamela Cress, 509-527-2270, Fax: 509-527-2253.

WALSH COLLEGE OF ACCOUNTANCY AND BUSINESS ADMINISTRATION, Troy, MI 48007-7006

General Information Independent, coed, upper-level institution. *Enrollment:* 106 full-time matriculated graduate/professional students (40 women), 2,025 part-time matriculated graduate/professional students (1,033 women). *Enrollment by degree level:* 2,131 master's. *Graduate faculty:* 14 full-time (4 women), 113 part-time/adjunct (26 women). *Tuition:* Part-time $435 per hour. *Required fees:* $119 per semester. One-time fee: $50. *Graduate housing:* On-campus housing not available. *Student services:* Campus employment opportunities, career counseling, disabled student services, international student services. *Library facilities:* Vollbrecht Library plus 1 other. *Online resources:* library catalog, web page, access to other libraries' catalogs. *Collection:* 26,300 titles, 8,210 serial subscriptions, 121 audiovisual materials.

Computer facilities: 300 computers available on campus for general student use. A campuswide network can be accessed from off campus. Internet access is available. *Web address:* http://www.walshcollege.edu/.

General Application Contact: Karen Mahaffy, Director of Admissions and Academic Advising, 248-823-1610, Fax: 248-689-0938, E-mail: kmahaffy@walshcollege.edu.

GRADUATE UNITS

Graduate Programs Students: 106 full-time (40 women), 2,025 part-time (1,033 women). Average age 34. 663 applicants, 90% accepted. *Faculty:* 14 full-time (4 women), 113 part-time/adjunct (26 women). Expenses: Contact institution. *Financial support:* In 2006–07, 732 students received support. Scholarships/grants available. Support available to part-time students. Financial award application deadline: 6/30; financial award applicants required to submit FAFSA. In 2006, 605 degrees awarded. *Degree program information:* Part-time and evening/weekend programs available. Offers accountancy (MSPA); business administration (MBA); business information technology (MSBIT); economics (MAE); finance (MSF); management (MSM); taxation (MST). *Application deadline:* For fall admission, 8/24 priority date for domestic students; for winter admission, 1/1 priority date for domestic students; for spring admission, 4/1 priority date for domestic students. Applications are processed on a rolling basis. *Application fee:* $25. Electronic applications accepted. *Application Contact:* Karen Mahaffy, Director of Admissions and Academic Advising, 248-823-1610, Fax: 248-689-0938, E-mail: kmahaffy@walshcollege.edu. *Vice President/Academic Dean,* Dr. Michael Hewlett, 248-689-8282, Fax: 248-689-0920.

WALSH UNIVERSITY, North Canton, OH 44720-3396

General Information Independent-religious, coed, comprehensive institution. *Enrollment:* 2,396 graduate, professional, and undergraduate students; 103 full-time matriculated graduate/professional students (76 women), 207 part-time matriculated graduate/professional students (142 women). *Enrollment by degree level:* 310 master's. *Graduate faculty:* 28 full-time (18 women), 10 part-time/adjunct (4 women). *Tuition:* Full-time $8,910; part-time $495 per credit. *Graduate housing:* Room and/or apartments available on a first-come, first-served basis to single students; on-campus housing not available to married students. Typical cost: $6,090 per year ($9,460 including board). Room and board charges vary according to board plan, campus/location and housing facility selected. Housing application deadline: 7/15. *Student services:* Campus employment opportunities, campus safety program, career counseling, disabled student services, exercise/wellness program, free psychological counseling, international student services, low-cost health insurance, multicultural affairs office, teacher training, writing training. *Library facilities:* Brother Edmond Drouin Library. *Online resources:* library catalog, web page, access to other libraries' catalogs. *Collection:* 199,543 titles, 5,586 serial subscriptions, 2,369 audiovisual materials.

Computer facilities: 262 computers available on campus for general student use. A campuswide network can be accessed from student residence rooms and from off campus. Internet access is available. *Web address:* http://www.walsh.edu/.

General Application Contact: Brett D. Freshour, Vice President of Enrollment Management, 330-490-7286, Fax: 330-490-7165, E-mail: bfreshour@walsh.edu.

GRADUATE UNITS

Graduate Programs Students: 103 full-time (76 women), 207 part-time (142 women); includes 15 minority (8 African Americans, 1 American Indian/Alaska Native, 1 Asian American or Pacific Islander, 5 Hispanic Americans), 7 international. Average age 33. 165 applicants, 68% accepted, 102 enrolled. *Faculty:* 28 full-time (18 women), 10 part-time/adjunct (4 women). Expenses: Contact institution. *Financial support:* In 2006–07, 64 students received support, including 23 research assistantships with partial tuition reimbursements available (averaging $4,672 per year); tuition waivers (partial) and unspecified assistantships also available. Support available to part-time students. Financial award application deadline: 12/31. In 2006, 75 degrees awarded. *Degree program information:* Part-time and evening/weekend programs available. Offers business administration (MBA); education (MA); mental health counseling (MA); physical therapy (M Sc); school counseling (MA); theology (MA). *Application deadline:* Applications are processed on a rolling basis. *Application fee:* $25. Electronic applications accepted. *Application Contact:* Brett D. Freshour, Vice President of Enrollment Management, 330-490-7286, Fax: 330-490-7165, E-mail: bfreshour@walsh.edu. *Academic Dean,* Dr. Laurence Bove, 330-490-7122, Fax: 330-490-7165, E-mail: lbove@walsh.edu.

WARNER PACIFIC COLLEGE, Portland, OR 97215-4099

General Information Independent-religious, coed, comprehensive institution. *Graduate housing:* Rooms and/or apartments available on a first-come, first-served basis to single and married students. Housing application deadline: 7/1.

GRADUATE UNITS

Graduate Programs *Degree program information:* Part-time programs available. Offers biblical and theological studies (MA); biblical studies (M Rel); education (M Ed); management/organizational leadership (MS); pastoral ministries (M Rel); religion and ethics (M Rel); theology (M Rel).

WARNER SOUTHERN COLLEGE, Lake Wales, FL 33859

General Information Independent-religious, coed, comprehensive institution.

GRADUATE UNITS

School of Business Offers business administration (MBA).

WARREN WILSON COLLEGE, Swannanoa, Asheville, NC 28815-9000

General Information Independent-religious, coed, comprehensive institution. *Graduate housing:* Room and/or apartments guaranteed to single students; on-campus housing not available to married students.

GRADUATE UNITS

MFA Program for Writers Postbaccalaureate distance learning degree programs offered (minimal on-campus study). Offers creative writing (MFA).

WARTBURG THEOLOGICAL SEMINARY, Dubuque, IA 52004-5004

General Information Independent-religious, coed, graduate-only institution. *Enrollment by degree level:* 138 first professional, 54 master's. *Graduate faculty:* 19 full-time (6 women), 9 part-time/adjunct (3 women). *Tuition:* Full-time $9,700; part-time $470 per credit. *Required fees:* $422; $50 per semester. *Graduate housing:* Rooms and/or apartments available on a first-come, first-served basis to single and married students. Typical cost: $2,300 per year for single students; $7,260 per year for married students. Room charges vary according to housing facility selected. Housing application deadline: 4/30. *Student services:* Campus employment opportunities, international student services, writing training. *Library facilities:* Reu Memorial Library. *Online resources:* library catalog, web page, access to other libraries' catalogs. *Collection:* 91,172 titles, 236 serial subscriptions, 596 audiovisual materials. *Research affiliation:* Menighetsfakultet (Oslo, Norway), Augustana Theologische Hochschule (Neuendettelsau, Germany).

Computer facilities: 19 computers available on campus for general student use. A campuswide network can be accessed from student residence rooms and from off campus. Internet access is available. *Web address:* http://www.wartburgseminary.edu/.

General Application Contact: Heather McClintuck, Director of Admissions, 563-589-0298, Fax: 563-589-0333, E-mail: admissions@wartburgseminary.edu.

GRADUATE UNITS

Graduate and Professional Programs Students: 159 full-time (76 women), 33 part-time (15 women); includes 2 minority (1 African American, 1 Hispanic American), 13 international. Average age 34. 86 applicants, 72% accepted, 50 enrolled. *Faculty:* 19 full-time (6 women), 9 part-time/adjunct (3 women). Expenses: Contact institution. *Financial support:* In 2006–07, 108 students received support, including 16 research assistantships with partial tuition reimbursements available (averaging $2,100 per year); career-related internships or fieldwork, Federal Work-Study, institutionally sponsored loans, and scholarships/grants also available. Support available to part-time students. Financial award application deadline: 6/15; financial award applicants required to submit FAFSA. In 2006, 30 M Divs, 5 master's awarded. *Degree program information:* Part-time programs available. Offers diaconal ministry (MA); theology (M Div, MA, MATDE, STM). *Application deadline:* For fall admission, 5/15 priority date for domestic students, 10/1 priority date for international students; for winter admission, 10/1 for international students; for spring admission, 12/15 priority date for domestic students, 10/1 for international students. Applications are processed on a rolling basis. *Application fee:* $0. Electronic applications accepted. *Application Contact:* Heather McClintuck, Director of Admissions, 563-589-0298, Fax: 563-589-0333, E-mail: admissions@wartburgseminary.edu. *Academic Dean,* Dr. Craig L. Nessan, 563-589-0207, Fax: 563-589-0333.

WASHBURN UNIVERSITY, Topeka, KS 66621

General Information City-supported, coed, comprehensive institution. *Enrollment:* 7,153 graduate, professional, and undergraduate students; 599 full-time matriculated graduate/professional students (298 women), 257 part-time matriculated graduate/professional students (178 women). *Enrollment by degree level:* 450 first professional, 406 master's. Tuition, state resident: full-time $4,338; part-time $241 per credit hour. Tuition, nonresident: full-time $8,820; part-time $490 per credit hour. *Required fees:* $62; $31 per semester. *Graduate housing:* Room and/or apartments available on a first-come, first-served basis to single students; on-campus housing not available to married students. Typical cost: $2,910 per year ($5,170 including board). Room and board charges vary according to board plan and housing facility selected. *Student services:* Campus employment opportunities, campus safety program, career counseling, disabled student services, exercise/wellness program, free psychological counseling, international student services, low-cost health insurance, multicultural affairs office, teacher training, writing training. *Library facilities:* Mabee Library plus 1 other. *Online resources:* library catalog, web page, access to other libraries' catalogs. *Collection:* 345,642 titles, 1,672 serial subscriptions, 3,141 audiovisual materials.

Computer facilities: 400 computers available on campus for general student use. A campuswide network can be accessed from off campus. Internet access and online class registration are available. *Web address:* http://www.washburn.edu/.

General Application Contact: Gordon McQuere, Dean, 785-670-1561, Fax: 785-670-1297, E-mail: gordon.mcquere@washburn.edu.

GRADUATE UNITS

College of Arts and Sciences Students: 31 full-time (20 women), 31 part-time (22 women). Average age 36. Expenses: Contact institution. *Financial support:* Research assistantships, career-related internships or fieldwork, Federal Work-Study, institutionally sponsored loans, and scholarships/grants available. Support available to part-time students. Financial award application deadline: 2/15; financial award applicants required to submit FAFSA. In 2006, 28 degrees awarded. *Degree program information:* Part-time and evening/weekend programs available. Offers arts and sciences (M Ed, MA, MLS); clinical psychology (MA); curriculum and instruction (M Ed); educational leadership (M Ed); liberal studies (MLS); reading (M Ed); special education (M Ed). *Application fee:* $0. *Dean,* Dr. Gordon McQuere, 785-670-1561, Fax: 785-670-1297, E-mail: gordon.mcquere@washburn.edu.

School of Applied Studies Offers applied studies (MCJ, MSW); clinical social work (MSW); criminal justice (MCJ).

School of Business Students: 19 full-time (13 women), 138 part-time (67 women); includes 13 minority (3 African Americans, 6 Asian Americans or Pacific Islanders, 4 Hispanic Americans). Average age 29. 40 applicants, 53% accepted, 21 enrolled. *Faculty:* 16 full-time (5 women), 3 part-time/adjunct (1 woman). Expenses: Contact institution. *Financial support:* In 2006–07, 21 students received support. Available to part-time students. Application deadline: 2/15; In 2006, 36 degrees awarded. *Degree program information:* Part-time and evening/weekend programs available. Offers business (MBA). *Application deadline:* For fall admission, 7/1 priority date for domestic and international students; for spring admission, 11/15 priority date for domestic and international students. Applications are processed on a rolling basis. *Application fee:* $40 ($60 for international students). Electronic applications accepted. *Application Contact:* Dr. Robert J. Boncella, MBA Program Director, 785-670-2047, Fax: 785-670-1063, E-mail: mba.advisor@washburn.edu. *Dean,* Dr. David L. Sollars, 785-670-1308, Fax: 785-670-1063, E-mail: david.sollars@washburn.edu.

School of Law Offers law (JD). Electronic applications accepted.

WASHINGTON AND LEE UNIVERSITY, Lexington, VA 24450-0303

General Information Independent, coed, comprehensive institution. *Enrollment:* 2,148 graduate, professional, and undergraduate students; 403 full-time matriculated graduate/professional students (165 women). *Enrollment by degree level:* 390 first professional, 13 other advanced degrees. *Graduate faculty:* 36 full-time (11 women), 6 part-time/adjunct (2 women). *Tuition:* Full-time $30,500. *Required fees:* $800. *Graduate housing:* Room and/or apartments available to single students. Typical cost: $15,695 (including board); $15,695 (including board) for married students. Housing application deadline: 4/15. *Student services:* Campus employment opportunities, campus safety program, career counseling, disabled student services, exercise/wellness program, free psychological counseling, international student services, low-cost health insurance, multicultural affairs office, writing training. *Library facilities:* James G. Leyburn Library plus 2 others. *Online resources:* library catalog, web page, access to other libraries' catalogs. *Collection:* 936,448 titles, 8,621 serial subscriptions, 17,224 audiovisual materials.

Computer facilities: Computer purchase and lease plans are available. 297 computers available on campus for general student use. A campuswide network can be accessed from student residence rooms and from off campus. Internet access and online class registration, e-mail are available. *Web address:* http://www.wlu.edu/.

General Application Contact: Andrea Hilton Howe, Director of Admissions, 540-458-8503, Fax: 540-458-8586, E-mail: hiltonhowea@wlu.edu.

GRADUATE UNITS

School of Law Students: 403 full-time (165 women); includes 62 minority (18 African Americans, 7 American Indian/Alaska Native, 31 Asian Americans or Pacific Islanders, 6 Hispanic Americans), 13 international. Average age 25. 2,764 applicants, 31% accepted, 126 enrolled. *Faculty:* 36 full-time (11 women), 6 part-time/adjunct (2 women). Expenses: Contact institution. *Financial support:* In 2006–07, 329 students received support, including 6 teaching assistantships (averaging $4,200 per year); fellowships, career-related internships or fieldwork, Federal Work-Study, institutionally sponsored loans, and scholarships/grants also available. Financial award application deadline: 2/15; financial award applicants required to submit FAFSA. In 2006, 129 JDs awarded. Offers law (JD); U.S. law (LL M). *Application deadline:* For fall admission, 1/15 priority date for domestic students. Applications are processed on a rolling basis. *Application fee:* $50. Electronic applications accepted. *Application Contact:* Andrea Hilton Howe, Director of Admissions, 540-458-8503, Fax: 540-458-8586, E-mail: hiltonhowea@wlu.edu. *Dean,* Rodney A. Smolla, 540-458-8502, Fax: 540-458-8488, E-mail: smollar@wlu.edu.

WASHINGTON COLLEGE, Chestertown, MD 21620-1197

General Information Independent, coed, comprehensive institution. *Enrollment:* 1,381 graduate, professional, and undergraduate students; 3 full-time matriculated graduate/professional students (2 women), 76 part-time matriculated graduate/professional students (42 women). *Enrollment by degree level:* 79 master's. *Graduate faculty:* 28 full-time (10 women), 7 part-time/adjunct (2 women). *Tuition:* Part-time $875 per course. Part-time tuition and fees vary according to program. *Graduate housing:* On-campus housing not available. *Student services:* Campus employment opportunities, career counseling, low-cost health insurance. *Library facilities:* Clifton M. Miller Library. *Online resources:* library catalog, web page, access to other libraries' catalogs. *Collection:* 243,030 titles, 4,667 serial subscriptions.

Computer facilities: Computer purchase and lease plans are available. 150 computers available on campus for general student use. A campuswide network can be accessed from student residence rooms and from off campus. Internet access, e-mail are available. *Web address:* http://www.washcoll.edu/.

General Application Contact: Dr. Christopher Ames, Provost/Dean, 800-422-1782 Ext. 7202, Fax: 410-778-7850, E-mail: cames2@washcoll.edu.

GRADUATE UNITS

Graduate Programs Students: 3 full-time (2 women), 76 part-time (42 women); includes 1 minority (African American), 1 international. *Faculty:* 28 full-time (10 women), 7 part-time/adjunct (2 women). Expenses: Contact institution. In 2006, 11 degrees awarded. *Degree program information:* Part-time and evening/weekend programs available. Offers English (MA); history (MA); psychology (MA). *Application deadline:* For fall admission, 8/1 priority date for domestic students; for winter admission, 12/1 priority date for domestic students; for spring admission, 4/15 priority date for domestic students. Applications are processed on a rolling basis. *Application fee:* $40. *Application Contact:* Dr. Kathryn W. Sack, Assistant Dean for Academic Affairs, 410-778-7213, Fax: 410-778-7850, E-mail: ksack2@washcoll.edu. *Provost/Dean,* Dr. Christopher Ames, 800-422-1782 Ext. 7202, Fax: 410-778-7850, E-mail: cames2@washcoll.edu.

WASHINGTON STATE UNIVERSITY, Pullman, WA 99164

General Information State-supported, coed, university. CGS member. *Enrollment:* 23,655 graduate, professional, and undergraduate students; 2,136 full-time matriculated graduate/professional students (1,074 women), 1,124 part-time matriculated graduate/professional

Washington State University (continued)

students (613 women). *Enrollment by degree level:* 1,891 master's, 1,247 doctoral, 120 other advanced degrees. *Graduate faculty:* 755 full-time (207 women), 34 part-time/adjunct (5 women). Tuition, state resident: full-time $7,066. Tuition, nonresident: full-time $17,204. *Graduate housing:* Rooms and/or apartments available on a first-come, first-served basis to single and married students. Housing application deadline: 3/1. *Student services:* Campus employment opportunities, campus safety program, career counseling, child daycare facilities, disabled student services, exercise/wellness program, free psychological counseling, grant writing training, international student services, low-cost health insurance, multicultural affairs office, teacher training, writing training. *Library facilities:* Holland Library plus 5 others. *Online resources:* library catalog, web page, access to other libraries' catalogs. *Collection:* 2.2 million titles, 31,590 serial subscriptions, 417,538 audiovisual materials. *Research affiliation:* Battelle Pacific Northwest Laboratories (biochemistry, engineering).

Computer facilities: 2,400 computers available on campus for general student use. A campuswide network can be accessed from student residence rooms and from off campus. Internet access and online class registration are available. *Web address:* http://www.wsu.edu/.

General Application Contact: Graduate School Admissions, 800-GRADWSU, Fax: 509-335-1949, E-mail: gradsch@wsu.edu.

GRADUATE UNITS

College of Veterinary Medicine Students: 383 full-time (296 women); includes 22 minority (3 African Americans, 3 American Indian/Alaska Native, 9 Asian Americans or Pacific Islanders, 7 Hispanic Americans). Average age 26. 784 applicants, 12% accepted, 96 enrolled. Expenses: Contact institution. *Financial support:* Fellowships, research assistantships with partial tuition reimbursements, teaching assistantships with partial tuition reimbursements, career-related internships or fieldwork, Federal Work-Study, institutionally sponsored loans, scholarships/grants, traineeships, and tuition waivers (partial) available. Support available to part-time students. Financial award application deadline: 3/1; financial award applicants required to submit FAFSA. In 2006, 70 DVMs, 5 master's, 6 doctorates awarded. *Degree program information:* Part-time programs available. Offers neuroscience (MS, PhD); veterinary and comparative anatomy, pharmacology, and physiology (MS, PhD); veterinary clinical sciences (MS); veterinary medicine (DVM, MS, PhD); veterinary microbiology and pathology (MS, PhD); veterinary science (MS, PhD). *Application deadline:* For fall admission, 10/2 for domestic and international students. Applications are processed on a rolling basis. *Application fee:* $40. Electronic applications accepted. *Application Contact:* Julie K. Smith, Principal Assistant, 509-335-3164, E-mail: jksmith@vetmed.wsu.edu. *Dean,* Dr. Warwick M. Bayly, 509-335-9515, Fax: 509-335-0160, E-mail: wmb@vetmed.wsu.edu.

Graduate School Students: 2,136 full-time (1,074 women), 1,124 part-time (613 women); includes 300 minority (46 African Americans, 43 American Indian/Alaska Native, 73 Asian Americans or Pacific Islanders, 138 Hispanic Americans), 623 international. Average age 31. 4,708 applicants, 28% accepted, 734 enrolled. *Faculty:* 721 full-time (160 women), 49 part-time/adjunct (13 women). Expenses: Contact institution. *Financial support:* In 2006–07, 2,309 students received support, including 266 fellowships with full tuition reimbursements available (averaging $3,939 per year), 583 research assistantships with full tuition reimbursements available (averaging $13,917 per year), 770 teaching assistantships with full tuition reimbursements available (averaging $13,056 per year); career-related internships or fieldwork, Federal Work-Study, institutionally sponsored loans, scholarships/grants, traineeships, tuition waivers (partial), unspecified assistantships, and staff assistantships, teaching associateships also available. Support available to part-time students. Financial award applicants required to submit FAFSA. In 2006, 169 first professional degrees, 650 master's, 172 doctorates, 15 other advanced degrees awarded. *Degree program information:* Part-time programs available. Offers interdisciplinary studies (PhD). Campuses also located at Spokane, Tri-Cities, and Vancouver. *Application deadline:* For fall admission, 2/1 priority date for domestic students, 3/1 for international students; for spring admission, 9/1 priority date for domestic students, 7/1 for international students. Applications are processed on a rolling basis. *Application fee:* $50. Electronic applications accepted. *Application Contact:* Graduate School Admissions, 800-GRADWSU, Fax: 509-335-1949, E-mail: gradsch@wsu.edu. *Dean,* Dr. Howard Grimes, 509-335-6424, Fax: 509-335-1949.

College of Agricultural, Human, and Natural Resource Sciences Students: 342 full-time (158 women), 51 part-time (28 women); includes 23 minority (2 African Americans, 5 American Indian/Alaska Native, 8 Asian Americans or Pacific Islanders, 8 Hispanic Americans), 145 international. Average age 30. 649 applicants, 23% accepted, 82 enrolled. Expenses: Contact institution. *Financial support:* In 2006–07, 278 students received support, including 26 fellowships (averaging $4,914 per year), 170 research assistantships with full and partial tuition reimbursements available (averaging $13,917 per year), 69 teaching assistantships with full and partial tuition reimbursements available (averaging $13,056 per year); career-related internships or fieldwork, Federal Work-Study, institutionally sponsored loans, tuition waivers (partial), unspecified assistantships, and staff assistantships, teaching associateships also available. Financial award application deadline: 4/1; financial award applicants required to submit FAFSA. In 2006, 53 master's, 21 doctorates awarded. *Degree program information:* Part-time programs available. Offers agribusiness (MA); agricultural economics (MA, PhD); agricultural, human, and natural resource sciences (MA, MS, MSLA, PhD, Certificate); agriculture (MS); animal sciences (MS, PhD); apparel, merchandising, design and textiles (MA); applied and theoretical options (MS); applied economics (MA); biological and agricultural engineering (MS, PhD); crop sciences (MS, PhD); economics (MA, PhD, Certificate); entomology (MS, PhD); environmental and natural resource sciences (PhD); food science (MS, PhD); horticulture (MS, PhD); human development (MA); human nutrition (MS); interdisciplinary (PhD); interior design (MA); international business economics (Certificate); landscape architecture (MSLA); molecular plant sciences (MS, PhD); natural resource sciences (MS); nutrition (PhD); plant pathology (MS, PhD); soil sciences (MS, PhD). *Application deadline:* For fall admission, 3/1 for international students; for spring admission, 7/1 for international students. Applications are processed on a rolling basis. *Application fee:* $50. Electronic applications accepted. *Application Contact:* Graduate School Admissions, 800-GRADWSU, Fax: 509-335-1949, E-mail: gradsch@wsu.edu. *Dean,* Dr. Daniel J. Bernardo, 509-335-4561.

College of Business Students: 124 full-time (48 women), 16 part-time (5 women); includes 3 minority (1 American Indian/Alaska Native, 2 Asian Americans or Pacific Islanders), 68 international. Average age 31. 384 applicants, 27% accepted, 43 enrolled. *Faculty:* 69. Expenses: Contact institution. *Financial support:* In 2006–07, 92 students received support, including 8 fellowships (averaging $6,326 per year), 8 research assistantships with full and partial tuition reimbursements available (averaging $13,917 per year), 67 teaching assistantships with full and partial tuition reimbursements available (averaging $13,056 per year); career-related internships or fieldwork, Federal Work-Study, institutionally sponsored loans, tuition waivers (partial), and teaching associateships also available. Financial award application deadline: 4/1; financial award applicants required to submit FAFSA. In 2006, 77 master's, 13 doctorates awarded. Offers accounting and business law (M Acc); accounting and information systems (M Acc); accounting and taxation (M Acc); business (M Acc, MBA, PhD, Certificate); business administration (MBA, PhD); finance, insurance and real estate (PhD). *Application deadline:* For fall admission, 2/1 priority date for domestic students, 2/1 for international students; for spring admission, 7/1 for domestic and international students. Applications are processed on a rolling basis. *Application fee:* $50. *Application Contact:* Graduate School Admissions, 800-GRADWSU, Fax: 509-335-1949, E-mail: gradsch@wsu.edu. *Dean,* Dr. Eric Spangenberg, 509-335-3596.

College of Education Students: 158 full-time (105 women), 74 part-time (49 women); includes 56 minority (15 African Americans, 4 American Indian/Alaska Native, 14 Asian Americans or Pacific Islanders, 23 Hispanic Americans), 14 international. Average age 34. 313 applicants, 35% accepted, 42 enrolled. *Faculty:* 88. Expenses: Contact institution. *Financial support:* In 2006–07, 12 fellowships (averaging $2,844 per year), 58 research assistantships with partial tuition reimbursements (averaging $13,917 per year), 39 teaching assistantships with partial tuition reimbursements (averaging $13,056 per year) were awarded; career-related internships or fieldwork, Federal Work-Study, institutionally sponsored loans, scholarships/grants, tuition waivers (partial), and staff assistantships, teaching associateships also available. Financial award application deadline: 4/1; financial award applicants required to submit FAFSA. In 2006, 174 master's, 19 doctorates awarded. Offers counseling psychology (Ed M, MA, PhD); curriculum and instruction (Ed D, PhD); diverse languages (M Ed, MA); education (Ed M, M Ed, MA, MIT, MS, Ed D, PhD); educational leadership (M Ed, MA, Ed D, PhD); educational psychology (Ed M, MA, PhD); elementary education (M Ed, MA, MIT); exercise science (MS); higher education (Ed M, MA, Ed D, PhD); higher education with sport management (Ed M); literacy education (M Ed, MA, PhD); math education (PhD); secondary education (M Ed, MA). *Application deadline:* For fall admission, 3/1 for domestic and international students; for spring admission, 10/1 for domestic students, 7/1 for international students. *Application fee:* $50. Electronic applications accepted. *Application Contact:* Graduate School Admissions, 800-GRADWSU, Fax: 509-335-1949, E-mail: gradsch@wsu.edu. *Dean,* Dr. Judy Mitchell, 509-335-4853.

College of Engineering and Architecture Students: 301 full-time (79 women), 145 part-time (33 women); includes 22 minority (1 African American, 2 American Indian/Alaska Native, 8 Asian Americans or Pacific Islanders, 11 Hispanic Americans), 181 international. Average age 31. 989 applicants, 14% accepted, 83 enrolled. *Faculty:* 99 full-time (13 women). Expenses: Contact institution. *Financial support:* In 2006–07, 287 students received support, including 21 fellowships with full and partial tuition reimbursements available (averaging $4,325 per year), 139 research assistantships with full and partial tuition reimbursements available (averaging $13,917 per year), 94 teaching assistantships with full and partial tuition reimbursements available (averaging $13,056 per year); career-related internships or fieldwork, Federal Work-Study, institutionally sponsored loans, tuition waivers (partial), and teaching associateships also available. Financial award application deadline: 4/1; financial award applicants required to submit FAFSA. In 2006, 82 master's, 27 doctorates awarded. Offers architecture (M Arch); architecture design theory (MS); chemical engineering (MS, PhD); civil engineering (MS, PhD); computer engineering (MS, PhD); computer science (MS, PhD); electrical engineering (MS, PhD); engineering and architecture (M Arch, MS, Dr DES, PhD); environmental engineering (MS); material science engineering (MS); mechanical engineering (MS, PhD). *Application deadline:* For fall admission, 3/1 priority date for domestic students, 3/1 for international students; for spring admission, 7/1 priority date for domestic students, 7/1 for international students. Applications are processed on a rolling basis. *Application fee:* $50. *Application Contact:* Graduate School Admissions, 800-GRADWSU, Fax: 509-335-1949, E-mail: gradsch@wsu.edu. *Dean,* Dr. Candis Claiborn, 509-335-5593.

College of Liberal Arts Students: 452 full-time (249 women), 80 part-time (36 women); includes 70 minority (14 African Americans, 13 American Indian/Alaska Native, 10 Asian Americans or Pacific Islanders, 33 Hispanic Americans), 61 international. Average age 31. 1,020 applicants, 21% accepted, 147 enrolled. *Faculty:* 247. Expenses: Contact institution. *Financial support:* In 2006–07, 458 students received support, including 26 fellowships with tuition reimbursements available (averaging $4,109 per year), 39 research assistantships with full and partial tuition reimbursements available (averaging $13,917 per year), 301 teaching assistantships with full and partial tuition reimbursements available (averaging $13,056 per year); career-related internships or fieldwork, Federal Work-Study, institutionally sponsored loans, scholarships/grants, tuition waivers (partial), and unspecified assistantships also available. Support available to part-time students. Financial award applicants required to submit FAFSA. In 2006, 93 master's, 34 doctorates awarded. Offers archaeology (MA, PhD); ceramics (MFA); clinical psychology (PhD); composition (MA); crime and deviance (MA, PhD); criminal justice (MA, PhD); cultural anthropology (MA, PhD); digital media (MFA); drawing (MFA); early and modern European history (MA, PhD); English (MA, PhD); environmental history (MA, PhD); environments, community and demographics (PhD); environments, community, and demographics (MA); ethnic studies (MA, PhD); evolutionary anthropology (MA, PhD); experimental psychology (PhD); feminist studies (MA, PhD); health communications (MA, PhD); history (MA, PhD); institutions and social organizations (MA, PhD); intercultural international communications (MA); intercultural/international communications (PhD); jazz (MA); Latin American history (MA, PhD); liberal arts (MA, MFA, MS, PhD); literature (MA, PhD); media and society (MA, PhD); media process and effects (MA, PhD); modern East Asia history (MA, PhD); music (MA); music education (MA); organizational communications (MA, PhD); painting (MFA); performance (MA); philosophy (MA); photography (MFA); political science (MA, PhD); political sociology (MA, PhD); print making (MFA); psychology (MS); public history (MA, PhD); sculpture (MFA); social inequality (MA, PhD); social psychology and life course (MA, PhD); Spanish (MA); teaching of English (MA); US history (MA, PhD); women's history (MA, PhD); world history (MA, PhD). *Application deadline:* For fall admission, 3/1 for international students; for spring admission, 7/1 for international students. *Application fee:* $50. Electronic applications accepted. *Application Contact:* Graduate School Admissions, 800-GRADWSU, Fax: 509-335-1949, E-mail: gradsch@wsu.edu. *Dean,* Dr. Eric Lear, 509-335-4581.

College of Pharmacy Students: 415 full-time (246 women), 14 part-time (9 women); includes 91 minority (6 African Americans, 6 American Indian/Alaska Native, 66 Asian Americans or Pacific Islanders, 13 Hispanic Americans), 8 international. Average age 26. 919 applicants, 10% accepted, 94 enrolled. *Faculty:* 30. Expenses: Contact institution. *Financial support:* In 2006–07, 206 students received support, including 32 fellowships (averaging $4,982 per year), 10 research assistantships with full and partial tuition reimbursements available (averaging $13,917 per year), 4 teaching assistantships with full and partial tuition reimbursements available (averaging $13,056 per year); Federal Work-Study, institutionally sponsored loans, tuition waivers (partial), and staff assistantships, teaching associateships also available. Financial award application deadline: 4/1; financial award applicants required to submit FAFSA. In 2006, 76 first professional degrees, 11 master's, 4 doctorates awarded. Offers health policy and administration (MHPA); pharmaceutical science (Pharm D); pharmacology and toxicology (MS, PhD); pharmacy (Pharm D, MHPA, MS, PhD). *Application deadline:* For fall admission, 2/1 for domestic students. Applications are processed on a rolling basis. *Application fee:* $35. *Application Contact:* Graduate School Admissions, 800-GRADWSU, Fax: 509-335-1949, E-mail: gradsch@wsu.edu. *Dean,* Dr. James P. Kehrer, 509-335-4750, E-mail: kehrer@wsu.edu.

College of Sciences Students: 371 full-time (160 women), 31 part-time (11 women); includes 20 minority (1 African American, 2 American Indian/Alaska Native, 7 Asian Americans or Pacific Islanders, 10 Hispanic Americans), 108 international. Average age 29. 788 applicants, 20% accepted, 96 enrolled. *Faculty:* 158. Expenses: Contact institution. *Financial support:* In 2006–07, 305 students received support, including 29 fellowships (averaging $4,199 per year), 105 research assistantships (averaging $13,917 per year), 166 teaching assistantships (averaging $13,056 per year); career-related internships or fieldwork, Federal Work-Study, institutionally sponsored loans, traineeships, tuition waivers (partial), and teaching associateships also available. Financial award applicants required to submit FAFSA. In 2006, 52 master's, 34 doctorates awarded. Offers applied mathematics (MS, PhD); biochemistry and biophysics (MS, PhD); biology (MS); botany (MS, PhD); chemistry (MS, PhD); environmental and natural resource sciences (MS, PhD); environmental science (MS, PhD); genetics and cell biology (MS, PhD); geology (MS, PhD); materials science (PhD); mathematics teaching (MS, PhD); microbiology (MS, PhD); molecular biosciences (MS, PhD); physics (MS, PhD); sciences (MS, PhD); zoology (MS, PhD). *Application deadline:* Applications are processed on a rolling basis. *Application fee:* $50. *Application Contact:* Graduate School Admissions, 800-GRADWSU, Fax: 509-335-1949, E-mail: gradsch@wsu.edu. *Dean,* Dr. Michael Griswold, 509-335-5548, E-mail: mgriswold@wsu.edu.

WASHINGTON STATE UNIVERSITY SPOKANE, Spokane, WA 99210-1495

General Information State-supported, coed, graduate-only institution. *Enrollment by degree level:* 429 first professional, 181 master's, 64 doctoral, 34 other advanced degrees. *Graduate faculty:* 258. Tuition, state resident: full-time $7,066. Tuition, nonresident: full-time $17,204. Tuition and fees vary according to program. *Student services:* Campus employment opportunities, campus safety program, career counseling, disabled student services, exercise/wellness program, free psychological counseling, grant writing training, international student services, low-cost health insurance. *Library facilities:* Cooperative Academic Library Service. *Online resources:* library catalog, web page, access to other libraries' catalogs. *Collection:* 2.3 million titles, 30,122 serial subscriptions, 426,737 audiovisual materials.

Computer facilities: 48 computers available on campus for general student use. A campuswide network can be accessed from off campus. Internet access and online class registration are available. *Web address:* http://www.spokane.wsu.edu/.

General Application Contact: Graduate School Admissions, 800-GRADWSU, Fax: 509-335-1949, E-mail: gradsch@wsu.edu.

GRADUATE UNITS

Graduate Programs Students: 167 full-time (109 women), 112 part-time (57 women); includes 34 minority (6 African Americans, 9 American Indian/Alaska Native, 8 Asian Americans or Pacific Islanders, 11 Hispanic Americans), 13 international. 249 applicants, 48% accepted, 70 enrolled. *Faculty:* 258. Expenses: Contact institution. *Financial support:* In 2006–07, 36 fellowships (averaging $4,207 per year), 22 research assistantships with tuition reimbursements (averaging $13,917 per year), 9 teaching assistantships with tuition reimbursements (averaging $13,056 per year) were awarded. Offers cellular physiology (MS); clinical exercise physiology (MS); clinical physiology (MS); criminal justice (MA, PhD); educational leadership (Ed M, MA); engineering management (M Eng Mgt); health policy and administration (MHPA); principal (Certificate); professional certification for teachers (Certificate); program administrator (Certificate); school psychologist (Certificate); speech and hearing sciences (MA); superintendent (Certificate); teaching (MIT). *Application deadline:* For fall admission, 2/1 priority date for domestic students, 3/1 for international students; for spring admission, 9/1 priority date for domestic students, 7/1 for international students. *Application fee:* $50. *Application Contact:* Graduate School Admissions, 800-GRADWSU, Fax: 509-335-1949, E-mail: gradsch@wsu.edu. *Chancellor,* Dr. Brian L. Pitcher, 509-358-7551, Fax: 509-358-7538.

Intercollegiate College of Nursing Students: 26 full-time (21 women), 36 part-time (35 women); includes 6 minority (3 American Indian/Alaska Native, 1 Asian American or Pacific Islander, 2 Hispanic Americans). 45 applicants, 64% accepted, 22 enrolled. *Faculty:* 64. Expenses: Contact institution. *Financial support:* In 2006–07, 62 students received support, including 11 fellowships (averaging $4,407 per year), 12 teaching assistantships with tuition reimbursements available (averaging $17,350 per year). Offers nursing (MN). *Application deadline:* For fall admission, 1/15 for domestic students; for spring admission, 8/5 for domestic students. *Application fee:* $50. *Application Contact:* Graduate School Admissions, 800-GRADWSU, Fax: 509-335-1949, E-mail: gradsch@wsu.edu. *Dean,* Dr. Patricia Butterfield, 509-324-7360, Fax: 509-858-7336.

Interdisciplinary Design Institute Students: 35 full-time (22 women), 5 part-time (3 women); includes 5 minority (2 American Indian/Alaska Native, 2 Asian Americans or Pacific Islanders, 1 Hispanic American), 2 international. Average age 35. 61 applicants, 67% accepted, 18 enrolled. *Faculty:* 11 full-time (3 women), 3 part-time/adjunct (2 women). Expenses: Contact institution. *Financial support:* In 2006–07, 30 students received support, including 10 research assistantships with full and partial tuition reimbursements available (averaging $13,917 per year), teaching assistantships with full and partial tuition reimbursements available (averaging $13,056 per year). *Degree program information:* Part-time programs available. Offers architecture (M Arch, MS); design (Dr DES); interior design (MA); landscape architecture (MS). *Application deadline:* For fall admission, 4/1 priority date for domestic students, 3/1 for international students. *Application fee:* $50. *Application Contact:* Graduate School Admissions, 800-GRADWSU, Fax: 509-335-1949, E-mail: gradsch@wsu.edu. *Director,* Dr. Nancy H. Blossom, 509-358-7920, E-mail: blossom@wsu.edu.

Program in Pharmacy Students: 415 full-time (246 women), 14 part-time (9 women); includes 91 minority (6 African Americans, 6 American Indian/Alaska Native, 66 Asian Americans or Pacific Islanders, 13 Hispanic Americans). Average age 29. 919 applicants, 10% accepted, 94 enrolled. *Faculty:* 29 full-time (11 women), 97 part-time/adjunct (39 women). Expenses: Contact institution. *Financial support:* In 2006–07, 156 students received support, including 17 fellowships (averaging $3,324 per year); career-related internships or fieldwork, Federal Work-Study, and scholarships/grants also available. Financial award application deadline:4/1. Offers pharmacy (Pharm D). *Application deadline:* For fall admission, 12/15 for domestic students. Applications are processed on a rolling basis. *Application fee:* $40. *Application Contact:* Graduate School Admissions, 800-GRADWSU, Fax: 509-335-1949, E-mail: gradsch@wsu.edu. *Interim Chair,* Dr. Linda Garretts, 509-335-8030.

WASHINGTON STATE UNIVERSITY TRI-CITIES, Richland, WA 99352-1671

General Information State-supported, coed, graduate-only institution. *Enrollment by degree level:* 242 master's, 23 doctoral, 13 other advanced degrees. *Graduate faculty:* 87. Tuition, state resident: full-time $7,066. Tuition, nonresident: full-time $17,204. *Graduate housing:* On-campus housing not available. *Student services:* Campus employment opportunities, career counseling, disabled student services, exercise/wellness program, low-cost health insurance, multicultural affairs office, writing training. *Library facilities:* Max E. Benitz Library plus 3 others. *Online resources:* library catalog, web page, access to other libraries' catalogs. *Collection:* 2.3 million titles, 30,122 serial subscriptions, 426,737 audiovisual materials.

Computer facilities: 50 computers available on campus for general student use. A campuswide network can be accessed from off campus. Internet access and online class registration are available. *Web address:* http://www.tricity.wsu.edu/.

General Application Contact: Graduate School Admissions, 800-GRADWSU, Fax: 509-335-1949, E-mail: gradsch@wsu.edu.

GRADUATE UNITS

Graduate Programs Students: 57 full-time (40 women), 221 part-time (124 women); includes 27 minority (1 African American, 1 American Indian/Alaska Native, 2 Asian Americans or Pacific Islanders, 23 Hispanic Americans). Average age 37. 157 applicants, 57% accepted, 52 enrolled. Expenses: Contact institution. *Financial support:* In 2006–07, 17 students received support, including 2 research assistantships (averaging $13,917 per year), 4 teaching assistantships (averaging $13,056 per year); Federal Work-Study, health care benefits, and unspecified assistantships also available. *Degree program information:* Part-time programs available. Offers applied environmental science (MS); atmospheric science (MS); biology (MS); chemistry (MS, PhD); counseling (Ed M); earth science (MS); educational leadership (Ed M, Ed D); environmental and occupational health science (MS); environmental regulatory compliance (MS); environmental science (PhD); environmental toxicology and risk assessment (MS); literacy (Ed M); secondary certification (Ed M); teaching (MIT); water resource science (MS). *Application deadline:* For fall admission, 3/1 for international students; for spring admission, 7/1 for international students. Applications are processed on a rolling basis. *Application fee:* $50. Electronic applications accepted. *Application Contact:* Graduate School Admissions, 800-GRADWSU, Fax: 509-335-1949, E-mail: gradsch@wsu.edu. *Chancellor,* Dr. Vicky Carwein, 509-372-7258, Fax: 509-372-7354.

College of Business Students: 6 full-time (2 women), 30 part-time (13 women); includes 4 minority (all Hispanic Americans) Average age 35. 27 applicants, 22% accepted, 4 enrolled. *Faculty:* 6 full-time (1 woman), 3 part-time/adjunct (2 women). Expenses: Contact institution. *Financial support:* In 2006–07, 17 students received support. *Degree program information:* Part-time and evening/weekend programs available. Offers business management (MBA); technology management (MTM). *Application deadline:* For fall admission, 2/1 priority date for domestic students, 3/1 for international students; for spring admission, 9/1 priority date for domestic students, 7/1 for international students. *Application fee:* $50. *Application Contact:* Graduate School Admissions, 800-GRADWSU, Fax: 509-335-1949, E-mail: gradsch@wsu.edu. *Graduate Program Director,* Dr. John Thornton, 509-372-7000, Fax: 509-372-7354.

College of Engineering and Computer Science Students: 3 full-time (2 women), 33 part-time (5 women); includes 5 minority (2 Asian Americans or Pacific Islanders, 3 Hispanic Americans), 7 international. Average age 34. 15 applicants, 33% accepted, 4 enrolled. *Faculty:* 34. Expenses: Contact institution. *Financial support:* In 2006–07, 6 students received support, including 3 research assistantships with tuition reimbursements available (averaging $13,917 per year). *Degree program information:* Part-time programs available. Offers computer science (MS, PhD); electrical and computer engineering (PhD); electrical engineering (MS); mechanical engineering (MS, PhD). *Application deadline:* For fall admission, 2/1 priority date for domestic students, 3/1 for international students; for spring admission, 9/1 priority date for domestic students, 7/1 for international students. *Application fee:* $50. *Application Contact:* Graduate School Admissions, 800-GRADWSU, Fax: 509-335-1949, E-mail: gradsch@wsu.edu. *Director,* Dr. Thomas Fischer, 509-335-8148.

Intercollegiate College of Nursing Students: 11 full-time (all women), 15 part-time (11 women); includes 1 minority (Hispanic American) 6 applicants, 100% accepted, 3 enrolled. *Faculty:* 10. Expenses: Contact institution. *Financial support:* In 2006–07, 24 students received support, including 5 fellowships (averaging $4,050 per year), 3 teaching assistantships with tuition reimbursements available (averaging $13,056 per year). *Degree program information:* Part-time programs available. Postbaccalaureate distance learning degree programs offered (minimal on-campus study). Offers nursing (MN). *Application deadline:* For fall admission, 1/15 for domestic students, 3/1 for international students; for spring admission, 8/5 for domestic students, 7/1 for international students. *Application fee:* $50. *Application Contact:* Graduate School Admissions, 800-GRADWSU, Fax: 509-335-1949, E-mail: gradsch@wsu.edu. *Unit Head,* Lorrie Dawson, 509-372-7000, Fax: 509-372-7354.

WASHINGTON STATE UNIVERSITY VANCOUVER, Vancouver, WA 98686

General Information State-supported, coed, graduate-only institution. *Enrollment by degree level:* 380 master's, 37 doctoral, 42 other advanced degrees. *Graduate faculty:* 87. Tuition, state resident: full-time $7,066. Tuition, nonresident: full-time $17,204. *Graduate housing:* On-campus housing not available. *Student services:* Campus employment opportunities, campus safety program, career counseling, disabled student services, free psychological counseling, grant writing training, low-cost health insurance, multicultural affairs office, teacher training, writing training. *Library facilities:* WSU Vancouver Library. *Online resources:* library catalog, web page, access to other libraries' catalogs. *Collection:* 2.3 million titles, 30,122 serial subscriptions, 426,737 audiovisual materials.

Computer facilities: 30 computers available on campus for general student use. A campuswide network can be accessed from off campus. Internet access and online class registration are available. *Web address:* http://www.vancouver.wsu.edu/.

General Application Contact: Graduate School Admissions, 800-GRADWSU, Fax: 509-335-1949, E-mail: gradsch@wsu.edu.

GRADUATE UNITS

Graduate Programs Students: 121 full-time (82 women), 338 part-time (227 women); includes 37 minority (4 African Americans, 3 American Indian/Alaska Native, 14 Asian Americans or Pacific Islanders, 16 Hispanic Americans), 8 international. Average age 38. 247 applicants, 59% accepted, 69 enrolled. *Faculty:* 87. Expenses: Contact institution. *Financial support:* In 2006–07, 224 students received support, including 17 fellowships (averaging $3,490 per year), 12 research assistantships with partial tuition reimbursements available (averaging $13,917 per year), 14 teaching assistantships with partial tuition reimbursements available (averaging $13,056 per year); Federal Work-Study, scholarships/grants, and unspecified assistantships also available. *Degree program information:* Part-time programs available. Offers business administration (MBA); education (Ed M, MIT, Ed D); environmental science (MS); history (MA, PhD); public affairs (MPA). *Application deadline:* For fall admission, 7/15 priority date for domestic students, 3/1 for international students; for spring admission, 10/15 priority date for domestic students, 7/1 for international students. *Application fee:* $50. *Application Contact:* Graduate School Admissions, 800-GRADWSU, Fax: 509-335-1949, E-mail: gradsch@wsu.edu. *Chancellor,* Dr. Hal Dengerink, 360-546-9581, Fax: 360-546-9043, E-mail: dengerin@wsu.edu.

Intercollegiate College of Nursing Students: 11 full-time (10 women), 76 part-time (72 women); includes 5 minority (1 American Indian/Alaska Native, 1 Asian American or Pacific Islander, 3 Hispanic Americans). 44 applicants, 68% accepted, 14 enrolled. *Faculty:* 20. Expenses: Contact institution. *Financial support:* In 2006–07, 52 students received support, including 8 fellowships with tuition reimbursements available (averaging $5,437 per year), 2 teaching assistantships with tuition reimbursements available (averaging $17,360 per year). Offers nursing (MN). *Application deadline:* For fall admission, 2/1 for domestic and international students; for spring admission, 10/1 for domestic students, 7/1 for international students. Applications are processed on a rolling basis. *Application fee:* $50. Electronic applications accepted. *Interim Academic Director,* Dr. Dawn Doutrich, 360-546-9752, Fax: 360-546-9038.

School of Engineering and Computer Science Students: 6 full-time (1 woman), 2 international. 15 applicants, 33% accepted, 2 enrolled. *Faculty:* 8. Expenses: Contact institution. *Financial support:* In 2006–07, 2 research assistantships with full tuition reimbursements (averaging $13,917 per year), 7 teaching assistantships with full tuition reimbursements (averaging $13,056 per year) were awarded; health care benefits and unspecified assistantships also available. *Degree program information:* Part-time programs available. Offers computer science (MS); mechanical engineering (MS). *Application deadline:* For fall admission, 2/1 priority date for domestic students, 2/1 for international students; for spring admission, 9/1 priority date for domestic students, 7/1 for international students. Applications are processed on a rolling basis. *Application fee:* $50. *Application Contact:* Peggy Moore, Academic Coordinator, 360-546-9638, Fax: 360-546-9438, E-mail: moorep@vancouver.wsu.edu. *Director,* Dr. Hakan Gurocak, 360-546-9639, Fax: 360-546-9438, E-mail: hgurocak@vancouver.wsu.edu.

WASHINGTON THEOLOGICAL UNION, Washington, DC 20012

General Information Independent-religious, coed, graduate-only institution. *Graduate housing:* Room and/or apartments available on a first-come, first-served basis to single students; on-campus housing not available to married students.

GRADUATE UNITS

Graduate and Professional Programs *Degree program information:* Part-time programs available. Offers theology (M Div, MA, MAPS).

WASHINGTON UNIVERSITY IN ST. LOUIS, St. Louis, MO 63130-4899

General Information Independent, coed, university. CGS member. *Graduate housing:* Rooms and/or apartments available on a first-come, first-served basis to single and married students.

GRADUATE UNITS

George Warren Brown School of Social Work Students: 369 full-time (322 women), 32 part-time (26 women); includes 84 minority (39 African Americans, 12 American Indian/Alaska Native, 17 Asian Americans or Pacific Islanders, 16 Hispanic Americans), 60 international. Average age 28. 524 applicants, 64% accepted, 166 enrolled. *Faculty:* 31 full-time (15 women), 49 part-time/adjunct (29 women). Expenses: Contact institution. *Financial support:* In 2006–07, 365 students received support, including 273 fellowships with partial tuition reimbursements available (averaging $5,432 per year), 43 research assistantships with full tuition reimbursements available (averaging $3,000 per year), 26 teaching assistantships with full tuition reimbursements available (averaging $1,000 per year); career-related internships or fieldwork, Federal Work-Study, institutionally sponsored loans, scholarships/grants, and tuition waivers (partial) also available. Support available to part-time students. Financial award applicants required to submit FAFSA. In 2006, 161 master's, 13 doctorates awarded. *Degree program information:* Part-time programs available. Offers social work (MSW, PhD). *Application deadline:* Applications are processed on a rolling basis. *Application fee:* $60. Electronic applications accepted. *Application Contact:* Janice Wells-White, Director of Admissions and Recruiting, 314-935-6676, Fax: 314-935-4859, E-mail: msw@gwbmail.wustl.edu. *Dean and William E. Gordon Professor,* Dr. Edward F Lawlor, 314-935-6693, Fax: 314-935-8511, E-mail: elawlor@wush.edu.

Graduate School of Arts and Sciences Offers American history (MA, PhD); anthropology (MA, PhD); art history (MA, PhD); arts and sciences (MA, MA Ed, MAT, MFAW, MM, PhD); Asian history (MA, PhD); Asian language (MA); Asian studies (MA); British history (MA, PhD); chemistry (MA, PhD); Chinese (MA, PhD); Chinese and comparative literature (PhD); classical archaeology (MA, PhD); classics (MA, MAT); clinical psychology (PhD); comparative literature (MA, PhD); earth and planetary sciences (MA); East Asian studies (MA); economics (MA, PhD); educational research (PhD); elementary education (MA Ed); English and American

Washington University in St. Louis (continued)

literature (MA, PhD); European history (MA, PhD); French (MA, PhD); general experimental psychology (MA, PhD); geochemistry (PhD); geology (MA, PhD); geophysics (PhD); Germanic languages and literature (MA, PhD); history (PhD); Islamic and Near Eastern studies (MA); Japanese (MA, PhD); Japanese and comparative literature (PhD); Jewish studies (MA); Jewish, Islamic, and Near Eastern studies (MA); Latin American history (MA, PhD); mathematics (MA, PhD); mathematics education (MAT); Middle Eastern history (MA, PhD); movement science (PhD); music (MA, MM, PhD); performing arts (MA); philosophy (MA, PhD); philosophy/neuroscience/psychology (PhD); physics (MA, PhD); planetary sciences (PhD); political economy and public policy (MA); political science (MA, PhD); Romance languages (MA, PhD); secondary education (MA Ed, MAT); social psychology (MA, PhD); social work (PhD); Spanish (MA, PhD); statistics (MA, PhD); writing (MFAW). Electronic applications accepted.

Division of Biology and Biomedical Sciences Offers biochemistry (PhD); chemical biology (PhD); computational biology (PhD); developmental biology (PhD); ecology (PhD); environmental biology (PhD); evolution, ecology and population biology (PhD); evolutionary biology (PhD); genetics (PhD); immunology (PhD); molecular biophysics (PhD); molecular cell biology (PhD); molecular genetics (PhD); molecular microbiology and microbial pathogenesis (PhD); neurosciences (PhD); plant biology (PhD). Electronic applications accepted.

Henry Edwin Sever Graduate School of Engineering and Applied Science *Degree program information:* Part-time and evening/weekend programs available. Offers biomedical engineering (MS, D Sc); chemical engineering (MS, D Sc); civil engineering (MSCE); computer engineering (MS, D Sc); computer science (MS, D Sc); construction management (MCM); electrical engineering (MS, D Sc, PhD); engineering and applied science (MCE, MCM, MEM, MIM, MS, MSCE, MSE, MSEE, MSEE, MTM, D Sc, PhD); environmental engineering (MS, D Sc); mechanical and aerospace engineering (MS, D Sc); structural engineering (MSCE, MSE, D Sc, PhD); systems science and mathematics (MS, D Sc, PhD). Electronic applications accepted.

John M. Olin School of Business Expenses: Contact institution. Offers accounting (MS); business (EMBA, M Acc, MBA, MS, PhD); business administration (EMBA, MBA); finance (MS). Electronic applications accepted.

Sam Fox School of Design and Visual Arts Offers design and visual arts (M Arch, MFA, MUD).

Graduate School of Architecture and Urban Design Students: 166 full-time (77 women); includes 12 minority (2 African Americans, 5 Asian Americans or Pacific Islanders, 5 Hispanic Americans), 33 international. Average age 25. 230 applicants, 80% accepted, 68 enrolled. *Faculty:* 21 full-time (7 women), 22 part-time/adjunct (7 women). Expenses: Contact institution. *Financial support:* In 2006–07, 145 students received support, including 5 research assistantships (averaging $2,000 per year), 35 teaching assistantships (averaging $2,500 per year); Federal Work-Study, scholarships/grants, tuition waivers (partial), and unspecified assistantships also available. Support available to part-time students. Financial award application deadline: 2/15; financial award applicants required to submit FAFSA. In 2006, 42 degrees awarded. Offers architecture (M Arch); architecture and urban design (M Arch, MUD); urban design (MUD). *Application deadline:* For fall admission, 2/1 priority date for domestic and international students; for spring admission, 10/1 for domestic and international students. *Application fee:* $50. *Application Contact:* Peter MacKeith, Director, Graduate Admissions, 314-935-6227, Fax: 314-935-7656, E-mail: mackeith@wustl.edu. *Dean,* Bruce Lindsey, 314-935-6200, Fax: 314-935-7656.

Graduate School of Art Students: 27 full-time (15 women); includes 3 minority (2 African Americans, 1 Hispanic American), 1 international. Average age 30. *Faculty:* 17 full-time (7 women), 3 part-time/adjunct (all women). Expenses: Contact institution. *Financial support:* In 2006–07, 26 students received support; fellowships with partial tuition reimbursements available, research assistantships with partial tuition reimbursements available, teaching assistantships with partial tuition reimbursements available, Federal Work-Study, institutionally sponsored loans, scholarships/grants, health care benefits, tuition waivers (partial), and unspecified assistantships available. Financial award application deadline: 2/1; financial award applicants required to submit FAFSA. In 2006, 14 master's awarded. Offers art (MFA). *Application deadline:* For fall admission, 1/15 for domestic and international students. *Application fee:* $75. *Application Contact:* Patricia Olynyk, Director of Graduate Studies, 314-935-5884, Fax: 314-935-6462, E-mail: olynyk@samfox.wustl.edu. *Dean,* Jeff Pike, 314-935-6500, Fax: 314-935-4862, E-mail: jpike@art.wustl.edu.

School of Law Students: 861 full-time (366 women), 29 part-time (8 women). Average age 27. 3,325 applicants, 27% accepted, 241 enrolled. *Faculty:* 59 full-time (28 women), 118 part-time/adjunct (24 women). Expenses: Contact institution. *Financial support:* Career-related internships or fieldwork, Federal Work-Study, institutionally sponsored loans, scholarships/grants, and health care benefits available. Support available to part-time students. Financial award application deadline: 3/1; financial award applicants required to submit FAFSA. In 2006, 251 degrees awarded. Offers law (JD, LL M, MJS, JSD). *Application deadline:* For fall admission, 3/1 priority date for domestic students. *Application fee:* $70. Electronic applications accepted. *Application Contact:* Mary Ann Clifford, Assistant Dean for Admissions, 314-935-4525, Fax: 314-935-8778, E-mail: admiss@wulaw.wustl.edu. *Dean,* Kent D Syverud, 314-935-6400.

School of Medicine Students: 971 full-time (605 women), 59 part-time (38 women); includes 278 minority (36 African Americans, 8 American Indian/Alaska Native, 203 Asian Americans or Pacific Islanders, 31 Hispanic Americans), 37 international. Average age 23. Expenses: Contact institution. *Financial support:* Fellowships, research assistantships, career-related internships or fieldwork, Federal Work-Study, and institutionally sponsored loans available. Support available to part-time students. Financial award applicants required to submit FAFSA. In 2006, 125 first professional degrees, 209 master's awarded. Offers audiology (Au D); clinical (MS); clinical investigation (MS); computational (MS); deaf education (MS); genetic epidemiology (Certificate); health administration (MHA); medicine (MD, MHA, MS, MSOT, Au D, DPT, OTD, PhD, Certificate, PPDPT); movement science (PhD); occupational therapy (MSOT, OTD); physical therapy (DPT, PhD, PPDPT); speech and hearing sciences (PhD). *Application Contact:* Dr. W. Edwin Dodson, Associate Dean, 314-362-6848, Fax: 314-362-4658, E-mail: wumscoa@msnotes.wustl.edu. *Dean,* Dr. William A. Peck, 314-362-6827.

See Close-Up on page 1141.

WAYLAND BAPTIST UNIVERSITY, Plainview, TX 79072-6998

General Information Independent-religious, coed, comprehensive institution. *Enrollment:* 1,072 graduate, professional, and undergraduate students; 7 full-time matriculated graduate/professional students (4 women), 95 part-time matriculated graduate/professional students (76 women). *Enrollment by degree level:* 102 master's. *Graduate faculty:* 16 full-time (6 women), 1 (woman) part-time/adjunct. *Tuition:* Full-time $6,120; part-time $340 per credit hour. *Required fees:* $50 per term. *Graduate housing:* Rooms and/or apartments available on a first-come, first-served basis to single and married students. Typical cost: $1,276 per year ($3,586 including board) for married students. Room and board charges vary according to board plan and housing facility selected. *Student services:* Campus employment opportunities, career counseling, free psychological counseling, teacher training. *Library facilities:* J.E. and L.E. Mabee Learning Resource Center. *Online resources:* library catalog, web page, access to other libraries' catalogs. *Collection:* 124,336 titles, 527 serial subscriptions, 12,247 audiovisual materials.

Computer facilities: 123 computers available on campus for general student use. A campuswide network can be accessed from student residence rooms and from off campus. Internet access is available. *Web address:* http://www.wbu.edu/.

General Application Contact: Dr. Bobby Hall, Vice President of Academic Services, 806-291-3410, Fax: 806-291-1953, E-mail: hallb@wbu.edu.

GRADUATE UNITS

Graduate Programs Students: 7 full-time (4 women), 95 part-time (76 women); includes 17 minority (3 African Americans, 2 American Indian/Alaska Native, 12 Hispanic Americans). Average age 34. 25 applicants, 100% accepted, 21 enrolled. *Faculty:* 16 full-time (6 women), 1 (woman) part-time/adjunct. Expenses: Contact institution. *Financial support:* Federal Work-Study, institutionally sponsored loans, and scholarships/grants available. Support available to part-time students. Financial award application deadline: 5/1; financial award applicants required to submit FAFSA. In 2006, 15 degrees awarded. *Degree program information:* Part-time and evening/weekend programs available. Postbaccalaureate distance learning degree programs offered. Offers Christian ministry (MCM); counseling (MA); education (M Ed); general business (MBA); government administration (MPA); health care administration (MBA); human resource management (MBA); international management (MBA); justice administration (MPA); management (MA, MBA); management information systems (MBA); multidisciplinary science (MS); religion (MA). *Application deadline:* Applications are processed on a rolling basis. *Application fee:* $35. *Vice President of Academic Services,* Dr. Bobby Hall, 806-291-3410, Fax: 806-291-1953, E-mail: hallb@wbu.edu.

WAYNESBURG COLLEGE, Waynesburg, PA 15370-1222

General Information Independent-religious, coed, comprehensive institution. *Graduate housing:* Room and/or apartments available on a first-come, first-served basis to single students; on-campus housing not available to married students. Housing application deadline: 8/1.

GRADUATE UNITS

Graduate and Professional Studies *Degree program information:* Part-time and evening/weekend programs available. Electronic applications accepted.

WAYNE STATE COLLEGE, Wayne, NE 68787

General Information State-supported, coed, comprehensive institution. CGS member. *Enrollment:* 3,407 graduate, professional, and undergraduate students; 49 full-time matriculated graduate/professional students (24 women), 492 part-time matriculated graduate/professional students (344 women). *Enrollment by degree level:* 503 master's, 38 other advanced degrees. *Graduate faculty:* 74 part-time/adjunct (39 women). Tuition, state resident: full-time $3,114; part-time $130 per credit hour. Tuition, nonresident: full-time $6,228; part-time $260 per credit hour. *Required fees:* $894; $37 per credit hour. Tuition and fees vary according to course load. *Graduate housing:* Room and/or apartments available to single students; on-campus housing not available to married students. Typical cost: $2,170 per year ($4,470 including board). Room and board charges vary according to board plan. *Student services:* Campus safety program, career counseling, disabled student services, free psychological counseling, international student services, low-cost health insurance, multicultural affairs office. *Library facilities:* U. S. Conn Library. *Online resources:* library catalog, web page, access to other libraries' catalogs. *Collection:* 245,259 titles, 14,975 serial subscriptions, 6,622 audiovisual materials. *Research affiliation:* Nebraska Business Development Center, Social Sciences Research Center.

Computer facilities: 365 computers available on campus for general student use. A campuswide network can be accessed from student residence rooms and from off campus. Internet access and online class registration are available. *Web address:* http://www.wsc.edu/.

General Application Contact: Dr. Carolyn Linster, Director of Graduate Studies, 402-375-7121, E-mail: calinst1@wsc.edu.

GRADUATE UNITS

School of Business and Technology Students: 3 full-time (2 women), 52 part-time (25 women); includes 1 Hispanic American. Average age 34. *Faculty:* 8 part-time/adjunct (4 women). Expenses: Contact institution. *Financial support:* In 2006–07, 2 teaching assistantships with full tuition reimbursements (averaging $4,000 per year) were awarded; unspecified assistantships also available. Financial award applicants required to submit FAFSA. In 2006, 16 degrees awarded. *Degree program information:* Part-time and evening/weekend programs available. Postbaccalaureate distance learning degree programs offered (minimal on-campus study). Offers business and technology (MBA). *Application deadline:* Applications are processed on a rolling basis. *Application fee:* $30. *Dean,* Dr. Vaughn Benson, 402-375-7245, E-mail: vabenso1@wsc.edu.

School of Education and Counseling Students: 29 full-time (18 women), 424 part-time (312 women); includes 13 minority (5 African Americans, 3 American Indian/Alaska Native, 2 Asian Americans or Pacific Islanders, 3 Hispanic Americans), 2 international. Average age 35. *Faculty:* 25 part-time/adjunct (15 women). Expenses: Contact institution. *Financial support:* In 2006–07, 4 teaching assistantships with full tuition reimbursements (averaging $4,000 per year) were awarded; career-related internships or fieldwork also available. Financial award applicants required to submit FAFSA. In 2006, 199 master's, 8 other advanced degrees awarded. *Degree program information:* Part-time and evening/weekend programs available. Offers counseling (MSE); counselor education (MSE); curriculum and instruction (MSE); education and counseling (MSE, Ed S); educational administration (MSE, Ed S); elementary administration (MSE); elementary and secondary administration (MSE); guidance and counseling (MSE); school counseling (MSE); secondary administration (MSE); special education (MSE). *Application deadline:* Applications are processed on a rolling basis. *Application fee:* $30. *Dean,* Dr. Anthony Koyzis, 402-375-7389, E-mail: ankoyzi1@wsc.edu.

WAYNE STATE UNIVERSITY, Detroit, MI 48202

General Information State-supported, coed, university. CGS member. *Enrollment:* 6,629 full-time matriculated graduate/professional students (3,575 women), 5,461 part-time matriculated graduate/professional students (3,448 women). *Enrollment by degree level:* 2,097 first professional, 7,970 master's, 1,683 doctoral, 340 other advanced degrees. *Graduate faculty:* 1,236 full-time (460 women), 155 part-time/adjunct (56 women). *Graduate housing:* Rooms and/or apartments available on a first-come, first-served basis to single and married students. Typical cost: $6,575 (including board) for single students. *Student services:* Campus employment opportunities, career counseling, child daycare facilities, disabled student services, exercise/wellness program, free psychological counseling, grant writing training, international student services, low-cost health insurance, writing training. *Library facilities:* David Adamany Undergraduate Library plus 6 others. *Online resources:* library catalog, web page, access to other libraries' catalogs. *Collection:* 1.9 million titles, 18,645 serial subscriptions, 70,131 audiovisual materials. *Research affiliation:* Henry Ford Health Systems, Detroit Medical Center, Southeastern Michigan Health Association, Michigan State University, University of Michigan, Van Andel Research Institute.

Computer facilities: 1,800 computers available on campus for general student use. A campuswide network can be accessed from student residence rooms and from off campus. Internet access and online class registration are available. *Web address:* http://www.wayne.edu/.

General Application Contact: Susan Zwieg, Director, 313-577-9753, Fax: 313-577-3536, E-mail: am4835@wayne.edu.

GRADUATE UNITS

College of Education Students: 766 full-time (551 women), 1,851 part-time (1,369 women); includes 1,008 minority (885 African Americans, 13 American Indian/Alaska Native, 49 Asian Americans or Pacific Islanders, 61 Hispanic Americans), 58 international. Average age 36. 619 applicants, 71% accepted, 325 enrolled. *Faculty:* 116 full-time (53 women), 14 part-time/adjunct (10 women). Expenses: Contact institution. *Financial support:* In 2006–07, fellowships with tuition reimbursements (averaging $34,919 per year), 9 research assistantships (averaging $12,939 per year), 2 teaching assistantships (averaging $13,222 per year) were awarded; career-related internships or fieldwork, Federal Work-Study, and institutionally sponsored loans also available. Support available to part-time students. In 2006, 625 master's, 40 doctorates, 79 other advanced degrees awarded. *Degree program information:* Evening/weekend programs available. Offers education (M Ed, MA, MAT, Ed D, PhD, Certificate, Ed S). *Application deadline:* For fall admission, 7/1 for domestic students, 6/1 for international students; for winter admission, 10/1 for international students; for spring admission, 2/1 for international students. Applications are processed on a rolling basis. *Application fee:* $30 ($50 for international students). Electronic applications accepted. *Application Contact:* Janice Green, Assistant Dean, 313-577-1605, E-mail: jwgreen@wayne.edu. *Dean,* Dr. Paula Wood, 313-577-1625, Fax: 313-577-3606, E-mail: ab2387@wayne.edu.

Division of Administrative and Organizational Studies Students: 153 full-time (103 women), 389 part-time (266 women); includes 252 minority (223 African Americans, 6 American

Indian/Alaska Native, 8 Asian Americans or Pacific Islanders, 15 Hispanic Americans), 19 international. Average age 38. 138 applicants, 79% accepted, 74 enrolled. *Faculty:* 24 full-time (13 women), 1 (woman) part-time/adjunct. Expenses: Contact institution. *Financial support:* In 2006–07, 4 research assistantships (averaging $12,797 per year) were awarded; career-related internships or fieldwork, Federal Work-Study, and institutionally sponsored loans also available. Support available to part-time students. In 2006, 116 master's, 30 doctorates, 64 other advanced degrees awarded. Offers administration and supervision-secondary (Ed S); college and university teaching (Certificate); curriculum and instruction (PhD); educational leadership (M Ed, Ed S); educational leadership and policy studies (Ed D, PhD); elementary education curriculum and instruction (MA, Ed S); general administration and supervision (Ed D, PhD, Ed S); higher education (Ed D, PhD); instructional technology (M Ed, Ed D, PhD, Ed S); secondary curriculum and instruction (M Ed, Ed S). *Application deadline:* For fall admission, 7/1 for domestic students, 6/1 for international students; for winter admission, 10/1 for international students; for spring admission, 2/1 for international students. *Application fee:* $30 ($50 for international students). Electronic applications accepted. *Assistant Dean*, Dr. JoAnne Holbert, 313-577-1721, E-mail: jholbert@wayne.edu.

Division of Kinesiology, Health and Sports Studies Students: 40 full-time (16 women), 73 part-time (24 women); includes 25 minority (22 African Americans, 1 Asian American or Pacific Islander, 2 Hispanic Americans), 6 international. Average age 31. 39 applicants, 95% accepted, 26 enrolled. *Faculty:* 9 full-time (2 women). Expenses: Contact institution. *Financial support:* In 2006–07, 3 research assistantships with tuition reimbursements (averaging $13,222 per year), 2 teaching assistantships with tuition reimbursements (averaging $13,222 per year) were awarded; career-related internships or fieldwork also available. In 2006, 39 degrees awarded. Offers health education (M Ed); kinesiology (M Ed); physical education (M Ed); recreation and park services (MA); sports administration (MA). *Application deadline:* For fall admission, 7/1 for domestic students, 6/1 for international students; for winter admission, 10/1 for international students; for spring admission, 2/1 for international students. *Application fee:* $30 ($50 for international students). Electronic applications accepted. *Application Contact:* John Wirth, Assistant Professor, 313-993-7972, Fax: 313-577-5999, E-mail: johnwirth@wayne.edu. *Assistant Dean*, Dr. Sally Erbaugh, 313-577-6210, Fax: 313-577-5999, E-mail: serbaugh@coe.wayne.edu.

Division of Teacher Education Students: 401 full-time (295 women), 1,021 part-time (784 women); includes 527 minority (452 African Americans, 6 American Indian/Alaska Native, 32 Asian Americans or Pacific Islanders, 37 Hispanic Americans), 18 international. Average age 36. 296 applicants, 81% accepted, 132 enrolled. *Faculty:* 41 full-time (22 women), 2 part-time/adjunct (both women). Expenses: Contact institution. *Financial support:* In 2006–07, 1 fellowship (averaging $34,919 per year) was awarded; research assistantships. In 2006, 386 master's, 1 doctorate awarded. Offers adult and continuing education (M Ed); art education (M Ed); bilingual/bicultural education (M Ed, MAT); business education (M Ed, MAT); career and technical education (M Ed, Ed D, PhD, Ed S); curriculum and instruction (Ed D, PhD, Ed S); distributive education (M Ed, MAT); early childhood education (M Ed); elementary education (M Ed, MAT, Ed D, PhD, Ed S); elementary education curriculum and instruction (M Ed); English education (M Ed); English education-secondary (M Ed, Ed S); foreign language education (M Ed); general education (Ed D, Ed S); health occupations education (M Ed); industrial education (M Ed); mathematics education (M Ed, Ed S); pre-school and parent education (M Ed); reading (M Ed, Ed D, Ed S); reading, languages and literature (Ed D); school music-vocal (M Ed); science education (M Ed, MAT, Ed S); secondary education (MAT); secondary school reading (M Ed); social studies education (M Ed, Ed S); special education (M Ed, Ed D, PhD, Ed S); teacher education (MAT, Ed D, PhD). *Application deadline:* For fall admission, 7/1 for domestic students, 6/1 for international students; for winter admission, 10/1 for international students; for spring admission, 2/1 for international students. *Application fee:* $30 ($50 for international students). Electronic applications accepted. *Application Contact:* Sharon Elliott, Assistant Dean, 313-577-0902, E-mail: sharon.elliott@wayne.edu. *Academic Director*, Dr. Joann Snyder, 313-577-1644, E-mail: joanne.snyder@wayne.edu.

Division of Theoretical and Behavioral Foundations Students: 156 full-time (125 women), 232 part-time (191 women); includes 146 minority (140 African Americans, 1 American Indian/Alaska Native, 5 Hispanic Americans), 14 international. Average age 35. 146 applicants, 38% accepted, 39 enrolled. *Faculty:* 51 full-time (18 women), 11 part-time/adjunct (7 women). Expenses: Contact institution. *Financial support:* In 2006–07, 2 research assistantships (averaging $12,797 per year) were awarded; fellowships, career-related internships or fieldwork, Federal Work-Study, and institutionally sponsored loans also available. In 2006, 84 master's, 8 doctorates awarded. *Degree program information:* Evening/weekend programs available. Offers counseling (M Ed, MA, Ed D, PhD, Ed S); education evaluation and research (M Ed, Ed D, PhD); educational psychology (M Ed, Ed D, PhD, Ed S); educational sociology (M Ed, Ed D, PhD, Ed S); history and philosophy of education (M Ed, Ed D, PhD); rehabilitation counseling and community inclusion (MA, Ed S); school and community psychology (MA, Ed S); school clinical psychology (Ed S). *Application deadline:* For fall admission, 7/1 for domestic students, 6/1 for international students; for winter admission, 10/1 for international students; for spring admission, 2/1 for international students. *Application fee:* $20 ($30 for international students). Electronic applications accepted. *Assistant Dean*, Dr. JoAnne Holbert, 313-577-1721, E-mail: jholbert@wayne.edu.

College of Engineering Students: 625 full-time (134 women), 362 part-time (84 women); includes 112 minority (36 African Americans, 63 Asian Americans or Pacific Islanders, 13 Hispanic Americans), 593 international. Average age 29. 1,198 applicants, 68% accepted, 250 enrolled. *Faculty:* 122 full-time (5 women), 3 part-time/adjunct (0 women). Expenses: Contact institution. *Financial support:* In 2006–07, 7 fellowships (averaging $45,596 per year), 83 research assistantships with tuition reimbursements (averaging $15,145 per year), 52 teaching assistantships with tuition reimbursements (averaging $15,655 per year) were awarded; career-related internships or fieldwork, Federal Work-Study, institutionally sponsored loans, scholarships/grants, and tuition waivers (full and partial) also available. Support available to part-time students. In 2006, 369 master's, 33 doctorates, 3 other advanced degrees awarded. *Degree program information:* Part-time programs available. Offers biomedical engineering (MS, PhD); chemical engineering (MS, PhD); civil engineering (MS, PhD); computer engineering (MS, PhD); electrical engineering (MS, PhD); electronics and computer control systems (MS); engineering (MS, PhD, Certificate); engineering management (MS); environmental auditing (Certificate); hazardous materials management on public lands (Certificate); hazardous waste (MS, Certificate); hazardous waste control (Certificate); hazardous waste management (MS); industrial engineering (MS, PhD); manufacturing engineering (MS); materials science and engineering (MS, PhD, Certificate); mechanical engineering (MS, PhD); metallurgical engineering (MS, PhD); polymer engineering (Certificate). *Application deadline:* For fall admission, 7/1 priority date for domestic students, 6/1 for international students; for winter admission, 10/1 for international students; for spring admission, 3/15 for domestic students, 2/1 for international students. Applications are processed on a rolling basis. *Application fee:* $30 ($50 for international students). *Application Contact:* Dr. Gerald O. Thompkins, Associate Dean, 313-577-3780. *Dean*, Dr. Ralph Kummler, 313-577-3861, Fax: 313-577-5300, E-mail: rkummler@eng.wayne.edu.

Division of Engineering Technology Students: 9 full-time (0 women), 11 part-time (1 woman); includes 3 minority (2 African Americans, 1 Asian American or Pacific Islander), 9 international. Average age 35. 10 applicants, 70% accepted, 4 enrolled. *Faculty:* 2 full-time (0 women), 1 part-time/adjunct (0 women). Expenses: Contact institution. *Financial support:* In 2006–07, 2 students received support. Career-related internships or fieldwork, Federal Work-Study, and institutionally sponsored loans available. In 2006, 2 degrees awarded. Offers engineering technology (MS). *Application deadline:* For fall admission, 7/1 priority date for domestic students, 6/1 for international students; for winter admission, 10/1 for international students; for spring admission, 3/15 for domestic students, 2/1 for international students. Applications are processed on a rolling basis. *Application fee:* $30 ($50 for international students). Electronic applications accepted. *Department Chair*, Dr. Chih-Ping Yeh, 313-577-8076, Fax: 313-577-1781, E-mail: aa4771@wayne.edu.

College of Fine, Performing and Communication Arts Students: 152 full-time (91 women), 187 part-time (131 women); includes 91 minority (74 African Americans, 1 American Indian/Alaska Native, 5 Asian Americans or Pacific Islanders, 11 Hispanic Americans), 33 international. Average age 34. 194 applicants, 56% accepted, 73 enrolled. *Faculty:* 152 full-time (37 women), 2 part-time/adjunct (0 women). Expenses: Contact institution. *Financial support:* In 2006–07, 47 research assistantships with tuition reimbursements (averaging $12,447 per year), 24 teaching assistantships with tuition reimbursements (averaging $12,503 per year) were awarded; fellowships with tuition reimbursements, career-related internships or fieldwork, Federal Work-Study, and institutionally sponsored loans also available. Support available to part-time students. In 2006, 81 master's, 10 doctorates awarded. Offers art (MA, MFA); art history (MA); choral conducting (MM); communication studies (MA, PhD); composition (MM); design and merchandising (MA); fine, performing and communication arts (MA, MFA, MM, PhD, Certificate); music (MA, MM); music education (MM); orchestral studies (Certificate); performance (MM); public relations and organizational communication (MA); radio-TV-film (MA, PhD); speech communication (MA, PhD); theatre (MA, MFA, PhD); theory (MM). *Application deadline:* For fall admission, 4/1 for domestic students, 6/1 for international students; for winter admission, 10/1 for international students; for spring admission, 2/1 for international students. Applications are processed on a rolling basis. *Application fee:* $30 ($50 for international students). Electronic applications accepted. *Application Contact:* John Vander Weg, Associate Dean, 313-577-5342. *Dean*, Sharon Vasquez, 313-577-5342, Fax: 313-577-5355, E-mail: au9925@wayne.edu.

College of Liberal Arts and Sciences Students: 1,058 full-time (599 women), 743 part-time (428 women); includes 332 minority (232 African Americans, 5 American Indian/Alaska Native, 57 Asian Americans or Pacific Islanders, 38 Hispanic Americans), 497 international. Average age 32. 1,789 applicants, 42% accepted, 440 enrolled. *Faculty:* 356 full-time (114 women), 3 part-time/adjunct (0 women). Expenses: Contact institution. *Financial support:* In 2006–07, 21 fellowships (averaging $35,246 per year), 134 research assistantships (averaging $16,546 per year), 377 teaching assistantships (averaging $15,235 per year) were awarded; career-related internships or fieldwork, Federal Work-Study, institutionally sponsored loans, scholarships/grants, and tuition waivers (full and partial) also available. Support available to part-time students. In 2006, 249 master's, 75 doctorates, 5 other advanced degrees awarded. *Degree program information:* Evening/weekend programs available. Offers anthropology (MA, PhD); applied mathematics (MA, PhD); audiology (MA, MS, Au D, PhD); behavioral and cognitive neuroscience (PhD); biological sciences (MA, MS, PhD); chemistry (MA, MS, PhD); classics (MA); clinical psychology (PhD); cognitive and social psychology (PhD); communication disorders and science (MA, PhD); comparative literature (MA); computer science (MA, MS, PhD); criminal justice (MPA); dispute resolution (MADR, Certificate); economic development (Certificate); economics (MA, PhD); English (MA, PhD); French (MA); geography (MA); geology (MA, MS); German (MA); history (MA, PhD); human development (MA); industrial relations (MAIR); industrial/organizational psychology (PhD); interdisciplinary studies (MIS, PhD); Italian (MA); language learning (MA); Latin (MA); liberal arts and sciences (MA, MADR, MAIR, MIS, MPA, MS, MUP, Au D, PhD, Certificate); linguistics (MA); mathematical statistics (MA, PhD); mathematics (MA, MS, PhD); modern languages (PhD); molecular biotechnology (MS); Near Eastern studies (MA); nutrition and food science (MA, MS, PhD); philosophy (MA, PhD); physics (MA, MS, PhD); political science (MA, PhD); psychology (MA, MS, PhD); public administration (MPA); Romance languages (MA); Russian (MA); scientific computing (Certificate); sociology (MA, PhD); Spanish (MA); speech-language pathology (MA, PhD); urban planning (MUP). *Application deadline:* For fall admission, 6/1 for international students; for winter admission, 10/1 for international students; for spring admission, 2/1 for international students. *Application fee:* $30 ($50 for international students). *Application Contact:* Janet Hankin, Professor, 313-577-0841, E-mail: janet.hankin@wayne.edu. *Dean*, Robert Thomas, 313-577-2519, Fax: 313-577-8971, E-mail: aa0817@wayne.edu.

College of Nursing Students: 60 full-time (56 women), 155 part-time (149 women); includes 50 minority (36 African Americans, 11 Asian Americans or Pacific Islanders, 3 Hispanic Americans), 15 international. Average age 38. 83 applicants, 76% accepted, 51 enrolled. *Faculty:* 83 full-time (80 women), 4 part-time/adjunct (all women). Expenses: Contact institution. *Financial support:* In 2006–07, 47 students received support, including 3 research assistantships with tuition reimbursements available (averaging $15,164 per year), 1 teaching assistantship; fellowships with tuition reimbursements available, Federal Work-Study, institutionally sponsored loans, scholarships/grants, and traineeships also available. Support available to part-time students. Financial award application deadline: 7/1; financial award applicants required to submit FAFSA. In 2006, 27 master's, 5 doctorates, 7 other advanced degrees awarded. *Degree program information:* Part-time programs available. Offers adult acute care nursing (MSN); adult primary care nursing (MSN); advanced practice nursing with women, neonates and children (MSN, Certificate); community health nursing (MSN); neonatal nurse practitioner (Certificate); nursing (MSN, PhD, Certificate); nursing education (Certificate); psychiatric mental health nurse practitioner (MSN, Certificate); transcultural nursing (MSN, Certificate). *Application deadline:* For fall admission, 6/1 for international students; for winter admission, 10/1 for international students; for spring admission, 2/1 for international students. Applications are processed on a rolling basis. *Application fee:* $30 ($50 for international students). Electronic applications accepted. *Application Contact:* Nancy Artinian, Professor, 313-577-4143, E-mail: n.artinian@wayne.edu. *Dean*, Dr. Barbara Redman, 313-577-4070, Fax: 313-577-4571, E-mail: ae9080@wayne.edu.

Eugene Applebaum College of Pharmacy and Health Sciences Students: 522 full-time (376 women), 100 part-time (75 women); includes 89 minority (27 African Americans, 2 American Indian/Alaska Native, 52 Asian Americans or Pacific Islanders, 8 Hispanic Americans), 119 international. Average age 27. 218 applicants, 42% accepted, 91 enrolled. *Faculty:* 110 full-time (43 women), 25 part-time/adjunct (6 women). Expenses: Contact institution. *Financial support:* In 2006–07, 11 fellowships (averaging $34,463 per year), 16 research assistantships (averaging $19,163 per year) were awarded; teaching assistantships, career-related internships or fieldwork and scholarships/grants also available. Support available to part-time students. In 2006, 50 first professional degrees, 117 master's, 1 doctorate, 2 other advanced degrees awarded. *Degree program information:* Part-time and evening/weekend programs available. Offers clinical laboratory science (MS); clinical laboratory sciences (MS, Certificate); experimental technology in pharmaceutical sciences (Certificate); health systems pharmacy management (MS); hospital pharmacy (MS); medical technology (Certificate); medicinal chemistry (MS, PhD); nurse anesthesia (MS); nursing anesthesia (MS, Certificate); occupational and environmental health sciences (MPH, MS, Certificate, Post-Master's Certificate); occupational therapy (MOT, MS); pediatric nurse anesthesia (Certificate); pharmaceutical administration (MS, PhD); pharmaceutical sciences (MS, PhD); pharmaceutics (MS, PhD); pharmacology (MS, PhD); pharmacy (Pharm D); pharmacy and health sciences (Pharm D, MOT, MPH, MPT, MS, PhD, Certificate, Post-Master's Certificate); physical therapy (MPT); physician assistant studies (MS). *Application deadline:* For fall admission, 6/1 for international students; for winter admission, 10/1 for international students; for spring admission, 2/1 for international students. Applications are processed on a rolling basis. *Application fee:* $30 ($50 for international students). Electronic applications accepted. *Application Contact:* William Lindblad, Associate Professor, 313-577-0513, E-mail: wlindbl@wayne.edu. *Dean*, Beverly J. Schmoll, 313-577-1574, Fax: 313-577-5589, E-mail: aj4682@wayne.edu.

Law School Students: 576 full-time (278 women), 177 part-time (81 women); includes 144 minority (78 African Americans, 3 American Indian/Alaska Native, 35 Asian Americans or Pacific Islanders, 28 Hispanic Americans), 13 international. Average age 27. 1,582 applicants, 42% accepted, 238 enrolled. *Faculty:* 56 full-time (21 women), 23 part-time/adjunct (3 women). Expenses: Contact institution. *Financial support:* In 2006–07, 460 students received support. Federal Work-Study available. Support available to part-time students. Financial award application deadline: 4/30; financial award applicants required to submit FAFSA. In 2006, 225 JDs, 25 master's awarded. *Degree program information:* Part-time and evening/weekend programs available. Offers law (JD, LL M, PhD). *Application deadline:* For fall admission, 4/15 for domestic students, 6/1 for international students; for winter admission, 10/1 for international students; for spring admission, 2/1 for international students. *Application fee:* $30 ($50 for international students). Electronic applications accepted. *Application Contact:* Linda Fowler Sims, Assistant Dean for Recruitment and Admissions, 313-577-3937, Fax: 313-577-9049, E-mail: ab2594@wayne.edu. *Dean*, Frank Wu, 313-577-3933, Fax: 313-577-2620, E-mail: aw7545@wayne.edu.

School of Business Administration Students: 218 full-time (92 women), 1,021 part-time (446 women); includes 313 minority (179 African Americans, 2 American Indian/Alaska

Wayne State University (continued)

Native, 111 Asian Americans or Pacific Islanders, 21 Hispanic Americans), 153 international. Average age 30. 526 applicants, 73% accepted, 276 enrolled. *Faculty:* 64 full-time (11 women), 5 part-time/adjunct (1 woman). Expenses: Contact institution. *Financial support:* In 2006–07, 10 research assistantships (averaging $13,222 per year) were awarded; career-related internships or fieldwork, Federal Work-Study, and scholarships/grants also available. Support available to part-time students. Financial award applicants required to submit FAFSA. In 2006, 386 degrees awarded. *Degree program information:* Part-time and evening/weekend programs available. Offers accounting (MS); business administration (MBA, PhD); interdisciplinary studies (PhD); taxation (MS). *Application deadline:* For fall admission, 8/1 for domestic students, 6/1 for international students; for winter admission, 10/1 for international students; for spring admission, 4/1 for domestic students, 2/1 for international students. Applications are processed on a rolling basis. *Application fee:* $30 ($50 for international students). Electronic applications accepted. *Application Contact:* Linda Zaddach, Assistant Dean, 313-577-4510, E-mail: l.s.zaddach@wayne.edu. *Dean,* Dr. Richard Gabrys, 313-577-4501, Fax: 313-577-4557, E-mail: az4994@wayne.edu.

School of Medicine Students: 2,208 full-time (1,027 women), 165 part-time (96 women); includes 711 minority (236 African Americans, 5 American Indian/Alaska Native, 436 Asian Americans or Pacific Islanders, 34 Hispanic Americans), 378 international. Average age 29. 1,044 applicants, 95% accepted, 123 enrolled. *Faculty:* 135 full-time (37 women), 2 part-time/adjunct (0 women). Expenses: Contact institution. *Financial support:* In 2006–07, 53 fellowships (averaging $35,605 per year), 143 research assistantships with tuition reimbursements (averaging $20,297 per year), 2 teaching assistantships with tuition reimbursements (averaging $15,866 per year) were awarded; career-related internships or fieldwork, Federal Work-Study, institutionally sponsored loans, scholarships/grants, and tuition waivers (full and partial) also available. Support available to part-time students. In 2006, 241 first professional degrees, 58 master's, 20 doctorates, 3 other advanced degrees awarded. *Degree program information:* Part-time and evening/weekend programs available. Offers medicine (MD, MPH, MS, PhD, Certificate). *Application deadline:* For fall admission, 6/1 for international students; for winter admission, 10/1 for international students; for spring admission, 2/1 for international students. Applications are processed on a rolling basis. *Application fee:* $30 ($50 for international students). Electronic applications accepted. *Application Contact:* Dr. Kenneth C. Palmer, Assistant Dean, 313-577-1455, E-mail: kpalmer@med.wayne.edu. *Dean,* Dr. Bernard Frank, 313-577-1450, Fax: 313-577-8777, E-mail: aa0946@wayne.edu.

Graduate Programs in Medicine Students: 266 full-time (137 women), 87 part-time (47 women); includes 77 minority (26 African Americans, 1 American Indian/Alaska Native, 44 Asian Americans or Pacific Islanders, 6 Hispanic Americans), 83 international. Average age 28. Expenses: Contact institution. *Financial support:* Fellowships, research assistantships, teaching assistantships, career-related internships or fieldwork, Federal Work-Study, institutionally sponsored loans, scholarships/grants, and tuition waivers (full and partial) available. Support available to part-time students. In 2006, 43 master's, 25 doctorates awarded. *Degree program information:* Part-time and evening/weekend programs available. Offers anatomy (MS, PhD); basic medical science (MS); biochemistry and molecular biology (MS, PhD); cancer biology (MS, PhD); cellular and clinical neurobiology (PhD); community health (MS); community health services (Certificate); immunology and microbiology (MS, PhD); medical physics (PhD); medical research (MS); medicine (MPH, MS, PhD, Certificate); pathology (MS, PhD); pharmacology (MS, PhD); physiology (MS, PhD); psychiatry and behavioral neurosciences (MS); public health (MPH); public health practice (Certificate); radiological physics (MS); rehabilitation science administration (Certificate); rehabilitation sciences (MS). *Application deadline:* For fall admission, 6/1 for international students; for winter admission, 10/1 for international students; for spring admission, 2/1 for international students. Applications are processed on a rolling basis. *Application fee:* $30 ($50 for international students). Electronic applications accepted. *Assistant Dean,* Dr. Kenneth C. Palmer, 313-577-1455, E-mail: kpalmer@med.wayne.edu.

School of Social Work Students: 293 full-time (257 women), 183 part-time (157 women); includes 180 minority (151 African Americans, 6 American Indian/Alaska Native, 14 Asian Americans or Pacific Islanders, 9 Hispanic Americans), 12 international. Average age 33. 318 applicants, 61% accepted, 144 enrolled. *Faculty:* 31 full-time (19 women), 19 part-time/adjunct (11 women). Expenses: Contact institution. *Financial support:* In 2006–07, 1 research assistantship with tuition reimbursement (averaging $15,475 per year), 1 teaching assistantship (averaging $13,222 per year) were awarded; career-related internships or fieldwork, institutionally sponsored loans, scholarships/grants, and tuition waivers (partial) also available. Support available to part-time students. Financial award application deadline: 5/1; financial award applicants required to submit FAFSA. In 2006, 205 master's, 13 other advanced degrees awarded. *Degree program information:* Part-time and evening/weekend programs available. Offers interdisciplinary studies (PhD); social work (MSW); social work practice with families and couples (Certificate). *Application deadline:* For fall admission, 3/31 for domestic students, 6/1 for international students; for winter admission, 10/1 for international students; for spring admission, 2/28 for domestic students, 2/1 for international students. Applications are processed on a rolling basis. *Application fee:* $20 ($30 for international students). Electronic applications accepted. *Application Contact:* Ann Alvarez, Associate Dean, 313-577-4441, E-mail: ann.r.alvarez@wayne.edu. *Dean,* Phyllis Vroom, 313-577-4400, Fax: 313-577-8770, E-mail: aa8773@wayne.edu.

WEBBER INTERNATIONAL UNIVERSITY, Babson Park, FL 33827-0096

General Information Independent, coed, comprehensive institution.

GRADUATE UNITS

Graduate School of Business *Degree program information:* Part-time and evening/weekend programs available. Offers accounting (MBA); management (MBA); sports management (MBA).

WEBER STATE UNIVERSITY, Ogden, UT 84408-1001

General Information State-supported, coed, comprehensive institution. *Enrollment:* 18,303 graduate, professional, and undergraduate students; 147 full-time matriculated graduate/professional students (33 women), 350 part-time matriculated graduate/professional students (196 women). *Enrollment by degree level:* 497 master's. *Graduate faculty:* 44 full-time (14 women), 26 part-time/adjunct (10 women). Tuition, state resident: full-time $3,950; part-time $203 per semester. Tuition, nonresident: full-time $10,371; part-time $518 per semester. *Required fees:* $544; $24 per semester. Tuition and fees vary according to course load and program. *Graduate housing:* Rooms and/or apartments available on a first-come, first-served basis to single students and available to married students. Typical cost: $2,142 per year ($5,328 including board) for single students; $7,200 per year for married students. *Student services:* Campus employment opportunities, campus safety program, career counseling, child daycare facilities, disabled student services, exercise/wellness program, free psychological counseling, grant writing training, international student services, low-cost health insurance, multicultural affairs office, teacher training, writing training. *Library facilities:* Stewart Library plus 1 other. *Online resources:* library catalog, web page, access to other libraries' catalogs. *Collection:* 734,487 titles, 19,881 audiovisual materials. *Research affiliation:* Raytheon Training Corporation (education).

Computer facilities: Computer purchase and lease plans are available. 558 computers available on campus for general student use. A campuswide network can be accessed from student residence rooms and from off campus. Internet access and online class registration, online grades are available. *Web address:* http://weber.edu/.

General Application Contact: Christopher C. Rivera, Director of Admissions, 801-626-6046, Fax: 801-626-6747, E-mail: crivera@weber.edu.

GRADUATE UNITS

College of Social and Behavioral Sciences Students: 8 full-time (2 women), 22 part-time (7 women). Average age 32. 16 applicants, 94% accepted, 13 enrolled. *Faculty:* 4 full-time (0 women), 2 part-time/adjunct (1 woman). Expenses: Contact institution. *Financial support:* In 2006–07, 1 student received support. In 2006, 20 degrees awarded. *Degree program information:* Part-time and evening/weekend programs available. Offers criminal justice (MCJ); social and behavioral sciences (MCJ). *Application deadline:* Applications are processed on a rolling basis. *Application fee:* $0. *Application Contact:* Dr. L. Kay Gillespie, Chair, 801-626-6245, Fax: 801-626-6145, E-mail: lgillespie1@weber.edu. *Dean,* Dr. Richard Sadler, 801-626-6232, Fax: 801-626-7130, E-mail: rsadler@weber.edu.

Jerry and Vickie Moyes College of Education Students: 4 full-time (all women), 168 part-time (129 women); includes 6 minority (2 Asian Americans or Pacific Islanders, 4 Hispanic Americans), 1 international. Average age 40. 37 applicants, 84% accepted, 31 enrolled. *Faculty:* 16 full-time (9 women), 7 part-time/adjunct (4 women). Expenses: Contact institution. *Financial support:* In 2006–07, 17 students received support. Institutionally sponsored loans, scholarships/grants, tuition waivers (full and partial), and unspecified assistantships available. Support available to part-time students. Financial award application deadline: 2/1. In 2006, 48 degrees awarded. *Degree program information:* Part-time and evening/weekend programs available. Offers curriculum and instruction (M Ed); education (M Ed). *Application deadline:* For fall admission, 5/1 priority date for domestic students; for spring admission, 11/1 priority date for domestic students. Applications are processed on a rolling basis. *Application fee:* $25. *Application Contact:* Dr. Claudia Eliason, Director, 801-626-7719, E-mail: eeliason@weber.edu. *Dean,* Dr. Jack L. Rasmussen, 801-626-6273, Fax: 801-626-7427, E-mail: jrasmussen@weber.edu.

John B. Goddard School of Business and Economics Students: 108 full-time (19 women), 111 part-time (24 women); includes 8 minority (1 African American, 4 Asian Americans or Pacific Islanders, 3 Hispanic Americans), 3 international. Average age 30. 181 applicants, 82% accepted, 129 enrolled. *Faculty:* 14 full-time (0 women), 6 part-time/adjunct (1 woman). Expenses: Contact institution. *Financial support:* In 2006–07, 29 students received support; research assistantships, teaching assistantships, Federal Work-Study, institutionally sponsored loans, scholarships/grants, and tuition waivers (full and partial) available. Financial award application deadline: 3/1. In 2006, 87 degrees awarded. *Degree program information:* Part-time and evening/weekend programs available. Postbaccalaureate distance learning degree programs offered. Offers accountancy (M Acc); business administration (MBA); business and economics (M Acc, MBA). *Application deadline:* Applications are processed on a rolling basis. *Application fee:* $60 ($75 for international students). Electronic applications accepted. *Dean,* Dr. Lewis R Gale, 801-626-6063, Fax: 801-626-6687, E-mail: lewisgale@weber.edu.

WEBSTER UNIVERSITY, St. Louis, MO 63119-3194

General Information Independent, coed, comprehensive institution. *Enrollment:* 3,894 full-time matriculated graduate/professional students (2,291 women), 11,651 part-time matriculated graduate/professional students (6,775 women). *Enrollment by degree level:* 15,267 master's, 42 doctoral, 236 other advanced degrees. *Graduate faculty:* 81 full-time (23 women), 1,689 part-time/adjunct (426 women). *Tuition:* Full-time $8,820; part-time $490 per credit. Tuition and fees vary according to degree level, campus/location and program. *Graduate housing:* Room and/or apartments available on a first-come, first-served basis to single students; on-campus housing not available to married students. Typical cost: $4,600 per year ($8,059 including board). Housing application deadline: 7/1. *Student services:* Campus employment opportunities, campus safety program, career counseling, disabled student services, exercise/wellness program, free psychological counseling, international student services, multicultural affairs office, writing training. *Library facilities:* Emerson Library. *Online resources:* library catalog, web page, access to other libraries' catalogs. *Collection:* 283,742 titles, 2,429 serial subscriptions. *Research affiliation:* Literacy Investment for Tomorrow.

Computer facilities: 330 computers available on campus for general student use. A campuswide network can be accessed. Internet access and online class registration are available. *Web address:* http://www.webster.edu/.

General Application Contact: Matt Nolan, Director of Graduate and Evening Student Admissions, 314-968-7089, Fax: 314-968-7462, E-mail: gadmit@webster.edu.

GRADUATE UNITS

College of Arts and Sciences Students: 1,090 full-time (904 women), 1,437 part-time (1,128 women); includes 1,363 minority (1,108 African Americans, 20 American Indian/Alaska Native, 26 Asian Americans or Pacific Islanders, 209 Hispanic Americans), 84 international. Average age 35. 473 applicants, 86% accepted, 348 enrolled. *Faculty:* 18 full-time (8 women), 246 part-time/adjunct. Expenses: Contact institution. *Financial support:* Career-related internships or fieldwork and Federal Work-Study available. Support available to part-time students. Financial award application deadline: 4/1; financial award applicants required to submit FAFSA. In 2006, 786 degrees awarded. *Degree program information:* Part-time and evening/weekend programs available. Postbaccalaureate distance learning degree programs offered. Offers arts and sciences (MA, MS, MSN); counseling (MA); gerontology (MA); international nongovernmental organizations (MA); international relations (MA); legal analysis (MA); legal studies (MA); nurse anesthesia (MS); nursing (MSN); patent agency (MA); professional science management and leadership (MA). *Application deadline:* Applications are processed on a rolling basis. *Application fee:* $25 ($50 for international students). *Application Contact:* Matt Nolan, Director of Graduate and Evening Student Admissions, 314-968-7089, Fax: 314-968-7462, E-mail: gadmit@webster.edu. *Dean,* Dr. David Carl Wilson, 314-968-7160, Fax: 314-963-6043, E-mail: wilson@webster.edu.

Leigh Gerdine College of Fine Arts Students: 11 full-time (8 women), 25 part-time (11 women), 2 international. Average age 31. 12 applicants, 92% accepted, 10 enrolled. Expenses: Contact institution. *Financial support:* Fellowships, teaching assistantships, career-related internships or fieldwork and Federal Work-Study available. Support available to part-time students. Financial award application deadline: 4/1; financial award applicants required to submit FAFSA. In 2006, 10 degrees awarded. *Degree program information:* Part-time and evening/weekend programs available. Offers art (MA); arts management and leadership (MFA); church music (MM); composition (MM); conducting (MM); fine arts (MA, MFA, MM); jazz studies (MM); music (MA); music education (MM); performance (MM); piano (MM). *Application deadline:* Applications are processed on a rolling basis. *Application fee:* $25 ($50 for international students). *Application Contact:* Director of Graduate and Evening Student Admissions, Fax: 314-968-7116, E-mail: gadmit@webster.edu. *Dean,* Peter Sargent, 314-968-7006, Fax: 314-963-6048, E-mail: sargenpe@webster.edu.

School of Business and Technology Students: 2,603 full-time (1,376 women), 8,990 part-time (4,348 women); includes 5,085 minority (3,847 African Americans, 74 American Indian/Alaska Native, 375 Asian Americans or Pacific Islanders, 789 Hispanic Americans), 623 international. Average age 35. 2,112 applicants, 99% accepted, 1818 enrolled. Expenses: Contact institution. *Financial support:* Career-related internships or fieldwork and Federal Work-Study available. Support available to part-time students. Financial award application deadline: 4/1; financial award applicants required to submit FAFSA. In 2006, 4,393 master's, 9 doctorates, 29 other advanced degrees awarded. *Degree program information:* Part-time and evening/weekend programs available. Postbaccalaureate distance learning degree programs offered (no on-campus study). Offers business (MA); business and organizational security management (MA, MBA); business and technology (MA, MBA, MS, DM, Certificate); computer resources and information management (MA, MBA); computer science/distributed systems (MS, Certificate); environmental management (MBA, MS); finance (MA, MBA); health care management (MA); health services management (MA, MBA); human resources development (MA, MBA); human resources management (MA, MBA); international business (MA, MBA); management (DM); management and leadership (MA, MBA); marketing (MA, MBA); procurement and acquisitions management (MA, MBA); public administration (MA); quality management (MA); space systems operations management (MS); telecommunications management (MA, MBA). *Application deadline:* Applications are processed on a rolling basis. *Application fee:* $25 ($50 for international students). *Application Contact:* Director of Graduate and Evening Student Admissions, Fax: 314-968-7116, E-mail: gadmit@webster.edu. *Dean,* Dr. Benjamin Ola Akande, 314-968-5951, Fax: 314-968-7077, E-mail: akandeb@webster.edu.

School of Communications Students: 43 full-time (25 women), 228 part-time (168 women); includes 96 minority (88 African Americans, 1 American Indian/Alaska Native, 1 Asian American or Pacific Islander, 6 Hispanic Americans), 17 international. Average age 30. 58 applicants, 95% accepted, 47 enrolled. *Faculty:* 4 full-time (2 women), 19 part-time/adjunct. Expenses: Contact institution. *Financial support:* Career-related internships or fieldwork and Federal

Work-Study available. Support available to part-time students. Financial award application deadline: 4/1; financial award applicants required to submit FAFSA. In 2006, 68 degrees awarded. *Degree program information:* Part-time and evening/weekend programs available. Postbaccalaureate distance learning degree programs offered. Offers advertising and marketing communications (MA); communications (MA); communications management (MA); media communications (MA); media literacy (MA); public relations (MA). *Application deadline:* Applications are processed on a rolling basis. *Application fee:* $25 ($50 for international students). *Application Contact:* Director of Graduate and Evening Student Admissions, Fax: 314-968-7116, E-mail: gadmit@webster.edu. *Dean,* Debra Carpenter, 314-968-7154, Fax: 314-963-6106, E-mail: carpenda@webster.edu.

School of Education Students: 147 full-time (127 women), 970 part-time (824 women); includes 224 minority (188 African Americans, 3 American Indian/Alaska Native, 16 Asian Americans or Pacific Islanders, 17 Hispanic Americans), 11 international. Average age 34. 237 applicants, 99% accepted, 210 enrolled. Expenses: Contact institution. *Financial support:* Career-related internships or fieldwork and Federal Work-Study available. Support available to part-time students. Financial award application deadline: 4/1; financial award applicants required to submit FAFSA. In 2006, 330 master's, 28 other advanced degrees awarded. *Degree program information:* Part-time programs available. Postbaccalaureate distance learning degree programs offered. Offers administrative leadership (Ed S); communications (MAT); early childhood education (MAT); education (MAT, Ed S); education leadership (Ed S); educational technology (MAT); mathematics (MAT); multidisciplinary studies (MAT); school systems, superintendency and leadership (Ed S); social science (MAT); special education (MAT). *Application deadline:* Applications are processed on a rolling basis. *Application fee:* $25 ($50 for international students). *Application Contact:* Director of Graduate and Evening Student Admissions, Fax: 314-968-7116, E-mail: gadmit@webster.edu. *Dean,* Dr. Brenda Fyfe, 314-968-6913, Fax: 314-968-7118, E-mail: fyfebv@webster.edu.

WESLEYAN COLLEGE, Macon, GA 31210-4462

General Information Independent-religious, Undergraduate: women only; graduate: coed, comprehensive institution. *Enrollment:* 636 graduate, professional, and undergraduate students; 33 full-time matriculated graduate/professional students (28 women), 60 part-time matriculated graduate/professional students (53 women). *Enrollment by degree level:* 93 master's. *Graduate faculty:* 9 full-time (7 women), 9 part-time/adjunct (6 women). *Tuition:* Full-time $14,500. Tuition and fees vary according to program. *Graduate housing:* Room and/or apartments available on a first-come, first-served basis to single students; on-campus housing not available to married students. Typical cost: $7,500 (including board). Housing application deadline: 5/1. *Student services:* Campus safety program, exercise/wellness program, teacher training, writing training. *Library facilities:* Lucy Lester Willet Memorial Library. *Online resources:* library catalog, web page. *Collection:* 117,547 titles, 630 serial subscriptions, 3,927 audiovisual materials.

Computer facilities: 24 computers available on campus for general student use. A campuswide network can be accessed from student residence rooms and from off campus. Internet access and online class registration are available. *Web address:* http://www.wesleyancollege.edu/.

General Application Contact: Danielle Lodge, Director, Recruiting and Non-Traditional Programs, 478-757-5263, Fax: 478-757-5148, E-mail: dlodge@wesleyancollege.edu.

GRADUATE UNITS

Department of Business and Economics Expenses: Contact institution. Offers business administration (EMBA); business and economics (EMBA).

Department of Education Students: 13 full-time (12 women), 36 part-time (35 women); includes 19 minority (18 African Americans, 1 Asian American or Pacific Islander), 1 international. Average age 37. *Faculty:* 4 full-time (3 women), 4 part-time/adjunct (all women). Expenses: Contact institution. *Financial support:* Scholarships/grants available. Financial award application deadline: 4/1; financial award applicants required to submit FAFSA. In 2006, 5 degrees awarded. *Degree program information:* Part-time programs available. Offers early childhood education (MA); middle-level mathematics and middle-level science education (MA). *Application deadline:* For fall admission, 7/1 priority date for domestic students; for spring admission, 12/1 priority date for domestic students. Applications are processed on a rolling basis. *Application fee:* $25. *Application Contact:* Amber E Poulson, MA Admissions Coordinator, 478-757-2480, E-mail: apoulson@wesleyancollege.edu. *Chair, Education Department,* Dr. Mae Sheftall, 478-757-5198, Fax: 478-757-5148, E-mail: msheft@wesleyancollege.edu.

WESLEYAN UNIVERSITY, Middletown, CT 06459-0260

General Information Independent, coed, university. CGS member. *Enrollment:* 3,220 graduate, professional, and undergraduate students; 182 full-time matriculated graduate/professional students (89 women). *Enrollment by degree level:* 47 master's, 135 doctoral. *Graduate faculty:* 97 full-time (20 women), 33 part-time/adjunct (10 women). *Tuition:* Full-time $26,133. *Required fees:* $20. *Graduate housing:* Rooms and/or apartments available to single and married students. Typical cost: $6,804 per year for single students; $8,004 per year for married students. Housing application deadline: 6/15. *Student services:* Campus employment opportunities, campus safety program, career counseling, child daycare facilities, exercise/wellness program, free psychological counseling, international student services, low-cost health insurance, multicultural affairs office, writing training. *Library facilities:* Olin Memorial Library plus 3 others. *Online resources:* library catalog, web page, access to other libraries' catalogs. *Collection:* 1.3 million titles, 6,789 serial subscriptions. *Research affiliation:* Cold Springs Marine Laboratory, Woods Hole Oceanographic Institution.

Computer facilities: Computer purchase and lease plans are available. 190 computers available on campus for general student use. A campuswide network can be accessed from student residence rooms and from off campus. Internet access and online class registration, electronic portfolio, online course drop/add, Blackboard course management system are available. *Web address:* http://www.wesleyan.edu/.

General Application Contact: Information Contact, 860-685-2000.

GRADUATE UNITS

Graduate Liberal Studies Program *Degree program information:* Part-time and evening/weekend programs available. Offers liberal studies (MALS, CAS).

Graduate Programs Students: 182 full-time (89 women); includes 11 minority (1 African American, 8 Asian Americans or Pacific Islanders, 2 Hispanic Americans), 70 international. Average age 27. *Faculty:* 97 full-time (20 women), 11 part-time/adjunct (2 women). Expenses: Contact institution. *Financial support:* Fellowships with tuition reimbursements, research assistantships with tuition reimbursements, teaching assistantships with tuition reimbursements, institutionally sponsored loans and tuition waivers (full and partial) available. Financial award application deadline: 4/15; financial award applicants required to submit FAFSA. In 2006, 30 master's, 10 doctorates awarded. Offers astronomy (MA); biochemistry (MA, PhD); cell biology (PhD); chemical physics (MA, PhD); comparative physiology (PhD); developmental biology (PhD); earth sciences (MA); ethnomusicology (PhD); genetics (PhD); inorganic chemistry (MA, PhD); mathematics (MA, PhD); molecular biology (PhD); music (MA); neurophysiology (PhD); organic chemistry (MA, PhD); physical chemistry (MA, PhD); physics (MA, PhD); population biology (PhD); psychology (MA); theoretical chemistry (MA, PhD). Electronic applications accepted. *Vice President and Provost for Academic Affairs,* Dr. Joseph W. Bruno, 860-685-2010, E-mail: jbruno@wesleyan.edu.

WESLEY BIBLICAL SEMINARY, Jackson, MS 39206

General Information Independent-religious, coed, graduate-only institution. *Graduate housing:* Room and/or apartments available on a first-come, first-served basis to single students; on-campus housing not available to married students.

GRADUATE UNITS

Graduate Programs *Degree program information:* Part-time programs available. Offers Biblical studies (MA); Christian education (MACE); Christian studies (MA); evangelism (M Div); family counseling (M Div); missions (M Div); pastoral ministry (M Div); theology (MA). Electronic applications accepted.

WESLEY COLLEGE, Dover, DE 19901-3875

General Information Independent-religious, coed, comprehensive institution. *Enrollment:* 2,306 graduate, professional, and undergraduate students; 68 full-time matriculated graduate/professional students (47 women), 110 part-time matriculated graduate/professional students (83 women). *Enrollment by degree level:* 178 master's. *Graduate faculty:* 12 full-time (8 women), 7 part-time/adjunct (4 women). *Tuition:* Full-time $6,120; part-time $340 per credit. *Required fees:* $60; $60 per year. *Graduate housing:* On-campus housing not available. *Student services:* Campus employment opportunities, campus safety program, career counseling, disabled student services, international student services, teacher training. *Library facilities:* Robert H. Parker Library. *Online resources:* library catalog, web page, access to other libraries' catalogs. *Collection:* 104,636 titles, 252 serial subscriptions, 946 audiovisual materials.

Computer facilities: Computer purchase and lease plans are available. 225 computers available on campus for general student use. A campuswide network can be accessed from student residence rooms and from off campus. Internet access and online class registration are available. *Web address:* http://www.wesley.edu/.

General Application Contact: G. R. Myers, Director of Graduate Admissions, 302-736-2343, E-mail: myersgr@wesley.edu.

GRADUATE UNITS

Business Program Students: 45 full-time (27 women), 32 part-time (19 women); includes 27 minority (21 African Americans, 4 Asian Americans or Pacific Islanders, 2 Hispanic Americans). Average age 30. 45 applicants, 93% accepted, 32 enrolled. *Faculty:* 3 full-time (2 women), 7 part-time/adjunct (4 women). Expenses: Contact institution. *Financial support:* Unspecified assistantships available. In 2006, 26 degrees awarded. *Degree program information:* Part-time and evening/weekend programs available. Offers environmental management (MBA); executive leadership (MBA); management (MBA). Executive leadership concentration also offered at New Castle, DE location. *Application deadline:* Applications are processed on a rolling basis. *Application fee:* $25. *Application Contact:* William H. Firman, Dean of Enrollment Management, 302-736-2400, Fax: 302-736-2301, E-mail: firmanwh@wesley.edu. *Director of Graduate Admissions,* G. R. Myers, 302-736-2343, E-mail: myersgr@wesley.edu.

Education Program Students: 9 full-time (6 women), 24 part-time (15 women), 3 international. Average age 30. 15 applicants, 67% accepted, 10 enrolled. *Faculty:* 4 full-time (3 women). Expenses: Contact institution. *Financial support:* In 2006–07, 7 students received support, including 7 teaching assistantships with full tuition reimbursements available (averaging $9,000 per year). In 2006, 12 degrees awarded. *Degree program information:* Part-time and evening/weekend programs available. Offers education (M Ed, MA Ed, MAT). *Application deadline:* Applications are processed on a rolling basis. *Application fee:* $25. *Application Contact:* Marie Cusick, Coordinator of Graduate and Evening Programs, 302-736-2352, E-mail: cusickma@wesley.edu. *Director of Graduate Admissions,* G. R. Myers, 302-736-2343, E-mail: myersgr@wesley.edu.

Environmental Studies Program Average age 25. 8 applicants, 75% accepted, 6 enrolled. *Faculty:* 1 full-time (0 women). Expenses: Contact institution. *Financial support:* Unspecified assistantships available. In 2006, 1 degree awarded. *Degree program information:* Part-time and evening/weekend programs available. Offers environmental studies (MS). *Application deadline:* Applications are processed on a rolling basis. *Application fee:* $25. *Application Contact:* William H. Firman, Dean of Enrollment Management, 302-736-2400, Fax: 302-736-2301, E-mail: firmanwh@wesley.edu. *Director of Graduate Admissions,* G. R. Myers, 302-736-2343, E-mail: myersgr@wesley.edu.

Nursing Program Students: 14 full-time (all women), 44 part-time (42 women); includes 15 minority (13 African Americans, 2 Hispanic Americans). Average age 36. 70 applicants, 86% accepted, 40 enrolled. *Faculty:* 4 full-time (3 women). Expenses: Contact institution. *Financial support:* Traineeships available. Financial award applicants required to submit FAFSA. In 2006, 14 degrees awarded. *Degree program information:* Part-time and evening/weekend programs available. Offers nursing (MSN). *Application deadline:* Applications are processed on a rolling basis. *Application fee:* $25. Electronic applications accepted. *Application Contact:* Marie Cusick, Coordinator of Graduate and Evening Programs, 302-736-2352, E-mail: cusickma@wesley.edu. *Director of Graduate Admissions,* G. R. Myers, 302-736-2343, E-mail: myersgr@wesley.edu.

WESLEY THEOLOGICAL SEMINARY, Washington, DC 20016-5690

General Information Independent-religious, coed, graduate-only institution. *Graduate housing:* Rooms and/or apartments available to single and married students. Housing application deadline: 7/1.

GRADUATE UNITS

Graduate and Professional Programs *Degree program information:* Part-time programs available. Offers theology (M Div, MA, MRE, MTS, D Min).

WEST CHESTER UNIVERSITY OF PENNSYLVANIA, West Chester, PA 19383

General Information State-supported, coed, comprehensive institution. CGS member. *Enrollment:* 12,882 graduate, professional, and undergraduate students; 547 full-time matriculated graduate/professional students (420 women), 1,514 part-time matriculated graduate/professional students (1,131 women). *Enrollment by degree level:* 2,061 master's. *Graduate housing:* Room and/or apartments available on a first-come, first-served basis to single students; on-campus housing not available to married students. *Student services:* Campus employment opportunities, campus safety program, career counseling, child daycare facilities, disabled student services, exercise/wellness program, free psychological counseling, grant writing training, international student services, low-cost health insurance, multicultural affairs office. *Library facilities:* Francis Harvey Green Library plus 1 other. *Online resources:* library catalog, web page, access to other libraries' catalogs. *Collection:* 752,451 titles, 7,755 serial subscriptions, 76,530 audiovisual materials. *Research affiliation:* Texas Instruments (mathematics), University Corporation for Atmospheric Research (geology and astronomy), Turner Biosystems (biology).

Computer facilities: 700 computers available on campus for general student use. A campuswide network can be accessed from student residence rooms and from off campus. Internet access and online class registration are available. *Web address:* http://www.wcupa.edu/.

General Application Contact: Information Contact, 610-436-2943, Fax: 610-436-2763, E-mail: gradstudy@wcupa.edu.

GRADUATE UNITS

Graduate Studies Students: 547 full-time (420 women), 1,514 part-time (1,131 women); includes 170 minority (106 African Americans, 1 American Indian/Alaska Native, 40 Asian Americans or Pacific Islanders, 23 Hispanic Americans), 47 international. Average age 31. 1,153 applicants, 84% accepted, 488 enrolled. Expenses: Contact institution. *Financial support:* In 2006–07, 132 research assistantships with full tuition reimbursements (averaging $5,000 per year) were awarded; career-related internships or fieldwork, Federal Work-Study, tuition waivers (full and partial), and unspecified assistantships also available. Support available to part-time students. Financial award application deadline: 2/15. In 2006, 523 degrees awarded. *Degree program information:* Part-time and evening/weekend programs available. Postbaccalaureate distance learning degree programs offered (minimal on-campus study). *Application deadline:* For fall admission, 4/15 priority date for domestic students; for spring admission, 10/15 for domestic students. Applications are processed on a rolling basis. *Application fee:* $35. *Application Contact:* 610-436-2943, Fax: 610-436-2763, E-mail: gradstudy@wcupa.edu. *Interim Dean,* Dr. Janet Hickman, 610-436-2943, Fax: 610-436-2763, E-mail: jhickman@wcupa.edu.

College of Arts and Sciences Students: 147 full-time (92 women), 238 part-time (156 women); includes 38 minority (15 African Americans, 1 American Indian/Alaska Native, 16 Asian Americans or Pacific Islanders, 6 Hispanic Americans), 21 international. Average age 31. 349 applicants, 88% accepted, 139 enrolled. Expenses: Contact institution. *Financial*

West Chester University of Pennsylvania (continued)

support: In 2006–07, 65 research assistantships with full tuition reimbursements (averaging $5,000 per year) were awarded; unspecified assistantships also available. Support available to part-time students. Financial award application deadline: 2/15; financial award applicants required to submit FAFSA. In 2006, 131 degrees awarded. *Degree program information:* Part-time and evening/weekend programs available. Offers arts and sciences (M Ed, MA, MS, MSA, Certificate); biology (MS); chemistry (M Ed, MS); clinical chemistry (MS); clinical psychology (MA); communication studies (MA); computer science (MS, Certificate); English (MA); French (M Ed, MA); general psychology (MA); German (M Ed); gerontology (Certificate); history (M Ed, MA); industrial organizational psychology (MA); Latin (M Ed); long term care (MSA); mathematics (MA); philosophy (MA); physical science (MA); Spanish (M Ed, MA); teaching English as a second language (MA). *Application deadline:* For fall admission, 4/15 priority date for domestic students; for spring admission, 10/15 for domestic students. Applications are processed on a rolling basis. *Application fee:* $35. *Interim Dean,* Dr. Gil Wiswall, 610-436-3521, Fax: 610-436-3150, E-mail: gwiswall@wcupa.edu.

College of Visual and Performing Arts Students: 14 full-time (9 women), 43 part-time (26 women); includes 2 Asian Americans or Pacific Islanders, 1 Hispanic American, 3 international. Average age 28. 48 applicants, 94% accepted, 21 enrolled. Expenses: Contact institution. *Financial support:* In 2006–07, 3 research assistantships with full tuition reimbursements (averaging $5,000 per year) were awarded; career-related internships or fieldwork and unspecified assistantships also available. Support available to part-time students. Financial award application deadline: 2/15; financial award applicants required to submit FAFSA. In 2006, 14 degrees awarded. *Degree program information:* Part-time and evening/weekend programs available. Offers music education (MM); music history (MA); performance (MM); visual and performing arts (MA, MM). *Application deadline:* For fall admission, 4/15 priority date for domestic students; for spring admission, 10/15 for domestic students. Applications are processed on a rolling basis. *Application fee:* $35. *Application Contact:* Dr. J. Bryan Burton, Graduate Coordinator, 610-436-2222, E-mail: jburton@wcupa.edu. *Dean,* Dr. Timothy Blair, 610-436-2739, Fax: 610-436-2873, E-mail: tblair@wcupa.edu.

School of Business and Public Affairs Students: 78 full-time (54 women), 137 part-time (63 women); includes 20 African Americans, 12 Asian Americans or Pacific Islanders, 4 Hispanic Americans, 10 international. Average age 32. 181 applicants, 81% accepted, 82 enrolled. Expenses: Contact institution. *Financial support:* In 2006–07, 12 research assistantships with full tuition reimbursements (averaging $5,000 per year) were awarded; career-related internships or fieldwork and unspecified assistantships also available. Support available to part-time students. Financial award application deadline: 2/15; financial award applicants required to submit FAFSA. In 2006, 111 degrees awarded. *Degree program information:* Part-time and evening/weekend programs available. Offers business and public affairs (MA, MBA, MS, MSA, MSW); criminal justice (MS); economics/finance (MBA); executive business administration (MBA); general business (MBA); geography (MA); health services (MSA); human research management (MSA); individualized (MSA); leadership for women (MSA); long-term care (MSA); management (MBA); public administration (MSA); regional planning (MSA); social work (MSW); sport and athletic training (MSA); technology and electronic commerce (MBA); training and development (MSA). *Application deadline:* For fall admission, 4/15 priority date for domestic students; for spring admission, 10/15 for domestic students. Applications are processed on a rolling basis. *Application fee:* $35. *Dean,* Dr. Christopher Fiorentino, 610-436-2930, E-mail: cfiorentino@wcupa.edu.

School of Education Students: 189 full-time (159 women), 536 part-time (460 women); includes 31 African Americans, 3 Asian Americans or Pacific Islanders, 7 Hispanic Americans, 2 international. Average age 29. 309 applicants, 94% accepted, 157 enrolled. Expenses: Contact institution. *Financial support:* In 2006–07, 25 research assistantships with full tuition reimbursements (averaging $5,000 per year) were awarded; unspecified assistantships also available. Support available to part-time students. Financial award application deadline: 2/15; financial award applicants required to submit FAFSA. In 2006, 173 degrees awarded. *Degree program information:* Part-time and evening/weekend programs available. Offers counseling and educational psychology (M Ed, MS); early childhood and special education (M Ed); educational research (MS); elementary education (M Ed); elementary school counseling (M Ed); higher education counseling (MS); literacy (M Ed); professional and secondary education (M Ed, MS); reading (M Ed); secondary education (M Ed); secondary school counseling (M Ed); special education (M Ed); teaching and learning with technology (Certificate). *Application deadline:* For fall admission, 4/15 priority date for domestic students; for spring admission, 10/15 for domestic students. Applications are processed on a rolling basis. *Application fee:* $35. *Dean,* Dr. Joseph Malak, 610-436-2428, E-mail: jmalak@wcupa.edu.

School of Health Sciences Students: 105 full-time (93 women), 181 part-time (143 women); includes 23 African Americans, 1 Asian American or Pacific Islander, 2 Hispanic Americans, 11 international. Average age 33. 266 applicants, 67% accepted, 89 enrolled. Expenses: Contact institution. *Financial support:* In 2006–07, 26 research assistantships with full tuition reimbursements (averaging $5,000 per year) were awarded; unspecified assistantships also available. Support available to part-time students. Financial award application deadline: 2/15; financial award applicants required to submit FAFSA. In 2006, 94 degrees awarded. *Degree program information:* Part-time and evening/weekend programs available. Postbaccalaureate distance learning degree programs offered (minimal on-campus study). Offers communicative disorders (MA); driver education (Certificate); emergency preparedness (Certificate); environmental health (MS); exercise and sport physiology (MS); gerontology (MS); health care administration (Certificate); health sciences (M Ed, MA, MPH, MS, MSA, MSN, Certificate); health services (MSA); integrative health (Certificate); nursing (MSN); nursing education (MSN); physical education (MS); public health (MPH, MS); school health (M Ed); sport and athletic administration (MSA). *Application deadline:* For fall admission, 4/15 priority date for domestic students; for spring admission, 10/15 for domestic students. Applications are processed on a rolling basis. *Application fee:* $35. *Dean,* Dr. Donald E. Barr, 610-436-2825, Fax: 610-436-2860, E-mail: dbarr@wcupa.edu.

See Close-Up on page 1143.

WESTERN CAROLINA UNIVERSITY, Cullowhee, NC 28723

General Information State-supported, coed, comprehensive institution. CGS member. *Graduate housing:* Rooms and/or apartments available to single students and guaranteed to married students. Housing application deadline: 6/1. *Research affiliation:* North Carolina Center for the Advancement of Teaching.

GRADUATE UNITS

Graduate School *Degree program information:* Part-time and evening/weekend programs available.

College of Applied Science *Degree program information:* Part-time and evening/weekend programs available. Offers applied science (MCM, MHS, MPT, MS, MSN); construction management (MCM); health sciences (MHS); nursing (MSN); physical therapy (MPT); technology (MS).

College of Arts and Sciences *Degree program information:* Part-time and evening/weekend programs available. Offers American history (MA); applied mathematics (MS); art education (MA Ed, MAT); arts and sciences (MA, MA Ed, MAT, MFA, MPA, MS); biology (MAT, MS); chemistry (MAT, MS); comprehensive education (MA Ed); comprehensive education—art (MA Ed); comprehensive education-biology (MA Ed); comprehensive education-chemistry (MA Ed); comprehensive education-English (MA Ed); comprehensive education-mathematics (MA Ed); English (MA, MAT); history (MA); mathematics (MAT); music (MA); public affairs (MPA); science and entrepreneurship (PSM); social sciences (MAT); studio art (MFA).

College of Business *Degree program information:* Part-time and evening/weekend programs available. Offers accountancy (M Ac); business administration (MBA); entrepreneurship (ME); project management (MPM).

College of Education and Allied Professions *Degree program information:* Part-time and evening/weekend programs available. Offers art education (MAT); behavioral disorders (MA Ed); biology (MAT); chemistry (MAT); clinical psychology (MA); communication disorders (MS); community college education (MA Ed); community counseling (MS); comprehensive education (MA Ed); comprehensive education-elementary education (MA Ed); comprehensive education-reading (MA Ed); comprehensive education-special education (MA Ed, MS); counseling (M Ed, MA Ed, MS); education and allied professions (M Ed, MA, MA Ed, MAT, MS, MSA, Ed D, Ed S); educational leadership (Ed D, Ed S); educational supervision (MA Ed); elementary education (MA Ed); English (MAT); family and consumer sciences (MAT); general special education (MA Ed, MAT); human resource development (MS); learning disabilities (MA Ed); mathematics (MAT); mental retardation (MA Ed); middle grades education (MA Ed, MAT); physical education (MA Ed, MAT); reading (MAT); reading education (M Ed, MA Ed, MAT); school administration (MSA); school counseling (M Ed, MA Ed); school psychology (MA); secondary education (MA Ed, MAT); social sciences (MAT); special education-learning disabilities (MAT).

WESTERN CONNECTICUT STATE UNIVERSITY, Danbury, CT 06810-6885

General Information State-supported, coed, comprehensive institution. *Enrollment:* 6,086 graduate, professional, and undergraduate students; 44 full-time matriculated graduate/professional students (32 women), 541 part-time matriculated graduate/professional students (345 women). *Enrollment by degree level:* 550 master's, 35 doctoral. *Graduate faculty:* 64 full-time (25 women), 9 part-time/adjunct (3 women). *Graduate housing:* Rooms and/or apartments available on a first-come, first-served basis to single and married students. Housing application deadline: 6/13. *Student services:* Campus employment opportunities, career counseling, child daycare facilities, disabled student services, free psychological counseling, international student services, low-cost health insurance, multicultural affairs office. *Library facilities:* Ruth Haas Library plus 1 other. *Online resources:* library catalog, web page, access to other libraries' catalogs. *Collection:* 182,915 titles, 1,273 serial subscriptions. *Research affiliation:* National Undergraduate Research Center.

Computer facilities: 400 computers available on campus for general student use. A campuswide network can be accessed from student residence rooms and from off campus. Internet access and online class registration are available. *Web address:* http://www.wcsu.edu/.

General Application Contact: Chris Shankle, Associate Director of Graduate Admissions, 203-837-8244, Fax: 203-837-8338, E-mail: shanklec@wcsu.edu.

GRADUATE UNITS

Division of Graduate Studies Students: 44 full-time (32 women), 541 part-time (345 women); includes 45 minority (14 African Americans, 1 American Indian/Alaska Native, 14 Asian Americans or Pacific Islanders, 16 Hispanic Americans), 5 international. Average age 34. *Faculty:* 64 full-time (25 women), 9 part-time/adjunct (3 women). Expenses: Contact institution. *Financial support:* Fellowships, teaching assistantships, career-related internships or fieldwork available. Support available to part-time students. Financial award application deadline: 5/1; financial award applicants required to submit FAFSA. In 2006, 239 degrees awarded. *Degree program information:* Part-time and evening/weekend programs available. Offers illustration (MFA); music education (MS); painting (MFA); visual and performing arts (MFA, MS). *Application deadline:* For fall admission, 8/1 priority date for domestic students. Applications are processed on a rolling basis. *Application fee:* $40. *Application Contact:* Chris Shankle, Associate Director of Graduate Admissions, 203-837-8244, Fax: 203-837-8338, E-mail: shanklec@wcsu.edu. *Dean Graduate Studies,* Dr. Ellen D. Durnin, 203-837-8244.

Ancell School of Business Students: 7 full-time (2 women), 89 part-time (38 women); includes 13 minority (6 African Americans, 5 Asian Americans or Pacific Islanders, 2 Hispanic Americans), 3 international. Average age 35. *Faculty:* 16 full-time (4 women), 1 part-time/adjunct (0 women). Expenses: Contact institution. *Financial support:* In 2006–07, 4 fellowships were awarded; career-related internships or fieldwork also available. Support available to part-time students. Financial award application deadline: 5/1; financial award applicants required to submit FAFSA. In 2006, 45 degrees awarded. *Degree program information:* Part-time and evening/weekend programs available. Offers accounting (MBA); business (MBA, MHA, MS); business administration (MBA); health administration (MHA); justice administration (MS). *Application deadline:* For fall admission, 8/1 priority date for domestic students. Applications are processed on a rolling basis. *Application fee:* $40. *Application Contact:* Chris Shankle, Associate Director of Graduate Admissions, 203-837-8244, Fax: 203-837-8338, E-mail: shanklec@wcsu.edu. *Dean,* Dr. Allen Morton, 203-837-8521.

School of Arts and Sciences Students: 4 full-time (3 women), 122 part-time (58 women); includes 2 African Americans, 4 Asian Americans or Pacific Islanders, 2 Hispanic Americans. Average age 38. *Faculty:* 25 full-time (8 women), 1 part-time/adjunct (0 women). Expenses: Contact institution. *Financial support:* Fellowships, teaching assistantships, career-related internships or fieldwork available. Support available to part-time students. Financial award application deadline: 5/1; financial award applicants required to submit FAFSA. In 2006, 44 degrees awarded. *Degree program information:* Part-time and evening/weekend programs available. Offers arts and sciences (MA); biological and environmental sciences (MA); earth and planetary sciences (MA); English (MA); history (MA); mathematics (MA); theoretical mathematics (MA). *Application deadline:* For fall admission, 8/1 priority date for domestic students. Applications are processed on a rolling basis. *Application fee:* $40. *Application Contact:* Chris Shankle, Associate Director of Graduate Admissions, 203-837-8244, Fax: 203-837-8338, E-mail: shanklec@wcsu.edu. *Dean,* Dr. Linda Vaden-Goad, 203-837-9400.

School of Professional Studies Students: 17 full-time (16 women), 305 part-time (235 women); includes 21 minority (5 African Americans, 1 American Indian/Alaska Native, 4 Asian Americans or Pacific Islanders, 11 Hispanic Americans), 2 international. Average age 34. *Faculty:* 23 full-time (13 women), 7 part-time/adjunct (3 women). Expenses: Contact institution. *Financial support:* Fellowships, career-related internships or fieldwork available. Support available to part-time students. Financial award application deadline: 5/1. In 2006, 150 degrees awarded. *Degree program information:* Part-time and evening/weekend programs available. Offers adult nurse practitioner (MSN); clinical nurse specialist (MSN); community counseling (MS); curriculum (MS); English education (MS); instructional leadership (Ed D); instructional technology (MS); mathematics education (MS); professional studies (MS, MSN, Ed D); reading (MS); school counseling (MS); special education (MS). *Application deadline:* For fall admission, 8/1 priority date for domestic students. Applications are processed on a rolling basis. *Application fee:* $40. *Application Contact:* Chris Shankle, Associate Director of Graduate Admissions, 203-837-8244, Fax: 203-837-8338, E-mail: shanklec@wcsu.edu. *Dean,* Dr. Lynne Clark, 203-837-9500.

WESTERN GOVERNORS UNIVERSITY, Salt Lake City, UT 84107

General Information Independent, coed, comprehensive institution. *Graduate housing:* On-campus housing not available.

GRADUATE UNITS

Programs in Business Postbaccalaureate distance learning degree programs offered. Offers information technology management (MBA); management and strategy (MBA); strategic leadership (MBA). Electronic applications accepted.

Teachers College *Degree program information:* Part-time and evening/weekend programs available. Postbaccalaureate distance learning degree programs offered (no on-campus study). Offers English language learning (K-12) (MA); learning and technology (M Ed, MA); management and innovation (M Ed); mathematics education (5-12) (MA); mathematics education (5-9) (MA); mathematics education (K-6) (MA); measurement and evaluation (M Ed); science (5-12) (MA); science education (5-9) (MA); teaching (MAT); technology for principals (Post-Graduate Certificate). Electronic applications accepted.

WESTERN ILLINOIS UNIVERSITY, Macomb, IL 61455-1390

General Information State-supported, coed, comprehensive institution. CGS member. *Enrollment:* 13,602 graduate, professional, and undergraduate students; 798 full-time matriculated graduate/professional students (387 women), 1,140 part-time matriculated graduate/professional students (750 women). *Enrollment by degree level:* 1,811 master's, 22 doctoral, 105 other advanced degrees. Tuition, state resident: part-time $200 per credit hour.

Tuition, nonresident: part-time $400 per credit hour. *Graduate housing:* Rooms and/or apartments available on a first-come, first-served basis to single and married students. Typical cost: $3,876 per year ($6,446 including board) for single students. *Student services:* Campus employment opportunities, campus safety program, career counseling, disabled student services, exercise/wellness program, free psychological counseling, international student services, low-cost health insurance, multicultural affairs office, writing training. *Library facilities:* Leslie Malpass Library plus 4 others. *Online resources:* library catalog, web page. *Collection:* 998,041 titles, 3,200 serial subscriptions. *Research affiliation:* Pollak Industries (physics), LiCor (biology), McDonalds Corporation (education), Earthwatch Institute (biology), Huron Mountain Foundation (biology), Energy Foundation (wind energy).

Computer facilities: 1,000 computers available on campus for general student use. A campuswide network can be accessed from student residence rooms and from off campus. Internet access and online class registration, course registration are available. *Web address:* http://www.wiu.edu/.

General Application Contact: Dr. Barbara Baily, Director of Graduate Studies/Associate Provost, 309-298-1806, Fax: 309-298-2345, E-mail: grad-office@wiu.edu.

GRADUATE UNITS

School of Graduate Studies Students: 798 full-time (387 women), 1,140 part-time (750 women); includes 123 minority (63 African Americans, 3 American Indian/Alaska Native, 15 Asian Americans or Pacific Islanders, 42 Hispanic Americans), 196 international. Average age 29. 1,224 applicants, 61% accepted. Expenses: Contact institution. *Financial support:* In 2006–07, 480 students received support, including 400 research assistantships with full tuition reimbursements available (averaging $6,568 per year), 49 teaching assistantships with full tuition reimbursements available (averaging $7,576 per year). Financial award applicants required to submit FAFSA. In 2006, 549 master's, 29 other advanced degrees awarded. *Degree program information:* Part-time programs available. Postbaccalaureate distance learning degree programs offered (no on-campus study). *Application deadline:* Applications are processed on a rolling basis. *Application fee:* $30. Electronic applications accepted. *Director of Graduate Studies/Associate Provost*, Dr. Barbara Baily, 309-298-1806, Fax: 309-298-2345, E-mail: grad-office@wiu.edu.

College of Arts and Sciences Students: 221 full-time (101 women), 120 part-time (66 women); includes 29 minority (17 African Americans, 5 Asian Americans or Pacific Islanders, 7 Hispanic Americans), 56 international. Average age 30. 317 applicants, 58% accepted. Expenses: Contact institution. *Financial support:* In 2006–07, 166 students received support, including 142 research assistantships with full tuition reimbursements available (averaging $6,568 per year), 24 teaching assistantships with full tuition reimbursements available (averaging $7,576 per year). Financial award applicants required to submit FAFSA. In 2006, 79 master's, 13 other advanced degrees awarded. *Degree program information:* Part-time programs available. Offers applied math (Certificate); arts and sciences (MA, MS, Certificate, SSP); biological sciences (MS); chemistry (MS); clinical/community mental health (MS); community development (Certificate); general psychology (MS); geography (MA); history (MA); literature and language (MA); mathematics (MS); physics (MS); political science (MA); psychology (MS, SSP); public and non-profit management (Certificate); school psychology (SSP); sociology (MA); writing (MA); zoo and aquarium studies (Certificate). *Application deadline:* Applications are processed on a rolling basis. *Application fee:* $30. Electronic applications accepted. *Application Contact:* Dr. Barbara Baily, Director of Graduate Studies/Associate Provost, 309-298-1806, Fax: 309-298-2345, E-mail: grad-office@wiu.edu. *Dean*, Dr. Inessa Levi, 309-298-1828.

College of Business and Technology Students: 185 full-time (49 women), 94 part-time (39 women); includes 12 minority (6 African Americans, 2 Asian Americans or Pacific Islanders, 4 Hispanic Americans), 106 international. Average age 26. 290 applicants, 68% accepted. Expenses: Contact institution. *Financial support:* In 2006–07, 74 students received support, including 64 research assistantships with full tuition reimbursements available (averaging $6,568 per year), 10 teaching assistantships with full tuition reimbursements available (averaging $8,584 per year). Financial award applicants required to submit FAFSA. In 2006, 102 degrees awarded. *Degree program information:* Part-time programs available. Offers accountancy (M Acct); business administration (MBA); business and technology (M Acct, MA, MBA, MS); computer science (MS); economics (MA); manufacturing engineering systems (MS). *Application deadline:* Applications are processed on a rolling basis. *Application fee:* $30. Electronic applications accepted. *Application Contact:* Dr. Barbara Baily, Director of Graduate Studies/Associate Provost, 309-298-1806, Fax: 309-298-2345, E-mail: grad-office@wiu.edu. *Dean*, Dr. Tom Erekson, 309-298-2442.

College of Education and Human Services Students: 275 full-time (154 women), 913 part-time (637 women); includes 74 minority (35 African Americans, 2 American Indian/Alaska Native, 8 Asian Americans or Pacific Islanders, 29 Hispanic Americans), 24 international. Average age 32. 433 applicants, 67% accepted. Expenses: Contact institution. *Financial support:* In 2006–07, 163 students received support, including 151 research assistantships with full tuition reimbursements available (averaging $6,568 per year), 12 teaching assistantships (averaging $7,576 per year). Financial award applicants required to submit FAFSA. In 2006, 329 master's, 16 other advanced degrees awarded. *Degree program information:* Part-time and evening/weekend programs available. Postbaccalaureate distance learning degree programs offered (no on-campus study). Offers college student personnel (MS); counseling (MS Ed); distance learning (Certificate); education and human services (MA, MAT, MS, MS Ed, Ed D, Certificate, Ed S); educational and interdisciplinary studies (MS Ed); educational leadership (MS Ed, Ed D, Ed S); elementary education (MS Ed); graphic applications (Certificate); health education (MS); health services administration (Certificate); instructional technology and telecommunications (MS); kinesiology (MS); law enforcement and justice administration (MA); multimedia (Certificate); police executive administration (Certificate); reading (MS Ed); recreation, park, and tourism administration (MS); secondary education (MAT); special education (MS Ed); sport management (MS); technology integration in education (Certificate); training development (Certificate). *Application deadline:* Applications are processed on a rolling basis. *Application fee:* $30. Electronic applications accepted. *Application Contact:* Dr. Barbara Baily, Director of Graduate Studies/Associate Provost, 309-298-1806, Fax: 309-298-2345, E-mail: grad-office@wiu.edu. *Dean*, Dr. Bonnie Smith, 309-298-1690.

College of Fine Arts and Communication Students: 117 full-time (83 women), 13 part-time (8 women); includes 8 minority (5 African Americans, 1 American Indian/Alaska Native, 2 Hispanic Americans), 10 international. Average age 27. 184 applicants, 44% accepted. Expenses: Contact institution. *Financial support:* In 2006–07, 77 students received support, including 74 research assistantships with full tuition reimbursements available (averaging $6,568 per year), 3 teaching assistantships with full tuition reimbursements available (averaging $7,576 per year). Financial award applicants required to submit FAFSA. In 2006, 39 degrees awarded. *Degree program information:* Part-time programs available. Offers acting (MFA); communication (MA); communication sciences and disorders (MS); costume design (MFA); directing (MFA); fine arts and communication (MA, MFA, MM, MS); lighting design/theatre technology (MFA); music (MM); scenic design (MFA). *Application deadline:* Applications are processed on a rolling basis. *Application fee:* $30. Electronic applications accepted. *Application Contact:* Dr. Barbara Baily, Director of Graduate Studies/Associate Provost, 309-298-1806, Fax: 309-298-2345, E-mail: grad-office@wiu.edu. *Dean*, Dr. Paul K. Kreider, 309-298-1552.

WESTERN INTERNATIONAL UNIVERSITY, Phoenix, AZ 85021-2718

General Information Proprietary, coed, comprehensive institution. *Enrollment:* 2,229 graduate, professional, and undergraduate students; 576 full-time matriculated graduate/professional students (281 women). *Enrollment by degree level:* 576 master's. *Graduate faculty:* 149 part-time/adjunct (49 women). *Tuition:* Full-time $9,600; part-time $400 per credit. One-time fee: $85 full-time. *Graduate housing:* On-campus housing not available. *Student services:* Disabled student services, international student services, writing training. *Library facilities:* Learning Resource Center. *Online resources:* web page. *Collection:* 7,500 titles, 125 serial subscriptions.

Computer facilities: 30 computers available on campus for general student use. A campuswide network can be accessed. Internet access is available. *Web address:* http://www.wintu.edu/.

General Application Contact: Karen Janitell, Director of Enrollment, 602-943-2311 Ext. 1063, Fax: 602-371-8637, E-mail: karen_janitell@apollogrp.edu.

GRADUATE UNITS

Graduate Programs in Business Students: 576 full-time (281 women); includes 136 minority (38 African Americans, 7 American Indian/Alaska Native, 32 Asian Americans or Pacific Islanders, 59 Hispanic Americans), 89 international. Average age 35. *Faculty:* 149 part-time/adjunct (49 women). Expenses: Contact institution. *Financial support:* In 2006–07, 103 students received support. Career-related internships or fieldwork and scholarships/grants available. Support available to part-time students. Financial award applicants required to submit FAFSA. In 2006, 140 degrees awarded. *Degree program information:* Evening/weekend programs available. Postbaccalaureate distance learning degree programs offered (no on-campus study). Offers business (MA, MBA, MPA, MS); finance (MBA); information systems engineering (MS); information technology (MBA, MS); innovative leadership (MA); international business (MBA); management (MBA); marketing (MBA); public administration (MPA). *Application deadline:* Applications are processed on a rolling basis. *Application fee:* $85 ($100 for international students). *Application Contact:* Karen Janitell, Director of Enrollment, 602-943-2311 Ext. 1063, Fax: 602-371-8637, E-mail: karen_janitell@apollogrp.edu. *Chief Academic Officer*, Dr. Deborah DeSimone, 602-943-2311 Ext. 1135, Fax: 602-749-0752, E-mail: deborah.desimone@apollogrp.edu.

WESTERN KENTUCKY UNIVERSITY, Bowling Green, KY 42101

General Information State-supported, coed, comprehensive institution. CGS member. *Enrollment:* 18,660 graduate, professional, and undergraduate students; 766 full-time matriculated graduate/professional students (467 women), 1,299 part-time matriculated graduate/professional students (941 women). *Enrollment by degree level:* 2,002 master's, 26 doctoral, 37 other advanced degrees. *Graduate faculty:* 230 full-time (100 women), 35 part-time/adjunct (15 women). *International tuition:* $15,820 full-time. Tuition, state resident: full-time $6,520; part-time $226 per hour. Tuition, nonresident: full-time $7,140; part-time $357 per hour. *Graduate housing:* Room and/or apartments guaranteed to single students; on-campus housing not available to married students. Typical cost: $3,400 per year ($4,572 including board). Room and board charges vary according to board plan. Housing application deadline: 4/1. *Student services:* Campus employment opportunities, career counseling, child daycare facilities, disabled student services, exercise/wellness program, free psychological counseling, grant writing training, international student services, low-cost health insurance, writing training. *Library facilities:* Helm-Cravens Library plus 3 others. *Online resources:* library catalog, web page, access to other libraries' catalogs. *Collection:* 1.2 million titles, 4,080 serial subscriptions, 23,068 audiovisual materials. *Research affiliation:* Bowling Green Field Station for Animal Studies (U.S. Fish and Wildlife Service), Roybal Center (gerontology).

Computer facilities: 1,300 computers available on campus for general student use. A campuswide network can be accessed from student residence rooms and from off campus. Internet access and online class registration, online grade reports are available. *Web address:* http://www.wku.edu/.

General Application Contact: Dean, Graduate Studies, 270-745-2446, Fax: 270-745-6950, E-mail: graduate.studies@wku.edu.

GRADUATE UNITS

Graduate Studies Students: 766 full-time (467 women), 1,299 part-time (941 women); includes 180 minority (117 African Americans, 7 American Indian/Alaska Native, 20 Asian Americans or Pacific Islanders, 36 Hispanic Americans), 338 international. Average age 31. *Faculty:* 265. Expenses: Contact institution. *Financial support:* In 2006–07, 88 research assistantships with partial tuition reimbursements (averaging $7,500 per year), 52 teaching assistantships with partial tuition reimbursements (averaging $7,500 per year) were awarded; career-related internships or fieldwork, Federal Work-Study, institutionally sponsored loans, tuition waivers (partial), and service awards also available. Support available to part-time students. Financial award application deadline: 4/1; financial award applicants required to submit FAFSA. In 2006, 713 master's, 11 other advanced degrees awarded. *Degree program information:* Part-time and evening/weekend programs available. Postbaccalaureate distance learning degree programs offered (minimal on-campus study). *Application deadline:* For fall admission, 7/1 priority date for domestic students, 4/1 for international students; for spring admission, 11/1 priority date for domestic students, 9/1 for international students. Applications are processed on a rolling basis. *Application fee:* $35. *Application Contact:* Crissy Priddy, Graduate Admissions Coordinator, 270-745-2446, Fax: 270-745-6950, E-mail: graduate.studies@wku.edu. *Interim Dean, Graduate Studies*, Dr. Richard G. Bowker, 270-745-3696, Fax: 270-745-6856, E-mail: richard.bowker@wku.edu.

College of Education and Behavioral Sciences Students: 183 full-time (138 women), 779 part-time (606 women); includes 61 minority (39 African Americans, 4 American Indian/Alaska Native, 6 Asian Americans or Pacific Islanders, 12 Hispanic Americans), 6 international. Average age 32. 354 applicants, 53% accepted, 136 enrolled. *Faculty:* 64 full-time (38 women), 19 part-time/adjunct (9 women). Expenses: Contact institution. *Financial support:* In 2006–07, 24 research assistantships with partial tuition reimbursements (averaging $8,000 per year), 1 teaching assistantship with partial tuition reimbursement (averaging $8,000 per year) were awarded; career-related internships or fieldwork, Federal Work-Study, institutionally sponsored loans, tuition waivers (partial), unspecified assistantships, and service awards also available. Support available to part-time students. Financial award application deadline: 4/1; financial award applicants required to submit FAFSA. In 2006, 351 master's, 11 other advanced degrees awarded. *Degree program information:* Part-time and evening/weekend programs available. Postbaccalaureate distance learning degree programs offered (no on-campus study). Offers business and marketing education (MA Ed, MAE); counseling (MA Ed); counselor education (Ed S); education and behavioral science (MA Ed); education and behavioral sciences (MA, MAE, MS, Ed S); educational administration (MAE); elementary education (MA Ed, MAE, Ed S); exceptional child education (MAE); interdisciplinary early child education (MAE); library media education (MS); literacy (MAE); middle grades education (MAE); middle years education (MA Ed); psychology (MA); school administration (Ed S); school psychology (Ed S); secondary education (MA Ed, MAE, Ed S); student affairs (MA Ed). *Application deadline:* For fall admission, 7/1 priority date for domestic students, 4/1 for international students; for spring admission, 11/1 priority date for domestic students, 9/1 for international students. Applications are processed on a rolling basis. *Application fee:* $35. *Dean*, Dr. Sam Evans, 270-745-4664, Fax: 270-745-6474, E-mail: sam.evans@wku.edu.

College of Health and Human Services Students: 230 full-time (154 women), 237 part-time (173 women); includes 70 minority (45 African Americans, 1 American Indian/Alaska Native, 7 Asian Americans or Pacific Islanders, 17 Hispanic Americans), 97 international. Average age 31. 309 applicants, 39% accepted, 75 enrolled. *Faculty:* 46 full-time (23 women), 7 part-time/adjunct (3 women). Expenses: Contact institution. *Financial support:* In 2006–07, 12 research assistantships with partial tuition reimbursements (averaging $9,400 per year), 3 teaching assistantships with partial tuition reimbursements (averaging $9,400 per year) were awarded; career-related internships or fieldwork, Federal Work-Study, institutionally sponsored loans, tuition waivers (partial), and unspecified assistantships also available. Support available to part-time students. Financial award application deadline: 4/1; financial award applicants required to submit FAFSA. In 2006, 165 degrees awarded. *Degree program information:* Part-time and evening/weekend programs available. Offers communication disorders (MS); health and human services (MHA, MPH, MS, MSN, MSW); healthcare administration (MHA); nursing (MSN); physical education (MS); public health (MPH); recreation (MS); social work (MSW). *Application deadline:* For fall admission, 7/1 priority date for domestic students, 4/1 for international students; for spring admission, 11/1 for domestic students, 9/1 for international students. Applications are processed on a rolling basis. *Application fee:* $35. *Dean*, Dr. John A Bonaguro, 270-745-7003, E-mail: john.bonaguro@wku.edu.

Gordon Ford College of Business Students: 36 full-time (22 women), 88 part-time (44 women); includes 10 minority (6 African Americans, 3 Asian Americans or Pacific Islanders, 1 Hispanic American), 41 international. Average age 30. 56 applicants, 41% accepted, 13 enrolled. *Faculty:* 9 full-time (1 woman). Expenses: Contact institution. *Financial support:* In 2006–07, 12 students received support, including 4 research assistantships with partial tuition reimbursements available (averaging $9,500 per year); Federal Work-Study, institution-

Western Kentucky University (continued)

ally sponsored loans, tuition waivers (partial), and service awards also available. Support available to part-time students. Financial award application deadline: 4/1; financial award applicants required to submit FAFSA. In 2006, 25 master's awarded. *Degree program information:* Part-time and evening/weekend programs available. Offers business (MBA); business administration (MBA). *Application deadline:* For fall admission, 2/1 priority date for domestic students, 4/1 for international students; for spring admission, 7/1 priority date for domestic students, 6/1 for international students. Applications are processed on a rolling basis. *Application fee:* $35. *Dean,* Dr. William Tallon, 270-745-6311, Fax: 270-745-3893.

Ogden College of Science and Engineering Students: 184 full-time (70 women), 64 part-time (36 women); includes 4 minority (1 American Indian/Alaska Native, 2 Asian Americans or Pacific Islanders, 1 Hispanic American), 147 international. Average age 25. 417 applicants, 58% accepted, 97 enrolled. *Faculty:* 57 full-time (14 women), 1 part-time/adjunct (0 women). Expenses: Contact institution. *Financial support:* In 2006–07, 22 research assistantships with partial tuition reimbursements (averaging $8,000 per year), 31 teaching assistantships with partial tuition reimbursements (averaging $8,000 per year) were awarded; career-related internships or fieldwork, Federal Work-Study, institutionally sponsored loans, traineeships, tuition waivers (partial), unspecified assistantships, and service awards also available. Support available to part-time students. Financial award application deadline: 4/1; financial award applicants required to submit FAFSA. In 2006, 91 master's awarded. *Degree program information:* Part-time and evening/weekend programs available. Offers agriculture (MA Ed, MS); biology (MA Ed, MS); chemistry (MA Ed, MS); computer science (MS); geography and geology (MAE, MS); mathematics (MA Ed, MS); science and engineering (MA Ed, MAE, MS). *Application deadline:* For fall admission, 7/1 priority date for domestic students, 4/1 for international students; for spring admission, 11/1 for domestic students, 9/1 for international students. Applications are processed on a rolling basis. *Application fee:* $35. *Dean,* Dr. Blaine R. Ferrell, 270-745-6371, Fax: 270-745-6471, E-mail: blaine.ferrell@wku.edu.

Potter College of Arts and Letters Students: 95 full-time (55 women), 112 part-time (73 women); includes 25 minority (17 African Americans, 1 American Indian/Alaska Native, 2 Asian Americans or Pacific Islanders, 5 Hispanic Americans), 10 international. Average age 30. 99 applicants, 76% accepted, 47 enrolled. *Faculty:* 53 full-time (24 women), 7 part-time/adjunct (3 women). Expenses: Contact institution. *Financial support:* In 2006–07, 10 research assistantships with partial tuition reimbursements (averaging $9,500 per year), 15 teaching assistantships with partial tuition reimbursements (averaging $9,500 per year) were awarded; career-related internships or fieldwork, Federal Work-Study, institutionally sponsored loans, tuition waivers (partial), unspecified assistantships, and service awards also available. Support available to part-time students. Financial award application deadline: 4/1; financial award applicants required to submit FAFSA. In 2006, 72 master's awarded. *Degree program information:* Part-time and evening/weekend programs available. Postbaccalaureate distance learning degree programs offered. Offers art education (MA Ed); arts and letter (MA, MA Ed, MPA); communication (MA); education (MA); English (MA Ed); folk studies (MA); history (MA, MA Ed); literature (MA); music (MA Ed); political science (MPA); sociology (MA); teaching English as a second language (MA); writing (MA). *Application deadline:* For fall admission, 7/1 priority date for domestic students, 4/1 for international students; for spring admission, 11/1 for domestic students, 9/1 for international students. Applications are processed on a rolling basis. *Application fee:* $35. *Dean,* Dr. David D Lee, 270-745-5204, Fax: 270-745-5734, E-mail: david.lee@wku.edu.

WESTERN MICHIGAN UNIVERSITY, Kalamazoo, MI 49008-5202

General Information State-supported, coed, university. CGS member. *Graduate housing:* Rooms and/or apartments available on a first-come, first-served basis to single and married students. Housing application deadline: 7/1. *Research affiliation:* Argonne National Laboratory (particle physics), Central States Universities, Inc., Ames Research Center (manufacturing education), Copper Development Association, Inc. (plastics extrusion), Pharmacia and Upjohn Company (electron microscopy), Flowserve Corporation (mechanical pumps and seals).

GRADUATE UNITS

Graduate College *Degree program information:* Part-time and evening/weekend programs available.

College of Arts and Sciences *Degree program information:* Part-time programs available. Offers anthropology (MA); applied behavior analysis (MA, PhD); applied economics (PhD); applied mathematics (MS); arts and sciences (MA, MDA, MFA, MPA, MS, DPA, PhD, Ed S); biological sciences (MS, PhD); biostatistics (MS); chemistry (MA, PhD); clinical psychology (MA, PhD); comparative religion (MA, PhD); computational mathematics (MS); creative writing (MFA); development administration (MDA); earth science (MS); economics (MA); English (MA, PhD); English education (MA, PhD); experimental analysis of behavior (PhD); experimental psychology (MA); geography (MA); geology (MS, PhD); graph theory and computer science (PhD); history (MA, PhD); industrial/organizational psychology (MA); mathematics (MA, PhD); mathematics education (MA, PhD); medieval studies (MA); molecular biotechnology (MS); organizational communication (MA); philosophy (MA); physics (MA, PhD); political science (MA, PhD); professional writing (MA); public affairs and administration (MPA, DPA); school psychology (PhD, Ed S); science education (PhD); sociology (MA, PhD); Spanish (MA); statistics (MS, PhD).

College of Education *Degree program information:* Part-time programs available. Offers administration (MA); athletic training (MA); career and technical education (MA); coaching and sports studies (MA); counseling psychology (PhD); counselor education (MA, Ed D, PhD); counselor education and counseling psychology (MA, PhD); counselor psychology (MA); early childhood education (MA); education (MA, Ed D, PhD, Ed S); education and professional development (MA); educational leadership (MA, Ed D, PhD, Ed S); educational studies (MA, Ed D); educational technology (MA); elementary education (MA); evaluation, measurement, and research (MA, PhD); exercise science (MA); family and consumer sciences (MA); human resources development (MA); marriage and family therapy (MA); middle school education (MA); motor development (MA); physical education (MA); reading (MA); socio-cultural foundations and educational thought (MA); special education for handicapped children (MA).

College of Engineering and Applied Sciences *Degree program information:* Part-time programs available. Offers computer engineering (MSE, PhD); computer science (MS, PhD); construction engineering and management (MS); electrical engineering (MSE, PhD); engineering and applied sciences (MS, MSE, PhD); engineering management (MS); industrial engineering (MSE); manufacturing engineering (MS); mechanical engineering (MSE, PhD); operations research (MS); paper and printing science and engineering (MS, PhD); structural engineering (MS); transportation engineering (MS).

College of Fine Arts *Degree program information:* Part-time programs available. Offers fine arts (MA, MFA, MM); graphic design (MFA); music (MA, MM); performing arts administration (MFA); textile design (MA, MFA).

College of Health and Human Services *Degree program information:* Part-time programs available. Offers audiology (MA); blind rehabilitation (MA); health and human services (MA, MS, MSW); occupational therapy (MS); physician assistant (MS); social work (MSW); speech pathology (MA).

Haworth College of Business *Degree program information:* Part-time programs available. Offers accountancy (MSA); business (MBA, MSA); business administration (MBA).

WESTERN NEW ENGLAND COLLEGE, Springfield, MA 01119

General Information Independent, coed, comprehensive institution. *Graduate housing:* On-campus housing not available.

GRADUATE UNITS

School of Arts and Sciences *Degree program information:* Part-time and evening/weekend programs available. Offers arts and sciences (M Ed, MAET, MAMT); elementary education (M Ed); English for teachers (MAET); mathematics for teachers (MAMT).

School of Business *Degree program information:* Part-time and evening/weekend programs available. Offers accounting (MSA); business (MBA, MSA); business administration (general) (MBA).

School of Engineering *Degree program information:* Part-time and evening/weekend programs available. Offers computer and engineering information systems (MSEE); computer engineering (MSEE); engineering (MSEE, MSEM, MSME); mechanical engineering (MSME); production management (MSEM).

School of Law *Degree program information:* Part-time and evening/weekend programs available. Offers estate planning/elder law (LL M); law (JD). Electronic applications accepted.

WESTERN NEW MEXICO UNIVERSITY, Silver City, NM 88062-0680

General Information State-supported, coed, comprehensive institution. *Enrollment:* 80 full-time matriculated graduate/professional students (49 women), 374 part-time matriculated graduate/professional students (265 women). *Enrollment by degree level:* 454 master's. *Graduate faculty:* 35 full-time (18 women), 32 part-time/adjunct (19 women). Tuition, state resident: full-time $1,329. Tuition, nonresident: full-time $4,779. *Graduate housing:* Rooms and/or apartments available on a first-come, first-served basis to single and married students. Housing application deadline: 6/30. *Student services:* Campus employment opportunities, campus safety program, career counseling, child daycare facilities, disabled student services, exercise/wellness program, free psychological counseling, low-cost health insurance, multicultural affairs office, writing training. *Library facilities:* Miller Library plus 2 others. *Online resources:* library catalog, web page, access to other libraries' catalogs. *Collection:* 245,146 titles, 236 serial subscriptions.

Computer facilities: 85 computers available on campus for general student use. Internet access and online class registration, online classes in Spanish are available. *Web address:* http://www.wnmu.edu/.

General Application Contact: Dan Tressler, Director of Admissions, 505-538-6106, Fax: 505-538-6127, E-mail: tresslerd@unmu.edu.

GRADUATE UNITS

Graduate Division *Degree program information:* Part-time programs available. Postbaccalaureate distance learning degree programs offered (minimal on-campus study). Offers business management (MBA); interdisciplinary studies (MA). Electronic applications accepted.

School of Education Offers counselor education (MA); elementary education (MAT); reading education (MAT); school administration (MA); secondary education (MAT); special education (MAT). Electronic applications accepted.

WESTERN OREGON UNIVERSITY, Monmouth, OR 97361-1394

General Information State-supported, coed, comprehensive institution. *Enrollment:* 4,885 graduate, professional, and undergraduate students; 173 full-time matriculated graduate/professional students (118 women), 529 part-time matriculated graduate/professional students (422 women). *Enrollment by degree level:* 702 master's. *Graduate faculty:* 33 full-time (20 women), 32 part-time/adjunct (19 women). Tuition, state resident: full-time $8,250; part-time $250 per credit. Tuition, nonresident: full-time $14,025; part-time $250 per credit. *Required fees:* $1,173. *Graduate housing:* Rooms and/or apartments available on a first-come, first-served basis to single and married students. Typical cost: $5,455 per year ($7,030 including board) for single students. Room and board charges vary according to board plan and housing facility selected. *Student services:* Campus employment opportunities, campus safety program, career counseling, child daycare facilities, disabled student services, exercise/wellness program, free psychological counseling, international student services, low-cost health insurance, multicultural affairs office, teacher training, writing training. *Library facilities:* Wayne and Lynn Hamersly Library. *Online resources:* library catalog, web page, access to other libraries' catalogs. *Collection:* 227,707 titles, 2,158 serial subscriptions, 8,010 audiovisual materials. *Research affiliation:* Teaching Research Institute (Education).

Computer facilities: 411 computers available on campus for general student use. A campuswide network can be accessed from student residence rooms and from off campus. Internet access and online class registration are available. *Web address:* http://www.wou.edu/.

General Application Contact: Dr. David McDonald, Dean of Admissions, Retention and Enrollment Management, 503-838-8919, Fax: 503-838-8067, E-mail: mcdonald@wou.edu.

GRADUATE UNITS

Graduate Programs Students: 173 full-time (118 women), 529 part-time (422 women); includes 64 minority (1 African American, 6 American Indian/Alaska Native, 24 Asian Americans or Pacific Islanders, 33 Hispanic Americans). Average age 36. 189 applicants, 74% accepted. *Faculty:* 33 full-time (20 women), 32 part-time/adjunct (19 women). Expenses: Contact institution. *Financial support:* In 2006–07, 164 students received support, including 15 research assistantships with full tuition reimbursements available (averaging $1,147 per year); teaching assistantships with full tuition reimbursements available, career-related internships or fieldwork, Federal Work-Study, scholarships/grants, tuition waivers (full and partial), and unspecified assistantships also available. Support available to part-time students. Financial award application deadline: 3/1; financial award applicants required to submit FAFSA. In 2006, 207 degrees awarded. *Degree program information:* Part-time and evening/weekend programs available. Postbaccalaureate distance learning degree programs offered (minimal on-campus study). *Application deadline:* Applications are processed on a rolling basis. *Application fee:* $50. *Application Contact:* Dr. David McDonald, Dean of Admissions, Retention and Enrollment Management, 503-838-8919, Fax: 503-838-8067, E-mail: mcdonald@wou.edu. *Unit Head,* Dr. Linda Stonecipher, 503-838-8492.

College of Education Students: 120 full-time (69 women), 202 part-time (149 women). Average age 36. *Faculty:* 20 full-time (14 women), 26 part-time/adjunct (18 women). Expenses: Contact institution. *Financial support:* In 2006–07, 6 research assistantships with full and partial tuition reimbursements (averaging $1,233 per year), 18 teaching assistantships with full and partial tuition reimbursements (averaging $870 per year) were awarded; career-related internships or fieldwork, Federal Work-Study, and tuition waivers (full and partial) also available. Support available to part-time students. Financial award application deadline: 3/1; financial award applicants required to submit FAFSA. In 2006, 237 degrees awarded. *Degree program information:* Part-time and evening/weekend programs available. Postbaccalaureate distance learning degree programs offered (minimal on-campus study). Offers bilingual education (MS Ed); deaf education (MS Ed); early childhood education (MS Ed); education (MAT, MS, MS Ed); health (MS Ed); humanities (MAT, MS Ed); information technology (MS Ed); initial licensure (MAT); learning disabilities (MS Ed); mathematics (MAT, MS Ed); multihandicapped education (MS Ed); rehabilitation counseling (MS); science (MAT, MS Ed); social science (MAT, MS Ed); teacher education (MAT, MS, MS Ed). *Application deadline:* Applications are processed on a rolling basis. *Application fee:* $50. *Application Contact:* Dr. David McDonald, Director of Admissions, 503-838-8919, Fax: 503-838-8067, E-mail: mcdonald@wou.edu. *Dean,* Dr. Hilda Rosselli, 503-838-8371, Fax: 503-838-8228, E-mail: rossellih@wou.edu.

College of Liberal Arts and Sciences Students: 7 full-time (3 women), 4 part-time (1 woman); includes 1 minority (American Indian/Alaska Native). Average age 35. *Faculty:* 96 full-time (30 women), 14 part-time/adjunct (6 women). Expenses: Contact institution. *Financial support:* In 2006–07, 2 teaching assistantships with full tuition reimbursements (averaging $676 per year) were awarded; research assistantships with full tuition reimbursements, career-related internships or fieldwork, Federal Work-Study, and tuition waivers (full and partial) also available. Support available to part-time students. Financial award application deadline: 3/1; financial award applicants required to submit FAFSA. In 2006, 5 degrees awarded. *Degree program information:* Part-time and evening/weekend programs available. Offers contemporary music (MM); criminal justice (MA, MS); liberal arts and sciences (MA, MM, MS). *Application deadline:* Applications are processed on a rolling basis. *Application fee:* $50. *Application Contact:* Dr. David McDonald, Dean of Admissions, Retention and Enrollment Management, 503-838-8919, Fax: 503-838-8067, E-mail: mcdonald@wou.edu. *Dean,* Dr. Stephen Scheck, 503-838-8226, Fax: 503-838-8034, E-mail: schecks@wou.edu.

WESTERN SEMINARY, Portland, OR 97215-3367

General Information Independent-religious, coed, graduate-only institution. *Graduate housing:* On-campus housing not available.

GRADUATE UNITS

Graduate Programs *Degree program information:* Part-time and evening/weekend programs available. Offers biblical studies (Certificate); church education (MA, D Min); counseling (MA); hospital chaplaincy (Certificate); intercultural ministry (M Div, MA, D Miss, Certificate); marriage and family counseling (MA, MFT); pastoral counseling (M Div); theology (MA, Th M); women's ministries (MA, Certificate).

WESTERN STATES CHIROPRACTIC COLLEGE, Portland, OR 97230-3099

General Information Independent, coed, graduate-only institution. *Graduate housing:* On-campus housing not available. *Research affiliation:* Oregon Center for Complimentary and Alternative Medicine in Craniofacial Disorders (complimentary and alternative medicine), Oregon Center for Complimentary and Alternative Medicine (complimentary and alternative medicine), Consortial Center for Chiropractic Research (Palmer Chiropractic College, Davenport, IA) (chiropractic).

GRADUATE UNITS

Professional Program Offers chiropractic (DC).

WESTERN STATE UNIVERSITY COLLEGE OF LAW, Fullerton, CA 92831-3000

General Information Proprietary, coed, graduate-only institution. *Enrollment by degree level:* 451 first professional. *Graduate faculty:* 22 full-time (9 women), 26 part-time/adjunct (9 women). *Tuition:* Full-time $27,220; part-time $9,160 per term. *Required fees:* $283; $130 per term. One-time fee: $23 part-time. *Graduate housing:* On-campus housing not available. *Student services:* Campus employment opportunities, campus safety program, career counseling, disabled student services, free psychological counseling, international student services, low-cost health insurance, writing training. *Library facilities:* Law Library. *Online resources:* library catalog, web page. *Collection:* 100,646 titles, 3,120 serial subscriptions, 74 audiovisual materials.

Computer facilities: 45 computers available on campus for general student use. A campuswide network can be accessed. Internet access and online class registration, Lexis, Westlaw, Dialog, Nexis, Cali, Authority, Hein Online are available. *Web address:* http://www.wsulaw.edu/.

General Application Contact: Gloria Switzer, Assistant Dean of Admission, 714-459-1101, Fax: 714-441-1748, E-mail: adm@wsulaw.edu.

GRADUATE UNITS

Professional Program Students: 310 full-time (162 women), 141 part-time (73 women); includes 156 minority (18 African Americans, 5 American Indian/Alaska Native, 83 Asian Americans or Pacific Islanders, 50 Hispanic Americans). Average age 30. 1,637 applicants, 40% accepted, 155 enrolled. *Faculty:* 22 full-time (9 women), 26 part-time/adjunct (9 women). Expenses: Contact institution. *Financial support:* In 2006–07, 434 students received support. Federal Work-Study and scholarships/grants available. Support available to part-time students. Financial award application deadline: 9/15; financial award applicants required to submit FAFSA. In 2006, 148 degrees awarded. *Degree program information:* Part-time and evening/weekend programs available. Offers law (JD). *Application deadline:* For fall admission, 5/1 priority date for domestic students; for spring admission, 10/1 priority date for domestic students. Applications are processed on a rolling basis. *Application fee:* $50. Electronic applications accepted. *Application Contact:* Gloria Switzer, Assistant Dean of Admission, 714-459-1101, Fax: 714-441-1748, E-mail: adm@wsulaw.edu.

WESTERN THEOLOGICAL SEMINARY, Holland, MI 49423-3622

General Information Independent-religious, coed, graduate-only institution. *Graduate housing:* Rooms and/or apartments available on a first-come, first-served basis to single and married students.

GRADUATE UNITS

Graduate and Professional Programs *Degree program information:* Part-time programs available. Postbaccalaureate distance learning degree programs offered (minimal on-campus study). Offers theology (M Div, M Th, D Min).

WESTERN UNIVERSITY OF HEALTH SCIENCES, Pomona, CA 91766-1854

General Information Independent, coed, graduate-only institution. *Enrollment by degree level:* 1,745 first professional, 385 master's. *Graduate faculty:* 136 full-time (58 women), 22 part-time/adjunct (14 women). *Graduate housing:* On-campus housing not available. *Student services:* Campus safety program, career counseling, disabled student services, exercise/wellness program, free psychological counseling, international student services, low-cost health insurance, teacher training. *Library facilities:* The Harriet K. and Philip Pumerantz Library and Learning Resources Cen plus 1 other. *Online resources:* library catalog, web page. *Collection:* 40,301 titles, 10,304 serial subscriptions, 2,945 audiovisual materials. *Research affiliation:* Watson Pharmaceuticals Inc. (pharmaceutical sciences).

Computer facilities: 27 computers available on campus for general student use. A campuswide network can be accessed from off campus. Internet access and online class registration are available. *Web address:* http://www.westernu.edu/.

General Application Contact: Audrey Navarro, Information Contact, 909-469-5335, Fax: 909-469-5570, E-mail: admissions@westernu.edu.

GRADUATE UNITS

College of Allied Health Professions Students: 304 full-time (213 women), 44 part-time (25 women); includes 172 minority (15 African Americans, 89 Asian Americans or Pacific Islanders, 68 Hispanic Americans), 2 international. Average age 30. 758 applicants, 35% accepted, 142 enrolled. *Faculty:* 19 full-time (11 women), 1 (woman) part-time/adjunct. Expenses: Contact institution. *Financial support:* Institutionally sponsored loans and scholarships/grants available. Financial award application deadline: 3/2; financial award applicants required to submit FAFSA. In 2006, 104 master's, 23 doctorates awarded. Offers allied health professions (MS, DPT); health sciences (MS); physical therapy (DPT); physician assistant studies (MS). *Application Contact:* Audrey Navarro, Information Contact, 909-469-5335, Fax: 909-469-5570, E-mail: admissions@westernu.edu. *Dean,* Dr. Stephanie Bowlin, 909-469-5383.

College of Graduate Nursing Students: 149 full-time (129 women), 7 part-time (all women); includes 83 minority (7 African Americans, 56 Asian Americans or Pacific Islanders, 20 Hispanic Americans), 1 international. Average age 33. 163 applicants, 48% accepted, 67 enrolled. *Faculty:* 8 full-time (all women), 9 part-time/adjunct (7 women). Expenses: Contact institution. *Financial support:* Institutionally sponsored loans, scholarships/grants, and Veterans Educational Benefits available. Financial award application deadline: 3/2; financial award applicants required to submit FAFSA. In 2006, 13 degrees awarded. *Degree program information:* Part-time and evening/weekend programs available. Postbaccalaureate distance learning degree programs offered. Offers family nurse practitioner (MSN). *Application deadline:* For fall admission, 3/1 priority date for domestic students. Applications are processed on a rolling basis. *Application fee:* $60. *Application Contact:* Audrey Navarro, Information Contact, 909-469-5335, Fax: 909-469-5570, E-mail: admissions@westernu.edu. *Dean,* Karen J. Hanford, 909-469-5243, Fax: 909-469-5521, E-mail: khanford@westernu.edu.

College of Osteopathic Medicine of the Pacific Students: 762 full-time (386 women); includes 344 minority (9 African Americans, 5 American Indian/Alaska Native, 300 Asian Americans or Pacific Islanders, 30 Hispanic Americans), 12 international. Average age 28. 2,631 applicants, 20% accepted, 218 enrolled. *Faculty:* 36 full-time (5 women), 6 part-time/adjunct (3 women). Expenses: Contact institution. *Financial support:* In 2006–07, 8 research assistantships (averaging $40,000 per year), 81 teaching assistantships (averaging $8,846 per year) were awarded; fellowships, institutionally sponsored loans, scholarships/grants, tuition waivers (full), unspecified assistantships, and Veterans Educational Benefits also available. Financial award application deadline: 3/2; financial award applicants required to submit FAFSA. In 2006, 150 degrees awarded. Offers osteopathic medicine (DO). *Application deadline:* For fall admission, 4/15 for domestic students. Applications are processed on a rolling basis. *Application fee:* $65. *Application Contact:* Audrey Navarro, Information Contact, 909-469-5335, Fax: 909-469-5570, E-mail: admissions@westernu.edu. *Dean,* Dr. Clinton Adams, 909-469-5423, Fax: 909-469-5535, E-mail: aclinton@westernu.edu.

College of Pharmacy Students: 505 full-time (368 women); includes 349 minority (6 African Americans, 1 American Indian/Alaska Native, 330 Asian Americans or Pacific Islanders, 12 Hispanic Americans), 31 international. Average age 29. 1,332 applicants, 18% accepted, 137 enrolled. *Faculty:* 31 full-time (12 women), 3 part-time/adjunct (2 women). Expenses: Contact institution. *Financial support:* Institutionally sponsored loans, scholarships/grants, and Veterans Educational Benefits available. Financial award application deadline: 3/2; financial award applicants required to submit FAFSA. In 2006, 110 Pharm Ds, 4 master's awarded. Offers pharmaceutical sciences (MS); pharmacy (Pharm D, MS). *Application deadline:* For fall admission, 11/1 for domestic and international students. *Application fee:* $65. *Application Contact:* Audrey Navarro, Information Contact, 909-469-5335, Fax: 909-469-5570, E-mail: admissions@westernu.edu. *Dean,* Dr. Daniel Robinson, 909-469-5581, Fax: 909-469-5539.

College of Veterinary Medicine Students: 359 full-time (285 women); includes 79 minority (1 African American, 4 American Indian/Alaska Native, 47 Asian Americans or Pacific Islanders, 27 Hispanic Americans), 5 international. Average age 29. 441 applicants, 42% accepted, 103 enrolled. *Faculty:* 42 full-time (21 women), 3 part-time/adjunct (1 woman). Expenses: Contact institution. *Financial support:* Institutionally sponsored loans, scholarships/grants, and Veterans Educational Benefits available. Financial award application deadline: 3/2; financial award applicants required to submit FAFSA. Offers veterinary medicine (DVM). *Application deadline:* For fall admission, 10/1 for domestic students. *Application fee:* $75. *Application Contact:* Audrey Navarro, Information Contact, 909-469-5335, Fax: 909-469-5570, E-mail: admissions@westernu.edu. *Interim Dean,* Dr. Phil Nelson, 909-469-5637, Fax: 909-469-5635.

WESTERN WASHINGTON UNIVERSITY, Bellingham, WA 98225-5996

General Information State-supported, coed, comprehensive institution. CGS member. *Enrollment:* 14,035 graduate, professional, and undergraduate students; 773 matriculated graduate/professional students. *Graduate faculty:* 457 full-time, 160 part-time/adjunct. Tuition, state resident: full-time $6,609; part-time $199 per credit. Tuition, nonresident: full-time $16,845; part-time $540 per credit. *Graduate housing:* Rooms and/or apartments available on a first-come, first-served basis to single and married students. Housing application deadline: 5/1. *Student services:* Campus employment opportunities, campus safety program, career counseling, child daycare facilities, disabled student services, exercise/wellness program, free psychological counseling, international student services, low-cost health insurance, multicultural affairs office, writing training. *Library facilities:* Wilson Library plus 1 other. *Online resources:* library catalog, web page, access to other libraries' catalogs. *Collection:* 1.3 million titles, 5,236 serial subscriptions. *Research affiliation:* Teck Cominco Ltd., Research Corporation, Dreyfus Foundation, Golden Associates, American Metals Technology.

Computer facilities: 1,874 computers available on campus for general student use. A campuswide network can be accessed from student residence rooms and from off campus. Internet access and online class registration are available. *Web address:* http://www.wwu.edu/.

General Application Contact: Graduate Office Admissions, 360-650-3170, Fax: 360-650-6811, E-mail: gradschool@wwu.edu.

GRADUATE UNITS

Graduate School Expenses: Contact institution. *Financial support:* In 2006–07, research assistantships with partial tuition reimbursements (averaging $9,000 per year), teaching assistantships with partial tuition reimbursements (averaging $9,000 per year) were awarded; career-related internships or fieldwork, Federal Work-Study, institutionally sponsored loans, scholarships/grants, tuition waivers (partial), and unspecified assistantships also available. Support available to part-time students. Financial award application deadline: 2/15; financial award applicants required to submit FAFSA. *Degree program information:* Part-time programs available. *Application deadline:* For fall admission, 6/1 for domestic students, 2/1 priority date for international students; for winter admission, 10/1 for domestic students; for spring admission, 2/1 for domestic students. Applications are processed on a rolling basis. *Application fee:* $50. *Application Contact:* 340-650-3170, Fax: 360-650-6811, E-mail: gradschool@wwu.edu. *Dean,* Dr. Moheb Ghali, 360-650-3170, Fax: 360-630-6811.

College of Business and Economics Students: 50 full-time (23 women), 6 part-time (3 women); includes 9 minority (2 African Americans, 6 Asian Americans or Pacific Islanders, 1 Hispanic American), 3 international. 26 applicants, 69% accepted, 13 enrolled. *Faculty:* 51. Expenses: Contact institution. *Financial support:* In 2006–07, 10 teaching assistantships with partial tuition reimbursements (averaging $9,339 per year) were awarded; Federal Work-Study, institutionally sponsored loans, scholarships/grants, tuition waivers (partial), and unspecified assistantships also available. Support available to part-time students. Financial award application deadline: 2/15; financial award applicants required to submit FAFSA. In 2006, 31 degrees awarded. *Degree program information:* Part-time and evening/weekend programs available. Offers business and economics (MBA). *Application deadline:* For fall admission, 5/1 for domestic students. Applications are processed on a rolling basis. *Application fee:* $50. *Application Contact:* Carrie Thurman, Graduate Program Coordinator, 360-650-3898, Fax: 360-650-4844, E-mail: carrie.thurman@wwu.edu. *Dean,* Dennis Murphy, 360-650-3896, Fax: 360-650-4844, E-mail: dennis.murphy@wwu.edu.

College of Fine and Performing Arts Expenses: Contact institution. *Financial support:* In 2006–07, teaching assistantships with partial tuition reimbursements (averaging $9,339 per year); Federal Work-Study, institutionally sponsored loans, scholarships/grants, and tuition waivers (partial) also available. Support available to part-time students. Financial award application deadline: 2/15; financial award applicants required to submit FAFSA. *Degree program information:* Part-time programs available. Offers fine and performing arts (M Mus, MA); music (M Mus); theatre arts (MA). *Application deadline:* For fall admission, 6/1 for domestic students; for winter admission, 10/1 for domestic students; for spring admission, 2/1 for domestic students. Applications are processed on a rolling basis. *Application fee:* $50. *Dean,* Dr. Carol D. Edwards, 360-650-3866, Fax: 360-650-3028.

College of Humanities and Social Sciences Expenses: Contact institution. *Financial support:* In 2006–07, 2 research assistantships with partial tuition reimbursements (averaging $9,339 per year), 106 teaching assistantships with partial tuition reimbursements (averaging $9,339 per year) were awarded; career-related internships or fieldwork, Federal Work-Study, institutionally sponsored loans, scholarships/grants, tuition waivers (partial), and unspecified assistantships also available. Support available to part-time students. Financial award application deadline: 2/15; financial award applicants required to submit FAFSA. *Degree program information:* Part-time programs available. Offers anthropology (MA); communication sciences and disorders (MA); English (MA); exercise science (MS); experimental psychology (MS); history (MA); humanities and social sciences (M Ed, MA, MS); mental health counseling (MS); political science (MA); school counseling (M Ed); sport psychology (MS). *Application deadline:* For fall admission, 6/1 for domestic students; for winter admission, 10/1 for domestic students; for spring admission, 2/1 for domestic students. Applications are processed on a rolling basis. *Application fee:* $50. *Dean,* Dr. Ronald Kleinknecht, 360-650-3763.

College of Sciences and Technology Expenses: Contact institution. *Financial support:* Research assistantships, teaching assistantships with partial tuition reimbursements, Federal Work-Study, institutionally sponsored loans, scholarships/grants, tuition waivers (partial), and unspecified assistantships available. Support available to part-time students. Financial award application deadline: 2/15. Offers biology (MS); chemistry (MS); computer science (MS); geology (MS); mathematics (MS); sciences and technology (MS). *Application fee:* $50. *Dean,* Dr. Arlan Norman, 360-650-6400, Fax: 360-650-2335.

Western Washington University (continued)

Huxley College of the Environment *Faculty:* 26. Expenses: Contact institution. *Financial support:* Teaching assistantships with partial tuition reimbursements, career-related internships or fieldwork, Federal Work-Study, institutionally sponsored loans, scholarships/grants, tuition waivers (partial), and unspecified assistantships available. Support available to part-time students. Financial award application deadline: 2/15; financial award applicants required to submit FAFSA. *Degree program information:* Part-time programs available. Offers environment (M Ed, MS); environmental science (MS); geography (MS); marine and estuarine science (MS); natural science/science education (M Ed). *Application deadline:* For fall admission, 2/1 for domestic students. *Application fee:* $50. *Application Contact:* Sally Elmore, Graduate Adviser, 360-650-3646. *Dean,* Dr. Bradley F. Smith, 360-650-3521.

Woodring College of Education Expenses: Contact institution. *Financial support:* In 2006–07, teaching assistantships with partial tuition reimbursements (averaging $9,339 per year); career-related internships or fieldwork, Federal Work-Study, institutionally sponsored loans, scholarships/grants, tuition waivers (partial), and unspecified assistantships also available. Support available to part-time students. Financial award application deadline: 2/15; financial award applicants required to submit FAFSA. *Degree program information:* Part-time programs available. Postbaccalaureate distance learning degree programs offered (minimal on-campus study). Offers advanced classroom practice (M Ed); continuing and college education (M Ed); education (M Ed, MA, MIT); educational administration (M Ed); elementary education (M Ed); rehabilitation counseling (MA); secondary education (MIT); special education (M Ed); student affairs administration (M Ed). *Application deadline:* For fall admission, 6/1 for domestic students; for winter admission, 10/1 for domestic students; for spring admission, 2/1 for domestic students. Applications are processed on a rolling basis. *Application fee:* $50. *Dean,* Dr. Stephanie Salzman, 360-650-3319.

WESTFIELD STATE COLLEGE, Westfield, MA 01086

General Information State-supported, coed, comprehensive institution. *Graduate housing:* On-campus housing not available.

GRADUATE UNITS

Division of Graduate and Continuing Education *Degree program information:* Part-time and evening/weekend programs available. Offers criminal justice (MS); early childhood education (M Ed); elementary education (M Ed); English (MA); history (M Ed); mental health counseling (MA); occupational education (M Ed, CAGS); physical education (M Ed); reading (M Ed); school administration (M Ed, CAGS); school guidance (MA); secondary education (M Ed); special education (M Ed); technology for educators (M Ed).

WESTMINSTER CHOIR COLLEGE OF RIDER UNIVERSITY, Princeton, NJ 08540-3899

General Information Independent, coed, comprehensive institution. *Enrollment:* 105 full-time matriculated graduate/professional students (72 women), 12 part-time matriculated graduate/professional students (9 women). *Graduate faculty:* 25 full-time (9 women), 8 part-time/adjunct (3 women). *Library facilities:* Talbott Library-Learning Center. *Collection:* 55,000 titles, 160 serial subscriptions.

Computer facilities: 60 computers available on campus for general student use. *Web address:* http://westminster.rider.edu/.

General Application Contact: Kate Shields, Director of Admissions, 609-921-7100 Ext. 8103, Fax: 609-921-2538, E-mail: wccadmission@rider.edu.

GRADUATE UNITS

Graduate Programs in Music Students: 105 full-time (72 women), 12 part-time (9 women); includes 31 minority (3 African Americans, 21 Asian Americans or Pacific Islanders, 7 Hispanic Americans). 127 applicants, 73% accepted, 47 enrolled. *Faculty:* 25 full-time (9 women), 8 part-time/adjunct (3 women). Expenses: Contact institution. *Financial support:* In 2006–07, 56 research assistantships (averaging $5,256 per year) were awarded; career-related internships or fieldwork, Federal Work-Study, and unspecified assistantships also available. Support available to part-time students. Financial award application deadline: 3/1; financial award applicants required to submit FAFSA. In 2006, 38 degrees awarded. *Degree program information:* Part-time programs available. Offers choral conducting (MM); composition (MM); music education (MM, MME); organ performance (MM); piano accompanying and coaching (MM); piano pedagogy and performance (MM); piano performance (MM); sacred music (MM); vocal pedagogy and performance (MM); vocal training (MVP). *Application deadline:* Applications are processed on a rolling basis. *Application fee:* $45. Electronic applications accepted. *Application Contact:* Kate Shields, Director of Admissions, 609-921-7100 Ext. 8103, Fax: 609-921-2538, E-mail: wccadmission@rider.edu. *Dean,* Robert L. Annis, 609-921-7100 Ext. 8206, Fax: 609-683-8856, E-mail: annis@rider.edu.

WESTMINSTER COLLEGE, New Wilmington, PA 16172-0001

General Information Independent-religious, coed, comprehensive institution. *Graduate housing:* On-campus housing not available.

GRADUATE UNITS

Programs in Education *Degree program information:* Part-time and evening/weekend programs available. Offers administration (M Ed, Certificate); general education (M Ed); guidance and counseling (M Ed, Certificate); reading (M Ed, Certificate).

WESTMINSTER COLLEGE, Salt Lake City, UT 84105-3697

General Information Independent, coed, comprehensive institution. *Enrollment:* 2,479 graduate, professional, and undergraduate students; 223 full-time matriculated graduate/professional students (92 women), 297 part-time matriculated graduate/professional students (132 women). *Enrollment by degree level:* 513 master's, 7 other advanced degrees. *Graduate faculty:* 43 full-time (23 women), 13 part-time/adjunct (9 women). *Graduate housing:* Room and/or apartments available on a first-come, first-served basis to single students; on-campus housing not available to married students. Typical cost: $3,370 per year ($6,140 including board). *Student services:* Campus employment opportunities, campus safety program, career counseling, disabled student services, free psychological counseling, grant writing training, low-cost health insurance, multicultural affairs office, teacher training, writing training. *Library facilities:* Giovale Library plus 1 other. *Online resources:* library catalog, web page, access to other libraries' catalogs. *Collection:* 154,069 titles, 695 serial subscriptions, 7,350 audiovisual materials.

Computer facilities: 400 computers available on campus for general student use. A campuswide network can be accessed from student residence rooms and from off campus. Internet access and online class registration are available. *Web address:* http://www.westminstercollege.edu/.

General Application Contact: Joel Bauman, Vice President of Enrollment Services, 801-832-2200, Fax: 801-832-3101, E-mail: admission@westminstercollege.edu.

GRADUATE UNITS

The Bill and Vieve Gore School of Business Students: 165 full-time (49 women), 189 part-time (56 women); includes 38 minority (3 African Americans, 1 American Indian/Alaska Native, 22 Asian Americans or Pacific Islanders, 12 Hispanic Americans), 12 international. Average age 32. 221 applicants, 71% accepted, 124 enrolled. *Faculty:* 23 full-time (7 women), 7 part-time/adjunct (5 women). Expenses: Contact institution. *Financial support:* In 2006–07, 167 students received support. Career-related internships or fieldwork and tuition remissions available. Support available to part-time students. Financial award applicants required to submit FAFSA. In 2006, 168 master's, 38 other advanced degrees awarded. *Degree program information:* Part-time and evening/weekend programs available. Postbaccalaureate distance learning degree programs offered (no on-campus study). Offers business administration (MBA, Certificate); technology management (MBATM). *Application deadline:* For fall admission, 8/1 priority date for domestic students. Applications are processed on a rolling basis. *Application fee:* $40. Electronic applications accepted. *Application Contact:* Joel Bauman, Vice President of Enrollment Services, 801-832-2200, Fax: 801-832-3101, E-mail: admission@westminstercollege.edu. *Dean,* James Clark, 801-832-2600, Fax: 801-832-3106, E-mail: jclark@westminstercollege.edu.

Program in Counseling Psychology Expenses: Contact institution. Offers counseling psychology (MSCP). *Director,* Janine Wanlass, 801-832-2428.

Program in Professional Communication Students: 8 full-time (6 women), 59 part-time (38 women); includes 2 minority (1 American Indian/Alaska Native, 1 Hispanic American). Average age 33. 32 applicants, 66% accepted, 13 enrolled. *Faculty:* 5 full-time (3 women), 2 part-time/adjunct (1 woman). Expenses: Contact institution. *Financial support:* In 2006–07, 35 students received support. Career-related internships or fieldwork and tuition remissions available. Support available to part-time students. Financial award applicants required to submit FAFSA. In 2006, 26 degrees awarded. *Degree program information:* Part-time and evening/weekend programs available. Offers professional communication (MPC). *Application deadline:* For fall admission, 8/1 priority date for domestic students. Applications are processed on a rolling basis. *Application fee:* $40. Electronic applications accepted. *Application Contact:* Philip J. Alletto, Vice President for Student Development and Enrollment Management, 801-832-2200, Fax: 801-832-3101, E-mail: admission@westminstercollege.edu. *Director,* Dr. Helen Hodgson, 801-832-2821, Fax: 801-832-3102, E-mail: hhodgson@westminstercollege.edu.

School of Education Students: 6 full-time (all women), 36 part-time (29 women); includes 2 minority (1 African American, 1 Hispanic American), 1 international. Average age 38. 27 applicants, 67% accepted, 12 enrolled. *Faculty:* 6 full-time (5 women), 4 part-time/adjunct (3 women). Expenses: Contact institution. *Financial support:* In 2006–07, 32 students received support. Career-related internships or fieldwork and tuition remissions available. Support available to part-time students. Financial award applicants required to submit FAFSA. In 2006, 30 degrees awarded. *Degree program information:* Part-time and evening/weekend programs available. Offers education (M Ed, MAT). *Application deadline:* For fall admission, 8/1 priority date for domestic students. Applications are processed on a rolling basis. *Application fee:* $40. Electronic applications accepted. *Application Contact:* Joel Bauman, Vice President of Enrollment Services, 801-832-2200, Fax: 801-832-3101, E-mail: admission@westminstercollege.edu. *Interim,* David Stokes, 801-832-2470, Fax: 801-832-3105.

School of Nursing and Health Sciences Students: 44 full-time (31 women), 13 part-time (9 women); includes 4 minority (1 African American, 2 Asian Americans or Pacific Islanders, 1 Hispanic American), 1 international. Average age 39. 57 applicants, 65% accepted, 32 enrolled. *Faculty:* 9 full-time (8 women). Expenses: Contact institution. *Financial support:* In 2006–07, 39 students received support. Career-related internships or fieldwork and tuition remissions available. Support available to part-time students. Financial award applicants required to submit FAFSA. In 2006, 5 degrees awarded. *Degree program information:* Part-time and evening/weekend programs available. Offers family nurse practitioner (MSN); nurse anesthesia (MSNA); nursing (MSN); nursing education (MSN). *Application deadline:* For fall admission, 8/1 priority date for domestic students. Applications are processed on a rolling basis. *Application fee:* $40. Electronic applications accepted. *Application Contact:* Joel Bauman, Vice President of Enrollment Services, 801-832-2200, Fax: 801-832-3101, E-mail: admission@westminstercollege.edu. *Dean,* Dr. Jean Dyer, 801-832-2168, Fax: 801-832-3110, E-mail: jdyer@westminstercollege.edu.

WESTMINSTER SEMINARY CALIFORNIA, Escondido, CA 92027-4128

General Information Independent-religious, coed, primarily men, graduate-only institution. *Graduate housing:* On-campus housing not available.

GRADUATE UNITS

Programs in Theology *Degree program information:* Part-time and evening/weekend programs available. Offers Biblical studies (MA); Christian studies (MA); historical theology (MA); theological studies (M Div, MA).

WESTMINSTER THEOLOGICAL SEMINARY, Philadelphia, PA 19118

General Information Independent-religious, coed, primarily men, graduate-only institution. *Enrollment by degree level:* 269 first professional, 241 master's, 206 doctoral, 85 other advanced degrees. *Graduate faculty:* 21 full-time (0 women), 40 part-time/adjunct (6 women). *Graduate housing:* Room and/or apartments available on a first-come, first-served basis to single students; on-campus housing not available to married students. Typical cost: $2,000 per year. *Student services:* Campus employment opportunities, campus safety program, international student services, low-cost health insurance, multicultural affairs office, writing training. *Library facilities:* Montgomery Library. *Online resources:* library catalog, web page. *Collection:* 128,449 titles, 685 serial subscriptions, 3,270 audiovisual materials.

Computer facilities: 16 computers available on campus for general student use. A campuswide network can be accessed. Internet access is available. *Web address:* http://www.wts.edu/.

General Application Contact: Daniel Cason, Director of Admissions, 215-887-5511, Fax: 215-887-5404, E-mail: admissions@wts.edu.

GRADUATE UNITS

Graduate and Professional Programs Students: 324 full-time (52 women), 477 part-time (132 women). Average age 36. 442 applicants, 78% accepted, 203 enrolled. *Faculty:* 21 full-time (0 women), 40 part-time/adjunct (6 women). Expenses: Contact institution. *Financial support:* In 2006–07, 271 students received support. Scholarships/grants and tuition waivers (partial) available. Financial award application deadline: 3/31; financial award applicants required to submit FAFSA. In 2006, 50 M Divs, 46 master's, 19 doctorates, 26 other advanced degrees awarded. *Degree program information:* Part-time programs available. Offers apologetics (Th M); Biblical and urban studies (Certificate); Biblical counseling (MA); biblical studies (MAR); Christian studies (Certificate); church history (Th M); counseling (M Div); general studies (M Div, MAR); hermeneutics and Bible interpretations (PhD); historical and theological studies (PhD); historical theology (Th M); New Testament (Th M); Old Testament (Th M); pastoral counseling (D Min); pastoral ministry (M Div, D Min); systematic theology (Th M); theological studies (MAR); urban missions (M Div, MA, MAR, D Min). *Application deadline:* For fall admission, 3/1 priority date for domestic students, 2/15 for international students; for spring admission, 9/30 priority date for domestic students. Applications are processed on a rolling basis. *Application fee:* $40. *Application Contact:* Daniel Cason, Director of Admissions, 215-887-5511, Fax: 215-887-5404, E-mail: admissions@wts.edu. *Acting Dean of Faculty,* Carl R. Trueman, 215-887-5511, Fax: 215-887-5404, E-mail: ctrueman@wts.edu.

WESTON JESUIT SCHOOL OF THEOLOGY, Cambridge, MA 02138-3495

General Information Independent-religious, coed, graduate-only institution. *Graduate housing:* Rooms and/or apartments available on a first-come, first-served basis to single and married students. Housing application deadline: 3/15.

GRADUATE UNITS

Graduate and Professional Programs *Degree program information:* Part-time programs available. Offers divinity (M Div); sacred theology (STD, STL); spiritual direction (MA); theological studies (MTS); theology (Th M, PhD). Electronic applications accepted.

WEST TEXAS A&M UNIVERSITY, Canyon, TX 79016-0001

General Information State-supported, coed, comprehensive institution. *Graduate housing:* Room and/or apartments available on a first-come, first-served basis to single students; on-campus housing not available to married students. *Research affiliation:* Pantex (chemistry), Agricultural Research (agricultural), Owens Corning (sports exercise), Agriculture Experiment Station (agriculture), Engineering Experiment Station (math/science).

GRADUATE UNITS

College of Agriculture, Nursing, and Natural Sciences *Degree program information:* Part-time and evening/weekend programs available. Offers agricultural business and economics (MS); agriculture (PhD); agriculture, nursing, and natural sciences (MS, MSN, PhD); animal science (MS); biology (MS); chemistry (MS); engineering technology (MS); environmental science (MS); mathematics (MS); nursing (MSN); plant science (MS). Electronic applications accepted.

College of Business *Degree program information:* Part-time and evening/weekend programs available. Postbaccalaureate distance learning degree programs offered (minimal on-campus study). Offers accounting (MP Acc); accounting/business administration (MPA); business (MBA, MP Acc, MPA, MS); business administration (MBA); finance and economics (MS); professional accounting (MPA). Electronic applications accepted.

College of Education and Social Sciences *Degree program information:* Part-time and evening/weekend programs available. Postbaccalaureate distance learning degree programs offered (minimal on-campus study). Offers administration (M Ed); counseling education (M Ed); criminal justice (MA); curriculum and instruction (M Ed); education and social sciences (M Ed, MA, MS); educational diagnostician (M Ed); educational technology (M Ed); history (MA); political science (MA); professional counseling (MA); psychology (MA); reading (M Ed); special education (M Ed); sports and exercise science (MS). Electronic applications accepted.

College of Fine Arts and Humanities *Degree program information:* Part-time and evening/weekend programs available. Offers art (MA); communication (MA); communication disorders (MS); English (MA); fine arts and humanities (MA, MFA, MM, MS); music (MA); performance (MM); studio art (MFA). Electronic applications accepted.

Program in Interdisciplinary Studies *Degree program information:* Part-time and evening/weekend programs available. Postbaccalaureate distance learning degree programs offered (minimal on-campus study). Offers interdisciplinary studies (MA, MS). Electronic applications accepted.

WEST VIRGINIA SCHOOL OF OSTEOPATHIC MEDICINE, Lewisburg, WV 24901-1196

General Information State-supported, coed, graduate-only institution. *Enrollment by degree level:* 503 first professional. *Graduate faculty:* 49 full-time (19 women), 93 part-time/adjunct (48 women). Tuition, state resident: full-time $18,886. Tuition, nonresident: full-time $46,736. *Graduate housing:* On-campus housing not available. *Student services:* Campus employment opportunities, campus safety program, career counseling, disabled student services, exercise/wellness program, multicultural affairs office. *Library facilities:* WVSOM Library. *Online resources:* library catalog, web page. *Collection:* 17,412 titles, 445 serial subscriptions, 1,709 audiovisual materials.

Computer facilities: 13 computers available on campus for general student use. A campuswide network can be accessed from off campus. Internet access is available. *Web address:* http://www.wvsom.edu.

General Application Contact: Donna S. Varney, Director of Admissions, 304-647-6373, Fax: 304-647-6384, E-mail: dvarney@wvsom.edu.

GRADUATE UNITS

Professional Program Students: 503 full-time (240 women); includes 71 minority (5 African Americans, 1 American Indian/Alaska Native, 57 Asian Americans or Pacific Islanders, 8 Hispanic Americans). Average age 26. 2,321 applicants, 26% accepted, 196 enrolled. *Faculty:* 49 full-time (19 women), 93 part-time/adjunct (48 women). Expenses: Contact institution. *Financial support:* In 2006–07, 479 students received support, including 9 teaching assistantships with full and partial tuition reimbursements available (averaging $10,560 per year); Federal Work-Study, scholarships/grants, tuition waivers (full), and unspecified assistantships also available. Financial award application deadline: 4/1; financial award applicants required to submit FAFSA. In 2006, 85 degrees awarded. Offers osteopathic medicine (DO). *Application deadline:* For fall admission, 2/15 for domestic students. Applications are processed on a rolling basis. *Application fee:* $155. Electronic applications accepted. *Application Contact:* Donna S. Varney, Director of Admissions, 304-647-6373, Fax: 304-647-6384, E-mail: dvarney@wvsom.edu. *President*, Dr. Olen E. Jones, 304-645-6270 Ext. 200, Fax: 304-645-4859.

WEST VIRGINIA STATE UNIVERSITY, Institute, WV 25112-1000

General Information State-supported, coed, comprehensive institution.

GRADUATE UNITS

Graduate Programs Offers biotechnology (MA, MS).

WEST VIRGINIA UNIVERSITY, Morgantown, WV 26506

General Information State-supported, coed, university. CGS member. *Enrollment:* 27,115 graduate, professional, and undergraduate students; 4,370 full-time matriculated graduate/professional students (2,240 women), 2,155 part-time matriculated graduate/professional students (1,394 women). *Enrollment by degree level:* 1,420 first professional, 3,352 master's, 1,280 doctoral, 473 other advanced degrees. *Graduate faculty:* 1,422 full-time (463 women), 448 part-time/adjunct (235 women). Tuition, state resident: full-time $4,926; part-time $276 per credit hour. Tuition, nonresident: full-time $14,278; part-time $796 per credit hour. Tuition and fees vary according to program. *Graduate housing:* Rooms and/or apartments available on a first-come, first-served basis to single students and available to married students. Typical cost: $6,422 (including board) for single students; $6,422 (including board) for married students. Room and board charges vary according to board plan and housing facility selected. Housing application deadline: 1/22. *Student services:* Campus employment opportunities, campus safety program, career counseling, disabled student services, exercise/wellness program, free psychological counseling, international student services, low-cost health insurance, teacher training, writing training. *Library facilities:* Downtown Library Complex plus 9 others. *Online resources:* library catalog, web page, access to other libraries' catalogs. *Collection:* 1.7 million titles, 9,107 serial subscriptions, 233,301 audiovisual materials. *Research affiliation:* Polymer Alliance Zone (polymer recycling research), NASA IV and V Center (GOCO addressing software verification/validation), Research Partnership for an Energy Secure America (energy research), Florida A & M (Plasma Physics), University of Pittsburgh and Carnegie Mellon University (Energy Research), National Energy Technology Laboratory (fossil energy and environmental research).

Computer facilities: Computer purchase and lease plans are available. 2,500 computers available on campus for general student use. A campuswide network can be accessed from student residence rooms and from off campus. Internet access and online class registration are available. *Web address:* http://www.wvu.edu/.

General Application Contact: Information Contact, 800-344-WVU1, Fax: 304-293-3080, E-mail: go2wvu@mail.wvu.edu.

GRADUATE UNITS

College of Business and Economics Students: 179 full-time (65 women), 181 part-time (79 women); includes 22 minority (13 African Americans, 3 American Indian/Alaska Native, 4 Asian Americans or Pacific Islanders, 2 Hispanic Americans), 49 international. Average age 30. 494 applicants, 55% accepted, 177 enrolled. *Faculty:* 56 full-time (11 women), 13 part-time/adjunct (5 women). Expenses: Contact institution. *Financial support:* In 2006–07, 222 students received support, including 2 fellowships with full tuition reimbursements available (averaging $16,000 per year), 15 research assistantships with full tuition reimbursements available (averaging $10,500 per year), 32 teaching assistantships with full tuition reimbursements available (averaging $10,500 per year); career-related internships or fieldwork, Federal Work-Study, institutionally sponsored loans, scholarships/grants, tuition waivers (full and partial), unspecified assistantships, and graduate administrative assistantships also available. Financial award application deadline: 2/1; financial award applicants required to submit FAFSA. In 2006, 198 master's, 12 doctorates awarded. *Degree program information:* Part-time programs available. Postbaccalaureate distance learning degree programs offered. Offers business administration (MBA); business and economics (MA, MBA, MPA, MSIR, PhD); industrial relations (MSIR). *Application deadline:* For fall admission, 10/15 priority date for domestic and international students; for spring admission, 3/1 priority date for domestic and international students. Applications are processed on a rolling basis. *Application fee:* $50. Electronic applications accepted. *Application Contact:* Dr. Cyril Logar, Associate Dean/Interim Director for Graduate Programs, 304-293-7956, Fax: 304-293-5652, E-mail: cyril.logar@mail.wvu.edu. *Dean*, Dr. R. Stephen Sears, 304-293-7800, Fax: 304-293-5652, E-mail: steve.sears@mail.wvu.edu.

Division of Accounting Students: 39 full-time (14 women), 4 part-time (3 women); includes 5 minority (1 African American, 1 American Indian/Alaska Native, 2 Asian Americans or Pacific Islanders, 1 Hispanic American), 4 international. Average age 25. 47 applicants, 87% accepted, 32 enrolled. *Faculty:* 9 full-time (2 women), 6 part-time/adjunct (4 women). Expenses: Contact institution. *Financial support:* In 2006–07, 30 students received support, including 2 research assistantships, 1 teaching assistantship; Federal Work-Study, institutionally sponsored loans, and unspecified assistantships also available. Financial award application deadline: 2/1; financial award applicants required to submit FAFSA. In 2006, 42 degrees awarded. *Degree program information:* Part-time and evening/weekend programs available. Offers accounting (MPA). *Application deadline:* For fall admission, 6/30 priority date for domestic students; for spring admission, 11/15 for domestic students. Applications are processed on a rolling basis. *Application fee:* $50. Electronic applications accepted. *Application Contact:* Dr. Cyril Logar, Associate Dean/Interim Director for Graduate Programs, 304-293-7956, Fax: 304-293-5652, E-mail: cyril.logar@mail.wvu.edu. *Director*, Prof. Timothy Pearson, 304-293-7847, Fax: 304-293-0635, E-mail: timothy.pearson@mail.wvu.edu.

Division of Economics and Finance Students: 46 full-time (15 women), 6 part-time (2 women); includes 2 minority (1 African American, 1 Asian American or Pacific Islander), 23 international. Average age 29. 84 applicants, 25% accepted, 15 enrolled. *Faculty:* 23 full-time (2 women), 2 part-time/adjunct (0 women). Expenses: Contact institution. *Financial support:* In 2006–07, 50 students received support, including 1 fellowship with full tuition reimbursement available (averaging $15,000 per year), 8 research assistantships with full tuition reimbursements available (averaging $9,300 per year), 23 teaching assistantships with full tuition reimbursements available (averaging $9,300 per year); Federal Work-Study, institutionally sponsored loans, and tuition waivers (full and partial) also available. Financial award applicants required to submit FAFSA. In 2006, 6 master's, 12 doctorates awarded. Offers business analysis (MA); econometrics (PhD); industrial economics (PhD); international economics (PhD); labor economics (PhD); mathematical economics (MA, PhD); monetary economics (PhD); public finance (PhD); public policy (MA); regional and urban economics (PhD); statistics and economics (MA). *Application deadline:* For fall admission, 3/1 priority date for domestic and international students. Applications are processed on a rolling basis. *Application fee:* $50. Electronic applications accepted. *Application Contact:* Dr. Brian Cushing, Director of Admissions and Financial Awards, 304-293-7881, Fax: 304-293-5652, E-mail: brian.cushing@mail.wvu.edu. *Director*, Dr. William N. Trumbull, 304-293-7860, Fax: 304-293-2233, E-mail: william.trumbull@mail.wvu.edu.

College of Creative Arts Students: 94 full-time (54 women), 42 part-time (18 women); includes 7 minority (5 African Americans, 2 Asian Americans or Pacific Islanders), 30 international. Average age 32. 138 applicants, 59% accepted, 41 enrolled. *Faculty:* 69 full-time (30 women), 20 part-time/adjunct (9 women). Expenses: Contact institution. *Financial support:* In 2006–07, 97 students received support, including 3 research assistantships, 51 teaching assistantships with full tuition reimbursements available (averaging $8,400 per year); career-related internships or fieldwork, Federal Work-Study, institutionally sponsored loans, tuition waivers (partial), and graduate administrative assistantships also available. Financial award applicants required to submit FAFSA. In 2006, 38 master's, 5 doctorates awarded. *Degree program information:* Part-time programs available. Offers acting (MFA); art education (MA); art history (MA); ceramics (MFA); creative arts (MA, MFA, MM, DMA, PhD); graphic design (MFA); music composition (MM, DMA); music education (MM, PhD); music history (MM); music performance (MM, DMA); music theory (MM); painting (MFA); printmaking (MFA); sculpture (MFA); studio art (MA); theatre design/technology (MFA). *Application deadline:* For fall admission, 3/1 priority date for domestic students, 2/15 for international students; for spring admission, 11/1 for domestic students, 9/15 for international students. Applications are processed on a rolling basis. *Application fee:* $50. *Application Contact:* Rachel Hanks, Records Officer, 304-293-4841, Fax: 304-293-2533, E-mail: rachel.hanks@mail.wvu.edu. *Dean*, Dr. Bernie Schultz, 304-293-4841 Ext. 3109, Fax: 304-293-6896, E-mail: bernie.schultz@mail.wvu.edu.

College of Engineering and Mineral Resources Students: 485 full-time (105 women), 198 part-time (31 women); includes 23 minority (5 African Americans, 1 American Indian/Alaska Native, 9 Asian Americans or Pacific Islanders, 8 Hispanic Americans), 345 international. Average age 28. 1,062 applicants, 43% accepted, 199 enrolled. *Faculty:* 113 full-time (6 women), 16 part-time/adjunct (1 woman). Expenses: Contact institution. *Financial support:* In 2006–07, 563 students received support, including 18 fellowships with full tuition reimbursements available (averaging $1,115 per year), 314 research assistantships with full tuition reimbursements available (averaging $1,009 per year), 81 teaching assistantships with full tuition reimbursements available (averaging $1,030 per year); career-related internships or fieldwork, Federal Work-Study, institutionally sponsored loans, tuition waivers (full and partial), and graduate administrative assistantships also available. Financial award application deadline: 2/1; financial award applicants required to submit FAFSA. In 2006, 241 master's, 30 doctorates awarded. *Degree program information:* Part-time programs available. Offers aerospace engineering (MSAE, PhD); chemical engineering (MS Ch E, PhD); civil engineering (MSCE, MSE, PhD); computer engineering (PhD); computer science (MSCS, PhD); electrical engineering (MSEE, PhD); engineering (MSE); engineering and mineral resources (MS, MS Ch E, MS Min E, MSAE, MSCE, MSCS, MSE, MSEE, MSIE, MSME, MSPNGE, MSSE, PhD); industrial engineering (MSE, MSIE, PhD); industrial hygiene (MS); mechanical engineering (MSME, PhD); mining engineering (MS Min E, PhD); occupational safety and health (PhD); petroleum and natural gas engineering (MSPNGE, PhD); safety management (MS); software engineering (MSSE). *Application deadline:* For fall admission, 4/1 for international students; for winter admission, 4/1 for international students; for spring admission, 10/1 for international students. Applications are processed on a rolling basis. *Application fee:* $50. *Application Contact:* Dr. Warren R. Myers, Associate Dean, Academic Affairs, 304-293-4821 Ext. 2210, Fax: 304-293-5024, E-mail: warren.myers@mail.wvu.edu. *Dean*, Dr. Eugene V. Cilento, 304-293-4821 Ext. 2237, Fax: 304-293-2037, E-mail: gene.cilento@mail.wvu.edu.

College of Human Resources and Education Students: 654 full-time (485 women), 715 part-time (551 women); includes 88 minority (51 African Americans, 5 American Indian/Alaska Native, 9 Asian Americans or Pacific Islanders, 23 Hispanic Americans), 57 international. Average age 34. 834 applicants, 71% accepted, 358 enrolled. *Faculty:* 81 full-time (48 women), 13 part-time/adjunct (11 women). Expenses: Contact institution. *Financial support:* In 2006–07, 780 students received support, including 2 fellowships with full tuition reimbursements available (averaging $15,000 per year), 20 research assistantships with full tuition reimbursements available (averaging $8,264 per year), 32 teaching assistantships with full tuition reimbursements available (averaging $8,265 per year); career-related internships or fieldwork, Federal Work-Study, institutionally sponsored loans, tuition waivers (full and partial), and graduate administrative assistantships also available. Financial award applicants required to submit FAFSA. In 2006, 481 master's, 32 doctorates awarded. *Degree program information:* Part-time and evening/weekend programs available. Postbaccalaureate distance learning degree programs offered (no on-campus study). Offers audiology (Au D); autism spectrum disorder (5-adult) (Ed D); autism spectrum disorder (K-6) (Ed D); child development and family studies (MA); counseling (MA); counseling psychology (PhD); curriculum and instruction (Ed D); early intervention (preschool) (MA); early intervention/early childhood special education (MA); educational leadership (Ed D); educational psychology (MA); elementary education (MA); gifted education (1-12) (MA); higher education administration (MA); higher education curriculum and teaching (MA); human resources and education (MA, MS, Au D, Ed D, PhD); information and communication systems (MA); instructional design and technology (MA); multicategorical special education (5-adult) (Ed D); multicategorical special education (K-6) (Ed D); professional development (MA); public school administration (MA); reading (MA); rehabilitation counseling (MS); secondary education (MA); severe/multiple disabilities (K-adult) (MA); special education (Ed D); speech-language pathology (MS); technology and society (MA); technology education (MA); vision impairments (PreK-adult) (Ed D). *Application fee:* $50. Electronic applications accepted. *Application Contact:* Dr. Jane Cardi, Director, Center for Student Advising and Records, 304-293-3441 Ext. 1323, Fax: 304-293-3802,

West Virginia University (continued)

E-mail: jane.cardi@mail.wvu.edu. *Dean,* Dr. Anne H. Nardi, 304-293-5703 Ext. 1811, Fax: 304-293-7565, E-mail: anne.nardi@mail.wvu.edu.

College of Law Students: 475 full-time (214 women), 6 part-time (4 women); includes 48 minority (31 African Americans, 2 American Indian/Alaska Native, 10 Asian Americans or Pacific Islanders, 5 Hispanic Americans), 4 international. Average age 26. 903 applicants, 30% accepted, 176 enrolled. *Faculty:* 25 full-time (8 women), 24 part-time/adjunct (10 women). Expenses: Contact institution. *Financial support:* In 2006–07, 405 students received support, including 5 research assistantships, 3 teaching assistantships; fellowships, career-related internships or fieldwork, Federal Work-Study, institutionally sponsored loans, scholarships/grants, tuition waivers (full), unspecified assistantships, and graduate administrative assistantships, graduate resident assistantships also available. Support available to part-time students. Financial award application deadline: 3/1. In 2006, 139 degrees awarded. *Degree program information:* Part-time programs available. Offers law (JD). *Application deadline:* For fall admission, 2/1 for domestic and international students. Applications are processed on a rolling basis. *Application fee:* $50. Electronic applications accepted. *Application Contact:* Janet Long Armistead, Assistant Dean for Admissions and Student Affairs, 304-293-7320, Fax: 304-293-6891, E-mail: janet.armistead@mail.wvu.edu. *Dean,* John W. Fisher, 304-293-3199, Fax: 304-293-6891, E-mail: john.fisher@mail.wvu.edu.

Davis College of Agriculture, Forestry and Consumer Sciences Students: 186 full-time (82 women), 41 part-time (21 women); includes 9 minority (3 African Americans, 2 American Indian/Alaska Native, 4 Asian Americans or Pacific Islanders), 49 international. Average age 29. 166 applicants, 64% accepted, 58 enrolled. *Faculty:* 88 full-time (17 women), 24 part-time/adjunct (15 women). Expenses: Contact institution. *Financial support:* In 2006–07, 8 fellowships (averaging $2,000 per year), 194 research assistantships (averaging $11,988 per year), 25 teaching assistantships (averaging $8,431 per year) were awarded; career-related internships or fieldwork, Federal Work-Study, institutionally sponsored loans, tuition waivers (full and partial), and unspecified assistantships also available. Financial award application deadline: 2/1; financial award applicants required to submit FAFSA. In 2006, 64 master's, 12 doctorates awarded. *Degree program information:* Part-time programs available. Offers agricultural and extension education (MS); agricultural and resource economics (MS); agricultural extension education (MS); agricultural sciences (PhD); agriculture, forestry and consumer sciences (M Agr, MS, MSF, PhD); agronomy (MS); animal and food sciences (PhD); animal and nutritional sciences (MS); animal breeding (MS, PhD); biochemical and molecular genetics (MS, PhD); breeding (MS); cytogenetics (MS, PhD); descriptive embryology (MS, PhD); developmental genetics (MS); entomology (MS); environmental microbiology (MS); experimental morphogenesis/teratology (MS); food sciences (MS); forest resource science (PhD); forestry (MSF); horticulture (MS); human genetics (MS, PhD); immunogenetics (MS, PhD); life cycles of animals and plants (MS, PhD); molecular aspects of development (MS, PhD); mutagenesis (MS, PhD); nutrition (MS); oncology (MS, PhD); physiology (MS); plant and soil sciences (PhD); plant genetics (MS, PhD); plant pathology (MS); population and quantitative genetics (MS, PhD); production management (MS); recreation, parks and tourism resources (MS); regeneration (MS, PhD); reproduction (MS); reproductive physiology (MS, PhD); resource management and sustainable development (PhD); teaching vocational-agriculture (MS); teratology (PhD); toxicology (MS, PhD); wildlife and fisheries resources (MS). *Application deadline:* For fall admission, 6/1 priority date for domestic students, 6/1 for international students; for spring admission, 1/5 for domestic and international students. Applications are processed on a rolling basis. *Application fee:* $50. Electronic applications accepted. *Application Contact:* Dr. Dennis K. Smith, Associate Dean, 304-293-2691, Fax: 304-293-3740, E-mail: dsmith3@wvu.edu. *Dean,* Dr. Cameron R. Hackney, 304-293-2395 Ext. 4530, Fax: 304-293-3740, E-mail: cameron.hackney@mail.wvu.edu.

Eberly College of Arts and Sciences Students: 770 full-time (424 women), 425 part-time (303 women); includes 83 minority (45 African Americans, 5 American Indian/Alaska Native, 16 Asian Americans or Pacific Islanders, 17 Hispanic Americans), 226 international. Average age 30. 1,235 applicants, 54% accepted, 395 enrolled. *Faculty:* 274 full-time (95 women), 150 part-time/adjunct (94 women). Expenses: Contact institution. *Financial support:* In 2006–07, 975 students received support, including 20 fellowships with full tuition reimbursements available (averaging $20,000 per year), 116 research assistantships with full tuition reimbursements available (averaging $18,000 per year), 333 teaching assistantships with full tuition reimbursements available (averaging $13,000 per year); career-related internships or fieldwork, Federal Work-Study, institutionally sponsored loans, health care benefits, tuition waivers (full and partial), and graduate administrative assistantships also available. Financial award application deadline: 2/1; financial award applicants required to submit FAFSA. In 2006, 325 master's, 43 doctorates awarded. *Degree program information:* Part-time and evening/weekend programs available. Postbaccalaureate distance learning degree programs offered (minimal on-campus study). Offers African history (MA, PhD); African-American history (MA, PhD); American history (MA, PhD); American public policy and politics (MA); analytical chemistry (MS, PhD); Appalachian/regional history (MA, PhD); applied mathematics (MS, PhD); applied physics (MS, PhD); arts and sciences (MA, MALS, MFA, MLS, MPA, MS, MSW, PhD); astrophysics (MS, PhD); behavior analysis (PhD); cell and molecular biology (MS, PhD); chemical physics (MS, PhD); clinical psychology (MA, PhD); communication in instruction (MA); communication theory and research (MA); comparative literature (MA); condensed matter physics (MS, PhD); corporate and organizational communication (MA); creative writing (MFA); development psychology (PhD); discrete mathematics (PhD); East Asian history (MA, PhD); elementary particle physics (MS, PhD); energy and environmental resources (MA); English (MA, PhD); environmental and evolutionary biology (MS, PhD); European history (MA, PhD); French (MA); geographic information systems (PhD); geography (MA, PhD); geography-regional development (PhD); geology (MS, PhD); geomorphology (MS, PhD); geophysics (MS, PhD); German (MA); GIS/cartographic analysis (MA); history of science and technology (MA, PhD); hydrogeology (MS); hydrology (PhD); inorganic chemistry (MS, PhD); integrative organismal biology (PhD); integrative organismal, biology (MS); interdisciplinary mathematics (MS); international and comparative public policy and politics (MA); Latin American history (MA); legal studies (MLS); liberal studies (MALS); linguistics (MA); literary/cultural studies (MA, PhD); materials physics (MS, PhD); mathematics for secondary education (MS); organic chemistry (MS, PhD); paleontology (MS, PhD); petrology (MS, PhD); physical chemistry (MS, PhD); plasma physics (MS, PhD); political science (PhD); psychology (MS); public policy analysis (PhD); pure mathematics (MS); regional development (MA); solid state physics (MS, PhD); Spanish (MA); statistical physics (MS, PhD); statistics (MS); stratigraphy (MS, PhD); structure (MS, PhD); teaching English to speakers of other languages (MA); theoretical chemistry (MS, PhD); theoretical physics (MS, PhD); writing (MA). *Application deadline:* For spring admission, 2/15 priority date for domestic and international students. Applications are processed on a rolling basis. *Application fee:* $45. Electronic applications accepted. *Application Contact:* Dr. Fred L. King, Associate Dean for Graduate Studies, 304-293-4611 Ext. 5205, Fax: 304-293-6858, E-mail: fred.king@mail.wvu.edu. *Dean,* Dr. Mary Ellen Mazey, 304-293-4611, Fax: 304-293-6858, E-mail: mary.mazey@mail.wvu.edu.

School of Applied Social Science Students: 177 full-time (121 women), 200 part-time (162 women); includes 35 minority (29 African Americans, 1 American Indian/Alaska Native, 2 Asian Americans or Pacific Islanders, 3 Hispanic Americans), 7 international. Average age 32. 275 applicants, 73% accepted, 147 enrolled. *Faculty:* 31 full-time (18 women), 23 part-time/adjunct (17 women). Expenses: Contact institution. *Financial support:* In 2006–07, 259 students received support, including 16 research assistantships (averaging $9,000 per year), 28 teaching assistantships (averaging $9,000 per year). In 2006, 96 degrees awarded. *Degree program information:* Part-time programs available. Offers aging and health care (MSW); applied social research (MA); applied social science (MA, MPA, MSW); children and families (MSW); community mental health (MSW); public administration (MPA). *Chair,* Dr. Christopher L. Plein, 304-293-2614 Ext. 3157, Fax: 304-293-8814, E-mail: chris.plein@mail.wvu.edu.

Perley Isaac Reed School of Journalism Students: 80 full-time (59 women), 126 part-time (82 women); includes 26 minority (15 African Americans, 2 American Indian/Alaska Native, 3 Asian Americans or Pacific Islanders, 6 Hispanic Americans), 5 international. Average age 31. 151 applicants, 77% accepted, 83 enrolled. *Faculty:* 11 full-time (5 women), 33 part-time/adjunct (16 women). Expenses: Contact institution. *Financial support:* In 2006–07, 121 students received support, including 2 research assistantships (averaging $8,500 per year), 5 teaching assistantships with full tuition reimbursements available (averaging $8,500 per year); career-related internships or fieldwork, Federal Work-Study, institutionally sponsored loans, tuition waivers (full and partial), and graduate administrative assistantships also available. Financial award application deadline: 2/1; financial award applicants required to submit FAFSA. In 2006, 37 degrees awarded. *Degree program information:* Part-time programs available. Postbaccalaureate distance learning degree programs offered (no on-campus study). Offers integrated marketing communications (MS); journalism (MSJ). MS program taught exclusively online. *Application deadline:* For fall admission, 3/1 priority date for domestic students, 3/1 for international students. *Application fee:* $50. Electronic applications accepted. *Application Contact:* Dr. R. Ivan Pinnell, Director of Graduate Studies and Associate Dean, 304-293-3505 Ext. 5404, Fax: 304-293-3072, E-mail: ivan.pinnell@mail.wvu.edu. *Dean,* Dr. Maryann Reed, 304-293-3505 Ext. 5409, Fax: 304-293-3072, E-mail: maryann.reed@mail.wvu.edu.

School of Dentistry Students: 210 full-time (94 women), 3 part-time (2 women); includes 16 minority (2 African Americans, 8 Asian Americans or Pacific Islanders, 6 Hispanic Americans), 6 international. Average age 26. 941 applicants, 8% accepted, 58 enrolled. *Faculty:* 38 full-time (9 women), 27 part-time/adjunct (8 women). Expenses: Contact institution. *Financial support:* In 2006–07, 180 students received support, including 1 research assistantship with partial tuition reimbursement available, 9 teaching assistantships with partial tuition reimbursements available (averaging $8,264 per year); Federal Work-Study, institutionally sponsored loans, scholarships/grants, and tuition waivers (partial) also available. Financial award application deadline: 3/1; financial award applicants required to submit FAFSA. In 2006, 43 DDSs, 6 master's awarded. Offers dentistry (DDS, MS); endodontics (MS); orthodontics (MS); prosthodontics (MS). *Application deadline:* For fall admission, 11/30 for domestic and international students. Applications are processed on a rolling basis. *Application fee:* $50. *Application Contact:* Dr. Sheila Price, Associate Dean for Admissions, Recruitment, and Access, 304-293-1980, E-mail: sprice@hsc.wvu.edu. *Dean,* Dr. James J. Koelbl, 304-293-2521, E-mail: jkoelbl@hsc.wvu.edu.

Division of Dental Hygiene Expenses: Contact institution. *Financial support:* In 2006–07, 1 research assistantship with partial tuition reimbursement was awarded; Federal Work-Study and institutionally sponsored loans also available. Financial award application deadline: 3/1; financial award applicants required to submit FAFSA. *Degree program information:* Part-time programs available. Offers dental hygiene (MS). *Application deadline:* For fall admission, 7/1 for domestic students; for spring admission, 11/15 priority date for domestic students. Applications are processed on a rolling basis. *Application fee:* $50. *Application Contact:* Loreen Hurley, Administrative Associate, 304-293-3417, E-mail: lhurley@hsc.wvu.edu. *Interim Director of Dental Hygiene,* Amy D. Funk, 304-293-3418, E-mail: afunk@hsc.wvu.edu.

School of Medicine Students: 564 full-time (265 women), 59 part-time (44 women); includes 66 minority (9 African Americans, 1 American Indian/Alaska Native, 55 Asian Americans or Pacific Islanders, 1 Hispanic American), 45 international. Average age 26. *Faculty:* 483 full-time (162 women), 179 part-time/adjunct (114 women). Expenses: Contact institution. *Financial support:* In 2006–07, 60 research assistantships, 53 teaching assistantships were awarded; fellowships, career-related internships or fieldwork, Federal Work-Study, institutionally sponsored loans, tuition waivers (full and partial), and graduate administrative assistantships also available. Financial award applicants required to submit FAFSA. In 2006, 74 MDs, 120 master's, 6 doctorates awarded. *Degree program information:* Part-time and evening/weekend programs available. Offers community health/preventative medicine (MPH); medicine (MD, MOT, MPH, MPT, MS, PhD); occupational therapy (MOT); physical therapy (MPT); public health (MPH); public health sciences (PhD). *Application fee:* $50. *Dean,* Dr. John E. Prescott, 304-293-6607, Fax: 304-293-6627, E-mail: john.prescott@hsc.wvu.edu.

Graduate Programs at the Health Sciences Center Students: 194 full-time (115 women); includes 2 minority (1 African American, 1 Hispanic American), 11 international. Average age 23. Expenses: Contact institution. *Financial support:* In 2006–07, 42 research assistantships, 41 teaching assistantships were awarded; fellowships, career-related internships or fieldwork, Federal Work-Study, institutionally sponsored loans, tuition waivers (full and partial), and graduate administrative assistantships also available. Financial award applicants required to submit FAFSA. In 2006, 38 master's, 18 doctorates awarded. *Degree program information:* Part-time and evening/weekend programs available. Postbaccalaureate distance learning degree programs offered (minimal on-campus study). Offers biochemistry and molecular biology (MS, PhD); cancer cell biology (PhD); cellular and integrative physiology (MS, PhD); exercise physiology (MS, PhD); health sciences (MS, PhD); immunology and microbial pathogenesis (MS, PhD); neuroscience (PhD); pharmaceutical and pharmacological sciences (MS, PhD). *Application deadline:* For spring admission, 3/15 for domestic students. *Application fee:* $50. *Application Contact:* Claire Noel, Assistant Director for Health Sciences Graduate Program, 304-293-7116, Fax: 304-293-9257, E-mail: cnoel@hsc.wvu.edu. *Associate Vice President, Health Sciences Center Research and Graduate Education,* Dr. Thomas Saba, 304-293-7206, Fax: 304-293-7038, E-mail: tsaba@hsc.wvu.edu.

School of Nursing Students: 47 full-time (46 women), 89 part-time (85 women); includes 1 minority (African American) Average age 36. 121 applicants, 74% accepted, 72 enrolled. *Faculty:* 40 full-time (38 women), 15 part-time/adjunct (all women). Expenses: Contact institution. *Financial support:* In 2006–07, 89 students received support, including 1 teaching assistantship; institutionally sponsored loans, tuition waivers (partial), and graduate administrative assistantships also available. Financial award application deadline: 2/1; financial award applicants required to submit FAFSA. In 2006, 20 degrees awarded. *Degree program information:* Part-time programs available. Postbaccalaureate distance learning degree programs offered (minimal on-campus study). Offers nurse practitioner (Certificate); nursing (MSN, PhD). *Application deadline:* For fall admission, 6/1 for domestic students. *Application fee:* $45. Electronic applications accepted. *Application Contact:* Dr. Mary Jane Smith, Associate Dean for Graduate Programs, 304-293-4298, Fax: 304-293-2546, E-mail: mjsmith@hsc.wvu.edu. *Dean,* Dr. E. Jane Martin, 304-293-4831, Fax: 304-293-6826, E-mail: ejmartin@hsc.wvu.edu.

School of Pharmacy Students: 350 full-time (227 women), 4 part-time (2 women); includes 15 minority (4 African Americans, 1 American Indian/Alaska Native, 8 Asian Americans or Pacific Islanders, 2 Hispanic Americans), 19 international. Average age 24. 255 applicants, 35% accepted, 84 enrolled. *Faculty:* 32 full-time (13 women), 2 part-time/adjunct (1 woman). Expenses: Contact institution. *Financial support:* In 2006–07, 326 students received support, including 13 research assistantships with full tuition reimbursements available (averaging $23,000 per year), 17 teaching assistantships with full tuition reimbursements available (averaging $23,000 per year); career-related internships or fieldwork, Federal Work-Study, institutionally sponsored loans, health care benefits, tuition waivers (full and partial), and unspecified assistantships also available. Financial award application deadline: 3/1; financial award applicants required to submit FAFSA. In 2006, 75 first professional degrees, 3 master's, 9 doctorates awarded. Offers administrative pharmacy (PhD); behavioral pharmacy (MS, PhD); biopharmaceutics/pharmacokinetics (MS, PhD); clinical pharmacy (Pharm D); industrial pharmacy (MS); medicinal chemistry (MS, PhD); pharmaceutical chemistry (MS, PhD); pharmaceutics (MS, PhD); pharmacology and toxicology (MS); pharmacy (MS); pharmacy administration (MS). *Application deadline:* For fall admission, 3/1 priority date for domestic and international students. *Application Contact:* Dr. Patrick S. Callery, Assistant Dean for Graduate Programs/Chair, 304-293-1482, Fax: 304-293-2576, E-mail: pcallery@hsc.wvu.edu. *Dean,* Dr. Patricia A. Chase, 304-293-5101, Fax: 304-293-5483, E-mail: pachase@hsc.wvu.edu.

School of Physical Education Offers athletic coaching (MS); athletic training (MS); exercise physiology (Ed D); physical education/teacher education (MS, Ed D); sport management (MS); sport psychology (MS, Ed D). Electronic applications accepted.

WEST VIRGINIA UNIVERSITY INSTITUTE OF TECHNOLOGY, Montgomery, WV 25136

General Information State-supported, coed, comprehensive institution. *Graduate housing:* Room and/or apartments available to single students; on-campus housing not available to married students.

GRADUATE UNITS

College of Engineering *Degree program information:* Part-time programs available. Offers control systems engineering (MS); engineering (MS).

WEST VIRGINIA WESLEYAN COLLEGE, Buckhannon, WV 26201

General Information Independent-religious, coed, comprehensive institution. *Graduate housing:* Room and/or apartments available to single students; on-campus housing not available to married students.

GRADUATE UNITS

Department of Business and Economics *Degree program information:* Part-time and evening/weekend programs available. Offers business and economics (MBA).

WHEATON COLLEGE, Wheaton, IL 60187-5593

General Information Independent-religious, coed, comprehensive institution. *Enrollment:* 2,924 graduate, professional, and undergraduate students; 284 full-time matriculated graduate/professional students (161 women), 275 part-time matriculated graduate/professional students (148 women). *Graduate faculty:* 26 full-time (5 women), 4 part-time/adjunct (1 woman). *Graduate housing:* Rooms and/or apartments available on a first-come, first-served basis to single and married students. Housing application deadline: 4/1. *Student services:* Campus employment opportunities, campus safety program, career counseling, exercise/wellness program, free psychological counseling, grant writing training, international student services, low-cost health insurance, multicultural affairs office, writing training. *Library facilities:* Buswell Memorial Library. *Online resources:* library catalog, web page, access to other libraries' catalogs. *Collection:* 461,249 titles, 4,012 serial subscriptions, 30,142 audiovisual materials.

Computer facilities: 238 computers available on campus for general student use. A campuswide network can be accessed from student residence rooms and from off campus. Internet access and online class registration, financial information, degree requirements evaluation are available. *Web address:* http://www.wheaton.edu/.

General Application Contact: Julie A. Huebner, Director of Graduate Admissions, 630-752-5195, Fax: 630-752-5935, E-mail: gradadm@wheaton.edu.

GRADUATE UNITS

Graduate School Students: 284 full-time (161 women), 275 part-time (148 women). Average age 29. 490 applicants, 62% accepted, 210 enrolled. *Faculty:* 41 full-time (10 women), 6 part-time/adjunct (1 woman). Expenses: Contact institution. *Financial support:* In 2006–07, 235 students received support, including 10 teaching assistantships; career-related internships or fieldwork, Federal Work-Study, scholarships/grants, and unspecified assistantships also available. Financial award application deadline: 3/1; financial award applicants required to submit FAFSA. Offers biblical and theological studies (MA, PhD); biblical archaeology (MA); biblical exegesis (MA); biblical studies (MA); Christian formation and ministry (MA); clinical psychology (MA, Psy D); counseling ministries (MA); elementary level (MAT); evangelism (MA); general history of Christianity (MA); historical and systematic theology (MA); intercultural studies (MA); intercultural studies/teaching English as a second language (MA); missions (MA); religion in American life (MA); secondary level (MAT); teaching English as a second language (Certificate). *Application deadline:* For fall admission, 3/1 priority date for domestic students, 1/1 for international students; for spring admission, 11/1 for domestic students. Applications are processed on a rolling basis. *Application fee:* $30. *Application Contact:* Julie A. Huebner, Director of Graduate Admissions, 630-752-5195, Fax: 630-752-5935, E-mail: gradadm@wheaton.edu.

See Close-Up on page 1145.

WHEELING JESUIT UNIVERSITY, Wheeling, WV 26003-6295

General Information Independent-religious, coed, comprehensive institution. *Enrollment:* 1,402 graduate, professional, and undergraduate students; 94 full-time matriculated graduate/professional students (53 women), 100 part-time matriculated graduate/professional students (81 women). *Enrollment by degree level:* 131 master's, 63 doctoral. *Graduate faculty:* 14 full-time (4 women), 9 part-time/adjunct (4 women). *Tuition:* Full-time $8,910; part-time $405 per credit hour. *Required fees:* $105 per semester. One-time fee: $380 full-time. Full-time tuition and fees vary according to course load, degree level and program. *Graduate housing:* Rooms and/or apartments available on a first-come, first-served basis to single and married students. Typical cost: $5,600 per year ($6,590 including board) for single students; $7,600 per year ($9,580 including board) for married students. Room and board charges vary according to board plan and housing facility selected. *Student services:* Campus employment opportunities, campus safety program, career counseling, disabled student services, exercise/wellness program, free psychological counseling, international student services, low-cost health insurance, multicultural affairs office. *Library facilities:* Bishop Hodges Library plus 1 other. *Online resources:* library catalog, web page, access to other libraries' catalogs. *Collection:* 144,242 titles, 456 serial subscriptions.

Computer facilities: 125 computers available on campus for general student use. A campuswide network can be accessed from student residence rooms and from off campus. Internet access is available. *Web address:* http://www.wju.edu/.

General Application Contact: Becky Forney, Associate Dean of Adult Education, 304-243-2250, Fax: 304-243-4441, E-mail: bforney@wju.edu.

GRADUATE UNITS

Department of Business Students: 19 full-time (5 women), 28 part-time (15 women), 2 international. Average age 31. 31 applicants, 97% accepted, 23 enrolled. *Faculty:* 6 full-time (0 women). Expenses: Contact institution. *Financial support:* In 2006–07, 38 students received support. Career-related internships or fieldwork, Federal Work-Study, and unspecified assistantships available. Financial award application deadline: 8/1; financial award applicants required to submit FAFSA. In 2006, 18 degrees awarded. *Degree program information:* Part-time and evening/weekend programs available. Offers accounting (MS); business administration (MBA). *Application deadline:* For fall admission, 8/1 priority date for domestic students, 8/1 for international students; for spring admission, 12/15 priority date for domestic students, 12/15 for international students. Applications are processed on a rolling basis. *Application fee:* $25. Electronic applications accepted. *Application Contact:* Becky Forney, Associate Dean of Adult Education, 304-243-2250, Fax: 304-243-4441, E-mail: bforney@wju.edu. *Director,* Dr. Edward W Younkins, 304-243-2255, Fax: 304-243-8703, E-mail: younkins@wju.edu.

Department of Nursing Students: 12 full-time (10 women), 62 part-time (59 women); includes 2 minority (1 African American, 1 Hispanic American). Average age 42. 28 applicants, 96% accepted, 21 enrolled. *Faculty:* 3 full-time (all women), 1 (woman) part-time/adjunct. Expenses: Contact institution. *Financial support:* Federal Work-Study, scholarships/grants, and unspecified assistantships available. Financial award application deadline: 8/1; financial award applicants required to submit FAFSA. In 2006, 11 degrees awarded. *Degree program information:* Part-time and evening/weekend programs available. Postbaccalaureate distance learning degree programs offered (minimal on-campus study). Offers nursing (MSN). *Application deadline:* For fall admission, 8/1 priority date for domestic students; for spring admission, 12/15 priority date for domestic students. Applications are processed on a rolling basis. *Application fee:* $25. Electronic applications accepted. *Application Contact:* Becky Forney, Associate Dean of Adult Education, 304-243-2250, Fax: 304-243-4441, E-mail: bforney@wju.edu. *Chair,* Dr. Rose M. Kutlenios, 304-243-2227, Fax: 304-243-4441, E-mail: rosekut@wju.edu.

Department of Physical Therapy Students: 63 full-time (38 women); includes 7 minority (3 African Americans, 1 American Indian/Alaska Native, 2 Asian Americans or Pacific Islanders, 1 Hispanic American). Average age 23. 66 applicants, 48% accepted, 32 enrolled. *Faculty:* 5 full-time (1 woman), 7 part-time/adjunct (2 women). Expenses: Contact institution. *Financial support:* Unspecified assistantships available. Financial award application deadline: 8/1; financial award applicants required to submit FAFSA. In 2006, 29 degrees awarded. Postbaccalaureate distance learning degree programs offered (no on-campus study). Offers physical therapy (DPT). *Application deadline:* For fall admission, 1/15 priority date for domestic and international students. Applications are processed on a rolling basis. *Application fee:* $25. Electronic applications accepted. *Director,* Dr. Luis G. Vargas, 504-243-2432, Fax: 504-243-2042.

WHEELOCK COLLEGE, Boston, MA 02215-4176

General Information Independent, coed, primarily women, comprehensive institution. *Graduate housing:* Room and/or apartments available on a first-come, first-served basis to single students; on-campus housing not available to married students. Housing application deadline: 5/1.

GRADUATE UNITS

Graduate Programs *Degree program information:* Part-time and evening/weekend programs available. Postbaccalaureate distance learning degree programs offered (minimal on-campus study). Offers education (MS, MSW).

Division of Arts and Sciences Offers human development (MS). Electronic applications accepted.

Division of Child and Family Studies *Degree program information:* Part-time programs available. Postbaccalaureate distance learning degree programs offered (minimal on-campus study). Offers family studies (MS); family support and parent education (MS); family, culture, and society (MS). Electronic applications accepted.

Division of Education Postbaccalaureate distance learning degree programs offered (minimal on-campus study). Offers early childhood education (MS); education leadership (MS); elementary education (MS); language, literacy, and reading (MS); teaching students with moderate disabilities (MS). Electronic applications accepted.

Division of Social Work Offers social work (MSW). Electronic applications accepted.

WHITTIER COLLEGE, Whittier, CA 90608-0634

General Information Independent, coed, comprehensive institution. *Graduate housing:* On-campus housing not available.

GRADUATE UNITS

Graduate Programs *Degree program information:* Part-time and evening/weekend programs available. Offers educational administration (MA Ed); elementary education (MA Ed); secondary education (MA Ed).

Whittier Law School *Degree program information:* Part-time and evening/weekend programs available. Offers foreign legal studies (LL M); law (JD). Electronic applications accepted.

WHITWORTH UNIVERSITY, Spokane, WA 99251-0001

General Information Independent-religious, coed, comprehensive institution. *Enrollment:* 2,504 graduate, professional, and undergraduate students; 58 full-time matriculated graduate/professional students (40 women), 190 part-time matriculated graduate/professional students (128 women). *Enrollment by degree level:* 213 master's, 35 other advanced degrees. *Graduate housing:* Room and/or apartments available on a first-come, first-served basis to single students; on-campus housing not available to married students. Housing application deadline: 5/1. *Student services:* Campus employment opportunities, career counseling, disabled student services, exercise/wellness program, free psychological counseling, international student services, low-cost health insurance, multicultural affairs office, teacher training, writing training. *Library facilities:* Harriet Cheney Cowles Library plus 2 others. *Online resources:* library catalog, web page. *Collection:* 17,982 titles, 773 serial subscriptions.

Computer facilities: Computer purchase and lease plans are available. 200 computers available on campus for general student use. A campuswide network can be accessed from student residence rooms and from off campus. Internet access and online class registration are available. *Web address:* http://www.whitworth.edu/.

General Application Contact: Office of Admissions, 509-777-1000.

GRADUATE UNITS

School of Education Expenses: Contact institution. *Financial support:* Career-related internships or fieldwork and Federal Work-Study available. Financial award application deadline:2/1. *Degree program information:* Part-time and evening/weekend programs available. Postbaccalaureate distance learning degree programs offered (minimal on-campus study). Offers education (M Ed, MAT, MIT). *Application deadline:* For fall admission, 9/1 priority date for domestic students; for spring admission, 2/1 priority date for domestic students. Applications are processed on a rolling basis. *Application fee:* $35. *Application Contact:* Pat Bailey, Program Assistant, 509-777-3228, Fax: 509-777-4753, E-mail: gse@whitworth.edu. *Dean,* Dr. Dennis Sterner, 509-777-3229.

Graduate Studies in Education *Faculty:* 2 full-time (both women), 25 part-time/adjunct (15 women). Expenses: Contact institution. *Financial support:* Fellowships with partial tuition reimbursements, career-related internships or fieldwork, institutionally sponsored loans, and scholarships/grants available. Financial award application deadline: 2/1. *Degree program information:* Part-time and evening/weekend programs available. Offers administration (M Ed); counseling (M Ed); elementary education (M Ed); gifted and talented (MAT); school counselors (M Ed); secondary education (M Ed); social agency/church setting (M Ed); special education (MAT); teaching (MIT). *Application deadline:* For fall admission, 9/1 priority date for domestic students; for spring admission, 2/1 priority date for domestic students. Applications are processed on a rolling basis. *Application fee:* $35. *Application Contact:* Pat Bailey, Program Assistant, 509-777-3228, Fax: 509-777-4753, E-mail: gse@whitworth.edu. *Director,* Dr. Sharon Mowry, 509-777-4393, Fax: 509-777-3785, E-mail: smowry@whitworth.edu.

School of Global Commerce and Management Students: 20 full-time (11 women), 5 part-time (3 women); includes 2 minority (both Asian Americans or Pacific Islanders), 4 international. Average age 35. 17 applicants, 65% accepted, 11 enrolled. *Faculty:* 4 full-time (3 women), 14 part-time/adjunct (11 women). Expenses: Contact institution. *Financial support:* In 2006–07, 9 students received support; fellowships with tuition reimbursements available, career-related internships or fieldwork, Federal Work-Study, institutionally sponsored loans, and scholarships/grants available. Support available to part-time students. Financial award application deadline: 3/1. In 2006, 9 degrees awarded. *Degree program information:* Part-time and evening/weekend programs available. Offers business administration (MBA); global commerce and management (MBA, MIM); international management (MBA). *Application deadline:* For fall admission, 8/20 priority date for domestic students; for spring admission, 1/8 priority date for domestic students. Applications are processed on a rolling basis. *Application fee:* $35. Electronic applications accepted. *Application Contact:* Bonnie Wakefield, Assistant Director, Graduate Studies in Business, 509-777-4606, Fax: 509-777-3723, E-mail: bwakefield@whitworth.edu. *Director, Graduate Studies in Business,* Mary Alberts, 509-777-4280, Fax: 509-777-3723, E-mail: malberts@whitworth.edu.

WICHITA STATE UNIVERSITY, Wichita, KS 67260

General Information State-supported, coed, university. CGS member. *Graduate housing:* Rooms and/or apartments available on a first-come, first-served basis to single and married students. *Research affiliation:* Boeing Aircraft Company (aeronautical engineering), Raytheon Aircraft Company (aeronautical engineering), Cessna Aircraft Company (aeronautical engineering), Bombardier (aeronautical engineering), Cisco Systems (computer engineering), Sikorsky Aircraft Corporation (aeronautical engineering).

GRADUATE UNITS

Graduate School *Degree program information:* Part-time and evening/weekend programs available. Electronic applications accepted.

College of Education *Degree program information:* Part-time and evening/weekend programs available. Offers communications sciences (MA, PhD); counseling (M Ed); curriculum and instruction (M Ed); education (M Ed, MA, Ed D, PhD, Ed S); education administration (M Ed, Ed D); educational psychology (M Ed); physical education (M Ed); school psychology (Ed S); special education (M Ed); sports administration (M Ed). Electronic applications accepted.

Wichita State University (continued)

College of Engineering *Degree program information:* Part-time and evening/weekend programs available. Offers aerospace engineering (MS, PhD); electrical engineering (MS, PhD); engineering (MEM, MS, PhD); industrial and manufacturing engineering (MEM, MS, PhD); mechanical engineering (MS, PhD). Electronic applications accepted.

College of Fine Arts *Degree program information:* Part-time programs available. Offers art education (MA); fine arts (MA, MFA, MM, MME); music (MM); music education (MME); studio arts (MFA). Electronic applications accepted.

College of Health Professions *Degree program information:* Part-time programs available. Offers clinical nurse specialist (MSN); health professions (MPH, MPT, MSN); nurse midwifery (MSN); nurse practitioner (MSN); nursing and health care systems administration (MSN); physical therapy (MPT); public health (MPH). Electronic applications accepted.

Fairmount College of Liberal Arts and Sciences *Degree program information:* Part-time and evening/weekend programs available. Offers anthropology (MA); applied mathematics (PhD); biological sciences (MS); chemistry (MS, PhD); communication (MA); community/clinical psychology (PhD); computer science (MS); creative writing (MA, MFA); criminal justice (MA); English (MA, MFA); environmental science (MS); geology (MS); gerontology (MA); history (MA); human factors (PhD); liberal arts and sciences (MA, MFA, MPA, MS, MSW, PhD); mathematics (MS); physics (MS); political science (MA); psychology (MA); public administration (MPA); social work (MSW); sociology (MA); Spanish (MA); statistics (MS). Electronic applications accepted.

W. Frank Barton School of Business *Degree program information:* Part-time and evening/weekend programs available. Offers accountancy (MPA); business (EMBA, MBA, MS); business economics (MA); economic analysis (MA); economics (MA); professional accountancy (MPA). Electronic applications accepted.

WIDENER UNIVERSITY, Chester, PA 19013-5792

General Information Independent, coed, comprehensive institution. CGS member. *Graduate housing:* Rooms and/or apartments available on a first-come, first-served basis to single students and available to married students. Housing application deadline: 5/30. *Research affiliation:* Advanced Technology Center (engineering), Riverfront Development Corporation (engineering, management), Small Business Administration.

GRADUATE UNITS

College of Arts and Sciences *Degree program information:* Part-time and evening/weekend programs available. Offers arts and sciences (MA, MPA); criminal justice (MA); liberal studies (MA); public administration (MPA).

Graduate Programs in Engineering *Degree program information:* Part-time and evening/weekend programs available. Offers chemical engineering (M Eng); civil engineering (M Eng); computer and software engineering (M Eng); engineering management (M Eng); management and technology (MSMT); mechanical engineering (M Eng); telecommunications engineering (M Eng).

School of Business Administration *Degree program information:* Part-time and evening/weekend programs available. Offers accounting information systems (MS); business administration (MBA, MHA, MHR, MS); health and medical services administration (MBA, MHA); human resource management (MHR, MS); taxation (MS). Electronic applications accepted.

School of Human Service Professions *Degree program information:* Part-time and evening/weekend programs available. Offers human service professions (M Ed, MS, MSW, DPT, Ed D, Psy D).

Center for Education *Degree program information:* Part-time and evening/weekend programs available. Offers adult education (M Ed); counseling in higher education (M Ed); counselor education (M Ed); early childhood education (M Ed); educational foundations (M Ed); educational leadership (M Ed); educational psychology (M Ed); elementary education (M Ed); English and language arts (M Ed); health education (M Ed); higher education leadership (Ed D); home and school visitor (M Ed); human sexuality (M Ed); mathematics education (M Ed); middle school education (M Ed); principalship (M Ed); reading and language arts (Ed D); reading education (M Ed); school administration (Ed D); science education (M Ed); social studies education (M Ed); special education (M Ed); technology education (M Ed). Electronic applications accepted.

Center for Social Work Education *Degree program information:* Part-time programs available. Offers social work education (MSW). Electronic applications accepted.

Institute for Graduate Clinical Psychology Offers clinical psychology (Psy D). Electronic applications accepted.

Institute for Physical Therapy Education Offers physical therapy education (MS, DPT).

School of Law *Degree program information:* Part-time programs available. Offers law (JD). Electronic applications accepted.

School of Law at Wilmington *Degree program information:* Part-time programs available. Offers corporate law and finance (LL M); health law (LL M, MJ, D Law); juridical science (SJD); law (JD).

School of Nursing *Degree program information:* Part-time and evening/weekend programs available. Offers nursing (MSN, DN Sc, PMC). Electronic applications accepted.

Announcement: Widener University has all the ingredients to make graduate studies a success. Students can choose from a wide variety of practically focused programs, most of which carry the highest possible accreditation. Small classes taught by experienced, dedicated faculty members provide the perfect environment to work in teams, learn from each other's experiences, and build professional networks. Flexible scheduling and convenient evening and Saturday classes are available with most programs of study. Extensive support is provided through Widener's state-of-the-art library and computing facilities and excellent Career Advising and Planning Services Office.

See Close-Up on page 1147.

WILFRID LAURIER UNIVERSITY, Waterloo, ON N2L 3C5, Canada

General Information Province-supported, coed, comprehensive institution. *Enrollment:* 14,796 graduate, professional, and undergraduate students; 550 full-time matriculated graduate/professional students, 513 part-time matriculated graduate/professional students. *Graduate faculty:* 545 full-time, 54 part-time/adjunct. *Graduate housing:* Rooms and/or apartments available on a first-come, first-served basis to single students and available to married students. Housing application deadline: 4/1. *Student services:* Campus employment opportunities, campus safety program, career counseling, disabled student services, free psychological counseling, international student services, low-cost health insurance, writing training. *Library facilities:* Wilfrid Laurier University Library. *Online resources:* web page. *Collection:* 891,400 titles, 15,900 serial subscriptions.

Computer facilities: 450 computers available on campus for general student use. A campuswide network can be accessed from off campus. Internet access is available. *Web address:* http://www.wlu.ca/.

General Application Contact: Dianne Duffy, Student Contact, 519-884-0710 Ext. 3127, Fax: 519-884-1020, E-mail: gradstudies@wlu.ca.

GRADUATE UNITS

Faculty of Graduate Studies Students: 550 full-time, 513 part-time. 1,280 applicants, 31% accepted, 394 enrolled. *Faculty:* 545 full-time, 54 part-time/adjunct. Expenses: Contact institution. *Financial support:* Fellowships, research assistantships, teaching assistantships available. In 2006, 385 master's, 5 doctorates awarded. Offers music (MMT). Electronic applications accepted. *Application Contact:* Dianne Duffy, Student Contact, 519-884-0710 Ext. 3127, Fax: 519-884-1020, E-mail: gradstudies@wlu.ca. *Dean,* Dr. Joan Norris, 519-884-1970 Ext. 3324.

Faculty of Arts Students: 144 full-time, 11 part-time. 268 applicants, 46% accepted, 75 enrolled. *Faculty:* 196 full-time, 14 part-time/adjunct. Expenses: Contact institution. *Financial support:* Fellowships, research assistantships, teaching assistantships available. In 2006, 59 master's, 3 doctorates awarded. Offers arts (MA, MES, MIPP, PhD); communication studies (MA); cultural analysis and social theory (MA); English (MA, PhD); geography and environmental studies (MA, MES, PhD); global governance (PhD); history (MA, PhD); international public policy (MIPP); philosophy (MA); political science (MA); religion and culture (MA, PhD); sociology (MA). *Application deadline:* For fall admission, 2/1 priority date for domestic students. *Application fee:* $75. Electronic applications accepted. *Application Contact:* Dianne Duffy, Student Contact, 519-884-0710 Ext. 3127, Fax: 519-884-1020, E-mail: gradstudies@wlu.ca. *Dean,* Dr. David Docherty, 519-884-1970 Ext. 3690.

Faculty of Science Students: 77 full-time, 3 part-time. 126 applicants, 44% accepted, 33 enrolled. *Faculty:* 73 full-time, 3 part-time/adjunct. Expenses: Contact institution. *Financial support:* Fellowships, research assistantships, teaching assistantships available. In 2006, 18 degrees awarded. Offers biology (M Sc); brain and cognition (M Sc, PhD); community psychology (MA, PhD); kinesiology and physical education (M Sc); mathematics (M Sc); science (M Sc, MA, PhD); social and developmental psychology (MA, PhD). *Application deadline:* For fall admission, 2/1 priority date for domestic students. *Application fee:* $75. Electronic applications accepted. *Application Contact:* Dianne Duffy, Student Contact, 519-884-0710 Ext. 3127, Fax: 519-884-1020, E-mail: gradstudies@wlu.ca. *Dean,* Dr. Deborah MacLatchy, 519-884-1970 Ext. 2401.

Faculty of Social Work Students: 209 full-time, 93 part-time. 402 applicants, 39% accepted, 120 enrolled. *Faculty:* 23 full-time, 30 part-time/adjunct. Expenses: Contact institution. *Financial support:* Fellowships, research assistantships, teaching assistantships available. In 2006, 108 master's, 2 doctorates awarded. *Degree program information:* Part-time programs available. Offers social work (MSW, PhD). *Application deadline:* For fall admission, 1/15 for domestic students. *Application fee:* $100. Electronic applications accepted. *Application Contact:* Dale Taylor, 519-884-1970, E-mail: socialwork@wlu.ca. *Dean,* Dr. Lesley Cooper, 519-884-1970.

School of Business and Economics Students: 108 full-time, 402 part-time. 473 applicants, 51% accepted, 159 enrolled. *Faculty:* 250 full-time, 4 part-time/adjunct. Expenses: Contact institution. *Financial support:* Fellowships, research assistantships, teaching assistantships, career-related internships or fieldwork available. In 2006, 193 degrees awarded. *Degree program information:* Part-time and evening/weekend programs available. Offers business (MBA); business and economics (MA, MBA, PhD); economics (MA); management (PhD). Electronic applications accepted. *Application Contact:* Dianne Duffy, Student Contact, 519-884-0710 Ext. 3127, Fax: 519-884-1020, E-mail: gradstudies@wlu.ca. *Dean,* Prof. Virginia Dybenko, 519-884-1970 Ext. 2671.

Waterloo Lutheran Seminary *Degree program information:* Part-time programs available. Offers Christian ethics (M Th); divinity (M Div); homiletics (M Th); ministry (D Min); pastoral counseling (M Th); theological studies (MTS).

WILKES UNIVERSITY, Wilkes-Barre, PA 18766-0002

General Information Independent, coed, comprehensive institution. *Enrollment:* 4,777 graduate, professional, and undergraduate students; 440 full-time matriculated graduate/professional students (265 women), 2,092 part-time matriculated graduate/professional students (1,439 women). *Enrollment by degree level:* 268 first professional, 2,264 master's. *Graduate housing:* On-campus housing not available. *Student services:* Career counseling, free psychological counseling, international student services, low-cost health insurance, multicultural affairs office. *Library facilities:* Eugene S. Farley Library. *Online resources:* library catalog, access to other libraries' catalogs.

Computer facilities: 700 computers available on campus for general student use. A campuswide network can be accessed from student residence rooms and from off campus. Internet access and online class registration are available. *Web address:* http://www.wilkes.edu/.

General Application Contact: Kathleen Houlihan, Director of Graduate Studies, 570-408-3235, Fax: 570-408-7846, E-mail: kathleen.houlihan@wilkes.edu.

GRADUATE UNITS

Graduate Studies and Continued Learning Students: 440 full-time (265 women), 2,092 part-time (1,439 women); includes 62 minority (14 African Americans, 6 American Indian/Alaska Native, 21 Asian Americans or Pacific Islanders, 21 Hispanic Americans), 40 international. Average age 32. Expenses: Contact institution. *Financial support:* Federal Work-Study and unspecified assistantships available. Financial award application deadline: 3/1; financial award applicants required to submit FAFSA. In 2006, 73 first professional degrees, 829 master's awarded. *Degree program information:* Part-time and evening/weekend programs available. Postbaccalaureate distance learning degree programs offered (minimal on-campus study). *Application deadline:* Applications are processed on a rolling basis. *Application fee:* $40. *Application Contact:* Kathleen Houlihan, Director of Graduate Studies, 570-408-3235, Fax: 570-408-7846, E-mail: kathleen.houlihan@wilkes.edu. *Interim Dean,* Dr. Michael Speziale, 570-408-4679, Fax: 570-408-4905, E-mail: michael.speziale@wilkes.edu.

College of Arts, Humanities and Social Sciences Students: 86 full-time (54 women), 1,593 part-time (1,109 women); includes 31 minority (6 African Americans, 4 American Indian/Alaska Native, 4 Asian Americans or Pacific Islanders, 17 Hispanic Americans). Average age 33. Expenses: Contact institution. *Financial support:* Federal Work-Study and unspecified assistantships available. Financial award application deadline: 3/1. In 2006, 754 degrees awarded. *Degree program information:* Part-time and evening/weekend programs available. Postbaccalaureate distance learning degree programs offered (minimal on-campus study). Offers arts, humanities and social sciences (MA, MS Ed); classroom technology (MS Ed); creative writing (MA); educational computing (MS Ed); educational development and strategies (MS Ed); educational leadership (MS Ed); elementary education (MS Ed); instructional technology (MS Ed); school business leadership (MS Ed); secondary education (MS Ed); special education (MS Ed). *Application fee:* $40. *Application Contact:* Kathleen Houlihan, Director of Graduate Studies, 570-408-3235, Fax: 570-408-7846, E-mail: kathleen.houlihan@wilkes.edu. *Dean,* Dr. Darin Fields, 570-408-4600, Fax: 570-408-7860, E-mail: dorin.fields@wilkes.edu.

College of Science and Engineering Students: 29 full-time (10 women), 17 part-time (4 women); includes 1 minority (Asian American or Pacific Islander), 35 international. Average age 25. Expenses: Contact institution. In 2006, 12 degrees awarded. *Degree program information:* Part-time programs available. Offers electrical engineering (MSEE); engineering operations and strategy (MS); mathematics (MS, MS Ed); science and engineering (MS, MS Ed, MSEE). *Application fee:* $40. *Application Contact:* Kathleen Houlihan, Director of Graduate Studies, 570-408-3235, Fax: 570-408-7846, E-mail: kathleen.houlihan@wilkes.edu. *Dean,* Dr. Dale Bruns, 570-408-4600, Fax: 570-408-7860, E-mail: dale.bruns@wilkes.edu.

Jay S. Sidhu School of Business and Leadership Students: 30 full-time (16 women), 149 part-time (73 women); includes 5 minority (1 African American, 2 Asian Americans or Pacific Islanders, 2 Hispanic Americans), 4 international. Average age 30. Expenses: Contact institution. *Financial support:* Federal Work-Study and unspecified assistantships available. Financial award application deadline: 3/1; financial award applicants required to submit FAFSA. In 2006, 48 degrees awarded. *Degree program information:* Part-time and evening/weekend programs available. Offers accounting (MBA); entrepreneurship (MBA); finance (MBA); human resource management (MBA); international business (MBA); management (MBA); marketing (MBA). *Application deadline:* Applications are processed on a rolling basis. *Application fee:* $40. *Application Contact:* Kathleen Houlihan, Director of Graduate Studies, 570-408-3235, Fax: 570-408-7846, E-mail: kathleen.houlihan@wilkes.edu. *Dean,* Dr. Paul Browne, 570-408-4701, Fax: 570-408-4700, E-mail: paul.browne@wilkes.edu.

Nesbitt College of Pharmacy and Nursing Students: 294 full-time (185 women), 13 part-time (12 women); includes 22 minority (6 African Americans, 1 American Indian/Alaska Native, 14 Asian Americans or Pacific Islanders, 1 Hispanic American), 1 international. Average age 25. Expenses: Contact institution. *Financial support:* Federal Work-Study and unspecified assistantships available. Financial award application deadline: 3/1. In 2006, 73 Pharm Ds, 15 master's awarded. *Degree program information:* Part-time and evening/

weekend programs available. Offers nursing (MSN); pharmacy (Pharm D); pharmacy and nursing (Pharm D, MSN). *Application deadline:* Applications are processed on a rolling basis. *Dean,* Dr. Bernard Graham, 570-408-4280, Fax: 570-408-7828, E-mail: bernard.graham@wilkes.edu.

WILLAMETTE UNIVERSITY, Salem, OR 97301-3931

General Information Independent-religious, coed, comprehensive institution. *Graduate housing:* Room and/or apartments available on a first-come, first-served basis to single students; on-campus housing not available to married students. Housing application deadline: 6/1.

GRADUATE UNITS

College of Law Students: 424 full-time (179 women); includes 36 minority (3 African Americans, 7 American Indian/Alaska Native, 18 Asian Americans or Pacific Islanders, 8 Hispanic Americans), 3 international. Average age 27. 1,329 applicants, 38% accepted, 159 enrolled. *Faculty:* 25 full-time (8 women), 20 part-time/adjunct (6 women). Expenses: Contact institution. *Financial support:* In 2006–07, 390 students received support; fellowships with partial tuition reimbursements available, research assistantships with partial tuition reimbursements available, Federal Work-Study, scholarships/grants, and tuition waivers (full and partial) available. Financial award application deadline: 3/1; financial award applicants required to submit FAFSA. In 2006, 137 JDs, 2 master's awarded. Offers law (JD, LL M). *Application deadline:* For fall admission, 4/1 priority date for domestic students, 4/1 for international students. Applications are processed on a rolling basis. *Application fee:* $50. Electronic applications accepted. *Application Contact:* Carolyn Dennis, Director of Admission, 503-370-6282, Fax: 503-370-6087, E-mail: law-admission@willamette.edu. *Dean,* Symeon C. Symeonides, 503-370-6402, Fax: 503-370-6828, E-mail: symeon@willamette.edu.

George H. Atkinson Graduate School of Management Students: 116 full-time (38 women), 7 part-time (2 women); includes 15 minority (1 African American, 2 American Indian/Alaska Native, 8 Asian Americans or Pacific Islanders, 4 Hispanic Americans), 28 international. Average age 25. 101 applicants, 95% accepted, 50 enrolled. *Faculty:* 15 full-time (3 women), 9 part-time/adjunct (2 women). Expenses: Contact institution. *Financial support:* In 2006–07, 115 students received support, including 12 research assistantships (averaging $1,500 per year); teaching assistantships, career-related internships or fieldwork, Federal Work-Study, scholarships/grants, and unspecified assistantships also available. Financial award application deadline: 5/1; financial award applicants required to submit FAFSA. In 2006, 56 degrees awarded. *Degree program information:* Part-time programs available. Offers business (MBA); government (MBA); not-for-profit management (MBA). *Application deadline:* For fall admission, 1/9 priority date for domestic and international students; for winter admission, 3/1 priority date for domestic and international students; for spring admission, 5/1 priority date for domestic and international students. Applications are processed on a rolling basis. *Application fee:* $50. Electronic applications accepted. *Application Contact:* Judy O'Neill, Director of Admission, 503-370-6167, Fax: 503-370-3011, E-mail: joneill@willamette.edu. *Interim Dean,* Debra J. Ringold, 503-370-6440, Fax: 503-370-3011, E-mail: dringold@willamette.edu.

School of Education Students: 66 full-time (44 women), 26 part-time (25 women); includes 5 minority (1 Asian American or Pacific Islander, 4 Hispanic Americans). Average age 28. 145 applicants, 72% accepted. *Faculty:* 12 full-time (9 women), 130 part-time/adjunct. Expenses: Contact institution. *Financial support:* In 2006–07, 75 students received support, including fellowships (averaging $4,000 per year); career-related internships or fieldwork, institutionally sponsored loans, scholarships/grants, and tuition waivers (partial) also available. Financial award application deadline: 2/1; financial award applicants required to submit FAFSA. In 2006, 78 degrees awarded. *Degree program information:* Evening/weekend programs available. Offers teaching (MAT). *Application deadline:* For winter admission, 2/1 priority date for domestic students. Applications are processed on a rolling basis. *Application fee:* $50. Electronic applications accepted. *Application Contact:* Debbie Harvey, Associate Director of Admissions, 503-375-5453, Fax: 503-375-5478, E-mail: dharvey@willamette.edu. Dr. Maureen Musser, Fax: 503-375-5478, E-mail: mmusser@willamette.edu.

WILLIAM CAREY UNIVERSITY, Hattiesburg, MS 39401-5499

General Information Independent-religious, coed, comprehensive institution. *Enrollment:* 2,493 graduate, professional, and undergraduate students; 319 full-time matriculated graduate/professional students (231 women), 534 part-time matriculated graduate/professional students (456 women). *Enrollment by degree level:* 838 master's, 15 other advanced degrees. *Graduate faculty:* 38 full-time (24 women), 35 part-time/adjunct (24 women). *Tuition:* Full-time $5,040; part-time $240 per credit hour. Tuition and fees vary according to course load. *Graduate housing:* Room and/or apartments available on a first-come, first-served basis to single students; on-campus housing not available to married students. Typical cost: $1,362 per year ($3,537 including board). Room and board charges vary according to board plan and housing facility selected. Housing application deadline: 8/15. *Student services:* Campus employment opportunities, campus safety program, career counseling, disabled student services, free psychological counseling. *Library facilities:* Smith-Rouse Library. *Online resources:* library catalog, web page, access to other libraries' catalogs. *Collection:* 92,290 titles, 662 serial subscriptions, 698 audiovisual materials.

Computer facilities: 50 computers available on campus for general student use. A campuswide network can be accessed from student residence rooms and from off campus. Internet access is available. *Web address:* http://www.wmcarey.edu/.

General Application Contact: Jason Douglas, Clerical Assistant, Graduate Admissions, 601-318-6774, Fax: 601-318-6765, E-mail: jason.douglas@wmcarey.edu.

GRADUATE UNITS

Graduate Studies *Degree program information:* Part-time programs available.

School of Business Students: 87 full-time (46 women), 35 part-time (23 women); includes 48 minority (42 African Americans, 1 Asian American or Pacific Islander, 5 Hispanic Americans). 45 applicants, 32 enrolled. *Faculty:* 9 full-time (4 women), 1 part-time/adjunct (0 women). Expenses: Contact institution. *Financial support:* In 2006–07, 60 students received support. Federal Work-Study and scholarships/grants available. Support available to part-time students. Financial award applicants required to submit FAFSA. In 2006, 88 degrees awarded. *Degree program information:* Part-time programs available. Offers business (MBA). *Application deadline:* For fall admission, 8/7 for domestic and international students; for winter admission, 10/30 for domestic and international students; for spring admission, 2/12 for domestic and international students. *Application fee:* $25. *Application Contact:* Jason Douglas, Clerical Assistant, Graduate Admissions, 601-318-6774, Fax: 601-318-6765, E-mail: jason.douglas@wmcarey.edu. *Dean,* Dr. Cheryl D. Dale, 601-318-6199, Fax: 601-318-6281, E-mail: cheryl.dale@wmcarey.edu.

School of Education Students: 142 full-time (111 women), 412 part-time (343 women); includes 123 minority (121 African Americans, 1 Asian American or Pacific Islander, 1 Hispanic American). *Faculty:* 19 full-time (12 women), 25 part-time/adjunct (17 women). Expenses: Contact institution. *Financial support:* In 2006–07, 371 students received support. Federal Work-Study and scholarships/grants available. Support available to part-time students. In 2006, 305 master's, 2 other advanced degrees awarded. *Degree program information:* Part-time programs available. Offers art education (M Ed); art of teaching (M Ed); elementary education (M Ed, Ed S); English education (M Ed); gifted education (M Ed); history and social science (M Ed); mild/moderate disabilities (M Ed); secondary education (M Ed). *Application deadline:* For fall admission, 8/7 for domestic and international students; for winter admission, 10/30 for domestic and international students; for spring admission, 2/12 for domestic and international students. *Application fee:* $25. *Application Contact:* Jason Douglas, Clerical Assistant, Graduate Admissions, 601-318-6774, Fax: 601-318-6765, E-mail: jason.douglas@wmcarey.edu. *Dean,* Dr. Patty Ward, 601-318-6139, Fax: 601-318-6185, E-mail: patty.ward@wmcarey.edu.

School of Nursing Students: 13 full-time (all women), 4 part-time (all women); includes 4 minority (all African Americans) 15 applicants, 12 enrolled. *Faculty:* 5 full-time (all women), 2 part-time/adjunct (both women). Expenses: Contact institution. *Financial support:* In 2006–07, 16 students received support. Federal Work-Study and scholarships/grants available. Support available to part-time students. Financial award applicants required to submit FAFSA. In 2006, 8 degrees awarded. *Degree program information:* Part-time programs available. Offers nursing (MSN). *Application deadline:* For fall admission, 8/7 for domestic and international students; for winter admission, 10/30 for domestic and international students; for spring admission, 2/12 for domestic and international students. *Application fee:* $25. *Application Contact:* Jason Douglas, Clerical Assistant, Graduate Admissions, 601-318-6774, Fax: 601-318-6765, E-mail: jason.douglas@wmcarey.edu. *Dean,* Dr. Mary Stewart, 601-318-6147, Fax: 601-318-6446, E-mail: mary.stewart@wmcarey.edu.

School of Psychology and Counseling Students: 77 full-time (61 women), 79 part-time (70 women); includes 71 minority (69 African Americans, 1 Asian American or Pacific Islander, 1 Hispanic American). 40 applicants, 95% accepted, 14 enrolled. *Faculty:* 5 full-time (3 women), 7 part-time/adjunct (5 women). Expenses: Contact institution. *Financial support:* In 2006–07, 142 students received support. Federal Work-Study, scholarships/grants, and unspecified assistantships available. Support available to part-time students. Financial award applicants required to submit FAFSA. In 2006, 39 degrees awarded. *Degree program information:* Part-time programs available. Offers counseling psychology (MS). *Application deadline:* For fall admission, 8/7 for domestic and international students; for winter admission, 10/30 for domestic and international students; for spring admission, 2/12 for domestic and international students. *Application fee:* $25. *Application Contact:* Jason Douglas, Clerical Assistant, Graduate Admissions, 601-318-6774, Fax: 601-318-6765, E-mail: jason.douglas@wmcarey.edu. *Dean, School of Psychology,* Dr. Frank G. Baugh, 601-318-6470, Fax: 601-582-6454, E-mail: frank.baugh@wmcarey.edu.

WILLIAM HOWARD TAFT UNIVERSITY, Santa Ana, CA 92704

General Information Proprietary, coed, graduate-only institution. *Web address:* http://www.taftu.edu/.

GRADUATE UNITS

Graduate Programs Expenses: Contact institution. Offers education (M Ed).

Bernard E. Witkin School of Law Expenses: Contact institution. Offers American jurisprudence (LL M); law (JD); taxation (LL M).

W. Edwards Deming School of Business Expenses: Contact institution. Offers taxation (MS).

WILLIAM MITCHELL COLLEGE OF LAW, St. Paul, MN 55105-3076

General Information Independent, coed, graduate-only institution. *Enrollment by degree level:* 1,103 first professional. *Graduate faculty:* 35 full-time (13 women), 212 part-time/adjunct (87 women). *Tuition:* Full-time $27,480; part-time $19,888 per year. *Required fees:* $50. *Graduate housing:* On-campus housing not available. *Student services:* Campus employment opportunities, campus safety program, career counseling, disabled student services, free psychological counseling, international student services, multicultural affairs office, writing training. *Library facilities:* Warren E. Burger Library. *Online resources:* library catalog, web page, access to other libraries' catalogs. *Collection:* 189,532 titles, 3,746 serial subscriptions, 654 audiovisual materials.

Computer facilities: 89 computers available on campus for general student use. A campuswide network can be accessed from off campus. Internet access and online class registration, wireless network for 1048 simultaneous users are available. *Web address:* http://www.wmitchell.edu/.

General Application Contact: Kendra Dane, Assistant Dean and Director of Admissions, 651-290-6343, Fax: 651-290-6414, E-mail: admissions@wmitchell.edu.

GRADUATE UNITS

Professional Program Students: 738 full-time (403 women), 365 part-time (184 women); includes 121 minority (33 African Americans, 5 American Indian/Alaska Native, 57 Asian Americans or Pacific Islanders, 26 Hispanic Americans), 7 international. Average age 29. 1,487 applicants, 55% accepted, 352 enrolled. *Faculty:* 35 full-time (13 women), 212 part-time/adjunct (87 women). Expenses: Contact institution. *Financial support:* In 2006–07, 621 students received support, including 62 research assistantships (averaging $1,487 per year); Federal Work-Study and scholarships/grants also available. Support available to part-time students. Financial award application deadline: 3/15; financial award applicants required to submit FAFSA. In 2006, 322 degrees awarded. *Degree program information:* Part-time and evening/weekend programs available. Offers law (JD). *Application deadline:* For fall admission, 5/1 for domestic and international students. Applications are processed on a rolling basis. *Application fee:* $50. Electronic applications accepted. *Application Contact:* Kendra Dane, Assistant Dean and Director of Admissions, 651-290-6343, Fax: 651-290-6414, E-mail: admissions@wmitchell.edu. *President/Dean,* Allen K. Easley, 651-290-6310, Fax: 651-290-6426, E-mail: allen.easley@wmitchell.edu.

WILLIAM PATERSON UNIVERSITY OF NEW JERSEY, Wayne, NJ 07470-8420

General Information State-supported, coed, comprehensive institution. CGS member. *Enrollment:* 10,600 graduate, professional, and undergraduate students; 326 full-time matriculated graduate/professional students, 1,411 part-time matriculated graduate/professional students. *Enrollment by degree level:* 1,737 master's. *Graduate housing:* Room and/or apartments available on a first-come, first-served basis to single students; on-campus housing not available to married students. *Student services:* Campus employment opportunities, campus safety program, career counseling, child daycare facilities, disabled student services, exercise/wellness program, free psychological counseling, international student services, low-cost health insurance, multicultural affairs office, teacher training, writing training. *Library facilities:* David and Lorraine Cheng Library. *Online resources:* library catalog, web page, access to other libraries' catalogs. *Collection:* 305,155 titles, 4,112 serial subscriptions.

Computer facilities: 700 computers available on campus for general student use. A campuswide network can be accessed from student residence rooms and from off campus. Internet access and online class registration are available. *Web address:* http://ww2.wpunj.edu/.

General Application Contact: Danielle Liautaud Watkins, Assistant Director, 973-720-3579, Fax: 973-720-2035, E-mail: liautaudd@wpunj.edu.

GRADUATE UNITS

College of Business Students: 14 full-time (8 women), 32 part-time (12 women); includes 11 minority (5 African Americans, 3 Asian Americans or Pacific Islanders, 3 Hispanic Americans). Expenses: Contact institution. *Financial support:* Research assistantships with full tuition reimbursements, unspecified assistantships available. Support available to part-time students. Financial award application deadline: 4/1; financial award applicants required to submit FAFSA. In 2006, 23 degrees awarded. *Degree program information:* Part-time and evening/weekend programs available. Offers business (MBA). *Application deadline:* Applications are processed on a rolling basis. *Application fee:* $50. Electronic applications accepted. *Application Contact:* Danielle Liautaud, Director, 973-720-3579, Fax: 973-720-2035, E-mail: liautaudd@wpunj.edu. *Dean,* Sam Basu, 973-720-2964.

College of Education Students: 632. Expenses: Contact institution. *Financial support:* Research assistantships with full tuition reimbursements, career-related internships or fieldwork, Federal Work-Study, and unspecified assistantships available. Support available to part-time students. Financial award application deadline: 4/1; financial award applicants required to submit FAFSA. Offers counseling (M Ed); counseling services (M Ed); education (M Ed, MAT); educational leadership (M Ed); elementary education (M Ed, MAT); reading (M Ed); special education (M Ed). *Application deadline:* Applications are processed on a rolling basis. *Application fee:* $50. Electronic applications accepted. *Application Contact:* Danielle Liautaud, Director, 973-720-3579, Fax: 973-720-2035, E-mail: liautaudd@wpunj.edu. *Dean,* Leslie Agard-Jones, 973-720-2413, Fax: 973-720-2955.

College of Science and Health Students: 49 full-time (46 women), 109 part-time (87 women); includes 23 minority (6 African Americans, 6 Asian Americans or Pacific Islanders, 11 Hispanic Americans). Expenses: Contact institution. *Financial support:* In 2006–07, 36 students received support; research assistantships with full tuition reimbursements available, career-related internships or fieldwork and unspecified assistantships available. Support

William Paterson University of New Jersey (continued)

available to part-time students. Financial award application deadline: 4/1; financial award applicants required to submit FAFSA. *Degree program information:* Part-time and evening/weekend programs available. Offers biotechnology (MS); general biology (MA); limnology and terrestrial ecology (MA); molecular biology (MA); nursing (MSN); physiology (MA); science and health (MA, MS, MSN); speech pathology (MS). *Application deadline:* Applications are processed on a rolling basis. *Application fee:* $50. Electronic applications accepted. *Application Contact:* Danielle Liautaud, Director, 973-720-3579, Fax: 973-720-2035, E-mail: liautaudd@wpunj.edu.

College of the Arts and Communication Students: 37 full-time (11 women), 35 part-time (14 women); includes 9 minority (5 African Americans, 4 Hispanic Americans). Expenses: Contact institution. *Financial support:* In 2006–07, 3 students received support; research assistantships with full tuition reimbursements available, career-related internships or fieldwork, Federal Work-Study, and unspecified assistantships available. Support available to part-time students. Financial award application deadline: 4/1; financial award applicants required to submit FAFSA. *Degree program information:* Part-time and evening/weekend programs available. Offers art (MFA); arts and communication (MA, MFA, MM); media studies (MA); music (MM); visual arts (MA). *Application deadline:* Applications are processed on a rolling basis. *Application fee:* $50. Electronic applications accepted. *Application Contact:* Danielle Liautaud, Director, 973-720-3579, Fax: 973-720-2035, E-mail: liautaudd@wpunj.edu. *Interim Dean,* Dr. Steve Marcone, 973-720-3128.

College of the Humanities and Social Sciences Students: 39 full-time (28 women), 107 part-time (73 women); includes 20 minority (9 African Americans, 2 Asian Americans or Pacific Islanders, 9 Hispanic Americans). Expenses: Contact institution. *Financial support:* In 2006–07, 13 students received support; research assistantships with full tuition reimbursements available, teaching assistantships with full tuition reimbursements available, unspecified assistantships available. Support available to part-time students. Financial award application deadline: 4/1; financial award applicants required to submit FAFSA. *Degree program information:* Part-time and evening/weekend programs available. Offers applied clinical psychology (MA); English (MA); history (MA); humanities and social sciences (MA); public policy and international affairs (MA); sociology (MA). *Application deadline:* Applications are processed on a rolling basis. *Application fee:* $50. Electronic applications accepted. *Application Contact:* Danielle Liautaud, Director, 973-720-3579, Fax: 973-720-2035, E-mail: liautaudd@wpunj.edu. *Dean,* Dr. Isabel Tirado, 973-720-2413, Fax: 973-720-2955.

See Close-Up on page 1149.

WILLIAMS COLLEGE, Williamstown, MA 01267

General Information Independent, coed, comprehensive institution. *Enrollment:* 2,049 graduate, professional, and undergraduate students; 23 full-time matriculated graduate/professional students (21 women). *Enrollment by degree level:* 23 master's. *Graduate faculty:* 24. *Tuition:* Full-time $34,275. *Graduate housing:* Room and/or apartments available on a first-come, first-served basis to single students; on-campus housing not available to married students. Typical cost: $4,540 per year. *Student services:* Campus employment opportunities, campus safety program, career counseling, disabled student services, exercise/wellness program, free psychological counseling, international student services, low-cost health insurance, multicultural affairs office, writing training. *Library facilities:* Sawyer Library plus 10 others. *Online resources:* library catalog, web page, access to other libraries' catalogs. *Collection:* 932,000 titles, 12,063 serial subscriptions, 38,076 audiovisual materials. *Research affiliation:* Clark Art Institute.

Computer facilities: 252 computers available on campus for general student use. A campuswide network can be accessed from student residence rooms and from off campus. Internet access and online class registration, wireless network are available. *Web address:* http://www.williams.edu/.

General Application Contact: Karen E. Kowitz, Program Administrator, 413-458-0596, Fax: 413-458-2317, E-mail: karen.kowitz@williams.edu.

GRADUATE UNITS

Program in the History of Art Students: 23 full-time (21 women), 3 international. Average age 26. 73 applicants, 26% accepted, 11 enrolled. *Faculty:* 24. Expenses: Contact institution. *Financial support:* In 2006–07, 18 students received support, including 4 fellowships with full and partial tuition reimbursements available (averaging $13,500 per year); tuition waivers (full and partial) also available. Support available to part-time students. Financial award application deadline: 4/1; financial award applicants required to submit FAFSA. In 2006, 11 degrees awarded. *Degree program information:* Part-time programs available. Offers history of art (MA). Offered jointly with Sterling and Francine Clark Art Institute. *Application deadline:* For fall admission, 1/1 for domestic students. *Application fee:* $50. *Application Contact:* Karen E. Kowitz, Program Administrator, 413-458-0596, Fax: 413-458-2317, E-mail: karen.kowitz@williams.edu. *Director of Graduate Art History,* Dr. Charles W. Haxthausen, 413-458-0598, Fax: 413-458-2317, E-mail: charles.w.haxthausen@williams.edu.

WILLIAM WOODS UNIVERSITY, Fulton, MO 65251-1098

General Information Independent-religious, coed, comprehensive institution. *Enrollment:* 2,893 graduate, professional, and undergraduate students; 1,944 full-time matriculated graduate/professional students (1,230 women). *Enrollment by degree level:* 1,641 master's, 303 other advanced degrees. *Graduate faculty:* 38 full-time (14 women), 174 part-time/adjunct (50 women). *Tuition:* Part-time $255 per credit hour. Tuition and fees vary according to program. *Graduate housing:* On-campus housing not available. *Student services:* Campus safety program, international student services. *Library facilities:* Dulany Library. *Online resources:* library catalog, web page, access to other libraries' catalogs. *Collection:* 139,986 titles, 11,713 serial subscriptions.

Computer facilities: Computer purchase and lease plans are available. 105 computers available on campus for general student use. A campuswide network can be accessed from student residence rooms. Internet access and online class registration are available. *Web address:* http://www.williamwoods.edu/.

General Application Contact: Linda Rembish, Administrative Assistant, 800-995-3199, Fax: 573-592-1164, E-mail: cgas@williamwoods.edu.

GRADUATE UNITS

Graduate and Adult Studies Students: 1,944 full-time (1,230 women); includes 71 minority (43 African Americans, 16 American Indian/Alaska Native, 7 Asian Americans or Pacific Islanders, 5 Hispanic Americans), 41 international. 824 applicants, 86% accepted, 631 enrolled. *Faculty:* 38 full-time (14 women), 174 part-time/adjunct (50 women). Expenses: Contact institution. *Financial support:* Institutionally sponsored loans available. Financial award applicants required to submit FAFSA. In 2006, 919 master's, 112 other advanced degrees awarded. *Degree program information:* Evening/weekend programs available. Offers administration (M Ed, Ed S); agribusiness (MBA); curriculum/instruction (M Ed); health management (MBA); human services (MBA); instructional leadership (Ed S). *Application deadline:* Applications are processed on a rolling basis. *Application fee:* $25. Electronic applications accepted. *Application Contact:* Linda Rembish, Administrative Assistant, 800-995-3199, Fax: 573-592-1164, E-mail: cgas@williamwoods.edu. *Dean of Graduate and Adult Studies Enrollment Services,* Sean Siebert, 573-592-4383, Fax: 573-592-1164.

WILMINGTON COLLEGE, New Castle, DE 19720-6491

General Information Independent, coed, comprehensive institution. *Enrollment:* 7,911 graduate, professional, and undergraduate students; 1,216 full-time matriculated graduate/professional students (832 women), 2,213 part-time matriculated graduate/professional students (1,615 women). *Enrollment by degree level:* 3,166 master's, 263 doctoral. *Graduate faculty:* 70 full-time (25 women), 507 part-time/adjunct (316 women). *Graduate housing:* On-campus housing not available. *Student services:* Career counseling, disabled student services, international student services, teacher training. *Library facilities:* Robert C. and Dorothy M. Peoples Library plus 1 other. *Online resources:* library catalog, access to other libraries' catalogs. *Collection:* 98,713 titles, 425 serial subscriptions.

Computer facilities: Computer purchase and lease plans are available. 516 computers available on campus for general student use. A campuswide network can be accessed. Internet access, online available in 6 months are available. *Web address:* http://www.wilmcoll.edu/.

General Application Contact: Chris Ferguson, Director of Admissions and Financial Aid, 302-356-4636 Ext. 256, Fax: 302-328-5164, E-mail: inquire@wilmcoll.edu.

GRADUATE UNITS

Division of Behavioral Science Students: 63 full-time (50 women), 170 part-time (125 women); includes 40 minority (34 African Americans, 1 Asian American or Pacific Islander, 5 Hispanic Americans). Average age 36. 78 applicants, 100% accepted, 39 enrolled. *Faculty:* 3 full-time (1 woman). Expenses: Contact institution. *Financial support:* Applicants required to submit FAFSA. In 2006, 69 degrees awarded. *Degree program information:* Part-time and evening/weekend programs available. Offers administration of human services (MS); administration of justice (MS); community counseling (MS). *Application deadline:* Applications are processed on a rolling basis. *Application fee:* $25. *Application Contact:* Chris Ferguson, Director of Admissions and Financial Aid, 302-328-9407 Ext. 256, Fax: 302-328-5164, E-mail: inquire@wilmcoll.edu. *Chair,* Dr. Thomas Cupples, 302-328-9401 Ext. 162, Fax: 302-328-5164, E-mail: thomas.b.cupples@wilmcoll.edu.

Division of Business Students: 230 full-time (138 women), 432 part-time (274 women); includes 109 minority (98 African Americans, 1 American Indian/Alaska Native, 3 Asian Americans or Pacific Islanders, 7 Hispanic Americans). Average age 34. 229 applicants, 100% accepted, 156 enrolled. *Faculty:* 3 full-time (0 women). Expenses: Contact institution. *Financial support:* Applicants required to submit FAFSA. In 2006, 273 degrees awarded. *Degree program information:* Part-time and evening/weekend programs available. Offers business administration (MBA); finance (MBA); health care administration (MBA, MS); human resource management (MS); management (MS); management information systems (MBA); organizational leadership (MS); public administration (MS); transportation and logistics (MBA, MS). *Application deadline:* Applications are processed on a rolling basis. *Application fee:* $25. *Application Contact:* Chris Ferguson, Director of Admissions and Financial Aid, 302-328-9407 Ext. 256, Fax: 302-328-5164, E-mail: inquire@wilmcoll.edu. *Chair,* Dr. Robert Edelson, 302-295-1147, Fax: 302-328-7021, E-mail: robert.e.edelson@wilmcoll.edu.

Division of Education Students: 609 full-time (447 women), 1,350 part-time (1,013 women); includes 144 minority (131 African Americans, 3 American Indian/Alaska Native, 1 Asian American or Pacific Islander, 9 Hispanic Americans). Average age 34. 818 applicants, 100% accepted, 599 enrolled. *Faculty:* 7 full-time (4 women). Expenses: Contact institution. *Financial support:* Applicants required to submit FAFSA. In 2006, 737 degrees awarded. *Degree program information:* Part-time and evening/weekend programs available. Offers applied education technology (M Ed); career and technical education (M Ed); elementary and secondary school counseling (M Ed); elementary special education (M Ed); elementary studies (M Ed); instruction: gifted and talented (M Ed); instruction: teaching and learning (M Ed); literacy (M Ed); reading (M Ed); school leadership (M Ed); secondary teaching (MAT). *Application deadline:* For fall admission, 4/30 for domestic students. Applications are processed on a rolling basis. *Application fee:* $25. *Application Contact:* Chris Ferguson, Director of Admissions and Financial Aid, 302-328-9407 Ext. 256, Fax: 302-328-5164, E-mail: inquire@wilmcoll.edu. *Chair,* Dr. Richard Gochnauer, 302-328-6795 Ext. 163, Fax: 302-328-7081.

Division of Information Technology and Advanced Communications Students: 21 full-time (10 women), 66 part-time (27 women); includes 11 minority (9 African Americans, 1 American Indian/Alaska Native, 1 Asian American or Pacific Islander). Average age 36. 28 applicants, 100% accepted, 19 enrolled. Expenses: Contact institution. In 2006, 26 degrees awarded. *Degree program information:* Part-time and evening/weekend programs available. Offers corporate training (MS); information systems technologies (MS); Internet web design (MS); management information systems (MS). *Application fee:* $25. *Head,* Dr. Jack Nold, 302-328-9401 Ext. 254.

Division of Nursing Students: 30 full-time (28 women), 195 part-time (176 women); includes 24 minority (19 African Americans, 3 Asian Americans or Pacific Islanders, 2 Hispanic Americans). Average age 39. 54 applicants, 100% accepted, 48 enrolled. Expenses: Contact institution. *Financial support:* In 2006–07, 28 fellowships with tuition reimbursements (averaging $2,200 per year) were awarded; traineeships also available. Financial award applicants required to submit FAFSA. In 2006, 58 degrees awarded. *Degree program information:* Part-time programs available. Offers adult nurse practitioner (MSN); family nurse practitioner (MSN); gerontology (MSN); leadership (MSN); nursing (MSN); women's nurse practitioner (MSN). *Application deadline:* For fall admission, 3/31 priority date for domestic students. Applications are processed on a rolling basis. *Application fee:* $25. *Application Contact:* Chris Ferguson, Director of Admissions and Financial Aid, 302-328-9407 Ext. 256, Fax: 302-328-5164, E-mail: inquire@wilmcoll.edu. *Chair,* Dr. Mary Letitia Gallagher, 302-328-9401 Ext. 161, Fax: 302-328-7081, E-mail: tgall@wilmcoll.edu.

Program in Innovation and Leadership Students: 263 full-time (159 women); includes 60 minority (52 African Americans, 2 Asian Americans or Pacific Islanders, 6 Hispanic Americans). Average age 41. 141 applicants, 101 enrolled. Expenses: Contact institution. In 2006, 45 degrees awarded. *Degree program information:* Part-time programs available. Offers education innovation (Ed D); organizational leadership (Ed D). *Application fee:* $25. *Application Contact:* 302-328-9407. *Head,* Dr. Joe Deardorff, 302-328-9401 Ext. 351.

WILMINGTON COLLEGE, Wilmington, OH 45177

General Information Independent-religious, coed, comprehensive institution. *Graduate housing:* On-campus housing not available.

GRADUATE UNITS

Department of Education *Degree program information:* Part-time programs available. Offers reading (M Ed); special education (M Ed).

WINEBRENNER THEOLOGICAL SEMINARY, Findlay, OH 45840

General Information Independent-religious, coed, graduate-only institution. *Enrollment by degree level:* 44 first professional, 44 master's, 7 doctoral. *Graduate faculty:* 8 full-time (1 woman), 4 part-time/adjunct (1 woman). *Tuition:* Full-time $9,180; part-time $380 per credit. *Graduate housing:* On-campus housing not available. *Student services:* Campus employment opportunities, career counseling, free psychological counseling, international student services. *Library facilities:* Winebrenner Collection within Shafer Library. *Online resources:* library catalog, access to other libraries' catalogs. *Collection:* 42,473 titles, 123 serial subscriptions, 657 audiovisual materials.

Computer facilities: 2 computers available on campus for general student use. A campuswide network can be accessed from off campus. Internet access is available. *Web address:* http://www.winebrenner.edu/.

General Application Contact: Jim Wilder, Admissions Counselor, 419-434-4220, Fax: 419-434-4267, E-mail: admissions@winebrenner.edu.

GRADUATE UNITS

Graduate Programs Students: 50 full-time (13 women), 45 part-time (17 women); includes 19 minority (17 African Americans, 2 Asian Americans or Pacific Islanders). Average age 41. 29 applicants, 100% accepted, 26 enrolled. *Faculty:* 8 full-time (1 woman), 4 part-time/adjunct (1 woman). Expenses: Contact institution. *Financial support:* In 2006–07, 62 students received support. Institutionally sponsored loans, scholarships/grants, and tuition waivers (partial) available. Support available to part-time students. Financial award application deadline: 7/1; financial award applicants required to submit FAFSA. In 2006, 12 M Divs, 5 master's, 4 doctorates awarded. *Degree program information:* Part-time and evening/weekend programs available. Offers church development (MA); family ministry (MA); theological study (MA); theological/ministerial studies (D Min); theology/ministerial studies (M Div). *Application deadline:* For fall admission, 8/15 priority date for domestic students; for winter admission, 12/15 priority date for domestic students; for spring admission, 4/15 priority date for domestic students. Applications are processed on a rolling basis. *Application fee:* $25. Electronic applications accepted. *Application Contact:* Jim Wilder, Admissions Counselor, 419-434-4220, Fax: 419-434-4267,

E-mail: admissions@winebrenner.edu. *Academic Dean,* Dr. M. John Nissley, 419-434-4247, Fax: 419-434-4267, E-mail: jnissley@winebrenner.edu.

WINGATE UNIVERSITY, Wingate, NC 28174-0159

General Information Independent-religious, coed, comprehensive institution. *Enrollment:* 1,809 graduate, professional, and undergraduate students; 243 full-time matriculated graduate/professional students (144 women), 177 part-time matriculated graduate/professional students (116 women). *Enrollment by degree level:* 244 first professional, 176 master's. *Graduate faculty:* 30 full-time (16 women), 6 part-time/adjunct (1 woman). *Tuition:* Full-time $3,330; part-time $185 per credit hour. *Graduate housing:* Rooms and/or apartments available on a first-come, first-served basis to single and married students. Typical cost: $3,375 per year ($6,750 including board) for single students. Housing application deadline: 8/15. *Student services:* Campus employment opportunities, career counseling, teacher training. *Library facilities:* Ethel K. Smith Library. *Online resources:* library catalog, web page. *Collection:* 107,187 titles, 15,325 serial subscriptions.

Computer facilities: 75 computers available on campus for general student use. A campuswide network can be accessed from student residence rooms and from off campus. Internet access is available. *Web address:* http://www.wingate.edu/.

General Application Contact: Dr. Greg Clemmer, Dean of Metro College, 704-849-2132, Fax: 704-849-2468, E-mail: clemmer@wingate.edu.

GRADUATE UNITS

Program in Business Administration Average age 29. 15 applicants, 93% accepted, 14 enrolled. *Faculty:* 3 full-time (0 women), 2 part-time/adjunct (0 women). Expenses: Contact institution. *Financial support:* In 2006–07, 9 students received support. Federal Work-Study and scholarships/grants available. Support available to part-time students. Financial award application deadline: 8/1; financial award applicants required to submit FAFSA. In 2006, 12 degrees awarded. *Degree program information:* Part-time and evening/weekend programs available. Offers business administration (MBA). *Application deadline:* For fall admission, 8/15 priority date for domestic students; for spring admission, 12/15 priority date for domestic students. Applications are processed on a rolling basis. *Application fee:* $50. Electronic applications accepted. *Application Contact:* Mary May, MBA Coordinator, 704-233-8148, Fax: 704-233-8146. *Dean,* Joseph M. Graham, 704-233-8148, Fax: 704-233-8146, E-mail: graham@wingate.edu.

Program in Education Students: 1 (woman) full-time, 127 part-time (96 women); includes 2 minority (both African Americans) Average age 35. 19 applicants, 58% accepted, 11 enrolled. *Faculty:* 4 full-time (3 women), 4 part-time/adjunct (1 woman). Expenses: Contact institution. *Financial support:* In 2006–07, 20 students received support. Scholarships/grants available. Support available to part-time students. Financial award applicants required to submit FAFSA. In 2006, 12 degrees awarded. *Degree program information:* Part-time and evening/weekend programs available. Offers educational leadership (MA Ed); elementary education (MA Ed, MAT); physical education (MA Ed); sport administration (MA Ed). *Application deadline:* For fall admission, 8/15 priority date for domestic students; for spring admission, 12/15 for domestic students. Applications are processed on a rolling basis. *Application fee:* $0. *Application Contact:* Marsha Luke, Secretary, Thayer School of Education, 704-233-8127, Fax: 704-233-8273, E-mail: mluke@wingate.edu. *Dean, Thayer School of Education,* Dr. Robert Shaw, 704-233-8128, Fax: 704-233-8273, E-mail: rshaw@wingate.edu.

School of Pharmacy Students: 242 full-time (143 women), 2 part-time; includes 27 minority (8 African Americans, 3 American Indian/Alaska Native, 14 Asian Americans or Pacific Islanders, 2 Hispanic Americans), 4 international. Average age 25. 771 applicants, 9% accepted, 60 enrolled. *Faculty:* 23 full-time (13 women). Expenses: Contact institution. *Financial support:* In 2006–07, 182 students received support; fellowships, research assistantships, teaching assistantships, career-related internships or fieldwork and scholarships/grants available. Financial award application deadline: 5/30. Offers pharmacy (Pharm D). *Application deadline:* For fall admission, 2/1 for domestic and international students. Applications are processed on a rolling basis. *Application fee:* $0. Electronic applications accepted. *Application Contact:* Erinn Nichols, Assistant to the Dean of Pharmacy, 704-233-8331, Fax: 704-233-8332, E-mail: enichols@wingate.edu. *Dean,* Dr. Robert Supernaw, 704-233-8015, Fax: 704-233-8332, E-mail: supernaw@wingate.edu.

WINONA STATE UNIVERSITY, Winona, MN 55987-5838

General Information State-supported, coed, comprehensive institution. *Enrollment:* 8,220 graduate, professional, and undergraduate students; 2 full-time matriculated graduate/professional students (both women), 390 part-time matriculated graduate/professional students (299 women). *Enrollment by degree level:* 392 master's. *Graduate faculty:* 57 full-time (38 women). *Graduate housing:* Room and/or apartments available to single students; on-campus housing not available to married students. Housing application deadline: 3/2. *Student services:* Campus employment opportunities, campus safety program, career counseling, child daycare facilities, disabled student services, exercise/wellness program, free psychological counseling, international student services, low-cost health insurance. *Library facilities:* Darrel W. Krueger. *Online resources:* library catalog, web page, access to other libraries' catalogs. *Collection:* 350,000 titles, 1,000 serial subscriptions, 8,000 audiovisual materials.

Computer facilities: Computer purchase and lease plans are available. 1,400 computers available on campus for general student use. A campuswide network can be accessed from student residence rooms and from off campus. Internet access and online class registration are available.

General Application Contact: Dr. Lee Gray, Director of Graduate Studies, 507-457-5346, E-mail: lgray@winona.edu.

GRADUATE UNITS

Graduate Studies Students: 2 full-time (both women), 390 part-time (299 women); includes 8 minority (6 Asian Americans or Pacific Islanders, 2 Hispanic Americans), 10 international. 114 applicants. *Faculty:* 57 full-time (38 women). Expenses: Contact institution. *Financial support:* Fellowships, research assistantships, career-related internships or fieldwork, Federal Work-Study, traineeships, and unspecified assistantships available. Support available to part-time students. In 2006, 162 master's, 10 other advanced degrees awarded. *Degree program information:* Part-time and evening/weekend programs available. *Application deadline:* Applications are processed on a rolling basis. *Application fee:* $20. Electronic applications accepted. *Director of Graduate Studies,* Dr. Lee Gray, 507-457-5346, E-mail: lgray@winona.edu.

College of Education Students: 2 full-time (both women), 273 part-time (196 women); includes 9 minority (1 American Indian/Alaska Native, 6 Asian Americans or Pacific Islanders, 2 Hispanic Americans). 117 applicants, 74% accepted, 70 enrolled. *Faculty:* 34 full-time (21 women). Expenses: Contact institution. *Financial support:* Fellowships, career-related internships or fieldwork, Federal Work-Study, and unspecified assistantships available. Support available to part-time students. In 2006, 125 master's, 5 other advanced degrees awarded. *Degree program information:* Part-time and evening/weekend programs available. Offers community counseling (MS); education (MS, Ed S); educational leadership (Ed S); general school leadership (MS); K-12 principalship (MS); professional development (MS); school counseling (MS); special education (MS); teacher leadership (MS). *Application deadline:* For fall admission, 8/8 priority date for domestic students; for spring admission, 2/17 for domestic students. Applications are processed on a rolling basis. *Application fee:* $20. *Acting Dean,* Lorene Olsen, 507-457-5570, E-mail: lolsen@winona.edu.

College of Liberal Arts 21 applicants, 67% accepted, 8 enrolled. Expenses: Contact institution. *Financial support:* Career-related internships or fieldwork, Federal Work-Study, and unspecified assistantships available. Support available to part-time students. Financial award applicants required to submit FAFSA. In 2006, 5 degrees awarded. *Degree program information:* Part-time programs available. Offers English (MA, MS); liberal arts (MA, MS). *Application deadline:* For fall admission, 7/26 priority date for domestic students; for spring admission, 12/8 for domestic students. Applications are processed on a rolling basis. *Application fee:* $20. *Dean,* Dr. Troy Paino, 507-457-5017, E-mail: tpaino@winona.edu.

College of Nursing and Health Sciences 70 applicants, 57% accepted, 32 enrolled. *Faculty:* 10 full-time (all women). Expenses: Contact institution. *Financial support:* In 2006–07, 3 research assistantships with partial tuition reimbursements (averaging $6,000 per year) were awarded; Federal Work-Study, traineeships, and unspecified assistantships also available. Support available to part-time students. Financial award applicants required to submit FAFSA. In 2006, 32 master's awarded. *Degree program information:* Part-time programs available. Offers adult nurse practitioner (MS); clinical nurse specialist (MS); family nurse practitioner (MS); nurse administrator (MS); nurse educator (MS). *Application deadline:* For fall admission, 2/1 for domestic students. *Application fee:* $20. *Graduate Director,* Dr. Timothy Gaspar, 507-457-5122, E-mail: tgaspar@winona.msus.edu.

WINSTON-SALEM STATE UNIVERSITY, Winston-Salem, NC 27110-0003

General Information State-supported, coed, comprehensive institution. *Enrollment:* 5,650 graduate, professional, and undergraduate students; 178 full-time matriculated graduate/professional students (142 women), 143 part-time matriculated graduate/professional students (94 women). *Enrollment by degree level:* 321 master's. *Graduate faculty:* 58 full-time (33 women), 7 part-time/adjunct (2 women). Tuition, state resident: full-time $2,010. Tuition, nonresident: full-time $10,502. Tuition and fees vary according to course load. *Graduate housing:* Room and/or apartments available on a first-come, first-served basis to single students; on-campus housing not available to married students. Typical cost: $3,270 per year ($5,476 including board). Room and board charges vary according to campus/location and housing facility selected. Housing application deadline: 5/15. *Student services:* Campus employment opportunities, campus safety program, career counseling, exercise/wellness program, free psychological counseling, international student services, teacher training. *Library facilities:* O'Kelly Library. *Online resources:* library catalog, web page. *Collection:* 197,765 titles, 1,010 serial subscriptions.

Computer facilities: 500 computers available on campus for general student use. A campuswide network can be accessed from student residence rooms and from off campus. Internet access and online class registration are available. *Web address:* http://www.wssu.edu/.

General Application Contact: Monica Elliot, Data Enrollment Communication Specialist, 336-750-3045, Fax: 336-750-3042, E-mail: elliottm@wssu.edu.

GRADUATE UNITS

Department of Occupational Therapy Students: 18 full-time (14 women); includes 8 minority (7 African Americans, 1 American Indian/Alaska Native). Average age 22. 22 applicants, 68% accepted, 15 enrolled. *Faculty:* 5 full-time (all women). Expenses: Contact institution. *Financial support:* In 2006–07, 15 students received support; research assistantships, teaching assistantships, career-related internships or fieldwork, institutionally sponsored loans, scholarships/grants, and tuition waivers (partial) available. Offers occupational therapy (MS). *Application deadline:* For fall admission, 3/15 for domestic and international students. Applications are processed on a rolling basis. *Application fee:* $40. Electronic applications accepted. *Application Contact:* 336-750-2102, Fax: 336-750-3042, E-mail: graduate@wssu.edu. *Chair and Associate Professor,* Dr. Dorothy P. Bethea, 336-750-3172, Fax: 336-750-3173, E-mail: betheadp@wssu.edu.

Department of Physical Therapy Students: 56 full-time (40 women); includes 19 minority (16 African Americans, 1 Asian American or Pacific Islander, 2 Hispanic Americans). 60 applicants, 43% accepted, 26 enrolled. *Faculty:* 7 full-time (5 women), 7 part-time/adjunct (2 women). Expenses: Contact institution. *Financial support:* In 2006–07, 26 students received support, including 7 teaching assistantships (averaging $2,500 per year); career-related internships or fieldwork, institutionally sponsored loans, scholarships/grants, and tuition waivers (partial) also available. In 2006, 18 degrees awarded. Offers physical therapy (MPT). *Application deadline:* For fall admission, 1/31 for domestic and international students. Applications are processed on a rolling basis. *Application fee:* $40. Electronic applications accepted. *Application Contact:* School of Graduate Studies and Research, 336-750-2102, Fax: 336-750-3042, E-mail: graduate@wssu.edu. *Chair and Professor,* Dr. Teresa Conner-Kerr, 336-750-2193, Fax: 336-750-2192, E-mail: connerkerrt@wssu.edu.

Program in Elementary Education 14 applicants, 71% accepted, 9 enrolled. *Faculty:* 4 full-time (1 woman). Expenses: Contact institution. *Financial support:* Research assistantships, teaching assistantships, career-related internships or fieldwork and institutionally sponsored loans available. In 2006, 9 degrees awarded. *Degree program information:* Part-time and evening/weekend programs available. Postbaccalaureate distance learning degree programs offered (minimal on-campus study). Offers elementary education (M Ed). *Application deadline:* For fall admission, 7/15 for domestic and international students. Applications are processed on a rolling basis. *Application fee:* $40. Electronic applications accepted. *Application Contact:* Graduate Studies and Research, 336-750-2102, Fax: 336-750-3042, E-mail: graduate@wssu.edu. *Chair, Education,* Dr. Cathy Griffin-Famble, 336-750-2550, Fax: 336-750-2335, E-mail: famblecg@wssu.edu.

WINTHROP UNIVERSITY, Rock Hill, SC 29733

General Information State-supported, coed, comprehensive institution. *Enrollment:* 6,292 graduate, professional, and undergraduate students; 306 full-time matriculated graduate/professional students (189 women), 395 part-time matriculated graduate/professional students (279 women). *Enrollment by degree level:* 691 master's, 10 other advanced degrees. *Graduate faculty:* 144 full-time (64 women), 79 part-time/adjunct (43 women). Tuition, state resident: full-time $9,148; part-time $383 per hour. Tuition, nonresident: full-time $16,864; part-time $704 per hour. *Graduate housing:* Rooms and/or apartments available to single and married students. Housing application deadline: 3/1. *Student services:* Campus employment opportunities, campus safety program, career counseling, disabled student services, exercise/wellness program, free psychological counseling, international student services, low-cost health insurance, multicultural affairs office. *Library facilities:* Dacus Library. *Online resources:* library catalog, web page, access to other libraries' catalogs. *Collection:* 425,648 titles, 1,545 serial subscriptions, 1,778 audiovisual materials.

Computer facilities: 250 computers available on campus for general student use. A campuswide network can be accessed from student residence rooms and from off campus. Internet access is available. *Web address:* http://www.winthrop.edu/.

General Application Contact: Information Contact, 800-411-7041, Fax: 803-323-2292, E-mail: graduatestu@withrop.edu.

GRADUATE UNITS

College of Arts and Sciences Students: 86 full-time (72 women), 62 part-time (46 women); includes 33 minority (25 African Americans, 1 American Indian/Alaska Native, 2 Asian Americans or Pacific Islanders, 5 Hispanic Americans), 1 international. Average age 29. *Faculty:* 57 full-time (24 women), 25 part-time/adjunct (13 women). Expenses: Contact institution. *Financial support:* Career-related internships or fieldwork, Federal Work-Study, scholarships/grants, and unspecified assistantships available. Support available to part-time students. Financial award application deadline: 2/1; financial award applicants required to submit FAFSA. In 2006, 39 master's, 9 other advanced degrees awarded. *Degree program information:* Part-time programs available. Offers arts and sciences (MA, MLA, MS, SSP); biology (MS); English (MA); history (MA); human nutrition (MS); liberal arts (MLA); psychology (MS, SSP); social work (MA); Spanish (MA). *Application deadline:* Applications are processed on a rolling basis. *Application fee:* $35 ($50 for international students). Electronic applications accepted. *Application Contact:* 800-411-7041, Fax: 803-323-2292, E-mail: graduatestu@winthrop.edu. *Dean,* Dr. Debra C. Boyd, 803-323-2183, E-mail: boydd@winthrop.edu.

College of Business Administration Students: 101 full-time (37 women), 95 part-time (51 women); includes 50 minority (36 African Americans, 1 American Indian/Alaska Native, 11 Asian Americans or Pacific Islanders, 2 Hispanic Americans), 24 international. Average age 28. *Faculty:* 33 full-time (10 women), 6 part-time/adjunct (3 women). Expenses: Contact institution. *Financial support:* Federal Work-Study, scholarships/grants, and unspecified assistantships available. Support available to part-time students. Financial award application deadline: 2/1; financial award applicants required to submit FAFSA. In 2006, 90 degrees awarded. *Degree program information:* Part-time and evening/weekend programs available. Postbaccalaureate distance learning degree programs offered (no on-campus study). Offers business administration (MBA, MS, Certificate); software development (MS); software project

Winthrop University (continued)

management (Certificate). *Application deadline:* For fall admission, 7/15 priority date for domestic students; for spring admission, 12/1 for domestic students. Applications are processed on a rolling basis. *Application fee:* $35 ($50 for international students). Electronic applications accepted. *Application Contact:* 800-411-7041, Fax: 803-323-2292, E-mail: graduatestu@winthrop.edu. *Dean,* Dr. Roger Weikle, 803-323-2186, Fax: 803-323-3960, E-mail: weikler@winthrop.edu.

College of Education Students: 105 full-time (71 women), 203 part-time (160 women); includes 81 minority (78 African Americans, 1 American Indian/Alaska Native, 1 Asian American or Pacific Islander, 1 Hispanic American), 2 international. Average age 29. *Faculty:* 32 full-time (20 women), 30 part-time/adjunct (20 women). Expenses: Contact institution. *Financial support:* Career-related internships or fieldwork, Federal Work-Study, scholarships/grants, and unspecified assistantships available. Support available to part-time students. Financial award application deadline: 2/1; financial award applicants required to submit FAFSA. In 2006, 112 degrees awarded. *Degree program information:* Part-time programs available. Offers agency counseling (M Ed); education (M Ed, MAT, MS); educational leadership (M Ed); middle level education (M Ed); physical education (MS); reading education (M Ed); school counseling (M Ed, MAT); secondary education (M Ed, MAT); special education (M Ed). *Application deadline:* For fall admission, 7/15 priority date for domestic students; for spring admission, 12/1 for domestic students. Applications are processed on a rolling basis. *Application fee:* $35 ($50 for international students). Electronic applications accepted. *Application Contact:* 800-411-7041, Fax: 803-323-2292, E-mail: graduatestu@winthrop.edu. *Dean,* Dr. Patricia Graham, 803-323-2151, Fax: 803-323-4369, E-mail: grahamp@winthrop.edu.

College of Visual and Performing Arts Students: 14 full-time (9 women), 33 part-time (21 women); includes 3 minority (2 African Americans, 1 American Indian/Alaska Native), 3 international. Average age 30. *Faculty:* 22 full-time (10 women), 18 part-time/adjunct (7 women). Expenses: Contact institution. *Financial support:* Federal Work-Study, scholarships/grants, and unspecified assistantships available. Support available to part-time students. Financial award application deadline: 2/1; financial award applicants required to submit FAFSA. In 2006, 20 degrees awarded. *Degree program information:* Part-time programs available. Offers art (MFA); art administration (MA); art education (MA); conducting (MM); music education (MME); performance (MM); visual and performing arts (MA, MFA, MM, MME). *Application deadline:* Applications are processed on a rolling basis. *Application fee:* $35 ($50 for international students). Electronic applications accepted. *Application Contact:* 800-411-7041, Fax: 803-323-2292, E-mail: graduatestu@winthrop.edu. *Dean,* Dr. Elizabeth Patenaude, 803-323-2255, Fax: 803-323-2333, E-mail: patenaude@winthrop.edu.

WISCONSIN SCHOOL OF PROFESSIONAL PSYCHOLOGY, Milwaukee, WI 53225-4960

General Information Independent, coed, graduate-only institution. *Graduate housing:* On-campus housing not available.

GRADUATE UNITS

Program in Clinical Psychology *Degree program information:* Part-time and evening/weekend programs available. Offers clinical psychology (MA, Psy D).

WITTENBERG UNIVERSITY, Springfield, OH 45501-0720

General Information Independent-religious, coed, comprehensive institution.

GRADUATE UNITS

Graduate Program

WOODBURY UNIVERSITY, Burbank, CA 91504-1099

General Information Independent, coed, comprehensive institution. *Enrollment:* 1,485 graduate, professional, and undergraduate students; 149 full-time matriculated graduate/professional students (87 women), 26 part-time matriculated graduate/professional students (12 women). *Enrollment by degree level:* 175 master's. *Graduate faculty:* 27 part-time/adjunct (6 women). *Tuition:* Full-time $8,052; part-time $671 per unit. Tuition and fees vary according to course load and campus/location. *Graduate housing:* Room and/or apartments available on a first-come, first-served basis to single students; on-campus housing not available to married students. Typical cost: $4,952 per year ($8,104 including board). Housing application deadline: 5/1. *Student services:* Campus employment opportunities, campus safety program, career counseling, free psychological counseling, international student services, low-cost health insurance, writing training. *Library facilities:* Los Angeles Times Library. *Online resources:* library catalog, web page, access to other libraries' catalogs. *Collection:* 69,515 titles, 363 serial subscriptions, 2,035 audiovisual materials.

Computer facilities: 135 computers available on campus for general student use. A campuswide network can be accessed from off campus. Internet access and online class registration are available. *Web address:* http://www.woodbury.edu/.

General Application Contact: Mauro Diaz, Director of Admissions, 800-784-9663, Fax: 818-767-7520, E-mail: admissions@woodbury.edu.

GRADUATE UNITS

Graduate Programs in Mediation and Applied Conflict Studies Offers conflict studies (Graduate Certificate); mediation (MM).

School of Architecture Students: 9 full-time (2 women); includes 5 minority (4 Asian Americans or Pacific Islanders, 1 Hispanic American). 14 applicants, 9 enrolled. *Faculty:* 7 part-time/adjunct (0 women). Expenses: Contact institution. In 2006, 6 degrees awarded. Offers real estate development (M Arch). *Application deadline:* For fall admission, 3/1 priority date for domestic and international students. *Application fee:* $60. *Application Contact:* Debra Abel, Administrative Director, 619-235-2900, Fax: 619-235-2901, E-mail: debra.abel@woodbury.edu. *Chair,* Norman Millar, 318-767-0888 Ext. 130, Fax: 318-504-9320, E-mail: norman.millar@woodbury.edu.

School of Business and Management Students: 120 full-time (75 women), 25 part-time (11 women); includes 41 minority (9 African Americans, 1 American Indian/Alaska Native, 10 Asian Americans or Pacific Islanders, 21 Hispanic Americans), 25 international. Average age 29. 80 applicants, 60% accepted, 37 enrolled. *Faculty:* 16 part-time/adjunct (4 women). Expenses: Contact institution. *Financial support:* In 2006–07, 2 fellowships with tuition reimbursements (averaging $12,000 per year) were awarded. Financial award application deadline: 7/15; financial award applicants required to submit FAFSA. In 2006, 54 degrees awarded. *Degree program information:* Part-time and evening/weekend programs available. Offers business administration (MBA); organizational leadership (MA). *Application deadline:* For fall admission, 8/1 priority date for domestic students; for spring admission, 12/1 for domestic and international students. Applications are processed on a rolling basis. *Application fee:* $35 ($50 for international students). *Application Contact:* Frank Frias, MBA Recruitment, 818-767-0888 Ext. 224, Fax: 818-767-7520, E-mail: frank.frias@woodbury.edu. *Dean,* Dr. Andre Van Niekerk, 818-767-0888 Ext. 264, Fax: 818-767-0032.

WOODS HOLE OCEANOGRAPHIC INSTITUTION, Woods Hole, MA 02543-1541

General Information Independent, coed, graduate-only institution. *Graduate housing:* Rooms and/or apartments guaranteed to single students and available on a first-come, first-served basis to married students.

GRADUATE UNITS

MIT/WHOI Joint Program in Oceanography/Applied Ocean Science and Engineering Offers applied ocean sciences (PhD); biological oceanography (PhD, Sc D); chemical oceanography (PhD, Sc D); civil and environmental and oceanographic engineering (PhD); electrical and oceanographic engineering (PhD); geochemistry (PhD); geophysics (PhD); marine biology (PhD); marine geochemistry (PhD, Sc D); marine geology (PhD, Sc D); marine geophysics (PhD); mechanical and oceanographic engineering (PhD); ocean engineering (PhD); oceanographic engineering (M Eng, MS, PhD, Sc D, Eng); paleoceanography (PhD); physical oceanography (PhD, Sc D). Electronic applications accepted.

WORCESTER POLYTECHNIC INSTITUTE, Worcester, MA 01609-2280

General Information Independent, coed, university. CGS member. *Enrollment:* 3,918 graduate, professional, and undergraduate students; 496 full-time matriculated graduate/professional students (133 women), 399 part-time matriculated graduate/professional students (75 women). *Enrollment by degree level:* 663 master's, 181 doctoral, 51 other advanced degrees. *Graduate faculty:* 203 full-time (38 women), 25 part-time/adjunct (4 women). *Tuition:* Part-time $1,042 per credit hour. *Required fees:* $1,009 per year. *Graduate housing:* On-campus housing not available. *Student services:* Campus employment opportunities, campus safety program, career counseling, disabled student services, exercise/wellness program, free psychological counseling, grant writing training, international student services, low-cost health insurance, multicultural affairs office, teacher training, writing training. *Library facilities:* George C. Gordon Library. *Online resources:* library catalog, web page, access to other libraries' catalogs. *Collection:* 310,265 titles, 23,591 serial subscriptions, 1,989 audiovisual materials. *Research affiliation:* Tufts University (veterinary medicine), University of Massachusetts Medical Center at Worcester, Alden Research Laboratory (hydraulics), Massachusetts Biomedical Initiatives, Massachusetts Extension Partnership, Manufacturing Advancement Center.

Computer facilities: 700 computers available on campus for general student use. A campuswide network can be accessed from student residence rooms and from off campus. Internet access and online class registration, online course content, wireless network are available. *Web address:* http://www.wpi.edu/.

General Application Contact: Lynne Dougherty, Administrative Assistant, 508-831-5301, Fax: 508-831-5717, E-mail: lmd@wpi.edu.

GRADUATE UNITS

Graduate Studies and Enrollment Students: 496 full-time (133 women), 399 part-time (75 women); includes 75 minority (12 African Americans, 1 American Indian/Alaska Native, 46 Asian Americans or Pacific Islanders, 16 Hispanic Americans), 235 international. 1,356 applicants, 64% accepted, 292 enrolled. *Faculty:* 203 full-time (38 women), 25 part-time/adjunct (4 women). Expenses: Contact institution. *Financial support:* In 2006–07, 305 students received support, including 21 fellowships with full tuition reimbursements available (averaging $20,437 per year), 92 research assistantships with full and partial tuition reimbursements available (averaging $21,416 per year), 121 teaching assistantships with full and partial tuition reimbursements available (averaging $15,003 per year); career-related internships or fieldwork, institutionally sponsored loans, scholarships/grants, tuition waivers (partial), and unspecified assistantships also available. Support available to part-time students. Financial award application deadline: 1/15. In 2006, 267 master's, 30 doctorates awarded. *Degree program information:* Part-time and evening/weekend programs available. Postbaccalaureate distance learning degree programs offered (no on-campus study). Offers applied mathematics (MS); applied statistics (MS); biochemistry (MS); biology (MS); biomedical engineering (M Eng, MS, PhD, Certificate); bioscience administration (MS); biotechnology (MS, PhD); building regulatory integration in construction management (Advanced Certificate); chemical engineering (MS, PhD); chemistry (MS, PhD); civil engineering (MS, PhD); clinical engineering (M Eng); computer based support systems for construction management (Advanced Certificate); computer science (MS, PhD, Advanced Certificate, Certificate); construction project management (MS, Certificate); customized management (Certificate); electrical and computer engineering (Advanced Certificate, Certificate); electrical engineering (MS, PhD); engineering (M Eng, MBA, MME, MS, PhD, Advanced Certificate, Certificate, Graduate Certificate); environmental engineering (MS, Certificate); financial mathematics (MS); fire protection engineering (MS, PhD, Advanced Certificate, Certificate); geotechnical engineering (Certificate); impact engineering (MS); industrial mathematics (MS); information security management (MS, Certificate); information technology (MS, Certificate); information technology and entrepreneurship (MS); information technology applications development (MS); information technology project management (MS); management of technology (Certificate); manufacturing and service information technology applications (MS); manufacturing engineering (MS, PhD, Certificate); manufacturing engineering management (MS); marketing and technological innovation (MS); marketing information technology applications (MS); master builder (Certificate); master builder environmental engineering (M Eng); materials process engineering (MS); materials science and engineering (MS, PhD, Certificate); materials/transportation (Certificate); mathematical sciences (PhD, Certificate); mathematics (MME); mechanical engineering (MS, PhD, Advanced Certificate); operations design and leadership (MS); physics (MS, PhD); power systems management (MS); process design (MS); social science (PhD); structural engineering (Certificate); supply chain management (MS); system dynamics (MS, Graduate Certificate); systems engineering (MS); systems modeling (MS); technology (MBA); technology marketing (Certificate); waste minimization and management (Advanced Certificate). *Application deadline:* For fall admission, 1/15 priority date for domestic and international students; for spring admission, 10/15 priority date for domestic and international students. Applications are processed on a rolling basis. *Application fee:* $70. Electronic applications accepted. *Application Contact:* Lynne Dougherty, Administrative Assistant, 508-831-5301, Fax: 508-831-5717, E-mail: lmd@wpi.edu. *Dean of Special Academic Programs,* Arlene R. Lowenstein, 508-831-5301, Fax: 508-831-5717, E-mail: grad_studies@wpi.edu.

See Close-Up on page 1151.

WORCESTER STATE COLLEGE, Worcester, MA 01602-2597

General Information State-supported, coed, comprehensive institution. *Enrollment:* 5,440 graduate, professional, and undergraduate students; 90 full-time matriculated graduate/professional students (83 women), 724 part-time matriculated graduate/professional students (528 women). *Enrollment by degree level:* 459 master's, 355 other advanced degrees. *Graduate faculty:* 42 full-time (27 women), 20 part-time/adjunct (9 women). Tuition, state resident: full-time $4,518; part-time $251 per credit hour. Tuition, nonresident: full-time $4,518; part-time $251 per credit hour. *Graduate housing:* On-campus housing not available. *Student services:* Campus safety program, career counseling, disabled student services, free psychological counseling, international student services, low-cost health insurance, multicultural affairs office, teacher training, writing training. *Library facilities:* Learning Resources Center. *Online resources:* library catalog, web page, access to other libraries' catalogs. *Collection:* 197,235 titles, 568 serial subscriptions, 3,326 audiovisual materials.

Computer facilities: Computer purchase and lease plans are available. 102 computers available on campus for general student use. A campuswide network can be accessed from student residence rooms. Internet access is available. *Web address:* http://www.worcester.edu/.

General Application Contact: Nicole Brown, Assistant Dean of Graduate and Continuing Education, 508-929-8787, Fax: 508-929-8100, E-mail: nbrown@worcester.edu.

GRADUATE UNITS

Graduate Studies Students: 90 full-time (83 women), 724 part-time (528 women); includes 38 minority (13 African Americans, 2 American Indian/Alaska Native, 6 Asian Americans or Pacific Islanders, 17 Hispanic Americans), 15 international. Average age 36. 493 applicants, 70% accepted, 179 enrolled. *Faculty:* 42 full-time (27 women), 20 part-time/adjunct (9 women). Expenses: Contact institution. *Financial support:* In 2006–07, 17 research assistantships with full tuition reimbursements (averaging $4,470 per year) were awarded; career-related internships or fieldwork, Federal Work-Study, institutionally sponsored loans, scholarships/grants, and unspecified assistantships also available. Support available to part-time students. Financial award application deadline: 3/1; financial award applicants required to submit FAFSA. In 2006, 171 master's awarded. *Degree program information:* Part-time and evening/weekend programs available. Offers accounting (MS); biotechnology (MS); community health nursing (MS); early childhood education (M Ed); elementary education (M Ed); English (M Ed); health care administration (MS); health education (M Ed); history (M Ed); leadership and administration (M Ed); middle school education (M Ed); moderate special needs (M Ed); non-profit management (MS); occupational therapy (MOT); organizational leadership (MS); reading (M Ed); secondary education (M Ed); Spanish (M Ed); speech-language pathology (MS). *Application fee:* $30. *Application Contact:* Nicole Brown, Assistant Dean of Continuing Education, 508-929-8787, Fax: 508-929-8100, E-mail: nbrown@worcester.edu. *Associate*

Vice President for Continuing Education and Outreach, Dean of the Graduate School, Dr. William H. White, 508-929-8125, Fax: 508-929-8100, E-mail: wwhite@worcester.edu.

WORLD MEDICINE INSTITUTE: COLLEGE OF ACUPUNCTURE AND HERBAL MEDICINE, Honolulu, HI 96828

General Information Independent, coed, graduate-only institution. *Graduate housing:* On-campus housing not available.

GRADUATE UNITS

Program in Acupuncture and Oriental Medicine *Degree program information:* Part-time and evening/weekend programs available. Offers acupuncture and Oriental medicine (M Ac OM).

WRIGHT INSTITUTE, Berkeley, CA 94704-1796

General Information Independent, coed, graduate-only institution. *Graduate housing:* On-campus housing not available.

GRADUATE UNITS

Program in Clinical Psychology Offers clinical psychology (Psy D). Electronic applications accepted.

WRIGHT STATE UNIVERSITY, Dayton, OH 45435

General Information State-supported, coed, university. CGS member. *Enrollment:* 16,207 graduate, professional, and undergraduate students; 2,169 full-time matriculated graduate/professional students (1,162 women), 1,365 part-time matriculated graduate/professional students (896 women). *Enrollment by degree level:* 366 first professional, 2,966 master's, 201 doctoral, 1 other advanced degree. *Graduate faculty:* 749 full-time (232 women), 354 part-time/adjunct (195 women). *Graduate housing:* Rooms and/or apartments available on a first-come, first-served basis to single students and available to married students. *Student services:* Campus employment opportunities, campus safety program, career counseling, child daycare facilities, disabled student services, exercise/wellness program, free psychological counseling, grant writing training, international student services, low-cost health insurance, multicultural affairs office, teacher training, writing training. *Library facilities:* Paul Laurence Dunbar Library plus 2 others. *Online resources:* library catalog, web page. *Collection:* 703,000 titles, 443,200 serial subscriptions, 29,800 audiovisual materials. *Research affiliation:* Wright-Patterson Air Force Base (research and development, systems and logistics), Wright-Patterson Air Force Base Medical Center, Veterans Administration Medical Center, Scott-Kettering Magnetic Resonance Research Laboratory (medical science), Edison Biotechnology Center, Edison Materials Technology Center (processing).

Computer facilities: 450 computers available on campus for general student use. A campuswide network can be accessed from student residence rooms and from off campus. *Web address:* http://www.wright.edu/.

General Application Contact: John Kimble, Associate Director of Graduate Admissions and Records, 937-775-2957, Fax: 937-775-2453, E-mail: john.kimble@wright.edu.

GRADUATE UNITS

School of Graduate Studies Students: 1,682 full-time (871 women), 1,359 part-time (890 women); includes 240 minority (170 African Americans, 8 American Indian/Alaska Native, 41 Asian Americans or Pacific Islanders, 21 Hispanic Americans), 556 international. Average age 31. 1,503 applicants, 75% accepted. *Faculty:* 735 full-time (226 women), 348 part-time/adjunct (155 women). Expenses: Contact institution. *Financial support:* In 2006–07, 300 fellowships with full tuition reimbursements, 170 research assistantships with full tuition reimbursements, 141 teaching assistantships with full tuition reimbursements were awarded; career-related internships or fieldwork, Federal Work-Study, institutionally sponsored loans, tuition waivers (full and partial), and unspecified assistantships also available. Support available to part-time students. Financial award applicants required to submit FAFSA. In 2006, 993 master's, 15 doctorates, 2 other advanced degrees awarded. *Degree program information:* Part-time and evening/weekend programs available. Offers interdisciplinary studies (MA, MS). *Application deadline:* Applications are processed on a rolling basis. *Application fee:* $25. Electronic applications accepted. *Application Contact:* John Kimble, Associate Director of Graduate Admissions and Records, 937-775-2957, Fax: 937-775-2453, E-mail: john.kimble@wright.edu. *Vice President for Research and Graduate Studies,* Dr. Jack A. Bantle, 937-775-3336, Fax: 937-775-2357, E-mail: jack.bantle@wright.edu.

College of Education and Human Services Students: 180 full-time (140 women), 627 part-time (509 women); includes 41 minority (36 African Americans, 1 American Indian/Alaska Native, 2 Asian Americans or Pacific Islanders, 2 Hispanic Americans), 2 international. Average age 34. 301 applicants, 95% accepted. Expenses: Contact institution. *Financial support:* In 2006–07, 40 fellowships with full tuition reimbursements were awarded; research assistantships, teaching assistantships, career-related internships or fieldwork, Federal Work-Study, institutionally sponsored loans, tuition waivers (full and partial), and unspecified assistantships also available. Support available to part-time students. Financial award applicants required to submit FAFSA. In 2006, 394 master's, 1 other advanced degree awarded. *Degree program information:* Part-time and evening/weekend programs available. Offers adolescent young adult (M Ed, MA); advanced curriculum and instruction (Ed S); advanced educational leadership (Ed S); career, technology and vocational education (M Ed, MA); chemical dependency (MRC); classroom teacher education (M Ed, MA); computer/technology education (M Ed, MA); counseling (M Ed, MA, MS); curriculum and instruction: teacher leader (MA); early childhood education (M Ed, MA); education and human services (M Ed, MA, MRC, MS, MST, Ed S); educational administrative specialist: teacher leader (M Ed); educational administrative specialist: vocational education administration (M Ed, MA); educational leadership (M Ed, MA); gifted educational needs (M Ed, MA); health, physical education, and recreation (M Ed, MA); higher education-adult education (Ed S); intervention specialist (M Ed, MA); library/media (M Ed, MA); middle childhood (M Ed); middle childhood education (MA); mild to moderate educational needs (M Ed, MA); moderate to intensive educational needs (M Ed, MA); multi-age (M Ed, MA); pupil personnel services (M Ed, MA); rehabilitation counseling (MRC); severe disabilities (MRC); student affairs in higher education-administration (M Ed, MA); superintendent (Ed S); vocational education (M Ed, MA); workforce education (M Ed, MA). *Application fee:* $25. *Application Contact:* John Kimble, Associate Director of Graduate Admissions and Records, 937-775-2957, Fax: 937-775-2453, E-mail: john.kimble@wright.edu. *Dean,* Dr. Gregory R. Bernhardt, 937-775-2822, Fax: 937-775-4855, E-mail: gregory.bernhardt@wright.edu.

College of Engineering and Computer Science Students: 478 full-time (119 women), 140 part-time (23 women); includes 21 minority (7 African Americans, 10 Asian Americans or Pacific Islanders, 4 Hispanic Americans), 401 international. Average age 29. 1,341 applicants, 61% accepted. Expenses: Contact institution. *Financial support:* In 2006–07, 65 fellowships with full tuition reimbursements, 106 research assistantships with full tuition reimbursements, 31 teaching assistantships with full tuition reimbursements were awarded; Federal Work-Study, institutionally sponsored loans, tuition waivers (full and partial), and unspecified assistantships also available. Support available to part-time students. Financial award applicants required to submit FAFSA. In 2006, 162 master's, 12 doctorates awarded. *Degree program information:* Part-time and evening/weekend programs available. Offers biomedical and human factors engineering (MSE); biomedical engineering (MSE); computer engineering (MSCE); computer science (MS); computer science and engineering (PhD); electrical engineering (MSE); engineering (PhD); engineering and computer science (MS, MSCE, MSE, PhD); human factors engineering (MSE); materials science and engineering (MSE); mechanical and materials engineering (MSE); mechanical engineering (MSE). *Application fee:* $25. *Dean,* Dr. Bor Z. Jang, 937-775-5001, Fax: 937-775-5009, E-mail: bor.jang@wright.edu.

College of Liberal Arts Students: 98 full-time (66 women), 80 part-time (49 women); includes 20 minority (17 African Americans, 1 American Indian/Alaska Native, 2 Hispanic Americans), 5 international. Average age 33. 113 applicants, 95% accepted. Expenses: Contact institution. *Financial support:* Fellowships with full tuition reimbursements, research assistantships with full tuition reimbursements, teaching assistantships with full tuition reimbursements, Federal Work-Study, institutionally sponsored loans, and unspecified assistantships available. Support available to part-time students. Financial award applicants required to submit FAFSA. In 2006, 73 degrees awarded. *Degree program information:* Part-time programs available. Offers composition and rhetoric (MA); criminal justice and social problems (MA); English (MA); history (MA); humanities (M Hum); international and comparative politics (MA); liberal arts (M Hum, M Mus, MA, MPA); literature (MA); music education (M Mus); performance (M Mus); public administration (MPA); teaching English to speakers of other languages (MA). *Application fee:* $25. *Dean,* Dr. Charles S. Taylor, 937-775-2225, Fax: 937-775-2707, E-mail: charles.taylor@wright.edu.

College of Nursing and Health Students: 46 full-time (45 women), 124 part-time (117 women); includes 16 minority (13 African Americans, 1 Asian American or Pacific Islander, 2 Hispanic Americans). Average age 39. 45 applicants, 100% accepted. Expenses: Contact institution. *Financial support:* In 2006–07, 15 fellowships with full tuition reimbursements were awarded; research assistantships, teaching assistantships, Federal Work-Study, institutionally sponsored loans, and unspecified assistantships also available. Support available to part-time students. Financial award application deadline: 6/1; financial award applicants required to submit FAFSA. In 2006, 64 degrees awarded. *Degree program information:* Part-time and evening/weekend programs available. Offers acute care nurse practitioner (MS); administration of nursing and health care systems (MS); adult health (MS); child and adolescent health (MS); community health (MS); family nurse practitioner (MS); nurse practitioner (MS); nursing and health (MS); school nurse (MS). *Application deadline:* For fall admission, 4/15 priority date for domestic students. *Application fee:* $25. *Application Contact:* Theresa A. Haghnazarian, Director of Student and Alumni Affairs, 937-775-2592, Fax: 937-775-4571, E-mail: theresa.haghnazarian@wright.edu. *Dean,* Dr. Patricia A. Martin, 937-775-3131, Fax: 937-775-4571, E-mail: patricia.martin@wright.edu.

College of Science and Mathematics Students: 231 full-time (110 women), 69 part-time (32 women); includes 26 minority (14 African Americans, 2 American Indian/Alaska Native, 7 Asian Americans or Pacific Islanders, 3 Hispanic Americans), 37 international. Average age 29. 337 applicants, 50% accepted. Expenses: Contact institution. *Financial support:* In 2006–07, 84 fellowships with full tuition reimbursements, 73 research assistantships with full tuition reimbursements, 77 teaching assistantships with full tuition reimbursements were awarded; career-related internships or fieldwork, Federal Work-Study, institutionally sponsored loans, tuition waivers (full and partial), and unspecified assistantships also available. Support available to part-time students. Financial award applicants required to submit FAFSA. In 2006, 106 master's, 9 doctorates awarded. *Degree program information:* Part-time and evening/weekend programs available. Offers anatomy (MS); applied mathematics (MS); applied statistics (MS); biochemistry and molecular biology (MS); biological sciences (MS); biomedical sciences (PhD); chemistry (MS); earth science education (MST); environmental sciences (MS); geological sciences (MS); geophysics (MS); human factors and industrial/organizational psychology (MS, PhD); mathematics (MS); medical physics (MS); microbiology and immunology (MS); physics (MS); physics education (MST); physiology and biophysics (MS); science and mathematics (MS, MST, PhD). *Application fee:* $25. *Dean,* Dr. Michele Wheatly, 937-775-2611, Fax: 937-775-3068, E-mail: michele.wheatly@wright.edu.

Raj Soin College of Business Students: 137 full-time (59 women), 297 part-time (125 women); includes 35 minority (21 African Americans, 1 American Indian/Alaska Native, 8 Asian Americans or Pacific Islanders, 5 Hispanic Americans), 71 international. Average age 30. 230 applicants, 89% accepted. Expenses: Contact institution. *Financial support:* In 2006–07, 32 fellowships with full tuition reimbursements, 1 research assistantship with full tuition reimbursement, 3 teaching assistantships with full tuition reimbursements were awarded; career-related internships or fieldwork, Federal Work-Study, institutionally sponsored loans, and unspecified assistantships also available. Support available to part-time students. Financial award applicants required to submit FAFSA. In 2006, 168 degrees awarded. *Degree program information:* Part-time and evening/weekend programs available. Offers accountancy (M Acc); accounting (MBA); business (M Acc, MBA, MIS, MS); business administration (MBA); business economics (MBA); finance (MBA); flexible business (MBA); health care management (MBA); information systems (MIS); international business (MBA); logistics and supply chain management (MS); management information technology (MBA); management, innovation and change (MBA); marketing (MBA); project management (MBA); social and applied economics (MS); supply chain management (MBA). *Application fee:* $25. *Application Contact:* Michael Evans, Director of MBA Programs, 937-775-2437, Fax: 937-775-3545, E-mail: michael.evans@wright.edu. *Dean,* Dr. Berkwood Farmer, 937-775-3242, Fax: 937-775-3545, E-mail: berkwood.farmer@wright.edu.

School of Medicine Students: 379 full-time (211 women), 2 part-time; includes 58 minority (35 African Americans, 19 Asian Americans or Pacific Islanders, 4 Hispanic Americans), 7 international. Average age 24. *Faculty:* 151 full-time (39 women), 17 part-time/adjunct (1 woman). Expenses: Contact institution. *Financial support:* In 2006–07, 3 research assistantships with full tuition reimbursements were awarded; fellowships, teaching assistantships, unspecified assistantships also available. Financial award applicants required to submit FAFSA. In 2006, 78 MDs, 5 master's awarded. Offers aerospace medicine (MS); health promotion and education (MPH); medicine (MD, MPH, MS, PhD); pharmacology and toxicology (MS); public health management (MPH); public health nursing (MPH). *Application Contact:* Dr. Paul G. Carlson, Associate Dean for Student Affairs and Admissions, 937-775-2934, Fax: 937-775-3672, E-mail: paul.carlson@wright.edu. *Dean,* Dr. Howard Part, 937-775-3010, Fax: 937-775-3672, E-mail: howard.part@wright.edu.

School of Professional Psychology Students: 121 full-time (90 women), 6 part-time (all women); includes 35 minority (24 African Americans, 5 Asian Americans or Pacific Islanders, 6 Hispanic Americans), 12 international. Average age 29. *Faculty:* 21 full-time (5 women), 2 part-time/adjunct (1 woman). Expenses: Contact institution. *Financial support:* In 2006–07, 30 fellowships with full tuition reimbursements were awarded; teaching assistantships, career-related internships or fieldwork, Federal Work-Study, institutionally sponsored loans, and unspecified assistantships also available. Financial award application deadline: 4/15; financial award applicants required to submit FAFSA. In 2006, 22 degrees awarded. Offers clinical psychology (Psy D). *Application deadline:* For fall admission, 12/15 for domestic students. *Application fee:* $30. *Application Contact:* Leona L. Gray, Director, Student Services/Admissions, 937-775-3492, Fax: 937-775-3493, E-mail: leona.gray@wright.edu. *Dean,* Dr. John R. Rudisill, 937-775-3490, Fax: 937-775-3434, E-mail: john.rudisill@wright.edu.

WYCLIFFE COLLEGE, Toronto, ON M5S 1H7, Canada

General Information Independent-religious, coed, graduate-only institution. *Graduate housing:* Rooms and/or apartments guaranteed to single students and available on a first-come, first-served basis to married students. Housing application deadline: 5/1.

GRADUATE UNITS

Division of Advanced Degree Studies *Degree program information:* Part-time programs available. Offers theology (MA, Th M, D Min, PhD, Th D).

Division of Basic Degree Studies *Degree program information:* Part-time programs available. Offers Christian Studies (Diploma); theology (M Div, M Rel, MTS).

XAVIER UNIVERSITY, Cincinnati, OH 45207

General Information Independent-religious, coed, comprehensive institution. *Enrollment:* 6,666 graduate, professional, and undergraduate students; 804 full-time matriculated graduate/professional students (506 women), 1,652 part-time matriculated graduate/professional students (957 women). *Graduate faculty:* 162 full-time (79 women), 133 part-time/adjunct (62 women). *Tuition:* Part-time $462 per credit hour. Part-time tuition and fees vary according to degree level, campus/location and program. *Graduate housing:* Room and/or apartments available on a first-come, first-served basis to single students; on-campus housing not available to married students. Housing application deadline: 5/1. *Student services:* Campus employment opportunities, campus safety program, career counseling, disabled student services, exercise/wellness program, international student services, low-cost health insurance, multicultural affairs office, teacher training, writing training. *Library facilities:* McDonald Library plus 1 other. *Online resources:* library catalog, web page, access to other libraries' catalogs. *Collection:* 227,200 titles, 21,650 serial subscriptions, 5,870 audiovisual materials.

Xavier University (continued)

Computer facilities: 210 computers available on campus for general student use. A campuswide network can be accessed from student residence rooms and from off campus. Internet access and online class registration are available. *Web address:* http://www.xu.edu/.

General Application Contact: Roger Bosse, Interim Director of Graduate Studies, 513-745-3357, Fax: 513-745-1048, E-mail: bosse@xavier.edu.

GRADUATE UNITS

College of Arts and Sciences Students: 7 full-time (2 women), 56 part-time (30 women); includes 3 minority (2 African Americans, 1 Asian American or Pacific Islander), 1 international. Average age 35. 57 applicants, 65% accepted, 20 enrolled. *Faculty:* 28 full-time (12 women). Expenses: Contact institution. *Financial support:* Scholarships/grants, tuition waivers (partial), and unspecified assistantships available. Support available to part-time students. Financial award applicants required to submit FAFSA. In 2006, 13 degrees awarded. *Degree program information:* Part-time and evening/weekend programs available. Offers arts and sciences (MA); English (MA); theology (MA). *Application deadline:* For fall admission, 8/15 priority date for domestic students. Applications are processed on a rolling basis. *Application fee:* $35. Electronic applications accepted. *Application Contact:* Roger Bosse, Interim Director of Graduate Studies, 513-745-3357, Fax: 513-745-1048, E-mail: bosse@xavier.edu. *Dean,* Dr. Janice B. Walker, 513-745-3101, Fax: 513-745-1099, E-mail: walker@xavier.edu.

College of Social Sciences, Health and Education Students: 549 full-time (417 women), 909 part-time (696 women); includes 169 minority (139 African Americans, 16 Asian Americans or Pacific Islanders, 14 Hispanic Americans), 36 international. Average age 32. *Faculty:* 75 full-time (45 women), 104 part-time/adjunct (54 women). Expenses: Contact institution. *Financial support:* In 2006–07, 16 research assistantships with partial tuition reimbursements, 4 teaching assistantships with partial tuition reimbursements were awarded; career-related internships or fieldwork, scholarships/grants, traineeships, unspecified assistantships, and residency stipends also available. Support available to part-time students. Financial award applicants required to submit FAFSA. In 2006, 552 master's, 16 doctorates awarded. *Degree program information:* Part-time and evening/weekend programs available. Offers clinical nurse leader (MSN); clinical psychology (Psy D); criminal justice (MS); forensic nursing (MSN); health services administration (MHSA); healthcare law (MSN); nursing administration (MSN); occupational therapy (MOT); psychology (MA); school nursing (MSN); social sciences, health and education (M Ed, MA, MHSA, MOT, MS, MSN, Psy D); sport administration (M Ed). *Application fee:* $35. *Application Contact:* Roger Bosse, Interim Director of Graduate Studies, 513-745-3357, Fax: 513-745-1048, E-mail: bosse@xavier.edu. *Dean,* Dr. Neil Heighberger, 513-745-3119, Fax: 513-745-1058, E-mail: heighber@xavier.edu.

School of Education Students: 312 full-time (242 women), 668 part-time (513 women); includes 110 minority (97 African Americans, 1 American Indian/Alaska Native, 4 Asian Americans or Pacific Islanders, 8 Hispanic Americans), 7 international. Average age 33. 448 applicants, 60% accepted, 245 enrolled. *Faculty:* 28 full-time (16 women), 69 part-time/adjunct (37 women). Expenses: Contact institution. *Financial support:* Career-related internships or fieldwork, scholarships/grants, and unspecified assistantships available. Support available to part-time students. Financial award applicants required to submit FAFSA. In 2006, 395 degrees awarded. *Degree program information:* Part-time and evening/weekend programs available. Offers community counseling (MA); education (M Ed, MA); educational administration (M Ed); elementary education (M Ed); human resource development (M Ed); Montessori (M Ed); multicultural literature for children (M Ed); reading specialist (M Ed); school counseling (MA); secondary education (M Ed); special education (M Ed). *Application deadline:* Applications are processed on a rolling basis. *Application fee:* $35. Electronic applications accepted. *Application Contact:* Roger Bosse, Interim Director of Graduate Studies, 513-745-3357, Fax: 513-745-1048, E-mail: bosse@xavier.edu. *Acting Dean,* Dr. James Boothe, 513-745-2951, Fax: 513-745-1052, E-mail: boothe@xavier.edu.

Williams College of Business Students: 227 full-time (66 women), 708 part-time (252 women); includes 99 minority (41 African Americans, 1 American Indian/Alaska Native, 43 Asian Americans or Pacific Islanders, 14 Hispanic Americans), 43 international. Average age 31. 486 applicants, 63% accepted, 229 enrolled. *Faculty:* 59 full-time (22 women), 29 part-time/adjunct (8 women). Expenses: Contact institution. *Financial support:* In 2006–07, 175 students received support, including 11 research assistantships with full and partial tuition reimbursements available; career-related internships or fieldwork, scholarships/grants, and tuition waivers (partial) also available. Support available to part-time students. Financial award application deadline: 4/30; financial award applicants required to submit FAFSA. In 2006, 294 degrees awarded. *Degree program information:* Part-time and evening/weekend programs available. Offers business (Exec MBA, MBA); business administration (Exec MBA, MBA); e-commerce (MBA); finance (MBA); international business (MBA); management information systems (MBA); marketing (MBA). *Application deadline:* For fall admission, 8/1 priority date for domestic students, 6/1 for international students; for winter admission, 12/1 priority date for domestic students; for spring admission, 4/1 priority date for domestic students, 10/1 for international students. Applications are processed on a rolling basis. *Application fee:* $35. Electronic applications accepted. *Application Contact:* Jennifer Bush, Executive Director, MBA Programs, 513-745-3525, Fax: 513-745-2929, E-mail: xumba@xavier.edu. *Dean,* Dr. Ali Malekzadeh, 513-745-3528, Fax: 513-745-2929, E-mail: malekzadeh@xavier.edu.

XAVIER UNIVERSITY OF LOUISIANA, New Orleans, LA 70125-1098

General Information Independent-religious, coed, comprehensive institution. CGS member. *Graduate housing:* On-campus housing not available.

GRADUATE UNITS

College of Pharmacy Students: 637 full-time (464 women); includes 499 minority (328 African Americans, 1 American Indian/Alaska Native, 161 Asian Americans or Pacific Islanders, 9 Hispanic Americans), 7 international. Average age 23. 704 applicants, 28% accepted, 163 enrolled. *Faculty:* 34 full-time (11 women), 4 part-time/adjunct (0 women). Expenses: Contact institution. *Financial support:* Career-related internships or fieldwork, Federal Work-Study, institutionally sponsored loans, and scholarships/grants available. Support available to part-time students. Financial award application deadline: 4/1; financial award applicants required to submit FAFSA. In 2006, 113 degrees awarded. Offers pharmacy (Pharm D). *Application deadline:* For fall admission, 12/15 for domestic students. *Application fee:* $25. Electronic applications accepted. *Application Contact:* Gwendolyn Hudson, Admissions Liaison, 504-520-7369, Fax: 504-520-7977, E-mail: ghudson@xula.edu. *Dean,* Dr. Wayne T. Harris, 504-520-7421, Fax: 504-520-7930, E-mail: wharris@xula.edu.

Graduate School *Degree program information:* Part-time and evening/weekend programs available. Offers curriculum and instruction (MA); education administration and supervision (MA); guidance and counseling (MA).

Institute for Black Catholic Studies *Degree program information:* Part-time programs available. Offers pastoral theology (Th M).

YALE UNIVERSITY, New Haven, CT 06520

General Information Independent, coed, university. CGS member. *Graduate housing:* Rooms and/or apartments available on a first-come, first-served basis to single and married students. Housing application deadline: 6/1. *Research affiliation:* Howard Hughes Medical Institute, J. B. Pierce Foundation (environmental physiology), Haskins Laboratories (speech, hearing, reading).

GRADUATE UNITS

Divinity School Students: 375 (190 women); includes 51 minority (27 African Americans, 19 Asian Americans or Pacific Islanders, 5 Hispanic Americans) 29 international. Average age 26. 407 applicants, 62% accepted, 136 enrolled. *Faculty:* 30 full-time, 10 part-time/adjunct. Expenses: Contact institution. *Financial support:* In 2006–07, 292 fellowships (averaging $12,436 per year) were awarded; career-related internships or fieldwork, Federal Work-Study, and scholarships/grants also available. Support available to part-time students. Financial award application deadline: 3/1; financial award applicants required to submit FAFSA. *Degree program information:* Part-time programs available. Offers divinity (M Div, MAR, STM). *Application deadline:* For fall admission, 1/15 priority date for domestic students. *Application fee:* $75. Electronic applications accepted. *Application Contact:* Anna T. Ramirez, Associate Dean of Admissions and Financial Aid, 203-432-9802, Fax: 203-432-7475, E-mail: anna.ramirez@yale.edu. *Dean,* Dr. Harold W. Attridge, 203-432-5306, Fax: 203-432-9712, E-mail: harold.attridge@yale.edu.

Graduate School of Arts and Sciences *Degree program information:* Part-time programs available. Offers African studies (MA); African-American studies (MA, PhD); American studies (MA, PhD); anthropology (MA, PhD); applied mathematics (M Phil, MS, PhD); applied mechanics and mechanical engineering (M Phil, MS, PhD); applied physics (MS, PhD); archaeological studies (MA); arts and sciences (M Phil, MA, MS, PhD); astronomy (MS, PhD); biophysical chemistry (PhD); cell biology (PhD); cellular and molecular physiology (PhD); chemical engineering (MS, PhD); classics (PhD); comparative literature (PhD); computer science (PhD); developmental biology (PhD); East Asian languages and literatures (PhD); East Asian studies (MA); ecology and evolutionary biology (PhD); economics (PhD); electrical engineering (MS, PhD); English language and literature (MA, PhD); environmental sciences (PhD); experimental pathology (PhD); forestry (PhD); French (MA, PhD); genetics (PhD); geochemistry (PhD); geophysics (PhD); Germanic language and literature (MA, PhD); history (MA, PhD); history of art (PhD); history of medicine and the life sciences (MS, PhD); immunobiology (PhD); inorganic chemistry (PhD); international and development economics (MA); international relations (MA); Italian language and literature (PhD); linguistics (PhD); mathematics (MS, PhD); mechanical engineering (M Phil, MS, PhD); medieval studies (MA, PhD); meteorology (PhD); mineralogy and crystallography (PhD); molecular biology (PhD); molecular biophysics and biochemistry (MS, PhD); music (MA, PhD); Near Eastern languages and civilizations (MA, PhD); neurobiology (PhD); neuroscience (PhD); oceanography (PhD); organic chemistry (PhD); paleoecology (PhD); paleontology and stratigraphy (PhD); petrology (PhD); pharmacology (PhD); philosophy (PhD); physical chemistry (PhD); physics (PhD); plant sciences (PhD); political science (PhD); psychology (PhD); religious studies (PhD); Renaissance studies (PhD); Russian and East European studies (MA); Slavic languages and literatures (PhD); sociology (PhD); Spanish and Portuguese (MA, PhD); statistics (MS, PhD); structural geology (PhD).

School of Architecture Students: 195 full-time (80 women); includes 33 minority (1 African American, 23 Asian Americans or Pacific Islanders, 9 Hispanic Americans), 40 international. 508 applicants, 20% accepted, 67 enrolled. *Faculty:* 15 full-time (6 women), 79 part-time/adjunct (21 women). Expenses: Contact institution. *Financial support:* In 2006–07, 165 students received support; fellowships, teaching assistantships, Federal Work-Study and institutionally sponsored loans available. Financial award application deadline: 2/1. In 2006, 68 degrees awarded. Offers architecture (M Arch, M Env Des, MEM). *Application deadline:* For fall admission, 1/3 for domestic students. *Application fee:* $70. *Application Contact:* 203-432-2291, Fax: 203-432-7175. *Dean,* Robert A. M. Stern, 203-432-2279, Fax: 203-432-7175.

School of Art Students: 119 full-time (61 women); includes 22 minority (4 African Americans, 1 American Indian/Alaska Native, 11 Asian Americans or Pacific Islanders, 6 Hispanic Americans), 21 international. Average age 27. 1,049 applicants, 6% accepted, 57 enrolled. *Faculty:* 11 full-time (3 women), 109 part-time/adjunct (44 women). Expenses: Contact institution. *Financial support:* In 2006–07, 90 students received support, including 56 teaching assistantships (averaging $1,500 per year); Federal Work-Study and scholarships/grants also available. Financial award application deadline: 3/1; financial award applicants required to submit FAFSA. In 2006, 56 degrees awarded. Offers graphic design (MFA); painting/printmaking (MFA); photography (MFA); sculpture (MFA). *Application deadline:* For fall admission, 1/9 for domestic and international students. *Application fee:* $75. *Application Contact:* Patricia Ann DeChiara, Director of Academic Affairs, 203-432-2600, E-mail: artschool.info@yale.edu. *Dean,* Robert Storr, 203-432-2606.

School of Drama Students: 199 full-time (95 women); includes 32 minority (15 African Americans, 10 Asian Americans or Pacific Islanders, 7 Hispanic Americans), 20 international. Average age 27. 1,037 applicants, 8% accepted, 72 enrolled. *Faculty:* 33 full-time (13 women), 57 part-time/adjunct (23 women). Expenses: Contact institution. *Financial support:* Career-related internships or fieldwork, Federal Work-Study, institutionally sponsored loans, and scholarships/grants available. Financial award application deadline: 2/15; financial award applicants required to submit FAFSA. Offers drama (MFA, DFA, Certificate). *Application deadline:* For fall admission, 1/3 for domestic and international students. *Application fee:* $95. Electronic applications accepted. *Application Contact:* Registrar's Office, 203-432-1507, Fax: 203-432-9668. *Dean/Artistic Director,* James Bundy, 203-432-1505.

School of Forestry and Environmental Studies Students: 244 full-time, 18 part-time; includes 24 minority (8 African Americans, 2 American Indian/Alaska Native, 4 Asian Americans or Pacific Islanders, 10 Hispanic Americans). Average age 28. 493 applicants, 45% accepted, 121 enrolled. *Faculty:* 32 full-time (8 women), 27 part-time/adjunct (7 women). Expenses: Contact institution. *Financial support:* In 2006–07, 158 fellowships (averaging $17,000 per year) were awarded; research assistantships, teaching assistantships, career-related internships or fieldwork, Federal Work-Study, institutionally sponsored loans, scholarships/grants, and health care benefits also available. Support available to part-time students. Financial award application deadline: 2/15; financial award applicants required to submit FAFSA. In 2006, 116 master's, 8 doctorates awarded. *Degree program information:* Part-time programs available. Offers forestry and environmental studies (MEM, MES, MF, MFS, PhD). *Application deadline:* For fall admission, 1/7 priority date for domestic and international students. *Application fee:* $70. Electronic applications accepted. *Application Contact:* Emly McDiarmid, Director of Admissions, 203-432-5138, Fax: 203-432-7297, E-mail: emly.mcdiarmid@yale.edu. *Dean,* James Gustave Speth, 203-432-5109, Fax: 203-432-5942.

School of Medicine *Degree program information:* Part-time programs available. Offers biological and biomedical sciences (PhD); computational biology and bioinformatics (PhD); immunology (PhD); medicine (MD, MM Sc, MPH, MS, PhD); microbiology (PhD); molecular biophysics and biochemistry (PhD); molecular cell biology, genetics, and development (PhD); neuroscience (PhD); pharmacological sciences and molecular medicine (PhD); physician associate (MM Sc); physiology and integrative medical biology (PhD). Electronic applications accepted.

School of Public Health Students: 209 full-time (169 women), 8 part-time (4 women); includes 77 minority (24 African Americans, 44 Asian Americans or Pacific Islanders, 9 Hispanic Americans), 21 international. Average age 26. 413 applicants, 71% accepted. *Faculty:* 67 full-time (37 women), 53 part-time/adjunct (18 women). Expenses: Contact institution. *Financial support:* In 2006–07, 21 fellowships with full tuition reimbursements (averaging $12,560 per year), 4 research assistantships with full tuition reimbursements (averaging $24,910 per year) were awarded; teaching assistantships with full tuition reimbursements, career-related internships or fieldwork, Federal Work-Study, institutionally sponsored loans, scholarships/grants, and tuition waivers (full and partial) also available. Support available to part-time students. Financial award application deadline: 3/1; financial award applicants required to submit FAFSA. In 2006, 124 master's, 8 doctorates awarded. *Degree program information:* Part-time programs available. Offers biostatistics (MPH, MS, PhD); chronic disease epidemiology (MPH, PhD); environmental health sciences (MPH, PhD); epidemiology of microbial diseases (MPH, PhD); global health (MPH); health management (MPH); health policy and administration (MPH, PhD); parasitology (PhD); social and behavioral sciences (MPH). MS and PhD offered through the Graduate School. *Application deadline:* For fall admission, 1/15 for domestic and international students. *Application fee:* $60. Electronic applications accepted. *Application Contact:* Jacqui Comshaw, Director of Admissions, 203-785-2844, Fax: 203-785-4845, E-mail: eph.admissions@yale.edu. *Dean and Chairman,* Dr. Paul D. Cleary, 203-785-2867, Fax: 203-785-6103, E-mail: paul.cleary@yale.edu.

School of Music Students: 214 full-time (97 women); includes 28 minority (1 African American, 18 Asian Americans or Pacific Islanders, 9 Hispanic Americans), 81 international. Average age 23. 1,362 applicants, 12% accepted, 126 enrolled. *Faculty:* 23 full-time (8 women), 32 part-time/adjunct (3 women). Expenses: Contact institution. *Financial support:* In 2006–07, 212 students received support, including 212 fellowships (averaging $24,700 per year); Federal Work-Study, institutionally sponsored loans, and scholarships/grants also available. Financial award application deadline: 5/1; financial award applicants required to submit FAFSA.

In 2006, 88 master's, 3 doctorates, 33 other advanced degrees awarded. Offers music (MM, MMA, DMA, AD, Certificate). *Application deadline:* For fall admission, 12/15 for domestic and international students. *Application fee:* $100. Electronic applications accepted. *Application Contact:* Suzanne M. Stringer, Registrar and Financial Aid Administrator, 203-432-1962, Fax: 203-432-7448, E-mail: suzanne.stringer@yale.edu. *Dean,* Robert Blocker, 203-432-4160, Fax: 203-432-7542.

School of Nursing *Degree program information:* Part-time programs available. Offers nursing (MSN, DN Sc, Post Master's Certificate).

Yale Law School Students: 586 full-time (260 women). Average age 24. 3,677 applicants, 7% accepted, 189 enrolled. *Faculty:* 71 full-time, 45 part-time/adjunct. Expenses: Contact institution. *Financial support:* Application deadline: 3/15; In 2006, 203 JDs, 29 master's, 10 doctorates awarded. Offers law (JD, LL M, MSL, JSD). *Application deadline:* For fall admission, 2/1 for domestic students. Applications are processed on a rolling basis. *Application fee:* $70. Electronic applications accepted. *Application Contact:* Asha Rangappa, Assistant Dean, 203-432-4995, E-mail: admissions.law@yale.edu. *Dean,* Harold Hongju Koh, 203-432-1660.

Yale School of Management Students: 450 full-time (160 women); includes 105 minority (18 African Americans, 71 Asian Americans or Pacific Islanders, 16 Hispanic Americans), 108 international. Average age 28. 2,520 applicants, 20% accepted, 212 enrolled. *Faculty:* 56 full-time (8 women), 22 part-time/adjunct (6 women). Expenses: Contact institution. *Financial support:* In 2006–07, 332 students received support. Institutionally sponsored loans and scholarships/grants available. Financial award application deadline: 3/1; financial award applicants required to submit FAFSA. In 2006, 215 master's, 6 doctorates awarded. Offers accounting (PhD); business administration (MBA, PhD); financial economics (PhD); management (MBA, PhD); marketing (PhD). *Application deadline:* For fall admission, 10/26 for domestic and international students; for winter admission, 1/11 for domestic and international students; for spring admission, 3/15 for domestic and international students. *Application fee:* $180. Electronic applications accepted. *Application Contact:* Anne Coyle, Director of Admissions, 203-432-5932, Fax: 203-432-7004, E-mail: mba.admissions@yale.edu. *Dean,* Joel M. Podolny, 203-432-6035, Fax: 203-432-5092, E-mail: joel.podolny@yale.edu.

YESHIVA BETH MOSHE, Scranton, PA 18505-2124

General Information Independent-religious, men only, comprehensive institution.

GRADUATE UNITS

Graduate Programs

YESHIVA DERECH CHAIM, Brooklyn, NY 11218

General Information Independent-religious, men only, comprehensive institution.

GRADUATE UNITS

Graduate Program

YESHIVA KARLIN STOLIN RABBINICAL INSTITUTE, Brooklyn, NY 11204

General Information Independent-religious, men only, comprehensive institution. *Graduate housing:* On-campus housing not available.

GRADUATE UNITS

Graduate Programs

YESHIVA OF NITRA RABBINICAL COLLEGE, Mount Kisco, NY 10549

General Information Independent-religious, men only, comprehensive institution.

GRADUATE UNITS

Graduate Programs

YESHIVA SHAAR HATORAH TALMUDIC RESEARCH INSTITUTE, Kew Gardens, NY 11418-1469

General Information Independent-religious, men only, comprehensive institution.

GRADUATE UNITS

Graduate Programs

YESHIVATH VIZNITZ, Monsey, NY 10952

General Information Independent-religious, men only, comprehensive institution.

GRADUATE UNITS

Graduate Programs

YESHIVATH ZICHRON MOSHE, South Fallsburg, NY 12779

General Information Independent-religious, men only, comprehensive institution.

GRADUATE UNITS

Graduate Programs *Degree program information:* Part-time programs available.

YESHIVA TORAS CHAIM TALMUDICAL SEMINARY, Denver, CO 80204-1415

General Information Independent-religious, men only, comprehensive institution.

GRADUATE UNITS

Graduate Programs

YESHIVA UNIVERSITY, New York, NY 10033-3201

General Information Independent, coed, university. CGS member. *Graduate housing:* On-campus housing not available.

GRADUATE UNITS

Azrieli Graduate School of Jewish Education and Administration *Degree program information:* Part-time and evening/weekend programs available. Offers Jewish education and administration (MS, Ed D, Specialist).

Benjamin N. Cardozo School of Law Students: 1,007 full-time (492 women), 101 part-time (62 women); includes 228 minority (42 African Americans, 3 American Indian/Alaska Native, 115 Asian Americans or Pacific Islanders, 68 Hispanic Americans), 60 international. Average age 25. 4,785 applicants, 29% accepted, 351 enrolled. *Faculty:* 50 full-time (20 women), 64 part-time/adjunct (15 women). Expenses: Contact institution. *Financial support:* In 2006–07, 944 students received support, including 65 research assistantships; career-related internships or fieldwork, Federal Work-Study, institutionally sponsored loans, scholarships/grants, health care benefits, and tuition waivers (full and partial) also available. Support available to part-time students. Financial award application deadline: 4/15; financial award applicants required to submit FAFSA. In 2006, 362 JDs, 65 master's awarded. *Degree program information:* Part-time programs available. Offers comparative legal thought (LL M); general studies (LL M); intellectual property law (LL M); law (JD). *Application deadline:* For fall admission, 4/1 for domestic students; for spring admission, 12/1 for domestic students. Applications are processed on a rolling basis. *Application fee:* $65. Electronic applications accepted. *Dean of Admissions,* David G. Martinidez, 212-790-0274, Fax: 212-790-0482, E-mail: lawinfo@yu.edu.

Bernard Revel Graduate School of Jewish Studies *Degree program information:* Part-time programs available. Offers Jewish studies (MA, PhD).

Ferkauf Graduate School of Psychology Students: 296 full-time (201 women), 64 part-time (44 women); includes 59 minority (16 African Americans, 14 Asian Americans or Pacific Islanders, 29 Hispanic Americans), 38 international. Average age 28. 570 applicants, 13% accepted. *Faculty:* 28 full-time (13 women), 73 part-time/adjunct (40 women). Expenses: Contact institution. *Financial support:* In 2006–07, 43 fellowships (averaging $5,000 per year), 26 research assistantships (averaging $2,000 per year), 79 teaching assistantships (averaging $2,000 per year) were awarded; career-related internships or fieldwork, Federal Work-Study, institutionally sponsored loans, and scholarships/grants also available. Support available to part-time students. Financial award application deadline: 4/15. In 2006, 13 master's, 83 doctorates awarded. *Degree program information:* Part-time programs available. Offers clinical psychology (Psy D); health psychology (PhD); mental health counseling psychology (MA); psychology (MA, PhD, Psy D); school/clinical-child psychology (Psy D). *Application fee:* $50. *Application Contact:* Elaine Schwartz, Assistant Director of Admissions, 718-430-3820, Fax: 718-430-3960, E-mail: eschwart@ymail.yu.edu. *Dean,* Dr. Lawrence J. Siegel, 718-430-3941, Fax: 718-430-3960, E-mail: lsiegel@aecom.yu.edu.

Wurzweiler School of Social Work Students: 273 full-time (182 women), 187 part-time (137 women); includes 217 minority (129 African Americans, 6 Asian Americans or Pacific Islanders, 82 Hispanic Americans). Average age 41. 444 applicants, 73% accepted, 223 enrolled. *Faculty:* 25 full-time (14 women), 38 part-time/adjunct (26 women). Expenses: Contact institution. *Financial support:* In 2006–07, 381 students received support, including 2 teaching assistantships (averaging $5,000 per year); career-related internships or fieldwork, Federal Work-Study, institutionally sponsored loans, and scholarships/grants also available. Financial award application deadline: 4/15; financial award applicants required to submit FAFSA. In 2006, 158 master's, 18 doctorates awarded. *Degree program information:* Part-time and evening/weekend programs available. Offers social work (MSW, PhD). *Application deadline:* For fall admission, 5/1 priority date for domestic students; for spring admission, 10/31 for domestic students. Applications are processed on a rolling basis. *Application fee:* $50. *Application Contact:* Ruth Bigman, Director of Admissions, 212-960-0811, Fax: 212-960-0822, E-mail: rbigman@yu.edu. *Dean,* Dr. Sheldon R. Gelman, 212-960-0820, Fax: 212-960-0822, E-mail: srgelman@yu.edu.

YORK COLLEGE OF PENNSYLVANIA, York, PA 17405-7199

General Information Independent, coed, comprehensive institution. *Graduate housing:* On-campus housing not available.

GRADUATE UNITS

Department of Business Administration *Degree program information:* Part-time and evening/weekend programs available. Offers business administration (MBA).

Department of Education *Degree program information:* Part-time and evening/weekend programs available. Offers education (M Ed). Electronic applications accepted.

Department of Nursing *Degree program information:* Part-time and evening/weekend programs available. Offers nursing (MS). Electronic applications accepted.

YORK UNIVERSITY, Toronto, ON M3J 1P3, Canada

General Information Province-supported, coed, university. *Enrollment:* 50,691 graduate, professional, and undergraduate students; 3,367 full-time matriculated graduate/professional students (1,822 women), 1,820 part-time matriculated graduate/professional students (1,004 women). *Enrollment by degree level:* 3,761 master's, 1,426 doctoral. *Graduate faculty:* 995 full-time, 166 part-time/adjunct. *Graduate housing:* Rooms and/or apartments available on a first-come, first-served basis to single and married students. *Student services:* Campus employment opportunities, campus safety program, career counseling, child daycare facilities, disabled student services, exercise/wellness program, free psychological counseling, grant writing training, international student services, low-cost health insurance, multicultural affairs office, teacher training, writing training. *Library facilities:* Scott Library plus 4 others. *Online resources:* library catalog, web page, access to other libraries' catalogs. *Collection:* 6.1 million titles, 540,000 serial subscriptions. *Research affiliation:* Imperial Oil LMT, National Palace Museum (Taiwan), Unicorn Children's Foundation (developmental and learning disorders), Smithsonian Institution (astronomy, physics, space), Beijing Municipality (management training), German Academic Exchange (German studies).

Computer facilities: 1,900 computers available on campus for general student use. A campuswide network can be accessed from student residence rooms and from off campus. Internet access and online class registration are available. *Web address:* http://www.yorku.ca/.

General Application Contact: Sharon Pereira, Student Affairs Officer, 416-736-5521, Fax: 416-736-5592, E-mail: sharonp@yorku.ca.

GRADUATE UNITS

Faculty of Graduate Studies Students: 3,367 full-time (1,822 women), 1,820 part-time (1,004 women). 5,408 applicants, 25% accepted, 1271 enrolled. *Faculty:* 1,622 full-time (689 women), 189 part-time/adjunct (72 women). Expenses: Contact institution. *Financial support:* Fellowships, research assistantships, teaching assistantships, career-related internships or fieldwork, institutionally sponsored loans, tuition waivers (partial), and fee bursaries available. In 2006, 676 master's, 111 doctorates awarded. *Degree program information:* Part-time and evening/weekend programs available. Offers communication and culture (MA, PhD); critical disability studies (MA, PhD); environmental studies (MES, PhD); French studies (MA); health (M Sc, M Sc N, MA, PhD); interdisciplinary studies (MA); kinesiology and health science (M Sc, MA, PhD); law (LL B, LL M, PhD); nursing (M Sc N); psychology (MA, PhD); public and international affairs (MA); translation (MA). *Application fee:* $80. Electronic applications accepted. *Application Contact:* Sharon Pereira, Student Affairs Officer, 416-736-5521, Fax: 416-736-5592, E-mail: sharonp@yorku.ca. *Interim Dean,* Ronald Pearlman, 416-736-5329.

Atkinson Faculty of Liberal and Professional Studies Expenses: Contact institution. Offers disaster and emergency management (MA); human resources management (MHRM, PhD); liberal and professional studies (MA, MHRM, MPPAL, MSW, PhD); public policy, administration and law (MPPAL); social work (MSW, PhD). *Application Contact:* Sharon Pereira, Student Affairs Officer, 416-736-5521, Fax: 416-736-5592, E-mail: sharonp@yorku.ca.

Faculty of Arts Students: 1,219 full-time (737 women), 212 part-time (123 women). 2,693 applicants, 19% accepted, 449 enrolled. *Faculty:* 879 full-time (382 women), 72 part-time/adjunct (28 women). Expenses: Contact institution. *Financial support:* Fellowships, research assistantships, teaching assistantships, tuition waivers (partial) and fee bursaries available. In 2006, 265 master's, 77 doctorates awarded. *Degree program information:* Part-time programs available. Offers arts (M Sc, MA, PhD); economics (MA, PhD); English (MA, PhD); geography (M Sc, MA, PhD); history (MA, PhD); humanities (MA, PhD); international development studies (MA); philosophy (MA, PhD); political science (MA, PhD); social and political thought (MA, PhD); social anthropology (MA, PhD); sociology (MA, PhD); theoretical and applied linguistics (MA, PhD); women's studies (MA, PhD). *Application fee:* $80. Electronic applications accepted. *Application Contact:* Sharon Pereira, Student Affairs Officer, 416-736-5521, Fax: 416-736-5592, E-mail: sharonp@yorku.ca. *Dean,* Robert Drummond, 416-736-5260.

Faculty of Education Students: 78 full-time (65 women), 244 part-time (206 women). 306 applicants, 29% accepted, 90 enrolled. *Faculty:* 63 full-time (39 women), 4 part-time/adjunct (2 women). Expenses: Contact institution. *Financial support:* In 2006–07, 23 fellowships (averaging $13,369 per year), 40 research assistantships (averaging $4,273 per year), 37 teaching assistantships (averaging $9,307 per year) were awarded; fee bursaries also available. In 2006, 70 master's, 4 doctorates awarded. *Degree program information:* Part-time programs available. Offers education (M Ed, PhD). *Application deadline:* For fall admission, 2/1 for domestic students. *Application fee:* $80. Electronic applications accepted. *Director,* Alison Griffith, 416-736-5018.

Faculty of Fine Arts Students: 183 full-time (105 women), 44 part-time (23 women). 504 applicants, 23% accepted, 106 enrolled. *Faculty:* 143 full-time (70 women), 50 part-time/adjunct (25 women). Expenses: Contact institution. *Financial support:* Fellowships, research assistantships, teaching assistantships, tuition waivers (partial) and fee bursaries available. In 2006, 44 master's, 2 doctorates awarded. *Degree program information:* Part-time programs available. Offers art history (MA, PhD); composition (MA); dance (MA, MFA); design (M Des); film (MA, MFA, PhD); fine arts (M Des, MA, MFA, PhD); musicology and

York University (continued)

ethnomusicology (MA, PhD); theatre (MFA); theatre studies (MA, PhD); visual arts (MFA, PhD). *Application fee:* $80. Electronic applications accepted. *Dean*, Phillip Silver, 416-736-5136.

Faculty of Science and Engineering Students: 322 full-time (119 women), 67 part-time (17 women). 520 applicants. *Faculty:* 218 full-time (30 women), 46 part-time/adjunct (7 women). Expenses: Contact institution. *Financial support:* Fellowships, research assistantships, teaching assistantships, career-related internships or fieldwork, tuition waivers (partial), and fee bursaries available. In 2006, 58 master's, 17 doctorates awarded. *Degree program information:* Part-time and evening/weekend programs available. Offers biology (M Sc, PhD); chemistry (M Sc, PhD); computer science (M Sc, PhD); earth and space science (M Sc, PhD); industrial and applied mathematics (M Sc); mathematics and statistics (MA, PhD); physics and astronomy (M Sc, PhD); science and engineering (M Sc, MA, PhD). *Application fee:* $80. *Dean*, Nick Cercone, 416-736-5051.

Schulich School of Business *Degree program information:* Part-time and evening/weekend programs available. Offers business (EMBA, IMBA, MBA, MPA, PhD). Electronic applications accepted.

YO SAN UNIVERSITY OF TRADITIONAL CHINESE MEDICINE, Los Angeles, CA 90066

General Information Private, coed, graduate-only institution. *Graduate housing:* On-campus housing not available.

GRADUATE UNITS

Program in Acupuncture and Traditional Chinese Medicine *Degree program information:* Part-time programs available. Postbaccalaureate distance learning degree programs offered (no on-campus study). Offers acupuncture and traditional Chinese medicine (MATCM).

YOUNGSTOWN STATE UNIVERSITY, Youngstown, OH 44555-0001

General Information State-supported, coed, comprehensive institution. CGS member. *Graduate housing:* Room and/or apartments available on a first-come, first-served basis to single students; on-campus housing not available to married students. *Research affiliation:* Ohio Supercomputer Center (computational chemistry and physics), Northeast Ohio Universities College of Medicine (medicine), Parker-Hannifin Corporation (engineering technology), Ohio Mass Spectrometry Consortium (chemistry and biology), BioRemedial Technologies Inc. (environmental bioremediation).

GRADUATE UNITS

Graduate School *Degree program information:* Part-time and evening/weekend programs available.

College of Arts and Sciences *Degree program information:* Part-time programs available. Offers arts and sciences (MA, MS, Certificate); biological sciences (MS); chemistry (MS); economics (MA); English (MA); environmental studies (MS); history (MA); industrial/institutional management (Certificate); mathematics (MS); risk management (Certificate).

College of Education *Degree program information:* Part-time and evening/weekend programs available. Offers counseling (MS Ed); early and middle childhood education (MS Ed); education (MS Ed, Ed D); educational administration (MS Ed); educational leadership (Ed D); gifted and talented education (MS Ed); secondary education (MS Ed); special education (MS Ed); teaching—elementary education (MS Ed); teaching—secondary reading (MS Ed).

College of Fine and Performing Arts *Degree program information:* Part-time and evening/weekend programs available. Offers fine and performing arts (MM); music education (MM); music history and literature (MM); music theory and composition (MM); performance (MM).

College of Health and Human Services *Degree program information:* Part-time and evening/weekend programs available. Offers criminal justice (MS); health and human services (MHHS); nursing (MSN); physical therapy (MPT); public health (MPH).

Warren P. Williamson Jr. College of Business Administration *Degree program information:* Part-time and evening/weekend programs available. Offers accounting (MBA); business administration (EMBA, MBA); executive business administration (EMBA); finance (MBA); management (MBA); marketing (MBA).

William Rayen College of Engineering *Degree program information:* Part-time and evening/weekend programs available. Offers civil, chemical, and environmental engineering (MSE); electrical engineering (MSE); engineering (MSE); mechanical and industrial engineering (MSE).

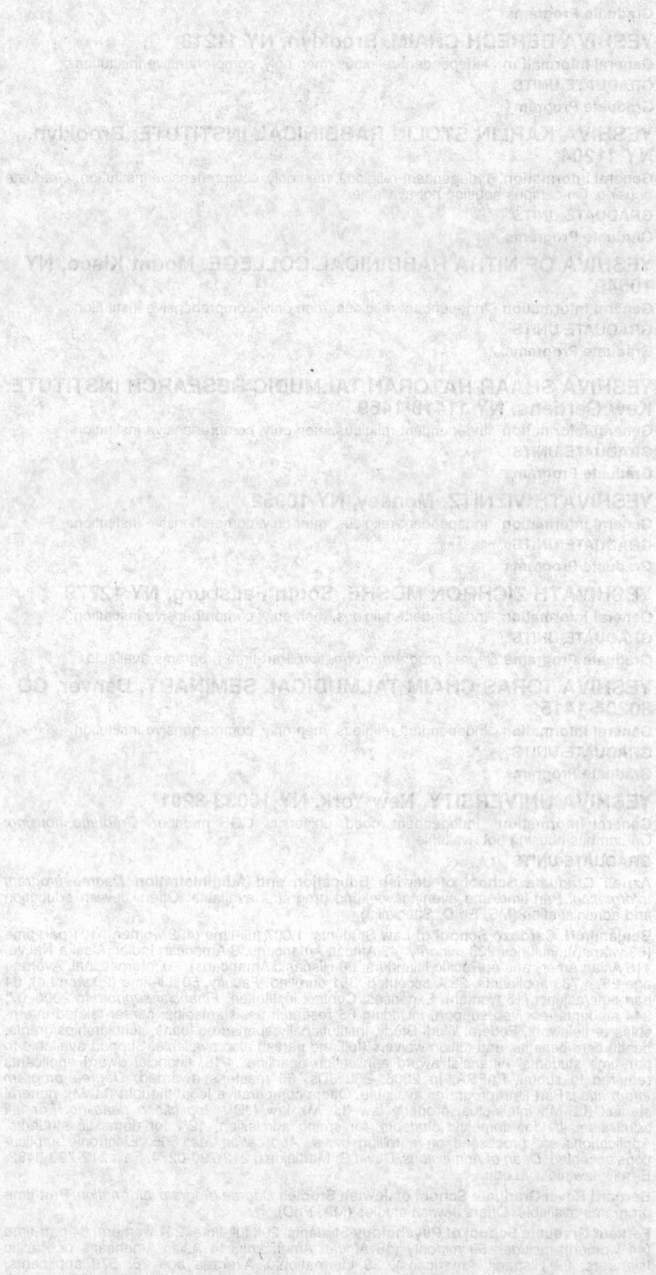

CLOSE-UPS OF INSTITUTIONS OFFERING GRADUATE AND PROFESSIONAL WORK

THE AMERICAN UNIVERSITY OF ATHENS

The School of Graduate Studies

Programs of Study

The School of Graduate Studies at The American University of Athens (AUA) offers a Master of Science in biomedical sciences, computer sciences, engineering and applied sciences, systems engineering, and telecommunications. The program in biomedical sciences prepares students for careers in the field of biology, linking it with medicine, drug design, and human disease diagnosis. The computer sciences program qualifies students for careers in computing research, business applications, and industrial progress. The Master of Science program in engineering and applied sciences prepares the student for a career in computing, research, business application, and industrial progress. The program of systems engineering equips students with the ability to utilize and become familiar with commercially available engineering software packages for solving complex problems. The mission of the program in telecommunications prepares students for careers in the area of telecommunications based on a strong knowledge of data communication, telecommunications principles, telecommunications management and regulations, network management, and wireless communications. The engineering and science degrees are research based in the labs of the internationally renowned Democritos Research Institute in Athens and the Pasteur Institute in central Athens as well as many others. In order to qualify for the M.S. degree, a student must complete 40 semester credit hours of course work and attain a minimum grade average of B-.

The School also offers a Master of Arts in business communication and a Master of Arts in politics and policymaking. A master's in business communication provides students with the tools for excelling in the ways of communicating and strengthens their skills in presentations, information technologies, and understanding the communication process. The program in politics and policymaking enables students to develop a critical understanding of the methods and epistemologies of political science, the art and science of policymaking, and the field of international relations. In order to qualify for the M.A. degree, a student must complete 40 semester credit hours of course work and attain a minimum grade average of B.

The Graduate School offers an M.B.A. with the following program specializations: international business, global financial analysis and management, and management with a focus on IT and e-commerce, operations, or people and organizations. The M.B.A. program enables students to develop skills and proficiencies essential to a dynamic professional and social environment. To qualify for an M.B.A. degree, a student must complete 44 semester credit hours of course work and attain a minimum grade average of B.

Graduate students in all programs must attend four noncredit seminars during the first semester. They are also required to submit a master's thesis at the end of their program that counts for 8 to 12 credit hours. The average duration of the master's programs is twelve months full-time and eighteen to twenty-four months part-time.

The doctorate programs of the School of Graduate Studies are biomedical sciences, business administration and international relations, computer sciences, general engineering, and politics and diplomacy. Any well-qualified person with a baccalaureate degree from a recognized college or university may apply for admission. A student's undergraduate program should include introductory studies in the humanities, social sciences, and natural sciences and engineering. The post-bachelor's doctorate program must be completed within seven years after the first registration for doctorate study. The post-master's doctorate program must be completed within five years.

Research Facilities

The library houses a wide variety of reference books and slides. Electronic data retrieval is also available, allowing access to the main European and American libraries and data banks. In addition to the library, there are several useful libraries in the area for use by graduate students. The Learning Resource Center is an academic service organization whose purpose is to enhance the teaching research mission at the University by creating and maintaining core resources, including library and information services, computing services, and telecommunications; facilitating and contributing to the development of AUA educational programs; and establishing global access to informational, educational, research, and management resources. Other facilities on campus include multimedia equipment and physics, biology, chemistry, and electronics laboratories with state-of-the-art equipment.

Financial Aid

Financial aid is available in the form of teaching, research, and other graduate assistantships, which are available in most programs. The total maximum workload for full-time graduate students is 15 hours per week. Graduate assistants must be full-time matriculated students with a GPA of 3.0 or higher.

Cost of Study

Spring and fall 2007 tuition for full-time students is €14,000 for M.A. or M.S. degree programs and €15,400 for the M.B.A. degree program. For part-time students, tuition is €350 per semester credit hour.

Spring and fall 2007 tuition for the post-bachelor's doctorate degree, the D.B.A. degree, and the post-master's doctorate degree is €500 per credit hour.

Living and Housing Costs

Graduate students are housed in fully equipped residence centers. Costs are €2900 (double) and €3400 (single) per academic year. Books and supplies cost about €250 per semester. Food and miscellaneous personal expenses for twelve months are approximately €2000 for a student with a conservative lifestyle. There is also a €400 insurance charge.

Student Group

The Graduate School has an enrollment of 38 students, 21 of whom are part-time. Thirty percent receive assistantships; 40 percent are international students. The School of Graduate Studies seeks to admit highly motivated, creative, intelligent, and career-focused aspiring leaders. An important criterion is a mix of previous work experience and educational background.

Location

The Graduate School is conveniently located in the heart of Athens, accessible to the Metro and bus transportation, public libraries, research centers, museums, and archeological sites. Athens is a warm and exciting city belonging to that privileged class of historic cities of antiquity that offers students a fascinating selection of cultural events. Greece has the reputation of being one of the safest and most hospitable countries of Europe.

The University

Founded in 1982, The American University of Athens was recently upgraded to the status of a teaching and research institution and has an enrollment of approximately 1,000 students. Coeducational in all divisions, AUA has students from the U.S., Greece, and thirty-eight other countries. The small-sized classes, the use of English instruction, the highly qualified faculty members, curricula, and teaching methodologies reflect the educational philosophy and structure of an American university.

AUA's distinguished graduate faculty members contribute to the University's growing reputation as a research university. Many faculty members serve as consultants to government and business, thus bringing their knowledge and experience into the classroom. They are accessible to assist, advise, and solve problems and are committed to meeting the learning needs of their students.

Applying

Applicants to the master's programs are required to submit an appropriate bachelor's degree from a recognized institution and evidence of capacity for productive work in the field selected, such as may be indicated by undergraduate grades. Some programs have additional requirements. Students whose native language is not English must submit a TOEFL score of at least 550. Students are admitted for any semester. The student's application, university degree (certified copy), two recommendation forms, resume, and application fee of €100 must be sent to the address listed in the contact information. A personal interview is also required. Transfer students are allowed to transfer no more than 8 credits with an average grade of B or higher. They are encouraged to file applications two months prior to the beginning of the semester of enrollment. Applicants must arrange for official transcripts of all previous college records to be sent directly to AUA. International students are required to submit additional documentation for immigration purposes.

Correspondence and Information

Office of Admissions
The School of Graduate Studies
The American University of Athens
Kifissias Avenue and 4 Sochou Street
Athens 11525
Greece

Phone: 30210-7259301-2
Fax: 30210-7259304
E-mail: info@aua.edu
Web site: http://www.aua.edu

THE FACULTY

Konstandinos Filis, Coordinator, Telecommunications Program; Ph.D. (electrical engineering), SMU, 1987.
Demetrios Gizelis, Professor; Ph.D. (economics), New School, 1983.
Donald Gordon, Associate Professor; Ph.D. (sociology), York, 1986.
Konstantinos Indounas, Professor; Ph.D. (marketing communication), Athens University of Economics and Business, 2003.
Michael Kabalouris, Professor; Ph.D. (economics), McMaster, 1985.
Achilles C. Kanellopoulos, Professor; Ph.D., Cape Town, 1978.
Nick C. Kanellopoulos, Professor; Ph.D. (chemical engineering), Rochester, 1975.
Athanasios Kapsalis, Professor; Ph.D. (computer science), East Anglia (England), 1996.
Eleftheria Laiou, Assistant Professor; Ph.D. (clinical chemistry), Wayne State, 2000.
George Miliaras, Associate Professor; Ph.D. (mathematics), Iowa State, 1988.
Tadeusz Olma, Associate Professor; Ph.D. (electronics), Wroclaw Technical (Poland), 1979.
Nic Panagopoulos, Associate Professor; Ph.D., (English and drama), Royal Holloway and Bedford New College (London), 1994.
Panagiotis Papadopoulos, Coordinator, Engineering and Systems Engineering Programs; Ph.D. (mechanical engineering), Illinois, 1991.
Elias Plakokefalos, Assistant Professor; Ph.D., (molecular biology), Thessalia (Greece), 2002.
Panagiota Plessa, Coordinator, Computer Science Program; Ph.D., (applied computer science), Athens University of Economics, 1993.
Rita Roussos, Director, Graduate School; Ph.D. (art history), London, 1999.
Wolfgang Schlyter, Professor; Ph.D. (aesthetics), Uppsala (Sweden), 1981.
Christina Sinou, Assistant Professor; Ph.D. (philosophy), Athens National Capodistrian, 2001.
Nickolas Siscoglou, Associate Professor; Ph.D. (applied management and decision science), Walden, 2001.
Maria Skolarikou, Assistant Professor; Ph.D. (political science), Southern Illinois, 2003.
Antonis Stamatakis, Coordinator, Biomedical Science Program; Ph.D. (biology and neurobiology), Crete (Greece), 2000.
Iraklis Varlamis, Professor; Ph.D. (computer science), Athens University of Economics and Business (Greece), 2003.
Athanasios Vasilakos, Associate Professor; Ph.D. (computer engineering), Patras (Greece), 1988.
Eleni Vernadou, Professor; Ph.D. (chemistry), Nottingham (England), 2004.
Angelis Vlahou, Professor; Ph.D. (political science), Southern Illinois, 2004.

ANGELO STATE UNIVERSITY

College of Graduate Studies

Programs of Study

Angelo State University offers programs in twenty-two areas of study, leading to Master of Arts, Master of Business Administration (M.B.A.), Master of Education, Master of Professional Accountancy, Master of Public Administration, Master of Physical Therapy (M.P.T.), Master of Science, and Master of Science in Nursing (M.S.N.) degrees as well as integrated B.B.A./M.B.A. (accounting), B.B.A./Master of Professional Accountancy, and RN-to-M.S.N. degrees.

Major areas of study include accounting, animal science, biology, business administration, communication, counseling psychology (with course work leading to Texas state licensure as a Licensed Professional Counselor or a psychological associate), curriculum and instruction, educational diagnostics, educational guidance and counseling, English (traditional research thesis and creative writing thesis options), general psychology, history, industrial/organizational psychology, interdisciplinary studies, kinesiology, nursing, physical therapy, public administration, reading specialization, school administration, and student development and leadership in higher education. Those programs in education that have Texas State Professional Certification meet the academic requirements to sit for the certification exam. The M.S.N. program is an online program.

Research Facilities

The Porter Henderson Library has comprehensive electronic resources, including an online catalog and a campuswide fiber-optic computer network with Internet connectivity. The total library holdings surpass 1 million items in a variety of formats. Resources include a partial depository for federal documents, a depository for Texas state documents, and the West Texas Collection, which contains numerous primary sources in the forms of diaries, journals, and memoirs of early settlers and pioneers from Texas.

The 6,000-acre Management, Instruction, and Research Center is a multipurpose agricultural production and wildlife management area. This multimillion-dollar complex includes four instructional and research laboratories for animal science, animal anatomy and physiology, animal reproduction, animal nutrition, wildlife management, wool and mohair technology, and plant and range sciences.

The graduate programs are supported by seven state-of-the-art microcomputer labs, more than 100 software packages, and a 20:1 student-computer ratio. Additional special facilities include the Small Business Development Center, International Trade Office, Language Learning Center, and school-based clinics.

Financial Aid

Academic Excellence Graduate Scholarships (AEGS), ranging from $800 to $5400 for the academic year, have summer extensions available and are awarded on a competitive basis to full-time or part-time graduate students. Carr Research Scholarships in the amount of $3000 plus itemized expenses up to $500 are available to support research projects.

Teaching assistantships paying $10,251 per academic year are available in some departments. Students must have completed 18 hours of graduate work in the field in which they teach and meet other criteria. Most graduate assistantships pay a maximum of $5413 per academic year, and they are available in most departments. Summer assistantships, residence hall assistantships, and student loans are also available.

Cost of Study

For the 2006–07 regular fall and spring semesters, tuition for students taking 9 semester credit hours per year was $3246.20 for Texas residents and $8196.20 for nonresidents. Additional expenses include the cost of books and supplies, parking fees, and special course fees. Tuition and fees are subject to change without notice.

Living and Housing Costs

Limited dormitory housing is available. Information about on-campus housing may be obtained from the Residence Life Office at 325-942-2035.

Student Group

Graduate student enrollment is approximately 450, and the total student population is 6,200. The graduate group is composed of 66 percent women, with approximately two thirds of all students attending part-time.

Location

Angelo State University is located in San Angelo, Texas (population 93,000). San Angelo, county seat of Tom Green County, is located in the heart of west Texas at the juncture of the Middle and North Concho Rivers. The city is a trading and shopping center for those in the ranching, farming, and oil industries and is an important medical and retirement center. Three lakes, a symphony orchestra, theaters, art galleries, museums, good shopping districts, proximity to the Texas hill country, and its famous friendly attitude make San Angelo an attractive place to live and study.

The University and The College

Angelo State University, which was established in 1965, is a regional comprehensive institution of higher learning offering programs in the liberal and fine arts, sciences, teacher education, education for the health professions, and business administration. The purpose of the College of Graduate Studies is to provide advanced specialized training that strengthens the academic and professional competence of its students. The graduate programs are designed to develop students' capacities for independent study, train students in the techniques of research, and acquaint them with research in their fields of study. Angelo State University is part of the Texas State University System.

Applying

All persons seeking admission to the College of Graduate Studies must complete and file an application and residency form, which is available on the Web or in the office of the College of Graduate Studies. An official copy of all transcripts of credits from all colleges and universities attended must be received directly from the institution(s). M.B.A. applicants must submit GMAT scores; applicants to all other programs must submit GRE scores. A $40 application fee is required of domestic students and $50 of international students. Students may apply for fall, spring, or summer admission, with the exception of Master of Physical Therapy and Master of Science in industrial/organizational psychology applicants. Applications for the M.P.T. program are accepted in the fall and spring preceding the summer when classes begin. Applications for the M.S. program have a February 1 deadline for classes beginning the following fall

Correspondence and Information

College of Graduate Studies
Angelo State University
ASU Station #11025
San Angelo, Texas 76909-1025

Phone: 325-942-2169
Fax: 325-942-2194
E-mail: graduate.school@angelo.edu
Web site: http://www.angelo.edu/gradschool

DEPARTMENT HEADS AND GRADUATE PROGRAM ADVISORS

Accounting, Economics, Finance: Dr. Tom Bankston, Department Head; Dr. Norman Sunderman, Program Advisor (telephone: 325-942-2046).
Animal Science: Dr. Gil Engdahl, Department Head; Dr. Cody Scott, Program Advisor (telephone: 325-942-2027).
Biology: Dr. J. Kelly McCoy, Department Head; Dr. Bonnie Amos, Program Advisor (telephone: 325-942-2189).
Business Administration: Dr. Tom Badgett, Department Head; Dr. Dan Khanna, Program Advisor (telephone: 325-942-2383).
Communications: Dr. June Smith, Department Head; Dr. Jeff Boone, Program Advisor (telephone: 325-942-2130 Ext. 359).
Education: Dr. Fritz Leifeste, Head, Department of Teacher Education (telephone: 325-942-2052 Ext. 266).
Curriculum and Instruction, Elementary Education: Dr. Judith Hakes, Program Advisor (telephone: 325-942-2052 Ext. 259).
Curriculum and Instruction, Instructional Technology: Dr. Nancy Hadley, Program Advisor (telephone: 325-942-2052 Ext. 252).
Curriculum and Instruction, Secondary Education: Dr. Nancy Hadley, Program Advisor (telephone: 325-942-2052 Ext. 252).
Curriculum and Instruction, Special Education: Dr. Mack McCoulskey, Program Advisor (telephone: 325-942-2052 Ext. 269).
Curriculum and Instruction, Reading: Dr. Cheryl Hines, Program Advisor (telephone: 325-942-2052 Ext. 283).
Guidance and Counseling: Dr. David Tarver, Program Advisor (telephone: 325-942-2052 Ext. 262).
Student Development and Leadership in Higher Education: Dr. David Tarver, Program Advisor (telephone: 325-942-2052 Ext. 262).
Reading Specialist: Dr. Cheryl Hines, Program Advisor (telephone: 325-942-2052 Ext. 283).
School Administration: Dr. Fritz Leifeste, Program Advisor (telephone: 325-942-2052 Ext. 266).
Superintendent Certificate: Dr. Lu Stephens, Program Advisor (telephone: 325-942-2052 Ext. 240).
English: Dr. Nancy Allen, Department Head; Dr. Terence A. Dalrymple, Program Advisor (telephone: 325-942-2273).
Government: Dr. Ed C. Olson, Department Head (telephone: 325-942-2262).
Public Administration: Dr. Jack Barbour, Program Advisor (telephone: 325-942-2262 Ext. 282).
History: Dr. Virginia Noelke, Department Head; Dr. Shirley Eoff, Program Director (telephone: 325-942-2203).
Interdisciplinary Studies: Dr. Carol Diminnie, Program Advisor (telephone: 325-942-2169).
Kinesiology: Dr. Doyle Carter, Department Head; Dr. Steven Snowden, Program Director (telephone: 325-942-2173).
Nursing: Dr. Leslie Mayrand, Department Head; Dr. Susan Wilkinson, Program Advisor (telephone: 325-942-2060 Ext. 290).
Physical Therapy: Dr. Shelly Weise, Department Head; Mark Pape, Program Advisor (telephone: 325-942-2545).
Psychology: Dr. William Davidson, Department Head.
Counseling Psychology: Dr. Sangeeta Singg, Program Advisor (telephone: 325-942-2068 Ext. 251).
General Psychology: Dr. James Forbes, Program Advisor (telephone: 325-942-2068 Ext. 249).
Industrial/Organizational Psychology: Dr. Kraig Schell, Program Advisor (telephone: 325-942-2766 Ext. 224).

ARCADIA UNIVERSITY

Graduate and Professional Studies

Programs of Study

The Master of Arts (M.A.) degree is offered in counseling psychology, English, and humanities. The M.A. in counseling psychology prepares students for work in schools (elementary and/or secondary) or in community, hospital, business, or industry settings. The M.A. in English offers three tracks in the following specializations: professional writing and teaching writing, writing and communications, and literary and critical studies. The M.A. in humanities provides an interdisciplinary study of one of the following areas: literature and modern language; fine arts, theater, and music; or history, philosophy, and religion. The Master of Arts in Education (M.A.Ed.) offers areas of concentrations in art, computer education, English, environmental education, history, mathematics, music, psychology, theater arts, and written communication. The environmental education program offered in cooperation with the Schuylkill Center for Environmental Education can also lead to Pennsylvania certification.

The Master of Education (M.Ed.) includes areas of concentration in art, computers and technology, early childhood education, educational leadership, elementary education, language arts, mathematics education, reading, school library science, science education, secondary education, and special education. Pennsylvania certification is available in all of the above areas except computer education and language arts. Secondary certification includes biology, chemistry, English, general science, mathematics, and social studies. Principal K–12, ESL, superintendent's letter of eligibility, and supervisory certification are also available. The Doctor of Education (Ed.D.) is offered in special education. This three-year, part-time program is designed to increase the level of professional expertise among practitioners in the field and find ways to effectively implement best-practices programs in school settings.

The Master of Science in Forensic Science (M.S.F.S.) is earned through a two-year, full-time program operated in partnership with the Fredric Rieders Family Renaissance Foundation (FRFRF) and in collaboration NMS Labs, one of the nation's premier forensic science laboratories. Arcadia's M.S.F.S. program focuses primarily on criminalistics, forensic toxicology, and forensic biology and, secondarily, on technical investigation. The Master of Science in Genetic Counseling (M.S.G.C.) is earned through a two-year, full-time program that includes a combination of scientific, medical, psychological, and clinical courses and practical experiences. The program, which is accredited by the American Board of Genetic Counseling, prepares counselors to deal with the new medical technologies related to human genetics and reproduction and to apply knowledge from the natural sciences and psychology in order to address the needs of patients, community lay groups, and health and human services professionals.

The Master of Science in Public Health (M.S.P.H.) is an entry-level degree in the field of public health. It trains graduates to work effectively as public-health professionals in a wide array of health-related organizations. Both the Master of Science (M.S.) degree in health education program and the Master of Arts (M.A.) degree in health education program are designed for school health and physical education teachers and community health educators. Both degree programs provide a breadth of knowledge in health education and train health educators to assess needs and plan and implement programs within the school and community settings. The Doctor of Physical Therapy (D.P.T.) is earned through a full-time, entry-level program that provides the academic study and clinical experience required by the American Physical Therapy Association (APTA) for work as a professional physical therapist. The program consists of 2½ academic years of formal course work integrated with clinical internships. The program is accredited by the APTA. The Transitional Doctor of Physical Therapy (T.D.P.T.) is a transitional pathway for practicing clinicians intending to make their final education congruent with students graduating from entry-level D.P.T. programs.

The Master of Arts in International Peace and Conflict Resolution (M.A.I.P.C.R.) features a year of study and fieldwork experience abroad and prepares students for career positions in nongovernmental organizations (NGOs) and intergovernmental organizations (IGOs). The Master of Medical Science (M.M.S.) physician assistant studies program consists of a two-year educational program, divided into didactic course work, clinical instruction, and clinical rotations. Dual-degree programs combine the M.M.S. degree with either the M.S.P.H. or M.S. degree in health education. The Certificate of Advanced Study (C.A.S.) program is a post-master's program that allows specialization and research in an area of education but does not lead to a graduate degree. The Master of Business Administration (M.B.A.) with an international perspective is a part-time, accelerated program that is completed in eighteen months. The program couples academic course work with leading industry technology and a focus on international business, which includes two separate one-week study-abroad sessions—one studying business in a developed economy and one in a developing economy.

Research Facilities

The Landman Library has 139,203 volumes, more than 57,000 units of microfilm, and 798 print periodical subscriptions. Students have access to several online bibliographical databases, and materials are made available through interlibrary loan and through membership in a cooperative group of academic libraries. For students of science and psychology, there are excellent laboratory facilities in Boyer Hall. Internet services for students include a campuswide wireless network, Telnet, file transfer protocol (ftp), and e-mail. Student laboratories are located in Boyer Hall, which houses three PC labs and one Macintosh lab; Landman Library; Brubaker Hall; and the Educational Enhancement Center in Taylor Hall. In addition, some academic departments (such as fine arts, biology, and psychology) maintain computer equipment for their specific disciplines. All instructional buildings house PC-equipped teaching classrooms. Specialized library material is available in different programs' resource centers as well as an online medical library.

Financial Aid

Arcadia offers several partial-tuition scholarships to its top applicants in each of the full-time graduate programs. A limited number of graduate assistantships are available to full-time students, and all students enrolled in one of the full-time programs or those matriculating in any graduate program and taking at least 6 credits per semester may apply for a Federal Stafford Student Loan. Several alternative loans are also available, as is a ten-month interest-free payment plan through Key Education Resources.

Cost of Study

Tuition for 2006–07 for part-time graduate programs was $550 per credit. Tuition for the physical therapy, genetic counseling, physician assistant, forensic science, and international peace and conflict resolution programs ranged from $21,840 to $28,500 per year.

Living and Housing Costs

There are a variety of housing options in proximity to the University.

Student Group

Graduate enrollment at Arcadia University consists of approximately 1,750 students. The majority of students study part-time. The genetic counseling, forensic science, international peace and conflict resolution, and physician assistant programs require a two-year, full-time commitment.The Doctor of Physical Therapy requires a 2½-year, full-time commitment.

Location

The University is located in Glenside, Pennsylvania, a suburb of Philadelphia, 14 miles from the center of the city. Theaters, museums, and the Philadelphia Orchestra are half an hour away by train or car. On campus, there are always a variety of lectures, concerts, and plays.

The University

Arcadia University, founded in 1853, is a comprehensive university committed to providing an education that integrates liberal learning with career preparation. The University operates one of the country's largest campus-based centers for study abroad and supports a wide array of cultural, intellectual, and recreational activities.

Applying

Admission to graduate programs is based on an overall evaluation of credentials, including the applicant's undergraduate record, which should show a B average or better in the major field. Applicants to programs other than genetic counseling, international peace and conflict resolution, and physical therapy should apply at least six weeks before the semester in which they plan to enroll. A $50 application fee must accompany the application. Applicants to the genetic counseling and physical therapy programs must apply by January 15. All applications for the physician assistant studies program are processed by the Centralized Application Service for Physician Assistants (CASPA) at http://www.caspaonline.org. Applications are not accepted by CASPA after January 15. The deadline for the doctorate in special education and the forensic science program is February 15 and the deadline for the international peace and conflict resolution program is April 1. Applicants who do not fulfill admission requirements or who have undergraduate deficiencies may be admitted conditionally.

Correspondence and Information

Office of Enrollment Management
Arcadia University
450 S. Easton Road
Glenside, Pennsylvania 19038-3295

Phone: 215-572-2910
877-272-2342 (toll-free)
Fax: 215-572-4049
E-mail: admiss@arcadia.edu
Web site: http://www.arcadia.edu

Arcadia University

FACULTY HEADS AND PROGRAM COORDINATORS

Michael L. Berger, Vice President for Academic Affairs and Provost; Ed.D., Columbia.
Mark P. Curchack, Dean of Graduate and Professional Studies; Ph.D., Berkeley.
Maureen Guim, Associate Dean of Graduate and Professional Studies; M.Ed., Arcadia.

Chairpersons

Business: Annette Halpin, Associate Professor; Ph.D., La Salle.
Counseling: Carol A. Lyman, Administrator; M.A., College of New Jersey.
Education: Steve Gulkus, Associate Professor; Ph.D., West Virginia.
English: Richard Wertime, Professor; Ph.D., Pennsylvania.
Forensic Science: Laurence Presley, Director; M.S., Pittsburgh.
Genetic Counseling: Kathleen D. Valverde, Assistant Professor; M.S., C.G.C., Sarah Lawrence.
Health Education: Andrea Crivelli-Kovach, Associate Professor; Ph.D., Temple.
Humanities: Richard Wertime, Professor; Ph.D., Pennsylvania.
International Peace and Conflict Resolution: Warren Haffar, Assistant Professor; Ph.D., Pennsylvania.
Physical Therapy: Rebecca Craik, Professor; Ph.D., Temple.
Physician Assistant: Michael Dryer, Assistant Professor; Dr.P.H., George Washington.
Public Health: Andrea Crivelli-Kovach, Associate Professor; Ph.D., Temple.

ARMSTRONG ATLANTIC STATE UNIVERSITY

A Unit of the University System of Georgia
School of Graduate Studies

Programs of Study

Armstrong Atlantic State University (AASU) offers a wide variety of master's-level degree programs through the College of Arts and Sciences, the College of Education, the College of Health Professions, and the School of Computing. The College of Arts and Sciences offers master's degrees in criminal justice, history, and liberal and professional studies. The College of Education offers master's degrees in adult education, curriculum and instruction, early childhood education, English education, middle grades education, secondary education (broad-field science education and mathematics education), special education (behavior disorders and learning disabilities), and a new Master of Arts in Teaching. The College of Health Professions offers master's degrees in communicative disorders, health services administration, nursing, nursing/health services administration (dual degree), physical therapy, public health, and sports medicine. The School of Computing offers a master's degree in computer science.

A minimum of half of the hours required for a degree must be earned in residence. AASU courses taken off campus as part of an approved external degree program are considered to have been completed in residence.

AASU also offers a doctorate in physical therapy as part of a consortium with the Medical College of Georgia and North Georgia College and State University.

Graduate certificates are offered in adult education, educational technology, heritage tourism, and strength and conditioning. Post-master's certificates are offered in adult-health nurse specialist studies, adult nurse practitioner studies, and nursing administration.

Research Facilities

The library collections consist of approximately 800,000 items, including 185,000 book volumes, 600,000 microforms, and 9,000 individual audiovisual titles, including compact discs, records, laser discs, slides, and video recordings. In addition, the library subscribes to 1,043 journals and newspapers. A special collection, the Florence Powell Minis Collection, contains publications of the University, published works by Savannah authors, and published material about Savannah and the surrounding area. The collection also includes first editions by Conrad Aiken, Flannery O'Connor, and other Savannah authors. Through participation in state, regional, and national resource-sharing agreements with other libraries, Lane Library is able to borrow and obtain for its clientele materials that are not available at Armstrong Atlantic. Interlibrary loan materials arrive by UPS, fax, and electronic delivery services. Off-campus library services for Armstrong Atlantic programs are supported by local libraries. Off-campus students may access library resources at home by accessing the online catalog, ORCA. Interlibrary loans may also be requested through ORCA. In addition, more than 100 databases are available on GALILEO, a system of databases shared among the thirty-four University System of Georgia libraries. GALILEO may be accessed by registered Armstrong Atlantic students from home via password. Laptop computers are available to graduate students. Computer labs are located at various sites on campus. A technology help desk facility is also available.

Financial Aid

Employment programs, grants, loans, out-of-state tuition waivers, scholarships, fellowship programs, and graduate assistantships are available. For more information, students should visit the Web site at http://gs.armstrong.edu/aid.html. Students may also request information via e-mail at graduate@mail.armstrong.edu.

Cost of Study

For the 2007–08 two-semester academic year, tuition and fees for full-time study (12 or more semester hours) are $3784 for Georgia residents and $13,460 for nonresidents.

Living and Housing Costs

AASU offers single-student housing in two- and four-bedroom furnished apartments with full kitchens. Each student has a private bedroom. For the 2005–06 academic year, housing in the residence halls on campus cost $5220 to $6600 per room per year. Many graduate students elect to live in apartments that are close to the campus or in historic Savannah.

Student Group

The total enrollment of 6,728 students in fall 2006 included 5,915 undergraduates and 642 graduate students. Of the 642 graduate students, 27.5 percent were enrolled full-time (9 or more semester hours) and 62.2 percent were enrolled part-time (8 or fewer semester hours). Approximately 87 percent were Georgia residents; the rest were either out-of-state or international students. The average age of the graduate students was 35 years.

The Graduate Student Coordinating Council provides representation for graduate students on campus. Many academic areas also offer graduate student associations.

Location

Armstrong Atlantic students find much to enjoy about living in the city of Savannah, the major urban area (population 280,000) of coastal Georgia. As Georgia's founding city, Savannah has all the historic and cultural variety of a metropolitan city, with the added advantage of the ocean at its back door. A temperate climate encourages year-round outdoor activities and recreation.

AASU is located on a 250-acre campus in a residential area of the city, which promotes a feeling of freedom and security on campus. Atlanta, Georgia, is a 4.5 hour's drive away, and Jacksonville, Florida, and Columbia, South Carolina, are each 2 hours away from AASU.

The University

Armstrong Atlantic was founded in 1935 as Armstrong Junior College to enhance educational opportunities in the community. Armstrong Atlantic State University now offers more than seventy-five academic programs and majors in the College of Arts and Sciences, the College of Health Professions, the College of Education, the School of Computing, and the School of Graduate Studies. AASU is a part of the University System of Georgia, which includes thirty-four state-operated institutions of higher education.

More than 400 full- and part-time faculty members teach at the University; 158 hold graduate faculty membership.

Applying

An application can be obtained by contacting the School of Graduate Studies or through the Graduate Admission's Web site at http://www.gs.armstrong.edu/admissions.html. The following additional graduate study information may be viewed online: the graduate catalog, financial aid guidelines, student services, assistantship guidelines, thesis guidelines, and faculty research interests.

Correspondence and Information

School of Graduate Studies
Armstrong Atlantic State University
11935 Abercorn Street
Savannah, Georgia 31419

Phone: 912-927-5377
Fax: 912-921-5586
E-mail: graduate@mail.armstrong.edu
Web site: http://www.gs.armstrong.edu

GRADUATE COORDINATORS

Adult Education: Patricia Coberly, Graduate Coordinator, Department of Special and Adult Education (phone: 912-961-3739; fax: 912-961-3054; e-mail: patricia.coberly@armstrong.edu). The Master of Education (M.Ed.) program in adult education and community leadership prepares participants to better disseminate their knowledge and expertise to others through a deeper, comprehensive understanding of the adult learner with a plan of study that builds upon prior professional preparation and experience. Three areas of study are available: human resource development, literacy education, and technology-based learning—all of which allow copious opportunities to develop and refine leadership skills with a focus on community development.

Communicative Disorders: Donna Brooks, Graduate Coordinator, College of Health Professions (phone: 912-961-3167; fax: 912-921-5591; e-mail: donna.brooks@armstrong.edu). The ASHA-accredited graduate program provides students with the academic and clinical education required for eligibility for the certificate of clinical competency.

Computer Science: Ray Hashemi, Graduate Coordinator, Department of Computer Science (phone: 912-921-2060; fax: 912-921-5606; e-mail: ray.hashemi@armstrong.edu). The M.S.C.S. degree provides students a solid foundation in the theory and practice of computer science so that graduates can have the fundamentals necessary to evolve with the discipline.

Criminal Justice: Zaphon Wilson, Head, Department of Criminal Justice, Social and Political Science (phone: 912-927-5938; fax: 912-921-5876; e-mail: zaphon.wilson@armstrong.edu). The criminal justice program is one of only three such programs in Georgia. The program is housed within University Hall, which is the same building that the Law Enforcement Training Center (Regional Police Academy) is housed, and in proximity to the Regional Office of the Georgia Bureau of Investigation and State Crime Lab. Upon completion of the M.S.C.J. degree, students are eligible for careers in criminal justice agency administration, planning, policy development and analysis, and management.

Curriculum and Instruction: Ed Strausser, Graduate Coordinator, College of Education (phone: 912-961-3070; fax: 912-921-5587; e-mail: ed.strausser@armstrong.edu). The Master of Education in Curriculum and Instruction Program is designed for practitioners in the field. It requires certified teachers to distribute courses across their subject disciplines and in areas of applied pedagogy. Several courses are either Web based or Web enhanced.

Early Childhood Education: John Hobe, Graduate Coordinator, College of Education (phone: 912- 927-5281; fax 912-921-5587; e-mail: john.hobe@armstrong.edu). The program in early childhood education prepares reflective master teachers who can address the academic, social, and emotional development of students in preschool through fifth grade (P–5). The program of study provides degree candidates with the skills to know the content they teach and to use variety of pedagogical strategies, including technology, to teach their P–5 students. The program of study also strives to ensure that degree candidates are committed and respectful of the diversity of all P–5 students and their learning, are responsible for managing and monitoring student learning, systematically reflect about their practice and learn from experience, and are professional members of a learning community.

Health Services Administration: Joey Crosby, Graduate Coordinator, Department of Health Science (phone: 912-921-7316; fax: 912-921-7350; e-mail: joey.crosby@armstrong.edu). Students wishing to design, implement, and manage health delivery systems learn the fundamentals of strategic planning, marketing, administration, and finance and the intricacies of the skills necessary to assist those who strive to maintain the health of others. The M.H.S.A. program at AASU is fully accredited by the Commission on Accreditation for Health Management Education (CAHME), one of only two such programs in the state of Georgia.

History: Christopher Hendricks, Graduate Coordinator, Department of History (phone: 912-927-5283; fax: 912-921-5581; e-mail: christopher.hendricks@armstrong.edu). Savannah provides an excellent laboratory for the student of history. Students may concentrate their graduate studies in one of the following three areas: American history, European history, or public history. Aside from a nationally recognized public history program that supports work in heritage tourism, museum studies, oral history, folklife, historic preservation, vernacular architecture, and other public history areas. Savannah contains the city and county legal and political records, the Georgia Historical Society and its archives, several noteworthy museums, and a cosmopolitan population that is interested in recording and learning about its various ethnic and religious cultures.

Liberal and Professional Studies: Richard Nordquist, Graduate Coordinator, Office of Liberal Studies (phone: 912-921-5991; fax 912-921-7355; e-mail: richard.nordquist@armstrong.edu). The M.A. in liberal and professional studies is an innovative interdisciplinary program for working professionals and recent college graduates who desire both personal enrichment and professional development. At the core of the program are four courses that focus on the values, research strategies, communication skills, and critical-thinking skills required for personal growth and career advancement. In addition, students elect to follow one of three tracks: gender and women's studies (coordinated by Teresa Winterhalter, teresa.winterhalter@armstrong.edu); international studies (coordinated by William Daugherty, william.daugherty@armstrong.edu); and leadership studies (coordinated by Richard Nordquist, richard.nordquist@armstrong.edu). All students in the program have opportunities to apply their knowledge and extend their professional experience through off-campus internships and guided projects.

Middle Grades Education: Mike Mink, Graduate Coordinator, College of Education (phone: 912-921-5547; fax: 912-921-5587; e-mail: michael.mink@armstrong.edu). The Master of Education (M.Ed.) middle grades program prepares a certified master teacher who can address the academic, social, and emotional development of the student in grades 4 through 8.

Nursing: Anita Nivens, Graduate Coordinator, Department of Nursing (phone: 912-927-5724; fax: 921-920-6579; e-mail: anita.nivens@armstrong.edu). The graduate program in nursing offers registered professional nurses the opportunity to pursue a master's degree in nursing in one of five tracks: adult clinical nurse specialist studies, adult nurse practitioner studies, advanced practice nursing, clinical nurse leader, and nursing administration. Post-master's nursing certificates are available in adult clinical nurse specialist studies, adult nurse practitioner studies, and nursing administration. The RN options track is available for nurses with a diploma or associate degree in nursing to enter and progress through the baccalaureate and the master's degrees.

Nursing/Health Services Administration (Dual Degree): Anita Nivens, Graduate Coordinator, Department of Nursing (phone: 912-927-5724; fax: 921-920-6579; e-mail: anita.nivens@armstrong.edu). The graduate programs in nursing and health services administration offer registered professional nurses the opportunity to pursue a dual master's degree with a specialty focus in nursing and health services administration.

Physical Therapy: David Lake, Graduate Coordinator, Department of Physical Therapy (phone: 912-921-2327; e-mail: david.lake@armstrong.edu). The physical therapy program is a full-time program involving nine semesters of study. It involves thirty weeks of full-time clinical practice and additional part-time clinical experiences. This program uses a modified problem-based learning (PBL) approach. The program maintains an active learning environment that promotes independent thinking and clinical problem-solving skills. The Department of Physical Therapy received the 2000 Regents' Teaching Excellence Award for Departments in the University System of Georgia.

Public Health: Michael Mink, Graduate Coordinator, Department of Health Science (phone: 912-921-5480; fax: 912-921-7350; e-mail: michael.mink@armstrong.edu). The M.P.H. degree provides the student with a mastery of the appropriate theory, content/knowledge, and application of skills in areas of public health specific to the student's interest, as well as the ability to plan, implement, and evaluate programs that influence behavioral change conducive to the positive health of the community.

Special Education: Pam Harwood-Bedwell, Intern Graduate Coordinator, College of Education (phone: 912-961-3066; fax 912-961-3054; e-mail: pamela.harwood@armstrong.edu). The Master of Education (M.Ed.) program in general special education is an initial certification program. Graduates are prepared to provide educational services for students with exceptional learning needs whose IEP indicates instruction using the general education curriculum and participation in general statewide assessment. Advanced degrees are also available in special education: learning disabilities and special education: behavior disorders.

Sports Medicine: Robert LeFavi, Graduate Coordinator, College of Health Professions (phone: 912-921-5480; fax: 912-921-7350; e-mail: robert.lefavi@armstrong.edu). The program of study prepares graduate students to advance in their chosen field related to sports medicine (exercise science, strength and conditioning, sports nutrition, etc.) and/or to extend their expertise in sports medicine.

AUBURN UNIVERSITY

Graduate School

Programs of Study The Graduate School offers programs leading to the Doctor of Philosophy in aerospace engineering, agronomy and soils, animal and dairy sciences, biological sciences, biomedical sciences, botany and microbiology, chemical engineering, chemistry, civil engineering, computer science and software engineering, counseling psychology, counselor education, curriculum and teaching, discrete and statistical sciences, economics, electrical and computer engineering, English, entomology, fisheries and allied aquacultures, forestry, health and human performance, history, horticulture, human development and family studies, industrial and systems engineering, management, materials engineering, mathematics, mechanical engineering, nutrition and food science, pharmaceutical sciences, physics, plant pathology, poultry science, psychology, public administration, rehabilitation and special education, wildlife science, and zoology. The Doctor of Education is also offered with major areas of specialization including counseling and counseling psychology; educational foundations, leadership, and technology; health and human performance; and vocational and adult education. The Specialist in Education degree may be earned in all departments of the College of Education. The M.S. and M.A. are available in many areas, along with nonthesis master's degrees in a number of fields. Minors also are available in biochemistry, community planning, ecology, economic development, environmental studies, molecular biology, sports management, and urban forestry. The Graduate Outreach Program offers graduate-level courses to off-campus students in engineering, business administration, accountancy, rehabilitation, and special education, and hotel and restaurant management.

Auburn University has identified seven areas as peaks of excellence in graduate education: cell and molecular biosciences, detection and food safety, fisheries and allied aquacultures, forest sustainability, information technology, poultry products' safety and quality, and transportation. Students in these areas receive special consideration and support.

Research Facilities The University, which has a graduate faculty of more than 1,100, provides various specialized facilities for graduate research. Among these are the Space Power Institute, the Alabama Microelectronics Science and Technology Center, the Advanced Manufacturing Technology Center, the Agricultural Experiment Station, the Engineering Experiment Station, the Scott-Ritchey Small Animal Research Facility, the Center for the Arts and Humanities, the Center for Aging Studies, the National Center for Asphalt Technology, the Truman Pierce Institute for the Advancement of Teacher Education, the Institute for Biological Detection Systems, the Pulp and Paper Research and Education Center, the Dauphin Island Sea and Gulf Coast Research Laboratories, and the International Center for Aquaculture. Auburn is a member of the Oak Ridge Associated Universities Research Participation Program and has access to the facilities of the National Laboratory at Oak Ridge, the Savannah River Laboratory, the laboratories of the Puerto Rico Nuclear Center, and the University of Tennessee Atomic Energy Commission Agricultural Research Laboratory.

The main library has more than 2 million bound books and more than 2 million other books and materials in microformat. Subscriptions are maintained for 20,800 serials, including 12,800 journals. High-speed computer searches may be made in approximately 750 fields. The catalog is Web-based, including data bases, full-text materials, electronic document delivery, and digitized collections. The library is a U.S. depository, receiving government publications and documents; a map reference library with a collection of more than 124,700 maps; and a depository for U.S. patents. University Archives has more than 900 manuscript collections, 150,000 photographs, 7,060 oral history tapes and audio cassettes, and 4,400 motion picture reels.

Auburn University has complete Internet access through the Alabama Research and Education Network and is a member of the Internet II/UCAID consortium. This includes supercomputing capabilities and a fiber optic Ethernet network linking all buildings and offices on campus. Auburn is ranked among the top twenty-five most-wired universities in the United States.

Financial Aid Auburn University funds approximately 1,700 graduate assistantships annually. Many additional assistantships are provided through grants and contracts from external sources. Graduate teaching and research fellowships cover tuition and fees for graduate assistants.

Cost of Study Full-time (10 to 15 hours) tuition and fees for 2006–07 were $2400 per semester for Alabama residents and $7200 per semester for out-of-state residents. Nonresident fees do not apply to out-of-state students receiving a one-fourth-time or greater appointment as a graduate teaching assistant, research assistant, or assistant.

Living and Housing Costs Off-campus housing is available to graduate students. Off-campus housing includes a wide selection of apartments, private dormitories, and mobile-home facilities, averaging $2000 per semester. The director of housing provides information. The estimated student cost for one calendar year, including fees and room and board, is $17,000 for in-state and $26,000 for out-of-state students.

Student Group The total enrollment is more than 23,500, of whom 3,200 are graduate students. The student population comprises more than 12,000 men and more than 11,000 women. Represented are every state, the District of Columbia, Puerto Rico, the Virgin Islands, and more than eighty countries. Graduate School enrollment includes more than 1,400 women and more than 1,000 students from minority groups and foreign countries. More than half of the graduate students are employed by the University as teaching or research assistants.

Location The main campus of 1,871 acres occupies the entire southwest quadrant of the city of Auburn. The city's population is about 38,000, including resident students, in an area of 23 square miles. Auburn is 50 miles northeast of Montgomery, 110 miles southeast of Birmingham, and 115 miles southwest of Atlanta. Interstate 85 provides convenient access to Montgomery and Atlanta. The area has brief, mild winters and abundant sunshine.

The University Auburn is a state-assisted, comprehensive, research university with a storied past dating from 1856. It has a long tradition of academic excellence and graduate education, awarding its first undergraduate degree in 1860 and its first graduate degree in 1870. Since then it has awarded more than 37,000 graduate degrees, including 5,500 doctorates. It is classified by the Carnegie Foundation as Research University (high research activity). The largest university in Alabama, Auburn has twelve colleges and schools in addition to the Graduate School—Agriculture, Architecture, Business, Education, Engineering, Forestry and Wildlife Sciences, Human Sciences, Liberal Arts, Nursing, Pharmacy, Sciences and Mathematics, and Veterinary Medicine. More than 120 buildings occupy a campus of Southern charm graced with stately trees and abundant flowers. Auburn is accredited by the Southern Association of Colleges and Schools.

Applying Minimum requirements include a baccalaureate degree from an accredited four-year college or university and competitive scores on the General Test of the GRE or, in business, the Graduate Management Admission Test (GMAT). All application materials should be received at least six weeks before planned enrollment.

Correspondence and Information

Dr. George T. Flowers and Dr. Joe F. Pittman
Interim Deans of the Graduate School
Hargis Hall
Auburn University
Auburn, Alabama 36849-5122

Phone: 334-844-4700
Fax: 334-844-4348
E-mail: gradadm@auburn.edu
Web site: http://www.grad.auburn.edu

AREAS OF INSTRUCTION

The names of the programs and the degrees offered are listed along with the contact name, e-mail address, and telephone number. The area code for all telephone numbers is 334.

Accountancy (M.Ac.): Amy B. Campbell, mac@auburn.edu (844-6207).
Aerospace Engineering (M.A.E., M.S., Ph.D.): David Cicci, ciccida@auburn.edu (844-6820).
Agricultural Economics (M.Ag., M.S., Ph.D.): Henry Thompson thomph1@auburn.edu (844-4800).
Agronomy and Soils (M.Ag., M.S., Ph.D.): Harold Walker, walkerh@auburn.edu (844-4100).
Anatomy, Physiology, and Pharmacology (M.S., Ph.D.): Lauren G. Wolfe, wolfelg@auburn.edu (844-4100).
Animal Sciences (M.Ag., M.S., Ph.D.): Russell Muntifering, muntirb@auburn.edu (844-4160).
Biological Sciences (M.S., Ph.D.): Jack Feminella, feminjw@auburn.edu (844-4830).
Biomedical Sciences (M.S., Ph.D.): Carl A. Pinkert, cap@vetmed.auburn.edu (844-3700).
Building Science (M.B.C.): Construction: Steve Williams, willi14@auburn.edu (844-4518); Design-Build: Dennis Ruth, ruthden@auburn.edu (844-4285).
Business Administration (M.S., M.B.A.): Kim Kuerten, kuertka@auburn.edu (844-4060).
Chemical Engineering (M.Ch.E., M.S., Ph.D.): Ram Gupta, guptarb@auburn.edu (844-4827).
Chemistry and Biochemistry (M.S., Ph.D.): Vince Cammarata, cammavi@auburn.edu (844-4043).
Civil Engineering (M.C.E., M.S., Ph.D.): Frazier Parker, parkefr@auburn.edu (844-6284).
Communication (M.A. M.Com.): Susan Brinson, brinssl@auburn.edu (844-2727).
Communication Disorders (M.C.D., M.S.): Michael Moran, moranmj@auburn.edu (844-9600).
Community Planning (M.C.P.): John Pittari , pittajj@auburn.edu (844-4516).
Computer Science and Software Engineering (M.S.W.E., M.S., Ph.D.): David Umphress, umphrda@auburn.edu (844-6335).
Consumer Affairs (M.S.): Carol Warfield, warficl@auburn.edu (844-4084).
Counselor Education, Counseling Psychology, and School Psychology (M.Ed., M.S., Ed.D., Ed.S., Ph.D.): Randolph Pipes, pipesrb@auburn.edu (844-2878).
Curriculum and Teaching (M.Ed., M.S., Ed.S., Ph.D.): Kim Walls, wallski@auburn.edu (844-6892).
Economics (M.S.): John Jackson, jacksjd@auburn.edu (844-4910).
Educational Foundations, Leadership, and Technology (M.Ed., M.S., Ed.D., Ed.S., Ph.D.): Maria Witte, wittemm@auburn.edu (844-4460).
Electrical and Computer Engineering (M.E.E., M.S., Ph.D.): Victor P. Nelson, nelsovp@auburn.edu (844-1800).
English (M.A., Ph.D.): Hilary Wyss, wysshil@auburn.edu (844-4620).
Entomology (M.Ag., M.S., Ph.D.): Wayne Clark, clarkwe@auburn.edu (844-2565).
Finance (M.S.): John Jahera, jaherjs@auburn.edu (844-5344).
Fisheries and Allied Aquacultures (M.Aq., M.S., Ph.D.): Yolanda Brady, ybrady@acesag.auburn.edu (844-4786).
Forestry and Wildlife Sciences (M.N.R., M.S., Ph.D.): Greg Somers, somergl@auburn.edu (844-1007).
Geology (M.S.): Charles Savrda, savrdce@auburn.edu (844-4282).
Health and Human Performance (M.Ed., M.S., Ed.S., Ed.D., Ph.D.): Mary Rudisill, rudisme@auburn.edu (844-4483).
History (M.A., Ph.D.): Patience Essah, essahpa@auburn.edu (844-4360).
Horticulture (M.Ag., M.S., Ph.D.): Gary Keever, keevegj@auburn.edu (844-3037).
Human Development and Family Studies (M.S., Ph.D.): Joe Pittman, pittmjf@auburn.edu (844-4151).
Industrial Design (M.I.D.): Clark E. Lundell, lundece@auburn.edu (844-2369).
Industrial and Systems Engineering (M.I.S.E., M.S., Ph.D.): Robert Buflin, bulfirl@auburn.edu (844-1422).
Integrated Textile and Apparel Science (Ph.D.): Carol Warfield, warficl@auburn.edu; Gisela Buschle-Diller, buschgi@auburn.edu (844-4084).
Landscape Architecture (M.L.A.): Charlene LeBleu, leblecm@auburn.edu (844-4967).
Large Animal Surgery and Medicine (M.S., Ph.D.): Lauren G. Wolfe, wolfelg@auburn.edu (844-6697).
Management (M.M.I.S., M.S., Ph.D.): Violet Lett, lettvio@auburn.edu (844-4071).
Materials Engineering (M.Mtl.E., M.S., Ph.D.): Jeffrey Fergus, ferguje@auburn.edu (844-4820).
Mathematics and Statistics (M.A.M., M.P.S., M.S., Ph.D.): Chris Rodger, rodgec1@auburn.edu (844-3746).
Mechanical Engineering (M.M.E., M.S., Ph.D.): George Flowers, flowegt@auburn.edu (844-4820).
Nursing (M.S.): Jennifer Hamner, hamnejb@auburn.edu (844-6757).
Nutrition and Food Science (M.S., Ph.D.): Sareen Gropper, groppss@auburn.edu (844-4261).
Pathobiology (M.S., Ph.D.): Lauren G. Wolfe, wolfelg@auburn.edu (844-4539).
Pharmacal Sciences (M.S., Ph.D.): Daniel Parsons, parsodl@auburn.edu (844-4037).
Pharmaceutical Sciences (Ph.D.): Daniel Parsons, parsodl@auburn.edu (844-4037); Salisa Westrick, westrsc@auburn.edu (844-8314).
Pharmacy Care Systems (M.S., Ph.D.): Salisa Westrick, westrsc@auburn.edu (844-8314).
Physics (M.S., Ph.D.): Joe Perez, perezjd@auburn.edu (844-4264).
Plant Pathology (M.Ag., M.S., Ph.D.): Wayne Clark, clarkwe@auburn.edu (844-5003).
Polymer and Fiber Engineering (M.S., Ph.D.): Gisela Buschle-Diller, buschgi@auburn.edu (844-4123).
Poultry Science (M.Ag., M.S., Ph.D.): Sarge Bilgili, bilgisf@auburn.edu (844-2612).
Psychology (M.S., Ph.D.): Thane Bryant, bryangt@auburn.edu (844-4412).
Public Administration (M.P.A., Ph.D.): Cal Clark, clarkcm@auburn.edu (M.P.A. Program); Linda Dennard, ldennard@aum.mail.edu (Ph.D. Program) (334-244-3646).
Radiology (M.S., Ph.D.): Lauren G. Wolfe, wolfelg@auburn.edu (844-5045).
Rehabilitation and Special Education (M.Ed., M.S., Ed.S., Ph.D.): Caroline Dunn, dunnca1@auburn.edu (844-2086).
Rural Sociology (M.S.): Conner Bailey, bailelc@auburn.edu (844-5632).
Small Animal Surgery and Medicine (M.S., Ph.D.): Lauren G. Wolfe, wolfelg@auburn.edu (844-6003).
Sociology (M.A., M.S.): Mark Konty, kontyma@auburn.edu (844-5049).
Spanish (M.A., M.H.S.): Tony Madrigal, madrija@auburn.edu (844-4345).
Sports Management (minor): Mary Rudisill, rudisme@auburn.edu (844-4483) (see Health and Human Performance).
Statistics: Chris Rodger, rodgec1@auburn.edu (844-3746) (see Mathematics and Statistics).
Technical and Professional Communication (M.T.P.C.): Hilary Wyss, wysshil@auburn.edu (844-4620) (see English).
Textile Science (M.S.): Gisela Buschle-Diller, buschgi@auburn.edu (844-4123) (see Polymer and Fiber Engineering).
Urban Forestry (minor): Greg Somers, somergl@auburn.edu (844-1007) (see Forestry and Wildlife Sciences).
Vocational and Adult Education (M.Ed., M.S., Ed.S., Ed.D.): Maria Witte, wittemm@auburn.edu (844-4460).
Wildlife Sciences (M.S., Ph.D.): Greg Somers, somergl@auburn.edu (844-1007) (see Forestry and Wildlife Sciences).
Zoology (M.S., Ph.D.): Jack Feminella, feminjw@auburn.edu (844-4830) (see Biological Sciences).

BARRY
UNIVERSITY
where you belong

BARRY UNIVERSITY

Graduate Programs

Programs of Study

Barry University offers more than fifty high-quality graduate degree programs that prepare students for career change and advancement. Classes are offered on evenings or Saturdays for many of the programs, thereby meeting the needs of the working professional. The faculty is well attuned to the learning styles of adult students. The experience at Barry is academically rewarding and challenging, with interaction with professionals who bring real-world experience to the classroom.

The School of Adult and Continuing Education offers the M.A. in administrative studies and liberal studies and the M.S. in information technology. The School of Arts and Sciences offers the M.A. in communication, pastoral ministry for Hispanics, and practical theology; the M.A. and M.F.A. in photography; the M.S. in clinical psychology and organizational communication; and the S.S.P. in school psychology. The M.A. in pastoral theology is offered in Venice, Florida. The Doctor of Ministry (D.Min.) is offered at the Miami Shores campus. The School of Business offers the Master of Business Administration (M.B.A.), with concentrations in accounting, finance, health services administration, international business, management, management information systems, and marketing. The School of Business also offers the M.S. in accounting and management. The School of Education offers programs in counseling (M.S. and Ed.S.), with specializations in guidance and counseling; marital, couple, and family counseling/therapy; mental health counseling; and rehabilitation counseling and a dual specialization in marital, couple, and family counseling/therapy and mental health counseling. The Ph.D. in counseling is also offered. The M.S. is offered in educational computing and technology, educational leadership, elementary education, exceptional student education, Montessori education, pre-K–primary education, reading, TESOL, and TESOL 3, with a specialization in international TESOL. The M.S. is also offered in higher education administration, human resource development and administration, and human resource development and administration with a specialization in not-for-profit/religious organizations. The Ed.S. is available in curriculum and instruction, educational computing and technology, educational leadership, exceptional student education, Montessori education, pre-K–primary education, and reading. The Ph.D. program in leadership and education has specializations in educational technology, exceptional student education, higher education administration, human resource development, and leadership. The Ph.D. is also offered in curriculum and instruction. The Ed.D. in educational leadership is also offered. The School of Graduate Medical Sciences offers programs leading to the Doctor of Podiatric Medicine and Surgery (D.P.M.) and the D.P.M./M.B.A. dual degree. Also available are the Master of Science in anatomy, a Physician Assistant Program leading to certification and the Master of Clinical Medical Science (M.C.M.Sc.), and the Professional Master of Public Health (M.P.H.). The School of Human Performance and Leisure Sciences offers the Master of Science in Sport Management (M.S.S.M.) and an M.S.S.M./M.B.A. dual degree program. The M.S. in movement science is also available, including options for specializations in athletic training, biomechanics, exercise science, and sport and exercise psychology. The School of Law offers the Juris Doctor (J.D.) degree and a joint J.D./M.S. in HRDA program. The School of Natural and Health Sciences offers the M.S. in anesthesiology, biology, biomedical sciences, health services administration, and occupational therapy and the Professional Master of Public Health (M.P.H.).The School of Nursing offers the M.S.N. in nurse practitioner studies, with concentrations in family practice or acute care, and the M.S.N. in nurse administrator studies; nurse educator studies, a dual program that leads to the M.S.N./M.B.A; and the Ph.D. in nursing. There are also bridge options for qualified RNs with bachelor's degrees in fields other than nursing to earn an M.S.N. and an accelerated option for qualified RNs to move seamlessly to the M.S.N. The School of Social Work offers programs that lead to the M.S.W. and the Ph.D. in social work. The Advanced Standing M.S.W. program is available to students with a recent B.S.W. from a school whose B.S.W. program is accredited by the Council on Social Work Education.

None of the graduate programs requires a foreign language for admission or graduation.

Research Facilities

Campus facilities include the Monsignor William Barry Library, photography and digital imaging labs, a human performance lab, an athletics training room, a biomechanics lab, a complete television production studio, an academic computing center, multimedia business classrooms, art studios, a performing arts center, a nursing lab, the Classroom of Tomorrow, and several other well-equipped science labs.

Financial Aid

Financial aid is available. Professional scholarships are available for full-time social work students, educators, nurses, or members of a religious community. Some schools offer scholarships and other forms of financial assistance. Barry University also participates in the Federal Family Loan Program and applicable State of Florida financial aid programs. Students should contact the specific school for details. Additional information is available from the Associate Director of Financial Aid (phone: 305-899-3673; e-mail: finaid@mail.barry.edu).

Cost of Study

Tuition for 2005–06 was $685 per credit hour for most programs, except those in the Schools of Graduate Medical Sciences, Education (Ph.D. program), Social Work (Ph.D. program), Nursing (Ph.D. program), and Law (J.D. program).

Living and Housing Costs

Campus housing is available for full-time graduate students, space permitting. Barry University provides assistance in locating off-campus housing.

Student Group

The total University enrollment for 2004–05 was 9,207, with 3,265 students registered in the graduate and professional programs. The majority of the graduate students are studying part-time in evening and weekend classes.

Location

The University's 122-acre campus is located in Miami Shores, which is between the cities of Miami and Fort Lauderdale. This ideal location provides students with access to one of the nation's most dynamic multicultural environments and all of its business, cultural, and recreational opportunities.

The University

Barry University is an independent, coeducational university, with a history of distinguished graduate programs. Founded in 1940, the University has grown steadily in size and diversity, while maintaining a low student-faculty ratio, thus providing for the individual needs of its academic community.

Applying

Applicants are expected to have earned a 3.0 cumulative GPA or above in undergraduate work and 3.25 or higher in graduate work for Ph.D. applicants. They are usually required to submit scores on standardized tests (such as the GRE, MAT, MCAT, or GMAT); the specific test requirement depends on the program. Some programs have additional requirements. Applicants who do not give evidence of being native English speakers are required to submit a TOEFL score of at least 550 (paper-based) or 213 (computer-based); the minimum acceptable score is 600 for the School of Graduate Medical Sciences. Students are admitted for most terms, depending on the program, except in the School of Graduate Medical Sciences and some programs in the School of Natural and Health Sciences. The student's application and credentials (transcripts, recommendations, and test scores) should be sent to the address listed in this description and should be received at least thirty days prior to the beginning of the term for which admission is desired. Students applying to Podiatric Medicine and the Physician Assistant Program are required to apply via the national application process.

Correspondence and Information

Office of Admission
Barry University
11300 Northeast Second Avenue
Miami Shores, Florida 33161-6695
Phone: 305-899-3100
800-695-2279 (toll-free)
Fax: 305-899-2971
E-mail: gradadmissions@mail.barry.edu
Web site: http://www.barry.edu/gradprograms

FACULTY HEADS

School of Adult and Continuing Education
Carol-Rae Sodano, Ed.D., Widener; Dean.
Arts and Administrative Studies: Lee Dutter, Ph.D., Rochester.
Informational Technology: Khaled Deeb, Ph.D., Florida International; Academic Coordinator.
Public Administration: Richard Orman, Ph.D., Maxwell.

School of Arts and Sciences
Christopher Starratt, Ph.D., Auburn; Interim Dean.
Clinical Psychology: Lenore T. Szuchman, Ph.D., Florida International; Chair.
Communication: Denis E. Vogel, Ph.D., Florida State; Chair.
Pastoral Ministry for Hispanics: Rev. Mario B. Vizcaino, Ph.D., Gregorian (Rome); Director, Southeast Pastoral Institute.
Photography: Stephen Althouse, M.F.A., Virginia Commonwealth; Chair.
School Psychology: Agnes Shine, Ph.D., Ball State; Program Director.
Theology: Mark Wedig, O.P., Ph.D., Catholic University; Chair.

School of Business
Jack Scarborough, Ph.D., Maryland; Dean.
Jeffrey Mello, Ph.D., Northeastern; Associate Dean for Faculty.
William Frank, M.B.A., DePaul; Assistant Dean for Students.

Adrian Dominican School of Education
Terry Piper, Ph.D., Alberta; Dean.
John Dezek, Ed.D., Western Michigan; Associate Dean for Graduate Professional Studies in Education.
Catheryn Weitman, Ph.D., Texas A&M; Associate Dean for Graduate Education and Research.
Catherina Eeltink, Ph.D., Florida State; Interim Assistant Dean for Curriculum and Graduate Programs and Counseling Program Coordinator—Orlando.
Maria Stallions, Ph.D., Barry; Assistant Dean for Outreach Programs.
Counseling (Ph.D.)—Miami Shores: Maureen Duffy, Ph.D., Nova Southeastern; Director and Chairperson for Counseling Programs, and Jeffrey Guterman, Ph.D., Florida State; Program Coordinator.
Counseling (Ph.D.)—Orlando: Steve Livingston, Ph.D., Florida State; Program Coordinator.
Curriculum and Instruction (Ed.S.)—Miami Shores (with specializations in culture, language, and literacy (TESOL); curriculum; evaluation and research; early childhood education; elementary education; reading, language, and cognition): Jill Farrell, Ed.D., Florida International; Program Director.
Curriculum and Instruction (Ph.D.)—Miami Shores (with specializations in accomplished teacher; early childhood education; elementary education; ESOL; gifted; Montessori; reading (Pre-K–primary or secondary focus): Rebecca P. Harlin, Ph.D., Florida; Program Director.
Educational Computing and Technology (M.S., Ed.S., Ph.D.)—Miami Shores: Joel Levine, Ed.D., Florida International; Program Director.
Educational Leadership (M.S., Ed.S.)—Miami Shores: Reid Bernstein, M.Ed., Miami (Florida); Administrative Director.
Educational Leadership (Ed.D.)—Miami Shores: Carmen McCrink, Ph.D., Miami (Florida); Director and Chairperson of Educational Leadership and Higher Education.
Educational Leadership (M.S., Ed.S., Ed.D.)—Orlando: Zorka Karaxha, Ed.D., Lehigh; Program Coordinator.
Elementary Education (M.S.)—Miami Shores: Victoria Giordano, Ph.D., Florida International; Program Director.
Elementary Education/ESOL (M.S.)—Miami Shores: Victoria Giordano, Ph.D., Florida International; Program Director.
Exceptional Student Education (M.S., Ed.S.)—Miami Shores: Judy Harris-Looby, Ph.D., Miami (Florida); Program Director.
Exceptional Student Education (Ph.D.)—Miami Shores: Clara Wolman, Ph.D., Minnesota; Program Coordinator.
Exceptional Student Education/ESOL (M.S.)—Miami Shores: Judy Harris-Looby, Ph.D., Miami (Florida); Program Director
Higher Education Administration (M.S., Ph.D.)—Miami Shores: Carmen McCrink, Ph.D., Miami (Florida); Director and Chairperson of Educational Leadership and Higher Education Administration.
Human Resource Development (Ph.D.)—Miami Shores: Betty Hubschman, Ed.D., Florida International; Program Director.
Human Resource Development (Ph.D.)—Orlando: Marilyn Lutz, Ed.D., Nova Southeastern; Program Coordinator.
Human Resource Development and Administration (M.S.)—Miami Shores: David Kopp, Ph.D., Barry; Program Coordinator.
Human Resource Development and Administration (M.S.)—Orlando: Marilyn Lutz, Ed.D., Nova Southeastern; Program Coordinator.
Leadership (Ph.D.)—Miami Shores: Carmen McCrink, Ph.D., Miami (Florida); Director and Chairperson of Educational Leadership and Higher Education Administration.
Leadership (Ph.D.)—Orlando: Zorka Karanxha, Ed.D., Lehigh; Program Coordinator.
Marital, Couple, and Family Counseling/Therapy (M.S., Ed.S.)—Miami Shores: James Rudes, Ph.D., Nova Southeastern, and Richard Tureen, Ph.D., Nova Southeastern; Program Coordinators.
Marital, Couple, and Family Counseling/Therapy (M.S., Ed.S.)—Orlando: Steve Livingston, Ph.D., Florida State, and J. Paul Gallant, Ph.D., Florida State; Program Coordinators.
Marital, Couple, Family Counseling/Therapy and Mental Health Counseling, Dual Specialization (M.S., Ed.S.)—Miami Shores: James Rudes, Ph.D., Nova Southeastern, and Richard Tureen, Ph.D., Nova Southeastern; Program Coordinators.
Marital, Couple, Family Counseling/Therapy and Mental Health Counseling, Dual Specialization (M.S., Ed.S.)—Orlando: Steve Livingston, Ph.D., Florida State, and Paul Gallant, Ph.D., Florida State; Program Coordinators.
Mental Health Counseling (M.S., Ed.S.)—Miami Shores: Jeffrey Guterman, Ph.D., Nova Southeastern; Program Coordinator.
Mental Health Counseling (M.S., Ed.S.)—Orlando: Eugene Tootle, Ed.D., Auburn; Program Coordinator.
Mental Health Counseling and Rehabilitation Counseling , Dual Specialization (M.S., Ed.S.)—Miami Shores: Jeffrey Guterman, Ph.D., Nova Southeastern; Program Coordinator.
Mental Health Counseling and Rehabilitation Counseling , Dual Specialization (M.S., Ed.S.)—Orlando: Eugene Tootle, Ed.D., Auburn; Program Coordinator.
Montessori Education, with specialization in early childhood education (M.S., Ed.S.)—Miami Shores: Ijya Tulloss, Ed.D., Nova Southeastern; Program Director.
Montessori, with specialization in elementary education (M.S., Ed.S.)—Miami Shores: Ijya Tulloss, Ed.D., Nova Southeastern; Program Director.
Pre-K–Primary (M.S.)—Miami Shores: Lilia DiBello, Ed.D., Florida International; Program Coordinator.
Pre-K–Primary/ESOL (M.S.)—Miami Shores: Lilia DiBello, Ed.D., Florida International; Program Coordinator.
Reading (M.S., Ed.S.)—Miami Shores: Joyce Warner, Ph.D., Pennsylvania; Program Director.
Reading, Language, and Cognition (Ph.D.)—Miami Shores: Jill Farrell, Ed.D., Florida International; Program Director.
Rehabilitation Counseling (M.S., Ed.S.)—Miami Shores: Jeffrey Guterman, Ph.D., Nova Southeastern; Program Coordinator.
Rehabilitation Counseling (M.S., Ed.S.)—Orlando: Eugene Tootle, Ed.D., Auburn; Program Coordinator.
School Counseling (M.S., Ed.S.)—Miami Shores: Sylvia Fernandez, Ph.D., Southern Illinois at Carbondale; Program Coordinator.
School Counseling (M.S., Ed.S.)—Orlando: Catherina Eeltink, Ph.D., Florida State; Program Coordinator and Counseling Program Coordinator.

School of Graduate Medical Sciences
Chet Evans, D.P.M., California College of Podiatric Medicine; Dean.
Physician Assistant Program: Doreen Parkhurst, M.D., Boston University; Program Director.

School of Human Performance and Leisure Sciences
G. Jean Cerra, Ph.D., Missouri; Dean.
Gayle Workman, Ph.D., Ohio State; Associate Dean and Department Chair.
Leta Hicks, Ed.D., Oklahoma State; Director of Graduate Programs.
Movement Science—Athletic Training and General Option: Carl Cramer, Ed.D., Kansas State; Program Director.
Movement Science—Biomechanics: Monique Mokha, Ph.D., Texas Woman's; Program Coordinator.
Movement Science—Exercise Science: Connie Mier, Ph.D., Texas; Program Coordinator.
Movement Science—Sport and Exercise Psychology: Gualberto Cremades, Ph.D., Houston; Program Coordinator.
Sport Management: Annie Clement, J.D., Cleveland State; Ph.D., Iowa; Program Coordinator.

School of Law
Glen-Peter Ahlers Sr., J.D., Washburn; Associate Dean for Information Services.
Leticia M. Diaz, J.D., Ph.D., Rutgers; Associate Dean of Academic Affairs.

School of Natural and Health Sciences
Sr. John Karen Frei, O.P., Ph.D., Miami (Florida); Associate Vice President and Dean.
Anesthesiology: John McFadden, M.S.N., Tennessee; Program Director.
Biology: Ralph Laudan, Ph.D., Rutgers; Associate Dean and Program Director.
Biomedical Sciences: Ralph Laudan, Ph.D., Rutgers; Associate Dean and Program Director.
Health Services Administration: Alan S. Whiteman, Ph.D., Walden; Program Director.
Occupational Therapy: Douglas Mitchell, M.S., Wayne State; Program Director.

School of Nursing
Pegge L. Bell, Ph.D., Virginia; Dean.
Claudette Spalding, Ph.D., Barry; Associate Dean of Graduate Programs.
Kathleen Papes, Ed.D., Florida Atlantic; Associate Dean for Administrative Affairs.
Linda Perkel, Ph.D., Barry; Associate Dean for Undergraduate Programs.

School of Social Work
Debra McPhee, Ph.D., Toronto; Dean.
Phyllis Scott, Ph.D., Barry; Interim Associate Dean.
M.S.W. Program: Carol Huffman, Interim Program Director.
Ph.D. Program: Elane Nuehring, Ph.D., Florida State, Director.

Barry's south Florida location gives students access to one of the nation's most dynamic multicultural environments.

Barry University's faculty is well attuned to the learning styles of adult students.

BELLEVUE UNIVERSITY

Graduate Programs

Program of Study

The Master of Business Administration (M.B.A.) degree program provides students the tools and methods required to run a business. The program requires 36 credit hours of course work. Students without an undergraduate business degree generally take the foundation of 9 credit hours, the core of 18 credit hours, and a concentration of 9 credit hours. Students with an undergraduate business degree typically have met the foundation requirements and instead take the core classes, a concentration, and complete 9 credit hours of graduate business electives (instead of the foundation). Concentrations are available in accounting, advanced programming, finance, health care, human resource management, interdisciplinary business, international management, management information systems, marketing, and supply chain management. The M.B.A., offered in the classroom and online, is open to any student with a bachelor's degree from an accredited college or university. The Master of Science in computer information systems (MSCIS) program, offered in the classroom and online, is designed to blend current foundational information technology skills with foundational managerial competencies. Students cover management-level training on project management as well as managerial competencies in IT accounting, personal communication, planning, and budgeting. Successful completion prepares students for management, consulting, and technical projects in both traditional and e-commerce-related businesses. Students with no computer background can access foundational principles through prerequisite classes. Students with undergraduate computer degrees typically complete the program with 36 credit hours of graduate work. A concentration is offered in business administration. The master's program in health-care administration (MHA), offered in the classroom and online, provides health-care professionals with an opportunity to study the various areas of planning, organizing, leading, and controlling as they provide administrative guidance to others within their health-related organizations. The program is designed to give students the ability to analyze the various knowledge and skill areas one needs to be effective in a rapidly changing environment. The external influences impacting health-care organizations are examined, with the intent to better manage the internal operations as various team members collaborate on efforts toward the optimum quality of care for consumers. The degree is a 39-credit-hour program that culminates in a 3-credit-hour capstone project. It is offered in an accelerated cohort format, which allows students to move through the program with the same class, completing it in eighteen months, followed by a 3-credit-hour capstone project. The Master of Arts in management (MAM) is a 36-credit-hour program that includes a directed independent research study of contemporary issues. The program is deliberately focused on students wanting to progress within a medium or large organization as well as those currently in a management position who seek to further their knowledge of the interworkings of business. It is offered in an accelerated, cohort format, which students can complete in approximately eighteen months. The goal of the Master of Arts in leadership (MAL) program is to enable students to develop and recognize their own unique styles, roles, and general philosophies of leadership and thus become prepared to accept expanding leadership roles. It is offered in an accelerated, cohort format, which students can complete in sixteen months. Work experience is an integral part of the program. The Master of Public Administration is a 48-credit-hour program, in the accelerated format, that prepares students to become outstanding managers and leaders who are prepared to handle the complexities and challenges that are present in the public sector. The Master of Science in human services (MSHS) program offers two options: a 36-credit-hour option in individual and community services and an expanded 48-credit-hour mental health counseling option. The individual and community services program is designed for students whose main goal is a master's degree, with emphasis on preparation for direct and administrative service roles. It includes all necessary courses to enable graduates to apply for Nebraska Provisionally Licensed Mental Health Practitioner (PLMHP) licensure. Additional courses in chemical dependency counseling make it possible for students in this option to meet Nebraska Certified Provisional Alcohol/Drug Abuse Counselor (CPADAC) standards. The expanded mental health counseling option serves the needs of those who are interested in pursuing career opportunities in therapy and counseling roles. It includes enhanced clinical course work and increased internship requirements. Graduates of this option benefit from a recommended, supervised experience of 450 contact hours in preparation for application for the Nebraska Department of Health and Human Services PLMHP and/or CPADAC. The program is offered in the classroom only. The communication studies master's program offers both the Master of Arts and the Master of Science degrees. The goal of the program, which is offered in the classroom only, is to give graduates the education necessary to meet internal training and development needs and to identify and use effective skills needed to bridge the modern workplace communication gap. The Master of Arts degree requires 38 credit hours (thesis optional), and the Master of Science requires 41 credit hours (thesis required). Students may complete all master's requirements in five semesters or may elect to take one course at a time. The Master of Science in security management program prepares students to function effectively at the director level in a broad spectrum of homeland security– and organizational-related occupations. The program, offered online and in the classroom, covers the broad spectrum of security issues, including the implementation of programs based on needs and contingencies derived from security vulnerability assessments. It is offered in an accelerated, cohort format, which students can complete in approximately sixteen months. The Master of Science in management of information systems (MSMIS) program was created for midlevel IT managers and future CIOs who need to retain currency in the rapidly changing world of enterprise technology as well as enhance their understanding of contemporary trends and emerging technologies. The MSMIS program requires 36 hours of course work. Students choose a concentration in business, computer information systems, health care, health-care information architecture, or information security. The Master of Science in information security management requires 36 credit hours of course work. Students with some computer education but without an undergraduate degree or equivalent experience in computer technology may learn any missing skills and concepts through additional courses. The Master of Arts in instructional technology (MAIT) is a 36-credit-hour program designed for community college instructors who want to apply cutting-edge instructional technology to both traditional and online classrooms. The MAIT combines theory and practice, emphasizing the integration of educational technology and active-learning principles.

Research Facilities

Renovated in 2002, the Freeman/Lozier Library houses a collection of approximately 105,000 volumes and 5,200 current periodical subscriptions, the Integrated Media Center, and the Collaborative Learning/Study Areas. The Integrated Media Center provides students access to computerized and Web-based resources along with the training facilities to educate students on how to effectively use these resources. Bellevue University and its professional librarians provide the academic services necessary to support and maintain high-quality undergraduate, graduate, and online education. Access to the library's entire collection is available electronically through an online catalog (iLink), along with nine other Nebraska Independent Library Collections. Online access to information is provided free of charge to all students and faculty members of Bellevue University through various database providers, such as ProQuest Direct, EBSCOhost, LexisNexis Academic Universe, OCLC, and netLibrary.

Additional online services and resources available are Virtual Reference Librarian (VRL), where students can converse directly with reference librarians online in real time; ERes, which allows the library to maintain an electronic reserve system; Periodicals Holdings List A–Z, which serves as a comprehensive list of the library's electronic and print titles; NoodleBib, a Web application that allows students to create and edit MLA- and APA-style source lists; and Turnitin.com, which is recognized worldwide as the standard in online plagiarism prevention.

Financial Aid

Financial assistance is available from the federal and state government, the University, and private sources. Financial aid includes scholarships, work-study programs, and student loans. Scholarships do not have to be repaid. The Federal Work-Study Program allows a student to work and earn money. Student loans must be repaid. In general, all U.S. citizens and eligible noncitizens who are enrolled in an approved degree program may apply for financial aid. For additional information, students may call 402-293-2000.

Cost of Study

Tuition for 2006–07 was $340 per credit hour. For example, tuition for the 39-credit-hour cohort online MHA program was $13,260, excluding books and fees.

Living and Housing Costs

Student housing is available for graduate students. Those who are interested can obtain more information by calling 402-557-7415.

Student Group

The total University enrollment for fall 2006 was 6,808, with 1,482 students registered in graduate programs. The majority of the graduate students are studying full-time in evening and online classes.

The University

Bellevue University is one of Nebraska's largest fully accredited independent colleges. Programs serve the needs of nearly 7,000 students annually and cater to working adult students as well as traditional undergraduates. Benefits include accelerated degree-completion programs, online programs, an online library, cooperative credit transfer agreements, and flexible corporate partnerships.

Applying

To apply, students must submit the application online or by mail, pay the appropriate fees, and submit transcripts for evaluation. Admissions counselors work with students to complete the official admissions process. An educational plan is completed for each student, defining requirements needed to achieve each student's degree goal.

Correspondence and Information

Admissions
Bellevue University
1000 Galvin Road South
Bellevue, Nebraska 68005
Phone: 402-293-2000
800-756-7920 (toll-free)
E-mail: info@bellevue.edu
Web site: http://www.bellevue.edu

THE FACULTY

The Bellevue University full-time and adjunct faculty consists of 246 men and 152 women, teaching students from freshman to graduate level. The student-faculty ratio is 22:1. For most classes and programs, Bellevue University employs adjunct faculty members who are professionals in their respective fields. Faculty members are screened to ensure that each is current on issues and technology.

BERNARD M. BARUCH COLLEGE OF THE CITY UNIVERSITY OF NEW YORK

Graduate Programs

Programs of Study

Baruch College offers graduate programs of study through its three schools: the Zicklin School of Business, the largest and one of the most respected business schools in the nation; the Mildred and George Weissman School of Arts and Sciences, an outstanding small school of the humanities and the natural and social sciences; and the School of Public Affairs, ranked by *U.S. News & World Report* among the top 20 percent of all public affairs programs in the nation for its Master of Public Administration program.

Flexible day, evening, and weekend class schedules are designed to accommodate both full-time and part-time students.

The Master of Business Administration (M.B.A.) is offered with specializations in accountancy (CPA program), computer information systems, decision sciences, economics, finance, industrial/organizational psychology, international business, management/entrepreneurship and small business management, management/operations management, management/organizational behavior-human resource management, marketing, real estate, statistics, and taxation. A general M.B.A. option is also offered.

Master of Science (M.S.) programs are offered in accountancy (CPA program), financial engineering, business computer information systems, industrial/organizational psychology, marketing, quantitative methods and modeling, statistics, and taxation. The Master of Arts (M.A.) degree is offered in corporate communication. The Master of Science in Education (M.S.Ed.) in educational leadership and in higher education administration is also offered. Master of Public Administration (M.P.A.) degrees are offered with specializations in health-care policy, nonprofit administration, policy analysis and evaluation, and public management. A joint M.S./M.P.A. degree program is offered with the Hunter-Bellevue School of Nursing.

Baruch College also offers an Executive M.B.A., Executive M.P.A., and the Baruch/Mt. Sinai M.B.A. in health-care administration as well as Executive M.S. degree programs in finance and industrial and labor relations. Two joint-degree programs (J.D./M.B.A.) are offered in conjunction with Brooklyn Law School and the New York Law School. Doctoral (Ph.D.) programs in business (with specializations available in accountancy, finance, information systems, marketing, and organizational behavior and human resource management) and in industrial/organizational psychology are based at Baruch College and offered through the CUNY Graduate Center.

Baruch College faculty members are among the most distinguished and most widely known in their fields. They combine outstanding academic credentials with significant real-world experience. About 95 percent hold a Ph.D. or other terminal degree. Faculty members are regularly recognized with fellowships and awards from notable foundations and public agencies, including the Guggenheim and Fulbright Foundations, the National Science Foundation, and the Henry Luce Foundation. There are more than 20 endowed chairs and professorships at Baruch College.

Research Facilities

Baruch College is committed to providing its students with the most modern learning environment and, to that end, has undertaken an ambitious campus-enhancement program over the past decade. The William and Anita Newman Library, named the top college library in the nation for 2003 by the Association of College and Research Libraries/American Library Association, is a 1,450-seat, 330,000-square-foot facility that provides the Baruch community with access to several hundred online databases and information resources in print and electronic formats. Users have access seven days a week to the library's on-site computing facilities, as well as remote access from off-campus locations to thousands of full-text journals, newspapers, and books, including a Web-based reference desk. Baruch College is home to many centers and institutes that support education and research in such key areas as business, finance, the global economy, public policy, social equity, and real estate and metropolitan development.

Financial Aid

Merit-based graduate assistantships are awarded by the individual schools to full- and part-time students. The amount of the stipend varies. Full-Time Honors M.B.A. students compete for merit-based scholarships valued at $2000 to $5000 annually. In addition, in the fall, the Mitsui USA Foundation awards $5000 scholarships to 2 newly admitted full-time students (U.S. citizens or permanent residents) pursuing an M.B.A. in international business. Full-time M.P.A. and M.S.Ed. students in the School of Public Affairs compete for a variety of merit-based scholarships in addition to $10,000–$12,000 graduate assistantships. Financial aid is also available to graduate students through state, federal, and College programs. International students are eligible to apply for graduate assistantships and College work-study. Support for graduate study in business journalism is provided by the Reuters Foundation and by alumnus Eric Kobren.

Cost of Study

In fall 2007, M.B.A. tuition for New York State residents was $4400 per term for full-time study and $400 per credit for part-time study. For out-of-state residents and international students, M.B.A. tuition was $600 per credit. M.S., M.A., M.P.A., and M.S.Ed./Certificate Program tuition for state residents was $3200 per semester for full-time study and $270 per credit for part-time study, and, for out-of-state residents and international students, it was $500 per credit. Students should contact the individual schools for tuition information on executive programs.

Living and Housing Costs

Baruch College does not offer student housing at this time. A single student should anticipate spending approximately $16,900 a year for housing, food, utilities, books, transportation, entertainment, and incidental expenses.

Student Group

Baruch College students come from more than ninety different cultural and ethnic backgrounds, reflecting the complex diversity of New York City itself. This mixture of people and life experiences creates a rich social and academic environment that enhances students' learning and truly prepares them for a global marketplace. Total enrollment is more than 15,000, including nearly 2,500 graduate students.

Location

Baruch College is situated on Lexington Avenue near the Flatiron/Gramercy Park district of Manhattan, in the heart of one of the world's most dynamic financial and cultural centers. The College is within easy reach of Wall Street, Midtown, the United Nations, and the global headquarters of major companies, firms, and organizations.

The College

In 2001, Baruch College opened its innovative, award-winning seventeen-floor Vertical Campus. Designed to recreate the atmosphere of a traditional college campus in an urban setting, it serves as the hub of the College. Covering nearly an entire square block between Lexington and Third Avenues and 24th and 25th Streets, the 800,000-square-foot structure houses more than 100 high-technology classrooms and research facilities, faculty and administrative offices, executive conference facilities, a three-level Athletics and Recreation Complex, an expanded student activities center, the Rose Nagelberg Theatre and Engelman Recital Hall, a 500-seat auditorium, a television studio, a food court, and a new campus bookstore. The Vertical Campus has been honored by the American Institute of Architects with the highest award it offers to an individual building.

Applying

Students should contact the appropriate school for application information.

Correspondence and Information

For M.B.A. and M.S. programs:
Zicklin School of Business
Baruch College
One Bernard Baruch Way, Box H-0820
New York, New York 10010-5585
Phone: 646-312-1300
E-mail: zicklingradadmissions@baruch.cuny.edu
Web site: http://zicklin.baruch.cuny.edu

For Ph.D. programs:
Zicklin School of Business
Baruch College
One Bernard Baruch Way, Box B13-255
New York, New York 10010-5585
Phone: 646-312-3090
E-mail: phd@baruch.cuny.edu
Web site: http://web.gc.cuny.edu/business

For M.P.A., M.S.Ed., and Advanced Certificate programs:
School of Public Affairs
Baruch College
One Bernard Baruch Way, Box D-0901
New York, New York 10010-5585
Phone: 646-660-6750
E-mail: spa_admissions@baruch.cuny.edu
Web site: http://www.baruch.cuny.edu/spa

For M.A. program:
Weissman School of Arts and Sciences
Baruch College
One Bernard Baruch Way, Box B8-211
New York, New York 10010-5585
Phone: 646-312-4490
E-mail: wsas_graduate_studies@baruch.cuny.edu
Web site: http://www.baruch.cuny.edu/wsas

RESEARCH CENTERS

The Bert W. and Sandra Wasserman Trading Floor/Subotnick Financial Services Center: Baruch College is now among an elite group of business schools that provide students with educational trading floor facilities. The Subotnick Center is the only business school resource of its kind in New York and one of a handful of comparable facilities at top educational institutions nationwide. Its centerpiece is the Bert W. and Sandra Wasserman Trading Floor, a fully equipped, simulated trading environment featuring forty-two high-end networked computer stations, continuous live data feeds, real-time market quotes, and computerized trading models. Actual market technology is used to teach students about markets and financial services—valuable experience for graduates seeking leading positions in the financial, banking, or accounting services industries. The center also features a sixty-seat seminar room and a twenty-five-seat development lab. An exciting and practical teaching resource, the center also functions as a laboratory for scholarly research. Faculty members and students from a number of disciplines, including economics, finance, statistics, and information systems, conduct research in market microstructure, investment management strategies, experimental economics, auditing, surveillance, and manipulation detection in financial markets.

Lawrence N. Field Center for Entrepreneurship and Small Business: The Field Center provides educational programs, a networking environment, and consulting help to more than 1,000 small and start-up businesses each year. The center links Zicklin School of Business faculty members and students with these entrepreneurs. Faculty members participate in the Field Center's programs in accounting and taxation, banking and finance, management and human resources, marketing and promotion, and technology assessment. Technical support services include assistance in developing business and marketing plans; evaluating and selecting funding alternatives, accounting systems, and technology; supervising employees; and studying the implications of business decisions.

Weissman Center for International Business: This center sponsors numerous programs, conferences, and forums for students, faculty members, and business professionals to enrich their understanding of critical issues in international business and the global economy. With guidance from an advisory board of distinguished executives, the center builds bridges between the worlds of academia and international business. Activities and programs include Global Market Breakfasts that introduce executives, investors, and professionals to key emerging markets and issues; Mitsui Lunchtime Forums, which feature experts who debate current issues in international business; the publication of the Official Directory of international firms and executives in New York City; International Business Alumni, an association of graduates of Baruch who have a professional interest in international business; international business internships with firms in the New York metropolitan area; study-abroad programs for Baruch students; and scholarships for graduate study in international business and international marketing and for study abroad and internships overseas.

Steven L. Newman Real Estate Institute: The Steven L. Newman Real Estate Institute offers professional education and continuing education; research and consulting, conducted by Baruch's business and public affairs faculties, that focuses on current real estate concerns of the New York metropolitan region; conferences and seminars that bring together the most forward-thinking real estate, government, nonprofit, and design professionals to discuss vital metropolitan development and real estate issues; and publications/exhibitions/Internet resources that explore the critical issues facing New York and its neighborhoods.

Baruch Survey Research Unit: Housed in the Baruch School of Public Affairs, the Baruch Survey Research Unit (BSRU) designs and conducts telephone and other surveys for government agencies, nonprofit organizations, and other partners on wide range of public affairs topics. Combining a state-of-the-art telephone center with the expertise of Baruch School of Public Affairs faculty members and graduate students, the BSRU specializes in careful, objective survey research on policy-relevant issues at both the national and local levels. In addition to fielding the research, the unit staff provides assistance with all stages of the survey research project—from questionnaire design to sample selection to the final report. Recent projects include an extensive survey for the New York City Department of Health on the health conditions and behaviors of New Yorkers (conducted in English, Spanish, Chinese, Korean, Russian, Polish, Greek, Yiddish, and Haitian Creole), a regular comprehensive survey of resident satisfaction with New York City government services conducted for the New York City Council, a community survey about youth violence in the Rockaways (Queens), and a survey of how nonprofit organizations utilize information technology in delivering services to their constituencies.

Center for Innovation and Leadership in Government: This center was created to preserve continuity and institutional memory in municipal government by preparing prospective and newly elected or appointed government officials for effective public service. The center also provides access to nonpartisan, interdisciplinary, scholarly, academically rigorous policy research that provides government officials with the ability to address complex issues without years of on-the-job experience. The center has adopted a broad range of activities and recently became the home of the archives on the New York City 1975 fiscal crisis. In addition, the center works to keep members of the civic community informed through public forums that debate some of the city's most difficult issues.

Center for the Study of Business and Government: This center is a research-based think tank in the Zicklin School of Business of Baruch College. Its goal is to sharpen and inform public decision making on an array of social and economic issues. Effective public policy requires objective analysis of underlying problems and of policies to remedy those problems. Yet, all too often, debate over policy issues is dominated by advocates and is based on inappropriate data and dubious analysis. The center helps to fill the need for objective high-quality analysis by conducting research that is theoretically well-grounded and tested empirically using sophisticated quantitative analysis. The center has made notable contributions in areas such as welfare reform, health policy, labor market policies, Social Security reform, and monetary policy and inflation. The center draws its faculty from the School of Public Affairs and the Zicklin School of Business at Baruch College as well as from other colleges in the New York area. Center scholars publish regularly in economics and other professional journals and present their work at professional meetings and seminars. In keeping with the goal of contributing to policy, they also write for more general audiences, give presentations at policy-oriented public forums, and provide congressional testimony. Several center scholars have had experience in important policy positions.

Center on Equality, Pluralism and Policy: The mission of the Center on Equality, Pluralism and Policy at Baruch College is to explore the opportunities and pitfalls associated with government policy in a racially, ethnically, and culturally diverse society. The primary objective of the center is to develop hard-nosed analytical approaches to issues of economic and social policies in societies (such as New York and the United States) where the government must formulate and implement policies that promote economic growth and equal opportunity for all persons: native born citizens, newly established citizens, and long-time noncitizen residents alike. In particular, the center encourages and supports scholarly research, popular writing, and curriculum projects that explore the contradictions among efficiency, diversity, and equality in the formulation and implementation of public policy, with special emphasis on the role of the public sector in divided societies, such as those in New York City and the entire United States; analyze the ways in which attention to diversity contributes to increased efficiency and equity in the delivery of public services; consider the ways that racial and ethnic conflict over access to public resources and public power can undermine the capacity of public policy to promote equal opportunity across racial and ethnic lines; develop safeguards against the possibility that diversity-sensitive public policy might inadvertently weaken civil society by reinforcing racial and ethnic division; and develop insights into the logic and limits of policy to promote social justice in a market society driven by permanent racial, ethnic, cultural, and religious conflict, with special attention to the consequences of market-based forms of economic equality for cooperation across racial and ethnic boundaries.

Center for Educational Leadership: The Center for Educational Leadership conducts policy research on issues pertinent to principals and other school leaders. This research serves as the basis for technical assistance to New York City public schools and policy monographs written for guidance of policy makers, practitioners, and researchers and for developing the curriculum of the Baruch School of Public Affairs programs for preservice and in-service training of principals and other school leaders.

Robert Zicklin Center for Corporate Integrity: The Robert Zicklin Center for Corporate Integrity is a forum for discussion of contemporary issues confronting U.S. corporations and capital markets. Its concerns include transparency of corporate reporting, corporate governance, resolving conflicting corporate stakeholder interests and responsibilities, and regulation. The Center aims to engage in timely discussion of corporate behavior; move the ethical climate of corporate America to a higher plane; increase the visibility of Baruch College and the Zicklin School; afford Baruch students and faculty members the opportunity to interact with business leaders and regulators; and increase the impact of ethics in the classroom and on the students' lives.

Direct and Interactive Marketing Center: The Direct and Interactive Marketing Center is a place for potential and current business professionals and entrepreneurs to find resources, advice, training, knowledge, and the opportunity to produce career and business results through integrated, interactive direct marketing. The center is the link between the academic world and the real business world. It is where the academic discipline of marketing merges with professional marketing resources. The center is New York's only academic resource center dedicated to preparing marketing students for marketing careers through the practical use of research tools, design tools, and consultation with fellow students and industry experts.

The Center for Nonprofit Strategy and Management: The Center for Nonprofit Strategy and Management offers lectures, public workshops, academic training, conferences on advocacy, management consultancy, and professional development opportunities for New York City's nonprofit community. Representatives of more than 2,000 nonprofit organizations come to campus each year, enriching the School of Public Affairs' study of nonprofit institutions and multiplying its students' networking opportunities.

The CUNY Institute for Demographic Research: The CUNY Institute for Demographic Research assembles scholars from across the University to study fertility, mortality, family dynamics, migration, race and ethnicity, spatial development, urban health, and aging. All of the School of Public Affairs' programs are informed by the powerful approach to population studies represented by the institute.

The New York Census Research Data Centers: Baruch College and Cornell University are two of the nine secure facilities in the country that provide researchers with the opportunity to engage in approved projects that use the confidential microdata collected by the U.S. Census Bureau.

BOSTON UNIVERSITY

Graduate School of Arts and Sciences

Programs of Study

The Graduate School of Arts and Sciences at Boston University offers forty-two M.A. programs and thirty-two Ph.D. programs in the humanities, social sciences, and natural sciences. There is, in addition, one division within the Graduate School that provides formal linkage to other professional graduate opportunities at Boston University: the Division of Religious and Theological Studies.

Freestanding M.A. programs within the Graduate School are offered through some research centers and institutes.

Additional academic options may be pursued through cross-registration in any of the University's other schools and colleges, including the University Professors' Program. Through an area consortium arrangement, students may also register for courses at many other graduate schools in the Boston area.

Research Facilities

The Boston University library system holds more than 4.5 million volumes in books and microform. Central service is provided by the Mugar Memorial Library. Among the units contained within this central facility are a music library, an African Studies library, and a Department of Special Collections, containing rare books and manuscripts. Numerous departmental libraries are located throughout the campus. An interlibrary loan system further extends the available resources, and a consortium arrangement enables graduate students to use the facilities of many Boston-area academic and research libraries.

The University provides laboratories for research and training in disciplines ranging from the physical sciences to the dramatic arts. The recently constructed Metcalf Center for Science and Engineering, for example, houses state-of-the-art facilities for science and engineering students. The University's Academic Computing Center, the Center for Computational Science, and individual departments provide computing resources, from parallel supercomputers to personal workstations, interconnected on a campuswide broadband network.

Financial Aid

Highly qualified graduate students are eligible for Presidential Fellowships and Dean's Fellowships, which include full-tuition scholarships and a stipend of $16,500 for the 2006–07 academic year. Teaching fellowships provide stipends that range from $15,500 to $16,000 for 2006–07, plus a tuition scholarship. The Martin Luther King Jr. Fellowships are available to students beginning graduate studies in any department who are committed to the principles espoused by Dr. King. Nominations are accepted from the department of application. A wide variety of grants and awards (e.g., graduate scholarships and research assistantships) are made annually by individual departments and centers. In addition, graduate students at Boston University are eligible to participate in a variety of federally funded programs.

Cost of Study

For 2006–07, full-time tuition is $33,330 for the academic year. Part-time tuition is $1042 per credit hour. The registration fee is $40 per semester, and the George Sherman Union fee is $90 per semester. Graduate students enrolled for continuing study pay $2084 per semester. The estimated cost of books and supplies is $1006 per year.

Living and Housing Costs

A limited number of rooms and apartments in University residences are available for graduate students. Information may be obtained from the Housing Office, 985 Commonwealth Avenue. The Office of Rental Property, 19 Deerfield Street, has information about off-campus housing.

Costs of living in Boston are comparable to those in any large metropolitan city. Average housing costs range from $850 to $1200 per month.

Student Group

The Graduate School has 1,910 students, of whom approximately 49 percent are women and 35 percent come from abroad.

Location

The character of Boston results from a rich blend of its historical heritage, active cultural life, and contemporary growth in business, technology, and medicine. Some sixty colleges and universities are located in greater Boston. Within Boston's compact central area are a host of galleries, the Public Garden, an active theater district, and the Freedom Trail, along which are located some of the most important landmarks in U.S. history. The Museum of Fine Arts, which is open without charge to Boston University students, has notable Oriental, Egyptian, American portrait, and French Impressionist collections. The Boston Symphony Orchestra, the Opera Company of Boston, and many fine chamber and jazz groups offer annual seasons; the Boston Pops season includes free outdoor summer concerts. Boston is the home of the Red Sox, the New England Patriots, the Celtics, and the Bruins.

The University

Boston University is an independent, coeducational, nonsectarian university. Founded by the Methodist Episcopal Church for the improvement of theological training, it has since its incorporation in 1869 been fully open to women and to all minorities. Its more than 24,020 full-time students and more than 3,500 faculty members contribute to its ranking as one of the world's largest independent universities. The main campus, on the south bank of the Charles River just west of downtown Boston, houses the Graduate School of Arts and Sciences, the College of Arts and Sciences, the School of Law, the School of Management, Metropolitan College, the College of Communication, Sargent College of Allied Health Professions, the School of Social Work, the School of Theology, and the University Professors' Program. On the medical campus are the School of Medicine, the School of Public Health, the Goldman School of Dental Medicine, and University Hospital.

Applying

Applications for admission with financial aid consideration for the fall semester must be received by January 15 for most programs; students should refer to the *Graduate School Bulletin* for exceptions. Some departments accept students in the spring semester, for which applications must be received by October 15 for financial aid consideration. Applications must include official transcripts from all colleges and universities attended, letters of recommendation from at least 2 faculty members in the proposed field of graduate study, and official results of the Graduate Record Examinations (General and Subject Tests) and/or the Miller Analogies Test, as required by the department to which the student is applying. Students from abroad must also submit the International Student Data Form and official English translations of all academic records. Students whose native language is not English must submit results of the Test of English as a Foreign Language (TOEFL). A nonrefundable application fee of $70 is required of all applicants. This fee cannot be waived.

Although financial aid competitions within individual programs begin in early January, students who wish to be considered for special Graduate School fellowships are urged to submit their application with all supporting documents by December 1.

Correspondence and Information

Graduate School of Arts and Sciences
Boston University
705 Commonwealth Avenue
Boston, Massachusetts 02215
Phone: 617-353-2696
E-mail: grartsci@bu.edu
Web site: http://www.bu.edu/grs

FACULTY HEADS

Departments, Divisions, and Programs
African American Studies Program: Ronald K. Richardson, Associate Professor; Ph.D., SUNY at Binghamton.
American and New England Studies Program: Marilyn Halter, Associate Professor; Ph.D., Boston University.
Anthropology Department: Thomas Barfield, Professor; Ph.D., Harvard.
Applied Linguistics Program: Mary Catherine O'Connor, Associate Professor; Ph.D., Berkeley.
Archaeology Department: Norman Hammond, Professor; Ph.D., Cambridge.
Art History Department: Fred Kleiner, Professor; Ph.D., Columbia.
Astronomy Department: James Jackson, Professor; Ph.D., MIT.
Biology Department: Geoffrey Cooper, Professor; Ph.D., Miami (Florida).
Biostatistics Program: Lisa Sullivan, Associate Professor; Ph.D., Boston University.
Cellular Biophysics Program: M. Carter Cornwall, Professor; Ph.D., Utah.
Chemistry Department: Guilford Jones, Professor; Ph.D., Wisconsin.
Classical Studies Department: Loren Samons, Associate Professor; Ph.D., Brown.
Cognitive and Neural Systems Program: Stephen Grossberg, Professor; Ph.D., Rockefeller.
Computer Science Department: Azer Bestavros, Associate Professor; Ph.D., Harvard.
Creative Writing: Leslie Epstein, Professor; D.F.A., Yale.
Earth Sciences Department: Guido Salvucci, Associate Professor; Ph.D., MIT.
Economics Department: Kevin Lang, Professor; Ph.D., MIT.
English Department: James Winn, Professor; Ph.D., Yale.
Geography Department: Mark Friedl, Associate Professor; Ph.D., California, Santa Barbara.
History Department: Charles Dellheim, Professor; Ph.D., Yale.
International Relations Department: Erik Goldstein, Professor; Ph.D., Cambridge.
Boston University Marine Program: Vincent Dionne, Professor; Ph.D., Arizona.
Mathematics and Statistics Department: Steven Rosenberg, Professor; Ph.D., Berkeley.
Modern Foreign Languages and Literatures Department: Christopher Maurer, Professor and Chair; Ph.D., Pennsylvania.
Music Department: André de Quadros, Professor; Graduate Certificate of Higher Education, Monash (Australia).
Neuroscience Department: William Eldred III, Professor; Ph.D., Colorado Health Science Center.
Philosophy Department: Charles Griswold, Professor; Ph.D., Penn State.
Physics Department: Bennett Goldberg, Professor; Ph.D., Brown.
Political Science Department: David Mayers, Professor; Ph.D., Chicago.
Preservation Studies: Claire Dempsey, Associate Professor and Director ad Interim; A.M., Boston University.
Program in Molecular Biology, Cell Biology, and Biochemistry: Kimberly McCall, Associate Professor and Director; Ph.D., Harvard.
Psychology Department: Howard Eichenbaum, Professor; Ph.D., Michigan.
Religious and Theological Studies Division: Stephen Prothero, Professor and Director; Ph.D., Harvard.
Sociology Department: John Stone, Professor; D.Phil., Oxford.
Sociology/Social Work (Interdisciplinary): Mary Ellen Collins, Professor; M.S.W., Ph.D., Chicago.
Women's Studies: Shahla Haeri, Assistant Professor and Director; Ph.D., UCLA.

Centers and Institutes
Center for Adaptive Systems: Stephen Grossberg, Professor; Ph.D., Rockefeller.
African Studies Center: James Pritchett, Associate Professor; Ph.D., Harvard.
Center for Anxiety and Related Disorders: David Barlow, Professor; Ph.D., Vermont.
Center for Archaeological Studies: James Wiseman, Professor; Ph.D., Chicago.
Institute for Astrophysical Research: James Jackson, Professor; Ph.D., MIT.
Institute for Classical Traditions: Wolfgang Haase, Professor; Ph.D., Tübingen (Germany).
Center for Computational Science: Claudio Rebbi, Professor; Ph.D., Turin.
Institute for the Study of Conflict, Ideology, and Policy: Uri Ra'anan, Professor; Ph.D., Oxford.
International Center for East Asian Archaeology and Cultural History: Robert Murowchick, Research Associate Professor; Ph.D., Harvard.
Center for Ecology and Conservation Biology: Thomas Kunz, Professor; Ph.D., Kansas.
Institute for Economic Development: Dilip Mookherjee, Professor; Ph.D., London School of Economics.
Editorial Institute: Christopher Ricks, Professor; D.Litt. (hon.), Oxford; Geoffrey Hill, Professor; D.Litt. (hon.), Oxford.
Center for Einstein Studies: John J. Stachel, Professor; Ph.D., Stevens.
Center for Energy and Environmental Studies: Cutler Cleveland, Associate Professor; Ph.D., Illinois.
International History Institute: Cathal Nolan, Associate Professor; Ph.D., Toronto.
Center for International Relations: Ambassador Husain Haggani, Associate Professor; M.A., Karachi (Pakistan).
Elie Weisel Center for Judaic Studies: Steven Katz, Professor; Ph.D., Harvard.
Center for Millennial Studies: Richard Landes, Associate Professor; Ph.D., Princeton.
Neuromuscular Research Center: Carlo De Luca, Professor; Ph.D., Queen's at Kingston.
Center for the Philosophy and History of Science: Alfred Tauber, Professor; M.D., Tufts.
Institute for Philosophy and Religion: M. David Eckel, Associate Professor; Ph.D., Harvard.
Center for Polymer Studies: H. Eugene Stanley, Professor; Ph.D., Harvard.
Institute on Race and Social Division: Glenn Loury, Professor; Ph.D., MIT.
Center for Remote Sensing: Farouk El-Baz, Research Professor; Ph.D., Missouri–Rolla.
Science and Mathematics Education Center: Kenneth Brecher, Professor; Ph.D., MIT.
Center for Space Physics: Supriya Chakrabarti, Professor; Ph.D., Berkeley.
Center for Transportation Studies: T. R. Lakshmanan, Professor; Ph.D., Ohio State.

Boston University along the Charles River.

Marsh Chapel.

The campus along Commonwealth Avenue.

BOWLING GREEN STATE UNIVERSITY

Graduate College

Programs of Study

Bowling Green State University (BGSU) offers Doctor of Philosophy (Ph.D.) programs in American culture studies (communication, English (rhetoric), history, popular culture, and sociology), applied philosophy, biological sciences, communication disorders, communication studies, English (rhetoric and composition), higher education administration, history, interdisciplinary studies, leadership studies, mathematics, photochemical sciences, psychology (clinical, developmental, experimental, industrial-organizational, and quantitative), sociology, and theater and film. A Doctor of Education (Ed.D.) degree is offered in leadership studies, along with a Doctoral of Musical Arts (D.M.A.). Other graduate and specialist programs include technology management (consortium degree), education specialist (administration and supervision, mathematics supervision, reading, and school psychology), and specialist in applied biology (immunohematology).

Graduate certificates are offered in ethnic studies, food and nutrition, gerontology, organizational change, quality systems, scientific and technical communication, and women's studies.

BGSU offers the Master of Accountancy (M.Acc.) degree. The Master of Arts (M.A.) degree is offered in American culture studies, art, art education, college student personnel, communication studies, cross-cultural and international education, economics, English (English literature and technical writing), French, German, guidance and counseling, history, mathematics, philosophy, political science (dual degree with German only), popular culture, psychology (clinical, developmental, experimental, industrial/organizational, and quantitative), sociology, Spanish, and theater and film. The Master of Arts in Teaching (M.A.T.) degree is offered in American culture studies, biological sciences, chemistry, French, geology, German, history, mathematics, physics, Spanish, and theater and film. The Master of Arts/Science is offered in interdisciplinary studies. The Master of Business Administration (M.B.A.) degree is offered in finance, management information systems, marketing, and supply chain management. The Master of Education (M.Ed.) degree is offered in business education; career and technology education; classroom technology; curriculum and teaching; educational administration and supervision; guidance and counseling; human movement, sport, and leisure studies (developmental kinesiology, recreation and leisure, and sport administration); interdisciplinary studies; reading; school psychology; and special education. BGSU also offers the Master of Family and Consumer Sciences (M.F.C.S.) degree. The Master of Fine Arts (M.F.A.) degree is offered in fine art and creative writing. The Master of Industrial Technology (M.I.T.) is offered in construction management and technology and manufacturing technology.BGSU also offers the Master of Music (M.M.) in composition, education, ethnomusicology, history, performance, and theory; Master of Organization Development (M.O.D.); Master of Public Administration (M.P.A.); Master of Public Health (M.P.H.); and Master of Rehabilitation Counseling (M.R.C.) degrees. The Master of Science (M.S.) degree is offered in applied statistics, biological sciences, chemistry, communication disorders, computer science, criminal justice, geology, and physics.

Ph.D. requirements include a minimum of 90 semester hours of graduate work beyond the baccalaureate. A minimum of 30 semester hours of graduate work beyond the baccalaureate is required for the master's degree; the choice of Plan I (thesis option) or Plan II (comprehensive examination option) is available in most programs. The Graduate College at BGSU is committed to helping students identify personal and professional goals. Through a comprehensive set of facilities and programs, opportunities are provided to pursue high-quality graduate education in an environment conducive to advanced study and research.

Research Facilities

The University libraries have approximately 2 million volumes and approximately 1.6 million microforms, including subscriptions to 6,000 periodicals and 600,000 government documents. In addition to providing a range of regular and specialized research facilities, the University supports a number of research centers and institutes. These include the Center for Archival Collections; the Center for Biomolecular Sciences; the Center for Family and Demographic Research; the Center for Neuroscience, Mind and Behavior; the Center for Photochemical Sciences; the Center for Regional Development; the Institute for the Study of Culture and Society; the Center for Microscopy and Microanalysis; the Institute for Great Lakes Research; the Institute for Psychological Research and Application; the Reading Center; the Social Philosophy and Policy Center; the National Institute for the Study of DigitalMedia; and the Statistical Consulting Center.

Financial Aid

Departmental assistantships in 2007–08 provide tuition scholarships and stipend payments totaling as much as $44,782 for master's assistantships and $49,716 for doctoral assistantships. About 80 percent of the University's full-time graduate students are awarded assistantship or fellowship support. Student employment and loans are available as sources of graduate student support.

Cost of Study

Tuition in 2007–08 is $535 per credit hour for Ohio residents and $884 per credit hour for nonresidents. Full-time students are assessed a combined fee of $641 per semester for general and registration fees.

Living and Housing Costs

On-campus housing is not available for graduate students. Numerous apartments and other housing are available near the campus. For more information, those interested should contact Off-Campus Housing at 419-372-2458 or go online at http://www.bgsu.edu/offices/sa/offcampus/housing.

Student Group

The University maintains an enrollment of about 16,000 undergraduates and approximately 3,100 graduate students on the main campus. Students represent all fifty states and fifty countries. The opportunities to meet people and exchange ideas at Bowling Green are greatly enhanced by the residential nature of the campus.

Location

Bowling Green is a northwestern Ohio community, located 23 miles south of Toledo and within a 100-mile radius of Ann Arbor, Detroit, Cleveland, and Columbus. The community offers numerous recreational and cultural programs that supplement the activities offered by the University.

The University

Bowling Green, a state-assisted university, was founded in 1910. The University has a 1,250-acre campus. Graduate programs are offered in six academic colleges—Arts and Sciences, Business Administration, Education and Human Development, Health and Human Services, Musical Arts, and Technology—within the Graduate College. Each year, the University invites visiting scholars, guest artists, and celebrities to lecture, perform, and meet informally with students to exchange ideas and information.

Applying

Applicants must have graduated with a baccalaureate degree from a regionally accredited college or university. Assistantships are awarded for the academic year beginning in the fall semester. Applicants for financial aid are encouraged to complete the admission process by January 15. The application for admission to the Graduate College should be submitted with a $30 nonrefundable application fee. Students should apply six months in advance for admission to a Ph.D. program and three months in advance for a master's program. International students should allow more time for the application process. Two official transcripts from all colleges attended are required. GRE General Test or GMAT scores must be submitted. TOEFL scores must be submitted by all applicants whose first language is not English. Three letters of recommendation must be forwarded to the department to which admission is requested.

Correspondence and Information

Office of Graduate Admissions
120 McFall Center
Bowling Green State University
Bowling Green, Ohio 43403-0180

Phone: 419-372-2791
Fax: 419-372-8569
E-mail: prospct@bgnet.bgsu.edu
Web site: http://www.bgsu.edu/colleges/gradcol

FACULTY HEADS

All telephone numbers are preceded by the area code 419.

GRADUATE COLLEGE

Heinz Bulmahn, Ph.D., Vice Provost for Research and Dean of the Graduate College, 372-7714.
Deanne Snavely, Ph.D., Associate Dean, 372-7710.
Lisa Chavers, Ph.D., Assistant Dean for Graduate Studies and Director of Project Search, 372-0343.
Terry Lawrence, Ph.D., Assistant Dean for Graduate Admissions, 372-7710.

ACADEMIC DEANS

Don Nieman, Ph.D., College of Arts and Sciences, 372-2340.
Rodney Rogers, Ph.D., College of Business Administration, 372-3411.
Rosalind Hammond, Ph.D., Interim Dean, College of Education and Human Development, 372-7403.
Linda Petrosino, Ph.D., College of Health and Human Services, 372-8243.
Richard Kennell, Ph.D., College of Musical Arts, 372-2188.
C. Wayne Unsell, Ph.D., College of Technology, 372-2438.
Thomas Atwood, J.D., College of University Libraries, 372-2106.
William Balzer, Ph.D., Continuing and Extended Education, 372-8183.

DEGREE PROGRAM GRADUATE COORDINATORS

College of Arts and Sciences

American Culture Studies: Don McQuarie, Ph.D., 372-0586 (dmcquar@bgsu.edu).
Art (School of): Shawn Morin, M.F.A., 372-7766 (morinsp@bgsu.edu).
Biology: Stan Smith, Ph.D., 372-8259 (stanlee@bgsu.edu).
Chemistry: Tom Kinstle, Ph.D., 372-2658 (tkinstl@bgsu.edu).
Communication Studies: Radhika Gajjala, Ph.D., 372-0528 (radhik@bgsu.edu).
Computer Science: Ron Lancaster, Ph.D., 372-8697 (rlancast@bgsu.edu).
Creative Writing: Larissa Celli, Ph.D., 372-7539 (slariss@bgsu.edu).
English: Piya Pal Lapinski, Ph.D., 372-7553 (piyapl@bgsu.edu).
Ethnic Studies: Timothy Messer-Kruse, Ph.D., 372-6056 (tmesser@bgsu.edu).
Geology: Peg Yacobucci, Ph.D., 372-7982 (mmyacob@bgsu.edu).
German, Russian, and East Asian Languages: Edgar Landgraf, Ph.D., 372-9517 (elandgr@bgsu.edu).
History: Walter Grunden, Ph.D., 372-8639 (wgrund@bgsu.edu).
Mathematics and Statistics: John Chen, Ph.D., 372-7481 (jchen@bgsu.edu).
Philosophy: Daniel Jacobson, Ph.D., 372-2117 (djacob@bgsu.edu).
Photochemical Sciences: Phil Castellano, Ph.D., 372-2033 (castell@bgsu.edu).
Physics and Astronomy: Lewis Fulcher, Ph.D., 372-2635 (fulcher@bgsu.edu).
Political Science/Public Administration: Shannon Orr, Ph.D., 372-7593 (skorr@bgsu.edu).
Popular Culture: Jeffrey Brown, Ph.D., 372-2982 (jabrown@bgsu.edu).
Psychology: Dale Klopfer, Ph.D., 372-2835 (klopfer@bgsu.edu).
Romance Languages/French: Deborah Schocket, Ph.D., 372-8632 (dschock@bgsu.edu).
Romance Languages/Spanish: Ernesto Delgrado, Ph.D., 372-7150 (eedelg@bgsu.edu).
Sociology: Steve Cernkovich, Ph.D., 372-2743 (scernko@bgsu.edu).
Technical Writing: Bill Coggin, Ph.D., 372-7552 (bcoggin@bgsu.edu).
Theater and Film: Jonathan Chambers, Ph.D., 372-9618 (jonathc@bgsu.edu).
Women's Studies: Vikki Krane, Ph.D., 372-2620 (vkrane@bgsu.edu).

College of Business Administration

Accounting/MIS: Alan Lord, Ph.D., 372-8045 (alord@bgsu.edu).
Applied Statistics/Operations Research: Jane Chang, Ph.D., 372-8683 (changj@bgsu.edu).
Economics: Peter VanderHart, Ph.D., 372-8070 (pvander@bgsu.edu).
Graduate Studies in Business (M.B.A.): Toby Swick, Ph.D., 372-2488 (tswick@bgsu.edu).
Organization Development: Angela Stoller, Ph.D., 372-8139 (astoll@bgsu.edu).

College of Education and Human Development

DIS/Guidance and Counseling: Gregory Garske, Ph.D., 372-7319 (ggarske@bgsu.edu).
DIS/Rehabilitation Counseling: Jay Stewart, Ph.D., 372-7301 (jstewar@bgsu.edu).
DIS/School Psychology: Audrey Ellenwood, Ph.D., 372-9848 (aellenw@bgsu.edu).
DIS/Special Education: Lessie Cochran, Ph.D., 372-7298 (llcochr@bgsu.edu).
DTL/Business Education: Bob Berns, Ph.D., 372-2904 (rberns@bgsu.edu).
DTL/Classroom Technology: Gregg Brownell, Ph.D., 372-9546 (gbrowne@bgnet.bgsu.edu).
DTL/Curriculum and Teaching: Larry Grasser, Ph.D., 372-9619 (larrygr@bgsu.edu).
DTL/Ed Administration and Leadership Studies: Patrick Pauken, Ph.D., 372-2550 (paukenp@bgsu.edu).
DTL/Reading: Cindy Hendricks, Ph.D., 372-7341 (cindyg@bgsu.edu).
Family and Consumer Sciences: Rebecca Pobocik, Ph.D., 372-7849 (pobocik@bgsu.edu).
Human Movement/Sport/Leisure Studies: Geoff Meek, D.A., 372-0501 (gmeek@bgsu.edu).
LPS/College Student Personnel: Michael Coomes, Ph.D., 372-7157 (mcoomes@bgsu.edu).
LPS/Ed Foundations and Inquiry Program: Rachel Vannatta, Ph.D., 372-7350 (rvanna@bgsu.edu).
LPS/Higher Education Administration: Michael Coomes, Ph.D., 372-7157 (mcoomes@bgsu.edu).
LPS/MACIE: Peggy Booth, Ph.D., 372-9950 (boothmz@bgsu.edu).

College of Health and Human Services

Communication Disorders: Lynne Hewitt, Ph.D., 372-7181 (lhewitt@bgsu.edu).
Criminal Justice: Bill King, Ph.D., 372-0373 (kingw@bgsu.edu).
Gerontology: Nancy Orel, Ph.D., 372-7768 (norel@bgsu.edu).
Public Health: Fleming Fallon, Ph.D., 372-8316 (ffallon@bgsu.edu).

College of Musical Arts

William Mathis, Ph.D., 372-8066 (wmathis@bgsu.edu).

College of Technology

Donna K. Trautman, Ph.D., 372-7575 (dktraut@bgsu.edu).

"Electric Falcon," the electric automobile developed by the College of Technology.

A professor with students and a telescope in the Physics and Astronomy Observatory.

Theater production of "The Good Times Are Killing Me."

BRANDEIS UNIVERSITY

Graduate School of Arts and Sciences

Programs of Study Doctoral study is the foundation of the Graduate School of Arts and Sciences (GSAS). Required teaching and research components are an integral part of the educational development of all doctoral students. Ph.D. degrees are offered in American and comparative history, anthropology, biochemistry, chemistry, computer science, English and American literature, mathematics, molecular and cell biology, musicology and music composition, Near East and Judaic studies, neuroscience, physics, politics, psychology, sociology, and structural biology and biophysics.

Terminal master's degrees are offered in most of the Ph.D. programs; master's and postbaccalaureate programs are offered in ancient Greek and Roman studies, coexistence and conflict, cultural production, genetic counseling, Jewish studies, premedical studies, studio art, teaching of Hebrew, and theater arts (acting and design). Joint master's degrees are offered in women's and gender studies with anthropology, English, Near Eastern and Judaic studies, or sociology. A Master of Arts in Teaching (M.A.T.) (elementary and secondary) is offered. A dual M.B.A./M.A. in Jewish professional leadership and a joint M.A. in Jewish professional leadership and Near Eastern and Judaic studies are also offered.

Research Facilities Research facilities include the International Center for Ethics, Justice, and Public Life; Women's Studies Research Center; the Volen National Center for Complex Systems; the Ashton Graybiel Spatial Orientation Laboratory; the Feminist Sexual Ethics Project; the Gordon Public Policy Center; the Andrei Sakharov Archives and Human Rights Center; the Lown School of Near Eastern and Judaic Studies; the Rosenstiel Basic Medical Sciences Research Center; the Tauber Institute for the Study of European Jewry; and the Goodman Institute for the Study of Zionism.

The University libraries offer a combined collection of more than 1 million print volumes, 880,000 microforms, 385,000 U.S. documents, and over 16,000 current serial and journal subscriptions (print and electronic), along with numerous other electronic resources. The Goldfarb/Farber Libraries house resources and services supporting the humanities, the social sciences, Judaica, creative arts, and intercultural studies. The Gerstenzang Library supports teaching and research in physics, chemistry, the life sciences, mathematics, and computing science. The Rapaporte Treasure Hall hosts many concerts and lectures and houses some of the special collections of rare books and materials. The Rose Art Museum includes daring exhibits by outstanding contemporary artists, as well as significant works from the University's permanent collection.

Financial Aid Most doctoral candidates are offered a 100 percent tuition scholarship and fellowship, renewable for at least four years. Advanced doctoral candidates may apply for a number of other awards, including the Dissertation Year Fellowship, a University Prize Instructorship, and the Sachar Awards for research and study abroad. A limited number of need-based and merit-based awards for up to 50 percent of tuition are available to master's candidates.

Cost of Study Tuition for the 2006–07 academic year was $32,951. Annual tuition for the postbaccalaureate studio art program was $17,500. Annual tuition for the Master of Arts in Teaching program was $20,250. Tuition for postbaccalaureate premedical studies and part-time residence was $4119 per course, per term.

Living and Housing Costs Most students live either in Waltham or Cambridge/Somerville. Both areas have large student populations; many local services are easily accessible to students without a car at Brandeis. On-campus housing is extremely limited, and preference is usually given to first-year international students from outside North America.

The coordinators of Graduate Student Services actively assist graduate students with their housing search. A large-scale house hunting weekend is held every July. In addition, Graduate Student Services monitors an e-mail list of available rental units and those seeking apartments and maintains a Web page that includes links to local housing Web sites and classified advertisements. The cost of living is comparable to that of most large metropolitan areas.

Student Group The Graduate School of Arts and Sciences student profile is a diverse one, with students from all parts of the United States and various countries around the world. More than 1,000 students are enrolled in the Graduate School, of whom 28 percent are international, 47 percent are women, and 90 percent are full-time students. The average age of the GSAS student is 30 years.

Student Outcomes After completing their programs, graduates regularly go on to positions in academics and in industry. Recent graduates have obtained tenure-track positions at Yale, Rutgers, Colgate, Boston College, University of California (Berkeley), and Virginia Commonwealth University. Postdoctoral positions have been held at Harvard Medical School, Yale Medical School, University of Pennsylvania Medical School, Massachusetts Institute of Technology, Boston College, the Joslin Clinic, and Beth Israel Hospital. Placements in the private sector include those at IBM, Chase Manhattan Bank, and Dupont-Merck.

Location The Greater Boston area is rich in culture, education, and opportunities. Brandeis University, located just 10 miles west of Boston, consists of more than 90 buildings on 235 acres of rolling land and is in proximity to museums, theaters, and other attractions of the city, as well as to ocean beaches, canoeing on the Charles River, historic towns, and countryside for hiking or cross-county skiing. Brandeis is easily accessible by major routes and by public transportation.

The University Brandeis University is a private, coeducational, and nonsectarian institution of high education and research. Founded in 1948, Brandeis brings to American higher education a unique cultural perspective reflecting Jewish traditions of scholarship and community service and the commitment to social justice personified by Louis Dembitz Brandeis, the distinguished Supreme Court Justice for whom the University is named. While Brandeis maintains a special relationship with the Jewish community, it is not affiliated with any religious organizations; it offers no theological instruction and it welcomes students and faculty members of all backgrounds and beliefs.

Applying The Graduate School generally accepts students for the fall semester, and electronic application is encouraged. The deadline for applications to the Ph.D. programs is January 15; deadlines to the master's and postbaccalaureate programs vary by department. The application fee is $55. Admission to the graduate programs is based on each applicant's prior scholastic achievement, statement of purpose, letters of recommendation, and for most programs, results of the GRE. Applications for the programs in theater or studio arts are evaluated on the basis of the applicant's portfolio. Nonnative speakers of English must submit official results of the TOEFL, with a minimum score of 600 on the paper-based test, 250 on the computer-based test, or 100 on the Internet-based test. Alternatively, applicants may submit the results of the IELTS, with a minimum score of 7.

Correspondence and Information

Graduate School of Arts and Sciences
Brandeis University
P.O. Box 9110 MS 031
Waltham, Massachusetts 02454-9110

Phone: 781-736-3410
Fax: 781-736-3412
E-mail: gradschool@brandeis.edu
Web site: http://www.brandeis.edu/gsas

THE FACULTY AND THEIR RESEARCH

The contributions of scholars and researchers at Brandeis are known throughout their fields. Ninety-eight percent of full-time faculty members hold the Ph.D. degree or highest terminal degree in their field. Many Brandeis scholars and researchers are members of the National Academy of Sciences and fellows of the American Association for the Advancement of Science. Others are members of the American Academy of Arts and Sciences. Each year Brandeis faculty members are awarded Fulbright Scholarships, Guggenheim Fellowships, National Institutes of Health, and other national and international awards, professional memberships, and National Science Foundation Grants. Several faculty members are recipients of the MacArthur Fellowship, also known as a "Genius Grant." The School of Creative Arts is home to an award-winning faculty in fine arts, music, and theater arts. The University is a member of the prestigious Association of American Universities.

American History: Office: 781-736-2270; Ph.D., M.A.: delorenzo@brandeis.edu.
Ancient Greek and Roman Studies: Office: 781-736-2180; Certificate; classics@brandeis.edu.
Anthropology: Office: 781-736-2210; Ph.D., M.A.: eschatt@brandeis.edu; joint M.A. with Women's and Gender Studies: slamb@brandeis.edu.
Biochemistry: Office: 781-736-2300; Ph.D.: lolsen@brandeis.edu.
Biophysics and Structural Biology: Office: 736-3100; Ph.D.: biophysics@brandeis.edu.
Chemistry: Office: 781-736-2500; Ph.D.: chemadm@brandeis.edu.
Coexistence and Conflict: Office: 781-736-5001; M.A.: coexistence@brandeis.edu.
Comparative History: Office: 781-736-2270; Ph.D., M.A.: delorenzo@brandeis.edu.
Computer Science: Office: 781-736-2701; Ph.D., M.A.: maf@cs.brandeis.edu.
Cultural Production: Office: 781-736-2210; M.A.: mausland@brandeis.edu.
Education, Elementary and Secondary: Office: 781-736-2002; M.A.T.: mat@brandeis.edu.
English and American Literature: Office: 781-736-2130; Ph.D., M.A., joint M.A. with Women's and Gender Studies: chaucer@brandeis.edu.
Genetic Counseling: Professor Judith Tsipis: 781-736-3165; M.S.: goldberg@brandeis.edu.
Jewish Professional Leadership: Office: 781-736-2990; dual M.A./M.B.A., joint M.A. with Near Eastern Judaic Studies: hornstein@brandeis.edu.
Mathematics: Office: 781-736-3051; Ph.D.: maths@brandeis.edu.
Molecular and Cell Biology: Biology Office: 781-736-3100; M.S., Ph.D.: cabral@brandeis.edu.
Music: Office: 781-736-3311; Composition and Theory Ph.D., M.F.A., M.A.; Musicology Ph.D., M.F.A., M.A., joint M.A. with Women's and Gender Studies: kagan@brandeis.edu.
Near Eastern and Judaic Studies: Office: 781-736-2957; Ph.D., M.A., Diploma, joint M.A. with Jewish Professional Leadership: judaica@brandeis.edu.; joint Ph.D. with Sociology: fishman@brandeis.edu; joint M.A. with Women's and Gender Studies: brooten@brandeis.edu.
Neuroscience: Biology Office: 781-736-3145; Ph.D., M.S.: cabral@brandeis.edu.
Physics: Office: 781-736-2800; Ph.D.: physics1@brandeis.edu.
Politics: Office: 781-736-2750; Ph.D., M.A.: omalleyk@brandeis.edu.
Premedical Studies: Office: 781-736-3465; Certificate: kfconnelly@brandeis.edu.
Psychology: Office: 781-736-3301; Ph.D.: dizio@brandeis.edu; M.A.: tcross@brandeis.edu.
Sociology: Office: 781-736-2631; Ph.D., M.A., joint M.A with Women's and Gender Studies: khansen@brandeis.edu.
Studio Art: Office: 781-736-2656; Certificate: wardwell@brandeis.edu.
Theater Arts: Office: 781-736-3340; M.F.A.: theater@brandeis.edu.

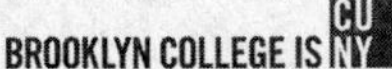

BROOKLYN COLLEGE OF THE CITY UNIVERSITY OF NEW YORK

Division of Graduate Studies

Programs of Study The Brooklyn College Division of Graduate Studies, founded in 1935, offers more than seventy-five full- and part-time master's degree and advanced certificate programs. These include programs leading to the Master of Arts, Master of Fine Arts, Master of Music, Master of Professional Studies, Master of Public Health, Master of Science, and Master of Science in Education degrees, as well as to a combined Bachelor of Science/Master of Professional Studies degree (in computer and information sciences and economics) and a Master of Arts/Doctor of Jurisprudence degree (offered jointly with Brooklyn Law School). In addition, on the Brooklyn College campus, doctoral students can pursue courses in biology, chemistry, computer and information science, earth and environmental sciences, physics, and psychology. The City University of New York Graduate Center (CUNY Graduate Center) administers doctoral programs in more than thirty disciplines, but, depending on the field, some courses are offered at the senior colleges of CUNY. The following Master of Arts programs are offered in the liberal arts and sciences: art history, biology, chemistry, community health (community health education, thanatology), computer and information science, economics, economics-accounting, English, French, geology, graphics/multimedia, history, Judaic studies, liberal studies, mathematics, music (musicology, performance practice), physics, political science, psychology (experimental, industrial/organizational), sociology, Spanish, speech (public communication), theater (history and criticism), and urban policy and administration. Programs leading to the Master of Fine Arts degree are offered in art (digital art, drawing and painting, photography, printmaking, sculpture), creative writing (fiction, playwriting, poetry), television production, and theater (acting, design and technical production, directing, dramaturgy, performing arts management). An interdisciplinary Advanced Certificate is offered in performance and interactive media arts. Programs leading to the Master of Music degree are offered in composition and performance. Programs leading to the Master of Public Health degree are offered in community health, health-care management, and health-care policy and administration. Programs leading to the Master of Science degree are offered in audiology, computer science and health science, exercise science and rehabilitation, information systems, nutrition, physical education (sports management), speech-language pathology, and television and radio. The teacher education program offers Master of Arts programs in art and music (all grades); biology, chemistry, English, French, general science (grades 5–9); and mathematics, physics, social studies, and Spanish (adolescent education, grades 7–12). The Master of Science in Education is offered with specializations in childhood education (bilingual teaching, liberal arts, mathematics, and science and environmental education, grades 1–6), early childhood education (birth–grade 2), health education (all grades), literacy education, middle childhood specialist studies (mathematics, grades 5–9), physical education (all grades), school counseling (bilingual studies extension may also be earned), school psychologist studies (bilingual extension may also be earned), and teaching students with disabilities in early childhood and childhood education and speech and language disabilities. Advanced Certificate programs are offered in school administration and supervision, guidance and counseling, music education, and school psychology.

Research Facilities The recently renovated library, the most technologically advanced facility in the CUNY system, includes a state-of-the-art book collection that houses more than 1.3 million volumes. Additional special libraries are available on campus for art, classics, economics, music, and speech communication arts and sciences. A number of campus research centers are available, and many of them publish their own scholarly research. These include the Africana Research Center, Archaeological Research Center, Center for Italian American Studies, Wolfe Institute for the Humanities, Center for Nuclear Theory, Applied Sciences Institute, Institute for Studies in American Music, Center for Latino Studies, Children's Studies Center, and Center for the Study of World Television. Other special facilities include solid-state and solar-energy laboratories, nuclear physics laboratories, an astronomical observatory, the Infant Study Center, Early Childhood Center, a greenhouse, an electronic music studio and Center for Computer Music, and the Speech and Hearing Center (and affiliated Center for Assistive Technology). The College maintains several large-scale computing facilities (more than 1,000 computers are available to students overall on the campus), including the Morton and Angela Topfer Library Café, the only CUNY facility open to students 24 hours a day, seven days a week. All campus computers are linked via high-speed networking to campus resources, the Internet, and CUNY's central mainframe facility, one of the largest academic computer centers in the country.

Financial Aid Federal and state aid programs available to eligible students include the Federal Perkins Loans program, Federal Work-Study Program, Federal Ford Direct Student Loan program, Veterans Administration Education Benefits program, and New York State Tuition Assistance Program. Fellowships, lectureships, and research assistantships are available through college funds, research grants, and outside agencies. Students may also apply through their departments for Fulbright scholarships and other international fellowships.

Cost of Study The Division of Graduate Studies at Brooklyn College provides advanced education of superior quality at a comparatively modest tuition. In 2006–07, graduate tuition for New York State residents was $3200 per semester full-time and $270 per credit part-time. Tuition for nonresidents and international students was $500 per credit, full-time or part-time. Tuition and fees are subject to change without notice.

Living and Housing Costs The following estimates of costs for graduate study for the 2003–04 academic year may help students determine if they need assistance. Full-time, independent students budgeted in excess of $11,000 for books, supplies, transportation, food, and living expenses for the nine-month academic year. Brooklyn College does not provide on-campus housing.

Student Group Students from all over the world attend the Division of Graduate Studies. About 65 to 70 percent are women, and about 90 percent attend part-time. The average age of students is 29. Many students are employed in the public schools in the greater New York City area.

Location Situated on one of the loveliest urban campuses in the country, the College encompasses 26 acres of broad lawns and tree-lined walkways and features a classic quadrangle surrounded by redbrick Georgian-style buildings. A second green quadrangle will extend the campus when a state-of-the-art student services and physical education building, currently under construction, is completed in 2008. The many different cultures of Brooklyn contribute to the wide ethnic diversity of the College's student and teacher population. Easy accessibility to a wide variety of New York City cultural events and institutions enriches students' educational experience. Subway and bus transportation to all points inside and outside the borough is easily accessible from the College. On-campus parking for students is available on a limited basis.

The College Brooklyn College, founded in 1930, was the first four-year, coeducational liberal arts college in New York City. In 1961, the College became part of the City University of New York. In fall 2006, approximately 12,000 undergraduate and 4,000 graduate students were enrolled in more than 125 degree and certificate programs. Brooklyn College is accredited by the Middle States Association of Colleges and Schools; its programs are registered by the New York State Department of Education and accredited by the Association of American Universities, the American Association of University Women, the Educational Standards Board of the American Speech-Language-Hearing Association, the Council on Education in Public Health, and the Northeastern Association of Graduate Schools.

Applying Admission to the Division of Graduate Studies is determined by graduate faculty, departmental, and/or program committees. All applicants are advised to review special admissions and matriculation requirements for each program, as stated in the *Brooklyn College Bulletin*. Applicants must have a baccalaureate degree from an accredited institution and have completed an approved program with a minimum average of B in the major and B– overall. Some programs require such specialized tests as the GRE. Applications and supporting credentials, including official transcripts, must be received by March 1 for the summer and fall terms, November 1 for the spring term, and March 1 for selected teacher education programs. Students educated outside the United States must file applications by February 1 for the summer and fall terms and by October 1 for the spring term. Late applicants may also submit their applications on a rolling basis; acceptance is determined solely by the department. Students may request an application from the Office of Admissions or apply online at the College's Web site.

Correspondence and Information

Office of Admissions
1103 James Hall
Brooklyn College
The City University of New York
2900 Bedford Avenue
Brooklyn, New York 11210-2889
Phone: 718-951-5001
Web site: http://www.brooklyn.cuny.edu

THE FACULTY

Christoph M. Kimmich, President; D.Phil., Oxford (England).
Louise Hainline, Dean of Research and Graduate Studies; Ph.D., Harvard.
Deborah A. Shanley, Dean of the School of Education; Ed.D., Columbia.
Kathleen McSorley, Assistant Dean; Ed.D., Syracuse.
Peter Taubman, Assistant Dean; Ed.D., Rochester.

DEPARTMENT AND PROGRAM HEADS

Art
Michael Mallory, Chairperson and Counselor for the Graduate M.A. Program in Art History; Ph.D., Columbia.
Janet Carlile, Graduate Deputy; M.F.A., Pratt.

Biology
John Blamire, Chairperson; Ph.D., Manchester (England).
Charlene Forest, Graduate Deputy; Ph.D., Indiana.

Chemistry
James Howell, Chairperson; Ph.D., Cornell.
Richard Magliozzo, Graduate Deputy; Ph.D., CUNY Graduate Center.

Computer and Information Science
Aaron M. Tenenbaum, Chairperson; Ph.D., NYU.
Keith Harrow, Graduate Deputy (Administrative); Ph.D., NYU.
Daniel Kopec, Graduate Deputy (Counseling); Ph.D., Edinburgh.

Conservatory of Music
Bruce MacIntyre, Director; Ph.D., CUNY Graduate Center.
Stephanie Jensen-Moulton, Graduate Deputy; M.M., Boston University.

Economics
Robert Bell, Chairperson; Ph.D., Brunel (England).
Emanuel Thorne, Graduate Deputy (Economics); Ph.D., Yale.
Merih Uctum, Graduate Deputy (Economics Programs); Ph.D., Queen's at Kingston.
Moishe Zelcer, Graduate Deputy (Accounting Admissions); Ph.D., CUNY Graduate Center.
Kreindel Giladi, Graduate Deputy (Accounting Programs); M.A., CUNY, Baruch.

School of Education
Deborah A. Shanley, Dean; Ed.D., Columbia Teachers College.
Educational Leadership (Advanced Certificate): David Bloomfield, J.D., Columbia.
Adolescence Education: Stephen Phillips, M.A., Stanford.
Childhood Bilingual Education: Alma Rubal-Lopez, Ph.D., Yeshiva.
Childhood Liberal Arts Education: Sharon O'Connor-Petruso, Ph.D., Ed.D., St. John's (New York).
Childhood Mathematics Education: Mary Chiusano, M.A., NYU.
Childhood Science and Environmental Education and Middle Childhood General Science Education: Konstantinos Alexakos, Ph.D., Columbia Teachers College.
Early Childhood Education: Mary DeBey, Ph.D., SUNY at Albany.
Middle Childhood Mathematics Education: Mary Chiusano, M.A., NYU.
School Counseling (Advanced Certificate and M.S. in Education): Lynda Sarnoff, Ph.D., CUNY, Staten Island.
School Psychology (Advanced Certificate and M.S. in Education): Florence Rubinson, Ph.D., Fordham.
Teacher of Students with Speech and Language Disabilities: Gail Gurland, Ph.D., CUNY Graduate Center.
Teacher of Students with Disabilities in Early Childhood and Childhood Education: Pauline Bynoe, Ed.D., Columbia Teachers College.

English
Ellen Tremper, Chairperson; Ph.D., Harvard.
Mark Patkowski, Graduate Deputy; Ph.D., NYU.

General Science
Eleanor Miele, Interdepartmental Coordinator; Ph.D., Columbia.

Geology
Wayne G. Powell, Chairperson; Ph.D., Queen's at Kingston.
Constantin Crânganu, Graduate Deputy; Ph.D., Oklahoma.

Health and Nutrition Sciences
Leslie Jacobson, Chairperson; Ph.D., NYU.
Kathleen Axen, Graduate Deputy (Nutrition); Ph.D., Columbia.
Jean Grassman, Graduate Deputy (Health); Ph.D., Berkeley.

History
David G. Troyansky, Chairperson; Ph.D., Brandeis.
Steven Remy, Graduate Deputy; Ph.D., Ohio.

Judaic Studies
Sara Reguer, Chairperson; Ph.D., Columbia.
Herbert Druks, Graduate Deputy; Ph.D., NYU.

Liberal Studies
George Brinton, Director; Ph.D., Washington (Seattle).

Mathematics
George Shapiro, Chairperson; Ph.D., Harvard.
William Miller, Graduate Deputy; M.A., CUNY, Brooklyn.

Modern Languages and Literatures
William M. Sherzer, Chairperson and Graduate Deputy; Ph.D., Princeton.

Physical Education and Exercise Science
Charles Tobey, Chairperson; Ed.D., Columbia.
Michael Hipscher, Graduate Deputy; M.A., NYU.

Physics
Peter Lesser, Chairperson; Ph.D., Rochester.
Ming-Kung Liou, Graduate Deputy; Ph.D., Manitoba.

Political Science
Sally Bermanzohn, Chairperson; Ph.D., CUNY Graduate Center.
Mark Ungar, Graduate Deputy; Ph.D., Columbia.
Joseph F. Wilson, Graduate Deputy (Worker Education Program); Ph.D., Columbia.

Psychology
R. Glen Hass, Chairperson; Ph.D., Duke.
Benzion Chanowitz, Graduate Deputy; Ph.D., CUNY Graduate Center.
Elisabeth Brauner, Ph.D. Subprogram Head (Mind, Brain, and Behavior); Dr.rer.nat., Göttingen (Germany).

Sociology
Kenneth A. Gould, Chairperson; Ph.D., Northwestern.
Alex Vitale, Graduate Deputy; Ph.D., CUNY Graduate Center.

Speech Communication Arts and Sciences
Timothy J. Gura, Chairperson; Ph.D., Northwestern.
Gail Gurland, Graduate Deputy (Teacher of Students with Speech and Language Disabilities); Ph.D., CUNY Graduate Center.
Michael Bergen, Director, Speech and Hearing Clinic; M.S., CUNY, Brooklyn.

Television and Radio
George R. Rodman, Chairperson; Ph.D., USC.
Katherine G. Fry, Graduate Deputy; Ph.D., Temple.

Theater
Rose Burnett Bonczek, Chairperson; M.F.A., CUNY, Brooklyn.
Tobie Stein, Graduate Deputy; Ph.D., CUNY Graduate Center.

DISTINGUISHED PROFESSORS

Edwin Burrows (History), Ph.D., Columbia.
Michael Cunningham (English), M.F.A., Iowa.
Jack Flam (Art), Ph.D., NYU.
Tania León (Music), M.A., NYU.
Rohit Parikh (Computer and Information Science), Ph.D., Harvard.
Theodore Raphan (Computer and Information Science), Ph.D., CUNY Graduate Center.
Anthony Sclafani (Psychology), Ph.D., Chicago.

BRYN MAWR COLLEGE

Graduate School of Arts and Sciences

Programs of Study Bryn Mawr's Ph.D. programs prepare candidates for academic and research careers in colleges and universities, museums, government and nongovernment agencies, and private enterprise. Graduates of the program in clinical developmental psychology are also prepared for counseling and for school and hospital administration. The Ph.D. is offered in chemistry; classical and Near Eastern archaeology; clinical developmental psychology; Greek, Latin, and classical studies; history of art; mathematics; physics; and Russian. The M.A. program in French prepares students for the best American Ph.D. programs as well as for teaching and many other professions using French.

A full-time course load is 3 units (courses) per semester; 6 units are required for the M.A. and 12 for the Ph.D. The M.A. can be earned in one or two years. Ph.D. preliminary examinations are normally taken in the fourth or fifth year, followed by two to three years on the dissertation. The program in clinical developmental psychology follows a somewhat different schedule and requires 18 units for completion.

Bryn Mawr is both teaching and research intensive. The science programs offer particularly close mentoring in teaching and research and are well suited to students who aim for a teaching career. The College's small scale and informality guarantee easy access to faculty mentors and facilitate participation in the academic offerings of other departments. Students typically take an active role in the design of their program of courses and their research. Good writing skills, independence, and originality are prized in all programs.

Research Facilities Collectively, the Mariam Coffin Canaday Library, the Lois and Reginald Collier Science Library, and the Rhys Carpenter Library contain more than 1 million volumes and provide access to more than 5,200 electronic journals. The tri-college consortium of Bryn Mawr, Haverford, and Swarthmore Colleges makes an additional 1 million volumes readily accessible. Rhys Carpenter Library is a specialized library for archaeology, classics, and the history of art and architecture, which contains more than 133,000 volumes, 250,000 electronic monographs, 153,000 e-books, and the Visual Resources Center, as well as 103 networked carrels for students, five classrooms, and a computer lab.

The Park Science complex includes state-of-the-art laboratories and the following major equipment for chemistry: a 300 MHz NMR spectrometer, a gas chromatograph-mass spectrometer, FT-IR spectrophotometer, fluorescence diode array UV-Vis spectrometers, high-pressure liquid chromatographs, ultracentrifuge, radioisotope facilities, a cold room, and four computer modeling workstations. In addition, faculty members' research laboratories contain the appropriate instrumentation to perform experiments in biological, organic, inorganic, and physical chemistry.

The Photo-Physics Laboratory houses three optical tables; three Nd:YAG pump lasers; two commercial, tunable dye lasers; two auto-tracking harmonic crystal systems; a differentially pumped vacuum chamber with two supersonic pulsed valves to produce molecular beams and time-of-flight mass and fluorescence detection capabilities; and a suite of computerized data acquisition equipment.

The Ultracold Rydberg Atom Laboratory houses three optical tables, a rubidium magnetooptical trap, a pulsed Nd:YAG laser pumping several dye lasers, a mode-locked and q-switched Nd:YAG laser, a high-vacuum atomic beam system, and a computerized data acquisition system.

Financial Aid Bryn Mawr offers fellowships and teaching assistantships for full-time study, as well as grants, tuition awards, and summer stipends. Fellowship stipends begin at $16,000, including a subsidy for health insurance and can be guaranteed for up to four years. Assistantship stipends are $16,000, including the subsidy. Summer stipends range from $2000 to $4000. The Marguerite N. Farley Fellowship is reserved for students who come from outside the U.S. and carries a stipend of $16,474. Opportunities for students in the Graduate Group in Archaeology, Classics, and History of Art include Fellowships for Multi-disciplinary Study with twelve-month stipends of $21,000; Areté (Excellence) Fellowships with stipends of $20,500, including the insurance subsidy and summer support; and (for advanced students) Curatorial or Exhibitions internships. Members of underrepresented American minorities are eligible for Dean's Fellowships, with stipends of $19,500.

Cost of Study Full-time tuition, consisting of six courses per year, is $28,980; part-time tuition is $4895 per course. Units of supervised work cost $785, and the fee for maintaining matriculation (continuing enrollment) is $395 per semester.

Living and Housing Costs Students live locally or in Philadelphia. Shared apartments can be rented for $600 to $900 per month; food costs are about $150 per month. Other expenses include transportation (about $120 per month if living in Philadelphia) and health insurance ($2460 per year for domestic students; $1104 for international students).

Student Group Total enrollment in the Graduate School of Arts and Sciences is 175, including 137 women and 38 men. Eleven percent of students are international. Thirty-nine percent of students are full-time; 67 percent receive some form of financial aid, including 49 percent who receive a stipend. Programs range in size from 3 to 34 students; the largest program is history of art followed by clinical developmental psychology.

Student Outcomes Of Ph.D. graduates in the past five years, 78 percent (51 of 65) are employed in the field of their degree. In science and mathematics, 82 percent are employed in the field of their degree; in the humanities, 74 percent; and in clinical developmental psychology, 77 percent. Occupations include college and university teachers, research scientists, museum curators, clinicians and counselors, editors, and academic and foundation administrators.

Location Bryn Mawr is a suburb of Philadelphia, the fifth-largest city in the U.S. It is well served by rail lines (the Main Line) and by bus. Philadelphia is renowned for music, museums, and sports, and it is also a culinary mecca with restaurants serving many cuisines. The metropolitan area has more than 100 museums and fifty colleges and universities, with a total population of 220,000 students.

The College and The School Bryn Mawr is a liberal arts college for women with two coeducational graduate schools: the Graduate School of Arts and Sciences and the Graduate School of Social Work and Social Research. Bryn Mawr was the first women's college in the U.S. to offer the Ph.D. to women in 1888, and graduate education continues to be a significant part of its mission. Total enrollment is 1,799, of whom 1,378 are undergraduates.

Applying The deadline for application for admission with financial aid is January 3. Applications for admission without aid are accepted up to June 30 in all programs except clinical developmental psychology. GRE scores, a writing sample, and three letters of recommendation are required. Nonnative speakers of English must submit a TOEFL score (minimum 600, paper-based; 250, computer-based). Other requirements vary by department.

Correspondence and Information

Graduate School of Arts and Sciences
Thomas Library
Bryn Mawr College
101 North Merion Avenue
Bryn Mawr, Pennsylvania 19010-2899
Phone: 610-526-5072
E-mail: gsas@brynmawr.edu
Web site: http://www.brynmawr.edu/gsas/prospective_students/

THE FACULTY AND THEIR RESEARCH

Chemistry

Sharon J. Nieter Burgmayer, Professor; Ph.D., North Carolina, 1984. Inorganic and bioinorganic chemistry: the role of transition metals in enzymes.
Michelle M. Francl, Professor and Chair; Ph.D., California, Irvine, 1983. Physical chemistry, computational chemistry and molecular architecture.
Jonas Goldsmith, Assistant Professor; Ph.D., Cornell, 2002. Electrochemistry, development and characterization of functional nanomaterials.
William Malachowski, Associate Professor; Ph.D., Michigan, 1993. Synthetic organic chemistry, peptidomimetic synthesis, development of new asymmetric synthetic methods.
Frank B. Mallory, Professor; Ph.D., Caltech, 1958. Organic chemistry, photochemistry and clear magnetic resonance spectroscopy.
Susan A. White, Professor; Ph.D., Johns Hopkins, 1988. Biochemistry, biochemical studies of RNA and RNA-protein interactions.

Classical and Near Eastern Archaeology

Mehmet-Ali Ataç, Assistant Professor; Ph.D., Harvard, 2003. Visual and intellectual traditions of the ancient Near East; Neo-Assyrian iconography, Near Eastern and Egyptian kingship.
A. A. Donohue, Professor; Ph.D., NYU, 1984. History and historiography of classical art.
Peter Magee, Associate Professor; Ph.D., Sydney, 1996. Archaeology of south Asia, Iran, and Arabia; field methods; materials analysis.
James C. Wright, Professor and Chair; Ph.D., Bryn Mawr, 1978. Prehistory of the Aegean basin, settlement forms and architecture of classical Greece, theory and method.

Clinical Developmental Psychology

Kimberly Wright Cassidy, Associate Professor; Ph.D., Pennsylvania, 1993. Cognition and education, children's theory of mind, pheriological/prosodic aspects of language, children's understanding of literature.
Clark R. McCauley, Professor; Ph.D., Pennsylvania, 1970. Social cognition, individual differences, health psychology, stereotype.
Leslie Rescorla, Professor; Ph.D., Yale, 1976. Preschool language development and language delay, child psychiatric disorders, ability and achievement in school children.
Marc Schulz, Associate Professor; Ph.D., Berkeley, 1994. Marital relationships and their effects on children, family child-rearing environments, work stress and its impact on family life, emotion regulation in adolescents and adults.
Anjali Thapar, Associate Professor; Ph.D., Case Western Reserve, 1994. Cognitive psychology.
Earl Thomas, Professor and Chair; Ph.D., Yale, 1967. Neurobiology and psychopharmacology, animal models of psychopathology.
Robert H. Wozniak, Professor; Ph.D., Michigan, 1971. Developmental theory, history of psychology, speech regulation of action, family belief systems.

French

Koffi Anyinéfa, Associate Professor (Haverford College); Ph.D., Bayreuth (Germany), 1989. Francophone African and Caribbean literature.
Grace M. Armstrong, Professor and Chair; Ph.D., Princeton, 1973. Medieval French literature, feminist studies, narrative techniques.
Francis Higginson, Associate Professor; Ph.D., Berkeley, 1997. Twentieth-century French and Francophone literature, critical theory.
Brigitte Mahuzier, Associate Professor; Ph.D., Cornell, 1988. Narrative and poetry of the nineteenth and twentieth centuries; feminist, gender, and queer theory; visual arts and aesthetic theory.
David Sedley, Associate Professor (Haverford College); Ph.D., Princeton, 1999. Sixteenth- and seventeenth-century literature, critical theory.

Greek, Latin, and Classical Studies

Annette Baertschi, Assistant Professor; Ph.D., Humboldt, 2006. Post-Augustan poetry, ancient magic, Latin meter, reception.
Catherine Conybeare, Associate Professor; Ph.D., Toronto, 1997. Late antique and early medieval Latin prose, cultural history, critical theory.
Radcliffe Edmonds, Associate Professor; Ph.D., Chicago, 1999. Greek myth, Greco-Roman religion and magic, Greek philosophy.
Richard Hamilton, Professor and Chair; Ph.D., Michigan, 1971. Greek lyric poetry, Greek drama, Greek religion.
Russell T. Scott, Professor; Ph.D., Yale, 1964. Roman history and historiography, Latin literature, Roman archaeology.

History of Art

David J. Cast, Professor and Chair; Ph.D., Columbia, 1970. Renaissance art and criticism, architecture post-1400, twentieth-century British art.
Christiane Hertel, Professor; Ph.D., Tübingen (Germany), 1985. German, Austrian, and Netherlandish art and architecture; German intellectual history; aesthetics and art theory.
Homay King, Assistant Professor; Ph.D., Berkeley, 2003. American film history; film, feminist, psychoanalytic, and rhetorical theory.
Dale Kinney, Professor; Ph.D., NYU, 1975. Late antique and medieval Italian art, medieval architecture, spolia.
Steven Z. Levine, Professor; Ph.D., Harvard, 1974. Sixteenth-to-twentieth-century French painting, psychoanalysis, self-portraiture, visual theory.
Gridley McKim-Smith, Professor; Ph.D., Harvard, 1974. Seventeenth-century Spanish painting and sculpture, scientific analysis of works of art, costume.
Lisa Saltzman, Professor; Ph.D., Harvard, 1994. Post–World War II art and theory, gender and identity, memory and trauma.

Mathematics

Leslie C. Cheng, Associate Professor; Ph.D., Pittsburgh, 1998. Fourier analysis on Euclidean spaces, oscillatory integrals, singular integrals, Hardy spaces.
Victor J. Donnay, Professor; Ph.D., NYU, 1986. Dynamical systems, ergodic theory, differential geometry.
Helen G. Grundman, Professor and Chair; Ph.D., Berkeley, 1989. Algebra, algebraic number theory, analytic number theory.
Rhonda Hughes, Professor; Ph.D., Illinois, 1975. Functional analysis, harmonic and wavelet analysis, operator theory.
Paul M. Melvin, Professor; Ph.D., Berkeley, 1977. Algebraic and differential topology, low-dimensional manifolds, quantum topology.
Lisa Traynor, Professor; Ph.D., SUNY at Stony Brook, 1992. Symplectic topology, contact geometry, differential geometry and topology.

Physics

Peter A. Beckmann, Professor and Chair; Ph.D., British Columbia, 1985. Chemical physics, condensed-matter physics.
Elizabeth F. McCormack, Professor; Ph.D., Yale, 1989. Atomic, molecular, and optical physics.
Michael W. Noel, Associate Professor; Ph.D., Rochester, 1996. Atomic, molecular, and optical physics.
Michael B. Schulz, Assistant Professor; Ph.D. Stanford, 2002. Theoretical physics with a focus on string theory and its applications to quantum field theory.

Russian

Elizabeth C. Allen, Professor and Chair; Ph.D., Yale, 1984. Nineteenth-century Russian and European literature, literary periodization, literary theory.
Dan E. Davidson, Professor; Ph.D., Harvard, 1972. Second-language acquisition, international language policy, Russian linguistics.
Linda G. Gerstein, Professor (Haverford College); Ph.D., Harvard, 1966. Russian history, modern European history, history of Russian art and architecture.
Timothy C. Harte, Associate Professor; Ph.D., Harvard, 2001. Russian avant-garde literature and painting, Russian and Soviet film, contemporary Russian culture.
George S. Pahomov, Professor; Ph.D., NYU, 1973. Nineteenth-century Russian literature, Russian drama, Russian culture.

CALDWELL COLLEGE

Graduate Programs

Programs of Study

Caldwell College offers master's degree programs (Master of Business Administration and Master of Arts) and postbaccalaureate and post-master's certificate programs in the areas of business, education, pastoral ministry, and psychology. All programs are designed to meet the scheduling needs of adult students and the accepted professional standards for each discipline.

The 39-credit-hour M.B.A. degree program is offered as a generalist degree or with an optional concentration in accounting or nonprofit management. This program is designed to prepare students to meet the demands of the twenty-first-century business world. Courses are offered evenings, Saturdays, and via distance learning.

The Master of Arts (M.A.) degree is offered in several areas, including three in education. The M.A. in curriculum and instruction comprises 36 credit hours, and students may elect to complete one of three optional specializations—educational technology, special education, or supervisor's certification. An M.A. in educational administration is offered for students who seek certification as a school principal, administrator, supervisor, or business administrator. Students can pursue this 36-credit-hour degree program on campus in a traditional program or in the innovative, dynamic one-year Off-Campus Leadership Development (OCLD) fast-track program. An M.A. in special education prepares students to teach in an inclusive or self-contained classroom or to work in a related field in special education. In this program, students choose one of three specializations: teacher certification, applied behavior analysis (ABA, with a focus on autism), or learning disabilities.

In psychology, the M.A. is offered in counseling psychology in a 48-credit-hour degree program, with optional specializations available in school counseling and in New Jersey's only graduate art therapy curriculum, which is accredited by the American Art Therapy Association. The M.A. in applied behavior analysis is a 39-credit-hour program that trains students to meet the educational needs of children with autism-spectrum disorders and cognitive delays. The ABA core is approved by the Behavior Analyst Certification Board, Inc.®

A 36-credit-hour M.A. in pastoral ministry prepares individuals to support the pastoral mission of the Roman Catholic or other churches. Its nontraditional format, with classes offered on Saturdays and optional weekend nights, meets the personal and professional scheduling needs of students. It also offers an optional concentration in church administration, a growing need in today's church.

Postbaccalaureate certificate programs are offered in the fields of education and psychology. The Post-Baccalaureate Teacher Certification Program enables individuals who have bachelor's degrees to earn their elementary (K–8 or K–8 with P–3) teacher certification or K–12 subject-specific certification. The Post-Baccalaureate Special Education Certification Program prepares current teachers to earn additional certification as a Teacher of Students with Disabilities. The College also offers an approved Post-Baccalaureate Certificate Program in Applied Behavior Analysis that focuses on the educational needs of people with autism-spectrum disorders.

The College also offers four post-master's programs. The 30-credit-hour Art Therapy Specialization Program meets national standards for the educational requirements for registration as an art therapist. The Professional Counselor Licensing Program is intended for those who hold a master's degree in counseling or a closely related field and who need additional credits to qualify as a Licensed Professional Counselor in New Jersey. The School Counseling Specialization is intended for those who hold a master's degree in education, psychology, or a related field and need additional credits to qualify for a New Jersey school counselor credential. A new post-master's program for Director of School Counseling certification is now also offered, pending state approval. The Supervisor's Certificate Program meets New Jersey certification requirements for the Supervisor's Certificate for educators and those in educational support services.

Research Facilities

Caldwell College's Jennings Library offers students approximately 145,000 volumes, more than 3,000 bound periodicals, and more than 5,000 microfilm reels. It also provides access to more than 9,000 journal and newspaper titles in a variety of formats: electronic, paper, and microform. The audiovisual collection numbers almost 2,000 items and contains videotapes and audiotapes, compact discs, filmstrips, etc. There is full Internet access through various workstation clusters and remote access 24 hours a day, seven days a week, which allows for continuous access to most online databases. Online access to the collection is available through the Dynix Automated System (CALCAT), which is available on and off campus via the Internet. The collections are developed continuously to support the curricular needs of students and the faculty. As a member of the OCLC (Online Computer Library Center) and the New Jersey Library Network, the library provides access to more than 30 million titles in more than 5,000 national and international libraries. A curriculum laboratory has texts for grades K–12, visual aids, and other resources.

Computer labs, which include up-to-date personal computers installed with current software and multimedia equipment, offer free scanning and laser printing. Other computer labs dedicated to specific areas of study include the Education, Business, Psychology, and Writing labs. Technology-enhanced classrooms are equipped with digital audio and video and computer equipment. All offices, classrooms, and labs are connected to the campus network and the Internet. Wide-screen video and computer graphic capability and satellite reception are available. Through an agreement with Microsoft Corporation, certain software is available for sale to registered students at greatly reduced prices.

Through an almost $2-million federal government grant to establish the Center for Excellence in Teaching on campus, Caldwell College recently renovated its biology, physics, and chemistry laboratories in order to implement innovative teacher preparation programs that emphasize the effective use of technology in classrooms, the refinement of math and science training, special education teacher training, and the development of programs for disadvantaged students. The Center for Educational Technology, which is supported by Caldwell College and AT&T, offers local teachers a variety of services to assist them in implementing technology into the teaching and learning experience.

Financial Aid

Financial aid in the form of federal aid, tuition discounts, and graduate assistantships is available to matriculated graduate students who are taking at least 6 credits; some aid requires full-time status (9 credits).

Cost of Study

For the 2006–07 academic year, graduate tuition was $607 per credit hour.

Living and Housing Costs

There is no on-campus housing for graduate students.

Student Group

Caldwell College enrolls approximately 600 graduate students.

Location

Wooded areas surround Caldwell College's campus, which is located in suburban Caldwell, New Jersey. The College is near major highways and public transportation and is only 20 miles from New York City. Within walking distance is the town center, which has a variety of shops and restaurants. Area and regional attractions include theaters, museums, parks, ski resorts, malls, the Meadowlands Sports Complex, and the New Jersey shore. Many corporate headquarters are easily accessible and provide a variety of internship opportunities.

The College

Founded in 1939 by the Sisters of Saint Dominic, Caldwell College is committed to serving a diverse student population of all ages. The College offers high-quality career-related programs that prepare graduates to take advantage of opportunities in an increasingly complex society. The integration of the arts, humanities, and sciences with the deepest expression of the contemplative and creative spirit of men and women forms the basis of the educational philosophy of Caldwell College. The hallmark of a Caldwell College education is small classes, quality, professional relevance, and scheduling that accommodates working adults.

Applying

Students should begin the application process by submitting the online application. Specific application requirements vary by program. Students should consult the College's Web site to determine the requirements for the program in which they are interested, or they should contact the Office of Graduate Studies for more information.

Correspondence and Information

Office of Graduate Studies
Caldwell College
9 Ryerson Avenue
Caldwell, New Jersey 07006

Phone: 973-618-3408
Fax: 973-618-3640
E-mail: graduate@caldwell.edu
Web site: http://www.caldwell.edu/graduate

THE CORE FACULTY

In addition to the following core graduate faculty members—all of whom are full-time members of the Caldwell College faculty—the graduate faculty also includes talented and accomplished adjuncts who bring both academic and professional experience into the classrooms.

Ann Marie Callahan, Associate Professor of Business; M.S., Seton Hall; M.B.A., Saint Peter's; CPA.
Walter Cmielewski, Associate Professor of Education; Ed.D., Seton Hall.
John Fanning, Associate Professor of Education; Ed.D., Maryland.
Lori Harris-Ransom, Professor of Business; M.A., J.D., Saint Louis.
Marie Hudson, Professor of Psychology; Ph.D., New School.
Joanne Jasmine, Assistant Professor of Education; Ed.D., Columbia.
Lynne Kalustian, Full-time Lecturer in Education; Ed.D., Rutgers.
Anatoly Kandel, Associate Professor of Business and Toohey Chair in Economics; Ph.D., Institute of World Economy (Moscow); Ph.D., Columbia.
Thomas R. Keen, Professor of Business; M.B.A., Fairleigh Dickinson; Ph.D., Walden.
John McIntyre, Professor of Education; Ed.D., Rutgers.
Barbara Moore, O.P., Assistant Professor of Theology and Pastoral Ministry; D.Min., Drew.
Dorothy Mutch, Associate Professor of Education; Ed.D., Seton Hall.
Alvin Neiman, Professor of Business; M.B.A., Seton Hall; CPA.
Donald Noone, Professor of Business; Ph.L., Fordham; Ph.D., Rutgers.
Bernard C. O'Rourke, Associate Professor of Business; M.B.A., Fordham; J.D., King's Inns Law School (Dublin).
Linda Patriarca, Professor of Education; Ph.D., Michigan State.
Joseph Pedoto, Associate Professor of Psychology; Ph.D., Seton Hall.
Marilyn Persico, Full-time Lecturer in Education; Ed.D., Columbia.
Patrick Progar, Associate Professor of Psychology; Ph.D., Wisconsin–Milwaukee; BCBA.
Kenneth F. Reeve, Associate Professor of Psychology; Ph.D., CUNY Graduate Center.
Sharon A. Reeve, Assistant Professor of Education and Psychology; Ph.D., CUNY Graduate Center; BCBA.
Edith Dunfee Ries, Associate Professor of Education; Ed.D., Rutgers.
Anthony Romano, Assistant Professor of Business; M.B.A., Adelphi.
Edward J. Schons, Professor of Business; M.B.A., Boston University; M.B.A., Ph.D., Rutgers.
Tina Sidener, Assistant Professor of Psychology; Ph.D., Western Michigan; BCBA.
Stacey M. Solomon, Assistant Professor of Psychology; Ph.D., Virginia.
Janice Stewart, Professor of Education; Ph.D., Illinois.
Sr. Catherine Waters, O.P., Associate Professor of Psychology; Ph.D., Fordham; LPC.
Marie Wilson, Associate Professor of Art Therapy; M.A., Norwich; ATR-BC, LPC.
Rita Wolpert, Professor of Psychology; Ed.D., Columbia.

CALIFORNIA LUTHERAN UNIVERSITY

Graduate and Adult Programs

Programs of Study

California Lutheran University (CLU) offers graduate students high-quality educational programs, small classes, and opportunities to interact directly with professors who are passionate about teaching with degrees and credential programs both on campus and at off-campus centers.

Degree programs include the doctorate (Ed.D.) in educational leadership; the Master of Arts (M.A.) in educational leadership combined with a Tier I administrative credential and specializations in school site leadership, teacher leader, leadership in educational technology, or leadership in reading education; the Master of Science (M.S.) in clinical psychology; the M.S. in counseling and guidance, with specializations in pupil personnel services or college student personnel; the M.S. in counseling psychology, with an emphasis in marital and family therapy; the M.S. in special education; the M.S. in computer science; the Master of Education (M.Ed.); the Master of Business Administration (M.B.A.), with professional tracks in finance, information technology, international business, management, management and organizational behavior, marketing, or small business/entrepreneurship; the M.B.A. in financial planning; and the Master of Public Policy and Administration (M.P.P.A.).

Certificates are available in child development, director permit, child welfare and attendance, CLAD, computer concepts and applications supplementary authorization, financial planning, post-M.B.A., and resource specialist (special education).

Resource specialist credentials are offered in Preliminary Level I: mild to moderate or moderate to severe emphases or Professional Level II: mild to moderate and moderate to severe emphases.

Evening graduate programs attract students from many of Southern California's most notable companies. Programs are stimulating, rigorous, and ethically insightful, and classes average around 15 to 20 students. Convenient evening and weekend classes are offered at the main campuses in Thousand Oaks, as well as graduate centers in Woodland Hills and Oxnard. Cal Lutheran's programs for working professionals are known for their low student-faculty ratio of 15:1, a personalized learning environment, and staff support as well as a network of industry and community partnerships that facilitate relevant and timely learning and career advancement opportunities. Evening and weekend classes are offered to meet the needs of working professionals who must balance their education goals with the demands of career and home life.

Research Facilities

Pearson Library houses a core book collection complemented by journals, microfilms, audiovisual software, and access to electronic databases. Through OCLC, a major information database provider, the library has access to more than 80 research databases, which cover every major field of inquiry. CLU offers access to more than 14,000 full-text journals to assist students with their research needs. These journal databases are served over the Internet through the campus network service, CLUnet. Students can access CLUnet through wireless connections across the campus or from the library, any of several computer laboratories on campus, or off campus via the Internet.

Financial Aid

Each semester, a limited number of assistantships, which offer a tuition remission award of up to 5 credits per semester, are offered to qualified graduate students. Graduate scholarships for students in the Teacher Preparation Program, for example, average about $500 per semester, and the Cal Grant T awards cover one year of tuition and fees. The Lutheran Teacher Award for Lutheran schoolteachers and administrators allows for a tuition reduction each semester based on their current employment at a Lutheran school. The Graduate Assumption Program of Loans for Education (Graduate APLE) provides loan assumption benefits for up to 500 students with financial need who are pursuing a recognized graduate degree and intend to become college-level faculty members. Students are awarded up to $2000 a year for up to three years' teaching service at an accredited California college or university.

Cost of Study

Tuition costs vary by program. In 2007–08, tuition costs range from $345 per credit for a certificate program to $695 per credit for a doctoral program. Counseling psychology students are assessed an $800 practicum fee per semester.

Living and Housing Costs

Private apartments and rooms are available for rent in the surrounding communities. The director of residence life may be contacted for housing assistance. Limited on-campus housing within the residence halls may be available for unmarried graduate and fifth-year students. The Residence Life Office is able to assist graduate students with finding off-campus housing in the Conejo Valley area.

Student Group

Originating from across the nation and around the world, CLU's student body represents a wide diversity of faiths and cultures. There are currently 1,500 graduate students enrolled in the University.

The University's International Student Services (ISS) and the International Programs Office (IPO) provide support and advisement for international students. The IPO serves as an educational resource for students and faculty and staff members and also offers immigration advisement, workshops, and social activities. Programs and activities sponsored by the office encourage interaction between international and American students and promote diversity both on and off campus.

Location

Located in Thousand Oaks, midway between Santa Barbara and Los Angeles, CLU puts students within reach of a variety of cultural experiences and the international business community. With a population of approximately 100,000, Thousand Oaks offers the conveniences of an urban area, a state-of-the-art performing arts center, a presidential library and public affairs center, regional shopping centers, and internship opportunities in high-tech industries while maintaining its scenic natural beauty enhanced by designated open space, rolling hills, and picturesque oak trees. Incorporated in 1964, Thousand Oaks is located in Ventura County, 15 miles inland from the Pacific Ocean. Recreational and cultural opportunities abound. In addition to the Thousand Oaks Civic Arts Plaza and CLU's on-campus Cultural Events Series, world-renowned museums, concert halls, and world premier productions are within an hour's drive. Sports enthusiasts—both spectators and participants—appreciate the variety and accessibility of events within driving distance. Winter ski resorts are just 3 hours away, and both ocean and freshwater sports are less than an hour away. Hiking on the nearby trails, biking along scenic corridors, and CLU's active intercollegiate and intramural sports programs provide ample opportunity for involvement. According to FBI statistics over the past ten years, Thousand Oaks is among the safest cities in the nation with populations of more than 100,000. Off-campus graduate centers are conveniently located in Oxnard and Woodland Hills.

The University

Founded in 1959, California Lutheran University is part of a 500-year-old tradition of Lutheran higher education. CLU is a diverse scholarly community dedicated to excellence in the liberal arts and professional studies through visionary academics, cutting-edge faculty members, and inspirational teaching and mentoring. The relationship between faith and reason is at the core of CLU's character as a university. Rooted in the Lutheran tradition of Christian faith, the University encourages critical inquiry into matters of both faith and reason. The mission of the University is to educate leaders for a global society who are strong in character and judgment, confident in their identity and vocation, and committed to service and justice.

California Lutheran University is accredited by the Accrediting Commission for Senior Colleges of the Western Association of Schools and Colleges. CLU's uncompromising standards of high-quality education at a reasonable cost have earned its place in the top tier of Western Regional Colleges and Universities in the *U.S. News & World Report*'s annual rankings.

Applying

Students must have a bachelor's (or higher) degree at a regionally accredited college or university, with a minimum grade point average of 3.0 (on a 4.0 scale). Applicants must submit the completed application for admission, the nonrefundable $50 application fee, all official transcripts from the colleges or universities attended, three letters of recommendation, a personal statement (no longer than two typewritten pages) that describes the reason for pursuing a graduate degree at CLU, and official test scores from the GRE (education, psychology, and M.P.P.A. students) or the GMAT (business students). International applicants must also submit an English translation of all official transcripts, TOEFL scores, and a current statement that verifies that the applicant has sufficient financial resources for academic and personal expenses while attending CLU. Some programs have additional requirements. Candidates are notified of the admission decision soon after their admission portfolio is complete.

Correspondence and Information

Graduate and Adult Programs
California Lutheran University
60 West Olsen Road #2300
Thousand Oaks, California 91360-2700

Phone: 805-493-3127
888-CLU-GRAD (toll-free)
Fax: 805-493-3542
E-mail: clugrad@callutheran.edu
Web site: http://www.callutheran.edu/fastforward

THE FACULTY

California Lutheran University's students benefit from young faculty members on the cutting-edge of their crafts who embrace students' contributions to the classroom and to society. In CLU's graduate programs, high-quality instructors teach from "real world" concepts, drawing upon their knowledge and the students' experiences and applying them to the classroom. CLU faculty members have excellent reputations. Their honors range from the President's Award for Teaching Excellence to Fulbright Scholarships. Recognition for their scholarship has come from such internationally known organizations as the U.S. Olympic Committee and the National Academy of Sciences.

Denise Aiani, Lecturer in Education; M.A., California Lutheran.
Ali Akbari, Professor of Business Administration; Ph.D., USC.
Jim Allyn, Lecturer in Business; M.B.A., California Lutheran.
Robert B. Amenta, Professor Emeritus of Education; Ed.D., USC.
Robert M. Arce, Lecturer in Education; Ph.D., California, Santa Barbara.
Jan Atkinson, Lecturer in Education; M.A., California State, Northridge.
Barry C. Barmann, Assistant Professor of Psychology; Ph.D., California, Santa Barbara.
Todd Barnum, Lecturer in Business; M.S., Naval Postgraduate School.
Jerry Barshay, Lecturer in Education; Ed.D., La Verne.
Somnath Basu, Associate Professor of Business; Ph.D., Arizona.
Richard J. Battaglia, Lecturer in Education; M.A., Loyola.
Rosalie Bell, Lecturer in Education; Ph.D., San Francisco.
Robert D. Benedetto, Lecturer in Public Policy and Administration; D.P.A., La Verne.
Robert R. Bergeson, Lecturer in Public Policy and Administration; M.P.A., San Diego State.
Julius Bianchi, Lecturer in Education; M.P.A., Indiana.
Caroline Broomand, Lecturer in Education; Ed.D., Nova.
Wendy S. Brown, Lecturer in Psychology; M.A., California Graduate Institute.
Beverly R. Bryde, Associate Professor of Education; Ed.D., Widener.
Linda Calvin, Lecturer in Education; Ph.D., USC.
Richard Canady, Lecturer in Education; Ed.D., La Verne.
Melinda Carrillo, Lecturer in Education; M.A., Chapman.
Julie Cavaliere, Lecturer in Education; Ed.D., La Verne.
Penny Cefola, Associate Professor of English; Ph.D., Georgetown.
Carol Lynn Coman, Assistant Professor of Business Administration; M.S., California State, Northridge.
Janet Cooper, Lecturer in Education; M.A., California Lutheran.
Judith A. Crowe, Assistant Professor of Education; Ph.D., La Verne.
Mary Ann Cummins-Prager, Lecturer in Education; Ed.D., UCLA.
Robert Cunha, Lecturer in Education; M.A., California State, Northridge.
Jamshid Damooei, Professor of Economics; Ph.D., Surrey.
Gerald Dannenberg, Lecturer in Education; Ed.D., USC.
Gary Delanoeye, Lecturer in Education; M.S., California Lutheran.
Harry A. Domicone, Associate Professor of Business; Ph.D., Cincinnati.
Randall D. Donohue, Assistant Professor of Business; Ph.D., South Australia (Adelaide).
Diana Linn Eastin, Lecturer in Marital and Family Therapy; M.S., California Lutheran.
Frederick George Elias, Lecturer in Business Administration; Ph.D., California, Santa Barbara.
Wendy Erlanger, Clinical Instructor in Education; M.A., California Lutheran.
Deborah Erickson, Assistant Professor of Education; Ed.D., University of the Pacific.
Charles Espalin, Lecturer in Education; Ed.D., USC.
Roy Farmer, Lecturer in Business Administration; M.B.A., California Lutheran.
Steve Feder, Lecturer in Business; L.L.M., South Dakota.
Eugene Ferkich, Lecturer in Education; Ed.D., Nova.
Patricia Finn, Lecturer in Education; Ph.D., UCLA.
Robert Fraisse, Lecturer in Education; M.A., M.S., California Lutheran.
R. Kirkland Gable, Professor of Psychology; Ed.D., J.D., Harvard.
Anita Garaway-Furtaw, Lecturer in Education; M.A., California Lutheran.
Joe Garcia, Lecturer in Business; Ph.D., Shelbourne.
Kenneth Gardner, Professor of Drama; M.F.A., Ohio.
Blas M. Garza, Assistant Professor of Education; Ed.D., USC.
Paul Gathercoal Jr., Associate Professor of Education; Ph.D., Oregon.
Farrell Gean, Lecturer in Business; Ph.D., Georgia State.
Marylie Gerson, Assistant Professor of Psychology; Ph.D., Princeton.
Michael J. Gerson, Lecturer in Psychology; Ph.D., California Graduate Institute.
Herbert E. Gooch III, Associate Professor of Political Science; Ph.D., UCLA.
Karen Gorback, Lecturer in Education; Ph.D., California, Santa Barbara.
Greg Gose, Lecturer in Business; J.D., UCLA.
Kathy Greaves, Lecturer in Education; M.S., M.A., California Lutheran.
Walton Greene, Lecturer in Education; M.S., Pepperdine.
Ronald E. Hagler, Professor of Business; Ed.D., USC.
Miriam Hamideh, Lecturer in Psychology; Ph.D., Belgrano.
Marsha Hanus, Lecturer in Business; M.B.A., Pepperdine.
Thomas Hardy, Lecturer in Business Administration; Ph.D., Oregon State.
Lisa Hayden, Lecturer in Psychology; Psy.D., Pepperdine.
Augie Herrera, Lecturer in Education; M.A., California State, Los Angeles.
Jacquelyn Herst, Lecturer in Education; M.A., Pepperdine.
Janice Hoffman, Lecturer in Psychology; Pharm.D., USC.
David Holmboe, Lecturer in Education; M.S., California Lutheran.
Joseph Huggins, Senior Lecturer in Business Administration; M.A., M.B.A., NYU.
Chandy Jacob, Lecturer in Business; M.S., Osmania.
Cynthia Jew, Associate Professor of Education; Ph.D., Denver.
Edward H. Julius, Professor of Business Administration; M.S., Pennsylvania.
Ronald Kaiser, Lecturer in Education; M.A., California State, Northridge.
Silva Karayan, Associate Professor of Education; Ph.D., California, Santa Barbara.
Harold Robert Keatinge, Lecturer in Education; M.A., California, Santa Barbara.
Jonathon Klein, Lecturer in Business Administration; Ph.D., USC.
James Konantz, Lecturer in Education; M.A., California State, Northridge.
Bernard Korenstein, Lecturer in Education; Ed.D., Nova Southeastern.
Timothy G. Kuehnel, Lecturer in Psychology; Ph.D., Texas at Austin.
Anna Kwong, Lecturer in Business Administration; M.B.A., California Lutheran.
Marjorie T. Lageman, Lecturer in Education; M.Ed., Boston University.
Stanley Levin, Lecturer in Education; Ed.D., Nova Southeastern.
Hans G. Lingens, Lecturer in Education; Ed.D., USC.
Michael Lodato, Associate Professor of Business Administration; Ph.D., Rutgers.
Kelvin Loh, Lecturer in Public Policy and Administration; M.D., Howard.
Yvonne Lux, Senior Lecturer in Education; Ed.D., USC.
Robert Maas, Lecturer in Business Administration; M.B.A., California Lutheran.
Laura Mageary, Lecturer in Education; M.A., California State, Northridge.
John A. Marshall, Professor Emeritus of Education; Ed.D., Northern Colorado.
Christine M. Martin, Lecturer in Business Administration; M.B.A., Pepperdine.
Deborah Martinez-Rambeau, Lecturer in Education; M.A., California State, Northridge; M.S., Pepperdine.
Ronald M. Maurer, Lecturer in Education; M.A., California State, Los Angeles.
Charles T. Maxey, Professor of Business Administration; Ph.D., Illinois at Urbana-Champaign.
Richard Bruce McAndrew, Lecturer in Business Administration; B.S., Arizona State.
Michael McCambridge, Assistant Professor of Education; Ed.D., San Francisco.
Thomas McCambridge, Assistant Professor of Education; Ph.D., UCLA.
Harry McCracken, Lecturer in Business Administration; J.D., Western State.
Robert Meadows, Associate Professor of Administration of Justice; Ed.D., Pepperdine; Ph.D., Claremont.
Cheryl Meyers, Lecturer in Education; M.S., California Lutheran.
Dree Miller, Lecturer in Psychology; Ph.D., Columbia Pacific.
Jody Miller, Lecturer in Education; M.A., Pacific Oaks.
Michael D. Miller, Lecturer in Business Administration; M.B.A., Loyola Marymount.
Penny Miller, Lecturer in Education; M.A., California State, Northridge.
Ron Minnehan, Lecturer in Business; J.D., Ventura College of Law.
Deborah Moore, Lecturer in Education; M.S., Washington (Seattle).
Lawrence Moore, Lecturer in Education; Ph.D., Claremont.
Susan M. Murphy, Assistant Professor of Business; Ph.D., Illinois at Chicago.
Christina Myren, Lecturer in Education; M.A., California State, Northridge.
Leanne M. Neilson, Professor of Psychology; Psy.D., Pepperdine.
Peggie Noisette, Lecturer in Education; M.A., Azusa Pacific.
Brian Oard, Lecturer in Business; B.A., California, Davis.
Carlo Ohanian, Lecturer in Business; M.A., Houston.
Terry F. Perkins, Lecturer in Marital and Family Therapy; Ph.D., USC.
David I. Reinstein, Lecturer in Education; Ed.D., UCLA.
Linda M. Rio, Lecturer in Psychology; M.A., US International.
Richard Roth, Lecturer in Education; M.A., California State, Los Angeles.
C. Douglas Saddler, Professor of Psychology; Ph.D., Texas.
Marlene Saddler, Lecturer in Education; M.Ed., Arkansas Tech.
Anthony M. Salzman, Lecturer in Business; M.B.A., US International.
Erika M. Schlomer-Fischer, Assistant Professor of Business; Ph.D., Washington State.
James Alan Schmidt, Lecturer in Marital and Family Therapy; M.A., San Jose State.
Sandra Shackelford, Lecturer in Education; M.Ed., Whittier.
Tobey Shaw, Lecturer in Education; M.A., California State, Northridge.
Susan Sheldon, Lecturer in Education; Ph.D., California Graduate Institute.
Jonathon F. Shepherd, Lecturer in Public Policy and Administration; M.P.L., M.P.A., USC.
Robert Shoup, Lecturer in Education; M.S., USC.
Julia Sieger, Assistant Professor of Education; Ed.D., San Francisco.
Scott Skellenger, Lecturer in Business; M.B.A., California Lutheran.
Beth Anderson Smith, Assistant Professor of Education; Ph.D., Colorado.
Claudia Spelman, Lecturer in Education; M.A., California Lutheran.
Henry Talifer, Senior Lecturer in Public Policy and Administration; J.D., Santa Clara; Ph.D., USC.
Susan Tandberg, Lecturer in Education; M.A., California State, Northridge.
Edgar Allen Terry, Lecturer in Business Administration; M.B.A., California Lutheran.
Mary Margaret Thomes, Professor of Sociology; Ph.D., USC.
Nathan L. Tierney, Professor of Philosophy; Ph.D., Columbia.
Maria Elena Tostado, Lecturer in Education; M.A., M.S., California Lutheran.
Hong Nhat (Sunny) Trihn, Lecturer in Business; M.B.A., California Lutheran.
Diana Tsaw, Assistant Professor of Business Administration; J.D., Loyola.
Kim Uebelhardt, Lecturer in Education; M.A., California Lutheran.
Gail E. Uellendahl, Associate Professor of Education; Ph.D., NYU.
Veronica Virgen-Heim, Clinical Instructor in Education; M.A., California Lutheran.
Valerie Wallace, Lecturer in Education; M.S., West Chester.
Charles Weingarten, Lecturer in Education; Ph.D., Purdue.
Diane Weis, Lecturer in Education; M.A., California Lutheran.
Jacqueline Williams, Lecturer in Education and Psychology; Psy.D., California School of Professional Psychology.
Paul R. Williams, Assistant Professor of Business Administration; Ph.D., Claremont.
Rita Wolenik, Assistant Professor of Education; Ph.D., USC.
Sidney Leon Yukelson, Lecturer in Education; M.A., California State, Los Angeles.

CALIFORNIA STATE UNIVERSITY, DOMINGUEZ HILLS

Graduate Studies

Programs of Study

Programs leading to the Master of Arts (M.A.) degree at California State University, Dominguez Hills (CSUDH), are offered in education (with options in counseling, curriculum and instruction, educational administration, multicultural education, physical education administration, technology-based education, and an individualized program); English; humanities; humanities external degree; negotiation, conflict resolution, and peacebuilding; psychology (clinical); sociology; and special education. A Master of Arts in teaching mathematics is also offered. Master of Science (M.S.) programs are offered in biology, computer science, health science (with options in gerontology and professional studies), marital and family therapy, nursing, and quality assurance. A Master of Business Administration (M.B.A.) program (with concentrations in finance, human resources management, international business, logistics management, management, marketing, and technology management), a Master of Public Administration (M.P.A.) program (with concentrations in criminal justice administration, nonprofit management, and public management), and a Master of Social Work (M.S.W.) program are also offered. The master's degree program in interdisciplinary studies is offered as either a Master of Arts or a Master of Science, depending on the program course work.

Programs of study are primarily focused on research, preparation for employment, and providing a solid foundation for doctoral studies. The average duration of a Dominguez Hills master's program is two years. Some programs require completion of a thesis, while others offer the alternative comprehensive exam or project. Opportunities exist for involvement in challenging research projects, both on and off campus.

Research Facilities

CSUDH has gained national recognition for student collaboration in externally funded faculty research.Graduate students have access to various research opportunities through a number of research facilities and laboratories.

Financial Aid

Sources of financial assistance include federal student loans, grants, and work-study opportunities. The University offers a limited number of fellowships and scholarships. Students should visit the Office of Financial Aid Web site at http://www.csudh.edu/fin_aid for more information. The Office of Graduate Studies offers support to students involved in mentored research through fellowships, a forgivable-loan program, and a predoctoral program. Support is available to enable students to present their work at professional meetings. Students should visit the Graduate Studies Web site at http://www.csudh.edu/graduatestudies for further information.

Cost of Study

Registration fees (including health services and other fees) for California residents in 2006–07 averaged $1600 per semester. Nonresidents paid tuition of $339 per semester unit in addition to registration fees.

Living and Housing Costs

University housing consists of 134 double- and triple-occupancy, fully furnished apartment units located at the east end of the campus. The average on-campus housing cost for the academic year is $5990. Off-campus monthly rental costs range from $600 to $1000 for a studio or one-bedroom apartment. Total off-campus living and housing costs average approximately $7615 per academic year.

Student Group

Graduate student enrollment averages about 3,100 out of 12,000 students; 50 percent are enrolled in master's programs and 50 percent are pursuing teaching credentials and other objectives. The master's programs with the highest enrollments are education, business administration, behavioral sciences, and the distance learning humanities program. The majority of students are part-time evening students with an average course load of 6 units. Campus diversity is strong, with a 74 percent minority population.

Location

California State University, Dominguez Hills, is a diverse, comprehensive public university located in the suburban city of Carson and primarily serving the greater Los Angeles metropolitan area. Carson sits just a few miles from the beaches, the Long Beach Aquarium, the L.A. County Museum of Art, the Getty Center, and Disneyland. CSUDH is known to have the safest campus in the CSU system.

The University

CSUDH is located on the historic Rancho San Pedro, the oldest Spanish land grant in the Los Angeles area. The land was in the Dominguez family from 1784 until its public acquisition to establish a university in 1960. CSUDH has a multicultural community that is committed to excellence and educating a student population of unprecedented diversity for leadership roles. University programs enable students to develop intellectually, personally, and professionally as they apply knowledge and hands-on expertise to real-world situations.

Applying

Applications are first accepted on November 1 for the following fall semester and September 1 for the following spring. Applicants should check with the individual department for application filing deadlines and for specific program requirements, such as supplemental applications, letters of recommendation, interviews, and test requirements. Applications for scholarships may be accessed through the Financial Aid Office on the Web at http://www.csudh.edu/fin_aid. The Free Application for Federal Student Aid (FAFSA) may be accessed on the Internet at http://www.fafsa.ed.gov.

Correspondence and Information

Students should address all inquiries to the Office of Graduate Studies via e-mail at lrobles@csudh.edu or by phone at 310-243-3693. Completed applications should be sent to the Admissions Office. Online applications are available at http://www.csumentor.edu/AdmissionApp.

Admissions Office
California State University, Dominguez Hills
1000 East Victoria Street
Carson, California 90747

Phone: 310-243-3696
Web site: http://www.csudh.edu
http://www.csudh.edu/graduatestudies (Graduate Studies)

THE FACULTY AND THEIR RESEARCH

Iris Baxter, Professor of Public Administration; Ph.D., USC. Health-care access for vulnerable populations.
James Cooper, Professor of Education; Ph.D., Iowa. Reading assessment reform, graduate retention, at-risk assessment.
Larry Ferrario, Professor of English; Ph.D., USC. Rhetoric and composition, effective teacher education.
Lois Feuer, Professor of English and Humanities; Ph.D., California, Irvine. Dramatic structure and intertextual relationships in Shakespeare.
Farah Fisher, Professor of Education; Ph.D., USC. Distance education, educational technology.
Ken Ganezer, Professor of Physics; Ph.D., UCLA. Neutrinos, biomedical research on bone density.
Thomas Giannotti, Professor of English; Ph.D., California, Riverside. Irish literature, rhetoric/composition.
Diane Henschel, Professor of Psychology; Ph.D., Berkeley. Child abuse, child development.
Pamela Krochalk, Professor of Health Science; Dr.P.H., UCLA. Aging, alternative health care, community disease prevention.
Donald Lewis, Professor of Philosophy; Ph.D., Southern Illinois. Postmodernism, continental philosophy.
Leonard Martinez, Professor of Chemistry; Ph.D., San Diego. Science education, physical chemistry, biophysics.
Helen Oesterheld, Professor of English; Ph.D., California, Irvine. Restoration literature, domestic and utopian fiction, the Gothic.
John W. Roberts, Professor of Biology; Ph.D., California, Santa Barbara. Environmental biology.
Laura Robles, Professor of Biology and Dean of Graduate Studies and Research; Ph.D., California, Santa Barbara. Biomedical research, cell signaling in the retina of the octopus.
Marilyn Sutton, Professor of English; Ph.D., Claremont. Medieval literature, death and dying.
A. Marco Turk, Professor of Behavioral Science; J.D., Southwestern Law. Crime prevention, international peace building.
Sara Waller, Professor of Philosophy; Ph.D., Loyola Chicago. Dolphin behavior, conceptual flexibility.
Andrea White, Professor of English; Ph.D., USC. Critical theory in modern British literature, Joseph Conrad.
Molly Youngkin, Professor of English; Ph.D., Ohio State. Victorian literature.

CENTRAL WASHINGTON UNIVERSITY

Graduate Studies and Research

Programs of Study

Central Washington University (CWU) offers programs that lead to the following degrees: Master of Arts, Master of Arts for Teachers, Master of Education, Master of Fine Arts, Master of Music, Master of Professional Accountancy, and Master of Science. Master of Arts programs include art (M.A. and M.F.A.), English (literature, TESOL), history, and theater production (summers only). Master of Science degree programs are available in biological sciences; chemistry; engineering technology; exercise science; experimental psychology; family and consumer sciences; geology; health, human performance, and nutrition; mental health counseling; and resource management. There is a Master of Professional Accountancy in accounting. A Master of Arts for Teachers of mathematics is available, in the summer only. Master of Education programs include master teacher, reading specialist, school administration, school counseling, school psychology, and special education.

A minimum of 45 quarter credits is needed for a master's degree, though some programs require more credits. As the capstone project, programs may require a thesis, a project, or a comprehensive examination in lieu of the thesis. A final oral examination is standard for most programs.

CWU encourages collaborative research among graduate students and faculty members. It is committed to ensuring that graduate students gain as much hands-on experience as possible in their programs. A measure of CWU's success is that graduate students regularly give conference presentations, exhibitions, and performances. Music students have performed with nationally recognized orchestras and at the Metropolitan Opera. Graduate students typically conduct research as part of federally sponsored grants in such areas as biological sciences, geographic information systems, geology, and resource management, and others have won awards for art.

Research Facilities

In addition to its library, CWU's massive science facility and the completely renovated education building augment CWU's instructional and research facilities. The Chimpanzee and Human Communications Institute is the home of world-famous, sign language–using chimpanzee, Washoe, and three other signing chimpanzees. The Geographic Information Systems Laboratory, Applied Social Data Center, and Community Psychology Services Clinic provide students with exceptional research opportunities. Computing services include access to the Internet, an online public catalog, and online bibliographic retrieval services. The James E. Brooks Library makes CWU the largest repository of state documents in central Washington.

Financial Aid

Graduate assistantships are available in each of CWU's departments offering graduate degrees. Approximately 45 percent of all full-time enrolled graduate students received appointments in 2005–06. About two thirds of the graduate assistants teach; the remainder serve as research assistants and a few perform service functions. The stipend package for a Washington State resident for the 2006–07 academic year was $15,385. Other financial support can be obtained through the Office of Financial Aid from federal and state sources for students demonstrating financial need. There are also employment opportunities on and off campus. Furthermore, graduate students may apply for travel and research funds on a competitive basis through the Office of Graduate Studies and Research.

Cost of Study

Graduate tuition for 2006–07 was $2104 per quarter for full-time (10–18 quarter credit hours) Washington State residents and $4704 per quarter for nonresidents. For resident part-time students, tuition was $210.40 per credit hour and $470.40 per credit hour for nonresidents. There is a $60 per quarter health service fee, a $35 per quarter athletic fee, a $25 per quarter technology fee, a $3 Central transit fee, and, for Ellensburg campus-based students, a $64 Student Union Building fee and a $95 recreation center fee. The cost of tuition for summer school 2006 was $175 per credit hour for both in-state and out-of-state graduate students.

Living and Housing Costs

University Housing Services offers a variety of apartments starting at $455 per month for a studio and running up to $600 for a three-bedroom apartment. Rents off campus range from $300 to $650 per month depending on the size and extras. The University also makes available rooms in residence halls for graduate students. Assistance with locating off-campus housing is available as well. Dining Services offers reasonably priced, quarterly contracts in its four dining halls. Meals vary at each location, and there are several meal plan options from which to choose.

Student Group

As of the fall quarter 2006, there were 543 graduate students at CWU enrolled in twenty-seven programs across nineteen departments; they make up almost 8 percent of the University's 10,286 students. Graduate classes are small and there are regular opportunities to work closely with professors and fellow students. The largest graduate programs are in education, psychology, and resource management. Other departments average between 12 and 30 enrolled graduate students.

Location

CWU's main campus is in Ellensburg, Washington. The community prides itself on quality living, and students experience a friendly and safe small-town atmosphere. This is complemented by diverse cultural and social fare offered by the University's proximity to the Cascade Mountains, Seattle, Puget Sound, Yakima, the Yakima River Valley, Spokane, and the Columbia River recreational areas. The Kittitas Valley boasts four distinct seasons and abundant sunshine.

The University

CWU is one of six state-assisted universities in the state. It was founded in 1890 as the Washington State Normal School and became a comprehensive university in 1977. Graduate programs were first offered in fall 1947. Fully accredited, CWU provides graduate programming at its instructional centers in Lynnwood, Moses Lake, Pierce County, Des Moines, Wenatchee, and Yakima, as well as Ellensburg. The campus is a mixture of traditional and modern architecture stretching across 380 acres of shaded lawns framed by evergreens and landscaped walkways. A nationally renowned Japanese garden in the center of the grounds offers a serene place to think, reflect, and relax. CWU is four blocks from historic downtown Ellensburg. Most shops and restaurants are within walking distance. The city and campus are accessible by wheelchairs, bicycles, and strollers. Other points of interest include an arts complex housing the Sarah Spurgeon Gallery, the contemporary music education building, a theater, a massive science facility, Nicholson Athletic Pavilion, and the new recreation center.

Applying

Application materials may be obtained from the University. The application fee is $50. Applicants should have earned at least a 3.0 GPA over the last 60 semester hours (90 quarter hours) of graded course work. Some programs require scores on the General Test of the GRE. The M.P.A. program requires GMAT scores. Students whose native language is not English must score at least 550 (paper-based), 213 (computer-based), or 79 (Internet-based) on the TOEFL. Students should contact the relevant department as they may need to supply other materials when submitting the application. Priority consideration is given to applications received by April 1 for fall quarter admissions. Assistantship applications should be submitted by February 15 for the following summer and academic year. Financial aid applications should be made directly to the Office of Financial Aid by March 1.

Correspondence and Information

Graduate Studies and Research
Central Washington University
400 East University Way
Ellensburg, Washington 98926-7510

Phone: 509-963-3103
Fax: 509-963-1799
E-mail: masters@cwu.edu
Web site: http://www.cwu.edu/~masters

GRADUATE AFFAIRS

The area code is 509 for all phone and fax numbers.

Graduate Studies and Research
(Phone: 963-3103; fax: 963-1799; e-mail: masters@cwu.edu)
Wayne S. Quirk, Associate Vice President; Ph.D., Washington State.
Roger S. Fouts, Director of University Research; Ph.D., Nevada, Reno.

Graduate Programs and Contacts

Accounting (M.P.A.): Professional accountancy. Ronald Tidd, Graduate Coordinator; Ph.D., Minnesota. (phone: 963-2466; fax: 963-2875; e-mail: mpa@cwu.edu)

Art (M.A., M.F.A.): Ceramics, computer art, drawing, jewelry and metal-smithing, painting, photography, sculpture, wood design. Brian Goeltzenleuchter, Graduate Coordinator; M.F.A., California, San Diego. (phone: 963-3150; fax: 963-1918; e-mail: goeltzeb@cwu.edu)

Biological Sciences (M.S.): Botany, microbiology-parasitology, stream ecology and fisheries, terrestrial ecology. Lixing Sun, Graduate Coordinator; Ph.D., SUNY Health Science Center at Syracuse. (phone: 963-2780; fax: 963-2730; e-mail: lixing@cwu.edu)

Chemistry (M.S.): Analytical, biological, inorganic, medicinal, organic, physical. Anne Johansen, Graduate Coordinator; Ph.D., Caltech. (phone: 963-2811; fax: 963-1050; e-mail: johansea@cwu.edu)

Education (M.Ed.): Master teacher, reading specialist, school administration, special education. Steven Schmitz, Department Chair and Graduate Coordinator; Ed.D., Washington State. (phone: 963-1461; fax: 963-1452; e-mail: henryv@cwu.edu)

English (M.A.): Literature, TESOL. Laila Abdalla, Graduate Coordinator; Ph.D., McGill. (phone: 963-1546; fax: 963-1561; e-mail: abadallal@cwu.edu)

Family and Consumer Sciences (M.S.): Family and consumer sciences education, family studies (on hold until 2007), recreation. Jan Bowers, Department Chair and Graduate Coordinator; Ph.D., Kansas State. (phone: 963-2766; fax: 963-2787; e-mail: bowersj@cwu.edu)

Geology (M.S.): Climate change, geomorphology, neotectonics, tectonics. Beth Pratt-Sitaula, Graduate Coordinator; Ph.D., California, Santa Barbara. (phone: 963-2702; fax: 963-2821; e-mail: psitaula@geology.cwu.edu)

Health, Human Performance, and Nutrition (M.S.): Exercise science, physical education teaching, and nutrition. Leo D'Aquisto, Graduate Coordinator; Ed.D., Northern Colorado. (phone: 963-1911; fax: 963-1848; e-mail: acquisto@cwu.edu)

History (M.A.): American women's history, Colonial America, East Africa, Latin America, modern Europe, modern Japan, Russia, Western America. Roxanne Easley, Graduate Coordinator; Ph.D., Oregon. (phone: 963-1655; fax: 963-1654; e-mail: easleyr@cwu.edu)

Industrial and Engineering Technology (M.S.): Engineering technology. Geoff Dean, Graduate Coordinator; Ph.D., Virginia Tech. (phone: 206-963-1756; fax: 206-963-1795; e-mail: deang@cwu.edu)

Mathematics (M.A.T.): Teaching mathematics (summer only). Mark Oursland, Graduate Coordinator; Ed.D., Montana State. (phone: 963-2103; fax: 963-3226; e-mail: oursland@cwu.edu)

Music (M.M.): Composition, conducting, music education, performance, performance pedagogy. Jeff Snedeker, Graduate Coordinator; D.M., Wisconsin–Madison. (phone: 963-1226; fax: 963-1239; e-mail: snedeker@cwu.edu)

Psychology (M.S., M.Ed.): Experimental psychology, mental health counseling psychology, organizational psychology (M.S.), school counseling, school psychology (M.Ed.). Robert Brammer, School Counseling and Mental Health Counseling Director; Ph.D., USC. (phone: 963-2381; fax: 963-2307; e-mail: brammerr@cwu.edu); Eugene Johnson, School Psychology Director; Ph.D., South Dakota. (phone: 963-2381, fax: 963-2307; email: johnsong@cwu.edu); Warren Street, Experimental Psychology Director; Ph.D., Claremont. (phone: 963-2381; fax 963-2307; email: warren@cwu.edu)

Resource Management (M.S.): Stream flow, water quality and riparian management, natural resources policy, wildlife and fisheries economics, resource systems, cultural resource management, geographic information systems, linkages between cultural and natural resource management. Patrick Lubinski, Co-Director; Ph.D., Wisconsin–Madison. (phone: 963-3201; fax: 963-2315; e-mail: lubinski@cwu.edu); Anthony Gabriel, Program Co-Director; Ph.D., Guelph. (phone: 963-1188; fax: 963-1047; e-mail: gabriela@cwu.edu)

Theatre Arts (M.A.): Theater production (summer only). George Bellah, Graduate Coordinator; M.F.A., North Carolina at Greensboro. (phone: 963-1766; fax: 963-1767; e-mail: bellahg@cwu.edu)

CHAPMAN UNIVERSITY

Graduate Studies

Programs of Study

Chapman offers the Juris Doctor (law), the Ph.D. in education, and the M.A. in education, educational psychology, English, film studies, psychology, school counseling, special education, and teaching (elementary or secondary). It offers the M.S. in food science. Also offered are a Master of Business Administration; a Master of Fine Arts in creative writing; a Master of Fine Arts in film production, film and television producing, production design, and screenwriting; and a Doctor of Physical Therapy. Dual degrees are offered for M.B.A./M.F.A. film production, J.D./M.B.A., and M.F.A. creative writing/M.A. English. Public school credential programs include multiple subjects/BCLAD, single subject, single subject CLAD, pupil personnel school counseling (PPS), special education credentials mild moderate and moderate severe Level 1, special education credentials mild moderate and moderate severe Level II, and preliminary administrative services credentials. Many of the degree programs offer specializations. Credential programs can be combined with one of the degree programs in education.

Required units vary with each degree; however, each program comprises courses that best prepare students to continue a career or enter a new profession. Program requirements include advancement to degree candidacy after the completion of 12 units. Some programs require a comprehensive examination, taken at the end of or during the final semester of course work. Some programs offer a thesis project option in place of the comprehensive examination. One or two internship courses that provide practical experience in the student's field are required for some programs. Course work from other accredited institutions may be transferred; a maximum of 6 credits may be applied to a program. At least 24 credits must be taken in residence.

Research projects are essential to many degree programs and are undertaken in research courses or through cooperative education. Because class sizes are kept small, students can readily communicate with faculty members about research projects and general academic work.

Research Facilities

Research facilities include the nationally recognized A. Gary Anderson Center for Economic Research, Albert Schweitzer Institute, Center for Non-Profit Leadership, Ludie and David C. Henley Social Science Research Laboratory, Walter Schmid Center for International Business, Ralph W. Leatherby Center for Entrepreneurship Business Ethics, Center for the Study of the Cold War Era, John Fowles Center for Creative Writing, Center for Educational and Social Equity, Barry and Phyllis Rodgers Center for Holocaust Education, Paulo Freire Democratic Project, a state-of-the-art human performance laboratory and research vivarium, food science and nutrition food-tasting and research laboratories, and a community clinic for psychological counseling and research. The computer lab has DEC MicroVAX and NCR Tower facilities, and there are also IBM PC and Apple Macintosh laboratories. The Chapman University Leatherby Libraries contain more than 170,000 volumes, more than 30,000 full text electronic journals, more than 8,000 electronic books, and 2,100 journal titles as well as DVDs, videos, CDs, and other media. Chapman has the largest collection of Albert Schweitzer memorabilia in the western United States; a permanent exhibit is on display in the Argyros Forum.

Financial Aid

Many financial aid opportunities are available for qualified students, including Chapman University Fellowships and loans, which are based on need and academic achievement; graduate assistantships; residence life positions; employment; California State Graduate Fellowships; Federal Stafford Student Loans; Benefits for Veterans and Dependents; and an employer-paid tuition plan. Students interested in any of these opportunities should contact the Financial Aid Office (714-997-6741).

Cost of Study

Tuition for 2007–08 varies by program. Part-time and full-time students, as well as California and non-California residents, are charged the same tuition rate. Tuition for a full-time student (9 credits per semester) is approximately $4545 to $8325 per academic year, depending on the student's program. Books and personal expenses add to annual costs.

Living and Housing Costs

Chapman offers limited housing for graduate students. Off-campus housing is available.

Student Group

Graduate study programs enroll more than 1,400 students each year on the Orange campus. Courses are scheduled so that both full- and part-time students can attend. Many students have been working in their field and bring practical experience to the classroom; they come from many states and countries, and about 50 percent of them are women. Students who choose to enroll at Chapman want a small-campus atmosphere, personalized attention, a superior faculty, and an education that enables them to succeed in a highly competitive professional world. Opportunities for graduates are plentiful due to the concentration of business and industry in Orange County and throughout southern California. People for whom graduates may eventually work sit on many College advisory boards.

Location

The beautiful tree-lined campus in Orange, California, is 35 miles southeast of Los Angeles. Ocean breezes are less than 10 miles away; mountains and deserts are within an hour's drive. Just minutes from the University are major recreation and entertainment venues, including Anaheim Convention Center, Orange County Performing Arts Center, Pacific Amphitheater, Verizon Wireless Amphitheater, Disneyland, Disney's California Adventure, Knott's Berry Farm, Angel Stadium, and Honda Center.

The University

Chapman is an independent, private institution and has provided liberal and professional education of distinction since it was founded in 1861 by the Christian Church (Disciples of Christ). It has continued to meet the needs of its students with fine academic programs and individualized attention. Undergraduate and graduate degree programs are offered on the main campus and at twenty-seven Academic Centers throughout California and Washington. The graduate curricula are designed to offer advanced study in specific disciplines to broaden and deepen a student's knowledge. Faculty members include distinguished academicians, a Nobel Laureate, and noted professional practitioners. Chapman is accredited by and is a member of the Western Association of Schools and Colleges. It is also a member of the Independent Colleges of Southern California, the College Entrance Examination Board, the Western College Association, the Association of Independent California Colleges and Universities, the American Council on Education, the American Association of Colleges for Teacher Education, the Division of Higher Education of the Christian Church (Disciples of Christ), and the American Assembly of Collegiate Schools of Business. It is also accredited by the Institute of Food Technologists. Its teacher training and credential programs are approved by the California State Department of Education. The school psychology program is approved by the National Association of School Psychologists. The physical therapy program is accredited by the Commission on Accreditation in the Physical Therapy Education of the American Physical Therapy Association and by the Physical Therapy Examining Committee of the Board of Medical Quality Assurance of the State of California. The M.B.A. program is fully accredited by AACSB International–The Association to Advance Collegiate Schools of Business. The School of Law is fully approved by the American Bar Association.

Applying

Students are admitted in the fall, spring, and summer for most programs. Applicants should submit an application fee and a completed Application for Graduate Studies; transcripts of all postsecondary work, showing the completion of a bachelor's degree; scores on the GMAT, GRE (General or Subject test), MAT, or CSET; TOEFL scores, for international students; two letters of recommendation; and a statement of intent. Departments, however, should be consulted for specific program requirements.

Correspondence and Information

Office of Graduate Admission
Argyros Forum, Room 304
Chapman University
Orange, California 92866

Phone: 714-997-6711
Fax: 714-997-6713
E-mail: gradadmit@chapman.edu
Web site: http://www.chapman.edu

PROGRAM DIRECTORS

Business Administration: Jon Kaplan, Assistant Dean for Graduate and Executive Programs, Argyros School of Business and Economics; M.B.A., UCLA.
Creative Writing: Richard Ruppel, Chair, Department of English and Comparative Literature; Ph.D., North Carolina at Chapel Hill.
Education: Mary McNeil, Professor and Associate Dean of Education; Ph.D., Boston University.
Educational Psychology: Michael Hass, Associate Professor and Coordinator of Educational Psychology Programs; Ph.D., California, Irvine.
English: Richard Ruppel, Chair, Department of English and Comparative Literature; Ph.D., North Carolina at Chapel Hill.
Film Production, Film and Television Producing, Screenwriting, Production Design, and Film Studies: Joe Slowensky, Associate Professor of Film and Television and Chair, Graduate Programs; M.F.A., USC.
Food Science: Anuradha Prakash, Associate Professor of Food Science and Program Director, Department of Physical Sciences; Ph.D., Ohio State.
Law: John C. Eastman, Dean; J.D., Chicago.
Physical Therapy: Jacklyn Heino Brechter, Chair, Division of Physical Therapy; Ph.D., USC.
Psychology: Georg Eifert, Professor of Psychology and Chair, Department of Psychology; Ph.D., Frankfurt (Germany).
School Counseling: John Brady, Associate Professor and Coordinator of School Counseling Programs; Ph.D., US International.
Special Education: Dawn Hunter, Associate Professor and Coordinator of Special Education Programs; Ph.D., Maryland, College Park.

Argyros Forum.

CHESTNUT HILL COLLEGE

Graduate Programs

Programs of Study

The School of Graduate Studies of Chestnut Hill College (CHC) offers the following master's degree and certificate programs: Clinical and Counseling Psychology, Education, Educational Leadership, Instructional Technology, Holistic Spirituality, and Administration of Human Services. The School also offers an APA-accredited Doctor of Psychology in Clinical Psychology (Psy.D.) degree, state certification programs, and a variety of post-master's programs.

The Clinical and Counseling Psychology program (M.A. and M.S. degrees) includes concentrations in child and adolescent therapy, marriage and family therapy, trauma studies, and addictions treatment. Students may also opt for a generalist curriculum. A post-master's certificate for licensure preparation prepares students for the licensure exam to become a LPC or LMFT in Pennsylvania and other states. Post-master's certificates are available in all areas of specialization. The APA-accredited Doctor of Psychology program is open to applicants who have a master's degree in counseling psychology or a closely related field. For applicants who have a bachelor's degree in psychology or 12 undergraduate credits in psychology, the combined M.S./Psy.D. track is available. All programs offered by the Department of Professional Psychology are practitioner based, and classes are taught by faculty members who are actively working in the field. Master's-level courses are also offered on the DeSales University campus in Center Valley, Pennsylvania.

The Education Department offers the M.Ed. in early childhood education, elementary education, secondary education, and educational leadership–accelerated/intensive format (with optional principal certification). Students may also opt for the following state certification programs: Elementary Education, Elementary Education with Certification in Special Education, Early Childhood Education, and various secondary education areas. Reading specialist and principal certification programs are available for qualified applicants. A Montessori specialization certificate (AMS) is also offered.

The Instructional Technology program offers M.S. degrees and various certificates in leadership and technology, education and technology, instructional design in e-learning, and instructional design specialist. CHC also offers Pennsylvania Department of Education (P.D.E.) Instructional Technology Specialist Certification. The Education and Technology program helps teachers develop new leadership skills and expertise in the use of technology in the achievement of curricular goals and applications of constructivist principles to today's changing classroom. The Instructional Design and Leadership and Technology programs are designed for students involved in technology who are challenged by cultural and technological changes. The e-learning track presents cutting-edge technology as the next wave in professional training, education, and design. The goal of the specializations is the preparation of professionals to assume leadership roles in the transformation of their work environments. The majority of course work for these programs is offered through a distance/on-site format.

The Holistic Spirituality program (M.A. degree) includes concentrations in spiritual direction and health care. Several certificate programs are also available. Each of the programs combine academic rigor with experiential learning in ways that promote the integration of theory and practice. The Holistic Spirituality program presents an annual summer Festival of Spirituality featuring nationally known theologians in public lectures, extended conversations, and intensive course formats. Each summer's festival is designed to advance the relationships between spirituality and the Bible, justice issues, and/or ecological concerns.

The Administration of Human Services program (M.S. degree) combines courses in management, public policy, and social issues to prepare students for supervisory and leadership positions in health and human-service organizations. With an emphasis on social change and diversity, this degree provides a comprehensive knowledge base about organizations, their philosophy and structure, and the specialized services that are provided. This program is offered in an accelerated format. Certificates are also available.

Research Facilities

Chestnut Hill College provides access to state-of-the-art hardware and software in five computer labs and a new building offering computer access from every workstation. The Logue Library offers an electronic research center, an online catalog, and nearly 140,000 volumes on three floors of open stacks. Among the electronic resources are ERIC, PsychINFO, LexisNexis, ProQuestReligion, JSTOR, EBSCOhost Elite, and Wilson OmniFile Mega, MLA. Specialized psychology demonstration rooms are available for live observation and taping of clinical sessions. Studio TV labs are used by the applied technology program; video editing and specialized multimedia development labs are used by other graduate programs.

Financial Aid

Chestnut Hill College offers a number of graduate assistantships for students at the master's and doctoral levels. The majority of students finance their education through student loans. The Financial Aid Office is available to assist students with the loan application process. Some graduate programs (Education and Holistic Spirituality) offer a discounted tuition to teachers and those in church-affiliated ministry.

Cost of Study

Tuition for 2007–08 is $485 per credit for the Administration of Human Services and Holistic Spirituality programs; $490 per credit for the Clinical and Counseling Psychology programs; $475 per credit for the Education programs; and $715 per credit for the doctoral program.

Living and Housing Costs

A variety of urban and suburban housing options are available within an easy commute to the campus.

Student Group

With classes primarily in the evening and on weekends, the School of Graduate Studies at Chestnut Hill College caters to the needs of the working professional. Degree programs should be completed within six years of matriculation. Within that time frame, students can choose their own pace for most programs; some opt to study full-time, while others take one or two courses per semester. Small classes and a welcoming atmosphere make Chestnut Hill College an excellent choice for traditional students as well as working professionals and those who wish to change careers.

Location

Chestnut Hill College is located in the northwestern corner of Philadelphia, easily accessible to all of the Philadelphia neighborhoods, outlying areas, and adjoining states. It is also near numerous cultural, athletic, and recreational activities in the region. The campus has a suburban feel, while remaining accessible through public transportation and major routes.

The College

Chestnut Hill College, founded by the Sisters of St. Joseph in 1924, is an independent Catholic institution that fosters equality through education and welcomes women and men of all backgrounds. The School of Graduate Studies provides a quality education that takes into equal account the academic, professional, and personal needs of both women and men. The aim of the graduate programs is to graduate professionals who are skilled, ethical, knowledgeable, and confident practitioners in their respective fields.

Applying

Applications for all programs are considered on a rolling admissions basis. Master's degree students may begin in any semester: fall, spring, or summer. Psy.D. and M.S./Psy.D. classes begin in the fall. All applicants are evaluated on the basis of the entire application packet, which includes the application, transcripts of all previous college study, three letters of recommendation, MAT or GRE General Test scores (PPST scores for education), and a 400–600-word statement of professional goals. Applicants with graduate degrees may be exempt from one or more requirements. Special admission requirements apply to the Holistic Spirituality, Psy.D., and M.S./Psy.D. programs. Interviews with department chairs are required for qualified applicants; tours and/or interviews with the director of graduate admissions or a graduate admissions counselor are available.

Correspondence and Information

For master's program information and all applications:

Jayne Mashett
Director of Graduate Admissions
Chestnut Hill College
9601 Germantown Avenue
Philadelphia, Pennsylvania 19118-2693
Phone: 215-248-7020
215-248-7170 (graduate office)
Fax: 215-248-7161
E-mail: mashetti@chc.edu or graddiv@chc.edu
Web site: http://www.chc.edu

For Psy.D. and M.S./Psy.D. program information:

Mary Steinmetz
Director of Psy.D. Admissions
Chestnut Hill College
9601 Germantown Avenue
Philadelphia, Pennsylvania 19118-2693
Phone: 215-248-7077
215-248-7170 (graduate office)
Fax: 215-248-7155
E-mail: profpsyc@chc.edu
Web site: http://www.chc.edu

THE FACULTY

Note: Research interests of the Psy.D. faculty members are available on the Web at http://www.chc.edu/graduate/psydfac.htm. Information on the entire faculty can be found at http://www.chc.edu/faculty/.

David Arena, Assistant Professor of Psychology; Psy.D., Widener.
Stephen Berk, Assistant Professor of Education; Ph.D., Temple.
Richard W. Black, Assistant Professor of Education; Ed.D., Temple.
David Borsos, Assistant Professor of Psychology; Ph.D., Temple.
Scott W. Browning, Professor of Psychology; Ph.D., Berkeley.
Melanie Cohen-Goodman, Assistant Professor of Education; Ph.D., Temple.
Dominic Cotugno, Associate Professor of Education; Ed.D., Temple.
Margery Covello, Assistant Professor of Education; Ed.D., Immaculata.
Carolynne Ervin, Coordinator of Spiritual Direction Program; M.A., Creighton.
Mary Kay Flannery, S.S.J., Associate Professor of Religious Studies; D.Min., Catholic Theological Union.
Elaine R. Green, Associate Professor of Sociology; Dean, School of Continuing Studies; and Chair, Administration of Human Services; Ed.D., Temple.
Barbara Hogan, Assistant Professor of Religious Studies and Chair, Holistic Spirituality; Ph.D., Temple.
Jessica Kahn, Associate Professor of Education; Ph.D., Pennsylvania.
Thomas E. Klee, Associate Professor of Psychology; Ph.D., Temple.
Mary M. Lindsay, S.S.J., Assistant Professor of Psychology; Ph.D., Temple.
Susan McGroarty, Assistant Professor of Psychology; Ph.D., Pennsylvania.
Joseph A. Micucci, Professor and Chair of Psychology; Ph.D., Minnesota.
Catherine Nerney, S.S.J., Associate Professor of Religious Studies; Ph.D., Catholic University.
Carol M. Pate, Assistant Professor and Chair, Education Department; Ed.D., Indiana.
Cheryll Rothery-Jackson, Associate Professor of Psychology; Psy.D., Rutgers.
Ralph E. Swan, Assistant Professor and Coordinator of Instructional Technology; Ph.D., Pennsylvania.
Margaret H. Vogelson, Professor of Education; Ph.D., Temple.

CITY COLLEGE OF THE CITY UNIVERSITY OF NEW YORK

Graduate Programs

Programs of Study

The City College of New York (CCNY) is similar to a small university offering a rich program of graduate study through the College of Liberal Arts and Science and the Schools of Architecture, Education, and Engineering. The College of Liberal Arts and Science offers the Master of Arts (M.A.) in art history, biochemistry, biology, chemistry, economics, English (English literature and language and literacy), history, international relations, mathematics (operations research, probability, pure mathematics, and statistics), museum studies, music, physics, psychology (general and mental health counseling), sociology, and Spanish and the Master of Fine Arts (M.F.A.) in art and creative writing. The School of Architecture, Urban Design and Landscape Architecture offers the Master of Architecture (M.Arch.), the Master of Landscape Architecture (M.L.A.), and the Master of Urban Planning (M.U.P.) in urban design. The Department of Media and Communication Arts offers professional studies leading to the M.F.A. in media arts production (film/video). The School of Education offers both the Master of Science in Education (M.S.Ed.) degree in administration and supervision, bilingual education K–12 (Chinese, Haitian-Creole, and Spanish), developmental and remedial reading, early childhood education, elementary education (curriculum and teaching), special education, special education–bilingual, and TESOL-bilingual. In addition, the Master of Arts in Education (M.A.Ed.) degree is offered in art education, English education, mathematics education, science education, and social studies. A bilingual component may be added to each of these programs. Advanced certificate programs are offered in administration and supervision and developmental and remedial reading. The Grove School of Engineering offers both the Master of Engineering (M.E.) and the Master of Science (M.S.) in biomedical, chemical, civil, electrical, and mechanical engineering and computer science. Interdepartmental programs are offered in air pollution control, engineering mechanics, and environmental engineering.

Research Facilities

The Morris Raphael Cohen Library in the North Academic Center houses more than 1 million volumes and is the largest in the CUNY system. Besides its general collection, it contains facilities for architecture, engineering, music, and science. Many library processes are computerized for rapid and efficient access to information. The University-wide Integrated Library System (CUNY Plus) provides online access to most holdings at both City College and all the libraries in the CUNY system. The Marshak Science Building houses more than 200 teaching and research laboratories, a planetarium, a weather station, an electron microscope, laser research facilities, a science and engineering library, and a physical education complex. The Grove School of Engineering houses the Benjamin Levich Institute for Physiochemical Hydrodynamics, the Center for Biomedical Engineering, the Clean Fuels Institute, the Center for Water Resources and Environmental Research, the Institute for Municipal Waste Research, the Earthquake Research Center, and the Institute for Ultrafast Spectroscopy and Lasers. The Grove School of Engineering also provides a wide range of networked computer facilities for both teaching and research.

Financial Aid

Graduate study at CCNY is supported by a combination of student fees, state funds, private and foundation contributions, and federal research grants. The Office of Financial Aid administers federal and state grants, loans, and work-study programs. The College offers a number of nonteaching assistantships and part-time teaching lectureships. These programs are administered by the Financial Aid Office. For more information, students should contact the Financial Aid Office at 212-650-5819 Ext. 6656.

Cost of Study

In the College of Liberal Arts and Science and the School of Education, tuition for state residents is $270 per credit; in the Schools of Engineering and Architecture, it is $315 per credit. For students from out of state and international students, tuition is $500 per credit in the College of Liberal Arts and Science and the School of Education; in the Schools of Engineering and Architecture, it is $555 per credit.

Living and Housing Costs

Campus housing is available in "The Towers." For information, students should phone 917-507-0070 or visit http://www.ccnytowers.com. Apartments and studios can also be found independently throughout the five boroughs of New York City. Estimated living expenses for one year is between $8500 and $10,000. For assistance, students can call 212-650-5370.

Student Group

The student body reflects a wide range of ethnic and cultural diversity. Students come from more than 100 different countries and speak more than ninety languages. Most are from Africa, Asia, the Caribbean, Latin America, and Europe. The students lend an international flavor to the campus and reflect the ethnic diversity of New York City. This has led City College to develop extensive international linkages. There are student and faculty exchanges with universities in Africa, Asia, Israel, and the Dominican Republic. The total student enrollment is approximately 13,245; of these, 2,930 are graduate students.

Location

The campus occupies 35 acres in upper Manhattan along Convent Avenue in an area known as Hamilton Heights in Harlem. It is an urban campus within easy commuting distance of midtown Manhattan.

The College

The City College of New York is the oldest institution in the City University of New York system. Founded in 1847 as the Free Academy, it was first housed at 23rd Street and Lexington Avenue. The name was changed in 1866 to the College of the City of New York; now it is called "City" or "CCNY." Although it originally granted only the bachelor's degree, CCNY began to expand its program offerings to advanced levels more than sixty years ago. Since 1961, it has offered a wide range of master's programs, and through the City University of New York offers doctoral study on campus in the sciences, all branches of engineering, computer science, and psychology. CCNY is known for its commitment to academic excellence combined with access to higher education. Immigrants and their children have historically used the College as a vehicle for upward mobility.

Applying

Graduate study is open to well-qualified students who possess a bachelor's degree from an accredited U.S. institution or the equivalent from an international institution and have an adequate background in the field of study they wish to pursue. Students are evaluated based on their previous academic record, generally with a minimum B average (3.0) required; letters of recommendation from scholars with whom they have studied; and writing samples, portfolios, Graduate Record Exams (GRE) test scores, and auditions (required by some programs only). International students whose native language is not English and who do not have a resident alien card must take the TOEFL (Test of English as a Foreign Language).

Correspondence and Information

Office of Graduate Admissions
Administration Building, Room 101
City College of the City University of New York
138th Street and Convent Avenue
New York, New York 10031

Phone: 212-650-6977
Fax: 212-650-6417
E-mail: gradadm@ccny.cuny.edu
Web site: http://www.ccny.cuny.edu

THE FACULTY

City College's faculty represents a broad range of disciplines, and many of its members have earned the nation's highest forms of recognition—Guggenheim and Fulbright awards—as well as grants amounting to millions of dollars in support of their research and scholarship. The faculty is internationally known for its research activities.

CITY UNIVERSITY

Graduate Division

Programs of Study

City University offers graduate education in five degree areas: Master of Business Administration (M.B.A.), Master of Science (M.S.), Master of Arts (M.A.), Master of Education (M.Ed.), and Master in Teaching (M.I.T.). Graduate certificate programs are also available in the areas of business, finance, technology, management, individual leadership, organizational leadership, and education. In keeping with City University's mission to make education accessible and convenient, graduate classes may be taken during the day, in the evening, or on weekends. Because classroom attendance is not always possible, City University also offers the majority of its graduate programs through online distance learning.

City University's M.B.A. program is created with input from industry leaders and incorporates such concepts as technology, marketing, finance, ethics, and global economies.

The M.A. program in counseling psychology prepares students to counsel individuals and families in a variety of capacities. This program involves classroom and field-based experience and requires 72 credit hours of course work.

The Master of Education program enables professionals to continue teaching while enhancing their skills and education. M.Ed. students may choose specialties in curriculum, technology, and instruction; literacy for diverse classroom; integrating arts and performance learning; reading and literacy; guidance and counseling; and educational leadership. The program also enables professionals to receive certification in elementary; special education; principal certification; curriculum, technology, and learning; guidance and counseling; and reading and literacy. Weekend classes are team-taught by practitioners offering experiential learning that can be applied directly to the classroom. The program requires 49–59 credit hours of course work, depending on the student's chosen specialty.

The Master in Teaching with Teacher Certification is a unique, 64-credit program that provides for career transition into the field of education for those who already hold a bachelor's degree but lack teacher certification. The program combines classroom teaching and course work and is complete in twelve months of full-time attendance. There is also a special two-year format available for para educators. The program prepares students to be teachers in Washington State and is not available through distance learning.

The Master of Science program offers majors in two areas: project management and computer systems. The project management program emphasizes systems, processes, and application of critical skills that pertain to the stages and concerns of project management as needed by industry and government. The computer systems program presents students with an in-depth study of the areas of importance to the professional working in informational technology today. Computer systems majors are available in five emphasis areas: C++ programming, Web development, individualized study, Web programming in e-commerce, or technology management. Master of Science programs require 45 credit hours of course work.

With the exception of the Master of Arts in counseling psychology degree, graduate programs generally do not require a thesis. M.Ed. candidates may elect to complete a thesis, project, or internship. M.B.A., M.S., and M.A. candidates complete a capstone course and project, with research embedded throughout the course of study.

Research Facilities

City University's library offers an abundance of information resources in paper, microfiche, and electronic formats. Its holdings include more than 800 print journal titles, access to 19,000 online journals, ERIC documents on microfiche and online, as well as more than 40,000 books and curriculum materials. Most resources are indexed on the University's Web site. Reference and interlibrary loan services are offered to all students through the library's toll-free telephone number and e-mail. To serve certain education programs, the library maintains branches in Bellevue, Everett, Tacoma, and Vancouver, Washington. In addition, City University has formed cooperative agreements with appropriate libraries to extend library privileges to students in selected cities.

Financial Aid

Whenever possible, City University strives to help its students meet the financial challenges associated with a high-quality education. Several financial assistance programs are available, including student loans, scholarships, federal grants, and the Federal Work-Study Program. More information on these programs and their application deadlines is available through the Student Financial Services Office.

Cost of Study

Graduate tuition for the 2006-07 academic year was $458 per credit, or $1374 for a 3-credit course. The tuition rate is the same for both in-class and distance learning study. Other fees may apply, depending on the specific course of study.

Living and Housing Costs

City University does not provide student housing, and the cost of living varies at each location. In the Seattle area, rental expenses for a one-bedroom apartment are approximately $850 per month.

Student Group

The graduate student body is diverse, ranging from students who have just completed baccalaureate work, to those holding advanced degrees, to mature adults returning to school after twenty or more years in the work force (or at home). The average age of the graduate students is 36. Most students are employed full-time and bring a wealth of experience to the classroom. More than 5,000 graduate students are enrolled at all locations. Of these, 52 percent are women and 32 percent are international students.

Location

City University's mission is to change lives for good by offering high-quality and relevant education to anyone with the desire to learn. This is accomplished by maintaining a decentralized campus and by establishing locations where there is a demonstrated interest in high-quality higher education. City University operates from locations throughout North America, Europe, and Asia. Students all over the United States as well as overseas may complete a degree through the distance learning format.

The University

City University is one of the largest not-for-profit private institutions of higher learning in the Pacific Northwest, with more than 41,000 graduates. The University upholds its philosophy that everyone should have access to high-quality higher education by offering programs that are credible and convenient, thus allowing people to enhance their lives through education without interrupting other personal and professional commitments. City University has been a respected member of the Northwest's academic community since 1973 and is accredited by the Northwest Commission on Colleges and Universities.

Applying

City University is a professional institution for a professional student body. Because of this, the University has an open-door admissions policy. Students may begin a degree program in any quarter, and there is no deadline for applications. The Office of Admissions and Student Services and the Office of International Student Services can provide more information on additional admissions requirements.

Correspondence and Information

Graduate Admissions
City University
11900 Northeast First Street
Bellevue, Washington 98005

Phone: 425-637-1010
800-426-5596 (toll-free)
425-450-4660 (TTY/TDD)
Fax: 425-709-5361
E-mail: info@cityu.edu
Web site: http://www.cityu.edu

THE FACULTY

The combination of academic strength and practical expertise is a characteristic of City University's faculty and ensures the relevancy, currency, and credibility of instruction. Leaders from the business community and law, government, human services, civic, and research organizations are members of the City University faculty. All have strong academic preparation, and most are active professionals in their particular fields.

The University's senior administration and faculty have a University-wide role in quality assurance, academic policies and standards, curricular development, and instructional quality. They oversee the University's hundreds of adjunct faculty members.

Senior Academic Staff

Marie Cini, Assistant Vice President, Academic Programs and Initiatives.
Margaret Davis, Dean, Gordon Albright School of Education.
Elizabeth Fountain, Dean, School of Arts and Sciences.
Fernando Leon Garcia, Executive Vice President, Academic Affairs.
David Griffin, Dean, Academic Affairs–Slovakia.
R. C. Arden Henley, Executive Director, Canadian Programs.
Branislav Lichardus, Rector, College of Management–Slovakia.
Scott Mason, Dean, Academic Affairs–Bulgaria.

Core Faculty–U.S. and Canada

Terry Allan, Senior Faculty, Master in Teaching.
John Armenia, Program Director, Educational Leadership, Principal Certification, and Superintendent Certification.
Dorothy Dee Bayne, Senior Faculty, Integrated Arts and Learning.
Stephanie Brommer, Senior Faculty, Undergraduate Arts and Sciences Programs.
Thomas Cary, Associate Dean, School of Management.
Jeff Chang, Program Director, Alberta Arts and Sciences Programs.
Anna Cholewinska, Program Director, Undergraduate Arts and Sciences Programs.
Kay Chomic, Senior Faculty, Marketing.
Margaret Chow, Program Director, Master in Teaching.
Angela Christofferson, Electronic Resources Librarian, Vi Tasler Library.
Avraham Cohen, Senior Faculty/Internship Coordinator, British Columbia Arts and Sciences Programs.
Thomas Culham, Senior Faculty, Canadian Management Programs.
Paul Dehnert, Senior Faculty, B.A. of Education.
Linda Fenster, Director of Library Services, Vi Tasler Library.
Nina Fenton, Senior Faculty, Finance and PFP Programs.
Virginia Fitch, Senior Faculty, B.A. of Education.
Roberta Fox, Senior Faculty, B.A. of Education.
Paul Ganalon, Academic Representative, Diversity Outreach and Continuing Education.
Theresa Gehrig, Educational Reference Librarian, Vi Tasler Library.
Mary L. Gokiert, Senior Faculty, Edmonton Arts and Sciences Programs.
Evelyn Grendahl, Senior Faculty, B.A. of Education, Master in Teaching, and Professional Certification.
Glenn Grigg, Senior Faculty, Vancouver (British Columbia) Arts and Sciences Programs.
Brian Guthrie, Senior Faculty, Calgary Arts and Sciences Programs.
Jay Hambly, Senior Faculty, Educational Leadership and Superintendent Certification.
Dan Hanson, Program Director, Master of Education and Senior Faculty, Educational Technology.
Karen Harrison, Technical Services Coordinator, Vi Tasler Library.
Judy Hinrichs, Associate Dean, Gordon Albright School of Education.
Sue Jackson, Senior Faculty, B.A. of Education.
Mary Jane Job, Senior Faculty, B.A. of Education.
Calvin Kam, Senior Faculty, Master in Teaching.
Christine Katayama, Senior Faculty, Professional Certification.
Mary Keller, Psychology and Canadian Programs Reference Librarian, Vi Tasler Library.
Daria Lall, Branch Librarian, Vancouver (Washington), Vi Tasler Library.
Karen Langer, Counseling Clinic Director, School of Arts and Sciences.
Cynthia Larson, Senior Faculty, B.A. of Education.
Lynda Lewis, Senior Faculty, Canadian Education Programs.
Jodey Lingg, Coordinator of Online Programs, School of Management.
David Lundsgaard, Senior Faculty, Educational Leadership.
Lauretta Main, Senior Faculty, Master in Teaching.
Mary Beth Mara, Branch Librarian, Tacoma, Vi Tasler Library.
Corll Morrissey, Senior Faculty, B.A. of Education.
Susan Mundy, Program Director, Accounting.
Neal Mutadi, Director, Canadian Education Programs.
Allen Nakano, Senior Faculty, Master in Teaching.
J. Patrick Naughton, Senior Faculty, Master in Teaching.
Fara Nizamani, Senior Faculty, Master in Teaching.
Peggy Paulson, Senior Faculty, B.A. of Education.
Gregory Pickering, Counseling Clinic Supervisor, Edmonton Arts and Sciences Programs.
T. Joseph Pierce, Senior Faculty, Master in Teaching.
Eduardo Razon, Senior Faculty, Computer Systems.
Mariella Remund, Senior Faculty, China.
Shirley Roberts, Senior Faculty, B.A. of Education.
Molly Ross, Senior Faculty, Master in Teaching.
Colin Sanders, Counseling Clinic Supervisor, British Columbia Arts and Sciences Programs.
Craig Scheiber, Program Director, B.A. in Education.
Mary Schroeder, Program Director, Guidance and Counseling.
Barbara Scott-Johnson, Senior Faculty, Master in Teaching.
Susan Seiber, Senior Faculty, B.A. of Education.
Nicole Sheldon, Counseling Clinic Supervisor, Calgary Arts and Sciences Programs.
Edward "Tad" Shipman, Senior Faculty, Master in Teaching.
Stephen Smith, Senior Faculty, Master in Teaching.
Candace Sorenson, Senior Faculty, Master in Teaching and Graduate Arts and Sciences Programs.
David Stewart, Counseling Clinic Supervisor, Victoria Arts and Sciences Programs.
Christa Stewart-Price, Senior Faculty, Master in Teaching.
Michael Theisen, Senior Faculty/Internship Coordinator, Washington State SAS Programs.
Karen Toler, Senior Faculty, Guidance and Counseling.
Ginny Tresvant, Senior Faculty, Master in Teaching.
Allan Wade, Senior Faculty, Victoria Arts and Sciences Programs.
Michael Walker, Senior Faculty, Master in Teaching.
Michael Weatherbie, Senior Faculty, Master in Teaching.
Theresa Raymer Wildt, Program Director, Graduate Arts and Sciences Programs.
Katherine Williams, Faculty Development Consultant.
Nicole Zeger, Certification and Placement Specialist.

CLARION UNIVERSITY OF PENNSYLVANIA

Division of Graduate Studies

Programs of Study

Clarion University awards the degrees of Master of Arts, Master of Business Administration, Master of Education, Master of Science, and Master of Science in Library Science. The Master of Arts is offered in English; the Master of Education in education, reading, and science education; and the Master of Science in biology, mass media arts and journalism, nursing, rehabilitative sciences, special education, and speech-language pathology. The M.S. in Nursing is a joint program offered by Clarion, Edinboro, and Slippery Rock University of Pennsylvania. In addition, the Division offers a Certificate of Advanced Studies in Library Science, school library media certification, and an Instructional Technology Specialist Certificate.

Clarion University is accredited by the Middle States Association of Colleges and Schools. The graduate program in business administration is accredited by AACSB International–The Association to Advance Collegiate Schools of Business. The graduate program in speech-language pathology is accredited by the Council on Academic Accreditation of the American Speech-Language-Hearing Association. The graduate program in library science is accredited by the American Library Association. The graduate program in nursing is accredited by the National League for Nursing Accrediting Commission. Clarion University of Pennsylvania is a member of the American Association of State Colleges and Universities and the American Association of Colleges for Teacher Education.

Research Facilities

Facilities supporting graduate programs at Clarion University include modern science laboratories supplied with excellent instrumentation, well-equipped clinical support areas for special education and communication sciences and disorders, a modern business administration building, technologically equipped classrooms for library science, radio and television studios and experimental audiovisual facilities in communication, and a fully equipped word processing lab.

The University libraries offer graduate students a broad collection of resources and services to support classwork and research. In addition to more than 400,000 print volumes, the University libraries provide electronic indexing and full-text access to thousands of periodicals, newspapers, and reference sources in a range of subject areas. The library offers access to a broad range of electronic databases, periodicals, and other services to distance education students through the library's Web site at http://www.clarion.edu/library. Interlibrary loan service further enables users to expand their research.

The Center for Computing Services is responsible for all telephone, data network, and central computing services. The center houses the University telephone system as well as various servers that support central technical services, such as the iClarion student portal, e-mail, Internet and Web access, Clarion's Web site, and Blackboard courseware for online course work. Computing Services also supports sixteen general access labs and smart classrooms located across the Clarion and Venango campuses.

Registered students automatically receive an e-mail account, the ability to create their own Web pages, and access to the Internet. Other academic services for instruction and research include support of the following computer languages and packages: COBOL, FORTRAN, BASIC, Pascal, SAS, C, C++, SPSS, and business simulations.

Financial Aid

Graduate assistantships are awarded on a competitive basis for the nine-month academic year and are renewable. In 2006–07, compensation for a graduate assistant was either $2000 for 10 hours per week and a waiver of one half tuition or $4000 for 20 hours per week and a waiver of full tuition. Interested students should apply to the appropriate academic office or to the Division of Graduate Studies. Additional information regarding financial aid is available through the Office of Financial Aid.

Cost of Study

In 2006–07, graduate tuition and fees for Pennsylvania residents were $4051 per semester for full-time study (9 to 15 hours) or $450 per hour part-time. Out-of-state students paid $5884 for full-time study or $654 per hour part-time. Tuition and fees are subject to change without notice. The cost of books is estimated at $500 per semester.

Living and Housing Costs

University-owned housing is available to graduate students for $2445 per semester. Housing throughout the town of Clarion, though at a premium, is available at costs ranging from $500 to $700 per month. The Office of Residence Life has information regarding private housing. In 2006–07, food service could be obtained in the University Dining Hall for $866 per semester.

Student Group

The total enrollment at Clarion University is more than 6,000 students, of whom more than 575 are graduate students. The graduate enrollment represents many states and several other countries.

Location

Clarion is located high on the Allegheny Plateau overlooking the Clarion River. The rural setting is one of Pennsylvania's most scenic resort areas. The rolling, wooded countryside, interspersed with small farms, offers some of the best outdoor recreational opportunities to be found anywhere in northwestern Pennsylvania, with the Clarion River and its tributaries providing an ideal setting for boating, swimming, and other aquatic sports.

The University

Founded in 1867 as Carrier Seminary, the institution has evolved to a state normal school, to Clarion State Teachers College, to Clarion State College, and finally to Clarion University of Pennsylvania of the State System of Higher Education. Clarion's 99-acre main campus has thirty-eight buildings. It is within the borough of Clarion, some 2 miles north of Interstate 80 at Exits 62 and 64, and is approximately 2 hours' driving time from the urban centers of Pittsburgh, Erie, and Youngstown. Clarion's 64-acre Venango Campus, located in Oil City, has four buildings, including the modern Suhr Library. The McKeever Environmental Education Center is located in Mercer County.

Applying

Admission materials may be obtained from the Division of Graduate Studies. The application for admission should be received at least thirty days prior to the semester for which the student seeks entrance. Assistantships are generally awarded in the spring for the following fall semester. Application for an assistantship should be made before March 1.

Correspondence and Information

Division of Graduate Studies
Clarion University of Pennsylvania
Clarion, Pennsylvania 16214
Phone: 814-393-2337
Fax: 814-393-2722
Web site: http://www.clarion.edu/graduatestudies

DEPARTMENT AND PROGRAM HEADS

Brenda Sanders Dédé, Assistant Vice President for Academic Affairs; Ed.D., Texas Southern.
Biology: Andrew Keth, Ph.D., Penn State.
Business: Soga Ewedemi, Ph.D., Pennsylvania.
Communication Sciences and Disorders (Speech-Language Pathology): Janis Jarecki-Liu, Ph.D., Kent State.
Education: Brian E. Maguire, Ph.D., Penn State.
English: Richard Lane, Ph.D., Miami (Ohio).
Library Science: Bernard Vavrek, Ph.D., Pittsburgh.
Mass Media Arts and Journalism: Susan Hilton, Ed.D., Nova Southeastern.
Nursing: Alice Conway, Ph.D., Pittsburgh.
Reading: Brian Maguire, Ph.D., Penn State.
Rehabilitative Sciences: Mark Kilwein, Ph.D., Ohio State.
Science Education: Bruce Smith, Ph.D., Penn State.
Special Education: Lorie Taylor, Ed.D., Southern Mississippi.

CLARK UNIVERSITY

Graduate School

Programs of Study

The Graduate School of Clark University offers the following degrees: Doctor of Philosophy, Master of Arts, Master of Arts in Education, Master of Arts in Liberal Arts, Master of Arts in Teaching, Master of Business Administration, Master of Public Administration, Master of Science in Finance, Master of Science in Professional Communications, and Master of Science in Information Technology.

The Doctor of Philosophy is conferred in biology, chemistry, economics, geography, history, physics, and psychology. Postdoctoral training is conducted in geography, psychology, and the sciences.

The Master of Arts is awarded in community development and planning; education; English; environmental science and policy; geographic information science, development, and environment (GISDE); information technology; international development; and communications. The Master of Business Administration and the Master of Science in Finance are offered in the Graduate School of Management. The Graduate School also offers accelerated B.A./M.A. programs (to qualifying Clark undergraduates) in biology, chemistry, communications, community development and planning, education, environmental science and policy, finance, geographic information science (GIS), history, international development, management, and physics.

An academic year of study in residence, which is eight courses, is a minimum requirement for a master's degree. One year of full-time study in residence, not less than eight courses beyond the master's, is required for the doctorate. Study in residence is broadly defined as graduate work done at Clark University under the immediate personal supervision of at least one member of the University faculty.

Research Facilities

The Arthur B. Sackler Science Center and Lasry Center for Bioscience emphasize the interdisciplinary nature of the sciences at Clark and provide teaching amphitheaters and seminar rooms, research laboratories, computer facilities, and a science library. The psychology department is also equipped with laboratory and computer facilities. The Graduate School of Geography maintains several GIS and remote sensing laboratories and the Guy H. Burnham Map and Aerial Photography Library. The George Perkins Marsh Institute provides research space and the J. X. Kasperson Library, a first-rate collection on human environment themes. Clark Labs provides specialized GIS research space for the production of IDRISI and related GIS software.

The Robert Hutchings Goddard Library provides fine quarters for large collections in all graduate fields. Most graduate departments provide study space for graduate students and maintain equipment necessary for study and research.

Financial Aid

Graduate fellowships and scholarships are provided by the University for well-qualified graduate students. Financial aid is also available through grants from special funds, sponsored research grants, and a University graduate loan fund. Several departments participate in national fellowship programs.

Cost of Study

Tuition for the academic year 2006–07 was $31,200. Special fees included health insurance, a diploma fee of $150 for the doctorate and $100 for the master's degree, a $30 activity fee, and a fee of $200 per semester for students who have completed all formal University and departmental residence requirements. Tuition waivers and stipends are offered to students in Ph.D. programs and many master's programs.

Living and Housing Costs

Living accommodations for both married and single graduate students are available a short distance from the campus at various costs. The University has a limited number of on-campus rooms available for single graduate students.

Student Group

During 2006–07, there were 610 full-time and 218 part-time graduate students in residence, of whom 332 were men and 496 were women. Approximately two thirds of the graduate students receive financial assistance in the form of remission of tuition and/or stipends in amounts that vary depending upon the field of study.

Location

Worcester, a city of diversified industry, is a rapidly emerging educational and cultural center. It has ten schools of higher learning with more than 10,000 students, as well as a modern medical school. Major cultural attractions include the Worcester Art Museum, Higgins Armory Museum, Worcester Historical Society, Worcester Public Library, and American Antiquarian Society. Worcester's Civic Center, the DCU Center, offers a wide variety of popular performing artists and athletic events. The Worcester Music Festival presents an annual series of concerts. Theatrical productions, symphonic concerts, light operas, folk festivals, and lecture series are offered regularly. Boston and Cambridge are less than an hour's drive away.

The University

Clark University was founded as a graduate institution in 1887 and awarded its first doctorate in 1891. Undergraduate liberal arts education was established in 1902. The University has twenty-eight major buildings situated on a 35-acre campus. The Robert Hutchings Goddard Library was opened in 1969 and is nationally known for its design as well as its holdings. It was named in honor of the father of the Space Age, who was a Clark alumnus and professor of physics at Clark from 1914 until 1942.

Applying

Applicants from American and other institutions should contact the department in which they expect to do their major work. Application deadlines for admission and financial aid vary by department. Students should contact the department or program of interest for the date. An application fee of $50 is charged. Further information can be obtained from the University's Web site.

Correspondence and Information

Chair, Department of (specify)
Clark University
950 Main Street
Worcester, Massachusetts 01610
Web site: http://www.clarku.edu/graduate

THE FACULTY

The chairpersons of departments and the directors of interdepartmental programs offering graduate work at Clark are listed below.

Biology: Dr. Susan Foster.
Chemistry: Dr. Mark Turnbull.
Community Development: Dr. William F. Fisher.
Economics: Dr. Wayne Gray.
Education: Dr. Thomas Del Prete.
English: Dr. Virginia Vaughan.
Environmental Science and Policy: Dr. William F. Fisher.
Finance: Dr. Edward J. Ottensmeyer.
Geographic Information Science (GISDE): Dr. William F. Fisher.
Geography: Dr. B. L. Turner II.
History: Dr. Drew McCoy.
Information Technology: Dr. Dennis Wadsworth.
International Development: Dr. William F. Fisher.
Management: Dr. Edward J. Ottensmeyer.
Physics: Dr. Charles Agosta.
Professional Communication: Dr. Max Hess.
Psychology: Dr. Michael Addis.
Public Administration: Dr. Brian Cook.

CLEMSON UNIVERSITY

Graduate School

Programs of Study Clemson University offers the following programs of study leading to degrees: accounting (M.P.Acc.); administration and supervision (M.Ed., Ed.S.); agricultural education (M.Ag.Ed.); animal and veterinary science (M.S., Ph.D.); applied economics (Ph.D.); applied economics and statistics (M.S.); applied psychology (M.S.); applied sociology (M.S.); architecture (M.S., M.Arch.); automotive engineering (M.S., Ph.D.); biochemistry and molecular biology (M.S., Ph.D.); bioengineering (M.S., Ph.D.); biological sciences (M.S., Ph.D.); biosystems engineering (M.S., Ph.D.); business administration (M.B.A.); chemical engineering (M.S., Ph.D.); chemistry (M.S., Ph.D.); city and regional planning (M.C.R.P.); civil engineering (M.S., Ph.D.); computer engineering (M.S., Ph.D.); computer science (M.S., Ph.D.); construction science and management (M.C.S.M., Cert.); counselor education (M.Ed.); curriculum and instruction (Ph.D.); digital production arts (M.F.A., Cert.); economics (M.A.); educational leadership (Ph.D.); electrical engineering (M.Engr., M.S., Ph.D.); elementary education (M.Ed.); English (M.A.); entomology (M.S., Ph.D.); environmental design and planning (Ph.D.); environmental engineering and science (M.Engr., M.S., Ph.D.); environmental toxicology (M.S., Ph.D.); graphic communications (M.S.); food technology (Ph.D.); food, nutrition, and culinary science (M.S.); forest resources (M.F.R., M.S., Ph.D.); genetics (M.S., Ph.D.); health communication (Cert.); historic preservation (M.S.H.P., Cert.); history (M.A.); human factors psychology (Ph.D.); human resource development (M.H.R.D.); hydrogeology (M.S.); industrial engineering (M.S., Ph.D.); industrial/organizational psychology (Ph.D.); international family and community studies (Ph.D.); landscape architecture (M.L.A.); management (M.S., Ph.D.); marketing (M.S.); materials science and engineering (M.S., Ph.D.); mathematical sciences (M.S., Ph.D.); mechanical engineering (M.S., Ph.D.); microbiology (M.S., Ph.D.); middle grades education (M.A.T.); nursing (M.S.); packaging science (M.S.); parks, recreation, and tourism management (M.P.R.T.M., M.S., Ph.D.); physics (M.S., Ph.D.); plant and environmental sciences (M.S., Ph.D.); policy studies (Ph.D., Cert.); polymer and fiber science (M.S., Ph.D.); professional communication (M.A.); public administration (M.P.A.); reading (M.Ed.); real estate development (M.R.E.D.); rhetorics, communication, and information design (Ph.D.); secondary education (M.Ed.); special education (M.Ed.); technology entrepreneurship (Cert.); visual arts (M.F.A.); wildlife and fisheries biology (M.S., Ph.D.); writing assessment (Cert.); and youth development leadership (M.S.).

Research Facilities Clemson's main library, the Robert M. Cooper Library, provides students with a variety of services and up-to-date collections. More than 1.6 million items are available, including books, periodicals, microforms, government publications, and electronic materials. On-campus branch libraries contain materials dealing with the special nature of their programs. Clemson University operates several institutes and centers dedicated to teaching and research in specific disciplines, such as the Center for Advanced Engineering Fibers and Films (CAEFF), the Clemson University Genomics Institute (CUGI), the Brooks Research Institute, the Robert J. Rutland Center for Ethics, and the South Carolina Institute for Energy Studies (SCIES). These centers encourage faculty members from several academic departments to bring their research skills to bear on multidisciplinary problems and issues. For more information on Clemson's Centers and Institutes, students should visit http://www.clemson.edu/centers.

Financial Aid The Federal Stafford Student Loan is available to most students regardless of income. Further information is available from the Office of Student Financial Aid. All other forms of assistance for graduate students are coordinated through the Graduate School. Awarding decisions rest with the departments. Traineeships and fellowships are available in many departments and do not require service to the University. Assistantships are available in many departments and provide competitive stipends. Graduate assistants pay a flat fee of $950 per semester for tuition and fees. Assistantships usually require half-time employment. Information about traineeships, fellowships, and assistantships should be obtained from the student's department of proposed study.

Cost of Study In October 2006, the Board of Trustees approved a four-tier tuition scale to reflect the broad array of programs the Graduate School offers. Each tier's tuition was set to be a realistic market rate based on peer programs at other institutions as identified by the program's department. This new tiered structure is in effect in fall 2007. For tuition rates by program and tier, students should visit http://www.grad.clemson.edu/Financial.php. Off-campus rates are $330 per hour for in-state students and $660 per hour for nonresidents. Graduate assistants pay a flat fee of $950 per semester and $315 per summer session. Graduate fellows pay South Carolina resident fees.

Living and Housing Costs On-campus housing is available; for information, students should visit http://www.housing.clemson.edu. The cost of living in Clemson is quite low compared to the national average; students who choose to live off-campus typically spend $300–$400 per month for rent, depending on location, amenities, and roommates.

Student Group Graduate enrollment for fall 2006 was 3,137 students, of whom 2,019 were classified as full-time and 1,118 as part-time. The graduate student population was made up of 1,623 men and 1,514 women.

Student Outcomes The University's career center offers assistance to students in identifying career interests through counseling, interest inventories, and computerized guidance systems. Graduate Student Career Workshops focus on career planning, preparing job-search and interview materials, and honing job-search and interviewing skills. The career library has information on employers, job outlooks, and salaries. An online recruiting system connects to employers through resume books, on-campus interviewing, and job postings.

Location Clemson is a small, beautiful, college town in upstate South Carolina. The Upstate is one of the country's fastest-growing areas and is an important part of the I-85 Corridor, a multi-state area along Interstate 85 that runs from the metro Atlanta area (home to nearly 5 million people) to Richmond, Virginia, and encompasses Charlotte, North Carolina, (the U.S.'s second-largest financial center) as well as North Carolina's Research Triangle. Atlanta and Charlotte are each a two hour drive away. Many financial institutions have regional offices located in the Upstate, including Wachovia and Bank of America. Other major industries of commerce in the Upstate include the automotive, healthcare, and pharmaceutical industries. Corporations based in or with a major presence in the Upstate include BMW, Bon Secours St. Francis Health System, Bosch North America, Bowater, Charter Communications, Ernst and Young, Fluor Corporation, IBM, Microsoft, Michelin of North America, and others.

The University Clemson is classified by the Carnegie Foundation as an RU/H: Research University (high research activity), a category comprising just 10 percent of all graduate degree-granting universities in America. The University's mission is to fulfill the covenant between its founder and the people of South Carolina to establish a "high seminary of learning" through its responsibilities of teaching, research, and extended public service. The University has identified eight areas of academic emphasis that create collaborations that, in turn, help fulfill the University's mission.

Applying Applicants may apply on the Web at http://www.grad.clemson.edu/Admission.php. Applications with a $50 nonrefundable fee should be received no later than five weeks prior to registration. Every required item in support of the application (completed application form, application fee, transcripts from each postsecondary school attended, letters of recommendation, and test scores) must be on file by that date. Students are advised to contact the department for the deadlines of the program of proposed study.

Correspondence and Information

Clemson University Graduate School
Clemson University
E-106 Martin Hall
Clemson, South Carolina 29634-5713

Phone: 864-656-3195
E-mail: graduate_school@clemson.edu
Web site: http://www.grad.clemson.edu

GRADUATE DEGREE PROGRAMS AND PROGRAM COORDINATORS

Bruce Rafert, Ph.D.; Dean of the Graduate School.

College of Agriculture, Forestry, and Life Sciences

Agricultural Education: Tom Dobbins. (tdbbns@clemson.edu; http://virtual.clemson.edu/groups/aged/graduate_overview.htm)

Animal and Veterinary Science: Tom Scott. (trscott@clemson.edu; http://www.clemson.edu/avs/graduate)

Applied Economics and Statistics: William Bridges. (wbrdgs@clemson.edu; http://cherokee.agecon.clemson.edu/ms_prog.htm)

Biochemistry and Molecular Biology: Kerry S. Smith and Lisa R. Pape. (kssmith@clemson.edu; lpape@clemson.edu; http://www.clemson.edu/genbiochem/gradprograms.html)

Biological Sciences: Margaret Ptacek. (mptacek@clemson.edu; http://www.clemson.edu/biosci/graduate)

Biosystems Engineering: Caye M. Drapcho. (cdrapch@clemson.edu; http://virtual.clemson.edu/groups/agbioeng/bio/deg.htm)

Entomology: John C. Morse. (jmorse@clemson.edu; http://entweb.clemson.edu/studentp/degrees/index.htm)

Environmental Toxicology: Tom Schwedler. (tschwdl@clemson.edu; http://www.clemson.edu/entox/academics/index.htm)

Food, Nutrition, and Culinary Sciences: Paul L. Dawson. (pdawson@clemson.edu; http://www.clemson.edu/foodscience/graduateprogram.htm)

Food Technology: Paul L. Dawson. (pdawson@clemson.edu; http://www.clemson.edu/foodscience/graduateprogram.htm)

Forest Resources: David C. Guynn. (dguynn@clemson.edu; http://www.clemson.edu/forestres/for_prog.html#grad)

Genetics: Lisa R. Pape and Jim Morris. (lpape@clemson.edu; jmorri2@clemson.edu; http://www.clemson.edu/genbiochem/gradstudents.html)

Microbiology: Margaret Ptacek. (mptacek@clemson.edu; http://www.clemson.edu/biosci/graduate)

Packaging Science: Kay D. Cooksey. (kcookse@clemson.edu; http://workgroups.clemson.edu/CAFLS0320_PACKAGING_SCIENCE/index.php?option=com_content&task=category§ionid=10&id=39&Itemid=72)

Plant and Environmental Sciences: Halina T. Knap and William V. Baird. (hskrpsk@clemson.edu; vbaird@clemson.edu; http://www.clemson.edu/plantenvgrad/INDEX.htm)

Wildlife and Fisheries Biology: David C. Guynn. (dguynn@clemson.edu; http://www.clemson.edu/forestres/aquaindex.html#MS)

College of Architecture, Arts, and Humanities

Architecture: Jori Erdman. (jerdman@clemson.edu; http://www.clemson.edu/caah/architecture/1.3.3.php)

City and Regional Planning: James D. London. (london1@clemson.edu; http://www.clemson.edu/caah/pla/planning/index.htm)

Construction Science and Management: Roger W. Liska. (riggor@clemson.edu; http://www.clemson.edu/caah/csm/GRAD/index.htm)

English: Alma Bennett. (balma@clemson.edu; http://www.clemson.edu/caah/english/graduate/malit.htm)

Environmental Design and Planning: Barry Nocks. (nocks2@clemson.edu; http://www.clemson.edu/caah/pla/edp)

Historic Preservation: Daniel J. Nadenicek. (dnadeni@clemson.edu; http://www.clemson.edu/caah/pla/mhp/index.htm)

History: Steve Marks. (msteven@clemson.edu; http://www.clemson.edu/caah/history/graduate/index.htm)

Landscape Architecture: Umit Yilmaz. (uyilmaz@clemson.edu; http://www.clemson.edu/caah/landscapearchitecture)

Professional Communications: Martin Jacobi. (mjacobi@clemson.edu; http://www.clemson.edu/caah/mapc)

Real Estate Development: Terry Farris. (jfarris@clemson.edu; http://www.clemson.edu/caah/pla/mred/index.htm)

Rhetorics, Communication, and Information Design: Victor Vitanza. (sophist@clemson.edu; http://www.clemson.edu/caah/rcid/index.htm)

Visual Arts: Dave Detrick. (ddavid@clemson.edu; http://www.clemson.edu/caah/art)

College of Business and Behavioral Sciences

Accounting: Thomas L. Dickens. (dickent@clemson.edu; http://business.clemson.edu/departments/acct/acct_about.htm)

Applied Economics: Michael Maloney. (maloney@clemson.edu; http://www.grad.clemson.edu/catalog/index.php?college=03&major=122)

Applied Psychology: Christopher C. Pagano. (cpagano@clemson.edu; http://www.clemson.edu/psych/?page_id=37)

Applied Sociology: Catherine F. Mobley. (camoble@clemson.edu; http://business.clemson.edu/departments/sociology/soc_grad.htm)

Business Administration: Martha J. Duke. (dmartha@clemson.edu; http://business.clemson.edu/mba/programs/academics.htm)

Economics: Michael Maloney. (maloney@clemson.edu; http://www.clemson.edu/economics/graduate/graduate.htm)

Graphic Communications: Nona Woolbright. (nwoolbr@clemson.edu; http://graphics.clemson.edu/graphics-site/grad-curric.htm)

Human Factors Psychology: Christopher C. Pagano. (cpagano@clemson.edu; http://www.clemson.edu/psych/?page_id=36)

Industrial/Organizational Psychology: Christopher C. Pagano. (cpagano@clemson.edu; http://www.clemson.edu/psych/?page_id=35)

Management: Russell Purvis. (rlpurvi@clemson.edu; http://business.clemson.edu/managemt/Acad_Overview/L1_msmgt.html)

Marketing: John D. Mittelstaedt. (jmittel@clemson.edu; http://business.clemson.edu/departments/marketing/mkt_grad.htm)

Public Administration: Robert W. Smith. (rws@clemson.edu; http://business.clemson.edu/MPA)

College of Engineering and Science

Automotive Engineering: Thomas Kurfess. (kurfess@clemson.edu; http://www.ces.clemson.edu/me/AutoEngineer)

Bioengineering: Robert A. Latour. (latourr@clemson.edu; http://www.ces.clemson.edu/bio/grad/grad-degrees.html)

Chemical Engineering: Graham Harrison. (grahamh@clemson.edu; http://www.ces.clemson.edu/chemeng/prospective_graduate_students.html)

Chemistry: Steve Stuart. (ss@clemson.edu; http://chemistry.clemson.edu/graduate/index.htm)

Civil Engineering: Ronald Andrus. (randrus@clemson.edu; http://www.clemson.edu/ce/graduate/index.php)

Computer Engineering: Darren M. Dawson. (ddarren@clemson.edu; http://www.ece.clemson.edu/ece/gradovvw.shtml)

Computer Science: Mark K. Smotherman. (mark@clemson.edu; http://www.cs.clemson.edu/Prospective/graduate.shtml)

EE&S–Environmental Health Physics: Cindy M. Lee. (lc@clemson.edu; http://www.ces.clemson.edu/ees/curriculum.html)

Electrical Engineering: Darren M. Dawson. (ddarren@clemson.edu; http://www.ece.clemson.edu/ece/gradovvw.shtml)

Environmental Engineering and Science: Cindy M. Lee and David Freeman. (lc@clemson.edu; dfreedm@clemson.edu http://www.ces.clemson.edu/ees/curriculum.html)

Hydrogeology: Jim Castle. (jcastle@clemson.edu; http://www.ces.clemson.edu/geology/hydro/mshydroinfo.htm)

Industrial Engineering: William G. Ferrell. (fwillia@clemson.edu; http://www.ces.clemson.edu/ie/academics/graduate/graduate.htm)

Materials Science and Engineering: Stephen Foulger. (foulger@clemson.edu; http://mse.clemson.edu/htm/degrees/MSEdegrees.htm)

Mathematical Sciences: KB Kulasekera. (mthgrad@clemson.edu; http://www.math.clemson.edu/graduate)

Mechanical Engineering: Richard S. Miller. (rm@clemson.edu; http://www.ces.clemson.edu/me/studentinfo/graduate/index.htm)

Physics: Mark Leising. (lmark@clemson.edu; http://physicsnt.clemson.edu/?main=p_grad&sub=programs)

Polymer and Fiber Science: Stephen Foulger. (foulger@clemson.edu; http://mse.clemson.edu/htm/degrees/TFPSdegrees.htm)

College of Health, Education, and Human Development

Administration and Supervision: Diane Ricciardi. (pdr@clemson.edu; http://www.hehd.clemson.edu/schoolofed/graduate.htm)

Counselor Education (Community Counseling): David Scott. (dscott2@clemson.edu; http://www.hehd.clemson.edu/schoolofed/graduate.htm)

Counselor Education (School Counseling): Robert Urofsky. (rurofsk@clemson.edu; http://www.hehd.clemson.edu/schoolofed/graduate.htm)

Counselor Education (Student Affairs): Pam Havice. (havice@clemson.edu; http://www.hehd.clemson.edu/schoolofed/graduate.htm)

Curriculum and Instruction: Victoria Ridgeway. (rvictor@clemson.edu; http://www.hehd.clemson.edu/schoolofed/g-c&i_po.htm)

Educational Leadership (Higher Education): Frankie Williams. (fkw@clemson.edu; http://www.hehd.clemson.edu/schoolofed/graduate.htm)

Educational Leadership (P-12): Jane Clark Lindle. (jlindle@clemson.edu; http://www.hehd.clemson.edu/schoolofed/graduate.htm)

Elementary Education: Dave Fleming. (dflemin@clemson.edu; http://www.hehd.clemson.edu/schoolofed/graduate.htm)

Human Resource Development: Phill McGee. (pmcgee@clemson.edu; http://www.hehd.clemson.edu/mhrd)

Middle-Grades Education: Lienne Medford. (lienne@clemson.edu; http://www.hehd.clemson.edu/schoolofed/graduate.htm)

Nursing: Margaret Wetsel and Julia Eggert. (mwetsel@clemson.edu; jaegger@clemson.edu; http://www.hehd.clemson.edu/nursing/ms.php)

Parks, Recreation, and Tourism Management: Fran McGuire. (lefty@clemson.edu; http://www.hehd.clemson.edu/PRTM/mprtm.htm)

Reading: Kathy Headley. (ksn1177@clemson.edu; http://www.hehd.clemson.edu/schoolofed/graduate.htm)

Secondary Education (English): Bea Bailey. (cbeatri@clemson.edu; http://www.hehd.clemson.edu/schoolofed/graduate.htm)

Secondary Education (History and Geography): Susan Pass. (spass@clemson.edu; http://www.hehd.clemson.edu/schoolofed/graduate.htm)

Secondary Education (Math): Robert Horton. (bhorton@clemson.edu; http://www.hehd.clemson.edu/schoolofed/graduate.htm)

Secondary Education (Natural Sciences): Robert Horton. (bhorton@clemson.edu; http://www.hehd.clemson.edu/schoolofed/graduate.htm)

Special Education: Antonis Katsiyannis. (antonis@clemson.edu; http://www.hehd.clemson.edu/schoolofed/graduate.htm)

Youth Development: William Quinn. (wquinn@clemson.edu; http://www.clemson.edu/youthdevelopment/)

Graduate Interdisciplinary Programs

Digital Production Arts: Tim Davis. (tdavis2@clemson.edu; http://www.fx.clemson.edu/)

International Family and Community Studies: Timothy Davis. (tdavis2@clemson.edu; http://virtual.clemson.edu/groups/ifnl/PhD_Program/content.html)

Policy Studies: Bruce W. Ransom. (bii@clemson.edu; http://www.strom.clemson.edu/policystudies/index.html)

COLLEGE OF MOUNT ST. JOSEPH

COLLEGE OF MOUNT ST. JOSEPH

Graduate Studies

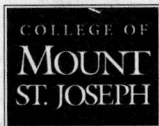

Programs of Study

The College of Mount St. Joseph (the Mount) offers five graduate degree programs: a Master of Arts (M.A.) in education with three accelerated teaching apprenticeships, a Master of Arts (M.A.) in religious studies, a Master of Science (M.S.) in organizational leadership, a Master of Nursing (M.N.) degree, and a Doctor of Physical Therapy (D.P.T.) degree.

The M.A. degree in education program meets the needs of college graduates who are prospective or experienced teachers. An intensive course of study integrates theory and field work in diverse educational settings. Classes meet during late afternoon, evening, summer, and occasionally on the weekend.

The TEAM (Teacher Education Apprenticeship Master's) programs prepare adults to enter the teaching profession through an intense learning and apprentice format. Three programs are offered: TEAM–IEC (Inclusive Early Childhood), TEAM–AYA (Adolescent/Young Adult), and TEAM–MSE (Multicultural/Special Education). The Mount TEAM programs lead to a Master of Arts degree in education, and all the programs can be completed in seventeen months. The programs are open to qualified students who have a bachelor's degree.

The M.A. degree in religious studies program, which concentrates on spiritual and pastoral care, is designed to enhance and integrate the interpersonal skills and theological knowledge of health-care professionals, educators, and ministers who serve in diverse populations and social contexts. Small classes, academic advising, and personal attention provide an environment conducive to the development of pastoral competence. Core courses are offered on weekends, enabling adult students to continue working while completing degree requirements in two years.

The M.S. degree in organizational leadership program takes a multidisciplinary approach and emphasizes values, spirituality, and ethics, while focusing on the development of effective leadership skills that can be used in any type of organization. Areas of study include leadership, people and organizations, organizational decision making, and technology. The M.S. degree can be completed in fewer than two years. All courses are offered on Saturdays.

The Master of Nursing degree program is an accelerated graduate-level program for individuals who have an undergraduate degree and who would like to become a nurse. The program prepares the student with advanced course work and offers the shortest path for college graduates who want to become nurses. This degree option is supported by the Ohio Board of Nursing.

The Doctor of Physical Therapy degree program is designed to prepare clinicians who can think critically and solve problems; apply scientifically validated therapeutic skills and techniques effectively; respect the dignity of individuals; and understand the responsibilities of the health-care provider in the twenty-first century. This program is fully accredited by the Commission on Accreditation in Physical Therapy Education. Upon completion, a graduate must apply for and successfully pass the National Physical Therapy Examination conducted by each state's licensing board.

Research Facilities

The Mount's Archbishop Alter Library owns more than 125,000 volumes, has access to more than 140 databases, online reference sources, and research assistance. Document delivery and interlibrary loan facilitate the prompt acquisition of materials available anywhere in the country. With FOCUS, the library's online public access catalog, patrons may search for materials available at the College library and other area libraries. OHIOLINK, a statewide network of public universities and private colleges, provides quick access to materials and full access to the Internet.

Financial Aid

Financial aid is available to all students enrolled at the Mount, with priority given to those in need of financial assistance. Students must complete a financial aid application. Five scholarships, each in the amount of $1000, are awarded annually to women who are graduate students in education and/or religious studies. To qualify, applicants must take at least 12 credit hours during the academic year.

A special grant is available to any individual enrolled in the religious studies graduate program who is a paid or volunteer minister serving in a congregation, hospital, health-care facility, social service agency, diocese, or educational institution. This grant reduces tuition during all semesters. Verification of employment/volunteer service and submission of a FAFSA form are required.

Cost of Study

Tuition for graduate programs is as follows: M.A. in education, $440 per hour; M.A. in religious studies, $440 per hour; M.S. in organizational leadership, $550 per hour; and D.P.T., $8,800 per semester. The tuition rates for TEAM Programs in Education are TEAM-IEC, $450 per hour; TEAM-MSE, $450 per hour; and TEAM-AYA, $450 per hour.

Living and Housing Costs

Apartments are for rent at reasonable rates in the immediate area.

Student Group

Total enrollment at the Mount exceeds 2,200. There are approximately 300 graduate students, with nearly 67 percent attending full-time.

Location

The Mount's campus is located in suburban Cincinnati, just 15 minutes from downtown cultural events, museums, entertainment, sports, shopping, and a variety of fine restaurants.

The College

The College of Mount St. Joseph is a Catholic college that provides its students with an interdisciplinary liberal arts and professional education emphasizing values, integrity, and social responsibility. Small class sizes encourage individualized learning, and students have opportunities for career experience, leadership development, service learning, and participation in a wide variety of activities. In addition to graduate programs, the Mount offers thirty-five undergraduate academic programs and ten associate degrees.

The Mount is fully accredited by the Higher Learning Commission of the North Central Association of Colleges and Schools and is consistently ranked among the top Midwest regional universities for quality, value, and a high graduation rate by *U.S. News & World Report* in its guide to America's Best Colleges. In addition, the Mount is one of a select group of 100 colleges and universities nationwide to be recognized in *The Templeton Guide* for building the character of its students. *Rugg's Recommendation on the Colleges* ranked the Mount as one of the nation's finest choices for programs in art, business, education, and nursing.

Applying

Students interested in applying should contact the Office of Graduate Admission to obtain application forms and other program materials.

Correspondence and Information

Office of Graduate Admission
College of Mount St. Joseph
5701 Delhi Road
Cincinnati, Ohio 45233

Phone: 513-244-GRAD
800-654-9314 (toll-free)
E-mail: admissions@mail.msj.edu
Web site: http://www.msj.edu

THE FACULTY

Education: Mifrando Obach, Ph.D., Chair; phone: 513-244-3263; fax: 513-244-4867; e-mail: mifrando_obach@mail.msj.edu.
Anne Broughton, Assistant Professor; Ed.D., Cincinnati.
Nancy Cavanaugh, Instructor; M.Ed., Cincinnati.
Tsila Evers, Assistant Professor; Ph.D., Michigan.
James Green, Assistant Professor; Ph.D., Ohio State.
Annie Hawkins, Assistant Professor; Ed.D., Cincinnati.
Kathleen Hulgin, Assistant Professor; Ph.D., Syracuse.
Angela Miller, Assistant Professor; M.Ed., Xavier.
Jay Parks, TEAM-IEC Coordinator; M.Ed., Cincinnati.
Clarissa Rosas, Associate Professor; Ph.D., New Mexico.
Paul Sallada, Director of Clinical Experiences; M.Ed., Cincinnati.
Linda Schoenstedt, Assistant Professor; Ed.D., Montana State.
Kim Shibinski, Assistant Professor; Ed.D., South Carolina.
Richard Sparks, Professor of Education; Ed.D., Cincinnati.
Mary West, Assistant Professor; Ph.D., Ohio State.
Health Services/M.N.: Darla Vale, D.N.Sc., Chair; phone: 513-244-4511; fax: 513-451-2547; e-mail: darla_vale@mail.msj.edu.
Susan Johnson, Associate Professor and Program Director; Ph.D., Cincinnati; RN.
Nezam Al-Nsair, Assistant Professor; Ph.D., Villanova; RN.
Mary Ellen Betz, Assistant Professor; Ed.D., International Graduate School; RN.
Gail Burns, Assistant Professor; M.S.N., Cincinnati; RN.
Agnes DiStasi, Assistant Professor; M.S.N., Cincinnati.
Donna Glankler, Assistant Professor; M.S.N., Cincinnati; RN.
Nancy Hinzman, Associate Professor; M.S.N., Indiana; RNC.
Mary Kishman, Associate Professor; Ph.D., Cincinnati; RN.
M. Kathleen Monahan, Assistant Professor; M.S.N., Akron; RN.
Patricia Sunderhaus, Instructor; M.S.N., Ball State.
Organizational Leadership: Jim Brodzinski, Ph.D., Department Chair; phone: 513-244-4918; fax: 513-244-4270; e-mail: jim_brodzinski@mail.msj.edu.
John Ballard, Associate Professor; Ph.D., Purdue.
Elizabeth Barkley, Professor; Ph.D., Cincinnati.
Missy Houlette, Assistant Professor; Ph.D., Delaware.
Kim Hunter, Assistant Professor and Director, Instructional Technology; M.B.A., Toledo.
Charles Kroncke, Assistant Professor; Ph.D., Auburn.
Tim Lawson, Professor; Ph.D., Miami (Ohio).
Judy Singleton, Assistant Professor; Ph.D., Cincinnati.
Scott Sportsman, Associate Professor and Director, Instructional and Market Research; Ph.D., Illinois.
Georgana Taggart, Associate Professor; J.D., Northern Kentucky.
Ron White, Professor; Ph.D., Kentucky.
Religious Studies: John Trokan, D.Min., Associate Professor and Chair; phone: 513-244-4496; fax: 513-244-4788; e-mail: john_trokan@mail.msj.edu.
Alan deCourcy, Associate Professor and Academic Dean; D.Min., United Theological Seminary (Ohio).
Sister Marge Kloos, Associate Professor; D.Min., United Theological Seminary (Ohio); SC.
Harriet Luckman, Associate Professor; Ph.D., Marquette.
Jozef D. Zalot, Assistant Professor; Ph.D., Marquette.

Adjunct Faculty
Georgiana Abplanalp, M.Ed., Xavier.
Christina Balogh, M.Ed., Mount St. Joseph.
John Berrens, Ph.D., Cincinnati.
Jerry Boyle, Ed.D., Cincinnati.
Bridget Brennan, M.Ed., Mount St. Joseph.
Lisa Campbell, Ed.D., Cincinnati.
Deborah Canter, Ed.D., Miami.
Kay Clifton, Professor; Ph.D., Iowa.
Elaine Crable, Ph.D., Georgia.
Yaping Gao, Ph.D., Purdue.
Barbara Garvin, M.Ed., Cincinnati.
John Miriam Jones, Ph.D., Notre Dame; SC.
Barbara Kalbli, M.Ed., Cincinnati.
James Kroeger, M.B.A., Cincinnati; CPA.
Gail Pitmon, M.Ed., South Carolina.
Anne Power, Ph.D., Columbia.
Peggy Riegel, M.Ed., Miami.
Rick Santoro, M.Ed., Cincinnati.
Amy Schlessman, Ph.D., Indiana.
Jane Shulman, M.Ed., Xavier.
Ann Slone, M.Ed., Miami.
Deborah Stroud, M.Ed., Wright State.

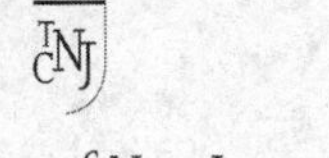

The College of New Jersey

THE COLLEGE OF NEW JERSEY

Graduate Programs

Programs of Study

The College of New Jersey (TCNJ) offers the following advanced degrees: Master of Arts (M.A.) in applied Spanish studies, counselor education, and English; Master of Arts in Teaching (M.A.T.) in early childhood education, elementary education, secondary education, special education, and technology education; Master of Education (M.Ed.) in educational leadership, elementary and secondary education (Global Program only), health education, instruction (a collaborative program in conjunction with the Regional Training Center), physical education, reading, special education, and teaching English as a second language; Master of Science (M.S.) in educational technology; Master of Science in Nursing (M.S.N.) in adult nurse practitioner studies, clinical nurse leader studies, family nurse practitioner studies, and neonatal nurse practitioner studies; and Educational Specialist (Ed.S.) in marriage and family therapy.

Graduate certificate programs are offered in bilingual education; educational leadership; family nurse practitioner; learning disabilities teacher/consultant studies; reading specialist; school licensure, preschool–grade 3; substance awareness coordinator; supervisor; teacher certification for international schools (Global Program only); teacher of the handicapped; and teaching English as a second language.

Global opportunities in education are also available for graduate students. Such global programs at TCNJ have been in existence for more than twenty-five years and provide course work leading toward a master's degree in education and state of New Jersey certification in teaching and administration. Courses are taught by TCNJ faculty members and other internationally recognized professors. Courses are offered June through July at TCNJ sites in Mallorca, Spain; Bangkok, Thailand; and Johannesburg, South Africa. During the academic year, courses are available in Kuwait City, Kuwait, and La Paz, Bolivia.

For the convenience of the majority of graduate students who pursue degrees while being employed full-time, graduate courses held on the Ewing campus are offered during the day and in the evening.

Research Facilities

TCNJ offers a state-of-the-art library that serves as an exciting intellectual, cultural, and social center for the College community. The five-story, 135,000-square-foot facility will provide cutting-edge services to the TCNJ community well into the twenty-first century. In addition to housing traditional library collections and services in an atmosphere that is both friendly and elegant, a key feature of the new library is its wide array of carefully considered and thoughtful amenities, which make using the facility both a pleasure and a convenience. The library provides twenty-four group-study rooms (one reserved for graduate students), ample and comfortable seating, tables and carrels, and both WiFi and LAN Internet access throughout, with power connections at every carrel and study table. Special design features include a café, a secure, late night/24-hour study area, and a 105-seat multipurpose auditorium. The library also houses the Instructional Technology Services facility, creating ideal one-stop shopping for students working on projects.

Library collections include more than 560,000 volumes and 200,000 microforms as well as subscriptions to more than 1,400 periodicals. The library also subscribes to more than seventy-five electronic indexes covering more than 14,000 scholarly journals, including full-text resources. A media facility offers viewing and listening equipment as well as sound recordings, videos, and interactive computer software. PCs are available for public access to electronic resources. Collections are constantly augmented by new acquisitions, and interlibrary loan and document delivery services are available as well. The library is also an active participant in a number of library networks and maintains cooperative arrangements with many regional academic libraries, from which students may borrow directly. TCNJ librarians are an important resource in and of themselves. In addition to advanced studies in library and information science, each subject-librarian has additional graduate degrees in one of the major academic areas, and students are encouraged to consult them in person and online.

In addition to providing new library facilities for the College community, TCNJ has met the challenge of the computer field's phenomenal growth with installations of computer facilities in each of its seven schools. The School of Education also houses a speech, language, and hearing center.

Financial Aid

The College of New Jersey offers financial aid to qualified matriculated students through a combination of loans, grants, and/or employment. To be considered for all financial aid programs, students must submit the Free Application for Federal Student Aid (FAFSA) to the College Financial Assistance Office. Graduate assistantships are available to qualified full-time students on a competitive basis.

Cost of Study

Tuition for graduate courses for 2006–07 was $525.45 per semester hour of credit for New Jersey residents and $782.60 per semester hour of credit for out-of-state residents. Additional fees include ID, student center, library, and health insurance for full-time students. Tuition and fees are subject to change by action of the New Jersey State Legislature.

Living and Housing Costs

As the majority of TCNJ's graduate students attend classes part-time in the evenings, the College does not offer on-campus housing for graduate students. Graduate students who seek housing in the area can get assistance from the Office of Residence Life.

Student Group

The College of New Jersey had an enrollment of approximately 5,900 undergraduate students and 1,000 graduate students in 2005–06.

Student Outcomes

The College of New Jersey's excellent reputation has afforded graduates outstanding opportunities when entering their professional fields. Many TCNJ graduates receive job placements through various on-campus recruitment programs sponsored by the Office of Career Services.

Location

The College of New Jersey is located on 289 tree-lined acres in suburban Ewing, New Jersey, 7 miles from the state capital in Trenton. Woodlands and two lakes surround the academic and residential buildings. More than thirty-five buildings make up the physical plant, most of which are built in the classic Georgian Colonial architecture. The campus is 30 miles from Philadelphia and 60 miles from New York's theaters, museums, and other attractions. The nearby towns of Princeton and New Hope offer additional cultural activities.

The College

Founded in 1855, the College has grown from its early years as a teachers' college to a multipurpose institution comprising seven schools: Art, Media, and Music; Business; Culture and Society; Education; Engineering; Nursing; and Science. Graduate study is available in the Schools of Culture and Society, Education, and Nursing.

TCNJ introduced its first advanced degree program, a Master of Science in elementary education, in 1947. Over the years, the number of graduate programs has steadily increased. At present there are more than fifty specialized graduate degree and certificate programs.

TCNJ's academic programs are accredited by the Middle States Association of Colleges and Schools, the National Council for Accreditation of Teacher Education (NCATE), and other appropriate professional associations.

Applying

Students of proven ability with undergraduate degrees in appropriate fields are eligible to apply for graduate study. Applications should be submitted online (http://www.tcnj.edu/~graduate) along with the $60 nonrefundable application fee. Transcripts of all previous college or university work and other supporting documentation as noted should be forwarded to the Office of Graduate Studies. Acceptable scores on the appropriate national standardized tests are required for all degree programs.

Application deadlines for matriculation are April 15 for the summer session and fall semester and October 15 for the spring semester, with the following exceptions. The fall semester deadline for the M.A.T. program for counselor education is March 1. Deadlines for the M.Ed. in instruction are August 1 for fall, October 15 for spring, and March 1 for summer. The special admission (nonmatriculated) deadlines are August 1 for the fall semester and December 1 for the spring semester.

Correspondence and Information

Susan L. Hydro, Assistant Dean
Office of Graduate Studies
The College of New Jersey
P.O. Box 7718
Ewing, New Jersey 08628
Phone: 609-771-2300
Fax: 609-637-5105
E-mail: graduate@tcnj.edu
Web site: http://www.tcnj.edu/~graduate

DEANS AND PROGRAM COORDINATORS

SCHOOL OF CULTURE AND SOCIETY

Susan Albertine, Dean; Ph.D., Chicago.

Graduate Program Coordinators

Applied Spanish Studies: Deborah Compte, Associate Professor; Ph.D., Princeton.
English: Jean Graham, Associate Professor; Ph.D., Case Western Reserve.

SCHOOL OF EDUCATION

William Behre, Dean; Ph.D., Michigan.

Graduate Program Coordinators

Counselor Education: Mark Woodford, Assistant Professor; Ph.D., Virginia. Mary Lou Ramsey, Professor; Ed.D., Fairleigh Dickinson. Charlene Alderfer, Associate Professor; Ed.D., Massachusetts Amherst.
Educational Leadership: Donald Leake, Associate Professor; Ph.D., Ohio State.
Educational Technology: Amy G. Dell, Professor; Ph.D., Rochester.
Early Childhood Education: Arti Joshi, Assistant Professor; M.S., Bombay (India).
Elementary Education: Brenda Leake, Associate Professor; Ph.D., Ohio State.
Health and Physical Education: Aristomen Chilakos, Professor; Ph.D., Temple.
Reading: Susan Blair-Larsen, Professor; Ed.D., Pennsylvania.
School Personnel Licensure
Secondary Education: Stuart Carroll, Professor; Ph.D., Syracuse. John Karsnitz, Professor; Ph.D., Ohio State.
Special Education: Shridevi Rao, Assistant Professor; Ph.D., Syracuse.
TESOL/Bilingual Education: Yiqiang Wu, Associate Professor; Ph.D., Texas A&M.

SCHOOL OF NURSING

Susan Bakewell-Sachs, Dean; Ph.D., Pennsylvania; CRNP.

Graduate Program Coordinator

Claire Lindberg, Associate Professor; Ph.D., Rutgers.

MAJOR RESEARCH PROJECTS

Grant Awards

Adaptive technology center; Dr. Amy G. Dell, School of Education.
Advanced education nursing traineeship program; Dr. Claire Lindberg, School of Nursing.
Infant functional status and discharge management; Dr. Susan Bakewell-Sachs, School of Nursing.
Preparing special and elementary educators to use inquiry and design-based learning; Dr. Amy Dell, School of Education.
Provisional teacher program; Dr. Anthony Evangelisto, School of Education.
TECH-NJ (Technology, Educators, and Children with Disabilities–New Jersey); Dr. Amy G. Dell, School of Education.
The New Jersey Teacher Quality Enhancement Recruitment Project; Dr. Sharon Sherman, School of Education and Dr. Cathy Liebars, School of Science.

Support of Scholarly Activity Awards (SOSA)

Conversation analysis of native/nonnative speakers; Dr. Jean Wong, School of Education.
Facilitating transition from school to employment for individuals with challenging behavior; Dr. Shridevi Rao, School of Education.
HIV symptom distress project; Dr. Claire Lindberg, School of Nursing.
Issues of literacy and teaching elementary students of color; Dr. Deborah Thompson, School of Education.
The reception of Dante and Chaucer within the work of their literary successors; Dr. Glenn Steinberg, School of Culture and Society.
When boys become parents: understanding and helping teen fathers; Dr. Mark Kiselica, School of Education.
Writing the republic; Dr. David Blake, School of Culture and Society.

The clock tower above Green Hall, the main administrative building on campus, is a well-known symbol of TCNJ tradition.

The College is made up of more than thirty-eight Georgian-style buildings all situated on a 289-acre suburban campus.

The College of New Jersey's tree-lined campus, which provides spectacular foliage, offers a beautiful setting for students all year long.

THE COLLEGE OF NEW ROCHELLE

Graduate School

Programs of Study

The dynamic community of the Graduate School of The College of New Rochelle, a professional school for men and women, provides students with the professional knowledge, personal advisement, and practical skills needed in today's world. The Graduate School's fine reputation is upheld by the alumni who are employed in schools, health-care institutions, the corporate world, and private practice. With the goal of education for service, a spirit of inquiry, and a blending of theory and practice, the Graduate School strives to develop the unique talents and aspirations of students in all professional areas. Providing a range of state-of-the-art courses, masters degrees and certificates are offered in human services, education, and the arts and communications studies.

The Division of Art and Communication Studies offers the M.A. degree in art education; the M.S. degree in art therapy, art therapy/counseling, communication studies, and studio art; and a certificate in communication studies. The Division of Education offers the M.S. in childhood education, creative teaching and learning, early childhood education, educational leadership, literacy education, multilingual/multicultural education, special education (childhood education), special education (early childhood education); dual certification in childhood education and childhood special education; dual certification in early childhood education and early childhood special education; professional diploma in school district leader; and certificates in bilingual education, education of the gifted, and school building leader. The Division of Human Services offers the M.S. in career development, gerontology, guidance and counseling, mental health counseling, and school psychology; it also offers certificates in guidance and counseling, long-term-care administration, and thanatology.

Classes are scheduled conveniently on weekends and evenings during six academic sessions each year. Admission is on a rolling basis. Small class size makes it possible for faculty members to respond to students' individual needs. Each student is assigned a faculty adviser in the student's program area. Students meet with their advisers every semester to plan course work, review progress, and discuss career goals.

Research Facilities

In addition to the libraries and museums of New York City, on-campus Gill Library houses one of the largest collections of print and nonprint resources in Westchester County. The library, which is newly renovated to meet the needs of the twenty-first century, subscribes to more than 1,400 periodicals and numerous online subscription databases. Collections of note include the ERIC Collection of educational documents, the Kutscher Collection of works in thanatology, and the Zierer Collection of materials in art therapy.

The Mooney Center provides technological support for all academic programs. Its facilities include a TV studio, photo labs, and model classroom. The center's desktop publishing, computer graphics, and Macintosh classrooms are available for work in graphic arts and communication studies. The computer laboratories are designed for individual student use and are open seven days a week.

The Castle Gallery, located in historic Leland Castle, opened its doors more than a decade ago. It enjoys an excellent reputation for the quality and diversity of its exhibitions and for its innovative programs that enhance campus activities and contribute to the academic experience. In addition, the Mooney Center Exhibit Hall features faculty and student art exhibits. These spaces function as a cultural resource for the entire community.

The Graduate Division of Education, through its Education Center, provides diagnostic and remedial services to students, children, and adults in the larger community.

Financial Aid

College-funded financial aid is available in the form of assistantships and partial scholarships, which are awarded on the basis of merit. Assistantships provide both a stipend and tuition for full-time students, and require 15 hours of service per week. New York State and federal grant and loan programs provide additional sources of assistance. Application deadlines are specified in the Financial Aid Information Packet.

Cost of Study

The Graduate School offers one of the most reasonable tuitions in the tristate area. Tuition is $575 per credit hour in 2006–07. Specific fees and tuition are listed in the Graduate School Catalog.

Living and Housing Costs

Off-campus housing is available for graduate students in the nearby residential community. A listing of available apartments is maintained by the Office of Student Life (telephone: 914-654-5365). The College's food service in the Student Campus Center offers a full range of dining options for commuter and residential students.

Student Group

The Graduate School, founded in 1969, continues its commitment to educate men and women for leadership in the service professions and the corporate world. Small in size (900-student enrollment) with ongoing academic advisement, students pursue a course of study to achieve their career goals. Graduate students earn degrees and certificates in programs that accommodate students on a full- or part-time basis.

Location

The College's location combines the advantages of a tranquil suburban campus and the cultural riches of New York City, a 30-minute train ride away. The 20-acre campus in Westchester County is located in a residential neighborhood of New Rochelle, within a few blocks of open green parks and the public beaches on the Long Island Sound. The College is easily reached by major highways from Queens, New York City, New Jersey, Connecticut, and upstate New York. The New Rochelle Metro North train station is a 30-minute ride from New York City, and buses from points in Westchester and the Bronx stop within a few blocks of the College.

The College

The College, founded in 1904, offers its various academic programs through four schools: Arts and Sciences, the Graduate School, the School of Nursing, and the School of New Resources (an undergraduate school for adult learners).

Applying

Admission to Graduate School programs takes place throughout the year, on a rolling basis. Applications and all supporting materials for admission must be submitted one month prior to the start of a session. A personal interview with the Assistant Dean and an on-site writing sample are required before a student is accepted into a program; both are scheduled upon receipt of the application packet. Interested students can access information at the Graduate School Web site at http://www.cnr.edu/gs.

Correspondence and Information

General inquiries:
Office of Enrollment Management
Phone: 914-654-5334
E-mail: gs@cnr.edu

Division of Art and Communication Studies
Dr. John Patton, Assistant Dean
Phone: 914-654-5279

Division of Education
Erin Churchill, Director of Education
Phone: 914-654-5322

Division of Human Services
Dr. Marie Ribarich, Assistant Dean
Phone: 914-654-5561

THE FACULTY

An outstanding faculty enlivens the students' learning experience through innovative teaching strategies, which are designed to challenge students to expand and grow. The faculty is composed of professional experts in their fields and is recognized nationally and internationally. Faculty members have published widely and are active in their respective areas and in professional organizations.

DIVISION HEADS

Division of Art and Communication Studies
Dr. John Patton, Assistant Dean; telephone: 914-654-5279.
Programs:
- Art Education
- Art Therapy
- Art Therapy/Counseling
- Communication Studies (Advertising, Corporate and Organizational Communication, Public Relations)
- Studio Art

Certificate Programs:
- Communication Studies

Division of Education
Erin Churchill, Director of Education; telephone: 914-654-5322.
Programs:
- Childhood Education
- Creative Teaching and Learning
- Dual Certification: Childhood Education/Childhood Special Education
- Dual Certification: Early Childhood Education/Childhood Education Special Education
- Early Childhood Education
- Educational Leadership
- Literacy Education
- Multilingual/Multicultural Education (TESOL)
- Special Education: Childhood Education
- Special Education: Early Childhood Education

Professional Diploma:
- School District Leader

Certificate Programs:
- Creative Teaching and Learning
- Multilingual/Multicultural Education (Bilingual)
- School Building Leader

Division of Human Services
Dr. Marie Ribarich, Assistant Dean; telephone: 914-654-5561
Programs:
- Career Development
- Gerontology
- Guidance and Counseling
- Mental Health Counseling
- School Psychology

Certificate Programs:
- Guidance and Counseling
- Long-term-care Administration
- Thanatology

THE COLLEGE OF SAINT ROSE

Programs of Study The College of Saint Rose offers graduate programs leading to the degrees of Master of Arts, Master of Science, Master of Science in Education, and Master of Business Administration as well as graduate certificates of advanced study. Graduate programs meet the needs of both part-time and full-time students. Courses are scheduled in the late afternoon and evening to accommodate the large number of students whose days are filled with other activities. Part-time students usually finish in two to three years, full-time students in 1½ years.

Fields of study include accounting, adolescence education, art education, business administration, business and marketing education, childhood education, college student services administration, communication sciences and disorders, computer information systems, counseling, early childhood education, educational leadership and administration, educational psychology, educational technology specialist studies, English, history and political science, literacy, music education, music technology, public communications, school psychology, special education, teacher education, and technology education. The College of Saint Rose also offers a joint J.D./M.B.A. degree with Albany Law School and a full-time, one-year M.B.A., in addition to the evening business program. The College also offers graduate certificates of advanced study in numerous fields, including educational computing, not-for-profit management, school building leadership, and school district leadership.

The objectives of Saint Rose graduate study are to encourage intellectual curiosity, foster creative thought, and promote careful research and professional competence. To these ends, programs are designed to provide essential core materials and to allow options for electives. The programs in adolescence education, childhood education, early childhood education, educational technology specialist studies, school counseling, special education, teacher education, and technology education also lead to professional education certification. In addition to a master's degree, certification only is available for adolescence education, applied technology, art education, business and marketing education, educational leadership and administration, literacy, and school psychology.

Small classes, opportunities for independent study, research assistantships, and, in many programs, internships or various practicum or fieldwork experiences facilitate the learning process. Through the College's membership in the Hudson-Mohawk Association of Colleges and Universities, full-time students may cross-register for graduate courses at other institutions in the Capital Region.

The College operates on an academic year of two 15-week semesters, fall and spring, and two 6-week summer sessions. The accounting and M.B.A. programs offer three 11-week sessions.

Research Facilities The Neil Hellman Library houses 211,000 volumes, 715 periodical subscriptions, 282,400 titles on microform, and a collection of rare books. Students requiring additional information can borrow books and articles through the College's membership in a nationwide interlibrary loan cooperative. Graduate students have access to computer labs featuring IBM and Macintosh computers with Internet access. The Patricia Standish Education and Curriculum Library, in the Thelma P. Lally School of Education, serves the educational and professional needs of preservice and practicing educators throughout the region and provides ready access to extensive research and curriculum materials. The Music Building provides state-of-the-art facilities for music majors at Saint Rose, including the Saints and Sinners Sound Studio, a sixteen-track professional recording studio, and the Henry and Alice Cooper Finks Music Library. In addition, the Thelma P. Lally School of Education's multidisciplinary Joy Emery Educational and Clinical Services Center includes ten treatment/assessment rooms, an audiology laboratory with sound booth, and a play area that allows clinicians to assess the cognitive and psychosocial development of children. In summer 2008, the College will open its new $14-million Massry Center for the Arts. This energy-efficient building will house an art gallery and a 400-seat recital hall.

Financial Aid Saint Rose serves graduate students through a variety of federal, state, and institutional programs, which include loans, grants, and employment opportunities. Graduate assistantships and merit, diversity, international, and second-chance scholarships are available to matriculated students. Matriculating graduate students may apply for campus-based assistance (assistantships and Federal Perkins Loans) by completing the Free Application for Federal Student Aid (FAFSA). The College deadline for the receipt of these documents is March 1 for fall admission and November 15 for spring admission.

Cost of Study The cost of graduate tuition in 2007–08 is $560 per credit hour. A technology fee of $20 per credit and a student records fee of $45 per year are also charged.

Living and Housing Costs The College's Office of Residence Life assists graduate students in locating suitable off-campus housing.

Student Group Saint Rose has a total enrollment of more than 5,000 students, of whom approximately 2,000 are graduate students. Approximately 60 percent of the graduate students attend part-time. Students come from colleges and universities throughout the United States and other countries, with the largest number from New York and neighboring states. In addition to students who are pursuing a degree, Saint Rose welcomes individuals who are taking courses toward teaching certification and students who seek personal or professional enrichment.

Location The Albany area, which is known as Tech Valley, offers extensive cultural and recreational opportunities. In addition to the many extracurricular activities offered by Saint Rose and several other colleges in the area, students may enjoy the Albany Symphony Orchestra, the Capital Repertory Theatre, the Albany Institute of History and Art, the New York State Museum, and other theater groups, museums, galleries, and historic sites. The College's location in the capital of New York State provides a special opportunity for students to seek involvement with the State Legislature and a large variety of government agencies. New York City, Boston, and Montreal are all less than a 4-hour drive from Saint Rose.

The College The College of Saint Rose, which was founded in 1920, is a private, coeducational liberal arts and sciences college with a strong tradition of academic excellence and service to the community. Located in Albany's Pine Hills residential neighborhood, the College enjoys all the advantages of a major metropolitan area. Its 25-acre campus, which is made up of a combination of more than eighty modern buildings and historic Victorian homes, creates an informal environment that is conducive to personal, as well as professional, growth and enrichment. Saint Rose supports educational innovation and faculty-student interaction. Faculty members and students often are engaged in joint research projects. The College is fully accredited by the Middle States Association of Colleges and Schools, the Board of Regents of the University of the State of New York, the National Association of Schools of Art and Design, the Council on Academic Accreditation of the American Speech-Language-Hearing Association, the Association of Collegiate Business Schools and Programs, the National Association of Schools of Music, the National Council for the Accreditation of Teacher Education, and the Council of Social Work Education.

Applying Applicants must file a graduate application, official transcripts of all postsecondary course work, a statement of purpose, two letters of recommendation for graduate study, and any other forms of evidence to support their credentials by the application deadline before the beginning of the semester in which they wish to begin study. The preferred application deadline for the fall semester is June 1; for the spring semester, it is October 15; and for the summer semesters, it is March 15. Candidates applying to the master's degree program in communication sciences and disorders must submit their applications by February 1 for fall and summer admission and by October 1 for spring admission. Candidates applying to the master's degree program in school psychology must submit their applications by March 1 for consideration for the fall semester. Applicants to the master's degree program in counseling or college student services administration must submit their applications by April 15 for the fall semester or by October 15 for the spring semester. Some applicants for the M.B.A. or the M.S. in accounting program are required to submit Graduate Management Admission Test scores. The nonrefundable application fee is $35. An online application is available at http://www.strose.edu/gradapply.

Correspondence and Information

Graduate and Continuing Education Admissions
The College of Saint Rose
432 Western Avenue
Albany, New York 12203-1490

Phone: 518-454-5143
800-637-8556 Ext. 2 (toll-free)
Fax: 518-458-5479
E-mail: grad@strose.edu
Web site: http://www.strose.edu/gradapply

DEANS OF SCHOOLS, PROGRAM CHAIRS, AND DESCRIPTIONS

SCHOOL OF ARTS AND HUMANITIES
Leslie Lewis, Dean; Ph.D., Indiana.

Art Education (Master of Science)
Karene Faul, Chair; M.F.A., Notre Dame.

Provides permanent certification for those who are provisionally certified in art education as well as those who have a background in fine arts but no teaching experience. Curriculum emphasizes studio work.

English (Master of Arts)
Barbara Ungar, Graduate Coordinator; Ph.D., CUNY Graduate Center.

With concentrations in literature and writing, this program can be tailored to meet students' personal and professional needs. Fulfills the academic requirement for permanent certification for those who are provisionally certified to teach English at the secondary level.

History/Political Science (Master of Arts)
Benjamin Clansy, Graduate Coordinator; Ph.D., Colorado.

Focuses on the historical, political, and international dimensions of the American experience. Fulfills the academic requirement for permanent certification for those who are provisionally certified to teach social studies at the secondary level.

Music Education (Master of Science)
Bruce Roter, Graduate Coordinator; Ph.D., Rutgers.

Prepares students to teach music in grades K–12 by providing a specialized, in-depth study of learning and teaching music. Meets the needs of current teachers pursuing permanent certification, as well as those who have undergraduate degrees in music but no teaching experience.

Music Technology (Master of Arts)
Bruce Roter, Graduate Coordinator; Ph.D., Rutgers.

Provides opportunities for personal and career enhancement by means of advanced study in music and music technology.

Public Communications (Master of Arts)
Karen McGrath, Graduate Coordinator; Ph.D., Southern Illinois.

Offers concentrations in journalism and public relations for communications professionals who want to build on skills that they use in the workplace.

SCHOOL OF BUSINESS
Severin C. Carlson, Dean; D.B.A., Indiana.

Accounting (Master of Science)
Barry Hughes, Chair; M.S., Saint Rose.

Qualifies students in New York State to take the CPA exam, provided they have 60 credits of liberal arts courses and 45 credits of undergraduate business courses. Also geared toward students who already work in accounting but want to advance in their field and those who want to enter the field of accounting for the first time.

Business/Economics (Master of Business Administration)
K. Michael Mathews, Chair; D.B.A., Louisiana Tech.

Provides students with the skills and knowledge to become effective managers in today's rapidly changing and competitive business environment. Offers an accelerated part-time option for working professionals and a one-year, full-time intensive option with an internship component.

SCHOOL OF EDUCATION
Margaret M. Kirwin, Dean; Ed.D., SUNY at Albany.

Adolescence Education (Master of Science in Education)
Designed for anyone who wants to teach at the middle or high school level. Fulfills all the education course work requirements for provisional certification to teach biology, business/marketing, chemistry, earth science, English, mathematics, social studies, or Spanish in grades 7–12.

Childhood Education (Master of Science in Education)
Designed for students who want to teach at the elementary school level (grades 1–6) and who are not yet provisionally certified.

College Student Services Administration (Master of Science in Education)
Michael Bologna, Chair; Ph.D., SUNY at Albany.

Prepares students for careers on college and university campuses, working in the offices of the registrar, financial aid, admissions, residence life, and student affairs.

Communication Sciences and Disorders (Master of Science in Education)
David DeBonis, Chair; Ph.D., SUNY at Albany.

Accredited by the American Speech-Language-Hearing Association and approved by New York State to license speech-language pathologists and to certify teachers of the speech and hearing handicapped.

Counseling (Master of Science in Education)
Michael Bologna, Chair; Ph.D., SUNY at Albany.

Offers concentrations in school counseling, community mental health counseling, and college mental health counseling.

Early Childhood Education (Master of Science in Education)
Designed for those who want to work with children in nursery schools, early childhood centers, Head Start programs, or elementary schools. Leads to initial New York State certification to teach through grade 2.

Educational Leadership and Administration (Master of Science in Education, Certificates of Advanced Study in School Building Leadership and School District Leadership)
Perry Berkowitz, Graduate Coordinator; Ed.D., Massachusetts.

Designed for educators who wish to become certified as administrators, principals, or superintendents at the school and/or school district levels.

Educational Psychology (Master of Science in Education)
Richard Brody, Chair; Ph.D., SUNY at Albany.

Designed for those with no prior experience in education and for those who have a background in education and want to expand their skills and expertise. Also fulfills the academic requirement for permanent certification for those who are provisionally certified in childhood, adolescence, or special education.

Literacy (Master of Science in Education)
Theresa Ward, Assistant Professor; Ed.D., Central Florida.

Designed for teachers who have provisional teaching certification in elementary education, secondary education, or special education and want additional certification in reading.

School Psychology (Master of Science in Education)
Maria Fast, Cochair; Ph.D., SUNY at Albany. Steven Hoff, Cochair; Ph.D., NYU.

Prepares students for careers as certified school psychologists.

Special Education (Master of Science in Education)
Theresa Ward, Assistant Professor; Ed.D., Central Florida.

Prepares teachers to address the variety of needs among students with disabilities and is designed for those with and without provisional certification in special education.

Teacher Education (Master of Science in Education)
Patricia Baldwin, M.S.Ed., SUNY at New Paltz.

Designed to provide a master's degree leading to professional teaching certification in grades K–12, under New York State requirements.

SCHOOL OF MATHEMATICS AND SCIENCES
Richard J. Thompson, Dean; Ph.D., Penn State.

Computer Information Systems (Master of Science)
John Avitabile, Chair; M.S., Rutgers.

A part-time or full-time evening program designed for students with some experience in computer technology and programming who wish to advance their skills and knowledge in areas such as software design and programming, computer architecture, and database theory.

COLLEGE OF STATEN ISLAND OF THE CITY UNIVERSITY OF NEW YORK

Graduate Degree Programs

Programs of Study

The College of Staten Island offers Master of Arts (M.A.) degrees in cinema and media studies, English, history, and liberal studies. Master of Science (M.S.) degrees are offered in biology, business management, computer science, environmental science, neuroscience, mental retardation and developmental disabilities, and nursing (adult health or gerontological). Master of Science in Education (M.S.Ed.) degrees are offered in childhood (elementary) education, adolescence (secondary) education (biology, English, mathematics, or social studies), and special education. The College offers an advanced certificate in educational leadership (elementary or secondary) and nursing (adult health and gerontological). Master's degree programs and the advanced certificate program generally require a minimum of 30 credits. Degree candidates are expected to meet the specific requirements of the graduate program to which they are accepted. The College of Staten Island also participates with the City University of New York (CUNY) Graduate School and University Center and Brooklyn College in a doctoral program in polymer chemistry and with the Graduate School and University Center in doctoral programs in computer science and physical therapy. In cooperation with the Center for Developmental Neuroscience and Developmental Disabilities, the College participates in CUNY doctoral subprograms in neuroscience (biology), learning processes (psychology), polymer chemistry, and computer science.

Research Facilities

The academic buildings house approximately 200 modern laboratories and classrooms. Academic and research programs are served by a computer network that allows students and faculty members full access to specialized software, the Internet, online library resources, and e-mail. All major computer languages and software packages are supported. The library holds up to 300,000 volumes, computer facilities for database searching, periodical subscriptions, and media services. The College library is a member of the City University of New York integrated library system. Students and faculty members have free access to ERIC as well as various databases on CD-ROM or via the Internet. The College's devotion to research is evident in its maintenance of the Center for Development Neuroscience and Developmental Disabilities and the Center for Environmental Science. In addition, the Center for the Arts, complete with a 900-seat concert hall, a 450-seat fully equipped theater, a recital hall, an experimental theater, an art gallery, a conference center, a lecture hall, and studios, provides facilities for teaching and public assembly.

Financial Aid

The Office of Student Financial Assistance administers federal and state grant, loan, and work-study programs to assist students with financial need to attend the College of Staten Island. Students should contact the Office of Student Financial Assistance early in the admissions process to discuss eligibility requirements and responsibilities. The College offers a limited number of tuition waivers for matriculated graduate students who demonstrate need. In some departments, graduate assistant positions are available for full-time graduate students, and information about these positions may be obtained from the individual program departments.

Cost of Study

In 2006–07, tuition for New York State residents was $270 per credit, or $3200 per semester for 12 or more credits. Tuition for nonresidents was $500 per credit.

Living and Housing Costs

For the 2006–07 academic year, dependent students budgeted a minimum of $850 for books and supplies, $820 for local transportation, $2600 for meals and personal expenses, and $1700 for living expenses. Independent students budgeted the same amounts for books, supplies, and transportation, plus $11,000 for food and living expenses for a nine-month academic year.

Student Group

More than 1,300 graduate students enrolled at the College of Staten Island in the 2007 fall semester. The graduate population reflects a wide range of ethnicity, social and economic backgrounds, educational and professional experiences, and aspirations.

Location

The College of Staten Island is located in New York City in the Borough of Staten Island. Completed in 1994, the 204-acre campus of the College of Staten Island is the largest one for a college in New York City. Set in a parklike landscape, the campus is centrally located on Staten Island and is accessible by automobile and public transportation.

The College

The College of Staten Island, a senior college of the City University of New York, was founded in 1976 through the union of two existing colleges, Richmond College and Staten Island Community College. Richmond College, an upper-division college that offered undergraduate and graduate degrees to students who had successfully completed the first two years of college at the Staten Island Community College (founded in 1955) or elsewhere, was founded in 1965. The College of Staten Island is the only public senior college of higher learning on Staten Island. The College offers fully accredited undergraduate and graduate programs.

Applying

Requirements for admission and application deadlines vary by program and department. Students should contact the Office of Recruitment and Admissions for additional information or to arrange an admissions interview or campus tour.

Correspondence and Information

Mary Beth Reilly, Director of Recruitment and Admissions
Office of Recruitment and Admissions
North Administration Building (2A), Room 103
College of Staten Island
2800 Victory Boulevard
Staten Island, New York 10314

Phone: 718-982-2010
Fax: 718-982-2500
E-mail: admissions@mail.csi.cuny.edu
Web site: http://www.csi.cuny.edu

College of Staten Island of the City University of New York

GRADUATE PROGRAM FACULTY HEADS

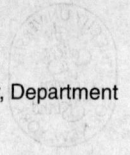

Adolescence Education: Brian Carolan, Ph.D., Assistant Professor, Department of Education; David Kritt, Ph.D., Assistant Professor, Department of Education.
Biology: Frank T. Burbrink, Ph.D., Assistant Professor, Department of Biology.
Business: John Sandler, Ph.D., Assistant Professor, Department of Business.
Childhood Education: Eileen Donoghue, Ed.D., Associate Professor, Department of Education; Vivian Shulman, Ph.D., Assistant Professor, Department of Education.
Cinema Studies: Matthew Solomon, Ph.D., Assistant Professor, Department of Media Culture.
Computer Science: Anatoliy Gordonov, Ph.D., Assistant Professor, Department of Computer Science.
Educational Leadership: Ruth Silverberg, Ed.D., Professor, Department of Education; Susan Sullivan, Ed.D., Assistant Professor, Department of Education.
English: Maryann Feola, Ph.D., Professor, Department of English.
Environmental Science: Alfred Levine, Ph.D., Professor, Department of Engineering Science and Physics; Center for Environmental Science.
History: Stephen Stearns, Ph.D., Associate Professor, Department of History.
Liberal Studies: David Traboulay, Ph.D., Professor, Department of History.
Neuroscience, Mental Retardation and Developmental Disabilities: Probal Banerjee, Ph.D., Associate Professor, Department of Chemistry; Andrzej Wieraszko, Ph.D., Professor, Department of Biology.
Nursing (Adult Health and Gerontology): Margaret Lunney, Ph.D., Professor, Department of Nursing.
Special Education: Jed Luchow, Ed.D., Associate Professor, Department of Education.

THE COLLEGE OF WILLIAM AND MARY

Graduate Studies

Programs of Study

The Faculty of Arts and Sciences offers M.A., M.S., and Ph.D. programs in a number of disciplines and the Master of Public Policy (M.P.P.). The Psy.D. in clinical psychology is offered in collaboration with neighboring institutions through the Virginia Consortium Program in Clinical Psychology, which awards the degree. Joint-degree programs leading to M.B.A./M.P.P., M.P.P/M.S. in marine science, M.P.P./M.S. in computational operations research, J.D./M.A. in American studies, and J.D. with M.P.P. are also offered. The School of Business offers a full-time M.B.A., an evening M.B.A., an Executive M.B.A., and a Master of Accounting (M.A.C.). Joint-degree programs in law (M.B. A./J.D.) and public policy (M.B.A./M.P.P.) are also offered. The School of Education offers an M.A.Ed. in elementary school teaching (with an emphasis in reading, language, and literacy), gifted education, and secondary school teaching; an M.Ed. in counseling, educational leadership (with emphases in general K–12 administration and higher education administration), school psychology, and special education; an Ed.S. in school psychology; and an Ed.D. and Ph.D. in counselor education and educational policy planning and leadership (with emphases in general K–12 administration, gifted education administration, higher education, and special education administration). *U.S. News & World Report* ranks William and Mary among the top fifty in a national survey of 191 doctoral degree–granting schools of education. The College was also ranked sixth in the country in terms of the quality of its teaching. The William and Mary School of Law offers the J.D. and LL.M. degrees as well as three joint degrees: J.D./M.A. in American studies, J.D./M.B.A., and J.D./M.P.P. The School of Marine Science offers M.S. and Ph.D. programs in marine science. Examples of areas of specialization available to students include biological, chemical, geological, and physical oceanography; marine fisheries science; marine resource management; and toxicology and pathology.

Research Facilities

The libraries of the College are the central Earl Gregg Swem Library; the chemistry, physics, geology, biology, and music libraries; the William and Mary School of Law Library; the School of Marine Science Library; the Professional Resource Center in the School of Business; and the Learning Resource Center/Curriculum Library in the School of Education. Specialized laboratories, equipment, publication organizations, collections, and other facilities are available in a variety of departments and institutes, including the Applied Research Center, which houses the Jefferson Lab library; the Omohundro Institute of Early American History and Culture; the Virginia Institute of Marine Science; the Center for Archaeological Research; the Archaeological Conservation Center; the Institute of Bill of Rights Law; Millington Life Sciences Hall; Muscarelle Museum; the Center for Public Policy Research; and the William Small Physical Laboratory. Research opportunities are extended in conjunction with neighboring organizations that include the Colonial Williamsburg Foundation, the Thomas Jefferson National Accelerator Facility, the Eastern State Hospital, the National Center for State Courts, and the Langley Research Center of the National Aeronautics and Space Administration (NASA). Graduate students and faculty members are working at national laboratories and accelerator installations throughout the world.

Financial Aid

Fellowships, scholarships, institutional and grant-funded assistantships, internships, apprenticeships, work-study arrangements, and loans are available. Duties are limited so that assistants can progress toward their degrees at the normal pace. Most of the funds are assigned through the departments and schools. While there is often some flexibility, early application is recommended.

Cost of Study

For the 2007–08 academic year, tuition and fees for two semesters of full-time study, by school, are as follows: Graduate Arts and Sciences, School of Marine Science, and Graduate School of Education, $9800 for Virginia residents and $23,014 for nonresidents; Virginia Consortium Program in Clinical Psychology, $10,368 for residents and $27,972 for nonresidents; School of Law, $18,336 for Virginia residents and $28,536 for nonresidents; full-time M.B.A. program, $18,124 for Virginia residents and $31,924 for nonresidents; and M.A.C. program, $18,124 for residents and $31,924 for nonresidents.

Living and Housing Costs

For academic year 2007–08, the estimated cost of living for a single student totals $12,290 plus tuition. Conveniently located College housing for graduate and professional students is available for between $2453 and $2503 per semester. Many graduate and professional students elect to live off campus.

Student Group

The total enrollment of 7,886 in fall 2006 included 5,651 undergraduates and 2,058 graduate and professional students (177 of these were unclassified). Most are full-time students who live on or in the vicinity of the campus. In each graduate school, there is an active graduate student association.

Location

Williamsburg is on a Chesapeake Bay peninsula between the York and James Rivers, on Interstate 64, 50 miles from Richmond, 45 miles from Norfolk, and 150 miles from Washington, D.C. The College is the center of a historic and popular tourist area that includes Colonial Williamsburg, Yorktown, Jamestown, a major water-sports region, and an exceptional concentration of cultural activities. Williamsburg has direct limousine service to the Newport News, Norfolk, and Richmond airports, and bus and railway service is also available.

The College

Although it retains the historic name under which it was chartered in 1693, the College of William and Mary has in fact been a small research university for a long time. In 1779, it established the first chair of law in the United States. The College is now organized as a Faculty of Arts and Sciences and Schools of Business, Education, Law, and Marine Science. The 1,200-acre main campus in Williamsburg encompasses most of the activities of the university and includes buildings ranging in age from those built around the time of the granting of the royal charter to recent construction. The School of Marine Science campus is located at Gloucester Point.

Applying

There are substantial variations in deadlines and procedures among the departments and schools, and applicants should request information from those in their areas of interest as soon as possible. Most programs are designed for students who wish to begin their studies in the fall semester. The financial aid deadline for the M.B.A. program is March 1; for all other graduate programs, it is March 15.

Correspondence and Information

For more information about the College of William and Mary, students can access its Web site at http://www.wm.edu/.

Office of Graduate Studies and Research
Faculty of Arts and Sciences
The College of William and Mary
P.O. Box 8795
Williamsburg, Virginia 23187-8795
Phone: 757-221-2467
Fax: 757-221-4874

Director of M.B.A. Admissions or M.A.C. Admissions
School of Business
The College of William and Mary
P.O. Box 8795
Williamsburg, Virginia 23187-8795
Phone: 757-221-2900 (M.B.A.)
757-221-2875 (M.A.C.)
Fax: 757-221-2958 (M.B.A.)
757-221-2937 (M.A.C.)

Dean of Graduate Studies
School of Marine Science
The College of William and Mary
P.O. Box 1346
Gloucester Point, Virginia 23062
Phone: 804-684-7106

Dean of Admissions
William and Mary School of Law
The College of William and Mary
P.O. Box 8795
Williamsburg, Virginia 23062
Phone: 757-221-3785

Associate Dean of Academic Programs
School of Education
The College of William and Mary
P.O. Box 8795
Williamsburg, Virginia 23187-8795
Phone: 757-221-2317

Virginia Consortium Program in Clinical Psychology
Virginia Beach Higher Education Center
1881 University Drive, Suite 259
Virginia Beach, Virginia 23543
Phone: 757-368-1820
Fax: 757-368-1823

DEPARTMENT CONTACTS AND RESEARCH AREAS

FACULTY OF ARTS AND SCIENCES

American Studies (M.A., M.A./Ph.D., Ph.D., J.D./M.A. with law): Jean Brown, Program Administrator (jxbrow@wm.edu). Program encourages students to use interdisciplinary approaches to explore the diverse past and present cultures of the peoples of the United States. The program has special strengths in African American studies, cultural studies, popular and material cultures, cultural and intellectual history, American history and literature, women's history, and the history of the book.

Anthropology (M.A., Ph.D.): Dr. Mary Voigt, Graduate Director (mmvoig@wm.edu or http://www.wm.edu/as/graduate/). The M.A. is designed as a terminal degree to prepare students for careers in cultural resource management and related professions. The Ph.D. program prepares students for long-term research and teaching in anthropology and strives to integrate social and cultural theory within historical studies in archaeology and anthropology. Faculty interests include comparative colonialism, the African diaspora, Native America, the Caribbean, and the archaeology of Colonial America. Students have access to unparalleled historical, archaeological, and museum resources, as well as opportunities to participate in a wide variety of ongoing projects in the mid-Atlantic region and the Caribbean areas.

Applied Science (M.S., Ph.D.): Dr. Mark Hinders, Graduate Director (hinders@as.wm.edu). Offers an interdisciplinary program in the physical sciences, which is cooperatively offered by the core faculty of applied science and participating faculty members from biology, chemistry, computer science, mathematics, and physics as well as NASA-Langley, Jefferson Lab, and Virginia Institute of Marine Science (VIMS). Research specializations of core and affiliated faculty members include thin films, computational materials, nanoscience, interface and surface science, processing materials with light and plasmas, nondestructive evaluation, medical imaging, computational biology, cell and systems neurophysiology, solid-state NMR, applied mathematics and modeling, and composite and polymer materials science.

Biology (M.A., M.S.): Dr. George Gilchrist, Graduate Director (gwgilc@wm.edu). Program is designed for students who desire an intensive, closely mentored research experience and advanced biology training. Graduates go on to doctoral programs, including medicine and law as well as traditional Ph.D. programs in biology, or find employment in environmental analysis or pharmaceuticals/biotechnology.

Chemistry (M.A., M.S., joint M.S./Ph.D. program with applied science): Dr. Chris Abelt, Graduate Director (cjabel@wm.edu). Program offers a thesis-based degree in areas of biochemistry and organic, inorganic, physical, polymer, and analytical chemistry. The program is designed for students who desire additional academic experience before pursuing an industrial career, a professional degree, or a Ph.D. degree.

Computer Science (M.S., Ph.D.): Dr. Evgenia Smirni, Graduate Director (esmirni@cs.wm.edu or http://www.wm.edu/computerscience). Research areas include computer systems and architecture, parallel and distributed processing, high-performance computing, performance modeling and simulation, software engineering, networked and embedded computer systems, numerical linear algebra and optimization, parallel mesh generation, cryptography, security, and algorithms. Interdisciplinary research opportunities can be found nearby at NASA-Langley, Jefferson Lab, VIMS, and the Applied Science Department. In addition to the traditional M.S. degree in computer science the department offers an M.S. degree specialization in computational operations research. Detailed information is available at http://www.math.wm.edu/~leemis/.

History (M.A., Ph.D.): Dr. Carol Sheriff, Graduate Director (gradap@wm.edu). Ph.D. students specialize in American history; M.A.-level students specialize in American or comparative history. In cooperation with the Institute of Early American History and Culture, Colonial Williamsburg, and Swem Library, the department offers students practical work experience through apprenticeships in archives and manuscripts, scholarly publishing, humanities computing, historical archaeology, architectural history, and teaching.

Physics (M.S., Ph.D.): Dr. Marc Sher, Graduate Admissions (grad@physics.wm.edu). Research specialties include accelerator physics; atomic, molecular, and optical physics; nuclear and particle physics; plasma theory and nonlinear dynamics; condensed matter physics; and computational physics. Collaborative research efforts and the proximity of NASA-Langley and Jefferson Lab bring graduate students into contact with the international community.

Psychology (M.A.): Dr. Peter M. Vishton, Graduate Director (pmvish@wm.edu). M.A. program includes core courses in all major subfields, a yearlong statistics sequence, a professional development seminar, and opportunities to conduct research with faculty members whose publications are on a par with faculties in the top quarter of Ph.D.-granting institutions.

Psychology (Psy.D.): Dr. Larry Ventis, Director of Clinical Training (wlvent@wm.edu or http://www.sci.odu.edu/vcpcp). The Psy.D. degree is offered by the Virginia Consortium Program in Clinical Psychology (the College of William and Mary, Eastern Virginia Medical School, Norfolk State University, and Old Dominion University) and provides education and training for the practice of clinical psychology.

Public Policy (M.P.P., J.D./M.P.P. with law, M.B.A./M.P.P. with business, M.S./M.P.P. with marine science): Professor Elaine McBeth, Admissions Director (mcbeth@wm.edu). Two-year interdisciplinary program prepares students for careers in public service by combining training in quantitative techniques and economic analysis with political analysis and law.

SCHOOL OF BUSINESS

M.B.A., M.B.A./J.D., M.B.A./M.P.P.: Kathy Pattison, Director of M.B.A. Admissions (admissions@business.wm.edu or http://mba.wm.edu). William and Mary provides a broad management education in a personalized environment that offers open access to faculty members and one-on-one interaction with some of today's most intriguing corporate leaders. Students achieve a thorough grounding in management theory and practice through the uniquely integrated curriculum, which addresses the complexities of multidisciplinary business issues. Elective courses and study-abroad opportunities provide concentrated study in specialized fields, while internships and field studies consulting projects provide hands-on experience in identifying, researching, and proposing solutions for real business problems. M.B.A. students have the unique advantage of a corps of corporate executives in the Executive Partners Mentorship Program.

M.A.C.: Lisa Margan, Associate Director of Admissions, Master of Accounting Program (mac@business.wm.edu or http://business.wm.edu/mac). A full-time, two-semester residential program, the M.A.C. program has been built upon the nationally recognized excellence in William and Mary's accounting and M.B.A. programs. Offering a unique curriculum that blends required accounting core courses with M.B.A. electives taught by highly respected faculty members, the M.A.C. program provides an extremely practical and valuable learning experience. The program accepts applications from accounting and nonaccounting majors alike. The following prerequisites are required prior to admission: Principles of Accounting, statistics, financial management, Introduction to Information Technology, and intermediate accounting I. Intermediate accounting is offered as an intensive course prior to the start of fall classes.

SCHOOL OF EDUCATION

M.Ed., M.A.Ed., Ed.D., Ed.S., Ph.D.: Thomas Ward, Associate Dean of Academic Programs (tjward@wm.edu or http://www.wm.edu/education). Programs prepare teachers for elementary, middle, and secondary education; prepare specialists in counseling, gifted education, and school psychology; and prepare students for educational policy, planning, and leadership roles for K–12 and higher education. Programs are organized into three divisions: curriculum and instruction; educational policy, planning, and leadership; and school psychology and counseling education.

WILLIAM AND MARY SCHOOL OF LAW

J.D., LL.M., J.D./M.A. in American Studies, J.D./M.B.A., J.D./M.P.P.: Faye F. Shealy, Associate Dean of Admission (lawadm@wm.edu or http://www.wm.edu/law/). Established in 1779, William and Mary School of Law is the nation's oldest, located near Colonial Williamsburg and within easy driving distance of Norfolk, Richmond, and Washington, D.C. A nationally recognized law school, William and Mary is well-known for the innovative Legal Skills Program—a nationally recognized model for teaching professional skills and ethics. The technologically advanced McGlothlin Courtroom is home of the Courtroom 21 Project. The Institute of Bill of Rights Law sponsors programs on emerging constitutional issues. The Supreme Court Preview, held each fall, includes nationally known journalists and academic commentators. The faculty members include nationally and internationally recognized experts in a wide range of subjects. Students, faculty members, administrators, and staff members maintain an exceptionally collegial learning and scholarly community.

SCHOOL OF MARINE SCIENCE

M.S., M.S./M.P.P., Ph.D.: Iris Anderson, Dean of Graduate Studies (iris@vims.edu or http://www.vims.edu). The School of Marine Science (SMS), the educational program of the Virginia Institute of Marine Sciences (VIMS), offers both M.S. and Ph.D. degrees in marine sciences. Although emphasis is on the study of estuarine and coastal ecosystems, research is performed in marine ecosystems worldwide. The school is organized into four departments: biological sciences, environmental and aquatic animal health, fisheries sciences, and physical science (including physical, chemical, and geological oceanography). In addition, SMS/VIMS offers a joint program in marine and environmental policy with the Thomas Jefferson program in public policy. SMS/VIMS also contributes to the College-wide environmental science and policy curriculum. Considerable attention is also paid to advisory services and outreach in response to both policy and private needs and interests.

COLORADO SCHOOL OF MINES

Graduate School

Programs of Study

The Colorado School of Mines (CSM) offers graduate education and research in areas related to the environment, energy, minerals, and materials. Advanced degrees are offered in chemical engineering, chemistry, engineering and technology management, engineering systems, environmental science and engineering, geochemistry, geology and geological engineering, geophysics and geophysical engineering, hydrology, international political economy of resources, materials science, mathematical and computer sciences, metallurgical and materials engineering, mineral economics, mining and earth systems engineering, petroleum engineering, and applied physics. Interdisciplinary programs can also be arranged to suit the student's particular career goals.

The Master of Science and Master of Engineering degrees require a minimum of 24 semester hours of acceptable course work and 12 hours of research credit plus a thesis or an engineering report. Nonthesis degree programs generally requiring 36 semester hours are available in most disciplines. The School accepts a maximum of 9 semester hours of transfer credit for thesis degree programs and 15 semester hours for nonthesis degrees. Course work requirements for master's degree programs are established by the major departments.

Like master's degree programs, course work requirements for Ph.D. degrees are established by the major department. The minimum credit hour requirement for the Ph.D. degree is 72 hours beyond the bachelor's degree, of which the Ph.D. thesis shall be no less than 24 hours. Each doctoral candidate is required to take a minimum of 12 semester hours of graduate credit in a minor field. Students with an earned master's degree may receive credit toward their Ph.D. requirements.

Professional master's degree programs emphasizing graduate-level work require a minimum of 36 hours of course work. These programs focus on emerging multidisciplinary fields of study and are designed to provide career-oriented skills and knowledge. Professional master's programs are offered in environmental geochemistry, mineral exploration and mining geosciences, and petroleum reservoir systems.

Graduate certificate programs are offered in international political economy through the Liberal Arts and International Studies Division. The program consists of two 15-hour certificates. Course work focuses in four areas: area studies; international political risk assessment and mitigation; geopolitics and economic geography; and global environmental politics and policies.

Research Facilities

CSM maintains twenty-five research centers and institutes dedicated to various aspects of research in the fields of environment, minerals, energy, and materials. Major areas include energy, exploration, mineral and petroleum production, environmental sciences and engineering, fuels science and engineering, materials science and engineering, automated and expert systems, and bioengineering (including bioenergy, biomaterials, and intelligent biomedical devices). Central Colorado is the home of numerous companies and high-tech industries working in these fields, and the nearby Rocky Mountains provide an excellent laboratory for educational fieldwork in the earth science disciplines. Located within a short distance of the CSM campus are valuable research facilities, including those of the U.S. Geological Survey, the National Park Service, the National Renewable Energy Laboratory, the U.S. Bureau of Reclamation, and the National Institute of Standards and Technology. CSM's proximity to the University of Colorado and Colorado State University provides opportunities for collaborative research and study in a wide variety of fields.

Financial Aid

Financial aid in the form of graduate research and teaching assistantships, as well as industrial, state, and federal fellowships, is available to full-time graduate students on a competitive basis. Financial assistance is provided to approximately 72 percent of all full-time graduate students.

Cost of Study

Tuition for the 2006–07 academic year was $4032 per semester for full-time state residents and $10,170 for full-time nonresidents. Part-time rates (between 3.5 and 10 credits) were $448 per credit for state residents and $1130 per credit for nonresidents. Student fees for all students are $491.70 per semester, and health insurance costs approximately $660 per semester.

Living and Housing Costs

Numerous options are available both on and off the campus. On-campus housing is available in the Mines Park complex. This apartment-style housing offers one-, two-, and three-bedroom apartments ranging from $650 to $1170 per month. Family housing is also available in this complex from $650 to $750 per month. There is a wide variety of private housing in the Golden and West Denver areas.

Student Group

The graduate enrollment of approximately 770 is composed of full- and part-time students. The latter are mainly practicing professionals working in the Denver area. Approximately 14 percent are international students, representing sixty-seven different nations. Approximately 26 percent of the graduate students are women.

Location

The School is located in Golden, a community of 15,000 people in the eastern foothills of the Rocky Mountains, about 15 minutes west of Denver. Colorado's world-famous ski resorts are a short drive from the campus, and the Rocky Mountains offer a variety of year-round outdoor activities. Hiking, backpacking, camping, fishing, hunting, bicycling, rock climbing, rafting, kayaking, and white-water canoeing are popular activities in Colorado. Golden's mild and dry climate has more than 300 sunny days a year.

The School

CSM offers engineering and applied science programs with a special focus on resource production and utilization. Founded in 1874 to support a growing mining industry in the Colorado territory, the school became the Colorado School of Mines when Colorado became a state in 1876. As the School grew, its mission widened from a focus on nonfuel minerals to encompass a broad range of engineering and science disciplines dealing with energy, minerals, materials, and the environment.

Applying

Interested individuals wishing to apply for graduate studies at the Colorado School of Mines should provide a duplicate set of transcripts from previous colleges, GRE scores, and three letters of recommendation along with the admissions application. Applications can be accessed online at the Web address listed in this In-Depth Description.

Correspondence and Information

Office of Graduate Studies
Colorado School of Mines
Golden, Colorado 80401
Phone: 303-273-3247
800-446-9488 (toll-free)
Fax: 303-273-3244
E-mail: grad-school@mines.edu
Web site: http://www.mines.edu/Admiss/grad

PROGRAMS, FACULTY HEADS, AND AREAS OF SPECIALIZATION

Chemical Engineering: Dr. James F. Ely, Head (303-273-3885). Advanced materials (nanocomposites, directed colloidal assemblies, microelectronics, photovoltaics, biobased materials), separation science and technologies (membranes for hydrogen separation, biorefining), theoretical and applied thermodynamics (molecular simulations, thermophysical properties), fuel cells (kinetic modeling, catalysts, membranes), computational chemistry, computer-aided process simulation, combustion science and engineering, mathematical modeling of transport processes, methane hydrates, microfluidics, microgravity combustion. Center for Hydrates, Center for Environmental Risk Assessment, Colorado Institute for Fuels and Energy Research, Colorado Institute for Macromolecular Science and Engineering, Center for Commercial Applications of Combustion in Space.

Chemistry and Geochemistry: Dr. Pat MacCarthy, Head (303-273-3626). Environmental chemistry, exploration geochemistry, biogeochemistry, inorganic/organometallic chemistry, fuel chemistry, catalysis and surface chemistry, polymer chemistry, materials chemistry, NMR, separation science, mass spectrometry, computational chemistry, laser spectroscopy.

Economics and Business: Dr. Roderick G. Eggert, Director (303-273-3981). Applied microeconomics; energy, mineral, and environmental economics; engineering and technology management; quantitative business methods; project management; international trade and economic development; technology entrepreneurship; business and investment decision making, including operations research/operations management; decision making under uncertainty; discounted cash flow analysis; managing new product development; simulation; financial risk management; corporate finance. International joint-degree program in petroleum economics and management with Institut Français du Pétrole.

Engineering: Dr. Terry Parker, Director (303-273-3657). Chemically reacting flow as applied to combustion and material processing; geotechnical engineering; earthquake and structural engineering; intelligent signal processing and control as applied to manufacturing, robotics, biomechanics, and telecommunications; static and dynamic behavior of solid-state and granular materials; analysis, design, and control of electric power systems. Power Systems Engineering Research Center; Center for Automation, Robotics and Distributed Intelligence; Center for Combustion and Environmental Research; Center for Intelligent Biomedical Devices and Musculoskeletal Systems. Web site: http://egweb.mines.edu

Environmental Science and Engineering: Dr. Robert L. Siegrist, Director (303-384-2158). Water and waste reclamation and reuse; environmental biotechnology; environmental chemistry and radiochemistry; site characterization and remediation; environmental systems modeling. Center for Experimental Study of Subsurface Environmental Processes, Environmental Engineering Pilot Laboratory, Laboratory for Applied and Environmental Radiochemistry, Environmental Biotechnology Lab, CSM/Golden Water Treatment Pilot Plant, Mines Park Water Reclamation Test Site, Integrated Environmental Teaching Lab. Web site: http://www.mines.edu/academic/envsci/

Geology and Geological Engineering: Dr. Murray W. Hitzman, Head (303-384-2127). Predictive sediment modeling, aquifer-contaminant flow modeling, waste management, water-rock interactions, petroleum geology, mineral deposits, economic geology, geotechnical engineering, environmental geology, groundwater engineering, petrology, structural geology. International Groundwater Modeling Center.

Geophysics and Geophysical Engineering: Dr. Terence K. Young, Head (303-273-3454). Applied geophysics, including seismic exploration, seismic data processing, gravity and geomagnetic fields, electrical and electromagnetic mapping and sounding, ground-penetrating radar, petrophysics, borehole geophysics, well logging, satellite remote sensing, groundwater exploration and exploitation, geohazard mitigation, mathematical geophysics, environmental and geotechnical geophysics. Center for Wave Phenomena, Reservoir Characterization Project, Center for Petrophysics, Center for Rock Abuse, Gravity and Magnetics Research Consortium, Near-Surface Seismology Group. Web site: http://www.mines.edu/Academic/geophysics

Liberal Arts and International Studies: Dr. Laura Pang, Director (303-273-3595). Program offers a master's degree program in international political economy of resources and graduate certificate programs in international political economy. International political economy of area studies, international political economy of resources and the environment, theories of globalization, case studies of global corporations, international political risk assessment and mitigation, theories of international political economy, comparative development theories of regions, political economy of ethnicity, theories and empirical case studies of comparative regimes, global political geography, comparative political cultures.

Materials Science: Dr. John J. Moore, Program Director (303-273-3660). Bonding theory, ceramics, coatings, composites, surface engineering, thin-films and advanced coatings, electronic materials, joining science, materials chemistry, mechanics of materials, metal and alloy systems, phase transformations, photovoltaic materials, polymeric materials, biomaterials, nuclear materials, solid-state physics, solid-state thermodynamics, structural and structured defects, surfaces/interfaces, transport and kinetics. Center for Computation and Simulation for Materials and Engineering, Center for Solar and Electronic Materials.

Mathematical and Computer Sciences: Dr. Graeme Fairweather, Head (303-273-3860). Applied mathematics: direct and inverse scattering, inverse problems, micro-local analysis, numerical analysis, scientific computing, symbolic computing, wave propagation. Computer science: algorithms, computational geometry, computer networks, databases, graphics, machine learning, mobile computing, sensor networks, visualization. Statistics: biostatistics, epidemiological methods, statistical seismic data processing, statistical regularization of inverse problems. Actively participates in Center for Wave Phenomena; Center for Automation, Robotics and Distributed Intelligence.

Metallurgical and Materials Engineering: Dr. John J. Moore, Head (303-273-3770); Dr. Gerard P. Martins, Graduate Affairs (303-273-3798); Physical and Mechanical Metallurgy: Dr. Stephen Liu (303-273-3796), Dr. David Matlock (303-273-3775); Physicochemical Processing of Materials: Dr. Patrick Taylor (303-384-2130); Ceramic Engineering: Dr. Dennis Readey (303-273-3437). Ceramics glasses and thin films; castings; coatings; composites, intermetallics, and smart materials; corrosion; electronic materials; extractive metallurgy, waste processing, and recycling; forming; advanced NDE methods; nuclear materials; photovoltaics; process modeling and control; surface engineering; synthesis and processing of materials; welding and joining. Five Research Centers: Advanced Coatings and Surface Engineering Laboratory; Advanced Steel Processing and Products Research Center; Center for Welding, Joining, and Coatings Research; Colorado Center for Advanced Ceramics; W. J. Kroll Institute for Extractive Metallurgy.

Mining Engineering: Dr. Tibor G. Rozgonyi, Head (303-273-3653). Mine evaluation, planning and design, mine productivity analysis, mine automation and robotics, underground excavation, tunneling and geotechnical engineering, rock fragmentation and explosive engineering, rock mechanics, bulk material handling, mineral processing and mine environmental remediation and sustainable development. Earth Mechanics Research Institute, Edgar Experimental Mine and Western Mining Resource Center.

Petroleum Engineering: Dr. Craig W. Van Kirk, Head (303-273-3740). Reservoir management; field development; computer simulation; geostatistics; interdisciplinary integration of petroleum engineering, geology, and geophysics; petroleum economics; enhanced oil and gas production; subsidence; drilling in space and laser drilling; well completion design; sand control; dynamic rock mechanics; petrophysics; geochemistry; hydrocarbon hydrates; multiphase flow in pipelines; fluid flow in porous media; and environmental issues.

Physics: Dr. James A. McNeil, Head (303-273-3844). Applied optics: lasers, ultrafast optics and X-ray generation, spectroscopy, near-field and multiphoton microscopy, nonlinear optics. Nuclear: low-energy reactions, nuclear astrophysics, nuclear theory, fusion plasma diagnostics. Electronic materials: photovoltaics, nanostructures and quantum dots, thin-film semiconductors, transparent conductors, amorphous materials, magnetic materials. Solid state: X-ray diffraction, Raman spectroscopy, electron microscopy, self-assembled systems, condensed-matter theory. Surface and interfaces: X-ray photoelectron and Auger spectroscopy, scanning probe microscopy. Center for Commercial Applications of Combustion in Space.

Environmental science class being held in the foothills outside campus.

Materials science and physics students work on solar cell research.

CONCORDIA UNIVERSITY

School of Graduate Studies

Programs of Study Concordia University offers programs leading to doctoral and master's degrees, graduate diplomas, and graduate certificates. Ph.D.'s are awarded in art education, art history, biology, building engineering, business administration, chemistry, civil engineering, communication, computer science, economics, educational technology, electrical and computer engineering, history, mathematics, mechanical engineering, political science, psychology, and religion. There are also interdisciplinary programs that lead to the Ph.D. in humanities and the Ph.D. in a special individualized program. The minimum residence requirement is two years of full-time study or the equivalent in part-time study. All Ph.D. programs are a minimum of 90 credits. Students entering without having completed a master's degree normally require more time. It is rare to complete a Ph.D. in less than three years. All Ph.D. programs require a thesis.

Master's degrees (M.A., M.A.Sc., M.Sc., M.Eng., M.Comp.Sc., M.Ap.Comp.Sc., M.B.A., M.I.M., M.T.M., or M.F.A.) are available in applied linguistics, art education, art history, biology, business administration (executive option, international aviation option, and professional), chemistry, child study, computer science, creative arts therapies, economics, educational studies, educational technology, engineering (aerospace, building, civil, electrical, and mechanical), English, exercise science, film studies, geography, planning and environment, history, history and philosophy of religion, human systems intervention, industrial engineering, information systems security, investment management, Judaic studies, littératures francophones et résonances médiatiques, mathematics, media studies, philosophy, psychology, public policy and public administration (with an option in geography), quality systems engineering, religion, social and cultural anthropology, sociology, software engineering, studio arts, teaching of mathematics, theological studies, and traductologie. Most master's programs require 45 credits and have a one year's minimum residence. Programs in business administration, creative arts therapies, studio arts, and educational technology require more than 45 credits and take proportionately longer. Many master's programs have a nonthesis option.

Diplomas are offered in administration, adult education, advanced music performance, aviation management, biotechnology and genomics, chartered accountancy, communication studies, community economic development, computer science, economics, environmental impact assessment, instructional technology, investment management, journalism, traduction, and sport administration. Diploma programs are 30 or more credits, normally take one year of full-time study, and do not require a thesis.

Graduate certificates are offered in anglais/français en langue et techniques de localisation, aviation management, building engineering, community organizational development, event management and fund-raising, digital technologies in design art practice, écriture, environmental engineering, management accounting, management of health-care organizations, mechanical engineering, service engineering and network management, software systems for mechanical and aerospace engineering, teaching English as a second language, and 3-D graphics and game development. Graduate certificates are normally 15 credits, can be completed in one year, and do not require a thesis.

One credit is deemed the equivalent of 45 hours of work by the student, which includes lectures, laboratory sessions, seminars, research, and preparation of assignments. The minimum full-time credit load for an individual graduate student is 24 credits over twelve months.

Research Facilities The Universities libraries have a rapidly expanding collection of reference and research materials and an extensive collection of government documents and newspapers on microfilm, microfiche, and microcard. The expanded Vanier Library houses unusual special collections. The main library has been designated a full depository library for Canadian federal government documents. Various cooperative arrangements exist with other research libraries in the Montreal area. Modern buildings house the well-equipped engineering and science laboratories, used for both teaching and research.

Financial Aid Scholarships and fellowships are available on a competitive basis; Concordia fellowships are currently valued at $2900 per term (master's level) and $3600 per term (doctoral level). All dollar amounts are in Canadian funds. Certain fellowships have a higher value. Work at the University in the form of part-time lecturer contracts, teaching assistantships, and research assistantships is limited. Information about the possibility of this kind of work is available from the graduate program in which the applicant hopes to enroll. The Graduate Awards Directory, available on the School of Graduate Studies Web site listed in the Correspondence and Information section, gives details about many awards tenable at Concordia and elsewhere. International students are strongly advised to apply for awards available to them from their own country or through agencies in their own country.

Cost of Study For 2007–08, tuition for Québec residents is $1251.24 per year (second- and third-cycle programs) and for non-Québec residents, $3309.39 per year (second-cycle programs) and $1251.24 per year (third-cycle programs); tuition for international students is $6876.24 per year. Students pay a number of miscellaneous fees, which are assessed at the time of registration. International students must also pay approximately $480 for health insurance.

Living and Housing Costs The expenses for a single student for an eight-month stay total approximately $21,000 (lodging, food, and transportation, $18,000; books and supplies, $1000; clothing, $500; and miscellaneous, $1500).

Student Group There are approximately 6,500 graduate students enrolled in the University. A significant number are bilingual and/or come from multicultural backgrounds.

Location Montreal is the second-largest city in Canada, with a population of nearly 3 million. Roughly three quarters of the population is French speaking. Montreal has all the attractions one would expect of a large cosmopolitan area: many theatres and museums, a rich musical life, numerous places of historic interest, and beautiful parks, including the famous Mount Royal Park. The climate is variable, with temperatures ranging from 30°C in summer to -20°C in winter.

The University Concordia University is one of four universities in the Montreal area. It was formed in 1974, when Sir George Williams University and Loyola College of Montreal merged the green spaces of the Loyola Campus and the urban downtown campus of Sir George Williams to complement each other. There are approximately 30,000 students enrolled in graduate and undergraduate programs. An interuniversity agreement makes it possible for graduate students to elect a certain number of their courses from any one of Montreal's four universities regardless of where they are enrolled.

Applying Applicants can apply online at http://welcome.concordia.ca/. There is a $75 application fee. Along with the application form, applicants must provide three academic assessments and arrange for official transcripts of university-level work to be sent directly by the registrar of the institution attended. Application deadlines vary for each program. While most students begin their degrees in the fall term, some programs accept students in the summer or the winter term. The deadline for financial aid applications is December 15.

Correspondence and Information

School of Graduate Studies
Concordia University
1455 de Maisonneuve Boulevard, West
Montreal, Québec H3G 1M8
Canada

Phone: 514-848-2424 Ext. 3800
Fax: 514-842-2812
Web site: http://graduatestudies.concordia.ca

FACULTY RESEARCH AREAS

Accountancy: financial and management accountancy, behavioural accountancy, accountancy education, auditing, management control in nonprofit organizations.
Administration: decision sciences and management information systems; finance; management; marketing; community services, public and parapublic; health and health-care delivery; arts, cultural affairs, and event management; sport administration.
Adult Education: staff development, literacy, learning in the workplace, professional development, self-directed learning, human relations training.
Aerospace: aeronautics and propulsion, avionics and control, structures and materials, space engineering.
Applied Human Sciences: applications of group development and small-group leadership, organizational development and change interventions, cross-cultural perspectives of management and leadership, coaching and mentoring relationships, community intervention.
Applied Linguistics: teaching English as a second/foreign language, second language learning, evaluation of language programs, teacher education for second/foreign language learning.
Art Education: development of symbolization and aesthetic response in children; the early development of artists; history of art education; museum education; adult education; multicultural and aboriginal issues; women in art and art education; built environment education; response to art; postmodernism; digital technologies and art education, ethnography; life history; oral history; action research; descriptive research; feminist research; video and photographic documentation; community-based video; studio-based inquiry; studio theory and practice.
Art History: Amerindian and Inuit art and architecture; North American architecture, craft, painting, photography, and sculpture, as well as other media, from the seventeenth to the twenty-first centuries; European art and theory from the Middle Ages to the present; art criticism; cultural studies; feminist and gender studies; industrial archaeology and museum studies.
Biology: animal biology and behaviour, cell biology/biochemistry, ecology and conservation, microbiology/molecular biology, plant biochemistry and biotechnology.
Building Engineering: computer-aided design, performance of building envelope and materials, building environment (HVAC, acoustics, illumination, air quality), building and energy, wind effects on buildings, building structures and construction management.
Business Administration: professional M.B.A., Executive M.B.A., International Aviation M.B.A.
Chemistry and Biochemistry: analytical and bioanalytical chemistry, biochemistry and biophysical chemistry, bioinorganic and physical inorganic chemistry, organic and physical organic chemistry, computational chemistry, materials and solid-state chemistry, synthetic inorganic chemistry.
Child Study: children's social behaviour in day-care settings, children and technology, historical perspectives on child care, early childhood curriculum, popular culture of youth and children, health and well-being, gender issues, teaching and teacher education, family and children, international issues in early childhood education, learning and cognition and educational psychology.
Civil Engineering: structural engineering, bridge engineering, structural mechanics, earthquake engineering, water resources, fluids engineering, geotechnical engineering, transportation.
Communication: information and communication technologies and society, media and cultural studies, discourse studies, organizational communication and networks of communication, international communication and development, media creation, design and practices.
Computer Science and Software Engineering: computer systems and VLSI architecture, database and information systems, parallel and distributed computing, mathematics of computation, pattern recognition, artificial intelligence, image processing, programming languages and methodology, software engineering, theoretical computer science.
Creative Arts Therapies: art psychotherapy, rehabilitation through art and drama, sand-play therapy, guided imagery in music, development and creative art therapy assessments, narrative therapy, storytelling as therapeutic process, art and psychoanalysis (postmodern theory French School of Thought).
Economics: economic theory, economic development and planning, financial economics, public economics, international economics, industrial economics, labour economics, econometrics, mathematical economics.
Educational Studies: education of immigrants and minorities, sociology of education and issues of difference in the classroom, political education, philosophy and history of education, women and development, curricular debate, various aspects of adult learning and professional development, literacy and education, education in developing countries.
Educational Technology: human performance technology, human resources development, educational cybernetics, systems analysis and design, media research and development, distance education.
Electrical and Computer Engineering: systems, control, and robotics; circuits and systems; communications; computer communications and protocols; signal processing; high-performance architecture; software engineering; VLSI systems; microelectronics; microwaves and optoelectronics; antennas and electromagnetic compatibility; power electronics and adjustable speed drives.
English: English literature from the Middle Ages to the present; European, Canadian, American, and postcolonial literature; genres; creative writing; composition; women's literature.
Etudes Françaises: littératures francophones, writing, translation, court interpretation.
Exercise Science: athletic therapy, clinical exercise physiology.
Film Studies: Canadian film, experimental film, gay and lesbian film making, experimental documentary and ethnography, Third World cinemas and auteur studies, film acting, film and philosophy, Japanese cinema, Indian cinema, documentary film, feminist theory, film theory and American cinema.
Finance: international financing consortia, efficiency of capital markets, financing of small and medium-sized businesses, corporate finance, capital markets, business economics.
Geography, Planning, and Environment: policy-oriented studies, with an emphasis on urban, environmental, and social issues, including watershed management, port development and planning, urban design, immigration, sustainable forestry, indigenous resource management, and metropolitan government.
History: Canadian, European, and American history and non-Western history (Africa, the Caribbean, China, India, the Middle East). Genres include genocide, anti-Semitism, and human rights; race and slavery in the Western hemisphere; colonialism; women's and gender history; urban history; pacifism; cultural history; intellectual history; religious history; and historiography.
Humanities: interdisciplinary doctoral studies in the humanities, social sciences, and fine arts.
Human Systems Intervention: applications of group development and small-group leadership, organizational development and change interventions, cross-cultural perspectives of management and leadership, coaching and mentoring relationships, community intervention and interventions with community workers.
Information Systems Engineering: information systems security, quality systems engineering, service engineering and network management, 3-D graphics and game development.
Journalism: ethics, Québec media, broadcast public affairs.
Mathematics: number theory–computational algebra, mathematical physics–differential geometry, dynamical systems, statistics–actuarial mathematics, mathematics education.
Mechanical Engineering: computational fluid dynamics, industrial control systems and robotics, composites, mechanical systems and manufacturing, microfabrication and micromechatronics, thermofluid and propulsion, biomedical and human factor engineering, vehicle systems engineering, industrial engineering.
Music: advanced music performance.
Philosophy: history of philosophy, logic and philosophy of logic, ethics, political philosophy and value theory, epistemology, metaphysics, philosophy of science and social sciences, contemporary philosophy.
Physics: quantum and high-energy physics, condensed-matter physics, theoretical physics, applied physics.
Political Science: public policy and public administration, Canadian and Québec politics, international politics, comparative politics, political theory.
Psychology: behavioural neuroscience, clinical and health research, human development and developmental processes, cognitive science
Religion: comparative religious ethics; ancient, medieval, and modern Judaism; women and religion; Christianity; Islam; Hinduism; Buddhism; sociology and philosophy of religion; new religious movements.
Social and Cultural Anthropology: gender from a cross-cultural perspective, economic anthropology, legal anthropology, anthropological linguistics, development, urban anthropology, community, ethnic studies, ethnographic writing, visual anthropology, information technologies, popular culture, youth culture, race, the politics of identity, globalization and transnationalism.
Sociology: research interests range from new rural economy and development to race and ethnic relations, comparative social history, social theory, and cultural sociology.
Specialized Individualized Programs: innovative studies that cross more than one recognized field.
Studio Arts: film production, open media, painting, photography, print media, sculpture, ceramics and fibres.
Theological Studies: Biblical periods, patristic age, fundamental and applied ethics, spirituality and contemporary theology.

DARTMOUTH COLLEGE

DARTMOUTH COLLEGE

Graduate School

Programs of Study

Dartmouth awards the A.M. degree in comparative literature and electroacoustic music and the M.S. degree in computer science, earth sciences, evaluative clinical sciences, and physics. The Ph.D. degree is awarded in biochemistry, biology, chemistry, computer science, earth sciences, engineering sciences, evaluative clinical sciences, experimental molecular medicine, genetics, mathematics, microbiology/immunology, pharmacology/toxicology, physics/astronomy, physiology, and psychological and brain sciences. A special program leading to the degree of Master of Arts in Liberal Studies (M.A.L.S.) is also offered. An interactive, cross-disciplinary program, the Molecular and Cellular Biology (MCB) program, is offered in the life sciences. It is comprised of faculty members from the College of Arts and Sciences, the Dartmouth Medical School, and the Thayer School of Engineering.

Graduate degrees are also offered by the professional Schools of Medicine (M.D.), Engineering (M.E.M., M.S., Ph.D.), and Business Administration (M.B.A.).

Dartmouth's graduate programs are small and selective and are designed to provide more flexibility than the traditional Ph.D. program usually allows. Breadth within the discipline, significant teaching experience, and a broadly conceived research-thesis project are the basic elements in each of the graduate programs. Research achievement is naturally the most fundamental aspect of the Ph.D. program, and the limited enrollment in each program ensures the student a close apprentice-colleague relationship with his or her research supervisor. Most students are expected to teach during part of their graduate career, and considerable emphasis is placed on carefully supervised teaching experience of increasing responsibility.

Research Facilities

Several significant research and teaching facilities at Dartmouth have been designed to encourage contact and intellectual exchange among scholars in related disciplines. The Sherman Fairchild Physical Sciences Center and the Burke Chemistry Laboratory building house programs in geology, chemistry, and physics and provide a common library, service shops, and computing facilities. Similarly, the Gilman Biomedical Center provides related facilities and space for the programs in biology, biochemistry, pharmacology, and physiology, and the Murdough Center serves as a connecting link for cooperative programs between engineering and business administration. Moore Hall, which houses the department of psychological and brain sciences, provides modern facilities for training in psychology and cognitive neuroscience, including the first MRI in the country dedicated to basic research.

All residence halls, classrooms, laboratories, and offices are networked at Dartmouth. Innovative ways are used to integrate personal computers into the curriculum, administration, and operation as well as the daily life of all members of the Dartmouth community. More than 12,000 network ports, a campuswide wireless network, and a variety of utilities make access to central computers and the Internet easy. The computing services group also maintains several clusters of personal computers and workstations throughout the campus for faculty student use. Berry Library, at the geographic and intellectual hub of the campus, houses the central machine room with a wide variety of computers for academic and administrative needs and general-purpose use. The center is open 24 hours a day, seven days a week and is a centrally located hub of information technology activity.

Financial Aid

Most students in the Ph.D. programs receive financial assistance through a program of scholarships, fellowships, and loans. These are made possible by Dartmouth funds and by federal and private fellowships and traineeships. Dartmouth is an authorized lender under the Federal Stafford Student Loan program. In 2006–07, fellowships for first-year students carried stipends of $1800 per month plus a scholarship covering full tuition. Insofar as is consistent with the duration of individual awards, each student's program of course work, teaching, and research is designed to promote most effectively his or her academic progress without reference to the source of financial support.

Cost of Study

Tuition for the academic year 2006–07 was $33,279. Full tuition scholarships are generally awarded to all admitted students.

Living and Housing Costs

The College assists graduate students in arranging for appropriate housing, either in College facilities or in private accommodations in the Hanover area. College-owned apartments are available at various rents for graduate students.

Student Group

Dartmouth is coeducational. The undergraduate student body numbers approximately 4,100. The graduate and professional school enrollment is about 1,670; approximately 600 of these students are enrolled in the graduate programs of arts and sciences.

Location

Dartmouth College is located in Hanover, New Hampshire, a town of about 6,000 on the border of New Hampshire and Vermont. Hanover is less than 3 hours' driving distance from Boston and Albany and about 4 hours from Montreal. The Hanover area provides excellent opportunities for hiking, canoeing, climbing, and skiing and is near many of northern New England's lake and skiing resorts.

The College

The Hopkins Center for the Performing Arts serves as the cultural focus of the College. The center sponsors an active film society, two full concert series, and a very active drama program. In addition, all students and faculty members have access to workshops for sculpture, painting, and various craft forms as well as to membership in various choral and instrumental music groups. Dartmouth also makes available to its graduate students the extensive facilities of the Dartmouth Outing Club and the Dartmouth College Athletic Council.

Applying

Each program has its own application form, which can be obtained by contacting the individual department. In general, an application requires a completed application, a college transcript, three letters of recommendation, and scores from the General Test of the Graduate Record Examinations. All application materials should be sent directly to the department in which the prospective student wishes to specialize. Particular details, as well as the application packet, can be obtained from each graduate program. Dartmouth College is committed to its policy of nondiscrimination. A statement of this policy and the mechanism for redress of grievances can be found in the College's *Affirmative Action Plan.* For a copy, interested students should call 603-646-3197.

Correspondence and Information

Department of (specify intended major)
Dartmouth College
Hanover, New Hampshire 03755-3526
Phone: 603-646-6578
E-mail: sandra.j.spiegel@dartmouth.edu
Web site: http://www.dartmouth.edu/~gradstdy/

DEANS AND DEPARTMENTAL CHAIRS

Charles K. Barlowe, Dean of Graduate Studies.
Gary L. Hutchins, Assistant Dean of Graduate Studies.

Biochemistry
Professor Ta Yuan Chang, Dartmouth Medical School, 7200 Vail Building, Room 405 (telephone: 603-650-1622).

Biological Sciences
Professor Thomas Jack, 6044 Gilman Hall (telephone: 603-646-3367).

Chemistry
Professor John Winn, 6128 Burke Hall (telephone: 603-646-3804).

Comparative Literature
Professor Graziella Parati, 6051 Reed Hall (telephone: 603-646-2912).

Computer Science
Professor Prasad Jayanti, 6211 Sudikoff Laboratory (telephone: 603-646-1292).

Earth Sciences
Professor Xiahong Feng, 6105 Fairchild Hall (telephone: 603-646-1712).

Evaluative Clinical Sciences
Professor Ann Flood, Dartmouth Medical School, 316 Strasenburgh (telephone: 603-650-1874).

Genetics
Professor Jay Dunlap, Dartmouth Medical School, 7400 Remsen Hall, Room 701 (telephone: 603-650-1494).

Master of Arts in Liberal Studies
Professor Don Pease, 6092 Wentworth Hall, Room 116 (telephone: 603-646-3592).

Mathematics
Professor Tom Shemanske, Bradley Hall (telephone: 603-646-3179).

Microbiology and Immunology
Professor William Green, Dartmouth Medical School, 7556 Borwell, Room 603W (telephone: 603-650-8607).

Molecular and Cellular Biology
Professor Charles Sentman, Dartmouth Medical School, 604E Borwell, (telephone: 603-650-8007).

Music
Professor Larry Polansky, 6187 Hopkins Center, Room 68A (telephone: 603-646-2139).

Pharmacology and Toxicology
Professor Ethan Dmitrovsky, Dartmouth Medical School, 7650 Remsen Hall, Room 523 (telephone: 603-650-1667).

Physics and Astronomy
Professor John Thorstensen, 6127 Wilder Laboratory, Room 239 (telephone: 603-646-2869).

Physiology
Professor Hermes Yeh, Dartmouth Medical School, 7700 Borwell (telephone: 603-660-7717).

Psychological and Brain Sciences
Professor Ann Clark, 353 Moore Hall (telephone: 603-646-3036).

Thayer School of Engineering
Professor Brian Pogue, 8000 Cummings Hall (telephone: 603-646-3861).

The Sherman Fairchild Physical Sciences Center.

Research lab in Sherman Fairchild Physical Sciences Center.

The Burke Chemistry Laboratory building.

DOMINICAN COLLEGE

Graduate Programs

Programs of Study

Dominican College offers a doctoral program in physical therapy (PT) as well as master's degree programs in nursing (family nurse practitioner), occupational therapy (OT), and special education. These programs are offered in formats that take into consideration the professional and personal commitments of working adults. The nursing program is offered in an evening format, with each class meeting once a week. The occupational therapy, physical therapy, and special education programs are offered on weekends; classes are offered approximately every third weekend.

The Doctor of Physical Therapy (D.P.T.) degree program, introduced in summer 2005, offers three options to accommodate students from a variety of educational backgrounds. Students who possess bachelor's degrees may apply directly to the entry-level D.P.T. program without first completing a master's degree program. Freshmen undergraduate students may enroll in a dual-degree option in biology and physical therapy (B.A./D.P.T. degree), which enables them to overlap their fourth year of undergraduate studies with the first year of doctoral studies. Licensed physical therapists can pursue the transitional doctoral degree (tD.P.T.) in two trimesters. Both the entry-level D.P.T. and the tD.P.T. are offered in a weekend format and are combined with online learning, allowing students to pursue other responsibilities during the week. The Doctor of Physical Therapy program at Dominican College is accredited by the National Commission on Physical Therapy Education and is registered by the New York State Education Department.

The M.S. in nursing, the family nurse practitioner program, is designed to prepare an advanced-practice family nurse practitioner. The curriculum for the master's degree program integrates current trends in nurse practitioner research, practice, and education. Emphasis is placed on integration of practice and theory across diverse settings where primary care is delivered within the context of family-centered care. Students engage in classroom instruction and experiential teaching and learning opportunities that prepare them in assessment, role development, and in-depth clinical practice. Students are encouraged to take electives that strengthen teaching, clinical practice, and/or research interests. The program is accredited by the Commission on Collegiate Nursing Education (CCNE).

The College offers an entry-level B.S./M.S. degree in occupational therapy for new college students, transfers, COTAs, and students holding other degrees. The program prepares its graduates for entry-level practice and provides graduates with the skills necessary to respond to societal trends and changes in human services. Its problem-solving approach develops the student's clinical reasoning and critical-thinking skills. The program is fully accredited by the Accreditation Council for Occupational Therapy Education (ACOTE) of the American Occupational Therapy Association (AOTA).

The College offers two M.S.Ed. degree programs. One program leads to certification as a teacher of students with disabilities, including those with multiple and severe disabilities. The second program focuses on certifying teachers of the blind and visually impaired.

Research Facilities

All the graduate programs require research by way of projects or papers. Dominican College has an Institutional Review Board that adheres to federal policy on all research activities involving human subjects. The College supports research activities by providing online databases that can be accessed in the library, computer laboratories, and the residence hall as well as from off-campus locations. These online databases include First Search, Proquest Direct, Country Watch, Ebscohest, Mergent Online, Inotrac, Serial Solution, and PubMedical. In addition, the new Center for Health and Science Education opened in 2005 and provides state-of-the-art labs and communication centers.

Financial Aid

The Financial Aid Office assists graduate students with obtaining various kinds of low-interest loans. Some students may be eligible for federal/state aid.

Cost of Study

For the academic year 2006–07, the tuition for the master's-level courses was $545 per credit.

Living and Housing Costs

Since most of the graduate programs meet in a weekend format and the participants are active professionals, students choose to commute from their homes.

Student Group

The College has a total student body of approximately 1,800 graduate and undergraduate students.

Student Outcomes

The programs are intended to prepare professionals in their respective fields. They provide significant enhancement of skills of those students who are already working in the field and allow for professional development and career enhancement.

Location

The College is located in Rockland County, New York. The beautiful Hudson Valley campus is located 17 miles north of New York City and 3 miles north of Bergen County, New Jersey. The College is easily reached by car or public transportation and from the major airports of New York and New Jersey.

The College

Dominican College, founded by the sisters of St. Dominic of Blauvelt, New York, in 1952, is chartered by the University of the State of New York and accredited by the Middle States Association of Colleges and Schools. Dominican College is an independent four-year liberal arts college offering undergraduate degrees in more than thirty disciplines, with graduate programs in four areas of study. The College does not discriminate on the basis of sex, race, color, religion, disability, or national or ethnic origin.

Applying

Applicants for master's degree programs must have a bachelor's degree from an accredited college or university. They should submit a completed application along with the application fee, three letters of recommendation, and transcripts from all institutions attended. Each program has specific additional admissions requirements.

Correspondence and Information

Joyce Elbe
Director of Admissions
Dominican College
470 Western Highway
Orangeburg, New York 10962
Phone: 866-4DC-INFO (toll-free)
Fax: 845-365-3150
E-mail: admissions@dc.edu
Web site: http://www.dc.edu

THE FACULTY

Sandra Countee, Associate Professor of Occupational Therapy and Program Director, Occupational Therapy Program; Ph.D., NYU.
Michael Galuchi, Associate Professor and Program Director, Physical Therapy Program; Ed.D., Columbia Teachers College.
Sr. Beryl Herdt, Professor of Allied Health and Coordinator of Graduate Studies; Ph.D., St. John's (New York).
Rona Shaw, Professor of Special Education and Coordinator of Graduate Education Programs; Ed.D., Columbia Teachers College.
Lynne Weissman, Assistant Professor of Nursing and Coordinator of the Graduate Family Nurse Practitioner Program; M.S., Columbia; PNP.

The fully equipped 25,000-square-foot Hennessy Center is available to all students and features a 1,000-seat gymnasium, physical fitness center, suspended track, locker rooms, athletic department offices, and a multipurpose room for student gatherings.

The Granito Center gives students access to a student health center, a video conferencing center and satellite downlink facility, a bookstore, and dining services.

Commencement.

DRAKE UNIVERSITY

Graduate Programs

Programs of Study

Drake University offers top-quality programs leading to master's, specialist, and doctoral degrees. The College of Business and Public Administration offers the Master of Business Administration (M.B.A.), the Master of Public Administration (M.P.A.), the Master of Accounting (M.Acc.), and the Master of Financial Management (M.F.M.). The M.B.A. and M.Acc. programs are accredited by AACSB International–The Association to Advance Collegiate Schools of Business. The M.B.A. and M.P.A. may be combined with a degree in law or pharmacy. Although the joint programs require full-time enrollment, students seeking graduate programs within the College of Business and Public Administration alone may enroll on either a full-time or part-time basis, since most courses are offered as evening classes. This past fall, Drake added a Master of Communication Leadership (M.C.L.) program. This is a unique and specialized master's-level program designed to prepare professionals working in communication-related jobs with the skill set to excel as leaders and decision makers in the communication profession. The program's curriculum blends course work from both the College of Business and Public Administration and the School of Journalism and Mass Communication.

The School of Education offers a variety of degree programs and numerous endorsements. A limited number of endorsements are offered online. Degrees include the Master of Arts in Teaching (M.A.T.) and Master of Science in Teaching (M.S.T.), which are designed to help individuals become certified elementary or secondary school teachers while earning a master's degree. Additional degrees include the Master of Science (M.S.) in adult learning, performance, and development; rehabilitation administration; and rehabilitation placement. Also offered is a Master of Science in counseling with concentrations in elementary and secondary school counseling, mental health counseling, and rehabilitation counseling.The Master of Science in Education (M.S.E.) is offered in educational leadership; effective teaching, learning, and leadership; and special education. The Educational Specialist (Ed.S.) and Doctor of Education (Ed.D.) are offered in education leadership.

The College of Pharmacy and Health Sciences offers the Doctor of Pharmacy (Pharm.D.) degree and joint programs. Through joint degree programs, students may obtain a Pharm.D. degree combined with advanced degrees in business, law, and public administration.

Drake Law School, one of the twenty-five oldest law schools in the country, offers the J.D. and joint programs. Through joint degree programs, students may obtain a degree in law combined with advanced degrees in business, public administration, political science, social work, or agricultural economics.

Research Facilities

State-of-the-art physical facilities are available in many disciplines. The Morgan E. Cline Hall of Pharmacy and Health Sciences provides students with technologically advanced research resources. Cowles Library collections include more than 550,000 books and journals, 94,000 federal and state government documents, 777,000 microform records, 80 electronic databases, and approximately 16,000 scholarly online journals. Computer labs are available in both the Cowles and Law Libraries and around campus. The Dwight D. Opperman Hall and Law Library is a wireless environment containing extensive computer and Web resources, numerous study areas and rooms, and more than 320,000 volumes.

Financial Aid

The Office of Student Financial Planning offers financial information and services to graduate students. Graduate assistantships are available in a limited number of fields and are administered and awarded through application to specific departments. Student loans (for U.S. citizens only) and part-time employment, both on- and off-campus, are also available. The Office of Student Financial Planning also has information about other scholarship possibilities. Students working for companies that offer tuition assistance may enroll in the Employer Tuition Deferment Plan. This plan provides the option of a delayed payment based on the anticipated tuition reimbursement provided by the student's employer.

Cost of Study

Tuition within the College of Business and Public Administration, the School of Journalism and Mass Communication, and the School of Education is charged on a per-credit-hour basis. The M.B.A., M.Acc., and M.F.M. programs are currently $450 per credit hour; the M.P.A. is $385, and programs within the School of Education are $355 per credit hour. Students attending the Pharm.D. and law degree programs are generally full-time students and are charged the current full-time tuition rates of $24,900 and $25,800, respectively.

Living and Housing Costs

The cost of living in the Des Moines area is low compared to many metropolitan areas, particularly in housing expenses. Numerous apartment options are available within the Drake neighborhood and are within walking distance of the campus. On-campus adult student housing is quite limited. Off-campus rent varies but generally ranges from $400 to $650 per month.

Student Group

Approximately 2,100 students are enrolled in Drake's graduate, law, and pharmacy programs. Of those, more than 950 are full-time law and pharmacy students. Graduate programs other than law and pharmacy offer the majority of courses either in the evening or on weekends, which allows many adults who are working full-time to pursue their degree while continuing to work. Students find that attendance with other professionals in the area brings an added dimension to their experience, as does attending class with 260 international students representing almost sixty countries. Faculty members are available to assist and advise students and to supervise their research. Classes are small enough to allow for maximum interaction.

Student Outcomes

Drake alumni live in all fifty states and many countries and hold positions as corporate CEOs, teachers, journalists, and state Supreme Court justices. Drake graduates are leaders in their fields, including education, business, journalism, pharmacy, and law. Upon graduation, students who are currently working and attending classes on a part-time basis are prepared to advance within their companies or to seek other opportunities. Those not yet in the work world are not only prepared for their first employment opportunity, but also for advancement beyond their first position. Drake is known for educating students for the variety of careers they may have throughout their lifetimes and for teaching students to be flexible and manage and create positive change. The graduating class of 2003–04 had an overall placement rate of 97 percent.

Location

Drake University's scenic campus is located in a residential neighborhood in Des Moines, a medium-sized city of 450,000 people. As Iowa's capital and largest city, Des Moines is a metropolitan center for business (especially insurance), government, publishing, broadcasting, advertising, and the arts. The quality of life is enriched by the people of Iowa, who are noted for their friendliness, honesty, strong work ethic, and educational values. The Des Moines International Airport, which is served by major airlines, is just 15 minutes by car from the safe campus, and the University's 150-acre community is within 10 minutes of downtown Des Moines. Des Moines was named by Kiplinger's *Personal Finance* as one of the country's fifteen "super cities" where "people are moving and opportunity is knocking." Because of its central U.S. location, the climate in Iowa has a cycle of four distinct seasons.

The University

Founded in 1881, Drake University is a highly ranked private, independent university that is nationally recognized for teaching excellence and academic reputation within a student-centered learning environment. The University is accredited by the North Central Association of Colleges and Schools, and professional programs are accredited by their corresponding professional associations. Drake's faculty members are very accessible for advising and mentoring, and the overall student-faculty ratio is 14:1. More than 95 percent of the faculty members hold the highest degree in their fields.

Applying

Applications may be obtained from the Office of Graduate Admission, or students may link to an online application or download the form at http://www.drake.edu/graduate/applying/. Most programs offer rolling admission; however, applications to the doctoral programs and certain other programs do have specific deadlines. Some programs also offer admission for the fall term only; most consider students for fall, spring, and summer admission. Students must submit the application for admission, application fee, official transcripts from each college or university previously attended, and appropriate entrance examination official score reports (when required), two letters of recommendation, an essay indicating why the applicant wishes to pursue the program, and a copy of a current resume, as well as any additional information specified by the department to which the student is applying.

Correspondence and Information

Ann J. Martin, Graduate Coordinator
Office of Graduate Admission
Drake University
2507 University Avenue
Des Moines, Iowa 50311

Phone: 515-271-3871
800-443-7253 Ext. 3871 (toll-free in the U.S.)
Fax: 515-271-2831
E-mail: gradadmission@drake.edu
ann.martin@drake.edu
Web site: http://www.drake.edu

Drake University

FACULTY HEADS

David Maxwell, President; Ph.D., Brown.
Ronald J. Troyer, Provost; Ph.D., Western Michigan.

Web Sites by School or College
College of Business and Public Administration: http://www.cbpa.drake.edu
College of Pharmacy and Health Sciences: http://pharmacy.drake.edu
Law School: http://www.law.drake.edu
School of Education: http://www.educ.drake.edu
School of Journalism and Mass Communication: http://www.drake.edu/journalism/sjmcsite/

DREW UNIVERSITY

The Caspersen School of Graduate Studies

Programs of Study

The Caspersen School of Graduate Studies offers students an opportunity to pursue graduate studies in a setting that emphasizes small class size, individual attention from faculty mentors, and the ability to explore a wide range of scholarly interests through intensive independent work and tutorials. The program in English literature (M.A., Ph.D.) offers courses in most areas of British and American literature, with particular emphasis on the modern period. The interdisciplinary modern history and literature program (M.A., Ph.D.), which covers the period from the early eighteenth century to the late twentieth century, provides students the ability to concentrate in American or European intellectual and cultural history or book history. The women's studies program (M.A., Ph.D. concentration) allows students to specialize in historical/literary or religious/theological perspectives. Drew also offers four programs in the field of religion and theology. Biblical studies and early Christianity (M.A., Ph.D.) encompasses two subfields: the New Testament and the religion of ancient Israel. The religion and society program (M.A., Ph.D.) offers students the ability to concentrate in anthropology and sociology, psychology, or ethics. The theological and philosophical studies program (M.A., Ph.D.) emphasizes constructive, philosophical, systematic, and ecumenical approaches to the study of religion. The liturgical studies program (M.A., Ph.D.) offers ecumenical study in the history and theology of Christian liturgy. The historical studies program (M.A., Ph.D.) offers students concentrations in U.S./American religious studies, as well as Wesleyan and Methodist studies.

Drew offers two additional degree programs. The interdisciplinary arts and letters program (M.Litt., D.Litt.) emphasizes broad competence in the liberal arts, while the innovative medical humanities program (C.M.H., M.M.H., D.M.H.), conducted jointly by Drew and Raritan Bay Medical Center, addresses topics such as biomedical ethics, medical narrative, and the history of medicine. Full- or part-time study is available.

The M.A. is designed to be completed in a minimum of one academic year and includes course work, demonstrated reading knowledge of one foreign language, and a thesis. The Ph.D. program includes two years of course work, demonstrated reading knowledge of two foreign languages, comprehensive examinations, and a dissertation. Requirements differ for the arts and letters and medical humanities programs. Students should contact Graduate Admissions for specific information.

Research Facilities

The Rose Memorial Library houses 499,417 volumes plus a large collection of manuscripts, journals, and other primary source material. It also has an unusually large collection of periodicals with special strengths in the basic areas of graduate study offered at Drew. The library is a depository for the publications of the federal government and the state of New Jersey. It also collects the official documents of the United Nations. The Center for Holocaust Studies is located on campus, and the United Methodist Archive and History Center, adjacent to the library, houses one of the most extensive collections of American religious history and Methodistica in the world.

Financial Aid

Financial aid may take the form of scholarships, loans, employment, or any combination of these. Both need and achievement are taken into account in determining the amount of assistance to be made available. Merit-based awards range from 40 percent of tuition to 100 percent of tuition plus stipend. Applicants must file financial aid forms.

Cost of Study

Tuition for full-time M.A. and Ph.D. students in the English literature, modern history and literature, and women's studies programs in 2006–07 was $30,744. Tuition for full-time M.A. and Ph.D. students in the biblical studies, historical studies, liturgical studies, religion and society, and theological and religious studies programs for 2006–07 was $29,070. Costs for part-time students are prorated. Arts and letters and medical humanities tuition was $790 per credit, with reduced rates for senior citizens and full-time educators.

Living and Housing Costs

Drew offers a variety of housing options in dormitories or apartments for both single and married students. For 2006–07, the cost was approximately $6100 to $12,000 for the academic year, depending on size requirements. Meal plans can be provided for an additional charge. Commuter rooms are also available.

Student Group

The total University enrollment is 2,627 students; of this number, 615 are in the Graduate School. Of the total number of graduate students, 55 percent are women, 12 percent are international students, and 13 percent are self-identified members of minority groups.

Student Outcomes

Drew seeks to actively place its graduates. Most Drew graduates from the doctoral program go on to teach in colleges and universities. Others choose to enter related fields; Drew graduates work for publishing houses, government and nonprofit agencies, church organizations, and similar employers.

Location

Drew is located on a beautiful, 186-acre campus in Madison, New Jersey (population 18,000), 25 miles west of Manhattan. Commuter rail and bus lines provide easy access to New York City and all its educational, cultural, and entertainment opportunities.

The University

One of the major characteristics of the Graduate School is the emphasis on interdisciplinary studies. Its size allows for graduate education on a personal level with many small seminars, one-to-one tutorials, and classes that encourage discussion and lively interaction. Faculty members excel in teaching as well as in scholarship and research.

Applying

Evaluation of an applicant's qualifications for admission is based upon previous course work and grade point average, three letters of recommendation from professors, a personal statement, and an academic writing sample. GRE General Test scores are required of U.S. and Canadian citizens. International students who are not native English speakers are required to submit recent TOEFL and TWE scores. To present a competitive application, students should have a grade point average of 3.5 (on a 4.0 scale) or better. M.A. and Ph.D. candidates are admitted for the fall semester only. Arts and letters and medical humanities candidates may be admitted for the fall, spring, or summer semester and have different application requirements. The deadline for receipt of financial aid forms for M.A. and Ph.D. candidates is February 15. Applicants to all other programs should contact Graduate Admissions for information on financial aid deadlines.

Prospective students are encouraged to attend the Graduate Open House held each fall.

Correspondence and Information

Director of Graduate Admissions
Drew University
Madison, New Jersey 07940
Phone: 973-408-3110
Fax: 973-408-3242
E-mail: gradm@drew.edu
Web site: http://www.drew.edu/grad

THE FACULTY

S. Wesley Ariarajah, Professor of Ecumenical Theology; Ph.D., London.
Fran Bernstein, Assistant Professor of History; Ph.D., Columbia.
Chris Bosel, Assistant Professor of Christian Theology; Ph.D., Emory.
Karen McCarthy Brown, Professor of Anthropology and Sociology of Religion; Ph.D., Temple.
Virginia Burrus, Associate Professor of Early Church History; Ph.D., Graduate Theological Union.
William Campbell, Affiliate Professor of Parasitology, RISE; Ph.D., Wisconsin.
Ashley Carter, Affiliate Professor of Physics and Mathematics, RISE; Ph.D., Brown.
Michael Christensen, Affiliate Assistant Professor of Spirituality; Ph.D., Drew.
Gabriel M. Coless, Affiliate Professor of Church History; S.Th.D., Pontificio Instituto Liturgico (Rome).
Robert Corrington, Associate Professor of Philosophic Theology; Ph.D., Drew.
David A. Cowell, Professor of Political Science; Ph.D., Georgetown.
Paolo Cucchi, Professor of French and Italian and Dean; Ph.D., Princeton.
Morris Davis, Assistant Professor of Wesleyan/Methodist Studies; Ph.D., Drew.
Lillie Edwards, Associate Professor of History and African-American Studies; Ph.D., Chicago.
Heather M. Elkins, Associate Professor of Worship and Liturgical Studies; Ph.D., Drew.
William Elkins, Affiliate Assistant Professor of Hermeneutics; Ph.D., Drew.
C. Wyatt Evans, Assistant Professor of History; Ph.D., Drew.
Danna Fewell, Professor of Old Testament; Ph.D., Emory.
Brett Gary, Assistant Professor of History; Ph.D., Pennsylvania.
David M. Graybeal, Professor of Church and Society; Ph.D., Yale.
James Paul Hala, Professor of English; Ph.D., Michigan.
Sara Henry-Corrington, Associate Professor of Art; Ph.D., Berkeley.
Herbert B. Huffmon, Professor of Old Testament; Ph.D., Michigan.
Ada-Maria Isasi-Diaz, Associate Professor of Theology and Ethics; Ph.D., Union Theological Seminary (New York).
Sandra Jamieson, Associate Professor of English; Ph.D., SUNY at Binghamton.
Laurel Kearns, Associate Professor of Sociology of Religion; Ph.D., Emory.
Catherine Keller, Professor of Constructive Theology; Ph.D., Claremont.
David Kohn, Professor of History of Science; Ph.D., Massachusetts.
Wendy Kolmar, Professor of English; Ph.D., Indiana.
Edwina Lawler, Associate Professor of German and Russian; Ph.D., Drew.
Perry Leavell Jr., Professor of History; Ph.D., Tulane.
John Lenz, Associate Professor of Classics; Ph.D., Columbia.
Neal Levi, Assistant Professor of English; Ph.D. Columbia.
Otto Maduro, Associate Professor of Latin American Christianity; Ph.D., Louvain.
Thomas Magnell, Professor of Philosophy; D.Phil., Oxford.
Jason Merrill, Assistant Professor of Russian History and Literature; Ph.D., Kansas.
William Messmer, Associate Professor of Political Science; Ph.D., Ohio State.
Jo Ann Middleton, Director of Medical Humanities; Ph.D., Drew.
Stephen Moore, Professor of New Testament Studies; Ph.D., Trinity College (Ireland).
A. Johan Noordsij, Affiliate Professor of Psychiatry; M.D., Leiden (Netherlands).
Frank Occhiogrosso, Professor of English; Ph.D., Johns Hopkins.
Thomas C. Oden, Henry Anson Buttz Professor of Theology; Ph.D., Yale.
James O'Kane, Professor of Sociology; Ph.D., NYU.
Nadine Ollman, Professor of English; Ph.D., Pennsylvania.
James H. Pain, Henry and Annie M. Pfeiffer Professor of Religion and Dean; D.Phil., Oxford.
Dale Patterson, Affiliate Assistant Professor of American Religious Studies; Ph.D., Drew.
Philip Peek, Professor of Anthropology; Ph.D., Indiana.
Virginia Phelan, Director of Arts and Letters; Ph.D., Rutgers.
Arthur Pressley, Associate Professor of Pastoral Care; Ph.D., Northwestern.
Jonathan W. Reader, Associate Professor of Sociology; Ph.D., Cornell.
Robert Ready, Professor of English; Ph.D., Columbia.
William B. Rogers, Affiliate Professor of History and Associate Dean; Ph.D., Drew.
Joseph Romance, Assistant Professor of Political Science; Ph.D., Rutgers.
Jonathan Rose, Assistant Professor of History; Ph.D., Pennsylvania.
Kenneth E. Rowe, Professor of Church History; Ph.D., Drew.
Ann Saltzman, Associate Professor of Psychology; Ph.D., CUNY Graduate Center.
Peggy Samuels, Associate Professor of English; Ph.D., CUNY Graduate Center.
Suzanne Selinger, Assistant Professor of Bibliography and Research; Ph.D., Yale.
Douglas W. Simon, Professor of Political Science; Ph.D., Oregon.
Merrill M. Skaggs, Professor of English; Ph.D., Duke.
Geraldine Smith-Wright, Professor of English; Ph.D., Rutgers.
William D. Stroker, Professor of Religion; Ph.D., Yale.
Shirley Sugerman, Affiliate Associate Professor of Religion; Ph.D., Drew.
Sharon Sundue, Assistant Professor of History; Ph.D., Harvard.
Jesse T. Todd Jr., Assistant Professor of American Religious Studies; Ph.D., Columbia.
Linda Van Blerkom, Associate Professor of Anthropology; Ph.D., Colorado.
Jeremy Varon, Assistant Professor of History; Ph.D., Cornell.
Traci West, Associate Professor of Ethics and African-American Studies; Ph.D., Union Theological Seminary (New York).
Lynne Westfield, Assistant Professor of Christian Education; Ph.D., Union.
James F. White, Thompson Visiting Professor of Liturgics; Ph.D., Duke.
Anne Bagnall Yardley, Associate Professor of Music; Ph.D., Columbia.
Charles Yrigoyen Jr., Affiliate Professor of Church History; Ph.D., Temple.

Drexel
UNIVERSITY

DREXEL UNIVERSITY

Graduate Studies

Programs of Study Drexel University offers graduate programs leading to the Doctor of Philosophy, Master of Arts, Master of Science, Master of Business Administration degrees, and certificates. Many programs include options for part-time studies; nondegree students are also welcome to pursue graduate course work in most programs.

Programs leading to the Doctor of Philosophy degree are offered in the College of Arts and Sciences (bioscience and biotechnology, chemistry, mathematics, clinical psychology, environmental science, law psychology, and physics), LeBow College of Business (business administration), College of Engineering (chemical, civil, electrical, environmental, materials, and mechanical engineering and computer science), and the College of Information Science and Technology. In addition, the Ph.D. may be earned through a multidisciplinary school. The School of Biomedical Engineering, Science and Health Systems offers the Ph.D. in biomedical engineering and biomedical science. The School of Education offers a Ph.D. in educational leadership and learning technologies.

Programs leading to the Master of Science degree are offered in the College of Arts and Sciences (bioscience and biotechnology, chemistry, communication, environmental policy, environmental science, human nutrition, mathematics, physics, psychology, publication management, and science, technology, and society), College of Business and Administration (M.B.A. and M.S. degrees in accounting, finance, and taxation), College of Media Arts and Design (arts administration, digital media, fashion design, interior design, and television management, as well as a postbaccalaureate certificate in digital media), College of Engineering (M.E. and M.S. degrees in biochemical, chemical, civil, computer, computer science, electrical, materials, mechanical, and telecommunications engineering and in environmental engineering and engineering management), College of Information Science and Technology (library and information science, and information systems), School of Biomedical Engineering, Science, and Health Systems (biomedical engineering and biomedical science), and through the multidisciplinary program in software engineering and television management (M.S./M.B.A.). The School of Education offers an M.S. in education administration, an M.S. in global and international education, an M.S. in higher education, an M.S. in science of instruction, an M.S. in teaching, learning, and curriculum, and numerous certificate programs. The Goodwin College of Professional Studies offers an M.S. program in sport management and an M.S. program in food science.

The Master of Business Administration degree program can include specialization in one of twelve areas of business study. All required course work for the M.B.A. degree may be completed in the evenings and online.

The College of Law offers a J.D. program with specializations in entrepreneurial business, health-care law, and intellectual property.

The College of Nursing and Health Professions offers programs leading to the Master of Science in Nursing (clinical trials, nurse anesthesia, nurse practitioner [adult acute care, family, psychiatric-mental health and women's health], nursing education, and nursing leadership and management); Doctor of Nursing Practice; Master of Family Therapy; post-master's certificate and Ph.D. in couple and family therapy; post-master's certificate and Master of Arts in art therapy, dance/movement therapy, and music therapy; Master of Science in emergency and public safety services, Master of Health Sciences (Physician Assistant: entry-level and advanced); Doctor of Physical Therapy: entry-level and postprofessional; a postbaccalaureate certificate in hand and upper quarter rehabilitation sciences; and a Ph.D. in rehabilitation sciences.

The School of Public Health offers programs leading to the Master of Public Health (M.P.H.) (full-time and executive programs), postbaccalaureate certificate in epidemiology and biostatistics, a Doctor of Public Health in community health and prevention as well as an M.D./M.P.H. degree in collaboration with the Drexel University College of Medicine.

The College of Medicine offers programs leading to the M.S. or Ph.D. degree (biochemistry, microbiology and immunology, molecular cell biology and genetics, molecular pathobiology, neuroscience, and pharmacology and physiology); a Master of Science in clinical research, research management and development, and pathologist's assistant; a Master of Laboratory Animal Science (M.L.S.); and a postbaccalaureate certificate in veterinary medical science, medical science preparatory studies, pathway to medical school, and an evening premedical program as well as a Master of Medical Science (interdepartmental medical science) and an M.S. in forensic science.

Research Facilities Drexel University is a major research institution, with basic and applied research complementing the studies listed above. A modern and expanding physical plant hosts research that is supported by a formal research grant program. Detailed descriptions of the research programs and the facilities that serve them may be found in specific program brochures and individual departments. Drexel's Web site and library also offer extensive resources.

Financial Aid Financial aid is available for matriculated students. This aid includes teaching and research assistantships, fellowships, work-study grants, student loans, and on-campus employment. Assistantships carry tuition remission benefits as well as monthly stipends.

Cost of Study In 2007–08, students are billed at the rate of $800 to $835 per credit hour, depending on their program of study. In addition, there is a general University fee of $210 per term for full-time students and $105 per term for part-time students.

Living and Housing Costs Ample off-campus housing is available in the neighborhoods bordering campus. For the nine-month academic year, transportation and living expenses for a single student are estimated at $15,285.

Student Group The University has a total enrollment of approximately 18,500 students, of whom 6,109 are graduate and professional students (3,469 full-time and 2,640 part-time).

Location Drexel University is located in the University City section of Philadelphia. The educational atmosphere is enhanced by Philadelphia's ample cultural, historical, corporate, and technological resources. The campus is within a 5-minute walk of Amtrak's 30th Street Station, which is adjacent to the Schuylkill Expressway (I-76). Drexel is also served by local bus, streetcar, and subway lines.

The University The University was founded in 1891 by Anthony J. Drexel, a Philadelphia financier and philanthropist, as Drexel Institute of Art, Science, and Industry. It later became Drexel Institute of Technology and finally, in 1970, Drexel University. Drexel operates under a four-term calendar, with graduate and undergraduate studies offered year-round.

Applying The application is available online at http://www.drexel.edu/apply. Some programs require admission tests (GRE, GMAT), and a few require interviews. At least two recommendations are required. International students must provide a TOEFL score that is less than two years old. Students typically enter in the fall term. However, for many programs, applicants may apply with the intention of enrolling in any of Drexel's four terms (these begin in January, March, June, and September). Application deadlines vary accordingly. The student is advised to confer with the Office of Graduate Admissions or the departmental adviser.

Drexel has a rolling admission review program. Those wishing consideration for assistantships, however, are encouraged to apply for the fall term and submit their credentials by January 1, as support decisions by departments are made soon thereafter. All paper applications require a nonrefundable $50 fee. The application fee is waived for online applications.

Correspondence and Information

Office of Graduate Admissions
Drexel University
3141 Chestnut Street
Philadelphia, Pennsylvania 19104-2876

Phone: 215-895-6700
E-mail: enroll@drexel.edu
Web site: http://www.drexel.edu
http://www.drexel.edu/apply (apply online)

PROGRAMS OF STUDY, DEPARTMENTAL GRADUATE ADVISERS, AND SELECTED AREAS OF RESEARCH

COLLEGE OF ARTS AND SCIENCES

Bioscience and Biotechnology (M.S., Ph.D.): Biochemistry, molecular biology, biotechnology, microbiology, ecology, physiological ecology. Susan Arfuso, 215-895-2905.

Chemistry (M.S., Ph.D.): Analytical chemistry, inorganic and bioinorganic chemistry, organic chemistry, physical chemistry, materials polymer chemistry, environmental chemistry, atmospheric chemistry. Dr. Reinhard Schweitzer-Stenner, 215-895-2268.

Clinical Psychology (Ph.D., Advanced Professional Certificate): Child psychology, neuropsychology, forensic psychology, and health psychology; scientist-practitioner model. Director: Dr. James Herbert, 215-762-1692.

Culture and Communication Communication (M.S.): Dr. Rachel Reynolds, 215-895-0498. Publication Management (M.S.): Professor Joan Blumberg, 215-895-6351.

Environmental Policy (M.S.): Dr. Rachel Reynolds, 215-895-0498.

Environmental Science (M.S., Ph.D.): Dr. Susan Kilham, 215-895-2905.

Human Nutrition (M.S., Ph.D.): Human nutrition, food science and nutrition. Susan Arfuso, 215-895-2905.

Mathematics (M.S., Ph.D.): Symbolic mathematic computation, functional analysis, parallel and distributed systems, software engineering, special functions and asymptotic analysis, biostatistics and biomathematics, combinatorics and differential equations. Dr. Robert Boyer, 215-895-1854.

Physics (M.S., Ph.D.): Nuclear and particle physics, atomic and molecular physics, condensed matter physics, biological physics, environmental and educational physics, atmospheric science, astrophysics. Dr. Michael Vogeley, 215-895-2710.

Science, Technology, and Society (M.S.): Integrates the study of history, science and technology, public policy, and contemporary social and political issues. Dr. Amy Slaton, 215-895-2061.

COLLEGE OF BUSINESS AND ADMINISTRATION

Business Administration (One-Year and Two-Year M.B.A., Professional M.B.A. full-time, Professional M.B.A. part-time, Anywhere M.B.A. Online, LEAD M.B.A., Executive M.B.A., General M.B.A. Online, M.S., Ph.D., Advanced Professional Certificate): Accounting, economics, financial management, health-care systems, international business, investment management, management information systems, marketing, organization management, production and operations management, taxation. Anna Serefeas, 215-895-0562.

Accounting (including Taxation) (M.S): Dr. David Campbell, 215-895-0222.

Finance (M.S.): Dr. Michael Gombola, 215-895-1743.

Ph.D.: Paul E. Jensen, Director, 215-895-6952. Accounting, decision sciences, economics, finance, marketing, organizational science, strategic management.

COLLEGE OF ENGINEERING

Chemical Engineering and Biochemical Engineering (M.S., Ph.D.): Process dynamics and control, environmental engineering, process design, semiconductor processing, biochemical engineering, heat and mass transfer, simulation and process modeling. Dr. Yossef Elabd, 215-895-0986.

Civil Engineering (M.S., Ph.D.): Environmental engineering, geosynthetic engineering, water and wastewater treatment, highway engineering, coastal engineering, hydrology, structural models and engineering, engineering geology, hazardous waste containment, construction materials. Dr. Patricia Gallagher, 215-895-6426.

Electrical and Computer Engineering (M.S., Ph.D.): Electrophysics, microwave-lightwave engineering, ultrasonics and ultrasound, signal processing, communications, controls, circuits, electromagnetic fields, image processing, computer vision, power systems, artificial intelligence, optics, superconductivity. Dr. Leon Hrebien, 215-895-6755.

Environmental Engineering (M.S., Ph.D.): Air pollution, applied ecology, environmental assessment, environmental chemistry, environmental health/industrial hygiene, environmental microbiology, hazardous waste, solid waste, water/wastewater treatment, water resources. Dr. Charles Haas, 215-895-2283.

Engineering Management Program (M.S.): Financial management, technical marketing, construction management, quality and manufacturing management, utility and energy management. Dr. Stephen Smith, 215-895-5809.

Materials Engineering (M.S., Ph.D.): Ceramics, polymer processing, biomaterials, powder and physical metallurgy, fibrous materials, composites. Dr. Wei-Heng Shih, 215-895-2338.

Mechanical Engineering (M.S., Ph.D.): Structural dynamics, biomechanics, dynamic systems and controls, CAD/CAM, thermal sciences, nuclear engineering, fluid mechanics, combustion and fuels chemistry, manufacturing, robotics, thermodynamics, aerodynamics, robotics. Dr. Alan Lau, 215-895-2377.

COLLEGE OF INFORMATION SCIENCE AND TECHNOLOGY

Library and Information Science (M.S., M.S.I.S., Ph.D., post-master's Certificate of Advanced Study, postbaccalaureate online certification in healthcare informatics). M.S.: library and information science. Master of Science in Information Systems. Ph.D.: information studies. 215-895-2474.

COLLEGE OF NURSING AND HEALTH PROFESSIONS

Art Therapy (M.A.): Nancy Gerber, 215-762-6928.

Couple and Family Therapy (post-master's, M.F.T., and Ph.D.): Dr. Marlene F. Watson, 215-762-6930.

Dance/Movement Therapy (M.A.): Ellen Schelly-Hill, 215-762-7851.

Hand and Upper Quarter Rehabilitation (Certificate of Advanced Practice): Jane Fedorczyk, 215-762-4680.

Music Therapy (M.A.): Paul Nolan, 215-762-6927.

Nursing (M.S.N.): Dr. Joanne Serembus, 215-762-8624.

Nursing (Dr.N.P.): Dr. H. Michael Dreher, 215-762-7481.

Physical Therapy: Entry-level (D.P.T.): Dr. Susan Smith, 215-762-1758.

Physical Therapy: Postprofessional (D.P.T.): Dr. Lisa Chiarello, 215-762-8805.

Physician Assistant: Entry-level (M.H.S.): Patrick Auth, 215-762-1432.

Physician Assistant: Advanced (M.H.S.): Geraldine Buck, 215-762-4625.

Rehabilitation Sciences (Ph.D.): Dr. Susan Smith, 215-762-1785.

COLLEGE OF MEDIA ARTS AND DESIGN

Arts Administration (M.S.): Professor Cecelia Fitzgibbon, 215-895-4913.

Digital Media (Post-baccalaureate certificate, M.S.): Glen Muschio, 215-895-2056.

Fashion Design (M.S.): Professor Kathi Martin, 215-895-4941.

Interior Design (M.S.): Debra Rubin, 215-895-1388.

Television Management (M.S., dual M.S./M.B.A.): Howard Hommonoff, 215-895-2180.

COLLEGE OF MEDICINE

Biochemistry, Microbiology and Immunology, Molecular Cell Biology and Genetics, Molecular Pathobiology, Neuroscience, and Pharmacology and Physiology (M.S. and Ph.D.): Dr. Barry Waterhouse, 215-991-8411.

Clinical Research, Research Management and Development, Pathologist's Assistant (M.S.): Dr. Julian Mesina, 215-762-8407.

Laboratory Animal Science (M.L.A.S.), **Veterinary Medical Science, Medical Science Preparatory, Pathway to Medical School, Evening Premedical program** (postbaccalaureate certificate), and **Interdepartmental Medical Science** (M.M.S.): Dr. Gerald Soslau, 215-762-7831.

MULTIDISCIPLINARY PROGRAM

Software Engineering (M.S.S.E.). Three tracks are available:
Computer Science: Dr. Spiros Mancoridis, 215-895-6824.
Engineering: Dr. Leon Hrebien, 215-895-6755.
Information Science and Technology: Dr. Michael E. Atwood, 215-895-6273.

SCHOOL OF BIOMEDICAL ENGINEERING, SCIENCE AND HEALTH SYSTEMS (M.S., Ph.D.)

Biomaterials/biotechnology, biomechanics, biomedical signal processing, biosensors, bioelectrodes and biotelemetry, biophysics, biostatistics, cardiovascular dynamics and instrumentation, computer applications to health care, medical imaging and image processing, medical ultrasound, neural networks and systems, sensory systems, clinical engineering, rehabilitation engineering. Dr. Kenneth Barbee, 215-895-2357.

SCHOOL OF EDUCATION (M.S., Ph.D.)

Educational Administration (M.S.): Aaron Preetam, 215-895-1865.

Global and International Education (M.S.): Stephanie McKissic, 215-895-1965.

Higher Education (M.S.): Stephanie McKissic, 215-895-1965.

Science of Instruction (M.S., Certificate program): Wendy Elliot-Pyle, 215-895-0376.

Teaching, Learning, and Curriculum (M.S.): Regina Ruane, 215-895-6692.

SCHOOL OF PUBLIC HEALTH

Community Health and Prevention (Dr.P.H.): Dr. Lisa Ulmer, 215-762-7034.

Epidemiology and Biostatistics (Postbaccalaureate certificate): Ray Lum, 215-762-4441.

Public Health (M.P.H.): Dr. Marcus Kolb, 215-762-1819.

DUQUESNE UNIVERSITY

McAnulty Graduate School of Liberal Arts

Programs of Study

The McAnulty Graduate School of Liberal Arts at Duquesne University offers a broad, diversified program of advanced study in a variety of academic disciplines. The graduate program gives qualified students the opportunity to broaden their knowledge in a chosen area of study, to acquire proficiency and experience in the traditional academic pursuits of scholarship and research, to contribute to the advancement of human knowledge as teachers and scholars in a personalized academic setting, to increase their professional competence, and to enhance their knowledge of current issues. Areas of study include traditional humanistic disciplines and newly designed interdisciplinary programs in liberal studies.

The Graduate School offers advanced degree programs in six disciplines at the doctoral level and in sixteen disciplines at the master's level. The Doctor of Philosophy is offered in English, health-care ethics, philosophy, psychology, rhetoric, and theology. The Master of Arts is offered in archival, museum, and editing studies; computational mathematics; conflict resolution; corporate communications; English; health-care ethics; history; multimedia technology; pastoral ministry; philosophy; psychology; rhetoric and philosophy of communication; social and public policy; and theology.

While no residence requirements are in effect for any master's program, all work toward this degree must be completed within six years. Doctoral candidates are expected to spend at least one year in full-time residence, during which they register for no less than 9 credits for two semesters. Doctoral students are also required to maintain continuous semester registration during their course of study at the University and to complete all degree requirements within four years of their qualifying examinations.

Research Facilities

The Gumberg Library serves the Duquesne community on campus and at a distance, offering access to a collection that includes both print and electronic resources. The library's collection has grown to more than 700,000 volumes, and it makes available more than 170 research databases that index newspapers, highly specialized research journals, and other publications. It also provides access to more than 6,000 electronic journals, newspapers, and other periodicals as well as electronic versions of books, reference works, poems, plays, and more. The library's catalog provides links to many scholarly electronic resources and to catalogs of other regional libraries. Graduate students have several options for obtaining materials not available at the Gumberg Library, including E-ZBorrow and ILLiad. The library is committed to using evolving technology to deliver the information that graduate students need in the most cost-effective manner. Professional librarians are available for on-site and remote consultation and assistance. The library participates in local, regional, and state consortia, which support reciprocal borrowing. It also maintains agreements with regional academic libraries and hospitals that allow graduate students to borrow books onsite at participating institutions.

Duquesne University has joined other universities working together to build a National Digital Library of Theses and Dissertations. Graduate students can attend training sessions at Gumberg Library to learn how to format documents, convert them to PDF files, and submit them online to meet University requirements.

The Gumberg Library provides a special graduate study room complete with wireless access and flexibility for individual study, group meetings, or seminars. Individual carrels are also available for 4-hour use. Prospective students can become better informed of the wealth of information available at the Gumberg Library by visiting the Web site at http://www.library.duq.edu.

Financial Aid

The various departments of the Graduate School award a limited number of graduate assistantships, both teaching and research, and tuition scholarships. Assigned on a competitive basis to students with outstanding academic records, these awards are made for an initial one-year period, with reappointments extended on the basis of proven competence and good academic standing. Assistantships normally provide a stipend along with waivers of both tuition and the University fee.

Cost of Study

Graduate tuition for 2007–08 is set at $848 per credit.

Living and Housing Costs

Students should contact the Graduate School for living and housing information.

Student Group

Duquesne University has a total enrollment of more than 10,000 students in its nine schools. With more than 700 students and 100 faculty members in its Graduate School of Liberal Arts, the University offers graduate students a highly personalized learning and advisement environment.

Location

One of the few private Catholic downtown universities in the United States, Duquesne University, from its position adjacent to Pittsburgh's main business section, offers ready access to the many cultural, social, and entertainment attractions of the city. Within walking distance of the campus are the Benedum Center and Heinz Hall for the Performing Arts (home of the symphony, opera, ballet, theater, and other musical and cultural institutions), the Mellon Arena (center for indoor sporting events and various exhibitions and conventions), Heinz Field and PNC Park (for outdoor sporting events), and South Side (an entertainment and nightlife center). The libraries, museums, art galleries, and music hall of the Carnegie Institute in the Oakland area are easily accessible by public transportation, whose routes pass immediately adjacent to the campus, or by private automobile. As one of the ten largest metropolitan areas in the United States, Pittsburgh also offers many professional career opportunities for its residents.

The University

Founded in 1878 by the Fathers and Brothers of the Congregation of the Holy Ghost, Duquesne University provides the opportunity for a superior private education for students from many backgrounds without regard to sex, race, creed, color, national or ethnic origins, nonperformance-related handicap, or veteran status. Duquesne's beautiful, 40-acre, self-contained campus on the bluff overlooking downtown Pittsburgh is the safest in Pennsylvania and one of the safest in the nation.

Applying

Applications for admission to graduate study with financial aid should be submitted no later than March 1 for the academic year beginning in the following September. Applications for admission without financial aid may be made up to one month prior to the beginning of the term in which the student desires to begin graduate work. All applications require official transcripts of previous undergraduate and graduate work, GRE scores, and three letters of recommendation. The Graduate School's bulletin and application forms are available by writing or calling the office of the Graduate School or by visiting the University's Web site at http://www.duq.edu.

Correspondence and Information

Linda L. Rendulic, Assistant to the Dean
McAnulty Graduate School of Liberal Arts
Duquesne University
Pittsburgh, Pennsylvania 15282

Phone: 412-396-6400
Fax: 412-396-5265
Web site: http://www.duq.edu/liberalarts/frontpage/graduate.html

THE FACULTY

The University faculty consists of more than 300 full-time members. The Graduate School faculty consists of more than 100 experienced teachers and scholars, of whom 90 percent or more have attained the highest degrees conferred in their academic disciplines.

Albert C. Labriola, Professor and Acting Dean, McAnulty Graduate School of Liberal Arts.
G. Evan Stoddard, Associate Dean of the Graduate School.
Ronald Arnett, Professor and Chair, Department of Communication and Rhetorical Studies.
Daniel Burston, Professor and Chair, Department of Psychology.
Aaron Mackler, Professor and Director, Health Care Ethics.
Holly Mayer, Professor and Chair, Department of History.
Mark Mazur, Professor and Director, Computational Mathematics.
Magali Michael, Professor and Chair, Department of English.
John Shepherd, Associate Professor and Director, Interactive Media.
James Swindal, Professor and Chair, Department of Philosophy.
George Worgul, Professor and Chair, Department of Theology.
Joseph Yenerall, Associate Professor and Director, Social and Public Policy.

Graduate classes at Duquesne are small, and students are ensured personal attention.

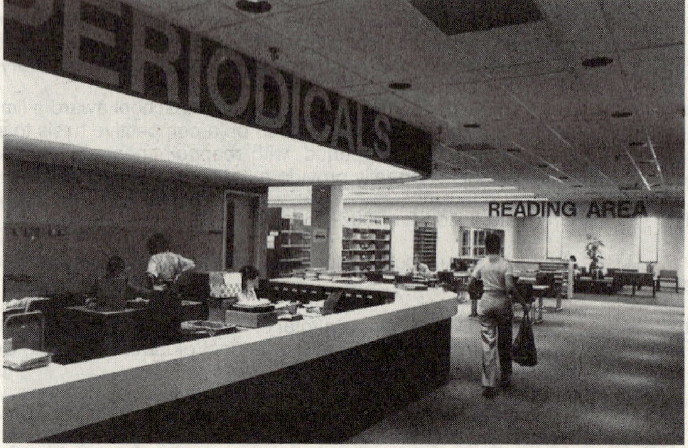

The Gumberg Library has more than half a million volumes and provides comfortable study areas.

D'YOUVILLE COLLEGE

Graduate Studies

Programs of Study

D'Youville College offers the Doctor of Education (Ed.D.) degree in educational leadership and health policy and health education. Doctor of Chiropractic (D.C.) and Doctor of Physical Therapy (D.P.T.) programs are also offered. Master of Science (M.S.) degrees are offered in clinical nurse specialist studies in community health nursing, education (early childhood, childhood, middle childhood (generalist and specialist), adolescence, and special education—including teacher certification), health services administration, business administration, international business, nurse practitioner studies (master's degree and post-master's certificate), nursing (with choice of clinical focus), occupational therapy, and physical therapy. Advanced certificate programs in clinical research associate studies, health services administration, long-term-care administration, and nursing and health-related professions education are also available. Five-year B.S./M.S. degrees are offered in dietetics, international business, nursing, and occupational therapy.

Research Facilities

D'Youville's Library Resources Center contains 101,000 volumes, including microtext and software, and subscribes to 630 periodicals and newspapers. The library also has access to 18,624 full-text journals via the Internet.

Financial Aid

In order to apply for federal aid, the Free Application for Federal Student Aid (FAFSA) must be completed. Graduate students must be matriculated for 6 or more credits in a degree program. Sources of federal aid include Federal Perkins Loans, the Federal Work-Study Program, Veterans' Benefits, Federal Stafford Student Loans, and Graduate Nursing Loans. The New York State Tuition Assistance Program (TAP) is available to full-time (at least 12 credit hours), matriculated graduate students who are residents of New York State. D'Youville College offers three forms of scholarships for graduate students matriculated in a master's degree program, including the Program Merit Scholarship, the Disadvantaged Student Scholarship, and the Retention Award. Nurse traineeship assistance is available to students enrolled for a minimum of 9 credit hours per semester in the Graduate Nursing Program. Canadian students (citizens and landed immigrants) are offered a 20 percent tuition reduction and may also apply for the Ontario Student Assistance Program (OSAP). Private education loans are also available to both U.S. and Canadian citizens.

Cost of Study

Graduate tuition for 2007–08 is $635 (M.S.) and $685 (Ed.D. and D.P.T.) per credit hour. The Doctor of Chiropractic is $8800 per semester. A general fee of between $30 and $60 is required and is based on credit hours taken. A Student Association fee of $2 per credit hour is applied toward concerts, yearbooks, activities, and guest lectures.

Living and Housing Costs

Marquerite Hall, the residence facility, houses men and women students on separate floors, with the exception of the designated coed floors. For 2007–08, room and board cost $4375 per semester. Overnight accommodations are available at a rate of $28 per night (space permitting). A new residence-apartment complex opened in 2005 and houses 175 junior, senior, and graduate students in one- and four-bedroom apartments. Rates for 2007–08 range around $3575 per semester, based on the type of apartment reserved.

Student Group

Graduate degree programs are enhanced by a 13:1 student-faculty ratio. The current enrollment is 1,113 full-time and 443 part-time graduate students. Seventy-three percent of the student population are women, 5 percent are from minority groups, and 62 percent are international students.

Location

D'Youville's location is ideally set in a residential community of Buffalo, New York. D'Youville College is minutes from the Peace Bridge to Canada and is approximately 90 minutes from Toronto and 25 minutes from Niagara Falls, making it a gateway to recreation areas in western New York and Ontario.

The College

D'Youville College is a private, coeducational liberal arts and professional college located in residential Buffalo, New York, approximately 1 mile from the Peace Bridge. The Grey Nuns founded D'Youville College in 1908. With a student population of just over 2,900, D'Youville offers its students the diversity and resources of a much larger college and the attention and accessibility that is usually attributed to a small college. The College's 7-acre campus offers students comprehensive facilities, modern computer labs, state-of-the-art medical labs, and modern classrooms.

Applying

Completed application files are reviewed on a rolling admissions basis for most programs. The Doctor of Physical Therapy program has a November 30 application deadline for entry the following fall. The Doctor of Chiropractic program requires a minimum of 90 credit hours of undergraduate course work for application to the professional phase of the program. All other program candidates must have earned a baccalaureate degree from an accredited college or university. Candidates for the Ed.D. programs must have completed a minimum of 30 credit hours of master's-level course work from an accredited college or university. A baccalaureate degree in nursing from an approved or accredited college or university and RN licensure are required for admission to the graduate nursing programs. Licensure as a registered nurse in New York State and a minimum of one year of experience as a registered nurse are required of candidates applying to the nurse practitioner studies programs. Admission to graduate programs is based on an overall evaluation of credentials, including the applicant's undergraduate record, which should show approximately a B average or better in the major field. Applicants who do not fulfill admission requirements may be admitted provisionally. Applicants to the Ed.D. programs should show a 3.25 GPA or better in their master's course work. Admission to Ed.D programs is competitive. Applicants whose native language is not English must submit a minimum TOEFL score of 500. The College does not require Graduate Record Examinations (GRE) or Miller Analogies Test (MAT) scores. Applicants for the M.B.A. program are required to take the GMAT.

Correspondence and Information

Linda E. Fisher
Director of Graduate Admissions
D'Youville College
One D'Youville Square
320 Porter Avenue
Buffalo, New York 14201-9985
Phone: 716-829-8400
800-777-3921 (toll-free)
Fax: 716-829-7900
E-mail: fisherl@dyc.edu
Web site: http://www.dyc.edu

THE FACULTY

Chiropractic
Geoff Gerow, Director of Chiropractic Program; D.C., National University of Health Sciences; DACBO.
Steven Zajac, Coordinator of Clinical Services; D.C., National University of Health Sciences; DACBO.

Education
Jamie DeWaters, Professor; Ph.D., SUNY at Buffalo.
Sheila G. Dunn, Associate Professor; Ed.D., SUNY at Buffalo.
Robert J. Gamble, Associate Professor; Ph.D., SUNY at Buffalo.
Mark Garrison, Associate Professor and Director of Doctoral Programs; Ph.D., SUNY at Buffalo.
Nancy M. Kaczmarek, GNSH, Associate Professor and Department Chair; Ph.D., SUNY at Buffalo.
James Lalley, Assistant Professor; Ph.D., SUNY at Buffalo.
Cathleen March, Assistant Professor; Ph.D., SUNY at Buffalo.
Robert Miller, Assistant Professor; Ph.D., SUNY at Buffalo.
Thomas Traverse, Assistant Professor; M.A., SUNY at Buffalo.
Stephen E. Williams, Assistant Professor; Ed.D., Clark.

Educational Leadership
Mark Garrison, Associate Professor and Director of Doctoral Programs; Ph.D., SUNY at Buffalo.

Health Policy and Health Education
Mark Garrison, Associate Professor and Director of Doctoral Programs; Ph.D., SUNY at Buffalo.

Health Services Administration
Walter Iwanenko, Assistant Professor and Department Chair; Ph.D., SUNY at Buffalo.
Elizabeth Miranda, Assistant Professor; J.D., SUNY at Buffalo.
James Notaro, Assistant Professor; Ph.D., North Carolina at Chapel Hill.
Judith H. Schiffert, Assistant Professor; Ed.D., SUNY at Buffalo.

International Business
Peter Eimer, Assistant Professor; M.B.A., Pittsburgh.
Joseph Fennell, Associate Professor; M.B.A., Columbia.
Bonnie Fox-Garrity, Assistant Professor; M.A., North Carolina at Chapel Hill.
Amable Pauline, Assistant Professor and Department Chair; Ph.D., Wisconsin–Madison.
Arup Sen, Assistant Professor; Ph.D candidate, SUNY at Buffalo.

Nursing
Joan Cookfair, Professor; Ed.D., SUNY at Buffalo. Community health nursing, HIV/AIDS, teaching strategies, transcultural nursing, strategies to facilitate critical thinking.
Carol A. Gutt, Associate Professor; Ed.D., SUNY at Buffalo. Wellness, child health, curriculum, women's health, women's issues, stress management, leadership roles.
Dorothy Hoehne, Associate Professor; Ph.D., SUNY at Buffalo. Pediatrics, hospice with adults and children, instruction, experimental/qualitative research, spouse and child abuse, wellness, rehabilitation, curriculum.
Verna Kieffer, Associate Professor and Department Chair; D.N.S., SUNY at Buffalo. Adult health, critical care, qualitative research, quality of life issues, professional practice issues.
Edith Malizia, Associate Professor and Assistant to the Chair; Ed.D., SUNY at Buffalo. Adult health, professional issues, professional socialization, leadership and management.
Pam Miller, Clinical Coordinator; M.S., SUNY at Buffalo; RN, Women's health NP.

Occupational Therapy
Merlene Gingher, Associate Professor and Department Chair; Ed.D., SUNY at Buffalo. Gerontic occupational therapy, range of motion in the elderly.
April Rockwood, Assistant Professor; M.S., SUNY at Buffalo. Pediatric practice, school-based OT, learning styles.
Elizabeth Stanton, Associate Professor; Ph.D., SUNY at Buffalo. Mental health issues, hospice care, culture and health.

Physical Therapy
James Karnes, Associate Professor; Ph.D., SUNY at Buffalo. Neuroanatomy/enruophysiology, gross anatomy, functional morphology.
Penelope Klein, Associate Professor; Ed.D., Syracuse. Tai chi, health-care systems and cost analysis.
Lynn Rivers, Associate Professor and Department Chair; Ph.D., SUNY at Buffalo. Health-care policy, physical activity health promotion for individuals with chronic disabilities with emphasis on African Americans.
John Rouselle, Associate Professor; Ed.D., SUNY at Buffalo. Exercise physiology, psychophysiology, wellness, health education.

EAST CAROLINA UNIVERSITY

Graduate School

Programs of Study East Carolina University (ECU) offers a wide range of graduate programs. There are seventy-four master's degree programs, seventeen doctoral degrees, and two first-professional degrees in ten colleges and professional schools, including the Brody School of Medicine. Post-master's programs leading to the Certificate of Advanced Study (C.A.S.) and Educational Specialist (Ed.S.) are also offered.

The minimum requirement for all master's, C.A.S., and Ed.S. programs is the successful completion of 30 semester hours and a comprehensive examination. A thesis and demonstrated proficiency in research skills are required in most M.A. and M.S. programs. Ph.D. programs in the biomedical sciences require completion of a minimum of 58 semester hours, candidacy examinations, and a dissertation. The Ed.D. program requires 60 semester hours, including an internship and a dissertation, and full-time residency for one year. Most master's, C.A.S., and Ed.S. programs can be completed in one calendar year of full-time study; part-time students can take up to six calendar years to complete their programs. Ph.D. students must complete all requirements no later than the end of the twelfth semester, including summers, following initial enrollment.

Research Facilities Joyner Library houses approximately 1.3 million bound volumes, more than 2.4 million pieces of microfilm, over 6,800 periodical subscriptions and 35,850 e-journals, 535,202 government documents, and 5,318 manuscript collections, as well as access to more than 200 online databases. The map collection now contains more than 100,000 maps and charts. The Music Library, a branch of Joyner, houses some 80,000 items, including books, periodicals, scores, software, and video and sound recordings of all types and periods of music. The William E. Laupus Health Sciences Library is located on ECU's West Campus and houses about 135,300 bound volumes, 16,400 units of microfilm, 725 print publications, and 6,337 e-journals.

Information Technology and Computing Services (ITCS) provides computing, network, and outreach support for academic education, research, and administrative programs on campus. East Carolina University is one of five universities holding membership in the Internet2 in North Carolina and is recognized throughout the region as a leader in incorporating technological advances in all phases of operation. The academic computing unit maintains various instructional and research software packages and provides technical assistance to faculty and graduate users. The campus has received national recognition for its computer networking infrastructure.

East Carolina University has renewed and strengthened its commitment to research, scholarship, and creative activity for both faculty and students. Extramural support for University activities has gone from $9.6 million to nearly $40 million in the last ten years. The faculty members have particular strengths in biomedical sciences, coastal studies, the fine arts, education, maritime history, and exercise physiology. The University continues to develop educational programs in response to regional needs in human service and health professions; endeavors draw on such cross-disciplinary research efforts as the Center on Aging and the Institute for Coastal and Marine Resources.

Financial Aid A limited number of graduate assistantships and fellowships, ranging in value from $800 to $21,000, are available. These are awarded through the departments and schools. A limited number of waivers are available for nonresident students that allow these students to pay the resident tuition rate. Inquiries about assistantships, fellowships, and fee waivers should be addressed to academic units. Information on loans, work-study programs, and other work opportunities is available from the Financial Aid Office.

Cost of Study For fall 2007, tuition and fees for a North Carolina resident for full-time graduate study were $2349.50 per semester; for a nonresident, the total was $7507.50. Tuition and fees are subject to change.

Living and Housing Costs Housing and board are available on campus for unmarried students at a cost of approximately $2075 per semester for room and $1650 per semester for board. All charges are subject to change. There are no University residences for married students, but rental accommodations are available in Greenville.

Student Group The University faculty of 1,700 provided instruction for 24,351 students in the fall of 2006, including 5,474 graduate students and 290 students in the School of Medicine. East Carolina University has seen a 29.2 percent increase in enrollment during the past ten years. Minority enrollment for the University at the graduate level is 18 percent. East Carolina University attracted a student body from all 100 North Carolina counties, forty-eight of the fifty states, the District of Columbia, and fifty-six other countries for fall 2006. There are more than 67,500 living alumni who reside in all fifty states and some thirty other countries.

Location The main campus is adjacent to the downtown area of Greenville, a city of more than 60,000 people. Greenville, the hub of the eastern North Carolina coastal plain and a business, medical, and university center, is located 80 miles east of Raleigh and is accessible by highway and nearby airports. It is within easy driving distance of coastal resorts and the Outer Banks. The campus of the School of Medicine is adjacent to Pitt County Memorial Hospital, a 734-bed facility that serves as the teaching hospital for the School of Medicine.

The University East Carolina University, North Carolina's third-largest institution of higher learning, was founded in 1907 as a state-supported teacher training school and became a liberal arts college in 1941. Developing and growing rapidly, ECU became a state university in 1967 and a constituent member of the University of North Carolina System in 1972. The University serves as a focal point in eastern North Carolina for higher education. The Division of Academic Affairs includes the Thomas Harriot College of Arts and Sciences, with seventeen departments; the Colleges of Business, Education, Health and Human Performance, Human Ecology, Technology and Computer Science; and Fine Arts and Communication, with Schools of Art, Music, Communication, and Social Work. The Division of Health Science comprises the Brody School of Medicine and the Schools of Nursing and Allied Health Sciences.

Applying Applications must be received by June 1 for fall enrollment and by October 15 for enrollment in the spring. Some academic units have earlier deadlines. Master's degree candidates planning to enroll in the fall who want to be considered for out-of-state tuition waivers must submit applications by February 1. All applications must include a completed application form, official transcripts of all prior academic work, letters of recommendation, appropriate standardized test scores, and a nonrefundable application fee of $50.

Correspondence and Information

Graduate School
131 Ragsdale Hall
East Carolina University
Greenville, North Carolina 27858-4353
Phone: 252-328-6012
Fax: 252-328-6071
E-mail: gradschool@mail.ecu.edu
Web site: http://www.ecu.edu/gradschool

GRADUATE DEGREE PROGRAMS AND PROGRAM DIRECTORS

Dr. Patrick Pellicane, Dean of the Graduate School. (pellicanep@ecu.edu)
Dr. Ron Newton, Associate Dean of the Graduate School. (newtonro@ecu.edu)
Dr. Belinda Patterson, Assistant Dean of the Graduate School. (pattersonb@ecu.edu)

Brody School of Medicine

Anatomy and Cell Biology (Ph.D.): Ronald Dudek, Ph.D. (252-744-2863; dudekr@ecu.edu)
Biochemistry and Molecular Biology (Ph.D.): George Kasperek, Ph.D. (252-744-2681; kasperekg@ecu.edu)
Microbiology and Immunology (Ph.D.): Richard Franklin, Ph.D. (252-744-2705; franklinr@ecu.edu)
Pharmacology and Toxicology (Ph.D.): M. Saeed Dar, Ph.D. (252-744-2885; darm@ecu.edu)
Physiology (Ph.D.): Alexander Murashov, Ph.D. (252-744-3654; murashoval@ecu.edu)

College of Arts and Sciences

Anthropology (M.S.): Linda Wolfe, Ph.D. (252-328-9453; wolfel@ecu.edu)
Biology (M.S.): Terry West, Ph.D. (252-328-1845; westt@ecu.edu)
Biomedical Physics (Ph.D.): Larry Toburen, Ph.D. (252-328-1861; toburenl@ecu.edu)
Chemistry (M.S.): Art Rodriguez, Ph.D. (252-328-9804; rodriguezar@ecu.edu)
Economics (M.S.): John Bishop, Ph.D. (252-328-6756; bishopj@ecu.edu)
English (M.A., M.A.Ed., Ph.D.): Janice Tovey, Ph.D. (252-328-1544; toveyj@ecu.edu)
Geography (M.A.): Jeff Popke, Ph.D. (252-328-6087; popkee@ecu.edu)
Geology (M.S.): Terri Woods, Ph.D. (252-328-6014; woodst@ecu.edu)
History (M.A., M.A.Ed.): Carl Swanson, Ph.D. (252-328-6485; swansonc@ecu.edu)
Maritime Studies (M.A., Ph.D.): Carl Swanson, Ph.D. (252-328-6485; swansonc@ecu.edu)
Mathematics (M.A., M.A.Ed.): Chal Benson, Ph.D. (252-328-6574; bensonf@ecu.edu)
Molecular Biology and Biotechnology (M.S.): Terry West, Ph.D. (252-328-1845; westt@ecu.edu)
Physics (M.S.): Edson Justiniano, Ph.D. (252-328-5275; justinianoe@ecu.edu)
Psychology, Clinical (M.A.): Beverly Harju, Ph.D. (252-328-1377; harjub@ecu.edu)
Psychology, General and Theoretic (M.A.): John Cope, Ph.D. (252-328-6497; copej@ecu.edu)
Psychology, Health (Ph.D.): Kathleen Rowe, Ph.D. (252-328-6492; rowek@ecu.edu)
Psychology, School (M.A./C.A.S.): Michael Brown, Ph.D. (252-328-4170; brownmi@ecu.edu)
Public Administration (M.P.A.): Carmine Scavo, D.P.A. (252-328-6130; scavoc@ecu.edu)
Sociology (M.A.): Ken Wilson, Ph.D. (252-328-4897; wilsonk@ecu.edu)

College of Business

Accounting (M.S.A.): Len Rhodes, M.B.A. (252-328-6970; rhodesl@ecu.edu)
Business Administration (M.B.A.): Len Rhodes, M.B.A. (252-328-6970; rhodesl@ecu.edu)

College of Education

Adult Education (M.A.Ed.): Vivian Mott, Ed.D. (252-328-6177; mottv@ecu.edu)
Business and Marketing Education (M.A.Ed., M.A.T.): Lilla Holsey, Ed.D. (252-328-6762; holseyl@ecu.edu)
Counselor Education (M.S.): J. Scott Glass, Ph.D. (252-328-6856; glassj@ecu.edu)
Educational Administration and Supervision (Ed.S.): Lynn Bradshaw, Ed.D. (252-328-6444; bradshawl@ecu.edu)
Educational Leadership (Ed.D.): Art Rouse, Ed.D. (252-328-6763; rousea@ecu.edu)
Elementary Grades Education (M.A.Ed.): Patricia Anderson, Ed.D. (252-328-4123; andersonp@ecu.edu)
Instructional Technology (M.S.): William Sugar, Ph.D. (252-328-1546; sugarw@ecu.edu)
Instructional Technology Education (M.A.Ed.): Carol Brown, Ph.D. (252-328-1624; browncar@ecu.edu)
Library Science (M.L.S.): Larry White, Ph.D. (252-328-2315; whitel@ecu.edu)
Library Science (C.A.S.): Jami Jones, Ph.D. (252-328-6621; jonesj@ecu.edu)
Master of Arts in Teaching (M.A.T.): Ann Bullock, Ed.D. (252-328-1126; bullockv@ecu.edu)
Middle Grades Education (M.A.Ed.): Patricia Anderson, Ed.D. (252-328-4123; andersonp@ecu.edu)
Reading Education (M.A.Ed.): Patricia Anderson, Ed.D. (252-328-4123; andersonp@ecu.edu)
School Administration (M.S.A.): Hal Holloman, Ph.D. (252-328-5315; hollomanh@ecu.edu)
Science Education (M.A., M.A.Ed.): Ronald Preston, Ph.D. (252-328-9353; prestonr@ecu.edu)
Special Education (Learning Disabilities and Mental Retardation) (M.A.Ed.): Patricia Anderson, Ed.D. (252-328-4123; andersonp@ecu.edu)
Vocational Education (M.S.): Lilla Holsey, Ed.D. (252-328-6762; holseyl@ecu.edu)

College of Fine Arts and Communication

Art (M.F.A., M.A., M.A.Ed.): Scott Eagle, M.F.A. (252-328-6285; eagles@ecu.edu)
Communication (M.A.): Laura Prividera, Ph.D. (252-328-5304; privideral@ecu.edu)
Music (M.M.): Tom Huener, Ph.D. (252-328-1247; huenert@ecu.edu)

College of Health and Human Performance

Environmental Health (M.S.E.H.): Alice Anderson, Ph.D. (252-328-4434; andersonj@ecu.edu)
Exercise and Sport Science (M.A., M.A.Ed.): James Decker, Ph.D. (252-328-0001; deckerj@ecu.edu)
Health Education (M.A.): Hans Johnson, Ph.D. (252-328-1818; johnsonh@ecu.edu)
Health Education (M.A.Ed.): Rick Barnes, Ph.D. (252-328-4238; barnesr@ecu.edu)
Recreation and Leisure Studies (M.S.): Hans Vogelsong, Ph.D. (252-328-0020; vogelsongh@ecu.edu)

College of Human Ecology

Child Development and Family Relations (M.S.): Cynthia Johnson, Ph.D. (252-328-6908; johnsoncy@ecu.edu)
Criminal Justice (M.S.): James F. Anderson, Ph.D. (252-328-4192; andersona@ecu.edu)
Family and Consumer Sciences Education (M.A.Ed., M.A.T.): Cynthia Johnson, Ph.D. (252-328-6908; johnsoncy@ecu.edu)
Marriage and Family Therapy (M.S.): Angela Lamson, Ph.D. (252-328-6908; lamsona@ecu.edu)
Medical Family Therapy (Ph.D.): Angela Lamson, Ph.D. (252-328-6908; lamsona@ecu.edu)
Nutrition (M.S.): William Forsythe, Ph.D. (252-328-6850; forsythew@ecu.edu)
Social Work (M.S.W.): Brenda Eastman, Ph.D. (252-328-4012; eastmanb@ecu.edu)

College of Technology and Computer Science

Computer Science (M.S.): Ronnie Smith, Ph.D. (252-328-9687; smithron@ecu.edu)
Construction Management (M.C.M.): David Batie, Ph.D. (252-328-1383; batied@ecu.edu)
Occupational Safety (M.S.): Michael Behm, Ph.D. (252-328-9674; behmm@ecu.edu)
Software Engineering (M.S.): John Placer, Ph.D. (252-737-9682; placerj@ecu.edu)
Technology Systems (M.S.): Andrew Jackson, Ph.D. (252-328-1468; jacksona@ecu.edu)

School of Allied Health Sciences

Communication Sciences and Disorders (M.S., Ph.D.): Monica Hough, Ph.D. (252-328-4460; houghm@ecu.edu)
Occupational Therapy (M.S.): Anne Dickerson, Ph.D. (252-328-9674; dickersona@ecu.edu)
Physical Therapy (D.P.T.): Blaise Williams, Ph.D. (252-328-4450; williamsdor@ecu.edu)
Physician Assistant (M.S.): Larry Dennis, Ph.D. (252-744-1705; dennisl@ecu.edu)
Rehabilitation Counseling and Administration (Ph.D.): Daniel Wong, Ph.D. (252-744-6298; wongd@ecu.edu)
Rehabilitation Counseling, Substance Abuse and Clinical Counseling, Vocational Evaluation (M.S.): Paul Alston, Ph.D. (252-328-4452; alstonp@ecu.edu)

School of Nursing

Nursing (M.S.N.): Mary Ann Rose, Ph.D. (252-744-6437; rosem@ecu.edu)
Nursing (Ph.D.): Nancy Alligood, Ph.D. (252-744-6422; alligoodn@ecu.edu)

Interdisciplinary and Multidisciplinary Programs

Bioenergetics (Ph.D.): James Decker, Ph.D. (252-328-0001; deckerj@ecu.edu)
Biological Sciences (Ph.D.): Donald Hoffman, Ph.D. (252-744-2807; hoffmand@ecu.edu)
Coastal Resources Management (Ph.D.): Lauriston King, Ph.D. (252-328-9372; kingl@ecu.edu)
International Studies (M.A.I.S.): Sylvie Henning, Ph.D. (252-328-6722; hennings@ecu.edu)
Public Health (M.P.H.): Lloyd Novick, Ph.D. (252-744-4079; novickl@ecu.edu)
Technology Management (Ph.D.): Andrew Jackson, Ph.D. (252-328-1468; jacksona@ecu.edu)

EASTERN ILLINOIS UNIVERSITY

Graduate Studies

Programs of Study

Eastern Illinois University offers programs of study leading to the Specialist degree in educational administration and school psychology. Students may also pursue the Master of Business Administration. The following programs of study lead to the Master of Arts degree: art, art with an art education option, clinical psychology, communication studies, communication studies with an option in community college pedagogy, economics, English, gerontology, history, history with a historical administration option, mathematics, mathematics with a mathematics education option, music, and political science. The following programs of study lead to the Master of Science degree: biological sciences, chemistry, college student affairs, communication disorders and sciences, counseling, family and consumer sciences (with an option in dietetics), and technology. The University offers the Master of Science in natural sciences with areas of emphasis in biological sciences, chemistry, geology/geography, and physics. Programs of study leading to the Master of Science in Education include educational administration, elementary education, and special education. The University also offers certificate programs in accountancy, computer technology, quality systems, technology security, and work performance improvement. Students may also pursue postbaccalaureate teacher certification or nondegree professional development courses.

Research Facilities

Following a $22.5-million renovation and expansion completed in 2002, Booth Library's patrons are enjoying many new enhancements, including study tables wired for data and power; new group-study rooms; improved accessibility throughout the building, including an atrium staircase and three elevators; and browsable media collections. The library collection consists of more than 926,000 cataloged volumes, approximately 1.3 million microtexts, as well as maps, music scores, and pamphlets selected to support the University's educational mission. The government documents collection includes United States and Illinois State publications. Booth Library is also home to the Coles Ballenger Teachers' Center, which houses K–12 curriculum materials, an extensive juvenile collection, and a variety of nonprint materials related to teachers and teaching. Leisure-time reading interests are served through materials from the general book, serial, and newspaper collections, as well as the latest bestsellers, films, and popular materials.

Booth Library's public catalog is available through ILLINET Online, the statewide network of forty-five academic libraries. The reference collection consists of 55,000 volumes. Library Technology Services provides students with computer labs, media equipment, and nonprint materials such as sound recordings and videotapes. Study carrels equipped for independent viewing and listening are provided, as are group listening/viewing rooms.

Currently under construction and slated for occupancy in late 2007, the Doudna Fine Arts Center is a $60-million project offering 138,000 square feet of space for the departments of art, music, and theater. Award-winning and world-renowned architect Antoine Predock has designed a facility that includes graphics design drafting labs and studios; studio space for metals, printmaking, drawing, painting, and sculpture; percussion labs; electric piano, music, and keyboard labs; movement studio; scene and costume shops; a 275-seat proscenium theater; and a 150-seat lecture hall.

Eastern provides several computer labs for student use. Individual departments also provide research facilities for graduate students.

Financial Aid

There is a strong history at Eastern of graduate students working with faculty members on a variety of sponsored research projects. The Graduate School provides a series of competitive grant programs to promote and support graduate research. Programs include Graduate School Research/Creative Activity Awards, Williams Travel Awards, and Master's Thesis Awards.

Graduate assistantships are available in the areas of teaching and research for qualified graduate students. The Housing Department offers residential assistantships. Service assistantships are offered in a limited number of nonacademic offices. Completed assistantship applications should be submitted to the appropriate department by February 15. Individual departments may establish other deadlines. The assistantships include a tuition waiver scholarship and a monthly stipend for the contract period. Program and service fees are not waived as part of the tuition waiver scholarship. As an additional benefit, a summer tuition waiver scholarship is offered to graduate assistants. Students interested in assistantships should contact individual departments for specific details.

In addition to graduate assistantships, students may qualify for the Federal Work-Study Program, student employment, federal loans, and various private scholarships. International students may qualify for a limited number of International Student Scholarships.

Cost of Study

Tuition for 2007–08 graduate study at Eastern Illinois University is $189.75 per credit hour for residents and $569.25 per credit hour for nonresidents. Fees per semester are approximately $900 for all full-time students and $66 per hour for part-time students. The fees cover health and accident insurance and programs and services. The textbook rental fee is $8.95 for each semester hour for all students.

Living and Housing Costs

Housing for families and single graduate students is available at a cost of $1902 per semester for a 1½-room apartment, $2000 per semester for a two-room apartment, and $1780 per semester for a super-efficiency apartment. These apartments are designed to provide inexpensive living facilities for graduate students.

Student Group

Total enrollment at Eastern Illinois University in fall 2006 was approximately 12,349 students. This number includes 1,757 graduate students. Graduate students are represented by the Graduate Student Advisory Council, an organization made up of student representatives from each program. A variety of activities are available for students at Eastern, including the use of the Student Recreation Center, which offers a fitness center, racquetball courts, basketball courts, volleyball courts, an indoor track, and a swimming pool. Numerous outdoor courts, playing fields, and a jogging trail are also available.

Location

Eastern Illinois University is located in Charleston, Illinois, the county seat of Coles County, in east-central Illinois. The city has a population of approximately 20,000. Two state highways, 16 and 130, go through Charleston and provide access to Interstates 57 and 70. Amtrak service is available in Mattoon, which is approximately 10 miles from Charleston. The larger communities of Champaign-Urbana, Decatur, and Terre Haute are within 1 hour's driving distance. Urban areas such as St. Louis, Chicago, and Indianapolis are within 2 to 3 hours' driving distance.

The University

The University was established as Eastern Illinois State Normal School in 1895 by the Illinois General Assembly. In response to growth and change, the institution became Eastern Illinois State Teachers College in 1921, Eastern Illinois State College in 1947, and Eastern Illinois University in 1957. The campus is located on 320 acres and consists of seventy-two buildings, including twelve residence halls and seventeen apartment buildings. The University also owns wooded tracts near Charleston, which are used for nature study and life science research.

Applying

Domestic applicants submit an application, a $30 application fee, and transcripts verifying completion of a baccalaureate degree from an accredited institution approved by Eastern Illinois University. Additional requirements such as test scores (GRE, GMAT, MAT) and departmental applications may be required by some degree programs. Admission and assistantship applications are available on the Web at http://www.eiu.edu/~graduate/.

International applicants must submit an international application, a $30 application fee, an approved financial affidavit form, an official raised-seal transcript, and required admission test scores (GRE, GMAT, MAT, TOEFL). TOEFL scores of at least 550 are required. International application materials are available on the Web at http://www.eiu.edu/~interntl/.

Correspondence and Information

The Graduate School
Eastern Illinois University
600 Lincoln Avenue
Charleston, Illinois 61920

Phone: 217-581-2220
Fax: 217-581-6020
Web site: http://www.eiu.edu/~graduate/

THE FACULTY AND THEIR RESEARCH

DEANS
Robert M. Augustine, Ph.D., Dean of the Graduate School, Research and Sponsored Programs, and International Programs.
Mary Anne Hanner, Ph.D., Dean of the College of Sciences.
Diane B. Hoadley, Ph.D., Dean of the Lumpkin College of Business and Applied Sciences.
James K. Johnson, M.F.A., Dean of the College of Arts and Humanities.
Diane H. Jackman, Ph.D., Dean of the College of Education and Professional Studies.

GRADUATE PROGRAMS AND FACULTY COORDINATORS
The area code for all phone numbers is 217.

College of Arts and Humanities
Master of Arts in Art: Mr. Chris Kahler (Telephone: 581-3410; E-mail: ckahler@eiu.edu)
Master of Arts in Communication Studies: Dr. Melanie Mills (Telephone: 581-3819; E-mail: mbmills@eiu.edu)
Master of Arts in English: Dr. Chris Hanlon (Telephone: 581-2428; E-mail: chanlon@eiu.edu)
Master of Arts in History: Dr. Edmund Wehrle (Telephone: 581-6372; E-mail: efwehrle@eiu.edu)
Master of Arts in History, Historical Administration Option: Dr. Nora Pat Small (Telephone: 581-6380; E-mail: npsmall@eiu.edu)
Master of Arts in Music: Dr. Peter Hesterman (Telephone: 581-3677; E-mail: pdhesterman@eiu.edu)

Lumpkin College of Business and Applied Sciences
Master of Arts in Gerontology: Dr. Jeanne Snyder (Telephone: 581-7843; E-mail: jrsnyder@eiu.edu)
Master of Business Administration: Dr. Cheryl Noll (Telephone: 581-3028; E-mail: clnoll@eiu.edu)
Postbaccalaureate Certificate in Accounting: Dr. Cheryl Noll (Telephone: 581-3028; E-mail: clnoll@eiu.edu)
Master of Science in Family and Consumer Sciences: Dr. Frances Murphy (Telephone: 581-6997; E-mail: flmurphy@eiu.edu)
Master of Science in Family and Consumer Sciences, Dietetics Option: Dr. Frances Murphy (Telephone: 581-6997; E-mail: flmurphy@eiu.edu)
Master of Science in Technology: Dr. Peter Ping Liu (Telephone: 581-6267; E-mail: pliu@ eiu.edu)
Certificate in Computer Technology
Certificate in Quality Systems
Certificate in Work Performance Improvement
Certificate in Technology Security

College of Education and Professional Studies
Master of Science in College Student Affairs: Dr. Richard Roberts (Telephone: 581-2400; E-mail: rlroberts@eiu.edu)
Master of Science in Counseling: Dr. Richard Roberts (Telephone: 581-2400; E-mail: rlroberts@eiu.edu)
Master of Science in Education in Elementary Education: Dr. Joy Russell (Telephone: 581-5315; E-mail: jlrussell@eiu.edu)
Master of Science in Education in Elementary Education: Dr. Nick Osborne (Telephone: 581-5728; E-mail: nrosborne@eiu.edu)
Master of Science in Education in Special Education: Dr. Kathlene Shank (Telephone: 581-5315; E-mail: ksshank@eiu.edu)
Master of Science in Physical Education: Dr. John Emmett (Telephone: 581-6363; E-mail: jemmett@eiu.edu)
Specialist in Education in Educational Administration: Dr. Linda Morford (Telephone: 581-2919; E-mail: lmmorford@eiu.edu)

College of Sciences
Master of Arts in Clinical Psychology: Dr. Anu Sharma (Telephone: 581-2127; E-mail: asharma@eiu.edu)
Master of Arts in Economics: Dr. Mukti Upadhyay (Telephone: 581-3812; E-mail: mpupadhyay@eiu.edu)
Master of Arts in Mathematics: Dr. Keith Wolcott (Telephone: 581-5902; E-mail: kwolcott@eiu.edu)
Master of Arts in Mathematics, Education Option: Dr. Marshall Lassak (Telephone: 581-6281; E-mail: mblassak@eiu.edu)
Master of Arts in Political Science: Dr. Ryan Hendrickson (Telephone: 581-6219; E-mail: rchendrickson@eiu.edu)
Master of Science in Biological Sciences: Dr. Charles Costa (Telephone: 581-2520; E-mail: cjcosta@eiu.edu)
Master of Science in Chemistry: Dr. Sean Peebles (Telephone: 581-3420; E-mail: sapeebles@eiu.edu)
Master of Science in Communication Disorders and Sciences: Dr. Tina Veale (Telephone: 581-7445; E-mail: tkveale@eiu.edu)
Master of Science in Natural Sciences
Emphasis in Biological Sciences: Dr. James McGaughey (Telephone: 581-2928; E-mail: jamcgaughey@eiu.edu)
Emphasis in Chemistry: Dr. Doug Klarup (Telephone: 581-2521; E-mail: dgklarup@eiu.edu)
Emphasis in Geology/Geography: Dr. John Stimac (Telephone: 581-2626; E-mail: jpstimac@eiu.edu)
Emphasis in Physics: Dr. Leonard Storm (Telephone: 581-3220; E-mail: lestorm@eiu.edu)
Specialist in School Psychology: Dr. J. Michael Havey (Telephone: 581-2127; E-mail: jmhavey@eiu.edu)

EASTERN MICHIGAN UNIVERSITY

Graduate School

Programs of Study Eastern Michigan University (EMU) offers programs of study leading to more than eighty graduate degrees, including the Master of Arts, Master of Science, Master of Fine Arts, specialist's, Ph.D., and Ed.D., as well as graduate and advanced graduate certificates in a variety of fields. A complete list of degree and certificate programs is found at the end of this summary.

Research Facilities Eastern Michigan's fully wireless, state-of-the-art Halle Library houses more than 600,000 volumes (more than 350,000 of which are stored in the Automated Retrieval Collection), more than 100,000 bound periodicals, 200,000 government documents, more than 50,000 maps, 665,000 microforms, and more than 7,500 videotapes and music CDs and subscribes to more than 4,300 journals. Computing facilities include a DEC VAX cluster mainframe system, and there are numerous computer labs on campus for student use in addition to specialized computer facilities in most departments.

All of the departments and programs have state-of-the-art facilities and equipment to support the students' fields of study. These range from research-quality Fourier-transform IR, UV, and visible spectrophotometers in the chemistry department; a fully equipped, 10-inch f/14 apochromatic refractor telescope for the study of astronomy; and an electron microscopy and photomicrography suite in the biology department to 200 computers and designated spaces for work in such areas as robotics and cluster computing in the computer science department to a counseling/reading/speech and hearing clinic to support studies in those areas of education and psychology.

There are also many organized research units at EMU. These include the Centers for Corporate Training, one of the leading University-based training operations in the nation, which comprises more than 100 program offerings for hundreds of major national and international companies; the Center for Environmental Information Technologies and Applications, an applied GIS research unit; the Center for Research Support; Coatings Research Institute and its affiliated NSF Center for Coatings Research; High Power Laser Laboratory; Institute for Community and Regional Development, which links faculty members and students to communities to address specific public-service needs; Institute for Diversity and Business Services, which provides practical assistance to minority businesses and communities; Institute for the Study of Children, Families, and Communities; the Linguist (international linguistics Web site dedicated to providing information on language and language analysis); Microbiology Research Facility; Molecular Biology Research Facility; National Institute for Consumer Education; Textiles Research and Training Institute; and the Urban Water Research Consortium.

Financial Aid Most full-time students receive some form of financial aid. The Graduate School administers scholarships, fellowships, and assistantship programs. Stipends vary by program. Assistantships also include full tuition and fees, free parking, faculty library privileges, and a bookstore discount. For information on need-based aid, applicants should contact the Office of Financial Aid.

Cost of Study In 2006–07, graduate tuition and fees for residents were $340.50 per credit hour and for nonresidents, $671. General and technical fees were $34 per credit hour; various other fees may apply to specific programs.

Living and Housing Costs Double rooms in residence halls (with eighteen meals a week) cost $6942 per school year. Single rooms are also available.

Student Group Total enrollment at EMU is approximately 23,000 students, including about 4,800 graduate students. About 65 percent are women. Students come from all fifty states and seventy-nine countries, but most are residents of southeast Michigan. The University has been recognized by *U.S. News & World Report* for fostering a favorable climate for diversity.

Location Ypsilanti is located in southeast Michigan, 15 minutes from the Detroit Metropolitan Airport, 35 miles west of Detroit, and 8 miles east of Ann Arbor, which is home to the University of Michigan. The regional economy is exceptionally strong, anchored by the auto industry but increasingly diversified with high-technology firms. Schools, health care, entertainment, parks, and recreational opportunities are outstanding.

The University Eastern Michigan University is one of fifteen state-supported institutions of higher learning in Michigan. It is accredited by the North Central Association of Colleges and Schools as well as the National Council for Accreditation of Teacher Education, AACSB International–The Association to Advance Collegiate School of Business, and many other accrediting agencies. Founded in 1849 as the first normal school west of the Allegheny Mountains, it remains among the top producers of education personnel in the U.S. In the past fifty years, EMU has become increasingly diversified and consists of five Colleges: Arts and Sciences, Business, Education, Health and Human Services, and Technology. The University emphasizes excellent teaching, applied research, and community service. More than 100 student organizations are available on campus, as are a student newspaper, two radio stations, and a television studio. EMU is a member of the NCAA Division I and competes in all major sports in the Mid-American Conference.

Applying The Graduate School's fall application deadline is May 15 (February 15 for students applying for financial aid), but individual programs may have different dates. Applicants are advised to contact specific programs directly for deadlines. The graduate application can be accessed online. All undergraduate transcripts are required; these, as well as any required standardized test scores, should be obtained well in advance of the deadline. An application fee of $35 must accompany the application.

Correspondence and Information

Office of Graduate Admissions (domestic applicants)
Office of International Admissions (international applicants)
400 Pierce Hall
Eastern Michigan University
Ypsilanti, Michigan 48197
Phone: 734-487-3060
E-mail: graduate_school@emich.edu
Web site: http://www.gradschool.emich.edu

GRADUATE PROGRAMS OF STUDY AND DEGREES

COLLEGE OF ARTS AND SCIENCES

African American Studies: African American Studies (Certificate).
Art: Art Education (M.A.), Studio Art (M.F.A.), Studio Art (M.A.).
Biology: Ecology and Organismal Biology (M.S.), Bioinformatics (M.S., Certificate), General Biology (M.S.), Molecular/Cellular Biology (M.S.), Water Resources (Certificate).
Chemistry: Chemistry (M.S.).
Communications and Theater Arts: Arts Administration (M.A.), Communication (M.A.), Interpretation/Performance Studies (M.A.), Drama/Theater for the Young (M.A., M.F.A.), Theater Arts (M.A.).
Computer Science: Artificial Intelligence (Certificate), Computer Science (M.S.).
Economics: Applied Economics (M.A.), Economics (M.A.), Health Economics (M.A.), International Economics and Development (M.A.), Trade and Development (M.A.).
English Language and Literature: Children's Literature (M.A.), Creative Writing (M.A.), English Linguistics (M.A.), Human Language Technology (Certificate), Literature (M.A.), Teaching of Writing (Certificate), Technical Communication (Certificate), Written Communication (M.A.).
Foreign Languages and Bilingual Studies: French (M.A.), German (M.A.), German for Business Practices (Certificate), Hispanic Language and Culture (Certificate), Japanese Business Practices (Certificate), Japanese Language Teaching (Certificate), Language and International Trade (M.A.), Spanish (M.A.), Spanish Bilingual/Bicultural Education (M.A.), TESOL (Certificate, M.A.).
Geography and Geology: Earth Science (M.S.), Geographic Information Systems (M.S.), Geographic Information Systems for Educators (Certificate), Geographic Information Systems for Professionals (Certificate), Geographic Information Systems–Planning (M.S.), Heritage Interpretation and Tourism (M.S.), Historic Preservation (Certificate, M.S.), Historic Preservation Conservation and Technology (M.S.), Historic Preservation Planning (M.S.), Water Resources–Geography (Certificate).
History and Philosophy: History (M.A.), Social Science (M.A.), Social Science and American Culture (M.L.S.), State and Local History (Certificate, Advanced Certificate).
Mathematics: Applied Statistics (M.A.), Mathematics (M.A.), Mathematics–Computer Science (M.A.), Mathematics Education (M.A.).
Music and Dance: Choral Music (M.A.), Music Education (M.A.), Music Performance (M.A.), Music Theory/Literature (M.A.), Piano Pedagogy (M.A.).
Physics and Astronomy: General Science (M.S.), Physics (M.S.), Physics Education (M.S.).
Political Science: General Public Management (Certificate), Local Government Management (Certificate), Management of Public Health Care Services (Certificate), Public Administration (M.P.A.), Public Budget Management (Certificate), Public Land Planning and Development Management (Certificate), Public Personnel Management (Certificate), Public Policy Analysis (Certificate).
Psychology: Clinical Behavioral Psychology (M.S.), Clinical Psychology (M.S., Ph.D.), General Experimental Psychology (M.S.).
Sociology, Anthropology, and Criminology: Criminology and Criminal Justice (M.A.), Schools Society and Violence (M.A.), Sociology (M.A.), Sociology–Family Specialty (M.A.).
Women's Studies: Women's and Gender Studies (M.L.S.).

COLLEGE OF BUSINESS

Master of Science Degrees: Accounting, Accounting 150-Hour Program, Accounting Information Systems 150-Hour Program, Computer Information Systems, Human Resource and Organizational Development, Integrated Marketing and Communications.
Graduate Business Programs: Master of Business Administration (M.B.A.). Program specializations in Computer Information Systems, E-business, Enterprise Business Intelligence, Entrepreneurship, Finance, Human Resource Management, International Business, Nonprofit Management, Supply Chain Management.
Graduate Certificates: Accounting–Financial and Operational Controls, Accounting–Taxation, Business Administration, Computer Information Systems, E-business, Entrepreneurship, Finance, Human Resources, International Business, Marketing Management, Nonprofit Management, Organizational Development, Strategic Quality Management, Supply Chain Management.

COLLEGE OF EDUCATION

Teacher Certification: Provisional Teacher Certificate–Elementary, Professional Teacher Certificate–Elementary, Provisional Teacher Certificate–Secondary, Professional Teacher Certificate–Secondary.
Leadership and Counseling: College Student Personnel (M.A.), College Counseling (M.A.), Community College Leadership (Certificate), Community Counseling (M.A.), Educational Leadership (M.A., Sp.A., Ed.D.), Helping Interventions in Multicultural Society (Certificate), Higher Education/General Administration (M.A.), Higher Education/Student Affairs (M.A.), K–12 Administration (M.A.), School Counseling (M.A.), School Counselor Licensure (Certificate).
Special Education: Administration and Supervision (Sp.A.), Cognitive Impairment (M.A.), Curriculum Development (Sp.A.), Emotional Impairment (M.A.), General (M.A.), Hearing Impairment (M.A.), Learning Disabilities (M.A.), Mentally Impaired (M.A.), Physical and Other Health Impairment (M.A.), Speech-Language Pathology (M.A.), Visual Impairment (M.A.).
Teacher Education: Curriculum and Instruction (M.A.); Early Childhood Education (M.A.); Educational Assessment (Certificate); Educational Media and Technology (M.A., Certificate); Educational Psychology Development and Personality (M.A.); Educational Psychology Research and Evaluation (M.A.); Elementary Education (M.A.); Interdisciplinary Cultural Studies (M.A.); K–12 Curriculum (M.A.); Middle School Education (M.A.); Reading (M.A.); Secondary School Education (M.A.); Schools, Society, and Violence (M.A., jointly taught with the Sociology Department); Social Foundations (M.A.).

COLLEGE OF HEALTH AND HUMAN SERVICES

Health Sciences: Clinical Research Administration (M.S., Certificate), Dietetics–Coordinated Program (M.S.), Health Administration (M.S., Certificate), Human Nutrition (M.S.), Occupational Therapy (M.O.T., M.S.).
Health Promotion & Human Performance: Adapted/Interdisciplinary Physical Education (M.S.), Community Building (Certificate), Exercise Physiology (M.S.), Health Education (M.S.), Orthotics (Certificate), Orthotics and Prosthetics (M.S.), Physical Education–Pedagogy (M.S.), Prosthetics (Certificate), Sports Management (M.S.).
Nursing: Adult Nurse Practitioner (Advanced Certificate), Nursing (M.S.N.), Quality Improvement Health Care (Certificate), Teaching in Health Care Systems (Certificate).
Social Work: Gerontology (Certificate), Community Building (Certificate), Dementia (Certificate), Family and Children's Services (M.S.W.), Mental Health and Chemical Dependency (M.S.W.), Services to the Aging (M.S.W.).

COLLEGE OF TECHNOLOGY

College of Technology: Technology: (Ph.D.).
Engineering Technology: Computer-Aided Engineering (M.S.), Construction (M.S.), Engineering Management (M.S.), Interior Design (M.S.), Polymer Technology (M.S.), Quality (M.S., Certificate).
Technology Studies: Apparel, Textiles & Merchandising (M.S.); Career, Technical and Workforce Education (M.S.); Hotel and Restaurant Management (M.S.); Information Security (M.L.S., Certificate); Interdisciplinary Technology (M.L.S.).

EAST STROUDSBURG UNIVERSITY OF PENNSYLVANIA

Graduate Studies

Programs of Study

East Stroudsburg University of Pennsylvania offers graduate studies leading to the M.A., M.Ed., M.P.H., and M.S. degrees. In cooperation with Indiana University of Pennsylvania, a doctorate of education degree in education administration leadership is offered on the East Stroudsburg (ESU) campus. In addition, graduate certification programs are available in twenty-four different areas of teacher certification. The Master of Arts degree is awarded with a major in history or political science. The Master of Education degree is awarded in biological sciences, elementary education, health and physical education, history, instructional technology, political science, reading, secondary education, and special education. All degrees and certificate programs in education are NCATE accredited. The Master of Public Health degree is awarded with a concentration in community health education. This program is accredited by the Council of Education for Public Health. The Master of Science degree is awarded with a major in biology, computer science, clinical exercise physiology, health and physical education, management and leadership (with concentrations in hotel restaurant, public administration, sport management, and tourism management), physical education, speech-language pathology, and sports management. The Certification Program includes, among others, the behavior analyst certification, the School Administration Program leading to the elementary and/or secondary principal certification and the cooperative program with Penn State University for the superintendent's letter of eligibility, the reading specialist certification, school nurse educational specialists, safety education/driver education certificate, and the special education supervisor certificate. Students may complete programs of study that lead to a Pennsylvania Instructional I or Instructional II teaching certificate. ESU's educational programs are accredited by NCATE. Graduate programs provide internship opportunities, well-equipped laboratories, computer facilities, and comprehensive Web-based research databases.

Research Facilities

Kemp Library (http://www.esu.edu/library/) houses more than 448,000 books and periodical volumes, and 1.3 million pieces of microform material. The library is a depository for both U.S. government documents and Pennsylvania state publications, totaling more than 80,000 documents. The library also has extensive electronic holdings, most of which are available both on and off campus. Full-text databases, such as Academic University (LexisNexis), American Chemical Society Web Editions, and BioOne, provide the full text to more than 7,500 journals. The Curriculum Materials Center provides teacher-trainees with a special collection of 7,600 items that includes a selection of textbooks currently used in schools throughout the country and a comprehensive collection of school courses of study. The Academic Computing network consists of fourteen UNIX or Windows NT-based servers that are connected to 600 microcomputers, which provide support instruction, Internet access, the World Wide Web, and e-mail. They are located in fifteen computer laboratories across the campus. Many academic departments maintain discipline-specific computer laboratories for their curricula. Stroud Hall contains classrooms, lecture halls, and computer and language laboratories. Beers Lecture Hall, which opened in 1998, seats 140 students and serves as a distance learning facility. The Fine and Performing Arts Center consists of two theaters, an art gallery, a concert hall, and classrooms. Other major classroom buildings include the Moore Biology building with laboratories for biological sciences, a large greenhouse, and a wildlife museum; the recently renovated Gessner Science Hall with laboratories for physics and chemistry; DeNike Center for Human Services with laboratory areas for recreation and leisure services management, nursing, and health; LaRue Hall with laboratories for speech pathology and audiology; and Rosenkrans Hall with offices and the media, communication, and technology department. Koehler Fieldhouse contains the human performance laboratories used for exercise science, cardiac rehabilitation, and sports medicine teaching and research.

Financial Aid

Financial aid, including the Federal Stafford Student Loan program, is available to graduate students. Nearly 150 graduate assistantships are offered to students each semester. Graduate assistantships provide a stipend of $2500 to $5000 for a nine-month appointment and waiver of tuition (including out-of-state tuition) for full-time graduate assistantships (20 hours per week) and partial waiver for half-time graduate assistantships. International students are eligible to apply for graduate assistantships. To receive full consideration for a graduate assistantship, applications should be submitted to the Graduate School prior to April 1 for the following fall semester.

Cost of Study

The basic tuition fee for the 2006–07 academic year for full-time Pennsylvania residents was $3700 per semester, including fees. Out-of-state tuition was $5547 per semester, including fees. All costs are subject to change.

Living and Housing Costs

On-campus housing is available, and the Office of Off-Campus Student Housing keeps listings of apartments and rooms, many within walking distance of the campus. Married student housing is not available. Students living off campus may take meals in the University dining facility.

Student Group

East Stroudsburg University of Pennsylvania has a total enrollment of about 6,000 students. About 1,000 are graduate students. Pennsylvania residents account for about 83 percent of the student body; women comprise 70 percent of the graduate enrollment, and more than 25 percent attend full-time.

Location

East Stroudsburg University is nestled in the foothills of the Pocono Mountains in northeastern Pennsylvania. The combination of quiet woodlands, mountain streams, and refreshing clean air has made the Poconos famous as a resort area for more than 100 years. Students take advantage of the scenic, historic, and recreational sites, including the Delaware Water Gap, Bushkill Falls, and the Pocono ski areas. The area offers fine restaurants and resorts, high-caliber entertainment, outstanding shopping, and year-round recreation, including hiking, skiing, and water sports. There is an excellent opportunity for weekend employment. The University, located in East Stroudsburg (Exit 308 off I-80), is within easy reach of major highway systems and commercial air services. The campus is approximately 75 miles west of New York City, 85 miles northeast of Philadelphia, 40 miles southeast of the Wilkes-Barre/Scranton area, and 40 miles northeast of the Allentown/Bethlehem/Easton area. Students and faculty members alike enjoy the opportunities of visits to the metropolitan areas.

The University

East Stroudsburg University is one of the fourteen institutions in the Pennsylvania State System of Higher Education. Founded in 1893 as a normal school to prepare teachers, the institution changed its name in 1927 to East Stroudsburg State Teachers College and again in 1960 to East Stroudsburg State College, reflecting the addition of a liberal arts and sciences curriculum. In 1983, it achieved university status. Today the University, with nearly 300 faculty members and 7,000 students (of which 1,100 are graduate students), awards the master's degree in twenty-one areas of specialization and, in cooperation with Indiana University of Pennsylvania, offers an on-campus doctorate degree in educational leadership. There are sixty campus buildings located on more than 200 acres. On-campus graduate housing is in a new apartment-suite style facility built in 2005. The Student Activity Association owns Stony Acres, a 119-acre off-campus student recreation area that includes a lodge and a small lake. There is a modern student recreation center located on the campus.

Applying

Application forms are available from the graduate school office at the address below. Students should submit an application for admission, a nonrefundable $50 application fee, and an official transcript of all undergraduate and postundergraduate course work. If courses were taken at more than one institution, a transcript is required from each institution attended. Applications for admission and graduate assistantships must be submitted before May 1 for full consideration for the fall semester and before December 15 for the spring semester. Earlier submission for international students and for some programs is required. Applications can be submitted online at the University's Web site (http://www.esu.edu). International students are required to submit TOEFL or ILETS scores and credential evaluation by World Education Services, Inc. (WES). Some programs require additional information for admission. Prospective students should visit the University's Web site for more information.

Correspondence and Information

Alberto Cradelle, M.P.H., Ph.D.
Dean, Graduate Studies and Research
East Stroudsburg University
East Stroudsburg, Pennsylvania 18301
Phone: 570-422-3536
866-837-6130 (toll-free)
Fax: 570-422-3711
E-mail: grad@po-box.esu.edu
Web site: http://www.esu.edu

East Stroudsburg University of Pennsylvania

GRADUATE PROGRAMS AND FACULTY CONTACTS

Biology
Dr. Jane Huffman, Program Graduate Coordinator (570-422-3716, jhuffman@po-box.esu.edu). Master of Science: thesis, nonthesis, nonresearch options. Master of Education: thesis, nonthesis, nonresearch options. Faculty areas of research include management of environmental resources, marine science, wildlife diseases/parasitology, animal behavior and migrating bird biology, protozoology, developmental biology of ferns/plant ecology, and molecular biology.

Computer Science
Professor Richard Amori, Program Graduate Coordinator (570-422-3779, ramori@po-box.esu.edu). Master of Science: research emphasis (highlights software engineering). Special areas of research include artificial intelligence, discrete algorithms, robotics, and expert systems.

Education Leadership, Ed.D. Cooperative Degree
Dr. Doug Lare, Program Coordinator (570-422-3431, dlare@po-box@esu.edu).

Elementary Education
Dr. Paula Kelberman, Graduate Program Coordinator (570-422-3365, pkelberman@po-box.esu.edu). Master of Education: thesis, project/portfolio, or extended programs options.

Exercise Science and Clinical Exercise Physiology
Dr. Shala Davis, Graduate Program Coordinator (570-422-3336, sdavis@po-box.esu.edu). Master of Education: major in health and physical education or sport management. Master of Science: clinical exercise physiology and exercise science. Thesis, research project, and comprehensive examination options. Additional departmental application and admission required for CRES program.

Health and Physical Education
Dr. Suzanne Mueller, Graduate Coordinator (570-422-3293, smueller@po-box.esu.edu). Master of Science.

Health Education
Dr. Kathy Hillman, Program Graduate Coordinator (570-422-3727, khillman@po-box.esu.edu). Master of Science: major in health education, with research and nonresearch options.

History
Dr. Larry Squeri, Department Chair/Graduate Program Coordinator (570-422-3284, lsqueri@po-box.esu.edu). Master of Arts: thesis required. Master of Education: thesis and nonthesis options.

Instructional Technology
Dr. Elzar Camper Jr., Graduate Coordinator (570-422-3646, ecamper@po-box.esu.edu). Master of Education in Instructional Technology. Instructional Technology Certificate (K–12). Prospective students should contact the department coordinator for details.

Management and Leadership
Dr. Robert Fleischman, Graduate Coordinator for sport management major (570-422-3316, rfleischman@po-box.esu.edu). Al Moranville, Graduate Coordinator for hotel restaurant management major (570-422-3049, amoranville@po-box.esu.edu). Dr. Jeff Weber, Graduate Coordinator for public administration major (570-422-3740, jweber@po-box.esu.edu). Master of Science in management and leadership: majors in hotel, restaurant, and tourism management; public administration; and sport management.

Political Science
Dr. Patricia Crotty, Department Chair and Graduate Program Coordinator (570-422-3286, pcrotty@po-box.esu.edu). Master of Arts: thesis required. Master of Education: thesis and nonthesis options.

Public Health
Dr. Lynn Woodhouse, M.P.H. Coordinator (570-422-3560, cwoodhouse@po-box.esu.edu). Master of Public Health: concentration in community health education. Program accredited by the Council on Education for Public Health. Internship option.

Reading
Dr. Jesse Moore, Department Chair and Graduate Program Coordinator (570-422-3751, jmoore@po-box.esu.edu). Master of Education: major in reading includes certification as a reading specialist. Certification as reading specialist also available without the M.Ed.

Secondary Education
Dr. Kathleen Foster, Graduate Program Coordinator (570-422-3373, kfoster@po-box.esu.edu). Master of Education: area of concentration required. Extended study option with comprehensive exam or research problem option available. Principal certification program for elementary and/or secondary. Cooperative doctoral program/superintendent's letter of eligibility with Temple University. Teacher intern program for college graduates to enter teaching profession in a secondary school of Pennsylvania.

Special Education
Dr. Teri Burcroff, Graduate Program Coordinator (570-422-3559, tburcroff@po-box.esu.edu). Master of Education: major in special education. Thirty-six-credit or thesis program option for holders of special education teaching certificate. Nonspecial education certified 36-credit or 31-credit research options available. Special education supervisor advanced certificate also available. Behavioral Analysis certificate.

Speech Pathology and Audiology
Dr. Jane Page, Graduate Program Coordinator (570-422-3684, jpage@po-box.esu.edu). Master of Science: major in speech-language pathology. Forty-two credits and appropriate clinical practicum and comprehensive examination.

Sports Management
Dr. Robert Fleischman, Graduate Coordinator (570-422-3316, rfleischman@po-box.esu.edu).

ETSU
East Tennessee State University

EAST TENNESSEE STATE UNIVERSITY

School of Graduate Studies

Programs of Study

The East Tennessee State University (ETSU) School of Graduate Studies offers almost 100 different program choices, including thirty master's degree programs (with many concentrations), twelve certificate programs, and eight doctoral programs. Graduate certificates are offered in archival studies, biostatistics, business administration, economic development, emerging technologies, entrepreneurial leadership, epidemiology, gerontology, health-care management, nursing, teaching English as a second language, and urban planning. Doctoral programs include the Au.D. in audiology, the Ph.D. in biomedical sciences, the Ed.D. in educational leadership and policy analysis, the Ph.D. in environmental health, the D.S.N. in nursing, the D.P.T. in physical therapy, the Ph.D. in clinical psychology, and the D.P.H. in public health. Beginning in the spring of 2007, ETSU's College of Pharmacy will offer the Pharm.D. In addition, the M.D. is offered through the James H. Quillen College of Medicine, recognized by national publications for its programs in rural, family, and primary-care medicine.

Research Facilities

The $28-million Sherrod Library, which opened in spring 1999, has 192,000 square feet, can hold 800,000 volumes, seats 1,800 students, has multiple computer stations, and houses 420 individual study carrels, including a limited number of private rooms for students who are working on theses or dissertations, all of which are network accessible. Twenty-five laptop computers are available for in-library use and 4-hour checkout. Four public microcomputer labs contain 160 PCs and twenty-six Macs, all of which provide access to the campus e-mail server, the Internet, and the library online catalog system. More than 700 terminals and nine open computer labs are also provided for student use. A large number of other departmental and dedicated labs and multimedia classrooms meet specialized needs of individual programs. The Archives of Appalachia and the law collection in Sherrod Library provide access to political, social, historical, and cultural records of the southern Appalachian Mountains.

Financial Aid

In addition to the wide range of private and federal aid offerings, ETSU has approximately 600 graduate assistantships and tuition scholarships. Graduate assistants are required to work 20 hours weekly in teaching, research, or administrative roles. Their stipends, which are set by individual programs, begin at $6000 (for a nine-month contract), and there is also in-state and out-of-state tuition remission. Tuition scholars are required to work 8 hours weekly for full-tuition remission, both in state and out of state. In addition to departmental assignments, assistantships and tuition scholarships are also available in nonacademic departments across the campus, such as University Housing, Sherrod Library, and various administrative offices. For information regarding all types of financial aid, students should visit the ETSU Web site at http://www.etsu.edu/gradstud/gasch/.

Cost of Study

For 2006–07, residential graduate students paid $280 per semester hour, which did not exceed $2659 per semester. Nonresident graduate students paid out-of-state tuition of $421 per semester hour, which did not exceed $4532.50 per semester. Graduate assistants and tuition scholars receive remission of graduate tuition. Additional fees, such as student activity and general access fees, are not included in the tuition rates listed. Prospective students can find a schedule of tuition and fees at http://www.etsu.edu/comptrol/bursar.htm.

Living and Housing Costs

For single students, residence halls (double occupancy) were available at costs ranging from $1136 to $1604 per semester in 2006–07; a furnished efficiency for single graduate students was $1461 per semester. BucRidge Apartments, Phase I, is a 300-bed apartment complex that offers 25 four-bedroom, two-bath units and 100 two-bedroom, two-bath apartments. BucRidge Apartments, Phase II, is a 112-bed apartment complex that offers 56 two-bedroom, two-bath apartments; all rooms are fully furnished with kitchens and washers and dryers, have common living rooms and balconies or patios, and have telephone, TV, and data jacks in each bedroom and living room. A clubhouse and recreational facilities are available to all occupants. Rent is variable, depending on occupancy and terms of lease.

Student Group

In fall 2006, more than 12,000 students were enrolled. Graduate students accounted for about 2,400 of that total.

Location

The main campus is located in Johnson City, 100 miles northeast of Knoxville, near the state lines of Virginia, Kentucky, West Virginia, North Carolina, and South Carolina. The University has locations in Kingsport, Bristol, Elizabethton, and Greeneville. With a population of more than 482,930, the Tri-Cities Tennessee/Virginia area is the nation's only region to be designated an All America City. Conveniently situated just a few miles off Interstates 81 and 26, ETSU is easily accessible by automobile and is served by Tri-Cities Regional Airport. The campus has more than 350 tree-shaded acres and more than sixty buildings. Recreational opportunities include biking, boating, climbing, fishing, golf, hiking, jogging, skiing (snow and water), tennis, and white-water rafting. This region provides tenancy to six major area hospitals affiliated with the University in various capacities, including the adjacent James H. Quillen Veterans Affairs Medical Center. The University's Division of Health Sciences (Medicine, Nursing, and Public and Allied Health) and the regional med-tech community make up the only center for health sciences between Knoxville and Roanoke, Virginia.

The University

Founded in 1911, ETSU is one of six state universities governed by the Tennessee Board of Regents (TBR) system, the largest higher-education system in Tennessee and the sixth-largest in the nation, providing programs to more than 180,000 students in ninety of Tennessee's ninety-five counties. Accredited by the Commission on Colleges of the Southern Association of Colleges and Schools, ETSU has seven colleges and two schools: the Colleges of Arts and Sciences, Business and Technology, Education, Medicine, Nursing, Pharmacy, and Public and Allied Health and the Schools of Continuing Studies and Graduate Studies. ETSU leads all TBR schools in the number of interactive television courses and leads the senior TBR institutions in Web-based instruction and in overall distance education course. ETSU offers a wide range of evening and online courses that support students who work full-time. Unique offerings include ETSU's internationally acclaimed advanced visualization computer animation, a 3-D design program housed in the Scott M. Niswonger Digital Media Center. ETSU is large enough to offer many choices in programs and activities but small enough to avoid the intimidation and anonymity of a larger university.

Applying

Application for admission to graduate study is open to any person with a bachelor's degree from a regionally accredited institution. All domestic application materials should be filed with the School of Graduate Studies at least six weeks prior to the semester in which the applicant plans to enroll. International applications must be received twelve weeks prior to the expected date of enrollment. Application forms are available online at http://www.etsu.edu/gradstud. Students can request a paper application by e-mail or by writing to the University's address. The current application fee is $25 for U.S. residents and $35 for international students.

Correspondence and Information

School of Graduate Studies
Box 70720
East Tennessee State University
Johnson City, Tennessee 37614-1710

Phone: 423-439-4221
E-mail: gradsch@etsu.edu
Web site: http://www.etsu.edu/gradstud

PROGRAM CONTACTS

Listed below are the graduate school administration and the graduate coordinators of the various programs with the graduate degree(s) available in each area.

Graduate School Administration
Wesley Brown, Dean, School of Graduate Studies and Vice Provost Academic Affairs (423-439-4431)

Cecilia McIntosh, Assistant Dean (423-439-6147)
Jeffrey Powers-Beck, Associate Dean (423-439-8638)
Wayne Gillespie, Assistant Dean (423-439-4707)
Queen Brown, Office Manager (423-439-6146)
David Moore, Admissions Counselor/Recruiter (423-439-6149)

College of Arts and Sciences
Gordon Anderson, Dean

Art (M.A., M.F.A.): Don Davis (423-439-7864)
Biology (M.S.): Hugh Miller (423-439-6919)
Chemistry (M.S.): Chu-Ngi Ho (423-439-6914)
Communication, Professional (M.A.): Jack Mooney (423-439-4168)
Criminal Justice and Criminology (M.A.): John Whitehead (423-439-5604)
English (M.A.): Robert Sawyer (423-439-6670)
History (M.A.): Dale Schmitt (423-439-6698)
Mathematical Sciences (M.A.): Robert Gardner (423-439-6977)
Microbiology (M.S.): Michael Trent (423-439-6293)
Psychology (M.A.):
  Clinical: Jon Ellis (423-439-6658)
  General: Russell Brown (423-439-5863)
Social Work (M.S.W.): Helene Halvorson (423-439-6006)
Sociology and Anthropology (M.A.): Leslie McCallister (423-439-4370)
Teaching English as a Second Language Certificate: Teresa McGarry (423-439-5995)

College of Business and Technology
Linda R. Garceau, Dean

Accountancy (M.Acc.): Gary Burkette (423-439-5314)
Business Administration Certificate: Martha Pointer (423-439-5314)
Clinical Nutrition (M.S.): Beth Lowe (423-439-7537)
Computer and Information Sciences (M.S.): Martin Barrett (423-439-7409); Phil Pfeiffer (423-439-5355)
Economic Development Certificate: Paul Trogen (423-439-6631)
Entrepreneurial Leadership Certificate: Andrew Czuchry (423-439-5314)
Master of Business Administration (M.B.A.): W. F. Mackara (423-439-5314)
Public Administration (M.P.M. and M.C.M.): Paul Trogen (423-439-6631)
Urban Planning Certificate: Paul Trogen (423-439-6631)

College of Education
Hal Knight, Dean

Counseling (M.A.): Clifton Mitchell (423-439-4197)
Early Childhood Education (M.A., M.Ed.): Laurelle Phillips (423-439-7903)
Educational Leadership and Policy Analysis (M.Ed., Ed.S., Ed.D): Louise MacKay (423-439-7615); Nancy McMurray (423-439-7619); Jasmine Renner (423-439-7629)
Educational Media and Educational Technology (M.Ed.): Lee Daniels (423-439-7843); Linda Turnbo (423-439-7851)
Elementary Education (M.Ed.): Leslie Perry (423-439-7602)
Elementary and Secondary Education (M.A.T.): Rhona Cummings (423-439-7588)
Exercise Physiology and Performance: Mike Stone (423-439-5796)
K–12 Physical Education: Diana Mozen (423-439-6157)
Reading Education (M.A., M.Ed.): Jane Melendez (423-439-7910)
Secondary Education (M.Ed.): Jean Shepherd Hamm (423-439-7595)
Special Education (M.Ed.): James Fox (423-439-7556)
Sports Management: Kevin Burke (423-439-4362)
Storytelling (M.A., M.Ed.): Joseph Sobol (423-439-7863)

College of Nursing
Patricia Smith, Dean

Advanced Nurse Practitioner Certificate: Jo-Ann Marrs (423-439-4624)
Nursing (M.S.N., D.S.N.): Jo-Ann Marrs (423-439-4624)
RODP (Regents Online Degree Program): Gail Gerding (423-439-4057)

College of Pharmacy
Dr. Larry D. Calhoun, Dean

Pharmacy (Pharm.D.): Alok Agrawal (423-439-6336)

College of Public and Allied Health
Randolph Wykoff, Dean

Allied Health (M.S.): Ester Verhovsek (423-547-0235)
Audiology (Au.D.): Marc Fagelson (423-439-4583)
Environmental Health (M.S.E.H.): Kurt Maier (423-439-7635)
Epidemiology Certificate: James Florence (423-439-6720)
Gerontology Certificate: James Florence (423-439-6720)
Health Care Management Certificate: Cynthia Taylor (423-439-8593)
Physical Therapy (D.P.T.): Dave Arnall (423-439-8787); Susan Epps (423-439-8275)
Public Health (M.P.H.): James Florence (423-439-6720)
Speech Pathology (M.S.): Kerry Proctor-Williams (423-439-7187)

James H. Quillen College of Medicine
Ronald Franks, Dean of Medicine and Vice President for Health Affairs

Biomedical Sciences (M.S., Ph.D.)
  Mitchell Robinson, Assistant Dean (423-439-2028)
  Anatomy and Cell Biology: Dennis DeFoe (423-439-2010)
  Biochemistry: Yue Zou (423-439-2124)
  Microbiology: Michael Stephen Trent (423-439-6293)
  Pharmacology: Alok Agrawal (423-439-6336)
  Physiology: Tom Ecay (423-439-2046)

School of Continuing Studies
Norma McRae, Dean

Archival Studies Graduate Certificate: Marie Tedesco (423-439-5792)
Liberal Studies (M.A.L.S.): Marie Tedesco (423-439-5792)
Professional Studies (M.A.P.S.): Jo Lobertini (423-439-4223)

EMORY UNIVERSITY

Graduate School

EMORY
GRADUATE
SCHOOL

Programs of Study

The Graduate School at Emory University offers the Master of Arts (M.A.) in educational studies, film studies, Jewish studies, music, and sacred music; the Master of Science (M.S.) in biostatistics, computer science, and mathematics; and the Master of Science in Clinical Research (MSCR) for physicians or Ph.D.'s in health-related sciences. Professional degrees awarded are the Master of Education (M.Ed.) and Master of Arts in Teaching (M.A.T.). A Diploma for Advanced Study in Teaching is also available.

The Doctor of Philosophy (Ph.D.) is offered in anthropology, art history, behavioral sciences and health education, biological and biomedical sciences, biomedical engineering, biostatistics, business, chemistry, comparative literature, computer science and informatics, economics, educational studies, English, epidemiology, French, health sciences research and health policy, history, liberal arts, mathematics, nursing, philosophy, physics, political science, psychology, religion, sociology, Spanish, and women's studies.

Programs within the Graduate Division of Biological and Biomedical Sciences include biochemistry, cell and developmental biology, genetics and molecular biology, immunology and molecular pathogenesis, microbiology and molecular genetics, molecular and systems pharmacology, neuroscience, nutrition and health sciences, and population biology, ecology, and evolution. A six-year Medical Scientist Program leads to a combined M.D./Ph.D. Programs in psychology include clinical psychology, cognitive and developmental psychology, and neuroscience and animal behavior. Courses of study within the Graduate Division of Religion include ethics and society; Hebrew Bible; historical studies in theology and religion; New Testament; person, community, and religious practices; theological studies; West and South Asian religion; and the J.D./Ph.D. program. The program in biomedical engineering is offered jointly with the Georgia Institute of Technology.

M.A. and M.S. degrees require a minimum of two semesters of residence; M.Ed. and M.A.T. degrees and the diploma require at least three semesters of residence; and the Ph.D. degree requires a minimum of four semesters of residence.

Research Facilities

Holdings of the five Emory libraries (Health Sciences Library, Law Library, Oxford College Library, Theology Library, and the General Libraries, made up of the Woodruff, Candler, Chemistry, and Math and Science Libraries) total approximately 2.7 million volumes. The libraries also offer access to thousands of electronic information resources. The Center for Library and Information Resources provides an integrated service environment that brings together technology and media specialists with librarians in a facility that includes an information commons, electronic classrooms, a distance learning classroom, the Center for Interactive Teaching, a state-of-the-art language lab and classrooms, the new high-tech Heilbrun Music and Media Library, the Electronic Services Data Center, group study rooms, and comfortable study spaces with data connections as well as wireless access throughout the building. The Special Collections and Archives Division of Woodruff Library contains modern literary manuscript archives, notable African-American collections, and other major archival and manuscript holdings.

Facilities in the biomedical sciences include a large number of specialized laboratories as well as the opportunities associated with a number of affiliated or adjacent research institutions: the Robert W. Woodruff Health Sciences Center, the Winship Cancer Institute, the Yerkes National Primate Research Center, the Emory Vaccine Center, the U.S. Centers for Disease Control and Prevention, and the American Cancer Society.

Additional facilities include the Information Technology Division and the Michael C. Carlos Museum. The Carter Center of Emory University provides resources for the study of national and international policy issues.

Financial Aid

All Emory University graduate fellowships are based on academic merit. They provide stipend and tuition scholarships for five years. All applications are due by January 3. Some programs have earlier deadlines; prospective students should check with the program. Tuition assistance grants are awarded to some teachers who are admitted to master's programs in the Division of Educational Studies. Information regarding extra-University financial aid (loans, work-study, or veterans' benefits) may be obtained from the Financial Aid Office.

Cost of Study

In 2007–08, full-time tuition is $15,400 (12 semester hours or more); the computing fee is $50 per semester; and the student activity and recreation fee is $188 per semester. Students must either join the Emory student health insurance plan, which costs $1896 per year, or demonstrate equivalent coverage under another policy. Many scholarships include a health insurance subsidy.

Living and Housing Costs

A variety of on- and off-campus housing is available. On-campus housing includes the Graduate Residential Center, which is located in a five-story complex, with one-, two-, and three-bedroom furnished and unfurnished (except three-bedroom) apartments. The apartments have central heat and air-conditioning and are equipped with a full kitchen, washer and dryer units, and full bathrooms (one per bedroom). All utilities are included in the rental price.

Student Group

Total University enrollment is more than 12,000. In fall 2006, total enrollment in degree programs in the Graduate School of Arts and Sciences was 1,626: 653 men and 973 women. Six percent were international students, and 90 percent of the students received merit awards.

Location

Emory University's wooded campus is located in an attractive residential section of Atlanta. Easily accessible by bus and metro from Emory, downtown Atlanta provides an exciting, progressive atmosphere with many recreational and cultural activities, often with reduced rates for students. Increased attention is being paid to the city's past and its historical development and the revitalization of the downtown area. With a population of 3 million, Atlanta is relatively close to the Appalachian Mountains, the Atlantic coast, and the Gulf coast.

The University

Founded by the Methodist Church in 1836, Emory received its university charter in 1915 and moved from Oxford, Georgia, to the northeast Atlanta campus. The University comprises the Graduate School, Emory College, Oxford College, and the schools of business, law, medicine, nursing, public health, and theology. The Graduate School was organized as a division of the University in 1919. Extracurricular activities are plentiful.

Applying

Minimum requirements for admission include a baccalaureate degree from an accredited four-year college, an undergraduate academic average of C, an academic average of B for the last two undergraduate years, and satisfactory scores on the General Test of the GRE. Applicants are considered without regard to race, color, national origin, religion, sex, sexual orientation, age, handicap, or veteran status. Applicants may apply online at http://www.emory.edu/GSOAS/. Applications are due by January 3. Some programs have earlier deadlines; students should check with the program.

Correspondence and Information

Emory University Graduate School
200 Candler Library
550 Asbury Circle
Atlanta, Georgia 30322

Phone: 404-727-6028
E-mail: gradschool-l@listserv.cc.emory.edu
Web site: http://www.emory.edu/GSOAS/

DIRECTORS OF GRADUATE STUDY AND THEIR RESEARCH

Anthropology: Patricia L. Whitten, Director of Graduate Studies; Ph.D., Harvard, 1982. Behavioral endocrinology, plant estrogens, reproductive ecology, diet and behavior, endocrine disruptors.

Art History: Eric R. Varner, Director of Graduate Studies; Ph.D., Yale, 1993. Roman portrait sculpture, Imperial iconography, Roman women, monuments and topography of ancient Rome.

Behavioral Sciences and Health Education: Gina Wingood, Sc.D., Harvard, 1995. Designing, implementing, and evaluating HIV prevention programs for many subpopulations of women, including female adolescents, young adult women, and heterosexual couples.

Biochemistry, Cell and Developmental Biology: Charles Saxe, Director of Graduate Studies; Ph.D., Arizona, 1980. G-protein-coupled receptor-mediated signal transduction and its role(s) in development.

Biological/Biomedical Sciences: Keith D. Wilkinson, Director; Ph.D., Michigan, 1977. Mechanism and regulation of protein synthesis and degradation.

Biomedical Engineering: Stephen P. DeWeerth, Associate Chair and Director of Graduate Studies; Ph.D., Caltech, 1991. Neuromorphic engineering, hybrid neural microsystems, modeling of biological sensorimotor systems, analog VLSI circuit design, nonlinear dynamical systems, distance learning and remote laboratories.

Biostatistics: Robert H. Lyles, Director of Graduate Studies; Ph.D., North Carolina, 1996. Adjustment methods for multiplicative measurement error in multiple linear regression, with applications in occupational epidemiology.

Business: Grace Pownall, Director of Doctoral Studies; Ph.D., Chicago, 1985. Information and global capital markets, voluntary disclosure incentives and practices, international accounting.

Chemistry: Tim Lian, Director of Graduate Studies; Ph.D., Pennsylvania, 1993. Electron transfer in nanomaterials, molecular solar cell, ultrafast dynamics in solid/liquid interface, physical chemistry of biological molecules.

Clinical Research: John R. Boring, Co-director; Ph.D., Florida, 1961. Infectious disease epidemiology, molecular microbiology.

Comparative Literature: Max Aue, Director of Graduate Studies; Ph.D., Stanford, 1973. German Modernism, Fin de siècle Vienna, the experimental novel, Romanticism.

Economics: Maria Arbatskaya, Director of Graduate Studies; Ph.D., Indiana, 1999. Industrial organization, applied game theory.

Educational Studies: Robert J. Jensen, Director of Graduate Studies; Ed.D., Georgia. Nonroutine problem solving and problem posing, mathematical thinking processes, integrating technology in the teaching of mathematics, the teaching and learning of algebra.

English: Michael A. Elliott, Director of Graduate Studies; Ph.D., Columbia, 1998. Literature and culture of the United States from the mid-nineteenth to early twentieth century, contemporary Native American literatures.

Epidemiology: Carolyn Drews-Botsch, Director of Graduate Studies; Ph.D., UCLA, 1988. Reproductive and ophthalmic epidemiology, methods.

Film Studies: Matthew Bernstein, Director of Graduate Studies; Ph.D., Wisconsin, 1987. History of American cinema, the American film industry, film research methods, film reception studies, African Americans in film, documentary film, Japanese cinema, postwar European cinema.

French: Valérie Loichot, Director of Graduate Studies; Ph.D., LSU, 1996. Twentieth-century French and Francophone literature and culture, Caribbean literature, postcolonial theory.

Genetics and Molecular Biology: Andreas Fritz, Director of Graduate Studies; Ph.D., Basel (Switzerland), 1988. Molecular and genetic mechanisms of the early patterning of the nervous system and segmentation of the mesoderm.

Health Services Research and Health Policy: David H. Howard, Director of Graduate Studies; Ph.D., Harvard, 2000. Differences in chronic disease rate between the U.S. and Europe, impact of poor health on receipt of cancer screening tests, waiting time as a price for deceased donor transplants.

History: Jonathan Prude, Director of Graduate Studies; Ph.D., Harvard, 1976. Nineteenth-century American social, labor, and cultural history; relations between culture and class during the "long" nineteenth century stretching from the founding of the United States to the early 1900s.

Immunology and Molecular Pathogenesis: Brian D. Evavold, Director of Graduate Studies; Ph.D., Chicago, 1989. T-cell activation, antigen recognition, EAE autoimmunity model, role of SHP-1 phosphatase in T-cell responses.

Institute of the Liberal Arts: Kevin Corrigan, Director of Graduate Studies; Ph.D., Dalhousie, 1980. Classics, philosophy, religion, patristics, literature, theory.

Jewish Studies: Eric Goldstein, Director of Graduate Studies; Ph.D., Michigan, 2000. Modern Jewish history, American Jewish history and culture, American social and cultural history.

Mathematics and Computer Science: James Nagy, Director of Graduate Studies; Ph.D., North Carolina State, 1991. Numerical linear algebra, scientific computation, numerical solution to ill-posed problems, image restoration and reconstruction.

M.D./Ph.D. Program: Allan I. Levey, Director; Ph.D., 1982, M.D., 1984, Chicago. Alzheimer's disease, Parkinson's disease, translational research in neurology, ApoE receptor LR11 in Alzheimer's etiopathogenesis, molecular analysis of presynaptic choline transporters.

Microbiology and Molecular Genetics: Tony Romeo, Director of Graduate Studies; Ph.D., Florida, 1986. Regulation of bacterial physiology and biofilm development, posttranscriptional regulatory mechanisms.

Molecular and Systems Pharmacology: John R. Hepler, Director of Graduate Studies; Ph.D., North Carolina, 1988. Cellular roles and regulation of novel signaling proteins/pathways used by neurotransmitters.

Music: Lynn Wood Bertrand, Director of Graduate Studies; Ph.D., Cincinnati, 1978. Contemporary Passion music.

Neuroscience: Larry J. Young, Director of Graduate Studies; Ph.D., Texas, 1994. Role of neuropeptide and neuropeptide receptor gene expression and social behavior in a variety of mammalian species.

Nursing: Kenneth Hepburn, Director of Graduate Studies; Ph.D., Washington (Seattle), 1968. Aging and geriatric medicine, family practice and community health.

Nutrition and Health Sciences: Lou Ann Brown, Director of Graduate Studies; Ph.D., Saint Louis, 1980. Impact of alcoholism (adult and fetal) on pulmonary oxidant injury.

Philosophy: Steven K. Strange, Director of Graduate Studies; Ph.D., Texas at Austin, 1981. Ancient philosophy, especially Platonism and Hellenistic philosophy, the history of Platonism, and the history of ethics.

Physics: Kurt Warncke, Director of Graduate Studies; Ph.D., Pennsylvania, 1990. Experimental biophysics.

Political Science: Clifford J. Carrubba, Director of Graduate Studies; Ph.D., Stanford, 1998. Legislative behavior and roll call vote analysis, the design and change of judicial institutions (with application to the European Court of Justice), statistical tests of game theoretic models.

Population Biology, Ecology, and Evolution: Mike Zwick, Director of Graduate Studies; Ph.D., California, 1998. Developing and applying a genomics-based framework to identify the genetic variation underlying phenotypic variation in organisms, autism susceptibility genes, *Drosophila* genomes, and rapid resequencing and characterization of biodefense pathogens.

Psychology: Lynne Nygaard, Director of Graduate Studies; Ph.D., Brown, 1991. Auditory imagery during reading, perceptual learning of voice and accent, emotional prosody and meaning.

Religion: Elizabeth M. Bounds, Director of Graduate Studies; Ph.D., Union Theological Seminary (New York), 1994. Communal dimensions of church and civil society, feminist and liberation ethics, the public voice of religion, transformative pedagogical practices.

Sociology: Irene Brown, Director of Graduate Studies; Ph.D., Yale, 1991. Gender, race/ethnicity, and inequality in urban labor markets.

Spanish: Maria M. Carrion, Chair; Ph.D., Yale. Spanish literature and culture from the sixteenth and seventeenth centuries, dramatic theory and performance, legal history and architectural theory and history, literature and culture of the Hispanic Caribbean.

Women's Studies: Lynne Huffer, Director of Graduate Studies; Ph.D., Michigan, 1989. Queer theory; gay, lesbian, bisexual, and transgender studies; modern French and Francophone literature; literary theory; ethics.

EMPORIA STATE UNIVERSITY

Graduate Studies

Programs of Study

Emporia State University (ESU) offers courses leading to the Master of Arts in biology, English, history, and teaching of English as a second language (TESOL). The Master of Science is offered in art therapy; biology; business education; clinical psychology; counselor education (school counseling); curriculum and instruction (pre-K–12 curriculum leadership, pre-K–12 effective practitioner, pre-K–12 national board certification); early childhood education; educational administration; health, physical education, and recreation; instructional design and technology; master teacher studies (elementary subject matter, reading specialist); mathematics; mental health counseling; physical sciences (chemistry, earth science, physical sciences, physics); psychology; rehabilitation counseling; school psychology; and special education. The Master of Arts in Teaching is offered in social sciences. The University also offers Master of Business Administration (accounting, general, information systems), Master of Legal Information Management, Master of Library Science, and Master of Music degree programs.

The Specialist in Education (Ed.S.) degree is offered in school psychology, and the Ph.D. is offered in library and information management.

The University conducts an academic year of two semesters plus a nine-week summer session in which graduate courses are offered in every field.

The University is accredited by the North Central Association of Colleges and Schools and is a member of the Council of Graduate Schools in the United States. Its programs are recognized by the AACSB International–The Association to Advance Collegiate Schools of Business, the American Chemical Society, and the National Association of Schools of Music and accredited by the National Council for Accreditation of Teacher Education, the American Library Association, the American Art Therapy Association, the Council on Rehabilitative Education, the Kansas State Department of Education, and the Council for Accreditation of Counseling and Related Educational Programs (CACREP).

Research Facilities

The William Allen White Library contains more than 1 million books, government documents, periodicals, theses, and nonprint materials. The library provides online access to a large number of bibliographic, full-text, and full-image databases. Other resources are available via the Internet at public access computers located in the library, via Web access through the home page, or through a proxy service for distance education students. Materials not available at ESU can be requested from other libraries throughout the world by utilizing the interlibrary loans service. Other key library resources are the Special Collections Department, located in White Library, and the University Archives, located in Anderson Library on the west campus.

The Departments of Biological Sciences and Physical Sciences have the Jones Biotechnology Laboratories and the Jones Environmental Chemistry Laboratories, with state-of-the-art equipment. The University operates four natural areas for biological research in tall grass prairie, upland and deciduous forest, and marshland. The Department of Psychology and Special Education has a state-of-the-art research laboratory for students and faculty members. The Department of Counselor Education and Rehabilitation Programs supports a state-of-the-art counseling clinic for training students and providing service to the community.

Financial Aid

Most departments offering graduate work, as well as numerous other units within the University, award graduate assistantships. During the academic year, the University employs at least 185 graduate assistants. To qualify for an assistantship, an applicant must have a minimum overall grade point average of 2.5 for four years or 2.75 for the last two years of undergraduate study, based on a 4.0 scale. Students may be eligible for tuition reductions during each term in which they hold an assistantship appointment. Nonresident full-time graduate assistants are assessed fees at the same rate as residents of Kansas.

Cost of Study

In 2006–07, fees for a full graduate course load were estimated at $2244 per semester for state residents and $5724 per semester for nonresidents. For the summer session, resident fees are $187 per credit hour, and nonresident fees are $477 per credit hour. Fees are subject to change by action of the Board of Regents.

Living and Housing Costs

The Department of Residential Life offers graduate students a number of cost-effective living arrangements. On-campus apartments rent for $258 per month (utilities included). The apartment complex five blocks east of campus features one- and two-bedroom units that rent for $525 to $862 per month, depending on furnishings. Students can contact the department by telephone at 620-341-5264 or by e-mail (reslife@emporia.edu) for more information.

Student Group

The total on-campus enrollment is 6,473, with 264 full-time and 1,751 part-time graduate students. About 30 percent of the full-time graduate students receive financial assistance of some kind; 6 percent are international students. In 2006, four Ed.S. degrees, 560 master's degrees, and two Ph.D. degrees were conferred.

Student Outcomes

Approximately 60 percent of the graduates find employment in their major fields of study within the state of Kansas, 29 percent of the graduates are employed in their major field of study outside the state of Kansas, 2 percent find employment outside their major field of study, 5 percent continue their education, and 4 percent are unemployed.

Location

Emporia, with a population of more than 26,000, is an educational, industrial, trade, and medical center serving 60,000 people in east-central Kansas. It is situated on the eastern edge of the famous Bluestem region of the Flint Hills and is surrounded by numerous lakes and recreational facilities. The city is located on the Kansas Turnpike, Interstate Highway 35. Three major metropolitan areas of the state—Topeka, Kansas City, and Wichita—are within 100 miles.

The University

The University, founded in 1863, has a long, diverse, and exciting history, which is reflected in its twenty-three different graduate programs in teaching, library science and information management, business, and liberal arts and sciences. Although all programs are of high quality, the University is particularly well known for its teacher education and library and information management programs. At ESU, small class sizes are the norm.

Applying

Applications for admission to the Graduate School should be made thirty days before the first day of an enrollment period. Some academic departments have earlier deadlines. For admission as a master's degree student, an applicant must have a minimum grade point average of 2.5 in the last 60 hours of undergraduate study. Applicants for the M.A. in English and the M.S. in special education must have at least a 2.75 grade point average or at least a 3.0 in the major. Applicants for the Specialist in Education degree must hold a master's degree from an accredited college or university with grades of B or better in three fourths of the credit hours taken for the degree. Applicants for the M.S. in psychology, school psychology, or art therapy must have a cumulative grade point average of at least 3.0 or at least 3.25 for the last 60 hours of an undergraduate program. Applicants for the M.A. in history must have a 3.0 GPA in 12 hours of history.

Correspondence and Information

Graduate Studies and Research
Campus Box 4003
Emporia State University
Emporia, Kansas 66801-5087

Phone: 620-341-5403
800-950-GRAD (toll-free)
Fax: 620-341-5909
E-mail: gradinfo@emporia.edu
Web site: http://www.emporia.edu/grad

FACULTY HEADS

The following list shows specializations, research, and/or exhibits of the faculty within each graduate program and the chair or graduate adviser of each department.

Biological Sciences (M.S., M.A.): Scott Crupper, Ph.D., Coordinator of Graduate Studies. Animal and plant ecology, animal behavior, cellular and molecular biology, ecology and physiology of grassland plants, endocrinology, entomology, environmental biochemistry and physiology, evolutionary biology, fisheries and wildlife management, ichthyology, immunology, invertebrate and vertebrate zoology, mammalogy, microbiology, ornithology, population and molecular genetics, plant and animal anatomy/physiology, plant and animal taxonomy/systematics, biology education, soil science, virology.

Business (M.B.A., M.S. in business education): Robert Hite, Ph.D., Dean. M.B.A. faculty research interests include accounting, computer information systems, finance, economics, international business, management, and marketing. The research interests of faculty members teaching in the Master of Science in business education program include business teacher education and vocational education.

Counselor Education and Rehabilitation Programs (M.S.): Patricia Neufeld, Ph.D., Chair. K–12 school counseling, rehabilitation counseling, student personnel services in higher education.

Early Childhood/Elementary Teacher Education (M.S.): Jean Morrow, Ph.D., Chair. Master teacher (elementary subject matter, reading specialist), early childhood education, postbaccalaureate teacher certification. Faculty specializations include authentic assessment, cooperative learning, curriculum integration, Reading Recovery, inclusion, and multicultural education. Distance learning is available for many courses in all programs.

English (M.A.): Mel Storm, Ph.D., Director of Graduate Studies. Emphases include rhetoric and composition, creative writing, and English and American literatures. Courses for in-service teachers and for those who wish to pursue careers in community college teaching are also available. Dual master's degrees are offered with the School of Library and Information Management. Faculty specializations include medieval literature and language, Renaissance literature, eighteenth- and nineteenth-century British literature, nineteenth-century American literature, twentieth-century American literature, contemporary literature, world literature, women's studies, American studies, young adult fiction, English education, creative writing, folklore, popular culture, gender and ethnic studies, critical theory, rhetoric and composition, linguistics, and journalism.

Health, Physical Education, and Recreation (M.S.): Kathy Ermler, Ed.D., Chair. Pedagogy, exercise physiology, technology in health and physical education, sports ethics, administration, psychology of sport and physical education, motor behavior, health promotion and health education. The entire Master of Science in physical education may be completed through the Internet.

History (M.A.): Deborah Gerish, Ph.D., Coordinator. World history (cultural, religious, and intellectual history of medieval and early modern Europe; military and political history of modern Germany, France, Russia, Eastern Europe), U.S. history (Native American cultures, colonial history, nineteenth-century U.S., political history of the South, women's history, twentieth-century political history, Kansas history, public history). Dual master's degrees are offered with the School of Library and Information Management.

Instructional Design and Technology (M.S.): Marcus Childress, Ph.D., Chair. Instructional design and technology. A number of courses are offered via the Internet (http://idt.emporia.edu).

Library and Information Management (M.L.S., Ph.D.): Robert Grover, Ph.D., Interim Dean. Analysis of information services and delivery systems, community analysis, economics of information, information brokering, information management, information transfer, library and information science education, management of library and information systems, organization and retrieval of information, psychology of information use, sociology of information, technology applications to information storage and retrieval. Dual master's degrees offered with the Departments of Music, History, Social Sciences, and English and the School of Business. School library media and information management certification is also available. Regional programs are offered in various locations in the western half of the country.

Mathematics (M.S.): Larry Scott, Ph.D., Chair. Applied mathematics, combinatorics, commutative algebra and field theory, computer science, functional analysis, mathematics education, numerical solutions of differential equations, optimization, probability and statistics, real and complex analysis, topology.

Music (M.M.): Marie C. Miller, Ph.D., Chair. Concentration in music education or performance. Areas of study and research include elementary and secondary music education; choral and instrumental conducting; vocal and instrumental methods and performance; jazz performance and instruction; applied studies in voice, keyboard, woodwinds, brass, strings, and percussion; music computer applications; digital audio recordings.

Physical Sciences (M.S.): DeWayne Backhus, Ph.D., Chair. Emphasis in chemistry, earth science (with an online option), physical science, or physics. All programs are designed to prepare students for additional degree work at the doctoral level, for industrial or government employment, or for teaching. Research opportunities are available in a number of areas within each discipline; NASA-funded research exists in each discipline emphasis.

Psychology and Special Education (M.S., Ed.S.): Kenneth A. Weaver, Ph.D., Chair. Clinical psychology; general and industrial/organizational psychology; mental health counseling; special education: adaptive and gifted, talented, and creative; art therapy; school psychology. Faculty specializations: teaching psychology at the secondary level; psychometrics; inclusion; assessment; neuropsychology; cognition/retrieval process; child abuse; special education attrition; behavioral toxicology, smoking, and stress; clinical applications of art; developmental psychology; psychology of gender; cheating; statistics learning; performance appraisal; control theory; language abilities; autobiographical memory; narrative development; adolescent art therapy; human resources practices in organizations; mental retardation; and autism. A number of courses are delivered via ITV, Telenet, and the Internet.

School Leadership/Middle and Secondary Teacher Education (M.S.): Jerry Will, Ph.D., Chair. Degree and certification programs in elementary and secondary school leadership (i.e., building, program, and district levels), curriculum and instruction (effective practitioner studies, national board certification, curriculum leadership), secondary education, and postbaccalaureate teacher certification. Varied courses are offered via ITV, the World Wide Web, Telenet, and ATM.

Social Sciences (M.A.T.): Darla Mallein, Ph.D., Coordinator. American history, world history, geography, political science, social studies education, anthropology, sociology.

Relaxing campus environment.

Interactive classes.

Technology in the classroom.

FAIRLEIGH DICKINSON UNIVERSITY

Graduate Studies

Programs of Study

Nearly fifty full- and part-time graduate programs are offered through Fairleigh Dickinson University's (FDU) four degree-granting colleges on its two northern New Jersey campuses. Graduate study is offered at the Maxwell Becton College of Arts and Sciences at the College at Florham; University College: Arts, Sciences, and Professional Studies and the Petrocelli College of Continuing Studies on the Metropolitan Campus, which both offer a number of programs on the College at Florham campus; and the Silberman College of Business, which offers programs accredited by AACSB International on both campuses. The majority of the University's graduate classes are scheduled during the evenings and on weekends for the convenience of working professionals. Not all programs are offered on both campuses.

Master of Science (M.S.) programs are offered in biology, chemistry (with a concentration in pharmaceutical chemistry), computer engineering, computer science, electrical engineering, electronic commerce, hospitality management studies, management information systems, medical technology, nursing (adult nurse practitioner studies with a concentration in administration or education), and systems sciences (with a concentration in environmental studies).

Master of Arts (M.A.) programs are offered in corporate and organizational communication, education for certified teachers, educational leadership, English and comparative literature, history, international studies, learning disabilities, mathematical foundations, media and professional communications, multilingual education, political science, psychology (clinical counseling, forensic, general-theoretical, industrial/organizational, organizational behavior, and school psychology), and science (with concentrations in cosmetic science, elementary science specialist studies, and science teaching specialist studies).

A Master of Fine Arts (M.F.A.) in creative writing is offered as a low-residency program, with concentrations in poetry, fiction, and creative nonfiction.

Master of Arts in Teaching (M.A.T.) programs are available in elementary education (with certification in grades K–5), English as a second language (with certification in grades K–12), and subject area certification grades K–12 in biological science, chemistry, earth science, English, mathematics, physical science, physics, social studies, and world languages.

Master of Business Administration (M.B.A.) programs are offered in entrepreneurial studies, finance, global business management, human resource management, international business, management (with concentrations in corporate communication, information systems, and management for executives and health-care and life sciences professionals), marketing, and pharmaceutical management. In addition, an M.S. in accounting and an M.S. in Taxation (M.S.T.) are offered.

Students may earn a joint M.A./M.B.A. degree in corporate and organizational communication and management and industrial psychology and human resource management.

Professional degree programs are available, such as the Master of Administrative Sciences (M.A.S.), featuring new online specializations in global security and terrorism studies, emergency management administration, and forensic administration, and a Master of Public Administration (M.P.A.), with specializations in health services administration, Jewish communal service, nursing management, public management, and global transportation studies

The University offers a nationally recognized, five-year, full-time Ph.D. program in clinical psychology that is fully accredited by the American Psychological Association. The program adheres to the scientist/practitioner model, requiring a number of clinical and research practicums in addition to an extensive classroom curriculum. A doctoral dissertation and a one-year clinical internship are required of all students. Program faculty interests include work in adult, child, and family therapy; childhood anxiety disorders; gerontology; quantitative methods; personality assessment; addictive behaviors; adult attachment processes; and gender bias. A doctoral program in school psychology leading to the Psy.D. is also available for the practicing professional.

A new Doctorate of Nursing Practice (D.N.P.) was launched in the spring of 2007. The 40-credit executive model prepares nursing professionals to be clinically expert as providers and educators. A joint-degree program leading to the Doctor of Physical Therapy (D.P.T.) is also offered in conjunction with the University of Medicine and Dentistry of New Jersey (UMDNJ).

Silberman College has educational partnerships with a growing network of international universities in Belize, Brazil, China, Costa Rica, France, Germany, Greece, India, and Monaco. Many programs offer the opportunity for students to participate in classes that incorporate a short-term study-abroad experience. Students may also opt to enroll for a semester-abroad experience at select partner schools. International seminars are held at FDU's Wroxton College in England in many areas of study, including the M.F.A. and M.A. programs in English and comparative literature and corporate and organizational communications and the M.A.S. with a specialization in global leadership.

Research Facilities

FDU offers a wide range of library, computer, health-care skills, and scientific laboratory equipment on both campuses to support student and faculty member research in virtually all graduate disciplines. A new, state-of-the-art cybercrime research laboratory, funded by the U.S. Department of Justice, is located on FDU's Metropolitan Campus. In addition, the University supports the dissemination of research activities through special departmental centers and research institutes.

Financial Aid

A limited number of research, honors research, teaching, and graduate administrative fellowships are available at FDU. Some programs, such as the Master of Arts in Teaching, the Master of Arts in corporate and organizational communication, and the Master of Public Administration, offer paid internships. Eligible domestic graduate students enrolled at least half-time may borrow up to a maximum of $20,500 annually in subsidized and unsubsidized loans under the Federal Stafford Student Loan program. In addition, FDU offers students a number of attractive flexible financing programs.

Cost of Study

Tuition for most nonbusiness graduate programs in 2007–08 is $869 per credit; most graduate business programs are $893 per credit. Fees include an annual technology fee of $288 for part-time students or $608 for full-time students. Several programs, such as the M.B.A programs for executives and health-care and life sciences professionals, the M.B.A. in global management, the M.A. in psychology (with a concentration in organizational behavior for managers), and doctoral-level programs, carry an inclusive full-program fee.

Living and Housing Costs

The University currently offers only limited on-campus housing for graduate students, offered on a first-come, first-served basis. The annual costs at the Metropolitan Campus are $6420 for a standard double room and $3508 for the standard eleven-meal plan, which includes $300 in flex dollars. International students should contact the University's international student organizations for assistance in locating housing.

Student Group

There are a total of 3,527 graduate students enrolled at Fairleigh Dickinson University. The College at Florham enrolls a total of 934 graduate students, and the Metropolitan Campus enrolls 2,593 graduate students.

Location

FDU has two major campus locations in northern New Jersey. The Metropolitan Campus is located less than 10 miles from New York City among seventy-three buildings on a modern, 88-acre site in Teaneck. The College at Florham is situated in the heart of New Jersey's growing corporate center. The campus's Georgian-style buildings span 166 acres of wooded grounds on what was once a private estate. Wroxton College, the University's British campus, is located near Banbury, between Oxford and Stratford-upon-Avon, which is 75 miles from London. In fall 2007, the University began offering select undergraduate degree programs at its FDU-Vancouver location in British Columbia, Canada.

The University

Founded in 1942, FDU is New Jersey's largest private university, with more than 11,000 students. In addition to its two major northern New Jersey campuses, FDU also offers graduate studies to residents of central New Jersey through its Fort Monmouth extension center in Eatontown, and the M.A.S. program is offered at more than fifty off-site locations throughout New Jersey.

Applying

Students can apply for graduate admission for the fall, spring, or summer semester. Requirements vary from program to program, but all require a baccalaureate degree from an accredited institution. To be considered for admission, an FDU application for graduate admission and official transcripts of previous college work must be filed. In some cases, letters of recommendation may be required. Depending on the college in which admission is sought, test scores on the Graduate Record Examinations, Graduate Management Admission Test, or Praxis must be submitted.

Correspondence and Information

Metropolitan Campus
Office of Graduate Admissions
Fairleigh Dickinson University
1000 River Road, T-KB1-01
Teaneck, New Jersey 07666
Phone: 201-692-2554
Fax: 201-692-2560
E-mail: grad@fdu.edu
Web site: http://www.fdu.edu

College at Florham
Office of Graduate Admissions
Fairleigh Dickinson University
285 Madison Avenue, M-MS1-01
Madison, New Jersey 07940
Phone: 973-443-8905
Fax: 973-443-8088
E-mail: grad@fdu.edu
Web site: http://www.fdu.edu

RESEARCH AREAS

COLLEGE OF ARTS AND SCIENCES, COLLEGE AT FLORHAM

The faculty of the Maxwell Becton College of Arts and Sciences offers master's degree programs that emphasize applied research in a variety of disciplinary and interdisciplinary areas. Becton faculty members also serve as the directors or editors of a journal of student research in psychology, two professional journals (*Literary Review* and the *Atlantic Journal of Communication*), and the Fairleigh Dickinson University Press.

Arts and Humanities: digital image processing, animation, and video; literary studies, including Shakespeare, nineteenth- and twentieth-century American authors, and world literature in English; history and theory of communications; corporate and organizational communication (language and social interaction, corporate relations, and quality management); and creative writing.

Biology, Chemistry, Computer Science, and Mathematics: pharmaceutical chemistry; biomedical sciences; ecology; implementation of programming languages, computational complexity, analysis, watermarking techniques, statistics, and actuarial science; quadratic and Hermitian forms.

Psychology: gambling, risk-taking behavior, and drive reduction theory; reduction of reinforcement frequency and increases in response-force requirements as aversive unconditioned stimuli; interpersonal power as an approach to conceptualizing psychopathology; bioenergetic techniques in treating psychopathology; neuropsychology of perception and cognitive processes; the effect of mass media on interpersonal awareness; organizational psychology, including managers' perceptions of problematic employee behavior and techniques for behavioral change; problems of the visibly handicapped.

Social Sciences and History: peaceful transitions to democracy, Japanese defense policy, campaign finance reform, campaign strategies and electoral behavior, race and gender in the antebellum South, the portrayal of sexual norms in women's magazines, anthropology of law, twentieth-century intellectual history, constitutional law and American politics, child soldiers, self-society relationships in the U.S. and the Middle East, concepts of culture in the U.S. in the Middle East, globalization and culture.

PETROCELLI COLLEGE OF CONTINUING STUDIES, METROPOLITAN CAMPUS AND COLLEGE AT FLORHAM

International School of Hospitality and Tourism Management: applied research in hospitality management, including internships with the Greater Atlantic City Hotel-Motel Association and numerous research opportunities with the properties in the New York/New Jersey area.

Public Administration Institute: applied research on problems in state and local government, administrative justice, emergency planning and management, administrative science, health services management, performance evaluation, and comparative health systems.

School of Administrative Science: degree and certificate programs for working professionals in government agencies and not-for-profit organizations; new online specializations in global security and terrorism studies, emergency management studies, and computer security and forensic administration.

SILBERMAN COLLEGE OF BUSINESS, METROPOLITAN CAMPUS AND COLLEGE AT FLORHAM

The faculty of the Silberman College of Business is committed to exemplary teaching and scholarship. Research activities are an integral part of accomplishing the mission of the college. Research work, which includes textbooks, journal articles, conference papers, and presentations before professional organizations, keeps the faculty current in its fields. The college also coordinates a number of applied research projects that are conducted for major corporations, manufacturing and industrial firms, and related organizations. The knowledge and experience gained through their research activities is adopted into lecture material and shared with students. Key research areas include entrepreneurship, both corporate and small ventures; enterprise resource planning; information systems management issues; integrated marketing communications; strategic pricing; and human resource management and development.

UNIVERSITY COLLEGE: ARTS, SCIENCES, AND PROFESSIONAL STUDIES, METROPOLITAN CAMPUS

There has been a growing emphasis on original research and scholarship by the faculty members and graduate students of the University College. Seasonal affective disorder, eating problems, personality development and psychological testing are among the research projects of the clinical psychology doctoral program. American writers of the nineteenth and twentieth centuries are the focus of the English and comparative literature department, while the Peter Sammartino School of Education conducts innovative research in learning disabilities and bilingual education. Science and engineering faculty members receive research funding for work in such diverse areas as high-temperature superconductivity, underwater digital imaging enhancement, digital image transmission, and ADA computer programming language. The campus's Wiener Library contains nearly 250,000 volumes and 1,600 periodicals and includes diverse special collections. The college also offers graduate students access to a wide range of computer resources and outstanding science research equipment in its biology, chemistry, and engineering laboratories.

Arts and Humanities: origins of civilization; the Middle East and its problems; Soviet studies; constitutional law and the Supreme Court; world regions and international relations; international law and organizations; study of American playwright Lanford Wilson; the star-spangled screen; American World War II films; popular culture in twentieth-century America; handling of time in William Faulkner; film history; media effects; advertising outcomes and effects; role of culture and language education at the school level; development of bicultural instructional materials for teaching; adult development as it concerns change agents, self-esteem; leadership related to learning by children with educational handicaps; use of ESL strategies in developing standard English among black English speakers; educational and research programs in cooperation with state and local agencies and school systems, as well as with the federal Department of Education.

Behavioral and Social Sciences: clinical psychology, personality assessment, psychological consequences of exposure to toxics, obesity, factors of sexual harassment, program evaluation, quantitative methods, jury selection.

Nursing and Allied Health: critical thinking; educational technology and pedagogy; obesity and stressful life events; parenting behaviors and perceived competence, perceived health status; ethnography of community health nursing.

Science and Engineering: aquatic ecology; prokaryotic and eukaryotic metabolism; protozoan genetics and ecology; industrial applications of bacterial enzymes; biofouling of reverse osmosis membranes; hormone function, using monoclonal antibodies; multimedia applications in histology and parasitology; enzyme inhibitors; cell culture media (growth factors); natural product antimicrobial testing; development of text systems to access environmental toxicity; physical and colloid chemistry (membranes); geochemistry (carbonate chemistry of water); theoretical organic chemistry (computational methods); consumer-provided cooperation in the transit-planning process; high-resolution, far-infrared spectroscopy; infrared optics (optical properties of solids and powders); computer simulation (sociological theory in pattern evasions); computer methods in engineering and statistical applications; software reuse; management information systems; operation systems; organizational memory; optics (light-wave technology); optical communications; parallel and fault-tolerant systems; electronic commerce; pattern recognition; computer engineering; wireless and digital communications; digital signal and image processing; computer networks.

FLORIDA INSTITUTE OF TECHNOLOGY

University College
Extended Studies and Distance Learning Divisions

Programs of Study

Florida Institute of Technology (Florida Tech) is a fully accredited university currently offering the following master's degree programs through the Extended Studies Division at its various sites: Professional Master of Business Administration, Master of Public Administration, and Master of Science (acquisition and contract management, aerospace engineering, computer information systems, computer science, electrical engineering, engineering management, human resources management, logistics management, management, materiel acquisition management, mechanical engineering, operations research, project management, quality management, software engineering, space science, space systems management, and systems management).

In addition to the above degrees, the Distance Learning Division's Virtual Campus also offers the following degree programs completely online: Professional Master of Business Administration, Master of Public Administration, and Master of Science (acquisition and contract management, computer information systems, human resources management, logistics management, management, materiel acquisition management, operations research, project management, and systems management).

Research Facilities

The Florida Tech Library can be accessed by University College students through the library's Web site for supplemental research sources.

Financial Aid

A graduate student must be registered for 5 semester hours per term and be a U.S. citizen or an eligible noncitizen to qualify for federal or state financial aid. A graduate student must complete a Free Application for Federal Student Aid (FAFSA). Forms are available through the Florida Tech off-campus sites.

The Federal Stafford Student Loan Program is available to all graduate students who apply for federal assistance and who maintain at least 5 semester hours in graduate-level courses per semester. Stafford loans are either subsidized or unsubsidized.

Cost of Study

The cost of Florida Tech's courses via online access or at the off-campus sites for the academic year 2007–08 is $475 per credit hour. Fees for students include application ($50), thesis binding ($75 for five copies), transcript ($5 per copy), and equivalency or currency examination ($80). Late fees include late graduation petitions ($30 after the deadline date but before the semester of graduation or $60 during the semester of graduation) and late payment ($30).

Student Group

The typical Extended Studies or Virtual Campus student is a full-time working professional. Students who work full-time and take two courses per semester can finish their master's degree program in two years.

Student Outcomes

Graduates have gone on to work for federal, state, and local governments; Aegon Equity; BCE Teleglobe; the Boeing Company; the Center for Disease Control; Colgate-Palmolive Company; Del Monte; Double Eagle Distributing, Inc.; General Dynamics; Harris Corporation; Lockheed Martin; Motorola; NASA; National Library of Medicine; Northrop Grumman; GVC, Inc.; Raytheon Corporation; Texaco Eastern Caribbean, Ltd.; Titan Corporation; U.S. Fish and Wildlife Services; United Space Alliance; Xerox Corporation; and the four United States military branches.

Location

Florida Tech offers programs at ten U.S. sites and the Virtual Campus. The sites include Orlando, Kennedy Space Center, and Patrick Air Force Base in Florida; Alexandria, the Hampton Roads area, and Fort Lee in Virginia; Aberdeen Proving Ground and Patuxent River in Maryland; Picatinny and Lakehurst, New Jersey; and Redstone Arsenal, Alabama. For more information about each site, prospective students should visit the Institute's Web site at http://uc.fit.edu/.

The main campus is located in Melbourne, Florida, and covers more than 175 acres. Nearly 5,500 graduate and undergraduate students are enrolled in university programs.

The Institute and The School

Florida Institute of Technology was founded in 1958, primarily as a graduate school to provide advanced scientific education for engineers and scientists at the Kennedy Space Center. Florida Tech has developed rapidly into a residential university, providing both undergraduate and graduate education in science, engineering, and management. It offers Ph.D. degrees in biology, electrical engineering, management, oceanography, physics, and science education as well as M.S. degrees in applied mathematics, biology, business, computer science, electrical engineering, environmental engineering, environmental science, management, mechanical engineering, ocean engineering, oceanography, operation research, physics, and science education.

University College consists of five divisions that include Applied Research, Distance Learning, Extended Studies, Florida Tech Consulting, and Professional Development. Extended Studies began in 1972 and has grown from 42 students to 1,425 students per year enrolled in over 30 degree programs. Extended Studies programs are conducted in a very traditional manner with admissions and graduation standards the same as those required on campus. Most courses offered are taught by instructors possessing terminal degrees. Curricula and course content are tailored to meet the needs of students and their employers, while maintaining the highest possible academic quality and integrity. For further information, prospective students should visit the University College Web page.

Applying

Applicants must have a bachelor's degree from a regionally accredited institution. Applicants are evaluated for admissions purposes on the basis of their undergraduate records, with consideration given to work experience. The GMAT requirement may be waived for qualified applicants in selected programs. Applications are accepted year-round. Studies for most degree programs may begin any term. Applications may be completed online through the university's Web site.

Correspondence and Information

University College
Florida Institute of Technology
150 West University Boulevard
Melbourne, Florida 32901
Phone: 321-674-8880
Fax: 321-674-7050
Web site: http://uc.fit.edu

Mary Ellen Roy
Director of Marketing
University College
Phone: 321-674-8882
E-mail: mroy@fit.edu

Vicky W. Knerly
Senior Administrator
Virtual Campus
Phone: 912-634-6336
888-225-2239 (toll-free)
Fax: 912-634-7783
E-mail: vgc@fit.edu

Florida Institute of Technology

THE FACULTY

Rhoda Baggs, Assistant Professor of Computer Science; Ph.D., Florida Tech.
Paul Battaglia, Associate Professor of Management; D.B.A., Nova Southeastern.
Richard O. Blalack, Associate Professor of Management; D.B.A., Georgia State.
Barry A. Bodt, Assistant Professor of Management; Ph.D., Delaware.
Norman W. Chlosta, Assistant Professor; M.P.A., USC.
David. E. Clapp, Associate Professor of Management; Ph.D., Arizona State.
John R. Clark, Professor of Space Systems; Ph.D., Maryland.
David W. Clay, Instructor; M.S., Florida Tech.
Arthur F. Dickinson, Adjunct Professor of Computer Science; Ph.D., Central Florida.
Catherine A. Elder, Assistant Professor of Management; Ph.D., Virginia Commonwealth.
John B. Foulkes, Assistant Professor of Management; Ph.D., Delaware.
Vernon Gordon, Associate Professor of Aeronautical Engineering; Ph.D., Naval Postgraduate School.
Dennis J. Kulonda, Professor of Management; Ph.D., North Carolina State.
Jennifer M. Long, Assistant Professor of Electrical Engineering; Ph.D., Johns Hopkins.
Atefeh S. McCampbell, Associate Professor of Management; D.B.A., Nova Southeastern.
Lloyd H. Muller, Associate Professor of Management; Ed.D., George Washington.
David W. Mutschler, Associate Professor of Computer Information Systems; Ph.D., Temple.
Terry W. Raney, Assistant Professor; M.B.A., William and Mary; J.D., Case Western Reserve.
M. Bala Subrahmanyam, Adjunct Professor; Ph.D., Iowa.
Daniel B. Weddle, Associate Professor of Computer Sciences; Ph.D., George Washington.
Kermit C. Zieg Jr., Professor of Finance and Management; Ph.D., Ohio State.

FLORIDA INSTITUTE OF TECHNOLOGY

Graduate School

Programs of Study The Graduate School offers master's, education specialist's (Ed.S.), and doctoral degree programs. The College of Business offers the M.B.A. degree. The College of Engineering offers Ph.D. and M.S. degrees in aerospace engineering, chemical engineering, civil engineering, computer engineering, computer science, electrical engineering, environmental science, mechanical engineering, ocean engineering, and oceanography. Master's programs are also offered in computer information systems, engineering management, environmental resources management, software engineering, and systems engineering. The College of Science offers master's and doctoral degrees in applied mathematics, biological sciences, chemistry, elementary science education, mathematics education, physics, science education, and space sciences. Master's degrees are offered in applied mathematics, computer education, environmental education, math education, operations research, and teaching. The Ed.S. degree in science education is also awarded. In the College of Psychology and Liberal Arts, the School of Psychology offers the Psy.D. degree in clinical psychology, the M.S. in applied behavior analysis, and the M.S. and Ph.D. in industrial/organizational psychology. A master's degree in technical and professional communication is offered through Liberal Arts Studies. The School of Aeronautics offers a Master of Science degree in aeronautics with specializations in airport development and management and aviation safety and a Master of Science degree in aviation human factors.

Research Facilities Laboratories on campus are equipped for research in the various programs of study. These are supplemented by the Life Science Research Complex, Applied Research Laboratories, Claude Pepper Institute for Aging and Therapeutic Research, Reproductive Biology Laboratory, Center for Energy Alternatives, and aquaculture and marine research facilities at Oceanside in Vero Beach. Additional facilities include a solar energy research laboratory and laboratories for optical and solid-state physics, environmental and water pollution analysis, electromagnetics, materials testing and research, electron microscopy, and cytogenetics, as well as in numerous other areas.

The Academic and Research Computing Services (ARCS) provides graduate students with a wide range of computing resources for course work and research. These resources include a Sun Enterprise 3000 and Harris Lab 5227 with several Sun SPARC and GSI Workstations. These machines are connected internally as part of the campus network and externally to the Internet. Many programs and departments have their own computing resources that are also connected to the campus network. Access to these computing resources is available in computer labs and academic units and through dial-up lines. Programming languages supported include C, Pascal, ADA, Fortran, and C++. A staff of professionals is available to assist users with consultation and documentation. In addition to these resources, ARCS maintains a large microcomputer center in the Library Pavilion.

Financial Aid Graduate student assistantships for instruction and research are available to well-qualified master's and doctoral degree students. Assistantships carry stipends plus a tuition waiver. In some cases, a tuition waiver alone may be awarded for a limited amount of service. Assistantships for master's degree students are normally for an academic year; assistantships for doctoral students are renewable on a yearly basis.

Cost of Study Tuition for graduate study is $945 per semester hour in 2007–08. A tuition deposit of $300 (deducted from the first semester's tuition charge) is required of all new students. Books are estimated to cost $800 per year.

Living and Housing Costs Room and board on campus cost approximately $3500 per semester in 2007–08. On-campus housing (dormitories and apartments) is available for full-time graduate students, but priority for dormitory rooms is given to undergraduate students. Many apartment complexes and rental houses are available near the campus.

Student Group Graduate students constitute more than one fourth of the students attending Florida Tech's Melbourne campus. Enrolled graduate and undergraduate students represent forty-nine states and more than eighty countries.

Location Melbourne is located on the central east coast of Florida. The area offers a delightful year-round subtropical climate and is 10 minutes from the ocean beaches. Kennedy Space Center and the massive NASA complex are just 45 minutes north of Melbourne. The city of Orlando, Walt Disney World, and EPCOT are 1 hour west of the Florida Tech main campus.

The Institute Florida Institute of Technology is a distinctive, independent university, founded in 1958 by a group of scientists and engineers to fulfill a need for specialized, advanced educational opportunities on the Space Coast of Florida. Florida Tech is the only comprehensive, independent scientific and technological university in the southeast. Supported by both industry and the community, Florida Tech is the recipient of many research grants and contracts, a number of which provide financial support for graduate students.

Applying Forms for applying to the Graduate School and for assistantships are sent on request. Applications for assistantships must be submitted by February 1. Department of Biology students must complete the application process by March 1. Doctor of Psychology applicants must complete the application process by January 15 and begin their program of study in the fall. Applied behavior analysis applicants must apply by March 1. Industrial/organizational psychology applicants must complete the application process by February 1. An online application and related forms are available on the graduate admissions page of the Florida Tech Web site at http://www.fit.edu/grad.

Correspondence and Information

Graduate Admissions Office
Florida Institute of Technology
150 West University Boulevard
Melbourne, Florida 32901-6975

Phone: 321-674-8027
800-944-4348 (toll-free)
Fax: 321-723-9468
E-mail: grad-admissions@fit.edu
Web site: http://www.fit.edu/grad

DEPARTMENT HEADS AND PROGRAM CHAIRS

The faculty members listed below will be pleased to answer inquiries concerning programs and degrees or to provide general university information.

COLLEGE OF AERONAUTICS
K. P. Stackpoole, Ph.D., Dean.
Airport Development and Management (M.S.): N. Villaire, Ed.D., Program Chairman.
Aviation Human Factors (M.S.): N. Villaire, Ed.D., Program Chairman.
Aviation Safety (M.S.): N. Villaire, Ed.D., Program Chairman.

COLLEGE OF BUSINESS
R. H. Fronk, Ph.D., Dean.
B. Pierce, Ph.D., Associate Dean.
Business Administration (M.B.A.)

COLLEGE OF ENGINEERING
T. D. Waite, Ph.D., Dean.
E. H. Kalajian, Ph.D., Associate Dean.
Chemical Engineering (M.S., Ph.D.): P. A. Jennings, Ph.D., Department Head.
Civil Engineering (M.S., Ph.D.): A. Pandit, Ph.D., Department Head.
Computer Sciences (M.S., Ph.D.): W. Shoaff, Ph.D., Department Head.
Electrical and Computer Engineering (M.S., Ph.D.): R. L. Sullivan, Ph.D., Department Head.
Engineering Systems (M.S.): M. Shiakh, Ph.D., Department Head.
Marine and Environmental Systems (M.S., Ph.D.): G. Maul, Ph.D., Department Head.
Mechanical and Aerospace Engineering (M.S., Ph.D.): P. Hsu, Ph.D., Department Head.

COLLEGE OF PSYCHOLOGY AND LIBERAL ARTS
School of Psychology
M. B. Kenkel, Psy.D., Dean.
Applied Behavior Analysis (M.S.): J. Martinez-Diaz, Ph.D., Department Head.
Clinical Psychology (Psy.D.): R. Krishnamurthy, Ph.D., Director Clinical Training.
Industrial/Organizational Psychology (M.S., Ph.D.): R. Griffith, Ph.D., Department Head.
Organizational Behavior Management (M.S.): D. A. Wilder, Ph.D., Department Head.
Liberal Arts Studies
Humanities and Communications (M.S.): N. Matar, Ph.D., Department Head.

COLLEGE OF SCIENCE
G. Nelson, Ph.D., Dean.
H. K. Rassoul, Ph.D., Associate Dean.
Biological Sciences (M.S., Ph.D.): G. N. Wells, Ph.D., Department Head.
Chemistry (M.S., Ph.D.): M. W. Babich, Ph.D., Department Head.
Mathematics Sciences (M.S., Ph.D.): V. Lakshmikatham, Ph.D., Department Head.
Physics and Space Sciences (M.S., Ph.D.): T. Oswald, Ph.D., Department Head.
Science and Mathematics Education (M.S., Ed.S., Ph.D.): D. Cook, Ph.D., Department Head.

FLORIDA INTERNATIONAL UNIVERSITY

University Graduate School

Programs of Study Graduate programs are offered at Florida International University (FIU) in the following fields (asterisks denote fields in which only a master's degree is offered): *accounting, adult education, *African–New World studies, *architecture, *art education, *Asian studies, biology, biomedical engineering, business administration, chemistry, civil engineering, comparative sociology, *computer engineering, computer science, *construction management, *counselor education, *creative writing, *criminal justice, curriculum and instruction, dietetics and nutrition, *early childhood education, economics, educational administration and supervision, educational leadership, electrical engineering, *elementary education, *engineering management, *English, *English education, *English for non-English speakers (TESOL), *environmental and urban systems, *environmental engineering, *environmental studies, *exercise and sports sciences, exceptional student education, *finance, *foreign language education: TESOL, *forensic science, *French education, geosciences, *health education, *health services administration, higher education administration, history, hospitality management, human resource development, *human resource management, industrial and systems engineering, *interior design, *international business, *international development education, international real estate, *international relations, international studies, *international and intercultural education, *landscape architecture, *Latin American and Caribbean studies, *liberal studies, *linguistics, management information systems, *mass communication, *materials science engineering, *mathematics education, *mathematical sciences, mechanical engineering, *modern language education, *music, *music education, nursing, *occupational therapy, *parks and recreation management, *physical education, physical therapy, physics, political science, psychology, *public administration, public health, public management, *reading education, *religious studies, school psychology, *science education, *social studies education, social welfare, *social work, Spanish, *Spanish education, *special education, speech-language pathology, statistics, *taxation, *technology education, *technology management, *telecommunications and networking engineering, tourism studies, *urban education, and *visual arts.

Research Facilities The libraries at University Park and the Biscayne Bay Campus house more than 1 million volumes, along with numerous periodicals, maps, microfilms, institutional archives, curriculum materials, and government documents. Access to 9,300 periodicals and serials is available. Interlibrary loan services offer access to holdings at major libraries throughout the country, and the online catalog gives information about the collections of all the libraries in the State University System of Florida. Special research centers and institutes include the following: the Academy for the Art of Teaching, the High-Performance Database Research Center, the Hemispheric Center for Environmental Technology, the International Hurricane Center, the Latin American and Caribbean Center, and the Southeast Florida Center on Aging.

Financial Aid Graduate students may qualify for assistantships and fellowships and other awards that are offered through FIU's schools, colleges, and departments. To apply, students should contact the departmental dean's office. A limited number of awards are available for students who demonstrate need through the Free Application for Federal Student Aid (FAFSA). The form is available at all U.S. colleges and universities.

Cost of Study The average tuition and fees for full-time, in-state graduate students were $2337.57 per semester. For the 2006–07 academic year, credit-hour fees for graduate students were $272.74 per credit hour for Florida residents and $776.81 per credit hour for out-of-state students. Tuition and fees are subject to change.

Living and Housing Costs Graduate student housing is available at University Park (telephone: 305-348-4190) and the Biscayne Bay Campus (telephone: 305-919-5587).

Student Group The graduate student community includes 6,500 students from all fifty states and more than 110 nations.

Student Outcomes Graduates of the University proceed to a wide variety of academic and professional careers in academic institutions, government agencies, nonprofit organizations, private industry, and entrepreneurial enterprises.

Location Located in suburban west Miami-Dade County, the 342-acre University Park campus is notable for its distinctive architecture, lush tropical landscape, and impressive outdoor sculpture park. The Biscayne Bay Campus is situated on 200 acres on Biscayne Bay in North Miami, which encompasses a natural mangrove preserve. FIU also operates an academic site in Pembroke Pines.

The University FIU is a public, multicampus research university and a member of the State University System of Florida. The University, designated by the Carnegie Foundation as a Doctoral/Research University–Extensive, offers more than 100 graduate and advanced academic and professional degrees.

Applying Applicants who have earned a bachelor or master's degree or the equivalent from a regionally accredited institution or a recognized institution of higher learning are welcome to apply. The Graduate Admissions Office must receive official transcripts, diplomas, and/or certificates directly from all previously attended institutions. Documents in a language other than English must be translated by an official translation agency. Applicants must submit GRE or GMAT scores. Students whose native language is not English must also submit TOEFL scores.

Correspondence and Information
Graduate Admissions Office
Florida International University
P.O. Box 659004
Miami, Florida 33265

Phone: 305-348-7442
Fax: 305-348-7441
E-mail: gradadm@fiu.edu
Web site: http://www.gradschool.fiu.edu

GRADUATE PROGRAMS

COLLEGE OF ARCHITECTURE AND THE ARTS
Architecture: http://www.fiu.edu/~soa
Landscape Architecture: http://www.fiu.edu/~soa

COLLEGE OF ARTS AND SCIENCES
African–New World Studies: http://www.fiu.edu/~africana
Asian Studies: http://asian.fiu.edu/
Biology: http://www.fiu.edu/~biology
Chemistry: http://www.fiu.edu/orgs/chemistry
Computer Science: http://www.cs.fiu.edu
Creative Writing: http://w3.fiu.edu/CRWRITING
Economics: http://www.fiu.edu/orgs/economics
English: http://www.fiu.edu/~english
Environmental Studies: http://www.fiu.edu/~envstud
Forensic Science: http://www.fiu.edu/~ifri
Geology: http://www.fiu.edu/orgs/geology
History: http://www.fiu.edu/~history
International Relations: http://www.fiu.edu/~intlrel
Latin American and Caribbean Studies: http://lacc.fiu.edu/
Liberal Studies: http://www.fiu.edu/~liberal
Linguistics: http://www.fiu.edu/~linguist
Mathematics: http://w3.fiu.edu/math
Modern Languages: http://www.fiu.edu/orgs/modlang
Music: http://www.fiu.edu/~music
Physics: http://www.fiu.edu/physics
Political Science: http://www.fiu.edu/~polsci
Psychology: http://w3.fiu.edu/psych
Religious Studies: http://www.fiu.edu/~religion
Sociology: http://www.fiu.edu/orgs/socant
Statistics: http://www.fiu.edu/~statdept
Visual Arts: http://www.fiu.edu/~visart

COLLEGE OF BUSINESS ADMINISTRATION
Accounting: http://business.fiu.edu/chapman/master_of_accounting.cfm
Business Administration: http://business.fiu.edu/chapman/phd_programs.cfm
Finance: http://business.fiu.edu/chapman/master_of_science_in_finance.cfm
International Business: http://business.fiu.edu/chapman/master_of_intl_business.cfm
International Real Estate: http://business.fiu.edu/chapman/master_of_science_in_intl_real_estate.cfm
Management: http://business.fiu.edu/chapman/master_of_science_in_hrm.cfm
Management Information Systems: http://business.fiu.edu/chapman/master_of_science_in_mis.cfm

COLLEGE OF EDUCATION
Adult Education and Human Resource Development: http://www.fiu.edu/~elps/aehrd.htm
Art Education: http://www.fiu.edu/~curricul/programs_ms_arted.html
Community Mental Health: http://fiu.edu/~edpsy/mentalhealth.htm
Counselor Education: http://www.fiu.edu/~edpsy/counseloredhome.htm
Curriculum and Instruction: http://www.fiu.edu/~curricul/
Early Childhood Education: http://education.fiu.edu/graduate_programs/ms_earlychilded.htm
Educational Administration/Supervision: http://education.fiu.edu/graduate_programs/phd_adminandsuper.htm
Elementary Education: http://www.fiu.edu/~curricul/admissionprocessEDS.htm
English Education: http://www.fiu.edu/~curricul/admissionprocessEDS.htm
English for Non-English Speakers (TESOL): http://education.fiu.edu/graduate_programs/ms_foreignlaned.htm
Exceptional Student Education: http://www.fiu.edu/%7Eedpsy/sped_graduate.htm
Health Education/Exercise Physiology: http://www.fiu.edu/~hper/graduate_degrees.htm
Higher Education/Community College Teaching: http://education.fiu.edu/graduate_programs/ms_highered.htm
Human Resource Development: http://education.fiu.edu/graduate_programs/ms_humanresource.htm
International Development Education: http://education.fiu.edu/graduate_programs/ms_intern_interculted.htm
Mathematics Education: http://education.fiu.edu/graduate_programs/ms_mathed.htm
Modern Languages: http://education.fiu.edu/graduate_programs/ms_modlanged.htm
Parks and Recreation Management: http://www.fiu.edu/~hper/parks&recreationalManagementMS.htm
Physical Education: http://www.fiu.edu/~hper/physicalEducationMS.htm
Reading Education: http://education.fiu.edu/graduate_programs/ms_readinged.htm
School Psychology: http://www.fiu.edu/~edpsy
Science Education: http://www.fiu.edu/~sste/sste_index.htm
Social Studies Education: http://education.fiu.edu/graduate_programs/ms_socistuded.htm
Special Education: http://www.fiu.edu/~edpsy/sped_graduate.htm
Technology Education: http://education.fiu.edu/graduate_programs/ms_urbaned.htm
Urban Education: http://education.fiu.edu/graduate_programs/ms_urbaned.htm

COLLEGE OF ENGINEERING AND COMPUTING
Biomedical Engineering: http://www.eng.fiu.edu/bmei
Civil Engineering: http://www.eng.fiu.edu/ce
Construction Management: http://www.cm.fiu.edu/
Electrical and Computer Engineering: http://www.eng.fiu.edu/ece
Engineering Management: http://www.eng.fiu.edu/ie
Environmental Engineering: http://www.eng.fiu.edu/ce
Industrial Engineering: http://www.eng.fiu.edu/ie
Materials Science Engineering: http://www.eng.fiu.edu/cec/CEC_MS_Material.htm
Mechanical Engineering: http://www.eng.fiu.edu/me

COLLEGE OF SOCIAL WORK, JUSTICE, AND PUBLIC AFFAIRS

SCHOOL OF CRIMINAL JUSTICE
Criminal Justice: http://swjpa.fiu.edu/cj/

SCHOOL OF SOCIAL WORK
Social Welfare: http://swjpa.fiu.edu/socialwork/PHDSW.htm
Social Work: http://swjpa.fiu.edu/socialwork/

SCHOOL OF PUBLIC ADMINISTRATION
Public Administration: http://swjpa.fiu.edu/pa/MPA.htm
Public Management: http://swjpa.fiu.edu/pa/PHDPM.htm

COLLEGE OF NURSING AND HEALTH SCIENCES
Health Services Administration: http://chua2.fiu.edu/hsa
Nursing: http://chua2.fiu.edu/nursing
Occupational Therapy: http://chua2.fiu.edu/ot
Physical Therapy: http://chua2.fiu.edu/physicaltherapy
Speech-Language Pathology: http://csd.fiu.edu

STEMPEL SCHOOL OF PUBLIC HEALTH
Dietetics and Nutrition: http://chua2.fiu.edu/dietetics-nutrition/
Public Health: http://chua2.fiu.edu/publichealth

SCHOOL OF HOSPITALITY AND TOURISM MANAGEMENT
Hotel and Food Service Management: http://hospitality.fiu.edu/

SCHOOL OF JOURNALISM AND MASS COMMUNICATION
Advertising/Public Relations: http://jmc.fiu.edu/sjmc
Journalism/Broadcasting: http://jmc.fiu.edu/sjmc
College of Law: law.fiu.edu
College of Medicine: medicine.fiu.edu

FLORIDA STATE UNIVERSITY

Graduate Studies

Programs of Study

Florida State University (FSU), a Carnegie Doctoral/Research-Extensive university, offers doctoral programs in seventy-three areas and master's programs in 112 areas. Advanced master's and specialist degrees are offered in twenty-eight programs. The University is composed of sixteen colleges: Arts and Sciences; Business; Communication; Criminology and Criminal Justice; Education; Engineering; Human Sciences; Information; Law; Medicine; Motion Pictures, Television, and Recording Arts; Music; Nursing; Social Sciences; Social Work; and Visual Arts, Theatre, and Dance. Students may pursue a number of interdisciplinary degrees, and several joint-degree programs are available.

FSU ranks among the top fifty public research universities in the country in the number of doctoral degrees awarded annually.

Research Facilities

Florida State University libraries contain approximately 2.9 million volumes, more than 52,000 serials, more than 8 million microfilms, and approximately 300,000 e-books. The libraries are committed to innovative use of new electronic technologies to enhance the research capabilities of students and faculty members. The University has more than eighty-six research centers, institutes, and special laboratories. Prominent among these are the National High Magnetic Field Laboratory, which is dedicated to research in supermagnetic fields and has application in the life sciences, transportation, and materials research. Among other research facilities are the Super FN Tandem Van de Graff Accelerator in Nuclear Research; the Institute for Molecular Biophysics; the Learning Systems Institute, which focuses on instructional systems design technology; the Institute for Science and Public Affairs, which focuses on assisting state and private agencies and the related units on aging, populations studies, family studies, and policy studies; the Marine Laboratory, which is located on the northern Gulf; the Geophysical Fluid Dynamics Institute; several centers devoted to atmospheric, oceanic, and climatic studies; the Center for Materials Research and Technology; and the Center for Music Research.

Financial Aid

Graduate students may compete for many forms of financial assistance for graduate study. There is an annual competition for nonduty University fellowships with stipends ranging from $18,000 to $23,000, plus tuition waivers with some departments supplementing this amount. In addition, a health insurance supplement of up to $1440 per student per academic year is offered toward the purchase of the University-sponsored student health insurance. All graduate programs offer teaching or research assistantships, with some programs funding many of their enrolled graduate students. Assistantship stipends vary from program to program, but in combination with tuition waivers they are competitive with other universities. Graduate assistants are eligible for a health insurance supplement of up to $500 per student per academic year toward the University-sponsored student health insurance. Student loans are available through the Office of Financial Aid, 4474 UCT, Florida State University, Tallahassee, Florida 32306 (Web site: http://www.ais.fsu.edu/finaid).

Cost of Study

Tuition and fees for an in-state resident for 2006–07 were $5822 for the academic year; this is based on 12 hours of graduate enrollment each term. The comparable amount for out-of-state graduate students was $20,976. Most students who receive a fellowship or an assistantship have both in-state and out-of-state tuition waived.

Living and Housing Costs

The University provides some housing for graduate students, but the majority of graduate students secure private housing, much of it within walking distance or free bus service of the University. There are many apartment complexes in Tallahassee and private dormitories near the University. For more information about housing, students can contact Housing, 108 CAW, Florida State University, Tallahassee, Florida 32306 (Web site: http://www.housing.fsu.edu). Generally, the cost of living in Tallahassee is moderate.

Student Group

Florida State enrolled more than 40,474 students in 2006–07, including more than 8,200 graduate students, of whom 66 percent were full-time. The overall student body is 56 percent women, and members of minority groups constitute 24.7 percent of all students. All fifty states and a large number of other countries are represented in the student body.

Student Outcomes

FSU awards more than 1,870 master's degrees and approximately 325 doctoral degrees each year. Students find many rewarding opportunities ranging from faculty positions in colleges and universities to postdoctoral appointments in other leading universities. The University has a Career Center to assist graduate students, and departments actively assist graduates in their search for employment.

Location

FSU is located in Tallahassee, the capital of Florida and the home of two other educational institutions, Florida A&M University, a historically black university, and Tallahassee Community College. Tallahassee is situated about 40 miles from the Gulf of Mexico, with some of the world's most beautiful beaches within an easy drive. The climate permits year-round outdoor activity. Recreation and sports activities abound for both participants and observers. Cultural activities are very rich as well. The outstanding College of Music and College of Visual Arts, Theatre, and Dance are the catalysts for several series of plays, musical performances, and operas, and the University operates both public television and radio stations. A new culture and science center is slated to open soon in downtown Tallahassee.

The University

FSU is a fully accredited public university and functions as a component of the ten-member State University System of Florida. While the University provides an extensive and high-quality undergraduate program, it has a central mission in graduate education and research. Its mission statement recounts that "the University's primary role is to serve as a center for advanced graduate and professional studies while emphasizing research and providing excellence in undergraduate programs." It has a distinguished faculty that has regularly included Nobel laureates and members of prestigious national academic societies. Its expenditures in sponsored research exceed $190 million per year. For more information about Florida State University, prospective students should visit the University Web site at http://www.fsu.edu.

Applying

Students may apply online at http://www.admissions.fsu.edu or fill out the general application for admission, which is available from Graduate Admissions; seek information about a program online at http://www.admissions.fsu.edu; and contact the academic department to which they are applying if they wish to be considered for financial assistance. While there are University-wide requirements for admission, the requirements for each program are set by the faculty members in that program and may be higher than University-wide requirements. The GRE General Test is required of all students (GMAT for business). Applications are carefully reviewed with due consideration to the academic record, test scores, letters of recommendation, and expressions of interest. A TOEFL score of 550 or better is required for applicants whose native language is not English. While admission deadlines vary by department, students should submit all materials by early January to be considered for all forms of financial assistance.

Correspondence and Information

For admissions:
Graduate Admissions
A2500 UCA
Florida State University
282 Champion Way
P.O. Box 3062400
Tallahassee, Florida 32306-2400
Phone: 850-644-3420
Fax: 850-644-0197
E-mail: admissions@admin.fsu.edu
Web site: http://www.fsu.edu

For specific programs:
(Department or Program)
Florida State University
Tallahassee, Florida 32306

For graduate studies:
Office of Graduate Studies
408 Westcott
Florida State University
222 S. Copeland Avenue
P.O. Box 3061410
Tallahassee, Florida 32306-1410
Phone: 850-644-3501
Fax: 850-644-2969
E-mail: gradstds@www.fsu.edu
Web site: http://www.gradstudies.fsu.edu

DIRECTORS OF GRADUATE PROGRAMS

COLLEGE OF ARTS AND SCIENCES

American and Florida Studies (M.A.): Dr. John Fenstermaker (850-644-0202; jfenstermaker@english.fsu.edu). **Anthropology (Ph.D./M.S.):** Dr. William A. Parkinson (850-644-7021; wparkins@mailer.fsu.edu). **Biological Science (Ph.D.):** Dr. George Bates (850-644-3023; bates@bio.fsu.edu). **Chemistry (Ph.D.):** Dr. Igor Alabugin (850-644-1897; alabugin@chem.fsu.edu). **Classics (Ph.D./M.A.):** Dr. James Sickinger (850-644-1091; jsicking@mailer.fsu.edu). **Computer Science (Ph.D.):** Dr. Sudhir Aggarwal (850-644-0164; admissions@cs.fsu.edu). **English (Ph.D.):** Dr. Stan Gontarski (850-644-6038; sgontarski@english.fsu.edu). **Geology (Ph.D./M.S.):** Dr. Vincent Salters (850-644-1934; salters@magnet.fsu.edu). **Geophysical Fluid Dynamics (Ph.D.):** Dr. Carol Ann Clayson (850-644-0922; clayson@met.fsu.edu). **History (Ph.D./M.A.):** Dr. Elna Green (850-644-9531; egreen@mailer.fsu.edu). **Interdisciplinary Humanities (Ph.D.):** Dr. Maricarmen Martinez (850-644-1401; mmartine@mailer.fsu.edu). **Mathematics (Ph.D./M.S.):** Dr. Betty Anne Case (850-644-1586; case@math.fsu.edu). **Meteorology (Ph.D.):** Dr. Guosheng Liu (850-644-6298; liug@met.fsu.edu). **Modern Languages (Ph.D.):** Dr. Brenda Cappuccio (850-644-2374; bcappucc@mailer.fsu.edu). **Molecular Biophysics (Ph.D.):** Dr. P. Bryant Chase (850-644-0056; chase@bio.fsu.edu). **Neuroscience (Ph.D.):** Dr. Robert Contreras (850-644-2040; contreras@psy.fsu.edu). **Oceanography (Ph.D.):** Ms. Michaela Lupiani (850-644-6700; admissions@ocean.fsu.edu). **Philosophy (Ph.D.):** Dr. Peter Dalton (850-644-0229; pdalton@mailer.fsu.edu). **Physics (Ph.D./M.S.):** Dr. Jorge Piekarewicz (850-644-6344; jorgep@scs.fsu.edu). **Psychology (Ph.D.):** Dr. Ellen Berler (850-644-2040; berler@psy.fsu.edu). **Psychology (Applied Behavioral Analysis) (M.S.):** Dr. Ellen Berler (850-644-2040; berler@psy.fsu.edu). **Religion (Ph.D.):** Amanda Porterfield (850-644-5433; aporterf@mailer.fsu.edu). **Statistics (Ph.D.):** Dr. Xufeng Niu (850-644-4008; niu@stat.fsu.edu).

COLLEGE OF BUSINESS

Accounting (Ph.D.): Dr. Allen Bathke (850-644-7888; abathke@cob.fsu.edu). **Business Administration (M.B.A.):** Dr. Pat Maroney (850-644-8217; pmaroney@cob.fsu.edu). **Finance (Ph.D.):** Dr. David Peterson (850-644-8200; dpeters@cob.fsu.edu). **Management (Ph.D.):** Dr. Jim Combs (850-644-7896; jcombs@cob.fsu.edu). **Management Information Systems (Ph. D.):** Dr. Ashley Bush (850-644-2779; abush@cob.fsu.edu). **(M.S.):** Dr. David Paradice (850-644-3888; paradice@cob.fsu.edu). **Marketing (Ph.D.):** Dr. Mike Brady (850-644-7853; mbrady@cob.fsu.edu). **Risk Management and Insurance (Ph.D.):** Dr. James Carson (850-644-5858; jcarson@cob.fsu.edu).

COLLEGE OF COMMUNICATION

Communications (Ph.D.): Dr. Arthur Raney (850-644-5034; art.raney@fsu.edu). **Communication Disorders (Ph.D.):** Dr. Amy Wetherby (850-488-4002; awetherb@garnet.acns.fsu.edu).

COLLEGE OF CRIMINOLOGY AND CRIMINAL JUSTICE (Ph.D.): Ms. Margarita Frankeberger (850-644-7373; mfrankeb@mailer.fsu.edu).

COLLEGE OF EDUCATION

Career Counseling (Specialist/M.S.): Dr. Robert Reardon (850-644-1249/9777; rreardon@admin.fsu.edu). **Counseling Psychology and School Psychology (combined Ph.D.):** Dr. Steven Pfeiffer (850-644-8796; Pfeiffer@coe.fsu.edu). **Early Childhood Education (Ph.D./Specialist/M.S.):** Dr. Charles Wolfgang (850-644-8484; wolfgang@coe.fsu.edu). **Educational Leadership and Policy (Ph.D.):** Dr. Jeffrey Milligan (850-644-8171; milligan@coe.fsu.edu). **Educational Leadership Administration (M.S.):** Dr. Judith Ervin (850-644-6447; irvin@coe.fsu.edu). **Educational Policy Studies and Evaluation (M.S.):** Dr. Sande Milton (850-644-8168; milton@coe.fsu.edu). **Education of Students with Disabilities (Ph.D./Specialist):** Dr. Stephanie Al Otaiba (850-644-8414; salotaiba@fsu.edu). **Education of Students with Disabilities (M.S.):** Dr. Frances Hanline (850-644-4880; mhanline@fsu.edu). **Elementary Education (Ph.D./Specialist/M.S.):** Dr. Diana Rice (850-645-4685; rice@coe.fsu.edu); **(Specialist/M.S.)** Dr. Jan Flake (850-644-8481; jflake@garnet.acns.fsu.edu). **English Education (Ph.D./Specialist/M.S.):** Dr. Susan Wood (850-644-1909; wood@coe.fsu.edu). **Health Education (M.S.):** Dr. Mary Sutherland (850-644-2122; sutherl@coe.fsu.edu). **Higher Education (Ph.D./M.S.):** Dr. Joseph Beckham (850-644-5553; jbeckham@coe.fsu.edu). **History & Philosophy of Education (M.S.):** Dr. Jeffrey Milligan (850-644- 8171; milligan@coe.fsu.edu). **Instructional Systems (Ph.D./M.S.):** Dr. Robert Reiser (850-644-4592; rreiser@mailer.fsu.edu). **Learning and Cognition (Ph.D./M.S.):** Dr. Susan Losh (850-644-8778; slosh@garnet.acns.fsu.edu). **Math Education (Ph.D./M.S.):** Dr. Elizabeth Jakubowski (850-644-8428; ejakubow@coe.fsu.edu); **(Ph.D./M.S.)** Dr. Leslie Aspinwall (850-644-8427; aspinwal@coe.fsu.edu). **Measurement & Statistics (Ph.D./M.S.):** Dr. Betsy Becker (850-645-2371; bjbecker@coe.fsu.edu). **Mental Health Counseling (Specialist/M.S.):** Dr. Michael Railey (850-644-9440; railey@coe.fsu.edu). **Multilingual/Multicultural Education (Ph.D./M.S.):** Dr. Deborah Hasson (850-644-2117; hasson@coe.fsu.edu). **Open & Distance Learning (M.S.):** Dr. Robert Reiser (850-644-4592; rreiser@mailer.fsu.edu). **Performance Improvement and Human Resource Development (M.S.):** Dr. Robert Reiser (850-644-4592; rreiser@mailer.fsu.edu). **Physical Education (Ph.D./M.S.):** Dr. Susan Lynn (850-644-3007; lynn@coe.fsu.edu). **Reading Education (Ph.D./Specialist/M.S.):** Dr. Carolyn Piazza (850-644-8476; cpiazza@garnet.acns.fsu.edu). **Recreation & Leisure Services (M.S.):** Dr. Joohyun Lee (850-644-3061; jlee@coe.fsu.edu). **Rehabilitation Counseling Services (Ph.D./Specialist/M.S.):** Dr. Jane Burkhead (850-644-6709; burkhead@coe.fsu.edu). **School Psychology (Specialist/M.S.):** Dr. Briley Proctor (telephone 850-644-3742; proctor@coe.fsu.edu). **Science Education (Ph.D./Specialist/M.S.):** Dr. Sherry Southerland (850- 645-4667; southerl@coe.fsu.edu). **Socio-Cultural Development (M.S.):** Dr. Jeffrey Milligan (850-644-8171; milligan@coe.fsu.edu). **Social Science Education (Ph.D./M.S.):** Dr. Toni Kirkwood-Tucker (850-644-6553; kirkwoodtf@aol.com). **Special Education (Ph.D./Specialist):** Dr. Stephanie Al Otaiba (850-644-0717; alotaiba@coe.fsu.edu). **Sport Psychology (Ph.D./M.S.):** Dr. Robert Eklund (850-645-2909; eklund@coe.fsu.edu). **Sport Management (Ph.D./M.S.): (Ph.D.):** Dr. Aubrey Kent (850-644-7174; kent@coe.fsu.edu); **(M.S.)** Dr. Cecile Reynaud (850-644-4298; reynaud@coe.fsu.edu). **Visual Disabilities (M.S.):** Dr. Sandra Lewis (850-644-8409; lewis@coe.fsu.edu).

COLLEGE OF ENGINEERING

Chemical Engineering (Ph.D.): Dr. Teng Ma (850-410-6558; teng@eng.fsu.edu). **Civil Engineering (Ph.D.):** Dr. Renatus Mussa (850-410-6125; mussa@eng.fsu.edu). **Electrical Engineering (Ph.D.):** Dr. Thomas Baldwin (850-410-6584; tbaldwin@eng.fsu.edu). **Industrial Engineering (Ph.D.):** Dr. Chun Zhang (850-410-6355; chzhang@eng.fsu.edu). **Mechanical Engineering (Ph.D.):** Dr. Cesar Luongo (850-410-6588; luongo@magnet.fsu.edu).

COLLEGE OF HUMAN SCIENCES

Family and Child Sciences (Ph.D.): Dr. Ron Mullis (850-644-3217; rmullis@garnet.acns.fsu.edu). **Marriage and the Family (Ph.D.):** Dr. Robert Lee (850-644-1412; relee@mailer.fsu.edu) **Nutrition, Food, and Exercise Sciences (Ph.D.):** Dr. Cathy Levenson (850-644-4800; utate@mailer.fsu.edu). **Textiles and Consumer Sciences (Ph.D.):** Dr. Jeanne Heitmeyer (850-644-5578; jheitmey@mailer.fsu.edu).

COLLEGE OF INFORMATION

Ph.D./M.A./M.S.: Dr. Corinne Jorgensen (850-644-8116; cjorgensen@lis.fsu.edu).

COLLEGE OF LAW

J.D.: Ms. Sharon Booker (850-644-3787; sbooker@law.fsu.edu).

COLLEGE OF MEDICINE

M.D.: Dr. Myra Hurt (850-644-8935; myra.hurt@med.fsu.edu).

COLLEGE OF MOTION PICTURE, TELEVISION, AND RECORDING ARTS

M.F.A.: Mr. Reb Braddock (850-644-8524; rbraddock@admin.fsu.edu).

COLLEGE OF MUSIC

Ph.D./D.M./Ed.D./M.M./M.A.: Dr. Seth Beckman (850-644-5848; sbeckman@admin.fsu.edu).

COLLEGE OF NURSING

M.S.N.: Dr. Dianne Speake (850-644-6846; dspeake@nursing.fsu.edu).

COLLEGE OF SOCIAL SCIENCES

Asian Studies (M.A./M.S.): Dr. Lee Metcalf (850-644-7328; lmetcalf@ fsu.edu). **Demography/Population Center (M.S.):** Dr. Isaac Eberstein (850-644-7108; leberstn@fsu.edu). **Economics (Ph.D./M.S.):** Dr. Thomas Zuehlke (850-644-7206; tzuehlke@fsu.edu). **Geography (Ph.D./M.S.):** Dr. Jay Anthony Stallins (850-644-8385; jastallins@fsu.edu). **International Affairs (M.A./M.S.):** Dr. Lee Metcalf (850-644-7328; lmetcalf@fsu.edu). **Political Science (Ph.D./M.A./M.S.):** Dr. Charles Barrilleaux (850-644-7643; cbarrilleaux@fsu.edu). **Public Administration and Policy (Ph.D.):** Dr. Mary Guy (850-644-9170; mguy@mailer.fsu.edu); **(M.P.A.):** Dr. Lee Metcalf (850-644-7328; lmetcalf@fsu.edu). **Russian and East European Studies (M.A./M.S.):** Dr. James Bowman (850-644-7605; jbowman@fsu.edu). **Sociology (Ph.D.):** Dr. John Reynolds (850-644-4321; jrreynolds@admin.fsu.edu). **Urban and Regional Planning (Ph.D.):** Dr. Rebecca Miles (850-644-7102; miles@fsu.edu); **(M.S.P.):** Dr. Tim Chapin (850-644-8515; tchapin@fsu.edu).

COLLEGE OF SOCIAL WORK

Ph.D.: Dr. Darcy Siebert (850-644-9704; dsiebert@mailer.fsu.edu); **M.S.W.:** Dr. Pam Graham (850-644-1201; pgraham@fsu.edu).

COLLEGE OF VISUAL ARTS, THEATRE, AND DANCE

Art (M.F.A.): Ms. Lilian Garcia-Roig (850-644-1326; lgarcia@fsu.edu). **Art Education (Ph.D./M.S.):** Dr. Marcia Rosal (850-644-2926; mrosal@fsu.edu). **Art History (Ph.D./M.A.):** Dr. Kathy Braun (850-644-8207; kbraun@mailer.fsu.edu **Arts Administration (M.A.):** Dr. Patricia Villeneuve (850-644-1915; pvillene@mailer.fsu.edu). **Arts Therapy (M.S.):** Dr. Marcia Rosal (850-644-2926; mrosal@fsu.edu).**Dance (M.F.A./M.A.):** Ms. Patricia Phillips (850-644-1023; pphillip@mailer.fsu.edu). **American Dance Studies (M.A.):** Ms. Tricia Young (850-644-1023; young@dance.fsu.edu). **Interior Design (M.F.A./M.A./M.S.):** Dr. Lisa Waxman (850-644-8326; lwaxman@fsu.edu). **Acting (M.F.A.):** Mr. Greg Leaming (910-951-9010 Ext. 2310; gleaming@conservatory.fsu.edu). **Costume Design (M.F.A.):** Ms. Colleen Muscha (850-644-7514; cmuscha@mailer.fsu.edu). **Directing (M.F.A.):** Mr. Fred Chappell (850-644-7237; fdchappe@fsu.edu). **Lighting Design (M.F.A.):** Ms. Sarah Maines (850-644-7251; smaines@mailer.fsu.edu). **Scene Design (M.F.A.):** Mr. Dale Jordan (850-644-4537; dfjordan@mailer.fsu.edu). **Technical Direction (M.F.A.):** Mr. Robert Coleman (850-644-4305; rcoleman@mailer.fsu.edu). **Theatre Management (M.F.A.):** Mr. David Rowell (850-645-1958; drowell@admin.fsu.edu). **Theatre (Ph.D./M.F.A.):** Dr. Mary Dahl (850-644-7238; mkdahl@admin.fsu.edu).

FORDHAM UNIVERSITY

Graduate School of Arts and Sciences

Programs of Study

The Graduate School of Arts and Sciences is committed to the education of talented men and women in the liberal arts and sciences and offers programs of advanced study in a number of academic disciplines. Areas of study include both the traditional humanistic and scientific disciplines and interdisciplinary programs that may be oriented academically, toward the achievement of career goals, or for personal enrichment.

Master's and doctoral degrees are offered in biological sciences, classics, economics, English, history, philosophy, psychology, sociology, and theology. Master's degrees are also offered in computer science, elections and campaign management, political science, and public communications. Interdisciplinary programs include master's degrees in humanities and sciences and international political economy and a master's degree and a doctoral-level certificate in medieval studies. Advanced certificate programs in emerging markets and risk analysis, financial econometrics and data analysis, health-care ethics, and Latin American and Latino studies are also offered.

Research Facilities

The combined libraries of the University contain more than 2 million bound volumes, over 15,500 periodicals, and more than 18,000 electronic journals. The main collection is in the William D. Walsh Family University Library, an open-stack library that seats 1,600 readers. The Law School library and the Gerald Quinn Library Lincoln Center may also be used by Fordham students. In addition to the University libraries, graduate students may use the New York Public Library system, and they also have access to the libraries of the City University of New York, Columbia University, New School University, and New York University through the New York City Doctoral Consortium. The library subscribes to several computerized online services and data search networks.

The Computing Center houses up-to-date equipment that is available for use by students, faculty members, and administrators at all times of the day and night. It also maintains an extensive array of software packages. Terminals located at various sites on all three campuses provide convenient access for users.

Separate laboratory facilities are maintained by a number of departments, including biology, communications, computer science, and psychology. The Louis Calder Center–Biological Field Station is a 113-acre forested preserve, supporting education and research by students and faculty members in a diverse range of ecological topics. State-of-the-art laboratories in proximity to forest, old field, wetland, and aquatic habitats provide opportunities to conduct experiments in natural ecological systems 40 miles north of the most populous urban region in North America, New York City. In addition, the University is affiliated with a number of outside agencies, including the New York Botanical Garden and the New York Zoological Society.

Financial Aid

The Graduate School awards a number of graduate assistantships and fellowships, both teaching and research, and some that require no service. All assistantships and fellowships include stipends, and recipients usually receive a separate tuition scholarship. They are assigned on a competitive basis to full-time students with outstanding academic records, and reappointments are extended on the basis of proven competence and good academic standing. Scholarships for members of underrepresented groups are also available.

Cost of Study

Tuition for the 2007–08 academic year is $995 per credit. Normally, a master's degree requires 30–36 credits and a doctoral degree 60–72 credits beyond the baccalaureate. Additional annual fees apply.

Living and Housing Costs

Rental costs for single students living in University apartments range from $7000 to $8000 a year. Shared rental units range from $600 to $750 per month in the immediate off-campus neighborhood. An up-to-date rental database is available on the Graduate Student Association Web site at http://www.fordham.edu/gasa/gsa.

Student Group

Of the approximately 15,000 students attending Fordham University, about 900 are enrolled in the various departments and programs of the Graduate School. Students come from all areas of the United States and many other countries. Many enroll either full-time or part-time in pursuit of a degree; some take individual courses for professional advancement or personal enrichment.

Location

New York City exposes students to the best the world has to offer in art, culture, and business and has the highly diversified atmosphere of a truly international city. Fordham encourages students to make the best possible use of the opportunities the city offers in class, at work, and during their leisure time. Professors draw upon the resources of the city to enrich their courses. Lectures, literary readings, Lincoln Center for the Performing Arts, museum exhibitions, art galleries, theaters, international film festivals, orchestras, and performances of every genre all combine to forge the intellects of Fordham students. Students can experience the city in their own personal and individual ways. The University is ideally located in a neighborhood bordered by the New York Bronx Zoo, the New York Botanical Garden, and "Arthur Ave," famous for Italian cuisine.

The University

Fordham is a university in the Jesuit tradition. Founded in 1841, it is governed as an institution under a charter granted by the State of New York. The Graduate School of Arts and Sciences is one of eleven colleges and schools at Fordham University. Founded in 1916, it carries on Fordham's oldest academic tradition, the education of talented men and women in the liberal arts and sciences, at the postgraduate level.

Applying

Online applications are available at the Fordham University Graduate School of Arts and Science Web site (http://www.fordham.edu/gsas). All applicants must submit a completed application form, official transcripts, Graduate Record Examinations (GRE) scores, three letters of recommendation, a resume, and a statement of intent. Some departments have additional requirements for which students should consult the individual department Web sites (http://www.fordham.edu/gsas). Students from abroad must have superior scholastic records and proficiency in written and spoken English. All international students are required to submit TOEFL scores. Transcripts should be comparable to the GPA grading system of 4.0.

Applications are accepted throughout the year for most programs, but they must be received by January 2, 2008, to be guaranteed consideration for financial aid. Psychology applications must be received by December 12, 2007.

Requests for program brochures and additional information should be directed to the Office of Admissions at the address provided.

Correspondence and Information

Office of Admissions
Graduate School of Arts and Sciences
216 Keating Hall
Fordham University
441 East Fordham Road
Bronx, New York 10458

Phone: 718-817-4416
Fax: 718-817-3566
E-mail: fuga@fordham.edu
Web site: http://www.fordham.edu/gsas/

FACULTY HEADS

Nancy Busch, Ph.D., Dean of GSAS and Associate Vice President for Academic Affairs/Chief Research Officer.
Department of Biological Sciences: William Thornhill, Ph.D., Chair.
Department of Classical Languages and Literature: Robert Penella, Ph.D., Chair.
Department of Communication and Media Studies: Paul Levinson, Ph.D., Chair.
Department of Computer and Information Science: Damian Lyons, Ph.D., Chair.
Department of Economics: Henry M. Schwalbenberg, Ph.D., Interim Chair.
Elections and Campaign Management: Costas Panagopoulos, Ph.D., Director.
Department of English Language and Literature: Nicola Pitchford, Ph.D., Chair.
Center for Ethics Education: Celia Fisher, Ph.D., Director.
Department of History: Doron Ben-Atar, Ph.D., Chair.
Humanities and Sciences Program: Hugo Benavides, Ph.D., Chair.
International Political Economy and Development: Henry M. Schwalbenberg, Ph.D., Director.
Latin American and Latino Studies: S. Elizabeth Penry, Ph.D., Director.
Medieval Studies Program: Maryanne Kowaleski, Ph.D., Director.
Philosophical Resources Program: Christopher Cullen, S.J., Ph.D., Director.
Department of Philosophy: John Drummond, Ph.D., Chair.
Department of Political Science: Bruce Berg, Ph.D., Chair.
Department of Psychology: Frederick J. Wertz, Ph.D., Chair.
Department of Sociology: Greta Gilbertson, Ph.D., Chair.
Department of Theology: Terrence Tilley, Ph.D., Chair.

RESEARCH

Biological Sciences. Two main areas of research are available: cell and molecular biology and ecology. Cell and molecular biology research programs include molecular and cellular analysis of immune response to cancer; immunomodulators and their molecular mechanisms of action; eukaryotic gene expression and RNA processing; genetic basis of aging; genetic toxicology; cytogenetic and molecular analysis of chromosomes; spermatogenesis and early development; cellular differentiation; regeneration in invertebrates; neuronal differentiation, structure, function, and analysis; role of growth factors. The ecology program spans behavioral, population, community, and ecosystem levels. Areas of emphasis include conservation biology, forest-microbial dynamics and function, ecology of phytoplankton and bacteria, insect-parasitoid interactions, medical entomology, paleoecology, plant-insect interactions, primate behavior and ecology, systematics and evolution of fishes, and vertebrate physiological ecology.

Classical Languages and Literature. Current research interests range widely over the following areas: Greek poetry, historiography, religion, archaeology, and philosophy; Latin lyric, elegiac, and epic poetry and historiography; Roman topography; textual criticism; the intellectual life of late antiquity; medieval and Renaissance Latin; and Latin paleography.

Communication and Media Studies. Support facilities provide a lab area for graduate study in interactive media, digital video, hypertext, computer graphics, Web page design, digital audio and video editing, news and magazine production, and public communications on the Internet as well as opportunities to work at the University's public radio station.

Computer and Information Science. Current research and concentrations are available in the following areas: information systems and applications, artificial intelligence, communications and networks, and computation and algorithms. Courses available include software system design, computer architecture, parallel computation, computer security and ethics, data communications and networks, graph theory and network design, internet computing and Java programming, data base systems, and artificial intelligence.

Economics. Research interests are broad, with perhaps slightly more emphasis given to areas of applied rather than theoretical economics. Topics include development economics, financial economics, international economics, monetary economics, and industrial organization.

Elections and Campaign Management. Current research interests focus on the theoretical and practical tools necessary to excel at managing political campaigns. Rigorous multidisciplinary instruction in voting behavior, candidate strategy, analysis of survey data, and media management is provided by leading academics and top industry professionals.

English Language and Literatures. The research interests of the faculty members are represented in virtually every field of English and American literature, from Old English literature to twentieth-century British and American literature as well as literary criticism and critical theory. The English department has particular strength in eighteenth-century literature and culture.

History. Current research interests range over diverse areas of medieval history, including England, France, Germany, Italy, and Spain, and include concentrations on the medieval Church, particularly liturgy, monasticism and canon law, medieval society and economy, notably women and family, towns, and trade; cultural history; and legal history. In European history the concentrations are Tudor-Stuart England; early modern and modern Britain, Ireland, France, and Germany; Protestant and Catholic reformations; European intellectual history; gender history; and Imperial and Soviet Russia. In American history research areas include women in colonial and modern America, Thomas Jefferson and the Republican era, the Civil War, the American South, the New Deal, foreign relations, African-American history, urban studies, immigration, and Latin America.

Humanities and Sciences. A unique course of study providing interdisciplinary approaches to individualized topics in areas that often cannot be addressed by more discipline-based graduate programs. Recent examples of study have explored the relationship between at least two fields or approaches to a particular topic. Such areas of study have included: the politics of culture, Native American approaches to science, and the historical economy of literature.

International Political Economy and Development. Current research efforts focus primarily on the interaction of political and economic institutions in the functioning of the global economy and their respective roles in facilitating political modernization and economic development. Ongoing research projects include the politics of economic stabilization programs, trade policies and economic growth, foreign assistance and economic reform efforts, and the political foundations of poverty. Participating faculty members have traditionally specialized in the following areas: corporative and international politics, development studies (project management, finance and development, economic and political development, community and social development), emerging markets and country risk analysis, international business and finance, and international and development economics.

Latin American and Latino Studies. The certificate program consists of three courses: an interdisciplinary course integrating the art, culture, and history of Latin Americans and Latinos in the United States; a course on the history of Latin America or Latinos in the U.S.; and an elective course on Latin American or Latino arts and humanities or social sciences.

Medieval Studies. The Center for Medieval Studies offers an interdisciplinary M.A. and a doctoral certificate in medieval studies, giving students the opportunity to broaden their knowledge of the Middle Ages and to integrate in a coherent whole the various facets of medieval civilization. Disciplines participating in the program include art, classics, English, history, modern languages and literature (French, German, Italian, and Spanish), music, philosophy, political science, and theology.

Philosophy. The department seeks to maintain a wide diversity of research interests and competencies. While strong in the history of philosophy, it has special capabilities in continental philosophy, analytic philosophy, classical American philosophy, medieval philosophy, and philosophy of religion. With respect to both historical and contemporary perspectives, it has strengths in epistemology and metaphysics as well as moral and political philosophy.

Political Science. Faculty members teach courses leading to the M.A. in the history of political philosophy, from classical to contemporary. Areas in American politics include institutions, political behavior, public policy, and urban politics. The department also offers M.A. and minor fields in political economy and comparative/international politics.

Psychology. Research is being undertaken in three areas: clinical, applied developmental, and psychometrics. Current clinical research interests are behavior therapy, family therapy, health psychology, neuropsychology, child therapy, social supports, and treatment planning and evaluation. Developmental research employs a life-span orientation in research on developmental processes and in the application of developmental principles to the design, implementation, and evaluation of prevention and intervention programs and to the assessment of children and families. Psychometrics research focuses on the quantitative aspects of psychology, especially test constructing, personnel selection, program evaluation, and advanced statistical procedures.

Sociology and Anthropology. Research centers on three specialization areas. Demography research includes family planning program efforts and fertility behavior; career histories and contraceptive behavior; gender, ethnic, and racial inequalities in the labor force; U.S. metropolitan migration; and residential segregation. Ethnic/minority research includes household structure among Dominican and Colombian immigrants, comorbidity of mental illness and problem behavior among Hispanic adolescents, and migration and adaptation of Hispanic groups. Sociology of religion research includes fundamentalist Catholic organizations, religion and social movements, and the abortion controversy and Catholic social thought. Other faculty research includes the sociology of emotions and the society of knowledge. The department also offers M.A. specialization in justice and criminology studies.

Theology. Faculty research represents the three areas of specialization in the department. In the biblical section, faculty research includes exegetical, theological, narrative, and historical interpretations. The historical theology faculty does research in Greek and Latin patristics, medieval theology, nineteenth- and twentieth-century European and American religious thought, and U.S. religious history. The systematic theology faculty, focusing on contemporary Catholic theology, is engaged in research in fundamental theology, Karl Rahner, liberation and feminist theologies, Christian social ethics, and moral theology.

GEORGE FOX UNIVERSITY

Graduate School

Programs of Study

The Doctor of Clinical Psychology (Psy.D.) (full-time: Newberg) is an APA–accredited, five-year program consisting of four years of study and a one-year internship. The program is based on the practitioner-scholar model and emphasizes clinical skills.

The Doctor of Education (Ed.D.) (part-time: Newberg, Portland) prepares educators to be leaders in their chosen specialties. Summer, weekend, and evening courses are designed for current educators.

The Master of Arts in Teaching (M.A.T.) (part-time: Portland, Salem, Redmond) is a sixteen- or twenty-month program that prepares early childhood and K–12 teachers for public and private schools. Evening, weekend, and summer programs are offered.

The Master of Education (M.Ed.) (part-time: multiple locations) is for educators seeking advanced training. Eight specializations are offered. Summer and evening courses are designed for current educators. Courses are offered on-site and online.

The Administrative License Program (part-time: multiple locations) is designed either as a stand-alone program or as part of the M.Ed. or Ed.D. programs. Curricula are offered leading to the Initial Administrative License, Continuing Administrator/Initial Superintendent License, and Continuing Superintendent's License.

The Master of Business Administration (M.B.A.) (part-time: Portland) is offered in two formats. The Executive M.B.A. is a two-year program scheduled in twenty-four Friday-Saturday blocks, with an online learning community. The Professional M.B.A. is a 26-month cohort program offering classes one night a week and some Saturdays.

The Master of Arts (M.A.) in counseling (full-time/part-time: Portland, Salem) prepares students to be licensed professional counselors. The program includes two semesters of internship.

The Master of Arts (M.A.) in marriage and family therapy (full-time/part-time: Portland, Salem) is designed to prepare students to be licensed marriage and family therapists. The program includes two semesters of internship.

The Master of Arts (M.A.) in school counseling (part-time: Portland) prepares students to obtain an Initial School Counseling License. Evening and weekend classes are designed for working professionals. The program includes two semesters of internship.

The Master of Science (M.S.) in school psychology (part-time: Portland) prepares students to obtain their Initial School Psychology License. Evening and weekend classes are designed for working professionals. The program includes two semesters of internship.

The Master of Arts (M.A.) in organizational leadership (part-time: Boise, Idaho) is a fifteen-month program designed to develop leaders for a broad range of organizations, including business, health care, education, the church, and the public sector.

Five programs are offered at the George Fox Evangelical Seminary in Portland.

The Doctor of Ministry (D.Min.) (full-time/part-time: Portland) is the highest professional degree for those in parish or related ministries. It is offered in two tracks: leadership in the emerging culture as well as leadership and spiritual formation.

The Master of Divinity (M.Div.) (full-time/part-time: Portland) prepares students for denominational ordination. Students may concentrate studies in chaplaincy, pastoral studies, biblical studies, Christian ministries, spiritual formation, marriage and family counseling, or Christian history and thought.

The Master of Arts (M.A.) in Christian ministries (full-time/part-time: Portland) prepares students for ordination or recording or for work as a lay minister. Studies may be concentrated in church leadership, adult ministries, urban ministries, spiritual formation, or family ministries.

The Master of Arts in Theological Studies (M.A.T.S.) program (full-time/part-time: Portland) prepares students for doctoral work in the field of theological studies with an emphasis on biblical studies or Christian history and thought.

The Master of Arts (M.A.) in spiritual formation is a 42-credit-hour degree designed to equip lay persons as spiritual directors or as guides for spiritual formation ministries in the church or parachurch organizations.

Research Facilities

The Newberg campus library and the Portland Center library house a combined total of nearly 200,000 print volumes and receive more than 1,100 print journal subscriptions. More than 19,000 journals are available in electronic format. The University is a member of the Portland Area Library System (PORTALS) and Summit, a consortium of academic libraries. Summit enables users to make requests from 22 million books held in all Oregon and Washington public colleges and eleven private colleges.

Financial Aid

Scholarships are available for selected programs. The University participates in Federal Stafford Student Loan programs.

Cost of Study

Tuition varies by program. Applicants should contact the Office of Graduate Admission for specific program costs.

Living and Housing Costs

A wide variety of housing is available in Newberg and the metropolitan Portland area. On-campus housing is not available for graduate students.

Student Group

Overall enrollment at George Fox University is more than 3,200 students. Of those, more than 1,300 are enrolled in graduate programs.

Location

George Fox's 77-acre campus is located in Newberg, Oregon, 23 miles southwest of Portland. Classes are held at the University's Portland Center, Salem Center, Boise (Idaho) Center, and at other teaching sites in Oregon.

The University

George Fox is a Christian university of the arts, sciences, and professional studies ranked by *U.S. News & World Report* as a top-tier regional university. The University was founded in 1891 by Quaker pioneers. From the beginning, its purpose has been to demonstrate the meaning of Jesus Christ by offering a caring educational community in which each individual can achieve the highest intellectual and personal growth and participate responsibly in the world's concerns.

Applying

To be admitted to any of the graduate programs, an applicant must have a baccalaureate degree from an accredited college or university, with at least a 3.0 GPA over the last two years of course work. Certain application requirements differ among the graduate programs. Information may be obtained by contacting the Office of Graduate Admissions. The application fee is a $40 (nonrefundable). A $200 matriculation deposit is required of all accepted applicants.

Correspondence and Information

Office of Graduate Admissions
George Fox University
414 North Meridian Street #6149
Newberg, Oregon 97132
Phone: 503-554-2260
800-631-0921 (toll-free)
E-mail: graduate.admission@georgefox.edu
Web site: http://georgefox.edu

DEGREE PROGRAMS AND DIRECTORS

SCHOOL OF BEHAVIORAL AND HEALTH SCIENCES
James D. Foster, Dean; Ph.D., Ohio State.
Doctor of Psychology (Psy.D.): Wayne V. Adams, Ph.D., Syracuse.

SCHOOL OF EDUCATION
James D. Worthington, Dean; Ph.D., Syracuse.
Doctor of Education (Ed.D.): Gary Railsback, Ph.D., UCLA.
Master of Arts in Counseling (M.A.): Karin B. Jordan, Ph.D., Georgia.
Master of Arts in Marriage and Family Therapy (M.A.): Karin B. Jordan, Ph.D., Georgia.
Master of Arts in Teaching (M.A.T.): Kevin Carr, Ph.D., Idaho.
Master of Education (M.Ed.): Judy Keeney, M.A., Oregon.
Master of Science in School Psychology (M.S.): Karin B. Jordan, Ph.D., Georgia.

SCHOOL OF MANAGEMENT
Dirk Barram, Interim Dean; Ph.D., Michigan State.
Master of Business Administration (M.B.A.) **Executive Track**: Jeff VandenHoek, M.A., Azusa Pacific.
Master of Business Administration (M.B.A.) **Professional Track**: Jim Steele, Ed.D., George Fox.

SCHOOL OF PROFESSIONAL STUDIES
Carol Green, Dean, Ph.D., Texas Tech.
Master of Arts in Organizational Leadership (M.A.): Mary Olson, Ph.D., Idaho.

GEORGE FOX EVANGELICAL SEMINARY
Jules Glanzer, Dean; D.Min., Fuller Theological Seminary.
Mark Weinert, Associate Dean; Ph.D., Vanderbilt.
Doctor of Ministry (D.Min.): Charles J. Conniry Jr., Ph.D., Fuller Theological Seminary.
Master of Divinity (M.Div.): MaryKate Morse, Ph.D., Gonzaga.
Master of Arts in Christian Ministries (M.A.): MaryKate Morse, Ph.D., Gonzaga.
Master of Arts in Spiritual Formation (M.A.): MaryKate Morse, Ph.D., Gonzaga.
Master of Arts in Theological Studies (M.A.T.S.): MaryKate Morse, Ph.D., Gonzaga.

GRAND VALLEY STATE UNIVERSITY

Graduate Studies

Programs of Study

Grand Valley State University (GVSU) offers twenty-six graduate programs and enrolls approximately 3,670 graduate students each year. Graduate programs include Master of Arts in English, Master of Business Administration, Master of Education (adult and higher education, advanced content specializations, college student affairs leadership, early childhood education, educational differentiation, educational leadership, educational technology integration, elementary education, graduate teacher certification, middle and secondary levels, reading–language arts, school counseling, school library media services, special education, and teaching English to speakers of other languages (TESOL)), Master of Health Administration, Master of Public Administration (criminal justice, health administration, nonprofit management and leadership, and public management/urban and regional affairs), Master of Science in Accounting, Master of Science in biology, Master of Science in biomedical sciences, Master of Science in biostatistics, Master of Science in cell and molecular biology, Master of Science in Communication, Master of Science in Computer Information Systems (database management, distributed computing, information systems management, object-oriented technology, and software engineering), Master of Science in Criminal Justice, Master of Science in Engineering (electrical and computer engineering, manufacturing operations, mechanical engineering, and product design and manufacturing engineering), Master of Science in medical and bioinformatics, Master of Science in Nursing (clinical emphases: adult/elderly, child, family, mental health, and women; functional roles: administration, case management, and education), Master of Science in Occupational Therapy, Doctor of Physical Therapy, Master of Science in Physician Assistant Studies, Master of Social Work, and Master of Science in Taxation. Certificates are also available in business (e-commerce), computer information systems, education, engineering, nursing, public administration, and social work.

Research Facilities

The Steelcase Library, which is located in the DeVos Center, has a computer-operated robotic retrieval system that holds the library's circulating collection and can accommodate 250,000 volumes. The 10,400-square-foot library also includes a circulation desk, a traditional reference desk, microfilm/fiche reader/printers, computers, a reading room, a photocopy room, a library instruction center with computers for database access, staff offices, and workspaces. Librarians staff the reference desk. The tables and carrels are wired for laptop computer use. The reading room holds the expanded reference collection and the current issue of 700 journal titles. This library also houses the Grand Rapids Bar Association's law collection. The entire GVSU library system houses more than 634,000 volumes, 5,000 periodical subscriptions in print and electronic format, and 23,200 reels of microfilm. Computer facilities are available throughout the campus, and all labs run on MS Office Suite, SPSS, SAS, SAP, and departmental-specific applications for course instruction. In addition to having wireless access in the main plaza, there are multiple network connections throughout the DeVos Center and wireless connectivity in all academic buildings. DeVos also has forty kiosk stations for access to e-mail, student records, and library resources.

Financial Aid

Grand Valley State University offers graduate assistantships through various departments to help students finance their education. Many assistantships cover tuition and include a stipend for hours worked in conjunction with faculty members. Domestic students may also apply for federal student aid. Tuition reimbursement options are available through some local employers.

Cost of Study

Tuition for 2006–07 is $325 per credit hour for in-state students and $600 per credit hour for out-of-state and international students. There are no additional fees charged to students for tuition or academic programs. Students who qualify for a graduate assistantship are considered Michigan residents for tuition purposes.

Living and Housing Costs

Grand Valley State University offers housing for graduate students at the Pew Campus, in downtown Grand Rapids. Housing 180 students, Secchia Hall has one-, two-, three-, and four-bedroom units and is located directly across the street from the academic facilities. Winter Hall features fully furnished one- and two-bedroom efficiencies. The most recent costs range from $2116 to $3176 per semester. Off-campus housing within walking distance of the campus is readily available in the Grand Rapids community.

Student Group

The graduate student population at Grand Valley State University ranges from full-time students directly out of an undergraduate program to part-time students with many years of professional experience. Approximately 65 percent of the students are women, and a small percentage are international students who represent more than thirty countries.

Location

The Pew Campus, which is located in downtown Grand Rapids, comprises the majority of Grand Valley's graduate programs. Located on a 15-acre site just west of the Grand River, Grand Valley is in the heart of the city. Grand Rapids is the second-largest city in Michigan, with a vibrant economy and a revitalized downtown that provides students numerous social and professional opportunities. As the University continues to grow, many regional sites offer graduate programs at locations such as Muskegon, Holland, and Traverse City.

The University

Grand Valley State University was established in 1963 in Allendale, Michigan. Grand Valley enrolls approximately 22,565 students, approximately 3,670 of whom are graduate students. The Pew Campus in downtown Grand Rapids is the only full-service campus in the city and houses the majority of Grand Valley's graduate programs. The DeVos Center is a 250,000-square-foot facility that includes a state-of-the-art library, more than sixty classrooms and laboratories, faculty and staff offices, and more than 320 computers for student use. The most recent project to add to the Grand Rapids skyline is the Cook-DeVos Center for Health Sciences. The five-story, 215,000-square-foot facility houses all of Grand Valley's health professions programs.

Correspondence and Information

Graduate Admissions
117B DeVos Center
Grand Valley State University
401 Fulton Street West
Grand Rapids, Michigan 49504
Phone: 616-331-7220
800-748-0246 (toll-free)
Fax: 616-331-6476
E-mail: go2gvsu@gvsu.edu
Web site: http://www.gvsu.edu

GRADUATE PROGRAM DIRECTORS

Priscilla Kimboko, Ph.D., Dean of Graduate Studies and Grants Administration.
Accounting: Claudia Bajema, M.B.A.
Biology: Mark Luttenton, Ph.D.
Biomedical Sciences: Debra Burg, Ph.D.
Biostatistics: Robert Downer, Ph.D.
Business: Claudia Bajema, M.B.A.
Cell and Molecular Biology: Mark Staves, Ph.D.
Communication: Michael Pritchard, Ed.D.
Computer Information Systems: D. Robert Adams, Ph.D.
Criminal Justice: Debra Ross, Ph.D.
Education: Douglas Busman, Ph.D.
Engineering: Charles Standridge, Ph.D.
English: Benjamin Lockerd, Ph.D.
Health Administration: Danny Balfour, Ph.D.
Medical and Bioinformatics: Paul Leidig, Ph.D.
Nursing: Jean Martin, D.N.Sc.
Occupational Therapy: Nancy Powell, Ph.D.
Physical Therapy: John Peck, Ph.D.
Physician Assistant Studies: Jane Toot, Ph.D.
Public Administration: Danny Balfour, Ph.D.
Social Work: George Grant, M.S.W.
Taxation: Claudia Bajema, M.B.A.

GREEN MOUNTAIN COLLEGE

Graduate Programs

Programs of Study

Green Mountain College (GMC) offers two master's degrees: a Master of Science (M.S.) in environmental studies and a Master of Business Administration (M.B.A.). The M.S. in Environmental Studies Program offers three concentrations: conservation biology, writing and communication, and a self-designed concentration. The M.B.A. emphasizes sustainable business practices (better known as a green M.B.A.), with an optional track in nonprofit organization management. Both programs are offered through a Web-based distance-learning model that allows students to live at home and continue their full-time professional careers while working toward their degree. These graduate programs emphasize professional development through applied skills and build a secure foundation of theory. The online graduate programs are accredited by the New England Association of Schools and Colleges. The normal time expected to complete each degree is two years, which includes two brief on-campus residencies.

The 39-credit M.S. in Environmental Studies Program is distinctive in that students apply the skills and knowledge learned to issues in their own regions. This enables students to go beyond conventional education and learn to identify and solve problems in their communities. Classes typically begin with a case study and then move to a relevant theory as students are asked to apply the theory to issues in their bioregions. Concentrations are offered in conservation biology and in writing and communications. Under special circumstances, students may be allowed to work with an adviser to craft an individually tailored curriculum (self-designed concentration).Students in the M.S. in Environmental Studies Program can expect to gain a solid foundation in environmental science, law, policy, and organizing principles. Students have ongoing interaction with the College's excellent faculty in disciplines as diverse as history, biology, business and economics, geology, communications, philosophy, law, education, English, and natural resource management.

The 37-credit M.B.A. program emphasizes sustainable business practices (better known as a green M.B.A.). Concentrations are available in general business administration and nonprofit organization management. Students learn how to achieve their economic objectives while addressing the needs of employees, their community, and other stakeholders. The program reflects the growing trend among successful companies to focus on the triple bottom line, seeking competitive advantages through practices that are socially responsible and environmentally sound. M.B.A. students gain a solid foundation in the core areas of business administration, including finance, accounting, marketing, organizational leadership, business law, and ethics. The program grounds this knowledge in the relationships that define the communities where students live and work. As one of the nation's pioneer environmental liberal arts colleges, Green Mountain is especially well prepared to produce business leaders who are able to focus on economic success—without losing sight of the bigger picture.

Research Facilities

Griswold Library, the Jose M. Calhoun Learning Center, and Computer Services occupy a spacious and modern four-story building situated at the southern end of the campus. The focus of the library's collection remains its bound collection of 72,000 volumes and accompanying periodicals. In recent years, access to the Internet and the addition of a number of electronic collections has significantly enhanced the library's available resources. The library's bound collection may be searched via the Web using the online catalog known as Quarry. More than 1,000 current and back-filed periodical titles in print, microform, and electronic format support the research efforts of students and faculty members, with electronic and print indexes providing access to these resources. The library's homepage provides further links to a host of electronic and online resources. Griswold Library is a national participant in interlibrary loan services through its membership in New England's library and information services network, NELINET. This association extends the College's borrowing privileges to libraries throughout the United States and Canada.

The Calhoun Learning Center, located on the building's top floor, actively uses the available resources provided by the library. Computer Services, located on the building's ground floor, provides assistance to students and faculty and staff members across the campus. Classrooms and computer labs, which provide electronic access to both the College's network system and to the Internet, are located in the library.

Financial Aid

Financial Aid is available to students in the College's graduate programs, and the Office of Financial Aid works with students to determine their eligibility. All students applying for federal financial aid must take at least 6 credits per term. For more information, students should contact Wendy Ellis, Director of Financial Aid (802-287-8209; ellisw@greenmtn.edu).

Cost of Study

Tuition is $475 per credit. M.B.A. students pay about $17,500 for 37 credits, while M.S. students pay around $18,500 for 39 credits.

Living and Housing Costs

Because these are distance-learning courses, student housing is not necessary. However, students attend two brief on-campus residencies, one at the beginning of each academic year. A list of local accommodations is available through the Office of Graduate Studies. The cost for lodging is not included in the tuition.

Student Group

There are about 700 undergraduate and graduate students; they come from thirty-three states and more than ten countries. About 47 percent are New England residents.

Location

Vermont's famously beautiful countryside provides the perfect backdrop for a college focused on the environment. Located in the historic town of Poultney, Vermont, the College is a rural campus positioned for convenient access to numerous metropolitan areas. Excellent interstate highways and public transportation connect the campus with New York City, Boston, and Montreal. Amtrak train service is 8 miles from the College. Several major ski resorts—Okemo, Killington, Pico, Bromley, and Stratton Mountain—are within an easy drive of the campus.

The College

Founded in 1834 by the Troy Conference of the Methodist Church, Green Mountain College is a coeducational, private college, accredited by the New England Association of Schools and Colleges, Inc. As an environmental liberal arts college, Green Mountain offers students a special opportunity to integrate modern environmental thought into a traditional liberal arts or preprofessional course of study, regardless of their major.

Applying

M.S. applicants must submit the completed application, all undergraduate- and graduate-level transcripts, a current resume, three letters of reference, and a portfolio that demonstrates interest and experience in the proposed field of study and includes a 500-word essay. Students interested in the conservation biology track are expected to have studied biology, ecology, chemistry, and statistics as undergraduates. M.B.A. applicants must submit the completed application, official transcripts from all colleges and/or professional schools, three letters of recommendation, GMAT scores, and a personal essay. Applications are processed on a rolling basis.

Correspondence and Information

Sue Whiting, Administrative Assistant
Office of Graduate Studies
Green Mountain College
One College Circle
Poultney, Vermont 05764

Phone: 802-287-8319
Fax: 802-287-8099
E-mail: whitings@greenmtn.edu
Web site: http://www.greenmtn.edu

THE FACULTY AND THEIR RESEARCH

Master of Science in Environmental Studies

Laird Christensen, Associate Professor of English and Environmental Studies and Program Director; Ph.D., Oregon. American literature, creative writing, poetry, Native American literatures, and natural history writing.

Meriel Brooks, Associate Professor of Biology; Ph.D., Arizona. Interface of science and policy, particularly as it plays out in recreational fisheries issues.

Greg Brown, Professor of Natural Resource Management; Ph.D., Idaho. Developing survey methods to expand public involvement in environmental decisions by including spatial measures of landscape values and special places.

Natalie Coe, Assistant Professor of Biology; Ph.D., Minnesota. Beech bark disease.

Theresa Coker, Assistant Professor of Environmental Education; Ph.D., Ohio State. Balancing the benefit and cost of outdoor learning.

Steven Fesmire, Associate Professor of Philosophy and Chair of Department of Environmental Studies; Ph.D., Southern Illinois. Ethics (especially environmental and animal ethics), history of American philosophy (including Henry David Thoreau, Ralph Waldo Emerson, William James, and John Dewey), social and political philosophy, philosophical psychology (especially theories of imagination and metaphor).

James Graves, Associate Professor of Botany and Environmental Studies; Ph.D., North Carolina at Chapel Hill. Biochemistry of secondary plant compounds, nutrient cycling in ecosystems, physiological ecology of plants, coevolution of fruits and avian frugivores.

James Harding, Assistant Professor of Recreation and Natural Resource Management; Ph.D., Montana. Environmental ethics as expressed through familiarity with place, decision making regarding low-impact recommendations, the ethics of rock climbing and rock climbers in the Bitterroot region of Montana.

Steven Letendre, Associate Professor of Management and Environmental Studies; Ph.D., Delaware. Economic analysis of emerging environmental technologies and the development of policies and regulations to promote a sustainable energy future.

Matthew Osborn, Assistant Professor of History and Environmental Studies; Ph.D., California, Santa Cruz. Modern European history, modern Britain, Latin American history, environmental studies.

Rebecca Purdom, Associate Professor of Environmental Studies, Law and Policy and Director, College Honors Program and Prelaw Advising Program; J.D., Vermont. Paradox of wilderness restoration: public participation and public virtue.

Ron Steffens, Associate Professor of Communications; M.F.A., Arizona. Journalism education, environmental communication, creative writing, creative writing in elementary and secondary schools, interdisciplinary education, computer-assisted instruction/distance education, natural resource management.

Susan Sutheimer, Associate Professor of Chemistry, Chair of Department of Natural and Mathematical Sciences, and Director, Service Learning; Ph.D., Kent State. Understanding aquatic ecosystems based on chemical analysis of freshwaters; development of analytical methods for the determination of environmentally important chemicals (natural and manmade); acid rain (its sources and its implications); nutrients and pharmaceuticals in lakes (sources and analysis); modeling aluminum, chromium and lead speciation, binding and toxicity in natural waters.

William Throop, Professor of Philosophy and Environmental Studies; Ph.D., Brown. Environmental ethics, theory of knowledge and contemporary Anglo-American philosophy.

John Van Hoesen, Assistant Professor of Geology; Ph.D., Nevada, Las Vegas. Glacial and periglacial geomorphology, using GIS and Visual Basic to evaluate natural earth processes, and addressing long- and short-term climate change gleaned from the geomorphic record.

Stefanie Wickstrom, Professor of Environmental Studies and Political Science; Ph.D., Oregon. Environmental politics and policy, Indian politics and policy, social movements and environmental justice in Latin America and the United States, the politics of identity, gender, and ethnicity.

Master of Business Administration

Bill Prado, Assistant Professor and Program Director; M.B.A., NYU. International business and finance: asset-based, credit-secured, and sales/export financing.

John F. Brennan, Professor of Business and President; M.B.A., Harvard. Executive leadership and business ethics.

Steven Fesmire, Associate Professor of Philosophy and Chair of Department of Environmental Studies; Ph.D., Southern Illinois. Ethics (especially environmental and animal ethics), history of American philosophy (including Henry David Thoreau, Ralph Waldo Emerson, William James, and John Dewey), social and political philosophy, philosophical psychology (especially theories of imagination and metaphor).

Karen Fleming, Visiting Professor of Business, M.B.A., Harvard.

Paul Hancock, Professor of Economics; Ph.D., New School for Social Research. Labor history, history of economic thought, migration theory.

Steven Letendre, Associate Professor of Management and Environmental Studies; Ph.D., Delaware. Economic analysis of emerging environmental technologies and development of policies and regulations to promote a sustainable energy future.

Jacob Park, Assistant Professor of Business and Public Policy; M.S., MIT. Global environment and business strategy, corporate social responsibility, business ethics, community-based entrepreneurship and innovation.

Frank Pauzé, Associate Professor of Business and Economics; M.B.A., Boston College. Strategy within the hospitality industry and small businesses within that service sector.

Rebecca Purdom, Associate Professor of Environmental Studies, Law and Policy and Director, College Honors Program and Prelaw Advising Program; J.D., Vermont. Paradox of wilderness restoration: public participation and public virtue.

HAMPTON UNIVERSITY

Graduate College

Programs of Study

The programs of the Graduate College are designed to prepare students for professional competence in a specific field and for prospective graduate study. Graduate programs leading to the Master in Teaching degree are offered for elementary, middle, and secondary education. The Graduate College also offers the Master of Arts (M.A.) degree in communicative sciences and disorders, counseling, elementary education, and special education. In addition, students may pursue the Master of Science (M.S.) degree in applied mathematics, biology, chemistry, computer science, medical science, nursing, and physics; the Master of Business Administration (M.B.A.); the Specialist in Education (Ed.S.) in counseling; the Ph.D. in nursing and physics; and the Doctor of Physical Therapy (D.P.T.).

Programs are planned in consultation with the student's faculty adviser. Specific requirements vary with the department, but in most instances, candidates for the Master of Arts degree must complete a minimum of 30–32 semester hours and take a comprehensive examination.

Candidates for the Master of Science degree in applied mathematics, biology, chemistry, and physics are required to complete a minimum of 32 semester hours, including a thesis. Medical Science majors must complete 50 semester hours, including a comprehensive examination. Nursing majors, who must complete a minimum of 45 semester hours, have a choice of a thesis or a comprehensive examination. The Master of Business Administration degree requires 36 semester hours, and the Ph.D. in physics requires a minimum of 72 semester hours.

Research Facilities

The William R. and Norma B. Harvey Library, which opened in 1992, is a major focal point of the academic environment of Hampton University. Besides housing an extensive collection of books and periodicals, it serves as a partial depository of U.S. government documents. The distinctive George Foster Peabody Collection, which consists of more than 25,000 items by and about African Americans, is housed in a specially designed room in the Harvey Library.

Other research facilities include computer resources with state-of-the-art mainframes, parallel processors and numerous microcomputers connected via a fiber-optic local area network. Selected research centers include the Center for Atmospheric Sciences, the Center for the Origin and Structure of Matter, the Center for Advanced Medical Instrumentation, the Nuclear/High Energy Physics Research of Excellence, the Research Center for Optical Physics, and the National Center for Minority Special Educational Research. The Hampton University Museum has an outstanding collection of art, including pieces from sub-Saharan Africa, Asia, Oceania, and American Indians.

Financial Aid

Financial aid is available in the form of fellowships; traineeships; teaching, research, laboratory, and residence hall assistantships; loans; and part-time employment. Assistantship and fellowship stipends generally range from $3200 to $20,000 per academic year and may include varying levels of tuition support.

Cost of Study

In 2006–07, tuition was $13,358 for two academic semesters for students taking 10–17 semester hours and $335 per semester hour for those taking 1–9 hours. Nonrefundable fees and book costs amounted to approximately $1000 per year.

Living and Housing Costs

Most graduate students live off campus. The University Office of Off-Campus Housing provides assistance in locating housing. Limited on-campus accommodations are available in University-owned apartments. Off-campus housing expenses for single students are estimated at $6750 per year.

Student Group

In 2005–06, the total University enrollment was more than 5,740 students, 362 of whom were enrolled in the Graduate College. The student body is drawn from forty-nine states, several U.S. territories, and other countries. Approximately 50 percent of the graduate students are enrolled full-time. About 95 percent of the Graduate College alumni are employed in their chosen fields.

Location

Hampton University is located in Hampton, Virginia, 27 miles north of Norfolk and 80 miles southeast of Richmond. The University was built on Virginia's peninsula, where the James and York rivers join. The region is richly steeped in early American history: a Kecoughtan native community once stood near the University grounds, and the historic communities of Jamestown, Yorktown, and Williamsburg are all within a 45-minute drive. The city of Hampton is the oldest community in the United States to be continuously occupied by English-speaking people. Hampton is accessible by car, bus, or train as well as direct airline service via Newport News/Williamsburg and Norfolk.

The University

Chartered in the city of Hampton, Elizabeth City County, Virginia, Hampton University was founded by Gen. Samuel Chapman Armstrong in April 1868, in the first days of Reconstruction, in order to assist recently freed slaves in obtaining an "education for life." In line with its broadening educational program, the University inaugurated graduate courses in 1928 and awarded its first master's degree in 1932. The graduate offerings have continued to expand with the addition of a Ph.D. in physics and in nursing as well as the D.P.T. in physical therapy.

Applying

Applications for admission should be mailed directly to the Graduate College. Students may be admitted to the Graduate College at the beginning of the fall or spring semester or at the beginning of the summer session.

Correspondence and Information

Dean
Graduate College
Hampton University
Hampton, Virginia 23668
Phone: 757-727-5454
Fax: 757-727-5498
E-mail: hugrad@hamptonu.edu
Web site: http://www.hamptonu.edu/academics/graduatecollege

THE FACULTY

Donald A. Whitney, Dean of the Graduate College; Ph.D., Virginia, 1977.
Karen D. Brown, Graduate College Counselor; M.S.M., Florida Tech, 2004.

Deans
Continuing Education: W. O. Lawton, Ed.D., George Washington, 1982.
School of Business: Sid Credle, Ph.D., Texas at Austin, 1989.
School of Engineering and Technology: Eric Sheppard, Sc.D., MIT, 1994.
School of Liberal Arts and Education: Mamie E. Locke, Ph.D., Miami (Florida), 1981.
School of Nursing: Constance Hendricks, Ph.D., Boston College, 1992.
School of Science: Claudia M. Rankins, Ph.D., Hampton, 1997.

Program Heads and Coordinators
Applied Mathematics: Carolyn Morgan, Professor and Chair; Ph.D., Union (New York), 1982.
Biology: Elaine Eatman, Professor; Ph.D., Howard, 1966.
Business Administration: Sid Credle, Associate Professor and Dean; Ph.D., Texas at Austin, 1989.
Chemistry: Isai T. Urasa, Professor; Ph.D., Colorado State, 1977.
Communicative Sciences and Disorders: Dorian Lee-Wilkerson, Associate Professor; Ph.D., Howard, 1988.
Computer Science: Stephen V. Providence, Assistant Professor; Ph.D., CUNY, 2000.
Counseling: Spencer R. Baker, Assistant Professor; Ph.D., Old Dominion, 2000.
Education: Martha M. Williams, Assistant Professor; Ph.D., Virginia Tech, 1979.
Master in Teaching: Martha M. Williams, Assistant Professor; Ph.D., Virginia Tech, 1979.
Medical Science: Mark G. Davis, Assistant Professor; Ph.D., Meharry Medical College, 1999.
Nursing: Arlene J. Montgomery, Associate Professor; Ph.D., Old Dominion, 1994.
Physical Therapy: Marilys Randolph, Associate Professor; Ph.D., Howard, 1991; PT.
Physics: Doyle A. Temple, Professor; Ph.D., MIT, 1989.

Academy Building, one of five national historic landmark buildings on campus.

The William R. and Norma B. Harvey Library, a state-of-the-art facility.

A view of the campus waterfront along the Hampton River.

HARVARD UNIVERSITY

Graduate School of Arts and Sciences

Programs of Study

The Graduate School of Arts and Sciences offers master's and Ph.D. degrees under fifty-four departments, committees, and divisions within the Harvard Faculty of Arts and Sciences (FAS). It also offers a joint M.D./Ph.D. program in cooperation with the Harvard Medical School and a special program in health science and technology with the Medical School and the Massachusetts Institute of Technology. In many departments, the master's degree is awarded only in progress to the doctorate, and applications for the master's degree only are not accepted. Common to all programs are a residence requirement, a tuition requirement, and a requirement of continuous registration from admission until completion of the degree program. Candidates for a master's degree must complete a minimum of one year of full-time study in residence at full tuition (see below). The requirements for the Ph.D. vary considerably from subject to subject, but in all departments a minimum of two years of full-time study in residence at full tuition is required. Candidates for the Ph.D. are normally expected to demonstrate language proficiency, pass general or qualifying examinations, and write a thesis based on original research. Application forms and pamphlets describing the requirements and programs of particular departments may be obtained from the Office of Admissions and Financial Aid.

Research Facilities

The University offers outstanding resources for study and research. The University library system has holdings of more than 11 million volumes and is composed of three main libraries—Widener Memorial, Lamont, and Hilles—and more than ninety other collections. These include special libraries in rare books and manuscripts, art, science, geology, Asian studies, government, music, and anthropology and separate libraries in many departments and research institutes. Several computing facilities with DEC and IBM mainframes and microcomputers are available for research, computing, thesis work, and word processing. Special research facilities in the sciences include the Center for Astrophysics, which combines the Harvard Observatory and the Smithsonian Astrophysical Observatory; the Center for Earth and Planetary Sciences; the Harvard Forest; the University Herbaria; and laboratories in chemistry, biology, biochemistry, physics, applied sciences, anthropology, and medical sciences. Facilities and institutes in the social sciences and humanities include the Harvard-Yenching Institute, the Fairbank Center for East Asian Research, the Edwin O. Reischauer Institute for Japanese Studies, the Center for Middle Eastern Studies, the Center for Jewish Studies, the Center for the Study of World Religions, the Center for European Studies, the Ukrainian Research Institute, the Russian Research Center, the Committee on Latin American and Iberian Studies, the Committee on African Studies, the Harvard Institute for International Development, the Center for International Affairs, the Center for American Political Studies, the W. E. B. DuBois Institute for Afro-American Studies, the Center for Urban Studies, the Carpenter Center for the Visual Arts, and the Loeb Drama Center. The University museums are also available for research and study; these include the Fogg and Arthur M. Sackler art museums, the Peabody Museum of Archaeology and Ethnology, the Semitic Museum, the Museum of Comparative Zoology, the Botanical Museum, and the Mineralogical Museum. Research affiliations are maintained with a variety of other institutions, including the Woods Hole Oceanographic Institute, the Arnold Arboretum, Dumbarton Oaks Library, the Center for Hellenic Studies, and Villa i Tatti.

Financial Aid

Assistance is available through Harvard and outside fellowships, assistantships, federal work-study, and loans. Financial aid is awarded based on both merit and need, as determined by the Office of Admissions and Financial Aid. Most admitted students are guaranteed full support for two or more years of study. In the third and following years, most students can support themselves through teaching and research. If necessary, loan funds are usually available to supplement these sources.

Cost of Study

All students must register for full-time study. For the academic year 2006–07, tuition and fees were $32,682 for those in the first two years of study. Reduced tuition of $10,476 was charged to students in the third and fourth years. Those in later years pay a facilities fee of $4608 per year if they are in residence. A health insurance fee of $1390 per year is included in the cost for students in residence. Students on leave to conduct research and advanced students living outside the Cambridge area pay an active file fee of $300 per year.

Living and Housing Costs

The standard student budget reflects the cost of living in the Boston area. For 2006–07, the average ten-month budget for a single student was approximately $20,300. Dormitory rooms rent for $3965 to $7729 per year; board is available at an additional cost in some cases. Rents for University-owned apartments range from $743 to $4132 per month.

Student Group

The Graduate School of Arts and Sciences has an enrollment of nearly 3,500. The student body is extremely diverse. Approximately 28 percent of the students are international; 45 percent are women. Approximately 24 percent are in humanities programs, while some 45 percent are in natural sciences and 31 percent in social sciences. Asian Americans constitute more than 4 percent of the student body, while the underrepresented minority community is nearly 10 percent. The wide range of interests of the students is reflected in a variety of organizations and activities.

Location

Most facilities of the University are located in Cambridge, adjacent to Boston. The two cities and their environs offer wide cultural and recreational opportunities. The University itself has excellent athletic facilities and sponsors numerous arts and public affairs activities. Within the area are many opportunities for public service. Other resources include museums, music, drama, dance, and sports. Recreational areas on the Atlantic coast and in the mountains and forests of New England are easily accessible.

The University

Harvard University is a complex of the Faculty of Arts and Sciences and nine other professional and graduate faculties. The FAS comprises Harvard College and the Graduate School of Arts and Sciences. Founded in 1636, Harvard College is the oldest college in the United States. Founded in 1872, the Graduate School of Arts and Sciences is the largest graduate institution in the University.

Applying

Students are admitted to graduate study only at the beginning of the academic year; there are no admissions for the spring term. The application deadlines are most natural sciences, December 8 or December 15; most social sciences and humanities, December 15 or January 2. The application fee is $90.

Correspondence and Information

Office of Admissions and Financial Aid
Graduate School of Arts and Sciences
Harvard University
1350 Massachusetts Avenue, 350
Cambridge, Massachusetts 02138
Phone: 617-495-5315
E-mail: admiss@fas.harvard.edu
Web site: http://www.gsas.harvard.edu

OFFICERS AND PROGRAMS IN THE GRADUATE SCHOOL OF ARTS AND SCIENCES

Theda R. Skocpol, Dean of the Graduate School of Arts and Sciences and Viktor S. Thomas Professor of Government and Sociology.
Margot N. Gill, Administrative Dean of the Graduate School of Arts and Sciences.

DEPARTMENTS AND COMMITTEES AND GRADUATE DEGREES AWARDED FOR 2005–06

Humanities
Department of African and African-American Studies (Ph.D.).
Department of Celtic Languages and Literatures (A.M., Ph.D.).
Department of Classics (Ph.D.).
Department of Comparative Literature (Ph.D.).
Department of East Asian Languages and Civilizations (Ph.D.).
Department of English and American Literature and Language (Ph.D.).
Department of Germanic Languages and Literatures (A.M., Ph.D.).
Committee on History and East Asian Languages (Ph.D.).
Committee on Inner Asian and Altaic Studies (Ph.D.).
Department of Linguistics (Ph.D.).
Department of Music (A.M., Ph.D.).
Department of Near Eastern Languages and Civilizations (A.M., Ph.D.).
Department of Philosophy (A.M., Ph.D.).
Committee on Regional Studies—East Asia (A.M.).
Committee on the Study of Religion (Ph.D.).
Department of Romance Languages and Literatures (A.M., Ph.D.).
Department of Sanskrit and Indian Studies (A.M., Ph.D.).
Department of Slavic Languages and Literatures (Ph.D.).

Natural Sciences
Department of Astronomy (Ph.D.).
Committee on Biological Sciences in Dental Medicine (Ph.D.).
Committee on Biological Sciences in Public Health (Ph.D.).
*Committee on Biophysics (Ph.D.).
Committee on Biostatistics (Ph.D.).
*Committee on Chemical Biology.
Committee on Chemical Physics (Ph.D.).
*Committee on Systems Biology.
*Department of Chemistry and Chemical Biology (Ph.D.).
Department of Earth and Planetary Sciences (Ph.D.).
Division of Engineering and Applied Sciences (S.M., M.E., Ph.D.).
The Harvard Forest (M.F.S.).
Division of Health Science and Technology (M.D./Ph.D., Ph.D.).
Department of Mathematics (Ph.D.).
*Division of Medical Sciences (Ph.D.).
*Department of Molecular and Cellular Biology (Ph.D.).
*Department of Organismic and Evolutionary Biology (Ph.D.).
Department of Physics (Ph.D.).
Department of Statistics (A.M., Ph.D.).

*Participating program in Harvard Integrated Life Sciences

Social Sciences
Department of Anthropology (A.M., Ph.D.).
Committee on Architecture, Landscape Architecture and Urban Planning (Ph.D.).
Committee on Business Economics (Ph.D.).
Department of Economics (Ph.D.).
Department of Government (Ph.D.).
Committee on Health Policy (Ph.D.).
Department of History (Ph.D.).
Committee on the History of American Civilization (Ph.D.).
Department of History of Science (A.M., Ph.D.).
Committee on Information Technology and Management (Ph.D.).
Committee on Middle Eastern Studies (A.M., Ph.D.).
Committee on Organizational Behavior (Ph.D.).
Committee on Political Economy and Government (Ph.D.).
Department of Psychology (Ph.D.).
Committee on Public Policy (Ph.D.).
Committee on Regional Studies—Russia, Eastern Europe, and Central Asia (A.M.).
Committee on Social Policy (Ph.D.).
Department of Sociology (Ph.D.).

HAWAI'I PACIFIC UNIVERSITY

Graduate Studies

Programs of Study Hawai'i Pacific University offers leading master's degree programs in business administration, communication, diplomacy and military studies, economics, global leadership and sustainable development, information systems, nursing, marine science, organizational change, teaching English as a second language, social work, and secondary education. The Master of Business Administration (M.B.A.) program offers concentrations in accounting, communications, economics, finance, human resource management, international business, management, marketing, organizational change, information systems, e-business, and travel industry management. The M.B.A. program requires 42 semester hours of graduate work. Prerequisite study in business subjects may be required.

The Master of Science in Information Systems (M.S.I.S.) is designed to create a generation of decision-makers and experts in information technology, systems design, and problem solving with automated resources. Students can individualize their program with elective courses or concentrations in information systems security, knowledge management, human-machine interfaces, telecommunications security, and software engineering, among others. Students lacking a background in the technical, scientific, and analytical realms are required to complete selected prerequisites to fully prepare for the program. Thirty-six semester hours of graduate work are required to complete the program.

The Master of Arts in human resource management (M.A./HRM) emphasizes the study and practices of human relations and managing personnel. These include human resource planning, recruitment and selection, compensation management and benefits, human resource development, labor-management relations, employment law, safety and health, and global perspective on human resources. Some undergraduate prerequisites may be required. The program requires completion of 42 semester hours of graduate work.

The Master of Arts in global leadership and sustainable development (M.A./GLSD) is designed to prepare students to become leaders in all types of organizations that include multinational, governmental, and not-for-profit organizations. Courses include Comparative Management Systems, Global Markets in Transition, International Business Management, and Systems Management. Some prerequisites may be required. Forty-two semester hours of graduate work are required to complete the program.

The Master of Arts in organizational change (M.A./OC) emphasizes the management, design, implementation, and application of organizational change. Courses include Organizational Change and Development, National and Community Change and Development, Culture and Human Organization, and Organizational Behavior. Some prerequisite courses may be required. Forty-two semester hours of graduate work are required to complete the program.

The Master of Science in Nursing (M.S.N.) offers concentrations for those interested in becoming family nurse practitioners or community-based health clinical nurse specialists. Students who have an RN but lack a Bachelor of Science in Nursing may enter the RN to M.S.N. Pathway. Forty-two semester hours are required to complete the M.S.N. with a clinical nurse specialist concentration, and 48 semester hours are required to complete the M.S.N. with a nurse educator or a family nurse practitioner concentration.

The Master of Science in Marine Science (M.S.M.S.) is designed to provide students with the knowledge and skills necessary to place them in marine-related technical positions in industry, government, and education or for entry into a doctoral marine science program. Courses include Cell and Molecular Biology, Aquatic Chemistry, Marine Ecology, and Toxicology. Some prerequisite courses may be required. The M.S.M.S. program requires 36 hours of graduate work.

The Master of Arts in communication (M.A./COM) is designed to prepare students for careers in business communication, marketing, advertising, mass media, public relations, entertainment, broadcast or print journalism, sales, the Internet, writing, or education. Some prerequisite courses may be required. Thirty-nine semester hours of graduate work are required to complete the program.

The Master of Arts in Teaching English as a Second Language (M.A.T.E.S.L.) requires 37 semester hours of graduate work. Courses include English Phonology and the Teaching of Pronunciation, English Syntax and the Teaching of Grammar, and Methods of Teaching Oral/Aural English. Some prerequisite courses may be required.

The Master of Arts in diplomacy and military studies (M.A./DMS) explores the complex relationships of politics, society, and the military. The M.A./DMS degree is useful for those who are professional military officers or work in government positions. Some prerequisites may be required. The M.A./DMS program requires 42 hours of graduate work.

The Master of Arts in Social Work (M.S.W.) program is built on a foundation of liberal arts and is committed to the preparation of professional social work practitioners who take pride in their careers. The program prepares social workers to become effective cross-cultural practitioners by focusing on direct planning, administration, and community practice. The M.S.W. program requires 61 semester hours of graduate work.

The Master of Education in Secondary Education (M.Ed.) program develops professional educators who are reflective practitioners dedicated to the scholarship of teaching and school renewal. The program is based on an innovative, standards-driven, field-based curriculum that employs cutting-edge educational technology to integrate content and pedagogy. The M.Ed. program requires 41 semester hours of graduate work.

Research Facilities To support graduate studies, University libraries, with a collection exceeding 153,000 volumes, add an average of 2,500 volumes annually, 15 percent of which are on business topics. A significant number of business reference books, including national and international business directories, investment and financial services, accounting and tax information sources, and a collection of annual reports, are available. Periodical titles number more than 1,700, and 205,000 pieces of microfiche and 5,300 rolls of microfilm are maintained. Dial-up access to local area databases of public and state university library catalogs, legislative information, and business-oriented statistical data is available in the library. Other in-house, business-related and commercial-vendor databases support specialized information needs. The University's accessible on-campus computer center houses more than 100 IBM-compatible microcomputers, with stand-alone support and networked configurations that support the graduate program's integrated computer applications approach.

Financial Aid The University participates in all federal financial aid programs designated for graduate students. These programs provide aid in the form of subsidized (need-based) and unsubsidized (non-need-based) Federal Stafford Student Loans. Through these loans, funds may be available to cover a student's entire cost of education. To apply for aid, students must submit the Free Application for Federal Student Aid (FAFSA) after January 1. Mailing of student award letters usually begins by the end of March. The University also offers several institutional scholarships and assistantships.

Cost of Study For the 2007–08 academic year, graduate tuition is $560 per credit hour. Books, supplies, and health insurance cost approximately $2560 for the academic year.

Living and Housing Costs The University has both on-campus residence halls and an apartment referral service. Cost of living for a single student for two semesters (nine months) is $25,840, including tuition, books, housing, food, health insurance, and miscellaneous expenses.

Student Group University enrollment currently stands at more than 9,000, including more than 1,200 graduate students. All fifty states and more than 100 countries are represented.

Location The University has three campuses linked by shuttle. Hawai'i Pacific combines the excitement of an urban, downtown campus with the serenity of the windward side of the island. The main campus is located in downtown Honolulu, the business and financial center of the Pacific. The Hawai'i Loa campus is 8 miles away situated in Kaneohe at the base of the Ko'olau Mountains; it is the site of the School of Nursing, the marine science program, and a variety of other course offerings. The third campus, Oceanic Institute, is an applied aquaculture research facility located on a 56-acre site at Makapu'u Point on the windward coast.

The University Hawai'i Pacific University is the largest private postsecondary institution in the state of Hawai'i. The University is coeducational, with a faculty of more than 300, a student-faculty ratio of 18:1, and an average class size of 20. A wide range of counseling and other student support services are available. There are more than ninety student organizations on campus, including the Graduate Student Organization.

Applying Hawai'i Pacific University seeks students with academic promise, outstanding career potential, and high motivation. Applicants should complete and forward a Graduate Admissions Application, have official transcripts sent from all colleges or universities attended, and forward two letters of recommendation. International students should submit scores from the TOEFL. Admissions decisions are made on a rolling basis, and applicants are notified between one and two weeks after all documents have been submitted. Applicants are encouraged to submit their applications online.

Correspondence and Information

Graduate Admissions
Hawai'i Pacific University
1164 Bishop Street, Suite 911
Honolulu, Hawaii 96813
Phone: 808-544-1135
866-GRAD-HPU (toll-free)
Fax: 808-544-0280
E-mail: graduate@hpu.edu
Web site: http://www.hpu.edu/grad

THE FACULTY

Valentina M. Abordonado, Associate Professor of English; Ph.D., Arizona.
Eric Abrams, Associate Professor of Economics; Ph.D., Iowa.
Jerome F. Agrusa, Professor of Travel Industry Management; M.H.M., Houston; Ph.D., Texas A&M.
Michelle Alarcon-Catt, Assistant Professor of Management; J.D., Loyola Marymount; M.B.A., Pepperdine.
Dale Allison, Professor of Nursing; Ph.D., Pennsylvania; RNC, APRN-Rx, FAAN.
Margaret Anderson, Associate Professor of Nursing; M.S.N., Ed.D., San Francisco; RN, APRN.
Wayne Andrews, Associate Professor of Philosophy; Ph.D., California, Santa Cruz.
John N. Barnum, Associate Professor of Public Relations; Ph.D., Texas at Austin.
Daniel Binkley, Professor of History and Humanities; Ph.D., Colorado.
Eric Brewe, Assistant Professor of Physics; Ph.D., Arizona State.
Patricia Burrell, Assistant Dean of Nursing for Students; Ph.D., Utah; RN, APRN, BC.
Brian Cannon, Assistant Professor in the College of Communication; Ph.D., Regent University (Virginia).
Kathleen J. Cassity, Assistant Professor of English; Ph.D., Hawai'i. English.
Grace Cheng, Assistant Professor of Political Science; Ph.D., Hawai'i at Manoa.
Richard Chepkevich, Instructor of Information Systems; M.S.S.M., USC.
Justin Gukhyun Cho, Assistant Professor of Management; Ph.D., MIT.
Yooncheong Cho, Assistant Professor of Marketing; Ph.D., Rutgers.
Jean Coffman, Associate Professor of English (ESL); M.A., Columbia Teachers College.
Steven Combs, Professor of Organizational Communication; Ph.D., USC.
Kenneth Cook, Professor of Linguistics; Ph.D., California, San Diego.
Leslie Correa, Associate Professor of Biology and Dean, Liberal Arts; Ed.D., Hawai'i at Manoa.
Rob Cranfill, Instructor of Management; M.S., Chapman.
Cheryl Ann Crozier-Garcia, Human Resource Management; M.B.A., Hawai'i Pacific; Ph.D., Walden.
Jon Davidann, Associate Professor of History; Ph.D., Minnesota.
ReNel Davis, Associate Professor of Nursing; Ph.D., Colorado; RN.
Dorothy Douthit, Assistant Professor of Education; Ph.D., Texas at Austin.
Eric Drabkin, Associate Professor of Economics; Ph.D., UCLA.
Antonina Espiritu, Associate Professor of Economics; Ph.D., Nebraska–Lincoln.
Hobie Etta Feagai, Professor of Nursing; Ed.D., M.S.N., Tennessee, Knoxville; RN, APRN, FNP, BC.
Daniel Flood, Assistant Professor of Marketing and Management; Ph.D., Union (Ohio).
Susan Fox-Wolfgramm, Professor of Management; M.P.A., Ph.D., Texas Tech.
W. Gerald Glover, Professor of Organizational Change; Ph.D., Florida.
Irene Rizkallah Gordon, Instructor of English (ESL) and Linguistics; M.A., Wayne State.
Joanne Gula, Assistant Professor in the College of Communication; Ph.D., Massachusetts.
Ken Guyette, Instructor of Accounting; M.S., North Dakota; M.B.A., Texas Tech; CPA.
Joseph Ha, Associate Professor of Marketing; Ph.D., Rutgers.
Ted Haggblom, Assistant Professor of Marketing; Ph.D., Michigan State.
Janice Haley, Associate Professor of Nursing; Ph.D., Hawai'i at Manoa.
Barbara Hannum, Assistant Professor of English (ESL); M.A., Hawai'i at Manoa.
John Hart, Professor and Assistant Dean, College of Communication; Ph.D., Kansas.
Russell Hart, Associate Professor of History; Ph.D., Ohio State.
Serena Hashimoto, Assistant Professor in the College of Communication; Ph.D., European Graduate School (Switzerland).
John Hawkins, Assistant Professor of Education; M.Ed., Hawai'i at Manoa.
Judith Holland, Assistant Professor of Nursing; Ph.D., Denver.
"Jade" Hsuan-Yuan Huang, Assistant Professor in the College of Communication; Ph.D., North Carolina at Chapel Hill.
Gordon L. Jones, Professor of Computer Science and Information Systems and Dean, College of Professional Studies; Ph.D., New Mexico.
Carlos Juarez, Associate Professor of Political Science and Dean, College of International Studies; Ph.D., UCLA.
Thomas Kam, Assistant Professor of Accounting and Finance; M.B.A., Hawai'i at Manoa; CPA.
John Karbens, Associate Professor of Accounting and Finance; M.B.A., Ed.D., Hawai'i at Manoa.
Lauren Kelly, Associate Professor of Accounting; Ph.D., Alabama.
Mary Kelly, Instructor of Economics; Ph.D., Greenwich.
Minjeong Kim, Assistant Professor in the College of Communication; Ph.D., North Carolina at Chapel Hill.
Jean Kirschenmann, Instructor of English (ESL); M.A., Hawai'i at Manoa.
Edward Klein, Professor of English (ESL) and Academic Coordinator, Applied Linguistics; Ph.D., Hawai'i at Manoa.
Jan Knight, Assistant Professor in the College of Communication; Ph.D. candidate, Ohio.
Wendy Lam, Assistant Professor of Marketing and Economics; M.B.A., Hawai'i at Manoa.
Mark A. Lane, Associate Professor of Finance; Ph.D., Missouri.
Teresa Lane, Assistant Professor of Spanish and TESL; M.A., Southern Mississippi; M.A.T.L., Hawai'i at Manoa.
Leroy Laney, Professor of Finance and Economics; Ph.D., Colorado.
Patricia Lange-Otsuka, Associate Dean of Nursing for Administration; M.S.N., Ed.D., Nova Southeastern.
Laurence LeDoux, Assistant Professor in the College of Communication and Faculty Editor, *Kalamalama*; D.A., Oregon.
Candis L. K. Lee, Assistant Professor of English (ESL); Ed.D., USC.
Binsheng Li, Assistant Professor in Economics; Ph.D., Hawai'i at Manoa.
Ernesto Lucas, Associate Professor of Economics; Ph.D., Hawai'i at Manoa.
Elaine Leilani Madison, Associate Professor of English; Ph.D., Yale.
Michelle Marineau, Assistant Professor of Nursing; Ph.D., M.S.N., Grand Valley State; RN, APRN, FNP.
Melvin Masuda, Associate Professor of Law and Public Administration; M.P.A., Harvard; J.D., Yale.
Gunter Meissner, Associate Professor of Finance; Ph.D., Christian Albrechts University Kiel (Germany).
Aytun Ozturk, Assistant Professor of Quantitative Methods; Ph.D., Pittsburgh.
Sterling Michael Pavelec, Assistant Professor of History and Program Chair, Diplomacy and Military Studies; Ph.D., Ohio State.
Steven Phillips, Instructor of Management; M.B.A., Central Michigan.
James Primm, Associate Professor of Political Science; Ph.D., Hawai'i at Manoa.
Evelyn Pua'a, Instructor of Mathematics; M.Ed., USC.
Mitchell Robertson, Associate Professor of Chemistry; Ph.D., Iowa State.
Kenneth Rossi, Assistant Professor of Information Systems; Ed.D., USC. Information systems.
Lawrence Rowland, Instructor of Information Systems; Ed.D., USC.
Catherine Ryan, Assistant Professor of Nursing; M.S.N., Georgetown; DNP, RN, APRN, CNM.
Catherine Sajna, Assistant Professor of English (ESL); M.A., Hawai'i at Manoa.
Dolly Samson, Professor of Computer Science/Computer Information Systems; Ph.D., George Mason.
Brett Saraniti, Associate Professor of Economics and Quantitative Methods; Ph.D., Northwestern.
Ken Schoolland, Associate Professor of Economics and Political Science; M.S.F.S., Georgetown.
Captain Carl O. Schuster (U.S. Navy Ret.), Adjunct Faculty, History; M.A., USC.
Michael Seiler, Associate Professor of Finance; D.B.A., Cleveland.
Mary Sheridan, Professor of Social Work and Program Chair for Social Work and Sociology; Ph.D., Hawai'i at Manoa; ACSW.
Joseph Smith, Assistant Professor of Management; Ed.D., USC.
Penny Pence Smith, Assistant Professor in the College of Communication; Ph.D., North Carolina at Chapel Hill.
William A. Sodeman, Associate Professor of Information Systems and Program Chair, M.S.I.S.; Ph.D., Georgia.
Edwin van Gorder, Associate Professor of Management and Mathematics; Ph.D., Stanford.
Niti Villinger, Associate Professor of Management; Ph.D., Cambridge.
James Waddington, Assistant Professor of Accounting; M.B.A., Hawai'i at Manoa; CPA.
Richard Ward, Affiliate Associate Professor of Management; Ed.D., USC.
Gary Waters, Associate Professor of Management; M.S.A., Central Michigan.
Warren Wee, Associate Professor of Accounting and Associate Dean, College of Business Administration; M.B.A., Hawai'i at Manoa; Ph.D., Washington (Seattle); CPA.
Arthur Whatley, Professor of Management; Ph.D., North Texas State.
Linda Wheeler, Assistant Professor of Education; Ed.D., Hawai'i at Manoa.
James Whitfield, Professor of Communication and Dean, College of Communication; Ph.D., Texas Tech.
Alfred Zimermann, Assistant Professor of Computer Science/Computer Information Systems; M.B.I.S., Georgia State.
Larry Zimmerman, Assistant Professor of Management; M.S., USC.

Programs of Study

Hebrew College offers two graduate degrees—a Master of Jewish Education (M.J.Ed.) and a Master of Arts in Jewish Studies (M.A.J.S.)—and several certificates. The College's five-year, full-time Rabbinical School offers Rabbinic Ordination within a transdenominational setting. The Cantor-Educator program culminates in Cantorial Ordination.

The M.J.Ed., offered through the Shoolman Graduate School of Jewish Education, prepares students to pursue careers or upgrade professional credentials in the expanding field of Jewish education. Students may pursue specialty tracks in adult Jewish education, early childhood Jewish education, Hebrew language teaching, informal Jewish education (including camp and youth leadership), Jewish day school education, Jewish family education, and Jewish special education. The M.J.Ed. program balances formal, academic study with independent work and practical internship experience. Students are required to develop a foundation in Jewish education, general education, and Jewish studies; the three-stage, 73-credit program is also individualized to support the needs and goals of each student. The Shoolman Graduate School of Jewish Education also offers certificates in early childhood Jewish education; early childhood Jewish education leadership; Hebrew language education; Jewish day school education; Jewish family education; Jewish informal education, youth leadership, and camping; and Jewish special education.

The 50-credit M.A.J.S. provides a solid academic base in Jewish studies, which may be used as a foundation for rabbinic or cantorial school, or for an advanced degree in Jewish scholarship. Curricula emphasize text study and Hebrew literacy; from the study of texts in the original Hebrew, students master the subject matter and develop the skills needed to continue independent scholarship. Through a sequence of framework, gateway, and advanced core-text courses that focus on primary sources of the biblical, rabbinic, medieval, and modern periods, students gain a broad understanding of Jewish thought, history, culture, and civilization. Students specialize in an area of interest—a discipline, period, or subject—and demonstrate mastery through a major project in their final semester.

Through its Jewish Music Institute, the College also offers certificates in Jewish liturgical music and Jewish music education.

Students benefit from the College's cross-registration agreements with several nearby colleges and universities, including Boston University, Boston College, Brandeis University, Andover Newton Theological School, Simmons College, the University of Massachusetts Boston, and Northeastern University.

Typically, graduate students complete their course work within two years, although part-time students may take additional time to complete the programs. The online M.A.J.S. covers the same curricula as the in-class degree program. The program, which can be completed in three years, combines online courses, independent study, and two 1-week summer seminars at Hebrew College.

The transdenominational **Rabbinical School of Hebrew College** offers a rigorous five-year, full-time course of study (six years with *mekhinah,* or preparatory year) within a *klal Yisrael* community of learners. Students are immersed in the religious, ethical, and intellectual pursuit of Jewish knowledge, sharing and debating views with classmates and teachers of divergent beliefs. An innovative curriculum integrates the study of primary texts with themes of Jewish living and daily rabbinic practice. In addition to participating in intensive text study, students have the opportunity to take graduate-level courses in subjects such as the psychology and sociology of religion, religion in America, contemporary Jewish life, and introductions to Christianity, Islam, and religions of the East. Students in the Rabbinical School earn a Master of Arts in Jewish Studies, with a concentration in rabbinics in conjunction with Rabbinic Ordination.

The **Cantor-Educator Program** was created in 2004 to train individuals to fulfill all aspects of Jewish leadership in the synagogue, including prayer leading, musical programming, lifecycle officiating, pastoral counseling, and congregational education. Through this five-year, full-time, 159-credit course of study, students earn an M.J.Ed. degree while fulfilling the requirements of cantorial ordination within Hebrew College's Jewish Music Institute and Shoolman Graduate School of Jewish Education. The text study and courses in pedagogy are balanced by intensive training in musicology, voice, choral conducting, and instrumental performance. The program's faculty team includes leading scholars and composers in the cantorial arts.

Research Facilities

The Rae and Joseph Gann Library contains more than 125,000 holdings, with special collections in modern Hebrew literature, Jewish medical ethics, Jewish education, Jewish genealogy, Holocaust studies, Hasidism, and Jewish children's literature. Through the Research Libraries Information Network, users can access a database of 53 million books, journals, maps, records, and cassettes drawn from Judaica collections across the country, including those of the Jewish Theological Seminary in New York, Harvard University, Yale University, Princeton University, and Brandeis University.

Financial Aid

The College works with each student to develop a financial aid package. Awards are made on the basis of financial need. Preference is given to students who apply for financial aid by December 15 (Early Decision) and February 15. The College participates in all federal programs as well as in numerous scholarship programs offered by various Jewish communal organizations. The Hebrew College Stone-Teplow Families' Fund provides Jewish educators working at least 12 hours a week—including teachers, youth leaders, family educators, educational leaders, and camp professionals—with a significant reduction in Hebrew College tuition on all courses taken for credit.

The Hebrew College Fellows Program encompasses several one-year, renewable fellowships for both full- and part-time study, awarded on a competitive basis to outstanding students enrolled in the College's Master of Jewish Education and Master of Arts in Jewish Studies degree programs. The Rose Bronstein Fellowship is awarded to an outstanding student in Jewish education who is committed to becoming a classroom teacher and is dedicated to the teacher/student encounter. The Betty and Irving Brudnick Fellowship is awarded to an outstanding student in the field of Jewish education. The Rabbi Carl and Barbara Benjamin Friedman Fellowship is awarded to a graduate student preparing for a career in Jewish education and is available as of spring 2007. The Ralph Goldman Fellowship in International and Professional Leadership is awarded to a student who is dedicated to working with Jewish communities outside of North America. The Dr. David M. Gordis Fellowship is granted to a student demonstrating exceptional potential for Jewish communal leadership. The Thelma Frisch Hoch Fellowship in Jewish Education is awarded to an outstanding student enrolled in a degree program in Jewish education. The Barbara and Leo Karas Fellowship in Jewish Education is granted to a graduate student in the Shoolman Graduate School of Jewish Education whose goal is postgraduate service in the Jewish community. Priority is given to those with a commitment to congregational religious schools. The Betty Laufer Fellowship is granted to a student enrolled in the M.J.Ed. program, pursuing a career in Jewish education. The Abraham and Sadie Shapiro Family Fellowships are given to students planning to pursue a career in Jewish education and committed to postgraduate service in the Jewish community. The Edith and Eliot Shoolman Fellowships are awarded to students who are currently active in the field of Jewish education as a teacher or administrator. The Rose and Morris Sokolove Rabbinical Fellowship is granted to an outstanding rabbinical student committed to strengthening Jewish life. The Betsy and Dr. Martin P. Solomon Graduate Fellowship is granted to an outstanding student in the field of Jewish education.

Cost of Study

Tuition for the 2006–07 academic year was $810 per credit hour.

Student Group

Although most students are drawn from the Jewish community, Hebrew College is nonsectarian and does not discriminate in admission or any matter in regard to age, gender, religion, handicap, race, color, national origin, or sexual orientation. Hebrew College students join the community of thousands of students enrolled at Boston-area colleges and universities.

Location

In 2001, Hebrew College moved to a 7-acre campus in Newton Centre, a beautiful Boston suburb within easy reach of Boston's many outstanding colleges, universities, and cultural institutions. The state-of-the-art campus, designed by architect Moshe Safdie, includes classrooms, lecture halls, administrative offices, parking facilities, a student center, cafeteria, and library.

The College

Founded in 1921, Hebrew College maintains a historical commitment to Jewish learning and scholarship within a transdenominational nonsectarian environment. Through intensive training in Jewish texts, history, literature, ethics, and Hebrew language, the College prepares students to become literate participants in the global Jewish community. Hebrew College offers graduate and undergraduate degrees and certificates in all aspects of formal and nonformal Jewish education as well as Jewish studies and Jewish music. The College also serves students of all ages through its Prozdor High School, Camp Yavneh, Ulpan, and Center for Adult Jewish Learning. In addition, the College created and directs Me'ah–One Hundred Hours of Adult Jewish Learning, a two-year program of adult study, and the Me'ah Graduate Institute. Hebrew College is also home to the National Center for Jewish Policy Studies, a policy research think-tank committed to the study of pivotal issues facing American Jews and the formulation of strategies to help ensure the continued growth and vitality of Jewish life. Hebrew College is a partner with Andover Newton Theological School in the Interreligious Center for Public Life.

Applying

The graduate programs of Hebrew College are open to qualified students holding a bachelor's degree from an accredited four-year college or university. Applicants are asked to provide three letters of recommendation, transcripts, and a personal statement. All applicants are also required to provide GRE scores. All prospective students are encouraged to contact the College early in the process to arrange for an interview and campus visit.

The deadline for Early Decision is December 15, with acceptance notification sent by January 15. For later applications, the deadlines are February 15 (for notification sent by March 15) and June 30 (for notification sent by July 15).

Correspondence and Information

Kate Nachman
Director of Admissions
Hebrew College
160 Herrick Road
Newton, Massachusetts 02459

Phone: 617-559-8610
800-866-4814 (toll-free)
Fax: 617-559-8601
E-mail: admissions@hebrewcollege.edu
Web site: http://www.hebrewcollege.edu

THE FACULTY

Martin Abramowitz, Adjunct Lecturer in Jewish Communal Studies; M.S.W., Michigan; Ph.D., Brandeis.
Tzvi I. Abusch, Visiting Professor of Biblical Languages and Civilizations; Ph.D., Harvard.
Howard Tzvi Adelman, Visiting Associate Professor of Jewish History; Ph.D., Brandeis.
Sharon Cohen Anisfeld, Dean, Rabbinical School; B.A., Brown; Rabbinic Ordination, Reconstructionist Rabbinical.
Moshe Bar Asher, Visiting Professor of Hebrew Language; Ph.D., Hebrew (Jerusalem).
Tzilla Barone, Instructor in Hebrew Language; B.A., SUNY at Albany.
Nurit Ben Yehuda, Instructor in Hebrew Language; M.A., Hebrew (Jerusalem).
David Bernat, Visiting Assistant Professor of Religion; Ph.D., Brandeis.
Avi Bernstein-Nahar, Assistant Professor of Jewish Thought and Dean of Educational Planning and Development; Ph.D., Stanford.
Harvey Bock, Adjunct Lecturer in Hebrew; J.D., Yale.
Edward Breuer, Visiting Associate Professor of Jewish History; Ph.D., Harvard.
Dvorah Buhr, Adjunct Instructor and Program Administrator, Jewish Music Institute; M.S.M., Diploma of Hazzan and Cantorial Investiture, Jewish Theological Seminary.
Shlomit Chayat, Adjunct Lecturer in Jewish Education; M.A., Hebrew (Jerusalem).
Helen Cohen, Adjunct Lecturer, Early Childhood Institute; M.S., Lesley.
Reuven Cohn, Adjunct Instructor in Rabbinics; J.D., Yale; Rabbinic Ordination, Yeshiva.
Steven Copeland, Assistant Professor of Jewish Thought and Education; Ed.D., Harvard.
Philip Cunningham, Visiting Professor of Theology; Ph.D., Boston College.
Sigalit Davis, Instructor in Hebrew Language; B.A., Hebrew (Jerusalem).
Nathan Ehrlich, Dean, Hebrew College Online; M.A., Lesley.
Leandra Elion, Adjunct Instructor in Jewish Special Education; M.S., LIU, C.W. Post.
Lewis Glinert, Visiting Professor of Hebrew Literature; Ph.D., London.
David M. Gordis, Professor of Rabbinics and President; Ph.D., Rabbinic Ordination, Jewish Theological Seminary.
Arthur Green, Professor of Jewish Mysticism and Rector, Rabbinical School; Ph.D., Brandeis; Rabbinic Ordination, Jewish Theological Seminary.
Marion Green, Adjunct Instructor in Jewish Special Education; M.A., Boston University.
Marion Gribetz, Adjunct Instructor in Jewish Education; M.A., Tufts.
Zvi Grumet, Adjunct Instructor in Jewish Education; M.A., Rabbinic Ordination, Yeshiva.
Shirah Hecht, Visiting Lecturer in Education; Ph.D., Chicago.
Sherry Israel, Visiting Associate Professor of Jewish Family Education; Ph.D., UCLA.
Sara Israeli, Adjunct Lecturer in Jewish Education; M.A., Hebrew (Jerusalem).
Joshua Jacobson, Visiting Professor of Jewish Music and Director, Zamir Chorale (Artists-in-Residence); D.M.A., Cincinnati.
Norman Janis, Associate Dean of Rabbinic School and Director, Rabbinical Student Life; Ph.D., Harvard. Private Rabbinic Ordination.
Kirk Jones, Visiting Professor of Ethics; D.Min., Emory; Ph.D., Drew.
Jane Kanarek, Instructor in Rabbinics; Ph.D. candidate, Chicago; Rabbinic Ordination, Jewish Theological Seminary.
Judith Kates, Professor of Jewish Women's Studies; Ph.D., Harvard.
Alvan Kaunfer, Visiting Instructor in Midrash; D.H.L., Rabbinic Ordination, Jewish Theological Seminary.
Jeff Klepper, Visiting Instructor in Jewish Music; M.A., Northeastern Illinois.
Hilla Kobliner, Adjunct Lecturer in Jewish Education; M.A., Harvard.
Yehuda Kurtzer, Adjunct Instructor in History; M.A., Brown; M.A., Harvard.
Karen Landy, Visiting Instructor in Pastoral Counseling; M.A., Brandeis; M.A., Rabbinic Ordination, Reconstructionist Rabbinical.
Ruth Langer, Visiting Associate Professor of Theology; Ph.D., Rabbinic Ordination, Hebrew Union–Jewish Institute of Religion.
Ebn Leader, Instructor in Rabbinics and Bet Midrash Director; M.A., Brandeis; Private Rabbinic Ordination.
Allan Lehmann, Adjunct Instructor of Liturgy; B.A., Columbia; Rabbinic Ordination, Reconstructionist Rabbinical.
Mark Leuchter, Adjunct Assistant Professor of Bible; Ph.D., Toronto.
Michal Levy, Instructor in Hebrew Language, Ulpan; M.Ed., Boston University.
Sarit Lisogorsky, Instructor in Hebrew Language and Ulpan; B.A., Hebrew (Jerusalem).
Natan Margalit, Adjunct Assistant Professor of Rabbinics; Ph.D., Berkeley; Rabbinic Ordination, Jerusalem Seminary.
Brian Mayer, Adjunct Associate Professor of Jewish Music; D.S.M., Cantorial Investiture, Jewish Theological Seminary.
Billy Mencow, Visiting Instructor in Jewish Education; B.A., Brandeis.
Barry Mesch, Stone-Teplow Families' Professor of Jewish Thought and Provost; Ph.D., Brandeis.
Jacob Meskin, Assistant Professor of Jewish Education; Ph.D., Princeton.
Gabi Mezger, Instructor in Hebrew Language, Ulpan; M.Ed., Boston State.
Sandra Miller-Jacobs, Adjunct Assistant Professor in Jewish Education; Ed.D., Boston College.
Shai Nathanson, Instructor in Hebrew Language and Director, Hebrew Language Programs and Ulpan; M.A., Lesley.
Joseph Ness, Adjunct Instructor in Jewish Music; M.M., Manhattan School of Music; Cantorial Investiture, Jewish Theological Seminary.
Charles Osborne, Adjunct Instructor of Jewish Music; B.M., Hartt School of Music; B.S.M., Diploma of Hazzan, Jewish Theological Seminary.
Ruti Peled, Adjunct Instructor in Hebrew Language, Ulpan; B.A., Gordon Teachers College (Israel).
Yaron Peleg, Visiting Assistant Professor in Hebrew Literature; Ph.D., Brandeis.
Carl Perkins, Adjunct Instructor of Rabbinics; J.D., Harvard; Rabbinic Ordination, Jewish Theological Seminary.
Nehemia Polen, Professor of Jewish Thought and Director, Hasidic Text Institute; Ph.D., Boston University; Rabbinic Ordination, Ner Yisrael Rabbinical.
Yehudah Potok, Bet Midrash Instructor, Academic Director, Prozdor, and Assistant Director, Camp Yavneh; M.S., Yeshiva; Rabbinical Ordination, Yeshivat Hamivtar.
Anat Green Ragen, Instructor in Hebrew Language and Ulpan; M.A., Education Diploma, Bar Ilan.
Miriam Raviv, Adjunct Instructor in Hebrew Language; Ph.D. candidate, Jewish Theological Seminary.
Ina Regosin, Lecturer in Jewish Education, Dean of Students, and Director, Early Childhood Institute and Early Childhood Directors Institute; M.S., Wheelock.
Ken Richmond, Adjunct Instructor of Jewish Music; M.S.M., Cantorial Investiture, Jewish Theological Seminary.
Susie Rodenstein, Lecturer in Early Childhood Education and Adjunct Lecturer in Jewish Education; M.A., Harvard.
Peretz Rodman, Visiting Lecturer in Hebrew Language and Literature; M.A., Brandeis; Rabbinic Ordination, Schechter Rabbinical Seminary of Jerusalem.
Or Rose, Instructor of Rabbinics and Jewish Thought and Coordinator of Informal Education, Rabbinical School; Ph.D. candidate, Brandeis. Private Rabbinic Ordination.
Rochelle Sorkin Rossman, Adjunct Instructor in Jewish Education; M.S.Ed., Lesley.
Lori Salzman, Adjunct Instructor in Jewish Music; M.S.M., Hebrew Union–Jewish Institute of Religion.
Sol Schimmel, Professor of Jewish Education and Psychology; Ph.D., Wayne State.
Judith Segal, Professor of Library Science and Director of the Library; D.L.S., Columbia.
Sanford Seltzer, Associate Dean for Communal and Rabbinic Relations, Rabbinical School; M.A.H.L., Rabbinic Ordination, Hebrew Union–Jewish Institute of Religion.
Harvey Shapiro, Associate Professor of Jewish Education and Dean, Shoolman Graduate School of Jewish Education; Ph.D., Hebrew Union–Jewish Institute of Religion.
Scott Sokol, Associate Professor of Jewish Music and Educational Psychology; Dean, Jewish Music Institute; Director, Cantor-Educator Program; and Director, Jewish Special Education; Ph.D., Johns Hopkins; Diploma of Hazzan, Cantorial Investiture, Jewish Theological Seminary.
David B. Starr, Assistant Professor in Jewish History; Ph.D., Columbia; Rabbinic Ordination, Jewish Theological Seminary.
Jonah Steinberg, Assistant Professor of Rabbinics; Ph.D., Columbia.
Joseph Stern, Assistant Professor of Jewish Law; Ph.D., Boston College; Rabbinic Ordination, Yeshiva.
Lynne Torgove, Adjunct Instructor of Jewish Music; M.U.S.M., Boston University.
Ilene Vogelstein, Adjunct Lecturer, Early Childhood Institute; M.S., Johns Hopkins.
Susan Wall, Adjunct Instructor in Jewish Education; D.H.L., Jewish Theological Seminary.
Arnold Wieder, Professor Emeritus of Rabbinic Literature; Ph.D., Brandeis; Rabbinic Ordination, Yeshiva.
Sara Zacharia, Bet Midrash Instructor; M.S., CUNY, Brooklyn; M.A., University of Judaism; Rabbinic Ordination, Ziegler School for Rabbinic Studies.
Alan Zaitchik, Visiting Assistant Professor of Jewish Thought; Ph.D., MIT.

Programs of Study

Hofstra University offers 155 graduate degree programs—each designed to give students the edge they need to succeed.

Hofstra College of Liberal Arts and Sciences (HCLAS) offers graduate programs in ten disciplines in the humanities, natural sciences, and social sciences. Master's degree programs, leading to the Master of Arts (M.A.) or the Master of Science (M.S.), are offered in biology, comparative literature and languages, computer science, English, humanities, mathematics, psychology, Romance languages and literatures, sociology, and speech-language-hearing. New College, a division of HCLAS, offers an M.A. in Interdisciplinary Studies.

The College offers the following doctoral programs: Ph.D. in applied organizational psychology, Ph.D. in clinical psychology, and Psy.D. in school-community psychology.

Building on the strength of its existing programs, HCLAS recently added two new graduate programs. The M.A. in applied social research and policy analysis, which is planned to launch in fall 2007, prepares students for a wide variety of jobs requiring research and analysis skills. The M.S. in physician assistant studies is designed to give physician assistants advanced training in patient care and health care delivery.

Accreditations include the M.A. program in speech-language pathology by the Council on Academic Accreditation of the American Speech-Language-Hearing Association (ASHA), the Ph.D. program in clinical psychology by the American Psychological Association (APA) (as a combined clinical and school psychology program), and the Psy.D. program in school-community psychology by the American Psychological Association (as a Psy.D. doctoral program in school psychology). The physician assistant studies program is accredited by the Accreditation Review Commission on Education for the Physician Assistant (ARC-PA, Inc.).

Research Facilities

Hofstra's graduate programs are supported by extensive academic resources and state-of-the-art facilities.

The Hofstra libraries contain 1.4 million print volumes and provide 24/7 electronic access to more than 50,000 journals and electronic books. The Hofstra Observatory, located atop the Chemistry and Physics Building, features Celestron telescopes and computerized CCD cameras. Biology research is conducted in Hofstra's unique six-laboratory aquaculture facility. Students in audiology, psychology, and speech pathology may conduct research in the Joan and Arnold Saltzman Community Services Center, which houses the Speech-Language-Hearing Clinic and the Psychological Evaluation Research and Counseling (PERC) Clinic. Among the arts resources are six theaters, including a new black-box theater, and an accredited museum. The Hofstra University Museum coordinates about 12 exhibitions annually and offers an extensive collection of outdoor sculpture.

Financial Aid

Financial aid is available in the form of fellowships, scholarships, grants, loans, and graduate assistantship positions. All applicants for financial assistance must file the Free Application for Federal Student Aid (FAFSA). Information about graduate financial aid may be obtained from the Office of Financial Aid or the graduate academic departments.

Cost of Study

Tuition is $790 per credit hour in 2007–08, with some program exceptions. University fees range from $78 to $300 each semester, depending on the number of credits taken.

Living and Housing Costs

The cost of housing in University residence halls for 2007–08 ranges from $2775 to $6000 per semester, depending on the type of accommodation. Board prices range from $495 to $1700 per semester, depending on the plan chosen. The Office of Residential Life maintains listings of available off-campus accommodations.

Student Group

The 2900 students enrolled in Hofstra's graduate programs form a dynamic group that is ethnically, culturally, and geographically diverse. These students represent twenty-six states and nineteen countries. About 15 percent are members of minority groups, 3 percent are international students, and 69 percent are women. Many students in these graduate programs have previous work experience.

Location

Hofstra's distinctive 240-acre campus, a registered arboretum, is located in suburban Long Island, just 25 miles from New York City.

With New York City just a short ride away, students take advantage of the museums, concerts, and professional sports as well as internships the city offers. Students can also explore Long Island, which offers spectacular beaches, museums, and internship opportunities.

The University

Hofstra University is a dynamic private institution where students find their edge to succeed in 140 undergraduate and 155 graduate programs in the liberal arts and sciences, business, communication, education and allied human services, and law.

With an outstanding faculty, advanced technological resources, and state-of-the-art facilities, Hofstra has a growing national reputation. Yet the average graduate class size is just 13, ensuring that students receive the personal attention they deserve.

Applying

Candidates generally are required to complete the graduate application and all supporting forms and to submit two letters of recommendation, a statement of professional objectives, official transcripts from every college or university attended, and scores obtained on the Graduate Record Examination (GRE). International students must also submit scores obtained on the TOEFL. Application requirements vary depending on the program. For further information, candidates should contact the Office of Graduate Admissions or individual departments. Applicants may file online or by mail.

Correspondence and Information

Office of Graduate Admissions
126 Hofstra University
105 Memorial Hall
Hofstra University
Hempstead, New York 11549-1260

Phone: 516-463-4723
800-HOFSTRA Ext. 624 (toll-free)
Fax: 516-463-4664
E-mail: graddean@hofstra.edu
Web site: http://www.hofstra.edu/graduate

DEPARTMENT AND PROGRAM HEADS

Biology
Robert W. Seagull, Professor and Chairperson; Ph.D., York, 1979.

Comparative Literature and Languages
Robert A. Leonard, Professor and Chairperson; Ph.D., Columbia, 1982.

Computer Science
Gerda L. Kamberova, Associate Professor and Chairperson; Ph.D., Pennsylvania, 1992.

English and Freshman Composition
Joseph Fichtelberg, Professor and Chairperson; Ph.D., Columbia, 1987.

Fine Arts, Art History, and Humanities
Warren R. Infield, Professor and Chairperson; M.A., CUNY, Hunter, 1964.

Mathematics
Marysia Weiss, Professor and Chairperson; Ph.D., CUNY Graduate Center, 1978.

New College Program
Barry N. Nass, Associate Professor and Vice Dean; Ph.D., Princeton, 1978.

Psychology
Charles Levinthal, Professor and Chairperson; Ph.D., Michigan 1971.

Romance Languages and Literatures
Marta Z. Bermudez, Special Assistant Professor and Chairperson; Ph.D., Arizona, 1988.

Sociology
Marc Silver, Professor and Chairperson; Ph.D., Columbia, 1981.

Speech-Language-Hearing Sciences
Ronald L. Bloom, Professor and Chairperson; Ph.D., CUNY Graduate Center, 1990.

Programs of Study

Graduate programs at Hollins are coeducational, and the number of students in each class is kept small to ensure maximum attention from the faculty. Hollins offers the following master's degrees: the Master of Arts (M.A.) and the Master of Fine Arts (M.F.A.) in children's literature and in screenwriting and film studies; the Master of Fine Arts in creative writing, dance, and playwriting; the Master of Arts in Teaching (M.A.T.); and the interdisciplinary Master of Arts in Liberal Studies (M.A.L.S.). Hollins also offers the Certificate of Advanced Studies (C.A.S.) for students who already hold both baccalaureate and master's degrees.

The M.A. and M.F.A. in either children's literature or screenwriting and film studies and the M.F.A. in playwriting are earned over the course of three to five summers during six-week sessions held from mid-June through July. Students must complete 40 credits for the M.A., consisting of eight 4-credit courses (usually two per summer) plus a thesis (8 credits). For the M.F.A. in children's literature or screenwriting, students must complete a total of 48 credits: ten 4-credit courses (usually two per summer) plus the thesis (8 credits). For the M.F.A. in playwriting, students must complete a total of 60 credits.

To earn the M.F.A. in creative writing, students must complete ten 4-credit courses plus an 8-credit thesis, which must consist of a book-length, original creative manuscript and must be completed by the end of year two.

The M.F.A. in dance program, the first of its kind, is in partnership with the renowned American Dance Festival (ADF) at Duke University. The highly selective 60-credit degree offers students an opportunity to immerse themselves for six weeks of the summer in the international community of ADF, followed by the intimate learning atmosphere at Hollins during the academic year. The program offers three tracks—the Year Residency Track, the Low Residency Track, and the Three-Summer Track.

The M.A.T. degree consists of ten graduate-level courses (40 credit hours), offered over a two- to three-year period. Courses are taught during summer, fall, and spring semesters. The program offers two tracks. Track 1 is for current teachers who wish to develop curriculum in collaborative teams and assume leadership within their school system. Track 2 offers students the opportunity to obtain initial licensure and the master's degree simultaneously. This track requires student teaching, for which Hollins is pleased to offer a grant.

The M.A.L.S. requires ten courses, two of which are heritage core seminars in humanities and social sciences. Five are required to form a concentration in the humanities, the social sciences, the visual and performing arts, or interdisciplinary studies. The final requirement is a capstone experience involving a research essay or creative project.

Research Facilities

Opened in spring 1999, the Wyndham Robertson Library collections consist of more than a half a million items, including books, print periodicals, e-texts, videos, screenplays, rare books, and manuscripts. More than 16,000 journals are available in print or through electronic database subscriptions. The library offers extensive media facilities, including a forty-seat screening room, a television studio, and a multimedia editing room with digital equipment. Hollins houses a notable selection of children's books, including items from the personal collections of Francelia Butler, former editor-in-chief of *Children's Literature*, the field's leading scholarly journal, and former poet laureate William Jay Smith. The University's Archives and Special Collections includes books and manuscripts from many famous faculty members and alumnae/i of Hollins, including Richard Dillard, George Garrett, Eudora Welty, Margaret Wise Brown, Lee Smith, and Annie Dillard. Through a Web-based library automation system shared with Roanoke College, readers are offered access to the combined materials in both collections.

The Richard Wetherill Visual Arts Center, which opened in 2004, centralizes into one dynamic building Hollins's already strong programs in studio art, art history, and film and photography. This comprehensive visual arts center combines spacious studio art facilities with contemporary teaching facilities for art history, film, and photography.

Financial Aid

The strong financial assistance program at Hollins combines merit- and need-based scholarships, grants, loans, campus jobs, and special financing plans. Hollins's scholarship and financial assistance program is made possible by the generosity of a number of foresighted individuals and organizations. William D. Ford Direct Loans are available to students enrolled in graduate-level programs. Students must be enrolled at least half-time (6 hours, fall and spring; 3 hours, summer). Student loan amounts vary according to need. The TAG Grant is available to Virginia students registering for a full-time course load in the fall and spring. The grant is limited to a maximum of three years (six semesters) of graduate studies and is currently estimated at $1900 per year.

Cost of Study

Tuition for M.F.A. in creative writing students for the 2007–08 academic year is $25,200. M.A.L.S courses are $265 per credit hour ($1060 per course). Those pursuing the M.A.T. degree are charged $265 per credit hour. Tuition for the M.F.A. in dance is $640 per credit ($2560 per course); tuition for the M.A. and the M.F.A. in screenwriting and film studies is $590 per credit ($2360 per course); tuition for the M.A. and the M.F.A. in children's literature is $590 per credit ($2360 per course); and tuition for the M.F.A. in playwriting is $590 per credit ($2360 per course).

Living and Housing Costs

Housing costs for the 2007–08 academic year are $5835 (no board available). Housing in summer term 2008, available in student apartments (private bedroom with shared living room, kitchen, and bath) and in other dormitories, will be $860 for the six-week term. Housing for the two-week dance term in 2008 will be $145 per week.

Location

Hollins's 475-acre campus is located in Roanoke, Virginia, a metropolitan area of 236,000 set in the heart of the Blue Ridge Mountains. The Roanoke Regional Airport is 10 minutes from the campus; the Appalachian Trail and Blue Ridge Parkway are minutes away.

The University

Hollins was founded in 1842 as Virginia's first chartered women's college. Coed graduate programs were established in 1958, and university status was granted in 1998. Over the years, Hollins has developed master's degree programs in children's literature, creative writing, dance, liberal studies, playwriting, screenwriting and film studies, and teaching. Hollins is accredited by the Commission on Colleges of the Southern Association of Colleges and Schools. The Hollins curricula and cocurricular programs prepare students for lives of active learning, fulfilling work, personal growth, achievement, and service to society.

Applying

Candidates must have a bachelor's degree from a regionally accredited college or university. Applicants must submit the completed application form, the $40 application fee, official transcripts from all universities attended, letters of recommendation, and writing samples or a portfolio. An interview may be required. Specific application requirements and deadlines vary by program.

Correspondence and Information

Hollins University
P.O. Box 9603
Roanoke, Virginia 24020

Phone: 540-362-6575
Fax: 540-362-6288
E-mail: hugrad@hollins.edu
Web site: http://www.hollins.edu/grad/coedgrad.htm

THE FACULTY

Children's Literature

Michelle Ann Abate, Assistant Professor of English at Hollins; Ph.D., CUNY Graduate Center.
Brian Attebery, Professor of English and Director of American Studies at Idaho State; Ph.D., Brown.
Susan Campbell Bartolletti, Ph.D., SUNY at Binghamton.
Rhonda Brock-Servais, Associate Professor of English at Longwood; Ph.D., South Carolina.
Amanda Cockrell, Director; M.A., Hollins.
Lisa Rowe Fraustino, Assistant Professor of English at Eastern Connecticut State; Ph.D., SUNY at Binghamton.
Tina Hanlon, Associate Professor of English at Ferrum College; Ph.D., Ohio State.
Len Hatfield, Associate Professor of English at Virginia Tech; Ph.D., Indiana.
Hillary Homzie, M.A., Hollins; M.Ed., Temple.
Alexandria LaFaye, Assistant Professor of English at California State, San Bernardino; M.A., Hollins and Mankato State; M.F.A., Memphis.
William Miller, Associate Professor of English at York College; Ph.D., SUNY at Binghamton.
Han Nolan, 1997 winner of the National Book Award and a 2002 writer-in-residence.
Julie Pfeiffer, Associate Professor of English at Hollins; Ph.D., Connecticut.
Klaus Phillips, Professor of German and Film at Hollins; Ph.D., Texas at Austin.
Kimberly Rhodes, Associate Professor of Art at Hollins; Ph.D., Columbia.
Ruth Sanderson, 1997 writer-in-residence.
Teri Sloat, author and illustrator of children's literature; B.S., Oregon State; B.A., Sonoma State; graduate study at Oregon College of Education and Sonoma State.
J. D. Stahl, Professor of English at Virginia Tech; Ph.D., Connecticut.
Morag Styles, Faculty of Education at Cambridge.
C. W. Sullivan III, Professor of English at East Carolina; Ph.D., Oregon.
Ernest Zulia, Assistant Professor of Theater at Hollins; M.F.A., Northwestern.

Creative Writing

T. J. Anderson, Associate Professor of English; Ph.D., SUNY at Binghamton.
Aaron Baker, Visiting Assistant Professor of English; M.F.A., Virginia.
Thomas Beller, Visiting Assistant Professor of English; M.F.A., Columbia.
R. H. W. Dillard, Professor of English; Ph.D., Virginia.
Cathryn Hankla, Professor of English; M.A., Hollins.
Wayne Johnston, Distinguished Chair in Creative Writing; M.A., New Brunswick.
Jeanne Larsen, Professor of English and Director; Ph.D., Iowa.
Thorpe Moeckel, Assistant Professor of English; M.F.A., Virginia.
Christine Schutt, Louis D. Rubin, Jr., Writer-in-Residence; M.F.A., Columbia.
Eric Trethewey, Professor of English; Ph.D., Tulane.

Dance

Jeffery N. Bullock, Associate Professor; M.F.A., Iowa.
Donna Faye Burchfield, Associate Professor, Director, and Artistic Director of Hollins Repertory Dance Company; M.F.A., Texas Christian.
Ben Pranger, Assistant Professor of Performance and New Media; M.F.A., Art Institute of Chicago.

Liberal Studies

Joseph D. Ametepe, Assistant Professor of Physics; Ph.D., William and Mary.
Lawrence C. Becker, Fellow; Ph.D., Chicago.
Sandra Boatman, Professor of Chemistry; Ph.D., Duke.
Jon Donald Bohland, Lecturer in Geography; M.A., Syracuse.
Kay R. Broschart, Professor of Sociology; Ph.D., Yale.
Jan Fuller Carruthers, Assistant Professor of Religious Studies and Chaplain of the University; D.Min., Wesley Theological Seminary.
Amanda Cockrell, Director of the Children's Literature Program; M.A., Hollins.
Peter F. Coogan, Associate Professor of History; Ph.D., North Carolina at Chapel Hill.
James Patrick Downey, Assistant Professor of Philosophy; Ph.D., Virginia.
Alison C. Hall, Lecturer in Art; M.F.A., American.
Richard Hensley, Lecturer in Art; M.F.A., Rhode Island School of Design.
Jan Knipe, Professor of Art; M.F.A., Minnesota.
George W. Ledger, Professor of Psychology; Ph.D., Notre Dame.
Joe W. Leedom, Professor of History; Ph.D., California, Santa Barbara.
Edward A. Lynch, Associate Professor of Political Science and Director, M.A.L.S.; Ph.D., Virginia.
Andrew Matzner, Lecturer in Women's Studies; M.A., Hawaii.
William P. Nye, Professor of Sociology; Ph.D., New School.
Klaus Phillips, Professor of German and Film; Ph.D., Texas at Austin.
Donna Polseno, Lecturer in Art; M.A.T., Rhode Island School of Design.
Ben Pranger, Lecturer in Art; M.F.A., Art Institute of Chicago.
Jong Oh Ra, Professor of Political Science; Ph.D., Illinois.
Wayne Reilly, Emeritus Professor of Political Science; Ph.D., Pittsburgh.
Theresia E. Reimers, Academic Advisor; Ph.D., Stanford.
Kimberly Rhodes, Assistant Professor of Art; Ph.D., Columbia.
Christopher J. Richter, Associate Professor of Communication Studies; Ph.D., Ohio State.
Brent Stevens, Lecturer in Humanities; Ph.D., South Carolina.
Karen Adams Sulkin, Lecturer in Literature; M.A., Hollins.
Robert M. Sulkin, Professor of Art; M.A., M.F.A., Iowa.
Eric Trethewey, Professor of English; Ph.D., Tulane.
Jane Tumas-Serna, Associate Professor of Communication Studies; Ph.D., Ohio.

Playwriting

Todd Ristau, Assistant Professor of Theater and Program Director; M.F.A., Iowa.
Stephen Sossaman, Professor Emeritus, Westfield State College; M.A., SUNY at Stony Brook; Ph.D. studies at NYU.

Screenwriting and Film Studies

Hal Ackerman, Assistant Professor of Screenwriting at UCLA.
Tim Albaugh, Assistant Professor of Screenwriting at UCLA; M.F.A., UCLA.
Reza Allamehzadeh, Iranian filmmaker and writer and publisher of novels and short stories in Farsi.
Edward Buscombe, leading authority on the Western, former head of publishing at the British Film Institute.
R. H. W. Dillard, Professor of English at Hollins; Ph.D., Virginia.
Doris Dörrie, diploma, Hochschule für Fernsehen; filmmaker.
Amy Gerber, M.F.A., California Institute of the Arts.
Jennifer Granville, teaches scriptwriting and producing at Leeds Metropolitan University in the United Kingdom.
Douglas Scott Hessler, professional screenwriter.
Jan-Christopher Horak, Ph.D., Westfalische Wilhelms (Germany).
Mary Johnson, Associate Professor of Film at Central Florida; Ph.D., Ohio State.
Jon Klein, Professor of Screenwriting and Playwriting at Ohio; M.F.A., UCLA.
Mari Kornhauser, UCLA Film School; screenwriter and producer.
Christa Maerker, screenwriter and filmmaker.
Adrienne McLean, Associate Professor of Film Studies at Texas at Dallas; Ph.D., Emory.
Gilberto Perez, Professor of Film Studies at Sarah Lawrence; Ph.D., Princeton.
Klaus Phillips, Professor of German and Film and Director, M.A. and M.F.A. in Screenwriting and Film Studies; Ph.D., Texas at Austin.
Stephen Prince, Associate Professor of Communication Studies at Virginia Tech; Ph.D., Pennsylvania.
Laura Shamas, Ph.D., Pacifica Graduate.
Ula Stöckl, graduate of the Institut für Filmgestaltung in Ulm.
Eric Trethewey, Professor of English; Ph.D., Tulane.

Teaching

Marcie Altice, Lecturer; M.A.T., Hollins.
Anna Baynum, Instructor in Education; M.Ed., Virginia.
Mitchell B. Bowman, Clinical Associate Professor; Ed.D., Virginia.
Kristi S. Fowler, Assistant Professor of Education and Director of Education Programs; Ph.D., Virginia.
Cathy Layman, Lecturer; M.A.T., Hollins.
Martha Moseley, Lecturer in English; M.S., Radford.
Jong Oh Ra, Professor of Political Science; Ph.D., Illinois.
Rebecca R. Reiff, Assistant Professor; Ph.D. candidate, Indiana.

ILLINOIS STATE UNIVERSITY

Graduate School

Programs of Study

Illinois State University offers degree and nondegree graduate programs in the Colleges of Applied Science and Technology, Arts and Sciences, Business, Education, Fine Arts, and Nursing.

Doctoral programs are offered in audiology, biological sciences, curriculum and instruction, educational administration, English studies, mathematics education, school psychology, and special education.

A specialist program is offered in school psychology, and Master of Fine Arts programs are offered in art and theater.

Master's programs are offered in accountancy, agribusiness, applied economics, art, arts technology, biological sciences, business, chemistry, clinical-counseling psychology, college student personnel administration, communication, criminal justice sciences, curriculum and instruction, educational administration, English, family and consumer sciences, foreign languages, historical archeology, history, hydrogeology, information technology, instructional technology and design, kinesiology and recreation, mathematics, music, nursing, political science, psychology, reading, social work, sociology, special education, speech pathology and audiology, technology, theater, and writing. An integrated B.S./M.P.A. program is available in accountancy.

Graduate certificates are offered in nurse educator; project management; training and development; social aspects of aging; women's studies; and the following learning behavior specialist certificates: LBS 2 behavior intervention specialist, LBS 2 curriculum adaptation specialist, LBS 2 multiple disabilities specialist, LBS 2 technology specialist, and LBS 2 transition specialist.

Postbaccalaureate graduate certificates are offered in teaching of writing in high school/middle school and alternative route to secondary teacher certification.

Post-master's graduate certificates are offered in chief school business official (CSBO) endorsement, family nurse practitioner, general administrative certification, superintendent endorsement in educational administration, and director of special education.

Research Facilities

The University library provides extensive access to state and national databases in addition to its own collection of more than 1.9 million volumes. The University maintains both an elementary and a secondary laboratory school in which graduate students may conduct educational research. Each department at Illinois State University provides students with both the laboratories and equipment needed for graduate study and access to the University's comprehensive computer services.

Financial Aid

Federal Perkins Loans, Federal Stafford Student Loans, and Federal Work-Study awards are offered to students with demonstrated financial need. State grants include Illinois Military Scholarships and various teacher shortage, minority, and administration scholarships. Both teaching and research assistantships, including tuition waivers, are arranged through individual academic and nonacademic units. GI bill benefits, plus fellowship/traineeship programs and several privately financed scholarships, are available.

Cost of Study

In 2006–07, tuition and fees for full-time (9 hours) state resident students were $2475 per semester; out-of-state students paid $4482.

Living and Housing Costs

The University offers a variety of room options in residence halls and a number of meal plans from which to choose. The 2006–07 cost of room and board was $6194 per year for a multiple-occupancy room and the basic meal plan. Single and married graduate students (with or without dependents) may qualify for University-owned apartments. Enrollment in a degree program is required. Rental rates in 2006–07 ranged from $347 to $476 per month. Early application for apartments is recommended.

Student Group

Illinois State University's total enrollment is approximately 20,000; of this number, about 3,000 are enrolled as full- or part-time graduate students. The graduate student population is diverse by gender, race/ethnicity, and state or country of origin.

Location

Illinois State University is located in the twin cities of Bloomington-Normal (population 100,000) and is easily accessible by car, bus, train, or plane. Amtrak offers train service to and from Chicago, Milwaukee, St. Louis, and points along the way, and various bus lines provide service to all points in the state. Airlines provide daily passenger service to Chicago, Atlanta, Detroit, Minneapolis, St. Louis, and points west. The Bloomington-Normal area is reached by one of the best highway systems in the state; the twin cities serve as the hub for Interstates 74, 55, and 39 and U.S. 51, the major north-south route in Illinois.

The University

Abraham Lincoln drafted the documents establishing Illinois State Normal University, which was founded in 1857 as the first public institution of higher education in Illinois. The University first began offering graduate work in several departments in 1943. In the 1960s, after more than a century as a single-purpose teacher-education institution, Illinois State began to offer liberal arts as well as teacher-education programs, introduced doctoral-level curricula, and renamed the institution Illinois State University.

Applying

Any student who has completed work for a bachelor's degree from a regionally accredited institution may apply for admission to the Graduate School. A GRE score is required for doctoral, specialist, and many master's programs. A GMAT score is required for accounting and business. Each program may have individual requirements. Admissions applications are electronic with an application fee of $30.

Correspondence and Information

Office of Admissions
Hovey Hall 201
Campus Box 2200
Illinois State University
Normal, Illinois 61790-2200

Phone: 309-438-2181
E-mail: admissions@ilstu.edu
Web site: http://www.IllinoisState.edu/admissions

IMMACULATA UNIVERSITY

College of Graduate Studies

Programs of Study

Immaculata University offers programs of study leading to the Master of Arts in counseling psychology, cultural and linguistic diversity (bilingual studies and teaching English to speakers of other languages), educational leadership, music therapy (accredited by National Association of Schools of Music), nutrition education (with an ADA Dietetic Internship), and organization leadership (with concentrations in health-care services and organizational effectiveness). Also available are curricula leading to the Master of Science in Nursing (M.S.N.), the Doctor of Education (Ed.D.) in educational leadership and administration, the Doctor of Psychology (Psy.D.) in clinical psychology, and the Doctor of Psychology (Psy.D.) in school psychology. The Doctor of Psychology in clinical psychology is accredited by the American Psychological Association. Pennsylvania certification for school nurses, school superintendents, elementary and secondary school teachers, school psychologists, elementary and secondary school guidance counselors, principals, special education, and supervisor for curriculum and instruction, special education, and specialty areas is also offered. Certificates are available in teaching English to speakers of other languages (TESOL), organizational effectiveness, health care, and existential humanistic psychotherapy.

The total semester hours required in each master's program vary from 36 to 60, depending on the program of study.

A unique feature of the master's programs is the required 9-credit integrative core curriculum. The core, along with course work in the area of specific concentration, provides an integrative, holistic, and humanistic approach to graduate education. Through close, ongoing advisement as well as the curriculum and career counseling, each student's personal development is assisted and monitored while he or she acquires the strong theoretical and practical preparation necessary for responsible professional practice.

The College of Graduate Studies is sensitive to the needs of the adult learner. Classes are offered in the late afternoon, evenings, and weekends to accommodate both part-time and full-time students. Innovative accelerated courses covering special topics are offered in intensive time blocks for elective credit or seminar experience.

Research Facilities

Gabriele Library is a freestanding 52,000-square-foot library that offers the latest advances in Internet and electronic access. Providing access to ERIC, PsycInfo, Academic Search, Business Source, Science Direct, MLA, CINAHL, FirstSearch, and LexisNexis databases, the Gabriele Library serves the needs of students who are conducting research in the areas of education, psychology, business, science, humanities, health, and many other fields. With online journal services, such as PsychArticles and Proquest Nursing, there is full-text availability of a wide variety of high-quality research journals. These resources are in addition to the online book catalog and interlibrary loan services. The library offers a computer/AV room with PCs and printers and VCRs, stereos, and DVD players; a fully equipped media classroom; a closed-circuit TV room; a video-editing room; group-study rooms; and a digital microfilm/fiche reader/printer.

Financial Aid

Thirty percent of the students receive financial aid. Federal Stafford Student Loans (subsidized and unsubsidized) and Federal Perkins Loans are available to students enrolled at least half-time in any discipline. Merit scholarships are awarded annually in a competitive process.

Cost of Study

Estimated tuition for 2007–08 is $500 per credit for 500- and 600-level courses and $700 per credit for 700-level courses. The practicum fee varies with the program. The graduation fee is approximately $100.

Living and Housing Costs

Limited on-campus housing is available. Most students commute to the campus. The University is located in a rapidly growing suburban area offering many off-campus housing options, the cost of which varies widely.

Student Group

Total enrollment at Immaculata University is approximately 3,200. The graduate student body of 1,200 women and men comprises recent college graduates, professionals with several years of experience in their field, and those returning to study after a number of years.

Student Outcomes

Students leaving Immaculata University's graduate programs typically are quickly engaged in positions with the helping professions. Many students come to Immaculata University's graduate programs to study part-time, while continuing their full-time employment with an eye toward advancement as a result of their studies. Other graduates report that their degree at Immaculata University has allowed them to make a complete career change and that they have generally found employment within a few months of graduation in fields that are closely allied to their studies. Employers frequently report their satisfaction with the quality and depth of preparation they find in the Immaculata graduates they hire.

Location

Immaculata's 390-acre campus overlooks the rapidly growing Chester Valley and is located in Frazer, Pennsylvania, on the Main Line, about 20 miles west of Philadelphia. Proximity to Philadelphia provides access to a great many cultural, academic, and recreational facilities. The University's close working relationships with the surrounding community offer excellent resources for internships, practicums, and professional experiences.

The University and The College

Immaculata University is fully accredited by the Middle States Association of Colleges and Schools Commission on Higher Education. Founded in 1920 by the Sisters, Servants of the Immaculate Heart of Mary, the University began the College of Graduate Studies in 1983.

The expansion of program offerings in the College of Graduate Studies is yet another example of Immaculata's continuing commitment to meeting the needs of a rapidly changing, highly complex, and diversified society. Immaculata's tradition of excellence and creative, responsive innovation is exemplified in its College of Graduate Studies.

Applying

The deadlines for those seeking admission to the Psy.D. programs in clinical psychology are January 15 for a May start or February 1 for a September start. Application deadlines for the Psy.D. in school psychology and the Ed.D. programs are November 1, March 1, and June 1. The application fee is $50. The Psy.D. programs in clinical and school psychology offer admission to students with B.A./B.S.- and M.A.-level degrees. Applications to the master's and certification/certificate programs are welcomed throughout the year and should be accompanied by a $35 application fee.

Applicants should forward official transcripts of all completed undergraduate and graduate work, two recommendations from academic and professional sources, and a writing sample. Application materials, interview appointments, and campus visit information are available by writing, calling, or e-mailing the College of Graduate Studies at Immaculata University. Open houses are held three times per year, usually in October, March, and July.

Additional requirements may include acceptable scores on either the Miller Analogies Test or the Graduate Record Examinations. Music therapy applicants are required to take a music entrance exam. M.S.N. applicants must have a bachelor's degree in nursing and be registered nurses. Educational leadership and administration program candidates must provide a copy of their teaching certificate, and school psychology doctoral students must provide a copy of their certification. Applicants should contact the graduate office for more specific program requirements and information.

Correspondence and Information

College of Graduate Studies
1145 King Road, Campus Box 500
Immaculata University
Immaculata, Pennsylvania 19345-0500

Phone: 610-647-4400 Ext. 3211 or 3212
Fax: 610-993-8550
E-mail: graduate@immaculata.edu
Web site: http://www.immaculata.edu

THE FACULTY

Faculty members are listed below according to department. Those who also teach in the core are indicated by an asterisk.

Sr. Ann M. Heath, Dean of the College of Graduate Studies; Ph.D., Bryn Mawr.

Core
Pamela Lunardi, Psy.D., Immaculata.
Sr. Jane Anne Molinaro, Ph.D., Ohio State.
Anne Reinsmith, D.Min., Eastern Baptist Theological Seminary.
Kathleen Soeder, Ed.D., Immaculata.
Suzann Steadman, Psy.D., Immaculata.

Cultural and Linguistic Diversity
Margaret van Naerssen, Coordinator; Ph.D., USC.
Diane Colom, Turabo (Puerto Rico).
Deborah Falk, M.A., Cabrini.
David Cassells Johnson, M.A., Northern Iowa.
Kalala Kabongo-Mianda, Ph.D., Pennsylvania.
Marcia Vega, M.S., Wilkes.

Educational Leadership
Sr. Carol Anne Couchara, Chair; Ed.D., Lehigh.
David Blozowich, Ed.D., Immaculata.
David Brennan, Ed.D., Immaculata.
Valerie Burnett, Ed.D., Immaculata.
Sr. Anne Marie Burton, Ed.D., Temple.
Mary Calderone, Ed.D., Immaculata.
Sr. Joseph Marie Carter, Ed.D., Immaculata.
*Christina Charnitski, Ph.D., Drexel.
Joseph J. Corabi, Ed.D., Widener.
Michael Kelly, Ed.D., Immaculata.
Thomas Kent, Ed.D., Pennsylvania.
David Morgan, Ed.D., Pennsylvania.
Kathleen Nolan, Ph.D., Saint Louis.
Thomas O'Brien, Ed.D., Immaculata.
Mary Rounds, Ed.D., Pennsylvania.
Thomas Scholvin, Ed.D., Nova Southeastern.
Charles F. Stefanski, Ed.D., Temple.
Robert Urzillo, Ed.D., West Virginia.
John Wingerter, Ed.D., Temple.

Music Therapy
Brian Abrams, Chair; Ph.D., Temple.
*William Carr, D.M.A., Catholic University.
Anthony Meadows, Ph.D., Temple.
Kathleen Murphy, M.M.T., Temple.

Nursing
Janice Cranmer, Chair; Ed.D., Temple.
Jean Klein, Graduate Director; D.N.Sc., Widener.
Marguerite Ambrose, D.N.Sc., Widener.
Susan Burke, D.N.Sc., Catholic University.
Margaret Lacey, Ph.D., Temple.
Kathleen Lawler, M.S.N., Temple.
Gail Lehner, M.S.N., Neumann.
Jane Tang, Ph.D., Iowa.
Stephanie Trinkl, D.N.Sc., Widener.

Nutrition Education
*Laura B. Frank, Chair; Ph.D., Temple; RD.
Sr. M. Carroll Isselmann, Ed.D., Rutgers; RD.
Susan W. Johnston, M.S., West Chester; RD.

Organization Studies
*Janice Jacobs, Chair; Ph.D., Temple.
Eric Anderson, Ph.D., Fuller Theological Seminary.
Johanna Bishop, M.S.Ed., Wilmington (Delaware).
Charlene Fitzwater, M.B.A., Kansas.
Glenn Forte, M.A., Villanova.
Donna Hammacher, J.D., Temple.
M. E. Jones, Ph.D., Drexel.
Valerie Martin, M.A.T., Hartford.
Rod Napier, Ph.D., Chicago.
Julie Roberts, Ph.D., Temple.
Julie Ryan, Ph.D., Capella.
Ed Travis, Ed.D., Massachusetts.

Psychology
Jed A. Yalof, Chair; Psy.D., ABPP, ABSNP, Illinois School of Professional Psychology.
Pamela Abraham, Psy.D., Baylor.
Donna Alberici, M.S., Villanova.
*Janet Belitsky, Psy.D., Immaculata.
Cris Chambers, Psy.D., Immaculata.
Maria Cuddy-Casey, Ph.D., Nova Southeastern.
Craig Cunningham, M.Ed., Villanova.
Barbara W. Domingos, Ph.D., Bryn Mawr.
Francien Dorliae, Psy.D., Immaculata.
Janet L. Etzi, Psy.D., Widener.
David Harman, Ph.D., Chicago.
Paul Haughton, Psy.D., Hahnemann.
Edward Jenny, Psy.D., Immaculata.
Angela Jones, Ph.D., Temple.
Matthew Leary, Ph.D., North Carolina at Chapel Hill.
Thomas Legere, Ph.D., Union (New York).
Todd Lewis, Ph.D., Drexel.
Marijo Lucas, Ph.D., Auburn.
Marie McGrath, Ph.D., Temple.
Nancy Mahoney, M.A., West Chester.
Edward Moon, Psy.D., Illinois School of Professional Psychology.
*Sr. Jeannine Marie O'Kane, Ph.D., Fordham.
Roger Osmun, Ph.D., Temple.
Michael Overtorf, M.A., Dayton.
Susan Platt, M.Ed., Temple.
Susan Proulx, Psy.D., Immaculata.
Louise Shuman, Psy.D., Immaculata.
Bonnie Socket, Ph.D., Temple.

RESEARCH

Cultural and Linguistic Diversity (M.A.): Second-language acquisition, sociolinguistics, phonology, ESL, TESOL, forensic linguistics.
Counseling Psychology (M.A.), Clinical Psychology (Psy.D.), and **School Psychology (Psy.D.):** Supervision, ethics, psychology of teaching, gender, spirituality, gerontology, sexuality, cultural diversity, women's issues, psychoanalytic psychotherapy, existentialism.
Educational Leadership/Administration (M.A., Ed.D.): Performance assessment, cooperative learning, school-based management, special education, whole language, educational theory and policy.
Music Therapy (M.A.): Music psychotherapy, behavioral music therapy, cultural music therapy, music healing.
Nutrition Education (M.A.): Obesity and weight control, nutrition counseling, mentoring of students in dietetics, multicultural nutrition, sports nutrition, school health and nutrition.

Immaculata University is committed to the principle of equal educational opportunity without discrimination by race, color, religion, gender, age, national origin, or condition of handicap.

INDIANA STATE UNIVERSITY

School of Graduate Studies

Programs of Study

Indiana State University (ISU) offers more than 100 graduate courses of study leading to a graduate certificate or a master's, education specialist's, or doctoral degree in the Colleges of Arts and Sciences, Business, Education, Health and Human Performance, Nursing, and Technology. The College of Arts and Sciences offers the Psy.D. in clinical psychology and the Ph.D. in ecology and organismal biology, geography, and life sciences. The Department of Art offers the M.F.A. The Department of Music offers the M.M. degree. The Department of Political Science offers the M.P.A. Both the M.A. and the M.S. are available in communication, criminology, ecology and organismal biology, English, history, life science, mathematics, political science, and psychology. The M.A. degree is offered in art; languages, literatures, and linguistics; and geography. The M.S. degree is offered in family and consumer sciences, geology, life sciences, and science education. The College of Business offers the M.B.A. degree. The College of Education offers the Ph.D. in counseling psychology, counselor education, curriculum and instruction, educational administration, and school psychology. The Ed.S. degree is offered in school administration and school psychology. The M.Ed. is offered in curriculum and instruction, early childhood education, elementary education, reading education, school administration, school counseling, and school psychology. The M.A. and M.S. are offered in communication disorders and special education. The M.S. is offered in educational technology, mental health counseling, and student affairs and higher education. The College of Health and Human Performance offers the M.A. and M.S. in health, safety, and environmental health sciences; physical education; and recreation and sport management. The M.S. is offered in athletic training. The College of Nursing offers the M.S. in nursing. The College of Technology offers the Ph.D. in technology management. The M.S. is offered in career and technical education teaching, electronics and computer technology, human resource development, industrial technology, and technology education.

Research Facilities

Indiana State University Cunningham Memorial Library houses more than 2.5 million items, subscribes to more than 5,000 periodicals, and provides access to more than 20,000 full-text electronic periodicals. These can be accessed through an online system that also connects with other college libraries in Terre Haute and Indiana. The ISU library provides collaborative workstations to facilitate group and collaborative research. All students enrolled at ISU have access to a wireless network that allows them to access the Internet from most locations on the campus. Several departments offer specialized research facilities. The Instructional and Research Technology Services offers services (at no cost to students) that include statistical design consultation, research design consultation, design and analysis of sample research surveys, and presentation of statistical graphs and tables. The Psychology Clinic serves as a training facility for clinical psychology doctoral students. The Porter School Psychology Center provides research opportunities for students in counseling and school psychology. The ISU Remote Sensing Laboratory specializes in earth resources analysis using computer-aided processing of satellite data. The Technology Services Center engages in cooperative research with industry using CAD/CAM and other related technologies. A radiation laboratory provides students experience with the latest technology. The Center for Research and Management Services utilizes students to provide research for local area and statewide businesses in fields of economic development and targeted industry studies.

Financial Aid

Eligible graduate students may apply for institutional graduate assistantships through the respective academic departments. ISU graduate assistantships include a stipend and a tuition fee waiver. The tuition fee waivers are exclusive of building and student services fees, for up to 18 hours per academic year. For policies regarding graduate assistantships and fee waivers, students should visit the School of Graduate Studies Web site.

There are also opportunities for graduates to apply for scholarships and fellowships at ISU, some of which include the Paul A. Witty Fellowships, which are available for eligible students specializing in educating gifted and creative children and the Gertrude and Theodore Debs Memorial Fellowships, available for eligible students specializing in American labor and reform movements. There are also the Kweku Bentil Awards, which recognize full-time students who have shown exceptional scholarship and leadership skills. The Noyce Scholarship Program provides an assistantship and fee waiver for students in the College of Arts and Sciences. In addition, the Charles and Kathleen Manatt Democracy Studies Fellowship program provides students an opportunity to conduct research in various aspects of the political process. Detailed information regarding the application process for these fellowships can be found online at the School of Graduate Studies Web site. Applications received prior to March 1 are given preference.

The Office of Student Financial Aid assists ISU graduate students in obtaining further educational funding opportunities through the Federal Perkins Loan (National Direct Student Loans) and Federal Stafford Student Loan programs, PLUS loans, or the College Work-Study Program. The office can be contacted at 812-237-2215 or at http://www.indstate.edu/finaid/.

Cost of Study

Tuition and fees for the 2007–08 academic year are $294 per semester hour for in-state students and $584 per semester hour for out-of-state students. The maximum load for fall and spring semesters is 12 semester hours. Summer Session I runs eight weeks, with three-, five-, and eight-week class options. A maximum of 9 credit hours may be earned during Session I. Summer Session II runs five weeks, and a maximum of 6 credit hours may be earned.

Living and Housing Costs

In addition to traditional residence halls, Indiana State University offers furnished and unfurnished apartment-style housing for graduate students at its University Apartments at reasonable and competitive rental rates. Each apartment is self-contained with its own bedroom(s), bathroom, living/dining area, and kitchen with an electric range, refrigerator, and garbage disposal. Utilities and free local telephone service are also included. Furnished apartments have one- or two-bedroom options and range from $540 to $606 per month. Unfurnished apartments have one-, two-, or three-bedroom options and range from $449 to $677 per month. Low-cost housing is also available in the surrounding community.

Student Group

Since 1927, ISU's graduate programs have prepared students for careers in a wide range of teaching, research, and service professions. The campus has the highest diversity of students among four-year institutions in Indiana. Both the areas of study and the student population are diverse. Graduate programs attract applicants from all over the United States and from forty-three countries around the world. Approximately 15 percent of the graduate students are international, 33 percent are out-of-state students, 13 percent are members of minority groups, and 58 percent are women. The average graduate student age is 33.

Location

The campus is located adjacent to the central business district of Terre Haute, Indiana, which is an industrial and commercial city of approximately 61,000 located in west-central Indiana. Cultural activities include amateur and professional theatrical productions, symphonies, and art exhibits. Excellent county and state parks are within easy driving distance. The city is convenient to the four major metropolitan areas of Indianapolis, St. Louis, Chicago, and Cincinnati.

The University and The School

Indiana State University is listed as one of the nation's best-value colleges by *The Princeton Review* in its 2007 edition of "America's Best Value Colleges." Indiana State University has grown during its 140-year history from Indiana State Normal School to Indiana State Teachers College and Indiana State College to full university status. With a graduate student population of approximately 2,000, students can be assured of a close mentoring experience and significant research opportunities within their academic program.

Applying

Applications to the School of Graduate Studies can be submitted online, by mail, or in person.

Prospective applicants should visit the School of Graduate Studies Web site at http://www.indstate.edu/sogs/and check with their respective departments for specific deadlines and additional required admissions materials, such as test scores, letters of recommendation, and other documents. Students generally receive a response acknowledging receipt of the application and other communication from the School of Graduate Studies within one to two weeks. Once admitted, students receive instructions regarding academic advisement and registration.

International students must submit a TOEFL score of 550 or better and an Affidavit of Financial Support. For additional requirements and documentation, students should visit the Graduate School Web site or the International Affairs Center at http://www.indstate.edu/IAC/.

Correspondence and Information

Dr. Jolynn Kuhlman, Interim Dean
School of Graduate Studies
Indiana State University
Terre Haute, Indiana 47809
Phone: 812-237-3005
800-444-GRAD (4723) (toll-free)
Fax: 812-237-8060
E-mail: grdstudy@isugw.indstate.edu
Web site: http://www.indstate.edu/sogs

For U.S. applicants, mail to:
School of Graduate Studies
Tirey Hall, Room 183
Indiana State University
Terre Haute, Indiana 47809
Phone: 812-237-3005
800-444-GRAD (4723) (toll-free)
Fax: 812-237-8060
E-mail: grdstudy@isugw.indstate.edu

For international applicants, mail to:
School of Graduate Studies
Indiana State University
Terre Haute, Indiana 47809
Phone: 812-237-3005
800-444-GRAD (4723) toll-free)
Fax: 812-237-8060
E-mail: grdstudy@isugw.indstate.edu
Web site: http://www.indstate.edu/sogs

THE FACULTY

Deans
Jolynn Kuhlman, Ph.D., Interim Dean, School of Graduate Studies.
Thomas Sauer, Ph.D.; Dean, College of Arts and Sciences.
Nancy J. Merritt, Ph.D.; Dean, College of Business.
Bradley Balch, Ph.D.; Dean, College of Education
Doug Timmons, Ph.D., and Esther Acree, M.S.N., RN, Sp.Cl.Nsg., FNP; Interim Co-Deans, College of Nursing, Health, and Human Services.
W. Tad Foster, Ph.D.; Dean, College of Technology.

Department Chairpersons and Directors of Graduate Degree Programs
Art: Charles Mayer, Ph.D., Professor and Interim Chairperson.
Athletic Training: Jeffrey Edwards, Ph.D., Professor and Interim Chairperson.
Business Administration: Dale Varble, Ph.D., Associate Dean and M.B.A. Director.
Center for Science Education: Susan Berta, Ph.D., Interim Program Director.
Clinical Psychology: Virgil Sheets, Ph.D., Professor and Interim Chairperson.
Communication: David Worley, Ph.D., Professor and Interim Chairperson.
Communication Disorders and Counseling, School, and Educational Psychology: Michele Boyer, Ph.D., Department Chairperson.
Communication Disorders: Vicki Hammen, Ph.D., Program Director.
Counseling Education: Debra Leggett, Ph.D., Program Director.
Counseling Psychology: James L. Campbell, Ph.D., Program Director.
Criminology and Criminal Justice: David Skelton, Ed.D., J.D., Professor and Interim Chairperson.
Curriculum, Instruction, and Media Technology: Susan Kiger, Ph.D., Interim Department Chairperson.
Ecology and Organismal Biology: Charles Amlaner, Ph.D., Professor and Chairperson.
Educational and School Psychology: Eric Hampton, Ph.D., Professor and Interim Chairperson.
Educational Leadership, Administration, and Foundations: Josh Powers, Ph.D., Professor and Chairperson.
Educational Technology: James Smallwood, Ph.D., Department Chairperson.
Electronics and Computer Technology: William Croft, Ph.D., Professor and Chairperson.
Elementary, Early, and Special Education: Diana Quatroche, Ph.D., Professor and Chairperson.
English: Robert Perrin, Ph.D., Professor and Chairperson.
Family and Consumer Sciences: Frederica Kramer, Ph.D., Professor and Chairperson.
Geography, Geology, and Anthropology: Susan Berta, Ph.D., Chairperson and Program Coordinator.
Health, Safety, and Environmental Health Sciences: Ernest Sheldon, Ph.D., Professor and Interim Department Chairperson.
History: William Griffin, Ph.D., Professor and Acting Chairperson.
Human Resource Development: James Smallwood, Ph.D., Professor and Chairperson.
Industrial Technology: Marion Schafer, Ph.D., Program Coordinator.
Languages, Literatures, and Linguistics: Ronald Dunbar, Ph.D., Professor and Chairperson.
Life Sciences: Swapan Ghosh, Ph.D., Professor and Interim Chairperson.
Mathematics and Computer Science: B. Rao Kopparty, Ph.D., Professor and Chairperson.
Mental Health Counseling: Matthew Draper, Ph.D., Program Director.
Music: Randall Mitchell, Ph.D., Professor and Interim Chairperson.
Nursing: Esther Acree, M.S.N., RN, Sp.Cl.Nsg., FNP; Professor and Interim Dean.
Physical Education: Jennifer Boothby, Ph.D., Professor and Acting Department Chairperson.
Political Science: Michael Chambers, Ph.D., Professor and Chairperson.
Psychology: Virgil Sheets, Ph.D., Professor and Chairperson.
Public Administration: Stan Buchanan, Ph.D., Assistant Professor and Program Coordinator.
Recreation and Sport Management: Steve Smidley, Ph.D., Interim Department Chairperson.
School Administration and Supervision: Joshua Powers, Ph.D., Professor and Interim Chairperson.
School Counseling, M.Ed., and Licensure Programs: Tonya Balch, Ph.D., Program Director.
School Psychology: Eric Hampton, Ph.D., Professor and Interim Chairperson.
Science Education: Susan Berta, Ph.D., Professor and Interim Coordinator.
Social Science Education: Daniel Clark, Ph.D., Interim Program Director.
Student Affairs and Higher Education: Denise Collins, Ph.D., Professor and Program Coordinator.
Technology Education: James Smallwood, Ph.D., Professor and Chairperson.
Technology Management: George Maughan, Ph.D., Program Director.

INDIANA UNIVERSITY OF PENNSYLVANIA

School of Graduate Studies and Research

Programs of Study

The School of Graduate Studies and Research at IUP offers programs of study leading to the Doctor of Education, Doctor of Psychology, and Doctor of Philosophy degrees in the areas of administration and leadership studies (educational administration track or human services track), clinical psychology, criminology, curriculum and instruction, English, and school psychology.

Master of Arts, Master of Science, Master of Business Administration, Master of Education, and Master of Fine Arts degrees are available in adult and community education, adult education and communications technology, applied mathematics, art, biology, business administration, business and workforce development, chemistry, community counseling, criminology, education, educational psychology, education of exceptional persons, elementary education, elementary and middle school mathematics education, secondary school mathematics education, elementary or secondary school counseling, English (English education, generalist English, literature, or teaching English to speakers of other languages), food and nutrition, geography, health and physical education, history, industrial and labor relations, information technology, literacy, music, nursing, physics, professional growth, public affairs, safety sciences, science for disaster response, sociology, speech-language pathology, sport science, and student affairs in higher education. IUP also offers graduate programs in the Pittsburgh area.

The School of Graduate Studies and Research offers specialization or certification in safety sciences, school counseling, reading specialist, school psychology, elementary/secondary principal, special education, supervisor of pupil services, and educational specialist.

Basic requirements for the doctoral degrees include spending a minimum of two semesters (or summer session equivalents) in residence at IUP, passing qualifying examinations, and presenting and defending a dissertation. The thesis is optional in most master's degree programs.

The University operates on an academic year of two semesters, plus summer sessions.

Research Facilities

The University library contains more than 852,000 book volumes, 1,700 periodical subscriptions, 14,500 electronic serials subscriptions, and 2.4 million units of microform materials and other documents and is a select federal depository. The computer center is housed in the same building as the School of Graduate Studies and Research and is available to members of the University community at all times. Specialized laboratories and research equipment are available for advanced master's, post-master's, and doctoral students. There are numerous research centers on campus.

Financial Aid

IUP offers a limited number of assistantships to degree-seeking graduate students. Full 20-hour assistantships currently pay a stipend of $4700 to $6330 for two semesters, plus a waiver of tuition for graduate course work. Various loan opportunities are available. Funds exist to support student research and attendance at professional meetings to present papers.

Cost of Study

In 2006–07, full-time graduate tuition was $3024 for in-state students and $4839 for out-of-state students. Tuition for part-time study was $336 per semester credit for in-state students and $538 per credit for out-of-state students. Full-time students paid an activity fee of $123 per semester; part-time students paid $51.50. Each semester, an instructional fee of $302 ($33.60 per credit hour for part-time students), a technology fee of $62.50 per semester for full-time in-state students, and a registration fee of $32 per semester were assessed. Costs are subject to change.

Living and Housing Costs

University residence halls and off-campus rooms and apartments are available. Costs vary depending upon room size, proximity, and whether or not meals are included in the arrangement.

Student Group

Approximately 2,270 students are enrolled in programs leading to the various graduate degrees. The total University enrollment is approximately 14,250. Students represent American minority groups, most states, and a number of countries.

Location

Indiana, Pennsylvania, a community of 28,000, is 59 miles northeast of Pittsburgh. A wide variety of cultural and recreational activities in urban, suburban, and rural settings are available in and near the town of Indiana and in Pittsburgh.

The University

Founded as a higher education institution in 1875 and designated a university in 1965, IUP is a Doctoral/Research University–Intensive institution with three campuses and more than 700 faculty members.

Applying

An admissions packet is available by request from the School of Graduate Studies and Research or online at the School's Web site (http://www.iup.edu/graduate). Brochures and other information describing individual programs are available directly from departmental graduate coordinators.

Correspondence and Information

School of Graduate Studies and Research
Stright Hall, Room 101
210 South Tenth Street
Indiana University of Pennsylvania
Indiana, Pennsylvania 15705-1048
Phone: 724-357-2222
Fax: 724-357-4862
E-mail: graduate-admissions@iup.edu
Web site: http://www.iup.edu/graduate

THE FACULTY

Listed below are IUP's graduate degree program areas. Each is followed by the name of the corresponding graduate coordinator and campus e-mail address.

PROGRAM AREAS
Administration and Leadership Studies, Education Track: Dr. Robert Millward (millward@iup.edu).
Administration and Leadership Studies, Human Services Track: Dr. Beth Mabry (mabry@iup.edu).
Adult and Community Education: Dr. Jeffrey Ritchey (Jeffrey.Ritchey@iup.edu).
Adult Education and Communications Technology: Dr. Gary Dean (gjdean@iup.edu).
Art: Ms. Susan Palmisano (palmisan@iup.edu).
Biology: Dr. Sandy Newell (sjnewell@iup.edu).
Business Administration: Dr. Krish Krishnan (Krishnan@iup.edu).
Business and Workforce Development: Dr. Dawn Woodland (woodland@iup.edu).
Chemistry: Dr. Charles Lake (lake@iup.edu).
Clinical Psychology: Dr. Beverly Goodwin (Goodwin@iup.edu).
Community Counseling: Dr. Claire Dandeneau (cdanden@iup.edu).
Counselor Education: Dr. Claire Dandeneau (cdanden@iup.edu).
Criminology, M.A.: Dr. Daniel Lee (danlee@iup.edu).
Criminology, Ph.D.: Dr. David Myers (david@iup.edu).
Curriculum and Instruction: Dr. Frank Corbett (fcorbett@iup.edu) and Dr. Mary Jalongo (mjalongo@iup.edu).
Education of Exceptional Persons: Dr. Jan Baker (jbaker@iup.edu).
Educational Psychology: Dr. Joseph Kovaleski (jkov@iup.edu).
Elementary Education: Dr. Mary Jalongo (mjalongo@iup.edu).
English, Generalist, Literature, and Literature and Criticism: Dr. Karen Dandurand (karenddd@iup.edu).
English, M.A.T.E., TESOL, and Composition: Dr. Ben Rafoth (Bennett.Rafoth@iup.edu).
Food and Nutrition: Dr. Stephanie Taylor-Davis (stdavis@iup.edu).
Geography: Dr. Kevin Patrick (kpatrick@iup.edu).
Health and Physical Education: Dr. Madeline Bayles (mpbayles@iup.edu) and Dr. Robert Kostelnik (bkostel@iup.edu).
History: Dr. Tami Whited (twhited@iup.edu).
Industrial and Labor Relations: Dr. Jennie Bullard (jbullard@iup.edu).
Information Technology: Dr. Dawn Woodland (woodland@iup.edu).
Literacy: Dr. Anne Creany (acreany@iup.edu).
Math, Applied: Dr. Frederick Morgan (fwmorgan@iup.edu).
Math Education, Elementary: Dr. James Myers (jrmyers@iup.edu).
Math Education, Secondary: Dr. Margaret Stempien (mmstemp@iup.edu).
Music, Performance, Education, Theory/Composition, History: Dr. Keith Young (kyoung@iup.edu).
Nursing, Education, Administration: Dr. Nashat Zuraikat (zuraikat@iup.edu).
Physics: Dr. Gregory Kenning (ccpm@iup.edu).
Principal Certification: Dr. Cathy Kaufman (ckaufman@iup.edu).
Professional Growth: School of Graduate Studies and Research Dean (graduate-admissions@iup.edu).
Professional Studies, Master of Education: Dr. Valeri Helterbran (vhelter@iup.edu).
Public Affairs: Dr. Gawdat Bahgat (gbahgat@iup.edu).
Safety Sciences, Management, Technical, Certificate of Recognition: Dr. Christopher Janicak (cjanicak@iup.edu).
School Psychology: Dr. Joseph Kovaleski (jkov@iup.edu).
Science for Disaster Response: Dr. Roberta Eddy (Roberta.Eddy@iup.edu).
Sociology: Dr. Kay Snyder (ksnyder@iup.edu).
Speech-Language Pathology: Dr. Shari Robertson (srobert@iup.edu).
Sport Science: Dr. Madeline Bayles (mpbayles@iup.edu) and Dr. Robert Kostelnik (bkostel@iup.edu).
Student Affairs in Higher Education: Dr. Ronald Lunardini (lunar@iup.edu).

IONA COLLEGE

School of Arts and Science and Hagan Business School Graduate Programs

Programs of Study

Iona College offers graduate programs leading to the degree of Master of Arts, Master of Science, Master of Science in Education, Master of Science in Teaching, and Master of Business Administration. Fields of study in the School of Arts & Science include computer science, criminal justice, education (childhood; childhood with literacy, science, multicultural; adolescence with subjects; educational leadership), educational technology, English, health services administration, history, journalism, marriage and family therapy, pastoral counseling, psychology (experimental, industrial/organizational, mental health counseling, school), public relations, Spanish, teaching for career changers (childhood, adolescence with subjects), and telecommunications. Certificate programs are available in educational technology, health services administration, long-term and post–acute care administration, marriage and family therapy, public relations, and telecommunications. From the Hagan School of Business, the M.B.A. degree is available with specializations in financial management, management, marketing, human resource management, and information and decision technology management. Certificates are available in business continuity and risk management, e-commerce, and international business.

Graduate programs at Iona College are taught on the main campus in New Rochelle and at the Rockland Graduate Center, the College's branch campus in Pearl River, New York. These programs are specially designed to meet the needs of part-time students, although many programs serve a student who would like to attend full-time. Classes are conveniently scheduled in the late afternoon and early evening to accommodate students' workdays. Depending on the number of credits required of a graduate program, a dedicated part-time student can expect to complete his or her degree in as little as two years. Each program is designed with a core requirement and elective courses. Internships and practicum experiences are built into many programs so students may gain hands-on experience.

Research Facilities

The heart of Iona's research facilities is its two libraries, the Ryan Library and the Arrigoni Technology Center. Ryan houses nearly 1,400 periodicals and 270,000 volumes, and Arrigoni is home to research and computer laboratories. Iona belongs to three interlibrary programs that allow online access to millions of volumes. Iona College features fully wireless facilities offering students high-speed access to the Internet and possesses more than 700 networked computers and two fully networked computer labs located at Iona's graduate center in Rockland County. Computer lab assistants are available to help students with their questions, and one lab stays open 24 hours a day, seven days a week. All students have e-mail accounts and access to the Internet.

Financial Aid

Iona College serves graduate students through a variety of state, federal, and institutional programs that include loans, scholarships, and assistantships. Scholarships are available based on undergraduate GPA or GRE or GMAT scores. To be eligible for federal loans, students must complete the FAFSA and the Iona College loan application.

Cost of Study

The cost of graduate tuition for the 2007–08 academic year is $712 per credit hour.

Living and Housing Costs

On-campus housing is not available to graduate students.

Student Group

There are approximately 885 students enrolled in graduate programs at Iona College. Most of these students are employed full-time and attend classes on a part-time basis in the evenings.

Student Outcomes

Some organizations that employ Iona graduates include American Express, Avon, Bristol-Meyers, Gannett Co., IBM, Lenox Hill and Sound Shore Hospitals, MasterCard, NBC, Sports Illustrated, top school districts, Verizon, Wyeth Pharmaceuticals, and Xerox.

Location

Iona's main campus is located in New Rochelle, New York, 15 miles north of Manhattan. New Rochelle is a beautiful suburb of 70,000 located on Long Island Sound and is well-served by mass transportation and highways. Iona's Rockland Graduate Center is 3 miles from the Palisades Parkway in Pearl River. Both campuses are safe and offer plentiful parking for evening students. The location of both campuses in the NYC metropolitan area allows students to take advantage of the many cultural, internship, and employment opportunities available.

The College

Iona College is a comprehensive, co-ed Catholic college, founded in 1940 by the Congregation of Christian Brothers. The overall enrollment is about 3,100 students, of whom 891 study at the graduate level.

Iona offers study in more than twenty graduate areas and is accredited by the Middle States Association of Colleges and Schools. In the School of Arts and Science, specialized recognitions are held by the following programs: education programs are accredited by NCATE: National Council for Accreditation of Teacher Education; public relations and journalism are accredited by ACEJMC: Accrediting Council of Education in Journalism and Mass Communication; and marriage and family therapy is in candidacy for accreditation by COAMFTE: Commission on Accreditation for Marriage and Family Therapy Education. Graduates of Mental Health Counseling and School Psychology are licensure-eligible. The Hagan School is accredited by AACSB International–The Association to Advance Collegiate Schools of Business.

Applying

Applications for Iona's School of Arts & Science graduate programs are available by mail or can be completed online at www.iona.edu/ionagrad/admission.html. To be considered, an applicant must submit the application and required application fee, official transcripts from all colleges attended, and three letters of recommendation. Interviews (in person or by phone) and other application materials may be required by some programs. Applications should be submitted at least a month before the intended start term. Applicants to Mental Health Counseling, School of Psychology, and Marriage and Family Therapy are strongly encouraged to apply by February 1, as enrollments in those programs are limited.

Candidates for the Hagan School of Business may enter the graduate program in the fall (September), winter (November), or spring (March) trimester or in the summer session. The completed application, with fee, must be accompanied by two letters of recommendation, official transcripts from all postsecondary schools, and GMAT scores. All documents must be received no later than two weeks prior to the start of the session for which the candidate is applying.

Correspondence and Information

Office of Graduate Admissions
School of Arts & Science
Iona College
715 North Avenue
New Rochelle, New York 10801
Phone: 914-633-2502
800-231-IONA (toll-free)
Fax: 914-633-2277
E-mail: admissions@iona.edu
Web site: http://www.iona.edu

Director of M.B.A. Admissions
Hagan School of Business
Iona College
715 North Avenue
New Rochelle, New York 10801
Phone: 914-633-2288
Fax: 914-633-2012
E-mail: hagan@iona.edu
Web site: http://www.iona.edu/hagan

Graduate Admissions Office
Rockland Graduate Center
Two Blue Hill Plaza
Concourse Level
Pearl River, New York 10965
Phone: 845-620-1350
Fax: 845-620-1260
E-mail: rockland@iona.edu
Web site: http://www.iona.edu/rockland

DEPARTMENT AND PROGRAM HEADS

Biology: Joseph Stabile, Associate Professor and Chair; Ph.D., CUNY Graduate Center.
Computer Science: Robert Schiaffino, Associate Professor and Chair; Ph.D., Polytechnic.
Criminal Justice: Robert Castelli, Assistant Professor and Chair; M.P.A., Harvard.
Education: Patricia A. Antonacci, Professor and Chair; Ph.D., Fordham.
English: Hugh Short, Associate Professor and Chair; Ph.D., Fordham.
Health Care Programs: Vincent Maher, Professor and Chair; J.D., CUNY, Queens.
History: Joseph G. Morgan, CFC, Associate Professor and Chair; Ph.D., Georgetown.
Mass Communication: Orly Shachar, Associate Professor and Chair; Ph.D., Boston University.
Mathematics: William Gratzer, Assistant Professor and Chair; Ed.D., Columbia.
Modern Languages: Victoria Ketz, Associate Professor and Chair; Ph.D., Columbia.
Pastoral Counseling and Marriage and Family Therapy: Robert A. Burns, Assistant Professor and Chair; Ph.D., St. John's (New York).
Psychology: Paul A. Greene, Associate Professor and Chair; Ph.D., Long Island.

IOWA STATE UNIVERSITY

Graduate College

Programs of Study Iowa State University provides outstanding facilities for graduate study and research in the Colleges of Agriculture, Business, Design, Engineering, Liberal Arts and Sciences, and Veterinary Medicine. Faculty members from more than 100 graduate programs offer advanced study opportunities. Advanced degrees include the research-oriented Master of Arts, Master of Science, and Doctor of Philosophy degrees; in certain fields, the Master of Science without thesis and the Master of Arts without thesis; and the advanced technical or professional degrees of Master of Accounting, Master of Agriculture, Master of Architecture, Master of Arts in Teaching, Master of Business Administration, Master of Community and Regional Planning, Master of Education, Master of Engineering, Master of Family and Consumer Sciences, Master of Fine Arts, Master of Landscape Architecture, Master of Public Administration, and Master of School Mathematics.

Although there is flexibility in planning each student's graduate program, certain minimum requirements are set for advanced degrees by the graduate faculty as well as by individual programs. Minimum Graduate College requirements include maintaining a B average and generally completing the degree requirements within five years for a master's degree and seven years for the Ph.D. Graduate students are advised by more than 1,500 graduate faculty members, who have been selected because their research activity, professional involvement, and publications qualify them to guide the research of graduate students.

Research Facilities Graduate assistants play an integral role in the research of numerous institutes, centers, and laboratories at Iowa State. Major research units associated with the University include the Ames Laboratory, the Plant Sciences Institute, the National Soil Tilth Laboratory, the National Animal Disease Center, the Institute for Physical Research and Technology, the Iowa Agriculture and Home Economics Experiment Station, Iowa State University's Biotechnology Program, the Leopold Center for Sustainable Agriculture, the Center for Agricultural and Rural Development, the Center for Transportation Research and Education, the Veterinary Medical Research Institute, the Institute for Social and Behavioral Research, the Center for Crops Utilization Research, the Statistical Laboratory, the Center for Food Security and Public Health, the Center for Designing Foods to Improve Nutrition, the Iowa Energy Center, and the Information Assurance Center.

The University library, with a collection exceeding 2 million volumes and an equally extensive number of nonprint holdings, is nationally recognized for its collections in the basic and applied fields of the biological and physical sciences. Its major strengths for research include holdings in agriculture, design arts, statistics, and veterinary medicine. An online catalog system provides computerized access to the collections from on and off campus.

Financial Aid Graduate assistantships, fellowships, and special research grants have been established to encourage graduate study and promote research. Information on these awards is available from individual programs. Other types of financial aid include a deferred-fee-payment plan, Federal Direct Student Loans (low-interest, deferred repayment), and University Emergency Loans.

Cost of Study In 2006–07, the graduate fees for a semester of full-time study totaled $2968 for state residents and $8175 for nonresidents. Fees for a partial schedule or for off-campus courses are determined on a per-hour basis. Students appointed to graduate assistantships are considered full-time students and are assessed the state resident fees. Most graduate assistants also qualify for a tuition scholarship award.

Living and Housing Costs The University provides housing for single and married graduate students. Costs for 2006–07 ranged from $4389 per academic year for a double-occupancy residence hall room to as low as $466 per month for a University student apartment. Students may also secure off-campus rooms, apartments, or duplexes in Ames and the surrounding communities. The cost for off-campus housing ranges from $500 to more than $1000 per month, depending on the size, amenities, and location.

Student Group In 2006–07, 25,462 students, including 4,783 graduate students, enrolled at the University. Most graduate students attend full-time; 42 percent are women, and 34 percent are international students. More than 50 percent are awarded graduate assistantships.

Location The University is situated on a 1,000-acre tract in Ames, Iowa (population 50,000), 35 miles north of the state capital of Des Moines. Ames is at the crossroads of three interstate highways: running north and south, I-35, and running east and west, U.S. 30 and (30 miles to the south) I-80. The city offers a calendar of social, cultural, and athletic activities that surpasses that of many other metropolitan areas. Students, faculty members, and Ames residents are a cosmopolitan group, representing more than 120 countries. The city maintains more than 700 acres of woods, streams, and open meadows as parks, and the general atmosphere of Ames is relaxed and friendly.

The University Iowa State was chartered in 1858 and became the land-grant institution for the state of Iowa after the passage of the Morrill Act. Graduate study was offered almost as soon as classes began in 1868, and the first graduate degree was conferred in 1877. The University's motto, "Science with Practice," suggests the importance placed on both the learning of theory and the discovery of applications in the many areas in which Iowa State excels.

Applying The Graduate College Web site (http://www.grad-college.iastate.edu) contains directions for applying, contacts, admission requirements for each graduate program, and access to the application. If financial assistance is a priority, the application, accompanied by a $30 application fee ($70 for international students) and an official transcript from each college attended, should be sent to the address for each major (listed at http://www.grad-college.iastate.edu/programs/APprograms.php). Applicants should correspond with the appropriate program, which provides guidance about application deadlines, graduate assistantships, fellowships, and special research grants.

Correspondence and Information

For program information:
Graduate Program of (specify)
Iowa State University
Ames, Iowa 50011

For general application information:
Office of Admissions
Alumni Hall
Iowa State University
Ames, Iowa 50011-2010
Phone: 800-262-3810 (toll-free)
E-mail: grad_admissions@iastate.edu
Web site: http://www.grad-college.iastate.edu

FIELDS OF STUDY

To request more information on Iowa State's major areas of study, students are encouraged to contact the following programs directly. The telephone area code for each program is 515.

Accounting: M.Acc. (294-8118).
Aerospace Engineering: M.Eng., M.S., Ph.D. (294-9669).
Agricultural Economics: M.S., Ph.D. (294-2702).
Agricultural Education: M.S., Ph.D. (294-5872).
Agricultural Engineering: M.Eng., M.S., Ph.D. (294-1033).
Agricultural History and Rural Studies: Ph.D. (294-1451).
Agricultural Meteorology: M.S., Ph.D. (294-1361).
Agronomy: M.S. (294-1361).
Analytical Chemistry: M.S., Ph.D. (294-2436).
Animal Breeding and Genetics: M.S., Ph.D. (294-2160).
Animal Ecology: M.S., Ph.D. (294-1626).
Animal Physiology: M.S., Ph.D. (294-2160).
Animal Science: M.S., Ph.D. (294-2160).
Anthropology: M.A. (294-7139).
Applied Linguistics and Technology: Ph.D. (294-2477).
Applied Mathematics: M.S., Ph.D. (294-0393).
Applied Physics: M.S., Ph.D. (294-5440).
Architectural Studies: M.S. (294-2187).
Architecture: M.Arch., M.Arch./M.B.A., M.Arch./M.C.R.P. (294-2187).
Art and Design: M.A. (294-6724).
Astrophysics: M.S., Ph.D. (294-5440).
Biochemistry: M.S., Ph.D. (294-3464).
Bioinformatics and Computational Biology: M.S., Ph.D. (294-5122).
Biomedical Sciences: M.S., Ph.D. (294-2440).
Biophysics: M.S., Ph.D. (294-3464).
Biorenewable Resources and Technology: M.S., Ph.D. (294-6555).
Business Administration: M.B.A., M.Arch./M.B.A., M.B.A./M.C.R.P., M.B.A./M.S. (Statistics) (294-8118).
Chemical Engineering: M.Eng., M.S., Ph.D. (294-7643).
Chemistry: M.S., Ph.D. (294-2436).
Civil Engineering: M.S., Ph.D. (294-5453).
Community and Regional Planning: M.C.R.P., M.Arch./M.C.R.P., M.B.A./M.C.R.P., M.L.A./M.C.R.P., M.P.A./M.C.R.P. (294-8958).
Computer Engineering: M.S., Ph.D. (294-2667).
Computer Science: M.S., Ph.D. (294-8361).
Condensed Matter Physics: M.S., Ph.D. (294-5440).
Creative Writing and Environment: M.F.A. (294-2477).
Crop Production and Physiology: M.S., Ph.D. (294-1361).
Earth Science: M.S., Ph.D. (294-7586).
Ecology and Evolutionary Biology: M.S., Ph.D. (294-6518).
Economics: M.S., Ph.D. (294-2702).
Education—Curriculum and Instruction: M.Ed., M.S., Ph.D. (294-7021).
Education—Educational Leadership and Policy Studies: M.Ed., M.S., Ph.D. (294-1241).
Education—Health and Human Performance: M.Ed. (294-8650).
Electrical Engineering: M.S., Ph.D. (294-2667).
Engineering Mechanics: M.Eng., M.S., Ph.D. (294-9669).
English: M.A. (294-2477).
Entomology: M.S., Ph.D. (294-7400).
Environmental Science: M.S., Ph.D. (294-6518).
Exercise and Sports Science: M.Ed., M.S. (294-8257).
Family and Consumer Sciences: M.F.C.S. (294-0211).
Family and Consumer Sciences Education: M.Ed., M.S., Ph.D. (294-5307).
Fisheries Biology: M.S., Ph.D. (294-1626).
Food Science and Technology: M.S., Ph.D. (294-6442).
Foodservice and Lodging Management: M.S., Ph.D. (294-7409).
Forestry: M.S., Ph.D. (294-1626).
Genetics: M.S., Ph.D. (294-7697).
Geology: M.S., Ph.D. (294-7586).
Graphic Design: M.F.A. (294-6724).
Health and Human Performance: Ph.D. (294-8257).
High Energy Physics: M.S., Ph.D. (294-5440).
History: M.A. (294-7266).
History of Technology and Science: M.A., Ph.D. (294-3828).
Horticulture: M.S., Ph.D. (294-2751).
Human Computer Interaction: M.S., Ph.D. (294-2089).
Human Development and Family Studies: M.S., Ph.D. (294-6321).
Immunobiology: M.S., Ph.D. (294-7252).
Industrial and Agricultural Technology: M.S., Ph.D. (294-7001).
Industrial Engineering: M.S., Ph.D. (294-1682).
Information Assurance: M.S. (294-8307).
Information Systems: M.S. (294-8118).
Inorganic Chemistry: M.S., Ph.D. (294-2436).
Integrated Visual Arts: M.F.A. (294-6724).
Interdisciplinary Graduate Studies: M.A., M.S. (294-1170).
Interior Design: M.F.A. (294-6724).
Journalism and Mass Communication: M.S. (294-0492).
Landscape Architecture: M.L.A., M.L.A./M.C.R.P. (294-8958).
Materials Science and Engineering: M.S., Ph.D. (294-9101).
Mathematics: M.S., M.S.M., Ph.D. (294-0394).
Meat Science: M.S., Ph.D. (294-2160).
Mechanical Engineering: M.S., Ph.D. (294-0368).
Meteorology: M.S., Ph.D. (294-4758).
Microbiology: M.S., Ph.D. (294-9052).
Molecular, Cellular, and Development Biology: M.S., Ph.D. (294-7252).
Neuroscience: M.S., Ph.D. (294-7252).
Nuclear Physics: M.S., Ph.D. (294-5440).
Nutritional Sciences: M.S., Ph.D. (294-6442).
Operations Research: M.S. (294-0126).
Organic Chemistry: M.S., Ph.D. (294-2436).
Physical Chemistry: M.S., Ph.D. (294-2436).
Physics: M.S., Ph.D. (294-5440).
Plant Breeding: M.S., Ph.D. (294-1361).
Plant Pathology: M.S., Ph.D. (294-7159).
Plant Physiology: M.S., Ph.D. (294-9052).
Political Science: M.A. (294-3764).
Professional Agriculture: M.Ag. (294-5872).
Psychology: M.S., Ph.D. (294-1743).
Public Administration: M.P.A., M.P.A./M.C.R.P., C.P.M. (294-3764).
Rhetoric and Professional Communication: Ph.D. (294-2477).
Rhetoric, Composition, and Professional Communication: M.A. (294-2477).
Rural Sociology: M.S., Ph.D. (294-6484).
School Mathematics: M.S.M. (294-0393).
Science Education: M.A.T. (294-7021).
Seed Technology and Business: M.S. (294-6821).
Sociology: M.S., Ph.D. (294-6484).
Soil Science: M.S., Ph.D. (294-1361).
Statistics: M.S., M.B.A./M.S., Ph.D. (294-3440).
Sustainable Agriculture: M.S., Ph.D. (294-6518).
Systems Engineering: M.Eng. (294-8731).
Teaching English as a Second Language/Applied Linguistics: M.A. (294-2477).
Textiles and Clothing: M.S., Ph.D. (294-9303).
Toxicology: M.S., Ph.D. (294-7697).
Transportation: M.S. (294-0814).
Veterinary Clinical Sciences: M.S. (294-6411).
Veterinary Microbiology: M.S., Ph.D. (294-5776).
Veterinary Pathology: M.S., Ph.D. (294-4682).
Veterinary Preventive Medicine: M.S. (294-3837).
Wildlife Biology: M.S., Ph.D. (294-1626).

ITHACA COLLEGE

Division of Graduate Studies

Programs of Study

All of Ithaca College's graduate degree programs promise an intellectual environment in which a close-knit group of similarly directed colleagues, both fellow students and nationally recognized faculty members, will work and walk alongside new students to help clarify their vision, guide their study, nurture their talent, and creatively and broadly help shape their future.

Perhaps most importantly, all of the College's graduate degrees feature one common and crucial component: students get the opportunity to experiment, practice, and hone real life and work skills in practical, hands-on, experiential learning, teaching, and working situations. Students who are at Ithaca College to perform will be on stage. Those there to gain credentials as a speech pathologist are responsible for real clients with real problems to solve. Students studying human performance work alongside real athletes. In research, internships, clinical placements, performance opportunities, and real-world applications, a student's journey and time at Ithaca is predicated on practice as well as on theory.

Since 1943, when Ithaca College offered its first master's degrees, it has awarded nearly 6,000 graduate diplomas to dedicated and talented professionals. The College offers master's degrees in adolescence education, business administration, childhood education, communications, exercise and sport sciences, health and physical education, music, physical and occupational therapy, speech-language pathology, and sport management. Its graduates are recognized leaders in their fields, enriching their professions and the world around them.

Ithaca College also offers a variety of professional development opportunities. Some offerings provide undergraduate or graduate credit and can be pathways toward degree programs. Others are noncredit programs offering continuing education units (CEUs). All offerings are designed to meet the needs of professionals in a variety of fields; some of these programs lead to a certificate from Ithaca College. For more information about current offerings, students should visit http://www.ithaca.edu/profdev or contact the Office of Certificate and Professional Programs in the Division of Graduate Studies at 607-274-3527.

Research Facilities

The library is open more than 100 hours a week to provide a complete range of information services and resources in both electronic and print formats. Information Technology Services (ITS) maintains an extensive collection of programming languages, data-analysis packages, and business programs to support the curriculum. Networked computers, both Macintosh and PCs, are available in thirty facilities across campus. One lab is open 24 hours a day and the rest are open from early morning to late at night throughout the fall and spring semesters. Laboratories are staffed by student consultants skilled at helping people use the computers.

Financial Aid

A limited number of assistantships are available in each of the master's degree programs on a competitive basis. Assistantships supplement tuition and offer a small salary in exchange for on-campus responsibilities.

Cost of Study

The 2007–08 graduate tuition rate varies by program: $650 per credit for business, $504 per credit for adolescence education and health and physical education, and $577 per credit for all other programs.

Living and Housing Costs

The College maintains no housing facilities for graduate students. Off-campus housing is available at various rates. Several meal plans are available in the College dining halls. Prices are as follows: $996 with $110 bonus dollars for seven meals per week, $2239 for ten meals per week, and $2463 for ten, fourteen, or twenty meals per week with bonus dollars.

Student Group

Approximately 500 students are enrolled in graduate programs.

Location

Ithaca, New York, is also the site of Cornell University. A majority of the city's 29,000 permanent residents are academically oriented, while a transient population of some 23,000 students, artists, scientists, and scholars enriches its unique academic atmosphere. Many visitors are drawn to Ithaca by the striking beauty of the scenery, the opportunities for outdoor life, and the cultural activity of a cosmopolitan community where there is extensive interest in the humanities, sciences, music, and drama. Students have frequent occasions to share in and contribute to these interests and opportunities.

The College

Constructed on a naturally terraced hillside, the unobstructed view of the surrounding countryside provides one of the finest vistas in the Finger Lakes region. The facilities were designed to take advantage of that view and to blend with the natural beauty of the terrain. Residence halls, dining halls, and academic buildings are located in spacious, closely knit units at the center of the site. Classrooms, laboratories, lecture halls, and specialized facilities have been designed to utilize modern teaching technology. The campus is surrounded by an abundance of recreational facilities, including an outdoor Olympic-size swimming pool, fitness trail, playing fields, and tennis courts. Recent construction includes additions to the Schools of Music and Health Sciences and Human Performance. A new fitness center has also recently been completed.

Applying

Applications for admission are available online at http://www.ithaca.edu/gradstudies. The deadlines for application, with the necessary transcripts and recommendations vary by program. The General Test of the Graduate Record Examinations is required by exercise and sport sciences, speech-language pathology, sport management, and teaching students with speech and language disabilities. The Graduate Management Admission Test (GMAT) is required for business administration.

Admission requirements include a bachelor's degree from an accredited college, a minimum 3.0 undergraduate GPA, and typically an undergraduate major or the equivalent in the proposed field. Application forms and catalogs are online at http://www.ithaca.edu/gradstudies.

Correspondence and Information

Division of Graduate Studies
Ithaca College
111 Towers Concourse
Ithaca, New York 14850-7142

Phone: 607-274-3527
Fax: 607-274-1263
E-mail: gradstudies@ithaca.edu
Web site: http://www.ithaca.edu/gradstudies

THE FACULTY

Business Administration
Emil Bóasson, Assistant Professor; Ph.D., SUNY at Buffalo.
Joanne Burress, Associate Professor; Ph.D., SUNY at Buffalo.
Joseph Cheng, Associate Professor; Ph.D., SUNY at Binghamton.
Mark Cordano, Assistant Professor; Ph.D., Pittsburgh.
Donald Eckrich, Professor and Chair; D.B.A., Kentucky.
G. Scott Erickson, Associate Professor; Ph.D., Lehigh.
Eileen Kelly, Professor; Ph.D., Cincinnati.
Eric Lewis, Associate Professor; Ph.D., Union (New York).
Patricia Libby, Associate Professor; Ph.D., Michigan.
Donald Lifton, Associate Professor; Ph.D., Cornell.
Jeffrey Lippitt, Associate Professor; Ph.D., Penn State.
Granger Macy, Associate Professor; Ph.D., Indiana.
Michael McCall, Professor; Ph.D., Arizona State.
Abraham Mulugetta, Professor; Ph.D., Wisconsin.
Margaret Nowicki, Assistant Professor; Ph.D., Colorado at Boulder.
David Saiia, Assistant Professor; Ph.D., Georgia.
Gwen Seaquist, Associate Professor; J.D., Mississippi.
Donald Simmons, Assistant Professor; Ph.D., SUNY at Binghamton.
William Tastle, Associate Professor; Ph.D., SUNY at Binghamton.
Fahri Unsal, Professor; Ph.D., Cornell.
M. Raquibuz Zaman, Professor; Ph.D., Cornell.

Communications
Dennis Charsky, Assistant Professor; Ph.D., Northern Colorado.
Marie Garland, Assistant Professor; Ph.D., Ohio State.
Diane M. Gayeski, Professor; Ph.D., Maryland.
Howard Kalman, Assistant Professor; Ph.D., Indiana.
Ari Kissiloff, Assistant Professor; M.S., Ithaca.
Gordon Rowland, Professor and Chair; Ph.D., Indiana.
Steven A. Seidman, Associate Professor; Ph.D., Indiana.
Tammy Shapiro, Assistant Professor; Ph.D., SUNY at Binghamton.

Exercise and Sport Sciences
Mary DePalma, Professor; Ph.D., Cornell.
Noah Gentner, Assistant Professor; Ph.D., Tennessee.
Jeff Ives, Associate Professor; Ph.D., Massachusetts.
Betsy A. Keller, Professor; Ph.D., Massachusetts.
Deborah King, Assistant Professor; Ph.D., Pennsylvania.
Tom Pfaff, Assistant Professor; Ph.D., Syracuse.
Kent Scribner, Professor; Ed.D., Syracuse.
Gary A. Sforzo, Professor; Ph.D., Maryland.
Greg Shelley, Associate Professor and Chair; Ph.D., Utah.
John Sigg, Associate Professor; Ph.D., Toledo.
Tom Swensen, Associate Professor; Ph.D., Tennessee.
Kent D. Wagoner, Assistant Professor; Ph.D., Georgia.

Health Promotion and Physical Education
Deborah A. Wuest, Professor and Chair; Ed.D., Boston University.
Stewart Auyash, Associate Professor; Ph.D., Penn State.
Srijana M. Bajracharya, Associate Professor; Ph.D., Auburn.
Mary K. Bentley, Associate Professor; Ph.D., Maryland.
Phoebe Constantinou, Assistant Professor; Ed.D., Columbia.
Ann Kolodji, Assistant Professor; Ph.D., Pennsylvania.
Prithwi Raj Subramaniam, Associate Professor; Ph.D., Illinois.

School of Humanities and Sciences
Linda Hanrahan, Associate Professor and Chair; Ed.D., Rutgers.
Ellen Cohen-Rosenthal, Instructor; Ph.D., Alfred.
M. Cathrene Connery, Assistant Professor; Ph.D., New Mexico.
Aaron Weinberg, Assistant Professor; Ph.D., Wisconsin–Madison.
Elizabeth Bleicher, Assistant Professor; Ph.D., USC.
Vicki Cameron, Professor; Ph.D., Colorado.
Edward Cluett, Associate Professor; Ph.D. Cornell.
Ellen Cohen-Rosenthal, Instructor; Ph.D., Alfred.
Vivian Bruce Conger, Professor; Ph.D., Cornell.
James Conklin, Associate Professor; Ph.D., Rochester.
Maria Di Francesco, Assistant Professor; Ph.D., SUNY at Buffalo.
Louise Donohue, Assistant Professor; M.A., SUNY at Binghamton.
Jason Freitag, Assistant Professor; Ph.D., Columbia.
Marian MacCurdy, Professor; Ph.D., Syracuse.
Thomas J. Pfaff, Associate Professor; Ph.D., Syracuse.
Eric Robinson, Professor; Ph.D., SUNY at Binghamton.
Margaret Robinson, Assistant Professor; M.S., SUNY at Binghamton.
Martin Sternstein, Professor; Ph.D., Cornell.
James Swafford, Associate Professor; Ph.D. Duke.
Michael Trotti, Associate Professor; Ph.D., North Carolina at Chapel Hill.
Michael Twomey, Professor; Ph.D., Cornell.
Kirsten Wasson, Assistant Professor; Ph.D., Wisconsin.
Zenon Wasyliw, Associate Professor; Ph.D., SUNY at Binghamton.
Aaron Weinberg, Assistant Professor; Ph.D., Wisconsin–Madison.

Music
Rebecca Ansel, Assistant Professor (Violin); D.M.A., Michigan.
Susan Avery, Assistant Professor (Music Education); Ph.D., Rochester (Eastman).
Diane Birr, Associate Professor (Piano); M.M., Indiana.
Leslie Black, Assistant Professor (Theory); Ph.D., Yale.
Randie Blooding, Associate Professor (Voice); D.M.A., Ohio State.
Stephen Brown, Professor (Guitar and Jazz Studies); M.M., Ithaca.
Verna Brummett, Associate Professor (Music Education) and Chair; Ed.D., Illinois.
Frank Campos, Professor (Trumpet and Music Education); M.M., North Texas State.
Pablo Cohen, Adjunct Assistant Professor (Classical Guitar); M.M., Temple.
Craig Cummings, Associate Professor (Music History); Ph.D., Indiana.
Charis Dimaras, Associate Professor (Performance); D.M.A., Manhattan School of Music.
Lawrence A. Doebler, Professor and Director of Chorale Music; M.M., Washington (St. Louis).
D. Kim Dunnick, Professor (Trumpet); D.M., Indiana.
Richard Edwards, Assistant Professor (Music Education); M.M., North Carolina at Greensboro.
Richard Faria, Associate Professor (Clarinet); M.M., Michigan State.
Mark Fonder, Professor (Music Education); Ed.D., Illinois.
Janet Galvan, Professor (Music Education); Ed.D., North Carolina.
Michael Galvan, Professor (Clarinet and Music Education); M.M., Illinois.
Jairo Geronymo, Assistant Professor (Music Performance); D.M.A., Washington (Seattle).
Lee Goodhew-Romm, Professor (Bassoon); M.M., SMU.
Jennifer Hayghe, Assistant Professor (Piano); D.M.A., Juilliard.
Jennifer Haywood, Assistant Professor (Music Education); Ph.D., Toronto.
Bradley Hougham, Assistant Professor (Voice); M.A., CUNY, Queens.
Daniel Isbell, Assistant Professor (Music Education); Ph.D., Colorado at Boulder.
Rebecca Jemian, Assistant Professor (Theory); Ph.D., Indiana.
Timothy A. Johnson, Associate Professor (Music Therapy, History, and Composition); Ph.D., SUNY at Buffalo.
Mark Kaczmarczyk, Assistant Professor (Opera and Musical Theater); D.M.A., Cincinnati.
Keith A. Kaiser, Associate Professor (Music Education); M.M., Redlands.
Jennifer Kay, Assistant Professor (Voice); D.M.A., Boston University.
Deborah Lifton, Adjunct Assistant Professor (Voice); M.M., Manhattan School of Music.
Deborah Martin, Associate Professor (Piano); D.M., Indiana.
Steven Mauk, Professor (Saxophone); D.M.A., Michigan.
Carol McAmis, Professor (Voice); M.M., Kansas.
Wendy Herbener Mehne, Professor (Flute); D.M.A., Wisconsin.
Phiroze Mehta, Professor (Piano); M.M., Massachusetts.
Jeffery Meyer, Assistant Professor and Director of Orchestras; D.M.A., SUNY at Stony Brook.
Deborah Montgomery, Professor (Voice); M.M., Illinois.
Debra Moree, Associate Professor (Viola and Violin); M.M., Indiana.
Paige Morgan, Associate Professor (Music Performance); D.M.A., Rochester (Eastman).
Timothy A. Nord, Associate Professor (Music Technology); Ph.D., Wisconsin.
David Pacun, Assistant Professor (Theory); Ph.D., Chicago.
David Parks, Professor (Voice); D.M.A., Arizona.
Patrice Pastore, Professor (Voice); M.M., New England Conservatory.
Elizabeth Peterson, Assistant Professor (Music Education); M.M., Northwestern.
Stephen G. Peterson, Associate Professor (Music Performance); Ph.D., Northwestern.
Mark Radice, Professor (Music History); Ph.D., Rochester (Eastman).
Sanford Reuning, Adjunct Assistant Professor (Suzuki Strings); B.M., Illinois.
Harold Reynolds, Professor (Trombone); D.M.A., Rochester (Eastman).
Deborah Rifkin, Assistant Professor (Theory); Ph.D., Rochester (Eastman).
Peter Rothbart, Professor (Electroacoustic); D.M.A., Cleveland Institute of Music.
Kelly Samarzea, Assistant Professor (Voice); D.M., Indiana.
Alex Shuhan, Associate Professor (French Horn); B.M., Rochester (Eastman).
Elizabeth P. Simkin, Associate Professor (Cello); M.M., Rochester (Eastman).
Gordon Stout, Professor (Percussion) and Chair of Performance Studies; M.M., Rochester (Eastman).
Edward Swenson, Professor; Ph.D., Cornell.
David Unland, Associate Professor (Baritone and Tuba); M.S., Illinois at Urbana-Champaign.
Nicholas Walker, Assistant Professor (Double Bass); D.M.A., Stony Brook, SUNY.
Susan Waterbury, Associate Professor; M.M., Rochester (Eastman).
John White, Assistant Professor; Ph.D., Indiana.
Dana Wilson, Professor (Composition); Ph.D., Rochester (Eastman).
Baruch Whitehead, Assistant Professor (Music Education); Ph.D., Capella.

Occupational Therapy
Melinda A. Cozzolino, Associate Professor (Associate Member) and Chair of Graduate Program; O.T.D., Creighton; OTR/L.
Carole W. Dennis, Associate Professor and Chair of Occupational Therapy; M.A., Connecticut; Sc.D., Boston University.
Rita Daly, Adjunct Instructor; M.S., D'Youville; OTR/L.
Catherine Y. Gordon, Associate Professor; Ed.D., SUNY at Buffalo; OTR.
Barbara P. Hansen, Clinical Assistant Professor (Associate Member); M.S., SUNY at Oswego; OTR.
Marilyn A. Kane, Assistant Professor; M.A., NYU; OTR.
Diane M. Long, Associate Professor and Curriculum Director; M.S., SUNY at Buffalo; OTR/L.
Meghan McNally, Lecturer (Adjunct Member); M.P.A., SUNY at Binghampton.
Kathleen Stoklosa, Clinical Assistant Professor (Adjunct Member); M.P.A., SUNY College at Brockport.
Sunny Winstead, Lecturer (Adjunct Member); M.S., Virginia Commonwealth; OTR/L.

Physical Therapy
Ernest Nalette, Associate Professor, Chair of the Graduate Program, and Director of the Rochester Unit; Ed.D., Vermont.
Katherine L. Beissner, Professor; Ph.D., Syracuse.
Christine Burns, Adjunct Professor; Ed.M., M.B.A., Rochester.
Lynda J. Dimitroff, Associate Professor; Ph.D., Southern Illinois, Carbondale.
Jeffrey Houck, Assistant Professor; Ph.D., Iowa; PT.
Helene Marie Larin, Associate Professor; Ph.D., Toronto.
Deborah A. Nawoczenski, Professor; Ph.D., Iowa; PT.
Karen W. Nolan, Assistant Professor; M.S., Rochester; PT.
Angela Rosenberg, Adjunct Professor; Dr.P.H., North Carolina at Chapel Hill.

Speech-Language Pathology/Audiology
Luanne Andersson, Assistant Professor; Ph.D., Connecticut.
Elizabeth Begley, Clinical Assistant Professor; M.A., California.
Christine M. P. Cecconi, Clinical Associate Professor; M.A., Bowling Green State.
Douglas E. Cross, Associate Professor; Ph.D., Tennessee.
Barbara Ann Johnson, Professor; Ph.D., Florida.
Mary Pitti, Instructor; M.S., Ithaca.
Marie Sanford, Clinical Associate Professor; M.S., Ithaca.
Richard J. Schissel, Associate Professor; Ph.D., Penn State.
John C. Stephens, Clinical Assistant Professor; M.S., Ithaca.
Kal M. Telage, Professor; Ph.D., Ohio.
E. W. Testut, Associate Professor and Chair; Ph.D., Oklahoma.

Sport Management
F. Wayne Blann, Professor; Ed.D., Boston University.
Annemarie Farrell, Assistant Professor; Ph.D., Ohio.
Stephen D. Mosher, Professor; Ph.D., Massachusetts Amherst.
Ellen J. Staurowsky, Professor and Chair; Ed.D., Temple.
John T. Wolohan, Associate Professor; J.D., Western New England.

THE JOHNS HOPKINS UNIVERSITY

Krieger School of Arts and Sciences

Programs of Study

Degree programs leading to the Ph.D. are offered in the Departments of Anthropology, Biology, Biophysics, Chemistry, Classics, Cognitive Science, Earth and Planetary Sciences, Economics, English, German and Romance Languages and Literatures, History, History of Art, History of Science and Technology, Mathematics, Near Eastern Studies, Philosophy, Physics and Astronomy, Political Science, Psychological and Brain Sciences, Sociology, and in the Humanities Center.

A degree program leading to the M.A. and M.F.A. is offered in the Writing Seminars. Master's degree programs are also offered in the Department of Public Policy.

Emphasis is placed on mastery of a field of study and on creative research. There are no formal schoolwide requirements measured in numbers of courses or credits. Each program is planned in consultation with a department or committee after reviewing the individual's attainments and areas of interest.

Specific requirements for the Ph.D. include a minimum of two consecutive semesters of registration as a full-time, resident graduate student; certification by a department or program committee that all departmental or committee requirements have been fulfilled; a dissertation approved by at least 2 referees appointed by the department or committee; and a Graduate Board oral examination.

The continuing process of education and research in the University setting requires involvement beyond the formal preparation for a degree. Postdoctoral training, therefore, is an integral part of many departmental programs.

Research Facilities

Major research activities and laboratories are integral to the Hopkins experience. The Milton S. Eisenhower Library houses the University's major collections. The quality and quantity of its collections and services make it one of the country's foremost research libraries. Other important Hopkins libraries include the Welch Medical Library, the Peabody Institute Library, and the Library of the School of Advanced International Studies (SAIS). The Homewood campus is also home to the Space Telescope Science Institute, administered for NASA by the Association of Universities for Research in Astronomy. Collaboration between the Institute and Hopkins scientists makes the University a world center for astronomical research. The Zanvyl Krieger Mind/Brain Institute is an interdisciplinary research center devoted to the study of neural mechanisms of higher mental functions, with emphasis on perception. Through the study of neuroanatomy, neurophysiology, computational neuroscience, neurology, and psychology, critical questions regarding the brain and how it operates are addressed.

Financial Aid

Most graduate students receive either full (teaching or research assistant) fellowships, which include a tuition waiver as well as a stipend or salary, or partial tuition fellowships. Also, there are fellowship awards made directly to students by government agencies, private foundations, and business and industrial corporations. Other aid, in the form of long-term student loans and employment, is administered by the Office of Student Financial Services. Notification of awards is made no later than the first week of April, and recipients are expected to respond to the offer no later than April 15.

Cost of Study

The matriculation fee, a one-time charge payable at the time of entrance, is $500. Tuition is approximately $35,900 for 2007–08; however, most graduate students receive a full or partial tuition fellowship.

Living and Housing Costs

During 2007–08, room and board costs are about $1126 for single students for a nine-month period. However, room and board costs vary depending on proximity to campus and choice of living arrangements. Other costs are books and supplies (up to $3500 per year) and travel expenses. All students are required to have health insurance either through the University or through a private insurer.

Student Group

Approximately 375–450 men and women representing a wide range of interests and a variety of backgrounds are selected each year for graduate study by the various academic departments. Students come from all areas of the United States as well as from many other countries. Approximately 40 percent of the graduate students are women.

Location

The campus is in a residential neighborhood of both single-family homes and apartments, located 4 miles from downtown Baltimore. There are churches, restaurants, drugstores, grocery stores, and other shops nearby. The 140-acre tree-lined Homewood campus offers a wide variety of areas for gatherings and recreation. Generally, graduate students find that their social as well as their academic lives tend to center on their departments. The three most widely used buildings are the Milton S. Eisenhower Library, the Ralph S. O'Connor Recreation Center, and the Hopkins Union, the University student center.

The University

Privately endowed, the Johns Hopkins University was founded in 1876 as the first American educational institution committed to the university idea of giving its students and faculty the freedoms of choice and opportunity that are necessary for learning and creativity to flourish. It remains committed to this idea. Johns Hopkins is a small coeducational university. The School of Arts and Sciences is located on the Homewood campus in north Baltimore. In order to preserve close intellectual association, the University community and the student-faculty ratio are intentionally small. Currently enrolled are approximately 4,000 undergraduate, 1,500 graduate, and 140 postdoctoral students. The faculty numbers about 380.

Applying

The online application and information regarding all the graduate programs can be found on the Web at http://www.grad.jhu.edu. Transcripts, letters of recommendation, and other supporting materials that are required should be sent directly to that department for processing. All applicants are advised to submit recent scores from the General Test of the Graduate Record Examinations. Although in most cases applications for fellowships must be made no later than January 15, application deadlines vary among departments; therefore, students should check the graduate admissions Web site for details.

Correspondence and Information

The Johns Hopkins University
Office of Graduate Admissions
Krieger School of Arts and Sciences
Whiting School of Engineering
101 Whitehead Hall
3400 North Charles Street
Baltimore, Maryland 21218
Phone: 410-516-8174
E-mail: graduateadmissions@jhu.edu
Web site: http://www.grad.jhu.edu

Academic Department (specify)
The Johns Hopkins University
3400 North Charles Street
Baltimore, Maryland 21218

DEANS AND DEPARTMENTAL CHAIRS

The mailing address for Deans and Departmental Chairs is: The Johns Hopkins University, 3400 North Charles Street, Baltimore, Maryland 21218. The area code for all numbers listed below is 410.

SCHOOL OF ARTS AND SCIENCES
Adam F. Falk, Dean.
Eaton E. Lattman, Dean of Research and Graduate Education.

Department, Location, Chair, Telephone, and E-mail (for admissions inquiries)
Anthropology: 404 Macaulay Hall, Veena Das, Chair; 516-7271 (bdaniels@jhu.edu).
Biology: 144 Mudd, Karen Beemon, 516-5502 (CMDBapplication@jhu.edu).
Biophysics: 101 Jenkins, Molecular and Computational Biophysics: David Draper, 516-5197 (pmb@jhu.edu).
Chemistry: 138 Remsen, John P. Toscano, 516-7429 (chem.grad.adm@jhu.edu).
Classics: 130 Gilman, Matthew B. Roller, 516-7556 (classics@jhu.edu).
Cognitive Science: 237 Krieger Hall, Barbara Landau, 516-5250 (inquire@cogsci.jhu.edu).
Earth and Planetary Sciences: 301 Olin, Peter Olsen, 516-7034 (kgaines@jhu.edu).
Economics: 440 Mergenthaler, Louis J. Maccini, 516-7601 (econ@jhu.edu).
English: 146 Gilman, Amanda Anderson, 516-4311 (english@jhu.edu).
German and Romance Languages: 407 Gilman, Stephen G. Nichols, 516-7226 (romance@jhu.edu).
History: 312 Gilman, Gabrielle Spiegel, 516-7575 (mzeller4@jhu.edu).
History of Art: 268 Mergenthaler, Stephen Campbell, 516-7117 (arthist@jhu.edu).
History of Science and Technology: 3505 North Charles Street, Sharon Kingsland, 516-7501 (danielle@jhu.edu).
Humanities Center: 113 Gilman, Ruth Leyes, 516-7368 (humanitiescenter@jhu.edu).
Mathematics: 404 Krieger, Richard Wentworth, 516-7399 (grad@math.jhu.edu).
Near Eastern Studies: 128 Gilman, Theodore Lewis, 516-7499 (nes@jhu.edu).
Philosophy: 347 Gilman, Michael Williams, 516-7525 (cc1@jhu.edu).
Physics and Astronomy: 366 Bloomberg, Jonathan Bagger, 516-7346 (admissions@pha.jhu.edu).
Political Science: 338 Mergenthaler, Jane Bennett, 516-7540 (political.science@jhu.edu).
Psychological and Brain Sciences: 204 Ames, Michela Gallagher, 516-6175 (rseitz@jhu.edu).
Public Policy: 540 Wyman, Sandra J. Newman, Director; 516-4167 (mpp@jhu.edu).
Sociology: 533 Mergenthaler, Karl Alexander, 516-7627 (sociology@jhu.edu).
Writing Seminars: 135 Gilman, Dave Smith, 516-6286 (regina@jhu.edu).

JOHNSON & WALES UNIVERSITY

Alan Shawn Feinstein Graduate School

Programs of Study

The Alan Shawn Feinstein Graduate School at Johnson & Wales University offers an M.B.A. degree in hospitality with concentration choices in event leadership, financial management, and marketing and an M.B.A. degree in global business with concentration choices in accounting, finance, international trade, marketing, and organizational leadership. The School also offers an M.A. degree in teacher education with certification in either business/food service education or elementary education and special education. An Ed.D. in educational leadership completes the programs offered at the Feinstein Graduate School. Classes are presented in both a day and evening schedule, and students with the appropriate business background can complete some programs in twelve months. The focus of all graduate programs is to provide students with the educational experiences that will help them attain employment in their chosen careers or enhance opportunities for advancement in their current employment. Very simply, the University's graduate programs teach people what they need to know to succeed in every economy.

Research Facilities

The main library, located on the first two floors of University Hall, is the central site of the Johnson & Wales University Library Network. This network currently includes the libraries of the following campuses: Denver, Colorado; and North Miami, Florida. The main Providence facility holds a collection of resource materials to serve the research needs of the University community, especially students in the School of Arts & Sciences, the College of Business, the Feinstein Graduate School, the Hospitality College, and the School of Technology. The College of Culinary Arts has its own library on the Harborside campus.

All graduate students have access to IBM computer labs, a multimedia center, and other specialized computer laboratories.

Financial Aid

The Feinstein Graduate School offers graduate assistantships as well as Federal Stafford Student Loans for those who qualify. International students, as well as domestic students, can apply for student employment on campus.

Cost of Study

Tuition for the 2007–08 academic year is $294 per quarter credit hour. (Three semester credits equal 4.5 quarter credits.) Total tuition is between $15,876 and $26,460. Payment options include term and monthly installment payment plans.

Living and Housing Costs

Graduate student housing is very limited, but an off-campus housing office maintains listings of apartments available locally. Students should anticipate costs of $8000 to $9000 per year for off-campus housing, food, and utilities.

Student Group

In 2006–07 there were approximately 785 students enrolled in graduate programs at Johnson & Wales University, the majority of whom are employed while pursuing their degree. Fifty-two percent of the student population are international students from sixty-four countries.

Student Outcomes

The objective of the Feinstein Graduate School is to meet the diverse needs of the global market. Graduates of the School's programs have entered positions that include management, administration, marketing, technology, accounting, and teaching. Organizations from around the globe, such as Sony, Ritz-Carlton, Citibank, and the Leromme Jerusalem Hotel, have hired the School's graduates.

Location

Johnson & Wales University is situated in Providence, Rhode Island, amidst a thriving business and academic community. Besides having a permanent population of 150,000, Providence is also a part-time home to more than 17,000 students from Johnson & Wales University, Brown University, Providence College, Rhode Island College, and Rhode Island School of Design. The arts are plentiful, from the plays of the Trinity Square Repertory Company to the musicals, ballets, operas, and current pop and comedy stars to be found at the Providence Performing Arts Center and the Civic Center. Providence is a reasonable driving distance from Newport, Rhode Island's beaches, and Boston, Massachusetts.

The University

Johnson & Wales University is a private, nonprofit, coeducational institution that offers students an opportunity to pursue practical career education in business, food service, hospitality, technology, and teacher education. Associate, bachelor's, and master's degree programs permit students to select the educational program most suited to their career interests and objectives.

Applying

Students are encouraged to apply early, as program enrollment is very limited. Applicants must submit a signed application, official transcripts documenting all undergraduate work, and two letters of recommendation. A statement of purpose is suggested. GMAT scores are recommended but not required. International applicants should also include documentation showing financial support and TOEFL score, unless they wish to enter the ESL program or they have graduated from an American university. New students may apply for the terms starting in September, December, March, and June.

Correspondence and Information

Alan Shawn Feinstein Graduate Admissions Office
Johnson & Wales University
8 Abbott Park Place
Providence, Rhode Island 02903
Phone: 401-598-1015
800-342-5598 Ext. 1015 (toll-free outside Rhode Island)
Fax: 401-598-1286
E-mail: admissions.grad@jwu.edu
Web site: http://www.jwu.edu

THE FACULTY

Administration

Frank Pontarelli, Ph.D., Professor and Dean, Alan Shawn Feinstein Graduate School.
Denise DeMagistris, Ph.D., Dean, School for Education and Ed.D. Program in Educational Leadership.

Faculty

Paul Boyd, Ph.D., Pennsylvania.
Paul Colbert, Ph.D., Boston College.
Caroline Cooper, Ed.D., Massachusetts; M.B.A., Bryant.
Joanne Crossman, Ed.D., Sarasota; C.A.G.S., Rhode Island College.
Ron DiBaptista, Ph.D., Arizona State.
Kevin Fountain, J.D., Suffolk; M.S.T., Bryant; CPA.
Robert Gable, Director, Educational Leadership Program; Ed.D.
Gary Gray, Ph.D., Salve Regina; M.B.A., C.A.G.S., Babson.
Ralph Jasparro, Ph.D., Clayton; C.A.G.S., Connecticut.
Stacey L. Kite, Associate Professor; D.B.A., Argosy; M.S., Johnson & Wales.
Alexander Portnyagin, Ph.D., Moscow State.
Thomas Rossi, M.S., Lesley.
Franklin Satterthwaite Jr., Ph.D., M.U.S., Yale.
Lisa Sisco, Ph.D., New Hampshire.
Martin Sivula, Ph.D., Connecticut; M.Ed., Fitchburg State.
Michael Timura, Ph.D., Connecticut; M.B.A., Bryant.

KANSAS STATE UNIVERSITY

The Graduate School

Programs of Study

Kansas State University's (KSU) Graduate School offers advanced study in sixty-two master's degree programs, forty-three doctoral programs, and twenty-six certificate programs, with more than 3,300 graduate students enrolled. There is an increasing emphasis on innovative interdisciplinary programs.

Opportunities exist for research and scholarly activities in the areas of agriculture, architecture and design, biochemistry, business administration, education, engineering, food science, genetics, human ecology, humanities and fine arts, natural sciences, social sciences, and veterinary medicine. Examples of areas for graduate study and research include atomic physics, automated manufacturing, software engineering, space biology, infectious disease research, prairie ecology, rural sociology, wheat genetics, molecular biology, nutrition and public health, theater, cancer biology, materials science, industrial and organizational psychology, military history, high-energy physics, milling science, functional foods, food service, and human development.

The Graduate School requires 30 semester hours beyond the bachelor's degree to obtain the master's degree, although some programs require more than 30 semester hours. Many programs require a substantial research project, although a nonthesis option is available in some programs. In the professional programs, that option predominates.

Doctoral programs require 90 semester hours beyond the bachelor's degree to obtain a Ph.D. and 94 semester hours beyond to obtain an Ed.D. Both programs include original research and a dissertation. Admission to candidacy requires the successful completion of the preliminary examinations.

The Division of Continuing Education offers many courses and degree programs through distance education, using a variety of delivery methods, including the World Wide Web, DVDs, videotapes, audiotapes, Telenet 2, and other technologies. KSU offers the following through distance learning: the Adult and Continuing Education Master's Program (Kansas City, Fort Leavenworth, or Wichita), an Agribusiness Master's Degree, the Classroom Technology Specialty, the Educational Administration and Leadership Master's Program, Engineering Degree Programs, English as a Second Language Specialty in Elementary/Secondary Education Program, Food Science, Gerontology, Industrial/Organization Psychology, Personal Financial Planning, and Youth Development. Several graduate certificate programs are also offered through the Division of Continuing Education.

Postbaccalaureate certificates provide a means to recognize mastery in a specialized area or to supplement a graduate degree. KSU currently offers twenty-one certificate programs in a variety of areas.

Research Facilities

KSU ranks among the nation's top seventy public research universities, with a growing foundation of research infrastructure to support vigorous training in scholarly research. The campus contains numerous specialized centers of interdisciplinary focused research, and these provide graduate students with dynamic training in their disciplines. Students should consult the KSU Research Facilities and Centers Web page at http://www.ksu.edu/Directories/research-facilities.html for a partial listing of these centers.

Financial Aid

Nearly half of KSU graduate students receive some type of financial assistance, including University graduate fellowships, teaching and research assistantships, or other forms of University employment and loans. Full-tuition waivers are given to graduate teaching assistants who receive at least a half-time appointment, and tuition reductions are available for graduate research assistants.

The KSU Office of Student Financial Assistance administers the federal assistance programs, work-study programs, and loans for which graduate students are eligible.

Cost of Study

For 2006–07, tuition for Kansas residents ranged from $239.50 for 1 graduate credit hour per semester to $2874 for 12 credit hours. Nonresident tuition ranged from $570.50 for 1 graduate credit hour per semester to $6846 for 12 credit hours. Fees in addition to tuition include campus privilege fees that range from $71 to $302. Some colleges have additional tuition surcharges and equipment fees.

Overall annual expenses, including living expenses, for a full-time student who completes 24 hours and is paying nonresident tuition are about $29,850.

Living and Housing Costs

KSU has 432 apartment units for graduate students. Married couples with children and single parents have priority. One-bedroom apartments on a semester basis range from $347 to $467 per month for traditional and newly constructed units, respectively, and two-bedroom apartments range from $409 to $914 per month for traditional and newly constructed units. On a yearly basis in William's Place, one-bedroom apartments range from $432 to $490 per month, and two-bedroom apartments range from $515 to $593 per month.

Student Group

The KSU graduate student population of more than 3,300 is made up of an almost-equal number of men and women. Approximately one fourth of the population is made up of international students from more than 100 countries. About two thirds of all graduate students are nontraditional (age 25 or older or married).

Student Outcomes

KSU graduates are highly sought after. They often receive multiple job offers, and many find employment well before graduation. They are leaders in public and private sectors, at government agencies, and at all levels of business and the private sector.

A sample of employers includes the National Institutes of Health, Argonne and Sandia National Labs, Nintendo, Merck, Pfizer, Cargill, Kellogg's, Hershey Foods, Anheuser-Busch, Motorola, AT&T Bell Labs, Texas Instruments, Rockwell International, and Sprint.

Location

KSU's picturesque 668-acre campus features many buildings of native limestone. KSU is centrally located in Manhattan (population 40,000), about 125 miles west of Kansas City. Manhattan has a new municipal airport, excellent schools, a daily newspaper, and numerous recreational facilities and cultural offerings. International festivals, Cinco de Mayo, Juneteenth, and Native American observances are held annually.

The University

Founded in 1863 as the first land-grant college, KSU is an internationally recognized, comprehensive research university with excellent academic programs carried out in a lively intellectual and cultural atmosphere.

In 1996, the University received the National Science Foundation's Recognition Award for the Integration of Research and Education. KSU was one of only ten universities selected.

Since 1974, KSU has ranked in the top 1 percent of all U.S. universities in the number of its graduates selected as Rhodes scholars.

Applying

Students should request admission applications and supplementary program information directly from the department or program coordinator. The Graduate School forwards correspondence to the appropriate program.

U.S. citizens should have all application materials on file by February 1 to receive priority consideration for full admission and for consideration for fellowships or graduate assistantships for the following fall semester. International students should apply no later than nine months prior to the term in which they wish to enroll.

Correspondence and Information

The Graduate School
103 Fairchild Hall
Kansas State University
Manhattan, Kansas 66506-1103

Phone: 785-532-6191
800-651-1816 (toll-free in the U.S.)
Fax: 785-532-2983
E-mail: grad@ksu.edu
Web site: http://www.k-state.edu/grad

PROGRAMS AND COORDINATORS

Students should contact the program coordinators listed below for more information.

COLLEGE OF AGRICULTURE

Agricultural Economics–Agribusiness (M.A.B.): Allen Featherstone.
Agricultural Economics (M.S., Ph.D.): Jeffery Williams.
Agronomy (M.S., Ph.D.): Bill Schapaugh.
Animal Sciences and Industry (M.S., Ph.D.): Ernest Minton.
Entomology (M.S., Ph.D.): James Nechols.
Grain Science and Industry (M.S., Ph.D.): David Wetzel.
Horticulture (M.S., Ph.D.): Channa Rajashekar.
Plant Pathology (M.S., Ph.D.): Bill Bockus.

COLLEGE OF ARCHITECTURE PLANNING AND DESIGN

Postprofessional Master's Program in Architecture (M.S.Arch.): Carol Martin Watts.
Professional Master's Programs. Architecture (M.Arch.): Carol Martin Watts. Landscape Architecture (M.L.A.): Dan Donelin. Regional and Community Planning (M.R.C.P.): Al Keithley. Community Development (M.S.): Al Keithley.

COLLEGE OF ARTS AND SCIENCES

Sciences and Mathematics

Biology (M.S., Ph.D.): S. Keith Chapes.
Chemistry (M.S., Ph.D.): Christer Aakeroy.
Geology (M.S., cooperative Ph.D. with the University of Kansas): C. G. (Jack) Oviatt.
Mathematics (M.S., Ph.D.): David Yetter.
Microbiology (M.S.): S. Keith Chapes.
Physics (M.S., Ph.D.): Zenghu Chang.
Statistics (M.S., Ph.D.): James Neill.

Humanities and Fine Arts

English (M.A.): Greg Eiselein.
Fine Arts (M.F.A.): Elliott Pujol.
History (M.A., Ph.D.): Louise Breen.
Modern Languages (M.A.): Claire Dehon.
Music (M.M.): Frederick Burrack.
Speech Communication, Theater, and Dance (M.A.). Speech: Bill Schenk-Hamlin. Theater: Sally Bailey.

Social Sciences

Economics (M.A., Ph.D.): William Blankenau.
Geography (M.A.): Kevin Blake.
Kinesiology (M.S.): Tom Barstow.
Mass Communication (M.S.): Robert Meeds.
Political Science (M.A.): Jeffrey Pickering.
Psychology (M.S., Ph.D.): Clive Fullagar.
Public Administration (M.P.A.): Krishna Tummala.
Sociology (M.A., Ph.D.): W. Richard Goe.

COLLEGE OF BUSINESS ADMINISTRATION

Accountancy (M.Acc.): Jeffrey Katz.
Business Administration (M.B.A.): Jeffrey Katz.

COLLEGE OF EDUCATION

Students should contact Marjorie Hancock for information related to the following programs.

Adult and Continuing Education (M.S., Ed.D., Ph.D.).
Counseling and Student Development (M.S., Ed.D., Ph.D.).
Curriculum and Instruction (M.S., Ed.D., Ph.D.).
Educational Administration and Leadership (M.S., Ed.D.).
Special Education (M.S., Ed.D.).

COLLEGE OF ENGINEERING

Architectural Engineering (M.S.): Kimberly Kramer.
Biological and Agricultural Engineering (M.S., Ph.D.): Naiqian Zhang.
Chemical Engineering (M.S., Ph.D.): Peter Pfromm.
Civil Engineering (M.S., Ph.D.): Mustaque Hossain.
Computing and Information Sciences (M.S., Ph.D.): Gurdip Singh.
Electrical and Computer Engineering (M.S., Ph.D.): Don Gruenbacher.
Engineering Management (M.E.M.): E. Stanley Lee.
Industrial Engineering (M.S., Ph.D.): E. Stanley Lee.
Mechanical Engineering (M.S., Ph.D.): Prakash Krishnaswami.
Nuclear Engineering (M.S., Ph.D.): Prakash Krishnaswami.
Operations Research (M.S.): E. Stanley Lee.
Software Engineering (M.S.E.): Gurdip Singh.

COLLEGE OF HUMAN ECOLOGY

Apparel and Textiles (M.S.): Jana Hawley.
Family Studies and Human Services (M.S.): Esther Maddux.
Food Service, Hospitality Management, and Dietetics Administration (M.S.): Deborah Canter.
Human Ecology (Ph.D.): Denis Medeiros.
Human Nutrition (M.S., Ph.D.). Food Science: Edgar Chambers IV. Nutrition: Denis Medeiros.

COLLEGE OF VETERINARY MEDICINE

Biomedical Sciences (M.S.): Lisa Freeman.
Pathobiology (Ph.D.): T. G. Nagaraja.
Physiology (Ph.D.): Michael Kenney.

GRADUATE CERTIFICATE PROGRAMS

Academic Advising: Stephen Benton.
Air Quality: Larry Erickson and Mo Hosni.
Applied Statistics: James Neill.
Business Administration: Jeffrey Katz.
Classroom Technology: Rosemary Talab.
Community Planning and Development: Al Keithley.
Complex Fluid Flows: Prakash Krishnaswami.
Conflict Resolution: Terrie McCants.
Entomology: James Nechols.
Feedlot Production Management: Dan Thomson.
Food Safety and Security: Thomas Herald.
Food Science: Thomas Herald.
Geoenvironmental Engineering: Lakshmi Reddi.
Geographic Information Science: J. M. Shawn Hutchinson.
Gerontology: Gayle Doll.
International Service: Jeffrey Pickering.
Occupational Health Psychology: Ron Downey.
Organizational Leadership: Jeffrey Katz.
Personal Financial Planning: Esther Maddux.
Public Administration: Krishna Tummala.
Real-Time Embedded System Design: Mitchell Neilsen.
Teaching Students with Autism Spectrum Disorders: Marilyn Kaff.
Technical Writing and Professional Communications: Gregory Eiselein.
Women's Studies: Angela Hubler.
Youth Development Administration: Elaine Johannes.
Youth Development Professional: Elaine Johannes.

INTERDISCIPLINARY PROGRAMS

Biochemistry: (M.S., Ph.D.): Larry Davis.
Environmental Design and Planning (Ph.D.): Wendy Ornelas.
Food Science (M.S., Ph.D.): Thomas Herald.
Genetics (M.S., Ph.D.): Barbara Valent.
Public Health (M.S.): Carol Ann Holcomb.
Security Studies (M.A., Ph.D.): Mark Parillo.

KEAN UNIVERSITY

Graduate School

Programs of Study The Nathan Weiss Graduate College of Kean University offers a wide variety of master's degree programs that address the needs of business, industry, education, and social services. Master of Arts degrees are available in the following areas: behavioral sciences, communication studies, counselor education, early childhood education, educational administration, educational psychology, fine arts education, Holocaust and genocide studies, instruction and curriculum, liberal studies, mathematics education, political science, reading specialization, school library media specialization, special education, and speech-language pathology. An M.B.A. in global management began offering courses in fall 2005, the Executive M.B.A. in spring 2006.

In addition to the M.A. degree programs, the University offers Master of Science degrees in accounting, biotechnology, computing, graphic communications technology management, management information systems, occupational therapy, political science, statistics and mathematics, and exercise science; the Master of Business Administration; the Master of Science in Nursing; the Master of Social Work; and the Master of Public Administration. The Master of Science in Nursing/Master of Public Administration is a dual-degree program. The Professional Diploma in School Psychology and in Marriage and Family Therapy as well as the post-master's Learning Disability Teacher Consultant certificate are also offered.

Students with an undergraduate liberal arts major may enter the Classroom Instruction or Early Childhood M.A. programs, which are special programs that grant an initial teaching certificate in early childhood, elementary, middle, and secondary education after the first year.

Most classes are scheduled during the evening to accommodate students who work full-time. Classes meet once a week during the fall and spring semesters; during the summer, students may take classes during the day or evening.

Research Facilities The Nancy Thompson Library is a comprehensive learning center with 271,000 volumes (including bound periodicals and 1,350 periodical subscriptions), 92,000 microfilms, and an extensive journal collection. Included are rare books and printed materials, the New Jersey Collection, and the papers of Congresswoman Florence P. Dwyer. Available materials are greatly expanded through an interlibrary loan system, and the University utilizes an online computerized retrieval system from several national databases that facilitates rapid bibliographic retrieval. In addition, the holdings of all institutions of the Consortium of East New Jersey are available to Kean University students through the Nancy Thompson Library. The Holocaust Resource Center contains a vast collection of encyclopedia and text on Holocaust survivors, all of which is indexed for use by scholars, historians, teachers, and students. This center is affiliated with the Video Archive for Holocaust Testimonies, Sterling Library, Yale University.

Laboratory facilities include the Teaching Performance Center, Reading Institute, Campus School, Institute of Child Study, and Comprehensive Evaluation Clinic (Clinic in Learning Disabilities and Clinic in Audiology Disabilities).

Research affiliates include the Cerebral Palsy Center, Camp Union, and Aid to Children with Learning Disabilities, as well as a statewide computer network that exceeds student needs in virtually all cases.

Financial Aid The University offers approximately 150 graduate assistantships, which are limited to full-time matriculated students (taking a minimum of 9 graduate credits per semester). Students receive a weekly stipend plus a waiver of tuition and fees.

A limited number of scholarships are available to graduate students as are institution-sponsored loans.

Cost of Study Full-time graduate tuition and fees are $5554.20 for the spring 2007 semester for New Jersey residents and $6754.20 for out-of-state students. Part-time graduate tuition and fees are $462.85 per credit for spring 2007 semester for New Jersey residents and $562.85 per credit for out-of-state students.

Student Group The 13,050 full- and part-time graduate and undergraduate students form a heterogeneous student body representing diverse cultural backgrounds. The graduate student population of 3,060 is primarily part-time, with approximately 20 percent attending on a full-time basis. The faculty-student ratio, which averages 1:15, allows for small classes and enables instructors to work closely with their students.

The graduate student community is diverse in terms of ethnic background and age. A number of graduate students return for purposes of making career changes or upgrading professional skills and competencies. Graduate students often work cooperatively in research seminars and study groups, exchanging ideas and questions and learning, to a considerable extent, from one another. Practical experience is provided through internships in many of the programs.

Student Outcomes Of the master's degree recipients in a recent year, approximately 61 percent went into teaching and education-related fields, 27 percent into administrative and business professions, and 12 percent into other occupations.

Location Kean University's location in Union, New Jersey, is accessible to all major highways and is minutes away from Newark Liberty International Airport. New York City is approximately 10 miles away.

The University Established in 1855 as Newark Normal School, Kean University celebrated its 150th year in 2005. It offers degrees in the humanities, education, sciences, government, technology, and business. The University observed the fiftieth year of its graduate programs in the academic year 1998–99.

The University has received national acclaim for its innovative assessment and retention programs. The University offers a wide variety of cultural and social events. The New Jersey Ballet offers several performances throughout the year.

A delightful contrast to the surrounding urban area, the campus is 122 acres of rolling lawns and wooded areas with a graceful, meandering stream. An additional 28 acres on Kean's East Campus are used for both intercollegiate and intramural recreation and student-oriented activities.

Applying A formal application; a $60 fee; scores on the GRE General Test, the GMAT, the Miller Analogies Test, or the PRAXIS exam; and official transcripts of all previous college work are required for admission in most programs. A personal interview and references may also be required.

Correspondence and Information

Office of Graduate Admissions
T-126
Kean University
1000 Morris Avenue
Union, New Jersey 07083

Phone: 908-737-3355
E-mail: grad-adm@kean.edu
Web site: http://www.kean.edu

FACULTY COORDINATORS

Kean University has 370 full-time faculty members, of whom 314 hold doctorates and 333 hold terminal degrees in their respective disciplines and also have distinguished themselves in their fields through research and publications. Adjunct faculty members drawn from the professions, business, and industry bring with them practical knowledge of their fields as well as academic qualifications. Graduate students receive personal attention, support, and guidance from the faculty and from the Office of Graduate Studies.

Accounting (M.S.): Dr. Eric Carlsen.
Behavioral Sciences (M.A.):
Option: Human Behavior and Organization Psychology. Dr. Henry L. Kaplowitz.
Option: Psychological Services. Dr. Muriel Singer.
Biotechnology (M.S.): Dr. Laura Lorentzen.
Business Administration (M.B.A.): Dr. David Shani.
Option: Executive M.B.A.
Option: M.B.A. in Global Management.
Communication Studies (M.A.): Dr. Jack Sargent.
Computing, Statistics and Mathematics (M.S.): Dr. Francine Abeles.
Counselor Education (M.A.): Dr. Juneau Gary.
Option: Alcohol and Drug Abuse Counseling.
Option: Business and Industry Counseling.
Option: Community/Agency Counseling.
*Option: School Counseling.
*Substance Awareness Coordinator (certification only).
Early Childhood Education (M.A.): Dr. Marjorie Kelly.
Option: Administration in Early Childhood and Family Studies.
Option: Advanced Curriculum and Teaching.
Option: Classroom Instruction with Initial P-3 Certification.
Option: Education for Family Living.
*Teacher of Preschool Through Third Grade (P-3) (certification only).
***Educational Administration (M.A.):** Dr. Effie Christie.
Option: School Business Administrators.
Option: Supervisor and Principle.
***Educational Psychology (M.A.):** Dr. Dennis Finger.
Exercise Science (M.S.): Dr. Walter Andzel.
Fine Arts Education (M.A.):
*Option: Initial Teaching Certification. Dr. Joseph Amorino.
*Option: Fine Arts Supervision. Dr. Joseph Amorino.
Option: Studio. Professor Jappie King Black.
Graphic Communications Technology Management (M.S.): Dr. Cyril Nwako.
Holocaust and Genocide Studies (M.A.): Dr. Bernard Weinstein.
Instruction and Curriculum (M.A.):
*Option: Bilingual/Bicultural Education. Dr. Gilda Del Risco.
*Option: Classroom Instruction. Dr. Dorothy Striplin.
*Option: Earth Science. Dr. Robert Mertz.
*Option: Educational Technology. Dr. Thomas Walsh.
Option: Mastery in Teaching. Dr. Suzanne Reynolds.
Option: Mathematics/Science/Computer Education. Dr. Suzanne Reynolds.
*Option: Teaching English as a Second Language. Professor Dr. Betsy Rodriguez-Bachiller.
Option: World Languages (Spanish). Dr. Pablo Pintado-Casas.
Liberal Studies (M.A.): Dr. John Gruesser.

Leads to New Jersey certification.

Management Information Systems (M.S.): Dr. Thomas Abraham and Dr. Jack Ryder.
Mathematics Education (M.A.): Dr. Francine Abeles.
Option: Computer Applications.
*Option: Supervision of Mathematics Education.
Option: Teaching of Mathematics.
Nursing (M.S.N.): Dr. Estelle Pisani.
Option: Clinical Management.
Nursing/Public Administration (M.S.N./M.P.A.): Dr. Estelle Pisani and Dr. Susan Ault.
Option: Clinical Management.
Option: Community Health.
Occupational Therapy (M.S.): Dr. Lynne Richard.
Political Science (M.A.): Dr. Larry Chang.
Public Administration (M.P.A.): Dr. Craig Donovan.
Option: Criminal Justice. Dr. Vanessa Garcia.
Option: Environmental Management. Jon Erickson.
Option: Health Services Administration. Dr. Susan Ault.
Option: Nonprofit Management. Dr. Patricia Moore.
***Reading Specialization (M.A.):** Dr. Joan Kastner.
Option: Adult Literacy.
Option: Basic Skills Specialist.
Option: Reading Specialist.
Reading Specialist (certification only).
Teacher of Reading (certification only).
***School Library Specialization (M.A.):** Dr. Joan Kastner.
***Social Work (M.S.W.):** Dr. Alan Lightfoot.
Option: Advanced Standing.
***Special Education (M.A.):** Dr. Beverly Kling.
Option: High Incidence Disabilities.
Option: Learning Disabilities.
Option: Low Incidence Disabilities.
Option: Teacher of Students with Disabilities (certification only).
***Speech-Language Pathology (M.A.):** Dr. Barbara Glazewski.
Post-Master's Programs:
Director of School Counseling (certification only).
*Learning Disabilities Teacher Consultant. Dr. Marie C. Segal.
Licensed Professional Counseling. Dr. Betty Dodd.
School Business Administrator (certification only).
School Counseling (certification only).
Professional Diplomas:
Marriage and Family Therapy: Dr. Muriel Singer.
*School Psychology: Dr. Dennis Finger.

Estabrook Fountain.

Harwood Arena.

Kean Hall.

KUTZTOWN UNIVERSITY OF PENNSYLVANIA

College of Graduate Studies

Programs of Study

The College of Graduate Studies at Kutztown University of Pennsylvania offers a variety of programs leading to the M.Ed., M.A., M.L.S. (Master of Library Science), M.B.A. (Master of Business Administration), M.P.A. (Master of Public Administration), and M.S. degrees. Certification programs are also offered.

The Master of Education degree is offered in art education; elementary education; elementary and secondary school counseling; instructional technology; reading; secondary education with cognate areas in biology, curriculum and instruction, English, mathematics, and social studies; and student affairs in higher education.

The Master of Science degree is offered in computer and information science, nursing, and electronic media.

The Master of Arts degree is offered in counseling psychology, with specialties in marital and family theory or agency counseling, and English.

It is possible to earn a graduate degree at Kutztown University while concurrently completing course work for teaching certification or extending a valid teaching certificate to include new fields. Pennsylvania maintains cooperative agreements with many states so that earning certification in Pennsylvania means that the candidate will be eligible for certification in some other states.

Research Facilities

The Rohrbach Library is the focal point of academic life at Kutztown University. The library houses collections of books, periodicals, pamphlets, newspapers, maps, microforms, nonprint media, and electronic resources. At present, the collection consists of 500,484 volumes, representative federal and state documents, 39,000 maps, 15,706 periodicals and newspapers, 18,113 units of nonprint media, and 1,323,162 units of various kinds of microforms. The library provides electronic access to several full-text databases and reference resources over the University's network. The map collection is one of the finest in the state and includes Braille maps, city plans, and topographic and raised relief maps. The library has a state-of-the-art facility with network access to the Web and the Internet and has installed Endeavor's Voyager integrated library system.

The Curriculum Materials Center provides a wide range of the newest teaching and learning resources for examination, evaluation, and curriculum revision.

The Audiovisual Center, located on the ground floor of the library, administers a comprehensive collection of audiovisual materials and equipment. In addition, the Audiovisual Center houses a microcomputer laboratory, microcomputer software collection, and a materials production area.

Rohrbach Library provides numerous services to faculty members and students. These include the circulation of open-collection and reserve materials, online database searching, interlibrary loan services, document delivery services, motion enhancement services, and electronic reference services.

The Rohrbach Library staff is responsible for developing and organizing the library collections and for administering programs of library orientation and bibliographic instruction. Librarians meet frequently with classes from all areas of curriculum to discuss specialized research tools.

Financial Aid

Various types of financial aid, in the form of grants and loans, are available to eligible graduate students who are enrolled either full-time or half-time (at least 6 hours). Financial aid in the form of Stafford loans is available to eligible students. Students should direct inquiries for information to the Financial Aid Office. A number of graduate assistantships are available. A stipend, accompanied by a tuition waiver, is offered to qualified students. Graduate assistants must take at least 9 semester hours for a full academic load. No more than 15 hours of course work are permitted for any one semester. Under supervision for a maximum of 20 hours each week, graduate assistants assume responsibilities that are related to their professional interests.

Cost of Study

Each full-time graduate student is charged a flat rate of either $3107 (Pennsylvania residents) or $4972 (out-of-state residents) per semester. Part-time students are assessed tuition at a rate of either $345 per credit (Pennsylvania residents) or $552 per credit (out-of-state residents).

Living and Housing Costs

Housing for graduate students in University residence halls is offered only during the summer session and on a space-available basis. Students should direct inquiries for information to the Office of Housing and Residence Life. Privately owned apartments and houses are available near the campus.

Student Group

In 2006–07, total enrollment was 10,000; 851 were graduate students. Most of the graduate students (68 percent) were studying part-time, and 71 percent were women.

Location

With access to both the Lehigh and Schuylkill River Valleys, Kutztown University is located in the heart of the Pennsylvania Dutch country of the Commonwealth of Pennsylvania. A short drive of 7 miles via Pennsylvania Route 737 provides easy access to Interstate Highway 78, connecting New York City and Harrisburg, Pennsylvania. Kutztown is equidistant (16 miles) from Reading and Allentown, Pennsylvania, along Route 222. Commercial bus transportation is available from Kutztown to Reading, Philadelphia, New York City, and Washington, D.C. The University is located 25 miles west of Lehigh Valley Airport and 18 miles east of Reading Airport.

The University

Established in 1866 as a school to prepare teachers, Kutztown was authorized to award the bachelor's degree in 1926. Teacher education, including elementary and secondary education and a variety of special fields, such as art education and library science, has always played an important part in the development of the institution. On January 8, 1960, the governor of the commonwealth approved legislation making Kutztown a center of learning that would offer the youth of Pennsylvania the best possible education in the arts and sciences as well as in teacher education. The year before, Kutztown State College had been authorized to grant master's degrees in art education and elementary education.

Under the new statement of mission, the College began to develop a richness and breadth that encompasses the liberal arts and sciences, the fine and performing arts, teacher education, and other professional programs at the undergraduate and graduate levels. In 1983, Kutztown State College became Kutztown University.

Applying

The Graduate Office coordinates the admissions process. All applications and instructions should be obtained from the College of Graduate Studies Office. The payment of a nonrefundable $35 fee must accompany the completed application. Brochures and other information describing graduate programs are available from the departments listed on the reverse of this page. Descriptions of programs and courses also are available in the graduate catalog or at the graduate Web site.

Correspondence and Information

Dr. Linda Matthews, Interim Dean, College of Graduate Studies
Mr. James Hubbard, Interim Assistant Dean, College of Graduate Studies
College of Graduate Studies
Kutztown University
Kutztown, Pennsylvania 19530

Phone: 610-683-4200 (Mr. Hubbard)
E-mail: hubbard@kutztown.edu
Web site: http://www.kutztown.edu/academics/graduate

Kutztown University of Pennsylvania

GRADUATE PROGRAMS AND CHAIRPERSONS

Art Education. John H. White, (610-683-4520).

Business Administration. Fidel Ikem, (610-683-4575).

Computer and Information Science. Linda Day, (610-683-4340).

Counselor Education/Counseling Psychology. Margaret A. Herrick, (610-683-4204).

Electronic Media. Joseph Chuk, (610-683-4492).

Elementary Education. Elsa Geskus, (610-683-4262).

English. Janice Chernekoff, (610-683-4353).

Instructional Technology. Eloise Long, (610-683-4300).

Library Science. Eloise Long, (610-683-4300).

Nursing. Mary Ann Dailey, (610-683-4326).

Public Administration. Jack Treadway, (610-683-4449).

Reading Specialist. Beth M. Herbine, (610-683-4271).

Secondary Education. Kathleen A. Dolgos, (610-683-4259).

LAMAR UNIVERSITY

Graduate School

Programs of Study

Doctoral degrees are offered in the following disciplines: deaf education (Ed.D.), audiology, educational leadership (Ed.D.), chemical engineering, civil engineering, industrial engineering, mechanical engineering, and electrical engineering (D.E.). Beginning in the fall 2005 semester, a Ph.D. is being offered in chemical engineering. A second Ph.D. will soon be offered in civil engineering.

Master's degrees are offered in applied criminology (M.S.), biology (M.S.), business administration (M.B.A.), chemical engineering (M.E. and M.E.S.), chemistry (M.S.), civil engineering (M.E. and M.E.S.), community and counseling psychology (M.S.), computer science (M.S.), counseling and development (M.Ed.), deaf studies/habilitation (M.S.), educational administration (M.Ed.), electrical engineering (M.E. and M.E.S.), elementary education (M.Ed.), engineering management (M.E.M.), English (M.A.), environmental engineering (M.S.), environmental studies (M.S.), family and consumer science (M.S.), history (M.A.), industrial engineering (M.E. and M.E.S.), industrial and organizational psychology (M.S.), kinesiology (M.Ed.), mathematics (M.S.), mechanical engineering (M.E. and M.E.S.), music (M.Mu.), music education (M.Mu.Ed.), nursing administration (M.S.), nursing education (M.S.), public administration (M.P.A.), secondary education (M.Ed.), special education (M.Ed.), speech-language pathology (M.S.), supervision (M.Ed.), theater (M.S.), and visual arts (studio art and art history) (M.A).

Teaching certification is available in the areas of counseling, educational diagnostician, elementary education, mental retardation, midmanagement administrator (principal), reading specialist, school superintendent, secondary education, special education supervisor, supervisor, and visiting teacher. The Early Childhood Development Center is a tool that provides University students direct observation of young children who exhibit typical and atypical development, as well as the opportunity to investigate effective teaching strategies for promoting optimal development among young children.

Research Facilities

The eight-story Mary and John Gray Library building dominates the campus from its central location. The library occupies seven floors and possesses an online public-access catalog to more than 1 million volumes and 3,000 periodicals. In addition to a collection of books and periodicals, the library provides access to state and federal government documents and participates in the library networks that extend access to information resources. The library coordinates multimedia programs on campus and has a basic collection of equipment and materials for central distribution.

The Research Office is administered by the Associate Vice President for Research, who chairs the research council. This office promotes and funds internal research; oversees sponsored programs and technology transfer, as well as patent, copyright, and intellectual property policies; establishes liaisons between the University and state and national funding sources; and ensures that proposed projects comply with institutional and governmental regulations. This office also provides assistance to faculty members in the development and submission of grant/project proposals by locating funding sources and providing editorial assistance in proposal preparation.

Financial Aid

Financial assistance in the form of loans, grants, scholarships, tuition fee waivers, and the Federal Work-Study Program is available for a number of qualified students. Details may be obtained upon request from the Director of Financial Aid, P.O. Box 10042, Beaumont, Texas 77710. Teaching and research assistantships are available in the various graduate departments. Additional information may be obtained either from the department chair or from the Dean of the College of Graduate Studies.

Cost of Study

Interested students can find the most current information about tuition and fees for the summer sessions and the fall and spring semesters at the Lamar University Web site at http://www.lamar.edu.

Living and Housing Costs

A variety of living options are available and include modern furniture, semiprivate rooms, carpet, central heating and air conditioning, and various color schemes in the dormitories. Apartment accommodations in newly remodeled buildings are also available. Questions concerning housing and rates can be directed to the Residence Life Office, Lamar University, P.O. Box 11950, Beaumont, Texas 77710 or Cardinal Village, P.O. Box 10040, Beaumont, Texas 77710.

Student Group

The student body consists of 9,726 undergraduate students, 1,117 master's students, and 101 doctoral students. The majority of undergraduate enrollment is from Jefferson and Orange Counties, while the Graduate School population is largely international. The average age of students is 27.

Student Outcomes

At the spring 2005 commencement, there were 126 master's degrees awarded, thirty-eight for arts and sciences, four for business, twenty-two for education, fifty for engineering, and twelve master's degrees in fine arts. There were also three doctoral degrees awarded, one for engineering and two for fine arts (deaf education). In addition, the fall 2005 commencement conferred 161 master's degrees.

Location

The Lamar University campus is located in Beaumont, Texas. With a population of more than 114,000, Beaumont is a diversified city, home to not only the University but also businesses and industry stemming from a strong petrochemical and agriculture base. World-renowned companies are located in Beaumont to take advantage of the area's resources and its educational workforce.

The University

Lamar University originated on March 8, 1923, with the plans for "a junior college of the first class." On June 8, 1942, classes were held for the first time on the present campus. In 1962, the Graduate School was established, and the Doctor of Engineering and the Doctor of Education in deaf education were established in 1971 and in 1993, respectively. Lamar is proud to be part of the Texas State University System and eagerly anticipates the evolving needs of its students.

Applying

General admission information can be found on the University Web site or in the graduate catalog. Graduate students must meet the general standards and may have to meet more stringent standards, depending upon the department. Domestic students must submit all materials at least thirty days before registration.

Correspondence and Information

Graduate Admissions
Lamar University
P.O. Box 10078
Beaumont, Texas 77710
Phone: 409-880-8356
Fax: 409-880-8414
E-mail: intladm@hal.lamar.edu
Web site: http://www.lamar.edu

FACULTY HEADS

College of Arts and Sciences
Brenda Nichols, Ph.D., Indiana.

College of Business
Enrique Venta, Ph.D., Northwestern.

College of Education and Human Development
Hollis Lowery-Moore, Ph.D., Houston.

College of Engineering
Jack R. Hopper, Ph.D., LSU.

College of Fine Arts and Communication
Russ Schultz, Ph.D., North Texas State.

Graduate Studies and Research/Admissions
Jerry Bradley, Ph.D., Texas Christian.

LONG ISLAND UNIVERSITY, C.W. POST CAMPUS

Graduate Programs

Programs of Study

The College of Liberal Arts and Sciences offers M.A. degrees in English, history, interdisciplinary studies, political science, psychology, and Spanish; M.S. degrees in applied mathematics, biology, environmental studies, and interdisciplinary studies; a Psy.D. degree in clinical psychology; and an advanced certificate in applied behavior analysis. The College of Liberal Arts and Sciences offers a number of accelerated five-year degree programs combining a broad-based liberal arts background at the bachelor's level with professional training at the master's level: B.S./M.S. (biology), B.A. (international studies)/M.B.A. (international business), B.A./M.A. (political science), and B.A. (political science)/M.P.A. (health-care administration). The College of Management offers the M.B.A. In addition, M.S. degrees are offered in accountancy, criminal justice, criminal justice (security administration concentration), and taxation; M.P.A. degrees are offered in health-care administration and public administration; and the M.S.W. (social work) degree is offered. Advanced certificates are also offered in business, gerontology, and nonprofit management. The College of Management also offers accelerated programs, including an M.P.A. (health-care administration)/J.D. and a J.D./M.B.A. in conjunction with Touro Law Center; B.S./M.S. (accountancy); B.S./M.B.A. (accountancy); B.A./M.S. (criminal justice); B.S./M.P.A. (health-care administration); and B.S./M.P.A. (public administration). The College of Information and Computer Science offers a Ph.D. in information studies; an M.S. in information systems, information technology education, library and information science, and management engineering; and advanced certificates in archives and records management and public library director. The School of Education offers M.S.Ed. degrees for literacy teachers, school building leaders, and teachers of special education; M.A. degrees in speech language pathology and teaching English to speakers of other languages (TESOL); M.S. degrees in early childhood and childhood education, educational technology specialist studies, mental health counseling, and school counseling; and M.S. degrees in the following areas of middle childhood (5–9) and adolescence (7–12) education: art (B–12), biology, earth science, English, mathematics, music (B–12), social studies, and Spanish. Advanced certificate programs are also offered in school building leader studies, school business district, and school district leader studies. C.W. Post also offers dual bachelor's/master's degree programs in education and dual certification master's degree programs in childhood/literacy and childhood/special education. The School of Visual and Performing Arts offers M.A. degrees in art, clinical art therapy, interactive media arts, music, and theater; an M.F.A. degree is offered in fine arts and design. The School of Health Professions and Nursing offers M.S. degrees in medical biology (with specializations in hematology, immunology, medical chemistry, or medical microbiology), cardiovascular perfusion, clinical laboratory management, clinical nurse specialist studies, family nurse practitioner studies, nursing education, and nutrition. An accelerated B.S./M.S. degree is offered in nutrition. Advanced certificates in family nurse practitioner studies and a dietetic internship are also offered. Master's degree students have five years in which to complete their course of study. For the College of Liberal Arts and Sciences there is a requirement of 30 to 42 credits, depending on the degree chosen. Entrance and thesis requirements vary, depending on the program. In the arts, the M.A. programs require 36 credits and a thesis; the M.F.A. program requires 60 credits, including a thesis. For all art programs a portfolio review is required. The M.B.A. program requires 36–48 credits. The M.P.A. is a 48-credit program; the M.S. in criminal justice is a 36-credit program, including a thesis. Most education degrees require at least 36 credits, and many require a thesis. Counseling degrees require 48–63 credits. The M.S. in library and information science requires 36 credits. Through weekend college, students may earn graduate credits toward degrees in criminal justice, education, health administration, medical biology, and public administration.

Research Facilities

The B. Davis Schwartz Memorial Library is one of the largest research libraries in New York and houses more than 2.8 million books and periodicals as part of a University-wide system. This multilevel library is a digital powerhouse with high-speed Web connections and wireless communications, online subscriptions, and more than 100 database services. It also features the nationally respected Center for Business Research, Media Center, and Government Information Collection. C.W. Post is home to the Center for Aging, the Financial Markets Center, and the Electronic Educational Village. Science, art, and education facilities are fully equipped.

Financial Aid

Various assistantships are available through each department. Financial aid is also available through federal financial aid programs, including the Federal William T. Ford Direct Loan, Federal Perkins Loan, and Federal Work-Study Program. In addition, full-time students may be eligible for state grants. A graduate scholarship provides awards of up to $125 per credit depending on the major and grade point average. The awarding of this scholarship is not based on financial need and does not prevent the student from applying for other types of financial assistance. Continuing graduate students who are high achievers may be considered for a Graduate Incentive Award. Deadline dates apply. Scholarships/grants are given on a funds-available basis.

Cost of Study

Tuition for 2006–07 was approximately $790 per credit plus college fees for all majors, except Psy.D. and Ph.D. students. Additional expenses include books and laboratory, thesis, and graduation fees. Fees are subject to change.

Living and Housing Costs

C.W. Post provides limited housing for graduate students.

Student Group

There are more than 3,700 graduate students from more than forty-five countries around the world. Students can enroll in either part-time or full-time study.

Location

C.W. Post is located on a beautiful 307-acre estate in the suburban Long Island community of Brookville. Major shopping centers in the immediate area include popular restaurants, movie theaters, and department stores. The campus is only 50 minutes from New York City. Bus transportation is available from the Long Island Railroad station in Hicksville.

The University

C.W. Post Campus is one of six campuses of Long Island University, one of the largest independent universities in the country. The many facilities available for student use include Tilles Center for the Performing Arts; the Hillwood Art Museum; the $18-million Pratt Recreation Center with fitness center, pool, gymnasium, and racquetball courts; an Interfaith Center; and several other art galleries, performance venues, and cafés.

Applying

Students who wish to apply for admission to any program should request a graduate bulletin and an application from the Office of Graduate Admissions. Deadlines exist for certain graduate degree programs. Interested applicants should contact the Office of Admissions for further information. An online application is available at http://www.liu.edu/postapp.

Correspondence and Information

Office of Graduate Admissions
Long Island University, C.W. Post Campus
720 Northern Boulevard
Brookville, New York 11548-1300

Phone: 516-299-2900
Fax: 516-299-2137
E-mail: enroll@cwpost.liu.edu
Web site: http://www.liu.edu/graduate

FACULTY HEADS

C.W. POST CAMPUS DEANS
College of Information and Computer Science: John Regazzi, Dean; Ph.D., Rutgers.
College of Liberal Arts and Sciences: Katherine C. Hill-Miller, Dean; Ph.D., Columbia.
College of Management: Matthew Cordaro, Ph.D., Cooper Union.
School of Education: Robert Manheimer, Dean; Ed.D., Columbia.
School of Health Professions and Nursing: Theodora Grauer, Ph.D., Adelphi.
School of Visual and Performing Arts: Rhoda Grauer, B.A., Vassar.

DEPARTMENT CHAIRPERSONS
Accounting: Charles A. Barragato, Ph.D., Baruch.
Administration and Leadership: Richard K. White, Ed.D., NYU.
Art: Donna Tuman, Ed.D., Columbia Teachers College.
Biology: Matthew Draud, Ph.D., Lehigh.
Biomedical Science: R. R. Modesto, Ph.D., IIT.
Clinical Psychology: Robert Keisner, Ph.D., Massachusetts.
Communication Science and Disorders: Dianne Slavin, Ph.D., NYU.
Computer Science: Susan Fife-Dorchak, Ph.D., Nova Southeastern. Seth Magot, Ph.D., St. John's (New York).
Counseling: A. Scott McGowan, Ph.D., Fordham.
Criminal Justice: Harvey Kushner, Ph.D., NYU.
Curriculum and Instruction: Anthony DeFalco, Ed.D., Rutgers.
Earth and Environmental Science: Margaret Boorstein, Ph.D., Columbia.
Educational Technology: Michael Byrne, Ph.D., Michigan State. Bette Schneiderman, Ph.D., Hofstra.
English: Edmund Miller, Ph.D., SUNY at Stony Brook.
Finance: Alan Murray, Ph.D., Columbia.
Foreign Languages: Sheila Gunther, M.A., Pennsylvania.
Health Care and Public Administration: Thomas Webster, Ph.D., Ohio State.
History: Jeanie Attie, Ph.D., Columbia.
Management: Biachun Xiao, Ph.D., Pennsylvania.
Marketing: T. Steven Chang, Ph.D., George Washington, National Chengchi (Taiwan).
Mathematics: Neo Cleopa, Ph.D., Adelphi.
Music: Chris Culver, D.A., Northern Colorado.
Nursing: Minna Kapp, Ed.D., Columbia.
Nutrition: Frances Gizis, Ph.D., NYU.
Political Science/International Studies: Roger Goldstein, Ph.D., Columbia.
Psychology: Gerald Lachter, Ph.D., CUNY, Queens.
Social Work: Ilene Nathanson, D.S.W., Adelphi.
Special Education and Literacy: James Vacca, Ph.D., Syracuse.
Theater and Film: Cara Gargano, Ph.D., CUNY Graduate Center.

LONG ISLAND UNIVERSITY, WESTCHESTER GRADUATE CAMPUS

Graduate Programs

Programs of Study

Since 1975, Long Island University has been offering graduate degree programs and certificates at its Westchester campus in Purchase, New York. The Westchester Graduate Campus (WGC) provides high-quality programs in diverse disciplines that encourage independent thought and advance academic growth in a career-oriented environment.

Central to the success of the Westchester campus is a distinguished and seasoned faculty whose members enrich and challenge students and shape the supportive atmosphere of the Westchester Graduate Campus. The faculty consists of active members and leaders of professional organizations who present at regional and national conferences, publish, and involve themselves in community-outreach efforts.

The Westchester Graduate Campus offers programs and certificates in the areas of teacher education, school counseling, school psychology, marriage and family therapy, mental health counseling, business administration (M.B.A.), and library and information science. Each curriculum is designed to help the student acquire and refine professional skills as well as to increase appreciation and understanding of cultural values. Classes are held in the late afternoons, evenings, and on Saturdays to accommodate the schedules of working adults.

For students without prior teaching certification, the Westchester Graduate Campus' M.S.Ed. degree in teacher education leads to Initial New York State certification. For those with prior teaching certification, the programs lead to Professional certification. WGC offers advanced certificates in these areas as well as a bilingual extension. The following education programs are offered: Early Childhood Education, Middle Childhood and Adolescence Education, Special Education, Teaching Literacy, and Teaching English to Speakers of Other Languages (TESOL).

The Early Childhood Education Program offers certificates in Early Childhood (birth–grade 2) and Childhood Education (grades 1–6); Early Childhood and Early Childhood Special Education (birth–grade 2); and Early Childhood (birth–grade 2) and Literacy (birth–grade 6).

The Childhood Education Program offers certificates in Childhood Education (grades 1–6), Childhood Education (grades 1–6) and Childhood Special Education (grades 1–6), Childhood Education (grades 1–6) and Literacy (birth–grade 6), and Childhood Education (grades 1–6) and TESOL (all grades).

The Middle Childhood and Adolescence Education Program offers certificates in Middle Childhood and Adolescence Education (grades 5–12): English, Social Studies, Mathematics, Science, and LOTE; Special Education (grades 5–12); and Middle Childhood and Adolescence Education: English, Social Studies, Mathematics, Science (grades 5–12).

The Special Education Program offers certificates in Special Education Childhood (grades 1–6), Special Education: Middle Childhood and Adolescence (grades 5–12), Special Education Childhood (grades 1–6), and Literacy (birth–grade 6).

The Teaching Literacy Program offers certificates in Teaching Literacy (birth–grade 6), Writing and Literacy (birth–grade 6), and Teaching Writing and Reading (grades 5–12).

The TESOL Program offers a certificate in TESOL (all grades).

Students who already hold a master's degree and/or prior teaching certification may elect to enroll in one of the sixteen advanced certificate programs offered at Westchester Graduate Campus of Long Island University in Early Childhood, Middle Childhood and Adolescence Education, Adolescence Education, Special Education, Literacy, and TESOL.

The M.S.Ed. in School Psychology Program fully prepares students to obtain provisional New York State certification as school psychologists. The program teaches the knowledge and skills necessary for today's practice of school psychology in diverse environments. Students may elect to take courses to qualify for the Bilingual Extension, which is designed to train bilingual psychologists to work with linguistically diverse children and their families. Upon completion of a two-year supervised work experience, students are eligible for permanent certification. Although the program is designed to be completed in three years, full-time and part-time study are possible.

The M.S.Ed. in School Counseling Program prepares students for counseling positions in public and private agencies as school counselors or personal counselors. Students may elect to take courses to qualify for the Bilingual Extension. Although the program is designed to be completed in three years, full-time and part-time study are possible.

The Marriage and Family Therapy and the Mental Health Counseling Graduate Programs complement the School Counseling and School Psychology Programs by training students to work in mental health and social service agencies, clinics, and hospitals and in private practice. In both these programs, graduate students are taught both theoretical models and clinical skills so that they emerge as true scholar-practitioners who understand current research in order to maximize their clinical effectiveness. The Mental Health Counseling students are trained in diagnosis, counseling techniques, and consultation. The Marriage and Family Therapy students are trained in counseling techniques and consultation skills that have been found to be effective with couples and families.

The M.B.A. Program is for men and women who wish to upgrade their professional credentials and enhance their management skills. This fast-track program can be completed in twenty-eight months and offers class schedules to accommodate the working adult. Students have extensive and direct contact with experienced faculty members who bring a real-world orientation to the classroom. Students learn to master skills in communication, teamwork, diversity management, financial analysis, strategic thinking, and leadership. Students entering the program at the same time take courses together. This cohort system affords students mutual support and fosters team leadership and project management skills. Individual arrangements are made to accommodate special scheduling needs.

The Master of Science in Library and Information Science Program offered at the WGC is accredited by the American Library Association (ALA). New York State certification for the School Library Media Specialist Program (SLMS) is also offered.

Research Facilities

The high-tech adult-learning facility on the campus of Purchase College offers classrooms wired for computers and the Internet and access to Long Island University's Brooklyn and C.W. Post computerized library catalog system that enables students to do research from home.

Financial Aid

The Westchester Graduate Campus offers three types of Credit Bank scholarships based on undergraduate academic performance; scholarships for Dominican and Concordia College alumni; Purchase Community Scholarships for alumni of colleges located in Purchase, New York; the City of Yonkers Employee Scholarships; the Westchester County Employee Scholarships; and the Bilingual Extension Certificate Tuition Scholarships. New York State residents and residents of other states are eligible for loans guaranteed by New York State. United States citizenship or permanent resident status is required. Matriculated students registering for at least 6 credits per semester are eligible to apply for the Federal Perkins Loan program. Generally, students do not begin repayment on federal student loans until six months after graduation. However, repayment provisions may vary with each type of loan.

Cost of Study

Tuition for 2006–07 was $790 per credit plus fees. Tuition and fees are subject to change.

Location

The Westchester Graduate Campus is located 30 minutes north of Manhattan in Purchase, New York. The town of Purchase borders Greenwich, Connecticut, and White Plains, New York. The campus is easily accessible from the Metro North train station in White Plains and from major highways, including I-287, I-684, and the Hutchinson River Parkway.

The University

The Westchester Graduate Campus is one of six campuses of Long Island University, the seventh-largest university in the United States. The WGC offers students an intimate, personal environment supported by the resources of a large university. The campus is located on the grounds of Purchase College, which also houses the Neuberger Museum of Art and the Performing Arts Center.

Applying

Students who wish to apply for admission to any program can request a *Graduate Bulletin* and an application from the Admissions Office by phone at 914-831-2700 or by e-mail at westchester@liu.edu, or they can download an application from the admissions page of the WGC Web site at http://www.liu.edu/westchester.

Correspondence and Information

Ellen Brief
Coordinator of Admissions, Student Services, Marketing, and Public Relations
The Westchester Graduate Campus of Long Island University
735 Anderson Hill Road
Purchase, New York 10577

Phone: 914-831-2700
800-GRAD-LIU (toll-free)
Fax: 914-251-5959
E-mail: westchester@liu.edu
Web site: http://www.liu.edu/westchester

FACULTY HEADS

Sylvia Blake, Associate Provost and Academic Dean; Ed.D., Columbia Teachers College.
Iris Goldberg, Early Childhood/Childhood; Ph.D., NYU.
Lynn Gunnar Johnson, Business Administration; Ph.D., Michigan.
Helaine Marshall, TESOL, Bilingual, and LOTE; Ph.D., Columbia Teachers College.
Rebecca Rich, Literacy Education; Ed.D., Columbia Teachers College.
Janet Simon, Special Education and Secondary Education; Ed.D., Cincinnati.
Beth Weiner, School Counseling, School Psychology, Marriage and Family Therapy, and Mental Health Counseling; Psy.D., Yeshiva.

LOYOLA MARYMOUNT UNIVERSITY

Programs of Study

The mission of the Graduate Division at Loyola Marymount University (LMU) is to provide high-quality postbaccalaureate degree programs that serve to expand knowledge and foster professional development. Consistent with the Jesuit and Marymount traditions, LMU's rigorous graduate programs share the common goal of educating the whole person and offer unparalleled opportunities to its students in order to prepare them for life and leadership in the twenty-first century.

Graduate students are taught by dedicated and talented faculty members, most of whom hold doctoral degrees. Although they are well-regarded academicians, researchers, and publishers, the faculty's primary objective is teaching. Classes are small, and faculty members are accessible. Furthermore, most of the graduate programs are planned with working individuals in mind; therefore, a majority of the graduate courses are held in the late afternoon or evening.

The Graduate Division offers curricula leading to the Doctor of Education (Ed.D.), Master of Arts (M.A.), Master of Arts in Teaching (M.A.T., in mathematics), Master of Business Administration (M.B.A.), Master of Fine Arts (M.F.A.), Master of Science (M.S.), and Master of Science in Engineering (M.S.E.). In addition, the School of Education offers credential and certificate programs in Administrative Services, Elementary Teaching, Literacy and Language Arts, Pupil Personnel Services (School Counseling and School Psychology), Reading and Language Arts, Secondary Teaching, and Special Education (Education Specialist).

The Ed.D. is awarded in educational leadership for social justice. The M.A. is offered in administration; biliteracy, leadership, and intercultural education; bioethics; Catholic inclusive education; Catholic school administration; child and adolescent literacy; educational psychology; elementary education; English (literature, creative writing, and rhetoric and composition); general education; literacy and language arts; marital and family therapy; pastoral theology; philosophy; school counseling (guidance and counseling, and Catholic school counseling); secondary education; special education; and theology. The M.A.T. degree is conferred in mathematics. The M.B.A. degree is offered with emphases in entrepreneurial organizations, financial decision systems, human resource management, information and decision sciences, international business systems, management and organizational behavior, and marketing management; the Executive M.B.A. is also offered. The M.F.A. is awarded in film production, screenwriting, and television production. The M.S. is conferred in computer science, environmental science, or systems engineering. The M.S.E. is available in civil engineering, electrical engineering, mechanical engineering, and systems engineering. Dual-degree programs include the M.B.A./J.D. in business administration and law and the M.S./M.B.A. in systems engineering and leadership.

Research Facilities

Loyola Marymount University is proud of its Von der Ahe Library, which contains approximately 486,000 volumes and bound periodicals, 14,900 media titles, 140,000 microforms, 3,050 current periodical subscriptions, and more than 16,000 electronic periodical subscriptions and provides network access to various online index databases, as well as the University of California's online library catalog. The University is also the home of a variety of centers and institutes dedicated to specialized research, including the Bioethics Institute; Center for Asian Business; Center for Ethics and Business; Center for Executive Learning; Center for Ignatian Spirituality; Center for Religion and Spirituality; Center for Service and Action; Center for the Study of Los Angeles; Center for Teaching Excellence; Leadership in Equity, Advocacy, and Diversity Center (LEAD); Marymount Institute for Faith, Culture, and Arts; Small Business Development Center; and Basil P. Caloyeras Center for Modern Greek Studies.

Financial Aid

In addition to the availability of a wide variety of federal and state financial aid programs, Loyola Marymount students may also benefit from several grant programs, program-specific scholarship offerings, graduate assistantships, and other graduate student employment opportunities.

Cost of Study

Tuition for the 2007–08 academic year for most programs is $809 per unit (most classes are 3 units). All programs in the School of Education cost $830 per unit, except the doctoral program, which costs $1048 per unit. Tuition for the College of Science and Engineering, Department of Marital Family Therapy, and School of Film and Television is approximately $845 per unit. Tuition is $982 per unit for the M.B.A. and the Systems Engineering Leadership Program.

Living and Housing Costs

Limited on-campus graduate student housing is available on a first-come, first-served basis. Room and board in the surrounding residential area averages $11,000 for the academic year.

Student Group

Loyola Marymount University is the home of more than 5,500 undergraduate and 1,900 graduate students and currently enrolls students from forty-five states and 150 other countries. LMU celebrates diversity in its students, which is reflected in the graduate student body. The graduate students represent a diverse mixture of religions, geographical origins, ethnicities, and interests. In keeping with these values, LMU oversees over 100 student clubs and organizations that provide a forum and social events for the wide variety of student interests.

Location

The Graduate Division at Loyola Marymount University is located in the Westchester area, a friendly, peaceful, residential neighborhood with easy access to the cultural richness of the cosmopolitan Southern California life. One mile from the Pacific Ocean, LMU's students enjoy ocean and mountain vistas as well as the moderate climate and crisp breezes characteristic of a coastal location. Loyola Marymount is situated in an ideal location for living and learning.

The University

Founded in 1911, Loyola Marymount University is one of the premiere Jesuit universities in the country. The strength of LMU is in its commitment to providing excellent academic programs in an environment that supports the needs of the whole student. Proof of Loyola Marymount's success can be found in its more than 53,000 alumni, each a living representative of the academic excellence, moral and ethical standards, and spirit of high achievement that personify the Loyola Marymount experience.

Applying

Loyola Marymount University welcomes applications from students without regard to race, color, gender, creed, national origin, disability, marital status, or religion. All prospective graduate students are expected to provide evidence of suitable preparation for graduate-level work. Individual programs have specific deadlines, prerequisites, or additional requirements. Interested students should visit LMU's Web site (http://graduate.lmu.edu) for more information.

The application for graduate admission to LMU can be completed in one of two ways. It is recommended that applicants apply using the online application at http://apply.embark.com/grad/lmu. However, hard copies of applications are also accepted. Students should contact Graduate Admissions for a paper application.

Correspondence and Information

Graduate Admissions
University Hall, Suite 2500
Loyola Marymount University
One LMU Drive
Los Angeles, California 90045-2659
Phone: 310-338-2721
888-946-5681 (toll-free)
Fax: 310-338-6086
E-mail: graduate@lmu.edu
Web site: http://graduate.lmu.edu

PROGRAM DIRECTORS

Bioethics Program: Dr. John Connolly Jr. (jconnoll@lmu.edu; 310-338-2754)
Civil Engineering and Environmental Science Program: Professor Joseph Reichenberger. (jreichenberger@lmu.edu; 310-338-2830)
Electrical Engineering and Computer Science Program: Dr. Stephanie August. (saugust@lmu.edu; 310-338-5973)
Marital and Family Therapy Program: Dr. Debra Linesch. (dlinesch@lmu.edu; 310-338-4562)
M.B.A. Program: Dr. Rachelle Katz. (rkatz@lmu.edu; 310-338-2848)
Mechanical Engineering Program: Dr. Bo Oppenheim. (boppenheim@lmu.edu; 310-338-2825)
Systems Engineering Leadership Program: Dr. Fred Brown. (fbrown@lmu.edu; 310-338-7878)
Teaching Mathematics Program (M.A.T.): Dr. Michael Grady. (mgrady@lmu.edu; 310-338-5107)
English Department: Dr. Paul Harris. (pharris@lmu.edu; 310-338-4452)
Philosophy Department: Dr. Mark Morelli. (mmorelli@lmu.edu; 310-338-7384)
Theology and Pastoral Theology Department: Dr. Michael Horan. (mhoran@lmu.edu; 310-338-2755)
School of Education: Dr. Beth Stoddard. (soeinfo@lmu.edu; 310-338-2863)
School of Education (Professional Services–Administration, Counseling, Educational Psychology, and Leadership for Social Justice): Dr. Mary McCullough. (soeinfo@lmu.edu; 310-338-2863)
School of Education (Bilingual Education, Child and Adolescent Literacy, Elementary Education, General Education, Secondary Education, Special Education, Teacher Education, and Teacher Certificates): Dr. Magaly Lavadenz. (soeinfo@lmu.edu; 310-338-2863)
School of Film and Television: Glenn Gebhard. (ggebhard@lmu.edu; 310-338-3025)

Loyola Marymount University campus.

LOYOLA UNIVERSITY CHICAGO

Graduate School

Programs of Study

The Graduate School is dedicated to the training of talented women and men who strive for understanding and truth in a humane environment. Programs of advanced study with academic and applied orientations are offered in the humanities, social sciences, and natural science disciplines, as well as in interdisciplinary science areas and dual-degree programs.

Master's and doctoral degrees are offered in administration and supervision, anatomy, biochemistry, chemistry, child development, clinical psychology, counseling, developmental psychology, cultural and educational policy studies, educational and school psychology, English, higher education, history, microbiology, molecular biology, neuroscience, nursing, pharmacology, philosophy, physiology, political science, research methodology, social psychology, social work, sociology, and theology. Master's degrees are offered in biology, community counseling, computer science, criminal justice, curriculum and instruction, mathematics and statistics, medical sciences, pastoral counseling, Spanish, and women's studies. The M.Div. degree is offered through the Institute of Pastoral Studies. Interdisciplinary areas include doctoral programs in neuroscience and in molecular biology. Dual degrees are available in M.D./Ph.D., M.D./M.S., and J.D./M.A. programs.

Research Facilities

The combined libraries of the University contain more than 1 million volumes, with standing orders for more than 7,800 serials, 650,000 microforms, and 21,000 pieces of audiovisual material. The library subscribes to several computerized online services, data search networks, and interlibrary access and loan programs.

The Academic Computing Service, with centers on all campuses, houses up-to-date equipment and software for use by students and faculty. To ensure convenient access to all users, programming advisers are housed on all campuses; terminals and personal computers are located throughout the University.

Specialized laboratory facilities are maintained in the basic medical science, science, and social science departments.

Financial Aid

In the 2004–05 academic year, Graduate School students at Loyola University Chicago received approximately $5.7 million in assistantship and fellowship stipends as well as about $3.5 million in tuition scholarships. These awards are assigned on a competitive basis for a period of one year to students with outstanding records. Reappointments are made on the basis of good academic standing and proven competence. In most instances, the award includes a full tuition scholarship and a stipend; teaching and/or research services are required in some departments and for some awards.

Cost of Study

Tuition for courses offered by the Graduate School for the 2005–06 academic year was approximately $645 per credit hour. Tuition rates for nursing, social work, medical sciences, pastoral studies, and all other graduate programs can be found at http://www.luc.edu/bursar/tuition/shtml.

Living and Housing Costs

There is limited graduate housing available on campus. Housing costs in the Chicago area vary considerably. Information is available through the Graduate School.

Student Group

Of the approximately 14,000 students attending Loyola University Chicago, more than 1,500 are enrolled in the various departments and programs of the Graduate School. Students come from all areas of the United States and many other countries.

Student Outcomes

More than 100,000 Loyola alumni are spread throughout every state of the nation and in at least 121 countries throughout the world. Among their ranks are hundreds of CEOs of major corporations and health-care institutions, dozens of state and national legislators, scores of circuit court and federal judges, and a number of presidents of nationally recognized universities.

Location

Chicago, the nation's third-largest city, is an international center for academics, art, business, culture, and sports. The University operates an academic medical center and four higher education campuses, three in the Chicago area and one in Rome, Italy.

The University

Founded in 1870, Loyola is a Jesuit, Catholic university dedicated to excellence in teaching, research, health care, and community service. Programs in the University's nine schools and colleges focus not only on intellectual growth but also on the social, cultural, and spiritual development of the students they serve.

Applying

All applicants must submit a completed application form and official transcripts. Most departments and programs also require the results of the Graduate Record Examinations. Additional material is required by some departments. Students should consult the *Graduate School Bulletin* for details. Applicants may apply online at http://www.luc.edu/gpem.

Applications are accepted throughout the year by most departments. Students who wish to be considered for need-based financial aid and merit awards must have their completed applications on file by February 1. Because there are some exceptions to this deadline, students should consult the *Graduate School Bulletin* for details.

Students from abroad must have proficiency in written and spoken English. Students for whom English is not the native language are required to submit scores from the TOEFL. Students from other countries are tested for competence in the English language and may have to take ESL courses.

Detailed descriptions of programs and procedures are found in the *Graduate School Bulletin.*

Correspondence and Information

Requests for additional information and applications should be directed to:

Graduate Enrollment Management
Loyola University Chicago
820 North Michigan Avenue, Suite 800
Chicago, Illinois 60611
Phone: 312-915-8964
Web site: http://www.luc.edu/gpem

GRADUATE PROGRAMS

Biomedical Sciences
Biochemistry, Molecular and Cellular (M.S., Ph.D.)
Bioethics and Health Policy (Online M.A., Online Certificate)
Cell and Molecular Physiology (M.S., Ph.D.)
Cellular Biology, Neurobiology, and Anatomy (M.S., Ph.D.)
Clinical Research Methods (M.S.)
Integrated Program in the Biomedical Sciences (Ph.D.)
M.D./Ph.D. Program with Stritch School of Medicine
Microbiology and Immunology (Ph.D.)
Molecular Biology (Ph.D.)
Neuroscience (M.S., Ph.D.)
Pharmacology and Experimental Therapeutics (M.S., Ph.D.)

Education
Administration and Supervision, Higher Education (Ed.D., M.Ed.)
Community Counseling (M.A., M.Ed.)
Counseling Psychology (Ph.D.)
Cultural and Educational Policy Studies (M.A., M.Ed., Ph.D.)
Curriculum and Instruction (M.Ed., Ed.D.)
Educational Psychology (M.Ed.)
Elementary Education (M.Ed.)
Higher Education (M.Ed., Ph.D.)
Instructional Leadership (M.Ed.)
Reading (M.Ed.)
Research Methodology (M.A., M.Ed., Ph.D.)
School Counseling (M.Ed., Type 73 Certificate)
School Psychology (Ed.S., M.Ed./Ed.S., Ph.D.)
School Technology (M.Ed.)
Science Education (M.Ed.)
Secondary Education (M.Ed.)
Special Education (M.Ed.)
Type 75 Principal (Certificate)
Type 75 Superintendent (Certificate)

Humanities
English (M.A., Ph.D.)
History (M.A., Ph.D.)
History: Public History (M.A.)
Philosophy (M.A., Ph.D.)
Philosophy: Applied (M.A.)
Spanish (M.A.)
Theology (M.A., Ph.D.)

Nursing
Nursing (Ph.D.) Interested students should see http://www.luc.edu/nursing for more information on the M.S. and M.S.N. degrees and numerous certificates offered by the Niehoff School of Nursing.

Pastoral Studies
Divinity (M.Div.)
Pastoral Counseling (M.A., Certificate)
Pastoral Studies (M.A., Online M.A.)
Religious Education (M.A., Certificate)
Social Justice (M.A., Certificate)
Spirituality (M.A.)

Mathematics and Sciences
Applied Statistics (M.S.)
Biology (M.S.)
Chemistry (M.S., Ph.D.)
Computer Science: Information Technology (M.S.)
Computer Science: Scientific and Technical Computing (M.S.)
Computer Science: Software Technology (M.S.)
Mathematics and Statistics (M.S.)
Medical Sciences (M.A.)

Social Sciences
Child Development (Ph.D.)
Criminal Justice (M.A.)
Political Science (M.A., Ph.D.)
Psychology: Applied Social (M.A., Ph.D.)
Psychology: Clinical (Ph.D.)
Psychology: Developmental (Ph.D.)
Social Work (Ph.D.) Interested students should see http://www.luc.edu/socialwork for more information on the M.S. and M.S.W. degrees and numerous certificate offered by the School of Social Work.
Sociology (M.A., Ph.D.)
Sociology: Applied (M.A.)
Urban Affairs and Public Policy (M.A.)
Women's Studies (M.A., Certificate)

MANHATTANVILLE COLLEGE

School of Graduate and Professional Studies

Programs of Study

Manhattanville's School of Graduate and Professional Studies offers career-oriented individuals the opportunity to acquire the skills they need to become effective leaders and advance their career tracks. The School offers part-time and accelerated programs at both the undergraduate and graduate levels.

Manhattanville offers six business programs of study. The five Master of Science (M.S.) programs (Leadership and Strategic Management, Organizational Management and Human Resource Development, Integrated Marketing Communications, International Management, and Sport Business Management) are offered in convenient one-weekend-per-month, weekday, and evening class schedules. A Certificate in Nonprofit Leadership program is also offered. The curriculum is designed and taught by executives presently employed in their field of expertise. Two Master of Arts (M.A.) programs are also offered (Liberal Studies and Writing). All master's programs have been developed to be completed within two years.

The Master of Science in Leadership and Strategic Management program is a 39-credit program providing advanced training in strategic management and planning and fostering the development of effective leadership skills. The learning is current, streamlined, and designed to allow managers and executives to excel in a rapidly changing and increasingly global work environment. Degree requirements include twelve courses and a final integrative project.

The Master of Science in Organizational Management and Human Resource Development program is a 36-credit program that provides training in human resources skills and organizational management for professionals who want to enter or already work in the human resources field. Emphasis is on a strong theoretical background as well as development of practical, administrative, and management skills for individuals in corporations, small businesses, government, education, and the not-for-profit sector. Degree requirements include eleven courses and a thesis or final project option.

The Master of Science in Integrated Marketing Communications program is a 36-credit program. It provides advanced training in developing a communications strategy that is integrated with an organization's marketing and financial objectives. Students learn the principles of effective communications in global settings and the communication issues involved in marketing brand management and public relations. Degree requirements include eleven courses and a final integrative project.

The Master of Science in International Management program is a 36-credit program designed to prepare business leaders to meet the evolving challenges of international management and to seize opportunities for business success in both mature and expanding markets. Courses are designed to emphasize the development of practical management skills against a strong background of theory and values-based leadership principles. The learning environment promotes a high level of interaction between faculty members and students and among students themselves. Degree requirements include eleven courses and a final integrative project.

The Master of Arts in Liberal Studies (M.A.L.S.), a 30-credit program, has been aptly described as a "time for your mind." This unique master's degree program cuts across many disciplines—art, literature, music, psychology, religion, sociology, philosophy, history, and politics. The M.A.L.S., designed for adult and part-time students, is self-paced and flexibly scheduled.

The Master of Arts in Writing program is a 32-credit program designed for writers and aspiring writers. The program enables students to develop skills in writing while deepening their knowledge of the humanities. All required courses are scheduled in the evening, with the exception of the intensive Summer Writers' Week and Writers' Weekend. A final project of an original piece of writing is required.

The Certificate in Nonprofit Leadership requires 18 credits and may be completed in nine months. Under the guidance of executives and consultants currently working in the nonprofit and private sectors, the program targets key topics of concern to the leaders of nonprofit organizations with a focus on its application to day-to-day decisions. The curriculum is also well suited to accelerate the understanding of the challenges facing leaders in the nonprofit sector for those aspiring to leadership positions.

For individuals who have not yet completed their undergraduate degrees, Manhattanville offers three accelerated programs for part-time students: Bachelor of Science (B.S.) in Behavioral Studies program, the B.S. in Communications Management program, and the B.S. in Organizational Management program. Students may pursue a dual degree in Creative Writing. Eligible students may take up to 8 credits in graduate-level courses, which can be applied toward both the undergraduate degree and the Master of Arts in Writing. This program is designed for students with a grade point average of 3.4 or better. Students may also pursue a dual-degree program with the School of Education. Eligible students may take up to five graduate-level education courses, which can be applied toward both the undergraduate degree and the Master of Arts in Teaching. These accelerated programs are designed for students who have earned an Associate of Arts degree or those who have accumulated 60–75 undergraduate credits with a grade point average of 2.5 or better and now want the personal and professional benefits of earning a degree. To enroll, students must have at least two years of work experience. Most of these programs may be completed within eighteen months.

Research Facilities

Manhattanville has been named one of the Top 100 Wired Colleges in the U.S. The Manhattanville Library capitalizes on the power of the Internet to connect students with information and analysis found in powerful subscription databases, electronic journals, and electronic books. Manhattanville is one of the first colleges in the U.S. to outsource a service that enables students to interact online with experienced reference librarians at any time of the day or night from anywhere in the world. The virtual research service, "Ask a Librarian 24/7," uses co-browsing to connect students with professional librarians who can answer questions about research and help students navigate the College's extensive array of subscription databases and other library resources. Manhattanville's teaching library, which supports the School of Education, ranks among the foremost undergraduate teaching libraries in the country. The Menendez Language Laboratory includes tapes and record libraries that provide materials for class instruction and individual practice in French, Spanish, Russian, Italian, German, Chinese, Japanese, Hindi, Marathi, modern Hebrew, and English as a second language. The College provides a writing clinic, a reading clinic, audiovisual facilities, and a bibliographic instruction program. The library building is open 24 hours a day, seven days a week through most of the fall and spring semesters, and it has computer labs, quiet study areas, group-study rooms, and a café, where students and faculty members can meet informally.

Financial Aid

Federal Stafford Student Loans, as well as a deferred payment plan, are available for graduate students. For further information, prospective students can contact the Office of Financial Aid, Reid Hall, Purchase, New York, 10577 (telephone: 914-323-5357).

Cost of Study

For 2006–07, tuition was $620 per credit for a Master of Science degree, $550 per credit for a Master of Arts degree, and $500 for a Bachelor of Science degree. There is a semester registration fee of $40.

Living and Housing Costs

Most School of Graduate and Professional Studies students live off campus and work in communities throughout Westchester and the surrounding counties. For campus housing information, students should call Residence Life at 914-323-5217.

Location

Manhattanville's 100-acre suburban campus is located in New York's Westchester County, just minutes from White Plains to the west and Greenwich, Connecticut, to the east. It is 30 miles from Manhattan. Many prominent corporate offices—IBM, MasterCard, Morgan Stanley, and PepsiCo—are headquartered nearby. The campus is accessible by public transportation.

The College

Manhattanville College is a coeducational, independent liberal arts college whose mission is to educate ethically and socially responsible leaders for the global community. Founded in 1841, the College has 1,600 undergraduate students and 1,000 graduate students. Manhattanville offers bachelor's and master's degrees in more than fifty academic concentrations in the arts and sciences. Its curriculum nurtures intellectual curiosity and independent thinking.

Applying

Applications to the School of Graduate and Professional Studies are reviewed on a continuing basis. Application requirements for the B.S. and M.S. programs include a completed application form, a resume, an autobiographical essay, an admissions interview, two recommendations, and official transcripts of all previous undergraduate and graduate college work.

For the Master of Arts in Writing program, submission of a 10- to 12-page creative writing sample, including at least five pages of prose, is substituted for the resume and letters of recommendation.

Correspondence and Information

Natalia Fernandez
Director of Admissions
Graduate and Professional Studies
Manhattanville College
2900 Purchase Street
Purchase, New York 10277

Phone: 914-694-3425
Fax: 914-323-1988
E-mail: gps@mville.edu
Web site: http://www.mville.edu

THE FACULTY

School of Graduate and Professional Studies Administration
Ruth Dowd, R.S.C.J., Professor of Philosophy and Dean; Ph.D. Fordham.
Donald J. Richards, Associate Dean; Ph.D., Notre Dame; M.B.A., LIU.
Andrea J. Covell, Assistant Dean; Ph.D., USC.

Master of Arts in Writing
Linda A. Simone, M.A.W., Manhattanville.

ADJUNCT FACULTY

Master of Science Programs (Integrated Marketing Communication, Leadership and Strategic Management, Organizational Management and Human Resource Development, International Management, and Sport Business Management)
Laurie J. Bilik, M.B.A., NYU. President, Global Human Resources, Inc.
Cynthia Brosnan, M.B.A., NYU. Management development consultant.
Harriet W. Cabell, Ed.D., Alabama, M.L.E., Harvard. Cabell & Associates.
Michael Crystal, M.B.A., Ph.D., Connecticut. Advanced Management Program, Stanford. Managing Principal, Myriad Development Group.
Gene Herbster, M.A., Seton Hall; M.S., Stevens. President, Gene A. Herbster & Associates, Inc.
David R. Lipsky, Ph.D., Hofstra. Manager in Organizational Effectiveness, Sony Electronics.
Mark Misercola, M.A., SUNY at Buffalo. Director of Internal Communications, Deutsche Bank.
Andy Paul, J.D., George Washington. Deputy Director, Metro North Railroad.
Thomas Schwartz, Ph.D., UCLA. President, Tri-State Nannies.
William Stopper, M.B.A., Connecticut. Partner, The Walker Group.
Robert Watson, M.B.A., USC. Consultant.
Morrison Webb, J.D., Harvard.
Rex W. Mixon Jr., J.D., Cornell, M.B.A., Cornell.

MARSHALL UNIVERSITY

Graduate College

Programs of Study

The Graduate College at Marshall University offers programs of study leading to the degrees of Master of Arts, Master of Science, Master of Business Administration, Master of Arts in Teaching, Master of Arts in Journalism, Master of Science in Nursing, Master of Science in Engineering, Doctor of Education, Doctor of Psychology, and Doctor of Philosophy in biomedical sciences. Education Specialist degrees are also available in school psychology and education (adult and technical education, counseling, leadership studies, and curriculum and instruction). Students should see the reverse side of this page for a detailed listing of graduate programs and the directors or department chairpersons involved in the programs. These graduate programs provide students with outstanding opportunities for advanced professional preparation, basic research, and applied research.

There are three basic requirements for most master's degrees: a minimum of 36 credit hours in graduate courses or 32 hours if a thesis option is chosen, including 6 hours for the thesis; a minimum grade point average of 3.0 (B) in all graduate courses applicable to the degree; and the comprehensive assessment, which can be written, oral, or both and which is taken when the student is nearing completion of all course work.

Since more than half of the graduate students at Marshall University attend on a part-time basis while working, a special effort is made to offer graduate courses in the late afternoon and evening. Full-time graduate students usually complete the master's degree requirements in one or two calendar years, part-time students in three or four years. The English as a Second Language Institute is available to international students.

Research Facilities

Marshall University Research Corporation is the contract and financial management agent for research/service contracts and grants of the University, with funding in excess of $50 million annually from such sources as the National Science Foundation, the National Institutes of Health, and the Economic Development Administration. Marshall maintains the University Computer Center, University Theater, Psychology Clinic, Speech Clinic, Writing Center, Learning Resources Center, language laboratory, chemistry and physics laboratories, mathematics laboratory, WMUL-FM, WPBY-TV, instructional television, extensive facilities in the Departments of Art and Music, and biomedical science facilities for DNA research. The John Deaver Drinko Library is a state-of-the-art electronic information center. The James Morrow Library houses one of the largest collections of materials from the antebellum South in the world. In addition, General Chuck Yeager has donated his memorabilia to Marshall.

Financial Aid

Graduate teaching and/or research assistantships are available in most departments offering graduate degrees. Information can be obtained from the individual department chairpersons. Inquiries about work-study opportunities, loans, and other forms of financial assistance should be directed to the Financial Aid Office. A brochure is available from the Dean of the Graduate College's office.

Cost of Study

Full-time West Virginia residents paid a base enrollment fee of $2193 per regular semester in 2006–07. Full-time nonresidents paid a base tuition of $6164 per regular semester. (Fees are subject to change.) Part-time students enrolling for 8 hours or less paid fees on the basis of a graduated hourly scale. Metro fees, a reduced fee structure for out-of-state students from certain counties of Ohio, Virginia, Maryland, and Kentucky, were $4046 per semester. There are additional fees for students in the health professions; the Colleges Business, Fine Arts, and Information Technology and Engineering; and the Ph.D. in psychology program.

Living and Housing Costs

The Huntington and Charleston areas offer a great variety of living accommodations, from $300 per month upward. Men's and women's residence halls are located on the main campus; room and board for a single student ranged from $1809 for a double room to $2818 for a single room (plus $1800 for nineteen meals weekly) per semester in 2006–07. (Fees are subject to change.) Married student housing units are located on the University Heights campus, within easy driving distance of the main campus. These furnished units range from $401 to $579 per month, including utilities.

Student Group

The University's total enrollment is approximately 14,000, of whom about 15 percent are out-of-state students. Enrollment in the Graduate College is approximately 4,000.

Location

Huntington, with a population of approximately 50,000, in a tristate metropolitan region with a population of 300,000, is situated on the banks of the Ohio River. There is a well-planned park system on the south side of the community. Several major industries are located in this area, including the CSX railway, Special Metals Company, and ACF Industries. There are two television stations, five radio stations, numerous theaters, an amusement park, boating facilities, and swimming pools. The community is noted for its friendliness.

The South Charleston campus is located just outside the state capital, a city of approximately 50,000 people. It is the political center of West Virginia and offers excellent restaurants, museums, and cultural centers.

The University

Founded in 1837, Marshall University is assisted by the state of West Virginia. The main campuses are located in Huntington and South Charleston. The Graduate College was authorized in 1948. The University provides a broad program of cultural programs through the Artists Series and the Departments of Art, Music, and English. The School of Medicine graduated its first class in 1981. The West Virginia Graduate College and Marshall University merged in 1997.

Marshall University is accredited by The Higher Learning Commission of the North Central Association of Colleges and Schools, and appropriate programs are accredited by the National Council for Accreditation of Teacher Education. It is a member of the Council of Graduate Schools. The business administration program is accredited by AACSB International–The Association to Advance Collegiate Schools of Business.

Applying

Admission is based on official transcripts of college credit; GRE, MAT, or GMAT scores; the information provided on the application form; and whatever examinations and conditions the Graduate College may require; some programs also require letters of recommendation. Applications are due at least two weeks prior to the beginning of the term of anticipated enrollment. Many departments have earlier application deadlines.

Correspondence and Information

Leonard J. Deutsch
Dean of the Graduate College
Marshall University
Huntington, West Virginia 25755-2100

Phone: 304-696-6606
E-mail: deutschl@marshall.edu
Web site: http://www.marshall.edu

FACULTY HEADS

College of Business

Business Administration (M.B.A.): Dr. Andrew Sikula, Associate Dean of Graduate Programs.
Human Resource Management (M.S.): Dr. Andrew Sikula, Associate Dean of Graduate Programs.
Health Care Management (M.S.): Dr. Andrew Sikula, Associate Dean of Graduate Programs.

College of Education

Adult and Technical Education (M.A., M.S.): Dr. LeVene A. Olson, Chairperson. Adult, business, career, cooperative, marketing, and vocational-technical education.
Counseling (M.A.): Dr. Michael Burton, Program Coordinator. Elementary, secondary school, higher education, and agency counseling.
Educational Administration (M.A., Ed.D.): Dr. Mike Cunningham, Program Coordinator. Elementary and secondary school principal studies, higher education, supervision, school superintendent studies.
Exercise Science (M.S.): Dr. William Marley, Program Coordinator.
Family and Consumer Science (M.A.): Dr. Mary Mhango, Program Coordinator. Foods and nutrition, home management, consumer economics, teacher education.
Sport Administration (M.S.): Dr. Dan Martin, Chairperson. Professional health education, professional physical education, athletic training, adult physical fitness, cardiac rehabilitation.
School Psychology (Ed.S.): Dr. Steve O'Keefe, Program Director. Advanced psychology and school psychology.
Teacher Education (M.A.): Dr. Carl Johnson, Division Head. Early childhood, elementary, middle childhood, secondary, reading, and special education in the areas of behavioral disorders, gifted, learning disabilities, mentally impaired, and physically handicapped.
Teaching (M.A.T.): Dr. James Sottile, Division Head. Certification for undergraduate content specialization.

College of Fine Arts

Art (M.A.): Professor Byron Clercx, Chairperson. Painting, drawing, sculpture, graphics, ceramics, weaving, art history, art education.
Music (M.A.): Dr. Stephen Lawson, Chairperson. Instrumental music, vocal music, church music, performance, history, literature, theory, composition, music supervision, teacher education.

College of Liberal Arts

Communication Studies (M.A.): Dr. Robert Edmunds, Chairperson. Speech communication.
Criminal Justice (M.S.): Professor Peggy Brown, Chairperson. Corrections and law enforcement.
English (M.A.): Dr. David Hatfield, Chairperson. American and English literature and language.
Geography (M.A., M.S.): Professor Larry Jarrett, Chairperson. Cultural geography, conservation, cartography.
History (M.A.): Dr. Donna Spindel, Chairperson. American, European, and Asian history.
Humanities (M.A.): Dr. Eric Lassiter, Director of Flexible Interdisciplinary Program.
Political Science (M.A.): Dr. Robert Behrman, Chairperson. American national and state government, comparative government, international governments, public administration, theory.
Psychology (M.A.): Dr. Marty Amerikaner, Chairperson. General-theoretical psychology, clinical psychology, and school psychology.
Sociology and Anthropology (M.A.): Dr. Ken Ambrose, Chairperson. General sociology, community development, industrial relations, sociology of the Appalachian region, medical anthropology.

College of Science

Biological Sciences (M.A., M.S.): Dr. Chuck Somerville, Chairperson. Environmental biology, plant and animal taxonomy, aquatic ecology, plant cell biology, evolutionary biology and systematics, plant and animal physiology, biological science education.
Chemistry (M.S.): Dr. Michael Castellani, Chairperson. Organic, physical, and analytical chemistry; interdisciplinary program in physical science.
Mathematics (M.A.): Dr. Ralph Oberste-Vorth, Chairperson. Algebra, topology, analysis, interdisciplinary program in physical science, teacher education.
Physical Science and Physics (M.A., M.S.): Dr. Ron Martino, Advisor. Interdisciplinary program in physical science, teacher education.

College of Information Technology and Engineering

Engineering (M.S.): Dr. William Pierson, PE, Chairperson. Areas of emphasis available in chemical engineering, engineering management, environmental engineering.
Environmental Science (M.S.): Dr. D. Allen Stern, PE, Chairperson. Breadth in dealing with environmental issues, analytical tools for addressing state and national issues.
Information Systems (M.S.): Dr. William Piersen, PE, Division Chair. Information system information analysis, design, development, effective use.
Safety Technology (M.S.): Dr. D. Allan Stern, Program Coordinator. Ergonomics, industrial hygiene, occupational safety and health, safety management, mine safety.
Technology Management (M.S.): Dr. D. Allen Stern. Technology planning, quality, and productivity management: information technology, environmental management, manufacturing systems, transportation systems, and technologies.

School of Medicine

Biomedical Science (M.S., Ph.D.): Dr. Richard Niles, Associate Dean. Biochemistry, anatomy, physiology, pharmacology, microbiology.
Forensic Science (M.S.): Dr. Terry Fenger. DNA and other forensic evidence from a scientific and legal perspective.

College of Nursing and Health Professionals

Communication Disorders (M.A.): Professor Kathy Chezik, Chairperson. Speech pathology and audiology.
Dietetics (M.S.): Dr. Kelli Williams, Graduate degree credential for those with licensure.
Nursing (M.S.N.): Dr. Shortie McKenzie, Dean. Family nurse practitioner studies.

School of Journalism and Mass Communication

Journalism (M.A.J.): Dr. Corley Dennison, Dean of the School. News-editorial writing, public relations, broadcast-TV journalism, advertising, teacher education.

Graduate School

Programs of Study

The Graduate School at Miami University offers programs leading to master's, specialist's, and doctoral degrees. Ph.D. programs are offered in botany, chemistry, educational leadership, English, geology, history, microbiology, political science, psychology, social gerontology, and zoology. The Ed.D. degree is offered in educational leadership. There are more than fifty different master's degree programs and fields of concentration offered by thirty-six departments in five academic divisions and the Institute of Environmental Sciences. The degrees offered are Master of Accountancy, Master of Architecture, Master of Arts, Master of Arts in Teaching, Master of Business Administration, Master of Education, Master of Environmental Science, Master of Fine Arts, Master of Gerontological Studies, Master of Music, Master of Science, Master of Science in Statistics, Master of Computer Science, and Master of Technical and Scientific Communication. A post-master's degree program leads to the Specialist in Education (Ed.S.) degree in school psychology.

The doctorate requires a minimum of 60 semester hours beyond the master's degree, the passing of a comprehensive examination, and the writing and defense of a dissertation. Language and research requirements for the doctorate are determined by individual departments. Both practice-oriented and research-oriented master's degree programs are offered, generally requiring a minimum of 30 semester hours, although some programs require more. Practice-oriented programs generally require internships or practicum experience in appropriate professional positions.

Research Facilities

The University libraries on the central campus at Oxford contain more than 1.8 million cataloged volumes, a government-documents collection of 90,000 volumes, and more than 2.1 million microforms. At present, the libraries receive more than 10,000 current periodicals and newspapers. The Edgar W. King Library building has a seating capacity of 2,000. Its facilities include rooms for the visually handicapped and for small-group study, a microform reading area, a record library with listening rooms, a student lounge, and special collections. The Brill Science Library houses more than 200,000 cataloged volumes and 1,800 journals in the science disciplines; it has a seating capacity of 700. The Walter E. Havighurst Special Collections Library includes the Edgar W. King Collection of Early Juvenile Books, the Samuel F. Covington Collection of Ohio Valley History, rare books, and special research materials and manuscripts. In addition, collections are housed in branch libraries for art and architecture and for music on the Oxford campus, in the Rentschler Library on the Hamilton campus, and in the Gardner-Harvey Library on the Middletown campus. The McGuffey Museum, designated a National Historic Landmark, has one of the finest collections of McGuffey Readers in the United States.

Other research facilities include the Institute of Environmental Sciences, the Scripps Gerontology Center, the Bachelor Wildlife Reserve, the Ecology Research Center, the Computer Centers, the Molecular Microspectroscopy Laboratory, the High Performance Computing cluster, child study and clinical psychology facilities, and a speech and hearing clinic. Major equipment (including electron microscopes, spectrophotometers, ultracentrifuges, nuclear magnetic resonators, and minicomputers), a greenhouse, and well-equipped laboratories support research in the science areas. Miami University will be the first North American institution to have an 850-mHz NMR, which researchers will use for disease biomarker studies.

Financial Aid

Financial support includes graduate assistantships, associateships, and grants-in-aid (tuition waivers). Stipends for full awards for assistantships and scholarships ranged from $4345 to $18,752 for the academic year 2006–07, plus a waiver of in-state and out-of-state instructional fees. Award holders also receive a waiver of summer instructional fees and a scholarship of up to $1800 for study during summer sessions. Inquiries about assistantships or associateships should be addressed to the appropriate academic department or program.

Cost of Study

In 2006–07, the instructional fee was $4548 per semester for a full load (12 hours) for Ohio residents and an additional $6065 for nonresidents. The student fees were $766 per semester. Graduate award holders paid reduced student fees of $383 per semester.

Living and Housing Costs

Students can call 513-529-5000 for housing information. Most graduate students live in apartments off campus in Oxford.

Student Group

Graduate students compose approximately 10 percent of the 16,000 enrollment at Miami's Oxford campus. A limited number of graduate courses are also offered at Miami's regional campuses in Hamilton and Middletown. Approximately 53 percent of Miami's full-time graduate students are women, 9 percent are members of ethnic minorities, and 16 percent are international scholars.

Location

Miami University is located in a small-town setting in southwestern Ohio, approximately 35 miles from Cincinnati and 45 miles from Dayton. Oxford has a resident population of 17,500.

The University

Miami University is a state-assisted university. It was established in 1809 and is the second-oldest institution of higher education in Ohio. The University has been engaged in graduate education since 1826, and its first earned master's degree was awarded in 1830. In 1947, graduate study was coordinated into the Graduate School. Doctoral programs began in 1967, with the first doctoral degrees awarded in 1969.

Applying

Applications for admission must be received at least one month before classes begin. Applications for financial support for the academic year must be received by March 1 for the following fall semester.

Correspondence and Information

Graduate School
102 Roudebush Hall
Miami University
Oxford, Ohio 45056

Phone: 513-529-3734
Fax: 513-529-3762
E-mail: gradschool@muohio.edu
Web site: http://www.miami.muohio.edu/graduate

FACULTY HEADS

The academic department chairpersons are listed below. Doctoral departments are indicated by an asterisk.

Accountancy: Mark Rubin, Ph.D., Texas at Austin.
Architecture and Interior Design: John Weigand (interim), Ph.D., Illinois at Urbana-Champaign.
Art/Art Education: dele jegede, Ph.D., Indiana.
*Botany: Linda Watson, Ph.D., Oklahoma.
*Chemistry and Biochemistry: Chris Makaroff, Ph.D., Purdue.
Communication: Gary Shulman, Ph.D., Purdue.
Comparative Religion: Liz Wilson, Ph.D., Chicago.
Computer Science and Systems Analysis: Douglas A. Troy, Ph.D., Waikato (New Zealand).
Decision Sciences: H. Jeff Smith, Ph.D., Cincinnati.
Economics: George Davis (Interim), Ph.D., SMU.
*Educational Leadership: Kate Rousmaniere, Ph.D., Columbia.
Educational Psychology: T. Stewart Watson, Ph.D., Nebraska–Lincoln.
*English: Keith Tuma, Ph.D., Chicago.
Environmental Sciences: Mark Boardman, Ph.D., North Carolina at Chapel Hill.
Family Studies and Social Work: Gary Peterson, Ph.D., Brigham Young.
Finance: Saul W. Adelman, Ph.D., Georgia.
French and Italian: Jonathan Strauss, Ph.D., Yale.
Geography: W. M. Renwick, Ph.D., Clark.
*Geology: William Hart, Ph.D., Case Western Reserve.
Gerontological Studies: C. Lee Harrington, Ph.D., California, Santa Barbara.
History: Mary Kupiec Cayton, Ph.D., Brown.
Management: Kay Snavely, Ph.D., Cincinnati.
Marketing: James Stearns, Ph.D., Florida State.
Mathematics and Statistics: Mark A. Smith, Ph.D., Illinois.
M.B.A. Program: Brad Bays, M.B.A., Indiana.
*Microbiology: Luis Actis (interim), Ph.D., Cordoba (Argentina).
Music: Richard Green, Ph.D., Illinois.
Paper Science and Engineering: Shashi Lalvani, Ph.D., Connecticut.
Philosophy: William McKenna, Ph.D., New School for Social Research.
Physical Education, Health, and Sport Studies: Melissa Chase (interim), Ph.D., Michigan State.
Physics: Michael Pechan, Ph.D., Iowa State.
*Political Science: Ryan Barilleaux. Ph.D., Texas.
*Psychology: Carl Paternite (interim), Ph.D., Iowa.
Spanish and Portuguese: Charles Ganelin, Ph.D., Chicago.
Speech Pathology and Audiology: Kathleen Hutchinson, Ph.D., Penn State.
Teacher Education: James Shiveley, Ph.D., Ohio State.
Technical and Scientific Communications: Jean Ann Lutz, Ph.D., Rensselaer.
Theater: Elizabeth Mullinex, Ph.D., Illinois at Urbana-Champaign.
*Zoology: Douglas B. Meikle, Ph.D., Bowling Green.

MICHIGAN STATE UNIVERSITY

Graduate School

Programs of Study

Michigan State University has thirteen graduate degree granting colleges with more than 100 departments offering approximately 300 programs of study leading to a master's and/or doctoral degree. Doctoral degree offerings are: African American and African studies; agricultural economics; agricultural technology and systems management; American studies; animal science; anthropology; applied mathematics; biochemistry and molecular biology; biosystems engineering; business administration (accounting, business information systems, finance, logistics, marketing, operations and sourcing management, organizational behavior and human resource management, and strategic management); cell and molecular biology; chemical engineering; chemical physics; chemistry; Chicano/Latino studies; civil engineering; communication; communication arts and sciences–media and information studies; community, agriculture, recreation, and resource studies; comparative medicine and integrative biology; computer science; construction management; criminal justice; crop and soil sciences; curriculum teaching and educational policy; ecology, evolutionary biology, and behavior; economics; educational policy; educational psychology and educational technology; electrical engineering; engineering mechanics; English; entomology; environmental engineering; environmental geosciences; epidemiology; family and child ecology; fisheries and wildlife; food science; forestry; French language and literature; genetics; geography; geological sciences; German studies; higher, adult, and lifelong education; Hispanic cultural studies; history; horticulture; human nutrition; industrial relations and human resources; K–12 educational administration; kinesiology; large- and small-animal clinical sciences; learning, technology, and culture; linguistics; materials science and engineering; mathematics; mathematics education; measurement and quantitative methods; mechanical engineering; microbiology; microbiology and molecular genetics; music (composition, conducting, education, performance, and theory); neuroscience; nursing; packaging; pathology; pharmacology and toxicology; philosophy; physics; physiology; plant biology; plant pathology; political science; psychology; rehabilitation counselor education; retailing; rhetoric and writing; school psychology; second language studies; social work; sociology; special education; statistics; and zoology. Interdepartmental doctoral degree programs that link environmental toxicology or plant breeding and genetics with a traditional academic discipline are also available.

Research Facilities

With a rapidly growing collection of more than 4.8 million volumes and tens of thousands of online resources, the University's libraries are well designed to serve educational and research programs. Fiber and broadband cable support a campuswide data and video network. Vector and parallel processing, geographic visualization, and database systems are available to all students and faculty members for both instruction and research. Shared facilities exist for electron and laser confocal microscopy, mass spectrometry, magnetic resonance, protein and nucleic acid sequencing, and materials fabrication.

A more complete listing of research facilities is found in the Academic Programs catalog.

Financial Aid

More than 3,000 assistantships are available in the various departments. In 2006–07, half-time assistantship stipends ranged from $1233 to $3148 per month. In addition to the stipend, substantial tuition waivers and health insurance are included for all assistants. During 2006–07, in addition to the above grants, more than 3,000 fellowships were held by graduate students. These included NSF fellowships, NIH and NIMH traineeships, Ford Foundation fellowships, and numerous other grants sponsored by industry, foundations, and government agencies as well as University graduate fellowships. Many of the fellowships pay tuition and fees in addition to stipends.

MSU Distinguished Fellowships and University Enrichment Fellowships are awarded each year in a University-wide competition. The stipend, beginning in fall 2008, is $24,000 per year plus tuition, fees, and health insurance.

MSU Student Aid Grants, Federal Perkins Loans, Supplemental Loans for Students (SLS), and Federal Stafford Student Loans are also available to graduate and professional students.

Cost of Study

The University operates on the semester system. In 2007–08, the tuition for out-of-state graduate students is $800 per credit, and the tuition for in-state graduate students is $378.75 per credit.

Living and Housing Costs

Housing for 872 graduate students is provided in Owen Hall, the graduate residence center, where charges are $2954 per semester for a single-occupancy room, $2529 per semester for a double-occupancy room, and $3328 per semester for a designated single (single in a double-occupancy room) for 2007–08. These charges include a $300 credit toward Owen Hall food purchases.

The University also operates 1,846 one- and two-bedroom apartments for graduate students and their families. These apartments rent for $630 per month for one bedroom and $699 per month for two bedrooms. This includes local telephone, cable television, Internet access, and all other utilities.

Off-campus housing costs vary widely.

Student Group

The University has an enrollment of 45,520 students on the East Lansing campus; 8,099 of these are graduate students and 1,600 are graduate professional students.

Student Outcomes

During the last five years, on average, 91 percent of the doctoral degree recipients and 91.5 percent of the master's degree recipients have secured job placement. Graduates have chosen the following career paths over the last five years: 36 percent of the doctoral graduates and 6.5 percent of the master's graduates are with hospital or medical services; 36 percent of the doctoral graduates and 7 percent of the master's graduates are employed by colleges or universities; 3.5 percent of the doctoral graduates and 12 percent of the master's graduates are attending graduate school or postdoctoral assignments; 2 percent of the doctoral graduates and 14 percent of the master's graduates are employed in elementary or secondary schools; 9 percent of the doctoral graduates and 8 percent of the master's graduates are with governmental agencies; plus other exciting career directions too numerous to mention.

Location

East Lansing offers the advantages of a small university town, with entertainment, sports, and cultural events provided by outstanding University programs. Contiguous with Lansing, the capital of Michigan, and within 2 hours' driving time of Detroit, East Lansing also provides the advantages of a larger metropolitan area.

The University

Founded in 1855, Michigan State University brought a new concept of higher education into being in the United States, combining education and research with public service as well as broad access to the citizenry. This approach set the pattern for the nation's land-grant institutions. The 5,200-acre campus, with 2,000 acres in existing or planned development, is essentially an arboretum park, providing a dynamic environment and an excellent atmosphere for study and research.

Applying

Applications for admission and supporting documents should be received by the graduate programs in time to meet appropriate departmental deadlines. Since these vary, students should correspond with a specific department prior to the date of desired enrollment. If a student is also applying for a graduate assistantship or fellowship, application materials should be received by December 31 prior to the fall semester of first enrollment.

Correspondence and Information

Department of (specify)
Michigan State University
East Lansing, Michigan 48824
Web site: http://grad.msu.edu/

Office of Admissions and Scholarships
Michigan State University
East Lansing, Michigan 48824
Phone: 517-355-8332

Michigan State University

FACULTY CHAIRS AND DIRECTORS

Graduate School
J. Ian Gray, Ph.D., Vice President for Research and Graduate Studies.
Karen L. Klomparens, Ph.D., Dean of the Graduate School and Associate Provost for Graduate Education.

Department of Accounting and Information Systems: Dr. Sanjay Gupta, Chairperson.
Department of Advertising, Public Relations, and Retailing: Dr. Richard T. Cole Chairperson.
Department of Agricultural Economics: Dr. Steven D. Hanson, Chairperson.
Department of Animal Science: Dr. Karen I. Plaut, Chairperson.
Department of Anthropology: Dr. Robert Hitchcock, Chairperson.
Department of Art and Art History: Thomas G. Berding, Chairperson.
Department of Biochemistry and Molecular Biology: Dr. S. Ferguson-Miller, Chairperson.
Department of Biosystems and Agricultural Engineering: Dr. Ajit Srivastava, Chairperson.
Program in Cell and Molecular Biology: Dr. Susan Conrad, Director.
Department of Chemical Engineering and Materials Science: Dr. Martin Hawley, Chairperson.
Department of Chemistry: Dr. John L. McCracken, Chairperson.
Program in Chicano Studies: Dr. Dionicio Valdes, Director.
Department of Civil and Environmental Engineering: Dr. R. S. Harichandran, Chairperson.
Department of Communication: Dr. Charles Atkin, Chairperson.
Department of Communicative Sciences and Disorders: Dr. Michael W. Casby, Chairperson.
Department of Community, Agriculture, Recreation, and Resource Studies: Dr. Scott G. Witter, Chairperson.
Program in Comparative Medicine and Integrative Biology: Dr. Vilma Yuzbasiyan-Gurkan, Director.
Department of Computer Science and Engineering: Dr. Laura K. Dillon, Chairperson.
Department of Counseling, Educational Psychology, and Special Education: Dr. Richard Prawat, Chairperson.
School of Criminal Justice: Dr. Edmund F. McGarrell, Director.
Department of Crop and Soil Sciences: Dr. James J. Kells, Chairperson.
Interdepartmental Program in Ecology, Evolutionary Biology and Behavior: Dr. Richard Lenski, Director.
Department of Economics: Dr. Carl Davidson, Chairperson.
Department of Educational Administration: Dr. Marilyn J. Amey, Chairperson.
Department of Electrical and Computer Engineering: Dr. Timothy Grotjohn, Chairperson.
Department of English: Dr. Stephen Arch, Chairperson.
Department of Entomology: Dr. Richard Merritt, Chairperson.
Doctoral Specialization in Environmental Science and Policy: Dr. Thomas Dietz, Director.
Department of Epidemiology: Dr. James C. Anthony, Chairperson.
Department of Family and Child Ecology: Dr. Karen Wampler, Chairperson.
Department of Finance: Dr. G. Geoffrey Booth, Chairperson.
Department of Fisheries and Wildlife: Dr. William W. Taylor, Chairperson.
Department of Food Science and Human Nutrition: Dr. Gale M. Strasburg, Chairperson.
Department of Forestry: Dr. Daniel E. Keathley, Chairperson.
Department of French, Classics, and Italian: Dr. John N. Rauk, Chairperson.
Program in Genetics: Dr. Barbara Sears, Director.
Department of Geography: Dr. Richard E. Groop, Chairperson.
Department of Geological Sciences: Dr. Ralph E. Taggart, Chairperson.
Department of History: Dr. Mark L. Kornbluh, Chairperson.
Department of Horticulture: Dr. Ronald L. Perry, Chairperson.
School of Hospitality Business: Dr. Ronald F. Cichy, Director.
Department of Human Environment and Design: Dr. Sally I. Helvenston, Chairperson.
School of Journalism: Dr. Jim Detjen, Director.
Department of Kinesiology: Dr. Deborah L. Feltz, Chairperson.
School of Labor and Industrial Relations: Professor Theodore Curry, Director.
Department of Large Animal and Clinical Sciences: Dr. Thomas Herdt, Chairperson.
Center for Latin American and Caribbean Studies: Dr. Peter Beattie, Acting Director.
Department of Linguistics and Germanic, Slavic, Asian, and African Languages: Dr. David K. Prestel, Chairperson.
Department of Management: Dr. Donald E. Conlon, Chairperson.
Department of Marketing and Supply Chain Management: Dr. Robert W. Nason, Chairperson.
Department of Mathematics: Dr. Peter W. Bates, Chairperson.
Department of Mechanical Engineering: Dr. Eann Patterson, Chairperson.
Program in Medical Technology: Dr. Kathryn M. Doig, Director.
Department of Microbiology and Molecular Genetics: Dr. Walter Esselman, Chairperson.
College of Music: Professor James B. Forger, Director.
College of Nursing: Dr. Mary Mundt, Dean.
School of Packaging: Dr. Susan Selke, Director.
Department of Pathobiology and Diagnostic Investigation: Dr. Jennifer Thomas, Acting Chairperson.
Department of Pharmacology and Toxicology: Dr. Joseph R. Haywood II, Chairperson.
Department of Philosophy: Dr. Richard Peterson, Chairperson.
Department of Physics and Astronomy: Dr. Wolfgang W. Bauer, Chairperson.
Department of Physiology: Dr. William S. Spielman, Chairperson.
School of Planning, Design, and Construction: Dr. Robert D. Von Bernuth, Director.
Department of Plant Biology: Dr. Richard E. Triemer, Chairperson.
Department of Plant Pathology: Dr. R. Hammerschmidt, Chairperson.
Department of Political Science: Dr. Richard C. Hula, Chairperson.
Department of Psychology: Dr. Neal Schmitt, Chairperson.
Program in Second Language Studies: Dr. Susan Gass, Director.
Department of Small Animal Clinical Sciences: Dr. Charles E. DeCamp, Chairperson.
School of Social Work: Dr. Gary R. Anderson, Director.
Department of Sociology: Dr. Janet L. Bokemeier, Chairperson.
Department of Spanish and Portuguese: Dr. Doug Noverr, Acting Chairperson.
Department of Statistics and Probability: Prof. Mark Meerschaert, Chairperson.
Department of Teacher Education: Dr. Suzanne Wilson, Chairperson.
Department of Telecommunication, Information Studies, and Media: Dr. Charles Steinfield, Chairperson.
Department of Theatre: Dr. George F. Peters, Chairperson.
Program in Urban and Regional Planning: Dr. Mark Wilson, Director.
Department of Zoology: Dr. Fred C. Dyer, Chairperson.

MICHIGAN TECHNOLOGICAL UNIVERSITY

Graduate School

Programs of Study

Michigan Technological University (MTU) offers graduate programs in many branches of engineering and science, as well as in related fields, including technical communication and business. M.S. degree programs are available in applied ecology, applied science education, biological sciences, business administration, chemical engineering, chemistry, civil engineering, computer science, electrical engineering, engineering mechanics, environmental engineering, environmental engineering science, environmental policy, forest ecology and management, forest molecular genetics and biotechnology, forestry, geological engineering, geology, geophysics, industrial archaeology, materials sciences and engineering, mathematical sciences, mechanical engineering, mineral economics, physics, and rhetoric and technical communication.

MTU offers a Master of Forestry degree, Master of Engineering options, and a graduate certificate in sustainability. In addition, the School of Forest Resources and Environmental Science, the Department of Civil and Environmental Engineering, and the Department of Geological and Mining Engineering Sciences offer master's international programs in cooperation with the Peace Corps.

The Ph.D. is offered in biological sciences, chemical engineering, chemistry, civil engineering, computer science, electrical engineering, engineering physics, forest molecular genetics and biotechnology, forest science, geological engineering, geology, industrial heritage and archaeology, materials science and engineering, mathematical sciences, mechanical engineering–engineering mechanics, physics, rhetoric and technical communication, and two nondepartmental engineering areas (computational science and environmental).

Research Facilities

The J. Robert Van Pelt Library provides books, periodicals, microfiche/film, and access to electronic information to complement instructional and research needs. Access to library resources is through the automated system, Voyager. The library contains more than 780,000 volumes, including government documents, and receives more than 10,000 serials and periodicals. The collection is particularly strong in the physical and natural sciences, mathematics, and engineering.

Individual departments maintain networked labs of PCs, Sun workstations, or other specialized computational or visualization systems tailored to their research needs. In addition to departmental facilities, campuswide computer and network services are offered by Informational Technology (IT). The campus network is connected to the Internet, allowing all faculty members and graduate students easy access to all network and information services from the desktop. Michigan Tech is an Internet2 university. All departments at Michigan Tech have the laboratories and equipment needed for graduate study as well as access to many other facilities, such as those of the National Park Service Cooperative Studies Unit, the Forestry Sciences Laboratory (USDA, Forest Service), the Remote Sensing Institute, the Center for Advanced Manufacturing and Materials Processing, and the Keweenaw Research Center.

Financial Aid

Financial aid is available to a limited number of qualified full-time students in the form of fellowships, research assistantships, and teaching assistantships. Aid packages include a stipend, tuition, and course and computer fees. The stipend for M.S. candidates is currently $4548 per semester and for Ph.D. candidates, $5280 per semester. In addition, a health insurance supplement is provided by the University. Funding may be available on a competitive basis for students to travel to professional conferences.

Cost of Study

Tuition and mandatory fees for full-time graduate students for the 2005–06 academic year were $4873 per semester; engineering and computer science majors paid $5373 per semester. Participants in the Peace Corps' master's international degree program and the master's in applied science education degree program paid $345 per credit hour. All students are responsible for student voted fees totaling approximately $127 per semester. Health insurance is required for all graduate students.

Living and Housing Costs

Michigan Tech residence halls have accommodations for single students, and applications may be obtained from the director of residential services. For married students, Michigan Tech has one- and two-bedroom furnished apartments; applications may be obtained from the manager of Daniell Heights Apartments. Because the cost of housing is subject to change, representative costs cannot be stated. Off-campus housing is also available in the surrounding community. *Yahoo!* lists the overall cost-of-living index for Houghton as eighty-three out of the national average of 100. For more information, students should visit the Web site at http://list.realestate.yahoo.com/realestate/neighborhood/main.html.

Student Group

The University has an enrollment of 6,538 students; 897 are graduate students.

Student Outcomes

Graduates attain positions in academia, industry, and government agencies as faculty members, research engineer/scientists, and project engineers. In past years, MTU graduates have gone to such institutions as Caltech, Michigan State, Notre Dame, Purdue, Wayne State, and the Universities of Central Florida and Missouri, as well as to corporations such as BASF, Ford, GE, GM, Kimberly Clark, and Tenneco. Master's program graduates have been accepted to doctoral programs at Illinois, Michigan State, Northern Arizona, Ohio State, Purdue, and SUNY at Stony Brook.

Location

Michigan Tech is located in Houghton on Michigan's scenic Keweenaw Peninsula. The Keweenaw stretches about 70 miles into Lake Superior, and the surrounding area is perfect for any outdoor activity. The campus is a 15-minute walk from downtown Houghton; public transportation is available from Houghton and Hancock. Houghton has been listed as the safest college town in Michigan and was ranked 8 out of 467 nationwide in the report "Crime at College: Student Guide to Personal Safety." The Houghton County Memorial Airport (CMX) serves the area with direct flights to Minneapolis via Northwest Airlink. Sawyer International Airport (SAW) at Marquette serves the area via Detroit and is approximately a 2-hour drive from Houghton.

The University

Michigan Tech was founded in 1885 as the Michigan Mining School to serve the nation's first major mining enterprises focused on copper and iron. Several name changes tracked the growth and diversification of the institution, and it was named Michigan Technological University in 1964. Today, the University offers a full range of associate, bachelor's, master's, and doctoral degrees in the sciences, engineering, forestry, business, communication, and technology. MTU has been rated one of the nation's "Top Ten" best buys for science and technology by *U.S. News & World Report.*

Applying

The application for admission and an official transcript of previous academic work at the undergraduate and graduate levels must be submitted to the Graduate School. A nonrefundable $40 application fee ($45 for international applications) must accompany the application. Applications should be submitted at least six weeks before the start of the applicant's desired semester of entrance.

Correspondence and Information

Graduate School
Michigan Technological University
1400 Townsend Drive
Houghton, Michigan 49931-1295

Phone: 906-487-2327
Fax: 906-487-2284
E-mail: gradadms@mtu.edu
Web site: http://www.gradschool.mtu.edu/

FACULTY CHAIRS

The administrative officers of the Graduate School and of the departments responsible for programs leading to graduate degrees are listed below.

Graduate School: Jacqueline E. Huntoon, Ph.D., Dean.
Department of Biological Sciences: John H. Adler, Ph.D., Chair.
Department of Biomedical Engineering: Michael Neuman, Ph.D., M.D., Chair.
School of Business and Engineering Administration (Mineral Economics): Christa Walck, Ph.D., Dean.
Department of Chemical Engineering: Michael E. Mullins, Ph.D., Chair.
Department of Chemistry: Sarah A. Green, Ph.D., Chair.
Department of Civil and Environmental Engineering: Neil Hutzler, Ph.D., Chair.
Department of Computer Science: Linda Ott, Ph.D., Chair.
Department of Electrical and Computer Engineering: Timothy J. Schulz, D.Sc., Chair.
School of Forest Resources and Environmental Science: Margaret R. Gale, Ph.D., Dean.
Department of Geological and Mining Engineering and Sciences: Wayne D. Pennington, Ph.D., Chair.
Department of Humanities (Rhetoric and Technical Communication): Robert R. Johnson, Ph.D., Chair.
Department of Materials Science and Engineering: Mark R. Plichta, Ph.D., Chair.
Department of Mathematical Sciences: A. H. Baartmans, Ph.D., Chair.
Department of Mechanical Engineering–Engineering Mechanics: W. W. Predebon, Ph.D., Chair.
Department of Physics: Ravindra Pandey, Ph.D., Chair.
Department of Social Science: Bruce E. Seely, Ph.D., Chair.
Computational Science and Engineering Ph.D. Committee: Phillip R. Merkey, Ph.D., Chair.

Students on MTU's campus.

MTU students have access to high-technology equipment.

A student works in one of MTU's many laboratories.

Michigan Technological University is an equal opportunity educational institution/equal opportunity employer.

MILLS

Programs of Study

Mills College offers certificate, master's, and doctoral programs to approximately 500 women and men each year. Mills graduate degrees include the Master of Arts (M.A.) in dance, early childhood education, education (child development, child life in hospitals, teaching), educational leadership, English and American literature, infant mental health, interdisciplinary computer science, and music composition; the Master of Business Administration (M.B.A.); the Master of Fine Arts (M.F.A.) in creative writing, dance (choreography and performance), music (music performance and literature, electronic music and recording media), and studio art; the Master of Public Policy (M.P.P.); and the Doctor of Education (Ed.D.).

In addition to its M.A. and Ed.D. program options, the Mills School of Education offers 6–12 single-subject and K–12 multiple-subject teaching credential programs and an administrative services credential program that focuses on educational leadership. Graduate students in the School of Education benefit from fieldwork in the Mills College Children's School, a laboratory school founded in 1926 that continues to maintain its reputation as a leader in the education of young children and the training of professionals in the field.

Mills also offers a range of specialized graduate certificates. The postbaccalaureate Pre-Medical Certificate Program is designed for college graduates who have decided to pursue a career in the health professions but need basic science courses. The New Horizons Certificate Program is available to college graduates who find barriers in their path to graduate study or employment because of a lack of exposure to sophisticated computer concepts. Mills also offers a certificate program in biochemistry and molecular biology for students who earned baccalaureate degrees in nonscience areas who wish to pursue advanced scientific study.

Most graduate degree programs require at least two years of full-time study, with degree completion within five years. The Master of Arts with an emphasis in teaching (MEET) allows a maximum of eight years for degree completion so that students can gain on-the-job classroom experience that will enhance their studies.

Mills is accredited by the Western Association of Schools and Colleges.

Research Facilities

The F. W. Olin Library offers a collection of more than 225,000 volumes and other media, with special emphases on literature, history, women's studies, art, and music. The library offers more than 60 online databases and is home to The Special Collections, containing more than 12,000 volumes and 10,000 manuscripts. Other facilities include the Mills College Art Museum, with more than 8,000 works of art—the largest permanent collection of any liberal arts college on the West Coast; the Center for Contemporary Music, the original home to the innovative San Francisco Tape Music Center; the Children's School, the first laboratory school founded west of the Mississippi for teacher training; and private art studios for M.F.A. candidates in art. The recently completed 26,000-square-foot Natural Sciences Building includes state-of-the-art equipment and laboratories and meets rigorous standards as a leadership in energy and environmental design (LEED) "green" building.

Financial Aid

Most graduate programs offer teaching assistantships that include both a stipend and partial tuition remission, particularly to second-year students. These awards are limited and are usually available for one or two semesters. Alumnae tuition scholarships are also available to help cover partial tuition costs. Graduate students are often eligible for state and federal assistance programs, including the Federal Stafford Student Loan Program.

Cost of Study

In 2007–08, tuition was $22,792 for the academic year. Tuition for the studio art program was $27,792.

Living and Housing Costs

Mills offers a variety of housing options on its lush, 135-acre campus—from Mediterranean-inspired residence halls to contemporary townhouses to cooperative residences. Students should visit http://www.mills.edu to learn more about options, rates, and meal plans.

Student Group

In 2006–07, the graduate student enrollment at Mills was approximately 500, with an undergraduate population of more than 900. Approximately 37 percent were students of color, 7 percent identified themselves as multiethnic, and 4 percent were international students. Mills is consistently recognized as one of the most diverse liberal arts colleges in the nation by *U.S. News & World Report*.

Location

Nestled in the foothills of Oakland, California, on the east shore of the San Francisco Bay, Mills is situated on a beautiful residential campus in one of the most culturally diverse cities in the United States. The campus is minutes away from Berkeley and downtown Oakland, 20 minutes from downtown San Francisco, and less than one hour from the beaches of the Pacific Ocean.

The College

Mills College is an innovative liberal arts institution offering undergraduate degrees to women and graduate degrees to women and men. Founded in 1852, Mills introduced its first graduate programs in the 1920s, establishing a national and international reputation based on groundbreaking work in fields such as electronic music, computer science, and education. Today, Mills continues the tradition of innovation by introducing new academic programs that fill unique needs. In 2005, Mills launched the Graduate School of Business, focused on the advancement of women in the professions. In fall 2007, Mills introduced the Public Policy Program, which is dedicated to preparing women to assume leadership roles in policy making and analysis, and the Infant Mental Health Program, which incorporates education and psychology in a one-of-a-kind interdisciplinary degree focused on child development.

Applying

Basic requirements for admission are an earned bachelor's degree or its equivalent from an accredited college or university and demonstrated intellectual potential or special performance in the field of study being sought. Application deadlines vary according to the program, with November 1 and February 1 being the standard deadlines for spring and fall admission, respectively. The dance, English, studio art, teaching credential, and postbaccalaureate pre-medical programs accept applicants for fall entry only.

Correspondence and Information

Office of Graduate Studies
Mills College
5000 MacArthur Blvd.
Oakland, California 94613

Phone: 510-430-3309
Fax: 510-430-2159
E-mail: grad-studies@mills.edu
Web site: http://www.mills.edu

GRADUATE PROGRAMS

Art
Hung Liu, M.F.A., California, San Diego.
Steve Matheson, M.F.A., California, San Diego. On leave 2007–08.
Anna Valentina Murch, M.A., Royal College of Art (London).
Ron Nagle, B.A., San Francisco State.
Catherine Wagner, M.A., San Francisco State.

Dance
Sonya Delwaide, B.F.A., York.
Molissa Fenley, B.A., Mills College. On leave 2007–08.
Judith Rosenberg, M.M., Rochester (Eastman).

Education
Jane B. Bowyer, Ph.D., Berkeley.
Ruth Cossey, Ph.D., Stanford.
David Donahue, Ph.D., Stanford.
Delaine Eastin, M.A., California, Santa Barbara.
Tomás Galguera, Ph.D., Stanford.
Joseph E. Kahne, Ph.D., Stanford.
Diane Ketelle, D.P.A., USC.
Linda Kroll, Ph.D., Berkeley.
Vicki LaBoskey, Ph.D., Stanford.
Linda Perez, Ph.D., Berkeley.
Anna Richert, Ph.D., Stanford.

English
Elmaz Abinader, Ph.D., Nebraska.
Diane Cady, Ph.D., Cornell.
Yiyun Li, M.F.A., Iowa.
Ajuan Mance, Ph.D., Michigan.
Cornelia Nixon, Ph.D., Berkeley.
Sarah Pollock, B.A., Berkeley.
Stephen Ratcliffe, Ph.D., Berkeley.
Kathryn Reiss, M.F.A., Michigan.
Kirsten Saxton, Ph.D., California, Davis.
Ruth Saxton, Ph.D., Berkeley.
Cynthia Scheinberg, Ph.D., Rutgers.
Juliana Spahr, Ph.D., SUNY at Buffalo.
Tom Strychacz, Ph.D., Princeton.

Interdisciplinary Computer Science
Almudena Konrad, Ph.D., Berkeley.
Barbara Li Santi, Ph.D., California, Santa Barbara.
Ellen Spertus, Ph.D., MIT. On leave 2007–08.
Susan Wang, Ph.D., Princeton.

Intermedia Arts
David Bernstein, Ph.D., Columbia.
Christopher Brown, M.F.A., Mills.
James Fei, M.A., Wesleyan.
Fred Frith, M.A., Cambridge.
Steven Matheson, M.F.A., California, San Diego.
Anna Valentina Murch, M.A., Royal College of Art (London).
Pauline Oliveros, B.A., San Francisco State.
Maggi Payne, M.Mus., Illinois at Urbana-Champaign.

Management M.B.A.
Eirik Evenhouse, Ph.D., Berkeley.
Siobhan Reilly, Ph.D., Berkeley.
Lorien Rice, Ph.D., California, San Diego.
David M. W. Roland-Holst, Ph.D., Berkeley.
Roger Sparks, Ph.D., California, Davis.
Nancy Thornborrow, Ph.D., California, San Diego.

Mathematics
Steven Givant, Ph.D., Berkeley.
Ellen Spertus, Ph.D., MIT. On leave 2007–08.
Zvezdelina Stankova, Ph.D., Harvard.
Susan Wang, Ph.D., Princeton.

Music
David Bernstein, Ph.D., Columbia.
John Bischoff, M.F.A., Mills.
Chris Brown, M.F.A., Mills.
Fred Frith, M.A., Cambridge.
Nalini Ghuman, Ph.D., Berkeley.
Maggi Payne, M.Mus., Illinois at Urbana-Champaign.

Postbaccalaureate Pre-Medical Program
Barbara Bowman, Ph.D., Berkeley.
John Brabson, Ph.D., Illinois at Urbana-Champaign.
Kristina Faul, Ph.D., California, Santa Cruz.
John Harris, Ph.D., California, Davis.
David Keeports, Ph.D., Washington (Seattle).
Bruce Pavlik, Ph.D., California, Davis.
Susan Spiller, Ph.D., Berkeley.
Lisa Urry, Ph.D., MIT.
John Vollmer, Ph.D., USC.
Elisabeth Wade, Ph.D., Berkeley.
Jared Young, Ph.D., California, San Diego.

Public Policy Program
Carol Chetkovich, Ph.D., Berkeley.

Mills College.

MISSOURI STATE UNIVERSITY

Graduate College

Programs of Study Missouri State University (MSU) offers forty-three graduate programs leading to the Master of Accountancy (M.Acc.), Master of Arts (M.A.), Master of Arts in Teaching (M.A.T.), Master of Business Administration (M.B.A.), Master of Health Administration (M.H.A.), Master of International Affairs and Administration (M.I.A.A.), Master of Music (M.M.), Master of Natural and Applied Science (M.N.A.S.), Master of Physical Therapy (M.P.T.), Master of Public Administration (M.P.A.), Master of Public Health (M.P.H.), Master of Science (M.S.), Master of Science in Education (M.S.Ed.), Master of Science in Nursing (M.S.N.), Master of Social Work (M.S.W.), Specialist in Education (Ed.S.), and Doctorate in Educational Leadership (Ed.D.), and Doctor of Audiology (Au.D.) degrees. Programs of study are available in accounting, administrative studies, audiology, biology, business administration, cell and molecular biology, chemistry, communication, communication sciences and disorders, computer information systems, counseling, criminology, defense and strategic studies, early childhood and family development, educational administration, elementary education, English, geospatial sciences, health administration, health promotion and wellness management, history, instructional media technology, international affairs and administration, materials science, mathematics, music, natural and applied science, nurse anesthesia, nursing, physical therapy, physician assistant studies, plant science, project management, psychology, public administration, public health, reading, religious studies, secondary education, social work, special education, student affairs, teaching, theater, and writing. All programs are accredited by the North Central Association of Colleges and Schools, and many programs are professionally accredited.

Missouri State University also offers twelve accelerated master's programs and sixteen for-credit graduate certificate programs. Accelerated master's programs enable outstanding MSU undergraduate students to begin graduate work while completing their undergraduate program. Accelerated master's programs are in the areas of accountancy, biology, business administration, cell and molecular biology, chemistry, geospatial sciences, materials science, mathematics, natural and applied science, nursing, public administration, and religious studies. Graduate certificate programs include autism spectrum disorders, conflict and dispute resolution, geospatial information sciences, instructional technology, internal auditing, orientation and mobility, Ozark studies, post-master's nurse educator studies, post-master's family nurse practitioner studies, project management, public management, religious studies for the professions, sports management, and technology management.

Research Facilities Missouri State University libraries have comprehensive electronic resources, including an online catalog, electronic indexes and full-text resources, and Internet accessibility. The University is a member of the Center for Research Libraries and is both a U.S. and United Nations document depository. Other facilities include a K–12 laboratory school and numerous research centers, including the Bull Shoals Field Station, the Center for Archaeological Research, the Center for Applied Science and Engineering, the Missouri State Fruit Experiment Station, and the Ozarks Environmental and Water Resources Institute.

Financial Aid Financial assistance is available through a variety of scholarships, graduate assistantships, grants, loans, and work-study programs. Most students who receive financial assistance do so through teaching or research graduate assistantships. Graduate assistantship stipends ranged from $6780 to $9000 for the nine-month academic year (2006–07) plus a full tuition scholarship (resident or nonresident) for up to 15 hours a semester. Students on academic-year assistantships also receive a 6-hour tuition scholarship for the summer term. To be eligible for an assistantship, a student must be admitted to a graduate program and have a minimum GPA of 3.0 (cumulative or in the last 60 hours of undergraduate course work). The Missouri Outreach Graduate Opportunity (MOGO) Scholarship provides a partial remission of out-of-state fees for full-time students in eligible graduate programs who are not Missouri residents. The MOGO Scholarship has a value of three-fourths of the nonresident graduate student fees for 9 credit hours (5 credits hours in the summer).

Cost of Study In 2006–07, graduate-level course fees were $199 per credit hour for instate residents and $388 per credit hour for nonresidents. Internet courses in the administrative studies program were $192–$258 per credit hour. Internet courses in computer information systems were $395 per credit hour. An additional student services fee is assessed per semester based on enrolled credit hours (courses taught via Internet excluded). This fee was $274 for full-time students (9 credit hours) in 2006–07.

Living and Housing Costs The average cost per year for room and board in residence halls was $5078 in 2006–07. Exact rates depend on room style and meal plan. Furnished apartments are available for graduate, married, and nontraditional students for $439 to $584 per month. University and privately owned apartments are within a reasonable distance of the campus.

Student Group The total student population is approximately 19,000, of which 15 percent are graduate students. Students come from across the United States and from more than sixty countries.

Location Missouri State University is located in Springfield, the third-largest city in Missouri with a metropolitan service region of 330,000. Located in the heart of the Ozarks recreational area, the University is within easy driving distance of numerous recreational lakes, streams, and parks. The community of Springfield is supported by an industrial/manufacturing base and an expanding service industry in tourism, with people drawn by the natural beauty and recreation of the Ozarks and the musical attractions in nearby Branson. Springfield has an extensive health and medical economy serving southwest Missouri, northwest Arkansas, southeast Kansas, and northeast Oklahoma.

The University Missouri State University founded in 1905 is a multicampus metropolitan university system with a statewide mission in public affairs. The University offers more than 150 undergraduate majors and forty-three graduate programs, many of which are the strongest of their kind in the state. The students experience college life at its best, with NCAA Division I athletics and more than 250 student organizations.

Applying Missouri State University invites applications from students with strong records of undergraduate performance. To apply to a program, prospective students must complete the Graduate College application as well as submit a $35 application fee. To complete the application, the Graduate College also requires students to submit two official copies of their transcripts, showing all prior academic work. Students should also contact the department or program to which they are applying to determine what additional materials (i.e., GRE, GMAT, letters of recommendation, resume, and/or other materials) are needed to complete their application. The application deadline to avoid a late fee is three weeks prior to the beginning of the desired semester of entrance; however, students are strongly encouraged to submit required paperwork before this date to allow for appropriate processing time. Many programs admit students only once a year and have specific deadlines. Prospective students should refer to program admission requirements. The graduate catalog and admission application can be accessed via the Web site listed in this description.

Correspondence and Information

Frank Einhellig, Dean
Graduate College
Missouri State University
901 South National Avenue
Springfield, Missouri 65897
Phone: 417-836-5335
417-836-4770 (MO Relay TDD)
866-767-4723 (toll-free)
Fax: 417-836-6888
E-mail: graduatecollege@missouristate.edu
Web site: http://graduate.missouristate.edu

FIELDS OF STUDY AND FACULTY ADVISERS

E-mail addresses of faculty members are in parentheses. All phone numbers are in area code 417.

Graduate College: Frank Einhellig, Dean (frankeinhellig@missouristate.edu); Barbara Bushman, Associate Dean (barbarabushman@missouristate.edu); 836-5335.
Administrative Studies (M.S.): John Bourhis, Program Director (johnbouris@missouristate.edu); 836-6390. This program is available on campus and as an Internet program. Options in applied communication, criminal justice, environmental management, project management, and sports management.
College of Arts and Letters: Dean; 836-5247.
Communication (M.A.): Carey Adams, Department Head (careyadams@missouristate.edu); 836-4423. Graduate certificate program in conflict and dispute resolution.
English (M.A.): W. D. Blackmon, Department Head (wdblackmon@missouristate.edu); 836-4226. Tracks in literature, creative writing, and TESOL, and graduate certificate programs in TESOL and Ozarks Studies.
Music (M.M.): Roger Stoner, Department Head (rogerstoner@missouristate.edu); Robert Quebbeman, Graduate Director (robertquebbeman@missouristate.edu); 836-5648. Program accredited by the National Association of Schools of Music (NASM). Options in conducting, theory and composition, pedagogy, performance, and education.
Theater (M.A.): Wade Thompson, Acting Department Head (wadethompson@missouristate.edu); 836-4400. Program accredited by the National Association of Schools of Theater.
Writing (M.A.): Department of English; W. D. Blackmon, Department Head (wdblackmon@missouristate.edu); 836-4226. Tracks in rhetoric and composition and technical and professional writing.
College of Business Administration: Ronald Bottin, Dean (ronaldbottin@missouristate.edu); 836-4408. Programs accredited by AACSB International–The Association to Advance Collegiate Schools of Business.
Accounting (M.Acc.): School of Accountancy; John R. Williams, Director (johnwilliams@missouristate.edu); 836-5414. Graduate certificate program in internal auditing.
Business Administration (M.B.A.): James Simmerman, Director of M.B.A. Program (jamessimmerman@missouristate.edu); 836-5646. Concentrations in accounting, computer information systems, finance, international management, management, and marketing.
Computer Information Systems (M.S.): Jerry Chin, Department Head (jerrychin@missouristate.edu); David Meinert, Graduate Director (davidmeinert@missouristate.edu); 836-4131.
Health Administration (M.H.A.): Department of Management; Barry Wisdom, Department Head (barrywisdom@missouristate.edu); Robert Lunn, Graduate Director (robertlunn@missouristate.edu); 836-5647.
Project Management (M.S.): Department of Industrial Management; Shawn Strong, Department Head (shawnstrong@missouristate.edu); 836-5121. Graduate certificate program.
College of Education: David Hough, Dean (davidhough@missouristate.edu); 836-5254. Programs accredited by the Department of Elementary and Secondary Education (DESE) and the National Council for Accreditation of Teacher Education (NCATE).
Counseling (M.S.): Charles Barké, Department Head (crbarke@missouristate.edu); 836-5449. Options in elementary, secondary, and community agency counseling.
Early Childhood and Family Development (M.S.): Suzanne George, Department Head (suegeorge@missouristate.edu); 836-3262.
Educational Administration (Ed.S. and M.S.Ed.): Gerald Moseman, M.S.Ed. Program Coordinator (geraldmoseman@missouristate.edu), 836-5490; Robert Watson, Ed.S. Program Coordinator (robertwatson@missouristate.edu); 836-6951. Options in elementary, principal, secondary principal, and superintendent.
Educational Leadership (Ed.D.): Cynthia MacGregor, Program Coordinator (cmacgregor@missouristate.edu); 836-6046. Cooperative program with the University of Missouri–Columbia (MU). Degree conferred by MU.
Elementary Education (M.S.Ed.): School of Teacher Education, Fred H. Groves, Director (fredgroves@missouristate.edu); Cynthia Wilson, Graduate Director (cindywilson@missouristate.edu); 836-6065.
Instructional Media Technology (M.S.Ed.): School of Teacher Education, Fred H. Groves, Director (fredgroves@missouristate.edu); 836-6769. Program accredited by the Association for Educational and Communications Technology (AECT). Graduate certificate program.
Reading (M.S.Ed.): School of Teacher Education, Fred H. Groves, Director (fredgroves@missouristate.edu); Deanne Camp, Graduate Director (deannecamp@missouristate.edu); 836-6983. Program accredited by the International Reading Association (IRA).
Secondary Education (M.S.Ed.): For information, students should contact the area of emphasis department or Tobin Bushman, Coordinator of Graduate Admissions and Recruitment (tobinbushman@missouristate.edu); 836-5331. Areas of emphasis include agriculture, art, biology, business, chemistry, earth science, English, family and consumer sciences, geography, history, industrial education, mathematics, modern and classical languages, music, natural science, physical education, physics, social science, and speech and theater.
Special Education (M.S.Ed.): School of Teacher Education, Fred H. Groves, Director (fredgroves@missouristate.edu); Paris DePaepe, Graduate Director (parisdepaepe@missouristate.edu); 836-4761. Program accredited by the Council for Exceptional Children (CEC). Graduate certificate programs in autism spectrum disorders and orientation/mobility.
Teaching (M.A.T.): School of Teacher Education, Fred H. Groves, Director (fredgroves@missouristate.edu); Emmett Sawyer, Coordinator (emmettsawyer@missouristate.edu); 836-3170.
College of Health and Human Services: Helen Reid, Acting Dean (helenreid@missouristate.edu); 836-4176.
Cell and Molecular Biology (M.S.): Department of Biomedical Sciences; Harold Falls, Department Head (haroldfalls@missouristate.edu); Christopher Field, Director of Graduate Studies (chrisfield@missouristate.edu); 836-5478.
Communication Sciences and Disorders (M.S.): Neil DeSarno, Department Head (neildesarno@missouristate.edu); 836-5368. Program options in audiology, education of the deaf/hard of hearing, and speech-language pathology. Audiology and speech-language pathology programs accredited by the American Speech-Language-Hearing Association. Education-of-the-deaf/hard-of-hearing program accredited by the Council of Education of the Deaf.
Health Promotion and Wellness Management (M.S.): Department of Health, Physical Education and Recreation, Gerald Masterson, Coordinator (jerrymasterson@missouristate.edu); 836-5251.
Nurse Anesthesia (M.S.): Department of Biomedical Sciences; Harold Falls, Department Head (haroldfalls@missouristate.edu); Michael Hendrix, Director of Graduate Studies (michaelhendrix@missouristate.edu); 836-4509. Program accredited by the Council on Accreditation of Nurse Anesthesia Education Programs.
Nursing (M.S.N.): Kathryn Hope, Department Head (kathrynhope@missouristate.edu); 836-5310. Program accredited by the National League for Nursing Accrediting Commission (NLNAC). Post-master's graduate certificate programs for nurse educator and family nurse practitioner.
Physical Therapy (M.P.T.): Akinniran Oladehin, Department Head (aoladehin@missouristate.edu); 836-6179; Scott Wallentine, Graduate Program Coordinator (swallentine@missouristate.edu); 836-4514. Program accredited by the Commission on Accreditation in Physical Therapy Education (CAPTE).
Physician Assistant Studies (M.S.): Steven T. Dodge, Department Head and Director (stevendodge@missouristate.edu); 836-6151. Program accredited by the Accreditation Review Commission on Education for the Physician Assistant (ARC-PA).
Psychology (M.S.): Robert G. Jones, Acting Department Head (robertjones@missouristate.edu); 836-5797. Options in industrial/organizational, clinical, and general psychology.
Public Health (M.P.H.): Dalen Duitsman, Program Coordinator (dalenduitsman@missouristate.edu); 836-5550.
Social Work (M.S.W.): Etta Madden, Acting Director, School of Social Work (ettamadden@missouristate.edu); Susan Dollar, M.S.W. Program Director (susandollar@missouristate.edu); 836-6359. Program accredited by the Council on Social Work Education.
Sports Management Certificate Program: Department of Health, Physical Education and Recreation; Gerald Masterson, Program Advisor (jerrymasterson@missouristate.edu); 836-5251.
College of Humanities and Public Affairs: Lorene H. Stone, Dean (lorenestone@missouristate.edu); 836-5529.
Criminology (M.S.): Department of Sociology, Anthropology, and Criminology; Karl Kunkel, Department Head (karlkunkel@missouristate.edu); 836-5640.
Defense and Strategic Studies (M.S.): Keith B. Payne, Department Head (kbpayne@missouristate.edu); 703-218-3565. Graduate certificate program. Program is located in Fairfax, Virginia.
History (M.A.): Michael Sheng, Department Head (michaelsheng@missouristate.edu); Thornton Miller, Graduate Director (ftmiller@missouristate.edu); 836-5511.
International Affairs and Administration (M.I.A.A.): Department of Political Science; Beat Kernen, Department Head (beatkernen@missouristate.edu), 836-5630; Dennis Hickey, Program Director (dennishickey@missouristate.edu); 836-5850.
Public Administration (M.P.A.): Department of Political Science; Beat Kernen, Department Head (beatkernan@missouristate.edu); James Kaatz, Program Director (jameskaatz@missouristate.edu); 836-6424. Program accredited by the National Association of Schools for Public Affairs and Administration.
Religious Studies (M.A.): James Moyer, Department Head (jimmoyer@missouristate.edu); Jack Llewellyn, Graduate Director (jllewellyn@missouristate.edu); 836-6681. Graduate certificate program.
College of Natural and Applied Sciences: Tamera Jahnke, Dean (tamerajahnke@missouristate.edu); 836-5249.
Biology (M.S.): S. Alicia Mathis, Department Head (aliciamathis@missouristate.edu); Thomas Tomasi, Graduate Director (tomtomasi@missouristate.edu); 836-5126.
Chemistry (M.S.): Paul Toom, Acting Department Head (paultoom@missouristate.edu); James Zimmerman, Graduate Director (jazimmerman@missouristate.edu); 836-5444.
Geospacial Sciences (M.S.): Department of Geography, Geology, and Planning; Thomas Plymate, Department Head (tomplymate@missouristate.edu); Bob Pavlowsky, Graduate Director (bobpavlowsky@missouristate.edu); 836-8473. Graduate certificate program.
Materials Science (M.S.): Department of Physics, Astronomy and Material Science; Pawan Kahol, Department Head (pawankahol@missouristate.edu); 836-5131.
Mathematics (M.S.): Yungchen Cheng, Department Head (yungchencheng@missouristate.edu); 836-5112.
Natural and Applied Science (M.N.A.S.): Dennis Schmitt, Program Director (dennisschmitt@missouristate.edu); 836-5091. An interdisciplinary program in which students select from of the following primary emphasis areas: agriculture, applied consumer science, astronomy, biology, chemistry, computer science, fruit science, geography, geology and planning, mathematics, physics, and materials science.
Plant Science (M.S.): Department of Agriculture; W. Anson Elliott, Department Head (ansonelliott@missouristate.edu); 836-5638; Dennis Schmitt, Program Coordinator (dennisschmitt@missouristate.edu); 836-5091.

where leaders look forward℠

MONMOUTH UNIVERSITY

Graduate School

Programs of Study

The Graduate School offers programs in several areas designed for students who wish to acquire advanced knowledge and skills in their chosen fields of study and engage in research and other scholarly activities. The programs are administered through the Wayne D. McMurray School of Humanities and Social Sciences; the Marjorie K. Unterberg School of Nursing and Health Studies; the School of Business Administration; the School of Science, Technology and Engineering; and the School of Education.

The School of Humanities and Social Sciences awards the Master of Arts (M.A.) in criminal justice, corporate and public communication, English, history, professional counseling, public policy, and psychological counseling; a Master of Arts in Liberal Arts (M.A.L.A.); and a Master of Social Work (M.S.W.). This school also offers post-master's certificates in play therapy and professional counseling and graduate certificates in criminal justice administration, public relations specialist studies, media studies, and human resources communication.

The School of Nursing and Health Studies offers a Master of Science in Nursing (M.S.N.) as well as advanced practice nursing post-master's certificates in adult nurse practitioner, adult psychiatric and mental health, family nurse practitioner, and nursing administration; a post-master's certificate in nursing education; and graduate certificates in forensic nursing, school nursing, and school nursing–noninstructional.

The School of Science, Technology and Engineering awards Master of Science (M.S.) degrees in computer science and software engineering. Certificates are available in computer science, software design and development, software development, and software engineering.

The School of Education offers three programs leading to master's degrees: the Master of Arts in Teaching (M.A.T.), the Master of Education (M.Ed.), and the Master of Science in Education (M.S.Ed.). The M.S.Ed. program offers concentrations in principal, special education, reading specialist, and educational counseling. Education endorsement certification programs are available in early childhood, ESL, substance awareness coordinator, and teacher of students with disabilities. Post-master's certification endorsement programs are offered in learning disabilities teacher-consultant, reading specialist, principal, supervisor, and counseling.

The School of Business Administration offers the Master of Business Administration (M.B.A.) program with optional tracks in accounting, finance, and real estate and the M.B.A. with a concentration in health-care management. The school also offers post-master's certificate programs in accounting and health-care management.

Monmouth also offers an accelerated degree program, the Graduate Scholars Program, to enable students to achieve both a bachelor's and master's degree in five years of study. This opportunity is available in the computer science, criminal justice, history, and nursing programs.

Research Facilities

The Monmouth University Library holds approximately 248,000 volumes and nearly 22,500 electronic journal subscriptions. Academic programs are amply supported by state-of-the-art computer hardware and software and classroom/laboratory facilities. The major components supporting Monmouth's academic programs include UNIX and Windows 2003 server systems connected by a sophisticated campus Ethernet network spanning twenty-three buildings and encompassing more than 1,200 workstations campuswide. Workstations that are specifically dedicated to student use are distributed among forty-five instructional and open-use laboratories and include Pentium-class workstations and Macintosh workstations. Laptop plug-in ports and wireless connectivity are available in convenient locations across the campus. A campus communications network (HawkNet) connects all Monmouth University computing resources to the Internet. All students receive a computer account that provides them with e-mail, World Wide Web browsing and authoring tools, and electronic access to the Monmouth University Library catalog.

Financial Aid

Financial aid is available in the form of fellowships, assistantships, and loans. Fellowships are awarded to qualified students on the basis of outstanding undergraduate cumulative grade point average. A limited number of assistantships are available to continuing students, with preference given to those maintaining a high grade point average. To determine eligibility for all other forms of aid, applicants must file the FAFSA form, which is available online at http://www.fafsa.gov or at the Financial Aid Office. Monmouth University participates in the Federal Direct Student Loan Program, which makes both need- and non-need-based loans available to students who file the FAFSA. Alternative loan funding sources are available to those students who might not otherwise qualify for federal funding.

Cost of Study

Tuition for study in 2006–07 was $673 per credit. A University fee is assessed each semester.

Living and Housing Costs

Due to Monmouth's proximity to the beach, there are ample off-campus housing opportunities that are conveniently located near the University. These accommodations are relatively inexpensive since the academic year is also the off-season for tourism. A file of off-campus residences for rent is maintained by the Office of Off-Campus and Commuter Services.

Student Group

Monmouth University enrolls approximately 6,000 students, about 1,800 of whom are enrolled in the Graduate School. The diverse student body includes many international students representing twenty-three different countries.

Location

Monmouth University is located less than 1 mile from the Atlantic Ocean on a 155-acre campus in the quiet, suburban town of West Long Branch, New Jersey. The campus is only 1½ hours from both New York City and Philadelphia. Both can be easily accessed by train. Commuter bus service is also available. The surrounding area has numerous activities, restaurants, and cultural events. Its proximity to high-technology firms, financial institutions, and a thriving business-industrial sector provides Monmouth students and graduates with a wide variety of employment possibilities.

The University

Monmouth University is a private, moderate-sized coeducational teaching university committed to providing a learning environment that enables men and women to pursue their educational goals and realize their full potential for making significant contributions to their community and society. Small classes that allow for individual attention and student-faculty dialogue, together with careful academic advising and career counseling, are hallmarks of a Monmouth education. The Rebecca Stafford Student Center houses the Office of Student Services, the Bookstore, placement services, computer laboratories, study lounges, a full-service cafeteria, and student activities meeting rooms and offices. The University's NCAA Division I intercollegiate athletics program includes nine men's and ten women's teams.

Applying

An application for admission to the Graduate School includes a completed application form with application fee, official transcript of the undergraduate record, score reports from the appropriate entrance examination, transcripts of any graduate work done elsewhere, and two letters of recommendation covering the candidate's personal and professional qualifications to pursue graduate work. Additional requirements may apply, based on the program. Students should contact the Office of Graduate Admission for details. International students must also provide evidence of English proficiency.

The application deadlines are July 15 for the fall term, November 15 for the spring term, and May 1 for the summer sessions. An initial review of the complete application for admission is conducted by the Office of Graduate Admission. The file is then forwarded to the faculty director of the program for an admission decision. All correspondence should be conducted with the Office of Graduate Admission.

Correspondence and Information

Kevin L. Roane
Director of Graduate Admission
Monmouth University
West Long Branch, New Jersey 07764-1898
Phone: 732-571-3452
800-320-7754 (toll-free)
Fax: 732-263-5123
E-mail: gradadm@monmouth.edu
Web site: http://www.monmouth.edu/admission

FACULTY HEADS AND PROGRAMS

Master of Arts in History (M.A.): Chris DeRosa, Program Director and Assistant Professor of History; Ph.D., Temple.

The program accommodates students who wish to specialize in European or United States history. The program is designed not only for recent college graduates but also for secondary school teachers of history and social studies and professionals in government, the military, and business. Thesis and nonthesis options are available.

Master of Arts in Psychological Counseling (M.A.): Frances K. Trotman, Program Director, Professor of Psychology, and Chair of the Department of Psychological Counseling; Ph.D., Columbia.

The program offers practical and theoretical courses in quantitative methods, intervention skills, and assessment methods. The program equips students with proficiencies in the traditional counseling field as well as in emerging areas. Upon completion of the program, students may pursue an advanced degree or enter the post-master's certification program.

Master of Science in Professional Counseling (M.S.): Frances K. Trotman, Program Director, Professor of Psychology, and Chair of the Department of Psychological Counseling; Ph.D., Columbia.

The program prepares students for the Professional Counselor Licensure Examination. Courses satisfy criteria prescribed by the New Jersey State Board of Professional Counselor Examiners. The curriculum concentrates on developing the basic course areas, specialty areas, research and evaluation skills, and practical experiences.

Master of Arts in Liberal Arts (M.A.L.A.): Richard Veit, Program Director and Associate Professor of Anthropology; Ph.D., Pennsylvania.

This program is an interdisciplinary approach to the graduate study of the humanities, the natural and applied sciences, and the social and behavioral sciences. Students are encouraged to cross disciplinary boundaries and to combine various areas into a degree program that satisfies personal curiosity and contributes to the achievement of professional objectives.

Master of Science in Software Engineering (M.S.): William Tepfenhart, Program Director and Associate Professor of Software Engineering; Ph.D., Texas at Dallas.

The software engineering program offers the first degree of its kind in New Jersey. Students learn to develop, validate, implement, and maintain high-quality software products. Specialization tracks are offered in embedded real-time systems, information management, organizational management, and telecommunications.

Master of Science in Computer Science (M.S.): Michiko Kosaka, Program Director and Associate Professor of Computer Science; Ph.D., NYU.

The program includes concentrations in computer networks, intelligent information systems, and telecommunications. The computer networks concentration includes study in analysis/modeling and simulation. The program is open to students with undergraduate degrees other than computer science (some preparatory work may be required).

Master of Science in Nursing (M.S.N.): Janet Mahoney, Associate Dean, Program Director, and Associate Professor of Nursing; Ph.D., NYU.

The nursing program is designed to prepare the professional nurse for advanced practice nursing. Tracks are offered in adult or family nurse practitioner, nursing administration, adult psychiatric and mental health, school nursing, nursing education, and forensic nursing.

Master of Education (M.Ed.): Judith Bazler, Program Director and Professor of Education; M.Ed., Ed.D., Montana.

The Master in Education program is designed for fully certified teachers and other experienced education professionals to increase their knowledge and skills in specific content areas and earn additional credentials in the field of education. Graduates of the program master educational research and curriculum design as well as progressive theory and approaches to teaching.

Master of Science in Education (M.S.Ed.): Lynn Andrews Romeo, Associate Dean, Program Director, and Associate Professor of Educational Leadership and Special Education; Ed.D., Rutgers.

The Department of Educational Leadership and Special Education provides research-based master's and endorsement programs that are linked to national, state, and local standards and effectively prepare individuals to serve as support specialists, leaders, literacy coaches, and master teachers in educational settings. Toward this end, faculty and staff members and students within the department value diversity; pursue reflective inquiry; apply problem-solving strategies; promote innovative, interdisciplinary educational practice; effectively integrate technology; and collaboratively support and assist colleagues within the professional areas of special education, reading, educational counseling, supervision, and educational administration.

Master of Arts in Teaching (M.A.T.): Shelia Baldwin, Program Director and Associate Professor of Education; Ph.D., Texas A&M. Sarah Moore, Program Coordinator; M.A.Ed., Georgian Court.

The Master of Arts in Teaching (M.A.T.) provides initial certification in four program areas: early childhood and elementary education (P3–K5), elementary education (K5), elementary education and middle school specialization (K5/6–8), and secondary content certification (9–12). Programs have been designed to emphasize state and national curriculum standards and research-based best practices. The M.A.T. program ensures that its candidates are well prepared with appropriate knowledge, skills, and understanding in order to improve learning in educational systems through a commitment to lifelong learning and responsiveness to communities that represent diverse viewpoints, cultures, and learning styles.

Master of Business Administration (M.B.A.): Donald R. Smith, Program Director of the M.B.A. Program and Associate Professor; Ph.D., Berkeley.

The comprehensive M.B.A. program provides a balance of theory and practice. Students learn the business disciplines as well as specific organizational functions. Current issues and realistic applications of skill and knowledge are discussed with prominent business executives who serve as visiting lecturers and adjunct professors. The program requires between 30 and 48 credit hours of study, depending on the student's background.

Master of Arts in Criminal Justice (M.A.): Gregory J. Coram, Program Director and Associate Professor; Psy.D., Indiana State.

The program offers a broad perspective on the criminal justice system and its various institutions and processes. The curriculum provides a concentration in administration, which prepares criminal justice professionals or pre-career students for supervisory and administrative roles.

Master of Arts in Corporate and Public Communication (M.A.): Eleanor Novek, Program Director and Associate Professor of Communication; Ph.D., Pennsylvania.

The program prepares students to become effective communication specialists in a number of fields, from interpersonal communication to mass media. Specialist certificates are available in human resources communication, public relations, and media studies.

Master of Social Work (M.S.W.): Robin Mama, Program Director and Professor and Chair of Social Work; Ph.D., Bryn Mawr.

The program prepares students for professional practice aimed at improving the quality of life for vulnerable individuals, families, and communities, both locally and internationally. Social workers with master's degrees gain access to a new world of career opportunities, including licensing (either the License of Social Work or the License of Clinical Social Work) and specialized practice. The program offers two concentrations—one in services to families and children and one in international and community development.

Master of Arts in English (M.A.): Heide Estes, Program Director and Associate Professor of English; Ph.D., NYU.

The courses at Monmouth provide a broad education in English literature and a sound foundation for further graduate study. Secondary school teachers can fulfill their continuing education requirements and accrue credits toward salary increases by taking courses in the program. Those interested in personal enrichment or career advancement find that the course work improves critical-thinking abilities along with reading, speaking, and writing skills.

Master of Arts in Public Policy (M.A.): Joseph Patten, Program Director and Associate Professor of Political Science; Ph.D., West Virginia.

The Master of Arts in public policy is a 30-credit program that appeals to those who wish to work in the public interest. The program focuses on the role of ethics in public policy and provides opportunities for experiential learning internships. Students can learn about the public policy process and policy analysis, improve critical thinking, increase oral and written communication skills, and develop research skills.

MONTCLAIR STATE UNIVERSITY

Graduate Programs

Programs of Study

Montclair State University is a major source of cultural, economic, and educational life in northern New Jersey. By foreseeing the ever-accelerating changes in the academic world, the University developed its first doctoral programs in pedagogy (Ed.D.), audiology (Sc.D.), and environmental management (D.Env.M.). Students have the opportunity to choose from more than eighty graduate programs, which include a variety of master's degree programs as well as teaching certifications and other certificate programs.

The College of the Arts offers the M.F.A. degree in studio arts and the M.A. degree in communication studies, fine arts, music, and theater. Concentrations include art education, arts management, museum management, music education, music therapy, organizational communication, performance, production stage management, public relations, and speech communication.

The College of Education and Human Services offers the Master of Arts (M.A.) in counseling, educational leadership, exercise science, health education, physical education, and reading. The Master of Science (M.S.) is offered in nutrition and food science. The Master of Arts in Teaching (M.A.T.) degree is offered in many areas of instructional certification. The Master of Education (M.Ed.) is offered in the fields of teacher leadership, early childhood and elementary education, early childhood special education, learning disabilities, and special education.

In addition, the College offers a number of certificate programs in certified alcohol and drug counselor, food safety instructor, health education, human sexuality education, nutrition and exercise science, and philosophy for children; a postbaccalaureate certificate in dietetics, approved by the American Dietetic Association (ADA); and post-master certificates in advanced counseling and school counseling.

The College of Humanities and Social Sciences offers the M.A. degree in applied linguistics, applied sociology, child advocacy, communication sciences and disorders, educational psychology, English, French, legal studies, psychology, social sciences, and Spanish.

The College of Sciences and Mathematics offers the Master of Science (M.S.) in biology and molecular biology, chemistry and biochemistry, computer science, geoscience, mathematics, and statistics. The College offers the M.A. degree in environmental studies and teaching middle grades mathematics.

The School of Business offers the Master of Business Administration (M.B.A.) with concentrations in accounting, finance, international business, management, management information systems, and marketing. An executive-style Saturday M.B.A. program is offered at the Brookdale Community College campus in Lincroft.

Research Facilities

Montclair State's fully computerized on-campus microcomputer laboratories offer Internet access, individual e-mail accounts for students in good standing, and specialized software in numerous fields. A comprehensive multimedia environment provides for the most sophisticated technological classes and conferences.

The Harry A. Sprague Library houses a superior collection of 1.5 million items, with more than 3,000 periodical subscriptions, 32,000 government documents, 430,000 books, and 1 million media items, which include government and reference reports on microfilm, corporate annual reports, spoken-word and music recordings, and classical and award-winning productions on videotape. Electronic databases provide access to many resources. The library is a designated government documents depository. For further information, students should visit the library Web site at http://www.montclair.edu/library.

Financial Aid

In addition to the Federal Stafford Student Loan Program, a limited number of students may be eligible for graduate assistantships or graduate scholarships. The graduate assistantships provide students with a $7000 master's-level stipend as well as covering University-wide tuition and fees. Students are required to work 20 hours per week during a ten-month academic year. A small number of graduate scholarships are also available. Students wishing to be considered for a graduate assistantship should indicate this preference on the admission application. Prospective students should visit the University's Web site or contact the Graduate School for additional information. For information on other assistance that may be available, prospective students should contact the Office of Student Financial Aid (telephone: 973-655-4461).

Cost of Study

In 2007–08, tuition and fees begin at $535.39 per credit for New Jersey residents and $767.24 per credit for nonresidents and international students. Tuition and fees vary depending on the program and are subject to change.

Living and Housing Costs

At Montclair State University, on-campus housing is available for a limited number of graduate students. For up-to-date housing costs and information, students should visit the Office of Residential Housing and Education Web site at http://www.montclair.edu/resed/residentialfacilities.html. Meal plans are available in flexible package and cost options, depending on individual needs.

Student Group

Of the total University enrollment of approximately 16,000 students, close to 4,000 are graduate students, with approximately 4 percent of the graduate population being international students. The majority of the graduate students are working professionals who enhance the programs by bringing a wealth of knowledge into the classrooms. Most graduate courses are offered in the evening hours to accommodate working students.

Location

The University is conveniently located on a beautiful 200-acre hilltop campus in Montclair, New Jersey. This suburban town is surrounded by a rich diversity of cultural and recreational opportunities in northern New Jersey and in New York City, which is located 14 miles from campus. Train and bus service to New York City are available from the campus.

The University

Since its establishment in 1908, Montclair State has been recognized for its high academic standards, outstanding faculty members, and vital academic programs. With more than 16,000 students and 492 full-time faculty members, Montclair State University is New Jersey's second-largest university, combining the breadth and scope of a large university with the small class size and individual attention of a small college. Montclair State began offering master's degrees in 1932, and two doctoral programs were recently added. The University has been designated a Center of Excellence for the Fine and Performing Arts and is the only institution in New Jersey to receive two Governor's Challenge for Excellence grants. The University is the home of the renowned Center of Pedagogy, which epitomizes the University's belief in the scholarship of application—the practical application of knowledge.

Applying

Admission credentials are processed as soon as they are received. Most programs do not have specific deadlines and utilize rolling admissions. For those programs without a specific deadline, the University recommends that students submit their credentials as far in advance as possible from the semester they plan to begin their studies to ensure a timely review of their application. Some programs have fixed deadlines (as early as February 15 for the fall semester and September 15 for the spring semester) and students should refer to the admission packet on the school's Web site for the most up-to-date information. The admission decision is based on a number of criteria, including the undergraduate grade point average, standardized test scores, letters of recommendation, and the statement of objectives. Some fine arts programs may also require a satisfactory portfolio review or a successful audition.

Correspondence and Information

Office of Graduate Admissions and Support Services
Montclair State University
Phone: 973-655-5147
800-955-GRAD (toll-free)
Fax: 973-655-7869
E-mail: graduate.school@montclair.edu
Web site: http://www.montclair.edu/graduate

GRADUATE PROGRAM COORDINATORS

DOCTORAL DEGREES

Audiology (Sc.D.)
Department of Communication Sciences and Disorders: 973-655-7072.

Pedagogy (Ed.D.)
Specialization in Philosophy for Children: 973-655-4262.

Mathematics Pedagogy (Ed.D)
Department of Mathematics Sciences: 973 655-7275.

Environmental Management (D.Env.M.)
Department of Environmental Science: 973-655-4448.

MASTER'S DEGREES

Master of Arts (M.A.)
Applied Linguistics: 973-655-4286.
Child Advocacy: 973-655-4188.
Child Advocacy/Public Child Welfare: 973-655-4188.
Communication Sciences and Disorders: 973-655-7946.
Communication Studies/Organizational Communications: 973-655-7471.
Communication Studies/Public Relations: 973-655-7471.
Communication Studies/Speech Communications: 973-655-7471.
Counseling: 973-655-7216.
Counseling/Addictions Counseling: 973-655-7216.
Counseling/Community Counseling: 973-655-7216.
Counseling/School Counseling: 973-655-7216.
Counseling/Student Affairs/Counseling in Higher Education: 973-655-7216.
Educational Leadership (formerly Administration and Supervision): 973-655-7216.
Educational Psychology: 973-655-5201.
Educational Psychology/Child/Adolescent Clinical Psychology: 973-655-5201.
Educational Psychology/Clinical Psychology for Spanish-English Bilinguals: 973-655-5201.
English: 973-655-4274.
Environmental Studies/Environmental Education: 973-655-4448.
Environmental Studies/Environmental Management: 973-655-4448
Environmental Studies/Environmental Science: 973-655-4448.
Exercise Science and Physical Education/Exercise Sciences: 973-655-7120.
Exercise Science and Physical Education/Sports Administration and Coaching: 973-655-7120.
Exercise Science and Physical Education/Teaching and Supervision of Physical Education: 973-655-7120.
Family and Child Studies: 973-655-6905.
Fine Arts: 973-655-4210.
Fine Arts/Museum Management: 973-655-4210.
Fine Arts/Studio: 973-655-4210.
French/French Literature: 973-655-5143.
French/French Studies: 973-655-5143.
Health Education: 973-655-5253.
Legal Studies: 973-655-4152.
Legal Studies/Dispute Resolution: 973-655-4152.
Legal Studies/Governance, Compliance and Regulation: 973-655-4152.
Legal Studies/Intellectual Property: 973-655-4152.
Legal Studies/Legal Management, Information and Technology: 973-655-4152.
Music/Music Education: 973-655-7212.
Music/Music Performance: 973-655-7212.
Music/Music Theory and Composition: 973-655-7212.
Music/Music Therapy: 973-655-7212.
Physical Education: 973-655-5253.
Psychology: 973-655-5201.
Psychology/Industrial and Organizational Psychology: 973-655-5201.
Reading: 973-655-5407.
Social Sciences–History: 973-655-5261.
Spanish: 973-655-4285.
Teaching Middle Grades Mathematics: 973-655-5132.
Theater/Arts Management: 973-655-4109.
Theater/Production/Stage Management: 973-655-4109.
Theater/Theater Studies: 973-655-4109.

Master of Arts in Teaching (M.A.T.)
Master of Arts in Teaching (Content Areas): 973-655-5187.
Master of Arts in Teaching (Early Childhood Education): 973-655-5407.
Master of Arts in Teaching (Elementary Education): 973-655-5407.
Early Childhood Education and Teacher of Students with Disabilities: 973-655-5187.
Elementary Education and Teacher of Students with Disabilities: 973-655-5187.

Master of Business Administration (M.B.A.)
M.B.A. Program Office: 973-655-4306.
M.B.A./Accounting Program Office: 973-655-4306.
M.B.A./Finance Program Office: 973-655-4306.
M.B.A./International Business Program Office: 973-655-4306.
M.B.A./Management Program Office: 973-655-4306.
M.B.A./Management Information Systems Program Office: 973-655-4306.
M.B.A./Marketing Program Office: 973-655-4306.

Master of Education (M.Ed.)
Early Childhood and Elementary Education: 973 655-5407.
Early Childhood Special Education: 973-655-5407.
Learning Disabilities: 973-655-5187.
Special Education: 973-655-7360.
Teacher Leadership: 973-655-5187.

Master of Fine Arts (M.F.A.)
Department of Art and Design: 973-655-7294.

Master of Science (M.S.)
Biology: 973-655-4397.
Biology/Biology Science Education: 973-655-4397.
Biology/Ecology and Evolution: 973-655-4397.
Biology/Physiology: 973-655-4397.
Chemistry: 973-655-5140.
Chemistry/Biochemistry: 973-655-5140.
Computer Science: 973-655-4166.
Computer Science/Informatics: 973-655-4166.
Geoscience: 973-655-4448.
Mathematics: 973-655-5132.
Mathematics/Mathematics Education: 973-655-5132.
Mathematics/Pure and Applied Mathematics: 973-655-5132.
Molecular Biology: 973-655-7178.
Nutrition and Food Science: 973-655-5253.
Statistics: 973-655-5132.

CERTIFICATE PROGRAMS

Accounting: 973-655-3306.
Advanced Counseling: 973-655-7216.
American Dietetics Association (ADA): 973-655-5253.
Artist Diploma: 973-655-7212.
Child Advocacy: 973-655-4188.
CISCO: 973-655-4166.
Conflict Management in the Workplace: 973-655-4157.
Food Safety Instructor: 973-655-5253.
Geographic Information Science: 973 655-7558.
Gifted and Talented Education: 973-655-4104.
Health Education: 973-655-5253.
Human Sexuality Education: 973-655-5254.
International Business: 973 655-3306.
Management: 973 655-3306.
Molecular Biology: 973-655-4397.
Music Therapy: 973-655-7212.
Nutrition and Exercise Science: 973-655-5253.
Object Oriented Computing: 973-655-4166.
Paralegal Studies: 973-655-4152.
Performer's Certificate: 973-655-7212.
Philosophy for Children: 973-655-5170.
Teaching English to Speakers of Other Languages (TESOL): 973-655-4286.
Teaching Middle Grades Mathematics: 973-655-5132.
Translation and Interpretation in Spanish: 973-655-4285.
Water Resource Management: 973-655-4448.

Educational Services Certification
Associate School Library Media Specialist: 973-655-5187.
Certified Drug and Alcohol Counselor (CADC) Eligibility: 973-655-6996.
Learning Disabilities Teacher-Consultant: 973-655-7361.
Principal: 973-655-5170.
Reading Specialist: 973-655-5407.
Speech-Language Specialist: 973-655-7946.
Substance Awareness Coordinator: 973 655-6996.
Supervisor: 973-655-5170.

NEW COLLEGE OF CALIFORNIA

Graduate Programs

Programs of Study

The Master of Arts (M.A.) in Humanities and Leadership program at New College of California offers emphases in a multitude of topics in leadership studies. The humanities and leadership seminars take place two Saturdays per month and offer many unique ways to discover techniques for successful leadership. The program is offered in a three-semester—one full year—program that challenges traditional notions of leadership studies. Students investigate the humanities for strong visions of leadership, relying heavily on ideas and methods that emerge mainly from literature, art, music, and history. Students are encouraged to seek a broad and humane understanding of leadership, which distinguishes the program in part from more scientific studies in management. The College initiates a lifelong process of exploration and questioning, linking the intuitive creative processes to the learning of leadership skills. The momentum built up in the year of classes, and the research and writing of a thesis encourage students to keep the process of learning alive in the home, in the work place, and in the world at large.

The M.A. in Humanities and Leadership program with an emphasis in activism and social change acts as a social justice think tank by placing the study of social change at the center of its curriculum. Students and faculty members representing a diverse array of social justice concerns come together to think, share, reflect, and strategize.

The M.A. in Humanities and Leadership program with an emphasis in culture, ecology, and sustainable community (North Bay campus) focuses on developing leaders in the field of culture, ecology, and sustainable community. Students learn from a platform of critical and systems thinking, practical applications, and personal inquiry; build leadership skills; apply learning to individual and collaborative projects; and advance their vocations into postgraduate work.

The M.A. in Media Studies program combines interdisciplinary theory with hands-on experience in independent journalism and media production. Offering an innovative media studies education for social change, the program is founded on the belief that vibrant alternative media are urgently needed to renew our democracy and achieve peace and social justice. The program encourages media makers to speak the truth to expose injustice and to power and enable marginalized communities to use media and create a forum for the practice of democracy. Questioning the notion that media can be objective, the program explores models of media making that challenge people to think critically, imagine alternatives, and embrace possibilities for a better world.

The M.A. in Clinical Psychology program, offered by the School of Graduate Psychology, is a two-year, two-evenings-a-week master's degree program that leads to marriage and family therapist (MFT) licensure in California. The curriculum and pedagogy address the politics of gender, culture, race, and sexuality. The curriculum focuses on a progressive learning community, cutting-edge research, enlightened scholarship, innovative practice, and deep self-inquiry. It leads to a meaningful career in the helping professions in community mental-health settings as well as private practice. This graduate psychology program offers two concentrations: feminist clinical and social clinical. The feminist clinical concentration is a full-time, two-year program and the only one of its kind in the country.

The M.A. in Women's Spirituality program features an innovative curriculum that explores women's roles in prehistory and history, women's spiritual and religious leadership, women's work in healing and social activism, and women's ritual, literary, social, and artistic contributions.

The Master of Arts/Master of Fine Arts (M.A./M.F.A.) in Poetics program is unique, combining a core curriculum in the history of poetry since the Renaissance with innovative writing seminars, individual manuscript work, and reflections on the deep questions of poetry making today.

The M.A./M.F.A. in Writing and Consciousness program is unlike most writing programs, which primarily emphasize the student's entry into the market economy. The writing and consciousness program, founded in 1998, offers writers a two-year M.F.A. program that emphasizes both craft and social engagement.

The M.A./M.F.A. in Creative Inquiry program with an emphasis in experimental performance combines the development of a traditional conservatory, the aesthetics of experimental theater, and the politics of activist and queer performance.

The M.F.A. in Creative Inquiry program with an emphasis in interdisciplinary arts emphasizes the interdependence of the arts while providing a unique path for each student. New College encourages experimentation, challenging students to begin an adventure that is personal, daring, and artistic.

The Master of Arts in Teaching (M.A.T.) program, emphasizing critical, environmental, and global literacy, is a one-year, 20- to 30-unit program intended for educators who are committed to providing their students with an understanding of the interdependence of the people and ecosystems around the globe.

The Master of Business Administration (M.B.A.) program in environmental entrepreneurship is a truly green, triple-bottom-line M.B.A. program, which means that environmental sustainability, social equity, and financial profitability are recognized as equally valuable components throughout the curriculum.

The Science Institute is an accredited weekend program that offers a breadth of science classes in an accelerated format. This program is ideal for working adults seeking to enter degree programs in the health professions.

The School of Law at New College of California is the oldest public-interest law school in the country. Through a combination of required and elective courses, skills-training seminars, clinics, and an apprenticeship, students are taught current legal doctrine and learn to challenge the assumptions embedded in the law.

New College M.A. programs, unless otherwise stated, require a minimum of 36 units and can be completed in three semesters. M.F.A. programs require 54 semester units and can be completed in five semesters.

Research Facilities

In addition to its resident collections, the Humanities Library offers access to other collections through a free online catalog and periodicals database search and through interlibrary loans. Students may also use the libraries at the nearby University of California at Berkeley as well as the San Francisco Public Library system.

Financial Aid

New College graduate students may obtain federally administered financial aid loans and work-study according to their assessed need and eligibility. New College also offers partial-tuition scholarships. For more information, students should visit http://www.newcollege.edu/finaid.

Cost of Study

Full-time tuition was $7571 per semester for the 2005–06 academic year. Some of the master's degree programs run year-round and enable a student to obtain a master's degree in one calendar year. The graduate psychology program runs on a trimester basis, and its tuition differs depending on the student's year. Applicants should refer to the College Web site for current tuition.

Living and Housing Costs

New College has no residence facilities for graduate students. Housing costs vary in the surrounding community. The College's Web site lists housing options.

Student Group

New College graduate students come from diverse backgrounds but share interests in creative thinking, creativity, and social justice. The total New College population is approximately 1,000.

Location

New College graduate programs, unless otherwise stated, are housed in three buildings on Valencia Street in the heart of the Mission District in San Francisco. This urban campus adds to its charm with neighborhood coffee houses, theaters, cultural centers, and bookstores.

The College

New College, founded in 1971, emphasized teacher-student dialogue and the study of the humanities without rigid disciplinary separations. Today, the College also links personal development with social responsibility and emphasizes critical thinking, collaborative learning, and a respect for diversity.

Applying

Admissions requirements vary with each program. All programs require a bachelor's degree from an accredited college or university. None of the School of Humanities graduate programs require any examination requirements, such as the GRE. There is a $50 application fee, along with other requirements.

Correspondence and Information

Violetta Babich
New College of California
777 Valencia Street
San Francisco, California 94110

Phone: 415-437-3460
E-mail: admissions@newcollege.edu
Web site: http://www.newcollege.edu

THE FACULTY AND THEIR RESEARCH

The following is a partial list of faculty members.

Activism and Social Change

Helene Vosters, M.A. Freelance journalist, artist, and activist. Her academic background is in art and social change and anthropology, with emphases in postcolonial theory, advocacy research, and emancipatory scholarship. She has worked extensively on issues of class and gender equality and on GLBT rights.

Humanities and Leadership

Gary Tombleson, Director, Ph.D., California, San Diego. He has written scholarly articles on interdisciplinary humanities, Poe, and architecture. He has a variety of teaching experiences in writing, literature, speech, and leadership.

Poetics

Tom Clark, M.A., Cambridge. Author, *White Thought, Like Real People, Junkets on a Sad Planet: Scenes from the Life of John Keats* (poetry), and of many other volumes of poetry, criticism, biography, and fiction. Scholarly interests include Charles Olson, Robert Creeley, Vietnam War literature, and the English Renaissance.

Adam Cornford, Chair; M.A., San Francisco State. Author, *Decision Forest, The Snarling Gift,* (in *Terminal Velocities*), *Animations* (poetry), and *O-Town* (prose memoir). Cofounded and coedited *Processed World* magazine, 1980–1992. Scholarly interests include William Blake, surrealism and negritude, and science fiction.

David Meltzer. Author, *Writing Jazz, Reading Jazz,* and *Arrows: Selected Poems 1957–92,* among many other books of poetry, criticism, and nonfiction. Scholarly interests include Kaballah, American popular fiction, children's literature, and the poetics of prophecy.

Teaching (CEGL)

Sudia Paloma McCaleb, Director and Founder, New College Teacher Education Program; Ph.D. Author, *Building Communities of Learners: A Collaboration Among Teachers, Students, Family, and Community.* Research interests include parent-teacher collaboration and the use of art and music across the curriculum.

Women's Spirituality

Judy Grahn. Internationally known poet, cultural theorist, and lesbian-feminist. Recipient, Lifetime Achievement Award in Lesbian Letters. Work centers on the desire for a reclamation of the values and aesthetics of the Sacred Feminine. Publications include *Blood, Bread, and Roses* and *Another Mother Tongue: Gay Words, Gay Worlds.*

Luisah Teish. Priestess of Oshun in the Yoruba tradition, actress, dancer, storyteller, feminist activist, choreographer, and teacher. Author, *Jambalaya: A Natural Woman's Book of Personal Charms* and *Practical Rituals and Carnival of the Spirit: Seasonal Celebrations and Rites of Passage.*

Writing and Consciousness

Juvenal Acosta, Ph.D. candidate, California, Davis. Author, *El Cazador de tatuajes (The Tattoo Hunter)* and *Tango de la cicatriz (Scar Tango). Light From a Nearby Window,* his anthology of 21 younger Mexican poets, won the PEN Oakland Award. Translator of Lawrence Ferlinghetti, Michael McClure, Jack Kerouac, and Louise Gluck.

NEW MEXICO INSTITUTE OF MINING AND TECHNOLOGY

Graduate Studies

Programs of Study

New Mexico Institute of Mining and Technology offers graduate courses and research opportunities leading to the M.S. degree in biology, chemistry, computer science, electrical engineering, engineering mechanics, environmental engineering, geochemistry, geology, geophysics, hydrology, materials engineering, mathematics, mineral engineering, petroleum engineering, and physics. A Master of Engineering Management is also offered, as is a Master of Science in Teaching for certified teachers of high school mathematics and science.

The Institute offers programs of study and research leading to the Ph.D. degree in chemistry, computer science, geochemistry, geology, geophysics, hydrology, materials engineering, mathematics, petroleum engineering, and physics.

The Institute is strongly research oriented in fields of study dealing with natural physical resources, such as the atmosphere and water. Some research topics are hydrology, geochemistry, volcanology (the Southwest and Antarctic), economic geology, stratigraphy and sedimentation, mineral exploration and recovery (including the biology and chemistry of leaching), fuel and energy research (production, use, and environmental considerations), nuclear and hazardous-waste hydrology, enhanced oil recovery, explosives (including the effect of high energized and strain rates on materials), mine ventilation and fire control, cave studies, seismological crustal studies, geotechnical and soil mechanics, environmental engineering, thunderstorm electrification and cloud physics, stellar and extragalactic processes, radio astronomy, and atmospheric chemistry.

Research Facilities

Graduate research opportunities are supported by a number of on-campus research groups, such as the Bureau of Geology, the Petroleum Recovery Research Center, and the Research and Development Office, including the Geophysical Research Center for geophysics, hydrology, and climatology and a Center for Explosives Technology Research. Special facilities include the Langmuir Laboratory for Atmospheric Research (for studies of lightning, atmospheric physics, chemistry, and air quality), the Magdalena Ridge Observatory, Waldo Experimental Mines, and the EMRTC Field Laboratory for explosives research. There are also materials characterization laboratories for structure/property correlation (TEM, SEM, EPMA, FIM, AFM, and mechanical testing). The Very Large Array Radio Telescope and the Very Large Baseline Array, both facilities of the National Radio Astronomy Observatory, are headquartered on the campus. Cooperative research opportunities are available with the Sandia National Laboratories and Kirtland Air Force Base in Albuquerque and with Los Alamos National Laboratories. Modern computer and library facilities and a wide range of analytical equipment are available, including a liquid scintillation spectrometer, a stable isotope mass spectrometer, automated XRF and XRD spectrometers, a microprobe, a geochronology Ar/Ar laboratory, NMR spectrometers, a quadruple mass spectrometer, FT-IR UV/vis, fluorescence and GC/M spectrometers, GCs, HPLCs, DSC, seismological equipment, a thunderstorm-penetrating airplane, instrumented balloons and rockets, cloud physics radar, and the space plasma laboratory, including a helicon plasma generator, a fluid inclusion laboratory, and a quantitative mineralogy laboratory.

Financial Aid

In 2007, minimum stipends vary from $15,970 for nine months for beginning M.S. assistants to $39,000 for doctoral students who are on twelve-month appointments and have completed candidacy requirements.

Cost of Study

Tuition (based on a 12-credit-hour load) per semester for 2007–08 is $1850.22 for residents and $5950.35 for nonresidents. Those with teaching/research appointments qualify for resident tuition.

Living and Housing Costs

The cost of room and board for single students living in residence halls in 2007–08 is approximately $5000 per semester. Housing for married students starts at approximately $500 per month for unfurnished one- or two-bedroom efficiency apartments. Housing in Socorro is also available.

Student Group

Tech has approximately 1,800 students, of whom about 445 are graduate students. About 51 percent of graduate students are women. International students from thirty-five countries constitute 10 percent of the student body.

Location

Socorro (population 9,000) is located in the Rio Grande Valley, in central New Mexico, 75 miles south of Albuquerque on Interstate 25. The campus is at an elevation of 1,400 meters. Nearby mountains reach 3,280 meters in elevation. The principal sources of income in New Mexico are scientific research, agriculture, minerals (including petroleum, copper, potash, and coal), lumbering, and tourism. New Mexico's cultural diversity provides an unusual political and social environment. Historic sites, ghost towns, and ancient Indian ruins are all within a short driving distance of the campus.

The Institute

New Mexico Tech, which started as the New Mexico School of Mines in 1889, has achieved international recognition in petroleum engineering, materials engineering, atmospheric physics, geosciences, mineral-resource engineering, and explosives technology. Its faculty is outstanding in such diverse areas as astrophysics, atmospheric physics, biomedical research, seismology, geochemistry, economic geology, mineral exploration, groundwater hydrology, bacteria leaching of ores, laser and ion surface modification, intermetallics, ceramic and metal matrix composites, solid oxide fuel cells, capacitor dielectrics and high-temperature superconductors, and all areas of chemistry and petroleum recovery.

Applying

Tech encourages interested people who have a bachelor's or master's degree from an accredited college and a record indicating potential for advanced study and research in science or engineering to apply for admission. Transcripts of previous college work, references from 3 professors and/or professionals, and GRE General Test and Subject Test scores are required. International students must also submit TOEFL scores.

Correspondence and Information

Dr. David B. Johnson
Dean of Graduate Studies
New Mexico Institute of Mining and Technology
801 Leroy Place
Socorro, New Mexico 87801
Phone: 505-835-5513
800-428-TECH (8324; toll-free)
E-mail: graduate@nmt.edu
Web site: http://www.nmt.edu

THE FACULTY AND THEIR RESEARCH

Biology. T. Kieft, Chairman: environmental biology, microbiology. K. Kirk: evolutionary ecology. J. Naik: vascular physiology, blood-flow control. R. Reiss: molecular biology and evolution. S. Rogelj: cell, cell adhesion, molecular biology, biosensors, nanoparticles, biofilms, antimicrobial materials, pathogen detection. S. Shors: viral immunology.

Chemistry. O. Wingenter, Chairman: atmospheric chemistry. J. Altig: physical chemistry, computational chemistry, chemical education. M. Heagy: organic chemistry, fluorescence, physical organic chemistry. I. Janser: organic chemistry, chemistry in aqueous media. A Kornienko: organic chemistry, medicinal chemistry. T. Pietrass: inorganic chemistry, physical chemistry, magnetic resonance spectroscopy. M. Pullin: environmental chemistry, geochemistry. W. Steelant: biochemistry, biomembrane structures, signal transduction. L. Werbelow: theoretical chemistry, chemical physics, spectroscopy. P. Zhang: bioanalytical chemistry, nanomaterials, fluorescence spectroscopy.

Civil and Environmental Engineering. M. P. Cal, Chairman: air pollution engineering, water treatment, plasma processing of gas streams, fate and transport of pollutants. P. V. Brady: aquatic chemistry, global change, groundwater remediation. F. Y. C. Huang: hazardous waste management, biological and chemical waste treatment, environmental systems modeling, risk assessment. C. P. Richardson: biological wastewater treatment, groundwater contamination, site remediation.

Computer Science. A. Sung, Chairman: computational intelligence and its applications, information assurance, modeling and simulation, algorithms. H. Clausen: operating systems and systems programming, broadband Internet, secure software construction. J.-L. Lassez: bioinformatics, search engines. L. Liebrock: parallel processing, high-performance computing, well-posedness analysis, software security testing, graphics and visualization, information security. S. Mazumdar: database systems, massive storage systems, computational logic. X. Qin: parallel and distributed systems, real-time computing, storage systems, embedded systems, fault tolerance, performance evaluation. D. Shin: authentication and identity management, access control and trust management, XML and Web services security, pki/pmi and secure e-commerce, software and security engineering. H. Soliman: computer networks, Internet protocols and security, image compression using neural wireless networks, fiber optics routing.

Earth and Environmental Science. R. S. Bowman, Chairman: surface chemistry, groundwater contamination, solute transport. R. C. Aster: earthquake and volcanic seismology and seismic structure. G. Axen: continental tectonics and fault mechanics; extensional, convergent, and wrench settings. S. Bilek: earthquake rupture processes, tsunami generation, fault-zone material properties. P. Boston: cave and karst studies, geomicrobiology. A. R. Campbell: metallic ore deposits, stable isotope geochemistry. K. Condie: trace element and isotope geochemistry, Precambrian studies. B. Harrison: soil properties, recurrence intervals of earthquakes, soil salinization in arid environments, soil stability. J. Hendrickx: soil water physics, vadose zone hydrology, soil contamination. D. B. Johnson: biostratigraphy, Pleozoic depositional environments. J. B. Johnson: seismicity, thermal, and acoustics of volcanic conduit processes. P. R. Kyle: igneous geochemistry, Antarctic geology, volcanology. W. C. McIntosh: argon geochronology, Cenozoic volcanism in southwestern united states, Antarctic volcanism. P. S. Mozley: environmental geology, sedimentary petrology, low-temperature geochemistry. D. I. Norman: metallic ore deposits, geochemistry of ore deposits, fluid inclusion studies. F. M. Phillips: groundwater chemistry, isotope hydrology, groundwater dating, quaternary studies. C. M. Snelson: exploration geophysics and seismicity. G. Spinelli: hydrogeology of oceanic lithosphere, groundwater–surface water interactions, sediment physical properties, sedimentology. E. Vivoni: surface water hydrology. J. L. Wilson: groundwater hydrology, numerical and analytic modeling, stochastic hydrology, colloid and bacterial transport.

Electrical Engineering. S. W. Teare, Chairman: experimental adaptive optics, radiation effects on semiconductors, directed energy. R. Arechiga: speech recognition. A. Jorgensen: optical interferometry techniques and instrumentation. R. Bond: design for test/manufacturability, teaching effectiveness. E. Calloni (adjunct): gravitational wave interferometry. A. El-Osery: wireless communications, control systems, soft computing. H. Erives: integration and calibration of hyperspectral and multispectralsensors, airborne and space-borne image analysis. P. Krehbiel (adjunct): lightning, thunderstorms, radar. G. Mansfield (adjunct): radar systems. J. Meason (adjunct): nuclear, electromagnetic, and space radiation effects and directed energy. D. Reicher (adjunct): physics and simulation of thin films. S. R. Restaino (adjunct): adaptive optics, novel optical systems. W. Rison: atmospheric electricity, instrumentation, lightning projection. R. Thomas: lightning, thunderstorms, and instrumentation. K. Wedeward: adaptive control, robotic systems, complex systems. D. Wick (adjunct): experimental adaptive and active optics. H. Xiao (adjunct): photonic/fiber sensors, intelligent sensor networks, optical communications, computer vision.

Engineering Mechanics. S. Bakhtiyarov, Chairman: non-Newtonian fluid mechanics, heat and mass transfer, oil recovery, rheology, metalcasting, materials processing, multiphase flows, instrumentation, fluidized beds, porous medium flows, nanotechnology, tribology, turbulence, microgravity. P. Cooper: explosives engineering. P. Gerity: robotics, system integration, technology turnkey and licensing. A. Ghosh: macrobehavior of composites, biomechanics, finite element analysis experimental mechanics and instrumentation, structural health monitoring and restoration construction materials and project management. C. Hockensmith: energetic materials, piezoelectrics and ferroelectrics phytoremediation, crystallography, and analytical techniques. J. Kennedy: science and applications of explosives. S. Lim: energetic materials, explosives technology, linear and conical shaped charges. W. Marcy: general aviation, conceptual design. J. Marshall: test measurement, process control systems. J. Meason: electromagnetic directed energy, nuclear, engineering. B. Melof: pyrotechnics, improvised explosives, fuel air explosions, explosive diagnostics. A. R. Miller: finite element analysis, explosive synthesis of materials, high-temperature system and simulation, actuators and actuator controls. W. Ostergren: mechanics of materials, structural anlaysis, machine design, propulsion and power systems. J. Stofleth: instrumentation techniques for explosives testing, experimentation and explosives. A. Watts: design and performance analysis of inertial navigation systems. N. Yilmaz: computational fluid dynamics, reactive flow, combustion and chemical kinetics, fire modeling, internal combustion engines. A. Zagrai: intelligent systems, structures and mechanisms, structural monitoring and infrastructure security.

Master of Engineering Management. Designed for engineers and applied scientists with work experience; offered both on campus and via Internet streaming.

Materials Engineering. D. Hirschfeld, Chairman: engineering ceramics and advanced composites, processing, protective coatings, thermal spray, solid free-form fabrication. G. M. Bond: electron microscopy, radiation damage, intermetallics, micromechanisms of deformation and fracture, hydrogen effects, CO_2 sequestration, bioimetic materials. T. D. Burleigh: corrosion mechanisms and mechanisms of corrosion protection. P. Fuierer: electronic ceramics, magnetic ceramics, sol-gel thin films. O. T. Inal: plasma-assisted (HCD and DC) CVD; design/modification of reactive solder/braze alloys; radiation-, shock-, and laser-induced defects; explosive ceramic and metal working; laser and plasma surface modification; enhancement of low-temperature ductility in ordered intermetallics; plasma spray deposition of oxide coatings. N. Kalugin: optoelectronics and nonlinear optics, nanostructures and nanotechnology, TeraHz lasers and photodetectors, solid-state physics of nanostructures, semiconductor materials and devices. P. Lu: electron microscopy and high-resolution electron microscopy, electronic thin film, chemical vapor deposition. B. Majumdar: mechanisms and mechanics of deformation and fracture, thin films and interfaces, composites, advanced alloys. J. McCoy: polymer blends, phase transitions, interfaces. Adjunct faculty: Adolph, Browning, Curro, Doughty, Hockensmith, Jacobson, Lowe, Ravi, Romig, Sickafus, Smith.

Mathematics. A. Hossain, Chairman: theory and applications of statistics, estimation, reliability and regression diagnostics. R. Aitbayev: numerical partial differential equations, numerical analysis. I. Avramidi: geometric analysis, mathematical physics, quantum field theory, differential geometry. B. Borchers: optimization, inverse problems. R. Ibragimov: fluid mechanics, geophysical fluid dynamics, multiphase flows, atmosphere-ocean dynamics, lie group analysis of differential equations, mathematical modeling. G. Kerr: thermoelasticity, integral equations. O. Makhnin: stochastic processes, spatial statistics, computational statistics, time series. S. Schaffer: applied mathematics, numerical analysis, control theory. J. Starrett: dynamical systems, physics models, knot theory. W. D. Stone: differential equations, mathematical biology, industrial mathematics. B. Wang: partial differential equations, dynamical systems, applied mathematics.

Mineral Engineering. N. Mojtabai, Chairman: rock blasting and fragmentation, ground vibration, geomechanics, mining applications. C. Aimone-Martin: rock blasting, ground vibration, soil mechanics, instrumentation, geostatistics. J. Barker: industrial minerals. W. S. Chavez Jr.: ore deposit genesis and natural resources utilization, mine waste assessment and remediation. A. Fakhimi: geomechanics, numerical modeling. I. Gundiler: hydrometallurgy, mineral processing. V. McLemore: economic geology. K. Oravescz: rock mechanics, surveying, instrumentation. I. Walder: geochemistry, mine waste assessment and remediation.

Petroleum and Chemical Engineering. H. Y. Chen, Chairman, Petroleum Engineering: well testing, reservoir mechanics. D. Weinkauf, Chairman, Chemical Engineering: polymer engineering, plasma polymerication, membrane separations, microsensors. R. Balch: geophysics, artificial intelligence, reservoir characterization. R. Bretz: transport phenomena, phase behavior, natural gas processing. J. Buckley: petrophysics and surface chemistry, reservoir wettability. T. Engler: formation evaluation, petrophysics, unconventional gas recovery. R. Grigg: gas flooding processes, phase behavior. R. Lee: natural gas storage, applied numerical methods, phase behavior. R. Seright: profile control, polymer, water and chemical flooding. J. Taber: oil recovery processes, mechanisms. M. Tartis: biomedical engineering. L. Teufel: rock mechanics, naturally fractured reservoir characterization in situ stresses, reservoir simulation including stress distribution, subsidence mechanisms.

Physics. D. Westpfahl, Chairman: dynamics of spiral and dwarf galaxies. I. Avramidi: mathematical physics, analysis on manifolds, quantum field theory. K. Balasubramanian: spectroscopy and polarized radiative transfer dynamics for solar active regions, vector magnetometry. D. Buscher: optical/IR interferometry, atmospheric seeing measurement, adaptive optics, early and late stages of stellar evolution. S. Colgate: astrophysics, plasma physics, atmospheric physics. M. Creech-Eakman: stellar astrophysics, mass loss, optical/IR interferometry, IR instrumentation. K. Eack: production of energetic particles and gamma rays in thunderstorms. J. Eilek: plasma astrophysics, quasars, radio galaxies, pulsars. M. Goss: radio astronomy, interstellar medium. C. Haniff: spatial interferometry at optical and near-infrared wavelengths, atmospheric turbulence, imaging theory, evolved stars. T. Hankins: radio astronomy of pulsars, instrumentation, signal processing. P. Hofner: star formation, interstellar medium, X-ray astronomy. R. M. Juberias: outer planets observations and atmospheric dynamics. D. Klinglesmith: asteroids, robotic telescope operations. P. Krehbiel: lightning studies, radar meteorology, thunderstorm electrification, remote sensing. G. Manney: atmospheric science, stratospheric dynamics/transport, stratospheric polar processes and ozone loss. J. Meason: nuclear physics, nuclear and space radiation effects, electromagnetic radiation effects and directed energy. K. Minschwaner: radiative transfer and climate, physics of the middle and upper atmosphere. S. Myers: cosmology, extragalactic radio astronomy, interferometric imaging algorithms. T. Pietrass: organic chemistry, organic synthesis, physical organic chemistry. D. Raymond: geophysical fluid dynamics, cloud physics, clouds and climate. W. Rison: atmospheric electricity, radar meteorology, instrumentation. V. Romereo: energetic materials, shock phenomena, high-energy physics. M. Rupen: gas and dust in galaxies, radio transients. E. Ryan: asteroid collisional physics, observational and theoretical studies. W. Ryan: asteroid astronomy, high-energy physics. S. Sessions: field theoretic approaches to atmospheric physics. R. Sonnenfeld: charge transport by lightning, embedded systems and instrumentation, tribocharging of ice. G. Taylor: very long baseline radio astronomy, active galactic nuclei. S. Teare: adaptive optics, instrumentation, astrophysics. R. Thomas: atmospheric physics, instrumentation. J. Ulvestad: compact radio sources, Seyfert galaxies, AGNs, space, VLBI techniques and future missions. W. Winn: thunderstorm electrification, electric discharges in gases, instrumentation. L. Young: star formation and the interstellar medium, dwarf and elliptical galaxies.

Macey Conference Center and Turtle Bay.

THE NEW SCHOOL: A UNIVERSITY

Graduate Overview

Programs of Study

The New School is a renowned progressive university comprising eight schools with a common goal: to prepare and inspire its 9,300 undergraduate and graduate students to effect positive change in the world.

The New School for General Studies was the first university in the United States for adults. Students can attend on a part-time or full-time basis and take advantage of hundreds of courses—many of which are taught in the evening—that are available to both degree and continuing education students. The degrees offered are the M.A. and M.S. in international affairs, the M.A. in media studies (online and on site), the M.A. in Teaching English to Speakers of Other Languages (M.A.T.E.S.O.L.) (online only), the M.S. in global finance, an M.F.A. in creative writing, an accelerated bachelor's/master's option, and graduate certificates in media management (online only) and documentary media studies.

The New School for Social Research is the University's graduate center for the core social sciences and philosophy. It began in 1933 as the University in Exile, a haven for refugee European scholars; today it maintains that progressive tradition by viewing world peace and global justice not as abstract ideals but as central and practical goals of every course of study. The school offers the M.A. and Ph.D. in anthropology, economics, historical studies, philosophy, political science, psychology, and sociology; the M.A. in global political economy and finance and liberal studies; the M.S. in economics; and accelerated bachelor's/master's options with Eugene Lang College.

Milano The New School for Management and Urban Policy trains students for leadership in the nonprofit, public, and private sectors. The superb faculty blends theory with practice and progressive analysis with hands-on activism. Milano students work on local and global issues affecting organizations and urban communities in New York City and around the world. The school offers the M.S. in health services management and policy, human resources management, nonprofit management, organizational change management, and urban policy analysis management; the Ph.D. in public and urban policy; accelerated bachelor's/master's options with Eugene Lang College; and graduate certificates.

At Parsons The New School for Design, students do not just learn about art and design—they redefine it. Successful alumni have paved the way for future graduates for a century, and the school remains committed to finding innovative design solutions to real-world problems. Parsons offers the M.A. in the history of decorative arts; the M.Arch.; the M.F.A. in design and technology, fine arts, lighting design, and photography; and certificate programs in fashion studies, fine art and foundation, graphic and digital design, and interior design.

Mannes College The New School for Music is an internationally renowned conservatory of classical music that provides a solid foundation for the serious graduate or undergraduate student of music to pursue a career in music. The instructors are top professionals in their fields and include scholars, composers, conductors, and performing artists from some of the world's most highly regarded orchestras, ensembles, and opera companies. Mannes offers the M.M. and diploma programs in music and performance or composition and arranging (for classical musicians).

The New School for Drama trains students for careers in the theater as actors, directors, and playwrights. Students work on full-scale productions with peers, faculty members, and guest artists, and classes and rehearsals often involve collaboration between students from all three concentrations. Over the course of three years, students are challenged by their classmates, mentored by a faculty of professional artists, and inspired to find their own voice. The school offers the M.F.A. in acting, directing, and playwriting.

Research Facilities

In addition to University-wide computer labs and a vast library system, each school offers its students unique resources. Students at The New School have access to a wide range of materials and resources from state-of-the-art practice rooms, multimedia labs, studios, and performance spaces to collections, archives, and institutes.

The New School is also a member of the Research Library Association of South Manhattan, one of the largest interuniversity library consortia in the country. Members of the consortium include The New School's Raymond Fogelman Library, which houses 173,000 volumes on the social sciences and philosophy; New York University's Elmer Holmes Bobst Library; and the Cooper Union Library. The total holdings of these libraries exceed 4.1 million volumes and 25,000 journals. Beyond the consortium are the rich resources of New York City, including 250 METRO-member libraries and the public library systems of the five New York boroughs.

Financial Aid

Many students in degree programs at The New School take advantage of financial aid programs. The University uses applications such as the FAFSA or Undergraduate International Student Scholarship Application to assess student eligibility for federal, state, and institutional financial aid. Graduate students should contact their academic department for separate applications for institutional awards, such as assistantships.

Cost of Study

The cost of attending The New School varies from program to program. For the cost of each program of study and information about on-campus housing charges, prospective students should visit http://www.newschool.edu/tuition/.

Living and Housing Costs

The University offers on-campus housing, University-run apartments, and assistance finding housing off campus. The cost of housing, food, transportation, books, and living expenses in New York City averages $17,000 annually. For more information, students should visit http://www.newschool.edu/studentservices.

Student Group

Students at The New School are talented, driven, and eager to effect change in their chosen fields. Students come from a variety of backgrounds and include undergraduates just out of high school; working professionals earning their bachelor's, master's, or doctoral degrees; and continuing education students and retired professionals eager to take advantage of the University's extensive and varied body of course offerings. Last year, the University enrolled 5,382 undergraduate students and 3,313 graduate students in addition to continuing education students. Together they represented 101 countries and all fifty states.

Location

The New School's location in New York City gives students access to an abundance of resources. Students are encouraged to take advantage of the city's many museums, performance venues, and other cultural institutions, which are only a walk or a subway ride away. An extension of the classroom, the city also offers excellent professional and networking opportunities, and some classes require that students work with outside businesses to complete assignments—giving them unparalleled real-world experience. Internships and apprenticeships with leading New York City companies and organizations in every field are also available, and many students have moved on from internships to successful careers with those companies and organizations upon graduation.

The University

From The New School's Greenwich Village campus come economists and actors, fashion designers and urban policy managers, dancers and anthropologists, orchestra conductors, filmmakers, political scientists, organizational experts, jazz musicians, scholars, psychologists, historians, journalists, and above all, world citizens—people whose ideas and innovations forge new paths in the arts, design, the humanities, public policy, and the social sciences. In addition to offering 70 graduate and undergraduate degrees, the University offers certificate programs and almost 1,000 continuing education courses to some 17,000 adult learners every year. Classes and degree programs are offered online and on site.

Applying

The New School is looking for talented and dedicated students who demand serious study, whatever their field. Because of the large number of programs offered at The New School, each school has its own application requirements. Students should visit the Web sites for detailed information.

Correspondence and Information

For general information, contact:
The New School
66 West 12th Street
New York, NY 10003
Phone: 212-229-5600
E-mail: Webmaster@newschool.edu
Web site: www.newschool.edu

For admissions, contact:

The New School for General Studies
Phone: 212-229-5630
E-mail: nsadmissions@newschool.edu

The New School for Social Research
Phone: 212-229-5710
E-mail: socialresearchadmit@newschool.edu

Milano The New School for Management and Urban Policy
Phone: 212-229-5462
E-mail: : milanoadmissions@newschool.edu

Parsons The New School for Design
Phone: 212-229-8910
E-mail: inquiry@newschool.edu

Eugene Lang College The New School for Liberal Arts
Phone: 212-229-5665
E-mail: lang@newschool.edu

Mannes College The New School for Music
Phone: 212-580-0210 Ext. 4862
E-mail: mannesadmissions@newschool.edu

The New School for Drama
Phone: 212-229-5859
E-mail: inquiry@newschool.edu

The New School for Jazz and Contemporary Music
Phone: 212-229-5896 Ext. 4589
E-mail: jazzadm@newschool.edu

GRADUATE PROGRAM FACULTY

The New School prides itself on its exceptional faculty. The University's strong academic programs and dedication to the arts attract leading professionals in their fields. Students should visit each school's Web site for faculty members' biographies and more information.

NEW YORK UNIVERSITY

Graduate School of Arts & Science

Programs of Study

The Graduate School of Arts & Science offers master's and doctoral degrees in fifty-three departments and programs within the Faculty of Arts & Science, including a wide range of interdisciplinary programs. The Graduate School also offers dual degrees with the faculties of the NYU School of Business, the School of Public Service, the School of Law, the School of Medicine, the School of Dentistry, and Long Island University's Palmer School of Library and Information Science. The NYU Institutes for Advanced Study allow distinguished visiting faculty members from throughout the world to join specialists and graduate students at NYU in research activities. Graduate students may also study at La Pietra, NYU's Italian research center on the outskirts of Florence, as well as participate in other global exchange programs.

Departmental requirements for the Ph.D. degree vary among disciplines, but all candidates for the doctoral degree are expected to demonstrate language proficiency and complete a thesis that makes an original contribution to their field of study. Students must also pass departmental qualifying or comprehensive examinations.

Research Facilities

The Elmer Holmes Bobst Library and Study Center houses 2.7 million volumes while providing seating for 3,500 students. The library integrates into one enormous collection more than 2.2 million books, journals, microfilms, and other materials from various libraries of the University. It is one of the world's largest open-stack libraries. With the introduction of BOBCAT (for BOBst Library CATalog), the first online catalog in a New York City library, students may search the library's collections using computer terminals. Among the noteworthy resources of the Bobst Library are special collections in education, science, music, Near Eastern and Ibero-American languages and literatures, and Judaica and Hebraica; the Tamiment Institute Library on the history of the U.S. labor movement; the Fales Library of English and American Literature since 1750; the Robert Frost Library; and numerous rare books and manuscripts. The Avery Fisher Electronics and Media Center, also in Bobst, is a center for research in music and film, with extensive holdings of videos, scores, and recordings. The Courant Institute of Mathematical Sciences has a highly specialized research collection consisting of more than 60,000 volumes in mathematics, computer science, and physics. CDC CYBER, IBM 4341, DEC, and other nonspecialized computer systems are also available in the Courant Institute of Mathematical Sciences.

The NYU art collection and the Grey Art Gallery and Study Center emphasize interdisciplinary study for students, instructors, artists, and scholars, and their exhibits also serve the community at large.

Financial Aid

The financial aid program of the Graduate School of Arts & Science seeks to ensure that outstanding, academically qualified students have financial support while they work toward their degrees. The Graduate School offers an extensive program of support. Awards for fully-funded students include support for tuition, fees, NYU health insurance, and a stipend. The Henry Mitchell MacCracken Program provides up to five years of full support for most entering doctoral students. This includes a one-time, $1000 Dean's Supplementary Fellowship grant for start-up research and educational expenses. New York University offers a full range of loan programs for students who require additional funding.

Cost of Study

In 2007–08, the cost of tuition is $1139 per credit, plus a registration fee of $57 per credit.

Living and Housing

University housing is available to some full-time students. Most students live off campus.

Student Group

The total enrollment at New York University is more than 50,000, with approximately 1,100 Ph.D. students and 1,800 master's students enrolled in the Graduate School of Arts & Science. Students come to NYU from more than 200 undergraduate institutions, all fifty states, and from more than 100 other countries.

Location

New York University is an integral part of the metropolis of New York City—a global city that is also arguably the cultural, artistic, intellectual, and financial center of the nation. The University's chief center for study is at Washington Square in Greenwich Village, which has long been famous for its contributions to the fine arts, literature, and drama and for its personalized, independent style of living. New York University makes a significant contribution to the creative activity of the Greenwich Village area through the high concentration of its faculty members and students residing within a few blocks of the University.

The University

New York University is a private, metropolitan university. Founded in 1831, the University now comprises twelve schools, colleges, and divisions at four centers in Manhattan, seven international campuses, and a 500-acre site at Sterling Forest near Tuxedo, New York, where certain of the University's facilities—notably the Institute of Environmental Medicine—are located. Courses for the Graduate School of Arts & Science are offered primarily at Washington Square; however, courses are also held at the University's Medical Center, the David B. Kriser Dental Center, Sterling Forest, the Institute of Fine Arts, and in the cities of Prague, Florence, London, Paris, Cracow, and Salamanca. Special arrangements have also been made to enable students to use the facilities of such nearby institutions as the Metropolitan Museum of Art, the New York Botanical Garden, the Museum of Modern Art, the Osborn Laboratories for Marine Science, the New York Zoological Society, and the Strang Clinic for Preventive Medicine.

NYU is a member of the distinguished Association of American Universities. The University is accredited by the Middle States Association of Colleges and Schools. Graduate and professional accrediting agencies recognize its degrees in many categories.

Applying

The Graduate School of Arts and Science prefers that applicants file the application online at http://www.nyu.edu/gsas/online. A complete application includes an application fee ($85 for the online application and $95 for paper), three letters of academic reference, GRE scores, and official college transcripts. Many departments also require a writing sample. Applications must be received by Graduate Enrollment Services before the published deadline date. Prospective students should consult the Graduate School of Arts & Science *Bulletin* or Web site to read about department deadline dates and program-specific application requirements.

Correspondence and Information

Graduate School of Arts & Science
New York University
Cooper Station, P.O. Box 907
New York, New York 10276-0907

Phone: 212-998-8050
E-mail: gsas.admissions@nyu.edu
Web site: http://gsas.nyu.edu

FACULTY HEADS

Catharine R. Stimpson, Dean, Graduate School of Arts & Science; Ph.D., Columbia.
Malcolm N. Semple, Vice Dean, Graduate School of Arts & Science; Ph.D., Monash.
Roberta S. Popik, Associate Dean, Graduate Enrollment Services, Graduate School of Arts & Science; Ph.D., Northwestern.
Kathleen T. Talvacchia, Assistant Dean, Academic and Student Life, Graduate School of Arts & Science; Ed.D., Columbia.
Vielka Holness, Director, Master's College, Graduate School of Arts & Science; M.P.A., Columbia.
Africana Studies: Awam Amkpa, Ph.D., Bristol.
American Studies: Carolyn Dinshaw, Ph.D., Princeton.
Ancient Near Eastern and Egyptian Studies: Mark Smith, Ph.D., Yale.
Anthropology: Fred R. Myers, Ph.D., Bryn Mawr.
Atmosphere Ocean Science: David Holland, Ph.D., McGill.
Basic Medical Sciences/Sackler Institute of Biomedical Sciences: Joel D. Oppenheim, Associate Dean; Ph.D., Loyola Chicago.
Bioethics: Life, Health, and Environment: William Ruddick, Ph.D., Harvard.
Biology: Gloria Coruzzi, Ph.D., NYU.
Biomaterials: Van P. Thompson, D.D.S., Maryland.
Biomedical Sciences/Mount Sinai School of Medicine: Diomedes Logothetis, Dean; Ph.D., Harvard.
Chemistry: Nicholas Geacintov, Ph.D., Syracuse.
Cinema Studies: Richard Allen, Ph.D., UCLA.
Classics: Michael Peachin, Ph.D., Columbia.
Comparative Literature: Nancy Ruttenburg, Ph.D., Stanford.
Computational Biology: Michael Shelley, Ph.D., Arizona.
Computer Science: Margaret Wright, Ph.D., Stanford.
Creative Writing: Deborah Landau, Ph.D., Brown.
East Asian Studies: Xudong Zhang, Ph.D., Duke.
Economics: David Pearce, Ph.D., Princeton.
English: John Guillory, Ph.D., Yale.
Environmental Health Sciences: Max Costa, Ph.D., Arizona.
Ergonomics and Biomechanics: Margareta Nordin, Med.Dr.Sci., Göteborg (Sweden).
European and Mediterranean Studies: K. Fleming, Ph.D., Berkeley.
Fine Arts: Mariet Westermann, Ph.D., NYU.
French: Judith Graves Miller, Ph.D., Rochester.
German: Ulrich Baer, Ph.D., Yale.
Hebrew and Judaic Studies: Lawrence Schiffman, Ph.D., Brandeis.
History: Michael Gomez, Ph.D., Chicago.
Humanities and Social Thought: Robin Nagle, Ph.D., Columbia.
Institute of French Studies: Edward Berenson, Ph.D., Rochester.
Irish Studies: John Waters, Ph.D., Duke.
Italian Studies: Ruth Ben-Ghiat, Ph.D., Brandeis.
Journalism: Brooke Kroeger, M.S., Columbia.
Latin American and Caribbean Studies: Thomas Abercrombie, Ph.D., Chicago.
Law and Society: Lewis Kornhauser, Ph.D., Berkeley.
Linguistics: Richard Kayne, Ph.D., MIT.
Mathematics: Jalal Shatah, Ph.D., Brown.
Middle Eastern and Islamic Studies: Zachary Lockman, Ph.D., Harvard.
Museum Studies: Bruce Altshuler, Ph.D., Harvard.
Music: Michael Beckerman, Ph.D., Columbia.
Near Eastern Studies: Michael Gilsenan, Ph.D., Oxford.
Neural Science: J. Anthony Movshon, Ph.D., Cambridge.
Performance Studies: José Esteban Muñoz, Ph.D., Duke.
Philosophy: Stephen Schiffer, Ph.D., Oxford.
Physics: David Grier, Ph.D., Michigan.
Politics: Nathaniel Beck, Ph.D., Yale.
Psychology: Marisa Carrasco, Ph.D., Princeton.
Religious Studies: Angela Zito, Ph.D., Chicago.
Russian and Slavic Studies: Eliot Borenstein, Ph.D., Wisconsin.
Sociology: Dalton Conley, Ph.D., Columbia.
Spanish and Portuguese: Gerard Aching, Ph.D., Berkeley.
Trauma and Violence Transdisciplinary Studies: Avital Ronell, Ph.D., Princeton.

The view north along Fifth Avenue seen from the center of New York University's Washington Square campus.

The entrance to the administrative offices of the Graduate School of Arts & Science, located at 6 Washington Square North.

NORTH CAROLINA AGRICULTURAL AND TECHNICAL STATE UNIVERSITY

School of Graduate Studies

Programs of Study

The School of Graduate Studies at North Carolina Agricultural and Technical State University (North Carolina A&T) offers more than forty academic programs in the broad categories of agriculture, business, education, engineering, humanities, and science and technology. The major areas of study and degrees conferred are agricultural economics (M.S., with concentrations in agricultural marketing and international trade and in rural development policy), agricultural education (M.S., with concentrations in professional licensure and professional service), animal health science (M.S.), biology (M.S. and M.S./secondary education), chemical engineering (M.S.), chemistry (M.S. and M.S./secondary education), civil and environmental engineering (M.S.), computational and science engineering (M.S.), computer science (M.S.), curriculum and instruction (M.A.E.D. in elementary and reading education and M.S. in instructional technology), electrical and computer engineering (M.S. and Ph.D.), energy and environmental studies (Ph.D.), English (M.A. in African-American and English literature and M.S. in English education), history (M.S. in history education), human development and services (M.S. in adult education, counselor education, human resources–agency counseling, human resources–rehabilitation counseling, and school administration), human environment and family sciences (M.S. in food and nutritional sciences), human performance and leisure studies (M.S. in physical education), human resources management (M.S.M.), industrial and systems engineering (M.S. and Ph.D.), industrial technology (M.S.I.T., with concentrations in construction management, electronics and computer technology, environmental and occupational safety and health, graphic communication systems, information technology, manufacturing systems, and occupational safety and health), leadership studies (Ph.D.), management information systems (M.S.M.), mathematics (M.S. in applied mathematics and secondary education), mechanical engineering (M.S. and Ph.D.), natural resources and environmental design (M.S. in plant and soil science, with concentrations in applied environmental biology, applied environmental chemistry, environmental horticulture, land use and management, plant biotechnology, soil and sustainable fertility, soil and water conservation, and soil mineralogy), physics (M.S., with concentrations in applied physics and professional physics), social work (joint M.S.W. with the University of North Carolina at Greensboro), teaching (M.A.T. in art education; biology education; business education, 7–12; chemistry education; elementary education, K–6; English education; family and consumer science education; history education; physical education, K–12; mathematics education; music education; special education, 9–12; technology education, 9–12; and trade and industrial education, 9–12), technology education (M.S., with concentrations in teaching, trade and industrial education teaching, training and development for industry, and workforce development), technology management (Ph.D. consortium with Indiana State University), and transportation and logistics (M.S.M.).

Research Facilities

The University library is a comprehensive, extensive facility that provides all the resources one would expect from a major research university. In addition, all of the schools, departments, and colleges of the University are supported by state-of-the-art computer laboratories and teaching and research laboratories and facilities. There are also many specialized facilities and equipment available on campus. In the College of Engineering, several researchers utilize UNIX-based workstations to provide robust simulation and multicomponent interactions for structural, thermal, mechanical, computational fluid dynamics, and electromagnetic analysis. Other research facilities include a well-equipped shop, a scanning electron microscope with X-ray energy-dispersive analyzer, VLSI design and solid-state materials laboratories, a solar collector laboratory, and a thermal-physical property laboratory with hot-wire/film, anemometry, and Schlieren systems. The Department of Physics operates a planetarium with a 30-foot hemispherical dome and an on-campus observatory with a 14-inch Celestron telescope. Much of the research activity in the School of Agriculture and Environmental Sciences is sponsored by the United States Department of Agriculture. It is conducted on the University farm and in on-campus laboratories, where investigations include such disciplines as agricultural economics, animal science, plant science, landscape architecture and design, human nutrition, housing, food science, and animal health. The Animal Science Department is housed in a $7-million facility that includes a closed-circuit television system and microcomputer labs. The department is also supported by a 600-acre farm that maintains modern research facilities in dairy and beef cattle, sheep, swine, and poultry. The Laboratory Animal Resources Unit provides housing for the laboratory animals that are used in instruction and research. The on-campus research labs are designed and equipped with modern instrumentation for studies in immunology, cell culture, microbiology, systemic toxicology, and therapeutic drug action.

Financial Aid

Graduate students can receive financial aid through graduate assistantships, stipends, scholarships, federal loan and work-study programs, and some grants.

Cost of Study

Tuition and fees for full-time students (9 or more semester hours) who are North Carolina residents are $3944 per academic year. For nonresidents, they are $13,529.

Living and Housing Costs

Graduate students normally find reasonably priced housing near the campus or in the city of Greensboro. Typical apartment rents range from $375 to more than $500 per month.

Student Group

There are about 1,310 full- and part-time graduate students enrolled at the University.

Location

Greensboro, Winston-Salem, High Point, and Burlington, all within a radius of 30 miles, are the major cities in the Piedmont Triad, the most heavily populated metropolitan area in North Carolina. Among the major industries and companies in the area are Burlington Industries, Jefferson Standard Life Insurance Company, Tyco Electronics, American Express, Analog Devices, Konica, Volvo-White Truck Corporation, and RF Micro Devices, Inc. Many professional and cultural activities flourish in the region. Greensboro has been noted for its outstanding quality of life in Rand-McNally surveys.

The University

North Carolina Agricultural and Technical State University is a public, comprehensive land-grant university committed to fulfilling its fundamental purposes through exemplary undergraduate and graduate instruction, scholarly and creative research, and effective public service. The University is a learner-centered community that develops and preserves intellectual capital through interdisciplinary learning, discovery, engagement, and operational excellence.

Applying

Applications for admission must be accompanied by two official transcripts from all colleges and universities previously attended; references from at least 3 people who know the applicant's academic record and potential for graduate study; an official report of GRE or, in some cases, other standardized test scores; and a letter of intent. Students whose native language is not English must submit TOEFL scores. Many programs have additional requirements that must be met by the student. Applications are not considered complete until all required materials are submitted. In general, application deadlines for master's students are July 1 for the fall semester, November 1 for the spring semester, and April 1 for the summer session; however, there are some programs that have different deadlines and only admit during certain times of the year. International students' application deadlines are April 1 for fall admission and September 1 for spring.

Correspondence and Information

School of Graduate Studies
120 Gibbs Hall
North Carolina Agricultural and Technical State University
1601 East Market Street
Greensboro, North Carolina 27411

Phone: 336-334-7920
Web site: http://www.ncat.edu/~gradsch

CENTERS AND INSTITUTES

Center for Advanced Materials and Smart Structures
The Center for Advanced Materials and Smart Structures (CAMSS) is an educational and research resource for the state of North Carolina and the nation in the field of advanced ceramic materials and their composites. It is a collaboration of academe, private industry, and the government in developing basic and applied research programs with a focus on an integration of research and education. Basic research in the technical thrust areas (advanced ceramics, advanced composites, electronic ceramic devices, sensors and smart structures, and III–V nitrides, ohmic contracts, and devices) drives the center's activities.

Center for Aerospace Research
The primary mission of the center is to conduct high-quality research in aeronautics and astronautics. The core research themes are aerospace structures, controls, and guidance; computational fluid dynamics; propulsion; and human-machine engineering. The center performs critical research that contributes to the development of technology necessary to support the development of NASA's High Speed Civil Transport programs and the improvement of the Single and Two Stage to Orbit missions. Ongoing research efforts are directed toward the support of NASA's exploration of space and long-term human presence in space as well as enhancement of life on Earth.

Center for Autonomous Control and Information Technology
The areas of concentration are soft computing, multiagent systems, artificial intelligence in general, control theory, genetic algorithms, and energy conservation and power electronics. The center conducts interdisciplinary research in demonstrative programs for the application of fuzzy logic–controlled power electronic building block systems in HVAC systems, nonlinear active control of dynamical systems, artificial potential field–based motion planning/navigation in two- and three-dimensional dynamic environments, and other relevant topics.

Center for Composite Materials Research
The major facilities of the center are the Computational Laboratory, Mechanical Testing Laboratory, Diagnostic Laboratory, and Composite Processing and Fabrication Laboratory. Research activities are focused on processing and fabrication of simple to complex composite components, use of textile fiber architectures in the fabrication of nontrivial lightweight composite components, testing and characterization of composite materials, analysis of composite structural components, study of cost-effective near net–shaped composite components, development of innovative processing techniques with textile fabrics, and training of students and engineers from industry in the fabrication and use of composites.

Center for Electronics Manufacturing
The goal of the center is to strengthen the manufacturing, service, and research arm of the electronics manufacturing industry with respect to productivity, quality, and timeliness of product and service delivered. Specifically, the center focuses on the need to reduce time to service or market, the need to access leading manufacturing technologies while reducing investments, the need to focus on core competencies, and the need to improve inventory management and purchasing power. This program develops expertise in the areas of electronics, manufacturing, safety, the environment, design, quality, computing, and management.

Center for Energy Research and Technology
The mission of the center is to enhance undergraduate and graduate education through energy-related research and to transfer this new knowledge to regional and national industries. The objective is to improve economic competitiveness while reducing the environmental impact that results from excessive energy consumption. The research focuses on energy use and energy efficiency in buildings and industrial processes as they relate to technological, economic, political, and environmental issues.

Center for International Trade
The primary mission of the center is to stimulate economic development and international trade. The educational activities are principally aimed at teaching students and providing research and related materials to small businesses as well as technical assistance and information to the agricultural business community. Program emphases include developing educational programs to enable farmers and processors to produce a broader range of products to boost local economic performance; identifying alternative markets; enhancing understanding of the linkages among national economies, world markets, and agriculture; conducting market-based research to understand factors that influence competitiveness; educating producers, processors, and other clients about trade policies, regulations, and world economic and political trends affecting U.S. trade competitiveness; and developing programs in North Carolina's rural communities to enhance entrepreneurial skills, create jobs, and diversify their economies.

Civil Infrastructure Research Institute
The institute conducts materials characterization, materials testing, load modeling, and structural health and durability research on concrete pavement materials and aircraft runway paving structures. The objective is to determine full-scale validation of airport pavement using field instrumentation and computer simulation, more accurate evaluation of asphalt and concrete elastic and viscoelastic properties, and more accurate simulation of the loading of new, heavier airplanes' landing gear on airfield pavements. Other focus areas are the structural health and durability of bridges and highways and dredging technology.

Institute for Human-Machine Studies
The field of human-machine system engineering emphasizes how users interact with machines, how usable machines are to users, and the impact of machines on user performance. The institute is a comprehensive, multidisciplinary program of basic and applied scientific research and technology development directed toward the understanding of the nature of human performance while interacting with complex technology-driven systems. It focuses on cognitive engineering and human-system interface sciences, aviation and transportation human factors, information and communication technology integration, and health-care and manufacturing applications.

Interdisciplinary Center for Entrepreneurship and E-Business
The Interdisciplinary Center for Entrepreneurship and E-Business (ICEEB) is dedicated to developing the entrepreneurial spirit at North Carolina A&T. ICEEB provides academic and experiential learning experiences for students interested in individual or corporate entrepreneurship and for local entrepreneurs interested in improving their businesses. The center's main goals are to promote entrepreneurship as a career option, increase student participation in e-business, provide an entrepreneurial environment and opportunities for students to successfully start their entrepreneurial careers, and encourage and support research in entrepreneurship and e-business. ICEEB is a joint project of the Schools of Business and Economics, Agriculture and Environmental Sciences, and Technology.

National Institute of Aerospace
The institute conducts and promotes leading-edge aerospace and atmospheric sciences research and develops innovative new technologies in the following seven technical areas: revolutionary aerospace systems, concepts, and analysis; planetary capture and entry technology; aerodynamics, aerothermodynamics, and acoustics; structures and materials; airborne systems; atmospheric and vehicle sensor system technology; and atmospheric chemistry and radiation science.

North Carolina Agromedicine Institute
The North Carolina Agromedicine Institute is a scientifically based organization whose focus is on environmental and occupational health and safety issues of agricultural, forestry, and fisheries producers and workers and their families. Its mission is to promote the health and safety of agricultural, forestry, and fisheries communities through research, education, and outreach.

Transportation Institute
The mission of the Transportation Institute is to coordinate and manage interdisciplinary research, training, and technology transfer activities involving faculty and staff members and students from various departments within the University. The activities of the institute include soliciting extramural funding, coordinating faculty development and student enrichment programs, facilitating technology transfer, providing technical assistance and public service, and coordinating other transportation-related programs. The Transportation Institute functions as a national and regional center for research and training and as an information clearinghouse.

Waste Management Institute
The Waste Management Institute is an interdisciplinary program that is designed to enhance awareness and understanding of waste management problems in society and to enhance instruction, research, and outreach aimed at improving quality of life and protecting the environment. The goals of the institute are to increase the number of professionals in environmental and waste management, enhance interdisciplinary research, increase public awareness, and facilitate cooperative and exchange programs among students, faculty members, government, and industry.

NORTH DAKOTA STATE UNIVERSITY

Graduate School

Programs of Study

North Dakota State University (NDSU) offers the Doctor of Philosophy (Ph.D.), Doctor of Nursing Practice (D.N.P.), Doctor of Education (Ed.D.), Doctor of Musical Arts (D.M.A.), Master of Arts (M.A.), Master of Business Administration (M.B.A.), Master of Education, Master of Music, Master of Science (M.S.), and Educational Specialist (Ed.S.) degrees.

The College of Agriculture, Food Systems, and Natural Resources offers the M.S. in agricultural economics, animal and range sciences, cereal science, entomology, food safety, horticulture, international agribusiness, microbiology, plant pathology, plant sciences, and soil science and the Ph.D. in animal and range sciences, cereal science, entomology, food safety, molecular pathogenesis, plant pathology, plant sciences, and soil science.

The College of Arts, Humanities, and Social Sciences offers the master's degree in criminal justice, emergency management, English, history, mass communication, music, political science, social science–anthropology, sociology, and speech communication; the Ph.D. is offered in communication, criminal justice, emergency management, and history; and the D.M.A. is offered in music.

The College of Business Administration offers the Master of Business Administration degree.

The College of Engineering and Architecture offers the M.S. in agricultural and biosystems engineering, civil engineering, electrical engineering, environmental and conservation science, environmental engineering, industrial engineering and management, manufacturing engineering, and mechanical engineering and the Ph.D. in agricultural and biosystems engineering, civil engineering, electrical and computer engineering, engineering, environmental and conservation science, industrial and manufacturing engineering, and mechanical engineering.

The College of Human Development and Education offers the master's degree in agricultural education, child development and family science, counseling and guidance, education, educational administration, family and consumer sciences education, nutrition and exercise sciences, and secondary education; the Ph.D. in human development and in education; and the Ed.D. in education.

The College of Pharmacy offers both the M.S. and Ph.D. in pharmaceutical sciences, the M.S. in nursing, and the D.N.P. in nursing practice.

The College of Science and Mathematics offers the M.S. in biochemistry, biology, botany, coatings and polymeric materials, chemistry, computer science, mathematics, physics, psychology, software engineering, statistics, and zoology and the Ph.D. in biochemistry, botany, chemistry, coatings and polymeric materials, computer science, mathematics, physics, psychology, software engineering, statistics, and zoology.

The following programs are offered as interdisciplinary degrees: M.S. and Ph.D. in environmental and conservation sciences, food safety, genomics, and natural resources management and Ph.D. in cellular and molecular biology, materials and nanotechnology, and transportation and logistics. The Educational Specialist may be earned in educational administration.

Research Facilities

NDSU possesses state-of-the-art facilities in magnetic resonance imaging, high-performance computing, electron microscopy, and computer chip assembly. Located on campus, a Research and Technology Park is expanding to house both academic research units and industrial partners, strengthening links between the University and technology-based companies. Research specializations in a wide variety of disciplines have resulted in the establishment of centers, some of which are the Center of Nanoscale Science and Engineering, NSF Coatings Cooperative Research Center, the Bio-imaging and Sensing Center, the Center for Protease Research, the Quentin Burdick Center for Cooperatives, the Center for Agricultural Policy and Trade Studies, the Great Plains Institute of Food Safety, the Upper Great Plains Transportation Institute, and the Institute for Regional Studies. As the state's land-grant institution, NDSU houses the North Dakota Agricultural Experiment Station and Extension Service, with eight research and extension centers located across the state. An Internet2 institution, NDSU provides high-speed network access to classrooms and desktops, an Access Grid facility for global virtual conferencing, and high-speed connections to other universities and federal agencies for research and distance education. Library resources include more than 518,921 bound volumes and 86,571 maps, 5,095 current electronic and print subscriptions, and an extensive array of specialized, full-text electronic databases, as well as an online catalog that interfaces with other regional, national, and international library catalogs.

Financial Aid

Graduate teaching and research assistantships are awarded to qualified students upon recommendations from individual departments and include tuition waivers for all graduate credits. Approximately half of the graduate students are awarded graduate assistantships. Student activity fees are not waived. Stipend amounts vary widely by discipline. The Graduate School has stipend enhancements available for outstanding applicants. North Dakota's very successful National Science Foundation EPSCoR program is centered at NDSU; it provides generous funding for graduate education through dissertation fellowships and stipends. For more information, students should contact the Financial Aid Office (phone: 701-231-7533).

Cost of Study

Tuition per credit, through 12 credits, was $213.34 for North Dakota residents; $261.88 for Minnesota residents; $320 for residents of Saskatchewan, Manitoba, South Dakota, and Montana; and $569.62 for other students in 2006–07. Student fees per credit, through 12 credits, were $39.49 in 2006–07.

Living and Housing Costs

Apartments for families, as well as single-occupancy units, are located near the University campus in University Village. For residence hall life, the combined room and meal plan cost approximately $5475 per academic year. Housing, utility, and food expenses for 2 people are estimated at $8075 on campus and $8500 off campus.

Student Group

Current enrollment at NDSU is more than 12,000 students on the central campus in Fargo. NDSU also serves several thousand people throughout the state in continuing education and extension programs. Graduate student enrollment is approximately 1,700 students. International students make up approximately 25 percent of the graduate student population, providing a wealth of diversity within both the academic and local communities.

Student Outcomes

North Dakota State University graduates more than 250 master's students and 50 Ph.D. students each year.

Location

With more than 160,000 people, Fargo-Moorhead is the largest metropolitan center between Minneapolis and Seattle and is nestled in the Red River Valley, which is rich in fertile farmlands. In Fargo-Moorhead, three universities and the technical colleges provide a wide variety of educational opportunities, while the community offers access to part-time jobs, internships, parks and other recreational facilities, entertainment, and cultural amenities.

The University

NDSU, the state's land-grant institution, was established in 1890. It is one of the two research institutions within North Dakota's university system of five 2-year schools, three 4-year schools, and three graduate institutions. NDSU is a comprehensive university that offers nationally recognized programs of study within a student-friendly community. Fifty-five master's programs, forty doctoral programs, eight certificate programs, and an Educational Specialist program are offered. Ninety-eight undergraduate majors are offered.

Applying

All application materials are due one month before registration for U.S. students; some departments have earlier deadlines. For international students, the completed application packet (application form, application fee, transcript evaluation fee if international transcripts are included in the application, official transcripts, three letters of reference, and personal statement) and required test scores should be received by the Graduate School by May 1 for the fall semester and August 1 for the spring semester.

Correspondence and Information

The Graduate School
North Dakota State University
P.O. Box 5790
Fargo, North Dakota 58105-5790

Phone: 701-231-7033
Fax: 701-231-6524
E-mail: ndsu.grad.school@ndsu.edu
Web site: http://www.ndsu.edu/gradschool
http://www.ndsu.edu

THE FACULTY

Listed below are North Dakota State University's deans, graduate degree programs, and corresponding phone numbers and e-mail addresses.

College of Agriculture, Food Systems, and Natural Resources: Ken Grafton, Ph.D.
Agribusiness and Applied Economics: 701-231-7466. (E-mail: agecinfo@ndsuext.nodak.edu)
Agricultural and Biosystems Engineering: 701-231-7274. (E-mail: leslie.backer@ndsu.edu)
Animal and Range Sciences: 701-231-8386. (E-mail: donald.kirby@ndsuext.nodak.edu)
Cellular and Molecular Biology: 701-231-8110. (E-mail: mark.sheridan@ndsu.edu)
Cereal and Food Sciences: 701-231-7712. (E-mail: james.venette@ndsu.edu)
Entomology: 701-231-7902. (E-mail: david.rider@ndsu.edu)
Food Safety: 701-231-6387. (E-mail: charlene.hall@ndsu.edu)
Genomics: 701-231-8443. (E-mail: phillip.mcclean@ndsu.edu)
Horticulture: 701-231-7971. (E-mail: albert.schneiter@ndsu.edu)
International Agribusiness: 701-231-7466. (E-mail: agecinfo@ndsuext.nodak.edu)
Microbiology: 701-231-7511. (E-mail: douglas.freeman@nsdu.edu)
Molecular Pathogenesis: 701-231-7511. (E-mail: douglas.freeman@ndsu.edu)
Natural Resources Management: 701-231-8180. (E-mail: carolyn.grygiel@ndsu.edu)
Plant Pathology: 701-231-8362. (E-mail: roberta.haspel@ndsu.edu)
Plant Sciences: 701-231-7971. (E-mail: albert.schneiter@ndsu.edu)
Soil Science: 701-231-8903. (E-mail: rod.lym@ndsu.edu)

College of Arts, Humanities, and Social Sciences: Thomas Riley, Ph.D.
Communication: 701-231-7705. (E-mail for Ph.D.: judy.pearson@ndsu.edu; e-mail for master's: mark.meister@ndsu.edu)
Criminal Justice: 701-231-8938. (E-mail: kevin.thompson@ndsu.edu)
Emergency Management: 701-231-8925. (E-mail: daniel.klenow@ndsu.edu)
English: 701-231-7144. (E-mail: dale.sullivan@ndsu.edu)
History: 701-231-8654. (E-mail: ndsu.history@ndsu.edu)
Musical Arts: 701-231-7932. (E-mail: ej.miller@ndsu.edu)
Political Science: 701-231-8938. (E-mail: kevin.thompson@ndsu.edu)
Sociology/Anthropology: 701-231-8925. (E-mail: daniel.klenow@ndsu.edu)

College of Business Administration: Ronald D. Johnson, Ph.D.
Business Administration: 701-231-7681. (E-mail: paul.brown@ndsu.edu)

College of Engineering and Architecture: Gary Smith, Ph.D.
Civil Engineering and Construction: 701-231-7245. (E-mail: kalpana.katti@ndsu.edu)
Electrical and Computer Engineering: 701-231-7019. (E-mail: jacob.glower@ndsu.edu)
Engineering: 701-231-7494. (E-mail: sheri.tomaszewski@ndsu.edu)
Environmental and Conservation Sciences: 701-231-8449. (E-mail: craig.stockwell@ndsu.edu)
Environmental Engineering: 701-231-7245. (E-mail: kalpana.katti@ndsu.edu)
Industrial and Manufacturing Engineering: 701-231-7287. (E-mail: susan.l.peterson.2@ndsu.edu)
Manufacturing Engineering: 701-231-7287. (E-mail: susan.l.peterson.2@ndsu.edu)
Mechanical Engineering: 701-231-8835. (E-mail: alan.kallmeyer@ndsu.edu)
Transportation and Logistics: 701-231-7190. (E-mail: denver.tolliver@ndsu.edu)

College of Human Development and Education: Virginia Clark Johnson, Ph.D.
Child Development and Family Science: 701-231-7568. (E-mail: jim.deal@ndsu.edu)
Education Ph.D.: 701-231-7210. (E-mail: ronald.stammen@ndsu.edu)
Health, Nutrition, and Exercise Sciences: 701-231-9718. (E-mail: bradford.strand@ndsu.edu)
Human Development: 701-231-8211. (E-mail: greg.sanders@ndsu.edu)
Merchandising: 701-231-8223. (E-mail: holly.bastow-shoop@ndsu.edu)
School of Education: 701-231-7202. (E-mail: william.martin@ndsu.edu)
- Agricultural Education: 701-231-7439. (E-mail: brent.young@ndsu.edu)
- Counseling Education: 701-231-7676. (E-mail: robert.nielsen@ndsu.edu)
- Educational Leadership: 701-231-9732. (E-mail: vicki.ihry@ndsu.edu)
- Family and Consumer Sciences Education: 701-231-7968. (E-mail: mari.borr@ndsu.edu)
- Secondary Education: 701-231-7108. (E-mail: justin.wageman@ndsu.edu)

College of Pharmacy: Charles Peterson, Ph.D.
Nursing: 701-231-7772. (E-mail: mary.mooney@ndsu.edu)
Pharmaceutical Sciences: 701-231-7943. (E-mail: jagdish.singh@ndsu.edu)

College of Science and Mathematics: Kevin McCaul, Ph.D.
Biochemistry: 701-231-8225. (E-mail: john.hershberger@ndsu.edu)
Botany/Biology: 701-231-7087. (E-mail: marinus.otte@ndsu.edu)
Chemistry: 701-231-8225. (E-mail: john.hershberger@ndsu.edu)
Coatings and Polymeric Materials: 701-231-7633. (E-mail: ndsu.polycoat@ndsu.edu)
Computer Science: 701-231-8562. (E-mail: carole.huber@ndsu.edu)
Mathematics: 701-231-8561. (E-mail: ndsu.math@ndsu.edu)
Physics: 701-231-7049. (E-mail: dan.kroll@ndsu.edu)
Psychology: 701-231-8622. (E-mail: ndsu.psych@ndsu.edu)
Software Engineering: 701-231-8197. (E-mail: kenneth.magel@ndsu.edu)
Statistics: 701-231-7532. (E-mail: ndsu.stats@ndsu.edu)
Zoology: 701-231-7087. (E-mail: marinus.otte@ndsu.edu)

NORTHEASTERN UNIVERSITY

Graduate School of Arts and Sciences

Programs of Study The Graduate School of Arts and Sciences at Northeastern University offers the Doctor of Philosophy degree in applied economics, biology, chemistry, English, history, mathematics, physics, psychology, public and international affairs, and sociology. An interdisciplinary program in law, policy, and society leads to the Doctor of Philosophy degree or to the Master of Science degree. A combined M.S./J.D. program of study is also available. The Master of Arts or Master of Science degree is awarded in applied mathematics, bioinformatics, biology, chemistry, economics, English, history, journalism, marine biology, mathematics, physics, political science, sociology, and writing. Also offered are the degrees of Master of Architecture, Master of Arts in Teaching (elementary or secondary), and Master of Public Administration. The Master of Science in Operations Research is offered in conjunction with the Graduate School of Engineering at Northeastern.

Research Facilities The University supports twenty-seven centers and institutes, including the Barnett Institute of Chemical and Biological Analysis, Institute for Molecular Biotechnology, Nano Manufacturing Research Institute, Institute on Race and Justice, Domestic Violence Institute, Electronic Materials Research Institute, Brudnick Center on Violence and Conflict, Center for Advanced Microgravity Materials Processing, Center for Subsurface Sensing and Imaging Systems, Center for Urban and Regional Policy, and the Institute for Complex Scientific Software. Special University facilities include the George J. Kostas Nanoscale Technology and Manufacturing Research Center, Electron Microscopy Center, and the Microfabrication Laboratory.

A high-speed data network links users and facilities on the central campus to three satellite campuses and to computing facilities around the world. Students have access to Compaq Alpha systems, public-access microcomputer labs (PC and Mac), a conferencing system, multimedia labs, and specialized computing equipment. Northeastern is also an Internet2 site.

University libraries contain more than 965,000 books, 2,300,000 microforms, 7,600 serial subscriptions, and 17,000 audiovisual materials. The libraries have licensed access to over 13,000 electronic information sources. A central and branch library contain technologically sophisticated services, including Web-based catalog and circulation systems and a Web portal to licensed electronic resources. The University is a member of the Boston Library Consortium and the Boston Regional Library System, giving students and faculty members access to the region's collections and information resources.

Financial Aid Northeastern University offers need-based financial aid to graduate students through the Federal Stafford Student Loan, Federal Perkins Loan, and Federal Work-Study programs. In addition, the University offers a wide variety of graduate assistantships, along with minority fellowships, such as the Martin Luther King Jr. Scholarship.

Cost of Study Tuition for the 2006–07 academic year in the Graduate School of Arts and Sciences cost $930 per semester hour of credit. Where applicable, special tuition charges are made for the thesis, the dissertation, teaching, practicums, or fieldwork. Other charges included the Student Center fee and health and accident insurance fee, which are required of all full-time students.

Living and Housing Costs On-campus housing for graduate students is limited and granted on a space-available basis. Meal plans are also available. For information about on- and off-campus housing options, students should refer to http://www.housing.neu.edu. A public transportation system serves the greater Boston area, and there are subway and bus services convenient to the University.

Student Group In fall 2005, 14,730 undergraduate and 4,811 graduate students were enrolled at Northeastern University, representing a wide variety of academic, professional, geographic, and cultural backgrounds. The Graduate School of Arts and Sciences has more than 900 students, 69 percent of whom attend on a full-time basis. Because graduate classes are offered primarily in the evening, many students pursue programs on a part-time basis while maintaining full-time employment.

Location Northeastern University is set in the heart of the ultimate college town—Boston, a high-energy hub of cultural, educational, and social activity. More than 300,000 college students from around the country and the world call Boston home, and the city is alive with people of every race, ethnicity, political persuasion, and religion. Within walking distance of Northeastern are the world-renowned Museum of Fine Arts, Symphony Hall, and stylish Newbury Street, with great shopping and dining.

The University Northeastern University is a world leader in practice-oriented education and is recognized for its expert faculty and first-rate academic and research facilities. Northeastern integrates challenging liberal arts and professional studies with the nation's largest cooperative education program. Northeastern has six undergraduate colleges, eight graduate and professional schools, two part-time undergraduate divisions, and an extensive variety of research institutes and divisions. Northeastern's graduate programs offer both professional and research degrees at the master's or doctoral level. Students have the opportunity for field experience through practicums, internships, and cooperative education, along with working closely with distinguished faculty members within their academic discipline. Northeastern's relationships with local and national organizations help students make professional contacts and explore career options. Among the University's alumni are the founders of some of the nation's most successful companies.

Applying The fall semester application deadline for Ph.D. programs (except for Biology and Psychology, whose deadlines are January 15) is February 1. The priority deadline for those master's degree applicants interested in assistantships is also February 1. Applicants are urged to view the Web site at http://www.cas.neu.edu/graduate for more information, including a list of required materials and admission deadlines and the online application.

Correspondence and Information

Graduate School of Arts and Sciences
124 Meserve Hall-PG
Northeastern University
360 Huntington Avenue
Boston, Massachusetts 02115
E-mail: gsas@neu.edu
Web site: http://www.cas.neu.edu/graduate

FACULTY HEADS, GRADUATE COORDINATORS, AND DEPARTMENTAL RESEARCH AREAS

Department e-mail and Web addresses are listed after the name of the department head.

Architecture. George Thrush, M.Arch., Harvard (gradarch@neu.edu; www.architecture.neu.edu).
Graduate Coordinator: George Thrush, M.Arch., 617-373-4637.

Urban architecture and design. Students must have earned a bachelor's degree in architecture to be eligible to apply to the M.Arch. program.

Biology. Edward L. Jarroll, Ph.D., West Virginia (gradbio@neu.edu; www.biology.neu.edu/graduate_programs.html).
Graduate Coordinator: Jacqueline M. Piret, Ph.D., 617-373-5266.

Biochemistry, bioinformatics, biotechnology, cell biology, developmental biology, ecology, immunology, marine biology, microbiology, molecular biology, neurobiology, physiology, vertebrate zoology.

Chemistry and Chemical Biology. Graham B. Jones, Ph.D., Imperial College (London) (chemistry-grad-info@neu.edu; www.chem.neu.edu).
Graduate Coordinator: David Forsyth, Ph.D., 617-373-2832.

Analytical biotechnology; analytical, inorganic, organic, and physical chemistry; bioorganic and medicinal chemistry; bioinorganic chemistry; computational chemistry; conducting polymers; fuel cells; green chemistry; magnetic resonance; mass spectrometry; materials science; molecular modeling; molecular spectroscopy; natural products; organic synthesis; proteomics; separation science; theoretical chemistry.

Economics. Steven A. Morrison, Ph.D., Berkeley (gradecon@neu.edu; www.economics.neu.edu).
Graduate Coordinator: Gregory H. Wassall, Ph.D., 617-373-2196.

Industrial organization, labor economics, urban economics, international economics, applied macroeconomics, transportation economics, economic history, natural resource economics, economics of nonprofit organizations, policy analysis.

Education. Thomas R. Gilbert, Ph.D., MIT (graded@neu.edu; www.education.neu.edu).
Graduate Coordinator: Peter Murrell, Ph.D., 617-373-4216.

Master of Arts in Teaching (M.A.T.) in elementary or secondary education.

English. Timothy Donovan, Ph.D., Wisconsin (gradenglish@neu.edu; www.english.neu.edu).
Graduate Coordinator: Laura Green, Ph.D., 617-373-3692.

British and American literature, literary theory, film and cultural studies, rhetoric, composition studies.

History. Laura Frader, Ph.D., Rochester (gradhistory@neu.edu; www.history.neu.edu).
Graduate Coordinator: Christina Gilmartin, Ph.D., 617-373-4449.

World history; American, European, African, Asian, environmental, and public history in a global perspective.

Journalism. Stephen Burgard, M.A., Boston University (gradjourn@neu.edu; www.journalism.neu.edu).
Graduate Coordinator: Laurel Leff, M.A., M.S.L., 617-373-3236.

Print and broadcast journalism, freedom of the press and democracy in Russia, journalism history, sports writing, media ethics, law of the press, Latin America, Holocaust studies, documentary film, online journalism.

Law, Policy and Society. Joan Fitzgerald, Ph.D., Penn State (lps@neu.edu; www.lps.neu.edu).
Graduate Coordinator: Joan Fitzgerald, Ph.D., 617-373-3644.

Criminal justice, culture diversity and gender issues, education policy, environmental policy, health policy, international development, labor market and workforce development policy, law and society, technology policy, urban policy.

Mathematics. Robert C. McOwen, Ph.D., Berkeley (mathdept@neu.edu; www.math.neu.edu/).
Graduate Coordinator: Christopher King, Ph.D., 617-373-3905.

Algebraic geometry, singularities, commutative algebra, representation theory, combinatorics, algebraic topology, applied mathematics, differential topology, K-theory, differential geometry, partial differential equations, probability theory, statistics, harmonic analysis, mathematical physics.

Physics. Robert P. Lowndes, Ph.D., London (gradphysics@neu.edu; www.physics.neu.edu).
Graduate Coordinator: George O. Alverson, Ph.D. 617-373-4240.

Astrophysics, biological physics, experimental particle astrophysics, experimental elementary particle physics, theoretical elementary particle physics, quantum field theory, cosmology, supersymmetry, experimental nanophysics, medical physics, microwaves, mesoscopic physics, spectroscopy, laser-light scattering, left-handed optical materials, photonic crystals, single-molecule–force spectroscopy, correlated electrons, low-dimensional quantum physics, high magnetic fields, femtosecond coherence spectroscopy, metal-insulator transitions, Quantum Hall effect, high-temperature superconductivity, quantum chaos, solid-state theory, many-body theory, statistical mechanics, theoretical biophysics, nanotribiology, quantum computing, nonlinear dynamics and pattern formation, electronic structure and spectroscopy of ordered and disordered materials, theoretical neurobiology and cell biology, nuclear-resonance spectroscopy of biomolecules.

Political Science. John Portz, Ph.D., Wisconsin (gradpolisci@neu.edu; www.polisci.neu.edu).
Graduate Coordinator: Amílcar Barreto, J.D., Ph.D., 617-373-4404.

Public policy and administration, political development and democratization, American politics and public policy, comparative politics, international relations, political behavior, state and urban politics, public management, political economy.

Psychology. Stephen G. Harkins, Ph.D., Missouri (psychology@neu.edu; www.psych.neu.edu).
Graduate Coordinator: Joanne L. Miller, Ph.D., j.miller@neu.edu.

Behavioral neuroscience, language/cognition, perception, personality/social.

Sociology. Thomas Koenig, Ph.D., California, Santa Barbara (gradsoc@neu.edu; www.casdn.neu.edu/~socant/).
Graduate Coordinator: Matthew Hunt, Ph.D., 617-373-2878.

Globalization and international studies, urban affairs and community studies, gender studies, race, ethnicity and social conflict, Center for Urban and Regional Policy.

OAKLAND UNIVERSITY

Graduate Study

Oakland UNIVERSITY

Programs of Study Oakland University (OU) offers ninety-nine graduate degree and certificate programs at the master's, doctoral, and specialist levels. Graduate programs are linked closely to research, scholarship, and public service activities. Students are assumed to be partners in the implementation of programs. In the process, they are educated in the methods of intellectual inquiry and critical analysis and trained in the skills needed for their chosen fields. Through this partnership, the goals and purposes of graduate education are fulfilled.

Doctoral degrees may be earned in applied mathematical sciences (Ph.D.), biological communication (Ph.D.), health and environmental chemistry (Ph.D.), medical physics (Ph.D.), computer science and informatics (Ph.D.), counseling (Ph.D.), early childhood education (Ph.D.), educational leadership (Ph.D.), mechanical engineering (Ph.D.), music education (Ph.D.), nursing practice (D.N.P.), physical therapy (D.P.T. and D.Sc.P.T.), reading education (Ph.D.), and systems engineering (Ph.D.). The post-master's degree of Education Specialist in leadership is also available.

Post-master's certificates are available in accounting, adult acute care, adult gerontological nurse practitioner studies, advanced reading and language arts, anesthesia, business economics, education administration, entrepreneurship, family nurse practitioner studies, finance, general management, higher education, human resources management, international business, local government management, management information systems, marketing, nonprofit organization and management, production/operations management, and reading, language arts, and literature.

Master's degrees are offered in accounting (M.Acc.), adult acute care clinical nurse specialist studies (M.S.N.), adult gerontological nurse practitioner studies (M.S.N.), anesthesia (M.S.N.), applied statistics (M.S.), biology (M.A. and M.S.), business administration (M.B.A.), chemistry (M.S.), computer science (M.S.), conducting (M.M.), counseling (M.A.), early childhood education (M.Ed.), educational leadership (M.Ed.), educational studies (M.Ed.), electrical and computer engineering (M.S.), embedded systems (M.S.), engineering management (M.S.), English (M.A.), exercise science (M.S.), family nurse practitioner studies (M.S.N.), history (M.A.), industrial applied mathematics (M.S.), industrial and systems engineering (M.S.), information technology management (M.S.), instrumental pedagogy (M.M.), instrumental performance (M.M.), liberal studies (M.A.L.S.), linguistics (M.A.), mathematics (M.A.), mechanical engineering (M.S.), music (M.M.), music education (M.M.), nursing education (M.S.N.), physical therapy (M.S.), physics (M.S.), piano pedagogy (M.M.), piano performance (M.M.), public administration (M.P.A.), reading and language arts (M.A.T.), reading and language arts with endorsement in early childhood education (M.A.T.), safety management (M.S.), software engineering and information technology (M.S.), special education (M.Ed.), systems engineering (M.S.), teacher leadership (M.Ed.), training and development (M.T.D.), vocal pedagogy (M.M.), and vocal performance (M.M.).

Graduate certificates in advanced microcomputer applications, clinical exercise science, complementary medicine and wellness, corporate and worksite wellness, exercise science, microcomputer applications, neurological rehabilitation, nursing education, orthopedic manual physical therapy, orthopedics, pediatric rehabilitation, statistical methods, teaching and learning for rehabilitation professionals, and teaching English as a second language are available. A teaching endorsement in autism impaired, early childhood education, English as a second language, and reading is also offered.

Research Facilities Most University library materials and services are housed in Kresge Library. The library's automated catalog allows patrons to identify resources held not only in the Kresge Library but also in the collections of Wayne State University, the University of Detroit Mercy, Detroit Public Library, and numerous other libraries in the area. These include the Center for Biomedical Research, the Center for Robotics and Advanced Automation, the Cumulative Trauma Research Institute, the Eye Research Institute, the Fastening and Joining Research Institute (FAJRI), the Human Systems Initiative, the Institute for Action Research, the Institute for Biochemistry and Biotechnology, the Michigan Center for Automotive Research, the Product Development and Manufacturing Center, and the Public Affairs Research Laboratory. Research dollars have increased every year for the past six years to the current level of $6.2 million.

Financial Aid In order to assist eligible graduate students in financing their education, the University participates in the following programs: King/Chavez/Parks Fellowships, a limited number of which are available for qualified members of minority groups; the Federal Perkins Loan program; the Federal Work-Study Program; and the William Ford Federal Direct Loan Program. Graduate assistants are appointed by departments offering graduate degree programs. Stipends vary by discipline.

Cost of Study The University operates on the semester system. For 2007–08, the tuition for in-state graduate students is $472.50 per credit hour, including fees, and the tuition for out-of-state graduate students is $814.50 per credit hour, including fees. Full-time graduate students normally carry 8 credits per semester.

Living and Housing Costs The 2007–08 rate for room and board is $6670 for the academic year. Facilities with a selected number of single rooms are available to graduate students. For students with families, a limited number of two-bedroom town houses and two- to four-bedroom student apartments are available.

Student Group Total enrollment for fall 2006 was 17,737. Twenty-three percent of the total enrollment is graduate students. Within the graduate enrollment, 66 percent are women and 11.4 percent are members of ethnic minority groups. The diverse student body includes international students representing many different countries.

Location Oakland University is located 25 miles north of Detroit in suburban Oakland County. OU is situated on 1,500 rolling acres near parks, recreational areas, and a large concentration of high-technology industries. Many Fortune 500 companies are located in proximity to the campus, which facilitates student research and internship opportunities.

The University Oakland University, founded in 1957, is a comprehensive state-supported institution of higher education. The University is organized into the College of Arts and Sciences and the Schools of Business Administration, Education and Human Services, Engineering and Computer Science, Health Sciences, and Nursing.

Applying Application for admission and supporting documents must be submitted to the Graduate Admissions Office in time to meet appropriate program deadlines for each semester. All application materials and deadline information may be obtained from the Graduate Admissions Office. International applicants should submit both a University application and an international student application at least one year before the date they wish to enter the University.

Correspondence and Information

Graduate Admissions
Oakland University
Rochester, Michigan 48309-4401

Phone: 248-370-3167
Fax: 248-370-4114
E-mail: gradmail@oakland.edu
Web site: http://www.oakland.edu/gograd

FACULTY/PROGRAM COORDINATORS

Accounting (M.Acc., post-master's certificate): Donna Free, M.Acc., CPA (phone: 248-370-3287).
Applied Mathematical Sciences (Ph.D.): Fiki Shillor, Ph.D. (phone: 248-370-3439).
Biology (M.S., M.A.): Rasul Chaudhry, Ph.D. (phone: 248-370-3550).
Business Administration (M.B.A.; Executive M.B.A.; M.S. in information technology management; post-master's certificates in business economics, finance, human resources management, international business, management information services, marketing, and production/operations management): Paul Trumbull, B.A. (phone: 248-370-3287).
Chemistry (M.S., Ph.D.): Kathleen Moore, Ph.D. (phone: 248-370-2320).
Counseling (Ph.D. in education): Lisa Hawley, Ph.D. (phone: 248-370-2841).
Counseling (M.A.; post-master's specializations in advanced career counseling, child and adolescent counseling, marriage and family counseling, mental health counseling, and substance-abuse counseling): Luellen Ramey, Ph.D. (phone: 248-370-4179).
Early Childhood Education (Ph.D. in education): Sherri Oden, Ph.D. (phone: 248-370-3027).
Early Childhood Education (M.Ed.): Ambika Bhargava, Ph.D. (phone: 248-370-3026).
Educational Leadership (Ph.D. in education): Julia Smith, Ph.D. (phone: 248-370-3082).
Educational Leadership (M.Ed.): Eric Follo, Ph.D. (phone: 248-370-3081).
Leadership (Ed.Spec.): Ilene Ingram, Ph.D. (phone: 248-370-3070).
Educational Studies (M.Ed.): Michael MacDonald, Ph.D. (phone: 248-370-2613).
Engineering (Ph.D. in systems engineering, Ph.D. in mechanical engineering, Ph.D. in computer science and informatics): Bhushan Bhatt, Ph.D. (phone: 248-370-2233).
Engineering (M.S. in computer science, M.S. in embedded systems, M.S. in software engineering and information technology): Ishwar Sethi, Ph.D. (phone: 248-370-2200).
Engineering (M.S. in engineering management): Sankar Sengupta, Ph.D. (phone: 248-370-2218).
Engineering (M.S. in industrial and systems engineering): Christian Wagner, Ph.D. (phone: 248-370-2215).
Engineering (M.S. in mechanical engineering): Gary Barber; Ph.D. (phone: 248-370-2184).
Engineering (M.S. in systems engineering, M.S. in electrical engineering and computer science): Monohar Das, Ph.D. (phone: 248-370-2237).
English (M.A.): Kevin Grimm, Ph.D. (phone: 248-370-2267).
Exercise Science (Graduate certificates in clinical exercise science, complementary medicine and wellness, corporate and worksite wellness, and exercise science): Brian Goslin, Ph.D. (phone: 248-370-4038).
Higher Education (Post-master's certificate): Sandra Packard, Ed.D. (phone: 248-370-3070).
History (M.A.): Don Matthews, Ph.D. (phone: 248-370-3525).
Liberal Studies (M.A.): Linda Benson, Ph.D. (phone: 248-370-3531).
Linguistics (M.A.; graduate certificates in teaching English as a second language and English as a second language teaching (ESL) endorsement): Madelyn Kissock, Ph.D. (phone: 248-370-2174).
Mathematics (M.S. in applied statistics, M.S. in industrial applied mathematics, M.A. in mathematics, graduate certificate in statistical methods, Ph.D. in applied mathematical science): Fiki Shillor, Ph.D. (phone: 248-370-3439).
Music (M.M. in piano performance, piano pedagogy, vocal performance, vocal pedagogy, instrumental performance, instrumental pedagogy, music education, and conducting): Joseph Shively, Ph.D. (phone: 248-370-2287).
Nursing (M.S.N. in adult acute care, adult gerontological nurse practitioner studies, family nurse practitioner studies, nurse anesthesia, and nursing education; post-master's specialization in adult gerontological nurse practitioner studies, family nurse practitioner studies, and nurse anesthesia): Patrina Carper (phone: 248-370-4068).
Physical Therapy (D.P.T): Tamra Bays, Ph.D. (phone: 248-370-3562).
Physical Therapy (Dr.Sc.P.T., M.S.): Kristine Thompson, Ph.D. (phone: 248-370-4096).
Physical Therapy (Graduate certificate in neurological rehabilitation): Cathy Larson, M.S. (phone: 248-370-4392).
Physical Therapy (Graduate certificate in orthopedic manual physical therapy): John Krauss, M.S.P.T.; OCS; FAAOMPT (phone: 248-370-4041).
Physical Therapy (Graduate certificate in pediatric rehabilitation): Chris Stiller Sermo, M.A.P.T. (phone: 248-370-4047).
Physical Therapy (Graduate certificate in teaching and learning for rehabilitation professionals): Kristine Thompson, Ph.D. (phone: 248-370-4096).
Physics (Ph.D.): Brad Roth, Ph.D. (phone: 248-370-4871).
Physics (M.S.): Gopalan Srinivasan, Ph.D. (phone: 248-370-3419).
Public Administration (Post-master's certificates in local government management and nonprofit organization and management; M.P.A.): Diane Hartmus, Ph.D. (phone: 248-370-2352).
Reading (Ph.D.): John McEneaney, Ph.D. (phone: 248-370-4155).
Reading (M.A.T.): Jim Cipielewski, Ph.D. (phone: 248-370-3054).
Reading (Graduate certificate in microcomputer applications): Ledong Li, Ph.D. (phone: 248-370-4373).
Special Education (M.Ed. in special education; teacher endorsements in autistic impairment, emotional impairment, and learning disability): Carol Swift, Ph.D. (phone: 248-370-3077).
Teacher Certification Sandra Deng, M.A. (phone: 248-370-4182).
Teacher Leadership Eric Follo, Ph.D. (phone: 248-370-3070).
Training and Development (M.T.D.): James Quinn, Ph.D. (phone: 248-370-3063).

OLD DOMINION UNIVERSITY

Graduate Programs

Programs of Study

The College of Arts and Letters at Old Dominion University (ODU) offers the Master of Arts (M.A.) in applied linguistics, applied sociology (in conjunction with Norfolk State University), English, history, humanities, international studies, and visual studies (in conjunction with Norfolk State); the Master of Fine Arts (M.F.A.) in creative writing and visual studies (in conjunction with Norfolk State); the Master of Music Education (M.M.E.); and the Doctor of Philosophy (Ph.D.) in English, international studies, and criminology and criminal justice.

The College of Business and Public Administration offers the Master of Arts (M.A.) in economics, the Master of Business Administration (M.B.A.), the Master of Public Administration (M.P.A.); the Master of Science (M.S.) in accounting, the Master of Urban Studies (M.U.S.), the Doctor of Philosophy (Ph.D.) in business administration, and the Doctor of Philosophy (Ph.D.) in public administration and urban policy.

The Darden College of Education offers the Master of Science (M.S.) in occupational and technical studies; the Master of Science in Education (M.S.Ed.) in biology, chemistry, counseling, early childhood education, educational leadership, elementary/middle education, English, higher education, physical education, reading, secondary education, special education, and speech-language pathology; the Education Specialist (Ed.S.) in counseling, educational leadership, and higher education; the Doctor of Philosophy (Ph.D.) in community college leadership, counseling, curriculum and instruction, early childhood education, educational leadership, higher education, human movement science, instructional design and technology, literacy leadership, occupational and technical studies, and special education. ODU also sponsors the Virginia Troops to Teachers Program and the Military Career Transition Program. These programs provide financial support and academic course work for military personnel seeking to transition into a teaching career.

The Frank Batten College of Engineering and Technology offers the Master of Science (M.S.) in aerospace, civil, computer, electrical, engineering management, environmental, mechanical, and modeling and simulation; the Master of Engineering (M.E.) in aerospace, civil, computer, electrical, environmental, experimental methods, mechanical engineering with a specialization option in design and manufacturing, modeling and simulation, motorsports engineering, and systems engineering; the Master of Engineering Management (M.E.M.); the Doctor of Philosophy (Ph.D.) in aerospace, civil, electrical and computer engineering, engineering management, environmental, mechanical, and modeling and simulation.

The College of Health Sciences offers the Master of Public Health (M.P.H.) as a generalist degree and with concentrations in environmental health, epidemiology, and health management/policy (in partnership with Eastern Virginia Medical School). The College also offers the Master of Science in Nursing (M.S.N.) with specialization options in family nurse practitioner, women's health nurse practitioner, nurse educator, nurse anesthetist, nurse administrator, and nurse midwifery (jointly with Shenandoah University); the Master of Science (M.S.) in environmental health/occupational health, health-care management, and long-term care administration; the Master of Science (M.S.D.H.) in dental hygiene, with specialization options in education, administration/management, research, marketing, and community health; the Doctor of Philosophy (Ph.D.) in health services research; and the Doctor of Physical Therapy (D.P.T.).

The College of Sciences offers the Master of Science (M.S.) in biology, chemistry, computational and applied mathematics, computer science, oceanography, physics, and psychology; the Doctor of Philosophy (Ph.D.) in biomedical sciences (in conjunction with Eastern Virginia Medical School), computational and applied mathematics, computer science, ecological sciences, industrial/organizational psychology, oceanography, and physics; and the Doctor of Psychology (Psy.D.) in clinical psychology (a consortium program in conjunction with Norfolk State University, Eastern Virginia Medical School, and the College of William and Mary).

For a full listing of graduate program directors and programs of study, students should refer to the University's Graduate Studies Web site at http://www.odu.edu/graduatestudies.

Research Facilities

The University provides a rich array of resources to support research and creative work. The Perry library provides a full complement of state-of-the-art services for all clientele with more than 2.8 million items. External research funding is approximately $50 million and utilizes state-of-the-art oceanographic research vessels, the world's largest university-run wind tunnel, the Virginia Modeling Analysis and Simulation Center, and significant high performance computing facilities. Many research projects involve partnerships with nearby premier research laboratories such as the Thomas Jefferson National Accelerator Facility, NASA-Langley Research Center, and NASA-Wallops Flight Center. There are also research opportunities in partnerships with local schools, institutions of higher learning, and agencies.

Financial Aid

Financial aid is available in the form of fellowships, research and teaching assistantships, and scholarships. Stipends generally ranged between $5000 and $18,000 for the 2006–07 academic year. In addition, full tuition scholarships are available in some programs. Low-interest, deferred-repayment graduate loans are also available to U.S. citizens who can demonstrate need.

Cost of Study

In-state tuition for 2007–08 is $304 per credit hour. Out-of-state tuition is $761 per credit hour. Other fees amount to approximately $99 per semester.

Living and Housing Costs

There are a wide range of affordable living and housing options on campus, close to campus, and in the Hampton Roads area. Campus residence halls with meal plans are also available.

Location

Old Dominion University's main campus is located in Norfolk, Virginia, one of seven major cities that make up Hampton Roads, an area with a population of 1.4 million. The campus is approximately 200 miles south of Washington, D.C.; within minutes of the world's largest naval base and the largest East Coast seaport; and 30 minutes from the Virginia Beach oceanfront. ODU also operates Higher Education Centers in Northern Virginia, Virginia Beach, Hampton, and the Tri-Cities of Portsmouth, Chesapeake, and Suffolk. Old Dominion sponsors fifty distance learning sites in Virginia, the District of Columbia, North Carolina, Georgia, Arizona, and Washington and delivers programs to Navy ships worldwide.

The University

Old Dominion University is a cutting-edge research university and an innovative educational institution that is home to more than 22,000 students. The University's 6,500 graduate students have the opportunity to take their education to the next level by working with world-class scholars who are pushing the boundaries of their disciplines. As Virginia's international university, top students from all fifty states and 108 countries have dynamic exchanges in seminars, laboratories, and studios.

Old Dominion University has been designated a Doctoral/Research University–Extensive institution by the Carnegie Foundation. This designation reflects the strong commitment to graduate studies and research in all six of its colleges: the College of Arts and Letters, the College of Business and Public Administration, the Darden College of Education, the Frank Batten College of Engineering and Technology, the College of Health Sciences, and the College of Sciences. Graduate students at Old Dominion can pursue their academic and professional interests from among sixty-five master's degree programs, two education specialist programs, twenty-three doctoral programs, and numerous opportunities for internships.

Applying

The application fee is $40. Applications and supporting credentials should be submitted well in advance of the preferred semester of entry to allow sufficient time for departmental review and processing. Deadlines, requirements, and financial aid information can vary significantly across departments so prospective students are encouraged to contact their department of interest as soon as possible. Financial awards are often made early in the admissions process. Applicants requesting financial aid are encouraged to submit all required credentials by February 15.

Correspondence and Information

For applications and admissions information:

Office of Admissions
108 Alfred B. Rollins Jr. Hall
Old Dominion University
Norfolk, Virginia 23529

Phone: 757-683-3685
800-348-7926 (toll-free)
Web site: http://admissions.odu.edu/graduate
http://www.odu.edu

GRADUATE PROGRAMS AND PROGRAM DIRECTORS

For the telephone numbers listed below, the area code is 757.

COLLEGE OF ARTS AND LETTERS

Applied Linguistics (M.A.): Dr. Janet M. Bing. 683-3879; linggpd@odu.edu.
Applied Sociology (M.A.): Dr. Dianne Carmody. 683-3801; socgpd@odu.edu.
Creative Writing (M.F.A.): Ms. Sheri Reynolds. 683-4010; cwgpd@odu.edu.
Criminology (Ph.D): Dr. Mona Danner. 683-5931; mdanner@odu.edu.
English (M.A., Ph.D.): Dr. Jeffrey Richards. 683-4032; englgpd@odu.edu.
History (M.A.): Dr. Jane Merritt. 683-3345; histgpd@odu.edu.
Humanities (M.A.): Dr. Dana Heller. 683-3719; humgpd@odu.edu.
International Studies (M.A., Ph.D.): Dr. Regina Karp. 683-5700; isgpd@odu.edu.
Music Education (M.M.E.): Dr. Nancy Klein. 683-4067; nklein@odu.edu.
Visual Studies (M.A., M.F.A.): Mr. Elliott Jones. 683-4047; artgpd@odu.edu.

COLLEGE OF BUSINESS AND PUBLIC ADMINISTRATION

Accounting (M.S.): Dr. Otto B. Martinson. 683-3505; acctgpd@odu.edu.
Business Administration (M.B.A.): Dr. Bruce L. Rubin. 683-3520; mbainfo@odu.edu.
Business Administration (Ph.D.): Dr. Sylvia Hudgins. 683-3551; busngpd@odu.edu.
Economics (M.A.): Dr. David Selover. 683-3541; dselover@odu.edu.
Public Administration (M.P.A.): Dr. William Leavitt. 683-5695; padmgpd@odu.edu.
Public Administration and Urban Policy (Ph.D.): Dr. John C. Morris. 683-6555; urbanphd@odu.edu.
Urban Services (Ph.D./Urban Management Concentration): Dr. John C. Morris. 683-6555; urbanphd@odu.edu.

DARDEN COLLEGE OF EDUCATION

Athletic Training: Dr. Bonnie Van Lunen. 683-4995; bvanlune@odu.edu.
Community College Leadership (Ph.D.): Dr. Ted Raspiller. 683-4375; eraspill@odu.edu.
Counseling (M.S.Ed., Ed.S., Ph.D. in Education Emphasis): Dr. Ted Remley. 683-3321; tremley@odu.edu.
Curriculum/Instruction (Ph.D.): Dr. Linda Bol. 683-4374; lbol@odu.edu.
Early Childhood Education (M.S.Ed., Ph.D. in Education Emphasis): Dr. Katharine Kersey. 683-4117; kkersey@odu.edu.
Educational Leadership (M.S.Ed., Ed.S., Ph.D. in Education Emphasis): Dr. Dana Burnett. 683-3221; dburnett@odu.edu.
Elementary/Middle Education (M.S.Ed.): Dr. Gail S. Taylor. 683-4374; gstaylor@odu.edu.
Exercise Science (M.S.Ed.): Dr. Elizabeth Dowling. 683-4995; ldowling@odu.edu.
Field-Based Master's Program in Education, Curriculum, and Instruction: Robert Lucking, 683-5545; rlucking@odu.edu.
Higher Education (M.S.Ed., Ed.S., Ph.D. in Education Emphasis): Dr. Dana Burnett. 683-3221; dburnett@odu.edu.
Human Movement Science (Ph.D. in Education Emphasis): Dr. Bonnie Van Lunen. 683-4995; bvanlune@odu.edu.
Instructional Design/Technology (M.S.Ed., Ph.D. in Education Emphasis): Dr. Gary Morrison. 683-4374; gmorriso@odu.edu.
Literacy Leadership (Ph.D. in Education Emphasis): Dr. Jane Hager. 683-4374; jhager@odu.edu.
Military Career Transition Program: Dr. Robert Lucking. 683-5545; rlucking@odu.edu.
Occupational and Technical Studies (M.S., Ph.D. in Education Emphasis): Dr. John M. Ritz. 683-4305; jritz@odu.edu.
Physical Education-Curriculum/Instruction (M.S.Ed.): Dr. Linda Gagen. 683-4995; lgagen@odu.edu.
Reading Education (M.S.Ed.): Dr. Charlene Fleener. 683-4374; cfleener@odu.edu.
Recreation and Tourism Studies (M.S.Ed.): Dr. Edward Hill. 683-4881; ehill@odu.edu.
Secondary Education (M.S.Ed.): Dr. Robert Lucking. 683-5545; rlucking@odu.edu.
Special Education (M.S.Ed., Ph.D. in Education Emphasis): Dr. Cheryl Baker. 683-4117; csbaker@odu.edu.
Speech-Language Pathology (M.S.Ed.): Dr. Nicholas Bountress. 683-4117; nbountre@odu.edu.
Sport Management (M.S.Ed.): Dr. Bob Case. 683-4995; rcase@odu.edu.

FRANK BATTEN COLLEGE OF ENGINEERING AND TECHNOLOGY

Aerospace Engineering (M.E., M.S., Ph.D.): Dr. Brett Newman. 683-5860; bnewman@odu.edu.
Civil Engineering (M.E., M.S., Ph.D.): Dr. Isao Ishibashi. 683-4641; cegpd@odu.edu.
Computer Engineering (M.E., M.S.): Dr. Sach Albin. 683-4967; ecegpd@odu.edu.
Electrical Engineering (M.E., M.S.): Dr. Sach Albin. 683-4967; ecegpd@odu.edu.
Electrical and Computer Engineering (Ph.D.): Dr. Sach Albin. 683-4967; ecegpd@odu.edu.
Engineering Management (M.S., M.E.M.): Dr. Robert Safford. 683-4558; enmagpd@odu.edu.
Engineering Management (Ph.D.): Dr. Ghaith Rabadi. 683-4558; grabadi@odu.edu.
Environmental Engineering (M.E., M.S., Ph.D.): Dr. Isao Ishibashi. 683-4641; cegpd@odu.edu.
Mechanical Engineering (M.E., M.S., Ph.D.): Dr. Gene Hou. 683-3428; megpd@odu.edu.
Modeling and Simulation (M.E., M.S., Ph.D.): Dr. Roland Mielke. 683-4570; rmielke@odu.edu.
Motorsports Engineering (M.E.): Dr. Brett Newman. 683-5860; bnewman@odu.edu.
Systems Engineering (M.E.): Dr. Robert Safford. 683-4558; enmagpd@odu.edu.

COLLEGE OF HEALTH SCIENCES

Community Health (M.S.): Dr. Brenda Stevenson Marshall. 683-4258; bmarshal@odu.edu.
Community Health (M.S. in Environmental Health Emphasis): Prof. James English. 683-6010; jenglish@odu.edu.
Dental Hygiene (M.S.): Prof. Michele Darby. 683-5232; dnthgpd@odu.edu.
Health Services Research (Ph.D.): Dr. Stacey Plichta. 683-4989; splichta@odu.edu.
Nursing (M.S.N.): Dr. Laurel Garzon. 683-5250; nursgpd@odu.edu.
Physical Therapy (D.P.T.): Dr. Martha Walker. 683-4519; mwalker@odu.edu.
Public Health (M.P.H. and all other inquiries): Prof. James English. 683-6010; jenglish@odu.edu.

COLLEGE OF SCIENCES

Biology (M.S.): Dr. Wayne Hynes. 683-3613; biolgpd@odu.edu.
Biomedical Sciences (Ph.D.): Dr. James R. Swanson. 683-3614; bimdgpd@odu.edu.
Chemistry (M.S.): Dr. Jennifer L. Radkiewicz-Poutsma. 683-4101; chemgpd@odu.edu.
Computational & Applied Mathematics (M.S., Ph.D.): Dr. Hideaki Kaneko. 683-4969; mathgpd@odu.edu.
Computer Science (M.S., Ph.D.): Dr. Hussein Abdel-Wahab. 683-4512; csgpd@odu.edu.
Ecological Sciences (Ph.D.): Dr. John Holsinger. 683-3606; ecolgpd@odu.edu.
Oceanography (M.S., Ph.D.): Dr. Fred Dobbs. 683-4285; oceangpd@odu.edu.
Physics (M.S., Ph.D.): Dr. Lepsha Vuskovic. 683-4611; physgpd@odu.edu.
Psychology (M.S.): Dr. Louis Janda. 683-4211; psycgpd@odu.edu.
Psychology Industrial/Organizational (Ph.D.): Dr. James Bliss. 683-4222; psychgpd@odu.edu.
Clinical Psychology (Psy.D.): Dr. Robin Lewis. 683-4210; psydgpd@odu.edu.

PACIFIC LUTHERAN UNIVERSITY

Graduate Studies

Programs of Study

Pacific Lutheran University (PLU) offers master's-level graduate degrees in five fields: business (M.B.A.), education (M.A.E.), nursing (M.S.N.), social sciences (M.A.), and creative writing (M.F.A.). Areas of specialization in education include classroom teaching, educational administration, and initial certification. The social sciences master's program offers a concentration in the area of marriage and family therapy. In nursing, concentrations include care and outcomes management, nurse practitioner studies, and entry-level nursing. The M.B.A. program offers a concentration in technology and innovative management. The M.F.A. in creative writing is a low-residency program.

Specific objectives for the University's graduate programs include increasing the breadth and depth of understanding of graduate students in their chosen disciplines, increasing students' knowledge of ongoing research in their fields of study, immersing students in research processes, developing students' abilities to do independent study and research, and preparing students to enter professional vocations or pursue advanced study leading to doctoral degrees.

The University offers a 4-1-4 calendar that consists of two 14-week semesters bridged by a 4-week January term. A minimum of 32 semester hours is required for each program. Individual programs may require more, depending upon prior preparation and specific degree requirements. Students must complete at least 24 of the required semester hours at PLU. Full-time students may complete most graduate programs in two years; however, some programs are designed to be completed in as little as fourteen months. Graduate students at PLU enjoy small classes and a high level of individual attention from the faculty.

Research Facilities

The Robert A. L. Mortvedt Library is the central multimedia learning resource center serving the entire University community. It contains more than 500,000 books and periodicals, microfilms, and audiovisual materials and receives more than 2,000 current magazines, journals, and newspapers. Computer access to other large libraries in the area combined with e-mail service allows students and faculty members rapid access to many other sources for research. A large computer lab, located in the University Center, provides IBM PCs, Macintosh computers, and access to the University's DEC Alpha 3400 computer.

Financial Aid

Financial assistance for graduate students is available in the form of Federal Perkins and Federal Stafford Student Loans, graduate assistantships, and scholarships. In addition, students may be eligible for a PLUS loan to a maximum of $3000. A limited number of graduate assistantships are awarded to full-time students in amounts up to $5000 per year.

Cost of Study

Graduate tuition is charged at the rate of $784 per semester credit hour in 2007–08. Some programs have special rates.

Living and Housing Costs

The University has a selection of residence halls that provide comfortable living arrangements. Although these are primarily undergraduate residences, any full-time student is welcome to apply for housing. One hall is designed to accommodate graduate students. Application may be completed through the Residential Life Office. In the surrounding area, there are numerous housing options available for off-campus living.

Student Group

The graduate student population for all programs totals approximately 250. Full-time students comprise about one half of the graduate population. Students come from throughout the United States and from several other countries.

Student Outcomes

More than 96 percent of recent M.B.A. graduates are employed and work in such diverse industries as manufacturing, aerospace, financial services, health care, accounting, and forest products. Graduates with the M.A.E. have accepted instructional and educational administrative positions across the state and region. Several graduates have been named Washington State Teacher of the Year. Graduates with the M.A. in social sciences (marriage and family therapy concentration) are employed, on average, one month after graduation as licensed/certified marriage and family therapists in mental health centers, social service organizations, group practices, and educational institutions. All students in the M.S.N. program who complete the care and outcomes management concentration have consistently been employed as managed-care coordinators and case managers. Graduates who complete the nurse practitioner studies concentration have been offered positions in ambulatory-care settings.

Location

Pacific Lutheran University is located on a 126-acre campus immediately adjacent to the city of Tacoma (population 193,556). The campus is 40 miles south of Seattle and 20 miles south of Seattle-Tacoma International Airport. Located in the midst of the Puget Sound region, the campus is in the heart of a wide variety of natural attractions, including Mt. Rainier, the Olympic and Cascade mountain ranges, and the Puget Sound.

The University

Pacific Lutheran University is an independent, comprehensive university affiliated with the Evangelical Lutheran Church in America. Total University enrollment is approximately 3,600. The faculty numbers approximately 260 and includes outstanding scholars known nationally and internationally for work in their fields. PLU has become a leader in global education through numerous study-away opportunities and a curriculum that integrates an international focus throughout academics and student life.

The University academic structure consists of five professional schools: Business, Education, Nursing, and Social Work and a College of Arts and Sciences, which has three divisions: Humanities, Social Sciences, and Natural Sciences. The curriculum also offers preprofessional advising in both health professions and law. Graduate students have the opportunity to work closely with faculty members and have access to superb academic facilities.

Applying

Further information and applications for graduate admission may be obtained from the Office of Admission or online. All application evaluations are based on scholastic qualifications, letters of recommendation, a statement of goals, and preparation in the proposed field of study. Certain programs require scores on standardized examinations and personal interviews. Applications for admission to most programs are acted upon throughout the year. However, all application documents should be received six weeks prior to the semester in which enrollment is sought.

Correspondence and Information

Office of Admission
Pacific Lutheran University
Tacoma, Washington 98447

Phone: 253-535-7151
800-274-6758 (toll-free)
Fax: 253-536-5136
E-mail: admission@plu.edu
Web site: http://www.plu.edu

PROGRAM ADMINISTRATION

Loren J. Anderson, President.
Patricia O'Connell Killen, Provost and Dean of Graduate Studies.

Graduate Studies
Patricia O'Connell Killen, Provost and Dean of Graduate Studies.

Division of Social Sciences (M.A.)
Charles York, Chair of Marriage and Family Therapy.

School of Business (M.B.A.)
Abby Wigstrom-Carlson, Director of Graduate Programs.

School of Education (M.A.E.)
Mike Hillis, Director of Graduate Programs.

School of Nursing (M.S.N.)
Susan Duis, Graduate Admissions Coordinator.

Department of English (M.F.A.)
Tom Campbell, Chair.

PENN STATE HARRISBURG

Graduate Programs

Programs of Study

Penn State Harrisburg offers the Master of Arts (M.A.) in American studies, which explores American civilization through history, philosophy, folklore, and the arts and their relationships to economic, political, and social institutions; the M.A. in humanities, an interdisciplinary program; the M.A. in criminal justice, which provides academic leadership for those working in corrections, victims' services, policing and law enforcement, human services, and courts; the Master of Business Administration (M.B.A.), a professionally oriented program for those seeking or holding management positions in business, engineering, scientific, technical, or health-care organizations; the Master of Education (M.Ed.), with a major in teaching and curriculum, designed for school teachers; the M.Ed., with a major in training and development, focusing on the special skills needed by training and development professionals in business, industry, health care, government, and human services; the M.Ed., with a major in health education, providing a broad background in health areas, the skills required to assess and deal with health educational needs, the theoretical basis for understanding health education research, and the knowledge to design, implement, and evaluate health education programs; the Master of Engineering (M.Eng.), with a major in engineering science, providing broad education in advanced aspects of engineering sciences and the opportunity for specialization; the M.Eng. in environmental engineering, offering opportunities for engineers to specialize in various environmental problems; the M.Eng. in electrical engineering, with concentrations in electronic communications systems, control systems, VLSI and computer engineering, and power systems; the Master of Environmental Pollution Control (M.E.P.C.) or Master of Science (M.S.) in environmental pollution control focuses on aspects of air and water pollution control and solid-waste disposal; the Master of Arts in community psychology and social change, which emphasizes the use of psychology and sociology to meet social needs in the community; the Master of Public Administration (M.P.A.), for those in or seeking professional careers in government, health-care, human service, or public service organizations; the Ph.D. in public administration combining the traditions of the doctoral degree with flexible class schedules for part-time students and scholar/practitioners; the Doctor of Education (D.Ed.) in adult education, a program in which adult education is merged with such areas as counseling and the behavioral sciences, business and organizational development, science and engineering, public affairs, the humanities, and health education; the M.A. in applied clinical psychology, which prepares students to work as mental health professionals in a variety of settings and provides the academic training necessary for graduates to apply for master's-level licensing as mental-health professionals in the Commonwealth of Pennsylvania; the M.A. in applied behavior analysis, which is designed to teach graduate-level students to become proficient in the clinical practice of applied behavior analysis and to meet certification standards set by the Association for Behavior Analysis and the Behavior Analyst Certification Board (BACB); the M.S. in applied psychological research, which focuses on the development of research skills within the context of scientific training in psychology; the Master of Science in Information Systems (M.S.I.S.), offered within the School of Business Administration for technically grounded, upper-level information resource managers with business organizations; the Master of Health Administration (M.H.A.), for careers in a variety of health-care organizations; and the Master of Science (M.S.) in computer science, for practical and theoretical applications. Penn State Harrisburg and the Dickinson School of Law of the Pennsylvania State University offer cooperative, concurrent programs leading to J.D./M.B.A., J.D./M.P.A., J.D./E.P.C., and J.D./M.S.I.S. degrees, as well as a program with the Penn State College of Medicine at Hershey leading to the Ph.D. degree in pharmacology and an M.B.A.

Research Facilities

The new campus library contains more than 275,000 volumes (growing by 6,000 a year) and subscribes to 1,300 periodicals. Microform holdings total 1 million units, including complete sets of ERIC, HRAF, Envirofiche, and Library of American Civilization. Wireless networking is available throughout the library. The resources of other libraries of the Penn State University are available through LIAS, an online integrated library system of the University libraries. Students also have access to the resources of the Associated College Libraries of Central Pennsylvania, a consortium of area college libraries.

The Computer Center provides support for instruction and research. Facilities include a nineteen-terminal microcomputer lab, a thirty-terminal microcomputer LAN, and a forty-terminal microcomputer LAN that accesses the library's online database search system and an IBM mainframe processing system located at Penn State's main campus. Programming support is available through the center's staff. Penn State Harrisburg is also home to the Pennsylvania State Data Center.

Financial Aid

Internships, fellowships, graduate assistantships, graduate work-study awards, grants-in-aid programs, Guaranteed Student Loans, and a minority graduate student assistantship are available.

Cost of Study

In 2006–07, resident tuition was $6612 per semester for full-time study (12 or more credits) and $551 per credit for part-time study (1 to 11 credits). Pennsylvania nonresident full-time tuition was $9326 per semester, and part-time tuition was $777 per credit. Pennsylvania resident M.B.A. tuition was $620 per credit. Pennsylvania nonresident M.B.A. tuition was $964 per credit. For business, science, IST, and engineering programs, resident tuition was $582 per credit. Pennsylvania nonresident tuition for business, science, IST, and engineering programs was $812 per credit.

Living and Housing Costs

Seventy-two new apartment-style units accommodate a minimum of 300 occupants. Housing is close to classrooms, the new library, recreation activities, and food and support services. Each unit contains four bedrooms, two full bathrooms, a kitchen, living area, and washers and dryers.

Student Group

Since the campus is a major graduate center, students are primarily mature individuals committed to continuing their education. The median age of graduate students is 29. There are approximately 1,500 graduate students, most of whom are employed full-time and attend classes on a part-time basis.

Location

The college is 8 miles from Harrisburg, the state capital. The resources of local, state, and federal agencies; museums; archives; and the state library are nearby. Within 30 miles are the urban centers of York and Lancaster, small towns such as Hershey, and rural settings in Lancaster and Lebanon Counties. Business, cultural, industrial, agricultural, residential, and service opportunities abound. Three interstate highways converge in Harrisburg and provide access to Philadelphia, Baltimore, New York City, and Washington, D.C., which also are accessible via nearby rail and air service.

The University

Penn State Harrisburg has a small-college atmosphere, with a student body of about 3,800, yet it has the resources, academic standards, and assets of the state's comprehensive land-grant research university. Graduate programs are designed primarily for persons employed full-time in area businesses, schools, government agencies, and industries, and most courses are held in the evening. A variety of programs and services are also offered through the Eastgate Center in Harrisburg.

Applying

Candidates must have a bachelor's degree from an accredited institution. Applicants generally are expected to have earned a GPA of at least 3.0 (4.0 scale). The GRE is required by some programs. The M.B.A. and M.S.I.S. programs require the GMAT. The M.P.A. program accepts scores from the GRE General Test, GMAT, LSAT, or MAT. The Adult Education Program accepts the GRE or MAT. Candidates from countries in which English is not the primary language must earn at least 550 (paper-based test) or 213 (computer-based test) on the TOEFL. International transcripts must be evaluated by the Educational Credential Evaluators (ECE). ECE evaluations should accompany the application and transcripts. Prospective students must submit an online application at http://www.hbg.psu.edu/hbg/admissapps.html.

Correspondence and Information

Enrollment Services
Penn State Harrisburg
777 West Harrisburg Pike
Middletown, Pennsylvania 17057

Phone: 717-948-6250
E-mail: hbgadmit@psu.edu
Web site: http://www.hbg.psu.edu

DEAN AND PROGRAM COORDINATORS

Marian R. Walters, Professor (physiology) and Associate Dean for Research and Graduate Studies; Ph.D., Houston.

Coordinators of Graduate Programs

Adult Education (D.Ed.): Elizabeth Tisdell, Associate Professor (adult education); D.Ed., Georgia.
Applied Behavior Analysis (M.A.): Kimberly Schreck, Associate Professor (psychology); Ph.D., Ohio State.
Applied Clinical Psychology (M.A.): Barbara Bremer, Associate Professor (psychology); Ph.D., Bryn Mawr.
Applied Psychological Research (M.A.): Barbara Bremer, Associate Professor (psychology); Ph.D., Bryn Mawr.
American Studies (M.A.): Charles J. Kupfer, Assistant Professor (American studies and history); Ph.D., Texas. Simon Bronner, Distinguished Professor (American studies and folklore); Ph.D., Indiana.
Business Administration (M.B.A.): Richard Young, Associate Professor (supply chain management); Ph.D., Penn State.
Community Psychology and Social Change (M.A.): Holly Angelique, Associate Professor (community psychology); Ph.D., Michigan State.
Computer Science (M.S.): Linda M. Null, Assistant Professor (computer science); Ph.D., Iowa State.
Criminal Justice (M.A.): Barbara Sims, Associate Professor (criminal justice); Ph.D., Sam Houston State.
Electrical Engineering (M.Eng.): Peter B. Idowu, Associate Professor (electrical engineering); Ph.D., Toledo.
Engineering Science (M.Eng.): Peter B. Idowu, Associate Professor (electrical engineering); Ph.D., Toledo.
Environmental Engineering (M.Eng.): Thomas Eberlein, Assistant Professor (chemistry); Ph.D., Wisconsin.
Environmental Pollution Control (M.E.P.C. and M.S.): Said Elnashaie, Professor (engineering); Ph.D., Edinburgh.
Health Administration (M.H.A.): Cynthia Mara, Associate Professor (health care administration and policy); Ph.D., Virginia Tech.
Health Education (M.Ed.): Samuel W. Monismith, Associate Professor (health education); D.Ed., Penn State.
Humanities (M.A.): Glenn A. Mazis, Professor (humanities and philosophy); Ph.D., Yale.
Information Systems (M.S.I.S.): Gayle J. Yaverbaum, Professor (information systems); Ph.D., Temple.
Public Administration (M.P.A.): Jeremy Plant, Professor (public administration and public policy); Ph.D., Virginia.
Public Administration (Ph.D.): Jeremy Plant, Professor (public administration and public policy); Ph.D., Virginia.
Teaching and Curriculum (M.Ed.): Steven A. Melnick, Associate Professor (education); Ph.D., Connecticut.
Training and Development (M.Ed.): Margaret C. Lohman, Associate Professor (training and development); Ph.D., Ohio State.

Vartan Plaza, with the college bookstore (left) and the Science and Technology Building (right).

The state-of-the-art library at Penn State Harrisburg.

PENNSTATE

PENN STATE UNIVERSITY PARK

Graduate School

Programs of Study Programs of graduate study are offered in the following fields (asterisks precede fields in which only a master's degree is offered; all other fields offer both master's and doctoral programs, except where noted): acoustics; adult education; aerospace engineering; agricultural, environmental, and regional economics; agricultural and extension education; agricultural and biological engineering; agronomy; *American studies; anatomy; animal science; anthropology; *applied behavior analysis; *applied clinical psychology; applied linguistics (Ph.D. only); *applied psychological research; *applied statistics; architectural engineering; *architecture; *art; *art education; art history; astronomy and astrophysics; biobehavioral health; biochemistry and molecular biology; biochemistry, microbiology, and molecular biology; bioengineering; biology; *biotechnology; business administration; cell and developmental biology; cell and molecular biology; chemical engineering; chemistry; civil engineering; *college student affairs; communication arts and sciences; communication sciences and disorders; *community psychology and social change; *community and economic development; comparative and international education; comparative literature; *composition/theory; computer science and engineering; *conducting; counseling psychology (Ph.D. only); counselor education; *criminal justice; crime, law, and justice; curriculum and instruction; demography; *earth sciences; ecology; economics; educational leadership; educational psychology; educational theory and policy; electrical engineering; energy and geo-environmental engineering; *engineering mechanics; *engineering science; engineering science and mechanics; English; entomology; *environmental engineering; *environmental pollution control; food science; *forensic science; forest resources; French; genetics; *geographic information systems; geography; geosciences; German; *health administration; health education; *health evaluation sciences; health policy and administration; higher education; history; horticulture; hotel, restaurant, and institutional management; human development and family studies; *humanities; industrial engineering; *industrial relations and human resources; *information science; information sciences and technology; *information systems; instructional systems; integrative biosciences; kinesiology; *laboratory animal medicine; *landscape architecture; *leadership development; leisure studies; *manufacturing systems engineering; mass communications (Ph.D. only); materials science and engineering; mathematics; mechanical engineering; *media studies; meteorology; microbiology and immunology; molecular medicine; molecular toxicology; music and music education; *music theory; *music theory and history; neuroscience; nuclear engineering; nursing; nutrition; *oil and gas engineering management; operations research; pathobiology; *performance; petroleum and mineral engineering; pharmacology; philosophy; physics; physiology; *piano pedagogy and performance; plant biology; plant pathology; political science; *project management; psychology; public administration; *public health preparedness; quality and manufacturing management; rural sociology; Russian and comparative literature; school psychology; sociology; software engineering; soil science; Spanish; special education; statistics; systems engineering; *teaching and curriculum; *teaching English as a second language; *telecommunications studies; *theater; *training and development; *voice performance and pedagogy; wildlife and fisheries science; women's studies; workforce education and development; and *youth and family education. Level I Instructional, Supervisory, Educational Specialist, and Administrative certificates are offered.

Research Facilities The University Libraries System has more than 5 million cataloged volumes, over 68,000 current serials, and 5.2 million microforms. Automated services are provided through the Library Information Access System developed at Penn State. The Center for Academic Computing (CAC) is the principal provider of central academic computing services. The center operates computers capable of providing not only numerically intensive computing but also electronic access to higher education facilities and research centers worldwide. Penn State and Internet resources include electronic bulletin boards, news and conferencing systems, publications, library catalogs, research databases, discussion groups, and much more. Public laboratories with terminals and desktop computers provide facilities for those without their own equipment.

Financial Aid Fellowships, traineeships, or assistantships are held by 69.3 percent of all University Park students. These awards involve remission of tuition and payment of stipends averaging $1580 per month. Awards are usually made by the student's department or on recommendation to another administrative unit. Student loans and work-study funds are available through the Office of Student Aid.

Cost of Study In 2006–07, tuition for full-time study (except for medical students) was $6612 per semester for residents and $12,032 per semester for nonresidents at all campuses except Penn State Great Valley and business, information sciences and technology, science, and engineering programs. Further information is available on the Web at http://www.bursar.psu.edu.

Living and Housing Costs Residence hall accommodations and University-owned apartments are available through the Assignment Office for Campus Residences (phone: 814-865-7501).

Student Group In fall 2006, 10,991 graduate students were enrolled. The University conferred 2,763 advanced degrees, including 674 doctorates, during the 2005–06 year.

Student Outcomes Graduates of the University typically proceed to a wide variety of academic and nonacademic professional careers in colleges and universities, private industry, government, and nonprofit organizations.

Location The main campus, University Park, is located in the center of the state in the borough of State College. Pittsburgh, Philadelphia, New York City, and Washington, D.C., are each within a few hours' travel by car and are readily accessible by bus or air. The beautiful mountain country surrounding the community offers seasonal recreation, including boating, camping, fishing, hiking, hunting, skiing, and swimming. Although Penn State is a major graduate and research institution, the community retains a collegiate atmosphere.

The Graduate School Graduate study is offered in more than 150 major programs, and twenty-seven types of advanced academic and professional degrees are conferred. The faculty of the Graduate School numbers about 2,800. In addition to the University Park campus, Penn State Great Valley near Philadelphia; Penn State Harrisburg; the College of Medicine at Hershey; and Penn State Erie, the Behrend College, offer graduate degree programs.

Applying Admission is granted jointly by the Graduate School and the department to which the student is applying. Applicants interested in programs at Penn State Erie, the Behrend College; Penn State Great Valley; and Penn State Harrisburg should apply directly to these campuses. Students should contact the Office of Certification and Educational Services, 181 Chambers Building, for information on Level I Instructional, Supervisory, Educational Specialist, or Administrative certificates. Students whose native language is not English or who have not received baccalaureate or master's degrees from an institution in which the language of instruction is English must submit TOEFL scores. Application materials and detailed information about specific graduate programs and GRE requirements are available from the individual graduate programs. Because the admission process is time consuming, applications should be submitted as early as possible.

Correspondence and Information

Graduate School
Penn State University
University Park Campus
114 Kern Graduate Building
University Park, Pennsylvania 16802

Phone: 814-865-1795 (Graduate Enrollment Services)
E-mail: gadm@psu.edu
Web site: http://www.gradsch.psu.edu

COLLEGES/CENTERS AND HEADS OF PROGRAMS

Unless otherwise indicated, the mailing address is The Pennsylvania State University, University Park, Pennsylvania 16802. (Penn State Harrisburg is in Middletown, Pennsylvania 17057; the Milton S. Hershey Medical Center, College of Medicine, is in Hershey, Pennsylvania 17033; Penn State Great Valley School of Graduate Professional Studies is in Malvern, Pennsylvania 19355; and Penn State Erie, the Behrend College, is in Erie, Pennsylvania 16563).

Agricultural Sciences
Agricultural and Biological Engineering: Roy Young, 249 Agricultural Engineering. Agricultural and Extension Education: Tracey Hoover, 323 Agricultural Administration. Agricultural, Environmental, and Regional Economics: Stephen Smith, 107 Armsby. Crop and Soil Sciences: David Sylvia, 116 Agricultural Sciences and Industries. Dairy and Animal Science: Terry Etherton, 324L Henning. Entomology: Gary Felton, 501 Agricultural Sciences and Industries. Food Science: John D. Floros, 202 Food Science. Forest Resources: Charles Strauss, 319 Forest Resources. Horticulture: Richard Marini, 102 Tyson. Pathobiology: C. Channa Reddy, 115 Henning. Plant Pathology: Barbara Crist, 211 Buckhout. Rural Sociology: Stephen Smith, 107 Armsby. Wildlife and Fisheries Science: Charles Strauss, 319 Forest Resources. Youth and Family Education: Tracey Hoover, 323 Agricultural Administration.

Arts and Architecture
Architecture: Daniel Willis, 121 Stuckeman. Art Education: Charles Garoian, 207 Arts Cottage. Art History: Craig Zabel, 229 Arts. Composing: Sue Haug, 233 Music. Composition/Theory: Sue Haug, 233 Music. Conducting: Sue Haug, 233 Music. Integrative Arts: William Kelly, 9 Brumbaugh Hall. Landscape Architecture: Brian Orland, 121 Stuckeman Family Building. Music and Music Education: Sue Haug, 233 Music. Music Theory: Sue Haug, 233 Music. Music Theory and History: Sue Haug, 233 Music. Performance: Sue Haug, 233 Music. Piano Pedagogy and Performance: Sue Haug, 233 Music. Theater: Dan Carter, 103 Arts. Art: C. Garoian, 210 Patterson. Voice Performance and Pedagogy: Sue Haug, 233 Music.

Business Administration
Business Administration (Ph.D., M.S.): Hans Baumgartner, 482 Business Building. Business Administration (M.B.A.): Dennis Sheehan, 220 Business Building.

Communications
Mass Communications: John Nichols, 201 Carnegie. Media Studies: John Nichols, 201 Carnegie. Telecommunications Studies: John Nichols, 201 Carnegie.

Earth and Mineral Sciences
Earth Sciences: Timothy Bralower, 507 Deike. Energy and Geoenvironmental Engineering: Yaw Yeboah, 110 Hosler. Geographic Information Systems: World Campus: Mark Gahegan, 2217 E.E.S. Geography: Roger Downs, 302 Walker. Geosciences: Timothy Bralower, 507 Dieke. Materials Science and Engineering: Gary Messing, 101 Steidle. Meteorology: William Brune, 503 Walker. Petroleum and Mineral Engineering: Yaw Yeborah, 110 Hosler.

Education
Adult Education: Edgar Farmer, 314 Keller; Elizabeth Tisdell, Penn State Harrisburg. College Student Affairs: Jacqueline Stefkovich, 300 Rackley. Counseling Psychology and Counselor Education: Spencer Niles, 327 Cedar. Curriculum and Instruction: Murry Nelson, 155 Chambers. Educational Leadership: Jacqueline Stefkovich, 300 Rackley. Educational Psychology: Kathy Ruhl, 125 Cedar. Educational Theory and Policy: Jacqueline Stefkovich, 300 Rackley. Higher Education: Jacqueline Stefkovich, 300 Rackley. Instructional Systems: Edgar Farmer, 314 Keller. School Psychology: Kathy Ruhl, 125 Cedar. Special Education: Kathy Ruhl, 125 Cedar; Arlene Mitchell, Great Valley. Workforce Education and Development: Edgar Farmer, 301 Keller.

Engineering
Aerospace Engineering: George Lesieutre, 229 Hammond. Agricultural and Biological Engineering: Roy Young, 249 Agricultural Engineering. Architectural Engineering: Richard Behr, 225 Engineering A. Chemical Engineering: A. Zydney, 158 Fenske. Civil Engineering: Peggy Johnson, 218 Sackett. Computer Science and Engineering: R. Acharya, 111 IST Building. Electrical Engineering: W. Kenneth Jenkins, 118 Electrical Engineering East. Engineering Mechanics: Judith Todd, 212 EES. Engineering Science: Judith Todd, 212 EES. Environmental Engineering: Andrew Scanlon, 218 Sackett. Industrial Engineering: Richard J. Koubek, 310 Leonhard. Mechanical Engineering: Karen Thole, 127 Reber. Nuclear Engineering: Karen Thole, 127 Reber.

Health and Human Development
Biobehavioral Health: Collins Airhihenbuwa, 315 Human Development East. Communication Sciences and Disorders: Gordon Blood, 110 Moore. Health Policy and Administration: Dennis Shea, 116N Henderson. Hotel, Restaurant, and Institutional Management: Hubert Van Hoof, 201 Mateer. Human Development and Family Studies: Steven Zarit, 211 South Henderson. Kinesiology: Philip Martin, 276 Recreation Building. Leisure Studies: John Dattilo, 201 Mateer. Nursing: Paula Milone-Nuzzo, 201 HHD East. Nutrition: M. Green, 126 South Henderson.

Hershey Medical Center
Anatomy: Patricia McLaughlin. Biochemistry and Molecular Biology: Judith Bond. Cell and Molecular Biology: Robert Donahue. Health Evaluation Sciences: Vernon Chinchilli. Laboratory Animal Medicine: Ronald Wilson. Microbiology and Immunology: Richard Courtney. Neuroscience: Robert Milner. Pharmacology: Kent Vrana. Physiology: Leonard S. Jefferson.

Intercollege Graduate Degree Programs
Acoustics: Anthony Atchley, 217A Applied Science. Bioengineering: Herbert Lipowsky, 205 Hallowell. Business Administration: John Fizel. Cell and Developmental Biology: Hong Ma, 201 Life Sciences. Demography: Gordon DeJong, 601 Oswald. Ecology: David Mortensen, 101 Life Sciences. Environmental Pollution Control: Said Elnashaie, Penn State Harrisburg. Genetics: Richard Ordway, 201 Mueller. Integrative Biosciences: Peter Hudson, 201 Life Sciences, University Park; Michael Verderame, Hershey. Molecular Medicine: Craig Meyers, Hershey. Molecular Toxicology: Jeffrey Peters, 312 Life Sciences. Operations Research: Susan Xu, 478 Business Building. Physiology: Leonard Jefferson, Hershey Medical Center. Plant Biology: Teh-hui Kao, 101 Life Sciences. Quality and Manufacturing Management: Jose Ventura, 344 Leonhard.

Liberal Arts
Anthropology: Nina Jablonski, 409 Carpenter. Applied Linguistics: Joan Kelly Hall, 305 Sparks. Communication Arts and Sciences: James Dillard, 234 Sparks. Comparative Literature: Caroline Eckhardt, 311 Burrowes. Crime, Law, and Justice: Paul Amato, 211 Oswald Tower. Economics: James Jordan, 604 Kern. English: Robert Caserio, 107 Burrowes. French: Thomas Hale, 211 Burrowes. German: Adrian Wanner, 311 Burrowes. History: Sally McMurry, 108 Weaver. Industrial Relations and Human Resources: Paul Clark, 133 Willard. Philosophy: Shannon Sullivan, 240 Sparks. Political Science: Donna Bahry, 202 Pond Lab. Psychology: Melvin Mark, 350 Moore. Sociology: Paul Amato, 201 Oswald Tower. Spanish: William Blue, 211 Burrowes. Teaching English as a Second Language: K. Johnson, 305 Sparks.

Penn State Erie, Behrend College
Business Administration: Margaret Thoms. Manufacturing Systems Engineering: Ralph Ford. Project Management: John Magenau.

Penn State Great Valley School of Graduate Professional Studies
Business Administration: Simon Pak. Information Science: James Nemes. Leadership Development: Simon Pak. Software Engineering: James Nemes. Systems Engineering: John McCool.

Penn State Harrisburg
Adult Education: Elizabeth Tisdell. American Studies: Kathryn Robinson. Applied Behavior Analysis: R. M. Foxx. Applied Clinical Psychology: B. Bremer. Applied Psychological Research: B. Bremer. Business Administration: Richard Young. Community Psychology and Social Change: Holly Angelique. Computer Science: Linda Null. Criminal Justice: Barbara Sims. Electrical Engineering: Peter Idowu. Engineering Science: Peter Idowu. Environmental Engineering: Thomas Eberlein. Environmental Pollution Control: Said Elnashaie. Health Administration: Cynthia Mara. Health Education: Samuel Monismith. Humanities: Glen Mazis. Information Systems: Gayle Yaverbaum. Public Administration: Jack Rabin. Teaching and Curriculum: Ernest Dishner. Training and Development: Margaret Lohman.

School of Information Sciences and Technology
Information Sciences and Technology: Joseph Lambert, 332 IST Building.

Science
Applied Statistics: J. L. Rosenberger, 326 Thomas. Astronomy and Astrophysics: Eric Feigelson, 525 Davey. Biochemistry, Microbiology, and Molecular Biology: Robert Schlegel, 108 Althouse. Biology: Douglas Cavener, 208 Mueller. Biotechnology: Robert Schlegel, 201 Life Sciences. Chemistry: Ayusman Sen, 104 Chemistry Building. Forensic Science: Robert Shaler, 107 Whitmore. Mathematics: John Roe, 104 McAllister. Physics: Jayanth Banavar, 104 Davey. Statistics: J. L. Rosenberger, 326 Thomas.

PEPPERDINE UNIVERSITY

Graduate School of Education and Psychology

Programs of Study

Pepperdine University's Graduate School of Education and Psychology offers degree and credential programs designed to prepare teachers and educational administrators, psychologists and counselors, mental health administrators, consultants, change agents, and technology specialists for lives of purpose, service, and leadership. At Pepperdine, a values-based commitment to improve the lives of others exists alongside a market-based commitment to deliver innovative, high-quality education.

Pepperdine offers a variety of graduate programs in education, leading to a Master of Science in administration, a Master of Arts in education, a Master of Arts in educational technology, and a Doctor of Education (Ed.D.). Several teaching credentials and Tier I and II administrative credentials are also offered.

The Doctor of Education program has four unique concentrations: educational leadership, administration, and policy; educational technology; organization change; and organizational leadership. Each doctoral concentration has its own format designed for working professionals. The Educational Leadership, Administration, and Policy Program offers classes that are 60 percent face-to-face sessions and 40 percent course work conducted online. The Educational Technology Program is a combination of 15 percent face-to-face sessions and 85 percent course work conducted online. The Organization Change Program has a sequence-oriented, seminar-style curriculum that is held at various conference locations. The Organizational Leadership Program offers traditional classes on weeknights and weekends.

Psychology programs include a Master of Arts in psychology; a Master of Arts in clinical psychology, with an emphasis in marriage and family therapy; and a Doctor of Psychology (Psy.D.). Master's programs are designed for students to work at their own pace, with evening classes available for working professionals and a daytime program offered for full-time students. The Psy.D. program, which is fully accredited by the American Psychological Association, consists of three years of course work in addition to an internship. A master's degree is required.

Research Facilities

A computer network links each of the University's libraries, which collectively contain more than 800,000 books, bound journals, and microforms. Each facility is fully supported with library services, wireless networking, and a computer center. The headquarters, located at the West Los Angeles Graduate Campus, houses a multimedia center.

Financial Aid

Scholarships, grants, and loans are available to qualified students. Veterans should follow regular admission procedures and secure the certificate of eligibility from the Veterans Administration or the state of California. More than 85 percent of students qualify for federal loans, and close to 70 percent are eligible for Pepperdine-funded assistance. Current information and all forms necessary to apply for financial aid are available on the financial aid Web site at http://gsep.pepperdine.edu/financialaid. For additional information, students should contact the Financial Aid Office at 310-568-5775 or gsepfaid@pepperdine.edu.

Cost of Study

Charges for one unit of instruction in 2006–07 varied from $795 to $1000, depending upon the program.

Living and Housing Costs

The Pepperdine University graduate campuses are in proximity to apartment buildings and residential areas. Students are assisted in finding housing near the campus at which they are enrolled, whether that housing is an apartment, town house, condominium, or guest room.

Student Group

Total University enrollment is approximately 7,360, and enrollment at the Graduate School of Education and Psychology is 1,600. Students range in age and experience, with many returning to the workforce or changing their careers and others entering the programs upon completion of their undergraduate degree.

Location

The headquarters for the Graduate School of Education and Psychology is the West Los Angeles Graduate Campus, located 30 minutes west of downtown Los Angeles. The Drescher Graduate Campus in Malibu overlooks the Pacific Ocean from the Santa Monica Mountains. The Encino Graduate Campus is located in the San Fernando Valley. The Irvine Graduate Campus is in Orange County, near the John Wayne Airport. The Westlake Village Graduate Campus is in Ventura County. Program offerings vary by location.

The University

Pepperdine, an independent, medium-sized Christian university, has two major campuses. Seaver College, the undergraduate residential college of letters, arts, and sciences; the School of Public Policy; and the School of Law are on an 830-acre campus overlooking the Pacific Ocean in Malibu. Headquarters for the Graduate School of Education and Psychology and the Graziadio School of Business and Management are in West Los Angeles, with additional graduate campuses in locations throughout Southern California.

Applying

Admission requirements vary by program. For more information, prospective students should contact the address listed in the Correspondence and Information section.

Correspondence and Information

Office of Admissions
Graduate School of Education and Psychology
Pepperdine University
6100 Center Drive
Los Angeles, California 90045

Phone: 800-347-4849
Web site: http://www.pepperdine.edu/GSEP

THE FACULTY

Education

Jeanmarie Hamilton Boone, Assistant Professor; Ph.D., Claremont.
Michael Botsford, Assistant Director of Student Teaching; Ed.D., USC.
Vance Caesar, Visiting Faculty; Ph.D., Walden.
Kathy Church, Assistant Professor; Ed.D., Ball State.
Anthony M. Collatos, Assistant Professor; Ph.D., UCLA.
Margot Condon, Assistant Director of Student Teaching; Ed.D., Pepperdine.
Kay Davis, Lecturer; Ed.D., Pepperdine.
Cynthia Dollins, Visiting Faculty; Ed.D., Pepperdine.
Saul Duarte, Visiting Faculty; Ph.D., UCLA.
Christopher Ellsasser, Visiting Faculty; Ed.D., Columbia.
John Fitzpatrick, Superintendent in Residence; Ed.D., USC.
J. L. Fortson, Lecturer; Ed.D., San Francisco.
Cara Garcia, Professor; Ph.D., Arizona.
Nancy Harding, Director of Student Teaching; Ph.D., UCLA.
Diana Hiatt-Michael, Professor; Ed.D., UCLA.
Martine Jago, Associate Professor; Ph.D., Kent (England).
Doug Leigh, Associate Professor; Ph.D., Florida State.
Farzin Madjidi, Professor of Leadership; Ed.D., Pepperdine.
Chester McCall Jr., Emeritus Professor; Ph.D., George Washington.
John McManus, Professor; Ph.D., Connecticut.
Robert Paull, Emeritus Professor; Ph.D., USC.
Linda Polin, Professor; Ph.D., UCLA.
Linda Purrington, Lecturer; Ed.D., Pepperdine.
Reyna Garcia Ramos, Associate Professor; Ph.D., California, Santa Barbara.
Elizabeth Orozco Reilly, Associate Professor; Ed.D., San Francisco.
Kent Rhodes, Visiting Faculty; Ed.D., Pepperdine.
Margaret Riel, Visiting Faculty; Ph.D., California, Irvine.
June Schmieder-Ramirez, Professor; Ph.D., Stanford.
Jack Scott, Distinguished Professor; Ph.D., Claremont.
Thomas Skewes-Cox, Visiting Faculty; Ph.D., UCLA.
Paul Sparks, Assistant Professor; Ph.D., USC.
Ronald Stephens, Professor; Ed.D., USC.
Sue Talley, Visiting Faculty; Ed.D., Pepperdine.
Margaret Weber, Professor and Dean; Ph.D., Missouri.

Psychology

Joy Keiko Asamen, Professor; Ph.D., UCLA.
Aaron Aviera, Clinical Faculty and Clinic Director, West Los Angeles; Ph.D., UCLA.
Thema Bryant-Davis, Assistant Professor; Ph.D., Duke.
Anat Cohen, Visiting Faculty; Ph.D., California School of Professional Psychology.
Louis John Cozolino, Professor; Ph.D., UCLA.
Robert deMayo, Professor and Associate Dean; Ph.D., UCLA.
Kathleen Eldridge, Assistant Professor; Ph.D., UCLA.
Drew Erhardt, Associate Professor; Ph.D., UCLA.
David Foy, Professor; Ph.D., Southern Mississippi.
Miguel Gallardo, Assistant Professor; Psy.D., California School of Professional Psychology.
Susan Hall, Assistant Professor; Ph.D., Arizona.
Pamela Harmell, Lecturer; Ph.D., California School of Professional Psychology.
Shelly Prillerman Harrell, Professor; Ph.D., UCLA.
Joanne Hedgespeth, Professor; Ph.D., Biola.
Susan Himelstein, Lecturer; Ph.D., UCLA.
Robert Hohenstein, Visiting Faculty; Ph.D., American Commonwealth.
Barbara Ingram, Professor; Ph.D., USC.
Caroline Keatinge, Lecturer; Ph.D., Illinois at Chicago.
David Levy, Professor; Ph.D., UCLA.
Dennis Lowe, Professor; Ph.D., Florida State.
Tomas Martinez, Professor; Ph.D., Michigan.
Cary Mitchell, Professor; Ph.D., Kentucky.
Daryl Rowe, Professor; Ph.D., Ohio State.
Edward Shafranske, Professor; Ph.D., US International; Ph.D., Southern California Psychoanalytic Institute.
Amy R. Tuttle, Assistant Professor; Ph.D., Loma Linda.
Duncan Wigg, Clinical Faculty and Clinic Director, Irvine; Ph.D., California School of Professional Psychology.
Stephanie Woo, Associate Professor; Ph.D., UCLA.

The Pepperdine University Malibu Campus.

The headquarters for the Graduate School of Education and Psychology in West Los Angeles.

QUEENS COLLEGE OF THE CITY UNIVERSITY OF NEW YORK

Graduate Programs in the Arts and Sciences

Programs of Study

Queens College offers programs of study leading to the Master of Arts in applied linguistics, art history, biology, chemistry, computer science, English, French, geology, history, Italian, mathematics, music, physics, psychology, psychology–clinical behavior, sociology, Spanish, speech pathology, and urban affairs. Master of Science degrees are offered in accounting, applied environmental geoscience, and nutrition and exercise science. The interdisciplinary degrees of Master of Arts in Liberal Studies and Master of Arts in Social Sciences are also offered. The Master of Fine Arts degree is offered in studio art. Master of Science in Education programs are available in bilingual elementary education, counselor education, elementary school education, family and consumer sciences, literacy education, school psychology, secondary school education (art; English; French; general science—biology, chemistry, earth science, and physics; Italian; mathematics; music; physical education; social studies; and Spanish), special education (B–2, 1–6, and 7–12), and teaching English to speakers of other languages. Professional diplomas in applied behavior analysis, education, school building leader, and school psychology at the elementary and secondary levels are also offered.

For applicants who seek New York State provisional teacher certification but whose undergraduate programs did not include a background in education, the College offers postbaccalaureate advanced certificate programs in elementary education and secondary education (art–visual arts, biology, chemistry, earth science, English, family and consumer science, French, general science, Italian, mathematics, music, physical education, physics, social studies, and Spanish). Bilingual certification programs are available in counselor education, school psychology, and special education.

The Master of Library Science degree is available for public librarianship and school media specialist. Also offered are advanced certificates in archives and records management preservation and childhood/youth public library and a post-master's advanced certificate in librarianship. All programs are accredited by the American Library Association. Concentrations in various areas also exist in a number of departments. Applicants should contact the Office of Graduate Admissions for more information.

Queens College is a major participant in the doctoral programs of the City University of New York (CUNY). Students interested in these programs should contact the CUNY Graduate Center, 365 Fifth Avenue, New York, New York 10016.

Research Facilities

The extensive laboratory facilities of the College house state-of-the-art scientific instruments for research in biology, chemistry, computer science, geology, physics, psychology, and health and physical education. There is also a low-temperature physics laboratory.Computing equipment ranges from cutting-edge, high-technology personal computers to highly specialized minicomputers. There are diverse computer laboratories, including a well-equipped social science research laboratory. The Graduate School of Library and Information Studies maintains a fully integrated computer-intensive facility.

Gertz Speech and Hearing Center provides a facility for research and clinical practice experience in communicative disorders. The College is home to an electronic music studio and to one of the best music libraries on the East Coast. It also shares facilities with the American Museum of Natural History, Brookhaven National Laboratory, the Lamont-Doherty Geological Observatory, and leading hospitals. The Benjamin S. Rosenthal Library holds 753,000 volumes, 3,860 print and electronic journal subscriptions, and an extensive collection of microform material. The library is a selective depository for many government publications. A reference area contains materials for research on a wide range of social science, humanities, education, and science topics. The library also houses significant collections of specialized materials. Access is provided via telephone page to electronic resources at http://www.qc.edu/library.

Financial Aid

A limited number of graduate fellowships, some requiring teaching and/or research, may be available from individual departments through the Office of the Assistant to the Provost for Graduate Admissions. Other kinds of financial aid include New York State Tuition Assistance Program grants, Board of Trustees partial tuition waivers, Federal Perkins Loans, the Federal Direct Student Loan Program, and Federal Work-Study Program awards. Applicants should contact the Financial Aid Office for information. The Cooperative Education Program helps students gain both academic credit and work experience in paid positions.

Cost of Study

In 2007–08, tuition per semester is $270 per credit (maximum $3200) for New York State residents and $500 per credit for nonresidents. Activities fees are additional.

Living and Housing Costs

Queens College does not provide housing for its students. Students who desire housing find it available in the surrounding neighborhood.

Student Group

Approximately 4,500 students are registered for master's and advanced certificate programs, and many CUNY doctoral students work under the direct supervision of Queens College faculty members. Students come from throughout the United States and from a number of countries. In 2003, 932 degrees and 97 certificates were awarded. The Graduate Student Association at Queens College, an elective body representing the interests of all graduate students, offers free help with income tax return preparation and legal counseling.

Location

Queens College is located close to the attractions of Manhattan. Opera, concerts, theater, and gallery and museum exhibits are accessible by public transportation; students can get tickets to many attractions at reduced prices. There are also parks and ocean beaches located nearby in Queens and on Long Island.

The College

Established in 1937, Queens College is a coeducational, publicly supported college with an emphasis on the liberal arts and sciences and education. Its attractive, tree-lined campus includes athletic fields, a gymnasium, a pool, tennis courts, and a performing arts center that schedules a lively calendar of events, with performances by internationally renowned artists. The College offers lectures, art exhibits, plays, concerts, dance recitals, and other cultural and educational programs to the community. An extensive construction program has recently added a music building, which includes a 500-seat recital hall with tracker organ; a science building that houses sophisticated laboratories and equipment; the Rosenthal Library, with shelf space for more than 1 million volumes and study carrels for 2,200 users; and a renovated art building. Queens College is registered by the New York State Department of Education and accredited by the Middle States Association of Colleges and Schools. The American Association of Colleges for Teacher Education includes the College in its list of member colleges.

Applying

The admission decision is based on the baccalaureate record and evidence of the ability to pursue graduate work. Scores from the General Test and Subject Test of the Graduate Record Examinations are required for admission to certain programs. For fall semester admission, applications should be filed by April 1. For spring semester admission, applications should be filed by November 1 (not all programs admit students in the spring). Applications for school psychology must be filed by March 15 for fall admission (spring applications are not accepted). Applications for fine arts must be filed by March 15 for fall admission and by October 15 for spring admission. Speech pathology applications must be filed by February 1 for fall admission (spring applications are not accepted). Counselor education applications must be submitted by March 1. Financial aid applications should be filed as early as possible. This information is subject to change.

Correspondence and Information

For information about a particular program:
Chair (listed overleaf)
Department of (specify)
Queens College
Flushing, New York 11367

For admission and registration information:
Graduate Admissions Office
Queens College
Flushing, New York 11367
Phone: 718-997-5200
Fax: 718-997-5193
E-mail: graduate_admissions@qc.edu

For other information:
Office of Graduate Studies
Queens College
Flushing, New York 11367
Phone: 718-997-5190
Fax: 718-997-5198
E-mail: steven.schwarz@qc.cuny.edu

THE FACULTY

From its beginnings in 1937, Queens College has made every effort to build a faculty of dedicated teachers and scholars. The list of institutions that have conferred degrees on members of the faculty includes every major university in the United States and several major European universities. Faculty members have received numerous national and international awards and fellowships as well as many sponsored research and training grants through the College's Office of Research and Sponsored Programs.

OFFICE OF GRADUATE STUDIES AND RESEARCH
Steven Schwarz, Ph.D., Dean of Research and Graduate Studies.

OFFICE OF GRADUATE ADMISSIONS
Mario Caruso, M.A., Director of Graduate Admissions.

The following is a list of the heads of departments that offer graduate programs at the College. An asterisk (*) indicates that there is no master's or advanced certificate program in this area, but faculty members participate in the Ph.D. program at the CUNY Graduate Center. A dagger (†) indicates that the program is not currently accepting students.

DIVISION OF THE ARTS AND HUMANITIES
Tamara Evans, Ph.D., Dean of the Faculty for the Arts and Humanities.
Art: Barbara Lane, Ph.D., Chair.
***Classical, Middle Eastern, and Asian Languages and Cultures:** William McClure, Ph.D., Chair.
***Comparative Literature:** Clare L. Carroll, Ph.D., Chair.
Drama, Dance, and Theatre: Susan Einhorn, Ph.D., Chair.
English: Nancy Comley, Ph.D., Chair.
***European Languages and Literatures:** Royal Brown, Ph.D., Chair.
Hispanic Languages and Literatures: Emilio de Torre, Ph.D., Chair.
Linguistics and Communication Disorders: Robert Vago, Ph.D., Chair.
†**Media Studies:** Richard Maxwell, Ph.D., Chair.
Music: Edward Smaldone, Ph.D., Chair and Director, Aaron Copland School of Music.

DIVISION OF MATHEMATICS AND THE NATURAL SCIENCES
Thomas Strekas, Ph.D., Dean of the Faculty for Mathematics and the Natural Sciences.
Biology: Corinne Michels, Ph.D., Chair.
Chemistry: William Hersh, Ph.D., Chair.
Computer Science: Jennifer Whitehead, Ph.D., Chair.
Earth and Environmental Sciences: Daniel Habib, Ph.D., Chair.
Family, Nutrition, and Exercise Sciences: Elizabeth Lowe, Ph.D., Chair.
Mathematics: Wallace Goldberg, Ph.D., Chair.
Physics: Alexander Lisyansky, Ph.D., Chair.
Psychology: Richard Bodnar, Ph.D., Chair.

DIVISION OF THE SOCIAL SCIENCES
Elizabeth Hendrey, Ph.D., Dean of the Faculty for the Social Sciences.
Accounting and Information Systems: Israel Blumenfrucht, Ph.D., Chair.
***Anthropology:** Sara Stinson, Ph.D., Chair.
†**Economics:** Harvey Gram, Ph.D., Chair.
History: Frank Warren, Ph.D., Chair.
Library Science: Virgil Blake, Ph.D., Chair and Director, Graduate School of Library and Information Studies.
Philosophy: Steven Hicks, Ph.D., Chair.
†**Political Science:** Patricia Rachal, Ph.D., Chair.
Sociology: Dean Savage, Ph.D., Chair.
Urban Studies: Leonard Rodberg, Ph.D., Chair.

DIVISION OF EDUCATION
Penny Hammerich, Ph.D., Dean of the Faculty for Education.
Educational and Community Programs: Jesse Vazquez, Ph.D., Chair.
Elementary and Early Childhood Education and Services: Myra Zarnowski, Ph.D., Chair.
Secondary Education and Youth Services: Eleanor Armour-Thomas, Ph.D., Chair.

INTERDISCIPLINARY STUDIES
Liberal Studies: James Jordon, Ph.D., Graduate Adviser.
Social Sciences: Martin Hanlon, Ph.D., Graduate Adviser.

REGENT UNIVERSITY

Graduate Programs

Programs of Study Regent University offers graduate programs leading to Master of Arts (M.A.), Master of Fine Arts (M.F.A.), Master of Business Administration (M.B.A.), Juris Doctor (J.D.), Master of Divinity (M.Div.), Doctor of Ministry (D.Min.), Master of Education (M.Ed.), Doctor of Education (Ed.D.), Education Specialist (Ed.S.), Doctor of Strategic Leadership (D.S.L.), Doctor of Clinical Psychology (Psy.D.), and Ph.D. degrees and to the Certificate of Graduate Studies (C.G.S.), Certificate of Advanced Graduate Studies (C.A.G.S.), and Certificate in Advanced Counseling Studies (C.A.C.S.). These graduate programs are offered in communication and the arts (M.A. in communication:cinema-TV, digital media, script and screenwriting; M.A. in journalism; M.A. in theater with emphasis in theater ministry or theater studies; M.F.A. in acting, with a directing concentration available; and the M.F.A. with majors in directing, producing (film/TV), or script and screen writing; Ph.D. in communication); divinity (Master of Arts with various concentrations, M.A. in missiology, M.A. in practical theology, M.Div., D.Min., Ph.D. in renewal studies); education (M.Ed., Ed.D., Ed.S. in special education leadership, Ph.D. in education, C.A.G.S. in education, TESOL certificate); entrepreneurial business (full-time and part-time M.A. in management, M.B.A., graduate certificate programs); global leadership studies (M.A. in organizational leadership, M.A. in strategic foresight, D.S.L., Ph.D. in organizational leadership, C.G.S. in leadership, C.A.G.S. in leadership); government (M.A. in government, C.G.S.); law (J.D.); and psychology and counseling (M.A. in counseling, M.A. in human services counseling, Psy.D., Ph.D. in counselor education and supervision, C.A.C.S.). All programs are fully accredited and, while all are offered on the Virginia Beach Campus, many are also offered online (distance education). Two education programs (M.Ed. and TESOL certificate) are also offered in the metro Washington, D.C., area. Virtually all master's-level programs are available as joint degrees, allowing students to earn two degrees in less time.

The following programs are offered online: M.A. in various concentrations, including M.A. in government, M.A. in human services counseling, M.A. in journalism, M.A. in management, M.A. in organizational leadership, and M.A. in practical theology; M.B.A. (full- and part-time); M.Ed.; Ed.D.; Ed.S.; C.A.G.S. in education; M.Div. (concentration in practical theology); D.S.L.; Ph.D. in communication; Ph.D. in counselor education and supervision; Ph.D. in organizational leadership; C.G.S. in a government concentration of choice; C.G.S. in leadership; C.A.G.S. in leadership; graduate certificates in business; and TESOL certificate. Some programs require on-campus courses and/or residencies.

Research Facilities The University Library collections consist of more than 270,000 printed volumes, 700,000 microforms, and 15,000 audiovisual items, including films, CDs, laser discs, audiocassettes, and videocassettes. In addition, the library subscribes to more than 1,700 journals related to Regent's curriculum and has access to more than 35,000 full-text journal titles online, over 120 article databases, and 70,000 electronic and downloadable audio books. The library provides access to more than 150 databases, including Academic Search Premier, WorldCat, ABI/Inform, NetLibrary, ATLA Religion Database, LexisNexis, CQ databases, Business Source Complete, ERIC Full Text, Education Full Text, Communication & Mass Media Complete, Historical Newspapers Online, Expanded Academic ASAP, Emerald Journals, JSTOR, Project Muse, PsycINFO and PsycArticles, International Index to the Performing Arts, Standard & Poor's, Dissertations & Theses, and many others.

Financial Aid The University financial aid is institutionally and federally funded. Approximately 75 percent of the graduate students receive some form of financial assistance. In addition to need-based assistance grants, Regent offers scholarship awards based on academic merit, potential in the chosen area of study, professional experience, spiritual maturity, and clarity of goals. Applications for most awards are due by April 1; however, some deadlines vary. Regent participates in the Virginia state Tuition Assistance Grant Program. Graduate assistantships, campus jobs, Federal Stafford Student Loans, and alternative private education loans are also available.

Cost of Study Tuition varies by program, as do additional fees. Tuition costs for the 2007–08 school year are as follows: M.A. in communication, M.A. in journalism, and M.F.A. in acting, communication, and script and screenwriting, $800 per credit hour; Ph.D. in communication, $850 per credit hour; M.A. (biblical studies), M.A. in missiology, M.A. in practical theology, and M.Div., $475 per credit hour; D.Min., $525 per credit hour; Ph.D. in divinity, $600 per credit hour; Ed.D., Ph.D. in education, and C.A.G.S. in education, $720 per credit hour; M.Ed. and TESOL certificate, $560 per credit hour; M.B.A. (full-time and part-time), M.A. in management, and graduate certificate programs in business, $700 per credit hour; Executive M.B.A., $880 per credit hour; M.A. in organizational leadership and C.G.S. in leadership, $575 per credit hour; Ph.D. in organizational leadership, D.S.L., and C.A.G.S. in leadership, $800 per credit hour; M.A. in government and C.A.G.S. with a government concentration, $655 per credit hour; J.D. and LL.M. in American legal studies (for international lawyers), $860 per credit hour; M.A. in counseling, M.A. in human services counseling, and C.A.C.S., $575 per credit hour; and Psy.D. in clinical psychology and Ph.D. in counselor education and supervision, $695 per credit hour.

Living and Housing Costs Student housing consists of two different complexes: Regent Commons and Regent Village. Regent Commons is located on campus and houses single students and married couples without children. This facility has 31 four-bedroom, two-bath suites; 80 studio apartments with one-bath; and 96 one-bedroom, one-bath apartments. Rental rates for Regent Commons range from $575 to $850 per month. Regent Village is less than 1 mile from the campus and is designated as family housing. It consists of 112 two-bedroom, one-bath apartments; 56 two-bedroom, two-bath apartments; and 56 three-bedroom, two-bath apartments. Rental rates for families range between $705 and $845 per month. Rent is subject to change.

Student Group Regent University has an enrollment of more than 4,000 students. In a typical year, this population represents all fifty states, forty-eight other countries, and more than 400 undergraduate institutions. Students range in age from 20 to 69, with the average age about 35. Approximately 50 percent are married.

Location The main campus of stately Georgian-style buildings is located in Virginia Beach, Virginia. Within a 2-hour drive of Regent University are historic Yorktown, Jamestown, and Colonial Williamsburg. Richmond, the state capital, and Washington, D.C., are less than a 4-hour drive by car. Regent University also offers programs online.

The University Regent University is accredited by the Commission on Colleges of the Southern Association of Colleges and Schools, 1866 Southern Lane, Decatur, Georgia 30033-4097 (telephone: 404-679-4501) to award the bachelor's, master's, and doctor's degrees. The School of Divinity is accredited by the Association of Theological Schools in the United States and Canada (ATS), The Commission on Accrediting of the Association of Theological Schools, 10 Summit Park Drive, Pittsburgh, Pennsylvania 15275. The School of Law is fully accredited by the American Bar Association. The School of Psychology and Counseling's Psy.D. program is accredited by the American Psychological Association (APA), Office of Program Consultation and Accreditation, 750 First Street, NE, Washington, D.C. 20002-4242, and its program areas of community counseling and school counseling (M.A.) are accredited by the Council for Accreditation of Counseling and Related Educational Programs (CACREP), 5999 Stevenson Avenue, Alexandria, Virginia 22304, a specialized accrediting body recognized by the Council for Higher Education Accreditation (CHEA).

Applying An application packet may be requested from the University. Some applications are available online at http://www.regent.edu/admissions. Application requirements include submission of transcripts, graduate test scores (GRE, GMAT, LSAT, or MAT), a nonrefundable fee of $50 ($25 for nondegree and one-time students), a personal goals statement, and three recommendations (clergy, faculty, and general). Requirements vary slightly for law school applicants. Application deadlines vary by program.

Correspondence and Information
Central Enrollment Management
Regent University
1000 Regent University Drive
Virginia Beach, Virginia 23464
Phone: 800-373-5504 (toll-free) (Central Admissions)
E-mail: inquire@regent.edu
admissions@regent.edu
Web site: http://www.regent.edu

DEPARTMENT CONTACTS AND RESEARCH AREAS

Regent University offers the knowledge and information needed to succeed—tools that will foster one's role as a leader in today's society—through graduate degrees that are critical in today's culture. Regent programs integrate rigorous academics with biblical principles—an approach that prepares students to succeed personally and professionally.

SCHOOL OF COMMUNICATION & THE ARTS
Michael Patrick, Dean. The Communication & Performing Arts Center opened in fall 2002. This state-of-the-art building features a 700-seat proscenium theater, camera acting labs, a dance studio, a Foley sound stage, a television production studio, a back lot, film screening rooms, a 200-seat experimental theater, an aircraft cable grid, a 2,500-square-foot scenographic lab with paint floor and prop shop, two 1,200-square-foot rehearsal/performance movement classrooms, and much more.

Department of Journalism
The M.A. in journalism offers areas of study in news journalism (print, broadcast, and Internet) and professional writing. Students may study at the Virginia Beach Campus or online. Research focus for the Ph.D. in communication may center on journalism.

Departments of Cinema, Television, and Theatre Arts
These departments offer the M.A. in communication, with a concentration from the following areas: cinema and television (animation, critical studies, directing, editing, or producing), script and screenwriting (writing for cinema-television or writing for theater), and theater arts (performance studies). Also available are the M.F.A. in acting (a general concentration or a concentration in directing), the cinema-television M.F.A. (directing, producing, or script and screenwriting), and the Ph.D. in communication, with a research concentration in any of the above areas.

Department of Communication Studies
The M.A. and Ph.D. in communication may be pursued with an emphasis in communication studies. Research areas for the Ph.D. depend upon the faculty members' areas of expertise and student interest.

SCHOOL OF DIVINITY
Dr. Michael Palmer, Dean. The school offers the Master of Arts (M.A.) with five emphases (biblical interpretation, Christian doctrine and history, English Bible, New Testament, and Old Testament); an M.A. in missiology and TESOL; and an M.A. in practical theology with emphases in church and ministry, interdisciplinary studies, and worship and renewal studies. The School of Divinity also offers the Master of Divinity (M.Div.), with emphases in missiology and practical theology with concentration tracks in biblical studies, biblical languages, church and ministry, interdisciplinary studies, and worship and renewal, and the Doctor of Ministry (D.Min.), with emphases in advanced clinical pastoral education, leadership and renewal, military ministry, community transformation, and leadership coaching. In addition, the school offers the Ph.D. in renewal studies. The School of Divinity is accredited by the Association of Theological Schools.

SCHOOL OF EDUCATION
Dr. Alan Arroyo, Dean. The school offers the M.Ed. with eight majors: Christian school program, cross-categorical special education, educational leadership, elementary education initial licensure (optional TESOL endorsement), individualized degree plan, master teacher program, master teacher program/English as a second language, and TESOL. The Ed.D. offers seven cognates: Christian education leadership. distance education, educational psychology, higher education, K–12 school leadership, special education, and staff development/adult education, Also offered are the Ed.S. in special education leadership and the Ph.D. in education. The C.A.G.S. in education and the TESOL certificate are also available.

SCHOOL OF GLOBAL LEADERSHIP & ENTREPRENEURSHIP
Dr. Bruce Winston, Dean. The School of Global Leadership & Entrepreneurship offers the following in the areas of business and leadership: M.A. in management, M.B.A., Executive M.B.A., graduate certificate programs, M.A. in organizational leadership* (church and ministry, coaching and mentoring, education administration, futures studies, health-care administration, human resource studies, information systems technology, interdisciplinary studies, international organizations, manufacturing, new business development, organizational communication, organizational development consulting, philanthropic and nonprofit organizations, public executive leadership, sales management, and virtual organizations), the C.G.S. in organizational leadership*, the Ph.D. in organizational leadership*, the Doctor of Strategic Leadership*, and the C.A.G.S. in organizational leadership*. The Ph.D. in organizational leadership requires three residencies at the Virginia Beach Campus for completion of the degree. (Programs with an * are available online.)

ROBERTSON SCHOOL OF GOVERNMENT
Dr. Charles W. Dunn, Dean. The school offers a Master of Arts in government, with nine concentrations: health care policy and administration, international politics, law and public policy, political leadership and management, political management, public administration, public policy, terrorism and homeland defense, and world economic and political development. In addition, the school offers a Certificate of Graduate Study in any of the nine concentrations as well.

SCHOOL OF LAW
Jeffrey Brauch, Dean. The school offers the J.D. (full- or part-time) with concentration tracks available: academic, commercial, dispute resolution, general practice, honors, public law, and Virginia law and the LL.M. in American legal studies (for non–U.S. lawyers). The School of Law is accredited by the American Bar Association.

SCHOOL OF PSYCHOLOGY & COUNSELING
Dr. Rosemarie Scotti Hughes, Dean. The school offers the M.A. in counseling and the Certificate of Advanced Counseling Studies (C.A.C.S.), both with concentrations in community counseling or school counseling; the M.A. in human services counseling; the Doctor of Clinical Psychology (Psy.D.); and the Ph.D. in counselor education and supervision. The Psy.D. program in the School of Psychology & Counseling is accredited by the American Psychological Association (APA) Committee for Accreditation, and the M.A. programs in school and community counseling are accredited by the Council for Accreditation of Counseling and Related Educational Programs (CACREP).

RENSSELAER POLYTECHNIC INSTITUTE

Graduate Studies

Programs of Study

Rensselaer awards advanced degrees in the Schools of Architecture, Engineering, Humanities and Social Sciences, Management, and Science.

The School of Architecture offers the M.Arch. as a first professional degree for students with bachelor's degrees in any field; this program requires 3½ years of study. The M.S. and Ph.D. in architectural sciences are also available, with concentrations in built ecologies, acoustics, and lighting. Additional programs include the M.S. in lighting and the M.S. in building conservation.

The School of Engineering ranks among the top engineering schools in the nation by the *U.S. News & World Report* survey. The school offers Master of Engineering (M.Eng.), Master of Science (M.S.), Doctor of Engineering (D.Eng.), and Doctor of Philosophy (Ph.D.) degrees. Programs include aeronautical engineering, biomedical engineering, chemical and biological engineering, civil engineering, computer and systems engineering, decision sciences and engineering systems, electrical engineering, electric power, environmental engineering, industrial and management engineering, materials engineering, mechanical engineering, nuclear engineering, and transportation engineering. The graduate program is primarily research oriented in areas such as biotechnology, nanotechnology, computation engineering, energy, and the environment.

The School of Science offers M.S. and Ph.D. programs in biology, biochemistry/biophysics, chemistry, computer science, geology, mathematics, multidisciplinary science, and physics. Master's degrees are also available in applied mathematics, applied science, astronomy, hydrogeology, information technology, and natural sciences.

The Lally School of Management grants M.B.A. (Executive, Full-time, and Pathfinder), M.S. in Management, M.S. in Management with a focus on financial technology or on technology commercialization and entrepreneurship, and Ph.D. degrees. The focus on innovation is concerned with organizational, financial, and technological innovation, while the emphasis on entrepreneurship involves both individually driven new start-ups and the launch of new businesses within larger corporations.

The School of Management is built around five streams of knowledge concentrating on the five following themes: creating and managing the enterprise; value creation, managing business/technology networks, and driving innovation; developing innovation new products and services; formulating and implementing competitive business strategy; and managing the business implications of emerging technologies.

The School of Humanities and Social Sciences offers the Master of Science degree in communication and rhetoric; ecological economics, economics, values, and policy; economics; electronic arts (M.F.A.); human-computer interaction; science and technology studies; and technical communication. A doctorate may be obtained in communication and rhetoric, cognitive science, ecological economics, electronic arts, and science and technology studies. Interdisciplinary programs are offered by most departments.

Research Facilities

Research is supported by state-of-the-art facilities and equipment, including the Rensselaer Libraries, whose electronic information system provides access to collections, databases, and the Internet from campus and remote terminals; the Rensselaer Computing System, which permeates the campus with a coherent array of more than 7,000 nodes of distributed laptops, desktops, advanced workstations, and servers; a shared toolkit of applications for interactive learning and research and high-speed Internet connectivity; one of the country's largest academically based, class 100 clean-room facilities; high-performance campuswide computing facilities that allow for serial or parallel computation; and five core laboratories for molecular biology, proteomics, bioimaging, and tissue engineering.

Rensselaer's research capabilities have been enhanced with the addition of the Computational Center for Nanotechnology Innovations (CCNI). The result of a $100-million collaboration with IBM and New York State, the CCNI is the world's most powerful university-based supercomputing center and a top 10 supercomputing center of any kind in the world. The CCNI is made up of massively parallel Blue Gene supercomputers, POWER-based Linux clusters, and Opteron-based clusters, providing more than 100 teraflops of computational muscle and approximately a petabyte of shared online storage.

Other facilities and research centers include the Center for Biotechnology and Interdisciplinary Studies; the George M. Low Center for Industrial Innovation; research centers for integrated electronics, terahertz science, nanotechnology, fuel-cell and hydrogen research, lighting research, science and technology policy, and infrastructure and transportation studies; the Geotechnical Centrifuge Research Center; the Darrin Fresh Water Institute; and the Scientific Computation Research Center.

In addition, academic departments and faculty laboratories have extensive discipline-specific research capabilities and equipment.

Financial Aid

Financial aid is available in the forms of teaching and research assistantships, which include tuition scholarships and stipends. Rensselaer assistantships and University, corporate, or national fellowships fund many of Rensselaer's full-time graduate students. Outstanding students may qualify for university-sponsored Rensselaer Graduate Fellowship Awards, which carry a minimum stipend of $20,000 and a full tuition and fees scholarship. All fellowship awards are calendar-year awards for full-time graduate students. Summer support is also available in many departments. Low-interest, deferred-repayment graduate loans are also available to U.S. citizens with demonstrated need.

Cost of Study

Full-time graduate tuition for the 2007–08 academic year is $34,900. Other costs (estimated living expenses, insurance, etc.) are projected to be about $12,500. Therefore, the cost of attendance for full-time graduate study is approximately $47,400. Part-time study and cohort programs are priced differently. Students should contact Rensselaer for specific cost information related to the program they wish to study.

Living and Housing Costs

Graduate students at Rensselaer may choose from a variety of housing options. On campus, students can select one of the many residence halls and immerse themselves in campus life or choose from a select number of apartments designed for graduate students only. There are abundant, affordable options off campus as well, many within easy walking distance.

Student Group

Of the 1,228 graduate students, 30 percent are women, 92 percent are full-time, and 72 percent study at the doctoral level.

Student Outcomes

Rensselaer's graduate students are hired in a variety of industries and sectors of the economy and by private and public organizations, the government, and institutions of higher education. Their starting salaries average $72,231 for master's degree recipients and $74,238 for Ph.D. recipients.

Location

Located just 10 miles northeast of Albany, New York State's capital city, Rensselaer's historic 275-acre campus sits on a hill overlooking the city of Troy, New York, and the Hudson River. The area offers a relaxed lifestyle with many cultural and recreational opportunities, with easy access to both the high-energy metropolitan centers of the Northeast—such as Boston, New York City, and Montreal, Canada—and the quiet beauty of the neighboring Adirondack Mountains.

The Institute

Recognized as a leader in interactive learning and interdisciplinary research, Rensselaer continues a tradition of excellence and technological innovation dating back to 1824. Rensselaer has five schools—Architecture, Engineering, Management, Science, and Humanities and Social Sciences—that offer more than 100 graduate programs in more than fifty disciplines, which attracts top students, researchers, and professors. The discovery of new scientific concepts and technologies, especially in emerging interdisciplinary fields, is the lifeblood of Rensselaer's culture and a core goal for the faculty, staff, and students. Fueled by significant support from government, industry, and private donors, Rensselaer provides a world-class education in an environment tailored to the individual.

Applying

Applications and all supporting credentials should be submitted well in advance of the preferred semester of entry to allow sufficient time for departmental review and processing. The admission deadline for the fall semester is January 1 and for the spring semester, August 15. Basic admission requirements are the submission of a completed application form (available online), the required application fee ($75), a statement of background and goals, official transcripts, resume, official scores on the GRE General Test, TOEFL or IELTS scores (if applicable), and two recommendations. Late applications are considered only with departmental approval.

Correspondence and Information

For written information about graduate work:

Department of (specify)
Graduate Admissions
Rensselaer Polytechnic Institute
110 Eighth Street
Troy, New York 12180-3590
Phone: 518-276-6216
Web site: http://admissions.rpi.edu/graduate/

For applications and admissions information:

Rensselaer Admissions
Rensselaer Polytechnic Institute
110 Eighth Street
Troy, New York 12180-3590
Phone: 518-276-6216
Web site: http://admissions.rpi.edu/graduate/

PROGRAMS AND AREAS OF RESEARCH

Aeronautical Engineering. Areas of research include computational and theoretical fluid dynamics, aerodynamics, advanced propulsion, experimental gas dynamics, energy conversion, structural dynamics, and optimal design.

Architecture. In addition to the first professional degree (Master of Architecture I), the School of Architecture offers rigorous, interdisciplinary postprofessional and research-based master's and doctoral degrees in architectural sciences. Current concentration areas are acoustics, building conservation, built ecologies, lighting, and other areas that integrate emerging technology with the discipline of architecture. The program emphasizes the theoretical, scientific, technical, and aesthetic potentials of modern spaces.

Bioinformatics. Design and applications of algorithms for sequence database searching, sequence alignment and sequence analysis, molecular modeling.

Biology. Research in biology focuses on molecular biology, biophysics, biochemistry, applied and environmental microbiology, plant biology, freshwater ecology, and bioinformatics.

Biomedical Engineering. Areas of advanced study and research include cell and tissue engineering, computational bioengineering, implantable sensors, orthopaedic engineering, biophysical regulation of cell function, musculoskeletal mechanics, wound healing and biophotonics.

Chemical and Biological Engineering. Research in these areas includes interfacial phenomena, nonlinear diffusion, thermodynamics, polymer engineering, biocatalysis and biochemical engineering, enzyme engineering, metabolic engineering, membrane and chromatographic separations, advanced materials, process control and design, and mesoscale/nanoscale engineering.

Chemistry. Research projects are conducted in the areas of biochemistry and biophysics, organic and bioorganic chemistry, carbohydrate chemistry, bioanalytical chemistry, medicinal chemistry, materials chemistry, polymer chemistry (synthesis and physical properties), analytical chemistry, inorganic chemistry, coordination and organometallic chemistry, photochemistry (including laser techniques), physical chemistry, physical organic chemistry, spectroscopy (laser, microwave, NMR, ESR, vibrational, fluorescence, and in situ environmental probes), and surface science.

Civil and Environmental Engineering. Research areas include geotechnical engineering; geotechnical centrifuge modeling; geoenvironmental, earthquake, structural, infrastructure, and transportation engineering; mechanics of composite materials and structures; and computational mechanics, environmental biotechnology, indoor air quality, and water quality. Research activities emphasize advanced computer-based modeling techniques with direct ties to simulation and state-of-the-art field and laboratory testing.

Cognitive Science. This doctoral program includes integrated cognitive systems, computational cognitive modeling, and cognitive engineering. Areas of research include machine and human reasoning, cognitive engineering, and perception and action. The program is designed to be interdisciplinary and hands-on with intensive theoretical studies.

Communication and Rhetoric. Research areas emphasize the interdisciplinary nature of communication in technologically mediated contexts, exploring the nature and impact of new communications technologies using insights from digital rhetoric, human-computer interaction, communication theory, game studies, and visual design.

Computer and Systems Engineering. Research and academic programs are available in intelligent network management, wireless networks, advanced image processing, parallel computation, digital signal processing, computer vision and pattern recognition, computational geometry, computer graphics and visualization, gigahertz microprocessor design, artificial intelligence and robotics, and distributed manufacturing systems.

Computer Science. Research and academic programs are available in bioinformatics, computer graphics, computer vision, concepts in software engineering, data mining, database systems, distributed systems, grid computing, machine and computational learning, pervasive computing, networking, network security, robotics, semantic Web, simulation, social networks, and theory.

Decision Sciences and Engineering Systems. Programs are offered in industrial and management engineering, manufacturing systems engineering, operations research and statistics, and information systems. The program in industrial and management engineering combines the quantitative and behavioral sciences with the classical approach to industrial engineering as applicable in both manufacturing and service systems. The program in service manufacturing systems engineering focuses on quality systems, information systems, management processes and technology, and systems modeling pertaining to services and manufacturing. The program in operations research and statistics offers advanced study in mathematical modeling optimization and statistical techniques applicable to a wide range of practical problems. Research at the doctoral level is conducted with particular emphasis on information systems, manufacturing systems engineering, operations research and statistics, industrial engineering, and systems engineering.

Ecological Economics, Values, and Policy. Program is focused on the theory and practice of sustainability: the economic, political, social, cultural, and ethical implications and interactions of science, technology, environment, and society.

Economics and Ecological Economics. The department offers an M.S. in economics and a Ph.D. in ecological economics. Areas of research include but are not limited to cost-benefit analysis, environmental valuation, natural resource economics, public sector economics, and regional economics. Ecological economics is concerned with the relationship between economic systems, society, and the environment.

Electrical Engineering. Research and academic programs are available in semiconductor device characterization, semiconductor power devices, multilevel interconnects, thermophotovoltaic devices, automation and robotics, multivariable and nonlinear control, agile manufacturing, communications and information processing, digital signal processing, advanced image processing, computer communication networks, gigahertz microprocessor design, multimedia systems, electronics manufacturing, and plasma diagnostics

Electric Power Engineering. Research includes high-voltage transmission and compaction of equipment, large electrical apparatus design, experimental machine analysis, circuit interruption technology, electromagnetics, economic studies of systems, modeling of power systems and component devices, insulation systems, power electronics, adjustable speed drives, and advanced power systems relaying.

Electronic Arts. The program's research focuses on creative work in an intermedia context, including computer music, digital video art, digital imaging and animation, interactive technologies, and performance and installation as well as historical and critical studies.

Engineering Physics. Current areas of research include applied radiation, radiation transport, medical physics, multiphase phenomena, sonoluminescence, and fusion plasma engineering.

Environmental Science. Active research studies involve groundwater studies, limnology, and aqueous geochemistry.

Geology. Research areas include geochemistry, petrology, structural geology, tectonics, geophysics, seismology, surficial geology, hydrogeology, and planetary science.

Hydrogeology. Research areas include geochemistry, igneous and metamorphic petrology, structural geology, tectonics, geophysics, seismology, groundwater systems and hydrogeology, chemical hydrology, and river and lake pollution.

Information Technology. Areas of research include database systems design, financial engineering, human-computer interaction, information security, information systems engineering, management information systems, networking, and software design.

Language, Literature, and Communication. The department offers an M.S. in human-computer interaction (HCI), an M.S. in technical communication, and an M.S. and Ph.D. in communication and rhetoric. These programs emphasize the interdisciplinary nature of communication and enable students to make contributions with rigor, depth, and creativity on issues related to technologically mediated contexts, exploring the nature and impact of new communications technologies using insights from digital rhetoric, human-computer interaction, communication theory, game studies, and visual design.

Management. The Lally School of Management and Technology offers an M.B.A., M.S., and Ph.D. in management. The theory and practice of integrating management and technology, of turning innovations into commercial or competitive advantages, is interwoven throughout the programs.

Materials Science and Engineering. Research areas include metallic and ceramic materials processing, composite materials and structures, electronic materials, ceramics and glass, melting and solidification, welding and joining, surface and interfacial phenomena, and nanostructured materials.

Mathematics. Research focuses on applied mathematics and analysis, including methods of applied mathematics, differential equations, numerical analysis, applied geometry, mathematical programming, operations research, inverse problems, data mining, and applications of mathematics in the physical sciences, biological sciences, and engineering.

Mechanical Engineering. Engineering computation, multiscale modeling, energy systems, nanotechnology, heat transfer, mechanics of materials, molecular and structural dynamics, solid and fluid mechanics, design and manufacturing, and tribology are some of the areas in which research is conducted.

Nuclear Engineering. Active research is undertaken in areas of nuclear data measurements, paramtric X-ray applications, biomedical applications of radiation, reactor thermal hydraulics, neatron and X-ray scattering, fusion systems design, and nuclear reactor safety.

Physics. Physics research includes experimental nuclear and particle physics, experimental and theoretical matter condensed-matter physics, astrophysics (interstellar matter and star formation), biological physics, optical physics, and educational research and development in physics.

Science and Technology Studies. The department's 16 faculty members come from anthropology, history, philosophy, political science, psychology, and sociology. Theoretical approaches and methodologies range widely, including feminist design and critical race theory, democratic decision theory, evolutionary psychology, social movement analysis, discourse analysis, ethnographic fieldwork, historical archival research, structured interviews, and simulation. Research clarifies barriers to a more democratic, environmentally sustainable, and socially just technological civilization. Current students are studying social movements, biomedicine, computer gaming, alternative design, postcolonial technoscience, information technology, nanotechnology, green chemistry, and robotics.

Transportation Engineering. Active research is underway in areas of intermodal transportation, urban goods modeling, transportation economics, network modeling, traffic engineering, transportation planning, response to extreme events, and intelligent transportation systems.

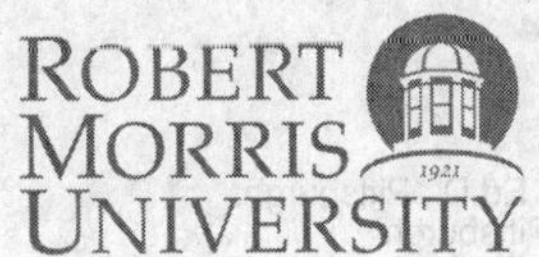

ROBERT MORRIS UNIVERSITY

Programs of Study

Robert Morris University (RMU) offers the Master of Business Administration (M.B.A.) degree and the Master of Science (M.S.) degree in business education, communications and information systems, competitive intelligence systems, engineering management, human resource management, information security and assurance, information systems management, information technology (IT) project management, instructional leadership, Internet information systems, nonprofit management, nursing, organizational studies, and taxation. The University also offers the Doctor of Science (D.Sc.) degree in information systems and communications, the Doctor of Nursing Practice (D.N.P.) degree, and the Doctor of Philosophy (Ph.D.) degree in engineering as well as instructional management and leadership. Postbaccalaureate certification programs are also offered for secondary and elementary teachers as well as instructional technology specialists.

Research Facilities

Facilities supporting the graduate programs at Robert Morris University include nine open-access computer laboratories, two physical libraries, and an electronic library offering an array of research databases. Twenty-eight classrooms have been equipped with advanced computer and presentation technology equipment to facilitate teaching and learning.

The University's two libraries house more than 125,000 volumes, more than 425,000 items on microfilm, nearly 1,000 periodical subscriptions, and a large collection of government documents. The library has a state-of-the-art searchable catalog system, which was installed in 1999. The RMU Electronic Library offers continual off-campus access to 9 major research databases. The library is a member of numerous resource-sharing consortia that greatly extend the amount of materials available to support graduate education.

Financial Aid

Graduate loans are available for those who qualify. Students are encouraged to file the Free Application for Federal Student Aid (FAFSA). Robert Morris University participates in the Federal Family Education Loan (FFEL) Program and also offers various interest-free payment plans.

Cost of Study

Tuition for the 2007–08 academic year for the M.B.A. and the M.S. programs in human resource management, nonprofit management, and taxation is $640 per credit; tuition for the M.S. programs in communications and information systems, competitive intelligence systems, information security and assurance, information systems management, information technology project management, and Internet information systems is $615 per credit; tuition for the M.S. programs in instructional leadership and business education and the postbaccalaureate teacher certification programs is $595 per credit; tuition for the M.S. in nursing is $650 per credit; tuition for the M.S. in engineering management is $660 per credit; and tuition for the M.S. in organizational studies is $550 per credit. Tuition for the D.Sc. in information systems and communications is $25,305 per year; tuition for the D.N.P. is $21,000 per year for full-time students, $700 per credit for part-time students, and $875 per credit for students in the completion option; tuition for the Ph.D. in engineering is $22,365 per year; and tuition for the Ph.D. in instructional management and leadership is $15,530 per year.

Living and Housing Costs

Students find an abundance of residential living opportunities. There are twelve residence halls on the Moon Township campus that house more than 1,300 students. The doctoral program fee includes the cost of the required residencies.

Student Group

Of a student body of more than 5,000, more than 1,100 are enrolled in graduate degree programs. The average age of graduate students is 32, with an age range of 21 to 62. Women make up 46 percent of the graduate student population. Students come from diverse professional and academic backgrounds.

Location

Robert Morris University has three locations. The main campus occupies 230 acres in suburban Moon Township, Pennsylvania, 17 miles northwest of downtown Pittsburgh and 15 minutes from Pittsburgh International Airport. RMU also has locations in downtown Pittsburgh and suburban Cranberry Township. Some graduate programs are offered exclusively at one location.

The University

Robert Morris University, founded in 1921, is a four-year, private, coeducational, independent institution. It has developed a national reputation for its strong business programs and offers thirty undergraduate degrees and nineteen master's and doctoral degree programs.

Applying

The graduate programs admit students on a rolling admission basis. However, students are encouraged to submit all required materials at least two months prior to the start of their desired term of entry. Applications can be filed for free through the University's Web site. Students should note that the M.S. in nonprofit management, the M.S. in nursing, the D.Sc. in information systems and communications, the D.N.P., the Ph.D. in engineering, and the Ph.D. in instructional management and leadership programs require an interview as part of the final selection process.

Correspondence and Information

Office of Graduate Admissions
Robert Morris University
6001 University Boulevard
Moon Township, Pennsylvania 15108-1189
Phone: 800-762-0097 (toll-free)
Web site: http://www.rmu.edu

THE FACULTY

SCHOOL OF ADULT AND CONTINUING EDUCATION
Kathleen V. Davis, Dean; Ph.D., South Carolina.

Organizational Studies Faculty
Peter J. Draus, Ed.D., Pittsburgh.
Elizabeth M. Stork, Ph.D., Pittsburgh.
Glenn Thiel, Ph.D., Pittsburgh.

SCHOOL OF BUSINESS
Derya A. Jacobs, Dean; Ph.D., Missouri–Rolla.
Lois D. Bryan, Associate Dean; D.Sc., Robert Morris; CPA.
Kurt C. Shimmel, Associate Dean; D.B.A., Cleveland State.

Accounting and Taxation Faculty
Gerald J. Berenbaum, M.B.A., Massachusetts; CPA.
Elise A. Boyas, Ph.D., Rutgers.
William G. Brucker, J.D., Duquesne; CPA.
Victoria A. Fratto, M.S., Robert Morris.
Jerry W. Hanwell, J.D., Duquesne.
David Hess, M.B.A., Ohio State; CPA.
Tanya M. Lee, Ph.D., Arizona State.
Kamala Raghavan, D.B.A., Cleveland State.
James E. Rebele, Ph.D., Indiana.
Ronald R. Rubenfield, M.B.A., Shippensburg; CPA, CMA.

Finance and Economics Faculty
Robert G. Beaves, Ph.D., Iowa.
Zane Dennick-Ream, M.B.A., Iowa.
Mark J. Eschenfelder, Ph.D., Missouri.
Frank R. Flanegin, Ph.D., Central Florida.
Adora D. Holstein, Ph.D., Penn State.
Denise C. Letterman, M.B.A., Shippensburg.
Patrick J. Litzinger, Ph.D., Pittsburgh.
J. Brian O'Roark, Ph.D., George Mason.
Stanko Racic, Ph.D., Pittsburgh.
Ralph R. Reiland, M.B.A., Duquesne.
Louis B. Swartz, J.D., Duquesne.
Joel A. Waldman, J.D., Miami.

Management Faculty
Frances M. Amatucci, Ph.D., Pittsburgh.
Artemesia Apostolopoulou, Ph.D., Massachusetts.
Scott Branvold, Ed.D., Utah.
John S. Clark, Ph.D., Massachusetts Amherst.
Michele T. Cole, J.D., Ph.D., Pittsburgh.
Daria Crawley, Ph.D., Michigan.
Gregory G. Dell'Omo, Ph.D., Wisconsin–Madison.
Jeffery K. Guiler, Ph.D., Pittsburgh.
Nell T. Hartley, Ph.D., Vanderbilt.
John Lipinski, M.B.A., Michigan.
Darlene Y. Motley, Ph.D., Pittsburgh.
Edward A. Nicholson, Ph.D., Ohio State.
Jodi A. Potter, Ph.D., Pittsburgh.
Yasmin S. Purohit, Ph.D., Drexel.
William F. Repack, M.S., Loyola.
David P. Synowka, Ph.D., Pittsburgh.
Michael A. Yahr, M.B.A., Pittsburgh.

Marketing Faculty
Steven R. Clinton, Ph.D., Michigan State.
Cathleen S. Jones, D.Sc., Robert Morris.
Ersem Karadag, Ph.D., Oklahoma State.
Jill K. Maher, Ph.D., Kent State.
Dean R. Manna, Ph.D., Pittsburgh.
Gayle J. Marco, Ph.D., Pittsburgh.
Charles Popovich, Ph.D., Pittsburgh.
Denis P. Rudd, Ed.D., Nevada, Las Vegas.
Norman V. Schnurr, M.B.A., Pittsburgh.
Alan D. Smith, Ph.D., Akron.
Yanbin Tu, Ph.D., Connecticut.

SCHOOL OF COMMUNICATIONS AND INFORMATION SYSTEMS
David Jamison, Dean; J.D., Michigan.
Frederick G. Kohun, Associate Dean; Ph.D., Carnegie Mellon.

Communication Faculty
Barbara Burgess-Lefebvre, M.F.A., Illinois State.
Dacia Charlesworth, Ph.D., Southern Illinois.
Rex L. Crawley, Ph.D., Ohio.
Michele Reese Edwards, Ph.D., Ohio State.
Seth Finn, Ph.D., Stanford.
Kenneth V. Gargaro, Ph.D., Pittsburgh.
Ann D. Jabro, Ph.D., Penn State.
John Lawson, Ph.D., Northern Illinois.
Barbara J. Levine, Ph.D., Wisconsin–Madison.
Marc Seamon, Ph.D., Penn State.
James A. Seguin, Ph.D., Ohio State.

Computer and Information Systems Faculty
Jeanne M. Baugh, Ed.D., West Virginia.
Donald J. Caputo, Ph.D., Pittsburgh.
Gary A. Davis, D.Sc., Robert Morris.
Seth Finn, Ph.D., Stanford.
Valerie J. Harvey, Ph.D., Texas at Austin.
Linda Kavanaugh, Ph.D., Pittsburgh.
Paul J. Kovacs, Ph.D., Pittsburgh.
Joseph Laverty, Ph.D., Pittsburgh.
G. James Leone, Ph.D., Pittsburgh.
Walter Pilof, M.B.A., Xavier (Cincinnati).
Karen Power, Ph.D., Pittsburgh.
Robert J. Skovira, Ph.D., Pittsburgh.
John Turchek, M.Ed., Duquesne.
David F. Wood, Ph.D., Pittsburgh.
Charles R. Woratschek, Ph.D., Pittsburgh.
Peter Wu, Ph.D., Rensselaer.
John Zeanchock, M.Ed., Indiana of Pennsylvania.

English Studies and Communications Skills Faculty
Diane Todd Bucci, Ph.D., Indiana of Pennsylvania.
Jay S. Carson, D.A., Carnegie Mellon.
Roger Gillan, M.A., Bucknell.
Arthur J. Grant, Ph.D., Wheaton (Illinois).
Rosemary Howley, M.A., Penn State.
Thomas A. Marshall, M.A., West Virginia.
John D. O'Banion, Ph.D., Northern Illinois.
Sylvia A. Pamboukian, Ph.D., Indiana Bloomington.
Constance M. Ruzich, Ph.D., Pennsylvania.
Jim Vincent, M.A., Indiana.

Media Arts Faculty
Lutz Bacher, Ph.D., Wayne State.
Ferris Crane, M.F.A., Academy of Arts.
Norma E. Gonzalez, M.F.A., Louisiana State.
Timothy J. Hadfield, M.F.A., Chelsea College of Art and Design (London).
Carolina Loyola-Garcia, M.F.A., Carnegie Mellon.
Jon A. Radermacher, M.F.A., Indiana.
Helena Vanhala, Ph.D., Oregon.
Hyla J. Willis, M.F.A., Carnegie Mellon.

SCHOOL OF EDUCATION AND SOCIAL SCIENCES
John E. Graham, Dean; Ed.D., Pittsburgh.
Donna Cellante, Associate Dean; Ed.D., Pittsburgh.

Elementary Education Faculty
Beatrice A. Gibbons, Ed.D., Pacific.
Michele N. Hipsky, Ed.D., Duquesne.
Anita Iaquinta, Ed.D., Indiana of Pennsylvania.
Daniel J. Shelley, Ph.D., Pittsburgh.

Secondary Education and Graduate Studies Faculty
Richard G. Fuller, D.Ed., Penn State.
Gretchen G. Generett, Ph.D., North Carolina.
Mary A. Hansen, Ph.D., Pittsburgh.
E. Gregory Holdan, Ph.D., Penn State.
Constance M. Ruzich, Ph.D., Pennsylvania.
George W. Semich, Ed.D., Pittsburgh.
Jon Shank, Ed.D., Pittsburgh.
Lawrence A. Tomei, Ed.D., Southern California.
John A. Zeanchock, Ed.D., Indiana of Pennsylvania.

Social Sciences Faculty
Daniel P. Barr, Ph.D., Kent State.
William R. Beaver, Ph.D., Carnegie Mellon.
Kathryn Dennick-Brecht, Ed.D., Duquesne.
Philip J. Harold, Ph.D., Catholic.
William E. Kelly, Ph.D., Louisiana Tech.
John M. McCarthy, Ph.D., Marquette.
Stephen T. Paul, Ph.D., Kansas.
David Wheeler, Ph.D., Washington (Seattle).

SCHOOL OF ENGINEERING, MATHEMATICS, AND SCIENCE
Winston F. Erevelles, Dean; Ph.D., Missouri–Rolla.
Maria V. Kalevitch, Associate Dean; Ph.D., Academy of Sciences (Lithuania).

Engineering Faculty
Sushil Acharya, D.Eng., Asian Institute of Technology (Thailand).
Zbigniew J. Czajkiewicz, Ph.D., Technical (Poland).
John Hayward, Ph.D., Penn State.
Priyadarshan A. Manohar, Ph.D., Wollongong (Australia).
Yildirim Omurtag, Ph.D., Iowa State.
Arif Sirinterlikci, Ph.D., Ohio State.
Murat Tiryakioglu, Ph.D., Missouri–Rolla; Ph.D., Birmingham (England).

Mathematics Faculty
Leonard A. Asimow, Ph.D., Washington (Seattle).
Mark A. Ciancutti, Ph.D., Carnegie Mellon.
Renato Clavijo, Ph.D., Arkansas.
Amy F. Hillen, Ed.D., Pittsburgh.
E. Gregory Holdan, Ph.D., Penn State.
David G. Hudak, Ph.D., Carnegie Mellon.
Richard J. Lesnak, M.Ed., Pittsburgh.
Allen R. Lias, Ph.D., Pittsburgh.
Mark M. Maxwell, Ph.D., Oregon.
Jeffrey J. Mitchell, Ph.D., Cornell.
Andris Niedra, Ph.D., Pittsburgh.
Monica M. VanDieren, Ph.D., Carnegie Mellon.
Charles W. Zimmerman, Ph.D., Ohio State.

Science Faculty
Paul D. Badger, Ph.D., Pittsburgh.
William J. Dress, Ph.D., Ohio State.
Kenneth A. Lasota, Ph.D., Pittsburgh.
Yildirim Omurtag, Ph.D., Iowa State.
Daniel Short, Ph.D., Liverpool (England).
Juliet E. Wynn, M.D., Buffalo, SUNY.

SCHOOL OF NURSING
Lynda J. Davidson, Dean; Ph.D., Pittsburgh; RN.
Lynn George, Associate Dean; Ph.D., Duquesne; RN.

Allied Health Faculty
Alphonso Baldwin, Ph.D., Alabama.
Angela M. Bires, Ed.D., Duquesne.
Donna L. Mason, M.S., Carlow.

Nursing Faculty
Nadine C. Englert, M.S.N., Pittsburgh; RN.
Patricia D. Fedorka, Ph.D., Pittsburgh; RN.
Valerie M. Howard, Ed.D., Pittsburgh; RN.
Lisa W. Locasto, M.S.N., Ohio State; RN.
Katherine Perozzi, M.S.N., Pittsburgh; RN.
Carl A. Ross, Ph.D., Duquesne; RN.
Kirstyn K. Zalice, M.S.N., Pittsburgh; CRNP, RN.

R·I·T

ROCHESTER INSTITUTE OF TECHNOLOGY

Graduate Studies

Programs of Study

The Rochester Institute of Technology (RIT) offers graduate programs of study in many areas.

Business, management, and communication programs are available in business administration (M.B.A., executive M.B.A., fast-track M.B.A.); communication and media technologies (M.S.); elements of health-care leadership (advanced certificate); facilities management (M.S.); finance (M.S.); health information resources (advanced certificate); health systems administration (M.S., advanced certificate); health systems finance (advanced certificate); hospitality-tourism management (M.S.); human resource development (M.S., advanced certificate); innovation management (M.S.); manufacturing management and leadership (M.S.); product development (M.S.); science, technology, and public policy (M.S.); senior-living management (advanced certificate); service leadership and innovation (advanced certificate); service management (M.S., advanced certificate); and technical information design (advanced certificate).

Computer science and information technology programs are offered in computer science (M.S.), computer security and information assurance (M.S.), computing and information sciences (Ph.D.), game design and development (M.S.), information assurance (advanced certificate), information technology (M.S.), interactive multimedia development (advanced certificate), learning and knowledge management systems (M.S., advanced certificate), networking and systems administration (M.S.), software development and management (M.S.), and software engineering (M.S.).

Education programs are available in art education (M.S.T.), school psychology (M.S.), and secondary education of students who are deaf and hard of hearing (M.S.).

Engineering and technology programs are offered in applied experimental and engineering psychology (M.S.), applied statistics (M.S.), computer engineering (M.S.), electrical engineering (M.S.), engineering management (M.E.), environmental health and safety management (M.S.), industrial engineering (M.E., M.S.), manufacturing and mechanical systems integration (M.S.), manufacturing engineering (M.E.), manufacturing leadership (M.S.), materials science and engineering (M.S., advanced certificate), mechanical engineering (M.E., M.S.), microelectronic engineering (M.S.), microelectronics manufacturing engineering (M.E., M.S.), microsystems engineering (Ph.D.), packaging science (M.S.), product development (M.S.), statistical methods for product and process improvement (advanced certificate), statistical quality (advanced certificate), systems engineering (M.E., M.S.), telecommunications engineering technology (M.S.) and vibrations engineering (advanced certificate).

Imaging arts programs are available in arts and design (M.F.A.), ceramics and ceramics sculpture (M.F.A.), computer animation and film (M.F.A.), computer graphics design (M.F.A.), cross-disciplinary professional studies (M.S.), fine arts studio (M.F.A.), glass and glass sculpture (M.F.A.), graphic design (M.F.A.), industrial design (M.F.A.), medical illustration (M.F.A.), metalcrafts and jewelry (M.F.A.), nontoxic intaglio printmaking (advanced certificate), photography (M.F.A.), print media (M.S.), and woodworking and furniture design (M.F.A.).

Science, mathematics, and imaging science programs are offered in bioinformatics (M.S.), chemistry (M.S.), clinical chemistry (M.S.), color science (M.S.), environmental science (M.S.), imaging science (M.S. and Ph.D.), industrial and applied mathematics (M.S.), and materials science and engineering (M.S.).

Programs in astrophysical sciences and technology (M.S. and Ph.D.), human-computer interaction (M.S.), and sustainability (M.S. and Ph.D.) are under development.

Research Facilities

State-of-the art technology in campus classrooms and laboratories reflects RIT's emphasis on career education. Six computer centers, a microchip-fabricating clean room, dedicated research laboratories, a student-operated restaurant, design studios, and more than 100 photography darkrooms provide students with the facilities they need to investigate and explore their academic fields. Wallace Library is the primary information source on campus, with full electronic access to research and data worldwide. It houses more than 750,000 items, including 350,000 books, 4,700 journals, 3,100 audio recordings, 6,700 film and video recordings, and 410,000 microforms. The online Infonet menu provides 24-hour access to a wide selection of resources, databases, the Internet, and the library's electronic catalog. Some of the nation's leading companies have supported research and teaching facilities that include the $22-million Center for Integrated Manufacturing Studies, the Sloan Printing Industry Center, and the Chester F. Carlson Center for Imaging Science. RIT's state-of-the-art Center for Excellence in Mathematics, Science and Technology showcases innovative teaching efforts using multimedia instructional technology. RIT offers opportunities to apply advanced technology to many areas of graduate study. Printing, design, and photography students merge these creative disciplines in the Electronic Still Photography Lab. Imaging science students analyze the latest in remote sensing capability from an on-campus remote-controlled observatory. Manufacturing management students evaluate production techniques in the manufacturing bays of the Center for Integrated Manufacturing Studies, and hospitality-tourism management students complete projects on their industry-standard SABRE computer system.

Financial Aid

Graduate scholarships and assistantships are available in most graduate departments. In addition, some departments offer externally funded stipends from corporate or government sources. Students should contact the appropriate department chairperson for additional information. Federal, state, and institutional aid are also available to those who qualify. Applicants seeking financial aid should submit the Free Application for Federal Student Aid (FAFSA) to the Office of Financial Aid by March 15 for consideration for entry for the following September.

Cost of Study

In 2007–08, the cost of full-time study (12–18 credit hours) is $9497 per quarter. The cost of part-time study (11 credit hours or fewer) is $800 per credit hour.

Living and Housing Costs

Housing Operations handles assignments for University-operated residence halls and more than 1,400 campus apartment units. Apartment rents begin at $829 per month for one-bedroom units for the academic year; reduced summer rates are available. In addition, there are several large local apartment complexes and individual living quarters within a short distance of the campus.

Student Group

The total enrollment at the Institute is 15,500. Enrollment in the graduate degree programs is approximately 2,500.

Location

RIT's campus in suburban Rochester occupies 400 acres on a 1,300-acre site and is located close to the cultural and entertainment districts of Rochester. Gallery and museum exhibits, a philharmonic orchestra, and theaters are located in metropolitan Rochester.

The Institute

RIT is accredited by the Middle States Association of Colleges and Schools and the New York State Board of Regents. It is a privately endowed, nonsectarian institution of higher education. RIT has been a pioneer in professional and career development programs since its founding in 1829. Its principal task is preparing men and women with the knowledge, skills, and attitudes required for technological, managerial, and aesthetic competence. It strives to assist them to mature as perceptive, skilled, and incisive professionals. Each graduate program is built as a freestanding unit and is designed to fill a specific demand in a given field. The thrust of the graduate programs is toward state-of-the-art technology and business, the aesthetic areas of the fine arts, photography, printing, and career-oriented programs in communication, school psychology, and public policy. As one of the pioneers of distance learning, RIT has a well-established and growing online learning division, with more than twenty graduate degrees and certificates available online.

Applying

Applicants should hold a bachelor's degree from a regionally accredited university and demonstrate, in the quality of undergraduate record, experience, and/or creative production, a genuine professional potential. Application deadlines vary by program, and applications must include all postsecondary official transcripts and degree certificates, a personal statement, two letters of recommendation, a $50 application fee, and a slide portfolio where applicable. In addition, some programs require GRE or GMAT scores, and a TOEFL score is required for students whose native language is not English.

Correspondence and Information

Office of Graduate Enrollment Services
Bausch & Lomb Center, Building 77, Room 1241
Rochester Institute of Technology
58 Lomb Memorial Drive
Rochester, New York 14623-5604

E-mail: gradinfo@rit.edu
Web site: http://www.rit.edu/grad

GRADUATE PROGRAM CONTACTS

Accounting
Ms. Peggy Tirrell. (585-475-2795; gradbus@rit.edu)

Applied Experimental and Engineering Psychology
Dr. Kathleen Chen. (585-475-2405; kccgss@rit.edu)

Applied Statistics
Dr. Joseph Voelkel. (585-475-6990; cqas@rit.edu)

Art Education
Ms. Carole Woodlock. (585-475-4556; cmwfaa@rit.edu)

Bioinformatics
Dr. Gary Skuse. (585-475-2532; grssbi@rit.edu)

Business Administration
Ms. Peggy Tirrell. (585-475-2795; gradbus@rit.edu)

Ceramics and Ceramic Sculpture
Ms. Julia Galloway. (585-475-2637; sacclay@rit.edu

Chemistry
Dr. Thomas Smith. (585-475-7982; twssch@rit.edu)

Clinical Chemistry
Dr. James Aumer. (585-475-2526; jcascl@rit.edu)

Color Science
Dr. Roy Berns. (585-475-2230; berns@cis.rit.edu)

Communication and Media Technologies
Dr. Rudy Pugliese. (585-475-5925; rrpgsl@rit.edu)

Computer Animation
Mr. Howard Lester. (585-475-7403; helpph@rit.edu)

Computer Engineering
Dr. Andreas Savakis. (585-475-2987; ce_chair@mail.rit.edu)

Computer Graphics Design
Ms. Marla Schweppe. (585-475-2754; mkspph@rit.edu)

Computer Science
Dr. Hans-Peter Bischof. (585-475-4994; csgradcoord@cs.rit.edu)

Computer Security and Information Assurance
Dr. Peter Lutz. (585-475-2669; peter.lutz@rit.edu)

Computing and Information Sciences
Dr. Evelyn Rozanski. (585-475-6193; phd@gccis.rit.edu)

Cross-Disciplinary Professional Studies
Dr. Samuel McQuade. (585-475-5230; scmcms@rit.edu)

Electrical Engineering
Dr. Soheil Dianat. (585-475-2165; sadeee@rit.edu)

Engineering Management
Dr. Michael Kuhl. (585-475-2134; mekeie@rit.edu)

Environmental, Health and Safety Management
Mr. Joseph Rosenbeck. (585-475-6469; jmrcem@rit.edu)

Environmental Science
Dr. Karl Korfmacher. (585-475-5554; kfkscl@rit.edu)

Executive M.B.A.
Dr. Brian O'Neil. (585-475-7435; boneil@rit.edu)

Film
Mr. Howard Lester. (585-475-7403; helpph@rit.edu)

Finance
Ms. Peggy Tirrell. (585-475-2795; gradbus@rit.edu)

Fine Arts Studio
Dr. Donald Arday. (585-475-4985; dkafaa@rit.edu)

Game Design and Development
Mr. Andrew Phelps. (585-475-6758; AMP@it.rit.edu)

Glass and Glass Sculpture
Ms. Julia Galloway. (585-475-2637; sacglass@rit.edu)

Graphic Design
Ms. Deborah Beardslee. (585-475-2664; dabfaa@rit.edu)

Health Systems Administration
Dr. Linda Underhill. (585-475-7359; lmuism@rit.edu)

Hospitality-Tourism Management
Dr. James Jacobs. (585-475-6017; jwjism@rit.edu)

Human Resource Development
Dr. Linda Underhill. (585-475-7359; lmuism@rit.edu)

Imaging Science
Dr. Maria Helguera. (585-475-7053; helguera@cis.rit.edu)

Industrial and Applied Mathematics
Dr. Hossein Shahmohamad. (585-475-7564; hxssma@rit.edu)

Industrial Design
Mr. David Morgan. (585-475-4769; dcmfaa@rit.edu)

Industrial Engineering
Dr. Michael Kuhl. (585-475-2134; mekeie@rit.edu)

Information Assurance
Dr. Peter Lutz. (585-475-2669; peter.lutz@rit.edu)

Informational Technology
Ms. Dianne P. Bills. (585-475-6179; itgradcoord@it.rit.edu)

Innovation Management
Ms. Peggy Tirrell. (585-475-2795; gradbus@rit.edu)

Interactive Multimedia Development
Ms. Dianne P. Bills. (585-475-6179; itgradcoord@it.rit.edu)

Learning and Knowledge Management System
Dr. Michael Yacci. (585-475-5416; may@it.rit.edu)

Manufacturing and Mechanical Systems Integration
Mr. Manian Ramkumar. (585-475-7024; smrmet@rit.edu)

Manufacturing Engineering
Dr. Jacqueline Mozrall. (585-475-2598; jrmeie@rit.edu)

Manufacturing Management and Leadership
Mr. Mark Smith. (585-475-7971; mmlmail@rit.edu)

Materials Science and Engineering
Dr. K.S.V. Santhanam. (585-475-2920; ksssch@rit.edu)

Mechanical Engineering
Dr. Edward Hensel. (585-475-2162; echeme@rit.edu)

Medical Illustration
Mr. Donald Arday. (585-475-4985; dkafaa@rit.edu)

Metalcrafts and Jewelry
Ms. Julia Galloway. (585-475-2637; sacglass@rit.edu)

Microelectronics Manufacturing Engineering
Dr. Santosh Kurinec. (585-475-6065; skkemc@rit.edu)

Microsystems Engineering
Dr. Mustafa Abushagur. (585-475-2295; maaeen@rit.edu)

Non-Toxic Print Making
Mr. Keith Howard. (585-475-2632; howard@mail.rit.edu)

Packaging Science
Ms. Deanna M. Jacobs. (585-475-6801; dmjipk@rit.edu)

Photography
Dr. Therese Mulligan. (585-475-2616; mtmpph@rit.edu)

Print Media
Dr. Twyla Cummings. (585-475-5567; tjcppr@rit.edu)

Product Development
Ms. Chris Fisher. (585-475-7971; mpdmail@rit.edu)

School Psychology
Dr. Scott Merydith. (585-475-7980; spmgsp@rit.edu)

Science, Technology, and Public Policy
Dr. Franz Foltz. (585-475-5368; mspolicy@rit.edu)

Secondary Education of Deaf or Hard of Hearing
Dr. Gerald Bateman. (585-475-6480; gcbnmp@rit.edu)

Senior Living Management
Dr. Linda Underhill. (585-475-7359; lmuism@rit.edu)

Service Management
Dr. James Jacobs. (585-475-6017; jwjism@rit.edu)

Service Leadership and Innovation
Dr. James Jacobs. (585-475-6017. jwjism@rit.edu)

Software Development and Management
Ms. Dianne P. Bills. (585-475-6179; itgradcoord@it.rit.edu)

Statistical Methods for Product and Process Improvement
Dr. Joseph Voelkel (585-475-6990; cqas@rit.edu)

Statistical Quality
Dr. Joseph Voelkel (585-475-6990; cqas@rit.edu)

Systems Engineering
Dr. Michael Kuhl. (585-475-2134; mekeie@rit.edu)

Technical Information Design
Mr. Thomas Moran. (585-475-4936; tfmcad@rit.edu)

Telecommunications Engineering Technology
Dr. Warren Koontz. (585-475-5706; telecom@cast-fc.rit.edu)

Vibrations Engineering
Dr. Edward Hensel. (585-475-2162; echeme@rit.edu)

Woodworking and Furniture Design
Ms. Julia Galloway. (585-475-2637; sacglass@rit.edu)

ROOSEVELT UNIVERSITY

Graduate Division

Programs of Study

The Graduate Division of Roosevelt University currently offers more than fifty graduate programs.

The College of Arts and Sciences offers the following programs: the Master of Arts (M.A.) in clinical psychology, clinical professional psychology, economics, English, history, industrial/organizational psychology, sociology, Spanish, and women's and gender studies; the Master of Fine Arts (M.F.A.) in creative writing; the Master of Public Administration (M.P.A.); the Master of Science (M.S.) in biotechnology and chemical science, computer science, mathematics/actuarial science, and telecommunications; the Master of Science in Journalism (M.S.J.); and the Master of Science in Integrated Marketing Communications (M.S.I.M.C.).

The Walter E. Heller College of Business Administration offers the following programs: Master of Business Administration (M.B.A.), the Master of Science in Accounting (M.S.A.), the Master of Science in Human Resource Management (M.S.H.R.M.), the Master of Science in Information Systems (M.S.I.S.), the Master of Science in International Business (M.S.I.B.), and the Master of Science in Real Estate (M.S.R.E.).

The College of Education offers the following programs: the Master of Arts (M.A.) in counseling and human services, early childhood education, early childhood professions, educational leadership, elementary education, reading, secondary education, special education, and teacher leadership.

The Evelyn T. Stone University College offers the following programs: the Master of Arts (M.A.) in training and development and the Master of Science (M.S.) in hospitality and tourism management.

The Chicago College of Performing Arts offers the following programs: the Master of Music (M.M.) in composition, musicology, orchestral studies, performance, and theory; the Master of Fine Arts (M.F.A.) in performance (theater); and the Master of Arts (M.A.) in general theater studies.

In addition, the Graduate Division offers two doctoral degrees: the Doctor of Education (Ed.D.) in educational leadership and the Doctor of Psychology (Psy.D.) in clinical psychology.

Certificate programs are available in biotechnology; chemical science; clinical child and family studies; computer science/telecommunications; e-learning; fraud examination; geographic information systems; health services management; hospitality and tourism; hospitality educator; information systems; instructional design; network computing and security; online teaching; paralegal studies; performance (diploma); performance consulting; real estate development; relaxation, meditation, and mindfulness programs; strategic management; training and development; and women and gender studies.

Research Facilities

The Murray-Green Library holds more than 225,000 volumes and a variety of research materials including periodicals and microforms. A full staff is on duty to assist student researchers at the downtown campus, and research services are also available at the Schaumburg Campus. Roosevelt University is a member of the Illinois Library Computer Services Organization (ILCSO), which operates a statewide online circulation system embracing forty-five of the largest libraries in Illinois. It is also backed up by the OCLC international bibliographic network and subscribes to numerous online electronic database services.

Financial Aid

Loans, grants, and scholarships are available for qualified students in all programs of the graduate division. Assistantships that pay stipends and carry tuition waivers are offered in most programs. Graduate students may also apply for college work-study. Partial tuition grants are available to qualified part-time students. Many graduate students finance their education through loans or are reimbursed by their employers. Those interested in financial aid should see the Applying section below for deadlines.

Cost of Study

For the College of Arts and Science, School of Business, and University College, the 2006-07 tuition was $688 per graduate-semester hour or $13,374 per year for full time students. Full-time tuition was $12,384 for the College of Education, and $21,590 for the Chicago College of Performing Arts. Fees included a general student fee of $150 per term and, in some programs, laboratory and other nominal fees.

Living and Housing Costs

The state-of-the-art University Center, an eighteen-floor multi-university residence hall, opened in 2004. It houses more than 1,700 students among three urban universities. The price starts at $7416. The University's Herman Crown Center provides reasonably priced housing for 350 students, starting at $5950. The cost of living in Chicago is about the same as in most other major cities. Chicago offers many job opportunities, myriad inexpensive services and activities, and a wide choice of living quarters at a variety of rent levels.

Student Group

Approximately 850 full-time and 2,200 part-time graduate students attend classes at Roosevelt. Students of varied multiracial and ethnic backgrounds and ages from many states and more than fifty other countries pursue graduate studies at the University. Most work part-time or full-time and find Roosevelt's scheduling flexibility well suited to their schedules.

Location

Roosevelt University's main campus has two campuses. The Michigan Avenue campus is in the heart of Chicago's downtown and is an easy commute by car or public transportation. Students can take advantage of the many events and activities in the city. The Albert A. Robin Campus is located in northwest suburban Schaumburg, approximately 30 miles from downtown Chicago. The University bus schedules daily transport to convenient public transportation. In addition to the two campus locations, Roosevelt is expanding its efforts to offer courses through partnerships with community colleges and corporations and through its Internet-based RU Online program. Currently, one entire degree program, the Master of Arts in Training and Development, is available in a fully online format as well as on campus.

The University

From its founding as a private university in 1945, Roosevelt pioneered the education of adults and nontraditional students, creating a diverse learning environment for all students, with an emphasis on social justice. Today, its educational programs are recognized nationwide, and students from all races and ethnicities throughout Metropolitan Chicago and from around the world pursue degrees at its two campuses. Roosevelt's characteristics provide a number of graduate educational benefits: small classes that encourage an open exchange of ideas, outstanding faculty, excellent academic programs, scheduling flexibility to accommodate students, and counseling and career planning services.

The Office of Career Services provides opportunities for students to engage in career exploration, career planning, internship experiences, and recruitment programs with major corporations and organizations. Students are able to meet one-on-one with career counselors for individualized sessions in order to clarify their major; assess their interests, skills, and values; engage in a job search; review resumes and cover letters; conduct mock interviews; and connect students to internship and employment opportunities. A number of the office's resources are online, including an online job and resume posting system, career education tools, a career resource library, and job development assessments.

Applying

Application for graduate study may be made to the Office of Graduate Admission on either campus or online. Applicants are urged to file their application one semester before the semester in which they plan to enroll; however the doctoral programs and a few other programs have earlier deadlines. Most priority deadlines for applications for admission are August 1 for the fall semester, December 1 for the spring semester, and April 15 for the summer terms. The priority application deadline for assistantships is March 31 for the following year, and for some scholarships, the priority deadline is May 1 for fall and October 15 for spring. There is a $25 fee for domestic applications and $35 for international applications. International students must apply at least three months prior to the intended semester, leaving additional time for visas.

Correspondence and Information

Chicago Campus
Roosevelt University
430 South Michigan Avenue
Chicago, Illinois 60605
Phone: 877-APPLY-RU (877-277-5978) (toll-free)
Fax: 312-341-3523
E-mail: applyRU@roosevelt.edu
Web site: http://www.roosevelt.edu

Schaumburg Campus
Roosevelt University
1400 North Roosevelt Road
Schaumburg, Illinois 60173
Phone: 877-APPLY-RU (877-277-5978) (toll-free)
Fax: 847-619-8636
E-mail: applyRU@roosevelt.edu
Web site: http://www.roosevelt.edu

GRADUATE PROGRAM DIRECTORS

Accounting: Deborah Pavelka, Ph.D., Missouri–Columbia. (dpavelka@roosevelt.edu)
Biotechnology and Chemical Science: Cornelius Watson, Ph.D., Wesleyan. (cwatson@roosevelt.edu)
Business Administration (Interdepartmental): Marilyn Nance, M.B.A., Roosevelt; CPA. (mnance@roosevelt.edu)
Computer Science and Telecommunications: Ken Mihavics, Ph.D., Illinois. (kmihavic@roosevelt.edu)
Counseling and Human Services: Roberto Clemente, Ph.D., Oregon State. (rclemente@roosevelt.edu)
Creative Writing: Janet Wondra, Ph.D., Louisiana State. (jwodra@roosevelt.edu)
Early Childhood Education: Ann Epstein, Ph.D., Maryland. (aepstein@roosevelt.edu)
Economics: June Lapidus, Ph.D., Massachusetts Amherst. (jlapidus@roosevelt.edu)
Educational Leadership (M.A.): Susan Katz, Ph.D., Indiana State. (skatz@roosevelt.edu)
Educational Leadership (Ed.D.): Martin Jason, Ed.D., Illinois at Urbana-Champaign. (mjason@roosevelt.edu)
Education/Teacher Leadership: Daniel White, Ph.D., Syracuse. (dlwhite@roosevelt.edu)
Elementary Education: Sharon Grant, Ph.D., Illinois at Chicago. (sgrant@roosevelt.edu)
English: Bonnie Gunzenhauser, Ph.D., Chicago. (bgunzenhauser@roosevelt.edu)
History: Susan Weininger, M.A., Chicago. (sweining@roosevelt.edu)
Hospitality and Tourism Management: Gerald Bober, Ed.D., Northern Illinois. (gbober@roosevelt.edu)
Human Resource Management: Ralph Haug, Ph.D., Wisconsin–Milwaukee. (rhaug@roosevelt.edu)
Information Systems: Joe Chan, Ph.D., Illinois. (jchan@roosevelt.edu)
Integrated Marketing Communications: Marian Azzaro, M.B.A., Chicago. (mazzaro@roosevelt.edu)
International Business: Alan Krabbenhoft, Ph.D., Wayne State. (akrabben@roosevelt.edu)
Journalism: Linda Jones, M.S., Northwestern. (ljones@roosevelt.edu)
Language and Literacy: Margaret Policastro, Ph.D., Northwestern. (mpolicas@roosevelt.edu)
Mathematics: John Currano, Ph.D., Chicago. (jcurrano@roosevelt.edu)
Music Conservatory: Linda Berna, Associate Dean; Ph.D., Northwestern. (lberna@roosevelt.edu)
Psychology: James Choca, Ph.D., Loyola Chicago. (jchoca@roosevelt.edu)
Psy.D.: Steven A. Kvaal, Ph.D., Ohio. (skvaal@roosevelt.edu)
Public Administration: David Hamilton, Ph.D., Pittsburgh. (dhamilto@roosevelt.edu)
Real Estate Development: Donald Swanton, Ph.D., Northwestern, (dswanton@roosevelt.edu)
Secondary Education: Linda Pincham, Ed.D., Virginia Tech. (lpincham@roosevelt.edu)
Sociology: Mike Maly, Ph.D., Loyola Chicago. (mmaly@roosevelt.edu)
Spanish: Pricilla Archibald, Ph.D., Stanford. (parchibald@roosevelt.edu)
Special Education: Sharon Grant, Ph.D., Illinois at Chicago. (sgrant@roosevelt.edu)
Theater Conservatory: Joel Fink, D.A., NYU; SEHNAP. (jfink@roosevelt.edu)
Training and Development: Deborah Colky, Ed.D., Northern Illinois. (dcolky@roosevelt.edu)
Women's and Gender Studies: Ann Brigham, Ph.D., Arizona. (abrigham@roosevelt.edu)

The Murray-Green Library, located at the downtown campus, offers panoramic views of Lake Michigan.

The Albert A. Robin Campus in Schaumburg is architecturally modern and decidedly horizontal, encompassing 225,000 square feet.

The downtown campus is located in the historic Auditorium Theatre building that overlooks Grant Park and Lake Michigan.

ROSEMONT COLLEGE

Schools of Graduate and Professional Studies

Programs of Study

Rosemont College offers programs leading to the Master of Arts in counseling psychology, curriculum and instruction, English and publishing, and English literature; the Master of Business Administration; the Master of Fine Arts in creative writing; and the Master of Science in Management. Postbaccalaureate elementary teacher certification and post-master's school counseling certification are also available. Addictions counseling certification is also offered.

Students may pursue graduate studies on a full-time or part-time basis. Summer sessions are offered for all programs. For more information on all programs, students should visit the College's Web site at http://www.rosemont.edu.

Research Facilities

The Rosemont College Library system spans several facilities and collections, including the Gertrude Kistler Memorial Library, the slide collection, and the Computer Centers, which are located both in the library and in the Dorothy McKenna Brown Science Center. The College's library program strives to meet the study and research needs of the students and faculty members by combining traditional library strengths with state-of-the-art access to electronic information and resource sharing.

Financial Aid

Graduate students are eligible to apply for tuition assistance in the form of Federal Stafford Student Loans if they are matriculated in a degree-granting program of study and are enrolled in at least half-time course work (two courses in the fall or spring; one course in each summer session). A limited number of competitive graduate assistantships are also available. Rosemont offers a tuition management option, so students can spread their payments out over the course of their program.

Cost of Study

Tuition for 2007–08 is $475 per credit hour for education programs and $525 per credit hour for business administration, counseling psychology, creative writing, English and publishing, English literature, and management programs. There are no registration fees.

Living and Housing Costs

On-campus housing is not available for graduate students; however, meal ticket options are available.

Student Group

The Schools of Graduate and Professional Studies serve working professional men and women in their mid-twenties to their mid-fifties. Total enrollment for the Schools is approximately 1,000 students.

Student Outcomes

Students who complete the education programs are employed in public and private schools as teachers, curriculum developers, staff developers, supervisors, counselors, and administrators. English literature and publishing graduates work in publishing houses or in organizations that require professionals who are skilled in publishing. English and creative writing program graduates teach at all levels; they also use their writing skills as entrepreneurs or in businesses that value employees with strong liberal arts backgrounds. Graduates in counseling psychology provide direct client services in schools, mental health centers, hospitals, social service agencies, the criminal justice system, and day treatment centers. Graduates of the business and management programs are employed by various private, public, and nonprofit organizations, corporations, and businesses in the local, regional, national, and international arenas.

Location

Rosemont College is located in Rosemont, Pennsylvania, one of several side-by-side college towns nestled among Philadelphia's historic Main Line suburbs. The College is easily accessible by car, train, or bus. Rosemont is ideally located within a 2-hour radius of New Jersey shore points, Longwood Gardens, the Pocono Mountains, New York City, Baltimore, and Washington, D.C.

The College

Rosemont College has a unique and progressive spirit of learning, engendered by an atmosphere of academic freedom and openness. Founded on the original Sinnott Estate, Rosemont received its charter as a college of liberal arts and was incorporated under the laws of the Commonwealth of Pennsylvania in 1922. Rosemont is accredited by the Middle States Association of Colleges and Schools.

Applying

Applications for admission to all master's degree and certification programs are reviewed throughout the year. No standardized test scores are required. The application fee is $50; this fee is waived for online applications.

Correspondence and Information

Schools of Graduate and Professional Studies
Rosemont College
1400 Montgomery Avenue
Rosemont, Pennsylvania 19010
Phone: 610-527-0200 Ext. 2213
888-2ROSEMONT (toll-free)
Fax: 610-526-2964
E-mail: admissions@rosemont.edu
Web site: http://www.rosemont.edu

FACULTY HEADS AND PROGRAM DIRECTORS

Rosemont College's faculty members are dedicated academicians and practitioners with a genuine commitment to teaching at the graduate level. For more information on the entire faculty, students should visit the College's Web site at http://www.rosemont.edu.

Liz Corcoran, Director of English Literature and Creative Writing; M. A., Temple.
Christine Erdner, Co-Director of Counseling Psychology; Ph.D., Temple.
Ann S. Hartsock, Director of Curriculum and Instruction; M.A.T., American.
Rebecca Mays, Director of English and Publishing; M.A., Pennsylvania.
Edward Samulewicz, Co-Director of Counseling Psychology; Ed.D., Lehigh.
Robert J. Siegfried, Director of Technology in Education; Ph.D., Pittsburgh.
Mary L. Sortino, Dean of Graduate and Continuing Studies; Psy.D., Widener.

RUTGERS, THE STATE UNIVERSITY OF NEW JERSEY, NEWARK

Graduate School

Programs of Study The Graduate School–Newark offers programs of study leading to a Doctor of Philosophy degree in American studies, biology*, chemistry, criminal justice, environmental science*, global affairs, management*, mathematical sciences*, integrative neuroscience, nursing, physics (applied)*, psychology, public administration, and urban systems. It offers programs leading to a master's degree in American studies, biology*, chemistry, computational biology*, economics, English, environmental geology, environmental science*, global affairs, history*, jazz history and research, liberal studies, nursing, physics (applied)*, and political science. The asterisks indicate joint/collaborative programs with NJIT and/or UMDNJ.

Other graduate programs available on the Rutgers–Newark campus are master's programs in criminal justice, public affairs and administration, public health, government accounting, management, professional accounting, and taxation and a J.D. degree through the School of Law. In general, doctoral students must satisfy the course requirements of their area of concentration, pass comprehensive examinations, present their research in an acceptable dissertation, and defend the dissertation in a public examination. Master's students pursue a course of study and must pass a comprehensive examination. While the master's thesis is an option in most programs, in some it is required. Specific requirements for both the doctoral and master's students are determined by the faculty of each program; additional information about these requirements should be obtained from the appropriate program director.

Opportunities for postdoctoral work are available in behavioral and neural sciences, biology, chemistry, and psychology. These programs also offer collaborative research opportunities for visiting scientists.

Research Facilities Scientific laboratories feature scanning and transmission electron microscopes, a confocal microscope, an automated DNA sequencer, ultracentrifuges, a phosphorimager, scintillation and gamma counters, a solid-phase peptide synthesizer, AVIV circular dichroism spectrophotometer, a time-correlated single photon counting instrument, fluorescence spectrometer, UV-vis NIR spectrometer, 20-MeV electron accelerator, excimer-isotopic carbon dioxide and semiconductor lasers, Auger spectrometer, quadrupole mass spectrometer, Allegra 3-Tesla functional magnetic resonance imaging instrument, and much more.

Financial Aid In 2007–08 University teaching assistantships provide a beginning annual salary of $18,347, remission of tuition, and other benefits. Fellowships and internships supported by federal, state, private, and University funds provide annual stipends of up to $18,000 and generally offer tuition remission. Program directors can provide information about support in their respective programs.

Cost of Study In 2007–08, per-credit tuition (1–11.5 credits) for New Jersey residents is $515.85 per semester. Twelve credits or more for New Jersey residents is $6190.20 per semester. Nonresident per-credit tuition (1–11.5 credits) is $766.90 per semester. Twelve credits or more for nonresidents is $9202.80 per semester. The full-time college fee (9 credits or more) is $548 per semester. The part-time college fee (fewer than 9 credits) is $168 per semester. The full-time computer fee is $137.50 per semester, and the part-time computer fee ranges from $55 to $107.50, based on credit hours.

Living and Housing Costs There is limited housing for graduate students in University-operated furnished apartments. The housing fee for the 2007–08 academic year (September 1 through about May 15) is $6896; for the calendar year (September 1 through about August 15), it is $8267.

Student Group The University's total enrollment is approximately 47,000 students, of whom 10,000 are in the nine schools and colleges on the Newark campus. The Graduate School–Newark enrolls approximately 1,300 students.

Location The Rutgers–Newark campus is conveniently located in the center of a diverse and thriving educational, professional, and cultural community in the downtown area of New Jersey's largest city. Located just a few minutes from the Newark campus, the New Jersey Performing Arts Center is a major cultural venue for the greater New York and Newark metropolitan areas and has restored Newark's historic role as the center for arts and culture in New Jersey. Because of its central location, Rutgers–Newark is accessible to a number of major metropolitan areas. New York City can be reached within 20 minutes by train, Philadelphia within an hour by train, and Washington, D.C., within an hour by plane.

The University Rutgers, The State University of New Jersey, was chartered in 1766 as Queen's College, the eighth institution of higher learning to be founded in the Colonies before the Revolutionary War. Queen's College opened its doors in New Brunswick in 1771 with one instructor and a handful of students. In 1825 the name of the college was changed to Rutgers to honor the former trustee and Revolutionary War veteran Col. Henry Rutgers. Rutgers College became the land-grant institution of New Jersey in 1864 and, almost 100 years later, after a period of phenomenal growth, was designated the State University of New Jersey in 1945. The University's Newark campus was created in 1946 when the University of Newark became part of Rutgers. The Graduate School–Newark was established in 1974. In addition to the Graduate School, Rutgers in Newark includes the College of Arts and Sciences, the College of Nursing, the Rutgers Business School, the School of Criminal Justice, the School of Law, and University College. The School of Public Affairs and Administration was established in 2006.

Applying Applications are available upon request from the Office of Graduate and Professional Admission, or they may be downloaded from http://www.gradstudy.rutgers.edu. Applicants may also apply online. The application fee is $60. All programs, except the program in management, require that applicants submit scores on the General Test of the Graduate Record Examinations (GRE); the management program requires scores on the Graduate Management Admission Test (GMAT). Programs in biology, chemistry, and psychology require scores on a GRE Subject Test as well as on the GRE General Test. International students and students whose native language is not English must provide scores on the Test of English as a Foreign Language (TOEFL).

By law and by purpose, Rutgers, The State University of New Jersey, is dedicated to serve all people on an equal and nondiscriminatory basis.

Correspondence and Information

Office of Graduate and Professional Admission
Rutgers, The State University of New Jersey
249 University Avenue
Newark, New Jersey 07102
Phone: 973-353-5205
Web site: http://gradstudy.rutgers.edu

Program Director (specify)
Rutgers, The State University of New Jersey
University Heights
Newark, New Jersey 07102
Web site: http://gsn.newark.rutgers.edu

PROGRAM DIRECTORS

Dr. Steven J. Diner, Dean of the Graduate School and Provost; Dr. Barry R. Komisaruk, Associate Dean (973-353-5834); Clara G. Bautista, Assistant Dean (973-353-5456); Adriana Afonso, Business Specialist (973-353-5197); and Virgen Reyes, Program Coordinator (973-353-5834; E-mail: gradnwk@newark.rutgers.edu).

American Studies (M.A., Ph.D.): Dr. Charles Russell (973-353-5279 Ext. 531). Newly established program to train students to become knowledgeable and productive scholars in a wide variety of academic, cultural, and public institutions. The doctoral program's Academic Profession track and Public Scholarship track each require 72 credits of course work and research, including core courses in the theory of American studies, substantial work in at least two of the six interdisciplinary fields of specialization, and the preparation of a dissertation. The master's program requires 24 course credits and 6 thesis credits. (http://americanstudies.newark.rutgers.edu/index.htm)

Biology (M.S., Ph.D.): Dr. Edward Bonder (973-353-1047). Research in neuroimmunology, cytoskeleton, signal transduction in animals and plants, computational neurobiology, molecular evolution, marine biology, environmental toxicology, and the parasitology of AIDS. Facilities are available for sophisticated techniques in molecular biology and biochemistry, microbial ecology, microscopic imaging, electron microscopy, woody plant physiology and development, and cell and tissue culture. Financial support is available to qualified candidates. (http://newarkbiosci.rutgers.edu)

Chemistry (M.S., Ph.D.): Dr. Phillip Huskey (973-353-5741). M.S. and Ph.D. degrees are offered on both a part-time and full-time basis in all major divisions of chemistry, including organic, inorganic, analytical, and physical chemistry and biochemistry. Financial support in the form of fellowships or assistantships is available to highly qualified applicants. (http://chemistry.rutgers.edu)

Computational Biology (M.S.): Dr. Michael Recce, NJIT (973-596-5535). Joint program offered by NJIT and Rutgers–Newark to address the need for personnel trained in both computer and biological sciences. Applicants with a background in either area gain expertise in the other, as well as take core courses that provide an understanding of computational biology. Areas of specialization are genomics, molecular modeling and drug discovery, computational neuroscience, biostatistics, and physiology. (http://catalog.njit.edu/graduate/programs/computationalbiology.php)

Criminal Justice (M.A., Ph.D.): Dr. Bonita Veysey (973-353-1929). Research: criminal justice theory, policy, and planning; situational crime prevention; community supervision of offenders; sentencing theory; violence; youth gangs; substance abuse and aggression; juvenile justice; organized crime; law and criminal justice; prosecution and the courts; comparative systems; maritime crime; policing; globalization of crime; business and crime. (http://www.newark.rutgers.edu/rscj/index.shtml)

Economics (M.A.): Dr. Sara J. Markowitz (973-353-5350). Research: transportation safety, financial markets and bubbles, decline of labor unions, household economics, gender differences in the labor market, school choice programs, real estate markets, alcohol and drug use among teenagers, foreign direct investment and the economic transformation of eastern Europe. (http://andromeda.rutgers.edu/~econnwk/mastersprogram.htm)

English (M.A.): Dr. Janet Larson (973-353-5279 Ext. 516). Research: medieval, Renaissance, and eighteenth-century literature; Romanticism; Victorian literature; nineteenth- and twentieth-century American and British literature; modernism; contemporary literature; Marxist, postcolonial, and feminist criticism; literature and technology; African-American literature. (http://english-newark.rutgers.edu/)

Environmental Geology (M.S.): Dr. Mitra Somenath, NJIT (973-596-5611). A collaborative program in environmental geology with the Departments of Geological Sciences of Rutgers–New Brunswick and Civil and Environmental Engineering of NJIT. Research: structural geology, radon, aqueous geochemistry, hydrogeology, stratigraphy, applied geophysics, mineralogy, and petrology. (http://www.andromeda.rutgers.edu/~geology/Programs/Programs-Masters.html)

Environmental Science (M.S., Ph.D.): Dr. Alexander Gates (973-353-5034). Joint M.S. and Ph.D. program with NJIT. Chemical engineering, coastal processes, ecology, environmental chemistry, environmental engineering, geochemistry, geology, geophysics, and microbiology with emphasis on urban problems. (http://andromeda.rutgers.edu/~geology/Programs/Programs-Masters.html) (http://andromeda.rutgers.edu/~geology/Programs/Programs-PhD.html)

Fine Arts (M.A.): Dr. Jayne Anne Phillips (973-353-5279 Ext. 622). Newly established 48-credit studio/research program. The program focuses strongly on 20 credit hours of a writing workshop in a declared genre and requires 7 thesis hours in which students work one-on-one with their mentor professors. Also requires 21 credit hours of graduate courses in literature. (http://mfa.newark.rutgers.edu/abouttheprogram.htm)

Global Affairs (M.S., Ph.D.): Dr. Alexander J. Motyl (973-353-3285). Offerings include an M.S. and a Ph.D. in global affairs. Programs are interdisciplinary, drawing on political science, history, economics, law, business, sociology, and anthropology to study the relationship between globalization and emerging forms of global governance. (http://dga.rutgers.edu/academics.html)

History (M.A., M.A.T.): Dr. Susan Carruthers (973-353-5410 Ext. 34). Joint M.A. and M.A.T. degrees offered with NJIT. American social, cultural, political, intellectual, legal, and diplomatic history; African-American history and the history of women; history of technology, the environment, medicine, and public health; European and American political culture; European history and the histories of Asia, Africa, Latin America, and the Near and Middle East; world history and comparative economic development. (http://history.newark.rutgers.edu/)

Integrative Neuroscience (Ph.D.): Dr. Ian Creese (Rutgers) (973-353-1080 Ext. 3300). Joint program with Rutgers–Newark and UMDNJ. The program offers specific research training in behavioral and cognitive neuroscience and molecular, cellular, clinical, and systems neuroscience. Research studies can emphasize either human, animal, or computational approaches. (http://ins.rutgers.edu)

Jazz History and Research (M.A.): Dr. Lewis Porter (973-353-5600 Ext. 30). This unique program prepares students to do research, publishing, and teaching by relying on the renowned Institute of Jazz Studies, the largest jazz library in the world. The required twelve courses focus on historiography and research, including transcribing, musical analysis, archival research, and interviewing. Applicants should have a bachelor's degree in any field and basic competence in playing and reading music. (http://gsn.newark.rutgers.edu/jazz/index.htm)

Liberal Studies (M.A.L.S.): Dr. Lillian Robbins (973-353-5440 Ext. 225). Conceptual and historical aspects of ethology; social theory; myth, drama, contemporary fiction, and film; bureaucracy; science and technology policy; poetry and criticism; history of philosophy; women's studies; ethics, philosophy of mind, and philosophy of religion; aesthetics; history of ideas from antiquity to the twenty-first century. (http://gsn.newark.rutgers.edu/liberal/index.htm)

Management (Ph.D.): Dr. Ronald D. Armstrong (973-353-5682). Research and doctoral training with majors possible in accounting, information systems, international business, finance, management science, and organization management. There are three majors in information systems: accounting information systems, computer information systems, and information technology. (http://business.rutgers.edu/default.aspx?id=107)

Mathematical Sciences (Ph.D.): Dr. Zhengya Mao (973-353-5156 Ext. 20). Joint program with NJIT. Research: low-dimensional topology, geometric group theory, Riemann surfaces, number theory, algebraic geometry, differential topology, representation theory, automorphic forms, harmonic analysis, Teichmuller theory. (http://andromeda.rutgers.edu/%7Emathcs/GradProg.html)

M.D./Ph.D.: Graduate School-Newark (973-353-5834 Ext. 10). Seven-year program leading to the M.D. from the New Jersey Medical School (NJMS)–University of Medicine and Dentistry of New Jersey (UMDNJ) and the Ph.D. from Rutgers–Newark. Students take two years of biomedical courses at NJMS, then conduct research at Rutgers–Newark for three years, and then return to NJMS for two years of clinical training. Students apply to both institutions simultaneously. Full tuition waiver plus annual salary support. Minority students encouraged to apply. (http://gsn.newark.rutgers.edu/md_phd/index.htm)

Nursing (M.S., Ph.D.): Dr. Wendy Nehring (973-353-5293 Ext. 606). Research: care and health promotion of children, adolescents, and adults/aged; symptom management in HIV/AIDS, CHF, and renal failure; pain control alternatives and exercise in hypertension; QOL issues for women in menopause and with breast cancer and persons with multiple sclerosis and surgeries that change appearance; sleep patterns of hospitalized cardiac patients; patient-care outcomes in vulnerable populations; and high-tech home care. (http://nursing.rutgers.edu/prospective_students/academic_programs)

Physics (Applied; M.S., Ph.D.): Dr. Zhen Wu, Rutgers–Newark (973-353-1311). Joint program offered by the Physics Departments of Rutgers (Newark) and NJIT. Research: applied optics, ultrafast optical phenomena, solid-state physics–microelectronics, MBE (molecular beam epitaxy), materials science, free electron laser, surface science, biophysics, astrophysics, plasma physics, laser spectroscopy, quantum electronics. (http://andromeda/rutgers.edu/~physics/index.html)

Political Science (M.A.): Dr. Mara Sidney (973-353-5787). International relations theory, public administration and bureaucracy, environmental politics and policy, policy formation and process evaluation, immigration policy, religion and politics, American human rights policy, generational ethnicity, ethics and international relations, gender and politics, international political economy. (http://politicalscience.newark.rutgers.edu/)

Psychology (Ph.D.): Dr. Kenneth Kressel (973-353-5440 Ext. 232). Graduate training and research focusing on basic issues in cognitive and behavioral sciences, with concentrations in the areas of perception, attention, visual cognition, language, cognitive neuroscience, cognitive and perceptual development, social psychology, connectionist modeling, learning and memory, emotion, hormones and behavior, adaptive behavior, and computational neuroimaging. (http://www.psych.rutgers.edu/)

Public Administration (Ph.D.): Dr. Norma Riccucci (973-353-5093 Ext. 16). The goal of the program is to train and educate public sector leaders, researchers, and educators. Areas of concentration in the doctoral program include productive public management, policy analysis, urban systems, and comparative public management, policy analysis, urban systems, and comparative public management and global governance. (http://spaa.newark.rutgers.edu/)

Public Health (M.P.H.): Dr. Evan Stark (973-353-5093 Ext. 22). Joint master's program offered by UMDNJ School of Public Health, NJIT, and Rutgers–Newark, in collaboration with the Public Health Research Institute. The program prepares students to work with communities to identify and assess health needs and problems, plan and implement solutions, monitor progress, and evaluate program outcomes. Specialty tracks are urban and environmental health, quantitative methods: biostatistics and epidemiology, and health policy and administration. All courses are offered in the late afternoon or evening. (http://sph.umdnj.edu/)

Urban Systems (Ph.D.): Dr. Karen A. Franck, NJIT (973-596-3092); Dr. Alan Sadovnik, Rutgers–Newark Urban Education Policy Coordinator (973-353-3532). Joint program offered by NJIT, UMDNJ, and Rutgers–Newark. The program is designed to prepare students to develop research-based knowledge in urban systems and to participate in the development, implementation, and evaluation of policy and services for urban populations. (http://www.umdnj.edu/urbsyweb/)

Women's & Gender Studies (Graduate Concentration): Dr. Jyl Josefson (973-353-1027). This four-course concentration can be taken through the programs in English, global affairs, history, liberal studies, political science, or public administration. (http://womenstudies.newark.rutgers.edu/)

SACRED HEART UNIVERSITY

Graduate Studies

Programs of Study

Sacred Heart University offers graduate degrees in ten fields of study: the Master of Arts in religious studies; the Master of Arts in criminal justice; the Master of Arts in Teaching (M.A.T.), which may lead to Connecticut public school teacher certification in elementary or secondary education; the Master of Business Administration (M.B.A.), with concentrations in accounting, finance, and general management; the Master of Science in chemistry; the Master of Science in computer science and information technology; the Master of Science in Nursing (M.S.N.), with concentrations in patient-care services administration, clinical nurse leader, or family nurse practitioner; the Master of Science in Occupational Therapy (M.S.O.T.); the online Master of Science in geriatric health and wellness; and the Doctor of Physical Therapy (D.P.T.).

Post-master's certificates are available in the educational administration and family nurse practitioner programs. Graduate certificates of study are available in accounting, database management, finance, interactive multimedia, international business, IT and network security, leadership, marketing, and Web development. The Center for Lay Ministry and Spirituality at Sacred Heart University offers graduate courses in conjunction with the graduate education and graduate religious studies programs.

A full-time M.B.A. program is available for those with bachelor's degrees in the liberal arts and sciences. Business prerequisites, internships, and an international experience are built into the graduate curriculum.

An accelerated RN-to-M.S.N. degree is offered to licensed RNs who wish to accelerate through the undergraduate curriculum and achieve the M.S.N. degree. M.S.N. courses are available both on campus and online.

The M.S. in Occupational Therapy program is offered through two years of full-time study on campus. The entry-level D.P.T. is offered through three years of full-time study. An online program for licensed physical therapists leads to the transitional Doctor of Physical Therapy (D.P.T.).

Each program is designed for students to maximize their potential through academic or internship experiences. Class sizes are generally small, allowing for frequent faculty-student contact. Most programs are available on a full-time and part-time basis. Courses are held locally throughout the calendar year in Fairfield, Stamford, and Griswold, Connecticut. The University currently offers the only U.S.-accredited M.B.A. program in the Grand Duchy of Luxembourg.

Research Facilities

The Ryan-Matura Library holds more than 263,000 volumes and maintains 2,100 periodical subscriptions. Additional materials are available through interlibrary loan with colleges and universities located throughout the area. A number of state-of-the-art chemistry, physical therapy, occupational therapy, and computer science laboratories are available for student use. The University sponsors the Center for Christian-Jewish Understanding, an educational and research resource on current religious thought in Christianity and Judaism. A 4,500-square-foot physical therapy clinic is housed in the William H. Pitt Health and Recreation Center.

Financial Aid

A limited number of research and staff assistantships are available to graduate students. Off-campus internship opportunities that provide tuition waivers and/or stipends are available on a competitive basis through the Office of Career Development. Teaching internships, which provide partial tuition waivers toward the teacher certification or the Master of Arts in Teaching program, are available in area school districts. Financial aid in the form of federal student loan programs, alternate private loans, and deferred payment plans are available through the Office of Student Financial Assistance.

Cost of Study

Tuition for most graduate students is charged on a per-credit-hour basis. Rates vary by program, but for the 2006–07 academic year, ranged from $465 to $575 per credit. Tuition for the Doctor of Physical Therapy program and for the Master of Science in Occupational Therapy program was approximately $25,000 for the 2006–07 academic year.

Living and Housing Costs

Graduate students commute to campus. Rent for off-campus housing in neighboring communities ranges from $500 to $900 per month for a one-bedroom apartment.

Student Group

There are approximately 5,800 undergraduate and graduate students enrolled at Sacred Heart University. Graduate enrollment for the 2006–07 academic year exceeded 1,600 full- and part-time students. Nearly 70 percent were women, and 9 percent represented minority groups. The graduate student body represents fifteen states from New England to the Pacific Northwest as well as thirteen countries.

Location

Established in 1639, Fairfield, Connecticut, is an attractive suburban community located 55 miles northeast of New York City. The community and surrounding area are considered one of the nation's more dynamic business and economic regions and are home to numerous Fortune 500 companies. The main campus is located on 56 acres near major thoroughfares and recreational areas.

The University

Sacred Heart University was founded in 1963 as a coeducational, independent, comprehensive institution in the Catholic intellectual tradition. Graduate programs are offered through the College of Arts and Sciences, the John F. Welch College of Business, and the College of Education and Health Professions. In recent years, the University has achieved unprecedented growth in its enrollment, faculty, and facilities. It is the second-largest Catholic university in New England.

Applying

A bachelor's degree from a regionally accredited four-year college or university or its equivalent is required for admission. Other requirements vary for each program. All applicants must submit a completed application to the Office of Graduate Admissions. International applicants must have a minimum TOEFL score of 550 on the paper-based exam or 213 on the computer-based exam and are required to demonstrate the ability to finance their education for F-1 Visa eligibility.

Correspondence and Information

Sacred Heart University
Office of Graduate Admissions
5151 Park Avenue
Fairfield, Connecticut 06825-1000

Phone: 203-365-7619
Fax: 203-365-4732
E-mail: gradstudies@sacredheart.edu
Web site: http://www.sacredheart.edu/graduate.cfm

THE FACULTY

College of Arts and Sciences
Claire Paolini, Dean; Ph.D., Tulane.
Chemistry: Dhia Habboush, Program Director; Ph.D., Southampton (England).
Computer Science and Information Technology: Domenick Pinto, Program Director; M.S., Polytechnic.
Criminal Justice: Pearl Jacobs, Program Director; Ph.D., Fordham.
Religious Studies: Christel Manning, Program Director; Ph.D., California, Santa Barbara.

College of Business
Stephen Brown, Dean; Ed.D., Boston University.
Business: Valerie Christian, M.B.A. Director; M.B.A., Dartmouth.

College of Education and Health Professions
Patricia Walker, Dean; Ed.D., Loyola.
Education: Edward Malin, Program Coordinator; Ph.D., Fordham.
Geriatric Health and Wellness: Michelle Lusardi, Program Director; Ph.D., Connecticut.
Nursing: Dori Sullivan, Program Director; Ph.D., Connecticut; RNC, CNA, CPHQ.
Occupational Therapy: Jody Bortone, Program Director; Ed.D., Fordham; OTR/L.
Physical Therapy: Michael Emery, Program Director; Ed.D., Vermont.

SAINT LOUIS UNIVERSITY

Graduate School

Programs of Study

The Graduate School offers more than forty programs of advanced study. In addition to the degree programs, certificates may be pursued parallel to degree study in empirical research methods in descriptive ethics, rhetorical studies/writing pedagogy, Renaissance studies, women's studies, university teaching skills, geographic information systems, organizational development, and health-care ethics. Post-master's certificates are available in marriage and family therapy and in a variety of nursing specialties. Opportunities for dual-degree programs that facilitate simultaneous training in one of the University's professional schools (e.g., law, medicine, business, or social service) also are available.

Research Facilities

Per the Carnegie Foundation rankings and listings, Saint Louis University (SLU) is a doctoral, research-extensive university with high research activity. SLU is one of only eight Catholic universities in the United States to achieve this designation. In 2006, the Medical Center received grants totaling $72 million. This includes funding from numerous governmental sources, such as the National Institutes of Health, and private industry. Researchers in areas outside medicine received grants totaling $7.3 million, approximately 80 percent of which support graduate students in a research role. In addition, more than $1 million was awarded for various graduate student training, assistantship, fellowship, and educational needs. The University is building a state-of-the-art research facility, which will strengthen Saint Louis University's ability to obtain important external funding and lead to additional clinical studies and innovative research programs.

The combined holdings of the University's four libraries total approximately 1.82 million volumes and 15,000 continuations. Through Saint Louis University's participation in the Online Computer Library Center, users have bibliographic access to more than 45 million titles in sixty-two countries in virtually any language. Special collections include 35 million pages of Vatican manuscripts and extensive theological holdings. The University is a member of the Center for Research Libraries (Chicago), and students also have access to the libraries of the University of Missouri and Washington University in St. Louis. Computer centers and research offices are staffed throughout the campus. The University's urban location has allowed the development of unique research opportunities with numerous public and private agencies and corporations.

Financial Aid

Financial assistance is available to qualified graduate students. Fellowships and teaching, research, and administrative assistantships are awarded in most fields of study; full-tuition scholarships accompany stipends in many instances. Assistantships and fellowships are awarded through individual departments. Federal and state (Missouri) grants and loans and Federal Work-Study Program eligibility may be sought through the University's Office of Financial Aid; a formal application and the need analysis are mandatory.

Cost of Study

The cost is $845 per Graduate School credit hour for the 2007–08 academic year.

Living and Housing Costs

Multiple options for off-campus living are available. Many apartments directly border SLU or are located within a short distance of the campus. SLU's surrounding neighborhoods offer a wide range of housing options and amenities, including the new downtown loft district. St. Louis County is within 10 miles of the campus and offers alternatives to city living.

Student Group

Of the 12,034 students attending Saint Louis University, 2,937 are students in the Graduate School pursuing advanced degrees.

Location

The University's main campus is located in the heart of midtown St. Louis, Missouri, and comprises nearly 300 well-manicured acres. The city of St. Louis and Saint Louis University have a long-standing commitment to each other's vitality and quality of life. The city offers a wide variety of urban entertainment and commerce. Saint Louis University is in the heart of the arts district, home to music and dance clubs, cafés, restaurants, performance theaters, and concert and opera halls.

The University

Saint Louis University is a Jesuit, Catholic university ranked among the top research institutions in the nation. The University fosters the intellectual and leadership development of more than 11,000 students on campuses in St. Louis and Madrid, Spain. Founded in 1818, it is the oldest university west of the Mississippi and the second-oldest Jesuit university in the United States. The University's first graduate degree was awarded in 1834. Through teaching, research, health care, and community service, Saint Louis University is the place where knowledge touches lives. Prospective students can find more information at the University's Web site (http://graduate.slu.edu).

Applying

Application forms for admission can be obtained from the Graduate School Admissions Office or online at http://graduate.slu.edu. General application deadlines are April 1 for the summer session, July 1 for the fall semester, and November 1 for the spring semester. February 1 is the deadline for applications to be considered for fellowships and is the recommended deadline for assistantship applications. Forms for need-based assistance can be obtained from the Office of Scholarship and Financial Aid or online at http://www.slu.edu/services/fin_aid.

International applicants are required to submit an official TOEFL score or other acceptable proof of English proficiency.

Correspondence and Information

Graduate School Admissions
Saint Louis University
3634 Lindell Boulevard
St. Louis, Missouri 63108
Phone: 314-977-2240
800-SLU-FOR-U (toll-free)
E-mail: gradadm@slu.edu
Web site: http://www.slu.edu/graduate/

Office of Scholarship and Financial Aid
Saint Louis University
221 North Grand Boulevard
St. Louis, Missouri 63103
Phone: 314-977-2350
Web site: http://www.slu.edu/services/fin_aid

GRADUATE PROGRAMS AND DEGREES AND CONTACT INFORMATION

American Studies: M.A., M.A.(R), Ph.D.; Dr. Matthew Mancini (heathcje@slu.edu; 314-977-2911).
Anatomy: M.S.(R), Ph.D.; Dr. Daniel Tolbert (anatomy@slu.edu; 314-977-8030).
Biochemistry and Molecular Biology: Ph.D.; Dr. William Sly (biochem@slu.edu; 314-977-9200).
Biology: M.S., M.S.(R), Ph.D.; Dr. Rob Wood (biology@slu.edu; 314-977-3910).
Biomedical Engineering: M.S., M.S.(R), Ph.D.; David W. Barnett (biomed@slu.edu; 314-977-8292).
Biosecurity and Disaster Preparedness: M.S., certificate; Dr. Greg Evans (bommarig@slu.edu; 314-977-8133).
Business Administration: Ph.D.; Dr. Steven Miller (jcsbphd@slu.edu; 314-977-2476).
Catholic School Leadership: M.A.; Dr. William Rebore (moorem@slu.edu; 314-977-2508).
Chemistry: M.S., M.S.(R); Dr. Shelley Minteer (chemdept@slu.edu; 314-977-2850).
Clinical Health Care Ethics Certificate: Dr. Jill Burkemper (chcecert@slu.edu; 314-977-6661).
Communication: M.A., M.A.(R); Dr. Paaige Turner (commdept@slu.edu; 314-977-3191).
Communication Sciences and Disorders: M.A., M.A.(R); Dr. Travis Threats (commdis@slu.edu; 314-977-2948).
Community Health: M.P.H.; Bernie Backer (sphinfo@slu.edu; 314-977-8100).
Counseling and Family Therapy: M.A., M.A.(R), Ph.D.; Dr. Craig Smith (cft@slu.edu; 314-977-7108).
Educational Administration: M.A., Ed.S., Ed.D., Ph.D.; Dr. William Rebore (moorem@slu.edu; 314-977-2508).
Educational Leadership: M.A.; Dr. William Rebore (moorem@slu.edu; 314-977-2508).
Educational Studies: M.A., M.A.T., Ed.D., Ph.D.; Dr. Dorothy Miles (miles2@slu.edu; 314-977-4062).
Endodontics: M.S.(R); Dr. John Hatton (cade@slu.edu; 314-977-8611).
English: M.A., M.A.(R), Ph.D.; Dr. Antony Hasler (hasleraj@slu.edu; 314-977-3010).
French: M.A.; Dr. Cassandra Hamrick (hamrick@slu.edu; 314-977-2450).
Geographic Information Systems Certificate: Dr. Robert Cropf (pps@slu.edu; 314-977-3934).
Geophysics: Ph.D.; Dr. Keith Koper (wise@eas.slu.edu; 314-977-3116).
Geoscience/Geology: M.S., M.S.(R); Dr. Keith Koper (wise@eas.slu.edu; 314-977-3116).
Health Care Ethics: Ph.D.; Dr. James DuBois (chcephd@slu.edu; 314-977-6661).
Health Management and Policy: M.H.A.; Bernie Backer (sphinfo@slu.edu; 314-977-8100).
Higher Education Administration: M.A., Ed.D., Ph.D.; Dr. William Rebore (moorem@slu.edu; 314-977-2508).
Historical Theology: M.A., Ph.D.; Dr. James Ginther (theology@slu.edu; 314-977-2881).
History: M.A., M.A.(R), Ph.D.; Dr. Thomas Madden (history@slu.edu; 314-977-2910).
Integrated and Applied Science: Ph.D.; Dr. Paul Jelliss (jellissp@slu.edu; 314-977-2834).
Mathematics: M.A., M.A.(R), Ph.D.; Fr. Michael K. May (mathweb@slu.edu; 314-977-2444).
Marriage and Family Therapy Certificate: Dr. Craig Smith (cft@slu.edu; 314-977-7108).
Meteorology: M.S., M.S.(R), Ph.D.; Dr. Charles Graves (wise@eas.slu.edu; 314-977-3116).
Molecular Microbiology and Immunology: Ph.D.; Dr. William Wold (mmigradprog@slu.edu; 314-977-8850).
Nursing–Doctoral: Ph.D.; Director, Ph.D.; Dr. Andrew Mills (slunurse@slu.edu; 314-977-8909).
Nursing–Master's: M.S.N., M.S.N.(R); Dr. Margie Edel (slunurse@slu.edu; 314-977-8909).
Nursing–Post-Master's Certificate: Dr. Margie Edel (slunurse@slu.edu; 314-977-8909).
Nutrition and Dietetics: M.S.; Dr. Mildred Mattfeldt-Beman (veggie@slu.edu; 314-977-8663).
Orthodontics: M.S.(R); Dr. Rolf Behrents (cade@slu.edu; 314-977-8611).
Organizational Leadership Certificate: Dr. Robert Mai (pps@slu.edu; 314-977-3934).
Pathology: Ph.D.; Dr. Jacki Kornbluth (kornblut@slu.edu; 314-268-5445).
Periodontics: M.S.(R); Dr. D. Douglas Miley (cade@slu.edu; 314-977-8611).
Pharmacological and Physiological Science: Ph.D.; Dr. Thomas Westfall (inquiry@slu.edu; 314-977-6400).
Philosophy: M.A., M.A.(R), Ph.D.; Fr. Theodore R. Vitali, C.P. (sluphilo@slu.edu; 314-977-3149).
Psychology–Clinical: M.S.(R), Ph.D.; Dr. Jeffrey Gfeller (slupsych@slu.edu; 314-977-2300).
Psychology–Experimental: M.S.(R), Ph.D.; Dr. James Churchill (psyappex@slu.edu; 314-977-2300).
Psychology–Industrial/Organizational: M.S.(R), Ph.D.; Dr. Edward Sabin (slupsych@slu.edu; 314-977-2300).
Public Administration: M.A.P.A.; Dr. Robert Cropf (pps@slu.edu; 314-977-3934).
Public Health Studies: Ph.D.; Bernie Backer (sphinfo@slu.edu; 314-977-8100).
Public Policy Analysis: Ph.D.; Dr. Robert Cropf (pps@slu.edu; 314-977-3934).
Spanish: M.A.; Dr. Mauricio Souza (gradsp@slu.edu; 314-977-2450).
Student Personnel Administration: M.A.; Dr. William Rebore (moorem@slu.edu; 314-977-2508).
Theology: M.A., Ph.D.; Dr. James Ginther (theology@slu.edu; 314-977-2881).
Urban Affairs: M.A.U.A.; Dr. Robert Cropf (pps@slu.edu; 314-977-3934).
Urban Planning and Real Estate Development: M.U.P.R.E.D.; Dr. Robert Cropf (pps@slu.edu; 314-977-3934).

OTHER PROGRAMS
M.B.A. Program: (mba@slu.edu; 314-977-MBA1).
School of Allied Health: Occupational Therapy (ot@slu.edu; 314-977-8580); Physical Therapy (ptdept@slu.edu; 314-977-8543); Physician Assistant Studies (majj@slu.edu; 314-977-8648).
School of Law: (admissions@law.slu.edu; 314-977-2800).
School of Medicine: (slumd@slu.edu; 314-977-9870).
School of Social Service: (socserv@slu.edu; 314-977-2722).

The clock tower in John E. Connelly Plaza is a focal point of the St. Louis campus.

The Billikens began competing as a full member of the Atlantic 10 Conference during the 2005–06 academic year.

St. Louis' rich civic offerings such as the Gateway Arch and the historic Old Courthouse provide students with great options for learning and recreation.

SAINT PETER'S COLLEGE

Graduate Studies

Programs of Study

Saint Peter's College offers selected graduate degrees and certification programs. The Master of Business Administration is a 48-credit program and runs on a trimester calendar. Students can choose from five areas of concentration: finance, management information systems, marketing, international business, and management. The Master of Science (M.S.) in accountancy is a 30-credit program and also runs on a trimester calendar. Upon graduation, M.S. in accountancy students will have completed the 150 credit hours of education that became a requirement in the year 2000 in the state of New Jersey to sit for the Certified Public Accountant (CPA) examination. The 36-credit Master of Arts in education runs on a semester calendar and offers concentrations in administration and supervision, reading, and teaching. For students who earned their undergraduate degrees in an area other than education and want to be certified to teach nursery through eighth grade or ninth through twelfth grade, a 26-credit teacher certification program is offered. The Master of Science in Nursing (M.S.N.) degree program offers two concentrations: a 37-credit concentration in case management and a 39-credit concentration in primary-care adult nurse practitioner studies. For students who already possess a master's degree in nursing and want to earn a certificate as an adult nurse practitioner, a 25-credit post-master's certificate is offered. Saint Peter's also offers an RN to M.S.N. Bridge Program for students who have bachelor's degrees in fields other than nursing and who have an RN license.

Research Facilities

The libraries of Saint Peter's College provide extensive services and research facilities to the College community at both campuses. The Theresa and Edward O'Toole Library in Jersey City is fully automated, and the catalog is accessible via the campus network. The Jersey City and Englewood Cliffs libraries hold more than 300,000 volumes. Every student has a computer ID that permits access to eighteen computer labs, the campus computer network, e-mail, and the Internet. All classrooms are wired for computer access. The Blackboard Classroom System makes class material available 24 hours a day, seven days a week. The College's campus is one of the first in New Jersey to offer students with remote-access-equipped laptops the ability to log onto the College system or the Internet at anytime or anywhere on campus.

Financial Aid

To make financing an education possible, Saint Peter's financial aid advisers help students explore the best means of affording their degree. Options include tuition deferment and installment plans, employer-sponsored tuition reimbursement plans, and student loans. Students should call a financial aid adviser at 201-915-9308 for more information.

Cost of Study

The cost of tuition for graduate study in 2006–07 was $780 per credit.

Student Group

Saint Peter's College has a total enrollment of more than 3,300 undergraduate and graduate students. The diverse student body includes many international students representing seventy different countries.

Location

Saint Peter's College offers two campuses in convenient locations. The main campus has long been a landmark on Kennedy Boulevard in Jersey City, New Jersey. The College's atmosphere, architecture, and activity reflect a dynamic, vital, urban institution that offers important intellectual resources to the community. The New York City skyline, visible from Jersey City, is a constant reminder of the College's proximity to a major cultural and financial center. The branch campus at Englewood Cliffs in Bergen County, New Jersey, was established as a college for adults. The campus is perched on a bluff overlooking northern Manhattan and the Hudson River, located on the Palisades 1 mile north of the George Washington Bridge.

An off-site location at the Jersey City Waterfront affords graduate students the opportunity to take business courses at a convenient location close to their place of employment in downtown Jersey City. It is also conveniently located close to PATH and ferry transportation. An additional off-site location in South Amboy, New Jersey, offers education and business courses.

The College

Saint Peter's College, founded in 1872, is a Jesuit, Catholic, coeducational liberal arts college in an urban setting that seeks to develop the whole person in preparation for a lifetime of learning, leadership, and service in a diverse and global society. Committed to academic excellence and individual attention, Saint Peter's College provides education informed by values.

Applying

To begin the graduate admissions process, students must submit an application, including official undergraduate transcripts. Additional admission requirements (if any) vary with each graduate program and can be requested by the admissions office after the initial application is received. International applicants must submit the same to begin applying. An initial review of the complete application for admission is conducted by the Office of Graduate Admissions. The office reserves the right to ask for additional application documentation at any time. The file is then forwarded to a graduate program director for an admission decision. All correspondence should be conducted with the Office of Graduate Admissions.

Correspondence and Information

Office of Graduate Admissions
Saint Peter's College
2641 Kennedy Boulevard
Jersey City, New Jersey 07306
Phone: 201-761-6470
Fax: 201-435-5270
E-mail: gradadmit@spc.edu
Web site: http://www.spc.edu

GRADUATE PROGRAMS

Master of Arts in Education (M.A.)
The Master of Arts in education program offers three areas of concentration: administration and supervision, reading, and teaching. Each concentration prepares teachers for certification by the state of New Jersey. The three concentrations have a set of foundation courses (9 credits), which are enhanced by specialized required courses and electives. The M.A. in education program is 36 credits and runs on a semester calendar.

For persons who earned their undergraduate degrees in an area other than education and want to be certified to teach nursery through eighth grade or ninth through twelfth grade, a 26-credit teacher certification program is offered. The program consists of six courses (18 credits) in addition to 8 credits in student teaching. The teacher certification program can be completed strictly in the evenings or strictly on the weekends. Students can also mix and match their class schedule by taking evening and weekend courses.

Master of Business Administration (M.B.A.)
The M.B.A. program at Saint Peter's has been designed to meet the changing requirements that are occurring in the business workplace. The M.B.A. program offers five areas of study: finance, management information systems, marketing, international business, and management. The M.B.A. is a 48-credit program. The M.B.A. student may receive credit for prior undergraduate and graduate work, up to 12 credits, with approval from the M.B.A. Coordinator and Adviser. Thus, individuals with undergraduate credit in accounting, statistics, computer science, or economics may complete the M.B.A. program in 36 credits. The program runs on a trimester calendar, with courses offered in the evenings and on weekends.

Master of Science in Accountancy (M.S.)
The 30-credit Master of Science in accountancy runs on a trimester calendar. This program keeps pace with changes in accounting practices and anticipates coming changes in the business environment. Furthermore, graduates of this program will have completed the 150 credit hours of education that became a requirement in the year 2000 by the state of New Jersey to sit for the Certified Public Accountant (CPA) examination. The M.S. in accountancy can be completed strictly in the evenings or strictly on the weekends. Students can also mix and match their class schedule by taking evening and weekend courses.

Master of Science in Nursing (M.S.N.)
The Master of Science in Nursing program offers two areas of specialization: primary-care adult nurse practitioner studies and case management with a functional concentration in nursing administration. Both options consist of core courses that provide a foundation for graduate study and theoretical and clinical practicum courses that prepare graduates for specialization in case management, nursing administration, or in primary care as adult nurse practitioners. The 37-credit M.S.N. in case management curriculum is offered on a trimester basis. The 39-credit M.S.N. adult nurse practitioner studies program is offered on a combined trimester/semester schedule.

For nurses who already possess a master's degree in nursing and want to earn a certificate as an adult nurse practitioner, a 25-credit, post-master's program is offered. Saint Peter's also offers an RN to M.S.N. Bridge Program for students who have bachelor's degrees in fields other than nursing and who have their RN license. Graduate study in nursing is offered exclusively at the Englewood Cliffs campus.

A professor at Saint Peter's College crosses campus on his way to class.

The Englewood Cliffs campus is specifically designed for adult learners and is conveniently located just 5 minutes from the George Washington Bridge.

SALVE REGINA UNIVERSITY

Graduate Programs

Programs of Study

Salve Regina University, a coeducational institution serving approximately 2,600 men and women, offers seven master's degree programs and a Ph.D. degree program. Courses typically are scheduled one evening per week in order to accommodate students who work full-time. In addition to on-campus courses at the main campus in Newport, Rhode Island, graduate courses are offered at the University's satellite location in Pawtucket, Rhode Island. For those interested in distance learning, four master's degree programs can be pursued online through Graduate Extension Study (eSalve).

Approximately 600 students are enrolled in the seven master's degree programs: business administration and management, health services administration, holistic counseling, humanities, international relations, justice/administration of justice, and rehabilitation counseling. Approximately 85 students are enrolled in the Ph.D. program in the humanities, which is devoted to the interdisciplinary study of the impact of technology on the world and the future. Some graduate students work full-time and take courses part-time, taking one or two courses each semester and during the summer. Some, who are too far away to take a course at one of Salve Regina's campuses, enroll in the GES program, which allows them to take advantage of the distance learning option and earn a degree in business administration, humanities, international relations, or management. Many on-campus students occasionally register for such courses when personal circumstances make it difficult to attend classes on campus.

Research Facilities

The McKillop Library provides seating for more than 450 students and has more than 250,000 holdings. The library is connected to a fiber-optic network and to the University's telecommunications system. Twenty-four intelligent terminals provide access to the University host, the library host, and external databases. The bibliographic research room is equipped with a local area network, fifteen intelligent workstations, an instructor's workstation, and four printers. Online public access catalog and circulation systems are available to the University community, and many CD-ROM databases are available to library and off-campus users. The University has four academic computer labs in the library that serve students and the faculty. The workstations in each lab are linked to a local area network and are open seven days a week.

Financial Aid

The Financial Aid Office assists graduate students with obtaining many different kinds of low-interest loans. A few part-time internship opportunities are also available.

Cost of Study

For the academic year 2007–08, the cost for a typical 3-credit master's-level course is $1095 ($365 per credit). The cost of a doctoral-level course was $1725 ($575 per credit).

Living and Housing Costs

On-campus housing is not available for graduate students. The Residence Office assists graduate students seeking off-campus housing, which is plentiful given that Newport is a worldwide tourist attraction.

Student Group

Approximately 600 full- and part-time students are enrolled in on-campus graduate courses, and 280 students are enrolled in distance learning classes, some of whom are also enrolled in on-campus courses.

Student Outcomes

Because many students are working professionals, the benefits derived from their participation in one of Salve Regina's graduate programs include professional advancement and greater opportunities for lateral movement within their professions. Younger students who enroll in the University with a recent bachelor's degree also benefit in two principal ways. They obtain the skills and education required for entrance into particular fields and positions as well as the additional education and experience they need to prepare themselves for doctoral education. Students also may enroll because they are interested in continuing their education in order to fuel their own personal development. This is particularly true of the students in the humanities and holistic counseling programs.

Location

Newport is a small resort city filled with architectural masterpieces, breathtaking natural beauty, and artistic delights. Tens of thousands of people visit Newport and its famous Bellevue Avenue mansions, seacoast, and shops each year. The main campus of Salve Regina is located next to the Breakers, the most famous of all Newport mansions, and is adjacent to the Cliff Walk, a magnificent, winding pathway that rises high above the Atlantic Ocean. It is comprised of historically important mansions and attractive landscaping, and it is considered by many to be among the most beautiful campuses in the U.S. Newport is about 2 hours from Boston, about 3 hours from New York, and about 40 minutes from T. F. Green International Airport in Providence.

The University

Salve Regina College was chartered by the state of Rhode Island in 1934. A 1991 amendment to its charter, reflecting in part the significant development of its graduate programs, changed the name of the institution to Salve Regina University. The University was founded by the Sisters of Mercy and operates as an independent Catholic university dedicated to the liberal education of its students. The University is accredited by the New England Association of Schools and Colleges and offers baccalaureate and postbaccalaureate degrees in several fields.

Applying

Applicants for master's degree programs must have a bachelor's degree from a regionally accredited college or university. They should submit a completed application along with the appropriate fee, a personal statement, two letters of recommendation, transcripts from all degree-granting institutions the applicant has attended, a transcript evaluation (if transcript is international), and official scores on the MAT, GRE, GMAT, or LSAT. Standardized testing may be waived based on GPA and work experience. Applicants should contact the graduate admissions office for details. Students may also enroll in a maximum of three courses without being formally admitted into the program. Formal admission into a program, however, requires submission of the above materials. There are additional requirements for applicants to the Ph.D. program in the humanities. Interested students should consult the graduate catalog or contact the dean of graduate studies for these additional requirements. Admission into all graduate programs is based on an overall assessment of each candidate, and no specific cut-offs or thresholds are used.

Correspondence and Information

Graduate Admissions
Salve Regina University
100 Ochre Point Avenue
Newport, Rhode Island 02840
Phone: 800-637-0002 (toll-free)
Fax: 401-341-2973
E-mail: graduate_studies@salve.edu
Web site: http://www.salve.edu/graduatestudies/index.html

AREAS OF RESEARCH

ADMINISTRATION OF JUSTICE: The focus of this program is on law enforcement leadership, justice (administration), and homeland security. Using a combination of current law enforcement research methodologies as well as practitioner-based curriculum, the program is designed to assist government agencies in meeting contemporary criminal justice issues. Program Director: Mr. Daniel Knight.

BUSINESS: The research interests of the business studies faculty include, but are not limited to, quality management, environmental management, and organizational development/effectiveness. Business faculty members work on pertinent and current issues including management issues in law enforcement leadership and homeland security. Finally, as global issues remain a key topic in business, the faculty members remain vibrant in the areas of global business and e-commerce (including e-marketing). Program Director: Dr. Myra Edelstein.

HEALTH SERVICES ADMINISTRATION: Quality of life for the elderly, biomedical ethics, nursing administration. Program Director: Dr. Joan Chapdelaine.

HOLISTIC COUNSELING: Psychoneuroimmunology as a means to heal oneself, Gestalt theory and family therapy, human development, expressive arts in healing. Program Director: Dr. Peter Mullen.

HUMANITIES: The meaning and effects of modern technology; mutual relations between art and technology; ethics and technology; human resources and technology; literature and technology; philosophy and technology; religion and technology; interdisciplinary perspective on technology and culture; the meaning and effects of technology in relation to art, religion, ethics, philosophy and history, literature, and social theory. Program Director: Dr. Michael Budd.

INTERNATIONAL RELATIONS: The program's emphasis is in international security and justice, ethnicity, nationalism and conflict, international development, and international criminal justice. The program relies on qualitative research and critical analysis to train graduates to meet the demands of an increasingly challenging international environment. Program Director: Dr. Symeon Giannakos.

REHABILITATION COUNSELING: Disability studies, sociology of disability, disability and employment, disability and inclusive practices, service quality and evaluation, training of direct service personnel. Program Director: Dr. Dimity Peter.

Many of the University's academic and administrative buildings look out on the Atlantic Ocean, guarded by Newport's world-famous Cliff Walk.

A student meets with a faculty member at the front entrance of McAuley Hall.

The McKillop Library has about 250,000 holdings and provides seating for more than 450 students.

Sarah Lawrence College

Programs of Study

Sarah Lawrence College has been a pioneer in several graduate fields, founding three outstanding programs in human genetics (genetic counseling), health advocacy, and women's history that have served as models nationwide. The College also offers master's degrees in areas where it has particular strength: the art of teaching, child development, creative writing, dance, and theater. The College believes in the importance of close and extensive collaboration with the faculty. Many of the graduate programs combine small seminar classes with individual student-faculty conferences. In all programs, opportunity for fieldwork is extensive and varied. Most graduate programs are for two years of full-time study and require 36 course credits. Part-time study may be arranged in all programs, with the exception of dance and theater.

The Art of Teaching Program leads to a Master of Science degree and recommendation for New York State certification in early childhood (birth–grade 2), childhood (grades 1–6), or dual certification (birth–grade 6). Special features of the program include study of child development, observation, and documentation; empirical courses in curriculum planning, with emphasis on language arts, mathematics, science, and social studies; and integration of theory with fieldwork from the first semester. Field placements and student teaching under master teachers are offered at the Sarah Lawrence Early Childhood Center and public schools in Westchester County and New York City.

The Child Development Program leads to an M.A. and is for students who seek in-depth understanding of childhood functioning in the context of contemporary society. Study of theoretical perspectives and research in developmental psychology is integrated with fieldwork experience. The program is unique in its ongoing combination of theory and fieldwork. Graduates of the program are prepared for direct work with young children in a variety of settings, for teaching child development at an intermediate level, or for pursuing more advanced study in psychology and related fields. In fall 2003, Sarah Lawrence College began offering a dual degree (M.A./M.S.W.) with the New York University School of Social Work and its Child Development Master's Program.

The Dance Program leads to an M.F.A. and is based on the premise that dance is a distinctive art form, calling for the integration of body, mind, and spirit. Daily modern and ballet technique classes are required of all graduate students. Basic physical skills, strength, and control are required for the central focus of the program, the creative use of the dance medium. The student is exposed to vital aspects of the art as a performer, creator, and observer, with music as an integral part. The curriculum centers on choreography, dance improvisation, music improvisation, composition, and the teaching of dance. The dance program offers dancers the opportunity to grow under the guidance of an excellent faculty made up of dancers and dance scholars with professional experience in the New York area and abroad.

The Human Genetics (Genetic Counseling) Program and the Health Advocacy Program, each leading to a master's degree, train health professionals devoted to the health concerns of patients. The interdisciplinary curriculum in each program consists of 40 academic course credits and 600 hours of clinical work or other fieldwork. The location of Sarah Lawrence College in the metropolitan New York area offers a rich network of settings—hospitals, clinics, and community agencies—in which on-site supervised training enables students to integrate theoretical knowledge with practice. The faculty includes professionals and academicians drawn from health and medical disciplines. Small classes and close faculty-student interaction offer a productive and stimulating environment for professional growth. Both programs make use of invited speakers, professional workshops, and community involvement to enrich the learning experience and expose students to new developments in the field. A joint degree in human genetics and health advocacy (M.S./M.A.) is also offered.

The Theatre Program leads to the M.F.A. and is based on the principle that learning comes through practical application, personal experience, and intensive workshops. Working with a faculty of New York City theater professionals, students explore playwriting, acting, directing, design, and technical work in small seminars, tutorials, and collaborative projects.

The Women's History Program leads to the M.A. It was the first in the nation to offer graduate study in the field and emphasizes the combination of scholarship and activism. A joint degree program in women's history and law is offered in cooperation with Pace University Law School.

The Writing Program leads to an M.F.A. This program offers an uncommon opportunity for students to develop as poets or creative nonfiction or fiction writers under the close attention of a nationally renowned faculty. At the center of the course of study are four successive seminars that students take during their two years in the program. In addition to the intensive student-faculty discussions in these seminars, students participate in individual conferences with faculty members every two weeks. This unique aspect of the Sarah Lawrence program provides further intensive scrutiny of students' writing and helps them create the substantial body of work needed to fulfill the program's requirements.

Research Facilities

The College's facilities include classrooms, laboratories, a computer center, and a state-of-the-art sports center; a modern library with 202,265 books and 880 periodicals, which is linked by computer to more than 6,000 other libraries; the Performing Arts Center, which consists of two theaters, a dance studio, and a concert hall; a music building, including a music library; a new Science Center; the Early Childhood Center; the Center for Graduate Studies; and the Center for Continuing Education.

Financial Aid

All graduate grants and loans are awarded based on financial need as determined by information provided on the Financial Aid PROFILE and the FAFSA. Applicants with financial need are considered for Sarah Lawrence College gift aid, Federal Perkins Loans, and Federal Stafford Student Loans. Sarah Lawrence College is unable to offer federal financial aid to students who are not citizens or permanent residents of the United States. However, international students may apply for Sarah Lawrence gift aid by filling out the PROFILE. International students are also advised to investigate other financing opportunities offered by their governments or through private institutions.

Cost of Study

Tuition varies according to program. For more information, prospective students should visit http://www.slc.edu/home.php.

Living and Housing Costs

Off-campus single rooms in local homes are available for $400 to $800 per month; sharing an apartment ranges from $400 to $800 per month. The minimum cost for an off-campus apartment in the area is $800 per month. Housing information is available from the Student Affairs Office and the Graduate Studies Office.

Student Group

Sarah Lawrence attracts students who seek a creative education and are eager to take responsibility for it. The College draws its approximately 320 graduate students from forty-nine states and thirty-one countries.

Location

The College is situated in the Bronxville/Yonkers community of Bronxville in southern Westchester County, just 15 miles north of midtown Manhattan in New York City. Highways and a commuter railroad make it possible to reach the city in about 30 minutes, enabling students to take advantage of its social, cultural, and intellectual riches and its internship possibilities.

The College

Founded in 1926, Sarah Lawrence is a small liberal arts college for men and women. It is a lively community of students, scholars, and artists, nationally renowned for its unique academic structure, which combines small classes with individual student-faculty conferences.

Applying

Applicants for graduate studies must have received a B.A. or an equivalent degree from an accredited college or university and have at least a 3.0 grade point average. They should request information on the program that interests them at the College address or by calling the College's telephone number. Applicants are asked to complete an application form and to furnish transcripts of all undergraduate work and two letters of recommendation, preferably from former teachers. Personal interviews may be arranged with the program directors and with the Director of Graduate Studies. The creative writing and the performing arts programs require demonstration of the candidate's ability. GRE scores are not required. Application deadlines vary according to program. The deadline for first consideration is February 1.

Correspondence and Information

Susan Guma
Dean of Graduate Studies
Sarah Lawrence College
1 Mead Way
Bronxville, New York 10708

Phone: 914-395-2371
Fax: 914-395-2664
E-mail: grad@sarahlawrence.edu
Web site: http://www.sarahlawrence.edu

THE FACULTY AND GRADUATE PROGRAM DIRECTORS

Art of Teaching
Sara Wilford, Director; M.S.Ed., M.Ed., Bank Street College of Education.
Mary Hebron, Associate Director; M.A., NYU.
Maggie Martinez DeLuca, M.S.Ed., Bank Street College of Education.
Jan Drucker, Ph.D., NYU.
Margery B. Franklin, Ph.D., Clark.
Linwood Lewis, Ph.D., CUNY.
Kathleen Ruen, Ph.D., NYU.

Child Development
Barbara Schecter, Director; Ph.D., Columbia Teachers College.
Carl Barenboim, Ph.D., Rochester.
Charlotte Doyle, Ph.D., Michigan.
Jan Drucker, Ph.D., NYU.
Jennifer Jipson, Ph.D., California, Santa Cruz.
Elizabeth Johnston, D.Phil., Oxford.
Linwood Lewis, Ph.D., CUNY.
Sara Wilford, M.S.Ed., M.Ed., Bank Street College of Education.

Dance
Sara Rudner, Director; M.F.A., Bennington.
Emmy Devine, B.A., Connecticut College.
Dan Hurlin, B.A., Sarah Lawrence.
Rose Anne Thom, B.A., McGill.
John Yannelli, M.F.A., Sarah Lawrence.

Health Advocacy
Laura Weil, Interim Director; M.A., Sarah Lawrence.
Peter S. Arno, Ph.D., New School.
Bruce Berg, Associate Professor and Chair, Department of Political Science at Fordham University; Ph.D., American.
Sayantani DasGupta, M.D./M.P.H., Johns Hopkins.
Rachel Grob, M.A., Sarah Lawrence.
Catherine M. Handy, Ph.D., NYU.
Alice Herb, J.D., LL.M., NYU.
Margaret Keller, J.D., M.S., Columbia.
Laura Long, M.S., Sarah Lawrence.
Terry Mizrahi, M.S.W., Columbia; Ph.D., Virginia.
Constance Peterson, M.A., Sarah Lawrence.

Human Genetics
Caroline Lieber, Director; M.S., Sarah Lawrence.
James W. Speer, Associate Director; M.S., Sarah Lawrence.
Jessica Davis, Director of Clinical Training; M.D., Columbia.
Jacob Canick, Ph.D., Brandeis.
Susanne Carter, M.S., Sarah Lawrence.
Peggy Cottrell, M.S., Sarah Lawrence.
Sayanti Dasgupta, M.D./Ph.D., Johns Hopkins.
Siobhan Dolan, M.D., Harvard.
Judith Durcan, M.S., Sarah Lawrence.
Marvin Frankel, Ph.D., Chicago.
Eva Bostein Griepp, M.D., NYU.
Susan Gross, M.D., Toronto.
Alice Herb, J.D., LL.M., NYU.
Laura Hercher, M.S., Sarah Lawrence.
Judith Hull, M.S., Sarah Lawrence.
David Kronn, M.D., Trinity College, Dublin.
Sharon LaVigne, M.S., Sarah Lawrence.
Laura Long, M.S., Sarah Lawrence.
Robert Marion, M.D., Yeshiva (Einstein).
Diana Punales Morejon, M.S., Sarah Lawrence.
Sally Nolin, Ph.D., SUNY Health Science Center at Brooklyn.
Elsa Reich, M.S., Sarah Lawrence.
Michael J. Smith, D.S.W., Columbia.
Jennifer Scalia Wilbur, M.S., Sarah Lawrence.

Theater
John Dillon, Director; M.F.A., Columbia (Danforth and Woodrow Wilson Fellow).
William D. McRee, Administrator; M.F.A., Sarah Lawrence.
Ernest Abuba, Member, Ensemble Studio Theatre; Rockefeller Foundation Fellowship.
Paul Austin, B.S., Emerson.
Edward Allen Baker, B.A., Rhode Island.
Lynn Book, M.F.A., Art Institute of Chicago.
Kevin Confoy, B.A., Rutgers.
Michael Early, M.F.A., Yale.
June Ekman, B.A., Goddard; ACAT, Alexander Technique.
Christine Farrell, M.F.A., Columbia.
Nancy Franklin, Member, Actors Studio and Ensemble Studio Theatre.
Dan Hurlin, B.A., Sarah Lawrence.
Chris Jones, M.F.A., Carnegie Mellon.
Shirley Kaplan, A.A., Briarcliff, Academie de la Grande Chaumiere (Paris).
Doug MacHugh, M.F.A., Sarah Lawrence.
Greg MacPherson, B.A., Vermont.
John McCormack, B.A., Hamilton.
Cassandra Medley, Michigan.
Kym Moore, M.F.A., Massachusetts Amherst.
Carol Ann Pelletier, B.A., Brandeis.
Paul Rudd, B.A., Fairfield.
Fanchon Miller Scheier, M.F.A., Sarah Lawrence.
James Shearwood, M.A., Smith.
Stuart Spencer, B.A., Sarah Lawrence.
Sterling Swann, B.A., Vassar.
John Yannelli, M.F.A., Sarah Lawrence.

Writing/Creative Nonfiction
Vijay Seshadri, Director; M.F.A., Columbia.
Gerald Albarelli.
Jo Ann Beard, M.A., Iowa.
Rachel Cohen, A.B., Harvard.
Stephen O'Connor, M.A., Berkeley.
Penny Wolfson, M.F.A., Sarah Lawrence.

Writing/Fiction
Mary La Chapelle, Director; M.F.A., Vermont.
Jo Ann Beard, M.F.A., Iowa.
Melvin Jules Bukiet, M.F.A., Columbia.
Carolyn Ferrell, M.A., CUNY, City College.
Myra Goldberg, M.A., CUNY Graduate Center.
Joshua Henkin, M.F.A., Michigan.
Amy Hempel.
Kathleen Hill, Ph.D., Wisconsin.
William Melvin Kelley, Writer; Harvard.
Ernesto Mestre, B.A., Tulane.
Mary Morris, Director; M.Phil., Columbia.
Brian Morton, B.A., Sarah Lawrence.
Victoria Redel, M.F.A., Iowa.
Lucy Rosenthal, M.F.A., Yale.
Joan Silber, M.A., NYU.

Writing/Poetry
Kate Knapp Johnson, Director; M.F.A., Sarah Lawrence.
Laure-Anne Bosselaar, M.F.A., National Institute for Performing Arts (Belgium).
Kurt Brown, M.A., Colorado.
Tina Chang, M.F.A., Columbia.
Suzanne Gardinier, M.F.A., Columbia.
Matthea Harvey, M.F.A., Iowa.
Cathy Park Hong, M.F.A., Columbia.
Marie Howe, M.F.A., Columbia.
Joan Larkin, M.A., Arizona.
Thomas Lux, B.A., Emerson; University of Iowa Writers Workshop.
Dennis Nurkse, B.A., Harvard.
Kevin Pilkington, M.A., Georgetown.
Victoria Redel, M.F.A., Iowa.
Vijay Seshadri, M.F.A., Columbia.

Women's History
Priscilla Murolo, Director; Ph.D., Yale. U.S. labor history.
Tara James, Associate Director; M.A., Sarah Lawrence.
Eileen Ka-may Cheng, Ph.D., Yale. Nineteenth-century America, with a focus on intellectual and political history.
Rachel Cohen, A.B., Harvard.
Lyde Cullen Sizer, Ph.D., Brown. Women's literary cultures, American popular culture, the American Civil War.
K. Komozi Woodard, Ph.D., Pennsylvania. African American history and culture, with emphasis on the black freedom movement, American urban history, and ghetto formation.

Affiliate Faculty in Women's History
Julie Abraham, Lesbian and Gay Studies.
Bella Brodzki, Literature.
Isabel De Sena, Spanish/Literature.
Mary Dillard, History.
Marsha Hurst, Health Advocacy.
Judith Kicinski, Literature.
Arnold Krupat, Literature.
Chikwenye Ogunyemi, Literature.
David Peritz, Political Science.
Mary Porter, Anthropology.
Marilyn Power, Economics.
Kasturi Ray, Global Studies.
Sandra Robinson, Asian Studies.
Judith Rodenbeck, Art History.
Shahnaz Rouse, Sociology.
Barbara Schecter, Psychology.
Pauline Watts, History.
Matilde Zimmermann, History.

The College is set on a 35-acre campus reminiscent of a rural English village.

SCHOOL FOR INTERNATIONAL TRAINING

Graduate and Professional Programs

Programs of Study

School for International Training (SIT), the higher education institution of World Learning, offers master's programs in language teaching (M.A.T.) and in intercultural service, leadership, and management (M.A. in conflict transformation, M.A. in international education (on-campus and low-residency options), M.A. in social justice in intercultural relations, M.A. in sustainable development, M.S. in management, and M.A. in intercultural service, leadership, and management). SIT also offers a variety of programs for working professionals who wish to enhance their careers and accelerate their professional development through distance education, low-residency options (Graduate Certificate in International Education), graduate or continuing education programs, short courses, and summer classes.

The academic programs that lead to the intercultural service, leadership, and management degrees develop the intercultural, managerial, and training skills necessary for careers in international and intercultural management. SIT alumni work in the fields of sustainable development, exchange management, global education, international student advising, cross-cultural training, and refugee relief. The program is based on the college's philosophy of learning through experience. It combines on-campus academic study with a minimum six-month professional-level internship and concludes with a capstone seminar. The organization that provides the internship can be located anywhere in the world and should be appropriate to the student's area of professional interest. Course work focuses on project management, development administration, training and organizational development, intercultural communication, and leadership and managerial skills.

With a focus on applied classroom practice, the academic program that leads to the M.A.T. degree is designed to prepare its graduates for a successful and effective career in language teaching. Concentrations offered are teaching English to speakers of other languages (TESOL), French, and Spanish, and the program can be taken as a one-academic-year program or in a two-summer format designed for working teachers. U.S. public school certification is available.

In the one-year program, the teaching internship, supervised by program faculty members during the winter quarter, is a period of rapid professional growth as the student is called upon to put theory into practice in the classroom and to make individual choices regarding teaching styles and approaches. The practical focus of the program serves to equip graduates to achieve a high professional standing in their field. Internship sites in the U.S. are located primarily in New England; overseas sites include Mexico, Morocco, Costa Rica, Haiti, Thailand, and South Africa. Students in the academic-year format are eligible for public school certification in ESL after a second teaching internship during the fall following the course work.

The Summer M.A.T. Program consists of two 8-week sessions in consecutive summers, with the teaching practicum supervised by program faculty members during the intervening year. This format brings together experienced TESOL, French, and Spanish teachers from all over the world who can earn the M.A.T. degree without taking time off from their jobs. The public school certification programs in French and Spanish feature an international field study and homestay and are completed in two summers, with an academic year of course work in between.

Research Facilities

The college's Donald B. Watt Library includes a specialized collection of some 30,000 volumes and 400 periodical titles and is supported by an interlibrary loan network. The library's reading and study areas are open 24 hours a day. The library also has various electronic and online databases that provide in-depth abstracting and indexing of more than 100,000 articles, journals, directories, and reports.

Financial Aid

The college participates in all federally sponsored financial aid programs, including the Federal Perkins Loan, Federal Work-Study, and Federal Stafford Student Loan programs. Institutional grants and scholarships are also offered. Financial aid is awarded based on need, with a few specific merit scholarships offered. Restricted scholarships are available for returned Peace Corps volunteers; staff members from development management, refugee assistance, population control, and exchange organizations; and members of minority groups.

Cost of Study

The total tuition and fees for graduate programs for the 2006–07 academic year were $27,000 for intercultural service, leadership, and management students and $24,770 for M.A.T. students. Summer M.A.T. students pay half their tuition each summer; the total is $25,138.

Living and Housing Costs

The 2006–07 on-campus room and board costs for intercultural service, leadership, and management students were $9017. For M.A.T. students, costs were $7716; summer M.A.T. students pay $2357 per summer. All costs depend on accommodations and length of enrollment in the program.

Student Group

The student body of the college is diverse, with an annual enrollment of about 300 students, who range in age from 20 to 45 or older. A typical group may include students from more than thirty countries and many regions of the United States, representing half a dozen basic language groups. The composition of the student body gives the campus a multicultural character that complements the academic programs. Many students have had extensive work experience, often in another culture, and are returning to school to acquire skills to help them advance professionally or change careers.

Location

School for International Training is located in Brattleboro, in southeastern Vermont. By car, Brattleboro is about 2 hours from Boston and 4 hours from New York City and Montreal. Skiing, hiking, canoeing, and climbing can be enjoyed nearby. In addition, the area is a center for a thriving arts community that includes the Brattleboro Music Center, the Yellow Barn Music Festival, the Marlboro Summer Music Festival, numerous community theater and dance groups, visual artists, and fine craftsmen.

The School

Established in 1964, School for International Training is an accredited college specializing in developing individual and institutional capacities for responsible leadership in global and local contexts. It began in 1932 as the Experiment in International Living and remains one of the oldest international education service organizations in the world.

SIT came into its own in the 1960s shortly after the Experiment provided the original language and culture training for the U.S. Peace Corps. In fact, through a special arrangement, SIT graduate programs continue to offer students the opportunity to combine Peace Corps service with other degree requirements.

Accredited by the New England Association of Schools and Colleges, SIT is a global leader in language education, intercultural training, human resource development, policy advocacy, conflict mediation, and nongovernmental organization (NGO) partnership and management.

SIT also maintains two centers for on-campus research, training, and project management: the Center for Professional Development and the Center for Teacher Education, Training and Research.

In addition to offering graduate degrees, SIT administers study-abroad programs (for credit) in more than forty countries for undergraduate students enrolled in other colleges and universities.

Applying

Application forms for admission and financial aid are available through the Admissions Office and also on the Web at http://www.sit.edu. Applications are accepted throughout the year; admission decisions are made on a rolling basis upon completion of the student's file. Applications must be accompanied by a $50 nonrefundable application fee. GRE scores are not required.

Correspondence and Information

Graduate and Professional Studies Admissions
School for International Training
Kipling Road
P.O. Box 676
Brattleboro, Vermont 05302-0676

Phone: 802-258-3510
800-336-1616 (toll-free within the U.S.)
Fax: 802-258-3500
E-mail: admissions@sit.edu
Web site: http://www.sit.edu

THE FACULTY

Master of Arts in Teaching
Lauren Alderfer, Ph.D.
Marti Anderson, Ph.D.
Francis Bailey, Ed.D.
Susan Barduhn, Ph.D.
Janis Birdsall, M.A.T.
Carmen Carracelas-Juncal, Ph.D.
Sean Conley, M.A.T.
William Conley, M.A.T.
Alvino Fantini, Ph.D.
Beatriz Fantini, M.A.T.
Donald Freeman, Ph.D.
Kathleen Graves, Ph.D.
Anne Katz, Ph.D.
Diane Larsen-Freeman, Ph.D.
Paul Levasseur, Ed.D.
Bonnie Mennell, M.A.T.
Patrick Moran, Ph.D.
Thomas Santos, M.A.T.
Alex Silverman, Ph.D.
Elizabeth Tannenbaum, M.A.T.
Elka Todeva, Ph.D.
Leslie Turpin, Ph.D.
Ronald White, M.A.
Tessa Woodward, M.Phil.

Master of International and Intercultural Management
Kanthie Athukorala, Ed.D.
Karen Blanchard, Ph.D.
James Breeden, Ed.D.
Charlie Curry-Smithson, Ph.D.
Mohammed Golam Samdani Fakir, Ph.D.
Sora Friedman, Ph.D.
Linda Drake Gobbo, M.Ed., M.B.A.
Paula Green, Ed.D.
Claire Halverson, Ph.D.
William Hoffa, Ph.D.
Maliha Khan, M.Sc.
Nikoi Kote-Nikoi, Ph.D.
Ralph Meima, Ph.D.
Janaki Natarajan, Ed.D.
Richard Rodman, Ph.D.
David Shallenberger, Ph.D.
Suzanne Simon, Ph.D.
Marla Solomon, Ed.D.
Syed Aqeel Tirmizi, Ph.D.
John Ungerleider, Ed.D.
Jeff Unsicker, Ph.D.
Ryland White, M.I.A.
Kenneth Williams, M.A., M.S.

Representing more than thirty-five countries, students in SIT's graduate and professional programs learn the theory and practice of responsible global citizenship on the School's idyllic 220-acre campus in southern Vermont.

SCHOOL OF VISUAL ARTS

Graduate Programs

Programs of Study

In 1983, the School of Visual Arts (SVA) introduced its first graduate offering, a Master of Fine Arts (M.F.A.) program in painting, drawing, and sculpture. Since that time, SVA has added eight more graduate programs: art criticism and writing, art education, art therapy, computer art, design, digital photography, illustration as visual essay, and photography, video, and related media. Each of these highly individual professional degree programs shares certain important characteristics that reflect the School of Visual Arts' unique approach to the education of artists.

The program in fine arts focuses on training students whose primary interest is the making of art. The program in art criticism and writing examines the visual arts within a philosophical and historical framework and incorporates intensive study in the writing of art criticism. The M.A.T. in art education offers rigorous academic study coupled with requisite teaching experience, which provides graduates with the essential knowledge and tools to teach art to children. The M.P.S. in art therapy curriculum examines a variety of approaches to the diagnosis and therapeutic treatment of challenged individuals while supporting the artistic development and creative endeavors of the artist-as-therapist. The College's program in computer art was the first in the country to base graduate training in computer art primarily upon the aesthetic concerns of this field. SVA's program in design perceives the designer not merely as a form giver but as a content creator; design is seen as more than the reorganization of existing elements. The M.P.S. program in digital photography is a concentrated one-year program focused on mastering the most current digital tools, techniques, and workflow strategies to create technically perfect and visually compelling photographic images. The program in illustration is predicated upon radical departure from the accepted methods of making illustration and focuses on the development of a strong personal vision. The program in photography seeks to develop individual talent within traditional and digital photography while investigating the impact of computer, film, and video technologies on the visual culture.

Research Facilities

SVA's location in New York City, extensive facilities, state-of-the-art equipment, faculty of professionals dedicated to excellence in the arts, and unique program philosophies offer graduate students the best opportunities for advanced study in the arts. SVA provides students the opportunity to exhibit their art in a number of campus galleries and in a professional gallery in Chelsea. The Offices of Career Development and Alumni Affairs provide resources for networking and job opportunities. In addition to networked studio environments and private graduate painting and sculpture studios, the campus features buildings dedicated to photography and sculpture. SVA has digital imaging and output centers and a commitment to maintaining technology that meets industry standards. Another invaluable resource to SVA students is the professional faculty members, who work to prepare graduates to meet the challenges of the industry. The Visual Arts Library maintains distinctive multimedia collections; a growing collection of books, periodicals, picture files, slides, exhibition catalogs, film scripts, and videos; and other materials.

Financial Aid

The School of Visual Arts offers scholarships and other financial aid based upon need and merit. Approximately 74 percent of students receive some sort of aid. The School of Visual Arts uses federal, state, and institutional guidelines to determine student need. The Office of Financial Aid is able to provide more information on need-based assistance. Students interested in financial aid are required to file the Free Application for Federal Student Aid (FAFSA).

Cost of Study

For the academic year 2007–08, the tuition fee for the art criticism and writing, art therapy, computer art, fine arts, illustration as visual essay, and photography, video, and related media programs is $26,120. Tuition for the design program is $28,900. Tuition for the digital photography program is $28,710. Tuition for the three-semester program in art education, including summer semester, is $31,340. Departmental fees range from $250 to $1200.

Living and Housing Costs

Housing costs range from $8500 to $14,500 for the 2007–08 academic year. The estimated cost for personal expenses for the nine-month academic year is $16,000.

Student Group

SVA has a full-time enrollment of approximately 3,000 undergraduate and 400 graduate students.

Student Outcomes

The thoroughly professional orientation of the graduate programs is reflected in the internationally renowned faculty. Ultimately, it is the extraordinary caliber of the faculty members with whom the graduate student works that makes the realization of personal goals and the development of personal vision possible. Students and graduates of SVA have had gallery exhibitions of their artwork and work published in newspapers, magazines, and a variety of print media. Graduates have also held internships with major multimedia, telecommunications, and production facilities in addition to winning numerous art awards nationally and abroad.

Location

Located in the heart of New York City, SVA offers students the opportunity to become involved in one of America's largest and most vibrant cities, the art and design capital of the world. The energy, the spirit, and the desire to be the best that characterize New York City constantly challenge and inspire students. The unparalleled leadership and accomplishment of the city's arts and design communities demand excellence, and the School of Visual Arts prepares students to compete successfully in this environment.

The School

Students who choose SVA are often attracted by the breadth and professional standing of the faculty members, the passion of the student body, the rigors of the curriculum, the industry standards within the studio facilities, and the energy and excitement that is New York City.

Applying

Applicants to the graduate degree program must have a bachelor's degree from a regionally accredited college or university or an equivalent diploma from a four-year professional art school. Applicants to the M.P.S. program in art therapy are required to have completed 12 credits in specific areas of psychology and 18 credits in studio art. Applicants to the M.A.T. program in art education are required to have completed a minimum of 30 credits in studio art (or to demonstrate an equivalent level of skill in visual art), a minimum of 12 credits in art history, and course work in a language other than English. Applicants must complete and submit all application requirements no later than February 1.

Correspondence and Information

Adam Rogers, Director of Admissions
School of Visual Arts
209 East 23rd Street
New York, New York 10010

Phone: 212-592-2100
800-436-4204 (toll-free)
Fax: 212-592-2116
E-mail: gradadmissions@sva.edu
Web site: http://www.sva.edu

THE FACULTY

Since the School of Visual Arts brings working professionals to its faculty, the 800 members comprise practicing artists, filmmakers, designers, and photographers. As a result of using working professionals to teach, the college has been able to attract some of the most prominent artists in New York.

M.A.T. Art Criticism and Writing
Thomas McEvilley, Chair
Suzanne Anker
William Beckley
Susan Bee
Roger Denson
Thyrza Nichols Goodeve
Tom Huhn
Donald Kuspit
Raphael Rubinstein
Mira Schor

M.A.T. Art Education
Rose Viggiano, Chair
Andrew Bencsko III
Sandra Edmonds
Michael Filan
Jerry M. James
Jo-Ann Wyke Hamilton
Barbara Salander
Natalie J. Schifano
Lynn Seeney
Virginia S. Stolarski

M.P.S. Art Therapy
Deborah Farber, Chair
Claudia Bader
Ted E. Becker Jr.
Irene Rosner David
Michael Fisher
Lisa Furman
Stephanie Gorski
Robert Abel Grant
Markus J. Kraebber
Eileen McGann
Basia Mosinski
Renee Obstfeld
Meagan O'Connell
Elaine Rapp
Anne Reilly
Valerie Sereno
Raquel Chapin Stephenson

M.F.A. Computer Art
Bruce Wands, Chair
Victor Acevedo
Timothy J. Anderson
Mike Barron
Ed Bowes
Kathy Brew
Todd Brous
Kevin Brownie
Yaron Canetti
Robert V. Cavaleri
Andy Deck
Joseph Dellinger
Sharon Denning
Carl Edwards
Joseph Ferrari
Peter Gluck
Thyrza Nichols Goodeve
Edgar David Grana
Christine Heun
Julia Heyward
In Pyo Hong
Mary Lynn Kirby
Russet Lederman
Barbara London
Jarryd Lowder
Gerald Marks
Nikita Mikros
Joseph Nechvatal
Christiane Paul
Kurt Ralske
Steve Rittler
Gae Savannah
Mathew Schlanger
Richard Shupe
Loretta Skeddle
Satre Stuelke
Grahame Weinbren
David Weisman

M.F.A. Design
Steven Heller, Co-chair
Lita Talarico, Co-chair
Gail Anderson
Randy Balsmeyer
Laurene Leon Boym
Nicholas Callaway
Brian Collins
Milton Glaser
Dorothy Twining Globus
Martin Kace
Maira Kalman
Warren Lehrer
Frank Martinez
Kevin T O'Callaghan
Howard W. Reeves
Stefan Sagmeister
Jeff Scher
Steven Schwartz
Bonnie Siegler
Scott Stowell
Alice Twemlow
Véronique Vienne

M.P.S. Digital Photography
Katrin Eismann, Chair
Thomas P. Ashe
David McLain
Chris Murphy
Jack Reznicki
Matthew B. Richmond
Kate Schaffer
Chris Tarantino

M.F.A. Fine Arts
David L. Shirey, Chair
Polly Apfelbaum
Perry Bard
Jake Berthot
Sam Cady
Dan Cameron
Petah Coyne
Kenji Fujita
Johan Grimonprez
Will Insley
Thomas Lanigan-Schmidt
Michelle Lopez
Suzanne McClelland
Marilyn Minter
Lucio Pozzi
James Siena
Gary Stephan
Julianne Swartz
Sarah Sze
Jacqueline Winsor

M.F.A. Illustration as Visual Essay
Marshall Arisman, Chair
N. C. Christopher Couch
Gregory Crane
Carol Fabricatore
Mikro Ilić
Viktor Koen
Matthew B. Richmond
David Sandlin
Carl Titolo
Mary Jo Vath
Michele Zackheim

M.F.A. Photography, Video, and Related Media
Charles Traub, Chair
Suzanne Anker
Shimon Attie
Robert Bowen
Ed Bowes
Chris Callis
Sarah Charlesworth
Charlotte Cotton
Yolanda Cuomo
Nancy Davenport
Liz Deschenes
Katrin Eismann
Marvin Heiferman
W. M. Hunt
Stephen Jablonsky
Ken Kobland
Richard Leslie
Paola Mieli
Andrew Moore
Mary M. Patierno
Philip Perkis
Nicholas Prior
Shelley Rice
Collier Schorr
Shelly Silver
Mark Stafford
Amy Taubin
Penelope Umbrico
Oliver Wasow
Grahame Weinbren
Jeff Weiss
Randy West
Sylvia Wolf
Bonnie Yochelson

SETON HILL UNIVERSITY

Graduate Programs

Programs of Study

Seton Hill University offers graduate programs in art therapy, business, genocide and holocaust studies, elementary and special education, inclusive education, instructional design, marriage and family therapy, physician assistant studies, and writing popular fiction.

The Master of Arts in Art Therapy with a specialization in counseling, approved by the American Art Therapy Association, is designed to teach students the theory and skills necessary for the effective practice of visual and verbal therapy in a variety of therapeutic settings.

The Master of Business Administration, accredited by the International Assembly for Collegiate Business Education, is designed to create a learning community committed to the study of both management theories and contemporary business practice. Students may choose to specialize in either entrepreneurship or management.

The Genocide and Holocaust Studies Program, developed with the support of the National Catholic Center for Holocaust Education, Seton Hill's graduate and international studies programs, and Seton Hill's Humanities Division, is a graduate certificate program.

Certification is simultaneously available in some options of the Master of Arts in elementary education and the Master of Arts in special education programs for those students with no previous background in teaching. The curricula for both education degrees meet the standards for certification established by the Pennsylvania Department of Education.

Master of Arts in Inclusive Education program is designed to expand teachers' skills to meet the demands of an ever-changing profession by preparing teachers for the present and the future by teaching them to adapt teaching methods to include students with a range of cognitive, affective, and physical disabilities in the learning process. This program is offered online.

The Master of Education in Instructional Design program offers advanced study for professionals in education, instruction, training, and development in a variety of settings. Professionals learn how to integrate technology into their teaching and training, whether in the classroom or in business. Specializations include classroom technology, workplace training, and instructional technology, which can lead to Pennsylvania certification as an instructional technology specialist. This program is offered online.

The Master of Arts in Marriage and Family Therapy program, which has been granted candidacy status by the American Association for Marriage and Family Therapy, is designed to expose students to the theory, practice, and research in psychology through a systems lens.

The Master of Science in Physician Assistant Studies program is fully accredited by the Accreditation Review Commission on Education for the Physician Assistant (ARC-PA). This 99-credit program qualifies students to complete 80 percent of the duties commonly handled by primary-care physicians.

The Master of Arts in Writing Popular Fiction program is one of the only programs in the country that teaches writers to produce fiction that sells and that reaches a wide audience—mysteries, romance, fantasy, horror, young adult literature, women's fiction, children's literature, and science fiction.

Research Facilities

Reeves Memorial Library serves as the University's information center. In the library, access to information is made convenient through an automated catalog, and online resources, such as EBSCOhost and LexisNexis. Wireless connectivity, a coffee bar, and comfortable study areas make it an inviting place for students. In addition, students have access to thirteen Pentium labs, a Power Mac lab, a multimedia lab, and a Silicon Graphics lab. All students receive an Internet account for e-mail, navigating the Web, and conducting research.

Financial Aid

An institutional scholar's discount, loan opportunities, and graduate-assistant opportunities are currently available to make education at Seton Hill University more affordable. For those students who prefer to pay the University bill in monthly installments, Seton Hill offers a tuition payment plan.

Cost of Study

Tuition for the 2007–08 academic year is $655 per semester hour. The tuition for the 2007–08 academic year is $695 per semester hour for the physician assistant program. A one-time application fee of $35 is also charged. Fees include a technology fee of $100 per semester, a graduation fee of $75, and a project-binding fee of $60. Books and supplies range from approximately $100 to $200 per course.

Living and Housing Costs

Room and board costs for the 2007–08 academic year range from $3870 to $4985 per semester. Room and board costs for the 2007 summer semester were $275 per week. Nightly room charges are $50. Parking permits are $70 per year.

Student Group

As of the spring 2007 semester, there were 357 graduate students enrolled at the University—35 art therapy students, 33 in elementary education, 9 in inclusive education, 37 in special education, 86 in business administration, 63 in writing popular fiction, 36 in marriage and family therapy, 12 in instructional design, and 46 in physician assistant studies. One hundred sixty-one of these students are full-time, while 196 students are enrolled on a part-time basis. Women comprise 281 of the total number of graduate students.

Location

Seton Hill University's 200-acre campus is located in Greensburg, Pennsylvania, which is easily accessible by car, train, or plane. Just 35 miles east of Pittsburgh, Greensburg enjoys all the advantages of a large city while maintaining a small-town atmosphere. The seat of Westmoreland County, Greensburg is home to the Westmoreland Museum of American Art, the Westmoreland Symphony Orchestra, Ohio Pyle recreation center, and Seven Springs ski resort.

The University

Seton Hill is a Catholic liberal arts university with a total enrollment of 1,700 students.

The graduate programs in Elementary Education and Art Therapy began in 1995. The Special Education program began in 1997. The Business Administration and Writing Popular Fiction programs were first offered in 1998. The Marriage and Family Therapy program began in 1999. The Instructional Design program began in 2000. The Physician Assistant Studies program became a master's degree program in 2004. The Inclusive Education and the Genocide and Holocaust Studies programs began in 2007.

Applying

All programs require a completed application and fee, official transcripts from all colleges and universities attended, three recommendation forms, and a current resume. In addition, the master's/certificate programs in genocide and holocaust studies, writing popular fiction, business administration, art therapy, instructional design, and marriage and family therapy require a letter of intent. The writing popular fiction program requires a writing sample. The art therapy program requires an art portfolio of fifteen to twenty slides. Admission to the education programs requires a copy of any teaching certification held. The physician assistant studies program requires students to apply online at http://www.caspaonline.org.

All nonnative English speakers are required to take the TOEFL. All international transcripts must be accompanied by a World Education Services (WES) evaluation.

Correspondence and Information

Christine E. Schaeffer, M.B.A.
Director of Graduate and Adult Studies
Seton Hill University
Seton Hill Drive
Greensburg, Pennsylvania 15601-1599

Phone: 724-838-4221
800-826-6234 (toll-free)
Fax: 724-830-1891
E-mail: gadmit@setonhill.edu
Web site: http://www.setonhill.edu

THE FACULTY

Students should visit the Seton Hill University Web site for a complete listing of the University's faculty members (http://www.setonhill.edu).

SHIPPENSBURG UNIVERSITY OF PENNSYLVANIA

School of Graduate Studies

Programs of Study

Shippensburg University of Pennsylvania offers programs of study leading to master's degrees (M.A., M.B.A., M.Ed., M.P.A., M.S., and M.S.W.) in administration of justice, applied history, biology, business administration, communication studies, computer science, counseling, curriculum and instruction, educational leadership and policy, geoenvironmental studies, information systems, organizational development and leadership, public administration, psychology, reading, social work, and special education. Students may also pursue postgraduate-level supervisory and certification credentials.

Research Facilities

The Ezra Lehman Memorial Library houses more than 1.8 million items and provides access to electronic resources, including books and articles, which are accessible from students' personal computers 24 hours a day. Via the Keystone Library and Pennsylvania Academic Library networks, students can access the collections of sixty academic libraries. The University maintains two general-purpose microcomputer laboratories (open 24 hours a day) and nineteen labs that have department- or major-specific software. The Center for Applied Research and Policy Analysis, the Center for Education and Human Services, the Center for Interdisciplinary Science, the Frehn-Center for Professional and Organizational Development, the Center for Juvenile Justice Training and Research, and the Center for Local and State Government offer students research opportunities in addition to department research projects.

Financial Aid

Graduate assistantships are awarded on a competitive basis without regard to financial need. They provide a tuition waiver as well as compensation on an hourly scale for work performed. Graduate assistants are required to work 250 hours during the semester and 150 hours during the summer. Applications should be filed by March 1. Residence director (RD) positions are available, with preference given to students enrolled in the counseling and college student personnel program. The RD position is a twelve-month appointment, compensated with a salary and a free apartment and meal plan. RDs also receive a tuition waiver for 6 credits per semester and 3 credits per summer. The University is approved for training veterans and administers a range of loan programs. Funds are available to support student research and attendance at professional meetings to present papers.

Cost of Study

Tuition for 2006–07 was $336 per credit hour for in-state students and $538 per credit hour for out-of-state students. Students also paid an educational services fee of $27 per credit hour. A health services fee of $85 and a technology fee of $62.50 are charged to full-time students. The technology fee for out-of-state students is $94. The student union fee is $102 for full-time students and $51 for those attending part-time.

Living and Housing Costs

Off-campus housing is available to graduate students during the fall and spring semesters. For information, students should visit the Web site at http://www.ship.edu/~deanstu/offcampus/. Housing is available on campus during the summer sessions. For summer housing information, students should contact the Dean of Students' office (phone: 717-477-1164; e-mail: deanstu@ship.edu). Various meal plans are available, including Flex Accounts, which can be used like cash in any of the campus dining locations.

Student Group

The University enrolls more than 1,000 graduate students and 6,500 undergraduate students. Most graduate students are part-time (78 percent) and women (69 percent). Graduate students represent various ethnicities, states, and countries. A Graduate Student Association Board represents the academic and social interests of graduate students. Student services include on-site day care, Women's Center, Multicultural Student Affairs, and Counseling Center.

Location

Shippensburg University is located in the Cumberland Valley of south-central Pennsylvania, 40 miles southwest of Harrisburg. It is easily accessible from exits 24 northward and 29 south of Interstate 81 and the Blue Mountain and Carlisle interchanges of the Pennsylvania Turnpike.

The University

Founded in 1871, Shippensburg is consistently rated as one of the best universities in the Northeast. Shippensburg has offered graduate education since 1959 and is one of fourteen universities in the Pennsylvania State System of Higher Education.

Applying

Applicants must present a bachelor's degree from an accredited college or university and an official transcript. In addition, some academic departments may require an interview, additional test scores, goal statements, or letters of recommendation. The application fee is $30. Students may apply and check the status of their application online at http://www.ship.edu/admiss/graduate/index.html.

Correspondence and Information

Office of Graduate Admissions
Shippensburg University
1871 Old Main Drive
Shippensburg, Pennsylvania 17257-2299
Phone: 717-477-1213
800-822-8028 (toll-free)
Fax: 717-477-4016
E-mail: admiss@ship.edu
Web site: http://www.ship.edu/admiss/graduate/index.html

THE FACULTY

Dean of Graduate Studies: Tracy A. Schoolcraft, Ph.D., Penn State.
Dean of Extended Studies: Anthony S. Winter, D.Ed., Penn State.
Dean of Enrollment Services: Thomas W. Speakman, Ed.D., Widener.
Administration of Justice: Robert M. Freeman, Ph.D., Maryland.
Applied History: David F. Godshalk, Ph.D., Yale.
Biology: Gregory Paulson, Ph.D., Washington State.
Business Administration: Robert Rollins, Ed.D., Penn State.
Communication Studies: Ted Carlin, Ph.D., Bowling Green State.
Computer Science and Information Systems: Carol Wellington, Ph.D., North Carolina State.
Counseling and College Student Personnel: Jan Arminio, Ph.D., Maryland.
Curriculum and Instruction, Reading, Special Education: Elizabeth Vaughn, Ph.D., South Florida.
Educational Leadership and Policy: Nancy Stankus, D.Ed., Penn State.
Geoenvironmental Studies: William Blewett, Ph.D., Michigan State.
Organizational Development and Leadership: Barbara Denison, Ph.D., Northwestern.
Psychology: Suzanne Morin, Ph.D., Connecticut.
Public Administration: Niel Brasher, Ph.D., American.
Social Work: Deb Jacobs, Ph.D., Brandeis.

SLIPPERY ROCK UNIVERSITY OF PENNSYLVANIA

Graduate School

Programs of Study

Slippery Rock University offers the Master of Arts degree in community counseling, English, history, and student affairs in higher education; the Master of Science degree in park and resource management, sport management, and sustainable systems (agroecology, built environment/energy management, permaculture, and sustainable resource management); the Master of Education degree in elementary education (elementary school mathematics/science and reading), physical education, school counseling, secondary education (mathematics/science), and special education (master teacher, mentally and physically handicapped, and supervision); the Master of Science in Nursing degree (nurse educator and nurse practitioner studies); and the Doctor of Physical Therapy degree. The physical therapy program takes 113 hours and requires eight semesters (which includes two summers) for completion.

Except for the physical therapy program, two semesters compose the academic year; summer sessions are arranged in one 3-week presession, two 5-week sessions, and one 7-week evening term. Up to 12 semester hours of graduate credit from an accredited institution may be transferred into most master's programs.

Research Facilities

More than 700,000 volumes, along with an extensive microfiche collection and major professional journals and newspapers, are housed in the Bailey Library. A large reference collection, including bibliographies, indexes, and abstracts, is available. A comprehensive materials center and an audiovisual center are also located in the library. One of the largest computer centers in western Pennsylvania is operated by the University. Slippery Rock University is part of a Marine Science Consortium with research facilities at Wallops Island in Virginia. In addition, the University operates a biology station at nearby Moraine State Park, is affiliated with the McKeever Environmental Learning Center near Sandy Lake, and owns 60 acres for environmental studies and research. Scanning and transmission electron microscopes, greenhouses, the Outdoor Recreational Instruction Laboratory, a planetarium, IBM and Apple computer laboratories, and modern equipment support research and instruction.

Financial Aid

For 2007–08, more than 100 graduate assistantships with waived tuition and stipends of $4000 are offered. Assistantships may be granted for up to two academic years, with full-time recipients working 17.5 hours a week and taking at least 9 graduate credits a semester. Application forms may be obtained from the Office of Graduate Admissions or via the University's Web site at http://www.sru.edu under "Graduate Students."

Educational loans are available to graduate students through the Federal Stafford Loan Program. Special Education Graduate Fellowships for special education majors are available through the Bureau of Education for the Handicapped. Information on additional sources of financial aid can be obtained from the Financial Aid Office.

Cost of Study

In 2007–08, Pennsylvania residents who study full-time pay $4087.67 in tuition and fees per semester; nonresidents pay $6276.92 per semester. The tuition per credit hour for part-time graduate students is $345 for residents and $552 for nonresidents. All fees are subject to change without notice.

Living and Housing Costs

On-campus housing for graduate students is available through the Office of Residence Life. For 2007–08, rooms on campus start at $1480 per semester. Information regarding off-campus housing and meal plans is also available.

Student Group

Total graduate enrollment for the fall semester of 2007 is approximately 700. Approximately 1 graduate student in 2 is enrolled on a full-time basis.

Student Outcomes

Recent graduates of Slippery Rock University have found employment in many different fields. More than 90 percent of graduates have obtained employment in their field of study. This statistic includes 100 percent placement in the fields of physical therapy, special education, and counseling. These graduates are employed in a variety of different agencies, including hospitals, social service agencies, and counseling centers.

Location

Slippery Rock, a borough of about 3,000 people, adjoins the University. Small shops and restaurants are within two or three blocks of the center of the campus. Pittsburgh, one of the country's largest cities, is about 50 miles to the south, and Erie, located on Lake Erie, is 75 miles to the north. Youngstown, Ohio, is 30 miles to the west. The borough is served by commercial buses from these cities and is located within 10 miles of two major interstate highways, I-80 and I-79. Cultural and recreational activities abound in the area.

The University

In 1889, the citizens of Slippery Rock borough founded the University and gave it their town's picturesque name. The University is one of fourteen state-owned institutions of higher education in Pennsylvania. Its undergraduate academic divisions include the Colleges of Business, Information, and Social Sciences; Education; Health, Environment, and Science; and Humanities, Fine and Performing Arts. The current enrollment of the University is approximately 7,200 undergraduates and 800 graduate students.

Slippery Rock University is fully accredited by the Middle States Association of Colleges and Schools, and appropriate programs are accredited by the National Council for Accreditation of Teacher Education.

Applying

The basic requirement for admission to graduate study is graduation from an accredited university or college with a major in the area proposed for graduate study, a grade point average of at least 2.75 (on a 4.0 scale) on all work attempted, and acceptable scores on either the General Test of the Graduate Record Examinations (GRE) or the Miller Analogies Test (MAT), depending upon the program of study. A nonrefundable fee of $25 must accompany applications for admission to graduate study. An official transcript must be submitted from the college or university at which the baccalaureate degree was earned. Applications should be filed two months prior to the opening of the semester for which admission is sought. Applications for financial aid should be filed at the financial aid office at least six months before the student is to begin graduate study. Application to the physical therapy and the master's in nursing programs require a $35 nonrefundable application fee.

Correspondence and Information

Office of Graduate Admissions
124 North Hall
Slippery Rock University
One Morrow Way
Slippery Rock, Pennsylvania 16057

Phone: 724-738-2051
877-SRU-GRAD (toll-free)
Fax: 724-738-2146
E-mail: graduate.admissions@sru.edu
Web site: http://academics.sru.edu/graduate/live/home.htm

GRADUATE PROGRAM COORDINATORS

The telephone numbers at the end of each entry below are equipped with voice mail.

Counseling and Development: Donald Strano, Ed.D., Texas Tech. (Telephone: 724-738-2035; e-mail: donald.strano@sru.edu)
Elementary Education/Early Childhood: Suzanne Rose, Ph.D., Penn State. (Telephone: 724-738-2042; e-mail: suzanne.rose@sru.edu)
English: Joseph McCarren, Ph.D., Indiana of Pennsylvania. (Telephone: 724-738-2043; e-mail: joseph.mccarren@sru.edu)
History: David Dixon, Ph.D., Kent State. (Telephone: 724-738-2053; e-mail: david.dixon@sru.edu)
Nursing: Joyce Penrose, Coordinator, M.S.N. program; Ph.D, Pittsburgh. (Telephone: 724-738-2065; e-mail: joyce.penrose@sru.edu); Alice Conway, Nursing Coordinator; Ph.D., Edinboro. (Telephone: 814-732-2285)
Parks and Recreational/Environmental Education: *Park and Resource Management, Environmental Education, Sustainable Systems:* Daniel Dziubek, Ed.D., Pittsburgh. (Telephone: 724-738-2068, e-mail: daniel.dziubek@sru.edu)
Physical Education: Betsy McKinley, Ph.D., Temple. (Telephone: 724-738-2072; e-mail: betsy.mckinley@sru.edu)
Physical Therapy: Carol Martin-Elkins, Ph.D., SUNY Health Science Center at Syracuse. (Telephone: 724-738-2080; e-mail: carol.martin-elkins@sru.edu)
Principalship: Joseph Merhaut, Ed.D., Duquesne. (Telephone: 724-738-2007; e-mail: joseph.merhaut@sru.edu)
Secondary Education/Foundations of Education: Jeffrey Lehman, Ph.D., Florida. (Telephone: 724-738-2041; e-mail: jeffrey.lehman@sru.edu)
Special Education: Dennis Fair, Ph.D., Pittsburgh. (Telephone: 724-738-2085; e-mail: dennis.fair@sru.edu)
Sport Management: Brian Crow, Ed.D., West Virginia. (Telephone: 724-738-2060; e-mail: brian.crow@sru.edu)

Sustainable energy sources are critical to the planet's future.

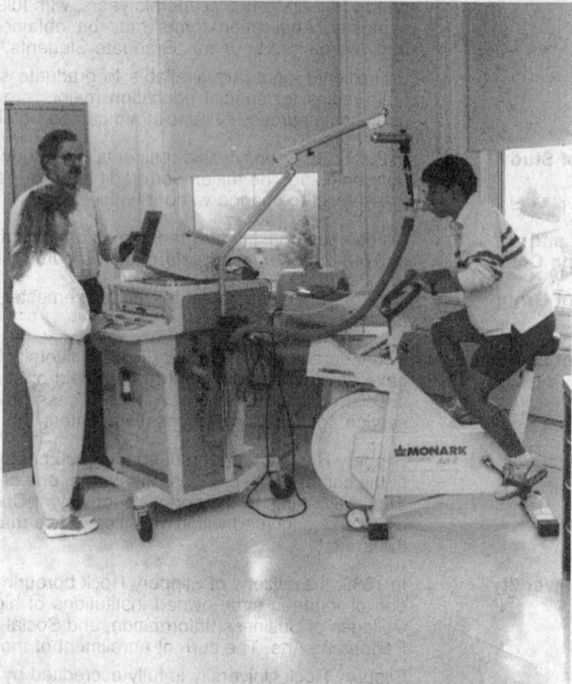

One of Slippery Rock's graduate degrees is the Doctor of Physical Therapy.

Teacher training programs are one of Slippery Rock's strengths.

SOUTH DAKOTA SCHOOL OF MINES AND TECHNOLOGY

Graduate Division

Programs of Study

Master of Science degrees are offered in atmospheric sciences, biomedical engineering, chemical engineering, civil engineering, computer science, electrical engineering, geology/geological engineering, materials engineering and science, mechanical engineering, paleontology, and technology management. A master's degree requires a minimum of 30 semester hours, including research and a thesis, or 32 hours without a thesis. The maximum graduate load is 15 credit hours per semester. Up to 12 hours of graduate credit may be transferred from another institution. The normal period required for completion of the M.S. degree ranges from one to two years for most students. Research credits may be earned during the summer.

Programs leading to a Ph.D. degree are offered in atmospheric and environmental sciences (AES; multidisciplinary program) in geology/geological engineering; biomedical engineering; chemical and biological engineering; materials engineering and science (MES); and nanoscience and nanoengineering. The Ph.D. program requires a minimum of 50 semester hours of course work and between 30 and 40 hours of research credits beyond the baccalaureate degree. (The AES program requires a total of 90 credits.) The Ph.D. programs also include qualifying and comprehensive examinations, language requirements, and a dissertation representing the culmination of between one and two academic years of full-time research. The residence requirement is two consecutive semesters.

The doctoral program in atmospheric and environmental sciences is offered jointly with South Dakota State University at Brookings. The master's and doctoral programs in biomedical engineering are offered jointly with the University of South Dakota.

Research Facilities

More than a hundred years after the School of Mines graduated its first students in1885, the School's commitment to research and development continues to result in powerful economic, social, and lifestyle benefits for the region, the state, and the nation. In fact, the School receives more than $17 million annually in research funding from a variety of organizations, including NASA, the Air Force Research Laboratory, the National Science Foundation, and the State of South Dakota.

Graduate students at the School of Mines work in high-tech laboratories and collaborate with faculty members on cutting-edge scientific research and development initiatives. They research everything from national defense to nanotechnology to remote sensing, global warming, fiber-reinforced composites, ultra-lightweight space systems, futuristic transportation, energy resource development, and mineral extraction and processing. Students design, build, and test alternative fuel vehicles at the School's Center of Excellence for Advanced Manufacturing and Production (CAMP), win international engineering competitions, make presentations at national conferences, and conduct research at off-campus sites as far away as Norway, Guatemala, Mozambique, and Mongolia.

Atmospheric sciences students conduct some of their research at the Institute of Atmospheric Sciences (IAS), while geological sciences and engineering students conduct their work at such places as the Black Hill Natural Sciences Field Station, the Engineering and Mining Experiment Station (EMES), the Museum of Geology, and the South Dakota Space Grant Consortium. Research facilities for students working in materials science and engineering program include the Additive Manufacturing Laboratory, the Advanced Materials Processing (AMP) and Joining Lab, The Center for Accelerated Applications at the Nanoscale (CAAN), the Center of Excellence for Advanced Manufacturing and Production (CAMP), the Computational Mechanics Laboratory, the Direct Write Laboratory, the Composite and Polymer Engineering Laboratory (CAPE), and the supersonic wind tunnel.

Financial Aid

Teaching and research assistantships, and various fellowships, are available. For the 2007–08 academic year, the minimum hourly pay for full-time teaching and research assistantships equates to $15.64 for the M.S. student and $16.74 for the Ph.D. student. Students who are interested in available assistantships and fellowships should apply early.

Information on other types of financial aid for U.S. students is available upon request from the Academic Enrollment Services Office at 605-394-2400.

Cost of Study

Graduate tuition in 2007–08 is $125.25 per credit hour for state residents and $369.30 for nonresidents. Assistants on state contract paid one third the graduate resident rate if registered for 9 credit hours or more. In addition, students are assessed fees of approximately $120 per credit hour depending on the type of course. Other fees are added for an application fee, guarantee deposit, parking, late registration, and health insurance, as applicable. International students pay an additional one-time enrollment fee of $113.70.

Students in master's programs enrolled in 24 credits per year pay estimated tuition and fees as follows: South Dakota resident, $5670; Minnesota resident, $8330; and other nonresidents, $11,750. A master's student who is a graduate assistant expects estimated tuition and fees of $3590. Books and supplies are estimated to cost $1200.

Students in doctoral programs enrolled in 18 credits per year pay estimated tuition and fees as follows: South Dakota resident, $4130; Minnesota resident, $6230; and other nonresidents, $8520. A doctoral student who is a graduate assistant expects estimated tuition and fees of $2630. Books and supplies are estimated to cost $1200.

Living and Housing Costs

Assistance in finding off-campus rooms and apartments is available from the director of housing. Apartments rent for a minimum of $350 per month. On-campus food is payable by the meal or is available through meal plans. When available to graduate students, on-campus room and board with the maximum meal plan is $4600 per year. The estimated cost of off-campus housing with the maximum meal plan is $7250. For commuters, the minimum-cost meal plan is $1620.

Student Group

Graduate enrollment averages 260 graduate students from forty states and twenty-seven countries. South Dakota School of Mines and Technology encourages women and members of minorities to apply.

Location

Rapid City has a population of more than 66,000. Described as the gateway to the Black Hills, homeland to the Lakota people, it is located a short distance from the Mount Rushmore and Crazy Horse Memorials and the White River Badlands. Climatic conditions are favorable in winter and summer for a variety of recreational activities—skiing, biking, hunting, fishing, hiking, and camping—with easy access to mountain streams and lakes.

The School

In 1885, the territorial legislature established the Dakota School of Mines in Rapid City, where it served the frontier communities of the Black Hills as a mining college and a prospectors' analytical laboratory. Since 1900, however, the educational emphasis has shifted to include a broad spectrum of engineering and scientific disciplines. Research capabilities have steadily improved. Modern teaching and research laboratories characterize the science and engineering departments with particular emphasis in the atmospheric sciences, hydrology, both natural and man-made materials, automated manufacturing, and computer networks. Recent staff additions include those in atmospheric sciences, biology, chemistry, civil engineering, geology, physics, and metallurgical engineering. Fifty to sixty graduate degrees are awarded annually. The School is accredited by the North Central Association of Colleges and Schools. The chemistry programs are approved by the American Chemical Society.

Applying

Applications from U.S. residents should be received sixty days before the beginning of the semester of desired admittance. International students should apply 150 days prior to their expected date of matriculation. All individuals who have graduated from institutions with accredited engineering and science curricula are encouraged to apply. The Graduate Record Examinations (GRE) is required of all applicants for admission except for School of Mines graduates. GMAT or GRE scores are required for technology management. A minimum score of 520 (paper-based test) or 190 (computer-based test) on the TOEFL is required (560/220 for admission without additional English tutoring) of applicants from non-English-speaking countries. English as a Second Language instruction is available on our campus beginning in fall semester 2007.

Correspondence and Information

Dr. John Helson, Jr., Dean of Graduate Education
South Dakota School of Mines and Technology
501 East Saint Joseph Street
Rapid City, South Dakota 57701-3995

Phone: 605-394-2493
E-mail: graduate.admissions@sdsmt.edu
Web site: http://graded.sdsmt.edu

PROGRAMS AND RESEARCH AREAS

Master of Science Program in Atmospheric Sciences
Acting John Helsdon Jr., Ph.D., SUNY at Albany. Telephone: 605-394-2291.

Research areas are listed below under Institute of Atmospheric Sciences.

Master of Science Program in Biomedical Engineering
Director: Mano Thubrikar, Ph.D., NYU. Telephone: 605-394-2401.

Biomaterials (nanomaterials, bioadhesives, and tissue engineering); computational biomedical engineering (biomechanics, imaging, advanced modeling/simulations); assistive technology/rehabilitation engineering (advanced prosthetics, control, biomimetics).

Master of Science Program in Chemical Engineering
Program Director: David Dixon, Ph.D., Texas. Telephone: 605-394-1235.

HPLC, NMR, FTIR, molecular modeling, biomass conversions, mining wastes characterization, hazardous waste incineration pollutants, environmental and forensic chemistries, combustion syntheses, natural products, synthetic plant growth regulators, organophosphorus chemistry, polymers and polymer/composites, kinetics and mechanisms of inorganic reactions, supermolecular assemblies, nanotechnology, supercritical fluids, process control.

Master of Science Program in Civil and Environmental Engineering
Program Director: Scott J. Kenner, Ph.D., Florida. Telephone: 605-394-2439.

Advanced materials, environmental engineering, geotechnical engineering, hazardous waste treatment and remediation, soil mechanics and hydraulics, structural engineering, water and wastewater treatment, water resources, and water quality engineering.

Master of Science Program in Computer Science
Program Director: Roger Johnson, Ph.D., California, San Diego. Telephone: 605-394-2471.

Artificial intelligence, fuzzy logic, neural networks, pattern recognition in satellite imagery, image processing, computer vision, computer graphics, database management systems, parallel and distributed systems, software engineering, mathematical foundations of computer science.

Master of Science Program in Electrical and Computer Engineering
Program Director: Brian T. Hemmelman, Ph.D., South Dakota School of Mines and Technology. Telephone: 605-394-1219.

Circuit and systems theory, communication theory, control systems, digital systems, electric power, electro optics, electromagnetics, instrumentation, material science, microcomputer/microprocessor applications, robotics, semiconductor processing.

Master of Science Program in Geology and Geological Engineering
Program Director: Maribeth Price, Ph.D., Princeton. Telephone: 605-394-1290.

Bioremediation, Black Hills geology, economic geology, engineering geophysics, geochemistry, geographic information systems, geohydrology, gold deposits, groundwater, igneous and metamorphic petrology, mineralogy, ore-forming systems, pegmatite petrogenesis, remote sensing, sedimentology, stratigraphy, surficial processes, tectonics, vertebrate paleontology.

Master of Science Program in Materials Engineering and Science
Program Director: Jon J. Kellar, Ph.D., Utah. Telephone: 605-394-2343.

Synthetic inorganic chemistry, polymer structure and properties, molecular modeling and dynamics, synthetic organic chemistry, supramolecular assembly, solid-phase microextraction technology, environmental chemistry, supercritical fluid extraction, metal ion activation of small molecules, electrochemistry, toxicity assessment, hydrometallurgy, interfacial phenomena, solution thermodynamics, metallurgic kinetics, transport phenomena, chlorination, polymer matrix composites, nanomechanics and micromechanics, phase transformation, strengthening mechanisms, fracture mechanics, X-ray diffraction, SEM/TEM microscopy, process control, artificial intelligence, NMR, FTIR, electronic and structural materials, electrical conductivity, photoconductivity, semiconductor materials, magnetic nanostructures, quantum wells, resonant tunneling devices.

Master of Science Program in Mechanical Engineering
Program Director: Michael Langerman, Ph.D., Idaho. Telephone: 605-394-2408.

Computational transport phenomena, natural convection, enhanced cooling of microelectronics, advanced structural analysis, fatigue life of composite materials, stress analysis by moire method, computer-integrated manufacturing.

Master of Science Program in Paleontology
Interim Program Director: Arden D. Davis, Ph.D., South Dakota Mines and Tech. Telephone: 605-394-2461.

Master of Science Program in Technology Management
Program Director: S. D. Kellogg, Ph.D., Texas at Austin. Telephone: 605-394-1271.

Engineering economics, management science, quality management, systems engineering.

Doctor of Philosophy Program in Atmospheric and Environmental Sciences
Program Director: Maribeth Price, Ph.D., Princeton. Telephone: 605-394-1290.

A joint program with South Dakota State University at Brookings. Separate degrees awarded in atmospheric, environmental, and water resources with research areas in atmospheric, groundwater, and surface water science and engineering; atmospheric chemistry; resource conservation; hydrologic mapping and modeling; remote sensing/satellite imagery; physical meteorology; meteorological modeling; and agricultural and urban waste treatment.

Doctor of Philosophy Program in Biomedical Engineering
Director: Mano Thubrikar, Ph.D., NYU. Telephone: 605-394-2401.

Research areas are listed above under the Master of Science Program.

Doctor of Philosophy Program in Chemical and Biological Engineering
Program Director: Jan A. Puszynski, Ph.D., Institute of Chemical Technology (Czech Republic). Telephone: 605-394-1230.

This chemical and biological engineering (CBE) Ph.D. program, new in 2007, is integral with the recently established 2010 Center for Bioprocessing Research and Development (CBRD) at the South Dakota School of Mines and Technology and the South Dakota State University (SDSU). Headquartered at the School of Mines campus, engineering and science collaborators from the School of Mines, South Dakota State University, and the Department of Energy's National Renewable Energy Laboratory, who are leading this effort, represent the fields of agricultural engineering, biochemical engineering, biochemistry, chemical engineering, mechanical engineering, and microbiology. Opportunities exist for CBE Ph.D. students to participate in cutting-edge research funded by the National Science Foundation, the Department of Energy, and Department of Defense, and industrial collaborators. CBRD's focus is on research that leads to new technologies for processing plant-derived lignocellulose materials into biomaterials such as ethanol and key building-block chemicals. The research foci of the CBRD is pretreatment, microbial conversions, separations, process simulation and economic analysis, and extremophiles from the Deep Underground Science and Engineering Laboratory. Because of the unique geographical location of the center, local industry by-products, such as agriwaste and logging waste, will play a significant part in providing the feedstock for the bio-derived chemicals and fuel research.

Doctor of Philosophy Program in Geology and Geological Engineering
Program Director: Maribeth Price, Ph.D., Princeton. Telephone: 605-394-1290.

Research areas are listed above under the Master of Science Program.

Doctor of Philosophy Program in Materials Engineering and Science
Program Director: Jon J. Kellar, Ph.D., Utah. Telephone: 605-394-2343.

Computational and continuum mechanics, composite materials, concrete technology, FT-IR spectroscopy, heterogeneous reaction kinetics, interfacial force microscopy, interfacial science, multiphase materials, polymer materials and processing, Raman spectroscopy, thermophysical and electronic properties.

Doctor of Philosophy Program in Nanoscience and Nanoengineering
Contact: Steve J. Smith, Ph.D., Michigan. Telephone: 605-394-5268.

A cross-disciplinary program in the emerging interdisciplinary field of nanoscience and nanotechnology, the curriculum integrates fundamental science principles with advances in nanoscience, nanoengineering, and nanotechnology. The focus of the program is aligned with the objectives of the state's 2010 Center for Accelerated Applications at the Nanoscale (CAAN). The program is oriented toward targeted applications of nanoscience, including such practical applications as the nanoscale utilization of regional minerals. Faculty expertise in theory and modeling and computational physics; theory and applications of nanocomposite materials; direct-write fabrication of sensors utilizing nano-inks; and synthesis and processing of inorganic and organic nano-scaled materials constitutes core expertise for the curricular thrust.

RESEARCH UNITS AND RESEARCH AREAS

Institute of Atmospheric Sciences
Acting Director: John Helsdon Jr., Ph.D., SUNY at Albany. Telephone: 605-394-2291.

Trace gas biogeochemistry, tropospheric chemistry, airborne measurements, atmospheric electricity, cloud physics, hailstorms, nucleation processes, mesoscale meteorology, numerical cloud modeling, radar meteorology, radiative transfer, land use and change, weather modification, climate change, hydrology.

South Dakota Space Grant Consortium
Director: Edward Duke, Ph.D., Dartmouth. Telephone: 605-394-2388.
Deputy Director and Outreach Coordinator: Thomas Durkin, M.S., South Dakota Mines and Tech. Telephone: 605-394-1975.

Remote sensing and image processing techniques and applications; satellite and balloon platform measurement technology; tropospheric sampling and measurement methodology; biogeochemistry of S, N, and C compounds; climate change; statistics and experimental design; and K–12 educational activities in space and earth sciences.

SOUTHERN CONNECTICUT STATE UNIVERSITY

School of Graduate Studies

Programs of Study

Southern Connecticut State University (SCSU) offers graduate programs leading to the degrees of Master of Arts, Master of Science, Master of Science in Education, Master of Science in Nursing, Master of Library Science, Master of Public Health, Master of Social Work, Master of Marriage and Family Therapy, and Master of Business Administration, as well as an Ed.D. in educational leadership. Graduate programs leading to the Sixth-Year Professional Diploma in special areas of education and library science are also offered.

The Master of Arts degree is awarded in English, history, psychology, Romance languages (French, Spanish, and Italian), and women's studies. The Master of Science degree is offered in biology; chemistry; communications disorders; computer science; instructional technology; recreation and leisure; research, measurement, and evaluation; sociology; and urban studies. The Master of Science in Education degree is awarded in art, bilingual/bicultural education, biology, chemistry, counseling, elementary education, English, environmental education, exercise science, foreign languages (French, Spanish, and Romance languages), history, mathematics, reading, school health education, school psychology, science education, and special education.

The Sixth-Year Professional Diploma is offered in counseling and school psychology, educational leadership, education—classroom teacher specialist studies, educational foundations, library information studies, reading, special education, and science education.

Most graduate programs are offered in the evening for the convenience of students, and some are offered online. Students follow a planned program that includes completing course requirements and taking a comprehensive examination, preparing a thesis, or completing a special project, as appropriate.

Research Facilities

The Hilton C. Buley Library, Southern Connecticut State University's center of education and research, plays an indispensable part in the academic experience of every student. Buley Library provides more than 600,000 print and media volumes and access to more than 100 electronic databases. An online shared catalog expands available print and media resources to more than 2 million volumes. The library also provides 2,000 current periodical titles, 60,000 bound periodicals, and nearly 100,000 microform volumes.

Financial Aid

There are a limited number of teaching and research assistantships available. The chief source of aid is the Federal Stafford Student Loan. Application forms for this loan are available from commercial banks. The School of Graduate Studies also offers competitive research fellowships of approximately $8000.

Cost of Study

Tuition for full-time study for the 2007–08 academic year is $8055 for state residents and $16,735 for out-of-state residents. Part-time study costs $428 per credit hour plus a $55 registration fee and an $8-per-credit-hour information technology fee each semester. Students in some programs are charged differential tuition. Full-time, in-state students in the M.B.A. program and the M.L.S. program are charged $4082 per semester, and out-of-state students in these programs are charged $8394 per semester. Part-time students in these programs are charged $482 per credit. Students enrolled in the doctoral program are charged $552 per credit.

Living and Housing Costs

On-campus housing is available for graduate students. Off-campus accommodations are also readily available close to the campus at a range of prices. Students may choose from a wide range of housing styles and options.

Student Group

Approximately 4,000 graduate students (including approximately 1,000 full-time) are enrolled in graduate programs in five schools of the University. SCSU has consistently ranked as one of the top ten graduate schools in New England in terms of enrollment.

Location

New Haven, Connecticut's third-largest city, is home to three universities, three colleges, and several private schools. New Haven serves as the gateway to New England, where I-95 and I-91 intersect and provide access to New York and Boston.

The University

Southern Connecticut State University is one of four institutions of the Connecticut State University System, which is authorized by the state of Connecticut. It receives its principal financial support from legislative appropriations. It is the policy of Southern Connecticut State University to accept students without regard to race, color, creed, sex, age, national origin, or physical disability.

Applying

Application forms for the School of Graduate Studies are available in the Graduate Office, which is located in Engleman Hall Room B110, or may be obtained by mail or telephone request. An online application is also available at http://www.gradstudies.SouthernCT.edu. Students are advised to send the completed, signed application and official transcripts from every college and graduate school attended, along with a $50 application fee, to the Graduate Office. International students must send also TOEFL scores to the Graduate Studies Office. All other documents, such as requested letters of recommendation or any departmental forms, should be sent directly to the academic department to which application is being made. A personal interview with the appropriate department chairperson or a designated faculty member in the major area of study is a requirement for admission. Requests for appointments must be made to the department. The application and credentials should be submitted well in advance of the semester for which the student seeks admission.

Correspondence and Information

School of Graduate Studies
Southern Connecticut State University
501 Crescent Street
New Haven, Connecticut 06515-1355
Phone: 203-392-5240
800-448-0661 (toll-free)
Web site: http://www.gradstudies.southernct.edu

FACULTY HEADS

Listed below is the chairperson or graduate coordinator of each department.

Art Education: Jesse Whitehead, Coordinator.
Biology: Rebecca Lerud, Coordinator.
Business Administration: Omid Nodoushani, Director.
Chemistry: Robert Snyder, Coordinator.
Communication Disorders: Deborah Weiss, Coordinator.
Computer Science: Lisa Lancor, Coordinator.
Counselor Education: Norris Haynes, Chair.
Education: Maria Diamantis, Chair.
Educational Foundations: Bernard Hayford, Coordinator.
Educational Leadership: Brian Perkins, Chair.
English: Kenneth Florey, Coordinator.
Exercise Science: Robert Axtell, Coordinator.
Foreign Languages: Carlos Arboleda, Chair.
History: Polly Beals, Coordinator.
Library Science and Instructional Technology: Josephine Sche, Chair.
Marriage and Family Therapy: J. Edward Lynch, Chair.
Mathematics: Richard Decesare, Coordinator.
Nursing: Eileen Crutchlow, Coordinator.
Psychology: Jerome Hauselt, Coordinator.
Public Health: Michael Perlin, Coordinator.
Reading: Nancy Boyles, Coordinator.
Recreation: James McGregor, Coordinator.
Research, Measurement, and Evaluation: William Diffley, Coordinator.
School Health: Doris Marino, Coordinator.
School Psychology: Joy Fopiano, Coordinator.
Science and Environmental Education: Susan Cusato, Chair.
Social Work: Todd Rofuth, Chair.
Sociology: Jon Bloch, Coordinator.
Special Education: Pamela Brucker, Chair.
Urban Studies: Peter Sakalowsky, Chair.
Women's Studies: Tricia Lin, Coordinator.

There are many opportunities for graduate students at SCSU to enroll in small classes and work closely with faculty members.

The Hilton C. Buley Library.

SOUTHERN ILLINOIS UNIVERSITY EDWARDSVILLE

Graduate Studies and Research

Programs of Study

Graduate Studies and Research awards the following degrees: Master of Arts in art therapy counseling, biological sciences, economics and finance, English, history, psychology, sociology, and speech communication; Master of Science in accountancy, biological sciences, chemistry, civil engineering, clinical nurse leader studies, computer management and information systems, computer science, economics and finance, electrical engineering, environmental sciences, geographical studies, health care and nursing administration, mass communications, mathematics, mechanical engineering, nurse anesthesia, nurse educator studies, nurse practitioner studies (adult, family, or dual), physics, psychology, public health nursing, and speech-language pathology; Master of Business Administration; Master of Fine Arts, with studio areas in ceramics, digital art, drawing, metalsmithing, painting, printmaking, sculpture, and textile art or with a specialization in art education; Master of Marketing Research; Master of Music in music education or music performance; Master of Public Administration; Master of Science in Education in educational administration, elementary education, instructional design and learning technologies, kinesiology, secondary education with concentrations in nine teaching areas, and special education; and Master of Social Work. The Specialist degree is offered in educational administration and in school psychology. Cooperative doctoral study is offered in some degree programs through special arrangements with Southern Illinois University Carbondale. Postbaccalaureate and post-master's certificates are also offered in several fields. For more information about these programs, students should visit http://www.siue.edu/graduate/.

Final examinations are required of all degree candidates. Projects that must be completed for master's programs include theses, research projects and papers, internships, practicums, exhibitions, or recitals.

Research Facilities

The University has laboratories for the technical sciences, education, human performance, anthropological studies, psychological studies, and urban studies, and it has practice facilities for fine arts, theater, and music. Lovejoy Library has more than 1 million bound volumes, 6,500 serials and periodicals, and 1.5 million microform units and maintains borrowing agreements with libraries locally and throughout the nation. Networked computers are available throughout the campus, including most offices, and numerous academic computing labs are available for use by graduate students. Problem-oriented programs have internship and practicum agreements with government, health, business, welfare, and educational agencies throughout the metropolitan St. Louis area.

Financial Aid

Teaching, research, and general assistantships are available, as are a number of special graduate awards, most of which carry stipends. Application for assistantships is made through department chairpersons. Application for some special awards is made through Graduate Studies and Research or Graduate Records. Student employment and various types of loans are available through the Office of Student Financial Aid.

Cost of Study

In 2006–07, tuition and fees for full-time graduate students were $6280 per academic year (fall and spring semesters) for Illinois residents and $14,380 for out-of-state students. Figures were based on 12 semester hours of enrollment each term and are subject to change. St. Louis–area residents taking 6 semester hours or fewer per term pay in-state tuition and fees.

Living and Housing Costs

In 2005–06, rent for on-campus apartments, managed by University Housing, ranged from $3200 for an academic year (fall through spring terms) for a single student sharing a furnished apartment with 3 other students to $1035 a month for a three-bedroom furnished apartment for a family. (Rates are subject to change.) A residence hall room shared with one other person is $3360 per academic year (fall through spring semester). The Housing Office also has lists of available off-campus housing. Reasonably priced meals are served in the University cafeteria, and restaurant and meal plans are available through the University's dining services. Special housing arrangements can be made for graduate students.

Student Group

More than 13,400 students are enrolled, including 2,200 full-time and part-time graduate students. Minority groups and other countries are well represented in the enrollment. Evening and weekend classes are offered to accommodate graduate students employed in area schools, businesses, and industries.

Location

The area surrounding the University is rich in cultural advantages. Three other major universities and a number of community colleges share with Southern Illinois University Edwardsville (SIUE) a responsibility for offering advanced educational opportunities to many thousands of people. Live theater, art shows, museums, public parks, Cahokia Mounds, Missouri Botanical Gardens, and the Gateway Arch are some of the attractions of the general area. The St. Louis Symphony Orchestra offers indoor and outdoor concerts. The area has a combination of farmland and urban concentrations. Thriving businesses and large industries offer opportunities for employment. Recreational opportunities for hikers, campers, and canoe enthusiasts exist in the wilderness preserves of the nearby Ozarks and southern Illinois. St. Louis, with its stadium, the Edward Jones Dome, the Scottrade Center, Municipal Opera, and Lambert International Airport, is a 25-minute drive from the University.

The University

The University is situated on 2,660 acres of rolling hills. The main campus consists of large, modern buildings housing classrooms, laboratories, administrative offices, four residence halls, an apartment complex, and a student center with cafeteria, restaurant, recreational facilities, bookstore, bowling alley, and lounge areas. An athletics complex offers a wide range of recreational opportunities, including an indoor pool and student fitness center. Tennis courts, playing fields, and other recreational facilities are located on the periphery of the main campus. Low-cost bus service connects the campus with many nearby Illinois and Missouri centers and the University apartment complex. Ample parking is provided for automobiles. An Art and Design Building opened in 1993, and an outstanding addition to campus music facilities opened in 1995. The School of Nursing has a simulated learning lab; the School of Engineering moved into a state-of-the-art building in 2000; and the School of Pharmacy opened new facilities in 2005.

Applying

Students should file an application for admission with the Office of Admissions. Admission requirements vary for different programs. Requests for application forms, program information, and financial aid information should be sent to Graduate Admissions, Box 1047. Graduate applications and information are also available on the Web at http://www.siue.edu/graduate/.

Correspondence and Information

Department Chairperson
Southern Illinois University Edwardsville
Edwardsville, Illinois 62026

Phone: 618-650-3160
Fax: 618-650-2081
Web site: http://www.siue.edu/graduate/

FACULTY HEADS

The Graduate School
Dr. Stephen L. Hansen, Graduate Dean.
Dr. Ron Schaefer, Associate Dean.
Christa Johnson, Assistant Dean.

College of Arts and Sciences
Dr. M. Kent Neely, Dean.
Dr. Carl Springer, Associate Dean.
Dr. Wendy Shaw, Associate Dean.
Art and Design: Ivy Cooper, Chair.
Art Therapy Counseling: Dr. Gussie Klorer, Program Director.
Biological Sciences: Dr. Steve McCommas, Chair.
Chemistry: Dr. Robert Dixon, Chair.
English Language and Literature: Dr. Charles Berger, Chair.
Environmental Sciences: Dr. Kevin Johnson, Program Director.
Geography: Dr. Randy Pearson, Chair.
Historical Studies: Dr. Anthony Cheeseboro, Chair.
Mass Communications: Dr. Patrick Murphy, Chair.
Mathematics: Dr. Krzysztof Jarosz, Chair.
Music: Dr. Prince Wells, Chair.
Physics: Dr. Kim Shaw, Chair.
Public Administration and Policy Analysis: Dr. T. R. Carr, Chair.
Social Work: Dr. Tom Regulus, Chair.
Sociology: Dr. Dave Kauzlarich, Chair.
Speech Communication: Dr. Laura Perkins, Chair.

School of Business
Dr. Timothy Schoenecker, Interim Dean.
Dr. Janice Joplin, Associate Dean.
Dr. Mary R. Sumner, Associate Dean.
Accounting: Dr. Michael Costigan, Chair.
Computer Management and Information Systems: Dr. Susan Yager, Chair; Dr. Jo Ellen Moore, Program Director.
Economics and Finance: Dr. Rik Hafer, Chair; Dr. Ali Kutan, Program Director.
Management/Marketing: Dr. Joseph Michlitsch.
Marketing Research: Dr. Joseph Michlitsch, Chair; Dr. Madhav Segal, Program Director.
M.B.A.: Janice Joplin, Program Director.

School of Education
Dr. L. Bill Searcy, Interim Dean.
Dr. Mary Weishaar, Associate Dean.
Dr. Curt Lox, Associate Dean.
Curriculum and Instruction: Dr. Randy Smith, Chair.
Educational Leadership: Dr. Wayne Nelson, Chair.
Kinesiology and Health Education: Dr. William Vogler, Chair.
Psychology: Dr. Bryce Sullivan, Chair.
Special Education and Communication Disorders: Dr. Jean Harrison, Chair.

School of Engineering
Dr. Hasan Sevim Hasan, Dean.
Dr. Jacob Van Roekel, Associate Dean.
Civil Engineering: Dr. Mark Rossow, Chair.
Computer Science: Dr. Jerry Weinberg, Chair.
Construction Management: Dr. Dianne Kay Slattery, Chair.
Electrical Engineering: Dr. Oktay Alkin, Chair.
Industrial and Manufacturing Engineering: Dr. S. Cem Karacal, Program Director.
Mechanical Engineering: Dr. Keqin Gu, Chair.

School of Nursing
Dr. Marcia Maurer, Dean.
Dr. Mary Ann Boyd, Associate Dean.
Dr. Jackie Clement, Graduate Program Director.

SPALDING UNIVERSITY

Graduate Programs

Programs of Study

Spalding University offers several levels of graduate study. Doctorates are offered in clinical psychology and education. The Doctor of Psychology (Psy.D.) in clinical psychology program is fully accredited by the American Psychological Association and includes emphasis areas in adult psychology; child, adolescent, and family psychology; and health psychology. The programs emphasize the acquisition of the professional skills and competencies required for the practice of psychology and are built upon a foundation of psychological theory and research. The Doctor of Education (Ed.D.) in leadership education emphasizes values and ethics in leadership and serves people in traditional educational roles as well as in business, technical, health, and other areas. Applicants must have a master's degree. Courses within this cohort-based program may be completed in two years, along with a third year for dissertation completion. Courses are structured in a fall, winter, and spring semester format. Master's degrees are offered in business communication, clinical psychology, creative writing, education, nursing, occupational therapy, and social work. Within the College of Education, the following options are available: the Master of Arts in Teaching (M.A.T.) in learning behavior disorders and in elementary, middle, high school, and dual middle and high school education; the Master of Arts (M.A.) in education with cognate areas in instructional computer technology, teaching English as a second language, and other approved areas; and certificate extension and Rank programs. All programs leading to teaching credentials are accredited by the National Council for Accreditation of Teacher Education (NCATE). The School of Professional Psychology offers an M.A. in clinical psychology, which qualifies the graduate to seek licensure as a psychological associate in Kentucky. The School of Social Work offers a Council on Social Work Education–accredited M.S.W. degree with a special focus on social justice and integrative practice. The program is designed specifically for the working student, with all classes held on weekends, in both a two-year and a one-year (for people who have the B.S.W.) program. Following the University's long-standing tradition of innovative education within the field of nursing, four Master of Science in Nursing (M.S.N.) tracks are offered within the School of Nursing: adult nurse practitioner studies, family nurse practitioner studies, leadership in nursing and health care, and pediatric nurse practitioner studies. A post-master's nurse practitioner studies program is also offered. The Auerbach School of Occupational Therapy offers an entry-level Master of Science (M.S.) in occupational therapy and is fully accredited by the Accreditation Council for Occupational Therapy Education (ACOTE) of the American Occupational Therapy Association (AOTA). The School of Social Sciences and Humanities offers a Master of Fine Arts (M.F.A.) in writing with concentrations in creative nonfiction, fiction, poetry, and writing for children. This brief residency program consists of intensive ten-day sessions in October and May that are attended by all faculty members and students as they begin each semester, after which students and faculty members return home to correspond on an individual basis. The School of Business and the School of Communication jointly offer the M.S. in business communication. This interdisciplinary degree is designed for working professionals, with courses offered in a weekend format.

Research Facilities

The library provides print and nonprint materials, audiovisual equipment, services, and facilities to support the educational and research programs. There are more than 200,000 volumes in the collection, which can be accessed via an automated catalog. These resources are augmented by external collections and services, particularly those of the Kentuckiana Metroversity, a consortium of seven colleges and universities in the metropolitan area that provides access to more than 3 million books and 20,000 journals. Access to further information is enhanced through online and CD-ROM databases and through Internet resources. Additional support is provided through document delivery services and SOLINET/OCLC. Study facilities include large loud-study rooms suitable for group work, while private study and research are supported by small rooms.

Financial Aid

The general types of financial assistance at Spalding University are graduate assistantships and scholarships, repayable aid (loans), work opportunities, and specific tuition remission programs in association with the School of Education/Jefferson County Public Schools, KHEAA, and Crusade for Children. Students should file the FAFSA for loans and work opportunities. Assistantship and scholarship information is available from the graduate office. Loan forgiveness, including interest, may be available for candidates who wish to teach math, science, and special education. This loan forgiveness may also apply to nursing candidates.

Cost of Study

In 2004–05, the cost per credit hour was $495 for 1-credit-hour master's programs and $560 per credit hour for the doctoral programs. The tuition for the M.F.A. in writing was $5040 for the first three semesters and $5640 for the last semester.

Living and Housing Costs

Housing for single students, both undergraduate and graduate, is available at Morrison Hall on the University campus for $1590 per semester, single occupancy. Married students find ample housing in the surrounding area at varying rates. Daily and weekly dormitory rates are also available for graduate students.

Student Group

More than 650 graduate students with diverse backgrounds and various experiences are enrolled at Spalding. The majority are older students who work full-time and are attracted by the flexibility of the programs.

Location

The Spalding University campus is located between the business section of the city and Old Louisville, a neighborhood of elegant Victorian mansions that was the center of gracious living in the latter half of the nineteenth century. The University is a participant in an effort to preserve and restore the rich architectural heritage of the Louisville Central Area. The campus is adjacent to the Louisville Free Public Library and is within walking distance of performances of the Louisville Orchestra, Kentucky Opera Association, Louisville Ballet, Bach Society, Actors Theatre, and other cultural activities. The campus is also convenient to the schools, hospitals, and agencies used for preprofessional, clinical, and practicum experiences of the students.

The University

Spalding University has its roots in Nazareth College and Academy, established by the Sisters of Charity of Nazareth in 1814 in Bardstown, Kentucky. The name of the University is derived from and honors Catherine Spalding, the founder of the Sisters of Charity of Nazareth. Since the establishment of the Louisville campus in 1920, Spalding University has occupied the Tompkins-Buchanan-Rankin Mansion as the core of its now-expanded campus. The University continues its tradition of service to the Louisville area by providing programs that include components of the liberal arts and sciences and professional education for men and women of all ages and from all sectors of society.

Historically, Spalding University has offered extensive programs for part-time students. Business and professional persons, in-service teachers, and others unable to attend college full-time have earned graduate degrees by attending evening and Saturday classes. Today, the University is maintaining its innovative stance at the cutting edge of educational service to the Louisville community and beyond.

Applying

Most graduate students may enter at the beginning of any term; however, students in psychology, the regular social work program, and the Ed.D. program are admitted only in the fall. Occupational therapy students are admitted in the spring. Advanced social work students begin in the summer. Prospective students should contact the Graduate Admissions Office to receive information and application materials.

Correspondence and Information

Office of University Admission
Spalding University
851 South Fourth Street
Louisville, Kentucky 40203-2188

Phone: 502-585-7111
800-896-8941 Ext. 2111
Fax: 502-992-2418
E-mail: gradadmissions@spalding.edu
Web site: http://www.spalding.edu

THE FACULTY

Administration
Jo Ann Rooney, University President; LL.M., Boston University; Ed.D., Pennsylvania; J.D., Suffolk.
L. Randy Strickland, Senior Vice President for Academic Affairs; Ed.D., North Carolina State.
Tori Murden McClure, Vice President for External Relations, Enrollment Management and Student Affairs; M.F.A., Spalding; M.Div., Harvard; J.D., Louisville.
Theresa Raidy, Vice President for Development.
Lynn Gillette, Vice President for Compliance, Institutional Effectiveness and Retention; Ph.D., Texas A&M.
James Laemmle, Chief Financial Officer.
Holli Lewis, Corporate General Counsel; J.D., Louisville.
Richard Hudson, M.R.C., Kentucky; Ph.D., Louisville. Educational and counseling psychology.
John James, Dean, College of Social Sciences and Humanities; Ph.D., Missouri–Columbia. Clinical psychology.
Margaret McCullough, Dean, College of Business and Communication; Ph.D., Cincinnati.
Betty Lindsey, Dean, College of Education; Ph.D., Louisville.

Business Communication
Robert Barraclough, Associate Professor of Communication and Chair of School of Communication; Ed.D., West Virginia.
Jeffrey Bile, Assistant Professor in Communication; M.A., Eastern Illinois.
Melissa Chastain, Assistant Professor in Communication; M.A., Duquesne.
Frances Ford, Assistant Professor of Accounting; M.B.A., Webster.
Lynn Gillette, Professor of Business; Ph.D., Texas A&M.
David J. Hudson, Assistant Professor of Business Administration; M.A., Webster.
Margaret McCullough, Professor of Accounting and Business Administration and Dean; Ph.D., Cincinnati.
Michelle Reiss, Assistant Professor of Marketing; D.B.A., Mississippi State.
Curtis Richards, Assistant Professor, School of Business, and Chair; M.B.A., Bellarmine.
Jo Ann Rooney, University President; LL.M., Boston University; Ed.D., Pennsylvania.
Iverson Warinner, Professor of Communication and Theater Arts; Ed.S., M.F.A., Louisville.

Education
Gladys M. Busch, Professor; Ph.D., Indiana.
Reginald Caldwell, Assistant Professor; M.Ed., Louisville.
Karen Dunnagan, Assistant Professor; Ph.D., Ohio State.
Barbara Foster, Assistant Professor; Ed.D., Spalding.
Robert Hay, Associate Professor; Ed.D., Louisville.
Betty Lindsey, Associate Professor and Dean; Ed.D., Louisville.
Paige Orman, Director of Field Experiences; M.A.T., Tennessee.
Anthony Owusu-Ansah, Assistant Professor; Ph.D., Ohio.
John G. Shaughnessy, C.F.X., Professor; Ed.D., Rutgers.
Mary Angela Shaughnessy, S.C.N., Professor; Ph.D., Boston College; J.D., Louisville.
Ella Simmons, Professor; Ed.D., Louisville.
Charles Wittenberg, Associate Professor; Ph.D., Miami (Ohio).
Jennifer Woods, Assistant Professor, School of Education, LBD Program; Louisville.
Veronica Wright, Assistant Professor; M.Ed., Louisville.

Master of Fine Arts in Writing
Kathleen Driskell, Associate Program Director; M.F.A., North Carolina at Greensboro.
Sena Jeter Naslund, Program Director; Ph.D., Iowa.

Nursing
Veronica Abdur-Rahman, Associate Professor; Ph.D., Houston.
Fran Anderson, Assistant Professor; Ph.D., Washington (Seattle).
Rebecca Gesler, Assistant Professor; M.S.N., Phoenix; RN.
Michael Huggins, Assistant Professor; Ph.D., Vanderbilt.
Karen Kinzer, Associate Professor; Ed.S., Spalding.
Shelia Kirk, Assistant Professor; M.S.N., Spalding; RN.
Ann Lyons, Professor; D.N.S., Indiana.
Jacquelyn Macmillian-Bohler, Assistant Professor; M.S.N., Vanderbilt.
Joseph Maloney, Professor; Ph.D., Maryland.
Marilyn Musacchio, Chair, School of Nursing; Ph.D., Case Western Reserve.
Dee Ann Totten, Assistant Professor; M.S.N., Louisville.
Pam White, Assistant Professor; M.S.N., Cincinnati.
Gracie Wishnia, Associate Professor; Ph.D., Louisville.
Pam Yancy, Associate Professor; M.S.N., Louisville.

Occupational Therapy
Jana Cason, Assistant Professor; M.H.S., Alabama; OTR/L.
Jeffrey Lederer, Assistant Professor; Ph.D., New Mexico.
Lori Reynolds, Assistant Professor; M.O.T., Texas Woman's; OTR/L.
Laura S. Strickland, Assistant Professor and Chair, Auerbach School of Occupational Therapy; Ed.D., Spalding.
L. Randy Strickland, Professor; Ed.D., North Carolina State.
Christine Wright, Assistant Professor; Ph.D., Texas Woman's; OTR/L.

Psychology
Abbie Beacham, Assistant Professor of Clinical Psychology; Ph.D., Louisville.
Barbara Beauchamp, Assistant Professor of Clinical Psychology; Psy.D., Spalding.
Thomas A. Bergandi, Professor; Ph.D., Ball State.
James Cooksey, Associate Professor; Ph.D., Louisville.
John A. James III, Associate Professor; Ph.D., Missouri.
Kenneth Linfield, Assistant Professor; Ph.D., Illinois.
David L. Morgan, Associate Professor; Ph.D., Auburn.
Thomas G. Titus, Professor; Ph.D., Louisville.
Diane Wohlfarth, Assistant Professor; Psy.D., Spalding.

Social Work
Desiree Brown-Daughtry, Director of Field, School of Social Work; M.S.S.W., Louisville.
Shannon Cambron, Instructor, School of Social Work; M.S.W., Spalding.
Robert Cooper, Assistant Professor; M.S.S.W., Louisville.
Helen Deines, Associate Professor; Ed.D., Spalding.
Elise Fullmer, Chair, School of Social Work; M.S.W., Ph.D., SUNY at Albany.
Erlene Grise-Owens, Assistant Professor and Director; Ed.D., Spalding.
David Peterson, Assistant Professor; M.S.S.W., Louisville.
Philip Schervish, Professor; Ph.D., Illinois.
Rita Valade, Assistant Professor; M.S.W., Catholic University.

University-Wide Studies
John Burden, Associate Professor of Natural Sciences and Interim Chair; Ph.D., Louisville.
Patricia Dillon, Assistant Professor of Social Sciences and Humanities; Ph.D. candidate, Mississippi.
Kathleen Driskell, Associate Professor of Liberal Studies; M.F.A., North Carolina.
Adeline Fehribach, Assistant Professor of Social Sciences and Humanities; Ph.D., Vanderbilt.
Frank Hutchins, Associate Professor of Liberal Studies; Ph.D., Wisconsin–Madison.
Youn-Kyung Kim, Assistant Professor of English; Ph.D., Oklahoma State.
Larry Wayne Lewis, Associate Professor of Mathematics; Ph.D., Louisville.
Kathleen Nesbitt, Professor and Chair of School of Social Sciences and Humanities; Ph.D., Michigan.
Joyce Ogden, Assistant Professor of Social Sciences and Humanities; M.F.A., Indiana.
Terry Wheeler, Associate Professor of Natural Sciences; Ph.D., Louisville.
John Wilcox, Professor of Social Sciences and Humanities; Ph.D., Notre Dame.
Marlene Will, Associate Professor of Natural Sciences; Ed.D., Spalding.

SPRINGFIELD COLLEGE

Graduate Programs

Programs of Study

Graduate study at Springfield College is designed to provide advanced professional preparation for qualified graduates of colleges and universities in the United States and abroad. Fourteen graduate programs, several with a number of subspecialty areas, are coordinated through the Graduate Studies Office. These programs are Art Therapy, Education (administration, early childhood, elementary, secondary, special education), Exercise Science and Sport Studies (athletic training, exercise physiology, health promotion and disease prevention, sport and exercise psychology, strength and conditioning), Health Studies (health education teacher licensure), Human Services, Occupational Therapy, Physical Education (adapted physical education, advanced-level coaching, athletic administration, physical education teacher licensure, sport performance), Physical Therapy, Psychology (athletic counseling, clinical mental health counseling, industrial/organizational psychology, marriage and family therapy, school guidance, student personnel in higher education), Rehabilitation Services (alcohol rehabilitation/substance abuse counseling, developmental disabilities, general counseling and casework, psychiatric rehabilitation/mental health counseling, special services, vocational evaluation/work adjustment), Social Work, and Sport Management and Recreation (recreational management, sport management, therapeutic recreational management). Graduate study is offered on three different levels, leading to the Master of Education, Master of Physical Education, Master of Science, Master of Social Work, Certificate of Advanced Graduate Study, Doctor of Philosophy, Doctor of Physical Therapy, and combined M.S.W./J.D. degrees.

For the Master of Science in Human Services, course work is offered on weekends. The program lasts sixteen months, and students meet one weekend each month. A five-year human services experience (paid or volunteer) is required for admission. Master of Social Work candidates attend classes on a part-time basis, every other weekend, or as full-time students two days a week.

Research Facilities

A well-equipped laboratory for physiology provides an area for student and faculty research. Experiments in the areas of kinesiology and exercise physiology are concerned with oxygen consumption and energy expenditure, strength, electrogoniometry, physical fitness, pulmonary function, and body density. Arrangements can also be made for work in cinematography and somatotyping. The Allied Health Center, the education curriculum laboratory, the College Counseling Center, a counseling laboratory with videotape facilities, a physical education tests and measurements laboratory, a biomechanics laboratory, the Computer Center, the College campgrounds, and the modern Babson Library offer campus opportunities for conducting research related to student interests and areas of study.

Financial Aid

Various types of financial assistance are available. Four All-College Tuition Scholarships are awarded each year. Teaching and research fellowships are offered in administrative and student affairs, art therapy, biology, chemistry, computer science, education, health studies, information and technology services, mathematics, multicultural affairs, occupational therapy, physical education, physical science, physics, psychology, recreation, rehabilitation services, and social sciences. These awards provide tuition waivers for a maximum of 24 semester hours per academic year and a stipend. Graduate assistantships are also available in teaching, coaching, laboratory supervision, research, and administrative areas. A limited number of scholarships, ranging from $200 to the full cost of tuition, are provided for international students. The Financial Aid Office administers federal loan programs.

Cost of Study

For a typical full-time graduate student at Springfield College, tuition and fees for two semesters (nine months) amount to $17,281 during the 2007–08 academic year. An ample schedule of courses is planned each summer, with the cost based mainly on the number of semester hours carried.

Living and Housing Costs

The College provides three meal plan options for resident students and two options for non-resident students. Both on- and off-campus housing are available. Entertainment costs and other personal expenses vary greatly from student to student. College-owned apartments cost approximately $6410 per academic year.

Student Group

During 2006–07, there were 1,493 full-time graduate students enrolled in the various programs. Sixty-eight percent were women. Students were drawn from twenty-four states and twenty-one countries.

Student Outcomes

Graduates consistently declare themselves well prepared and qualified for employment in the professional fields of art; occupational and physical therapy; education; counseling psychology; sport, wellness, and recreation; and health and human services. The positions include teacher, coach, trainer, counselor, administrator, director, consultant, entrepreneur, and hands-on practitioner. Employers who have recently hired Springfield graduates include the YMCA, Old Sturbridge Village, Veterans Affairs Medical Centers, Baystate Health Systems, Goodwill Industries, Motorola, Harvard University, the National Football League, the American Hockey League, Converse, Advantage Health Corp., the United States Olympic Committee, Disney Wide World of Sports, Hamilton Sundstrand, Merrill Lynch, Morgan Stanley, NBC Sports, Six Flags, United Cerebral Palsy, and Yale New Haven Hospital.

Location

The campus is located on Lake Massasoit, about 3 miles from the downtown area of Springfield, Massachusetts, offering the advantages of a small-town setting within a metropolitan area. The campus site covers 156 acres, including the 56-acre campground fronting on the lake.

The College is within a day's drive of major centers in the northeastern United States. Boston, the largest city in New England, is less than a 2-hour drive away, and New York City is only 3 hours away. The Green Mountains of Vermont and the White Mountains of New Hampshire are easily reached via modern highways going north. The entire area abounds in lakes, mountains, resorts, historic sites, museums, and other attractions.

The College

Springfield College is, and has been since its founding more than 100 years ago, concerned with the preparation of the total person—in spirit, in mind, and in body. Its professional curriculum has been specifically designed to prepare students for careers in what have come to be known as the "human-helping" professions. The College lists more than 30,000 alumni whose professional education at Springfield has enabled them to assume leadership positions in virtually all areas of community service, including recreation, physical education, counseling, psychological services, education, commerce and industry, community leadership and development, rehabilitation services, health promotion, and physical, art, occupational, and recreational therapy.

Applying

Applications for the Physical Therapy and Occupational Therapy Programs are reviewed on a rolling admissions basis beginning December 1 and January 1, respectively. Applications are due by March 1 for the Master of Social Work degree. All other programs follow a rolling admissions process, in which files are reviewed as they become complete. The general application deadline is January 15. The financial aid application deadline is March 1. Notification usually takes a minimum of six weeks from receipt of an application. Candidates lacking undergraduate prerequisites must make up their deficiencies without earning graduate credit for these. Standardized tests and interviews are not a regular part of the admission process for most master's and certificate students. However, the General Test of the GRE is required of exercise science and sport studies, physical education, physical therapy, and sport management and recreation applicants. In some programs, personal interviews are a prerequisite to action on the application. Scores on the General Test of the GRE are also required of doctoral students.

Correspondence and Information

Donald J. Shaw Jr.
Director of Graduate Admissions
Box P.G.
Springfield College
Springfield, Massachusetts 01109

Phone: 413-748-3225
Fax: 413-748-3694
E-mail: graduate@springfieldcollege.edu
Web site: http://www.springfieldcollege.edu

THE FACULTY

There are more than 100 faculty members teaching graduate-level courses. They hold degrees from colleges and universities in the United States and abroad, and approximately two thirds of them have doctorates. Many are authorities in their fields, and all members of the graduate faculty teach. In addition, many engage in research or writing projects as their teaching loads permit.

GRADUATE PROGRAMS
Dean: Betty L. Mann, Associate Professor of Physical Education; D.P.E., Springfield, 1984.
Director of Graduate Admissions: Donald J. Shaw Jr., M.Ed., Springfield, 1970.

Program Coordinators
Art Therapy: Simone Alter-Muri, Professor of Art; Ed.D., Massachusetts, 1994.
Education: Gerard P. Thibodeau, Associate Professor of Education; Ph.D., Connecticut, 1978.
Exercise Science and Sport Studies: Charles J. Redmond, Associate Professor of Physical Education; M.S.P.T., Boston University, 1981.
Healthcare Management: John J. Doyle Jr., Professor of Economics; Ph.D., Clark, 1976.
Human Services: Ann Marie Frisbe, Coordinator of Admissions, School of Human Services; B.A., St. Michael's, 1993.
Occupational Therapy: Katherine M. Post, Associate Professor of Occupational Therapy; Ph.D., Connecticut, 2004.
Physical Education: Stephen Coulon, Associate Professor of Physical Education; Ph.D., Ohio State, 1987.
Physical Therapy: Linda Tsoumas, Associate Professor of Physical Therapy; Ph.D., Hartford, 2002.
Psychology: Anna Moriarty, Associate Professor of Psychology; Ph.D., US International, 1979.
Rehabilitation Services: Thomas J. Ruscio, Professor of Rehabilitation; C.A.S., Springfield, 1966.
Social Work: Francine Vecchiolla, Dean, School of Social Work; Ph.D., Brandeis, 1987.
Sport Management and Recreation: Donald R. Snyder, Professor of Sport Management and Recreation; Ph.D., Connecticut, 1987.

SUNY BROCKPORT

STATE UNIVERSITY OF NEW YORK COLLEGE AT BROCKPORT

Graduate Studies

Programs of Study

SUNY College at Brockport is accredited by the Middle States Association of Colleges and Universities and the Board of Regents of the University of the State of New York. The College offers twenty-seven graduate programs, including M.A. degrees in communication, dance, English, history, liberal studies, mathematics, and psychology; M.S. degrees in biological sciences, computational science, environmental science and biology, and recreation and leisure; M.F.A. degrees in dance and visual studies; an M.P.A. in public administration; M.S.Ed. degrees in counseling, education (including graduate teacher certification programs), educational administration, health education, physical education, and additional teacher certification areas; a Master of Science in Social Work (M.S.W., in collaboration with Nazareth College of Rochester); and Certificates of Advanced Study (C.A.S.) in school counseling, educational administration, and school business administration.

Graduate teacher certification programs include bilingual education, biology and general science 5–12, chemistry and general science 5–12, childhood education 1–6, childhood literacy birth to grade 2, dance pre-K–12, earth sciences and general science 5–12, English 5–12, health education pre-K–12, mathematics 5–12, physical education pre-K–12, physics and general science 5–12, school building leader, school business leader, school counselor, school district leader, and social studies 5–12.

Research Facilities

SUNY Brockport's Drake Memorial Library offers a full range of services and houses a collection of more than 472,000 books, 101,000 bound periodicals, 2 million microforms, 9,000 media items, 25,000 cataloged government documents, subscriptions to more than 800 journals and magazines in print form, and online database subscriptions to more than 27,000 periodical titles. Students can access electronic reserves, conduct online searches, and download publications from remote sites or from more than 100 PCs in the library. The library's extended hours are particularly helpful for students whose classes meet in the evenings. Students studying primarily at the downtown SUNY Brockport MetroCenter can use the MetroCenter's three computer labs, or they can use the SUNY Student Resource Center in the Bausch & Lomb Building of the Rochester Public Library, which provides PCs that are linked to the Internet and Drake Memorial Library. The on-campus two-story computing center is augmented by twenty satellite computing labs, providing more than 700 public access workstations to students and offering standard and specialized software as well as Internet access.

SUNY Brockport is home to several centers, institutes, and unique academic endeavors that enrich the academic enterprise, including the Center for Philosophic Exchange, sponsoring programs of philosophic inquiry on academic and public issues; the Child and Adolescent Stress Management Institute, offering preventive health programming to campus and public audiences; the Congress on Research in Dance, providing opportunities for dance scholars, professionals, and graduate students to exchange ideas and methodologies through publication, conferences, and workshops; the Institute for Leadership Development in Public Safety and Criminal Justice, providing interactive training and workshops, conducting agency needs assessments, and sponsoring other organizational and employee development programs that include planning and evaluation services; the Monroe County Historian's Office, providing assistance with local history projects to county and village historians and the general public; the Visual Studies Workshop, an affiliate of SUNY Brockport, offering courses and the M.F.A. program for Brockport graduate art students; and the Writers Forum and Videotape Library, advancing the appreciation for and practice of the art of writing through sponsored public readings by writers of local, national, and international reputation.

Financial Aid

Of the 1,215 matriculated graduate students enrolled for fall 2006, 438 full- and part-time students (36 percent) received financial aid. Some graduate students hold teaching, graduate, and research assistantships. A competitive fellowship program provides opportunities for students who have been admitted to graduate study and who will contribute to the diversity of the student body in the graduate program in which enrollment is sought. Full or partial tuition scholarships accompany most assistantships and fellowships. Graduate Opportunity Tuition Scholarships are available to students who participated in undergraduate EOP, HEOP, or SEEK programs, as funding permits.

Cost of Study

Full-time tuition for 2006–07 was $6900 per academic year for New York State residents and $10,920 per academic year for nonresidents. Part-time tuition was $288 per credit for residents and $455 per credit for nonresidents. All tuition rates are subject to adjustment by the Board of Trustees. College fees total $706 per academic year for full-time graduate students and $29.23 per credit for part-time students. Because the M.S.W. program operates as a bi-institutional collaborative program, the tuition structure for this program varies from the tuition of SUNY Brockport. For current tuition rates, applicants may contact the program directly by phone at 585-395-8450 or by e-mail at grcmsw@brockport.edu.

Living and Housing Costs

Housing is offered to graduate students on a first-come, space-available basis. On-campus housing offers easy access to computing facilities, the library, recreational and dining facilities, and cultural events. All standard services are provided, including Internet and cable TV access and free laundry facilities. A double-occupancy room is $5090 per person per academic year. Meal plans currently range from $2400 to $3400 per academic year.

Student Group

SUNY Brockport's total enrollment for fall 2006 was 8,312 (3,452 men and 4,860 women), with a graduate student population of 1,396 (493 men and 903 women), of whom 355 (108 men and 247 women) were engaged in full-time study.

Location

SUNY Brockport is located in the village of Brockport, 16 miles west of Rochester, New York. Brockport combines the familiarity and friendliness of a charming college town with easy access to the opportunities of a metropolitan city. The College's 435-acre campus is only 10 miles from the southern shores of Lake Ontario, with its many parks and beaches; within short driving distance of New York State's renowned Finger Lakes; and within easy reach of area ski resorts. The College is 20 minutes by car from the Monroe County International Airport, 1 hour from Niagara Falls, and 3 hours from Toronto.

The College

Student success is at the heart of the College's mission statement: "Brockport has the success of its students as its highest priority, emphasizing student learning and committed to advancing teaching, scholarship, creative endeavors, and service." The foundation for today's comprehensive institution was laid in 1841 with the opening of the Brockport Collegiate Institute. Over the years, the College has expanded beyond its sole focus on teacher education to become a comprehensive institution offering both baccalaureate and master's programs. Since the College began sponsoring graduate education over half a century ago, the graduate alumni now number more than 12,000.

The campus includes sixty-eight buildings, professional-quality athletic fields, and open and wooded land. Recent renovations include Hartwell Hall ($10 million), which houses several departments, including the Department of Dance, with theater and performance spaces; Lennon Hall Science Complex ($20 million); and the Seymour College Union, with expanded dining facilities, 24-hour computer lab, and enhanced student activity space.

Applying

Applications should be filed directly with the Office of Graduate Admissions. Deadlines for filing applications vary by department. Application forms and information describing the credentials required for admission to SUNY Brockport's graduate programs are available at the Web site or the school.

Correspondence and Information

The Office of Graduate Admissions
SUNY College at Brockport
350 New Campus Drive
Brockport, New York 14420

Phone: 585-395-5465
585-395-2525
E-mail: gradadmit@brockport.edu
Web site: http://www.brockport.edu/graduate

State University of New York College at Brockport

GRADUATE PROGRAM ADMINISTRATORS AND DIRECTORS

The area code for all numbers is 585.

ADMINISTRATORS

Dean of Graduate Studies: Susan Stites-Doe, Ph.D., 395-2525, sstites@brockport.edu.
Assistant Director of Graduate Admissions: Mr. Julian Ortiz, 395-5465, jortiz@brockport.edu.
School of Arts and Performance: Francis X. Short, P.E.D., Dean, 395-2350, fshort@brockport.edu.
School of Letters and Sciences: Stuart Appelle, Ph.D., Dean, 395-2394, sappelle@brockport.edu.
School of Professions: Christine Murray, Ph.D., Dean, 395-2510, cmurray@brockport.edu.

GRADUATE PROGRAM DIRECTORS/CONTACTS

School of Arts and Performance
Communication (M.A.): Matthew Althouse, Ph.D., 395-5203, malthous@brockport.edu.
Dance (M.A./M.F.A.): Darwin Prioleau, Ed.D., 395-2023, dpriolea@brockport.edu.
Physical Education (M.S.Ed.): William Stier, Ed.D., 395-5331, bstier@brockport.edu.
Visual Studies Workshop (M.F.A.): Christopher Burnett, M.F.A., 442-8676, cburnett@brockport.edu.

School of Letters and Sciences
Biological Sciences (M.S.): Adam Rich, Ph.D., 395-5740, arich@brockport.edu.
Computational Sciences (M.S.): Osman Yasar, Ph.D., 395-2595, oyasar@brockport.edu.
English (M.A.): Miriam E. Burstein, Ph.D., 395-5827, mburstei@brockport.edu
Environmental Science and Biology (M.S.): Joseph Makarewicz, Ph.D., 395-5747, jmakarew@brockport.edu.
History (M.A.): Jennifer Lloyd, Ph.D., 395-5680, jlloyd@brockport.edu.
Liberal Studies (M.A.): Kulathur Rajasethupathy, Ph.D., 395-2262, kraja@brockport.edu.
Mathematics (M.A.): Dawn Jones, Ph.D., 395-5174, djones@brockport.edu.
Psychology (M.A.): Janet Gillespie, Ph.D., 395-2433, jgillesp@brockport.edu.

School of Professions
Counselor Education (M.S.Ed./C.A.S.): Susan Rachel Seem, Ph.D., 395-2258, sseem@brockport.edu.
Educational Administration (M.S.Ed./C.A.S.): Sandra Graczyk, Ed.D., 395-5802, slgraczyk@aol.com.
Education and Human Development (M.S.Ed.): Sandra Selden, M.S., 395-2326, sselden@brockport.edu.
Health Science (M.S.Ed.): Patti Follansbee, Ph.D., 395-5483, pfollans@brockport.edu.
Public Administration (M.P.A.): James Fatula, Ph.D., 395-2375, jfatula@brockport.edu.
Recreation and Leisure (M.S.): Joel Frater, Ed.D., 395-5338, jfrater@brockport.edu.
Social Work (M.S.W.): Carol Brownstein-Evans, Ph.D., 395-8450, grcmsw@brockport.edu.

STATE UNIVERSITY OF NEW YORK INSTITUTE OF TECHNOLOGY

School of Business, School of Information Systems and Engineering Technology, School of Arts and Sciences, and School of Nursing and Health Systems

Programs of Study

Full-time or part-time graduate students at the State University of New York Institute of Technology (SUNYIT) can pursue the Master of Business Administration (M.B.A.) degree in technology management or a Master of Science (M.S.) degree in one of twelve programs, some of which have online options.

In the School of Business, the M.B.A. degree in technology management prepares managers for careers in the high-tech business world. The M.B.A. degree offers both a broad and integrative perspective across business functions as well as a chance to specialize in a field of one's choice. The program, which is available online, offers the following concentrations: accounting and finance, e-commerce and marketing, health services, human resource management, and an individually designed concentration. SUNYIT's School of Business also offers three M.S. degree programs in accountancy, business management, and health services administration, with concentrations available in accounting and finance, health services management, human resources management, and marketing. The accounting program, which is also available online and is registered in New York State to satisfy the 150-hour licensure requirement, prepares students for careers in public, corporate, not-for-profit, and government accounting. Graduates are prepared to sit for professional accounting examinations that lead to credentials such as the CPA and CMA designations. The focus of course work in the business management program is on the use of quantitative and qualitative analysis in conjunction with financial, accounting, and economic principles to solve current and future business challenges. The health services administration program, which is also available online, prepares students for management positions in the health-care industry.

The School of Information Systems and Engineering Technology offers three graduate degrees. The M.S. degree in computer and information science is designed to provide students with a strong theoretical and application-oriented education. Course offerings stress principles of problem-solving methodology that are required of computer professionals working in industry and education or those pursuing advanced degrees. The M.S. degree in advanced technology is an interdisciplinary program with an emphasis on practical applications and is designed for part-time students. A number of Internet-based online courses are available. The M.S. degree in telecommunications is based on a solid core of telecommunications courses combined with computer science/information systems and business-related components to provide a broad knowledge of design, management, and maintenance of complex telecommunication systems.

SUNYIT's School of Arts and Sciences offers two Master of Science degree programs. The M.S. in information design and technology (IDT) meets the needs of professionals who use communication technologies to design and manage information. Students use a variety of computer-based tools to create original materials, including Web pages, multimedia presentations, newsletters, and related desktop publishing documents in fields such as education, technical communication, public relations, marketing, instructional design and technology, government service, publications, and corporate communication. The M.S. in applied sociology promotes the application of anthropological and sociological theory and research to design, implement, and evaluate organizationally based interventions. Students learn to integrate various methods of data collection and analysis to use in evaluating social programs.

The School of Nursing and Health Systems offers five M.S. degree programs: adult nurse practitioner, family nurse practitioner, gerontological nurse practitioner, nursing administration, and nursing education. Graduates of the nurse practitioner programs are prepared to focus on health assessments, disease prevention, health promotion, and the monitoring of chronic conditions with appropriate emphasis on the specific patient groups. Advanced certificates are offered in all programs. The nursing administration program is specifically designed to prepare registered nurses to effectively manage the delivery of nursing services through the synthesis of theories of organization, leadership, and management with nursing theory, practice, and research. The nursing education program promotes the core application of theory, research, and health-care policy to the role of the nurse educator within the academic and in-service settings. Graduates of the master's program are qualified to take the American Nurses Association's certification exam.

Research Facilities

Research facilities include the Cayan Library's 192,425 bound volumes, 65,396 microforms, and an extensive collection of professional journals, newspapers, and other national publications. The library serves as a depository for selected state and federal documents. The library participates in SUNYConnect, the State University's virtual library, which offers many online resources. Graduate students also have access to interlibrary loans. SUNYIT's computing facilities include numerous laboratory environments consisting of more than 380 personal computers and workstations in a networked environment that extends to every classroom, office, and dormitory room. Internet access is provided through a fractional T-3 connection. The master's degree program in telecommunications is supported by three voice, data, and network operations laboratories possessing more than $5 million in industry-donated equipment. The IDT program is supported by a networked computer lab and related technologies, including workstations designed for collaborative project work.

Financial Aid

Matriculated graduate students who are enrolled for at least 6 credit hours each semester and are in good academic standing are eligible to apply for aid from the following sources: Federal Work-Study Program, Federal Perkins Loan Program, and Federal Direct Student Loan Program. New York State residents who are enrolled for at least 12 hours are eligible to apply for aid from the Tuition Assistance Program. Graduate assistantships are awarded each academic year to selected students and generally include a state tuition waiver for work performed as a teaching assistant, research assistant, or administrative assistant. A limited number of Graduate Minority Fellowships, which include a state tuition waiver and stipend, are available to full-time students who are members of underrepresented groups.

Cost of Study

Full-time graduate tuition for New York State residents for the 2006–07 academic year was $3450 per semester for all programs except the M.B.A., which was $3550 per semester. The comprehensive student fee was $463.50 per semester. For nonresidents, full-time graduate tuition was $5460 per semester in all programs except the M.B.A., which was $5670 per semester. Part-time graduate tuition costs for the 2005–06 academic year were $288 per credit hour ($296 for the M.B.A.) for residents and $455 per credit hour ($473 for the M.B.A.) for nonresidents.

Living and Housing Costs

SUNYIT provides town-house-style residence halls for 584 students at $8250 (single rate) for room and board. Residence halls are available on a first-come, first-served basis. Assistance in locating off-campus housing is provided. Complete housing rate information is available online at http://www.catalog.sunyit.edu.

Student Group

SUNYIT offers a small-college atmosphere, enrolling 2,587 undergraduate and graduate students in the fall 2006 semester. There were 125 full-time and 393 part-time graduate students. The ratio of men to women was approximately 1:1. Ten percent of the students were from minority groups; 3.6 percent were international students. Students work closely with faculty members and receive individual attention. Nearly 100 percent of students who have completed graduate programs at SUNYIT are working full-time in their professional field.

Location

SUNYIT is situated in the geographic center of New York State. The campus is just north of the city of Utica, which is a cultural and recreational center for the Mohawk Valley Region. Museums, theaters, and restaurants are available nearby.

The Institute

SUNYIT was established in 1966 by the SUNY Board of Trustees to provide upper-division and graduate-level education in sciences and technologies and now offers undergraduate and graduate degree programs in technology, professional studies, and selected liberal arts disciplines. The campus includes three major academic, administrative, and student life buildings; two town-house-style residential complexes; a facilities building; and a $14-million library, dedicated in 2003. Planning is underway for two buildings: a $20-million field house and a $13.7-million student services building.

Applying

Applications to one of the graduate programs should be completed by June 1 for the fall semester and November 1 for spring. While SUNYIT does offer rolling admission in most programs, these application deadlines are required for international students. Students seeking admission to the adult nurse practitioner, advanced technology, computer science, family nurse practitioner, and nursing administration programs are required to take the Graduate Record Examinations (GRE) General Test. The Graduate Management Admissions Test (GMAT) is required for accountancy and the M.B.A. in technology management. Scores from the GMAT follow the recommended guidelines of AACSB International–The Association to Advance Collegiate Schools of Business. For complete admissions criteria, students should consult the SUNYIT graduate catalog, available online at http://www.catalog.sunyit.edu.

Correspondence and Information

Director of Admissions
State University of New York Institute of Technology
P.O. Box 3050
Utica, New York 13504-3050

Phone: 866-2-SUNYIT (toll-free)
E-mail: admissions@sunyit.edu
Web site: http://www.sunyit.edu

THE FACULTY AND THEIR RESEARCH

School of Arts and Sciences (Information Design and Technology, Applied Sociology)

Maarten Heyboer, Associate Professor; Ph.D., Virginia Tech. Computer-mediated communication and distance learning via the Internet.
Walter Johnston, Associate Professor; Ph.D., Cornell. Technical writing and editing.
Russell Kahn, Associate Professor; Ph.D., SUNY at Albany. Social implications of the Web, graphic design, Web design, and computer software documentation.
Kenneth Mazlen, Associate Professor; Ph.D., SUNY at Albany. Social theory, white-collar crime, unemployment and crime.
Alphonse Sallett, Associate Professor; Ph.D., Syracuse. Social theory, criminology and the sociology of drug use.
Steven Schneider, Professor; Ph.D., MIT. Computer-mediated communication and computer-mediated instructional systems.
Veronica Tichenor, Assistant Professor; Ph.D., Michigan. Marriages and families, sociology of community, violence and identity construction.
Linda Weber, Associate Professor; Ph.D., North Texas. Social practice, medical sociology, social psychology, health promotion, at-risk youth.

School of Business (M.B.A. in Technology Management; M.S. in Accountancy, Business Management, and Health Services Administration)

John Barnes, Associate Professor; Ph.D., Arizona State. Marketing.
Lisa Berardino, Associate Professor; Ph.D., Virginia Tech. Human resource management in small businesses, adult learning and needs assessment.
Sema Dube, Assistant Professor; Ph.D., George Washington. Firm acquisitions and mergers.
Laura Francis-Gladney, Assistant Professor; Ph.D., Southern Illinois Carbondale. Accounting.
Joseph Gerard, Assistant Professor; Ph.D., Georgia. Technology management.
J. Allen Hall, Associate Professor; Ph.D., Iowa. Communications for business.
Kimberly Jarrell, Assistant Professor; Ph.D., Syracuse. Marketing and technology.
Peter Karl, Associate Professor; J.D., Albany Law; M.B.A., Rensselaer; CPA. Tax, business law, real estate transactions, federal taxation.
William Langdon, Professor; Ph.D., Syracuse. Quantitative methods and finance.
Hoseoup Lee, Assistant Professor; Ph.D., Connecticut. Capital markets and accounting information systems.
David McLain, Assistant Professor; Ph.D, Wisconsin-Madison. Technology management.
Edward Petronio, Associate Professor; Ph.D., Syracuse. Business policy and organizational behavior.
Rafael F. Romero, Associate Professor; Ph.D., West Virginia. Emerging capital markets, international economics.
Gary Scherzer, Associate Professor; M.P.H., Tennessee. Public health, planning, marketing, health policy.
Maureen Smith-Gaffney, Assistant Professor; Ph.D., Ohio State. Accounting.
Janice Welker, Assistant Professor; Ph.D., St. Louis. Managed care, economics.
Robert Yeh, Assistant Professor; Ph.D., Purdue. Quantitative marketing models, statistical applications and mathematical modeling in product designing and product improvement.

School of Information Systems and Engineering Technology (Advanced Technology, Computer Information Science, and Telecommunications)

Bruno Andriamanalimanana, Associate Professor; Ph.D., Lehigh. Combinatorics, coding theory and cryptography.
Daniel Benincasa, Assistant Professor; Ph.D., Rensselaer. Digital signal processing, electrooptic systems, RF systems, communication intelligence systems.
Roger Cavallo, Professor; Ph.D., SUNY at Binghamton. Systems theory, systems methodology, conceptual modeling, probabilistic database theory.
Digendra Kumar Das, Associate Professor; Ph.D., Manchester (England). CAD/CAM/CIM, fluid/prognostics, turbomachinery and thermal sciences and MEMS.
Heather Dussault, Assistant Professor; Ph.D., Rensselaer. Nuclear engineering and science.
Larry Hash, Associate Professor of Telecommunications; Ph.D., North Carolina State. Wireless networks and services, LAN-WAN.
Atlas Hsie, Associate Professor; M.S., Michigan; M.S., Akron; CmfgE, CQE, CRE. Quality and reliability engineering, engineering economics, production management, CAM and robotics.
Raymond G. Jesaitis, Professor; Ph.D., Cornell. Distributed systems, UNIX operating system, numerical methods.
Daniel K. Jones, Assistant Professor; Ph.D., Pittsburgh; PE. Rehabilitation engineering and assistive technology, experimental fluid mechanics and FMS.
Michael J. Medley, Assistant Professor; Ph.D., Rensselaer. Lapped transform domain excision, adaptive nonlinear/linear filtering, RA -OFDM, wireless information assurance, integrated transmission and exploitation.
Rosemary Mullick, Associate Professor; Ph.D., Wayne State. Operating systems, artificial intelligence, computer networks, parallels between human cognition and artificial intelligence and human engineering.
Eugene J. Newman, Professor of Telecommunications; Ph.D., Wisconsin. International telecommunications policy and trade issues, project management.
Jorge Novillo, Professor; Ph.D., Lehigh. Combinatorics, complexity, artificial intelligence.
Michael Pittarelli, Professor; Ph.D., SUNY at Binghamton. Systems science, artificial intelligence, statistics, database theory.
Salahuddin Qazi, Associate Professor; Ph.D., Loughborough (England). Fiber optics, optical and wireless communications.
Mohamed Rezk, Associate Professor; D.Eng., Concordia. Circuit theory, computer-aided circuit design, and digital filters.
Ronald Sarner, Distinguished Service Professor; Ph.D., SUNY at Binghamton. Data modeling, statistical inference in the social sciences, instructional computing.
Saumendra Sengupta, Professor; Ph.D., Waterloo. Systems modeling, computer networks and distributed systems, pattern recognition.
Scott Spetka, Associate Professor; Ph.D., UCLA. Distributed database systems and distributed query processing.
Anglo-Kamel Tadros, Associate Professor; Ph.D., Bradford (England). Mechanics of sheet metal forming, computer-aided engineering, finite element analysis.

School of Nursing and Health Systems (Nursing Administration, Nursing Education, Gerontological Nurse Practitioner, Family Nurse Practitioner, Adult Nurse Practitioner)

Esther G. Bankert, Associate Professor; Ph.D., SUNY at Albany. Critical thinking and instruction, ethical decision making models and moral development in the RN student.
Louise Dean-Kelly, Associate Professor; D.N.S., SUNY at Buffalo. Definition of health and health-care practices through cross-cultural studies.
Deborah A. Hayes, Clinical Assistant Professor; M.S., SUNY at Binghamton. Family health.
Christeen Liang, Clinical Assistant Professor; M.S., SUNY at Binghamton. Women's health.
Gina Myers, Ph.D., SUNY at Binghamton, Nursing education.
Kathleen F. Sellers, Assistant Professor; Ph.D., Adelphi. Nursing systems.
Amy Shaver, M.S., SUNY Technology. Nursing administration and community health nursing.
Pat Zawko, M.S., SUNY Technology. Nursing administration and community health nursing.

STONY BROOK UNIVERSITY, STATE UNIVERSITY OF NEW YORK

Graduate School

Programs of Study

The Graduate School at Stony Brook University offers more than 102 master's and forty doctoral degrees in a wide range of academic disciplines. In addition, the University offers Advanced Graduate Degree Certificates and Postdoctoral Certificates in a variety of areas of study.

Located just 50 miles east of Manhattan, Stony Brook has been recognized as a leading research university in the Northeast. In 2004, *London Times Higher Education Supplement* ranked Stony Brook in the top 150 universities in the world and tenth among U.S. public universities. The Graduate School is also a recent recipient of Peterson's Award for Innovation in Promoting an Inclusive Graduate Community, which is given to a university that demonstrates the importance of campuswide diversity initiatives to advance a multicultural perspective among faculty members, students, and staff members and to enhance learning.

The diversity and excellence of the faculty are key to the University's research accomplishments and the scholarly advances of its students. Stony Brook's faculty includes several scientists from Brookhaven National Laboratory and Cold Spring Harbor Laboratory, who serve as advisers to more than 100 graduate students. World-renowned scholars come to Stony Brook regularly as visiting professors and lecturers, further adding to its academic offerings. Richard Leakey, the famed anthropologist and environmental activist, joined the Department of Anthropology in 2003. The Emerson String Quartet, one of the world's foremost chamber ensembles, joined the Department of Music as Quartet-in-Residence in fall 2002, and internationally known intellectuals such as Noam Chomsky and Angela Davis have been visitors to the Department of Philosophy.

For a complete listing and description of Stony Brook's graduate degree programs, students should visit the Graduate School's Web site at http://www.grad.sunysb.edu or call 631-632-GRAD.

Research Facilities

Research support is provided by the Frank Melville Jr. Memorial Library, the Health Sciences Library, and six branch science libraries, holding more than 2 million volumes and 3 million publications in microformat. Sun, IBM, and DEC computers in the Division of Information Technology and in other academic departments are available for general research use. There are more than 800 publicly available state-of-the-art computers for student use. E-mail and Internet accounts are provided to all full-time students. Campus facilities extend to New York City with Stony Brook Manhattan, a facility on Park Avenue that offers graduate courses as well as special events and lectures. The University also includes Stony Brook Southampton, a new college focusing on environmental sustainability, public policy, and natural resource management. Many graduate students also conduct research at nearby Cold Spring Harbor Laboratories and Brookhaven National Laboratories. Other research facilities include the Institute for Theoretical Physics, the Humanities Institute, and the Marine Science Research Center.

Financial Aid

Because Stony Brook is committed to attracting high-quality students, the Graduate School provides two competitive fellowships for U.S. citizens and permanent residents. Graduate Council fellowships are for outstanding doctoral candidates studying in any discipline, and the W. Burghardt Turner Fellowships target outstanding African-American, Hispanic American, and Native American students entering either a doctoral or master's degree program. For doctoral students, both fellowships provide an annual stipend of at least $17,572 for up to five years, as well as a full-tuition scholarship. For master's students, the Turner Fellowship provides an annual stipend of $10,000 for up to two years, along with a full-tuition scholarship. Health insurance subsidies are also provided within a scale, depending on the size of the fellow's dependent family. Departments and degree programs award approximately 900 teaching and graduate assistantships and approximately 600 research assistantships on an annual basis. Full assistantships carry a stipend amount that usually ranges from $15,145 to more than $25,000, depending on the department.

Cost of Study

In 2006–07, full-time tuition for 12 credits for entering in-state residents was $3450 per semester, while out-of-state residents and international students paid $5460. Additional fees for each semester, including (but not limited to) the infirmary, activity, technology, and transportation fees, total about $430. International students also pay a service fee of $35 per semester and an orientation fee of $50. Fees for the mandatory Student Health Insurance Plan vary, depending on citizenship and employment status.

Living and Housing Costs

For 2006–07, Stony Brook calculated the cost of education, excluding tuition, fees, and insurance, to be $13,520 per year. On-campus apartments range in cost from approximately $315 per month to approximately $1455 per month, depending on the size of the unit and the number of students sharing the space. Off-campus housing options include rooms, houses, and apartments that can be rented for $350 to $2500 per month. Costs such as books, food, and transportation may vary, depending on academic program and/or personal circumstances.

Student Group

Stony Brook University's Graduate School attracts a diverse array of students from across the country and around the world. Stony Brook's current enrollment is 22,527 students. Graduate students number more than 6,220 and come from all states in the nation as well as from some seventy-five countries. International students, both graduate and undergraduate, represent about 10 percent of the total student body. Stony Brook graduate students have won awards as researchers and teachers in the arts, sciences, social sciences, engineering, and the humanities. Many have attained prestigious doctoral fellowships and faculty positions in the nation's finest universities.

Location

Stony Brook's campus is approximately 60 miles east of Manhattan on the north shore of Long Island. The cultural offerings of New York City and Suffolk County's countryside and seashore are conveniently located nearby. Cold Spring Harbor Laboratories and Brookhaven National Laboratories are easily accessible from, and have close relationships with, the University.

The University

The University, which was established in 1957, achieved national stature within a generation. Founded at Oyster Bay, Long Island, the school moved to its present location in 1962. Stony Brook has grown to encompass more than 123 buildings on 1,100 acres. There are more than 1,900 faculty members, and the annual budget is more than $1.6 billion. Stony Brook's prominence as a leading research institution was recognized when the University was invited to join the prestigious Association of American Universities in 2001. The Graduate Student Organization oversees the spending of the student activity fee for graduate student campus events. International students find the additional four-week Summer Institute in American Living very helpful. The Intensive English Center offers classes in English as a second language. The Career Development Office assists with career planning and has information on permanent full-time employment. Disabled Student Services has a Resource Center that offers placement testing, tutoring, vocational assessment, and psychological counseling. The Counseling Center provides individual, group, family, and marital counseling and psychotherapy. Day-care services are provided in four on-campus facilities. The Writing Center offers tutoring in all phases of writing.

Applying

Applicants are judged on the basis of distinguished undergraduate records (and graduate records, if applicable), thorough preparation for advanced study and research in the field of interest, candid appraisals from those familiar with the applicant's academic/professional work, potential for graduate study, and a clearly defined statement of purpose and scholarly interest germane to the program. A baccalaureate degree is required, with a minimum overall grade point average of 2.75 and average grade of B in the major and related courses. Some programs require a higher GPA. Students should submit admission and financial aid applications by January 15 for the fall semester and by October 1 for the spring semester. Decisions are made on a rolling basis as space permits. The $60 application fee may be waived in some circumstances.

Correspondence and Information

For further information, students should contact the graduate program director listed in the Faculty section of this description (area code is 631) or phone or write:

Graduate School
State University of New York at Stony Brook
Stony Brook, New York 11794-4433

Phone: 631-632-4723
Fax: 631-632-7243
E-mail: graduate.school@sunysb.edu
Web site: http://www.grad.sunysb.edu

THE FACULTY

According to the most recent independent, quantitative study, Stony Brook ranked among the top three public research universities in the nation on the basis of faculty productivity in research and scholarship. With the total research volume nearly doubling in the last decade and now exceeding $150 million annually, Stony Brook's researchers have propelled the University to the top position among all of New York's public institutions in federally sponsored project funding. Adjusted for size, Stony Brook can claim more members of the most selective national bodies of scholars than any other public university in the Northeast. Stony Brook faculty members are part of the National Academy of Sciences, the National Academy of Engineering, and the American Academy of Arts and Sciences. Distinguished faculty members and some of their most outstanding accomplishments include C. N. Yang, Physics (emeritus), Nobel laureate; applied mathematician James Glimm, Dannie Heineman Prize for mathematics; mathematician James Milnor, Fields Medal, Wolf Prize; the Emerson String Quartet and Ani Kavafian, Artists-in-Residence in Music; neuroscientist Paul Adams, MacArthur Award; anatomist John Fleagle, MacArthur Award; George C. Williams, Ecology and Evolution (emeritus), Royal Swedish Academy of Sciences Crafoord Prize; anthropologist Patricia Wright, whose work was recently featured in the award-winning documentary *Me and Isaac Newton,* MacArthur Award; mathematician Dennis Sullivan, King Faisal International Prize of Science; and neuroscientist Gail Mandel, Howard Hughes Medical Institute Investigator.

BASIC HEALTH SCIENCES Craig Malbon, Vice Dean.
Anatomical Sciences: Maureen O'Leary, Director, 444-3114, moleary@stonybrook.edu; William Jungers, Chairperson.
Molecular and Cellular Pharmacology: Stella Tsirka, Director, 444-3057, stella.tsirka@stonybrook.edu; Jeffrey Pessin, Chairperson.
Molecular Genetics and Microbiology: Janet Hearing, Director, 632-8812, janet.hearing@stonybrook.edu; Jorge Benach, Chairperson.
Oral Biology and Pathology: Marcia Simon, Director, 632-8923, marcia.simon@stonybrook.edu; Israel Kleinberg, Chairperson.
Physiology and Biophysics: Suzanne Scarlata, Director, 444-2299, suzanne.scarlata@stonybrook.edu; Peter Brink, Chairperson.
Medical Scientist Training Program (M.D./Ph.D.): Michael A. Frohman, 632-1476, michael.frohman@stonybrook.edu.

DENTISTRY Barry Rifkin, Dean, 632-8950.
Debra Cinotti, Assistant Dean for Admissions and Student Affairs, 632-3745, debra.cinotti@stonybrook.edu.

HEALTH TECHNOLOGY AND MANAGEMENT Craig Lehmann, Dean.
Health Policy, Management and Education: Nanci Rice, Director, 444-3240, nanci.rice@stonybrook.edu; Alan Leiken, Chairperson.

MEDICINE Richard N. Fine, Dean.
Grace Agnetti, Assistant Dean for Admissions, 444-2113, grace.agnetti@stonybrook.edu.

NURSING Lenora J. McClean, Dean.
Philip Tarantino, Student Affairs and Continuing Professional Education, 444-3200, philip.tarantino@stonybrook.edu.

SOCIAL WELFARE Frances Brisbane, Dean.
Ph.D. Program: Joel Blau, Director, 444-8361, joel.blau@stonybrook.edu.
M.S.W. Program: Linda Francis, Director, 444-3141, linda.francis@stonybrook.edu.

COLLEGE OF ARTS AND SCIENCES James Staros, Dean.
Anthropological Science (Ph.D.): Elizabeth Stone, Director, 632-7606, elizabeth.stone@stonybrook.edu; Diane Doran, Chairperson.
Anthropology (M.A.): Karen Kramer, Director, 632-7606, karen.kramer@stonybrook.edu; Fred Grine, Chairperson.
Art: Michele Bogart, Director, 632-7270, michele.bogart@stonybrook.edu; Mel Pekarsky, Chairperson.
Biochemistry and Structural Biology: Erwin London, Director, 632-8533, erwin.london@stonybrook.edu; William Lennarz, Chairperson.
Chemistry: Dale Drueckhammer, Director, 632-7912, dale.drueckhammer@stonybrook.edu; Michael White, Chairperson.
Comparative Literature: Sandy Petrey, Director, 632-7456, sandy.petrey@stonybrook.edu; Robert Harvey, Chairperson.
Ecology and Evolution (Ph.D.): Geeta Bharathan, Director, 632-8604, geeta.bharathan@stonybrook.edu; Jessica Guervitch, Chairperson.
Ecology and Evolution (M.A.): Lev Ginzburg, Director, 632-8604, lev.ginzburg@stonybrook.edu.
Economics: Sandro Brusco, Director, 632-7530, sandro.brusco@stonybrook.edu; Warren Sanderson, Chairperson.
English: Celia Marshik, Director, 632-7373, celia.marshik@stonybrook.edu; Peter Manning, Chairperson.
European Languages, Literatures, and Cultures: Andrea Fedi, Director, 632-7442, timothy.westphalen@stonybrook.edu; Nicholas Rzhevsky, Chairperson.
Genetics: Gerald Thomsen, Director, 632-8812, gerald.h.thomsen@stonybrook.edu.
Geosciences: Lianxing Wen, Director, 632-8554, lianxing.wen@stonybrook.edu; Teng-Fong Wang, Chairperson.
Hispanic Languages and Literature: Lou Deutsch, Director, 632-6935, lou.deutsch@stonybrook.edu; Victoriano Roncero-Lopez, Chairperson.
History: Tom Klubock, Director, 632-7490, thomas.klubock@stonybrook.edu; Ned Landsman, Chairperson.
Linguistics: Alice Harris, Director, 632-1901, alice.harris@stonybrook.edu; Daniel Finer, Chairperson.
Mathematics: Michael Anderson, Director, 632-8282, michael.anderson@stonybrook.edu; David Ebin, Chairperson.
Mathematics (Secondary Teaching Option): Bernard Maskit, Director, 632-8282, bernard.maskit@stonybrook.edu.
Molecular and Cellular Biology: Rolf Sternglanz, Director, 632-8533, rolf.sternglanz@stonybrook.edu; William Lennarz, Chairperson.
Music: Peter Winkler, Director, 632-7352, peter.winkler@stonybrook.edu; Daniel Weymouth, Chairperson.
Neurobiology and Behavior: Lonnie Wollmuth, Director, 632-8630, lonnie.wollmuth@stonybrook.edu; Simon Halegoua, Chairperson.
Philosophy: Jeff Edwards, Director, 632-7580, b.edwards@stonybrook.edu; Robert Crease, Chairperson.
Physics and Astronomy: Laszlo Mihaly, Director, 632-8080, laszlo.mihaly@stonybrook.edu; Peter Koch, Chairperson.
Political Science (Ph.D.): Charles Taber, Director, 632-7667, charles.taber@stonybrook.edu; Jeffrey Segal, Chairperson.
Psychology: Arthur Samuel, Director, 632-7855, arthur.samuel@stonybrook.edu; Nancy Squires, Chairperson.
Public Policy (M.A.): Scott Basinger, Director, 632-7667, scott.basinger@stonybrook.edu.
Public Health (M.P.H.): Raymond L. Goldsteen, Director, 444-2074, raymond.goldsteen@stonybrook.edu.
Sociology: Timothy Moran, Director, 632-7730, tpmoran@stonybrook.edu; Diane Barthel-Bouchier, Chairperson.
Theater Arts: Steve Marsh, Director, 632-4596, steve.marsh@stonybrook.edu; Peggy Morin, Chairperson.
Women's Studies: Oyeronke Oyewumi, Director, 632-9176, oyeronke.oyewumi@stonybrook.edu.

COLLEGE OF BUSINESS Bill Turner, Dean.
Business Administration: Owen Carroll, Director, 632-7171, tcarroll@stonybrook.edu; Joe McDonnell, Chairperson.

COLLEGE OF ENGINEERING AND APPLIED SCIENCE Yacov Shamash, Dean.
Applied Math and Statistics: Xiaolin Li, Director, 632-8360, xiaolin.li@stonybrook.edu; James Glimm, Chairperson.
Biomedical Engineering: Michael Hadjiargyrou, Director, 444-2303, michael.hadjiargyrou@stonybrook.edu; Clinton Rubin, Chairperson.
Computer Science: I. V. Ramakrishnan, Director, 632-8462, iv.ramakrishnan@stonybrook.edu; Arie Kaufman, Chairperson.
Electrical and Computer Engineering: Yuanyuan Yang, Director, 632-8400, yuanyuan.yang@stonybrook.edu; Serge Luryi, Chairperson.
Information Systems Management: Rob Kelly, Director, 632-7543, robert.kelly@stonybrook.edu.
Materials Science: Dilip Gersappe, Director, 632-4986, dilip.gersappe@stonybrook.edu; Michael Dudley, Chairperson.
Mechanical Engineering: Peisen Huang, Director, 632-8340, peisen.huang@stonybrook.edu; Fu-Pen Chiang, Chairperson.
Technology and Society: Sheldon J. Reaven, Director, 632-8765, sheldon.reaven@stonybrook.edu; David Ferguson, Chairperson.

MARINE SCIENCE RESEARCH CENTER David Conover, Dean.
Marine Sciences: Anne McElroy, Director, 632-8681, anne.mcelroy@stonybrook.edu.

SCHOOL OF PROFESSIONAL DEVELOPMENT Paul Edelson, Dean, 632-7050.
Graduate Degrees and Advanced Graduate Certificates for Evening, Part-Time, and Online Study: Veronica Bersamin, Director of Admission and Advisement, 632-7050, veronica.bersamin@stonybrook.edu.

TEACHERS COLLEGE COLUMBIA UNIVERSITY

Programs of Study

Teachers College is the world's largest and most comprehensive graduate school of education, applied psychology, and health professions. Programs lead to Master of Arts, Master of Science, Master of Education, Doctor of Education, and Doctor of Philosophy degrees. The College comprises the Departments of Arts and Humanities; Biobehavioral Studies; Counseling and Clinical Psychology; Curriculum and Teaching; Health and Behavioral Studies; Human Development; International and Transcultural Studies; Mathematics, Science, and Technology; and Organization and Leadership. These nine departments are augmented by centers, institutes, and projects that reinforce instructional areas with research, service, and experiential initiatives. Teachers College puts strong emphasis on consultation and field research and on close faculty-student relationships. Day and evening classes are available.

Areas of study are administration of special education; adult education; adult learning and leadership; anthropology and education; applied anthropology; applied behavior analysis; applied linguistics; applied physiology; applied physiology and nutrition; art and art education; arts administration; bilingual/bicultural education; blindness and visual impairment; clinical psychology; cognitive studies in education; communication and education; community nutrition education; comparative and international education; computing and education; conflict resolution; counseling psychology; cross-categorical studies; curriculum and teaching; curriculum and teaching in physical education; deaf and hard of hearing; developmental psychology; early childhood education; early childhood special education; economics and education; educational leadership; educational leadership and management (with Columbia Business School); educational policy; elementary/childhood education; English education; gifted education; guidance and habilitation; health-care human resources; health education; higher and postsecondary education; history and education; instructional practice; instructional technology and media; interdisciplinary studies in education; international educational development; kinesiology; learning disabilities; mathematics education; measurement, evaluation, and statistics; mental retardation; motor learning and control; music and music education; neuroscience and education; nurse executive studies; nursing education; nutrition education; philosophy and education; physical disabilities; physical education; politics and education; psychological counseling; psychology in education; reading and learning disabilities; reading specialist studies; school psychology; science education; social-organizational psychology; social studies; sociology and education; speech and language pathology; supervision of special education; teaching American Sign Language as a foreign language; and teaching English to speakers of other languages.

Research Facilities

The Gottesman Libraries, with more than a million books and materials, is one of the nation's largest and most comprehensive research libraries in education, psychology, and health services. Students also have access to the 5.5 million volumes in the Columbia University library system. Organized research and service activities at Teachers College, in addition to being carried out by individual professors, are conducted through special projects and major institutes. Many of these centers of research are listed later in this description.

Data, voice, and video outlets are found in every classroom, office, and residence on the main portion of the campus, and laptops and projectors may be borrowed from Media Services. The Microcomputer Center provides students with PCs and Macintoshes, software, printers, and other peripherals. The center's software library includes PC and Mac programs for word processing, Web development, graphics, statistical analysis, and qualitative analysis and databases. The Instructional Media Lab (IML) is a facility in which students and faculty members create rich content for classes, online learning, student teaching, and research. Digital cameras and other equipment are loaned. Workstations allow computer-based full-motion video from camera, VCR, or videodisc to be edited and integrated with animation, digitized voice, and music and to be written to CD, DVD, or tape. IML also provides satellite downlink. Computer classrooms for hands-on instruction include both a PC and a Macintosh room, and the Goodman Family Computer Classroom suite includes a classroom with thirty-two notebook computers on tables that can be reconfigured for varying work groups.

Financial Aid

Each year, Teachers College awards approximately $6 million of its own funds in scholarship and stipend aid and $2 million of endowed funds to new and continuing students. There are no separate scholarship applications; faculty members nominate new students based upon their admission application. Financial assistance is also available through federal aid programs. All students are encouraged to file the FAFSA regardless of eligibility for aid; 51 percent of students receive financial aid.

Cost of Study

For the 2006–07 academic year, tuition was $975 per point, with 12 or more points considered full-time. Fees included the Teachers College, $320; Teachers College research, $320; health service, $356; continuous doctoral advisement registration, $2925; and Ph.D. oral defense, $4319. The tuition deposit was $300. Medical insurance ranged from about $553 to $1218.

Living and Housing Costs

Teachers College offers a variety of on-campus housing options that are unique to the area and convenient to the campus. Housing for a single student ranges from $3100 to $8000 per semester, depending upon the type of setting selected. Family housing ranges from $6875 to $8200 per semester. Teachers College has approximately 705 spaces available for single students and 150 apartments for students with families. The buildings are located in the vibrant and historic urban neighborhood of Morningside Heights. Current residence halls are historic buildings similar to other apartment-style buildings that were in New York City in the early 1900s.

Student Group

There are approximately 5,000 students enrolled at Teachers College. About 77 percent are women, 12 percent are African American, 11 percent are Asian American, and 7 percent are Latino/a. The student body is composed of 13 percent international students from eighty different countries and 87 percent domestic students from all fifty states.

Location

The College is located in the Morningside Heights section of Manhattan's Upper West Side. Home to such venerable New York landmarks as Lincoln Center, the Cathedral of St. John the Divine, Grant's Tomb, Morningside Park, and the Manhattan School of Music, the Upper West Side is bounded by Central Park on the east and the Hudson River on the west. Because the College is located in New York City, students have access to an outstanding array of learning organizations, including museums, libraries, galleries, corporate learning centers, and K–12 schools.

The College and The University

Teachers College was founded in 1887 to provide a new form of schooling for teachers of children from low-income families of New York—one that combined a humanitarian concern to help others with a scientific approach to human development. For more than 100 years, Teachers College has conducted research on the central issues facing education, prepared generations of education leaders, and shaped debate and public policy in education. The College provides programs of study in administration, counseling, curriculum development, and school health care and continues its efforts to strengthen teaching skills, prepare leaders to develop and administer psychological and health-care programs, and develop new teaching software. In 1898, the College became affiliated with Columbia.

Columbia University was founded in 1754 as King's College by royal charter of King George II of England. It is the oldest institution of higher learning in the state of New York and the fifth oldest in the United States. From its beginnings in a schoolhouse in lower Manhattan, the University has grown to encompass two principal campuses: the historic, neoclassical campus in Morningside Heights and the modern Medical Center in Washington Heights. Today, Columbia is one of the top academic and research institutions in the world, conducting research in medicine, science, the arts, and the humanities. It includes three undergraduate schools, thirteen graduate and professional schools, and a school of continuing education. Sixty-four Nobel laureates have taught or studied at Columbia. Each year, the faculty of approximately 4,000 teaches more than 23,000 students from more than 150 countries.

Applying

Teachers College welcomes applicants who wish to pursue graduate study associated with the education, psychological, and health service professions. All applicants receive consideration for admission without regard to race, color, creed, religion, sex, national origin, age, or disability. In order to be considered for scholarships, students must meet the priority deadline. Admission applications received after the priority deadlines may be considered on a space-available basis. Certain programs have special application deadlines. The final and early deadline for Ph.D. and all psychology doctoral programs is December 15. The early deadline for Ed.D. programs is January 2, with a final deadline of April 1. The early deadline for master's programs is January 15, with a final deadline of April 15. The early deadline is November 1 for the spring semester. Teachers College requests that applicants collect the required documents for the application process and submit the entire package to the Office of Admission at one time. Admission application deadlines always refer to the date by which the Teachers College Office of Admission must have received the application components and any other supporting material required by the department.

Correspondence and Information

Teachers College Columbia University
525 West 120th Street, Box 302
New York, New York 10027

Phone: 212-678-3710
Web site: http://www.tc.columbia.edu

RESEARCH CENTERS AND INSTITUTES

The **Center for Adult Education** is interested in research on adult and organizational learning and on transformative learning for adults in a variety of settings. The center has conducted award-winning research on literacy and has pioneered an innovative Action Research Professional Development program.

The **Center for Arts Education Research** is an interdisciplinary arts group that engages in basic and applied research in the arts and human development, art education, and the arts in education. The center calls upon expertise from professionals in visual, music, dance, theater, and media arts and also philosophy, psychology, education, and technology. Studies explore the role of the arts in diverse educational settings.

The **Center for Children and Families** advances the policy, education, and development of children and their families. The center produces and applies interdisciplinary research to improve practice and to raise public awareness of social issues that affect the well-being of America's children and families. This work is accomplished through cutting-edge research and analysis; the systematic training of future leaders, scholars, and policy scientists; and dissemination of information to the media, policy makers, and practitioners on the front lines.

The **Center on Chinese Education** is aimed at contributing to a better understanding of education in China and to educational exchange between the United States and China.

The **Center for Educational and Psychological Services** is both a training and research center for the College and a community resource that provides help to people of all ages with educational and personal problems. Several hundred psychoeducational assessment and evaluation instruments, as well as a growing library of materials for reading remediation, are available for use by the students attending practicums affiliated with the center.

The **Center for Health Promotion** comprises diverse working groups of faculty members and students who are interested in stimulating research and development efforts responsive to national priorities in health promotion and disease prevention.

The **Center for Opportunities and Outcomes for People with Disabilities** confronts the challenges facing special education today and broadens the scope of research at Teachers College. The center is committed to producing knowledge and professional expertise that enhances the quality of life for people with disabilities.

The **Center for Social Imagination, the Arts, and Education** is committed to the development of alternative modes of inventing, creating, and interpreting. Working in the tradition of Dewey, James, and the Existentialists, the center brings schoolchildren, artists, academics, and social activists together in conferences and workshops to explore possibilities of reform and transformation in schools and social communities.

The **Center for Technology and School Change** helps schools integrate technology into their curricula and daily lives by planning for the use of technology with schools, educating teachers how to use it, planning curriculum projects that include technology, helping teachers to implement projects, and assessing the effect of technology on schools.

The **Community College Research Center** carries out and promotes research on major issues affecting the development, growth, and changing roles of community colleges in the United States.

The **Creative Arts Laboratory** prepares teachers of economically disadvantaged and educationally challenged students to change school cultures by integrating the arts into core curricula of public elementary and middle schools.

The **Edward D. Mysak Speech-Language and Hearing Center** provides advanced students in the Speech and Language Pathology and Audiology Program practical experience in a professional setting. The center offers evaluation and therapy services to individuals who have speech, voice, language, or hearing problems.

The **Elbenwood Center for the Study of the Family as Educator** pursues various lines of systematic research and inquiry that bring the behavioral sciences to bear in illuminating the educational functions of the family and the relationships between the family and other educative institutions. Recent topics include social networks and educative styles of teenagers, the mediation of television by the family and television in cross-cultural perspective, multigenerational education, grandparents as educators, and immigration.

The **Rita Gold Early Childhood Center** supports and promotes the growth and development of infants, toddlers, and preschoolers and their families through supportive early care and education; transdisciplinary professional preparation for students; ongoing research to improve practice and inform theory in early development, care, and education for young children and families; and outreach. The center is a resource for students across the College who are engaged in observation, teaching, and research with young children and families.

The **Hechinger Institute on Education and the Media** endeavors to help journalists who cover education to do a better job. The institute carries out its mandate primarily through seminars for journalists held at Teachers College and at locales around the country.

Hollingworth Center is a service, research, and demonstration site designed to provide internship and training opportunities for the graduate students at Teachers College. The center develops model programs in early childhood education and offers enriching educational services for children and educators in the neighboring communities.

The **J. M. Huber Institute for Learning in Organizations** conducts research on learning and change in organizations. The institute works through partnerships with organizations, including businesses, not-for-profits, and government agencies, to assist those who want to improve their ability to use learning strategically to address business and organizational challenges.

The **Institute for Higher Education** promotes and supports scholarly activity on the range of purposes, practices, policies, problems, and perspectives framing the higher education enterprise. The institute views postsecondary teaching, learning, and scholarly and creative endeavors in social, political, economic, and historic perspectives and promotes efforts to strengthen and enrich these core activities for all participants in the higher education enterprise.

The **Institute for Learning Technologies (ILT)** uses digital communications technologies to advance innovation in education and society. Rapid change in information technology is reconfiguring social, cultural, and intellectual possibilities. ILT is a major element of Columbia University's effort to shape these transitions.

The **Institute for Urban and Minority Education** is committed to better understanding and influencing the educational, psychological, and social development of urban and minority-group students and the schools that serve them.

The **Institute of International Studies** helps to formulate and coordinate the College's international effort, to serve as both catalyst and repository for grants and gifts in aid of international studies at the College, to strengthen instructional programs with comparative and international thrusts, and to upgrade the quality of research on international or cross-national themes.

The **Institute of Research and Service in Nursing Education** carries on a program of research and course work on questions in the education of nurse professors, deans, chief executive officers, and developers of human resources. Institute members examine theory-based questions within nursing's history and provide consultant services to professionals involved in nursing research.

The **Institute on Education and Government** develops ideas and implementation strategies for education innovations.

The **Institute on Education and the Economy (IEE)** is an interdisciplinary policy research center that focuses its attention on the interaction between education and the economy. IEE's research agenda includes issues such as the changes in the nature, organization, and skill requirements of work; education reforms designed to address the changing needs of the workplace; work-based learning; employer participation in education; and academic and industry-based skill standards.

The **International Center for Cooperation and Conflict Resolution** helps individuals as well as institutions better understand the nature of conflict and how to achieve its constructive resolution. The center particularly emphasizes the importance of the social, cultural, organizational, and institutional contexts within which conflicts occur.

The **Esther A. and Joseph Klingenstein Center for Independent School Education** sponsors programs aimed at the professional development of independent school teachers and administrators and research activities that contribute to the advancement of independent school education.

The **National Center for Restructuring Education, Schools, and Teaching** supports restructuring efforts by documenting successful school improvement initiatives, creating reform networks to share new research findings with practitioners, and linking policy to practice.

The **National Center for the Study of Privatization in Education** serves as a nonpartisan venue to analyze and disseminate information about the contentious private initiatives in education, including vouchers, charter schools, and educational contracting.

The **Research Center for Arts and Culture** provides data and ideas for applied research, education, advocacy, policymaking, and action. Collaboration and cooperation with service organizations, trade publishers, and arts institutions strengthen the center's unique position and enable it to translate its findings into useful, practical forms.

The **Teachers College Reading and Writing Project** is a staff development organization that works in intimate and long-lasting ways with educators in the metropolitan area and provides more limited assistance to educators all over the U.S. to establish reading and writing workshops.

Programs of Study

Doctor of Philosophy programs are offered in the following fields: African American studies, anatomy, anthropology, art history, biochemistry, biology, biomedical neuroscience, business administration, chemistry, communication sciences, computer and information science, counseling psychology, criminal justice, dance, economics, educational psychology, engineering, English, health studies (public health, therapeutic recreation), history, kinesiology, mass media and communication, mathematics, microbiology and immunology, molecular biology/genetics, music education, music therapy, pathology, pharmaceutical sciences (medicinal chemistry, pharmaceutics, pharmacodynamics), pharmacology, philosophy, physical therapy, physics, physiology, political science, psychology, religion, school psychology, sociology, Spanish, statistics, and urban education.

The Doctor of Musical Arts is offered in music composition and music performance. Doctor of Education degrees are offered in curriculum, instruction, and technology in education (language arts education, math and science education) and in educational administration.

Master's degree programs are offered in accounting and financial management; actuarial science; adult and organizational development; African American studies; applied behavioral analysis; art education; art history; biochemistry; bioengineering; biology; biomedical neuroscience; broadcasting, telecommunications, and mass media; business administration; career and technical education; cell biology; chemistry; choral conducting; civil engineering; communication management (media management, government and social policy, strategic and corporate communication management); community and regional planning; community health education; computer and information science; counseling psychology; creative writing; criminal justice; curriculum, instruction, and technology in education; dance; early childhood education; economics; educational administration; educational psychology; electrical engineering; elementary education; English; English education; environmental health; epidemiology; finance; financial engineering; geography; geology; healthcare financial management; healthcare management; history; human resource management; information technology management; international business; journalism; kinesiology; liberal arts; linguistics; management information systems; marketing; mathematics; mathematics education; mechanical engineering; microbiology and immunology; music composition; music education; music history; music performance; music theory; music therapy; nursing; occupational therapy; opera; oral biology; pharmaceutical sciences (medicinal chemistry, pharmaceutics, pharmacodynamics); philosophy; physics; physiology; piano accompanying (chamber music, opera coaching); piano pedagogy; political science; quality assurance/regulatory affairs; religion; school health education; school psychology; science education; second and foreign language education; social work; sociology; Spanish; special education; speech, language and hearing science; sport and recreation administration; statistics; string pedagogy; teaching English as a second language; therapeutic recreation; tourism and hospitality management; urban education; and urban studies. Also offered are an executive M.A. in criminal justice, an executive M.B.A., and an international M.B.A.

Master of Fine Arts degree programs are available in ceramics/glass, dance, fibers and fabric design, film and media arts, graphic and interactive design, metals/jewelry/CAD-CAM, painting, photography, printmaking, sculpture, and theater (acting, design, directing, playwriting).

Research Facilities

The University libraries contain nearly 2.5 million volumes and provide reading space for 2,500 students. Across the main campus, numerous research centers and laboratories offer facilities where faculty members and students engage in collaborative research. In addition, less than 2 miles north of the main academic campus is the Health Sciences Center at Broad and Ontario Streets. This campus houses the Schools of Medicine, Dentistry, and Pharmacy; the College of Health Professions; the Temple University Hospital; and the Medical Research Building, all of which offer excellent and varied facilities for research in many fields.

Financial Aid

Graduate students are eligible for various kinds of financial assistance from private, University, state, and federal sources. The Office of Student Financial Services (http://www.temple.edu/SFS) administers loans, grants, work-study, and other forms of financial aid. Students should visit the Web site or contact the SFS office directly at 215-204-2244 for additional information about financial assistance.

Cost of Study

Resident tuition for the 2006–07 academic year was $511 per credit hour for most graduate programs, $528 per credit hour for the Tyler School of Art, $531 per credit hour for the Fox School of Business and Management, $532 per credit hour for the College of Health Professions, and $700 per credit hour for courses in the School of Pharmacy's Department of Pharmaceutical Sciences. Nonresident tuition was $746 per credit hour for most graduate programs, $777 per credit hour for the College of Health Professions and the Tyler School of Art, $788 per credit hour for the Fox School of Business and Management, and $928 per credit hour for courses in the School of Pharmacy's Department of Pharmaceutical Sciences.

Living and Housing Costs

On-campus housing is limited. Students should contact the Office of University Housing at 215-204-7184 or visit http://www.temple.edu/housing.

Student Group

With a student body of more than 30,000 students, Temple University is the twenty-sixth-largest university in the country. Since becoming a part of the Commonwealth System of Higher Education, it has placed increased emphasis on upper-division and graduate work. Although the institution has historically served the greater metropolitan area of southeastern Pennsylvania, a significant and growing portion of the student body is from outside Philadelphia.

Location

Philadelphia is the fifth-largest city in the country and has a regional population of more than 6.1 million. It offers a variety of cultural attractions. The city has a world-renowned symphony orchestra, a ballet company, two professional opera companies, and a chamber music society. Besides attracting touring plays, Philadelphia enjoys a professional repertory theater and many amateur productions. All facilities for sports and recreation are easy to reach. The city is world famous for its historic shrines, parks, and eighteenth-century charm, which is carefully maintained in its oldest section. The climate is temperate, with an average winter temperature of 33 degrees and an average summer temperature of 75 degrees.

The University

The development of Temple University has been in line with the ideal of "educational opportunity for the able and deserving student of limited means." With a rich heritage of populist tradition, Temple provides students with an opportunity for education of high quality without regard to race, creed, or station in life. Affiliation with the Commonwealth System of Higher Education undergirds Temple's character as a public institution.

Temple's academic programs are conducted on seven campuses in central and north Philadelphia and its nearby suburbs. These locations, as well as numerous extension centers throughout eastern Pennsylvania, give Temple University the distinction of being a fast-growing institution with many superior facilities.

The main campus, located at Broad Street and Montgomery Avenue, is the site of the Colleges of Education, Engineering, Liberal Arts, and Science and Technology; the Esther Boyer College of Music and Dance; the Schools of Communications and Theater, Social Administration, and Tourism and Hospitality Management; the Beasley School of Law; and the Fox School of Business and Management.

Applying

Departmental deadlines for admissions and financial aid vary. Applicants should consult the Graduate Bulletin (http://www.temple.edu/gradbulletin) and the Web site of the program in which they are interested. Notification regarding admission and financial aid is made following the screening of the application.

Correspondence and Information

Aquiles Iglesias, Ph.D.
Dean of the Graduate School
Temple University
501 Carnell Hall
1803 North Broad Street
Philadelphia, Pennsylvania 19122-6095
Phone: 215-204-1380
Fax: 215-204-8781
Web site: http://www.temple.edu/grad

FACULTY HEADS

Graduate School: Aquiles Iglesias, Ph.D., Dean.
Ambler College: James W. Hilty, Ph.D., Interim Dean.
College of Education: C. Kent McGuire, Ph.D., Dean.
College of Engineering: Keyanoush Sadeghipour, Ph.D., Dean.
College of Health Professions: Ronald T. Brown, Ph.D., Dean.
College of Liberal Arts: Carolyn Adams, Ph.D., Interim Dean.
College of Science and Technology: Hai-Lung Dai, Ph.D., Dean.
Esther Boyer College of Music and Dance: Robert T. Stroker, Ph.D., Dean.
James E. Beasley School of Law: Robert J. Reinstein, J.D., Dean.
Richard J. Fox School of Business and Management: M. Moshe Porat, Ph.D., Dean.
School of Communications and Theater: Concetta M. Stewart, Ph.D., Dean.
School of Dentistry: Martin F. Tansy, Ph.D., Dean.
School of Medicine: John M. Daly, M.D., Dean.
School of Pharmacy: Peter H. Doukas, Ph.D., Dean.
School of Podiatric Medicine: John A. Mattiacci, D.P.M., Dean.
School of Social Administration: Linda Mauro, D.S.W., Interim Dean.
School of Tourism and Hospitality Management: M. Moshe Porat, Ph.D., Dean.
Tyler School of Art: Keith Morrison, M.F.A., Dean.

A time for quiet study in Mitten Hall.

The view from Founder's Garden at Temple's main campus.

TEXAS A&M UNIVERSITY–KINGSVILLE

College of Graduate Studies

Programs of Study

Through the College of Graduate Studies, fifty-seven master's degrees and four doctoral degrees are offered from five academic colleges.

The College of Agriculture, Natural Resources, and Human Sciences offers a Doctor of Philosophy (Ph.D.) in wildlife science; a cooperative Doctor of Philosophy in horticulture; Master of Science (M.S.) degrees in agribusiness, agriculture science, animal science, plant and soil science, and range and wildlife management; and a Master of Science in Human Sciences (M.S.H.S.).

The College of Arts and Sciences offers many degrees in a vast range of disciplines. Graduate degrees include the cooperative Doctor of Philosophy in Hispanic studies; Master of Arts (M.A.) in bilingual education, English, history and politics, psychology, sociology, and Spanish; Master of Science in art, biology, chemistry, communication science and disorders, English, history and politics, mathematics, psychology, and sociology; and the Master of Music in music education.

The College of Business Administration offers the Master of Business Administration (M.B.A.), M.S. with a major in business administration, and Master of Professional Accountancy (M.P.A.) in accounting.

The College of Education offers Doctor of Education (Ed.D.) degrees in bilingual education and educational leadership (the latter jointly with Texas A&M–Corpus Christi); Master of Education (M.Ed.) in adult education, early childhood, English as a second language, and special education; M.S. in reading specialization; and M.A. and M.S. degrees in bilingual education, counseling and guidance, educational administration, instructional technology, and kinesiology.

The Frank H. Dotterweich College of Engineering offers several interdisciplinary courses of study leading to M.S. and Master of Engineering (M.E.) degrees in chemical engineering, civil engineering, electrical engineering, environmental engineering, industrial management, mechanical engineering, and natural gas engineering; M.S. degrees in computer science and industrial engineering; and the Doctor of Philosophy in environmental engineering.

Research Facilities

Graduate study is supported by University and departmental attitudes and facilities. The James C. Jernigan Library contains more than 500,000 volumes and 700,000 microfiche documents, subscribes to 2,200 periodicals, and is a depository for selected U.S. government documents. Electronic information resources offer online and CD-ROM databases. Graduate students have interlibrary loan privileges, providing access to nationwide library collections. Research is conducted through such centers, institutes, and laboratories as the Caesar Kleberg Wildlife Research Institute, the Citrus Center, the Natural Toxins Research Center, the King Ranch Institute for Ranch Management, and the Caesar Kleberg Wildlife Center at the Tio and Janell Wildlife Research Park.

Financial Aid

Graduate students taking at least 9 semester hours of graduate courses are eligible for a variety of fellowships and research or teaching assistantships. Financial aid is available for up to 48 semester hours of graduate credit. The University participates in most federal and state grant, loan, and work-study programs. Non-Texas residents receiving approved fellowships or assistantships may be eligible to pay Texas resident tuition. University teaching and research assistantships provide annual stipends, while fellowships and internships supported by federal, state, and University funds provide stipends of $1000 to $14,000. International students are required to guarantee their support but are eligible, after enrollment, for in-state tuition rates if awarded competitive scholarships valued at a minimum of $1000. Inquiries about the availability of support should be addressed to the graduate coordinator of the various disciplines.

Cost of Study

Tuition and fees for 9 semester hours are $1497 per semester for full-time graduate students who are Texas residents and $3981 per semester for non-Texas residents and international students.

Living and Housing Costs

The cost of living in south Texas is relatively low when compared to other areas of the country. Apartments and homes rent for $450 to $550 per month and up. Several apartment complexes and rental properties are within walking or short driving distance of the University. Dormitory rooms for unmarried students as well as family apartments are available at the University. Dorm residents may purchase optional meal plans. Student family apartments rent for less than $390 per month.

Student Group

The University enrollment is approximately 6,200; 1,100 are enrolled as graduate students. International students make up 30 percent of the graduate student enrollment. The overall student population, a multicultural mix of thirty-two countries and forty-three states, is 62 percent Hispanic, 24 percent Anglo-American, 4 percent African American, less than 1 percent Asian American and American Indian, and 9 percent international.

Location

Texas A&M University–Kingsville is located in semitropical south Texas. Kingsville is about 40 miles southwest of Corpus Christi, 153 miles southeast of San Antonio, and 120 miles north of Mexico. Kingsville (population 25,000) is in a semirural area that is easily accessible to urban areas. The King Ranch, one of the largest commercial ranches in the world, provides tours. Water sports and outdoor activities can be found nearby along the coastline. Corpus Christi offers many social and cultural activities, including museums, concerts, and plays, as well as shopping malls.

The University

Texas A&M University–Kingsville (formerly Texas A&I University) was established in 1925 as Texas State Teachers College and has since evolved into a comprehensive institution of higher education. The University became a part of the Texas A&M University System in 1989 and changed its named to Texas A&M University–Kingsville in 1993.

Applying

Candidates must submit admissions applications to the Admissions Office. Students must be admitted both to the College of Graduate Studies and to a specific program to take courses for graduate credit. The application fee is $35 for United States residents and $50 for international students. Students must have a GRE score of at least 1000 (verbal plus quantitative) and an undergraduate GPA of at least 3.0 on a 4.0 scale. International students are required to score a minimum of 500 on the Test of English as a Foreign Language (TOEFL), with engineering and business graduate programs requiring a TOEFL score of at least 550. Application deadlines for U.S. students are July 1 for fall, November 15 for spring, and April 15 for summer. Application deadlines for first-time international students are June 1 for fall, October 1 for spring, and April 1 for summer.

Correspondence and Information

Dr. Alberto M. Olivares, Dean
College of Graduate Studies
MSC 118–700 University Boulevard
Texas A&M University–Kingsville
Kingsville, Texas 78363-8202

Phone: 361-593-2808
Fax: 361-593-3412
E-mail: international.inquiries@tamuk.edu (international application forms and application status inquiries)
l-knippers@tamuk.edu (U.S. application forms and catalogs)
kalmh00@tamuk.edu (U.S. application graduate admission status inquiries)
Web site: http://www.tamuk.edu/grad

COLLEGE DEANS AND GRADUATE COORDINATORS

Graduate School: Alberto M. Olivares, Dean; Ph.D., Texas A&M. (Telephone: 361-593-2808)

Agriculture, Natural Resources, and Human Sciences: Allen Rasmussen, Interim Dean; Ph.D., Texas Tech. (Phone: 361-593-3712)
Agricultural Programs (Master's in Agribusiness, Agriculture Science, Animal Science, Plant and Soil Science, Range and Wildlife Science): Steven Lukefahr, Ph.D., Oregon State. kfsdl00@tamuk.edu
Human Sciences: Anna P. McArthur, Ph.D., Texas Tech. kfapm00@tamuk.edu
Horticulture (Doctoral): Duane T. Gardiner, Ph.D., Oregon State. duane.gardiner@tamuk.edu
Wildlife Science (Doctoral): Scott Henke, Ph.D., Texas Tech. scott.henke@tamuk.edu

Arts and Sciences: Ronald J. Hy, Dean; Ph.D., Miami (Ohio). (Phone: 361-593-2761)
Art: Charles Wissinger, M.F.A., Ohio State. chuckwissinger@yahoo.com
Biology: Enrique Massa, Ph.D., Michigan. e-massa@tamuk.edu
Chemistry: Nicholas R. Beller, Ph.D., New Mexico. kfnrb00@tamuk.edu
Communication Sciences and Disorders: Shari Schlehuser Beams, Ph.D., Purdue. kfsls01@tamuk.edu
English: David Sabrio, Ph.D., South Carolina. d-sabrio@tamuk.edu
Geosciences: Daniel Suson, Ph.D., Texas at Dallas. daniel.suson@tamuk.edu
History: Leslie G. Hunter, Ph.D., Arizona. kflgh00@tamuk.edu
Mathematics: Stephen A. Sedory, Ph.D., Oklahoma State. s.sedory@tamuk.edu
Music: Nancy KingSanders, D.M.A., Illinois at Urbana-Champaign. kfnks00@tamuk.edu
Physics (Minor): Lionel D. Hewett, Ph.D., Missouri–Rolla. l-hewett@tamuk.edu
Political Science: Jimmie D. Phaup, Ph.D., Arizona. j-phaup@tamuk.edu
Psychology: Lloyd Dempster, Ph.D., Pittsburgh. kflvd00@tamuk.edu
Sociology: Jieming Chen, Ph.D., Michigan. jmchen@tamuk.edu
Spanish (Master's and Doctoral): Michelle Johnson Vela, Ph.D., Indiana. kfrgv00@tamuk.edu

Business Administration: Robert Diersing, Dean; Ph.D., Texas A&M. (Phone: 361-593-3801)
Business Administration and Professional Accountancy: Robert Diersing, Dean; Ph.D., Texas A&M. r-diersing@tamuk.edu

Education: Mike Daniel, Dean; Ed.D., Arkansas. (Phone: 361-593-2801)
Adult Education: Rebecca Davis, Ph.D., Texas A&M. rebecca.davis@tamuk.edu
Bilingual Education (Master's): Roberto Torres, Ph.D., Colorado. kfrlt00@tamuk.edu
Bilingual Education (Doctoral): Lento Maez, Ph.D., Texas at Austin. kflfm00@tamuk.edu
Certification Programs: Glenna S. Cannon, Ph.D., Texas at Austin. kfgsc00@tamuk.edu
Counseling and Guidance: Karen Furgerson, Ph.D., Alabama. kfklf00@tamuk.edu
Early Childhood: Karen Sue Bradley, Ed.D., Texas A&M. kfksb00@tamuk.edu
Educational Administration: Ronald McKenzie, Ph.D., Texas at Austin. kfrfm00@tamuk.edu
Educational Leadership (Doctoral): Gary Low, Ph.D., East Texas State. gary.low@tamuk.edu
Kinesiology: Christopher Hearon, Ph.D., LSU. christopher.hearon@tamuk.edu
Reading Specialization: Shirley Ermis, Ed.D., Texas A&M–Kingsville. kfsoe00@tamuk.edu
Special Education: Grace A. Hopkins, Ph.D., Illinois. g-hopkins1@tamuk.edu

Engineering: William Heenan, Dean; D.Engr., Detroit. (Phone: 361-593-2001)
Chemical Engineering: Robert W. Serth, Ph.D., SUNY at Buffalo. r-serth@tamuk.edu
Civil Engineering: Joseph Sai, Ph.D., Texas A&M. jsai@tamuk.edu
Computer Science: Barbara Schreur, Ph.D., Florida State. bschreur@tamuk.edu
Electrical Engineering: Raj Challoo, Ph.D., Wichita State. r-challoo@tamuk.edu
Environmental Engineering: Alvaro Martinez, Ph.D., Central Florida. alvaro.martinez@tamuk.edu
Industrial Engineering: Kai Jin, Ph.D., Texas Tech. kfkj000@tamuk.edu
Industrial Management: Farzin Heidari, Ph.D., Idaho. kffh000@tamuk.edu
Mechanical Engineering: Selahattin Ozcelik, Ph.D., Rensselaer. sozcelik@tamuk.edu
Natural Gas Engineering: Ali Pilehvari, Ph.D., Tulsa. a-pilehvari@tamuk.edu

TEXAS TECH UNIVERSITY

Graduate School

Programs of Study

Through its Graduate School, School of Law, School of Allied Health, School of Nursing, School of Pharmacy, and School of Medicine, Texas Tech offers a diverse range of graduate studies. The Graduate School offers degrees from eight academic colleges. The College of Agriculture offers the Doctor of Philosophy (Ph.D.), Master of Science (M.S.), Doctor of Education (Ed.D.), and Master of Agriculture (M.Ag.) in a variety of disciplines. In addition, the college offers the Master of Landscape Architecture (M.L.A.). The College of Architecture offers the Master of Architecture (M.Arch.), Master of Science in architecture, and Ph.D. degrees. The College of Arts and Sciences offers many degrees in a vast range of disciplines, including the Ph.D. in eighteen academic disciplines, the Master of Arts (M.A.) in eighteen fields, and the Master of Science in twelve fields. Texas Tech's College of Business Administration offers the Ph.D. in business administration, M.S. in business administration, Master of Science in Accounting (M.S.A.), and Master of Business Administration (M.B.A.) degree programs. Each degree offers concentrations in various areas. An M.B.A. is available as a joint degree with foreign languages, law, nursing, and medicine and also with architecture. The College of Education offers the Master of Education (M.Ed.) in twelve fields, the Doctor of Education, and the Ph.D. The College of Engineering offers the Ph.D. in seven engineering fields, the M.S. in ten fields, the Master of Engineering (M.Eng.), the Master of Science in Environmental Engineering (M.S.Env.E.), and the Master of Science in Environmental Technology Management (M.S.E.T.M.). The College of Human Sciences offers the M.S. as well as the Ph.D. in various fields. The College of Visual and Performing Arts offers Ph.D., M.A., Master of Fine Arts (M.F.A.), Master of Music (M.M.), and Master of Music Education (M.M.Ed.) degrees. In addition, the college offers the Doctor of Musical Arts (D.M.A.).

Interdisciplinary degrees housed in the Graduate School include predesigned programs or self-designed programs that are coordinated to meet individual needs. Predesigned programs include applied linguistics, heritage management, museum science, public administration, sports health, and multidisciplinary science. Self-designed programs may be generated from any of the courses listed in the graduate catalog. Some of the more common minors or areas of interest include comparative literature, environmental evaluation, ethnic studies, fine arts management, land-use planning management and design, Latin American studies, legal studies, neural and behavioral science, risk-taking behavior, and women's studies. The School of Law offers the Doctor of Jurisprudence degree and joint-degree programs with the M.P.A., M.S. in agricultural economics; M.S. in accounting; and M.B.A. The School of Allied Health offers an M.S. in three disciplines: communication disorders (speech-language pathology or audiology), occupational therapy, and physical therapy. The School of Nursing offers a Ph.D. in Nursing, a Master of Science in Nursing, and a joint-degree program with the M.B.A. The School of Pharmacy offers the Doctor of Pharmacy (Pharm.D.). The School of Medicine offers the Doctor of Medicine, medical education in thirty residency programs, Ph.D. and M.S. degrees in six disciplines, and a joint M.B.A./M.D. degree.

Research Facilities

Graduate study is strongly supported by the University and its departments. The library houses more than 4 million volumes and more than 27,000 serials. The high-performance computer center provides students with up-to-date computing facilities. The Advanced Technology Learning Center gives students comprehensive access to the latest computer technology and software. Many departments feature their own library and computer facilities. Consistent dedication to quality and research has earned national and international respect for numerous departments. Every department has its own strengths, and each college possesses its special resources, centers for investigation, and research opportunities. A small sample of the numerous centers and institutes includes the Institute for Ergonomics Research, Institute for Banking and Financial Studies, Child Development Center, Center for Petroleum Mathematics, Southwest Center for German Studies, Institute for Disaster Research, International Center for Arid and Semi-Arid Land Studies, Center for the Study of Addiction, Center for Professional Development, and Institute of Environmental and Human Health. In the new Carnegie classification, Texas Tech was rated as an RU/H: Research University (high research activity), the highest category for graduate degree–granting institutions.

Financial Aid

Graduate students are eligible for an array of scholarships, fellowships, and research or teaching assistantships in many academic disciplines. Part-time employment is readily available both on and off campus. The University participates in most federal and state grant, loan, and work-study programs. Texas Tech University's Gelin Emergency Loan Fund is a special benefit for students in need. Non-Texas residents receiving approved scholarships, fellowships, or assistantships may be eligible to pay Texas resident tuition, which is among the lowest in the nation.

Cost of Study

Graduate School tuition and fees for the 2007–08 academic year for Texas residents are approximately $390 per semester credit hour. Students employed at least half-time as teaching or research assistants pay the same tuition as Texas residents. The graduate nonresident tuition rate for residents of New Mexico and Oklahoma who are legal residents of a county adjacent to Texas is $179 per semester credit hour. Nonresident student tuition is $665 per semester credit hour. Fees may vary but generally include the Texas Tech University identification fee, laboratory fee, informational technology fee, library fee, and general fees. Most fees are waived for half-time teaching and research assistants. Tuition and fees for law, nursing, pharmacy, allied health, and medicine vary and may be confirmed in the course catalog or by contacting the school directly. Texas has no state income tax. Tuition and fees are subject to change.

Living and Housing Costs

Characteristics of Lubbock are low unemployment, low housing costs, and a low cost of living. On-campus living, meals included, in upperclass halls costs about $7000 per academic year. Abundant privately owned housing in the city meets most price and amenity demands.

Student Group

More than 50 percent of Texas Tech's 28,000 students have permanent homes more than 300 miles away, making Tech a residential campus. Students come from all parts of Texas, the nation, and more than 100 other countries. Tech's growing graduate and professional student population is about 4,300, most of whom are full-time students.

Location

With a population of approximately 200,000, Lubbock enjoys all the services of a major city. The city has more than sixty parks, numerous cultural and civic events, and a modern and convenient international airport that hosts several major airlines. Lubbock is the principal trade, medical, and financial center in a rich agricultural and petroleum area. Situated on the high plains of west Texas, Lubbock is about an hour's flight from Dallas, Houston, Albuquerque, and Denver. Lubbock enjoys 265 days of sunshine each year, a warm and dry climate, and pleasant weather year-round.

The University

Founded in 1923, Texas Tech is a state-assisted major research university. Texas Tech's campus features expansive lawns and impressive landscaping with unique Spanish Renaissance architecture. The beautiful, spacious campus—one of the largest in the nation—is well-equipped not only for research and study but also for cultural and recreational activities. A fulfilling after-study-hours life can be achieved by participating in the wide array of campus and community activities.

Applying

Application forms for admission can be provided upon request or accessed electronically through the Graduate School Web site. Applications are accepted throughout the year for the fall, spring, and two summer terms. The Graduate School requires a $50 application fee for U.S. citizens and permanent residents and $60 for international applicants.

Correspondence and Information

Shannon Samson
Coordinator for Graduate School Recruitment
Graduate Admissions
Texas Tech University
P.O. Box 41030
Lubbock, Texas 79409-1030

Phone: 806-742-2787 Ext. 239
E-mail: shannon.samson@ttu.edu
Web site: http://www.gradschool.ttu.edu

DEANS AND FACULTY HEADS

Graduate School: John Borrelli, Dean; Ph.D., Penn State (phone: 806-742-2781).

Agricultural Sciences: Marvin Cepica, Dean; Ed.D., Oklahoma State (phone: 806-742-2810).
Agricultural and Applied Economics: Don Etheridge, Ph.D., North Carolina State.
Agricultural Education and Communication: Matt Baker, Ph.D., Ohio State.
Animal Science and Food Technology: Kevin Pond, Ph.D., Texas A&M.
Landscape Architecture: Alon Kvashny, Ed.D., West Virginia.
Plant and Soil Science: Dick Auld, Ph.D., Montana State.
Range and Wildlife Management: Ernest Fish, Ph.D., Arizona.

Architecture: Andrew Vernooy, Dean; M.Arch., Texas at Austin (phone: 806-742-3136).
Associate Dean (Academics): David Driskill, M.Arch., Catholic University.
Associate Dean (Research): Glenn Hill, M.Arch., Colorado.

Arts and Sciences: Jane L. Winer, Dean; Ph.D., Ohio State (phone: 806-742-3833).
Biological Sciences: John Zak, Ph.D., Calgary.
Chemistry and Biochemistry: Dominick J. Casadonte Jr., Ph.D., Purdue.
Classical and Modern Languages and Literature: Frederick Suppe, Ph.D., Montana.
Communication Studies: K. David Roach, Ed.D., Texas Tech.
Economics and Geography: Joseph E. King, Ph.D., Illinois at Urbana-Champaign.
English: Sam Dragga, Ph.D., Ohio.
Environmental Toxicology: Ronald J. Kendall, Ph.D., Virginia Tech.
Geosciences: George B. Asquith, Ph.D., Wisconsin–Madison.
Health, Exercise, and Sports Sciences: Steve Richards, Ph.D., SUNY at Stony Brook.
History: Jorge Iber, Ph.D., Utah.
Mathematics and Statistics: Lawrence Schovanec, Ph.D., Indiana.
Philosophy: Peder G. Christiansen, Ph.D., Wisconsin–Madison.
Physics: Lynn Hatfield, Ph.D., Arkansas.
Political Science: Phillip D. Marshall, Ph.D., Illinois at Urbana-Champaign.
Psychology: M. David Rudd, Ph.D., Texas.
Sociology, Anthropology, and Social Work: Paul Johnson, Ph.D., Illinois at Urbana-Champaign.

Business Administration: Allen McInnes, Dean; Ph.D., Texas (phone: 806-742-3188).
Accounting: Robert Ricketts, Ph.D., North Texas.
Finance: Paul Goeble, Ph.D., Georgia.
Information and Quantitative Sciences (MIS): James Hoffman, Ph.D., Nebraska.
Management: Kimberly Boal, Ph.D., Wisconsin–Madison.
Marketing: Robert Wilkes, Ph.D., Alabama.

Education: Sheryl Santos, Dean; Ph.D., Kansas State (phone: 806-742-1837).
Curriculum and Instruction: Margaret Johnson, Ph.D., Florida.
Educational Psychology and Leadership: Gerald Parr, Ph.D., Colorado.

Engineering: Pamela Eibeck, Dean; Ph.D., Stanford (phone: 806-742-3451).
Chemical Engineering: M. Nazmul Karim, Ph.D., Manchester.
Civil Engineering: H. Scott Norville, Ph.D., Purdue; PE.
Computer Science: Noé López-Benitez, Ph.D., Purdue.
Electrical Engineering: Jon Bredeson, Ph.D., Northwestern.
Engineering Physics: Lynn Hatfield, Ph.D., Arkansas.
Engineering Technology: Larry Masten, Ph.D., Texas Tech.
Industrial Engineering: Milton Smith, Ph.D., Texas Tech.
Mechanical Engineering: Jharna Chaudhuri, Ph.D., Rutgers.
Petroleum Engineering: Lloyd R. Heinze, Ph.D., Missouri–Rolla; PE.

Human Sciences: Linda Hoover, Dean; Ph.D., Texas Woman's (phone: 806-742-3031).
Food and Nutrition: Debra B. Reed, Ph.D.,Texas; RD, LD.
Restaurant, Hotel, and Hospitality Management: Lynn Huffman, Ph.D., Texas A&M.
Human Development and Family Studies: Anisa Zvonkovic, Ph.D., Penn State.
Merchandising, Environmental Design, and Consumer Economics: JoAnn Shroyer, Ph.D., Oklahoma State.

Mass Communications: Michael Parkinson, Ph.D., Oklahoma (phone: 806-742-6500).

School of Law: Walter Huffman, Dean; J.D., Texas Tech (phone: 806-742-3793).

Visual and Performing Arts: Jonathon Marks, Dean; D.F.A., Yale (phone: 806-742-3825).
Art: Tina Fuentes, M.F.A., North Texas.
Music: William Ballenger, M.A., Northeast Missouri State.
Theater: Fred Christoffel, M.F.A., Illinois at Urbana-Champaign.

Interdisciplinary Studies: Clifford Fedler, Ph.D., Illinois; Wendell Aycock, Coordinator; Ph.D., South Carolina (phone: 806-742-2787).
Applied Linguistics: James E. Holland, Ph.D., Missouri–Columbia.
Heritage Management: Gary Edson, M.F.A., Tulane.
Multidisciplinary Science: Julie Thomas, Ph.D., Nebraska–Lincoln.
Museum Science: Gary Edson, M.F.A., Tulane.
Public Administration: Brian K. Collins, Ph.D., Indiana.

Allied Health: Paul Brooke, Dean; Ph.D., Iowa; FACHE (phone: 806-743-3223).
Communication Disorders: Rajinder Koul, Ph.D., Iowa.
Diagnostic and Primary Care: Hal S. Larsen, Ph.D., Nebraska.
Rehabilitation Services: Steven Sawyer, Ph.D., San Diego.

Graduate School of Biomedical Sciences: Richard Homan, Dean; M.D., SUNY (phone: 806-743-3000).
Cell Biology and Biochemistry: Harry Weitlauf, M.D., Washington (Seattle).
Macrobiology and Biochemistry: Ronald Kennedy, Ph.D., Baylor College of Medicine.
Pharmacology: Reid Norman (Interim), Ph.D., Kansas.

Nursing: Alexia Green, Dean; Ph.D., Texas Woman's; RN (phone: 806-743-2737).

Medicine: Richard Homan, Dean; M.D., SUNY (phone: 806-743-3000).

Pharmacy: Arthur A. Nelson Jr., Dean; R.Ph., Ph.D., Iowa (phone: 806-356-4011).

THOMAS EDISON STATE COLLEGE

Graduate Programs

Programs of Study

Thomas Edison State College offers four graduate degree programs that have broad appeal to adult students who desire to build professional expertise by completing high-quality, online degrees.

The Master of Science in Human Resources Management (M.S.H.R.M.) degree serves human resources professionals who wish to become strategic partners in their organizations. This program uses a cohort model and is designed to position human resources professionals as leaders within their organizations. The 36-credit program provides practitioners with technical human resources skills in staffing, providing professional development, managing organizational culture, and measuring and rewarding performance. Skills in assessing and using research and best-practice standards from the human resources field to improve their practice are integrated.

The Master of Science in Management (M.S.M.) degree serves employed adults with three to five years' professional experience in management. Designed in partnership with major corporations, the M.S.M. degree program integrates the theory and practice of management. The 36-credit program is typically completed within eighteen months.

The College's Master of Arts in Liberal Studies (M.A.L.S.) degree provides working professionals an opportunity to study the liberal arts from an applied perspective. Students work from the context of their ongoing professional work. Their study of professionalism, community, and change infuses their professional lives with a deeper understanding of the workplace and their responsibilities as professionals. Students acquire leadership tools as they gain a deeper appreciation of the value and relevance of the arts, sciences, and humanities to the practical concerns of the workplace. The M.A.L.S. program attracts a diverse student body working in positions such as museum curator, college business manager, computer networking specialist, nuclear engineer, and teacher. M.A.L.S. students add depth by designing their own professional focus through the learner-designed area of study.

The Master of Science in Nursing (M.S.N.) degree in nurse education serves registered nurses with a current RN license valid in the United States who have already completed a Bachelor of Science in Nursing degree. Graduates of the 36-credit M.S.N. degree program are awarded a Nurse Educator Certificate in addition to the diploma and are prepared for teaching positions in schools of nursing and health-care settings.

Thomas Edison State College also offers graduate certificates. Graduate certificates are available to students who have earned baccalaureate degrees. Students who successfully complete certificates may apply the credits earned toward a graduate degree at Thomas Edison State College. The College offers graduate certificates in human resources management, online learning and teaching, public service leadership, homeland security, and clinical trials management. The Nurse Educator Certificate is only available to students who have earned a Master of Science in Nursing degree.

Research Facilities

Thomas Edison State College students utilize the rich library research facilities of the New Jersey State Library, which is an affiliate of Thomas Edison State College. Students have access to VALE, the Virtual Academic Libraries Environment, a system that provides access to a network of research libraries.

Financial Aid

Graduate students support their studies with employer tuition aid and loans. Unsubsidized loans are available to all accepted applicants. The Thomas Edison State College Office of Financial Aid & Veterans' Affairs is available to assist students.

Cost of Study

Tuition for the M.S.H.R.M., M.S.M., and M.A.L.S. is $422 per credit in 2006–07. Fees and tuition are specified in the *Graduate Prospectus.* Books and materials are estimated at $200 to $300 per semester. Tuition for the M.S.N. program is $433 per credit in 2006–07.

Living and Housing Costs

Thomas Edison State College graduate students complete course work through distance education. There are no college-based living and housing costs associated with an education through Thomas Edison State College.

Student Group

Students are working adults who maintain membership in their current professional associations. Graduates are invited to become active in the Thomas Edison State College Alumni Association.

Location

Thomas Edison State College is located in the capital city of Trenton, New Jersey. Students live and study in all fifty states and more than seventy other countries. The College's campus embraces the Kelsey Building at 101 West State Street and the adjacent Townhouse Complex, the Academic Center at 167 West Hanover Street, the Canal Banks Building at 221 West Hanover Street, and the Kuser Mansion at 315 West State Street. The College's state-of-the-art facilities, from electronic classrooms and computer labs to a corporate-style education conference room and other amenities, allow Thomas Edison State College to link students and mentors at dozens of colleges throughout the country and around the world.

The College

Founded in 1972, Thomas Edison State College specializes in providing flexible, high-quality collegiate learning opportunities for self-directed adults. One of New Jersey's twelve senior public institutions of higher education, the College offers four online graduate degrees as well as twelve associate and baccalaureate degrees. Thomas Edison State College, a pioneer in the assessment of adult learning and use of educational technologies, enrolls more than 11,200 students. Undergraduate students earn degrees through assessment of their college-level learning, transfer credit, independent study, and online courses. Graduate study is primarily online. Online courses require student interaction and collaboration; intensive communication with mentors is the norm. *Forbes* magazine identified the College as one of the top twenty colleges and universities in the nation in the use of technology to create learning opportunities for adults. The College is home to The John S. Watson Institute for Public Policy, which provides public policy analysis and other assistance to government, community groups, and the private sector.

Applying

Admission is competitive for the M.S.H.R.M., M.S.M., and M.A.L.S. The programs are open to students with baccalaureate degrees in any field and three to five years' experience appropriate to the program. The application requires a statement of professional goals and analytic essays to demonstrate graduate writing skills, transcripts documenting the earned degree, a resume, and two letters of recommendation. Students are required to have computer access and be proficient in computer use. A minimum TOEFL score of 550 is required for applicants whose primary language in not English. The application fee of $75 is nonrefundable. Applications are accepted throughout the year, and students may apply online.

Admission for the M.S.N., in addition to a current RN license valid in the U.S., requires a baccalaureate degree in nursing. The M.S.N. application requires receipt of an official transcript from the institution where the B.S.N. degree was awarded. Students are required to have computer access and be proficient in computer use. Two years' experience in nursing is recommended. The application fee of $75 is nonrefundable. Applications are accepted throughout the year, and students may obtain a printable application online at the College's Web site.

Correspondence and Information

Renee San Giacomo
Director of Admissions
Thomas Edison State College
101 West State Street
Trenton, New Jersey 08608-1176
Phone: 888-442-8372
Fax: 609-984-8447
E-mail: info@tesc.edu
Web site: http://www.tesc.edu

ABOUT THE FACULTY

Thomas Edison State College mentors are selected for their strong academic credentials in the subject area in which they work with students and for their extensive practical experience. Ninety percent of the mentors have earned their doctoral degrees from institutions such as Rutgers, the State University of New Jersey; Temple University; Columbia University; the University of California; and the Union Institute and University. M.S.M. mentors have worked in a variety of industries such as health care, telecommunications, manufacturing, market research, and financial services management. M.S.H.R.M. mentors include attorneys, professors, human resources management specialists, and organizational development practitioners. M.A.L.S. mentors have worked in occupations as diverse as corporate consultants, performing artists, librarians, novelists, and public relations executives.

M.S.N. mentors, who are offsite independent contractors, hold a minimum of a master's degree in nursing; approximately 85 percent hold doctoral degrees. Mentors are experienced nurse educators from baccalaureate and higher-degree nursing programs and settings who guide the development, implementation, and evaluation of the programs.

THOMAS JEFFERSON UNIVERSITY

Programs of Study

Thomas Jefferson University (TJU) is an academic health center that comprises Jefferson Medical College (JMC), Jefferson College of Graduate Studies (JCGS), and Jefferson College of Health Professions (JCHP) and shares its campus with Thomas Jefferson University Hospital. Faculty members and alumni are published researchers, clinical practitioners, chairs of professional organizations, and leaders in advocacy groups.

The M.D. curriculum at Jefferson Medical College provides opportunities for students to acquire basic knowledge and skills in the biomedical sciences as well as to develop appropriate professional behaviors. Several joint programs are available: M.D./Ph.D., in conjunction with Jefferson College of Graduate Studies; M.D./M.P.H., in conjunction with Johns Hopkins Bloomberg School of Public Health; and M.D./M.B.A. in Health Administration, in partnership with Widener University.

Jefferson College of Graduate Studies offers the Master of Science (M.S.) degree in biomedical sciences, cell and developmental biology, microbiology, pharmacology, and public health. A J.D./M.P.H. and M.J./M.P.H. are offered in partnership with Widener University.The College offers Ph.D. degrees in biochemistry and molecular biology, cell and developmental biology, genetics, immunology and microbial pathogenesis, molecular pharmacology and structural biology, molecular physiology and biophysics, neuroscience, and tissue engineering and regenerative medicine. Graduate certificates are available in clinical research/trials and public health/health systems research.

Jefferson College of Health Professions offers graduate-level programs in the bioscience technologies (biotechnology, cytotechnology, and medical technology), couple and family therapy, nursing, occupational therapy, pharmacy, radiologic sciences, and physical therapy.

Research Facilities

The Bluemle Life Sciences Building, with 157,000 square feet of laboratory space, serves as the primary research facility for molecular biology and genetics, molecular virology, microbiology, and immunology. The Farber Institute for Neurosciences is housed in the Jefferson Hospital for Neuroscience building and Jefferson Alumni Hall. Students have access to modern research equipment for molecular analysis of gene expression and functional aspects of the immune system, sophisticated studies of cell physiology, and in-depth studies of embryonic development and all aspects of drug metabolism.

The Center for Translational Medicine is the focal point for research in the Department of Medicine at Thomas Jefferson University. At the forefront of academic health care, the center aims to bridge basic scientific discoveries with physicians' needs for their patients. It focuses on cutting-edge basic molecular biomedical research and its translation into the most efficient and tailored forms of diagnosis and treatment as well as modes of prevention.

The Scott Memorial Library's collection includes approximately 210,000 books and bound print journals, more than 2,600 electronic journal subscriptions, leisure reading materials, the University Archives, and significant holdings of rare books dating to the fifteenth century. JEFFLINE, the University's academic information system, allows 24-hour access to the world's medical literature, including MEDLINE, the premier database for medical literature, and Micromedex CCIS, an extensive drug and chemical resource. Electronic access to full-text articles is available for more than 1,100 journals, electronic textbooks, and other critical knowledge-based resources.

AISR Learning Resources Centers provide access to videos, slides, anatomical models, human skeletons, and a wide variety of education technologies. Computing labs and electronic classrooms include digital-scanning equipment, PDA synchronizing workstations, laptop computers with wireless capabilities, and more than 250 computers.

Financial Aid

The University Office of Student Financial Aid assists students in securing federal, state, institutional, and private funding. A limited number of fellowships are available from the Jefferson College of Graduate Studies on a competitive basis for the support of full-time Ph.D. students with a strong academic background and research potential. The awards provide for the full cost of tuition and a stipend for the student's essential living expenses. The stipend for the 2006–07 academic year was $24,500. More information about general financial aid is available from the financial aid office. Additional information about financial support for Ph.D. students may be obtained from the Jefferson College of Graduate Studies.

Cost of Study

For the 2007–08 academic year, medical school tuition is $40,701 and fees are $400. The comprehensive fee for full-time Ph.D. students is $20,340; however, Ph.D. students are generally awarded fellowship support, which covers tuition and stipend for educational and living expenses. Tuition for M.S. basic science and public health programs and JCGS certificate programs is $818 per credit. JCHP's master's degree programs have a comprehensive fee ranging from $25,821 to $29,012.

Living and Housing Costs

University apartments are available. Room and board average $15,000 per year. Reasonable alternative housing near the University can also be found.

Location

Thomas Jefferson University's 13-acre campus is centrally located in Philadelphia, within walking distance of many places of cultural interest, including concert halls, theaters, museums, art galleries, and historic sites. Convenient bus and subway lines connect the University with other local universities and several outstanding libraries.

The University

Thomas Jefferson University was founded as Jefferson Medical College in 1824. JMC has awarded more than 26,000 medical degrees and has more living graduates than any other medical school in the nation. Existing basic medical sciences and allied health programs were formally organized within JCGS and JCHP when the two colleges were established in 1969. Public and private funding of Jefferson research exceeds $140 million annually.

Applying

Jefferson Medical College participates in the American Medical College Application Service (AMCAS). After completing this application, prospective students must submit the Jefferson Medical College Secondary Application Form, the nonrefundable $80 application fee, MCAT scores, and letters of recommendation. The deadline for receipt of all supporting materials is January 1.

Admission to all programs in Jefferson College of Graduate Studies requires a bachelor's degree from an accredited institution; strong academic performance, as demonstrated by grade point average; and GRE results. Individual programs have additional or alternate requirements.

Admission to Jefferson College of Health Professions is on a rolling basis and is divided into Admissions Review Periods beginning October 31. The final date to apply is July 15. Admission is competitive, as there are a limited number of seats in each class. Students need not complete all prerequisites before applying, but all course work must be completed before matriculation. In addition to the application, students must submit a nonrefundable $50 fee (reduced to $25 for online application), official transcripts, two letters of recommendation, a personal statement, and GRE or MAT scores, if applicable. English language proficiency is required of all non-U.S. citizens. JCHP interviews all academically eligible students. Applicants should contact the program to which they are applying for specific application guidelines.

Correspondence and Information

Office of Admissions
Jefferson Medical College
1015 Walnut Street, Room 110
Philadelphia, Pennsylvania 19107
Phone: 215-955-6983
E-mail: JMC.admissions@jefferson.edu
Web site: http://www.jefferson.edu/jmc

Office of Admissions
Jefferson College of Health Professions
130 South 9th Street, Suite 100
Philadelphia, Pennsylvania 19107
Phone: 215-503-8890
E-mail: JCHP@jefferson.edu
Web site: http://www.jefferson.edu/jchp

Office of Admissions
Jefferson Alumni Hall M-60
Jefferson College of Graduate Studies
1020 Locust Street
Philadelphia, Pennsylvania 19107-6799
Phone: 215-503-4400
E-mail: jcgs-info@jefferson.edu
Web site: http://www.jefferson.edu/jcgs

THE DEPARTMENTS

Anesthesiology
Zvi Grunwald, James D. Wentzler M.D. Professor and Chair, M.D. (215-955-6161; zvi.grunwald@jefferson.edu)

Biochemistry and Molecular Biology
Jeffrey L. Benovic, Professor and Chair; Ph.D. (215-503-4607; benovic@mail.jci.tju.edu)

Bioscience Technologies
Shirley E. Greening, Professor and Chair; M.S., J.D., CT(ASCP), CFIAC (shirley.greening@jefferson.edu)

Dermatology and Cutaneous Biology
Jouni Uitto, Professor and Chair; M.D., Ph.D. (jouni.uitto@jefferson.edu)

Emergency Medicine
Theodore Arthur Christopher, Associate Professor and Chair; M.D., FACEP (215-955-6844; theodore.christopher@jefferson.edu)

Family Medicine
Richard C. Wender, Chair; M.D. (215-955-2356; richard.wender@jefferson.edu)

Health Policy
David B. Nash, Chair; M.D., M.B.A., FACP (215-955-6969; david.nash@jefferson.edu)

Medicine
Arthur Michael Feldman, Chair; M.D., Ph.D. (arthur.feldman@jefferson.edu)

Microbiology and Immunology
Timothy L. Manser, Professor and Chair; Ph.D. (215-503-4669; manser@mail.jci.tju.edu)

Neurology
A. M. Rostami, Professor and Chair; M.D., Ph.D. (a.m.rostami@jefferson.edu)

Neurosurgery
Robert H. Rosenwasser, Professor and Chair; M.D., FACS (215-955-7000; robert.rosenwasser@jefferson.edu)

Nursing
Mary G. Schaal, Professor and Dean of Jefferson School of Nursing; Ed.D., RN (215-503-5090; mary.schaal@jefferson.edu)

Obstetrics and Gynecology
Louis Weinstein, Chair; M.D. (louis.weinstein@jefferson.edu)

Occupational Therapy
Janice P. Burke, Professor, Chair of the Department of Occupational Therapy, and Dean of Jefferson School of Health Professions; Ph.D., OTR/L, FAOTA (215-503-9606; janice.burke@jefferson.edu)

Ophthalmology
William Tasman, Chair; M.D. (215-928-3073; william.tasman@jefferson.edu)

Oral and Maxillofacial Surgery
Robert J. Diecidue, Chair; M.D., D.M.D. (215-955-5131; robert.diecidue@jefferson.edu)

Orthopaedic Surgery
Todd J. Albert, James Edwards Professor and Chairman; M.D. (267-339-3617; tjsurg@aol.com)

Otolaryngology
William Keane, Chair; M.D. (215-955-6760; william.keane@jefferson.edu)

Pathology; Anatomy and Cell Biology
Fred Gorstein, Chair; M.D. (215-955-5110; fred.gorstein@jefferson.edu)

Pediatrics
Jay Greenspan, Acting Chair; M.D. (215-955-0710; jay.greenspan@jefferson.edu)

Pharmacology and Experimental Therapeutics
Scott A. Waldman, Professor and Chair; M.D. (215-955-6086; scott.waldman@jefferson.edu)

Pharmacy
Rebecca S. Finley, Founding Dean of Jefferson School of Pharmacy; Pharm.D., M.S. (215-503-9082; rebecca.finley@jefferson.edu)

Physical Therapy
Margaret Rinehart Ayres, Associate Professor and Acting Chair; Ph.D., PT (215-503-1647; margaret.ayres@jefferson.edu)

Physiology
Marion J. Siegman, Chair; Ph.D. (215-503-3975; marion.siegman@jefferson.edu)

Psychiatry and Human Behavior
Michael Vergare, Daniel Lieberman Professor and Chair; M.D. (215-955-6912; mjv002@jefferson.edu)

Radiation Oncology
Walter J. Curran Jr., Professor and Chair; M.D. (215-955-6702; walter.curran@jefferson.edu)

Radiologic Sciences
Frances H. Gilman, Assistant Professor and Chair; M.S., RT(R)(CT)(MR)(CV) (215-503-1865; frances.gilman@jefferson.edu)

Radiology
Vijay M. Rao, Professor and Chair; M.D. (215-955-7264; vijay.rao@jefferson.edu)

Rehabilitation Medicine
John Melvin, Chair; M.D. (215-955-7446; john.melvin@jefferson.edu)

Surgery
Charles J. Yeo, Samuel D. Gross Professor and Chair; M.D. (215-955-8643; charles.yeo@jefferson.edu)

Urology
Leonard G. Gomella, Bernard W. Godwin Jr. Professor of Prostate Cancer and Chair; M.D. (215-955-1702; leonard.gomella@jefferson.edu)

Programs of Study

Truman State, Missouri's public liberal arts and sciences university, offers six selective graduate programs leading to the Master of Accountancy, Master of Arts, Master of Arts in Education (including teacher certification), and Master of Science degrees. Areas of study include accountancy, biology, communication disorders, education, English, and music.

Most programs require a thesis or other capstone project. For example, the M.A.E. program offers a reflective case study option. Programs range from 30 to 48 semester hours.

Programs with special accreditation include accountancy, accredited by AACSB International–The Association to Advance Collegiate Schools of Business; communication disorders, accredited by the American Speech-Language-Hearing Association (ASHA); education, accredited by the National Council for Accreditation of Teacher Education (NCATE); and music, accredited by the National Association of Schools of Music (NASM).

Research Facilities

Truman's graduate programs offer a combination of theory and practical application. The University Library supports faculty and student research with a collection of 427,286 volumes, 1,509,988 microforms, and 3,700 serial subscriptions; interlibrary loan services; and access to bibliographic databases online and on compact disc.

Academic computer facilities include seven computer classrooms with 219 stations and 328 workstations in student labs, some available 24 hours a day. Internet access is available at no charge.

A $20.4-million renovation of the Ophelia Parrish Building became home to Truman's Fine Arts Division in 2000–01.

Truman's close association with the birthplace of osteopathic medicine, A. T. Still University, formerly the Kirksville College of Osteopathic Medicine, offers students access to additional graduate-level faculty members and research opportunities. The science facilities have undergone a $24-million renovation and expansion.

Financial Aid

Graduate teaching and research assistantships are available in many programs. Most assistantships include an $8000 stipend for a nine-month contract as well as a waiver of in-state or out-of-state graduate tuition for up to 9 credit hours per academic semester. In addition, the University offers some divisional fellowships and private scholarships and participates in all major federal financial aid programs.

Cost of Study

Full-time graduate tuition for 2007–08 is $6720 per academic year for Missouri residents and $11,460 for nonresident students.

Living and Housing Costs

In 2007–08, room and board in residence halls costs from $5995.50 to $6200 per person per year for a double room. Apartments rent from $3350 to $6070 per person per year. University family student housing is available for $5650 per year for a one-bedroom apartment and $6850 per year for a two-bedroom apartment. The apartments and the University family student housing include most utilities. Many privately owned apartment complexes close to the University are available to single students and families.

Student Group

Total enrollment at Truman State University is approximately 5,800, of whom about 200 are graduate students. International students and American students who are members of minority groups are encouraged to apply.

Location

Truman's campus comprises 140 acres, located in the heart of Kirksville, Missouri. Kirksville offers numerous social and cultural opportunities, including a variety of recreation areas, shops, restaurants, theaters, and churches. Recreation areas include Thousand Hills State Park and the 700-acre Forest Lake.

The University

Founded in 1867, Truman provides a world-class liberal arts and sciences education to a select number of high-ability students. The University offers forty-two undergraduate and six graduate majors.

Truman is recognized nationally for offering top-quality education at an affordable cost to students. The University's achievements have been featured in such publications as *USA Today, Time, Money, IBM Viewpoint, The Chronicle of Higher Education, U.S. News & World Report, Kiplinger's Personal Finance,* and *Changing Times.*

Applying

Truman State University invites applications from students with outstanding records of undergraduate performance. There is no application fee for American citizens. Application deadlines vary. Official transcripts from each college or university attended are required. In addition, scores on the appropriate entrance exam or exams must be submitted to the Graduate Office. Accountancy majors must submit GMAT scores. The GRE General Test is required by all other programs. Prospective students are advised to take the required exam(s) prior to filing for admission.

Correspondence and Information

Graduate Office
203 McClain Hall
Truman State University
100 East Normal
Kirksville, Missouri 63501

Phone: 660-785-4109
Fax: 660-785-7460
E-mail: gradinfo@truman.edu
Web site: http://gradschool.truman.edu

PROGRAM DIRECTORS AND FACULTY RESEARCH AREAS

Accountancy (AACSB accredited)
Program Director: Dr. Scott Fouch, Professor of Accounting.

Areas of Faculty Research: EDP influences on internal auditing, accounting education, informational impacts on audit reports, managerial accounting, FASB's conceptual framework, accounting standards overload, applications of federal tax laws.

Biology
Program Director: Dr. Scott Burt, Assistant Professor of Biology.

Areas of Faculty Research: Ecology, systematics, and evolution (plant/insect/fungus interactions, plant reproductive ecology, ecological genetics, plant population biology, conservation biology, microbial ecology, fungal ecology, microbe-vertebrate interactions, plant taxonomy, biosystematics, aquatic ecology, rare plant ecology, evolution of Caribbean birds, ornithology, paleobotany, evolution of seed plants, evolution and ecology of marine invertebrates); cellular and molecular biology (maize genetics, nerve cell biology, carotenoid genetics, DNA repair, genetics of sperm development, microbial genetics, plant cell biology, membrane transport, steroid receptor biochemistry); physiology and anatomy (plant stress physiology, physiology of drug abuse, neurophysiology, parasitology/immunology, respiratory physiology); biology education (teaching technology and laboratory investigations).

Communication Disorders (ASHE accredited)
Program Director: Dr. Janet Gooch, Associate Professor of Communication Disorders.

Areas of Faculty Research: Speech and language characteristics of geriatric populations, microcomputer-assisted language intervention, orofacial anomalies, augmentative communication systems, child phonology, bilingual phonology.

Education (NCATE accredited)
Program Director: Dr. Wendy Miner, Professor and Education Department Chair.

Areas of Teaching Specialty: Communication (speech, theater, journalism), English, elementary education, exercise science, foreign language (French, Spanish), history, mathematics, music, science, special education, visual arts.

English
Program Director: Dr. Alanna Pruessner, Professor of English.

Areas of Faculty Research: Composition and rhetorical theory, writing poetry and fiction, world literature, postcolonial literature, Old English language and literature, medieval drama, Chaucer and his contemporaries, Shakespeare and his contemporaries, British period literature from medieval through contemporary, Irish literature, Germanic literature, Joyce and his contemporaries, William Blake, Walt Whitman, William Faulkner, American period literature from early through contemporary, literary theory, film studies, cold war culture, cultural studies.

Music (NASM accredited)
Program Director: Dr. Warren Gooch, Professor of Music.

Specialty Areas: Musicology, theory, composition, music education, conducting, orchestral instruments, piano, voice. Emphases: Research (thesis), performance (recital), composition (recital), conducting (recital).

TUFTS UNIVERSITY

Graduate School of Arts and Sciences

Programs of Study

The Graduate School of Arts and Sciences offers master's and doctoral programs in selected areas of the natural sciences, social sciences, and the humanities.

The Doctor of Philosophy degree is offered in biology, chemistry, chemistry/biotechnology, child development, drama, education, English, history, mathematics, physics, and psychology. A highly selective interdisciplinary doctorate is available in other areas. Tufts also offers a Doctor of Occupational Therapy.

The Master of Arts degree may be earned in art history, art history and museum studies, child development, classical archaeology, classics, drama, economics, education, English, French, German, history, history and museum studies, mathematics, museum education, music, occupational therapy, philosophy, school psychology, and urban and environmental policy and planning. The Master of Science is offered in biology, chemistry, chemistry/biotechnology, education, mathematics, occupational therapy, physics, and psychology. The Master of Arts in Teaching is available with concentrations in art, early childhood, elementary, and secondary education. The Master of Fine Arts degree is awarded in conjunction with the School of the Museum of Fine Arts, Boston. Tufts also offers the Master of Public Policy degree. A Certificate of Advanced Graduate Study may be earned in child development or school psychology.

Full-time students can take one course per semester, for both a grade and credit, through cross-registration agreements with Boston College, Boston University, and Brandeis University.

Research Facilities

The University library system includes the Tisch Library, the Music Library, and the Edward Ginn Library of the Fletcher School. Through Tufts' membership in the Boston Library Consortium, graduate students also have library privileges at Boston College, Boston University, Brandeis University, Brown University, Massachusetts Institute of Technology, Northeastern University, University of Massachusetts, and Wellesley College. Drama students have access to the Harvard Theatre Collection.

Special research facilities for science and engineering students include the campus-based Science and Technology Center, which houses selected areas of research in physics and electrical and chemical engineering, as well as laboratory facilities in biology, chemistry, psychology, and electrical and civil engineering. Students are encouraged to pursue collaborative research at off-site facilities, which have included Fermilab, the Woods Hole Oceanographic Institute, and Brookhaven Laboratories. Many researchers carry out collaborative research with colleagues at nearby Boston universities.

Financial Aid

In 2006–07, the School awarded more than $9 million in tuition scholarships. Teaching and research assistantships are available, as are some fellowships. Tufts also awards need-based financial aid through the Federal Perkins Loan, Federal Work-Study, and Federal Stafford Student Loan programs.

Cost of Study

Tuition for 2007–08 is $35,052, which covers the full cost of one-year master's programs and one third the cost of most doctoral programs. Tuition for two-year master's programs (occupational therapy and urban and environmental policy and planning) is $26,288 for the 2007–08 academic year. Tuition for the school psychology program is $30,670 and tuition for the studio art program is $30,704. Part-time tuition is $3504 per course. Other charges include student health insurance, a health service fee, and a student activity fee.

Living and Housing Costs

Living expenses are estimated at about $1200 a month. There is limited on-campus housing for graduate students. Rents for one-bedroom apartments in Medford and Somerville begin at approximately $900 per month. The cost of sharing an apartment averages about $600 per person. A public transportation system serves the greater Boston area and provides easy access to and from the campus.

Student Group

In 2006–07, 1,532 students were enrolled in the Graduate School of Arts and Sciences and graduate programs offered by the School of Engineering. Of these, 59 percent were women and 16 percent were international students.

Location

The main campus, which spans the Medford-Somerville city line, is 7 miles from downtown Boston, a city where the arts (music, drama, and dance), museums, and sporting events abound. Cape Cod beaches and the mountains and forests of Maine, New Hampshire, and Vermont can be easily reached.

The University

Chartered as a liberal arts college in 1852, today Tufts is a small, selective, private university offering opportunities for undergraduate, graduate, and professional education to more than 7,500 students. The Graduate School of Arts and Sciences, the Fletcher School of Law and Diplomacy, the School of Engineering, the Friedman School of Nutrition Science and Policy, the Sackler School of Graduate Biomedical Sciences, the Cummings School of Veterinary Medicine, and the Schools of Dental Medicine and Medicine offer graduate and/or professional education. The University is accredited by the New England Association of Schools and Colleges.

Applying

Deadlines for applications vary by program. Applicants are required to submit three letters of recommendation, official transcripts from all colleges and universities attended, and a personal statement. Most departments also require the results of the Graduate Record Examinations (GRE). Students whose native language is not English must submit official results of the Test of English as a Foreign Language (TOEFL). A minimum score of 550 (or 213 CBT) is required.

Correspondence and Information

Graduate Studies Office
Tufts University
Ballou Hall, First Floor
Medford, Massachusetts 02155

Phone: 617-627-3395
Fax: 617-627-3016
Web site: http://gradstudy.tufts.edu

FIELDS OF STUDY AND FACULTY ADVISERS

Art and Art History: Cristelle Baskins (M.A. program); Andrew McClellan (Museum Studies); David Brown (M.F.A. program).
Biology: Juliet Fuhrman.
Chemistry: Samuel Kounaves.
Child Development: Anne Easterbrooks.
Classics: Peter Reid (Classics); Jodi Magness (Classical Archaeology).
Drama: Laurence Senelick.
Economics: Marcelo Bianconi.
Education: Linda Beardsley (Teacher Education); Barbara Brizuela (Educational Studies); Analucia Schliemann (Museum Education); Caroline Wandle (School Psychology); Patty Bode (Art Education).
English: Joseph Litvak.
French: Vincent Pollina.
German: Ron Salter.
History: Reed Ueda.
Interdisciplinary Doctorate: Robin Kanarek.
Mathematics: Zbigniew Nitecki.
Music: Jane Bernstein (Musicology); David Locke (Ethnomusicology); John McDonald (Composition); Janet Schmalfeldt (Theory).
Occupational Therapy: Linda Tickle-Degnen.
Philosophy: Nancy Bauer.
Physics: Krzysztof Sliwa.
Psychology: Holly Taylor.
Urban and Environmental Policy and Planning: Julian Agyeman.

UNIVERSITY AT BUFFALO, THE STATE UNIVERSITY OF NEW YORK

Graduate School

Programs of Study The Graduate School offers 185 master's degree programs, seventy-eight doctoral degree programs, and four professional programs, as well as a number of certificate and dual-degree programs. Interdisciplinary research is available through more than forty centers and graduate groups. The graduate programs and departments fashion individual curricula to meet specific objectives. Each program establishes its own requirements for admission, its own assessment of satisfactory student progress, and its own mandates for satisfactory completion of the degree offered under a broad institutional mandate for excellence. Each department is responsible for admitting its own students. For the master's degree, one year of residence is required, as is a comprehensive test, a thesis based on independent research, or an appropriate special project. For the doctoral degree, the residence requirement is one year; other requirements include an evaluation of the student's work in the doctoral program, an original dissertation, and an oral defense.

Research Facilities The University at Buffalo (UB) has become a leader in developing and deploying an IT environment that empowers University members to accomplish their goals. Students and faculty members have multimedia e-mail; access to campus high-speed networks in laboratories, classrooms, and University residence halls and apartments; wireless access points on campus; Web access to extensive library resources; easy Web publishing; and extensive technical support and training. Through its digital initiative, the University libraries offer online access to major full-text information products covering journal literature, books, statistical data, worldwide newspapers, and hundreds of databases supporting research in the sciences, social sciences, humanities, and interdisciplinary studies. More than 2,200 personal computers and high-performance workstations are available to students in more than ninety public and departmental computing labs. Students also have access to computing on powerful clusters on UNIX time-sharing machines and to computational resources at one of the leading academic supercomputing sites in the U.S., the Center for Computational Research (CCR).

More than a dozen investigative centers and institutes are part of a research effort that exceeded $297 million in expenditures last year. In addition to governmental and private foundation support for research, UB receives considerable industrial support through research collaborations and affiliations. The University enjoys an international reputation, attracting students from all over the world and maintaining scholarly exchanges with institutions in several nations. Leading-edge interdisciplinary research centers integrating the fields of medicine, engineering, and physical sciences provide students with a unique environment to conduct research at the interfaces of disciplines. Some examples include the Center for Single-Molecule Biophysics; the Center for Spin Effects and Quantum Information in Nanostructures; the Institute for Lasers, Photonics, and Biophotonics; the Research Institute on Addictions; the Center for Hearing and Deafness; and the Toshiba Stroke Research Center. The Center of Excellence in Bioinformatics and Life Sciences, which is a 129,000-square-foot, state-of-the-art interdisciplinary research facility, opened its doors in 2006 on the Buffalo-Niagara Medical Campus after a commitment of more than $200 million from New York State and private industry. UB is also a founding member of the New York Structural Biology Center, providing investigators access to high-field NMR and cryoelectron microscopy for the elucidation of protein structures.

Other specialized centers include the Center for Studies in American Culture, Baldy Center for Law and Social Policy, Center for Urban Studies, Regional Institute, Center for Excellence in Global Enterprise Management, Great Lakes Institute, National Center for Geographic Information and Analysis, Humanities Institute, Center for Assistive Technology, MCEER, Institute for Research and Education on Women and Gender, Center for Excellence for Document Analysis and Recognition, and Center for Unified Biometrics and Sensors.

Financial Aid Many students hold teaching, graduate, or research assistantships. A number of competitive fellowship programs are also available, including opportunities for students who are members of underrepresented minority groups. Full- or partial-tuition scholarships accompany most assistantships and fellowships. Graduate Opportunity Tuition Scholarships are available to students who participated in undergraduate EOP, HEOP, or SEEK programs. Students should contact the department for information and applications. The most up-to-date contact information for all of UB's graduate and professional programs can be found on the School's Web site.

Cost of Study Full-time tuition for 2006–07 was $3450 per semester for New York State residents and $5460 per semester for nonresidents. Part-time tuition was $288 per credit hour for residents and $455 per credit hour for nonresidents. Tuition in the professional schools is higher. All tuition rates are subject to adjustment by the Board of Trustees.

Living and Housing Costs The University at Buffalo has four apartment complexes that house graduate students. There are two complexes that are two-bedroom town houses. One is for graduate and married students only and is located off campus. The proposed rate for 2007–08 is $920 per month plus utilities for the entire unit. The second town-house complex is for graduate students only and is on campus. This apartment complex is fully furnished; the proposed rate is $720 per student per month, including all utilities. The two other apartment complexes that house graduate and undergraduate students consist of four-bedroom, two-bedroom, single, and studio apartments. Both of these apartment complexes are located on campus and are fully furnished. The rents include all utilities. Proposed rents for four bedrooms range from $555 to $658 per student per month, two bedrooms range from $625 to $695 per student per month, singles range from $715 to $776 per student per month, and studios are $740 per month.

Student Group The total enrollment of 27,823 consists of 14,429 men and 13,394 women. Graduate students number 9,317. The student body includes representatives from more than 100 countries.

Location Buffalo is a Great Lakes city on an international border with a metropolitan population of more than 1 million. It is a city of friendly neighborhoods with big-city recreation for all tastes: professional sports (football, hockey, indoor soccer, lacrosse, and Triple-A baseball), the Buffalo Philharmonic Orchestra, a celebrated theater district, the renowned twentieth-century collection in the Albright-Knox Art Gallery, and a lively club scene. Buffalo enjoys four distinct seasons in a dramatic setting on Lake Erie and the Niagara River. Skiing, hiking, camping, sailing, boating, and Lake Erie beaches on both the U.S. and Canadian shores and the natural wonder of Niagara Falls are all nearby.

The University The University at Buffalo is the largest and most comprehensive public research university in New York and New England. The University's two campuses make up the largest unit of the sixty-four-campus SUNY system. Its North Campus, the seat of most of its non–medical sciences academic programs, occupies 2 square miles of fields and woods in suburban Amherst. It is one of the most modern university campuses in the nation. More than 5 million square feet of academic space, laboratories, libraries, residence halls, and recreation facilities have been built there since 1972. An expanded 30,000-seat football stadium, a $45-million Center for the Arts, an expanded Student Union, and apartment-style accommodations for students and families are recent additions to the North Campus. The University's South Campus, 3 miles away in the residential northeast corner of Buffalo, is now largely devoted to the health sciences. Buffalo's rapid-transit system connects that campus with the city center and the waterfront.

Applying Applications should be filed directly with the appropriate department. The quickest and easiest way to apply is online. Deadlines for filing applications vary by department.

Correspondence and Information

Graduate Enrollment Management Services
408 Capen Hall
University at Buffalo, the State University of New York
Buffalo, New York 14260-1606

Phone: 716-645-3482
Fax: 716-645-6998
Web site: http://www.grad.buffalo.edu/admissions

GRADUATE AND PROFESSIONAL PROGRAMS

Acting Vice Provost for Graduate Education and Dean of the Graduate School: Dr. John Ho, 716-645-3786.
Associate Provost and Executive Director of the Graduate School: Dr. Myron A. Thompson, 716-645-6227.

Accounting (M.S.)
Acute Health Nursing (M.S., Adv. Cert., post-master's)
Adult/Medical Surgical–Surgical Clinical Nurse Specialist (M.S.)
Adult Health Nursing (M.S., Adv. Cert., post-master's)
Aerospace Engineering (M.S., Ph.D.)
American Studies (Concentration in Women's Studies) (M.A., Ph.D.)
Anatomical Sciences (M.A., Ph.D.)
Anthropology (M.A., Ph.D.)
Applied Economics: Financial Economics (Adv. Cert.)
Applied Economics: Health Services (Adv. Cert.)
Applied Economics: Information and Internet Economics (Adv. Cert.)
Applied Economics: International Economics (Adv. Cert.)
Applied Economics: Law and Regulation (Adv. Cert.)
Applied Economics: Urban and Regional Economics (Adv. Cert.)
Architecture (M.Arch., M.Arch./M.B.A., M.Arch./M.U.P., M.Arch./M.F.A.)
Art History (M.A.)
Assistive and Rehabilitative Technology (Adv. Cert.)
Audiology (Au.D.)
Behavioral Neuroscience (Ph.D.)
Biochemical Pharmacology (B.S./M.S.)
Biochemistry (M.A., Ph.D.)
Biological Sciences (M.A., M.S., Ph.D.)
Biological Sciences (Cellular and Molecular Biology) (Roswell) (Ph.D.)
Biology Education: Adolescence (5–12 or 7–12) (Ed.M., Adv. Cert.)
Biomaterials (M.S.)
Biophysical Sciences (M.S., Ph.D.)
Biophysics (Molecular and Cellular) (Roswell) (M.S., Ph.D.)
Biostatistics (Concentration in Biostatistics) (M.A., Ph.D., M.P.H.)
Biotechnology (M.S.)
Business Administration (Concentrations in Accounting, Biotechnology Management, Finance, Information Assurance, Information Systems and E-business, Marketing Management, International Management, Management Consulting, and Supply Chains and Operations Management) (M.B.A., J.D./M.B.A., M.Arch./M.B.A., M.A./M.B.A., M.D./M.B.A., B.S./M.B.A.)
Chemical and Biological Engineering (M.E., M.S., Ph.D.)
Chemistry (M.A., Ph.D.)
Chemistry Education: Adolescence (5–12 or 7–12) (Ed.M., Adv. Cert.)
Child Health Nursing (M.S.)
Childhood Education (1–6) (Ed.M., Adv. Cert.)
Childhood Education with Bilingual Extension (1–6) (Ed.M., Adv. Cert.)
Civil, Structural and Environmental Engineering (M.E., M.S., Ph.D.)
Classics (M.A., Ph.D.)
Clinical Psychology (Ph.D.)
Cognitive Psychology (Ph.D.)
Communication (M.A., Ph.D.)
Communicative Disorders and Sciences (M.A., Ph.D., Au.D.)
Comparative Literature (M.A., Ph.D.)
Computational Science (Adv. Cert.)
Computer Science and Engineering (M.S., Ph.D.)
Counseling/School Psychology (Ph.D.)
Counselor Education (Ph.D.)
Criminal Law (LL.M.)
Critical Museum Studies (Adv. Cert.)
Dentistry (D.D.S., B.S./D.D.S.)
Early Childhood Education (Birth–grade 2) (Adv. Cert., Ed.M.)
Early Childhood Education with Bilingual Extension (Birth–grade 2) (Ed.M., Adv. Cert.)
Earth Science Education: Adolescence (5–12 or 7–12) (Ed.M., Adv. Cert.)
Ecology, Evolution and Behavior (Adv. Cert., M.S., Ph.D.)
Economics (M.A., M.S., Ph.D., B.A./M.S.)
Educational Administration (Ed.M., Ed.D., Ph.D., Adv. Cert.)
Educational Psychology (M.A., Ph.D.)
Electrical Engineering (M.E., M.S., Ph.D., B.S./M.B.A.)
Elementary Education (Ed.D., Ph.D.)
Endodontics (Adv. Cert.)
English (M.A., Ph.D.)
English Education (Ph.D.)
English Education: Adolescence (5–12 or 7–12) (Ed.M., Adv. Cert.)
English for Speakers of Other Languages (Ed.M., Adv. Cert.)
Epidemiology (M.S.)
Epidemiology and Community Health (Ph.D.)
Executive M.B.A. (M.B.A.)
Exercise Science (M.S., Ph.D., B.S./M.S.)
Family Nurse Practitioner (M.S., Adv. Cert., post-master's)
Finance (M.S.)
Fine Arts (M.F.A.)
Foreign and Second Language Education (Ph.D.)
French Education: Adolescence (5–12 or 7–12) (Adv. Cert., Ed.M.)
French Language and Literature (M.A., Ph.D.)
General Education (Ed.M.)
General Education: Educational Leadership and Policy (Ed.M.)
General Education: Learning and Instruction (Ed.M.)
Geographic Information Science (Adv. Cert.)
Geography (M.A., M.S., Ph.D.)
Geological Sciences (M.A., M.S., Ph.D.)
Geriatric Clinical Nurse Specialist (M.S.)
Geriatric Nurse Practitioner (M.S., Adv. Cert., post-master's)
German Education: Adolescence (5–12 or 7–12) (Ed.M., Adv. Cert.)
Higher Education Administration (Concentration in Student Affairs) (Ph.D., Ed.M.)
History (M.A., Ph.D.)
Humanities: Interdisciplinary with a concentration in African American Studies (M.A.)
Humanities: Interdisciplinary with a concentration in Arts Management (M.A.)
Humanities: Interdisciplinary with a concentration in Caribbean Cultural Studies (M.A.)
Humanities: Interdisciplinary with a concentration in Computational Linguistics (M.A.)
Humanities: Interdisciplinary with a concentration in Film Studies (M.A.)
Industrial Engineering (M.E., M.S., Ph.D.)
Information Assurance (Adv. Cert.)
Interdisciplinary Graduate Program in Biomedical Sciences (Ph.D.)
Italian Education: Adolescence (5–12 or 7–12) (Adv. Cert., Ed.M.)
Latin Education: Adolescence (5–12 or 7–12) (Adv. Cert., Ed.M.)
Law (J.D., LL.M. General LL.M. program for international students)
Library and Information Science (M.L.S., Adv. Cert.)
Linguistics (M.A., Ph.D.)
Literacy Specialist (Ed.M.)
Management (Ph.D.)
Management Information Systems (M.S.)
Maternal and Women's Health Nurse Practitioner (M.S., Adv. Cert., post-master's)
Mathematics (M.A., Ph.D.)
Mathematics Education (Ph.D.)
Mathematics Education: Adolescence (5–12 or 7–12) (Ed.M., Adv. Cert.)
Maxillofacial Prosthodontics (Adv. Cert.)
Mechanical Engineering (M.S., Ph.D.)
Media Arts Production (M.F.A.)
Medical Scientist Training Program (M.D./Ph.D.)
Medicinal Chemistry (M.S., Ph.D.)
Medicine (M.D.)
Mentoring Teachers (Adv. Cert.)
Microbiology and Immunology (M.A., Ph.D.)
Microbiology and Immunology (Roswell) (Ph.D.)
Molecular and Cellular Biology (Adv. Cert.)
Music (M.A., Ph.D.)
Music Composition (M.A., Ph.D.)
Music Education (Adv. Cert., Ed.M.)
Music History (M.A.)
Music Performance (M.M.)
Music Theory (M.A., Ph.D.)
Music: Historical Musicology (M.A., Ph.D.)
Natural Sciences: Interdisciplinary (M.S.)
Natural Sciences: Interdisciplinary: Natural and Biomedical Sciences (Roswell) (M.S.)
Neonatal Nurse Practitioner (Adv. Cert., M.S.)
Neuroscience (M.S., Ph.D.)
New Media Design (Adv. Cert.)
Nurse Anesthetist (M.S.)
Nursing (Ph.D.)
Nursing Education (Adv. Cert.)
Nutrition (M.S.)
Occupational Therapy/Early Intervention (M.S.)
Occupational Therapy/Physical/Developmental Disabilities (M.S.)
Oral and Maxillofacial Pathology (Adv. Cert.)
Oral and Maxillofacial Surgery (Adv. Cert.)
Oral Biology (Ph.D.)
Oral Sciences (M.S.)
Orthodontics (M.S., Adv. Cert.)
Part-Time Professional M.B.A. (M.B.A.)
Pathology (M.A., Ph.D.)
Pathology (Roswell) (Ph.D.)
Pediatric Dentistry (Adv. Cert.)
Pediatric Nurse Practitioner (Adv. Cert.)
Periodontics (Adv. Cert.)
Pharmaceutical Sciences (M.S., Ph.D.)
Pharmacology and Toxicology (M.A., Ph.D.)
Pharmacology (Molecular Pharmacology and Cancer Therapeutics) (Roswell) (Ph.D.)
Pharmacy Practice (Pharm.D.)
Philosophy (M.A., Ph.D.)
Physical Therapy (D.P.T.)
Physics (M.S., Ph.D.)
Physics Education: Adolescence (5–12 or 7–12) (Ed.M., Adv. Cert.)
Physiology (M.A., Ph.D.)
Political Science (M.A., Ph.D.)
Prosthodontics (Adv. Cert.)
Psychiatric–Mental Health Nurse Practitioner (M.S., Adv. Cert., post-master's)
Psychology (M.A., Ph.D.)
Public Health (M.P.H.)
Reading Education (Ph.D.)
Rehabilitation Counseling (M.S.)
Rehabilitation Science (Ph.D.)
Removable Prosthodontics (Adv. Cert.)
School Business and Human Resource Administrator (Adv. Cert.)
School Counseling (Ed.M., Adv. Cert.)
School District Business Leader (Adv. Cert.)
School Media Specialist (M.L.S.)
School Psychology (M.A.)
Science Education (Ph.D.)
Social Foundations (Ph.D.)
Social Sciences: Interdisciplinary (M.S.)
Social Studies Education: Adolescence (5–12 or 7–12) (Ed.M., Adv. Cert.)
Social Welfare (Ph.D.)
Social Work (M.S.W., J.D./M.S.W., M.B.A./M.S.W., B.A./M.S.W.)
Social-Personality Psychology (Ph.D.)
Sociology (M.A., Ph.D.)
Spanish Education: Adolescence (5–12 or 7–12) (Adv. Cert., Ed.M.)
Spanish Language and Literature (M.A., Ph.D.)
Special Education (Ph.D.)
Structural Biology (M.S., Ph.D.)
Supply Chains and Operations Management (M.S.)
Teaching and Leading for Diversity (Adv. Cert.)
Teaching English to Speakers of Other Languages (Ed.M.)
Temporomandibular Disorders and Orofacial Pain (Adv. Cert.)
Transportation and Business Geographics (Adv. Cert.)
Urban Planning (M.U.P., M.Arch./M.U.P.)

THE UNIVERSITY OF ALABAMA AT BIRMINGHAM

Graduate School

Programs of Study

The University of Alabama at Birmingham (UAB) offers doctoral degrees in administration health services, applied mathematics, biochemistry and molecular genetics, biology, biomedical engineering, biostatistics, cell biology, cellular and molecular physiology, chemistry, civil engineering, computer and information sciences, computer engineering, early childhood education, educational leadership, electrical engineering, environmental health engineering, environmental health sciences, epidemiology, genetics, health education/health promotion, materials engineering, materials science, mechanical engineering, medical sociology, microbiology, neurobiology, nursing, nutrition science, pathology, pharmacology/toxicology, physical therapy, physics, psychology (medical, developmental, and behavioral neuroscience), public health, and vision science.

Master's degrees are offered in accounting, anthropology, art history, biology, biomedical engineering, biostatistics, business administration, chemistry, civil engineering, clinical laboratory sciences, clinical nutrition, communication management, computer and information sciences, criminal justice, dentistry, education (all areas), electrical engineering, English, forensic science, health administration, health informatics, history, materials engineering, mathematics, mechanical engineering, nurse anesthesia, nursing, occupational therapy, oral biology, physician assistant studies, physics, public administration, public health, sociology, and vision science.

Interdisciplinary training and certification programs that add to traditional doctoral programs are available in cellular and molecular biology, forensic science, gerontology, integrative biomedical sciences, neuroscience, and toxicology. Combined degree programs are available in many areas, including the M.D./Ph.D., M.D./M.S.B.M.S., M.P.A./J.D., M.P.A./M.P.H., O.D./M.S., O.D./Ph.D., M.B.A./M.P.H., and M.S. H.A./M.B.A.

Research Facilities

UAB is one of the top research universities in the country. Research funding has doubled every decade at UAB. Today, UAB receives more than $433 million in grants and contracts. In funding from the National Institutes of Health (NIH), UAB ranks twentieth overall, with five schools in the top twenty: Health Related Professions (first), Optometry (fourth), Public Health (tenth), Nursing (seventeenth), and Medicine (sixteenth).

UAB's research enterprise is highly interdisciplinary. University-wide research centers house active basic and translational research programs in the areas of aging, arthritis, and musculoskeletal diseases; AIDS; biophysical sciences and engineering; cancer; clinical nutrition; cystic fibrosis; free-radical biology; health promotion; metabolic bone disease; outcomes and effectiveness research and education; women's health; and vision science. Other schoolwide centers focus their research efforts on Alzheimer's disease, cell adhesion and matrix, labor education and research, neuroimmunology, nuclear magnetic resonance, urban affairs, telecommunications, and educational accountability. Many centers house special research facilities such as the transgenic animal/embryonic stem cell facility, the hybridoma core facility, the digital microscopy facility, and a 4.1 Tesla magnet for functional NMR imaging. Two major research libraries, the Mervyn H. Sterne Library and the Lister Hill Library of the Health Sciences, provide online access to the research literature in all areas of graduate study.

A major focus of UAB research is moving technology into the marketplace. The OADI Technology Center is a business incubator facility that houses new advanced-technology companies in areas such as biotechnology, robotics, software development, and medical devices. The UAB Research Foundation serves as a conduit of information, discoveries, and inventions from researchers to business. In partnership with industry, it guides technology through laboratory observation, product development, and marketing. Other University-industry partnerships include student organizations such as the Industry Roundtable, which introduces students to career options outside academia by providing information and networking opportunities with business and industry.

Financial Aid

Each year, approximately 190 students are appointed as Graduate School fellows or assistants. Stipends range from approximately $10,000 to $23,000 plus full payment of tuition and fees. The individual graduate programs also offer similar awards. Some programs need teaching or laboratory assistants, some have federal and state research grants that are budgeted to include student assistants, and many need graders or lab tutors. UAB currently has substantial training support from federal agencies. The Comprehensive Minority Faculty and Student Development Program offers four years of support to minority students enrolled in doctoral programs.

Cost of Study

Tuition in 2006–07 was $170 per semester hour for Alabama residents and $425 per semester hour for nonresident students.

Living and Housing Costs

UAB offers two residence halls geared toward the needs of graduate students. The Housing Office also provides information on off-campus housing, including listings for short- and long-term lease facilities. Many reasonably priced apartments are located within easy walking distance of UAB.

Student Group

More than 4,300 graduate students are enrolled in UAB's forty-four doctoral programs and forty-three master's programs. Many of these programs unite different disciplines and cross departmental and school lines, illustrating the strong interdisciplinary character of the University.

Location

Birmingham is located in the geographic heart of the Southeast, 2½ hours by interstate from Atlanta, 4 hours from Nashville, 6 hours from New Orleans, 5 hours from the Smoky Mountains, and 5 hours from the beaches of the Gulf of Mexico. Birmingham is a dynamic, progressive urban center of great natural beauty. More than 1 million people live in the metropolitan area.

The University

The University of Alabama at Birmingham is a comprehensive, urban university and medical center that encompasses eighty-two city blocks and has a student enrollment of more than 16,000. UAB is the home of a large graduate school, a world-renowned health-care complex, and more than seventy research centers focusing on such diverse issues as AIDS, business development, and biodefense and emerging infections.

The University comprises thirteen schools as well as hospitals and clinics that house internationally renowned patient-care programs. UAB includes the Schools of Arts and Humanities, Business, Dentistry, Education, Engineering, Health Professions, Medicine, Natural Sciences and Mathematics, Nursing, Optometry, Public Health, and Social and Behavioral Sciences and the Graduate School.

Applying

UAB's admission process has two levels of review. The Graduate School sets general admission requirements, and each graduate program specifies its particular requirements. In general, the Graduate School welcomes applications from students who have earned a bachelor's degree from a regionally accredited academic institution, have favorable letters of evaluation, and have scored well on a recognized standardized test (usually the Graduate Record Examinations General Test). Each application is evaluated by the program faculty on the basis of all information available about the applicant.

Applications for admission are not processed until all credentials required by the Graduate School have been received. Prospective students can submit an application via the Internet from the Graduate School's Web page.

Correspondence and Information

The Graduate School
The University of Alabama at Birmingham
HUC 511
1530 Third Avenue South
Birmingham, Alabama 35294-1150
E-mail: gradschool@uab.edu
Web site: http://www.uab.edu/graduate

GRADUATE PROGRAM DIRECTORS

Accounting: Dr. Richard A. Turpen.
Administrative Health Services: Dr. Robert Hernandez.
Anthropology: Dr. Christopher Taylor.
Art History: Dr. Heather McPherson.
Biochemistry and Molecular Genetics: Dr. Thomas Ryan.
Biology: Dr. Steven Watts.
Biostatistics: Dr. Christopher Coffey.
Business–M.B.A.: Melody Lake.
Cell Biology: Dr. James Collawn.
Cellular and Molecular Biology: Dr. Harald W. Sontheimer.
Cellular and Molecular Physiology: Dr. Lisa Schwiebert.
Chemistry: Dr. David E. Graves.
Clinical Laboratory Sciences: Dr. Pat Greenup.
Clinical Nutrition: Dr. M. Amanda Brown.
Communication Management: Dr. Jonathan H. Amsbary.
Computer and Information Sciences: Dr. John K. Johnstone.
Criminal Justice: Dr. Kathryn Morgan.
Dentistry–Oral Biology: Dr. Firoz Rahemtulla.
Education–Curriculum and Instruction: Dr. Charles Calhoun.
Education–Human Studies: Dr. David Macrina.
Educational Leadership–Special Education: Dr. Boyd Rogan.
English: Dr. Kyle Grimes.
Engineering, Biomedical: Dr. Richard Gary.
Engineering, Civil: Dr. Fouad H. Fouad.
Engineering, Computer: Dr. Thomas Jannett.
Engineering, Electrical: Dr. Thomas Jannett.
Engineering, Environmental Health: Dr. Melinda Lalor.
Engineering, Materials: Dr. Burton R. Patterson.
Engineering, Mechanical: Dr. Bharat Soni.
Environmental Health Science: Dr. Shannon Bailey.
Epidemiology: Dr. Gerald McGwin.
Forensic Science: Dr. John Sloan.
Genetics: Dr. Ada Elgavish.
Gerontology: Dr. Patricia L. Sawyer.
Health Administration: Dr. Steven O'Connor.
Health Education/Health Promotion: Dr. David Macrina (Education); Dr. Patricia Lee (Public Health).
Health Informatics: Dr. Gerald Glandon.
History: Dr. Michael McConnell.
Integrative Biomedical Sciences: Dr. Coral Lamartiniere.
Materials Science: Dr. Gregg Janowski.
Mathematics, Applied Mathematics: Dr. Ioulia Karpechina.
M.D./Ph.D. Program: Dr. R. Pat Bucy.
Microbiology: Dr. Peter Burrows.
Neurobiology: Dr. Anne Theibert.
Neuroscience: Dr. Lori McMahon.
Nurse Anesthesia: Dr. Joe Williams.
Nursing: Dr. Marguerite Kinney.
Nutrition Sciences: Dr. Tim Nagy.
Occupational Therapy: Dr. Penelope Moyers.
Pathology: Dr. Scott W. Ballinger.
Pharmacology/Toxicology: Dr. Coral Lamartiniere.
Physical Therapy: Dr. Sharon Shaw, D.P.T.; Dr. Cecilia L. Graham, D.Sc.P.T.
Physician Assistant Studies: Dr. Herbert Ridings.
Physics: Dr. Yogesh Vohra.
Psychology–Behavioral Neuroscience: Dr. Alan Randich.
Psychology–Developmental: Dr. Karlene Ball.
Psychology–Medical: Dr. Jesse Milby.
Public Administration: Dr. Akhlaque Haque.
Sociology/Medical Sociology: Dr. Patricia Drentea.
Toxicology Feeder Program: Dr. Coral Lamartiniere.
Vision Science: Dr. Kent Keyser.

UNIVERSITY of ARKANSAS 1871

UNIVERSITY OF ARKANSAS

Graduate School

Programs of Study

The University of Arkansas is a nationally competitive, student-centered research university serving Arkansas and the world. Recognized as the only comprehensive doctoral degree–granting institution in the state, the University is the major center in Arkansas for graduate-level instruction as well as basic and applied research. Firmly positioned as Arkansas's premier research institution, the University of Arkansas offers more than 140 graduate degree programs leading to advanced degrees conferred within the University's six colleges and the Graduate School.

The Dale Bumpers College of Agriculture, Food and Life Sciences offers doctoral programs in animal science; crop, soil, and environmental sciences; entomology; food science; plant science; and poultry science and master's degree programs in agricultural education; agricultural and extension education; agricultural economics; agricultural, food and life sciences; animal science; crop, soil, and environmental sciences; entomology; food science, horticulture; human environmental sciences; plant pathology; and poultry science.

The J. William Fulbright College of Arts and Sciences has doctoral programs in anthropology, biology, chemistry, comparative literature, computer science, English, environmental dynamics, history, mathematics, philosophy, physics, and psychology and master's degree programs in anthropology, applied physics, art, biology, chemistry, communications, communication disorders, comparative literature, computer science, creative writing, drama, English, French, geography, geology, German, history, journalism, mathematics, music, nursing, philosophy, physics, political science, psychology, public administration, social work, sociology, Spanish, statistics, and translation.

The Sam M. Walton College of Business offers doctoral programs in accounting, economics, finance, information systems, management, and marketing and master's degree programs in accounting, business administration economics, and information systems.

The College of Education and Health Professions has doctoral programs in counselor education, curriculum and instruction, educational administration, educational foundations, health science, higher education, kinesiology, recreation, rehabilitation education and research, and workforce development education and master's degree programs in counseling, educational administration, educational technology, educational foundations, elementary education, health science, higher education, kinesiology, middle-level education, physical education, recreation, rehabilitation, secondary education, speech-language pathology, special education, statistics, and workforce development education.

In the College of Engineering, there are doctoral programs in biological engineering, chemical engineering, civil engineering, computer systems engineering, electrical engineering, environmental engineering, industrial engineering, and mechanical engineering and master's degree programs in biological engineering, chemical engineering, civil engineering, computer systems engineering, electrical engineering, environmental engineering, industrial engineering, mechanical engineering, operations management, operations research, telecommunications engineering, and transportation engineering.

The Graduate School offers doctoral programs in cell and molecular biology, microelectronics-photonics, public policy, and space and planetary science.

Research Facilities

The University library contains nearly 1.5 million volumes, approximately 14,170 subscriptions to periodicals and journals, 3.2 million titles on microform, and more than 19,400 recordings. The University of Arkansas also provides computer labs with both IBM and Macintosh stations at locations across the campus, some open around the clock. Recent renovations in the fine arts center provide stunning gallery and theater facilities. The Center of Excellence for Poultry Science is a $22-million facility offering the finest training in the U.S. for poultry scientists. Other facilities include the Center for Sensing Technology and Research, which features a 9.4-Tesla Fourier-transform mass spectrometer (FTMS); the Chemical Hazards Research Center; the High Density Electronics Center; the Center for Advanced Spatial Technologies, which was recognized nationally for its data storage and retrieval warehouse, GeoStor, by the Urban and Regional Information Systems Association (URISA); and other state-of-the-art science labs.

Financial Aid

Graduate assistant positions are available for master's and doctoral students who have been accepted into a degree program. Application is made directly to the department; appointments are awarded by the department. Several fellowships are available for graduate students. Students may apply directly to the Graduate School for the Paul Kuroda Fellowship and the Harry and Jo Leggett Chancellor's Fellowship. The Benjamin Franklin Lever Graduate Tuition Fellowship is a tuition-only fellowship for qualified underrepresented students. Doctoral fellowships, Doctoral Academy Fellowships, and Distinguished Doctoral Fellowships are available for exceptional incoming graduate students.Nominations for fellowships are submitted by the department head/graduate coordinator; fellowships are awarded by the Graduate School.

Cost of Study

For the 2006–07 school year, tuition was $269.99 per credit hour for Arkansas residents and $638.71 for out-of-state residents. Other, miscellaneous fees ranged from $67 to $287. For international students, tuition, fees, housing, health insurance, books and supplies, equipment fees, and personal expenses range from $22,322 to $25,971, depending on the department.

Living and Housing Costs

On-campus housing is not available for graduate students. Apartments rates in Fayetteville average about $450 to $800 per month for two bedrooms.

Student Group

In 2006–07, the University enrolled 3,576 graduate professional students. Fayetteville's 345-acre campus is home to students from all counties in Arkansas, every state in the U.S., and more than 100 countries throughout the world. Total University enrollment for 2006–07 was approximately 17,925 students and included a diverse student population, with more than 940 international students representing 100 countries. The University has targeted advanced-degree enrollment to grow to 5,500 by 2010.

Location

Fayetteville is nestled in the Ozark Mountains and is accessible to major metropolitan amenities, making it an excellent place for a well-balanced college experience. The community has a population of more than 65,000. In recent years, Fayetteville has been named "One of America's Most Livable Cities," one of the "Top 10 Best Places to Retire," "One of America's Hottest' Cities," one of the nation's "least stressful" metro areas, and among the "Best Places to Live in America" by publications such as *Frommer's Guide* 2004 and *Money* magazine.

The University

Established in 1871, the University of Arkansas is the state's flagship campus. The Graduate School was established in 1927 and is now benefiting from a $100-million endowment, part of the historic $300-million gift from the Walton Family Charitable Foundation, which was announced in April 2002. The gift supports endowed fellowships and an endowed research fund for graduate students. The campus is also graced by the unique, much-loved tradition of Senior Walk. Since the University's founding, the names of all graduates have been etched into more than 5 miles of campus sidewalks, their names arranged by year of graduation.

Applying

To earn graduate-level credit as a degree-seeking student, students must make formal application to and be officially admitted by the Graduate School. Applications for admission to the Graduate School must be accompanied by two official copies of the student's academic record, including all courses, grades, and credits attempted and indication of degree(s) earned from each college or university that the student has previously attended, and a $40 application fee ($50 for international applicants). Applicants are encouraged to apply online at http://www.uark.edu/grad.

Correspondence and Information

For program information, applicants can write to the Graduate Coordinator, (specific department or program), 1 University of Arkansas, Fayetteville, Arkansas 72701.

Office of Graduate and International Recruitment and Admissions
119 Ozark Hall
1 University of Arkansas
Fayetteville, Arkansas 72701
Phone: 479-575-5869
866-234-3957 (toll-free)
E-mail: gradinfo@uark.edu
Web site: http://www.uark.edu/grad

Sam M. Walton College of Business
1 University of Arkansas
Fayetteville, Arkansas 72701
Phone: 479-575-2851
E-mail: gsb@walton.uark.edu
Web site: http://gsb.uark.edu/

School of Law
Waterman Hall 107
1 University of Arkansas
Fayetteville, Arkansas 72701
Phone: 479-575-5601
Web site: http://law.uark.edu

FACULTY CONTACTS

DALE BUMPERS COLLEGE OF AGRICULTURE, FOOD AND LIFE SCIENCES
(http://bumperscollege.uark.edu/)

Agricultural Economics: Dr. Lucas Parsch, lparsch@uark.edu; **Agricultural Education:** Freddie Scott, fscott@uark.edu; **Agriculture and Extension Education:** Dr. George Wardlow, wardlow@uark.edu; **Agricultural, Food and Life Sciences:** Randy Lutrell, luttrell@uark.edu. **Animal Science:** Dr. Wayne Kellog, wkellog@uark.edu. **Crop, Soil, and Environmental Sciences:** Derrick Oosterhuis, gfry@uark.edu. **Entomology:** Robert Wiedenmann, jfunk@uark.edu. **Food Science:** Dr. Jean-Francois Meullenet, jfmeull@uark.edu. **Horticulture:** Dr. J. Brad Murphy, jbmurph@uark.edu. **Human Environmental Sciences:** Dr. Mary Warnock, mwarnock@uark.edu. **Plant Pathology:** Rose Gergerich, gergeric@uark.edu. **Poultry Science:** Dr. Mike Slavik, mslavik@uark.edu.

J. WILLIAM FULBRIGHT COLLEGE OF ARTS AND SCIENCES
(http://fulbright.uark.edu)

Anthropology: Dr. Mary Jo Schneider, maryjo@uark.edu. **Applied Physics:** Dr. Rajendra Gupta, rgupta@uark.edu. **Art:** Dr. Michael Peven, mpeven@uark.edu. **Biology:** Cindy Sagers, csagers@uark.edu. **Chemistry:** Dr. Bill Durham, lizwill@uark.edu. **Communication Disorders:** Dr. Barbara Shadden, bshadde@uark.edu. **Communications:** Ron Warren, ronw@uark.edu. **Comparative Literature and Cultural Studies:** Luis Restrepo, lrestr@uark.edu. **Computer Science:** Gordon Beavers, tijacks@uark.edu. **Creative Writing:** Davis McCombs, dmccomb@uark.edu. **Drama:** D. Andrew Gibbs, dagibbs@uark.edu. **English:** Dr. Keith Booker, kbooker@uark.edu. **Environmental Dynamics:** Dr. Stephen K. Boss, sboss@uark.edu. **French:** Dr. Nancy Arenberg, arenberg@uark.edu. **Geography:** Dr. David Stahle, dstahle@uark.edu. **Geology:** Dr. Doy Zachry, dzachry@uark.edu. **German:** Todd Hanlin, thanlin@uark.edu. **History:** Richard Sonn, rsonn@uark.edu. **Journalism:** Jan Wicks, jwicks@uark.edu. **Mathematics:** Graduate Advisor, gradmath@uark.edu. **Music:** Dr. Ronda Mains, rmains@uark.edu. **Philosophy:** Jack Lyons, jclyons@uark.edu. **Physics:** Dr. Rajendra Gupta, rgupta@uark.edu. **Political Science:** Dr. Margaret Reid, mreid@uark.edu. **Psychology:** Dr. Dough Behrend, psycapp@uark.edu. **Public Administration:** Dr. Margaret Reid, mreid@uark.edu. **Social Work:** Carol Tucker, cstucke@uark.edu. **Sociology:** Anna Zajicek, azajicek@uark.edu. **Spanish:** Reina Ruiz, rruiz@uark.edu. **Statistics:** Dr. Laurie Meaux, lmeaux@uark.edu. **Translation:** Dr. John Duval, jduval@uark.edu.

SAM M. WALTON COLLEGE OF BUSINESS
(http://waltoncollege.uark.edu/)

Accounting (M.Acc.): Gary Peters, peters@uark.edu. **Accounting (Ph.D.):** Dr. Carolyn Callahan, cmcall@uark.edu. **Economics:** Raja Kali, rkali@uark.edu. **Finance:** Dr. Pu Liu, pliu@uark.edu. **Information Systems (M.I.S.):** Dr. Paul Cronan, cronan@uark.edu. **Information Systems (Ph.D.):** Dr. Bill Hardgrave, whardgra@uark.edu. **Management:** John Delery, jdelery@uark.edu. **Marketing:** Dr. Jeff Murray, jmurray@uark.edu.

COLLEGE OF EDUCATION AND HEALTH PROFESSIONS
(http://coehp.uark.edu)

Childhood Education: Tom Smith, cweaver@uark.edu. **Counseling:** Michael Miller, gchilder@uark.edu. **Counselor Education:** Michael Miller, gchilder@uark.edu. **Curriculum and Instruction:** Tom Smith, tecsmith@uark.edu. **Educational Administration:** Michael Miller, gchilder@uark.edu. **Educational Foundations:** Michael Miller, gchilder@uark.edu. **Educational Technology:** Michael Miller, gchilder@uark.edu. **Elementary Education:** Tom Smith, tecsmith@uark.edu. **Health Science:** Dr. Dean Gorman, dgorman@uark.edu. **Higher Education:** Michael Miller, gchilder@uark.edu. **Kinesiology:** Dr. Dean Gorman, dgorman@uark.edu. **Middle-Level Education:** Tom Smith, tecsmith@uark.edu. **Physical Education:** Dr. Dean Gorman, dgorman@uark.edu. **Recreation:** Dr. Dean Gorman, dgorman@uark.edu. **Rehabilitation:** Dr. Dean Gorman, dgorman@uark.edu. **Secondary Education:** Tom Smith, tecsmith@uark.edu. **Special Education:** Tom Smith, tecsmith@uark.edu. **Workforce Development Education:** Fredrick Nafukho, nafukho@uark.edu.

COLLEGE OF ENGINEERING
(http://www.engr.uark.edu)

Biological Engineering: Indrajeet Chaubey, mlw001@uark.edu. **Chemical Engineering:** Dr. Richard Ulrich, rulrich@uark.edu. **Civil Engineering:** Kelvin Wang, kcw@uark.edu. **Computer Science:** Gordon Beavers, gordonb@uark.edu. **Electrical Engineering:** Dr. Randy Brown, rlb02@uark.edu. **Environmental Engineering:** Kelvin Wang, kcw@uark.edu. **Industrial Engineering:** Dr. Scott Mason, mason@uark.edu. **Mechanical Engineering:** Dr. Rick Couivillion, rjc@uark.edu. **Operations Management:** Sandra Parker, nsloan@engr.uark.edu. **Operations Research:** Scott Mason, mason@uark.edu. **Telecommunications Engineering:** Randy Brown, rlb02@uark.edu. **Transportation Engineering:** Kelvin Wang, kcw@uark.edu.

GRADUATE SCHOOL
(http://www.uark.edu/depts/gradinfo)

Cell and Molecular Biology: Dr. Doug Rhoads, drhoads@uark.edu. **Microelectronics-Photonics:** Professor Ken Vickers, vickers@uark.edu; microep.uark.edu. **Public Policy:** Dr. Will Miller, policy@uark.edu. Space and **Planetary Science:** Derek Sears, hsears@uark.edu.

UNIVERSITY OF CENTRAL MISSOURI

The Graduate School

Programs of Study

The University of Central Missouri offers programs leading to the Master of Arts, Master of Arts in Teaching, Master of Business Administration, Master of Science, Master of Science in Education, Education Specialist, and cooperative doctoral degrees. Areas of study include accountancy, aviation safety, biology, business administration, college student personnel administration, counseling, criminal justice, curriculum and instruction, educational technology, English, environmental studies, history, industrial hygiene, industrial management, industrial technology, information technology, library science and information services, literacy education, mass communication, mathematics (applied mathematics), music, occupational safety management, physical education (exercise and sport science), psychology, rural family nursing, school administration, social gerontology, sociology, special education, speech communication, speech-language pathology, teaching English as a second language, technology and occupational education, and theater. The University also offers Education Specialist degrees in administration (elementary school principalship, secondary school principalship, and superintendency), curriculum and instruction, and human services (guidance and counseling, learning resources, special education, and technology and occupational education). The two cooperative doctoral programs include the Ph.D. in technology management, with Indiana State University as the degree-granting institution, and the Ed.D. in educational leadership, with the University of Missouri–Columbia as the degree-granting institution.

Research Facilities

The Office of Sponsored Programs in the Graduate School provides research support for students and faculty members.

The James C. Kirkpatrick Library houses more than 2.4 million items in print and nonprint formats, CD-ROM databases, a historical children's literature collection, an online public access catalog, and a variety of information networks.

Information Services provides academic computing support using an ATM-based high-speed network with more than 2,000 attached workstations. The network is connected to a Windows NT network domain supported by a cluster of network servers for application, Web, data, and mail services. The networked environment provides high-speed Internet connectivity. Research support is provided through products such as SPSS. Information Services also provides a help desk and basic consulting services.

Financial Aid

Graduate assistantships, providing a competitive stipend and a scholarship covering academic fees, are available to qualified students under the terms of a nine-month contract. Scholarships include the Graduate Student Achievement Award, the State Line Grant Program, the Warren C. Lovinger Graduate Student Scholarship, the President's Diversity Scholarship, and the Graduate Non-Resident Scholarship. The University participates in a full range of federal financial-aid programs, including grants, loans, and student employment.

Cost of Study

Graduate tuition for 2007–08 is $235.65 per credit hour for Missouri residents and $471.30 for nonresident students. Rates for Extended Campus are variable.

Living and Housing Costs

In 2007–08, double rooms cost $1873 per semester and single rooms cost $2473 per semester. One- and two-bedroom apartments and town houses are available at prices ranging from $474 to $598 per month. The University has beautiful accommodations for students with families. Graduate students can select from various meal plan packages. An unlimited-access meal plan is $1050 per semester.

Student Group

Total enrollment at the University of Central Missouri is about 11,000 students, nearly 1,800 of whom are doing postgraduate work. The student-faculty ratio is 18:1. International students and ethnic minority students are encouraged to apply. Students attend the University from all fifty states and approximately sixty countries. Enrolled graduate students automatically become members of the Graduate Student Association.

Location

The University of Central Missouri is located 50 miles southeast of Kansas City, in Warrensburg, Missouri. It is easily accessible by highway, bus, and passenger rail service.

The University

Founded in 1871, Central is a public university with a statewide mission in professional technology that has been fully integrated into a comprehensive liberal arts curriculum. Four colleges offer degree programs encompassing more than 150 areas of study at the undergraduate and graduate levels. Providing top-quality education at affordable cost is one of the institution's top priorities, as is its commitment to rigorous academic standards and thorough career preparation. The campus includes instructional buildings, residence halls, full-service dining, superb athletic facilities, and a spacious University Union. Other facilities on the 1,240-acre campus include a 300-acre recreational and biological research area with fishing lakes, a heated outdoor pool, and an 18-hole golf course; the Max B. Swisher Skyhaven Airport; 100,000-watt public television and radio stations; and the University Farm.

Applying

A nonrefundable fee of $50 is required for U.S. and international students applying for admission to a graduate program.

Correspondence and Information

The Graduate School
The University of Central Missouri
Ward Edwards 1800
Warrensburg, Missouri 64093
Phone: 660-543-4621 (admissions information)
660-543-4621 (enrollment information)
877-729-8266 (toll-free)
E-mail: gradinfo@ucmo.edu
Web site: http://www.ucmo.edu/graduate

Master's Degree Programs and Coordinators
Accountancy: Kenneth Stone, Ph.D. (660-543-4816)
Aviation Safety: John Horine, Ed.D. (660-543-4457)
Biology: Selene Nikaido, Ph.D. (660-543-8796)
Business Administration: Paul Engelmann, Ph.D. (660-543-4324)
College Student Personnel Administration: Robert Bowman, Ph.D. (660-543-8628)
Communication: Wendy Geiger, Ph.D. (660-543-4469)
Counseling: Janelle Cowles, Ph.D. (660-543-8204)
Criminal Justice: Gene Bonham, Ph.D. (660-543-4950)
Curriculum and Instruction: Wayne Williams, Ed.D. (660-543-8701)
Educational Technology: Odin Jurkowski, Ed.D. (660-543-8387)
English: Daniel Schierenbeck, Ph.D. (660-543-8696)
Environmental Studies: James Loch, Ph.D. (660-543-8804)
History: Sara Sundberg, Ph.D. (660-543-8698)
Industrial Hygiene: John Zey, M.S. (660-543-4410)
Industrial Management: Ron Woolsey, Ph.D. (660-543-4340)
Industrial Technology: Ron Woolsey, Ph.D. (660-543-4340)
Information Technology: Sam S. Ramanujan, Ph.D. (660-543-8565)
Library Science and Information Services: Odin Jurkowski, Ph.D. (660-543-8387)
Literacy Education: Carol Mihalevich, Ph.D. (660-543-8731)
Master of Arts in Teaching: Wayne Williams, Ph.D. (660-543-8701)
Mathematics: Shing So, Ph.D. (660-543-8839)
Music: J. Franklin Fenley, Ed.D. (660-543-4974)
Occupational Safety Management: Omer Frank, Ph.D. (660-543-4412)
Physical Education, Exercise, and Sport Science: Scott Strohmeyer, Ph.D. (660-543-8191)
Psychology: Jonathan Smith, Ph.D. (660-543-4378)
Rural Family Nursing: Linda Mulligan, Ph.D. (816-802-2226)
School Administration: Doug Thomas, Ph.D. (660-543-8834)
Social Gerontology: Jean Nuernberger, Ph.D. (660-543-8758)
Sociology: Musa Ilu, Ph.D. (660-543-8790)
Special Education: Jerry Neal, Ph.D. (660-543-8797)
Speech-Language Pathology: Carl Harlan, Ph.D. (660-543-4918)
Teaching English as a Second Language: Dennis Muchisky, Ph.D. (660-543-8711)
Technology and Occupational Education: Barton Washer, Ph.D. (660-543-4580)
Theater: Julie Pratt, Ph.D. (660-543-4020)

Education Specialist Degree Programs and Coordinators
Administration (Elementary School Principalship, Secondary School Principalship, Superintendency): Doug Thomas, Ph.D. (660-543-8834)
Curriculum and Instruction: Wayne Williams, Ph.D. (660-543-8701)
Human Services
  Guidance and Counseling: Janelle Cowles, Ph.D. (660-543-8204)
  Learning Resources: Odin Jurkowski, Ph.D. (660-543-8387)
  Special Education: Jerry Neal, Ph.D. (660-543-8497)
  Technology and Occupational Education: Barton Washer, Ph.D. (660-543-4580)

Cooperative Doctoral Degree Programs and Coordinators
Ph.D. in Technology (Indiana State University): John Sutton, Ph.D. (660-543-4439)
Ed.D. in Educational Leadership (University of Missouri–Columbia): Sandy Hutchinson, Ph.D. (660-543-4720)

UNIVERSITY OF CONNECTICUT

Graduate School

Programs of Study

The Graduate School of the University of Connecticut offers programs leading to the degrees of Master of Arts, Master of Science, Master of Business Administration, Master of Dental Science, Master of Engineering, Master of Fine Arts (offered in art and dramatic arts), Master of Music, Master of Professional Studies (offered in human resources management, homeland security leadership, humanitarian services administration, and in occupational safety and health management), Master of Public Administration, Master of Public Health, and Master of Social Work, as well as to the degrees of Doctor of Audiology, Doctor of Education (educational leadership), Doctor of Musical Arts, Doctor of Physical Therapy, and Doctor of Philosophy.

Study leading to the degree of Master of Arts or Master of Science is offered in accounting; agricultural and resource economics; allied health; animal science; anthropology; applied financial mathematics; applied genomics; applied microbial systems analysis; art history; biochemistry; biodiversity and conservation biology; biomedical engineering; biotechnology; botany; cell biology; chemical engineering; chemistry; civil engineering; communication sciences; comparative literary and cultural studies; computer science and engineering; dramatic arts; ecology; economics; education; electrical engineering; English; entomology; environmental engineering; French; genetics and genomics; geography; geological sciences; German; history; human development and family studies; international studies; Italian; Judaic studies; linguistics; materials science; mathematics; mechanical engineering; medieval studies; metallurgy and materials engineering; microbiology; music; natural resources—land, water, and air; nursing; nutritional science; oceanography; pathobiology; pharmaceutical science; philosophy; physics; physiology and neurobiology; plant science; political science; polymer science; psychology; sociology; Spanish; statistics; structural biology and biophysics; survey research; and zoology.

Study leading to the degree of Doctor of Philosophy is offered in adult learning; agricultural and resource economics; animal science; anthropology; biochemistry; biomedical engineering; biomedical science; botany; business administration; cell biology; chemical engineering; chemistry; civil engineering; communication sciences; comparative literary and cultural studies; computer science and engineering; curriculum and instruction; ecology; economics; educational administration; educational psychology; educational technology; electrical engineering; English; entomology; environmental engineering; French; genetics and genomics; geography; geological sciences; German; history; human development and family studies; Italian; kinesiology; linguistics; materials science; mathematics; mechanical engineering; medieval studies; metallurgy and materials engineering; microbiology; music; natural resources–land, water, and air; nursing; nutritional science; oceanography; pathobiology; pharmaceutical science; philosophy; physics; physiology and neurobiology; plant science; political science; polymer science; psychology; public health; social work; sociology; Spanish; special education; statistics; structural biology and biophysics; and zoology.

Research Facilities

The Homer Babbidge Library at Storrs seats 2,300 people in a wide variety of study facilities, including individually assigned research studies, group studies, and areas designed for the use of computers, videos, and microtext. The building contains more than 2 million volumes of the system's total of more than 3 million volumes, as well as microtext, maps, manuscripts, archives, recordings, and other materials. The library's book and journal holdings as well as many periodical indexes are accessible through HOMER, the online information system. A wide array of electronic resources is available in the reference area of the Babbidge Library. The Thomas J. Dodd Research Center is a fully equipped research facility and a major archive for historic papers. The University has several dozen centers and institutes that promote research in specialized areas of study.

Financial Aid

Available are graduate assistantships for teaching and research, tuition remission awards, Special Graduate Student Fellowships, University predoctoral fellowships, doctoral dissertation fellowships, summer fellowships for doctoral and predoctoral students, and aid in a variety of forms for students in specific programs.

Cost of Study

Course-related fees in 2007–08 for full-time students total $5026 per semester for in-state students and $11,767 per semester for out-of-state students. Fees for part-time study are prorated. Fees are subject to change without notice.

Living and Housing Costs

On-campus housing for graduate students is limited. In 2007–08, students living in the Graduate Residence are charged $2672 per semester, or approximately $8000 for the calendar year. Information about other on-campus housing options is available online at http://www.reslife.uconn.edu. The comprehensive board plan provides three meals a day while classes are in session at a cost of $2076 per semester. Other options are available. Fees are subject to change without notice.

Student Group

Approximately 5,000 students are enrolled in graduate degree programs. About 2,000 are working toward doctoral degrees.

Location

Most graduate degree programs offered by the University are located at the Storrs campus, which is 25 miles northeast of Hartford. Storrs is a scenic, agricultural area. Degree programs in the biomedical sciences and the marine sciences are offered at the University of Connecticut Health Center in Farmington (near Hartford) and at the Marine Sciences Institute at Avery Point (on Long Island Sound), respectively.

The University

The University of Connecticut grew out of the Storrs Agricultural School, which was founded in 1881 as a direct result of the gift of land, money, and buildings presented to the Connecticut General Assembly by Charles and Augustus Storrs of Mansfield. Master's degree study was offered by 1920. The Graduate School was established officially in 1939, and the University conferred its first Ph.D.'s a decade later.

Applying

Applicants should consult the academic department or program of their choice concerning application deadlines. Applicants are encouraged to apply online. Many programs have early closing dates. Application to some programs may require scores on one or more graduate admission tests, an interview or audition, or demonstrated proof of adequate facility in English for international applicants (the TOEFL is generally required for international applicants whose native language is not English). The application packet contains a complete summary of these requirements.

Correspondence and Information

The Graduate School
Unit 1006
University of Connecticut
438 Whitney Road Extension
Storrs, Connecticut 06269-1006

Phone: 860-486-3617
E-mail: gradschool@uconn.edu
Web site: http://www.grad.uconn.edu/

FACULTY HEADS

Accounting: A. J. Rosman, Ph.D.
Adult and Vocational Education: B. G. Sheckley, Ph.D.
Agricultural and Resource Economics: E. Pagoulatos, Ph.D.
Allied Health: K. Kerr, Ph.D.
Animal Science: D. Fletcher, Ph.D.
Anthropology: W. P. Handwerker, Ph.D.
Applied Financial Mathematics: J. G. Bridgeman, M.A.
Applied Genomics: L. Strausbaugh, Ph.D.
Applied Microbial Systems Analysis: P. L. Yeagle, Ph.D.
Art: J. Thorpe, M.F.A.
Art History: J. Thorpe, M.F.A.
Biochemistry: P. L. Yeagle, Ph.D.
Biodiversity and Conservation Biology: K. E. Holsinger, Ph.D.
Biomedical Engineering: J. D. Enderle, Ph.D.
Biomedical Science: G. D. Maxwell, Ph.D.
Biophysics: P. L. Yeagle, Ph.D.
Biotechnology: P. L. Yeagle, Ph.D.
Botany: K. E. Holsinger, Ph.D.
Business Administration: M. E. Hussein, Ph.D.
Cell Biology: P. L. Yeagle, Ph.D.
Chemical Engineering: D. J. Cooper, Ph.D.
Chemistry: S. Suib, Ph.D.
Civil Engineering: M. Accorsi, Ph.D.
Communication Science: C. A. Coehlo, Ph.D.
Comparative Literary and Cultural Studies: L. McNeece, Ph.D.
Computer Science and Engineering: R. A. Ammar, Ph.D.
Curriculum and Instruction: M. A. Doyle, Ph.D.
Dental Science: R. L. MacNeil, D.D.S., M.Dent.Sc.
Dramatic Arts: G. M. English, M.F.A.
Ecology: K. E. Holsinger, Ph.D.
Economics: D. R. Heffley, Ph.D.
Education: R. L. Schwab, Ph.D.
Educational Administration: B. G. Sheckley, Ph.D.
Educational Psychology: H. Swaminathan, Ph.D.
Educational Technology: M. Young, Ph.D.
Electrical Engineering: P. Luh, Ph.D.
Engineering: E. Smith, Ph.D.
English: R. S. Tilton, Ph.D.
Entomology: K. E. Holsinger, Ph.D.
Environmental Engineering: A. C. Bagtzoglou, Ph.D.
French: N. Bouchard, Ph.D.
Genetics: P. L. Yeagle, Ph.D.
Geography: J. P. Osleeb, Ph.D.
Geological Sciences: P. Visscher, Ph.D.
German: N. Bouchard, Ph.D.
History: S. A. Roe, Ph.D.
Human Development and Family Studies: R. M. Sabatelli, Ph.D.
International Studies: B. E. Bravo-Ureta, Ph.D.
Italian: N. Bouchard, Ph.D.
Judaic Studies: A. M. Dashefsky, Ph.D.
Kinesiology: C. M. Maresh, Ph.D.
Linguistics: D. C. Lillo-Martin, Ph.D.
Materials Science: H. L. Marcus, Ph.D.
Mathematics: M. Neumann, Ph.D.
Mechanical Engineering: B. Cetegen, Ph.D.
Medieval Studies: T. J. Jambeck, Ph.D.
Metallurgy and Materials Engineering: M. Aindow, Ph.D.
Microbiology: P. L. Yeagle, Ph.D.
Music: R. W. Bass, Ph.D.
Natural Resources: J. C. Clausen, Ph.D.
Nursing: E. C. Polifroni, Ed.D.
Nutritional Science: S. Koo, Ph.D.
Oceanography: A. C. Bucklin, Ph.D.
Pathobiology: H. J. Van Kruiningen, D.V.M., Ph.D., M.D.
Pharmaceutical Science: R. McCarthy, Ph.D.
Philosophy: C. L. Elder, Ph.D.
Physical Therapy: R. W. Bohannon, D.Ed.
Physics: W. C. Stwalley, Ph.D.
Physiology and Neurobiology: A. de Blas, Ph.D.
Plant Science: M. Musgrave, Ph.D.
Political Science: H. L. Reiter, Ph.D.
Polymer Science: T. A. P. Seery, Ph.D.
Professional Studies: S. Nesbit, Ph.D.
Psychology: C. A. Lowe, Ph.D.
Public Administration: M. D. Robbins, Ph.D.
Public Health (M.P.H. Program): D. Gregorio, Ph.D.
Public Health (Ph.D. Program): A. M. Ferris, Ph.D.
Social Work: D. Cournoyer, Ph.D.
Sociology: D. S. Glasberg, Ph.D.
Spanish: N. Bouchard, Ph.D.
Special Education: H. Swaminathan, Ph.D.
Statistics: D. Dey, Ph.D.
Survey Research: M. D. Robbins, Ph.D.
Zoology: K. E. Holsinger, Ph.D.

A study area in the Homer Babbidge Library on the Storrs campus.

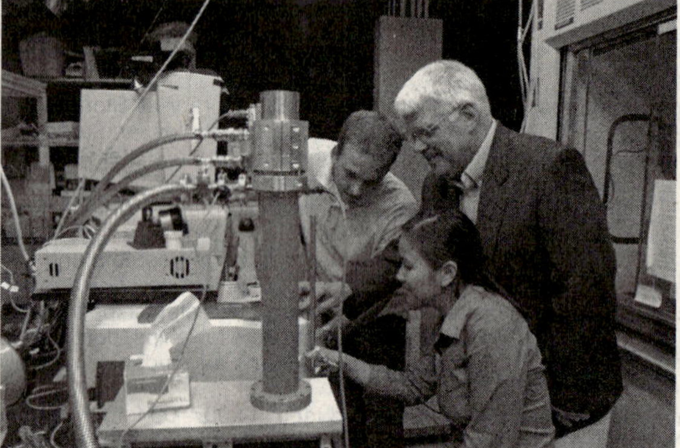

A faculty member works with graduate students in the lab.

Many new buildings on campus have been completed in the past ten years, including the Chemistry Building as shown above.

UNIVERSITY OF DENVER

Graduate Studies

Programs of Study

The University of Denver offers programs of study leading to master's, doctoral, and specialist degrees. The Doctor of Philosophy (Ph.D.) is available from many programs in the Arts and Humanities, Social Sciences, and the Natural Sciences and Mathematics; the School of Engineering and Computer Science; the College of Education; the Graduate School of International Studies; and the Graduate School of Social Work. A joint Ph.D. in religious and theological studies is available through the University and the Iliff School of Theology. The Doctor of Psychology (Psy.D.) is available from the Graduate School of Professional Psychology.

An Education Specialist (Ed.S.) degree is available from the College of Education. The Juris Doctor (J.D.) is available from the College of Law.

Master's degrees can be pursued in the Arts and Humanities, Social Sciences, and the Natural Sciences and Mathematics; the School of Engineering and Computer Science; Daniels College of Business; the College of Education; the Graduate School of International Studies; University College; the Graduate School of Professional Psychology; the Conflict Resolution Institute; and the Graduate School of Social Work.

Various joint and interdisciplinary degrees, which combine study with two or more programs, are also available.

The College of Law, Daniels College of Business, the Graduate School of International Studies, the Graduate School of Social Work, the College of Education, the Department of Human Communication Studies, and the Department of Psychology offer various dual degrees, which combine study in two programs and award two degrees.

In addition, the University of Denver offers students the opportunity to simultaneously enroll in any two master's degree programs, thus creating flexible dual degrees. These programs must make academic and/or career preparation sense, and no more than 15 credits of each program can be counted toward the other program.

Research Facilities

The University of Denver libraries provide an extensive collection of volumes, periodical subscriptions, and microforms in all subjects covered by University courses and research. Penrose Library has been a U.S. government document depository since 1909. Penrose has numerous online search capabilities that include the Colorado Alliance of Research Libraries (CARL), LexisNexis, Dialog, and other business and humanities indexes. In addition, Penrose has been selected by Higher Education Resource Services to provide scholarly information to the western United States. Students also have access to many other academic and public libraries. The University also possesses excellent media and computer facilities and state-of-the-art research laboratories on campus.

Financial Aid

Two kinds of financial aid are available for graduate students: need-based aid and merit-based aid. Students applying for either kind of aid must be accepted into an eligible graduate program at the University. Need-based financial aid consists of Direct Loans, Federal Perkins Loans, Federal Work-Study Program awards, and Colorado Graduate Grants. Merit-based financial aid consists of graduate tuition scholarships, graduate teaching and research assistantships, and Graduate Studies Doctoral Fellowships. A student who seeks state and federal financial assistance to pursue graduate studies at the University must file the Free Application for Federal Student Aid (FAFSA). For more information, students should contact the graduate school or department in which they wish to enroll.

Cost of Study

For the 2007–08 academic year, tuition is $873 per credit hour. Full-time tuition per quarter (12 to 18 hours) was $10,476. There is an additional technology fee of $4 per credit hour with a maximum of $144 per academic year and an activity fee of $40 per quarter. In addition, there is an optional health services fee per quarter and a University insurance fee per six months (which is waived with proof of alternate insurance).

Living and Housing Costs

The yearly rate in 2007–08 for an on-campus, unfurnished one-bedroom apartment is $7554 ($6048 for a studio). The yearly rate for 1 person in an on-campus unfurnished two-bedroom apartment (double occupancy) is $5652. Off-campus apartments are available nearby and range from $650 to $725. A liberal estimate of total monthly living expenses (e.g., rent, board, books, and personal spending) is $1200.

Student Group

Approximately 5,570 graduate students attend the University and compose more than one half of the University's total student enrollment of 10,791 students. Approximately 14 percent of the total graduate student population consists of members of diverse domestic ethnic groups, and an additional 7 percent of the total graduate student population is composed of international students.

Student Outcomes

Students who have received their doctoral degrees from the University have obtained teaching and research positions at universities throughout the U.S. and the world. Master's degree recipients have pursued work in various business sectors and with governments throughout the world. The University has a Career Center that actively works with students and alumni who are seeking employment.

Location

Mile-high Denver, with a population of about 555,000, is the financial, administrative, commercial, and sports center of the Rocky Mountain region. Denver offers many cultural and intellectual attractions, including numerous theater groups, an outstanding symphony orchestra, and fine museums. Denver has a mild climate, with an average of 300 sunny days a year. Excellent outdoor recreation of all kinds, especially skiing, may be enjoyed within an hour's drive of the University.

The University

In 1864, John Evans, second governor of the Colorado Territory, signed the charter establishing Colorado's first private university—the University of Denver. Founded in the spirit of westward expansion, the University is one of the few major private universities between Chicago and the West Coast. The University of Denver is nationally recognized for graduate programming and the quality of the professional schools.

Applying

Each graduate program provides specific information about admission to that school and/or department. Application fees, deadlines, and requirements vary by school and department.

Correspondence and Information

For general information, students should contact:

Graduate Studies, Admissions and Records
University of Denver
2197 South University Boulevard, Room 216
Denver, Colorado 80208

Phone: 303-871-2831
877-871-3119 (toll-free)
Fax: 303-871-4942
E-mail: grad-info@du.edu
Web site: http://www.du.edu

SCHOOLS, PROGRAMS, AND FACULTY

The University of Denver's deans, graduate degree programs, and admissions phone numbers are listed below.

Arts and Humanities: Interim Dean George Potts, Ph.D., Indiana.
Art and Art History: 303-871-2846 (e-mail: saah-gradinfo@du.edu).
English: 303-871-2266 (e-mail: engl-info@du.edu).
Music: 303-871-6973 (e-mail: marhuels@du.edu).
Religious Studies: 303-871-2740 (e-mail: rlgs@du.edu).

Natural Sciences and Mathematics: Dean Jim Fogleman, Ph.D., Cornell.
Biological Sciences: 303-871-3661 (e-mail: tquinn@du.edu).
Chemistry and Biochemistry: 303-871-2435 (e-mail: cheminfo@du.edu).
Geography: 303-871-2513 (e-mail: geog-info@du.edu).
Mathematics: 303-871-3344 (e-mail: info@math.du.edu).
Physics and Astronomy: 303-871-2238 (e-mail: phys-gradinfo@du.edu).

School of Engineering and Computer Science: Dean Rahmat A. Shoureshi, Ph.D., MIT.
Computer Science: 303-871-2453 (e-mail: info@cs.du.edu).
Engineering: 303-871-2102 (e-mail: engrinfo@du.edu).

Social Sciences: Interim Dean George Potts, Ph.D., Indiana.
Anthropology: 303-871-2406 (e-mail: anth02@du.edu).
Economics: 303-871-2685 (e-mail: econ04@du.edu).
Psychology: 303-871-3803 (e-mail: phoughta@du.edu).
Public Policy: 303-871-2468 (e-mail: ipps@du.edu)
School of Communication:
- **Digital Media Studies:** 303-871-7716 (e-mail: treddell@du.edu).
- **Human Communication Studies:** 303-871-2385 (e-mail: joasmith@du.edu).
- **International and Intercultural Communication:** 303-871-2088 (e-mail: iic@du.edu).
- **Mass Communication and Journalism Studies:** 303-871-2166 (e-mail: jparks@du.edu).
- **Public Relations and Advertising:** 303-871-2166 (e-mail: jparks@du.edu).

College of Education: Dean Virginia R. Maloney, Ph.D., George Washington. Contact: 303-871-2509; 800-835-1607 (toll-free) (e-mail: edinfo@du.edu).

College of Law: Dean José Roberto Juárez Jr., J.D., Texas. Contact: 303-871-6135 (e-mail: admissions@law.du.edu).

Conflict Resolution Institute: Karen Feste, Director; Ph.D., Minnesota. Contact: 303-871-6477 (e-mail: cri@du.edu).

Daniels College of Business: Dean Karen Newman, Ph.D., Chicago. Contact: 303-871-3416; 800-622-4723 (toll-free) (e-mail: dcb@du.edu).

Graduate School of International Studies: Dean Tom Farer, J.D., Harvard. Contact: 303-871-2544; 877-474-7236 (toll-free) (e-mail: gsisadm@du.edu).

Graduate School of Professional Psychology: Dean Peter Buirski, Ph.D., Adelphi. Contact: 303-871-3873 (e-mail: gsppinfo@du.edu).

Graduate School of Social Work: Interim Dean Christian Molidor, Ph.D., Illinois at Chicago. Contact: 303-871-2841 (e-mail: gssw-admission@du.edu).

Graduate Tax Program: Mark Vogel, Director; J.D., Notre Dame; CPA. Contact: 303-871-6239 (e-mail: gtp@du.edu).

Intermodal Transportation Institute: Cathryne Johnson. Contact: 303-871-4146 (e-mail: du-iti@du.edu).

University College: Dean James Davis, Ph.D., Michigan. Contact: 303-871-2291; 800-347-2042 (toll-free) (e-mail: uc-admission@du.edu).

UNIVERSITY OF FLORIDA

Graduate School

Programs of Study

The University of Florida (UF) Graduate School offers the Ph.D. in eighty-six disciplines, in addition to the Doctor of Audiology, Doctor of Education, and Doctor of Plant Medicine degrees. There are master's programs in 111 disciplines, fourteen Engineer degree programs, and twelve Specialist in Education programs. In addition, a number of interdisciplinary concentrations are available at the doctoral level, and there are many successful joint-degree programs. Professional postbaccalaureate degrees are offered in dentistry, law, medicine, pharmacy, physician assistance, and veterinary medicine.

Research Facilities

UF major research centers include the Archie Carr Center for Sea Turtle Research, the Center for Environmental Systems Commercial Space Technology, the Center for Applied Optimization, the Database Systems Research and Development Center, the Engineering Research Center for Particle Science and Technology, the Florida Museum of Natural History, the Genetics and Cancer Research Center, the McGuire Center for Lepidoptera and Biodiversity, the McKnight Brain Institute, the National High Magnetic Field Laboratory partnership with Florida State University and Los Alamos, the Proton-beam Therapy Center, and the new Public Health and Health Professions, Nursing, and Pharmacy Building.

UF's nine libraries offer more than 4 million catalogued volumes and links to fulltext articles in more than 34,000 journals. Of national significance are the Baldwin Library of Historical Children's Literature, the Latin American Collection, the Map and Imagery Library, the P. K. Yonge Library of Florida History (preeminent Floridiana collection), the Price Library of Judaica, and holdings on architectural preservation and eighteenth-century American architecture, late nineteenth- and early twentieth-century German state documents, rural sociology of Florida, and tropical and subtropical agriculture.

Financial Aid

The Graduate Fellowship Initiative (http://www.aa.ufl.edu/fellows) offers Alumni Graduate Fellowships to superior students entering Ph.D. and M.F.A. programs. In addition, qualified graduate students are eligible for other fellowships, assistantships, and awards (http://gradschool.rgp.ufl.edu/students/financial-aid.html). UF also has a substantial number of fellowships targeted specifically for underrepresented students (http://gradschool.rgp.ufl.edu/diversity/introduction.html#ogmp). Applications for these awards should be made to the appropriate department chair on or before February 15 of each year.

Non-Florida tuition payments and in-state tuition payments are available to eligible graduate students who hold assistantships or certain fellowships. These payments cover most tuition charges.

Cost of Study

Tuition and fees for new in-state residents in 2007–08 are $9348 per year, based on 30 hours of graduate enrollment. The comparable amount for new out-of-state graduate students is $28,254 per year. Near graduation, there are expenses for typing and duplicating a thesis (dissertation) and fees for library processing, microfilming, and publishing the dissertation abstract.

Living and Housing Costs

UF provides some variety in types of accommodations. The double room for 2 students is the most common. Air-conditioned dormitory rooms range from $1893 to $2840 per person per semester. Accommodations for single graduate or professional students in Diamond Apartment Village begin at $453 per person per month. At present, a one-bedroom unfurnished apartment off campus rents for about $650 per month.

Student Group

UF's 50,000 students are from all sixty-seven Florida counties (86 percent), the remaining forty-nine states (9 percent), and 100 other countries (5 percent). The University of Florida is the fifth-largest university in the U.S. and the largest university in the Southeast. UF is the number one Florida recruiter and the number two U.S. recruiter of National Merit Scholars. Of fall freshmen, 25 percent have GPAs above 4.0 and SAT I scores above 1340. UF's student body is made up of 47 percent men. Eighteen percent (9,300) are members of minority groups. Seventy-two percent are undergraduate students (36,000), 21 percent are graduate students (10,400), and 8 percent are professional students (4,200).

Location

An hour from each coast, the Gainesville metropolitan statistical area's population is near 240,000. One of the 100 best U.S. cities, Gainesville's urban forest makes its home in Florida's heart. Highs average 76°F to 82°F in the spring and fall, 89°F to 91°F in the summer, and 69°F in the winter. Alachua County delights nature lovers with its 965 square miles, 65 percent of which are made up of wilderness, lakes, wetlands, and trails.

The University

The University of Florida is a major, public, land-grant, research university. The state's oldest, largest, and most comprehensive university, UF is among the nation's most academically diverse. One of only seventeen land-grant universities in the Association of American Universities, UF has a long history of established programs in international education, research, and service. UF also has an outstanding intercollegiate sports program.

Applying

First-time UF graduate students need a B average or better for all upper-division undergraduate work, a GRE score acceptable to the program to which they have applied, and a baccalaureate degree from a regionally accredited college, university, or equivalent. Individual departments may have additional requirements. Applicants whose native language is not English need a TOEFL score of at least 550 on the paper-based test, 213 on the computer-based test, or 80 on the Internet-based test, an IELTS score of at least 6 or an MELAB score of 77, or successful completion of the University of Florida English Language Institute program. Deadlines can be found in the graduate catalog and at either http://www.registrar.ufl.edu/catalog/adsumac0506.html or at http://www.registrar.ufl.edu.

Correspondence and Information

For general information:
Graduate Admissions Office
201 Criser Hall
University of Florida
P.O. Box 114000
Gainesville, Florida 32611-4000
Phone: 352-392-1365 Ext. 7172
Web site: http://www.admissions.ufl.edu/grad

For program information:
Department of
(specify department or program)
College of (specify)
University of Florida
Gainesville, Florida 32611
E-mail: gradschool@rgp.ufl.edu
Web site: http://gradschool.rgp.ufl.edu

COLLEGES AND PROGRAMS

College of Agricultural and Life Sciences (http://www.cals.ufl.edu). Master of Agribusiness: Food and Resource Economics. Master of Agriculture: Agriculture Education and Communication, Animal Sciences, Botany, Food and Resource Economics, Soil and Water Science. Master of Family, Youth, and Community Sciences. Master of Fisheries and Aquatic Sciences. Master of Forest Resources and Conservation: Forest Resources and Conservation. Master of Science: Agricultural and Biological Engineering; Agricultural Education and Communication (Farming Systems); Agronomy; Animal Sciences; Botany; Entomology and Nematology; Family, Youth, and Community Sciences; Fisheries and Aquatic Sciences; Food and Resource Economics; Food Science and Human Nutrition (Nutritional Sciences); Forest Resources and Conservation; Horticultural Science (Environmental Horticulture, Horticultural Sciences); Interdisciplinary Ecology; Microbiology and Cell Science; Plant Molecular and Cellular Biology; Plant Pathology; Soil and Water Science; Wildlife Ecology and Conservation. Doctor of Philosophy: Agricultural and Biological Engineering, Agricultural Education and Communication, Agronomy, Animal Sciences, Botany, Entomology and Nematology, Fisheries and Aquatic Sciences, Food and Resource Economics, Food Science and Human Nutrition (Food Science, Nutritional Sciences), Forest Resources and Conservation, Horticultural Science (Environmental Horticulture, Horticultural Sciences), Interdisciplinary Ecology, Microbiology and Cell Science, Plant Molecular and Cellular Biology, Plant Pathology, Soil and Water Science, Wildlife Ecology and Conservation. Doctor of Plant Medicine.

Warrington College of Business Administration (http://www.cba.ufl.edu). Master of Accounting. Master of Arts: Business Administration (Insurance, Marketing), Economics. Master of Business Administration (M.B.A.): Arts Administration, Business Strategy and Public Policy, Competitive Strategy, Decision and Information Sciences, Electronic Commerce, Entrepreneurship, Finance, General Business, Global Management, Graham-Buffet Security Analysis, Health Administration, Human Resource Management, International Studies, Latin American Business, Management, Marketing, Real Estate and Urban Analysis, Sports Administration. Master of Science: Business Administration (Entrepreneurship, Insurance, Marketing, Retailing), Decision and Information Sciences, Finance, Management, Real Estate. Doctor of Philosophy: Business Administration (Accounting, Decision and Information Sciences, Finance, Insurance, Management, Marketing, Real Estate and Urban Analysis), Economics.

College of Dentistry (http://www.dental.ufl.edu). Master of Science: Dental Sciences (Endodontics, Orthodontics, Periodontics, Prosthodontics), Oral Biology.

College of Design, Construction, and Planning (http://www.dcp.ufl.edu). Master of Architecture. Master of Arts in Urban and Regional Planning. Master of Building Construction: Building Construction (Sustainable Construction). Master of Interior Design. Master of International Construction Management. Master of Landscape Architecture. Master of Science in Architectural Studies. Master of Science in Building Construction (Sustainable Construction). Doctor of Philosophy: Design, Construction, and Planning (Architecture, Building Construction, Interior Design, Landscape Architecture, Urban and Regional Planning).

College of Education (http://www.coe.ufl.edu). Master of Arts in Education: Curriculum and Instruction, Early Childhood Education, Educational Leadership, Educational Psychology, Elementary Education, English Education, Foundations of Education, Marriage and Family Counseling, Mathematics Education, Mental Health Counseling, Reading Education, Research and Evaluation Methodology, School Counseling and Guidance, School Psychology, Science Education, Social Studies Education, Special Education. Master of Education (majors: same as Master of Arts in Education degree). Specialist in Education (special degree requiring one year of graduate work beyond the master's degree): Curriculum and Instruction, Educational Leadership, Educational Psychology, Foundations of Education, Higher Education Administration, Marriage and Family Counseling, Mental Health Counseling, Research and Evaluation Methodology, School Counseling and Guidance, School Psychology, Special Education. Doctor of Education: Curriculum and Instruction, Educational Leadership, Educational Psychology, Foundations of Education, Higher Education Administration, Marriage and Family Counseling, Mental Health Counseling, Research and Evaluation Methodology, School Counseling and Guidance, School Psychology, Special Education. Doctor of Philosophy: Curriculum and Instruction, Educational Leadership, Educational Psychology, Foundations of Education, Higher Education Administration, Marriage and Family Counseling, Mental Health Counseling, Research and Evaluation Methodology, School Counseling and Guidance, School Psychology, Special Education.

College of Engineering (http://www.eng.ufl.edu). Master of Civil Engineering. Master of Engineering: Aerospace Engineering, Agricultural and Biological Engineering, Biomedical Engineering, Chemical Engineering, Civil Engineering, Coastal and Oceanographic Engineering, Computer Engineering, Electrical and Computer Engineering, Environmental Engineering Sciences, Industrial and Systems Engineering, Materials Science and Engineering, Mechanical Engineering, Nuclear Engineering Sciences. Master of Science: Aerospace Engineering, Biomedical Engineering, Chemical Engineering, Civil Engineering, Coastal and Oceanographic Engineering, Computer Engineering, Digital Arts and Sciences, Electrical and Computer Engineering, Environmental Engineering Sciences, Industrial and Systems Engineering, Materials Science and Engineering, Mechanical Engineering, Nuclear Engineering Sciences. Engineer (special degree requiring one year of graduate work beyond the master's degree: same programs as for Master of Engineering degree, except Biomedical Engineering, Civil Engineering, and Coastal and Oceanographic Engineering). Doctor of Philosophy: Aerospace Engineering, Agricultural and Biological Engineering, Biomedical Engineering, Chemical Engineering, Civil Engineering, Coastal and Oceanographic Engineering, Computer Engineering, Electrical and Computer Engineering, Environmental Engineering Sciences, Industrial and Systems Engineering, Materials Science and Engineering, Mechanical Engineering, Nuclear Engineering Sciences.

College of Fine Arts (http://www.arts.ufl.edu). Master of Arts: Art Education, Art History, Digital Arts and Sciences, Museology (Museum Studies). Master of Fine Arts: Art, Theater. Master of Music: Music (Choral Conducting, Composition, Instrumental Conducting, Music History and Literature, Music Theory, Performance, Sacred Music), Music Education. Doctor of Philosophy: Art History, Music (Composition, Music History and Literature), Music Education.

College of Health and Human Performance (http://www.hhp.ufl.edu). Master of Science: Applied Physiology and Kinesiology (Athletic Training/Sport Medicine, Biomechanics, Clinical Exercise Physiology, Exercise Physiology, Human Performance, Motor Learning/Control, Sport and Exercise Psychology); Health Education and Behavior; Recreation, Parks, and Tourism; Sport Management. Doctor of Philosophy: Health and Human Performance (Athletic Training/Sport Medicine, Biomechanics, Exercise Physiology, Health Behavior, Motor Learning/Control, Natural Resource Recreation, Sport and Exercise Psychology, Sport Management, Therapeutic Recreation, Tourism).

College of Journalism and Communications (http://www.jou.ufl.edu). Master of Advertising. Master of Arts in Mass Communication. Doctor of Philosophy: Mass Communication.

Levin College of Law (http://www.law.ufl.edu). Master of Laws in Comparative Law. Master of Laws in International Taxation. Master of Laws in Taxation.

College of Liberal Arts and Sciences (http://www.clas.ufl.edu). Master of Arts: Anthropology, Classical Studies, Communication Sciences and Disorders, Criminology and Law, English, French, Geography (Applications of Geographic Technologies), German, History, Latin, Latin American Studies, Linguistics, Mathematics, Philosophy, Political Science, Political Science—International Relations, Psychology, Religion, Sociology, Spanish, Women's Studies. Master of Arts in Teaching: Anthropology, French, Geography, Latin, Latin American Studies, Linguistics, Mathematics, Philosophy, Political Science, Political Science—International Relations, Psychology, Spanish. Master of Fine Arts: Creative Writing. Master of Latin. Master of Science: Astronomy, Botany, Chemistry, Computer Science, Geography, Geology, Mathematics, Physics, Psychology, Zoology. Master of Science in Statistics. Master of Science in Teaching: Astronomy, Botany, Chemistry, Geography, Geology, Mathematics, Physics, Psychology, Zoology. Master of Statistics. Master of Women's Studies. Doctor of Audiology. Doctor of Philosophy: Anthropology, Astronomy, Botany, Chemistry, Classical Studies, Communication Sciences and Disorders, Counseling Psychology, Criminology and Law, English, Geography, Geology, German, History, Linguistics, Mathematics, Philosophy, Physics, Political Science, Psychology, Religious Studies, Romance Languages (French, Spanish), Sociology, Statistics, Zoology.

College of Medicine (http://www.med.ufl.edu). Master of Science: Biochemistry and Molecular Biology, Epidemiology (Biostatistics, Health Policy), Medical Sciences (Clinical Investigation). Doctor of Philosophy: Biochemistry and Molecular Biology, Medical Sciences (Biochemistry and Molecular Biology, Genetics, Imaging Science and Technology, Immunology and Microbiology, Molecular Cell Biology, Neuroscience, Physiology, Pharmacology, and Toxicology).

College of Nursing (http://con.ufl.edu). Master of Science in Nursing. Doctor of Philosophy: Nursing Sciences.

College of Pharmacy (http://www.cop.ufl.edu). Master of Science in Pharmacy: Pharmaceutical Sciences (Forensic Drug Chemistry, Forensic Science, Forensic Serology and DNA, Medicinal Chemistry, Pharmacodynamics, Pharmacy, Pharmacy Health Care Administration). Doctor of Philosophy: Pharmaceutical Sciences (Medicinal Chemistry, Pharmacodynamics, Pharmacy, Pharmacy Health Care Administration, Toxicology).

College of Public Health and Health Professions (http://www.phhp.ufl.edu): Master of Health Administration. Master of Health Science: Occupational Therapy. Rehabilitation Counseling. Master of Occupational Therapy. Master of Public Health: Public Health (Biostatistics, Environmental Health, Epidemiology, Public Health Management and Policy, Social and Behavioral Sciences). Doctor of Philosophy: Health Services Research, Psychology (Clinical Psychology), Rehabilitation Science.

College of Veterinary Medicine (http://www.vetmed.ufl.edu): Master of Science: Veterinary Medical Sciences (Forensic Toxicology). Doctor of Philosophy: Veterinary Medical Sciences.

Innovative Program Options (http://www.distancelearning.ufl.edu). UF's Web site for distance education resources and opportunities provides information about the various degrees, certificates, and courses offered.

Interdisciplinary Concentrations and Certificates (http://gradschool.rgp.ufl.edu/students/catalog.html). African Studies, Agroforestry, Animal Molecular and Cellular Biology, Biological Sciences, Chemical Physics, Ecological Engineering, Geographic Information Sciences, Gerontological Studies, Historic Preservation, Hydrologic Sciences, Latin American Studies, Medical Physics, Quantitative Finance, Quantum Theory Project, Toxicology, Translation Studies, Tropical Agriculture, Tropical Conservation and Development, Tropical Studies, Vision Sciences, Wetland Sciences, Women's and Gender Studies.

Combined, Concurrent, and Joint Programs (http://admissions.ufl.edu/ugrad/combdegree.html). Prospective students should check with the major department on the availability of combined (bachelor's/master's), concurrent (simultaneous study toward two graduate degrees), and joint (coupling of graduate and professional degrees) programs.

Programs of Study

The Graduate School of the University of Louisville offers programs of study leading to the degree of Doctor of Philosophy in thirty different disciplines. A Doctor of Audiology degree and a Doctor of Education degree in educational leadership and organizational development are also offered. Degree programs combining medicine, dentistry, or law with a number of disciplines are also offered. Programs of study leading to the master's degree are available in more than sixty different areas, including interdisciplinary studies. The Master of Arts in Teaching and Master of Education degrees are offered for prospective elementary, secondary, and junior college teachers.

Each student is expected to take those courses required for advancement of general knowledge in his or her discipline as well as courses in a field of specialization. Although guidelines for study have been established by each department, curricula may be tailored to meet the needs, abilities, and interests of the student. All appropriate courses offered by the University are open to the doctoral student, with permission of the instructor. The doctoral degree is awarded in recognition of creative scholarship and research, and therefore some degree of flexibility exists regarding curricular requirements. In general, a thesis or dissertation of significant value and quality, developed under the supervision of a faculty preceptor, is required. The doctoral student usually completes the program in about four to five years of full-time work, whereas the master's programs usually require two years of study.

Research Facilities

The University has a number of outstanding on-campus research facilities and, as a member of ORAU, provides access to the facilities and educational programs of Oak Ridge National Laboratory. The Kentucky Institute for the Environment and Sustainable Development provides an exciting venue for interdisciplinary research in environmental science, policy, and education. The Urban Studies Institute is in direct contact with the community through public service and research related to problems of urban life, community development, and city planning. New, state-of-the-art research buildings have been constructed on the Health Sciences and Belknap campuses and house numerous centers and institutes, including Nanotechnology, Cellular Therapeutics, Genetics and Molecular Medicine, and Molecular Cardiology. The Kentucky Lions Eye Research Institute is a modern 75,000-square-foot facility equipped for molecular biological, biochemical, physicochemical, electrophysiological, morphometric, and transgenic studies of the eye and the visual system. The General Electric Factory Automation Laboratory provides a model factory environment and includes a rapid prototyping center, industrial robots, computer-aided engineering facilities, and space for research and development projects.

The University Libraries, a member of the Association of Research Libraries, has holdings of more than 2 million volumes and microtexts and nearly 25,000 serials. The library system collection ranges from the most extensive academic music holdings in the state to a vast collection of Edgar Rice Burrough's work. The main library even has a robotic book retrieval system. Students also have access to the collections of six other area institutions.

Financial Aid

A number of awards are available. In general, teaching and research assistantships for 2007–08 vary from $12,000 to $18,000 in stipend and include full tuition and health insurance. Doctoral fellowships are available and carry a stipend of $18,000–$22,000 plus full tuition and health insurance. Prestigious Grawemeyer Award Fellowships are also available in music, education, and psychology.

Cost of Study

For 2007–08, full-time tuition and fees are $24,120 per year for nonresidents and $10,042 per year for Kentucky residents. Student fees are prorated on a credit-hour basis; however, full-time is considered 9 credit hours each semester and 6 credit hours in the summer.

Living and Housing Costs

Housing is available for single and married students on the University of Louisville's main campus (Belknap campus), 10 minutes from the Health Sciences Center. For 2007–08, an efficiency apartment is $7548 per year. Partially furnished apartments for married students cost $9612 per year for a two-bedroom apartment, including utilities.

Student Group

More than 4,900 graduate students are enrolled in various departments of the University. Approximately one fourth are working toward doctorates. Students come from all areas of the United States and a number of other countries. The total student population is nearly 22,000.

Location

The Louisville Metro area, situated on the Ohio River, includes more than three quarters of a million people and is the sixteenth-largest city in the nation. Resident opera, art, theater, choral, ballet, and orchestral societies provide Louisville with cultural resources beyond those typically available in cities of comparable size. The surrounding countryside is rich in natural resources; many local and state parks provide a variety of outdoor activities. Each May, the famed Kentucky Derby is held at Churchill Downs in Louisville.

The University

The University traces its history to 1798 with the founding of the Jefferson Seminary. It became the University of Louisville in 1846 and a part of the state university system in 1970. Among its major divisions are the College of Arts and Sciences, College of Business, Graduate School, Raymond A. Kent School of Social Work, J. B. Speed School of Engineering, Louis D. Brandeis School of Law, School of Music, and College of Education and Human Development, which are located on the main campus (Belknap campus) about 2 miles from the downtown area. The School of Medicine, School of Dentistry, School of Nursing, and School of Public Health and Information Sciences are located in the heart of a growing sixteen-square-block Health Sciences Center. The University of Louisville is a member of the Kentuckiana Metroversity, which aims at cooperative ventures among the six institutions of higher education in the area, and is a Research University (High Research Activity) in the Carnegie classifications.

Applying

For application information and deadline dates, students should contact the department to which they wish to apply or the Graduate School.

Correspondence and Information

Graduate School
University of Louisville
Louisville, Kentucky 40292
E-mail: graduate@louisville.edu
Web site: http://graduate.louisville.edu

FACULTY HEADS

ADMINISTRATION

Ronald M. Atlas, Ph.D., Dean.
Richard W. Stremel, Ph.D., Associate Dean.
Michael J. Cuyjet, Ed.D., Associate Dean.
Paul J. DeMarco, Ph.D., Assistant Dean.

PROGRAMS AND AREAS OF ADVANCED TRAINING

Anatomical Sciences and Neurobiology: http://www.louisville.edu/medschool/anatomy/. Fred Roisen, Ph.D., Chair (e-mail: fjrois01@gwise.louisville.edu).
Audiology: http://www.louisville.edu/medschool/surgery/com-disorders/audiology. Ian M. Windmill, Ph.D., Director (e-mail: imwind01@gwise.louisville.edu).
Biochemistry and Molecular Biology: http://www.biochemistry.louisville.edu. Kenneth Ramos, Ph.D., Chair (e-mail: ksramo01@gwise.louisville.edu).
Bioethics and Medical Humanities: http://www.med.louisville.edu/humanism/masters.htm. David J. Doukas, M.D., and Robert Kimball, Ph.D., Co-Directors (e-mail: djdouk01@gwise.louisville.edu and rhkimb01@gwise.louisville.edu).
Biology: http://www.louisville.edu/a-s/biology/. Ronald Fell, Ph.D., Chair (e-mail: rfell@louisville.edu). Advanced training: biosystematics, biotechnology, ecology, environmental biology, microbiology, molecular biology, physiology.
Biostatistics–Decision Science: http://www.sphis.louisville.edu/bb_home.cfm. Rudolph S. Parrish, Ph.D., Chair (e-mail: rsparr01@gwise.louisville.edu).
Chemical Engineering: http://www.louisville.edu/speed/chemical. James C. Watters, Ph.D., Chair (e-mail: jcwatt01@gwise.louisville.edu). Advanced training: advanced process control, advanced materials, catalysis, pollution prevention, polymer processing, chemical vapor deposition, chemical sensors, thin-film applications.
Chemistry: http://www.louisville.edu/a-s/chemistry. George Pack, Ph.D., Chair (e-mail: george.pack@louisville.edu). Advanced training: analytical chemistry, inorganic chemistry, organic chemistry, physical chemistry, chemical physics.
Civil Engineering: http://www.louisville.edu/speed/civil. J. P. Mohsen, Ph.D., Director (e-mail: jpmohs01@louisville.edu). Advanced training: Civil and environmental engineering.
Classical and Modern Languages: http://modernlanguages.louisville.edu/. Mary Makris, Ph.D., Chair (e-mail: m0makr01@louisville.edu). Advanced training: French, Spanish.
Clinical Investigation Sciences: http://louisville.edu/sphis/. Susan Muldoon, Ph.D., M.P.H., Director and Associate Dean for Student Affairs (e-mail: susan.muldoon@louisville.edu).
Communication: http://comm.louisville.edu/department/index.php. Allan Futrell, Ph.D., Chair (e-mail: awfutr01@gwise.louisville.edu).
Communicative Disorders: http://www.louisville.edu/medschool/surgery/com-disorders. David R. Cunningham, Ph.D., Chair (e-mail: drcunn01@gwise.louisville. edu).
Computer Engineering and Computer Science: http://www.louisville.edu/speed/cecs. Adel S. Elmaghraby, Ph.D., Chair (e-mail: aselma01@gwise. louisville.edu).
Computer Science and Engineering: http://www.louisville.edu/speed/cecs. Rammohan K. Ragade, Ph.D., Coordinator of CSE Ph.D. Program (e-mail: rkraga01@gwise.louisville.edu). Advanced training: computationally intensive applications, hardware engineering, software engineering.
Education: http://www.louisville.edu/edu. Robert Felner, Ph.D., Dean, College of Education and Human Development (e-mail: r0feln01@louisville.edu). Teacher certification in multiple disciplines and advanced studies in education at the master's level, both M.Ed. and M.A.T.; Doctoral training in:
Counseling and Personnel Services: Sam Stringfield, Ph.D., Director (e-mail: scstri01@gwise.louisville.edu).
Curriculum and Instruction: Thomas Tretter, Ph.D., Director (e-mail: trtret01@gwise.louisville.edu).
Educational Leadership and Organizational Development: Joseph Petrosko, Ph.D., Director (e-mail: jmpetr01@louisville.edu).
Electrical and Computer Engineering: http://www.ece.louisville.edu. Jacek Zurada, Ph.D., Chair (e-mail: jmzura02@gwise.louisville.edu).
English: http://coldfusion.louisville.edu/webs/a-s/english/index.cfm. Susan Ryan, Ph.D., Director of Graduate Studies (e-mail: smryan01@gwise.louisville.edu). Advanced training: computer-assisted instruction, critical theory, professional writing, rhetoric and composition, rhetoric of science, writing assessment, literature, literature with creative writing emphasis.
Epidemiology: http://www.sphis.louisville.edu/. Richard Baumgartner, Ph.D., Director (e-mail: rnbaum01@gwise.louisville.edu).
Entrepreneurship: see: http://business.louisville.edu/entrepreneurshipphd/. James Fiet, Ph.D., Director (e-mail: jofiet01@gwise.louisville.edu).
Exercise Physiology: http://www.louisville.edu/edu/hpes/exphys. Jennifer Olive, Ph.D., Director (e-mail jloliv05@gwise.louisville.edu).
Fine Arts: http://www.louisville.edu/a-s/finearts. James T. Grubola, M.F.A., Chair (e-mail: grubola@louisville.edu); Thomas Buser, Ph.D., Art History Program Director (e-mail: tabuse01@gwise.louisville.edu). Advanced training: architectural history, art history.
Higher Education Administration: http://louisville.edu/education/degrees/ma-hed.html. Paul Winter, Ph.D., Director (e-mail: pawint01@gwise.louisville.edu).
History: http://www.louisville.edu/a-s/history/. John E. McLeod, Ph.D., Chair (e-mail: jemcle01@gwise.louisville.edu). Advanced training: ancient-medieval, modern European, U.S. history, U.S. history with oral-public history concentration.
Human Resource Education: http://louisville.edu/education/degrees/ms-hre.html. Carolyn Rude-Parkins, Ph.D., Director (e-mail: cparkins@louisville.edu).
Humanities: http://www.louisville.edu/a-s/humanities. Annette Allen, Ph.D., Director of Graduate Studies (e-mail: acalle01@gwise.louisville.edu).
Industrial Engineering: http://www.louisville.edu/speed/industrial. Suraj M. Alexander, Ph.D., Chair (e-mail: suraj.alexander@louisville.edu). Advanced training: ergonomics and human factors, manufacturing engineering, production systems engineering, operations research and logistics.
Interdisciplinary Studies: http://graduate.louisville.edu. Paul J. DeMarco, Ph.D., Assistant Dean, Graduate School (e-mail: paul.demarco@louisville.edu).
Justice Administration: http://www.louisville.edu/a-s/ja. Deborah G. Wilson, Ph.D., Chair (e-mail: dgwilson@louisville.edu).
Mathematics: http://www.math.louisville.edu.Thomas Riedel, Ph.D., Chair (e-mail: t0ried01@gwise.louisville.edu). Advanced training: applied analysis, combinatorics and graph theory, financial and actuarial mathematics, functional equations.
Mechanical Engineering: http://www.louisville.edu/speed/mechanical. Glen Prater Jr., Ph.D., Chair (e-mail: gprater@louisville.edu).
Microbiology and Immunology: http://www.louisville.edu/medschool/microbiology. Robert D. Stout, Ph.D., Chair. (e-mail: bobstout@louisville.edu). Advanced training: cellular and molecular immunology, genetics and pathogenesis, microbial physiology, molecular virology.
Music: http://www.louisville.edu/music. Christopher P. Doane, Ph.D., Dean, School of Music (e-mail: cpdoan01@louisville.edu); Jean M. Christensen, Ph.D., Chair, Music History (e-mail: jmchri01@gwise.louisville.edu). Advanced training: music history (Spanish medieval renaissance theory, early music performance, and twentieth-century music history), music education, music performance, theory and composition; Robert Amchin, Ph.D., Chair (e-mail: robamchin@aol.com). Music education.
Nursing: http://www.louisville.edu/nursing. Cynthia McCurren, Ph.D., Acting Dean, School of Nursing (e-mail: camccu01@gwise.louisville.edu). Advanced training: adult nurse practitioner, adult acute-care clinical specialist, neonatal nurse practitioner, psychiatric–mental health clinical specialist.
Oral Biology: http://www.dental.louisville.edu/future_students/postdoc_oralbio.htm. David Scott, Ph.D., Director (e-mail: dascot07@louisville.edu).
Pan African Studies: http://www.louisville.edu/a-s/pas/. Ricky L. Jones, Ph.D., Chair (e-mail: rljone01@gwise.louisville.edu).
Pharmacology and Toxicology: http://www.louisville.edu/medschool/pharmacology. David Hein, Ph.D., Chair (e-mail: d.hein@louisville.edu).
Physics: http://www.physics.louisville.edu. David N. Brown, Ph.D., Acting Chair (e-mail: dnbrow01@louisville.edu).
Physiology and Biophysics: http://www.louisville.edu/medschool/physiology. Irving G. Joshua, Ph.D., Chair (e-mail: igjosh01@gwise.louisville.edu). Advanced training: cardiopulmonary physiology, hypertension, microcirculation, microvascular control mechanisms, smooth-muscle function.
Political Science: http://www.louisville.edu/a-s/polsci/. Charles E. Ziegler, Ph.D., Chair (e-mail: cezieg01@gwise.louisville.edu). Advanced training: American politics, urban politics, comparative politics and international relations, policy and administration.
Psychological and Brain Sciences: http://www.louisville.edu/a-s/psychology. Barbara Burns, Ph.D., Chair (e-mail: bburns@louisville.edu). Advanced training: clinical psychology (anxiety disorders, behavioral medicine, forensics, mental health and aging), experimental psychology (cognition, perception and sensory physiology, social psychology, visual science).
Public Administration: http://supa.louisville.edu/. Steven C. Bourassa, Ph.D., Director (e-mail: steven.bourassa@louisville.edu). Advanced training: labor and public management, public policy and administration, urban development and environment.
Public Health Sciences: http://www.sphis.louisville.edu/. W. Paul McKinney, M.D., Director (e-mail: wpmcki01@gwise.louisville.edu).
Social Work: http://www.louisville.edu/kent/. Terry Singer, Ph.D., Dean, Kent School of Social Work (e-mail: terry.singer@louisville.edu); Ruth Huber, Ph.D., Director, Doctoral Program (e-mail: ruth.huber@louisville.edu).
Sociology: http://www.louisville.edu/a-s/soc. L. Allen Furr, Ph.D., Acting Chair (e-mail: lafurr01@louisville.edu).
Sports Administration: http://louisville.edu/education/degrees/ms-spad.html. May Hums, Ph.D., Director (e-mail: mahums01@gwise.louisville.edu).
Theater Arts: http://www.louisville.edu/a-s/ta. Russell J. Vandenbroucke, D.F.A., Chair (e-mail: rjvand01@louisville.edu). Advanced training: acting, design/technical theater, directing, African American theater.
Urban Planning: http://supa.louisville.edu. David Simpson, Ph.D., Director (e-mail: dmsimp01@gwise.louisville.edu). Advanced training: administration of planning organizations, land use and environmental planning, spatial analysis for planning.
Urban and Public Affairs: http://supa.louisville.edu. Steven Bourassa, Ph.D., Director (e-mail: steven.bourassa@louisville.edu). Advanced training: environmental policy and planning, urban planning and development, urban policy and administration.
Women's and Gender Studies: http://www.louisville.edu/a-s/ws. Nancy Theriot, Ph.D., Chair (e-mail: nmther01@gwise.louisville.edu).

AN HONORS UNIVERSITY IN MARYLAND

UNIVERSITY OF MARYLAND, BALTIMORE COUNTY

Graduate Studies

Programs of Study

The University of Maryland, Baltimore County (UMBC) Graduate School offers more than forty graduate degrees at the master's and doctoral levels and a number of postbaccalaureate certificates. Graduate degrees are offered in computer science and information systems, aging services, economics, education, emergency health services, engineering, the liberal arts and humanities, modern languages (French, German, Spanish), the natural sciences and mathematics, biotechnology, public policy, social sciences, and the visual arts. A wide range of disciplinary, interdisciplinary, and professional programs prepare students for further graduate study, new careers, and career advancement.

More than 400 graduate faculty members, over 2,200 graduate students, and more than $85 million in external support for research and training provide a rich environment for graduate education. Graduates go on to careers in such fields as university teaching and research, business, industry, government, the arts, and education. Opportunities for interdisciplinary collaboration are encouraged through more than twenty UMBC research centers and institutes, as well as interdepartmental collaborations. Graduate students take advantage of the University's proximity to the vast array of Baltimore-Washington research sites. Research innovations are actively shared with industry and government partners through collaborative studies, joint training programs, shared facilities, and technology transfer.

The University of Maryland Graduate School, Baltimore, created in 1985, represents the combined graduate and research programs at UMBC and the University of Maryland, Baltimore (UMB). This combined graduate school provides UMBC students access to courses, practical experiences, and research opportunities—including the schools of law, medicine, pharmacy, dentistry, nursing, and social work—at the UMB campus.

Research Facilities

Exceptional research facilities are available to graduate students in all disciplines at UMBC. The University offers state-of-the-art computer facilities and well-equipped laboratories for research in the social, physical, and biological sciences. Departmental Web sites provide detailed descriptions of research facilities.

The Albin O. Kuhn Library has a collection of more than 800,000 books and bound journals, more than 4,200 current journals and subscriptions, and more than 3 million photographs, slides, maps, music scores, recordings, microforms, and government documents. In addition, graduate students have access to the other libraries of the University System of Maryland campuses as well as to the Peabody Library and the Enoch Pratt Free Library in Baltimore, the Library of Congress, and other outstanding libraries in the Baltimore-Washington area.

Financial Aid

Graduate assistantships (research, teaching, and administrative) are available to qualified, full-time, degree-seeking students and are awarded and administered through the departments. Doctoral assistantship levels are competitive with other major research universities. Financial aid for students who demonstrate need is available in the form of government loans, work-study opportunities, and grants-in-aid.

Cost of Study

Tuition for graduate courses for the 2007–08 academic year is $412 per credit hour for Maryland residents and $681 per credit hour for nonresidents. (Students in the Erickson School for Aging Services have a different tuition structure; please refer to the school's Web site for more information.) Nonrefundable fees are approximately $864 per semester (or $96 per credit hour) for a graduate student carrying a full 9-credit load.

Living and Housing Costs

Limited on-campus housing is available for graduate students. Graduate students are also able to find reasonably priced apartments in the Baltimore area with monthly rentals starting at about $650. Several apartment developments are located near campus.

Student Group

UMBC has a current graduate school enrollment of approximately 2,300 students who come from forty states and fifty-nine countries. A wide variety of cultural events enrich campus life. There is an active Graduate Student Association and an Office of Graduate Student Life.

Location

UMBC is situated approximately 6 miles from downtown Baltimore on a 474-acre suburban site. A convenient shuttle bus links the campus to the surrounding residential neighborhoods, the downtown campus of UMB, the nearby Baltimore–Washington International Airport, and the Amtrak and commuter train stations. Students profit from the immense concentration of academic, cultural, and recreational facilities in the Baltimore-Washington urban centers.

The University

UMBC is a medium-sized research university. When founded in 1966, UMBC joined the state's oldest campus, the University of Maryland, Baltimore, in serving the public higher education and research needs of the Baltimore area. With almost 12,000 undergraduate, graduate, and postdoctoral students, UMBC is large enough to provide students with excellent training and research opportunities and small enough for close student-faculty interaction.

Applying

The application process involves submitting the completed application form, official college transcripts, and three letters of recommendation. Graduate Record Examinations (GRE) scores are required for most programs. International students are generally required to submit TOEFL scores. Details are available with the application materials. The application fee of $50 for the online application is neither waived nor deferred.

For information on programs or applications for assistantships, students may write to the appropriate Graduate Program Director. Program and course descriptions, class schedules, application forms, faculty research interests, and other campus information are available on the UMBC Web site at http://www.umbc.edu/gradschool. For applications and general admission information, students should contact the Office of Graduate Enrollment.

Correspondence and Information

Office of Graduate Enrollment
University of Maryland, Baltimore County
1000 Hilltop Circle
Baltimore, Maryland 21250

Phone: 410-455-2537
Fax: 410-455-1130
E-mail: umbcgrad@umbc.edu
Web site: http://www.umbc.edu/gradschool

THE FACULTY

Dean, Graduate School: Dr. Scott A. Bass. Telephone: 410-455-2199.
Dean, College of Arts, Humanities, and Social Sciences: Dr. John Jeffries. Telephone: 410-455-2385.
Dean, College of Engineering and Information Technology: Dr. Warren DeVries. Telephone: 410-455-3270.
Dean, College of Natural and Mathematical Sciences: Dr. Geoffrey Summers. Telephone: 410-455-5827.
Dean, Erickson School of Aging Studies: Dr. Kevin Eckert. Telephone: 443-543-5622.

GRADUATE PROGRAM DIRECTORS

COMPUTER SCIENCE AND INFORMATION SYSTEMS

Computer Science (M.S., Ph.D.): Dr. Krishna Sivalingam. Telephone: 410-455-1433; e-mail: cmscgrad@CSEE.umbc.edu; Web site: http://www.cs.umbc.edu/CSEE/grad/index.html

Information Systems (M.S., Ph.D., certificate in electronic government): Dr. Aryya Gangopadhyay. Telephone: 410-455-2650; e-mail: ifsm-gradinfo@umbc.edu; Web site: http://www.is.umbc.edu/

ECONOMICS

Economic Policy Analysis (M.A.): Dr. David Mitch. Telephone: 410-455-2157; e-mail: econ-masters@umbc.edu; Web site: http://www.umbc.edu/economics/grad_intro.html

EDUCATION

Master of Arts in Teaching (M.A.T.): Postbaccalaureate teacher education in early childhood, elementary, or secondary education for beginning teachers. Dr. Susan Blunck. Telephone: 410-455-3388; e-mail: blackwel@umbc.edu; Web site: http://www.umbc.edu/education/

Master of Arts in Education (M.A.): Postbaccalaureate teacher education for advanced teachers. Dr. Susan Blunck. Telephone: 410-455-3388; e-mail: blackwel@umbc.edu; Web site: http://www.umbc.edu/education/

Master of Arts in Instructional Systems Development (M.A. and certificate in Teaching English for Speakers of Other Languages): English as a second language. Dr. John Nelson. Telephone: 410-455-3056; e-mail: jnelson@umbc.edu; Web site: http://www.umbc.edu/isd/

ENGINEERING

Chemical and Biochemical Engineering (M.S., Ph.D., certificate in bio-chemical regulatory engineering): Dr. Theresa Good. Telephone: 410-455-3400; e-mail: kedziers@umbc.edu; Web site: http://www.umbc.edu/cbe

Civil and Environmental Engineering (M.S., Ph.D.): Dr. Upal Ghosh. Telephone: 410-455-8665; e-mail: ughosh@umbc.edu; Web site: http://www.umbc.edu/engineering/cee

Computer Engineering (M.S., Ph.D.): Dr. John Pinkston. Telephone: 410-455-1433; e-mail: gmarieg@umbc.edu; Web site: http://www.cs.umbc.edu/CSEE/grad/index.html

Electrical Engineering (M.S., Ph.D., certificate in systems engineering): Dr. Gary Carter. Telephone: 410-455-1433; e-mail: cmscgrad@CSEE.umbc.edu; Web site: http://www.cs.umbc.edu/CSEE/grad/index.html

Engineering Management (M.S.): Dr. Ted Foster. Telephone: 410-455-3357; e-mail: ccsmithso@umbc.edu; Web site: http://www.umbc.edu/engineering/eng-man.html

Mechanical Engineering (M.S., Ph.D., certificates in computer thermal/fluid dynamics and mechatronics): Dr. Tim Topoleski. Telephone: 410-455-3330; e-mail: csmithso@umbc.edu; Web site: http://www.umbc.edu/engineering/me/

HEALTH

Emergency Health Services (M.S., certificate in Emergency Management): Dr. Rick Bissell. Telephone: 410-455-3223; e-mail: lgordon@umbc.edu; Web site: http://ehs.umbc.edu/

INTERDISCIPLINARY PROGRAMS

Gerontology (Ph.D.): Dr. Leslie Morgan. Telephone: 410-706-4926; e-mail: jgolden@epi.umaryland.edu; Web site: http://www.gerontologyphd.umaryland.edu/

Language, Literacy, and Culture (Ph.D.): Dr. JoAnn Crandall. Telephone: 410-455-1417; e-mail: llc@umbc.edu; Web site: http://www.umbc.edu/llc/

Marine, Estuarine, and Environmental Science (M.S., Ph.D.): Dr. Thomas Cronin. Telephone: 410-455-3669; e-mail: biograd@umbc.edu; Web site: http://www.umbc.edu/biosci/Graduate/mees.html/

Neuroscience and Cognitive Sciences (Ph.D.): Dr. Phyllis Robinson. Telephone: 410-455-3669; e-mail: biograd@umbc.edu; Web site: http://www.umbc.edu/biosci/Graduate/neuro.html/

INSTRUCTIONAL SYSTEMS DEVELOPMENT

Master of Arts in Instructional Systems Development—Training and Development (M.A.; certificates in Distance Education, Instructional Technology, and/or Instructional Systems Development): Dr. Greg Williams. Telephone: 410-455-8670; e-mail: gregw@umbc.edu; Web site: http://continuinged.umbc.edu/isd

LIFE SCIENCES

Biochemistry (Ph.D.): Dr. Michael Summers. Telephone: 410-706-8417; e-mail: chemgrad@umbc.edu; Web site: http://www.umbc.edu/chem/

Biological Sciences (M.S., Ph.D.): Dr. Phyllis Robinson. Telephone: 410-455-3669; e-mail: biograd@umbc.edu; Web site: http://www.umbc.edu/biosci/Graduate/

Molecular and Cell Biology (Ph.D.): Dr. Phyllis Robinson. Telephone: 410-455-3669; e-mail: biograd@umbc.edu; Web site: http://www.umbc.edu/biosci/Graduate/mocb.html/

Molecular Biology (Applied) (M.S.): Dr. Richard Wolf. Telephone: 410-455-3669; e-mail: biograd@umbc.edu; Web site: http://www.umbc.edu/biosci/Graduate/amb.html/

MODERN LANGUAGES AND INTERCULTURAL COMMUNICATION

Intercultural Communication (M.A.): Dr. Ed Larkey. Telephone: 410-455-2109; e-mail: fbateman@umbc.edu; Web site: http://www.umbc.edu/mll/incc/

NATURAL SCIENCES AND MATHEMATICS

Chemistry (M.S., Ph.D.): Dr. James Fishbein. Telephone: 1-866-743-8622; e-mail: chemgrad@umbc.edu; Web site: http://www.umbc.edu/chem/

Mathematics (Applied) (M.S., Ph.D.): Dr. Muddappa Gowda. Telephone: 410-455-2412; e-mail: grad_info@math.umbc.edu; Web site: http://www.math.umbc.edu/

Physics (Applied) (M.S., Ph.D.): Dr. Terrance Worchesky. Telephone: 410-455-2513; e-mail: physics@umbc.edu; Web site: http://physics.umbc.edu/Graduate/grad.htm

Physics, Atmospheric (M.S., Ph.D.): Dr. Wallace McMillan. Telephone: 410-455-3615; e-mail: mcmillan@umbc.edu; Web site: http://physics.umbc.edu/Graduate/grad.htm

Statistics (M.S., Ph.D.): Dr. Muddappa Gowda. Telephone: 410-455-2412; e-mail: grad_info@math.umbc.edu; Web site: http://www.math.umbc.edu/

PUBLIC POLICY

Public Policy (M.P.P., Ph.D., certificate in electronic government): Dr. Dave Marcotte. Telephone: 410-455-3201; e-mail: gradpubpol@umbc.edu; Web site: http://www.umbc.edu/pubpol/

SOCIAL SCIENCES

Historical Studies (M.A.): Dr. Constantine Vaporis. Telephone: 410-455-4178; e-mail: ison@umbc.edu; Web site: http://www.umbc.edu/history/programs/program2.html/

Psychology, Applied Developmental (Ph.D.): Dr. Susan Sonnenschein. Telephone: 410-455-2614; e-mail: psychdept@umbc.edu; Web site: http://www.umbc.edu/psyc/grad/adpflyerfinal.html

Psychology, Human Services Psychology (M.A., Ph.D.): Dr. Steve Pitts. Telephone: 410-455-2614; e-mail: psychdept@umbc.edu; Web site: http://www.umbc.edu/psyc/grad/hsp/html

Sociology, Applied (M.A., certificate in the Nonprofit Sector): Dr. William Rothstein. Telephone: 410-455-3365; e-mail: marmstro@umbc.edu; Web site: http://www.umbc.edu/sociology/

VISUAL ARTS

Imaging and Digital Arts (M.F.A.): Vin Grabill. Telephone: 410-455-2150; e-mail: imda@umbc.edu; Web site: http://art.umbc.edu/

UNIVERSITY OF MARYLAND EASTERN SHORE

Graduate School

Programs of Study

The Graduate School offers the following degrees: Master of Science (M.S.), Master of Education (M.Ed.), Doctor of Physical Therapy (D.P.T.), Master of Arts in Teaching (M.A.T.), Doctor of Philosophy (Ph.D.), and Doctor of Education (Ed.D.). The M.S. programs offered are applied computer science, criminology and criminal justice, food and agricultural sciences, marine-estuarine-environmental sciences, rehabilitation counseling, and toxicology. The M.Ed. programs are in guidance and counseling, career and technology education, and special education. The M.A.T. program is for initial teacher certification in secondary schools. The D.P.T. program is in physical therapy. Ph.D. programs are offered in food science and technology, marine-estuarine-environmental sciences, organizational leadership, and toxicology. The Doctor of Education (Ed.D.) program is offered in education leadership.

For most master's programs, a minimum of 30 semester hours is required in acceptable course work and research credit toward a graduate degree. The M.S. programs in marine-estuarine-environmental sciences and toxicology require a thesis. The master's programs in criminology and criminal justice and food and agricultural sciences offer a thesis or nonthesis option. The D.P.T. program is a three-year program. Two doctoral programs (marine-estuarine-environmental sciences and toxicology) are interdisciplinary and intercampus (within the University System of Maryland). Applicants should consult the individual programs for specific requirements. The three-year organizational and educational leadership programs are offered in a weekend format.

Research Facilities

Students have the opportunity to participate directly in ongoing research, development, and training projects. UMES is an 1890 land-grant and historically black institution, which conducts research and creative endeavors in the agricultural, environmental, and marine sciences; mathematics and computer applications; education and allied health; and other fields. Federal agency support includes the following: U.S. Departments of Agriculture, Commerce, Defense, Education, Energy, Health and Human Services, and the Interior; the National Science Foundation; the National Aeronautics and Space Administration; and the Agency for International Development.

There are a number of research and applications laboratories and facilities on campus and on the University's farm. Students also have access to other University System of Maryland, federal, and state facilities and field sites located throughout the state and region. Library and information resources may be accessed locally through the University System of Maryland Web site and the Internet.

Financial Aid

Limited financial assistance is available for qualified students, on the basis of merit and/or need, from institutional and sponsored funding. Examples of financial assistance are teaching, research and other types of assistantships, fellowships, scholarships, grants, Federal Work-Study, and loan programs.

Cost of Study

In 2006–07, tuition was $225 per semester credit hour for Maryland students and $408 per semester credit hour for out-of-state students.

Living and Housing Costs

Current monthly housing rates range from $200 for a room in a private or group home to $500 for an apartment in the local area. University housing is generally unavailable.

Student Group

UMES has a current graduate enrollment of 434 students, both full- and part-time. More than half the students are women.

Student Outcomes

Students find employment in school systems as special, agriculture, or technology educators and guidance counselors as well as other certified middle and high school teachers; in state agencies and private practice as guidance and rehabilitation counselors; in computer firms and educational settings as computer applications specialists and academic leaders; in private practice as physical therapists; and in federal, state, and local agencies and private businesses as marine, environmental, agricultural, and food scientists, and criminology and criminal justice specialists and administrative heads.

Location

UMES is located in Princess Anne, a small town on the eastern shore of Maryland. The town dates back to 1733 and has many buildings and landmarks of historic interest. The area is quiet and ideally suited for a learning environment, yet it is only 2½ hours by car from the abundant cultural and recreational facilities of Washington, D.C., and Baltimore, Maryland. The state's famous seaside resort, Ocean City, is only 45 minutes from the campus. The campus is 13 miles south of the town of Salisbury, which provides shopping and recreational facilities.

The School

The University of Maryland Eastern Shore Graduate School has more than 150 graduate faculty members, who, through an elected Graduate Council, determine the policies, procedures, and degree requirements for the various graduate programs. Approved specialists from industry, government, and academia may also serve on student research committees as graduate faculty members.

The University of Maryland Eastern Shore Graduate School is a public research school that admits students without regard to sex, race, creed, or ethnic origin.

Applying

Completed application and other pertinent forms, official college/university transcripts, and three letters of evaluation are required. Some graduate programs have additional admission requirements. Admission deadlines vary by graduate program. There is an application fee of $30. International applicants need TOEFL scores or an equivalent and a certification of available finances for study. GRE General Test scores may be required in some cases for the programs in marine-estuarine-environmental sciences, food and agricultural sciences, special education, criminology and criminal justice, food science and technology, and applied computer science. Other programs may use the GRE as a criterion for admission. Education programs may require the PRAXIS examinations.

Correspondence and Information

Dr. Ejigou Demissie
Graduate Studies Office
University of Maryland Eastern Shore
Princess Anne, Maryland 21853-1299
Phone: 410-651-6507 or 7966
Fax: 410-651-7571
E-mail: edemissie@umes.edu
vcshockley@umes.edu
Web site: http://www.umes.edu

THE FACULTY

Emmanuel Acquah, Professor; Ph.D., Ohio State, 1976.
Mary L. Agnew, Assistant Professor; Ph.D., Georgia, 1994.
Isoken T. Aighewi, Lecturer; Ph.D., Minnesota, 1988.
Ayodele J. Alade, Professor; Ph.D., Utah, 1981.
Arthur L. Allen, Associate Professor; Ph.D., Illinois, 1971.
David Alston Jr., Assistant Professor; Ph.D., North Carolina State, 2001.
Brenda Anderson, Assistant Professor; Ed.D., American, 1979.
Joseph O. Arumula, Professor; Ph.D., Clemson, 1982.
Kathryn Barrett-Gaines, Assistant Professor; Ph.D., Stanford, 2001.
Eugene L. Bass, Professor; Ph.D., Massachusetts Amherst, 1970.
Joseph Beatus, Associate Professor; Ph.D., Maryland College Park, 1996.
Sarah B. Bing, Associate Professor; Ph.D., Georgia, 1976.
Lowell Jay Bishop, Associate Professor; Ph.D., Case Western Reserve, 1988.
Raymond Blakely, Professor; Ph.D., NYU, 1977.
Dwayne Boucaud, Associate Professor; Ph.D., SUNY at Buffalo, 1999.
Cheryl Bowers, Assistant Professor; Ph.D., Pennsylvania, 1997.
Eddie Boyd Jr., Assistant Professor; Ph.D., Oklahoma State, 1977.
Ramona Brockett, Associate Professor; Ph.D., Rutgers, 1998.
Carolyn B. Brooks, Professor; Ph.D., Ohio State, 1977.
Henry M. Brooks, Associate Director, Co-op Extension; Ph.D., Ohio State, 1975.
Nicole Buzzetto-More, Assistant Professor; Ed.D., Columbia, 2004.
Albert Casavant, Assistant Professor; Ph.D., Illinois, 1984.
E. William Chapin, Assistant Professor; Ph.D., Princeton, 1969.
Leon L. Copeland, Professor; Ed.D., Virginia Tech, 1977.
Clement L. Counts, Assistant Professor; Ph.D., Delaware, 1983.
Leon N. Coursey, Professor; Ph.D., Ohio State, 1971.
I. K. Dabipi, Professor; Ph.D., Louisiana State, 1987.
Robert Dadson, Professor; Ph.D., McGill, 1969.
Gerald F. Day, Associate Professor; Ph.D., Maryland, 1976.
Ejigou Demissie, Professor; Ph.D., Oklahoma State, 1982.
Stanley DeViney Jr., Professor; Ph.D., Rutgers, 1983.
Joseph N. D. Dodoo, Assistant Professor; Ph.D., King's College (London), 1979.
Joseph J. Dudis, Assistant Professor; Ph.D., Johns Hopkins, 1970.
Clayton W. Faubion, Associate Professor; Ph.D., Arkansas, 1998.
Tao Gong, Research Analyst; Ph.D., Tennessee State, 2005.
Thomas Handwerker, Professor; Ph.D., Cornell, 1972.
Jeannine M. Harter-Dennis, Associate Professor; Ph.D., Illinois, 1977.
Fawzy Hashem, Research Associate Professor; Ph.D., Maryland, 1988.
George Heath, Associate Professor; Ph.D., Minnesota, Twin Cities, 1985.
Harry Hoffer, Director, Educational Leadership Program; Ph.D., Union (Ohio), 1991.
Nancy A. Horton, Assistant Professor; Ph.D., SUNY at Albany, 1995.
Gurdeep Singh Hura, Professor; Ph.D., Roorkee (India), 1984.
C. Dennis Ignasias, Associate Professor; Ph.D., Michigan State, 1967; Ph.D., Wisconsin–Madison, 1973.
Ali Ishaque, Associate Professor; Ph.D., Free University of Brussels, 1998.
Iqbal Javaid, Research Associate Professor; Ph.D., Zambia, 1989.
Jongdae Jin, Professor; Ph.D., Arizona, 1989.
Andrea K. Johnson, Assistant Professor; Ph.D., North Carolina State, 2004.
Linda P. Johnson, Associate Professor; Ph.D., Temple, 1995.
Robert Johnson Jr., Associate Professor; Ph.D., St. Louis, 1997.
Gerald E. Kananen, Assistant Professor; Ph.D., Duquesne, 1968.
Richard Kennan, Professor; Ph.D., Temple, 1974.
Wilbert C. Larson, Assistant Professor; Ph.D., Nebraska, 1990.
Joseph Love, Postdoctoral Research Scientist; Ph.D., Mississippi State, 2004.
Kelly Mack, Professor; Ph.D., Howard, 1995.
Malik B. Malik, Associate Professor; Ph.D., Essex, 1985.
Lurline Marsh, Professor; Ph.D., Minnesota, 1984.
Dorothy M. Mattison, Associate Professor; Ph.D., George Washington, 1990.
Eric B. May, Associate Professor; Ph.D., Oregon State, 1982.
Madhumi Mitra, Assistant Professor; Ph.D., North Carolina State, 2002.
Theodore A. Mollett, Associate Professor; Ph.D., Purdue, 1980.
Thomas S. Mosely, Associate Professor; Ph.D., Howard, 1997.
Abhijit Nagchandhuri, Professor; Ph.D., Duke, 1992.
Anthony K. Nyame, Professor; Ph.D., Georgia, 1987.
Stanley Nyirenda, Director, Institutional Research, Assessment, and Evaluation; Ph.D., Pittsburgh, 1991.
Okeleke Nzeogwu, Associate Professor; Ph.D., Missouri–Columbia, 1988.
Joseph Okoh, Professor; Ph.D., Howard, 1982.
Emmanuel Onyeozili, Assistant Professor; Ph.D., Florida State, 1998.
Salina Parveen, Assistant Professor; Ph.D., Florida, 1997.
Joseph Pitula, Lecturer; Ph.D., SUNY at Buffalo, 2001.
Kimberly Poole, Assistant Professor; Rh.D., Southern Illinois at Carbondale, 2000.
Michael Rabel, Assistant Professor; D.Sc., Maryland, Baltimore, 2006.
Maryam Rahimi, Associate Professor; Ph.D., Florida State, 1987.
Howard M. Rebach, Professor; Ph.D., Michigan State, 1968.
Douglas E. Ruby, Associate Professor; Ph.D., Michigan, 1976.
Jurgen Schwarz, Associate Professor; Ph.D., Cornell, 1993.
Barbara Seabrook, Assistant Professor; Ed.D., Wilmington (Delaware), 1996.
Daniel Seaton, Assistant Professor; Ed.D., Virginia Tech, 1991.
Dinesh Sharma, Professor; Ph.D., Chaudhary Charan Singh (India), 1999.
Anugrah Shaw, Professor; Ph.D., Texas Woman's, 1984.
George S. Shorter, Assistant Professor; Ph.D., Iowa State, 1981.
Bernita Sims-Tucker, Associate Professor; Ph.D., Maryland, 1988.
Gurbax Singh, Professor; Ph.D., Maryland College Park, 1971.
Jeurel Singleton, Lecturer; Ph.D., Ottawa, 1980.
Voranuch Suvanich, Assistant Professor; Ph.D., Mississippi State, 1997.
William B. Talley, Associate Professor; Rh.D., Southern Illinois at Carbondale, 1987.
Margarita Treuth, Associate Professor; Ph.D., Maryland College Park, 1992.
Karen A. Verbeke, Professor; Ph.D., Maryland College Park, 1982.
Yan Waguespack, Associate Professor; Ph.D., Tulane, 1990.
Shawn R. White, Assistant Professor; Ph.D., Clemson, 1997.
Niki C. Whitley, Associate Professor; Ph.D., Mississippi State, 1998.
James W. Wiley, Assistant Professor; Ph.D., Miami, 1982.
Allen B. Williams, Assistant Professor; Ph.D., California, Santa Barbara, 1995.
Mark Williams, Assistant Professor; Ph.D., Cincinnati, 1986.
Emin Yilmaz, Professor; Ph.D., Michigan, 1970.
Sehwan Yoo, Lecturer; Ph.D., Kansas, 1996.

UNIVERSITY OF MASSACHUSETTS BOSTON

Graduate Studies

Programs of Study

The University of Massachusetts Boston (UMass Boston) offers master's and doctoral degree programs through the Colleges of Liberal Arts, Management, Nursing and Health Sciences, Public and Community Service, and Science and Mathematics; the Graduate College of Education; and the McCormack Graduate School of Policy Studies. The Master of Arts (M.A.) is awarded in American studies, applied linguistics (with four concentrations: bilingual education, English as a second language, foreign language pedagogy, and Latin and classical humanities), applied sociology, critical and creative thinking, dispute resolution, English, historical archaeology, and history (with two concentrations: history and history teaching). The Master of Fine Arts (M.F.A.) is offered in creative writing. The B.A./M.A. accelerated program in applied sociology allows UMass Boston students to earn both a bachelor's degree in their field of interest and a master's degree in sociology in five years. The Master of Education (M.Ed.) degree is offered in educational administration, instructional design, school counseling, school psychology, special education (with one concentration: teaching of the visually impaired), and teacher education. The Master of Science degree (M.S.) is offered in accounting, biology, biotechnology and biomedical science, chemistry, computer science, environmental sciences, family therapy, gerontology, human services, mental health counseling, nursing (with three concentrations: adult/gerontological nurse practitioner studies, family nurse practitioner studies, and acute/critical care clinical nurse specialist studies), physics (applied), public affairs (with one concentration: international relations), and rehabilitation counseling. An intercampus M.S. in marine sciences and technology is also offered in cooperation with other campuses within the University of Massachusetts system. The Master of Business Administration (M.B.A.) is offered in business administration. The B.A./M.B.A. accelerated program allows students to earn both a bachelor's degree in liberal arts and the M.B.A. in five years. Also offered are the Master of Science in Accounting (M.S.A.) and the Master of Science in Information Technology (M.S.I.T.). A Certificate of Advanced Graduate Study (C.A.G.S.) is offered in counseling, educational administration, and school psychology. The Doctor of Philosophy (Ph.D.) is offered in biology (with two concentrations: environmental biology and molecular, cellular, and organismal biology), chemistry (with one concentration: green chemistry), clinical psychology, computer science, environmental sciences (with one concentration: environmental, earth, and ocean sciences), gerontology, nursing, and public policy. Intercampus Ph.D. programs are also offered in biomedical engineering and biotechnology and in marine sciences and technology, in cooperation with other campuses within the University of Massachusetts system. The Doctor of Education (Ed.D.) is offered in higher education administration and leadership in urban schools. Graduate certificates in adapting the curriculum frameworks, applied behavioral analysis, biotechnology, critical and creative thinking, database technology, dispute resolution, forensic services, geographic information science, instructional technology design, nursing (post-master's certificate: family nurse practitioner studies and adult/gerontological nurse practitioner studies), orientation and mobility, and women in politics and public policy are also offered.

Research Facilities

The University holds a collection of more than 575,000 volumes and subscribes to 3,120 domestic and international journals and newspapers. The Joseph P. Healey Library is centrally located on the campus, easily accessible from the bridgeway connecting all buildings. UMass Boston is a member of the Boston Library Consortium, which includes the libraries of Boston College, Boston University, Brandeis University, Brown University, Massachusetts Institute of Technology, Northeastern University, Tufts University, all five campuses of the University of Massachusetts, Wellesley College, and the Woods Hole Oceanographic Institute. Graduate students may use materials on site at any of these libraries and are eligible for cards granting borrowing privileges at these institutions. UMass Boston's Computing Services provides students with seven-day-a-week access to desktop labs with some 250 Dell Pentium III and Apple McIntosh G5 computers, as well as other specialized, course-related facilities. A wide variety of information technology and data communications resources are available, with network connections in every office and classroom. The campus network is fiber-optic based, with ATM protocol. Computing Services houses equipment from Data General, Dell, Compaq, Sun, and Apple and operating systems include NT, UNIX, Linux, Apple OS, and VMS. Wide-area access to worldwide computing and information resources is provided through Internet services. The John F. Kennedy Presidential Library, a public institution for education and research, stands on the coastal edge of the campus. Designed by the architectural firm of I. M. Pei, the facility was established to preserve and provide access to the documents and memorabilia of President Kennedy and his contemporaries in politics and government. Its archival collections contain approximately 28 million pages of documents, 6.5 million feet of film, and more than 100,000 still photographs. The JFK Library is linked to the University by a series of educational programs enabling students and their instructors to share its rich resources. The Archives of the Commonwealth are also adjacent to the UMass Boston campus, and members of the University community benefit greatly from this additional rich repository of research materials covering the past three centuries.

Financial Aid

Assistantships carrying stipends, tuition waivers, partial fee waivers and a health insurance payment are available to qualified graduate students in all programs. The Office of Financial Aid Services assists students through the Federal Work-Study Program, Federal Perkins Loans program, and Federal Stafford Student Loans program. UMass Boston uses the FAFSA. A limited number of tuition waivers are available to international students who have completed at least one semester of study.

Cost of Study

Academic year 2007–08 costs for a full-time student (twelve state-supported courses per semester for two semesters) are $6437 for Massachusetts residents and $11,690 for residents of other states and international students. This estimate included both mandatory fees and tuition and do not include one-time, course-related, and optional fees; medical insurance; room and board; transportation; or books.

Living and Housing Costs

The University of Massachusetts Boston does not have on-campus housing, and all students are responsible for their own living arrangements. However, referral assistance is available from the campus's Office of Student Housing.

Student Group

Of the 2,648 graduate students enrolled in 2006, approximately 69 percent were women. Reported members of minority groups represented some 41 percent of the total student population. About 11 percent of the campus's total graduate student population was made up of international students. The mean graduate student age was 31.

Location

UMass Boston's proximity to the educational, professional, and cultural riches of Boston's urban milieu provides resources that greatly enhance students' educational experience.

The University

The University of Massachusetts Boston was founded in 1964 to provide superb educational opportunities for the people of the commonwealth, especially those of the greater Boston area. Since its founding, the University has demonstrated a deep commitment to serving students and the community. Situated on a peninsula reaching into Dorchester Bay and Boston Harbor, the campus is easily accessible by both public and private transportation. The campus consists of eight connected buildings on about 100 acres of waterfront property. A Campus Center provides enhanced student services and various student and community venues. Life at the University is as rich and varied as the city of Boston itself. Students on campus can attend plays, musical recitals, films, and lectures; use outstanding specimen collections and facilities for research; navigate the bay in one of the University's sailboats; or conduct research on the various harbor islands and at the University's field station on Nantucket Island.

Applying

Deadlines for submission of domestic applications and application fees ($50 for Massachusetts residents and $60 for all others) range from January 1 to June 1 for fall semester (September) enrollment, and from October 1 to November 1 for spring semester (January) enrollment. Some programs have specific earlier or later deadlines. For many programs, submission of GRE scores is required. The M.B.A. program requires GMAT scores. Other programs, especially in education, require the Miller Analogies Test (MAT) and/or the Massachusetts Test for Educator Licensure (MTEL). The Test of English as a Foreign Language (TOEFL) or the International English Language Testing System (IELTS) exam is required of all applicants from countries whose native language is not English. Unless otherwise specified, completed applications from international students must be received by UMass Boston by May 1 for September enrollment and October 1 for January enrollment.

Correspondence and Information

For information about programs and admissions:
Enrollment Information Services
University of Massachusetts Boston
100 Morrissey Boulevard
Boston, Massachusetts 02125-3393
Phone: 617-287-6000
617-287-6010 (TTY/TDD)
Fax: 617-287-7173
Web site: http://www.umb.edu

For information about research and service activities:
Office of Public Information
University of Massachusetts Boston
100 Morrissey Boulevard
Boston, Massachusetts 02125-3393
Phone: 617-287-5380
Fax: 617-287-5393
E-mail: news@umb.edu

PROGRAM DIRECTORS

College of Liberal Arts
American Studies (M.A.): Judith Smith, Ph.D.
Applied Linguistics (M.A.): Donaldo Macedo, Ed.D., Ph.D.
Applied Sociology (M.A.): Russell Schutt, Ph.D.
Clinical Psychology (Ph.D.): Joan Liem, Ph.D.
English (M.A.): Pamela Annas, Ph.D.
History (M.A.): Paul Bookbinder, Ph.D.
History/Historical Archaeology (M.A.): Stephen Silliman, Ph.D.
History/Teaching History (M.A.): Paul Bookbinder, Ph.D.

College of Management
Business Administration (M.B.A.): William Koehler, Ph.D.

College of Nursing and Health Sciences
Adult-Gerontological Nurse Practitioner Studies (certificate): Karen Dick, Ph.D.
Family Nursing (certificate): Karen Dick, Ph.D.
Nursing (M.S.): Karen Dick, Ph.D.
Nursing (Ph.D.): Carol Ellenbecker, Ph.D.
RN-to-M.S. (M.S.): Karen Dick, Ph.D.

College of Public and Community Service
Dispute Resolution (M.A.): David Matz, J.D.
Human Services (M.A.): Sylvia Mignon, Ph.D.

College of Science and Mathematics
Applied Physics (M.S.): Gopal Rao, Ph.D.
Biology (M.S.): Rick Kesseli, Ph.D.
Biomedical Engineering and Biotechnology (Ph.D.): Manickam Sugumaran, Ph.D.
Biotechnology (certificate): Rick Kesseli, Ph.D.
Biotechnology and Biomedical Science (M.S.): Gregory Beck, Ph.D.
Chemistry (M.S.): Michelle Foster, Ph.D.
Computer Science (M.A., M.S., Ph.D.): Daniel Simovici, Ph.D.
Database Technology (certificate): Daniel Simovici, Ph.D.
Environmental Sciences (M.S.): Eugene Gallagher, Ph.D.
Environmental Sciences/Environmental Biology (Ph.D.): Rick Kesseli, Ph.D.
Environmental Sciences/Environmental, Coastal, and Ocean Sciences (Ph.D.): Eugene Gallagher, Ph.D.
Environmental Sciences/Green Chemistry (Ph.D.): Michelle Foster, Ph.D.
Environmental Sciences/Marine Science and Technology (M.S., Ph.D.): Eugene Gallagher, Ph.D.
Environmental Sciences/Molecular, Cellular, and Organismal Biology (Ph.D.): Rick Kesseli, Ph.D.
Forensic Services (certificate): Stephanie Hartwell, Ph.D.

Graduate College of Education
Adapting the Curriculum Frameworks (certificate): Mary Brady, Ph.D.
Applied Behavioral Analysis (certificate): Mary Brady, Ph.D.
Boston Writing Project (certificate): Joseph Check, Ph.D.
Counseling (M.Ed., C.A.G.S.): Gonzalo Bacigalupe, Ph.D.
Critical and Creative Thinking (certificate): Nina Greenwald, Ph.D.
Critical and Creative Thinking (M.A.): Nina Greenwald, Ph.D.
Educational Administration (M.Ed., C.A.G.S.): Joseph Check, Ph.D.
Education/Higher Education Administration (Ed.D.): Jay Dee, Ph.D.
Education/Leadership in Urban Schools (Ed.D.): Joseph Check, Ed.D.
Education/Teacher Education (elementary, middle, physical education, secondary) (M.Ed.): Lisa Gonsalves, Ph.D.
Instructional Design (M.Ed.): Canice McGarry, M.Ed.
Instructional Technology Design (certificate): Canice McGarry, M.Ed.
Orientation and Mobility (certificate): Laura Bozeman, Ph.D.
School Psychology (M.Ed., C.A.G.S.): Virginia Smith-Harvey, Ph.D.
Special Education (M.Ed.): E. Glenn Mitchell, Ph.D.
Special Education/Teacher of the Visually Impaired (M.Ed., certificate): Laura Bozeman, Ph.D.
Teaching Writing in the Schools (certificate): Mary Ann Byrnes, Ed.D.
Teaching Spanish (certificate): Clara Estow, Ph.D.

McCormack Graduate School of Public and Social Policy
Gerontology (M.S.): Ellen Bruce, Ph.D.
Gerontology (Ph.D.): Ellen Bruce, Ph.D.
Gerontology/Aging and Management Services (certificate): Lillian Glickman, Ph.D.
Public Affairs (M.S.): James Ward, Ph.D.
Public Affairs/International Relations (M.S.): Robert Weiner, Ph.D.
Public Policy (Ph.D.): Connie Chan, Ph.D.
Women in Politics and Public Policy (certificate): Carol Hardy-Fanta, Ph.D.

UMass Boston graduate students are exposed to a wide array of cultural and intellectual viewpoints, providing for a thorough exploration of all subject matter.

A state-of-the-art Campus Center provides enhanced student services, social and cultural opportunities, and dining services for all UMass Boston students.

UNIVERSITY OF MASSACHUSETTS LOWELL

Graduate School

Programs of Study

The University of Massachusetts (UMass) Lowell offers more than 100 areas of graduate study in eighteen doctoral degree, over forty master's degree, and more than fifty graduate certificate programs, which are regionally and nationally accredited. Lowell's internationally renowned research faculty members take a deep personal interest in the professional development of their students.

The Doctor of Philosophy (Ph.D.) is offered in biomedical engineering and biotechnology (intercampus), chemistry (with options in biochemistry, environmental studies, polymer science, and polymer science/plastics engineering), marine sciences and technology (intercampus), nursing (health promotion–intercampus), physics (with areas of study in atomic physics, elementary particle physics, experimental and theoretical condensed matter physics, experimental and theoretical nuclear physics, laser physics, optics, and photonics, or with options in applied mechanics, atmospheric sciences, energy engineering (nuclear and solar), and radiological sciences), and polymer science (with an option in polymer science/plastics engineering, offered jointly with the chemistry department). The Doctor of Science (Sc.D.) is offered in computer science (biochemical informatics, computational math) and work environment (with options in cleaner production and pollution prevention, epidemiology, occupational and environmental hygiene, occupational ergonomics and safety, and work environment policy). Both the Doctor of Engineering (D.Eng.) and the Doctor of Philosophy (Ph.D.) are available with options in chemical engineering, civil and environmental engineering, computer engineering, electrical engineering, energy engineering, mechanical engineering, and plastics engineering. A Doctor of Physical Therapy (D.P.T.) is offered by the School of Health and Environment. The Doctor of Education (Ed.D.) is available in language arts and literacy, leadership in schooling, and mathematics and science education. The Certificate of Advanced Graduate Study (CAGS) is offered in curriculum and instruction, educational administration, planning and policy, and reading and language.

The Master of Arts (M.A.) is offered in community and social psychology, criminal justice, and economic and social development of regions. The Master of Science (M.S.) is available in biological sciences (with an option in biotechnology), biomedical engineering and biotechnology, chemistry, clinical laboratory sciences, computer science (biochemical informatics), environmental studies (atmospheric science), health management and policy, marine sciences and technology (intercampus), mathematics (applied mathematics, mathematics for teachers, scientific computing, statistics and operations research), nursing (adult psychiatric/mental health, family health, and gerontological), physics (with areas of study in atomic physics, elementary particle physics, experimental and theoretical condensed matter physics, experimental and theoretical nuclear physics, laser physics, optics, photonics, or with an option in optical sciences), radiological sciences and protection, and work environment (cleaner production and pollution prevention, epidemiology, occupational and environmental hygiene, occupational ergonomics and safety, and work environment policy). The Master of Science in Engineering (M.S.Eng.) is offered in chemical engineering, civil engineering (environmental, geoenvironmental, geotechnical, structural, and transportation), computer engineering, electrical engineering, energy engineering (nuclear and solar), mechanical engineering, and plastics engineering (elastomeric materials, materials design, medical, and processing materials). The Master of Education (M.Ed.) is offered in curriculum and instruction, educational administration, initial and advanced licensure, reading and language, and science education (online). The Master of Music (M.M.) is available in music education (teaching) and sound recording technology. Also available is the accredited Master of Business Administration (M.B.A.) (with options in accounting, finance, general business, and information technology).

UMass Lowell is among the national leaders in graduate certificate education. Graduate certificates are designed to provide knowledge and expertise vital to today's changing and complex needs in the workplace. In most cases, courses may be applied toward a master's degree program. Most certificates consist of four courses and 12 graduate credits. Graduate certificates are offered in four area clusters: biomedical, health, and social sciences; computers, communications, and information systems; engineering and management; and environmental studies. A number of programs are also offered online.

Research Facilities

All graduate departments are equipped to support scholarly research through collaboration with twenty-eight campus research centers and institutes. More than $25 million in sponsored research was realized in 2006. The University of Massachusetts system is ranked fourteenth among all universities in the United States for monies received for intellectual property licensed to the commercial sector. Industrial-community relations are nurtured and enhanced through research collaborations, technology exchange, student internships, and advisory boards. Faculty members routinely interact with industry, business, community groups, and government agencies. Computer and e-mail accounts are issued to all students. The University has hundreds of workstations, PCs, and terminals connected to multiple servers via a state-of-the-art network infrastructure. Multimedia labs, distance learning classrooms, and online programs are available. Lowell's electronic library includes more than 300 databases, more than 28,000 journals, and ninety computer workstations and wireless systems. The library has consortium arrangements with other major libraries, and remote computer access is available.

Financial Aid

Nearly 400 teaching and research assistantships (TAs/RAs) were awarded in 2006–07; interested students should contact the graduate coordinator or chair of the department to which they are applying. Low-interest student loans are also available for citizens of Massachusetts and Canada through the Massachusetts Educational Financing Authority (MEFA). Federal Direct, Stafford, Perkins, and supplemental loans are available.

Cost of Study

In 2006–07, approximate tuition and fees for a 3-credit graduate course were $1338 for Massachusetts residents and $2636 for out-of-state students. New England Regional Tuition is available for some programs of study in which qualified out-of-state students pay 150 percent of the Massachusetts resident tuition charges.

Living and Housing Costs

Costs for on-campus graduate housing were $4241 per year for single students in 2006–07 (meal plans were extra and cost $2410). Married student housing was $735–$793 per month (unfurnished). Unfurnished efficiencies were $604 per month (no utilities). Furnished and unfurnished rooms/apartments are available within walking distance of the campus. Apartments commonly require a one-month's security deposit.

Student Group

The fall 2006 total enrollment was 11,208, of whom 2,559 were graduate students and 8,649 were undergraduates. UMass Lowell enrolled approximately 465 international students.

Student Outcomes

UMass Lowell awards a significant percentage of its total degrees at the graduate level. Response from both graduate student alumni and industry-employers reveals high satisfaction with education received and level of preparedness and professional perspective. Graduate students are highly sought by major corporations, both as interns during the course of their studies and as full-time employees upon graduation.

Location

In the heart of the birthplace of America's Industrial Revolution, Lowell, Massachusetts, is 25 miles from Boston and home to the first urban national park in the U.S. The Merrimack River runs through this city of 105,000, which hosts professional baseball and hockey adjacent to the campus. Access to Boston is easy via car or commuter train. New Hampshire, Vermont, and Maine, as well as the shores and beaches of the Atlantic Ocean and Cape Cod, are short driving distances away.

The University

The University of Massachusetts Lowell is one member of the five-campus University of Massachusetts system. Graduate students have access to selected courses at other UMass campuses through the UMass Graduate Studies Consortium. Both the University's Annual Campus Crime and Safety Report and the results and information on the Massachusetts Tests for Educator Licensure are available on the Web site and by request.

Applying

Applications (except for computer science) can be submitted at any time; however, early applications ensure that all materials are processed on time and that due consideration is given to those seeking TAs. GRE General Test, GMAT (for the M.B.A.), and TOEFL (for international students) scores; official transcripts; a statement of purpose; an application fee ($40 for Massachusetts residents, $60 for all others); and three letters of reference are required. Some departments have deadlines and additional requirements. Complete application packages with step-by-step instructions and course catalogs are available upon request. Online applications (at a reduced fee) are recommended and are available on the Graduate Admissions' Web site.

Correspondence and Information

Linda Southworth, Director, Graduate Admissions Office
Jay DeFrank, Assistant Director, Graduate Admissions

Graduate Admissions
University of Massachusetts Lowell
883 Broadway Street, Dugan Hall
Lowell, Massachusetts 01854-5130
Phone: 978-934-2390
800-656-GRAD (toll-free)
Fax: 978-934-4058
E-mail: graduate_admissions@uml.edu
Web site: http://www.uml.edu/grad

THE FACULTY

COLLEGE DEANS
E-mail format for faculty members: first name_last name@uml.edu.

Arts and Sciences
Dr. Robert Tamarin (Dean, Sciences Division), Olney 524; 978-934-3847.
Dr. Charles Carroll (Dean, Humanities, Fine Arts, and Social Sciences Division), Durgin 112; 978-934-3843.

Continuing Studies and Corporate Education
Dr. Jacqueline Moloney, Southwick 308A; 978-934-2260.

Education
Dr. Donald Pierson, O'Leary Library 510D; 978-934-4601.

Engineering
Dr. John Ting, Kitson 311; 978-934-2576.

Health and Environment
Dr. David Wegman, Weed 104; 978-934-4461.

Intercampus Graduate School of Marine Sciences and Technology
Dr. Robert R. Gamache, Olney 302A; 978-934-3904.

Management
Dr. Kathryn Carter, Pasteur 305; 978-934-2741.

GRADUATE PROGRAM COORDINATORS AND DEPARTMENT CHAIRS

Biological Sciences
Dr. Susan Braunhut, Coordinator, Olsen 415B; 978-934-2876.
Dr. Mark Hines, Chair, Olsen 517; 978-934-2867.

Biomedical Engineering and Biotechnology
Dr. Bryan Buchholz, Director, Kitson 204D; 978-934-3241.

Chemical Engineering
Dr. Francis Bonner, Coordinator, Engineering 306; 978-934-3154.
Dr. Alfred Donatelli, Chair, Engineering 104; 978-934-3171.

Chemistry/Polymer Science
Dr. Eugene Barry, Chair and Coordinator, Olney 313; 978-934-3669.

Civil and Environmental Engineering
Dr. Chronis Stamatiadis, Coordinator, Pasteur 113; 978-934-2283.
Dr. Nathan Gartner, Chair, Falmouth 108; 978-934-2280.

Clinical Laboratory and Nutritional Sciences
Dr. Eugene Rogers, Coordinator, Weed 309A; 978-934-4478.
Dr. Kathleen Doyle, Chair, Weed 308; 978-934-4425.

Computer Science
Dr. James Canning, Coordinator, Olsen 231; 978-934-3633.
Dr. Thomas Costello, Chair, Olsen 313; 978-934-3620.

Criminal Justice
Dr. April Pattavina, Coordinator, Mahoney 203A; 978-934-4145.
Dr. Eve Buzawa, Chair, Mahoney 214; 978-934-4262.

Education
Dr. Anita Greenwood, Chair and Coordinator (M.Ed.), O'Leary 525; 978-934-4658.
Dr. Michaela Colombo, Coordinator (CAGS/Ed.D.), O'Leary 518; 978-934-4617.
Dr. Vera Ossen, Coordinator (M.Ed./Licensure/Certification), O'Leary 510E; 978-934-4604.

Electrical and Computer Engineering
Dr. Anh Tran, Coordinator (M.S.), Ball 317; 978-934-3322.
Dr. Dikshitulu Kalluri, Coordinator (D.Eng.), Ball 421C, 978-934-3318.
Dr. Craig Armiento, Chair, Ball 301; 978-934-3395.

Energy Engineering (M.E.)
Dr. John Duffy, Coordinator (solar), Engineering 330A; 978-934-2968.
Dr. Gilbert Brown, Coordinator (nuclear), Engineering 220; 978-934-3166.

Environmental Studies
Dr. Clifford Bruell, Coordinator, Engineering 105; 978-934-2284.

Health Management and Policy
Dr. Michael O'Sullivan, Coordinator, Weed 300; 978-934-4480.
Dr. Beverly Volicer, Chair, Weed 320; 978-934-4479.

Management (M.B.A.)
Dr. Gary Mucica, Coordinator, Pasteur 303; 978-934-2853.

Marine Sciences and Technology
Dr. Frank Colby, Coordinator, Olney 302C; 978-934-3906.

Mathematical Sciences
Dr. Charles Byrne, Coordinator, Olney 428W; 978-934-2447.
Dr. James Graham-Eagle, Chair, Olney 428W; 978-934-2712.

Mechanical Engineering
Dr. Majid Charmchi, Coordinator, Ball 224; 978-934-2969.
Dr. John McKelliget, Chair, Engineering 331; 978-934-2974.

Music
Dr. Nicholas Tobin, Coordinator, Durgin 328; 978-934-3879.
Dr. Paula Telesco, Chair, Durgin 107; 978-934-3850.

Nursing
Dr. Susan Houde, Coordinator (M.S.), O'Leary 313Q; 978-934-4426.
Dr. Lin Zhan, Coordinator (Ph.D.), Weed 224A; 978-934-4537.
Dr. Karen Melillo, Chair, O'Leary 312; 978-934-4417.

Physical Therapy
Dr. Barbara Cocanour, Coordinator, Weed 208; 978-934-4413.
Dr. Susan O'Sullivan, Chair, Weed 220; 978-934-4412.

Physics
Dr. Kunnat Sebastian, Coordinator, Olney 134; 978-934-3767.
Dr. James Egan, Chair, Olney 136; 978-934-3780.

Plastics Engineering
Dr. Stephen McCarthy, Coordinator (M.S.Eng.), Ball 207A; 978-934-3417.
Dr. Jim Huang, Coordinator (D.Eng.), Ball 213; 978-934-3428.
Dr. Robert Malloy, Chair, Ball 204; 978-934-3435.

Psychology
Dr. Sharon Wasco, Co-Coordinator, Mahoney 6; 978-934-3964.
Dr. Khanh Dinh, Co-Coordinator, Mahoney 103A; 978-934-3916.
Dr. Nina Coppens, Chair, Mahoney 110; 978-934-3954.

Radiological Sciences (Physics)
Dr. Clayton French, Coordinator, Pinanski 207; 978-934-3286.

Regional Economic and Social Development
Dr. Chris Tilly, Coordinator, O'Leary 500-O; 978-934-2796.
Dr. Philip Moss, Chair, O'Leary 500N; 978-934-2787.

Work Environment
Dr. David Kriebel, Coordinator, Kitson 202D; 978-934-3271.
Dr. Rafael Moure-Eraso, Chair, Kitson 200; 978-934-3250.

Sailing on the Merrimack River.

Riverside walk adjacent to the two campuses.

The University of Massachusetts Lowell is an Equal Opportunity/Affirmative Action, Title IX, H/V, ADA 1990 Employer.

UNIVERSITY OF MEMPHIS

Graduate School

Programs of Study

The Graduate School of the University of Memphis (U of M) awards the Doctor of Philosophy degree in audiology and speech-language pathology, biology, biomedical engineering, business administration, chemistry, communication, computer science, counseling psychology, earth sciences, educational psychology and research, engineering, English, history, mathematics, music, philosophy, and psychology. The degrees of Doctor of Audiology, Doctor of Education, and Doctor of Musical Arts are awarded by the School of Audiology and Speech-Language Pathology, the College of Education, and the College of Communication and Fine Arts, respectively. The College of Education also offers the degree of Education Specialist. Master's degrees are offered in fifty-three major areas through six colleges and one school. The degrees are Master of Science, Master of Arts, Master of Fine Arts, Master of Arts in Teaching, Master of Business Administration, International Master of Business Administration, Master of Liberal Arts, Master of Music, Master of City and Regional Planning, Master of Health Administration, Master of Education, Master of Public Administration, and Master of Science in Nursing. Master's degree majors are accounting, advanced studies in teaching and learning, ancient Egyptian history, anthropology, applied computer science, art, art history, audiology and speech-language pathology, biology, bioinformatics, biomedical engineering, business administration, chemistry, city and regional planning, civil engineering, clinical nutrition, communication, computer science, consumer science and education, counseling and personnel services, creative writing, criminal justice, earth sciences, economics, educational psychology and research, electrical engineering, engineering technology, English, health administration, health and sports sciences, history, instruction and curriculum leadership, international business, journalism, leadership and policy studies, mathematical sciences, mechanical engineering, music, philosophy, physics, political science, public and nonprofit administration, psychology, Romance languages, school psychology, sociology, theater, and women's studies. Graduate certificates are offered in college teaching, community college teaching and learning, geographic information systems, instructional computer applications, museum studies, teaching English as a second language, and women's studies. The Master of Education and Master of Science in Nursing degrees and the family nurse practitioner studies certificate are also offered through the Regents Online Degree Program.

Research Facilities

The University of Memphis Libraries contain more than 1 million bound volumes and 3.4 million microformat items in the Ned R. McWherter Library and five branch libraries (Audiology and Speech-Language Pathology, Chemistry, Earth Sciences, Mathematics, and Music). The libraries' Web site (http://exlibris.memphis.edu) offers access to the holdings of the libraries and more than 90 electronic databases (some full-text) from all on-campus workstations and via proxy server from all off-campus sites. Reciprocal-use agreements with other academic libraries within the region allow University of Memphis students and faculty members to access additional library collections with the appropriate University of Memphis ID card. The University of Memphis is a full partner and early adopter of Internet2 technology for research and instruction. A network of computer labs provides U of M students with opportunities to tap numerous computing resources: software, utilities, the Internet, PCs, Macintoshes, and laser printers. Consulting, training, and help desk services are available as well.

Specialized research units include the Bureau of Business and Economic Research, Center for Earthquake Research and Information, Center for Humanities, Center for the Study of Higher Education, Institute for Intelligent Systems, Regional Economic Development Center, Center for Research on Women, and, at off-campus sites, the Edward J. Meeman Biological Station (a biological research center), the Chucalissa Indian Village and Museum, and the Center for Community Health. Various service units maintained by the University, such as the Psychological Services Center, the Speech and Hearing Center, and the Integrated Microscopy Center, offer additional facilities. The University is affiliated with the Gulf Coast Research Laboratory, Oak Ridge Associated Universities, the National Center for Toxicological Research, and the St. Jude Children's Research Hospital; it maintains joint programs with the University of Tennessee, Memphis. The University receives special funding from the state to support Centers of Excellence in the following areas: audiology and speech pathology, earthquake research, educational policy, Egyptology, and psychology.

Financial Aid

A limited number of fellowships, assistantships, and scholarships are available. Stipends for graduate assistants vary among departments and include tuition and fees. Inquiries regarding assistantships and fellowships should be addressed to the department chair or director of graduate studies of the appropriate college. Financial aid is also available through the Federal Perkins Loan program, the Federal Stafford Student Loan program, and the Federal Work-Study Program. Information about student loans and work-study programs should be requested through the Office of Student Aid.

Cost of Study

The 2006–07 tuition and fees for full-time study on campus were $3189 per semester for Tennessee residents and $8422 per semester for nonresidents. Tuition for part-time students in 2006–07 was $349 per credit hour for Tennessee residents and $797 per credit hour for nonresidents. There are additional fees for Regents Online Degree Program courses and a $20-per-credit-hour surcharge for art, business, and engineering courses.

Living and Housing Costs

The 2006–07 rates for residence halls on campus ranged from $1290 to $2250 per semester. Single-student apartments and town houses ranged from $2445 to $2520 per semester. The University has 150 apartments on the South Campus for student families, with some units specifically built for students with disabilities; the 2006–07 rates ranged from $490 to $690 per month. Utilities are paid by the tenant. Numerous housing facilities also exist off campus in the Memphis community.

Student Group

In the spring of 2007, the University of Memphis had an enrollment of 19,199 students, including 4,029 graduate students. Of the total graduate student population, 2,536 (63 percent) were women and 23 percent were members of minority groups. The majority of students were from Tennessee, but the University attracts students from other states and countries as well.

Location

The Memphis metropolitan area has a population of over 1 million and is one of the South's largest and most attractive cities. As a primary medical, educational, communication, and transportation center, Memphis offers a full range of research opportunities and cultural experiences. The city, known worldwide for its musical heritage, has many fine restaurants, museums, and theaters, as well as one of the nation's largest urban park systems. The Memphis Medical Center is the South's largest and one of the nation's foremost centers of medical research. A public transportation system serves the University and other parts of the city.

The University

The University's modern and beautifully landscaped campus is centrally located in an attractive residential area of Memphis, with shopping, recreation, and entertainment centers nearby. In addition to the facilities on the Main Campus, the University has research and athletic training facilities and housing for student families on the South Campus and research and clinical facilities in the medical center.

Applying

Electronic applications for graduate admission are available at https://apply.embark.com/Grad/Memphis. Hard-copy applications are available from the individual graduate programs. Completed forms must be returned with a $35 nonrefundable application fee for domestic applicants or a $60 nonrefundable fee for international students three to six weeks prior to the beginning of the semester. Individual programs may have earlier deadlines. Consideration for admission requires satisfactory scores on the General Test of the Graduate Record Examinations (GRE) or the Graduate Management Admission Test (GMAT) and an acceptable grade point average. Individual programs may have additional requirements. Students who do not hold degrees from colleges or universities in which English is the classroom language or for whom English is not the native language are also required to provide a satisfactory score on the TOEFL. Applicants whose highest degree is from an international university must have their credentials evaluated by World Education Services (P.O. Box 745, Old Chelsea Station, New York, New York 10113-0745; Web site: http://wes.org). The course-to-course report is required.

Correspondence and Information

Graduate School
215 Administration Building
University of Memphis
Memphis, Tennessee 38152-3370

Phone: 901-678-2531
Web site: http://www.memphis.edu/gradschool/

FACULTY HEADS

GRADUATE SCHOOL
Karen Weddle-West, Ph.D., Vice Provost for Graduate Studies.

COLLEGE OF ARTS AND SCIENCES
Henry Kurtz, Ph.D., Dean.
Linda Bennett, Ph.D., Associate Dean and Director of Graduate Studies.
Anthropology (M.A.): Ruthbeth Finerman, Ph.D., Chair (901-678-2080).
Biology (M.S., Ph.D.): Melvin Beck, Ph.D., Interim Chair (901-678-2581).
Chemistry (M.S., Ph.D.): Peter Bridson, Ph.D., Chair (901-678-2622).
City and Regional Planning (M.C.R.P.): Gene Pearson, M.U.R.P., Director (901-678-2057).
Computer Science (M.S., Ph.D.): Sajjan G. Shiva, Ph.D., Chair (901-678-5465).
Criminal Justice (M.A.): Randolph Dupont, J.D., Chair (901-678-2737).
Earth Sciences (M.A., M.S., Ph.D.): M. Jerry Bartholomew, Ph.D., Chair (901-678-4358).
English (M.A., M.F.A., Ph.D.): Stephen Tabachnik, Ph.D., Chair (901-678-2651).
Foreign Languages and Literatures (M.A.): Ralph Albanese, Ph.D., Chair (901-678-2506).
Health Administration (M.H.A.): Lutchmie Narine, Ph.D., Director (901-678-5552).
History (M.A., Ph.D.): Janann Sherman, Ph.D., Chair (901-678-2515).
Mathematics (M.S., Ph.D.): James Jamison, Ph.D., Chair (901-678-2482).
Philosophy (M.A., Ph.D.): Nancy Simco, Ph.D., Chair (901-678-2535).
Physics (M.S.): M. Shah Jahan, Ph.D., Chair (901-678-2410).
Political Science (M.A.): Shannon Blanton, Ph.D., Interim Chair (901-678-2395).
Psychology (M.S., Ph.D.): Arthur C. Graesser, Ph.D., Chair (901-678-2145).
Public Administration (M.P.A.): Dorothy Norris-Tirrell, Ph.D., Director (901-678-3368).
Sociology (M.A.): Larry Peterson, Ph.D., Chair (901-678-2611).
Women's Studies (M.A.): Leigh Anne Duck, Ph.D., Interim Director (901-678-3550).

FOGELMAN COLLEGE OF BUSINESS AND ECONOMICS
John J. Pepin, Ph.D., Dean.
Carol Danehower, D.B.A., Associate Dean for Academic Programs (901-678-3721).
Accountancy (M.S., Ph.D.): Kenneth Lambert, Ph.D., Director (901-678-4022).
Economics (M.A., Ph.D.): Julia Heath, Ph.D., Chair (901-678-5243).
Finance, Insurance, and Real Estate (M.S., Ph.D.): Ronald H. Spahr, Ph.D., Chair (901-678-5930).
Management (M.S., Ph.D.): Robert Taylor, Ph.D., Chair (901-678-4551).
Management Information Systems (M.S., Ph.D.): Jasbir Dhaliwal, Ph.D., Chair (901-678-4613).
Marketing and Supply Chain Management (M.S., Ph.D.): Marla Stafford, Ph.D., Interim Chair (901-678-2667).

COLLEGE OF COMMUNICATION AND FINE ARTS
Richard Ranta, Ph.D., Dean.
Moira Logan, M.F.A., Associate Dean and Director of Graduate Studies.
Art (M.A., M.F.A.): Jed Jackson, M.F.A., Chair (901-678-2216).
Communication (M.A., Ph.D.): Michael Leff, Ph.D., Chair (901-678-2565).
Journalism (M.A.): James Redmond, Ph.D., Chair (901-678-2401).
Rudi E. Scheidt School of Music (M.Mu., D.M.A., Ph.D.): Patricia J. Hoy, D.M.A., Director (901-678-3764).
Theater and Dance (M.F.A.): Robert A. Hetherington, M.A., Chair (901-678-2565).

COLLEGE OF EDUCATION
Ric Hovda, Ph.D., Dean.
Ernest Rakow, Ph.D., Associate Dean for Administration and Graduate Programs.
Counseling, Educational Psychology and Research (M.S., Ed.D., Ph.D.): Douglas C. Strohmer, Ph.D., Chair (901-678-2841).
Health and Sport Sciences (M.S.): Michael H. Hamrick, Ed.D., Chair (901-678-2324).
Instruction and Curriculum Leadership (M.S., M.A.T., Ed.D.): Rebecca Anderson, Ph.D., Chair (901-678-2365).
Leadership (M.S., Ed.D.): Larry McNeal, Ph.D., Chair (901-678-2368).

HERFF COLLEGE OF ENGINEERING
Richard C. Warder, Ph.D., Dean.
Steven M. Slack, Ph.D., Associate Dean and Director of Graduate Studies.
Biomedical Engineering (M.S., Ph.D.): Eugene Eckstein, Ph.D., Chair (901-678-3733).
Civil Engineering (M.S., Ph.D.): Martin Lipinski, Ph.D., Chair (901-678-2746).
Electrical and Computer Engineering (M.S., Ph.D.): David Russomanno, Ph.D., Chair (901-678-2175).
Engineering Technology (M.S.): Deborah Hochstein, M.S.E., Chair (901-678-2238).
Mechanical Engineering (M.S., Ph.D.): John Hochstein, Ph.D., Chair (901-678-2173).

LOEWENBERG SCHOOL OF NURSING
Marjorie F. Luttrell, Ph.D., Interim Dean.
Robert Koch, Ph.D., Director of Graduate Studies.
Nursing (M.S.N.).

SCHOOL OF AUDIOLOGY AND SPEECH-LANGUAGE PATHOLOGY
Maurice I. Mendel, Ph.D., Dean.
David Wark, Ph.D., Director of Graduate Studies (901-678-5800).
Audiology and Speech Pathology (M.A., Ph.D., Au.D.).

UNIVERSITY COLLEGE
Dan Lattimore, Ph.D., Dean.
M. David Arant, Ph.D., Coordinator of M.A.L.S. Program.
Consumer Science and Education (M.S.).
Interdisciplinary (M.A.L.S.).

UNIVERSITY OF MIAMI

Graduate School

Programs of Study

The Graduate School of the University of Miami offers programs of study leading to the Doctor of Philosophy (Ph.D.) degree in biology, chemistry, communications, economics, education (counseling psychology, educational research, educational research/exercise physiology, elementary education, TESOL, special education, and reading), engineering (biomedical, civil, electrical and computer, industrial, and mechanical), English, ergonomics, history, international studies, marine and atmospheric sciences (applied marine physics, marine and atmospheric chemistry, marine biology and fisheries, marine geology and geophysics, and meteorology and physical oceanography), mathematics, medicine (biochemistry and molecular biology, epidemiology, microbiology and immunology, molecular cell and developmental biology, molecular and cellular pharmacology, neuroscience, and physiology and biophysics), music education, nursing, philosophy, physical therapy, physics, psychology, Romance languages (French and Spanish), and sociology.

Interdepartmental doctoral programs, tailored to the needs of the individual student, are available to qualified applicants. The Master of Architecture, Master of Arts, Master of Arts in Liberal Studies, Master of Business Administration, Master of Fine Arts, Master of Music, Specialist in Music Education, Master of Professional Accounting, Master of Public Administration, Master of Public Health, Master of Science, Master of Science in Education, Specialist in Education (Ed.S.), Master of Science in Engineering (architectural, biomedical, civil, electrical and computer, industrial, and mechanical), Master of Science in Music Engineering, Master of Science in Nursing, Master of Science in Taxation, and Doctor of Physical Therapy are offered in the areas cited for doctoral study and through other programs.

The Doctor of Musical Arts (D.M.A.) is offered with concentrations in applied music, composition, conducting, and accompanying and chamber music. The Doctor of Arts (D.A.) degree, an interdisciplinary degree designed for community college and four-year college teachers, is offered in the Department Mathematics.

The basic requirements for the completion of the Ph.D. include a minimum of 60 credits beyond the bachelor's degree, including 12–24 credits of dissertation research; a minimum residence of two consecutive academic semesters at the University of Miami beyond the first year of graduate work, wherever taken; qualifying examinations; and the presentation and defense of a dissertation. Individual programs have their own requirements. The academic year consists of two semesters (fall and spring) and two 5-week summer sessions.

Research Facilities

In addition to providing a range of regular and specialized laboratories and libraries, the University has developed advanced facilities for study and research in tropical and subtropical ecology, marine and atmospheric sciences, and studies relating to the Caribbean and Latin America. The University operates or cooperates in teaching and research stations in the Caribbean, the Florida Keys, the Everglades, and Central and South America. Extensive research facilities exist at the University's Ungar Computing Center. Several major research centers—the North-South Center, the Center for Social Research in Aging, the Behavioral Medicine Division of Psychology, the Mailman Center for Child Development, the Miami Project to Cure Paralysis, the South Campus for Applied Research, the Rosenstiel School of Marine and Atmospheric Science, the Parkinson Research Foundation, and the Comprehensive Cancer Center—are available to qualified doctoral and postdoctoral students.

Financial Aid

Financial assistance is available to qualified graduate students. In 2007–08, this includes fellowships, with stipends ranging from $9000 to $20,000 plus tuition; teaching, research, and graduate assistantships, with stipends ranging from $5000 to $21,000 plus tuition; and a variety of additional financial aids in the form of endowed fellowships and service assistantships. Various loan programs, work-study, and part-time employment opportunities are also available. Those interested should direct inquiries to the Office of Financial Assistance Services for loans and employment information and to the appropriate graduate department for assistantships and fellowships.

Cost of Study

Graduate tuition is $1350 per credit hour in 2007–08. The University fee is $82, and the student activity fee is $35.

Living and Housing Costs

A limited number of University rooms are available for single graduate students. Inquiries should be addressed to the director of housing. Generally, graduate students arrange for their own housing in the community. The cost of living varies with the accommodations desired and the needs and resources of the individual.

Student Group

During 2006–07, approximately 3,175 graduate students were enrolled for studies and programs leading to various degrees. This number includes students from all the states and from more than 100 other countries.

Location

The suburb of Coral Gables is one of the municipalities that make up the southeastern Florida metropolitan region. This subtropical area, which stretches from the Palm Beaches to the Florida Keys, is an exciting cosmopolitan community offering substantial cultural and recreational attractions. The University supports a full calendar of social, cultural, and academic events throughout the year. For those interested in outdoor recreation, the Atlantic Ocean, the Florida Keys, and Everglades National Parks are nearby.

The University

The University is an independent, nonprofit, nonsectarian, international institution open to all qualified individuals. Founded in Coral Gables in 1925, its schools, colleges, centers, and institutes now occupy four campuses: the Main Campus in Coral Gables, the Medical Campus in Miami, the Marine and Atmospheric Sciences Campus on Virginia Key, and the South Campus for medical research in Dade County.

Applying

Applicants for admission to the Graduate School must file application forms provided by the University. For the 2007–08 academic year, the application fee is $50, but is subject to change. Applicants are required to furnish transcripts of all postsecondary education, official Graduate Record Examinations scores, three letters of recommendation, and any other requirements of the program in which they seek admittance. The deadline for receiving applications for admission for the fall semester varies by department but is generally no later than June 15; for fellowship and assistantship consideration, February 1; and for other financial aid, March 1. Some departments may require an earlier deadline. For Graduate School information, students should visit the Web site or write to the Graduate School.

Correspondence and Information

For specific admission information:
Graduate Admissions
Department of (specify)
University of Miami
Coral Gables, Florida 33124

For general information:
Graduate School
University of Miami
P.O. Box 248125
Coral Gables, Florida 33124-3220
Phone: 305-284-4154
Fax: 305-284-5441
E-mail: graduateschool@miami.edu
Web site: http://www.miami.edu/grad

DEGREE PROGRAMS AND GRADUATE PROGRAM DIRECTORS

Accounting (M.P.Acc.; M.S.Tax.): Kay W. Tatum, Ph.D. Auditing and financial reporting, federal tax, accounting, information systems, financial information in the health-care industry, managerial accounting, internal control structure.

Architecture (M.Arch.): Teofilo Victoria, M.Arch. Town and suburb design, urban design and development, computer-aided urban and suburban design.

Art and Art History (M.A.; M.F.A.): Lise Drost, M.F.A., Chair. Studio art-painting, sculpture, graphic design/illustration, printmaking, photography/digital imaging, and ceramics; art history.

Biochemistry and Molecular Biology (Ph.D.): Rudolf Werner, Ph.D. Macromolecular structure, gene expression and regulation, developmental biology, protein engineering, reproductive endocrinology, protein interactions and function, tumor biology, growth factors, hormones and signal transduction, extracellular matrix, macromolecular synthesis, cytoskeleton, neurobiology, oncogenes, retroviruses.

Biology (M.S.; Ph.D.): Leo Sternberg, Ph.D. Environmental biology, organismic biology, developmental biology, genetics, animal behavior, ecology, subtropical and tropical studies, cellular and molecular biology.

Business Administration (M.B.A.; M.S.): Anuj Mehrotra, Ph.D., Vice Dean; David Green, Assistant Dean. Accounting, computer information systems, economics, finance, international business, legal implications, management, management science, marketing, M.B.A. for executives and professionals, political science.

Chemistry (M.S.; Ph.D.): Francisco M. Raymo, Ph.D. Inorganic chemistry, organic chemistry, physical chemistry.

Communication (M.A.; M.F.A.; Ph.D.): Leonardo C. Ferreira, Ph.D. Communication studies, public relations, communications, motion pictures, journalism.

Computer Information Systems (M.S.): Joel Stutz, Ph.D. Database, information systems analysis and design, microcomputer applications, expert systems, telecommunications, computer network security, project management, object-oriented programming.

Computer Science (M.S.): Dilip Sarkar, Ph.D.

Creative Writing (M.F.A.): Manette Ansay, M.F.A.

Economics (M.A.; Ph.D.): Pedro Gomis Porqueras, Ph.D. International and developmental economics, microeconomic and macroeconomic theory, law and economics, human resources and health economics, public-sector economics, industrial organization, labor economics.

Education (M.S.Ed.; Ed.S.; Ph.D.): Andy Gillentine, Ph.D. Special education and reading, teaching and learning, counseling and counseling psychology, educational leadership, higher education, educational research, exercise and sport sciences.

Engineering (M.S.; D.A.; Ph.D.): Helene Solo-Gabriele, Ph.D. Biomedical, civil and architectural, electrical and computer, industrial, and mechanical engineering.

English (M.A.; Ph.D.): Mihoko Suzuki, Ph.D. Renaissance, neoclassical, Romantic, Victorian, American, Anglo-Irish, and modern British literatures; feminist literary theory.

Epidemiology and Public Health (M.P.H.; M.S.P.H.; Ph.D.): Jay Wilkinson, Ph.D. Epidemiology and biostatistics, public health administration, environmental health, health education, international health.

Ergonomics (M.S.; Ph.D.): Shihab Asfour, Ph.D.

Modern Languages and Literatures (Ph.D.): Gema Perez-Sanchez, Ph.D. Spanish, French, Romance languages, comparative literature, critical theory.

History (M.A.; Ph.D.): Michael Miller, Ph.D. American, Asian, and European history (M.A. degree only); Latin American history (M.A. and Ph.D. degrees).

International Studies (M.A.): Bruce Bagley, Ph.D. International affairs, comparative development, international security and conflict, international economics, international business, inter-American studies, European studies (including former Soviet states), Middle East studies.

Liberal Studies (M.A.L.S.): Eugene Clasby, Ph.D. Interdisciplinary studies in the arts and sciences.

Management Science (M.S.): Howard Gitlow, Ph.D. Applied statistics, computer applications, logistics, operations research, systems analysis and man-machine systems, mathematical programming simulation.

Marine and Atmospheric Sciences (M.A.; M.S.; Ph.D.): Larry Peterson, Ph.D. Physical oceanography, chemical oceanography, atmospheric science, marine affairs, marine geology and geophysics, marine biological science-including fisheries science.

Mathematics (M.S.; M.A.; D.A.; Ph.D.): Marvin Mielke, Ph.D. Pure mathematics-algebra, analysis, and topology; applied mathematics; statistics.

Microbiology and Immunology (Ph.D.): Larry Boise, Ph.D. Microbial genetics, microbial chemistry and physiology, molecular and cellular immunology, virology and tissue culture, mycology, pathogenic bacteriology, applied and industrial microbiology, environmental microbiology, marine microbiology.

Molecular and Cellular Pharmacology (Ph.D.): Kerry Burnstein, Ph.D. Mechanism of drug action at the molecular and cellular level, receptor pharmacology, signal transduction, cardiovascular biology, neuropharmacology, molecular neurobiology.

Molecular Cell and Developmental Biology (Ph.D): Pedro Salas, Ph.D.

Music (M.M.; Spec.M.; D.M.A.; Ph.D.): Edward Asmus, Ph.D. Theory and composition; music education and music therapy; musicology; applied music-conducting, voice, piano, organ, harp, woodwind, brass, percussion, and stringed instruments; studio music and jazz; accompanying; music media and industry.

Neuroscience (Ph.D.): Charles W. Luetji, Ph.D. Study of brain and nervous systems from diverse vantage points-including cell and molecular biology, physiology, pharmacology, anatomy, and immunology. Includes 55 faculty members from throughout the University.

Nursing (M.S.N.; Ph.D.): Gail McCain, Ph.D., Doctoral Level; JoAnn T. Trybulski, Ph.D., Master's Level. Nursing; primary health care, including adult nurse practitioner, family nurse practitioner, nurse midwifery; psychiatric/mental-health nursing; women's health.

Philosophy (M.A.; Ph.D.): Otavio Bueno, Ph.D. History of philosophy, epistemology, metaphysics, logic, philosophy of language, ethics, political philosophy, aesthetics.

Physical Therapy (D.P.T.; Ph.D.): Sherrill Hayes, Ph.D., P.T. Physical therapy, evidence-based practice, entry-level postprofessional. Offers academic and professional programs of study leading to the entry-level clinical doctorate (Doctor of Physical Therapy, D.P.T.) and a post-professional Ph.D. program emphasizing research, teaching, and the study of human motion.

Physics (M.S.; D.A.; Ph.D.): Joshua Cohn, Ph.D. Plasma physics, optics, solid-state physics, nonlinear phenomena and chaos, optical oceanography, environmental optics.

Physiology and Biophysics (Ph.D.): David Landowne, Ph.D. Cell physiology; membrane biophysics; muscle cell physiology; neurobiology-including molecular biology, developmental biology, and neuroimmunology.

Political Science (M.P.A.): Jonathan West, Ph.D. Public administration, public-sector manpower management, budgetary and fiscal management, nonprofit management, environmental policy, international politics.

Psychology (M.S./Ph.D.): A. Rodney Wellens, Ph.D. Clinical psychology-adult, child, and health; experimental psychology-applied developmental, behavioral medicine, and behavioral neuroscience.

Sociology (M.A.; Ph.D.): Robert J. Johnson, Ph.D. Medical sociology, criminology, race and ethnic studies, sociology of education, sociological theory, sociology of science.

UNIVERSITY OF MICHIGAN–DEARBORN

Graduate Studies

Programs of Study

The University of Michigan–Dearborn (UM–Dearborn) is the campus of choice for more than 8,500 students in southeastern Michigan, including over 2,000 graduate students who value accessibility, flexibility, affordability, and preeminence in education. The University is distinguished by its commitment to the provision of exceptional educational opportunities in an interactive, student-centered environment. All of the programs reflect the traditions of excellence, innovation, and leadership that distinguish a University of Michigan degree.

The University of Michigan–Dearborn offers more than twenty-six graduate degrees oriented toward working professionals who seek further educational opportunities for career advancement and/or intellectual enrichment. Classes are offered in the late afternoon and evening or on Saturdays for the convenience of those wishing to pursue graduate studies while working full-time.

The College of Arts, Sciences, and Letters offers a Master of Arts in liberal studies, a Master of Science in applied and computational mathematics, a Master of Science in environmental studies, a Master of Science in psychology with specializations in health psychology and clinical psychology, and a Master of Public Policy. The College of Engineering and Computer Science offers Master of Science in Engineering degrees in automotive systems engineering, computer engineering, electrical engineering, industrial and systems engineering, manufacturing systems engineering, and mechanical engineering. Master of Science degrees are offered in computer and information science, engineering management, information systems and technology, and software engineering. The Doctor of Engineering in Manufacturing degree is offered in collaboration with the Program in Manufacturing, College of Engineering, University of Michigan at Ann Arbor. The School of Education offers Master of Arts degrees in education and teaching as well as a Master of Education degree in special education, a Master of Public Administration degree, and a Master of Science in science education. The School of Management, accredited by AACSB International–The Association to Advance Collegiate Schools of Business, offers a Master of Business Administration (M.B.A.) degree and a Web-based M.B.A. as well as a Master of Science in accounting and a Master of Science in finance. The College of Engineering and Computer Science and the School of Management offer a dual degree M.B.A./M.S.E. in industrial and systems engineering.

Research Facilities

The University of Michigan–Dearborn's excellent facilities encourage a high level of student-faculty interaction both in the classroom and the laboratory. The Mardigian Library houses a collection of more than 300,000 bound volumes and approximately 1,200 current periodicals. In addition, students have access to the library collections of the University of Michigan–Ann Arbor, and both on-campus and off-campus access to many online resources, including full-text periodicals, reference sources, and abstracting and indexing services. The campus maintains two general purpose computer laboratories with the latest PC workstations. Each school also has dedicated computer laboratories equipped with PCs, Macs, and Sun Workstations, all networked and accessible from remote locations. The College of Engineering and Computer Science operates numerous laboratories, including specialized ones dedicated to manufacturing, machine vision, materials, engines, vehicle electronics, and networks.

Financial Aid

Graduate students may apply for scholarships, loans, internships, and employment. The College of Engineering and Computer Science has a limited number of assistantships available. Many current students obtain support for their graduate education through their employer's educational assistance programs.

Cost of Study

Graduate tuition for 2007–08 can be found on the University of Michigan–Dearborn Web site at http://www.umd.umich.edu/rr_tuition-fees/.

Living and Housing Costs

No on-campus housing is available. A Housing Referral Office is available for locating housing in the area.

Student Group

In fall 2006, the University had an approximate enrollment of 8,500, of whom 1,954 were graduate students. Of these graduate students, 51 percent were women, 3.4 percent were international, and 19 percent were members of minority groups.

Student Outcomes

Graduate students at UM–Dearborn come from all professions. Most have worked for several years and have gained valuable experience in their particular occupations. The graduate experience enhances their productivity and effectiveness in the workplace. Many report successful promotions within their organizations or higher-paying job offers after graduating. The automotive industry in southeastern Michigan provides worldwide employment opportunities for graduates.

Location

Located in the heart of one of the world's premier manufacturing regions, the University of Michigan–Dearborn campus is approximately 15 miles from downtown Detroit and 15 miles from the Detroit Metropolitan International Airport and is easily accessible from major area freeways. The Henry Ford Estate-Fair Lane, former home of the automotive pioneer, is a National Historic Landmark and is located on campus.

The University

The Dearborn campus is part of the University of Michigan system. It was established in 1956 through a gift from the Ford Motor Company consisting of 196 acres of land, which includes 70 acres of the Henry Ford Estate-Fair Lane and the funds for the construction of four buildings. The campus opened its doors in 1959 as a senior college serving the local engineering and business community. In 1971, UM–Dearborn began admitting freshmen and expanded its programs to focus on master's-level education. The campus recently completed a significant infrastructure growth with new buildings for the engineering and management schools and renovations in the School of Education building.

Applying

Criteria and deadline dates are included in the University's informational materials. Applications for admission and supporting documents should be sent directly to the program(s) of interest.

Correspondence and Information

Graduate Studies Office
University of Michigan–Dearborn
4901 Evergreen Road, 1080 AB
Dearborn, Michigan 48128-1491

Phone: 313-593-1494
Fax: 313-436-9156
E-mail: umdgrad@umd.umich.edu
Web site: http://www.umd.umich.edu/graduatestudies/

THE FACULTY

Teaching is at the core of the University of Michigan–Dearborn's mission; thus, members of the faculty are dedicated professionals who place great emphasis on their role as teachers. Faculty members strive to train students, mentor them, and interact with them both inside and outside the classroom. In addition, original works of the faculty in research and scholarship, as well as in creativity, enrich the teaching and educational experience the students receive and contribute to advancing their knowledge. More information about University faculty members may be found on UM–Dearborn's Web site.

UNIVERSITY OF MISSOURI–ST. LOUIS

Graduate School

Programs of Study The University of Missouri–St. Louis (UM–St. Louis) offers programs of study leading to the Ph.D.: applied mathematics, biology, business administration, chemistry, criminology and criminal justice, education, nursing, physics, physiological optics, political science, and psychology. The Ed.D. and Ed.S. in education are also administered by the Graduate School. The O.D. in optometry is administered by the School of Optometry.

Master's degrees are offered in the areas of accounting, adult and higher education, biochemistry and biotechnology, biology, business administration, chemistry, communication, computer science, counseling, creative writing, criminology and criminal justice, economics, educational administration, elementary education, English, gerontology, history, information systems, mathematics, museum studies, music education, nursing, philosophy, physics, physiological optics, political science, psychology, public policy administration, secondary education, social work, sociology, and special education. The University also offers numerous graduate certificate programs.

Research Facilities The three libraries at the University of Missouri–St. Louis (Thomas Jefferson, Ward E. Barnes, and Mercantile) hold more than 1 million volumes, 3,264 periodical subscriptions, and 1 million government documents and provide access to approximately 3,000 full-text, online journals. The Mercantile Library, with collection strengths in Western Americana, holds two distinguished transportation collections: the Barringer Collection, which focuses on American railroad history, and the Pott Waterways Collection, which focuses on United States river and inland waterways history. The Center for Molecular Electronics conducts research to understand and control actions at the atomic and molecular levels that are essential for state-of-the-art materials and devices. The International Center for Tropical Ecology promotes research in biodiversity, conservation, and sustainable use of tropical ecosystems. The Center for Neurodynamics conducts research on the effects of stochastic noise on information transfer in natural and artificial neurological systems. The Center for Trauma Recovery conducts research on the assessment and treatment of post-traumatic stress disorder. The Center for Business and Industrial Studies investigates managerial problems and performs applied research. The Center for International Studies supports academic programs, seminars, and conferences designed to promote and improve research in international studies and the methods of teaching international studies in schools and colleges. The Public Policy Research Center conducts research in the areas of employment, education, housing, and law and offers training experiences for students in urban research. The Center for Transportation Studies is pioneering a new program in supply chain management, developing funds for research into the role private-sector transportation plays in the provision of public transportation services.

Financial Aid Financial assistance is available to graduate students primarily through assistantships. Departments determine the stipend level for teaching and research assistants. Appointments range from $5000 to $18,000 for master's students and from $7500 to $30,000 for doctoral students.

Cost of Study Tuition and fees per semester (full-time, 9 credit hours) for 2007–08 are $3000 for residents and $7089 for nonresidents. Estimated annual living and health insurance expenses for international students are $10,003 for the academic year.

Living and Housing Costs Traditional residence hall or apartment housing is available. Full information is available online at http://www.umsl.edu/html/housing.html.

Student Group Enrollment in fall 2006 was 15,540 students, of whom 2,897 were graduate students. Sixty-three percent of the graduate students were women, and 12.5 percent were African American.

Location The University occupies a suburban campus of more than 300 acres northwest of St. Louis, the major metropolitan area in the state. The campus has easy access to the airport and the downtown area via the MetroLink, which has stops on both the north and south campuses. St. Louis has an abundance of cultural, sports, and entertainment opportunities.

The University UM–St. Louis is one of four campuses of the University of Missouri System. It was established in 1963 and is the third-largest university in the state. In addition to its role in advancing knowledge as part of a comprehensive research university, UM–St. Louis has a special mission determined by its urban location and its shared land-grant tradition. It works in partnership with other key community institutions to help the St. Louis region progress and prosper.

Applying Doctoral applications have deadlines as early as January 5 and no later than July 15. Master's degree student applications are generally due July 15 for the fall semester, December 15 for the winter/spring semester, and May 1 for the summer session. Applicants requesting financial aid should submit their applications by March 15. Additional information is available online at the Web address listed in this description.

Correspondence and Information

Graduate Admissions
217 Millennium Student Center
University of Missouri–St. Louis
One University Boulevard
St. Louis, Missouri 63121-4499

Phone: 314-516-5458
Fax: 314-516-6996
E-mail: gradadm@umsl.edu
Web site: http://www.umsl.edu/divisions/graduate

FACULTY RESEARCH

Biology. Animal behavior/behavioral ecology, biochemistry, biogeography, community/evolutionary ecology, conservation biology, evolutionary developmental biology, ecophysiology, evolution of sociality, history of biology, membrane biology and signal transduction, molecular biology, molecular and morphological systematics, microbial genetics, neuroethology of aquatic organisms, plant-animal/insect-microbe interactions, plant biochemical/cellular/molecular biology, plant population genetics/biology, RNA processing and metabolism, studies in tropical and temperate ecosystems, taxonomy.

Business. Accounting, accounting regulation, auditor judgment and decision making, taxation, commercial banking, corporate finance, investments and portfolio management, government regulations, telecommunications, client/server, IS sourcing, decision support systems, international information systems, management of information systems, production/operations management, mathematical programming, transportation routing and scheduling, logistics systems, freight consolidation, simulation, supply chain management, human resources, international management, strategic management, marketing strategy, new product development, advertising, consumer behavior.

Chemistry and Biochemistry. Organometallic chemistry, supramolecular chemistry, transition metal–catalyzed reactions, redox enzymes based on cyclodextrin, serum transferrin chemistry, natural products chemistry, carbohydrate chemistry, organic synthesis, phosphorus chemistry, silicon chemistry, physical organic chemistry, structure-function studies of enzymes, biophysical chemistry, structural studies using NMR spectroscopy and X-ray diffraction, cell model systems, drug discovery and medicinal chemistry, biological polymers, microscopy, chemical education, materials chemistry, nanoscience, nanomaterials and nanocatalysis, elucidation of nanostructures.

Communication. Theory and methodology, intercultural, interpersonal, mass, and organizational.

Computer Science. Computer graphics, scientific computation, CAGD, image processing, computer vision, sensor simulation, knowledge-based information retrieval and classification, artificial intelligence, evolutionary computation, genetic algorithms and genetic programming, fuzzy reasoning, clustering algorithms, machine learning, Bayesian networks, stochastic optimization, software engineering.

Criminology and Criminal Justice. Criminological theory, social control, crime prevention, crime and social institutions, delinquency, violence, gangs, gender, race and ethnicity, victimization, offender decision making, policing, courts, corrections, prisoner re-entry, criminal and juvenile justice policy analysis, evaluation research, qualitative and quantitative methods.

Economics. Applied econometrics; microeconomics; macroeconomics; monetary theory; international trade and comparative systems; urban, state, and local finance; public sector; labor; public policy; law and economics; forensic economics; property rights; industrial organization; telecommunications; health economics; economics of aging; gender; poverty; science and technology.

Education. Instructional strategies; inclusion; ethics and character education; motivation in learning; evaluation of educational programs; counseling (school, community, and marriage/family); remedial and corrective reading; literacy; action research on teacher development; technology and learning; mathematics education (manipulatives); constructivism; behavioral disorder; performance-based assessment; motor development; postmodern thought and deconstruction; higher, adult, and vocational education; methodology, measurement, and assessment; urban education; school-university partnerships and community collaboration; positive behavior support; schoolwide systems of discipline.

English (M.A.) and Creative Writing (M.F.A.). Chaucer, Milton, Shakespeare, medieval, early modern, eighteenth-century, Victorian, American, modern British, and Jewish literature; literary theory; feminist theory; composition theory; creative writing in fiction and poetry; linguistics.

Gerontology. Social security and other pension policies; caregiving and other informal support of the elderly; mental health assessment and treatment; ethnic differences, particularly in health-care behavior; cross-cultural comparisons of retirement patterns and policies; driving assessment and intervention in older adults.

History. United States social and political; nineteenth-century; twentieth-century; African-American; women; slavery and emancipation; urban; environmental; military; St. Louis, Missouri; Native American; German-American ethnic; American West; Roman Empire; European-medieval; eighteenth-century French, German, Spanish, English; economic; women; Renaissance and Reformation; medieval; African; East Asian—Japan, China, Asian-Pacific Rim; Latin American colonial; nineteenth- and twentieth-century sports; museum studies.

Mathematics. Wavelets and computational harmonic analysis, splines and approximation theory, subdivision methods for computer graphics, medical imaging, computational mathematics, string theory, algebraic geometry, differential geometry, transformation groups, statistics, stochastic processes.

Music Education. Psychology of music, application of technology in music education, tests and measurements in music, conducting, choral and instrumental performance, music education curriculum design, affective response to music, music supervision and administration, music software design, urban music education, arts education.

Nursing. Adherence to health treatment, catastrophic stress, exercise and hypertension, informatics and telemetry in health care, psychosocial nursing interventions, quantitative methods in nursing research, injuries and violence as a health problem, women's health.

Philosophy. Ethics (contemporary ethical theory and bioethics), philosophy and history of science (philosophy of medicine and ancient Greek and medieval Arabic traditions), history of philosophy, aesthetics (aesthetic appreciation and environmental aesthetics).

Physics. Astrophysics, observational astronomy, experimental atomic physics, biophysics, theoretical elementary particle physics, experimental and theoretical solid-state physics, nanoscale microscopy.

Physiological Optics (vision science). Aging and Alzheimer's disease, binocular vision in children and adults, contact lenses, control of eye movements, electrophysiology in healthy and diseased visual systems, low vision, mathematical approaches to vision, neurophysiology of visual and oculomotor pathways, public health, theoretical and applied visual optics, theoretical and applied visual psychophysics.

Political Science. American government and politics; political economy; public administration and public policy; urban politics and urban economic development; program evaluation; public law and judicial politics; public opinion and elections; methodology; labor relations; political thought; international law and organization; civil liberties; comparative politics; comparative health policy; environmental politics; interpersonal politics; minority politics; policy implementation and evaluation; political communication; African, Chinese, Japanese, and Latin American politics; Western and Eastern European politics.

Psychology–Clinical. Role of culture in mental health, anxiety disorders, post-traumatic stress disorder, relationship between anxiety and physical health, childhood problems, psychology and religion, development of ACT use with children/adolescents, women and sexuality, interventions for family dementia caregiving, issues of aging in place.

Psychology–Behavioral Neuroscience. Neuroendocrinology, neuropharmacology, cognitive processes, cognitive aging, neuropsychology, neuroimaging, psychophysiology, animal cognition.

Psychology–Industrial/Organizational. Recruitment, interviewing, personality, performance appraisal, compensation and benefits, diversity and discrimination, global issues, work-family conflict, time management, job attitudes, motivation, person by situation fit, competitive climate, mentoring, group processes, leadership, psychometrics, statistics, applied measurement issues, research methodology, social psychology, nonverbal communication.

Public Policy Administration. Managing human resources and organization, policy research and analysis, local government management, health policy, nonprofit organization management and leadership, metropolitan governance, urban and regional planning, welfare policy, social security policy, organization theory, government contracting for services, performance measurement, program evaluation, conflict resolution, defense conversion, labor economics, public-sector microeconomics.

Social Work. Urban-related research issues, family violence, social welfare, gerontology, child abuse and neglect, immigration, substance abuse and minorities, community economic development, international social welfare, addiction, disabilities.

Sociology. Minority groups, stratification, deviance, comparative social organization, health, social psychology, conflict intervention, aging, race and ethnic relations, education, interpersonal violence.

Women's and Gender Studies. Women's and gender issues, feminist and gender theory.

Programs of Study

The Graduate College at the University of Nevada, Las Vegas (UNLV), strives to advance its mission of becoming a premier metropolitan research university by supporting excellent graduate programs that focus on student interests, as well as issues of importance to the community, state, and region. Graduate education at UNLV is guided by an institutional commitment to the support of students through both the provision of administrative and financial assistance and the creation of enhanced learning opportunities through research, scholarly endeavors, and creative activity. Through its ten schools and colleges, UNLV offers more than 100 graduate degree programs, including thirty-four doctoral and professional degrees.

The College of Business offers the following programs and degrees: accountancy, M.S.; business administration, M.B.A., Executive M.B.A.; business administration/dental medicine, dual M.B.A./D.M.D.*; business administration/hotel administration, dual M.B.A./M.S.*; business administration/law, dual M.B.A./J.D.*; economics, M.A.; management information systems, M.S.; and management information systems/business administration, dual M.S./M.B.A.* The College of Education offers the following programs and degrees: curriculum and instruction, M.Ed., M.S., Ed.S., Ed.D., Ph.D.; counseling, M.S., M.Ed.; early childhood education, M.Ed.; educational leadership, M.Ed., M.S., Ed.S., Ed.D., Ph.D., Executive Ed.D.; educational psychology, M.S., Ed.S., Ph.D.; learning and technology, Ph.D.; special education, M.Ed., M.S., Ed.S., Ed.D., Ph.D.; and sports education leadership/physical education, M.Ed., M.S., Ph.D. The College of Engineering offers the following programs and degrees: aerospace engineering, M.S.; biomedical engineering, M.S.; civil and environmental engineering, M.S., Ph.D.; computer science, M.S., Ph.D.; construction management, M.S.; electrical and computer engineering, M.S., Ph.D.; informatics, M.S., Ph.D.; materials and nuclear engineering, M.S.; mechanical engineering, M.S., Ph.D.; and transportation, M.S. The College of Fine Arts offers the following programs and degrees: architecture, M.Arch.; art, M.F.A.; film/screenwriting, M.F.A.; music, M.M.; musical arts, D.M.A.; and theater, M.A., M.F.A. The Division of Health Sciences offers the following programs and degrees: dental medicine, D.M.D.; dental medicine/business administration, dual D.M.D./M.B.A.*; exercise physiology, M.S.; health-care administration, M.H.A.; health physics, M.S.; health promotion, M.Ed.; kinesiology, M.S.; nursing, M.S.N., Ph.D.; physical therapy, D.P.T.; and public health, M.P.H. The College of Hotel Administration offers the following programs and degrees: executive hospitality administration, M.H.A.; hospitality administration, Ph.D.; hotel administration, M.S.; hotel administration/business administration, dual M.S./M.B.A.*; and recreation and sports management, M.S. The William S. Boyd School of Law offers the following programs and degrees: juris doctorate, J.D.; juris doctorate/social work, dual J.D./M.S.W.*; and juris doctorate/business administration, dual J.D./M.B.A.* The College of Liberal Arts offers the following programs and degrees: anthropology, M.A., Ph.D.; creative writing, M.F.A.; English, M.A., Ph.D.; ethics and policy studies, M.A.; foreign languages and literature, M.A.; history, M.A., Ph.D.; political science, M.A.; psychology, M.A., Ph.D.; and sociology, M.A., Ph.D. The College of Sciences offers the following programs and degrees: astronomy, M.S., Ph.D.; biochemistry, M.S.; biological sciences, M.S., Ph.D.; chemistry, M.S., Ph.D.; geoscience, M.S., Ph.D.; mathematical sciences, M.S., Ph.D.; physics, M.S., Ph.D.; radiochemistry, Ph.D.; science, M.A.; and water resource management, M.S. The College of Urban Affairs offers the following programs and degrees: communication studies, M.A.; criminal justice, M.A.; crisis and emergency management, M.S.; environmental studies, M.S., Ph.D.; journalism and media studies, M.A.; juris doctorate/social work, dual J.D./M.S.W.*; public administration, M.P.A.; public affairs, Ph.D.; and social work, M.S.W. Graduate certificate programs are offered in addiction studies, family nurse practitioner studies, food and beverage management, forensic social work, marriage and family therapy, nursing education, public management, rehabilitation counseling, Spanish translation, and women's studies.

* These programs are offered jointly with other departments and require full admission into each program.

Research Facilities

The integration of the University's research and graduate program management into the Division of Research and Graduate Studies supports UNLV's commitment to high-quality graduate education. This structure strategically links the ongoing development of UNLV's research infrastructure with the Graduate College directly and enhances research opportunities for graduate students. UNLV has nearly seventy research centers, laboratories, and museums, including, but not limited to, the International Institute of Modern Letters, International Gaming Institute, Harry Reid Center for Environmental Studies, Nevada Institute for Children, Nevada Center for Advanced Computation Methods, Nevada Small Business Development Center, Center for American Indian Research and Education, Center for Energy Research, Center for Business and Economic Research, Center for Health Disparities Research, Center for Urban Horticulture and Water Conservation, Center for Urban Partnerships, and Center for Volcanic and Tectonic Studies.

UNLV also houses the National Supercomputing Center for Energy and the Environment (NSCEE). Funded through the Department of Energy, the NSCEE has national network accessibility. It provides supercomputing training and services to academic and research institutions and government and private industry for research and development related to energy, the environment, medical informatics, and health-care delivery.

The computer facility located on the campus is part of the University of Nevada System Computing Network. UNLV computers are linked through the network to computers at the University of Nevada, Reno, and at Clark County Community College. Time-sharing terminals, remote batch terminals, and local batch terminals give students and faculty members access to the computer network.

UNLV's new, state-of-the-art Lied Library, one of the most technologically sophisticated in the U.S., contains more than 1 million volumes and occupies more than 300,000 square feet within five stories. UNLV has additional libraries for the disciplines of curriculum and instruction, music, and architecture.

Financial Aid

Financial assistance for graduate students is available in a variety of forms, including competitive graduate teaching and research assistantships that provide partial tuition waivers, generous stipends, optional health insurance, and valuable teaching, administrative, and/or research experience. Generally, assistantships are valued at $10,000 to $12,000 per academic year. In addition, fellowships, scholarships, fee waivers, Federal Work-Study Program awards, Federal Perkins Loans, Federal Stafford Student Loans, Nevada Incentive Grants, and many other opportunities are also available.

Cost of Study

For the 2007–08 academic year, residents and nonresidents pay a $173-per-credit fee for graduate courses. Full-time nonresident tuition (7 or more credits) is $5405 per semester, plus a $173-per-credit fee for graduate courses.

Living and Housing Costs

On-campus housing costs include room and board. Nine dorms are available. Off-campus housing can be found close to the University; the cost of rent averages between $600 and $1000 per month.

Student Group

Graduate and professional students make up more than 6,000 of UNLV's 28,000 students. UNLV has a socially and ethnically diverse student population, as students who are members of minority groups make up more than 30 percent of the student body, and more than 56 percent of students are women. Graduate students come from all fifty states in the U.S. and fifty-eight other countries. UNLV's programs are designed for traditional and nontraditional, full-time and part-time students. The median age for graduate and professional students is 29 years, and many work full-time while attending UNLV.

Location

Las Vegas is on the southern tip of Nevada in a desert valley surrounded by mountains. The main campus is surrounded by apartments, restaurants, shopping centers, parks, libraries, hospitals, and other facilities of this dynamic city of more than 1.3 million residents.

Within a 30-mile radius lie the shores of Lake Mead, the massive Hoover Dam, the Colorado River recreation area, the snow-skiing and hiking trails of 12,000-foot Mount Charleston, and a panorama of red-rock mountains and eroded sandstone landscapes. In addition, the city is only 4 to 5 hours by car from the beaches of southern California and the national parks of Utah and Arizona.

The University

UNLV's beautiful, modern main campus is located on 340 acres in dynamic southern Nevada. The University has grown dramatically since its founding in 1957. Recently, the University has expanded to include the Shadow Lane Campus and the UNLV Harry Reid Research and Technology Park, both of which are also located in Las Vegas. The University is a member of the American Association of State Colleges and Universities, the Council of Graduate Schools, the Western Association of Graduate Schools, the American Council on Education, and the Western College Association. All programs are fully accredited by the Northwest Association of Schools and Colleges, and many have disciplinary and professional accreditation as well. UNLV's more than 800 full-time professors bring degrees and teaching experience from leading universities around the world. Faculty members are involved in important research for government and public service agencies and for scholarly books and journals. Many faculty members have won major awards. UNLV has two semesters (fall and spring) of approximately sixteen weeks each and three summer sessions.

Applying

Minimum requirements for admission include a completed admissions application, official transcripts from all postsecondary institutions attended, a bachelor's degree from an accredited four-year college or university, and a minimum cumulative GPA of 2.75 for the bachelor's degree or 3.0 for the last two years of work. Each academic department has its own additional admissions requirements, such as letters of recommendation, adequate undergraduate prerequisite courses, and/or a writing sample. Many programs require acceptable scores from standardized tests, including scores from the Graduate Record Examinations, Graduate Management Admission Test, or Miller Analogies Test. International students must achieve a minimum score of 80 on the Internet-based Test of English as a Foreign Language.

Correspondence and Information

Graduate College
University of Nevada, Las Vegas
4505 Maryland Parkway, Box 1017
Las Vegas, Nevada 89154-1017

Phone: 702-895-3320
E-mail: gradcollege@ccmail.nevada.edu
Web site: http://graduatecollege.unlv.edu

FACULTY HEADS AND DEPARTMENT CONTACT NUMBERS

Graduate College
Ron Smith, Ph.D., Vice President for Research and Graduate Dean.
Kate Hausbeck, Ph.D., Senior Associate Dean.
Harriet E. Barlow, Ph.D., Associate Dean for Graduate Student Services.

College of Business
Richard Flaherty, Ph.D., Dean.
Accounting: 702-895-1559.
Business Administration: 702-895-1025.
Economics: 702-895-3776.
Management Information Systems: 702-895-3796.

College of Education
Christopher Brown, Ph.D., Dean.
Counselor Education: 702-895-5994.
Curriculum and Instruction: 702-895-3241.
Educational Leadership: 702-895-3491.
Educational Psychology: 702-895-3253.
Special Education: 702-895-3250.
Sports Education Leadership: 702-895-5057.

College of Engineering
Eric Sandgren, Ph.D., Dean.
Civil and Environmental Engineering: 702-895-3071.
School of Computer Science: 702-895-3681.
Electrical and Computer Engineering: 702-895-4183.
School of Informatics: 702-895-3699.
Mechanical Engineering: 702-895-1331.

College of Fine Arts
Jeff Koep, Ph.D., Dean.
Architecture: 702-895-3031.
Art: 702-895-3237.
Film: 702-895-3547.
Music: 702-895-3332.
Theater: 702-895-3666.

Division of Health Sciences
School of Allied Health Sciences: 702-895-3693.
School of Dental Medicine: 702-774-2500.
Environmental and Occupational Health: 702-895-5420.
Health-Care Administration: 702-895-5410.
Health Physics: 702-895-4320.
Health Promotion: 702-895-4030.
Kinesiology: 702-895-3289.
School of Nursing: 702-895-3906.
Physical Therapy: 702-895-3003.
School of Public Health: 702-895-5090.

College of Hotel Administration
Stuart H. Mann, Ph.D., Dean.
Graduate Studies: 702-895-3321.
Sport and Leisure Service Management: 702-895-1188.

William S. Boyd School of Law
John Valery White, J.D., Dean.

College of Liberal Arts
Christopher Hudgins, Ph.D., Interim Dean.
Anthropology: 702-895-3590.
English: 702-895-3533.
Ethics and Policy Studies: 702-895-3307.
Foreign Languages: 702-895-3431.
History: 702-895-3349.
Political Science: 702-895-3307.
Psychology: 702-895-3305.
Sociology: 702-895-3322.

College of Science
Ronald Yasbin, Ph.D., Dean.
Chemistry: 702-895-3510.
Geoscience: 702-895-3262.
School of Life Sciences: 702-895-3390.
Mathematical Sciences: 702-895-0396.
Physics: 702-895-3563.

College of Urban Affairs
Martha Watson, Ph.D., Dean.
Communication Studies: 702-895-5125.
Criminal Justice: 702-895-0236.
Environmental Studies: 702-895-4440.
Journalism and Media Studies: 702-895-3270.
Marriage and Family Therapy: 702-895-1867.
Public Administration: 702-895-4828.
School of Social Work: 702-895-3311.

The central corridor of the campus contains (from left to right) Grant Hall, Dungan Humanities Building, Dickinson Library, Carlson Education Building, and Ham Hall.

UNIVERSITY OF NEW HAMPSHIRE

Graduate School

Programs of Study

The University of New Hampshire (UNH) Graduate School offers the Doctor of Philosophy degree in animal and nutritional sciences, biochemistry, chemistry (education), computer science, earth and environmental sciences (geology, oceanography), economics, education, engineering (chemical, civil, electrical, materials, mechanical, ocean, systems design), English, genetics, history, mathematics, mathematics education, microbiology, natural resources and environmental studies, physics, plant biology, psychology, sociology, and zoology.

Master's degree programs include the Master of Arts in counseling, economics, English (language and linguistics, literature), environmental education, history (museum studies), justice studies, music (music education, music studies), political science, sociology, and Spanish; Master of Arts in Liberal Studies; Master of Science in accounting, animal sciences, biochemistry, chemical engineering, chemistry, civil engineering, communication science and disorders (language and literacy, early childhood intervention), computer science, earth sciences (geology, ocean mapping, oceanography), electrical engineering, family studies (marriage and family therapy), genetics, hydrology, kinesiology, materials science, mathematics (applied mathematics, statistics), mechanical engineering, microbiology, natural resources (environmental conservation, forestry, soil science, water resources, wildlife), nursing, nutritional sciences, occupational therapy, ocean engineering (ocean mapping), physics, plant biology, recreation management and policy (recreation administration, therapeutic recreation administration), resource administration and management, resource economics, and zoology; Master of Education in administration and supervision, counseling, early childhood education (special needs), elementary education, reading, secondary education, special education, and teacher leadership; Master of Arts in Teaching in elementary education and secondary education; Master of Science for Teachers in chemistry, college teaching, English, and mathematics (summer only); Master of Business Administration (day, evening, and executive programs); Master of Fine Arts (painting, writing); Master of Public Administration; Master of Public Health; and Master of Social Work.

The Certificate of Advanced Graduate Study is offered in educational administration and supervision.

Research Facilities

Modern research facilities for both basic and applied research are extensive. Organized research units include: the Agricultural Experiment Station; the Biomolecular Interaction Technologies Center (BITC); the Center for Business and Economic Research; the Center for Coastal and Ocean Mapping Joint Hydrographic Center; the Center for Freshwater Biology; the Center for Humanities; the Center for Venture Research; the Center to Advance Molecular Interaction Science (CAMIS); the Cooperative Institute for Coastal and Estuarine Environmental Technology (CICEET); the Crimes Against Children Research Center; the Environmental Research Group (ERG) (Bedrock Bioremediation Center, Recycled Materials Resource Center, Water Treatment Technology Assistance Center); the Family Research Laboratory; the Hamel Center for the Management of Technology and Innovation; the Hubbard Center for Genome Studies; the Institute for Policy and Social Science Research; the Institute for the Study of Earth, Oceans, and Space EOS (Climate Change Research Center, Complex Systems Research Center, Ocean Process Analysis Laboratory, Space Science Center); the Institute on Disability; the Instrumentation Center; the Joint Hydrographic Center; Justiceworks; the Marine Program (Center for Marine Biology, Center for Ocean Engineering, Center for Ocean Sciences); the New Hampshire Industrial Research Center; the New Hampshire Institute for Health Policy and Practice; the Nanostructured Polymers Research Center (Advanced Polymer Laboratory, Polymer Nanoparticle Laboratory, Polymer Research Group); the Research Computing Center (CATlab, InterOperability Lab); the Robotics Laboratory; the Sea Grant College Program; the Shoals Marine Laboratory; the UNH Survey Center; the Water Resource Research Center; and the William Rosenberg International Center of Franchising.

The Dimond Library houses more than 1.1 million volumes, more than 6,500 periodicals, and substantial microfilm collections. Specialized collections are housed in the chemistry, engineering and mathematics, biological sciences, and physics departments.

Financial Aid

Graduate assistantships paid a base stipend of $13,500 for the 2006–07 academic year. Students on assistantships receive a tuition waiver and health insurance. Tuition scholarships are available to both full- and part-time students.

Cost of Study

Tuition for the 2006–07 academic year was $8540 for New Hampshire residents and $20,990 for nonresidents. Engineering and computer science students pay an additional $533 for the academic year. Accounting and economics students pay an additional $583 for the academic year. Mandatory fees are $1400 per year. Tuition and fees for part-time students are prorated.

Living and Housing Costs

Babcock House, the graduate residence hall, provides single rooms at a cost of $5654 for the academic year. Meal contracts are available, and students may remain in the house during the summer at special reduced rates. Limited on-campus housing for married students is provided at Forest Park. Prices for studio and one- or two-bedroom apartments range from $608 to $993 per month. Off-campus apartments are available at a wide range of prices.

Student Group

The University enrolls approximately 11,500 undergraduate students and 2,400 graduate students.

Location

The University is located in Durham, one of the oldest towns in northern New England. Its easy accessibility to Boston's cultural opportunities (65 miles south); to the unsurpassed skiing, hiking, and scenery in the White Mountains (60 miles northwest); and to the sandy beaches and rocky coast of New Hampshire and Maine (10 miles east) makes it an ideal location.

The University

The University was founded in 1866 as a land-grant college. In 1980, it was designated jointly with the University of Maine as a sea-grant college. In 1991, it was designated as a space-grant college together with Dartmouth. The University occupies a picturesque 200-acre campus, with seventy-four buildings devoted to teaching, research, and service; it serves as the cultural and scientific center for southeastern New Hampshire. Graduate education has been carefully planned by the faculty to provide programs of moderate size and high quality. The Graduate School is nationally recognized for its Preparing Future Faculty program.

Applying

Application deadlines vary by program. Applications from international students are considered for admission for the fall session only and must be completed by April 1. The application for admission also serves as the application for assistantships and scholarships. Prospective graduate students applying for financial assistance should file an application before February 15 to ensure consideration for the following year. Individual programs may require the GRE or GMAT. Scores on the TOEFL are required of all applicants whose native language is not English. Students should apply early since many programs are filled before the published deadlines.

Correspondence and Information

Graduate School
University of New Hampshire
105 Main Street
Durham, New Hampshire 03824-3547

Phone: 603-862-3000
E-mail: grad.school@unh.edu
Web site: http://www.gradschool.unh.edu

DEANS AND PROGRAM COORDINATORS

Harry J. Richards, Dean; Ph.D., Florida State.
Cari Moorhead, Associate Dean; Ph.D., New Hampshire.
Dovev L. Levine, Coordinator for Recruitment and Retention; M.S., Northeastern.

The following individuals should be contacted for specific information on admissions and financial assistance in their respective program.

Accounting: George T. Abraham, Director of Graduate and Executive Programs; M.Ed., New Hampshire.
Animal Science: Dennis J. Bobilya, Associate Professor; Ph.D., Missouri.
Biochemistry: Clyde L. Denis, Professor; Ph.D., Washington.
Business Administration: George T. Abraham, Director of Graduate and Executive Programs; M.Ed., New Hampshire.
Chemical Engineering: Stephen S. T. Fan, Professor; Ph.D., Stanford.
Chemistry: Sterling A. Tomellini, Professor; Ph.D., Rutgers.
Civil Engineering: Michael R. Collins, Professor; Ph.D., Arizona.
Communication Sciences and Disorders: Frederick C. Lewis, Associate Professor; Ph.D., Ohio.
Computer Science: James L. Weiner, Associate Professor; Ph.D., UCLA.
Earth Sciences (Geology, Hydrology, Ocean Mapping, Oceanography): William C. Clyde, Professor; Ph.D., Michigan.
Economics: George T. Abraham, Director of Graduate and Executive Programs; M.Ed., New Hampshire.
Education: Ruth M. Wharton-McDonald, Associate Professor; Ph.D., SUNY at Albany.
Electrical Engineering: Kent A. Chamberlin, Professor; Ph.D., Ohio.
English: Michael K. Ferber, Professor; Ph.D., Harvard.
Environmental Education: Ruth M. Wharton-McDonald, Associate Professor; Ph.D., SUNY at Albany.
Family Studies (Marriage and Family Therapy): Kerry Kazura, Associate Professor; Ph.D., Auburn.
Genetics: Estelle M. Hrabak, Associate Professor; Ph.D., Wisconsin.
History: Ellen Fitzpatrick, Professor; Ph.D., Brandeis.
Justice Studies: Todd DeMitchell, Professor; Ph.D., USC.
Kinesiology: Ronald V. Croce, Professor; Ph.D., New Mexico.
Liberal Studies: David Andrew, Professor; Ph.D., Washington (St. Louis).
Materials Science: Olof Echt, Professor; Ph.D., Konstanz (Germany).
Mathematics: Rita A. Hibschweiler, Professor; Ph.D., SUNY at Albany.
Mathematics Education: Karen Graham, Professor; Ph.D., New Hampshire.
Mechanical Engineering: Igor Tsukrov, Associate Professor; Ph.D., Tufts.
Microbiology: Cheryl A. Whistler, Assistant Professor; Ph.D., Oregon State.
Music: Robert Stibler, Professor; D.M.A., Catholic University.
Natural Resources (Environmental Conservation, Forestry, Soil Science, Water Resources, Wildlife): Russell Congalton, Professor; Ph.D., Virginia Tech.
Natural Resources and Earth Systems Science: Sara Head, Program Coordinator; M.Ed., Plymouth.
Nursing: Lynette Ament, Associate Professor; Ph.D., Wisconsin.
Nutritional Sciences: Dennis J. Bobilya, Associate Professor; Ph.D., Missouri.
Occupational Therapy: Elizabeth L. Crepeau, Professor; Ph.D., New Hampshire.
Ocean Engineering (Ocean Mapping): Kenneth C. Baldwin, Professor; Ph.D., Rhode Island.
Painting: Craig A. Hood, Associate Professor; M.F.A., Indiana Bloomington; and Jennifer K. Moses, Associate Professor; M.F.A., Indiana Bloomington.
Physics: Per Berglund, Assistant Professor; Ph.D., Texas.
Plant Biology: James E. Pollard, Associate Professor; Ph.D., Florida.
Political Science: Aline M. Kuntz, Associate Professor; Ph.D., Cornell; and Stacy VanDeveer, Associate Professor; Ph.D., Maryland.
Psychology: Robert C. Drugan, Associate Professor; Ph.D., Colorado.
Public Administration: Melvin Dubnick, Professor; Ph.D., Colorado.
Public Health: James B. Lewis, Associate Professor; Ph.D., Johns Hopkins.
Recreation Management and Policy (Recreation Administration, Therapeutic Recreation): Lou G. Powell, Professor; Re.D., Indiana Bloomington.
Resource Administration and Management: John M. Halstead, Professor; Ph.D., Virginia Tech.
Resource Economics: Douglas E. Morris, Associate Professor; Ph.D., Oklahoma State.
Social Work: Jerry D. Marx, Associate Professor; Ph.D., Boston College.
Sociology: Michele Dillon, Associate Professor; Ph.D., Berkeley.
Spanish: Marti-Olivella, Assistant Professor; Ph.D., Illinois.
Systems Design: Igor Tsukrov, Associate Professor; Ph.D., Tufts.
Zoology: Michelle P. Scott, Professor; Ph.D., Harvard.

UNIVERSITY OF NEW HAVEN

UNIVERSITY OF NEW HAVEN

Graduate Studies

Programs of Study

The University of New Haven (UNH) offers Master of Arts degree programs in community psychology and industrial/organizational psychology. The Master of Business Administration program has eight available areas of concentration, including options in accounting, business policy and strategic leadership, finance, global marketing and e-commerce, human resource management, sports management, a fifth-year CPA exam track, and a track for prospective chartered financial analyst (CFA) candidates. Dual-degree programs allow students to earn both the M.B.A. and the Master of Science in Industrial Engineering and both the M.B.A. and the Master of Public Administration. An Executive M.B.A. degree program is also offered by the University. This program is designed for experienced, upper-level executives and managers.

The Master of Science degree is offered in the areas of cellular and molecular biology, computer science, criminal justice, education, electrical engineering, environmental engineering, environmental science, engineering management, fire science, forensic science, health-care administration, human nutrition, industrial engineering, labor relations, management of sports industries, mechanical engineering, national security and public safety, and taxation. The Master of Public Administration degree is also offered.

Research Facilities

The holdings of the Marvin K. Peterson Library include more than 244,000 volumes and 1,400 print journals and newspaper subscriptions; electronic access to more than 17,940 full-text journal and newspaper titles; U.S. government documents; and numerous corporate annual reports, pamphlet files, and microfilm as well as current and extensive back-issue files of periodicals. Interlibrary loan search and other resources are available through OCLC, First Search, LexisNexis, Dialog, Dow Jones News/Retrieval, and CD-ROM systems.

The UNH Center for Computing Services provides both administrative and academic computing support. Administrators, faculty members, and students have access to the latest in computer technology. Personal computers for student use are spread throughout the campus, with the largest concentration located at the Center for Computing Services. In addition, the Computer-Aided Engineering Center laboratory in the Tagliatela College of Engineering houses workstations plus micros connected by an Ethernet LAN. Graphics, printing and plotting devices, laser printing, and a wide variety of data files, software, and simulation packages are also available.

Financial Aid

Financial aid is available for graduate students through assistantships and loans. The University participates in Federal Stafford Student Loan programs.

Cost of Study

Tuition for master's degree students for the 2006–07 academic year was $595 per graduate credit or $1785 per course for most graduate courses. The Graduate Student Council fee is $45 per year, and there is a $20 technology fee each term. All charges and fees are subject to change.

Living and Housing Costs

There is no on-campus housing for graduate students, but the Office of Residential Life maintains a listing of apartments in the local area at a variety of costs.

Student Group

Many students are from Connecticut, but each year an increasing number come from other states and many other countries. The graduate student body of more than 1,700 ranges from recent college graduates to professionals with several years of experience in their fields. About 51 percent of the graduate students are women, about 12 percent receive some sort of financial aid, approximately 12 percent are international students, and nearly 12 percent are members of minority groups. Graduates are employed in government service, teaching, private agencies, and business.

Location

The University of New Haven maintains a close relationship with the surrounding community. Although the campus is located in West Haven, it is less than 3 miles from downtown New Haven and students can easily take advantage of the cultural offerings of the city. New Haven has rail, bus, and air service, and its location at the junction of two major interstate highways places the school within easy driving distance of New York, Boston, and Providence.

The University

The University of New Haven was founded in 1920 and is accredited as a general-purpose institution by the New England Association of Schools and Colleges. A number of graduate classes are held at several off-campus locations across the state as well as in Virginia and California. Most graduate classes are held in the early evening to accommodate both part-time and full-time students.

Applying

Applicants must hold a baccalaureate degree from an accredited college or university. An applicant for admission to the Graduate School must submit the following before the initial registration: a formal application; a nonrefundable $50 application fee; letters of recommendation; final official transcripts from all previous college work. In addition, a satisfactory TOEFL score (except for students whose native language is English) and certified financial support forms are required for all international students. In some programs, students may be required to take a specific standardized test as part of the application process. All correspondence and requests for materials should be directed to the Graduate Admissions Office. Descriptions of programs and procedures are available in the *Graduate Catalog*. Information about the University of New Haven is available on the Web site.

Correspondence and Information

Office of Graduate Admissions
University of New Haven
300 Boston Post Road
West Haven, Connecticut 06516
Phone: 203-932-7133 (option 5)
800-DIAL-UNH (toll-free)
Fax: 203-932-7137
E-mail: gradinfo@newhaven.edu
Web site: http://www.newhaven.edu

FACULTY HEADS

The faculty consists of approximately 470 full- and part-time professors. The coordinators for the various graduate programs and the Associate Provost for Graduate Studies are listed below.

Graduate School: Ira Kleinfeld, Associate Provost for Graduate Studies, Research, and Faculty Development; Eng.Sc.D., Columbia.
Business Administration/Industrial Engineering (dual degree): Alexis N. Sommers, Ph.D., Purdue.
Business Administration/Public Administration (dual degree): Charles N. Coleman, M.P.A., West Virginia.
Cellular and Molecular Biology: Eva Sapi, Ph.D., Eötvös Loránd (Budapest).
Community Psychology: Michael Morris, Ph.D., Boston College.
Computer Science: Tahany Fergany, Ph.D., Connecticut.
Criminal Justice: James Cassidy, Ph.D., Hahnemann.
Education: Paulette Pepin, Ph.D., Fordham.
Electrical Engineering: Bouzid Aliane, Ph.D., Polytechnic.
Engineering Management: Barry J. Farbrother, C.Eng., Hertfordshire (UK).
Environmental Engineering: Agamemnon D. Koutsospyros, Ph.D., Polytechnic.
Environmental Science: Roman N. Zajac, Ph.D., Connecticut.
Executive Master of Business Administration: Raja Nag, Ph.D., Connecticut.
Fire Science: Robert E. Massicotte Jr., M.S., New Haven.
Forensic Science: Carol A. Scherczinger, Ph.D., Connecticut.
Health-Care Administration: Charles N. Coleman, M.P.A., West Virginia.
Human Nutrition: Rosa Mo, Ed.D., Columbia.
Industrial Engineering: Alexis Sommers, Ph.D., Purdue.
Industrial/Organizational Psychology: Stuart Sidle, Ph.D., DePaul.
Labor Relations: Charles N. Coleman, M.P.A., West Virginia.
Management of Sports Industries: Allen Sack, Ph.D., Penn State.
M.B.A./Business Administration: Charles N. Coleman, Coordinator; M.P.A., West Virginia.
Mechanical Engineering: Konstantine C. Lambrakis, Ph.D., Rensselaer.
National Security and Public Safety: Thomas A. Johnson, D.Crim., Berkeley.
Public Administration: Charles N. Coleman, M.P.A., West Virginia.

Students enjoy easy access to laboratory facilities furnished with modern equipment, data acquisition systems, and software.

UNH engineering students have access to the latest technology in several fully equipped, state-of-the-art learning environments.

The Forensic Science Program, one of the finest in the world, supports extensive well-equipped labs for hands-on work with modern equipment and instruments used in this profession.

UNIVERSITY OF NEW MEXICO

Graduate Studies

Programs of Study

The University of New Mexico (UNM) offers programs of study leading to the Ph.D. in American studies; anthropology; art history; biology; biomedical sciences; chemistry and chemical biology; communication; computer science; counseling; earth and planetary sciences; economics; educational linguistics; educational psychology; engineering; English; family studies; French studies; history; language, literature, and sociocultural studies (LLSS); Latin American studies; linguistics; mathematics; multicultural teacher and childhood education; nanoscience and microsystems; nursing; optical sciences and engineering; organizational learning and instructional technology; pharmaceutical sciences; philosophy; physical education, sports, and exercise science (PESES); physics; political science; psychology; sociology; Spanish and Portuguese; special education; and statistics. The Doctor of Education (Ed.D.) is offered in educational leadership, multicultural teacher and childhood education, and special education. Master of Fine Arts degrees include concentrations in art studio, creative writing, dance, and dramatic writing. Master's degrees are offered in all of the above programs except educational linguistics; physical education, sports, and exercise science; and multicultural teacher education as well as the following: accounting and business administration, architecture, art education, chemical and nuclear engineering, civil engineering, clinical laboratory science, community and regional planning, comparative literature, computer engineering, construction management, electrical engineering, elementary education, French, geography, German studies, hazardous-waste engineering, health education, landscape architecture, manufacturing engineering, mechanical engineering, music, nursing, nutrition, occupational therapy, physical education, physical therapy, Portuguese, public administration, public health, secondary education, Spanish, speech-language pathology, theater and dance, and water resources.

There are four Educational Specialist Certificates in the College of Education (sixth-year program): curriculum and instruction (elementary and secondary), educational leadership, organizational learning and instructional technologies, and special education.

Transcripted certificate programs include computational science and engineering, historic preservation and regionalism, post-M.B.A. in management, post-master's in nursing, system engineering, town design, and women's studies.

Formalized and individualized dual-degree programs are also offered. The University operates on an academic year of two semesters and two summer sessions.

Research Facilities

The University Libraries comprise the Zimmerman Library, the Center for Academic Program Support, the Center for Southwest Research, the Centennial Science and Engineering Library, the Fine Arts Library, and the William J. Parish Business and Economics Library. The University Libraries' collections contain 1.6 million cataloged volumes, 17,000 currently received journals, 5 million microform items, and vast quantities of archival material of all types. These resources provide study and research facilities for graduate students in specialized fields in which graduate work is offered. Library faculty members teach graduate courses. In addition, the Law Library, the Health Sciences Center Library, and the Tireman Learning Materials Library provide excellent reference sources. Specialized research facilities include the Centers for Alcohol and Substance Abuse, Learning and Research in Integrative Studies, Health Sciences, Mental Illness and Neuroscience Discovery Institute, High Performance Computing and Education and Research, the Robert Wood Johnson Center for Health Policy, High Technology Materials, Microelectronics Research, Micro-Engineering Ceramics, and Radioactive Waste Management. Other research units include the Institute for Applied Research Services, Institute for Astrophysics, Addiction and Substance Abuse Programs, BRaIN Imaging Center, Cancer Research & Treatment Center, Center for Disaster Medicine, Center for Environmental Health Sciences, Center for Telehealth, Center of Biomedical Research Excellence, Center on Aging, Children's Hospital Heart Center, Clinical Trials Center, General Clinical Research Center, Geriatric Education Center, HSC Institute for Ethics, New Mexico AIDS Education and Training Center, New Mexico Immunization Coalition, New Mexico Poison Center, Sleep Disorders Center, School of Medicine Center for Community Partnerships, Speech/Language/Swallow Center, Institute for Environmental Education, Latin American and Iberian Institute, New Mexico Engineering Research Institute, Institute of Meteoritics, Institute for Organizational Communication, Training and Research Institute for Plastics, Institute for Public Policy, Institute for Social Research, Institute for Space and Nuclear Power Studies, Southwest Hispanic Research Institute, and UNM Business Link. Special research opportunities exist with the Air Force Research Laboratories and the Sandia and Los Alamos National Laboratories, which are located in Albuquerque and Los Alamos, respectively.

Financial Aid

Stipends for teaching and graduate assistantships range from $12,223 to $18,338 and post-master's stipends, from $13,445 to $20,167. These assistantships may also include a tuition waiver. In addition, research and project assistantships are available, with stipends based upon departmental guidelines and funding agency stipulations. The University of New Mexico also provides full payment of the assistantship recipient's insurance coverage. Interested students should contact the academic department or the Graduate Studies office concerning assistantships. A limited number of fellowships are also available.

Cost of Study

As of spring 2007, state residents paid $209.30 per credit hour, and nonresidents paid $640.05 per credit hour. Nonresident students taking 6 credit hours or fewer paid the resident rate of $209.30 per credit hour. For tuition and fees for the law, Pharm.D., and medicine programs, students should consult the UNM Bursar's Web site at http://unm.edu/~bursar. Tuition for dissertation students is $562 per semester for residents; nonresident dissertation students pay $562 for 1–6 credit hours, plus an additional $640.05 for each hour above 6 credit hours. All graduate, law, and medical students pay a fee of $25 per semester to the Graduate and Professional Student Association.

Living and Housing Costs

A limited number of residence hall accommodations are available for graduate students. The University also has 200 apartments for student families. Eligibility is limited to students enrolled for at least 6 credit hours. Annual living costs range from approximately $11,500 to $16,500 per year. Additional information may be obtained by contacting the Housing Reservations Office (505-277-2606).

Student Group

As of fall 2006, the total University student population on the main and branch campuses was approximately 32,350, with more than 5,844 (4,366 graduate only) graduate and professional degree–seeking students drawn from fifty states and seventy-five other countries. The average age of graduate students is 34. Numerous graduate courses are offered in the late afternoon and evening to accommodate the working student population. The University encourages and welcomes applications from members of U.S. groups that are underrepresented in higher education and from other countries.

Location

The University is situated in Albuquerque, a metropolitan area of more than 816,811 people and the center of much of the scientific development contributed by New Mexico to the atomic age. In a setting rich with the traditions of Indian, Spanish, Anglo, and African American cultures, the University of New Mexico continues to strive for new levels of excellence in its teaching, research, and service.

The University

Created by an act of the territorial legislature in 1889, the University of New Mexico began full-term instruction in 1892. In 1916, a Committee on Graduate Study was formed at the University to structure postgraduate programs that would allow students an opportunity to continue beyond their undergraduate education. The University is committed to providing its graduate students with a dedicated and distinguished faculty, up-to-date laboratories and libraries, and leading facilities that are equal to any in the region. The University has strong academic connections in the sciences and engineering with some of the world's best research laboratories, which are in proximity; these connections build on the state's historical association with advanced science and technology. The University and its programs are accredited by twenty-three separate accrediting bodies, and it is a charter member of both the Council of Graduate Schools in the United States and the Western Association of Graduate Schools.

Applying

Applicants for admission must submit a completed application, which may be obtained from the graduate unit in which the student is interested or completed online. A $50 application fee must be sent to the Office of Admissions or included with the online application, allowing sufficient time to meet departmental application deadlines. These deadlines vary; early application is encouraged. Information on graduate programs and assistantships may be obtained from the department of interest.

Correspondence and Information

To contact the Office of Graduate Studies:

Graduate Studies
MSC03 2180
1 University of New Mexico
Albuquerque, New Mexico 87131-0001
Phone: 505-277-2711
Web site: http://www.unm.edu/grad/

To send application materials:

Office of Admissions
ATTN: Graduate Admissions
University of New Mexico
P.O. Box 4849
Albuquerque, New Mexico 87196-4849
Web site: http://www.unm.edu/grad/admissions/onlineapps.html

FACULTY HEADS

Provost: Reed Dasenbrock, Ph.D., Johns Hopkins, 1982.
Acting Dean of Graduate Studies: Charles Fleddermann, Ph.D., Illinois at Urbana-Champaign, 1985.

Listed below are the chairpersons of the graduate departments, directors of divisions and programs, and deans of nondepartmentalized colleges.

Architecture and Planning
Dean: Roger Schluntz, M.Arch., Berkeley, 1968.
Architecture: Professor Geraldine Forbes Isais, M.Arch., California Polytechnic, San Luis Obispo, 1988.
Community and Regional Planning: Associate Professor David Henkel, Ph.D., Cornell, 1984.
Landscape Architecture: Associate Professor Alf Simon, Ph.D., Arizona State, 2002.

Arts and Sciences
Dean: Brenda Claiborne, Ph.D., California, San Diego.
American Studies: Professor Gabriel Meléndez, Ph.D., New Mexico, 1984.
Anthropology: Professor Michael W. Graves, Ph.D., Arizona, 1981.
Biology: Professor Eric Samuel Loker, Ph.D., Iowa State, 1979.
Chemistry: Professor Cary Morrow, Ph.D., Tulane, 1972.
Communication and Journalism: Associate Professor John Oetzel, Ph.D., Iowa, 1995.
Earth and Planetary Sciences: Professor Leslie M. McFadden, Ph.D., Arizona, 1982.
Economics: Professor Philip Ganderton, Ph.D., California, Santa Barbara, 1989.
English: Professor David Jones, Ph.D., Princeton, 1968.
Foreign Languages and Literatures: Professor Natasha Kolchevska, Ph.D., Berkeley, 1981.
Geography: Professor Olen P. Matthews, Ph.D., Washington (Seattle), 1980.
History: Professor Patricia Risso, Ph.D., McGill, 1982.
Latin American Studies: Associate Professor Kimberly Gauderman, Ph.D., UCLA, 1998.
Linguistics: Professor Sherman Wilcox, Ph.D., New Mexico, 1988.
Mathematics and Statistics: Professor Alejandro Aceves, Ph.D., Arizona, 1989.
Philosophy: Professor John Taber, Ph.D., Hamburg, 1983.
Physics and Astronomy: Professor Bernd Bassalleck, Ph.D., Karlsruhe (Germany), 1977.
Political Science: Professor Mark Peceny, Ph.D., Stanford, 1993.
Psychology: Professor Ronald Yeo, Ph.D., Texas, 1984.
Sociology: Professor Phillip Gonzales, Ph.D., Berkeley, 1985.
Spanish and Portuguese: Professor J. Clancy Clements, Ph.D., Washington (Seattle), 1985.
Speech and Hearing Sciences: Professor Phillip Dale, Ph.D., Michigan, 1982.

Education
Dean: Viola Florez, Ed.D., Texas A&M, 1980.
Educational Leadership and Organizational Learning: Professor Carolyn Wood, Ph.D., Washington (St. Louis), 1977.
Educational Specialties: Professor Ruth Luckasson, J.D., New Mexico, 1980.
Individual, Family, and Community Education: Associate Professor Deborah Rifenbary, Ph.D., Virginia, 1989.
Language, Literacy, and Sociocultural Studies: Associate Professor Rebecca Blum-Martinez, Ph.D., Berkeley, 1993.
Physical Performance and Development: Associate Professor David Scott, Ed.D., Northern Colorado, 1997.

Engineering
Dean: Joseph L. Cecchi, Ph.D., Harvard, 1972.
Chemical and Nuclear Engineering: Professor Julia E. Fulghum, Ph.D., North Carolina, 1987.
Civil Engineering: Professor Arup Maji, Ph.D., Northwestern, 1984.
Computer Science: Professor Stephanie Forrest, Ph.D., Michigan, 1985.
Electrical and Computer Engineering: Professor Chaouki Abdallah, Ph.D., Georgia Tech, 1988.
Mechanical Engineering: Professor Juan Heinrich, Ph.D., Pittsburgh, 1975.
Manufacturing Engineering: Professor John E. Wood, Ph.D., MIT.

Fine Arts
Dean: Christopher Mead, Ph.D., Pennsylvania, 1986.
Art and Art History: Professor Martin Facey, M.F.A., UCLA, 1974.
Music: Associate Professor Steven Block, Ph.D., Pittsburgh, 1981.
Theater and Dance: Professor Judith Chazin-Bennahum, Ph.D., New Mexico, 1981.

Robert O. Anderson Graduate School of Management
Interim Dean: Amy Wohlert, Ph.D., Northwestern, 1989.
Public Administration (interim): Professor Emeritus F. Lee Brown, Ph.D., Purdue, 1969.

HEALTH SCIENCES

Medicine
Dean and Executive Vice President for Health Sciences: Paul Roth, M.D., George Washington, 1976.

Biomedical Sciences
Biomedical Sciences: Professor Angela Wandinger-Ness, Ph.D., UCLA.
Occupational Therapy: Professor Janet Poole, Ph.D., Pittsburgh.
Physical Therapy: Associate Professor Susan Queen, Ph.D., New Mexico, 1987; PT.
Public Health: Professor Nina Wallerstein, Dr.P.H., Berkeley, 1988.

Nursing
Interim Dean: Karen Carlson, Ph.D., Texas at Austin, 1991; RN.

Pharmacy
Dean: John A. Pieper, Pharm.D., SUNY at Buffalo, 1979.

University College
Dean: Peter L. White, Ph.D., Penn State, 1976.
Water Resources: Professor Bruce Thompson, Ph.D., Rice, 1985.

UNIVERSITY OF NORTH CAROLINA AT GREENSBORO

The Graduate School

Programs of Study

The University of North Carolina at Greensboro (UNCG) offers programs of study leading to the Ph.D., Ed.D., Dr.P.H., and D.M.A. degrees. The Ph.D. is offered in consumer, apparel, and retail studies; communication sciences and disorders; counseling and counselor education; curriculum and teaching; economics; educational research, measurement, and evaluation; English; exercise and sport science; geography; history; human development and family studies; information systems; music education; nursing; nutrition; psychology; and special education. Programs leading to the Ed.D. degree are offered in community counseling, educational leadership, exercise and sport science, school counseling, and student development in higher education. The Dr.P.H. is offered in community health education. A D.M.A. degree in music performance is offered with three areas of study: accompanying and chamber music, orchestral instrument or instrumental conducting, and voice, keyboard, or choral conducting.

Sixth-year programs are available in counseling and development, educational leadership, and higher education, leading to the Ed.S. degree. Post-master's certificates are offered in adult clinical nurse specialist, adult nurse practitioner/gerontological nurse practitioner, advanced school counseling, financial analysis, general nursing, gerontological counseling, information technology, international studies in business administration, management, marriage and family counseling, music theory pedagogy, nurse anesthesia, school counseling, and teaching of adult learners. Postbaccalaureate certificates are offered in business administration, conflict resolution, geographic information science, gerontological nursing, gerontology, historic preservation, information technology, museum studies, nonprofit management, nursing administration, nursing case management, nursing education, special endorsement in computer education, statistics, teaching English as a second language, technical writing, urban and economic development, and women's and gender studies.

Master's degrees include M.A., M.B.A., M.Ed., M.F.A., M.L.I.S., M.M., M.P.A., M.P.H., M.S., M.S.A., M.S.N., M.S.W., and dual programs leading to the M.S.N./M.B.A. and the M.S.(gerontology)/M.B.A. Programs are offered in more than sixty specializations, including accounting; applied economics; biochemistry; biology; business administration; business education; chemistry; communication studies; community counseling; computer science; conflict resolution; consumer, apparel, and retail studies, creative writing; curriculum and instruction (chemistry, elementary education, English as a second language (ESL), French, instructional technology, mathematics, middle grades education, reading, science, social studies, Spanish); dance; dance education; drama; education research, measurement, and evaluation; educational supervision; English; exercise and sport science; genetic counseling; geography; gerontology; gerontology/business administration; health management; higher education; history; human development and family studies; information technology and management; interior architecture; Latin; liberal studies; library and information studies; mathematics; music composition; music education; music performance; music theory; nursing; nutrition; parks and recreation management; political science; psychology; public affairs; public health; public history; romance languages (French and Spanish literature); school administration; school counseling; social work; sociology; special education; speech-language pathology; student development in higher education; studio arts; theater education; and women's and gender studies. (Details are contained in the *Graduate School Bulletin,* which is available online at the Graduate School Web site.)

Research Facilities

The University's research facilities are substantial and constantly growing. In addition to research occurring within departments, the campus supports centers for research in educational research and evaluation, global business education, legislative studies, immigrant populations, women's health and wellness, youth, family and community partnerships, collaborative early intervention, family research, and other areas. Library holdings total more than 3.4 million books, federal and state documents, microforms, and other formats, with approximately 4,400 serial publications in paper form, over 30,000 full-text electronic journals, and more than 225,000 electronic books. Special collections include historical physical education materials, cello music, materials on the history of dance, and others, as well as a notable collection of rare books in several fields. State-of-the-art information technology is available for use with large computer centers that provide access to the library's catalog, a broad array of electronic databases, and full-text resources. Cooperative borrowing programs and interlibrary loan services provide ready access to university libraries within the state and beyond.

Financial Aid

More than half of the University's full-time graduate students hold assistantships of one kind or another. In 2007–08, these stipends average approximately $11,000 a year and require such duties of the student as grading or assisting with teaching or research. Those interested in such appointments should apply as early as possible to the head of their prospective department (listed in the Faculty Heads section of this description). A limited number of fellowships are also available to new doctoral students who demonstrate outstanding promise and ability. Other fellowships designated for specific disciplines are also available. Fellowships range from $2000 to $18,000 for the academic year. It is not necessary to apply separately for these fellowships, since all doctoral applicants are routinely considered for them. Funds also are available to increase campus diversity.

Cost of Study

In 2007–08, a North Carolina resident's tuition and academic fees total $2037.39 per semester for a full course load; for a nonresident, the total is $7562.39. Nonresident students who have been recruited for their special talents and who perform substantial academic duties for their department or school as teaching or research assistants may, in some cases, be eligible for tuition waivers. A health insurance fee of $109 per semester may be required, depending upon the course load and whether the student lives on or off campus. All charges are subject to change.

Living and Housing Costs

Housing is available on campus for unmarried students. The cost in 2007–08 for a standard (non–air-conditioned) double room is $1599 per semester. Single rooms are available at a higher cost. A variety of meal plans are also available; graduate students most often opt for the $825 per semester declining balance option, which is accepted at all dining facilities on campus. No University accommodations are designated for married students, but apartments and houses may be rented in Greensboro at reasonable rates. All charges are subject to change. Students should contact the Office of Housing and Residence Life for additional information (telephone: 336-334-5636).

Student Group

The total enrollment of the University is approximately 15,920 students, of whom 3,900 are graduate students. Many countries and nationalities are represented, but the majority of students are from North Carolina.

Location

Greensboro is an attractive city of approximately 236,000, with a mild climate and a variety of cultural advantages. It has an active musical and theatrical life, and the University's Weatherspoon Gallery has an impressive collection of modern art. The Great Smoky Mountains to the west and the Atlantic beaches to the east are within a few hours' drive.

The University

Third in seniority among the sixteen institutions of the University of North Carolina System, the University of North Carolina at Greensboro was established in 1891. It has offered graduate work since 1920.

Applying

Early application is encouraged. Many programs have specific deadlines for fall admission and admit students only for the fall term. Applicants are strongly encouraged to apply using the online application located at the Graduate School's Web site. In addition to a completed application form, three letters of recommendation, transcripts of earlier work, and, in most cases, appropriate test scores are required as a part of the application. A nonrefundable application fee of $45 is required.

Correspondence and Information

The Graduate School
The University of North Carolina at Greensboro
241 Mossman Building
1202 Spring Garden Street
Greensboro, North Carolina 27412

Phone: 336-334-5596
E-mail: inquiries@uncg.edu
Web site: http://www.uncg.edu/grs

FACULTY HEADS

James C. Petersen, Ph.D., Dean of the Graduate School.
Rebecca Saunders, Ph.D., Associate Dean of the Graduate School.
J. Scott Hudgins, Assistant Dean of the Graduate School.

COLLEGE OF ARTS AND SCIENCES
Timothy D. Johnston, Ph.D., Dean.
Art: Patricia Wasserboehr, M.F.A.
Biology: John Lepri, Ph.D.
Broadcasting and Cinema: David A. Cook, Ph.D.
Chemistry: Patricia H. Reggio, Ph.D.
Classical Studies: Susan Shelmerdine, Ph.D.
Communication: Pete Kellett, Ph.D.
Computer Sciences: Stephen R. Tate, Ph.D.
English: Anne Wallace, Ph.D.
Geography: Jeffrey C. Patton, Ph.D.
History: Charles Bolton, Ph.D.
Liberal Studies: Kathleen Forbes, M..Div.
Mathematics and Statistics: Alex Chigogidze, Ph.D.
Political Science: Ruth DeHoog, Ph.D.
Psychology: George Michel, Ph.D.
Romance Languages: Carmen Sotomayor, Ph.D.
Sociology: Julie V. Brown, Ph.D.
Theater Education: Jim Fisher.
Women's and Gender Studies: Katherine Jamieson, Ph.D.

BRYAN SCHOOL OF BUSINESS AND ECONOMICS
James K. Weeks, Ph.D., Dean.
Accounting and Finance: Daniel T. Winkler, Ph.D.
Economics: Stuart Allen, Ph.D.
Information Systems and Operations Management: Kwasi Amoako-Gyampah, Ph.D.
M.B.A. Program: Vidyaranya B. Gargeya, Ph.D.

SCHOOL OF EDUCATION
Dale H. Schunk, Ph.D., Dean.
Counseling and Educational Development: DiAnne Borders, Ph.D.
Curriculum and Instruction: Samuel Miller, Ph.D.
Educational Leadership and Cultural Foundations: Carol Mullen, Ph.D.
Educational Research Methodology: Terry Ackerman, Ph.D.
Library Science and Information Studies: Lee Shiflett, Ph.D.
Specialized Education Services: J. David Smith, Ph.D.

SCHOOL OF HEALTH AND HUMAN PERFORMANCE
Celia R. Hooper, Ph.D., Interim Dean.
Communication Science and Disorders: Robert Mayo, Ph.D.
Dance: Jan E. Van Dyke, Ed.D.
Exercise and Sports Science: Jennifer L. Etnier, Ph.D.
Public Health Education: Dan Bibeau, Ph.D.
Recreation, Parks, and Tourism: Stuart Schleien, Ph.D.

SCHOOL OF HUMAN ENVIRONMENTAL SCIENCES
Laura S. Sims, Ph.D., Dean.
Consumer, Apparel, and Retail Studies: Gwendolyn O'Neal, Ph.D.
Interior Architecture: Tom Lambeth, M.L.A.
Human Development and Family Studies: Dan Perlman, Ph.D.
Nutrition: Debbie Kipp, Ph.D.
Social Work: Cathryne Schmitz, Ph.D.

INTERDISCIPLINARY PROGRAMS
Conflict Resolution: Cathie Witty, Ph.D.
Genetic Counseling: Nancy Callanan, M.S., C.G.C.
Gerontology: Janice Wassel, Ph.D.

SCHOOL OF MUSIC
John J. Deal, Ph.D., Dean.

SCHOOL OF NURSING
Lynne G. Pearcey, Ph.D., Dean.

UNIVERSITY OF NORTHERN COLORADO

Graduate School

Programs of Study

The University of Northern Colorado (UNC) Graduate School offers programs of study leading to master's, specialist, and doctoral degrees. There are thirty-one master's programs (several of which have optional fields of emphasis). The post-master's Specialist in Education (Ed.S.) degree is offered in educational leadership and school psychology.

At the doctoral level, the Doctor of Arts (D.A.) in music is offered. The Doctor of Education (Ed.D.) is offered in educational leadership, elementary education, and special education. The Doctor of Philosophy (Ph.D.) is offered in applied statistics and research methods, biological education, chemical education, counselor education, educational mathematics, educational psychology, educational technology, higher education and student affairs leadership, nursing education, school psychology, and sport and exercise science. The Doctor of Psychology (Psy.D.) is offered in counseling psychology. The Doctor of Audiology (Au.D.) is also offered. Doctoral programs all require the completion of a dissertation.

Master's degrees require a minimum of 30 semester hours. M.S. degrees offered include applied statistics, biology, chemistry, and nursing. M.A. degrees offered include communication, community counseling, earth sciences, educational leadership, educational technology, English, gerontology, history, and mathematics. Individually designed graduate interdisciplinary programs may be approved for the M.A. and M.S. degrees. All degrees require the passing of a comprehensive examination or an approved equivalent capstone project. Many of the research-oriented master's programs require a thesis, while practice-oriented programs usually require internships or practicums.

Research Facilities

The University libraries contain more than 1.5 million catalogued pieces, including hardbound volumes, periodicals, monographs, government documents, archival materials, filmstrips, slides, maps, software programs, videos, and microforms. A new integrated library system, The Source, provides users with online access to library collections worldwide. Other research facilities include the herbarium and greenhouses available for biological research and laboratories for chemistry, biology, and neuropsychology research in the College of Natural and Health Sciences, the Center for Educational Leadership, the Bresnahan-Halstead Center of Mental Retardation and Developmental Disabilities, the Kephart Memorial Child Study Center, National Center on Low-Incidence, and the Research Consulting Lab in the College of Education and Behavioral Sciences; multidisciplinary health clinics and human performance laboratories and the Rocky Mountain Cancer Rehabilitation Institute in the College of Natural and Health Sciences; and the Music Technology Center in the College of Performing and Visual Arts.

Financial Aid

Financial support includes graduate teaching and research assistantships, fellowships, and scholarships, as well as need-based grants and loans. The University uses the Free Application for Federal Student Aid (FAFSA) for need-based awards and loans. The deadline for priority consideration for all financial awards is March 1. Some programs have earlier deadlines. Full assistantships (appointments of .40 full-time equivalent (FTE) or greater) usually include tuition scholarships and have stipends that vary by nature of assignment, discipline, and relevant expertise. Most assistantships are available through academic program areas and some administrative units. Inquiries should be directed to the appropriate unit for assistantships. Application for graduate scholarships or fellowships should be submitted to the appropriate office upon admission.

Cost of Study

In 2006–07, the graduate student tuition for a full load (9 hours) per semester was $1919.25 for Colorado residents and $5562 for nonresidents. In addition, student fees were $303.30 per semester and student health insurance $788 per semester.

Living and Housing Costs

UNC has on-campus housing for graduate students, offered on a space-available basis. Applications for on-campus housing are sent to admitted graduate students on request. Apartment-style units range in rent from $1400 and up per semester. Family student apartments rent for about $350 per month ($250 housing deposit). Most graduate students live in off-campus apartments or houses near the campus at rents of approximately $400 and up per month.

Student Group

In fall 2007, UNC expects to enroll nearly 1,770 graduate students, constituting 15 percent of the total student body. Seventy percent of the graduate students are women, 9 percent are members of ethnic minority groups, and 5 percent are international students. Fifty-five percent of the graduate students are enrolled part-time, and 86 percent are Colorado residents (it takes one full year to establish residency). An active Graduate Student Association participates in student government and in the Graduate Council and supports graduate student initiatives.

Student Outcomes

Graduates of the UNC master's, specialist, and doctoral programs find leadership positions in public schools; in nonprofit and for-profit health, human services, or arts agencies; and in universities and colleges. Others work in private practice or in professional roles in their chosen fields. Many master's graduates go on to doctoral programs in their disciplines.

Location

Nestled between the snow-capped Rocky Mountains and the sprawling high plains just an hour's drive north of Denver, Greeley is a growing city of nearly 100,000. Its pace is comfortable, its personality eclectic, its population diverse. Graduate students find an abundance of housing choices, job opportunities, and cultural, recreational, and entertainment amenities. Greeley also provides easy access to a wide variety of Colorado adventures such as skiing, hiking, camping, horseback riding, shopping, and exploring new vistas.

The University

The University of Northern Colorado commits to the success of its students by providing a solid liberal arts foundation, relevant professional course work, and real-world experiences in an environment where faculty and staff members value personal attention as a key to learning. Its five colleges include a nationally recognized business school, innovative health and natural science programs, and award-winning theater arts and teacher education programs, all supported by a cornerstone curriculum in the humanities and social sciences. With its rich 118-year history, dedicated faculty members, active students, and Division I athletic teams, the University of Northern Colorado is large enough to provide true university opportunities and small enough to treat students as individuals.

Applying

The Graduate School Office is responsible for coordinating graduate admissions at UNC. Applications may be submitted at any time. Under UNC's student-administered application process the student is responsible for collecting and submitting all materials required for admission at one time, with the application fee ($50 for domestic and $60 for international students) to the Graduate School. Students may also apply online. Most programs have established application and financial aid deadlines. Applicants should contact the specific department of interest to them for information about such deadlines and admission requirements. Program specifics are available at the University of Northern Colorado Web site (http://www.unco.edu).

Correspondence and Information

For applications or general information:

Graduate School/International Admissions
Campus Box 135
University of Northern Colorado
Greeley, Colorado 80639

Phone: 970-351-2831
Fax: 970-351-2371
E-mail: gradsch@unco.edu
Web site: http://www.unco.edu/grad

SCHOOLS, PROGRAMS, AND FACULTY

COLLEGE OF EDUCATION AND BEHAVIORAL SCIENCES
Eugene Sheehan, Dean

School of Educational Research, Leadership and Technology
Dan Mundfrom, Director
- **Applied Statistics and Research Methods (M.S., Ph.D.):** Susan Hutchinson, Coordinator
- **Educational Leadership (M.A., Ed.S., Ed.D.):** Kathy Whitaker, Coordinator
- **Educational Media (M.A.):** Berlinda Saenz and Heng-Yu Ku, Coordinators
- **Educational Technology (M.A., Ph.D.):** Heng-yu Ku, Coordinator
- **Higher Education and Student Affairs Leadership (Ph.D.):** Michael Gimmestad, Coordinator

School of Applied Psychology and Counselor Education
Fred Hanna, Director
- **Clinical Counseling (M.A.):** Sandy Magnuson, Coordinator
  - Couples and Family Therapy
- **Counseling Psychology (Psy.D.):** Brian Johnson, Coordinator
- **Counselor Education and Supervision (Ph.D.):** Linda Black and Sean O'Halloran
- **School Counseling (M.A.):** Sandy Magnuson, Coordinator
- **School Psychology (Ed.S., Ph.D.):** Michelle Athanasiou, Coordinator

School of Psychological Sciences
Mark Acorn, Director
- **Educational Psychology (M.A., Ph.D.):** Marilyn Welsh and Steven Pulos Coordinators

School of Special Education
Harvey Rude, Director
- **Special Education (M.A., Ed.D.):**
  - Deaf and Hard of Hearing Emphasis: John Luckner, Coordinator
  - Early Childhood Special Education Emphasis: Hannah Schertz, Coordinator
  - Generalist Emphasis: Diane Basset, Coordinator
  - Gifted and Talented Education Emphasis: George Betts, Coordinator
  - Vision Impairment Emphasis: Paula Conroy, Coordinator

School of Teacher Education
Alexander Sidorkin, Director
- **Educational Studies (Ed.D.):**Alexander Sidorkin, Coordinator
- **Educational Studies (M.A.T.):**
  - Curriculum Studies Emphasis: Fred Bartelheim, Coordinator
- **Reading (M.A.):** Michael Opitz, Coordinator

COLLEGE OF HUMANITIES AND SOCIAL SCIENCES
David Caldwell, Dean

School of Communication
Thomas Endres, Director
- **Communication: Human Communication**
  - Thesis Option (M.A.): James Keaton, Coordinator
  - Nonthesis Option (M.A): James Keaton, Coordinator

School of English Language and Literature
Joonok Huh, Director
- **English (M.A.):** Marcus Embry, Coordinator

School of History, Philosophy and Political Science
Barry Rothaus, Director
- **History (M.A.):** Michael Welsh, Coordinator

School of Modern Languages and Cultural Studies
Elizabeth Franklin, Director
- **Foreign Languages (M.A.)**
  - Spanish Teaching Emphasis: Joy Landeira, Coordinator

School of Social Sciences
Robert Brunswig, Director
- **Social Sciences (M.A.)**
  - Clinical Sociology Emphasis: Karen Jennison, Coordinator

COLLEGE OF NATURAL AND HEALTH SCIENCES
Denise Battles, Dean

School of Biological Sciences
Catherine Gardiner, Director
- **Biological Education (Ph.D.):** Susan Keenan, Coordinator
- **Biological Sciences (M.S.):** Susan Keenan, Coordinator
  - Thesis Option
  - Nonthesis Option

School of Chemistry, Earth Sciences and Physics
William Hoyt, Director
- **Chemistry Education (M.S.):** Richard Schwenz and David Pringle, Coordinators
- **Chemistry Research (M.S.):** Richard Schwenz and David Pringle, Coordinators
- **Chemical Education (Ph.D.):** Richard Schwenz and David Pringle, Coordinators
- **Earth Sciences (M.A.):** William Neese or Gary Huffines, Coordinators

School of Human Sciences
Sherrie Frye, Director
- **Audiology (Au.D.):** Katie Bright, Coordinator
- **Gerontology (M.A.):** Susan Collins, Coordinator
- **Public Health (M.P.H.)**
  - Community Health Education Emphasis: Stuart Zisman, Coordinator
- **Rehabilitation Counseling (M.A.):** Sherrie Frye, Coordinator
- **Speech Language Pathology (M.A.):** Julie Hanks, Coordinator

School of Mathematical Sciences
Dean Allison, Director
- **Educational Mathematics (Ph.D.):** Jodie Novak, Coordinator
- **Mathematics: Liberal Arts (M.A.):** Dean Allison, Coordinator
- **Mathematics Teaching (M.A.):** Dean Allison, Coordinator

School of Nursing
Debra Leners, Director
- **Nursing (M.S.):** Deb Leners, Coordinator
  - Clinical Nurse Specialist in Chronic Illness Emphasis: Carol Roehrs, Coordinator
  - Education Emphasis: Carol Roehrs, Coordinator
  - Family Nurse Practitioner Emphasis: Debra Leners, Coordinator
- **Nursing Education (Ph.D.):** Nancy White, Coordinator

School of Sport and Exercise Science
David Stotlar, Director
- **Sport and Exercise Science (M.S., Ed.D.)**
  - Exercise Science Emphasis: Jim Stiehl and Gary Heise, Coordinators
  - Sport Administration Emphasis: Jim Stiehl and Gary Heise, Coordinators
  - Sport Pedagogy Emphasis: Jim Stiehl and Gary Heise, Coordinators

COLLEGE OF PERFORMING AND VISUAL ARTS
Andrew Svedlow, Dean

School of Music
David Caffey, Director
- **Music (M.M., D.A.):** Robert Ehle, Coordinator
  - Collaborative Keyboard (M.M.)
  - Conducting (M.M., D.A.)
  - Education (M.M., D.A.)
  - History and Literature (M.M., D.A.)
  - Instrumental Performance (M.M.)
  - Jazz Studies(M.M.)
  - Performance (D.A.)
  - Theory and Composition (M.M., D.A.)
  - Vocal Performance (M.M.)

School of Visual Arts
Dennis Morimoto, Director
- **Art and Design (M.A.):** Tom Stephens, Coordinator

GRADUATE SCHOOL
Robbyn Wacker, Assistant Vice President for Research and Extended Studies, Dean of the Graduate School

UNIVERSITY OF NORTH TEXAS

Toulouse School of Graduate Studies

Programs of Study

The University of North Texas (UNT) offers graduate study in 111 master's degree programs and fifty doctoral programs.

Doctoral degrees are offered in accounting, art education, applied gerontology, audiology, biological sciences, business computer information science, chemistry, computer science, counseling, education (applied technology and performance improvement, curriculum and instruction, early childhood education, educational administration, educational computing, educational research, higher education, reading education, and special education), English, environmental science, finance, history, information science, management, management science, marketing, materials science, mathematics, molecular biology, music composition, music education, musicology, music performance, music theory, philosophy, physics, political science, psychology (including clinical, counseling, experimental, and health psychology/behavioral medicine), public administration, and sociology.

Master's degrees are offered in most of the above areas plus the following: administration of long-term care and retirement facilities, applied anthropology, applied economics, applied geography, art (including ceramics, communication design, drawing and painting, fashion design, fibers, history, interior design, metalsmithing and jewelry, photography, printmaking, sculpture, and watercolor), behavior analysis, communications studies, computer education and cognitive systems, computer engineering, creative writing, criminal justice, decision technologies, delivery of community-based services for the aging, economics, electrical engineering, human development and family studies, educational psychology, engineering technology, English, English as a second language, French, general studies in aging, health services management, hospitality management, information technologies, journalism, kinesiology, labor and industrial relations, library science, linguistics, merchandising, music (including jazz studies), organizational behavior and human resource management, philosophy, psychology, public administration, public health, radio/television/film, strategic management, real estate, recreation, rehabilitation counseling, secondary education, Spanish, speech/language pathology, taxation, and technical writing.

Master's and doctoral degree programs in several areas are offered in cooperation with the Federation of North Texas Area Universities.

Research Facilities

The University libraries contain more than 5.8 million cataloged holdings and provide diverse, rapidly growing electronic resources. The libraries provide all of the services traditionally associated with academic research libraries, plus services provided by membership in national consortia and electronic access/searching of academic and commercial information resources.

The University's information resources infrastructure includes both central and distributed computing, combining personal computers and several major host computer systems. The campus backbone system combines high-speed fiber optics linking approximately thirty-five buildings, a broadband cable network linking video capabilities at more than 2,000 locations in approximately sixty buildings, and a developing wireless capacity. The campus network is linked to a variety of external networks, including the Internet and World Wide Web, and students and faculty members have access to computer resources both on and off campus through dial-in procedures.

In addition to departmental facilities, specialized or interdisciplinary research facilities are housed in a variety of centers, institutes, and laboratories. Science and technology centers focus on the applied sciences, environmental archaeology, forensic anthropology, ion-beam modification and analysis, nanostructural materials research, network neuroscience, organometallic chemistry, parallel and distributed computing, remote sensing and geographic information systems, and water research. Business research includes centers for information systems research, quality and productivity, and small business. The fine arts include centers for experimental music and intermedia and visual arts education. Humanities, social sciences, and educational research centers focus on inter-American studies, diplomatic and military history, local history, aging, economic development, environmental economic studies, peace studies, sport psychology, public and international affairs, self-managed work teams, labor and industrial relations, addiction, minority aging, survey research, developmental studies, play therapy, public support of nonprofit agencies, educational reform, educational research, and the school-to-work transition.

Financial Aid

More than 1,000 assistantships are available. The stipends vary according to the amount and level of work required and the background of the student. Half-time appointments and University-awarded scholarships and fellowships of $1000 or more qualify graduate students for in-state tuition rates. The graduate school annually awards a growing number of fellowships to new doctoral and master's students who are departmental nominees. Doctoral awards are $20,000; master's awards are $10,000. Many departments also award scholarships and fellowships.

Loans, including Federal Perkins Loans and Federal Stafford Student Loans, are also available to graduate students.

Cost of Study

For 2006–07, tuition and fees for out-of-state graduate students were estimated at $1732 per 3-credit course, and tuition and fees for in-state graduate students were estimated at $907 per 3-credit course (subject to change).

Living and Housing Costs

Graduate students attending the Toulouse School of Graduate Studies may live in University-owned residence halls for approximately $5600 for two semesters. Nearby off-campus housing is also available at reasonable rates.

Student Group

More than 6,000 of the University's approximately 32,000 students are in the graduate school. UNT serves students from every state in the nation and almost 100 other countries.

Location

The University of North Texas is located in Denton, Texas, about 35 miles north of Dallas–Fort Worth. With a population of approximately 54 million, the metropolitan area is the largest in Texas and the ninth largest in the United States. There is a wide range of employment, cultural, and sports opportunities.

The University

Founded in 1890, the University of North Texas is one of Texas's five major research and graduate institutions and the only comprehensive graduate and research university in the region. The University began offering graduate work at the master's level in 1935 and at the doctoral level in 1950. Approximately 1,200 master's degrees and 150 doctoral degrees are awarded annually. UNT has awarded more than 147,000 degrees at the undergraduate and graduate levels. The Denton campus consists of 140 buildings on 756 acres on the main campus and one building on 200 acres at the Research Park.

Applying

Applications for admission and supporting documents should be received at least six weeks before entrance. For many departments an earlier deadline must be met. Since deadlines vary, students should correspond with a specific department prior to the date of desired enrollment. If a student is also applying for a graduate teaching or research assistantship, fellowship, or scholarship, application materials should be received several months earlier and at least by the deadline established by the award committee.

Correspondence and Information

Toulouse School of Graduate Studies
354 Eagle Student Services Building
University of North Texas
Box 305459, NT Station
Denton, Texas 76203-5459

Phone: 940-565-2383
Fax: 940-565-2141
E-mail: gradschool@unt.edu
Web site: http://www.tsgs.unt.edu

FACULTY HEADS

GRADUATE SCHOOL
Sandra L. Terrell, Dean.
Lawrence J. Schneider, Associate Dean.
Donna Hughes, Director of Graduate Services and Admissions.

COLLEGE OF ARTS AND SCIENCES
Warren Burggren, Dean.
Jean B. Schaake, Associate Dean.
Kathryn Gould Cullivan, Associate Dean.
Michael Monticino, Associate Dean.

Audiology: Kamakshi Gopal.
Biological Sciences: Art J. Goven, Chair; Beth Chaplek and Thomas LaPoint, Advisers.
Chemistry: Ruthanne Thomas, Chair; Angela Wilson, Adviser.
Communication Studies: Jay Allison, Chair and Adviser.
Economics: Steven L. Cobb, Chair; Margie Tieslau, Adviser.
English: Brenda Sims, Graduate Chair; Marshall Armintor, Adviser.
Foreign Languages: Marie Christine Koop, Chair; Michel Sirvent, French Adviser; Pierina Beckman; Spanish Adviser.
Geography: Paul Hudak, Chair; Donald Lyons, Adviser.
History: Adrian R. Lewis, Chair; F. Todd Smith, Adviser.
Journalism: Susan C. Zavoina, Chair; Mitch Land, Adviser.
Labor/Industrial Relations: Margie Tieslau, Adviser.
Mathematics: Neal Brand, Chair; Matt Douglass, Adviser.
Philosophy: Robert Frodeman, Chair and Adviser.
Physics: Floyd D. McDaniel, Chair; William D. Deering, Adviser.
Political Science: James D. Meernik, Chair; Steve Forde, Adviser.
Psychology: Linda L. Marshall, Chair; Joseph Critelli, Adviser.
Radio/TV/Film: Alan B. Albarran, Chair; Ben Levin, Adviser.
Speech and Hearing: Jeffrey A. Cokely, Chair; Maria Jimenez-Castro, Adviser.

COLLEGE OF BUSINESS ADMINISTRATION
Kathleen B. Cooper, Dean.
Mary Thibodeaux, Associate Dean.
Cengiz Capan, Associate Dean.

Accounting: O. Finley Graves, Chair; Tom Klammer, M.B.A. Adviser; Barbara Merino, Doctoral Adviser.
Business (General): Denise Galubenski, Adviser.
Finance, Insurance, Real Estate, and Law: James A. Conover, Interim Chair; Foster Roden, M.B.A./M.S.-Finance Adviser; John Baen, M.S.-Real Estate Adviser; John Kensinger, Doctoral Finance Adviser.
Information Technology and Decision Sciences: Mary C. Jones, Interim Chair; Shailesh Kulkarni, M.B.A./M.S. Adviser; John Windsor, Doctoral Adviser.
Management: Nancy Boyd-Lillie, Interim Chair; Kathy Voelker, M.B.A. Adviser; Dr. Mark Davis, Health Services Management Adviser; Dr. Richard White, Doctoral Adviser.
Marketing and Logistics: David Strutton, Chair; Jeffrey Lewin, M.B.A. Adviser; Audhesh Paswan, Doctoral Adviser.

COLLEGE OF EDUCATION
M. Jean Keller, Dean.
Judith A. Adkison, Associate Dean.
Michael F. Sayler, Associate Dean.

Counseling, Development and Higher Education: Ron Newsom, Interim Chair.
Kinesiology, Health Promotion, and Recreation: Jeff E. Goodwin, Chair; Noreen Goggin, Adviser.
Teacher Education and Administration: Mary Harris, Interim Chair.
Technology and Cognition: Robin Henson, Interim Chair.

COLLEGE OF ENGINEERING
Oscar N. Garcia, Dean.
Reza Mirshams, Associate Dean.
Kathleen Swigger, Associate Dean.

Computer Science and Engineering: Krishna Kavi, Chair; Armin Mikler, Adviser.
Electrical Engineering: Murali Varanasi, Chair.
Engineering Technology: Albert Grubbs, Chair; Michael Kozak, Adviser.
Materials Science and Engineering: Michael Kaufman, Chair; Nandika D'Souza, Adviser.

COLLEGE OF MUSIC
James C. Scott, Dean.
Warren Henry, Associate Dean
Jon C. Nelson, Associate Dean
John Scott, Associate Dean

COLLEGE OF PUBLIC ADMINISTRATION AND COMMUNITY SERVICE
David W. Hartman, Dean.
Dr. Ann Jordan, Associate Dean.

Anthropology: Tyson Gibbs, Chair; Lisa Henry, Adviser.
Applied Economics: Bernard Weinstein, Director; Terry Clower, Adviser.
Behavioral Analysis: Richard G. Smith, Chair; Janet Ellis, Adviser.
Criminal Justice: Robert W. Taylor, Chair; Eric Fritsch, Adviser.
General Studies in Aging: Richard Lusky, Chair; Phyllis Eccleston, Adviser.
Public Administration: Bob Bland, Chair; Lisa Dicke, Master's Adviser; Al Bavon, Doctoral Adviser.
Rehabilitation Studies: Paul Leung, Chair and Adviser.
Sociology: David A. Williamson, Chair; Rudy Seward, Adviser.

SCHOOL OF LIBRARY AND INFORMATION SCIENCES
Herman L. Totten, Dean.
Linda Schamber, Associate Dean.

SCHOOL OF MERCHANDISING AND HOSPITALITY MANAGEMENT
Judith C. Forney, Dean.
Johnny Sue Reynolds, Associate Dean.
Tammy Kinley, Adviser.

SCHOOL OF VISUAL ARTS
Robert Milnes, Dean.
Don Schol, Associate Dean.

Art History and Art Education Division: Kelly Donahue-Wallace, Interim Chair.
Design Division: Cynthia Mohr, Chair.
Studio Division: Jerry Austin, Chair.

UNIVERSITY OF OKLAHOMA

Graduate College

Programs of Study

The University of Oklahoma (OU) combines a mixture of academic excellence, varied social cultures, and a blend of scholarly and creative activities that offer exceptional opportunities for graduate study. Graduate education is offered in more than 100 master's programs and fifty-three doctoral programs on the Norman campus. At the OU Health Sciences Center (OU-HSC), located 19 miles away in Oklahoma City, graduate degrees are offered in twenty-nine master's programs and sixteen doctoral programs. In addition to the Doctor of Philosophy, the University confers the Doctor of Education, Doctor of Engineering, Doctor of Musical Arts, and Doctor of Public Health. The University of Oklahoma also offers graduate programs at the Tulsa Graduate Research and Education Center located approximately 120 miles northeast of the main campus in the city of Tulsa, Oklahoma. On the Tulsa campus, OU offers graduate programs in architecture, urban studies, human relations, library and information studies, organization dynamics, public administration, social work, and telecomputing. Interdisciplinary degree programs are available at both the master's and doctoral levels on all three campuses. Master's degree programs require a minimum of 30 semester hours of course work. Doctoral programs require a minimum of 90 semester hours of course work and are awarded for excellence in research scholarship. Doctoral students are also required to complete general written and oral examinations and defend the results of their dissertation research.

Research Facilities

OU is in the process of establishing a new research campus with a center for genomic and biogenetic research, a field in which OU is a national leader. Research and scholarly activity take place on the well-landscaped 567-acre main campus in Norman, which houses most of the University's academic colleges and research buildings. The University of Oklahoma provides an exceptional networking and computational environment for students and faculty and staff members. All graduate students at the University of Oklahoma have access to electronic mail service, digital libraries, the Internet, a central help desk, campus software and licensing, and many other benefits to enhance their graduate experiences. The academic areas of campus are part of the University intranet system that provides computer access in residence halls, classrooms, student computer labs, and University offices. The University maintains an OC-3 high-speed connectivity to the commercial Internet, allowing seamless access to graduate resources elsewhere in the world. The University is a charter member of the Internet2 and vBNS initiatives and continues to expand the technological possibilities for research. The $50-million Sarkeys Energy Center has 200 teaching and research laboratories, as well as classrooms and offices and the Youngblood Energy Library. There are central advanced analytical services, including the Electron Microprobe Library and Samuel Robert Noble Electron Microscopy Laboratory.

The Norman campus houses Bizzell Memorial Library, the largest in the state, with more than 4.2 million volumes, 17,000 periodicals, 1.6 million documents, 3 million microforms, and 400,000 photographs. Special collections include the internationally known History of Science Collections, the Western History Collections, and the Political Commercial Archives. There are also six specialized branch libraries. The new Sam Noble Museum of Natural History opened in 2000. The 195,000-square-foot facility is the largest university-based museum in the country. The museum is home to 6 million artifacts including the longest Apatosaurus, and priceless Native American objects. The Fred Jones Jr. Art Center, the Catlett Music Center, and the Rupel L. Jones Theatre provide excellent facilities for graduate studies in the College of Fine Arts. In 2005, the Fred Jones Jr. Art Center opened a new addition, designed by acclaimed architect Hugh Newell Jacobsen of Washington, D.C. Named in honor of Mary and Howard Lester of San Francisco, the wing adds more than 34,000 square feet to the earlier 27,000-square-foot building. The University of Oklahoma Press and *World Literature Today* are two internationally recognized agencies for research and scholarship. The University's 622-acre south campus includes the Oklahoma Center for Continuing Education (OCCE) and the research programs of the Institute for Community and Economic Development.The White Forum Building at OCCE supports research symposia and teleconferencing. The OCCE is fully equipped with AV equipment and satellite communications capability. The University also has a north campus of 1,675 acres, which includes the University Research Park, incubator firms, NOAA's National Severe Storms Laboratory, and the National Weather Service's advanced weather forecasting office. OU's Health Sciences Center includes a 200-acre complex of educational, research, and health-care facilities operated by nineteen public and private entities along with an 11-acre College of Medicine campus in Tulsa. The OU-HSC is the recipient of an $8.7-million grant, which established the Oklahoma Center for Molecular Medicine.

Financial Aid

Nearly one third of all graduate students attending the University are employed by their departments as either teaching or research assistants. Salaries for these positions vary from unit to unit, but the University average for 2006 was $9124 for graduate teaching assistants and $12,165 for graduate research assistants. Out-of-state tuition is waived for all students holding a half-time teaching or research assistantship up to 9 credit hours.

Cost of Study

Tuition for Oklahoma residents was $190.30 per graduate credit hour in 2005–06; nonresident tuition was $514 (nonresidents appointed as at least half-time graduate assistants pay the in-state rate). In addition, a $54 health fee and a $50 student facilities fee were charged each semester.

Living and Housing Costs

The monthly rent for University-owned apartments ranges from $515 to $734. There are a large number of privately owned apartments, duplexes, and houses available in Norman, many of which are served by the University's Campus Area Rapid Transit (CART) system.

Student Group

Enrollment was 24,500 students on the Norman campus and 2,693 at the Health Sciences Center during the 2005–06 academic year. More than 3,200 of these students were enrolled in the Graduate College in Norman and nearly 1,000 in the Graduate College at the Health Sciences Center. Approximately one third of the graduate students at the University of Oklahoma are enrolled in doctoral programs. Approximately one fifth of the student body comes from out of state, with students from every state. In addition, international students from seventy-two nations make up nearly 20 percent of the graduate student body.

Location

As part of the dynamic Southwest, Oklahoma benefits from both its rich historic heritage and the vital and modern growth of its metropolitan areas. Although by location a suburb of Oklahoma City, Norman is an independent community with a permanent population of more than 95,000. Norman residents enjoy extensive parks and recreation programs and a 10,000-acre lake and park area.

The College

The Graduate College is the center of advanced study, research, and creative activity for the University. Faculty members and students share an obligation to achieve greater knowledge in their chosen fields and to present their achievements to the scholarly community. Students were first accepted at the University of Oklahoma in 1892. Graduate instruction was offered as early as 1899, and the first master's degree was conferred in 1900. The Graduate School was formally organized in 1909, and the first doctorate was awarded in 1929.

Applying

Application procedures vary depending on the student's academic background. There is a $40 application fee for U.S. citizens and permanent residents and a $75 application fee for international students. Applications for assistantships, fellowships, and other forms of financial aid should be directed to the academic units. Deadlines vary from department to department, but applications should generally be filed no later than January for students desiring admission in the fall term.

Correspondence and Information

Graduate College
731 Elm Avenue, Room 100
University of Oklahoma
Norman, Oklahoma 73019

Phone: 800-522-0772 (toll-free)
E-mail: gradinfo@ou.edu
Web site: http://gradweb.ou.edu/

AREAS OF INSTRUCTION

The graduate faculty consists of more than 600 active scholars in residence on the Norman campus and another 270 at the Health Sciences Center. In addition, the graduate faculty is supplemented by visiting scholars from other institutions and by specialists from government and industry. The names of the programs and the degrees offered are listed along with the telephone number. The area code for all numbers is 405 except for the nursing program, which is a toll-free number.

Norman Campus
Accounting (M.Ac.): telephone: 325-4221; e-mail: fayres@ou.edu.
Accounting (Ph.D.): telephone: 325-4221; e-mail: rlipe@ou.edu.
Aerospace and Mechanical Engineering (M.S., Ph.D.): telephone: 325-1735; e-mail: rparthasarathy@ou.edu.
Anthropology (M.A., Ph.D.): telephone: 325-2490; e-mail: pgilman@ou.edu.
Architecture (M.Arch., M.L.A., M.R.C.P., M.S.C.A.): telephone: 325-2444; e-mail: tpatterson@ou.edu.
Art (M.A., M.F.A.): telephone: 325-2691; e-mail: alphelan@ou.edu.
Botany and Microbiology (M.S., Ph.D.): telephone: 325-6281; e-mail: guno@ou.edu.
Business Administration (M.B.A., Ph.D.): telephone: 325-2931; e-mail: rdauffen@ou.edu.
Chemical Engineering (M.S., Ph.D.): telephone: 325-4366; e-mail: nollert@ou.edu.
Chemistry and Biochemistry (M.S., Ph.D.): telephone: 325-2967; e-mail: lblank@chemdept.ou.edu.
Civil Engineering and Environmental Science (M.S., Ph.D.): telephone:325-4253; e-mail: gamiller@ou.edu.
Communication (M.A., Ph.D.): telephone: 325-1571; e-mail: sragan@ou.edu.
Computer Science (M.S., Ph.D.): telephone: 325-0566; e-mail: thulasi@ou.edu.
Dance (M.F.A.): telephone: 325-4051; e-mail: marymholt@ou.edu.
Drama (M.A., M.F.A.): telephone: 325-4021; e-mail: torr@ou.edu.
Economics (M.A., Ph.D.): telephone: 325-2861; e-mail: dsutter@ou.edu.
Education (M.Ed., Ph.D., Ed.D.): telephone: 325-5976; e-mail: gnoley@ou.edu.
Electrical and Computer Engineering (M.S., Ph.D.): telephone: 325-4721; e-mail: zelby@ou.edu.
Engineering (M.S., Ph.D.): telephone: 325-2621; e-mail: hkumin@ou.edu.
Engineering Physics (M.S., Ph.D.): telephone: 325-3961; e-mail: msantos@ou.edu.
English (M.A., Ph.D.): telephone: 325-6219; e-mail: schleifer@ou.edu.
Geography (M.A., Ph.D.): telephone: 325-5325; e-mail: jgreene@ou.edu.
Geology and Geophysics (M.S., Ph.D.): telephone: 325-3253; e-mail: mengel@ou.edu.
Health and Sports Sciences (M.S.): telephone: 325-2717; e-mail: agardner@ou.edu.
History (M.A., Ph.D.): telephone: 325-6058; e-mail: wmetcalf@ou.edu.
History of Science (M.A., Ph.D.): telephone: 325-2213; e-mail: ktaylor@ou.edu.
Human Relations (M.H.R.): telephone: 325-1756; e-mail: smmendoza@ou.edu.
Industrial Engineering (M.S., Ph.D.): telephone: 325-3721; e-mail: pulat@ou.edu.
International Studies (M.A.): telephone: 325-8893; e-mail: rhcox@ou.edu.
Journalism and Mass Communication (M.A., Ph.D.): telephone: 325-5206; e-mail: dcraig@ou.edu.
Landscape Architecture (M.L.A.): telephone: 325-2444; e-mail: schurch@ou.edu.
Liberal Studies (M.L.S.): telephone: 325-1061; e-mail: tgabert@ou.edu.
Library and Information Studies (M.L.I.S.): telephone: 325-3921; e-mail: dwallace@ou.edu.
Mathematics (M.A., M.S., M.S./M.B.A., Ph.D.): telephone: 325-3971; e-mail: ozaydin@ou.edu.
Meteorology (M.S., Ph.D.): telephone: 325-6097; e-mail: ashapiro@ou.edu.
Modern Languages (French, German, Spanish for M.A., Ph.D.): telephone: 325-6181; e-mail:hmadland@ou.edu.
Music (M.Mus., D.M.A.): telephone: 325-5344; e-mail: iwagner@ou.edu.
Music Education (M.Mus.Educ., Ph.D.): telephone: 325-5344; e-mail: iwagner@ou.edu.
Natural Science (M.Nat.Sci.): telephone: 325-1498; e-mail: eamarek@ou.edu.
Petroleum and Geological Engineering (M.S., Ph.D.): telephone: 325-2921; e-mail: crai@ou.edu.
Philosophy (M.A., Ph.D.): telephone: 325-6491; e-mail: lzagzebski@ou.edu.
Physics and Astronomy (M.S., Ph.D.): telephone: 325-3961; e-mail: kmullen@ou.edu.
Political Science (M.A., Ph.D.): telephone: 325-5517; e-mail: alfranklin@ou.edu.
Professional Meteorology (M.S.): telephone: 325-6097; e-mail: ashapiro@ou.edu.
Psychology (M.S., Ph.D.): telephone: 325-4599; e-mail: ltoothaker@ou.edu.
Public Administration (M.P.A.): telephone: 325-5517; e-mail: alfranklin@ou.edu.
Regional and City Planning (M.R.C.P.): telephone: 325-2399; e-mail: rmarshment@ou.edu.
Social Work (M.S.W.): telephone: 325-2821; e-mail: rwright@ou.edu.
Sociology (M.A., Ph.D.): telephone: 325-1571; e-mail: estjohn@ou.edu.
Zoology (M.S., Ph.D.): telephone: 325-5271; e-mail: bmatthews@ou.edu.

Health Sciences Campus (e-mail: grad-college@ouhsc.edu)
Biochemistry and Molecular Biology (Ph.D.): telephone: 271-2227.
Biological Psychology (M.S., Ph.D.): telephone: 271-2011.
Biostatistics and Epidemiology (M.S., M.P.H., Ph.D., Dr.P.H.): telephone:271-2229.
Cell Biology (M.S., Ph.D.): telephone: 271-2377.
Communication Sciences and Disorders (M.S., Ph.D.): telephone: 271-4124.
Health Administration and Policy (M.H.A., M.P.H., M.P.A./M.P.H., M.P.H./M.B.A., M.P.H./J.D., M.P.H./M.D., Dr.P.H.): telephone: 271-2114.
Health Promotion Sciences (M.S., M.P.H., Dr.P.H.): telephone: 271-2017.
Microbiology and Immunology (M.S., Ph.D.): telephone: 271-2133.
Neuroscience (M.S., Ph.D.): telephone: 271-2406.
Nursing (M.S., M.S./M.B.A.): telephone: 877-367-OURN (toll-free).
Nutritional Sciences (M.S.): telephone: 271-2113.
Occupational and Environmental Health (M.S., M.P.H., M.S./J.D., Ph.D., Dr.P.H.): telephone: 271-2070.
Orthodontics (M.S.): telephone: 271-6087.
Pathology (Ph.D.): telephone: 271-2693.
Periodontics (M.S.): telephone: 271-6531.
Pharmaceutical Sciences (M.S., M.S./M.B.A., Ph.D.): telephone: 271-3830.
Physiology (M.S., Ph.D.): telephone: 271-2226.
Radiological Sciences (M.S., Ph.D.): telephone: 271-5132.
Rehabilitation Sciences (M.S.): telephone: 271-2131.

Students change class on OU's campus.

UNIVERSITY OF PENNSYLVANIA

Graduate Studies

Programs of Study Penn's research doctoral and master's programs enroll students across twelve schools, engaging graduate faculty members and students from across disciplinary boundaries. The Doctor of Philosophy degree (Ph.D.) is conferred in recognition of marked ability and high attainment in a specific branch of learning. Penn's students are prepared to teach and do research that will advance the frontiers of knowledge in their respective fields. Many of the University's nearly sixty graduate groups are, by design, interdisciplinary and include faculty members from multiple departments and schools. Penn is committed to providing graduate students with the widest range of opportunities for interdisciplinary learning.

Penn's distinct success in interdisciplinary pursuits is sustained through the location of its twelve schools on one self-contained campus; everything is within walking distance. Penn is home to graduate students earning professional master's and doctorates in these twelve top-ranked schools: the Schools of Arts and Sciences, Design, Education, Engineering and Applied Science, Law, Medicine, Dental Medicine, Veterinary Medicine, Nursing, and Social Policy and Practice, the Annenberg School for Communication, and The Wharton School. Penn pioneered professional education in America and continues to set the pace today with outstanding professional programs. Professional degree programs prepare students to become leading practitioners in their fields.

The University has 4,822 members of the Standing and Associated Faculty, among them members of the Academy of Arts and Sciences (65), the Institute of Medicine (55), the National Academy of Sciences (33), American Philosophical Society (26), Guggenheim Fellows (112), National Academy of Engineering (9), MacArthur Award recipients (7), National Medal of Science recipients (6), Nobel Prize recipients (5), and Pulitzer Prize (5) winners.

Research Facilities The University is a major research enterprise, with $790 million in competitive sponsored research awards in 2006. Its interdisciplinary character is reflected in the more than 100 on-campus research institutes and centers. The collections of Penn's fifteen libraries total more than 5.5 million printed volumes and access to one of the premier digital libraries in North America. As the birthplace of modern computing, the campus is home to a vast array of scientific workstations, computer-controlled instruments, and computer labs. All on-campus student residences are connected by high-speed network, and much of the campus is wireless.

Financial Aid More than 90 percent of incoming doctoral students are awarded full support, including tuition, fees, health insurance, and a maintenance stipend. Applicants who indicate on the application form that they wish to be considered for financial assistance are automatically considered for all awards for which they are eligible, including University fellowships and teaching and research assistantships. In general, financial aid is available in the form of need-based grants and loans. The University of Pennsylvania is committed to making a Penn education accessible for all talented and qualified students. For details, students should visit http://www.sfs.upenn.edu.

Cost of Study Tuition and fees for 2007–08 Ph.D. study is $35,640. Tuition for professional degree programs differs according to the school.

Living and Housing Costs Living on campus is a great option for students new to Penn or the Philadelphia area. Off campus there are many options in terms of location, convenience, cost, and type of unit; the Off-Campus Living Office assists students and maintains an extensive database of rental properties at http://www.upenn.edu/housing and http://www.upenn.edu/offcampusliving.

Student Group Penn is home to more than 23,700 students; nearly half are graduate and professional students, more than one third are international students, and 20 percent are members of U.S. minority groups. Women account for almost half of all graduate students. The hub of Penn's vibrant graduate and professional student community is the Graduate Student Center. Located in the heart of the campus, it is home to a wide range of social and intellectual programming (http://www.upenn.edu/gsc).

Location Penn is situated in West Philadelphia, an international multicultural area full of offerings that reflect its diverse populace. West Philadelphia is home to the Philadelphia Zoo, Bartram's Gardens, parks, cultural institutions, ethnic restaurants, and many types of nineteenth- and early twentieth-century architecture. The University is also situated adjacent to Center City Philadelphia, near the heart of the Boston–Washington, D.C., corridor, affording nearly unlimited possibilities for linkages with industry, government, and other centers of research. Philadelphia is ranked among the most livable cities in the nation. Area cultural resources include the Philadelphia Museum of Art, the Rodin Museum, the Barnes Foundation, the Academy of Natural Sciences, and the Athenaeum.

The University Founded in 1740 by Benjamin Franklin, the University of Pennsylvania is a private research university and a member of the Ivy League. The University of Pennsylvania is an Equal Opportunity/Affirmative Action educator and employer.

Applying To be ensured of receiving full consideration for fellowships and scholarships, completed applications, including the results of the Graduate Record Examinations (GRE), should be received no later than December 15. Most doctoral programs admit students for September only. Applicants should apply online.

Correspondence and Information Students should browse the University Web site and contact the appropriate program office at http://www.upenn.edu/grad

Office of Graduate Education
University of Pennsylvania
122 College Hall
Philadelphia, Pennsylvania 19104-6303

E-mail: graded@pobox.upenn.edu
Web site: http://www.upenn.edu/grad

SCHOOLS, AREAS OF STUDY, AND CONTACTS

The School of Arts and Sciences: Dr. Jack Nagel, Associate Dean for Graduate Studies, 3401 Walnut Street, 322A, Philadelphia, Pennsylvania 19104-6228; phone: 215-898-7444; e-mail: gdasadmis@sas.upenn.edu; Web site: http://www.sas.upenn.edu.

Ancient history, anthropology, art and archaeology of the Mediterranean world, biology, chemistry, classical studies, comparative literature and literary theory, criminology, demography, earth and environmental science, East Asian languages and civilization, economics, English, Germanic languages and literatures, governmental administration, history, history and sociology of science, history of art, international studies (M.B.A./A.M.), liberal arts, linguistics, mathematics, music, Near Eastern languages and civilization, organizational dynamics, philosophy, physics and astronomy, political science, psychology, public finance, religious studies, Romance languages, sociology, and South Asia regional studies.

Biomedical Graduate Studies: Dr. Susan Ross, Director, University of Pennsylvania, 240 John Morgan Building, Philadelphia, Pennsylvania 19104-6064; phone: 215-898-1030; e-mail: bgs@mail.med.upenn.edu; Web site: http://www.med.upenn.edu/bgs/.

Biochemistry and molecular biophysics, bioethics, cell and molecular biology, clinical epidemiology, epidemiology and biostatistics, genomics and computational biology, immunology, neuroscience, pharmacological sciences, and public health.

School of Engineering and Applied Science: Dr. Sampath Kannan, Associate Dean, Graduate Education and Research, University of Pennsylvania, 113 Towne Building, Philadelphia, Pennsylvania 19104-6391; phone: 215-898-4542; e-mail: engadmis@seas.upenn.edu; Web site: http://www.seas.upenn.edu.

Bioengineering, chemical and biomolecular engineering, computer and information science, electrical and systems engineering, materials science and engineering, and mechanical engineering and applied mechanics. Master's programs are available in biotechnology, computer and information technology, technology management, and telecommunications and networking.

The Wharton School: Ms. Mallory Hiatt, Associate Director, Wharton Doctoral Programs, University of Pennsylvania, 1150 SH-DH, Philadelphia, Pennsylvania 19104-6302; phone: 215-898-4877; e-mail: hiattm@wharton.upenn.edu; Web site: http://www.wharton.upenn.edu.

Accounting, business and public policy, ethics and legal studies, finance, health-care systems, insurance and risk management, management, marketing, operations and information management, real estate, and statistics.

The Graduate School of Education: Manager of Admissions, The Graduate School of Education, University of Pennsylvania, Philadelphia, Pennsylvania 19104-6216; phone: 877-PENNGSE (toll-free); e-mail: admissions@gse.upenn.edu; Web site: http://www.gse.upenn.edu.

The School of Design: Dr. Gary Hack, Dean, University of Pennsylvania, 102 Meyerson Hall, Philadelphia, Pennsylvania 19104-6321; phone: 215-898-6213; e-mail: admissions@design.upenn.edu; Web site: http://www.design.upenn.edu.

Architecture, city and regional planning, fine arts, historic preservation, landscape architecture, and urban design.

The Annenberg School for Communication: Assistant Dean of Graduate Studies, The Annenberg School for Communication, University of Pennsylvania, 3620 Walnut Street–Room 315, Philadelphia, Pennsylvania 19104-6220; phone: 215-573-6349; Web site: http://www.asc.upenn.edu.

The School of Nursing: Associate Director of Graduate Enrollment Management, The School of Nursing, University of Pennsylvania, 420 Guardian Drive, Philadelphia, Pennsylvania 19104-6096; phone: 866-867-6877 (toll-free); e-mail: phd@nursing.upenn.edu; Web site: http://www.nursing.upenn.edu.

The School of Social Policy and Practice: Mary Mazzolla, Director of Recruitment and Admissions, The School of Social Policy and Practice, University of Pennsylvania, 3701 Locust Walk, Philadelphia, Pennsylvania 19104-6214; phone: 215-898-5550; e-mail: sswadmissions@sp2.upenn.edu; Web site: http://www.sp2.upenn.edu.

RICHMOND

UNIVERSITY OF RICHMOND

Arts and Sciences Graduate School

Programs of Study

The Arts and Sciences Graduate School offers programs of study leading to the degrees of Master of Arts (M.A.), Master of Science (M.S.), and Master of Liberal Arts (M.L.A.).

The M.A. degree is offered in English, history, and psychology. Course work requirements range from 30 to 36 semester hours. The psychology program requires a thesis based on original research; students in history and English may choose between thesis and nonthesis tracks.

The M.S. degree is offered in biology. Degree requirements include 30 semester hours of course work and a thesis. The program has a strong research orientation.

The M.L.A. program is cross disciplinary in nature, consisting of courses taught by faculty members from a variety of disciplines, such as art, history, literature, music, philosophy, politics, and religion. Ten courses, a minimum of 30 semester hours, are required.

Students may enroll on either a full-time or part-time basis in all programs except those in biology and psychology, which accept only full-time students.

Research Facilities

The libraries of the University contain more than 800,000 volumes and microforms. Collections in various Richmond-area libraries are also available for research and consultation, including those in the Richmond Public Library, Virginia State Library and Archives, Virginia Historical Society, and Virginia Baptist Historical Society Library (located on the campus). The Gottwald Science Center houses well-equipped laboratories and a science library. Computing support for research and instruction is provided by the University Computing Center.

Financial Aid

The Graduate School offers assistantships and a limited number of service-free scholarships to full-time graduate students who qualify on the basis of academic background and promise. Full-time students from Virginia may apply for a Virginia Tuition Assistance Grant. Various work-study and loan programs are also available to eligible graduate students. A special tuition remission, which results in substantially reduced fees, is provided for part-time students who enroll in one course per semester. Funds to support graduate student research are available through the Graduate Research Program.

Cost of Study

Tuition for full-time students for the two-semester academic year was $27,590 in 2006–07. Part-time students were charged at the reduced rate of $470 per credit hour for the first course taken each semester and at the full rate of $1380 per credit hour for additional courses.

Living and Housing Costs

The University has no on-campus housing for graduate students; however, accommodations for both single and married students are available within the Richmond community at various costs. Graduate students are welcome to purchase a meal plan or a plan on a pay as you go basis to eat in the University dining hall.

Student Group

The total University enrollment is approximately 4,700, of whom one fifth are graduate and professional students. About 100 students are enrolled in arts and sciences graduate programs each semester. Graduate students vary widely in age and background. Although the majority are from the states along the Atlantic seaboard, other parts of the nation and various other countries are represented. More than 80 percent of the full-time students receive financial aid.

Location

The University is located at the western edge of Richmond, Virginia, about 15 minutes by automobile from the city's center. Richmond is the state's capital and a major financial, business, and industrial center. The Richmond metropolitan area offers a full range of social, religious, cultural, and educational opportunities. Among cultural highlights are the Virginia Museum of Fine Arts, Richmond Symphony Orchestra, Virginia Opera, and Science Museum of Virginia. Eight other institutions of higher education are located within the metropolitan area. Richmond is only 2-hour drive away from Washington, D.C., and an hour from the Blue Ridge Mountains and Williamsburg.

The University

Founded in 1830, the University of Richmond has developed into the second-largest private university in the state. Currently among the fifty most heavily endowed universities in the nation, the University possesses the financial resources to further enhance its tradition of academic quality and humane values. The Arts and Sciences Graduate School is one of several schools and colleges that constitute the University. Other divisions include the T. C. Williams School of Law; the E. Claiborne Robins School of Business; School of Continuing Studies for summer and continuing education programs; and the Jepson School of Leadership Studies.

Applying

Applicants are required to submit a completed application form, a $30 nonrefundable processing fee, official transcripts of all previous college work, three letters of recommendation, GRE scores (for most programs), and a statement of purpose. For most programs, applications must be received by March 15. Psychology applications are due February 10. Those students wishing an assistantship or scholarship in any program should have their applications and supporting documents on file by March 15.

Correspondence and Information

Arts and Sciences Graduate School
28 Westhampton Way
University of Richmond, Virginia 23173
Phone: 804-289-8417
E-mail: asgrad@richmond.edu
Web site: http://asgraduate.richmond.edu/

THE FACULTY AND THEIR RESEARCH

Kathy W. Hoke, Director; Ph.D., North Carolina.

Biology
Linda Boland, Ph.D., North Carolina at Chapel Hill. Cell biology, neuroscience.
Rafael de Sá, Graduate Coordinator; Ph.D., Texas. Amphibian systematics.
Joseph Gindhart, Ph.D., Indiana. Genetics, bioinformatics.
W. John Hayden, Ph.D., Maryland. Plant anatomy, plant systematics.
April Hill, Ph.D., Houston. Genetics.
Malcolm Hill, Ph.D., Houston. Ecology.
Roni J. Kingsley, Chair; Ph.D., South Carolina. Invertebrate mineralization.
Valerie M. Kish, Ph.D., Michigan. Cell biology.
Scott Knight, Ph.D., Montana. Genetics.
Gary P. Radice, Ph.D., Yale. Developmental anatomy.
Laura Runyen-Janecky, Ph.D., Wisconsin. Genetics.
Peter Smallwood, Ph.D., Arizona. Ecology, evolutionary biology.
Krista Jane Stenger, Ph.D., Virginia Commonwealth. Immunology.
Aparna Telang, Ph.D., Arizona. Animal physiology.
Amy Treonis, Ph.D., Colorado State. Soil ecology, microbiology.
John Warrick, Ph.D., Temple. Genetics.

English
Bertram D. Ashe, Ph.D., William and Mary. American literature and African American literature.
Abigail Cheever, Ph.D., Johns Hopkins. Film studies.
Daryl Cumber Dance, Ph.D., Virginia. African American literature and folklore, Caribbean literature and folklore.
Terryl L. Givens, Ph.D., North Carolina. Romanticism, literary theory.
Elisabeth R. Gruner, Ph.D., UCLA. The novel, nineteenth- and twentieth-century British literature, women's literature.
Brian Henry, M.F.A., Massachusetts. Creative writing, poetry, contemporary literature.
Kathleen Hewett-Smith, Ph.D., California, Irvine. Medieval English literature, Piers Plowman, allegorical theory.
Dona J. Hickey, Ph.D., Wisconsin–Milwaukee. Rhetoric and composition, twentieth-century American and British poetry.
Raymond F. Hilliard, Ph.D., Rochester. British novel, eighteenth-century English literature, modern novel.
Suzanne W. Jones, Ph.D., Virginia. Southern fiction, women writers, feminist theory, narrative theory, the novel.
Alan S. Loxterman, Ph.D., Ohio State. Literary criticism, seventeenth-century poetry.
Joyce B. MacAllister, Ph.D., Texas. Rhetoric and composition.
Anthony P. Russell, Ph.D., Yale. Shakespeare, English Renaissance.
Ilka Saal, Ph.D., Duke. Theater and performance art, American literature.
Louis Schwartz, Graduate Coordinator; Ph.D., Brandeis. Sixteenth- and early seventeenth-century British nondramatic literature, John Milton.
David Stevens, Ph.D., Emory. Creative writing, nineteenth- and twentieth-century American literature, fiction and nonfiction writing
Louis B. Tremaine, Chair; Ph.D., Indiana. African literature, cultural studies.

History
Joan L. Bak, Ph.D., Yale. Latin America, modern Brazil.
David Brandenberger, Ph.D., Harvard. Russia and Soviet bloc.
Joanna H. Drell, Ph.D., Brown. Medieval Europe.
John L. Gordon Jr., Graduate Coordinator; Ph.D., Vanderbilt. Modern Britain and empire, Canada.
Woody Holton, Ph.D., Duke. Colonial/Revolutionary America.
Robert C. Kenzer, Ph.D., Harvard. Civil War and Reconstruction, nineteenth-century America, American South.
Tze Loo, Ph.D., Cornell. East Asia.
Kibibi Mack-Shelton, Ph.D., SUNY at Binghamton. African American.
David Routt, Ph.D., Ohio State. Medieval Europe, England.
Nicole Sackley, Ph.D., Princeton. Twentieth-century United States.
L. Carol Summers, Ph.D., Johns Hopkins. Africa.
John D. Treadway, Ph.D., Virginia. European diplomatic, Central and Eastern Europe.
Sydney Watts, Ph.D., Early modern Europe, eighteenth-century France.
Hugh A. West, Ph.D., Stanford. Modern European intellectual.
Yucel Yanikdag, Ph.D., Ohio State. Middle East, Ottoman Empire.
Eric Yellin, Ph.D., Princeton. Twentieth-century United States.

Liberal Arts
Frank E. Eakin Jr., Graduate Coordinator; Ph.D., Duke.

Psychology
Scott T. Allison, Ph.D., California, Santa Barbara. Social, decision making, social inference.
Catherine L. Bagwell, Ph.D., Duke. Developmental psychopathology, social development.
Jane M. Berry, Ph.D., Washington (St. Louis). Adult development, aging and memory.
Cindy M. Bukach, Ph.D., Victoria. Cognitive neuroscience.
Mary Churchill, Ph.D., Cincinnati. Clinical, ethics.
L. Elizabeth Crawford, Ph.D., Chicago. Spatial cognition, categorization, memory, emotion.
Craig H. Kinsley, Ph.D., SUNY at Albany. Behavioral neuroscience.
David Leary, Ph.D., Chicago. History and philosophy of psychology.
Peter O. LeViness, Ph.D., Boston College. College student mental health, positive psychology.
Ping Li, Graduate Coordinator; Ph.D., Leiden. Psycholinguistics, cognitive science.
Andrew F. Newcomb, Ph.D., Minnesota. Child clinical, developmental.
Elizabeth Stott, Ph.D., Virginia Commonwealth. Clinical, eating disorders.

UNIVERSITY OF SAN DIEGO

Graduate Programs

Programs of Study

The University of San Diego (USD) offers programs leading to both doctoral and master's degrees. The College of Arts and Sciences offers the M.A. in history, international relations, and pastoral care and counseling. A Certificate of Advanced Studies in pastoral counseling is offered for licensed health and mental health care givers. A joint-degree program leading to the J.D./M.A. in international relations is also offered in conjunction with the USD School of Law. The Globe Theatre/University of San Diego Professional Actor Training Program offers an M.F.A. in dramatic arts. The M.S. is offered in marine science, a research-based thesis program, with opportunities for research in biological, physical, chemical, and geological oceanography for students with a bachelor's degree in natural science.

The newly established Joan B. Kroc School of Peace Studies offers the M.A. in peace studies and houses the Institute for Peace & Justice and the Trans-Border Institute.

The School of Business Administration offers the M.B.A. degree, with areas of emphasis in accountancy and financial, e-commerce, finance and banking, general management, information management, international management, IT management, marketing, supply chain management, and venturing and venture capital. The M.B.A. offers both an evening and full-time option. The International Master of Business Administration (I.M.B.A.) degree is also offered as a separate program. A dual-degree program is available in conjunction with the Instituto Tecnológico y de Estudios Superiores de Monterrey (ITESM), Mexico. Joint-degree programs leading to the J.D./M.B.A., M.S.N./M.B.A., and J.D./I.M.B.A. are offered in conjunction with the USD School of Law or School of Nursing and Health Science. Other degree programs include the M.S. in accountancy and financial management, executive leadership, global leadership, supply chain management, taxation, and real estate. The business administration programs are fully accredited by AACSB International–The Association to Advance Collegiate Schools of Business.

The School of Leadership and Education Sciences offers the Doctor of Philosophy (Ph.D.) in leadership studies and has a joint doctoral program (Ed.D.) with San Diego State University. The school awards the M.A. in marital and family therapy, leadership studies, and counseling. The M.A. program in marital and family therapy is accredited by the Commission on Accreditation for Marriage and Family Therapy Education (COAMFTE). The Master of Arts in Teaching is also available. The Master of Education is awarded in learning and teaching. The University is authorized by the California Commission on Teacher Credentialing (CCTC) to recommend candidates for credentials at USD in multiple subject, multiple subject (bilingual emphasis), CLAD and BCLAD certificates, preliminary administrative services, single subject, pupil personnel services in school counseling, special education (mild/moderate, moderate/severe, deaf/hard of hearing), TESOL (teaching English to speakers of other languages) certificate, character education certificate, and the early childhood special education certificate.

The Hahn School of Nursing and Health Science offers a Master's Entry Program in Nursing (MEPN) for non-RNs, the Master of Science in Nursing (M.S.N.), a joint-degree program combining the Master of Business Administration and Master of Science in Nursing (M.B.A./M.S.N.), and the Doctor of Philosophy (Ph.D.) in nursing. The School Nurse Health Services Credential, Post-Master's Health Care Systems Certificate, and Post-M.S.N. Nurse Practitioner Certificate are also offered. The M.S.N. program prepares family, pediatric, and adult nurse practitioners and nurse administrators for a variety of health-care settings and prepares nurse case managers for specific client groups in acute, long-term community, and home-health settings.

The School of Law offers the Juris Doctor (J.D.); Master of Law (LL.M.) in business and corporate law, comparative law, international law, and taxation; and Master of Laws (LL.M.) general as well as the joint-degree programs mentioned above.

Research Facilities

Copley Library features more than 714,080 books and 10,450 current journal subscriptions as well as newspapers, government documents, reference books, rare books, and access to many databases. The Media Center has an extensive audiovisual collection. The Legal Research Center in the School of Law maintains a collection in excess of 450,000 volumes.

Financial Aid

For application materials, students should contact the Office of Financial Aid Services, University of San Diego, Hughes Administration Center, 5998 Alcalá Park, San Diego, California 92110-2492 (telephone: 619-260-4514 or 800-248-4873 (toll-free); Web site: http://www.sandiego.edu/admissions/financialaid). Students interested in applying for graduate assistantships should contact the graduate schools to which they are applying. Applications for financial aid should be received by April 1 for the fall semester. However, applications are accepted during the year for any portion of the year remaining.

Cost of Study

For the 2007–08 academic year, master's and credential tuition costs are $1010 per semester unit. Doctoral tuition costs are $1085 per semester unit.

Living and Housing Costs

Information on graduate housing can be obtained by contacting the Department of Housing and Residence Life, University of San Diego, Mission Crossroads, 5998 Alcalá Park, San Diego, California 92110 (telephone: 619-260-4777; Web site: http://www.housing.sandiego.edu).

Student Group

The student population in 2006–07 was approximately 7,483, including approximately 1,376 graduate and 1,145 law students. Students come from all over the U.S., and international students represent about 5 percent of the graduate enrollment.

Student Outcomes

Graduate degree recipients report employment in areas related to their fields of study. For example, in the College of Arts and Sciences, students with international relations degrees secured employment in international business, teaching, and corporate relations; practical theology degrees led to teaching, campus, and catechetical ministries. School of Business graduates were hired in areas such as e-commerce, finance development, project management, and supply chain management. School of Leadership and Education Sciences graduates are employed in teaching at all levels and in counseling, administrative, nonprofit management, and consulting careers. School of Nursing graduates entered clinical, educational, and research settings as well as advanced degree programs.

Location

San Diego, a city of more than 1 million people, is the second-largest city in California and sixth largest in the country. Just 30 minutes north of the border with Mexico, it offers spectacular views of the Pacific Ocean and surrounding mountains. USD's 180-acre campus provides access to business, cultural, residential, and recreational areas by its proximity to air and rail terminals, city bus stops, and freeways.

The University

USD is an independent, Roman Catholic university that was founded in 1949. The University comprises six academic schools: the College of Arts and Sciences, the School of Peace Studies, the School of Business, School of Leadership and Education Sciences, School of Law, and School of Nursing and Health Science. Class size averages 18 students, facilitating close rapport with faculty members.

Applying

Application for admission is made to the Office of Graduate Admissions. There are several different applications, depending on the program, and most are available online, through the graduate admissions Web site. All applicants must submit the application form, application fee, one official copy of all postsecondary transcripts, three letters of recommendation, and applicable standardized test scores. Application deadlines vary. Students should contact Graduate Admissions for program deadlines.

Correspondence and Information

Office of Graduate Admissions
University of San Diego
5998 Alcalá Park
San Diego, California 92110-2492
Phone: 619-260-4524; 800-248-4873 (toll-free)
Fax: 619-260-4158
E-mail: grads@sandiego.edu
Web site: http://www.sandiego.edu/admissions/graduate

Office of Admissions and Financial Aid
School of Law
University of San Diego
Warren Hall, Room 203
5998 Alcalá Park
San Diego, California 92110-2492
Phone: 619-260-4528; 800-248-4873 (toll-free)
E-mail: jdinfo@sandiego.edu
Web site: http://www.sandiego.edu/usdlaw

FACULTY HEADS

DEANS

College of Arts and Sciences: Nicholas M. Healy, Ph.D.
School of Business (interim): Andrew T. Allen, Ph.D.
School of Law: Kevin Cole, J.D.
School of Leadership and Education Sciences: Paula A. Cordeiro, Ed.D.
School of Nursing and Health Science: Sally Hardin, Ph.D.
School of Peace Studies: Fr. William Headley

GRADUATE PROGRAM COORDINATORS

College of Arts and Sciences
Dramatic Arts: Richard Seer, M.F.A.
History: Michael Gonzalez, Ph.D.
International Relations: Emily Edmonds, Ph.D.
Marine Science: Ronald Kaufmann, Ph.D.
Pastoral Care and Counseling: Ellen Colangelo, Ph.D.
Peace and Justice Studies: Lee Ann Otto, Ph.D.

School of Business
Ahler's Center for International Business: Denise Dimon, Ph.D.
Business Administration: Kacy Kilner, M.B.A.

School of Leadership and Education Sciences
American Humanics: Theresa Van Horn, M.A.
Counseling: Susan Zgliczynski, Ph.D.
Leadership Studies: Cheryl Getz, Ed.D.
Learning and Teaching: Judy Mantle, Ph.D.
Marital and Family Therapy: Todd Edwards, Ph.D.
Master of Arts in Teaching: Judy Mantle, Ph.D.
Multiple Subjects Credentials: Judy Mantle, Ph.D.
Single Subject Credentials: Judy Mantle, Ph.D.

School of Nursing and Health Science
Accelerated B.S.N./M.S.N.: Susan Instone, D.N.Sc.
Adult Clinical Nurse Specialist: Susan Instone, D.N.Sc.
Adult Nurse Practitioner: Susan Instone, D.N.Sc.
Doctor of Philosophy (Ph.D.) in Nursing: Patricia Roth, Ph.D.
Family Nurse Practitioner: Susan Instone, D.N.Sc.
Health Care Systems Administration: Susan Instone, D.N.Sc.
Joint M.B.A./M.S.N.: Susan Instone, D.N.Sc.
Master's Entry Program in Nursing: Anita Hunter, Ph.D.
Pediatric Nurse Practitioner: Susan Instone, D.N.Sc.
Post–FNP Urgent/Emergent Care Certificate: Susan Instone, D.N.Sc.
Post–M.S.N. Adult Clinical Nurse Specialist Certificate: Susan Instone, D.N.Sc.
Post–M.S.N. Adult, Family, and Pediatric Nurse Practitioner Certificates: Susan Instone, D.N.Sc.
RN-B.S.N.: Anita Hunter, Ph.D.
Web-Enhanced Family Nurse Practitioner: Susan Instone, D.N.Sc.

UNIVERSITY OF SOUTH ALABAMA

Graduate School

Programs of Study The Graduate School offers a wide range of graduate degrees, including an interdisciplinary M.S. in environmental toxicology, the M.S. in occupational therapy and in speech and hearing sciences, and an M.H.S. in physician assistant studies (College of Allied Health Professions); the M.A. in communication, English, history, and sociology; the M.S. in biological sciences, mathematics, marine sciences, and psychology; and the Master of Public Administration in the Department of Political Science (College of Arts and Sciences); the Master of Business Administration and the Master of Accounting (Mitchell College of Business); the M.S. in computer and information sciences (School of Computer and Information Sciences); the Master of Education, with concentrations in alternative education, alternative secondary education, early childhood education, educational leadership, educational media, elementary education, health education, physical education, school counseling, school psychometry, and secondary education, as well as a collaborative program; the M.S. in community counseling, exercise technology, instructional design and development, recreation administration, rehabilitation counseling, and therapeutic recreation; and the Educational Specialist degree in counselor education, early childhood education, educational leadership, educational media, elementary education, health education, physical education, secondary education, and special education as well as a collaborative program (College of Education); the M.S. in electrical engineering, chemical engineering, and mechanical engineering (College of Engineering); and the Master of Science in Nursing, with concentrations in adult health nursing, clinical nurse specialist studies, community–mental health nursing, executive and midlevel nursing administration, nursing education, and woman and child health nursing (College of Nursing). The Doctor of Audiology (Au.D.), the Doctor of Nursing Practice (D.N.P.), and the Doctor of Physical Therapy are offered. The Ph.D. is offered in communication sciences and disorders, instructional design and development, marine sciences, and the basic medical sciences, with specializations available in biochemistry, microbiology/immunology, pharmacology, physiology, and structural and cellular biology.

Research Facilities The graduate program in the basic medical sciences is housed in the College of Medicine, which has the Primate Center, Laboratory of Molecular Biology, Electron Microscopy Center, Mass Spectroscopy Center, Flow Cytometry Center, DNA-Protein Sequencing and Synthesis Center, Sickle-Cell Center, and Cancer Center. The graduate program in nursing has access to the clinical facilities of the two University of South Alabama (USA) hospitals and numerous outpatient clinics. The graduate program in marine sciences is housed in the College of Arts and Sciences, which has the Big Creek Biological Station available during the entire year for field research on reservoirs and streams. The University is a member of the Alabama Marine and Environmental Sciences Consortium and has full access to the consortium's extensive research facilities, which are located on the Gulf of Mexico on Dauphin Island, Alabama. The University is also a member of the Mississippi-Alabama Sea Grant Consortium and the Oak Ridge Associated Universities Consortium. The University libraries consist of the University (main) Library, USA Archives on the Spring Hill Avenue Campus, the Biomedical Library, two hospital libraries, and library services offered at the Baldwin County campus. The Biomedical Library system serves the information needs of students and faculty members in the Colleges of Medicine, Nursing, and Allied Health Professions, while the main library serves the remaining colleges (Arts and Sciences, Business, Computer and Information Sciences, Continuing Education, Education, and Engineering). Collectively, they provide access to more than 500,000 monographic titles, nearly 3,000 print subscriptions, about 1 million government documents, and an ever-expanding array of Internet-accessible information databases, including full-text article databases that provide electronic access to thousands of additional, unique journal titles or serial publications. The Archives houses one of the largest photographic collections in the region, as well as many important collections, including the papers of Congressmen Jack Edwards and Sonny Callahan, and material from the civil rights era. The Psychological Teaching Clinic is operated in support of the master's degree program in psychology, and the Business Resources Center is available to students in the M.B.A. program. A modern, fully equipped Speech and Hearing Clinic provides research facilities for graduate students in that program.

Financial Aid The major University awards are assistantships in master's programs in all fields, with stipends of $6000 to $15,000 for the academic year plus tuition fellowships and remission of out-of-state tuition. Assistants are expected to pay other specific fees. Stipends of $10,000 to $17,000 per year, a remission of out-of-state tuition, plus tuition fellowships and remission of out-of-state tuition are awarded to students in the Ph.D. programs.

Cost of Study The basic fees for fall 2006 amounted to $265 per semester plus course fees of $167 per semester hour; thus, a regular student carrying a 9-semester-hour load paid course fees of $1503 per semester, or $3006 for the academic year. Out-of-state rates were $334 per semester hour; thus, a regular student carrying a 9-semester-hour load paid course fees of $3006 per semester, or $6012 for the academic year. There is no tuition fee for Ph.D. students in basic medical sciences.

Living and Housing Costs The University has extensive housing near the campus for single and married students; rent is about $240 to $485 per month. Single students may live in dorms; the cost ranges from about $960 per semester for a suite to about $1936 per semester for a one-person efficiency apartment. A board plan is available, with options from $935 to $1049 per semester. The cost of living in Mobile is slightly below the national average.

Student Group In 2006–07, the University enrolled 13,303 students, 2,736 of them as graduate students. Sixty-two percent of the students were from Alabama, 26 percent from other states, and 12 percent from other countries.

Student Outcomes The University of South Alabama awards approximately 650 master's degrees each academic year. Graduates are currently enrolled in Ph.D. programs at Arizona State, Emory, Michigan, Missouri–Columbia, Rutgers, Texas A&M, Washington University in St. Louis, Wisconsin, Yale, and a number of other institutions. Education graduates have found teaching and administrative positions in all fifty states and in Australia, Bahrain, Canada, Germany, Hong Kong, Mexico, Nigeria, Russia, Venezuela, and the Virgin Islands. Others find employment in business and industry, government agencies, and hospitals and clinics throughout the country.

Location The University is in Mobile, Alabama, a port city and metropolitan area with a population of 476,000. While summers are warm, the overall climate is pleasantly mild. The nearby Gulf of Mexico beaches and extensive water resources of Mobile Bay and its tributaries provide outstanding recreational opportunities.

The University Founded in 1964, the University comprises the Graduate School; the Colleges of Allied Health Professions, Arts and Sciences, Education, Engineering, Medicine, and Nursing; Mitchell College of Business; the School of Continuing Education and Special Programs; and the School of Computer and Information Sciences. There are three specialized departments: cooperative education, military science, and aerospace studies. The University has two major teaching hospitals in Mobile. All facilities are entirely modern.

Applying The University deadlines for applications and all supporting documents are July 15 for fall, December 1 for spring, and May 1 for summer. Some programs may have earlier deadlines; the requirements for a specific program may be found in the University Bulletin. The admission decision is based on the applicant's previous academic record and on evidence of the ability to pursue work on the graduate level.

Correspondence and Information

For admission information:
Director of Admissions
Meisler Hall 2500
University of South Alabama
Mobile, Alabama 36688-0002
Phone: 800-872-5247 (toll-free)

For the basic medical sciences program:
Graduate Director
Graduate Program in Basic Medical Sciences
College of Medicine (MSB 3316)
University of South Alabama
Mobile, Alabama 36688-0002
Phone: 251-460-6153

For other graduate programs:
Dean of the Graduate School
Mobile Townhouse 222
University of South Alabama
Mobile, Alabama 36688-0002
Phone: 251-460-6310
E-mail: dpatters@usouthal.edu
Web site: http://www.southalabama.edu

DEANS AND DIRECTORS

Graduate School: B. Keith Harrison, Interim Dean; Ph.D., Missouri.
College of Allied Health Professions: Richard E. Talbott, Dean; Ph.D., Oklahoma. Julio Turrens, Director of Graduate Studies; Ph.D., Buenos Aires (Argentina).
College of Arts and Sciences: G. David Johnson, Dean; Ph.D., Southern Illinois at Carbondale. S. L. Varghese, Director of Graduate Studies; Ph.D., Yale.
Mitchell College of Business: Carl Moore, Dean; Ph.D., Alabama. John E. Gamble, Director of Graduate Studies; Ph.D., Alabama.
School of Computer and Information Sciences: David Feinstein, Dean; Ph.D., Stanford. Roy Daigle, Director of Graduate Studies; Ph.D., Georgia.
College of Education: Richard L. Hayes, Dean; Ed.D., Boston University. Abigail Baxter, Director of Graduate Studies; Ph.D., Vanderbilt.
College of Engineering: John W. Steadman, Dean; Ph.D., Colorado State. Thomas G. Thomas Jr., Director of Graduate Studies; Ph.D., Alabama in Huntsville.
College of Medicine: Samuel J. Strada, Interim Dean; Ph.D., Vanderbilt. Ronald D. Balczon, Director of Graduate Studies; Ph.D., Baylor.
College of Nursing: Debra C. Davis, Dean; D.S.N., Alabama at Birmingham. Rosemary Rhodes, Director of Graduate Studies; D.N.S., LSU.

A lecture at sea for marine science students at the University of South Alabama.

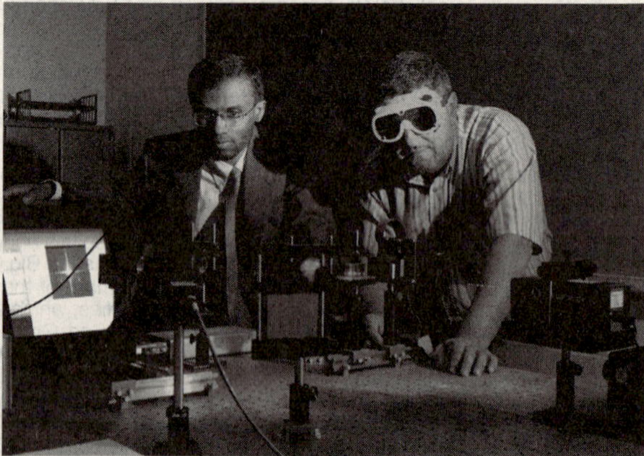

Ultrafast optical processor used for pattern recognition and tracking applications developed in the electrical and computer engineering department at USA.

USA basic medical science researchers at work.

UNIVERSITY OF SOUTH CAROLINA

The Graduate School

Programs of Study

The University of South Carolina offers the doctorate, with specializations in anthropology, biology, biomedical science, business administration, chemistry, communication sciences and disorders, comparative literature, computer science, economics, education, engineering, English, geography, geology, history, journalism, library and information science, linguistics, marine science, mathematics, music, nursing, pharmacy, philosophy, physical education, physical therapy, physics, political science, psychology, public health, social work, sociology, and statistics.

Master's degrees are offered in all the above fields. Students can also earn master's degrees in accountancy; creative writing; criminology and criminal justice; earth resources management; fine arts; French; genetic counseling; German; hotel, restaurant, and tourism management; human resources; international business; library and information science; media arts; nurse anesthesia; the professional master's program in the sciences; public administration; religious studies; retailing; Spanish; sports management; teaching; and theater.

Research Facilities

The University's Thomas Cooper Library provides access to more than 7.5 million volumes, periodicals, microfilm entries, and manuscripts in the University system through the USCAN integrated information system. Outstanding research facilities are maintained in the sciences, humanities, and professional disciplines. Computer facilities include an Intel Paragon high-performance parallel computer system and an IBM 3090-400E mainframe computer. An extensive fiber-optic network connects local area networks to the Internet's global resources. A number of areas of particular research excellence are supported by research centers and institutes, including the Baruch Institute for Marine Biology and Coastal Research, the Institute for Biological Research and Technology, the Center for Family in Society, the Southeast Manufacturing Technology Center, the Research Division of the Moore School of Business Administration, the Institute for International Studies, and the Institute for Southern Studies.

Financial Aid

Fellowships are available in many departments. Graduate assistantships are available in most departments and provide competitive stipends. Information about fellowships and assistantships should be obtained from the department of interest.

Cost of Study

Academic fees for full-time study in 2006–07 were $4144 per semester for South Carolina residents and $8958 per semester for nonresidents. Part-time resident students' academic fees were $411 per hour; part-time nonresident students' academic fees were $874 per hour. Academic fees for students in the health professions differ from the above-stated charges. Health-services fees are included for students taking 12 or more hours. Optional activity, athletic, and health-services fees are based on the student's full- or part-time status. The University reserves the right to alter its charges without notice.

Living and Housing Costs

Graduate students normally live in off-campus housing. For 2006–07, a room in a private home averaged $500 per month. An unfurnished apartment without utilities averaged $575 per month (one bedroom) to $675 per month (two bedrooms). The Off-Campus Student Services Office assists students in locating off-campus housing. Total costs per academic year for a single resident student were estimated at $16,500 for tuition, room, board, and general expenses.

Student Group

During the 2006–07 academic year, graduate enrollment averaged about 7,000. Approximately 32 percent of the graduate students were from out of state, representing every state and ninety other countries.

Student Outcomes

Doctoral and master's program graduates are nationally competitive for academic, research, and leadership positions in national and multinational corporations, public and private institutions, and government agencies and are actively recruited on campus. Graduates seeking placement in the Southeast find positions in the rapidly expanding technology and manufacturing industries, major tourism and service industries, and educational and research institutions.

Location

Columbia, the capital of the state, has a population of approximately 500,000 residents within the metropolitan area. The University is located near the main downtown areas and the state government complex of buildings. Greater Columbia offers a wide range of cultural attractions and entertainment, including the Koger Center for the Arts, the Colonial Center, the South Carolina Orchestra Association, the Columbia City Ballet, the Columbia Art Museum, South Carolina State Museum, several excellent community and children's theaters, and the nationally known Riverbanks Zoo. The city is located in the center of the state, and an excellent network of roads makes it easy to drive to the ocean and the mountains. Lake Murray, one of the largest lakes in the state and the setting for a range of aquatic activities, is only 15 miles from Columbia. Golf and tennis may be enjoyed the year round.

The University

The University was founded in 1801, the first state college to be supported by annual public appropriations. Having expanded through the years around the original horseshoe-shaped campus, the University today is the state's largest public institution of higher learning. Expansion in the last twenty years has been particularly rapid, and some of the most striking architecture of the region can be found on the campus. The University has launched the first phase of its research campus in downtown Columbia.

Applying

Application must be made on Graduate School forms, which must be accompanied by a nonrefundable fee of $40. Applications should be submitted by July 1 for the fall semester, November 15 for the spring semester, May 1 for the first summer session, and June 1 for the second summer session. Some programs have earlier application deadlines; therefore, students should contact the academic unit to which they intend to apply. Earlier submission is necessary if financial aid is requested. An application cannot receive final consideration until all required credentials reach the Graduate School, including official transcripts, letters of recommendation, and test scores. Detailed admission requirements are given in the *Graduate Studies Bulletin.*

Correspondence and Information

The Graduate School
University of South Carolina
Columbia, South Carolina 29208
Phone: 803-777-4243
Fax: 803-777-2972
E-mail: gradapp@gwm.sc.edu
Web site: http://www.gradschool.sc.edu/

University of South Carolina

DEANS OF COLLEGES AND HEADS OF DEPARTMENTS

Graduate School: Christine Ebert, Associate Provost and Dean.
Anthony Edwards, Assistant Dean.
Dale Moore, Director of Graduate Admissions.

Moore School of Business: Joel A. Smith, Dean.

College of Education: Les Sternberg, Dean.
Department of Educational Leadership and Policies.
Department of Educational Studies: Alan Wieder, Chair.
Department of Instruction and Teacher Education: Ed Dickey, Chair.
Department of Physical Education: Murray Mitchell, Chair.

College of Engineering and Information Technology: Michael Amiridis, Dean.
Department of Chemical Engineering: Harry Ploehn, Interim Chair.
Department of Civil Engineering: M. Hanif Chaudhry, Chair.
Department of Computer Science and Engineering: Manton M. Mattews, Interim Chair.
Department of Electrical Engineering: M. Asif Kahn, Chair.
Department of Mechanical Engineering: Abdel Bayoumi, Chair.

School of the Environment: Madilyn M. Fletcher, Director.

College of Hospitality, Retail, and Sport Management: Patricia Moody, Dean.
School of Hotel, Restaurant, and Tourism Management: Carl Boger, Chair.
Department of Retailing: Marianne Bickle, Chair.
Department of Sport and Entertainment Management: Tom H. Regan, Chair.

College of Arts and Sciences: Mary Anne Fitzpatrick, Dean.
Department of Anthropology: Thomas Leatherman, Chair.
Department of Art: Cynthia Colbert, Chair.
Department of Biology: Sarah Woodin, Chair.
Department of Chemistry and Biochemistry: Daniel L. Reger, Chair.
Program in Comparative Literature: Allen Miller, Director.
Department of Criminology and Criminal Justice: Geoffrey Alpert, Chair.
Department of English: Steve Lynn, Chair.
Department of Geography: David J. Cowen, Chair.
Department of Geological Sciences: James N. Kellogg, Chair.
Department of History: Patrick Maney, Chair.
Department of Languages, Literatures, and Cultures: William Edmiston, Chair.
Program in Linguistics: D. Eric Holt, Director.
Program in Marine Science: Robert C. Thunell, Director.
Department of Mathematics: Manfred Stoll, Chair.
Department of Philosophy: Jerry Hackett, Chair.
Department of Physics and Astronomy: Fred Myrer, Chair.
Department of Political Science: Harvey Starr, Chair.
Department of Psychology: Charles F. Mactutus, Chair.
Department of Religious Studies: Carl D. Evans, Chair.
Department of Sociology: Barry Markovsky, Chair.
Department of Statistics: Don Edwards, Chair.
Department of Theatre, Speech, and Dance: Jim O'Connor, Chair.

Law School: Walter F. Pratt Jr., Dean.

College of Mass Communications and Information Studies: Charles Bierbauer, Dean.
School of Journalism and Mass Communications: Shirley Staples Carter, Director.
School of Library and Information Science: Samantha K. Hastings, Director.

School of Medicine: Larry R. Faulkner, Dean.

School of Music: Tayloe Harding, Dean

College of Nursing: Peggy Hewlett, Dean.

College of Pharmacy: Farid Sadik, Dean.

Arnold School of Public Health: Donna Richter, Dean.
Department of Communication Sciences and Disorders: Elaine Frank, Chair.
Department of Environmental Health Science: G. Thomas Chandler, Chair.
Department of Epidemiology and Biostatistics: John Vena, Chair.
Department of Exercise Science: J. Larry Durstine, Chair.
Department of Health Services Policy and Management: Jan Probst, Chair.
Department of Health Promotion, Education, and Behavior: Ken Watkins, Interim Chair.

College of Social Work: Dennis Poole, Dean.

The University of South Carolina is committed to a policy of affirmative action that ensures equal opportunity in education and employment to all qualified persons regardless of race, sex, religion, creed, handicap, disability, veteran status, national origin, or ancestry.

The University of South Dakota.

THE UNIVERSITY OF SOUTH DAKOTA

Graduate School

Programs of Study

The Graduate School of the University of South Dakota offers programs leading to the degrees of Master of Arts, Master of Business Administration, Master of Fine Arts, Master of Music, Master of Natural Science, Master of Professional Accountancy, Master of Public Administration, and Master of Science as well as to the degrees of Specialist in Education, Doctor of Education, Doctor of Philosophy, Juris Doctor, and Doctor of Medicine.

Majors leading to the degree of Master of Arts are offered in biology; communication studies; counseling and psychology in education; educational administration; elementary education; English; health, physical education, and recreation; history; interdisciplinary studies; mathematics; political science; psychology; secondary education; special education; and theater.

Majors leading to the degree of Master of Science are offered in administrative studies, basic biomedical sciences, biology, chemistry, computer science, occupational therapy, and technology for education and training.

Majors leading to the Specialist in Education are counseling and psychology in education, curriculum and instruction, and educational administration.

Majors leading to the degree of Doctor of Education include curriculum and instruction and educational administration.

Majors leading to the degree of Doctor of Philosophy are offered in basic biomedical science, biological science, computational science and statistics; counseling and psychology in education, English, and psychology.

The University of South Dakota also offers clinical doctorate degrees in communication disorders and in physical therapy, and a joint M.D./Ph.D. program.

Variations exist in the requirements of the graduate degree programs offered by respective departments. It is important for students to become acquainted with the specific requirements of their departments, because these, as well as certain University requirements, must be satisfied.

The University's academic year is divided into two semesters of approximately sixteen weeks each and a summer session of twelve weeks. By regular attendance during the summer sessions only, a student may earn a master's degree in four summers in some areas of the Graduate School.

Research Facilities

The University of South Dakota places great emphasis on the integration of research and teaching; consequently, graduate students have access to essentially all of the University's research facilities. There are a number of specialized research institutes, such as the Human Factors Laboratory, the Archaeology Laboratory, the Oral History Center, the Missouri River Institute, and the Business Research Bureau. Scientific instrumentation includes state-of-the-art equipment in the biological, physical, and computational sciences. Supporting on-campus organizations include the National Music Museum, which houses one of the world's largest collections of historic musical instruments; the W. H. Over Museum; the South Dakota State Geological Survey; and the Allen H. Neuharth Center for Excellence in Journalism.

Financial Aid

Financial assistance is available through a variety of graduate assistantships, grants, loans, scholarships, and work-study programs. During the 2005–06 school year, graduate assistantships ranged from $4600 to $18,000 for the nine-month academic year. Assistantships qualify the student for a two-thirds tuition reduction. Summer assistantships are available in a variety of areas. To be eligible for an assistantship, a student must be fully admitted to a graduate degree program, have a minimum GPA of 3.0, and maintain full-time status with 9 or more credit hours per semester.

Cost of Study

Graduate tuition in 2007–08 is $125.25 per credit hour for state residents and $369.30 for nonresidents. Graduate assistants pay one third the graduate resident rate if registered for 9 credit hours or more. Other fees are added accordingly, which are the general activity fee, $23.80 per credit hour, and the university support fee, $73.35 per credit hour.

Living and Housing Costs

Assistance in finding off-campus rooms and apartments is available from the Director of Housing. Dormitory rooms are also available. For the 2007–08 school year, single-occupant rooms cost $1557 per semester. Double-occupant rooms cost $1251.65 per semester. Graduate students who reside in the dorms are not required to carry a meal plan; however, COYOTE CA$H is recommended. Married student housing is also available at the rate of $401.10 per month.

Student Group

There were approximately 6,500 undergraduate students and 2,300 graduate students enrolled during the 2006–07 fall semester. Sixty-one percent of all enrolled students are women; approximately 25 percent of students are either nonresident or international.

Location

The University of South Dakota, authorized by the first territorial legislature in 1862, is located in Vermillion, a community of 10,000 people that is situated in the southeastern corner of the state. Vermillion overlooks the scenic and historic Missouri River Valley and is home to a special blend of agriculture, retail business, and light industry.

The University and The School

The University is accredited by the North Central Association of Colleges and Schools to offer master's, specialist's, and doctoral programs. The individual graduate programs are accredited by the appropriate agencies.

Applying

Students who wish to take graduate-level courses must register through the Graduate School of the University of South Dakota. A completed application packet must be sent to the Graduate School Office. The packet should include an application form, a $35 nonrefundable fee, three recommendation forms, purpose statement, two official transcripts (sent by the institution to USD's Graduate School), and official test score results. Applicants should be aware that several programs, including physical therapy, physician assistant studies, and occupational therapy, have their own application forms.

Correspondence and Information

Graduate School
Slagle Hall, Room 107
The University of South Dakota
414 East Clark Street
Vermillion, South Dakota 57069

Phone: 605-677-6287
877-COYOTES (toll-free)
E-mail: gradsch@usd.edu
Web site: http://www.usd.edu/gradsch

GRADUATE PROGRAMS AND DIRECTORS

Direct telephone contacts may be made by dialing the number listed for each program.

MASTER OF ARTS
Basic Biomedical Sciences: Steven Waller (605-677-5157).
Biology: Paula Mabee (605-605-677-5211).
Chemistry: Ranjit Koodali (605-677-5487).
Communication Studies: Clark Callahan (605-677-8818).
Computer Science: Richard McBride (605-677-5388).
Counseling and Psychology in Education: Hee-sook Choi (605-677-5250).
Educational Administration: Mark Baron (605-677-5260).
Elementary Education: Garreth Zalud (605-677-5451).
English: John Dudley (605-677-5981).
Health, Physical Education and Recreation: Garreth Zalud (Interim) (605-677-5336).
History: Robert Hilderbrand (605-677-5218).
Interdisciplinary Studies: John Day (605-677-5481).
Mathematics: Nan Jiang (605-677-5262).
Political Science: Rich Braunstein (605-677-5242).
Psychology: Barbara Yutrzenka (605-677-5351).
Clinical Psychology: Barbara Yutrzenka (605-e-mail: byutrzyen@usd.edu).
Human Factors: Jan Berkhout (605-e-mail: berkhout@usd.edu).
Secondary Education: Garreth Zalud (605-677-5451).
Special Education: Garreth Zalud (605-677-5451).
Theater: Ron Moyer (605-677-5418).

MASTER OF BUSINESS ADMINISTRATION: Angeline Lavin (605-677-5232).

MASTER OF FINE ARTS
Art: Cory Knedler (605-677-5636).
Theater: Ron Moyer (605-677-5418).

MASTER OF MUSIC: David Moskowitz (605-677-5274).

MASTER OF NATURAL SCIENCE: Miles Koppang (605-677-5211 or 5487).

MASTER OF PUBLIC ADMINISTRATION: Rich Braunstein (605-677-5242).

MASTER OF SCIENCE
Administrative Studies: Tony Molina (605-677-6405).
Biology: Paula Mabee (605-677-5211).
Occupational Therapy: Barbara Brockevelt (605-677-5600).
Physician Assistant Studies: Wade Nilson (605-677-5128).
Technology for Education and Training: Leslie Moller (605-677-5448).

SPECIALIST IN EDUCATION
Counseling and Psychology in Education: Hee-Sook Choi (605-677-5250).
Curriculum and Instruction: Garreth Zalud (605-677-5210).
Educational Administration: Mark Baron (605-677-5260).

DOCTOR OF EDUCATION
Curriculum and Instruction: Garreth Zalud (605-677-5210).
Educational Administration: Mark Baron (605-677-5260).

DOCTOR OF PHILOSOPHY
Basic Biomedical Sciences: Steven Waller (605-677-5170).
Computational Science and Statistics: Asai Asaithambi (605-677-5388).
Counseling and Psychology in Education: Frank Main (605-677-5250).
English: John Dudley (605-677-5981).
Psychology: Barbara Yutrzenka (605-677-5351).
Clinical Psychology: Barbara Yutrzenka (605-e-mail: byutrzyen@usd.edu).
Human Factors: Jan Berkhout (605-e-mail: berkhout@usd.edu).
M.D./Ph.D. in Medicine: Paul Bunger (605-677-6886)

JURIS DOCTOR: Tom Sorenson (605-677-5444).

DOCTOR OF MEDICINE
Clinical Doctorate in Communication Disorders: Teresa Bellis (605-677-5474)
Clinical Doctorate in Physical Therapy: Lana Svien (605-677-5915)

UNIVERSITY OF SOUTH FLORIDA

Graduate School

Programs of Study

University of South Florida (USF) graduate programs address significant national, regional, and local issues. For example, USF hosts the only interdisciplinary program in aging studies in the nation and an interdisciplinary cancer biology Ph.D. with the H. Lee Moffitt Cancer Center. USF offers 136 master's degrees, three education specialist programs, and thirty-eight separate doctoral degrees. More than eighty-five graduate certificates are also available. Some of USF's nationally recognized doctoral programs are applied anthropology, biology, chemistry, communication, computer science, education, electrical engineering, marine science, medical sciences, nursing, psychology, and public health.

Research Facilities

The University of South Florida is one of the nation's top sixty-three public research universities, as designated by the Carnegie Foundation for the Advancement of Teaching. In the last five years, research funding at USF has grown from $186 million to $310 million, and USF is ranked by the National Science Foundation as one of the nation's fastest-growing universities in terms of federal research and development expenditures. Outstanding among USF's more than seventy interdisciplinary research and education centers, bureaus, and institutes are the H. Lee Moffitt Cancer Center, the Florida Mental Health Institute, the Center for Urban Transportation and Research, the Institute on Black Life, and the Florida Institute of Oceanography.

Financial Aid

Qualified graduate students may be eligible for a number of presidential fellowships, assistantships, and other awards. Interested students should contact the program director for information and applications. Additional information is available from the Web site of the Graduate School. USF also has a substantial number of fellowships targeted specifically at underrepresented minority students; minority applicants can contact the Graduate School Office at 813-974-2846 for details. Tuition waivers are available to eligible graduate students who hold assistantships or certain fellowships.

Cost of Study

Tuition, including activity fees, for in-state residents at the Tampa Campus for 2007–08 is $275.11 per credit hour, or $3301.32 per semester, based on 12 hours of graduate enrollment. The comparable amount for out-of-state graduate students is $919.04 per credit hour, or $11,028.48 per semester, based on 12 hours of graduate enrollment.

Living and Housing Costs

Many graduate students choose to live in Magnolia Apartments, where two buildings are designated for students who are 21 years of age and older. In addition, one building is designed for families. Magnolia opened in fall 2001 and offers two-bedroom family apartments as well as three- and four-bedroom apartments for single students. Dining plans are available, offering all-you-can-eat dining in two dining halls on campus. For additional information regarding the residence halls and meal plans, students should visit http://www.reserv.usf.edu.

Student Group

The 44,251 University of South Florida students in fall 2006 came from 156 countries (of 3,718 international students, about 21 percent are graduate students), all fifty states and the District of Columbia, and nearly all of the sixty-seven counties in Florida. The ratio of men to women is 2:3. Approximately 77 percent of the students are undergraduates, 18 percent are graduate students, and 6 percent are in the professional programs or unclassified. About 5,056 African-American students, 4,902 Hispanic-American students, and 2,418 Asian-American students attend USF.

Location

Strategically located in the Tampa Bay metropolitan area, this multicultural metropolis offers a wealth of arts and leisure activities: a professional orchestra, Broadway theatrical productions, world-class concert halls, art museums, big-city nightlife, bountiful ethnic restaurants, and professional sports teams. In job opportunities, cost of living, education, climate, health care, and arts and recreation, this area ranks among the top five best places to live in the country, according to *Places Rated Almanac.*

The University

Established in 1956, the University of South Florida is a rising star in American education. The first of a new breed of universities created to meet America's urban higher education needs, this young, dynamic institution has experienced explosive growth. With a $1.3-billion annual budget, USF is one of the largest metropolitan universities in the Southeast, serving nearly 45,000 students on campuses in Tampa, St. Petersburg, Sarasota, and Lakeland. USF is a member of the Big East Athletic Conference.

Applying

Admission requirements vary among USF's graduate programs; applicants should contact the program of interest for specific admission requirements. For a complete list of colleges, graduate programs, and application materials, prospective students should visit the Graduate School's Web site or contact the USF Graduate School.

Correspondence and Information

For general information:
USF Graduate School
4202 East Fowler Avenue, BEH304
University of South Florida
Tampa, Florida 33620-8470
Phone: 813-974-2846
866-974-8800 (toll-free)
Fax: 813-974-5762
E-mail: admissions@grad.usf.edu
Web site: http://www.grad.usf.edu

For program information:
Graduate Coordinator
(specify college and department or program)
University of South Florida
4202 East Fowler Avenue
Tampa, Florida 33620

COLLEGES, DEANS, AND PROGRAMS

Graduate Studies (http://www.grad.usf.edu). Delcie Durham, Associate Provost for Research and Graduate Dean. Applied behavior analysis, cancer biology, entrepreneurship in applied technologies.

School of Architecture and Community Design (http://www.arch.usf.edu). Charles C. Hight, Dean.

College of Arts and Sciences (http://www.cas.usf.edu). John Skvoretz, Dean. Aging studies, American studies, anthropology, applied anthropology, applied physics, audiology, aural rehabilitation, biology, chemistry, classics and classical language, communication, communication sciences and disorders, criminology, English, English as a second language, environmental science and policy, French, geography, geology, gerontology, history, Latin American and Caribbean studies, liberal arts, library and information science, linguistics, mass communication, mathematics, microbiology, philosophy, physics, political science, psychology, public administration, rehabilitation and mental health counseling, religious studies, social work, sociology, Spanish, speech-language pathology, women's studies.

College of Business (http://www.coba.usf.edu). Robert Forsythe, Dean. Accountancy, business administration (M.B.A. and Ph.D.), business economics, executive M.B.A., finance, management, management information systems.

College of Education (http://www.coedu.usf.edu). Colleen Kennedy, Dean. Adult education, business and office education, career and technical education, college student affairs, counselor education, early childhood education, educational leadership (college leadership), educational leadership (K–12), elementary education, English education, foreign language education, gifted education, guidance/counselor education, higher education, instructional technology, interdisciplinary education, mathematics education, measurement and evaluation, physical education, reading education, reading/language arts education, school psychology, science education, second language acquisition/instructional technology, social science education, special education (specializations in behavior disorders, exceptional student education, gifted, mental retardation, specific learning disabilities, and varying exceptionalities), vocational education.

College of Engineering (http://www.eng.usf.edu). Sunil Saigal, Interim Dean. Biomedical engineering, chemical engineering, civil engineering, computer engineering, computer science, electrical engineering, engineering management, engineering science, environmental engineering, industrial engineering, mechanical engineering.

College of Marine Sciences (http://www.marine.usf.edu). Peter Betzer, Dean. Marine sciences: biological oceanography, chemical oceanography, geological oceanography, physical oceanography.

College of Medicine (http://www.med.usf.edu). Stephen K. Klasko, Vice President for Health Sciences and Dean. Medical sciences: anatomy, biochemistry and molecular biology, bioethics and humanities, bioinformatics and computational biology, microbiology and immunology, neuroscience, pathology and lab medicine, pharmacology and therapeutics, physical therapy, physiology and biophysics.

College of Nursing (http://www.hsc.usf.edu/nursing). Patricia Burns, Dean. Nursing master's: acute-care nurse practitioner studies, adult nurse practitioner studies, clinical nurse leader (CNL) studies, family nurse practitioner studies, gerontological nurse practitioner studies, gerontological-psychiatric nurse practitioner studies, nurse anesthesia program, nursing education, occupational health nursing dual degree with the College of Public Health (M.S./M.P.H.), oncology nurse practitioner studies, pediatric nurse practitioner studies, psychiatric nurse practitioner studies. Graduate certificate: hospice and palliative care, nurse education, nurse practitioner studies, nursing informatics. Nursing doctoral: Bachelor of Science (nursing) to Ph.D., Master of Science (nursing) to Ph.D., Doctor of Nursing Practice.

College of Public Health (http://www.publichealth.usf.edu). Donna Petersen, Dean. Dual degrees in applied anthropology, medicine, occupational health nursing, physical therapy, and social work; public health degrees in behavioral health, biostatistics, community and family health, environmental health, epidemiology, executive M.P.H. for health professionals, global communicable disease, global health practice, health administration, health-care organizations and management, health policies and programs, health policy and management, industrial hygiene, maternal and child health, nurse practitioner studies and public health, occupational health for health professionals, occupational medicine residency, public health, public health practice (online), public health education, safety management, socio-health sciences, toxicology and risk assessment.

College of Visual and Performing Arts (http://www.arts.usf.edu/). Ronald Jones Jr., Dean. Art, art history, music, music education.

A typical scene at USF.

THE UNIVERSITY OF TOLEDO

College of Graduate Studies

Programs of Study

The College of Graduate Studies at The University of Toledo (UT) offers the Master of Arts in counselor education, criminal justice, economics, English, foreign language (French, German, Spanish), geography and planning, history, mathematics, philosophy, political science, psychology, recreation and leisure, school psychology, social work, sociology and anthropology, and speech language pathology.

The Master of Science is offered in accounting, bioengineering, biology (cell-molecular biology, ecology), chemical engineering, chemistry, civil engineering, computer science, electrical engineering, exercise science, geology, industrial engineering, mathematics (applied, statistics), mechanical engineering, medicinal chemistry, pharmacology toxicology, pharmacy (administrative pharmacy, industrial pharmacy), and physics and astronomy.

The Master of Business Administration; Master of Education; Master of Liberal Studies; Master of Public Administration; Master of Music in Music Education and Music Performance; and Master of Studies in Law are also offered.

Doctoral programs are offered in biology (cell-molecular biology, ecology), biomedical sciences (cell-molecular neurobiology, molecular basis of disease, molecular and cellular biology), chemistry, counselor education (Ph.D. and Ed.S.), curriculum and instruction (educational media, elementary, gifted and talented, secondary, special education), educational administration and supervision, engineering science, exercise science, foundations of education (educational psychology, educational research and measurement, educational sociology, history of education, and philosophy of education), health education, higher education, history, manufacturing management, mathematics, medicinal chemistry, occupational therapy, pharmacy (Pharm.D.), physical therapy, physics, and psychology.

Research Facilities

The University of Toledo has been classified as Doctoral/Research University-Extensive by the Carnegie Foundation for the Advancement in Teaching. It has nearly 2500 graduate students enrolled in more than 100 degree-granting programs. In 2000, The University of Toledo embraced an aggressive program to identify areas of research focus, accelerate technology transfer, expand research activities, and increase its role in community economic development. The Toledo Science and Technology Corridor is an initiative of The University of Toledo and its partners to enhance Toledo's innovation-based economy through investments that promote linkages and collaboration among the region's academic institutions, businesses, and government entities. In January 2005, the University purchased a 35,000 square foot building to house the Toledo Science and Technology Alternative Energy Incubation Center. Identified research focus areas include advanced films and coatings, astrophysical search for origins, biotechnology, environmental sustainability science and engineering/bioremediation, geographic information systems and applied geographics, and science education teaching, learning and reform.

Carlson Library, the main library at the University, contains more than 1.6 million volumes, 1.4 million microforms, 150,000 maps, and 5,000 periodicals. The library is a federal depository for government documents and is a charter member of the statewide cooperative program OhioLINK.

Financial Aid

Most full-time graduate students receive some financial support. College fellowships, teaching assistantships, and research assistantships, which include a stipend and a tuition waiver, are available for qualified students on a competitive basis.

The out-of-state tuition surcharge normally charged to out-of-state and international students is waived for students whose permanent address is within one of the following Michigan counties: Hillsdale, Lenawee, Macomb, Oakland, Washtenaw, and Wayne.

In addition, the University of Toledo offers an out-of-state tuition surcharge waiver to cities and regions that are a part of the Sister Cities Agreement. These regions include Toledo, Spain; Londrina, Brazil; Qinhuangdao, China; Csongrad County, Hungary; Delmenhorst, Germany; Toyohashi, Japan; Tanga, Tanzania; Bekaa Valley, Lebanon; and Poznan, Poland. The University of Toledo Graduate College offers a variety of memorial and minority scholarship awards, including the Ronald E. McNair Postbaccalaureate Achievement Scholarship, the Graduate Minority Assistantship Award, and two full University fellowships.

Cost of Study

The graduate tuition rate for the 2006–07 academic year was $390.05 per semester credit hour for in-state students. For nonresidents, the out-of-state surcharge was $367.15 per semester credit hour. Additional fees are required and include the general fee, technology fee, and mandatory insurance.

Living and Housing Costs

The University of Toledo has a diverse offering of student housing options, including suite-style and traditional residential halls. Housing is offered to graduate students through Residence Life or contracted individually by the student. Affordable, high-quality off-campus apartment-style housing within walking distance of campus is abundant.

Student Group

There are approximately 20,000 students at the University of Toledo. About 4,000 are graduate and professional students. The University has a rich diversity of student organizations. Students join groups that are organized around common cultural, religious, athletic, and educational interests.

Location

The University of Toledo has several campus sites in the city of Toledo. Graduate students take classes on the main campus, which is located in suburban western Toledo, and the Health Science Campus, which is located in South Toledo. With a population of more than 330,000, Toledo is the fiftieth-largest city in the United States. It is located on the western shores of Lake Erie, within a 2-hour drive of Cleveland and Detroit.

The University

The University of Toledo was founded by Jessup W. Scott in 1872 as a municipal institution and became part of the state of Ohio's system of higher education in 1967. On July 1, 2006, The University of Toledo merged with the Medical University of Ohio becoming one of only seventeen American universities to offer professional and graduate academic programs in medicine, law, pharmacy, nursing, health sciences, engineering, and business. Students benefit from cooperative educational (COOP) experiences. Students enrolled at UT may take courses at Bowling Green State University through the cooperative enrollment program and benefit from internship opportunities, the diverse job market in the community, and the activities and excitement of the city of Toledo.

UT boasts nearly twenty student service-related offices and programs, more than 200 student organizations, more than forty intramural/sport programs, a $17.3-million Student Recreation Center, an honors-academic center residence hall, a housing village for members of fraternities and sororities, a visual arts building on the grounds of the world-renowned Toledo Museum of Art, the $25-million College of Engineering complex, and a $33-million pharmacy, chemistry, and life sciences complex. The graduate student association supports the academic, social, and administrative needs of graduate students throughout the University.

The University's faculty includes nearly 700 members, of which more than 80 percent hold doctorates. Faculty members are active within the University, as well as in community programs, research projects, and publication of professional articles and textbooks. University faculty members take an interest in students and commit to providing the best possible learning experience and environment.

The College of Graduate Studies is accredited by the North Central Association of Colleges and Schools. The University is a member of the Council of Graduate Schools in the United States, the Midwest Association of Graduate Schools, and the National Association of State Universities and Land-Grant Colleges. The College of Education is approved by the National Council for Accreditation of Teacher Education. The Master of Business Administration program is approved by the American Assembly of Collegiate Schools of Business. The Accreditation Board for Engineering and Technology has approved all undergraduate engineering programs. The University is a member of the American Society for Engineering Education and its Engineering College Council and Engineering Research Council.

Applying

To be admitted as a graduate student at the University of Toledo, an applicant must have received a bachelor's degree from an accredited college or university and must have compiled a minimum undergraduate grade point average of 2.7 on a 4.0 scale, (some colleges require a higher minimum GPA). Some departments require scores on the Graduate Record Examinations (General Test and/or Subject Tests), or the Graduate Management Admission Test. All requirements for admission must be met at least two weeks prior to registration.

Correspondence and Information

College of Graduate Studies
The University of Toledo
2801 West Bancroft Street
Toledo, Ohio 43606-3390

Phone: 419-530-4723
Fax: 419-530-4724
E-mail: grdsch@utnet.utoledo.edu
Web site: http://www.gradschool.utoledo.edu

FACULTY HEADS

Martin Abraham, Ph.D.; PE; Dean of the College of Graduate Studies.

Arts and Sciences

Sue Ott Rowlands, M.F.A.; Interim Dean, College of Arts and Sciences.
David Guip, Ph.D.; Chair, Department of Art Education.
Patricia Komuniecki, Ph.D.; Chair, Department of Biological Sciences.
Alan Pinkerton, Ph.D.; Chair, Department of Chemistry.
James Benjamin, Ph.D.; Chair, Department of Communication.
Michael Phillips, Ph.D.; Chair, Department of Earth, Ecological and Environmental Sciences.
Michael Dowd, Ph.D.; Chair, Department of Economics.
Sara Lundquist, Ph.D.; Chair, Department of English Language and Literature.
Antonio Varela, Ph.D.; Chair, Department of Foreign Languages.
Peter Lindquist, Ph.D.; Chair, Department of Geography and Planning.
Timothy Messer-Kruse, Ph.D.; Chair, Department of History.
Geoffrey Martin, Ph.D.; Chair, Department of Mathematics.
Lee Heritage, D.M.A.; Chair, Department of Music and Dance.
Eric Snider, Ph.D.; Chair, Department of Philosophy.
Alvin Compaan, Ph.D.; Chair, Department of Physics and Astronomy.
Mark Denham, Ph.D.; Chair, Department of Political Science and Public Administration.
Joseph Hovey, Ph.D.; Chair, Department of Psychology.
Barbara Chesney, Ph.D.; Chair, Department of Sociology and Anthropology.
Holly Monsos, M.F.A.; Interim Chair, Department of Theatre and Film.
Nandini Bhattacharya, Ph.D.; Chair, Department of Women's and Gender Studies.

Business Administration

Thomas Gutteridge, Ph.D.; Dean, College of Business.
Diana Franz, Ph.D.; Interim Chair, Department of Accounting.
Andrew Solocha, Ph.D.; Interim Chair, Department of Finance and Business Economics.
T. S. Ragu-Nathan, Ph.D.; Interim Chair, Department of Information Operations and Technology Management.
Ron Zallocco, Ph.D.; Interim Chair, Department of International Business and Marketing.
Dale Dwyer, Ph.D.; Interim Chair, Department of Management.

Education

Thomas Switzer, Ph.D.; Dean, College of Education.
William Weber, Ph.D.; Interim Chair, Curriculum and Instruction.
Laurie Dinnebeil, Ph.D.; Chair, Early Childhood, Physical, and Special Education.
Ronald D. Opp, Ph.D.; Chair, Educational Leadership.
Dale Snauwaert, Ph.D.; Chair, Foundations of Education.

Engineering

Naganathan Ganapathy, Ph.D.; Dean, College of Engineering.
Vijay A. Goel, Ph.D.; Chair, Department of Bioengineering.
Glenn Lipscomb, Ph.D.; Chair, Department of Chemical Engineering.
Ashok Kumar, Ph.D.; Chair, Department of Civil Engineering.
Roger J. King, Ph.D.; Interim Chair, Department of Electrical Engineering.
Abdollah Afjeh, Ph.D.; Chair, Department of Mechanical, Industrial, and Manufacturing Engineering.
Mohamed Samir Hefzy, Ph.D.; PE; Graduate Director/Interim Associate Dean of Graduate Studies.

Health and Human Services

Jerome M. Sullivan, Ph.D.; Dean, College of Health and Human Services.
Paula Dupuy, Ed.D.; Chair, Department of Counseling and Mental Health Services.
Eric Lambert, Ph.D.; Chair, Department of Criminal Justice.
Suzanne Wambold, Ph.D.; RN, RDCS; Chair, Department of Health Professions.
Charles Armstrong, Ph.D.; Chair, Department of Kinesiology.
Ruthie Kucharewski, Ph.D.; Chair, Department of Public Health and Rehabilitative Services.
Terry Cluse-Tolar, Ph.D.; Chair, Department of Social Work

Pharmacy

Johnnie L. Early II, R.Ph., Ph.D.; Dean, College of Pharmacy.
Marcia McInerney, Ph.D.; Chair, Department of Medicinal Chemistry.
William Messer, Ph.D.; Chair, Department of Pharmacology.
Curtis D. Black, R.Ph., Ph.D.; Chair, Department of Pharmacy Practice.

UNIVERSITY OF TULSA

Graduate School

Programs of Study The Graduate School offers graduate study leading to master's degrees in thirty programs and to Ph.D.'s in nine programs. Interdisciplinary degree programs are also available.

Doctoral degrees conferred are the Doctor of Philosophy, with specialization in biological science, chemical engineering, clinical psychology, computer science, English language and literature, geosciences, industrial/organizational psychology, mechanical engineering, and petroleum engineering.

Master's degrees conferred are the Master of Arts, Master of Business Administration, Master of Engineering, Master of Fine Arts, Master of Science, Master of Science in Engineering, Master of Science in Finance, Master of Science in Math/Science Education, Master of Taxation, and Master of Teaching Arts.

The master's degree is offered in anthropology, art, biochemistry, biological science, business administration (traditional and online programs), chemical engineering, chemistry, clinical psychology, computer science, education (with certification in elementary education and secondary education), electrical engineering, engineering physics, English language and literature, finance, fine art, geosciences, history, industrial/organizational psychology, mathematics, math/science education, mechanical engineering, petroleum engineering, physics, speech-language pathology, and taxation. Interdisciplinary joint-degree programs include a Master of Science in Finance/M.S. in applied mathematics program and an M.B.A./Master of Science in Finance program. Joint master's/Juris Doctor degree programs leading to J.D./M.A. degrees with specialization in anthropology, clinical psychology, English language and literature, history, and industrial/organizational psychology are offered in conjunction with the College of Law; the J.D./M.S. degree in biological science, computer science, and geosciences; a J.D./Master of Taxation degree; a J.D./Master of Science in Finance degree; and the J.D./M.B.A. degree are also offered.

Research Facilities The University libraries house more than 3 million books, bound periodical volumes, microforms, state and federal depository government documents, sound and video recordings, CD-ROM abstracts and indexes, and maps. McFarlin Library, the central facility, orders and catalogs 10,000 new titles each year, subscribes to 2,200 periodicals in paper and fiche formats, and, by way of an online service, provides full-text access to 2,000 more (as well as indexing for a further 10,000). A computerized catalog maintains both bibliographic and circulation records, which currently number more than 650,000. It can be accessed through more than eighty-five terminals in the libraries or remotely by way of campus networks and personal computers. It also acts as a gateway to other databases and, via the Internet, to several hundred library catalogs in this country and abroad. The libraries are also linked electronically to two national utilities (OCLC and RLIN) to facilitate an active interlibrary loan program that borrows about 10,000 items each year from other libraries and loans a slightly smaller number to them.

The College of Law library contains 280,000 volumes, with extensive holdings in natural resources and energy law. Special collections in three areas are recognized internationally for their quality and distinctiveness: twentieth-century American, British, and Irish literature (with holdings that include comprehensive collections for Faulkner, Graves, Joyce, Lawrence, Whitman, and many other writers and 3,500 feet of manuscripts, among them the papers of Richard Ellmann, Richard Murphy, 2001 Nobel laureate V. S. Naipaul, Jean Rhys, and Rebecca West); Native American history and law, with exceptional strength for the Cherokee, Creek, and Osage; and holdings related to petroleum exploration and production in all parts of the world, among them the source documents abstracted for *Petroleum Abstracts,* which has been published at the University since 1960.

The University maintains a robust fiber-optic network that interconnects computing and information resources in all of the University's buildings. The University also offers a ubiquitous wireless network, giving campus community members access to the Internet and campus computing resources while anywhere on campus, either indoors or outside. Centralized and decentralized computing services are provided by numerous servers that are networked to a full complement of peripheral devices. The servers are used for a variety of instructional and research activities, which include accessing the University's library database and other worldwide information resources that are available on the Internet. McFarlin Library reflects the convergence of traditional print and electronic media and provides a cyber café, an open-computing student laboratory, an information/research laboratory, a training laboratory, and a faculty development center. Modern student computing laboratories and high-technology classrooms are located in the College of Arts and Sciences, the College of Business Administration, the College of Engineering and Natural Sciences, and the College of Law. The College of Engineering and Natural Sciences has numerous engineering workstations to support the computer-intensive applications required by scientists and engineers.

Financial Aid A number of assistantships and fellowships are available for full-time graduate students. The stipends vary according to the amount of work required and the experience of the student. Most appointments provide 9 credit hours of tuition scholarship per semester in addition to the monthly stipend. Other scholarships are available through the sponsorship of corporations, businesses, and individuals. Recipients of these scholarships are often chosen only from applicants who are interested in fields prescribed by the donors. Government-directed student aid is available through the Office of Financial Services.

Cost of Study All graduate students at the University of Tulsa graduate school pay tuition at the rate of $778 per credit hour in 2007–08.

Living and Housing Costs The University offers a variety of housing and dining options, several of which are specifically tailored to the needs of single as well as married graduate students. These options include modern market-quality apartments designated specifically for graduate and law students. Room and board for two semesters in a double-occupancy room average $6700 in 2007–08.

Student Group Approximately 670 of the University's 4,200 students are in the Graduate School; women make up more than 40 percent of that population. More than 10 percent of graduate students are members of minority groups. International students from dozens of nations constitute more than 30 percent of the graduate population.

Location The University of Tulsa is located in a residential neighborhood just 2 miles from a renovated downtown area. Tulsa has a population of more than 700,000. Symphonies, theater, art galleries, opera, ballet, museums, and outdoor sports are all accessible to students. Guest performers and lecturers regularly visit the campus and the city.

The University The University was founded in 1894 as Henry Kendall College in Muskogee, Indian Territory. Moving to Tulsa in 1907, the University of Tulsa was chartered in 1921. The University of Tulsa began offering graduate course work in 1933 and was fully accredited through the doctoral level by 1972.

Applying Applicants for admission to the graduate school must complete a Graduate School Application and provide official transcripts, three letters of recommendation, and all appropriate test scores. Admitted students may apply for financial aid by contacting the Financial Services Office. Full-time admitted students who wish to apply for a graduate assistantship must complete a graduate assistantship application.

Correspondence and Information

Dean, Graduate School
University of Tulsa
600 South College Avenue
Tulsa, Oklahoma 74104

Phone: 918-631-2336
800-882-4723 (toll-free)
E-mail: grad@utulsa.edu
Web site: http://www.utulsa.edu/graduate

FACULTY HEADS

GRADUATE SCHOOL

Janet Haggerty, Dean.
Richard Redner, Associate Dean.
John Bury, Assistant Dean.

College of Arts and Sciences

Thomas Benediktson, Dean.
Anthropology: Lamont Lindstrom, Chairperson; Michael Whalen, Adviser.
Art: Susan Dixon, Chairperson; Whitney Forsyth, Adviser.
Clinical Psychology: Judy Berry, Chairperson; Elana Newman, Adviser.
Education: Thomas Benediktson, Chairperson; Tao Wang, Adviser.
English Language and Literature: Lars Engle, Chairperson; Sean Latham, Adviser.
History: Joseph Bradley, Chairperson; Christine Ruane, Adviser.
Industrial/Organizational Psychology: Judy Berry, Chairperson; John McNulty, Adviser.
Speech-Language Pathology: Paula Cadogan, Chairperson; Mary Moody, Adviser.

College of Business Administration

Gale Sullenberger, Dean.
Stephen Rockwell, Director of Graduate Business Programs and Adviser.
Accounting: Karen Cravens, Director.
Finance: Roger P. Bey, Chairperson.
Management: Ralph Jackson, Chairperson.
Marketing: Ralph Jackson, Chairperson.
Operations Management: Roger P. Bey, Chairperson.

College of Engineering and Natural Sciences

Steven Bellovich, Dean.
Biochemistry: Dale Teeters, Chairperson; Robert Sheaff, Adviser.
Biological Science: Estelle Levetin, Chairperson; Kenton Miller, Adviser.
Chemical Engineering: Geoffrey Price, Chairperson; Laura Ford, Adviser.
Chemistry: Dale Teeters, Chairperson and Adviser.
Computer Science: Roger Wainwright, Chairperson; Rose Gamble, Adviser.
Electrical Engineering: Gerald Kane, Chairperson; Heng-Ming Tai, Adviser.
Geosciences: Bryan Tapp, Chairperson; Peter Michael, Adviser.
Mathematics: Roger Wainwright, Chairperson; Christian Constanda, Adviser.
Mathematics and Science Education: Robert Howard and Tao Wang, Program Coordinators.
Mechanical Engineering: Edmund Rybicki, Chairperson; Siamack Shirazi, Adviser.
Petroleum Engineering: Mohan Kelkar, Chairperson; Holden Zhang, Adviser.
Physics and Engineering Physics: George Miller, Chairperson.

RESEARCH OPPORTUNITIES

Anthropological research projects range from archaeological research investigating Stone Age sites in Jordan to Pithouse and Pueblo sites in the southwestern United States and northwestern Mexico. The department is home to the journal *Lithic Technology.*

Current projects in **biochemistry** address the biochemical basis of human diseases such as cancer and neurodegeneration, new diagnostic tools using nanotechnology, and detecting heavy metals or other toxins in soil and groundwater. There are also active collaborations with chemists to develop and characterize novel antitumor drugs.

Research in **biological science** includes projects in molecular, cell, environmental, and comparative biology. Projects in molecular and cell biology include studies of lymphocyte development, glycobiology, development of the mammalian nervous system, molecular and developmental genetics, and structure-function relationships of microbial light harvesting proteins. Projects in environmental biology include behavioral ecology of colonial birds, population and pollination biology of bees, and microbial population biology. Projects in comparative biology include the evolutionary biology of reptilian viviparity, molecular systematics of algae and fish, aerobiology, and mammalian and invertebrate reproductive biology. The Mervin Bovaird Center for Molecular Biology and Biotechnology augments and promotes graduate training in molecular techniques.

Research in **chemical engineering** is largely experimentally based, involving laboratory and pilot-scale programs. A major focus of activities is in the environmental field. Areas of current research include reaction kinetics and catalysis, supercritical fluids, multiphase chemical reactors and multiphase flows, capillary hydrodynamics, combustion, biological treatment of hazardous wastes and bioremediation of petroleum hydrocarbons, petroleum and natural gas processing, thermodynamics and phase equilibria, fuel-cell technology, and particulate science.

Chemistry research involves synthetic, organic, bioanalytic, environmental, and natural product chemistry; solution kinetics; molecular protective films; and nanotechnology.

Computer science faculty members are involved in research related to network and information systems security, genetic algorithms, medical imaging, parallel and scientific computation, artificial intelligence, distributed artificial intelligence, software engineering, and networking. The Center for Information Security is a National Security Agency "Center of Excellence" and the home of the University's Cyber Corps and Information Assurance programs.

Research opportunities are available in **English language and literature.** The *James Joyce Quarterly, Tulsa Studies in Women's Literature,* and *Nimrod* are published at the University, and the department collaborates with Brown University on the Modernist Journals Project.

Geoscience research is balanced in areas of petroleum exploration/production and environmental science, including clastic sedimentology, petroleum seismology, seismic stratigraphy, structural geology, geochemistry, and biogeoscience. There are also active programs in marine geology, including the petrogenesis of midocean ridge basalts.

Research in **history** concerns early American and Native American history, Russian social and cultural history, late Imperial China, comparative urban history of the Americas, and American diplomacy.

Mechanical engineering research is being conducted in thermal fluid sciences, solid mechanics, erosion/corrosion, composite materials, biologically inspired materials, fatigue, manufacturing, thermal spray coatings, and residual stress analysis.

Petroleum engineering research opportunities derive from nine continuing, cooperative industry/University energy-related projects, including artificial lift, drilling, fluid flow, erosion/corrosion in the oil and gas industry, horizontal well completion, reservoir exploration, delayed coking, sand probes, separation technology, and wax deposition. Other petroleum-related projects include the impact of earthquakes on pipelines and phase behavior of CO_2 and heavy oils.

Research in **physics** and **engineering physics** draws on active research in fluid dynamics, artificial lift technology, carbon nanotubes, nanotechnology, optics, solid-state physics, and plasma physics theory.

Research in **psychology** involves issues in theory and measurement of personality and social behavior as applied to problems in clinical and organizational psychology. Active areas of research in clinical psychology include trauma studies, randomized control trials of exposure treatments, pain modulation, social-cognitive processing of delusional disorders, psychological assessments, and MMPI studies. Industrial/organizational psychology projects currently focus on assessing personality disorders in the workplace, leadership, and managerial performance.

Speech-language pathology research includes neurogenic communication disorders, fluency disorders, aphasia, speech articulation problems, swallowing impairments, and delayed language and literacy development.

UNIVERSITY OF WISCONSIN–LA CROSSE

Graduate Studies

Programs of Study

Graduate programs at the University of Wisconsin–La Crosse (UW–L) are offered in each of the three colleges that comprise the University: the College of Business Administration (CBA); the College of Liberal Studies (CLS); and the College of Science and Health (CSAH).

The College of Business Administration offers a Master of Business Administration degree that is fully accredited by AACSB International–The Association to Advance Collegiate Schools of Business.

The College of Science and Health offers a Doctor of Physical Therapy and the Master of Science degree in biology (with concentrations in aquatic science, cellular and molecular biology, clinical microbiology, microbiology, nurse anesthesia–CRNA, and physiology), clinical exercise physiology, health education (with options in community health education and school health education), human performance (with an emphasis in strength conditioning or a concentration in athletic training), occupational therapy, physician assistant studies, physical education teaching (with concentrations in adventure/outdoor pursuits, health as a lifestyle, and special populations), recreation management, sport administration, and therapeutic recreation. In addition, the College of Science and Health offers the only nationally accredited Master of Public Health in community health education in the University of Wisconsin System. The college also offers a Master of Software Engineering.

The College of Liberal Studies offers an education specialist degree in school psychology through its School of Psychology and the Master of Science in Education degree in reading and special education through the School of Education. A Master of Education Professional Development degree (with initial teacher certification options) is also offered by the School of Education. In addition, the college offers a master's-level program in college student development and administration.

Research Facilities

UW–L is the home of a number of research facilities for graduate student researchers. Murphy Library is an extensive research facility and contains more than 550,000 volumes; the online catalog allows users to search local and other University of Wisconsin catalogs. Modern microcomputer laboratories are available campuswide. Wing Technology Center is completely dedicated to advanced technology initiatives. The River Studies Center conducts research in aquatic ecology, watershed ecology, fisheries, aquatic parasitology, aquatic microbiology, aquatic toxicology, and water quality. The College of Science and Health, the administrative home of the La Crosse Medical Health Science Consortium, Inc., which is a public/private partnership with regional health-care providers and local colleges, has constructed the 168,000-square-foot La Crosse Medical Health Science Education and Research Center. The Center focuses on applied clinical research activities in microbiology, immunology, molecular diagnostics, virology, and human physiology. The Human Performance Laboratory, the La Crosse Exercise and Health Program, the Musculoskeletal Research Center, the Center for Diversity and Community Renewal, and the Special Populations Exercise Program provide extensive opportunities for clinical work and basic and applied research in exercise and sport science and education. The Leisure Lifestyle Center provides research opportunities for therapeutic recreation students. The Small Business Development Center is affiliated with the CBA and is part of a statewide organization that provides counseling to small business managers related to business start-up and management. The Bureau of Business and Economic Research is a University contract research facility for area businesses. The CBA also serves as a US-AID training site for large numbers of managers and public administrators from Central Europe.

Financial Aid

Merit- and need-based financial aid is offered in the form of graduate assistantships and nonresident tuition waivers. Additional assistantships are available for qualified U.S. citizens who are members of minority groups. Interested students should contact the appropriate graduate program director for assistantship application procedures. Information on need-based financial aid such as the Stafford and Perkins Loan Programs, Federal Work-Study, Advanced Opportunity Program grants, and partial tuition grants may be obtained from the Office of Financial Aid, 215 Graff Main Hall (608-785-8604; finaid@uwlax.edu).

Cost of Study

Tuition for 2006–07 (applicable to both Wisconsin and Minnesota residents, with reciprocity) was $331.41 per credit hour. Out-of-state tuition was $920.84 per credit hour. Students from Kansas, Michigan, Missouri, Nebraska, and North Dakota may be eligible for the Midwest Student Exchange Program, which offers reduced out-of-state tuition through a special application process (students should contact the admissions office for details). A limited number of full or partial nonresident tuition waivers are available to out-of-state and international graduate students with superior academic credentials or documented need. Certain programs may have different tuition and fees.

Living and Housing Costs

Most graduate students live in private apartments and homes near the campus. Limited University-owned housing is available for single graduate students. No University-owned housing is available for married students. Further information about housing can be obtained from the Office of Residence Life, 213 Wilder Hall (608-785-8075). The cost of living in La Crosse is moderate and slightly below the national average.

Student Group

The University annually enrolls more than 1,000 graduate students; about 60 percent of the students are women. The Office of Career Services (http://www.uwlax.edu/CareerServices/) serves graduate students from all schools and colleges who are seeking professional employment upon degree completion.

Location

La Crosse is famous for its exceptional natural beauty. The city (population about 53,000) is located on the east bank of the Mississippi River below towering bluffs. The metro area population is 121,800. Abundant water and woodlands provide year-round recreation sites for skiing, hunting, bicycling, hiking, camping, and other outdoor activities. La Crosse is also home to two other colleges, a symphony orchestra, excellent theatrical and cultural events, superb health-care facilities, and first-class elementary and secondary schools. For more information on La Crosse, prospective students should visit the Web site at http://www.explorelacrosse.com/home/index.asp.

The University

The University of Wisconsin–La Crosse, founded in 1909, is a public institution governed by the Board of Regents of the University of Wisconsin System. With a faculty and academic staff of more than 450, UW–L serves more than 9,000 students from Wisconsin, Minnesota, Iowa, Illinois, and forty other states and forty-two other countries. The 119-acre campus is located within easy walking distance of downtown La Crosse in a residential section of the city. UW–La Crosse has an extensive NCAA Division III athletic program.

Applying

Applicants from the U.S. may request admissions materials from the Office of Admissions, 115 Graff Main Hall (608-785-8939; admissions@uwlax.edu). International applicants may request complete application packets from the Office of International Education, 116 Graff Main Hall (phone: 608-785-8016, fax: 608-785-8923, e-mail: uwlworld@uwlax.edu). All applicants must submit a completed application form, transcripts of all undergraduate course work, and a $45 application fee. M.B.A. students are required to submit a GMAT score. Applicants should check with specific graduate program directors regarding other required admission tests and application deadline dates.

Correspondence and Information

Dr. Vijendra K. Agarwal, Associate Vice Chancellor for Academic Affairs and Director of University Graduate Studies
145 Graff Main Hall
University of Wisconsin–La Crosse
La Crosse, Wisconsin 54601

Phone: 608-785-8124 (Graduate Studies)
608-785-8939 (Admissions Office)
Fax: 608-785-8046 (Graduate Studies)
608-785-8940 (Admissions Office)
E-mail: admissions@uwlax.edu
uwlworld@uwlax.edu (international student graduate admissions)
Web site: http://www.uwlax.edu/graduate

THE FACULTY

Director of University Graduate Studies: Dr. Vijendra K. Agarwal, 145 Graff Main Hall (608-785-8124; agarwal.vije@uwlax.edu).

ASSOCIATE DEANS OF THE COLLEGES
College of Business Administration: Dr. Bruce May, 223 Wimberly Hall (608-785-8090; may.bruc@uwlax.edu).
College of Liberal Studies: Dr. Charles Martin-Stanley, 227 Graff Main Hall (608-785-8113; martin-s.char@uwlax.edu).
College of Science and Allied Health: Dr. Karen McLean, 105 Graff Main Hall (608-785-8459; mclean.kare@uwlax.edu).

GRADUATE PROGRAM DIRECTORS
MASTER OF SCIENCE
Biology (all concentrations except Clinical Microbiology): Dr. Tom Volk, 3024 Cowley Hall (608-785-6972; volk.thom@uwlax.edu).
Biology–Clinical Microbiology: Dr. Mike Hoffman, 3023 Cowley Hall (608-785-6984; hoffman.mic2@uwlax.edu).
Clinical Exercise Physiology: Dr. John P. Porcari, 141 Mitchell Hall. (608-785-8684; porcari.john@uwlax.edu).
Exercise and Sport Science
Adventure/Outdoor Pursuits Option: Dr. Jeff Steffen, 218 Mitchell Hall (608-785-6535; steffen.jeff@uwlax.edu).
Athletic Training Concentration: Dr. Brian Udermann, 149 Mitchell Hall (608-785-8181; udermann.brian@uwlax.edu).
Health as a Lifestyle Option: Dr. Dan Duquette, 203 Mitchell Hall (608-785-8162; duquette.rode@uwlax.edu).
Human Performance: Dr. Glenn Wright, 142 Mitchell Hall (608-785-8689; wright.glen@uwlax.edu).
Physical Education Teaching: Dr. Jeff Steffen, 218 Mitchell Hall (608-785-6535; steffen.jeff@uwlax.edu).
Special Populations (Adapted/Special Physical Education) Option: Dr. Patrick DiRocco, 137 Mitchell Hall (608-785-8173; dirocco.patr@uwlax.edu).
Sport Administration: Dr. David Waters, 152 Mitchell Hall (608-785-8167; waters.davi@uwlax.edu).
Health Education and Health Promotion
Community Health Education: Dr. Gary Gilmore, 201 Mitchell Hall (608-785-8163; gilmore.gary@uwlax.edu).
School Health Education: Dr. Tracey Caravella, 200 Mitchell Hall (608-785-6788; caravell.trac@uwlax.edu).
Occupational Therapy: Peggy Denton, 4043 Health Science Center (608-785-6620; denton.pegg@uwlax.edu).
Physician Assistant Studies: Mr. Mary Rathgaber, 4053 Health Science Center (608-785-5061; rathgabe.mary@uwlax.edu).
Recreation Management: Dr. Steve Simpson, 136 Wittich Hall (608-785-8216; simpson.stev@uwlax.edu).
Therapeutic Recreation: Dr. Steve Simpson, 136 Wittich Hall (608-785-8216; simpson.stev@uwlax.edu).

MASTER OF SCIENCE IN EDUCATION
College Student Development and Administration: Dr. Chris Bakkum, 235 Morris Hall (608-785-8113; bakkum.chris@uwlax.edu).
Reading: Dr. Delores Heiden, 240C Morris Hall (608-785-8149; heiden.delo@uwlax.edu).
Special Education: Dr. Jeanne Danneker, 240B Morris Hall (608-785-8147; danneker.jean@uwlax.edu).

DOCTOR OF PHYSICAL THERAPY (D.P.T.)
Physical Therapy: Dr. Michele Thorman, 4063 Health Science Center (608-785-8466; thorman.mich@uwlax.edu).

MASTER OF PUBLIC HEALTH
Community Health Education: Dr. Gary Gilmore, 201 Mitchell Hall (608-785-8163; gilmore.gary@uwlax.edu).

MASTER OF BUSINESS ADMINISTRATION (M.B.A.)
Business Administration: Dr. Bruce May, 223 Wimberly Hall (608-785-8090; may.bruc@uwlax.edu).

MASTER OF EDUCATION–PROFESSIONAL DEVELOPMENT
Professional Development: Dr. Teri Staloch, 269 Morris Hall (608-785-8142; staloch.teri@uwlax.edu).

EDUCATION SPECIALIST
School Psychology: Dr. Rob Dixon, 349D Graff Main Hall (608-785-6893; dixon.robe@uwlax.edu).

MASTER OF SOFTWARE ENGINEERING
Software Engineering: Dr. Kasi Periyasamy, 222 Wing (608-785-6823; periyasa.kas2@uwlax.edu).

Graduate students have clinical and Preceptorship experiences in a variety of settings, including schools, hospitals, community agencies, and health-care organizations.

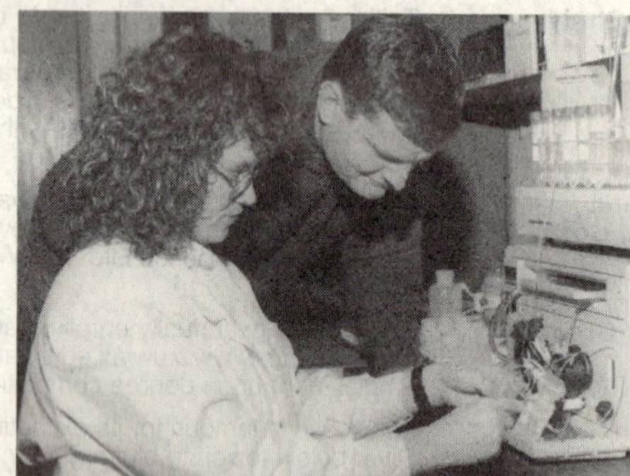

Graduate students at UW–L are guided in research by dedicated faculty members.

M.B.A. students bring real-world work experiences to their graduate courses and seminars.

Programs of Study

Master's degrees and certificates are offered in the following areas: biology, communication, computer science, counseling and human relations (community, elementary, and secondary), education (elementary, educational leadership, and secondary), English, Hispanic studies, history, human resource development, liberal studies, mathematics, political science, public administration, and theater. Master's degrees only are offered in the following areas: applied statistics, chemistry, classical studies, criminal justice, psychology, software engineering, and theology. Doctoral degrees are offered in the area of philosophy only.

The academic year consists of two semesters. The first semester begins in mid-August and ends in mid-December. The second semester begins in mid-January and ends in mid-May. In addition, there are three summer sessions—two successive monthlong day sessions and a third evening session that is offered over a two-month period.

Research Facilities

The University library contains more than 780,000 volumes and 5,600 current periodicals. Special library holdings include the collection of the Augustinian Historical Institute and an extensive collection of works in contemporary Continental philosophy.

The Office of University Information Technologies provides data and voice communication, computing services, and access to remote computing and information services over the Internet; offers noncredit seminars and workshops on popular computer software and the use of the Villanova phone system; and maintains state-of-the-art computer labs for students on campus.

Financial Aid

Graduate assistantships are awarded on a competitive basis. The assistantship stipend begins at approximately $12,656 in 2007–08 and carries with it a waiver of all tuition and academic fees. A few research fellowships are also awarded each year. A number of tuition scholarships are available; they provide a waiver of all tuition and academic fees.

In addition, the office of the director of financial aid administers the Federal Stafford Student Loan Program.

Cost of Study

Graduate tuition ranges from approximately $585 to $650 per credit hour in 2007–08. In addition, there is a University fee of $30 each semester.

Living and Housing Costs

The University does not maintain accommodations for graduate students, but second-year students are eligible for positions as resident counselors in the dormitories. The area has a wide selection of living quarters that are convenient to the campus.

Student Group

Approximately 2,290 graduate students were enrolled for the fall 2006 term, of whom 1,074 were in liberal arts and sciences programs. Total University enrollment is approximately 12,000, including 7,472 full-time undergraduates, 1,000 part-time evening (undergraduate and continuing studies) students, and 1,000 students in the School of Law. There are about equal numbers of men and women graduate students.

Location

Located in the heart of the Delaware Valley's Main Line, the University occupies more than 200 handsomely landscaped acres in the town of Villanova, 12 miles west of Philadelphia. The location combines the advantages of a tranquil suburban setting with proximity to a large metropolitan city that is known for its outstanding contributions in the areas of culture, education, history, recreation, religion, and sport.

The University

Villanova University is a private institution that was founded in 1842 by the Augustinian Fathers. Graduate programs were first administered separately in 1931. Currently, there are six academic units in addition to Graduate Studies—the Colleges of Arts and Sciences, Commerce and Finance, Engineering, and Nursing; the Division of Part-Time Studies; and the School of Law.

Applying

Application forms and the *Graduate Studies Viewbook* may be obtained from the Graduate Studies Office. Due dates for submission of credentials vary by program. In addition to forwarding the completed application form and official college transcripts, applicants must also arrange to have three letters of recommendation submitted on their behalf. There is an application fee of $50. GRE scores are required by some departments. Descriptions of programs and procedures are found in the *Graduate Studies Viewbook* and on the University's Web site.

Correspondence and Information

Dean, Graduate Studies
College of Liberal Arts and Sciences
Villanova University
800 Lancaster Avenue
Villanova, Pennsylvania 19085-1688
Phone: 610-519-7090
E-mail: gradinformation@villanova.edu
Web site: http://www.gradartsci.villanova.edu/

THE FACULTY

Gerald M. Long, Dean; Ph.D., Stanford.

Listed below are the chairpersons and/or directors for the University's graduate programs.

Master's Programs

Applied Statistics: Douglas Norton, Ph.D., Minnesota.
Biology: Russell M. Gardner, Ph.D., Indiana.
Chemistry: W. Scott Kassel, Ph.D., Florida.
Classical and Modern Languages and Literatures (Hispanic Studies): Mercedes Juliá, Ph.D., Chicago.
Communication: Bryan Crable, Ph.D., Purdue Calumet.
Computer Science: Robert E. Beck, Ph.D., Pennsylvania.
Counseling (Community, Elementary, Secondary): Connie Titone, Ed.D., Harvard.
Criminal Justice: Thomas Arvanites, Ph.D., SUNY at Albany.
Education: Connie Titone, Ed.D., Harvard.
Educational Leadership: Connie Titone, Ed.D., Harvard.
Elementary and Secondary Graduate Teacher Education: Connie Titone, Ed.D., Harvard.
English: Evan Radcliffe, Ph.D., Cornell.
History: Marc S. Gallicchio, Ph.D., Temple.
Human Resource Development: David F. Bush, Ph.D., Purdue.
Liberal Studies: Eugene McCarraher, Ph.D., Rutgers.
Mathematics: Douglas Norton, Ph.D., Minnesota.
Political Science: Lowell Gustafson, Ph.D., Virginia.
Psychology: Thomas C. Toppino, Ph.D., New Mexico.
Public Administration: Christine Kelleher, Ph.D., North Carolina.
Theatre: Rev. Richard G. Cannuli, O.S.A., M.F.A., Pratt.
Theology: Bernard Prusak, Ph.D., Lateran (Rome).

Ph.D. Program

Philosophy: John Carvalho, Ph.D., Duquesne.

VCU

VIRGINIA COMMONWEALTH UNIVERSITY

Graduate School

Programs of Study

Virginia Commonwealth University (VCU) offers master's and doctoral degrees in anatomy, art history, biochemistry, biomedical engineering, biostatistics, business, chemistry, educational leadership, engineering, human genetics, microbiology/immunology, nursing, pharmaceutical sciences, pharmacology/toxicology, and physiology. Doctoral degrees are offered in education; health-related sciences; health services organization/research; integrative life sciences; media, art, and text; medical physics; psychology; public policy and administration; rehabilitation and movement science; and social work. Master's degrees are offered in accountancy; adult education; adult learning; art education; bioinformatics; biology; business administration; clinical laboratory sciences; computer science; counselor education; creative writing; criminal justice; curriculum/instruction; dentistry; design; economics; English; environmental studies; fine arts; forensic science; genetic counseling; gerontology; health administration; health and movement sciences; history; information systems; interdisciplinary studies; mass communications; mathematical sciences; music; nurse anesthesia; occupational therapy (postprofessional, professional); physics; public health; reading; recreation, parks, and sport leadership; rehabilitation counseling; social work; sociology; special education; taxation; teaching; theater; and urban and regional planning. The University also offers first professional degrees in medicine, dentistry, pharmacy, and physical therapy as well as a variety of cooperative, interdisciplinary, and combined-degree programs.

Research Facilities

VCU libraries provide a combined capacity of more than 1.7 million volumes and 10,200 periodical titles and an online bibliographic search service accessing hundreds of databases. In addition, the Virginia State and Richmond Public Libraries are within walking distance of both VCU campuses. Academic Computing provides a variety of microcomputer, minicomputer, and mainframe computing services to support the research and instructional endeavors of its faculty and students, including consultation, instruction, and computer acquisition. Other research facilities operated by VCU include the Anderson Art Gallery Conservation Laboratory, Burn Trauma Clinic, Virginia Institute for Developmental Disabilities, Massey Cancer Center, Pharmacokinetics Laboratory, School of the Arts Library and Slide Collections, Sickle Cell Anemia Clinic, Survey Research Laboratory, Virginia Center on Aging, Virginia Biotechnology Research Park, and Virginia Real Estate Research Center. VCU is a member of the Oak Ridge Associated Universities and is fully accredited by the Southern Association of Colleges and Schools.

Financial Aid

A number of departmental and University stipends and tuition awards are available. Students also may apply for need-based assistance with the University's Financial Aid Office. Part-time employment is often available.

Cost of Study

For full-time study in 2007–08, Virginia residents pay tuition and fees of $4452 per semester; nonresidents, $8876 per semester. For part-time study, Virginia residents pay tuition and fees of $401.30 per hour; nonresidents, $884 per hour. Some graduate programs require additional fees.

The tuition and fee structure is different on the Medical College of Virginia (MCV) Campus. The medicine, Pharm.D., nurse anesthesia, dentistry, and School of Allied Health programs vary in tuition, fees, and other expenses.

Living and Housing Costs

Graduate student housing is available on both the MCV Campus and the academic campus of Virginia Commonwealth University. Many graduate students live in off-campus housing, which is reasonably priced and readily available in a variety of styles and settings in nearby residential areas or within easy commuting distance. On- and off-campus housing information is available on the Web at http://www.students.vcu.edu/housing.

Student Group

VCU enrolls 30,452 students, 7,611 of whom are graduate students. More than 200 clubs and organizations reflect the diverse social, recreational, educational, political, and religious interests of the student body.

Location

Richmond is Virginia's capital and a major East Coast financial and manufacturing center that offers students a wide range of cultural, educational, and recreational activities. Richmond is located in central Virginia at the intersection of Interstates 95 and 64, 2 hours south of Washington, D.C., and nestled between the Blue Ridge Mountains and the Atlantic coast. The Richmond region is easily accessible by plane, car, and train. With nearly 1 million residents, the city combines big-city offerings with small-town hospitality. Applicants are encouraged to explore http://www.visit.richmond.com/ for more information on the city.

The University

VCU is a state-supported, coeducational university with a graduate school, a major teaching hospital, and twelve academic and professional units that offer fifty-two undergraduate, twenty-two postbaccalaureate certificate, sixty-five master's, six post-master's certificate, and twenty-nine Ph.D. programs. VCU also offers M.D., D.D.S., D.P.T., and Pharm.D. programs as well as cooperative degree programs with other major Virginia colleges and universities. VCU has one of the largest evening colleges in the United States. The academic campus is located in Richmond's historic Fan District. The health sciences campus and hospital are located 2 miles east in the downtown business district. A University bus service provides free intercampus transportation for faculty members and students.

The Carnegie Foundation for the Advancement of Teaching ranks Virginia Commonwealth University as one of the nation's top research universities, with more than $211 million in annual research funding. More than 29,000 undergraduate, certificate, graduate, post-master's, professional, and doctoral students are enrolled in 162 academic programs, forty of which are unique in the commonwealth of Virginia.

The faculty members at VCU represent the finest American and international graduate institutions and enhance the University's position among the important institutions of higher learning in the United States and the world via their work in the classroom, laboratory, studio, and clinic and in their scholarly publications.

Applying

Admission procedures and program requirements are detailed in the *Graduate Bulletin*. Application deadlines and materials, including the application and the *Graduate Bulletin*, are available online at the Graduate School Web site (http://www.graduate.vcu.edu).

Virginia Commonwealth University is an equal-opportunity/affirmative-action institution, providing access to education and employment without regard to age, race, color, national origin, gender, religion, sexual orientation, veteran's status, political affiliation, or disability.

Correspondence and Information

Graduate School
Virginia Commonwealth University
P.O. Box 843051
Richmond, Virginia 23284-3051

Phone: 804-828-6916
Fax: 804-828-6949
Web site: http://www.graduate.vcu.edu

FACULTY HEADS

Dr. F. Douglas Boudinot, Dean, Graduate School.
Dr. Sherry T. Sandkam, Associate Dean, Graduate School.

DEANS

Center for the Study of Biological Complexity: Dr. Gregory A. Buck.
Center for Environmental Studies: Dr. Gregory C. Garman.
College of Humanities and Sciences: Dr. Robert D. Holsworth, Acting Dean.
L. Douglas Wilder School of Government and Public Affairs: Dr. Robert D. Holsworth.
School of Allied Health Professions: Dr. Cecil B. Drain.
School of the Arts: Dr. Richard Toscan.
School of Business: Dr. Michael Sesnowicz.
School of Dentistry: Dr. Ronald J. Hunt.
School of Education: Dr. Beverly J. Warren, Interim Dean.
School of Engineering: Dr. Russell Jamison.
School of Mass Communications: Dr. Judy VanSlyke Turk.
School of Medicine: Dr. Jerome F. Strauss III.
School of Nursing: Dr. Nancy F. Langston.
School of Pharmacy: Dr. Victor A. Yanchick.
School of Social Work: Dr. Frank R. Baskind.
School of World Studies: R. McKenna Brown.
VCU Life Sciences: Dr. Richard Rezba.

GRADUATE PROGRAM DIRECTORS

For the telephone numbers listed below, the area code is 804.

Center for Public Policy
Public Policy and Administration, Ph.D.: Dr. Michael D. Pratt, 828-6837.

College of Humanities and Sciences
Adcenter: Ashley Sommardahl, 800-311-3341 (toll-free).
Biology: Dr. John F. Pagels, 828-1562.
Chemistry: Dr. Maryann Collinson, 828-1298.
Creative Writing: David Wojahn, 828-1331.
Criminal Justice: Dr. Jay Albanese, 828-2292.
English: Dr. Katherine Bassard, 828-1331.
Forensic Science: Dr. Tracey Dawson Cruz, 828-8420.
History: Dr. Tim Thurber, 828-4670.
Mass Communications: Dr. Ernest F. Martin, 828-2660.
Physics: Dr. Alison A. Baski, 828-1818.
Psychology, Biopsychology: Dr. Wendy L. Kliewer, 828-1793.
Psychology, Clinical: Dr. Wendy L. Kliewer, 828-1793.
Psychology, Counseling: Dr. Wendy L. Kliewer, 828-1793.
Psychology, Social: Dr. Wendy L. Kliewer, 828-1793.
Public Administration, Master's: Dr. Janet Hutchinson, 828-8041.
Sociology: Dr. Sarah Jane Brubaker, 828-1026.
Statistics and Operations Research: Dr. James A. Davenport, 828-1301.
Urban and Regional Planning: Dr. John Accordino, 827-0525.

School of Allied Health Professions
Clinical Laboratory Sciences: Dr. Theresa S. Nadder, 828-9469.
Gerontology: Dr. Ayn Welleford, 828-1565.
Health Administration: Dr. Kenneth R. White, 828-0719.
Health Administration, Professional M.S.H.A. Program Online: Dr. Dolores G. Clement, 828-9466.
Health-Related Sciences: Monica White, 828-7247.
Health Services Organization and Research: Dr. Michael McCue, 828-5218.
Nurse Anesthesia: Dr. Michael D. Fallacaro, 828-9808.
Occupational Therapy, Entry-Level: Sandra H. Cash, 828-2219.
Occupational Therapy, Post-Professional: Dr. Jayne T. Shepherd, 828-2219.
Patient Counseling: Dr. Alexander F. Tartaglia, 828-0540.
Physical Therapy, D.P.T.: Laura S. Spittle, 828-0234.
Rehabilitation Counseling: Dr. Allen Lewis, 828-1132.

School of the Arts
Art History, Ceramics, Fibers, Furniture Design, Glassworking, Interior Environments, Jewelry/Metalworking, Music, Painting and Printmaking, Photography and Film, Sculpture, Theater and Visual Communications: Joseph H. Seipel, 828-2787.

School of Business
Accountancy, Business Administration (Master's), Decision Sciences, Economics, Finance, Financial Economics, Human Resources Management, Information Systems, Marketing, Real Estate Valuation, Risk Management, Taxation: Jana P. McQuaid, 828-1741.
Fast Track M.B.A.: Dr. William J. Miller, 828-3939.

School of Dentistry
Dentistry: Dr. Laurie Carter, 828-9184.

School of Education
Administration/Supervision; Curriculum/Instruction; Physical Education; Recreation, Parks, and Sport Leadership; Special Education; Teaching; Ph.D. in Education: Jennifer R. Burruss, 828-3382.

School of Engineering
Biomedical Engineering: Dr. Gary L. Bowlin, 828-2592.
Computer Science: Dr. James E. Ames IV, 828-0575.
Engineering, M.S., Ph.D.: Dr. Rosalyn Hobson, 828-8308.

Graduate School
Interdisciplinary Studies Program: Dr. Sherry T. Sandkam, 828-6916.

School of Medicine
Anatomy: Dr. George R. Leichnetz, 828-9512; Dr. Bill Buido, 828-9623.
Biochemistry: Dr. Suzanne E. Barbour, 828-9762; Dr. Tomaz Kordula, 828-0771.
Biostatistics: Dr. Russell M. Boyle, 828-9824; Dr. Robert Johnson, 828-2036.
Epidemiology: Dr. R. Leonard Vance, 628-2513.
Human Genetics: Dr. Linda A. Corey, 828-9632; Dr. Rachel Gannaway, 828-9632; Dr. Rita Shiang, 828-9632.
Medicine, M.D./Ph.D.: Dr. Gordon L. Archer, 828-7380.
Microbiology and Immunology: Dr. Guy Cabral, 828-9728.
Molecular Biology and Genetics: Dr. Gail E. Christie, 828-9093.
Neuroscience: Dr. Les Satin, 828-7823.
Pathology: Dr. Shawn E. Holt, 828-0458.
Pharmacology and Toxicology: Dr. Stephen T. Sawyer, 828-8400.
Physiology: Dr. George D. Ford, 828-9501.
Pre-Medical Basic Health Science Certificate Programs: Dr. Jan F. Chlebowski, 828-8366.
Public Health: Dr. R. Leonard Vance, 628-2513.

School of Nursing
Nursing (Certificate, Master's, and Ph.D.): Susan L. Lipp, 828-5171.

School of Pharmacy
Medicinal Chemistry: Dr. Susanna Wu-Pong, 828-4328.
Pharmaceutics: Dr. Susanna Wu-Pong, 828-4328.
Pharmacotherapy, Pharmacy Administration: Dr. Susanna Wu-Pong, 828-4328.

School of Social Work
Social Work (Certificate and M.S.W.): Elizabeth Dungee-Anderson, 828-1043.
Social Work (Ph.D.): Dr. Kia J. Bentley, 828-0453.

VCU Life Sciences
Bioinformatics: Dr. Herschell S. Emory, 827-5600.
Environmental Studies: Dr. Gregory Garman, 828-7202.
Integrative Life Sciences: Dr. Robert Tombes, 827-0141.

Graduate School of Arts and Sciences

Programs of Study

The Wake Forest University Graduate School of Arts and Sciences offers courses of study leading to the M.A., M.A.Ed., M.A.L.S., M.S., M.S.A., and Ph.D. degrees. Master's degrees may be earned in accountancy, biology, biomedical engineering, chemistry, communication, comparative medicine, computer science, counseling, education, English, health and exercise science, health services research, liberal studies, mathematics, molecular medicine, physics, psychology, and religion.

There are Ph.D. programs in biochemistry and molecular biology, biology, biomedical engineering, cancer biology, chemistry, microbiology and immunology, molecular and cellular pathobiology, molecular genetics and genomics, molecular medicine, neurobiology and anatomy, neuroscience, physics, and physiology and pharmacology. Combined M.D./Ph.D. and Ph.D./M.B.A. programs are also offered.

Residence requirements vary, but a master's program can generally be completed in two years and a Ph.D. program in approximately five years. Foreign language and special skill requirements vary with each program. Graduate programs are tailored to the individual. The Graduate School's educational philosophy encourages students to pursue an area of specialization in depth and to broaden their training while filling in any gaps in their earlier education. A Ph.D. scholar should be able to carry out teaching and research independently and competently. Various special programs of an interdisciplinary or tutorial nature enhance students' opportunities to develop their full potential.

Research Facilities

The Graduate School of Arts and Sciences conducts its programs on two campuses, the Reynolda Campus and the Bowman Gray Campus. Both campuses have excellent library resources open to all students. Each graduate program has the facilities and equipment needed for its research programs.

Financial Aid

Financial support is available to qualified students. On the Bowman Gray campus, scholarships ($27,285 in 2006–07) and fellowships ($48,057) are awarded annually in the biomedical sciences. On the Reynolda Campus, scholarships ($26,985), fellowships ($30,985), and assistantships ($32,985–$48,985) are awarded annually in the arts and sciences. In addition, a number of miscellaneous grants are available each year to students on both campuses.

Cost of Study

In 2006–07, tuition for full-time students was $26,985 per year for students taking courses on the Reynolda campus and $27,285 for students taking courses on the Bowman Gray campus. Part-time students registered at $960 per semester hour. There is also a graduation fee.

Living and Housing Costs

The Graduate School does not require that students live in University housing. Most students make their own arrangements for housing off campus.

Student Group

Wake Forest University attracts superior students. In 2005–06, undergraduate enrollment was 4,263, and graduate and professional enrollment was 2,453. Members of underrepresented minority groups and international students constitute a portion of the student body.

Location

Wake Forest University is located in the city of Winston-Salem, in the Piedmont section of North Carolina, about 75 miles from the Blue Ridge Mountains and 225 miles from the beaches of the Atlantic Ocean. The city's early Moravian heritage is reflected in its many cultural programs and community activities. Tanglewood Park, with its championship golf courses and recreational facilities, is nearby. Technology, health services, tobacco, textiles, transportation, and banking are the main business activities of Winston-Salem. Within 100 miles are the universities and research institutions associated with the Research Triangle.

The University

Wake Forest University is coeducational and has a strong academic orientation. It was founded in 1834 in Wake County, North Carolina. The School of Law was established in 1894; the School of Medicine, in 1902; the Graduate School of Arts and Sciences, in 1961; the Babcock Graduate School of Management, in 1969; the School of Business and Accountancy, in 1980 (in 1995, the name was changed to the Wayne Calloway School of Business and Accountancy); and the School of Divinity, in 1999. In 1941, the School of Medicine moved to Winston-Salem, where it became affiliated with North Carolina Baptist Hospital and was renamed the Bowman Gray School of Medicine of Wake Forest College. In 1997, the name was changed to Wake Forest University School of Medicine. The remaining divisions of the institution moved to Winston-Salem in 1956, following acceptance of a Z. Smith Reynolds Foundation proposal to build a new campus under substantial continuing endowment. In 1967, the college's augmented character was recognized by the change in name to Wake Forest University. The University prides itself on its strong arts and sciences and basic medical sciences programs, all of which emphasize close student-professor interaction.

Applying

Applications for admission should be directed to the Dean of the Graduate School at the Reynolda Campus or to the Dean of the Graduate School at the Bowman Gray Campus. There is a $45 application fee for domestic applicants, $55 for international applicants, and $35 for MALS applicants. Completed applications should be received by January 15. The Master Teacher Programs begin with the first summer session. Scores on the Graduate Record Examinations are required. Scores on the Graduate Management Admission Test are required for the accountancy program. International applicants whose native language is not English must submit their scores on the Test of English as a Foreign Language. Further details are available on the Graduate School Web site.

Correspondence and Information

Dean of the Graduate School
Wake Forest University
P.O. Box 7487 Reynolda Station
Winston-Salem, North Carolina 27109-7487
Phone: 336-758-5301
800-257-3166 (toll-free)
Fax: 336-758-4230
E-mail: gradschl@wfu.edu
Web site: http://www.wfu.edu/graduate

Dean of the Graduate School
Biomedical Sciences
Bowman Gray Campus
Wake Forest University
Medical Center Boulevard
Winston-Salem, North Carolina 27157-1001
Phone: 336-716-4303
800-438-4723 (toll-free)
Fax: 336-716-0185
E-mail: bggrad@wfubmc.edu
Web site: http://www.wfu.edu/graduate

PROGRAM DIRECTORS

The graduate faculty of Wake Forest University consists of 507 members on all University campuses. Departmental chairs, who may be addressed concerning graduate study, are listed below. The administrative officials of the Graduate School are Nathan O. Hatch, President; William B. Applegate, Senior Vice President and Dean of the School of Medicine; William C. Gordon, Provost; and Cecilia H. Solano, Interim Dean of the Graduate School.

Accountancy: Yvonne Hinson, Ph.D., Tennessee.
Biochemistry and Molecular Biology: Suzy Torti, Ph.D., Tufts.
Biology: Brian Tague, Ph.D., California, San Diego.
Biomedical Engineering: Craig Hamilton, Ph.D., North Carolina State.
Cancer Biology: Steven Akman, M.D., Albert Einstein College of Medicine.
Chemistry: S. Bruce King, Ph.D., Cornell.
Communication: Ananda Mitra, Ph.D., Illinois at Champaign-Urbana.
Comparative Medicine: Carol A. Shively, Ph.D., California, Davis.
Computer Science: Stan William Turkett, Ph.D., South Carolina.
Counseling: Samuel T. Gladding, Ph.D., North Carolina at Greensboro.
Education: Leah McCoy, Ed.D., Virginia Tech.
English: Scott Klein, Ph.D., Yale.
Health and Exercise Science: Anthony Marsh, Ph.D., Arizona State.
Health Services Research: Michelle J. Naughton, Ph.D., Iowa; Ronny A. Bell, Ph.D., North Carolina at Chapel Hill.
Liberal Studies: Cecilia H. Solano, Ph.D., Johns Hopkins.
Mathematics: Edward Allen, Ph.D., California, San Diego.
M.D./Ph.D.: Paul Laurienti, M.D., Ph.D., Texas; Charles McCall, M.D., Wake Forest.
Microbiology and Immunology: Martha Alexander-Miller, Ph.D., Washington (St. Louis).
Molecular and Cellular Pathobiology: John S. Parks, Ph.D., Wake Forest.
Molecular Genetics and Genomics: Donald Bowden, Ph.D., Berkeley.
Molecular Medicine: Linda McPhail, Ph.D., Wake Forest; Kevin High, M.D., Virginia.
Neurobiology and Anatomy: Emilio Salinas, Ph.D., Brandeis.
Neuroscience: Ronald W. Oppenheim, Ph.D., Washington (St. Louis).
Ph.D./M.B.A.: Dr. Dwayne Godwin, Ph.D., Alabama at Birmingham.
Physics: Keith Bonin, Ph.D., Maryland, College Park.
Physiology and Pharmacology: Sara Jones, Ph.D., North Carolina; Jeff Weiner, Ph.D., Toronto.
Psychology: Catherine Seta, Ph.D., North Carolina at Greensboro.
Religion: Simeon Ilesanmi, Ph.D., SMU.

Programs of Study

Since 1970, Walden University has offered working professionals the opportunity to earn advanced degrees through distance learning. Today, this comprehensive, accredited online university offers master's and doctoral degrees in education, health and human services, management, psychology, and public policy and administration, as well as master's programs in engineering and IT and bachelor's completion programs in business. For more information, prospective students should visit http://www.waldenu.edu.

Walden University's online doctoral, master's, and bachelor's programs are designed to help students achieve their goals of personal enrichment and professional advancement and make a difference in the lives of others.

Walden's degree programs combine high-quality curricula, expert faculty members, and innovative distance-delivery models to offer highly applied, rigorous programs that allow adult learners to pursue an advanced degree while maintaining their personal and professional commitments.

Walden University is accredited by the Higher Learning Commission and a member of the North Central Association (http://www.ncahlc.org or 312-263-0456).

Research Facilities

Dedicated Walden librarians are available year-round to help students identify, evaluate, and obtain books, journal articles, and other resources. Online databases are always accessible. Through a partnership with Indiana University, students may request books and copies of journal articles owned by libraries on the Bloomington campus. Walden's Research Center provides assistance in pursuing grants, fellowships, and other sources of research funding; resources for publishing and presenting research; guidelines and rubrics for developing the thesis and dissertation; and access to the Institutional Review Board (IRB), which is responsible for ensuring that Walden research complies with the University's ethical standards and federal regulations.

Financial Aid

Walden University offers financial assistance in the form of federal student loans and payment plans. The financial aid office also assists students in securing tuition benefits from employers and other agencies. Several merit-based and need-based scholarships as well as competitive fellowships are available.

The U.S. Department of Education has certified Walden University as being eligible to participate in Federal Family Educational Loan Programs (formerly Guaranteed Student Loan Programs) under the Higher Education Act of 1965, as amended. Eligible students may apply for Federal Stafford Student Loans, Federal Unsubsidized Loans, and Veterans Administration benefits.

Cost of Study

For the 2007–08 academic year, the tuition for Walden programs is as follows: Ed.D. is $645 per semester credit hour; Ph.D. in applied management and decision sciences, education, health services, human services, or public policy and administration is $4175 per quarter; Ph.D. in psychology is $420 per quarter credit hour; Ph.D. in public health is $390 per quarter credit hour; M.B.A. is $685 per quarter credit hour (including books); M.P.A. is $405 per quarter credit hour; M.P.H. is $370 per quarter credit hour; M.S. in computer engineering, computer science, electrical engineering, software engineering, or systems engineering is $865 per semester credit hour; M.S. in Education is $392 per semester credit hour; M.S. in mental health counseling is $330 per quarter credit hour; M.S. program in Nursing is $395 per semester credit hour; and M.S. in psychology is $345 per quarter credit hour. For residency, materials, and other fees that apply to each program, prospective students should visit the University Web site at http://www.waldenu.edu.

Living and Housing Costs

Walden doctoral students should anticipate travel and room and board expenses for the dispersed academic residencies.

Student Group

Walden students are generally midcareer professionals who seek to make a difference in their organizations and communities as well as in their careers.

Location

Walden's academic office is located in Minneapolis, and its administrative office is in Baltimore. Residency requirements for doctoral students at Walden are met by attendance at regional sessions held in professional conference and instructional centers throughout the country.

The University

Founded in 1970, Walden University was conceived as and remains an institution dedicated to providing the established professional an opportunity to complete a challenging degree while maintaining family and career commitments. Social betterment is important to Walden's philosophy, as is helping the mature student understand change within his or her chosen field. Program formats emphasize self-paced learning and flexibility, which allow learners to create professionally relevant approaches to their graduate studies.

Applying

Walden University accepts students on a rolling admissions basis, depending on the program. Applicants submit an application form and a nonrefundable fee ($50), official transcripts from previous degree programs, a resume, a goal statement, and, in some cases, letters of recommendation.

Correspondence and Information

For further information:
Office of Student Enrollment
Walden University
1001 Fleet Street
Baltimore, Maryland 21202
Phone: 866-492-5336 (toll-free)
Fax: 410-843-8780
E-mail: info@waldenu.edu
Web site: http://www.waldenu.edu

THE ADMINISTRATION AND FACULTY

Walden attracts esteemed scholars, researchers, and distinguished professionals as faculty members. The distance-delivery model allows students to fully benefit from the diverse talents and experiences of the finest faculty members, regardless of where they reside. Some are deans or faculty members at major universities, while others are corporate executives, educators, clinicians, and military leaders. Their specializations range from entrepreneurship and strategic planning to change theory and individual coherence theory. All faculty members are credible subject experts who demonstrate vast experience and a profound commitment to adult learners.

Jonathan Kaplan, J.D., President.
Denise DeZolt, Ph.D., Provost.
Marcia Moody, Ph.D., Vice Provost for Faculty Development.
David Brigham, Ph.D., Vice Provost for Student Development.

College of Education
Susan E. Saxton, Ph.D., Acting Dean.
Kelley Costner, Ed.D., Associate Dean, Master's Programs.
Linda S. Gatlin, Ph.D., Assistant Dean, Faculty Development and Assessment of Education.
Cheryl Keen, Ed.D., Assistant Dean, Student Success.
José A. Quiles, Ph.D., Interim Associate Dean, Doctoral Programs.
Beate R. Baltes, Ed.D., Faculty Chair, Faculty Development, Doctoral Programs.
Steve Canipe, Ed.D., Faculty Chair.
Alice Duhon-Ross, Ph.D., Faculty Chair.
Leslie Van Gelder, Ph.D., Faculty Chair.
Sherry L. Harrison, Ed.D., Faculty Chair.
Carol R. Philips, Ed.D., Faculty Chair.
Daniel W. Salter, Ph.D., Faculty Chair.
Dia Sekayi, Ph.D., Faculty Chair.
Barbara Weschke, Ph.D., Faculty Chair.
Amie A. Beckett, Ph.D., Program Director.
Patricia R. Brewer, Ed.D., Program Director.
Dan Farrell, Ed.D., Program Director.
Joe Ann Hinrichs, Ed.D., Program Director.
Laura Lynn, Ph.D., Program Director.
Joseph E. Nolan, Ph.D., Program Director.
Kurt W. Schoch, Ed.D., Program Director.
Mary Friend Shepard, Ph.D., Program Director.
Thomas A. Stapléford, Ed.D., Program Director.

College of Social, Behavioral, and Health Sciences
Gary J. Burkholder, Ph.D., Dean.
Rebecca L. Jobe, Ph.D., Assistant Dean for Student Success.
Peter Anderson, Ph.D., Assistant Dean for Faculty Development.
George Smeaton, Ph.D., Assistant Dean for Research and Evaluation.

School of Psychology
Nina Nabors, Ph.D., Associate Dean and Interim Faculty Chair, Clinical Psychology.
Ivonne Chirino-Klevans, Ph.D., Faculty Chair, Organizational Psychology.
Harris Friedman, Ph.D., Faculty Chair, Clinical Psychology.
Bonnie K. Nastasi, Ph.D., Faculty Chair, School Psychology.
Rachel L. Piferi, Ph.D., Faculty Chair, Health Psychology.
Sreeroopa Sarkar, Ph.D., Faculty Chair, M.S. Programs.
Beth A. Venzke, Ph.D., Faculty Chair, General.
Heather Walen-Frederick, Ph.D., Faculty Chair, General.
Miguel Ybarra, Ph.D., Faculty Chair, Counseling.

Mental Health Counseling
Savitri V. Dixon-Saxon, Ph.D., Program Director, M.S. in Mental Health Counseling.

School of Social Service
Nina Nabors, Ph.D., Interim Associate Dean.
Elaine Spaulding, Ph.D., Faculty Chair.

School of Health Sciences
Jorg Westermann, Ph.D., Faculty Chair, Ph.D. in Public Health and Health Services.
Regina A. Galer-Unti, Ph.D., Interim Faculty Chair, M.P.H. Program.

School of Nursing
Barbara Brown, Ed.D., Interim Associate Dean.

School of Management
Kathy O. Simmons, M.S., Faculty Chair, Bachelor of Science in Business Administration.
Rebecca Sidler, Ph.D., Faculty Chair, Master of Business Administration.
Elizabeth Hirst, Ed.D., Faculty Chair, Faculty Development and Student Experience.
James Stahley, Ph.D., Faculty Chair, Ph.D. in Applied Management and Decision Sciences.

School of Public Policy and Administration
Gary Kelsey, Ph.D., Interim Associate Dean.
Stan Amaladas, Ph.D., Faculty Chair.
Gloria J. Billingsley, Ph.D., Faculty Chair, Mentoring and Research.

NTU College of Engineering and Applied Science
Ahmed Naumaan, Ph.D., Faculty Chair, M.S. in Electrical Engineering.

WASHINGTON UNIVERSITY IN ST. LOUIS

Graduate School of Arts and Sciences

Programs of Study The Graduate School of Arts and Sciences offers more than thirty programs leading to the doctorate (Ph.D.) and to the Master of Arts (A.M.). In addition, programs are offered leading to the Master of Arts in Education (M.A.Ed.), Master of Arts in Teaching (M.A.T.), Master of Fine Arts in Writing (M.F.A.W.), Master in Music (M.M.), and Master of Liberal Arts (M.L.A.).

Opportunities for combining a degree available through the Graduate School of Arts and Sciences with a degree from one of the University's professional schools (business, engineering, law, medicine) are also available.

Research Facilities The Washington University community is served by a network of libraries designed to meet the instructional and research needs of faculty members, students, and staff members. Washington University libraries contain the largest collection of any private academic library system between the Mississippi River and California. John M. Olin Library, the central University library, and twelve school and departmental libraries house many important and unique collections and provide state-of-the-art computerized information retrieval. The combined holdings include more than 3 million books and bound periodicals, 18,000 current serial subscriptions, and access to thousands of electronic journals and databases. For more information, students can visit http://library.wustl.edu.

More than thirty centers and institutes provide a spectrum of research opportunities. They include Center for Air Pollution Impact and Trend Analysis; Center for the Study of American Business; Center for American Indian Studies; Business, Law, and Economics Center; Arts and Sciences Computing Center; Institutes for Biomedical Computing; McDonnell Center for Cellular and Molecular Neurobiology; Construction Management Center; Carolyne Roehm Electronic Media Center; Center for Engineering Computing; Center for Genetics in Medicine; McDonnell Center for Studies of Higher Brain Function; Center for the History of Freedom; Office of International Studies; International Writers Center; Center for the Study of Islamic Societies and Civilizations; Management Center; Fred Gasche Laboratory for Microstructured Materials Technologies; Markey Center for Research in Molecular Biology of Human Disease; Center for Optimization and Semantic Control; Center for Plant Science and Biotechnology; Center for Political Economy; Center for the Study of Public Affairs; Center for Robotics and Automation; Social Work Research Development Center; McDonnell Center for Space Sciences; Center for the Application of Information Technology; and Urban Research and Design Center.

Financial Aid The majority of full-time students receive financial support. Financial assistance in the form of scholarships, fellowships, and traineeships is offered annually on a competitive basis through the Graduate School from government, private, or endowed sources. Also available are scholarships, teaching assistantships, research assistantships, and, in applied social sciences, clinical internships; grants and fellowships in national competition; and loans. Specific information may be obtained from the departmental or administrative unit to which the student intends to apply.

Cost of Study Tuition for the 2007–08 academic year for the Graduate School is $34,500. The cost per credit unit is $1438.

Living and Housing Costs Many graduate students live in University-owned apartments, some with data connections and shuttle bus service. Listing information for these units as well as non-University housing is available through the University's Apartment Referral Service (http://offcampushousing.wustl.edu/). Rent ranges from $450 to $950 per month for one- to three-bedroom units, respectively.

Student Group Of the more than 14,000 people attending Washington University, more than 5,000 are graduate students; approximately 2,000 of those are enrolled in the Graduate School of Arts and Sciences. Students come to Washington University from all fifty states and more than eighty international locations.

Location Washington University has two campuses that lie at opposite ends of Forest Park (one of the largest municipal parks in the nation). The campuses are approximately 5 miles west of downtown St. Louis. The Danforth campus is the location of the Graduate School of Arts and Sciences and all other schools of the University except Medicine. The latter is located on the east, or medical, campus. The Division of Biology and Biomedical Sciences is also located on the medical campus. Free shuttle buses run between the campuses on a regular schedule.

The St. Louis area has nearly 2.4 million residents. The cost of living is affordable. The University's central location provides easy access to the zoo, museums, Science Center, Missouri Botanical Gardens, St. Louis Symphony, Opera Theatre, St. Louis Repertory Theatre, Black Repertory Theatre, Blues hockey, Rams football, and Cardinals baseball. Outdoor adventure beyond the city can be found in the Ozark Mountains and on the rivers of Missouri. Camping, hiking, floating, rock climbing, and spelunking are among the many possibilities within a few hours' drive of St. Louis.

The Graduate School The Graduate School of Arts and Sciences is a charter member of both the Association of Graduate Schools and the Council of Graduate Schools. The School provides a physical and academic environment in which inquiry, intellectual growth, and discovery can thrive and flourish.

Applying Prospective students may apply online. Application forms for admission and financial aid can also be obtained from either the Graduate School office or individual departments. Applicants should check with the department or program to which they are applying as application deadlines vary. For international students whose native language is not English, most programs require an official copy of a TOEFL or TSE score. Most programs require GRE scores.

Correspondence and Information

Graduate School of Arts and Sciences
Campus Box 1187
Washington University in St. Louis
One Brookings Drive
St. Louis, Missouri 63130-4899

Phone: 314-935-6880
Fax: 314-935-4887
E-mail: graduateschool@artsci.wustl.edu
Web site: http://www.artsci.wustl.edu/GSAS/

FACULTY HEADS, DEGREES OFFERED, AND DEPARTMENTAL INTERESTS

Anthropology (Ph.D.): Erik Trinkaus (trinkaus@artsci.wustl.edu). Archaeology, physical anthropology, primate studies, sociocultural anthropology, medical anthropology.
Art History and Archaeology (A.M., Ph.D.): William E. Wallace (wwallace@wustl.edu). Classical and Chinese archaeology; ancient, medieval, Renaissance, Baroque, and modern American art history.
Asian and Near Eastern Languages and Literatures (A.M., Ph.D.): Robert Hegel (anell@artsci.wustl.edu). Chinese, Japanese (A.M.); Chinese fiction, theater (joint Ph.D.).
Division of Biology and Biomedical Sciences (Ph.D.): Rebecca Riney (800-852-9074 (toll-free); e-mail: dbbs-admissions@dbbs.wustl.edu).
Biochemistry: Kathleen Hall (kathleenhal@gmail.com). Metabolic regulation/signal transduction, membranes, nucleic acid–protein structure interactions and function, replication/repair/recombination, transcription/translation enzyme kinetics.
Computational Biology: David Sept (dsept@biomed.wustl.edu). Bioinformatics, sequence analysis, structural biology, modeling of complex systems.
Developmental Biology: Kerry Kornfeld (kornfeld@wustl.edu) and James Skeath (jskeath@genetics.wustl.edu). Stem-cell biology, cell-fate determination, gene expression, growth control/morphogenesis, neural development, signal transduction, evolution and development.
Evolution, Ecology, and Population Biology: Barbara Schaal (schaal@wustl.edu). Experimental and theoretical population genetics; population and community ecology; phylogenetics, systematics, and evolution in plants and animals; primate evolutionary biology.
Human and Statistical Genetics: Anne Bowcock (bowcock@genetics.wustl.edu) and D. C. Rao (rao@wubios.wustl.edu). Human genetics, statistical genetics, genetic epidemiology, linkage analysis, human disease and complex traits.
Immunology: Barry Sleckman (sleckman@immunology.wustl.edu). Cellular and molecular immunology, immunopathology, inflammatory mediators, immunogenetics.
Molecular Biophysics: Nathan Baker (baker@ccb.wustl.edu). Protein and nucleic acid kinetics and thermodynamics, single-molecule enzymology, biomolecular folding, macromolecular structure determination, ion channels and lipid membranes, computational biophysics.
Molecular Cell Biology: Maurine Linder (mlinder@.wustl.edu). Cell adhesion, protein trafficking and organelle biogenesis, cell cycle, receptors, signal transduction, gene expression, metabolism, cytoskeleton and motility, membrane excitability.
Molecular Genetics and Genomics: Tim Schedl (ts@genetics.wustl.edu) and James Skeath (jskeath@genetics.wustl.edu). Gene expression and regulation, genome structure and analysis, gene regulatory networks, molecular evolution, model organism genetics, genetic basis of disease.
Molecular Microbiology and Microbial Pathogenesis: Tamara Doering (doering@wustl.edu) and Joseph Vogel (jvogel@borcim.wustl.edu). Molecular microbiology, microbial physiology, infectious disease, microbial pathogenesis, bacteriology, mycology, parasitology, virology, host defense.
Neurosciences: Dora Angelaki (angelaki@wustl.edu) and Paul Taghert (taghertp@pcg.wustl.edu). Central nervous system structure and function; cellular and molecular neurobiology; development and plasticity; neuropharmacology; motor systems sensory transduction.
Plant Biology: Eric Richards (richards@wustl.edu). Plant genetics; biochemistry; cell biology; development; molecular evolution, physiology, and epigenitics.
Business (Ph.D.): Cretta Wilson (wilsonc@wustl.edu). Accounting, business economics, finance, marketing, organizational behavior/strategy, operations and manufacturing management.
Chemistry (A.M., Ph.D.): Joseph Ackerman (ackerman@wuchem.wustl.edu). Bioinorganic, biological, bioorganic, biophysical, materials, nuclear, organic, organometallic, physical, polymer, radiochemistry, theoretical.
Classics (A.M.): Robert Lamberton (classics@artsci.wustl.edu). Greek and Latin language; Greek and Roman literature, philosophy, history, and material culture.
Comparative Literature (A.M., Ph.D.): Harriet Stone (hastone@wustl.edu). Literary theory, East-West comparison, translation, global and multicultural theory, comparative drama, interarts and intermediality, narrative theory, film.
Earth and Planetary Sciences (A.M., Ph.D.): Raymond E. Arvidson (epscinfo@levee.wustl.edu). Planetary sciences, geology, geobiology, geochemistry, geodynamics.
East Asian Studies (A.M., A.M./J.D., A.M./M.B.A.): Robert Hegel (eas@artsci.wustl.edu). Economic development, law, political, economic, intellectual history, literature and culture, art history and archaeology, anthropology.
Economics (Ph.D.): Michele Boldrin (mboldrin@artsci.wustl.edu). Economic theory, industrial organization, political economy, public economics, macroeconomics, public finance, development economics.
Education (M.A.Ed., M.A.T., Ph.D.): William F. Tate (wtate@wustl.edu). Teacher education, educational studies, urban education, policy studies, science and math education, literacy studies, learning science.
English and American Literature (M.A., Ph.D.): David Lawton (dalawton@wustl.edu). Medieval and early modern literature, nineteenth-century British literature, late nineteenth-century and modern American literature, African American literature, twentieth-century Irish poetry.
Germanic Languages and Literatures (A.M., Ph.D.): Stephan K. Schindler (german@artsci.wustl.edu). Contemporary German literature, German literature and culture prior to 1700, literature and history, film studies, gender studies, German-European literary and cultural relations.
History (Ph.D.): Hillel J. Kieval (hkieval@wustl.edu). British, American, African American, world and empire, Europe, Latin American, gender.
Islamic and Near Eastern Studies (A.M.): Pamela Barmash (pbarmash@wustl.edu). Islamic history, Arabic language and literature, Persian language and literature, modern Middle East history.
Jewish and Near Eastern Studies (A.M.): Pamela Barmash (pbarmash@wustl.edu). Hebrew bible, rabbinic literature, medieval Jewish history, modern Hebrew literature, modern Jewish history.
Mathematics (A.M., Ph.D.): David Wright (wright@math.wustl.edu). Algebra, polynomials, polynomial rings and automorphisms, algebraic geometry, geometry of affine space, combinatorics.
Movement Science (Ph.D.): Michael Mueller (muellerm@wustl.edu). Philosophy of human movement function and dysfunction, with special emphasis on bioenergetics, biomechanics, and biocontrol.
Music (M.M., A.M., Ph.D.): Craig Monson (camonson@artsci.wustl.edu). Piano, voice, composition, musicology, ethnomusicology, theory.
Philosophy (A.M., Ph.D.): Mark Rollins (mark@wustl.edu). Ethics, social and political philosophy, history of philosophy, philosophy of law, philosophy of science philosophy of mind, philosophy of language, theory of knowledge, aesthetics.
Philosophy/Neuroscience/Psychology (Ph.D.): José Bermúdez (bermudez@wustl.edu). Philosophy of mind and language, with a special emphasis on the philosophical dimensions of psychology, neuroscience, and linguistics.
Physics (A.M., Ph.D.): John W. Clark (jcw@wustl.edu). Experimental, theoretical, and computational physics; condensed matter and materials; magnetic resonance; many-body systems; nuclear physics; particles and fields; relativity and cosmology; astrophysics; space physics; biological physics; ultrasonics; biomedical physics.
Political Economy (A.M.): Norman Schofield (schofield@wustl.edu). International political economy, public policy.
Political Science (Ph.D.): Andrew Martin (admartin@wustl.edu). American politics, comparative politics, formal theory, international political economy, policy.
Psychology (Ph.D.): Deanna Barch (dbarch@wustl.edu). Behavior/brain/cognition, clinical, development and aging, social/personality.
Romance Languages and Literatures (A.M., Ph.D.): Elzbieta Sklodowska (esklodow@wustl.edu). French literature, Spanish and Latin American literature.
Social Work (Ph.D.): Wendy Auslander (phdsw@wustl.edu). Mental health, social development, addictions, aging, child welfare, civic service, disabilities, health, poverty and social policy, youth development and schools.
Speech and Hearing (Ph.D.): William Clark (clarkw@wustl.edu). Speech and hearing sciences, clinical audiology, deaf education, speech and language, sensory neuroscience.
Statistics (A.M.): Steven Krantz (sk@wustl.edu). Mathematical statistics, biostatistics.
The Writing Program (M.F.A.W.): Mary JoBang (english@wustl.edu). Two-year program: fiction or poetry-writing workshops and academic courses.

WEST CHESTER UNIVERSITY OF PENNSYLVANIA

Graduate Studies

Programs of Study

West Chester University of Pennsylvania offers graduate study leading to the M.A., M.B.A., M.Ed., M.M., M.P.H., M.S., M.S.W., M.S.N., and M.S.A. degrees. The Master of Arts is offered in communication studies, communicative disorders, English, French, geography, history, Holocaust and genocide studies, mathematics, music history, philosophy, physical sciences (earth science), psychology (general, clinical, and industrial/organizational psychology), Spanish, and teaching English as a second language. The Master of Business Administration is awarded in four concentrations: economics/finance, general business administration, management, and technology and electronic commerce. The Master of Education and/or certification is available in early childhood education, elementary and secondary school counseling, elementary education, French, history, reading, school health, secondary education, Spanish, and special education. The Master of Music is offered in accompanying, music education, music theory or composition, performance, and piano pedagogy. The Master of Science is offered in biology, computer science, criminal justice, educational research, environmental health, higher education counseling, and health and physical education. The Master of Science in Administration is awarded in eight concentrations: health services, human resource management, leadership for women, long-term care, public administration, sport and athletic administration, training and development, and urban and regional planning. West Chester University also offers the Master of Public Health, the Master of Social Work, the Master of Science in Nursing, and the Master of Science in applied statistics degrees. Certificate programs are offered in administration, computer science, geography, gerontology, Holocaust and genocide studies, integrative health, leadership for women, literacy, music, teaching English as a second language, and teaching and learning with technology.

Research Facilities

The Francis Harvey Green Library houses more than 500,000 volumes and a micromedia collection of more than 350,000 titles and subscribes to more than 2,800 periodicals. Its services include interlibrary loans, reference advice, computerized online literature searches, and an instructional materials center. The University's state-of-the-art computer facilities include an Ethernet Local Area Network, which connects all 1,400 computer workstations on campus. The LAN provides access to mainframe data, the library's online catalog, the Internet, and e-mail. Each student has an e-mail account and access to the Academic Computing Center 24 hours a day. The University makes Braille printers, translators, and speech synthesizers available to its visually impaired students. The Schmucker Science Center houses a fully equipped observatory and planetarium and extensive, well-equipped laboratories. Boucher Hall has state-of-the-art science labs for electronics, mineral spectroscopy, optics, and liquid crystal studies as well as an animal facility and greenhouse.

Financial Aid

A limited number of graduate assistantships are available on a competitive basis. In 2006–07, each carried an annual stipend of $5000 plus remission of tuition. In addition, some summer assistantships are available. Frederick Douglass Graduate Assistantships are also available. Scholarships and awards are offered by individual departments as well. West Chester University also participates in the Federal Perkins Loan and the Federal Stafford Student Loan programs.

Cost of Study

The basic per-semester tuition for full-time in-state residents taking 9 to 15 credits in 2006–07 was $3570 plus a $484 general fee; part-time and overload students were billed at a per-credit rate of $336 for tuition and a $47 general fee for fewer than 9 credits or for credits beyond 15. Out-of-state students paid $5417 for 9 to 15 credits and the general fee; part-time students were billed at the per-credit rate of $538.

Living and Housing Costs

West Chester University offers limited on-campus housing for single graduate students. Choices include designated quiet and honors dormitories, as well as apartment living in a 4- or 5-person fully furnished unit, with each bedroom having either single or double occupancy. Current costs (subject to change) are $2815 (single) in the residence hall and $2118 (double) or $2665 (single) in the apartments.

Many meal plans are available to students and range in cost from $538 to $1061 per semester.

The Office of Off-Campus and Commuter Services can provide assistance in identifying available off-campus housing. The office maintains listings and evaluations of apartments and rooms, many within walking distance of the campus.

Student Group

The student body at West Chester University numbers 12,822, of whom 2,100 are graduate students. The Graduate Student Association represents graduate students. The School of Education sponsors an active chapter of Phi Delta Kappa, the international graduate honor society. African-American and Hispanic student unions are active at West Chester. In addition, graduate students are invited to participate in the activities of undergraduate honor societies in which they hold membership. These include Alpha Lambda Delta, Alpha Mu Gamma, Alpha Psi Omega, Gamma Theta Upsilon, Kappa Delta Pi, Pi Gamma Mu, Pi Kappa Delta, Pi Mu Epsilon, Sigma Alpha Iota, Psi Chi, Phi Alpha Theta, Phi Delta Kappa, Phi Epsilon Kappa, Phi Eta Sigma, Phi Kappa Delta, Phi Mu Alpha Sinfonia, and Sigma Delta Pi.

Location

The University is located in West Chester, a community in southeastern Pennsylvania strategically located at the center of the mid-Atlantic corridor. The seat of Chester County government for almost two centuries, West Chester retains much of its historical charm in its buildings and unspoiled countryside while offering the twenty-first-century advantages of a town in the heart of an expanding economic area. West Chester is just 25 miles west of Philadelphia and 17 miles north of Wilmington, Delaware.

The interstate highway system and rail connections make the town accessible from many directions. Philadelphia is just an hour away, and travel to New York or Washington is possible in less than 3 hours.

The University

West Chester University is the second-largest of the fourteen institutions in the Pennsylvania State System of Higher Education and the fourth-largest in the Philadelphia metropolitan area. Officially founded in 1871, the University traces its heritage to the West Chester Academy, which existed from 1812 to 1869. The University's quadrangle buildings, part of the original campus, are on the National Register of Historic Places, and its 385-acre campus features well-maintained facilities, including eight modern residence halls.

In 2005–06, the University awarded 545 advanced degrees in fifty-nine graduate programs.

Applying

Application forms are available from the Office of Graduate Studies and Extended Education. Students should apply by April 15 or October 15 prior to the desired semester of entry. Earlier deadlines exist for some programs and for eligibility for assistantships and financial aid. Students are required to submit two official transcripts from all postsecondary institutions they have attended. Letters of recommendation; scores on the General Test and any applicable Subject Test of the Graduate Record Examinations, Graduate Management Admission Test, or Miller Analogies Test; and/or an interview are required for most programs.

Correspondence and Information

Janet Hickman, Interim Dean of Graduate Studies and Extended Education
Office of Graduate Studies and Extended Education
McKelvie Hall, 102 Rosedale Avenue
West Chester University
West Chester, Pennsylvania 19383

Phone: 610-436-2943
E-mail: gradstudy@wcupa.edu
Web site: http://www.wcupa.edu/

GRADUATE PROGRAM INFORMATION AND COORDINATORS

Listed below are West Chester University's graduate degree programs and the program coordinators. For information concerning a specific degree program, students should contact the graduate coordinator listed; for applications and general information, they should contact the Office of Graduate Studies.

Administration (M.S.A. with concentrations in health services administration, leadership for women, long-term-care administration, human resource management, training and development, public administration, sport and athletic administration, and regional planning; certificate in administration): Dr. Duane Milne (610-436-2438).
Applied Statistics (M.S.): Dr. Randall Reiger (610-436-2893).
Biology (M.S.): Dr. Judith Greenamyer (610-436-1023).
Business (M.B.A. with concentrations in economics/finance, general studies, management, and technology and electronic commerce): Dr. Paul Christ (610-425-5000).
Communication Studies (M.A. with emphasis on organizational studies, cross-cultural interaction, interpersonal relationships, communication education, language, group decision making, forensics, rhetorical theory and criticism, mass communication, and nonverbal communication): Dr. David Levasseur (610-436-2180).
Communicative Disorders (M.A.): Dr. Michael Weiss (610-436-3403).
Computer Science (M.S., certificate): Dr. Elaine Milito (610-436-2690).
Counselor Education (M.Ed. in elementary and secondary school counseling, M.S. in higher education/postsecondary studies, Specialist I certificate): Dr. Angelo Gadaleto (610-436-2559).
Criminal Justice (M.S.): Dr. Mary Brewster (610-436-2630).
Early Childhood Education: Dr. George Drake (610-436-2867).
Elementary Education (M.Ed. and certification; concentrations in general elementary education, creative teaching-learning, human development, and language arts; Certificate of Advanced Graduate Study): Dr. Connie DiLucchio (610-436-3323).
English (M.A.): Dr. Karen Fitts (610-436-2853).
Foreign Languages (M.Ed. or M.A. in French or Spanish): Dr. Rebecca Pauly (610-436-2382).
Geography (M.A. certificate): Dr. Joan Welch (610-436-2940).
Geology (M.A. in physical science, with a concentration in earth science) and Astronomy: Dr. Steve Good (610-436-2230).
Health (M.Ed. in school health and M.P.H.): Dr. Bethann Cinelli (610-436-2267).
History (M.A. in history, M.Ed. in social science): Dr. Maria Boes (610-436-2201).
History (M.A. in Holocaust and genocide studies): Dr. John Friedman (610-436-2972).
Mathematics (M.A.): Dr. John Kerrigan (610-436-2351).
Music (M.A. in music history and M.M. in music education, instrumental performance, keyboard performance, music theory and composition, and vocal/choral performance): Dr. Bryan Burton (610-436-2739).
Nursing (M.S.N. in community health nursing, with options in nursing education and nursing administration): Dr. Ann Stowe (610-436-2258).
Philosophy (M.A.): Dr. Thomas Platt (610-436-2857).
Physical Education (M.S. in physical education, with concentrations in general physical education, exercise, and sport physiology): Dr. Raymond Zetts (610-436-2146).
Psychology (M.A. in clinical, industrial/organizational, and general psychology): Dr. Loretta Rieser-Danner (610-436-3154).
Reading (M.Ed. and reading specialist certification): Dr. Deena Beeghly (610-436-2944).
Secondary Education (M.Ed. and M.S. in educational research): Dr. Cynthia Haggard (610-436-6934); postbaccalaureate certification (in biology, chemistry, earth and space science, English, French, German, Latin, math, physics, social studies, and Spanish): Dr. James Pugh (610-436-3063).
Special Education (M.Ed. and certificate programs): Dr. George Drake (610-436-1060).
Social Work (M.S.W.): Dr. Ann Abbott (610-738-0351).
TESL (M.A. in teaching English as a second language): Dr. Charles Grove (610-436-2916).

Students walking across the campus of West Chester University of Pennsylvania.

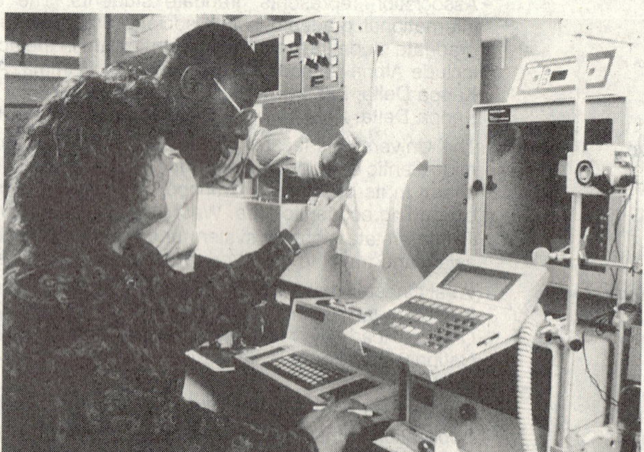

Research is an integral part of the graduate school experience at West Chester University.

WHEATON COLLEGE

Graduate School

Programs of Study

Wheaton College offers a Doctor of Philosophy (Ph.D.) in biblical and theological studies, a Doctor of Clinical Psychology (Psy.D.), and the Master of Arts (M.A.) degree in biblical archaeology, biblical exegesis, biblical studies, Christian formation and ministry, clinical psychology, counseling ministries, evangelism and leadership, historical and systematic theology, history of Christianity, intercultural studies, intercultural studies and teaching English to speakers of other languages (TESOL), missions, and primary and secondary education (M.A.T.). All of the graduate programs have core curriculum requirements, but elective options give students flexibility in arranging a program that suits their individual interests and goals.

In addition, nondegree certificates are available in teaching English as a second language, urban studies, and urban missions.

Research Facilities

The Buswell Memorial Library contains more than 1 million items, including books, records, scores, audiovisuals, microforms, and curriculum materials. The library belongs to LIBRAS, a consortium of sixteen metropolitan-area college libraries; the Association of Chicago Theological Schools, a consortium of Chicago-area seminaries; ILLINET; and OCLC.

The Billy Graham Center's mission is to stimulate world evangelism. The center includes a museum featuring educational exhibits on the evangelical message and the history of evangelism. The archives of the Billy Graham Center contain a rich collection of documents on North American Protestant nondenominational missions and the history of evangelism. They include the files of organizations such as National Religious Broadcasters, the Billy Graham Evangelistic Association, and Youth for Christ as well as the private papers of evangelical leaders, including Billy Sunday, Donald McGavran, and Charles Colson.

Special collections, housed in the Wade Center, consist of the books and papers of C. S. Lewis, G. K. Chesterton, George MacDonald, Dorothy Sayers, J. R. R. Tolkien, Charles Williams, and Owen Barfield.

Financial Aid

There is more than $500,000 in grant money available to full-time, degree-seeking graduate students. Nearly two thirds of that sum is directed toward American and international applicants involved in missionary work. Financial aid is awarded on the basis of need, as demonstrated on the Free Application for Federal Student Aid (FAFSA) and the Wheaton College Institutional Form. Assistantships are available in the various academic departments and are paid on a per-hour basis.

The Federal Stafford Student Loan Program is available to full- and part-time graduate students. Information and application forms may be acquired through the College Financial Aid Office, a local bank, savings and loan association, or credit union.

Cost of Study

Tuition for 2007–08 is $580 per semester hour for the master's degree, for which full-time study is 12 hours per semester. Tuition is $760 per semester hour for the Psy.D. degree and $706 per semester hour for the Ph.D. degree (including summer courses), for which full-time study is 10 hours per semester.

Living and Housing Costs

For 2007–08, a single graduate student should budget $13,868 for room, board, books, and personal expenses. Married students should plan on a budget of $17,868, plus $6000 for each dependent. These figures should be viewed as estimates.

Student Group

Total enrollment at Wheaton College is approximately 2,700 students. The graduate student body of 557 represents twenty-seven states, twelve countries, 110 colleges, and more than twenty denominations. About 50 percent of the graduate students are women and 8 percent are international students.

Location

Wheaton's 80-acre campus is located in Wheaton, Illinois, a residential suburb 25 miles west of Chicago with a population of 50,000. The educational and cultural resources of the Chicago metropolitan area are easily accessible. The Wheaton area is the home of approximately twenty Christian organizations.

The Graduate School

The Graduate School is an integral part of Wheaton College's distinguished history. It was founded in 1937 as the result of a generous gift. The emphasis of the Graduate School throughout its history has been on practical scholarship—scholarship that is totally rooted in the final authority of Scripture but is also practical, so that educated and trained Christian leaders are equipped to relate to the needs of modern man.

Applying

Application materials may be obtained by sending a request to the Graduate Admissions Office or via the Web site at http://www.wheatongrad.com. A nonrefundable application fee—$30 for the master's degree and $50 for the Psy.D. or Ph.D.—must be submitted with the application. The following materials are required for M.A. applicants: official transcripts of all academic work since high school graduation, three recommendations (one each from the applicant's pastor, an employer, and a college professor or academic adviser), employment resume, and scores from the General Test of the Graduate Record Examinations (GRE) or Miller Analogies Test (MAT). Biblical archaeology M.A. applicants must also submit a ten-page research paper. Applicants to the three psychology degree programs cannot submit the Miller Analogies Test and must submit a fourth recommendation from a mental health professional. Psy.D. applicants must also submit a ten-page research paper. Ph.D. applicants must submit three academic recommendations, one pastoral reference, and a 20- to 30-page research paper. Personal interviews are required for those who are finalists in the process for Ph.D. and Psy.D. admission.

Application deadlines for the fall semester are January 1 (Ph.D., M.A. in biblical archaeology, and international applicants), January 15 (Psy.D.), March 1 (M.A. in clinical psychology and the early deadline for all other M.A. degree programs), and May 1 (final deadline). Psychology, Ph.D., and international students are admitted only in the fall semester. Biblical archaeology applicants are admitted for the summer, with the application deadline being January 1.

Correspondence and Information

Graduate Admissions Office
Wheaton College
Wheaton, Illinois 60187
Phone: 630-752-5195
800-888-0141 (toll-free)
E-mail: gradadm@wheaton.edu
Web site: http://www.wheatongrad.com

THE FACULTY AND THEIR RESEARCH

(* denotes undergraduate faculty members who regularly teach graduate-level courses.)

Biblical and Theological Studies/Biblical Archaeology

* Vincent Bacote, Associate Professor of Theology; Ph.D., Drew.
Gregory Beale, Kenneth T. Wessner Professor of Biblical Studies; Ph.D., Cambridge.
Henri Blocher, Gunther H. Knoedler Professor of Theology; D.D., Gordon-Conwell Theological Seminary.
Daniel Block, Professor of Old Testament; D.Phil., Liverpool.
* Edith Blumhofer, Professor of History; Ph.D., Harvard.
* C. Hassell Bullock, Franklin S. Dyrness Professor of Biblical Studies; Ph.D., Hebrew Union–Jewish Institute of Religion. Old Testament theology, Old Testament criticism.
* Gary M. Burge, Professor of New Testament; Ph.D., Aberdeen (Scotland).
* Lynn Cohick, Associate Professor of New Testament; Ph.D., Pennsylvania.
* Gene Green, Professor; Ph.D., Aberdeen (Scotland). Macedonian and Anatolian Christianity.
Jeffrey Greenman, Professor of Christian Ethics and Associate Dean of Biblical and Theological Studies; Ph.D., Virginia.
* Andrew Hill, Professor of Old Testament; Ph.D., Michigan. Hebrew and Old Testament.
* Leroy Huizenga, Assistant Professor of New Testament; Ph.D., Duke.
Karen Jobes, Gerald Hawthorne Professor of New Testament Greek and Exegesis; Ph.D., Westminster.
* George Kalantzis, Associate Professor of Theology; Ph.D., Northwestern.
Jon Laansma, Associate Professor of Ancient Languages and New Testament; Ph.D., Aberdeen (Scotland).
Timothy Larsen, McManis Professor of Christian Thought; Ph.D., Stirling (Scotland).
* David Lauber, Assistant Professor of Theology; Ph.D., Princeton.
* Kathryn Long, Associate Professor of History; Ph.D., Duke. History of Christianity in North America, nineteenth-century Protestantism, women in religion.
* Daniel Master, Associate Professor of Archaeology; Ph.D., Harvard.
* Laura Miguelez, Assistant Professor of Theology; M.Div., Gordon-Conwell Theological Seminary.
* John Monson, Associate Professor of Archaeology; Ph.D., Harvard. Archaeology and Old Testament.
Douglas Moo, Blanchard Professor of New Testament; Ph.D., St. Andrews.
Nicholas Perrin, Assistant Professor of New Testament; Ph.D., Marquette.
* Arthur A. Rupprecht, Professor of Classical Languages; Ph.D., Pennsylvania.
* Richard Schultz, Carl Armerding and Hudson T. Armerding Professor of Biblical Studies; Ph.D., Yale.
Stephen Spencer, Blanchard Professor of Theology; Ph.D., Michigan State.
* Daniel Treier, Associate Professor of Theology; Ph.D., Trinity Evangelical Divinity School.
John Walton, Professor of Old Testament; Ph.D., Hebrew Union–Jewish Institute of Religion.

Christian Formation and Ministry

Scottie May, Assistant Professor of Christian Formation and Ministry; Ph.D., Trinity Evangelical Divinity School. Children's ministries, family studies, curriculum development.
Barrett McRay, Associate Professor of Christian Formation and Ministry and Department Chair; Psy.D., Wheaton (Illinois). Youth ministry, pastoral care and counseling in ministry, community mental health.
* Donald E. Ratcliff, Price-LeBar Professor of Christian Education; Ph.D., Georgia. Human development and ministry, research methods, children's spirituality.
Thomas Schwanda, Associate Professor of Christian Formation and Ministry; D.Min., Fuller Theological Seminary; Ph.D., Durham (England). Worship and spirituality.
David Setran, Associate Professor of Christian Formation and Ministry; Ph.D., Indiana. History and philosophy of Christian education, college/young adult ministry, small-group discipleship.
David Sveen, Adjunct Assistant Professor of Christian Formation and Ministry; Ph.D., Trinity Evangelical Divinity School. Ministry leadership, intercultural education/ministry, history/philosophy of ministry.
* James C. Wilhoit, Scripture Press Professor of Christian Formation & Ministry; Ph.D., Northwestern. Christian education, dynamics of spiritual growth, Bible and ministry, prayer. Author and editor of numerous books on Christian education.

Clinical Psychology

Keith A. Baird, Adjunct Instructor of Psychology; Ph.D., Loyola Chicago.
* Trey Buchanan, Associate Professor of Psychology; Ph.D., New Hampshire. Developmental psychology.
Richard E. Butman, Professor of Psychology; Ph.D., Fuller Theological Seminary. Psychological assessment.
Sally Canning, Associate Professor of Psychology; Ph.D., Pennsylvania. Child and adolescent psychology, community psychology, research.
Kenneth Davison, Adjunct Instructor of Psychology; Psy.D., Wheaton.
Helen DeVries, Professor of Psychology and Director, Psy.D. Program; Ph.D., Virginia Commonwealth. Geropsychology, neuropsychology, marital and family functioning.
Kelly S. Flanagan, Assistant Professor; Ph.D., Penn State. Child clinical psychology.
Robert Gregory, Professor of Psychology and Department Chair; Ph.D., Minnesota. Neuropsychological assessment, psychodiagnosis.
* Darlene Hannah, Assistant Professor; Ph.D., Northwestern. Social psychology.
* Cynthia J. Neal Kimball, Associate Professor of Psychology; Ph.D., New Mexico. High-risk families.
Michael W. Mangis, Associate Professor of Psychology; Ph.D., Wyoming. Psychodynamic psychology, assessment and treatment of adolescents.
J. Derek McNeil, Associate Professor of Psychology and Coordinator of Diversity; Ph.D., Northwestern. Identity development of African American men.
* Raymond Phinney, Assistant Professor; Ph.D., Washington State. Sensory psychology.
* William Struthers, Associate Professor of Psychology; Ph.D., Illinois at Chicago. Behavioral psychology.
* John Vessey, Associate Professor of Psychology; Ph.D., Northwestern. Statistics, experimental design.
Robert Watson, Associate Professor of Psychology; Psy.D., Illinois School of Professional Psychology. Psychodynamic and psychoanalytic psychology.
Terri Watson, Associate Professor of Psychology and Coordinator, M.A. Program; Psy.D., Illinois School of Professional Psychology. Child and adolescent therapy and child play therapy.
Natalia Yangarber-Hicks, Assistant Professor of Psychology; Ph.D., Cincinnati.

Education

* Laura Barwegen, Assistant Professor of Education; Ed.D., Northern Illinois. Neuropsychology and teacher efficacy.
* Andrew Brulle, Professor of Education; Ed.D., Northern Illinois. Special education and teacher preparation.
* Paul C. Egeland, Associate Professor of Education; Ed.D., Northern Illinois. Authentic assessment in social studies and science education and technology.
* Jillian Lederhouse, Professor of Education and Department Chair; Ph.D., Illinois at Chicago. Urban education and teacher development.
* Steven Loomis, Assistant Professor of Education; Ph.D., Claremont. Educational economics and policy and philosophical foundations of education.
* Sally E. Morrison, Associate Professor of Education; Ed.D., Northern Illinois. Moral development of teachers and mentorship.

Intercultural Studies

Lon Allison, Adjunct Associate Professor of Evangelism and Leadership; D.Min., Gordon-Conwell Theological Seminary.
John Armstrong, Adjunct Instructor of Evangelism and Leadership; D.Min., Luther Rice.
Evvy Hay Campbell, Associate Professor of Missions and Intercultural Studies and Chair; Ph.D., Michigan State.
Lonna Dickerson, Adjunct Instructor of Intercultural Studies and TESOL; Ph.D., Illinois at Urbana-Champaign.
Rob Gallagher, Associate Professor of Missions and Intercultural Studies; Ph.D., Fuller Theological Seminary.
Nancy Grisham, Adjunct Instructor of Evangelism and Leadership; Ph.D., Trinity Evangelical Divinity School.
Laura Hahn, Adjunct Instructor of Intercultural Studies and TESOL; Ph.D., Illinois at Urbana-Champaign.
A. Scott Moreau, Professor of Missions and Intercultural Studies; D.Miss., Trinity Evangelical Divinity School.
Cheri Pierson, Assistant Professor of Intercultural Studies and TESOL; Ed.D., Northern Illinois.
Rick Richardson, Associate Professor of Evangelism and Leadership; M.Div., Northern Baptist Theological Seminary.
Jerry Root, Adjunct Assistant Professor of Evangelism and Leadership; Ph.D., Open University (England).
Alan Seaman, Associate Professor of Intercultural Studies and TESOL; Ph.D., Virginia.
Timothy Sisk, Adjunct Instructor of Missions and Intercultural Studies; D.Min., Fuller Theological Seminary.

WIDENER UNIVERSITY

Graduate Studies

Programs of Study

Widener University awards the degrees of Doctor of Education (Ed.D.), Doctor of Juridical Science (S.J.D.), Doctor of Laws (D.L.), Doctor of Nursing Science (D.N.Sc.), Doctor of Philosophy (Ph.D.) in social work, Doctor of Physical Therapy (D.P.T.), Doctor of Psychology (Psy.D.), Juris Doctor (J.D.), Master of Arts (M.A.) in criminal justice, Master of Arts in Liberal Studies (M.L.S.), Master of Business Administration (M.B.A.), Master of Business Administration in health and medical services administration (M.B.A.-HMSA), Master of Education (M.Ed.), Master of Engineering (M.Eng.), Master of Jurisprudence (M.J.), Master of Laws (LL.M.), Master of Public Administration (M.P.A.), Master of Science in Hospitality Management (M.S.H.M.), Master of Science in Nursing (M.S.N.), and Master of Social Work (M.S.W.).

Master of Science degrees are also offered in the following business disciplines: Accounting Information Systems (M.S.A.I.S.), Information Systems (M.S.I.S.), Management and Technology (M.S.M.T.), and Taxation (M.S.T.). The M.Ed. program offers more than twenty majors, including counselor education, educational leadership, elementary education, human sexuality education, reading, special education, and supervision. The M.S.N. program offers concentrations in the advanced practice roles of adult health nursing, community-based nursing, emergency/critical care nursing, family nurse practitioner studies, nurse educator studies, and psychiatric/mental health nursing. Post-master's certificates are available in all clinical specialty areas as well as nursing education. The M.Eng. program offers specializations in engineering management and chemical, civil, computer and software, mechanical, and telecommunications engineering. An environmental engineering option is also available.

Dual-degree programs include the M.Eng./M.B.A., J.D./M.B.A., J.D./Psy.D., Psy.D./M.B.A., Psy.D./M.B.A.–HMSA, Psy.D./M.A. in criminal justice, Psy.D./M.P.A., M.Ed. in human sexuality education/Psy.D., M.S.W./M.Ed. in human sexuality education, M.S.W./Ed.D. in human sexuality, and M.Ed. in adult education/Ed.D. in human sexuality.

Research Facilities

The Wolfgram Memorial Library has a fine collection that includes more than 240,000 volumes, 175,000 microforms, and nearly 2,000 periodical titles. Services include online access to bibliographic information, full-text electronic journals, Web-based databases, audiovisual-media collections and facilities, and access to other libraries' resources through interlibrary loans. Computing facilities are available to meet students' needs.

The Center for Education runs a full-time laboratory preschool and early childhood center. It also has an extensive collection of curriculum materials, a reading laboratory, and a personal computer laboratory for computer-assisted instruction and interactive video.

The School of Law library maintains a collection of more than 600,000 volumes. Contained in the collection are legal publications and journals, treatises, reports, and statutes. Access to a wide range of supporting materials is available through LexisNexis and WESTLAW online legal research services.

Financial Aid

More than 85 percent of the law students receive some form of financial aid. Applicants should complete the Free Application for Federal Student Aid (FAFSA) form at the time of application.

Students in graduate programs other than law can apply for financial aid programs through the Financial Aid Office on the Main Campus. A limited number of graduate assistantships are available to full-time students in graduate programs other than law, and a number of loan programs are available to all eligible students.

Cost of Study

Tuition for Widener's graduate programs is as follows: $700 per credit for Ed.D. courses, $855 per credit for S.J.D. and LL.M. courses, $675 per credit for D.N.Sc. courses, $22,165 per year for the D.P.T. program, $20,490 per year for the Psy.D. program, and $29,330 per year for Regular Division J.D. students; $21,950 per year for first-, second-, third-year Extended Division students; $20,400 per year for fourth-year Extended Division students; and $525 per credit for graduate criminal justice and M.P.A. courses, $475 per credit for M.L.S. courses, $680 per credit for graduate business courses, $550 per credit for M.Ed. courses, $750 per credit for M.Eng. courses, $725 per credit for M.J. and D.L. courses, $600 per credit for M.S.H.M. courses, $595 for M.S.W. courses, and $650 per credit for M.S.N. courses. Part-time law courses (flex program, seven credits or less) are $975 per credit.

Living and Housing Costs

Affordable rental apartments are available within a 3-mile radius of all three campuses.

Student Group

Approximately 3,200 students are pursuing graduate or professional degrees at the University. About 57 percent are women. The student population is largely drawn from the mid-Atlantic region; about 5 percent of the graduate and professional students are from other countries. Students enter with a variety of undergraduate majors, including liberal arts, engineering, business, and nursing.

Location

Widener's Main Campus, occupying more than 100 acres in Chester, Pennsylvania, is easily accessible from Interstate 95. Located in Delaware County, one of the oldest counties in Pennsylvania, the campus is near historic and commercial areas; Philadelphia is just 15 miles north.

The 40-acre Delaware Campus (15 miles southwest of the Main Campus) is located on Route 202 (Concord Pike), north of Wilmington, and is only a short distance from Interstate 95. It houses the School of Law and is also a course site for the School of Business Administration. A branch of the School of Law is located on the 21-acre Harrisburg Campus in central Pennsylvania. Graduate social work, nursing, and education courses are also offered on this campus.

In fall 2004, Widener opened its fourth campus in Exton, Pennsylvania, which houses adult undergraduate education and the Osher Lifelong Learning Institute, a learning cooperative for area retirees. The Institute is the first facility of its kind in the Philadelphia metropolitan region.

The University

Widener University is a multicampus, independent, metropolitan institution located in and accredited by the commonwealth of Pennsylvania and the state of Delaware. The University distinguishes itself by connecting curricula to societal issues through civic engagement, inspiring its students to be citizens of character as well as professional and civic leaders.

Applying

Applicants for admission must file forms provided by the University, submit official transcripts of records covering all academic work beyond high school, and submit the standardized test scores (e.g., scores on the GMAT, GRE, or LSAT) appropriate to the program they wish to enter. An application fee is required. Final selection is based on the quality of the total application, as determined by the student's record of achievement and his or her personal qualification for graduate study and professional practice.

Correspondence and Information

For the Juris Doctor program:
Office of Admissions
Widener University School of Law
4601 Concord Pike
Wilmington, Delaware 19803
Phone: 302-477-2160
E-mail: law.admissions@law.widener.edu
Web site: http://www.law.widener.edu

For other graduate programs:
Office of Graduate Studies
Widener University
One University Place
Chester, Pennsylvania 19013
Phone: 610-499-4372
E-mail: gradmc@mail.widener.edu
Web site: http://www.widener.edu

FACULTY HEADS

Associate Provost for Graduate Studies: Stephen C. Wilhite, D.Phil.

Deans
College of Arts and Sciences: Mathew Poslusny, Ph.D.
School of Business Administration: Savas Ozatalay, Ph.D.
School of Engineering: Fred A. Akl, Ph.D.
School of Human Service Professions: Stephen C. Wilhite, D.Phil.
School of Law: Linda L. Ammons, J.D.
School of Nursing: Marguerite M. Barbiere, M.S.N., Ed.D.

WILLIAM PATERSON UNIVERSITY OF NEW JERSEY

Graduate Programs

Programs of Study

William Paterson University offers nineteen degree programs in the University's five colleges. Eight degrees are awarded: Master of Arts (M.A.), Master of Fine Arts (M.F.A.), Master of Science (M.S.), Master of Education (M.Ed.), Master of Business Administration (M.B.A.), Master of Arts in Teaching (M.A.T.), Master of Music (M.M.), and Master of Science in Nursing (M.S.N.). Degree requirements vary. The M.A. is offered in applied clinical psychology, English (with concentrations in literature and writing), history, media studies, public policy and international affairs, and sociology (with concentrations in crime and justice and diversity studies). The M.F.A. in art offers concentrations in fine arts, media arts, and design arts, with studio courses in ceramics, computer arts and animation, fibers, foundry, furniture design, graphic design, painting, photography, printmaking, and sculpture. The M.S. is offered in biology, biotechnology, and communication disorders (speech-language pathology). The M.Ed. is offered in counseling services (with concentrations in agency counseling and school counseling), education (with concentrations in bilingual/English as a second language, early childhood, educational media, language arts, learning technologies, social studies, and teaching children mathematics), educational leadership, reading, and special education (with specializations in developmental disability and learning disability). The M.M. is offered in music, with concentrations in jazz studies, music education, and music management. The M.B.A. is offered with concentrations in finance, general business, management, and marketing. The M.S.N. is offered in community-based nursing, with tracks in administrative, advanced practice, and educational. The M.A.T. is offered in elementary education. The College of Education also offers teacher certification programs for college graduates who wish to obtain initial teaching certification in New Jersey, as well as endorsement programs for certified teachers who wish to obtain additional teaching certification.

Research Facilities

The biological science facilities include scanning and transmission electron microscopes; fully equipped biochemistry, molecular biology, and neurobiology laboratories; computer, animal-care, and instrument rooms; NMR, IR, UV-visible, and AA spectrometers; GC and HPLC equipment; an amino acid analyzer; an ecology laboratory; and a greenhouse. Biotechnology facilities include an automated DNA sequencer, a DNA synthesizer, a DNA thermal coupler, gel electrophoresis equipment, and high-speed and ultracentrifuges; a modern tissue culture laboratory; a radioisotope laboratory; and a computer-assisted image-processing system. Hobart Hall houses two broadcast-quality TV studios, a multipurpose computer lab, a film studio, an FCC-licensed FM radio station, an uplink and four downlink satellite dishes, a cable system, and a computerized telephone system for voice and data transmission. The Atrium is a state-of-the-art technology center on campus that holds more than 100 multimedia computers arranged in classrooms with video projection capacity. The media center, which supports multimedia and Internet development, includes scanners, CD-ROM writers, digitizers, and related software tools. A multiphasic on-site clinic provides practical experience for special education, reading, and communication disorders program participants. William Paterson University is a member of the VALE Consortium, a nonprofit organization of colleges and universities fostering the growth of video, voice, and data networking in the state. VALE has offices at Rutgers University, Stevens Institute of Technology, and William Paterson University. University administrative computer facilities consist of a Digital Equipment Corporation Alpha cluster and interactive time-sharing terminals running VMS. The campus has a fiber-optic ATM backbone interconnecting all faculty offices, classrooms, and laboratories. There are currently more than 1,500 nodes on WPUNJnet. The David and Lorraine Cheng Library is open seven days a week when classes are in session and includes more than 350,000 volumes, more than 1,700 periodical titles, and an extensive collection of nonprint media. Services include professional reference assistance, online bibliographic searching, an interlibrary loan program, viewing facilities, and the latest in end-use searching. Nonprint resource materials include a microcomputer software collection and an audiovisual collection of film and videocassettes. The library has added an electronic resource center and a graduate research center equipped with RJ-45 Ethernet data jacks so that laptops can be plugged into the William Paterson network and has doubled its seating capacity.

Financial Aid

The University is participating in the Federal Family Education Loan Program. This program consists of Federal Stafford Student Loans (subsidized and unsubsidized) and the Federal PLUS program. Students must file the Free Application for Federal Student Aid (FAFSA) to determine their eligibility. The University makes a limited number of graduate assistantships available each year. Assistantships normally carry a stipend of $6000 and a waiver of tuition and fees. Graduate assistants must carry a minimum of 9 credits in each of the fall and spring semesters and work 20 hours per week in an assigned area. Graduate assistantships require a minimum grade point average of 3.0 and are awarded on the basis of availability and applicants' qualifications. Application forms are available in the Office of Graduate Studies.

Cost of Study

In 2006–07, full-time graduate tuition and fees were $514 per credit for New Jersey residents and $799 per credit for out-of-state students. Other fees apply for books, parking, the Student Center, information technology, and general services. Tuition and fees are subject to change in accordance with policies established by the Board of Trustees.

Living and Housing Costs

On-campus housing is available for single graduate students. Housing options include suite-style, single, and double accommodations or apartment-style living offered in a grouping of 4 students to an apartment. Currently, on-campus housing costs range from $3120 to $3750 per semester, with meal plans available at an additional cost of $690 to $1940 per semester. The University does not offer family student housing; however, the Office of Residence Life provides an off-campus living listing service. These dwellings are not preapproved by the University and may include listings for shared homes or apartments as well as private rooms. A graduate student selecting such off-campus housing may expect room and board costs of $7000 for the combined fall and spring semesters. Students are also advised to include $1100 in their budgets for travel as well as an additional $1500 for miscellaneous and personal expenses.

Student Group

The University has 10,600 students, of whom 1,737 (16 percent) are graduate students. Eighty-one percent of the students enrolled in graduate programs pursue their studies on a part-time basis. The traditional service area of the University consists of New Jersey's northernmost counties.

Location

Set on a 370-acre wooded hilltop, the University commands a breathtaking view of the surrounding communities. Located 20 miles west of New York City, the campus is easily accessible from major highways that provide access to the cultural and educational resources available within the metropolitan area.

The University

Founded in the city of Paterson in 1855, William Paterson is one of nine institutions in the New Jersey State Higher Education system. The University moved to the Wayne campus in 1951. In 1966, the University became a comprehensive institution offering undergraduate, graduate, and professional degrees. In 1997, William Paterson was awarded university status by the New Jersey Commission on Higher Education. Governed by a local board of trustees, William Paterson is accredited by the Middle States Association of Colleges and Schools. An on-campus state-certified center provides child care for eligible dependents of full- and part-time students. The Career Development and Advisement Center helps matriculated students and alumni who seek professional advancement or career changes.

Applying

To receive application information and materials, students should contact the Office of Graduate Studies.

Correspondence and Information

Office of Graduate Studies
William Paterson University of New Jersey
300 Pompton Road, R139
Wayne, New Jersey 07470-2103
Phone: 973-720-2237
E-mail: graduate@wpunj.edu
Web site: http://www.wpunj.edu

GRADUATE PROGRAMS AND DIRECTORS

Applied Clinical Psychology: Dr. Kathleen Torsney (973-720-3395). The program prepares students for the professional practice of psychological counseling, assessment, and mental health research in nonschool settings.

Art: David Horton (973-720-2401). The M.F.A. program is designed as the professional degree for the fine artist, craftsperson, designer, or media artist or for those wishing to teach at the college or university level. Concentrations are available in fine arts, design arts, or media arts.

Bilingual/English as a Second Language: Dr. Bruce Williams (973-720-3654).

Biology: Dr. Robert Chesney (973-720-3455). Neuroscience, image processing, transmission electron microscopy, protozoology, neuroendocrinology, teratogenic agents and development, animal behavior, behavior genetics, scanning electron microscopy, palynology, muscle physiology, invertebrate zoology, aquatic ecology, ecology and entomology, wetland ecology, and endocrinology.

Biotechnology: Dr. Robert Chesney (973-720-3455). Microbial genetics, molecular biology, protein biochemistry, neurochemistry, algal biochemistry, plant genetic engineering, parasitology, immunochemistry, mycology, molecular biology development, marine biochemistry, and gene activation.

Business Administration: Dr. Francis Cai (973-720-2178). The M.B.A. program is designed to provide students with both the background and perspective necessary for success in today's and tomorrow's business environments. Emphasis is placed on preparing students for the competitive global marketplace. Computer courses are designed to enhance students' skills by providing up-to-date software packages. The major areas of concentration are marketing, management, finance, and general business.

Certification Programs: College of Education (973-720-2138). Certification programs are intended for graduates who wish to obtain initial certification or endorsement in the state of New Jersey.

Communication Disorders: Dr. Jennifer Hsu (973-720-3352). This ASHA-accredited program provides students the training required to work as speech/language pathologists. The program is affiliated with the ASHA-accredited William Paterson University Speech and Hearing Clinic, which offers clinical services in the diagnosis or treatment of speech, language, and hearing disorders. Students have the opportunity to work with state-of-the-art equipment in audiometric testing, auditory brain stem–evoked responses, and speech and hearing science.

***Counseling Services (Agency):** Dr. Paula Danzinger (973-720-3085).

***Counseling Services (School):** Dr. Henry Heluk (973-720-3130).

Education: Dr. Rochelle Kaplan (973-720-2598). The M.Ed. program offers concentrations in bilingual/English as a second language, early childhood, language arts, learning technologies, school library media, social studies, and teaching children mathematics.

Education Leadership: Dr. Michael Chirichello (973-720-2130). This graduate program is designed for teachers who aspire to leadership positions in schools.

***Elementary Education:** Andrew Pachtman (973-720-3146). The Master of Arts in Teaching degree also enables graduates to obtain elementary (N–8) teacher certification.

English: Dr. Andrew Barnes (973-720-2837). Literature concentration: modern English and its background, major authors, early drama, and the novel; seventeenth- and eighteenth-century, romantic, Victorian, and modern British literature; nineteenth- and twentieth-century American literature; and related literature, including women's studies and film. Writing concentration: creative writing, advanced critical writing, writing for the magazine market, fiction writing, poetry writing, book and magazine editing, teaching writing as process, journalism, and script writing for the media.

History: Dr. Krista O'Donnell (973-720-2146). Through an innovative curriculum that focuses on historical analysis and the integration of information technology into historical research and teaching, program graduates acquire the skills necessary to communicate historical insights in a diverse and technologically advanced society.

Media Studies: Dr. Jay Ludwig (973-720-2743). The program encompasses theory, philosophy, and applications in the various areas of communication, including interpersonal communication, mass communication, and telecommunication. Research areas are cable access policy, intercultural communication, legal communication, and film and broadcast theory.

Music: Dr. Stephen Marcone (973-720-2314).

Nursing: Dr. Kem Louie (973-720-3215). The M.S.N. program is designed to provide students the training to work as advanced practitioners, educators, or administrators in nursing. The program combines course work and clinical practice in a variety of settings and includes courses in advanced nursing, health-care systems, health assessment, legislation and social policy, financial management, and labor law.

Public Policy and International Affairs: Dr. Sheila Collins (973-720-3424). The program provides the foundation for understanding how contemporary public policy crosses and supersedes national boundaries in an increasingly global environment of trade and information.

***Reading:** Dr. Kathleen Malu (973-720-2679) and Geraldine Mongillo (973-720-3139).

Sociology: Dr. Charley Flint (973-720-2368). The program consists of two interrelated tracks: diversity studies and crime and justice.

***Special Education:** Dr. Marjorie Goldstein (Certification) (973-720-3092); Dr. Christopher Mulrine (Developmental Disability) (973-720-3123); Jacqueline McConnell (Learning Disability) (973-720-3442).

**Teacher education programs are fully approved by the National Council of Accreditation of Teacher Education and meet the standards of the National Association of State Directors of Teacher Education and Certification.*

A view of the campus at William Paterson University of New Jersey.

William Paterson University offers abundant study space.

WORCESTER POLYTECHNIC INSTITUTE

Graduate Programs

Programs of Study

Worcester Polytechnic Institute (WPI) offers M.S. and Ph.D. programs in the following sciences: biology and biotechnology, chemistry and biochemistry, computer science, mathematics, and physics. Programs are also offered in the following areas of engineering: biomedical, chemical, civil and environmental, electrical and computer, fire protection, manufacturing, materials science, materials process, and mechanical. The university also offers an M.S. degree in system dynamics, M.S. and Ph.D. degrees in interdisciplinary studies, and M.S. and M.B.A. programs in management.

A biomedical engineering/medical physics joint Ph.D. program is sponsored by WPI and the University of Massachusetts Medical School.

The programs for the M.S. degree require a minimum of 30 credit hours. Although the specific requirements vary, most departments require a thesis of at least 6 semester hours. Arrangements may be made with local industries for thesis research.

The Ph.D. degree requires a minimum of 90 credit hours beyond the bachelor's degree, with a minimum of one year of full-time residence at the Institute.

Research Facilities

In addition to the extensive facilities for research available in all departments, graduate students have the opportunity to conduct research in a number of research institutes, centers, and laboratories, including the Metal Processing Institute, the largest industry-university alliance in North America, and the Bioengineering Institute (BEI), an interdisciplinary life sciences–based research and development organization. BEI and WPI's life sciences–based graduate research programs are located in the new 124,600-square-foot WPI Life Sciences and Bioengineering Center.

Other research centers include the Aerodynamics Laboratory, Analog/Digital Microelectronics Laboratory, Artificial Intelligence Laboratory, Assistive Technology Resource Center, Atomic Force Microscopy Laboratory, Biological Interaction Forces Laboratory, Bioprocess Technology Center, Center for Advanced Integrated Radio Navigation, Center for Entrepreneurship and Innovation, Center for Holographic Studies and Laser Micromechatronics, Center for Industrial Mathematics and Statistics, Center for Inorganic Membrane Studies, Center for Sensory and Physiologic Signal Processing, Center for Research in Electronic Commerce Technology, Center for Wireless Information Network Studies, Computer-Aided Manufacturing Laboratory, Convergent Technology Center, Cryptography and Information Security Research Laboratory, Environmental Laboratory, Fire Science Laboratory, Fuel Cell Center, Global Clean Energy Center, Hydrodynamics Laboratory, IPG Photonics Laboratory, Magnetic Resonance Imaging Facility, Materials Testing Laboratory, Microfluidics and Biosensors Laboratory, Nanomaterials and Nanomanufacturing Laboratory, Nondestructive Evaluation and Electromagnetics Research Laboratory, Pavement Research Laboratory, Polymer Laboratory, Robotics Laboratory, Structural Mechanics Impact Laboratory, Surface Metrology Laboratory, Tissue Engineering Laboratory, and Ultrasound Research Laboratory.

WPI is one of only 210 universities nationwide connected to Internet2 (the next generation Internet) and is one of only six institutions in New England with a node on the Access Grid, a worldwide high-speed multimedia conference network.

Central and departmental computation facilities include parallel processing mainframes and UNIX-based engineering workstations/minicomputers connected by a campuswide fiber-optic-linked Ethernet network. There are approximately 1,000 Windows-based personal computers on campus, many in open-access laboratories.

Financial Aid

Graduate assistantships are available for teaching or research. For the academic year 2007–08, teaching assistantships carry a stipend of $1722 per month, and research assistantship stipends vary between $1722 and $2500 per month. Both assistantships provide remission of tuition for up to 20 credits. Additional assistance may be available for the summer. U.S. citizens with exceptional qualifications are encouraged to apply for the Robert H. Goddard Fellowship. This prestigious award offers full-time tuition for one year (up to 20 credits) and a stipend of $1722 per month for twelve months. Other fellowship opportunities are also available. For more information, students should visit http://www.wpi.edu/Admin/FA/.

Cost of Study

Graduate tuition for the 2007–08 academic year is $1042 per credit hour. Full-time students are expected to enroll in 9 credit hours per semester (fall and spring).

Living and Housing Costs

On-campus graduate student housing is limited to a space-available basis. There is no on-campus housing for married students. Apartments and rooms in private homes near the campus are available at varying costs. For further information and apartment listings students should visit the Residential Services Office online at http://www.wpi.edu/Admin/RSO/Offcampus/.

Student Group

Worcester Polytechnic Institute has a student body of 3,903, of whom 877 are full- or part-time graduate students. Most states and nearly fifty countries are represented.

Location

The university is located on an 80-acre campus in a residential section of Worcester. The city, the second largest in New England, has many colleges and an unusual variety of cultural opportunities. Located three blocks from the campus, the nationally famous Worcester Art Museum contains one of the finest permanent collections in the country. From the renowned Worcester Music Festival to Foothills Theatre, the community provides outstanding programs in music and theater. The DCU Center offers rock concerts and hosts the American Hockey League's Worcester Sharks. The Tornadoes, of baseball's Can Am League, play at nearby Fitton Field. Easily reached for recreation are Boston and Cape Cod to the east and the Berkshires to the west; good skiing is nearby to the north. Complete athletic and recreational facilities and a program of concerts and special events are available on campus to graduate students.

The University

Worcester Polytechnic Institute, founded in 1865, is the third-oldest independent university of engineering and science in the United States. Graduate study has been a part of the Institute's activity for more than 100 years. Classes are small and provide for close student-faculty relationships. Graduate students frequently interact in research with undergraduates participating in WPI's innovative project-enriched curriculum.

Applying

Applicants must submit WPI application forms, official college transcript(s), three letters of recommendation, and a $70 application fee (waived for WPI alumni). Submission of GRE scores or other materials may be required depending on the academic department. International students whose primary language is not English must also submit proof of English language proficiency. WPI accepts either the TOEFL (Test of English as a Foreign Language) or the IELTS (International English Language Testing System). A paper-based TOEFL score of at least 550 (computer-based equivalent: 213, or Internet-based equivalent: 79–80) or an IELTS overall band score of 6.5 with no band score below 6.0 is required for admission. To be considered for funding (assistantships and fellowships), complete applications must be on file by January 15 for fall admission and October 15 for spring admission. Files completed after those deadlines are reviewed on a rolling basis and may not be considered for funding. Some fellowships require an additional application. Students should visit http://www.wpi.edu/Admin/FA/ for more information. Inquiries should be directed to the head of the degree program of interest or to the Office of Graduate Studies and Enrollment.

Correspondence and Information

Office of Graduate Studies and Enrollment
Worcester Polytechnic Institute
100 Institute Road
Worcester, Massachusetts 01609

Phone: 508-831-5301
Fax: 508-831-5717
E-mail: grad_studies@wpi.edu
Web site: http://www.grad.wpi.edu/

FACULTY HEADS AND RESEARCH AREAS

Biology and Biotechnology: Professor Eric W. Overstrom, Head. The department offers a Master of Science (M.S.) degree in biology and biotechnology and a Doctor of Philosophy (Ph.D.) degree in biotechnology. These full-time degree programs require students to successfully complete a set of required core courses in the field and a thesis project or dissertation that applies the basic principles of biology and biotechnology using hypothesis-driven experimental methods to study research problems or questions. Major research strengths in the department target areas of cell, molecular, and developmental/regenerative biology; ecology/evolution; computational biology; plant science; and applied microbial systems. Students graduate with a broad knowledge of the field of biology and biotechnology and demonstrate detailed knowledge and applied research skills in their area of specialization. Students who complete these programs are well prepared for further graduate education or for employment in academics or industry.

Biomedical Engineering: Professor Yitzhak Mendelson, Interim Head. Major research areas include biomaterials, biomechanics, biofluids, tissue engineering, stem cell and regenerative engineering tissue mechanics, regenerative medicine, nuclear magnetic resonance imaging and spectroscopy, biomedical sensors, biological signal processing, and biomedical instrumentation.

Chemical Engineering: Professor David DiBiasio, Head. The Chemical Engineering Department's research effort is concentrated in the following major areas: nanotechnology/nanomaterials, environmental engineering, energy research, bioengineering, process control, and reaction engineering.

Chemistry and Biochemistry: Professor Kristin K. Wobbe, Interim Head. The three major areas of research in the department are biochemistry and biophysics, including heavy-metal transport and metal homeostasis of both plants and bacteria, plant-pathogen interactions, enzyme structure and function, and others; molecular design and synthesis, encompassing supramolecular materials, photovoltaic materials, polymorphism in pharmaceutical drugs, spectroscopy of heterocyclic molecules, photophysical properties of cumulenes, host-guest chemistry, and more; and nanotechnology, including photonic and nonlinear optical materials, nanoporous and microporous crystals of organic and coordination compounds, molecular interactions at surfaces, and others.

Civil and Environmental Engineering: Professor Tahar El-Korchi, Head. Research areas include impact analysis; vehicle crashworthiness; transportation safety and roadside safety; asphalt technology; materials, biological, chemical, and physical aspects of water and wastewater treatment; water quality and distribution; integration of design and construction; groundwater flow; and contaminant distribution and hazardous waste. Environmental graduate courses are offered on campus and via distance learning.

Computer Science: Professor Michael A. Gennert, Head. Departmental research includes analysis of algorithms, artificial intelligence, computer graphics, computer vision, database systems, data mining, distributed systems, graph theory, human-computer interaction, intelligent tutoring systems, mobile and wireless communication, multimedia, networks, network and computer security, performance evaluation, programming languages, robotics, software engineering, user interfaces, virtual reality, and visualization. The department is housed in Fuller Laboratories, which was designed specifically for multimedia, high-technology education. The department has numerous general-purpose and specialized computing laboratories, with special devices and printers, a Linux-running cluster, and scores of high-end personal computers and workstations.

Electrical and Computer Engineering: Professor Fred Looft, Head. M.S. and Ph.D. Research areas include wireless networking, cryptography and network security, multimedia networks, the global positioning system, image processing, computational methods for electromagnetics and ultrasonics, analog microelectronics, medical imaging, power quality, and power system state estimation. Approximately $1 million in external research support is received annually. Major facilities include an extensive network of UNIX workstations and PCs, a wireless networks lab, VLSI design and test facilities, RF/microwave laboratories, and power electronics and power systems laboratories.

Fire Protection Engineering: Professor Kathy Notarianni, Head. Faculty research interests cover a wide range of topics in fire protection engineering and related areas. Research is directed toward fundamental understanding (theoretical and empirical), modeling of phenomena, and the development of practical engineering methods. Research areas include structural fire behavior, computer fire modeling, and fire-related combustion: flame spread and dust explosions; fire characteristics of materials: property estimation and study of complex systems such as composites, risk analysis, and regulatory reform; and protective clothing, composite materials, building fire safety, protective clothing, structural fire behavior, fire detection, and explosion protection. The combustion and materials research is supported by the Fire Science Laboratory, which contains state-of-the-art bench-scale apparatuses (Cone and 2 FPAs) and a residential-scale fire-test compartment, as well as exhaust hood space for bench- and residential-scale experiments. WPI offers both the master's and doctoral degrees in fire protection engineering as well as a five-year dual-degree program for high school graduates. Graduate courses are offered on campus and via distance learning.

Management: Professor McRae C. Banks, Head. WPI offers leading-edge management programs at the intersection of business and technology. Concentration areas include entrepreneurship, information security management, information technology, operations management, process design, supply chain management, technological innovation, and technology marketing. Graduate degree programs include the Master of Business Administration (M.B.A.), the Master of Science in marketing and technological innovation, the Master of Science in information technology, and the Master of Science in operations design and leadership. Graduate courses are offered on campus and online via WPI's Advanced Distance Learning Network.

Manufacturing Engineering: Professor Richard D. Sisson, Director, and Professor Yiming Rong, Associate Director. Research areas include fixturing, computer-integrated manufacturing, machining dynamics, tool wear, grinding, and surface metrology. Resources include the Haas Technical Center for computer-controlled machining, with eight CNC tool and UNIX workstations. The program also has a dedicated surface metrology laboratory with conventional profiling, a scanning laser microscope, and software for area-scale fractal analysis. The M.S. program includes thesis and nonthesis options. There are no required courses for the Ph.D.; however, residency, a comprehensive exam, and a dissertation are required.

Materials Science and Engineering: Professor Richard D. Sisson Jr., Director, and Professor Yiming Rong, Associate Director. Graduate study ranges over various engineering and science disciplines after focusing on fundamental work in materials science and materials engineering. Close ties with mechanical engineering, manufacturing, and other engineering and science programs are maintained. Facilities and equipment include optical microscopy, X-ray diffraction, casting, welding, mechanical testing, fatigue and fracture mechanics, materials characterization laboratories, and scanning and transmission electron microscopes. There is the nation's only dedicated Surface Metrology Laboratory, with conventional profiling, scanning laser microscope, and fractal analysis software supporting surface engineering. The Metals Processing Institute, a major university-industry consortium with more than 100 industrial members, is also an integrated part of the program. The Metals Processing Institute is made up of six research centers: the Advanced Casting Research Center, Powder Metallurgy Research Center, Center for Heat Treating Excellence, Non-Destructive Evaluation Center, Aerospace Materials Education Research Innovation Center, and Sloan Industry Center.

Mathematical Sciences: Professor Bogdan Vernescu, Head. The department offers an M.S. in applied mathematics, which emphasizes analysis, differential equations, numerical methods, mathematical modeling, and discrete mathematics; an M.S. in applied statistics, which emphasizes scientific applications for industry and government; professional M.S. degrees in industrial mathematics and financial mathematics for students interested in industrial careers; a Master of Mathematics for Educators; and a Ph.D. in mathematical sciences, which emphasizes mathematical modeling, scientific computing, and industrial, scientific, and engineering applications. Research interests of the 33 full-time faculty members include Bayesian statistics, biomathematics, biostatistics, composite materials and optimal design, computational fluid dynamics, computational mathematics, cryptography, discrete mathematics, graph theory, mathematical physics, matroid theory, numerical analysis, operations research, optimization, parallel computing, statistical computing, stochastic control, and time-series analysis.

Mechanical Engineering: Professor Gretar Tryggvason, Head. Departmental research includes theoretical, numerical, and experimental work in rarefied gas and plasma dynamics, propulsion, multiphase flows, turbulent flows, fluid-structure interactions, structural analysis, nonlinear dynamics and control, random vibrations, biomechanics and biomaterials, materials processing, mechanics of granular materials, laser holography, MEMS, computer-aided engineering systems, reconfigurable machine design, compliant mechanism design, and other areas of engineering design. Facilities include the Aerospace Laboratory, Biomechanical Engineering Laboratory, the Center for Holographic Studies and Laser Technology, the Heat Transfer Laboratory, the Vibrations and Dynamics Laboratory, the Fluid Dynamics Laboratory, the Metal Processing Institute, the Advanced Casting Research Center, the Center for Heat Treating Excellence, the Powder Metallurgy Research Center, the HAAS Center for Computer-Controlled Machining, and the Robotics Laboratory.

Physics: Associate Professor Germano Iannacchione, Interim Head. Current research interests include theoretical and experimental work in optics, quantum physics, chemical physics, statistical mechanics, and nuclear physics. Specializations include optical properties of semiconductor superlattices, as measured by inelastic light scattering, luminescence, and excitation spectroscopies; laser spectroscopy of impurity ions in fiber-optic glasses; nonlinear and quantum optics; coherent and squeezed states; light-scattering spectroscopy of transport phenomena in complex fluids, such as polymer and biomacromolecular solutions; magnetic systems and tunneling states; low-temperature behavior of glassy and amorphous materials; electronic properties of diluted magnetic semiconductors; lattice dynamics of dielectric crystals; and proton microbeam development.

Social Science and Policy Studies: Associate Professor James K. Doyle, Head. Major research areas include system dynamics, retrofitting and decentralization of electricity distribution networks, telecom infrastructure development, peer-to-peer markets, environmental mitigation, institutional development, and success and failure of political systems.

APPENDIXES

Institutional Changes Since the 2007 Edition

Following is an alphabetical listing of institutions that have recently closed, moved, merged with other institutions, or changed their names or status. In the case of a name change, the former name appears first, followed by the new name.

Alliant International University–San Francisco Bay (San Francisco, CA): name changed to Alliant International University–San Francisco.

American Academy of Nutrition, College of Nutrition (Knoxville, TN): name changed to Huntington College of Health Sciences.

American InterContinental University (Atlanta, GA): name changed to American InterContinental University Buckhead Campus.

American InterContinental University (Atlanta, GA): name changed to American InterContinental University Dunwoody Campus.

Antioch New England Graduate School (Keene, NH): name changed to Antioch University New England.

Argosy University/Atlanta (Atlanta, GA): name changed to Argosy University, Atlanta Campus.

Argosy University/Chicago (Chicago, IL): name changed to Argosy University, Chicago Campus.

Argosy University/Dallas (Dallas, TX): name changed to Argosy University, Dallas Campus.

Argosy University/Denver (Denver, CO): name changed to Argosy University, Denver Campus.

Argosy University/Hawai'i (Honolulu, HI): name changed to Argosy University, Hawai'i Campus.

Argosy University/Nashville (Franklin, TN): name changed to Argosy University, Nashville Campus.

Argosy University/Orange County (Santa Ana, CA): name changed to Argosy University, Orange County Campus.

Argosy University/Phoenix (Phoenix, AZ): name changed to Argosy University, Phoenix Campus.

Argosy University/San Diego (San Diego, CA): name changed to Argosy University, San Diego Campus.

Argosy University/San Francisco Bay Area (Point Richmond, CA): name changed to Argosy University, San Francisco Bay Area Campus.

Argosy University/Santa Monica (Santa Monica, CA): name changed to Argosy University, Santa Monica Campus.

Argosy University/Sarasota (Sarasota, FL): name changed to Argosy University, Sarasota Campus.

Argosy University/Schaumburg (Schaumburg, IL): name changed to Argosy University, Schaumburg Campus.

Argosy University/Seattle (Seattle, WA): name changed to Argosy University, Seattle Campus.

Argosy University/Tampa (Tampa, FL): name changed to Argosy University, Tampa Campus.

Argosy University/Twin Cities (Eagan, MN): name changed to Argosy University, Twin Cities Campus.

Argosy University/Washington D.C. (Arlington, VA): name changed to Argosy University, Washington DC Campus.

Arizona State University West (Phoenix, AZ): name changed to Arizona State University at the West Campus.

Central Missouri State University (Warrensburg, MO): name changed to University of Central Missouri.

Chatham College (Pittsburgh, PA): name changed to Chatham University.

Chicago School of Professional Psychology (Chicago, IL): name changed to The Chicago School of Professional Psychology.

David N. Myers University (Cleveland, OH): name changed to Myers University.

The Dickinson School of Law of The Pennsylvania State University (Carlisle, PA): name changed to Penn State Dickinson School of Law.

Dominican House of Studies (Washington, DC): name changed to Dominican House of Studies, Pontifical Faculty of the Immaculate Conception.

Embry-Riddle Aeronautical University, Extended Campus (Daytona Beach, FL): name changed to Embry-Riddle Aeronautical University Worldwide.

Evangelical School of Theology (Myerstown, PA): name changed to Evangelical Theological Seminary.

The Feinstein Institute for Medical Research (Manhasset, NY): name changed to North Shore–LIJ Graduate School of Molecular Medicine.

Franklin Pierce College (Rindge, NH): name changed to Franklin Pierce University.

International College (Naples, FL): name changed to Hodges University.

Methodist College (Fayetteville, NC): name changed to Methodist University.

Nevada College of Pharmacy (Las Vegas, NV): name changed to University of Southern Nevada.

North American Baptist Seminary (Sioux Falls, SD): name changed to Sioux Falls Seminary.

North Greenville College (Tigerville, SC): name changed to North Greenville University.

The Pennsylvania State University at Erie, The Behrend College (Erie, PA): name changed to Penn State Erie, The Behrend College.

The Pennsylvania State University Great Valley Campus (Malvern, PA): name changed to Penn State Great Valley.

The Pennsylvania State University Harrisburg Campus (Middletown, PA): name changed to Penn State Harrisburg.

The Pennsylvania State University Milton S. Hershey Medical Center (Hershey, PA): name changed to Penn State Hershey Medical Center.

The Pennsylvania State University University Park Campus (University Park, PA): name changed to Penn State University Park.

Piedmont Baptist College (Winston-Salem, NC): name changed to Piedmont Baptist College and Graduate School.

Rutgers, The State University of New Jersey, New Brunswick/Piscataway (New Brunswick, NJ): name changed to Rutgers, The State University of New Jersey, New Brunswick.

Santa Barbara College of Oriental Medicine (Santa Barbara, CA): closing December 2007.

Southwestern University School of Law (Los Angeles, CA): name changed to Southwestern Law School.

State University of New York at Buffalo (Buffalo, NY): name changed to University at Buffalo, the State University of New York.

State University of New York, Fredonia (Fredonia, NY): name changed to State University of New York at Fredonia.

Texas A&M University System Health Science Center (College Station, TX): name changed to Texas A&M Health Science Center.

Thunderbird, The Garvin School of International Management (Glendale, AZ): name changed to Thunderbird School of Global Management.

University of Colorado at Denver and Health Sciences Center–Downtown Denver Campus (Denver, CO): name changed to University of Colorado at Denver and Health Sciences Center.

University of Judaism (Bel Air, CA): name changed to American Jewish University.

University of Maryland (Baltimore, MD): name changed to University of Maryland, Baltimore.

University of Phoenix–Idaho Campus (Boise, ID): name changed to University of Phoenix–Magic View.

University of Phoenix–Nevada Campus (Las Vegas, NV): name changed to University of Phoenix–Las Vegas Campus.

University of Phoenix–South Florida Campus (Fort Lauderdale, FL): name changed to University of Phoenix–Fort Lauderdale Campus.

University of Phoenix–Spokane Campus (Spokane Valley, WA): name changed to University of Phoenix–Eastern Washington Campus.

Whitworth College (Spokane, WA): name changed to Whitworth University.

William Carey College (Hattiesburg, MS): name changed to William Carey University.

Abbreviations Used in the Guides

The following list includes abbreviations of degree names used in the profiles in the 2008 edition of the guides. Because some degrees (e.g., Doctor of Education) can be abbreviated in more than one way (e.g., D.Ed. or Ed.D.), and because the abbreviations used in the guides reflect the preferences of the individual colleges and universities, the list may include two or more abbreviations for a single degree.

Degrees

A Mus D	Doctor of Musical Arts
AC	Advanced Certificate
AD	Artist's Diploma
ADP	Artist's Diploma
Adv C	Advanced Certificate
Adv M	Advanced Master
AGSC	Advanced Graduate Specialist Certificate
ALM	Master of Liberal Arts
AM	Master of Arts
AMRS	Master of Arts in Religious Studies
APC	Advanced Professional Certificate
App Sc	Applied Scientist
App Sc D	Doctor of Applied Science
Au D	Doctor of Audiology
B Th	Bachelor of Theology
CAES	Certificate of Advanced Educational Specialization
CAGS	Certificate of Advanced Graduate Studies
CAL	Certificate in Applied Linguistics
CALS	Certificate of Advanced Liberal Studies
CAMS	Certificate of Advanced Management Studies
CAPS	Certificate of Advanced Professional Studies
CAS	Certificate of Advanced Studies
CASPA	Certificate of Advanced Study in Public Administration
CASR	Certificate in Advanced Social Research
CATS	Certificate of Achievement in Theological Studies
CBHS	Certificate in Basic Health Sciences
CBS	Graduate Certificate in Biblical Studies
CCJA	Certificate in Criminal Justice Administration
CCMBA	Cross-Continent Master of Business Administration
CCSA	Certificate in Catholic School Administration
CE	Civil Engineer
CEM	Certificate of Environmental Management
CET	Certificate in Educational Technologies
CG	Certificate in Gerontology
CGS	Certificate of Graduate Studies
Ch E	Chemical Engineer
CM	Certificate in Management
CMH	Certificate in Medical Humanities
CMM	Master of Church Ministries
CMS	Certificate in Ministerial Studies
CNM	Certificate in Nonprofit Management
CP	Certificate in Performance
CPASF	Certificate Program for Advanced Study in Finance
CPC	Certificate in Professional Counseling Certificate in Publication and Communication
CPH	Certificate in Public Health
CPM	Certificate in Public Management
CPS	Certificate of Professional Studies
CScD	Doctor of Clinical Science
CSD	Certificate in Spiritual Direction
CSS	Certificate of Special Studies
CTS	Certificate of Theological Studies
CURP	Certificate in Urban and Regional Planning
D Arch	Doctor of Architecture
D Ed	Doctor of Education
D Eng	Doctor of Engineering
D Engr	Doctor of Engineering
D Env	Doctor of Environment
D Env M	Doctor of Environmental Management
D Law	Doctor of Law
D Litt	Doctor of Letters
D Med Sc	Doctor of Medical Science
D Min	Doctor of Ministry
D Min PCC	Doctor of Ministry, Pastoral Care, and Counseling
D Miss	Doctor of Missiology
D Mus	Doctor of Music
D Mus A	Doctor of Musical Arts
D Phil	Doctor of Philosophy
D Ps	Doctor of Psychology
D Sc	Doctor of Science
D Sc D	Doctor of Science in Dentistry
D Sc IS	Doctor of Science in Information Systems
D Th	Doctor of Theology
D Th P	Doctor of Practical Theology
DA	Doctor of Arts
DA Ed	Doctor of Arts in Education
DAOM	Doctorate in Acupuncture and Oriental Medicine
DAST	Diploma of Advanced Studies in Teaching
DBA	Doctor of Business Administration
DBS	Doctor of Buddhist Studies
DC	Doctor of Chiropractic
DCC	Doctor of Computer Science
DCD	Doctor of Communications Design
DCL	Doctor of Comparative Law
DCM	Doctor of Church Music
DCN	Doctor of Clinical Nutrition
DCS	Doctor of Computer Science
DDN	Diplôme du Droit Notarial
DDS	Doctor of Dental Surgery
DE	Doctor of Education Doctor of Engineering
DEIT	Doctor of Educational Innovation and Technology
DEM	Doctor of Educational Ministry
DEPD	Diplôme Études Spécialisées
DES	Doctor of Engineering Science
DESS	Diplôme Études Supérieures Spécialisées
DFA	Doctor of Fine Arts
DGP	Diploma in Graduate and Professional Studies
DH Ed	Doctor of Health Education
DH Sc	Doctor of Health Sciences
DHA	Doctor of Health Administration
DHCE	Doctor of Health Care Ethics
DHL	Doctor of Hebrew Letters Doctor of Hebrew Literature

DHS	Doctor of Health Science Doctor of Human Services
DHSc	Doctor of Health Science
DIBA	Doctor of International Business Administration
Dip CS	Diploma in Christian Studies
DIT	Doctor of Industrial Technology
DJ Ed	Doctor of Jewish Education
DJS	Doctor of Jewish Studies
DM	Doctor of Management Doctor of Music
DMA	Doctor of Musical Arts
DMD	Doctor of Dental Medicine
DME	Doctor of Manufacturing Management Doctor of Music Education
DMEd	Doctor of Music Education
DMFT	Doctor of Marital and Family Therapy
DMH	Doctor of Medical Humanities
DML	Doctor of Modern Languages
DMM	Doctor of Music Ministry
DN Sc	Doctor of Nursing Science
DNP	Doctor of Nursing Practice
DNS	Doctor of Nursing Science
DO	Doctor of Osteopathy
DPA	Doctor of Public Administration
DPC	Doctor of Pastoral Counseling
DPDS	Doctor of Planning and Development Studies
DPE	Doctor of Physical Education
DPH	Doctor of Public Health
DPM	Doctor of Plant Medicine Doctor of Podiatric Medicine
DPS	Doctor of Professional Studies
DPT	Doctor of Physical Therapy
DPTSc	Doctor of Physical Therapy Science
Dr DES	Doctor of Design
Dr PH	Doctor of Public Health
Dr Sc PT	Doctor of Science in Physical Therapy
DrNP	Doctor of Nursing Practice
DS	Doctor of Science
DS Sc	Doctor of Social Science
DSJS	Doctor of Science in Jewish Studies
DSL	Doctor of Strategic Leadership
DSM	Doctor of Sport Management
DSN	Doctor of Science in Nursing
DSW	Doctor of Social Work
DTL	Doctor of Talmudic Law
DV Sc	Doctor of Veterinary Science
DVM	Doctor of Veterinary Medicine
EAA	Engineer in Aeronautics and Astronautics
ECS	Engineer in Computer Science
Ed D	Doctor of Education
Ed DCT	Doctor of Education in College Teaching
Ed M	Master of Education
Ed S	Specialist in Education
Ed Sp	Specialist in Education
Ed Sp PTE	Specialist in Education in Professional Technical Education
EDBA	Executive Doctor of Business Adminstration
EDM	Executive Doctorate in Management
EDSPC	Education Specialist
EE	Electrical Engineer
EJD	Executive Juris Doctor
EM	Mining Engineer
EMBA	Executive Master of Business Administration
EMCIS	Executive Master of Computer Information Systems
EMHA	Executive Master of Health Administration
EMIB	Executive Master of International Business
EMPA	Executive Master of Public Affairs
EMS	Executive Master of Science
EMTM	Executive Master of Technology Management
Eng	Engineer
Eng Sc D	Doctor of Engineering Science
Engr	Engineer
Ex Doc	Executive Doctor of Pharmacy
Exec Ed D	Executive Doctor of Education
Exec MBA	Executive Master of Business Administration
Exec MPA	Executive Master of Public Administration
Exec MPH	Executive Master of Public Health
Exec MS	Executive Master of Science
GBC	Graduate Business Certificate
GCE	Graduate Certificate in Education
GDM	Graduate Diploma in Management
GDPA	Graduate Diploma in Public Administration
GDRE	Graduate Diploma in Religious Education
GEMBA	Global Executive Master of Business Administration
Geol E	Geological Engineer
GMBA	Global Master of Business Administration
GPD	Graduate Performance Diploma
GSS	Graduate Special Certificate for Students in Special Situations
IMA	Interdisciplinary Master of Arts
IMBA	International Master of Business Administration
ITMA	Master of Instructional Technology
JCD	Doctor of Canon Law
JCL	Licentiate in Canon Law
JD	Juris Doctor
JD/DVM	Juris Doctor/Doctor of Veterinary Medicine
JD/MAP	Juris Doctor/Master of Applied Politics
JD/MCS	Juris Doctor/Master of Computer Science
JD/MHRIR	Juris Doctor/Master of Human Resources and Industrial Relations
JSD	Doctor of Juridical Science Doctor of Jurisprudence Doctor of the Science of Law
JSM	Master of Science of Law
L Th	Licenciate in Theology
LL B	Bachelor of Laws
LL CM	Master of Laws in Comparative Law
LL D	Doctor of Laws
LL M	Master of Laws
LL M T	Master of Laws in Taxation
M Ac	Master of Accountancy Master of Accounting Master of Acupuncture
M Ac OM	Master of Acupuncture and Oriental Medicine
M Acc	Master of Accountancy Master of Accounting
M Acct	Master of Accountancy Master of Accounting
M Accy	Master of Accountancy
M Actg	Master of Accounting
M Acy	Master of Accountancy
M Ad	Master of Administration

M Ad Ed	Master of Adult Education
M Adm	Master of Administration
M Adm Mgt	Master of Administrative Management
M ADU	Master of Architectural Design and Urbanism
M Adv	Master of Advertising
M Aero E	Master of Aerospace Engineering
M AEST	Master of Applied Environmental Science and Technology
M Ag	Master of Agriculture
M Ag Ed	Master of Agricultural Education
M Agr	Master of Agriculture
M Anesth Ed	Master of Anesthesiology Education
M App Comp Sc	Master of Applied Computer Science
M App St	Master of Applied Statistics
M Appl Stat	Master of Applied Statistics
M Aq	Master of Aquaculture
M Ar	Master of Architecture
M Arch	Master of Architecture
M Arch I	Master of Architecture I
M Arch II	Master of Architecture II
M Arch E	Master of Architectural Engineering
M Arch H	Master of Architectural History
M Arch UD	Master of Architecture in Urban Design
M Arch/SMRED	Master of Architecture/Master of Science in Real Estate Development
M Bio E	Master of Bioengineering
M Biomath	Master of Biomathematics
M Ch	Master of Chemistry
M Ch E	Master of Chemical Engineering
M Chem	Master of Chemistry
M Cl D	Master of Clinical Dentistry
M Cl Sc	Master of Clinical Science
M Comp E	Master of Computer Engineering
M Comp Sc	Master of Computer Science
M Coun	Master of Counseling
M Dent	Master of Dentistry
M Dent Sc	Master of Dental Sciences
M Des	Master of Design
M Des S	Master of Design Studies
M Div	Master of Divinity
M E Com	Master of Electronic Commerce
M Ec	Master of Economics
M Econ	Master of Economics
M Ed	Master of Education
M Ed T	Master of Education in Teaching
M En	Master of Engineering
M En S	Master of Environmental Sciences
M Eng	Master of Engineering
M Eng Mgt	Master of Engineering Management
M Eng Tel	Master of Engineering in Telecommunications
M Engr	Master of Engineering
M Env	Master of Environment
M Env Des	Master of Environmental Design
M Env E	Master of Environmental Engineering
M Env Sc	Master of Environmental Science
M Fin	Master of Finance
M Fr	Master of French
M Geo E	Master of Geological Engineering
M Geoenv E	Master of Geoenvironmental Engineering
M Geog	Master of Geography
M Hum	Master of Humanities
M Hum Svcs	Master of Human Services
M Kin	Master of Kinesiology
M Land Arch	Master of Landscape Architecture
M Lit M	Master of Liturgical Music
M Litt	Master of Letters
M Man	Master of Management
M Mat SE	Master of Material Science and Engineering
M Math	Master of Mathematics
M Med Sc	Master of Medical Science
M Mgmt	Master of Management
M Mgt	Master of Management
M Min	Master of Ministries
M Mtl E	Master of Materials Engineering
M Mu	Master of Music
M Mus	Master of Music
M Mus Ed	Master of Music Education
M Nat Sci	Master of Natural Science
M Nurs	Master of Nursing
M Oc E	Master of Oceanographic Engineering
M Pharm	Master of Pharmacy
M Phil	Master of Philosophy
M Phil F	Master of Philosophical Foundations
M Pl	Master of Planning
M Pol	Master of Political Science
M Pr A	Master of Professional Accountancy
M Pr Met	Master of Professional Meteorology
M Prob S	Master of Probability and Statistics
M Prof Past	Master of Professional Pastoral
M Psych	Master of Psychology
M Pub	Master of Publishing
M Rel	Master of Religion
M Sc	Master of Science
M Sc A	Master of Science (Applied)
M Sc AHN	Master of Science in Applied Human Nutrition
M Sc BMC	Master of Science in Biomedical Communications
M Sc CS	Master of Science in Computer Science
M Sc E	Master of Science in Engineering
M Sc Eng	Master of Science in Engineering
M Sc Engr	Master of Science in Engineering
M Sc F	Master of Science in Forestry
M Sc FE	Master of Science in Forest Engineering
M Sc Geogr	Master of Science in Geography
M Sc N	Master of Science in Nursing
M Sc OT	Master of Science in Occupational Therapy
M Sc P	Master of Science in Planning
M Sc Pl	Master of Science in Planning
M Sc PT	Master of Science in Physical Therapy
M Sc T	Master of Science in Teaching
M Soc	Master of Sociology
M Sp Ed	Master of Special Education
M Stat	Master of Statistics
M Sw En	Master of Software Engineering
M Sys Sc	Master of Systems Science
M Tax	Master of Taxation
M Tech	Master of Technology
M Th	Master of Theology
M Th Past	Master of Pastoral Theology
M Tox	Master of Toxicology
M Trans E	Master of Transportation Engineering
M Vet Sc	Master of Veterinary Science

MA	Master of Administration Master of Arts
MA Comm	Master of Arts in Communication
MA Ed	Master of Arts in Education
MA Ed Ad	Master of Arts in Educational Administration
MA Ext	Master of Agricultural Extension
MA Islamic	Master of Arts in Islamic Studies
MA Min	Master of Arts in Ministry
MA Missions	Master of Arts in Missions
MA Past St	Master of Arts in Pastoral Studies
MA Ph	Master of Arts in Philosophy
MA Ps	Master of Arts in Psychology
MA Psych	Master of Arts in Psychology
MA Sc	Master of Applied Science
MA Sp	Master of Arts (Spirituality)
MA Th	Master of Arts in Theology
MA-R	Master of Arts (Research)
MAA	Master of Administrative Arts Master of Applied Anthropology Master of Arts in Administration
MAAA	Master of Arts in Arts Administration
MAAE	Master of Arts in Art Education
MAAT	Master of Arts in Applied Theology Master of Arts in Art Therapy
MAB	Master of Agribusiness
MABC	Master of Arts in Biblical Counseling Master of Arts in Business Communication
MABE	Master of Arts in Bible Exposition
MABL	Master of Arts in Biblical Languages
MABM	Master of Agribusiness Management
MABS	Master of Arts in Biblical Studies
MABT	Master of Arts in Bible Teaching
MAC	Master of Accounting Master of Addictions Counseling Master of Arts in Communication Master of Arts in Counseling
MACAT	Master of Arts in Counseling Psychology: Art Therapy
MACC	Master of Arts in Christian Counseling
MACCM	Master of Arts in Church and Community Ministry
MACCT	Master of Accounting
MACE	Master of Arts in Christian Education
MACFM	Master of Arts in Children's and Family Ministry
MACH	Master of Arts in Church History
MACJ	Master of Arts in Criminal Justice
MACL	Master of Arts in Classroom Psychology
MACM	Master of Arts in Christian Ministries Master of Arts in Church Music Master of Arts in Counseling Ministries
MACN	Master of Arts in Counseling
MACO	Master of Arts in Counseling
MAcOM	Master of Acupuncture and Oriental Medicine
MACP	Master of Arts in Counseling Psychology
MACPC	Master of Clinical Pastoral Counseling
MACS	Master of Arts in Catholic Studies Master of Arts in Christian Service
MACSE	Master of Arts in Christian School Education
MACT	Master of Arts in Christian Thought Master of Arts in Communications and Technology
MACY	Master of Arts in Accountancy
MAD	Master in Educational Institution Administration Master of Art and Design
MADR	Master of Arts in Dispute Resolution
MADS	Master of Animal and Dairy Science Master of Applied Disability Studies
MAE	Master of Aerospace Engineering Master of Agricultural Economics Master of Architectural Engineering Master of Art Education Master of Arts in Economics Master of Arts in Education Master of Arts in English Master of Automotive Engineering
MAEd	Master of Arts Education
MAEE	Master of Agricultural and Extension Education
MAEL	Master of Arts in Educational Leadership Master of Arts in Executive Leadership
MAEM	Master of Arts in Educational Ministries
MAEN	Master of Arts in English
MAEP	Master of Arts in Economic Policy
MAES	Master of Arts in Environmental Sciences
MAESL	Master of Arts in English as a Second Language
MAET	Master of Arts in English Teaching
MAF	Master of Arts in Finance
MAFE	Master of Arts in Financial Economics
MAFLL	Master of Arts in Foreign Language and Literature
MAFM	Master of Accounting and Financial Management
MAFS	Master of Arts in Family Studies
MAG	Master of Applied Geography
MAGC	Master of Arts in Global Communication
MAGP	Master of Arts in Gerontological Psychology
MAGU	Master of Urban Analysis and Management
MAH	Master of Arts in Humanities
MAHA	Master of Arts in Humanitarian Assistance Master of Arts in Humanitarian Studies
MAHCM	Master of Arts in Health Care Mission
MAHG	Master of American History and Government
MAHL	Master of Arts in Hebrew Letters
MAHN	Master of Applied Human Nutrition
MAHS	Master of Arts in Human Services
MAHT	Master of Arts in History Teaching
MAIA	Master of Arts in International Administration
MAIB	Master of Arts in International Business
MAICS	Master of Arts in Intercultural Studies
MAIDM	Master of Arts in Interior Design and Merchandising
MAIPCR	Master of Arts in International Peace and Conflict Management
MAIR	Master of Arts in Industrial Relations
MAIS	Master of Accounting and Information Systems Master of Arts in Intercultural Studies Master of Arts in Interdisciplinary Studies Master of Arts in International Studies
MAIT	Master of Administration in Information Technology Master of Applied Information Technology
MAJ	Master of Arts in Journalism
MAJ Ed	Master of Arts in Jewish Education
MAJCS	Master of Arts in Jewish Communal Service
MAJE	Master of Arts in Jewish Education
MAJS	Master of Arts in Jewish Studies
MAL	Master in Agricultural Leadership
MALA	Master of Arts in Liberal Arts
MALD	Master of Arts in Law and Diplomacy
MALER	Master of Arts in Labor and Employment Relations

MALM	Master of Arts in Leadership Evangelical Mobilization
MALP	Master of Arts in Language Pedagogy
MALPS	Master of Arts in Liberal and Professional Studies
MALS	Master of Arts in Liberal Studies
MALT	Master of Arts in Learning and Teaching
MAM	Master of Acquisition Management Master of Agriculture and Management Master of Applied Mathematics Master of Applied Mechanics Master of Arts in Management Master of Arts in Ministry Master of Arts Management Master of Avian Medicine
MAMB	Master of Applied Molecular Biology
MAMC	Master of Arts in Mass Communication Master of Arts in Ministry and Culture Master of Arts in Ministry for a Multicultural Church
MAME	Master of Arts in Missions/Evangelism
MAMFC	Master of Arts in Marriage and Family Counseling
MAMFCC	Master of Arts in Marriage, Family, and Child Counseling
MAMFT	Master of Arts in Marriage and Family Therapy
MAMM	Master of Arts in Ministry Management
MAMS	Master of Applied Mathematical Sciences Master of Arts in Ministerial Studies Master of Arts in Ministry and Spirituality Master of Associated Medical Sciences
MAMT	Master of Arts in Mathematics Teaching
MAN	Master of Applied Nutrition
MANM	Master of Arts in Nonprofit Management
MANT	Master of Arts in New Testament
MAO	Master of Arts in Organizational Psychology
MAOA	Master of Arts in Organizational Administration
MAOL	Master of Arts in Organizational Leadership
MAOM	Master of Acupuncture and Oriental Medicine Master of Arts in Organizational Management
MAOT	Master of Arts in Old Testament
MAP	Master of Applied Psychology Master of Arts in Planning Master of Public Administration Masters of Psychology
MAP Min	Master of Arts in Pastoral Ministry
MAPA	Master of Arts in Public Administration
MAPC	Master of Arts in Pastoral Counseling
MAPE	Master of Arts in Political Economy
MAPM	Master of Arts in Pastoral Ministry Master of Arts in Pastoral Music Master of Arts in Practical Ministry
MAPP	Master of Arts in Public Policy
MAPPS	Master of Arts in Asia Pacific Policy Studies
MAPS	Master of Arts in Pastoral Counseling/Spiritual Formation Master of Arts in Pastoral Studies Master of Arts in Public Service
MAPT	Master of Practical Theology
MAPW	Master of Arts in Professional Writing
MAR	Master of Arts in Religion
Mar Eng	Marine Engineer
MARC	Master of Arts in Rehabilitation Counseling
MARE	Master of Arts in Religious Education
MARL	Master of Arts in Religious Leadership
MARS	Master of Arts in Religious Studies
MAS	Master of Accounting Science Master of Actuarial Science Master of Administrative Science Master of Advanced Study Master of Aeronautical Science Master of American Studies Master of Applied Science Master of Applied Statistics Master of Archival Studies
MAS/JD	Master of Accounting Science/Juris Doctor
MASA	Master of Advanced Studies in Architecture
MASAC	Master of Arts in Substance Abuse Counseling
MASC	Master of Arts in School Counseling
MASD	Master of Arts in Spiritual Direction
MASE	Master of Arts in Special Education
MASF	Master of Arts in Spiritual Formation
MASJ	Master of Arts in Systems of Justice
MASL	Master of Arts in School Leadership
MASLA	Master of Advanced Studies in Landscape Architecture
MASM	Master of Arts in Special Ministries Master of Arts in Specialized Ministries
MASP	Master of Applied Social Psychology Master of Arts in School Psychology
MASPAA	Master of Arts in Sports and Athletic Administration
MASS	Master of Applied Social Science Master of Arts in Social Science
MAST	Master of Arts Science Teaching
MASW	Master of Aboriginal Social Work
MAT	Master of Arts in Teaching Master of Arts in Theology Master of Athletic Training Master in Administration of Telecommunications
Mat E	Materials Engineer
MATCM	Master of Acupuncture and Traditional Chinese Medicine
MATDE	Master of Arts in Theology, Development, and Evangelism
MATE	Master of Arts for the Teaching of English
MATESL	Master of Arts in Teaching English as a Second Language
MATESOL	Master of Arts in Teaching English to Speakers of Other Languages
MATF	Master of Arts in Teaching English as a Foreign Language/Intercultural Studies
MATFL	Master of Arts in Teaching Foreign Language
MATH	Master of Arts in Therapy
MATI	Master of Administration of Information Technology
MATL	Master of Arts in Teaching of Languages Master of Arts in Transformational Leadership
MATM	Master of Arts in Teaching of Mathematics
MATS	Master of Arts in Theological Studies Master of Arts in Transforming Spirituality
MATSL	Master of Arts in Teaching a Second Language
MAUA	Master of Arts in Urban Affairs
MAUD	Master of Arts in Urban Design
MAUM	Master of Arts in Urban Ministry
MAURP	Master of Arts in Urban and Regional Planning
MAW	Master of Arts in Writing
MAWL	Master of Arts in Worship Leadership
MAWS	Master of Arts in Worship/Spirituality
MAWSHP	Master of Arts in Worship
MAYM	Master of Arts in Youth Ministry

MB	Master of Bioinformatics
MBA	Master of Business Administration
MBA-EP	Master of Business Administration–Experienced Professionals
MBA/M Stat	Master of Business Administration/Master of Statistics
MBA/MEE	Master of Business Administration/Master of Electrical Engineering
MBA/MNO	Master of Business Administration/Master of Nonprofit Organization
MBAA	Master of Business Administration in Aviation
MBAE	Master of Biological and Agricultural Engineering Master of Biosystems and Agricultural Engineering
MBAH	Master of Business Administration in Health
MBAi	Master of Business Administration–International
MBAICT	Master of Business Administration in Information and Communication Technology
MBAIM	Master of Business Administration in International Management
MBAPA	Master of Business Administration–Physician Assistant
MBATM	Master of Business Administration in Technology Management Master of Business in Telecommunication Management
MBC	Master of Building Construction
MBE	Master of Bilingual Education Master of Bioengineering Master of Biological Engineering Master of Biomedical Engineering Master of Business and Engineering Master of Business Economics Master of Business Education
MBET	Master of Business, Entrepreneurship and Technology
MBI	Master in Business Informatics
MBIOT	Master of Biotechnology
MBIT	Master of Business Information Technology
MBL	Master of Business Law
MBLE	Master in Business Logistics Engineering
MBMSE	Master of Business Management and Software Engineering
MBOL	Master of Business and Organizational Leadership
MBS	Master of Behavioral Science Master of Biological Science Master of Biomedical Sciences Master of Bioscience Master of Building Science
MBSI	Master of Business Information Science
MBT	Master of Biblical and Theological Studies Master of Biomedical Technology Master of Business Taxation
MC	Master of Communication Master of Counseling Master of Cybersecurity
MC Ed	Master of Continuing Education
MC Sc	Master of Computer Science
MCA	Master of Arts in Applied Criminology Master of Commercial Aviation
MCALL	Master of Computer-Assisted Language Learning
MCAM	Master of Computational and Applied Mathematics
MCC	Master of Computer Science
MCCS	Master of Crop and Soil Sciences
MCD	Master of Communications Disorders Master of Community Development
MCE	Master in Electronic Commerce Master of Christian Education Master of Civil Engineering Master of Control Engineering
MCEM	Master of Construction Engineering Management
MCH	Master of Community Health
MCHE	Master of Chemical Engineering
MCIS	Master of Communication and Information Studies Master of Computer and Information Science
MCIT	Master of Computer and Information Technology
MCJ	Master of Criminal Justice
MCJA	Master of Criminal Justice Administration
MCL	Master in Communication Leadership Master of Canon Law Master of Civil Law Master of Comparative Law
MCM	Master of Christian Ministry Master of Church Management Master of Church Ministry Master of Church Music Master of City Management Master of Communication Management Master of Community Medicine Master of Competitive Manufacturing Master of Construction Management Master of Contract Management Master of Corporate Media
MCMS	Master of Clinical Medical Science
MCP	Master in Science Master of City Planning Master of Community Planning Master of Counseling Psychology Master of Cytopathology Practice
MCPD	Master of Community Planning and Development
MCRP	Master of City and Regional Planning
MCRS	Master of City and Regional Studies
MCS	Master of Christian Studies Master of Clinical Science Master of Combined Sciences Master of Communication Studies Master of Computer Science
MCSE	Master of Computer Science and Engineering
MCSL	Master of Catholic School Leadership
MCSM	Master of Construction Science/Management
MCST	Master of Science in Computer Science and Information Technology
MCTP	Master of Communication Technology and Policy
MCVS	Master of Cardiovascular Science
MD	Doctor of Medicine
MD/CM	Doctor of Medicine and Master of Surgery
MD/MSBS	Doctor of Medicine/Master of Science in Biomedical Science
MDA	Master of Development Administration Master of Dietetic Administration
MDE	Master of Developmental Economics Master of Distance Education
MDH	Master of Dental Hygiene
MDR	Master of Dispute Resolution
MDS	Master of Defense Studies Master of Dental Surgery
ME	Master of Education Master of Engineering Master of Entrepreneurship Master of Evangelism
ME Sc	Master of Engineering Science

MEA	Master of Educational Administration Master of Engineering Administration
MEAP	Master of Environmental Administration and Planning
MEBT	Master in Electronic Business Technologies
MEC	Master of Electronic Commerce
MECE	Master of Electrical and Computer Engineering
Mech E	Mechanical Engineer
MED	Master of Education of the Deaf
MEDL	Master of Educational Leadership
MEDS	Master of Environmental Design Studies
MEE	Master in Education Master of Electrical Engineering Master of Environmental Engineering
MEEM	Master of Environmental Engineering and Management
MEENE	Master of Engineering in Environmental Engineering
MEEP	Master of Environmental and Energy Policy
MEERM	Master of Earth and Environmental Resource Management
MEH	Master in Humanistics Studies
MEHS	Master of Environmental Health and Safety
MEIM	Master of Entertainment Industry Management
MEL	Master of Educational Leadership Master of English Literature
MEM	Master of Ecosystem Management Master of Electricity Markets Master of Engineering Management Master of Environmental Management Master of Marketing
MEME	Master of Engineering in Manufacturing Engineering Master of Engineering in Mechanical Engineering
MEMS	Master of Engineering in Manufacturing Systems
MENG	Master of Arts in English
MENVEGR	Master of Environmental Engineering
MEP	Master of Engineering Physics Master of Environmental Planning
MEPC	Master of Environmental Pollution Control
MEPD	Master of Education–Professional Development
MEPM	Master of Environmental Protection Management
MER	Master of Employment Relations
MES	Master of Education and Science Master of Engineering Science Master of Environmental Science Master of Environmental Studies Master of Environmental Systems Master of Special Education
MESM	Master of Environmental Science and Management
MET	Master of Education in Teaching Master of Educational Technology Master of Engineering Technology Master of Entertainment Technology Master of Environmental Toxicology
Met E	Metallurgical Engineer
METM	Master of Engineering and Technology Management
MEVE	Master of Environmental Engineering
MF	Master of Finance Master of Forestry
MFA	Master of Financial Administration Master of Fine Arts
MFAM	Master in Food Animal Medicine
MFAS	Master of Fisheries and Aquatic Science
MFAW	Master of Fine Arts in Writing
MFC	Master of Forest Conservation
MFCC	Marriage and Family Counseling Certificate
MFCS	Master of Family and Consumer Sciences
MFE	Master of Financial Engineering Master of Forest Engineering
MFG	Master of Functional Genomics
MFHD	Master of Family and Human Development
MFM	Master of Financial Mathematics
MFMS	Masters in Food Microbiology and Safety
MFP	Master of Financial Planning
MFPE	Master of Food Process Engineering
MFR	Master of Forest Resources
MFRC	Master of Forest Resources and Conservation
MFS	Master of Financial Services Master of Food Science Master of Forensic Sciences Master of Forest Science Master of Forest Studies Master of French Studies
MFSA	Master of Forensic Sciences Administration
MFT	Master of Family Therapy Master of Food Technology
MFWB	Master of Fishery and Wildlife Biology
MFWS	Master of Fisheries and Wildlife Sciences
MFYCS	Master of Family, Youth and Community Sciences
MG	Master of Genetics
MGA	Master of Government Administration
MGE	Master of Gas Engineering Master of Geotechnical Engineering
MGF	Master of Global Finance
MGH	Master of Geriatric Health
MGIS	Master of Geographic Information Science
MGM/MBA	Master in Global Management/Master of Business Administration
MGP	Master of Gestion de Projet
MGS	Master of Gerontological Studies Master of Global Studies
MH	Master of Humanities
MH Ed	Master of Health Education
MH Sc	Master of Health Sciences
MHA	Master of Health Administration Master of Healthcare Administration Master of Hospital Administration Master of Hospitality Administration
MHCA	Master of Health Care Administration
MHCI	Master of Human-Computer Interaction
MHCL	Master of Health Care Leadership
MHE	Master of Health Education
MHE Ed	Master of Home Economics Education
MHHS	Master of Health and Human Services
MHI	Master of Health Informatics
MHIIM	Master of Health Informatics and Information Management
MHIS	Master of Health Information Systems
MHK	Master of Human Kinetics
MHL	Master of Hebrew Literature
MHM	Master of Hospitality Management
MHMS	Master of Health Management Systems
MHP	Master of Health Physics Master of Heritage Preservation Master of Historic Preservation
MHPA	Master of Heath Policy and Administration
MHPE	Master of Health Professions Education

MHR	Master of Human Resources
MHRD	Master in Human Resource Development
MHRDL	Master of Human Resource Development Leadership
MHRIM	Master of Hotel, Restaurant, and Institutional Management
MHRIR	Master of Human Resources and Industrial Relations
MHRIR/JD	Master of Human Resources and Industrial Relations/Juris Doctor
MHRIR/MBA	Master of Human Resources and Industrial Relations/Master of Business Administration
MHRLR	Master of Human Resources and Labor Relations
MHRM	Master of Human Resources Management
MHROD	Master of Human Resources and Organization Development
MHRTM	Master of Hotel, Restaurant, and Tourism Management
MHS	Master of Health Sciences Master of Health Studies Master of Hispanic Studies Master of Humanistic Studies
MHSA	Master of Health Services Administration
MHSM	Master of Health Sector Management Master of Health Systems Management Master of Human Services Management
MI	Master of Instruction
MI Arch	Master of Interior Architecture
MI St	Master of Information Studies
MIA	Master of Interior Architecture Master of International Affairs
MIAA	Master of International Affairs and Administration
MIAM	Master of International Agribusiness Management
MIB	Master of International Business
MIBA	Master of International Business Administration
MICM	Master of International Construction Management
MID	Master of Industrial Design Master of Industrial Distribution Master of Interior Design Master of International Development
MIE	Master of Industrial Engineering
MIEM	Master of Industrial Engineering and Management
MIJ	Master of International Journalism
MILR	Master of Industrial and Labor Relations
MIM	Master of Information Management Master of International Management
MIMLAE	Master of International Management for Latin American Executives
MIMS	Master of Information Management and Systems Master of Integrated Manufacturing Systems
MIP	Master of Infrastructure Planning Master of Intellectual Property
MIPER	Master of International Political Economy of Resources
MIPP	Master of International Policy and Practice Master of International Public Policy
MIPS	Master of International Planning Studies
MIR	Master of Industrial Relations Master of International Relations
MIS	Master of Industrial Statistics Master of Information Science Master of Information Systems Master of Integrated Science Master of Interdisciplinary Studies Master of International Service Master of International Studies
MISE	Master of Industrial and Systems Engineering
MISKM	Master of Information Sciences and Knowledge Management
MISM	Master of Information Systems Management
MIT	Master in Teaching Master of Industrial Technology Master of Information Technology Master of Initial Teaching Master of International Trade Master of Internet Technology
MITA	Master of Information Technology Administration
MITE	Master of Information Technology Education
MITM	Master of International Technology Management
MITO	Master of Industrial Technology and Operations
MJ	Master of Journalism Master of Jurisprudence
MJ Ed	Master of Jewish Education
MJA	Master of Justice Administration
MJS	Master of Judicial Studies Master of Juridical Science
MKM	Master of Knowledge Management
ML	Master of Latin
ML Arch	Master of Landscape Architecture
MLA	Master of Landscape Architecture Master of Liberal Arts
MLAS	Master of Laboratory Animal Science
MLAUD	Master of Landscape Architecture in Urban Development
MLBLST	Master of Liberal Studies
MLD	Master of Leadership Development Master of Leadership Studies
MLE	Master of Applied Linguistics and Exegesis
MLER	Master of Labor and Employment Relations
MLERE	Master of Land Economics and Real Estate
MLHR	Master of Labor and Human Resources
MLI	Master of Legal Institutions
MLI Sc	Master of Library and Information Science
MLIS	Master of Library and Information Science Master of Library and Information Studies
MLM	Master of Library Media
MLOS	Master in Leadership and Organizational Studies
MLRHR	Master of Labor Relations and Human Resources
MLS	Master of Leadership Studies Master of Legal Studies Master of Liberal Studies Master of Library Science Master of Life Sciences
MLS/PMC	Master of Library Science/Graduat Certificate in Public Management
MLSP	Master of Law and Social Policy
MLT	Master of Language Technologies
MLW	Master of Studies in Law
MM	Master of Management Master of Mediation Master of Ministry Master of Missiology Master of Music
MM Ed	Master of Music Education
MM Sc	Master of Medical Science
MM St	Master of Museum Studies
MMA	Master of Marine Affairs Master of Media Arts Master of Musical Arts
MMAE	Master of Mechanical and Aerospace Engineering
MMAS	Master of Military Art and Science

MMB	Master of Microbial Biotechnology
MMBA	Managerial Master of Business Administration
MMC	Master of Competitive Manufacturing Master of Mass Communications Master of Music Conducting
MMCM	Master of Music in Church Music
MMCSS	Master of Mathematical Computational and Statistical Sciences
MME	Master of Manufacturing Engineering Master of Mathematics for Educators Master of Mechanical Engineering Master of Medical Engineering Master of Mining Engineering Master of Music Education Mater of Mathematics Education
MMFT	Master of Marriage and Family Therapy
MMG	Master of Management
MMH	Master of Management in Hospitality Master of Medical History Master of Medical Humanities Master of Military History
MMIS	Master of Management Information Systems
MMM	Master of Manufacturing Management Master of Marine Management Master of Medical Management
MMME	Master of Metallurgical and Materials Engineering
MMMP	Master of Music in Music Performance
MMP	Master of Marine Policy Master of Music Performance
MMPA	Master of Management and Professional Accounting
MMQM	Master of Manufacturing Quality Management
MMR	Master of Marketing Research
MMRM	Master of Marine Resources Management
MMS	Master of Management Science Master of Manufacturing Systems Master of Marine Studies Master of Materials Science Master of Medical Science Master of Medieval Studies Master of Modern Studies
MMSE	Master of Manufacturing Systems Engineering
MMSM	Master of Music in Sacred Music
MMT	Master in Marketing Master of Music Teaching Master of Music Therapy Masters in Marketing Technology
MMus	Master of Music
MN	Master of Nursing Master of Nutrition
MN Sc	Master of Nursing Science
MNA	Master of Nonprofit Administration Master of Nurse Anesthesia
MNAL	Master of Nonprofit Administration and Leadership
MNAS	Master of Natural and Applied Science
MNCM	Master of Network and Communications Management
MNE	Master of Network Engineering Master of Nuclear Engineering
MNL	Master in International Business for Latin America
MNM	Master of Nonprofit Management
MNO	Master of Nonprofit Organization
MNO/MSSA	Master of Nonprofit Organization/Master of Arts
MNPL	Master of Not-for-Profit Leadership
MNPS	Master of New Professional Studies
MNR	Master of Natural Resources
MNRES	Master of Natural Resources and Environmental Studies
MNRM	Master of Natural Resource Management
MNRS	Master of Natural Resource Stewardship
MNS	Master of Natural Science
MO	Master of Oceanography
MOA	Maître d'Orthophonie et d'Audiologie
MOD	Master of Organizational Development
MOGS	Master of Oil and Gas Studies
MOH	Master of Occupational Health
MOL	Master of Organizational Leadership
MOM	Master of Manufacturing Master of Oriental Medicine
MOR	Master of Operations Research
MOT	Master of Occupational Therapy
MP	Master of Physiology Master of Planning
MP Ac	Master of Professional Accountancy
MP Acc	Master of Professional Accountancy Master of Professional Accounting Master of Public Accounting
MP Aff	Master of Public Affairs
MP Th	Master of Pastoral Theology
MPA	Master of Physician Assistant Master of Professional Accountancy Master of Professional Accounting Master of Public Administration Master of Public Affairs
MPA-URP	Master of Public Affairs and Urban and Regional Planning
MPAC	Master in Professional Accounting
MPAID	Master of Public Administration and International Development
MPAP	Master of Physician Assistant Practice Master of Public Affairs and Politics
MPAS	Master of Physician Assistant Science Master of Physician Assistant Studies Master of Public Art Studies
MPC	Master of Pastoral Counseling Master of Professional Communication Master of Professional Counseling
MPD	Master of Product Development Master of Public Diplomacy
MPDS	Master of Planning and Development Studies
MPE	Master of Physical Education
MPEM	Master of Project Engineering and Management
MPH	Master of Public Health
MPHE	Master of Public Health Education
MPHTM	Master of Public Health and Tropical Medicine
MPIA	Master of Public and International Affairs
MPL	Master of Pastoral Leadership
MPM	Master of Pastoral Ministry Master of Pest Management Master of Practical Ministries Master of Project Management Master of Public Management
MPNA	Master of Public and Nonprofit Administration
MPOD	Master of Positive Organizational Development
MPP	Master of Public Policy
MPPA	Master of Public Policy Administration Master of Public Policy and Administration
MPPAL	Master of Public Policy, Administration and Law
MPPM	Master of Public and Private Management Master of Public Policy and Management
MPPPM	Master of Plant Protection and Pest Management

MPPUP Master of Public Policy and Urban Planning
MPRTM Master of Parks, Recreation, and Tourism Management
MPS Master of Pastoral Studies
Master of Perfusion Science
Master of Political Science
Master of Preservation Studies
Master of Professional Studies
Master of Public Service
MPSA Master of Public Service Administration
MPSRE Master of Professional Studies in Real Estate
MPT Master of Pastoral Theology
Master of Physical Therapy
MPVM Master of Preventive Veterinary Medicine
MPW Master of Professional Writing
Master of Public Works
MQF Master of Quantitative Finance
MQM Master of Quality Management
MQS Master of Quality Systems
MR Master of Recreation
MRC Master of Rehabilitation Counseling
MRCP Master of Regional and City Planning
Master of Regional and Community Planning
MRD Master of Rural Development
MRE Master of Religious Education
MRED Master of Real Estate Development
MRLS Master of Resources Law Studies
MRM Master of Rehabilitation Medicine
Master of Resources Management
MRP Master of Regional Planning
MRP/JD Master of Regional Planning/Juris Doctor
MRRA Master of Recreation Resources Administration
MRS Master of Religious Studies
MRSc Master of Rehabilitation Science
MS Master of Science
MS Kin Master of Science in Kinesiology
MS Acct Master of Science in Accounting
MS Aero E Master of Science in Aerospace Engineering
MS Ag Master of Science in Agriculture
MS Arch Master of Science in Architecture
MS Arch St Master of Science in Architectural Studies
MS Bio E Master of Science in Bioengineering
Master of Science in Biomedical Engineering
MS Bm E Master of Science in Biomedical Engineering
MS Ch E Master of Science in Chemical Engineering
MS Chem Master of Science in Chemistry
MS Cp E Master of Science in Computer Engineering
MS Eco Master of Science in Economics
MS Econ Master of Science in Economics
MS Ed Master of Science in Education
MS El Master of Science in Educational Leadership and Administration
MS En E Master of Science in Environmental Engineering
MS Eng Master of Science in Engineering
MS Engr Master of Science in Engineering
MS Env E Master of Science in Environmental Engineering
MS Exp Surg Master of Science in Experimental Surgery
MS Int A Master of Science in International Affairs
MS Mat E Master of Science in Materials Engineering
MS Mat SE Master of Science in Material Science and Engineering
MS Met E Master of Science in Metallurgical Engineering
MS Metr Master of Science in Meteorology
MS Mgt Master of Science in Management
MS Min Master of Science in Mining
MS Min E Master of Science in Mining Engineering
MS Mt E Master of Science in Materials Engineering
MS Otol Master of Science in Otolaryngology
MS Pet E Master of Science in Petroleum Engineering
MS Phr Master of Science in Pharmacy
MS Phys Master of Science in Physics
MS Phys Op Master of Science in Physiological Optics
MS Poly Master of Science in Polymers
MS Psy Master of Science in Psychology
MS Pub P Master of Science in Public Policy
MS RSS Master of Science in Recreation and Sport Sciences
MS Sc Master of Science in Social Science
MS SEng Master of Science in Systems Engineering
MS Sp C Master of Science in Space Science
MS Sp Ed Master of Science in Special Education
MS Stat Master of Science in Statistics
MS Surg Master of Science in Surgery
MS Tax Master of Science in Taxation
MS Tc E Master of Science in Telecommunications Engineering
MS-R Master of Science (Research)
MSA Master of School Administration
Master of Science Administration
Master of Science in Accountancy
Master of Science in Accounting
Master of Science in Administration
Master of Science in Aeronautics
Master of Science in Agriculture
Master of Science in Anesthesia
Master of Science in Architecture
Master of Science in Aviation
Master of Sports Administration
MSA Phy Master of Science in Applied Physics
MSAA Master of Science in Astronautics and Aeronautics
MSAAE Master of Science in Aeronautical and Astronautical Engineering
MSABE Master of Science in Agricultural and Biological Engineering
MSAC Master of Science in Acupuncture
MSACC Master of Science in Accounting
MSaCS Master of Science in Applied Computer Science
MSAE Master of Science in Aeronautical Engineering
Master of Science in Aerospace Engineering
Master of Science in Agricultural Engineering
Master of Science in Applied Economics
Master of Science in Architectural Engineering
Master of Science in Art Education
MSAH Master of Science in Allied Health
MSAL Master of Sport Administration and Leadership
MSAM Master of Science in Applied Mathematics
MSAOM Master of Science in Agricultural Operations Management
MSAPM Master of Security Analysis and Portfolio Management
MSAS Master of Science in Administrative Studies
Master of Science in Applied Statistics
Master of Science in Architectural Studies
MSAT Master of Science in Advanced Technology
MSB Master of Science in Bible
Master of Science in Business
MSBA Master of Science in Business Administration

MSBAE	Master of Science in Biological and Agricultural Engineering Master of Science in Biosystems and Agricultural Engineering
MSBC	Master of Science in Building Construction
MSBE	Master of Science in Biological Engineering Master of Science in Biomedical Engineering Master of Science in Business Education
MSBENG	Master of Science in Bioengineering
MSBIT	Master of Science in Business Information Technology
MSBM	Master of Sport Business Management
MSBME	Master of Science in Biomedical Engineering
MSBMS	Master of Science in Basic Medical Science
MSBS	Master of Science in Biomedical Sciences
MSC	Master of Science in Commerce Master of Science in Communication Master of Science in Computers Master of Science in Counseling Master of Science in Criminology
MSCC	Master of Science in Christian Counseling Master of Science in Community Counseling
MSCD	Master of Science in Communication Disorders Master of Science in Community Development
MSCE	Master of Science in Civil Engineering Master of Science in Clinical Epidemiology Master of Science in Computer Engineering Master of Science in Continuing Education
MSCEE	Master of Science in Civil and Environmental Engineering
MSCES	Master of Science in Computer and Engineering Sciences
MSCF	Master of Science in Computational Finance
MSCH	Master of Science in Chemical Engineering
MSChE	Master of Science in Chemical Engineering
MSCI	Master of Science in Clinical Investigation Master of Science in Curriculum and Instruction
MSCIS	Master of Science in Computer and Information Systems Master of Science in Computer Information Science Master of Science in Computer Information Systems
MSCIT	Master of Science in Computer Information Technology
MSCJ	Master of Science in Criminal Justice
MSCJA	Master of Science in Criminal Justice Administration
MSCLS	Master of Science in Clinical Laboratory Studies
MSCM	Master of Science in Conflict Management Master of Science in Construction Management
MScM	Master of Science in Management
MSCP	Master of Science in Clinical Psychology Master of Science in Computer Engineering Master of Science in Counseling Psychology
MSCPharm	Master of Science in Pharmacy
MSCRP	Master of Science in City and Regional Planning Master of Science in Community and Regional Planning
MSCS	Master of Science in Computer Science Master of Science in Construction Science
MSCSD	Master of Science in Communication Sciences and Disorders
MSCSE	Master of Science in Computer Science and Engineering Master of Science in Computer Systems Engineering
MSCST	Master of Science in Computer Science Technology
MSCTE	Master of Science in Career and Technical Education
MSD	Master of Science in Dentistry Master of Science in Design
MSDD	Master of Software Design and Development
MSDM	Master of Design Methods
MSDR	Master of Dispute Resolution
MSE	Master of Science Education Master of Science in Education Master of Science in Engineering Master of Science in Engineering Managment Master of Software Engineering Master of Structural Engineering
MSE Mgt	Master of Science in Engineering Management
MSECE	Master of Science in Electrical and Computer Engineering
MSED	Master of Sustainable Economic Development
MSEE	Master of Science in Electrical Engineering Master of Science in Environmental Engineering
MSEH	Master of Science in Environmental Health
MSEL	Master of Science in Educational Leadership Master of Science in Executive Leadership Master of Studies in Environmental Law
MSEM	Master of Science in Engineering Management Master of Science in Engineering Mechanics Master of Science in Environmental Management
MSENE	Master of Science in Environmental Engineering
MSEO	Master of Science in Electro-Optics
MSEP	Master of Science in Economic Policy
MSES	Master of Science in Embedded Software Engineering Master of Science in Engineering Science Master of Science in Environmental Science Master of Science in Environmental Studies
MSESM	Master of Science in Engineering Science and Mechanics
MSET	Master of Science in Education in Educational Technology Master of Science in Engineering Technology
MSETM	Master of Science in Environmental Technology Management
MSEV	Master of Science in Environmental Engineering
MSEVH	Master of Science in Environmental Health and Safety
MSF	Master of Science in Finance Master of Science in Forestry Master of Social Foundations
MSFA	Master of Science in Financial Analysis
MSFAM	Master of Science in Family Studies
MSFCS	Master of Science in Family and Consumer Science
MSFE	Master of Science in Financial Engineering
MSFOR	Master of Science in Forestry
MSFP	Master of Science in Financial Planning
MSFS	Master of Science in Financial Sciences Master of Science in Forensic Science
MSFT	Master of Science in Family Therapy
MSGC	Master of Science in Genetic Counseling
MSGL	Master of Science in Global Leadership
MSH	Master of Science in Health Master of Science in Hospice
MSHA	Master of Science in Health Administration
MSHCA	Master of Science in Health Care Administration
MSHCI	Master of Science in Human Computer Interaction

MSHCPM	Master of Science in Health Care Policy and Management
MSHCS	Master of Science in Human and Consumer Science
MSHE	Master of Science in Health Education
MSHES	Master of Science in Human Environmental Sciences
MSHFID	Master of Science in Human Factors in Information Design
MSHFS	Master of Science in Human Factors and Systems
MSHP	Master of Science in Health Professions
MSHR	Master of Science in Human Resources
MSHRM	Master of Science in Human Resource Management
MSHROD	Master of Science in Human Resources and Organizational Development
MSHS	Master of Science in Health Science
	Master of Science in Health Services
	Master of Science in Health Systems
MSHT	Master of Science in History of Technology
MSI	Master of Science in Instruction
MSIA	Master of Science in Industrial Administration
	Master of Science in Information Assurance and Computer Security
	Master of Science in Interior Architecture
MSIB	Master of Science in International Business
MSIDM	Master of Science in Interior Design and Merchandising
MSIDT	Master of Science in Information Design and Technology
MSIE	Master of Science in Industrial Engineering
	Master of Science in International Economics
MSIEM	Master of Science in Information Engineering and Management
MSIM	Master of Science in Information Management
	Master of Science in Investment Management
MSIMC	Master of Science in Integrated Marketing Communications
MSIO	Master of Science of Industrial-Organizational Psychology
MSIR	Master of Science in Industrial Relations
MSIS	Master of Science in Information Science
	Master of Science in Information Systems
	Master of Science in Interdisciplinary Studies
MSISE	Master of Science in Infrastructure Systems Engineering
MSISM	Master of Science in Information Systems Management
MSISPM	Master of Science in Information Security Policy and Management
MSIST	Master of Science in Information Systems Technology
MSIT	Master of Science in Industrial Technology
	Master of Science in Information Technology
	Master of Science in Instructional Technology
MSITM	Master of Science in Information Technology Management
MSJ	Master of Science in Journalism
	Master of Science in Jurisprudence
MSJE	Master of Science in Jewish Education
MSJFP	Master of Science in Juvenile Forensic Psychology
MSJJ	Master of Science in Juvenile Justice
MSJPS	Master of Science in Justice and Public Safety
MSJS	Master of Science in Jewish Studies
MSK	Master of Science in Kinesiology
MSL	Master of School Leadership
	Master of Science in Limnology
	Master of Studies in Law
MSLA	Master of Science in Landscape Architecture
	Master of Science in Legal Administration
MSLD	Master of Science in Land Development
MSLS	Master of Science in Legal Studies
	Master of Science in Library Science
	Master of Science in Logistics Systems
MSLT	Master of Second Language Teaching
MSM	Master of Sacred Ministry
	Master of Sacred Music
	Master of School Mathematics
	Master of Science in Management
MSMA	Master of Science in Marketing Analysis
MSMAE	Master of Science in Materials Engineering
MSMC	Master of Science in Mass Communications
MSME	Master of Science in Mechanical Engineering
MSMFE	Master of Science in Manufacturing Engineering
MSMIS	Master of Science in Management Information Systems
MSMIT	Master of Science in Management and Information Technology
MSMM	Master of Science in Manufacturing Management
MSMO	Master of Science in Manufacturing Operations
MSMOT	Master of Science in Management of Technology
MSMS	Master of Science in Management Science
MSMSE	Master of Science in Manufacturing Systems Engineering
	Master of Science in Material Science and Engineering
	Master of Science in Mathematics and Science Education
MSMT	Master of Science in Management and Technology
	Master of Science in Medical Technology
MSN	Master of Science in Nursing
MSN-R	Master of Science in Nursing (Research)
MSN/Ed D	Master of Science in Nursing/Doctor of Education
MSN/M Div	Master of Science in Nursing/Master of Divinity
MSNA	Master of Science in Nurse Anesthesia
MSNE	Master of Science in Nuclear Engineering
MSNM	Master of Science in Nonprofit Management
MSNS	Master of Science in Natural Science
	Master's of Science in Nutritional Science
MSOD	Master of Science in Organizational Development
MSOEE	Master of Science in Outdoor and Environmental Education
MSOES	Master of Science in Occupational Ergonomics and Safety
MSOL	Master of Science in Organizational Leadership
MSOM	Master of Science in Organization and Management
	Master of Science in Oriental Medicine
MSOR	Master of Science in Operations Research
MSOT	Master of Science in Occupational Technology
	Master of Science in Occupational Therapy
MSP	Master of Science in Pharmacy
	Master of Science in Planning
	Master of Speech Pathology
MSP Ex	Master of Science in Exercise Physiology
MSPA	Master of Science in Physician Assistant
	Master of Science in Professional Accountancy
MSPAS	Master of Science in Physician Assistant Studies

MSPC	Master of Science in Professional Communications
	Master of Science in Professional Counseling
MSPE	Master of Science in Petroleum Engineering
MSPG	Master of Science in Psychology
MSPH	Master of Science in Public Health
MSPHR	Master of Science in Pharmacy
MSPM	Master of Science in Professional Management
MSPNGE	Master of Science in Petroleum and Natural Gas Engineering
MSPS	Master of Science in Pharmaceutical Science
	Master of Science in Psychological Services
MSPT	Master of Science in Physical Therapy
MSpVM	Master of Specialized Veterinary Medicine
MSQFE	Master of Science in Quantitative Financial Economics
MSR	Master of Science in Radiology
	Master of Science in Rehabilitation Sciences
MSRA	Master of Science in Recreation Administration
MSRC	Master of Science in Resource Conservation
MSRE	Master of Science in Real Estate
	Master of Science in Religious Education
MSRED	Master of Science in Real Estate Development
MSREM	Master of Science in Real Estate Management
MSRLS	Master of Science in Recreation and Leisure Studies
MSRMP	Master of Science in Radiological Medical Physics
MSRS	Master of Science in Rehabilitation Science
MSS	Master of Science in Software
	Master of Social Science
	Master of Social Services
	Master of Software Systems
	Master of Sports Science
	Master of Strategic Studies
MSSA	Master of Science in Social Administration
MSSE	Master of Science in Software Engineering
MSSEM	Master of Science in Systems and Engineering Management
MSSI	Master of Science in Strategic Intelligence
MSSL	Master of Science in Strategic Leadership
MSSLP	Master of Science in Speech-Language Pathology
MSSM	Master of Science in Sports Medicine
MSSPA	Master of Science in Student Personnel Administration
MSSS	Master of Science in Safety Science
	Master of Science in Systems Science
MSST	Master of Science in Systems Technology
MSSW	Master of Science in Social Work
MST	Master of Science and Technology
	Master of Science in Taxation
	Master of Science in Teaching
	Master of Science in Technology
	Master of Science in Telecommunications
	Master of Science Teaching
MSTC	Master of Science in Telecommunications
MSTCM	Master of Science in Traditional Chinese Medicine
MSTE	Master of Science in Telecommunications Engineering
	Master of Science in Transportation Engineering
MSTM	Master of Science in Technical Management
	Master of Science in Technology Management
MSTOM	Master of Science in Traditional Oriental Medicine
MSUD	Master of Science in Urban Design
MSUESM	Master of Science in Urban Environmental Systems Management
MSW	Master of Social Work
MSWE	Master of Software Engineering
MSWREE	Master of Science in Water Resources and Environmental Engineering
MSX	Master of Science in Exercise Science
MT	Master of Taxation
	Master of Teaching
	Master of Technology
	Master of Textiles
MTA	Master of Arts in Teaching
	Master of Tax Accounting
	Master of Teaching Arts
	Master of Tourism Administration
MTCM	Master of Traditional Chinese Medicine
MTD	Master of Training and Development
MTE	Master in Educational Technology
	Master of Teacher Education
MTEL	Master of Telecommunications
MTESL	Master in Teaching English as a Second Language
MTHM	Master of Tourism and Hospitality Management
MTI	Master of Information Technology
MTIM	Masters of Trust and Investment Management
MTL	Master of Talmudic Law
MTLM	Master of Transportation and Logistics Management
MTM	Master of Technology Management
	Master of Telecommunications Management
	Master of the Teaching of Mathematics
MTMH	Master of Tropical Medicine and Hygiene
MTOM	Master of Traditional Oriental Medicine
MTP	Master of Transpersonal Psychology
MTPC	Master of Technical and Professional Communication
MTS	Master of Teaching Science
	Master of Theological Studies
MTSC	Master of Technical and Scientific Communication
MTSE	Master of Telecommunications and Software Engineering
MTT	Master in Technology Management
MTX	Master of Taxation
MUA	Master of Urban Affairs
MUD	Master of Urban Design
MUEP	Master of Urban and Environmental Planning
MUP	Master of Urban Planning
MUPDD	Master of Urban Planning, Design, and Development
MUPP	Master of Urban Planning and Policy
MUPRED	Masters of Urban Planning and Real Estate Development
MURP	Master of Urban and Regional Planning
	Master of Urban and Rural Planning
MUS	Master of Urban Studies
Mus Doc	Doctor of Music
Mus M	Master of Music
MVP	Master of Voice Pedagogy
MVPH	Master of Veterinary Public Health
MVTE	Master of Vocational-Technical Education
MWC	Master of Wildlife Conservation
MWE	Master in Welding Engineering
MWPS	Master of Wood and Paper Science
MWR	Master of Water Resources

MWS	Master of Women's Studies
MZS	Master of Zoological Science
Nav Arch	Naval Architecture
Naval E	Naval Engineer
ND	Doctor of Naturopathic Medicine
NE	Nuclear Engineer
Nuc E	Nuclear Engineer
OD	Doctor of Optometry
OTD	Doctor of Occupational Therapy
PBME	Professional Master of Biomedical Engineering
PD	Professional Diploma
PDD	Professional Development Degree
PE Dir	Director of Physical Education
PGC	Post-Graduate Certificate
Ph L	Licentiate of Philosophy
Pharm D	Doctor of Pharmacy
PhD	Doctor of Philosophy
PhD Otol	Doctor of Philosophy in Otolaryngology
Phd Surg	Doctor of Philosophy in Surgery
PhDEE	Doctor of Philosophy in Electrical Engineering
PM Sc	Professional Master of Science
PMBA	Professional Master of Business Administration
PMC	Post Master Certificate
PMD	Post-Master's Diploma
PMS	Professional Master of Science
PPDPT	Postprofessional Doctor of Physical Therapy
PSM	Professional Master of Science
Psy D	Doctor of Psychology
Psy M	Master of Psychology
Psy S	Specialist in Psychology
Psya D	Doctor of Psychoanalysis
Re Dir	Director of Recreation
Rh D	Doctor of Rehabilitation
S Psy S	Specialist in Psychological Services
Sc D	Doctor of Science
Sc M	Master of Science
SCCT	Specialist in Community College Teaching
ScDPT	Doctor of Physical Therapy Science
SD	Doctor of Science Specialist Degree
SJD	Doctor of Juridical Science
SLPD	Doctor of Speech-Language Pathology
SLS	Specialist in Library Science
SM	Master of Science
SM Arch S	Master of Science in Architectural Studies
SM Arch S/MCP	Master of Science in Architectural Studies/Master of City Planning
SM Arch S/ SMRED	Master of Science in Architectural Studies/Master of Science in Real Estate Development
SM Vis S	Master of Science in Visual Studies
SMBT	Master of Science in Building Technology
SP	Specialist Degree
Sp C	Specialist in Counseling
Sp Ed	Specialist in Education
Sp LIS	Specialist in Library and Information Science
SPA	Specialist in Arts
SPCM	Special in Church Music
Spec	Specialist's Certificate
Spec M	Specialist in Music
SPEM	Special in Educational Ministries
SPS	School Psychology Specialist
Spt	Specialist Degree
SPTH	Special in Theology
SSP	Specialist in School Psychology
STB	Bachelor of Sacred Theology
STD	Doctor of Sacred Theology
STL	Licentiate of Sacred Theology
STM	Master of Sacred Theology
TDPT	Transitional Doctor of Physical Therapy
Th D	Doctor of Theology
Th M	Master of Theology
VMD	Doctor of Veterinary Medicine
WEMBA	Weekend Executive Master of Business Administration
XMBA	Executive Master of Business Administration

INDEXES

Profiles, Announcements, and Close-Ups

Directories and Subject Areas in Books 2–6

Following is an alphabetical listing of directories and subject areas in Books 2–6. Also listed are cross-references for subject area names not used in the directory structure of the guides, for example, "Arabic (*see* Near and Middle Eastern Languages)."